MICRO STRONG'S EXHAUSTIVE CONCORDANCE
OF THE KING JAMES BIBLE

JAMES STRONG, S.T.D., LL.D first published this Concordance in 1890. It lists every word in the "King James Bible" in each location and gives the Hebrew and Greek "root" meaning at most occurences—the understanding which a native speaker would have. This is a wonderful insight for understanding the text being read, whether you speak any Hebrew or Greek at all! The Micro version enables anyone to carry it with him in the back of his Bible—at his fingertips. **Directions:** 1.)To find where a verse is in the Bible, look up the most striking, significant word you can remember. Be sure to spell the word exactly as in the King James Bible. If you can't find it, try a different word. Because the Micro Strong's omits the phrase from the text for each word, you are forced to familiarize yourself with where that word occurs in the entire Bible—this is a rewarding word study exercise. 2.)The numbers beside each reference are where the word is found in the Hebrew or Greek Dictionaries in the rear of the concordance. If no number is given for that reference, then it is the number given for "all=". If the word in your verse is not listed in the Concordance, it was "supplied" by the translators (and often printed in *italics* in the Bible), meaning that it is implied or required by the grammatical form. 3.)The small superscripts (for example, ^{2}, etc.) that appear following some verse numbers indicate the number of times the word appears in the verse. 4.)In the Hebrew and Greek Dictionaries, each definition is followed by ":–" and then is written every way that word is translated in the King James Bible; this gives you an exhaustive list of everywhere that Hebrew or Greek word is found in the Bible. 5.) "sup"=supplied; "subscri"=subscript; "t"=title.

Look in the APPENDIX for **persons, places,** and **races,** as well as for the following 49 words which are seldom looked up: a , all, an, and, are, as, be, but, by, for, from, he, her, him, his, I, if, in, is, it, me, my, not, O, of, our, out, shall, shalt, she, that, the, thee, their, them, they, thou, thy, to, unto, up, upon, us, was, we, were, with, ye, you.

ABBREVIATIONS OF THE NAMES OF THE BOOKS OF THE BIBLE

GE =	Genesis	JOB =	Job	NA =	Nahum	PH'P =	Philippians
EX	Exodus	PS	Psalms	JON	Jonah	COL	Colossians
LE	Leviticus	PR	Proverbs	HAB	Habakkuk	1TH	1 Thessalonians
NU	Numbers	EC	Ecclesiastes	ZEP	Zephaniah	2TH	2 Thessalonians
DE	Deuteronomy	SONG	Song of Solomon	HAG	Haggai	1TI	1 Timothy
JOS	Joshua	IS	Isaiah	ZEC	Zechariah	2TI	2 Timothy
J'G	Judges	JER	Jeremiah	MAL	Malachi	TIT	Titus
RU	Ruth	LA	Lamentations	M'T	Matthew	PH'M	Philemon
1SA	1 Samuel	EZE	Ezekiel	M'R	Mark	HEB	Hebrews
2SA	2 Samuel	DA	Daniel	LU	Luke	JAS	James
1KI	1 Kings	HO	Hosea	JOH	John	1PE	1 Peter
2KI	2 Kings	JOE	Joel	AC	Acts	2PE	2 Peter
1CH	1 Chronicles	AM	Amos	RO	Romans	1JO	1 John
2CH	2 Chronicles	OB	Obadiah	1CO	1 Corinthians	2JO	2 John
EZR	Ezra	MIC	Micah	2CO	2 Corinthians	3JO	3 John
NE	Nehemiah			GA	Galatians	JUDE	Jude
ES	Esther			EPH	Ephesians	RE	Revelation

Because Hebrew in its essential elements and vocabulary is much simpler than Greek or Latin, it is possible to have access to the majestic Hebrew tongue–which conveys to us the greater portion of the oracles of God. A good start would be the Handbook of Biblical Hebrew by Sanford LaSor (Eerdman's Publ, 1980). (This is actually a delightful verse by verse study of the book of Esther.) With what you learn from LaSor, you will then be able to have a depth of understanding of the grammatical analysis from Benjamin Davidson's Analytical Hebrew and Chaldee Lexicon (Hendrickson Publ. Co). It is necessary to memorize the Hebrew alphabet (listed on the first page of the Hebrew Dictionary) in order to use Davidson, but knowing the Hebrew "aleph-bets" will actually give you beginning access to the Hebrew Bible and to all Hebrew references. Also consider Do It Yourself Hebrew and Greek by Ed Goodrick, Multnomah Press). Lasor, Goodrick, and Davidson are helpful friends.

A

ABASE-JOB-40:11(8213)-IS-31:4(6031)-EZE-21:26(8213)-DA-4:37(8214)

ABASED-all=5013-M'T-23:12-LU-14:11■18:14-PH'P-4:12

ABASING-2CO-11:7(5013)

ABATED-GE-8:3(2637),8(7043),11(7043)-LE-27:18(1639)-DE-34:7(5127)-J'G-8:3(7503)

ABHOR-all=8581&marked-LE-26:11(1602),15(1602),30(1602),44(1602)-DE-7:26■23:7^2-1SA-27:12(887)-JOB-9:31■30:10■42:6(3988)-PS-5:6■119:163-PR-24:24(2194)-JER-14:21(5006)-AM-5:10■6:8(8374)-MIC-3:9■N.T.-RO-12:9(655)

ABHORRED-EX-5:21(887)-LE-20:23(6973)■26:43(1602)-DE-32:19(5006)-1SA-2:17(5006)-2SA-16:21(887)-1KI-11:25(6973)-JOB-19:19(8581)-PS-22:24(8262)■78:59(3988)■89:38(3988)■106:40(8581)-PR-22:14(2194)-LA-2:7(5010)-EZE-16:25(8581)-ZEC-11:8(973)

ABHORREST-IS-7:16(6973)■N.T.-RO-2:22(948)

ABHORRETH-JOB-33:20(2092)-PS-10:3(5006)■36:4(3988)■107:18(8581)-IS-49:7(8581)

ABHORRING-IS-66:24(1860)

ABIDE-all=3427&marked-GE-19:2(3885)■22:5■24:55■29:19■44:33-EX-16:29-LE-8:35■19:13(3885)-NU-22:5■31:19(2583),23(935)■35:25-DE-3:19-JOS-18:5^2(5975)-RU-2:8(1692)-1SA-1:22■5:7■19:2■22:5,23■30:21-2SA-11:11■15:19■16:18-1KI-8:13-2CH-25:19■32:10-JOB-24:13■38:40■39:9(3885)-PS-15:1(1481)■61:4(1481),7■91:1(3885)-PR-7:11(7937)■19:23(3885)-EC-8:15(3867)-JER-10:10(3557)■42:10■49:18,33■50:40-HO-3:3,4■11:6(2342)-JOE-2:11(3557)-MIC-5:4-NA-1:6(6965)-MAL-3:2(3557)■N.T.-all=3306&marked-M'T-10:11-M'R-6:10-LU-9:4■19:5■24:29-JOH-12:46■14:16■15:4^3,6,7,10^2-AC-15:34(1961)■16:15■20:23■27:31-RO-11:23(1961)-1CO-3:14■7:8,20,24,40■16:6(3887)-PH'P-1:24(1961),25-1TI-1:3(4357)1JO-2:24,27,28

ABIDETH-all=3427&marked-NU-31:23(935)-2SA-16:3-JOB-39:28(3885)-PS-49:12(3885)■55:19■119:90(5975)■125:1-PR-15:31(3885)-EC-1:4(5975)-JER-21:9■N.T.-all=3306-JOH-3:36■8:35^2■12:24,34■15:5-1CO-13:13-2TI-2:13-HEB-7:3-1PE-1:23-1JO-2:6,10,14,17,27■3:6,14,24-2JO-1:9^2

ABIDING-NU-24:2(7931)-J'G-16:9(3427),12(3427)-1SA-26:19(5596)-1CH-29:15(4723)■N.T.-LU-2:8(63)-JOH-5:38(3306)-AC-16:12(1304)-1JO-3:15(3306)

ABILITY-LE-27:8(5381)-EZR-2:69(3581)-NE-5:8(1767)-DA-1:4(3581)■N.T.-M'T-25:15(1411)-AC-11:29(2141)-1PE-4:11(2479)

ABJECTS-PS-35:15(5222)

ABLE-all=3201,a=3318&marked-GE-13:6(5375)■15:5■33:14(7272)-EX-10:5■18:18,21(2428),23,25(2428)■40:35-LE-5:7(5060,1767),11(5381)■12:8(4672,1767)■14:22(5381),31(5381),32(5381)■25:26(5381),28(4672,1767),49(5381)-NU-1:3a,20a,22a,24a,26a,28a,30a,32a,34a,36a,38a,40a,42a,45a■11:14■13:30,31■14:16■22:11,37■26:2a-DE-1:9■7:24(3320)■9:28■11:25(3320)■14:24■16:17(4979,3027)-JOS-1:5(3320)■23:9(5975)-J'G-8:3-1SA-6:20■17:9,33-1KI-3:9■9:21-2KI-3:21(2296)■18:23,29-1CH-5:18(5375)■9:13(2428)■26:8(2428)■29:14(6113,3581)-2CH-2:6(6113,3581)■7:7■20:37(6113)■32:13,14,15-EZR-10:13(3581)-NE-4:10-PS-18:38■21:11■36:12■40:12-EC-8:17-IS-36:8,14■47:11,12-JER-10:10■11:11■49:10-LA-1:14-EZE-7:19■33:12■46:5(4991,3027),11(4991,3027)-DA-2:26(3546)■3:17(3202)■4:18(3202),18(3546),37(3202)■6:20(3202)-AM-7:10-ZEP-1:18■N.T.-all=1410,a=1415&marked-M'T-3:9■9:28■10:28^2■19:12■20:22^2■22:46■26:61-M'R-4:33-LU-1:20■3:8■12:26■13:24(2480)■14:29(2480),30(2480),31a■21:15-JOH-10:29■21:6(2480)-AC-6:10(2480)■15:10(2480)■20:32■25:5a-RO-4:21a■8:39■11:23a■14:4a■15:14-1CO-3:2^2■6:5■10:13^2-2CO-1:4■3:6(2427)■9:8a-EPH-3:18(1840),20■6:11,13,16-PH'P-3:21-2TI-1:12a■2:2(2425)■3:7,15-TIT-1:9a-HEB-2:18■5:7■7:25■11:19a-JAS-1:21■3:2a■4:12-2PE-1:15(2192)-JUDE-24-RE-5:3■6:17■13:4■15:8

ABOARD-AC-21:2(1910)

ABODE-all=3427&marked-GE-29:14■49:24-EX-24:16(7931)■40:35(7931)-NU-9:17(7931),18(7931),20(2583),21(1961),22(2583)■11:35(1961)■20:1■22:8■25:1-DE-1:46^2■3:29■9:9-JOS-2:22■5:8■8:9-J'G-5:17^2(7931)■11:17■19:4■20:47■21:2-1SA-1:23■7:2■13:16■22:6■23:14,18,25■25:13■26:3■30:10(5975)-2SA-1:1■11:12■15:8-1KI-17:19-2KI-19:27-EZR-8:15(2583),32-IS-37:28-JER-38:28■N.T.-all=3306&marked-M'T-17:22(390)-LU-1:56■8:27■21:37(835)-JOH-1:32,39■4:40■7:9■8:44(2476)■10:40■11:6■14:23(3438)-AC-1:13(2650)■12:19(1304)■14:3(1304),28(1304)■17:14(5278)■18:3■20:3(4160),6(1304)■21:7,8-GA-1:18(1961)-2TI-4:20

ABODEST-J'G-5:16(3427)

ABOLISH-IS-2:18(2498)

ABOLISHED-IS-51:6(2865)-EZE-6:6(4229)■N.T.-all=2673-2CO-3:13-EPH-2:15-2TI-1:10

ABOMINABLE-all=8581&marked-LE-7:21(8263)■11:43(8262)■18:30(8441)■19:7(6292)■20:25(8262)-DE-14:3(8441)-1CH-21:6-2CH-15:8(8251)-JOB-15:16-PS-14:1■53:1-IS-14:19■65:4(6292)-JER-16:18(8441)■44:4(8441)-EZE-4:14(6292)■8:10(8263)■16:52-MIC-6:10(2194)-NA-3:6(8251)■N.T.-TIT-1:16(947)-1PE-4:3(111)-RE-21:8(948)

ABOMINABLY-1KI-21:26(8581)

ABOMINATION-all=8441,a=8263&marked-GE-43:32■46:34-EX-8:26^2-LE-7:18(6292)■11:10a,11a,11(8262),12a,13(8262),13a,20a,23a,41a,42a■18:22■20:13-DE-7:25,26■12:31■13:14■17:1,4■18:12■22:5■23:18■24:4■25:16■27:15-1SA-13:4(887)-1KI-11:5(8251),7^2(8251)-2KI-23:13^2(8251),13-PS-88:8-PR-3:32■6:16■8:7■11:1,20■12:22■13:19■15:8,9,26■16:5,12■17:15■20:10,23■21:27■24:9■28:9■29:27^2-IS-1:13■41:24■44:19■66:17a-JER-2:7■6:15■8:12■32:35-EZE-16:50■18:12■22:11■33:26-DA-11:31(8251)■12:11(8251)-MAL-2:11■N.T.-all=946-M'T-24:15-M'R-13:14-LU-16:15-RE-21:27

ABOMINATIONS-all=8441,a=8251&marked-LE-18:26,27,29-DE-18:9,12■20:18■29:17a■32:16-1KI-14:24-2KI-16:3■21:2,11■23:24a-2CH-28:3■33:2■34:33■36:8,14-EZR-9:1,11,14-PR-26:25-IS-66:3a-JER-4:1a■7:10,30a■13:27a■32:34a■44:22-EZE-5:9,11■6:9,11■7:3,4,8,9,20■8:6^2,9,13,15,17■9:4■11:18,21■12:16■14:6■16:2,22,36,43,47,51^2,58■18:13,24■20:4,7a,8a,30a■22:2■23:36■33:29■36:31■43:8■44:6,7,13-DA-9:27a-HO-9:10a-ZEC-9:7a■N.T.-RE-17:4(946),5(946)

ABOUND-PR-28:20(7227)■N.T.-all=4052&marked-M'T-24:12(4129)-RO-5:20(4121),20(5248)■6:1(4121)■15:13-2CO-1:5■8:7^2■9:8^2-PH'P-1:9■4:12^2,17(4121),18-1TH-3:12■4:1-2PE-1:8(4121)

ABOUNDED-all=4052&marked-RO-3:7■5:15,20(4121)-2CO-8:2-EPH-1:8

ABOUNDETH-PR-29:22(7227)■N.T.-2CO-1:5(4052)-2TH-1:3(4121)

ABOUNDING-PR-8:24(8513)■N.T.-1CO-15:58(4052)-COL-2:7(4052)

ABOUT-all=5437,a=5439,b=5921&marked-GE-41:42b-EX-13:18■19:23(854)-LE-6:5b-NU-2:2a■4:14b■11:8(7751)■16:24a,49b-DE-17:14a■31:21(6213)■32:10-JOS-6:11(5362)■16:6-J'G-20:43(3803)-RU-1:19b-1SA-5:8^2,9,10■15:12,27■17:42(5027)■22:6b,7b,17b-2SA-3:12■14:20■18:15■22:6■24:6a-1KI-2:15■5:3■6:29(4524)■7:15■18:32a-2KI-3:25■6:14(5362)■8:21(413)■11:7(413)■11:11b-2CH-13:13■14:7■17:9■23:2-EZR-1:6a■10:15b-NE-13:21(5048)JOB-1:5(5362),10(1157)■8:17(5440)■11:18a■29:5a■30:18(247)-PS-48:12a■55:10■89:7a■139:11(1157)-PR-3:3b■6:21b■20:19(1980)-EC-2:20■12:5-SONG-3:2,3,7a■5:7■7:2(5473)-IS-23:16■26:20(1157)-JER-2:36(235)■14:18(5503)■17:26a■31:22(2559)■32:44a■33:13a■41:14■48:17a,39a■49:5a-LA-3:7(1157)-EZE-1:4a■5:2a■12:14a■32:22a■36:7a■43:17^{2}a■47:2-DA-5:7(5922),16(5922),29(5922)■9:16a-HO-7:2-JON-2:6(1157)-ZEC-12:6(1157)■14:14(1157)■N.T.-all=4012,a=5616,b=4066,c=5613&marked-M'T-1:11(1909)■3:4,5b■4:23(4013)■8:18■9:22(1994),35(4013)■14:21(5616),35b■18:6(1909)■20:3,5,6,9■21:33(4060)■27:46-M'R-1:6,28b■2:2(4314)■3:5(4017),8,32,34(2945),34■4:10■5:13c,30(1994),32(4017)■6:6(2945),36(2945),44a,48,55b,55(4064)■8:9c,33(1994)■9:8(4017),14,42■10:23(4017)■11:11(4017)■12:1(5418)■14:51(1909)■15:17(4060)-LU-1:56a,65(4037)■2:9(4034),37c,49(1722)■3:3b,23a■4:14b,37b■6:10(4017)■7:9(4762),17b■8:37b,42c■9:12(2945),14a,28a■10:40,41■12:35(4024)■13:8■17:2■19:43(4016)■22:41a,49,59a■23:44a-JOH-1:39c■3:25■4:6a■6:10a,19c■7:19(2212),20(2212)■10:24(2944)■11:18c,44(4019)■19:14a,39a■20:7(1909)■21:20(1994)-AC-1:15c■2:10(2596),41a■3:3(3195)■4:4a■5:7c,16(4038),36a■9:3(4015),29(2021)■10:3a,9,38(1330)■11:19(1909)■12:1(2596),8(4016)■13:11(4013),18c,20c■14:6b,20(2944)■15:2■18:14(3195)■19:7a,23,34c■20:3(3195)■21:31(2212)■22:6^2■24:6(3985)■25:7(3936),15,24■26:13(4034),21(3985)■27:27(2596),30(2212)-RO-4:19(4225)■10:3(2212)■15:19(2945)-1CO-9:5(4013)-2CO-4:10(4064)-EPH-4:14(4064)■6:14(4024)-1TI-5:13(4022)■6:4-TIT-3:9(3163)-HEB-8:5(3195)■9:4(3840)■11:30(2944),37(4022)■12:1(4029)■13:9(4064)-JAS-3:3(3329),4(3329)-1PE-5:8(4043)-JUDE-1:7,9,12(4064)-RE-1:13(4024)■4:3(2943),4(2943),6(2943),8(2943)■5:11(2943)■7:11(2943)■8:1c■10:4(3195)■16:21c■20:9(2944)

ABOVE-all=5921,a=4605&marked-GE-1:7,20■6:16a■7:17■27:39■28:13■48:22■49:25,26-EX-18:11■20:4a■25:21a,22■26:14a,24■28:27a,28a■29:13■30:14a■36:19a■39:20a,21■40:19a,20a-LE-3:4,10,15■4:9■7:4■9:10(4480),19■11:21a■27:7a-NU-3:49■4:25a■16:3-DE-4:39a■5:8a■25:3■26:19■28:1,13a,43-JOS-2:11a■3:13a,16a-2SA-22:17(4791)-1KI-7:3a,11a,20a,25a,29a,31a■8:7a,23a-2KI-25:28-1CH-16:25■23:27a■27:6■29:3a-2CH-4:4a■5:8a■24:20■25:5a■34:4-NE-8:5■9:5■12:37,39^2-ES-3:1■5:11-JOB-3:4a■18:16■31:2a,28a-PS-8:1■10:5(4791)■18:16(4791)■27:6■50:4■57:5^2,11^2■78:23a■95:3■96:4■97:9^2■99:2■103:11■104:6■108:4,5^2■113:4^2■136:6■137:6■138:2■144:7(4791)■148:4(4791),13(4791)-PR-8:28a■15:24a-EC-3:19(4480)-IS-6:2a■7:11a■14:13a,14■45:8a-JER-4:28a■31:37a■35:4a■52:32a-LA-1:13(4791)-EZE-1:22a,26^{2}a■10:1,

19a▪11:22a▪16:43▪29:15▪37:8a▪41:17,20-DA-6:3(5922)▪11:5,36,37-AM-2:9a▪**N.T.**-all=5228&marked-M'T-10:24^2-LU-3:20(1909)▪6:40▪13:2(3844),4(3844)-JOH-3:31(509),31(1883)▪8:23(507)▪19:11(509)-AC-2:19(507)▪4:22(4117)▪26:13-RO-14:5(3844)-1CO-4:6▪10:13▪15:6(1883)-2CO-1:8▪11:23▪12:2(4253),6-GA-1:14▪4:26(507)-EPH-1:21(5231)▪3:20▪4:6(1909),10(5231)▪6:16(1909)-PH'P-2:9-COL-3:1(507),2(507),14(1909)-2TH-2:4(1909)-PH'M-16-HEB-1:9(3844)▪10:8(511)-JAS-1:17(509)▪3:15(509),17(509)▪5:12(4253)-1PE-4:8(4253)-3JO-2(4012)

ABROAD-all=2351&marked-GE-10:18(5310)▪11:4(6527),8(6527),9(6527)▪15:5▪19:17▪28:14(6555)-EX-5:12(6527)▪9:29(6566),33(6566)▪12:46▪21:19▪40:19(6566)-LE-13:7(6581),12(6524),22(6581),27(6581)▪14:8▪18:9-NU-11:32(7849)-DE-23:10,12,13▪24:11^2▪32:11(6566)-J'G-12:9^2-1SA-9:26▪30:16(5203)-2SA-22:43(7554)-2KI-4:3-1CH-13:2(6555)▪14:13(6584)-2CH-26:15(7350)▪29:16▪31:5(6555)-NE-1:8(6327)-ES-1:17(3318)▪3:8(6340)-JOB-4:11(6504)▪15:23(5074)▪40:11(6327)-PS-41:6▪77:17(1980)-PR-5:16-IS-24:1(6327)▪28:25(6327)▪44:24(7554)-JER-6:11-LA-1:20-EZE-34:21-ZEC-1:17(6527)▪2:6(6566)▪**N.T.**-all=1831&marked-M'T-9:26,31(1310),36(4496)▪12:30(4650)▪26:31(1287)-M'R-1:28,45(1310)▪4:22(1519,5318)▪6:14(1519,1096)-LU-1:65(1255)▪2:17(1232)▪5:15(1330)▪8:17(1519,5318)-JOH-11:52(1287)▪21:23-AC-2:6(1096,5456)▪8:1(1289),4(1289)▪11:19(1289)-RO-5:5(1632)▪16:19(864)-2CO-9:9(4650)-1TH-1:8-JAS-1:1(1290)

ABSENCE-LU-22:6(817)-PH'P-2:12(666)

ABSENT-GE-31:49(5641)▪**N.T.**-all=548&marked-1CO-5:3-2CO-5:6(1553),8(1553),9(1553)▪10:1,11▪13:2▪13:10-PH'P-1:27-COL-2:5

ABSTAIN-all=567-AC-15:20,29-1TH-4:3▪5:22-1TI-4:3-1PE-2:11

ABSTINENCE-AC-27:21(776)

ABUNDANCE-all=7230&marked-DE-28:47▪33:19(8228)-1SA-1:16-2SA-12:30(7235)-1KI-1:19,25▪10:10,27▪18:41(1995)-1CH-22:3^2,4(369,4557),14,15▪29:2,21-2CH-1:15▪2:9▪4:18▪9:1,9,27▪11:23▪14:15▪15:9▪17:5▪18:1,2▪20:25▪24:11▪29:35▪31:5(7235)▪32:5,29-NE-9:25-ES-1:7(7227)-JOB-22:11(8229)▪36:31(4342)▪38:34(8229)-PS-37:11▪52:7▪72:7▪105:30(8317)-EC-5:10(1995),12(7647)-IS-7:22▪15:7(3502)▪47:9(6109)▪60:5(1995)▪66:11(2123)-JER-33:6(6283)-EZE-16:49(7962)▪26:10(8229)-ZEC-14:14▪**N.T.**-all=4052&marked-M'T-12:34(4051)▪13:12▪25:29-M'R-12:44-LU-6:45(4051)▪12:15▪21:4-RO-5:17(4050)-2CO-8:2(4050),14^2(4051),20(100)▪12:7(5236)-RE-18:3(1411)

ABUNDANT-EX-34:6(7227)-IS-56:12(1419)-JER-51:13(7227)▪**N.T.**-all=4055&marked-1CO-12:23^2,24-2CO-4:15(4121)▪7:15(4056)▪9:12(4052)▪11:23(4056)-PH'P-1:26(4052)-1TI-1:14(5250)-1PE-1:3(4183)

ABUNDANTLY-all=8317&marked-GE-1:20,21▪8:17▪9:7-EX-1:7▪8:3-NU-20:11(7227)-1CH-12:40(7230)▪22:5(7230),8(7230)-2CH-31:5(7230)-JOB-36:28(7227)-PS-36:8(7301)▪65:10(7301)▪132:15(1288)▪145:7(5042)-SONG-5:1(7937)-IS-15:3(3381)▪35:2(6524)▪55:7(7235)▪**N.T.**-all=4056&marked-JOH-10:10(4053)-1CO-15:10(4054)-2CO-1:12▪2:4▪10:15(1519,4050)▪12:15-EPH-3:20(1537,4053)-1TH-2:17-TIT-3:6(4146)-HEB-6:17(4054)-2PE-1:11(4146)

ABUSE-1SA-31:4(5953)-1CH-10:4(5953)▪**N.T.**-1CO-9:18(2710)

ABUSED-J'G-19:25(5953)

ABUSERS-1CO-6:9(733)

ABUSING-1CO-7:31(2710)

ACCEPT-all=7521&marked-GE-32:20(5375)-EX-22:11(3947)-LE-26:41,43-DE-33:11-1SA-26:19(7306)-2SA-24:23-JOB-13:8(5375),10(5375)▪32:21(5375)▪42:8(5375)-PS-20:3(1878)▪82:2(5375)▪119:108-PR-18:5(5375)-JER-14:10,12-EZE-20:40,41▪43:27-AM-5:22-MAL-1:8(5375),10,13▪**N.T.**-AC-24:3(588)

ACCEPTABLE-all=7522&marked-LE-22:20-DE-33:24-PS-19:14▪69:13-PR-10:32▪21:3(977)-EC-12:10(2656)-IS-49:8▪58:5▪61:2-JER-6:20-DA-4:27(8232)**N.T.**-all=2101&marked-LU-4:19(1184)-RO-12:1,2▪14:18▪15:16(2144)-EPH-5:10(2101)-PH'P-4:18(1184)-1TI-2:3(587)▪5:4(587)-1PE-2:5(2144),20(5485)

ACCEPTABLY-HEB-12:28(2102)

ACCEPTANCE-IS-60:7(7522)

ACCEPTATION-1TI-1:15(594)▪4:9(594)

ACCEPTED-all=7521&marked-GE-4:7(7613)▪19:21(5375)-EX-28:38(7522)-LE-1:4▪7:18▪10:19(3190)▪19:7▪22:21(7522),23,25,27▪23:11(7522)-1SA-18:5(3190)▪25:35(5375)-ES-10:3-JOB-42:9(5375)-IS-56:7(7522)-JER-37:20(5307)▪42:2(5307)▪**N.T.**-all=2144&marked-LU-4:24(1184)-AC-10:35(1184)-RO-15:31-2CO-5:9(2101)▪6:2(1184),2▪8:12,17(1209)▪11:4(1209)-EPH-1:6(5487)

ACCEPTEST-LU-20:21(2983)

ACCEPTETH-JOB-34:19(5375)-EC-9:7(7521)-HO-8:13(7521)▪**N.T.**-GA-2:6(2983)

ACCEPTING-HEB-11:35(4327)

ACCESS-all=4318-RO-5:2-EPH-2:18▪3:12

ACCOMPANIED-AC-10:23(4905)▪11:12(2064,4862)▪20:4(4902),38(4311)

ACCOMPANY-HEB-6:9(2192)

ACCOMPANYING-2SA-6:4(5973)

ACCOMPLISH-all=3615&marked-LE-22:21(6381)-1KI-5:9(6213)-JOB-14:6(7521)-PS-64:6(8552)-IS-55:11(6213)-JER-44:25(6965)-EZE-6:12▪7:8▪13:15▪20:8,21-DA-9:2(4390)▪**N.T.**-LU-9:31(4137)

ACCOMPLISHED-all=4390&marked-2CH-36:22(3615)-ES-2:12-JOB-15:32-PR-13:19(1961)-IS-40:2-JER-25:12,34▪29:10-LA-4:11(3615),22(8552)-EZE-4:6(3615)▪5:13^2(3615)-DA-11:36(3615)▪12:7(3615)▪**N.T.**-4130&marked-LU-1:23▪2:6,21,22▪12:50(5055)▪18:31(5055)▪22:37(5055)-JOH-19:28(5055)-AC-21:5(1822)-1PE-5:9(2005)

ACCOMPLISHING-HEB-9:6(2005)

ACCOMPLISHMENT-AC-21:26(1604)

ACCORD-LE-25:5(5599)-JOS-9:2(6310)▪**N.T.**-all=3661&marked-AC-1:14▪2:1,46▪4:24▪5:12▪7:57▪8:6▪12:10(844),20▪15:25▪18:12▪19:29-2CO-8:17(830)-PH'P-2:2(4861)

ACCORDING-all=5921,a=6310&marked-GE-33:14(7272)▪41:40▪43:7▪45:21▪47:12a▪49:28(834)▪50:12(3651)-EX-6:26▪12:4sup,4a▪16:16sup,16a,18a,21a▪17:1▪28:21,21sup▪38:21▪39:14^3-LE-4:35▪5:12▪25:16^{2}a,51a,52a▪27:8a,16a,18(5921)a-NU-2:34sup,34▪3:16,51▪4:37,41,45,49^3▪6:21a▪7:5a,7a,8a▪9:20^2▪10:13▪26:54a,56(5921),a▪35:8a,24▪36:5-DE-17:10(5921)a,11^2▪25:2(1767)▪34:5-JOS-15:13(413)▪17:4(413)▪18:4a▪19:50▪22:9-1KI-6:3(5921,6440)▪8:39(3605)▪17:1a-2KI-23:35-1CH-25:2,6-2CH-3:4,8▪31:2a-EZR-6:13(6903),14(4481)-PR-12:8a-EC-1:6-IS-59:18▪63:7-ZEC-5:3^2(3644)-MAL-2:9a▪**N.T.**-all=2596&marked-M'T-1:t▪2:16▪9:29▪16:27▪25:15-M'R-1:t▪7:5-LU-1:t,9,38▪2:22,24,29,39▪12:47(4314)▪23:56-JOH-1:t▪7:24▪18:31-AC-2:30▪4:35(2530)▪7:44▪11:29(2531)▪13:23▪22:3,12▪24:6-RO-1:3,4▪2:2,6,16▪4:18▪8:27,28▪9:3,11▪10:2▪11:5,8(2531)▪12:6^2▪15:5▪16:25^2,26-1CO-1:31(2531)▪3:8,10▪15:3,4-2CO-1:17▪4:13▪5:10(4314)▪8:12(2526)▪9:7(2531)▪10:2,13,15▪11:15▪13:10-GA-1:4▪2:14(4314)▪3:29-EPH-1:4(2531),5,7,9,11,19▪2:2^2▪3:7,11,16,20▪4:7,16,22▪6:5-PH'P-1:20▪3:21▪4:19-COL-1:11,25,29▪3:22-2TH-1:12-1TI-1:11,18▪6:3-2TI-1:1,8,9▪2:8▪4:14-TIT-1:1,3▪3:5,7-HEB-2:4▪7:5▪8:4,5,9▪9:19-JAS-2:8-1PE-1:2,3,14,17▪3:7▪4:6^2,19-2PE-1:3(5613)▪3:13,15-1JO-5:14-RE-2:23▪18:6▪20:12,13▪22:12(5613)

ACCORDINGLY-IS-59:18(5922)

ACCOUNT-1CH-27:24(4557)-2CH-26:11(6486)-JOB-33:13(6030)-PS-144:3(2803)-EC-7:27(2808)▪**N.T.**-all=3056&marked-M'T-12:36▪18:23-LU-16:2-AC19:40-RO-14:12-1CO-4:1(3049)-PH'P-4:17-PH'M-18(1677)-HEB-13:17-1PE-4:5-2PE-3:15(2233)

ACCOUNTED-all=2803&marked-DE-2:11,20-1KI-10:21-2CH-9:20-PS-22:30(5608)-IS-2:22▪**N.T.**-M'R-10:42(1380)-LU-20:35(2661)▪21:36(2661)▪22:24(1380)-RO-8:36(3049)-GA-3:6(3049)

ACCOUNTING-HEB-11:19(3049)

ACCOUNTS-DA-6:2(2941)

ACCURSED-all=2764&marked-DE-21:23(7045)-JOS-6:17,18,18(2763),18▪7:1^2,11,12^2,13^2,15▪22:20-1CH-2:7-IS-65:20(7043)▪**N.T.**-all=331-RO-9:3-1CO-12:3-GA-1:8,9

ACCUSATION-EZR-4:6(7855)▪**N.T.**-all=2724&marked-M'T-27:37(156)-M'R-15:26(156)-LU-6:7(2724)▪19:8(4811)-JOH-18:29(2724)-AC-25:18(156)-1TI-5:19(2724)-2PE-2:11(2920)-JUDE-9(2920)

ACCUSE-PR-30:10(3960)▪**N.T.**-all=2723&marked-M'T-12:10-M'R-3:2-LU-3:14(4811)▪11:54▪23:2,14-JOH-5:45▪8:6-AC-24:2,8,13▪25:5▪25:11▪28:19-1PE-3:16(1908)

ACCUSED-DA-3:8(399,7170)▪6:24(399,7170)▪**N.T.**-all=2723&marked-M'T-27:12-M'R-15:3-LU-16:1(1225)▪23:10-AC-22:30▪23:28(1458),29(1458)▪25:16▪26:2(1458),7(1458)-TIT-1:6(1722,2724)-RE-12:10

ACCUSER-RE-12:10(2725)

ACCUSERS-all=2725&marked-JOH-8:10-AC-23:30,35▪24:8▪25:16,18-2TI-3:3(1228)-TIT-2:3(1228)

ACCUSETH-JOH-5:45(2723)

ACCUSING-RO-2:15(2723)

ACCUSTOMED-JER-13:23(3928)

ACKNOWLEDGE-all=5234&marked-DE-21:17▪33:9-PS-51:3(3045)-PR-3:6(3045)-IS-33:13(3045)▪61:9▪63:16-JER-3:13(3045)▪14:20(3045)▪24:5-DA-11:39▪**N.T.**-all=1921-1CO-14:37▪16:18-2CO-1:13^2

ACKNOWLEDGED-GE-38:26(5234)-PS-32:5(3045)▪**N.T.**-2CO-1:14(1922)

ACKNOWLEDGETH-supplied

ACKNOWLEDGING-all=1922-2TI-2:25-TIT-1:1-PH'M-6

ACKNOWLEDGMENT-COL-2:2(1922)

ACQUAINT-JOB-22:21(5532)

ACQUAINTANCE-all=3045&marked-2KI-12:5(4378),7(4378)-JOB-19:13▪42:11-PS-31:11▪55:13▪88:8,18▪**N.T.**-LU-2:44(1110)▪23:49(1110)-AC-24:23(2398)

ACQUAINTED-PS-139:3(5532)-IS-53:3(3045)

ACQUAINTING-EC-2:3(5090)

ACQUIT-JOB-10:14(5352)-NA-1:3(5352)

ACRE-1SA-14:14(4618)

ACRES-IS-5:10(6776)

ACT-IS-28:21(5656)■59:6(6467)■N.T.-JOH-8:4(1888)

ACTIONS-1SA-2:3(5949)

ACTIVITY-GE-47:6(2428)

ACTS-all=1697&marked-DE-11:3(4639),7(4639)-2SA-23:20(6467)-1KI-10:6■11:41^2■14:19,29■15:7,23,31■16:5,14,20,27■22:39,45-2KI-1:18■8:23■10:34■12:19■13:8,12■14:15,18,28■15:6,11,15,21,26,31,36■16:19■20:20■21:17,25■23:19(4640),28■24:5-1CH-11:22(6467)■29:29-2CH-9:5,29■12:15■13:22■16:11■20:34■25:26■26:22■27:7■28:26■32:32■33:18■35:26■36:8-ES-10:2(4640)-PS-103:7(5949)■N.T.-AC-1:t(4234)

ADAMANT-EZE-3:9(8068)-ZEC-7:12(8068)

ADD-all=3254&marked-GE-30:24-LE-5:16■6:5■27:13,15,19,27,31-NU-5:7■35:6(5414)-DE-4:2■12:32■19:9■29:19(5595)-2SA-24:3-1KI-12:11,14-2KI-20:6-1CH-22:14-2CH-10:14■28:13-PS-69:27(5414)-PR-3:2■30:6-IS-29:1(5595)■30:1(5595)■38:5■N.T.-M'T-6:27(4369)-LU-12:25(4369)-PH'P-1:16(2018)-2PE-1:5(2023)-RE-22:18^2(2007)

ADDED-all=3254&asmarked-DE-5:22-1SA-12:19-JER-36:32■45:3-DA-4:36(3255)■N.T.-all=4369&asmarked-M'T-6:33-LU-3:20■12:31■19:11-AC-2:41,47■5:14■11:24-GA-2:6(4323)■3:19

ADDER-GE-49:17(8207)-PS-58:4(6620)■91:13(6620)-PR-23:32(6848)

ADDERS'-PS-140:3(5919)

ADDETH-all=3254-JOB-34:37-PR-10:22■16:23■N.T.-GA-3:15(1928)

ADDICTED-1CO-16:15(5021)

ADDITION-1KI-7:30(3914)

ADDITIONS-all=3914-1KI-7:29,36

ADJURE-1KI-22:16(7650)-2CH-18:15(7650)■N.T.-M'T-26:63(1844)-M'R-5:7(3726)-AC-19:13(3726)

ADJURED-JOS-6:26(7650)-1SA-14:24(422)

ADMINISTERED-2CO-8:19(1247),20(1247)

ADMINISTRATION-2CO-9:12(1248)

ADMINISTRATIONS-1CO-12:5(1248)

ADMIRATION-N.T.-JUDE-16(2296)-RE-17:6(2295)

ADMIRED-2TH-1:10(2296)

ADMONISH-all=3560-RO-15:14-1TH-5:12-2TH-3:15

ADMONISHED-EC-4:13(2094)■12:12(2094)-JER-42:19(5749)■N.T.-AC-27:9(3867)-HEB-8:5(5537)

ADMONISHING-COL-3:16(3560)

ADMONITION-all=3559-1CO-10:11-EPH-6:4-TIT-3:10

ADO-M'R-5:39(2350)

ADOPTION-all=5206-RO-8:15,23■9:4-GA-4:5-EPH-1:5

ADORN-1TI-2:9(2885)-TIT-2:10(2885)

ADORNED-JER-31:4(5710)■N.T.-all=2885-LU-21:5-1PE-3:5-RE-21:2

ADORNETH-IS-61:10(5710)

ADORNING-1PE-3:3(2889)

ADULTERER-all=5003-LE-20:10-JOB-24:15-IS-57:3

ADULTERERS-all=5003-PS-50:18-JER-9:2■23:10-HO-7:4-MAL-3:5■N.T.-all=3432-LU-18:11-1CO-6:9-HEB-13:4-JAS-4:4

ADULTERESS-LE-20:10(5003)-PR-6:26(802,376)-HO-3:1(5003)■N.T.-RO-7:3^2(3428)

ADULTERESSES-all=5003-EZE-23:45^2(5003)■N.T.-JAS-4:4(3428)

ADULTERIES-JER-13:27(5004)-EZE-23:43(5004)-HO-2:2(5005)■N.T.-M'T-15:19(3430)-M'R-7:21(3430)

ADULTEROUS-PR-30:20(5003)■N.T.-all=3428-M'T-12:39■16:4-M'R-8:38

ADULTERY-all=5003-EX-20:14-LE-20:10^2-DE-5:18-PR-6:32-JER-3:8,9■5:7■7:9■23:14■29:23-EZ-16:32■23:37^2-HO-4:2,13,14■N.T.-all=3431&marked-M'T-5:27,28,32^2(3429)■19:9^2(3429),18-M'R-10:11(3429),12(3429),19-LU-16:18^2■18:20-JOH-8:3(3430),4-RO-2:22^2■13:9-GA-5:19(3430)-JAS-2:11^2-2PE-2:14(3428)-RE-2:22

ADVANCED-1SA-12:6(6213)-ES-3:1(5375)■5:11(5375)■10:2(1431)

ADVANTAGE-JOB-35:3(5532)■N.T.-RO-3:1(4053)-2CO-2:11(4122)-JUDE-16(5622)

ADVANTAGED-LU-9:25(5623)

ADVANTAGETH-1CO-15:32(3786)

ADVENTURE-DE-28:56(5254)■N.T.-AC-19:31(1325)

ADVENTURED-J'G-9:17(7993)

ADVERSARIES-all=6862&marked-EX-23:22(6696)-DE-32:27,43-JOS-5:13-1SA-2:10(7378)-2SA-19:22(7854)-EZR-4:1-NE-4:11-PS-38:20(7853)■69:19(6887)■71:13(7853)■81:14■89:42■109:4(7853),20(7853),29(7853)-IS-1:24■9:11■11:13(6887)■59:18■63:18■64:2-JER-30:16■46:10■50:7-LA-1:5,7,17■2:17-MIC-5:9-NA-1:2■N.T.-all=480&marked-LU-13:17■21:15-1CO-16:9-PH'P-1:28-HEB-10:27(5227)

ADVERSARY-all=7854&marked-EX-23:22(6887)-NU-22:22-1SA-1:6(6869)■29:4-1KI-5:4■11:14,23,25-ES-7:6(6862)-JOB-31:35(376,7379)-PS-74:10(6862)-IS-50:8(1166,4941)-LA-1:10(6862)■2:4(6862)-4:12(6862)-AM-3:11(6862)■N.T.-all=476&marked-M'T-5:25^2-LU-12:58■18:3-1TI-5:14(480)-1PE-5:8

ADVERSITIES-1SA-10:19(7451)-PS-31:7(6869)

ADVERSITY-all=6869&marked-2SA-4:9-2CH-15:6-PS-10:6(7451)■35:15(6761)■94:13(7451)-PR-17:17■24:10-EC-7:14(7451)-IS-30:20(6862)■N.T.-HEB-13:3(2558)

ADVERTISE-NU-24:14(3289)-RU-4:4(1540,241)

ADVICE-all=1697&marked-J'G-19:30(5779)■20:7-1SA-25:33(2940)-2SA-19:43-2CH-10:9(3289),14(6098)■25:17(3289)-PR-20:18(8458)■N.T.-2CO-8:10(1106)

ADVISE-2SA-24:13(3045)-1KI-12:6(3289)-1CH-21:12(7200)

ADVISED-PR-13:10(3289)■N.T.-AC-27:12(1012,5087)

ADVISEMENT-1CH-12:19(6098)

ADVOCATE-1JO-2:1(3875)

AFAR-all=7350&marked-GE-22:4■37:18-EX-2:4■20:18,21■24:1■33:7(7368)-NU-9:10-1SA-26:13-2KI-2:7■4:25(5048)-EZR-3:13-NE-12:43-JOB-2:12■36:3,25■39:25,29-PS-10:1■38:11■65:5■138:6(4801)■139:2-PR-31:14(4801)-IS-23:7■59:14■66:19-JER-23:23■30:10■31:10(4801)46:27■51:50-MIC-4:3■N.T.-all=3113&marked-M'T-26:58■27:55-M'R-5:6■11:13■14:54■15:40-LU-16:23■17:12(4207)■18:13■22:54■23:49-AC-2:39(3112)-EPH-2:17(3112)-HEB-11:13(4207)-2PE-1:9(3467)-RE-18:10,15,17

AFFAIRS-1CH-26:32(1697)-PS-112:5(1697)-DA-2:49(5673)■3:12(5673)■N.T.-EPH-6:21(2596),22(4012)-PH'P-1:27(4012)-2TI-2:4(4230)

AFFECT-GA-4:17^2(2206)

AFFECTED-AC-14:2(2559)-GA-4:18(2206)

AFFECTETH-LA-3:51(5953)

AFFECTION-1CH-29:3(7521)■N.T.-RO-1:31(794)-2CO-7:15(4698)-COL-3:2(5426),5(3806)-2TI-3:3(794)

AFFECTIONATELY-1TH-2:8(2442)

AFFECTIONED-RO-12:10(5387)

AFFECTIONS-RO-1:26(3806)-GA-5:24(3804)

AFFINITY-all=2859-1KI-3:1-2CH-18:1-EZR-9:14

AFFIRM-RO-3:8(5346)-1TI-1:7(1226)-TIT-3:8(1226)

AFFIRMED-all=1340&marked-LU-22:59-AC-12:15■25:19(5335)

AFFLICT-all=6031&marked-GE-15:13■31:50-EX-1:11■22:22,23-LE-16:29,31■23:27,32-NU-24:24■29:7■30:13-J'G-16:5,6,19-2SA-7:10-1KI-11:39-2CH-6:26-EZR-8:21-JOB-37:23-PS-44:2(7489)■55:19■89:22■94:5■143:12(6887)-IS-9:1(3513)■51:23(3013)■58:5■64:12-JER-31:28(7489)-LA-3:33-AM-5:12(6887)■6:14(3905)-NA-1:12-ZEP-3:19

AFFLICTED-all=6031,a=6041&marked-EX-1:12-LE-23:29-NU-11:11(7489)-DE-26:6-RU-1:21(7489)-2SA-22:28a-1KI-2:26^2-2KI-17:20-JOB-6:14(4523)■30:11■34:28a-PS-18:27a■22:24a■25:16a■82:3a■88:7,15a■90:15■102:ta■107:17■116:10■119:67,71,75,107■129:1(6887),2(6887)■140:12a-PR-15:15a■22:22a■26:28(1790)■31:5(6040)-IS-9:1(7043)■49:13a■51:21a■53:4,7■54:11a■58:3,10■60:14■63:9(6862)-LA-1:4(3013),5(3013),12(3013)-MIC-4:6(7489)-NA-1:12-ZEP-3:12a■N.T.-all=2346&marked-M'T-24:9(2347)-2CO-1:6-1TI-5:10-HEB-11:37-JAS-4:9(5003)■5:13(2553)

AFFLICTEST-1KI-8:35(6031)

AFFLICTION-all=6040&marked-GE-16:11■29:32■31:42■41:52-EX-3:7,17■4:31-DE-16:3■26:7-1SA-1:11-2SA-16:12(5869)-1KI-22:27^2(3905)-2KI-14:26-2CH-18:26^2(3905)■20:9(6869)■33:12(6887)-NE-1:3(7451)■9:9-JOB-5:6(205)■10:15■30:16,27■36:8,15,21-PS-22:24(6039)■25:18■44:24■66:11(4157)■88:9■106:44(6862)■107:10,39(7451),41■119:50,92,153-IS-30:20(3905)■48:10■63:9(6869)-JER-4:15(205)■15:11(6869)■16:19(6869)■30:15(7667)■48:16(7451)-LA-1:3,7,9■3:1,19-HO-5:15(6862)-AM-6:6(7667)-OB-13(7451)-JON-2:2(6869)-NA-1:9(6869)-HAB-3:7(205)-ZEC-1:15(7451)■8:10(6862)■10:11(6869)■N.T.-all=2347&marked-M'R-4:17■13:19-AC-7:11,34(2561)-2CO-2:4■4:17■8:2-PH'P-1:16■4:14-1TH-1:6■3:7-HEB-11:25(4797) JAS 1:27■5:10(2552)

AFFLICTIONS-PS-34:19(7451)■132:1(6031)■N.T.-all-2347&marked-AC-7:10■20:23-2CO-6:4-COL-1:24-1TH-3:3-2TI-1:8(4777)■3:11(3804)■4:5(2553)-HEB-10:32(3804),33-1PE-5:9(3804)

AFFORDING-PS-144:13(6329)

AFFRIGHT -2CH-32:18(3372)

AFFRIGHTED-DE-7:21(6206)-JOB-18:20(270,8178)■39:22(2865)■39:22(2865)-IS-21:4(1204)-JER-51:32(926)■N.T.-M'R-16:5(1568),6(1568)-LU-24:37(1719)-RE-11:13(1719)

AFOOT-M'R-6:33(3979)-AC-20:13(3978)

AFORE-2KI-20:4(3808)-PS-129:6(6924)-IS-18:5(6440)-EZE-33:22(6440)■N.T.-RO-1:2(4279)■9:23(4282)-EPH-3:3(4270)

AFOREHAND-M'R-14:8(4301)

AFORETIME-NE-13:5(6440)-JOB-17:6(6440)-IS-52:4(7223)-JER-30:20(6924)-DA-6:l0(4481,6928,1836)■N.T.-JOH-9:13(4218)-RO-15:4(4270)

AFRAID-all=3372&marked-GE-3:10■18:15■20:8■28:17■31:31■32:7■42:28(2729),35■43:18-EX-3:6■14:10■15:14(7264)■34:30-LE-26:6(2729)-NU-12:8■22:3(1481)-DE-1:17(1481),29■2:4■5:5■7:18,19(3373)■9:19(3025)■18:22(1481)■20:1■28:10,60(3025)■31:6(6206)-JOS-1:9(6206)■9:24■11:6-J'G-

7:3(2730)-RU-3:8(2729)-1SA-4:7■7:7■17:11,24■18:12,15(1481),29■21:1(2729),12■23:3(3373)■28:5,13,20■31:4-2SA-1:14■6:9■14:15■17:2(2729)■22:5(1204),46(2296)-1KI-1:49(2729)-2KI-1:15■10:4■19:6■25:26-1CH-10:4■13:12■21:30(1204)-2CH-20:15■32:7-NE-2:2■4:14■6:9,13-ES-7:6(1204)-JOB-3:25(3025)■5:21,22■6:21■9:28(3025)■11:19(2729)■13:11(1204),21(1204)■15:24(1204)■18:11(1204)■19:29(1481)■21:6(926)■23:15(6342)■32:6(2119)■33:7(1204)■39:20(7493)■41:25(1481)-PS-3:6■18:4(1204),45(2727)■27:1(6342)■49:16■56:3,11■65:8■77:16(2342)■83:15(926)■91:5■112:7,8■119:120-PR-3:24(6342),25■31:21-EC-12:5-IS-8:12(6206)■10:24,29(2729)■12:2(6342)■13:8(926)17:2(2729)■19:16(2729),17(6342)■20:5(2865)■31:4(2865),9(2865)■33:14(6342)■37:6■40:9■41:5(2729)■44:8(7297)■51:7(2865),12■57:11(1672)-JER-1:8■2:12(8175)■10:5■26:21■30:10(2729)■36:16(6342),24(6342)■38:19(1672)■39:17(3025)■41:18■42:11,11(3373),11,16(1672)■46:7(2729)-EZE-2:6[3]■27:35(8175)■30:9(2729)■32:10(8175)■34:28(2729)■39:26(2729)-DA-4:5(1763)■8:17(1204)-JOE-2:22-AM-3:6(2729)-JON-1:5,10-MIC-4:4(2729)■7:17(6342)-NA-2:11(2729)-HAB-2:17(2865)■3:2-ZEP-3:13(2729)-MAL-2:5(2865)■N.T.-all=5399-M'T-2:22■14:27,30■17:6,7■25:25■28:10-M'R-5:15,36■6:50■9:6(1630),32■10:32■16:8-LU-2:9■8:25,35■12:4■24:5(1719)-JOH-6:19,20■14:27(1168)■19:8-AC-9:26■10:4(1719)■18:9■22:9(1719),29-RO-13:3,4-GA-4:11-HEB-11:23-1PE-3:6,14-2PE-2:10(5141)

AFRESH-HEB-6:6(388)

AFTER-all=310,a=5921&marked-GE-5:4,7,10,13,16,19,22,26,30■6:4■9:9,28■10:1,32■11:10,11,13,15,17,19,21,23,25■13:14■14:17■15:1■16:3(7093),13■17:7[2],8,9,10,19■18:5,12,19■19:6■22:1,20■23:19■24:55,67■25:11,26■26:18■31:23,36■33:2(314),7■35:5,12■37:17■39:7■40:1■41:3,6,19,23,27,30■44:4■45:15■48:1,4,6,6a■50:14-EX-3:20■7:25■10:14■11:8■14:4,8,9,10,23,28■15:20■18:2■23:2■28:43■29:29■33:8■34:15,16[2],27a-LE-13:7,35,55,56■14:8,43[3],48■15:28■16:1■17:7■19:31(413)■20:5,6(413),6■25:15,46,48■26:33■27:18-NU-4:15■6:19,20,21a■7:88■8:15,22■9:17■12:14■13:25(7093)■15:13(3602),39[2]■25:8,13■26:1■30:15■32:15■35:28-DE-1:4,8■3:14a■4:37,40■6:14■8:19■10:15■11:4,28■12:25,28,30■13:2,4■21:13■24:4■28:14■29:22■31:16,27,29-JOS-1:1■2:5,7[2]■3:2(7097),3■6:9,13■8:6,16[2],17■9:16■10:14,19■20:5■22:27■23:1■24:6,20,29-J'G-1:1,6■2:10,17■3:22,28[2],31■4:14,16[2]■5:14■6:34,35■7:23■8:5,12,27,33■10:1,3■12:8,11,13■13:11■15:7■16:22(834)■19:3■20:45-RU-1:15,16■2:2,3,7,9■4:4-1SA-1:9[2]■5:9■6:12■7:2■8:3■10:5■11:5,7[2]■12:21■13:4■14:12,13[2],22,36,37■15:31■17:35,53■18:30(167)■20:37(311),38(311)■22:20■23:25,28■24:8,14[3],21■25:13,19,42(7272),42■26:3,18■30:8-2SA-1:1,10■2:1,19,24,25,28■3:26■5:13■7:12■8:1■10:1■12:28a■13:1,17,18■15:1,7(7093),13,16(7272),17(7272),18(7272)■17:1,21■18:16,18a,22■20:2,6,7[2],10,11,13,14■21:1,14,18■23:9,10,11■24:10-1KI-1:6,13,14,17,20,24,27,30,35,40■2:28[2]■3:12■9:21■11:2,4,5[2],6,10■13:14,23,31,33■15:4■16:24a■17:7(7093),13(314),17■19:11,12[2],20,21■20:15■21:1-2KI-1:1■5:20,21[2]■6:24■7:14,15■9:25,27■10:29■14:17,19,22■17:15■18:5■23:3,25■25:5-1CH-2:24■5:25■8:8(4480)■10:2■11:12■14:14■17:11■18:1■19:1■20:1(6256),4■27:7,34■28:8-2CH-1:12■2:17■8:8■11:16,20■13:19■18:2(7093),19[2](3602)■20:1,35■21:18■22:4■24:4,17■25:14,25,27sup,27■26:2,17■31:2a■32:1,9■33:14■34:31,14■35:20-EZR-2:61a■3:10a■5:12(4481)■7:1■9:10,13-NE-3:16,17,18,20,21,22,23[2],24,25,27,29[2],30[2],31■5:8(1767)■7:63a■11:8■12:32,38■13:6(7093),19-ES-2:1,12(7093)■3:1■9:26a-JOB-3:1■18:20(314)■19:26■21:3,21,33■29:22■30:5a■31:7■37:4■39:8,10■41:32■42:7,16-PS-42:1a,1(413)■49:17■51:t(834)■63:8■68:25■110:4a-PR-7:22■20:7,25-EC-1:11(314)■2:12,18■3:22■4:16(314)■6:12■7:14■9:3■10:14■12:2-SONG-1:4-IS-43:10■45:14■65:2-JER-2:2,5,8,23,25■3:7,17■5:8(413)■7:6,9■8:2■9:14,14,16,22■11:10■12:6,15■13:6(7093),9(3602),10■16:11,12,16■18:12■24:1■25:6,26■28:12■29:2,10(6310)■30:18a■31:19[2],33■32:18,39■34:8■35:15■36:27■39:5■40:1■41:16■42:7(7093),16■49:37■50:21■51:46■52:8-EZE-5:2,12■6:9■9:5■12:14■16:23■20:16,24,30sup,30■23:30■29:16■33:31■40:1■44:10,26■46:12■48:31a-DA-2:39(870)■3:29(1836)■4:26(1767)■7:6(870),7(870),24(311)■8:1■9:26■11:13(7093)-HO-2:5,13■5:8,11■11:10-JO-2:2-AM-2:4,7a■7:1-ZEC-2:8■6:6■7:14■N.T.-all=3326,a=2596,b=3694&marked-M'T-1:12■3:11(3694)■6:9(3779),32(1934)■10:38b■12:39(1934)■15:23(3693)■16:4(1934),24b■17:1(3326)■23:3a■24:29■25:19■26:2,32,73■27:31(3753),53,63-M'R-1:7b,14,17b,20b,36(2614)■2:1(1223)■4:28(1534)■8:12(1934),25(1534),31,34b■9:2■12:34(3765)■13:24■14:1,28,70■16:12,19-LU-1:24,59(1909)■2:27a,42a,46■5:27■6:1(1207)■7:11(1836)■9:23b,28■10:1■12:4,5,30(1934)■13:9(1519,3195)■14:27b■15:4(1909),13■19:14b■20:40(2089)■21:8b,26(4329)■22:20,58■23:26(3693),55(2628)-JOH-1:15b,27b,30b,35(1887)■2:6a,12■3:22■4:43■5:1,4■6:1■7:1■8:15a■11:7,11■12:19b■13:5(1534),12(3753),27■19:28,38■20:26■21:1-AC-1:3■3:24(2517)■5:37,37b■7:5,7,45■9:23(5613)■10:24,37,41■12:4■13:15,20,22a,25■15:13,16,17(1567),36■16:10(5613)■18:1■19:4,21(5613),21■20:1,6,18(4459),29,30b■21:1(5613),15■23:3a,25(4023)■24:1,14a,17(1223),24,27(4137)■25:1,13(1230)■26:5a■27:21(5225)■28:11,13,17-RO-2:5a■3:11(1567)■5:14(1909)■7:22a■8:1a,4a,5[2]a,12a,13a■10:20(1905)■14:19(1377)-1CO-1:21(1894),26a■7:7(3779),40a■10:6(1938),18a■11:25(5615)■12:28(1899)■15:6(1899),7(1899),32a-2CO-5:16[2]a■7:9a,11a■9:14(1971)■10:3a,7a■11:17a,18a-GA-1:11a,18a■2:1(1223)■3:15a,17■4:23a,29[2]a-EPH-1:11a■4:24a-PH'P-1:8(1971)■2:26(1971)-COL-2:8[3]a,22a■3:10a-2TH-2:9a■3:6a-1TI-5:15(3694),24(1872)-2TI-4:3a-TIT-1:1a,4a■3:4(3753),10-HEB-4:7,11(1722)■5:6a,10a■6:20a■7:2(1899),11[2]a,15a,16[2]a,17a,21a■8:10■9:3,27■10:15,16,26■11:8(3195)■12:10a-JAS-3:9a-1PE-3:5(3779)■-2PE-1:15■2:6(3195),10b■3:3a-2JO-6a-3JO-6(516)-JUDE-7b,16a,18a-RE-4:1■7:1,9■11:11■12:15b■13:3b■15:5■18:1■19:1■20:3

AFTERNOON-J'G-19:8(5186,3117)

AFTERWARD-all=310,a=310,3651&marked-GE-10:18■15:14a■32:20a■38:30-EX-5:1■34:32a-LE-14:19,36a■16:26a,28a■22:7-NU-5:26■12:16■19:7■31:2,24■32:22-DE-17:7(314)■24:21-JOS-2:16■8:34a■10:26a■24:5-J'G-1:9■7:11■16:4a■19:5-1SA-24:5a,8a-2SA-3:28a-1CH-2:21-2CH-35:14-EZR-3:5a-PS-73:24-IS-1:26a■9:1(314)-JER-21:7a■34:11a■46:26a■49:6a-HO-3:5-JOE-2:28a■N.T.-all=5305&marked-M'T-4:2■21:29,32■25:11-M'R-4:17(1534)■16:14-LU-4:2■8:1(2517)■17:8(3326,5023)■18:4(3326,5023)-JOH-5:14(3326,5023)-AC-13:21(2547)-1CO-15:23(1899),46(1899)-HEB-4:8(3326,5023)■12:11(5305),17(3347)-JUDE-5(1208)

AFTERWARDS-all=310&marked-GE-30:21-EX-11:1(310,3651)-DE-13:9(314)-1SA-9:13(310,3651)-JOB-18:2-PR-20:17■24:27■28:23■29:11(268)■N.T.-JOH-13:36(5305)-GA-1:21(1899)

AGAIN-all=7725,a=5750,b=3254&marked-GE-4:2b,25a■8:10b,12b,21[2]b■14:16■15:16■18:29b■22:5■24:5,6,8,20■25:1b■26:18■28:15,21■29:3,33a,34a,35a■30:7a,19a,31■35:9a■37:14,22■38:4a,5a,26b■40:21■42:24,37■43:2,12[2],13,21■44:8,25■48:21■50:5-EX-4:7[3]■10:8,29b■14:13b,26■15:19■23:4■24:14■33:11■34:35-LE-13:6(8145),7(8145),16■14:39,43■25:51,52■26:26-NU-11:4■17:10■22:8,15b,25b,34■23:16■32:15b■33:7■35:32-DE-1:22,25■5:30■13:16a■18:16b■22:1,2■24:4,13,19,20(310)■28:68,68b■30:9-JOS-5:2■8:21■14:7■18:8■22:32-J'G-3:12b,19■4:1b■6:18■8:9,33■9:37b,a■10:6b■11:8,9,13,14b,a■13:1b,8a,9■15:19■19:3,7■20:22b,23b,25a,28b,48■21:14-RU-1:11,12,14a,21■4:3-1SA-3:5,6b,6,8b,21b■5:3,11■6:21■9:8b■15:25,30,31■17:30■19:8b,21b■20:17b■23:4b,23■25:12■27:4b■29:4■30:12-2SA-2:22b,a■3:11a,26b,34b■5:22b■6:1a■12:23a■14:13,21,29a■15:8,25,29■16:19(8145)■18:22b■19:30,37■20:10(8138)■21:15a,18a,19a■22:38■24:1b-1KI-2:30,41■8:33:34■12:5,12,20,21,27[2]■13:4,6[2],9,17,33■17:21,22■18:37(322),43■19:6,7,20■20:5,9-2KI-1:6,11,13■2:18■4:22,31,38■5:10,14■7:8■9:18,20,36■13:25■19:9,30b■20:5■21:3■22:9,20■24:7b-1CH-13:3(5437)■14:13b,14a■20:5a,6a■21:12,27-2CH-6:25■10:5,12■11:1■12:11■13:20a■18:32■19:4■20:27■24:11,19■28:17■30:6,9[2]■32:25■33:3,13■34:16a,28-EZR-2:1■6:5(1946),21■9:14-NE-7:6■8:17■9:28,29■13:9,21(3138)-ES-6:12■7:2(1571)■8:3b-JOB-6:29a■10:9,16■14:7a■29:22(8138)■34:15-PS-18:37■37:21(7999)■60:1■68:22[2]■71:20[2]■78:39■80:3,7,19■85:6,8■104:9■126:4-PR-2:19■3:28■19:17(7999),19b,24■23:35a■26:15-EC-1:6,7■3:20■4:11(1571)-IS-7:10b■8:5b■10:20b■11:11b■24:20b■37:31b■38:8■46:8■49:5,20a■51:2■52:8-JER-3:1a■12:15■15:19■16:15■18:4■19:11a■23:3■24:6■25:5■27:16■28:3,4,6■29:14■30:3,18■31:4[2]a,16,17,21,23■32:15a,37■33:10a,12a,13a■36:28■37:8■41:16■46:16■48:47■49:6,39■50:19-LA-3:40-EZE-3:20■4:6(8145)■5:4a■7:7(1906)■8:6a,13a,15a■16:53■26:21a■29:14■33:15(7999)■34:4,16■39:25,27■47:1-DA-2:7(8579)■9:25■10:18b-HO-1:6a-JOE-3:1-AM-7:8b,13■8:2b,14a■9:14-JON-2:4b-MIC-7:19-HAG-2:20(8145)-ZEC-2:12a■4:1,12(8145)■8:15■10:6,9,10■12:6a-MAL-2:13(8145)■N.T.-all=3825,a=450&marked-M'T-2:8(518)■4:7,8■5:33■7:2(488),6(4762)■11:4(518)■13:44,45,47■16:21(1453)■17:9a,23(1453)■18:19■19:24■20:5,19a■21:36■22:1,4■26:32(1453),42,43,44,52(654),7■27:3(654),50,63(1453)-M'R-2:1,13■3:1,20■4:1■5:21■7:31■8:13,25,31a■10:1[2],10,24,32,34a■11:27■12:4,5■13:16(1994)■14:39,40,61,69,70[2]■15:4,12,13-LU-2:34(386),45(5290)■4:20(591)■6:30(523)34(618),35(560),38(488)■8:37(5290),55(1994)■9:8a,19a,39(3326),42(591)■10:6(344),17(5290),35(1880)■13:20■14:6(470),12(479)■15:24(326),32(326)■17:4(1994)■18:33a■20:11(4388),12(4388)■23:11(375),20■24:7a-JOH-1:35■3:3(509),7(509)■4:3,13,46,54■6:15,39a■8:2,8,12,21■9:15,17,24(1537,1208),26,27■10:7,17,18,19,31,39,40■11:7,8,23a,24a,38■12:22,28,39■13:12■14:3■16:16■17,19,22,28■18:7,27,33,38,40■19:4,9,37■20:9a,10,21,26■21:1,16-AC-1:6(600)■7:26(1515),39(4762)■10:15,16■11:9(1537,1208),10■13:33a,37(1453)

14:21(5290)■15:16^{2}(456),36(1994)■17:3a,
32■18:21■21:6(5290)■22:17(5290)■
27:28-RO-4:25(1453)■8:15,34(1453)■
10:7(321)■11:23,35(467)■15:10,11,12
-1CO-3:20■7:5■12:21■15:4(1453)
-2CO-1:16■2:1■3:1■5:12,15(1453)■
10:7■11:16■12:19,21■13:2-GA-
1:9,17■2:1,18■4:9^{2},19■5:1,3-PH'P-
1:26■2:28■4:4,10(330),16(1364)
-1TH-2:18(1364)■3:9(467)■4:14a-TIT-
2:9(483)-PH'M-12(375)-HEB-1:5,6■
2:13^{2}■4:5,7■5:12■6:1,6■10:3(364),30■
11:35(386)■13:20(321)-JAS-5:18-1PE-
1:3(313),23(313)■2:23(486)-2PE-2:20,
22(1994)-1JO-2:8-RE-10:8,11■19:3
(1208)■20:5(326)

AGAINST-all=5921,a=413,b=7125,
c=4136,d=5973,e=5048,f=5980,g=6440,
h=5227&marked-GE-4:8a■14:15■15:10b■
21:16^{2}c■34:30■37:18(834)■40:2^{3}■42:36■
43:18,25(5704)■50:20-EX-7:15b■9:17■14:2g,
5a,27b■15:7(6965),24■16:2,7^{2},8^{2}■17:3■
23:29■25:27f,37(5676)g■26:17a■35h■
28:27f■37:14f■39:20f■40:24h-LE-4:14■
19:16-NU-8:2c,g,3cg■10:9,21(5704),
13:31(431)■14:2,27^{2},29,35,36■16:3^{2},
11^{2},19,41^{2},42^{2}■17:5■20:2,18b,20b,24
(4775)■21:23b,33b■22:5c,25a,34b■
24:10a■25:4e■26:9^{3}■27:3■30:9■31:3,
7-DE-1:1c,44b■2:19c,32b■3:1b■3:29c■
4:46c■9:7d,19,24d■11:30c■15:9sup,9■
19:11■20:1,3,4d,10,12d,19^{2},20■21:10■
22:26■23:4,9■24:15■28:7,7a,25a,49■
29:7b■31:21g,27d■32:49g■34:1g,6c
-JOS-3:16e■5:13e■8:5b,14b,22b,33c■9:1c,
18■10:5,6a,29d,31,34,36,38■11:5d,7,20b■
18:17h,18c■19:47d■22:11c,12,33-J'G-
1:10a,11a■3:10,12■4:24■5:20d■6:2,3,4,31■
7:2,24b■9:18,31,33a,34,43,50a■11:4d,5d,
12a,20d,25^{2}d■12:3a■14:5b■15:10,14b■
18:9■19:2,10h■20:5,9,11a,14d,18d,19,20,
20sup,23d,23a,24a,25b,28d,30^{2}a,31b,
34e,43h-1SA-3:12a■4:1b,2b■7:7a■
9:14b■11:1■12:12■14:5^{2}c,52■15:7g■
17:2b,21b,33a,35,55b■22:8^{2},13,13a■
23:3a,9,28b■24:7a■25:17a,17,20b■
27:10^{2}b,10a■30:23■31:3a-2SA-
5:23c■10:9a,9b,10b,17b■11:23,25a■
12:11,28■14:7,13■16:13f■17:21■18:6b,
12a,13e,31,32■20:15a■23:8,18■24:4a,4
-1KI-6:5,5sup,10■7:4a,5c,a,20f,39c■8:44■
12:21d,24d■13:2,4^{2},32^{2}■14:25■15:17,
20,27■16:1,7^{2}a,9,12a,15■20:12,22,26d,
27b,29h■22:6,15a,32,35h-2KI-3:7sup,
7a,27■7:6■8:28d■9:14a,21b■10:9■
12:17■13:12d■14:19■15:10,19,25,30■
16:7,9a,11(5704)■17:3,9■18:9,13,25^{2}■
19:8,20a,22^{2},27a,28a,32■21:23,24■
22:19^{2}■23:17,29,29b■24:11■25:1^{2},4
-1CH-5:11e,20■8:32e,9:38e■10:1,3,
13sup,13■11:11,20■12:19,21■14:8
(6640),10,14c■19:10a,10b,11b,17a,17b■
21:1,4■24:31^{2}(5980)■25:8(5980)■26:12
(5984),16(5984)■27:24-2CH-4:10c■
6:34■8:3■9:29■11:1d,4d,4a■12:2,
9■13:3(5973),6,7,12,12d■14:9a,10g,11,
11d■16:1,4a■17:1,10d■18:22,34h■
20:1,2,12g,12,16,17g,22,22sup,23,
29d,37■21:16■22:5,7a■24:21,23,25,
26■25:27■26:7^{2},13■27:5■28:12,13sup,
13■32:1,2,9,16^{2},17,19a,19■33:24,25■
34:27^{2}■35:20sup,20b,21,21a■36:6
-EZR-4:5,6,8(5922),19(5922)■7:23
(5922)■8:22sup,22,-NE-2:19■3:10e,
16e,19e,23e,25e,26e,27e,28e,29e,
30e,31e■4:9■5:1a,7■6:12■7:3e■
9:10■12:9e,24e,24f,37e,38c■
13:2-ES-2:1■5:1^{2}h,9■7:7a■8:3■9:24,25
-JOB-9:4a■10:17e,17d■11:5d■13:26■
15:13a,25^{2}a■16:4,10■17:8■18:9■19:5^{2},
11,12■21:27■23:6(5978)■30:12■31:21,
38■32:14a■33:10,13a■34:6,29■39:23
-PS-2:2^{2}■3:1,6■15:3,5■21:11,12■27:3^{2}■
31:13,18■35:3b,15,20,21,26■38:16■41:7^{2},
9■54:3■55:12■56:5■59:3■62:3■81:14■
83:3^{2},5■86:14■92:11■94:16^{2}d,21■109:2,
20■119:69■124:2■137:9a■138:7-PR-3:29■
19:3■21:30e■30:31d-EC-7:14f■9:14a,
14■10:4-IS-2:4a■3:8■5:25sup,25,30■
7:1^{2},5■9:11,21■10:6sup,6,15^{2},24■13:17■
14:4,8,22■19:17■23:8,11a■29:3^{3},7,
7sup,8■31:2^{2},4■32:6a■36:1,10,10a■37:8,
21a,23,23a,28a,29a,33■42:13■54:15,17,
17sup,■57:4^{2}-JER-1:15^{2},16,18,18^{3}sup,
19a,19sup■4:16^{2},17,17sup■6:3,4,6,23■
11:17,17sup,19■12:8,9,14■13:14a■
15:6,8,20a■16:10,10sup■18:8,11,18,23■
19:15■21:2,13a,13■22:7■23:2,30,31,32■
25:9^{3},13^{2},30^{2}a■26:9a,11a,12^{2}a,13,19^{2},20■
27:13a■28:8a,8,16a■29:32■31:39e■
32:24,29■34:1,7^{2},7a,22■35:17■36:2^{2},7a,
31a■37:8,19^{2}■39:1a■44:7a,29■46:1■
47:1a,7a■48:2,26,42■49:14,19a,20^{2}a,
30^{2},34a■50:1^{2}a,3,9,9sup,14,14sup,
15,21^{2},21a,29a,29,29a,31a,42,45^{2}a■51:1,
1a,2,3^{2}a,11,12a,14,25a,27^{3},28,29,46,60a,
62a■52:4^{2}-LA-1:15■2:16■3:5,46,61,
62sup,62■5:22-EZE-1:20f,21f■3:8^{2}f,
13f■4:2^{4},3a,3,7■5:8■6:2a■11:4■13:2a,
8a,17a,17,20a■16:37,40,44■19:8■
20:46a■21:2a,3a,4a,15,22,31■22:3■
23:22^{2},24^{2}■24:2a■25:2a,2,3^{3}a,6a■26:2,3^{2},
8^{3}■27:30■28:7,21a,21,22■29:2^{2},3,10^{2}a,
18a,18■30:11,22a■34:2,10a■35:2^{2},3a,3,
12,13^{2}■36:2,5^{2}■38:2a,2,3a,8,16^{2},17,18,
21,21sup■39:1,1a■40:13e,18f,23e■
41:15g,16e■42:1e,3^{2}e,7f,10^{2}g■44:12■
45:6f,7f■46:9h■47:20(5704)h■48:13f,
15(5921)g,18^{2}f,21a,g,21(5921)g,21f-DA-
3:19(5922),29(5922)■5:5(6903),23(5922)■
6:5(5922),5sup■7:25(6655)■8:7a,12,25■
9:12^{2}■11:14,16a,24,25^{2},28,30,36,40-HO-
7:13sup,13,15a■8:1^{2}■10:9,10-AM-1:8■3:1^{2}■
5:1,9^{2}■6:14■7:9,10,16^{2}-OB-1-JON-1:2,
13-MIC-2:3,4■3:5■4:3a,11■5:1,5-NA-
1:9a,11■2:13a■3:5-HAB-2:6-ZEP-
1:16^{2}■2:5,8,10,13-ZEC-9:13■10:3■12:2^{2},
3,7,9■13:7^{2}■14:2a,12,13,16-MAL-
3:13^{2}■N.T.-all=2596,a=1909,b=1519,
c=4314&marked-M'T-4:6c■5:11,23■
10:21a,35^{3}■12:14,25^{2},26a,30,32^{2}■16:18
(2729)■18:15b,21b■20:11,24(4012)■
21:2(561)■23:13(1715)■24:7^{2}a■26:55a,
59,62(2649)■27:1,61(561)-M'R-3:6,24a,
25a,26a,29b■9:40■10:11a■11:2(2713),
25■12:12c,41(2713)■13:3(2713),8^{2}a,
12a■14:5(1690),48a,55,56,57■15:39(1537,
1727)-LU-2:34(483)■4:11c■5:30c■6:49
(4366)■7:30b■8:26(495)■9:5a,50■
11:17^{2}a,18a,23■12:10^{2}b,52a,53^{6}a■
14:31sup,31a■15:18b,21b■17:3b,
4b■19:30(2713)■20:19c■21:10^{2}a■
22:52a,53a,65b-JOH-12:7b■13:18b■
18:29sup,29■19:11,12(483)-AC-
4:14(471),26^{2},27a■6:1c,11b,13■8:1a■
9:1b,5c,29c■13:45(483),50a,51a■
14:2■16:22■19:16,36(386),38c■
20:15(481)■21:28■22:24(2019)■
23:30c■24:1,19c■25:2,3,7,8^{3}b,15,18
(4012),19c,27■26:10(2702),11(1693),
14c■27:7^{2},14■28:17(1727),19(483),22
(483)-RO-1:18a,26(3844)■2:2a,5(1722)■
4:18(3844)■7:23(497)■8:7b,31■9:20(470)■
11:2,18(2620)-1CO-4:6■6:1c,18b■
8:12^{2}b■9:17(210)-2CO-10:2a,5■13:8
-GA-3:21■5:17^{2},23-EPH-6:11c,12^{4}c
-COL-2:14■3:13c,19c-1TI-5:11(2691),
19■6:19b-2TI-1:12b-HEB-12:3b,4c
-JAS-2:13(2620)■3:14■5:9-1PE-2:11,12a■
3:12a-2PE-2:11■3:7b-3JO-10(5396)
-JUDE-9(2018),15-RE-2:4,14,16(3326),
20■11:7(3326)■12:7■13:6c■19:19^{2}(3326)

AGATE-EX-28:19(7618)■39:12(7618)
-EZE-27:16(3539)

AGATES-IS-54:12(3539)

AGE-all=3117&marked-GE-15:15
(7872)■18:11■24:1■25:8(7872)■47:28■
48:10(2207)-NU-8:25(1121)-JOS-23:1,
2-J'G-8:32(7872)-RU-4:15(7872)-1SA-
2:33(582)-1KI-14:4(7869)-1CH-23:3
(1121),24(1121)■29:28(7872)-2CH-36:17
(3486)-JOB-5:26(3624)■8:8(1755)■11:17
(2465)■30:2(3624)-PS-39:5(2465)■
92:14(7872)-IS-38:12(1755)■46:4(2209)
-ZEC-8:4■N.T.-all=2244&marked
-LU-2:36(2250)-JOH-9:21,23-1CO-7:36
(5230)-HEB-5:14(5046)■11:11

AGED-all=2205&marked-2SA-19:32
(2204)-JOB-12:20■15:10(3453)■29:8■
32:9-JER-6:11■N.T.-TIT-2:2(4246),3
(4247)-PH'M-9(4246)

AGES-EPH-2:7(165)■3:5(1074),21
(1074)-COL-1:26(165)

AGO-all=7350&marked-1SA-9:20
(3117)-2KI-19:25-EZR-5:11(6928)
-IS-22:11■37:26■N.T.-all=575&marked
-M'T-11:21(3819)-LU-10:13(3819)-AC-
10:30■15:7-2CO-8:10■9:2■12:2(4253)

AGONE all supplied

AGONY-LU-22:44(74)

AGREE-all=4856&marked-M'T-5:25
(2132)■18:19■20:13-M'R-14:59(2470)
-AC-15:15-1JO-5:8(1526)-RE-17:17
(4160,3391,1106)

AGREED-AM-3:3(3259)■N.T.
-M'T-20:2(4856)-M'R-14:56(2470)
-JOH-9:22(4934)-AC-5:9(4856),40(3982)■
23:20(4934)■28:25(800)

AGREEMENT-IS-28:15(2374),
18(2380)-DA-11:6(4339)-2CO-6:16(4783)

AGREETH-M'R-14:70(3662)
-LU-5:36(4856)

AGROUND-AC-27:41(2027)

AGUE-LE-26:16(6920)

AH-all=162&marked-PS-35:25(253)
-IS-1:4(1945),24(1945)-JER-1:6■4:10■
14:13■22:18^{2}(1945)■32:17■34:5(1945)
-EZE-4:14■9:8■11:13■20:49■21:15
(253)■N.T.-M'R-15:29(3758)

AHA-all=253-PS-35:21■40:15■70:3
-IS-44:16-EZE-25:3■26:2■36:2

AIDED-J'G-9:24(2388,3027)

AILED-all supplied

AILETH-all supplied

AIR-all=8064&marked-GE-1:26,28,
30■2:19,20■6:7■7:3■9:2-DE-4:17■
28:26-1SA-17:44,46-2SA-21:10-1KI-
14:11■16:4■21:24-JOB-12:7■28:21■
41:16(7307)-PS-8:8-PR-30:19-EC-10:20■
N.T.-all=3772,a=109&marked-M'T-
6:26■8:20■13:32-M'R-4:4,32-LU-8:5■
9:58■13:19-AC-10:12■11:6■22:23a
-1CO-9:26a■14:9a-EPH-2:2a-1TH-
4:17a-RE-9:2a■16:17a

ALABASTER-all=211-M'T-26:7
-M'R-14:3-LU-7:37

ALARM-all=8643&marked-NU-10:5,
6^{2},7(7321)9(7321)-2CH-13:12(7321)-JER-
4:19■49:2-JOE-2:1(7321)-ZEP-1:16

ALAS-all=162&marked-NU-12:11
(994)■24:23(188)-JOS-7:7-J'G-6:22■
11:35-1KI-13:30(1945)-2KI-3:10■6:5,15
-JER-30:7(1945)-EZE-6:11(253)-JOE-
1:15-AM-5:16(1930)■N.T.-all=3759
-RE-18:10,16,19

ALBEIT-PH'M-19(2448)

ALGUM-all=418-2CH-2:8■9:10,11

ALIEN-all=2537&marked-EX-18:3
(1616)-DE-14:21-JOB-19:15-PS-69:8
-IS-61:5(5236)

ALIENATE-EZE-48:14(5674)

ALIENATED-all=5361&marked
-EZE-23:17(3363),18(3363),18,22,28■
N.T.-EPH-4:18(526)-COL-1:21(526)

ALIENS-LA-5:2(5237)■N.T.-EPH-
2:12(526)-HEB-11:34(245)

ALIKE-all=3126&marked-DE-12:22■
15:22-1SA-30:24-JOB-21:26-PS-33:15
-PR-20:10(1571)■27:15(7737)-EC-9:2
(834)■11:6(259)

ALIVE-all=2421,a=2416&marked
-GE-6:19,20■7:3■12:12■43:7a,27a,28a■
45:26a,28a■46:30a■50:20-EX-1:17,18,
22■4:18a-LE-14:4a■16:10a-NU-16:33a■
21:35(8300)■22:33■31:15,18-DE-4:4a■
5:3■6:24■20:16■31:27a■32:39-JOS-
2:13■6:25a■8:23a■14:10-J'G-8:19■
21:14-1SA-2:6■15:8a■27:9,11-2SA-8:2■
12:18a,21a,22a■18:14a-1KI-18:5■20:18^{2}a,
32a■21:15a-2KI-5:7■7:4,12a■10:14^{2}a
-2CH-25:12a-PS-22:29■30:3■33:19■
41:2-PR-1:12a-EC-4:2a-JER-49:11
-EZE-7:13a■13:18,19■18:27-DA-5:19
(2418)■N.T.-all=2198&marked-M'T-

27:63-**M'R**-16:11-**LU**-15:24(326),32(326)■24:23-**AC**-1:3■9:41■20:12■25:19-**RO**-6:11,13■7:9-**1CO**-15:22(2227)-**1TH**-4:15,17-**RE**-1:18■2:8■19:20

ALLEGING-**AC**-17:3(3908)

ALLEGORY-**GA**-4:24(238)

ALLELUIA-all=239-**RE**-19:1,3,4,6

ALLIED-**NE**-13:4(7138)

ALLOW-**LU**-11:48(4909)-**AC**-24:15(4327)-**RO**-7:15(1097)

ALLOWANCE-**2KI**-25:30(737)

ALLOWED-**1TH**-2:4(1381)

ALLOWETH-**RO**-14:22(1381)

ALLURE-**HO**-2:14(6601)■**N.T.**-**2PE**-2:18(1185)

ALMIGHTY-all=7706-**GE**-17:1■28:3■35:11■43:14■48:3■49:25-**EX**-6:3-**NU**-24:4,16-**RU**-1:20,21-**JOB**-5:17■6:4,14■8:3,5■11:7■13:3■15:25■21:15,20■22:3,17,23,25,26■23:16■24:1■27:2,10,11,13■29:5■31:2,35■32:8■33:4■34:10,12■35:13■37:23■40:2-**PS**-68:14■91:1-**IS**-13:6-**EZE**-1:24■10:5-**JOE**-1:15■**N.T.**-all=3841-**2CO**-6:18-**RE**-1:8■4:8■11:17■15:3■16:7,14■19:15■21:22

ALMOND-**EC**-12:5(8247)-**JER**-1:11(8247)

ALMONDS-all=8246&marked-**GE**-43:11(8247)-**EX**-25:33^{2},34■37:19^{2},20-**NU**-17:8(8247)

ALMOST-all=4592-**EX**-17:4-**PS**-73:2■94:17■119:87-**PR**-5:14■**N.T.**-**AC**-13:44(4975)■19:26(4975)■21:27(3195)■26:28(1722,3641),29(1722,3641)-**HEB**-9:22(4975)

ALMS-all=1654-**M'T**-6:1,2,3,4-**LU**-11:41■12:33-**AC**-3:2,3,10■10:2,4,31■24:17

ALMSDEEDS-**AC**-9:36(1654)

ALMUG-**1KI**-10:11(484),12^{2}(484)

ALOES-all=174-**NU**-24:6-**PS**-45:8-**PR**-7:17-**SONG**-4:14■**N.T.**-**JOH**-19:39(250)

ALONE-all=905&marked-**GE**-2:18■32:24■42:38■44:20-**EX**-14:12(2308)■18:14,18■24:2-**LE**-13:46(909)-**NU**-11:14,17■23:9(909)-**DE**-1:9,12■9:14(7503)■32:12(909)■33:28(909)-**JOS**-22:20(259)-**J'G**-3:20■11:37(7503)-**1SA**-21:1-**2SA**-18:24,25,26-**1KI**-11:29-**2KI**-4:27(7503)■19:15■23:18sup,18(4422)-**1CH**-29:1-**EZR**-6:7(7662)-**NE**-9:6-**ES**-3:6-**JOB**-1:15,16,17,19■7:16(2308),19(7503)■9:8■10:20(7896)■15:19■31:17-**PS**-83:18■86:10■102:7(909)■136:4■148:13-**PR**-9:12-**EC**-4:10(259)-**IS**-2:11,17■5:8■14:31(909)■37:16■44:24■49:21■51:2(259)■63:3-**JER**-15:17(909)■49:31(909)-**LA**-3:28-**DA**-10:7,8-**HO**-8:9(909)■**N.T.**-all=3441&marked-**M'T**-4:4■14:23■15:14(863)■18:15-**M'R**-1:24(1439)■4:10(2651),34(2596,2398)■6:47■14:6(863)■15:36(863)-**LU**-4:4,34(1439)■5:21■6:4■9:18(2651),36■10:40■13:8(863)-**JOH**-6:15,22■8:9,16,29■11:48(863)■12:7(863),24■16:32^{2}■17:20(3440)-**AC**-5:38(1439)■19:26(3440)-**RO**-4:23(3440)■11:3-**GA**-6:4-**1TH**-3:1-**HEB**-9:7-**JAS**-2:17(2596,1438)

ALONG-all=1980&marked-**1SA**-6:12■28:20(4393,6967)-**2SA**-3:16-**JER**-41:6

ALOOF-**PS**-38:11(5048)

ALOUD-all=7442&marked-**GE**-45:2(5414,854,6963)-**1KI**-18:27(6963,1419),28(1419,3605)-**EZR**-3:12(7311,1419)-**JOB**-19:7(7768)-**PS**-51:14■55:17(1993)■59:16■81:1■132:16■149:5-**IS**-24:14(6670)■54:1(6670)■58:1(1627)-**DA**-3:4(2429)■4:14(2429)■5:7(2429)-**HO**-5:8(7321)-**MIC**-4:9(7452)■**N.T.**-**M'R**-15:8(310)

ALREADY-all=3528-**EC**-1:10■2:12■3:15■4:2■6:10■**N.T.**-all=2235&marked-**M'T**-5:28■17:12-**M'R**-15:44-**LU**-12:49-**JOH**-3:18■4:35■9:22,27■11:17■19:33-**AC**-27:9-**1CO**-5:3-**2CO**-12:21(4258)-**PH'P**-3:12^{2},16(5348)-**2TH**-2:7-**1TI**-5:15-**2TI**-2:18-**1JO**-4:3

ALSO-all=1571,a=637&marked-**GE**-3:6,22■4:4,22,26■6:3(7683),4■7:3■10:21■13:5,16■14:7,16^{2}■15:14■16:13■17:16■18:23a,24a■19:21,34,35■20:4,6■24:14,19,44,46^{2}■26:21■27:31,34,38,45■29:27,30^{2},33■30:3,6,15,30■31:15■32:6,18■33:7■35:17■38:10,11,22,24■40:15,16a■42:22■43:8■44:9,10,16,29■46:4,34■47:3■48:11,19^{2}■50:18,23-**EX**-1:10■2:19■3:9■4:9,14■6:4,5■7:11^{2},23■8:21,32■10:24,25,26■12:32^{2},38■18:23■19:22■21:29,35■33:12,17-**LE**-23:27(389),39(389)■26:16a,24a,39,39a,40a,41a,42^{2}a-**NU**-4:22■11:4■12:2■16:10■18:2,3,28■22:19,33■24:12,24,25■27:13-**DE**-1:37■2:6,11a,20a■3:3,20■9:19,20■10:10■15:17a■26:13■28:61■33:28a-**JOS**-1:15■2:12■7:11^{2}■10:30■22:7■24:18-**J'G**-1:22■2:3,10,21■3:22,31■5:4,15(3651)■6:35■7:18■8:9,22,31■9:19,49■10:9■15:5(5704)■17:2■19:19-**RU**-1:5,12,17(3541)■2:16-**1SA**-1:6,28■2:15,26■3:17(3541)■4:17^{2}■8:8,20■10:11,12,26■12:14■13:4■14:15,21,22,44(3541)■15:29■18:5■19:20,21,22,23,24^{2}■22:17■23:17■25:13,22(3541)■26:25■28:19^{2},22-**2SA**-1:4^{2}■2:2,6,7■3:9(3541),19^{2},35(3541)■4:2■5:2■7:19■11:12,17,21,24■12:13,14■13:36■14:7■15:19^{2},24■17:5,10■18:2,22,26■19:13(3541),40,43■20:14a,26■21:20-**1KI**-1:6,46,48■2:5,23(3541)■3:13,18■4:15■7:20,31■10:11■13:18■14:23,24■15:13■16:7,16■18:35■19:2(3541)■20:10(3541)■21:19,23■22:22-**2KI**-6:31(3541)■8:1■9:27■13:6■17:19■21:11■22:19■23:19,27■24:4-**1CH**-8:32a■9:38a■10:13■12:38■16:30(637)■18:11■20:6■23:26■29:9-**2CH**-9:10■12:12■14:15■15:16■18:21■21:4,13,17■22:3,5■23:13■24:7,12■26:20■28:2,8■29:7,35■30:1,12■31:6■34:27■36:13,22-**EZR**-1:1■5:10(638),14(638)■6:5(638)-**NE**-2:18a■5:13,16■6:7,19■13:15a,22,23-**ES**-1:9■4:16■5:12■7:8,9■9:13,15-**JOB**-1:6■2:1■13:2,16■16:4,19■31:28■32:10a,17^{2}■33:6■36:29a,33a■37:1,11■40:8a,14-**PS**-16:7a,9a■19:13■38:10■65:13sup,13a■68:8a,18a■71:18,22,24■74:16a■77:16a,17a■78:20,21■83:8■84:6■89:5a,11a,21a,27a,43a■93:1(389)■96:10a■119:3a,23■132:12a-**PR**-1:26■9:2a■11:25■17:26■18:3,9■19:2■21:13■23:28a■24:23a■25:1a■26:4■30:31(176)-**EC**-1:17■2:1,7,8,9a,14,15,19,21,23,24,26■3:11,13■4:4,8,14,16^{2}■5:10,16,17,19■6:3,9■7:6,14,18,21,22■8:10,14,16■9:3,6,12,13■10:3■11:2■12:5-**SONG**-1:16a-**IS**-5:2■7:13,20■13:3■14:10■21:12■23:12■26:12■28:7,29■30:5■31:2■33:2a■34:14sup,14(389),15(389)■40:24■44:19a■45:16■46:11^{2}a■48:12a,13a■66:4,21-**JER**-2:16,33,34,36■3:8■4:12■10:5■13:23■14:5■25:14■26:20■27:6■28:14■31:36,37■33:21■36:6■46:21^{2}■48:2,7,26sup,26,34■50:24^{2}■52:10-**LA**-2:9■3:8■4:21-**EZE**-5:11■8:18■9:10■10:16■16:41,43,52^{2}■20:12,15,23,25■21:9,17■23:35,37■24:3,5■31:17■39:16-**DA**-6:22(638)■11:8,22-**HO**-3:3■4:3,5,6sup,6■5:5■6:11■9:12■10:6-**JO**-1:12,20■2:12,29-**AM**-4:6,7-**MIC**-6:13-**NA**-3:10,11^{2}-**HAB**-2:5a,15a,16-**ZEP**-2:12-**ZEC**-3:7^{2}■8:6,21■9:2,11■11:8■13:2■14:14-**MAL**-2:9■**N.T.**-all=2532,a=2504-**M'T**-2:8a■3:10■5:39,40■6:14,21■10:4,32a,33a■12:45■13:22(1161),23(1211),26,29(260)■15:3,16■16:1,18(1161)■17:12■18:33,35■19:3,28■20:4,7■21:21(2579),24a■22:26,27■23:26,28■24:27,37,39,44■25:11,17,22,41,44■26:13,35,69,71,73■27:41(1161),44,57-**M'R**-1:19,38(2546)■2:15,21,26,28■3:19■7:18■8:7,38■11:25,29a■12:6,22■14:9,31,67■15:31,40,41,43-**LU**-1:3a,35,36■2:4,35■3:9,12,21■4:23,41,43■5:10,36,39■6:4,5,6,13,14,16,29^{2},31,32,33,34,36■7:8,49■8:36■9:61■10:1,39■11:1,4,18,30,34^{2},40,45,46,49■12:8(1161),8,34,40,54■13:6(1161),8■14:12^{2},26■16:1,10^{2},14,22,28■17:24,26,28■18:15■19:9,19■20:3a,11(2528),12,31,32■21:2■22:20,24,39,56,58,59,68■23:7,27,32,35,36,38,51,55■24:22,23-**JON**-3:23■4:45■5:18,19,27■6:24,36,67■7:3,10,47,52■8:17,19■9:15,27,40■10:16(2548)■11:16,33,52■12:9,10,18,26,42■13:9,14,32,34■14:1,3,7,12(2548),19■15:20^{2},23,27■17:1,18a,19,20,21,24(2548)■18:2,5,17,25■19:23,39■20:8■21:3,20,25-**AC**-1:3,11■2:22,26■3:17■5:2,16,32,37(2548)■7:45■8:13,19a■9:32■10:26a,45■11:1,18,30■12:3■13:5,9,22,33,35■14:1,5,15,21■15:27,32,35(1161),35■17:6,12,13(2546),28^{2}■19:17,19(1161)21,27■20:21,30■21:13,16,24,28■22:5^{2},20,29■23:11,30,33,35■24:6,9,15,26(260,1161,2532)■25:22,24■26:10,26,29■27:10,12(2547),36■28:9,10-**RO**-1:6,13,15,16,24,27■2:9,10,12,15(4828)■3:7a,29^{2}■4:6,9,11,12,16,21,24■5:2,3,11,15■6:4,5,8,11■7:4■8:11,17,21,23,26,29,30^{3},32,34■9:1(4828),10,24,25,27(1161)■11:1,5,16,21(3761),22,23(1161),31■13:5,6■15:7,14^{3},22,27■16:2,4,7-**1CO**-1:8,16■2:13■4:8■5:12■6:14■7:3,4,22,40a■9:8■10:6(2548),9,10,13■11:1a,6,12,19,23,25■12:12■13:12■14:15^{2},19,34■15:1,2,3,8a,14,18,21,28,40,42,48^{2},49■16:4a,10-**2CO**-1:5,6,7,11,14^{2},22■2:9,10■3:6■4:10,11,13,14■5:5,11■6:1,13■8:6^{2},7,10,11,14,19,21■9:6^{2},12■10:11,14■11:15,18a,21a■13:4,9-**GA**-2:1,10,13,17■5:21,25■6:1,7-**EPH**-1:11,13^{2},15a,21■2:3,22■4:9,10■5:2,25■6:9,21-**PH'P**-1:15,20,29■2:4,5,9,18,19a,24,27■3:4,12,20■4:3^{2},10,15-**COL**-1:6,7,8,9,29■2:11,12■3:4,7,8,13,15■4:1,3^{2},16-**1TH**-1:5,8■2:8,10,13^{2},14■3:6■4:6,8,14■5:11,24-**2TH**-1:5,11-**1TI**-2:9■3:10■5:13,20,25■6:12-**2TI**-1:5,12■2:2,5,10,11,12,12(2548),20,22(1161)■3:1(1161),8,9■4:8,15-**TIT**-3:3,14-**PH'M**-9,21,22-**HEB**-1:2■2:4(4901),14■3:2■4:10■5:2,3,5,6■7:2^{2},9,12,25■8:3,6■9:1,16■10:15■11:11,19,32(5037)■12:1,26■13:3,12-**JAS**-1:11■2:2,11,19,25,26■3:2,4■5:8-**1PE**-2:5,6,8,18,21■3:1,5,18,19,21■4:6,13■5:1^{2}-**2PE**-1:19■2:1■3:10,15,16^{2},17(4879)-**1JO**-1:3■2:2,6,23,24■3:4■4:11,21■5:1^{2}-**2JO**-1-**3JO**-12-**JUDE**-8,14-**RE**-1:9■2:6a,15■3:10a,21a■6:11■11:8■14:7

ALTAR-all=4196&marked-**GE**-8:20^{2}■12:7,8■13:4,18■22:9^{2}■26:25■33:20■35:1,3,7-**EX**-17:15■20:24,25,26■21:14■24:4,6■27:1^{2},5^{2},6,7■28:43■29:12^{2},13,16,18,20,21,25,36,37^{3},38,44■30:1,18,20,27,28■31:8,9■32:5■35:15,16■37:25■38:1,3,4,7,7sup,30^{2}■39:38,39■40:5,6,7,10^{3},26,29,30,32,33-**LE**-1:5,7,8,9,11^{2},12,13,15^{3},16,17■2:2,8,9,12■3:2,5,8,11,13,16■4:7^{2},10,18^{2},19,25^{2},26,30^{2},31,34^{2},35■5:9^{2},12■6:9^{2},10^{2},12,13,14,15■7:2,5,31■8:11^{2},5^{3},16,19,21,24,28,30■9:7,8,9^{2},10,12,13,14,17,18,20,24■10:12■14:20■6:12,18^{2},20,25,33■17:6,11■21:23■2:22-**NU**-3:26■4:11,13,14,26■5:25,26■7:1,10^{2},11,84,88■16:38,39,46■18:3,5,7,17■23:2,4,14,30-**DE**-12:27^{2}■16:21■26:4■27:5^{2},6■33:10-**JOS**-8:30,31■9:27■22:10,11,16,19^{2},23,26,28,29^{2},34-**J'G**-6:24,25,26,28^{2},30,31,32■13:20^{2}■21:4-**1SA**-2:28,33■7:17■14:35^{2}-**2SA**-24:18,21,25-**1KI**-1:50,51,53■2:28,9■3:4■6:20,22■7:48■8:22,31,54,64■9:25^{2}■12:32,33^{2}■13:1,2^{2},3,4^{2},5^{2},32■16:32■18:26,30,32^{2},35-**2KI**-11:11■12:9■16:10^{2},11,12^{2},13,14^{3},15^{2}■18:22■23:9,15^{2},16,17-**1CH**-6:49^{2}■16:40■21:18,22,26^{2},29■22:1■28:18-**2CH**-1:5,6■4:1,19■5:12■6:12,22■7:7,9■8:12■15:8■23:10■26:16,19■29:18,19,21,22^{3},24,27■32:12■33:16■35:16-**EZR**-3:2,3■7:17(4056)-**NE**-10:34-**PS**-26:6■43:4■51:19■118:27-**IS**-6:6■19:19■27:9■36:7■56:7■60:7-**LA**-2:7-**EZE**-8:5,16■9:2■40:46,47■41:22■43:13^{2},15^{2}(741),16(741),18,22,26,27■45:19■47:1-**JOE**-1:13■2:17-**AM**-2:8■3:14■9:1-**ZEC**-9:15■14:20-**MAL**-1:7,10■2:13■**N.T.**-all=2379&marked-**M'T**-5:23,24■23:18,19,20,35-**LU**-1:11■11:51-**AC**-17:23(1041)-**1CO**-9:13^{2}■10:18-**HEB**-

7:13■13:10-JAS-2:21-RE-6:9■8:3^{2},5■9:13■11:1■14:18■16:7

ALTARS-all=4196-EX-34:13-NU-3:31■23:1,4,14,29-DE-7:5■12:3-J'G-2:2-1KI-19:10,14-2KI-11:18^{2}■18:22■21:3,4,5■23:12^{2},20-2CH-14:3■23:17^{2}■28:24■30:14,14sup■31:1■32:12■33:3,4,5,15■34:4,5,7-PS-84:3-IS-17:8■36:7-JER-11:13^{2}■17:1,2-EZE-6:4,5,6,13-HO-8:11^{2}■10:1,2,8■12:11-AM-3:14■N.T.-RO-11:3(2379)

ALTER-LE-27:10(2498)-EZR-6:11(8133),12(8133)-PS-89:34(8138)

ALTERED-ES-1:19(5674)■N.T.-LU-9:29(1096,2087)

ALTERETH-DA-6:8,12(5709)

ALTHOUGH-all=3588&marked-EX-13:17-2SA-23:5^{2}-1KI-20:5-ES-7:4-JOB-5:6■35:14(637,3588)-EZE-11:16,16(272)-HAB-3:17(272)■N.T.-M'R-14:29(2532,1487)-HEB-4:3(2543)

ALTOGETHER-all=3162&marked-GE-18:21(3617)-EX-11:1(3617)■19:18(3605)-NU-16:13(1571)-2CH-12:12(3617)-PS-19:9■39:5(3605)■53:3■62:9■139:4(3605)-SONG-5:16(3605)-IS-10:8-JER-5:5■10:8(259)■N.T.-JOH-9:34(3650)-AC-26:29(1722,4183)-1CO-5:10(3843)■9:10(3843)

ALWAY-all=3065,3117&marked-EX-25:30(8548)-NU-9:16(8548)-DE-11:1■28:33-2SA-9:10(8548)-1KI-11:36-2KI-8:19(3605,3117)-JOB-7:16(5769)-PS-9:18(5331)■119:112(5769)-PR-28:14(8548)■N.T.-all=104&marked-M'T-28:20(3956,2250)-JOH-7:6(3842)-AC-10:2(1275)-RO-11:10(1275)-2CO-4:11■6:10-PH'P-4:4-COL-4:6-1TH-2:16-2TH-2:13-TIT-1:12-HEB-3:10

ALWAYS-all=8548&marked-GE-6:3(5769)-EX-27:20■28:38-DE-5:29(3605,3117)■6:24(3605,3117)■11:12■14:23(3605,3117)-1CH-16:15(5769)-2CH-18:7(3606,3117)-JOB-27:10(3605,6256)-PS-10:5(3605,6256)■16:8■103:9(5331)-PR-5:19■8:30(3605,6256)-EC-9:8(3605,6256)-IS-57:16(5331)-JER-20:17(5769)-EZE-38:8■N.T.-all=3842&marked-M'T-18:10(1223,3956)■26:11^{2}-M'R-5:5(1275)■14:7^{2}-LU-8:1■21:36(1722,3956,2540)-JOH-8:29■11:42■12:8^{2}■18:20-AC-2:25(1223,3956)■7:51(104)■24:3(3839),16(1275)-RO-1:9-1CO-1:4■15:58-2CO-2:14■4:10■5:6■9:8-GA-4:18-EPH-5:20■6:18(1722,3956,2540)-PH'P-1:4,20■2:12-COL-1:3■4:12-1TH-1:2■3:6-2TH-1:3,11■3:16(1223,3956)-PH'M-4-HEB-9:6(1275)-1PE-3:15(104)-2PE-1:12(104),15(1539)

AM-all=1961-EX-3:14^{2}-JOB-12:3-PS-88:4sup,4■102:6^{2}■N.T.-all=1510&marked-M'T-3:11■8:8,9■11:29■16:13(1511),15(1511)■18:20■20:15■22:32■24:5■27:24,43■28:20-M'R-1:7■8:27(1511),29(1511)■13:6■14:62-LU-1:19■3:16■5:8■7:6,8■9:18(1511),20(1511)■15:19,21■18:11■21:8■22:27,33,58,70-JOH-1:20,21,27■3:28^{2}■4:9(5607),26■6:35,41,48,51■7:28,29,33,34,36■8:12,16,18,23^{2},24,28,58■9:5^{2},9■10:7,9,11,14■11:25■12:26■13:13,19,33■14:3,6■15:1,5■16:32■17:11,14,16,24■18:5,6,8,17,25,35,37■19:21-AC-9:5■10:21,26■13:25(1511),25^{2}■18:10■21:39,39sup■22:3,8■23:6■26:15,29■27:23-RO-1:14■7:14■11:1,13-1CO-1:12■3:4■9:1^{2},2■12:15^{2},16^{2}■13:2■15:9^{2},10-2CO-12:10^{2}-PH'P-4:11-COL-2:5-1TI-1:15-1PE-1:16-2PE-1:13-RE-1:8,11,17,18^{2}■2:23■3:17■18:7■19:10■21:6■22:9,13,16

AMAZED-EX-15:15(926)-J'G-20:41(926)-JOB-32:15(2865)-IS-13:8(8539)-EZE-32:10(8074)■N.T.-all=1839&marked-M'T-12:23■19:25(1605)-M'R-1:27(2284)■2:12■6:51■9:15(1568)■10:32(2284)■14:33(1568)■16:8(1611)-LU-2:48(1605)■4:36(1096,2285)■5:26(1611,2983)■9:43(1605)-AC-2:7,12■9:21

AMAZEMENT-AC-3:10(1611)-1PE-3:6(4423)

AMBASSADOR-all=6735-PR-13:17-JER-49:14-OB-1■N.T.-EPH-6:20(4243)

AMBASSADORS-all=4397&marked-JOS-9:4(6735)-2CH-32:31(3887)■35:21(4397)-IS-18:2(6735)■30:4■33:7-EZE-17:15■N.T.-2CO-5:20(4243)

AMBASSAGE-LU-14:32(4242)

AMBER-all=2830-EZE-1:4,27■8:2

AMBUSH-all=693-JOS-8:2,7,9,12,14,19,21

AMBUSHES-JER-51:12(693)

AMBUSHMENT-2CH-13:13^{2}(3993)

AMBUSHMENTS-2CH-20:22(693)

AMEN-all=543-NU-5:22-DE-27:15,16,17,18,19,20,21,22,23,24,25,26-1KI-1:36-1CH-16:36-NE-5:13■8:6-PS-41:13■72:19■89:52■106:48-JER-28:6■N.T.-all=281-M'T-6:13■28:20-M'R-16:20-LU-24:53-JOH-21:25-RO-1:25■9:5■11:36■15:33■16:20,24,27-1CO-14:16■16:24-2CO-1:20■13:14-GA-1:5■6:18-EPH-3:21■6:24-PH'P-4:20,23-COL-4:18-1TH-5:28-2TH-3:18-1TI-1:17■6:16,21-2TI-4:18,22-TIT-3:15-PH'M-25-HEB-13:21,25-1PE-4:11■5:11,14-2PE-3:18-1JO-5:21-2JO-13-JUDE-25-RE-1:6,7,18■3:14■5:14■7:12^{2}■19:4■22:20,21

AMEND-all=3190&marked-2CH-34:10(2388)-JER-7:3,5■26:13■35:15■N.T.-JOH-4:52(2192,2866)

AMENDS-LE-5:16(7999)

AMERCE-DE-22:19(6064)

AMETHYST-EX-28:19(306)■39:12(306)■N.T.-RE-21:20(217)

AMIABLE-PS-84:1(3039)

AMISS-2CH-6:37(5753)-DA-3:29(7955)■N.T.-LU-23:41(824)-JAS-4:3(2560)

AMONG-all=8432,a=7130,b=996&marked-GE-23:6,10■24:3a■35:2■40:20■42:5-EX-2:5■7:5■12:31,49■17:7a■25:8■28:1■29:45,46■30:13(5921),14(5921)■31:14a■34:9a,10a-LE-11:13(4480)■15:31■16:16(854),29■17:4a,8,10,10a,12,13■18:26,29a■19:34(854)■20:3a,5a,6a,14,18a■22:32■23:30a■24:10■25:33■26:11,12,25-NU-1:47,49■2:33■3:12■4:2,18■5:21,27a■8:6,14,16,19■9:7,14(854)■11:4a,20a,21a■14:11a,13a,14a,42a■15:14,26,29sup,29,30a■16:3,21,33,45■17:6■18:6,20^{2},23,24■19:10,20■25:7,11■26:62^{2}■27:4^{2},7■32:30■35:6(854),15,34-DE-1:42a■2:14a,15a,16a■4:3a■6:15a■7:21a■13:1a,11a,13a,14a■16:11a■17:2a,7a,15a■18:2a,18a■19:19a,20a■21:9a,21a■22:21a,24a■23:16a■24:7a■26:11a■31:16a,17a■32:51-JOS-3:5a,10a■4:6a■7:12a,13a■8:9,35a■9:7a,16a,22a■10:1a■13:13a,22(413)■14:3■15:13■16:9,10a■17:4^{2},6,9■18:7a■19:49■20:4(5973),9■22:7(5973),19,31■23:12(854)■24:5a,23a-J'G-1:16(854),29a,30a,32a,33a■3:5a■5:16b■10:16a■12:4^{2}■18:1-RU-2:7b■4:10(5973)-1SA-2:8(5973)■4:3a■7:3■10:10,11(5973),23■15:6^{2}■31:9(854)-1KI-6:13■11:20■14:7-2KI-4:13■9:2■11:2■23:9-1CH-11:25(4480)■21:6■26:30(5921)-2CH-22:11■24:16(5973)■33:19(5921)-NE-4:11■5:17(4480)■9:17(5973)-ES-3:8b■9:21(5921),28-JOB-1:6■2:1,8■15:19■30:5(1460),7b■33:23(4480)■34:4b,37b■39:25(1767)■41:6b■42:15-PS-55:15a■57:4,4sup■68:13b,25■74:9(854)■82:1■104:10b,12b■109:30■136:11-PR-1:14■6:19b■14:9■15:31a■17:2■27:22■31:23(5973)-EC-6:1(5921)-SONG-2:2^{2}b,3sup,3b-IS-2:4b■24:13■44:4■61:9sup,9-JER-4:3(413)■12:14■25:16b,27b■29:32■37:4■39:14■40:1,5,6■41:8sup,8-LA-1:17b-EZE-1:1,13b■2:5,6(413)■3:15,25■6:13■9:2■11:1■12:10,12■13:19(413)■18:18■19:2b,2,6,11(5921)b■20:9■22:26■29:12sup,12■31:3b,10b,14(413)■33:33■34:12,24■37:21b■39:28(413)■44:9■47:22^{2},22sup,22-DA-7:8(997)-HO-13:15b-OB-4b-MIC-3:11a■4:3b-HAG-2:5-ZEC-1:8b,10b,11b■3:7b■7:14(5921)■N.T.-all=1722,a=4314,b=1519&marked-M'T-2:6■4:23■9:35■11:11■12:11(1537)■13:7(1909),22b,25(303,3319),49(3319)■16:7,8■20:26^{2},27■21:38■26:5■27:56■28:15-M'R-1:27a■4:7b,18b■5:3■6:4■8:16a,19b,20b■9:33a,34a■10:26a,43^{2}■12:7a■13:10b■15:31a,40■16:3a-LU-1:1,25,28,42■2:44■4:36a■7:16,28■8:7(1722,3319),14b■9:46,48■10:3(1722,3319),30(4045),36b■16:15■20:14a■22:23a,24,26,27(1722,3319),37(3326),55(3319)■24:5(3326),47b-JOH-1:14,26(1722,5216)■6:9b,43(3326),52a■7:12,35a,43■9:16■10:19■11:54,56(3326)■12:19a,20(1537),42(1537)■15:24■16:17a,19(3326)■19:24a■21:23b-AC-1:21(1909)■2:22b■4:12,15(4315),17b,34■5:12■6:3(1537),8■10:22(5259)■12:18■13:26■14:14b■15:7,12,19(575),22■17:33(3319),34■18:11■20:25,29b,32■21:19,21(2596),34■23:10(3319)■24:21■25:5,6■26:3(2596),4,18■27:22(1537),28:4a,25a,29-RO-1:5,6,13^{2},24■8:29■11:17■12:3■15:9■16:7-1CO-1:10,11■2:2,6■3:3,18■5:1^{2},2(3319)■6:5,7■11:18,19^{2},30■15:12-2CO-1:19■6:17(3319)■10:1■11:6b,26■12:12,21a-GA-1:16■2:2■3:1,5-EPH-2:3■3:8■5:3-PH'P-2:15-COL-1:27■4:16(3844)-1TH-1:5■2:7(1722,3319)■5:12,13,15b-2TH-1:10(1909)■3:7,11-2TI-2:2(1223)-HEB-5:1(3319)-JAS-1:26■3:6,13■4:1■5:13,14-1PE-2:12■4:8b■5:1,2-2PE-2:1^{2},8-3JO-9-RE-2:13(3844)■7:15(1909)

AMONGST-GE-3:8(8432)■23:9(8432)

AMOUNTING-all supplied

ANATHEMA-1CO-16:22(331)

ANCESTORS-LE-26:45(7223)

ANCHOR-HEB-6:19(45)

ANCHORS-AC-27:29(45),40(45)

ANCIENT-all=6924&marked-DE-33:15-J'G-5:21(6917)-2KI-19:25-1CH-4:22(6267)-EZR-3:12(2204)-JOB-12:12(3453)-PS-77:5(5769)-PR-22:28(5769)-IS-3:2(2204),5(2204)■19:15(2204)■19:11■23:7■37:26■44:7(5769)■45:21■46:10■47:6(2204)■51:9-JER-5:15(5769)■18:15(5769)-EZE-9:6(2204)■36:2(5769)-DA-7:9(6268),13(6268),22(6268)

ANCIENTS-all=2204&marked-1SA-24:13(6931)-PS-119:100-IS-3:14■24:23-JER-19:1^{2}-EZE-7:26■8:11,12■27:9

ANCLE-AC-3:7(4974)

ANCLES-EZE-47:3(657)

ANGEL-all=4397&marked-GE-16:7,9,10,11■21:17■22:11,15■24:7,40■31:11■48:16-EX-3:2■14:19■23:20,23■32:34■33:2-NU-20:16■22:22,23,24,25,26,27,31,32,34,35-J'G-2:1,4■5:23■6:11,12,20,21^{2},22^{2}■13:3,6,9,13,15,16^{2},17,18,20,21^{2}-2SA-14:17,20■19:27■24:16^{3},17-1KI-13:18■19:5,7-2KI-1:3,15■19:35-1CH-21:12,15^{3},16,18,20,27,30-2CH-32:21-PS-34:7■35:5,6-EC-5:6-IS-37:36■63:9-DA-3:28(4398)■6:22(4398)-HO-12:4-ZEC-1:9,11,12,13,14,19■2:3^{2}■3:1,3,5,6■4:1,4,5■5:5,10■6:4,5■12:8■N.T.-all=32-M'T-1:20,24■2:13,19■28:2,5-LU-1:11,13,18,19,26,28,30,34,35,38■2:9,10,13,21■22:43-JOH-5:4■12:29-AC-5:19■6:15■7:30,35,38■8:26■10:3,7,22■11:13■12:7,8,9,10,11,23■23:8,9■27:23-2CO-11:14-GA-1:8■4:14-RE-1:1■2:1,8,12,18■3:1,7,14■5:2■7:2■8:3,5,7,8,10,12,13■9:1,11,13,14■10:1,5,7,8,9■11:1,15■14:6,8,9,15,17,18,19■16:3,4,5,8,10,12,17■17:7■18:1,21■19:17■20:1■21:17■22:6,8,16

ANGEL'S-RE-8:4(32)■10:10(32)

ANGELS-all=4397&marked-GE-19:1,15■28:12■32:1-JOB-4:18-PS-8:5(430)■68:17(8136)■78:49■91:11■103:20■104:4■148:2■**N.T.**-all=32&marked-M'T-4:6,11■13:39,41,49■16:27,18:10,22:30■24:31,36■25:31,41■26:53-M'R-1:13■8:38■12:25■13:27,32-LU-2:15■4:10■9:26■12:8,9■15:10■16:22■20:36(2465)■24:23-JOH-1:51■20:12-AC-7:53-RO-8:38-1CO-4:9■6:3■11:10■13:1-GA-3:19-COL-2:18-2TH-1:7-1TI-3:16■5:21-HEB-1:4,5,6,7^{2},13■2:2,5,7,9,16■12:22■13:2-1PE-1:12■3:22-2PE-2:4,11-JUDE-6-RE-1:20■3:5■5:11■7:1,2,11■8:2,6,13■9:14,15■12:7^{2},9■14:10■15:1,6,7,8■16:1■17:1■21:9,12

ANGELS'-PS-78:25(47)

ANGER-all=639,a=3707&marked-GE-27:45■30:2■44:18■49:6,7-EX-4:14■11:8■32:19,22-NU-11:1,10■12:9■22:22,27■24:10■25:3,4■32:10,13,14-DE-4:25a■6:15■7:4■9:18a,19■13:17■29:20,23,24,27,28■31:17,29a■32:16a,21a,21sup,22-JOS-7:1,26■23:16-J'G-2:12a,14,20■3:8■6:39■8:3(7307)■9:30■10:7■14:19-1SA-11:6■17:28■20:30,34-2SA-6:7■12:5■24:1-1KI-14:9a,15a■15:30a■16:2a,7a,13a,26a,33a■21:22a■22:53a-2KI-13:3■17:11a,17a■21:6a,15a■22:17a■23:19a,26■24:20-1CH-13:10-2CH-25:10^{2},15■28:25a■33:6a■34:25a-NE-4:5a■9:17-ES-1:12(2534)-JOB-9:5,13■18:4■21:17■35:15-PS-6:1■7:6■21:9(6440)■27:9■30:5■37:8■38:3(2195)■56:7■69:24■74:1■77:9■78:21,38,49,50,58a■85:3,4(3708),5■90:7,11■103:8■106:29a■145:8-PR-15:1,18■16:32■19:11■20:2(5674)■21:14■22:8(5678)■27:4-EC-7:9(3708)-IS-1:4(5006)■5:25^{2}■7:4■9:12,17,21■10:4,5,25■12:1■13:3,9,13■14:6■30:27,30■42:25■48:9■63:3,6■65:3a■66:15-JER-2:35■3:12,12sup(6440)■4:8,26■7:18a,19a,20■8:19a■10:24■11:17a■12:13■15:14■17:4■18:23■21:5■23:20■25:6a,7a,37,38■30:24■32:9a,30a,31,32a,37■33:5■36:7■42:18■44:3a,6■49:37■51:45■52:3-LA-1:12■2:1^{2},3,6,21,22■3:43,66■4:11,16(6440)-EZE-5:13,15■7:3,8■8:17a■13:13■16:26a■20:8,21■22:20■25:14■35:11■43:8-DA-9:16■11:20-HO-8:5■11:9■12:14a■13:11■14:4-JOE-2:13-AM-1:11-JON-3:9■4:2-MIC-5:15■7:18-NA-1:3,6-HAB-3:8,12-ZEP-2:2^{2},3■3:8-ZEC-10:3■**N.T.**-all=3709&marked-M'R-3:5-RO-10:19(3949)-EPH-4:31-COL-3:8

ANGERED-PS-106:32(7107)

ANGLE-IS-19:8(2443)-HAB-1:15(2443)

ANGRY-all=599&marked-GE-18:30(2734),32(2734)■45:5(2734)-LE-10:16(7107)-DE-1:37■4:21■9:8,20-J'G-18:25(4751,5315)-2SA-19:42(2734)-1KI-8:46■11:9-2KI-17:18-2CH-6:36-EZR-9:14-NE-5:6(2734)-PS-2:12■7:11(2194)■76:7(639)■79:5■80:4(6225)■85:5-PR-14:17(639)■21:19(3708)■22:24(639)■25:23(2194)■29:22(639)-EC-5:6(7107)■7:9(3707)-SONG-1:6(2734)-IS-12:1-EZE-16:42(3707)-DA-2:12(1149)-JON-4:1(2734),4(2734),9^{2}(2734)■**N.T.**-all=3710&marked-M'T-5:22-LU-14:21■15:28-JOH-7:23(5520)-EPH-4:26-TIT-1:7(3711)-RE-11:18

ANGUISH-all=6869&marked-GE-42:21-EX-6:9(7115)-DE-2:25(2342)-2SA-1:9(7661)-JOB-7:11(6862)■15:24(4961)-PS-119:143(4689)-PR-1:27(6695)-IS-8:22(6695)■30:6(6695)-JER-4:31■6:24■49:24■50:43■**N.T.**-JOH-16:21(2347)-RO-2:9(4730)-2CO-2:4(4928)

ANISE-M'T-23:23(432)

ANOINT-all=4886&marked-EX-28:41■29:7,36■30:26,30■40:9,10,11,13,15^{2}-LE-16:32-DE-28:40(5480)-J'G-9:8,15-RU-3:3(5480)-1SA-9:16■15:1■16:3,12-2SA-14:2(5480)-1KI-1:34■19:15,16^{2}-IS-21:5-DA-9:24■10:3(5480)-AM-6:6-MIC-6:15(5480)■**N.T.**-all=218&marked-M'T-6:17-M'R-14:8(3462)■16:1-LU-7:46-RE-3:18(1472)

ANOINTED-all=4886,a=4899&marked-EX-29:2,29(4888)-LE-2:4■4:3a,5a,16a■6:20,22a■7:12,36■8:10,11,12-NU-3:3■6:15■7:1^{2},10,84,88■35:25-1SA-2:10a,35a■10:1■12:3a,5a■15:17■16:6a,13■24:6^{2}a,10a■26:9a,11a,16a,23a-2SA-1:14a,16a,21a■2:4,7■3:39■5:3,17■12:7,20(5480)■19:10,21a■22:51a■23:1a-1KI-1:39,45■5:1-2KI-9:3,6,12■11:12■23:30-1CH-11:3■14:8■16:22a■29:22-2CH-6:42a■22:7■23:11■28:15-PS-2:2a■18:50a■20:6a■28:8a■45:7■84:9a■89:20,38a,51a■92:10(1101)■105:15a■132:10a,17a-IS-45:1a■61:1-LA-4:20a-EZE-16:9(5480)■28:14(4473)-HAB-3:13a-ZEC-4:14(1121,3323)■**N.T.**-all=5548&marked-M'R-6:13(218)-LU-4:18■7:38(218),46(218)-JOH-9:6(2025,1909),11(2025)■11:2(218)■12:3(218)-AC-4:27■10:38-2CO-1:21-HEB-1:9

ANOINTEDST-GE-31:13(4886)

ANOINTEST-PS-23:5(1878)

ANOINTING-all=4888&marked-EX-25:6■29:7,21■30:25,31■31:11■35:8,15,28■37:29■39:38■40:9,15-LE-7:35^{2}■8:2,10,12,30■10:7■21:10,12-NU-4:16■18:8-IS-10:27(8081)■**N.T.**-JAS-5:14(218)-1JO-2:27^{2}(5545)

ANON-M'T-13:20(2117)-M'R-1:30(2112)

ANOTHER-all=312,a=259,b=7453,c=250&marked-GE-4:25■11:3b■15:10b■26:21,22■29:19■30:24■31:49b■37:9,19c■42:21c,28c■43:33b-EX-10:23c■16:15c■18:16b■21:10,18b■22:5■25:20c■26:3^{2}(269),5(269),17(269),19a,21a,25a■36:10^{2}a,12a,13a,22a,24a,26a■37:8a,9c,19a-LE-7:10c■19:11(5997)■25:14c,17(5997),46c■26:37c■27:20-NU-8:8(8145)■14:4c,24■23:13,27■36:9-DE-20:5,6,7■21:15a,24:2■25:11c■28:30,32■29:28-J'G-2:10■6:29b■9:37a■10:18b■16:7a,11a-RU-2:8■3:14b-1SA-2:25(376)■10:3^{2}a,6,9■10:11b■13:18^{2}a■17:30■20:41^{2}b-2SA-11:25(2090)■18:20,26,26sup-1KI-6:27(3671)■7:8■13:10■14:5(5234),6(5234)■18:6a■20:37■22:20(2088)-2KI-1:11■3:23b■7:3b,6c,8,9b-1CH-2:26■16:20■26:12(251)-2CH-18:19(2088)■20:23b■32:5-NE-3:19(8145),21(8145),24(8145),27(8145),30(8145)■4:19c-ES-1:19(7468)■4:14■9:19b,22b-JOB-1:16(2088),17(2088),18(2088)■19:27(2114)■21:25(2088)■31:8,10■41:16a,17c-PS-16:4■75:7(2088)■105:13sup,13■109:8-PR-25:9■27:2(2114)-EC-4:10(8145)-IS-6:3(2088)■13:8b■28:11■42:8■44:5^{2}(2088)■48:11■65:15,22^{2}-JER-3:1■13:14c■18:4,14(2114)■22:26■25:26c■36:28,32■46:16b-EZE-1:9(269),11(376)■3:13(269)■4:17c■10:9^{2}a■12:3■17:7a■19:5a■22:11^{2}(376)■24:23c■33:30a■37:16a,17a■40:26a,49a■41:11a■47:14c-DA-2:39^{2}(317),43(1836)■5:6(1668),17(321)■7:3(1668),5(317),6(317),8(317),24(321)■8:13a-HO-4:4(376)-JOE-1:3■2:8c-AM-4:7(259)-NA-2:4(8264)-ZEC-2:3■8:21a■11:9(7468)-MAL-3:16b■**N.T.**-all=240,a=243,b=2087&marked-M'T-2:12a■8:9a,21b■10:23a■11:3b■13:24a,31a,33a■19:9a■21:33a,35(3739)■24:10^{2}■25:15(3739),32■26:71a■27:38(1520)-M'R-4:41■9:10(1438),50■10:11a,12a■12:4a,5a■14:19a,58a■16:12b-LU-2:15■6:6b,11■7:8a,19a,20a,32■8:25■9:56b,59b,61b■12:1■14:19b,20b,31b■16:7b,12(245),18b■19:20b■20:11b■22:58b,59a■24:17,32-JOH-4:33,37a■5:7a,32a,43a,44■13:22,34^{2},35■14:16a■15:12,17■18:15a■19:37b■21:18a-AC-1:20b■2:7,12a■7:18b,26■10:28(246)■12:17b■3:35b■17:7b■19:32a,38■21:6,34a-RO-1:27■2:1b,15,21b■7:3^{2}b,4b,23b■9:21(3739)■12:5,10^{2},16■13:8,8b■14:2(3739),4(245),5sup,5(3739),13,19■15:5,7,14,20(245)■16:16-1CO-3:4b,10^{3}a,10b,10a■4:6b■6:1b,7(1438)■7:7(3588)■10:29a■11:21(3739),33■12:8a,9b,9a,10^{4}a,10b,25■14:30a■15:39^{2}a,40b,41^{2}a,41sup■16:20-2CO-10:16(245)■11:4a,4^{2}b■13:12-GA-1:6b,7a■5:13,15^{2},26■6:4b-EPH-4:2,25,32,32(1438)■5:21-COL-3:9,13,13(1438),16(1438)-1TH-3:12■4:9,18■5:11(1520)-1TI-5:21(4299)-TIT-3:3-HEB-3:13(1438)■4:8a■5:6b■7:11b,13b,15b■10:24-JAS-2:25b■4:11,12b■5:9,16^{2}-1PE-1:22■3:8(4835)■4:9,10(1438)■5:5,14-1JO-1:7■3:11,23■4:7,11,12-2JO-5-RE-6:4a,4■7:2a■8:3a■10:1a■11:10■12:3a■13:11a■14:6a,8a,15a,17a,18a■15:1a■16:7a■18:1a,4a■20:12a

ANOTHER'S-GE-11:7(7453)-EX-21:35(7453)■**N.T.**-JOH-13:14(240)-1CO-10:24(2087)-GA-6:2(240)

ANSWER-all=6030,a=7725&marked-GE-30:33■41:16■45:3-DE-20:11■21:7■25:9■27:15-JOS-4:7(559)-J'G-5:29(559)-1SA-2:16(559)■20:10-2SA-3:11a■24:13(1697)-1KI-9:9(559)■12:6(7725,1697),7,9(7725,1697)■18:29-2KI-4:29■18:36-2CH-10:6(1697),9(1697),10(559)-EZR-4:17(6600)■5:5(8421),11(6600)-NE-5:8(1696)-ES-4:13a-JOB-5:1■9:3,14,15,32■13:22,22a■14:15■19:16■20:2a,3■23:5■31:14a,35■32:1,3(4617),5(4617),14a,17,20■33:5a,12,32a■35:4(7725,4405),12■38:3(3045)■40:2,4a,5-PS-27:7■65:5■86:7■91:15■102:2■108:6■119:42■143:1-PR-1:28■15:1(4617),23(4617),28■16:1(4617)■22:21a■24:26a(1697)■26:4,5■27:11a(1697)■29:19(4617)-SONG-5:6-IS-14:32■30:19■36:21■41:28a■46:7■50:2■58:9■65:12,24■66:4-JER-5:19(559)■7:27■22:9(559)■33:3■42:4■44:20-EZE-14:4,7■21:7(559)-DA-3:16(8421)-JOE-2:19-MIC-3:7(4617)-HAB-2:1a,11-ZEC-13:6(559)■**N.T.**-all=611&marked-M'T-22:46■25:37,40,44,45-M'R-11:29,30■14:40-LU-11:7■12:11(626)■13:25■14:6(470)■20:3(2036),26(612)■21:14(626)■22:68-JOH-1:22(612)■19:9(612)-AC-24:10(626)■25:16(627)■26:2(626)-RO-11:4(5538)-1CO-9:3(627)-COL-4:6-2TI-4:16(627)-1PE-3:15(627),21(1906)

ANSWERABLE-EX-38:18(5980)

ANSWERED-all=6030,a=559,b=6032&marked-GE-18:27■23:5,10,14■24:50■27:37,39■31:14,31,36,43■34:13■35:3■40:18■41:16■42:22■43:28a-EX-4:1■15:21■19:8,19■24:3-NU-11:28■22:18■23:12,26■32:31-DE-1:14,41-JOS-1:16■2:14a■7:20■9:24■15:19a■17:15a■22:21■24:16-J'G-5:29■7:14■8:8^{2},18a,25a■11:13a■15:6a,10a■18:14■19:28■20:4-RU-2:4a,6,11■3:9a-1SA-1:15,17■3:4a,6a,10a,16a■4:17,20■5:8a■6:4a■9:8,12,19,21■10:12,22a■11:2a■12:5a■14:12,28,37,39,44a■16:18■17:27a,30(7725,1697),58a■18:7■19:17a■20:28,32■21:4,5■22:9,12a,14■23:4■25:10■26:6,14,22■28:6,15■29:9■30:8a,22-2SA-1:4a,7a,8a,13a■2:20a■4:9■9:6a■13:12a,32■14:5a,18,19,32a■15:21■18:3a,29a,32a■19:21,26a,38a,42,43■20:17^{2}a,20■21:1a,5a■22:42-1KI-1:28,36,43■2:22,30■3:27■11:22a■12:13,16(7725,1697)13:6■18:8a,18a,21,24,26■20:4,11,14a■21:6a,20a■22:15a-2KI-1:8a,10,11,12■2:5a■3:8a,11■4:13a,14a,26a■6:2a,3a,16a,22a,28a■7:2,13,19■8:12a,13a,14a■9:19a,22a■10:13a,15a■18:36■20:10a,15-1CH-12:17■21:3a,26,28-2CH-2:11a■7:22a■10:13,14(1697),16(7725)■18:3a■25:9a■29:31■31:10a■34:15,23a-EZR-10:2,12-NE-2:20(7725,1697)■6:4(7725)■8:6-ES-1:16a■5:4a,7(6039)■6:7a■7:3,5a-JOB-1:7,9■2:2,4■4:1■6:1■8:1■9:1,16■11:1,2■12:1■15:1■16:1■18:1■19:1■20:1■21:1■22:1■23:1■25:1■26:1■32:6,12,15,16■34:1■38:1■40:1,3,6■42:1-PS-18:41■81:7■99:6■118:5-IS-6:11a■21:9■36:21■39:4a-JER-7:13■11:5■23:35,37■35:17■36:18a■44:15-EZE-24:20a■37:3a

-DA-2:5b,7b,8b,10b,14(8421),15b,20b,26b,27b,47b■3:16b,24b,25b■4:19b■5:17b■6:12b,13b-AM-7:14-MIC-6:5-HAB-2:2-HAG-2:12,13,14-ZEC-1:10,11,12,13,19a■3:4■4:4,5,6,11,12,13a■5:2a■6:4,5■N.T.-all=611&marked-M'T-4:4■8:8■11:4,25■12:38,39,48■13:11,37■14:28■15:3,13,15,23,24,26,28■16:2,16,17■17:4,11,17■19:4,27■20:13,22■21:21,24,27,29,30■22:1,29■24:4■25:9,12,26■26:23,25,33,63,66■27:12,14,21,25■28:5-M'R-3:33■5:9■6:37■7:6,28■8:4,28■9:5,12,17,38■10:3,5,20,29,51■11:14,29,33■12:28,29,34,35■14:20,48,61■15:3,5,9,12-LU-1:35,60■3:16■4:4,8■7:43■8:21,50■9:49■10:28,41■11:45■13:14,15■14:5■17:20,37■19:40■20:3,7,24■22:51■23:3,9-JOH-1:21,26,48,49,50■2:18,19■3:3,5,9,10,27■4:10,13,17■5:7,11,17,19■6:7,26,29,43,68,70■7:16,20,21,46,47,52■8:14,19,33,34,39,48,49,54■9:3,11,20,25,27,30,34,36■10:25,32,33,34■11:9■12:23,30,34■13:7,8,26,36,38■14:23■16:31■18:5,8,20,23,30,34,35,36,37■19:7,11,15,22■20:28■21:5-AC-3:12■4:19■5:8,29■8:24,34,37■9:13■10:46■11:9■15:13■19:15■21:13■22:8,28■24:10,25■25:4,8(626),9,12,16,■26:1(626)-RE-7:13

ANSWEREDST-PS-99:8(6030)■138:3(6030)

ANSWEREST-1SA-26:14(6030)-JOB-16:3(6030)■N.T.-all=611-M'T-26:62-M'R-14:60■15:4-JOH-18:22

ANSWERETH-all=6030&marked-1SA-28:15-1KI-18:24-JOB-12:4-PR-18:13(7725),23-EC-5:20■10:19■N.T.-all=611&marked-M'R-8:29■9:19-LU-3:11-GA-4:25(4960)

ANSWERING-all=611&marked-M'T-3:15-M'R-11:22,33■12:17,24■13:2,5■15:2-LU-1:19■4:12■5:5,22,31■6:3■7:22,40■9:19,20,41■10:27,30(5274)■13:2,8■14:3■15:29■17:17■20:34,39■23:40■48:18-TIT-2:9(488)

ANSWERS-JOB-21:34(8666)■34:36(8666)■N.T.-LU-2:47(612)

ANT-PR-6:6(5244)

ANTICHRIST-all=500-1JO-2:18,22■4:3-2JO-7

ANTICHRISTS-1JO-2:18(500)

ANTIQUITY-IS-23:7(6927)

ANTS-PR-30:25(5244)

ANVIL-IS-41:7(6471)

ANY-all=3605,a=376,b=259&marked-GE-3:1■4:15■8:12(5750),21^2(5750)■9:11^2(5750)■14:23■17:5(5750),12■19:12(4310)■22:12^2(3972)■30:31(3972)■35:10(5750)■39:9(3972),23(3972)■43:34-EX-8:29(3254)■9:29(5750)■10:15,23a■11:6(3254),7■20:4sup,4,4sup,10,17■22:9,10,22■31:14,15■34:10■35:24,33,35■36:6(5750)-LE-2:1(5315),11,11sup■4:2,2b,13b,22,27(5315),27b■5:2,17b■6:3b,7b■7:19,21,21sup,21,24,26,27■11:10,32sup,32,37sup,37,43,44■13:48,49,51,52,53,57,59■15:2a,10,10sup22■17:10■18:6a,23,24,26,29■20:16,25■21:9a,11a■22:4,5,25■23:30■24:17■25:32(5769)■27:11-NU-5:6,12a■6:3■9:10a■14:23■15:27b■19:11,13■29:7■30:5■35:22,23■36:3b-DE-2:37■4:16,17^2,18^2,23,25■5:8,14^2,21■7:7■8:9■12:17■13:11(1697)■14:3,21■15:7b,21sup,21■16:5b,21■17:1sup,1,2b,3■18:6b■19:15^2,20(1697)■22:6■23:18,19■24:5,7(5315),10(3972)■27:21■28:14,55b■29:23-JOS-11:11,14■13:33■21:45-J'G-13:4,7,14^2■16:17■18:10■19:19■20:8^{2}a■21:1a-1SA-2:13■5:5■9:2■10:23■13:22■14:24sup,24,52■20:26(3972),39(3972)■21:2(3972)■22:15■25:15(3972)■27:1sup,1■30:2a,19-2SA-2:1b■7:7b■9:3a■13:2(3972)■15:2,11■21:5-1KI-3:13a■5:6a■6:7■8:38■10:20■15:5,29-2KI-4:2,29sup,29a■10:5a,14a■12:5a■18:33a-1CH-17:6b■23:26■27:1■28:21■29:25-2CH-2:14■6:29■8:15■9:19,20(3972)■23:19■32:15■34:13-EZR-1:4■7:24(3606)-JOB-8:12■33:13■34:27■37:24-PS-34:10■59:5■115:17■119:133■147:20-PR-1:17■6:35■30:30■31:5-EC-2:10■9:5(3972),5sup,6sup,6-IS-33:20■36:18a■56:2-JER-9:4■17:22■18:18■23:24a■32:27■36:24■42:21■44:26-EZE-7:11(1991),13a■9:6■12:28■15:2,3sup,3■16:5b■18:7a,11,16a,■31:8■37:23sup,23■44:9,13,21,31■46:16a-DA-2:10(3606),30sup,30(3606)■3:28(3606)■6:4,5,7,12(3606)■11:37-AM-8:7-JON-3:7(3792)-HAG-2:12,13-ZEC-13:3a■N.T.-all=5100,a=1536&marked-M'T-4:6(3379)■5:25(3379)■11:27■12:19■13:15(3379),19(3956)■16:24a■18:19(3956),21:3■22:16(3762),46,46(3765)■24:17,23-M'R-1:44(3367)■4:12(3379),22,23a■5:4(3762),35(2089)■7:16a■8:26■9:8(3765),22a,30,35a■11:3a,13a,16a,16sup,25a■13:5,15,21■14:31(3364),63(2089)■16:8^2(3762),18-LU-4:11(3379)■8:43(3762)■9:23,36(3762)■10:19(3364)■11:11■14:8,26(1536)■15:29(3763)■19:8,8(1536),31■20:27(3361),28,36(2089),40(3762)■21:34(3379)■22:16(3765),35,71(2089)■24:41-JOH-1:3(1520),18(4455),46■2:25■4:33(3387)■5:37(4455)■6:46,51■7:4,17,37,48(3387),51(3588)■8:33(3762)■9:22,31,32■10:9,28■11:9,57■12:26^2,47■14:14■16:30■18:31(3762)■21:5(3387)-AC-4:12(3762),32(1520),34■9:2■10:14(3956),28(3367),47■11:8(3763)■13:15(5150)■17:25■19:38,39■24:12,20a■25:5a,8,11,16,17(3362),24(3370)■27:12(4458),22(3762),34(3762),42■28:21^2-RO-1:10(4458)■6:2(2089)8:9,39■9:11■11:14(4458)■13:8(3367),9■14:13(3370),14,21(3362)■15:18-1CO-1:15(3387),16a■2:2■3:7,12,14a,15a,17a,18a■5:11■6:1,12■7:12a,18^2,36■8:2,3,9(3381),10■9:7(4218),15,27(3381)■10:19^2,27,28■11:16,34■14:27,35,37a,38a■16:22a-2CO-1:4(3956)■2:5,10,10a■3:5■5:17a■6:3(3367)■7:14a■10:7■11:3(3381),21■12:6,17-GA-1:9a■2:2(3381)■5:6■6:15-EPH-2:9■5:27■6:8(1538)-PH'P-2:1^{4}a■3:4a,11(4458),15a■4:8a-COL-2:4(3387),8(3387),23■3:13-1TH-1:8■2:5(4218),9■5:15-2TH-2:3(3367)■3:8^2,10a,14-1TI-1:10a■5:4,8,16a■6:3a-TIT-1:6a-HEB-1:5(4218),13(4218)■2:1(3379)■3:12,13■4:1,11,12(3956)■12:15^2,16,19(2089)-JAS-1:5,7,13(3762),23a,26a■3:2a■5:12,13^2,14,19a-1PE-3:1,6a■4:11^{2}a-2PE-3:9-1JO-2:1,15,27■4:12(4455)■5:14,16a-2JO-10a-RE-3:20a■7:1(3956),16(2089),16(3956)■9:4^2(3956)■11:5^{2}a■12:8(2089)■13:9a■14:9a■18:11(3765),22(2089)■21:4(2089),27(3956)■22:18,19

ANYTHING-supplied

APACE-all supplied

APART-all=905&marked-EX-13:12(5674)-LE-15:19(5079)■18:19(5079)-PS-4:3(6395)-EZE-22:10(5079)-ZEC-12:12^5,13^4,14^2■N.T.-all=2596,2398&marked-M'T-14:13,23■17:1,19■20:17-M'R-6:31■9:2-JAS-1:21(659)

APES-1KI-10:22(6971)-2CH-9:21(6971)

APIECE-1KI-7:15(5982,259)-EZE-10:21(259)■N.T.-LU-9:3(303)-JOH-2:6(303)

APOSTLE-all=652-RO-1:t,1■11:13-1CO-1:t,1■9:1,2■15:9-2CO-1:t,1■12:12-GA-1:t,1-EPH-1:t,1-PH'P-1:t-COL-1:t,1-1TH-1:t-2TH-1:t-1TI-1:t,1■2:7-2TI-1:t,1,11-TIT-1:1-HEB-1:t■3:1-1PE-1:1-2PE-1:1

APOSTLES-all=652&marked-M'T-10:2-M'R-6:30-LU-6:13■9:10■11:49■17:5■22:14■24:10-AC-1:t(40,652),2,26■2:37,43■4:33,36■5:12,18,29,34,40■6:6■8:1,14■9:27■11:1■14:4,14■15:2,4,6,22,23■16:4-RO-16:7-1CO-4:9■9:5■12:28,29■15:7,9-2CO-11:5,13(5570),13■12:11-GA-1:17,19-EPH-2:20■3:5■4:11-1TH-2:6-2PE-3:2-JUDE-17-RE-2:2■18:20■21:14

APOSTLES'-all=652-AC-2:42■4:35,37■5:2■8:18

APOSTLESHIP-all=651-AC-1:25-RO-1:5-1CO-9:2-GA-2:8

APOTHECARIES-NE-3:8(7543)

APOTHECARIES'-2CH-16:14(4842)

APOTHECARY-all=7543-EX-30:25,35■37:29-EC-10:1

APPAREL-all=3830&marked-J'G-17:10(899)-1SA-27:9(899)-2SA-1:24■12:20(8071)■14:2(899)-1KI-10:5(4403)-2CH-9:4^2(4403)-EZR-3:10(3847)-ES-6:8,9,10,11■8:15-IS-3:22(4254)■4:1(8071)■63:1,2-EZE-27:24(1264)-ZEP-1:8(4403)-ZEC-14:14(899)■N.T.-all=2066&marked-AC-1:10■12:21■20:33(2441)-1TI-2:9(2689)-JAS-2:2-1PE-3:3(2440)

APPARELLED-2SA-13:18(3847)■N.T.-LU-7:25(2441)

APPARENTLY-NU-12:8(4758)

APPEAL-all=1941-AC-25:11■28:19

APPEALED-all=1941-AC-25:12,21,25■26:32

APPEAR-all=7200&marked-GE-1:9■30:37(4286)-EX-23:15,17■34:20,23,24-LE-9:4,6■13:57■16:2-DE-6:16^2■31:11-J'G-13:21-1SA-1:22■2:27(1540)-2CH-1:7-PS-42:2■90:16■102:16-SONG-2:12■4:1(1570)■6:5(1570)■7:12(6524)-IS-1:12■66:5-JER-13:26-EZE-21:24■N.T.-all=5316&marked-M'T-6:16,18■23:27,28■24:30-LU-11:44(82)■19:11(398)-AC-22:30(2064)■26:16(3700)-RO-7:13-2CO-5:10(5319)■7:12(5319)■13:7-COL-3:4^2(5319)-1TI-4:15(5318,5600)-HEB-9:24(1718),28(3700)■11:3-1PE-4:18■5:4(5319)-1JO-2:28(5319)■3:2^2(5319)-RE-3:18(5319)

APPEARANCE-all=4758-NU-9:15,16-1SA-16:7(5869)-EZE-1:5,13^2,14,16^2,26^2,27^4,28^3■8:2^3■10:1,9■40:3,41:21■42:11■43:3-DA-8:15■10:6,18-JOE-2:4■N.T.-JOH-7:24(3799)-2CO-5:12(4383)■10:7(4383)-1TH-5:22(1491)

APPEARANCES-EZE-10:10(4758),22(4758)

APPEARED-all=7200&marked-GE-12:7^2■17:1■18:1■26:2,24■35:1,7(1540),9■48:3-EX-3:2,16■4:1,5■6:3■14:27(6437)■16:10-LE-9:23-NU-14:10■16:19,42■20:6-DE-31:15-J'G-6:12■13:3,10-1SA-3:21-2SA-22:16-1KI-3:5■9:2^2■11:9-2CH-3:1■7:12-NE-4:21(3318)-JER-31:3-EZE-10:1,8■19:11-DA-1:15■8:1■N.T.-all=3700&marked-M'T-1:20(5316)■2:7(5316)■13:26(5316)■17:3■27:53(1718)-M'R-9:4■16:9(5316),12(5319),14(5319)-LU-1:11■9:8(5316),31■22:43■24:34-AC-2:3■7:2,30,35■9:17■16:9■26:16■27:20(2014)-TIT-2:11(2014)■3:4(2014)-HEB-9:26(5319)-RE-12:1,3

APPEARETH-all=7200&marked-LE-13:14,43(4758)-PS-84:7-PR-27:25(1540)-JER-6:1(8259)-MAL-3:2(7200)■N.T.-all=5316-M'T-2:13,19-JAS-4:14

APPEARING-all=2015&marked-1TI-6:14-2TI-1:10■4:1,8-TIT-2:13-1PE-1:7(602)

APPEASE-GE-32:20(3722,6440)

APPEASED-ES-2:1(7918)■N.T.-AC-19:35(2687)

APPEASETH-PR-15:18(8252)

APPERTAIN-JER-10:7(2969)

APPERTAINED-all supplied

APPERTAINETH-all supplied

APPETITE-all=5315&marked-JOB-38:39(2416)-PR-23:2-EC-6:7-IS-29:8(8264)

APPLE-all=8598&marked-DE-32:10(380)-PS-17:8(380,1323)-PR-7:2(380)-SONG-2:3■8:5-LA-2:18(1323)-JOE-1:12-ZEC-2:8(892)

APPLES-all=8598-PR-25:11-SONG-2:5■7:8

APPLIED-EC-7:25(5437)■8:9(5414),16(5414)

APPLY-PS-90:12(935)-PR-2:2(5186)■22:17(7896)■23:12(935)

APPOINT-all=7760,a=6485&marked-GE-30:28(5344)■41:34a-EX-21:13■30:16(5414)-LE-26:16a-NU-1:50a■3:10a■4:19,27a■35:6(5414),11(7136)-JOS-20:2(5414)-1SA-8:11,12-2SA-6:21(6680)■7:10■15:15(977)-1KI-5:6(559),9(7971)-1CH-15:16(5975)-NE-7:3(5975)-ES-2:3a-JOB-14:13(7896)-IS-26:1(7896)■61:3-JER-15:3a■49:19a,19(3259)■50:44a,44(3259)■51:27a-EZE-21:19,20,22^2■45:6(5414)-HO-1:11■N.T.-M'T-24:51(5087)-LU-12:46(5087)■22:29(1303)-AC-6:3(2525)

APPOINTED-all=4150&marked-GE-4:25(7896)■18:14■24:14(3198),44(3198)-EX-9:5(7760)■23:15-NU-9:2,3,7,13-JOS-8:14■20:7(6942),9(4152)-J'G-18:11(2296),16(2296),17(2296)■20:38-1SA-13:11■19:20(5324)■20:35■21:2(3045)■25:30(6680)■29:4(6485)-2SA-17:14(6680)■20:5(3259)■24:15-1KI-1:35(6680)■11:18(559)■12:12(1696)■20:42(2764)-2KI-7:17(6485)■8:6(5414)■10:24(7760)■11:18(7760)■18:14(7760)-1CH-6:48(5414)■9:29(4487)■15:17(5975)■16:4(5414)-2CH-8:14(5975)■20:21(5975)■23:18(7760)■31:2(5975)■33:8(5975)-EZR-3:8(5975)■8:20(5414)■10:14(2163)-NE-5:14(6680)■6:7(5975)■7:1(6485)■9:17(5414)■10:34(2163)■12:31(5975),44(6485)■13:30(5975),31(2163)-ES-1:8(3245)■2:15(559)■4:5(5975)-JOB-7:1(6635),3(4487)■14:5(6213),14(6635)■20:29(561)■23:14(2706)■30:23-PS-78:5(7760)■79:11(1121)■81:3(3677)■102:20(1121)■104:19(6213)-PR-7:20(3677)■8:29(2710)■31:8(1121)-IS-1:14■14:31(4151)■28:25(5567)■44:7(7760)-JER-5:24(2708)■8:7■33:25(7760)■46:17■47:7(3259)-EZE-4:6(5414)■36:5(5414)■43:21(4662)-DA-1:5(4487),10(4487)■8:19■10:1(6635)■11:27,29,35-MIC-6:9(3259)-HAB-2:3■N.T.-all=5087&marked-M'T-26:19(4929)■27:10(4929)■28:16(5021)-LU-3:13(1299)■10:1(322)■22:29(1303)-AC-1:23(2476)■7:44(1299)■17:26(4384),31(2476)■20:13(1299)■22:10(5021)■28:23(5021)-1CO-4:9(1935)-GA-4:2(4287)-1TH-3:3(2749)■5:9-2TI-1:11-TIT-1:5(1299)-HEB-1:2■9:27(606)-1PE-2:8

APPOINTETH-DA-5:21(6966)

APPOINTMENT-NU-4:27(6310)-2SA-13:32(6310)-EZR-6:9(3983)-JOB-2:11(3259)

APPREHEND-2CO-11:32(4084)-PH'P-3:12(2638)

APPREHENDED-AC-12:4(4084)-PH'P-3:12(2638),13(2638)

APPROACH-all=7126&marked-LE-18:6,14,19■20:16■21:17,18-NU-4:19(5066)-DE-20:2(5066),3■31:14-JOS-8:5-JOB-40:19(5066)-PS-65:4-JER-30:21^2(5066)-EZE-42:13(7138),14■43:19(7138)■N.T.-1TI-6:16(676)

APPROACHED-2SA-11:20(5066)-2KI-16:12(7126)

APPROACHETH-LU-12:33(1448)

APPROACHING-IS-58:2(7132)■N.T.-HEB-10:25(1448)

APPROVE-PS-49:13(7520)■N.T.-1CO-16:3(1381)-PH'P-1:10(1381)

APPROVED-all=1384&marked-AC-2:22(584)-RO-14:18■16:10-1CO-11:19-2CO-7:11(4921)■10:18■13:7-2TI-2:15

APPROVEST-RO-2:18(1381)

APPROVETH-LA-3:36(7200)

APPROVING-2CO-6:4(4921)

APRONS-GE-3:7(2290)■N.T.-AC-19:12(4612)

APT-2KI-24:16(6213)■N.T.-1TI-3:2(1317)-2TI-2:24(1317)

ARCHANGEL-1TH-4:16(743)-JUDE-9(743)

ARCHER-GE-21:20(7198)-JER-51:3(1869)

ARCHERS-all=3384&marked-GE-49:23(1167,2671)-J'G-5:11(2686)-1SA-31:3(3384,376,7198),3-1CH-8:40(1869,7198)■10:3(3384,7198),3-2CH-35:23-JOB-16:13(7228)-IS-21:17(7198)■22:3(7198)-JER-50:29(7228)

ARCHES-all=361-EZE-40:16,21,22,24,25,26,29^2,30,31,33^2,34,36

ARGUING-JOB-6:25(3198)

ARGUMENTS-JOB-23:4(8433)

ARIGHT-PS-78:8(3559)-PR-15:2(3190)■23:31(4339)-JER-8:6(3651)

ARISE-all=6965&marked-GE-13:17■19:15■21:18■27:19,31,43■28:2■31:13■35:1,3■41:30■43:8,13-DE-9:12■10:11■13:1■17:8sup,8-JOS-1:2■8:1-J'G-5:12■7:9,15■18:9■20:40(5927)-1SA-9:3■16:12■23:4-2SA-2:14^2■3:21■11:20(5927)■13:15■15:14■17:1,21■19:7■22:39-1KI-3:12■14:2,12■17:9■19:5,7■21:7,15,18-2KI-1:3■8:1■9:2-1CH-22:16,19-2CH-6:41-EZR-10:4-NE-2:20-ES-4:14(5975)-JOB-7:4■25:3-PS-3:7■7:6■9:19■10:12■12:5■17:13■44:23(6974),26■68:1■74:22■78:6■82:8■88:10■89:9(7721)■102:13■109:28■132:8-PR-6:9■31:28-SONG-2:13-IS-21:5■23:12■26:19■31:2■49:7■52:2■60:1,2(2224)-JER-1:17■2:27,28■6:4,5■8:4■13:4,6■18:2■31:6■46:16■49:28,31-LA-2:19-EZE-3:22-DA-2:39(6966)■7:5(6966),17(6966),24(6966)-HO-10:14-AM-7:2,5-OB-1-JON-1:2,6■3:2■4:8(2224)-MIC-2:10■4:13■6:1■7:8-HAB-2:19(5782)-MAL-4:2(2224)■N.T.-all=450,a=1453&marked-M'T-2:13a,20a■9:5a,6a■17:7a■24:24a-M'R-2:9a,11a■5:41a-LU-5:24a■7:14a■8:54a■15:18■17:19■24:38(305)-JOH-14:31a-AC-8:26■9:6,11,34,40■10:20■11:7■12:7■20:30■22:10,16-EPH-5:14-2PE-1:19(393)

ARISETH-all=2224&marked-1KI-18:44(5927)-PS-104:22■112:4-EC-1:5-IS-2:19(6965),21(6965)-NA-3:17■N.T.-M'T-13:21(1096)-M'R-4:17(1096)-JOH-7:52(1453)-HEB-7:15(450)

ARISING-ES-7:7(6965)

ARK-all=727,a=8392&marked-GE-6:14^{2}a,15a,16^{2}a,18a,19a■7:1a,7a,9a,13a,15a,17a,18a,23a■8:1a,4a,6a,9^{2}a,10a,13a,16a,19a■9:10a,18a-EX-2:3a,5a■25:10,14^2,15,16,21^2,22■26:33,34■30:6,26■31:7■35:12■37:1,5■39:35■40:3^2,5,20^3,21^2-LE-16:2-NU-3:31■4:5■7:89■10:33,35■14:44-DE-10:1,2,3,5,8■31:9,25,26-JOS-3:3,6^2,8,11,13,14,15^2,17■4:5,7,9,10,11,16,18■6:4,6^2,8,9,11,12,13^2■7:6■8:33^2-J'G-20:27-1SA-3:3■4:3,4^2,5,6,11,13,17,18,19,21,22■5:1,2,3,7,8^3,10^3,11■6:1,2,3,8,11,13,15,18,19,21■7:1^2,2■14:18^2-2SA-6:2,3,4^2,6,7,9,10,11,12^2,13,15,16,17■7:2■11:11■15:24^2,25,29-1KI-2:26■3:15■6:19■8:1,3,4,5,6,7^2,9,21-1CH-6:31■13:3,5,6,7,9,10,12,13,14■15:1,2^2,3,12,14,15,23,24^2,25,26,27,28,29■16:1,4,6,37^2■17:1■22:19■28:2,18-2CH-1:14■5:2,4,5,6,7,8^2,9sup,9,10■6:11,41■8:11■35:3-PS-132:8-JER-3:16■N.T.-all=2787-M'T-24:38-LU-17:27-HEB-9:4■11:7-1PE-3:20-RE-11:19

ARM-all=2220&marked-EX-6:6■15:16-NU-31:3(2502)-DE-4:34■5:15■7:19■9:29■11:2■26:8■33:20-1SA-2:31^2-2SA-1:10-1KI-8:42-2KI-17:36-2CH-6:32■32:8-JOB-26:2■31:22(3802),22(248)■35:9■38:15■40:9-PS-10:15■44:3^2■77:15■89:10,13,21■98:1■136:12-SONG-8:6-IS-9:20■17:5■30:30■33:2■40:10,11■48:14■51:5,9■52:10■53:1■59:16■62:8■63:5,12-JER-17:5■21:5■27:5■32:17,21(248)■48:25-EZE-4:7■20:33,34■30:21■31:17-DA-11:6^2-ZEC-11:17^2■N.T.-all=1023&marked-LU-1:51-JOH-12:38-AC-13:17-1PE-4:1(3695)

ARMED-all=2502&marked-GE-14:14(7324)-NU-31:5■32:17,20,21,27,29,30,32-DE-3:18-JOS-1:14(2571)■4:12(2571)■6:7,9,13-J'G-7:11(2571)-1SA-17:5(3847),38^2(3847)-1CH-12:2(5401),23,24-2CH-17:17(5401)■28:14-JOB-39:21(5402)-PS-78:9(5401)-PR-6:11(4043)■24:34(4043)-IS-15:4■N.T.-LU-11:21(2528)

ARMHOLES-JER-38:12(679,3027)-EZE-13:18(679,3027)

ARMIES-all=6635&marked-EX-6:26■7:4■12:17,51-NU-1:3■2:3,9,10,16,18,24,25■10:14,18,22,28■33:1-DE-20:9-1SA-17:1(4264),8(4634),10(4634),23(4630),26(4634),36(4634),45(4634)■23:3(4634)■28:1(4264)■29:1(4264)-2KI-25:23(2428),26(2428)-1CH-11:26(2428)-2CH-16:4(2428)-JOB-25:3(1416)-PS-44:9■60:10■68:12-SONG-6:13(4264)-IS-34:2■N.T.-all=4753&marked-M'T-22:7-LU-21:20(4760)-HEB-11:34(3925)-RE-19:14,19

ARMOUR-all=3627&marked-1SA-14:1,6■17:38(4055),39(4055),54■31:9,10-2SA-2:21(2488)■18:15(3627)-1KI-10:25(5402)■22:38(2185)-2KI-3:21(2290)■10:2(5402)■20:13-1CH-10:9,10-IS-22:8(5402)■39:2■N.T.-all=3833&marked-LU-11:22-RO-13:12(3696)-2CO-6:7(3696)-EPH-6:11,13

ARMOURBEARER-all=5375,3627-J'G-9:54-1SA-14:7,12^2,13^2,14,17■16:21■31:4^2,5,6-2SA-23:37-1CH-10:4^2,5■11:39

ARMOURY-NE-3:19(5402)-SONG-4:4(8530)-JER-50:25(214)

ARMS-all=2220&marked-GE-49:24-DE-33:27-J'G-15:14■16:12-2SA-22:35-2KI-9:24-JOB-22:9-PS-18:34■37:17-PR-31:17-IS-44:12■49:22(2684)■51:5-EZE-13:20■30:22,24^2,25^2-DA-2:32(1872)■10:6■11:15,22,31-HO-7:15■11:3■N.T.-M'R-9:36(1723)■10:16(1723)-LU-2:28(43)

ARMY-all=2428&marked-GE-26:26(6635)-EX-14:9-DE-11:4-J'G-4:7(6635)■8:6(6635)■9:29(6635)-1SA-4:2(4634),12(4634),16^2(4634)■17:21(4634),22(4634),48(4634)-1KI-20:19,25^2-2KI-25:5^2,10-1CH-20:1(6635)■27:34(6685)-2CH-13:3■14:8■20:21(2502)■24:24■25:7(6635),9(1416),10(1416),13(1416)■26:13(2426,6635)-NE-2:9■4:2-JOB-29:25(1416)-IS-36:2(2426)■43:17-JER-32:2■34:1,7,21■35:11^2■37:5,7,10,11^2■38:3■39:1,5■46:2,22■52:4,8^2,14-EZE-17:17■27:10,11■29:18^2,19■32:31■37:10■38:4,15-DA-3:20(2429)■4:35(2429)■11:7,13,25^2,26-JOE-2:11,25-ZEC-9:8(4675)■N.T.-all=4753-AC-23:27-RE-9:16■19:19

AROSE-all=6965&marked-GE-19:15(5927),33,35^2■24:10,61■37:7■38:19-EX-1:8-DE-34:10-JOS-8:3,19■18:8■24:9-J'G-2:10■3:20■4:9■5:7^2■6:28(7925)■8:21■10:1,3■13:11■16:3■19:3,5(7925),8(7925)■20:8,18-RU-1:6-1SA-3:6,8■5:3(7925),4(7925)■9:26(7925),26■13:15■17:35,48,52■18:27■20:25,34,41,42■21:10■23:13,16,24■24:4,8■25:1,41,42■26:2,5■27:2■28:23■31:12-2SA-2:15■6:2■11:2■12:17,20■13:29,31■14:23,31■15:9■17:22,23■19:8■23:10-1KI-1:50■2:40■3:20■8:54■11:18,40■14:4,17■17:10■19:3,8,21-2KI-1:15■4:30■7:7,12■8:2■9:6■10:12■11:1■12:20■19:35(7925)■23:25■25:26-1CH-10:12■20:4(5975)-2CH-22:10■29:12■30:14,27■36:16(5927)-EZR-9:5■10:5-NE-2:12-ES-8:4-JOB-1:20■19:18■29:8-PS-76:9-EC-1:5(2224)-IS-37:36(7925)-JER-41:2-EZE-3:23-DA-6:19(6966)-JON-3:3,6■N.T.-all=450,a=1453&marked-M'T-2:14a,21a■8:15a,24(1096),26a■9:7a,9,19a,25a■25:7a■26:62■27:52a-M'R-2:12a,14■4:37(1096),39(1326)■5:42■7:24■9:27■10:1■14:57-LU-1:39■4:38,39■6:8,48(1096)■8:24a,55■9:46(1525)■15:14(1096)■20■23:1■24:12-JOH-3:25(1096)■6:18(1326)■11:29a-AC-5:6■6:1(1096),9■7:18■8:27■9:8a,18,34,39■11:19(1096)■19:23(1096)■23:7

(1096),9(1096),9,10(1096)■27:14(906)-RE-9:2(305)

ARRAY-all=6186&marked-J'G-20:20,22^{2},30,33-1SA-4:2■17:2,8,21-2SA-10:8,9,10,17-1CH-19:9,10,11,17^{2}-2CH-13:3(631),3■14:10-ES-6:9(3847)-JOB-6:4■40:10(3847)-IS-22:7(7896)-JER-6:23■43:12(5844)■50:9,14,42-JOE-2:5■N.T.-1TI-2:9(2441)

ARRAYED-all=3847-GE-41:42-2CH-5:12■28:15-ES-6:11■N.T.-all=4016&marked-M'T-6:29-LU-12:27■23:11-AC-12:21(1746)-RE-7:13■17:4■19:8

ARRIVED-LU-8:26(2668)-AC-20:15(3846)

ARROGANCY-all=1347&marked-1SA-2:3(6277)-PR-8:13-IS-13:11-JER-48:29

ARROW-all=2671&marked-1SA-20:36(2678),37^{2}(2678)-2KI-9:24(2678)■13:17^{2}■19:32-JOB-41:28(1121,7198)-PS-11:2■64:7■91:5-PR-25:18-IS-37:33-JER-9:8-LA-3:12-ZEC-9:14

ARROWS-all=2671&marked-NU-24:8-DE-32:23,42-1SA-20:20,21^{2},22,36,38(2678)-2SA-22:15-2KI-13:15^{2},18-1CH-12:2-2CH-26:15-JOB-6:4-PS-7:13■18:14■38:2■45:5■57:4■58:7■64:3■76:3(7565)■77:17(2687)■120:4■127:4■144:6-PR-26:18-IS-5:28■7:24-JER-50:9,14■51:11-LA-3:13(1121)-EZE-5:16■21:21■39:3,9-HAB-3:11

ART-all=4640&marked-EX-30:25,35-2CH-16:14-DA-2:26(383)■N.T.-all=1488&marked-M'T-2:6■5:25■11:3■14:33■16:16,17,18,23■22:16■25:24■26:73■27:11-M'R-1:11,24sup,24■3:11■8:29■12:14,34■14:61,70■15:2-LU-3:22■4:34,41■7:19,20■15:31■22:58,67,70■23:3,40-JOH-1:19,21^{2},22,42,49^{2}■3:10■4:12,19■6:69■7:52■8:25,48,53,57(2192)■9:28■11:27■18:17,25,33,37■19:9,12■21:12-AC-9:5■13:33■17:29(5078)■21:38■22:8,27■26:15-RO-2:1^{2}■9:20■14:4-GA-4:7(1488)-HEB-1:5,12■5:5-JAS-4:11,12-RE-2:9■3:1,15,16,17■4:11■5:9■11:17,17sup(5607)■16:5(1488),5(5607)

ARTIFICER-GE-4:22(2794)-IS-3:3(2796)

ARTIFICERS-1CH-29:5(2796)-2CH-34:11(2796)

ARTILLERY-1SA-20:40(3627)

ARTS-AC-19:19(4021)

ASCEND-all=5927-JOS-6:5-PS-24:3■135:7■139:8-IS-14:13,14-JER-10:13■51:16-EZE-38:9■N.T.-all=305-JOH-6:62■20:17-RO-10:6-RE-17:8

ASCENDED-all=5927-EX-19:18-NU-13:22-JOS-8:20,21■10:7■15:3-J'G-13:20■20:40-PS-68:18-PR-30:4■N.T.-all=305-JOH-3:13■20:17-AC-2:34■25:1-EPH-4:8,9,10-RE-8:4■11:12

ASCENDETH-RE-11:7(305)■14:11(305)

ASCENDING-GE-28:12(5927)-1SA-28:13(5927)■N.T.-all=305-LU-19:28-JOH-1:51-RE-7:2

ASCENT-NU-34:4(4608)-2SA-15:30(4608)-1KI-10:5(5930)-2CH-9:4(5944)

ASCRIBE-DE-32:3(3051)-JOB-36:3(5414)-PS-68:34(5414)

ASCRIBED-1SA-18:8^{2}(5414)

ASH-IS-44:14(766)

ASHAMED-all=954&marked-GE-2:25-NU-12:14(3637)-J'G-3:25-2SA-10:5(3637)■19:3(3637)-2KI-2:17■8:11-1CH-19:5(3637)-2CH-30:15(3637)-EZR-8:22■9:6-JOB-6:20(2659)■11:3(3637)■19:3-PS-6:10^{2}■25:2,3^{2},20■31:1,17^{2}■34:5(2659)■35:26■37:19■40:14■69:6■70:2■74:21(3637)■86:17■109:28■119:6,46,78,80,116■127:5-PR-12:4-IS-1:29■20:5■23:4■24:23■26:11■29:22■30:5■33:9(2659)■41:11■42:17■44:9,11^{2}■45:16,17,24■49:23■50:7■54:4■65:13■66:5-JER-2:26(1322),26,36^{2}■3:3(3637)■6:15^{2}■8:9,12^{2}■12:13■14:3,4■15:9■17:13■20:11■22:22■31:19■48:13^{2}■50:12(2659)-EZE-16:27(3637),61(3637)32:30■36:32■43:10(3637),11(3637)-HO-4:19■10:6-JOE-1:11■2:26,27-MIC-3:7-ZEP-3:11-ZEC-9:5■13:4■N.T.-all=1870&marked-M'R-8:38^{2}-LU-9:26^{2}■13:17(2617)■16:3(153)-RO-1:16■5:5(2617)■6:21■9:33(2617)■10:11(2617)-2CO-7:14(2617)■9:4(2617)■10:8(153)-PH'P-1:20(153)-2TH-3:14(1788)-2TI-1:8,12,16■2:15(422)-TIT-2:8(1788)-HEB-2:11■11:16-1PE-3:16(2617)■4:16(153)-1JO-2:28(153)

ASHES-all=665&marked-GE-18:27-EX-9:8(6368),10(6368)■27:3(1878)-LE-1:16(1880)■4:12^{2}(1880)■6:10(1880),11(1880)-NU-4:13(1878)■19:9,10,17(6083)-2SA-13:19-1KI-13:3(1880),5(1880)■20:38,41-2KI-23:4(6083)-ES-4:1,3-JOB-2:8■13:12■30:19■42:6-PS-102:9■147:16-IS-44:20■58:5■61:3-JER-6:26■31:40(1880)-LA-3:16-EZE-27:30■28:18-DA-9:3-JON-3:6-MAL-4:3■N.T.-all=4700&marked-M'T-11:21-LU-10:13-HEB-9:13-2PE-2:6(5077)

ASIDE-all=5186&marked-NU-5:12(7847),19(7847),20(7847),29(7847)■22:23-DE-28:14(5493)-1SA-8:3-2SA-2:21■3:27■6:10■18:30^{2}(5437)-2KI-4:4(5265)■22:2(5493)-1CH-13:13-JOB-6:18(3943)-PS-14:3(5493)■40:4(7847)■78:57(2015)■101:3(7750)■125:5-SONG-1:7(5844)■3:1(6437)-IS-10:2■29:21■30:11■44:20-JER-14:8■15:5(5493)-LA-3:35-AM-2:7■5:12-MAL-3:5■N.T.-all=402&marked-M'T-2:22-M'R-7:8(863),33(2596,2398)-LU-9:10(5298)-JOH-13:4(5087)-AC-4:15(565)■23:19■26:31-1TI-1:6(1824)■5:15(1824)-HEB-12:1(659)-1PE-2:1(659)

ASK-all=7592&marked-GE-32:29-NU-27:21-DE-4:32■13:14■32:7-JOS-4:6,21■15:18-J'G-1:14■18:5-1SA-12:19■25:8■28:16-2SA-14:18■20:18-1KI-2:16,20,22^{2}■3:5■14:5(1875)-2KI-2:9-2CH-1:7■20:4(1245)-JOB-12:7-PS-2:8-IS-7:11^{2},12■45:11■58:2-JER-6:16■15:5■18:13■23:33■30:6■38:14■48:19■50:5-LA-4:4-DA-6:7(1156),12(1156)-HO-4:12-HAG-2:11-ZEC-10:1■N.T.-all=154,a=2065&marked-M'T-6:8■7:7,9,10,11■14:7■18:19■20:22■21:22,24a■22:46(1905)■27:20

20:22■21:22,24a■22:46(1905)■27:20

-M'R-6:22,23,24■9:32(1905)■10:38■11:29(1905)■12:34(1905)-LU-6:9(1905),30(523)■9:45a■11:9,11,11sup12,13■12:48■19:31a■20:3a,40(1905)■22:68-JOH-1:19a■9:21a,23a■11:22■13:24(4441)■14:13,14■15:7,16■16:19a,23a,23,24,26,30a■18:21(1905)■21:12(1833)-AC-3:2■10:29(4441)-1CO-14:35(1905)-EPH-3:20-JAS-1:5,6■4:2,3^{2}-1JO-3:22■5:14,15,16

ASKED-all=7592&marked-GE-24:47■26:7■32:29■37:15■38:21■40:7■43:7,27■44:19-EX-18:7-JOS-9:14■19:50-J'G-1:1■5:25■6:29(1245)■13:6■20:18,23-1SA-1:17,20,27■8:10■14:37■19:22■20:6,28-1KI-3:10,11^{5},13■10:13-2KI-2:10■8:6-2CH-1:11^{3}■9:12-EZR-5:9(7593),10(7593)-NE-1:2-JOB-21:29-PS-21:4■105:40-IS-30:2■41:28■65:1-JER-36:17■37:17■38:27-DA-2:10(7593)■7:16(1156)■N.T.-all=1905,a=2065&marked-M'T-12:10■16:13a■17:10■22:23,35,41■27:11-M'R-4:10a■5:9■6:25(154)■7:5,17■8:5,23,27■9:11,16,21,28,33■10:2,10,17■12:18,28■13:3■14:60,61■15:2,4,44-LU-1:63(154)■3:10■8:9,30■9:18■15:26(4441)■18:18,36(4441),40■20:21,27■21:7■22:64■23:3,6-JOH-1:21a,25a■4:10(154)■5:12a■9:2a,15a,19a■16:24(154)■18:7,19a-AC-1:6■3:3a■4:7(4441)■5:27■10:18(4441)■23:19a,34■25:20(3004)-RO-10:20

ASKEST-J'G-13:18(7592)■N.T.-JOH-4:9(154)■18:21(1905)

ASKETH-all=7592-GE-32:17-EX-13:14-DE-6:20-MIC-7:3^{2}■N.T.-all=154&marked-M'T-5:42■7:8-LU-6:30■11:10-JOH-16:5(2065)-1PE-3:15

ASKING-all=7592-1SA-12:17-1CH-10:13-PS-78:18■NT.-LU-2:46(1905)-JOH-8:7(2065)-1CO-10:25(350),27(350)

ASLEEP-J'G-4:21(7290)-1SA-26:12(3463)-SONG-7:9(3463)-JON-1:5(7290)■N.T.-all=2837&marked-M'T-8:24(2518)■26:40(2518),43(2518)-M'R-4:38(2518)■14:40(2518)-LU-8:23(879)-AC-7:60-1CO-15:6,18-1TH-4:13,15-2PE-3:4

ASP-IS-11:8(6620)

ASPS-all=6620-DE-32:33-JOB-20:14,16■N.T.-RO-3:13(785)

ASS-all=2543,a=860&marked-GE-22:3,5■42:27■44:13■49:14-EX-4:20■13:13■20:17■21:33■22:4,9,10■23:4,5,12■34:20-NU-16:15■22:21a,22a,23^{3}a,25a,27^{2}a,28a,29a,30^{2}a,32a,33a-DE-5:14,21■22:3,4,10■28:31-JOS-6:21■15:18-J'G-1:14■6:4■10:4(5895)■12:14(5895)■15:15,16^{2}■19:28-1SA-12:3■15:3■16:20■25:20,23,42-2SA-17:23■19:26-1KI-2:40■13:13^{2},23,24,27,28^{2},29-2KI-4:24a-JOB-6:5(6501)■24:3■39:5(6501),5(6171)-PR-26:3-IS-1:3■32:20-JER-2:24(6501)■22:19-HOS-8:9(6501)-ZEC-9:9,9a■14:15■N.T.-all=3688&marked-M'T-21:2,5,5(5268),7-LU-13:15■14:5-JOH-12:14(3678)-2PE-2:16(5268)

ASSAULT-ES-8:11(6696)■N.T.-AC-14:5(3730)

ASSAULTED-AC-17:5(2186)

ASSAY-JOB-4:2(5254)

ASSAYED-DE-4:34(5254)-1SA-17:39(2974)■N.T.-AC-9:26(3987)■16:7(3985)

ASSAYING-HEB-11:29(3984,2983)

ASSEMBLE-all=622&marked-NU-10:3(3259)-2SA-20:4(2199),5(2199)-IS-11:12■45:20(6908)■48:14(6908)-JER-4:5■8:14■12:9■21:4-EZE-11:17■39:17(6908)-DA-11:10-HO-7:14(1481)-JOE-2:16(6908)■3:11(5789)-AM-3:9-MIC-2:12■4:6-ZEP-3:8(6908)

ASSEMBLED-all=6950&marked-EX-38:8(6633)-NU-1:18-JOS-18:1-J'G-10:17(622)-1SA-2:22(6633)■14:20(2199)-1KI-8:1,2,5(3259)■12:21-1CH-15:4(622)■28:1-2CH-5:2,3,6(3259)■20:26■30:13(622)-EZR-9:4(622)■10:1(6908)-NE-9:1(622)-ES-9:18-PS-48:4(3259)-IS-43:9(622)-JER-5:7(1413)-EZE-38:7-DA-6:6(7284),11(7284),15(7284)■N.T.-all=4863&marked-M'T-26:3,57■28:12-M'R-14:53(4905)-JOH-20:19-AC-1:4(4871)■4:31■11:26■15:25(1096)

ASSEMBLIES-PS-86:14(5712)-EC-12:11(627)-IS-1:13(4744)■4:5(4744)-EZE-44:24(4150)-AM-5:21(6116)

ASSEMBLING-EX-38:8(6633)■N.T.-HEB-10:25(1997)

ASSEMBLY-all=6951&marked-GE-49:6-EX-12:6■16:3-LE-4:13■8:4(5712)■23:36(6116)-NU-8:9(5712)■10:2(5712),3(5712)■14:5■16:2(5712)■20:6,8(5712)■29:35(6116)-DE-5:22■9:10■10:4■16:8(6116)■18:16-J'G-20:2■21:8-1SA-17:47-2KI-10:20(6116)-2CH-7:9(6116)■30:23-NE-5:7(6952)■8:18(6116)-PS-22:16(5712)■89:7(5475)■107:32(4186)■111:1(5475)-PR-5:14(5712)-JER-6:11(5475)■9:2(6116)■15:17(5475)■26:17■50:9-LA-1:15(4150)■2:6(4150)-EZE-13:9(5475)■23:24-JOE-1:14(6116)■2:15(6116)-ZEP-3:18(4150)■N.T.-all=1577&marked-AC-19:32,39,41-HEB-12:23(3831)-JAS-2:2(4864)

ASSENT-2CH-18:12(6310)

ASSENTED-AC-24:9(4934)

ASS'S-GE-49:11(860)-2KI-6:25(2543)-JOB-11:12(6501)■N.T.-JOH-12:15(3688)

ASSES-all=2543,a=860&marked-GE-12:16,16a■24:35■30:43■32:5,15a■34:28■36:24■42:26■43:18,24■44:3■45:23,23a■47:17-EX-9:3-NU-31:28,30,34,39,45-JOS-7:24■9:4-J'G-5:10a■19:3,10,19,21-1SA-8:16■9:3^{2}a,5a,20a■10:2^{2}a,14a,16a■22:19■25:18■27:9-2SA-16:1,2-2KI-4:22a■7:7,10-1CH-5:21■12:40■27:30a-2CH-28:15-EZR-2:67-NE-

7:69■13:15-JOB-1:3a,14a■24:5(6501)■42:12a-PS-104:11(6501)-IS-21:7■30:6(5895),24(5895)■32:14(6501)-JER-14:6(6501)-EZE-23:20-DA-5:21(6167)

ASSIGNED-JOS-20:8(5414)-2SA-11:16(5414)

ASSIST-RO-16:2(3936)

ASSOCIATE-IS-8:9(7489)

ASSURANCE-DE-28:66(539)-IS-32:17(983)■N.T.-all=4136&marked-AC-17:31(4102)-COL-2:2-1TH-1:5-HEB-6:11■10:22

ASSURE-1JO-3:19(3982)

ASSURED-LE-27:19(6966)-JER-14:13(571)■N.T.-2TI-3:14(4104)

ASSUREDLY-all=3588&marked-1SA-28:1(3045)-1KI-1:13,17,30-JER-32:41(571)■38:17(3318)■49:12(8354)■N.T.-AC-2:36(806)-16:10(4822)

ASSWAGE-JOB-16:5(2820)

ASSWAGED-GE-8:1(7918)-JOB-16:6(2820)

ASTONIED-all=8074&marked-EZR-9:3,4-JOB-17:8■18:20-IS-52:14-JER-14:9(1724)-EZE-4:17-DA-3:24(8429)■4:19(8075)■5:9(7672)

ASTONISHED-all=8074&marked-LE-26:32-1KI-9:8-JOB-21:5■26:11(8539)-JER-2:12■4:9■18:16■19:8■49:17■50:13-EZE-3:15■26:16■27:35■28:19-DA-8:27■N.T.-all=1605&marked-M'T-7:28■13:54■22:33-M'R-1:22■5:42(1839)■6:2■7:37■10:24(2284),26■11:18-LU-2:47(1839)■4:32■5:9(4023,2285)■8:56(1839)■24:22(1839)-AC-9:6(2284)■10:45(1839)■12:16(1839)■13:12

ASTONISHMENT-all=8047&marked-DE-28:28(8541),37-2CH-7:21(8074)■29:8-PS-60:3(8653)-JER-8:21■25:9,11,18■29:18■42:18■44:12,22■51:37,41-EZE-4:16(8078)■5:15■12:19(8078)■23:33-ZEC-12:4(8541)■N.T.-M'R-5:42(1611)

ASTRAY-all=8582&marked-EX-23:4-DE-22:1(5080)-PS-58:3■119:67(7683),176-PR-5:23(7686)■7:25■28:10(7686)-IS-53:6-JER-50:6-EZE-14:11■44:10^2,15■48:11^3■N.T.-all=4105-M'T-18:12^2,13-1PE-2:25-2PE-2:15

ASTROLOGER-DA-2:10(826)

ASTROLOGERS-all=826&marked-IS-47:13(1895,8064)-DA-1:20(825)■2:2(825),27■4:7■5:7,11,15

ASUNDER-2KI-2:11(996)■N.T.-M'T-19:6(5563)■24:51(1371)-M'R-5:4(1288)■10:9(5563)-AC-1:18(2997)■15:39(673)-HEB-11:37(4249)

AT-all=5921,a=413&marked-GE-6:6a■14:17a■20:13a■24:30,55(176)■26:8(1157)■27:41(7126)■43:33a-EX-2:5■16:12(996)■19:15a■28:7a■29:39(996),41(996)■30:8(996)■36:29a-LE-1:3a,15■4:7a,18a,25a,30a,34a■5:9a■8:15,33(3117)■9:9a■23:5(996)■26:32-NU-3:39■4:27■6:6■9:3(996),5(996),11(996),18^2,23^3■10:3a■27:21■28:4(996),8(996)■31:12a■33:38-DE-7:21(6440),22(4118)■15:9(7126)■16:6a,16^{2}sup■17:6^2■19:15^2■32:35(7138)■33:8,8sup-JOS-5:3a■8:29a■11:5a■15:5(5704),7■18:14a■21:3a■22:11a-J'G-3:2(7535)■5:27^2(996),28(1157)■12:6a■19:22■20:16a-1SA-20:33■21:4(389)■22:14a■25:24-2SA-9:7,10,11,13■16:13(5980)■20:8(5973)-1KI-13:20a-2KI-4:37■9:30(1157)■24:3-1CH-12:32■15:29(1157)-2CH-8:17■15:15■23:13,19■26:9^2-EZR-8:21-NE-5:17■6:1(5704)■12:37■13:19-ES-8:3(6440)-JOB-17:8■18:20■27:23■29:21(3926)■31:9a■39:27-PS-39:12a■52:6■68:29■74:6(3162)■81:7■104:7^2(4480)■106:7^2,32■109:6■110:5■119:162-PR-1:25(6544)■7:12(681)■8:3^2,3sup(3027),34,34sup■14:19■23:30a-EC-5:6,8■12:6,6a-SONG-2:9(4480)■7:13-IS-7:3a■13:6(7138),8a■19:19(681)■30:17^2(6440)■42:14(3162)■60:4,14■66:2,5a-JER-2:12■32:20(5704)■49:17■50:13,14a-LA-1:7■2:15^2-EZE-12:23(7126)■16:25a,46■21:21a■22:13a,13■27:3,35,36■28:19■32:10,10sup■36:8(7126)■39:20■40:40a,44^{2}a■44:11a,17a,25a■46:2,19■47:7a■49:28a,32a-DA-4:8(5705)■8:27■11:27a-HO-11:7(3162)-JOE-1:15(7138)■2:9(1157)-ZEC-3:1■N.T.-all=1722,a=1909,b=1519&marked-M'T-3:2(1448)■4:6(3379),17(1448)■5:25(3379),34(2527),40(2919)■7:13(1223),28a■8:6■9:9a,10(345)■10:7(1448),35(1369)■11:22,25■12:1,41b■13:15(3379),49■14:1,9(4873)■15:17b,30(3844)■18:1,29b■19:4(575)■22:33a■23:6,24(1368)■24:33,41■26:7(345),18(1451),18(4314),45(1448),46(1448)■27:15(2596)-M'R-1:15(1448),22a,33(4314)■2:14a,15(2621)■4:12(3379)■5:22(4314)■6:3■7:25(4314)■9:12(1847)■10:22a,24a■11:1(4314),18a■12:17a,39■13:29a,29■14:3(2621),42(1448),54(4314)■15:6(2596)■16:14(345)-LU-1:14a■2:18(4012),33a,47a■4:11(3379),18,22a,32a■5:5a,8(4363),9a,27a■7:37(345),38(3844),49(345)■8:19b,26b,35(3844),41(3844)■9:31,43^{2}a,61sup,61b■10:14,32(2596),39(3844)■11:5(3317),32b■12:46■13:1,24(1223)■14:10(4873),14,15(4873)■15:29(3763)■16:20(4314)■17:16(3844)■19:5,29(4314),30(1531),37(4314),42(1065)■20:10,26a,37a,46■21:30(1451),31(1451),34(3379),37(3571)■22:27^2,(345),30a,40a■23:7^2,11(1848),12,17(2596),18(3826)■24:22a,27(575),30(2625),47(575)-JOH-1:18(4455)■2:10(4412),13(1451),23■4:21,45^2,46,47(3195,53■5:2,4(2596),37(4455)■6:21a,39,41(4012),61(4012)■7:2(1451),11■8:7a,9(575),59a■10:22■11:24,32b,49(3762),55(1451)■12:2(4873),16(4412),20■13:28(345),14:20■16:4(1537),26■18:16(4314),39■19:42(1451)■20:11(4314),12(4314)■21:1a,20-AC-1:6■2:5■3:1a,2(4314),10^{2}a,12a■4:6b,11(1848),18(2527),35(3844),37(3844)■5:2(3844),9a,10(3844),15(2579)■7:13,26b,29,58(3844)■8:1^2,14,35(575),40b■9:10,13,19,22,27,28,36■10:25a■11:8(3763),15■13:1,5,12a,27■14:8■16:2,4,25(2596)■17:13,16■18:22b■19:1,27b■20:5,14b,15b,15,16b■21:3b,11,13b,24(1159)■22:3(3844)■23:11b,23(575)■25:4,10a,15b,24■26:4(575),4,32(630)■27:3b■28:12b-RO-1:10(4218),15■3:26■4:20b■8:34■9:9(2596)■11:5■13:12(1448)■14:10(1848)■15:26■16:1-1CO-1:2■7:39(1657)■8:10(2621)■9:7(4218)■11:34■14:16a,35■15:6(2178),23,29(3654),32,52■16:8,12(3843),12(3568)-2CO-1:1■4:18^2(4648)■5:6■8:14-GA-4:12(3762)-EPH-1:1,20■2:12■3:13-PH'P-1:1■2:10■4:5(1451),10(4218)-COL-1:2■2:1-1TH-2:2,5(4218),19■3:1,13■5:13-2TH-2:2(1764)■3:11(3367)-1TI-1:3-2TI-1:18■2:26b■3:11■4:1(2596),6(2186),8,13,16,20^2-TIT-2:5(3626)-HEB-1:5(4218),13(4218)■2:1(3379)■9:17(3379)■12:2■13:23(630)-JAS-3:11(1537)-1PE-1:7,13■4:7(1448),17^2(575)■5:13-1JO-1:5(3762)■2:28■4:12(4455)-RE-1:3(1451),17(4314)■3:20a■8:3a■19:2(1537),10(1715)■21:12a■22:10(1451)

ATE-PS-106:28(398)-DA-10:3(398)■N.T.-RE-10:10(2719)

ATHIRST-all=6770-J'G-15:18-RU-2:9■N.T.-all=1372-M'T-25:44-RE-21:6■22:17

ATONEMENT-all=3722&marked-EX-29:33,36(3725),36,37■30:10^2,15,16(3725),16■32:30-LE-1:4■4:20,26,31,35■5:6,10,13,16,18■6:7■7:7■8:34■9:7^2■10:17■12:7,8■14:18,19,20,21,29,31,53■15:15,30■16:6,10,11,16,17^2,18,24,27,30,32,33^3,34■17:11^2■19:22■23:27(3725),28(3725),28■25:9(3725)-NU-5:8(3725),8■6:11■8:12,19,21■15:25,28^2■16:46,47■25:13■28:22,30■29:5,11(3725)■31:50-2SA-21:3-1CH-6:49-2CH-29:24-NE-10:33■N.T.-RO-5:11(2643)

ATONEMENTS-EX-30:10(3725)

ATTAIN-PR-1:5(7069)-EZE-46:7(5381)-HO-8:5(3201)■N.T.-AC-27:12(2658)-PH'P-3:11(2658)

ATTAINED-all=935&marked-GE-47:9(5381)-2SA-23:19,23-1CH-11:21,25■N.T.-RO-9:30(2638)31(5348)-PH'P-3:12(2983),16(5348)-1TI-4:6(3877)

ATTEND-all=7181&marked-ES-4:5(6440)-PS-17:1■55:2■61:1■86:6■142:6-PR-4:1,20■5:1■7:24■N.T.-1CO-7:35(2145)

ATTENDANCE-1KI-10:5(4612)-2CH-9:4(4612)■N.T.-1TI-4:13(4337)-HEB-7:13(4337)

ATTENDED-JOB-32:12(995)-PS-66:19(7181)■N.T.-AC-16:14(4337)

ATTENDING-RO-13:6(4342)

ATTENT-2CH-6:40(7183)■7:15(7183)

ATTENTIVE-all=7183-NE-1:6,11-PS-130:2■N.T.-LU-19:48(1582)

ATTENTIVELY-JOB-37:2(8085)

ATTIRE-PR-7:10(7897)-JER-2:32(7196)-EZE-23:15(2871)

ATTIRED-LE-16:4(6801)

AUDIENCE-all=241-GE-23:10,13,16-EX-24:7-1SA-25:24-1CH-28:8-NE-13:1■N.T.-all=191&marked-LU-7:1(189)■20:45-AC-13:16■15:12■22:22

AUGMENT-NU-32:14(5595)

AUL-EX-21:6(4836)-DE-15:17(4836)

AUNT-LE-18:14(1733)

AUSTERE-LU-19:21(840),22(840)

AUTHOR-HEB-5:9(159)■12:2(747)

AUTHORITIES-1PE-3:22(1849)

AUTHORITY-ES-9:29(8633)-PR-29:2(7235)■N.T.1849&marked-M'T-7:29■8:9■20:25(2715)■21:23^2,24,27-M'R-1:22,27■10:42(2715)■11:28^2,29,33■13:34-LU-4:36■7:8■9:1■19:17■20:2^2,8,20■22:25(1850)-JOH-5:27-AC-8:27(1413)■9:14■26:10,12-1CO-15:24-2CO-10:8-1TI-2:2(5247),12(831)-TIT-2:15(2003)-RE-13:2

AVAILETH-ES-5:13(7737)■N.T.-all=2480-GA-5:6■6:15-JAS-5:16

AVENGE-all=5358&marked-LE-19:18■26:25-NU-31:2(5358,5360),3(5414,5360)-DE-32:43-1SA-24:12-2KI-9:7-ES-8:13-IS-1:24-JER-46:10-HO-1:4(6485)■N.T.-all=1556&marked-LU-18:3,5,7(4160,3588,1557),8(4160,3588,1557)-RO-12:19-RE-6:10

AVENGED-all=5358&marked-GE-4:24-JOS-10:13-J'G-15:7■16:28-1SA-14:24■18:25■25:31(3467)-2SA-4:8(5414,5360)■18:19,(8199),31(8199)-JER-5:9,29■9:9■N.T.-AC-7:24(4160,1557)-RE-18:20(2919,3588,2917)■19:2(1556)

AVENGER-all=1350&marked-NU-35:12-DE-19:6,12-JOS-20:3,5,9-PS-8:2(5358)■44:16(5358)■N.T.-1TH-4:6(1558)

AVENGETH-2SA-22:48(5414,5360)-PS-18:47(5414,5360)

AVENGING-J'G-5:2(6544,6546)-1SA-25:26(3467),33(3467)

AVERSE-MIC-2:8(7725)

AVOID-PR-4:15(6544)■N.T.-RO-16:17(1578)-1CO-7:2(1223)-2TI-2:23(3868)-TIT-3:9(4026)

AVOIDED-1SA-18:11(5437)

AVOIDING-2CO-8:20(4724)-1TI-6:20(1624)

AVOUCHED-DE-26:17(559),18(559)

AWAIT-AC-9:24(1917)

AWAKE-all=5782,a=6974&marked-J'G-5:12-JOB-8:6■14:12a-PS-7:6■17:15a■35:23a■44:23■57:8^3■59:4,5a■108:2^2■139:18a-PR-23:35a-SONG-2:7■3:5■4:16■8:4-IS-26:19a■51:9^2,17■52:1-DA-12:2a-JOE-1:5a-HAB-2:7a,19a-ZEC-13:7■N.T.-M'R-4:38(1326)-LU-9:32(1235)-JOH-11:11(1852)-RO-13:11(1453)-1CO-15:34(1594)-EPH-5:14(1453)

AWAKED-all=6974&marked-GE-28:16(3364)-J'G-16:14(3364)-1SA-26:12-1KI-18:27(3364)-2KI-4:31-PS-3:5■78:65(3364)-JER-31:26

AWAKEST-PS-73:20(5782)-PR-6:22(6974)

AWAKETH-PS-73:20(69743)-IS-

29:8^{2}(6974)

AWAKING-AC-16:27(1096,1853)

AWARE-SONG-6:12(3045)-JER-50:24(3045)■N.T.-M'T-24:50(1097)-LU-11:44(1492)■12:46(1097)

AWAY-all=5493,a=1197,b=1540&marked-EX-19:24(3212)-NU-14:43(310)■27:4(1639)-DE-13:5sup,5a■15:16(3318)■17:7a,12a■19:13a,19a■21:9a,21a■22:21a,22a,24a■24:7a■26:13a,14a-JOS-24:14,3-J'G-10:16■16:3(5265),14(5265)■20:13a-1SA-1:14■7:3,4■20:29(4422)■23:26(3212)■24:19(1870)■26:12(3212)■28:3-2SA-4:7(3212)■5:6■7:15sup,15■12:13(5674)■23:6(5704)■24:10(5674)-1KI-2:31■8:46(7617),48(7617)■20:41■22:43-2KI-3:2■12:3■14:4■17:6b,11b,23b,28b,33b■18:11b,22■23:11(7673),19,24a■24:14b,15b■25:11sup,11b,21b-1CH-5:6,21(7617),26b■6:15b■8:13(1272)■9:1b■17:13■21:8(5674)-2CH-6:36(7617)■14:3,5,15(7617)■15:8(5674),17■17:6■19:3a■20:33■21:17(7617)■28:5(7617)■30:14^{2}■32:12■33:15■34:33■35:23(5674)■36:20b-EZR-2:1(1473),1b■5:12(1541)■8:35(1473)■9:4(1473)■10:3(3318)■6(1473),8(1473),19(3318)-NE-7:6(1473),6(1546)-ES-2:6^{3}(1546)■4:4■8:3(5674)-JOB-4:21(5265)■7:21(5674)■9:12(2862),34■12:24■20:19(1497)■21:18(1589)■22:23(7368)■27:2■27:8(7953)■34:5,20sup,20■36:18(5496)-PS-18:22■27:9(5186)■52:5(2846)■69:4(1497)■88:8(7368)-PR-4:16(1497),24■10:3(1920)■25:4(1898),5(1898)■25:20(5710)-EC-11:10-IS-1:1,6sup,6,25■3:1,18■5:5,23■6:7■10:2(1497),27■17:1■18:5■25:8sup,8■27:9■30:22(2219)■31:7(3988)■36:7■58:9-JER-4:1,4■5:10■48:9(3318)-EZE-11:18■16:50■23:25■26:16■36:26■43:9(7368)■45:9(7311)-DA-4:14(5111)■7:12(5709),14(5709),26■8:11(7311)■11:31,44(2763)■12:11-HO-2:2,17-AM-4:10(7628)■5:23■6:3(5077)-MIC-2:2(7726)-NA-2:7b■3:10(1473)-ZEP-3:11,15-ZEC-3:4■9:7-MAL-3:7■N.T.-all=630,a=565,b=520&marked-M'T-1:11(3350),17^{2}(3350),19■5:31,32,42(654)■8:31a■13:12(142),19(726),36(863),48(1854)■14:15,22,23■15:23,32,39■19:3,7,8,9^{2},22a■22:13(142)■24:35^{2}(3928),39(142)■25:29(142),46a■26:42a,42(3928),44a,57b■27:2b,31b-M'R-1:43(1544)■2:20(522),21(142)■4:15(142),36(863)■5:10(649)■6:36,45,46(657)■8:3,9,26(649)■10:2,4,11,12,22a,50(577)■12:3(649),4(649)■13:31^{2}(3928)■14:36(3911),39a,44b,53b■15:1(667),16b■16:3(617),4(617)-LU-1:25(851),53(1821)■2:15a■5:35(851)■6:29(142),30(142)■8:12(142),13(868),38■9:12sup,12,25(2210)■10:42(851)■13:15b■16:3(851),18^{2}■20:10(1821),11(1821)■23:26b■24:2(617)-JOH-4:8a■5:13(1593)■6:22a,67(5217)■10:40a■12:11(5217)■14:28(5217)■16:7^{2}a■18:13b■19:15(142),16b■20:10a-AC-3:26(654)■5:37(868)■7:27(683),43(3351)■8:39(726)■10:23(1831)■13:3,8(1294)■17:10(1599),14(1821)■19:26(3179)■20:6(1602),30(645)■21:36(142)■22:16(628),22(142)■24:7b■27:20(4014)-RO-11:1(683),2(683),15(580),26(654),27(851)-1CO-5:13(1808)■7:11(863),12(863)■12:2b■13:8(2673),10(2673),11(2673)-2CO-3:7(2673),11(2673),14(343),14(2673),16(4014)-GA-2:13(4879)-EPH-4:25(659)-COL-1:23(3334)-2TH-2:3(646)-1TI-1:19(683)-2TI-1:15(654)■3:5(665)■4:4(654)-HEB-6:6(3895)■9:26(115)■10:4(851),9(337),11(4014),35(577)■12:25(654)-1PE-1:24(1601)■3:21(595)-2PE-3:17(4879)-RE-7:17(1813)■17:3(667)■21:4(1813),4(565),10(667)■22:19^{2}(851)

AWE-PS-4:4(7264)■33:8(1481)■119:161(6342)

AWOKE-all=3364-GE-9:24■41:4,7,21-J'G-16:20-1KI-3:15■N.T.-M'T-8:25(1453)-LU-8:24(1326)

AX-all=1631&marked-DE-19:5■20:19-J'G-9:48(7134)-1SA-13:20(7134)-1KI-6:7-2KI-6:5(1270)-IS-10:15-JER-10:3(4621)■51:20(4661)■N.T.-M'T-3:10(513)

AXE-LU-3:9(513)

AXES-all=7134&marked-1SA-13:21-2SA-12:31(4037)-1CH-20:3(4050)-PS-74:5,6(3781)-JER-46:22-EZE-26:9(2719)

AXLETREES-1KI-7:32(3027),33(3027

B

BABBLER-EC-10:11(1167,3956)■N.T.-AC-17:18(4691)

BABBLING-PR-23:29(7879)

BABBLINGS-1TI-6:20(2757)-2TI-2:16(2757)

BABE-EX-2:6(5288)■N.T.-all=1025&marked-LU-1:41,44■2:12,16-HEB-5:13(3516)

BABES-PS-8:2(5768)■17:14(5768)-IS-3:4(8586)■N.T.-all=3516&marked-M'T-11:25■21:16-LU-10:21-RO-2:20-1CO-3:1-1PE-2:2(1025)

BABYLONISH-JOS-7:21(8152)

BACK-all=7725,a=268&marked-GE-14:16■19:9(1973)■38:29■39:9(2820)-EX-23:4■33:23a-NU-9:7(1639)■13:26■22:34■24:11(4513)-DE-23:13-JOS-8:20(2015),26■11:10■23:12-J'G-11:35■18:26-RU-1:15■2:6-1SA-10:9(7926)■15:11■25:34(4513)-2SA-1:22a■12:23■15:20,25■17:3■18:16(2820)■19:10,11,12,37,43-1KI-13:18,19,20,22,23,26,29■14:9(1458),28■18:37(322)■19:20,21■22:26,33-2KI-1:5^{2}■2:13,24(310)■8:29■15:20■19:28■20:9-1CH-21:20-2CH-13:14(6437)■18:25,32■19:4■25:13■34:16-NEH-2:15-JOB-23:12(4185)■33:18(2820),30■34:27(5493)■39:22-PS-9:3a■14:7■19:13(2820)■21:12(7926)■35:4a■44:10a,18a■53:3(5472),6■56:9a■70:3■78:9(2015),41,57(5472)■80:18(5472)■85:1■114:3a,5a■129:3(1354),5a-PR-10:13(1458)■19:29(1458)■26:3(1458)-IS-14:27■31:2(5493)■37:29■38:17(1458)■42:17a■43:6(3607)■50:5a,6(1458)-JER-2:27(6203)■4:8,28■6:9■8:5■11:10■18:17(6203)■21:4(5437)■32:33(6203)■38:22a■40:5^{2}■42:4(4513)■46:5a,5(6437),21(6437)■47:3(6437)■48:10(4513),39(6203)■49:8(6437)-LA-1:13a■2:3a-EZE-23:35(1458)■24:14(6544)■38:4,8■39:2■44:1-DA-7:6(1355)-HO-4:16(5637)-NA-2:8(6437)-ZEP-1:6(5253)■3:20■N.T.-M'T-24:18(3694)■28:2(617)-M'R-13:16(617)-LU-2:45(5290)■8:37(5290)■9:62(3694)■17:15(5290),31(3694)-JOH-6:66(3694)■20:14(3694)-AC-5:2(3557),3(3557)■7:39(4762)■20:20(5288)-RO-11:10(3577)-HEB-10:38(5288),39(5289)-JAS-5:4(650)

BACKBITERS-RO-1:30(2637)

BACKBITETH-PS-15:3(7270)

BACKBITING-PR-25:23(5643)

BACKBITINGS-2CO-12:20(2636)

BACKBONE-LE-3:9(6096)

BACKS-all=6203&marked-EX-23:27-JOS-7:8,12-2CH-29:6-NE-9:26(1458)-EZE-8:16(268)■10:12(1354)

BACKSIDE-EX-3:1(310)■26:12(268)■N.T.-RE-5:1(3693)

BACKSLIDER-PR-14:14(5472)

BACKSLIDING-all=4878&marked-JER-3:6,8,11,12,14(7726),22(7726)■8:5■31:22(7728)■49:4(7728)-HO-4:16(5637)■11:7■14:4

BACKSLIDINGS-all=4878-JER-2:19■3:22■5:6■14:7

BACKWARD-all=268&marked-GE-9:23(322),23(322)■49:17-1SA-4:18(322)-2KI-20:10(322),11(322)-JOB-23:8-PS-40:14■70:2-IS-1:4■28:13■38:8(322)■44:25■59:14-JER-7:24■15:6-LA-1:8■N.T.-JOH-18:6(1519,3588,3694)

BAD-all=7451&marked-GE-24:50■31:24,29-LE-27:10^{2},12,14,33-NU-13:19■24:13-2SA-13:22■14:17-1KI-3:9-EZR-4:12(873)-JER-24:2■N.T.-M'T-13:48(4550)■22:10(4190)-2CO-5:10(2556)

BADE-all=559&marked-GE-43:17-EX-16:24(6680)-NU-14:10-JOS-11:9-RU-3:6(6680)-1SA-24:10-2SA-1:18■14:19(6680)-2CH-10:12(1696)-ES-4:15■N.T.-all=2564&marked-M'T-16:12(2036)-LU-14:9,10,12,16-AC-11:12(2036)■18:21(657)■22:24(2036)

BADEST-GE-27:19(1696)

BADGERS'-all=8476-EX-25:5■26:14■35:7,23■36:19■39:34-NU-4:6,8,10,11,12,14,25-EZE-16:10

BADNESS-GE-41:19(7455)

BAG-all=3599&marked-DE-25:13-1SA-17:40(3627),49(3627)-JOB-14:17(6872)-PR-7:20(6872)■16:11-IS-46:6-MIC-6:11-HAG-1:6(6872)■N.T.-JOH-12:6(1101)■13:29(1101)

BAGS-2KI-5:23(2754)■12:10(6696)■N.T.-LU-12:33(905)

BAKE-all=644&marked-GE-19:3-EX-16:23-LE-24:5■26:26-1SA-28:24-2SA-13:8(1310)-EZE-4:12(5746)■46:20

BAKED-EX-12:39(644)-NU-11:8(1310)-IS-44:19(644)

BAKEMEATS-GE-40:17(3978,4639,644)

BAKEN-all=644&marked-LE-2:4■6:17,21(7246),21(8601)■7:9■23:17

BAKETH-IS-44:15(644)

BAKER-all=644-GE-40:1,5,16,20,22■41:10-HO-7:4,6

BAKERS-GE-40:2(644)-1SA-8:13(644)

BAKERS'-JER-37:21(644)

BALANCE-all=3976&marked-JOB-31:6-PS-62:9-PR-11:1■16:11■20:23-IS-40:12,15■46:6(7070)

BALANCES-all=3976&marked-LE-19:36-JOB-6:2-JER-32:10-EZE-5:1■45:10-DA-5:27(3977)-HO-12:7-AM-8:5-MIC-6:11

BALANCINGS-JOB-37:16(4657)

BALD-all=7139&marked-LE-11:22(5556)■13:40(7142),41(1371),42(7146),42(1372),43(7146),43(1372)-2KI-2:23(7142)-JER-16:6■48:37(7144)-EZE-27:31■29:18-MIC-1:16

BALDNESS-all=7144-LE-21:5-DE-14:1-IS-3:24■15:2■22:12-JER-47:5-EZE-7:18-AM-8:10-MIC-1:16

BALL-IS-22:18(1754)

BALM-all=6875-GE-37:25■43:11-JER-8:22■46:11■51:8-EZE-27:17

BAND-all=1416&marked-EX-39:23(8193)-1SA-10:26(2428)–1KI-11:24-2KI-13:21-1CH-12:18,21-2CH-22:1-EZR-8:22(2428)-JOB-39:10(5688)-DA-4:15(613),23(6:13)■N.T.-all=4686-M'T-27:27-M'R-15:16-JOH-18:3,12-AC-10:1■21:31■27:1

BANDED-AC-23:12(4160,4963)

BANDS-all=1416&marked-GE-32:7(4264),10(4264)-LE-26:13(4133)-J'G-15:14(612)-2SA-4:2-2KI-6:23■13:20■23:33(631)■24:2^{4}-1CH-7:4■12:23(7218)-2CH-26:11-JOB-1:17(7218)■38:31(4189)■39:5(4147)-PS-2:3(4147)■73:4(2784)■107:14(4147)■119:61(2256)-PR-30:27(2686)-EC-7:26(612)-IS-28:22(4147)■52:2(4147)■58:6(2784)-JER-2:20(4147)-EZE-3:25(5688)■4:8(5688)■12:14(102)■17:21(102)■34:27(4133)■38:6^{2}(102),9(102),22(102)■39:4(102)-HO-11:4(5688)-ZEC-11:7(2256),14(2256),■N.T.-all=1199-LU-8:29-AC-16:26■22:30■27:40(2202)-COL-2:19(4886)

BANISHED-2SA-14:13(5080),14(5080)

BANISHMENT-EZR-7:26(8331)-LA-2:14(4065)

BANK-all=8193&marked-GE-41:17-DE-4:48-JOS-12:2■13:9,16-2SA-20:15(5550)-2KI-2:13■19:32(5550)-IS-37:33(5550)-EZE-47:7,12-DA-12:5^{2}■N.T.-LU-19:23(5132)

BANKS-all=1415&marked-JOS-3:15■4:18-1CH-12:15(1428)-IS-8:7

BANNER-PS-60:4(5251)-SONG-

2:4(1714)-IS-13:2(5251)

BANNERS-all=1713-PS-20:5-SONG-6:4,10

BANQUET-all=4960&marked-ES-5:4,5,6,8,12,14■6:14■7:1(8354),2,7,8-JOB-41:6(3738)-DA-5:10(4961)-AM-6:7(4797)

BANQUETING-SONG-2:4(3196)

BANQUETINGS-1PE-4:3(4224)

BAPTISM-all=908-M'T-3:7■20:22,23■21:25-M'R-1:4■10:38,39■11:30-LU-3:3■7:29■12:50■20:4-AC-1:22■10:37■13:24■18:25■19:3,4-RO-6:4-EPH-4:5-COL-2:12-1PE-3:21

BAPTISMS-HEB-6:2(909)

BAPTIZE-all=907-M'T-3:11^{2}-M'R-1:4,8-LU-3:16^{2}-JOH-1:26,33-1CO-1:17

BAPTIZED-all=907-M'T-3:6,13,14,16■20:22^{2},23^{2}-M'R-1:5,8,9■10:38^{2},39^{2}■16:16-LU-3:7,12,21^{2}■7:29,30■12:50-JOH-3:22,23■4:1,2■10:40-AC-1:5^{2}■2:38,41■8:12,13,16,36,38■9:18■10:47,48■11:16^{2}■16:15,33■18:8■19:3,4,5■22:16-RO-6:3^{2}-1CO-1:13,14,15,16^{2}■10:2■12:13■15:29^{2}-GA-3:27

BAPTIZEST-JOH-1:25(907)

BAPTIZETH-JOH-1:33(907)■3:26(907)

BAPTIZING-all=907-M'T-28:19-JOH-1:28,31■3:23

BAR-all=1280&marked-EX-26:28■36:33-NU-4:10(4132),12(4132)-J'G-16:3-NE-7:3(270)-AM-1:5

BARBARIAN-1CO-14:11^{2}(915)-COL-3:11(915)

BARBARIANS-AC-28:4(915)-RO-1:14(915)

BARBAROUS-AC-28:2(915)

BARBED-JOB-41:7(7905)

BARBER'S-EZE-5:1(1532)

BARE-all=3205,a=5375-GE-4:1,2,17,20,22,25■6:4■7:17a■16:1■16:15^{2},16■19:37,38■20:17■21:2,3■22:24■24:24,36,47■25:2,12,26■29:32,33,34,35■30:1,5,7,10,12,17,19,21,23■31:8^{2},39(2398)■34:1■36:4^{2},5,12,14,■38:3,4,5^{2}■41:50■44:27■46:15,18,20,25-EX-2:2,22■6:20,23,25■19:4a-LE-13:45(6544),55(7146)-NU-13:23a■26:59^{2}-DE-1:31a■31:9a,25a-JOS-3:15^{2}a,17a■4:9a,10a,18a■8:33a-J'G-3:18a■8:31■11:2■13:2,24-RU-4:12,13-1SA-1:20■2:21■14:1a,6a■17:41a-2SA-6:13a■11:27■12:15,24■18:15a■21:8-1KI-5:15a■9:23(7287)■10:2a■11:20■14:28a-2KI-4:17■5:23-1CH-1:32a■2:4,17,19,21,24,29,35,46,48,49■4:6,9,17(2029),18■7:14^{2},16,18,23■12:24a■15:15a,26a,27a-2CH-8:10(7287)■9:1a■11:19,20■14:8^{2}a-NE-4:17a■5:15(7980)-PR-17:25■23:25-SONG-6:9■8:5-IS-8:3■22:6a■32:11(6209)■47:2(2834)■51:2(2342)■52:10(2834)■53:12a■63:9(5190)-JER-13:22(2554)■16:3■20:14■22:26■49:10(2834)■50:12-EZE-12:7a■16:7(6181),22(6181),39(6181)■19:11(4910)■23:4,29(6181),37-HO-1:3,6,8-JOE-1:7(2834)■N.T.-all=3140-M'T-8:17(941)-M'R-14:56(5576),57(5576)-LU-4:22■7:14(941)■8:8(4160)■11:27(941)■23:29(1080)-JOH-1:15,32,34■2:8(5342)■5:33■12:6(941),17■19:35-AC-15:8-1CO-15:37(1131)-1PE-2:24(399)-RE-1:2■22:2(4160)

BAREFOOT-all=3182-2SA-15:30-IS-20:2,3,4

BAREST-1KI-2:26(5375)-IS-63:19(4910)■N.T.-JOH-3:26(3140)

BARK-IS-56:10(5024)

BARKED-JOE-1:7(7111)

BARLEY-all=8184-EX-9:31^{2}-LE-27:16-NU-5:15-DE-8:8-J'G-7:13-RU-1:22■2:17,23■3:2,15,17-2SA-14:30■17:28■21:9-1KI-4:28-2KI-4:42■7:1,16,18-1CH-11:13-2CH-2:10,15■27:5-JOB-31:40-IS-28:25-JER-41:8-EZE-4:9,12■13:19■45:13-HO-3:2^{2}-JOE-1:11■N.T.-JOH-6:9(2916),13(2916)-RE-6:6(2915)

BARN-JOB-39:12(1637)-HAG-2:19(4035)■N.T.-M'T-13:30(596)-LU-12:24(596)

BARNFLOOR-2KI-6:27(1637)

BARNS-PR-3:10(618)-JOE-1:17(4460)■N.T.-M'T-6:26(596)-LU-12:18(596)

BARREL-all=3537-1KI-17:12,14,16

BARRELS-1KI-18:33(3537)

BARREN-all=6135-GE-11:30■25:21■29:31-EX-23:26-DE-7:14-J'G-13:2,3-1SA-2:5-2KI-2:19(7921),21(7921)-JOB-24:21■39:6(4420)-PS-113:9-PR-30:16(6115)-SONG-4:2(7909)■6:6(7909)-IS-54:1-JOE-2:20(6723)■N.T.-all=4723&marked-LU-1:7,36■23:29-GA-4:27-2PE-1:8(692)

BARRENNESS-PS-107:34(4420)

BARS-all=1280&marked-EX-26:26,27^{2},29^{2}■35:11■36:31,32^{2},34^{2}■39:33■40:18-NU-3:36■4:31-DE-3:5-1SA-23:7-1KI-4:13-2CH-8:5■14:7-NE-3:3,6,13,14,15-JOB-17:16(905)■38:10■40:18(4300)-PS-107:16■147:13-PR-18:19-IS-45:2-JER-49:31■51:30-LA-2:9-EZE-38:11-JON-2:6-NA-3:13

BASE-all=4350-2SA-6:22(8217)-1KI-7:27,29(3653),30,31(3653),32,34^{2},35^{2}-JOB-30:8(1097,8034)-IS-3:5(7034)-EZE-17:14(8217)■29:14(8217)-ZEC-5:11(4369)-MAL-2:9(8217)N.T.-1CO-1:28(36)-2CO-10:1(5011)

BASER-AC-17:5(60)

BASES-all=4350&marked-1KI-7:27,28,37,38,39■43^{2}-2KI-16:17■25:13,16-2CH-4:14^{2}-EZR-3:3-JER-27:19(4369)■52:17,20

BASEST-EZE-29:15(8217)-DA-4:17(8215)

BASKET-all=5536&marked-GE-40:17^{2}-EX-29:3^{2},23,32-LE-8:2,26,31-NU-6:15,17,19-DE-26:2(2935),4(2935)■28:5(2935),17(2935)-J'G-6:19-JER-24:2^{2}(1731)-AM-8:1(3619),2(3619)■N.T.-AC-9:25(4711)-2CO-11:33(4553)

BASKETS-GE-40:16(5536),18(5536)-2KI-10:7(1731)-JER-6:9(5552)■24:1(1736)■N.T.all=2894&marked-M'T-14:20■15:37(4711)■16:9,10(4711)-M'R-6:43(2894)■8:8(4711),19,20(4711)-LU-9:17-JOH-6:13

BASON-EX-12:22^{2}(5592)-1CH-28:17^{2}(3713)■N.T.-JOH-13:5(3537)

BASONS-all=4219&marked-EX-24:6(101),27:3■38:3-NU-4:14-2SA-17:28(5592)-1KI-7:40,45,50-2KI-12:13-1CH-28:17(3713)-2CH-4:8,11,22-EZR-1:10^{2}(3713)■8:27(3713)-NE-7:70-JER-52:19(5592)

BASTARD-DE-23:2(4464)-ZEC-9:6(4464)

BASTARDS-HEB-12:8(3541)

BAT-LE-11:19(5847)-DE-14:8(5847)

BATH-all=1324-IS-5:10-EZE-45:10,11^{2},14^{2}

BATHE-all=7364-LE-15:5,6,7,8,10,11,13,18,21,22,27■16:26,28■17:15,16-NU-19:7,8,19

BATHED-IS-34:5(7301)

BATHS-all=1324-1KI-7:26,38-2CH-2:10^{2}■4:5-EZR-7:22(1325),22-EZE-45:14^{2}

BATS-IS-2:20(5847)

BATTERED-2SA-20:15(7843)

BATTLE-all=4421&marked-GE-14:8-NU-21:33■31:14(6635,4421),21,27(6635),28(6635)■32:27,29-DE-2:9,24■3:1■20:1,2,3,5,6,7■29:7-JOS-4:13■8:14■11:19,20■22:33(6635)-J'G-8:13■20:14,18,20,22,23,28,34,39^{2},42-1SA-4:1,2■7:10■13:22■14:20,22,23■17:1,2,8,13^{2},20,28,47■26:10■28:1(4264)■29:4^{2},9■30:24■31:3-2SA-1:4,25■2:17■3:30■10:8,9,13■11:15,25■17:11(7128)■18:6,8■19:3,10■21:17,18,19,20■22:40■23:9-1KI-8:44■20:14,29,39■22:4,6,15,30^{2},35-2KI-3:7,26-1CH-5:20■7:11,40■10:3■11:13■12:8,19,33(6635),36(6635),37■14:15■19:7,9,10,14,17sup,sup-2CH-13:3^{2},14■14:10■18:5,14,29^{2},34■20:1,15■25:8,13-JOB-15:24(3593)■38:23(7128)■39:25■41:8-PS-18:39■24:8■55:18(7128)■76:3■78:9(7128)■89:43■140:7(5402)-PR-21:31-EC-9:11-IS-9:5(5430)■13:4■22:2■27:4■28:6■42:25-JER-8:6■18:21■46:3■49:14■50:22,42■51:20(4661)-EZE-7:14■13:5-DA-11:20,25-HO-1:7■2:18■10:9,14-JOE-2:5-AM-1:14-OB-1-ZEC-9:10■10:3,4,5■14:2,3(7128)■N.T.all=4171-1CO-14:8-RE-9:7,9■16:14■20:8

BATTERING-all supplied

BATTLEMENT-DE-22:8(4624)

BATTLEMENTS-JER-5:10(5189)

BATTERING-all supplied

BATTLES-all=4421-1SA-8:20■18:17■25:28-1CH-26:27-2CH-32:8-IS-30:32

BAY-all=3956&marked-JOS-15:2,5■18:19-PS-37:35(249)-ZEC-6:3(554),7(554)

BDELLIUM-GE-2:12(916)-NU-11:7(916)

BEACON-IS-30:17(8650)

BEAM-all=4500&marked-J'G-16:14(708)-1SA-17:7-2SA-21:19-1KI-7:6(5646)-2KI-6:2(6982),5(6982)-1CH-11:23■20:5-HAB-2:11(3714)■N.T.-all=1385-M'T-7:3,4,5-LU-6:41,42^{2}

BEAMS-all=7136&marked-1KI-6:9(1356),36(3773)■7:2(3773),3(6763),12(3773)-2CH-3:7(6982)-NE-2:8■3:3,6-PS-104:3-SONG-1:17(6982)

BEANS-2SA-17:28(6321)-EZE-4:9(6321)

BEAR-all=5375,a=3205,b=1677&marked-GE-4:13■13:6■16:11a■17:17a,19a,21a■18:13a■22:23a■30:3a■36:7■43:9(2398)■44:32(2398)■49:15(5445)-EX-18:22■20:16(6030)■25:27■27:7■28:12,29,30,38,43■30:4■37:5,14,15,27■38:7-LE-5:1,17■7:18■10:17■12:5a■16:22■17:16■19:8,18(5201)■20:17,19,20■22:9,16■24:15-NU-1:50■4:15,25■5:31■7:9■9:13■11:14,17^{2}■14:33,34■18:1^{2},22,23,32■30:15-DE-1:9,12,31■5:20(6030)■10:8■28:57a-JOS-3:8,13■4:16■6:4,6-J'G-13:3a,5a,7a-RU-1:12a-1SA-17:34b,36b,37b-2SA-17:8b■18:19(1319),20^{3}(1319)-1KI-3:21a■21:10(5749)-2KI-18:14■19:30(6213)-1CH-5:18-2CH-2:2(5445)-ES-1:22(8323)-PS-75:3(8505)■89:50■91:12-PR-9:12■12:24(4910)■17:12b■18:14■28:15b■30:21-SONG-4:2(8382)-IS-1:14■7:14a■11:7b■37:31(6213)■46:4,7■52:11■53:11(5445)■54:1(3205)-JER-5:31(7287)■10:19■17:21,27■29:6a■31:19■44:22-LA-3:10b,27-EZE-4:4,5,6■12:6,12■14:10■16:52^{2},54■17:8,23(6213)■18:19,20^{2}■23:35,49■32:30■34:29■36:7,15■44:10,12,13■46:20(3318)-DA-2:39(7981)■7:5(1678)-HO-9:16(6213)■13:8b-AM-5:19b■7:10(3557)-MIC-6:16■7:9-ZEP-1:11(5187)-HAG-2:12-ZEC-5:10(3212)■6:13■N.T.-all=3140,a=941&marked-M'T-3:11a■4:6(142)■19:18(5576)■27:32(142)-M'R-10:19(5576)■15:21(142)-LU-1:13(1080)■4:11(142)■11:48■13:9(4160)■14:27a■18:7(3114),20(5576)■23:26(5342)-JOH-1:7,8■2:8■(5342)■3:28■5:31,36■8:14,18■10:25■15:4(5342),8(5342),27■16:12a■18:23,37-AC-9:15a■15:10a■18:14(430)■22:5■23:11■27:15(503)-RO-10:2■13:9(5576)■15:1a-1CO-10:13(5297)■15:49(5409)-2CO-8:3■11:1^{2}(430),4(430)-GA-4:15■5:10a■6:2a,5a,17a-COL-4:13-1TI-5:14(5041)-HEB-9:28(399)-JAS-3:12(4160)-1JO-1:2■5:7,8-RE-2:2a■13:2(715)

BEARD-all=2206&marked-LE-13:29,30■14:9■19:27■21:5-1SA-17:35■21:13-2SA-19:24(8222)■20:9-EZR-9:3-PS-133:2^{2}-IS-7:20■15:2-JER-48:37-EZE-5:1

BEARDS-all=2206-2SA-10:4,5-1CH-19:5-JER-41:5

BEARERS-all=5449-2CH-2:18■34:13-NE-4:10

BEAREST-J'G-13:3(3205)■N.T.-JOH-8:13(3140)-RO-11:18(941)-GA-4:27(5088)

BEARETH-all=5375&marked-LE-11:25,28,40■15:10-NU-11:12-DE-25:6(3205)■29:18(6509),23(6779)■32:11

-JOB-16:8(6030)■24:21(3205)-PR-25:18 (6030)■29:2(4910)-SONG-6:6(8382) -JOE-2:22■N.T.-M'T-13:23(2592) -JOH-5:32(3140)■8:18(3140)■15:2^2(5342) -RO-8:16(4828)■13:4(5409)-1CO-13:7 (4722)-HEB-6:8(1627)-1JO-5:6(3140)

BEARING-all=5375&marked-GE-1:29(2232)■16:2(3205)■29:35(3205)■30:9(3205)■37:25-NU-10:17,21-JOS-3:3,14■6:8,13-1SA-17:7-2SA-15:24-PS-126:6■N.T.-all=941&marked-M'R-14:13-LU-22:10-JOH-19:17-RO-2:15 (4828)■9:1(4828)-2CO-4:10(4064) -HEB-2:4(4901)■13:13(5342)

BEARS-2KI-2:24(1677)-IS-59:11(1677)

BEAST-all=929,a=2416&marked -GE-1:24a,25a,30a■2:19a,20a■3:1a,14a■6:7■7:2,14a,21a■8:19a,20■9:2a,5a,10^{2}a■34:23■37:20a,33a-EX-8:17,18■9:9,10, 19,22,25■11:7■12:12■13:2,12,15■19:13■22:5(1165),10,19■23:29a-LE-5:2a■7:21, 24(5038),25,26■11:26,39,47^{2}a■17:13a■18:23^2■20:15^2,16^2,25■24:18(5315,929),18 (5315),21■25:7a■27:9,10,11^2,27,28-NU-3:13■8:17■31:26,47-DE-4:17■14:6■27:21-J'G-20:48-2KI-14:9a-2CH-25:18a -NE-2:12^2,14-JOB-39:15a-PS-36:6■50:10a■73:22■80:13(2123)■104:11a■135:8■147:9-PR-12:10-EC-3:19,21-IS-35:9a■43:20a■63:14-JER-7:20■9:10■21:6■27:5■31:27■32:43■33:10^2,12■36:29■50:3■51:62-EZE-14:13,17,19,21a,21■25:13■29:8,11■34:8a,28a■36:11■39:17a■44:31-DA-7:5(2423),6(2423),7(2423),11 (2423),19(2423),23(2423)-HO-13:8a -JON-3:7,8-MIC-1:13(7409)-ZEP-1:3 -ZEC-8:10■N.T.-all=2342&marked -LU-10:34(2934)-AC-28:4,5-HEB-12:20-RE-4:7^4(2226)■6:3(2226),5(2226), 7(2226)■11:7■13:1,2,3,4^3,11,12^2,14^2,15^3, 17,18■14:9,11■15:2■16:2,10,13■17:3, 7,8^2,11,12,13,16,17■19:19,20^2■20:4,10

BEAST'S-DA-4:16(2423)

BEASTS-all=929,a=2416,b=2423& marked-GE-7:2,8■31:39(2966)■36:6■45:17(1165)-EX-11:5■22:31(2966)■23:11a-LE-7:24(2966)■11:2a,2,3,27a, 46■17:15(2966)■20:25■22:8(2966)■26:6a, 22a■27:26-NU-18:15^2■20:8(1165),11 (1165)■31:11,30■35:3a-DE-7:22a■14:4, 6■28:26■32:24-1SA-17:44,46a-2SA-21:10a -1KI-4:33■18:5-2KI-3:17-2CH-32:28 -EZR-1:4,6-JOB-5:22a,23a■12:7■18:3■35:11■37:8a■40:20a-PS-8:7■49:12,20■50:11(2123)■79:2a■104:20a,25a■148:10a -PR-9:2(2874)■30:30-EC-3:18,19-IS-1:11 (4806)■13:21(6728),22(338)■18:6^2■30:6■34:14(6728),14(338)■40:16a■46:1a■56:9^{2}a■66:20(3753)-JER-7:33■12:4,9a■15:3■16:4■19:7■27:6a■28:14a■34:20■50:39 (6728),39(338)-EZE-5:17a■8:10■14:15^{2}a■29:5a■31:6a,13a■32:4a,13^2■33:27a■34:5a, 25a■38:20a■39:4a-DA-2:38b■4:12b,14b, 15b,21b,23b,25b,32b■5:21b■7:3b,7b,12b, 17b■8:4a-HO-2:12a,18a■4:3a-JOE-1:18,20■2:22-AM-5:22(4806)-MIC-5:8-HAB-2:17-ZEP-2:14a,15a-ZEC-14:15■N.T.-all=2226&marked-M'R-1:13(2342)-AC-7:42(4968)■10:12(5074), 12(2342)■11:6(5074),6(2342)■23:24 (2934)-RO-1:23(5074)-1CO-15:32(2341), 39(2934)-TIT-1:12(2342)-HEB-13:11 -JAS-3:7(2342)-2PE-2:12-JUDE-10-RE-4:6,8,9■5:6,8,11,14■6:1,6,8(2342)■7:11■14:3■15:7■18:13(2934)■19:4

BEAT-all=5221&marked-EX-30:36 (7833)■39:3(7554)-NU-11:8(1743)-DE-25:3-J'G-8:17(5422)■9:45(5422)■19:22 (1849)-RU-2:17(2251)-2SA-22:43(7833) -2KI-3:25(2040)■13:25■23:12(5422) -PS-18:42(7833)■89:23(3807)-PR-23:14 -IS-2:4(3807)■3:15(1792)■27:12(2251)■41:15(1854)-JOE-3:10(3807)-JON-4:8 -MIC-4:3(3807),13(1854)■N.T.-all= 1194&marked-M'T-7:25(4363),27(4350)■21:35-M'R-4:37(1911)■12:3-LU-6:48 (4366),49(4366)■12:45(5180)■20:10,11 -AC-16:22(4463)■18:17(5180)■22:19

BEATEN-all=4749&marked-EX-5:14(5221),16(5221)■25:18,31,36■27:20 (3795)■29:40(3795)■37:7,17,22-LE-2:14(1643),16(1643)■16:12(1851)■24:2 (3795)-NU-8:4^2■28:5(3795)-DE-25:2^2 (5221)-JOS-8:15(5060)-2SA-2:17(5062) -1KI-10:16(7820),17(7820)-2CH-2:10 (4347)■9:15^2(7820),16(7820)■34:7(3807) PR-23:35(1986)-IS-27:9(5310)■28:27 (2251)■30:31(2865)-JER-46:5(3807)MIC-1:7(3807)■N.T.-all=1194&marked M'R-13:9-LU-12:47,48-AC-5:40■16:37 2CO-11:25(4463)

BEATEST-DE-24:20(2251)-PR-23:13 (5221)

BEATETH-1CO-9:26(1194)

BEATING-1SA-14:16(1986)N.T. -M'R-12:5(1194)-AC-21:32(5180)

BEAUTIES-PS-110:3(1926)

BEAUTIFUL-all=3303&marked -GE-29:17(3303,8389)-DE-21:11(3303, 8389)-1SA-16:12■25:3-2SA-11:2(2896) -ES-2:7(2896,4758)-PS-48:2-EC-3:11 -SONG-6:4■7:1-IS-4:2(6643)■52:1 (8597),7(4998)■64:11(8597)-JER-13:20 (8597)■48:17(8597)-EZE-16:12(8597), 13■23:42(8597)■N.T.-all=5611-M'T-23:27-AC-3:2,10-RO-10:15

BEAUTIFY-all=6286-EZR-7:27 -PS-149:4-IS-60:13

BEAUTY-all=3308,a=8597& marked-EX-28:2a,40a-2SA-1:19(6643)■14:25(3303)1CH-16:29(1927)-2CH-3:6a■20:21(1927)-ES-1:11-JOB-40:10(1926) -PS-27:4(5278)■29:2(1927)■39:11(2530)■45:11■49:14(6736)■50:2■90:17(5278)■96:6a,9(1927)-PR-6:25■20:29(1926)■31:30-IS-3:24■13:19a■28:1a,4a,5a■33:17■44:13a■53:2(4758)■61:3(6287) -LA-1:6(1926)■2:1a,15-EZE-7:20(6643)■16:14,15,25■27:3,4,11■28:7,12,17■31:8■32:19(5276)-HO-14:6(1935)-ZEC-9:17■11:7(5278),10(5278)

BECAME-all=1961&marked-GE-2:7,10■19:26■20:12■21:20■24:67■26:13 (1431)■44:32(6148)■47:20,26■49:15 -EX-2:10■4:3,4■7:10,12■8:17^2■9:10, 24■36:13-NU-26:10-DE-26:5-JOS-7:5■14:14■24:32-J'G-1:30,33,35■8:27■15:14■17:5,12-RU-4:16-1SA-10:12■16:21■18:29■22:2■25:37,42-2SA-2:25■4:4 (6452)■8:2,6,14■11:27-1KI-11:24■12:30■13:6,33,34-2KI-17:3,15(1891)■24:1-1CH-18:2,6,13■19:19(5647)-2CH-27:6(2388) -NE-9:25(8080)-ES-8:17(3054)-PS-69:11■83:10■109:25-JER-51:30 -EZE-17:6^2■19:3,6■23:10■31:5(748)■34:5,8■36:4-DA-2:35(1934),35(1934)■8:4 (1431)■10:15(481)-OB-12(5235)■N.T. -all=1096&marked-M'T-28:4-M'R-9:3 -AC-10:10-RO-1:21(3154),22(3471)■6:18(1402)-1CO-9:20,22■13:11-2CO-8:9 (4433)-PH'P-2:8-1TH-1:6■2:14-HEB-2:10(4241)■5:9■7:26(4241)■10:33■11:7-RE-6:12^2■8:8,11(1096,1519)■16:3,4

BECAMEST-1CH-17:22(1961) -EZE-16:8(1961)

BECAUSE-all=3588,a=5921,b=6440, c=3282,d=834&marked-GE-2:3,23■ -GE-2:3,23■3:10,14,17,20■5:29(4480)■7:7b■11:9■12:13(1558),17(1697)■16:11■18:20^2■19:13■20:11,18a(1697)■21:11a (182)12^{2}a,13,25a(182),31■22:16c,d, 18(6118)d■25:21,28■26:5(6119),7,9, 20■27:20,23,41a,46b■28:11■29:15,33, 34■30:18d,20■31:30,31■32:32■33:11^2■34:7,13d,19,27d■35:7■36:7b■37:3■38:15,26■39:9d,23d■41:32,57■43:18, 18a(1697),32■46:30■47:20■49:4-EX-1:12b,19,21■2:10■5:21d■8:12a(1697)■9:11b■12:39■13:8(5668)■14:11(1115)■17:7^{2}a,16■18:15■19:18b,d■29:33,34■32:35a,d■40:35-LE-6:4,9a■10:13■11:4,5,6■14:18■19:8,20■20:3■21:23■22:7, 25■26:10b,35(854)d■43c-NU-3:13■6:7, 12■7:9■9:13■11:3,14,20c,34■12:1(a,182)■13:24a(182)■14:16(1115),22,24(6118),43a (3588,3651)■15:31,34■19:13,20■20:12c, 13d,24a,d■22:3,3(6640),22,29,32■25:13d (8478)■26:62■27:4■30:5,14■32:11,17b,19■35:28-DE-1:36c,d■2:5,9,19,25b■4:37(8478, 3588)■7:8,8sup■8:20(6118)■9:18a, 25■12:20■13:5,10■14:8,29■15:2,10,16^2■16:15■18:12(1558)■19:6■20:3b■21:14 (8478,d)■22:19,21,24^{2}a(1697,843),29d (8478)■23:4a,d(1697),5,7■24:1■27:20■28:20b,45,47d(8478),62■29:25a,d■31:17a,(3588),29■32:3,47,51^{2}a,d■33:21 -JOS-2:9b,11b,24b■5:1b,6d,7■6:1b, 17,25■7:12,15^2■9:18,20a,24,24b■10:2^2, 42■11:6b■14:9,14c■17:1,6■20:5■22:31d■23:3b-J'G-1:19■2:18b,20c■3:12a(3588)■5:23■6:2b,6b,7a(182),22a(3651),27d,30^2, 31,32■8:20,24■9:18■10:10■11:13■12:4■13:22■14:17■15:6■18:28■20:36■21:15,22 -1SA-1:6,20■2:1,25■3:13■4:21^2(413)■6:19^2■8:18b■9:13,16■10:1■12:10,22■13:11,14■14:29■ 15:23c,24■16:7■17:32a■18:12,16■19:4^2■20:18,34■21:8■22:17^2■24:5a,d■25:28■26:12,16d,21(8478)d■28:18d■30:6, 13,22c-2SA-1:9,10,12■2:6d,30a,d■6:8a,d, 12(5668)■8:10a,d■10:5■12:6(6118)d, 6ad,10(6118,3588),14,25(5668)■13:22a (1697)d■14:15,26■16:8,10■18:20(3588)a■19:21,26,42■21:1a,d,7a■22:8,20■23:6 -1KI-1:50b■2:7b,26^2■3:2,11c,19d■8:11b, 33d,35,64■9:9a,d■11:9,33c,d,34d■14:13c, 15d,16(1558)■15:5d,13d,30a■16:7d■17:7■19:7,14■20:28c,d,36c,d,42c■21:2, 4a,6■23:20c,29c(3588)-2KI-1:17■5:1■8:12, 29■9:14b■10:30c,d■13:4,23(4616)■15:16■17:26d■18:12c,d■19:28c■21:11c,d, 15c,d■22:7,13c,d,17(8478)d,19c■23:26a -1CH-1:19■4:9,41■5:9,20,22■7:21,23■9:27■12:1b■13:10a,d,11■14:2(5668)■15:13,22■16:33,41■18:10a,d■19:2■21:8d, 30b■22:8■23:28■27:23■28:3■29:9-2CH-1:11c,d■6:24,26■7:2,6,7,22c,d■8:11■12:2,5 (6448),14■13:18■14:6,7■15:16d■16:10a■17:3■21:3,10,7c,10,12(8478)d■22:6^2,9■24:16,20,24■25:16,20■26:20■27:6■28:19 (5668),23■30:3■34:21c,d,25(8478)d,27c■35:14■36:15-EZR-3:11,11a■4:14(3606, 6903,1768)■8:22■9:4a,15a■10:6a,9a -NE-4:9b■5:15b,18■6:18■8:12■13:2,29a -ES-1:15a,d■8:7a,d■9:3,24-JOB-3:10■6:20■8:9■11:16,18■15:27■17:12b■20:19■23:17■29:12■30:11■31:25^2■32:1,2a,3a,d, 4■34:27d,a(3651),36a■35:12b,15■36:18■38:21■39:11,17-PS-5:8(4616)■8:2(4616)■13:6■14:6■16:8■18:7,19■27:11(4616)■28:5,6■33:21■37:40■38:3^{2}b,5b,20(8478)■39:9■41:11■44:3■45:4a(1697)■48:11 (4616)■52:9■53:5■55:3sup,3b,19d■60:4b■8a■63:3,7■69:7,18(4616)■78:22■86:17■91:9,14^2■97:8(4616)■102:10b■106:33■107:11,17(1870),17sup,30■109:16c,21■116:1,2■118:1■119:56,62a, 74,100,136a,139,158d,164a■122:9(4616) -PR-1:24c■21:7■22:22■24:13-EC-2:17■4:9d■5:20■8:6,11d,13d,15d,17d■10:15d■12:3,5-IS-2:6■3:8,16c(3588)■5:24■6:5■7:5c(3588),24■8:20d■10:27b■14:20,29■15:1^2■17:9b,10■19:16b,17b,20b■22:4a■24:5■26:3■28:15,28■30:12c■31:1^2■32:14■37:29c■40:7■43:20■49:7 (4616)■51:13b■53:9a,12(8478)d■55:5 (4616)■60:5,9■61:1c■64:7(3027)■65:12c,16^2■66:4c-JER-2:35,35a■4:4b, 17,18,19,28a(3588)■5:6,14c■6:19 (3588)a(1697),30■7:13c■8:14■9:10,13a,19^2■10:5■12:4,11■13:17, 25d■14:4(5668),5,6,16b■15:4(1558), 17b■16:11a,d,18a■17:13■18:15■19:4c,d,8a,13(3605),15■20:8,17d■21:12b■22:9a,d,15■23:9sup,9b,10b, 38c■25:8c,d,16b,27b,37b,38^{2}b■26:3b■28:16■29:15■29:19(8478)d, 23c,d,25c,d,31c,d,32■30:17■31:15, 19■32:24b,32a■35:16,17c,18c,d■39:18■40:3■41:9(3027),18b,18■44:3b,22^{2}b■23b,d,23■46:15,21,23■47:4a■48:7(3588)c, 36a(3651),42(3588)a■50:7(8471)d,11^2,24■51:11,51,55,56-LA-1:8,16^2■3:22,28■5:9b, 10b,18a-EZE-3:20,21■5:7c,9c,11c■6:9d■

7:19▪13:8c,10c,22c▪14:5d,15b▪15:8c▪16:15a,28(1115),36c,43c,d▪63b▪18:18▪20:16c,24c▪21:7,13,24^{2}c,28(4616)▪22:19c▪23:30sup,30ad,35c,45▪24:13c▪25:3c,6c,8c,12c,15c▪26:2c▪28:2c,6▪29:6c,9c,20d▪31:10c,d▪33:29a▪34:8c,8sup,21c▪35:5c,10c,15a▪36:2c,3c,6c,13c▪39:23a,d▪44:2(3588),7(413),12c,d▪47:9,12-DA-2:8(3606,6903,1768)▪3:22(4481,1768)▪3:29(3606,6903,1768)▪4:9(1768)▪6:3(3606,6903,1768),23(1768)▪7:11(4481)▪9:8d,11,16(3588)▪11:35(3588,5750)-HO-4:1,6,10,13▪5:1,11▪7:13▪8:1c,11▪9:17▪10:3,5sup,5,13,15b▪11:5-JOE-1:5a,11,12,18▪2:20▪3:5d,19-AM-1:3a,6a,9a,11a,13a▪2:1a,4a,6a,4:12(6118,3588)-JON-1:10-MIC-2:1,10(5668)▪6:13a▪7:9,13a,18-HAB-1:16▪2:3,5,8-ZEP-1:17▪2:10-HAG-1:9c-ZEC-8:10(4480)▪10:2,5▪11:2d-MAL-2:2,14a(3588)▪N.T.-all=3754,a=1223&marked-M'T-2:18▪5:36▪7:14▪9:36▪11:20,25▪12:41▪13:5a,6a,11,13,21a,58a▪14:5▪15:32▪16:7,8▪17:20a▪18:7(575),32(1893)▪19:8(4314)▪20:7,15,31(2443)▪21:46(1894)▪23:29▪24:12a▪26:31(1722),33(1722)▪27:6(1893),19a-M'R-1:34▪3:9a,30▪4:5a,6a,29▪5:4a▪6:6a,34▪7:19▪8:2,16,17▪9:38,41▪11:18▪14:27(1722)▪15:42(1893)▪16:14-LU-1:7(2530),20(473,3759)▪2:4a,7(1360)▪4:18(3739,1752)▪5:19a▪8:6a,30▪9:7a,49,53▪10:20▪11:8^{2}a,18▪12:17▪13:2,14▪15:27▪16:8▪17:9▪18:5a▪19:3,11^{2}a,17,21,31,44(473,3739)▪23:8a-JOH-1:50▪2:24a▪3:18,19(1063),23,29a▪4:41a,42a▪5:16,18,27,30▪6:2,26^{2},41▪7:1,7,22,23,30,39,43a▪8:22,37,43,44,45,47▪9:16,22▪10:13,17,26(1063),33,36▪11:9,10,42a▪12:6,11,30a,39,42a▪13:29(1893)▪14:12,17,19,28▪15:19,21,27▪16:3,4,6,9,10,11,16,17,21,27,32▪17:14▪19:7,31(1893),42a▪20:13,29▪21:17-AC-2:6,24(2530),27▪4:21a▪6:1▪8:11a,20▪10:45▪12:20a,23(473,3739)▪14:12(1894)▪16:3a▪17:18,31(1360)▪18:2a,3a▪20:16(3704)▪22:29▪27:4a,9a▪28:2^{2}a,18a,20(1063)-RO-1:19(1360),21(1360)▪3:2▪4:15(1063)▪5:5▪6:15,19a▪8:7(1360),10^{2}a,21,27▪9:7,28,32▪14:23▪15:15a-1CO-1:25▪2:14▪3:13▪6:7▪11:10a▪12:15,16▪15:9(1360),15-2CO-7:13▪11:7,11-GA-2:4a,11▪3:19(5484)▪4:6-EPH-4:18a▪5:6a,16-PH'P-1:7a▪2:26(1360),30▪4:17-1TH-2:8(1360),9(4314),13▪4:6(1360)-2TH-1:3,10▪2:10(473,3739),13▪3:9-1TI-1:13▪4:10▪5:12▪6:2^{2},-PH'M-7-HEB-3:19a▪4:6a▪6:13(1893)▪7:23a,24a▪8:9▪10:2a▪11:5(1360),11(1893),23(1360)-JAS-1:10▪4:2a,3(1360)-1PE-1:16(1360)▪2:21▪5:8-1JO-2:8,11,12,13^{3},14^{2},21^{2}▪3:1,9,12,14,16,22▪4:1,4▪4:9,13,17,18,19▪5:6,10-3JO-7(1063)-JUDE-16(5484)-RE-1:7(1909)▪2:4,14,20▪3:10,16,17▪5:4▪8:11▪11:10,17▪14:8▪16:5,11(1537),21(1537)

BECKONED-LU-1:22(1269)▪5:7(2656)-JOH-13:24(3506)-AC-19:33(2678)▪21:40(2678)▪24:10(3506)

BECKONING-AC-12:17(2678)▪13:16(2678)

BECOME-all=1961&marked-GE-3:22▪9:15▪18:18▪24:35(1431)▪32:10▪34:16▪37:20▪48:19^{2}-EX-4:9▪7:9,19▪8:16▪9:9▪15:2,6(142)▪23:29▪32:1,23-LE-19:29(4390)-DE-27:9▪28:37-JOS-9:13(1086)-J'G-16:17(2470)-1SA-28:16-2SA-7:24-1KI-2:15▪14:3-2KI-21:14▪22:19-ES-2:11(6213)-JOB-7:5(3988)▪21:7(6275)▪30:19(4911),21(2015)-PS-14:3(444)▪28:1(4911)▪53:3(444)▪62:10(1891)▪69:8,22,22sup▪79:4▪109:7▪118:14,21,22▪119:83-PR-29:21-IS-1:21,22▪7:24▪12:2▪14:10(2470),10(4911)▪19:11(1197),13(2973)▪29:11▪34:9▪35:7▪59:6▪60:22-JER-2:5(1891)▪3:1▪5:13,27(6238)▪7:11▪10:21(1197)▪22:5▪26:18▪49:13▪50:23,37▪51:37,41-LA-1:1^{2},2,6,11▪4:1(6004),8-EZE-22:4(816),18,19▪26:5▪36:35,35sup▪37:17-DA-4:22(8631)▪11:23(6105)-HO-12:8(6238),13:16(816)-JON-4:5-MIC-3:12-ZEP-1:13▪2:15▪N.T.-all=1096&marked-M'T-18:3▪21:42(1096,1519)-M'R-1:17▪12:10(1096,1519)-LU-20:17(1096,1519)-JOH-1:12-AC-4:11(1096,1519)▪7:40▪12:18-RO-3:12(889),19▪4:18▪6:22(1402)▪7:4(2289),13-1CO-3:18▪7:18(1986)▪8:9▪13:1▪15:20-2CO-5:17▪12:11-GA-4:16▪5:4(2673)-TIT-2:1(4241)-PH'M-6-HEB-5:12-JAS-2:4,11-RE-11:15▪18:2

BECOMETH-PS-93:5(4998)-PR-17:7(5000),18(6148)▪N.T.-all=1096&marked-M'T-3:15(4241)▪13:22,32-M'R-4:19,32-RO-16:2(516)-EPH-5:3(4241)-PH'P-1:27(516)-1TI-2:10(516)-TIT-2:3(2412)

BED-all=4904,a=4296&marked-GE-48:2▪49:4,33a-EX-8:3a▪21:18-LE-15:4,5,21,23,24,26^{2}-1SA-19:13a,15a,16a▪28:23a-2SA-4:5,7a,11▪11:2,13▪13:5-1KI-1:47▪17:19a▪21:4a-2KI-1:4a,6a,16a▪4:10a,21a,32a-1CH-5:1(3326)-2CH-16:14▪24:25a-ES-7:8a-JOB-7:13(6210)▪17:13(3326)▪33:15,19-PS-4:4▪6:6a▪36:4▪41:3(6210),3▪63:6(3326)▪132:3(6210,3326)▪139:8(3331)-PR-7:16(6210),17▪22:27▪26:14a-SONG-1:16(6210)▪3:1,7a▪5:13(6170)-IS-28:20(4702)▪57:7,8^{2}-EZE-23:17,41a▪32:25-DA-2:28(4903),29(4903)▪4:5(4903),10(4903),13(4903)▪7:1(4903)-AM-3:12a▪N.T.-all=2895&marked-M'T-9:2(2825),6(2825)-M'R-2:4,9,11,12▪4:21(2825)▪7:30(2825)-LU-5:18(2825)▪8:16(2825)▪11:7(2845)▪17:34(2825)-JOH-5:8,9,10,11,12-AC-9:33,34(4766)-HEB-13:4(2845)-RE-2:22(2825)

BEDCHAMBER-EX-8:3(2315,4904)-2SA-4:7(2315,4904)-2KI-6:12(2315,4904)▪11:2(2315,4296)-2CH-22:11(2315,4296)-EC-10:20(2315,4296)

BED'S-GE-47:31(4296)

BEDS-all=4904&marked-2SA-17:28-ES-1:6(4296)-PS-149:5-SONG-6:2(6170)-IS-57:2-HO-7:14-AM-6:4(4296)-MIC-2:1▪N.T.-M'R-6:55(2895)-AC-5:15(2825)

BEDSTEAD-DE-3:11(6210)

BEE-IS-7:18(1682)

BEEN-all=1961&marked-GE-13:3▪31:5,42▪46:34▪47:9-EX-2:22▪9:18▪18:3-DE-4:32▪9:7,24▪31:27-1SA-4:7,17▪14:38▪20:13▪29:3,8-2SA-13:20,32▪15:34-1KI-1:37▪14:8▪17:7-1CH-17:8▪29:25-EZR-4:20(1934)▪9:2-NE-2:1-ES-2:12-JOB-3:16▪10:19^{2}-PS-27:9▪37:25▪42:3▪59:16▪61:3▪63:7▪73:14▪90:1▪119:54▪124:1,2-EC-1:9,10,16▪3:15^{2}▪4:3,16▪6:10-IS-1:9,9sup▪25:4▪26:17▪48:18,19,19sup▪60:15▪66:2-JER-2:31▪3:3sup,3▪20:17▪28:8▪32:31▪50:6-EZE-2:5▪10:10▪16:31▪22:13▪28:13▪29:6▪33:33▪38:8-HO-5:1-JOE-1:2▪2:2-OB-1:16-MAL-1:9▪N.T.-all=1906,a=2258&marked-M'T-23:30^{2}a▪25:21a,23a,▪26:24a-M'R-6:49(1511)▪8:2(4357)▪16:10-LU-2:44(1511)▪10:11▪16:12▪19:17▪24:21(2076)-JOH-5:6(2192)▪9:18a▪11:21a,32a,39(2076)▪14:9(1510)▪15:27(2075)-AC-4:13a▪7:52▪15:7▪19:21▪20:18▪24:10(5607),19(3918)▪25:14(1304)▪26:32-RO-9:29▪11:34▪16:2-2CO-11:25(4160)-GA-3:21sup,21a-COL-4:11-1TI-5:9-HEB-8:7a-2PE-2:21a-1JO-2:19a

BEES-all=1682-DE-1:44-J'G-14:8-PS-118:12

BEETLE-LE-11:22(2728)

BEEVES-all=1241-LE-22:19,21-NU-31:28,30,33,38,44

BEFALL-all=7122-GE-42:4,38▪44:29(7136)▪49:1-DE-31:17(4672),29-PS-91:10(579)-DA-10:14(7136)▪N.T.-AC-20:22(4876)

BEFALLEN-all=4672&marked-LE-10:19(7122)-NU-20:14-DE-31:21-J'G-6:13-1SA-20:26(4745)-ES-6:13(7136)▪N.T.-M'T-8:33(4876)

BEFALLETH-EC-3:19^{2}(4745)

BEFELL-GE-42:29(7136)-JOS-2:23(4672)-2SA-19:7(935)▪N.T.-M'R-5:16(1096)-AC-20:19(4819)

BEFORE-all=6440,a=2962,b=5921,c=5048,d=6925&marked-GE-2:5^{2}a▪6:11,13▪7:1▪10:9^{2},11:28▪(b,6440)▪12:15(413)▪13:9,10▪17:1,18▪18:8,22▪19:4a,13(854),27(854,6440)▪20:15▪23:3b,6440,12,17,19▪24:7,15a,33,40,45a,51▪25:9b,(6440),18b(6440)▪27:4a,7,10,33a▪29:26▪30:30,38(5227)39(413)▪31:2(8543,8032),5(8543,8032),32c,35,37c▪32:3,16,17,20,21▪33:3,12c,14^{2},18(854,6440)▪34:10▪36:31▪37:18a▪40:9▪41:43,46,50a▪43:9,14,15,33,34▪44:14▪45:5,7,28a▪46:28▪47:6,7,10▪48:5(5704),15,20▪49:30b(6440)▪50:13b(6440),16,18-EX-4:3,21▪6:12,30▪7:9,10^{2}▪8:20▪9:10,11,13▪10:1(7130),3,10,14▪11:10▪12:34a▪13:21,22▪14:2,2(5226),9,19^{2}▪16:9,33,34▪17:5,6▪18:12▪19:2c▪20:3b(6440),20b▪21:1▪22:9(5703)▪23:15,17(413,6440),20,23,27,28^{2},29,30,31▪25:30▪27:21b,21▪28:12,25(434,4136,6440),29,30^{2},35,38▪29:10,11,23,24,25,26,42▪30:6^{2},8,16,36▪32:1,5,23,34▪33:2,19^{2}▪34:3(413,4136),6b(6440)10c,11,20,23,24,24(413,6440),34▪39:18(413,4136,6440)▪40:5,6,23,25,26-LE-1:3,5,11▪3:1,7,8,12,13▪4:4^{2},6^{2},7,14,15^{2},17^{2},18,24▪6:7,14,25▪7:30▪8:26,27,29▪9:2,4,5(413,6440),5,21,24▪10:1,2,3b(6440),4,15,17,19▪12:7▪14:11,12,16,18,23,24,27,29,31,36a▪15:14,15,30▪16:1,2(413,6440),7,10,12,13,14,15,18,30▪17:4▪18:23,24,27,28,30▪19:14,22,32▪20:23▪23:11,20,28,40▪24:3,4,6,8▪26:7,8,17,37^{2}▪27:8,11-NU-3:4^{2},6,7,38^{2}▪5:16,18,25,30▪6:12(7223)16,20▪7:3^{2},10▪8:9,10,11,13,21,22▪9:6▪10:9,10,33,35▪11:20▪13:22,30(413)▪14:5,10(413),14,37,42,43▪15:15,25,28▪16:2,7,9,16,17,38,40,43(413,6440)▪17:4,7,9,10▪18:2,19▪19:3,4▪20:3,9,10(413,6440)▪21:11b(6440)▪22:32c▪26:61▪27:2^{3},5,17^{2},19,21^{2},22▪31:50,54▪32:4,17,20,21^{2},22,22sup,22,27,29^{2},32▪33:7b(6440),7,8,47,52,55▪35:12▪36:1-DE-1:8,21,22,30,30sup,33,38,42,45▪2:12,21,22,31,33▪3:18,28▪4:8,10,32,38,44▪5:7▪6:19,25▪7:1,2,22,24▪9:2,3,3sup,4^{2},5,18,25▪10:8,11▪11:23,25,26,32▪12:7,12,18^{2},29,30▪14:23,26▪15:20▪16:11,16^{2}(854,6440)▪17:12(854),18▪18:7,12▪19:17^{2}▪21:16▪22:6,17▪23:14▪24:4,13▪26:4,5,10^{2},13▪27:7▪28:7sup,7,25^{2},66c▪29:10,15▪30:1,15,19▪31:3^{3},8,11(854,6440),11c,21a▪32:52c▪33:1,10(639),27-JOS-1:5,14▪2:8a▪3:1a,6^{2},10,11,14▪4:5,7,12,13,18(8543,8032),23^{2}▪5:1▪6:4,5c,6,7,8,9,13^{2},20c,26▪7:4,5,6,8,12^{2},13,23▪8:5,6^{2},10,11c,14,15,33c,33(7223),35c▪9:24▪10:5b,8,10,11,12,14▪11:6▪13:3b(6440),6,25b(6440)▪14:15▪15:7(5227),8b(6440),15(6440▪17:4^{3},7b(6440)▪18:1,6,8,10,14b(6440)16b(6440)▪19:11b(6440),46(4136),51▪20:6,9▪21:44▪22:27,29▪23:5,9^{2},13▪24:1,8,12^{2},18-J'G-1:10,11,23▪2:3,14,21▪3:2,27▪4:14,15,23▪5:5^{2}▪6:9,18▪8:13(4608),28▪9:39,40▪11:9,11,23,24,33▪14:16b,17b,18a▪16:3b(6440),20(6471)▪18:6(5227),21▪20:23,26^{2},28,32,35,39,42▪21:2-RU-3:14(2958)▪4:4^{2}c-1SA-1:12,15,19,2(854,6440)▪2:11(854,6440),15a,17(854,6440),18(854,6440),21(5973),28,30,35▪3:1▪4:2,3,17▪5:3,4▪6:20▪7:6▪8:11,20▪9:12,13a,15,19,24^{2},27▪10:5,8,19,25▪11:15^{2}▪12:2^{2},3^{2}c,7▪14:13,21(865)▪15:30^{2}c,33▪16:6c,8,10,16,21,22▪17:7,31,41,57▪18:13,16▪19:24▪20:1^{2}▪21:6,7,13(5869)▪22:4(854,6440)▪23:18,24▪25:19,23(639)▪26:1b(6440),3b(6440),19,20c▪28:22,25^{2}▪30:20▪31:1-2SA-2:14,17,24b(6440)▪3:28(5973),31,34▪5:3,20,24▪6:4,5,14,16,17,21,21^{2}sup▪7:15,16,18,23,26,29,10:9,13,14,15,16,18,19▪11:13▪12:12^{2}c▪13:9▪14:33▪15:1,18b(6440)▪18:7▪19:8,13,

17,18■20:8■21:9■22:13c,23c■24:13 -1KI-1:2,5,23,25,28,32■2:4,26■45■ 3:6,12,15,16,22,24■6:3^{2}b(6440),7 (4551),17(3942),21■7:6^{2}b(6440),49■ 8:5,8b(6440),22,23,25^2,28,31,33,50,54, 59,62,64^2,65■9:3,4,6,25■10:8■11:7b (6440),36■12:6(854,6440),8,30■13:6 (7223)■14:9,24■15:3■16:25,30,33■17:1, 3,5■18:15,46■19:11^2,19■20:27c■21:10c, 13c,26,29^2■22:10,21-2KI-1:13c■2:9a■ 3:14,24■4:12,31,38,43,44■5:15,16,23, 25(413)■6:22,32■8:9■10:4■11:18■14:12■ 15:10(6905)■16:3,14■17:2,8,11■18:5, 22■19:14,15,26,32(6924)■20:3■21:2,9, 11■22:10,19^2■23:3,13b(6440),25■25:29 -1CH-1:43■5:25■6:32■10:1■11:3,13■13:8, 10■14:15■15:24■16:1,4,6,29,30,37^2,39■ 17:8,13,16,21,24,25,27■19:7,10,14^2,15, 16^2,18,19■21:12,30■22:5,18^2■23:13,31■ 24:2,6,6sup■29:10(5869),15,22,25 -2CH-1:5,6,10,12,13■2:4,6■3:15,17■ 4:20■5:6,9b(6440)■6:12,13c,14,16,19, 22,24^2,36■7:4,6c,7,17,19■8:12,14c■ 9:7,11■10:6,8■13:13,14,15,16■14:5, 7,12^2,13^2■15:8■18:9,20■19:2,11■20:5, 7,9,13,16,18,21■23:17■24:14■25:8, 14,22■26:19■27:6■28:3,9,14■29:11, 19,23■30:9■31:20■32:12■33:2,9, 12(854,6440),19,23■34:18,24,27^3,31, 36:12-EZR-3:12■4:18d,23d■7:19d,28^2■ 8:21,29■9:15^2■10:1,6-NE-1:4,6■2:1,13(413, 6440)■4:2,5,5c■5:15■6:19■8:1,2,3^2,3c■ 9:8,11,24,28,32,35■12:36■13:4,19-ES- 1:3,11,16,17,19■2:11,23■3:7■4:2,6,8■ 6:1,9,11,13^2■7:6,8(5973),9■8:1,3,4,5■ 9:11,25-JOB-1:6b■2:1b■3:24■4:15b,16c, 19■8:12,16■10:21a■13:15(413,6440),16■ 15:4,7,32(3808)■18:20(6931)■21:18,33■ 23:4,17■26:6c■30:11■33:5■35:14■41:10, 22■42:11-PS-16:8c■18:6,12c,22c,23 (5973),42b(6440)■22:27,29■23:5■ 26:3c■31:19c,22c■34:t■35:5■36:1c■ 38:9c,17c■39:1c,5c,13a■42:2■44:15c■ 50:3,8c■51:3c■52:9c■54:3■56:13■ 57:6■58:9a■61:7■62:8■68:1,2,3,4,7,25 (6924)■69:19c,22■72:9■73:22(5973)■ 78:55■79:11■80:2,9■83:13■84:7 (413)■85:13■86:9,14c■88:1c,2■90:2a, 8c■95:2(6924),6■96:6,9,13■97:3■98:6,9■ 101:3c■102:t,28■105:17■106:23■109:15c■ 116:9■119:46c■67a,168c,169,170■138:1c■ 139:5(6924)■141:2■142:2^2■147:17-PR- 4:25c■5:21(5227)■8:22(6924),25a,25, 30■14:19■15:11c,33■16:18^2■17:14,24 (854,6440)■18:12^2,13a,16■22:29^2■23:1■ 25:5,26■27:4■30:7a-EC-1:10,16■2:7,9, 26■3:14■4:16■5:2,6,6:8c■7:17(3808)■ 8:12,13■9:1-SONG-8:12-IS-1:12,16c■ 7:16a■8:4a,4■9:3,12(6924)■17:13^2,14^{2}a■ 3:18■24:23c■28:4a■30:8(854),11■36:7■ 37:14,27,33(6924)■38:3■40:10,17c■ 41:1(413),2■42:9a,16■43:10■45:1^2, 2■47:14c■48:5a,7,19■49:16c■52:12■ 53:2,7■55:12■57:16■58:8■59:12c■ 61:11c■62:11■63:12■65:6,24a■66:7^{2}a, 22,23-JER-1:5^{2}a,17■2:22■6:7b(6440), 21(413)■7:10■9:13■13:16^{2}a■15:1,9, 19■17:16(5227,6640)■18:17,20,23■ 19:7■21:8■24:1■26:4■28:8^2■30:20■ 31:36^2■32:12(5869),13(5869),30(5869), 31b■33:18,24■34:5,15,18■35:5,19■36:7, 9,22■37:20■38:10a,26■39:16■40:4■ 42:2,9■44:10■47:1a■49:19,37^2■50:8,44■ 52:33-LA-1:5,6,22■2:3,19(5227)■3:35c -EZE-2:10■3:20■4:1■6:4,5■8:1,11■9:6■ 14:1,3(5227),4(5227),7(5227)■16:18,19, 50,57a■20:1,9(5869),14(5869),41(5869)■ 22:30■23:24,41■28:9,17■30:24■32:10b (6440)■33:31■36:17■40:12,22,26,47■ 41:4(413,6440),12(413,6440),22■42:1c, 2(413,6440),4,8b(6440),11,12,13 (413,6440)■43:24■44:3,4(413,6440), 11,12,15■45:7^2(413,6440)■46:3,9 -DA-1:5,13,18,19■2:2,9d,10d,11d, 24d,25d,31(6903),36d■3:3(6903), 13d■4:6d,7d,8^2(5922,6925)■5:1(6903), 13d,15d,17d,19d(4481),23d■6:10d,11d, 12d,13d,18d,22^{2}d,26d(4481)■7:7d,8d, 10^{2}d,13d,20d(4481)■8:3,4,6,7,15a■9:10, 13(854,6440),18,20■10:12,16c■11:16,22 -HO-7:2c-JOE-1:16c■2:3^2,10,11,31 -AM-1:1■2:9■4:3(5084)■9:4-JON- 1:2■4:2(6924)-MIC-1:4■2:13^2■6:1(854), 4,6sup,6(6924)-NA-1:6■2:1b-HAB- 1:3c■2:20■3:5-ZEP-2:2a,2sup,2^{2}a(3808) -HAG-1:12■2:14,15c-ZEC-2:13■3:1,3, 4,8,9■4:7■6:5b■7:2(854,6440)■8:10, 21(854,6440),22(854,6440)■12:8■ 14:4b(6440),5,20-MAL-2:5■3:1,14,16■ 4:5■N.T.-all=1715,a=1799,b=4253, c=1909,d=4254&marked-M'T- 1:18(4250,2228)■2:9d■5:12b,16,24■ 6:1,2,8b■7:6■8:29b■10:18c,32^2,33^2■ 11:10b,10■14:6(3319),8(4264),22d■17:2■ 21:9d,31d■24:25(4280),38b■25:32■ 26:32d,34(4250),70,75(4250)■27:11,2 (561),29■28:7d-M'R-1:2b,2,35(1773) 2:12(1726)■3:11(4363)■5:33(4363)■6:4 (3908),45d■8:6^2(3908),7(3908)■9:2■1 0:32d■11:9d■13:9c■14:28d,30(4250, 2228),72(4250)■15:42(4315)■16:7d -LU-1:6a,8(1725),17a,75a,76b■2:21b, 26(4250,2228),31(2596)■5:18a,19,25a■ 7:27b,27■8:28(4363),47(4363),47a■ 9:16(3908),52b■10:1b,8(3908)■11:6 (3908),38b■12:6a,8^2,9^{2}a■14:2■15:18a■ 16:15a■18:39d■19:4,27,28■20:26 (1726)■21:12b,12c,14(4304),36■22:15b, 34(4250,2228),47(4281),61(4250)■ 23:12(4391),14a,53(3764)■24:19(1726), 43a-JOH-1:15,15(4413),27,30,30 (4413),48b■3:28■5:7b■6:62(4386)■7:51 (3362,4386)■8:58(4250)■9:8(4386)■ 10:4,8b■11:55b■12:1b,37■13:1b,19b■ 14:29(4250)■15:18(4412)■17:5b,24b -AC-1:16(4277)■2:20(4250,2228),25a, 31(4275)■3:18(4293),20(4296)■4:10a, 28(4309)■5:23b,27(1722),36b■6:6a■ 7:2(4250,2228),40(4313),45(575),46a, 52(4293)■8:32(1726)■9:15a■10:4a, 17c,30a,33a,41(4401)■12:6b,14b■13:24b (4383)■14:13b■16:29(4363),34(3908)■ 17:26(4384)■18:17■19:9a,19a■20:5(4281), 13(4281)■21:29(4308),38b■22:30 (1519),30c■24:19c,20c■25:9c,16(4250), 26^{2}c■26:2c,26(4314)■27:24(3936) -RO-2:13(3844)■3:9(4256),18(561)■4:2 (4314),17(2713)■9:29(4280)■14:10(3936), 22a■16:7b-1CO-2:7b■4:5b■6:1^{2}c,6c■ 10:27(3908)■11:21(4301)-2CO-1:15 (4386)■5:10■7:3(4280),14c■8:10(4278), 24(1519,4383)■9:5(4281),5(4293)■12:19 (2714)■13:2(4280)-GA-1:9(4280),17b, 20a■2:12b,14■3:1(2596),8(4283),17 (4300),23b■5:21(4302)-EPH-1:4b,4 (2714)■2:10(4282)-PH'P-3:13-COL- 1:5(4257),17b-1TH-2:2(4310)■3:4(4302), 9,13-1TI-1:13(4386),18(4254)■5:4a,19c, 20a,21a,21(4299),24d■6:12a,13sup,13c -2TI-subscr(3936)■1:9b■2:14a■4:1a, 21b-TIT-1:2b-HEB-6:18(4295)■ 7:18d■10:15(4280)■11:5b■12:1(4295), 2(4295)-JAS-1:27(3844)■2:6(1519)■5:9b -1PE-1:20b-2PE-2:11(3844)■3:2(4280), 17(4267)-1JO-2:28(575)■3:19-3JO-6a -JUDE-4(4270),17(4280),24(2714)-RE- 1:4a■2:14a■3:2a,5a,8a,9a■4:5a,6a,6■10^{2}a■ 5:8a■7:9a,11a,15a■8:2a,3a,4a■9:13a■ 10:11c■11:4a,16a■12:4a,10a■13:12a■14:3a, 5a■15:4a■16:19a■19:20a■20:12a■22:8

BEFOREHAND-M'R-13:11(4305) -2CO-9:5(4294)-1TI-5:24(4271),25(4271) -1PE-1:11(4303)

BEFORETIME-all=6440&marked -DE-2:12-JOS-11:10■20:5(8543,8032) -1SA-9:9^2■10:11(865,8032)-2SA-7:10 (7223)-2KI-13:5(8543,8032)-IS-41:26■ N.T-AC-8:9(4391)

BEG-PS-109:10(7592)-PR-20:4(7592)■ N.T.-LU-16:3(1871)

BEGAN-all=2490■&marked-GE- 4:26■6:1■9:20■10:8■41:54■44:12-NU- 25:1-DE-1:5(2974)-J'G-13:25■16:19,22■ 19:25(5927)■20:31,39,40-1SA-3:2-2KI- 10:32■15:37-1CH-1:10■27:24-2CH- 3:1,2■20:22■29:17,27^2■31:7,10,21■ 34:3^2-EZR-3:6,8■5:2(8271)■7:9(3246) -NE-4:7■13:19(6751)-EZE-9:6-JON- 3:4■N.T.-all=756&marked-M'T-4:17■ 11:7,20■12:1■16:21,22■26:22,37,74■ 28:1(2020)-M'R-1:45■2:23■4:1■5:17,20■ 6:2,7,34,55■8:11,31,32■10:28,32,41,47■ 11:15■12:1■13:5■14:9,33,65,69,71■15:8, 18-LU-3:23■4:21■5:21■7:15,24,38,49■ 9:12■11:29,53■12:1■14:18,30■15:14, 24■19:37,45■20:9■22:23■23:2-JOH- 4:52(2192)■13:5■-AC-1:1■2:4■8:35■ 10:37■11:15■18:26■24:2■27:35-HEB- 2:3(746,2983)

BEGAT-all=3205-GE-4:18^3■5:3,4,6, 7^2,9,10^2,12,13^2,15,16^2,18,19^2,21,22^2,25,26^2, 28,30^2,32■6:10■10:8,13,15,24^2,26■11:10, 11^2,12,13^2,14,15^2,16,17^2,18,19^2,20,21^2, 22,23^2,24,25^2,26,27^2■22:23■25:3,19-LE- 25:45-NU-26:29,58-DE-32:18-J'G-11:1 -RU-4:18,19,20^2,21,22-1CH-1:10,11,13, 18^2,20,34■2:10^2,11,12,13,18,20,22,36,37, 38,39,40,41^2,44^2,46■4:2^2,8,11,12,14^2■ 6:4^2,5^2,6^2,7^2,8^2,9^2,10,11^2,12^2,13^2,14^2■7:32■ 8:1,7,8,9,11,32,33^2,34,36^3,37■9:38,39^2,40, 42^3,43■14:3-2CH-11:21■13:21■24:3 -NE-12:10^3,11^2-PR-23:22-JER-16:3 -DA-11:6-ZEC-13:3^2■N.T.-all=1080& marked-M'T-1:2^3,3^3,4^3,5^3,6^2,7^3,8^3,9^3,10^3, 11,12^2,13^3,14^3,15^3,16-AC-7:8,29-JAS- 1:18(616)-1JO-5:1

BEGET-all=3205-GE-17:20-DE- 4:25■28:41-2KI-20:18-EC-6:3-IS- 39:7-JER-29:6-EZE-18:10,14■47:22

BEGETTEST-GE-48:6(3205)-IS- 45:10(3205)

BEGETTETH-all=3205-PR-17:21■ 23:24-EC-5:14

BEGGAR-1SA-2:8(34)N.T.-LU- 16:20(4434),22(4434)

BEGGARLY-GA-4:9(4434)

BEGGED-M'T-27:58(154)-LU- 23:52(154)-JOH-9:8(4319)

BEGGING-PS-37:25(1245)■N.T. -M'R-10:46(4319)-LU-18:35(4319)

BEGIN-all=2490&marked-GE-11:6 -DE-2:24,25,31■16:9-JOS-3:7-J'G-10:18■ 13:5-1SA-3:12■22:15-NE-11:17(8462) -JER-25:29-EZE-9:6■N.T.-all=756 -M'T-24:49-LU-3:8■12:45■13:25,26■ 14:9,29■21:28■23:30-2CO-3:1-1PE- 4:17,17sup-RE-10:7(3195)

BEGINNEST-DE-16:9(2490)

BEGINNING-all=7225,a=8462, b=7218-GE-1:1■10:10■13:3a■41:21a■ 49:3-EX-12:2b-DE-11:12■21:17■32:42b -J'G-7:19b-RU-1:22a■3:10(7223) -2SA-21:9a,10a-2KI-17:25a-1CH-17:9 (7223)-EZR-4:6a-JOB-8:7■42:12-PS- 111:10■119:160b-PR-1:7■8:22,23b■ 9:10a■17:14■20:21(7223)-EC-3:11b■ 7:8■10:13a-IS-1:26a■18:2(1931),7 (1931)■40:21b■41:4b,26b■46:10■48:3 (227),5(227),7(227),16b■64:4(5769) -JER-17:12(7223)■26:1■27:1■28:1■49:34 -LA-2:19b-EZE-40:1b-DA-9:21a,23a -HO-1:2a-AM-7:1a-MIC-1:13■N.T.- all=746&marked-M'T-14:30(756)■ 19:4,8■20:8(756)■24:8,21-M'R-1:1■ 10:6■13:19-LU-1:2■23:5(756)■24:27 (756),47(756)-JOH-1:1,2■2:10(4412), 11■6:64■8:9(756),25,44■15:27■16:4 -AC-1:22(756)■11:4(756),15■26:5(509) -PH'P-4:15-COL-1:18-2TH-2:13-HEB- 1:10■3:14■7:3-2PE-2:20(4413)■3:4-1JO- 1:1■2:7^2,13,14,24^2■3:8,11-2JO-5,6-RE- 1:8■3:14■21:6■22:13

BEGINNINGS-NU-10:10(7218)■ 28:11(7218)-EZE-36:11(7221)■N.T. -M'R-13:8(746)

BEGOTTEN-all=3205&marked -GE-5:4-LE-18:11(4138)-NU-11:12 -DE-23:8-J'G-8:30(3318)-JOB-38:28 -PS-2:7-IS-49:21-HO-5:7■N.T.-all= 1080&marked-JOH-1:14(3439),18(3439)■ 3:16(3439),18(3439)-AC-13:33-1CO- 4:15-PH'M-10-HEB-1:5■5:5■11:17 (3439)-1PE-1:3(313)-1JO-4:9(3439)■ 5:1,18-RE-1:5(4416)

BEGUILE-COL-2:4(3884),18(2603)
BEGUILED-GE-3:13(5377)▪29:25(7411)-NU-25:18(5230)-JOS-9:22(7411)▪N.T.-2CO-11:3(1818)
BEGUILING-2PE-2:14(1185)
BEGUN-all=2490-NU-16:46,47-DE-2:31▪3:24-ES-6:13▪9:23▪N.T.-M'T-18:24(756)-2CO-8:6(4278),10(4278)-GA-3:3(1728)-PH'P-1:6(1728)-1TI-5:11(2691)
BEHALF-EX-27:21(854)-2SA-3:12(8478)-2CH-16:9(5973)▪N.T.-all=5228&marked-RO-16:19(1909)-1CO-1:4(4012)-2CO-1:11▪5:12▪8:24▪9:3(3313)-PH'P-1:29-1PE-4:16(3313)
BEHAVE-DE-32:27(5234)-1CH-19:13(2388)-PS-101:2(7919)-IS-3:5(7292)▪N.T.-1CO-13:5(807)-1TI-3:15(390)
BEHAVED-all=7919&marked-1SA-18:5,14,15,30-PS-35:14(1980)▪131:2(7737)-MIC-3:4(7489)▪N.T.-1TH-2:10(1096)-2TH-3:7(812)
BEHAVETH-1CO-7:36(807)
BEHAVIOUR-1SA-21:13(2940)-PS-34:t(2940)▪N.T.-1TI-3:2(2887)-TIT-2:3(2688)
BEHEADED-DE-21:6(6202)-2SA-4:7(5493,7218)▪N.T.-all=607&marked-M'T-14:10-M'R-6:16,27-LU-9:9-RE-20:4(3990)
BEHELD-all=7200&marked-GE-12:14▪13:10▪19:28▪31:2▪48:8-NU-21:9(5027)▪23:21(5027)-J'G-16:27-1SA-26:5-1CH-21:15-JOB-31:26-PS-119:158▪142:4-PR-7:7-EC-8:17-IS-41:28-JER-4:23,24,25,26▪31:26-EZE-1:15▪8:2▪37:8-DA-7:4(2370,934),6(2370,934),9(2370,934),11^{2}(2370,934),21(2370,934)-HAB-3:6▪N.T.-all=1492&marked-M'T-19:26(1689)-M'R-9:15▪12:41(2334)▪15:47(2334)-LU-10:18(2334)▪19:41▪20:17(1689)▪22:56▪23:55(2300)▪24:12(991)-JOH-1:14(2300),42(1689)-AC-1:9(991)▪17:23(333)-RE-5:6,11▪6:5,12▪7:9▪8:13▪11:12(2334)▪13:11
BEHEMOTH-JOB-40:15(930)
BEHIND-all=310&marked-GE-18:10▪19:17,26▪22:13▪32:18,20-EX-11:5▪14:19^{2}-NU-3:23-DE-25:18-JOS-8:2,4,14,20-J'G-18:12▪20:40-1SA-21:9▪24:8▪30:9(3498),10(5975)-2SA-1:7,2:20,23▪3:16▪5:23▪10:9(268)▪13:34-1KI-10:19▪14:9-2KI-6:32▪9:18,19▪11:6-1CH-19:10(268)-2CH-13:13^{2},14(268)-NE-4:13,16▪9:26-PS-50:17▪139:5(268)-SONG-2:9-IS-9:12(268)▪30:21▪38:17▪57:8▪66:17-EZE-3:12▪23:35▪41:15-JOE-2:3^{2},14-ZEC-1:8▪N.T.-all=3693&marked-M'T-9:20▪16:23(3694)-M'R-5:27▪8:33(3694)▪12:19(2641)-LU-2:43(5278)▪4:8(3694)▪7:38(3694)▪8:44-1CO-1:7(5302)-2CO-11:5(5302)▪12:11(5302)-PH'P-3:13(3694)-COL-1:24(5303)-RE-1:10(3694)▪4:6
BEHOLD-all=2009,a=2005,b=7200&marked-GE-1:29,31▪3:22a▪4:14a▪6:12,13a,17a▪8:13▪9:9a▪11:6a▪12:11,19▪15:3a,4,17▪16:2,6▪11,14▪17:4,20▪18:9,27,31▪19:2,8,19,20,34a▪20:3,15,16^{2}▪22:1,7,13,20▪24:15,30,43,45,51,63▪25:24,32▪26:8,9▪27:1,2,6▪11a,36,37a,39,42▪28:12^{2},13,15▪29:2,6,25▪30:3,34a▪31:2,10,51▪32:18,20▪33:1▪34:21▪37:7^{2},9^{2},15,19,25,29▪38:13,23,24,27,29▪39:8a▪40:6,9,16▪41:1,2,3,5,6,7,17a,18,19,22,23,29▪42:2,13,22,27,35▪43:21▪44:8a,16▪45:12▪47:1,23▪48:1,2,4a,21▪50:18-EX-1:9a;2:6,13,3:2,9▪13▪4:1a,6,7,14,23▪5:5a,16▪6:12a,30a▪7:16,17▪8:2,21a,29▪9:3,7,18a▪10:4a,14:10,17a▪16:4a,10,14▪17:6a▪23:20▪24:8,14▪31:6▪32:9,34▪33:21▪34:10▪11a,30▪39:43-LE-10:16,18a,19a▪13:5,6,8,10,13,17,20,21,25,26,30,31,32,34,36,39,43,53,55,56▪14:3,37,39,44,48▪25:20a-NU-3:12▪12:8(5027),10^{2}▪16:42,47▪17:8,12a▪18:6,18,21▪20:16▪22:5^{2},11,32▪23:9(7789),11,17,20,24a▪24:10,14a,17(7789)▪25:6,12a▪31:16a▪32:1,14,23-DE-1:8b,10,21b▪2:24b,31b▪3:11,27b▪4:5b▪5:24a▪9:13,16▪10:14a▪11:26b▪13:14▪17:4▪19:18▪26:10▪31:14a,16,27a▪32:49b-JOS-2:2,18▪3:11▪5:13▪7:21,22▪8:4b,20▪9:12,13,25a▪14:10▪22:11,28b▪23:4b,14▪24:27-J'G-1:2▪3:24,25^{2}▪4:22^{2}▪6:15,28,37▪7:13^{2},17▪8:15▪9:31^{2},33,36,43▪11:34▪13:3,7,10▪14:5,8,16▪16:10▪17:2▪18:9,12▪19:9^{2},16,22,24,27▪20:7,40▪21:8,9,19,21-RU-1:15,2:4▪3:2,8▪4:1-1SA-2:31▪3:11▪5:3,4▪8:5▪9:6,7,8,12,14,17,24▪10:8,10,11,22▪11:5▪12:1,2^{2},3,13^{2}▪13:10▪14:7a,8,11,16,17,20,26,33▪15:22▪16:11,15,18▪17:23▪18:17,22▪19:16,19,22▪20:2,5,12,21^{2},22,23▪21:9▪23:1,3▪24:1,4^{2},9,10,20▪25:14,19a,20,36,41▪26:7,21,22,24▪28:7,9,21▪30:3,16,26-2SA-1:2,6,18▪3:12,22,24▪4:8,10▪5:1a▪9:4,6▪12:11a,18▪13:24,34,35,36▪14:7,21,32▪15:15,26a,32,36▪16:1,3,4,5,8,11▪17:9▪18:10,11,24,26,31▪19:1,8,20,37,41▪20:21▪24:22b-1KI-1:14,18,23,25,42,51▪2:8,29,39▪3:12,15,21^{2}▪5:5a▪8:27▪10:7▪11:22,31a▪12:28▪13:1,2,3,25▪14:2,5,10a,19▪15:19▪16:3a▪17:9,10,12a▪18:7,8,11,14,44▪19:5,6,9,11,13▪20:13,13a,31,36,39▪21:18,21a▪22:13,23,25-2KI-1:9,14▪2:11,16,19▪3:20▪4:9,13,25,32▪5:6,11,15,20,22▪6:1,13,15,17,20,25,30,33^{2}▪7:2^{2},5,10,13^{2},19^{2}▪8:5▪9:5▪10:4,9▪11:14▪13:21▪15:11,15▪26,31▪17:26▪18:21▪19:7a,9,11,35▪20:5a,17▪21:12▪22:16a,20a-1CH-9:1▪11:1,25▪22:9,14▪28:21▪29:29-2CH-2:4,8,10▪6:18▪9:6▪13:12,14▪16:3,11▪18:12,22,24▪19:11▪20:2,10,11,16,24,34▪21:14▪23:3,13▪24:27▪25:26▪26:20▪28:9,26▪29:19▪32:32▪33:18,19▪34:24a,28a▪35:25,27▪36:8-EZR-9:15a-NE-9:36^{2}-ES-6:5▪7:9▪8:7-JOB-1:12,19▪2:6▪4:3,18a▪5:17▪8:19a,20a▪9:12a▪12:14a,15a▪13:18▪15:15a▪16:19▪19:7a,27b▪20:9(7789)▪21:27a▪22:12b▪23:8a,9(2372)▪24:5a▪25:5a▪27:12a▪28:28a▪31:35a▪32:11a,12,19▪33:2,6a,7,10a,12a▪34:29(7789)▪35:5(7789)▪36:5a,22a,24(7891),25(5027),26a,30a▪39:29(5027)▪40:4a,11b,15,23a▪41:9a-PS-7:14▪10:14(5027)11:4(2372),7(2372)▪17:2(2372),15(2372)▪27:4(2372)▪33:18▪37:37b▪39:5▪46:8(2372)▪51:5a,6a▪54:4▪59:4b,7▪66:7(6822)▪73:12,15▪78:20a▪80:14b▪84:9b▪87:4▪91:8(5027)▪102:19(5027)▪113:6b▪119:18(5027),40▪121:4▪123:2▪128:44▪133:1▪134:1▪139:8-PR-1:23▪7:10▪11:31a▪23:33b▪24:12a-EC-1:14▪2:1,11,12b▪4:1▪5:18▪7:27b▪11:7b-SONG-1:15^{2},16▪2:8,9▪3:7,11b▪4:1^{2}-IS-3:1▪5:7^{2},26,30▪7:14▪8:7,18,22▪10:33▪12:2▪13:9▪17a▪17:1,14▪19:1▪20:6▪21:9▪22:13,17▪23:13a▪24:1▪26:10b,21▪28:2,16a▪29:8^{3},14a▪30:27▪32:1a▪33:7a,17b▪34:5▪35:4▪37:7a,11,36▪38:5a,8a,11b,17▪39:6▪40:9,10^{2},15^{2}a,26b▪41:11a,15,23b,24a,27,29a▪42:1a,9▪43:19a▪44:11a▪47:14▪48:7,10▪49:12,16a,18b,21a,22▪50:1a,2a,9a,11a▪51:22▪52:6,13▪54:11,15a,16a▪55:4a,5a▪56:3a▪58:3a,4a▪59:1a,9▪60:2▪62:11^{3}▪63:15b▪64:5a,9a▪65:1,6,13^{3},14,17a,18a▪66:12a,15-JER-1:6,9,18▪2:35a▪3:5,22a▪4:13,16▪5:14a,6:10^{2},19,21a,22▪7:8,11,20,32▪8:15,17a,19▪9:7a,15a,25▪10:18a,22▪11:11a,22a▪12:14a▪13:7,13a,20b▪14:13,18^{2},19▪16:9a,12,14,16a,21a▪17:15▪18:3,6,11▪19:3a,6,15a▪20:4a,4b▪21:4a,8a,13a▪23:2a,5,7,15a,19,30a,31a,32a,39a▪24:1▪25:9a,32▪26:14a▪27:16▪28:16a▪29:17a,32a,32b▪30:18a,23▪31:8a,27,31,38▪32:3a,4b,7,17,24^{2},27,28a,37a▪33:6a,14▪34:2a,3b,17a,22a▪35:17a▪37:7a▪38:5,22▪39:16a▪40:4,4b,10a▪42:2b,4a▪43:10a▪44:2,11a,26a,27a,30a▪45:4,5a▪46:25a,27a▪47:2▪48:12,40▪49:2,5a,12,19,22,35a▪50:12,18a,31a,41,44▪51:1a,25a,36a,47,52-LA-1:9b,12(5027),18b,20b▪2:20b▪3:50b,63(5027)▪5:1b-EZE-1:4,15▪2:9▪3:8,23,25▪4:8,14,16a▪5:8a▪6:3a▪7:5,6,10▪8:4,5,7,8,9b,10,14,16,9:2,11,10:1,9▪11:1▪12:27▪13:8a,20a▪14:22^{2}▪15:4,5▪16:8,27,37a,43(1887),44,49▪17:7,10,12▪18:4a▪20:47a▪21:3a,7▪22:6,13,19a▪23:22a,28a▪24:16a,21a▪25:4a▪7a,8,9a,16a▪26:3a,7a▪28:3,7a,17b,18b,22a▪29:3a,8a,10a,19a▪30:22a▪31:3▪34:10a,11a,17a,20a▪35:3a▪36:6a,9a▪37:2,5,7,11,12,19,21▪38:3a▪39:1a,8▪40:3,4b,5,24▪43:2,5,12▪44:4,5b▪46:19,21▪47:1,2,7-DA-2:31(431)▪4:10(431),13(431)▪7:2(718),5(718),7(718),8^{2}(431),13(718)▪8:3,5,15,19a▪9:18b▪10:5,10,16▪11:2▪12:5-HO-2:6a,14-JOE-2:19a▪3:1,7a-AM-2:13▪3:9b▪6:11,14a▪7:1,4,7,8a▪8:1,11▪9:8,13-OB-2-MIC-1:3▪2:3a▪7:9b,10-NA-1:15(2209)▪2:13(2205)▪3:5(2205),13-HAB-1:3(5027),5b,13b▪2:4,13,19-ZEP-3:19a-ZEC-1:8,11,18▪2:1,3,9a▪3:4b,8a,9,9a▪4:2a▪5:1,7,9▪6:1,8b,12▪8:7a▪9:4,9▪12:2▪14:1-MAL-1:13▪2:3a▪3:1a,1▪4:1,5▪N.T.-all=2400,a=2396&marked-M'T-1:20,23▪2:1,13,19▪4:11▪6:26(1689)▪7:3(991),4▪8:2▪24,29,32,34▪9:2,3,10,18,20,32▪10:16▪11:8,10,19▪12:2,10,18,41,42,46,47,49▪13:3▪15:22▪17:3▪5^{2}▪18:10(991)▪19:16,27▪20:18,30▪21:5▪22:4▪23:34,38▪24:25,26^{2}▪25:6,20a,22a▪26:45,46,51,65a▪27:51▪28:2,7,9▪11-M'R-1:2▪2:24a▪3:32a,34a▪4:3▪5:22▪10:33▪11:21a▪13:23▪14:41▪15:4a,35▪16:6a-LU-1:20,31,36,38,48▪2:10,25,34,48▪5:12,18▪6:23,41(991),42(991)▪7:12,25,27,34,37▪8:41▪9:30,38▪10:3,19,25▪11:31,32,41▪13:7,11,30,32,35▪14:2,29(2334)▪17:21,18:31▪19:2,8,20▪21:6(2334),29(1492)▪22:10,21,31,38,47▪23:14,29,50▪24:4,13,39(1492),49-JOH-1:29a,36a,47a▪3:26a▪4:35▪5:14a▪11:3a,36a▪12:15,19a▪16:32▪17:24(2334)▪18:21a▪19:4a,5a,14a,26,27▪20:27a-AC-1:10▪2:7▪4:29(1896)▪5:9,25,28▪7:31(2657),32(2657),56▪8:27▪9:10,11▪10:17,19,21,30▪11:11▪12:7▪13:11,25,41(1492)▪16:1▪20:22,25-RO-2:17a▪9:33▪11:22(1492)-1CO-10:18(991)▪15:51-2CO-3:7(816)▪5:17▪6:2^{2},9▪7:11▪12:14-GA-1:20▪5:2a-HEB-2:13▪8:8-JAS-3:3,4,5▪5:4,7,9,11-1PE-2:6,12(2029)▪3:2(2029)-1JO-3:1(1492)-JUDE-14-RE-1:7,18▪2:10,22▪3:8,9^{2},11,20▪4:1,2▪5:5▪6:2,8▪9:12▪11:14▪12:3▪14:14▪15:5▪16:15▪17:8(991)▪19:11▪21:3,5▪22:7,12
BEHOLDEST-PS-10:14(5027)▪N.T.-M'T-7:3(991)▪-LU-6:41(991),42(991)
BEHOLDETH-JOB-4:18(6437)▪41:34(7200)-PS-33:13(7200)▪N.T.-JAS-1:24(2657)
BEHOLDING-PS-119:37(7200)-PR-15:3(6822)-EC-5:11(7200)▪N.T.-all=2334&marked-M'T-27:55-M'R-10:21(1689)-LU-23:35,48,49(3708)-AC-4:14(991)▪8:13▪14:9(816)▪23:1(816)-2CO-3:18(2734)-COL-2:5(991)-JAS-1:23(2657)
BEHOVED-LU-24:46(1163)-HEB-2:17(3784)
BEING-1KI-2:27(1961)▪16:7(1961)-PS-104:33(5750)▪146:2(5750)-JER-31:36(1961)▪N.T.-all=5607,a=5225&marked-M'T-1:19▪7:11▪12:34-M'R-8:1▪9:33(1096)▪14:3-LU-2:5▪3:2(1909),23▪11:13a▪13:16▪16:23a▪20:36▪22:3,44(1096)-JOH-4:9▪5:13▪6:71▪7:50▪10:33▪11:49,51▪18:26▪19:38-AC-2:30a▪7:55a▪14:8a▪15:32▪16:20a,21(5605),37a▪17:28(2070)▪19:40a▪27:2-RO-11:17-1CO-8:7▪9:21▪12:12-2CO-8:17a▪12:16a-GA-1:14a▪2:3,14a-EPH-2:20▪4:18-PH'P-2:6a-COL-2:13-1TI-3:10-TIT-1:16▪3:11-PH'M-9-HEB-13:3-JAS-1:25(1096)-1PE-1:7(1096)▪5:3sup,3(1096)-RE-12:2(2192)
BEKAH-EX-38:-26(1235)
BELCH-PS-59:7(5042)
BELIED-JER-5:12(3584)
BELIEF-2TH-2:13(4102)
BELIEVE-all=539&marked-EX-4:1,5,8^{2},9▪19:9-NU-14:11-DE-1:32-2KI-17:14-2CH-20:20^{2}▪32:15-JOB-9:16▪39:12-PR-26:25-IS-7:9▪43:10-JER-12:6-HAB-1:5▪N.T.-all=4100&marked-MT-9:28▪18:6▪21:25,32▪24:23,26▪27:42-M'R-1:15(4100,1722)▪5:36▪9:23,24,42▪11:23,24,31▪13:21▪15:32▪16:17-LU-8:12,13,

50▪22:67▪24:25(4100,1909)-**JOH**-1:7, 12▪3:12^2▪4:21,42,48▪5:38,44,47^2▪6:29, 30,36,64,69▪7:5,39▪8:24,45,46▪9:18,35, 36,38▪10:26,37,38^3▪11:15,27,40,42,48▪ 12:36,39,47▪13:19▪14:1,11^2,29▪16:9,30, 31▪17:20,21▪19:35▪20:25,31-**AC**-8:37▪ 13:39,41▪15:7,11▪16:31▪19:4▪21:20,25▪ 27:25-**RO**-3:3(569),22▪4:11,24▪6:8▪ 10:9,14▪15:31(544)-**1CO**-1:21▪10:27(571)▪ 11:18▪14:22,22^2(571),22-**2CO**-4:4(571), 13-**GA**-3:22-**EPH**-1:19-**PH'P**-1:29 -**1TH**-1:7▪2:10,13▪4:14-**2TH**-1:10▪2:11 -**1TI**-1:16▪4:3(4103),10(4103)-**2TI**-2:13 (569)-**HEB**-10:39(4102)▪11:6-**JAS**-2:19 -**1PE**-1:21▪2:7-**1JO**-3:23▪4:1▪5:13^2

BELIEVED-all=539&marked-**GE**-15:6▪45:26-**EX**-4:31▪14:31-**NU**-20:12-**DE**-9:23-**1SA**-27:12-**1KI**-10:7-**2CH**-9:6 -**JOB**-29:24-**PS**-27:13▪78:22,32▪106:12, 24▪116:10▪119:66-**IS**-53:1-**JER**-40:14 -**LA**-4:12-**DA**-6:23(540)-**JON**-3:5(539)▪ **N.T.**-all=4100&marked-**M'T**-8:13▪ 21:32^2-**M'R**-16:11(569),13,14-**LU**-1:1 (4135),20,45▪20:5▪24:11(569),41(569) -**JOH**-2:11,22,23▪3:18▪4:39,41,50,53▪ 5:46^2▪6:64▪7:31,48▪8:30,31▪10:25,42▪ 11:45▪12:11,37,38,42▪14:10▪16:27▪ 17:8▪20:8,29^2-**AC**-2:44▪4:4,32▪8:12,13▪ 9:26,42▪10:45(4103)▪11:17,21▪13:12,48▪ 14:1,23▪15:5▪16:1(4103)▪17:4(3982),5(544), 12,34▪18:8^2,27▪19:2,9(544),18▪22:19▪ 27:11(3982)▪28:24(3982),24sup-**RO**-4:3(569,4100),17,18▪10:14,16▪11:30(544) ,31(544)▪13:11-**1CO**-3:5▪15:2,11-**2CO**-4:13 -**GA**-2:16▪3:6-**EPH**-1:13-**2TH**-1:10▪ 2:12-**1TI**-3:16-**2TI**-1:12-**TIT**-3:8 -**HEB**-3:18(544)▪4:3▪11:31(544)-**JAS**-2:23-**1JO**-4:16-**JUDE**-5

BELIEVERS-**AC**-5:14(4100)-**1TI**-4:12(4103)

BELIEVESTall=4100-**LU**-1:20 -**JOH**-1:50▪11:26▪14:10-**AC**-8:37▪26:27^2 -**JAS**-2:19

BELIEVETH-all=539-**JOB**-15:22▪ 39:24-**PR**-14:15-**IS**-28:16▪**N.T.**-all= 4100&marked-**M'R**-9:23▪16:16,16(569) -**JOH**-3:15,16,18^2,36,36(544)▪5:24▪6:35, 40,47▪7:38▪11:25,26▪12:44,46▪14:12 -**AC**-10:43-**RO**-1:16▪3:26(1537,4102)▪ 4:5▪9:33▪10:4,10,11▪14:2-**1CO**-7:12 (571),13(571)▪13:7▪14:24(571)-**2CO**-6:15(4103)-**1TI**-5:16(4103)-**1PE**-2:6 -**1JO**-5:1,5,10^3

BELIEVING-all=4100&marked -**M'T**-21:22-**JOH**-20:27(4103),31-**AC**-16:34▪24:14-**RO**-15:13-**1TI**-6:2(4103) -**1PE**-1:8

BELL-all=6472-**EX**-28:34^2▪39:26

BELLIES-**TIT**-1:12(1064)

BELLOW-**JER**-50:11(6670)

BELLOWS-**JER**-6:29(4647)

BELLS-**EX**-28:33(6472)▪39:25 -**ZEC**-14:20(4698)

BELLY-all=990&marked-**GE**-3:14 (1512)-**LE**-11:42(1512)-**NU**-5:21,22,27▪ 25:8(6897)-**J'G**-3:21,22-**1KI**-7:20-**JOB**-3:11▪15:2,35▪20:15,20,23▪32:19▪40:16 -**PS**-17:14▪22:10▪31:9▪44:25-**PR**-13:25▪ 18:8,20▪20:27,30▪26:22-**SONG**-5:14(4578)▪ 7:2-**IS**-46:3-**JER**-1:5▪51:34(3770)-**EZE**-3:3-**DA**-2:32(4577)-**JON**-1:17(4578)▪2:1 (4578),2-**HAB**-3:16▪**N.T.**-all=2836 -**M'T**-12:40▪15:17-**M'R**-7:19-**LU**-15:16 -**JOH**-7:38-**RO**-16:18-**1CO**-6:13^2-**PH'P**-3:19-**RE**-10:9,10

BELONG-**M'R**-9:41(1510)

BELONGED-**ES**-2:9(4490)▪**N.T.** -**LU**-23:7(1510)

BELONGEST-supplied

BELONGETH-**HEB**-5:14(1510)

BELONGING-all supplied

BELOVED-all=1730&marked-**DE**-21:15^2(157),16(157)▪33:12(3039)-**NE**-13:26(157)-**PS**-60:5(3039)▪108:6 (3039)▪127:2(3039)-**SONG**-1:14, 16(157)▪2:3,8,9,10,16,17▪4:16▪5:1,2,4, 5,6,8,9^2,10,16▪6:1^2,2,3▪7:9,11,13▪8:5,14 -**IS**-5:1-**JER**-11:15(3039)▪12:7(3033) -**DA**-9:23(2530)▪10:11(2530),19(2530) -**HO**-3:1(157)▪9:16(4261)▪**N.T.**-all= 27&marked-**M'T**-3:17▪12:18▪17:5 -**M'R**-1:11▪9:7-**LU**-3:22▪9:35▪20:13 -**AC**-15:25-**RO**-1:7▪9:25(25)▪11:28▪ 12:19▪16:8,9,12-**1CO**-4:14,17▪10:14▪ 15:58-**2CO**-7:1▪12:19-**EPH**-1:6(25)▪ 6:21-**PH'P**-2:12▪4:1^2-**COL**-3:12(25)▪ 4:7,9,14-**1TH**-1:4(25)-**2TH**-2:13(25)-**1TI**-6:2-**2TI**-1:2-**PH'M**-1,2,16-**HEB**-6:9 -**JAS**-1:16,19▪2:5-**1PE**-2:11▪4:12-**2PE**-1:17▪3:1,8,14,15,17-**1JO**-3:2,21▪4:1,7,11 -**3JO**-2,5,11-**JUDE**-3,17,20-**RE**-20:9(25)

BELOVED'S-**SONG**-6:3(1730)▪ 7:10(1730)

BEMOAN-all=5110-**JER**-15:5▪ 16:5▪22:10▪48:17-**NA**-3:7

BEMOANED-**JOB**-42:11(5110)

BEMOANING-**JER**-31:18(5110)

BENCHES-**EZE**-27:6(7175)

BEND-all=1869&marked-**PS**-11:2▪ 64:3-**JER**-9:3▪46:9▪50:14,29▪51:3 -**EZE**-17:7(3719)

BENDETH-**PS**-58:7(1869)-**JER**-51:3(1869)

BENDING-**IS**-60:14(7817)

BENEATH-all=8478&marked -**GE**-35:8-**EX**-20:4▪26:24(4295)▪27:5 (4295)▪32:19▪36:29(4295)▪38:4(4295) -**DE**-4:18,39▪5:8^2▪28:13(4295)▪33:13 -**JOS**-2:11-**J'G**-7:8-**1KI**-4:12▪7:29▪8:23 -**JOB**-18:16-**PR**-15:24(4295)-**IS**-14:9▪ 51:6-**JER**-31:37(4295)-**AM**-2:9▪**N.T.** -all=2736-**M'R**-14:66-**JOH**-8:23-**AC**-2:19

BENEFACTORS-**LU**-22:25(2110)

BENEFIT-**2CH**-32:25(1576)-**JER**-18:10(3190)▪**N.T.**-**2CO**-1:15(5485) -**1TI**-6:2(2108)-**PH'M**-14(18)

BENEFITS-**PS**-103:2(1576)▪116:12 (8408)

BENEVOLENCE-**1CO**-7:3(2133)

BENT-all=1869&marked-**PS**-7:12▪ 37:14-**IS**-5:28▪21:15▪-**LA**-2:4▪3:12 -**HO**-11:7(8511)-**ZEC**-9:13

BEREAVE-all=7921&marked-**EC**-4:8(2637)-**JER**-15:7-**EZE**-5:17▪36:12, 14(3782,7921)-**HO**-9:12

BEREAVED-**GE**-42:36(7921)▪ 43:14(7921)-**JER**-18:21(7909)-**EZE**-36:13 (7921)-**HO**-13:8(7909)

BEREAVETH-**LA**-1:20(7921)

BERRIES-**IS**-17:6(1620)-**JAS**-3:12 (1636)

BERYL-all=8658-**EX**-28:20▪39:13 -**SONG**-5:14-**EZE**-1:16▪10:9▪28:13-**DA**-10:6▪**N.T.**-**RE**-21:20(969)

BESEECH-all=4994&marked -**EX**-3:18▪33:18-**NU**-12:11,13▪14:17,19 -**1SA**-23:11-**2SA**-13:24▪24:10-**2KI**-19:19▪ 20:3(577)-**1CH**-21:8-**2CH**-6:40-**NE**-1:5 (577),8,11(577)-**JOB**-10:9▪42:4-**PS**-80:14▪ 116:4(577)▪118:25^2(577)▪119:108-**IS**-38:3(577)▪64:9-**JER**-38:4,20▪42:2-**DA**-1:12▪9:16-**AM**-7:2,5-**JON**-1:14(577)▪ 4:3-**MAL**-1:9(2470,6440)▪**N.T.**-all= 3870&marked-**M'R**-7:32-**LU**-8:28(1189)▪ 9:38(1189)-**AC**-21:39(1189)▪26:3 (1189)-**RO**-12:1▪15:30▪16:17-**1CO**-1:10▪ 4:16▪16:15-**2CO**-2:8▪5:20▪6:1▪10:1, 2(1189)-**GA**-4:12(1189)-**EPH**-4:1 -**PH'P**-4:2-**1TH**-4:1(2065),10▪5:12 (2065)-**2TH**-2:1(2065)-**PH'M**-9,10 -**HEB**-13:19,22-**1PE**-2:11-**2JO**-5(2065)

BESEECHING-**M'T**-8:5(3870) -**M'R**-1:40(3870)-**LU**-7:3(2065)

BESET-all=5437&marked-**J'G**-19:22▪ 20:5-**PS**-22:12(3803)▪139:5(6696)-**HO**-7:2▪**N.T.**-**HEB**-12:1(2139)

BESIDE-all=905,a=5921-**GE**-26:1▪ 31:50a-**EX**-12:37▪14:9a▪29:12(413) -**LE**-1:16(681)▪6:10(681)▪9:17▪10:12 (681)▪18:18a▪23:38^4-**NU**-5:8,20(1107)▪ 6:21▪11:6(1115)▪16:49▪24:6a▪28:10a, 15a,23,24a,31▪29:6,11,34,38,39▪31:8a -**DE**-3:5▪4:35▪11:30(681)▪18:8▪19:9a▪ 29:1-**JOS**-3:16(6654)▪7:2(5973)▪12:9 (6654)▪17:5▪22:19(1107),29-**J'G**-7:1a▪ 8:26^2▪20:15,17,36(413),-**RU**-2:14(6654)▪ 4:4(2108)-**1SA**-2:2(1115)▪4:1a▪19:3 (3027)-2--**SA**-7:22(2108)▪13:23(5973)▪ 15:2a(3072)▪18a(3027)-**1KI**-3:20(681)▪ 4:23▪5:16▪9:26(854)▪10:13,15,19(681)▪ 11:25(854)▪13:31(681)-**2KI**-12:9(681)▪ 21:16-**1CH**-3:9▪17:20(2108)-**2CH**-9:12, 14▪17:19▪26:19a▪31:16-**EZR**-1:4(5973), 6(905)a▪2:65-**NE**-5:15(310)▪7:67▪8:4 (681)-**JOB**-1:14a(3027)-**PS**-23:2a▪73:25 (5973)-**SONG**-1:8a-**IS**-26:13(2108)▪ 32:20a▪43:11(1107)▪44:6(1107),8(1107), 45:5(2108),6(1107),21(1107),21(2108)▪ 47:8(657),10(657)▪64:4(2108)-**JER**-36:21a-**EZE**-9:2(681)▪10:6(681),16 (681),19(5980)▪11:22(5980)▪32:13a-**DA**-11:4-**HO**-13:4(1115)-**ZEP**-2:15(657)▪ **N.T.**-all=1909&marked-**M'T**-14:21 (5565)▪15:38(5565)▪25:20,22-**M'R**-3:21(1839)-**LU**-16:26▪24:21(4862)-**AC**-26:24(3105)-**2CO**-5:13(1839)▪11:28 (5565)-**2PE**-1:5(846)

BESIDES-all=5750&marked-**GE**-19:12▪46:26(905)-**LE**-7:13(5921)-**1KI**-22:7-**2CH**-18:6-**JER**-36:32▪**N.T.**-**1CO**-1:16(3063)-**PH'M**-19(4359)

BESIEGE-all=6696&marked-**DE**-20:12,19▪28:52^2(6887)-**1SA**-23:8-**1KI**-8:37(6887)-**2KI**-24:11-**2CH**-6:28-**IS**-21:2-**JER**-21:4,9

BESIEGED-all=6696&marked -**2SA**-11:1▪20:15-**1KI**-16:17▪20:1-**2KI**-6:24,25▪16:5▪17:5▪18:9▪19:24(4693)▪ 24:10(935,4692)▪25:2(935,4692)-**1CH**-20:1-**EC**-9:14(5437)-**IS**-1:8(5341)▪37:25 (4693)-**JER**-32:2▪37:5▪39:1▪52:5(935, 4692)-**EZE**-4:3(4692)▪6:12(5341)-**DA**-1:1

BESOM-**IS**-14:23(4292)

BESOUGHT-all=2470&marked -**GE**-42:21(2603)-**EX**-32:11-**DE**-3:23 (2603)-**2SA**-12:16(1245)-**1KI**-13:6-**2KI**-1:13(2603)▪13:4-**2CH**-33:12-**EZR**-8:23 (1245)-**ES**-8:3(2603)-**JER**-26:19▪**N.T.**-all=3870&marked-**M'T**-8:31,34▪14:36▪ 15:23(2065)▪18:29-**M'R**-5:10,12,23▪6:56▪ 7:26(2065)▪8:22-**LU**-4:38(2065)▪5:12 (1189)▪7:4▪8:31,32,37(2065),38(1189), 41▪9:40(1189)▪11:37(2065)-**JOH**-4:40 (2065),47(2065)▪19:31(2065),38(2065) -**AC**-13:42▪16:15,39▪21:12▪25:2▪27:33 -**2CO**-12:8-**1TI**-1:3

BEST-all=2896&marked-**GE**-43:11 (2173)▪47:6(4315),11(4315)-**EX**-22:5^2(4315) -**NU**-18:12^2(2459),29(2459),30(2459),32 (2459)▪36:6-**DE**-23:16-**1SA**-8:14▪15:9 (4315),15(4315)-**2SA**-18:4(3190)-**1KI**-10:18 (6338)-**2KI**-10:3-**ES**-2:9-**PS**-39:5(5324) -**SONG**-7:9-**EZE**-31:16-**MIC**-7:4▪**N.T.** -**LU**-15:22(4413)-**1CO**-12:31(2909)

BESTEAD-supplied

BESTIR-**2SA**-5:24(2782)

BESTOW-**EX**-32:29(5414)-**DE**-14:26(5414)-**2CH**-24:7(6213)-**EZR**-7:20^2(5415)▪**N.T.**-**LU**-12:17(4863),18 (4863)-**1CO**-12:23(4060)▪13:3(5595)

BESTOWED-**1KI**-10:26(3240)-**2KI**-5:24(6485)▪12:15(5414)-**1CH**-9:25(5414) -**2CH**-9:25(3240)-**IS**-63:7^2(1580)▪**N.T.**-**JOH**-4:38(2872)-**RO**-16:6(2872)-**2CO**-8:1(1325)-**GA**-4:11(2872)-**1JO**-3:1(1325)

BETHINK-**1KI**-8:47(7725,413,3820) -**2CH**-6:37(7725,413,3820)

BETIMES-**GE**-26:31(7925)-**2CH**-36:15(7925)-**JOB**-8:5(7836)▪24:5(7836) -**PR**-13:24(7836)

BETRAY-**1CH**-12:17(7411)-**IS**-16:3 (1540)▪**N.T.**-all=3860-**M'T**-24:10▪ 26:16,21,23,46-**M'R**-13:12▪14:10, 11,18-**LU**-22:4,6-**JOH**-6:64,71▪12:4▪ 13:2,11,21

BETRAYED-all=3860-**M'T**-10:4▪ 17:22▪20:18▪26:2,24,25,45,48▪27:3,4 -**M'R**-3:19▪14:21,41,44-**LU**-21:16▪22:22 -**JOH**-18:2,5-**1CO**-11:23

BETRAYERS-**AC**-7:52(4273)

BETRAYEST-**LU**-22:48(3860)

BETRAYETH-all=3860-**M'R**-14:42 -**LU**-22:21-**JOH**-21:20

BETROTH-all=781-**DE**-28:30

-**HO**-2:19^2,20
BETROTHED-all=781&marked-**EX**-21:8(3259),9(3259)▪22:16-**LE**-19:20(2778)-**DE**-20:7▪22:23,25,27,28
BETTER-all=2896&marked-**GE**-29:19-**EX**-14:12-**NU**-14:3-**J'G**-8:2▪9:2▪11:25▪18:19-**RU**-4:15-**1SA**-1:8▪15:22,28▪27:1-**2SA**-17:14▪18:3-**1KI**-1:47(3190)▪2:32▪19:4▪21:2-**2KI**-5:12-**2CH**-21:13-**ES**-1:19-**PS**-37:16▪63:3▪69:31(3190)▪84:10▪118:8,9▪119:72-**PR**-3:14▪8:11,19▪12:9▪15:16,17▪16:8,16,19,32▪17:1▪19:1,22▪21:9,19▪25:7,24▪27:5,10▪28:6-**EC**-2:24▪3:22▪4:3,6,9,13▪5:5▪6:3,9,11(3148)▪7:1,2,3,3(3190),5,8^2,10▪8:15▪9:4,16,18▪10:11(3504)-**SONG**-1:2▪4:10-**IS**-56:5-**LA**-4:9-**EZE**-36:11-**DA**-1:20(3027)-**HO**-2:7-**AM**-6:2-**JON**-4:3,8-**NA**-3:8(3190)▪**N.T.**-all=2909&marked-**M'T**-6:26(1308)▪12:12(1308)▪18:6(4851),8(2570),9(2570)-**M'R**-9:42(2570,3123),43(2570),45(2570),47(2570)-**LU**-5:39(5543)▪12:24(1308)▪17:2(3081)-**RO**-3:9(4284)-**1CO**-7:9,38(2573)▪8:8(4052)▪9:15(2570,3123)▪11:17-**PH'P**-1:23▪2:3(5242)-**HEB**-1:4▪6:9▪7:7,19,22▪8:6^2▪9:23▪10:34▪11:16,35,40▪12:24-**1PE**-3:17-**2PE**-2:21
BETTERED-**M'R**-5:26(5623)
BETWEEN-all=996&marked-**GE**-3:15^2▪9:12,13,15,16,17▪10:12▪13:3,7,8▪15:17▪16:5,14▪17:2,7,10▪20:1▪31:44,48,49▪48:12(5973)▪49:10,14-**EX**-8:23▪9:4▪11:7▪13:9,16▪14:2,20▪16:1▪18:16▪22:11▪25:22▪26:33▪28:33(8432)▪30:18▪31:13,17▪39:25^2(8432)▪40:7,30-**LE**-10:10^2▪11:47^2▪20:25^2▪26:46-**NU**-7:89▪11:33▪13:23▪16:48▪21:13▪26:56▪30:16^2▪31:27^2▪35:24-**DE**-1:1,16^2▪5:5▪6:8▪11:18▪14:1▪17:8^2▪25:1▪28:57▪33:12-**JOS**-3:4▪8:9,11,12▪18:11▪22:25,27,28,34▪24:7-**J'G**-4:5,17▪9:23▪11:10,27▪13:25▪15:4▪16:25,31▪20:38(5973)-**1SA**-7:12,14▪14:4,42▪17:1,3,6▪20:3,23,42▪24:12,15▪26:13-**2SA**-3:1,6▪18:9,24▪19:35▪21:7-**1KI**-3:9▪5:12▪7:28,29,46▪14:30▪15:6,7,16,19^2,32▪18:21(5921),42▪22:1,34-**2KI**-9:24▪11:17^2▪16:14▪25:4-**1CH**-21:16-**2CH**-4:17▪13:2▪16:3^2▪18:33▪19:10▪23:16^3-**NE**-3:32-**JOB**-41:16-**PR**-18:18-**IS**-22:11▪59:2-**JER**-7:5▪34:18,19▪42:5▪52:7-**LA**-1:3-**EZE**-4:3▪8:3,16▪10:2^2,6,7^2▪18:8▪20:12,20▪22:26^2▪34:17,17sup,20^2,22▪40:7▪41:10,18▪42:20▪43:8▪44:23^2▪47:16▪48:22-**DA**-7:5(997)▪8:5,16,21▪11:45-**HO**-2:2-**JOE**-2:17-**JON**-4:11-**ZEC**-5:9▪6:1,13▪9:7▪11:14-**MAL**-2:14▪3:18^2▪**N.T.**-all=3342&marked-**M'T**-18:15▪23:35-**LU**-11:51▪16:26▪23:12(4314)-**JOH**-3:25(1537,3326)-**AC**-12:6▪15:9▪26:31(4314)-**RO**-1:24(1722)-**1CO**-6:5(303,3319)▪7:34(3307)
BETWIXT-all=996&marked-**GE**-17:11▪23:15▪26:28▪30:36▪31:37,50,51,53▪32:16-**JOB**-9:33▪36:32(6293)-**SONG**-1:13-**IS**-5:3-**JER**-39:4▪**N.T.**-**PH'P**-1:23(1537)
BEWAIL-all=1058-**LE**-10:6-**DE**-21:13-**J'G**-11:37-**IS**-16:9▪**N.T.**-**2CO**-12:21(3996)-**RE**-18:9(2799)
BEWAILED-**J'G**-11:38(1058)▪**N.T.**-**LU**-8:52(2875)▪23:27(2875)
BEWAILETH-**JER**-4:31(3306)
BEWARE-all=8104&marked-**GE**-24:6-**EX**-23:21-**DE**-6:12▪8:11▪15:9-**J'G**-13:4,13-**2SA**-18:12-**2KI**-6:9-**PR**-19:25(6191)▪**N.T.**-all=4337&marked-**M'T**-7:15▪10:17▪16:6,11,12-**M'R**-8:15(991)▪12:38(991)-**LU**-12:1,15(5442)▪20:46-**AC**-13:40(991)-**PH'P**-3:2^2(991)-**COL**-2:8-**2PE**-3:17(5442)
BEWITCHED-**AC**-8:9(1839),11(1839)-**GA**-3:1(940)
BEWRAY-**IS**-16:3(1540)
BEWRAYETH-**PR**-27:16(7121)29:24(5046)▪**N.T.**-**M'T**-26:73(1212,4160)
BEYOND-all=5676&marked-**GE**-35:21(1973)▪50:10,11-**LE**-15:25(5921)-**NU**-22:18(5674)▪24:13(5674)-**DE**-3:20,25▪30:13-**JOS**-9:10▪13:8▪18:7-**J'G**-3:26(5674)▪5:17-**1SA**-20:22(1973),36(5674),37(1973)-**2SA**-10:16-**1KI**-4:12▪14:15-**1CH**-19:16-**2CH**-20:2-**EZR**-4:17(5675),20(5675)▪6:6^2(5675),8(5675)▪7:21(5675),25(5675)-**NE**-2:7,9▪12:38(5921)-**IS**-7:20▪9:1▪18:1-**JER**-22:19(1973)▪25:22-**AM**-5:27(1973)-**ZEP**-3:10▪**N.T.**-all=4008&marked-**M'T**-4:15,25▪19:1-**M'R**-3:8▪6:51(1537,4058)▪7:37(5249)-**JOH**-1:28▪3:26▪10:40-**AC**-7:43(1900)-**2CO**-8:3(5228)▪10:14(5239),16(5238)-**GAL**-1:13(2596,5236)-**1TH**-4:6(5233)
BID-all=559&marked-**NU**-15:38-**JOS**-6:10-**1SA**-9:27-**2SA**-2:26-**2KI**-4:24▪5:13(1696)▪10:5-**JON**-3:2(1696)-**ZEP**-1:7(6942)▪**N.T.**-**M'T**-14:28(2753)▪22:9(2564)▪23:3(2036)-**LU**-9:61(657)▪10:40(2036)▪14:12(479)-**1CO**-10:27(2564)-**2JO**-10(3004)
BIDDEN-**1SA**-9:13(7121),22(7121)-**2SA**-16:11(559)▪**N.T.**-all=2564&marked-**M'T**-1:24(4367)▪22:3,4,8-**LU**-7:39▪14:7,8^2,10,17,24
BIDDETH-**2JO**-11(3004)
BIDDING-**1SA**-22:14(4928)
BIER-**2SA**-3:31(4296)▪**N.T.**-**LU**-7:14(4673)
BILL-all=5612-**DE**-24:1,3-**IS**-50:1-**JER**-3:8▪**N.T.**-**M'R**-10:4(975)-**LU**-16:6(1121),7(1121)
BILLOWS-**PS**-42:7(1530)-**JON**-2:3(4867)
BIND-all=631,a=7194&marked-**EX**-28:28(7405)▪39:21(7405)-**NU**-30:2,3-**DE**-6:8a▪11:18a▪14:25(6887)-**JOS**-2:18a-**J'G**-15:10,12,13▪16:5,7,11-**JOB**-31:36(6029)▪38:31a▪39:10a▪40:13(2280)▪41:5a-**PS**-105:22▪118:27▪149:8-**PR**-3:3a▪6:21a▪7:3a-**IS**-8:16(6887)▪49:18a▪61:1(2280)-**JER**-51:63(7164)-**EZE**-3:25▪5:3(6887)▪24:17(2280)▪30:21(2280)▪34.16(2280)-**DA**-3:20(3729)-**HO**-6:1(2280)▪10:10-**MIC**-1:13(7573)▪**N.T.**-all=1210&marked-**M'T**-12:29▪13:30▪16:19▪18:18▪22:13▪23:4(1195)-**M'R**-3:27▪5:3-**AC**-9:14▪12:8(5265)▪21:11
BINDETH-all=2280&marked-**JOB**-5:18(2280)▪26:8(6887)▪28:11(2280)▪30:18(247)▪36:13(631)-**PS**-129:7(6014)▪147:3(2280)-**PR**-26:8(6887)-**IS**-30:26(2280)
BINDING-**GE**-37:7(481)▪49:11(631)-**EX**-28:32(8193)-**NU**-30:13(632)▪**N.T.**-**AC**-22:4(1195)
BIRD-all=6833&marked-**GE**-7:14-**LE**-14:6^2,7,51^2,52^2,53-**JOB**-41:5-**PS**-11:1▪124:7-**PR**-1:17(1167,3671)▪6:5▪7:23▪26:2▪27:8-**EC**-10:20(5775)▪12:4-**IS**-16:2(5775)▪46:11(5861)-**JER**-12:9(5861)-**LA**-3:52-**HO**-9:11(5775)▪11:11-**AM**-3:5▪**N.T.**-**RE**-18:2(3732)
BIRD'S-**DE**-22:6(6833)
BIRDS-all=6833&marked-**GE**-15:10▪40:17(5775),19(5775)-**LE**-14:4,5,49,50-**DE**-14:11-**2SA**-21:10(5775)-**PS**-104:17-**EC**-9:12-**IS**-31:5-**JER**-4:25(5775)▪5:27(5775)▪12:4(5775)▪12:9(5861)-**EZE**-39:4▪**N.T.**-all=4071&marked-**M'T**-8:20▪13:32-**LU**-9:58-**RO**-1:23-**1CO**-15:39(4421)-**JAS**-3:7
BIRDS'-**DA**-4:33(6853)
BIRTH-all=5309&marked-**EX**-28:10(8435)-**2KI**-19:3(4866)-**JOB**-3:16-**PS**-58:8-**EC**-6:3▪7:1(3205)-**IS**-37:3(4866)▪66:9(7665)-**EZE**-16:3(4351)-**HO**-9:11(3205)▪**N.T.**-**M'T**-1:18(1083)-**LU**-1:14(1083)-**JOH**-9:1(1079)-**GA**-4:19(5605)-**RE**-12:2(5605)
BIRTHDAY-**GE**-40:20(3117,3205)▪**N.T.**-**M'T**-14:6(1077)-**M'R**-6:21(1077)
BIRTHRIGHT-all=1062-**GE**-25:31,32,33,34▪27:36▪43:33-**1CH**-5:1^2,2▪**N.T.**-**HEB**-12:16(4415)
BISHOP-all=1985&marked-**1TI**-3:1(1984),2-**2TI**-subscr.-**TIT**-1:7,subscr.-**1PE**-2:25
BISHOPRICK-**AC**-1:20(1984)
BISHOPS-**PH'P**-1:1(1985)
BIT-**NU**-21:6(5391)-**PS**-32:9(4964)-**AM**-5:19(5391)
BITE-all=5391-**EC**-10:8,11-**JER**-8:17-**AM**-9:3-**MIC**-3:5-**HAB**-2:7▪**N.T.**-**GA**-5:15(1143)
BITETH-**GE**-49:17(5391)-**PR**-23:32(5391)
BITS-**JAS**-3:3(5469)
BITTEN-**NU**-21:8(5391),9(5391)
BITTER-all=4751&marked-**GE**-27:34-**EX**-1:14(4843)▪12:8(4844)▪15:23-**NU**-5:18,19,23,24^2,27▪9:11(4844)-**DE**-32:24(4815),32(4846)-**2KI**-14:26(4784)-**ES**-4:1-**JOB**-3:20▪13:26(4846)▪23:2(4805)-**PS**-64:3-**PR**-5:4▪27:7-**EC**-7:26-**IS**-5:20▪24:9(4843)-**JER**-2:19▪4:18▪6:26(8563)▪31:15(8563)-**EZE**-27:31-**AM**-8:10-**HAB**-1:6▪**N.T.**-all=4087&marked-**COL**-3:19-**JAS**-3:11(4089),14(4089)-**RE** 8:11▪10:9,10
BITTERLY-**J'G**-5:23(779)-**RU**-1:20(4843)-**IS**-22:4(4843)▪33:7(4751)-**EZE**-27:30(4751)-**HO**-12:14(8563)-**ZEP**-1:14(4751)▪**N.T.**-**M'T**-26:75(4090)-**LU**-22:62(4090)
BITTERN-all=7090-**IS**-14:23▪34:11-**ZEP**-2:14
BITTERNESS-all=4751&marked-**1SA**-1:10▪15:32-**2SA**-2:26-**JOB**-7:11▪9:18(4472)▪10:1▪21:25-**PR**-14:10▪17:25(4470)-**IS**-38:15,17(4843)-**LA**-1:4(4843)▪3:15(4844)-**EZE**-3:14▪21:6(4814)▪27:31-**ZEC**-12:10^2(4843)▪**N.T.**-all=4088-**AC**-8:23-**RO**-3:14-**EPH**-4:31-**HEB**-12:15
BLACK-all=7838&marked-**LE**-13:31,37-**1KI**-18:45(6937)-**ES**-1:6(5508)-**OB**-30:30(7835)-**PR**-7:9(380)-**SONG**-1:5,6(7840)▪5:11-**JER**-4:28(6937)▪8:21(6937)▪14:2(6937)-**LA**-5:10(3648)-**ZEC**-6:2,6▪**N.T.**-all=3189-**M'T**-5:36-**RE**-6:5,12
BLACKER-**LA**-4:8(2821)
BLACKISH-**JOB**-6:16(6937)
BLACKNESS-**JOB**-3:5(3650)-**IS**-50:3(6940)-**JOE**-2:6(6289)-**NA**-2:10(6289)▪**N.T.**-**HEB**-12:18(1105)-**JUDE**-13(2217)
BLADE-**J'G**-3:22^2(3851)-**JOB**-31:22(7929)▪**N.T.**-**M'T**-13:26(5528)-**M'R**-4:28(5528)
BLAINS-**EX**-9:9(76),10(76)
BLAME-**GE**-43:9(2398)▪44:32(2398)▪**N.T.**-**2CO**-8:20(3469)-**EPH**-1:4(299)
BLAMED-**2CO**-6:3(3469)-**GA**-2:11(2607)
BLAMELESS-**GE**-44:10(5355)-**JOS**-2:17(5355)-**J'G**-15:3(5352)▪**N.T.**-all=410&marked-**M'T**-12:5(338)-**LU**-1:6(273)-**1CO**-1:8-**PH'P**-2:15(273)▪3:6(273)-**1TH**-5:23(274)-**1TI**-3:2(483),10▪5:7(483)-**TIT**-1:6,7-**2PE**-3:14(298)
BLASPHEME-**2SA**-12:14(5006)-**1KI**-21:10(1288),13(1288)-**PS**-74:10(5006)▪**N.T.**-all=987-**M'R**-3:28,29-**AC**-26:11-**1TI**-1:20-**JAS**-2:7-**RE**-13:6
BLASPHEMED-all=1442&marked-**LE**-24:11(5344)-**2KI**-19:6,22-**PS**-74:18(5006)-**IS**-37:6,23▪52:5(5006)▪65:7(2778)-**EZE**-20:27▪**N.T.**-all=987-**AC**-18:6-**RO**-2:24-**1TI**-6:1-**TIT**-2:5-**RE**-16:9,11,21
BLASPHEMER-**1TI**-1:13(989)
BLASPHEMERS-**AC**-19:37(987)-**2TI**-3:2(989)
BLASPHEMEST-**JOH**-10:36(987)
BLASPHEMETH-**LE**-24:16^2(5344)-**PS**-44:16(1442)▪**N.T.**-**M'T**-9:3(987)-**LU**-12:10(987)
BLASPHEMIES-**EZE**-35:12(5007)▪**N.T.**-all=988-**M'T**-15:19-**M'R**-2:7▪3:28-**LU**-5:21-**RE**-13:5
BLASPHEMING-**AC**-13:45(987)
BLASPHEMOUS-**AC**-6:11(989),13(989)
BLASPHEMOUSLY-**LU**-22:65(987)
BLASPHEMY-**2KI**-19:3(5007)-**IS**-37:3(5007)▪**N.T.**-all=988&marked-**M'T**-

12:31^{2}■26:65(987),65-M'R-7:22■14:64-JOH-10:33-COL-3:8-RE-2:9■13:1,6■17:3

BLAST-all=7307&marked-EX-15:8-2SA-22:16(5397)-2KI-19:7-JOB-4:9(5397)-PS-18:15(5397)-IS-25:4■37:7

BLASTED-all=7710&marked-GE-41:6,23,27-2KI-19:26(7711)-IS-37:27(7709)

BLASTING-all=7711-DE-28:22-1KI-8:37-2CH-6:28-AM-4:9-HAG-2:17

BLAZE-M'R-1:45(1310)

BLEATING-1SA-15:14(6963)

BLEATINGS-J'G-5:16(8292)

BLEMISH-all=8549,a=3971&marked-EX-12:5■29:1-LE-1:3,10■3:1,6■4:3,23,28,32■5:15,18■6:6■9:2,3■14:10^{2}■21:17a,18a,20(8400),21^{2}a,23a■22:19,20a,21a■23:12,18■24:19a,20a-NU-6:14^{3}■19:2a■28:19,31■29:2,8,13,20,23,29,32,36-DE-15:21^{2}a■17:1a-2SA-14:25a-EZE-43:22,23^{2},25■45:18,23■46:4^{2},6^{2},13-DA-1:4a■N.T.-EPH-5:27(299)-1PE-1:19(299)

BLEMISHES-LE-22:25(3971)■N.T.-2PE-2:13(3470)

BLESS-all=1288-GE-12:2,3■17:16^{2}■22:17■26:3,24■27:4,7,10,19,25,31,34,38■28:3■32:26■48:9,16,20■49:25-EX-12:32■20:24■23:25-NU-6:23,24,27■23:20,25■24:1-DE-1:11■7:13^{2}■8:10■10:8■14:29■15:4,10,18■16:15■21:5■23:20■24:13,19■26:15■27:12■28:8,12■29:19■30:16■33:11-JOS-8:33-J'G-5:9-RU-2:4-1SA-9:13-2SA-6:20■7:29■8:10■21:3-1KI-1:47-1CH-4:10■16:43■17:27■23:13■29:20-NE-9:5-PS-5:12■16:7■26:12■28:9■29:11■34:1■62:4■63:4■66:8■67:1,6,7■68:26■96:2■100:4■103:1,1sup,2,20,21,22^{2}■104:1,35■109:28■115:12^{2},13,18■128:5■129:8■132:15■134:1,2,3■135:19^{2},20^{2}■145:1,2,10,21-PR-30:11-IS-19:25■65:16-JER-4:2■31:23-HAG-2:19■N.T.-all=2127-M'T-5:44-LU-6:28-AC-3:26-RO-12:14-1CO-4:12■10:16■14:16-HEB-6:14-JAS-3:9

BLESSED-all=1288,a=835&marked-GE-1:22,28■2:3■5:2■9:1,26■12:3■14:19^{2},20■17:20■18:18■22:18■24:1,27,31,35,48,60■25:11■26:4,12,29■27:23,27^{2},29,33^{2},41■28:1,6^{2},14■30:13(833),27,30■31:55■32:29■35:9■39:5■47:7,10■48:3,15,20■49:28^{2}-EX-18:10■20:11■39:43-LE-9:22,23-NU-22:6,12■23:11,20■24:9,10-DE-2:7■7:14■12:7■14:24■15:14■16:10■28:3^{2},4,5,6^{2}■33:1,13,20,24-JOS-14:13■17:14■22:6,7,33■24:10-J'G-5:24^{2}■13:24■17:2-RU-2:19,20■3:10■4:14-1SA-2:20■15:13■23:21■25:32,33^{2},39■26:25-2SA-2:5■6:11,12,18■7:29■13:25■18:28■19:39■22:47-1KI-1:48■2:45■5:7■8:14,15,55,56,66■10:9-1CH-13:14■16:2,36■17:27■26:5■29:10^{2},20-2CH-2:12■6:3,4■9:8■20:26■30:27■31:8,10-EZR-7:27-NE-8:6■9:5■11:2-JOB-1:10,21■29:11(833)■31:20■42:12-PS-1:1a■2:12a■18:46■21:6(1293)■28:6■31:21■32:1a,2a■33:12■34:8■37:22,26(1293)■40:4a■41:1a,2(833),13■45:2■49:18■65:4a■66:20■68:19,35■72:17,17(833),18,19■84:4a,5a,12a■89:15a,52■94:12a■106:3a,48■112:1a,2■113:2■115:15■118:26^{2}■119:1a,2a,12■124:6■128:1a,4■135:21■144:1■147:13-PR-5:18■8:32a,34a■10:7(1293)■20:7a,21■22:9■31:28(833)-EC-10:17a-SONG-6:9(833)-IS-19:25■30:18a■32:20a■51:2■56:2a■61:9■65:23■66:3-JER-17:7■20:14-EZE-3:12-DA-2:19(1289),20(1289)■3:28(1289)■4:34(1289)■12:12a-ZEC-11:5-MAL-3:12(833)■N.T.-all=3107,a=2127&marked-M'T-5:3,4,5,6,7,8,9,10,11■11:6■13:16■14:19a■16:17■21:9a■23:39a■24:46■25:34a■26:26a-M'R-6:41a■8:7a■10:16a■11:9a,10a■14:22a,61(2128)-LU-1:28a,42^{2}a,45,48(3106),68(2128)■2:28a,34a■6:20,21^{2},22■9:16a■10:23■11:27,28■12:37,38,43■13:35a■14:14,15■19:38a■23:29■24:30a,50a,51a-JOH-12:13a■20:29-AC-3:25(1757)■20:35-RO-1:25(2128)■4:7,8■9:5(2128)-2CO-1:3(2128)■11:31(2128)-GA-3:8(1757),9a-EPH-1:3(2128),3a-1TI-1:11■6:15-TIT-2:13-HEB-7:1a,6a,7a■11:20a,21a-JAS-1:12,25-1PE-1:3(2128)-RE-1:3■14:13■16:15■19:9■20:6■22:7,14

BLESSEDNESS-all=3108-RO-4:6,9-GA-4:15

BLESSEST-all=1288-NU-22:6-1CH-17:27-PS-65:10

BLESSETH-all=1288-GE-27:29-NU-24:9-DE-15:6-PS-10:3■107:38-PR-3:33■27:14-IS-65:16

BLESSING-all=1293&marked-GE-12:2■22:17(1288)■27:12,30,35,36^{2},38,41■28:4■33:11■39:5■49:28-EX-32:29-LE-25:21-DE-11:26,27,29■12:15■16:17■23:5■28:8■30:1,19■33:1,23-JOS-15:19-J'G-1:15-1SA-25:27-2SA-7:29-2KI-5:15-NE-9:5■13:2-JOB-29:13-PS-3:8■24:5■109:17■129:8■133:3-PR-10:22■11:11,26■24:25-IS-19:24■44:3■65:8-EZE-34:26^{2}■44:30-JOE-2:14-ZEC-8:13-MAL-3:10■N.T.-all=2129&marked-LU-24:53(2127)-RO-15:29-1CO-10:16-GA-3:14-HEB-6:7,14■12:17-JAS-3:10-1PE-3:9^{2}-RE-5:12,13■7:12

BLESSINGS-all=1293-GE-49:25^{3},26^{2}-DE-28:2-JOS-8:34-PS-21:3-PR-10:6■28:20-MAL-2:2■N.T.-EPH-1:3(2129)

BLEW-all=8628-JOS-6:8,9,13,16,20-J'G-3:27■6:34■7:19,20,22-1SA-13:3-2SA-2:28■18:16■20:1,22-1KI-1:39-2KI-9:13■11:14■N.T.-M'T-7:25(4154),27-JOH-6:18(4154)-AC-27:13(5285)■28:13(1920)

BLIND-all=5787&marked-EX-4:11-LE-19:14■21:18■22:22(5788)-DE-15:21■16:19(5786)■27:18■28:29-1SA-12:3(5956)-2SA-5:6,8^{2}-JOB-29:15-PS-146:8-IS-29:18■35:5■42:7,16,18,19^{3}■43:8■56:10■59:10-JER-31:8-LA-4:14-ZEP-1:17-MAL-1:8■N.T.-all=5185-M'T-9:27,28■11:5■12:22^{2}■15:14^{3},30,31■20:30■21:14■23:16,17,19,24,26-M'R-8:22,23■10:46,49,51-LU-4:18■6:39■7:21,22■14:13,21■18:35-JOH-5:3■9:1,2,6,8,13,17,18,19,20,24,25,32,39,40,41■10:21■11:37-AC-13:11-RO-2:19-2PE-1:9-RE-3:17

BLINDED-JOH-12:40(5186)-RO-11:7(4456)-2CO-3:14(4456)■4:4(5186)-1JO-2:11(5186)

BLINDETH-EX-23:8(5786)

BLINDFOLDED-LU-22:64(4028)

BLINDNESS-GE-19:11(5575)-DE-28:28(5788)-2KI-6:18^{2}(5575)-ZEC-12:4(5788)■N.T.-RO-11:25(4457)-EPH-4:18(4457)

BLOCK-IS-57:14(4383)

BLOOD-all=1818&marked-GE-4:10,11■9:4,5,6■37:22,26,31■42:22■49:11-EX-4:9■7:17,19^{2},20,21■12:7,13^{2},22^{2},23■22:2,3■23:18■24:6^{2},8^{2}■29:12^{2},16,20^{2},21■30:10■34:25-LE-1:5,11,15■3:2,8,13,17■4:5,6^{2},7^{2},16,17,18^{2},25^{2},30^{2},34^{2}■5:9^{2}■6:27,30■7:2,14,26,27,33■8:15^{2},19,23,24^{2},30■9:9^{3},12,18■10:18■12:4,5,7■14:6,14,17,25,28,51,52■15:19,25■16:14^{2},15^{3},18^{2},19,27■17:4^{2},6,10^{2},11^{2},12^{2},13,14^{3}■19:16,26■20:9,11,12,13,16,18,27-NU-18:17■19:4^{2},5■23:24■35:19,21,24,25,27^{3},33^{3}-DE-12:16,23^{2},27^{2}■15:23■17:8■19:6,10^{2},12,13■21:7,8^{2},9■22:8■32:14,42^{2},43-JOS-2:19^{2}■20:3,5,9-J'G-9:24-1SA-14:32,33,34■19:5■25:26,31,33■26:20-2SA-1:16,22■3:27,28■4:11■14:11■16:8■20:12■23:17-1KI-2:5^{2},9,31,32,33,37■18:28■21:19^{2}■22:35,38-2KI-3:22,23■9:7^{2},26^{2},33■16:13,15^{2}■21:16■24:4^{2}-1CH-11:19■22:8^{2}■28:3-2CH-19:10■24:25■29:22^{3},24■30:16-JOB-16:18■39:30-PS-9:12■16:4■30:9■50:13■58:10■68:23■72:14■78:44■79:3,10■94:21■105:29■106:38^{3}-PR-1:11,16,18■6:17■12:6■28:17■30:33-IS-1:11,15■4:4■9:5■15:9■26:21■33:15■34:3,6^{2},7■49:26■59:3,7■63:3(5332)■66:3-JER-2:34■7:6■19:4■22:3,17■26:15■46:10■48:10■51:35-LA-4:13,14-EZE-3:18,20■5:17■9:9■14:19■16:6^{3},9,22,36,38^{2}■18:10,13■19:10■21:32■22:3,4,6,9,12,13,27■23:37,45^{2}■24:7,8■28:23■32:6■33:4,5,6,8,25^{2}■35:6^{3}■36:18■38:22■39:17,18,19■43:18,20■44:7,15■45:19-HO-1:4■4:2■6:8■12:14-JOE-2:30,31■3:19,21-JON-1:14-MIC-3:10■7:2-HAB-2:8,12,17-ZEP-1:17-ZEC-9:7,11■N.T.-all=129&marked-M'T-9:20(131)■16:17■23:30,35^{3}■26:28■27:4,6,8,24,25-M'R-5:25,29■14:24-LU-8:43,44■11:50,51^{2}■13:1■22:20,44-JOH-1:13■6:53,54,55,56■19:34-AC-1:19■2:19,20■5:28■15:20,29■17:26■18:6■20:26,28■21:25■22:20-RO-3:15,25■5:9-1CO-10:16■11:25,27■15:50-GA-1:16-EPH-1:7■2:13■6:12-COL-1:14,20-HEB-2:14■9:7,12^{2},13,14,18,19,20,21,22^{2}(130),25■10:4,19,29■11:28■12:4,24■13:11,12,20-1PE-1:2,19-1JO-1:7■5:6^{2},8-RE-1:5■5:9■6:10,12■7:14■8:7,8■11:6■12:11■14:20■16:3,4,6^{2}■17:6^{2}■18:24■19:2,13

BLOODGUILTINESS-PS-51:14(1818)

BLOODTHIRSTY-PR-29:10(582,1818)

BLOODY-all=1818-EX-4:25,26-2SA-16:7,8■21:1-PS-5:6■26:9■55:23■59:2■139:19-EZE-7:23■22:2■24:6,9-NA-3:1■N.T.-AC-28:8(1420)

BLOOMED-NU-17:8(6692)

BLOSSOM-all=6524&marked-NU-17:5-IS-5:24(6525)■27:6(6692)■35:1,2-HAB-3:17

BLOSSOMED-EZE-7:10(6692)

BLOSSOMS-GE-40:10(5322)-NU-17:8(6731)

BLOT-all=4229&marked-EX-32:32,33-NU-5:23-DE-9:14■25:19■29:20-2KI-14:27-JOB-31:7(3971)-PS-51:1,9-PR-9:7(371)-JER-18:23■N.T.-RE-3:5(1813)

BLOTTED-all=4229-NE-4:5-PS-69:28■109:13,14-IS-44:22■N.T.-AC-3:19(1813)

BLOTTETH-IS-43:25(4229)

BLOTTING-COL-2:14(1813)

BLOW-all=8628&marked-EX-15:10(5398)-NU-10:3,4,5,6^{2},7,8,9(7321),10■31:6(8643)-JOS-6:4-J'G-7:18^{2},20-1KI-1:34-1CH-15:24(2690)-PS-39:10(8409)■78:26(5265)■81:3■147:18(5380)-SONG-4:16(6315)-IS-40:24(5398)-JER-4:5■6:1■14:17(4347)■51:27-EZE-21:31(6315)■22:20(5301),21(5301)■33:3,6-HO-5:8-JOE-2:1,15-HAG-1:9(5301)-ZEC-9:14■N.T.-LU-12:55(4154)-RE-7:1(4154)

BLOWETH-IS-18:3(8628)■40:7(5380)■54:16(5301)■N.T.-JOH-3:8(4154)

BLOWING-LE-23:24(8643)-NU-29:1(8643)-JOS-6:9(8628),13(8628)

BLOWN-all=8628&marked-JOB-20:26(5301)-IS-27:13-EZE-7:14-AM-3:6

BLUE-all=8504&marked-EX-25:4■26:1,4,31,36■27:16■28:5,6,8,15,28,31,33,37■35:6,23,25,35■36:8,11,35,37■38:18,23■39:1,2,3,5,8,21,22,24,29,31-NU-4:6,7,9,11,12■15:38-CH-2:7,14■3:14-ES-1:6■7:6(8336)■8:15-JER-10:9-EZE-23:6■27:7,24

BLUENESS-PR-20:30(2250)

BLUNT-EC-10:10(6949)

BLUSH-all=3637-EZR-9:6-JER-6:15■8:12

BOAR-PS-80:13(2386)

BOARD-all=7175-EX-26:16^{2},17,19^{2},21^{2},25^{2}■36:21^{2},22,24^{2},26^{2},30

BOARDS-all=7175&marked-EX-26:15,17,18^{2},19,20,22,23,25,26,27^{2},28,29■27:8(3871)■35:11■36:20,22,23^{2},24,25,27,28,30,31,32^{2},33,34■38:7(3871)■39:33■40:18-NU-3:36■4:31-1KI-6:9(7713),15(6763),16(6763)-SONG-8:9(3871)-EZE-27:5(3871)■N.T.-AC-27:44(4548)

BOAST-all=1984&marked-1KI-20:11-2CH-25:19(3513)-PS-34:2■44:8■49:6■94:4(559)■97:7-PR-27:1-IS-10:15(6286)■61:6(3235)■N.T.-all=2744&

marked-RO-2:17,23■11:18(2620),18sup-2CO-9:2■10:8,13,16■11:16-EPH-2:9

BOASTED-EZE-35:13(1431)■N.T.-2CO-7:14(2744)

BOASTERS-RO-1:30(213)-2TI-3:2(213)

BOASTEST-PS-52:1(1984)

BOASTETH-all=1984-PS-10:3-PR-20:14■25:14■N.T.-JAS-3:5(3166)

BOASTING-all=2746&marked-AC-5:36(3004)-RO-3:27-2CO-7:14■8:24■9:3(2745),4■10:15(2744)■11:10,17

BOASTINGS-JAS-4:16(212)

BOAT-2SA-19:18(5679)■N.T.-all=4627&marked-JOH-6:22^{2}(4142)-AC-27:16,30,32

BOATS-JOH-6:23(4142)

BODIES-all=1472&marked-GE-47:18-1SA-31:12-1CH-10:12(1480)-2CH-20:24(6297),25(6297)-NE-9:37-JOB-13:12(1354)-PS-79:2(5038)■110:6-JER-31:40(6297)■33:5(6297)■34:20(5038)■41:9(6297)-EZE-1:11,23-DA-3:27(1655),28(1655)-AM-8:3(6297)■N.T.-all=4983&marked-M’T-27:52-JOH-19:31-RO-1:24■8:11■12:1-1CO-6:15■15:40-EPH-5:28-HEB-10:22■13:11-RE-11:8(4430),9^{2}(4430)

BODILY-LU-3:22(4984)-2CO-10:10(4983)-COL-2:9(4985)-1TI-4:8(4984)

BODY-all=5315&marked-EX-24:10(6106)-LE-21:11-NU-6:6■9:6,7,10■19:11,13,16-DE-21:23(5038)■28:4(990),11(990),18(990),53(990)■30:9(990)-J’G-8:30(3409)-1SA-31:10(1472),12(1472)-1CH-10:12(1480)-JOB-19:17(990)■20:25(1465)-PS-132:11(990)-PR-5:11(7607)-IS-10:18(1320)■26:19(5038)■51:23(1460)-JER-26:23(5038)■36:30(5038)-LA-4:7(6106)-EZE-10:12(1320)-DA-4:33(1655)■5:21(1655)■7:11(1655),15(5085)■10:6(1472)-MIC-6:7(990)-HAG-2:13(5315)■N.T.-all=4983&marked-M’T-5:29,30■6:22^{2},23,25^{2}■10:28^{2}■14:12■26:12,26■27:58^{2},59-M’R-5:29■14:8,22,51■15:43,45-LU-11:34^{3},36■12:4,22,23■17:37■22:19■23:52,55■24:3,23-JOH-2:21■19:38^{2},40■20:12-AC-9:40■19:12(5559)-RO-4:19■6:6,12■7:4,24■8:10,13,23■12:4,5-1CO-5:3■6:13^{2},16,18^{2},19,20■7:4^{2},34■9:27■10:16,17■11:24,27,29■12:12^{3},13,14,15^{2},16^{2},17,18,19,20,22,23,24,25,27■13:3■15:35,37,38^{2},44^{4}-2CO-4:10^{2}■5:6,8,10■12:2^{2},3-GAL-6:17-EPH-1:23■2:16■3:6(4954)■4:4,12,16^{2}■5:23,30-PH’P-1:20■3:21^{2}-COL-1:18,22■2:11,17,19,23■3:15-1TH-5:23-HEB-10:5,10■13:3-JAS-2:16,26■3:2,3,6-1PE-2:24-JUDE-9

BODY’S-COL-1:24(4983)

BOIL-all=7822&marked-EX-9:9,10,11-LE-8:31(1310)■13:18,19,20,23-2KI-20:7-JOB-41:31(7570)-IS-38:21■64:2(1158)-EZE-24:5(7570)■46:20(1310)■24^{2}(1310)

BOILED-1KI-19:21(1310)-2KI-6:29(1310)-JOB-30:27(7570)

BOILING-EZE-46:23(4018)

BOILS-EX-9:11(7822)-JOB-2:7(7822)

BOISTEROUS-M’T-14:30(2478)

BOLD-PR-28:1(982)■N.T.-all=5111&marked-AC-13:46(3955)-RO-10:20(662)-2CO-10:1(2292),2(2292),2■11:21^{2}-PH’P-1:14-1TH-2:2(3955)-PH’M-8(3954)

BOLDLY-GE-34:25(983)■N.T.-all=3955&marked-M’R-15:43(5111)-JOH-7:26(3954)-AC-9:27,29■14:3■18:26■19:8-RO-15:15(5112)-EPH-6:19(3954),20-HEB-4:16(3954)■13:16(2292)

BOLDNESS-EC-8:1(5797)■N.T.-all=3954-AC-4:13,29,31-2CO-7:4-EPH-3:12-PH’P-1:20-1TI-3:13-HEB-10:19-1JO-4:17

BOLLED-EX-9:31(1392)

BOLSTER-all=4763-1SA-19:13,16■26:7,11,12,16

BOLT-2SA-13:17(5274)

BOLTED-2SA-13:18(5274)

BOND-all=632&marked-NU-30:2,3,4^{2},10,11,12-JOB-12:18(4148)-EZE-20:37(4562)■N.T.-all=1401&marked-LU-13:16(1199)-AC-8:23(4886)-1CO-12:13-GA-3:28-EPH-4:3(4886)■6:8-COL-3:11,14(4886)-RE-13:16■19:18

BONDAGE-all=5650&marked-EX-1:14(5656)■2:23(5656),23(5656)■6:5(5647),6(5656),9(5656)■13:3,14■20:2-DE-5:6■6:12■8:14■13:5,10■26:6(5656)-JOS-24:17-J’G-6:8-EZR-9:8(5659),9(5659)-NE-5:5^{2}(3533),18(5656)■9:17(5659)-IS-14:3(5656)■N.T.-all=1397&marked-JOH-8:33(1398)-AC-7:6(1402),7(1398)-RO-8:15,21-1CO-7:15(1402)-2CO-11:20(2615)-GA-2:4(2615)■4:3(1402),9(1398),24,25(1398)■5:1-HEB-2:15-2PE-2:19(1402)

BONDMAID-LE-19:20(8198)■N.T.-GA-4:22(3814)

BONDMAIDS-LE-25:44^{2}(519)

BONDMAN-all=5650-GE-44:33-DE-15:15■16:12■24:18,22■N.T.6:15(1401)

BONDMEN-all=5650&marked-GE-43:18■44:9-LE-25:42,44^{2},46(5647)■26:13-DE-6:21■7:8■28:68-JOS-9:23-1KI-9:22-2KI-4:1-2CH-28:10-EZR-9:9-ES-7:4-JER-34:13

BONDS-all=4147&marked-NU-30:5(632),7(632),14(632)-PS-116:16-JER-5:5■27:2■30:8-NA-1:13■N.T.-all=1199&marked-AC-20:23■23:29■25:14(1198)■26:29,31-EPH-6:20(254)-PH’P-1:7,13,14,16-COL-4:3(1210),18-2TI-2:9-PH’M-10,13-HEB-10:34■11:36■13:3(1198)

BONDSERVANT-LE-25:39(5656,5650)

BONDSERVICE-1KI-9:21(5647)

BONDWOMAN-all=519-GE-21:10^{2},12,13■N.T.-all=3814-GAL-4:23,30^{2},31

BONDWOMEN-all=8198-DE-28:68-2CH-28:10-ES-7:4

BONE-all=6106&marked-GE-2:23■29:14-EX-12:46-NU-9:12■19:16,18-J’G-9:2-2SA-5:1■19:13-1CH-11:1-JOB-2:5■19:20■31:22(7070)-EZE-37:7■39:15■N.T.-JOH-19:36(3747)

BONES-all=6106&marked-GE-2:23■50:25-EX-13:19^{2}-NU-24:8-JOS-24:32-J’G-19:29-1SA-31:13-2SA-19:12■21:12^{2},13^{2},14-1KI-13:2,31-2KI-13:21■23:14,16,18^{2},20-1CH-10:12-2CH-34:5-JOB-4:14■10:11■20:11■21:24■30:17,30■33:19,21■40:18,18(1634)-PS-6:2■22:14,17■31:10■32:3■34:20■35:10■38:3■42:10■51:8■53:5■102:3,5■109:18■141:7-PR-3:8■12:4■14:30■15:30■16:24■17:22(1634)■25:15(1634)-EC-11:5-IS-38:13■58:11■66:14-JER-8:1^{5}■20:9■23:9■50:17-LA-1:13■3:4■4:8-EZE-6:5■24:4,5^{2},10■32:27■37:1,3,4^{2},5,7,11^{2}-DA-6:24(1635)-AM-2:1■6:10-MIC-3:2,3-HAB-3:16-ZEP-3:3(1633)■N.T.-all=3747&marked-M’T-23:27-LU-24:39-AC-3:7(4974)-EPH-5:30(3747)-HEB-11:22(3747)

BONNETS-all=4021&marked-EX-28:40■29:9■39:28-LE-8:13-IS-3:20(6287)-EZE-44:18(6287)

BOOK-all=5612&marked-GE-5:1-EX-17:14■24:7■32:32,33-NU-5:23■21:14-DE-17:18■28:58,61■29:20,21,27■30:10■31:24,26-JOS-1:8■8:31,34■10:13■18:9■23:6■24:26-1SA-10:25-2SA-1:18-1KI-11:41■14:19,29■15:7,23,31■16:5,14,20,27■22:39,45-2KI-1:18■8:23■10:34■12:19■13:8,12■14:6,15,18,28■15:6,11,15,21,26,31,36■16:19■20:20■21:17,25■22:8^{2},10,11,13^{2},16■23:2,3,21,24,28■24:5-1CH-9:1■29:29^{3}(1697)-2CH-9:29(1697)■12:15(1697)■16:11■17:9■20:34(1697),34■24:27■25:4,26■27:7■28:26■32:32■33:18(1697)■34:14,15^{2},16,18,21^{2},24,30,31■35:12,27■36:8-EZR-4:15^{2}(5609)■6:18(5609)-NE-8:1,3,5,8,18■9:3■12:23■13:1-ES-2:23■6:1■9:32■10:2-JOB-19:23■31:35-PS-40:7■56:8■69:28■139:16-IS-29:11,12,18■30:8■34:16-JER-25:13■30:2■32:12■36:2,4,8,10,11,13,18,32■45:1■51:60,63-EZE-2:9-DA-12:1,4-NA-1:1-MAL-3:16■N.T.-all=975,a=976&marked-M’T-1:1a-M’R-12:26a-LU-3:4a■4:17^{2},20■20:42a-JOH-20:30-AC-1:20a■7:42a-GAL-3:10-PH’P-4:3a-HEB-9:19■10:7-RE-1:11■3:5a■5:1,2,3,4,5,7,8,9■10:2(974),8(974),9(974),10(974)■13:8a■17:8a■20:12^{2}a,15a■21:27■22:7,9,10,18^{2},19^{2}a,19

BOOKS-EC-12:12(5612)-DA-7:10(5609)■9:2(5612)■N.T.-all=975&marked-JOH-21:25-AC-19:19(976)-2TI-4:13-RE-20:12^{2}

BOOTH-JOB-27:18(5521)-JON-4:5(5521)

BOOTHS-all=5521-GE-33:17-LE-23:42^{2},43-NE-8:14,15,16,17^{2}

BOOTIES-HAB-2:7(4933)

BOOTY-NU-31:32(4455)-JER-49:32(957)-ZEP-1:13(4933)

BORDER-all=1366&marked-GE-10:19(1366)■49:13(3411)-EX-19:12(7097)■25:25^{2}(4526),27(4526)■28:26(8193)■37:12^{2}(4526),14(4526)■39:19(8193)-NU-20:16,21■21:13,15,23,24■22:36■33:44■34:3,4,5,6^{3},7,8sup,8,9^{2},10,11,12■35:26-DE-3:16^{2}■12:20-JOS-4:19(7097)■12:2,5^{2}■13:10,11,23^{2},26,27■15:1,2,5^{2},6^{2},7^{2},8^{2},9^{2},10,11^{3},12,47■16:5^{2},6^{2},8■17:7,8,10■18:12^{2},13^{2},14,15,16,19^{2},20(1379)■19:10,11,12,14,18,22,25,46■22:25■24:30-J’G-2:9■7:22(8193)■11:18^{2}-1SA-6:12■10:2■13:18-2SA-8:3(3027)-1KI-4:21-2KI-3:21-2CH-9:26-PS-78:54-PR-15:25-IS-19:19■37:24(7093)-JER-31:17■50:26(7093)-EZE-11:10,11■29:10■43:13,17,20■45:7■47:13,15,16^{2},17^{3},18,20■48:1,2,3,4,5,6,7,8,12,13,21^{2},22^{2},24,25,26,27,28^{2}-JOE-3:6-AM-1:13■6:2-OB-7-ZEP-2:8-ZEC-9:2(1379)-MAL-1:4,5■N.T.-M’R-6:56(2899)-LU-8:44(2899)

BORDERS-all=1366&marked-GE-23:17■47:21-EX-8:2■16:35(7097)■34:24-NU-15:38^{2}(3671)■20:17■21:22■35:27-JOS-11:2(5299)■13:2(1552),3,4■16:2■22:10(1552)■11(1552)-1KI-7:28(4526),28(4526),29(4526),31(4526),32(4526),35(4526),36(4526)-2KI-16:17(4526)■18:8■19:23(7093)-1CH-5:16(8444)■7:29(3027)-PS-74:17(1367)■147:14-SONG-1:11(8447)-IS-15:8■54:12■60:18-JER-15:13■17:3-EZE-27:4■45:1-MIC-5:6■N.T.-M’T-4:13(3725)■23:5(2899)-M’R-7:24(8181)

BORE-EX-21:6(7527)-JOB-41:2(5344)

BORED-2KI-12:9(5344)

BORN-all=3205,a=249&marked-GE-4:18,26■6:1■10:1,21,25■14:14(3211)■15:3(1121)■17:12(3211),13(3211),17,23(3211),27(3211)■21:3,5,7,9■22:20■24:15■29:34■30:20,25■31:43■35:26■36:5■41:50■46:20,22,27■48:5-EX-1:22(3209)■12:19a,48a■21:4-LE-12:2,7■18:9^{2}(4138)■19:34a■22:11(3211)■23:42a■24:16a-NU-9:14a■15:13a,29a,30a■26:60-DE-21:15-JOS-5:5(3209)■8:33a-J’G-13:8■18:29-RU-4:15,17-1SA-2:5■4:20-2SA-3:2,5■5:13,14(3209)■12:14(3209)■14:27■21:20,22-1KI-13:2-1CH-1:19■2:3,9■3:1,4,5■7:21■20:8■22:9■26:6-EZR-10:3-JOB-1:2■3:3■5:7■11:12■14:1■15:7,14■25:4■38:21-PS-22:31■58:3(990)■78:6■87:4,5,6-PR-17:17-EC-2:7(1121)■3:2■4:14-IS-9:6■66:8-JER-16:3■20:14,15■22:26-EZE-16:4,5■47:22a-HO-2:3■N.T.-all=1080&marked-M’T-1:16■2:1,2(5088),4■11:11(1084)■19:12■26:24-M’R-14:21-LU-1:35■2:11(5088)■7:28(1084)-JOH-1:13■3:3,4^{2},5,6^{2},7,8■8:41■9:2,19,20,32,34■16:21■18:37-AC-2:8■7:20■18:2(1085),24(1085)■22:3,28-RO-9:11-1CO-15:8(1626)-GA-4:23,29-HEB-11:23-1PE-1:23(313)-1JO-2:29■3:9^{2}■4:7■5:1,4,18-RE-12:4(5088)

BORNE-all=5375&marked-**EX**-25:14, 28-**J'G**-16:29(5564)-**JOB**-34:31-**PS**-55:12■ 69:7-**IS**-46:3(6006)■53:4■66:12-**JER**-10:5■15:9(3205),10(3205)-**LA**-3:28(5190)■ 5:7(5445)-**EZE**-16:20(3205),58■32:24,25■ 36:6■39:26-**AM**-5:26■**N.T.**-**M'T**-20:12 (941)■23:4(1418)-**M'R**-2:3(142)-**LU**-11:46 (1418)-**JOH**-20:15(941)-**AC**-21:35(941) -**1CO**-15:49(5409)-**RE**-2:3(941)

BORROW-all=7592&marked-**EX**-3:22■11:2■22:14-**DE**-15:6(5670)■28:12 (3867)-**2KI**-4:3■**N.T.**-**M'T**-5:42(1155)

BORROWED-**EX**-12:35(7592) -**2KI**-6:5(7592)-**NE**-5:4(3867)

BORROWER-**PR**-22:7(3867)-**IS**-24:2(3867)

BORROWETH-**PS**-37:21(3867)

BOSOM-all=2436&marked-**GE**-16:5 -**EX**-4:6^{2},7^{3}-**NU**-11:12-**DE**-13:6■28:54, 56-**RU**-4:16-**2SA**-12:3,8-**1KI**-1:2■3:20^{2}■ 17:19-**JOB**-31:33(2243)-**PS**-35:13■74:11■ 79:12■89:50■129:7(2683)-**PR**-5:20■6:27■ 17:23■19:24(6747)■21:14■26:15(6747) -**EC**-7:9-**IS**-40:11■65:6,7-**JER**-32:18 -**LA**-2:12-**MIC**-7:5■**N.T.**-all=2859-**LU**-6:38■16:22,23-**JOH**-1:18■13:23

BOSSES-**JOB**-15:26(1354)

BOTCH-**DE**-28:27(7822),35(7822)

BOTH-all=8147,a=1571&marked -**GE**-2:25■3:7■9:23■19:36■21:27,31■22:6, 8■24:25a■27:45■31:37■40:5■43:8a■44:16a■ 46:34a■47:3a,19a■48:13■50:9a-**EX**-5:14a■ 12:31a■18:18a■22:9,11■26:24■32:15■ 36:29^{2}-**LE**-16:21■20:11,12,13,18-**NU**-7:13,19,25,31,37,43,49,55,61,67,73,79■ 12:5■25:8-**DE**-19:17■22:22a,(8147),24■ 23:18■32:25a-**J'G**-8:22a■19:6,8,19a-**RU**-1:5-**1SA**-2:26a,34■3:11■5:4■9:26■12:14a, 25a■14:11■17:36a■20:11(8174),42(8174)■ 25:16a,43■26:25a-**2SA**-9:13■16:23a■17:18 -**1KI**-3:13a■6:25-**2KI**-2:11■17:41a■21:12■ 23:15a-**ES**-2:23-**JOB**-9:33■15:10a-**PS**-4:8 (3162)■49:2a-**PR**-17:15■20:10,12■24:22■ 27:3■29:13-**EC**-4:3■11:6-**IS**-1:31■7:16■ 8:14-**JER**-14:18a■23:11a■36:16(413)■ 46:12■51:12a■15:4■23:13-**DA**-11:27-**ZEP**-2:14a-**ZEC**-6:13■12:2a■**N.T.**-all=2532, a=5037,b=297&marked-**M'T**-9:17b■10:28■ 12:22■13:30b■15:14b■22:10a-**M'R**-6:30a■ 7:37a-**LU**-1:6b,7b■2:46■5:7b,36,38b■ 6:39b■7:42b■21:16■22:33-**JOH**-2:2■ 4:36■7:28■9:37■11:48,57■12:28■15:24■ 20:4(1417)-**AC**-1:1a,8a,13a■2:29,36■4:27a■ 5:14a■8:12a,38b■38a■10:39a■14:1sup,1a,5a■ 19:10a■20:21a■21:12a■22:4a■23:8b■ 24:15a■25:24a■26:16a,22a,29■28:23a -**RO**-1:12a,14^{2}a■3:9a■11:33■14:9^{2}-**1CO**-1:2a,24a■4:5,11■6:13,14■7:29,34-**2CO**-9:10-**EPH**-1:10a■2:14b,16b,18b-**PH'P**-1:7a■2:13■4:9,12^{2}-**1TH**-2:15■5:15-**2TH**-3:4-**1TI**-4:10,16-**TIT**-1:9-**PH'M**-16-**HEB**-2:4a,11a■5:1a,14a■6:19a■9:9a,19a,21■ 10:33a■11:21(1538)-**2PE**-3:18-**2JO**-9 -**JUDE**-25-**RE**-13:15■19:18a,18,20(1417)

BOTTLE-all=2573&marked-**GE**-21:14,15,19-**J'G**-4:19(4997)-**1SA**-1:24 (5035)■10:3(5035)■16:20(4997)-**2SA**-16:1(5035)-**PS**-56:8(4997)■119:83(4997) -**JER**-13:12^{2}(5035)■19:1(1228),10(1228) -**HAB**-2:15

BOTTLES-**JOS**-9:4(4997),13(4997) -**1SA**-25:18(5035)-**JOB**-32:19(178)■38:37 (5035)-**JER**-48:12(5035)-**HO**-7:5(2573)■ **N.T.**-all=779-**M'T**-9:17^{4}-**M'R**-2:22^{4} -**LU**-5:37^{3},38

BOTTOM-all=3247&marked-**EX**-15:5(4688)■29:12-**LE**-4:7,18,25,30,34■ 5:9■8:15■9:9-**JOB**-36:30(8328)-**SONG**-3:10(7507)-**EZE**-43:13(2436),14(2436), 17(2436)-**DA**-6:24(773)-**AM**-9:3(7172) -**ZEC**-1:8(4699)■**N.T.**-**M'T**-27:51 (2736)-**M'R**-15:38(2736)

BOTTOMS-**JON**-2:6(7095)

BOTTOMLESS-all=12-**RE**-9:1,2, 11■11:7■17:8■20:1,3

BOUGH-**GE**-49:22^{2}(1121)-**J'G**-9:48 (7754),49(7754)-**IS**-10:33(6288)■17:6 (534),9(2793)

BOUGHS-all=5688&marked-**LE**-23:40(6529),40(6057)-**DE**-24:20(6288) -**2SA**-18:9(7730)-**JOB**-14:9(7105)-**PS**-80:10(6057),11(7105)-**SONG**-7:8(5577) -**IS**-27:11(7105)-**EZE**-17:23(6057)■31:3, 5(5634),6(5589),8(5589),10,12(6288),14-**DA**-4:12(6056)

BOUGHT-all=7069&marked-**GE**-17:12(4736),13(4736),23(4736),27(4736)■ 33:19■39:1■47:14(7666),20,22,23■49:30■ 50:13-**EX**-12:44(4736)-**LE**-25:28,30,50, 51(4736)■27:22(4736),24-**DE**-32:6-**JOS**-24:32-**RU**-4:9-**2SA**-12:3■24:24-**1KI**-16:24 -**NE**-5:16-**IS**-43:24-**JER**-32:9,43-**HO**-3:2(3739)■**N.T.**-all=59&marked-**M'T**-13:46■21:12■27:7-**M'R**-11:15■15:46■16:1 -**LU**-14:18,19■17:28■19:45-**AC**-7:16 (5608)-**1CO**-6:20■7:23-**2PE**-2:1

BOUND-all=631&marked-**GE**-22:9 (6123)■38:28(7194)■39:20■40:3,5■42:19, 24■44:30(7194)■49:26(8379)-**EX**-12:34 (6887)-**LE**-8:7(640)-**NU**-19:15(6616)■ 30:4^{2},5,6,7,8,9,10,11-**JOS**-2:21(7194)■ 9:4(6887)-**J'G**-15:13■16:6,8,10,12,13,21 -**1SA**-25:29(6887)-**2SA**-3:34-**2KI**-5:23 (6887)■17:4■25:7-**2CH**-33:11■36:6 -**JOB**-36:8■38:20(1366)-**PS**-68:6(615)■ 104:9(1366)■107:10(615)-**PR**-22:15(7194)■ 30:4(6887)-**IS**-1:6(2280)■22:3^{2}■61:1 -**JER**-5:22(1366)■30:13(4205)■39:7■40:1■ 52:11-**LA**-1:14(8244)-**EZE**-27:24(2280)■ 30:21(2280)■34:4(2280)-**DA**-3:21(3729), 23(3729),24(3729)-**HO**-4:19(6887)■5:10 (1366)■7:15(3256)■13:12(6887)-**NA**-3:10 (7576)■**N.T.**-all=1210&marked-**M'T**-14:3■16:19■18:18■27:2-**M'R**-5:4■6:17■ 15:1,7-**LU**-8:29(1196)■10:34(2611)■13:16 -**JOH**-11:44,44(4019)■18:12,24-**AC**-9:2,21■ 12:6■20:22■21:11,13,33■22:5,25(4385), 29■23:12(332),14(332),21(332)■24:27■ 28:20(4029)-**RO**-7:2-**1CO**-7:27,39-**2TH**-1:3(3784)■2:13(3784)-**2TI**-2:9-**HEB**-13:3 (4887)-**RE**-9:14■20:2

BOUNDS-**EX**-19:12(1379),23 (1379)■23:31(1366)-**DE**-32:8(1367) -**JOB**-14:5(2706)■26:10(2706)-**IS**-10:13(1367)■**N.T.**-**AC**-17:26(3734)

BOUNTIFUL-**PR**-22:9(2896)-**IS**-32:5(7771)

BOUNTIFULLY-all=1580-**PS**-13:6■ 116:7■119:17■142:7■**N.T.**-**2CO**-9:6(2129)

BOUNTIFULNESS-**2CO**-9:11(572)

BOUNTY-**1KI**-10:13(3027)■**N.T.** -**2CO**-9:5^{2}(2129)

BOW-all=7198,a=7812&marked-**GE**-9:13,14,16■27:3,29^{2}a■37:10a■41:43(86)■ 48:22■49:8a,24-**EX**-11:8a■20:5a■23:24a -**LE**-26:1a-**DE**-5:9a-**JOS**-23:7a■24:12 -**J'G**-2:19a-**1SA**-18:4-**2SA**-1:18,22■22:35 -**1KI**-22:34-**2KI**-5:18^{2}a■6:22■9:24■ 13:15^{2},16■17:35a■19:16(5186)-**1CH**-5:18■12:2-**2CH**-17:17■18:33-**JOB**-20:24■29:20■31:10(3766)■39:3(3766) -**PS**-7:12■11:2■18:34■22:29(3766)■ 31:2(5186)■37:14■44:6■46:9■72:9 (3766)■76:3■78:57■86:1(5186)■95:6 (3766)■144:5(5186)-**PR**-5:1(5186)■14:19 (7817)■22:17(5186)-**EC**-12:3(5791)-**IS**-10:4(3766)■21:15■41:2■45:23(3766)■ 46:2(3766)■49:23a■51:23a■58:5(3721)■ 60:14a■65:12(3766)■66:19-**JER**-6:23■ 9:3■46:9■49:35■50:14,29,42■51:3-**LA**-2:4■3:12-**EZE**-1:28■39:3-**HO**-1:5,7■ 2:18■7:16-**AM**-2:15-**MIC**-6:6(3721) -**HAB**-3:6(7817),9-**ZEC**-9:10,13■10:4■ **N.T.**-**RO**-11:10(4781)■14:11(2578) -**EPH**-3:14(2578)-**PH'P**-2:10(2578) -**RE**-6:2(5115)

BOWED-all=7812,a=6915&marked -**GE**-18:2■19:1■23:7,12■24:26a,48a■33:3, 6,7^{2}■42:6■43:26,28a■47:31■48:12■49:15 (5186)-**EX**-4:31a■12:27a■34:8a-**NU**-22:31a■25:2-**JOS**-23:16-**J'G**-2:12,17■ 5:27^{3}(3766)■7:6(3766)■16:30(5186)-**RU**-2:10-**1SA**-4:19(3766)■20:41■24:8■25:23, 41■28:14-**2SA**-9:8■14:22,33■18:21■19:14 (5186)■22:10(5186)■24:20-**1KI**-1:16a, 23,31a,47,53■2:19■19:18(3766)-**2KI**-2:15■4:37-**1CH**-21:21■29:20a-**2CH**-7:3 (3766)■20:18a■25:14■29:29(3766),30a -**NE**-8:6a-**ES**-3:2^{2}(3766),5(3766)-**PS**-18:9 (5186)■35:14(7817)■38:6(7817)■44:25 (7743)■57:6(3721)■145:14(3721)■146:8 (3721)-**IS**-2:11(7817),17(7817)■21:3 (5791)■**N.T.**-**M'T**-27:29(1120)-**LU**-13:11(4794)■24:5(2827)-**JOH**-19:30 (2827)-**RO**-11:4(2578)

BOWELS-all=4578&marked-**GE**-15:4■25:23■43:30(7358)-**NU**-5:22-**2SA**-7:12■16:11■20:10-**1KI**-3:26(7358)-**2CH**-21:15,18,19■32:21-**JOB**-20:14■30:27 -**PS**-22:14■71:6■109:18(7130)-**SONG**-5:4-**IS**-16:11■48:19■49:1■63:15-**JER**-4:19■31:20-**LA**-1:20■2:11-**EZE**-3:3■ 7:19■**N.T.**-all=4698-**AC**-1:18-**2CO**-6:12 -**PH'P**-1:8■2:1-**COL**-3:12-**PH'M**-7,12, 20-**1JO**-3:17

BOWETH-**J'G**-7:5(3766)-**IS**-2:9 (7817)■46:1(3766)

BOWING-**PS**-17:11(5186)■62:3 (5186)■**N.T.**-**M'R**-15:19(5087)

BOWL-all=4219&marked-**NU**-7:13, 19,25,31,37,43,49,55,61,67,73,79,85 -**J'G**-6:38(5602)-**EC**-12:6(1543)-**ZEC**-4:2(1543),3(1543)

BOWLS-all=1375&marked-**EX**-25:29 (4518),31,33^{2},34■37:16(4518),17,19^{2},20-**NU**-4:7(4518)■7:84(4219)-**1KI**-7:41^{2}(1543), 42(1543),50(5592)-**2KI**-12:13(5592)■ 25:15(4219)-**1CH**-28:17(4219)-**JER**-52:18 (4219),19(4219)-**AM**-6:6(4219)-**ZEC**-9:15 (4219)■14:20(4219)

BOWMEN-**JER**-4:29(7411,7198)

BOWS-all=7198-**1SA**-2:4-**1CH**-12:2 -**2CH**-14:8■26:14-**NE**-4:13,16-**PS**-37:15■ 78:9-**IS**-5:28■7:24■13:18-**JER**-51:56 -**EZE**-39:9(7198)

BOWSHOT-**GE**-21:16(2909,7198)

BOX-**2KI**-9:1(6378),3(6378)-**IS**-41:19 (8391)■60:13(8391)■**N.T.**-all=211-**M'T**-26:7 -**M'R**-14:3^{2}-**LU**-7:37

BOY-**JOE**-3:3(3206)

BOYS-**GE**-25:27(5288)-**ZEC**-8:5(3206)

BRACELET-**2SA**-1:10(685)

BRACELETS-all=6781&marked -**GE**-24:22,30,47■38:18(6616),25(6616) -**EX**-35:22(2397)-**NU**-31:50-**IS**-3:19 (8285)-**EZE**-16:11■23:42

BRAKE-all=7665,a=5422-**EX**-9:25■ 32:3(6561),19-**DE**-9:17-**J'G**-7:19(5310), 20■9:53(7533)■16:9(5423),12(5423)-**1SA**-4:18-**2SA**-23:16(1234)-**1KI**-19:11-**2KI**-10:27^{2}a■11:18a,18■14:13(6555)■18:4,4 (3807)■23:7a,8a,12(7323),14■23:15a■ 25:10a-**1CH**-11:18(1234)-**2CH**-14:3■ 21:17(1234)■23:17a,17■25:23(6555)■ 26:6(6555)■31:1■34:4a,4■36:19a-**JOB**-29:17■38:8(1518),10-**PS**-76:3■105:16,33■ 106:29(6555)■107:14(5423)-**JER**-28:10■ 31:32(6565)■39:8a■52:14a,17-**EZE**-17:16 (6565)-**DA**-2:1(1961),34(1855),45(1855)■ 6:24(1855)■7:7(1855),19(1855)■8:7■**N.T.**-all=2806&marked-**M'T**-14:19■15:36■ 26:26-**M'R**-6:41(2622)■8:6,19■14:3 (4937),22-**LU**-5:6(1284)■8:29(1284)■9:16 (2622)■22:19(2806)■24:30(2806)-**JOH**-19:32(2608),33(2608)-**1CO**-11:24

BRAKEST-all=7665&marked-**EX**-34:1 -**DE**-10:2-**PS**-74:13,14(7533)-**EZE**-29:7

BRAMBLE-**J'G**-9:14(329),15^{2}(329)■ **N.T.**-**LU**-6:44(942)

BRAMBLES-**IS**-34:13(2336)

BRANCH-all=7070&marked-**EX** 25:33^{2}■37:17,19^{2}-**NU**-13:28(2156)-**JOB**-8:16(3127)■15:32(3712)■18:16(7105)■ 29:19(7105)-**PS**-80:15(1121)-**PR**-11:28 (5929)-**IS**-4:2(6780)■9:14(3712)■11:1 (5342)■14:19(5342)■17:9(534)■19:15 (3712)■25:5(2158)■60:21(5342)-**JER**-23:5(6780)■33:15(6780)-**EZE**-8:17(2156)■ 15:2(2156)■17:3(6788),22(6788)-**DA**-11:7 (5342)-**ZEC**-3:8(6780)■6:12(6780) -**MAL**-4:1(6057)■**N.T.**-all=2814& marked-**M'T**-24:32(2798)-**M'R**-13:28 (2798)-**JOH**-15:2,2sup,4,6

BRANCHES-all=7070&marked

-GE-40:10(8299),12(8299)■49:22(1121)-EX-25:31,32^{3},33,35^{4},36■37:18^{3},19,21^{4},22-LE-23:40(3709)-NE-8:15^{3}(5929)-JOB-15:30(3127)-PS-80:11(3127)■104:12(6073)-IS-16:8(7976)■17:6(5585)■18:5(5189)■27:10(5585)-JER-11:16(1808)-EZE-17:6(1808),36(905),7(1808),8(6057),23(1808)■19:10(6058)■11(5688),11(1808),14(905)■31:3(6057),5(6288),6(6288),7(1808),8(6288),9(1808),12(1808),13(6288)■6:8(6057)-DA-4:14^{2}(6056),21(6056)-HO-11:6(905)■14:6(3127)-JOE-1:7(8299)-NA-2:2(2156)-ZEC-4:12(7641)■N.T.-all=2798&marked-M'T-13:32■21:8-M'R-4:32■11:8(4746)-LU-13:19-JOH-12:13(902)■15:5(2814)-RO-11:16,17,18,19,21

BRAND-ZEC-3:2(181)

BRANDISH-EZE-32:10(5774)

BRANDS-J'G-15:5(3940)

BRASEN-all=5178-EX-27:4■35:16■38:4,10,30■39:39-LE-6:28-NU-16:39-1KI-4:13■7:30■8:64■14:27-2KI-16:14,15,17■18:4■25:13-1CH-18:8-2CH-1:5,6■6:13■7:7-JER-1:18■15:20■52:17,20-EZE-9:2■N.T.-M'R-7:4(5478)

BRASS-all=5178&marked-GE-4:22-EX-25:3■26:11,37■27:2,3,4,6,10,11,17,18,19■30:18^{2}■31:4■35:5,24,32■36:18,38■38:2,3,5,6,8^{2},11,17,19,20,29■39:39-LE-26:19(5154)-NU-21:9^{2}■31:22-DE-8:9■28:23■33:25-JOS-6:19,24■22:8-J'G-16:21-1SA-17:5^{2},6^{2},38-2SA-8:8,10■21:16-1KI-7:14^{2},15,16,27,30,38,45,47-2KI-25:7,13^{2},14,16,17^{2}-2CH-15:19■18:8^{2},10■22:3,14,16■29:2,7-2CH-2:7,14■4:1,9,16,18■12:10■24:12-JOB-6:12(5153)■28:2(5154)■40:18(5154)■41:27(5154)-PS-107:16-IS-45:2(5154)■48:4(5154)■60:17^{2}-JER-6:28■52:17^{2},18,20,22^{2}-EZE-1:7■22:18,20■24:11■27:13■40:3-DA-2:32(5174),35(5174),39(5174),45(5174)■4:15(5174),23(5174)■5:4(5174),23(5174)■7:19(5174)■10:6-MIC-4:13(5154)-ZEC-6:1■N.T.-all=5475&marked-M'T-10:9-1CO-13:1-RE-1:15(5474)■2:18(5474)■9:20(5470)■18:12

BRAVERY-IS-3:18(8597)

BRAWLER-1TI-3:3(269)

BRAWLERS-TIT-3:2(269)

BRAWLING-PR-21:9(4090)■25:24(4090)

BRAY-JOB-6:5(5101)-PR-27:22(3806)

BRAYED-JOB-30:7(5101)

BREACH-all=6556&marked-GE-38:29-LE-24:20(7667)-NU-14:34(8569)-J'G-21:15-2SA-5:20■6:8-2KI-12:5(919)-1CH-13:11■15:13(6555)-NE-6:1-JOB-16:14-PS-106:23-PR-5:4(7667)-IS-7:6(1234)■30:13,26(7667)■58:12-JER-14:17(7667)-LA-2:13(7667)-EZE-26:10(1234)

BREACHES-all=919&marked-J'G-5:17(4664)-1KI-11:27(6556)-2KI-12:5,6,7^{2},8,12■22:5-NE-4:7(6555)-PS-60:2(7667)-IS-22:9(1233)-AM-4:3(6556)■6:11(7447)■9:11(6556)

BREAD-all=3899-GE-3:19■14:18■18:5■21:14■25:34■27:17■28:20■31:54^{2}■37:25■39:6■41:54,55■43:25,31,32■45:23■47:12,13,15,17^{2},19■49:20-EX-2:20■16:3,4,8,12,15,22,29,32,■18:12■23:25■29:2,23,23sup,32,34■34:28■40:23-LE-7:13■8:31,32■21:6,8,17,21,22■22:25■23:14,18,20■24:7■26:5,26^{3}-NU-4:7■14:9■15:19■21:5^{2}■28:2-DE-8:3,9■9:9,18■16:3^{2}sup,3■23:4■29:6-JOS-9:5,12-J'G-7:13■8:5,6,15■13:16■19:5,19-RU-1:6■2:14-1SA-2:5,36^{2}■9:7■10:3,4■16:20■21:3,4^{2},6sup,6^{2}■22:13■25:11■28:20,22■30:11,12-2SA-3:29,35■6:19■9:7,10■12:17,20,21■16:1,2-1KI-13:8,9,15,16,17,18,19,22^{2},23■17:6^{2},11■18:4,13■21:4,5,7■22:27-2KI-4:8^{2},42■6:22■18:32■25:3,29-1CH-12:40■16:3-2CH-18:26-EZR-10:6-NE-5:14,15,18■9:15■13:2-JOB-15:23■22:7■27:14■28:5■33:20■42:11-PS-14:4■37:25■41:9■53:4■78:20■80:5■102:4,9■104:15■105:16,40■127:2■132:15-PR-4:17■6:26■9:5,17■12:9,11■20:13,17■22:9■23:6■25:21■28:19,21■31:27-EC-9:7,11■11:1-IS-3:1,7■4:1■21:14■28:28■30:20,23■33:16■36:17■44:15,19■51:14■55:2,10■58:7-JER-5:17■37:21^{2}■38:9■41:1■42:14■52:6,33-LA-1:11■4:4■5:6,9-EZE-4:9,13,15,16^{2},17■5:16■12:18,19■13:19■14:13■16:49■18:7,16■24:17,22■44:3,7-DA-10:3-HO-2:5■9:4^{2}-AM-4:6■7:12■8:11-OB-7-HAG-2:12-MAL-1:7■N.T.all=740-M'T-4:3,4■6:11■7:9■15:2,26,33■16:5,7,8,11,12■26:26-M'R-3:20■6:8,36,37■7:2,5,27■8:4,14,16,17■14:22-LU-4:3,4■7:33■9:3■11:3,11■14:1,15■15:17■22:19■24:30,35-JOH-6:5,7,23,31,32^{2},33,34,35,41,48,50,51^{3},58^{2}■13:18■21:9,13-AC-2:42■20:7,11■27:35-1CO-10:16,17^{2}■11:23,26,27,28-2CO-9:10-2TH-3:8,12

BREADTH-all=7341&marked-GE-6:15■13:17-EX-25:10,17,23,25(2948)■26:2,8,16■27:12,13,18■28:16■30:2■36:9,15,21■37:1,6,10,25■38:1,18■39:9-DE-2:5(4096)■3:11-1KI-6:2,3^{2},20■7:2,6,26(2947),27-2CH-3:3,4,8^{2}■4:1-EZR-6:3(6613)-JOB-37:10■38:18(7338)-IS-8:8-EZE-40:5(2948),5,11,13,19,20,21,25,36,48,49■41:1,2^{2},3,4,5,7,11,14■42:2,4■43:13(2948),13,14^{2}■45:1,2,3,5■48:8,9,10^{2},13^{2},15-DA-3:1(6613)-HAB-1:6(4800)-ZEC-2:2■5:2■N.T.-all=4114-EPH-3:18-RE-20:9■21:16^{2}

BREAK-all=7665,a=6565,b=5310&marked-GE-19:9■27:40(6561)-EX-12:46■13:13(6202)■19:21(2040),22(6555),24(2040),24(6555)■22:6(3318)■23:24■32:2(6561),24(6561)■34:13,20(6202)-LE-11:33■13:12(6524)■14:43(6524),45(5422)■26:15a,19,44a-NU-9:12■24:8(1633)■30:2(2490)-DE-7:5■12:3■31:16a,20a-J'G-2:1a■8:9(5422)-1SA-25:10(6555)-2SA-2:32(215)-1KI-15:19a-2KI-3:26(1234)■25:13-2CH-16:3a-EZR-9:14a-NE-4:3a-JOB-13:25(6206)■19:2(1792)■34:24(7489)■39:15(1758)-PS-2:3(5423),9(7489)■10:15■58:6(2040),6(5422)■72:4(1792)■74:6(1986)■89:31(2490),34(2490)■94:5(1792)■141:5(5106)-EC-3:3(6555)-SONG-2:17(6315)■4:6(6315)-IS-5:5(6555)■14:7(6476),25■28:24(7702),28(2000)■30:14■35:6(1234)■38:13■42:3■44:23(6476)■45:2■49:13(6476)■52:9(6476)■54:1(6476),3(6555)■55:12(6476)■58:6(5423),8(1234)-JER-1:14(6605)■4:3(5214)■14:21a■15:12(7489)■19:10,11■28:4,11■30:8■31:28(5422)■33:20a■43:13■45:4(2040)■48:12b■49:35■51:20b,21^{2}b,22^{3}b,23^{3}b-EZE-4:16■5:16■13:14(2040)■14:13■16:38(5003),39(5422)■17:15a■23:34(1633)■26:4(2040),9(5422),12(2040)■29:7(7533)■30:18,22,24-DA-2:40(1854),44(1854)■4:27(6562)■7:23(1854)-HO-1:5■2:18■4:2(6555)■10:2(6202),11(7702),12(5214)-JOE-2:7(5670)-AM-1:5■5:6(6743)-MIC-3:3(6476)-NA-1:13-ZEC-11:10a,14a■N.T.-M'T-5:19(3089)■6:19(1358),20(1358)■9:17(4486)■12:20(2608)-AC-20:7(2806),11(827)■21:13(4919)-1CO-10:16(2806)-GA-4:27(4486)

BREAKER-MIC-2:13(6555)■N.T.-RO-2:25(3848)

BREAKEST-PS-48:7(7665)

BREAKETH-all=7665&marked-GE-32:26(5927)-JOB-9:17(7779)■12:14(2040)■16:14(6555)■28:4(6555)-PS-9:5^{2}■46:9■119:20(1638)-PR-25:15-EC-10:8(6555)-IS-59:5(1234)-JER-19:11■23:29(6327)-LA-4:4(6566)-DA-2:40(1855),40(7490)

BREAKING-all=6556&marked-GE-32:24(5927)-EX-9:9(6524),10(6524)■22:2(4290)-1CH-14:11-JOB-30:14-PS-144:14-IS-22:5(6979)■30:13(7667),14(7667)-EZE-16:59(6565)■17:18(6565)■21:6(7670)-HO-13:13(4866)■N.T.-LU-24:35(2800)-AC-2:42(2800),46(2806)-RO-2:23(3847)

BREAKINGS-JOB-41:25(7667)

BREAST-all=2373&marked-EX-29:26,27-LE-7:30^{2},31,34■8:29■10:14,15-NU-6:20■18:18-JOB-24:9(7699)-IS-60:16(7699)-LA-4:3(7699)-DA-2:32(2306)■N.T.-all=4738-LU-18:13-JOH-13:25■21:20

BREASTPLATE-all=2833&marked-EX-25:7■28:4,15,22,23^{2},24,26,28^{2},29,30■29:5■35:9,27■39:8,9,15,16,17,19,21^{2}-LE-8:8^{2}-IS-59:17(8302)■N.T.-EPH-6:14(2382)-1TH-5:8(2382)

BREASTPLATES-RE-9:9(2382),17(2382)

BREASTS-all=7699&marked-GE-49:25-LE-9:20(2373),21(2373)-JOB-3:12■21:24(5845)-PS-22:9-PR-5:19(1717)-SONG-1:13■4:5■7:3,7,8■8:1,8,10-IS-28:9■66:11-EZE-16:7■23:3,8(1717),34-HO-2:2■9:14-JOE-2:16-NA-2:7(3824)■N.T.-LU-23:48(4738)-RE-15:6(4738)

BREATH-all=7307&marked-GE-2:7(5397)■6:17■7:15,22(5397)-2SA-22:16-1KI-17:17(5397)-JOB-4:9■9:18■12:10■15:30■17:1■19:17■27:3(5397)■33:4(5397)■34:14(5397)■37:10(5397)■41:21(5315)-PS-18:15■33:6■104:29■135:17■146:4■150:6(5397)-EC-3:19-IS-2:22(5397)■11:4■30:28,33(5397)■33:11■42:5(5397)-JER-10:14■51:17-LA-4:20-EZE-37:5,6,8,9,10-DA-5:23(5396)■10:17(5397)-HAB-2:19■N.T.-AC-17:25(4157)

BREATHE-JOS-11:11(5397),14(5397)-PS-27:12(3307)-EZE-37:9(5301)

BREATHED-GE-2:7(5301)-JOS-10:40(5397)-1KI-15:29(5397)■N.T.-JOH-20:22(1720)

BREATHETH-DE-20:16(5397)

BREATHING-LA-3:56(7309)■N.T.-AC-9:1(1709)

BRED-EX-16:20(7311)

BREECHES-all=4370-EX-28:42■39:28-LE-6:10■16:4-EZE-44:18

BREED-GE-8:17(8317)-DE-32:14(1121)

BREEDING-ZEP-2:9(4476)

BRETHREN-all=251&marked-GE-9:22,25■13:8■16:12■19:7■24:27■25:18■27:29,37■29:4■31:23,25,32,37,46,54■34:11,25■37:2,4^{2},5,8,9,10^{2},11,12,13,14,16,17,23,26,27,30■38:1,11■42:3,4,6,7,8,13,19,28,32,33■44:14,33■45:1,3^{2},4,15^{2},16,17,24■46:31^{2}■47:1,2,3,5,6,11,12■48:6,22■49:5,8,26■50:8,14,15,17,18,24-EX-1:6■2:11^{2}■4:18-LE-10:4,6■21:10■25:46,48-NU-8:26■16:10■18:2,6■20:3■25:6■27:4,7,9,10^{2},11■32:6-DE-1:16,28■2:4,8■3:18,20■10:9■15:7■17:15,20■18:2,7,15,18■24:7,14■25:5■33:9,16,24-JOS-1:14,15■2:13,18■6:23■14:8■17:4^{2}■22:3,4,7,8-J'G-8:19■9:1,3,5,24,26,31,41,56■11:3■14:3■16:31■18:8^{2},14■19:23■20:13■21:22-RU-4:10-1SA-16:13■17:17^{2},18,22■20:29■22:1■30:23-2SA-2:26■3:8■15:20■19:12,41-1KI-1:9■12:24-2KI-9:2■10:13^{2}■23:9-1CH-4:9,27■5:2,7,13■6:44,48■7:5,22■8:32■9:6,9,13,17,19,25,32,38^{2}■12:2,32,39■13:2■15:5,6,7,8,9,10,12,16,17^{2},18■16:7,37,38,39■23:22,32■24:31^{2}■25:7,9,10,11,12,13,14,15,16,17,18,19,20,21,22,23,24,25,26,27,28,29,30,31■26:7,8,9,11,25,26,28,30,32■27:18■28:2-2CH-5:12■11:4,22■19:10^{2}■21:2,4,13■22:8■28:8,11,15■29:15,34■30:7,9■31:15■35:5,6,9,15-EZR-3:2^{2},8,9^{2}■6:20■7:18(252)■8:17,18,19,24■10:18-NE-1:2■3:1,18■4:2,14,23■5:1,5,8^{2},10,14■10:10,29■11:12,13,14,17,19■12:7,8,9,24,36■13:13-ES-10:3-JOB-6:15■19:13■42:11,15-PS-22:22■69:8■122:8■133:1-PR-6:19■17:2■19:7-IS-66:5,20-JER-7:15■12:6■29:16■35:3■41:8■49:10-EZE-11:15^{2}-HO-2:1■13:15-MIC-5:3■N.T.-all=80&marked-M'T-1:2,11■4:18,21■5:47■12:46,47,48,49■13:55■19:29■20:24■22:25■23:8■25:40■28:10-M'R-3:31,32,33,34■10:29,30■12:20-LU-8:19,20,21■14:12,26■16:28■18:29■20:29■21:16■22:32-JOH-2:12■7:3,5,10■20:17■21:23-AC-1:14,16■2:29,37■3:17,22■6:3■7:2,13,23,25,26,37■9:30■10:23■11:1,12,29■12:17■13:15,26,38■14:2■15:1,3,7,13,22,23^{2},32,33,36,40■16:2,40■17:6,10,14■18:18,27■20:32■21:7,17■22:1,5■23:1,5,6■28:14,15,17,21-RO-1:13■7:1,4■8:12,29■

9:3■10:1■11:25■12:1■15:14,15,30■16:14,17-1CO-1:10,11,26■2:1■3:1■4:6■6:5,8■7:24,29■8:12■9:5■10:1■11:2,33■12:1■14:6,20,26,39■15:1,6,50,58■16:11,12,15,20-2CO-1:8■8:1,23■9:3,5■11:9,26(5569)■13:11-GA-1:2,11■2:4(5569)■3:15■4:12,28,31■5:11,13■6:1,18-EPH-6:10,23-PH'P-1:12,14■3:1,13,17■4:1,8,21-COL-1:2■4:15-1TH-1:4■2:1,9,14,17■3:7■4:1,10^{2},13■5:1,4,12,14,25,26,27-2TH-1:3■2:1,13,15■3:1,6,13-1TI-4:6■5:1■6:2-2TI-4:21-HEB-2:11,12,17■3:1,12■7:5■10:19■13:22-JAS-1:2,16,19■2:1,5,14■3:1,10,12■4:11■5:7,9,10,12,19-1PE-1:22(5360)■3:8(5361)■5:9(81)-2PE-1:10-1JO-2:7■3:13,14,16-3JO-3:5,10-RE-6:11■12:10■19:10■22:9

BRETHREN'S-DE-20:8(251)

BRIBE-1SA-12:3(3724)-AM-5:12(3724)

BRIBERY-JOB-15:34(7810)

BRIBES-1SA-8:3(7810)-PS-26:10(7810)-IS-33:15(7810)

BRICK-all=3843&marked-GE-11:3(3835),3-EX-1:14■5:7(3835),14(3835),16-IS-65:3

BRICKILN-all=4404-2SA-12:31-JER-43:9-NA-3:14

BRICKS-all=3843-EX-5:8,18,19-IS-9:10

BRIDE-all=3618&marked-IS-49:18■61:10■62:5-JER-2:32■7:34■16:9■25:10■33:11-JOE-2:16■N.T.-all=3565-JOH-3:29-RE-18:23■21:2,9■22:17

BRIDECHAMBER-all=3567-M'T-9:15-M'R-2:19-LU-5:34

BRIDEGROOM-all=2860-PS-19:5-IS-61:10■62:5-JER-7:34■16:9■25:10■33:11-JOE-2:16■N.T.-all=3566-M'T-9:15^{2}■25:1,5,6,10-M'R-2:19^{2},20-LU-5:34,35-JOH-2:9■3:29^{2}-RE-18:23

BRIDEGROOM'S-JOH-3:29(3566)

BRIDLE-all=7448&marked-2KI-19:28(4964)-JOB-30:11■41:13-PS-32:9■39:1(4269)-PR-26:3(4964)-IS-30:28■37:29(4964)■N.T.-JAS-3:2(5469)

BRIDLES-RE-14:20(5469)

BRIDLETH-JAS-1:26(5468)

BRIEFLY-RO-13:9(346)-1PE-5:12(1223,3641)

BRIER-IS-55:13(5636)-EZE-28:24(5544)-MIC-7:4(2312)

BRIERS-all=8068&marked-J'G-8:7(1303),16(1303)-IS-5:6■7:23,24,25■9:18■10:17■27:4■32:13-EZE-2:6(5621)■N.T.-HEB-6:8(5146)

BRIGANDINE-JER-51:3(5630)

BRIGANDINES-JER-46:4(5630)

BRIGHT-all=934&marked-LE-13:2,4,19,23,24,25,26,28,38^{2},39■14:56-1KI-7:45(4803)-2CH-4:16(4838)-JOB-37:11(216),21(925)-SONG-5:14(6247)-JER-51:11(1305)-EZE-1:13(5051)■21:15(1300),21(7043)■27:19(6219)■32:8(3974)-NA-3:3(3851)-ZEC-10:1(2385)■N.T.-M'T-17:5(5460)-LU-11:36(796)-AC-10:30(2986)-RE-22:16(2986)

BRIGHTNESS-all=5051&marked-2SA-22:13-JOB-31:26(3368)-PS-18:12-IS-59:9(5054)■60:3,19■62:1-EZE-1:4,27,28■8:2(2096)■10:4■28:7(3314),17(3314)-DA-2:31(2122)■4:36(2122)■12:3(2096)-AM-5:20-HAB-3:4■N.T.-AC-26:13(2987)-2TH-2:8(2015)-HEB-1:3(541)

BRIM-all=8193&marked-JOS-3:15(7097)-1KI-7:23,24,26^{2}-2CH-4:2,5^{2}■N.T.-JOH-2:7(507)

BRIMSTONE-all=1614&marked-GE-19:24-DE-29:23-JOB-18:15-PS-11:6-IS-30:33■34:9-EZE-38:22■N.T.-all=2303&marked-LU-17:29-RE-9:17(2306),17,18■14:10■19:20■20:10■21:8

BRING-all=935,a=7725,b=3318,c=5927,d=7126,e=3381,f=3205,g=3947,h=5066&marked-GE-1:11(1876),20(8317),24b■3:16f,18(6779)■6:17,19■8:17b■9:7(8317),14(6049)■18:16(7971),19■19:5b,8b,12b■24:5a,6a,8a■27:4,5,7,10,12,25h■28:15a■37:14a■38:24b■40:14b■41:32(6213)■42:20,34,37,37a,38e■43:7e,9,16■44:21e,29e,31e,32■45:13e,19(5375)■46:4c■48:9g,21a■50:20(6213),24c-EX-3:8c,10b,11b,17c■6:6b,8,13,26b,27b■7:4b,5b■8:3(8317),18b■10:4■11:1■12:51b■13:5,11■15:17■16:5■18:19,22■21:6^{2}h■22:13■23:4a,19,20,23■25:2g■26:33■27:20g■29:3d,4d,8d■32:2,12b■33:12c■34:26■35:5■36:5■40:4^{2},12d,14d-LE-1:2^{2}d,5d,10d,13d,14d,15d■2:2,4d,8,8h,11d■4:3d,4,5,14,16,23,28,32^{2}■5:6,7(5060),7,8,11e,11,12,15,18■6:6,21■7:29,30^{2}■10:15■12:6,8(4672),8g■14:23■15:29■16:9d,11d,12,15,20d■17:5^{2}■18:3■19:21■20:22■23:10,17■24:2g,14b,23b■25:21(6213)■26:10b,21(3254),25,31(8074),32(8074)■27:9d-NU-3:6d■5:9d,15^{2},16d■6:10,12,16d■8:9d,10d■11:16g■13:20g■14:8,16,24,31,37b■15:4d,9d,10d,18,25,27d■16:9d,17d■17:10a■18:2d,13,15d■19:2g,3b■20:5,8b,12,25c■22:8a■23:27g■27:17■28:26d■32:5(5674)-DE-1:17d,22a■4:38■6:23■7:1,26■9:3(3665),28■12:6,11■14:28b■17:5b■21:4(2381),12,19b■22:1a,2(622),8(7760),14b,15b,21b,24b■23:18■24:11b■26:2■28:36(3212),49(5375),60a,61c,63(8045),68a■29:27■30:5,12g,13g■31:23■33:7-JOS-2:3b,18(622)■6:22b■10:22b■18:6■23:15-J'G-6:13c,18b,30b■7:4(338)■11:9a■19:3a,22b,24b-RU-3:15(3051)-1SA-1:22■4:4(5375)■6:7a■9:7^{2},23(5414)■11:12(5414)■13:9h■14:18h,34h■15:32h■16:17■19:15c■20:8■23:9h■27:11■28:8c,11^{2}c,15c■30:7h,15^{2}e-2SA-2:3c■3:12(5437),13■6:2c■9:10■12:23a■13:10■14:10,21a■15:8a,14(5080),25a■17:3a,13(5375),14■19:11a,12a■22:28(8213)-1KI-1:33e■2:9e■3:24g■5:9e■8:1c,4c,32(5414),34a■10:29b■12:21a■13:18a■14:10■17:11g,13b■20:33g■21:21,29^{2}-2KI-2:20g■3:15g■4:6h,41g■6:19(3212)■10:22b■12:4■19:3f■22:16,20■23:4b-1CH-9:28(935)b■13:3(5437),5,6c,12■15:3c,12c,14c,25c■16:29(5375)■21:2,12a■22:19-2CH-2:16■5:2c,5c■6:25a■11:1a■24:6,9,19a■28:13■29:31■31:10■34:24,28-EZR-1:8b,11c■3:7■8:17,30-NE-1:9■5:5(3533)■8:1■9:29a■10:31,34,35,36,37,38c,39■11:1■12:27■13:18^{2}-ES-1:11■3:9■6:1,9(7392),14-JOB-6:22(3051)■10:9a■14:4(5414),9(6213)■15:35f■18:14(6805)■30:23a■33:30a■38:32b■39:1f,2f,3(6398),12a■40:12(3665),20(5375)-PS-18:27(8213)■25:17b■37:5(6213),6b,38:t(2142)■43:3■55:23e■59:11e■60:9(2986)■68:22^{2}a,29(2986),70:t(2142)■71:20c■72:3(5375),10a■76:11(2986)■81:2(5414)■92:14(5107)■94:23a■96:8(5375)■104:14b■108:10(2986)■142:7b■143:11b■144:13(503)-PR-4:8(3513)■19:24a■26:15a■27:1f■29:8(6315),23(8213)-EC-3:22■11:9■12:14-SONG-8:2,11-IS-1:13■5:2(6213),4(6213)■7:17■14:2■15:9(7896)■23:4f,4(7311),9(7034)■25:5(3665),11(8213),12(7817),12(5060)■28:21(5647)■31:2■33:11f■37:3f■38:8a■41:21h,22h■42:1b,3b,7b,16(3212)■43:5,6,8b,9(5414)■45:8(6509),21h■46:8a,11,13d■49:5a,22■52:8a■55:10f■56:7■58:7■59:4f■60:6(5375),9,11,17^{2}■63:6e■65:9b,23f■66:4,8(2342),9(7665),9^{2}f,20^{2}-JER-3:14■4:6■5:15■6:19■8:1b■11:8,11,23■12:2(6213),15a■15:19a■16:15a■17:18,21,24■18:22■19:3,15■23:3a,12,40(5414)■24:6a■25:9,13■26:15(5414)■27:11,12,22c■28:3a,4a,6a■29:14a■30:3a,18a■31:8,23a,32b■32:37a,42■33:6(4608),11■35:2,17■36:31■38:23(4672)■39:16■41:5■42:17■45:5■48:44,47a■49:5,6a,8,16e,32,36,37,39a■50:19a■51:40e,44b,64-LA-1:21-EZE-5:17■6:3■7:24■11:7b,8,9b■12:4b,13■13:14(5060)■14:17■16:40c,53a■17:8(6213),20,23(5375)■20:6b,15,34b,35,37,38b,41b,42■21:29(5414)■23:22,46c■24:6b■26:7,19c,20e■28:7,8e,18b,18(5414)■29:4c,8,14a■31:6f■32:3c,9■33:2■34:13b,13,16a■36:11(6509),24■37:6c,12,21■38:4b,16,17■39:2,25a■47:12(1069)-DA-1:3,18■2:24(5924)■3:13(858)■4:6(5924)■5:2(858),7(5924)■9:24-HO-2:14(1980)■7:12e■9:12(1431),13b,16f-JOE-3:1a,2e-AM-3:11e■4:1,4■6:10b■8:10c■9:2e,14a-OB-3e,4e-JON-1:13a-MIC-1:15■4:10(1518)■7:9b-ZEP-2:2f■3:5(5414),10(2986),20-HAB-1:6,8-ZEC-3:8■4:7b■5:4b■8:8■10:6a,10a,10■13:9-MAL-3:10■N.T.-all=71,a=5342&marked-M'T-1:21(5088),23(5088)■2:8(518),13(2036)■3:8(4160)■5:23(4374)■7:18^{2}(4160),■14:18a■17:17a■21:2■28:8(518)-M'R-4:20(2592)■7:32a■8:22a■9:19a■11:2■12:15a■15:22a-LU-1:31(5088)■2:10(2097)■3:8(4160)■5:18(1533),19(1533)■6:43(4160)■8:14(5062),15(2592)■9:41(4317)■12:11(4374)■14:21(1521)■15:22(1627),23a■19:27,30-JOH-10:16■14:26(5179)■15:2a,16a■18:29a■19:4■21:10a-AC-5:28(1863)■7:6(1402)■9:2,21■12:4(321)■17:5■22:5■23:10,15(2609),17(520),18,20(2609),24(1295)■24:17(4160)-RO-7:4(2592),5(2592)■10:6(2609),7(321),15(2097)-1CO-1:19(114),28(2673)■4:5(5461),17(363)■9:27(1396)■16:3(667),6(4311)-2CO-11:20(2615)-GA-2:4(2615)-EPH-6:4(1625)-1TH-4:14-2TI-4:11,13a-TIT-3:13(4311)-1PE-3:18(4317)-2PE-2:1(3919),1(1863),11a-2JO-10a-3JO-6(4311)-JUDE-9(2018)-RE-21:24a,26a

BRINGERS-2KI-10:5(539)

BRINGEST-1KI-1:42(1319)-JOB-14:3(935)-IS-40:9^{2}(1319)■N.T.-AC-17:20(1533)

BRINGETH-all=3318&marked-EX-6:7-LE-11:45(5927)■17:4(935),9(935)-DE-8:7(935)■14:22-1SA-2:6(3381),6(5927),7(8213)-2SA-18:26(1319)■22:48(3381),49-JOB-12:6(935),22■28:11-PS-1:3(5414)■14:7(7725)■33:10(6331)■37:7(6213)■53:6(7725)■68:6■107:28,30(5148)■135:7-PR-10:31(5107)■16:30(3615)■18:16(5148)■19:26(2659)■20:26(7725)■21:27(935)■29:21(6445),25(5414)■30:33^{3}■31:14(935)-EC-2:6(6779)-IS-8:7(5927)■26:5(7817),5(5060)■40:23(5414),26■41:27(1319)■43:17■52:7^{2}(1319)■54:16■61:11-JER-4:31(1069)■10:13■51:16-EZE-29:16(2142)-HO-10:1(7737)-NA-1:15(1319)-HAG-1:11■N.T.-all=4160&marked-M'T-3:10■7:17^{2},19■12:35^{2}(1544)■13:23,52(1544)■17:1(399)-M'R-4:28(2592)-LU-3:9■6:43,45^{2}(4393)-JOH-12:24(5342)■15:5(5342)-COL-1:6(2592)-TIT-2:11(4992)-HEB-1:6(1521)■6:7(5088)-JAS-1:15(616),15(5088)

BRINGING-all=935&marked-EX-12:42(3318)■36:6-NU-5:15(2142)■14:36(3318)-2SA-19:10(7725),43(7725)-1KI-10:22(5375)-2KI-21:12-2CH-9:21(5375)-NE-13:15-PS-126:6(5375)-JER-17:26^{2}-EZE-20:9(3318)-DA-9:12■N.T.-M'T-21:43(4160)-M'R-2:3(5342)-LU-24:1(5342)-AC-5:16(5342)-RO-7:23(163)-2CO-10:5(163)-HEB-2:10(71)■7:19(1898)-2PE-2:5(1863)

BRINK-all=8193&marked-GE-41:3-EX-2:3■7:15-DE-2:36-JOS-3:8(7097)-EZE-47:6

BROAD-all=7341&marked-EX-27:1-NU-16:38(7555),39(7554)-1KI-6:6^{3}-2CH-6:13-NE-3:8(7342)■12:38(7342)-JOB-36:16(7338)-PS-119:96(7342)-SONG-3:2(7339)-IS-33:21(7338,3027)-JER-5:1(7339)■51:58(7342)-EZE-40:6^{2},7,29,30,33,42,47■41:1^{2},12■42:11(7342),20■43:16,17■45:6■46:22-NA-2:4(7339)■N.T.-M'T-7:13(2149)■23:5(4115)

BROADER-JOB-11:9(7342)

BROIDED-1TI-2:9(4117)

BROIDERED-all=7553&marked-EX-28:4(8665)-EZE-16:10,13,18■26:16■27:7,16,24

BROILED-LU-24:42(3702)

BROKEN-all=7665,a=6555&marked-GE-7:11(1234)■17:14(6565)■

38:29a-**LE**-6:28■11:35(5422)■13:20 (6524),25(6524)■15:12■21:20(4790)■ 22:22,24(5423)■26:13,26-**NU**-15:31 (6565)-**J'G**-5:22(1986)■16:9(5423)-**1SA**-2:4(2844),10(2865)-**2SA**-5:20a■22:35 (5181)-**1KI**-18:30(2040)■22:48-**2KI**-11:6(4535)■25:4(1234)-**1CH**-14:11a -**2CH**-20:37a,37■24:7a■25:12(1234)■ 32:5a■33:3(5422)■34:7(5422)-**NE**-1:3a■2:13a-**JOB**-4:10(5421)■7:5(7280)■ 16:12(6565)■17:11(5423)■22:9(1792)■ 24:20■31:22■38:15-**PS**-3:7■18:34(5181)■ 31:12(6)■34:18,20■37:15,17■38:8(1794)■ 44:19(1794)■51:8(1794),17^{2}■55:20(2490)■ 60:2(6480)■69:20■80:12a■89:10(1792), 40a■107:16■109:16(5218)■124:7■ 147:3-**PR**-3:20(1234)■6:15■15:13(5218)■ 17:22(5218)■24:31(2040)■25:19(7465), 28a-**EC**-4:12(5423)■12:6(7533),6,6(7533) -**IS**-5:27(5423)■7:8(2844)■8:9^{3}(2844), 15■9:4(2865)■14:5,29■16:8(1986)■19:10 (1792)■21:9■22:10(5422)■24:5(6565), 10,19(7489)■27:11■28:13■30:14(3807)■ 33:8(6565),20(5423)■36:6(7533)-**JER**-2:13,16(7462),20■4:26(5422)■5:5■10:20 (5423)■11:10(6565),16(7489)■14:17■ 22:28(5310)■23:9■28:2,12,13■33:21 (6565)■37:11(5927)■39:2(1234)■48:17, 20(2865)25,38,39(2865)■50:2(2844),2 (2865),17(6105),23■51:30,56(2865),58 (6209)■52:7(1234)-**LA**-2:9■3:4,16 (1638)-**EZE**-6:4,6,9■17:19(6331)■19:12 (6531)■26:2■27:26,34■30:4(2040),21,22■ 31:12■32:28■34:4,16,27■44:7(6565) -**DA**-2:35(1854),42(8406)■8:8,22,25■ 11:4,22-**HO**-5:11(7533)■8:6(7616)-**JOE**-1:17(2040)-**JON**-1:4-**MIC**-2:13a-**ZEC**-11:11(6565),16■**N.T.**-all=3089&marked -**M'T**-15:37(2801)■21:44(4917)■24:43 (1358)-**M'R**-2:4(1846)■5:4(4937)■8:8 (2801)-**LU**-12:39(1358)■20:18(4917) -**JOH**-5:18■7:23■10:35■19:31(2608),36 (4937)■21:11(4977)-**AC**-13:43■20:11 (2806)■27:35(2806),41-**RO**-11:17(1575), 19(1575),20(1575)-**1CO**-11:24(2806) -**EPH**-2:14-**RE**-2:27(4937)

BROKENFOOTED-**LE**-21:19 (7667,7272)

BROKENHANDED-**LE**-21:19 (7667,3027)

BROKENHEARTED-**IS**-61:1 (7665,3820)■**N.T.**-**LU**-4:18(4937,2588)

BROOD-**LU**-13:34(3555)

BROOK-all=5158&marked-**GE**-32:23 -**LE**-23:40-**NU**-13:23,24-**DE**-2:13^{2},14■ 9:21-**1SA**-17:40■30:9,10,21-**2SA**-15:23■ 17:20(4323)-**1KI**-2:37■15:13■17:3,4,5,6, 7■18:40-**2KI**-23:6^{2},12-**2CH**-15:16■ 20:16■29:16■30:14■32:4-**NE**-2:15-**JOB**-6:15■40:22-**PS**-83:9■110:7-**PR**-18:4-**IS**-15:7-**JER**-31:40■**N.T.**-**JOH**-18:1(5493)

BROOKS-all=5158&marked-**NU**-21:14, 15-**DE**-8:7-**2SA**-23:30-**1KI**-18:5-**1CH**-11:32-**JOB**-6:15■20:17■22:24-**PS**-42:1 (650)-**IS**-19:6(2975),7^{3}(2975),8(2975)

BROTH-**J'G**-6:19(4839),20(4839) -**IS**-65:4(6564)

BROTHER-all=251&marked-**GE**-4:2,8^{2},9■9:5■10:21■14:13,14,16■20:5,13, 16■22:20,21,23■24:15,29,53,55■25:26■ 27:6,11,23,30,35,40,41,42,43■28:2,5■ 29:10^{3},12,15■32:3,6,11,13,17■33:3,9■ 35:1,7■36:6■37:26,27■38:8,9,29,30■42:4, 15,16,20,21,34^{2},38■43:3,4,5,6,7^{2},13,14, 29^{2},30■44:19,20,23,26^{2}■45:4,12,14■48:19 -**EX**-4:14■7:1,2■28:1,2,4,41■32:27,29 -**LE**-16:2■18:14■19:17■21:2■25:25^{2},35, 36,39,47-**NU**-6:7■20:8,14■27:13■36:2 -**DE**-1:16■13:6■15:2,3,7,9,11,12■17:15■ 19:18,19■22:1,2^{2}■23:7,19,20■24:10 (7453)■25:3,5(2993),5(2992)6,7(2993), 7,7(2992)■28:54■32:50-**JOS**-15:17-**J'G**-1:3,13,17■3:9■9:3,18,21,24■20:23,28■ 21:6-**RU**-4:3-**1SA**-14:3■17:28■20:29■ 26:6-**2SA**-1:26■2:22,27■3:27,30^{2}■4:6,9■ 10:10■13:3,4,7,8,10,12,20^{4},26,32■14:7^{2}■ 18:2■20:9,10■21:21■23:18,24-**1KI**-1:10■ 2:7,21,22■9:13■13:30■20:32,33-**2KI**-24:17-**1CH**-2:32,42■4:11■6:39■7:16,35■ 8:39■11:20,26,38,45■19:11,15■20:5,7■ 24:25(1730)■26:22■27:7-**2CH**-31:12, 13■36:4^{2},10-**NE**-5:7■7:2-**JOB**-22:6■ 30:29-**PS**-35:14■49:7■50:20-**PR**-17:17■ 18:9,19,24■27:10-**EC**-4:8-**SONG**-8:1 -**IS**-3:6■9:19■19:2■41:6-**JER**-9:4^{2}■ 22:18■23:35■31:34■34:9,14,17-**EZE**-18:18■33:30■38:21■44:25-**HO**-12:3 -**AM**-1:11-**OB**-10,12-**MIC**-7:2-**HAG**-2:22-**ZEC**-7:9,10-**MAL**-1:2■2:10■**N.T.**-all=80&marked-**M'T**-4:18,21■5:22^{2}, 23,24■7:4■10:2^{2},21■12:50■14:3■17:1■ 18:15^{2},21,35■22:24^{2},25-**M'R**-1:16,19■ 3:17,35■5:37■6:3,17■12:19^{3}■13:12-**LU**-3:1,19■6:14,42■12:13■15:27,32■17:3■ 20:28^{3}-**JOH**-1:40,41■6:8■11:2,19,21,23, 32-**AC**-9:17■12:2■21:20■22:13-**RO**-14:10^{2},15,21■16:23-**1CO**-1:1■5:11■6:6■ 7:12,15■8:11,13^{2}■16:12-**2CO**-1:1■2:13■ 8:18,22■12:18-**GA**-1:19-**EPH**-6:21-**PH'P**-2:25-**COL**-1:1■4:7,9-**1TH**-3:2■4:6-**2TH**-3:6,15-**PH'M**-1,7,16,20-**HEB**-8:11■ 13:23-**JAS**-1:9■2:15■4:11-**1PE**-5:12 -**2PE**-3:15-**1JO**-2:9,10,11■3:10,12,14,15, 17■4:20^{2},21■5:16-**JUDE**-1-**RE**-1:9

BROTHERHOOD-**ZEC**-11:14 (264)■**N.T.**-**1PE**-2:17(81)

BROTHERLY-**AM**-1:9(251)■ **N.T.**-all=5360-**RO**-12:10-**1TH**-4:9 -**HEB**-13:1-**2PE**-1:7

BROTHER'S-all=251&marked -**GE**-4:9,10,11,21■10:25■12:5■14:12■ 24:48■27:44,45■38:8,9-**LE**-18:16^{2}■ 20:21^{2}-**DE**-22:1,3,4■25:7^{2}(2994),9(2994), 9-**1KI**-2:15-**1CH**-1:19-**JOB**-1:13,18 -**PR**-27:10■**N.T.**-all=80-**M'T**-7:3,5 -**M'R**-6:18■6:41,42-**RO**-14:13-**1JO**-3:12

BROTHERS'-**NU**-36:11(1730)

BROUGHT-all=935,a=3318,b=7725, c=5927,d=7126,e=3381,f=5375,g= 3205,h=5066&marked-**GE**-1:12a,21 (8317)■2:19,22■4:3,4■14:16^{2}b,18a■ 15:5a,7a■19:16a,17a■20:9■24:53a,67■ 26:10■27:14,20(7136),25h,25,31,33■ 29:13,23■30:14,39g■31:39■33:11■37:2, 28,32■38:25a■39:1^{2}e,14,17■40:10(1310)■ 41:14(7323),47(6213)■43:2,12b,17,18^{2}, 21b,22e,23a,24,26■44:8b■46:7,32■ 47:7,14,17■48:10h,12a,13h■50:23g-**EX**-2:10■3:12a■8:7c,12(7760)■9:19(622)■ 10:8b,13(5090),13f■12:17a,39a■13:3a, 9a,14a,16a■15:19b,22(5265),26(7760)■ 16:3a,6a,32a■17:3c■18:1a,26■19:4,17a■ 20:2a■22:8d■29:10d,46a■32:1c,3,4c, 6h,8c,11a,21,23c■33:1c■35:21,22,23,24^{2}, 25,27,29■36:3^{2}■39:33■40:21-**LE**-6:30■ 8:6d,13d,14h,18d,22d,24d■9:5(3947),9d, 15d,16d,17d■10:18■13:2,9■14:2■ 16:27■19:36a■22:27g,33a■23:14,15,43a■ 24:11■25:38a,42a,55a■26:13a,41,45a -**NU**-6:13■7:3,3d■9:13d■11:31(1468)■ 12:15(622),26b,32a■14:3■15:33d,36a, 41a■16:10d,13c,14■17:8a,9a■20:4,16a■ 21:5c■22:41c■23:7(5148),14(3947),22a, 28(3947)■24:8a■25:6d■27:5d■31:12, 50d,54■32:17-**DE**-1:25e,25b,27a■4:20a, 37a■5:6a,15a■6:10,12a,21a,23a■7:8a, 19a■8:14a,15a■9:4,12a,26a,28a■11:29■ 13:5a.10a■16:1a■20:1c■22:19a■26:8a,9, 10,13(1197)■29:25a■31:20,21-**JOS**-2:6c■ 6:23^{2}a■7:7(5674),14d,16d,17^{2}d,18d,23, 24c■8:23d■10:23a,24a■14:7b■22:32b■ 24:5a,6a,7,8,17c,32c-**J'G**-1:7■2:1,12a■ 3:17d■5:25d■6:8c,8a,19a■7:5e,25■11:35 (3766)■14:11(3947)■15:13c■16:8c,18c, 21e,31c■18:3■19:3,21,25a■21:12-**RU**-1:21b■2:18a-**1SA**-1:24,25■2:14c,19c■ 5:1,2,10(5437)■6:21b■7:1■8:8c■9:22■ 10:18c,27■12:6c,8a■14:34h■15:15,20■ 16:12■17:54,57■18:27■19:7■20:8■ 21:8(3947),14,15■22:4(5148)■23:5 (5090)■25:27,35■28:25h■30:7h,11(3947), 16e-**2SA**-1:10■2:8(5674)■3:22,26b■4:8, 10(1319)■6:3f,4f,12c,15c,17■7:6c,18■ 8:2f,6f,7,10(1961)■10:16a■12:30a,31a■ 13:10,11h,18a■14:23■17:28h■19:41 (5674)■21:8g,13c■22:20a■23:16-**1KI**-1:3,38(3212),53e■2:30b,40■3:1,24■ 4:21h,28■5:17(5265)■6:7(4551)■7:51■ 8:4c,6,16a,21a■9:9a,9,28■10:11f,11,25, 28(4161)■12:28c■13:20b,23b,26b,29b■ 14:28b■15:15■17:6,23e■18:40e■20:9b, 39■22:37-**2KI**-2:20(3947)■4:5h,20,42■ 5:2(7617),6,20■10:1(539),6(1431),8,22a, 24,26a■11:4,12a,19e■12:4,9,13,16■ 14:20f■16:14d■17:4c,7c,24,27(1540),36c■ 19:25■20:11b,20■22:4,9b,20b■23:6a,8, 30■24:16■25:6c,20(3212)-**1CH**-5:26■ 10:12■11:18,19■12:40■13:13(5493)■14:17 (5414)■15:28c■16:1■17:5c,16■18:2f,6f, 7,8(3947),11f■20:2a,3a■22:4-**2CH**-1:4c, 16(4161),17^{2}a■5:1,5c,7■6:5a■7:22a,22■ 8:11c,18■9:10,12,14^{2},24,28a■10:8(1431), 10(1431)■12:11b■13:18(3665)■15:11, 18■16:2a■17:5(5414),11^{2}■19:4b■22:9■ 23:11a,14a,20e■24:10,11,14■25:12,14, 23,28f■28:5,8,15,19(3665),27■29:4,16a, 21,23h,31,32■30:15■31:5^{2},6,12■32:23,30 (3474)■33:11,13b■34:9,14a,14,16b,28b■ 35:24(3212)■36:10,17c,18-**EZR**-1:7^{2}a, 11c■4:2c,10(1541)■5:14(2987)■6:5(2987), 5(1946)■8:18-**NE**-4:15(6565)■5:5(3533)■ 8:2,16■9:18c,33■12:31c■13:9b,12,15,16, 19-**ES**-1:17■2:7(539),8(3947),20(539)■ 6:8,11(7392)■9:11-**JOB**-4:12(1589)■ 10:18a■14:21(6819)■21:30(2986),32 (2986)■24:24(4355)■31:18(1431)■ 42:11-**PS**-7:14g■18:19a■20:8(3766)■ 22:15(8239)■30:3c■35:4(2659),26(2659)■ 40:2c■45:14(2986),14,15(2986)■71:24 (2659)■78:16a■26(5090),54,71■79:8 (1809)■80:8(5265)■81:10c■85:1b■89:40 (7760)■90:2g■105:30(8317),37a,40,43a■ 106:42(3665),43(4355)■107:12(3665),14a, 39(7817)■116:6(1809)■136:11a■142:6 (1809)-**PR**-8:24(2342),25(2342),30(539) -**EC**-12:4(7817)-**SONG**-1:4■2:4■3:4■8:5^{2} (2254)-**IS**-1:2(7311)■2:12(8213)■5:2 (6213),4(6213),15(7817)■14:11e,15e■15:1^{2} (1820)■18:7(2986)■21:14(857)■23:13 (7760)■25:5(6030)■26:18g■29:4(8213),20 (656)■37:26■43:14e,23■45:10(2342)■ 48:15■49:21(1431)■51:18g,18(1431)■ 53:7(2986)■59:16(3467)■60:11(5090)■ 62:9(6908)■63:5(3467),11c■66:7g,8g -**JER**-2:6c,7,27g■7:22a■10:9■11:4a,7c, 19(2986)■15:8■16:14c,15c■20:3a,15 (1319)■23:7c,8c■24:1■26:23■27:16b■ 32:21a,42■34:11(3533),13a,16(3533)■ 35:4■37:14■38:22a■39:5c■40:3■41:16b■ 44:2■50:25a■51:10a■52:26(3212),31 (3218)-**LA**-2:2(5060),22(7235)■ 3:2(3212)■4:5(539)-**EZE**-8:3,7,14, 16■11:1,24■12:7^{2}a■14:22a,22^{2}■17:6f,24 (8213)■19:3c,4,9^{2}■20:10,14a,22a,28■ 21:7(1961)■23:42■27:15b,26■29:5(622)■ 30:11■31:18e■34:4b■37:13c■38:8b,8a■ 39:27b■40:1,2,3,4,17,24(3212),28,32,35, 48■41:1■42:1a,1,15a■43:1(3212),5■ 44:1b,4,7■46:19,21a■47:1b,2a,3(5674),4^{2} (5674),6(3212),8a-**DA**-1:2,9(5414),18■ 2:25(5954)■3:13(858)■5:3(858),13(5954), 13(858),15(5954),23(858)■6:16(858),17 (858),18(5954),24(858)■7:13(7127)■9:14, 15a■11:6-**HO**-12:13c-**AM**-2:10c■3:1c■ 9:7c-**OB**-7(7971)-**JON**-2:6c-**MIC**-5:3g■6:4c-**NA**-2:7c-**HAG**-1:9■2:19f -**ZEC**-10:11e-**MAL**-1:13^{2}■**N.T.**-all= 71,a=5342,b=4374&marked-**M'T**-1:12 (3350),25(5088)■4:24b■8:16b■9:2b,32b■ 10:18■11:23(2601)■12:22b,25(2049)■13:8 (1325),26(4160)■14:11^{2}a,35b■16:8(2989)■ 17:16b■18:24b■19:13b■21:7■22:19b■ 25:20b■27:3(654)-**M'R**-1:32a■4:8a,21 (2064),29(3860)■6:27a,28a■9:17a,20a■ 10:13^{2}b■11:7■12:16a■13:9(2476)-**LU**-1:57(1080)■2:7(5088),22(321),7(1521)■ 3:5(5013)■4:9,16(5142),40■5:11(2609),18a■ 7:37(2865)■10:34■11:17(2049)■12:16 (2164)■18:15(4374),40■19:35■21:12■22:54 (1521)■23:14-**JOH**-1:42■4:33a■7:45■ 8:3■9:13■18:16(1521)■19:13,39a-**AC**-4:34a,37a■5:2a,15(1627),19(1806),21, 26,27,36(1096)■6:12■7:36(1806),40 (1806),45(1521)■9:8(1521),27,30(2609),

39(321)■11:26■12:6(4254),17(1806)■13:1(4939),17(1806)■14:13a■15:3(4311)■16:16(3930),20(4317),30(4254),34(321),39(1806)■17:15,19■18:12■19:12(2018),19(4851),24(3930),37■20:12■21:5(4311),16,28(1521),29(1521)■22:3(397),24,30(2609)■23:18,28(2609),31■25:6,17,18(2018),23,26(4254)■27:24(3936)-RO-15:24(4311)-1CO-6:12(1850)■15:54(1096)-2CO-1:16(4311)-GA-2:4(3920)-1TH-3:6(2097)-1TI-5:10(5044)■6:7(1533)-2TI-1:10(5461),subscr(5936)-HEB-13:11(1533),20(321)-JAS-5:18(985)-1PE-1:13a-2PE-2:19(1402)-RE-12:5(5088),13(5088)

BROUGHTEST-all=3318&marked-EX-32:7(5927)-NU-14:13(5927)-DE-9:28,29-2SA-5:2(935)-1KI-8:51,53-1CH-11:2(935)-NE-9:7,15,23(935)-PS-66:11(935),12

BROW-IS-48:4(4696)■N.T.-LU-4:29(3790)

BROWN-all=2345-GE-30:32,33,35,40

BRUISE-GE-3:15^{2}(7779)-IS-28:28(1854)■53:10(1792)-JER-30:12(7667)-DA-2:40(7490)-NA-3:19(7667)■N.T.-RO-16:20(4937)

BRUISED-LE-22:24(4600)-2KI-18:21(7533)-IS-28:28(1854)■42:3(7533)■53:5(1792)-EZE-23:3(6213),8(6213)■N.T.-M'T-12:20(4937)-LU-4:18(2352)

BRUISES-IS-1:6(2250)

BRUISING-EZE-23:21(6213)■N.T.-LU-9:39(4937)

BRUIT-JER-10:22(8052)-NA-3:19(8088)

BRUTE-2PE-2:12(249)-JUDE-10(249)

BRUTISH-all=1197-PS-49:10■92:6■94:8-PR-12:1■30:2-IS-19:11-JER-10:8,14,21■51:17-EZE-21:31

BUCKET-IS-40:15(1805)

BUCKETS-NU-24:7(1805)

BUCKLER-all=4043&marked-2SA-22:31-1CH-5:18■12:8(7420)-PS-18:2,30■35:2(6793)■91:4(5507)-PR-2:7-JER-46:3-EZE-23:24(6793)■26:8(6793)

BUCKLERS-all=4043&marked-2CH-23:9-JOB-15:26-SONG-4:4-EZE-38:4(6793)■39:9(6793)

BUD-all=6779&marked-JOB-14:9(6524)■38:27(4161)-PS-132:17-SONG-7:12(5132)-IS-18:5(6525)■27:6(6524)■55:10■61:11-EZE-16:7■29:21-HO-8:7

BUDDED-GE-40:10(6524)-NU-17:8(6524)-SONG-6:11(5132)-EZE-7:10(6524)■N.T.-HEB-9:4(985)

BUDS-NU-17:8(6525)

BUFFET-M'R-14:65(2852)-2CO-12:7(2852)

BUFFETED-all=2852-M'T-26:67-1CO-4:11-1PE-2:20

BUILD-all=1129&marked-GE-11:4,8-EX-20:25-NU-23:1,29■32:16,24-DE-20:20■25:9■27:5,6■28:30-JOS-22:26,29-J'G-6:26-RU-4:11-1SA-2:35-2SA-7:5,7,13,27■24:21-1KI-2:36■5:3,5^{2},18■6:1■8:16,17,18,19^{2}■9:15,19,24■11:7,38■16:34-1CH-14:1■17:4,10,12,25■21:22■22:2,6,7,8,10,11,19■28:2,3,6,10■29:16,19-2CH-2:1,3,4,5,6^{2},9,12■3:1,2■6:5,7,8,9^{2}■8:6■14:7■35:3■36:23-EZR-1:2,3,5■4:2,3^{2}■5:2(1124),3(1124),9(1124),13(1124),11(1124)17(1124)■6:7(1124)-NE-2:5,17,18,20■3:3■4:3,10-PS-28:5■51:18■69:35■89:4■102:16■127:1^{2}■147:2-PR-24:27-EC-3:3-SONG-8:9-IS-9:10■45:13■58:12■60:10■61:4■65:21,22■66:1-JER-1:10■18:9■22:14■24:6■29:5,28■31:4,28■33:7■35:7,9■42:10-EZE-4:2■11:3■21:22■28:26■36:36-DA-9:25-AM-9:11,14-MIC-3:10-ZEP-1:13-HAG-1:8-ZEC-5:11■6:12,13,15■9:3-MAL-1:4^{2}■N.T.-all=3618&marked-M'T-16:18■23:29■26:61-M'R-14:58-LU-11:47,48■12:18■14:28,30-AC-7:49■15:16^{2}(456)■20:32(2026)-RO-15:20-1CO-3:12(2026)-GA-2:18

BUILDED-all=1129,a=1124&marked-GE-4:17■8:20■10:11■11:5■12:7,8■26:25-EX-24:4-NU-32:38-JOS-22:16-1KI-8:27,43■15:22-2KI-23:13-1CH-22:5-EZR-3:2■4:1a,13a,16a,21a■5:8a,11^{2}a,15a■6:3a,14^{2}a-NE-3:1,2^{2}■4:1,17,18■6:1■7:4■12:29-JOB-20:19-PS-122:3-PR-9:1■24:3-EC-2:4-SONG-4:4-JER-30:18-LA-3:5-EZE-36:10,33■N.T.-LU-17:28(3618)-EPH-2:22(4925)-HEB-3:3(2680),4(2680)

BUILDEDST-DE-6:10(1129)

BUILDER-HEB-11:10(5079)

BUILDERS-all=1129-1KI-5:18-2KI-12:11■22:6-2CH-34:11-EZR-3:10-NE-4:5,18-PS-118:22-EZE-27:4■N.T.-all=3618-M'T-21:42-M'R-12:10-LU-20:17-AC-4:11-1PE-2:7

BUILDEST-all=1129-DE-22:8-NE-6:6-EZE-16:31■N.T.-M'T-27:40(3618)-M'R-15:29(3618)

BUILDETH-all=1129-JOS-6:26-JOB-27:18-PR-14:1-JER-22:13-HO-8:14-AM-9:6-HAB-2:12■N.T.-1CO-3:10^{2}(2026)

BUILDING-all=1129&marked-JOS-22:19-1KI-3:1■6:7^{2},12,38■7:1■9:1■15:21-1CH-28:2-2CH-3:3■16:5,6-EZR-4:4,12(1124)■5:4(1147),16(1124)■6:8(1124)-EC-10:18(4746)-EZE-17:17■40:5(1146)■41:12^{2}(1146),13(1140),15(1146)■42:1(1146),5(1146)■42:10(1146)■N.T.-JOH-2:20(3618)-1CO-3:9(3619)-2CO-5:1(3619)-EPH-2:21(3619)-HEB-9:11(2937)-JUDE-20(2026)-RE-21:18(1739)

BUILDINGS-all=3619-M'T-24:1-M'R-13:1,2

BUILT-all=1129&marked-GE-13:18■22:9■33:17■35:7-EX-1:11■17:15■32:5-NU-13:22■21:27■23:14■32:34,37-DE-8:12■13:16■20:5-JOS-8:30■19:50■22:10,11,23■24:13-J'G-1:26■6:24,28■18:28■21:4-1SA-7:17■14:35^{2}-2SA-5:9,11■24:25-1KI-3:2■6:2,5,7,9,10,14,15,16^{2},36■7:2■8:13,20,44,48■9:3,10,17,24,25■10:4■11:27,38■12:25^{2}■14:23■15:17,22,23■16:24^{2},32■18:32■22:39-2KI-14:22■15:35■16:11,18■17:9■21:3,4,5■25:1-1CH-6:10,32■7:24■8:12■11:8■17:6■21:26■22:19-2CH-6:2,10,18,33,34,38■8:1,2,4^{2},5,11,12■9:3■11:5,6■14:6,7■16:1,6■17:12■20:8■26:2,6,9,10■27:3^{2},4^{2}■32:5■33:3,4,5,14,15,19-NE-3:13,14,15■4:6■7:1-JOB-3:14■12:14■22:23-PS-78:69■89:2-EC-9:14-IS-5:2■25:2■44:26,28-JER-7:31■12:16■19:5■31:4,38■32:31,35■45:4■52:4-EZE-13:10■16:24,25■26:14-DA-4:30(1124)■9:25-AM-5:11-MIC-7:11-HAG-1:2■1:16■8:9■N.T.-all=3618&marked-M'T-7:24,26■21:33-M'R-12:1-LU-4:29■6:48,49■7:5-AC-7:47-1CO-3:14(2026)-EPH-2:20(2026)-COL-2:7(2026)-HEB-3:4(2680)-1PE-2:5

BULL-JOB-21:10(7794)-IS-51:20(8377)

BULLOCK-all=6499,a=7794&marked-EX-29:1,3,10^{2},11,12,14,36-LE-1:5(1121,1241)■4:3,4^{2},7,8,10a,11,12,14,15^{2},20^{2},21^{2}■8:2,14^{2},17■9:4a,18a,19a■16:3,6,11^{2},14,15,18,27■22:23a,27a■23:18-NU-7:15,21,27,33,39,45,51,57,63,69,75,81■8:8^{2}■15:8(1121,1241),9(1121,1241),11a,24■23:2,4,14,30■28:12,14,20,28■29:2,3,8,9,14,36,37-DE-15:19a■17:1a■33:17a-J'G-6:25^{2},26,28-1SA-1:25-1KI-18:23^{2},25,26,33-2CH-13:9-PS-50:9■69:31-IS-65:25(1241)-JER-31:18(5695)-EZE-43:19,21,22,23,25■45:18,22,24■46:6,7,11

BULLOCK'S-all=6499-LE-4:4,5,16

BULLOCKS-all=6499&marked-NU-7:87,88■8:12■23:29■28:11,19,27■29:13,14,17,18,20,21,23,24,26,27,29,30,32,33-1SA-1:24-1KI-18:23-1CH-15:26■29:21-2CH-29:21,22(1241),32(1241)■30:24^{2}■35:7(1241)-EZR-6:9(8450),17(8450)■7:17(8450)■8:35-JOB-42:8-PS-51:19■66:15(1241)-IS-1:11■34:7-JER-46:21(5695)■50:27-EZE-39:18■45:23-HO-12:11(7794)

BULLS-all=47&marked-GE-32:15(6499)-PS-22:12(6499),12sup■50:13■68:30-IS-34:7-JER-50:11■52:20(1241)■N.T.-HEB-9:13(5022)■10:4(5022)

BULRUSH-IS-58:5(100)

BULRUSHES-EX-2:3(1573)-IS-18:2(1573)

BULWARKS-DE-20:20(4692)-2CH-26:15(6438)-PS-48:13(2430)-EC-9:14(4685)-IS-26:1(2426)

BUNCH-EX-12:22(92)

BUNCHES-2SA-16:1(6778)-1CH-12:40(6778)-IS-30:6(1707)

BUNDLE-GE-42:35(6872)-1SA-25:29(6872)-SONG-1:13(6872)■N.T.-AC-28:3(4128)

BUNDLES-GE-42:35(6872)■N.T.-M'T-13:30(1197)

BURDEN-all=4853&marked-EX-23:5-NU-4:15,19,31,32,47,49■11:11,17-DE-1:12-2SA-15:33■19:35-2KI-5:17■8:9■9:25-2CH-35:3-NE-13:19-JOB-7:20-PS-38:4■55:22(3053)■81:6(5449)-EC-12:5(5445)-IS-9:4(5448)■10:27(5448)■13:1■14:25(5448),28■15:1■17:1■19:1■21:1,11,13■22:1,25■23:1■30:6,27(4858)■46:1,2-JER-17:21,22,24,27■23:33^{2},34,36^{2},38^{3}-EZE-12:10-HO-8:10-NA-1:1-HAB-1:1-ZEP-3:18(4864)-ZEC-9:1■12:1,3(6006)-MAL-1:1■N.T.-M'T-11:30(5413)■20:12(922)-AC-15:28(922)■21:3(1117)-2CO-12:16(2599)-GA-6:5(5413)-RE-2:24(922)

BURDENED-2CO-5:4(916)■8:13(2347)

BURDENS-all=5450&marked-GE-49:14(4942)-EX-1:11■2:11■5:4,5■6:6,7-NU-4:24(4853),27^{2}(4853)-1KI-5:15(5449)-2CH-2:2(5449),18(5449)■24:27(4853)■34:13(5449)-NE-4:10(5449),17(5447)■13:15(4853)-IS-58:6(92)-LA-2:14(4864)-AM-5:11(4864)■N.T.-M'T-23:4(5413)-LU-11:46^{2}(5413)-GA-6:2(922)

BURDENSOME-ZEC-12:3(4614)■N.T.-2CO-11:9(4)■12:13(2655),14(2655)-1TH-2:6(1722,922)

BURIAL-all=6900-2CH-26:23-EC-6:3-IS-14:20-JER-22:19■N.T.-M'T-26:12(1779)

BURIED-all=6912-GE-15:15■23:19■25:9,10■35:8,19,29■48:7■49:31^{3}■50:13,14-NU-11:34■20:1■33:4-DE-10:6■34:6-JOS-24:30,32,33-J'G-2:9■8:32■10:2,5■12:7,10,12,15■16:31-RU-1:17-1SA-25:1■28:3■31:13-2SA-2:4,5,32■3:32■4:12■17:23■21:14-1KI-2:10,34■11:43■13:31^{2}■14:18,31■15:8,24■16:6,28■22:37,50-2KI-8:24■9:28■10:35■12:21■13:9,13,20■14:16,20■15:7,38■16:20■21:18,26■23:30-1CH-10:12-2CH-9:31■12:16■14:1■16:14■21:1,20■22:9■24:16,25^{2}■25:28■26:23■27:9■28:27■32:33■33:20■35:24-JOB-27:15-EC-8:10-JER-8:2■16:4,6■20:6■22:19■25:33-EZE-39:15■N.T.-all=2290&marked-M'T-14:12-LU-16:22-AC-2:29■5:6,9,10-RO-6:4(4916)-1CO-15:4(2290)-COL-2:12(4916)

BURIERS-EZE-39:15(6912)

BURN-all=6999,a=8313,b=1197&marked-GE-11:3a■44:18(2734)-EX-12:10a■27:20(5927)■29:13,14a,18,25,34a■30:1(4729),7^{2},8,20-LE-1:9,13,15,17■2:2,9,11,16■3:5,11,16■4:10,12a,19,21a,26,31,35■5:12■6:12b,12,15■7:5,31■8:32a■13:52a,55a,57a■16:25,27a■17:6■24:2(5927)-NU-5:26■18:17■19:5^{2}a-DE-5:23b■7:5a,25a■12:3a■13:16a■32:22(3344)-JOS-11:6a,13a-J'G-9:52a■12:1a■14:15a,-1SA-2:16,28-1KI-13:1,2-2KI-16:15■18:4■23:5-1CH-23:13-2CH-2:4,6■4:20b■13:11,11b■26:16,18^{2},19■28:25■29:11■32:12-NE-10:34b-PS-79:5b■89:46b-IS-1:31b■10:17b■27:4(6702)■

40:16b■44:15b■47:14a-**JER**-4:4b■7:9,20b■31a■11:13■15:14(3344)■17:4(3344)■19:5a■21:10a,12b■32:29a■34:2a,5a,22a■36:25a■37:8a,10a■38:18a■43:12a,13a■44:3,5,17,18,25-**EZE**-5:2b,4a■16:41a■23:47a■24:5(1754),11(2787)■39:9(5400),9b,10b■43:21a-**HO**-4:13-**NA**-2:13b-**HAB**-1:16-**MAL**-4:1b,1(3857)■**N.T.**-all=2618&marked-**M'T**-3:12■13:30-**LU**-1:9(2370)■3:17■24:32(2545)-**1CO**-7:9(4448)-**2CO**-11:29(4448)-**RE**-17:16

BURNED-all=8313,a=6999&marked-**EX**-3:2(1197)-**LE**-4:21■8:16a-**DE**-4:11(1197)■9:15(1197)-**JOS**-7:25■11:13-**1SA**-30:1,3,14-**2SA**-5:21(5375)■23:7-**2KI**-10:26■15:35a■22:17a■23:4,5a,6,8a,11,15^{2},16,20-**1CH**-14:12-**2CH**-25:14a■29:7a■34:25a-**NE**-1:3(3341)■2:17(3341)■4:2-**ES**-1:12(1197)-**JOB**-1:16(1197)■30:30(2787)-**PS**-39:3(1197)■74:8■80:16■102:3(2787)■106:18(3857)-**PR**-6:27,28(3554)-**IS**-1:7■24:6(2787)■33:12(3341)■42:25(1197)■43:2(3554)■44:19(8314)■64:11(8316)■65:7a-**JER**-1:16a■2:15(3341)■6:29(2787)■9:10(3341),12(3341)■18:15a■19:4a,13a■36:27,28,29,32■38:17,23■39:8■44:15a,19a,21a,23a■49:2(3341)■51:30(3341),32,58(3341)■52:13^{2}-**LA**-2:3(1197)-**EZE**-15:4(2787),5(2787)■20:47(6866)■24:10(2787)-**HO**-2:13a■11:2a-**JOE**-1:19(3857)-**AM**-2:1-**MIC**-1:7-**NA**-1:5(5375)■**N.T.**-all=2618&marked-**M'T**-3:40■22:7(1714)-**JOH**-15:6(2545)-**AC**-19:19-**RO**-1:27(1572)-**1CO**-3:15■13:3(2545)-**HEB**-6:8(2740)■12:18(2545)■13:11-**2PE**-3:10-**RE**-1:15(4448)■18:18

BURNETH-all=1197&marked-**LE**-13:24(4348)■16:28(8313)-**NU**-19:8(8313)-**PS**-46:9(8313)■83:14■97:3(3857)-**IS**-9:18■44:16(8313)■62:1■64:2(6919)■65:3(6999),5(3344)■66:3(2142)-**JER**-48:35(6999)-**HO**-7:6-**JOE**-2:3(3857)-**AM**-6:10(5635)■**N.T.**-**RE**-21:8(2545)

BURNING-all=3345&marked-**GE**-15:17(784)-**EX**-21:25(3555)-**LE**-6:9(4169),9(3344),12(3344),13(3344)■10:6(8316)■13:23(6867),24(4348),25(4348),28^{2}(4348)■16:12(784)■26:16(6920)-**NU**-16:37(8316)■19:6(8316)-**DE**-28:22(2746)■29:23(8316)-**2CH**-16:14(8316)■21:19^{2}(8316)-**JOB**-41:19(3940)-**PS**-140:10(784)-**PR**-16:27(6867)■26:21(1513),23(1814)-**IS**-3:24(3587)■4:4(1197)■9:5(8316)■10:16(3350)■30:27(1197)■34:9(1197)-**JER**-20:9(1197)■36:22(1197)■44:8(6999)**EZE**-1:13(1197)-**DA**-3:6,11,15,17,20,21,23,26■7:9(1815),11(3346)-**AM**-4:11(8316)-**HAB**-3:5(7565)■**N.T.**-all=2545&marked-**LU**-12:35-**JOH**-5:35-**JAS**-1:11(2742)-**RE**-4:5■8:8,10■18:9(4451),18(4451)19:20

BURNINGS-**IS**-33:12(4955),14(4168)-**JER**-34:5(4955)

BURNISHED-**EZE**-1:7(7044)

BURNT-all=5930,a=8313,b=6999&marked-**GE**-8:20■22:2,3,6,7,8,13■38:24a-**EX**-3:3(1197)■10:25■18:12■20:24■24:5■29:18,25,42■30:9,28■31:9■32:6,20a■35:16■38:1■40:6,10,27b,29^{2}-**LE**-1:3,4,6,9,10,13,14,17■2:12(5927)■3:5■4:7,10,12a,18,24,25^{2},29,30,33,34■5:7,10■6:9^{2},10,12b,22b,25,30a■7:2,8^{2},17a,19a,37■8:17a,18,20b,21b,21,28b,28■9:2,3,7,10,11a,12,13,13b,14b,14,16,17b,17,20b,22,24■10:16a,19■12:6,8■13:52a■14:13,19,20,22,31■15:15,30■16:3,5,24^{2}■17:8■19:6a■20:14a■21:9a■22:18■23:12,18,37-**NU**-6:11,14,16■7:15,21,27,33,39,45,51,57,63,69,75,81,87■8:12■10:10■11:1(1197),3(1197)■15:3,5,8,24■16:39a■19:17(8316)■23:3,6,15,17■28:3,6,10^{2},11,13,14,15,19,23^{2},24,27,31■29:2,6^{2},8,11,13,16,19,22,28,31,34,36,38,39■31:10a-**DE**-9:21a■12:6,11,13,14,27,31a■27:6■32:24(4198)■33:10(3632)-**JOS**-6:24a■7:15a■8:28a,31■11:9a,11a■22:23,26,27,28,29-**J'G**-6:26■11:31■13:16,23■15:5(1197),6a,14(1197)■18:27a■20:26■21:4-**1SA**-2:15b■6:14,15■7:9,10■10:8■13:9^{2},10,12■15:22■31:12a-**2SA**-6:17,18■24:22,24,25-**1KI**-3:3b,4,15■8:64^{2}■9:16a,25,25b■11:8b■12:33b■13:2a■15:13a■16:18a■18:33,38■22:43b-**2KI**-1:14(398)■3:27■5:17■10:24,25■12:3b■14:14b■15:4b■16:4b,13,15^{4}■17:11b,31a■25:9^{2}a-**1CH**-6:49■16:1,2,40^{2}■21:23,24,26^{2},29■22:1■23:31■29:21-**2CH**-1:6■2:4■4:6■7:1,7^{2}■8:12■13:11■15:16a■23:18■24:14■28:3b,3(1197),4b■29:7,18,24,27^{2},28,31,32^{2},34,35^{2}■30:15■31:2,3^{3}■34:5a■35:12,14,16■36:19^{2}a-**EZR**-3:2,3^{2},4,5,6■6:9(5928)■8:35^{2}-**NE**-10:33-**JOB**-1:5■42:8-**PS**-20:3■40:6■50:8■51:16,19■66:13,15-**IS**-1:11■40:16■43:23■56:7■61:8-**JER**-6:20■7:21,22■14:12■17:26■19:5■33:18■51:25(8316)-**EZE**-40:38,39,42^{2}■43:18,24,27■44:11■45:15,17^{2},23,25■46:2,4,12^{2},13,15-**HO**-6:6-**AM**-5:22-**MIC**-6:6■**N.T.**-all=3646&marked-**M'R**-12:33-**HEB**-10:6,8-**RE**-8:7^{2}(2618)

BURST-all=5423&marked-**JOB**-32:19(1234)-**PR**-3:10(6555)-**JER**-2:20■5:5■30:8-**NA**-1:13■**N.T**-2:22(4486)-**LU**-5:37(4486)-**AC**-1:18(2997)

BURSTING-**IS**-30:14(4386)

BURY-all=6912-**GE**-23:4,6^{2},8,11,13,15■47:29,30■49:29■50:5^{2},6,7,14-**DE**-21:23-**1KI**-2:31■11:15■13:29,31■14:13-**2KI**-9:10,34,35-**PS**-79:3-**JER**-7:32■14:16■19:11^{2}-**EZE**-39:11,13,14-**HO**-9:6■**N.T.**-all=2290&marked-**M'T**-8:21,22■27:7(5027)-**LU**-9:59,60-**JOH**-19:40(1779)

BURYING-**2KI**-13:21(6912)-**EZE**-39:12(6912)■**N.T.**-**M'R**-14:8(1780)-**JOH**-12:7(1780)

BURYINGPLACE-all=6913-**GE**-23:4,9,20■47:30■49:30■50:13-**J'G**-16:31

BUSH-all=5572-**EX**-3:2^{3},3,4-**DE**-33:16■**N.T.**-all=942-**M'R**-12:26-**LU**-6:44■20:37-**AC**-7:30,35

BUSHEL-all=3426-**M'T**-5:15-**M'R**-4:21-**LU**-11:33

BUSHES-**JOB**-30:4(7880),7(7880)-**IS**-7:19(5097)

BUSHY-**SONG**-5:11(8534)

BUSIED all supplied

BUSINESS-all=4399&marked-**GE**-39:11-**DE**-24:5(1697)-**JOS**-2:14(1697),20(1697)-**J'G**-18:7(1697),28(1697)-**1SA**-20:19(4639)■21:2^{2}(1697),8(1697)-**1CH**-26:29,30-**2CH**-13:10■17:13-**NE**-11:16,22■13:30-**ES**-3:9-**PS**-107:23-**PR**-22:29-**EC**-5:3(6045)■8:16(6045)-**DA**-8:27■**N.T.**-**AC**-6:3(5532)-**RO**-12:11(4710)■16:2(4229)-**1TH**-4:11(2398)

BUSY-**1KI**-20:40(6213)

BUSYBODIES-**2TH**-3:11(4020)-**1TI**-5:13(4021)

BUSYBODY-**1PE**-4:15(244)

BUTLER-all=4945-**GE**-40:1,5,9,13,20,21,23■41:9

BUTLERS-**GE**-40:2(4945)

BUTLERSHIP-**GE**-40:21(4945)

BUTTER-all=2529&marked-**GE**-18:8-**DE**-32:14-**J'G**-5:25-**2SA**-17:29-**JOB**-20:17■29:6-**PS**-55:21(4260)-**PR**-30:33-**IS**-7:15,22^{2}

BUTTOCKS-**2SA**-10:4(8357)-**1CH**-19:4(4667)-**IS**-20:4(8357)

BUY-all=7069,a=7666&marked-**GE**-41:57a■42:2a,3a,5a,7a,10a■43:2a,4a,20a,22a■44:25a■47:19-**EX**-21:2-**LE**-22:11■25:15,44,45-**DE**-2:6a,6(3739)■28:68-**RU**-4:4,5,8-**2SA**-24:21,24-**2KI**-12:12■22:6-**1CH**-21:24-**2CH**-34:11-**EZR**-7:17(7066)-**NE**-5:3(3947)■10:31(3947)-**PR**-23:23-**IS**-55:1^{2}a-**JER**-32:7^{2},8^{2},25,44-**AM**-8:6■**N.T.**-all=59&marked-**M'T**-14:15■25:9,10-**M'R**-6:36,37-**LU**-9:13■22:36-**JOH**-4:8■6:5■13:29-**1CO**-7:30-**JAS**-4:13(1710)-**RE**-3:18■13:17

BUYER-all=7069-**PR**-20:14-**IS**-24:2-**EZE**-7:12

BUYEST-**LE**-25:14(7069)-**RU**-4:5(7069)

BUYETH-**PR**-31:16(3947)■**N.T.**-**M'T**-13:44(59)-**RE**-18:11(59)

BYWAYS-**J'G**-5:6(734,6128)

BYWORD-all=3148-**DE**-28:37-**1KI**-9:7-**2CH**-7:20-**JOB**-17:6(4914)■30:9(4405)-**PS**-44:14(4912)

C

CAB-**2KI**-6:25(6894)

CABINS-**JER**-37:16(2588)

CAGE-**JER**-5:27(3619)■**N.T.**-**RE**-18:2(5438)

CAKE-all=2471&marked-**EX**-29:23-**LE**-8:26^{2}■24:5-**NU**-6:19■15:20-**J'G**-7:13(6742)-**1SA**-30:12(1690)-**2SA**-6:19(2471)-**1KI**-17:12(4580),13(5692)■19:6(5692)-**HO**-7:8(5692)

CAKES-all=2471&marked-**GE**-18:6(5692)-**EX**-12:39(5692)■29:2-**LE**-2:4■7:12^{2},13■24:5-**NU**-6:15■11:8(5692)-**JOS**-5:11(4682)-**J'G**-6:19(4682),20(4682),21(4682)-**1SA**-25:18(1690)-**2SA**-13:6(3834),8(3823),8(3834),10(3834)-**1CH**-12:40(1690)■23:29(7550)-**JER**-7:18(3561)■44:19(3561)-**EZE**-4:12(5692)

CALAMITIES-**PS**-57:1(1942)■141:5(7451)-**PR**-17:5(343)

CALAMITY-all=343&marked-**DE**-32:35-**2SA**-22:19-**JOB**-6:2(1942)■30:13(1942)-**PS**-18:18-**PR**-1:26■6:15■19:13(1942)■24:22■27:10-**JER**-18:17■46:21■48:16■49:8,32-**EZE**-35:5-**OB**-13^{3}

CALAMUS-all=7070-**EX**-30:23-**SONG**-4:14-**EZE**-27:19

CALDRON-all=5518&marked-**1SA**-2:14(7037)-**JOB**-41:20(100)-**EZE**-11:3,7,11-**MIC**-3:3(7037)

CALDRONS-**2CH**-35:13(1731)-**JER**-52:18(5518),19(5518)

CALF-all=5695&marked-**GE**-18:7(1121,1241),8(1121,1241)-**EX**-32:4,8,19,20,24,35-**LE**-9:2,3,8-**DE**-9:16,21-**1SA**-28:24-**NE**-9:18-**PS**-29:6■106:19-**IS**-11:6■27:10-**JER**-34:18,19-**HO**-8:5,6■**N.T.**-all=3448&marked-**LU**-15:23,27,30-**AC**-7:41(3447)-**RE**-4:7

CALF'S-**EZE**-1:7(5695)

CALKERS-**EZE**-27:9(2388,919),27(2388,919)

CALL-all=7121&marked-**GE**-2:19■4:26■16:11■17:15,19■24:57■30:13(833)■46:33-**EX**-2:7,20■34:15-**NU**-16:12■22:5,20,37-**DE**-2:11,20■3:9^{2}■4:7,26(5749)■25:8■30:1(7725),19(5749)■31:14,28(5749)■33:19-**J'G**-12:1■16:25■21:13-**RU**-1:20,21-**1SA**-3:6,8,9■12:17■16:3■22:11-**2SA**-17:5■22:4-**1KI**-1:28,32■8:52■17:18(2142)■18:24^{2},25■22:13-**2KI**-4:12,15,36■5:11■10:19-**1CH**-16:8-**2CH**-18:12-**JOB**-5:1■13:22■14:15■27:10-**PS**-4:1,3■14:4■18:3■20:9■49:11■50:4,15■55:16■72:17(833)■77:6(2142)■80:18■86:5,7■91:15■99:6■102:2■105:1■116:2,13,17■145:18^{2}-**PR**-1:28■7:4■8:4■9:15■31:28(833)-**IS**-5:20(559)■7:14■8:3■12:4■22:12,20■31:2(5493)■34:12■41:25■44:5,7■45:3■48:2,13■55:5,6■58:5,9,13■60:14,18■61:6■62:12■65:15,24-**JER**-1:15■3:17,19■6:30■7:27■9:17■10:25■25:29■29:12■33:3■50:29(8085)■51:27(8085)-**LA**-2:15(559)-**EZE**-21:23(2142)■36:29■38:21■39:11-**DA**-2:2-**HO**-1:4,6,9■2:16^{2}■7:11-**JOE**-1:14■2:15,32^{2}-**AM**-5:16-**JON**-1:6-**ZEP**-3:9-**ZEC**-3:10■13:9-**MAL**-1:4■3:12(833),15(833)■**N.T.**-all=2564&marked-**M'T**-1:21,23■9:13■20:8■22:3,43,45■23:9-**M'R**-2:17■10:49(5455)■15:12(3004),16(4779)-**LU**-1:13,31,48(3106)■5:32■6:46■14:12(5455),13-**JOH**-4:16(5455)■13:13(5455)■15:15(3004)-**AC**-2:21(1941),39(4341)■9:14(1941)■10:5(3343),15(2840),28(3004),32(3333)■11:9(2840),13(3343)■19:13(3687)■24:14(3004),25(3333)-**RO**-9:25■10:12(1941),13(1941),14(1941)-**1CO**-1:2(1941)-**2CO**-1:23(1941)-**2TI**-1:5(2983)■2:22(1941)-**HEB**-2:11■10:32(363)-**JAS**-5:14(4341)-**1PE**-1:17(1941)

CALLED-all=7121&marked-**GE**-

1:5^2,8,10^2■2:19,23■3:9,20■4:17,25,26■5:2,3,29■11:9■12:8,18■13:4■16:13,14,15■17:5■19:5,22,37,38■20:8,9■21:3,12,17,31,33■22:11,14,15■24:58■25:25,26,30■26:9,18^2,20,21,22,25,33■27:1,42■28:1,19,19sup,■29:32,33,34,35■30:6,8,11,13,18,20,21,24■31:4,47^2■31:48,54■32:2,28(559),30■33:17,20■35:7,8,10^2,15,18^2■38:3,4,5,29,30■39:14■41:8,14,45,51,52■47:29■48:6■49:1■50:11-**EX**-1:18■2:8,10,22■3:4■7:11■8:8,25■9:27■10:16,24■12:21,31■15:23■16:31■17:7,15■19:3,7,20■24:16■31:2■33:7■34:31■35:30■36:2-**LE**-1:1■9:1■10:4-**NU**-11:3,34■12:5■13:16,24■21:3■24:10■25:2■32:41,42-**DE**-3:13,14■5:1■15:2■25:10■28:10■29:2■31:7-**JOS**-4:4■5:9■6:6■7:26■8:16(2199)■9:22■10:24■19:47■22:1,34■23:2■24:1,9-**J'G**-1:17,26■2:5■4:6,10(2199)■6:24,32■8:31(7760)■9:54■10:4■12:2(2199)■13:24■14:15■15:17,18,19■16:18,19,25,28■18:12,29-**RU**-4:17-**1SA**-1:20■3:4,5,6^2,8^2,10,16■6:2■7:12■9:9,26■10:17(6817)■12:18■13:4(6817)■16:5,8■19:7■23:8(8085),28■28:15■29:6-**2SA**-1:7,15■2:16,26■5:9,20■6:2,8■9:2,9■11:13■12:24,25,28■13:17■14:33■15:2,11■18:18^2,26,28■21:2■22:7-**1KI**-1:9,10,19^2,25,26■2:36,42■7:21^2■8:43■9:13■12:3,20■16:24■17:10,11■18:3,26■20:7■22:9-**2KI**-3:10,13■4:12,15,22,36^2■6:11■7:10,11■8:1■9:1■12:7■14:7■18:4,18-**1CH**-4:9,10■6:65■7:16,23■11:7■13:6,11■14:11■15:11■21:26■22:6-**2CH**-3:17■6:33■7:14■10:3■18:8■20:26■24:6-**EZR**-2:61-**NE**-5:12■7:63-**ES**-2:14■3:12■4:5,11^2■5:10(935)■8:9■9:26-**JOB**-1:4■9:16■19:16■42:14-**PS**-17:6■18:6■31:17■50:1■53:4■79:6■88:9■99:6■105:16■116:4■118:5-**PR**-1:24■16:21■24:8-**SONG**-5:6-**IS**-1:26■4:1,3(559)■9:6■13:3■19:18(559)■31:4■32:5■35:8■41:2,9■42:6■43:1,7,22■45:4■47:1,5■48:1,8,12,15■49:1■50:2■51:2■54:5,6■56:7■58:12■61:3■62:2,4,12■63:19■65:1,12■66:4-**JER**-7:10,11,13,14,30,32(559)■11:16■12:6■14:9■15:16■19:6■20:3■23:6■25:29■30:17■32:34■33:16■34:15■35:17■36:4■42:8-**LA**-1:15,19,21■2:22■3:55,57-**EZE**-9:3■20:29-**DA**-5:12(7123)■8:16■9:18,19■10:1-**HO**-11:1,2,7-**AM**-7:4■9:12-**HAG**-1:11-**ZEC**-8:3■11:7^2■**N.T.**-all=2564,a=3004,b=4341,c=5455&marked-**M'T**-1:16a,25■2:7,15,23a,23■4:18a,21■5:9,19^2■10:1b,2a,25■13:55a■15:10b,32b■18:2b,32b■20:16(2822),25b,32c■21:13■22:14(2822)■23:7,8,10■25:14■26:3a,14a,36a■27:8,16a,17a,22a,33a-**M'R**-1:20■3:23b■6:7b■7:14b■8:1b,34b■9:35c■10:42b,49c■11:17■12:43b■14:72(363)■15:16(3739,2076)-**LU**-1:32,35,36,59,60,61,62,76■2:4,21,23■6:13(4377),15■7:11■8:2,54c■9:1(4779),10■10:39■13:12(4377)■15:19,21,26b■16:2c,5b■18:16b■19:13,15c,29■21:37■22:1a,25,47a■23:13(4779),33■24:13(3686)-**JOH**-1:42,48c■2:2,9c■4:5a,25a■5:2(1951)■9:11a,18c,24c■10:35(2036)■11:16a,28c,54a■12:17c■15:15(2046)■18:33c■19:13a,17^{2}a■20:24a■21:2a-**AC**-1:12,19,23■3:2a,11■4:18■5:21(4779),40b■6:2b,9a■7:14(3333)■8:9(3686)■9:11,11(3686),21(1941),36a,41c■10:1(3686),1,7c,18c,23(1528),24(4779)■11:26(5537)■13:1,2b,7b■14:12■15:17(1941)■16:10b,29(154)■19:25(4867),40(1458)■20:1b,17(3333)■23:6(2919),17b,18b,23b■24:2,21(2919)■27:8,14,16■28:1,17(4779),20(3870)-**RO**-1:1(2822),6(2822),7(2822)■2:17(2028)■7:3(5537)■8:28(2822),30^2■9:7,24,26-**1CO**-1:1(2822),2(2822),9,24(2822)■5:11(3687)■7:15,17,18^2,20,21,22^2,24■8:5a■15:9-**GA**-1:6,15■5:13-**EPH**-2:11^{2}a■4:1,4-**COL**-3:15■4:11a-**1TH**-2:12■4:7-**2TH**-2:4a,14-**1TI**-6:12,20(5581)-**2TI**-1:9-**HEB**-3:13■5:4,10(4316)■7:11a■9:2a,3a,15■11:8,16(1941),18,24a–**JAS**-2:7(1941),23-**1PE**-1:15■2:9,21■3:9■5:10-**2PE**-1:3-**1JO**-3:1-**JUDE**-1(2822)-**RE**-1:9■8:11a■11:8■12:9■16:16■17:14(2822)■19:9,11,13

CALLEDST-all=7121&marked-**J'G**-8:1-**1SA**-3:5-**PS**-81:7-**EZE**-23:21(6485)

CALLEST-all=3004-**M'T**-19:17-**M'R**-10:18-**LU**-18:19

CALLETH-all=7121-**1KI**-8:43-**2CH**-6:33-**JOB**-12:4-**PS**-42:7■147:4-**PR**-18:6-**IS**-21:11■40:26■59:4■64:7-**HO**-7:7-**AM**-5:8■9:6■**N.T.**-all=2564,a=3004,b=5455-**M'T**-27:47b-**M'R**-3:13(4341)■10:49b■12:37(3004)■15:35b-**LU**-15:6(4779),9(4779)■20:37a,44-**JOH**-10:3■11:28(5455)-**RO**-4:17■9:11-**1CO**-12:3a-**GA**-5:8-**1TH**-5:24-**RE**-2:20a

CALLING-all=7121&marked-**NU**-10:2(4744)-**IS**-1:13■41:4■46:11-**EZE**-23:19(2142)■**N.T.**-all=2821&marked-**M'T**-11:16(4377)-**M'R**-3:31(5455)■11:21(363)■15:44(4341)-**LU**-7:19(4341),32(4377)-**AC**-7:59(1941)■22:16(1941)-**RO**-11:29-**1CO**-1:26■7:20-**EPH**-1:18■4:4-**PH'P**-3:14-**2TH**-1:11-**2TI**-1:9-**HEB**-3:1-**1PE**-3:6(2564)-**2PE**-1:10

CALM-**PS**-107:29(1827)-**JON**-1:11(8367),12(8367)■**N.T.**-all=1055-**M'T**-8:26-**M'R**-4:39-**LU**-8:24

CALVE-**JOB**-39:1(2342)-**PS**-29:9(2342)

CALVED-**JER**-14:5(3205)

CALVES-all=5695&marked-**1SA**-6:7(1121),10(1121)■14:32(1121,1241)-**1KI**-12:28,32-**2KI**-10:29■17:16-**2CH**-11:15■13:8-**PS**-68:30-**HO**-10:5(5697)■13:2(5697)■14:2(6499)-**AM**-6:4-**MIC**-6:6-**MAL**-4:2■**N.T.**-**HEB**-9:12(3448),19(3448)

CALVETH-**JOB**-21:10(6403)

CAME-all=935,a=1961,b=3318,c=5927,d=3381&marked-**GE**-4:3a,8a■6:1a,4■7:10a■8:6a,11,13a■10:14b■11:2a,5d,31■12:5,11a,14a■13:18■14:1a,5,7,13■15:1a,11d,17a■19:1,5,8,9,9(5066),17a,29a,34a■20:3,13a■21:22a■22:1a,9,20a■23:2■24:15a,15b,16c,22a,30a,30,32,42,45b,52a,■25:11a,25b,26b,29■26:8a,32a,32■27:1a,18,27(5066),30a,30,35■29:1(3212),9,10a,13a,23a,25a■30:16,25a,38^2,41a■31:10a,24■32:6,13■33:1,3(5066),6(5066),7^2(5066),18^2■34:7,20,25a,25,27■35:6,9,17a,18a,22a,27■37:14,18(7126),23a,25■38:1a,9a,18,24a,27a,28a,28b,29a,29b,30b■39:5a,7a,10a,11a,13a,14,15a,16,17,18a,19a■40:1a,6,20a■41:1a,2c,3c,5c,8a,13a,14,18c,19c,22c,27c,50,57■42:5,6,29,35a■43:2a,19(5066),20d,21a,21,25,26■44:14,18(5066),24a,24c■45:4(5066),25■46:1,6,8,26,26b,27,28■47:1,15,18■48:1a,5,7■50:10-**EX**-1:1^2,5b,21a■2:5d,11a,16,17,18,23a,23c■3:1■4:24a■5:15,20b,23■6:28a■8:6c,24■10:3■12:29a,41^{2}a,51a■13:3b,4b,8b,15a,17a■14:20,20(7126),24a,28■15:23,27■16:1,10a,13a,13c,22a,22,27a,35^2■17:8,11a■18:5,7,12,13a■19:1,7,16a,20d■21:3■22:15■24:3■32:19(7126),24b,30a■33:7a,8a,9a■34:29a,29^{2}d,32(5066),34^{2}b■35:21,22■36:4■40:17a,32(7126)-**LE**-9:1a,22d,23b,24b-**NU**-4:47■7:1a■9:6(7126)■10:11a,21,35a■11:20b,25d,25a■12:4b,5d,5b■13:22,23,26,27■14:45d■16:27b,31a,35b,42a,43■17:8a■19:2c■20:1,11b,20b,22,28d■21:1,7,9a,23■22:7,9,16,20,39,41a■23:17■24:2a■25:6■26:1a■27:1(7126)■31:14,48(7126)■32:2,11c,16(5066)■33:9■36:1(7126)-**DE**-1:3a,19,22(7126),24,31,44b■2:14(1980),16a,23b,32b■3:1b■4:11(7126),45b■5:23a,23(7126)■9:7,11a,15d■10:5d■11:5,10b■22:14(7126)■23:4b■29:7,7b,16(5674)■31:24a■32:17,44■33:2,2(857),21(857)-**JOS**-1:1a■2:1,2,4,5a,8c,10b,22,23■3:1,2a,14a,16^{2}d■4:1a,11a,18a,19c,22(5674)■5:1a,4^{2}b,5^{2}b,6b,8a,13a■6:1,8a,9(1980),11,13(1980),15a,16a,20a■8:11,14a,24a■9:1a,12b,16a,17■10:1a,9,11a,20a,24a,24(7126),27a,33c■11:1,5,7,21■14:6(5066)■15:18a,18■16:7(6293)■17:4(7126),13a■18:9,11c,11b,16d■19:1b,10c,17b,24b,32b,40b■21:1(5066),4b,45■22:10,15■23:1a■24:6,11,29a-**J'G**-1:1a,14a,14,28a■2:1c,4a,19a■3:10a,20,22b,24,27a■4:5c,22b,22■5:14d,19,23■6:3^{2}c,5c,5,7a,11,25a,34(3847),35c■7:9a,13,19■8:4,15,33a■9:25(5674),26,42a,52,57■11:4a,13c,16c,16,18^2,29a,34,34b,35a,39a■13:6^2,9,10,11,20a■14:2c,5,6(6743),9(1980),11a,14^{2}b,15a,17a,19(6743)■15:1a,6c,14,14(6743,935),17a,19b,19(7725)■16:4a,5c,16a,18c,25a,31d■17:8■18:2,7,8,13,15,17,27■19:1a,5a,10,16,22,26,30c■20:4,21b,24(7126),26,33(1518),34,48^2(4672)■21:2,4a,5^{2}c,8c,8,14(7725)-**RU**-1:1a,2,19,19a,22■2:3,4,6(7725),7■3:7,8a,14,16■4:1(5674)-**1SA**-1:12a,19,20a■2:13,14,15,19c,27■3:2a,10■4:1a,5,12,13^2,14,16,18a,19(2015)■5:10a,10■6:14■7:1,2a,13■8:1a,4■9:12,14b,15,26a■10:9,10,10(6743),11a,13,14■11:1c,4,5,6(6743),7b,9^2,11,11a■12:12■13:5c,8,10a,10,17b,22a■14:1a,19a,20,25■15:2c,5,6c,10a,12,13,32(1980)■16:4,6a,13(6743),21,23a■17:20,22,23c,34,41(3212),48a,48(3212)■18:1a,6a,6,6b,10a,10(6743),13,16,19a,30a■19:18,22,23■20:1,27a,35a,38■21:1,5b■22:5,11■23:6a,6d,19c,25d,27■24:1a,3,5a,16a■25:9,12,20^{2}d,36,37(1916),38(1916)■26:1,3,5,7,15■27:9■28:1a,4,8,21■30:1a,3,9,12(7725),21,21(5066),23,26■31:7,8a,8,12-**2SA**-1:1,2^3■2:1a,4,23b,23,29,32■3:6a,20,22,23,24^2,25,35■4:4,4a,5,6,7■5:1,3,17c,18,20,22c■6:6,16,20d■7:1a,4^{2}a■8:1a,5■10:1a,2,8b,14,16,17■11:1a,2a,4,14a,16a,22,23b■12:1,4,18a,20^2■13:1a,23a,24,30a,30,34(1980),36a,36■14:31,33^2■15:1a,2,5(7126),6,7a,13,18,32a,37^2■16:5,5^{3}b,11b,14,15,16a■17:18,20,21a,21c,24,27a■18:4b,25(3212),31■19:5,8,15^2,16d,24d,24,25a,31d,41■20:3,12,15■21:18a■22:10d■23:13■24:6^2,7,8,11a,13,18-**1KI**-1:22,28,32,40c,42,47,53(7126)■2:7,8d,13,28,30,39a■3:15,16,18a■4:27(7131),34■5:7a■6:1a,11a■7:14■8:3,9b,10a■9:1a,10a,12b,24c,28■10:1,2,7,10,12,14,22,29c■11:4a,15a,18^2,29a■12:2a,3,12,20a,22a■13:1,4a,10,11,12,20^{2}a,21,23a,25,29,31a■14:4,6,17^2,25a,25c■15:21a,29a■16:1a,7a,11a,18a,31a■17:2a,7a,8a,10,17a,22(7725)■18:1^{2}a,17a,21(5066),27a,29a,30(5066),31a,36a,36(5066),44a,45a■19:3,4,7(7725),9,9sup■20:5(7725),12a,13(5066),19b,22(5066),26a,28(5066),30,32,33b,43■21:1a,4,5,13,15a,16a,17a,27a,28a■22:2a,2d,15,21b,32a,33a-**2KI**-1:6c,7c,10d,12d,13,14d■2:1a,3b,4,5(5066),9a,11a,15,18(7725),23b,24b■3:5a,15^{2}a,20a,20,24■4:6a,7,11,25,25a,27,27(5066),38(7725),39,40a,42■5:7a,9,13(5066),14(7725),15,24■6:4,14,18d,20a,23,24a,30a,32,33d■7:8,8(7725),10^2,17d,18a■8:3a,5a,7,9,14,15a■9:5,11b,11,17,18,19,20,22a,36(7725)■10:7a,7,8,9a,12(1980),17,21^3,25a■11:9,13,16(3996),19■12:10c■13:14d,21a■14:5a,13■15:12a,14,19,29■16:5c,6,11■17:3c,5c,28■18:1a,9a,9c,17^2,18b,37■19:1a,5,33,35a,37a■20:1,4^{2}a,14^2■21:15b■22:3a,9,11a■23:9c,17,18,34■24:1c,3a,7b,10c,11,20a■25:1a,1,8,23,25a,25,26,27a-**1CH**-1:12b■2:53b,55■4:41■7:21d,22■10:7,8a,8■11:3■12:1,16,18(3847),19,22,23,38■13:9■14:9,11c■15:26a,29a,29■17:1a,3a,3,16■18:1a,5■19:1a,2,7^2,9b,15,17■20:1a,1,4a■21:4,11,21■22:8a■24:7b■25:9b■26:14b■27:1-**2CH**-1:13■5:4,10b,11a,13a■7:1d,3d,11■8:1a■9:1,6,13,21■10:2a,3,12■11:2a,14(3212),16■12:1a,2a,2c,3,4,5,7a,9c,11■13:15a■14:9b,9,14a■15:1a,5■16:1c,5a,7■18:20b,23(5066),31a,32a■20:1a,1,2,4,10,14a,24,25,28■21:12,17c,19a■22:1,8a■23:2,12,20■24:4a,11a,11,17,18a,20(3847),23a,23c,23,24■25:3a,7,14a,16a■28:9,12,20■29:15,17■30:11,25^2,27■31:5(6555),8■32:1,21(3329),26■34:9,19a■35:20c,22■36:6c-**EZR**-2:1(7725),2,68■4:2(5066),12(5559)■5:3(858),5(1946),16(858)■7:8,9■8:32■9:1(5066)■10:6(3212)-**NE**-1:1a,2,4a■2:1a,9,11■4:1a,7a,12a,12,15a,16a■5:17■6:1a,10,16a,17■7:1a,5c,6(7725),7,73(5060)■13:3a,6,7,19a,21-**ES**-1:1a,17■2:8a,13,14■3:4a■4:2,3(5060),4,9■5:1a,5,10■6:6,12(7725),14■7:1■8:1,17(5060)■

9:25-**JOB**-1:6^{2},14,16,17,18,19,21b■2:1^{2}, 11■3:11b,26■4:14(7122)■6:20■26:4b■ 29:13■30:14(857),26^{2}■38:29b■42:11 -**PS**-18:6,9d■27:2(7126)■51:t■52:t■54:t■ 78:21c,31c■88:17(5437)■105:19,23,31, 34-**PR**-7:15b-**EC**-5:15b,15,16■9:14 -**SONG**-4:2c-**IS**-7:1a■11:16c■20:1■ 30:4(5060)■36:1a,1c,3b,22■37:1a,5,34, 38a■38:1,4a■39:3^{2}■41:5(857)■48:3,5■ 50:2■66:7-**JER**-1:2a,3a,4a,11a,13a■ 2:1a■3:9a■7:1a,25b,31c■11:1a■13:3a, 6a,8a■14:1a,3■16:1a■17:16(4161)■18:1a, 5a■19:5c,14■20:3a,18b■21:1a■24:4a■ 25:1a■26:1a,8a■10c■27:1a■28:1a,12a■ 29:30a■30:1a■32:1a,6a,8,23,26a,35c■ 33:1a,19a,23a■34:1a,8a,12a■35:1a,11a, 11c,12a■36:1^{2}a,9a,9,14,16a,23a,27a■ 37:4,6a,11a■38:27■39:1,3,4a,15a■ 40:1a,8,12,13■41:1a,1,4a,5,6a,7,13a■42:1 (5066),7^{2}a■43:1a,7^{2},8a■44:1a,21c■46:1a■ 47:1a■49:34a■52:3a,4a,4,12,31a-**LA**-1:9d-**EZE**-1:1a,3a,4,■3:15,16^{2}a■4:14■ 6:1a■7:1a■8:1a■9:2,8a■10:6a■11:13a, 14a■12:1a,8a,17a,21a,26a■13:1a■14:1,2a, 12a■15:1a■16:1a,23a■17:1a,3,11a■18:1a■ 20:1a,1,2a,45a■21:1a,8a,18a■22:1a,17a, 23a■23:1a,17,39,40■24:1a,15a,20a■ 25:1a■26:1^{2}a■27:1a■28:1a,11a,20a■ 29:1a,17^{2}a■30:1a,20^{2}a■31:1^{2}a■32:1^{2}a, 17^{2}a■33:1a,21a,21,22^{2},23a■34:1a■35:1a■ 36:16a■37:7(7126),8c,10,15a■38:1a■ 40:6■43:2,3,4■46:9■47:1d-**DA**-1:1■ 2:2,29(5559)■3:8(7127),26(7127),26 (5312)■4:7(5954),8(5954),13(5182),28 (4291)■5:5(5312),8(5954),10(5954)■ 6:12(7127),20(7127),24(4291)■7:3 (5559),8(5559),10(5312),13(858,1934), 13(4291),16(7127),20(5559),22(858), 22(4291)■8:2a,3c,5,6,8c,9b,15a,17^{2}■9:2a, 23b■10:3,13-**HO**-1:1a■2:15c-**JO**-1:1a -**AM**-6:1■7:2a-**OB**-5^{2}-**JON**-1:1a,6(7126)■ 2:7■3:1a,6(5060)■4:8a,10a-**MIC**-1:1a,11b,12d-**HAB**-3:3-**ZEP**-1:1a-**HAG**-1:1a,3a,14■2:1a,5b,10a,16^{2},20a-**ZEC**-1:1a,7a■4:1(7725),8a■5:9b■6:1b,9a■7:1^{2}, 1a,4a,8a,12a■8:1a,10,18a■10:4b■14:16■ **N.T.**-all=2064,a=4334,b=1096,c=1831 -**M'T**-1:18(4905)■2:1(3854),9,21,23■3:1 (3854)■4:3a,11a,13■5:1a■7:25,27,28b■ 8:2,5a,19a,25a,34c■9:1,10b,10,14a,18,20a, 23,28a■10:34■11:1b,18,19■12:42,44c■ 13:4,10a,25,27a,36a,53b■14:12a,15a,33, 34■15:1a,12a,22c,23a,25,29,30a,39■16:1a, 13■17:7a,9(2597),14a,19a,24a■18:1a,21a, 31■19:1b,1,3a,16a■20:9,10,20a,28■21:14a, 19,23a,28a,30a,32■22:11(1525),23a■24:1a, 3a,39■25:10,11,20a,22a,24a,36,39■26:1b, 7a,17a,43,47,49a,50a,60^{2}a,69a,73a■27:32c, 53c,57,62(4863)■28:1,2a,9a,11,13,18a -**M'R**-1:9b,9,11b,14,26c,31a,38c,40,45■ 2:15b,17,23b■3:8,13(565),22(2597),31■ 4:4b,4■5:1,27,33,35■6:1,22(1525),25 (1525),29,33(4905),34c,35a,53■7:1(4863), 1,25,31■8:3(2240),10,11c■9:7,9(2597), 14,21b,25(1998),26c,33■10:2a,17(4370), 45,46,50■11:1(1448),13^{2},12:28a,42■ 14:3,16,32■15:41(4872),43■16:2-**LU**-1:8b,22c,23b,28(1525),41b,57(4130),59b, 59,65b■2:1b,9(2186),15b,16,27,46b,51■ 3:2b,3,7(1607),12,21b,22b■4:16,31(2718), 35c,41c,42■5:1b,7,12b,15(4905),17b,32■ 6:1b,6b,12b,17(2597),17■7:4(3854),11b, 12(1448),14a,16(2983),33,45(1525)■ 8:1b,19(3854),22b,23(2597),24a,35,40b, 41,44a,47,51(1525),55(1994)■9:12a,18b, 28b,33b,34b,35b,37b,51b,57b■10:31 (2597),32,33,38b,40(2186)■11:1b,14b, 24c,27b,31■13:6,31a■14:1b,21(3854)■ 15:17,20,25,28c■16:21,22b■17:11b,14b, 27■18:3,35b■19:5,6(2597),15b,16(3854) 18,20,29b■20:1b,1(2186),27a■21:38 (3719)■22:7,39c,66(4863)■23:48(4836), 55(4905)■24:1,4b,15b,23,30b,51b-**JOH**-1:7,11,17b,39■3:2,13(2597),22,23(3854), 26■4:27,30,46■6:23,24,38(2597),41(2597), 42(2597),51(2597),58(2597)■7:45,50■ 8:2(3854),2,14,42(2240),42■9:7■10:8,24 (2944),35b■11:17,19,29,33(4905),44c, 45■12:1,9,20(305),21a,27,28,30b,47■ 16:27c,28c■17:8c■18:37■19:5c,32,33,34c, 38,39^{2}■20:3,4,8,18,19,24,26■21:8-**AC**-2:2b,6(4905),43b■4:1(2186),5b■5:5b,7 (1525),10(1525),11b,16(4905),21(3854), 22(3854),25(3854)■6:12(2186)■7:4c,11, 23(305),31,45(1237)■8:7c,36,40■9:3b, 21,32b,32,(2718)37b,43b■10:13b,29,45 (4905)■11:5,22(191),23(3854),26b,27 (2718),28b■12:7(2186),10,12,13a,20 (3918)■13:13,14(3854),31(4872),44(4863), 51■14:1b,19(1904),20(1525),24■15:1 (2718),6(4863),30■16:1(2658),8(2597), 11(2113),16b,18c,29b,39■17:1,13■18:1, 2a,19(2658),24(2658)■19:1b,1,6,18■ 20:2,6,7(4869),14,15,15(2658),18(1910)■ 21:1b,1,7(2658),8,10(2718),31(305),33 (1448),35b■22:6b,11,13,17b,27a■23:14a, 27(2186),33(1525)■24:7(3928),17(3854), 24(3854),27(2983,1240)■25:7(2597),13 (2658)■27:5(2718),8,44b■28:3c,8b,9a,13 (2658),13,15c,16,17b,21(3854),23(2240), 30(1531)-**RO**-7:9-**1CO**-2:1^{2}■14:36c,36 (2658)-**2CO**-1:8b,23■2:3,12■11:9-**GA**-1:21■2:4(3922),12■3:23-**EPH**-2:17 -**1TH**-1:5b■3:4b,6-**1TI**-1:15-**2TI**-3:11b -**HEB**-3:16c■11:15c-**2PE**-1:17(5342), 18(5342),21(5342)-**1JO**-5:6-**3JO**-3-**RE**-5:7■7:13,14■8:3■9:3c■14:15c,17c,18c, 20c■15:6c■16:17c,19(3415)■17:1■19:5c■ 20:9(2597)■21:9

CAMEL-all=1581-**GE**-24:64-**LE**-11:4-**DE**-14:7-**1SA**-15:3-**ZEC**-14:15■ **N.T.**-all=2574-**M'T**-19:24■23:24-**M'R**-10:25-**LU**-18:25

CAMEL'S-**GE**-31:34(1581)■**N.T.** -**M'T**-3:4(2574)-**M'R**-1:6(2574)

CAMELS-all=1581&marked-**GE**-12:16■24:10,11,14,19,20,22,30,31,32^{2}, 35,44,46^{2},61,63■30:43■31:17■32:7,15■ 37:25-**EX**-9:3-**J'G**-6:5■7:12-**1SA**-27:9■ 30:17-**1KI**-10:2-**1CH**-5:21■12:40■27:30 -**2CH**-9:1■14:15-**EZR**-2:67-**NE**-7:69 -**ES**-8:10(327),14(327)-**JOB**-1:3,17■ 42:12-**IS**-21:7■30:6■60:6-**JER**-49:29, 32-**EZE**-25:5

CAMELS'-all=1581-**J'G**-8:21,26 -**2KI**-8:9

CAMEST-all=935&marked-**GE**-16:8■24:5(3318)■27:33-**EX**-23:15(3318)■ 34:18(3318)-**NU**-22:37(1980)-**DE**-2:37 (7126)■16:3^{2}(3318),6(3318)-**1SA**-13:11■ 17:28(3381)-**2SA**-11:10■15:20-**1KI**-13:9 (1980),14,17(1980),22(7725)-**2KI**-19:28 -**NE**-9:13(3381)-**IS**-37:29■64:3(3381) -**JER**-1:5(3318)-**EZE**-32:2(1518)■**N.T.** -**M'T**-22:12(1525)-**JOH**-6:25(1096)■ 16:30(1831)-**AC**-9:17(2064)

CAMP-all=4264&marked-**EX**-14:19, 20^{2}■16:13■19:16,17■29:14■32:17,19, 26,27■33:7^{2},11■36:6-**LE**-4:12,21■6:11■ 8:17■9:11■10:4,5■13:46■14:3,8■16:26, 27,28■17:3^{2}■24:10,14,23-**NU**-1:52■2:3, 9,10,16,17^{2},18,24,25,31■4:5,15■5:2,3,4■ 10:14,18,22,25,34■11:1,9,26^{2},27,30,31^{2}, 32■12:14,15■14:44■15:35,36■19:3,7,9■ 31:12,13,19,24-**DE**-23:10^{2},11,12,14^{2}■ 29:11-**JOS**-5:8■6:11,14,18,23■9:6■10:6, 15,21,43-**J'G**-7:17,18,19,21■13:25■21:8, 12-**1SA**-4:3,5,6^{2},7■13:17■14:21■17:4,17■ 26:6-**2SA**-1:2,3-**1KI**-16:16-**2KI**-3:24■ 6:8(8466)■7:5^{2},7,8,10,12■19:35-**2CH**-22:1■32:21-**PS**-78:28■106:16-**IS**-29:3 (2583)■37:36-**JER**-50:29(2583)-**EZE**-4:2-**JOE**-2:11-**NA**-3:17(2583)■**N.T.**-all=3925-**HEB**-13:11,13-**RE**-20:9

CAMPED-**EX**-19:2(2583)

CAMPHIRE-**SONG**-1:14(3724)■ 4:13(3724)

CAMPS-all=4264&-**NU**-2:32■5:3■ 10:2,5,6,25-**AM**-4:10

CAN-all=3201&marked-**GE**-13:16■ 44:1-**DE**-7:17■31:2-**2SA**-12:23-**ES**-8:6^{2} -**JOB**-4:2-**PS**-78:19,20^{2}-**EC**-7:13-**IS**-56:11 (3045)-**JER**-5:22sup,22■38:5-**DA**-2:10 (3202)■3:29(3202)■10:17■**N.T.**-all=1410&marked-**M'T**-6:24,27■9:15■12:29, 34■16:3(1097),3■19:25■27:65(1492) -**M'R**-2:7,19■3:23,27■7:15■8:4■9:3,29, 39■10:26,38,39-**LU**-5:21,34■6:39■ 12:25,56(1492)■16:13,26■18:26■20:36 -**JOH**-1:46■3:2,4^{2},9,27■5:19,30,44■ 6:44,52,60,65■9:4,16■10:21■14:5■15:5 -**AC**-8:31■10:47■24:13-**RO**-8:7-**1CO**-2:14■ 3:11■12:3-**2CO**-13:8-**PH'P**-4:13(2480) -**1TH**-3:9■-**1TI**-6:7,16sup,16-**HEB**-5:2■10:1,11-**JAS**-2:14■3:8,12,12sup -**1JO**-4:20-**RE**-3:8■9:20

CANDLE-all=5216-**JOB**-18:6■ 21:17■29:3-**PS**-18:28-**PR**-20:27■ 24:20■31:18-**JER**-25:10■**N.T.**-all=3088-**M'T**-5:15-**M'R**-4:21-**LU**-8:16■ 11:33,36■15:8-**RE**-18:23■22:5

CANDLES-**ZEP**-1:12(5216)

CANDLESTICK-all=4501&marked -**EX**-25:31^{2},32^{2},33,34,35■26:35■30:27■ 31:8■35:14■37:17^{2},18^{2},19,20■39:37■ 40:4,24-**LE**-24:4-**NU**-3:31■4:9■8:2, 3,4^{2}-**2KI**-4:10-**1CH**-28:15^{2}-**2CH**-13:11 -**DA**-5:5(5043)-**ZEC**-4:2,11■**N.T.**-all=3087-**M'T**-5:15-**M'R**-4:21-**LU**-8:16■ 11:33-**HEB**-9:2-**RE**-2:5

CANDLESTICKS-all=4501-**1KI**-7:49-**1CH**-28:15^{2}-**2CH**-4:7,20-**JER**-52:19■ **N.T.**-all=3087-**RE**-1:12,13,20^{2}■2:1■11:4

CANE-**IS**-43:24(7070)-**JER**-6:20(7070)

CANKER-**2TI**-2:17(1044)

CANKERED-**JAS**-5:3(2728)

CANKERWORM-all=3218-**JOE**-1:4^{2}■ 2:25-**NA**-3:15^{2},16

CANNOT-all=3808,a=3808,3201&marked-**GE**-19:19a,22a■24:50a■29:8a■ 31:35a■32:12a■34:14a■38:22■43:22■ 44:22a,26a-**EX**-10:5■19:23a-**LE**-14:21 (369,3027)-**NU**-22:18a■23:20■24:13a■ 35:33-**DE**-28:35a-**JOS**-24:19a-**J'G**-11:35a■14:13a-**RU**-4:6^{2}a-**1SA**-12:21 (3308)■17:39,55(518)-**2SA**-5:6■14:14■ 23:6-**1KI**-3:8■8:27■18:12-**2CH**-2:6■6:18■ 24:20-**EZR**-9:1305-**NE**-6:3(369)-**JOB**-5:12a■6:30■9:3■12:14■14:5■17:10■ 19:8■23:8,9^{2}■28:15,16,17■31:31■33:21■ 36:18■37:5(408),19,23■41:17,23(1077), 26(1097),28-**PS**-40:5(408)■77:4■88:8■ 93:1(1077)■125:1■139:6a-**PR**-30:21a-**EC**-1:8a,15^{2}a■8:17a■10:14(3045)-**SONG**-8:7a-**IS**-1:13a■29:11a■38:18^{2},44:20■ 45:20■56:10a,11(3808,3045)■57:20a■ 59:1^{2},14a-**JER**-1:6■4:19■5:22■6:10a■7:8 (1115)■10:5^{2}■14:9a■18:6a■19:11a■24:3, 8■29:17■33:22■36:5a■46:23■49:23a -**LA**-3:7■4:18-**DA**-2:27(3809,3202)-**HO**-1:10-**JON**-4:11-**HAB**-2:5■**N.T.**-all=3756,1410&marked-**M'T**-5:14■6:24■ 7:18■19:11(3756)■21:27(3756,1492)■ 26:53■27:42-**M'R**-2:19■3:24,25,26■ 7:18■11:33(3756,1492)■15:31-**LU**-11:7■ 13:33(3756,1735)■14:14(3756,2192),20, 26,27,33■16:3(3756,2480),13,26(3361, 1410)-**JOH**-3:3,5■7:7,34,36■8:14(3756, 1492)■21,22,43■10:35■13:33,37■14:17■ 15:4■16:12,18(3756,1492)-**AC**-4:16, 20■5:39■15:1■19:36(368)■27:31-**RO**-8:8,26(215)-**1CO**-7:9(3756)■10:21^{2}■12:21■ 15:50-**2CO**-12:2^{2}(3756,1492),3(3756, 1492)-**GA**-3:17(3756)■5:17(3361)-**1TI**-5:25-**2TI**-2:13-**TIT**-1:2(893)■2:8(176) -**HEB**-4:15(3361,1410)■9:5■12:27(3361), 28(761)-**JAS**-1:13(551)■4:2-**2PE**-1:9 (3467)■2:14(180)-**1JO**-3:9

CANST-all=3201&marked-**EX**-33:20 -**DE**-28:27-**JOS**-7:13-**JOB**-33:5■42:2 -**DA**-5:16^{2}(3202)-**HAB**-1:13■**N.T.**-all=1410&marked-**M'T**-5:36■8:2-**M'R**-1:40■9:22,23-**LU**-5:12■6:42-**JOH**-3:8 (1492)■13:36-**AC**-21:37(1097)-**RE**-2:2

CAPTAIN-all=8269,a=7227,b=5387 &marked-**GE**-21:22,32■26:26■37:36■ 39:1■40:3,4■41:10,12-**NU**-2:3b,5b,7b, 10b,12b,14b,18b,20b,22b,25b,27b,29b■ 14:4(7218)-**JOS**-5:14,15-**J'G**-4:2,7■11:6 (7101)■11(7101)-**1SA**-9:16(5057)■10:1 (5057)■12:9■13:14(5057)■14:50■17:18, 55■18:13■22:2■26:5-**2SA**-2:8■5:2(5057)■ 10:16,18■17:25(5921)■19:13■23:19■24:2 -**1KI**-1:19■2:32^{2}■11:15,21,24■16:9,16

-2KI-1:9,10,11,13^{2}■4:13■5:1■9:5^{2},25 (7991)■15:25(7991)■18:24(6346)■20:5 (5057)■25:8a,10a,11a,12a,15a,18a,20a -1CH-11:6,21,42(7218)■19:16,18■27:5,8 -2CH-13:12(7218)■17:15-NE-9:17(7218) -IS-3:3■36:9(6346)-JER-37:13(1167)■ 39:9a,11a,13a■40:1a,2a,5a■41:10a■43:6a■ 51:27(2951)■52:12a,14a,15a,16a,19a,24a, 26a,30a-DA-2:14(7229),15(7990)■N.T.-all=5506&marked-JOH-18:12-AC-4:1 (4755)■5:24(4755),26(4755)■21:31,32, 33,37■22:24,26,27,28,29■23:10,15,17,18, 19,22■24:7,22■28:16(4759)-HEB-2:10(747)

CAPTAINS-all=8269&marked-EX-14:7(7991)■15:4(7991)-NU-31:14^{2},48^{2}, 52^{2},54-DE-1:15^{4}■20:9■29:10(7218)-JOS-10:24(7101)-1SA-8:12^{2}■22:7^{2}-2SA-4:2■ 18:1^{2},5■23:8(7991)■24:4^{2}-1KI-1:25■2:5■ 9:22(7991)■15:20■20:24(6346)■22:31, 32,33-2KI-1:14■8:21■9:5■10:25^{2}(7991)■ 11:4(3746),9,10,15,19(3746)■25:23,26 -1CH-4:42(7218)■11:11(7991),15(7218)■ 12:14(7218),18(7991),18(7218),20(7218), 21,28,34■13:1■15:25■25:1■26:26^{2}■27:1, 3■28:1^{3}■29:6-2CH-1:2■8:9(7991),9■ 11:11(5057)■16:4■17:14■18:30,31,32■ 21:9■23:1,9,14,20■25:5^{2}■26:11■32:6,21■ 33:11,14-NE-2:9-JOB-39:25-JER-13:21 (441)■40:7,13■41:11,13,16■42:1,8■43:4, 5■51:23(6346)■28(6346),57(6346) -EZE-21:22(3733)■23:6(6346),12(6346), 23(6346)-DA-3:2(6347),3(6347),27(6347)■ 6:7(6347)-NA-3:17(2951)■N.T.-all=5506 &marked-M'R-6:21-LU-22:4(4755), 52(4755)-AC-25:23-RE-6:15■19:18

CAPTIVE-all=7617,a=1540& marked-GE-14:14■34:29-EX-12:29 (7628)-NU-24:22-DE-21:10-J'G-5:12 -1KI-8:48,50-2KI-5:2■6:22■15:29a■ 16:9a■24:16(1473)-1CH-5:6a-2CH-6:37■25:12■28:8,11■30:9-PS-68:18■ 137:3-IS-49:21(1473),24(7628)■ 51:14(6808)■52:2(7628)-JER-1:3a■ 13:17,19^{2}a■20:4a■22:12a■24:1a,5(1546)■ 27:20a■28:6(1473)■29:1(1473),14a■39:9a■ 40:1(1546),1a,7a■41:10^{2},14■52:15a,27a, 28a,29a,30a-AM-1:6a■6:7^{2}a■7:11a-OB-11-NA-2:7a■N.T.-LU-21:24(163)-EPH-4:8(162)-2TI-2:26(2221)■3:6(162)

CAPTIVES-all=7617&marked-GE-31:26-NU-31:9,12(7628),19(7628)-DE-21:11(7633)■32:42(7633)-1SA-30:2,3,5 -1KI-8:46,47^{2}-2KI-24:14(1540)-2CH-6:36,38■28:5(7633),11(7633),13(7633),14 (7633),15(7633),17(7628)-PS-106:46 -IS-14:2^{2}■20:4(1546)■45:13(1546)■ 49:25(7628)■61:1(7628)-JER-28:4(1546)■ 29:1(1473),4(1473),7(1540)■43:3(1540), 12■48:46(7628),46(7633)■50:33-EZE-1:1(1473)■6:9■16:53(7628)-DA-2:25 (1123,1547)■11:8(7628)■N.T.-LU-4:18(164)

CAPTIVITY-all=7622,a=7628, b=1473,c=1546&marked-NU-21:29a -DE-21:13(7633)■28:41a■30:3-J'G-5:12a■18:30c-2KI-24:15b■25:27c-1CH-5:22b-2CH-6:37(7633),38(7633)■29:9a -EZR-1:11b■2:1a■3:8a■4:1b■6:16(1547), 19b,20b,21b■8:35a■9:7a■10:7b,16b -NE-1:2a,3a■4:4(7633)■7:6a■8:17a-ES-2:6b-JOB-42:10-PS-14:7■53:6■68:18a■ 78:61a■85:1■126:1,4-IS-5:13(1540)■ 22:17(2925)■46:2a-JER-15:2a■20:6a■ 22:22a■29:14,16b,20b,22c,31b■30:3,10a, 16(7633),18■31:23■32:44■33:7^{2},11,26■ 43:11a■46:19b,27(7633)■48:7b,11b,47■ 49:3b,6,39■52:31c-LA-1:3(1540),5a,18a■ 2:14■4:22(1540)-EZE-1:2c■3:11b,15b■ 11:24b,25b■12:4b,7b,11a■16:53^{4}■25:3b■ 29:14■30:17a,18a■33:21c■39:28(1540), 25,28b■40:1c-DA-5:13(1547)■6:13 (1547)■11:33a-HO-6:11-JOE-3:1 -AM-1:5(1540),6c,9c,15b■5:5(1540),27 (1540)■7:17(1540)■9:4a,14-OB-20^{2}c -MIC-1:16(1540)-NA-3:10a-HAB-1:9a -ZEP-2:7■3:20-ZEC-6:10b■14:2b■N.T.-RO-7:23(163)-2CO-10:5(163)-EPH-4:8(161)-RE-13:10(161)

CARBUNCLE-all=1304-EX-28:17■ 39:10-EZE-28:13

CARBUNCLES-IS-54:12(68,688)

CARCASE-all=5038&marked-LE-5:2^{3}■11:8,24,25,27,28,35,36,37,38,39,40^{2} -DE-14:8■28:26-JOS-8:29-J'G-14:8(4658), 8(1472),9(1472)-1KI-13:22,24^{2},25^{2},28^{3}, 29,30-2KI-9:37-IS-14:19(6297)■N.T. -M'T-24:28(4430)

CARCASES-all=6297&marked-GE-15:11-LE-11:11(5038)■26:30-NU-14:29, 32,33-1SA-17:46-IS-5:25(5038)■34:3■ 66:24-JER-7:33(5038)■9:22(5038)■16:4 (5038),18(5038)■19:7(5038)-EZE-6:5■ 43:7,9-NA-3:3■N.T.-HEB-3:17(2966)

CARE-1SA-10:2(1697)-2SA-18:3^{2} (7760,3820)-2KI-4:13(2731)-JER-49:31 (983)-EZE-4:16(1674)■N.T.-all=3199 &marked-M'T-13:22(3308)-LU-10:34 (1959),35(1959),40-1CO-7:21■9:9■12:25 (3309)-2CO-7:12(4710)■8:16(4710)■ 11:28(3308)-PH'P-2:20(3309)■4:10 (5426)-1TI-3:5(1959)-1PE-5:7(3308)

CARED-PS-142:4(1875)■N.T.-JOH-12:6(3199)-AC-18:17(3199)

CAREFUL-2KI-4:13(2729)-JER-17:8(1672)-DA-3:16(2818)■N.T.-LU-10:41(3309)-PH'P-4:6(3309),10(5426) -TIT-3:8(5431)

CAREFULLY-DE-15:5(8085)-MIC-1:12(2470)■N.T.-PH'P-2:28(4708) -HEB-12:17(1567)

CAREFULNESS-EZE-12:18(1674), 19(1674)■N.T.-1CO-7:32(275)-2CO-7:11(4710)

CARELESS-all=982&marked-J'G-18:7(983)-IS-32:9,10,11-EZE-30:9(983)

CARELESSLY-all=983-IS-47:8 -EZE-39:6-ZEP-2:15

CARES-all=3308-M'R-4:19-LU-8:14■21:34

CAREST-all=3199-M'T-22:16-M'R-4:38■12:14

CARETH-DE-11:12(1875)■N.T.-all=3309&marked-JOH-10:13(3199) -1CO-7:32,33,34^{2}-1PE-5:7(3199)

CARING-all supplied

CARNAL-all=4559&marked-RO-7:14■ 8:7(4561)■15:27-1CO-3:1,3^{2},4■9:11-2CO-10:4-HEB-7:16■9:10(4561)

CARNALLY-LE-18:20(7903,2233)■ 19:20(7902,2233)-NU-5:13(7902,2233)■ N.T.-ROM-8:6(4561)

CARPENTER-IS-41:7(2796)■44:13 (2796,6086)■N.T.-M'R-6:3(5045)

CARPENTER'S-M'T-13:55(5045)

CARPENTERS-all=2796&marked -2SA-5:11(2796,6086)-2KI-12:11(6086)■ 22:6-1CH-14:1(2796,6086)-2CH-24:12 -EZR-3:7-JER-24:1■29:2-ZEC-1:20

CARRIAGE-J'G-18:21(3520)■ -1SA-17:22^{2}

CARRIAGES-IS-10:28(3627)■46:1 (5385)■N.T.-AC-21:15(643)

CARRIED-all=1540,a=5375,b=935, c=7617&marked-GE-31:18(5090),26 (5090)■46:5a■50:13a-LE-10:5a-JOS-4:8(5674)-J'G-16:3(5927)-1SA-5:8^{2} (5437),9(5437)■30:2(5090),18(3947) -2SA-6:10(5186)■15:29(7725)-1KI-8:47^{2}c, 50c■17:19(5927)■21:13(3318)-2KI-7:8^{2}a■ 9:28(7392)■15:29■16:9■17:6,11,23,28, 33■20:17a■23:4a,30(7392)■24:13(3318), 14,15,15(1980)■25:7b,13a,21-1CH-5:6,26■6:15■9:1■13:7(7392),13(5186) -2CH-6:37c,38c■12:9(3947)■14:13a,15c■ 16:6a■21:17c■24:11(7725)■28:5c,8c,15 (5095),17c■33:11(3212)■34:16b■36:4b, 7b,20(1473)-EZR-2:1^{2}■5:12(1541)■ 8:35(1473)■9:4(1473)■10:6(1473),8 (1473)-NE-7:6(1473),6-ES-2:6^{3}-JOB-1:17(3947)■5:13(4116)■10:19(2986) -PS-46:2(4131)■106:46c■137:3c-IS-39:6a■ 46:3a■49:22a■53:4(5445)■63:9a-JER-13:17c,19^{2}a■24:1,5(1546)■27:20(1546), 22b■28:3b,6(1473)■29:1(1473),1,4(1473), 4,7,14■39:9■40:1(1546),1,7■41:10^{2}c,14c■ 52:9(5927),11b,15,17a,27,28-EZE-6:9c■ 17:4b■37:1(3318)-DA-1:2b■2:35(5376) -HO-10:6(2986)■12:1(2986)-JOE-3:5b -AM-1:6-OB-11c-NA-3:10(1473)■ N.T.-M'T-1:11(3350)-M'R-15:1(667) -LU-7:12(1580)■16:22(667)■24:51(399) -AC-3:2(941)■5:6(1627)■7:16(3346)■ 8:2(4792)■21:34(71)-1CO-12:2(520) -GA-2:13(4879)-EPH-4:14(4064)-HEB-13:9(4064)-2PE-2:17(1643)-JUDE-12(4064)-RE-12:15(4216)■17:3(667)■ 21:10(667)

CARRIEST-PS-90:5(2229)

CARRIETH-JOB-21:18(1589)■27:21 (5375)■N.T.-RE-17:7(941)

CARRY-all=5375,a=3318&marked -GE-37:25(3381)■42:19(935)■43:11 (3381),12(7725)■44:1■45:27■46:5■ 47:30■50:25(5927)-EX-12:46a■ 13:19(5927)■14:11a■33:15(5927) -LE-4:12a,21a■6:11a■10:4■14:45a■ 16:27a-NU-11:12■24:22(7617)-DE-14:24■28:38a-JOS-4:3(5674)-1SA-17:18 (935)■20:40(935)-2SA-15:25(7725)■ 19:18(5674)-1KI-8:46(7617)■18:12■21:10a■ 22:26(7725),34a-2KI-4:19■9:2(935)■ 17:27(1980)■18:11(1540)■25:11(1540) -1CH-10:9(1319)■15:2^{2}■23:26-2CH-2:16(5927)■6:36(7617)■18:25(7725),33a■ 20:25(4853)■25:12(7617)■29:5a,16a■ 36:6(3212)-EZR-5:15(5182)■7:15(2987) -JOB-15:12(3947)-PS-49:17(3947)-EC-5:15(3212)■10:20(3212)-IS-5:29(6403)■ 15:7■22:17(2904)■23:7(2986)■30:6■ 40:11■41:16■46:4^{2}(5445),7(5445)■ 57:13-JER-17:22a■20:4(1540),5(935)■ 39:7(935),14a■43:3(1540),12(7617) -LA-4:22(1540)-EZE-12:5a,6a,12a■22:9 (7400)■38:13-DA-11:8(935)■N.T. -M'R-6:55(4064)■11:16(1308)-LU-10:4 (941)-JOH-5:10(142)■21:18(5342)-AC-5:9(1627)■7:43(3351)-1TI-6:7(1627)

CARRYING-all=5375&marked -1SA-10:3^{3}-PS-78:9(7411)-JER-1:3(1540)■ N.T.-M'T-1:17^{2}(3350)-AC-5:10(1627)

CART-all=5699-1SA-6:7^{2},8,10,11,14^{2} -2SA-6:3^{2}-1CH-13:7^{2}-IS-5:18■28:27, 28-AM-2:13

CARVED-all=7049&marked-J'G-18:18(6459)-1KI-6:18(4734),29,29(6603), 32,35,35(2707)-2CH-33:7(6459),22 (6456)■34:3(6456),4(6456)-PS-74:6 (6603)-PR-7:16(2405)

CARVING-EX-31:5(2799)■35:33(2799)

CARVINGS-1KI-6:32(4734)

CASE-DE-19:4(1697)■22:1(7725)■ 24:13(7725)-PS-144:15(3602)■N.T. -M'T-5:20(3364)■19:10(156)

CASES-suppliws

CASEMENT-PR-7:6(822)

CASSIA-EX-30:24(6916)-PR-45:8 (7102)-EZE-27:19(6916)

CAST-all=7993,a=5307,b=7971,c= 2186,d=3332,e=3423,f=7412,g=3988 &marked-GE-21:10(1644),15■31:38 (7921),51(3384)■37:20,22,24■39:7 (5375)-EX-1:22■4:3^{2},25(5060)■7:9,10, 12■10:19(8628)■15:4(3384),25■22:31■ 23:26(7921)■25:12e■26:37e■32:19,24■ 34:24f■36:36e■37:3e,13e■38:5e,27e -LE-1:16■14:40■16:8(5414)■18:24b■ 20:23b■26:30(5414),44h-NU-19:6■35:22, 23a-DE-6:19(1920)■7:1(5394)■9:4(1920), 17,21■28:40(5394)■29:28-JOS-8:29■ 10:11,27■13:12f■18:6(3384),8,10-J'G-6:28(5422),30(5422),31(5422)■8:25■9:53■ 15:17-1SA-14:42a■18:11(2904)■20:33 (2904)-2SA-1:21(1602)■11:21■16:6 (5619),13(6080)■18:17■20:12,15(8210), 22-1KI-7:15(6696),24e,24(3333),46e■ 9:7b■13:24,25,28■14:9,24f■18:42(1457)■ 19:19■21:26f-2KI-2:16,21■3:25■4:41■ 6:6■7:15■9:25,26■10:25■13:21,23■16:3f■ 17:8f,20■19:18(5414),32(8210)■21:2f■ 23:6,12,27h■24:20-1CH-24:31a■25:8a■ 26:13a,14a■28:9c-2CH-4:3e,3(4166), 17e■7:20■11:14c■13:9(5080)■20:11(1644)■ 24:10■25:8(3782),12■28:3f■29:19c■ 30:14■33:2f,15-NE-1:9(5080)■6:16a■

9:26■10:34a■11:1a■13:8-**ES**-3:7a■9:24a-**JOB**-8:4b,20h■15:33■18:7,8b■20:15f,23b■22:29(8213)■27:22■29:24a■30:19(3384)■39:3b■40:11(6327)■41:9(2904)-**PS**-2:3■5:10(5080)■17:13(3766)■18:42(7324)■22:10,18a■36:12(1760)■37:14a,24(2904)■42:5(7817),6(7817),11(7817)■43:2c,5(7817)■44:2b,9c,23c■51:11■55:3(4131),22■56:7(3381)■60:1c,8,10c■62:4(5080)■71:9■74:1c,7b■76:6(7290)■77:7c■78:49b,55(1644)■80:8(1644)■89:38c,44(4048)■94:14(5203)■102:10■108:9,11c■140:10a■144:6(1299)-**PR**-1:14a■7:26a■16:33(2904)■22:10(1644)-**EC**-3:5,6■11:1b-**IS**-2:20■5:24h■6:13(7995)■14:19■16:2b■19:8■25:7(3874)■26:19a■28:2(3240),25(6327),25(7760)■30:22(2219)■31:7h■34:3,17a■37:19(5414),33(8210)■38:17■41:9h■57:14(5549),20(1644)■58:7(4788)■62:10(5549)■66:5(5077)-**JER**-6:6(8210),15(3782)■7:15^{2},29■8:12(3782)■9:19■14:16■15:1b■16:13(2904)■18:15(5549)■22:19,26(2904),28,28(2904)■26:23■28:16b■31:37h■33:24h,26h■36:23,30■38:6,9,11(5499),12(5499)■41:9,14(5437)■50:26(5549)■51:34(1740),63■52:3-**LA**-2:1,7c,10(5927)■3:31c,53(3034)-**EZE**-4:2(8210)■5:4■6:4a■7:19■11:16(7368)■15:4(5414)■16:5■18:31■19:12■20:7,8■21:22(8210)■23:35■26:8(8210)■27:30(5927)■28:16(2490),17■31:16(3381)■32:4(2904),18(3381)■36:5(4054)■43:24-**DA**-3:6g,11g,15g,20g,21g,24g■6:7g,12g,16g,24g■7:9g■8:7,10a,11,12■11:12a,15(8210)-**HO**-8:3c,5c■9:17h■14:5(5221)-**JOE**-1:7■3:3(3032)-**AM**-1:11(7843)■4:3■8:3,8(1644)-**OB**-11(3032)-**JON**-1:5(2904),7^{2}a,12(2904),15(2904)■2:3,4(1644)-**MIC**-2:5,9(1644)■4:7(1972)■7:19-**NA**-3:6,10(3032)-**ZEP**-3:15(6437)-**ZEC**-1:21(3034)■5:8^{2}■9:4f■10:6c■11:13^{2}-**MAL**-3:11(7921)■**N.T.**-all=906,a=1544&marked-**M'T**-3:10■4:6,12(3860)■5:13,25,29^{2},30^{2}■6:30■7:5^{2}a,6,19,22a■8:12a,16a,31a■9:33a■10:1a,8a■12:24a,26a,27^{2}a,28a■13:42,47,48,50■15:17a,26,30(4496)■17:19a,27■18:8^{2},9^{2},30■21:12a,21,39a■22:13a■25:30a■27:5(4496),35,44(3679)-**M'R**-1:34a,39a■3:15a,23a■4:26■6:13a■7:26a,27■9:18a,22,28a,42,45,47■11:7(1911),15a,23■12:4(3036),8a,41^{2},43^{2},44^{2}■14:51(4016)■16:9a,17a-**LU**-1:29(1260)■3:9■4:9,29(2630)■6:22a,42a■9:25(2210),40a■11:18a,19^{2}a,20a■12:5(1685),28,58■13:19,32a■14:35■17:2(4496)■19:35(1977),43(4016),45a■20:12a,15a■21:3,4^{2}■22:41(1000)■23:19,25,34-**JOH**-3:24■6:37a■8:7,59■9:34a,35a■12:31a■15:6^{2}■19:24(2975),24■21:6^{2},7-**AC**-7:19(4160,1570),21(1620),58a■12:8(4016)■16:23,37■22:23(4496)■27:19(4496),26(1601),29(4496),30(1614),38a,43(641)-**RO**-11:1(683),2(683)■13:12(656)-**1CO**-7:35(1911)-**2CO**-4:9(2598)■7:6(5011)-**GA**-4:30a-**1TI**-5:12(114)-**HEB**-10:35(577)-**2PE**-2:4(5020)-**RE**-2:10,14,22■4:10■8:5,7,8■12:4,9^{3},10(2598),13,15,16■14:19■18:19,21■19:20■20:3,10,14,15

CASTAWAY-**1CO**-9:27(96)

CASTEDST-**PS**-73:18(5307)

CASTEST-**JOB**-15:4(6565)-**PS**-50:17(7993)■88:14(2186)

CASTETH-**JOB**-21:10(7921)-**PS**-147:6(8213),17(7993)-**PR**-10:3(1920)■19:15(5037)■21:22(3381)■26:18(3384)-**IS**-40:19(6884)-**JER**-6:7^{2}(6979)■**N.T.**-all=1544&marked-**M'T**-9:34-**M'R**-3:22-**LU**-11:15-**1JO**-4:18(906)-**3JO**-10-**RE**-6:13(906)

CASTING-**2SA**-8:2(7901)-**1KI**-7:37(4165)-**EZR**-10:1(5307)-**JOB**-6:21(2866)-**EZE**-17:17(8210)-**MIC**-6:14(3445)■**N.T.**-all=906&marked-**M'T**-4:18■27:35-**M'R**-1:16■9:38(1544)■10:50(577)■15:24-**LU**-9:49(1544)■11:14(1544)■21:1,2-**RO**-11:15(580)-**2CO**-10:5(2507)-**1PE**-5:7(1977)

CASTLE-**1CH**-11:5(4686),7(4679)-**PR**-18:19(759)■**N.T.**-all=3925-**AC**-21:34,37■22:24■23:10,16,32

CASTLES-all=2918&marked-**GE**-25:16-**NU**-31:10-**1CH**-6:54■27:25(4026)-**2CH**-17:2(1003)■27:4(1003)

CATCH-**EX**-22:6(4672)-**J'G**-21:21(2414)-**1KI**-20:33(2480)-**2KI**-7:12(8610)-**PS**-10:9(2414)■35:8(3920)■109:11(5367)-**JER**-5:26(3920)-**EZE**-19:3(2963),6(2963)-**HAB**-1:15(1641)■**N.T.**-**M'R**-12:13(64)-**LU**-5:10(2221)■11:54(2340)

CATCHETH-**LE**-17:13(6679)■**N.T.**-**M'T**-13:19(726)-**JOH**-10:12(726)

CATERPILLER-all=2625-**1KI**-8:37-**PS**-78:46-**IS**-33:4-**JOE**-1:4■2:25

CATERPILLERS-all=3218&marked-**2CH**-6:28(2625)-**PS**-105:34-**JER**-51:14,27

CATTLE-all=4735,a=929,b=6629&marked-**GE**-1:24a,25a,26a■2:20a■3:14a■4:20■6:20a■7:14a,21a,23a■8:1a,17a■9:10a■13:2,7^{2}■29:7■30:29,32^{2}(7716),39b,40b,41^{2}b,42b,43b■31:8^{2}b,9,10^{2}b,12b,18^{2},41b,43b■33:14(4399),17■34:5,23■36:6,7■46:6,32,34■47:6,16^{2},17^{3},18a-**EX**-9:3,4^{2},6^{2},7,19,20,21■10:26■12:29a,38■17:3■20:10a■34:19-**LE**-1:2a■5:2a■19:19a■25:7a■26:22a-**NU**-3:41^{2}a,45■20:4(1165),19■31:9a■32:1^{2},4^{2},16,26a■35:3a-**DE**-2:35a■3:7a,19^{2}■5:14a■7:14a■11:15a■13:15a■20:14a■28:4a,11a,51a■30:9a-**JOS**-1:14■8:2a,27a■11:14a■14:4■21:2a■22:8-**J'G**-6:5■18:21-**1SA**-23:5■30:20-**1KI**-1:9(4806),19(4806),25(4806)-**2KI**-3:9a,17-**1CH**-5:9,21a■7:21a-**2CH**-14:15a■26:10a-**NE**-9:37a■10:36a-**JOB**-36:33-**PS**-50:10a■78:48(1165)■104:14a■107:38a■148:10a-**EC**-2:7-**IS**-7:25(7716)■30:23■43:23(7716)■46:1a-**JER**-9:10■49:32(4734)-**EZE**-34:17(7716),20^{2}(7716),22(7716)■38:12,13-**JOE**-1:18(1241)-**JON**-4:11a-**HAG**-1:11a-**ZEC**-2:4a■13:5(7069)■**N.T.**-**LU**-17:7(4165)-**JOH**-4:12(2353)

CAUGHT-all=2388&marked-**GE**-22:13(270)■39:12(8610)-**EX**-4:4-**NU**-31:32(962)-**J'G**-1:6(270)■8:14(3920)■15:4(3920)■21:23(1497)-**1SA**-17:35-**2SA**-2:16■18:9-**1KI**-1:50,51(270)■2:28■11:30(8610)-**2KI**-4:27-**2CH**-22:9(3920)-**PR**-7:13-**EC**-9:12(270)-**JER**-50:24(8610)■**N.T.**-all=4884&marked-**M'T**-14:31(1949)■21:39(2983)-**M'R**-12:3(2983)-**LU**-8:29-**JOH**-21:3(4084),10(4084)-**AC**-6:12■8:39(726)■16:19(1949)■19:29■26:21(4815)■27:15-**2CO**-12:2(726),4(726),16(2983)-**1TH**-4:17(726)-**RE**-12:5(726)

CAUL-all=3508&marked-**EX**-29:13,22-**LE**-3:4,10,15■4:9■7:4■8:16,25■9:10,19-**HO**-13:8(5458)

CAULS-**IS**-3:18(7636)

CAUSE-all=7379,a=2600&marked-**EX**-9:16(5668)■22:9(1697)■23:2,3,6-**LE**-24:19(5414)-**NU**-16:11(3651)■27:5(4941)-**DE**-1:17(1697)■28:7(5414),25(5414)-**JOS**-5:4(1697)■20:4(1697)-**1SA**-17:29(1697)■19:5a■24:15■25:39-**2SA**-15:4(4941)-**1KI**-8:45(4941),49(4941),59^{2}(4941)■11:27(1697)■12:15(5438)-**2CH**-6:35(4941)■39(4941)■10:15(5252)■19:10-**JOB**-2:3a■5:8(1700)■9:17a■13:18(4941)■23:4(4941)■29:16■31:13(4941)-**PS**-7:4(7387)■9:4(1779)■25:3(7387)■35:7^{2}a,19a,23■43:1■69:4a■74:22■109:3a■119:78(8267),154,161a■140:12(1779)-**PR**-1:11a■3:30a■18:17■22:23■23:11,29a■24:28a■25:9■29:7(1779)■31:8(1779)-**EC**-7:10(1961)-**IS**-1:28■41:21■52:4(657)-**JER**-5:28(1779)■11:20■15:4(5414)■20:12■22:16(1779)■30:13(1779)■32:35(4616)■50:34■51:36-**LA**-3:36■52a,59(4941)-**EZE**-14:23a■26:17(5414)-**DA**-2:12(3606,6903,1836)-**JON**-1:7(7945),8(834)-**MIC**-7:9■**N.T.**-all=1223&marked-**M'T**-5:22(1500),32(3056)■10:21(2289)■19:3(156),5(1752)-**M'R**-10:7(1752)■13:12(2289)-**LU**-8:47(156)■21:16(2289)■23:22(158)-**JOH**-12:18,27■15:25(1432)-**AC**-10:21(156)■13:28(156)■19:40(158)■23:28(156)■25:14(3588,2596)■28:18(156),20(156)-**RO**-1:26■13:6■15:9,22(1352)■16:17(4160)-**1CO**-4:17■11:10,30-**2CO**-4:16(1352)■7:12^{2}(1752)-**EPH**-3:1(5484),14(5484)■5:31(873)-**PH'P**-2:18(846)-**COL**-1:9(1223,5124)■4:16(4160)-**1TH**-2:13■3:5-**2TH**-2:11-**1TI**-1:16-**2TI**-1:12(156)-**TIT**-1:5(5484)-**HEB**-2:11(156)■9:15-**RE**-12:15(4160)■13:15(4160)

CAUSED-all=5414&marked-**LE**-24:20-**NU**-31:16(1961)-**EZE**-16:7■32:23,24,25,26,32■**N.T.**-**JOH**-11:37(4160)-**AC**-15:3(4160)-**2CO**-2:5(3076)

CAUSELESS-**1SA**-25:31(2600)-**PR**-26:2(2600)

CAUSES-**EX**-18:19(1697),26(1697)-**JER**-3:8(182)-**LA**-3:58(7379)■**N.T.**-**AC**-26:21(1752)

CAUSEST-all supplied

CAUSETH-**PR**-10:10(5414)■**N.T.**-all=4160&marked-**M'T**-5:32-**2CO**-2:14(2358)■9:11(2716)-**RE**-13:12,16

CAUSEWAY-**1CH**-26:16(4546),18(4546)

CAUSING-all supplied

CAVE-all=4631-**GE**-19:30■23:9,11,17,19,20■25:9■49:29,30,32■50:13-**JOS**-10:16,17,18,22^{2},23,27-**1SA**-22:1■24:3^{2},7,8,10-**2SA**-23:13-**1KI**-18:4,13■19:9,13-**1CH**-11:15-**PS**-57:t■142:t■**N.T.**-**JOH**-11:38(4693)

CAVE'S-**JOS**-10:27(4631)

CAVES-all=4631&marked-**J'G**-6:2-**1SA**-13:6-**JOB**-30:6(2356)-**IS**-2:19(4247)-**EZE**-33:27■**N.T.**-**HEB**-11:38(3692)

CEASE-all=7673,a=2308&marked-**GE**-8:22-**EX**-9:29a-**NU**-8:25(7725)■11:25(3254)■17:5(7918)-**DE**-15:11a■32:26-**JOS**-22:25-**J'G**-15:7a■20:28a-**1SA**-7:8(2790)-**2CH**-16:5-**EZR**-4:21(989),23(989)■5:5(989)-**NE**-4:11■6:3-**JOB**-3:17a■10:20a■14:7-**PS**-37:8(7503)■46:9■85:4(6565)■89:44-**PR**-18:18■19:27a■20:3(7674)■22:10■23:4a-**EC**-12:3(988)-**IS**-1:16a■2:22a■10:25(3615)■13:11■16:10■17:3■21:2■30:11■33:1(8552)-**JER**-7:34■14:17(1820)■16:9■17:8(4185)■31:36■36:29■48:35-**LA**-2:18(1826)-**EZE**-6:6■7:24■12:23■16:41■23:27,48■26:13■30:10,13,18■33:28■34:10,25-**DA**-9:27■11:18-**HO**-1:4■2:11-**AM**-7:5a■**N.T.**-all=3973&marked-**AC**-13:10-**1CO**-13:8-**EPH**-1:16-**COL**-1:9-**2PE**-2:14(180)

CEASED-all=7673&marked-**GE**-18:11(2308)-**EX**-9:33(2308),34(2308)-**JOS**-5:12-**J'G**-2:19(5307)■5:7(2308)-**1SA**-2:5(2308)■25:9(5117)-**EZR**-4:24(989),24(1934,989)-**JOB**-32:1-**PS**-35:15(1826)■77:2(6313)-**IS**-14:4^{2}-**LA**-5:14,15-**JON**-1:15(5975)■**N.T.**-all=3973&marked-**M'T**-14:32(2869)-**M'R**-4:39(2869)■6:51(2869)-**LU**-7:45(1257)■8:24■11:1-**AC**-5:42■20:1,31■21:14(2270)-**GA**-5:11(2673)-**HEB**-4:10(2664)■10:2-**1PE**-4:1

CEASETH-all=7673&marked-**PS**-12:1(1584)■49:8(2308)-**PR**-26:20(8367)-**IS**-16:4(3615)■24:8^{2}■33:8-**LA**-3:49(1820)-**HO**-7:4■**N.T.**-**AC**-6:13(3973)

CEASING-**1SA**-12:23(2308)■**N.T.**-all=89&marked-**AC**-12:5(1618)-**RO**-1:9-**1TH**-1:3■2:13■5:17-**2TI**-1:3(83)

CEDAR-all=730&marked-**LE**-14:4,6,49,51,52-**NU**-19:6■24:6-**2SA**-5:11■7:2,7-**1KI**-4:33■5:6,8,10■6:9,10,15,16,18^{2},20,36■7:2^{2},3,7,12■9:11-**2KI**-14:9■19:23-**1CH**-22:4^{2}-**2CH**-1:15■2:8■9:27■25:18-**EZR**-3:7-**JOB**-40:17-**PS**-92:12-**SONG**-1:17■8:9-**IS**-41:19-**JER**-22:14,15-**EZE**-17:3,22,23■27:24(729)■31:3-**ZEP**-2:14(731)-**ZEC**-11:2

CEDARS-all=730-**J'G**-9:15-**1KI**-7:11■10:27-**1CH**-14:1■17:1,6-**2CH**-2:3

-PS-29:5^2■80:10■104:16■148:9-SONG-5:15-IS-2:13■9:10■14:8■37:24■44:14-JER-22:7,23-EZE-27:5■31:8-AM-2:9-ZEC-11:1

CELEBRATE-LE-23:32(7673),41(2287)-IS-38:18(1984)

CELESTIAL-1CO-15:40^2(2032)

CELLARS-1CH-27:27(214),28(214)

CENSER-all=4829&marked-LE-10:1■16:12-NU-16:17^3,18,46-2CH-26:19(4730)-EZE-8:11(4730)■N.T.-HEB-9:4(2369)-RE-8:3(3031),5(3031)

CENSERS-all=4829-NU-4:14■16:6,17,37,38,39-1KI-7:50-2CH-4:22

CENTURION-all=1543&marked-M'T-8:5,8,13■27:54-M'R-15:39(2760),44(2760),45(2760)-LU-7:6■23:47-AC-10:1,22■22:25,26■24:23■27:1,6,11,31,43■28:16

CENTURION'S-LU-7:2(1543)

CENTURIONS-all=1543&marked-AC-21:32■23:17,23

CEREMONIES-NU-9:3(4941)

CERTAIN-GE-38:1(376),2(376)-EX-16:4(1697)-NU-16:2(582)-DE-3:14(3559)■17:4(3559)-J'G-9:53(259)■13:2(259)■19:1(376),22(582)-1SA-1:1(259)-2SA-18:10(259)-1KI-2:37(3045),42(3045)■11:17(582)■20:35(259)-2KI-4:1(259)■8:6(259)-2CH-8:13(1697)■28:12(582)-EZR-10:16(582)-NE-13:25(582)-ES-2:5(376)■3:8(259)-JER-26:15(3045),17(582)■41:5(582)-EZE-14:1(582)■20:1(582)-DA-2:45(3330)■3:8(1400),12(1400)■8:13(6422)■10:5(259)■11:13(6256)■N.T.-all=5100&marked-M'T-8:19(1520)■9:3■12:38■17:14■18:23(444)■20:20■21:33(444,5100)■22:2(444)-M'R-2:6■5:25■7:1■11:5■12:13,42(1520)■14:51,57-LU-1:5■5:12(1520),17(1520)■6:2■7:2,41■8:2,22(1520),27■9:57■10:25,30,31,33,38^2■11:1,27,37■12:16■13:6,31■14:2,16■15:11■16:1,19,20■17:12■18:9,18,35■19:12■20:9,27,39■21:2■22:56■23:19■24:22,24-JOH-4:46■5:5■11:1■12:20-AC-3:2■5:1,2■6:9■8:9,36■9:10,19,33,36■10:1,11,23,48■11:5■12:1■13:1,6■14:8■15:1,2,5,24■16:1^2,12,14,16■17:5,6,18,20,28,34■18:2,7,24■19:1,13,24,31■20:9■21:10,16■23:12,17■24:1,18,24■25:13,14,19,26(804)■27:1,16,26,39-RO-15:26-1CO-4:11(790)-GA-2:12-1TI-6:7(1212)-HEB-2:6(4225)■4:4(4225),7■10:27-JUDE-4

CERTAINLY-EX-3:12(3588)-JER-8:8(403)-LA-2:16(389)■N.T.-LU-23:47(3689)

CERTAINTY-1SA-23:23(3559)-PR-22:21(7189)-DA-2:8(3330)■N.T.-LU-1:4(803)-AC-21:34(804)■22:30(804)

CERTIFIED-EZR-4:14(3046)-ES-2:22(559)

CERTIFY-all=3046&marked-2SA-15:28(5046)-EZR-4:16■5:10■7:24-GA-1:11(1107)

CHAFED-2SA-17:8(4751)

CHAFF-all=4671&marked-JOB-21:18-PS-1:4■35:5-IS-5:24(2842)■17:13■29:5■33:11(2842)■41:15-JER-23:28(8401)-DA-2:35(5784)-HO-13:3-ZEP-2:2■N.T.-M'T-3:12(892)-LU-3:17(892)

CHAIN-all=2002&marked-GE-41:42(7242)-1KI-7:17(8333)-PS-73:6(6059)-SONG-4:9(6060)-LA-3:7(5178)-EZE-7:23(7569)■16:11(7242)-DA-5:7,16,29■N.T.-all=254-AC-28:20-2TI-1:16-RE-20:1

CHAINS-all=8333&marked-EX-28:14^2,22(8331),24(5688)■39:15,17(5688),18(5688)-NU-31:50(685)-J'G-8:26(6060)-1KI-6:21(7569)-2CH-3:5,16^2-PS-68:6(3574)■149:8(2131)-PR-1:9(6060)-SONG-1:10(2737)-IS-3:19(5188)■40:19(7569)■45:14(2131)-JER-39:7(5178)■40:1(246),4(246)■52:11(5178)-EZE-19:4(2397),9(2397)-NA-3:10(2131)■N.T.-all=254&marked-M'R-5:3,4^2-LU-8:29-AC-12:6,7■21:33-2PE-2:4(4577)-JUDE-6(1199)

CHALCEDONY-RE-21:19(5472)

CHALKSTONES-IS-27:9(68,1615)

CHALLENGETH-EX-22:9(559)

CHAMBER-all=2315,a=3957&marked-GE-43:30-J'G-3:24■15:1■16:9,12-2SA-13:10^2■18:33(5944)-1KI-1:15■6:6(3326),8(6763)■14:28(8372)■17:23(5944)■20:30■22:25-2KI-1:2(5944)■4:10(5944),11(5944)■9:2■23:11a,12(5944)-2CH-12:11(8372)■18:24-EZR-10:6a-NE-3:30(5393)■13:4a,5a,7(5393),8a-PS-19:5(2646)-SONG-3:4-JER-35:4^{3}a■36:10a,12a,20a,21a-EZE-40:7(8372),13(8372),45a,46a■41:5(6763),9(6763)■42:1a-DA-6:10(5952)-JOE-2:16■N.T.-all=5253-AC-9:37,39■20:8

CHAMBERING-RO-13:13(2845)

CHAMBERLAIN-all=5631-2KI-23:11-ES-2:3,14,15■N.T.-AC-12:20(1909,3588,2846)-RO-16:23(3623)

CHAMBERLAINS-all=5631-ES-1:10,12,15■2:21■4:4,5■6:2,14■7:9

CHAMBERS-all=3957&marked-1KI-6:5(3326),5(6763),10(3326)-1CH-9:26,33■23:28■28:11(5944),12-2CH-3:9(5944)■31:11-EZR-8:29-NE-10:37,38,39■12:44(5393)■13:9-JOB-9:9(2315)-PS-104:3(5944),13(5944)■105:30(2315)-PR-7:27(2315)■24:4(2315)-SONG-1:4(2315)-IS-26:20(2315)-JER-22:13(5944),14(5944)■35:2-EZE-8:12(2315)■21:14(2315)■40:7(8372),10(8372),12^2(8372),16(8372),17^2,21(8372),29(8372),33(8372),36(8372),38,44■41:6^2(6763),7(6763),8(6763),9(6763),10,11(6763),26(6763)■42:4,5,7^2,8,9,10,11,12,13^2■44:19■45:5■46:19■N.T.-M'T-24:26(5009)

CHAMELEON-LE-11:30(3581)

CHAMOIS-DE-14:5(2169)

CHAMPAIGN-DE-11:30(6160)

CHAMPION-1SA-17:4(376,1143),23(376,1143),51(1368)

CHANCE-DE-22:6(7122)-1SA-6:9(4745)-2SA-1:6(7122)-EC-9:11(6294)■N.T.-LU-10:31(4795)-1CO-15:37(5177)

CHANCELLOR-all=1169,2942-EZR-4:8,9,17

CHANCETH-DE-23:10(4745)

CHANGE-all=4171&marked-GE-35:2(2498)-LE-27:10^2,33^2,33(8545)-J'G-14:12(2487),13(2487),19(2487)-JOB-14:14(2487)■17:12(7760)-PS-102:26(2498)-PR-24:21(8138)-IS-9:10(2498)-JER-2:36(8138)■13:23(2015)-DA-7:25(8133)-HO-4:7-HAB-1:11(2498)-ZEC-3:4(4254)-MAL-3:6(8138)■N.T.-AC-6:14(236)-RO-1:26(3337)-GA-4:20(236)-PH'P-3:21(3345)-HEB-7:12(3331)

CHANGEABLE-IS-3:22(4254)

CHANGED-all=8133&marked-GE-31:7(2498),41(2498)■41:14(2498)-LE-13:16(2015),55(2015)-NU-32:38(5437)-1SA-21:13(8138)-2SA-12:20(2498)-2KI-24:17(5437)■25:29(8132)-JOB-30:18(2664)-PS-34t■102:26(2498)■106:20(4171)-EC-8:1(8132)-IS-24:5(2498)-JER-2:11^2(4171)■48:11(4171)■52:33(8138)-LA-4:1(8132)-EZE-5:6(4171)-DA-2:9■3:19,27,28■4:16■5:6,9,10■6:8,15,17■7:28-MIC-2:4(4171)■N.T.-all=236&marked-AC-28:6(3328)-RO-1:23,25(3337)-1CO-15:51,52-2CO-3:18(3339)-HEB-1:12■7:12(3346)

CHANGERS-JOH-2:14(2773)

CHANGERS'-JOH-2:15(2855)

CHANGES-all=2487-GE-45:22^2-2KI-5:5,22,23-JOB-10:17-PS-55:19

CHANGEST-JOB-14:20(8138)

CHANGETH-PS-15:4(4171)-DA-2:21(8133)

CHANGING-RU-4:7(8545)

CHANNEL-IS-27:12(7641)

CHANNELS-all=650-2SA-22:16-PS-18:15-IS-8:7

CHANT-AM-6:5(6527)

CHAPEL-AM-7:13(4720)

CHAPITER-all=3805&marked-1KI-7:16^2,17^2,18,20,31-2KI-25:17^3-2CH-3:15(6858)-JER-52:22^2(3805)

CHAPITERS-all=3805&marked-EX-36:38(7218)■38:17(7218),19(7218),28(7218)-1KI-7:16,17,18,19,20,41^2,42-2CH-4:12^2,13-JER-52:22

CHAPMAN-2CH-9:14(582,8446)

CHAPT-JER-14:4(2865)

CHARGE-all=4931,a=6680&marked-GE-26:5■28:6a-EX-6:13a■19:21(5749)-LE-8:35-NU-1:53■3:7^2,8,25,28,31,32,36,38^2■4:27,28,31,32■5:19(7650),21(7650)■8:26^2■9:19,23■18:3,4,5^2,8■27:19a,23a■31:30,47,49(3027)-DE-3:28a■11:1■21:8(7130)■31:14a,23a-JOS-22:3-2SA-14:8a■18:5a-1KI-2:3■4:28(4941)■11:28(5447)-2KI-7:17(5921)-1CH-9:27,28(5921)■22:12a■23:32^3-2CH-13:11■30:17(5921)-NE-7:2a■10:32(5414)-ES-3:9(6213)■4:8a-JOB-34:13(6485)-PS-35:11(7592)■91:11a-SONG-2:7(7650)■3:5(760)■5:8(7650),9(7650)■8:4(7650)-IS-10:6a-JER-39:11a■47:7a■52:25(6496)-EZE-9:1(6486)■40:45,46■44:8^2,11(6486),14,15,16■48:11-ZEC-3:7■N.T.-all=3853&marked-M'T-4:6(1781)-M'R-9:25(2004)-LU-4:10(1781)-AC-7:60(2476)■8:27(1909)■16:24(3852)■23:29(1462)-RO-8:33(1458,2596)-1CO-9:18(77)-1TH-5:27(3726)-1TI-1:3,18(3852)■5:7,21(1263)■6:13,17-2TI-4:1(1263),16(3049)

CHARGEABLE-2SA-13:25(3513)-NE-5:15(3513)■N.T.-2CO-11:9(2655)-1TH-2:9(1912)-2TH-3:8(1912)

CHARGED-all=6680&marked-GE-26:11■28:1■40:4(6485)■49:29-EX-1:22-DE-1:16■24:5(5674,5921)■27:11-JOS-18:8■22:5-RU-2:9-1SA-14:27(7650),28(7650)-2SA-11:19■18:12-1KI-2:1,43■13:9-2KI-17:15,35-1CH-22:6,13-2CH-19:9■36:23(6485)-EZR-1:2(6485)-NE-13:19(559)-ES-2:10,20-JOB-1:22(5414)■4:18(7760)-JER-32:13■35:8■N.T.-all=1291&marked-M'T-9:30(1690)■12:16(2008)■16:20■17:9(1781)-M'R-1:43(1690)■3:12(2008)■5:43■7:36^2■8:15,30(2008)■9:9■10:48(2008)-LU-5:14(3853)■8:56(3853)■9:21(2008)-AC-23:22(3853)-1TH-2:11(3143)-1TI-5:16(916)

CHARGEDST-EX-19:23(5749)

CHARGER-all=7086-NU-7:13,19,25,31,37,43,49,55,61,67,73,79,85■N.T.-all=4094-M'T-14:8,11-M'R-6:25,28

CHARGERS-NU-7:84(7086)-EZR-1:9^2(105)

CHARGES-all=4931-2CH-8:14■31:16,17■35:2■N.T.-AC-21:24(1159)-1CO-9:7(3800)

CHARGEST-2SA-3:8(6485)

CHARGING-AC-16:23(3853)-2TI-2:14(1263)

CHARIOT-all=7393,a=4818&marked-GE-41:43a■46:29a-EX-14:6,25a-J'G-4:15a■5:28-2SA-8:4-1KI-7:33a■10:29a■12:18a■20:25,33a■22:34(7395),35a,35,38-2KI-2:11,12■5:9,21a,26a■7:14■9:21^2,24,27a■10:15a,16■13:14-1CH-18:4■28:18a-2CH-1:14,17a■8:6■9:25■10:18a■18:33(7395),34a■35:24a,24-PS-46:9(5699)■76:6■104:3(7398)-SONG-3:9(668)-IS-21:7^2,9■43:17-JER-51:21-MIC-1:13a-ZEC-6:2^{2}a,3^{2}a■9:10■N.T.-all=716-AC-8:28,29,38

CHARIOTS-all=7393,a=4818&marked-GE-50:9-EX-14:7^2,9,17,18,23,26,28■15:4a,19-DE-11:4■20:1-JOS-11:4,6a,9a■17:16,18■24:6-J'G-1:19■4:3,7,13^2,15,16■5:28a-1SA-8:11^{2}a,12■13:5-2SA-1:6■8:4sup,4■10:18■15:1a-1KI-1:5■4:26(4817)■9:19,22■10:26^3■16:9■20:1,21■22:31,32,33-2KI-6:14,15,17■7:6■8:21^2■10:2■13:7■18:24■19:23■23:11-1CH-18:4^2■19:6,7,18-2CH-1:14^2■8:9■9:25a■12:3■14:9a■16:8■18:30,31,32■21:9^2-PS-20:7■68:17-SONG-1:9■6:12a-IS-2:7a■22:6,7,18a■31:1■36:9■37:24■66:15a,20-JER-4:13a■17:25■22:4■46:9■47:3■50:37-EZE-23:24(2021)■

26:7,10▪27:20(7396)▪39:20-**DA**-11:40 -**JOE**-2:5a-**MIC**-5:10a-**NA**-2:3,4,13▪ 3:2a-**HAB**-3:8a-**HAG**-2:22a-**ZEC**-6:1a▪ **N.T.**-**RE**-9:9(716)▪18:13(4480)

CHARITABLY-**RO**-14:15(2596,26)

CHARITY-all=26-**1CO**-8:1▪13:1,2, 3,4^2,8,13^2▪14:1▪16:14-**COL**-3:14-**1TH**-3:6-**2TH**-1:3-**1TI**-1:5▪2:15▪4:12-**2TI**-2:22▪3:10-**TIT**-2:2-**1PE**-4:8^2▪5:14 -**2PE**-1:7-**3JO**-6-**JUDE**-12-**RE**-2:19

CHARMED-**JER**-8:17(3908)

CHARMER-**DE**-18:11(2266,2267)

CHARMERS-**PS**-58:5(3907)-**IS**-19:3(328)

CHARMING-**PS**-58:5(2266,2267)

CHASE-all=7291&marked-**LE**-26:7, 8,36-**DE**-32:30-**JOS**-23:10-**PS**-35:5(1760)

CHASED-all=7291&marked-**DE**-1:44-**JOS**-7:5▪8:24▪10:10▪11:8-**J'G**-9:40▪20:43-**NE**-13:28(1272)-**JOB**-18:18(5074)▪20:8(5074)-**IS**-13:14 (5080)▪17:13-**LA**-3:52(6679)

CHASETH-**PR**-19:26(1272)

CHASING-**1SA**-17:53(1814)

CHASTE-all=53-**2CO**-11:2-**TIT**-2:5-**1PE**-3:2

CHASTEN-all=3256&marked-**2SA**-7:14(3198)-**PS**-6:1▪38:1-**PR**-19:18-**DA**-10:12(6031)▪**N.T.**-**RE**-3:19(3811)

CHASTENED-**DE**-21:18(3256) -**JOB**-33:19(3198)-**PS**-73:14(8433)▪ 118:18(3256)▪**N.T.**-all=3811-**1CO**-11:32-**2CO**-6:9-**HEB**-12:10

CHASTENEST-**PS**-94:12(3256)

CHASTENETH-**DE**-8:5^2(3256) -**PR**-13:24(4148)▪**N.T.**-**HEB**-12:6 (3811),7(3811)

CHASTENING-all=4148-**JOB**-5:17-**PR**-3:11-**IS**-26:16▪**N.T.**-all= 3809-**HEB**-12:5,7,11

CHASTISE-all=3256-**LE**-26:28 -**DE**-22:18-**1KI**-12:11,14-**HO**-7:12▪ 10:10▪**N.T.**-**LU**-23:16(3811),22(3811)

CHASTISED-all=3256-**1KI**-12:11, 14-**2CH**-10:11,14-**JER**-31:18

CHASTISEMENT-all=4148-**DE**-11:2-**IS**-53:5-**JER**-30:14▪**N.T.**-**HEB**-12:8(3809)

CHASTISETH-**PS**-94:10(3256)

CHATTER-**IS**-38:14(6850)

CHECK-**JOB**-20:3(4148)

CHECKER-**1KI**-7:17(7639)

CHEEK-all=3895&marked-**1KI**-22:24-**2CH**-18:23-**JOB**-16:10-**PS**-3:7 -**LA**-3:30-**JOE**-1:6(4973)-**MIC**-5:1▪**N.T.**-**M'T**-5:39(4600)-**LU**-6:29(4600)

CHEEKS-all=3895-**DE**-18:3-**SONG**-1:10▪5:13-**IS**-50:6-**LA**-1:2

CHEER-**DE**-24:5(8055)-**EC**-11:9 (3190)▪**N.T.**-all=2293&marked-**M'T**-9:2▪14:27-**M'R**-6:50-**JOH**-16:33-**AC**-23:11▪27:22(2114),25(2114),36(2114)

CHEERETH-**J'G**-9:13(8055)

CHEERFUL-**PR**-15:13(3190) -**ZEC**-8:19(2896)▪9:17(5107)▪**N.T.**-**2CO**-9:7(2431)

CHEERFULLY-**AC**-24:10(2115)

CHEERFULNESS-**RO**-12:8(2432)

CHEESE-**2SA**-17:29(8194)-**JOB**-10:10(1385)

CHEESES-**1SA**-17:18(2757,2461)

CHERISH-**1KI**-1:2(5532)

CHERISHED-**1KI**-1:4(5532)

CHERISHETH-**EPH**-5:29(2282) -**1TH**-2:7(2282)

CHERUB-all=3742-**EX**-25:19^2▪ 37:8^2-**2SA**-22:11-**1KI**-6:24^2,25,26^2,27 -**2CH**-3:11sup,11,12^2-**PS**-18:10-**EZE**-9:3▪10:2,4,7,9^2,14▪28:14,16▪41:18^2

CHERUBIMS-all=3742-**GE**-3:24 -**EX**-25:18,19,20^2,22▪26:1,31▪36:8,35▪ 37:7,8^2,9^2-**NU**-7:89-**1SA**-4:4-**2SA**-6:2 -**1KI**-6:23,25,27^2,28,29,32^2,35▪7:29,36▪ 8:6,7^2-**2KI**-19:15-**1CH**-13:6▪28:18-**2CH**-3:7,10,11,13,14▪5:7,8^2-**PS**-80:1▪99:1 -**IS**-37:16-**EZE**-10:1,2,3,6,7^2,8,9,15, 16^2,18,19,20▪11:22▪41:18,20,25▪**N.T.** -**HEB**-9:5(5502)

CHERUBIMS'-**EZE**-10:5(3742)

CHESTNUT-**GE**-30:37(6196) -**EZE**-31:8(6196)

CHEST-all=727-**2KI**-12:9,10-**2CH**-24:8,10,11^2

CHESTS-**EZE**-27:24(1595)

CHEW-all=5927-**LE**-11:4-**DE**-14:7^2

CHEWED-**NU**-11:33(3772)

CHEWETH-all=5927-**LE**-11:3,4, 5,6,7(1641),26-**DE**-14:6

CHICKENS-**M'T**-23:37(3556)

CHIDE-all=7378-**EX**-17:2^2-**J'G**-8:1 -**PS**-103:9

CHIDING-**EX**-17:7(7379)

CHIEF-all=7218,a=5329,b=8269& marked-**GE**-40:2^{2}b,9b,16b,20b,21b,22b, 23b▪41:9b,10b-**LE**-21:4(1167)-**NU**-3:24 (5387),30(5387),32(5387),35(5387)▪4:34 (5387),46(5387)▪25:14(1),15(1)▪31:26▪ 32:28▪36:1^2-**DE**-1:15▪33:15-**JOS**-22:14 (1)-**J'G**-20:2(6438)-**1SA**-14:38(6438)▪ 15:21(7225)-**2SA**-8:18(3548)▪20:26 (3548)▪23:8,13,18-**1KI**-5:16b▪8:1(5387)▪ 9:23b▪14:27b-**2KI**-25:18-**1CH**-5:2(5057), 7,12,15▪7:3,40▪8:28▪9:9,17,26(1368),33, 34▪11:6^2,10,11,20▪12:3,18▪15:5b,6b,7b, 8b,9b,10b,11,12,16b,22b▪16:5▪18:17(7223)▪ 23:8,9,11,16,17,18,24▪24:4^2,6,31▪26:10^2, 12,21,26,31,32▪27:1,3,5▪29:6b,22(5057) -**2CH**-1:2▪5:2(5387)▪8:9b,10b▪11:22▪ 12:10b▪17:14▪19:8,11▪23:2▪24:6▪26:12, 20▪31:10▪35:9b▪36:14b-**EZR**-1:5▪2:68▪ 3:12▪4:2,3▪5:10(7217)▪7:5,28▪8:1,16, 17,24b,29^{2}b▪9:2(7223)▪10:5b,16-**NE**-7:70,71▪8:13▪10:14▪11:3,13,16▪12:7, 12,22,23,24,46-**JOB**-12:24▪29:25▪40:19 (7225)-**PS**-4:ta▪5:ta▪6:ta▪9:ta▪11:ta▪ 12:ta▪13:ta▪14:ta▪18:ta▪19:ta▪20:ta▪ 21:ta▪22:ta▪31:ta▪36:ta▪39:ta▪40:ta▪ 41:ta▪42:ta▪44:ta▪45:ta▪46:ta▪47:ta▪ 49:ta▪51:ta▪52:ta▪53:ta▪54:ta▪55:ta▪ 56:ta▪57:ta▪58:ta▪59:ta▪60:ta▪61:ta▪ 62:ta▪64ta▪65:ta▪66:ta▪67:ta▪68:ta▪ 69:ta▪70:ta▪75:ta▪76:ta▪77:ta▪78:51 (7225)▪80:ta▪81:ta▪84:ta▪85:ta▪88:ta▪ 105:36(7225)▪109:ta▪137:6▪139:ta▪ 140:ta-**PR**-1:21▪16:28(441)-**SONG**-4:14-**IS**-14:9(6260)▪41:9(678)-**JER**-13:21▪20:1(5057)▪31:7▪49:35(7225)▪ 52:24-**LA**-1:5-**EZE**-27:22▪38:2,3▪39:1 -**DA**-2:48(7229)▪10:13(7223)▪11:41 (7225)-**AM**-6:1(7225),6(7225)-**HAB**-3:19a▪**N.T**-all=749,a=5506&marked -**M'T**-2:4▪16:21▪20:18,27(4413)▪ 21:15,23,45▪23:6(4410)▪26:3,14,47,59▪ 27:1,3,6,12,20,41,62▪28:11-**M'R**-6:21 (4413)▪8:31▪10:33▪11:18,27▪12:39(4410)▪ 14:1,10,43,53,55▪15:1,3,10,11,31-**LU**-9:22▪11:15(758)▪14:1(758),7(4411)▪19:2 (754),47,47(4413)▪20:1,19,46(4411)▪ 22:2,4,26(2283),52,66▪23:4,10,13,23▪ 24:20-**JOH**-7:32,45▪11:47,57▪12:10,42 (758)▪18:3,35▪19:6,15,21-**AC**-4:23▪5:24▪ 9:14,21▪13:50(4413)▪14:12(2233)▪15:22 (2233)▪16:12(4413)▪17:4(4413)▪18:8 (752),17(752)▪19:14,31(775)▪21:31a,32a, 33a,37a▪22:24a,26a,27a,28a,29a,30▪ 23:10a,14,15a,17a,18a,19a,22a▪24:7a,22a▪ 25:2(4413),15,23a▪26:10,12▪28:7(4413), 17(4413)-**EPH**-2:20(204)▪-**1TI**-1:15 (4413)-**1PE**-2:6(204)▪5:4(750)-**RE**-6:15a

CHIEFEST-**1SA**-2:29(7725)▪9:22 (7218)▪21:7(47)-**2CH**-32:33(4608) -**SONG**-5:10(1713)-**M'R**-10:44(4413) -**2CO**-11:5(5228,3029)▪12:11(5228, 3029)-**1TI**-subscr.(3390)

CHIEFLY-**RO**-3:2(4412)-**PH'P**-4:22(3122)-**2PE**-2:10(3122)

CHILD-all=5288,a=3206,b=2030, c=1121&marked-**GE**-11:30(2056)▪ 16:11b▪19:36(2029)▪21:8a,14a,15a,16a▪ 37:30a▪38:24b,25b▪42:22a▪44:20a-**EX**-2:3a,6a,7a,9^{2}a,10a▪21:22b-**LE**-22:13 (2233)-**DE**-25:5c-**J'G**-11:34(3173)▪13:5, 7,8,12,24-**RU**-4:16a-**1SA**-1:11(2233),22, 24,25,27▪2:11,18,21,26▪3:1,8▪4:19b, 21-**2SA**-6:23a▪11:5b▪12:14c,15a,16, 18^{4}a,19^{2}a,21^{2}a,22^{2}a-**1KI**-3:7,17(3205), 19c,20c,21c,25a,26c,26(3205),27(3205)▪ 11:17▪13:2c▪14:3,12a,17▪17:21a,22a, 23a-**2KI**-4:14c,18a,26a,29,30,31^2,32,34a, 34sup,34a,35^{2}a▪5:14▪8:12b▪15:16b-**PR**-20:11▪22:6,15▪23:13▪29:15,21(5290) -**EC**-4:8c,13a,15a▪10:16▪11:5(4392)-**IS**-3:5▪7:16▪8:4▪9:6a▪10:19▪11:6▪26:17b,18 (2029)▪65:20-**JER**-1:6,7▪20:15c▪30:6 (3205)▪31:8b,8(3205),20a▪44:7(5768) -**HO**-11:1▪13:16b-**AM**-1:13b▪**N.T.**-all=3813&marked-**M'T**-1:18(1722,1064, 2192),23(1722,1064,2192)▪2:8,9,11,13^2, 14,20,21▪10:21(5043)▪17:18(3816)▪ 18:2,4,5▪23:15(5207)▪24:19(1722,1064, 2192)-**M'R**-9:21(3812),24,36▪10:15▪ 13:17(1722,1064,2192)-**LU**-1:7(5043),59, 66,76,80▪2:5(1471),17,21,27,40,43 (3816)▪9:38(3439),42(3816),47,48▪ 18:17▪21:23(1722,1064,2192)-**JOH**-4:49▪16:21-**AC**-4:27(3816),30▪7:5 (5043)▪13:10(5207)-**1CO**-13:11^3(3516) -**GA**-4:1(3516)-**1TH**-5:3(1722,1064,2192) -**2TI**-3:15(1025)-**HEB**-11:11(5088),23 -**RE**-12:2(1722,1064,2192),4(5043),5 (5207),5(5043)

CHILDBEARING-**1TI**-2:15(5042)

CHILDHOOD-**1SA**-12:2(5271) -**EC**-11:10(3208)

CHILDISH-**1CO**-13:11(3516)

CHILDLESS-all=6185&marked -**GE**-15:2-**LE**-20:20,21-**1SA**-15:33^2(7921) -**JER**-22:30(6185)-**LU**-20:30(815)

CHILDREN-all=1121a=3206& marked-**GE**-3:16▪10:21,22,23▪11:5▪ 16:2(1129)▪18:19▪19:38▪21:7▪22:20▪ 23:5,7,10^2,18▪25:4,22▪30:1,3(1129),26a▪ 31:43^2▪32:11,32▪33:1a,2^{2}a,5^{2}a,6a,7a,13a, 14a,19▪36:21,22,23,24,25,26,27,28,31▪ 37:3▪45:10,21▪46:8▪59:8,32▪50:23^2,25 -**EX**-1:1,7,9,12,13,17a,18a▪2:6a,23,25▪ 3:9,10,11,13,14,15▪4:29,31▪5:14,15,19▪ 6:5,6,9,11,12,13^2,26,27▪7:2,4,5▪9:6,26, 35▪10:20,23▪11:7,10▪12:26,27,28,31,35, 37,37(2945),40,42,50,51▪13:2,13,15,18, 19▪14:2,3,8^2,10^2,15,16,22,29▪15:1,19▪ 16:1,2,3,6,9,10,12,15,17,35▪17:1,3,7▪19:1, 3,6▪20:5,22▪21:4a,5▪22:24▪24:5,11,17▪ 25:2,22▪27:20,21▪28:1,9,11,12,21,29,30, 38▪29:28^2,43,45▪30:12,16^2,31▪31:13,16, 17▪32:20,28▪33:5,6▪34:7,7sup,30,32,34,35▪ 35:1,4,20,29,30▪36:3▪39:6,7,14,32,42▪ 40:36-**LE**-1:2▪4:2▪6:18▪7:23,29,34^2,36, 38▪9:3▪10:11,14▪11:2▪12:2▪15:2,31▪ 16:5,16,19,21,34▪17:2,5,12,13,14▪18:2▪ 19:2,18▪20:2^2▪21:24▪22:2,3,15,18,32▪ 23:2,10,24,34,43,44▪24:2,8,10,15,23^2▪ 25:2,33,41,45,46^2,54,55▪26:46▪27:2,34 -**NU**-1:2,10,20,22,24,26,28,30,32^2,34,36, 38,40,42,45,49,52,53,54▪2:2,3,5,7,10,12, 20,25,27,29,32,33,34▪3:4,8,9,12^2,15,38, 40,41^2,42,45,46,50▪5:2,4^2,6,9,12▪6:2, 23,27▪7:24,30,36,42,48,54▪7:60,66,72, 78▪8:6,9,10,11,14,16^2,17,18,19^5,20^2▪9:2, 4,5,7,10,17^2,18,19,22▪10:12,14,15,16,19, 20,22,23,24,25,26,27,28▪11:4▪13:2,3,22 (3211),24,26,28(3211),32▪14:2,3(2945), 5,7,10,18,27,33,39▪15:2,18,25,26, 29,32,38▪16:2,27(2945),38,40,41▪ 17:2,5,6,9,12▪18:5,6,8,11,19,20,21, 22,23,24^2,26,28,32▪19:2,9,10▪20:1, 12,13,19,22,24▪21:10,24^2▪22:1, 3,5▪24:17▪25:6^2,8,11^2,13▪26:2,4,5, 11,15,18,44,51,62^2,63,64▪27:8,11,12,20, 21▪28:2▪29:40▪30:1▪31:2,9,12,16,18 (2945),30,42,47,54▪32:1^2,2,6^2,7,9,17,18, 25,28,29,31,33^2,34,37,39▪33:1,3,5,38,40,51▪ 34:2,13,14^2,20,22,23^2,24,25,26,27,28,29▪ 35:2,8,10,15,34▪36:1^2,2,3,4,5,7^2,8^2,9,13 -**DE**-1:3,36,39▪2:4,8,9,12,19^3,22,29,37▪ 3:6,(2945),11,16,18▪4:10,25,40,44,45, 46▪5:9,29▪6:7▪9:2^2▪10:6^2▪11:2,19,21▪ 12:25,28▪13:13▪14:1▪17:20▪21:15▪ 23:8▪24:7,16^2▪28:54,55,57▪29:1,22,29▪ 30:2▪31:12(2945),13,19^2,22,23▪32:5,8, 20,46,49,51^2,52▪33:1,9,24▪34:8,9-**JOS**-1:2▪2:2▪3:1,9▪4:4,5,6,7,8^2,12^3,21^2,22▪ 5:1^2,2,3,6,7,10,12▪6:1▪7:1^2,12,23▪8:31, 32▪9:17,18,26▪10:4,11,12,20,21▪11:14,

19,22■12:1,2,6,7■13:6,10,13,15,22,23^{2},24,25,28,29,31^{2}■14:1^{2},4,5,6■15:1,12,13,14,(3211),20,21,63^{2}■16:1,4,5,8,9^{2}■17:2^{8},8,12,13,14,16■18:1,2,3,10,11^{3},14,20,21,28■19:1^{2},8,9^{4},10,16,17,23,24,31,32^{2},39,40,47^{2},48,49,51■20:2,9■21:1,3,4,5,6,7,8,9^{2},10^{2},13,19,20^{2},26,27,34,40,41■22:9^{3},10,11^{4},12^{2},13^{3},15^{2},21^{2},24,25^{2},27,30^{3},31^{4},32^{3},33^{3},34^{2}■24:4,32^{2}-**J'G**-1:1,8,9,16^{2},21^{2},34■2:4,6,11■3:2,5,7,8,9^{2},12,13,14,15^{2},27■4:1,3^{2},5,6^{2},11,23,24■6:1,2,3,6,7,8,33■7:12■8:10,18,28,33,34■10:6^{2},7,8^{2},9,10,11^{2},15,17^{2},18■11:4,5,6,8,9,12,13,14,15,27,28,29,30,31,32,33^{2},36■12:1,2,3■13:1■14:16,17■18:2,16,22,23,25,26,30■19:12,30■20:1,3^{3},7,13^{3},14^{2},15,18^{2},19,21,23^{2},24^{2},25,26,27,28,30^{2},31,32^{2},35,36,48■21:5,6,10(2945),13,18,20,23,24-**1SA**-1:2a,3a■2:5,28■7:4,6,7^{2},8■9:2■10:18,27■11:8■12:12■14:18,47■15:6■16:11(5288)■17:53■22:19(5768)■26:19■30:22-**2SA**-1:18■2:25■4:2,7:6,7,10■7:14■8:12■10:1,2,3,6^{2},8,10,11,14^{2},19■11:1■12:3,9,26,31■17:27■21:2^{3}■23:29-**1KI**-2:4■4:30■6:1,13■8:1,9,25,39,63■9:6,20,21^{2},22■11:2,7,33■12:17,24,33■14:24■18:20■19:10,14■20:3,5,7,15,27^{2},29■21:13,26-**2KI**-2:23(5288),24a■4:7■8:12,12(6768),19■9:1■10:13^{2},30■13:5■14:6^{3}■16:3■17:7,8,9,22,24,31,34,41■18:4■19:3,12■21:2,9■23:6,10,13■24:2-**1CH**-1:43■2:10,30,31,32■4:27^{2}■5:11,14,23■6:3,33,64,65^{3},77■7:12,29^{2},33,40■9:3^{3},4,18,23■11:31■12:16,24,25,26,29,30,32■14:4(3205)■15:4,15■16:13■17:9■18:11■19:1,2,3,6^{2},7,9,11,12,15,19■20:1,3,4(3211)■24:2■26:10■27:1,3,10,14,20■28:8-**2CH**-5:2,10■6:11,16,30■7:3■8:2,8^{2},9■10:17,18■11:19,23■13:7,12,16,18^{2}■20:1,10,13,19^{2},22,23■21:14■25:4^{3},7,11,12,14■27:5^{2}■28:3^{2},8,10,12■30:6,9,21■31:1,5,6■33:2,6,9■34:33■35:17-**EZR**-2:1,2,3,4,5,6^{2},7,8,9,10,11,12,13,14,15,16,17,18,19,20,21,24,25,26,29,30,31,32,33,34,35,36,37,38,39,40^{2},41,42^{4},43^{2},44^{2},45^{3},46^{2},47^{2},48^{2},49^{2},50^{2},51^{2},52^{2},53^{2},54,55^{3},56^{2},57^{4},58,60^{2},61^{3}■3:1■4:1■6:16^{2},19,20,21■7:7■8:35■9:12■10:1a,7,16,44-**NE**-1:6^{2}■2:10■5:5■7:6,8,9,10,11^{2},12,13,14,15,16,17,18,19,20,21,22,23,24,25,34,35,36,37,38,39,40,41,42,43^{2},44,45^{3},46^{2},47^{2},48^{2},49^{2},50^{2},51^{2},52^{2},53^{2},54^{2},55^{2},56,57^{3},58^{2},59^{4},60,62^{2},63^{2},73■8:14,17■9:1,23,24■10:39■11:3,4^{3},24,25,31■12:43a,47■13:2,16,24-**ES**-3:13(2945)■5:11-**JOB**-5:4■8:4■17:5■20:10■21:11a,19■24:5(5288)■27:14■29:5(5288)■30:8■41:34-**PS**-11:4■12:1■14:2■17:14■21:10■34:11■36:7■45:2,16■53:2■66:5■69:8■72:4■73:15■78:4,5,6^{2},9■82:6■83:8■89:30■90:3,16■102:28■103:7,13,17■105:6■107:8,15,21,31■109:9,10■113:9■115:14,16■127:3,4■128:3,6■132:12^{2}■137:7■144:7,11■147:13■148:12(5288),14■149:2-**PR**-4:1■5:7■7:24■8:32■13:22■14:26■15:11■17:6^{2}■20:7■31:28-**SONG**-1:6-**IS**-1:2,4■2:6a■3:4(5288),12(5768)■8:18a■11:14■13:16(5768),18■14:21■17:3,9■21:17■27:12■29:23a■30:1,9■31:6■37:3,12■38:19■49:17,20,25■54:1^{2},13^{2}■57:4a,5a■63:8■66:8,20-**JER**-2:9,16,30■3:14,19,21,22■4:22■5:7■6:1,11(5768)■7:18,30■9:21(5768),26■10:20,16:14,15■17:2,19■18:21■23:7■25:21■30:20■31:15^{2},17■32:18,30^{3},32,39■38:23■40:7(2945)■41:16(2945)■43:6(2945),47:3■49:6,11■50:4^{2},33-**LA**-1:5(5768),16■2:11(5768),20(5768)■3:33■4:4(5768),10a■5:13(5288)-**EZE**-2:3,4■3:11■4:13■6:5■9:6(2945)■16:21,36,45^{2}■20:18,21■23:39■31:14■33:2,12,17,30■35:5■37:16,18,21,25■43:7■44:9,15■47:22^{2}■48:11-**DA**-1:3,4a,6,10a,13a,15a,17a■2:38(1123)■5:13(1123)■6:13(1123),24(1123)■11:41■12:1-**HO**-1:2a,10,11■2:4^{2}■3:1,4,5■4:1,6■5:7■9:12,13■10:9,14■11:10■13:13-**JOE**-1:3^{3}■2:16(5768),23■3:6^{2},8,16,19-**AM**-1:13■2:11■3:1,12■4:5■9:7^{2}-**OB**-12,20-**MIC**-1:16■2:9(5768)■5:3-**NA**-3:10(5768)-**ZEP**-1:8■2:8,9-**ZEC**-10:7,9-**MAL**-4:6^{2}■**N.T.**-all=5043,a=5207,b=3813&marked-**M'T**-2:16(3816),18■3:9■5:9a,45a■7:11■8:12a■9:15a■10:21■11:16(3808),19■12:27a■13:38^{2}a■14:21b■15:38b■17:25a,26a■18:3b,25■19:13b,14b,29■20:20a■21:15(3816)■22:24■23:31a,37■27:9a,25,56a-**M'R**-2:19a■7:27■9:37b■10:13b,14b,24,29,30■12:19■13:12-**LU**-1:16a,17■3:8■5:34a■6:35a■7:32b,35■11:7b,13■13:34■14:26■16:8^{2}a■18:16b,29■19:44■20:28(815),29(815),31,34a,36^{2}a■23:28-**JOH**-4:12a■8:39■11:52■12:36a■13:33(5040)■21:5b-**AC**-2:39■3:25a■5:21a■7:19(1025),23a,37a■9:15a■10:36a■13:26a,33■21:5,21-**RO**-8:16,17,21■9:7,8^{3},26,27-**1CO**-7:14■14:20b,20(3515)-**2CO**-3:7a,13a■6:13■12:14^{2}-**GA**-3:7a,26a■4:3(3516),19(5040),25,27,28,31-**EPH**-1:5(5206)■2:2a,3■4:14(3516)■5:1,6a,8■6:1,4-**COL**-3:6a,20,21-**1TH**-2:7,11■5:5^{2}a-**1TI**-3:4,12■5:4,10(5044),14(5041)-**TIT**-1:6■2:4(5388)-**HEB**-2:13b,14b■11:22a■12:5a-**1PE**-1:14-**2PE**-2:14-**1JO**-2:1(5040),12(5040),13b,18b,28(5040)■3:7(5040),10^{2},18(5040)■4:4(5040)■5:2,21(5040)-**2JO**-1,4,13-**3JO**-4-**RE**-2:14a,23■7:4a■21:12a

CHILDREN'S-all=1121-**GE**-31:16■45:10-**EX**-9:4■34:7-**JOS**-14:9-**1KI**-17:41-**JOB**-19:17-**PS**-103:17■128:6-**PR**-13:22■17:6-**JER**-2:9■31:29-**EZE**-18:2■37:25■**N.T.**-**M'T**-15:26(5043)-**M'R**-7:27(5043),28(3813)

CHILD'S-**EX**-2:8(3206)-**1KI**-17:21(3206)-**JOB**-33:25(5290)■**N.T.**-**M'T**-2:20(3813)

CHIMNMEY-**HO**-13:3(699)

CHODE-**GE**-31:36(7378)-**NU**-20:3(7378)

CHOICE-all=4005&marked-**GE**-23:6■49:11(8321)-**DE**-12:11-**1SA**-9:2(970)-**2SA**-10:9(977)-**2KI**-3:19■19:23-**1CH**-7:40(1305)■19:10(970)-**2CH**-25:5(970)-**NE**-5:18(1305)-**PR**-8:10(977),19(977)■10:20(977)-**SONG**-6:9(1249)-**IS**-37:24-**JER**-22:7-**EZE**-24:4,5■31:16■**N.T.**-**AC**-15:7(1586)

CHOICEST-**IS**-5:2(8321)■22:7(4005)

CHOKE-**M'T**-13:22(4846)-**M'R**-4:19(4846)

CHOKED-all=638&marked-**M'T**-13:7-**M'R**-4:7(4846)■5:13(4155)-**LU**-8:7,14(4846),33

CHOLER-**DA**-8:7(4843)■11:11(4843)

CHOOSE-all=977&marked-**EX**-17:9-**NU**-16:7■17:5-**DE**-7:7■12:5,11,14,18,26■14:23,24,25■15:20■16:2,6,7,15,16■17:8,10,15■18:6■23:16■26:2■30:19■31:11-**JOS**-9:27■24:15-**1SA**-2:28■17:8(1262)-**2SA**-16:18■17:1■21:6(972)■24:12-**1KI**-14:21■18:23,25-**1CH**-21:10,11(6901)-**NE**-9:7-**JOB**-9:14■34:4,33-**PS**-25:12■47:4-**PR**-1:29■3:31-**IS**-7:15,16■14:1■49:7■56:4■65:12■66:4-**EZE**-21:19(1254)-**ZEC**-1:17■2:12■**N.T.**-**PH'P**-1:22(138)

CHOOSEST-**JOB**-15:5(977)-**PS**-65:4(977)

CHOOSETH-all=977-**JOB**-7:15-**IS**-40:20■41:24

CHOOSING-**HEB**-11:25(138)

CHOP-**MIC**-3:3(6566)

CHOSE-all=977-**GE**-6:2■13:11-**EX**-18:25-**DE**-4:37■10:15-**JOS**-8:3-**J'G**-5:8-**1SA**-13:2■17:40-**2SA**-6:21■10:9-**1KI**-8:16^{2}■11:34-**1CH**-19:10■28:4-**2CH**-6:5^{2}-**JOB**-29:25-**PS**-78:67,68,70-**IS**-66:4-**EZE**-20:5■**N.T.**-all=1586&marked-**LU**-6:13■14:7-**AC**-6:5■13:17■15:40(1951)

CHOSEN-all=977,a=970&marked-**EX**-14:7a■15:4(4005)-**NU**-16:5-**DE**-7:6■12:21■14:2■16:11■18:5■21:5-**JOS**-24:22-**J'G**-10:14■20:15a,16a,34a-**1SA**-8:18■10:24■12:13■16:8,9,10■20:30■24:2a■26:2a-**2SA**-6:1a-**1KI**-3:8■8:44,48■11:13,32,36■12:21a-**2KI**-21:7■23:27-**1CH**-9:22(1305)■15:2■16:13(972),41(1305)■28:4,5,6,10■29:1-**2CH**-6:6^{2},34,38■7:12,16■11:1a■12:13■13:3^{2}a,17■29:11■33:7-**NE**-1:9-**JOB**-36:21-**PS**-33:12■78:31a■89:3(972),19a■105:6(972),26,43(972)■106:5(972),23(972)■119:30,173■132:13■135:4-**PR**-16:16■22:1-**IS**-1:29■41:8,9■43:10,20(972)■44:1,2■48:10■58:5,6■65:15(972)■66:3-**JER**-8:3■33:24■48:15(4005)■49:19a■50:44a-**EZE**-23:7(4005)-**DA**-11:15(4005)-**HAG**-2:23-**ZEC**-3:2■**N.T.**-all=1586&marked-**M'T**-12:18(140)■20:16(1588)■22:14(1588)-**M'R**-13:20-**LU**-10:42■23:35(1588)-**JOH**-6:70■13:18■15:16^{2},19-**AC**-1:2,24■9:15(1589)■10:41(4401)■15:22,25■22:14(4400)-**RO**-16:13(1588)-**1CO**-1:27^{2},28-**2CO**-8:19(5500)-**EPH**-1:4-**2TH**-2:13(138)-**2TI**-2:4(4758)-**JAS**-2:5-**1PE**-2:4(1588),9(1588)-**RE**-17:14(1588)

CHRONICLES-all=1697,3117-**1KI**-14:19,29■15:7,23,31■16:5,14,20,27■22:39,45-**2KI**-1:18■8:23■10:34■12:19■13:8,12■14:15,18,28■15:6,11,15,21,26,31,36■20:20■21:17,25■23:28■24:5-**1CH**-1:t(1697,3117)■27:24-**2CH**-1:t(1697,3117)-**NE**-12:23-**ES**-2:23■6:1■10:2

CHRYSOLITE-**RE**-21:20(5555)

CHRYSOPRASUS-**RE**-21:20(5556)

CHURCH-all=1577-**M'T**-16:18■18:17^{2}-**AC**-2:47■5:11■7:38■8:1,3■11:22,26■12:1,5■13:1■14:23,27■15:3,4,22■18:22■20:17,28-**RO**-16:1,5,23,subcsr.-**1CO**-1:2■4:17■6:4■10:32■11:18,22■12:28■14:4,5,12,19,23,28,35■15:9■16:19-**2CO**-1:1-**GA**-1:13-**EPH**-1:22■3:10,21■5:23,24,25,27,29,32-**PH'P**-3:6■4:15-**COL**-1:18,24■4:15,16-**1TH**-1:1-**2TH**-1:1-**1TI**-3:5,15■5:16-**2TI**-subscr.-**TI**-subscr.-**PH'M**-2-**HEB**-2:12■12:23-**JAS**-5:14-**1PE**-5:13-**3JO**-6,9,10-**RE**-2:1,8,12,18■3:1,7,14

CHURCHES-all=1577&marked-**AC**-9:31■15:41■16:5■19:37(2417)-**RO**-16:4,16-**1CO**-7:17■11:16■14:33,34■16:1,19-**2CO**-8:1,18,19,23,24■11:8,28■12:13-**GA**-1:2,22-**1TH**-2:14-**2TH**-1:4-**RE**-1:4,11,20^{2}■2:7,11,17,23,29■3:6,13,22■22:16

CHURL-**IS**-32:5(3596),7(3596)

CHURLISH-**1SA**-25:3(7186)

CHURNING-**PR**-30:33(4330)

CIELED-**2CH**-3:5(2645)-**JER**-22:14(5608)-**EZE**-41:16(7824)-**HAG**-1:4(5603)

CIELING-**1KI**-6:15(5604)

CINNAMON-all=7076-**EX**-30:23-**PR**-7:17-**SONG**-4:14■**N.T.**-**RE**-18:13(2792)

CIRCLE-**IS**-40:22(2329)

CIRCUIT-**1SA**-7:16(5437)-**JOB**-22:14(2329)-**PS**-19:6(8622)

CIRCUITS-**EC**-1:6(5439)

CIRCUMCISE-all=4135&marked-**GE**-17:11(5243)-**DE**-10:16■30:6-**JOS**-5:2,4-**JER**-4:4■**N.T.**-all=4059-**LU**-1:59-**JOH**-7:22-**AC**-15:5■21:21

CIRCUMCISED-all=4135-**GE**-17:10,12,13,14,23,24,25,26,27■21:4■34:15,17,22^{2},24-**EX**-12:44,48-**LE**-12:3-**JOS**-5:3,5^{2},7^{2}-**JER**-9:25■**N.T.**-all=4059&marked-**AC**-7:8■15:1,24■16:3-**RO**-4:11(203)-**1CO**-7:18^{2}-**GA**-2:3■5:2,3■6:12,13^{2}-**PH'P**-3:5(4061)-**COL**-2:11

CIRCUMCISING-**JOS**-5:8(4135)■**N.T.**-**LU**-2:21(4059)

CIRCUMCISION-**EX**-4:26(4139)■**N.T.**-all=4061-**JOH**-7:22,23-**AC**-7:8■10:45■11:2-**RO**-2:25^{2},26,27,28,29■3:1,30■4:9,10^{2},11,12^{2}■15:8-**1CO**-7:19-**GA**-2:7,8,9,12■5:6,11,15-**EPH**-2:11-**PH'P**-3:3-**COL**-2:11^{2}■3:11■4:11-**TIT**-1:10

CIRCUMSPECT-**EX**-23:13(8104)

CIRCUMSPECTLY-**EPH**-5:15(199)

CISTERN-all=953-**2KI**-18:31-**PR**-5:15-**EC**-12:6-**IS**-36:16

CISTERNS-**JER**-2:13(877)

CITIES-all=5892&marked-**GE**-13:12■19:25^{2},29^{2}■35:5■41:35,48■47:21-**EX**-1:11-**LE**-25:32^{2},33,34■26:25,31,33-**NU**-13:19,28■21:2,3,25^{2}■31:10■32:16,17,24,26,33^{2},36,38■35:2^{2},3,4,5,6^{3},7^{2},8^{2},11^{2},12,13^{2},14^{3},15-**DE**-1:22,28■2:34,35,37■3:4^{2},

5,7,10^{2},12,19■4:41,42■6:10■9:1■13:12■19:1,2,5,7,9,11■20:15^{2},16■21:2-JOS-9:17^{2}■10:2,19,20,37,39■11:12,13,14,21■13:10,17,21,23,25,28,30,31■14:4,12■15:9,21,32,36,41,44,51,54,57,59,60,62■16:9^{2}■17:9^{2},12■18:9,21,24,28■19:6,7,8,15,16,22,23,30,31,35,38,39,48■20:2,4,9■21:2,3,4,5,6,7,8,9,16,18,19^{2},20,22,24,25,26,27,29,31,32,33^{2},35,37,39,40^{2},41^{2},42^{2}■24:13-J'G-10:4■11:26,33■12:7■20:14,15,42,48■21:23-1SA-6:18^{2}■7:14■18:6■30:29^{2}■31:7-2SA-2:1,3■8:8■10:12■12:31■20:6■24:7-1KI-4:13■8:37(8179)■9:11,12,13,19^{3}■10:26■12:17■13:32■15:20,23■20:34■22:39-2KI-3:25■13:25^{2}■17:6,9,24^{2},26,29■18:11,13■19:25■23:5,8,19-1CH-2:22,23■4:31,32,33■6:57,60^{2},61sup,61,62,63,64,65,66,67■9:2■10:7■13:2■18:8■19:7,13■20:3■27:25-2CH-1:14■6:28(8179)■8:2,4,5,6^{3}■9:25■10:17■11:5,10■12:4■13:19■14:5,6,7,14^{2}■15:8■16:4^{2}■17:2^{2},7,9,12,13,19■19:5,10■20:4■21:3■23:2■24:5■25:13■26:6■27:4■28:18■31:1^{2},6,15,19■32:1,29■33:14■34:6-EZR-2:70^{2}■3:1■4:10(7141)■10:14-NE-7:73^{2}■8:15■9:25■10:37■11:1,3^{2},20■12:44-ES-9:2-JOB-15:28-PS-9:6■69:35-IS-1:7■6:11■14:17,21■17:2,9■19:18■33:8■36:1■37:26■40:9■42:11■44:26■54:3■61:4■64:10-JER-1:15■2:15,28■4:5,7,16,26■5:6,17■7:17,34■8:14■9:11■10:22■11:6,12,13■13:19■17:26■20:16■22:6■25:18■26:2■31:21,23,24■32:44^{4}■33:10,12,13^{3}■34:1,7^{3},22■36:6,9■40:5,10■44:2,6,17,21■48:9,15,24,28■49:1,13■50:32■51:43-LA-5:11-EZE-6:6■12:20■19:7■25:9^{2}■26:19■29:12^{2}■30:7^{2}■35:4,9■36:4,10,33,35,38■39:9-DA-11:15-HO-8:14^{2}■11:6■13:10-AM-4:6,8■9:14-OB-20-MIC-5:11,14■7:12-ZEP-1:16■3:6-ZEC-1:12,17■7:7■8:20■N.T.-all=4172-M'T-9:35■10:23■11:1,20■14:13-M'R-6:33,56-LU-4:43■13:22■19:17,19-AC-5:16■8:40■14:6■16:4■26:11-2PE-2:6-JUDE-7-RE-16:19

CITIZEN-LU-15:15(4177)■-AC-21:395(4177)

CITIZENS-LU-19:14(4177)

CITY-all=5892,a=7151&marked-GE-4:17^{2}■10:11,12■11:4,5,8■18:24,26,28■19:4,12,14,15,16,20,21,22■23:10,18■24:10,11,13■26:33■28:19■33:18^{2}■34:20^{2},24^{2},25,27,28■35:27a■36:32,35,39■41:48■44:4,13-EX-9:29,33-LE-14:40,41,45,53■25:29,30,33-NU-20:16■21:26,27,28a■22:36■24:19■35:4,5^{2},25,26,27,28,32-DE-2:34,36,36a■3:4a,6■13:13,15,16■19:12■20:10,14,19,20■21:3^{2},4,6,19,20,21■22:15,17,18,21,23,24^{2}■25:8■28:3,16■34:3-JOS-3:16■6:3^{2},4,5,7,11,14,15^{2},16,17,20^{2},21,24,26■8:1,2,4^{3},5,6,7,8^{2},11,12,13^{2},14^{2},16,17,18,19^{2},20,21^{2},22,27,29■10:2■11:19■13:9,16■15:13a,13sup,62■18:14■19:29,50^{2}■20:4^{3},6^{3},21:11a,11sup,12,13,21,27,32,38-J'G-1:8,16,17,23,24^{2},25^{2},26■3:13■6:27,28,30■8:16,17,27■9:30,31,33,35,43,44,45^{3},51^{2}■14:18■16:2,3■17:8■18:27,28,29^{2}■19:11,12,15,17,22■20:11,31,32,37,38,40^{2},48-RU-1:19■2:18■3:11(8179),15■4:2-1SA-1:3■4:13^{2}■5:9^{2},11,12■8:22■9:6,10,11,12,13,14^{2},25,27■10:5■15:5■20:6,29,40,42■22:19■23:10■27:5■28:3■30:3-2SA-5:7,9■6:10,12,16■10:3,14■11:16,17,20,25■12:1,26,27,28^{2},30■15:2,12,14,24,25,27,34,37■17:13^{2},17,23■18:3■19:3,37■20:15,16,19,21,22■24:5-1KI-1:41a,45a■2:10■3:1■8:1,16,44,48■9:16,24■11:27,32,36,43■13:25,29■14:11,12,21,31■15:8,24■16:4,18,24■17:10■20:2,12,19,30^{2}■21:8,11^{2},13,24■22:26,36,50-2KI-2:19^{2},23■3:19^{2}■6:14,15,19■7:4^{2},10,12■7:12■8:24■9:15,28■10:2,5,6,25■11:20■12:21■14:20■15:7,38■16:20■17:9■18:8,30■19:13,32,33,34■20:6^{2},20■23:8^{2},17,27■24:10,11■25:2,3,4^{2},11,19^{3}-1CH-1:43,46,50■6:56■11:5,7,8^{2}■13:13■15:1,29■19:9,15■20:2-2CH-5:2■6:5,34,38■8:11■9:31■11:12,23■12:13,16■14:1■15:6■16:14■18:25■19:5■21:1,20■23:21■24:16,25■25:28■27:9■28:15,25,27■29:20■30:10■31:19■32:3,5,6,18,30■33:14,15■34:8-EZR-2:1■4:12(7149),13(7149),15^{2}(7149),16(7149),19(7149),21(7149)■10:14-NE-2:3,5,8■3:15■7:4,6■11:1,9,18■12:37■13:8-ES-3:15■4:1,6■6:9,11■8:11,15,17■9:28-JOB-24:12■29:7(7176)■39:7a-PS-31:21■46:4■48:1,2a,8^{2}■55:9■59:6,14■60:9■72:16■87:3■101:8■107:4,7,36■108:10■122:3■127:1-PR-1:21■8:3(7176)■9:3(7176),14(7176)■10:15a■11:10a,11(7176)■16:32■18:11a,19a■21:22■25:28■29:8a-EC-7:19■8:10■9:14,15■10:15-SONG-3:2,3■5:7-IS-1:8,21a,26,26a■14:4(4062),31■17:1■19:2,18■22:2,2a,9■23:16■24:10a,12■25:2^{2},2a,2,3a■26:1,5a■27:10■29:1a■32:13a,14,19■33:20a■36:15■37:13,33,34,35■38:6^{2}■45:13■48:2■52:1■60:14■62:12■66:6-JER-1:18■3:14■4:29^{2}■6:6■8:16■14:18■15:8■17:24,25^{2}■19:8,11,12,15■20:5■21:4,6,7,9,10■22:8^{2}■23:39■25:29■26:6,9,11,12,15■26:20■27:17,19■29:7,16■30:18■31:38■32:3,24^{2},25,28,29^{2},31,36■33:4,5■34:2,22■37:8,10,21■38:2,3,4,9,17,18,23■39:2,4,9,16■41:7■46:8■47:2■48:8^{2}■49:25,25a■51:31■52:5,6,7^{3},15,25^{3}-LA-1:1,19■2:11a,12,15■3:51-EZE-4:1,3■5:2■7:15,23■9:1,4,5,7,9■10:2■11:2,3,6,23^{2}■17:4■21:19■22:2,3■24:6,9■26:10,17,19■33:21■39:16■40:1,2■43:3■45:6,7^{2}■48:15^{2},17,18,19,20,21,22,30,31,35-DA-9:16,18,19,24,26-HO-6:8a■11:9-JOE-2:9-AM-3:6^{2}■4:7^{2},8■5:3■6:8■7:17-JON-1:2■3:2,3,4■4:5^{3},11-MIC-4:10a■6:9-NA-3:1-HAB-2:8a,12a,17a-ZEP-2:15■3:1-ZEC-8:3,5■14:2^{3}■N.T.-all=4172&marked-M'T-2:23■4:5■5:14,35■8:33,34■9:1■10:5,11,14,15,23■12:25■21:10,17,18■22:7■23:34■26:18■27:53■28:11-M'R-1:33,45■5:14■6:11■11:19■14:13,16-LU-1:26,39■2:3,4^{2},11,39■4:26,29^{2},31■5:12■7:11,12^{2},37■8:1,4,27,34,39■9:5,10■10:1,8,10,11,12■14:21■18:2,3■19:41■22:10■23:19,51■24:29-JOH-1:44■4:5,8,28,30,39■11:54■19:20-AC-7:58■8:5,8,9■9:6■10:9■11:5■12:10■13:44,50■14:4,13,19,20,21■15:21,36■16:12^{2},13,14,20,39■17:5,6(4173),8(4173),16■18:10■19:29■19:35■20:23■21:5,29,39■22:3sup,3■24:12■25:23■27:8-RO-16:23-2CO-11:26,32-1TI-subscr.(3390)-TIT-1:5-HEB-11:10,16■12:22■13:14-JAS-4:13-RE-3:12■11:2,8,13■14:8,20■16:19■17:18■18:10,16,18,19,21■20:9■21:2,10,14,15,16^{2},18,19,21,23■22:14,19

CLAD-1KI-11:29(3680)-IS-59:17(5844)

CLAMOROUS-PR-9:13(1993)

CLAMOUR-EPH-4:31(2906)

CLAP-JOB-27:23(5606)-PS-47:1(8628)■98:8(4222)-IS-55:12(4222)-LA-2:15(5606)-NA-3:19(8628)

CLAPPED-2KI-11:12(5221)-EZE-25:6(4222)

CLAPPETH-JOB-34:37(5606)

CLAVE-all=1234&marked-GE-22:3■34:3(1692)-NU-16:31-J'G-15:19-RU-1:14(1692)-1SA-6:14-2SA-20:2(1692)■23:10(1692)-1KI-11:2(1692)-2KI-18:6(1692)-NE-10:29(2388)-PS-78:15-IS-48:21■N.T.-AC-17:34(2853)

CLAWS-DE-14:6(6541)-ZEC-11:16(6541)

CLAY-all=2563&marked-1KI-7:46(4568)-2CH-4:17(4568)-JOB-4:19■10:9■13:12■27:16■33:6■38:14-PS-40:2(2916)-IS-29:16■41:25(2916)■45:9■64:8-JER-18:4,6■43:9(4423)-DA-2:33(2635),34(2635),35(2635),41^{2}(2635),42(2635),43^{2}(2635),45(2635)-NA-3:14(2916)-HAB-2:6(5671)■N.T.-all=4081-JOH-9:6^{2},11,14,15-RO-9:21

CLEAN-all=2889,a=2891&marked-GE-7:2^{2},8^{2}■8:20■35:2a-LE-4:12■6:11■7:19■10:10,14■11:36,37,47■12:8a■13:6^{2}a,13a,13,17a,17,23a,28a,34^{2}a,37,37a,38a,39,40,41,58a,59a■14:4,7a,8a,9a,11^{2}a,20a,48a,53a,57■15:8,13a,28a■16:30a■17:15a■20:25^{2}■22:4a,7a-NU-5:28■8:7a■9:13■18:11,13■19:9^{2},12^{2}a,18,19,19a■31:23a,24a-DE-12:15,22■14:11,20■15:22■23:10-JOS-3:17(8552)■4:1(8552),11(8552)-1SA-20:26-2KI-5:10a,12a,13a,14a-2CH-30:17-JOB-9:30(2141)■11:4(1249)■14:4■15:14(2135),15(2141)■17:9a■25:4(2135)■33:9(2134)-PS-19:9■24:4(5355)■51:7a,10■73:1(1249)■77:8(656)-PR-14:4(1249)■16:2(2134)■20:9(2135)-EC-9:2-IS-1:16(2135)■24:19(6565)■30:24(2548)■52:11(1305)■66:20-JER-13:27a-EZE-22:26■36:25,25a■44:23■N.T.-all=2513&marked-M'T-8:2(2889),3(2889)■23:25(2889),26■27:59-M'R-1:40(2511),41(2511)-LU-5:12(2511),13(2511)■11:39(2511),41-JOH-13:10^{2},11■15:3-AC-18:6-2PE-2:18(3689)-RE-19:8,14

CLEANNESS-all=1252&marked-2SA-22:21,25-PS-18:20,24-AM-4:6(5356)

CLEANSE-all=2891&marked-EX-29:36(2398)-LE-14:49(2398),52■16:19,30-NU-8:6,7,15,21-2CH-29:15,16-NE-13:22-PS-19:12(5352)■51:2(5352)■119:9(2135)-JER-4:11(1305)■33:8-EZE-36:25■37:23■39:12,14,16■43:20(2398),22^{2}(2398)■45:18(2398)-JOE-3:21(5352)■N.T.-all=2511-M'T-10:8■23:26-2CO-7:1-EPH-5:26-JAS-4:8-1JO-1:9

CLEANSED-all=2891&marked-LE-11:32■12:7■14:4,7,8,14,17,18,19,25,28,29,31■15:13,28-NU-35:33(3722)-JOS-22:17-2CH-29:18■30:18■34:5-NE-13:9,30-PS-73:13(2135)-EZE-22:24■36:33■44:26(2893)-DA-8:14(6663)-JOE-3:21(5352)■N.T.-all=2511-M'T-8:3■11:5-M'R-1:42-LU-4:27■7:22■17:14,17-AC-10:15■11:9

CLEANSETH-JOB-37:21(2891)-PR-20:30(8562)-1JO-1:7(2511)

CLEANSING-all=2893-LE-13:7,35■14:2,23,32■15:13-NU-6:9-EZE-43:23■N.T.-M'R-1:44(2512)-LU-5:14(2512)

CLEAR-all=5352&marked-GE-24:8,41,41(5355)■44:16(6663)-EX-34:7-PS-51:4(2135)-SONG-6:10(1249)-IS-18:4(6703)-AM-8:9(216)-ZEC-14:6(3368)■N.T.-2CO-7:11(53)-RE-21:11(2929),18(2513)■22:1(2986)

CLEARER-JOB-11:17(6965)

CLEARING-NU-14:18(5352)■N.T.-2CO-7:11(627)

CLEARLY-JOB-33:3(1305)■N.T.-M'T-7:5(1227)-M'R-8:25(5081)-LU-6:42(1227)-RO-1:20(2529)

CLEARNESS-EX-24:10(2892)

CLEAVE-all=1692&marked-GE-2:24-LE-1:17(8156)-DE-4:4(1695)■10:20■11:22■13:4,17■28:21,60■30:20-JOS-22:5■23:8,12-2KI-5:27-JOB-38:38-PS-74:15(1234)■101:3■102:5■137:6-IS-14:1(5596)-JER-13:11-EZE-3:26-DA-2:43(1693)■11:34(3867)-HAB-3:9(1234)-ZEC-14:4(1234)■N.T.-all=4347&marked-M'T-19:5-M'R-10:7-AC-11:23-RO-12:9(2853)

CLEAVED-all=1692-2KI-3:3-JOB-29:10■31:7

CLEAVETH-all=1692&marked-DE-14:6(8157)-JOB-16:13(6398)■19:20-PS-22:15■41:8(3332)■44:25■119:25■141:7(1234)-EC-10:9(1234)-JER-13:11-LA-4:4,8(6821)■N.T.-LU-10:11(2853)

CLEFT-DE-14:6(8156)-MIC-1:4(1234)

CLEFTS-all=2288&marked-SONG-2:14-IS-2:21(5366)-JER-49:16-AM-6:11(1233)-OB-3

CLEMENCY-AC-24:4(1932)

CLIFF-2CH-20:16(4608)

CLIFFS-JOB-30:6(6178)

CLIFT-EX-33:22(5366)

CLIFTS-IS-57:5(5585)

CLIMB-all=5927-JER-4:29-JOE-2:7,9-AM-9:2

CLIMBED-1SA-14:13(5927)■N.T.-LU-19:4(305)

CLIMBETH-JOH-10:1(305)

CLIPPED-**JER**-48:37(1639)
CLODS-**JOB**-7:5(1487)■21:33(7263)■38:38(7263)-**IS**-28:24(7702)-**HO**-10:11(7702)-**JOE**-1:17(4053)
CLOKE-**IS**-59:17(4598)■**N.T.**-**M'T**-5:40(2440)-**LU**-6:29(2440)-**JOH**-15:22(4392)-**1TH**-2:5(4392)-**2TI**-4:13(5341)-**1PE**-2:16(1942)
CLOSE-**NU**-5:13(5956)-**2SA**-22:46(4526)-**1CH**-12:1(6113)-**JOB**-28:21(5641)■41:15(6862)-**PS**-18:45(4526)-**JER**-42:16(1692)-**DA**-8:7(681)-**AM**-9:11(1443)■**N.T.**-**LU**-9:36(4601)-**AC**-27:13(788)
CLOSED-**GE**-2:21(5462)■20:18(6113)-**NU**-16:33(3680)-**J'G**-3:22(5462)-**IS**-1:6(2115)■29:10(6105)-**DA**-12:9(5640)-**JON**-2:5(5437)■**N.T.**-**M'T**-3:15(2576)-**LU**-4:20(4428)-**AC**-28:27(2576)
CLOSER all supplied
CLOSEST-**JER**-22:15(8474)
CLOSET-**JOE**-2:16(2646)■**N.T.**-**M'T**-6:6(5009)
CLOSETS-**LU**-12:3(5009)
CLOTH-all=899&marked-**NU**-4:6,7,8,9,11,12,13-**DE**-22:17(8071)-**1SA**-19:13■21:9(8071)-**2SA**-20:12-**2KI**-8:15(4346)■**N.T.**-all=4616&marked-**M'T**-9:16(4470)■27:59-**M'R**-2:21(4470)■14:51,52
CLOTHE-all=3847-**EX**-40:14-**ES**-4:4-**PS**-132:16,18-**PR**-23:21-**IS**-22:21■49:18■50:30-**EZE**-26:16■34:3-**HAG**-1:6-**ZEC**-3:4■**N.T.**-**M'T**-6:30(294)-**LU**-12:28(294)
CLOTHED-all=3847&marked-**GE**-3:21-**LE**-8:7-**2SA**-1:24-**1CH**-15:27(3736)■21:16(3680)-**2CH**-6:41■18:9■28:15-**ES**-4:2(3830)-**JOB**-7:5■8:22■10:11■29:14■39:19-**PS**-35:26■65:13■93:1^2■104:1■109:18,29■132:9-**PR**-31:21-**IS**-61:10-**EZE**-7:27■9:2,3,11■10:2,6,7■16:10■23:6,12■38:4■44:17-**DA**-5:7(3848),16(3848),29(3848)■10:5■12:6,7-**ZEP**-1:8-**ZEC**-3:3,5■**N.T.**-all=4016&marked-**M'T**-6:31■11:8(294)■25:36,38,43-**M'R**-1:6(1746)■5:15(2439)■15:17(1746)■16:5-**LU**-7:25(294)■8:35(2439)■16:19(1737)-**2CO**-5:2(1902),3(1746),4(1902)-**1PE**-5:5(1463)-**RE**-1:13(1746)■3:5,18■4:4■7:9■10:1■11:3■12:1■15:6(1746)■18:16■19:13,14(1746)
CLOTHES-all=899&marked-**GE**-37:29,34(8071)■44:13(8071)■49:11(5497)-**EX**-12:34(8071)■19:10(8071),14(8071)-**LE**-10:6■11:25,28,40^2■13:6,34,45■14:8,9,47^2■15:5,6,7,8,10,11,13,21,22,27■16:26,28,32■17:15■21:10-**NU**-8:7,21■14:6■19:7,8,10,19,21■21:24-**DE**-29:5(8008)-**JOS**-7:6(8071)-**J'G**-11:35-**1SA**-4:12(4055)■19:24-**2SA**-1:2,11■3:31■13:31■19:24-**1KI**-1:1■21:27-**2KI**-2:12■5:7,8^2■6:30■11:14■18:37■19:1■22:11,19-**2CH**-23:13■34:19,27-**NE**-4:23■9:21(8008)-**ES**-4:1-**JOB**-9:31(8008)-**PR**-6:27-**IS**-36:22■37:1-**JER**-41:5-**EZE**-16:39■23:26■27:20,24(1545)-**AM**-2:8■**N.T.**-all=2440&marked-**M'T**-21:7■24:18■26:65-**M'R**-5:28,30■14:63(5509)■15:20-**LU**-2:7(4683),12(4683)■8:27■19:36■24:12(3608)-**JOH**-19:40(3608)■20:5(3608),6(3608),7(3608)-**AC**-7:58■14:14■16:22■22:23
CLOTHEST-**JER**-4:30(3847)
CLOTHING-all=3830&marked-**JOB**-22:6(899)■24:7,10■31:19-**PS**-35:13■45:13-**PR**-27:26■31:22,25-**IS**-3:6(8071),7(8071)■23:18(4374)■59:17(8516)-**JER**-10:9■**N.T.**-**M'T**-7:15(1742)-**M'R**-12:38(4749)-**AC**-10:30(2066)-**JAS**-2:3(2066)
CLOTHS-all=899-**EX**-31:10■35:19■39:1,41
CLOUD-all=6051&marked-**GE**-9:13,14^2,16-**EX**-13:21,22■14:19,20,24■16:10■19:9,16■24:15,16^2,18■34:5■40:34,35,36,37,38-**LE**-16:2,13-**NU**-9:15,16,17^2,18,19,20,21^3,22■10:11,12,34■11:25■12:5,10■14:14^2■16:42-**DE**-1:33■5:22■31:15^2-**1KI**-8:10,11■18:44(5645)-**2CH**-5:13,14-**NE**-9:19-**JOB**-3:5(6053)■7:9■22:13(6205)■26:8,9■30:15(5645)■37:11(5645),11,15■38:9-**PS**-78:14■105:39-**PR**-16:15(5645)-**IS**-4:5■18:4(5645)■19:1(5645)■25:5(5645)■44:22(5645),22■60:8(5645)-**LA**-2:1(5743)■3:44-**EZE**-1:4,28■8:11■10:3,4■30:18■32:7■38:9,16-**HO**-6:4■13:3■**N.T.**-all=3507&marked-**M'T**-17:5^2-**M'R**-9:7^2-**LU**-9:34^2,35■12:54■21:27-**AC**-1:9-**1CO**-10:1,2-**HEB**-12:1(3509)-**RE**-10:1■11:12■14:14^2,15,16
CLOUDS-all=5645&marked-**DE**-4:11(6051)-**J'G**-5:4-**2SA**-22:12■23:4-**1KI**-18:45-**JOB**-20:6■22:14■26:8■35:5(7834)■36:28(7834),29,32(3709)■37:16,21(7834)■38:34,37(7834)-**PS**-18:11,12■36:5(7834)■57:10(7834)■68:34(7834)■77:17■78:23(7834)■97:2(6051)■104:3■108:4(7834)■47:8-**PR**-3:20(7834)■8:28(7834)■25:14(5387)-**EC**-11:3,4■12:2-**IS**-5:6■14:14-**JER**-4:13(6053)-**DA**-7:13(6050)-**JOE**-2:2(6051)-**NA**-1:3(6051)-**ZEP**-1:15(6051)-**ZEC**-10:1(2385)■**N.T.**-all=3507-**M'T**-24:30■26:64-**M'R**-13:26■14:62-**1TH**-4:17-**2PE**-2:17-**JUDE**-12-**RE**-1:7
CLOUDY-all=6051-**EX**-33:9,10-**NE**-9:12-**PS**-99:7-**EZE**-30:3■34:12
CLOUTED-**JOS**-9:5(2921)
CLOUTS-**JER**-38:11(5499),12(5499)
CLOVEN-**DE**-14:7(8156)■**N.T.**-**AC**-2:3(1266)
CLOVENFOOTED-all=8156,8157,6541-**LE**-11:3,7,26
CLUSTER-all=811-**NU**-13:23,24-**SONG**-1:14-**IS**-65:8-**MIC**-7:1
CLUSTERS-all=811&marked-**GE**-40:10-**DE**-32:32-**1SA**-25:18(6778)■30:12(6778)-**SONG**-7:7,8-**RE**-14:18(1009)
COAL-**2SA**-14:7(1513)-**IS**-6:6(7531)■47:14(1513)-**LA**-4:8(7815)
COALS-all=1513&marked-**LE**-16:12-**2SA**-22:9,13-**1KI**-19:6(7529)-**JOB**-41:21-**PS**-18:8,12,13■120:4■140:10-**PR**-6:28■25:22■26:21(6352),21-**SONG**-8:6(7565)-**IS**-44:12(6352),19■54:16(6352)-**EZE**-1:13■10:2■24:11-**HAB**-3:5(7565)■**N.T.**-**JOH**-18:18(439)■21:9(439)-**RO**-12:20(440)
COAST-all=1366&marked-**EX**-10:4-**NU**-13:29(3027)■20:23■22:36■24:24(3027)■34:3(3027),3(7097),11-**DE**-2:4,18■3:17■11:24■16:4■19:8-**JOS**-1:4■12:4,23(5299)■13:16,25,30■15:1,4^2,12^2,21■16:3■17:7,9^2■18:5,11,19■19:22,29^2,29(2256)33,34,41,47-**J'G**-1:18^3,36■11:20-**1SA**-6:9■7:13■27:1-**2KI**-14:25-**1CH**-4:10-**EZE**-25:16(2348)■47:16■48:1^2(3027)-**ZEP**-2:5(2256),6(2256),7(2256)■**N.T.**-**M'T**-4:13(3864)-**LU**-6:17(3882)
COASTS-all=1366&marked-**EX**-10:14,19-**NU**-21:13■32:33(1367)■34:2(1367),12(1367)-**DE**-3:14■19:3■28:40-**JOS**-9:1(2348)■18:5,20(1367)■19:49(1367)-**J'G**-11:22,26(3027)■18:2(7098)■19:29-**1SA**-5:6■7:14■11:3,7-**2SA**-21:5-**1KI**-1:3-**2KI**-10:32■15:16-**1CH**-6:54,66■21:12-**2CH**-11:13-**PS**-105:31,33-**JER**-25:32(3411)■31:8(3411)■50:41(3411)-**EZE**-33:2(7097)-**JOE**-3:4(1552)■**N.T.**-all=3725&marked-**M'T**-2:16■8:34■15:21(3313),22,39■16:13(3313)■19:1-**M'R**-5:17■7:31^2■10:1-**AC**-13:50■19:1(3313)■26:20(5561)■27:2(5117)
COAT-all=3801&marked-**GE**-37:3,23,31^2,32^2,33-**EX**-28:4,39■29:5-**LE**-8:7■16:4-**1SA**-2:19(4598)■17:5^2(8302),38(8302)-**2SA**-15:32-**JOB**-30:18-**SONG**-5:3■**N.T.**-all=5509&marked-**M'T**-5:40-**LU**-6:29-**JOH**-19:23■21:7(1903)
COATS-all=3801&marked-**GE**-3:21-**EX**-28:40■29:8■39:27■40:14-**LE**-8:13■10:5-**DA**-3:21(5622),27(5622)■**N.T.**-all=5509-**M'T**-10:10-**M'R**-6:9-**LU**-3:11■9:3-**AC**-9:39
COCK-all=220-**M'T**-26:34,74,75-**M'R**-14:30,68,72^2-**LU**-22:34,60,61-**JOH**-13:38■18:27
COCKATRICE-**IS**-14:29(6848)
COCKATRICE'-**IS**-11:8(6848)■59:5(6848)
COCKATRICES-**JER**-8:17(6848)
COCKCROWING-**M'R**-13:35(219)
COCKLE-**JOB**-31:40(890)
COFFER-all=712-**1SA**-6:8,11,15
COFFIN-**GE**-50:26(727)
COGITATIONS-**DA**-7:28(7476)
COLD-all=7135&marked-**GE**-8:22(7120)-**JOB**-24:7■37:9-**PS**-147:17-**PR**-20:4(2779)■25:13(6793),20,25(7119)-**JER**-18:14(7119)-**NA**-3:17■**N.T.**-all=5593&marked-**M'T**-10:42■24:12(5594)-**JOH**-18:18(5592)-**AC**-28:2(5592)-**2CO**-11:27(5592)-**RE**-3:15^2,16
COLLAR-**JOB**-30:18(6310)
COLLARS-**J'G**-8:26(5188)
COLLECTION-**2CH**-24:6(4864),9(4864)■**N.T.**-**1CO**-16:1(3048)
COLLEGE-**2KI**-22:14(4932)-**2CH**-34:22(4932)
COLLOPS-**JOB**-15:27(6371)
COLONY-**AC**-16:12(2862)
COLOUR-all=5869-**LE**-13:55-**NU**-11:7-**PR**-23:31-**EZE**-1:4,7,16,22,27■8:2■10:9-**DA**-10:6■**N.T.**-**AC**-27:30(4392)
COLOURED-all supplied
COLOURS-all=6446&marked-**GE**-37:3,23,32-**J'G**-5:30^3(6648)-**2SA**-13:18,19-**1CH**-29:2(7553)-**IS**-54:11(6320)-**EZE**-16:16(2921)■17:3(7553)
COLT-**GE**-49:11(1121)-**JOB**-11:12(5895)-**ZEC**-9:9(5895)■**N.T.**-all=4454-**M'T**-21:2,5,7-**M'R**-11:2,4,5,7-**LU**-19:30,33^2,35-**JOH**-12:15
COLTS-**GE**-32:15(1121)-**J'G**-10:4(5895)■12:14(5895)
COME-all=935,a=1961,b=3318,c=3381,d=5927,e=3212,f=5066,g=7725,h=7126&marked-**GE**-4:14a■6:13,18,20■7:1■9:14a■12:11h,14■15:4b,14b,16g■17:6b■18:5(5674),21■19:22,31,32e■20:4h,13■22:5g■24:13b,14a,31,43a■26:27■27:21f,26f,40a■28:21g■30:16,33(4279),33■31:44e■32:8,11■33:14■34:5■35:11b,16■37:10,13e,20e,23,27e■38:16^2■41:29,35,54■42:7,9,10,12,15,21■44:23c,30,31a,34(4672)■45:4f,9c,16,18,19■46:31,33a■47:1,4,5,24a■48:7■49:6,10■50:5g-**EX**-1:10(3051),10a,19■2:18■3:8c,9,10e,13,18,21a■4:8a,9a■7:15(7125)■8:3,4d,5d■9:19c■10:12d,26■11:8c■12:23,25a,25,26a,48h■13:14(4279)■14:26g■16:5a,9h■17:6b■18:6,8(4672),15,16■19:2,9,11c,13d,15f,22f,23d,24^{2}d■20:20,24■22:9,27a■23:27■24:1d,2^{2}f,12d,14g,14f■25:32b,33b■28:43,43f■30:20f■32:1c■33:5d,22a■34:2d,3d,30f■35:10■36:2h-**LE**-4:23(3045),28(3045)■10:3(7138),4h■12:4■13:16■14:8,34,35,39g,43g,44,48■15:14■16:2,3,17b,23,24b,26,28■19:19d,23■21:21^{2}f,23f■23:10■25:2,22,25-**NU**-1:1b■4:5,15■5:14^2(5674),27a■6:5(5674),6■8:19f■9:1b■10:29e■11:17c,20b,23(7136)■12:4b■13:21■14:30■15:2,18■16:5^{2}h,12d,14d,40h■17:5a■18:3h,4h,22h■19:7,14■20:5d,18b■21:8a,27■22:5b,6e,11b,11e,14(1980),17e,20,36,38■23:3(7136),7e,13e,27e■24:14e,17(1869),19c■27:21■31:24■33:38b,55a,56a■34:2■35:10(5674),26b,32g-**DE**-1:20,22■2:14(5674)■4:30(4672),46b■6:20(4279)■7:12a■10:1d■11:13a,29a■12:5,9■13:2■14:29■15:19(3205)■17:9,14■18:6^2,9,19a,22■20:2h■21:2b,5f■23:10,11■24:1a,9b■25:1f,9f,17b■26:1,3■27:12(5674)■28:1a,2,7b,15a,15,24c,43c,45,52c,63a■29:19a,22(314),22■30:1a,1■31:2,11,17(4672),21a■32:35(6264)■33:16-**JOS**-2:3^2,18■3:4h,8,9f,13a,13c,15■4:6(4279),16d,17d,18d,21(4279)■5:14■6:5a,19■7:14^{2}h■8:5a,5b,6b■9:6,8,9■10:4d,6d,24h■11:20(7122)■14:11■18:4,8g■20:6■22:24(4279),27(4279),28(4279)■23:7,14,15a,15-**J'G**-1:3d,24b,34c■3:27■4:20,22e■6:4,18,18g■7:13,17,24c■8:9g■9:10e,12e,14e,15,15b,20^{2}b,24,29b,31,33b,36c,37c,37,43b■11:6e,7,12,33■12:3d■13:5d,8,12,17■15:10^{2}d,12c■16:2,17d,18d■18:10■

19:11e,13e,23,29■20:10,41(5060)■21:3a,21^{2}b,22-**RU**-1:19■2:11(1980),12,14(5060)■4:3g,11-**1SA**-1:11d,20(8622)■2:3b,31,34,36a,36■4:3,6,7■5:5■6:7d,21c■9:5,5e,9e,10e,13^2,14,16,25c■10:3,5,5a,6(6743),7,8c,8,11a,20h,21h,22■11:3b,10b,14e■12:8■13:12c■14:1e,6e,9(5060),10d,11b,12^{2}d,26■16:2,5^2,6,11,16a■17:8b,8c,25^{2}d,28c,44e,45,52■19:16■20:9,11e,19,21,24a,37■21:15■22:3b■23:3e,7,10,11^{2}c,15b,20^{2}c,23g,23a,27e■24:14b■25:8,19,30a,34,40■26:4,10,20b,22(5674)■29:10■30:1■31:4-**2SA**-1:9(270)■2:24■3:23,26b■5:6^2,8,13,23,25■6:9■9:6■10:11(1980)■11:7■12:4^2■13:5,6^2,11,35■14:3,15,29^2,32^2■15:4,28,32■16:7b,16■17:2,6,9a,12,17,27■19:11,18(5674),20,25,30,33(5674),39(5674)■20:16h,17h■24:13,21-**1KI**-1:12e,14,21a,23,35d,35,42,45d■2:30b,41g■3:7■6:1b■8:10b,19b,31,42■10:2■11:2■12:1,5g,12g,20g,21■13:7,15e,22,32a■14:6,13■15:17,19e■17:18,21g■18:12a,12,30f■19:17a■20:17b,18^{2}b,22d,33sup33d■22:27-**2KI**-1:4c,6c,9c,10c,11c,12c,16c■3:21d■4:1,4,22g,32,36■5:6,8,10g,11b,22■6:9(5185),20■7:4e,5,6,9(4672),9e,12b■8:1,7■9:16c,30,34■10:6,16e,25c■11:9■14:8e■16:7d,12■18:13d,17d,25d,31b,32■19:3,9b,23d,28d,32,32(6923),33■20:14,17-**1CH**-9:25■10:4■11:5■12:17,31■14:14■16:29■17:11a■19:3,9■24:19-**2CH**-1:10■5:11b■6:9b,22,32^2■8:11■9:1■10:1,5g,12g■11:1■13:13■16:1■18:14■19:10,10a■20:11,16d,22■22:7■23:6,8,15■25:10,14,17e■28:17■29:31f■30:1,5,9g■32:2,4,21-**EZR**-3:1(5060),8■4:12(858)■6:21g■8:35■9:13■10:8,14-**NE**-2:7,10,17e■4:8,11■6:2e,3^{2}c,7e,10^2■8:17g■9:32(4672)■13:1,22-**ES**-1:12,17b,19■2:12(5060),15(5060)■4:11^2,14(5060)■5:4,8,12■6:4,5■8:6(4672)■9:26(5060)-**JOB**-2:11^2■3:6,7,25(857),25■4:5■5:26■7:9d■9:32■13:13(5674),16■14:14■15:21■16:22(857)■17:10■19:12■20:22■22:21■23:3,10b■34:28■37:13(4672)■38:11■41:13,16-**PS**-5:7,16c■17:2b■22:31■24:7,9■32:6(5060),9h■34:11e■35:8■36:11■40:7■41:6■42:2■44:17■46:8e■50:3■52:t■55:5■65:2■66:5e,16e■68:31(857)■69:1,2,27■71:18■72:6c■78:4(314),6(314)■79:1,11■80:2e■83:4e■86:9■88:2,8b■91:7f,10h■95:1e,2(6923),6■96:8■100:2■101:2■102:1,13,18(314)■109:17,18■119:41,77,169h,170■126:6■132:3■144:5c-**PR**-1:11e■3:28g■5:8h■6:3,11,15■7:18e,20■9:5e■10:24■11:27■12:13b■24:25,34■25:4b,7d■26:2■28:22■31:25(314)-**EC**-1:7(1980),11(314),11a■2:16■4:16(314)■7:18b■8:10■12:1-**SONG**-2:10e,12(5060),13e■4:8,16^2■5:1■7:11e-**IS**-1:12,18e,23■2:2a,3e,5e■3:24a■4:3a■5:6d,19,26■7:7a,17,18a,19,21a,22a,23a,24,25■8:7d,21a■10:3,12a,20a,27a,28■11:1b,11a■13:5,6,22■14:3a,8d,24a,29b,31■16:8(5060),12a,12■17:4a■19:1,23■21:12(857)■22:7a,20a■23:15a,17a■24:10,18a,21a■26:20e■27:6,11,12a,13a,13■28:15■29:24(3045),8(314),29■31:4c■32:10,13d■34:1h,1(6631),3d,5c,7c,13d■35:4^2,10■36:10d,16b,17■37:3,9b,24d,29d,33,33(6923),34■39:3,6■40:10■41:1f,1h,22,23(857),25(857),25■42:9■44:7■45:11(857),14(5674),14e,14(5674),20,24■47:1c,9^2,11^2,13■48:1b,16h■49:12,18■50:8f■51:11,19(7122)■52:1■54:14h■55:1^{3}e,3e,13^{2}d■56:1,9(857),12(857)■59:19,20■60:1,3(1980),4^2,5,6,7d,13,14(1980)■63:4■64:1c■65:5f,17d,24a■66:15,18^2,23a,23-**JER**-1:15■2:3,31■3:16a,16d,18,22(857)■4:4b,7,9a,12,13d,16■5:12,19a■6:3,26■7:10,32■8:16■9:17^2,21d,25■10:22■12:9e,9(857),12,15a,16a■13:18c,20,22(7122)■15:2a■16:10a,14,19■17:15,19,24a,26,18^{2}e■19:6■20:6■21:13(5181)■22:23■23:5,7,17■25:3a,12a,31■26:2■27:3,7,8a■28:9■30:3,8a■31:9,12,16g,17g,27,28a,31,38■32:7,23(7122),24,24a,29■33:5,14■35:11■36:6,14e,29■37:5b,7b,8g,19■38:25■40:3a,4^3,10■41:6■42:4a,16a■46:9d,9b,13,18,21,22■47:5■48:2e,8,12,16,18c,18d,21,45b■49:2,4,9,14,19d,22d,36,39a■50:4,5,9d,26,27,31,41,44d■51:10,13,27d,33,42d,46,47,48,50d,51,52,53,56,60-**LA**-1:4,14d,22■3:47a■4:18■5:1a-**EZE**-5:4b■7:2,5,6^2,7^2,10,12,26■9:6f■11:5(4609),16,18■12:16,25(6213)■14:22b■16:7,16,33■17:12■18:6h■20:3■21:19,19b,20,25,27,29■22:3,4■23:24,40■24:8d,14(835),26(835)■26:3^{2}d,16c■27:29c■30:4,6c,9a■32:11■33:3,4,6^2,30,31,33■34:26c■36:8■37:9,12d■38:8,9,10a,10d,13,15,16d,18a,18,18d■39:2d,8,11a,17■40:46(7131)■44:13^{2}f,15h,16h,17a,17d,25■45:4(7131)■46:9■47:9a,9^2,10a,20,22a,23a-**DA**-2:29^2(1934),45(1934)■3:2(858),26(5312),26(858)■4:24(4291)■8:7(5060)■9:13,22b,23,26■10:12,14,20^2■11:6,7,9,10,11b,13,15,21,23d,29,30■11:40(8175),45-**HO**-1:5a,10a,11d,■2:21a■4:15■6:1e,3■9:4,7^2■10:8d,12■13:13,15,15d-**JOE**-1:6d,13,15■2:20^{2}d,23c,28a,31,32a■3:9d,11,11(5181),12d,13,18a,18b-**AM**-4:2,4,10d■5:5a,9■6:3f,9a■8:2,9a,11■9:13-**OB**-21d-**JON**-1:2d,7e■4:6d-**MIC**-1:3c,9,9(5060),15■2:13d■3:11■4:1a,2(1980),2e,8(857),8■5:2b,5,10a■6:6^2(6923)■7:12-**NA**-1:11b■2:1d■3:7a-**HAB**-1:8,9■2:3-**ZEP**-1:8a,10a,12a■2:2^2-**HAG**-1:2■2:7,22c-**ZEC**-1:21^2,10■6:10,15,15a■7:13a■8:13a,20sup,20,22■11:2c■12:9a,9■13:2a,3a,4a,8a■14:5,6a,7a,13a,16a,17d,18,18d,19d,21-**MAL**-3:1^2,5h■4:6■**N.T.**-all=2064,a=1096,b=1831,c=2240,d=1525,e-3854&marked-**M'T**-2:2,6b,8,11■3:7,7(3195)■5:17^2,24,26b■6:10■7:15■8:1(2597),7,8d,9,11c,14,16a,28,29,32b■9:13,15,18,28■10:12d,13,23,34,35■11:3,14,28(1205)■12:28(5348),32(3195),44■13:32,49b,54■14:23a,28,29,29(2597),32(1684)■15:18b■16:5,24,27■17:10,11,12,14,24,25d■18:7,11■19:14,21(1204)■20:8a■21:1,10d,23,38(1205)■22:3,4(1205)■23:35,36c■24:5,6a,14c,17(2597),42,43,50c■25:31,34(1205)■26:20a,50(3918),55b■27:1a,33,40(2597),42(2597),49,57a,64■28:6(1205),14(191)-**M'R**-1:17(1205),24,25b,29b■2:3,4(4331),18,20■4:22,29(3936),35a■5:2b,8b,15,18(1684),23,39d■6:2a,21a,31(1205),47a,54b■7:15(1607),23(1607),30(565)■8:34■9:1,11,13,25b,28d,29b■10:14,21(1204),30,35(4365)■11:11(1511),12b,15,19a,23a,27^2■12:7(1205),9,14,18■13:6,29a■14:8(4301),41,45,48b■15:30(2597),33a,36,42a■16:1-**LU**-1:35(1904),43■2:15a■3:7(3195)■4:34,35b,36b■5:7,17,35■7:3,7,8,19,20e,20,34■8:4(1975),17,19(4940),29b,41d■9:23,26,37(2718),51(4845),54(2597),56■10:1,9(1448),11(1448),35(1880)■11:2,6e,20(5348),22(1904),33(1531)■12:37(3928),38^2,39,46c,49,51e■13:7,14,29c,35c■14:9,17,20,23d,26,27■15:27c,30■16:28■17:1^2,7d,20,22,31(2597)■18:16,22(1204),30,35(1448),40(1448)■19:5(2597),9a,10,13,29(1448),37(1448),41(1448),43c■20:14(1205),16■21:6,7a,8,9a,28a,31a,34(2186),35(1904),36a■22:14a,18,45,52e,52b■23:33(565)■24:12a,18a-**JOH**-1:31,39,46(1511),46■2:4c■3:2,19,26■4:15,16,25,29(1205),40,45,47c,47(2597),49(2597),54■5:14a,24,29(1607),40,43^2■6:5,14,15,16a,17,37c,44,65■7:6(3918),8(4137),28,30,34,36,37,41■8:14,20,21,22■9:39■10:10■11:27,28(3918),30,32,34,43(1204),48,56■12:12,23,35(2638),46■13:1,3b,19^{2}a,33■14:3,18,23,28,29a■15:22,26■16:4,7,8,13^2,21,28,32■17:1,11,13■18:4■21:4a,9(576),12(1205),22,23-**AC**-1:6(4905),8(1904),11,13d■2:1(4845),17(1511),20,21(1511)■3:19,23(1511)■5:38(2647)■7:3(1204),7(1834),34(2597),34(1204)■8:15(2597),24(1904),27,31(305),39(305)■9:26e,38(1330),39e■10:4(305),21(3918),27(4905),28(4334),33e■11:2(305),11(2186),20d■12:11a■13:40(1904)■14:11(2597),27e■15:4e■16:7,9(1224),15d,18b,37■17:6(3918),15■18:2,5(2718),27e■19:4,32(4905)■20:11(305),18e■21:11,17a,22(4905),22■22:6(1448),17(5290)■23:15(1448),35e■24:8,22(2597),23(4334),25(3195,1511)■25:1(1910),7e,17(4905),23■26:7(2658),22a■27:7a,16(4031)a,27a■28:6a,17(4905)-**RO**-1:10,13■3:8,23(5302)■5:14(3195)■8:38(3195)■9:9,26(1511),25d,26c■15:23,24,28(565),29,32■16:19(864)-**1CO**-1:7(5302)■2:6(2673)■3:22(3195)■4:5,18,19,21■7:5(4905)■10:11(2658)■11:17(4905),18(4905),20(4905),26,33(4905),34(4905),34■13:10■14:6,23(4905),23d,24d,26(4905)■15:35■16:2,3e,5,10,11,12^3-**2CO**-1:15,16■2:1■6:17b■7:5■9:4■10:14(5348)■12:1,14,20,21■13:2-**GA**-2:11,12■3:14a,19,25■4:4-**EPH**-1:21(3195)■2:7(1904)■4:13(2658)-**PH'P**-1:27■2:24-**COL**-1:6(3918)■2:17(3195)■4:10-**1TH**-1:10■2:16(5348),18-**2TH**-1:10■2:3^2-**1TI**-2:4■3:14■4:8(3195),13■6:19(3195)-**2TI**-3:1(1764),7■4:3(1511),9,21-**TIT**-3:12-**HEB**-2:5(3195)■4:1(5302),16(4334)■6:5(3195)■7:5b,25(4334)■8:8■9:11e,11(3195)■10:1(3195),7c,9c,37,37c■11:20(3195),24a■12:18(4334),22(4334)■13:14(3195),23-**JAS**-2:2^{2}d■5:1(1904)-**2PE**-3:3,9(5562),10c-**1JO**-2:18■4:2,3^2■5:20c-**2JO**-7,10,12-**3JO**-10-**RE**-1:1a,4,8■2:5,16,25c■3:3^{2}c,9c,10,11,20d■4:1(305),8■6:1,3,5,7,17■9:12■10:1(2597)■11:12(305),17,18■12:10a,12(2597)■13:13(2597)■14:7,15■15:4c,16:15■17:1(1204),10■18:1(2597),4b,8c,10,17(2049)■19:7,17(1205)■20:1(2597)■21:9(1204)■22:7,12,17^3,20^2

COMELINESS-all=1926&marked-**IS**-53:2-**EZE**-16:14■27:10-**DA**-10:8(1935)■**N.T.**-**1CO**-12:23(2157)

COMELY-all=5000&marked-**1SA**-16:18(8389)-**JOB**-41:12(2433)-**PS**-33:1■147:1-**PR**-30:29(3190)-**EC**-5:18(3303)-**SONG**-1:5,10(4998)■2:14■4:3■6:4-**IS**-4:2(8597)-**JER**-6:2■**N.T.**-**1CO**-7:35(2158)■11:13(4241)■12:24(2158)

COMERS-**HEB**-10:1(4334)

COMEST-all=935&marked-**GE**-10:19■13:10■24:41-**DE**-2:19(7126)■20:10(7126)■23:24,25■28:6,19-**J'G**-17:9■18:23(2199)■19:17-**1SA**-15:7■16:4■17:43,45-**2SA**-1:3■3:13-**1KI**-2:13■19:15-**2KI**-9:2-**JOB**-1:7■2:2-**JER**-51:61-**JON**-1:8■**N.T.**-all=2064-**M'T**-3:14-**LU**-23:42-**2TI**-4:13

COMETH-all=935,a=3318&marked-**GE**-24:43a■29:6■30:11■32:6(1980)■37:19■48:2-**EX**-4:14a■8:20a■13:12(7698)■28:35a■29:30-**LE**-11:34-**NU**-1:51(7131)■3:10(7131)■38(7131)■5:30(5674)■12:12a■17:13(7131)■18:7(7131)■21:13a-**DE**-23:11(6437),13(6627)■28:57a-**J'G**-11:31a■13:14a-**1SA**-4:3■9:6■11:7a■20:27,29■25:8(4672)■28:14(2927)-**2SA**-13:5■18:27-**1KI**-8:41■14:5^2-**2KI**-4:10■6:32■9:18(7725),20(7725)■10:2■11:8^2■12:4(5927),9-**1CH**-16:33-**2CH**-13:9■20:2,9,12■23:7^2-**JOB**-3:24■5:6a,21,26(5927)■14:2a,18(5034)■20:25a,25(1980)■21:17■27:9■28:5a,20■36:32(6293)■37:9,22(857)-**PS**-78:39(7725)■96:13■98:9■118:26■121:1-**PR**-1:26,27,27(857)27■3:25■11:2,8■13:10(5414),12■18:3,17■-**EC**-1:4■2:12■4:14a■5:3■6:4■11:8-**SONG**-2:8■3:6(5927)■8:5(5927)-**IS**-13:9■21:1,9,12(857)■24:18(5927)■26:21a■28:29a■30:13,27■42:5(6631)■55:10(3381)■62:11■63:1-**JER**-6:20,22■17:6,8■43:11■46:7(5927),20■47:4■50:3(5927)-**LA**-3:37(1961)-**EZE**-4:12(6627)■7:25■14:4^2,7■20:32(5927)■21:7^2■24:24■30:9■33:30a,31,33■47:9-**DA**-11:16■12:12(5060)-**HO**-7:1-**JOE**-2:1-**MIC**-1:3a■5:6■7:4-**HAB**-3:16(5927)-**ZEC**-9:9■14:1-**MAL**-4:1^2■**N.T.**-all=2064&marked-**M'T**-3:11,13(3854)■5:37(1511)■8:9■13:19■15:11(1607)■17:27(305)■18:7■21:5,9,40■23:39■24:27(1831),44,46■25:6,13,19■26:36,40,45-**M'R**-1:7■

3:20(4905)▪4:15▪5:22,38▪6:48▪7:20 (1607)▪8:22,38▪9:12▪10:1▪11:9,10▪ 13:35▪14:17,37,41,43(3854),66-LU-3:16▪6:47▪7:8▪8:12,49▪11:25▪12:36, 37,40,43,54,55(1096)▪13:35▪14:10▪31▪ 15:6▪17:20▪18:8▪19:38-JOH-1:9,15,30▪ 3:8,20,21,31^{2}▪4:5,7,21,23,25,35▪6:33 (2597),35,37,45,50(2597)▪7:27,31,42▪ 9:4▪11:38▪12:13,15,22▪13:6▪14:6,30▪ 16:2,25,32▪18:3▪20:1,2,6▪21:13-AC-10:32(3854)▪13:25▪18:21-2CO-11:4, 28(1999)EPH-5:6-COL-3:6-1TH-5:2, 3(2186)-1TI-6:4(1096)-HEB-6:7▪11:6 (4334)-JAS-1:17(2591)-JUDE-14-RE-1:7▪3:12(2597)▪11:14▪17:10

COMFORT-all=5162&marked-GE-5:29▪18:5(5582)▪27:42▪37:35-J'G-19:5 (5582),8(5582)-2SA-10:2-1CH-7:22▪ 19:2^{2}-JOB-2:11▪6:10(5165)▪7:13▪9:27 (1082)▪10:20(1082)▪21:34-PS-23:4▪ 71:21▪119:50,76,82-SONG-2:5(7502) -IS-22:4▪40:1▪51:3^{2},19▪57:6▪61:2▪ 66:13-JER-8:18(4010)▪16:7▪31:13-LA-1:2,17,21▪2:13-EZE-14:23▪16:54-ZEC-1:17▪10:2▪N.T.-all=3870&marked -M'T-9:22(2293)-M'R-10:49(2293)-LU-8:48(2293)-JOH-11:19(3888)-AC-9:31 (3874)-RO-15:4(3874)-1CO-14:3(3889) -2CO-1:3(3874),4,4(3874)▪2:7▪7:4(3874), 13(3874)▪13:11-EPH-6:22-PH'P-2:1 (3890),19(2174)-COL-4:8,11(3931)-1TH-3:2▪4:18▪5:11,14(3888)-2TH-2:17

COMFORTABLE-2SA-14:17 (4496)-ZEC-1:13(5150)

COMFORTABLY-all=5921,3820 &marked-2SA-19:7-2CH-30:22▪32:6 (5921,3824)-IS-40:2-HO-2:14

COMFORTED-all=5162-GE-24:67▪37:35▪38:12▪50:21-RU-2:13-2SA-12:24▪13:39-JOB-42:11-PS-77:2▪86:17▪ 119:52-IS-49:13▪52:9▪54:11▪66:13 -JER-31:15-EZE-5:13▪14:22▪31:16▪ 32:31▪N.T.-all=3870&marked-M'T-2:18▪5:4-LU-16:25-JOH-11:31(3888) -AC-16:40▪20:12-RO-1:12(4837)-1CO-14:31-2CO-1:4,6▪7:6,7,13-COL-2:2 -1TH-2:11(3888)▪3:7

COMFORTEDST-IS-12:1(5162)

COMFORTER-EC-4:1(5162),1sup -LA-1:9(5162),16(5152)▪N.T.-all=3875 -JOH-14:16,26▪15:26▪16:7

COMFORTERS-all=5162-2SA-10:3-1CH-19:3-JOB-16:2-PS-69:20-NA-3:7

COMFORTETH-all=5162&marked -JOB-29:25-IS-51:12▪66:13▪N.T. -2CO-1:4(3870)▪7:6(3870)

COMFORTLESS-JOH-14:18(3737)

COMFORTS-PS-94:19(8575)-IS-57:18(5150)

COMING-all=935&marked-GE-24:63▪30:30(7272)-NU-22:16(1980)▪ 33:40-J'G-5:28-1SA-10:5(3381)▪16:4 (7122)▪22:9▪25:26,33▪29:6^{2}-2SA-3:25 (4126)▪24:20(5674)-2KI-13:20▪19:27 -2CH-22:7-EZR-3:8-PS-19:5(3318)▪ 37:13▪121:8-PR-8:3(3996)-IS-14:9▪ 32:19(3381)▪37:28▪44:7(857)-JER-8:7 -DA-4:23(5182)-MIC-7:15(3318)-MAL-3:2▪4:5▪N.T.-all=2064,a=3952& marked-M'T-8:28(1831)▪16:28▪24:3a, 27a,30,37a,39a,48▪25:27▪26:64-M'R-1:10(305)▪6:31▪13:26,36▪14:62▪15:21 -LU-2:38(2186)▪9:42(4334)▪12:45▪ 18:5▪19:23▪21:26(1904),27▪23:26,29, 36(4334)-JOH-1:27,29,47▪5:7,25,28▪ 10:12▪11:20▪12:12-AC-7:52(1660)▪ 9:12(1525),28(1531)▪10:3(1525),25 (1525)▪13:24(1529)▪17:10(3854)▪27:33 (3195,1096)-RO-15:22-1CO-1:7(602)▪ 15:23a▪16:17a-2CO-7:6a,7a▪13:1-PH'P-1:26a-1TH-2:19a▪3:13a▪4:15a▪5:23a -2TH-2:1a,8a,9a-JAS-5:7a,8a-1PE-2:4 (4334)-2PE-1:16a▪3:4a,12a-1JO-2:28a -RE-13:11(305)▪21:2(2597)

COMINGS-EZE-43:11(4126)

COMMAND-all=6680&marked -GE-18:19▪27:8▪50:16-EX-7:2▪8:27 (559)▪18:23▪27:20▪34:11-LE-6:9▪ 13:54▪14:4,5,36,40▪24:2▪25:21-NU-5:2▪ 9:8▪28:2▪34:2▪35:2▪36:6-DE-2:4▪4:2^{2}, 40▪6:2,6▪7:11▪8:1,11▪10:13▪11:8,13, 22,27,28▪12:11,14,28,32▪13:18▪15:5,11, 15▪18:18▪19:7,9▪24:18,22▪27:1,4,10▪ 28:1,8,13,14,15▪30:2,8,11,16▪32:46 -JOS-1:11▪3:8▪4:3,16▪11:15-1SA-16:16 (559)-1KI-5:6▪11:38-2CH-7:13-JOB-39:27(6310)-PS-42:8▪44:4-IS-5:6▪ 45:11-JER-1:7,17▪11:4▪26:2▪27:4▪34:22 -LA-1:10-AM-9:3,4,9▪N.T.-all=3853& marked-M'T-4:3(2036)▪19:7(1781)▪27:64 (2753)-M'R-10:3(1781)-LU-4:3(2036)▪ 8:31(2004)▪9:54(2036)-JOH-15:14 (1781),17(1781)-AC-5:28▪15:5▪16:18 -1CO-7:10-2TH-3:4,6,12-1TH-4:11

COMMANDED-all=6680,a=559, b=560&marked-GE-2:16▪3:11,17▪6:22▪ 7:5,9,16▪12:20▪21:4▪32:4,17,19▪42:25▪ 44:1▪45:19▪47:11▪50:2,12-EX-1:17 (1696)▪4:28▪5:6▪7:6,10,20▪12:28,50▪ 16:16,34▪19:7▪23:15▪29:35▪31:6,11▪ 32:8▪34:4,18,34▪35:1,4,10,29▪36:1,5▪ 38:22▪39:1,5,7,21,26,29,31,32,42,43▪ 40:16,19,21,23,25,27,29,32-LE-7:36,38^{2}▪ 8:4,5,9,13,17,21,29,31,34,35,36▪9:5,6,7, 10,21▪10:1,13,15,18▪16:34▪17:2▪24:23▪ 27:34-NU-1:19,54▪2:33,34▪3:16,42,51▪ 4:49▪8:3,20,22▪9:5▪15:23^{2},36▪16:47 (1696)▪17:11▪19:2▪20:9,27▪26:4▪ 27:11,22,23(1696)▪29:40▪30:1,16▪31:7, 21,31,41,47▪32:28▪34:13^{2},29▪36:2^{2},5, 10,13-DE-1:18,19,41▪3:18,21▪4:5,13, 14▪5:12,15,16,32,33▪6:1,17,20,24,25▪ 9:12,16▪10:5▪12:21▪13:5▪17:3▪18:20▪ 20:17▪24:8▪26:13,14,16▪27:1▪28:45▪ 29:1▪31:5,10,25,29▪33:4▪34:9-JOS-1:7, 9,10,13▪3:3▪4:8,10^{2},17▪6:10▪7:11▪8:4, 8,27,29,31,33,35▪9:24▪10:27,40▪11:12, 15^{2},20▪13:6▪14:2,5▪17:4▪21:2,8▪22:2^{2}▪ 23:16-J'G-2:20▪3:4▪4:6▪13:14▪21:10, 20-RU-2:15-1SA-2:29▪13:13,14^{2}▪17:20▪ 18:22▪20:29▪21:2^{2}-2SA-4:12▪5:25▪7:7, 11▪9:11▪13:28^{2},29▪18:5▪21:14▪24:19 -1KI-2:46▪5:17▪8:58▪9:4▪11:10^{2},11▪ 13:21▪15:5▪17:4,9▪22:31-2KI-11:5,9, 15▪14:6▪16:15,16▪17:13,27,34▪18:6,12▪ 21:8^{2}▪22:12▪23:4,21-1CH-6:49▪14:16▪ 15:15▪16:15,40▪17:6,10▪21:17a,18a,27a▪ 22:2a,17▪24:19-2CH-7:17▪8:14(4687)▪ 14:4a▪18:30▪23:8▪25:4▪29:21a,24a,27a, 30a▪31:4a,11a▪32:12a▪33:8,16a▪34:20▪ 35:21a-EZR-4:3,19(7761,2942)▪5:3 (7761,2942),9(7761,2942)▪7:23(4480, 2941)▪9:11-NE-8:1,14▪13:5(4687),9a, 19a,22a-ES-1:10a,17a▪3:2,12▪4:13a, 17▪6:1a▪8:9▪9:14a,25a-JOB-38:12▪ 42:9(1696)-PS-7:6▪33:9▪68:28▪78:5, 23▪105:8▪106:34a▪111:9▪119:4,138▪ 133:3▪148:5-IS-13:3▪34:16▪45:12▪ 48:5-JER-7:22,23^{2},31▪11:4,8▪13:5,6▪ 14:14▪17:22▪19:5▪23:32▪26:8▪29:23▪ 32:35▪35:6,10,14,16,18▪36:5,8,26▪37:21▪ 38:10,27▪50:21▪51:59-LA-1:17▪2:17 -EZE-9:11▪10:6▪12:7▪24:18▪37:7,10 -DA-2:2a,12b,46b▪3:4b,13b,19b,20b▪ 4:26b▪5:2b,29b▪6:16b,23b,24b-AM-2:12 -ZEC-1:6-MAL-4:4▪N.T.-all=2753,a= 3853&marked-M'T-8:4(4367)▪10:5a▪ 14:9,19▪15:4(1781),35▪18:25▪21:6 (4367)▪27:58▪28:20(1781)-M'R-1:44 (4367)▪5:43(2036)▪6:8a,27(2004),39 (2004)▪8:6a,7(2036)▪10:49(2036)▪ 11:6(1781)▪13:34(1781)▪-LU-5:14 (4367)▪8:29a,55(1299)▪9:21a▪14:22 (2004)▪17:9(1299),10(1299)▪18:40▪ 19:15(2036)-JOH-8:5(1781)-AC-1:4a▪ 4:15,18a▪5:34,40a▪8:38▪10:33(4367), 42a,48(4367)▪12:19▪13:47(1781)▪16:22▪ 18:2(1299)▪21:33,34▪22:24,30▪23:2 (2004),10,31(1299),35▪24:23(1299)▪25:6, 17,21▪27:43-2CO-4:6(2036)-1TH-4:11a -2TH-3:10a-HEB-12:20(1291)-RE-9:4(4483)

COMMANDEDST-all=6680-NE-1:7,8▪9:14-JER-32:23

COMMANDER-IS-55:4(6680)

COMMANDEST-JOS-1:16,18▪ N.T.-AC-23:3(2753)

COMMANDETH-all=6680& marked-EX-16:32-NU-32:25-JOB-9:7 (559)▪36:10(559),32▪37:12-PS-107:25 (559)-LA-3:37-AM-6:11▪N.T.-all= 2004&marked-M'R-1:27-LU-4:36▪ 8:25-AC-17:30(3853)

COMMANDING-GE-49:33(6680)▪ N.T.-M'T-11:1(1299)-AC-24:8(2753)

COMMANDMENT-all=4687, a=6310,b=1697&marked-GE-45:21a -EX-17:1a▪25:22(6680)▪34:32(6680)▪ 36:6(6680)▪38:21a-NU-3:39a▪4:37a, 41a,49a▪9:18^{2}a,20^{2}a,23^{3}a▪10:13a▪13:3a▪ 14:41a▪15:31(4687)▪24:13a▪27:14a▪ 33:2a,38a-DE-1:3(6680),26a,43a▪9:23a▪ 17:20▪30:11-JOS-1:18a▪8:8b▪15:13a▪ 17:4a▪21:3a▪22:3,5-1SA-12:14a,15a▪ 13:13▪15:13b,24a-2SA-12:9b-1KI-2:43▪ 13:21-2KI-17:34,37▪18:36▪23:35a▪ 24:3a-1CH-12:32a▪14:12(559)▪28:21b -2CH-8:13,15▪14:4▪19:10▪24:8(559), 21▪29:15,25^{2}▪30:6,12▪31:5b,13(4662)▪ 35:10,15,16-EZR-4:21(2942),21(2941)▪ 6:14(2941),14(2942)▪8:17(3318)▪10:3 -NE-11:23▪12:24,45-ES-1:12b,15(3982), 19b▪2:8b,20(3982)▪3:3,14(1881),15b▪ 4:3b,5(6680),10(6680)▪8:13(1881),14b, 17b▪9:1b-JOB-23:12-PS-19:8▪71:3(6680)▪ 119:96▪147:15(565)-PR-6:20,23▪8:29a▪ 13:13▪19:16-EC-8:2a,5-IS-23:11(6680)▪ 36:21-JER-35:14,16,18-LA-1:18a-DA-3:22(4406)▪9:23b,25b-HO-5:11(6673) -NA-1:14(6680)-MAL-2:1,4▪N.T.-all= 1785&marked-M'T-8:18(2753)▪15:3,6▪ 22:36,38-M'R-7:8,9▪12:28,30,31-LU-15:29▪23:56-JOH-10:18▪11:57▪12:49, 50▪13:34▪14:31(1781)▪15:12-AC-15:24 (1291)▪17:15▪23:30(3853)▪25:23(2753) -RO-7:8,9,10,11,12,13▪13:9▪16:26(2003) -1CO-7:6(2003),25(2003)-2CO-8:8(2003) -EPH-6:2-1TI-1:1(2003),5(3852)▪6:14 -TIT-1:3(2003)-HEB-7:5,16,18▪11:22 (1781),23(1297)-2PE-2:21▪3:2-1JO-2:7^{3},8▪3:23^{2}▪4:21-2JO-4,5,6

COMMANDMENTS-all=4687 &marked-GE-26:5-EX-15:26▪16:28▪ 20:6▪24:12▪34:28(1697)-LE-4:2,13, 22,27▪5:17▪22:31▪26:3,14,15▪27:34 -NU-15:22,39,40▪36:13-DE-4:2,13 (1697),40▪5:10,29,31▪6:1,2,17,25▪7:9, 11▪8:1,2,6,11▪10:4(1697),13▪11:1,8,13, 22,27,28▪13:4,18▪15:5▪19:9▪26:13^{2}, 17,18▪27:1,10▪28:1,9,13,15,45▪30:8, 10,16▪31:5-JOS-22:5-J'G-2:17▪3:4 -1SA-15:11(1697)-1KI-2:3▪3:14▪6:12▪ 8:58,61▪9:6▪11:34,38▪14:8▪18:18-2KI-17:13,16,19▪18:6▪23:3-1CH-28:7,8▪ 29:19-2CH-7:19▪17:4▪24:20▪31:21▪ 34:31-EZR-7:11▪9:10,14-NE-1:5,7▪9:13, 16,29,34▪10:29-PS-78:7▪89:31▪103:18 (6490),20(1697)▪111:7(6490)▪112:1▪ 119:6,10,19,21,32,35,47,48,60,66,73,86, 98,115,127,131,143,151,166,172,176 -PR-2:1▪3:1▪4:4▪7:1,2▪10:8-EC-12:13 -IS-48:18-DA-9:4-AM-2:4(2706)▪ N.T.-all=1785&marked-M'T-5:19▪ 15:9(1778)▪19:17▪22:40-M'R-7:7 (1778)▪10:19▪12:29-LU-1:6▪18:20 -JOH-14:15,21▪15:10^{2}-AC-1:2(1781) -1CO-7:19▪14:37-EPH-2:15-COL-2:22(1778)▪4:10-1TH-4:2(3852)-TIT-1:14-1JO-2:3,4▪3:22,24▪5:2,3^{2}-2JO-6 -RE-12:17▪14:12▪22:14

COMMEND-all=4921&marked -LU-23:46(3908)-AC-20:32(3908)-RO-3:5▪16:1-2CO-3:1▪5:12▪10:12

COMMENDATION-2CO-3:1^{2} (4956)

COMMENDED-GE-12:15(1984) -PR-12:8(1984)-EC-8:15(7623)▪N.T. -LU-16:8(1867)-AC-14:23(3908)-2CO-12:11(4921)

COMMENDETH-RO-5:8(4921) -1CO-8:8(3936)-2CO-10:18^{2}(4921)

COMMENDING-2CO-4:2(4921)

COMMISSION-AC-26:12(2011)

COMMISSIONS-EZR-8:36(1881)

COMMIT-all=6213&marked-EX-20:14(5003)-LE-5:15(4600),17■6:2(4600)■18:26,29^{2},30■20:5(2181)-NU-5:6,6sup,12(4600)■25:1(2181)■31:16(4560)-DE-5:18(5003)■19:20-JOS-22:20(4600)-2SA-7:14(5753)-2CH-21:11(2181)-JOB-5:8(7760)-PS-31:5(6485)■37:5(1556)-PR-16:3(1556),12-IS-22:21(5414)■23:17(2181)-JER-7:9(5003)■9:5(5753)■23:14(5003)■37:21(6485)■44:7-EZE-3:20■8:17^{2}■16:17(2181),34(2181),43■20:30(2181)■22:9■23:43(2181)■33:13-HO-4:10(2181),13(2181),13(5003),14(2181),14(5003)■6:9(6313)■7:1(6466)■N.T.-all=3431&marked-M'T-5:27,32(3429)■19:9(3429),18-M'R-10:19-LU-12:48(4160)■16:11(4100)■18:20-JOH-2:24(4100)-RO-1:32(4238)■2:2(4238),22^{2},22(2416)■13:9(3431)-1CO-10:8(4203)-1TI-1:18(3908)-2TI-2:2(3908)-JAS-2:9(2038),11^{2}-1PE-4:19(3908)-1JO-3:9(4160)-RE-2:14(4203),20(4203),22(3431)

COMMITTED-all=6213&marked-GE-39:8(5414),22(5414)-LE-4:35(2398)■5:7(2398)■18:30■20:13,23-NU-15:24-DE-17:5■21:22(1961)-JOS-7:1(4600)■22:16,31-J'G-20:6-1KI-8:47(7561)■14:22(2398),27(6485)-1CH-10:13(4600)-2CH-12:10(6485)■34:16(5414)-PS-106:6(5753)-JER-2:13■3:8(5003),9(5003)■5:7(5003),30(1961)■6:15■8:12■16:10(2398)■29:23^{2}■39:14(5414)■40:7(6485)■41:10(6485)■44:3,9,22-EZE-6:9■15:8(4600)■16:26(2181),50,51(2398),52(8581)■18:12,21,22,27,28■20:27(4600),43■22:11■23:3^{2}(2181),7(5414),37^{2}(5003)■33:13,16(2398),29■43:8■44:13-DA-9:5(5753)-HO-1:2(2181)■4:18(2181)-MAL-2:11■N.T.-all=4100&marked-M'T-5:28(3431)-M'R-15:7(4160)-LU-12:48(3908)-JOH-5:22(1325)-AC-8:3(3860)■25:11(4238),25(4238)■27:40(1439),28:17(4160)-RO-3:2-1CO-9:17■10:8(4203)-2CO-5:19(5087)■11:7(4160)■12:21(4238)-GA-2:7-1TI-1:11■6:20(3872)-2TI-1:12(3866),14(3872)-TIT-1:3-JAS-5:15(4160)-1PE-2:23(3860)-JUDE-15(764)-RE-17:2(4203)■18:3(4203),9(4203)

COMMITTEST-HO-5:3(2181)

COMMITTETH-all=5003&marked-LE-20:10^{2}-PS-10:14(5800)-PR-6:32-EZE-8:6(6213)■16:32■18:24(6213),26(6213)■33:18(6213)■N.T.-all=3429&marked-M'T-5:32■19:9-M'R-10:11,12-LU-16:18^{2}(3431)-JOH-8:34(4160)-1CO-6:18(4203)-1JO-3:4(4160),8(4160)

COMMITTING-EZE-33:15(6213)-HO-4:2(5003)

COMMODIOUS-AC-27:12(428)

COMMON-LE-4:27(776)-1SA-21:4(2455),5(2455)-EC-6:1(7227)-JER-26:23(1121)■31:5(2490)-EZE-23:42(7230)■N.T.-all=2839&marked-M'T-27:27(4232)-M'R-12:37(4183)-AC-2:44■4:32■5:18(1219)■10:14,15(2840),28■11:8,9-1CO-10:13(442)-TIT-1:4-JUDE-3

COMMONLY-M'T-28:15(1310)-1CO-5:1(3654)

COMMONWEALTH-EPH-2:12(4174)

COMMOTION-JER-10:22(7494)

COMMOTIONS-LU-21:9(181)

COMMUNE-all=1696&marked-GE-34:6-EX-25:22-1SA-18:22■19:3-JOB-4:2(1697)-PS-4:4(559)■64:5(5608)■77:6(7878)

COMMUNED-all=1696-GE-23:8■34:8,20■42:24■43:19-J'G-9:1-1SA-9:25■25:39-1KI-10:2-2KI-22:14-2CH-9:1-EC-1:16-DA-1:19-ZEC-1:14■N.T.-LU-6:11(1255)■22:4(4814)■24:15(3656)-AC-24:26(3656)

COMMUNICATE-GA-6:6(2841)-PH'P-4:14(4790)-1TI-6:18(2843)-HEB-13:16(2842)

COMMUNICATED-GA-2:2(394)-PH'P-4:15(2841)

COMMUNICATION-2SA-3:17(1697)-2KI-9:11(7879)■N.T.-M'T-5:37(3056)-EPH-4:29(3056)-COL-3:8(148)-PH'M-6(2842)

COMMUNICATIONS-LU-24:17(3056)-1CO-15:33(3657)

COMMUNION-all=2842-1CO-10:16^{2}-2CO-6:14■13:14

COMMUNING-GE-18:33(1696)-EX-31:18(1696)

COMPACT-PS-122:3(2266)

COMPACTED-EPH-4:16(4822)

COMPANIED-AC-1:21(4905)

COMPANIES-all=7218&marked-J'G-7:16,20■9:34,43,44-1SA-11:11■13:17-2KI-5:2(1416)-1CH-9:18(4264)■28:1(4256)-JOB-6:19(1979)-IS-21:13(736)-EZE-26:7(6951)■N.T.-M'R-6:39(4849)

COMPANION-all=4828&marked-EX-32:27(7453)-J'G-14:20■15:2,6-1CH-27:33(7453)-JOB-30:29(7453)-PS-119:63(2270)-PR-13:20(7462)■28:7(7462),24(2270)-MAL-2:14(2278)■N.T.-PH'P-2:25(4904)-RE-1:9(4791)

COMPANIONS-all=3675&marked-J'G-11:38(7464)■14:11(4828)-EZR-4:7,9,17,23■5:3,6■6:6,13-JOB-35:4(7453)■41:6(2271)-PS-45:14(7464)-SONG-1:7(2270)■8:13(2270)-IS-1:23(2270)-EZE-37:16^{2}(2270)-DA-2:17(2269)■N.T.-AC-19:29(4898)-HEB-10:33(2844)

COMPANIONS'-PS-122:8(7453)

COMPANY-all=6951,a=5712&marked-GE-32:8^{2}(4264),21(4264)■35:11(6951)■37:25(736)■50:9(4264)-NU-14:7a■16:5a,6a,11a,16a,40a■22:4■26:9a,10a■27:3^{2}a-J'G-9:37(7218),44(7218)■18:23(2199)-1SA-10:5(2256),10(2256)■13:17(7218),18^{2}(7218)■19:20(3862)■30:15^{2}(1416),23(1416)-2KI-5:15(4264)■9:17^{2}(8229)-2CH-9:1(2428)■20:12(1995)-JOB-16:7a■34:8(2274)-PS-55:14(7285)■68:11(6635),30(2416)■106:17a,18a-PR-29:3(7462)-SONG-6:13(4246)JER-31:8-EZE-16:40■17:17■23:46,47■27:6(1323),27,34■32:3,22,23■38:4,7,13,15-HO-6:9(2267)■N.T.-all=3793&marked-LU-2:44(4923)■5:29■6:17■9:14(2828),38■11:27■12:13■23:27(4128)-JOH-6:5-AC-4:23(2398)■6:7■10:28(2853)■13:13(3588,4012)■17:5(3792)■21:8(4012)-1CO-5:9(4874),11(4874)-2TH-3:14(4874)-HEB-12:22(3461)-RE-8:17(3658)

COMPARABLE-LA-4:2(5537)

COMPARE-IS-40:18(6186)■46:5(4911)■N.T.-M'R-4:30(3846)-2CO-10:12(4793)

COMPARED-PS-89:6(6186)-PR-3:15(7737)■8:11(7737)-SONG-1:9(1819)

COMPARING-1CO-2:13(4793)-2CO-10:12(4793)

COMPARISON-HAG-2:3(3644)■N.T.-M'R-4:30(3850)

COMPASS-all=5437&marked-EX-27:5(3749)■38:4(3749)-NU-21:4■34:5-JOS-6:3,4,7■15:3-2SA-5:23-1KI-7:15,23,35(5439)-2KI-3:9■11:8(5362)-2CH-4:2(5439),2,3■23:7(5362)-JOB-16:13■40:22-PS-5:12(5849)■7:7■17:9(5362)■26:6■32:7,10■49:5■140:9(4524)■142:7(3803)-PR-8:27(2329)-IS-44:13(4230)■50:11(247)-JER-31:22,39■52:21-HAB-1:4(3803)■N.T.-M'T-23:15(4013)-LU-19:43(4033)-AC-28:13(4022)

COMPASSED-all=5437&marked-GE-19:4-DE-2:1,3-JOS-6:11,14,15^{2}■15:10■18:14-J'G-11:18■16:2-1SA-23:26(5849)-2SA-18:15■22:5(661),6-2KI-6:14(5362),15■8:21-2CH-18:31■21:9■33:14-JOB-19:6(5362)■26:10(2328)-PS-17:11■18:4(661),5■22:12,16■40:12(661)■88:17(5362)■109:3■116:3(661)■118:10,11,12-LA-3:5(5362)-JON-2:3,5(661)■N.T.-all=2944&marked-LU-21:20-HEB-5:2(4029)■11:30■12:1(4029)-RE-20:9

COMPASSEST-PS-139:3(2219)

COMPASSETH-all=5437&marked-GE-2:11,13-JOS-19:14-PS-73:6(6059)-HO-11:12

COMPASSING-1KI-7:24(5437),24(5362)-2CH-4:3(5362)

COMPASSION-all=7355&marked-EX-2:6(2550)-DE-13:17■30:3-1SA-23:21(2550)-1KI-8:50(7356),50-2KI-13:23-2CH-30:9(7356)■36:15(2550),17(2550)-PS-78:38(7349)■86:15(7349)■111:4(7349)■112:4(7349)■145:8(7349)-IS-49:15-JER-12:15-LA-3:32-EZE-16:5(2550)-MIC-7:19■N.T.-all=4697&marked-M'T-9:36■14:14■15:32■18:27,33(1653)■20:34-M'R-1:41■5:19(1653)■6:34■8:2■9:22-LU-7:13■10:33■15:20-RO-9:15(3627)-HEB-5:2(3356)■10:34(4834)-1PE-3:8(4835)-JUDE-22(1653)

COMPASSIONS-LA-3:22(7355)-ZEC-7:9(7356)

COMPEL-LE-25:39(5647)-ES-1:8(597)■N.T.-M'T-5:41(29)-M'R-15:21(29)-LU-14:23(315)

COMPELLED-1SA-28:23(6555)-2CH-21:11(5080)■N.T.-all=315&marked-M'T-27:32(29)-AC-26:11-2CO-12:11-GA-2:3

COMPELLEST-GA-2:14(315)

COMPLAIN-J'G-21:22(7378)-JOB-7:11(7878)■31:38(1058)-LA-3:39(596)

COMPLAINED-NU-11:1(596)-PS-77:3(7878)

COMPLAINERS-JUDE-16(3202)

COMPLAINING-PS-144:14(6682)

COMPLAINT-all=7879-1SA-1:16-JOB-7:13■9:27■10:1■21:4■23:2-PS-55:2■102:t■142:2

COMPLAINTS-AC-25:7(157)

COMPLETE-LE-23:15(8549)■N.T.-COL-2:10(4137)■4:12(4137)

COMPOSITION-EX-30:32(4971),37(4971)

COMPOUND-EX-30:25(4842)

COMPOUNDETH-EX-30:33(7543)

COMPREHEND-JOB-37:5(3045)-EPH-3:18(2638)

COMPREHENDED-IS-40:12(3557)■N.T.-JOH-1:5(2638)-RO-13:9(346)

CONCEAL-GE-37:26(3680)-DE-13:8(3680)-JOB-27:11(3582)■41:12(2790)-PR-25:2(5641)-JER-50:2(3582)

CONCEALED-JOB-6:10(3582)-PS-40:10(3582)

CONCEALETH-PR-11:13(3680)■12:23(3680)

CONCEIT-all=5869&marked-PR-18:11(4906)■26:5,12,16■28:11

CONCEITS-RO-11:25(3844,1438)■12:16(3844,1438)

CONCEIVE-all=3179&marked-GE-30:38,41^{2}-NU-5:28(2232)-J'G-13:3(2029),5(2030),7(2030)-JOB-15:35(2029)-PS-51:5-IS-7:14(2030)■33:11(2029)■59:4(2029)■N.T.-LU-1:31(4815)-HEB-11:11(2602)

CONCEIVED-all=2029&marked-GE-4:1,17■16:4^{2},5■21:2■25:21■29:32,33,34,35■30:5,7,17,19,23,39(3179)■31:10(3179)■38:3,4,5(3254),18-EX-2:2-LE-12:2(2232)-NU-11:12-1SA-1:20■2:21-2SA-11:5-2KI-4:17-1CH-7:23-JOB-3:3-PS-7:14-SONG-3:4-IS-8:3-JER-49:30(2803)-HO-1:3,6,8■2:5■N.T.-all=4815&marked-M'T-1:20(1080)-LU-1:24,36■2:21-AC-5:4(5087)-RO-9:10(2845,2192)-JAS-1:15(4815)

CONCEIVING-IS-59:13(2029)

CONCEPTION-all=2032-GE-3:16-RU-4:13-HO-9:11

CONCERN-AC-28:31(4012)-2CO-11:30(4012)

CONCERNETH-PS-138:8(1157)

CONCERNING-all=5921,a=413&marked-GE-12:20■24:9■26:32(5921,182)■42:21-EX-24:8■5:18-NU-8:22■10:29-JOS-14:6(5921,182)■23:14

-RU-4:7-1SA-3:12a▪25:30-2SA-7:25▪13:39▪14:8▪18:5(5921,1697)-1KI-2:4,27▪8:41a▪11:10▪22:8,18,23-2KI-10:10▪19:21,32a▪22:13^2-1CH-11:10▪17:23^2▪19:2▪22:12,13-2CH-6:32a▪31:9▪34:21-EZR-5:5(5922),17(5922)▪7:14(5922)▪10:2-NE-1:2^2▪11:23▪13:14-ES-9:26-JOB-36:33^2-PS-7:t▪90:13▪135:14-EC-1:13▪3:18▪7:10-IS-1:1▪2:1▪16:13a▪29:22a▪37:9,22,33a▪45:11-JER-7:22(5921,1697)▪14:1(5921,1697),15▪16:3^3▪18:7,9▪22:18a▪23:15▪25:1▪27:19^2,21▪29:31a▪30:4a▪32:36a▪33:4^2▪39:11▪42:19▪44:1a-EZE-13:16a▪14:7,22,22(854)▪18:2▪21:28^{2}a▪36:6-DA-2:18(5922)▪5:29(5922)▪6:4(6655),12(5922)-AM-1:1-MIC-1:1▪3:5-NA-1:14▪N.T.-all=4012&marked-M'T-4:6▪11:7▪16:11-M'R-5:16▪7:17-LU-2:17▪7:24▪22:37▪24:19,27,44-JOH-7:12,32▪9:18▪11:19-AC-1:16▪2:25(1519)▪8:12▪13:34(3754)▪19:8,39▪21:24▪22:18▪23:15▪24:24▪25:16▪28:21,22,23-RO-1:3▪9:5(2596),27(5228)▪11:28(2596)▪16:19(1519)-1CO-7:1,25▪8:4▪12:1▪16:1-2CO-8:23(1519)▪11:21(2596)-EPH-4:22▪5:32(1519)-PH'P-3:6(2596)▪4:15(1519,3056)-1TH-3:2▪4:13▪5:18(1519)-1TI-1:19▪6:21-2TI-2:18▪3:8-HEB-7:14▪11:20,22-1PE-4:12-2PE-3:9(4314)-1JO-2:26

CONCISION-PH'P-3:2(2699)

CONCLUDE-RO-3:28(3049)

CONCLUDED-AC-21:25(2919)-RO-11:32(4788)-GA-3:22(4788)

CONCLUSION-EC-12:13(5490)

CONCORD-2CO-6:15(4857)

CONCOURSE-PR-1:21(1993)▪N.T.-AC-19:40(4963)

CONCUBINE-all=6370-GE-22:24▪35:22▪36:12-J'G-8:31▪19:1,2,9,10,24,25,27,29▪20:4,5,6-2SA-3:7^2▪21:11-1CH-1:32▪2:46,48▪7:14

CONCUBINES-all=6370&marked-GE-25:6-2SA-5:13▪15:16▪16:21,22▪19:5▪20:3-1KI-11:3-1CH-3:9-2CH-11:21^2-ES-2:14-SONG-6:8,9-DA-5:2(3904),3(3904),23(3904)

CONCUPISCENCE-all=1939-RO-7:8-COL-3:5-1TH-4:5

CONDEMN-all=7561&marked-EX-22:9-DE-25:1-JOB-9:20▪10:2▪34:17▪40:8-PS-37:33▪94:21▪109:31(8199)-PR-12:2-IS-50:9▪54:17▪N.T.-all=2632&marked-M'T-12:41,42▪20:18-M'R-10:33-LU-6:37(2618)▪11:31,32-JOH-3:17(2919)▪8:11-2CO-7:3(2633)-1JO-3:20(2607),21(2607)

CONDEMNATION-all=2917&marked-LU-23:40-JOH-3:19(2920)▪5:24(2920)-RO-5:16(2631),18(2631)▪8:1(2631)-1CO-11:34-2CO-3:9(2633)-1TI-3:6-JAS-3:1▪5:12(5272)-JUDE-4

CONDEMNED-2CH-36:3(6064)-JOB-32:3(7561)-PS-109:7(3318,7563)-AM-2:8(6064)▪N.T.-all=2632&marked-M'T-12:7(2613),37(2613)▪27:3-M'R-14:64-LU-6:37(2613)▪24:20(1519,2917)-JOH-3:18^2(2919)▪8:10-RO-8:3-1CO-11:32-TIT-2:8(176)▪3:11(843)-HEB-11:7-JAS-5:6(2613),9-2PE-2:6

CONDEMNEST-RO-2:1(2632)

CONDEMNETH-JOB-15:6(7561)-PR-17:15(7561)▪N.T.-RO-8:34(2632)▪14:22(4314)

CONDEMNING-1KI-8:32(7561)▪N.T.-AC-13:27(2919)

CONDESCEND-RO-12:16(4879)

CONDITION-all supplied

CONDITIONS-LU-14:32(4314)

CONDUCT-2SA-19:15(5674),31(7971)-1CO-16:11(4311)

CONDUCTED-2SA-19:40(5674)▪N.T.-AC-17:15(2525)

CONDUIT-all=8585-2KI-18:17▪20:20-IS-7:3▪36:2

CONEY-LE-11:5(8227)-DE-14:7(8227)

CONFECTION-EX-30:35(7545)

CONFECTIONARIES-1SA-8:13(7543)

CONFEDERACY-IS-8:12^2(7195)-OB-7(1285)

CONFEDERATE-GE-14:13(1167,1285)-PS-83:5(1285,3772)-IS-7:2(5117)

CONFERENCE-GA-2:6(4323)

CONFERRED-1KI-1:7(1961,1697)▪N.T.-AC-4:15(4820)▪25:12(4814)-GA-1:16(4323)

CONFESS-all=3034-LE-5:5▪16:21▪26:40-NU-5:7-1KI-8:33,35-2CH-6:24,26-NE-1:6-JOB-40:14-PS-32:5▪N.T.-all=3670&marked-M'T-10:32^2-LU-12:8^2-JOH-9:22▪12:42-AC-23:8▪24:14-RO-10:9▪14:11(1843)▪15:9(1843)-PH'P-2:11(1843)-JAS-5:16(1843)-1JO-1:9▪4:15-2JO-7-RE-3:5(1843)

CONFESSED-all=3034-EZR-10:1-NE-9:2,3▪N.T.-JOH-1:20^2(3670)-AC-19:18(1843)-HEB-11:13(3670)

CONFESSETH-PR-28:13(3034)▪N.T.-1JO-4:2(3670),3(3670)

CONFESSING-DA-9:20(3034)▪N.T.-M'T-3:6(1843)-M'R-1:5(1843)

CONFESSION-JOS-7:19(8426)-2CH-30:22(3034)-EZR-10:11(8426)-DA-9:4(3034)▪N.T.-RO-10:10(3670)-1TI-6:13(3671)

CONFIDENCE-all=4009&marked-J'G-9:26(982)-2KI-18:19(986)-JOB-4:6(3690)▪18:14▪31:24-PS-65:5▪118:8(982),9(982)-PR-3:26(3689)▪14:26▪21:22▪25:19-IS-30:15(985)▪36:4(986)-JER-48:13-EZE-28:26(983)▪29:16-MIC-7:5(982)▪N.T.-all=3954&marked-AC-28:31-2CO-1:15(4006)▪2:3(3982)▪7:16(2292)▪8:22(4006)▪10:2(4006)▪11:17(5287)-GA-5:10(3982)-EPH-3:12(4006)-PH'P-1:25(3982)▪3:3(3982)▪3:4(4006)-2TH-3:4(3982)-PH'M-21(3982)-HEB-3:6,14(5287)▪10:35-1JO-2:28▪3:21▪5:14

CONFIDENCES-JER-2:37(4009)

CONFIDENT-PS-27:3(982)-PR-14:16(982)▪N.T.-all=3982&marked-RO-2:19-2CO-5:6(2292),8(2292)▪9:4(5287)-PH'P-1:6,14

CONFIDENTLY-LU-22:59(1340)

CONFIRM-all=6965&marked-RU-4:7-1KI-1:14(4390)-2KI-15:19(2388)-ES-9:29,31-PS-68:9(3559)-IS-35:3(553)-EZE-13:6-DA-9:27(1396)▪11:1(2388)▪N.T.-RO-15:8(950)-1CO-1:8(950)-2CO-2:8(2964)

CONFIRMATION-PH'P-1:7(951)-HEB-6:16(951)

CONFIRMED-2SA-7:24(3559)-2KI-14:5(2388)-1CH-14:2(3559)▪16:17(5975)-ES-9:32(6965)-PS-105:10(5975)-DA-9:12(6965)▪N.T.-AC-15:32(1991)-1CO-1:6(950)-GA-3:15(2964),17(4300)-HEB-2:3(950)▪6:17(3315)

CONFIRMETH-all=6965-NU-30:14-DE-27:26-IS-44:26

CONFIRMING-M'R-16:20(950)-AC-14:22(1991)▪15:41(1991)

CONFISCATION-EZR-7:26(6065)

CONFLICT-PH'P-1:30(73)-COL-2:1(73)

CONFORMABLE-PH'P-3:10(4832)

CONFORMED-RO-8:29(4832)▪12:2(4964)

CONFOUND-GE-11:7(1101),9(1101)-JER-1:17(2865)▪N.T.-1CO-1:27^2(2617)

CONFOUNDED-all=954,a=3637&marked-2KI-19:26-JOB-6:20-PS-22:5▪35:4▪40:14(2659)▪69:6a▪70:2(2659)▪71:13,24▪83:17▪97:7▪129:5-IS-1:29(2659)▪19:9▪24:23(2659)▪37:27▪41:11a▪45:16a,17a▪50:7a▪54:4a-JER-9:19▪10:14(3001)▪14:3a▪15:9(2659)▪17:18^2▪22:22a▪31:19a▪46:24(3001)▪48:1^2(3001),20(3001)▪49:23▪50:2^2(3001),12▪51:17(3001),47,51-EZE-16:52,54a,63▪36:32a-MIC-3:7(2659)▪7:16-ZEC-10:5(3001)▪N.T.-AC-2:6(4797)▪9:22(4797)-1PE-2:6(2617)

CONFUSED-IS-9:5(7494)-AC-19:32(4797)

CONFUSION-all=3639&marked-LE-18:23(8397)▪20:12(8397)-1SA-20:30(1322)-EZR-9:7(1322)-JOB-10:15(7036)-PS-35:4(2659),26(2659)▪44:15▪70:2(3637)▪71:1(954)▪109:29(1322)-IS-24:10(8414)▪30:3▪34:11(8414)▪41:29(8414)▪45:16▪61:7-JER-3:25▪7:19(1322)▪20:11-DA-9:7(1322),8(1322)▪N.T.-AC-19:29(4799)-1CO-14:33(181)-JAS-3:16(181)

CONGEALED-EX-15:8(7087)

CONGRATULATE-1CH-18:10(1288)

CONGREGATION-all=4150,a=5712,b=6951&marked-EX-12:3a,6a,19a,47a▪16:1a,2a,9a,10a,22a▪17:1a▪27:21▪28:43▪29:4,10,11,30,32,42,44▪30:16,18,20,26,36▪31:7▪33:7^2▪34:31a▪35:1a,4a,20a,21▪33:8,25a,30▪39:32,40▪40:2,6,7,12,22,24,26,29,30,32,34,35-LE-1:1,3,5▪3:2,8,13▪4:4,5,7^2,13a,14b,14,15a,16,18^2,21b▪6:16,26,30▪8:3a,3,4,5a,31,33,35▪9:5,5a,23▪10:7,9,17a▪12:6▪14:11,23▪15:14,29▪16:5a,7,16,17,17b,33sup,33b▪17:4,5,6,9▪19:2a,21▪24:3,14a,16a-NU-1:1,2a,16a,18a,53a▪2:2,17▪3:7a,7,8,25^2,38▪4:3,4,15,23,25^2,28,30,31,33,34a,35,37,39,41,43,47▪6:10,13,18▪7:5,89▪8:9,15,19,20a,22,24,26▪10:3,7b▪11:16▪12:4▪13:26^{2}a▪14:1a,2a,5a,10a,10,27a,35a,36a▪15:15b,24^{2}a,25a,26a,33a,36a▪16:2,3a,3b,9^{2}a,18,19^{2}a,19,21a,22a,24a,26a,33b,41a,42a,42,43,45a,46a,47b,50▪17:4▪18:4,6,21,22,23,31▪19:4,9a,20b▪20:1a,2a,4b,6,8a,10b,11a,12b,22a,27a,29a▪25:6a,6,7a▪26:2a,9a▪27:2a,2,14a,16a,17a,19a,20a,21a,22a▪31:12a,13a,16a,26a,27a,43a,54▪32:2a,4a▪35:12a,24a,25^{2}a-DE-23:1b,2b,3^{2}b,8b▪31:14^2,30▪33:4(6952)-JOS-8:35b▪9:15a,18^{2}a,19a,21a,27a▪18:1a,1▪19:51▪20:6a,9a▪22:12a,16a,17a,18a,20a,30a-J'G-20:1a▪21:5b,10a,13a,16a-1SA-2:22-1KI-8:4,5a,14^{2}b,22b,55b,65b▪12:3b,20a-1CH-6:32▪9:21▪13:2b,4b▪23:32▪28:8b▪29:1b,10b,20^{2}b-2CH-1:3b,3,5b,6,13▪5:5,6a▪6:3^{2}b,12b,13b▪7:8b▪20:5b,14b▪23:3b▪24:6b▪28:14b▪29:23b,28b,31b,32b▪30:2b,4b,13b,17b,24^{2}b,25^{2}b▪31:18b-EZR-2:64b▪10:1b,8b,12b,14b-NE-5:13b▪7:66b▪8:2b,17b▪13:1b-JOB-15:34a▪30:28b-PS-1:5a▪7:7a▪22:2b,25b▪26:5b▪35:18b▪40:9b,10b▪58:1(482)▪68:10(2416)▪74:2a,19(2416)▪75:2▪82:1a▪89:5b▪107:32b▪111:1a▪149:1b-PR-5:14b▪21:16b▪26:26b-IS-14:13-JER-6:18a▪30:20a-LA-1:10b-HO-7:12a-JOE-2:16b-MIC-2:5b▪N.T.-AC-13:43(4864)

CONGREGATIONS-PS-26:12(4721)▪68:26(4721)▪74:4(4150)

CONIES-PS-104:18(8227)-PR-30:26(8227)

CONQUER-RE-6:2(3528)

CONQUERING-RE-6:2(3528)

CONQUERORS-RO-8:37(5245)

CONSCIENCE-all=4893-JOH-8:9-AC-23:1▪24:16-RO-2:15▪9:1▪13:5-1CO-8:7^2,10,12▪10:25,27,28,29^2-2CO-1:12▪4:2-1TI-1:5,19▪3:9▪4:2-2TI-1:3-TIT-1:15-HEB-9:9,14▪10:2,22▪13:18-1PE-2:19▪3:16,21

CONSCIENCES-2CO-5:11(4893)

CONSECRATE-all=4390,3027&marked-EX-28:3(6942),41▪29:9,33,35▪30:30(6942)▪32:29-LE-8:33▪16:32-NU-6:12(5144)-1CH-29:5-2CH-13:9-EZE-43:26-MIC-4:13(2763)

CONSECRATED-all=4390,3027&marked-EX-29:29-LE-21:10-NU-3:3-JOS-6:19(6944)-J'G-17:5,12-1KI-13:33-2CH-26:18(6942)▪29:31,33(6942)▪31:6(6942)-EZR-3:5(6942)▪N.T.-HEB-7:28(5048)▪10:20(1457)

CONSECRATION-all=4394&marked-EX-29:22,26,27,31-LE-8:22,29,33-NU-6:7(5145),9(5145)

CONSECRATIONS-all=4394

-EX-29:34-LE-7:37■8:28,31

CONSENT-all=14&marked-GE-34:15(225),22(225),23(225)-DE-13:8-J'G-11:17-1SA-11:7(376)-1KI-20:8-PS-83:5(3820)-PR-1:10-HO-6:9(7926)-ZEP-3:9(7926)■N.T.-RO-7:16(4852)-1CO-7:5(4859)-1TI-6:3(4334)

CONSENTED-2KI-12:8(225)-DA-1:14(8085)■N.T.-LU-23:51(4784)-AC-18:20(1962)

CONSENTEDST-PS-50:18(7521)

CONSENTING-AC-8:1(4909)■22:20(4909)

CONSIDER-all=995,a=7200&marked-EX-33:13a-LE-13:13a-DE-4:39(7725)■8:5(3045)■32:7,29-J'G-18:14(3045)■19:30(7760)-1SA-12:24a■25:17a-2KI-5:7(3045)-JOB-11:11■23:15■34:27(7919)■37:14-PS-5:1■8:3a■9:13a■13:3(5027)■25:19a■37:10■45:10a■48:13(6448)■50:22■64:9(7919)■119:95,153a,159a-PR-6:6a■23:1■24:12-EC-5:1(3045)■7:13a,14a-IS-1:3■5:12a■14:16■18:4(5027)■41:20(7760),22(776,3820)■43:18■52:15-JER-2:10■9:17■23:20■30:24-LA-1:11(5027)■2:20(5027)■5:1(5027)-EZE-12:3a-DA-9:23-HO-7:2(559)-HAG-1:5(7760,3820,5921),7(7760,3820,5921)■2:15(7760,3820),18^{2}(7760,3820)■N.T.-all=2657&marked-M'T-6:28(2648)-LU-12:24,27-JOH-11:50(1260)-AC-15:6(1492)-2TI-2:7(3539)-HEB-3:1■7:4(2334)■10:24■12:3(357)

CONSIDERED-all=7200&marked-1KI-3:21(995)■5:8(8085)-JOB-1:8(7760,3820)■2:3(7760,3820)-PS-31:7■77:5(2803)-PR-24:32(7896,3820)-EC-4:1,4,15■9:1(5414)-DA-7:8(7920)■N.T.-M'R-6:52(4920)-AC-11:6(2657)■12:12(4894)-RO-4:19(2657)

CONSIDEREST-JER-33:24(7200)■N.T.-M'T-7:3(2657)

CONSIDERETH-PS-33:15(995)■41:1(7919)-PR-21:12(7919)■28:22(3045)■29:7(3045)■31:16(2161)-IS-44:19(7725)-EZE-18:14(7200),28(7200)

CONSIDERING-IS-57:1(995)-DA-8:5(995)■N.T.-GA-6:1(4648)-HEB-13:7(333)

CONSIST-COL-1:17(4921)

CONSISTETH-LU-12:15(2076)

CONSOLATION-JER-16:7(8575)■N.T.-all=3874-LU-2:25■6:24-AC-4:36■15:31-RO-15:5-2CO-1:5,6^{2},7■7:7-PH'P-2:1-2TH-2:16-PH'M-7-HEB-6:18

CONSOLATIONS-all=8575&marked-JOB-15:11■21:2-IS-66:11

CONSORTED-AC-17:4(4345)

CONSPIRACY-all=7195&marked-2SA-15:12-2KI-12:20■14:19■15:15,30■17:4-2CH-25:27-JER-11:9-EZE-22:25■N.T.-AC-23:13(4945)

CONSPIRATORS-2SA-15:31(7194)

CONSPIRED-all=7194&marked-GE-37:18(5230)-1SA-22:8,13-1KI-15:27■16:9,16-2KI-9:14■10:9■15:10,25■21:23,24-2CH-24:21,25,26■33:24,25-NE-4:8-AM-7:10

CONSTANT-1CH-28:7(2388)

CONSTANTLY-PR-21:28(5331)■N.T.-AC-12:15(1340)-TIT-3:8(1226)

CONSTELLATIONS-IS-13:10(3685)

CONSTRAIN-GA-6:12(315)

CONSTRAINED-2KI-4:8(2388)■N.T.-M'T-14:22(315)-M'R-6:45(315)-LU-24:29(3849)-AC-16:15(3849)■28:19(315)

CONSTRAINETH-JOB-32:18(6693)■N.T.-2CO-5:14(4912)

CONSTRAINT-1PE-5:2(317)

CONSULT-PS-62:4(3289)

CONSULTATION-M'R-15:1(4824)

CONSULTED-all=3289&marked-1KI-12:6,8-1CH-13:1-2CH-20:21-NE-5:7(4427)-PS-83:3,5-EZE-21:21(7592)-DA-6:7(3272)-MIC-6:5-HAB-2:10■N.T.-M'T-26:4(4823)-JOH-12:10(1011)

CONSULTER-DE-18:11(7592)

CONSULTETH-LU-14:31(1011)

CONSUME-all=3615&marked-GE-41:30-EX-32:10,12■33:3,5-LE-26:16-NU-16:21,45-DE-5:25(398)■7:16(398),22■28:38(2628),42(3423)■32:22(398)-JOS-24:20-1SA-2:33-2KI-1:10,12(398)-NE-9:31-ES-9:24(2000)-JOB-15:34(398)■20:26(398)■24:19(1497)-PS-37:20■39:11(4529)■49:14(1086)■59:13■78:33-IS-7:20(5595)■10:18■27:10-JER-8:13(5486)■14:12■49:27(398)-EZE-4:17(4743)■13:13■20:13■21:28(398)■22:15(8552)■24:10(8552)■35:12(402)-DA-2:44(5487)■7:26(8046)-HO-11:6-ZEP-1:2(5486),3^{2}(5486)-ZEC-5:4■14:12^{3}(5743)■N.T.-LU-9:54(355)-2TH-2:8(355)-JAS-4:3(1159)

CONSUMED-all=3615,a=8552,b=398&marked-GE-19:15(5595),17(5595)■31:40b-EX-3:2b■15:7b■22:6b-LE-6:10b■9:24b-NU-11:1b■12:12b■14:35a■16:26(5595),35b■17:13a■21:28b■25:11■32:13a-DE-2:15a,16a■28:21-JOS-5:6a■8:24a■10:20a-J'G-6:21b-1SA-12:25(5595)■15:18-2SA-21:5■22:38,39-1KI-18:38b■22:11-2KI-1:10b,12b■7:13a■13:17,19-2CH-7:1b■8:8■18:10-EZR-9:14-NE-2:3b,13b-JOB-1:16b■4:9■6:17(1846)■7:9■19:27■33:21-PS-6:7(6244)■18:37■31:9(6244),10(6244)■39:10■71:13■73:19a■78:63b■90:7■102:3■104:35a■119:87,139(6789)-PR-5:11-IS-1:28■16:4a■29:20■64:7(4127)■66:17(5486)-JER-5:3■6:29a■9:16■10:25■12:4(5595)■14:15a■16:4■20:18■24:10a■27:8a■36:23a■44:12^{2}a,18a,27a■49:37-LA-2:22■3:22a-EZE-5:12■13:14■19:12b■22:31■24:11a■34:29(622)■43:8b■47:12a-DA-11:16-MAL-3:6■N.T.-GA-5:15(355)

CONSUMETH-JOB-13:28(1086)■22:20(398)■31:12(398)-IS-5:24(7503)

CONSUMING-DE-4:24(398)■9:3(398)■N.T.-HEB-12:29(2654)

CONSUMMATION-DA-9:27(3617)

CONSUMPTION-LE-26:16(7829)-DE-28:22(7829)-IS-10:22(3631),23(3617)■28:22(3617)

CONTAIN-all=3557&marked-1KI-8:27■18:32(1004)-2CH-2:6■6:18-EZE-45:11(5375)■N.T.-JOH-21:25(5562)-1CO-7:9(1467)

CONTAINED-1KI-7:26(3557),38(3557)■N.T.-1PE-2:6(4023)

CONTAINETH-EZE-23:32(3557)

CONTAINING-JOH-2:6(5562)

CONTEMN-PS-10:13(5006)-EZE-21:13(3988)

CONTEMNED-PS-15:4(959)■107:11(5006)-SONG-8:7(936)-IS-16:14(7034)

CONTEMNETH-EZE-21:10(3988)

CONTEMPT-all=937&marked-ES-1:18(963)-JOB-12:21■31:34-PS-107:40■119:22■123:3,4-PR-18:3-IS-23:9(7043)-DA-12:2(1860)

CONTEMPTIBLE-all=959-MAL-1:7,12■2:9■N.T.-2CO-10:10(1848)

CONTEMPTUOUSLY-PS-31:18(937)

CONTEND-all=7378&marked-DE-2:9(1624),24(1624)-JOB-9:3■13:8-PR-28:4(1624)-EC-6:10(1777)-IS-49:25■50:8■57:16-JER-12:5(8474)■18:19(3401)-AM-7:4-MIC-6:1■N.T.-JUDE-3(1864)

CONTENDED-all=7378&marked-NE-13:11,17,25-JOB-31:13-IS-41:12(4695)■N.T.-AC-11:2(1252)

CONTENDEST-JOB-10:2(7378)

CONTENDETH-JOB-40:2(7378)-PR-29:9(8199)-IS-49:25(3401)

CONTENDING-JUDE-9(1252)

CONTENT-all=2974&marked-GE-37:27(8085)-EX-2:21(2974)-LE-10:20(3190,5869)-JOS-7:7-J'G-17:11■19:6-2KI-5:23■6:3-JOB-6:28-PR-6:35(14)■N.T.-all=714&marked-M'R-15:15(2425,3588,4160)-LU-3:14-PH'P-4:11(842)-1TI-6:8-HEB-13:5-3JO-10

CONTENTION-all=4066&marked-PR-13:10(4683)■17:14(7379)■18:6(7379)■22:10-JER-15:10-HAB-1:3■N.T.-AC-15:39(3948)-PH'P-1:16(2052)-1TH-2:2(73)

CONTENTIONS-all=4079-PR-18:18,19■19:13■23:29■N.T.-1CO-1:11(2054)-TIT-3:9(2054)

CONTENTIOUS-all=4066-PR-21:19■26:21■27:15■N.T.-RO-2:8(1537,2052)-1CO-11:16(5380)

CONTENTMENT-1TI-6:6(841)

CONTINUAL-all=8548&marked-EX-29:42-NU-4:7■29:3,6,10,15,23,24,31■29:11,16,19,22,25,28,31,34,38-2KI-25:30-2CH-2:4-EZR-3:5-NE-10:33^{2}-PR-15:15■19:13(2956)■27:15(2956)-IS-14:6(1115,5627)-JER-52:34-EZE-39:14■46:15■N.T.-LU-18:5(1519,5056)-RO-9:2(88)

CONTINUALLY-all=8548,a=3605,3117&marked-GE-6:5a■8:3(1980,7725),5(1980)-EX-28:29,30■29:38-LE-24:2,3,4,8-JOS-6:13(1980)-1SA-18:29a-2SA-9:7,13■15:12(1980)■19:13a-1KI-10:8-2KI-4:9■25:29-1CH-16:6,11,37,40■23:31-2CH-9:7■12:15a■24:14-JOB-1:5a-PS-34:1■35:27■38:17■40:11,16■42:3a■44:15a■50:8■52:1a■69:23■70:4■71:3,6,14■72:15■73:23■74:23■109:10,15,19■119:44,109,117■140:2a-PR-6:14(3605,6256),21-IS-21:8■49:16■51:13■52:5■58:11■60:11■65:3-JER-6:7■33:18a■52:33-EZE-46:14-DA-6:16(8411),20(8411)-HO-12:6-OB-16-NA-3:19-HAB-1:17■N.T.-all=4342&marked-LU-24:53(1725)-AC-6:4■10:7-RO-13:6-HEB-7:3(1519,1336)■10:1(1519,1336)■13:15(1275)

CONTINUANCE-DE-28:59(539),59(539)-PS-139:16(3117)-IS-64:5(5769)■N.T.-RO-2:7(5281)

CONTINUE-all=6965&marked-EX-21:21(5975)-LE-12:4(3427),5(3427)-1SA-12:14(1961)■13:14-2SA-7:29(1961)-1KI-2:4-JOB-15:29■17:2(3885)-PS-36:10(4900)■102:28(7931)■119:91(5975)-IS-5:11(309)-JER-32:14(5975)-DA-11:8(5975)■N.T.-all=3306&marked-M'T-15:32(4357)-JOH-8:31■15:9-AC-13:43(1961)■14:22(1696)■26:22(2476)-RO-6:1(1961)■11:22(1961)-GAL-2:5(1265)-PH'P-1:25(4839)-COL-1:23(1961)■4:2(4342)-1TI-2:15■4:16(1961)-2TI-3:14-HEB-7:23(3887)■13:1-JAS-4:13(4160)-2PE-3:4(1265)-1JO-2:24-RE-13:5(4160)■17:10

CONTINUED-all=3427&marked-GE-40:4(1961)-J'G-5:17-RU-1:2(1961)■2:7(5975)-1SA-1:12(7235)-2SA-6:11-1KI-22:1-NE-5:16(2388)-JOB-27:1(3254),29:1(3254)-PS-72:17(5125)-DA-1:21(1961)■N.T.-all=4342&marked-LU-6:12(1273)■22:28(1265)-JOH-2:12(3306)■8:7(1961)■11:54(1304)-AC-1:14■2:42■8:13■12:16(1961)■15:35(1304)■18:11(2523)■19:10(1096)■20:7(3905)■27:33(1300)-HEB-8:9(1696)-1JO-2:19(3306)

CONTINUETH-JOB-14:2(5975)■N.T.-GAL-3:10(1696)-1TI-5:5(4357)-HEB-7:24(3306)-JAS-1:25(3887)

CONTINUING-JER-30:23(1641)■N.T.-AC-2:46(4342)-RO-12:12(4342)-HEB-13:14(3306)

CONTRADICTING-AC-13:45(483)

CONTRADICTION-HEB-7:7(485)■12:3(485)

CONTRARIWISE-all=5121-2CO-2:7-GA-2:7-1PE-3:9

CONTRARY-all=7147&marked-LE-26:21,23,24,27,28,40,41-EZE-16:34^{2}(2016)■N.T.-all=1727&marked-M'T-14:24-M'R-6:48-AC-17:7(561)■18:13(3844)■23:3(3891)■26:9■27:4-RO-11:24(3844)■16:17(3844)-GA-5:17(480)-COL-2:14(5227)-1TH-2:15-1TI-1:10(480)-TIT-2:8

CONTRIBUTION-RO-15:26

(2842)

CONTRITE-PS-34:18(1793)■51:17(1794)-IS-57:15(1793),15(1792)■66:2(5223)

CONTROVERSIES-2CH-19:8(7379)

CONTROVERSY-all=7379-DE-17:8■19:17■21:5■25:1-2SA-15:2-IS-34:8-JER-25:31-EZE-44:24-HO-4:1■12:2-MIC-6:2[2]■N.T.-1TI-3:16(3672)

CONVENIENT-PR-30:8(2706)-JER-40:4(3477),5(3477)■N.T.-M'R-6:21(2121)-AC-24:25(2540)-RO-1:28(2520)-1CO-16:12(2119)-EPH-5:4(433)-PH'M-8(433)

CONVENIENTLY-M'R-4:11(2122)

CONVERSANT-JOS-8:35(1980)-1SA-25:15(1980)

CONVERSATION-PS-37:14(1870)■50:23(1870)■N.T.-all=391&marked-2CO-1:12(390)-GA-1:13-EPH-2:3(390)■4:22-PH'P-1:27(4176)■3:20(4175)-1TI-4:12-HEB-13:5(5158),7-JAS-3:13-1PE-1:15,18■2:12■3:1,2,16-2PE-2:7■3:11

CONVERSION-AC-15:3(1995)

CONVERT-IS-6:10(7725)-JAS-5:19(1994)

CONVERTED-PS-51:13(7725)-IS-60:5(2015)■N.T.-all=1994&marked-M'T-13:15■18:3(4762)-M'R-4:12-LU-22:32-JOH-12:40-AC-3:19■28:27

CONVERTETH-JAS-5:20(1994)

CONVERTING-PS-19:7(7725)

CONVERTS-IS-1:27(7725)

CONVEY-1KI-5:9(7760)-NE-2:7(5674)

CONVEYED-JOH-5:13(1593)

CONVICTED-JOH-8:9(1651)

CONVINCE-TIT-1:9(1651)-JUDE-15(1827)

CONVINCED-JOB-32:12(3198)■N.T.-AC-18:28(1246)-1CO-14:24(1651)-JAS-2:9(1651)

CONVINCETH-JOH-8:46(1651)

CONVOCATION-all=4744-EX-12:16[2]-LE-23:3,7,8,21,24,27,35,36-NU-28:18,25,26■29:1,7,12

CONVOCATIONS-all=4744-LE-23:2,4,37

COOK-1SA-9:23(2876),24(2876)

COOKS-1SA-8:13(2876)

COOL-GE-3:8(7307)■N.T.-LU-16:24(2711)

COPIED-PR-25:1(2675)

COPING-1KI-7:9(2947)

COPPER-EZR-8:27(5178)

COPPERSMITH-2TI-4:14(5471)

COPULATION-all=7902-LE-15:16,17,18

COPY-all=6573,a=6572&marked-DE-17:18(4932)-JOS-8:32(4932)-EZR-4:11,23■5:6■7:11-ES-3:14a■4:8a■8:13a

COR-EZR-45:14(3734)

CORAL-JOB-28:18(7215)-EZR-27:16(7215)

CORBAN-M'R-7:11(2878)

CORD-all=2256&marked-JOS-2:15-JOB-30:11(3499)■41:1-EC-4:12(2339)■12:6-MIC-2:5

CORDS-all=2256&marked-EX-35:18(4340)■39:40(4340)-NU-3:26(4340),37(4340)■4:26(4340),32(4340)-J'G-15:13(5688),14(5688)-ES-1:6-JOB-36:8-PS-2:3(5688)■118:27(5688)■129:4(5688)■140:5-PR-5:22-IS-5:18■33:20■54:2(4340)-JER-10:20(4340)■38:6,11,12,13-EZE-27:24-HO-11:4■N.T.-JOH-2:15(4979)

CORIANDER-EX-16:31(1407)-NU-11:7(1407)

CORMORANT-LE-11:17(7994)-DE-14:17(7994)-IS-34:11(6893)-ZEP-2:14(6893)

CORN-all=1715&marked-GE-27:28,37■41:35(1250),49(1250)■42:1(7668),2(7668),3(1250),19(7668),25(1250),26(7668)■43:2(7668)■44:2(7668)■45:23(1250)■47:14(7668)-EX-22:6sup,6(7054)-LE-2:14sup,14(1643),16(1643)-NU-18:27-DE-7:13■11:14■12:17■14:23■16:9(7054),13(1637)■18:4■23:25[2](7054)■28:51■33:28-JOS-5:11(5669),11sup,12(5669)-J'G-15:5[2](7054)-RU-3:7(6194)-2SA-17:19(7383)-2KI-4:42(3759)■18:32-2CH-31:5■32:28-NE-5:2,3,10,11■10:39■13:5,12-JOB-24:6(1098)■39:4(1250)-PS-4:7■65:9,13(1250)■72:16(1250)■78:24-PR-11:26(1250)-IS-17:5(7054)■21:10(1121)■36:17■62:8-LA-2:12-EZE-36:29-HO-2:8,9,22■7:14■14:7-JOE-1:10,17■2:19-AM-8:5(7668)-HAG-1:11-ZEC-9:17■N.T.-all=4702&marked-M'T-12:1,1(4719)-M'R-2:23,23(4719)■4:28(4621)-LU-6:1,1(4719)-JOH-12:24(2848)-AC-7:12(4621)

CORNER-all=6438&marked-EX-36:25(6285)-LE-21:5(6285)-JOS-18:14(6285)-2KI-11:11[2](3802)■14:13-2CH-25:23(6437)■26:9■28:24-NE-3:24,31,32-JOB-38:6-PS-118:22■144:12(2106)-PR-7:8,12■21:9■25:24-IS-28:16■30:20(3671)-JER-31:38,40■48:45(6285)■51:26-EZE-46:21(4742)-AM-3:12(6285)-ZEC-10:4■14:10(6434)■N.T.-all=1137&marked-M'T-21:42-M'R-12:10-LU-20:17-AC-4:11■26:26-EPH-2:20(204)-1PE-2:6(204),7

CORNERS-all=6285&marked-EX-25:12(6471),26■26:23(4742),24(4742)■27:2(6438),4(7098)■30:4(6763)■36:28(4742),29■37:3(6471),13,27(6763)■38:2(6438)-LE-19:9,27[2]■23:22-NU-24:17-DE-32:26(6284)-1KI-7:30(6471),34(6438)-NE-9:22-JOB-1:19(6438)-IS-11:12(3671)-JER-9:26■25:23■49:32-EZE-7:2(3671)■41:22(4740)■43:20(6438)■45:19(6348)■46:21(4742),22(4742),22(7106)-ZEC-9:15(2106)■N.T.-M'T-6:5(1137)-AC-10:11(746)■11:5(746)-RE-7:1(1137)

CORNET-all=7162&marked-1CH-15:28(7782)-PS-98:6(7782)-DA-3:5,7,10,15-HO-5:8(7782)

CORNETS-2SA-6:5(4517)-2CH-15:14(7782)

CORNFLOOR-HO-9:1(1637,1715)

CORPSE-M'R-6:29(4430)

CORPSES-2KI-19:35(6297)-IS-37:36(6297)-NA-3:3(1472)

CORRECT-all=3256&marked-PS-39:11■94:10(3198)-PR-29:17-JER-2:19■10:24■30:11■46:28

CORRECTED-PR-29:19(3256)■N.T.-HEB-12:9(3810)

CORRECTETH-JOB-5:17(3198)-PR-3:12(3198)

CORRECTION-all=4148&marked-JOB-37:13(7626)-PR-3:11(8433)■7:22■15:10■22:15■23:13-JER-2:30■5:3■7:28-HAB-1:12(3198)-ZEP-3:2■N.T.-2TI-3:16(1882)

CORRUPT-all=7843&marked-GE-6:11,12-DE-4:16,25■31:29-JOB-17:1(2254)-PS-14:1■38:5(4743)■53:1■73:8(4167)-PR-25:26-EZE-20:44■23:11-DA-2:9(7844)■11:32(2610)-MAL-1:14■2:3(1605)■N.T.-all=4550&marked-M'T-6:19(853),20(853)■7:17,18■12:33-LU-6:43[2]-1CO-15:33(5351)-2CO-2:17(2585)-EPH-4:22(5351),29-1TI-6:5(1311)-2TI-3:8(2704)-JUDE-10(5351)-RE-19:2(5351)

CORRUPTED-all=7843&marked-GE-6:12-EX-8:24■32:7-DE-9:12■32:5-J'G-2:19-EZE-16:47■28:17-HO-9:9-ZEP-3:7-MAL-2:8■N.T.-2CO-7:2(5351)■11:3(5351)-JAS-5:2(4595)

CORRUPTERS-IS-1:4(7843)-JER-6:28(7843)

CORRUPTETH-LU-12:33(1311)

CORRUPTIBLE-all=5349&marked-RO-1:23-1CO-9:25■15:53,54-1PE-1:18,23■3:4(862)

CORRUPTING-DA-11:17(7843)

CORRUPTION-all=7845-LE-22:25(4893)-2KI-23:13(4889)-JOB-7:14-PS-16:10■49:9-IS-38:17(1097)-DA-10:8(4889)-JON-2:6■N.T.-all=5356&marked-AC-2:27(1312),31(1312)■13:34(1312),35(1312),36(1312),37(1312)-RO-8:21-1CO-15:42,50-GA-6:8-2PE-1:4■2:12,19

CORRUPTLY-2CH-27:2(7843)-NE-1:7(2254)

COST-2SA-24:24(2600)-1CH-21:24(2600)■N.T.-LU-14:28(1160)

COSTLINESS-RE-18:19(5094)

COSTLY-all=3368-1KI-5:17■7:9,10,11■N.T.-JOH-12:3(4186)-1TI-2:9(4185)

COTES-2CH-32:28(220)

COTTAGE-IS-1:8(5521)■24:20(4412)

COTTAGES-ZEP-2:6(3741)

COUCH-GE-49:4(3326)-JOB-7:13(4904)■38:40(7742)-PS-6:6(6210)-AM-3:12(6210)■N.T.-LU-5:19(2826),24(2826)

COUCHED-GE-49:9(7257)-NU-24:9(3766)

COUCHES-AM-6:4(6210)-AC-5:15(2895)

COUCHETH-DE-33:13(7257)

COUCHING-GE-49:14(7257)

COUCHINGPLACE-EZE-25:5(4769)

COULD-all=3201&marked-GE-13:6■36:7■37:4■45:1,3■48:10-EX-2:3■7:21,24■8:18■9:11■12:39■15:23-NU-9:6-JOS-7:12■15:63■17:12-J'G-2:14■14:14-1SA-3:2■4:15-2SA-3:11-1KI-5:3■8:11■13:4■14:4-2KI-3:26■4:40■16:5-1CH-21:30-2CH-5:14■7:2■29:34■30:3■32:14-EZR-2:59-NE-7:61■13:24(5234)-ES-6:1(5074)-JOB-31:23-IS-7:1■46:2-JER-6:15(3045)■8:12(3045)■20:9■44:22-LA-4:14-EZE-47:5,5sup-DA-5:8(3546),15(3546)■6:4(3202)-HO-5:13-JON-1:13■N.T.-all=1410&marked-M'T-17:16,19■26:40(2480)-M'R-1:45■2:4■3:20■5:3,4(2480)■6:5,19■7:24■9:18(2489),28■14:8(2192)-LU-1:22■6:48(2480)■8:19,43(2480)■9:40■13:11■14:6(2480)■19:3■20:7(5342),26(2480)-JOH-9:33■11:37■12:39-AC-4:14(2192)■11:17(1415)■13:39■21:34■25:7(2480)■27:15,43-RO-8:3(102)-1CO-3:1-2CO-3:7-GA-3:21-HEB-3:19■6:13(2192)■9:9-RE-7:9■14:3

COULDEST-JER-3:5(3201)-DA-2:47(3202)■N.T.-M'R-14:37(2480)

COULTER-1SA-13:20(855)

COULTERS-1SA-13:21(855)

COUNCIL-PS-68:27(7277)■N.T.-all=4892&marked-M'T-5:22■12:14(4824)■26:59-M'R-14:55■15:1-LU-22:66-JOH-11:47-AC-4:15■5:21,27,34,41■6:12,15■22:30■23:1,6,15,20,28■24:20■25:12(4824)

COUNCILS-M'T-10:17(4891)-M'R-13:9(4892)

COUNSEL-all=6098,a=3289&marked-EX-18:19a-NU-31:16(1697)-DE-32:28-J'G-20:7-2SA-15:31,34■16:20,23[2]■17:7,11a,14[3],15a,23-1KI-1:12■12:8,9a,13,14,28a-2KI-6:8a■18:20-2CH-10:6[2]a,8,8a,13■22:5■25:16a,16■30:2a,23a■32:3a-EZR-10:3,8-NE-4:15■6:7a-JOB-5:13■10:3■12:13■18:7■21:16■22:18■29:21■38:2■42:3-PS-1:1■2:2(3245)■13:2■14:6■16:7a■20:4■31:13(3245)■33:10,11■55:14(5475)■64:2(5475)■71:10a■73:24■83:3(5475)■106:13,43■107:11-PR-1:25,30■8:14■11:14(8458)■12:15■15:22(5475)■19:20,21■20:5,18■21:30■24:6(8458)■27:9-IS-5:19■7:5a■8:10■11:2■16:3■19:3,11,17■23:8a■28:29■29:15■30:1■36:5■40:14a■44:26■45:21a■46:10,11-JER-18:18,23■19:7■23:18(5475),22(5475)■32:19■38:15a■49:7,20,30■50:45-EZE-7:26■11:2-DA-2:14(5843)■4:27(4431)-HO-10:6-MIC-4:12-ZEC-6:13■N.T.-all=1012&marked-M'T-22:15(4824)■27:1(4824),7(4824)■28:12(4824)-M'R-3:6(4824)-LU-7:30■

23:51-**JOH**-11:53(4823)■18:14(4823)-**AC**-2:23■4:28■5:33(1011),38■9:23(4823)■20:27■27:42-**EPH**-1:11-**HEB**-6:17-**RE**-3:18(4823)

COUNSELLED-all=3289-**2SA**-16:23■17:15,21-**JOB**-26:3

COUNSELLER-all=3289&marked-**2SA**-15:12-**1CH**-26:14■27:32,33-**2CH**-22:3-**IS**-3:3■9:6■40:13(6098)■41:28-**MIC**-4:9-**NA**-1:11

COUNSELLERS-all=3289&marked-**2CH**-22:4-**EZR**-4:5■7:14(3272),15(3272),28■8:25-**JOB**-3:14■12:17-**PS**-119:24(6098)-**PR**-11:14■12:20■15:22■24:6-**IS**-1:26■19:11-**DA**-3:2(1884),3(1884),24(1907),27(1907)■4:36(1907)■6:7(1907)

COUNSELLOR-**M'R**-15:43(1010)-**LU**-23:50(1010)-**RO**-11:34(4825)

COUNSELS-all=4156&marked-**JOB**-37:12(8458)-**PS**-5:10■81:12-**PR**-1:5(8458)■12:5(8458)■22:20-**IS**-25:1(6098)■47:13(6098)-**JER**-7:24-**HO**-11:6-**MIC**-6:16■**N.T.**-**1CO**-4:5(1012)

COUNT-all=5608&marked-**EX**-12:4(3699)-**LE**-23:15■25:27(2803),52(2803)-**NU**-23.10(4487)-**1SA**-1:16(5414)-**JOB**-19:15(2803)■31:4-**PS**-87:6■139:18,22(1961)■**N.T.**-all=2233&marked-**AC**-20:24(2192)-**PH'P**-3:8^2,13(3049)-**2TH**-1:11(515)■3:15-**1TI**-6:1-**PH'M**-17(2192)-**JAS**-1:2■5:11(3106)-**2PE**-2:13■3:9-**RE**-13:18(5585)

COUNTED-all=2803&marked-**GE**-15:6■31:15-**EX**-38:21(6485)-**LE**-25:31-**NU**-18:30-**JOS**-13:3-**1KI**-3:8(5608)-**1CH**-21:6(6485)■23:24(6485)-**NE**-13:13-**JOB**-18:3■41:29-**PS**-44:22■88:4■106:31-**PR**-17:28■27:14-**IS**-5:28■32:15■33:18(5608)■40:15,17-**HO**-8:12■**N.T.**-all=3049&marked-**M'T**-14:5(2192)-**M'R**-11:32(2192)-**AC**-5:41(2661)■19:19(4860)-**RO**-2:26■4:3,5■9:8-**PH'P**-3:7(2233)-**2TH**-1:5(2661)-**1TI**-1:12(2233)■5:17(515)-**HEB**-3:3(515)■7:6(1075)■10:29(2233)

COUNTENANCE-all=6440&marked-**GE**-4:5,6■31:2,5-**EX**-23:3(1921)-**NU**-6:26-**DE**-28:50-**J'G**-13:6(4758)-**1SA**-1:18■16:7(4758),12(5869)■17:42(4758)■25:3(8389)-**2SA**-14:27(4758)-**2KI**-8:11-**NE**-2:2,3-**JOB**-14:20■29:24-**PS**-4:6■10:4(639)■11:7■21:6■42:5,11■43:5■44:3■80:16■89:15■90:8-**PR**-15:13■16:15■25:23■27:17-**EC**-7:3-**SONG**-2:14^2(4758)■5:15(4758)-**IS**-3:9-**EZE**-27:35-**DA**-1:13(4758)■5:6(2122),9(2122),10(2122)■7:28(2122)■8:23■**N.T.**-all=4383&marked-**M'T**-6:16(4659)■28:3(2397)-**LU**-9:29-**AC**-2:28-**2CO**-3:7-**RE**-1:16(3799)

COUNTENANCES-**DA**-1:13(4758),15(4758)

COUNTERVAIL-**ES**-7:4(7737)

COUNTETH-**JOB**-19:11(2803)■33:10(2803)■**N.T.**-**LU**-14:28(5585)

COUNTING-all supplied

COUNTRIES-all=776&marked-**GE**-10:20■26:3,4■41:57-**JOS**-17:11(5316)-**2KI**-18:35-**1CH**-22:5■29:30-**2CH**-11:23■12:8■15:5■20:29■34:33-**EZR**-3:3-**PS**-110:6-**IS**-8:9■37:18-**JER**-23:3,8■28:8■32:37■40:11-**EZE**-5:5,6■6:8■11:16^2,17■12:15■20:23,32,34,41■22:4,15■25:7■29:12^2■30:7,23,26■32:9■34:13■35:10■36:19,24-**DA**-9:7■11:40,42■**N.T.**-**LU**-21:21(5561)

COUNTRY-all=776&marked-**GE**-12:1■14:7(7704)■19:28■20:1■24:4,62■25:6■29:26(4725)■30:25■32:3(7704),9■34:2■36:6■42:30,33■47:27-**LE**-16:29(249)■17:15(249)■24:22(249)■25:31-**NU**-15:13(249)■20:17■21:20(7704)■32:4,33-**DE**-3:14(2256)■4:43■26:3-**JOS**-2:2,3,24■6:22,27■7:2■9:6,9,11■10:40,41■12:7■13:21■19:51■22:9-**J'G**-8:28■11:21■12:12■16:24■18:14■20:6(7704)-**RU**-1:1,2,6^2,22■2:6■4:3-**1SA**-6:1,18(6521)■27:5(7704),7(7704),11(7704)-**2SA**-15:23■18:8■21:14-**1KI**-4:19^2■8:41■10:13,15■11:21,22■20:27■22:36-**2KI**-3:20■18:35■20:14-**1CH**-8:8(7704)■20:1-**2CH**-6:32■9:14■30:10-**PR**-25:25-**IS**-1:7■13:5■22:18■39:3■46:11-**JER**-2:7■4:16■6:20,22■8:19■10:22■22:10,26■23:8■31:8■32:8■44:1■46:10■47:4(339)■48:21■50:9■51:9-**EZE**-20:38,42■25:9■32:15■34:13■47:8(1552),22(249)-**HO**-12:12(7704)-**JON**-1:8■4:2(127)-**ZEC**-6:6^2,8^2■8:7^2■**N.T.**-all=5561&marked-**M'T**-2:12■8:28■9:31(1093)■13:54(3968),57(3968)■14:35(4066)■21:33(589)■25:14(589)-**M'R**-5:1,10,14(68)■6:1(3968),4(3968),36(68),56(68)■12:1(589)■15:21(68)■16:12(68)-**LU**-2:8■3:3(4066)■4:23(3968),24(3968),37(4066)■8:26,34(68),37(4066)■9:12(68)■15:13,15■19:12■20:9(589)■23:26(68)-**JOH**-4:44(3968)■11:54,55-**AC**-4:36(1085)■7:3(1093)■12:20■18:23■27:27-**HEB**-11:14(3968)

COUNTRYMEN-**2CO**-11:26(1085)-**1TH**-2:14(4853)

COUPLE-all=2266&marked-**EX**-26:6,9,11■36:18■39:4-**J'G**-19:3(6776)-**2SA**-13:6(8147)■16:1(6776)-**IS**-21:7(6776),9(6776)

COUPLED-all=2266&marked-**EX**-26:3^2,24(8382),24(8535)■36:10^2,13,16,29(8382),29(8535)■39:4

COUPLETH-**EX**-26:10(2279)■36:17(2279)

COUPLING-all=4225&marked-**EX**-26:4(2279),4,5,10(2279)■28:27■36:11^2,12,17■39:20

COUPLINGS-**2CH**-34:11(4226)

COURAGE-all=553&marked-**NU**-13:20(2388)-**DE**-31:6,7,23-**JOS**-1:6,9,18■2:11(7307)■10:25-**2SA**-10:12(2388)-**1CH**-19:13(2388)■22:13■28:20-**2CH**-15:8(2388)-**EZR**-10:4(2388)-**PS**-27:14(2388)■31:24(2388)-**IS**-41:6(2388)-**DA**-11:25(3824)■**N.T.**-**AC**-28:15(2294)

COURAGEOUS-**JOS**-1:7(553)■23:6(2388)-**2SA**-13:28(2388)-**2CH**-32:7(553)**AM**-9:16(533,3820)

COURAGEOUSLY-**2CH**-19:11(2388)

COURSE-all=4256&marked-**1CH**-27:1,2^2,4^3,5,6,7,8,9,10,11,12,13,14,15■28:1-**2CH**-5:11-**PS**-82:5(4131)-**JER**-8:6(4794)■23:10(4794)■**N.T.**-all=1408&marked-**LU**-1:5(2183),8(2183)-**AC**-13:25■16:11(2113)■20:24■21:1(4144),7(4144)-**1CO**-14:27(3313)-**EPH**-2:2(165)-**2TH**-3:1(5143)-**2TI**-4:7(1408)-**JAS**-3:6(5164)

COURSES-all=4256&marked-**J'G**-5:20(4546)-**1KI**-5:14(2487)-**1CH**-23:6■27:1■28:13,21-**2CH**-8:14^2■23:8■31:2^2,15,16,17■35:4,10-**EZR**-6:18(4255)-**IS**-44:4(2988)

COURT-all=2691&marked-**EX**-27:9^2,12,13,16,17,18,19■35:17^2,18■38:9^2,15,16,17,18^2,20,31^3■39:40^2■40:8^2,33^2-**LE**-6:16,26-**NU**-3:26^2,37■4:26^2,32-**2SA**-17:18-**1KI**-6:36■7:8,9,12^2■8:64-**2KI**-20:4(5892)-**2CH**-4:9,9^2(5835)■6:13(5835)■7:7■20:5■24:21■29:16-**NE**-3:25-**ES**-1:5■2:11■4:11■5:1,2■6:4^2,5-**IS**-34:13(2681)-**JER**-19:14,26:2■32:2,8,12■33:1■36:10,20■37:21^2■38:6,13,28■39:14,15-**EZE**-8:7,16■10:3,4,5■40:14,17^2,19,20,23,27,28,31,32,34,37,44,47■41:15■42:1,3^2,7,8,9,10,14■43:5■44:17^2,19^2,21,27■45:19■46:1,20,21^3,22-**AM**-7:13(1004)■**N.T.**-**RE**-11:2(833)

COURTEOUS-**1PE**-3:8(5391)

COURTEOUSLY-**AC**-27:3(5364)■28:7(5390)

COURTS-all=2691-**2KI**-21:5■23:12-**1CH**-23:28■28:6,12-**2CH**-23:5■33:5■8:16^2■13:7-**PS**-65:4■84:2,10■92:13■96:8■100:4■116:19■135:2-**IS**-1:12■62:9-**EZE**-9:7■42:6■46:22-**ZEC**-3:7

COUSIN-**LU**-1:36(4773)

COUSINS-**LU**-1:58(4773)

COVENANT-all=1285-**GE**-6:18■9:9,11,12,13,15,16,17■15:18■17:2,4,7^2,9,10,11,3^2,14,19^2,21■21:27,32■26:28■31:44-**EX**-2:24■6:4,5■19:5■23:32■24:7,8■31:16■34:10,12,15,27,28-**LE**-2:13■24:8■26:9,15,25,42^3,44,45-**NU**-10:33■14:44■18:19■25:12,13-**DE**-4:13,23,31■5:2,3■7:2,9,12■8:18■9:9,11,15■10:8■17:2■29:1^2,9,12,14,21,25■31:9,16,20,25,26■33:9-**JOS**-3:3,6^2,8,11,14,17■4:7,9,18■6:6,8■7:11,15■8:33■23:16■24:25-**J'G**-2:1,20■20:27-**1SA**-4:3,4^2,5■11:1■18:3■20:8■23:18-**2SA**-15:24■23:5-**1KI**-3:15■6:19■8:1,6,21,23■11:11■19:10,14■20:34^2-**2KI**-11:4,17■13:23■17:15,35,38■18:12■23:2,3^3,21-**1CH**-11:3■15:25,26,28,29■16:6,15,16,17,37■17:1■22:19■28:2-**2CH**-5:2,7■6:11,14■13:5■15:12■21:7■23:1,3,16■29:10■34:30,31^2,32-**EZR**-10:3-**NE**-1:5■9:8,32■13:29-**JOB**-31:1■41:4-**PS**-25:10,14■44:17■50:5,16■55:20■74:20■78:10,37■89:3,28,34,39■103:18■105:8,10■106:45■111:5,9■132:12-**PR**-2:17-**IS**-24:5■28:15,18■33:8■42:6■49:8■54:10■55:3■56:4,6■59:21■61:8-**JER**-3:16■11:2,3,6,8,10■14:21■22:9■31:31,32^2,33■32:40■33:20^2,21,25■34:8,10,13,15,18^2■50:5-**EZE**-16:8,59,60^2,61,62■17:13,14,15,16,18,19■20:37■34:25■37:26^2■44:7-**DA**-9:4,27■11:22,28,30^2,32-**HO**-2:18■6:7■8:1■10:4■12:1-**AM**-1:9-**ZEC**-9:11■11:10-**MAL**-2:4,5,8,10,14■3:1■**N.T.**-all=1242-**LU**-1:72-**AC**-3:25■7:8-**RO**-11:27-**GA**-3:15,17-**HEB**-8:6,7,8,9^2,10■9:4^2■10:16,29■12:24■13:20

COVENANTBREAKERS-**RO**-1:31(802)

COVENANTED-**2CH**-7:18(3772)-**HAG**-2:5(3772)■**N.T.**-**M'T**-26:15(2476)-**LU**-22:5(4934)

COVENANTS-all=1242-**RO**-9:4-**GA**-4:24-**EPH**-2:12

COVER-all=3680&marked-**EX**-10:5■21:33■25:29(5258)■26:13■28:42■33:22(5526)■37:16(5258)■40:3(5526)-**LE**-13:12■16:13■17:13-**NU**-4:5,7(5258),8,9,11,12■22:5-**DE**-23:13(2645)■33:12(2645)-**1SA**-24:3(5526)-**1KI**-7:18,41,42-**2CH**-4:12,13-**NE**-4:5-**JOB**-16:18■21:26■22:11■38:34■40:22(5526)-**PS**-91:4(5526)■104:9■109:29(5844)■139:11(7779)■140:9-**IS**-11:9■14:11(4374)■22:17(5844)■26:21■30:1(5258)■58:7■59:6■60:2,6-**JER**-46:8-**EZE**-7:18■12:6,12■24:7,17(5844),22(5844)■26:10,19■30:18■32:7^2■37:6(7159)■38:9,16-**HO**-2:9■10:8-**OB**-10-**MIC**-3:7(5844)■7:10-**HAB**-2:14,17■**N.T.**-**M'R**-14:65(4028)-**LU**-23:30(2572)-**1CO**-11:7(2619)-**1PE**-4:8(2572)

COVERED-all=3680&marked-**GE**-7:19,20■9:23■24:65■38:14,15-**EX**-8:6■10:15■14:28■15:5,10■16:13■24:15,16■37:9(5526)■40:21(5526),34-**LE**-13:13-**NU**-4:20(1104)■7:3(6632)■9:15,16■16:42-**DE**-32:15(3780)-**JOS**-24:7-**J'G**-4:18,19-**1SA**-19:13■28:14(5844)-**2SA**-15:30^2(2645)■19:4(3813)-**1KI**-1:1■6:9(5603),15^2(6823),20(6823),35(6823)■7:3(5603),7(5603)■8:7(5526)-**2KI**-19:1,2-**1CH**-28:18(5526)-**2CH**-5:8-**NE**-3:15(2926)-**ES**-6:12(2645)■7:8(2645)-**JOB**-23:17■31:33-**PS**-32:1■44:15,19■65:13(5848)■68:13(2645)■69:7■71:13(5844)■80:10■85:2■89:45(5844)■106:11,17■139:13(5526)■140:7(5526)-**PR**-24:31■26:23(6823),26-**EC**-6:4-**IS**-6:2^2■29:10■37:1,2■51:16■61:10(3271)-**JER**-14:3(2645),4(2645)■51:42,51-**LA**-2:1(5743)■3:16(3728),43(5526),44(5526)-**EZE**-1:11,23^2■16:8,10■18:7,16■24:8■27:7(4374)■31:15■37:8(7159)■41:16-**JON**-3:6,8-**HAB**-3:3■**N.T.**-**M'T**-8:24(2572)■10:26(2572)-**LU**-12:12(4780)-**RO**-4:7(1943)-**1CO**-11:4(2596),6^2(2619)

COVEREDST-**PS**-104:6(3680)

COVEREST-**DE**-22:12(3680)-**PS**-104:2(5844)

COVERETH-all=3680&marked-**EX**-29:13,22-**LE**-3:3,9,14■4:8■7:3■9:19

(4374)-NU-22:11-J'G-3:24(5526)-JOB-9:24(4374)▪15:27▪36:30,32-PS-73:6(5848)▪109:19(5844)▪147:8-PR-10:6,11,12▪12:16▪17:9▪28:13-JER-3:25-EZE-28:14(5526)-MAL-2:16▪N.T.-LU-8:16(2572)

COVERING-all=4372&marked-GE-8:13▪20:16(3682)-EX-22:27(3682)▪25:20(5526)▪26:7(168),14^{2}▪35:11,12(4539)▪36:19^{2}▪39:34^{2},34(4539)▪40:19,21(4539)-LE-13:45(5844)-NU-3:25▪4:5(4539),6(3681),8,10,11,12,14(3681),15(3680),25▪16:38(6826),39(6826)▪19:15(6781)-2SA-17:19(4539)-JOB-22:14(5643)▪24:7(3682)▪26:6(3682)▪31:19(3682)-PS-105:39(4539)-SONG-3:10(4817)-IS-22:8(4539)▪25:7(3875)▪28:20(4541)▪30:1(4541),22(6826)▪50:3(3682)-EZE-28:13(4540),16(5526)-MAL-2:13(3680)▪N.T.-1CO-11:15(4018)

COVERINGS-PR-7:16(4765)▪31:22(4765)

COVERS-all=7184-EX-25:29▪37:16-NU-4:7

COVERT-all=5643&marked-1SA-25:20-2KI-16:18(4329)-JOB-38:40(5521)▪40:21-PS-61:4-IS-4:6(4563)▪16:4▪32:2-JER-25:38(5520)

COVET-all=2530-EX-20:17^{2}-DE-5:21(183)-MIC-2:2▪N.T.-RO-7:7(1937)▪13:9(1937)-1CO-12:31(2206)▪14:39(2206)

COVETED-JOS-7:21(2530)▪N.T.-AC-20:33(1937)-1TI-6:10(3713)

COVETETH-PR-21:26(183)-HAB-2:9(1214)

COVETOUS-PS-10:3(1214)▪N.T.-all=4132&marked-LU-16:14(5366)-1CO-5:10,11▪6:10-EPH-5:5-1TI-3:3(866)-2TI-3:2(5366)-2PE-2:14(4124)

COVETOUSNESS-all=1215-EX-18:21-PS-119:36-PR-28:16-IS-57:17-JER-6:13▪8:10▪22:17▪51:13-EZE-33:31-HAB-2:9▪N.T.-all=4124&marked-M'R-7:22-LU-12:15-RO-1:29-2CO-9:5-EPH-5:3-COL-3:5-1TH-2:5-HEB-13:5(866)-2PE-2:3(4124)

COW-LE-22:28(7794)-NU-18:17(7794)-JOB-21:10(6510)-IS-7:21(5697)▪11:7(6510)

COW'S-EZE-4:15(1241)

CRACKLING-EC-7:6(6963)

CRACKNELS-1KI-14:3(5350)

CRAFT-DA-8:35(4820)▪N.T.-M'R-14:1(1388)-AC-18:3(3673)▪19:25(2039),27(3313)-RE-18:22(5078)

CRAFTINESS-JOB-5:13(6193)▪N.T.-all=3834-LU-20:23-1CO-3:19-2CO-4:2-EPH-4:14

CRAFTSMAN-DE-27:15(2796)▪N.T.-RE-18:22(5079)

CRAFTSMEN-all=2796-2KI-24:14,16-1CH-4:14-NE-11:35-HO-13:2▪N.T.-AC-19:24(5079),38(5079)

CRAFTY-JOB-5:12(6175)▪15:5(6175)-PS-83:3(6191)▪N.T.-2CO-12:16(3835)

CRAG-JOB-39:28(8127)

CRANE-IS-38:14(5483)-JER-8:7(5483)

CRASHING-ZEP-1:10(7667)

CRAVED-M'R-15:43(154)

CRAVETH-PR-16:26(404)

CREATE-all=1254-PS-51:10-IS-4:5▪45:7^{2}▪57:19▪65:17,18^{2}

CREATED-all=1254-GE-1:1,21,27^{3}▪2:3,4▪5:1,2^{2}▪6:7-DE-4:32-PS-89:12▪102:18▪104:30▪148:5-IS-40:26▪41:20▪42:5▪43:1,7▪45:8,12,18^{2}▪48:7▪54:16^{2}-JER-31:22-EZE-21:30▪28:13,15-MAL-2:10▪N.T.-all=2936-M'R-13:19-1CO-11:9-EPH-2:10▪3:9▪4:24-COL-1:16^{2}▪3:10-1TI-4:3-RE-4:11^{2}▪10:6

CREATETH-AM-4:13(1254)

CREATION-all=2937-M'R-10:6▪13:19-RO-1:20▪8:22-2PE-3:4-RE-3:14

CREATOR-all=1254-EC-12:1-IS-40:28▪43:15▪N.T.-RO-1:25(2936)-1PE-4:19(2939)

CREATURE-all=5315&marked-GE-1:20(8318),21,24▪2:19▪9:10,12,15,16-LE-11:46^{2}-EZE-1:20(2416),21(2416),22(2416)▪10:15(2416),17(2416),20(2416)▪N.T.-all=2937&marked-M'R-16:15-RO-1:25▪8:19,20,21,39-2CO-5:17-GA-6:15-COL-1:15,23-1TI-4:4(2938)-HEB-4:13-RE-5:13(2938)

CREATURES-all=2416&marked-IS-13:21(255)-EZE-1:5,13^{2},14,15^{2},19^{2}▪3:13▪N.T.-JAS-1:18(2938)-RE-8:9(2938)

CREDITOR-DE-15:2(1167,4874,3027)-2KI-4:1(5383)▪N.T.-LU-7:41(1157)

CREDITORS-IS-50:1(5383)

CREEK-AC-27:39(2859)

CREEP-LE-11:20(8318),29(8317),31(8318),42(8317)-PS-104:20(7430)-EZE-38:20(7430)▪N.T.-2TI-3:6(1744,1519)

CREEPETH-all=7430&marked-GE-1:25(7431),26,30▪7:8,14,21(8317)▪8:17,19-LE-11:41(8317),43(8317),44,46(8317)▪20:25-DE-4:18

CREEPING-all=7431,a=8318&marked-GE-1:24,26▪6:7,20▪7:14,21a,23▪8:17,19-LE-5:2a▪11:21a,23a,29a,41a,42a,43a,44a▪22:5a-DE-14:19a-1KI-4:33-PS-104:25▪148:10-EZE-8:10▪38:20-HOS-2:18-HAB-1:14▪N.T.-all=2062-AC-10:12▪11:6-RO-1:23

CREPT-JUDE-4(3921)

CREW-all=5455-M'T-26:74-M'R-14:68,72-LU-22:60-JOH-18:27

CRIB-all=18-JOB-39:9-PR-14:4-IS-1:3

CRIED-all=7121,a=2199,b=6817,c=7768&marked-GE-27:34b▪39:14,15,18▪41:43,55b▪45:1-EX-2:23a▪5:15b▪8:12b▪14:10b▪15:25b▪17:4b-NU-11:2b▪12:13b▪14:1(5414)▪20:16b-DE-22:24b,27b▪26:7b-JOS-24:7b-J'G-3:9a,15a▪4:3b▪5:28(2980)▪6:6a,7a▪7:20,21(7321)▪9:7a▪10:10a,12b▪18:23-1SA-4:13a▪5:10a▪7:9a▪12:8a,10a▪15:11a▪17:8▪20:37,38▪24:8▪26:14▪28:12a-2SA-18:25▪19:4a▪20:16▪22:7-1KI-13:2,4,21,32▪17:20,21▪18:28▪20:39b▪22:32a-2KI-2:12b▪4:1b,40b▪6:5b,26b▪8:5b▪11:14▪18:28▪20:11-1CH-5:20a-2CH-13:14b▪14:11▪18:31a▪32:18,20a-NE-9:4a,27b,28a-EC-4:1a-JOB-29:12c▪30:5(7321),28c-PS-3:4▪18:6c,41c▪22:5a,24c▪30:2c,8▪31:22c▪34:6▪66:17▪77:1b▪88:1b,13c▪107:6b,13a▪119:145,146,147c▪120:1▪130:1▪138:3▪142:1a,5a-IS-6:3,4▪21:8▪30:7▪36:13-JER-4:20▪20:8a,8-LA-2:18b▪4:15-EZE-9:1,8a▪10:13▪11:13a-DA-3:4(7123)▪4:14(7123)▪5:7(7123)▪6:20(2200)-HO-7:14a-JON-1:5a,14▪2:2,2c▪3:4-ZEC-1:4▪6:8a▪7:7,13^{2}▪N.T.-all=2896&marked-M'T-8:29▪14:26,30▪15:22(2905)▪20:30,31▪21:9▪27:23,46(310),50-M'R-1:23(349),26▪3:11▪5:7▪6:49(349)▪9:24,26▪10:48▪11:9▪15:13,14,34(994),37(863),39-LU-4:33(349)▪8:8(5455),28(349)▪9:38(310)▪16:24(5455)▪18:38(994),39▪23:18(349),21(2019),46(5455)-JOH-1:15▪7:28,37▪11:43(2095)▪12:13,44▪18:40(2905)▪19:6(2905),12,15(2095)-AC-7:57,60▪16:17,28(5455)▪19:28,32,34▪21:34(994)▪22:23(2905),24(2019)▪23:6▪24:21-RE-6:10▪7:2,10▪10:3^{2}▪12:2▪14:18(5455)▪18:2,18,19▪19:17

CRIES-JAS-5:4(995)

CRIEST-EX-14:15(6817)-1SA-26:14(7121)-PR-2:3(7121)-IS-57:13(2199)-JER-30:15(2199)

CRIETH-all=7121&marked-GE-4:10(6817)-EX-22:27(6817)-JOB-24:12(7768)-PS-72:12(7768)▪84:2(7442)-PR-1:20(7442),21▪8:3(7442)▪9:3-IS-26:17(2199)▪40:3-JER-12:8(5414,6963)-MIC-6:9▪N.T.-all=2896-M'T-15:23-LU-9:39-RO-9:27-JAS-5:4

CRIME-JOB-31:11(2154)▪N.T.-AC-25:16(1462)

CRIMES-EZE-7:23(4941)▪N.T.-AC-25:27(156)

CRIMSON-all=3758&marked-2CH-2:7,14▪3:14-IS-1:18(8438)-JER-4:30(8144)

CRIPPLE-AC-14:8(5560)

CRISPING-IS-3:22(2754)

CROOKBACKT-LE-21:20(1384)

CROOKED-DE-32:5(6618)-JOB-26:13(1281)-PS-125:5(6128)-PR-2:15(6141)-EC-1:15(5791)▪7:13(5791)-IS-27:1(6129)▪40:4(6121)▪42:16(4625)▪45:2(1921)▪59:8(6140)-LA-3:9(5753)▪N.T.-LU-3:5(4646)-PH'P-2:15(4646)

CROP-LE-1:16(4760)-EZE-17:22(6998)

CROPPED-EZE-17:4(6998)

CROSS-all=4716-M'T-10:38▪16:24▪27:32,40,42-M'R-8:34▪10:21▪15:21,30,32-LU-9:23▪14:27▪23:26-JOH-19:17,19,25,31-1CO-1:17,18-GA-5:11▪6:12,14-EPH-2:16-PH'P-2:8▪3:18-COL-1:20▪2:14-HEB-12:2

CROSSWAY-OB-14(6563)

CROUCH-1SA-2:36(7812)

CROUCHETH-PS-10:10(1794)

CROW-all=5455-M'T-26:34,75-M'R-14:30,72-LU-22:34,61-JOH-13:38

CROWN-all=5850,a=2213,b=5145&marked-GE-49:26(6936)-EX-25:11a,24a,25a▪29:6b▪30:3a,4a▪37:2a,11a,12a,26a,27a▪39:30b-LE-8:9b▪21:12b-DE-33:20(6936)-2SA-1:10b▪12:30▪14:25(6936)-2KI-11:12b-1CH-20:2-2CH-23:11b-ES-1:11(3804)▪2:17(3804)▪6:8(3804)▪8:15-JOB-2:7(6936)▪19:9▪31:36-PS-21:3▪89:39b▪132:18b-PR-4:9▪12:4▪14:24▪16:31▪17:6▪27:24b-SONG-3:11-IS-3:17(6936)▪28:1,3,5▪62:3-JER-2:16(6936)▪13:18▪48:45(6936)-LA-5:16-EZE-16:12▪21:26-ZEC-9:16b▪N.T.-all=4735-M'T-27:29-M'R-15:17-JOH-19:2,5-1CO-9:25-PH'P-4:1-1TH-2:19-2TI-4:8-JAS-1:12-1PE-5:4-RE-2:10▪3:11▪6:2▪12:1▪14:14

CROWNED-PS-8:5(5849)-PR-14:18(3803)-SONG-3:11(5849)-NA-3:17(4502)▪N.T.-2TI-2:5(4737)-HEB-2:9(4737)

CROWNEDST-HEB-2:7(4737)

CROWNEST-PS-65:11(5849)

CROWNETH-PS-103:4(5849)

CROWNING-IS-23:8(5849)

CROWNS-all=5850-EZE-23:42-ZEC-6:11,14▪N.T.-all=4735&marked-RE-4:4,10▪9:7▪12:3(1238)▪13:1(1238)▪19:12(1238)

CRUCIFIED-all=4717&marked-M'T-26:2▪27:22,23,26,35,38,44(4957)▪28:5-M'R-15:15,24,25,32(4957)▪16:6-LU-23:23,33▪24:7,20-JOH-19:16,18,20,23,32(4957),41-AC-2:23(4362),36▪4:10-RO-6:6(4957)-1CO-1:13,23▪2:2,8-2CO-13:4-GA-2:20(4957)▪3:1▪5:24▪6:14-RE-11:8

CRUCIFY-all=4717&marked-M'T-20:19▪23:34▪27:31-M'R-15:13,14,20,27-LU-23:21-JOH-19:6^{2},10,15^{2}-HEB-6:6(388)

CRUEL-all=394&marked-GE-49:7(7185)-EX-6:9(7185)-DE-32:33(393)-JOB-30:21(393)-PS-25:19(2555)▪71:4(2556)-PR-5:9▪11:17▪12:10▪17:11▪27:4(395)-IS-13:9▪19:4(7186)-JER-6:23▪30:14▪50:42-LA-4:3(393)

CRUELLY-EZE-18:18(6233)

CRUELTY-all=2555&marked-GE-49:5-J'G-9:24-PS-27:12▪74:20-EZE-34:4(6531)

CRUMBS-all=5589-M'T-15:27-M'R-7:28-LU-16:21

CRUSE-all=6835&marked-1SA-26:11,12,16-1KI-14:3(1228)▪17:12,14,16▪19:6-2KI-2:20(6746)

CRUSH-JOB-39:15(2115)-LA-1:15(7665)▪3:34(1792)-AM-4:1(7533)

CRUSHED-LE-22:24(3807)-NU-22:25(3905)-DE-28:33(7533)-JOB-4:19(1792)▪5:4(1792)-IS-59:5(2116)-JER-51:34(2000)

CRY-all=7121,a=2199,b=2201,c=6818,d=6817,e=7440,f=7775&marked-GE-18:20b,21c▪19:13c▪27:34c-EX-2:23f▪3:7c,9c▪5:8d▪11:6c▪12:30c▪22:23d,23c▪32:18(6030)-LA-13:45-NU-16:34(6963)-DE-15:9▪24:15-J'G-10:14a-1SA-5:12f▪7:8a▪8:18a▪9:16c-2SA-19:28a▪22:7f-1KI-8:28e▪18:27-2KI-8:3d-2CH-6:19e▪13:12(7321)▪20:9a

-NE-5:1c,6b■9:9b-ES-4:1b■9:31b -JOB-16:18b■19:7d,7(7768)■27:9c■ 30:20(7768),24(7769)■31:38a■34:28^{2}c■ 35:9a,9(7768),12d■36:13(7768)■38:41 (7768)-PS-5:2(7773)■9:12c■17:1e■18:6f■ 22:2■27:7■28:1,2(7768)■34:15f,17d■ 39:12f■40:1f■55:17(1993)■56:9■57:2■ 61:1e,2■86:3■88:2e■89:26■102:1f■ 106:44e■107:19a,28d■119:169e■141:1^2■ 142:6e■145:19f■147:9-PR-8:1■ 21:13b,13-EC-9:17b-IS-5:7c■8:4■12:6 (6670)■13:22(6030)■14:31a■15:4a,4(7321), 5a,5b,8b■19:20d■24:14(6670)■29:9(8173)■ 30:19b■33:7d■34:14■40:2,6^2■42:2d,13 (7321),14(6463)■43:14e■46:7d■54:1 (6670)■58:1,9(7768)■65:14d-JER-2:2■ 3:4■4:5■7:16e■8:19f■11:11a,12a,14e,14■ 14:2(6682),12e■18:22b■20:16b■22:20^{2}d■ 25:34a,36c■31:6■46:12(6682),17■47:2a■ 48:4b,5c,20a,31a,34b■49:3d,21c,29■ 50:46b■51:54b-LA-2:19(7442)■3:8a,56f -EZE-8:18■9:4(602)■21:12a■24:17(602)■ 26:15(602)■27:28b,30a-HO-5:8(7321)■ 8:2a-JOE-1:14a,19,20(6165)-AM-3:4 (5414,6963)-JON-1:2■3:8-MIC-3:4a,5■ 4:9(7321)-HAB-1:2(7768),2a■2:11a-ZEP- 1:10c,14(6873)-ZEC-1:14,17■N.T.-all= 2906&marked-M'T-12:19(2905)■25:6 -M'R-10:47(2896)-LU-18:7(994)■19:40 (2896)-AC-23:9-RO-8:15(2896)-GA- 4:27(994)-RE-4:18

CRYING-1SA-4:14(6818)-2SA-13:19 (2201)-JOB-39:7(8663)-PS-69:3(7121) -PR-19:18(4191)-IS-22:5(7771)■24:11 (6682)■65:19(2201)-JER-48:3(6818) -MAL-2:13(603)■N.T.-all=2896& marked-M'T-3:3(994)■9:27■21:15 -M'R-1:3(994)■5:5■15:8(310)-LU-3:4(994)■ 4:41-JOH-1:23(994)-AC-8:7(994)■ 14:14■17:6(994)■21:28,36■25:24(1916) -GA-4:6-HEB-5:7(2906)-RE-14:15■ 21:4(2906)

CRYSTAL-JOB-28:17(2137)-EZE-1:22 (7140)■N.T.-RE-4:6(2930)■21:11(2929)■ 22:1(2930)

CUBIT-all=520&marked-GE-6:16 -EX-25:10^2,17,23^2■26:13^2,16■30:2^2■36:21■ 37:1^2,6,10^2,25^2-DE-3:11-J'G-3:16(1574) -1KI-7:24,31^2,32,35-2CH-4:3-EZE-40:5, 12^2,42^3■42:4■43:13^3,14^2,17^2■N.T.-M'T- 6:27(4083)-LU-12:25(4083)

CUBITS-all=520&marked-GE-6:15^3■ 7:20-EX-25:10,17,23■26:2^2,8^2,16■27:1^2,9, 11,12,13,14,16,18^2■30:2■36:9^2,15^2,21■37:1, 6,10,25■38:1^3,9,11,12,13,14,15,18^2-NU- 11:31■35:4,5^4-DE-3:11^2-JOS-3:4-1SA- 17:4-1KI-6:2,2sup,2,3^2,6^3,10,16,17,20^3,23, 24^3,25,26■7:2^3,6^2,10,15^2,16^2,19,23^3,27^3, 38-2KI-14:13■25:17^2-1CH-11:23-2CH- 3:3^3,4,8^2,11^3,12^2,13,15^2■4:1^3,2^3■6:13^2■ 25:23-EZR-6:3^2(521)-NE-3:13-ES- 5:14■7:9-JER-52:21^2,22-EZE-40:5,7,9^2, 11^2,12^2,13,14,15,19,21^2,23,25^2,27,29^2,30^2, 33^2,36^2,47^2,48^4,49^2■41:1^2,2^5,3^2,4^2,5^2,8,9, 10,11,12^3,13^2,14,15,22^2■42:2^2,4,7,8^2■ 43:13,14^2,15■45:2■47:3-DA-3:1^2(521) -ZEC-5:2^2■N.T.-JOH-21:8(4088) -RE-21:17(4088)

CUCKOW-LE-11:16(7828)-DE- 14:15(7828)

CUCUMBERS-NU-11:5(7180) -IS-1:8(4750)

CUD-all=1625&marked-LE-11:3,4^2, 5,6,7,26-DE-14:6,7^2,8

CUMBERED-LU-10:40(4049)

CUMBERETH-LU-13:7(2673)

CUMBRANCE-DE-1:12(2960)

CUMI-M'R-5:41(2891)

CUMMIN-all=3646&marked-IS- 28:25,27^2■N.T.-M'T-23:23(2951)

CUNNING-all=2803,a=2450& marked-GE-25:27(3045)-EX-26:1,31■ 28:6,15■31:4(4284)■35:33(4284),35,35 (4284)■36:8,35■38:23■39:3,8-1SA-16:16 (3045),18(3045)-1KI-7:14(1847)-1CH- 22:15a■25:7(995)-2CH-2:7^{2}a,13a,14^{2}a■ 26:15-SONG-7:1(542)-IS-3:3a■40:20a -JER-9:17a■10:9a-DA-1:4(3045)

CUNNINGLY-all supplied

CUP-all=3563&marked-GE-40:11^3, 13,21■44:2(1375),12(1375),16(1375), 17(1375)-2SA-12:3-1KI-7:26-2CH-4:5 -PS-11:6■16:5■23:5■75:8■116:13-PR- 23:31(3599)-IS-51:17^2,22^2-JER-16:7■ 25:15,17,28■49:12■51:7■LA-4:21-EZE- 23:31,32,33^2-HAB-2:16-ZEC-12:2(5592)■ N.T.-all=4221-M'T-10:42■20:22,23■ 23:25,26■26:27,39,42-M'R-9:41■10:38, 39■14:23,36-LU-11:39■22:17,20^2,42 -JOH-18:11-1CO-10:16,21^2■11:25^2,26, 27,28-RE-14:10■16:19■17:4■18:6

CUPBEARER-NE-1:11(4945)

CUPBEARERS-1KI-10:5(4945) -2CH-9:4(4945)

CUPS-1CH-28:17(7184)-IS-22:24 (101)-JER-35:5(3563)■52:19(4518)■ N.T.-M'R-7:4(4221),8(4221)

CURDLED-JOB-10:10(7087)

CURE-JER-33:6(4832),6(7495)-HO- 5:13(1455)■N.T.-M'T-17:16(2323) -LU-9:1(2323)

CURED-JER-46:11(8585)■N.T.-all= 2323-M'T-17:18-LU-7:21-JOH-5:10

CURES-LU-13:32(2392)

CURIOUS-EX-35:32(4284)■N.T. -AC-19:19(4021)

CURIOUSLY-PS-139:15(7551)

CURRENT-GE-23:16(5674)

CURSE-all=7045,a=7043,b=779& marked-GE-8:21a■12:3b■27:12,13-EX- 22:28b-LE-19:14a-NU-5:18b,19b,21 (423),22b,24^{2}b,27b,27(423)■22:6b,11 (6895),12b,17(6895)■23:7b,8(5344),11 (6895),13(6895),25(6895),27(6895)■24:10 -DE-11:26,28,29■23:4a,5■27:13■29:19 (423)■30:1-JOS-6:18(2764)■24:9a-J'G- 5:23^{2}b■9:57-2SA-16:9a,10^{2}a,11a-1KI- 2:8-2KI-22:19-NE-10:29(423)■13:2a,2 -JOB-1:11(1288)■2:5(1288),9(1288)■ 3:8(5344),8b■31:30(423)-PS-62:4a■ 109:28a■3:33(3994)■11:26(5344)■24:24 (5344)■26:2■27:14■28:27(3994)■30:10a -EC-7:21a■10:20^{2}a-IS-8:21a■24:6(423)■ 34:5(2764)■43:28(2764)■65:15(7621) -JER-15:10a■24:9■25:18■26:6■29:18 (423),22■42:18■44:8,12,22■49:13-LA- 3:65(8381)-DA-9:11(423)-ZEC-5:3 (423)■8:13-MAL-2:2(3994),2b■3:9 (3994)■4:6(2764)■N.T.-all=2672& marked-M'T-5:44■26:74(2653)-M'R- 14:71(332)-LU-6:28-AC-23:12(332), 14(332)-RO-12:14-GA-3:10(2671),13^2 (2671)-JAS-3:9-RE-22:3(2652)

CURSED-all=779,a=7043&marked -GE-3:14,17■4:11■5:29■9:25■27:29■ 49:7-LE-20:9a■24:11a,14a,23a-NU- 22:6■23:8(6895)■24:9-DE-7:26^2(2764)■ 13:17(2764)■27:15,16,17,18,19,20,21, 22,23,24,25,26■28:16^2,17,18,19^2-JOS- 6:26■9:23-J'G-9:27a■21:18-1SA-14:24, 28■17:43a■26:19-2SA-16:5a,7a,13a■ 19:21a-1KI-2:8a-2KI-2:24a■9:34 -NE-13:25a-JOB-1:5(1288)■3:1a■5:3 (5344)■24:18a-PS-37:22a■119:21-EC- 7:22a-JER-11:3■17:5■20:14,15■48:10^2 -MAL-1:14■2:2■3:9■N.T.-all=1944& marked-M'T-25:41(2672)-JOH-7:49 -GA-3:10,13-2PE-2:14-(2671)

CURSEDST-J'G-17:2(422)■N.T. -M'R-11:21(2672)

CURSES-all=423&marked-NU-5:23 -DE-28:15(7045),45(7045)■29:20,21,27 (7045)■30:7-2CH-34:24

CURSEST-NU-22:6(779)

CURSETH-all=7043&marked-GE- 12:3■27:29(779)-EX-21:17-LE-20:9■ 24:15-NU-24:9(779)-PR-20:20■30:11■ N.T.-M'T-15:4(2551)-M'R-7:10(2551)

CURSING-all=7045&marked-NU- 5:21(423)-DE-28:20(3994)■30:19-2SA- 16:12-PS-10:7(423)■59:12(423)■109:17, 18-PR-29:24(423)■N.T.-RO-3:14(685) -HEB-6:8(2671)-JAS-3:10(2671)

CURSINGS-JOS-8:34(7045)

CURTAIN-all=3407&marked-EX- 26:2^2,4^2,5^2,8^2,9,10^2,12■36:9^2,11^2,12^2,15^2,17^2 -NU-3:26(4539)-PS-104:2-IS-40:22(1852)

CURTAINS-all=3407-EX-26:1,2, 3^2,6,7^2,8,9^2,12,13■36:8,9,10^2,13,14^2,15, 16-NU-4:25-2SA-7:2-1CH-17:1-SONG-1:5 -IS-54:2-JER-4:20■10:20■49:29-HAB-3:7

CUSTODY-all=3027&marked-NU- 3:36(6486)-ES-2:3,8^2,14

CUSTOM-GE-31:35(1870)-J'G- 11:39(2706)-1SA-2:13(4941)-EZR-3:4 (4941)■4:13(1983),20■7:24(1983)-JER- 32:11(2706)■N.T.-all=5058&marked -M'T-9:9■17:25(5056)-M'R-2:14-LU- 1:9(1485)■2:27(1480),42(1485)■4:16 (3588,1486)■5:27-JOH-18:39(4914) -RO-13:7(5056)-1CO-11:16(4914)

CUSTOMS-LE-18:30(2708)-JER- 10:30(2708)■N.T.-all=1485-AC-6:14■ 16:21■21:21■26:3■28:17

CUT-all=3772,a=1438,b=7112marked -GE-9:11■17:14-EX-4:25■9:15(3582)■ 12:15,19■23:23(3582)■29:17(5408)■ 30:33,38■31:14■34:13■39:3b-LE-1:6 (5408),12(5408)■7:20,21,25,27■8:20 (5408)■17:4,9,10,14■18:29■19:8■20:3,5, 6,17,18■22:3,24■23:29■26:30-NU-4:18■ 9:13■13:23,24■15:30,31■19:13,20-DE- 7:5a■12:29■14:1(1413)■19:1,5■20:19, 20■23:1■25:12b-JOS-3:13,16■4:7^2■7:9■ 11:21■17:15(1254),18(1254)■23:4-J'G- 1:6b,7b■6:25,26,28,30■9:48,49■20:6 (5408)■21:6a-RU-4:10-1SA-2:31a,33■ 5:4■17:51■20:15^2■24:4,5,11,21■28:9■ 31:9-2SA-4:12b■7:9■10:4■20:22-1KI- 9:7■11:16■13:34(3582)■14:10,14■18:4, 23(5408),28(1413),33(5408)■21:21-2KI- 6:4(1504),6(7094)■9:8■10:32(7096)■ 16:17b■18:4,16b■19:23■23:14■24:13b -1CH-17:8■19:4■20:3(7787)-2CH-2:8, 10,16■14:3a■15:16■22:7■26:21(1504)■ 28:24b■31:1a■32:21(3582)■34:4,7a-JOB- 4:7(3582)■6:9(1214)■8:12(6998),14 (6990)■11:10(2498)■14:2(5243),7■18:16 (5243)■21:21(2686)■22:16(7059),20(3582)■ 23:17(6780)■24:24(5243)■30:4(6998)■ 36:20(5927)-PS-12:3■31:22(1629)■34:16■ 37:2(5243),9,22,28,34,38■54:5(6789)■ 58:7(4135)■75:10a■76:12(1219)■80:16 (3683)■83:4(3582)■88:5(1504),16(6789)■ 90:6(4135),10(1504)■94:23^2(6789)■ 101:5(6789),8■107:16a■109:13,15■ 129:4b■143:12(6789)-PR-2:22■10:31■ 23:18■24:14-IS-9:10a,14■10:7,34(5362)■ 11:13■14:12a,22■15:2a■18:5,5(8456)■ 22:25a,25■29:20■33:12(3683)■37:24■ 38:12(7088),12(1214)■45:2a■48:9,19■ 51:9(2672)■53:8(1504)■55:13■56:5-JER- 7:28,29(1494)■9:21■11:19■16:6(1413)■ 22:7■25:37(1826)■34:18■36:23(7167)■ 41:5(1413)■44:7,8,11■46:23■47:4,5(1820), 5(1413)■48:2,2(1826),25a■49:26(1826)■ 50:16,23a,30(1826)■51:6(1826),62-LA- 2:3a■3:53(6789),54(1504)-EZE-6:6a■ 14:8,13,17,19,21■16:4■17:9(7082),17■ 21:3,4■25:7,13,16■29:8■30:15■31:12■ 35:7■37:11(1504)■39:10(2404)-DA-2:5 (5648)34(1505),45(1505)■3:29(5648)■ 4:14(7113)■9:26-HO-8:4■10:7(1820), 15(1820)-JOE-1:5,9,16-AM-1:5,8■2:3■ 3:14a■9:1(1214)-OB-,5(1820),9,10,14 -MIC-5:9,10,11,12,13-NA-1:12(1494),14, 15■2:13■3:15-HAB-3:17(1504)-ZEP- 1:3,4,11(1820),11■3:6,7-ZEC-5:3^2(5352)■ 9:6,10^2■11:8(3582),9^2(3582),10a,14a,16 (3582)■12:3(8295)■13:2,8■14:2-MAL- 2:12■N.T.-all=1581&marked-M'T- 5:30■18:8■21:8(2875)■24:51(1371) -M'R-9:43(609),45(609)■11:8(2875)■ 14:47(851)-LU-12:46(1371)■13:7,9■ 22:50(851)-JOH-18:10(609),26(609) -AC-5:33(1282)■7:54(1282)■27:32(609) -RO-9:2(4932)■11:22,24-2CO-11:12 -GAL-5:12(609)

CUTTEST-DE-24:19(7114)

CUTTETH-JOB-28:10(1234)-PS- 46:9(7112)■141:7(6398)-PR-26:6(7096) -JER-10:3(3772)■22:14(7167)

CUTTING-EX-31:5(2799)■35:33 (2799)-IS-38:10(1824)-HAB-2:10(7096)■

N.T.-M'R-5:5(2629)

CUTTINGS-LE-19:28(8296)■21:5 (8296)-JER-48:37(1417)

CYMBAL-1CO-13:1(2950)

CYMBALS-all=4700&marked-2SA-6:5(6767)-1CH-13:8■15:16,19,28■16:5, 42■25:1,6-2CH-5:12,13■29:25-EZR-3:10-NE-12:27-PS-150:5^{2}(6767)

CYPRESS-IS-44:14(8645)

D

DAGGER-all=2719-J'G-3:16,21,22

DAILY-all=3117&marked-EX-5:13,19■16:5-NU-4:16(8548)■28:24■ 29:6(8548)-J'G-16:16-2KI-25:30-2CH-31:16-EZR-3:4-NE-5:18(3117,259) -ES-3:4-PS-13:2(3119)■42:10(3605, 3117)■56:1(3605,3117),2(3605,3117)■ 61:8■68:19■72:15(3605,3117)■74:22 (3605,3117)■86:3(3605,3117)■88:9 (3605,3117),17(3605,3117)-PR-8:30, 34-IS-58:2-JER-7:25■20:7(3605, 3117),8(3605,3117)■37:21-EZE-30:16 (3119)■45:23^{2}■46:13-DA-1:5■8:11 (8548),12(8548),13(8548)■11:31(8548)■ 12:11(8548)-HO-12:1(3605,3117)■ N.T.-all=2596,2250&marked-M'T-6:11(1967)■26:55-M'R-14:49-LU-9:23■ 11:3(1967)■19:47■22:53-AC-2:46,47■ 3:2■5:42(3956,2250)■6:1(2522)■16:5■ 17:11,17(2596,3956,2550)■19:9-1CO-15:31-2CO-11:28-HEB-3:13(2596, 1538,2250)■7:27■10:11-JAS-2:15(2184)

DAINTIES-GE-49:20(4574)-PS-141:4(4516)-PR-23:3(4303)

DAINTY-JOB-33:20(8378)-PR-23:6(4303)■N.T.-RE-18:14(3045)

DALE-GE-14:17(6010)-2SA-8:18(6010)

DAM-all=517-EX-22:30-LE-22:27 -DE-22:6^{2},7

DAMAGE-EZR-4:22(2257)-ES-7:4(5143)-PR-26:6(2555)-DA-6:2(5142)■ N.T.-AC-27:10(2209)-2CO-7:9(2210)

DAMNABLE-2PE-2:1(684)

DAMNATION-all=2917&marked -M'T-23:14,33(2920)-M'R-3:29(2920)■ 12:40-LU-20:47-JOH-5:29(2920)-RO-3:8■13:2-1CO-11:29-1TI-5:12-2PE-2:3(684)

DAMNED-M'R-16:16(2632)-RO-14:23(2632)-2TH-2:12(2919)

DAMSEL-all=5291&marked-GE-24:14,16,28,55,57■34:3^{2},4(3207),12-DE-22:15,19,20,21,23,24,25,26^{2},27,28-J'G-5:30(7356)■19:3-RU-2:5,6-1KI-1:3,4■ N.T.-all=2877&marked-M'T-14:11■ 26:69(3814)-M'R-5:39(3813),40^{2}(3813)■ 41(3813),41,42■6:22,28^{2}-JOH-18:17 (3814)-AC-12:13(3814)■16:16(3814)

DAMSEL'S-all=5291-DE-22:15,16, 29-J'G-19:4,5,6,8,9

DAMSELS-GE-24:61(5291)-2SA-25:42(5291)-PS-68:25(5959)

DANCE-all=4234&marked-J'G-21:21 (2342)-JOB-21:11(7540)-PS-149:3■ 150:4-EC-3:4(7540)-IS-13:21(7540) -JER-31:13-LA-5:15

DANCED-J'G-21:23(2342)-2SA-6:14(3769)■N.T.-all=3738-M'T-11:17■ 14:6-M'R-6:22-LU-7:32

DANCES-all=4246-EX-15:20-J'G-11:34■21:21-1SA-21:11■29:5-JER-31:4

DANCING-EX-32:19(4246)-1SA-18:6(4246)■30:16(2287)-2SA-6:16 (3769)-1CH-15:29(7540)-PS-30:11 (4234)■N.T.-LU-15:25(5525)

DANDLED-IS-66:12(8173)

DANGER-all=1777&marked-M'T-5:21,22^{3}-M'R-3:29-AC-19:27(2793), 40(2793)

DANGEROUS-AC-27:9(2000)

DARE-all=5111-RO-5:7■15:18-1CO-6:1-2CO-10:12

DARK-all=2822&marked-GE-15:17 (5939)-LE-13:6(3544),21(5344),26(3544), 28(3544),56(3544)-NU-12:8(2420) -JOS-2:5-2SA-22:12(2841)-NE-13:19 (6751)-JOB-3:9(2821)■12:25■18:6 (2821)■22:13(6205)■24:16-PS-18:11 (2824)■35:6■49:4(2420)■74:20(4285)■ 78:2(2420)■88:12■105:28(2821)-PR-1:6(2420)■7:9(653)-IS-29:15(4285)■ 49:19-JER-13:16(5399)-LA-3:6(4285) -EZE-8:12■32:7(6937),8(6937)■34:12 (6205)-DA-8:23(2420)-JOE-2:10(6937) -AM-5:8(2821),20(651)-MIC-3:6(2821), 6(6937)-ZEC-14:6(7087)■N.T.-LU-11:36(4652)-JOH-6:17(4653)■20:1 (4653)-2PE-1:19(850)

DARKEN-AM-8:9(2821)

DARKENED-all=2821&marked -EX-10:15-PS-69:23-EC-12:2,3-IS-5:30■9:19(6272)■13:10■24:11(6150) -EZE-30:18-JOE-3:15(6937)-ZEC-11:17(3543)■N.T.-all=4654-M'T-24:29-M'R-13:24-LU-23:45-RO-1:21■ 11:10-EPH-4:18-RE-8:12■9:2

DARKENETH-JOB-38:2(2821)

DARKISH-LE-13:39(3544)

DARKLY-1CO-13:12(1722,135)

DARKNESS-all=2822,a=6205& marked-GE-1:2,4,5,18■15:12(2825) -EX-10:21^{2},22■14:20■20:21a■-DE-4:11,11a■5:22a,23■28:29(653)-JOS-24:7(3990)-1SA-2:9-2SA-22:10a,12,29 -1KI-8:12a-2CH-6:1a-JOB-3:4,5,6(652)■ 5:14■10:21,22(5890),22^{2}(652)■12:22■ 15:22,23,30■17:12,13■18:18■19:8■ 20:26■22:11■23:17,17(652)■28:3,3(652)■ 29:3(2822)■30:26(652)■34:22■37:19■ 38:9a,19-PS-18:9a,11,28■82:5(2825)■ 88:6(4285),18(4285)■91:6(652)■97:2a■ 104:20■105:28■107:10,14■112:4■ 139:11,12,12(2825)■143:3(4285)-PR-2:13■4:19(653)■20:20-EC-2:13,14■ 5:17■6:4^{2}■11:8-IS-5:20,30■8:22(2825), 22(653)■9:2■29:18■42:7,16(4285)■ 45:3,7■47:5■49:9■50:10(2825)■58:10 (653)■59:9(653)■60:2,2a-JER-2:31(3991)■ 13:16(2821),16a■23:12(653)-LA-3:2 -EZE-32:8-DA-2:22(2816)-JOE-2:2,2a, 31-AM-4:13(5890)■5:18,20-MIC-7:8 -NA-1:8-ZEP-1:15,15a■N.T.-all=4655& marked-M'T-4:16■6:23,(4652),23■8:12■ 10:27(4653)■22:13■25:30■27:45-M'R-15:33-LU-1:79■11:34(4652),35■12:3 (4653)■22:53■23:44-JOH-1:5^{2}(4653)■ 3:19■8:12■12:35^{2},46-AC-2:20■13:11■ 26:18-RO-2:19■13:12-1CO-4:5-2CO-4:6■6:14-EPH-5:8,11■6:12-COL-1:13 -1TH-5:4,5-HEB-12:18-1PE-2:9-2PE-2:4(2217),17-1JO-1:5(4653),6■2:8(4653), 9(4653),11^{2}(4653)-JUDE-6(2217),13 -RE-16:10(5656)

DARLING-PS-22:20(3173)■35:17(3173)

DART-JOB-41:26(4551)-PR-7:23 (2671)-HEB-12:20(1002)

DARTS-2SA-18:14(7626)-2CH-32:5 (7973)-JOB-41:29(8455)■N.T.-EPH-6:16(956)

DASH-2KI-8:12(7376)-PS-2:9(5310)■ 91:12(5062)-IS-13:18(7376)-JER-13:14 (5310)■N.T.-M'T-4:6(4350)-LU-4:11(4350)

DASHED-all=7376&marked-EX-15:6(7492)-IS-13:16-HO-10:14■ 13:16-NA-3:10

DASHETH-PS-137:9(5310)-NA-2:1(6327)

DAUB-EZE-13:11(2902)

DAUBED-all=2902&marked-EX-2:3(2560)-EZE-13:10,12,14,15^{2}■22:28

DAUBING-EZE-13:12(2915)

DAUGHTER-all=1323,a=3618 &marked-GE-11:29,31a■20:12^{2}■24:23, 24,47^{2},48■25:20■26:34^{2}■28:9■29:6■ 29:10,18,23,24,28,29■30:21■34:1,3,5,7, 8,17,19■36:2^{2},3,14^{2},18,25,39■38:2,11a, 12,16a,24a■41:45,50■46:15,18,20,25 -EX-1:16,22■2:1,5,7,8,9,10,21■6:23■ 20:10■21:7,31-LE-12:6■18:9,10^{2},11,15a, 17^{3}■19:29■20:12a,17^{2}■21:2,9■22:12,13■ 24:11-NU-25:15,18■26:46,59■27:8,9■ 30:16■36:8-DE-5:14■7:3^{2}■12:18■13:6■ 16:11,14■18:10■22:16,17■27:22■28:56 -JOS-15:16,17-J'G-1:12,13■11:34^{2},35, 40■19:24■21:1-RU-1:22a■2:2,8,20a,22a, 22■3:1,10,11,16,18■4:15a-1SA-1:16■4:19a■ 14:50a■17:25■18:17,19,20,27,28■25:44 -2SA-3:3,7,13■6:16,20,23■11:3■12:3■ 14:27■17:25■21:8^{2},10,11-1KI-3:1■4:11, 15■7:8■9:16,24■11:1■15:2,10■16:31■ 22:42-2KI-8:18,26■9:34■11:2■14:9■ 15:33■18:2■19:21^{2}■21:19■22:1■23:10, 31,36■24:8,18-1CH-1:50■2:3,4a,21■35, 49■3:2,5■4:18■7:24■15:29-2CH-8:11■ 11:18(1121),18,20,21■13:2■20:31■21:6■ 22:2,11sup,11■25:18■27:1■29:1-NE-6:18-ES-2:7^{2},15^{2}■9:29-PS-9:14■45:10, 12,13■137:8-SONG-7:1-IS-1:8■10:30, 32(1004)■16:1■22:4■23:10,12■37:22^{2}■ 47:1^{2},5■52:2■62:11-JER-4:11,31■6:2,23, 26■8:11,19,21,22■9:1,7■14:17■31:22■ 46:11,19,24■48:18■49:4■50:42■51:33■ 52:1-LA-1:6,15■2:1■2:2,4,5,8,10,11, 13^{2},15,18■3:48■4:3,6,10,21,22^{2}-EZE-14:20■16:44,45■22:11a,11■44:25-DA-11:6,17-HO-1:3,6-MIC-1:13■4:8^{2},10, 13■5:1■7:6,6a-ZEP-3:10,14^{2}-ZEC-2:7,10■9:9^{2}-MAL-2:11■N.T.-all= 2364&marked-M'T-9:18,22■10:35,35 (3565),37■14:6■15:22,28■21:5-M'R-5:23(2365),34,35■6:22■7:25(2365),26, 29,30-LU-2:36■8:42,48,49■12:53,53 (3565)■13:16-JOH-12:15-AC-7:21 -HEB-11:24

DAUGHTER'S-all=1323-LE-18:10, 17-DE-22:17

DAUGHTERS-all=1121&marked -GE-5:4,7,10,13,16,19,22,26,30■6:1,2,4■ 11:11,13,15,17,19,21,23,25■19:8,12,14, 15,16,30^{2},36■24:3,13,37■27:46^{3}■28:1,2, 6,8■29:16■30:13■31:26,28,31,41,43^{2},50^{2}, 55■34:1,9^{2},16^{2},21^{2}■36:2,6■37:35■46:7, 15-EX-2:16,20■3:22■6:25■10:9■21:4,9■ 32:2■34:16^{2}-LE-10:14■26:29-NU-18:11, 19■21:29■25:1■26:33^{2}■27:1^{2},7■36:2,6, 10,11-DE-12:12,31■23:17■28:32,41,53■ 32:19-JOS-7:24■17:3^{2},6-J'G-3:6^{2}■11:40■ 12:9^{2}■14:1,2,3■21:7,18,21^{2}-RU-1:6(3618), 7(3618),8(3618),11,12,13-1SA-1:4■2:21■ 8:13■14:49■30:3,6,19-2SA-1:20^{2},24■ 5:13■13:18■19:5-2KI-17:17-1CH-2:34■ 4:27■7:15■14:3■23:22■25:5-2CH-2:14■ 11:21■13:21■24:3■28:8■29:9■31:18 -EZR-2:61■9:2,12^{2}-NE-3:12■4:14■5:2, 5^{2}■7:63■10:28,30^{2}■13:25^{2}-JOB-1:2,13, 18■42:13,15-PS-45:9■48:11■97:8■ 106:37,38■144:12-PR-30:15■31:29-EC-12:4-SONG-1:5■2:2,7■3:5,10,11■5:8,16■ 6:9■8:4-IS-3:16,17■4:4■16:2■32:9■ 43:6■49:22■56:5■60:4-JER-3:24■5:17■ 7:31■9:20■11:22■14:16■16:2,3■19:9■ 29:6^{3}■32:35■35:8■41:10■43:6■48:46■ 49:2,3-LA-3:51-EZE-13:17■14:16,18, 22■16:20,27,46^{2},48^{2},49,53^{2},55^{3},57^{2}, 61■23:2,4,10,25,47■24:21,25■26:6, 8■30:18■32:16,18-HOS-4:13,14-JOE-2:28■3:8-AM-7:17■N.T.-all=2364& marked-LU-1:5■23:28-AC-2:17■21:9 -2CO-6:18-1PE-3:6(5043)

DAWN-M'T-28:1(2020)-2PE-1:19(1306)

DAWNING-JOS-6:15(5927)-J'G-19:26 (6437)-JOB-3:9(6079)■7:4(5399)-PS-119:147(5399)

DAY-all=3117,a=3119&marked-GE-1:5^{2},8,13,14,16,18,19,23,31■2:2^{2},3,4,17■ 3:5,8■4:14■5:1,2■7:11^{2},13■8:4,14,22■ 15:18■17:23,26■18:1■19:37,38■21:8, 26■22:4,14■24:12,42■25:31,33■26:32, 33■27:2,45■29:7■30:32,35■31:22■ 39,40,43,48■32:24(7837),26(7837),32■ 33:13,16■34:25■35:3,20■39:10■40:7, 20■41:9■42:13,18,32■47:23,26■48:15, 20■50:20-EX-2:13,18■5:6,14■6:28■8:22■ 10:6^{2},13,28■12:6,14,15^{2},16^{2},17^{2},18^{2},41, 51■13:3,4,6,8,21^{2}a,22a■14:13^{2},30■16:1, 4,5,22,25^{2},26,27,29^{2},30■19:1,10,11^{2},15, 16■20:8,10,11^{2}■21:21■22:30■23:12■ 24:16■29:36,38■31:15,17■32:28,29^{2},34■ 34:11,21■35:2,3■40:2,37,38a-LE-6:5a, 20a■7:15a,16a,17a,18a,35a,36a,38a■8:34, 35a■9:1,4■10:19^{2}■12:3■13:5,6,27,32,34,

51■14:2,9,10,23,39■15:14,29■16:30■
19:6^{2},7■22:27,28,30■23:3,6,7,8,12,14,
15,21,27sup,27,28^{2},29,30,34,35,
36,37,39^{3},40■25:9sup,9■27:23
-**NU**-3:1,13■6:9^{2},10,11■7:1,10,11,12,18,
24,30,36,42,48,54,60,66,72,78,84■8:17■
9:3,5,6^{2},11,15,21a■10:10,34a■11:19,32^{2}■
14:14a,34■15:23,32■19:12^{4},19^{3}■22:30■
25:18■28:3,9,16,17,18,25,26■29:1sup,
1,12,17,20,23,26,29,32,35■30:5,7,8,12,
14^{2}■31:19^{2},24■33:3-**DE**-1:10,33a,39■
2:18,22,25,30■3:14■4:4,8,10,15,20,
26,32,38,39,40■5:1,3,12,14,15,24■
6:6,24■7:11■8:1,11,18,19■9:1,3,7,
10,24■10:4,8,13,15■11:2,4,8,13,26,27,
28,32■12:8■13:18■15:5,15■16:3,4,8■
18:16■19:9■20:3■21:23■24:15■26:3,
16,17,18■27:1,2,4,9,10,11■28:1,13,
14,15,32,66a■29:4,10,12,13,15^{2},18,28■
30:2,8,11,15,16,18,19■31:2,17^{2},18,22,27■
32:35,46,48■33:12■34:6-**JOS**-1:8a■3:7■
4:9,14■5:9^{2},10,11■6:4,10,14,15,15(7837),15,
25■7:25,26^{2}■8:25,28,29■9:12,17,27^{2}■
10:12,13,14,27,28,32,35^{2}■13:13■14:9,
10,11,12^{2},14■15:63■16:10■22:3,16^{2},17,
18^{2},22,29,31■23:8,9,14■24:15,25-**J'G**-
1:21,26■3:30■4:14,23■5:1■6:24,27a,32■
9:18,19,45■10:4,15■11:27■12:3■13:7,10■
14:15,17,18■15:19■16:2(1242)■18:1,12,
30■19:5,8,9^{2},11,25(7837),26(1242),30^{2}■
20:21,22,24,25,26,30,35,46■21:3,6-**RU**-
2:19^{2}■3:18■4:5,9,10,14-**1SA**-2:34■3:12■
4:3,12,16■5:5■6:15,16,18■7:6,10■8:8^{2},
18^{2}■9:12^{2},15,19,24,26(7837)■10:2,9,19■
11:11,13^{2}■12:2,5,17,18■13:22■14:1,23,
24,28,30,31,33,37,38,45■15:28,35■16:13■
17:10,46^{2}■18:2,9,21■19:24■20:5,12,
26,27sup,27,34■21:5,6,7,10■22:8,
13,18,22■23:14■24:4,10^{2},18,19■
25:8,16a,32,33■26:8,10,19,21,23,
24■27:1,6^{2},10■28:18,20■29:3,6,8■30:1,
17(4283),25^{2}■31:6-**2SA**-1:2■2:17,32(215)■
3:8^{2},35,37,38,39■4:3,5,8■5:8■6:8,9,20^{2},
23■7:6■11:12^{2}■12:18■13:4(1242),32,37■
14:22■15:20■16:3,12■18:7,8,18,20^{3},31■
19:2^{2},3,5^{2},6^{3},19,20,22^{3},24^{2},35■20:3■
21:10a■22:1,19■23:10■24:18-**1KI**-1:25,
30,48,51■2:8,24,37,42■3:6,18■4:22■5:7■
8:8,16,24,28,29,59a,61,64,66■9:13,21■
10:12■12:7,12^{2},19,32,33■13:3,11■14:14■
16:16■17:14■18:15,36■20:13,29^{2}■22:5,
25,35-**2KI**-2:3,5,22■4:8,11,18,23■6:28,
29,31■7:9■8:6,22■10:27■14:7■15:5■16:6■
17:23,34,41■19:3■20:5,8,17■21:15^{2}■25:30
-**1CH**-4:41,43■5:26■9:33a■11:22■12:22■
13:11,12■16:7,23■17:5^{2}■26:17^{2}■28:7■29:5,
21,22-**2CH**-5:9■6:5,15,20a■7:9,10■8:8,
13,14,16■10:12^{2},19■18:4,24,34■20:26^{2}■
21:10,15■24:11■26:21■28:6■30:21■35:16,
21,25-**EZR**-3:4,6■6:9(3118),15(3118)■
8:33■9:7^{2},15■10:13,16,17-**NE**-1:6a,11■
4:2,9a,22■5:11■8:2,9,10,11,13,17,18^{3}■
9:1,3,10,12a,19a,32,36■10:31^{2}■11:23■
12:43,47■13:1,15^{2},17,19,22-**ES**-1:10,
18■2:11■3:7,12,13,14■4:16■5:1,4,9■
7:2■8:1,12,13,17■9:1^{2},11,15,17,17sup,

17,18^{2},sup,18,19,19sup,19,21^{2},22-**JOB**-
1:4,6,13■2:1■3:1,3,4,5,8,9(7837)■7:4
(5399)■14:6■15:23■17:12■18:20■
20:28■21:30^{2}■23:2■26:10(216)■38:23
-**PS**-1:2a■2:7■7:11,18:t,18■19:2■20:1■
25:5■32:3,4a■35:28■37:13■38:6,12■
42:3a■44:8,22■50:15■55:10a■56:5■59:16■
71:8,15,24■73:14■74:16■77:2■78:9,42■
81:3■84:10■86:7■88:1■89:16■91:5a,
92:t■95:7,8■96:2■102:2^{2},8■110:3,5■
118:24■119:91,97,164■121:6a■136:8■
137:7■138:3■139:12■140:7■145:2■
146:4-**PR**-4:18■6:34■7:14,20■11:4■
16:4■21:26,31■22:19■23:17■24:10■27:1,
10,15-**EC**-7:1,14^{2}■8:8,16■12:3-**SONG**-
2:17■3:11^{2}■4:6■8:8-**IS**-2:11,12,17,
20■3:7,18■4:1,2,5a■5:30■7:17,18,20,21,
23■9:4,14■10:3,17,20,27,32■11:10,11,
16■12:1,4■13:6,9,13■14:3■17:4,7,9,11^{2}■
19:16,18,19,21,23,24■20:6■22:5,8,12,
20,25■23:15■24:21■25:9■26:1■27:1,2,3,
8,12,13■28:5,19,24■29:18■30:23,25,26■
31:7■34:8,10a■37:3■38:12,13,19■39:6■
43:13■47:9■48:7■49:8■51:13■52:5,6■
56:12■58:3,4,5^{2},13■60:11a,19a■61:2■
62:6■63:4■65:2,5■66:8-**JER**-1:10,18■
3:25■4:9■6:4■7:22,25^{2}■9:1a■11:4,5,7^{2}■
12:3■14:17a■15:9a■16:13a,19■17:6,17,18,
21,22^{2},24^{2},27^{2}■18:17■20:14^{2}■25:3,18,33■
27:22■30:7,8■31:6,32,35a■32:20^{2}a,31a■
33:20,20a,25a■34:13■35:14■36:2^{2},6,30■
38:28■39:16,17■40:4■41:4■42:19,21■
44:2,6,10,22,23■46:10^{2},21■47:4■48:41■
49:22,26■50:27,30,31■51:2■52:11,34
-**LA**-1:12,13,21■2:1,7,16,18a,21,22^{2}■3:3,
14,57,62-**EZE**-1:28■2:3■4:6,10■7:7,
10,12,19■12:3a,4a,7a■13:5■16:4,5,56■
20:5,6,29,31■21:25,29■22:24■23:38,39■
24:2^{3},25,26,27■26:18■27:27■28:13,15■
29:21■30:2,3^{2},9^{2},18,20■31:15■32:10■
33:12^{3}■34:12^{2}■36:33■38:14,19■39:8,11,
13,22■40:1sup,1■43:18,22,25,27■44:27■
45:21,22,25■46:1,4,6,12■48:35-**DA**-
6:10(3118),13(3118)■9:7,15■10:4,12
-**HO**-1:5,11■2:3,15,16,18,21■4:5■5:9■
6:2■7:5■9:5^{2}■10:14-**JOE**-1:15■2:1,2^{2},
11,31■3:14,18-**AM**-1:14^{2}■2:16■3:14■
5:8,18^{2},20■6:3■8:3,9^{2},10,13■9:11
-**OB**-8,11^{2},12^{3},13^{3},14,15-**JON**-4:7
(4283)-**MIC**-2:4■3:6■4:6■5:10■7:4,11^{2},
12-**NA**-1:7■2:3■3:17-**HAB**-3:16-**ZEP**-
1:7,8,9,10,14^{2},15^{5},16,18■2:2^{2},3■3:8,
11,16-**HAG**-1:1,15■2:15,18^{3},19,23
-**ZEC**-1:7■2:11■3:9,10■4:10■6:10■
8:9■9:12,16■11:11■12:3,4,6,8^{2},9,
11■13:1,2,4■14:1,3,4,6,7^{2},8,9,13,20,21
-**MAL**-3:2,17■4:1^{2},3,5■**N.T.**-all=2250,
a=4594&marked-**M'T**-6:11a,30a,34■
7:22■10:15■11:22,23a,24■12:36■13:1■
16:3a,21■17:23■20:2,6,12,19■21:28a■
22:23,46■24:36,38,50■25:13■26:29■27:8a,
19a,62(1887),64■28:15a-**M'R**-1:35(1773),
4:27,35■5:5■6:11,21,35(5610)■9:31■
10:34■13:32■14:12,25,30a-**LU**-1:20,59,
80■2:11a,37■4:16,21a,42■5:17,26a■6:13,
23■7:11■8:22■9:12,22,37■10:12■11:3■

12:28a,46■13:14sup,14,16,31,32sup,
32a,33a,33sup■14:5■16:19■17:4^{2},24,
27,29,30,31■18:7,33■19:5a,9a,42■
21:34,37■22:7,34a,66■23:12,43a,54■
24:7,13,21a,21,29,46-**JOH**-1:29(1887),
35(1887),39,43(1887)■2:1■5:9■6:22
(1887),39,40,44,54■7:37■8:56■9:4■
11:9sup,9,24,53■12:7,12(1887),48■
14:20■16:23,26■20:19^{2}-**AC**-1:2,22■
2:1,15,20,29,41■4:3(839),9a■7:8,26■
9:24■10:3,40■12:18,21■13:33a■14:20
(1887)■16:35■17:31■20:11(827),
16,18,26a,31■21:7,26■22:3a■23:1,
12■24:21a■25:6(1887)■26:2a,7,22,
29a■27:29,33,33a,33,39■28:13,23
-**RO**-2:5,16■8:36■10:21■11:8a(2250)■
13:12,13■14:5^{2},6^{2}-**1CO**-1:8■3:13■4:13(737)■
5:5■10:8■15:4-**2CO**-1:14■3:14a,15a■
4:16■6:2^{2}■11:25(3574)-**EPH**-4:30■6:13
-**PH'P**-1:5,6,10■2:16■3:5-**COL**-1:6,9
-**1TH**-2:9■3:10■5:2,4,5,8-**2TH**-1:10■2:2■
3:8-**1TI**-5:5-**2TI**-1:3,12,18■4:8-**HEB**-1:5a■
3:7a,8,13a,15a■4:4sup,4,7,7^{2}a,8■5:5a■8:9■
10:25■13:8a-**JAS**-4:13a■5:5-**1PE**-2:12-**2PE**-
1:19,19a■2:8,9,13■3:7,8^{2},10,12-**1JO**-4:17
-**JUDE**-6-**RE**-1:10■4:8■6:17■7:15■8:12■
9:15■12:10■14:11■16:14■18:8■20:10■
21:25

DAY'S-all=3117-**NU**-11:31^{2}-**1KI**-19:4
-**1CH**-16:37-**ES**-9:13-**JON**-3:4■**N.T.**-
LU-2:44(2250)-**AC**-19:40(4594)

DAYS-all=3117&marked-**GE**-1:14■
3:14,17■5:4,5,8,11,14,17,20,23,27,31■
6:3,4■7:4^{2},10,12,17,24■8:3,6,10,12■
9:29■10:25■11:32■14:1■17:12■21:4,34■
24:55■25:7,24■26:1,15,18■27:41,44■
29:20,21■30:14■35:28,29■37:34■40:12,
13,18,19■42:17■47:9^{4}■49:1■50:3^{3},4,10
-**EX**-2:11■7:25■10:22,23■12:15,19■13:6,
7■15:22■16:26,29■20:9,11,12■22:30■
23:12,15,26■24:16,18■29:30,35,37■31:15,
17■34:18,21,28■35:2-**LE**-8:33^{2},35■
12:2^{2},4^{2},5,6■13:4,5,21,26,31,33,46,50,54■
14:8,38■15:13,19,24,25^{3},26,28■22:27■
23:3,6,8,16,34,36,39,40,41,42-**NU**-6:4,5^{2},
6,8,12^{2},13■9:19,20,22■11:19^{2}■12:14^{2},15■
13:25■14:34^{2}■19:11,14,16■20:29■24:14■
28:17,24■29:12■31:19-**DE**-1:46^{2}■2:1■
4:9,10,26,30,32,40■5:13,16,33■6:2■9:9,
11,18,25■10:10■11:9,21^{3}■12:1■16:3^{2},
4,8,13,15■17:9,19,20■19:17■22:7,19,29■
23:6■25:15■26:3■30:18,20■31:14,29■32:7,
47■33:25■34:8^{2}-**JOS**-1:5,11■2:16,22■3:2■
4:14■6:3,14■9:16■20:6■22:3■24:31^{2}
-**J'G**-2:7^{2},18■5:6^{2}■8:28■11:40■14:12,14,
17■15:20■17:6■18:1^{2}■19:1,4■20:27,28■
21:25-**RU**-1:1-**1SA**-1:11■2:31■3:1■7:13,
15■9:20■10:8■13:8,11■14:52■17:12,16■
18:26■21:5(8543)■25:10,28,38■28:1■29:3■
30:12,13■31:13-**2SA**-1:1■7:12■16:23■
20:4■21:1■24:8-**1KI**-2:1,11,38■3:2,13,
14■4:21,25■8:40,65■10:21■11:12,25,
34■12:5■14:20,30■15:5,6,14,16,32■
16:15,34■17:15■18:1■19:8■20:29■21:29■
22:46-**2KI**-2:17■8:20■10:32■12:2■13:3,
22■15:18,29,37■18:4■20:1,6,17,19■

23:22^{2},29■24:1■25:29,30-**1CH**-1:19■
4:41■5:10,17^{2}■7:2,22■9:25■10:12■12:39■
13:3■17:11■21:12■22:9■23:1■29:15,28
-**2CH**-7:8,9■9:20■10:5■13:20■14:1■
15:17■20:25■21:8■24:2,14,15■26:5■
29:17■30:21,22,23^{2}■32:24,26■34:33■
35:17,18■36:9-**EZR**-4:2,5,7■6:22■8:15,
32■9:7■10:8,9-**NE**-1:4■2:11■5:18■
6:15,17■8:17,18■12:7,12,22,23,26^{2},46,
47^{2}■13:6,15,23-**ES**-1:1,2,4^{2},5^{2}■2:12,21■
4:11,16■9:22^{2},26,27,28^{2},31-**JOB**-1:5■2:13■
3:6■7:1,6,16■8:9■9:25■10:5^{2},20■12:12■
14:1,5,14■15:20■17:1,11■21:13■24:1■
29:2,4,18■30:16,27■32:7■33:25■36:11■
38:12,21■42:17-**PS**-21:4■23:6■27:4■
34:12■37:18,19■39:4,5■44:1■49:5■55:23■
72:7■77:5■78:33■89:29,45■90:9,10,12,
14,15■94:13■102:3,11,23,24■103:15■
109:8■119:84■128:5■143:5■144:4-**PR**-
3:2,16■9:11■10:27■15:15■28:16■31:12
-**EC**-2:3,16,23■5:17,18,20■6:3,12■7:10,
15■8:13,15■9:9^{2}■11:1,8,9■12:1^{2}-**IS**-
1:1■2:2■7:1,17■13:22■23:7,15■24:22■
30:26■32:10■38:1,5,10,20■39:6,8■51:9■
53:10■60:20■63:9,11■65:20^{2},22-**JER**-
1:2,3■2:32■3:6,16,18■5:18■6:11■7:32■
9:25■13:6■16:9,14■17:11■19:6■20:18■
22:30■23:5,6,7,20■25:34■26:18■30:3,
24■31:27,29,31,33,38■32:14■33:14,15,
16■35:1,7^{2},8■36:2■37:16■42:7■46:26■
48:12,47■49:2,39■50:4,20■51:47,52■
52:33,34-**LA**-1:7^{2}■2:17■4:18■5:21
-**EZE**-3:15,16■4:4,5^{2},6,8,9^{2}■5:2■12:22,
23,25,27■16:22,43,60■22:4,14■23:19■
38:8,16,17■43:25,26,27■44:26■45:21,23^{2},
25■46:1-**DA**-1:12,14,15,18■2:28(3118),
44(3118)■4:34(3118)■5:11(3118)■6:7
(3118),12(3118)■7:9(3118),13(3118),22
(3118)■8:14(6153,1242),26,27■10:2,
13,14^{2}■11:20,33■12:11,12,13-**HO**-1:1^{2}■
2:13,15■3:3,4,5■6:2■9:7^{2},9■10:9■12:9
-**JOE**-1:2■2:29■3:1-**AM**-1:1^{2}■4:2■8:11■
9:11,13-**JON**-1:17■3:4-**MIC**-1:1■4:1■
7:14,15,20-**HAB**-1:5-**ZEP**-1:1-**ZEC**-
8:6,9,10,11,15,23■14:5-**MAL**-3:4,7■
N.T.-all=2250&marked-**M'T**-2:1■
3:1■4:2■9:15■11:12■12:40^{2}■15:32■
17:1■23:30■24:19,22^{2},29,37,38■26:2,
61■27:40,63-**M'R**-1:9,13■2:1,20^{2},26
(1909)■8:1,2,31■9:2■13:17,19,20^{2},24■
14:1,58■15:29-**LU**-1:5,23,24,25,39,75■
2:1,6,21,22,43,46■4:2^{2},25■5:35^{2}■6:12■
9:28,36■13:14■15:13■17:22^{2},26^{2},28■
19:43■20:1■21:6,22,23■23:29■24:18
-**JOH**-2:12,19,20■4:40,43■11:6,17,39
(5066)■12:1■20:26-**AC**-1:3,5,15■2:17,
18■3:24■5:36,37■6:1■7:41,45■9:9,19,
23,37,43■10:30,48■11:27,28(1909)■12:3■
13:31,41■15:36■16:12,18■20:6^{2}■21:4,5,
10,15,26,27,38■24:1,11,24■25:1,6,13,14■
27:7,20■28:7,12,14,17-**GA**-1:18■4:10
-**EPH**-5:16-**2TI**-3:1-**HEB**-1:2■5:7■
7:3■8:8,10■10:16,32■11:30■12:10-**JAS**-
5:3-**1PE**-3:10,20-**2PE**-3:3-**RE**-2:10,13■
9:6■10:7■11:3,6,9,11■12:6

DAYS'-all=3117-**GE**-30:36■31:23-**EX**-

3:18■5:3■8:27-NU-10:33^2■33:8-DE-1:2-1SA-11:3-2SA-24:13-2KI-3:9-JON-3:3

DAYSMAN-JOB-9:33(3198)

DAYSPRING-JOB-38:12(7837)■N.T.-LU-1:78(395)

DAYTIME-all=3119-JOB-5:14■24:16-PS-22:2■42:8■78:14-IS-4:6■21:8

DEACON-1TI-3:10(1247),13(1247)

DEACONS-all=1249-PH'P-1:1-1TI-3:8,12

DEAD-all=4191&marked-GE-20:3■23:3,4,6^2,8,11,13,15■42:38■44:20■50:15-EX-4:19■9:7■12:30,33■14:30■21:34,35,36-LE-11:31(4194),32(4194)■19:28(5315)■21:1(5315),11■22:4(5315)-NU-5:2(5315)■6:6,11(5315)■9:6(5315),7(5315),10(5315)■12:12■16:48■19:11,13^2,16,18■20:29(1478)-DE-2:16■14:1,8(5038)■25:5,6■26:14-JOS-1:2-J'G-2:19■3:25■4:1,22■5:27(7703)■8:33■9:55■16:30■20:5-RU-1:8■2:20■4:5,10^2-1SA-4:17,19■17:51■24:14■25:39■28:3■31:5,7-2SA-1:4^2,5■2:7■4:1,10■9:8■11:21,24^2,26■12:18^2,19^3,21,23■13:32,33^2,39■14:2,5■16:9■18:20■19:10,28(4194)-1KI-3:20,21,22^2,23^2■11:21■13:31■21:14,15^2,16-2KI-3:5(4194)■4:1,32■8:5■11:1■19:35■23:30-1CH-1:44,45,46,47,48,49,50■2:19,24(4194)■10:5,7-2CH-20:24(6297),25(6297)-ES-2:7(4194)-JOB-1:19■26:5(7496)-PS-31:12■79:2(5038)■88:5,10,10(7496)■106:28■110:6(1472)■115:17■143:3-PR-2:18(7496)■9:18(7496)■21:16(7496)-EC-4:2■9:3,4,5■10:1(4194)-IS-8:19■14:9(7496)■22:2■26:14,19,19(5038),19(7496)■37:36■59:10-JER-16:7■22:10■26:23(5038)■31:40(6297)■33:5(6297)■34:20(5038)■36:30(5038)■41:9(6297)-LA-3:6-EZE-24:17■44:25,31(5038)-AM-8:3(6297)■N.T.-all=3498,a=599&marked-M'T-2:19(5053),20(2348)■8:22■9:18(5053),24a■10:8■11:5■14:2■17:9■22:31,32■23:27■27:64■28:4,7-M'R-5:35a,39a■6:14,16■9:9,10,26,26a■12:25,26,27■15:44(2348),44a-LU-7:12(2348),15,22■8:49(2348),52a,53a■9:7,60■10:30(2258)■15:24,32■16:30,31■20:35,37,38■24:5,46-JOH-2:22■5:21,25■6:49a,58a■8:52a,53^{2}a■11:14a,25a,39(2348),39sup,41(2348),44(2348)■12:1(2348),1,9,17■19:33(2348)■20:9■21:14-AC-2:29(5053)■3:15■4:2,10■5:10■7:4a■10:41,42■13:30,34■14:19(2348)■17:3,31,32■20:9■23:6■24:15,21■25:19(2348)■26:8,23■28:6-RO-1:4■4:17,19(3499),24■5:15a■6:2a,4,7a,8a,9,11,13■7:2a,3a,4(2289),4,6a,8■8:10,11^2■10:7,9■11:15■14:9-1CO-7:39(2837)■15:12^2,13,15,16,20,21,29^3,32,35,42,52-2CO-1:9■5:14a-GA-1:1■2:19a,21a-EPH-1:20■2:1,5■5:14-PH'P-3:11-COL-1:18■2:12,13,20a■3:3a-1TH-1:10■4:16-1TI-5:6(2348)-2TI-2:8,11(4880)■4:1-HEB-6:1,2■9:14,17■11:4a,12(3499),19,35■13:20-JAS-2:17,20,26^2-1PE-1:3,21■2:24(581)■4:5,6-JUDE-12a-RE-1:5,17,18■2:8■3:1■11:8(4430),9^2(4430),18■14:13■16:3■20:5,12^2,13^2

DEADLY-1SA-5:11(4194)-PS-17:9(5315)■N.T.-M'R-16:18(2286)-JAS-3:8(2287)-RE-13:3(2288),12(2288)

DEADNESS-RO-4:19(3500)

DEAF-all=2795&marked-EX-4:11-LE-19:14-PS-38:13■58:4-IS-29:18■35:5■42:18,19■43:8-MIC-7:16(2790)■N.T.-all=2794-M'T-11:5-M'R-7:32,37■9:25-LU-7:22

DEAL-all=6213&marked-GE-24:49■34:31■47:29-EX-21:9■23:11-NU-11:15-DE-7:5-JOS-2:14-RU-1:8-1SA-20:8-2CH-2:3■19:11-JOB-42:8-PS-119:17(1580),124■142:7(1580)-PR-12:22-IS-58:7(6536)-JER-18:23■21:2-EZE-8:18■16:59■18:9■22:14■23:25,29■31:11-DA-1:13■11:7■N.T.-M'R-7:36(4054)

DEALER-all supplied

DEALERS-all supplied

DEALEST-EX-5:15(6213)

DEALETH-all=6213-J'G-18:4-PR-10:4■13:16■14:17■21:24-JER-6:13■8:10■N.T.-HEB-12:7(4374)

DEALING-all supplied

DEALINGS-1SA-2:23(1697)■N.T.-JOH-4:9(4798)

DEALS-all supplied

DEALT-all=6213&marked-EX-14:11-J'G-9:16,19-RU-1:8-1SA-24:18-2SA-6:19(2505)-2KI-12:15■21:6■22:7-1CH-16:3(2505)■20:3-PS-13:6(1580)■103:10■116:7(1580)■119:65■147:20-EZE-22:7■25:12,15-JOE-2:26-ZEC-1:6■N.T.-LU-1:25(4160)■2:48(4160)-AC-7:19(2686)■25:24(1793)-RO-12:3(3307)

DEAR-JER-31:20(3357)■N.T.-all=27&marked-LU-7:2(1784)-AC-20:24(5093)-EPH-5:1-COL-1:7,13(26)-1TH-2:8

DEARLY-all supplied

DEARTH-all=7458&marked-GE-41:54^2-2KI-4:38-2CH-6:28-NE-5:3-JER-14:1(1226)■N.T.-AC-7:11(3042)■11:28(3042)

DEATH-all=4194,a=4191,b=6757&marked-GE-21:16■25:11■26:11a,18■27:2,7,10-EX-10:17■19:12a■21:12a,15a,16a,17a,29a■22:19a■31:14a,15a■35:2a-LE-16:1■19:20a■20:2a,9a,10a,11a,12a,13a,15a,16a,27a■24:16^{2}a,17a,21a■27:29a-NU-1:51a■3:10a,38a■15:35a■16:29■18:7a■23:10■35:16a,17a,18a,21a,25,28^2■35:30(7523)■31^{2}a,32-DE-13:5a,9a■17:6^{3}a,7a■19:6■21:22,22a■22:26■24:16^{3}a■30:15,19■31:27,29■33:1-JOS-1:1,18a■2:13■20:6-J'G-1:1■5:18a■6:31a■13:7■16:16a,30■20:13a■21:5a-RU-1:17■2:11-1SA-4:20a■11:12a,13a■15:32,35■20:3-2SA-1:1,23■6:23■8:2a■15:21■19:21a,22a■20:3a■21:9a■22:5,6-1KI-2:8a,24a,26,26a,■11:40-2KI-1:1■2:21■4:40■14:6^{3}a,17■15:5■20:1a-1CH-22:5-2CH-15:13a■22:4■23:7a■24:17■25:25■26:21■32:24,33-EZR-7:26(4193)-ES-4:11a-JOB-3:5b,21■5:20■7:15■10:21b,22b■12:22b■16:16b■18:13■24:17^{2}b■27:15■28:3b,22■30:23■34:22b■38:17,17b-PS-6:5■7:13■9:13■13:3■18:4,5■22:15■23:4b■33:19■44:19b■48:14(4192)■49:14■55:4,15■56:13■68:20■73:4■78:50■89:48■102:20(8546)■107:10b,14b,18■116:3,8,15■118:18-PR-2:18■5:5■7:27■8:36■10:2■11:4,19■12:28■13:14■14:12,27,32■16:14,25■18:21■21:6■24:11■26:18-EC-7:1,26■8:8-SONG-8:6-IS-9:2b■25:8■28:15,18■38:1a,18■53:9,12-JER-2:6b■8:3■9:21■13:16b■15:2■18:21■21:8■26:15a,19a,21a,24a■38:4a,15a,16a,25a■43:3a,11■52:11,27a,34-LA-1:20-EZE-18:32■31:14■33:11-HO-13:14-AM-5:8b-JON-4:9-HAB-2:5■N.T.-all=2288&marked-M'T-2:15(5054)■4:16■10:21,21(2289)■14:5(615)■15:4■16:28■20:18■26:38,59(2289),66■27:1(2289)-M'R-5:23(2079)■7:10■9:1■10:33■13:12,12(2289),14:1(615),34,55(2289),64-LU-1:79■2:26■9:27■18:33(615)■21:16(2289)■22:33■23:15,22,32(337)■24:20-JOH-4:47(599)■5:24■8:51,52■11:4,13,53(615)■12:10(615),33■18:31(615),32■21:19-AC-2:24■8:1(336)■12:19(520)■13:28■22:4,20(336)■23:29(336)■25:11(336),25(336)■26:10(337),31■28:18-RO-1:32■5:10,12,14,17,21■6:3,4,5,9,16,21,23■7:5,10,13^2,24■8:2,6,38-1CO-3:22■4:9(1935)■11:26■15:21,26,54,55,56-2CO-1:9,10■2:16■3:7■4:11,12■7:10-PH'P-1:20■2:8^2,27,30■3:10-COL-1:22-2TI-1:10-HEB-2:9^2,14^2,15■5:7■7:23■9:15,16■11:5-JAS-1:15■5:20-1PE-3:18(2289)-1JO-3:14^2■5:16^3,17-RE-1:18■2:10,11,23■6:8^2■9:6^2■12:11■13:3■18:8■20:6,13,14^2■21:4,8

DEATHS-JER-16:4(4463)-EZE-28:8(4463),10(4194)■N.T.-2CO-11:23(2288)

DEBASE-IS-57:9(8213)

DEBATE-PR-25:9(7378)-IS-27:8(7378)■58:4(4683)■N.T.-RO-1:29(2054)

DEBATES-2CO-12:20(2054)

DEBT-1SA-22:2(5378)-2KI-4:7(5386)-NE-10:31(3027)■N.T.-M'T-18:27(1156),30(3784),32(3782)-RO-4:4(3783)

DEBTOR-EZE-18:7(2326)■N.T.-M'T-23:16(3784)-RO-1:14(3781)-GA-5:3(3781)

DEBTORS-all=3781&marked-M'T-6:12-LU-7:41(5533)■16:5(5533)-RO-8:12■15:27

DEBTS-PR-22:26(4859)■N.T.-M'T-6:12(3783)

DECAY-LE-25:35(4131)

DECAYED-NE-4:10(3782)-IS-44:26(2723)

DECAYETH-JOB-14:11(2717)-EC-10:18(4355)■N.T.-HEB-8:13(3822)

DECEASE-LU-9:31(1841)-2PE-1:15(1841)

DECEASED-IS-26:14(7496)-M'T-22:25(5053)

DECEIT-all=4820&marked-JOB-15:35■27:4(7423)■31:5-PS-10:7■36:3■50:19■55:11(8496)■72:14(8496)■101:7(7423)■119:118(8649)-PR-12:5,17,20■14:8■20:17(8267)■26:24,26(4860)-IS-53:9-JER-5:27■8:5(8649)■9:6^2,8■14:14(8649)■23:26(8649)-HO-11:12■12:7-AM-8:5-ZEP-1:9■N.T.-M'R-7:22(1388)-RO-1:29(1388)■3:13(1387)-COL-2:8(539)-1TH-2:3(4106)

DECEITFUL-all=4820&marked-PS-5:6■35:20■43:1■52:4■55:23■78:57(7423)■109:2■120:2(7423)-PR-11:18(8267)■14:25■23:3(3577)■27:6(6280)■29:13(8501)■31:30(8267)-JER-17:9(6121)-HO-7:16(7423)-MIC-6:11,12(7423)-ZEP-3:13(8649)■N.T.-2CO-11:13(1386)-EPH-4:22(539)

DECEITFULLY-all=4820&marked-GE-34:13-EX-8:29(2048)■21:8(898)-LE-6:4(6231)-JOB-6:15(898)■13:17(7423)-PS-24:4■52:2(7423)-JER-48:10(7423)■11:23■N.T.-2CO-4:2(1389)

DECEITFULNESS-all=539-M'T-13:22-M'R-4:19-HEB-3:13

DECEITS-PS-38:12(4820)-IS-30:10(4123)

DECEIVABLENESS-2TH-2:10(539)

DECEIVE-all=5377&marked-2SA-3:25(6601)-2KI-4:28(7952)■18:29■19:10-2CH-32:15-PR-24:28(6601)-IS-36:14■37:10-JER-9:5(2048)■29:8■37:9-ZEC-13:4(3584)■N.T.-all=4105&marked-M'T-24:4,5,11,24-M'R-13:5,6-RO-16:18(1818)-1CO-3:18(1818)-EPH-4:14(4106)■5:6(538)-2TH-2:3(1818)-1JO-1:8■3:7-RE-20:3,8

DECEIVED-all=7411&marked-GE-31:7(2048)-LE-6:2(6231)-DE-11:16(6601)-1SA-19:17■28:12-2SA-19:26-JOB-12:16(7683)■15:31(8582)■31:9(6601)-PR-20:1(7686)-IS-19:13(5377)■44:20(2048)-JER-4:10(5377)■20:7(6601)■49:16(5377)-LA-1:19-EZE-14:9^2(6601)-OB-3(5377),7(5377)■N.T.-all=4105&marked-LU-21:8-JOH-7:47-RO-7:11(1818)-1CO-6:9■15:33-GA-6:7-1TI-2:14^2(538)-2TI-3:13-TIT-3:3-RE-18:23■19:20■20:10

DECEIVER-GE-27:12(8591)-JOB-12:16(7686)-MAL-1:14(5230)■N.T.-M'T-27:63(4108)-2JO-7(4108)

DECEIVERS-2CO-6:8(4108)-TIT-1:10(5423)-2JO-7(4108)

DECEIVETH-PR-26:19(7411)■N.T.-all=4105&marked-JOH-7:12-GA-6:3(4522)-JAS-1:26(538)-RE-12:9■13:14

DECEIVING-2TI-3:13(4105)-JAS-1:22(3884)

DECEIVINGS-2PE-2:13(539)

DECENTLY-1CO-14:40(2156)

DECIDED-1KI-20:40(2782)

DECISION-JOE-3:14^2(2742)

DECK-JOB-40:10(5710)-JER-10:4(3302)

DECKED-all=5710&marked-PR-7:16(7234)-EZE-16:11,13-HO-2:13■N.T.-RE-17:4(5558)■18:6(5558)

DECKEDST-EZE-16:16(6213)■

23:40(5710)

DECKEST-JER-4:30(5710)

DECKETH-IS-61:10(3547)

DECLARATION-ES-10:2(6575)-JOB-13:17(262)■N.T.-LU-1:1(1335)

DECLARE-all=5046,a=5608&marked-GE-41:24-DE-1:5(874)-JO-20:4(1696)-J'G-14:12,13,15-1CH-16:24a-ES-4:8-JOB-12:8a■15:17a■21:31■28:27a■31:37■38:4,18■40:7(3045)■42:4(3405)-PS-2:7a■9:11■19:1a■22:22a,31■30:9■38:18■40:5■50:6,16a■64:9■66:16a■73:28a■75:1a,9■78:6a■96:3■97:6■102:21a■107:22a■118:17a■145:4,3a-EC-9:1(952)-IS-3:9■12:4(3045)■21:6■41:22(8085)■42:9,12■43:9,26a■44:7■45:19■48:6,20■53:8(7878)■57:12■66:19-JER-4:5■5:20■9:12■31:10■38:15,25■42:4,20■46:14■50:2,28■51:10a-EZE-12:16a■23:36■40:4-DA-4:18(560)-MIC-1:10■3:8-ZEC-9:12■N.T.-all=1107&marked-M'T-13:36(5419)■15:15(5419)-JOH-17:26-AC-8:33(1334)■13:32(2097),41(1555)■17:23(2605)■20:27(312)-RO-3:25(1732),26(1732)-1CO-3:13(1213)■11:17(3853)■15:1-COL-4:7-HEB-2:12(518)■11:14(1718)-1JO-1:3(518),5(312)

DECLARED-all=5046&marked-EX-9:16(5608)-LE-23:44(1696)-NU-15:34(6567)-DE-4:13-2SA-19:6-NE-8:12(3045)-JOB-26:3(3045)-PS-40:10(559)■71:17(5046)■77:14(3045)■88:11(5608)■119:13(5608),26(5608)-IS-21:2,10■41:26■43:12■44:8■45:21(8085)■48:3,5,14-JER-36:13■42:21■N.T.-all=1834&marked-LU-8:47(518)-JOH-1:18■17:26(1107)-AC-9:27(1334)■10:8■12:17(1334)■15:4(312),14■21:19■25:14(394)-RO-1:4(3724)■9:17(1229)-1CO-1:11(1213)-2CO-3:3(5319)-COL-1:8(1213)-RE-10:7(2097)

DECLARETH-all=5046-IS-41:26-JER-4:15-HO-4:12-AM-4:13

DECLARING-IS-46:10(5046)■N.T.-AC-15:3(1555),12(1834)-1CO-2:1(2605)

DECLINE-all=5186&marked-EX-23:2-DE-17:11(5493)-PS-119:157-PR-4:5■7:25(7847)

DECLINED-all=5186&marked-2CH-34:2(5493)-JOB-23:11-PS-44:18■119:51

DECLINETH-PS-102:11(5186)■109:23(5186)

DECREASE-PS-107:38(5491)■N.T.-JOH-3:30(1642)

DECREASED-GE-8:5(2637)

DECREE-all=2942&marked-2CH-30:5(1697)-EZR-5:13,17■6:1,3,8,11,12■7:13,21-ES-1:20(6599)■2:8(1881)■3:15(1881)■4:3(1881),8(1881)■8:14(1881),17(1881)■9:1(1881),13(1881),14(1881),32(3982)-JOB-22:28(1504)■28:26(2706)-PS-2:7(2706)■148:6(2706)-PR-8:15(2710),29(2706)-IS-10:1(2710)-JER-5:22(2706)-DA-2:9(1882),13(1882),15(1882)■3:10,29■4:6,17(1510),24(1510)■6:7(633),8(633),9(633),12^{2}(633),13(633),15(633),26-JON-3:7(2940)-MIC-7:11(2706)-ZEP-2:2(2706)■N.T.-LU-2:1(1378)

DECREED-ES-2:1(1504)■9:31(6965)-JOB-38:10(2706)-IS-10:22(2782)■N.T.-1CO-7:37(2919)

DECREES-IS-10:1(2711)■N.T.-AC-16:4(1378)■17:7(1378)

DEDICATE-all=6942&marked-DE-20:5(2596)-2SA-8:11-1CH-26:27-2CH-2:4

DEDICATED-all=6944&marked-DE-20:5(2596)-J'G-17:3(6942)-2SA-8:11(6942)-1KI-7:51■8:63(2596)■$15:15^{2}$-2KI-12:4,18(6942)-1CH-18:11(6942)■26:20,26,26(6942),28^{2}(6942)■28:12-2CH-5:1■7:5(2596)■$15:18^{2}$■24:7■31:12-EZE-44:29(2764)■N.T.-HEB-9:18(1457)

DEDICATING-NU-7:10(2598),11(2598)

DEDICATION-all=2598&marked-NU-7:84,88-2CH-7:9-EZR-6:16(2597),17(2597)-NE-$12:27^{2}$-PS-30:t-DA-3:2(2597),3(2597)■N.T.-JOH-10:22(1456)

DEED-all=1697&marked-GE-44:15(4639)-EX-9:16(199)-1SA-25:34(199)■26:4(3559)-2SA-12:14-ES-1:17,18■N.T.-all=2041&marked-LU-23:51(4234)■24:19-AC-4:9(2108)-RO-15:18-1CO-5:2-2CO-10:11-COL-3:17-JAS-1:25(4162)-1JO-3:18

DEEDS-GE-20:9(4639)-1CH-16:8(5949)-2CH-35:27(1697)-EZR-9:13(4639)-PS-28:4(6467)■105:1(5949)-IS-59:18(1578)-JER-5:28(1697)■25:14(6467)■N.T.-all=2041&marked-LU-11:48■23:41(3739,4238)-JOH-3:19,20,21■8:41-AC-7:22■19:18(4234)■24:2(2735)-RO-2:6■3:20,28■8:13(4234)-2CO-12:12(1411)-COL-3:9(4234)-2PE-2:8-2JO-11-3JO-10-JUDE-15-RE-2:6,22■16:11

DEEMED-AC-27:27(5282)

DEEP-all=8415&marked-GE-1:2■2:21(8639)■7:11■8:2■15:12(8639)■49:25-DE-33:13-1SA-26:12(8639)-JOB-4:13(8639)■12:22(6013)■33:15(8639)■38:30■41:31(4688),32-PS-36:6■42:7■64:6(6013)■69:2(4688),2(4615),14(4615),15(4688)■80:9(8328)■92:5(6009)■95:4(4278)■104:6■107:24(4688)■135:6■140:10(4113)-PR-8:28■18:4(6013)■19:15(8639)■20:5(6013)■22:14(6013)■23:27(6013)-EC-7:24(6013)-IS-29:10(8639),15(6009)■30:33(6009)■44:27(6683)■51:10■63:13-JER-49:8(6009),30(6009)-EZE-23:32(6013)■26:19■31:4,15■32:14(8257)■34:18(4950)-DA-2:22(5994)■8:18(7290)■10:9(7290)-AM-7:4-JON-2:3(4688)-HAB-3:10■N.T.-all=899&marked-LU-5:4■6:48(2532,900)■8:31(12)-JOH-4:11(901)-AC-20:9(901)-RO-10:7(12)-1CO-2:10-2CO-8:2■11:25(1037)

DEEPER-all=6013&marked-LE-13:3,4,25,30,31,32,34-JOB-11:8-IS-33:19(6012)

DEEPLY-IS-31:6(6009)-HO-9:9(6009)■N.T.-M'R-8:12(389)

DEEPNESS-M'T-13:5(899)

DEEPS-all=4688&marked-NE-9:11-PS-88:6■148:7(8415)-ZEC-10:11

DEER-DE-14:5(3180)

DEFAMED-1CO-4:13(987)

DEFAMING-JER-20:10(1681)

DEFEAT-2SA-15:34(6565)■17:14(6565)

DEFENCE-all=4869&marked-NU-14:9(6738)-2CH-11:5(4692)-JOB-22:25(1220)-PS-7:10(4043)■31:2(4686)■59:9,16,17■62:2,6■89:18(4043)■94:22-EC-7:12(6738)-IS-4:5(2646)■19:6(4692)■33:16-NA-2:5(5526)■N.T.-all=627&marked-AC-19:33(626)■22:1-PH'P-1:7,17

DEFENCED-all=1219&marked-IS-25:2■27:10■36:1■37:26-JER-1:18(4013)■4:5(4013)■8:14(4013)■34:7(4013)-EZE-21:20

DEFEND-all=1598&marked-J'G-10:1(3467)-2KI-19:34■20:6-PS-20:1(7682)■59:1(7682)■82:3(8199)-IS-31:5■37:35■38:6-ZEC-9:15■12:8

DEFENDED-2SA-23:12(5337)■N.T.-AC-7:24(292)

DEFENDEST-PS-5:11(5526)

DEFENDING-IS-31:5(1598)

DEFER-EC-5:4(309)-IS-48:9(748)-DA-9:19(309)

DEFERRED-GE-34:19(309)-PR-13:12(4900)■N.T.-AC-24:22(306)

DEFERRETH-PR-19:11(748)

DEFIED-all=2778&marked-NU-23:8(2194)-1SA-17:36,45-2SA-21:21■23:9-1CH-20:7

DEFILE-all=2930&marked-LE-11:44■15:31■18:20,23,24,28,30■20:3■21:4,11■22:8-NU-5:3■35:34-2KI-23:13-SONG-5:3(2936)-IS-30:22-JER-32:34-EZE-7:22(2490)■9:7■20:7,18■22:3■28:7(2490)■33:26■37:23■43:7■44:25-DA-$1:8^{2}$(1351)■N.T.-all=2840&marked-M'T-15:18,20-M'R-$7:15^{2}$,18,23-1CO-3:17(5351)-1TI-1:10(733)-JUDE-8(3392)

DEFILED-all=2930&marked-GE-34:2(6031),5,13,27-LE-5:3■11:43(2933)■13:46■15:32■18:24,25,27■19:31■21:1,3-NU-5:2(2931),13,14^{2},20,27,28,29■6:9,12■9:6(2931),7(2931)■19:20-DE-21:23■22:9(6942)■24:4-2KI-23:8,10-1CH-5:1(2490)-NEH-13:29(1351)-JOB-16:15(5953)-PS-74:7(2490)■79:1■106:39-IS-24:5(2610)■59:3(1351)-JER-2:7■3:9(2610)■16:18(2490)■19:13(2931)-EZE-4:13■5:11■7:24(2490)■18:6,11,15■20:43■22:4,11■23:7,13,17,38■28:18(2490)■36:17■43:8-HOS-5:3■6:10-MIC-4:11(2610)■N.T.-all=3392&marked-M'R-7:2(2839)-JOH-18:28-1CO-8:7(3435)-TIT-$1:15^{2}$-HEB-12:15-RE-3:4(3435)■14:4(3435)

DEFILEDST-GE-49:4(2490)

DEFILETH-EX-31:14(2490)-NU-19:13(2930)■35:33(2610)■N.T.-all=2840&marked-M'T-$15:11^{2}$,20-M'R-7:20-JAS-3:6(4695)-RE-21:27

DEFRAUD-LE-19:13(6231)■N.T.-all=650&marked-M'R-10:19-1CO-6:8■7:5-1TH-4:6(4122)

DEFRAUDED-1SA-12:3(6231),4(6231)■N.T.-1CO-6:7(650)-2CO-7:2(4122)

DEFY-all=2778&marked-NU-23:7(2194),8(2194)-1SA-17:10,25,26

DEGENERATE-JER-2:21(5494)

DEGREE-LU-1:52(5011)-1TI-3:13(898)-JAS-1:9(5011)

DEGREES-all=4609-2KI-$20:9^{2}$,10^{2},11-PS-120:t,121:t,122:t,123:t,124:t,125:t■126:t■127:t■128:t■129:t■130:t■131:t■132:t■133:t■134:t-IS-$38:8^{3}$

DELAY-EX-22:29(309)■N.T.-AC-9:38(3635)■25:17(311)

DELAYED-EX-32:1(954)-PS-119:60(4102)

DELAYETH-M'T-24:48(5549)-LU-12:45(5549)

DELECTABLE-IS-44:9(2530)

DELICACIES-RE-18:3(4764)

DELICATE-all=6028&marked-DE-28:54,56-IS-47:1-JER-6:2(6026)-MIC-1:16(8588)

DELICATELY-1SA-15:32(4574)-PR-29:21(6445)-LA-4:5(4574)■N.T.-LU-7:25(5172)

DELICATENESS-DE-28:56(6026)

DELICATES-JER-51:34(5730)

DELICIOUSLY-RE-18:7(4763),9(4763)

DELIGHT-all=2654&marked-GE-34:19-NU-14:8-DE-10:15(2836)■21:14-1SA-15:22(2656)■18:22-2SA-15:26■24:3-ES-6:6-JOB-22:26(6026)■27:10(6026)■34:9(7521)-PS-1:2(2656)■16:3(2656)■37:4(6026),11(6026)■40:8■62:4(7521)■68:30■94:19(8173)■119:16(8173),24(8191),35,47(8173),70(8173),77(8191),174(8191)-PR-1:22(2531)■2:14(1523)■8:30(8191)■11:1(7522),20(7522)■12:22(7522)■15:8(7522)■16:13(7522)■18:2■19:10(8588)■24:25(5276)■29:17(4574)-SONG-2:3(2530)-IS-1:11■13:17■55:2(6026)■$58:2^{2}$,13(6027),14(6026)-JER-6:10■9:24-MAL-3:1(2655)■N.T.-RO-7:22(4913)

DELIGHTED-all=2654&marked-1SA-19:2-2SA-22:20-1KI-10:9-2CH-9:8-NE-9:25(5727)-ES-2:14-PS-18:19■22:8■109:17-IS-65:12■66:4,11(6026)

DELIGHTEST-PS-51:16(7521)

DELIGHTETH-all=2654&marked-ES-6:6,7,9^{2},11-PS-37:23■112:1■147:10-PR-3:12(7521)-IS-42:1(7521)■62:4■66:3-MIC-7:18-MAL-2:17

DELIGHTS-all=8191&marked-2SA-1:24(5730)-PS-119:92,143-PR-8:31-EC-2:8(8588)-SONG-7:6(8588)

DELIGHTSOME-MAL-3:12(2656)

DELIVER-all=5414,a=5337&

marked-GE-32:11a■37:22(7725)■40:13■42:34,37-EX-3:8a■5:18■21:13(579)■22:7,10,26(7725)■23:31-LE-26:26(7725)-NU-21:2■35:25a-DE-1:27■2:30■3:2■7:2,16,23,24■19:12■23:14a,15(5462)■24:13(7725)■25:11a■32:39a-JOS-2:13a■7:7■8:7■11:6■20:5(5462)-J'G-4:7■7:7■10:13(3467),14(3467),15a■11:9,30■13:5(3467)■15:12,13■20:13,28-1SA-4:8a■7:3a,14a■12:10a,21a■14:37■17:37a,46(5462)■23:4,11(5462),12[2](5462),20(5462)■24:4,15(8199)■26:24a■28:19[2]■30:15(5462)-2SA-3:14■5:19[2]■14:7,16a■20:21-1KI-8:46■18:9■20:5,13,28■22:6,12,15■2KI-3:10,13,18■12:7■17:39a■18:23,29a,30a,32a,35a■20:6a■21:14■22:5-1CH-14:10[2]■16:35a-2CH-6:36■18:5,11■25:15a,20■28:11(7725)■32:11a,13a,14[2]a,15[2]a,17a-EZR-7:19(8000)-NE-9:28a-JOB-5:4a,19a■6:23(4422)■10:7a■22:30(4422)■33:24(6308),28(6299)■36:18(5186)-PS-6:4(2502)■7:1a,2a■17:13(6403)■22:4(6403),8(6403),8a,20a■25:20a■27:12■31:1(6403),2a,15a■33:17(4422),19a■37:40(6403)■39:8a■40:13a■41:1(4422),2■43:1(6403)■50:15(2502),22a■51:14a■56:13a■59:1a,2a■69:14a,18(6299)■70:1a■71:2a,4(6403),11a■72:12a■74:19■79:9a■82:4(6403)■89:48(4422)■91:3a,14(6403),15(2502)■106:43a■109:21a■116:4(4422)■119:134(6299),153(2502),154(1350),170a■120:2a■140:1(2502)■142:6a■143:9a■144:7a,11a-PR-2:12a,16a■4:9(4042)■6:3a,5a■11:6a■12:6a■19:19a■23:14a■24:11a-EC-8:8(4422)-ISA-5:29a■19:20a■29:11■31:5a■36:14a,15a,18a,20a■38:6a■43:13a■44:17a,20a■46:2(4422),4(4422)■47:14a■50:2a■57:13a-JER-1:8a,19a■15:9,20a,21a■18:21■20:5■21:7,12a■22:3a■24:9■29:18,21■38:19,20■39:17a,18(4422)■42:11a■43:3■46:26■51:6(4422),45(4422)-LA-5:8(6561)-EZE-7:19a■11:9■13:21a,23a■14:14a,16a,18a,20[2]a■21:31a■23:28■25:4,7■33:5(4422),12a■34:10a,12a-DA-3:15(7804),17[2](7804),29(5338)■6:14(7804),14(5338),16(7804),20(7804)■8:4a,7a-HO-2:10a■11:8(4042)-AM-1:6(5462)■2:14(4422),15[2](4422)■6:8(5462)-JON-4:6a-MIC-5:6a,8a■6:14(6403)-ZEP-1:18a-ZEC-2:7(4422)■11:6(4672),6a■**N.T.**-all=3860&marked-M'T-5:25[2]■6:13(4506)■10:17,19,21■20:19■24:9■26:15■27:43(4506)-M'R-10:33■13:9,11-LU-11:4(4506)■12:58■20:20-AC-7:25(1325),34(1807)■21:11■25:11(5483),16(5483)-RO-7:24(4506)-1CO-5:5-2CO-1:10[2](4506)-GA-1:4(1807)-2TI-4:18(4506)-HEB-2:15(525)-2PE-2:9(4506)

DELIVERANCE-all=8668&marked-GE-45:7(6413)-J'G-15:18-2KI-5:1■13:17[2]-1CH-11:14-2CH-2:7(6413)-EZ-9:13(6413)-ES-4:14(2020)-PS-18:50(3444)■32:7(6405)-IS-26:18(3444)-JOE-2:32(6413)-OB-17(6413)■**N.T.**-LU-4:18(859)-HEB-11:35(629)

DELIVERANCES-PS-44:4(3444)

DELIVERED-all=5414,a=5337-GE-9:2■14:20(4042)■25:24(3205)■32:16■37:21a-EX-1:19(3205)■2:19a■5:23a■12:27a■18:4a,8a,9a,10[2]a-LE-6:2(6487),4(6487)■26:25-NU-21:3,34■31:5(4560)-DE-2:33,36■3:3■5:22■9:10■20:13■21:10■31:9-JOS-2:24■9:26a■10:8,12,19,30,32■11:8■21:44■22:31a■24:10a,11-J'G-1:2,4■2:14,16(3467),18(3467),23■3:9(3467),10,28,31(3467)■4:14■6:1,9a,13■7:9,14,15■8:3,7,22(3467),34a■9:17a■10:12(3467)■11:21,32■12:2(3467),3(3467),3■13:1■16:23,24-1SA-4:19(3205)■10:18a■12:11a■14:10,12,48a■17:35a,37a■23:7(5234),14■24:10,18(5462)■26:8(5462),23■30:23-2SA-3:8(4672)■10:10■12:7a■16:8■18:28(5462)■19:9(4422)■21:6,9■22:1a,18a,20(5202),44(6403),49a-1KI-3:17(3205),18[2](3205)■13:26■15:18■17:23-2KI-12:15■13:3■17:20■18:30,33a,34a,35a■19:10,11a,12a■22:7,9,10-1CH-5:20■11:14a■16:7■19:11-2CH-13:16■16:8■18:14■23:9■24:24■28:5[2],9■29:8■32:17a■34:9,15,17-EZR-5:14(3052)■8:31a,36■9:7-ES-6:9-JOB-16:11(5462)■22:30(4422)■23:7(6403)■29:12(4422)-PS-7:4(2502)■18:ta,17a,19(2502),43(6403),48a■22:5(4422)■33:16a■34:4a■54:7a■55:18(6299)■56:13a■60:5(2502)■69:14a■78:42(6299),61■81:6(5674),7(2502)■86:13a■107:6a,20(4422)■108:6(2502)■116:8(2502)-PR-11:8(2502),9(2502),21(4422)■28:26(4422)-EC-9:15(4422)-IS-20:6a■29:12■34:2■36:15,18a,19a,20a■37:11a,12a■49:24(4422),25(4422)■66:7(4422)-JER-7:10a■20:13a■32:4,16,36■34:3■37:17■46:24-LA-1:14-EZE-3:19a,21a■14:16a,18a■16:21,27■17:15(4422)■23:9■31:11,14■32:20■33:9a■34:27a-DA-3:28(7804)■6:27(7804)■12:1(4422)-JOE-2:32(4422)-AM-1:9(5462)■9:1(4422)-OB-14(5462)-MIC-4:10a-HAB-2:9a-MAL-3:15(4422) **N.T.**-all=3860&marked-M'T-11:27■18:34■25:14■27:2,18,26,58(591)-M'R-7:13■9:31■10:33■15:1,10,15-LU-1:2,57(5088),74(4506)■2:6(5088)■4:6,17(1929)■7:15(1325)■9:42(591),44■10:22■12:58(252)■18:32■19:13(1325)■23:25■24:7,20-JOH-16:21(1080)■18:30,35,36■19:11,16-AC-2:23(1560)■3:13■6:14■7:10(1807)■12:4,11(1807)■15:30(1929)■16:4■23:33(325)■27:1■28:16,17-RO-4:25■6:17■7:6(2673)■8:21(1659),32■15:31(4506)-1CO-11:2,23■15:3,24-2CO-1:10(4506)■4:11-COL-1:13(4506)-1TH-1:10(4506)-2TH-3:2(4506)-1TI-1:20-2TI-3:11(4506)■4:17(4506)-HEB-11:11(5088)-2PE-2:4,7(4506),21-JUDE-3-RE-12:2(5088),4(5088)■20:13(1325)

DELIVEREDST-NE-9:27(5414)■**N.T.**-M'T-25:20(3860),22(3860)

DELIVERER-all=6403&marked-J'G-3:9(3467),15(3467)■18:28(5337)-2SA-22:2-PS-18:2■40:17■70:5■144:2■**N.T.**-AC-7:35(3086)-RO-11:26(4506)

DELIVEREST-PS-35:10(5337)-MIC-6:14(6403)

DELIVERETH-all=5337&marked-JOB-36:15(2502)-PS-18:48(6403)■34:7(2502),17,19■97:10■144:10(6475)-PR-10:2■11:4■14:25■31:24(5414)-IS-42:22-DA-6:27(7804)

DELIVERING-LU-21:12(3860)-AC-22:4(3860)■26:17(1807)

DELIVERY-IS-26:17(3205)

DELUSION-2TH-2:11(4106)

DELUSIONS-IS-66:4(8586)

DEMAND-all=7592&marked-JOB-38:3■40:7■42:4-DA-4:17(7595)

DEMANDED-EX-5:14(559)-2SA-11:7(7592)-DA-2:27(7593)■**N.T.**-M'T-2:4(4441)-LU-3:14(1905)■17:20(1905)-AC-21:33(4441)

DEMONSTRATION-1CO-2:4(585)

DEN-all=1358-PS-10:9(5520)-IS-11:8(3975)-JER-7:11(4631)■9:11(4583)■10:22(4583)-DA-6:7,12,16,17,19,20,23[2],24[2]-AM-3:4(4585)■**N.T.**-all=4693&marked-M'T-21:13-M'R-11:17-LU-19:46

DENIED-GE-18:15(3584)-1KI-20:7(4513)-JOB-31:28(3584)■**N.T.**-all=720&marked-M'T-26:70,72-M'R-14:68,70-LU-8:45■12:9(533)■22:57-JOH-1:20■13:38(533)■18:25,27-AC-3:13,14-1TI-5:8-RE-2:13■3:8

DENIETH-all=720-LU-12:9-1JO-2:22[2],23

DENOUNCE-DE-30:18(5046)

DENS-all=4585&marked-J'G-6:2(4492)-JOB-37:8(695)■38:40-PS-104:22-SONG-4:8-IS-32:14(4631)-NA-2:12■**N.T.**-HEB-11:38(4693)-RE-6:15(4693)

DENY-JOS-24:27(3584)-1KI-2:16(7725)-JOB-8:18(3584)-PR-30:7(4513),9(3584)■**N.T.**-all=533&marked-M'T-10:33[2](720)■16:24■26:34,35,75-M'R-8:34■14:30,31,72-LU-9:23■20:27(483)■22:34,61-AC-4:16(720)-2TI-2:12(720),13(720)-TIT-1:16(720)

DENYING-all=720-2TI-3:5-TIT-2:12-2PE-2:1-JUDE-4

DEPART-all=5493,a=3212&marked-GE-49:10-EX-8:11,29■18:27(7971)■21:22(3318)■33:1a-LE-25:41(3318)-NU-10:30a■16:26-DE-4:9■9:7(3318)-JOS-1:8(4185)■24:28(7971)-J'G-6:18(4185)■7:3(6852)■19:5a,7a,8a,9a-1SA-15:6■22:5a■29:10a,11a■30:22a-2SA-7:15■11:12(7971)■12:10■15:14a■20:21a■22:23-1KI-11:21(7971)■12:5a,24a■15:19(5927)-2CH-16:3(5927)■35:15-JOB-7:19(8159)■15:30■20:28(1540)■21:14■22:17■28:28-PS-6:8■34:14■37:27■55:11(4185)■101:4■119:115■139:19-PR-3:7,21(3868)■4:21(3868)■5:7■13:14,19■14:27■15:24■16:6,17■17:13(4185)■22:6■27:22-IS-11:13■14:25[2]■52:11■54:10[2](4185)■59:21-JER-6:8(3363)■17:13(3249)■31:36(4185)■32:40■37:9[2](1980)■50:3(1980)-LA-4:15[2]-EZE-16:42-HOS-9:12-MIC-2:10a-ZEC-10:11■**N.T.**-all=1831&marked-M'T-7:23(672)■8:18(565)■34(3327)■10:14■14:16(565)■25:41(4198)-M'R-5:17(565)■6:10,11(1607)-LU-2:29(630)■4:42(4198)■5:8■8:37(565)■9:4■12:59■13:27(868),31(4198)■21:21(1633)-JOH-7:3(3327)■13:1(3327)■16:7(4198)-AC-1:4(5562)■16:36,39■18:2(5562)■20:7(1826)■22:21(4198)■23:22(630)■25:4(1607)■27:12(321)-1CO-7:10(5562),11(5562),15(5562)-2CO-12:8(868)-PH'P-1:23(360)-1TI-4:1(868)-2TI-2:19(868)-JAS-2:16(5217)

DEPARTED-all=3212,a=5265,b=5493&marked-GE-12:4,4(3318)■14:12■21:14■24:10■26:17,31■31:40(5074),55■37:17a■42:26■45:24-EX-19:2a■33:11(4185)■35:20(3318)-LE-13:58b-NU-10:33a■12:9,10b■14:9b,44(4185)■22:7■33:3a,6a,8a,13a,15a,17a,18a,19a,20a,27a,30a,31a,35a,41a,42a,43a,44a,45a,48a-DE-1:19a■24:2(3318)-JOS-2:21■22:9-J'G-6:21(1980)■9:55■16:20b■17:8■18:7,21■19:10■21:24(1980)-1SA-4:21(1540),22(1540)■6:6■10:2■15:6b■16:14b,23b■18:12b■20:42■22:1,5■23:13(3318)■28:15b,16b-2SA-6:19■11:8(3318)■12:15■17:21■19:24-1KI-12:5,16■14:17■19:19■20:9,36(1980),36,38-2KI-1:4■3:3b,27a■5:5,19,24■8:14■10:12(935),15,29b,31b■13:2b,6b,11b■14:24b■15:9,18b,24b,28b■17:22b■18:6b■19:8a,36a-1CH-16:43■21:4(3318)-2CH-8:15b■10:5■20:32b■21:20■24:25■34:33b-EZR-8:31a-NE-9:19b-PS-34:t■105:38(3318)■119:102b-IS-7:17b■37:8a,37a■38:12a-JER-29:2(3318)■37:5(5927)■41:10,17-LA-1:6(3318)-EZE-6:9b■10:18(3318)-DA-4:31(5709)-HO-10:5(1540)-MAL-2:8b■**N.T.**-all=565,a=1831&marked-M'T-2:9(4198),12(402),13(402),14(402)■4:12(402)■9:7,27(3855),31a■11:1(3327),7(4198)■12:9(3327)■13:53(3332)■14:13(402)■15:21(402),29(3327)■16:4■17:18a■19:1(3332),15(4198)■20:29(1607)■24:1(4198)■27:5(402),60■28:8a-M'R-1:35,42■5:20■6:32,46■8:13■9:30a-LU-1:23,38■2:37(868)■4:13(868),42a■5:13,25■7:24■8:35a,38a■9:6a,33(1316)■10:30,35a■24:12-JOH-4:3,43■5:15■6:15(402)■12:36-AC-5:41(4198)■10:7■11:25a■12:10(868),17a■13:4(2718),14(1330)■14:20a■15:38(868)■39(673),40a■16:40a■17:15(1826),33a■18:1(5562),7a,23a■19:9(868),12(525)■20:1a,11a■21:5,8■22:29(868)■28:10(321),11(321),25(630),29-PH'P-4:15a-PH'M-15(5563)-2TI-4:10(4198)-RE-6:14(673)■18:14[2]

DEPARTETH-all=5493&marked-JOB-27:21(3212)-PR-14:16-EC-6:4(3212)-IS-59:15-JER-17:5-NA-3:1(4185)■**N.T.**-LU-9:39(672)

DEPARTING-GE-35:18(3318)-EX-16:1(3318)-IS-59:13(5253)-DA-9:5(5493),11(5493)■**N.T.**-M'R-6:33

(5217)■7:31(1831)-**AC**-13:13(672)■20:29(867)-**HEB**-3:12(868)■11:22(1841)

DEPARTURE-**EZE**-26:18(3318)-**2TI**-4:6(359)

DEPOSED-**DA**-5:20(5182)

DEPRIVED-**GE**-27:45(7921)-**JOB**-39:17(5382)-**IS**-38:10(6485)

DEPTH-all=8415&marked-**JOB**-28:14■38:16-**PS**-33:7-**PR**-8:27■25:3(6012)-**IS**-7:11(6009)-**JON**-2:5(8415)■**N.T.**-all=899&marked-**M'T**-18:6(3989)-**M'R**-4:5-**RO**-8:39■11:33-**EPH**-3:18

DEPTHS-all=8415&marked-**EX**-15:5,8-**DE**-8:7-**PS**-68:22(4688)■71:20■77:16■78:15■106:9■107:26■130:1(4615)-**PR**-3:20■8:24■9:18(6010)-**IS**-51:10(4615)-**EZE**-27:34(4615)-**MIC**-7:19(4688)■**N.T.**-**RE**-2:24(899)

DEPUTED-all supplied

DEPUTIES-**ES**-8:9(6346)■9:3(6346)■**N.T.**-**AC**-19:38(446)

DEPUTY-**1KI**-22:47(4324)■**N.T.**-all=446&marked-**AC**-13:7,8,12■18:12

DERIDE-**HAB**-1:10(7832)

DERIDED-**LU**-16:14(1592),23:35(1592)

DERISION-all=7814&marked-**JOB**-30:1(7832)-**PS**-2:4(3932)■44:13(7047)■59:8(3932)■79:4(7047)■119:51(3887)-**JER**-20:7,8(7047)■48:26,27,39-**LA**-3:14-**EZE**-23:32(3932)■36:4(3932)-**HOS**-7:16(3932)

DESCEND-all=3381&marked-**NU**-34:11-**1SA**-26:10-**PS**-49:17-**IS**-5:14-**EZE**-26:20■31:16■**N.T.**-all=2597-**M'R**-15:32-**AC**-11:5-**RO**-10:7-**1TH**-4:16

DESCENDED-all=3381-**EX**-19:18■33:9■34:5-**DE**-9:21-**JOS**-2:23■17:9■18:13,16[2],17-**PS**-133:3-**PR**-30:4■**N.T.**-all=2597-**M'T**-7:25,27■28:2-**LU**-3:22-**AC**-24:1-**EPH**-4:9,10

DESCENDETH-**JAS**-3:15(2718)

DESCENDING-**GE**-28:12(3381)■**N.T.**-all=2597-**M'T**-3:16-**M'R**-1:10-**JOH**-1:32,33,51-**AC**-10:11-**RE**-21:10

DESCENT-**LU**-19:37(2600)-**HEB**-7:3(35),6(1075)

DESCRIBE-all=3789-**JOS**-18:4,6,8[2]

DESCRIBED-**JOS**-18:9(3789)-**J'G**-8:14(3789)

DESCRIBETH-**RO**-4:6(3004)■10:5(1125)

DESCRIPTION-all supplied

DESCRY-**J'G**-1:23(8446)

DESERT-all=4057&marked-**EX**-3:1■5:3■19:2■23:31-**NU**-20:1■27:14■33:16-**DE**-32:10-**2CH**-26:10-**JOB**-24:5-**PS**-28:4(1576)■78:40(3452)■102:6(2723)■106:14(3452)-**IS**-13:21(6728)■21:1[2](4057)■34:14(6728)■35:1(6160),6(6160)■40:3(6160)■41:19(6160)■43:19(3452),20(3452)■51:3(6160)-**JER**-17:6(6160)■25:24■50:12(6160),39(6728)-**EZE**-47:8(6160)■**N.T.**-all=2048-**M'T**-14:13,15■24:26-**M'R**-1:45■6:31,32,35-**LU**-4:42■9:10,12-**JOH**-6:31-**AC**-8:26

DESERTS-**IS**-48:21(2723)-**JER**-2:6(6160)-**EZE**-7:27(4941)■13:4(2723)■**N.T.**-**LU**-1:80(2048)-**HEB**-11:38(2047)

DESERVE-all supplied

DESERVETH-all supplied

DESERVING-**J'G**-9:16(1576)

DESIRABLE-all=2531-**EZE**-23:6,12,23

DESIRE-all=8378&marked-**GE**-3:16(8669)■4:7(8669)-**EX**-10:11(1245)■34:24(2530)-**DE**-5:21(2530)■7:25(2530)■18:6(183)■21:11(2836)-**J'G**-8:24(7592)-**1SA**-9:20(2532)■23:20(183)-**2SA**-23:5(2656)-**1KI**-2:20(7592)■5:8(2656),9(2656),10(2656)■9:1(2837),11(2656)■10:13(2656)-**2KI**-4:28(7592)-**2CH**-9:12(2656)■15:15(7522)-**NE**-1:11(2655)-**JOB**-13:3(2654)■14:15(3700)■21:14(2654)■31:16(2656),35(8420)■33:32(2654)■34:36(15)■36:20(7602)-**PS**-10:3,17■21:2■38:9■40:6(2654)■45:11(183)■70:2(2655)■73:25(2654)■78:29■112:10■145:16(7522),19(7522)-**PR**-3:15(2656)■10:24■11:23■13:12,19■18:1■19:22■21:25■23:6(183)■24:1(183)-**EC**-6:9(5315)■12:5(35)-**SONG**-7:10(8669)-**IS**-26:8■53:2(2530)-**JER**-22:27(5375,5315)■42:22(2654)■44:14(5375,5315)-**EZE**-24:16(4261),21(4261),25(4261)-**DA**-2:18(1156)■11:37(2532)-**HO**-10:10(183)-**AM**-5:18(183)-**MIC**-7:3(5315)-**HAB**-2:5(5315)-**HAG**-2:7(2532)■**N.T.**-all=2309&marked-**M'R**-9:35■10:35(154)■11:24(154)■15:8(154)-**LU**-17:22(1937)■20:46■22:15(1939)-**AC**-23:20(2065)■28:22(515)-**RO**-10:1(2107)■15:23(1974)-**1CO**-14:1(2206)-**2CO**-7:7(1972),11(1972)■11:12■12:6-**GA**-4:9,20,21■6:12,13-**EPH**-3:13(154)-**PH'P**-1:23(1939)■4:17[2](1934)-**COL**-1:9(154)-**1TH**-2:17(1939)-**1TI**-3:1(3713)-**HEB**-6:11(1937)■11:16(3713)-**JAS**-4:2(2206)-**1PE**-1:12(1937)■2:2(1971)-**RE**-9:6(1937)

DESIRED-all=2530&marked-**GE**-3:6-**1SA**-12:13(7592)-**1KI**-9:19(2836)-**2CH**-8:6(2836)■11:23(7592)■21:20(2532)-**ES**-2:13(559)-**JOB**-20:20-**PS**-19:10■27:4(7592)■107:30(2656)■132:13(183),14(183)-**PR**-8:11(2656)■21:20-**EC**-2:10(7592)-**IS**-1:29■26:9(183)-**JER**-17:16(183)**DA**-2:16(1156),23(1156)-**HO**-6:6(2654)-**MIC**-7:1(183)-**ZEP**-2:1(3700)■**N.T.**-all=154&marked-**M'T**-13:17(1939)■16:1(1905)-**M'R**-15:6-**LU**-7:36(2065)■9:9(2212)■10:24(2309)■22:15(1937),31(1809)■23:25-**JOH**-12:21(2065)-**AC**-3:14■7:46■8:31(3870)■9:2■12:20■13:7(1934),21,28■16:39(2065)■18:20(2065)■25:3■28:14(3870)-**1CO**-16:12(3870)-**2CO**-8:6(3870)■12:18(3870)-**1JO**-5:15

DESIREDST-**DE**-18:16(7592)■**N.T.**-**M'T**-18:32(3870)

DESIRES-**PS**-37:4(4862)■140:8(3970)■**N.T.**-**EPH**-2:3(2307)

DESIREST-**PS**-51:6(2654),16(2654)

DESIRETH-all=8378&marked-**DE**-14:26(7592)-**1SA**-2:16■18:25(2656)■20:4(559)-**2SA**-3:21-**1KI**-11:37-**JOB**-7:2(7602)■23:13(183)-**PS**-34:12(2655)■68:16(2530)-**PR**-22:12(2530)■13:4(183)■21:10(183)-**EC**-6:2(183)■**N.T.**-**LU**-5:39(2309)■14:32(2065)-**1TI**-3:1(1937)

DESIRING-all=1971&marked-**M'T**-12:46(2212),47(2212)■20:20(154)-**LU**-8:20(2309)■16:21(1937)-**AC**-9:38(3870)■19:31(3870)■25:15(154)-**2CO**-5:2-**1TH**-3:6-**1TI**-1:7(2309)-**2TI**-1:4

DESIROUS-**PR**-23:3(183)■**N.T.**-all=2309&marked-**LU**-23:8-**JOH**-16:19-**2CO**-11:32-**GAL**-5:26(2755)-**1TH**-2:8(2442)

DESOLATE-all=8077,a=8074,b=8047&marked-**GE**-47:19(3456)-**EX**-23:29-**LE**-26:22a,33,34a,35a,43a-**2SA**-13:20(8076)-**2CH**-36:21a-**JOB**-3:14(2723)■15:28(3582),34(1565)■16:7a■30:3(7722)■38:27(7722)-**PS**-25:16(3173)■34:21(816),22(816)■40:15a■69:25a■109:10(2723)■143:4a-**IS**-1:7[2]■3:26(5352)■5:9b■6:11■7:19(1327)■13:9b,22(490)■15:6(4923)■24:6(816)■27:10(910)■49:8(8076),19a,21(1565)■54:1a,3■59:10(820)■62:4-**JER**-2:12(2717)■4:7b,27■6:8■7:34(2723)■9:11■10:22,25a■12:10,11a,11,11a■18:16b■19:8b■25:38b■26:9(2717)■32:43■33:10(2717),10a,12(2717)■44:6■46:19(3341)■48:9b,34(4923)■49:2,20a■50:3b,13,45a■51:26,62-**LA**-1:4(8076),13(8076),16(8076)■3:11(8076)■4:5a■5:18a-**EZE**-6:4a,6(3456),6(816),14,14b■12:19(3456),20■14:15,16■15:8■19:7(490),7(3456)■20:26a■25:3a,13(2723)■26:19(2717),20(2723)■29:9,10,12,12a,12■30:7[2]a,14a■32:15■33:28,28a,29■35:3,4,7,12a,14,15a,15■36:3a,4(8076),34a,34,35[2]a,36a■38:12(2723)-**DA**-9:17a,27a,27(8076)■11:31a■12:11a-**HO**-5:9b■13:16(816)-**JOE**-1:17a,18(816)■2:3,20■3:19-**AM**-7:9a-**MIC**-1:7■6:13a■7:13-**ZEP**-3:6a-**ZEC**-7:14a,14b-**MAL**-1:4(2723)■**N.T.**-all=2048&marked-**M'T**-23:38-**LU**-13:35-**AC**-1:20-**GAL**-4:27-**1TI**-5:5(3443)-**RE**-17:16(2049)-**RE**-18:19(2049)

DESOLATION-all=8077,a=8047&marked-**LE**-26:31(8074),32(8074)-**JOS**-8:28-**2KI**-22:19a-**2CH**-30:7a-**JOB**-30:14(7722)-**PS**-73:19a-**PR**-1:27(7584)■3:25(7722)-**IS**-10:3(7722)■17:9■24:12a■47:11(7722)■51:19(7701)■64:10-**JER**-22:5(2723)■25:11(2723),18(2723)■34:22■44:2(2723),22(2723)■49:13a,17a,33■50:23a■51:29a,43a-**LA**-3:47(7612)-**EZE**-7:27■23:33-**DA**-8:13(8074)-**HO**-12:1(7701)-**JOE**-3:19-**MIC**-6:16a-**ZEP**-1:13a,15(4875)■2:4,9,13,14(2721),15a■**N.T.**-all=2050&marked-**M'T**-12:25(2049)■24:15-**M'R**-13:14-**LU**-11:17(2049)■21:20

DESOLATIONS-all=8074&marked-**EZR**-9:9(2723)-**PS**-46:8(8047)■74:3(4876)-**IS**-61:4[2]-**JER**-25:9(2723),12(8077)-**EZE**-35:9(8077)-**DA**-9:2(2723),18,26

DESPAIR-**1SA**-27:1(2976)-**EC**-2:20(2976)■**N.T.**-**2CO**-4:8(1820)

DESPAIRED-**2CO**-1:8(1820)

DESPERATE-**JOB**-6:26(2976)-**IS**-17:11(605)

DESPERATELY-**JER**-17:9(605)

DESPISE-all=959&marked-**LE**-26:15(3988)-**1SA**-2:30-**2SA**-19:43(7043)-**ES**-1:17-**JOB**-5:17(3988)■9:21(3988)■10:3(3988)■31:13(3988)-**PS**-51:17■73:20■102:17-**PR**-1:7(936)■3:11(3988)■6:30(936)■23:9(936),22(936)-**IS**-30:12(3988)-**JER**-4:30(3988)■23:17(5006)-**LA**-1:8(2107)-**EZE**-16:57(7590)■28:26(7590)-**AM**-5:21(3988)-**MAL**-1:6■**N.T.**-all=2706&marked-**M'T**-6:24■18:10-**LU**-16:13-**RO**-14:3(1848)-**1CO**-11:22■16:11(1848)-**1TH**-5:20(1848)-**1TI**-4:12■6:2-**TIT**-2:15(4065)-**HEB**-12:5(3643)-**2PE**-2:10-**JUDE**-8(114)

DESPISED-all=959,a=3988&marked-**GE**-16:4(7043),5(7043)■25:34-**LE**-26:43a-**NU**-11:20a■14:31a■15:31-**J'G**-9:38a-**1SA**-10:27-**2SA**-6:16■12:9,10-**2KI**-19:21-**1CH**-15:29-**2CH**-36:16-**NE**-2:19■4:4(939)-**JOB**-12:5(937)■19:18a-**PS**-22:6,24■53:5a■106:24a■119:141-**PR**-1:30(5006)■5:12(5006)■12:8(937),9(7034)-**EC**-9:16-**SONG**-8:1(937)-**IS**-5:24(5006)■33:8a■37:22■53:3[2]■60:14(5006)-**JER**-22:28■33:24(5006)■49:15-**LA**-2:6(5006)-**EZE**-16:59■17:16,18,19■20:13a,16a,24a■22:8■28:24(7590)-**AM**-2:4a-**OB**-2-**ZEC**-4:10(937)-**MAL**-1:6■**N.T.**-all=1848&marked-**LU**-18:9-**AC**-19:27(1519,3762,3049)-**1CO**-1:28■4:10(820)-**GA**-4:14-**HEB**-10:28(114)-**JAS**-2:6(818)

DESPISERS-**AC**-13:41(2707)-**2TI**-3:3(865)

DESPISEST-**RO**-2:4(2706)

DESPISETH-all=959&marked-**JOB**-36:5(3988)-**PS**-69:33-**PR**-11:12(936)■13:13(936)■14:2(959),21(936)■15:5(5006),20,32(3988)■19:16■30:17(936)-**IS**-33:15(3988)■49:7(960)■**N.T.**-**LU**-10:16[2](114)-**1TH**-4:8(114)

DESPISING-**HEB**-12:2(2706)

DESPITE-**EZE**-25:6(7589)■**N.T.**-**HEB**-10:29(1796)

DESPITEFUL-**EZE**-25:15(7589)■36:5(7589)■**N.T.**-**RO**-1:30(5197)

DESPITEFULLY-**M'T**-5:44(1908)-**LU**-6:28(1908)-**AC**-14:5(5195)

DESTITUTE-**GE**-24:27(5800)-**PS**-102:17(6199)■141:8(6168)-**PR**-15:21(2638)-**EZE**-32:15(8047)■**N.T.**-**1TI**-6:5(650)-**HEB**-11:37(5302)-**JAS**-2:15(3007)

DESTROY-all=7843,a=6,b=8045,c=2763&marked-**GE**-6:7(4229),13,17■

7:4(4229)■9:11,15■18:23(5595),24(5595),28^{2},31,32■19:13^{2},14-**EX**-8:9(3772)■12:13(4889)■15:9(3423)■23:27(2000)■34:13(5422)-**LE**-23:30a■26:22(3772),30b,44(3615)-**NU**-21:2c■24:17(6979),19a■32:15■33:52^{2}a-**DE**-1:27b■2:15(2000)■4:31■6:15b■7:2c,4b,5(5422),10a,23(2000),24a■9:3b,3a,14b,19b,25b,26■10:10■12:2a,3a■20:17c,19,20■28:63a■31:3b■32:25(7921)■33:27b-**JOS**-7:7a,12b■9:24b■11:20c,20b■22:33-**J'G**-6:5■21:11c-**1SA**-15:3c,6(622),9c,18c■23:10■24:21b■26:9,15-**2SA**-1:14■14:7b,11,11b,16b■20:19(4191),20■22:41(6789)■24:16-**1KI**-9:21c■13:34b■16:12b-**2KI**-8:19■10:19a■13:23■18:25^{2}■24:2a-**1CH**-21:15-**2CH**-12:7,12■20:23b,23(4889)■21:7■25:16■35:21-**EZR**-6:12(4049),12(2255)-**ES**-3:6b,13b■4:7a,8b■8:5a,11b■9:24^{2}a-**JOB**-2:3(1104)■6:9(1792)■8:18(1104)■10:8(1104)■19:26(5362)-**PS**-5:6a,10(816)■18:40(6789)■21:10a■28:5(2040)■40:14(5595)■52:5(5422)■55:9(1104)■63:9(7722)■69:4(6789)■74:8(3238)■101:8(6789)■106:23b,23,34b■118:10(4135),11(4135),12(4135)■119:95a■143:12a■144:6(1949)■145:20b-**PR**-1:32a■11:3(7703)■15:25(5255)■21:7(1641)-**EC**-5:6(2254)■7:16(8074)-**IS**-3:12(1104)■10:7b■11:9,15c■13:5(2254),9b■19:3(1104)■23:11b■25:7(1104)■32:7(2254)■36:10^{2}■42:14(5395)■51:13■54:16(2254)■65:8^{2},25-**JER**-1:10a■5:10■6:5■11:19■12:17a■13:14■15:3,6,7a■17:18(7665)■18:7a■23:1a■25:9c■31:28a■36:29■46:8a■48:18■49:9,38a■50:21c,26c■51:3c,11,20-**LA**-2:8■3:66b-**EZE**-5:16■6:3a■9:8■14:9b■21:31(4889)■22:27a,30■25:7b,15(4889),16(9)■26:4,12(5422)■28:16a■30:11,13a■32:13a■34:16b■43:3-**DA**-2:12(7),24^{2}(7)■4:23(2255)■7:26(7)■8:24^{2},25■9:26■11:26(7665),44b-**HO**-2:12(8074)■4:5(1820)■11:9-**AM**-9:8^{2}-**OB**-8a-**MIC**-2:10(2254)■5:10a,14b-**ZEP**-2:5a,13a-**HAG**-2:22b-**ZEC**-12:9b-**MAL**-3:11■N.T.-all=622&marked-**M'T**-2:13■5:17^{2}(2647)■10:28■12:14■21:41■26:61(2647)■27:20-**M'R**-1:24■3:6■9:22■11:18■12:9■14:58(2647)-**LU**-4:34■6:9■9:56■19:47■20:16-**JOH**-2:19(3089)■10:10-**AC**-6:14(2647)-**RO**-14:15■14:20(2647)-**1CO**-1:19■3:17(5351)■6:13(2673)-**2TH**-2:8(2673)-**HEB**-2:14(2673)-**JAS**-4:12-**1JO**-3:8(3089)-**RE**-11:18(1311)

DESTROYED-all=8045,a=2763,b=6,c=7843&marked-**GE**-7:23^{2}(4229)■13:10c■19:29c■34:30-**EX**-10:7b■22:20a-**NU**-21:3a-**DE**-1:44(3807)■2:12,21,22,23,34a■3:6a■4:3,26■7:20b,23,24■9:8,20■11:4b■12:30■28:20,24,45,48,51,51b,61■31:4-**JOS**-2:10a■6:21a■8:26a■10:1a,28a,35a,37a,39a,40a■11:12a,14,21a■23:15■24:8-**J'G**-1:17a■4:24(3772)■6:4c■20:21c,25c,35c,42c■21:16,17(4229)-**1SA**-5:6(8074)■15:8a,9a,15a,20a,21(2764)-**2SA**-11:1c■21:5■22:38■24:16c-**1KI**-15:13(3772),29-**2KI**-10:17,28■11:1b■13:7b■19:12(843),17(2717),18b■21:3b,9-**1CH**-4:41a■5:25■20:1(2040)■21:12(5595),15-**2CH**-14:13(7665)■15:6(3807)■20:10■22:10(1696)■24:23c■31:1(3615)■32:14a■33:9■34:11c■36:19c-**EZR**-4:15(2718)■5:12(5642)-**ES**-3:9b■4:14b■7:4■9:6b,12b-**JOB**-4:20(3807)■19:10(5422)■34:25(1792)-**PS**-9:5b,6b(5428)■11:3(2040)■37:38■73:27(6789)■78:38c,45c,47(2026)■92:7■137:8(7703)-**PR**-13:13(2254)■13:20(7321),23(5595)■29:1(7665)-**IS**-9:16(1104)■10:27(2254)■14:17(2040),20c■26:14■34:2a■37:12c,19a■48:19-**JER**-12:10c■22:20(7665)■48:4(7665),8,42■51:8(7665)■51:55b-**LA**-2:5c,6c,9b-**EZE**-26:17b■27:32(1822)■30:8(7665)■32:12-**DA**-2:44(2255)■6:26(2255)■7:11(7),14(2255)■11:20(7665)-**HO**-4:6(1820)■10:8■13:9c-**AM**-2:9^{2}-**ZEP**-3:6(6658)■N.T.-all=622&marked-**M'T**-22:7-**LU**-17:27,29-**AC**-3:23(1842)■9:21(4199)■13:19(2507)■19:27(2507)-**RO**-6:6(2673)-**1CO**-10:9,10■15:26(2673)-**2CO**-4:9-**GA**-1:23(4199)■2:18(2647)-**HEB**-11:28(3645)-**2PE**-2:12(5356)-**JUDE**-5-**RE**-8:9(1311)

DESTROYER-all=7843&marked-**EX**-12:23-**J'G**-16:24(2717)-**JOB**-15:21(7703)-**PS**-17:4(6530)-**PR**-28:24-**JER**-4:7■N.T.-**1CO**-10:10(3644)

DESTROYERS-**JOB**-3:22(4191)-**IS**-49:17(2040)-**JER**-22:7(7843)■50:11(8154)

DESTROYEST-**JOB**-14:19(6)-**JER**-51:25(7843)■N.T.-**M'T**-27:40(2647)-**M'R**-15:29(2647)

DESTROYETH-all=6&marked-**DE**-8:20-**JOB**-9:22(3615)■12:23-**PR**-6:32(7843)■11:9(7843)■31:3(4229)**EC**-7:7■9:18

DESTROYING-all=2763&marked-**DE**-3:6■13:15-**JOS**-11:11-**2KI**-19:11-**1CH**-21:12(7843),15(7843)-**IS**-28:2(6986)■37:11-**JER**-2:30(7843)■51:1(7843),25(4889)-**LA**-2:8(1104)-**EZE**-9:1(4892)■20:17(7843)

DESTRUCTION-all=7667&marked-**DE**-7:23(4103)32:24(6986)-**1SA**-5:9(4103),11(4103)-**1KI**-20:42(2764)-**2CH**-22:4(4889),7(8395)■26:16(7843)-**ES**-8:6(13)■9:5(12)-**JOB**-5:21(7701),22(7701)■18:12(343)■21:17(343),20(3589),30(343)■26:6(11)■28:22(11)■30:12(343),24(6365)■31:3(343),12(11),23(343),29(6365)-**PS**-35:8(7722),8(7722)■55:23(7845)■73:18(4876)■88:11(11)■90:3(1793)■91:6(6986)■103:4(7845)-**PR**-1:27(343)■10:14(4288),15(4288),29(4288)■13:3(4288)■14:28(4288)■15:11(11)■16:18■17:19■18:7(4288),12■21:15(4288)■24:2(7701)■27:20(10)■31:8(2475)-**IS**-1:28■10:25(8399)■13:6(7701)■14:23(8045)■15:5■19:18(2041)■24:12(7591)■49:19(2035)■51:19■59:7■60:18-**JER**-4:6,20■6:1■17:18(7670)■46:20(7171)■48:3,5■50:22■51:54-**LA**-2:11■3:47,48■4:10-**EZE**-5:16(4889)■7:25(7089)■32:9-**HO**-7:13(7701)■9:6(7701)■13:14(6987)-**JOE**-1:15(7701)-**OB**-12(6)-**MIC**-2:10(2256)-**ZEC**-14:11(2764)■N.T.-all=684&marked-**M'T**-7:13-**RO**-3:16(4938)■9:22-**1CO**-5:5(3639)-**2CO**-10:8(2506)■13:10(2506)-**PH'P**-3:19-**1TH**-5:3(3639)-**2TH**-1:9(3639)-**1TI**-6:9(3639)-**2PE**-2:1■3:16

DESTRUCTIONS-**PS**-9:6(2723)■35:17(7722)■107:20(7825)

DETAIN-**J'G**-13:15(6113),16(6113)

DETAINED-**1SA**-21:7(6113)

DETERMINATE-**AC**-2:23(3724)

DETERMINATION-**ZEP**-3:8(4941)

DETERMINE-all supplied

DETERMINED-all=2782&marked-**1SA**-20:7(3615),9(3615)■20:33(3615)■25:17(3615)-**2SA**-13:32(7760)-**2CH**-2:1(559)■25:16(3289)-**ES**-7:7(3615)-**JOB**-14:5-**IS**-10:23■19:17(3289)■28:22-**DA**-9:24(2852),26,27■11:36■N.T.-all=2919&marked-**LU**-22:22(3724)-**AC**-3:13■4:28(4309)■11:29(3724)■15:2(5021),37(1011)■17:26(3724)■19:39(1956)■20:16■25:25■27:1-**1CO**-2:2-**2CO**-2:1-**TIT**-3:12

DETEST-**DE**-7:26(8262)

DETESTABLE-all=8251-**JER**-16:18-**EZE**-5:11■7:20■11:18,21■37:23

DEVICE-all=4284&marked-**2CH**-2:14-**ES**-8:3■9:25-**EC**-9:10(2808)-**JER**-18:11■51:11(4209)-**LA**-3:62(1902)■N.T.-**AC**-17:29(1761)

DEVICES-all=4284&marked-**JOB**-5:12■21:27(4209)-**PS**-10:2(4209)■33:10■37:7(4209)-**PR**-1:31(4156)■12:2(4209)■14:17(4209)-**PR**-19:21-**IS**-32:7(2154)-**JER**-11:19■18:12,18-**DA**-11:24,25■N.T.-**2CO**-2:11(3540)

DEVIL-all=1228,a=1140marked-**M'T**-4:1,5,8,11■9:32(1139),33a■11:18a■12:22(1139)■13:39■15:22(1139)■17:18a■25:41-**M'R**-5:15(1139),16(1139),18(1139)■7:26a,29a,30a-**LU**-4:2,3,5,6,13,33a,35a■7:33a■8:12,29(1142)■9:42a■11:14^{2}a-**JOH**-6:70■7:20a■8:44,48a,49a,52a■10:20a,21(1139),21a■13:2-**AC**-10:38■13:10-**EPH**-4:27■6:11-**1TI**-3:6,7-**2TI**-2:26-**HEB**-2:14-**JAS**-4:7-**1PE**-5:8-**1JO**-3:8^{3},10-**JUDE**-9-**RE**-2:10■12:9,12■20:2,10

DEVILISH-**JAS**-3:15(1141)

DEVILS-**LE**-17:7(8163)-**DE**-32:17(7700)-**2CH**-11:15(8163)-**PS**-106:37(7700)■N.T.-all=1140&marked-**M'T**-4:24(1139)■7:22■8:16(1139),28(1139),31(1142),33(1139)■9:34^{2}■10:8■12:24^{2},27,28-**M'R**-1:32(1139),34^{2},39■3:15,22^{2}■5:12(1142)■6:13■9:38■16:9,17-**LU**-4:41■8:2,27,30,33,35,36(1139),38■9:1,49■10:17■11:15^{2},18,19,20■13:32-**1CO**-10:20^{2},21^{2}-**1TI**-4:1-**JAS**-2:19-**RE**-9:20■16:14(1142)■18:2(1142)

DEVISE-all=2803&marked-**EX**-31:4■35:32,35-**2SA**-14:14-**PS**-35:4,20■41:7-**PR**-3:29(2790)■14:22^{2}(2790)■16:30-**JER**-18:11,18-**EZE**-11:2-**MIC**-2:1,3

DEVISED-all=2803&marked-**2SA**-21:5(1819)-**1KI**-12:33(908)-**ES**-8:3,5(4284)■9:24,25-**PS**-31:13(2161)-**JER**-11:19■48:2■51:12(2161)-**LA**-2:17(2161)■N.T.-**2PE**-1:16(4679)

DEVISETH-all=2803&marked-**PS**-36:4■52:2-**PR**-6:14(2790),18(2790)■16:9■24:8-**IS**-32:7(3289),8(3289)

DEVOTE-**LE**-27:28(2763)

DEVOTED-all=2764&marked-**LE**-27:21,28^{2},29,29(2763)-**NU**-18:14(2764)

DEVOTIONS-**AC**-17:23(4574)

DEVOUR-all=398&marked-**GE**-49:27-**DE**-32:42-**J'G**-9:15,20^{2}-**2SA**-2:26-**2CH**-7:13-**JOB**-18:13^{2}-**PS**-21:9■50:3■80:13(7462)-**PR**-30:14-**IS**-1:7■9:12,18■10:17■26:11■31:8■33:11■42:14(7602)■56:9-**JER**-2:3■5:14■12:9(402),12■15:3■17:27■21:14■30:16■46:10,14■48:45■50:32-**EZE**-7:15■15:7■20:47■23:37(402)■28:18■34:28■36:14-**DA**-7:5(399),23(399)-**HO**-5:7■8:14■11:6■13:8-**AM**-1:4,7,10,12,14■2:2,5■5:6-**OB**-18-**NA**-2:13■3:13,15-**HAB**-3:14-**ZEC**-9:15■11:1■12:6■N.T.-all=2719&marked-**M'T**-23:14-**M'R**-12:40-**LU**-20:47-**2CO**-11:20-**GA**-5:15-**HEB**-10:27(2068)-**1PE**-5:8(2666)-**RE**-12:4

DEVOURED-all=398&marked-**GE**-31:15■37:20,33■41:7(1104),24(1104)-**LE**-10:2-**NU**-26:10-**DE**-31:17■32:24(3898)-**2SA**-18:8^{2}■22:9-**PS**-18:8■78:45■79:7■105:35-**IS**-1:20■24:6-**JER**-2:30■3:24■8:16■10:25■30:16■50:7,17■51:34-**LA**-4:11-**EZE**-15:5■16:20■19:3,6,14■22:25■23:25■33:27■39:4(402)-**DA**-7:7(399),19(399)-**HO**-7:7,9-**JOE**-1:19,20-**AM**-4:9■7:4-**NA**-1:10-**ZEP**-1:18■3:8-**ZEC**-9:4■N.T.-all=2719-**M'T**-13:4-**M'R**-4:4-**LU**-8:5■15:30-**RE**-20:9

DEVOURER-**MAL**-3:11(398)

DEVOUREST-**EZE**-36:13(398)

DEVOURETH-all=398&marked-**2SA**-11:25-**PR**-19:28(1104)■20:25(3216)-**IS**-5:24-**LA**-2:3-**EZE**-15:4-**JOE**-2:3,5-**HAB**-1:13(1104)-**RE**-11:5(2719)

DEVOURING-all=398&marked-**EX**-24:17-**PS**-52:4(1105)-**IS**-29:6■30:27,30■33:14

DEVOUT-all=2152&marked-**LU**-2:25(2126)-**AC**-2:5(2126)■8:2(2126)■10:2,7■13:50(4576)■17:4(4576),17(4576)■22:12

DEW-all=2919&marked-**GE**-27:28,39-**EX**-16:13,14-**NU**-11:9-**DE**-32:2■33:13,28-**J'G**-6:37,38,39,40-**2SA**-1:21■17:12-**1KI**-17:1-**JOB**-29:19■38:28-**PS**-110:3-**PR**-3:20■19:12-**SONG**-5:2-**IS**-18:4■26:19-**DA**-4:15(2920),23(2920),25(2920),33(2920)■5:21(2920)-**HO**-6:4■13:3■14:5-**MIC**-5:7-**HAG**-1:10-**ZEC**-8:12

DIADEM-**JOB**-29:14(6797)-**IS**-28:5(6843)■62:3(6797)-**EZE**-21:26(4701)

DIAL-**2KI**-20:11(4609)-**IS**-38:8(4609)

DIAMOND-all=3095&marked-**EX**-

28:18■39:11-**JER**-17:1(8068)-**EZE**-28:13

DID-all=6213&marked-**GE**-6:22^{2}■7:5■21:1■29:28■38:10■39:3,19,22,23■42:20,25■43:17■44:2■45:21■50:12,15(1580),17(1580)-**EX**-1:17■4:30■7:6^{2},10,11,20,22■8:7,13,17,18,24,31■9:6■11:10■12:28^{2},35,50^{2}■13:8■14:4,31■16:17■17:6,10■18:14,24■19:4■32:21,28■36:29■39:32^{2}■40:16^{2}-**LE**-4:20■8:4,36■10:7■16:15,34■24:23-**NU**-1:54^{2}■2:34■5:4^{2}■8:3,20^{2},22■9:5■14:22■17:11^{2}■20:27■21:14(2052)■23:2,30■27:22■31:31■32:8■36:10-**DE**-1:30■2:12,22,29■3:6■4:3,34■7:18■11:3,4,5,6,7■24:9■25:17■29:2■31:4■34:9-**JOS**-2:10■4:8,23■5:15■6:14■9:4,9,10,26■10:23,28,30,39■11:9,15■14:5■24:5,17-**J'G**-2:7,11,17■3:7,12■4:1■6:1,20,27^{2},40■9:56■10:6■11:39■13:1,19■15:11■17:6■21:23,25-**RU**-3:6-**1SA**-1:7■2:11(1961),14,22■6:10■12:7■15:2■16:4■27:11-**2SA**-3:36■5:25■11:7(7965)■12:6,31■13:29■15:6■23:17,22-**1KI**-2:5^{2}■7:18■11:6,6sup,8,38,41■12:32■14:4,22,24,29■15:5,7,11,11sup,23,26,31,34■16:5,7,14,19,27,30,33■17:5,15■18:13■20:25■21:11,26sup,26■22:39,52-**2KI**-1:18■8:2,18^{2},23,27,27sup■10:19,34■11:9■12:2,11,19■13:2,8,11■14:3^{3},15,24,28■15:3,6,9,18,21,24,26,28,31,34^{2},36■16:2,16,19■17:2,22,40sup,40,41■18:3^{2}■21:2,3,11,17,20^{2},25■22:2■23:19,28,32,37■24:3,5,9,19-**1CH**-11:19,24■14:16■23:24■27:26-**2CH**-12:14■14:2■20:35sup,35■21:6■22:4■23:8■24:2,11,12■25:2■26:4^{2}■27:2^{2},2sup■28:1■29:2■31:20,21■32:33■33:2,22^{2}■34:2,12,32■36:5,8,9,12-**EZR**-10:16-**NE**-2:16^{2}■5:13,15■9:28■11:12■13:7,10-**ES**-1:21■2:4,11(7965),20■4:17■9:5-**JOB**-1:5■42:9-**PS**-78:12■135:6-**IS**-20:2■48:3■58:2■65:12■66:4^{2}sup,4-**JER**-7:12■11:8■15:4■36:8■38:12■52:2-**EZE**-12:7■18:18■24:18■46:12-**DA**-6:10(5648)■8:4,27-**JON**-3:10-**HAG**-1:14■**N.T.**-all=4160&marked-**M'T**-1:24■12:3■13:58■20:5■21:6,15,31,36■25:45^{2}■26:12,19■28:15-**M'R**-2:25■3:8■6:20-**LU**-6:3,10,23,26■9:15,43,54■12:47■17:9-**JOH**-2:11,23■4:29,39,45,54■6:2,14■8:40■9:26■10:41■11:45■15:24■19:24sup,24■20:30■21:25-**AC**-2:22■3:17(4238)■6:8■7:27(91)■8:6■9:36■10:39■11:30■12:8■14:17(15)■16:18■19:14■26:10-**2TI**-4:14(1731)-**HEB**-7:27■9:9(3000)-**1PE**-2:22

DIDDEST-**AC**-7:28(337)

DIDST-all=6213&marked-**GE**-20:6-**DE**-3:2-**JOS**-8:2-**1SA**-15:19^{2}sup,19-**2SA**-12:12■13:16-**1KI**-2:44-**NE**-9:17-**PS**-39:9■44:1(6466)-**IS**-64:3

DIE-all=4191&marked-**GE**-2:17■3:3,4■6:17(1478)■19:19■20:7■25:32■26:9■27:4■30:1■33:13■38:11■42:2,20■43:8■44:9,22,31■45:28■46:30■47:15,19^{2},29■48:21■50:5,24-**EX**-7:18■9:4,19■10:28■11:5■14:11,12■20:19■21:12,14,18,20,28,35■22:2,10,14■28:35,43■30:20,21-**LE**-8:35■10:6,7,9■11:39■15:31■16:2,13■20:20■22:9-**NU**-4:15,19,20■6:7(4194),9■14:35■16:29■17:10,12(1478),13■18:3,22,32■20:4,26■21:5■23:10■26:65■27:8■35:12,16,17,18,20,21,23^{2},30-**DE**-4:22■5:25^{2}■13:10■17:5,12■18:16,20■19:5,11,12■20:5,6,7■21:21■22:21,22,24,25■24:3,7■25:5■31:14■32:50■33:6-**JOS**-20:9-**J'G**-6:23,30■13:22■15:18■16:30-**RU**-1:17-**1SA**-2:33,34■12:19■14:39,43,44,45■20:2,14,31■22:16■26:10,16(4194)■28:9-**2SA**-11:15■12:5(4194),13,14■14:14■18:3■19:23,37-**1KI**-1:52■2:1,30,37,42■14:12■17:12■19:4■21:10-**2KI**-1:4,6,16■7:3,4^{3}■8:10■18:32■20:1-**2CH**-25:4^{3}■32:11-**JOB**-2:9■4:21■12:2■14:8,14■27:5(1478)■29:18(1478)■34:20■36:12(1478),14-**PS**-41:5■49:10■79:11(8546)■82:7■88:15(1478)■104:29(1478)■118:17-**PR**-5:23■10:21■15:10■19:16■23:13■30:7-**EC**-3:2■7:17■9:5-**IS**-22:13,14,18■38:1■51:6,12,14■65:20■66:24-**JER**-11:21,22^{2}■16:4,6■20:6■21:6,9■22:12,26■26:8,11(4194),16(4194)■27:13■28:16■31:30■34:4,5■37:20■38:2,9,10,24,26■42:16,17,22■44:12-**EZE**-3:18^{2},19,20^{2}■5:12■6:12■7:15■12:13■13:19■17:16■18:4,13,17,18,20,21,23(4194),24,26,28,31■28:8,10■33:8^{2},9,11,13,14,15,18,27-**AM**-2:2■6:9■7:11,17■9:10-**JON**-4:3(4194),8^{2}-**HAB**-1:12-**ZEC**-11:9■13:8(1478)■**N.T.**-all=599&marked-**M'T**-15:4(5053)■22:24■26:35-**M'R**-7:10(5053)■12:19■14:31(4880)-**LU**-7:2(5053)■20:28^{2},36-**JOH**-4:49■6:50■8:21,24^{2}■11:16,26,50,51■12:24^{2},33■18:14(622),32■19:7■21:23^{2}-**AC**-21:13■25:11,16(684)-**RO**-5:7^{2}■8:13■14:8^{2}-**1CO**-9:15■15:22,31,32,36-**2CO**-7:3(4880)-**PH'P**-1:21-**HEB**-7:8■9:27-**RE**-3:2■9:6■14:13

DIED-all=4191&marked-**GE**-5:5,8,11,14,17,20,27,31■7:21(1478),22■9:29■11:28,32■23:2■25:8,17,18(5307)■35:8,18,19,29■36:33,34,35,36,37,38,39■38:12■46:12■48:7■50:16(4194),26-**EX**-1:6■2:23■7:21■8:13■9:6^{2}■16:3-**LE**-10:2■16:1■17:15(5038)-**NU**-3:4■14:2^{2},37■15:36■16:49^{2}■20:1,3^{2}(1478),28■21:6■25:9■26:10(4194),11,19,61■27:3^{2}■33:38,39(4194)-**DE**-10:6■32:50■34:5,7(4194)-**JOS**-5:4■10:11^{2}■24:29,33-**J'G**-1:7■2:8,21■3:11■4:21■8:32■9:49,54■10:2,5■12:7,10,12,15-**RU**-1:3,5-**1SA**-4:18■5:12■14:45■25:1,37,38■31:5,6-**2SA**-1:15■2:23^{2},31■3:27,33■6:7■10:1,18■11:17,21■12:18■17:23■18:33■19:6■20:10■25:15-**1KI**-2:25,46■3:19■12:18■14:17■16:18,22■21:13■22:35,37-**2KI**-1:17■4:20■7:17,20■8:15■9:27■12:21■13:14,20,24■23:34■25:25-**1CH**-1:51■2:30,32■10:5,6^{2},13■13:10■19:1■23:22■24:2■29:28-**2CH**-10:18■13:20■16:13■18:34■21:19■24:15,15(4194),22,25■35:24-**JOB**-3:11■42:17-**IS**-6:1(4194)■14:28(4194)-**JER**-28:17-**EZE**-11:13■24:18-**HO**-13:1■**N.T.**-all=599&marked-**M'T**-22:27-**M'R**-12:21,22-**LU**-16:22^{2}■20:29,30,31,32-**JOH**-11:21,32,37-**AC**-7:15(5053)■9:37-**RO**-5:6,8■6:10■7:9■8:34■14:9,15-**1CO**-8:11■15:3-**2CO**-5:14,15^{2}-**1TH**-4:14■5:10-**HEB**-10:28■11:13,22(5053)-**RE**-8:9,11■16:3

DIEST-**RU**-1:17(4191)

DIET-**JER**-52:34^{2}(737)

DIETH-all=4191&marked-**LE**-7:24(5038)■22:8(5038)-**NU**-19:14-**DE**-14:21(5038)-**2SA**-3:33(4194)-**1KI**-14:11^{2}■16:4^{2}■21:24^{2}-**JOB**-14:10■21:23,25-**PS**-49:17(4194)-**PR**-11:7(4194)-**EC**-2:16■3:19(4194)-**IS**-50:2■59:5-**EZE**-4:14(5038)■18:26,32-**ZEC**-11:9■**N.T.**-all=5053&marked-**M'R**-9:44,46,48-**RO**-6:9(599)■14:7(599)

DIFFER-**1CO**-4:7(1252)

DIFFERENCE-all=914&marked-**EX**-11:7(6395)-**LE**-10:10■11:47■20:25■**N.T.**-**AC**-15:9(1252)-**RO**-3:22(1293)■10:12(1293)-**1CO**-7:34(3307)-**JUDE**-22(1252)

DIFFERENCES-**1CO**-12:5(1243)

DIFFERETH-**1CO**-15:41(1308)-**GA**-4:1(1308)

DIFFERING-**RO**-12:6(1313)

DIG-all=2864&marked-**EX**-21:33(3738)-**DE**-8:9(2672)■23:13(2658)-**JOB**-3:21(2658)■6:27(3738)■11:18(2658)■24:16-**EZE**-8:8■12:5,12-**AM**-9:2■**N.T.**-**LU**-13:8(4626)■16:3(4623)

DIGGED-all=2658&marked-**GE**-21:30■26:15,18^{2},19,21,22,25(3738),32■49:6(6131)■50:5(3738)-**EX**-7:24-**NU**-21:18,18(3738)-**DE**-6:11(2672)-**2KI**-19:24(5365)-**2CH**-26:10(2672)-**NE**-9:25(2672)-**PS**-7:15■35:7■57:6(3738)■94:13(3738)■119:85(3738)-**IS**-5:6(5737)■7:25(5737)■37:25(5365)■51:1(5365)-**JER**-13:7■18:20(3738),22(3738)-**EZE**-8:8(2864)■12:7(2864)■**N.T.**-all=3736&marked-**M'T**-21:33■25:18-**M'R**-12:1-**LU**-6:48(4626)-**RO**-11:3(2679)

DIGGEDST-**DE**-6:11(2672)

DIGGETH-**PR**-16:27(3738)■26:27(3738)-**EC**-10:8(2658)

DIGNITIES-**2PE**-2:10(1391)-**JUDE**-8(1391)

DIGNITY-**GE**-49:3(7613)-**ES**-6:3(1420)-**EC**-10:6(4791)-**HAB**-1:7(7613)

DILIGENCE-**PR**-4:23(4929)■**N.T.**-all=4710&marked-**LU**-12:58(2039)-**RO**-12:8-**2CO**-8:7-**2TI**-4:9(4704),21(4704)-**HEB**-6:11-**2PE**-1:5,10-**JUDE**-3

DILIGENT-all=2742&marked-**DE**-19:18(3190)-**JOS**-22:5(3966)-**PR**-10:4■12:24,27■13:4■21:5■22:29(4106)■**N.T.**-**2CO**-8:22(4705),22(4707)-**TIT**-3:12(4704)-**2PE**-3:14(4704)

DILIGENTLY-all=3966&marked-**DE**-4:9■6:7(8150)■13:14(3190)■17:4(3190)■24:8-**1KI**-20:33(5172)-**EZR**-7:23(149)-**PS**-37:10(995)■119:4-**PR**-7:15(7836)■11:27(7836)-**IS**-21:7(7182)-**JER**-2:10■**N.T.**-**M'T**-2:8(199)-**LU**-15:8(1960)-**AC**-18:25(199)-**2TI**-1:17(4706)-**TIT**-3:13(4709)-**HEB**-11:6(1567)

DIM-all=3543&marked-**GE**-27:1■48:10(3513)-**DE**-34:7-**1SA**-3:2(3544)■4:15(6965)-**JOB**-17:7-**IS**-32:3(8159)-**LA**-4:1(6004)■5:17(2821)

DIMINISH-all=1639&marked-**EX**-5:8■21:10-**LE**-25:16(4591)-**DE**-4:2■12:32-**JER**-26:2-**EZE**-5:11■29:15(4591)

DIMINISHED-all=4591&marked-**EX**-5:11(1639)-**PR**-13:11-**IS**-21:17-**JER**-29:6-**EZE**-16:27(1639)

DIMINISHING-**RO**-11:12(2275)

DIMNESS-**IS**-8:22(4588)■9:1(4155)

DINE-**GE**-43:16(398)■**N.T.**-**LU**-11:37(709)-**JOH**-21:12(709)

DINED-**JOH**-21:15(709)

DINNER-**PR**-15:17(737)■**N.T.**-all=712-**M'T**-22:4-**LU**-11:38■14:12

DIP-all=2881-**EX**-12:22-**LE**-4:6,17■14:6,16,51-**NU**-19:18-**DE**-33:24-**RU**-2:14■**N.T.**-**LU**-16:24(911)

DIPPED-all=2881&marked-**GE**-37:31-**LE**-9:9-**JOS**-3:15-**1SA**-14:27-**2KI**-5:14■8:15-**PS**-68:23(4272)■**N.T.**-**JOH**-13:26(911),26(1686)-**RE**-19:13(911)

DIPPETH-**M'T**-26:23(1686)-**M'R**-14:20(1686)

DIRECT-all=3474&marked-**GE**-46:28(3384)-**PS**-5:3(6186)-**PR**-3:6■11:5-**EC**-10:10(3787)-**IS**-45:13■61:8(5414)-**JER**-10:23(3559)■**N.T.**-**1TH**-3:11(2720)-**2TH**-3:5(2720)

DIRECTED-**JOB**-32:14(6186)-**PS**-119:5(3559)-**IS**-40:13(8505)

DIRECTETH-**JOB**-37:3(3474)-**PR**-16:9(3559)■21:29(3559)

DIRECTION-all supplied

DIRECTLY-**NU**-19:4(413,5227)-**EZE**-42:12(1903)

DIRT-**J'G**-3:22(6574)-**PS**-18:42(2916)-**IS**-57:20(2916)

DISALLOW-**NU**-30:5(5106)

DISALLOWED-all=5106-**NU**-30:5,8,11■**N.T.**-**1PE**-2:4(593),7(593)

DISANNUL-**JOB**-40:8(6565)-**IS**-14:27(6565)■**N.T.**-**GA**-3:17(208)

DISANNULED-**IS**-28:18(3722)

DISANNULLETH-**GA**-3:15(114)

DISANNULLING-**HEB**-7:18(115)

DISAPPOINT-**PS**-17:13(6923)

DISAPPOINTED-**PR**-15:22(6565)

DISAPPOINTETH-**JOB**-5:12(6565)

DISCERN-all=5234&marked-**GE**-31:32■38:25-**2SA**-14:17(8085)■19:35(3045)-**1KI**-3:9(995),11(8085)-**EZR**-3:13-**JOB**-4:16■6:30(995)-**EZE**-44:23(3045)-**JON**-4:11(3045)-**MAL**-3:18(7200)■**N.T.**-**M'T**-16:3(1252),3sup-**LU**-12:56(1381)-**HEB**-5:14(1258)

DISCERNED-**GE**-27:23(5234)-**1KI**-20:41(5234)-**PR**-7:7(995)■**N.T.**-**1CO**-2:14(350)

DISCERNER-**HEB**-4:12(2924)

DISCERNETH-**EC**-8:5(3045)

DISCERNING-1CO-11:29(1252)▪12:10(1253)

DISCHARGE-EC-8:8(4917)

DISCHARGED-1KI-5:9(5310)

DISCIPLE-all=3101&marked-M'T-10:24,25,42▪27:57(3100)-LU-6:40▪14:26 27,33-JOH-9:28▪18:15,16▪19:26,27^2,38▪20:2,3,4,8▪21:7,20,23,24-AC-9:10,26,36 (3102)▪16:1▪21:16

DISCIPLES-IS-8:16(3928)▪N.T.-all=3101-M'T-5:1▪8:21,23,25▪9:10,11,14^2,19,37▪10:1▪11:1,2▪12:1,2,49▪13:10,36▪14:12,15,19,22,26▪15:2,12,23,32,33,36^2▪16:5,13,20,21,24▪17:6,10,13,16,19▪18:1▪19:10,13,23,25▪20:17▪21:1,6,20▪22:16▪23:1▪24:1,3▪26:1,8,17,18,19,26,35,36,40,45,56▪27:64▪28:7,8,9,13,16-M'R-2:15,16,18^3,23▪3:7,9▪4:34▪5:31▪6:1,29,35,41,45▪7:2,5,17▪8:1,4,6,10,27^2,33,34▪9:14,18,28,31▪10:10,13,23,24,46▪11:1,14▪12:43▪13:1▪14:12,13,14,16,32▪16:7-LU-5:30,33▪6:1,13,17,20▪7:11,18,19▪8:9,22▪9:1,14,16,18,40,43,54▪10:23▪11:1^2▪12:1,22▪16:1▪17:1,22▪18:15▪19:29,37,39▪20:45▪22:11,39,45-JOH-1:35,37▪2:2,11,12,17,22▪3:22,25▪4:1,2,8,27,31,33▪6:3,8,11,12,16,22^3,24,60,61,66▪7:3▪8:31▪9:2,27,28▪11:7,8,12,54▪12:4,16▪13:22,23,35▪15:8▪16:17,29▪18:1^2,2,17,19,25▪20:10,18,19,20,25,26,30▪21:1,2,4,8,12,14-AC-1:15▪6:1,2,7▪9:1,19,25,26,38▪11:26,29▪13:52▪14:20,22,28▪15:10▪18:23,27▪19:1,9,30▪20:1,7,30▪21:4,16

DISCIPLES'-JOH-13:5(3101)

DISCIPLINE-JOB-36:10(4149)

DISCLOSE-IS-26:21(1540)

DISCOMFITED-all=1949&marked-EX-17:13(2522)-NU-14:45(3807)-JOS-10:10-J'G-4:15(2000)▪8:12(2729)-1SA-7:10-2SA-22:15(2000)-PS-18:14-IS-31:8(4522)

DISCOMFITURE-1SA-14:20(4103)

DISCONTENTED-1SA-22:2 (4751,5315)

DISCONTINUE-JER-17:4(8058)

DISCORD-PR-6:14(4066),19(4090)

DISCOURAGE-NU-32:7(5106)

DISCOURAGED-NU-21:4(7114)▪32:9(5106)-DE-1:21(2865),28(4549)-IS-42:4(7533)▪N.T.-COL-3:21(120)

DISCOVER-all=1540&marked-DE-22:30-1SA-14:8-JOB-41:13-PR-18:2▪25:9-IS-3:17(6168)-JER-13:26(2834)-LA-4:22-EZE-16:37-HO-2:10-MIC-1:6-NA-3:5

DISCOVERED-all=1540&marked-EX-20:26▪20:18(6168)-1SA-14:11▪22:6 (3045)-2SA-22:16-PS-18:15-IS-22:8▪57:8-JER-13:22-LA-2:14-EZE-13:14▪16:36,57▪21:24▪22:10▪23:10,18,29-HO-7:1▪N.T.-AC-21:3(398)▪27:39(2657)

DISCOVERETH-JOB-12:22(1540)-PS-29:9(2834)

DISCOVERING-HAB-3:13(6168)

DISCREET-GE-41:33(995),39(995)-TIT-2:5(4998)

DISCREETLY-M'R-12:34(3562)

DISCRETION-all=4209&marked-PS-112:5(4941)-PR-1:4▪2:11▪3:21▪5:2▪11:22(2940)▪19:11(7922)-IS-28:26 (4941)-JER-10:12(8394)

DISDAINED-1SA-17:42(959)-JOB-30:1(3988)

DISEASE-all=2483&marked-2KI-1:2▪8:8,9-2CH-16:12^2▪21:15(4245),18-PS-41:8(1697)-EC-6:2▪N.T.-all=3119&marked-M'T-4:23▪9:35▪10:1-JOH-5:4(3553)

DISEASED-1KI-15:23(2470)-2CH-16:12(2470)-EZE-34:4(2456),21(2456)▪N.T.-M'T-14:35(2560,2192)-M'R-1:32 (2560,2192)-JOH-6:2(770)

DISEASES-EX-15:26(4245)-DE-7:15(4064)▪28:60(4064)-2CH-21:19 (8463)▪24:25(4251)-PS-103:3(8463)▪N.T.-all=3554&marked-M'T-4:24-M'R-1:34-LU-4:40▪6:17▪9:1-AC-19:12▪28:9(769)

DISFIGURE-M'T-6:16(853)

DISGRACE-JER-14:21(5034)

DISGUISE-1KI-14:2(8138)▪22:30 (2664)-2CH-18:29(2664)

DISGUISED-all=2664-1SA-28:8-1KI-20:38▪22:30-2CH-18:29▪35:22

DISGUISETH-JOB-24:15(5643)

DISH-J'G-5:25(5602)-2KI-21:13 (6747)▪N.T.-M'T-26:23(5165)-M'R-14:20(5165)

DISHES-all=7086-EX-25:29▪37:16-NU-4:7

DISHONEST-EZE-22:13(1215),27(1215)

DISHONESTY-2CO-4:2(152)

DISHONOUR-all=3639&marked-EZR-4:14(6173)-PS-35:26▪69:19▪71:13-PR-6:33(7036)▪N.T.-all=819&marked-JOH-8:49(818)-RO-1:24(818)▪9:21-1CO-15:43▪-2CO-6:8-2TI-2:20

DISHONOUREST-RO-2:23(818)

DISHONOURETH-MIC-7:6(5034)▪N.T.-1CO-11:4(2617),5(2617)

DISINHERIT-NU-14:12(3423)

DISMAYED-all=2865&marked-DE-31:8-JOS-1:9▪8:1▪10:25-1SA-17:11-2KI-19:26-1CH-22:13▪28:20-2CH-20:15,17▪32:7-IS-21:3(926)▪37:27▪41:10 (8159),23(8159)-JER-1:17▪8:9▪10:2^2▪17:18▪23:4▪30:10▪46:5(2844),27▪48:1▪49:37▪50:36-EZE-2:6▪3:9-JOB-9

DISMAYING-JER-48:39(4288)

DISMISSED-2CH-23:8(6362)▪N.T.-AC-15:30(630)▪19:41(630)

DISOBEDIENCE-all=543&marked-RO-5:19(3876)-2CO-10:6(3876)-EPH-2:2▪5:6-COL-3:6-HEB-2:2(3876)

DISOBEDIENT-1KI-13:26(4784)-NE-9:26(4784)▪N.T.-all=545&marked-LU-1:17-AC-26:19-RO-1:30▪10:21(544)-1TI-1:9(506)-2TI-3:2-TIT-1:16▪3:3-1PE-2:7(544),8(544)▪3:20(544)

DISOBEYED-1KI-13:21(4784)

DISORDERLY-2TH-3:6(814),7 (812),11(814)

DISPATCH-EZE-23:47(1254)

DISPENSATION-all=3622-1CO-9:17-EPH-1:10▪3:2-COL-1:25

DISPERSE-all=2219&marked-1SA-14:34(6327)-PR-15:7-EZE-12:15▪20:23▪22:15▪29:12▪30:23,26

DISPERSED-2CH-11:23(6555)-ES-3:8(6504)-PS-112:9(6340)-PR-5:16 (6327)-IS-11:12(5310)-EZE-36:19 (2219)-ZEP-3:10(6327)▪N.T.-JOH-7:35(1290)-AC-5:37(1287)-2CO-9:9(4650)

DISPERSIONS-JER-25:34(8600)

DISPLAYED-PS-60:4(5127)

DISPLEASE-all=7489,5869&marked-GE-31:35(2734)-NU-22:34-1SA-29:7(6213,7451,5869)-2SA-11:25-PR-24:18

DISPLEASED-all=7489,5869&marked-GE-38:10▪48:17-NU-11:1 (7451,241),10(5869,7541)-1SA-8:6▪18:8-2SA-6:8(2734)▪11:27-1KI-1:6(6087)▪20:43(2198)▪21:4(2198)-1CH-13:11(2734)▪21:7(3415,5869)-PS-60:1(599)-IS-59:15-DA-6:14(888)-JON-4:1-HAB-3:8(2734)-ZEC-1:2(7107),15^2(7107)▪N.T.-all=23&marked-M'T-21:15-M'R-10:14,41-AC-12:20(2371)

DISPLEASURE-all=2534&marked-DE-9:19-J'G-15:3(7451)-PS-2:5 (2740)▪6:1▪38:1

DISPOSED-JOB-34:13(7760)▪37:15 (7760)▪N.T.-AC-18:27(1014)-1CO-10:27(2309)

DISPOSING-PR-16:33(4941)

DISPOSITION-AC-7:53(1296)

DISPOSSESS-NU-33:53(3423)-DE-7:17(3423)

DISPOSSESSED-NU-32:39 (3423)-J'G-11:23(3423)

DISPUTATION-AC-15:2(4803)

DISPUTATIONS-RO-14:1(1253)

DISPUTE-JOB-23:7(3198)

DISPUTED-all=1256&marked-M'R-9:33(1260),34-AC-9:29(4802)▪17:17-JUDE-9

DISPUTER-1CO-1:20(4804)

DISPUTING-all=1256&marked-AC-6:9(4802)▪5:7(4803)▪19:8,9▪24:12

DISPUTINGS-PH'P-2:14(1261)-1TI-6:5(3859)

DISQUIET-JER-50:34(7264)

DISQUIETED-all=1993&marked-1SA-28:15(7264)-PS-39:6▪42:5,11▪43:5-PR-30:21(7264)

DISQUIETNESS-PS-38:8(5100)

DISSEMBLED-JOS-7:11(3584)-JER-42:20(8582)▪N.T.-GA-2:13(4942)

DISSEMBLERS-PS-26:4(5956)

DISSEMBLETH-PR-26:24(5234)

DISSENSION-all=4714-AC-15:2▪23:7,10

DISSIMULATION-RO-12:9(505)-GA-2:13(5272)

DISSOLVE-DA-5:16(8271)

DISSOLVED-all=4127&marked-PS-75:3-IS-14:31▪24:19(6565)▪34:4 (4743)-NA-2:6(4127)▪N.T.-2CO-5:1 (2647)-2PE-3:11(3089),12(3089)

DISSOLVEST-JOB-30:22(4127)

DISSOLVING-DA-5:12(8271)

DISTAFF-PR-31:19(6418)

DISTANT-EX-36:22(7947)

DISTIL-DE-32:2(5140)-JOB-36:28 (7491)

DISTINCTION-1CO-14:7(1293)

DISTINCTLY-NE-8:8(6567)

DISTRACTED-PS-88:15(6323)

DISTRACTION-1CO-7:35(563)

DISTRESS-all=6869&marked-GE-35:3▪42:21-DE-2:9(6696),19(6696)▪28:53(6693),55(6693),57(6693)-J'G-11:7 (6887)-1SA-22:2(4689)-2SA-22:7(6862)-1KI-1:29(6869)-2CH-28:22(6887)-NE-2:17(7451)▪9:37(6869)-PS-4:1(6862)▪18:6(6862)▪118:5(4712)▪120:1-PR-1:27-IS-25:4(6862)▪29:2(6693),7(6693)-JER-10:18(6887)-LA-1:20(6887)-OB-12,14-ZEP-1:15(4691),17(6887)▪N.T.-all=318&marked-LU-21:23,25(4928)-RO-8:35(4730)-1CO-7:26-1TH-3:7

DISTRESSED-all=3334&marked-GE-32:7-NU-22:3(6973)-J'G-2:15▪10:9-1SA-13:6(5065)▪14:24(5065)▪28:15 (6887)▪30:6-2SA-1:26(6887)-2CH-28:20(6696)▪N.T.-2CO-4:8(4729)

DISTRESSES-all=4691&marked-PS-25:17▪107:6,13,19,28-EZE-30:16 (6862)▪N.T.-2CO-6:4(4730)▪12:10(4730)

DISTRIBUTE-JOS-13:32(5157)-2CH-31:14(5414)-NE-13:13(2505)▪N.T.-LU-18:22(1239)-1TI-6:18(2130)

DISTRIBUTED-JOS-14:1(5157)-1CH-24:3(2505)-2CH-23:18(2505)▪N.T.-JOH-6:11(1239)-1CO-7:17(3307)-2CO-10:13(3307)

DISTRIBUTETH-JOB-21:17(2505)

DISTRIBUTING-RO-12:13(2841)

DISTRIBUTION-AC-4:35(1239)-2CO-9:13(2842)

DITCH-JOB-9:31(7845)-PS-7:15 (7845)-PR-23:27(7745)-IS-22:11(4724)▪N.T.-M'T-15:14(999)-LU-6:39(999)

DITCHES-2KI-3:16(1356)

DIVERS-all=6648&marked-DE-22:9 (3610),11(8162)-J'G-5:30^3-2SA-13:18 (6446),19(6446)-1CH-29:2(7553)-2CH-30:11(582)-EZE-16:16(2921)▪17:3 (7553)▪N.T.-all=4164&marked-M'T-4:24-M'R-1:34▪8:3(5100)-LU-4:40--AC-19:9(5100)-2TI-3:6-TIT-3:3-HEB-1:1(4187)▪2:4▪9:10(1313)▪13:9-JAS-1:2

DIVERSE-all=8133&marked-LE-19:19(3610)-ES-1:7(8138)▪3:8(8138)-DA-7:3,7,19,23,24

DIVERSITIES-1CO-12:4(1243)6 (1243),28(1085)

DIVIDE-all=2505&marked-GE-1:6 (914),14(914),18(914)▪49:7,27-EX-14:16 (1234)▪15:9▪21:35^2(2673)▪26:33(914)-LE-1:17(914)▪5:8(914)▪11:4(6536),7(6536)-NU-31:27(2673)▪33:54(5157)▪

34:17(5157),18(5157)-DE-14:7^2(6536)-JOS-13:6(5307),7■18:5■22:8-2SA-19:29-1KI-3:25(1504),26(1504)-NE-9:11(1234),22-JOB-27:17-PS-55:9(6385)■60:6■74:13(6565)■108:7-PR-16:19-IS-9:3■53:12^2(5312)-EZE-5:1■45:1(5307)■47:21,22(5307)■48:29(5307)-DA-11:39■N.T.-LU-12:13(3307)■22:17(1266)

DIVIDED-all=2505&marked-GE-1:4(914),7(914)■10:5(6504),25(6385),32(5504)■14:15■15:10^2(1334)■32:7(2673)■33:1(2673)-EX-14:21(1234)-NU-26:53,55,56■31:42(2673)-DE-4:19-JOS-14:5■18:10■23:4(5307)-J'G-5:30■7:16(2673)■9:43(2673)■19:29(5408)-2SA-1:23(6504)-1KI-16:21■18:6-2KI-2:8(2673)-1CH-1:19(6385)■23:6■24:4,5-2CH-35:13(7323)-JOB-38:25(6385)-PS-68:12■78:13(1234),55(5307)■136:13(1504)-IS-33:23■34:17■51:15(7280)-LA-4:16-EZE-37:22(2673)-DA-2:41(6386)■5:28(6537)■11:4(2673)-HO-10:2-AM-7:17-MIC-2:4-ZEC-14:1■N.T.-all=3307&marked-M'T-12:25^2,26-M'R-3:24,25,26■6:41-LU-11:17(1266),18(1266)■12:52(1266),53(1266)■15:12(1244)-AC-13:19(2624)■14:4(4977)■23:7(4977)-1CO-1:13-RE-16:19(1096)

DIVIDER-LU-12:14(3312)

DIVIDETH-all=6536&marked-LE-11:4,5,6,26-DE-14:8-JOB-26:12(7280)-PS-29:7(2672)-JER-31:35(7280)■N.T.-M'T-25:32(873)-LU-11:22(1239)

DIVIDING-JOS-19:51(2505)-IS-63:12(1234)-DA-7:25(6387)■N.T.-1CO-12:11(1244)-2TI-2:15(3718)-HEB-4:12(3311)

DIVINATION-all=7081&marked-NU-22:7■23:23-DE-18:10-2KI-17:17-JER-14:14-EZE-12:24(4738)■13:6,7(4738)■21:21,22,23(7080)■N.T.-AC-16:16(4436)

DIVINATIONS-EZE-13:23(7081)

DIVINE-all=7080&marked-GE-44:15(5172)-1SA-28:8-PR-16:10(7081)-EZE-13:9,23(7081)■21:29-MIC-3:6,11■N.T.-HEB-9:1(2999)-2PE-1:3(2304),4(2304)-RE-1:t(2312)

DIVINERS-all=7080-DE-18:14-1SA-6:2-IS-44:25-JER-27:9■29:8-MIC-3:7-ZEC-10:2

DIVINETH-GE-44:5(5172)

DIVINING-EZE-22:28(7080)

DIVISION-EX-8:23(6304)-2CH-35:5(2515)■N.T.-all=4978&marked-LU-12:51(1267)-JOH-7:43■9:16■10:19

DIVISIONS-all=4256&marked-JOS-11:23■12:7■18:10-J'G-5:15(6391),16(6391)-1CH-24:1■26:1,12,19-2CH-35:5(6391),12(4653)-EZR-6:18(6392)-NE-11:36■N.T.-RO-16:17(1370)-1CO-1:10(4978)■3:3(1370)■11:18(4978)

DIVORCE-JER-3:8(3748)

DIVORCED-all=1644-LE-21:14■22:13-NU-30:9■N.T.-M'T-5:32(630)

DIVORCEMEMT-all=3748-DE-24:1,3-IS-50:1■N.T.-all=647-M'T-5:31■19:7-M'R-10:4

DO-all=6213&marked-GE-11:6^2■16:6■18:5,17,19,25^2,29,30■19:8^2,22■21:23■22:12■26:29■27:37■30:31■31:16,29,43■34:14,19■39:9,11■41:25,28,34,55■42:18■43:11■44:7,17■45:17,19■47:30-EX-3:20■4:15,17,21■6:1■8:26■9:5■15:26■17:4■18:20,23■19:8■20:9,10■21:7(3318),11■22:30■23:12,22,24■24:3,7,14(1167)■29:1,35,41■31:11■32:14■33:5,17■34:10^2■35:1,35■36:2-LE-4:2,20^2■8:34■9:6■16:15,16,29■18:3^2,4,5■19:15,35,37■20:8,22■22:31■23:3,7,8,21,25,28,31,35,36■25:18^2■26:3,14,15,16-NU-3:7(5647),8(5647)■4:3,19,23(5647),30(5647),37(5647),41(5647),47(5647)■5:6■6:21■7:5(5647)■8:7,15(5647),19(5647),22(5647),26(5647),26■9:14■10:32^2(3190)■14:28,35■15:12,13,14,39,40■16:6,9(5647)28■18:6,23(5647)■21:34■22:17,18,20,30■23:19,26■24:13,14,18■28:18,25,26■29:1,7,12,35,39■30:2■32:20,23,24,25,31■33:56-DE-1:14,18,44■3:2,21,24■4:1,5,6,14,25■5:1,13,14,27,31,32■6:1,3,18,24,25■7:11,12,19■8:1■11:22,32■12:1,4,8,14,25,30,31,32■13:11,18■15:5,17■16:8,12■17:10^2,11,12,19■18:9,12■19:9,19■20:15,18■21:9■22:3^2,5■24:8^2,18,22■25:16^2■26:16^2■27:10,26■28:1,13,15,20,58■29:9^2,29■30:8,12,13,14■31:4,5,12,29■32:46■34:11-JOS-1:7,8,16■3:5■6:3■7:9■8:2,8■9:20,25■10:25■22:5,27(5647)■23:6-J'G-6:27■7:17^2■8:3■9:33,48^2■10:15■11:10,36■13:8,12(4640)■14:10■15:3,10■18:14sup,14,18■19:23sup,23,24^2■20:9,10■21:7,11,16-RU-1:17■3:4,5,11■4:11-1SA-1:23■2:23,35■3:11,17,18■5:8■6:2■8:8■10:2,7,8■11:10■12:16■14:7,36,40,44■16:3■20:2,4,13,13sup■22:3■24:4,6■25:17,22■26:25■28:2,15■30:23-2SA-3:8,9^2,18,35■7:3,23,25■9:11■10:12■11:11■12:9,12■13:2,12■15:26■16:20■17:6■18:4■19:13,18,27,37,38^2■21:3,4■23:17■24:12-1KI-1:30■2:6,9,23,31,38■3:28■5:8■8:32,39,43,43sup■9:1,4■10:9■11:12,33,38■12:27■14:8■17:13■19:2■20:9,10,24■22:22-2KI-2:9■4:2■6:15,31■7:9■8:12,13■10:5^2■11:5■17:12,15,17,34^2,37,41■18:12■19:31■20:9■21:8,9■22:9,13-1CH-11:19■12:32■13:4■17:2,23■19:13■21:8(5674),10,23■28:7,10,20■29:19-2CH-6:23,33■7:17■9:8■14:4■18:21■19:6,7,9,10■20:12■23:4■25:8,9■30:12■33:8,9■34:16,21■35:6-EZR-4:22(5648)■6:8(5648)■7:10,18^2(5648),26(5648)■10:4,5,11,12-NE-1:9■2:12,19■4:2■5:9,12^2■6:2,13■9:24,29■10:29■13:17,27-ES-1:8,15■3:11■5:5,8■6:6,10■7:5■9:13,23-JOB-7:20(6466)■11:8(6466)■13:20■15:3(6953)■22:17(6466)■34:32(6466)■37:12(6467)-PS-11:3(6466)■34:14,16■37:3,27■40:8■56:4,11■60:12■83:9■103:18,20,21■107:23■108:13■109:21■111:10■118:6■119:3(6466)■143:10-PR-2:14■3:27■6:3■10:23■21:3,7,15■24:29■25:8■31:12(1580)-EC-2:3,11■3:12■5:1■8:11,12■9:10-SONG-8:8-IS-5:5■10:3,11■19:15,21(5647)■28:21■37:32■38:7■42:16■43:19■45:7■46:10,11■48:11,14■56:1■65:8-JER-4:30■5:31■7:10,14,17■9:7■11:4,6,8■12:5■14:7■17:22,24■18:6,8,10,12■19:12■22:4,15,17■26:3,14■28:6■29:32■32:23,35■33:9,18■36:3■39:12■40:16■42:3,5,20■44:4,17■50:15,21,29-LA-1:22(5953)-EZE-5:9^2■6:10■7:27■8:6,9,12,13■11:20■15:3■16:5■18:5,21■20:11,13,19,21■22:14■23:48■24:14,22,24■25:14■33:14,19,31,32■35:11,15■36:22,27,32,36,37■37:24■43:11■45:20,25-DA-9:19■11:3,16,17,24,28,30,32^{2}sup,32,36,39-HO-6:4^2■9:5■10:3,15-JOE-2:21-AM-3:7,10■4:12^2-JON-1:11■3:10-MIC-6:8-ZEP-3:5,13-ZEC-1:6,21■8:16-MAL-4:1,3■N.T.-all=4160&marked-M'T-5:19,44,46,47^2■6:1,2sup,2■7:12^2■8:9■9:28■12:2^2,12,50■13:41■18:35■19:16■20:13(91),15,32■21:21,24,27,40■23:3^3,5■27:22-M'R-2:24■3:4(15),4(2554)■6:5■7:8,12,13■9:39■10:17,35,36,51■11:3,5,28,29,33■12:9■14:7■15:12-LU-2:27■3:10,11,12,14,14(1286)■4:23■6:2^2,9(15),9(2554)11,27,31^2,33sup,33(15),33,35(15),46■7:4(3930),8■8:21■10:25,28,37■12:4,17,18■13:32(2005)■16:3,4■17:10■18:18,41■19:48■20:8,13,15■22:19,23(4238)■23:31,34-JOH-2:5■3:2■4:34■5:19^2,30,36■6:6,28,38■7:4,17,31■8:28,29,38,39,41,44■9:16,33■10:25,37,38■11:12(4982),47■13:7,15,17,27■14:12^2,13,14,31■15:5,14,21■16:3■17:4-AC-1:1■2:37■4:16,28■5:35(4238)■7:26(91)■9:6^2■10:6■14:15■15:29(4238),36(2192)■16:28(4238),30■17:7■19:36■21:23■22:10^2■25:9(2698)■26:9(4238),20(4238)-RO-1:28,32sup,32(4238)■2:3(4238),14■3:8■7:15(2716),15(4238),15,16,17(2716),19,19(4238),20,20(2716),21■13:3,4-1CO-7:36■9:17(4238),23■10:31■11:24,25■15:29■16:1-2CO-8:1(1107),10■11:12■13:7-GA-2:10■3:10■5:3,17,21(4238)■6:10(2038)-EPH-3:20■6:9,21(4238)-PH'P-2:13(1754),14■4:9(4238),13(2480)-COL-3:17,23,23(2038)-1TH-4:10,11(4238)■5:11,24-2TH-3:4-1TI-6:2(1398),18(14)-2TI-4:5,9(4704),21(4704)-PH'M-14,21-HEB-4:13(3588,3056)■6:3■10:7,9■13:16(2140),17,19,21-JAS-2:8,12■4:15,17-1PE-2:14(17),20(15)■3:6(15),11,12-2PE-1:10,19-1JO-1:6■3:22■3JO-6-RE-2:5■13:14■22:14

DOCTOR-AC-5:34(3547)

DOCTORS-LU-2:46(1320)■5:17(3547)

DOCTRINE-all=3948&marked-DE-32:2-JOB-11:4-PR-4:2-IS-28:9(8052)■29:24-JER-10:8(4148)■N.T.-all=1322,a=1319&marked-M'T-7:28■16:12■22:33-M'R-1:22,27■4:2■11:18■12:38-LU-4:32-JOH-7:16,17■18:19-AC-2:42■5:28■13:12■17:19-RO-6:17■16:17-1CO-14:6,26-EPH-4:14a-1TI-1:10a■4:6a,13a,16a■5:17a■6:1a,3a-2TI-3:10a,16a■4:2,3a-TIT-1:9a■2:1a,7a,10a-HEB-6:1(3056),2-2JO-9^2,10-RE-2:14,15,24

DOCTRINES-all=1319&marked-M'T-15:9-M'R-7:7-COL-2:22-1TI-4:1-HEB-13:9(1322)

DOER-all=6123-GE-39:22-2SA-3:39-PS-31:23■N.T.-all=4163&marked-2TI-2:9(2557)-JAS-1:23,25■4:11

DOERS-2KI-22:5^2(6213)-PS-101:8(6466)■N.T.-RO-2:13(4163)-JAS-1:22(4163)

DOEST-all=6213&marked-GE-21:22-EX-18:14,17-DE-12:28■14:29■15:18-J'G-11:27-2SA-3:25-1KI-2:3■20:22-JOB-9:12■35:6(6466),6-PS-77:14■86:10-EC-8:4■15:5(7965)-EZE-12:9■16:30■24:19-DA-4:35(5648)■N.T.-all=4160-M'T-6:2,3■21:23-M'R-11:28-LU-20:2-JOH-2:18■3:2■7:3■13:27-AC-22:26-RO-2:1(4238),3-JAS-2:19-3JO-5

DOETH-all=6213-GE-31:12-EX-31:14,15■35:2-LE-4:27■6:3■23:30-NU-15:30■24:23(7760)-JOB-5:9■9:10■23:13■37:5-PS-1:3■14:1,3■15:3,5■53:1,3■72:18■106:3■118:15,16■136:4-PR-6:32■11:17(1580)-EC-2:2■3:14^2■7:20■8:3-IS-56:2-JER-5:19■48:10-EZE-17:15■18:10,11,14,24^2,27-DA-4:35(5648)■9:14-AM-9:12-MAL-2:12,17■N.T.-all=4160-M'T-6:3■7:21,24,26■8:9-LU-6:47,49■7:8(4238)-JOH-3:20,21■5:19^2,20■7:4,51■9:31■11:47■14:10■15:15■16:2(4374)-AC-15:17■26:31(4238)-RO-3:12■10:5■13:4(4238)-1CO-6:18■7:37,38^2-GA-3:12-EPH-6:8-COL-3:25(91)-JAS-4:17-1JO-2:17,29■3:7,10-3JO-10,11(15),11(2554)-RE-13:13

DOG-all=3611-EX-11:7-DE-23:18-J'G-7:5-1SA-17:43■24:14-2SA-9:8■16:9-2KI-8:13-PS-22:20■59:6,14-PR-26:11,17-EC-9:4■N.T.-2PE-2:22(2965)

DOG'S-2SA-3:8(3611)-IS-66:3(3611)

DOGS-all=3611-EX-22:31-1KI-14:11■16:4■21:19^2,23,24■22:38-2KI-9:10,36-JOB-30:1-PS-22:16■68:23-IS-56:10,11-JER-15:3■N.T.-all=2965&marked-M'T-7:6■15:26(2952),27(2952)-M'R-7:27(2952),28(2952)-LU-16:21-PH'P-3:2-RE-22:15

DOING-all=6213&marked-GE-31:28■44:5-EX-15:11-DE-9:18-1KI-7:40■16:19■22:43-2KI-21:16-1CH-22:16-2CH-20:32-NE-6:3-PS-64:9(4640)■66:5(5949)■118:23(854)-IS-56:2■58:13^2■N.T.-all=4160&marked-M'T-21:42(1096)■24:46-M'R-12:11(1096)-LU-12:43-AC-10:38(2109)■24:20(92)-RO-2:7(2041)■12:20-2CO-8:11-GA-6:9-EPH-6:6,7(1398)-2TH-3:13(2569)-1TI-4:16■5:21-1PE-2:15(15)■3:17(15),17(2554)■4:19(16)

DOINGS-all=4611,a=5949&marked

-LE-18:3^{2}(4640)-DE-28:20-J’G-2:19-1SA-25:3-2CH-17:4(4640)-PS-9:11a■77:12a-PR-20:11-IS-1:16■3:8,10■12:4a-JER-4:4,18■7:3,5■11:18■17:10■18:11■21:12,14■23:2,22■25:5■26:3,13■32:19■35:15■44:22-EZE-14:22a,23a■20:44a■21:24a■24:14a■36:17a,19a,31-HOS-4:9■5:4■7:2■9:15■12:2-MIC-2:7■3:4■7:13-ZEP-3:7a,11a-ZEC-1:4,6

DOLEFUL-IS-13:21(255)-MIC-2:4(5093)

DOMINION-all=7985&marked-GE-1:26(7287),28(7287)■27:40(7300)■37:8(4910)-NU-24:19(7287)-J’G-5:13^{2}(7287)■14:4(4910)-1KI-4:24(7287)■9:19(4475)-2KI-20:13(4475)-1CH-4:22(1166)■18:3(3027)-2CH-8:6(4475)■21:8(3027)-NE-9:28(7287),37(4910)-JOB-25:2(4910)■38:33(4896)-PS-8:6(4910)■19:13(4910)■49:14(7287)■72:8(7287)■103:22(4475)■114:2(4475)■119:133(7980)■145:13(4475)-IS-26:13(1166)■39:2(4475)-JER-34:1(4475)■51:28(4475)-DA-4:3,22,34■6:26^{2}■7:6,12,14^{2},26,27■11:3(4474),4(4915),5(4910),5(4474),5(4475)-MIC-4:8(4475)-ZEC-9:10(4915)■N.T.-all=2961&marked-M’T-20:25(2634)-RO-6:9,14■7:1-2CO-1:24-EPH-1:21(2963)-1PE-4:11(2904)■5:11(2904)-JUDE-8(2963),25(2904)-RE-1:6(2904)

DOMINIONS-DA-7:27(7985)-COL-1:16(2963)

DONE-all=6213,a=6466&marked-GE-3:13,14■4:10■8:21■9:24■12:18■18:21■20:5,9^{3},10■21:23,26■22:16■24:15(3615),19^{2}(3615),22(3615),45(3615),66■26:10,29■27:19,45■28:15■29:25,26■30:26(5647)■31:26■34:7■40:15■42:28■44:15-EX-1:18■2:4■3:16■10:2(7760)■12:16^{2}■14:5■18:1,8,9■21:31■31:15■34:10(1254),33(3615)■35:2■39:43^{2}-LE-4:2,13^{2},22^{2},27■5:17■6:7■8:5,34■11:32■18:27■23:3■24:19,20(5414)-NU-5:7■15:11,34■22:2,28■23:11■27:4(1639)■32:13-DE-3:21■10:21■12:31■19:19■25:9■26:14■29:24■32:27(6466)-JOS-5:8(8552)■7:19,20■9:3,24■10:1^{2},32,35,37,39^{2}■22:24■23:3,8■24:7,31-J’G-1:7■2:2,10■3:12■6:29^{2}■8:2■9:16^{2}■11:37■14:6■15:6,7,10,11^{2}■19:30(1961)■20:12(1961)-RU-2:11■3:3(3615),16-1SA-4:16(1697)■6:9■8:8■11:7■12:17,20■13:11■14:43■17:26,27,29■19:18■20:1,32■24:19■25:30■26:16,18■28:9,17,18■29:8■31:11-2SA-2:6■3:24■7:21■11:27■12:5,21■13:12■14:20,21■15:24(8552)■16:10■21:11■23:20■24:10,10sup,17sup,17-1KI-1:6■3:12■8:66■9:8■13:11■14:9,22■15:3■18:36■19:1,20■22:53-2KI-4:13,14■5:13■7:12■8:4■10:10,30■15:3,9,34■19:11,25■20:3■21:11^{2},15■23:17,19,32,37■24:9,19-1CH-10:11■16:12■17:19■21:8,8sup,17sup,17-2CH-7:21■24:16,22■25:16■29:2,6■30:5■32:13-EZR-6:12(5648)■7:21(5648),23(5648)■9:1(3615)■10:3-NE-5:19■6:9■8:17■9:33,33sup■13:14-ES-2:1■4:1■6:3^{2},6,9,11■9:12^{2},14-JOB-21:31■34:32a-PS-7:3■22:31■40:5■50:21■51:4■52:9■66:16■71:19■78:4■98:1■105:5■106:6■109:27■111:8■115:3■119:121,166■120:3(3254)■126:2,3-PR-3:30(1580)■24:29■30:20(466)■31:29a-EC-1:9a,13a,14a■2:12a■4:1a,3a■8:9a,10a,14a,16a,17a■9:3a,6a-IS-5:4^{2}a■10:11,13a■12:5a■24:13(3615)■25:1■33:13■37:11,26■38:3,15■41:4,20■44:23■46:10■48:5■53:9-JER-2:23■3:5,6,7,16■5:13■7:13,14,30■8:6■11:17■16:12■18:13■22:8■30:15,24■31:37■32:23,30,32■34:15■35:10,18■38:9■40:3■41:11■42:10■44:17■50:15,29■51:12,24■52:2-LA-1:12(5953),21,22(5953)■2:17,20(5953)-EZE-3:20■5:7,9■9:4,11■11:12■12:11,28■14:23^{2}■16:47,48^{2},51,54,59,63■17:18,24■18:13,14,19^{2},22,24,26■23:38,39■24:22,24■33:16■39:24■43:11■44:14-DA-6:22(5648)■9:12■11:24,36-JOE-2:20-AM-3:6-OB-1:15-JON-1:10,14-MIC-6:3-ZEC-7:3-MAL-2:13■N.T.-all=1096,a=4160-M‘T-1:22■6:10■7:22a■8:13■11:20,21^{2},23^{2}■13:28a■17:12a■18:19,31^{2}■21:4,21sup,21■23:23a,40^{2}a■26:13a,42,56■27:23a,54■28:11-M‘R-4:11■5:14,19a,20a,32a,33■6:30a■7:37a■9:13a■13:30■14:8a,9a■15:8a,14a-LU-1:49a■3:19a■4:23■5:6a■8:34,35,39^{2}a,56■9:7,10a■10:13^{2}■11:2,42a■13:17■14:22■16:8a■17:10^{2}a■22:42■23:8,15(4238),22a,31,41(4238),47,48■24:21-JOH-1:28■5:16a,29a,29(4238)■7:21a,31a■11:46a■12:16a,18a,37a■13:12a,15a■15:7,24a■18:35a■19:36-AC-2:43■4:7a,16,21,28,30■5:7■8:13■9:13a■10:16,33a■11:10■12:9■13:12■14:3,11a,27a■15:4a■21:14,33a■24:2■25:10(91)■26:26(4238)■28:9-RO-9:11(4238)-1CO-5:2a,3(2716)■9:15■13:10(2673)■14:26,40■16:14-2CO-3:7(2673),11(2673),14(2673)■5:10sup,10(4238)■7:12(91)-EPH-5:12■6:13(2716)-PH’P-4:14a-COL-3:25(91)-TIT-3:5a-HEB-10:29(1796),36a-RE-16:17■21:6■22:6

DOOR-all=6607,a=1817&marked-GE-4:7■6:16■18:1,2,10■19:6,6a,9a,10a,11^{2}■43:19-EX-12:7(4947),22,23■21:6a,6(4201)■26:36■29:4,11,32,42■33:8,9,10^{2}■35:15,17(8179)■36:37■38:8,30■39:38■40:5,6,12,28,29-LE-1:3,5■3:2■4:4,7,18■8:3,4,31,33,35■10:7■12:6■14:11,23,38■15:14,29■16:7■17:4,5,6,9■19:21-NU-3:25,26■4:25,26■6:10,13,18■10:3■11:10■12:5■16:18,19,27,50■20:6■25:6■27:2-DE-11:20(4201)■15:17a■22:21■31:15-JOS-19:51-J’G-4:20■9:52■19:22a,26,27-1SA-2:22-2SA-11:9■13:17a,18a-1KI-6:8(6907),33(6907),34^{2}a■14:6,17(1004),27-2KI-4:4a,5a,15,33a■5:9■6:32a■9:3a,10a■12:9(5592)■22:4(5592)■23:4(5592)■25:18(5592)-1CH-9:21-NE-3:20,21-ES-2:21(5592)■6:2(5592)-JOB-31:9,34-PS-141:3a-PR-5:8■9:14■26:14a-SONG-8:9a-IS-6:4(5592)-JER-35:4(5592)■52:24(5592)-EZE-8:3,7,8,14,16■10:19■11:1■40:13■41:2^{2},3^{3},11^{2},16^{2}(5592),17,20,24a■42:2,12■46:3■47:1-HO-2:15■N.T.-all=2374&marked-M’T-6:6■25:10■27:60■28:2-M’R-1:33■2:2■11:4■15:46■16:3-LU-11:7■13:25^{2}-JOH-10:1,2,7,9■18:16,16(2377),17(2377)-AC-5:9■12:6■14:27-1CO-16:9-2CO-2:12-COL-4:3-JAS-5:9-RE-3:8,20^{2}■4:1

DOORKEEPER-PS-84:10(5605)

DOORKEEPERS-1CH-15:23(7778),24(7778)

DOORS-all=1817&marked-JOS-2:19-J’G-3:23,24,25■11:31■16:3■19:27-1SA-3:15■21:13-1KI-6:31,32,34■7:5(6607),50^{2}-2KI-18:16-1CH-22:3-2CH-3:7■4:9^{2},22^{2}■23:4(5592)■28:24■29:3,7■34:9(5592)-NE-3:1,3,6,13,14,15■6:1,10■7:1,3-JOB-3:10■31:32■38:8,10,17(8179)■41:14-PS-24:7(6607),9(6607)■78:23-PR-8:3(6607),34(6607)-EC-12:4-IS-26:20■57:8-EZE-33:30(6607)■41:11(6607),23,24,25■42:4(6607),11(6607),12(6607)-MIC-7:5(6607)-ZEC-11:1-MAL-1:10■N.T.-all=2374-M’T-24:33-M’R-13:29-JOH-20:19,26-AC-5:19,23■16:26,27■21:30

DOST-all supplied

DOTE-JER-50:36(2973)

DOTED-all=5689-EZE-23:5,7,9,12,16,20

DOTH-all supplied

DOTING-1TI-6:4(3552)

DOUBLE-all=4932&marked-GE-43:12,15-EX-22:4(8147),7(8147),9(8147)■26:9(3717)■39:9(3717)-DE-15:18■21:17(8147)-2KI-2:9(8147)-JOB-11:6(3718)■41:13(3718)-IS-40:2(3718)■61:7^{2}-JER-16:18■17:18-ZEC-9:12■N.T.-1TI-5:17(1362)-JAS-1:8(1374)■4:8(1374)-RE-18:6(1363),6(3588,1362),6(1362)

DOUBLED-all=3717&marked-GE-41:32(8138)-EX-28:16■39:9-EZE-21:14

DOUBLETONGUED-1TI-3:8(1351)

DOUBT-JOB-12:2(551)■N.T.-M’T-14:31(1365)■21:21(1252)-M’R-11:23(1252)-LU-11:20(686)-JOH-10:24(142,5590)-AC-2:12(1280)■28:4(3843)-1CO-9:10(1063)-GA-4:20(639)

DOUBTED-M’T-28:17(1365)-AC-5:24(1280)■10:17(1280)■25:20(639)

DOUBTETH-RO-14:23(1252)

DOUBTFUL-LU-12:29(3349)-RO-14:1(1261)

DOUBTING-JOH-13:22(639)-AC-10:20(1252)■11:12(1252)-1TI-2:8(1261)

DOUBTLESS-NU-14:30(518)-IS-63:16(3588)■N.T.-1CO-9:2(1065)-2CO-12:1(1211)-PH’P-3:8(3304)

DOUBTS-DA-5:12(7001),16(7001)

DOUGH-all=1217&marked-EX-12:34,39-NU-15:20(6182),21(6182)-NE-10:37(6182)-JER-7:18-EZE-44:30(6182)-HO-7:4

DOVE-all=3123-GE-8:8,9,10,11,12-PS-55:6■68:13-SONG-2:14■5:2■6:9-IS-38:14-JER-48:28-HO-7:11■11:11■N.T.-all=4058-M’T-3:16-M’R-1:10-LU-3:22-JOH-1:32

DOVE’S-2KI-6:25(1686)

DOVES-all=3123-SONG-5:12-IS-59:11■60:8-EZE-7:16-NA-2:7■N.T.-all=4058-M’T-10:16■21:12-M’R-11:15-JOH-2:14,16

DOVES’-SONG-1:15(3123)■4:1(3123)

DOWN-all=3381,a=7901,b=7812,c=5422,d=2040,e=935,f=7257&marked-GE-11:5,7■12:10■15:11,12e,17e■18:21■23:12b■24:11(1288),14(5186),16,18,26(6915),45,46,48(6915)■26:2■7:29^{2}b■37:10b,25sup,25,35■38:1■39:1^{2}■42:2,3,6b,38■43:4,5,7,11,15,20,22,28(6915)■44:11,21,23,26^{2},29,31■45:9,13■46:3,4■49:6(6131),8b-EX-2:5■3:8■9:19■11:8,8b■17:11(5117),12e■19:11,14,20,21,24,25■20:5b■22:26e■23:24b,24(7665)■32:1,7,15■34:29^{2}-LE-9:22■11:35c■14:45c■18:23(7250)■20:16(7250)■22:7e■26:1b-NU-1:51■4:5■10:17■11:17,25■12:5■14:45■16:30,33■20:15,28■21:15(5186)■22:27f,31(6915)■23:24a■24:9a■25:2b■33:52(8045)■34:11,12-DE-1:25■5:9b■6:7a■9:3(3665),12,15■10:5,22■11:30(3996)■12:3(1438)■16:6e■21:4■23:11e■24:13e,15e■26:5■28:24,43,52■33:3(8497),28(6201)-JOS-1:4(3996)■2:8a,15,18■3:13,16^{2}■7:5(4174)■8:29e,29■10:11(4174),11sup,27sup,27■15:10■16:3,7■18:16,18■24:4-J’G-1:9,34■2:2c,19b,27,28■4:14,15■5:11,14,27a,27sup■6:25d,25sup,28c,31c,32c■7:4,5,9,10^{2},11^{2},24■8:9(5242),17(5242)■9:36,37,45c■11:37■14:1,5,7,10,19■15:8,12■16:21,31-RU-3:3,4^{2}a,6,7^{2}a,13a-1SA-2:6■3:2a,3a,5a,6a,9^{2}a■6:15,21■9:25,27■10:5,8^{2}■13:12,20■14:36,37■15:6,12■17:8,28^{2}■19:12■20:19■21:13■22:1■23:4,6,8,11^{2},20^{2},25■25:1,20^{2}■26:2,6^{2}■29:4■30:15^{2},16,24-2SA-3:35e■5:17■8:2a■11:8,9,10^{2},13■13:5a,6a,8a■15:20(5128),24(3332)■17:18■18:28b■19:16,20,24,31■20:15(5307)■21:15■22:10,28,48(8213)■23:13,20,21-1KI-1:25,33,38,53■2:6,8,9■5:9■17:23,40(3281),42(1457),44■19:6a,10d,14d■21:4a,16,18^{2}■22:2,-2KI-1:4,6,9,10^{2},11,12^{2},14,15^{2},16■2:2■3:12,25d■5:14,18b■6:9(5181),18,33■7:17■8:29■9:16,33(8058)■10:13,27^{2}c■11:6(4535),18c,19■12:20■13:14,21(3212)■16:17■19:16(5186)■20:10(5186),11■23:5(7673),7c,12c,12(7323),15c■25:10c-1CH-7:21■11:15,22,23■29:20(6915)-2CH-7:1,3■18:2■20:16■22:6■23:17c,20■25:8(3782),14(7812)■31:1(1438),1c■32:30(4295)■33:3c■34:4c,4(1438),7c,7(1438)■36:3(5493),19c-EZR-10:1(5307)-NE-3:15■6:3^{2},16(5307)■9:13-JOB-7:4a,9■11:19f■12:14d■14:12a,16■20:11a■21:13(5181),26a,29(8213)■27:19a■29:24(5307)■

31:10(3766)▪33:24▪41:1(8257),9(2904)
-PS-3:5a▪4:8a▪7:16▪17:11(5186),13
(3766)▪18:9,27(8213)▪20:8(3766)▪
22:29▪23:2f▪28:1▪30:3,9▪31:2(5186)▪
35:14(7817)▪36:12(1760)▪37:2(5243),14
(5307),24(2904)▪38:6(7817)▪42:5(7817),
6(7817),11(7817)▪43:5(7817),25(7743)▪
55:15,23▪59:11▪72:6,11b▪73:18(5307)▪
75:7(8213)▪78:31(3766)▪86:1(5186)▪
88:4▪95:6(3766)▪104:8,22f▪107:12
(3665),12(3782),23,26▪115:17▪133:2^2▪
139:3(7252),143:7▪144:5▪147:6(8213)-PR-
1:12▪3:20(7491),24^{2}a▪5:5,27▪14:1
(8045)▪18:8▪21:22▪22:17(5186)▪23:34a▪
24:31d▪26:22-SONG-6:2,11-IS-2:9
(7817),11(7817),17(7817),5:15(7817),9:10
(1438)▪10:4(3766),13,33(1438)▪
11:6f,7f▪14:8a,11,12(1438),15,19,30f▪
17:2f▪22:10c,25(1438)▪25:5(3665),11
(8213),12(7817)▪26:5(7817)▪27:10f▪
29:4(8213)▪30:2,30(5183)▪31:1,4▪
32:19▪34:5,7▪38:18▪42:10▪43:14,17▪
44:15(5456),17(5456),19(5456),45:14b▪
46:1(3766),2(3766),6(5456)▪47:1▪
49:23b▪50:11a▪51:23b▪52:4▪55:10▪
56:10a▪60:14b▪63:14▪64:1,1sup,3▪
65:10(7257),12(3766)-JER-1:10sup,
10d▪3:25a▪4:26c▪6:15(3782)▪8:12
(3782)▪13:18sup,18▪18:2,3▪21:13
(5181)▪22:1▪31:28c,28d,40d▪33:4c,
12a▪36:12▪38:6(7971),11(7971)▪39:8c▪
45:4d▪48:5(4174),15,18▪49:16▪50:15d,
27▪51:40▪52:14c-LA-1:9▪2:2d,2sup,10,
17d-EZE-1:24(7503),25(7503)▪
6:4(5307),6(1438)▪13:14d▪16:39d,
39c▪17:24(8213)▪19:2(7257)▪26:4d,
9c,11sup,11,12d,16,20^2▪27:29▪
28:8▪30:4d,6▪31:14,15,16,17,18▪
32:18^2,19,21,24^2,25,27,29,30^2▪34:15a,
26▪38:20d▪47:1,8-DA-4:13(5182),
23(5182)▪5:19(8214)▪6:14(4606)▪
8:10(5307)▪11:12(5307),26-HO-2:18a▪
7:12-JOE-1:17d▪2:23▪3:2,11(5181),13
-AM-3:11▪6:2▪9:2-OB-3,4-JON-1:3^2,5▪
2:6-MIC-1:3,12▪5:11d-NA-1:6c-ZEP-2:7
(7257),14(7257),15(4769)▪3:13(4769)
-HAG-2:22-ZEC-10:11▪11:2-MAL-1:4d▪
N.T.-all=2597&marked-M'T-2:11
(4098)▪3:10(1581)▪4:6(2736),9(4098)▪
7:19(1581)▪8:1,11(347),32(2596)▪9:10
(347)▪11:23(2601)▪13:48(2523)▪14:19,
29▪15:29(2521),30(4496),35(377)▪17:9▪
21:8(2875)▪24:2(2647),17▪26:20(345)▪
27:5(4496),19(2521),36(2521),40,42
-M'R-2:4(2465),22▪5:13(2596)▪6:39
(347),40(377)▪8:6(377)▪9:9,35(2523)▪
11:8(2875)▪13:2(2647),15▪15:30,36
(2507),46(2507)-LU-1:52(2507)▪:51▪
3:9(1581)▪4:9(2736),20(2523),29(2630),
31(2718)▪5:3(2523),4(2565),5(2565),
19(2524),29(2621)▪6:17▪7:36(347)▪
8:5(2662),23,33(2596)▪9:14(2625),
15(347),37(2778),54▪10:15(2601),30,
31▪11:37(377)▪12:18(2507),37(347)▪
13:7(1581),9(1581),29(347)▪14:8(2625),
10(377),28(2523),31(2523)▪16:6(2523)▪
17:7(377),31▪18:14▪19:5,6▪21:6(2647)▪
22:14(377),44,55(4776),55(2521)▪
23:53(2507),24:12(3879)-JOH-2:12▪
3:13▪4:47,49,51▪5:4,7▪6:10^2(377),11(345),
16,33,38,41,42,50,51,58▪8:2(2523),6
(2736),8(2736)▪13:12(377)▪19:13
(2523)▪20:5(3879),11(3879)-AC-7:15,
34▪8:5(2718),15,26,38▪9:25(2524),
30(2609),32(2718)▪10:11(2524),20,21▪
11:5(2524)▪12:19(2718)▪13:14(2523),29
(2507)▪14:11,25▪15:1(2718)▪16:8,13(2523)▪
17:6(387)▪18:22▪20:9(2736),10▪21:10
(2718),32(2701)▪22:30(2609)▪23:10,15
(2609),20(2609)▪24:22▪25:5(4782),6,7▪
27:27(1308),30(5465)▪28:6(2667)-RO-
10:6(2609)▪11:3(2679),10(4781)▪16:4
(5294)-1CO-10:7(2523)▪15:24(2673)
-2CO-4:9(2598)▪7:6(5011)▪10:4(2506),
5(2504)▪11:33(5465)-EPH-4:26(1931)
-HEB-1:3(2523)▪10:12(2597)▪12:2
(3935),12(3935)-JAS-1:17-1JO-3:16
-RE-3:12,21(2523)▪10:1▪12:10(2598),
12▪13:13▪18:1▪20:1,9▪21:2

DOWNSITTING-PS-139:2(3427)

DOWNWARD-all=4295-2KI-19:30
-EC-3:21-IS-37:31-EZE-1:27▪8:2

DOWRY-all=4119&marked-GE-
30:20(2065)▪34:12-EX-22:17-1SA-18:25

DRAG-HAB-1:15(4365),16(4365)

DRAGGING-JOH-21:8(4951)

DRAGON-all=8577-NEH-2:13
-PS-91:13-IS-27:1▪51:9-JER-51:34
-EZE-29:3▪N.T.-all=1404-RE-12:3,
4,7^2,9,13,16,17▪13:2,4,11▪16:13▪20:2

DRAGONS-all=8577&marked
-DE-32:33-JOB-30:29-PS-44:19▪74:13▪
148:7-IS-13:22▪34:13▪35:7▪43:20
-JER-9:11▪10:22▪14:6▪49:33▪51:37
-MIC-1:8-MAL-1:3(8568)

DRAMS-all=1871&marked-1CH-
29:7(150)-EZR-2:69▪8:27(150)-NE-
7:70,71,72

DRANK-all=8354&marked-GE-
9:21▪24:46▪27:25▪43:34-NU-20:11
-DE-32:38-2SA-12:3-1KI-13:19-DA-
1:5(4960),8(4960)▪5:1(8355),3(8355),4
(8355)▪N.T.-all=4095-M'R-14:23
-LU-17:27,28-JOH-4:12-1CO-10:4

DRAUGHT-2KI-10:27(4280)▪
N.T.-M'T-15:17(856)-M'R-7:19(856)
-LU-5:4(61),9(61)

DRAVE-all=5090&marked-EX-
14:25-JOS-16:10(3423)▪24:12(1644),18
(1644)-J'G-1:19(3423)▪6:9(1644)-1SA-
30:20-2SA-6:3-2KI-16:6(5394)▪17:21
(5071)-1CH-13:7▪N.T.-AC-7:45(1856)▪
18:16(556)

DRAW-all=7579&marked-GE-24:11,
13,19,20,43,44-EX-12:21(4900)▪15:9
(7324)-LE-26:33(7324)-J'G-3:22(8025)▪
4:6(4900),7(4900)▪9:54(8025)▪20:32
(5423)-1SA-9:11▪31:4(8025)-2SA-17:13
(5498)-1CH-10:4(8025)-JOB-21:33
(4900)▪40:23(1518)▪41:1(4900)-PS-
28:3(4900)▪35:3(7324)▪85:5(4900)-PR-
20:5(1802)-SONG-1:4(4900)-IS-5:18
(4900)▪12:3▪57:4(748)▪58:10(6329)▪
66:19(4900)-JER-49:20(5498)▪50:45
(5498)-LA-4:3(2502)-EZE-5:2(7324),
12(7324)▪12:14(7324)▪21:3(3318)▪28:7
(7324)▪30:11(7324)▪32:20(4900)-NA-
3:14-HAG-2:16(2834)▪N.T.-all=1670
&marked-JOH-2:8(501)▪4:7(501),11
(502),15(501)▪6:44▪12:32▪21:6-AC-
20:30(645)-HEB-10:22(4334),38
(5288),39(5289)-JAS-2:6

DRAWER-DE-29:11(7579)

DRAWERS-all=7579-JOS-9:21,23,27

DRAWETH-J'G-19:19(7503)-JOB-
24:22(4900)-PS-10:9(4900)

DRAWING-J'G-5:11(4857)▪N.T.-
JOH-6:19(1096)

DRAWN-all=8388&marked-NU-
22:23(8025),31(8025)-DE-21:3(4900)▪
30:17(5080)-JOS-5:13(8025)▪8:6
(5423),16(5423)▪15:9^2,11▪18:14,17
-J'G-20:31(5423)-RU-2:9(7579)-1CH-
21:16(8025)-JOB-20:25(8025)-PS-
37:14(6605)▪55:21(6609)-PR-24:11
(3947)-IS-21:15(5203)▪28:9(6267)
-JER-22:19(5498)▪31:3(4900)-LA-2:3
(7725)-EZE-21:5(3318),28(6605)▪
N.T.-AC-11:10(385)-JAS-1:14(1828)

DREAD-all=6343&marked-GE-
9:2(2844)-EX-15:16-DE-1:29(6206)▪
2:25▪11:25(4172)-1CH-22:13(3372)
-JOB-13:11,21(367)-IS-8:13(6206)

DREADFUL-all=3372&marked
-GE-28:17-JOB-15:21(6343)-EZE-1:18
(3374)-DA-7:7(1763),19(1763)▪9:4
-HAB-1:7-MAL-1:14▪4:5

DREAM-all=2472,a=2493&marked
-GE-20:3,6▪31:10,11,24▪37:5,6,9^2,10▪
40:5^3,8,9^2,16▪41:7,8,11^2,12,15^2,17,22,
25,26,32-NU-12:6-J'G-7:13^2,15-1KI-
3:5,15-JOB-20:8▪33:15-PS-73:20▪
126:1-EC-5:3-IS-29:7-JER-23:28^2
-DA-2:3^2,4a,5a,6^{2}a,7a,9^{2}a,26a,28a,36a,
45a▪4:5a,6a,7a,8a,9a,18a,19^{2}a▪7:1^{2}a
-JOE-2:28(2492)▪N.T.-all=3677&
marked-M'T-1:20▪2:12,13,19,22▪
27:19-AC-2:17(1798)

DREAMED-all=2492-GE-28:12▪
37:5,6,9^2,10▪40:5,8▪41:1,5,11^2,15▪42:9
-J'G-7:13-JER-23:25▪29:8-DA-2:1,3

DREAMER-all=2492&marked
-GE-37:19(1167,2472)-DE-13:1,3,5

DREAMERS-JER-27:9(2492)▪
N.T.-JUDE-8(1797)

DREAMETH-IS-29:8^2(2492)

DREAMS-all=2472&marked-GE-
37:8,20▪41:12▪42:9-DE-13:1,3,5-1SA-
28:6,15-JOB-7:14-EC-5:7-JER-23:27,
32▪29:8-DA-1:17▪2:1,2▪5:12(2493)-JOE-
2:28-ZEC-10:2▪N.T.-AC-2:17(1797)

DREGS-PS-75:8(8105)-IS-51:17
(6907),22(6907)

DRESS-all=6213&marked-GE-2:15
(5647)▪18:7-DE-28:39(5647)-2SA-
12:4▪13:5,7-1KI-17:12▪18:23,25

DRESSED-all=6213-GE-18:8-LE-
7:9-1SA-25:18-2SA-12:4▪19:24-1KI-
18:26▪N.T.-HEB-6:7(1090)

DRESSER-LU-13:7(289)

DRESSERS-2CH-26:10(3755)

DRESSETH-EX-30:7(3190)

DREW-all=8025&marked-GE-24:20,
45(7579)▪37:28(4900)▪38:29(7725)
-EX-2:10(4871),16(1802),19(1802)
-JOS-8:26(7725)-J'G-8:10,20▪20:2,
15,17,25,35,37(4900),46-RU-4:8-1SA-
7:6(7579)▪17:51-2SA-22:17(4871)▪
23:16(7579)▪24:9-1KI-8:8(748)▪22:34
(4900)-2KI-3:26-1CH-11:18(7579)▪
19:16(3318)▪21:5^2(8025)-2CH-5:9
(748)▪14:8(1869)▪18:33(4900)-PS-18:16
(4871)-JER-38:13(4900)-HO-11:4(4900)▪
N.T.-all=1670&marked-M'T-13:48
(307)▪26:51(645)-M'R-6:53(4358)▪
14:47(4685)-LU-23:54(2020)-JOH-
2:9(501)▪18:10▪21:11-AC-5:37(868)▪
7:31(4334)▪14:19(4951)▪16:19,27(4635)▪
17:6(4951)▪19:33(4264)▪21:30▪27:27
(4317)-RE-12:4(4951)

DREWEST-all supplied

DRIED-all=3001&marked-GE-8:7,
13(2717),14-LE-2:14(7033)-NU-6:3
(3002)▪11:6-JOS-2:10▪4:23^2▪5:1-J'G-
16:7(2717),8(2717)-1KI-13:4▪17:7-2KI-
19:24(2717)-JOB-18:16▪28:4(1809)
-PS-22:15▪69:3(2787)▪106:9(2717)-IS-
5:13(6704)▪19:5,6(2717)▪37:25(2717)▪
51:10(2717)-JER-23:10▪50:38-EZE-
17:24▪19:12▪37:11-HO-9:16▪13:15
(2717)-JOE-1:10,12,20-ZEC-11:17▪
N.T.-all=3583-M'R-5:29▪11:20-RE-6:12

DRIEDST-PS-74:15(3001)

DRIETH-JOB-14:11(3001)-PR-17:22
(3001)-NA-1:4(2717)

DRINK-all=8354,a=5262,b=8248,c=
7941&marked-GE-19:32b,33b,34b,35b▪
21:19b▪24:14^2,14b,17(1572),18,18b,19b,
43b,44,45b,46,46b,54▪25:34▪26:30▪
30:38^2▪35:14a-EX-7:18,21,24^2▪15:23,
24▪17:1,2,6▪24:11▪29:40a,41a▪30:9a▪32:6,
20b▪34:28-LE-10:9,9c▪11:34(4945)▪
23:13a,18a,37a-NU-5:24b,26b,27b▪6:3c,
3,3c,3,15a,17a,20▪15:5a,7a,10a,24a▪20:5,
8b,17,19▪21:22▪23:24▪28:7^{2}a,8a,9a,10a,
14a,15a,24a,31a▪29:6a,11a,16a,18a,19a,
21a,22a,24a,25a,27a,28a,30a,31a,33a,34a,
37a,38a,39a▪33:14-DE-2:6,28▪9:9,18▪
14:26c▪28:39▪29:6c▪32:14,38(5257)-J'G-
4:19^{2}b▪7:5,6▪9:27▪13:4,4c,7c,7,14,14c▪
19:4,6,21-RU-2:9-1SA-1:15c▪30:11b
-2SA-11:11,13▪16:2▪19:35▪23:15b,16,17
-1KI-1:25▪13:8,9,16,17,18,22▪17:4,10▪
18:41,42▪19:6,8-2KI-3:17▪6:22▪7:8▪9:34▪
16:13a,15a▪18:27,31-1CH-11:17b,18,
19^2▪29:21a,22(8353)-2CH-28:15b▪29:35a
-EZR-3:7(4960)▪7:17(5261)▪10:6-NE-
8:10,12-ES-1:7b▪3:15▪4:16-JOB-1:4▪
21:20▪22:7b-PS-16:4a▪36:8b▪50:13▪
60:3b▪69:21b▪75:8▪78:15b,44▪80:5b▪
102:9(8249)▪104:11b▪110:7-PR-4:17▪
5:15▪9:5▪20:1c▪23:7▪25:21b▪31:4,4c,
5,6c,7-EC-2:24▪3:13▪5:18▪8:15▪9:7
-SONG-5:1,5(7937)▪8:2b-IS-5:11c,22,

22c■21:5■22:13■24:9,9c,9■28:7^{3}c■29:9c■32:6(4945)■36:12,16■43:20b■51:22■56:12c■57:6(5262)■62:8,9■65:11(4469),13-**JER**-2:18^2■7:18a■8:14b■9:15b■16:7b,8■19:13a■22:15■23:15b■25:15b,16,17b,26,27,28^2■32:29a■35:2b,5,6^2,8,14^2■44:17a,18a,19^{2}a,25a■49:12^2-**EZE**-4:11^2,16■12:18,19■20:28a■23:32,34■25:4■31:14,16■34:19■39:17,18,19■44:21■45:17a-**DA**-1:10(4960),12,16(4960)■5:2(8355)-**HO**-2:5(8250)■4:18(5435)-**JOE**-1:9a,13a■2:14a■3:3-**AM**-2:8,12b■4:1,8■5:11■6:6■9:14-**OB**-16^2-**JON**-3:7-**MIC**-2:11c■6:15-**HAB**-2:15b,16-**ZEP**-1:13-**HAG**-1:6,6(7937)-**ZEC**-7:6^2■9:15■**N.T.**-all=4095&marked-**M'T**-6:25,31■10:42(4222)■20:22,23■24:49■25:35(4222),37(4222),42(4222)■26:27,29^2,42■27:34^2-**M'R**-9:41(4222)■10:38,39■14:25^2■15:23,36(4222)■16:18-**LU**-1:15,15(4608)■5:30,33■12:19,29,45■17:8■22:18,30-**JOH**-4:7,9,10■6:53,55(4213)■7:37■18:11-**AC**-9:9■10:41(4844)■23:12,21-**RO**-12:20(4222)■14:17(4213),21-**1CO**-9:4■10:4,4(4188),7,21,31■11:22,25,26,27,28■12:13(4222)■15:32-**COL**-2:16(4213)-**1TI**-5:23(5202)-**RE**-14:8(4222),10■16:6

DRINKERS-**JOE**-1:5(8354)

DRINKETH-all=8354&marked-**GE**-44:5-**DE**-11:11-**JOB**-6:4■15:16■34:7■40:23(6231)-**PR**-26:6-**IS**-29:8■44:12■**N.T.**-all=4095-**M'T**-2:16-**JOH**-4:13,14■6:54,56-**1CO**-11:29^2-**HEB**-6:7

DRINKING-all=8354&marked-**GE**-24:19,22-**RU**-3:3-**1SA**-30:16-**1KI**-4:20■10:21(4945)■16:9■20:12,16-**1CH**-12:39-**2CH**-9:20(4945)-**ES**-1:8(8360)-**JOB**-1:13,18-**IS**-22:13■**N.T.**-all=4095-**M'T**-11:18,19■24:38-**LU**-7:33,34■10:7

DRINKS-**HEB**-9:10(4188)

DRIVE-all=3423,a=1644&marked-**EX**-6:1a■23:28a,29a,30a,31a■33:2a■34:11a-**NU**-22:6a,11a■33:52,55-**DE**-4:38■9:3,4,5■11:23■18:12-**JOS**-3:10■13:6■14:12■15:63■17:12,13,18■23:5,13-**J'G**-1:19,21,27,28,29,30,31,32,33■2:3(1644),21■11:24-**2KI**-4:24(5090)-**2CH**-20:7-**JOB**-18:11(6327)■24:3(5090)-**PS**-44:2■68:2(5086)-**IS**-22:19(1920)-**JER**-24:9(5080)■27:10(5080),15(5080)■46:15(1920)-**EZE**-4:13(5080)-**DA**-4:25(2957),32(2957)-**HO**-9:15a-**JOE**-2:20(5080)-**ZEP**-2:4(1644)■**N.T.**-**AC**-27:15(1929)

DRIVEN-all=5080&marked-**GE**-4:14(1644)-**EX**-10:11(1644)■22:10(7617)-**NU**-32:21(3423)-**DE**-4:19■30:1,4-**JOS**-23:9(3423)-**1SA**-26:19(1644)-**JOB**-6:13■13:25(5086)■18:18(1920)■30:5(1644)-**PS**-40:14(5472)■68:2(5086)■114:3(5437),5(5437)-**PR**-14:32(1760)-**IS**-8:22■19:7(5086)■41:2(5086)-**JER**-8:3■16:15■23:2,3,8■23:12(1760)■29:14,18■32:37■40:12■43:5■46:28■49:5■50:17-**EZE**-31:11(1644)■34:4,16-**DA**-4:33(2957)■5:21(2957)■9:7-**HO**-13:3(5590)-**MIC**-4:6-**ZEP**-3:19■**N.T.**-**LU**-8:29(1643)-**AC**-27:17(5342),27(1308)-**JAS**-1:6(416)■3:4(1643)

DRIVER-**1KI**-22:34(7395)-**JOB**-39:7(5065)

DRIVETH-**2KI**-9:20(5090)-**PS**-1:4(5086)-**PR**-25:23(2342)■**N.T.**-**M'R**-1:12(1544)

DRIVING-**J'G**-2:23(3423)-**2KI**-9:20(4491)-**1CH**-17:21(1644)

DROMEDARIES-**1KI**-4:28(7409)-**ES**-8:10(7424)-**IS**-60:6(1070)

DROMEDARY-**JER**-2:23(1072)

DROP-all=5197&marked-**DE**-32:2(6201)■33:28(6201)-**JOB**-36:28(5140)-**PS**-55:11(7491),12(7491)-**PR**-3:20(7491)■5:3-**SONG**-4:11-**IS**-40:15(4752)■45:8(7491)-**EZE**-20:46■21:2-**JOE**-3:18-**AM**-7:16■9:13

DROPPED-all=5197&marked-**J'G**-5:4-**1SA**-14:26(1982)-**2SA**-21:10(5413)-**JOB**-29:22-**PS**-68:8-**SONG**-5:5

DROPPETH-**EC**-10:18(1811)

DROPPING-**PR**-19:13(1812)■27:15(1812)-**SONG**-5:13(5197)

DROPS-**JOB**-36:27(5197)■38:28(96)-**SONG**-5:2(7447)■**N.T.**-**LU**-22:44(2361)

DROPSY-**LU**-14:2(5203)

DROSS-all=5509-**PS**-119:119-**PR**-25:4■26:23-**IS**-1:22,25-**EZE**-22:18^2,19

DROUGHT-all=2721&marked-**GE**-31:40-**DE**-8:15(6774)-**JOB**-24:19(6723)-**PS**-32:4(2725)-**IS**-58:11(6710)-**JER**-2:6(6723)■17:8(1226)■50:38-**HO**-13:5(8514)-**HAG**-1:11

DROVE-all=1644&marked-**GE**-3:24■15:11(5380)■32:16^2(5739)■33:8(4264)-**EX**-2:17-**NU**-21:32(3423)-**JOS**-15:14(3423)-**1CH**-8:13(1272)-**PS**-34t-**HAB**-3:6(5425)■**N.T.**-**JOH**-2:15(1544)

DROVES-**GE**-32:19(5739)

DROWN-**SONG**-8:7(7857)■**N.T.**-**1TI**-6:9(1036)

DROWNED-**EX**-15:4(2883)-**AM**-8:8(8248)■9:5(8248)■**N.T.**-**M'T**-18:6(2670)-**HEB**-11:29(2666)

DROWSINESS-**PR**-23:21(5124)

DRUNK-all=8354&marked-**LE**-11:34-**DE**-29:6■32:42(7937)-**J'G**-15:19-**RU**-3:7-**1SA**-1:9,15■30:12-**2SA**-11:13(7937)-**1KI**-13:22,23■16:9(7910)■20:16(7910)-**2KI**-6:23■19:24-**SONG**-5:1-**IS**-37:25■51:17■63:6(7937)-**JER**-46:10(7301)■51:57(7937)-**EZE**-34:18-**DA**-5:23(8355)-**OB**-16■**N.T.**-**LU**-5:39(4095)■13:26(4095)-**JOH**-2:10(3184)-**EPH**-5:18(3182)-**RE**-17:2(3182)

DRUNKARD-**DE**-21:20(5435)-**PR**-23:21(5435)■26:9(7910)-**IS**-24:20(7910)■**N.T.**-**1CO**-5:11(3183)

DRUNKARDS-all=7910&marked-**PS**-69:12(8354,7941)-**IS**-28:1,3-**JOE**-1:5-**NA**-1:10(5435)■**N.T.**-**1CO**-6:10(3183)

DRUNKEN-all=7937&marked-**GE**-9:21(7943)-**1SA**-1:13(7910),14■25:36(7910)-**JOB**-12:25(7910)-**PS**-107:27(7910)-**IS**-19:14(7910)■29:9■49:26■51:17(8354),21-**JER**-23:9(7910)■25:27■48:26■49:12■51:7,7(8354),39-**LA**-3:15(7301)■4:21■5:4(8354)-**EZE**-39:19(7943)-**NA**-1:10(5435)■3:11-**HAB**-2:15■**N.T.**-all=3184&marked-**M'T**-24:49-**LU**-12:45(3182)■17:8(4095)-**AC**-2:15-**1CO**-11:21-**1TH**-5:7-**RE**-17:6

DRUNKENNESS-**DE**-29:19(7302)-**EC**-10:17(8358)-**JER**-13:13(7943)-**EZE**-23:33(7943)■**N.T.**-all=3178-**LU**-21:34-**RO**-13:13-**GA**-5:21

DRY-all=3004,a=3001&marked-**GE**-1:9,10■7:22(2724)■8:13(2720)-**EX**-4:9,9(3006)■14:16,21(2724),22,29■15:19-**LE**-7:10(2720)■13:30(5424)-**JOS**-3:17^2(2724)■4:18(2724),22■9:5a,12a-**J'G**-6:37(2721),39(2721),40(2721)-**2KI**-2:8(2724)-**NE**-9:11-**JOB**-12:15a■13:25(3002)■15:30a-**PS**-63:1(6723)■66:6■68:6(6707)■95:5(3006)■105:41(6723)■107:33(6774),35(6723)-**PR**-17:1(2720)-**IS**-25:5(6724)■32:2(6724)■41:18(6723)■42:15^{2}a■44:3,27(2717),27a■50:2(2717)■53:2(6723)■56:3(3002)-**JER**-4:11(6703)■50:12(6723)■51:36(2717),36a,43(6723)-**EZE**-17:24(3002)■19:13(6723)■20:47(3002)■19:13(6723)■20:47(3002)■30:12(2724)■37:2(3002),4(3002)-**HO**-2:3(6723)■9:14(6784)■13:15(954)-**JON**-1:9■2:10-**NA**-1:4a,10(3002)-**ZEP**-2:13(6723)-**HAG**-2:6(2724)-**ZEC**-10:11a■**N.T.**-**M'T**-12:43(504)-**LU**-11:24(504)■23:31(3584)-**HEB**-11:29(3584)

DRYSHOD-**IS**-11:15(5275)

DUE-**LE**-10:13(2706),14(2706)-**DE**-18:3(4941)-**NE**-11:23(1697)-**PR**-3:27(1167)■**N.T.**-all=2398&marked-**M'T**-18:34(3784)-**LU**-23:41(514)-**1CO**-7:3(3784)-**GA**-6:9-**1TI**-2:6-**TIT**-1:3

DUES-**RO**-13:7(3782)

DUKE-all=441-**GE**-36:15^2,16,17^2,18,29^2,30,40,41,42,43-**1CH**-1:51,52,53,54

DUKES-all=441&marked-**GE**-36:15,16,17,18,19,21,29,30^2,40,43-**EX**-15:15-**JOS**-13:21(5257)-**1CH**-1:51

DULCIMER-all=5481-**DA**-3:5,10,15

DULL-**M'T**-13:15(917)-**AC**-28:27(917)-**HEB**-5:11(3576)

DUMB-all=481&marked-**EX**-4:11(483)-**PS**-38:13(483)■39:2,9-**PR**-31:8(483)-**IS**-35:6(483)■53:7■56:10(483)-**EZE**-3:26■24:27■33:22-**DA**-10:15-**HAB**-2:18(483),19(1748)■**N.T.**-all=2974&marked-**M'T**-9:32,33■12:22^2■15:30,31-**M'R**-7:37(216)■9:17(216),25(216)-**LU**-1:20(4623)■11:14^2-**AC**-8:32(880)-**1CO**-12:2(880)-**2PE**-2:16(880)

DUNG-all=6569&marked-**EX**-29:14-**LE**-4:11■8:17■16:27-**NU**-19:5-**1KI**-14:10(1557)-**2KI**-6:25(2755)■9:37(1828)■18:27(2716,6675)-**NE**-2:13(830)■3:13(830),14(830)■12:31(830)-**JOB**-20:7(1561)-**PS**-83:10(1828)-**IS**-36:12(2716,6675)-**JER**-8:2(1828)■9:22(1828)■16:4(1828)■25:33(1828)-**EZE**-4:12(1561),15(6832),15(1561)-**ZEP**-1:17(1561)-**MAL**-2:3^2■**N.T.**-**LU**-13:8(906,2874)-**PH'P**-3:8(4657)

DUNGEON-all=953&marked-**GE**-40:15■41:14-**EX**-12:29(104,953)-**JER**-37:16(104,953)■38:6^2,7,9,10,11,13-**LA**-3:53,55

DUNGHILL-**1SA**-2:8(830)-**EZR**-6:11(5122)-**PS**-113:7(830)-**IS**-25:10(4087)-**DA**-2:5(5122)■3:29(5122)■**N.T.**-**LU**-14:35(2874)

DUNGHILLS-**LA**-4:5(830)

DURABLE-**PR**-8:18(6276)-**IS**-23:18(6266)

DURETH-**M'T**-13:21(2076)

DURST-**JOB**-32:6(3372)■**N.T.**-all=5111-**M'T**-22:46-**M'R**-12:34-**LU**-20:40-**JOH**-21:12-**AC**-5:13■7:32-**JUDE**-9

DUST-all=6083&marked-**GE**-2:7■3:14,19^2■13:16^2■18:27■28:14-**EX**-8:16,17^2■9:9(80)-**LE**-14:41■17:13-**NU**-5:17■23:10-**DE**-9:21^2■28:24■32:24-**JOS**-7:6-**1SA**-2:8-**2SA**-16:13■22:43-**1KI**-16:2■18:38■20:10-**2KI**-13:7■23:12-**2CH**-1:9■34:4(1854)-**JOB**-2:12■4:19■5:6■7:5,21■10:9■14:19■16:15■17:16■20:11■21:26■22:24■27:16■28:6■30:19■34:15■38:38■39:14■40:13■42:6-**PS**-7:5■18:42■22:15,29■30:9■44:25■72:9■78:27■102:14■103:14■104:29■113:7■119:25-**PR**-8:26-**EC**-3:20■12:7-**IS**-2:10■5:24(80)■25:12■26:5,19■29:4^2,5(80)■34:7,9■40:12,15(7834)■41:2■47:1■49:23■52:2■65:25-**LA**-2:10■3:29-**EZE**-24:7■26:4,10(80),12■27:30-**DA**-12:2-**AM**-2:7-**MIC**-1:10■7:17-**NA**-1:3(80)-**HAB**-1:10-**ZEP**-1:17-**ZEC**-9:3■**N.T.**-all=2868&marked-**M'T**-10:14-**M'R**-6:11(5522)-**LU**-9:5■10:11-**AC**-13:51■22:23-**RE**-18:19(5522)

DUTY-**2CH**-8:14(1697)-**EZR**-3:4(1697)■**N.T.**-**LU**-17:10(3784)-**RO**-15:27(3784)

DWARF-**LE**-21:20(1851)

DWELL-all=3427,a=7931&marked-**GE**-4:20■9:27a■13:6^2■16:12a■19:30■20:15■24:3,37■26:2a■30:20(2082)■34:10^2,16,21,22,23■35:1■36:7■45:10■46:34■47:4,6^2■49:13a-**EX**-2:21■8:22(5975)■15:17■23:33■25:8a■29:45a,46a-**LE**-13:46■20:22■23:42^2,43■25:18,19■26:5,32-**NU**-5:3a■13:19^2,28,29^3■14:30a■23:9a■32:17■33:53,55■35:2,3,32,34^{2}a-**DE**-2:4,29^2■11:30,31■12:10^2,11a■13:12■17:14■23:16■25:5■28:30■30:20■33:12^{2}a,28a-**JOS**-9:7,22■10:6■13:13■14:4■15:63■16:10■17:12,16■20:4,6■21:2■24:13,15-**J'G**-1:21,27,35■6:10■9:41■17:10,11■18:1-**1SA**-12:8■27:5^2-**2SA**-7:2,5,10a-**1KI**-2:36■3:17■6:13a■8:12a,13(2073),27■17:9-**2KI**-4:13■6:1,2■17:27■25:24-**1CH**-17:1,4,9a■23:25a-**2CH**-2:3■6:1a,18■8:2,11■19:10-**EZR**-4:17(3488)■6:12(7932)-**NE**-8:14■11:1,2-**JOB**-3:5a■4:19a■11:14a■18:15a■19:15(1481)■30:6a-**PS**-4:8■5:4(1481)■15:1a■23:6■24:1■25:13(3885)■

27:4■37:3a,27a,29a■65:4a,8■68:6a,16,16a,18a■69:25,35,36a■78:55a■84:4,10(1752)■85:9a■98:7■101:6,7■107:4(4186),34,36■120:5a■132:14■133:1■139:9a■140:13■143:3-PR-1:33a■2:21a■8:12a■12:9,19■25:24-IS-6:5■9:2■11:6(1481)■13:21a■16:4(1481)■23:18■24:6■26:5,19a■30:19■32:16a■33:14^2(1481),16a,24■34:11a,17a■40:22■49:20■51:6■57:15a■58:12■65:9a-JER-4:29■7:3a,7a■8:16■9:26■12:4■20:6■23:6a,8■24:8■25:5,24a■27:11■29:5,28,32■31:24■32:37■33:16a■35:7,9,11,15■40:5,9,10^2■42:13,14■43:4,5(1481)■44:1^2,8(1481),13,14,26■47:2■48:9,28,28a■49:1,8,18(1481),30,31a,33(1481)■50:3,39^2,40(1481)■51:1-EZE-2:6■12:19■16:46■17:23^{2}a■28:25,26^2■32:15■34:25,28■36:28,33■37:25^2■38:8,11,12■39:6,9■43:7a,9a-DA-2:38(1753)■4:1(1753)■6:25(1753)-HO-9:3■12:9■14:7-JOE-3:20-AM-3:12■5:11-MIC-4:10a■7:13,14a-NA-1:5■3:18a-HAB-2:8,17-ZEP-1:18-HAG-1:4-ZEC-2:10a,11a■8:3a,4,8a■9:6■14:11■N.T.-all=2730&marked-M'T-12:45-LU-11:26■21:35(2521)-AC-1:20■2:14■4:16■7:4■13:27■17:26■28:16(3306)-RO-8:9(3611),11(3611)-1CO-7:12(3611),13(3611)-2CO-6:16(1774)-EPH-3:17-COL-1:19■3:16(1774)-1PE-3:7(4924)-1JO-4:13(3306)-RE-3:10■6:10■7:15(4637)■11:10^2■12:12(4637)■13:6(4637),8,12,14^2■14:6■17:8■21:3(4637)

DWELLED-all=3427&marked-GE-13:7,12^2■20:1-RU-1:4-1SA-12:11

DWELLERS-IS-18:3(7931)■N.T.-AC-1:19(2730)■2:9(2730)

DWELLEST-all=3427&marked-DE-12:29■19:1■26:1-2KI-19:15-PS-80:1■123:1-SONG-8:13-IS-10:24■37:16■47:8-JER-49:16(7931)■51:13(7931)-LA-4:21-EZE-7:7■12:2-OB-3(7931)-ZEC-2:7■N.T.-JOH-1:38(3306)-RE-2:13(2730)

DWELLETH-all=3427&marked-LE-19:34(1481)-NU-13:18-DE-33:20(7931)-JOS-6:25■22:19(7931)-1SA-4:4■27:11-2SA-6:2■7:2-1CH-13:6-JOB-15:28(7931)■38:19(7931)■39:28(7931)-PS-9:11■26:8(4908)■91:1■113:5■135:21(7931)-PR-3:29-IS-8:18(7931)■33:5(7931)-JER-29:16■44:2■49:31■51:43-LA-1:3-EZE-16:46■38:14-DA-2:22(8271)-HO-4:3-JOE-3:21(7931)-AM-8:8■N.T.-all=3306&marked-M'T-23:21(2730)-JOH-6:56■14:10,17-AC-7:48(2730)■17:24(2730)-RO-7:17(3611),18(3611),20(3611)■8:11(1774)-1CO-3:16(3611)-COL-2:9(2730)-2TI-1:14(1774)-JAS-4:5(2730)-2PE-3:13(2730)-1JO-3:17,24■4:12,15,16-2JO-2-RE-2:13(2730)

DWELLING-all=3427&marked-GE-10:30(4186)■25:27■27:39(4186)-LE-25:29(4186)-NU-21:15-JOS-13:21-1KI-8:30,39,43,49■21:8-2KI-17:25-1CH-6:32(4908),54(4186)-2CH-6:2,21,30,33,39■30:27(4583)■36:15(4583)-JOB-8:22(168)■21:28(4908)-PS-49:11(4908),14(2073)■52:5(168)■74:7(4908)■76:2(4585)■79:7(5116)■90:1(4583)■91:10(168)-PR-21:20(5116)■24:15(5116)-IS-4:5(4349)■18:4(4349)-JER-46:19■49:33(4583)-EZE-38:11■48:15(4816)-DA-2:11(4070)■4:25(4070),32(4070)■5:21(4070)-JOE-3:17(7931)-NA-2:11(4583)-ZEP-3:7(4583)■N.T.-all=2730&marked-M'R-5:3(2731)-AC-2:5■19:17-1TI-6:16(3611)-HEB-11:9(2730)-2PE-2:8(1460)

DWELLINGPLACE-NU-24:21(4186)-JER-51:37(4583)■N.T.-1CO-4:11(790)

DWELLINGPLACES-all=4908&marked-JER-30:18■51:30-EZE-6:6(4186)■37:23(4186)-HAB-1:6(4908)

DWELLINGS-all=4186&marked-EX-10:23-LE-3:17■7:26■23:3,14,21-LE-23:31-NU-35:29-JOB-18:19(4033),21(4908)■39:6(4908)-PS-55:15(4033)■87:2(4908)-IS-32:18(4908)-JER-9:19(4908)-EZE-25:4(4908)-ZEP-2:6(5116)

DWELT-all=3427&marked-GE-4:16■11:2,31■13:18■14:7,12,13(7931)■16:3■19:29,30^2■21:20,21■22:19■23:10■24:62■25:11,18(7931)■26:6,17■35:22(7931)■36:8■37:1■38:11■47:27■50:22-EX-2:15■12:40-LE-18:3■26:35-NU-14:25,45■20:15■21:1,25,31,34■31:10(4186)■32:40■33:40-DE-1:4^2,6,44■2:8,10,12^2,20,21,22^2,23^2■3:2■4:46■8:12■29:16■33:16(7931)-JOS-2:15■7:7■9:16■12:2,4■16:10■19:47,50■21:43■22:33■24:2,7,8,18-J'G-1:9,10,16,29^2,30,32,33■3:3,5■4:2,5■8:11(7931),29■9:21,41■10:1■11:3,26■15:8■18:7,28■21:23-RU-2:23-1SA-19:18■22:4■23:29■27:3,7■31:7-2SA-2:3■5:9■7:6■9:12(4186),13■14:28-1KI-2:38■4:25■7:8■9:16■11:24■12:2,17,25■13:11,25■15:18,21■17:5-2KI-13:5■15:5■16:6■17:24,28,29■19:36■22:14-1CH-2:55■4:23^2,28,40,41,43■5:8,10,11,16,22,23■7:29■8:28,29,32■9:3,16,34,35,38■10:7■11:7■17:5-2CH-10:17■11:5■16:2■19:4■20:8■26:7,21■28:18■30:25■31:4,6■34:22-EZR-2:70-NE-3:26■4:12■7:73■11:1,3^2,4,6,21,25,30(2583)■13:16-ES-9:19-JOB-22:8■29:25(7931)-PS-68:10■74:2(7931)■94:17(7931)■120:6(7931)-IS-13:20(7931)■29:1(2583)■37:37-JER-2:6■35:10■39:14■40:6■41:17■44:15■50:39(7931)-EZE-3:15■31:6,17■36:17■37:25■39:26-DA-4:12(1753),21(1753)-ZEP-2:15■N.T.-all=2730&marked-M'T-2:23■4:13-LU-1:65(4039)■13:4-JOH-1:14(4637),39(3306)-AC-7:2,4■9:22,32,35■11:29■13:17(3940)■19:10■22:12■28:30(3306)-2TI-1:5(1774)-RE-11:10

DYED-IS-63:1(2556)-EZE-23:15(2871)

DYING-NU-17:13(1478)■N.T.-all=599&marked-M'R-12:20-LU-8:42-2CO-4:10(3500)■6:9-HEB-11:21

E

EACH-all=259&marked-GE-15:10(376)-EX-30:34(905)-NU-1:44(376)■7:11,85^2■16:17(376)■29:14,15-JOS-22:14-RU-1:8(802),9(802)-1KI-4:7■22:10(376)-2KI-9:21(376)■15:20-2CH-4:13-IS-6:2■N.T.-LU-13:15(1538)-AC-2:3(1538)-PH'P-2:3(240)-2TH-1:3(240)-RE-4:8(303)

EAGLE-all=5404&marked-LE-1:13,18(7360)-DE-14:12,17(7360)■28:49■32:11-JOB-9:26■39:27-PR-23:5■30:19-JER-48:40■49:16,22-EZE-1:10■10:14■17:3,7-HO-8:1-OB-4-MIC-1:16-HAB-1:8■N.T.-RE-4:7(105)■12:14(105)

EAGLE'S-PS-103:5(5404)-DA-7:4(5403)

EAGLES-all=5404-2SA-1:23-PR-30:17-IS-40:31-JER-4:13-LA-4:19■N.T.-M'T-24:28(105)-LU-17:37(105)

EAGLES'-EX-19:4(5404)-DA-4:33(5403)

EAR-all=241,a=238&marked-EX-9:31(24)■15:26a■21:6■29:20^2-LE-8:23,24■14:14,17,25,28-DE-1:45a■15:17■32:1a-J'G-5:3a-1SA-8:12(2790)■9:15-2KI-19:16-2CH-24:19a-NE-1:6,11■9:30a-JOB-4:12■12:11■13:1■29:11,21(8085)■32:11a■34:2a,3■36:10■42:5-PS-5:1a■10:17■17:1a,6■31:2■39:12a■45:10■49:1a,4■54:2a■55:1a■58:4■71:2■77:1a■78:1a■80:1a■84:8a■86:1,6a■88:2■94:9■102:2■116:2■141:1a■143:1a-PR-2:2■4:20■5:1,13■15:31■17:4a■18:15■20:12■22:17■25:12■28:9-EC-1:8-IS-1:2a,10a■8:9a■28:23a■30:24(5647)■32:9a■37:17■42:23a■48:8■50:4,5■51:4a■55:3■59:1■64:4a-JER-6:10■7:24,26■9:20■11:8■13:15a■17:23■25:4■34:14■35:15■44:5-LA-3:56-DA-9:18-HO-5:1a-JOE-1:2a-AM-3:12■N.T.-all=3775&marked-M'T-10:27■26:51(5621)-M'R-4:28^2(4719)■14:47(5621)-LU-12:3■22:50,51(5621)-JOH-18:10(5621),26(5621)-1CO-2:9■12:16-RE-2:7,11,17,29■3:6,13,22■13:9

EARED-DE-21:4(5647)

EARING-GE-45:6(2758)-EX-34:21(2758)

EARLY-all=7925&marked-GE-19:2,27■20:8■21:14■22:3■28:18■31:55-EX-8:20■9:13■24:4■32:6■34:4-NU-14:40-JOS-3:1■6:12,15■7:16■8:10,14-J'G-6:28,38■7:1,3(6852)■9:33■19:5,8,9■21:4-1SA-1:19■5:3,4■9:26■15:12■17:20■29:10^2,11-2SA-15:2-2KI-3:22■6:15■19:35-2CH-20:20■29:20-JOB-1:5-PS-46:5(1242)■57:8(7837)■63:1(7836)■78:34(7836)■90:14(1242)■101:8(1242)■108:2(7837)■127:2-PR-1:28(7836)■8:17(7836)■27:14-SONG-7:12-IS-5:11■26:9(7836)■37:36-JER-7:13,25■11:7■25:3,4■26:5■29:19■32:33■35:14,15■44:4-DA-6:19(8238)-HO-5:15(7836)■6:4■13:3-ZEP-3:7■N.T.-all=260,4404&marked-M'T-20:1-M'R-16:2,9-LU-21:38(3719)■24:1(3722),22(3721)-JOH-8:2(3722)■18:28(4405)■20:1(4404)-AC-5:21(3722)-JAS-5:7(4406)

EARNEST-all=728&marked-RO-8:19(603)-2CO-1:22■5:5■7:7(1972)■8:16(4710)-EPH-1:14-PH'P-1:20(603)-HEB-2:1(4056)

EARNESTLY-NE-3:20(2734)-MIC-7:3(3190)■N.T.-all=816&marked-LU-22:44(1617),56-AC-3:12■23:1-1CO-12:31(2206)-2CO-5:2(1971)-JAS-5:17(4335)-JUDE-3(1864)

EARNETH-HAG-1:6(7936)

EARRING-all=5141-GE-24:22,30,47-JOB-42:11-PR-25:12

EARRINGS-all=5141&marked-GE-35:4-EX-32:2,3■35:22-NU-31:50(5694)-J'G-8:24^2,25,26-IS-3:20(3908)-EZE-16:12(5694)-HO-2:13

EARS-all=241,a=7641&marked-GE-20:8■35:4■41:5a,6a,7^{2}a,22a,23a,24a,26a,27a■44:18■50:4-EX-10:2■11:2■17:14■32:2,3-LE-2:14(24),14(3759)■23:14(3759)-NU-11:18■14:28-DE-5:1■23:25(4425)■29:4■31:28,30■32:44-JOS-20:4-J'G-7:3■9:2,3■17:2-RU-2:2a-1SA-3:11■8:21■11:4■15:14■18:23-2SA-3:19^2■7:22■22:7-2KI-4:42(3759)■18:26■19:28■21:12■23:2-1CH-17:20-2CH-6:40■7:15■34:30-NE-8:3-JOB-13:17■15:21■24:24a■28:22■33:16■36:15-PS-18:6■34:15■40:6■44:1■78:1■92:11■115:6■130:2■135:17-PR-21:13■23:9,12■26:17-IS-5:9■6:10^2■11:3■17:5^{2}a■22:14■30:21■32:3■33:15■35:5■36:11■37:29■42:20■43:8■49:20-JER-2:2■5:21■19:3■26:11,15■28:7^2■29:29■36:6^2,10,13,14,15^2,20,21^2-EZE-3:10■8:18■9:1■12:2■16:12■23:25■24:26■40:4■44:5-MIC-7:16-ZEC-7:11■N.T.-all=3775&marked-M'T-11:15■12:1(4719)■13:9,15^2,16,43■28:14(191)-M'R-2:23(4719)■4:9,23■7:16,33,35(189)■8:18-LU-1:44■4:21■6:1(4719)■8:8■9:44■14:35-AC-7:51,57■11:22■17:20(189)■28:27^2-RO-11:8-2TI-4:3(189),4(189)-JAS-5:4-1PE-3:12

EARTH-all=776,a=127,b=772&marked-GE-1:1,2,10,11^2,12,15,17,20,22,24^2,25,25a,26^2,28^2,29,30^2■2:1,4^2,5^2,6■4:11a,12,14a■6:1a,4,5,6,7a,11^2,12^2,13^2,17^2,20a■7:3,4,4a,6,8a,10,12,14,17^2,18,19,21^2,23,24■8:1,3,7,9,11,13,14,17^3,19,22■9:1,2,2a,7,10^2,11,13,14,16,17,19■10:8,25,32■11:1,4,8,9^2■12:3a■13:16^2■14:19,22■18:18,25■19:23,31^2■22:18■24:3,52■26:4,15(6083)■27:28,39■28:12,14,14a■37:10■41:47,56■42:6■43:26■45:7■48:12,16-EX-8:17,22■9:14,15,16,29,33■10:5^2,6a,15■15:12■19:5■20:4^2,11,24a■31:17■32:12a■33:16a■34:8,10-LE-11:2,21,29,41,42,44,46■15:12(2789)■26:19-NU-11:31■12:3a■14:21■16:30a,32,33,34■22:5,11■26:10-DE-3:24■4:10a,40a,17,18,26,32,36,39,40a■5:8^2■6:15a■7:6a■10:14■11:6,21■12:1a,16,19a,24■13:7^2■14:2a■26:2a■28:1,10,23,25,26,49,64■30:19■31:28■32:1,13,22■33:16,17-JOS-

2:11■3:11,13■4:24■5:14■7:6,9,21■23:14-**J'G**-3:25■5:4■6:4,37■18:10-**1SA**-2:8,10■4:5,12a■5:3■14:15■17:46^2,49■20:15a■24:8■25:41■26:8,20■28:13,20,23■30:16-**2SA**-1:2a,2■4:11■7:9,23■12:16,17,20■13:31■14:7a,11,20■15:32a■18:19,28■22:8,43■23:4-**1KI**-1:31,40,52■2:2■4:34■8:23,27,43,53,60■10:23,24■13:24a■17:14a■18:1a,42-**2KI**-5:15,17a■10:10■19:15^2,19-**1CH**-1:10,19■16:14,23,30,31,33■17:8,21■21:16■22:8■29:11,15-**2CH**-1:9■2:12■6:14,18,33■9:22,23■16:9■20:24■32:19■36:23-**EZR**-1:2■5:11b-**NE**-9:1a,6-**JOB**-1:7,8■2:2,3■3:14■5:10,22,25■7:1■8:9,19 6083)■9:6,24■11:9■12:8,15,24■14:8,19■15:19,29■16:18■18:4,17■19:25(6083)■20:4,27■22:8■24:4,18■26:7■28:2(6083),5,24■30:6(6083),8■34:13■35:11■37:3,6,12,17■38:4,13,18,24,26,33■39:14■41:33(6083)-**PS**-2:2,8,10■7:5■8:1,9■10:18■12:6■16:3■17:11■18:7■19:4■21:10■22:29■24:1■25:13■33:5,8,14■34:16■37:9,11,22■41:2■44:25■45:16■46:2,6,8,9,10■47:2,7,9■48:2,10■50:1,4■57:5,11■58:2,11■59:13■60:2■61:2■63:9■65:5,9■66:4■67:2,4,6,7■68:8,32■69:34■71:20■72:6,8,16^2,19■73:9,25■74:12,17,20■75:3,8■76:8,9,12■77:18■78:69■79:2■82:5,8■83:10a,18■85:11■89:11,27■90:2■94:2■95:4■96:1,9,11,13■97:1,4,5,9■98:3,4,9■99:1■102:15,19,25■103:11■104:5,9,13,14,24,30a,32,35■105:7■106:17■108:5■109:15■112:2■113:6■114:7■115:15,16■119:19,64,87,90,119■121:2■124:8■134:3■135:6,7■136:6■138:4■139:15■140:11■141:7■146:4a,6■147:8,15■148:7,11^2,13-**PR**-2:22■3:19■8:16,23,26,29,31■10:30■11:31■17:24■25:3■30:4,14,16,21,24-**EC**-1:4■3:21■5:2,9■7:20■8:14,16■10:7■11:2,3■12:7-**SONG**-2:12-**IS**-1:2■2:19(6083),19,21■4:2■5:8,26■6:3■8:22■10:14■11:4^2,9,12■12:5■13:13■14:7,9,16,26■18:3,6^2■23:8,9,17a■24:1,4^2,5,6^2,16,17,18,19^2,20,21a■25:8■26:9,15,18,19,21^2■28:2,22■30:23a■33:9■34:1■37:16^2,20■40:12,21,22,23,24,28■41:5,9■42:4,5,10■43:6■44:23,24■45:8,9a,12,18,19,22■48:13,20■49:6,8,13,23■51:6^2,13,16■52:10■54:5,9■55:9,10■58:14■60:2■61:11■62:7■63:6■65:16^2,17■66:1,8,22-**JER**-4:23,28■6:19,22■7:33■8:2a■9:3,24■10:10,11(778),11b,12,13■14:4■15:3,4,10■16:4a,4,19■17:13■19:7■22:29■23:5,24■24:9■25:26a,29,30,31,32,33^2■26:6■27:5■28:16a■29:18■31:8,22,37■32:17■33:9,25■34:1,17,20■44:8■46:8■49:21■50:23,41,46■51:7,15,16,25,41,48,49-**LA**-2:1,11,15■3:34■4:12-**EZE**-1:15,19,21■7:21■8:3,12■9:9■10:16,19■26:20■27:33■28:18■31:12,14,16,18■32:4,18,24■34:6,27■35:14■38:20^{2}a■39:14,18■43:2-**DA**-2:10(3007),35b,39b■4:1b,10b,11b,15^{2}b,20b,22b,23b,35^{2}b■6:25b,27b■7:4b,17b,23^{2}b■8:5■12:2a-**HO**-2:18,21,22,23■6:3-**JOE**-2:10,30■3:16-**AM**-2:7■3:2a,5,5a■4:13■5:7,8■8:9■9:6^2,8a,9-**JON**-2:6-**MIC**-1:2,3■4:13■5:4■6:2■7:2,17-**NA**-1:5■2:13-**HAB**-2:14,20■3:3,6,9-**ZEP**-2:3,11■3:8,20-**HAG**-1:10■2:6,21-**ZEC**-1:10,11^2■4:10,14■5:3,6,9■6:5,7^3■9:10■12:1,3■14:9,17-**MAL**-4:6■N.T.-all=1093&marked-**M'T**-5:5,13,18,35■6:10,19■9:6■10:34■11:25■12:40,42■13:5^2■16:19^2■17:25■18:18^2,19■23:9,35■24:30,35■25:18,25■27:51■28:18-**M'R**-2:10■4:5^2,28,31^2■9:3■13:27,31-**LU**-2:14■5:24■6:49■10:21■11:2,31■12:49,51,56■16:17■18:8■21:25,26(3625),33,35■23:44■24:5-**JON**-3:31^2■12:32■17:4-**AC**-1:8■2:19■3:25■4:24,26■7:49■8:33■9:4,8■10:11,12■11:6■13:47■14:15■17:24,26■22:22■26:14-**RO**-9:17,28■10:18-**1CO**-8:5■10:26,28■15:47-**EPH**-1:10■3:15■4:9■6:3-**PH'P**-2:10(1919),10(2709)-**COL**-1:16,20■3:2,5-**2TI**-2:20(3749)-**HEB**-1:10■6:7■8:4■11:13,38■12:25,26^2-**JAS**-5:5,7,12,17,18-**2PE**-3:5,7,10,13-**1JO**-5:8-**RE**-1:5,7■3:10■5:3,6,10,13■6:4,8^2,10,13,15■7:1^3,2,3■8:5,7,13■9:1,3^2,4■10:2,5,6,8■11:4,6,10^2,18■12:4,9,12,13,16^2■13:8,11,12,13,14^2■14:3,6,7,15,16^2,18,19^2■16:1,2,14,18■17:2^2,5,8,18■18:1,3^2,9,11,23,24■19:2,19■20:8,9,11■21:1^2,24

EARTHEN-all=2789&marked-**LE**-6:28■11:33■14:5,50-**NU**-5:17-**2SA**-17:28(3335)-**JER**-19:1■32:14-**LA**-4:2■N.T.-**2CO**-4:7(3749)

EARTHLY-all=1919&marked-**JOH**-3:12,31(1537,3588,1093)-**2CO**-5:1-**PH'P**-3:19-**JAS**-3:15

EARTHQUAKE-all=7494-**1KI**-19:11^2,12-**IS**-29:6-**AM**-1:1-**ZEC**-14:5■N.T.-all=4578-**M'T**-27:54■28:2-**AC**-16:26-**RE**-6:12■8:5■11:13^2,19■16:18^2

EARTHQUAKES-all=4578-**M'T**-24:7-**M'R**-13:8-**LU**-21:11

EARTHY-all=5517-**1CO**-15:47,48^2,49

EASE-all=7600-**DE**-23:13(3427)■28:65(7280)-**J'G**-20:43(4496)-**2CH**-10:4(7043),9(7043)-**JOB**-7:13(5375)■12:5■16:12(7961)■21:23(7946)-**PS**-25:13(2896)■123:4-**IS**-1:24(5162)■32:9,11-**JER**-46:27(7599)■48:11(7599)-**EZE**-23:42(7961)-**AM**-6:1-**ZEC**-1:15■N.T.-**LU**-12:19(373)

EASED-**JOB**-16:6(1980)■N.T.-**2CO**-8:13(425)

EASIER-**EX**-18:22(7043)■N.T.-all=2123-**M'T**-9:5■19:24-**M'R**-2:9■10:25-**LU**-5:23■16:17■18:25

EASILY-all supplied

EAST-all=6921,a=6924,b=4217&marked-**GE**-2:14(6926)■3:24a■4:16(6926)■10:30a■11:2a■12:8^{2}a■13:11a■25:6a■28:14a■29:1a■41:6,23,27-**EX**-10:13^2■14:21■27:13a■38:13a-**LE**-1:16a-**NU**-2:3a■3:38a■10:5a■23:7a■34:10a,11a■35:5a-**JOS**-4:19b■7:2a■11:3b■12:1,3^{2}b■15:5a■16:1b,5b,6b■17:10b■18:7b,20a■19:13a-**J'G**-6:3a,33a■7:12a■8:10a,11a■11:18b(8121)■21:19b(8121)-**1KI**-4:30a■7:25b-**1CH**-4:39b■5:10b■6:78b■9:24b■12:15b-**2CH**-4:4b,10a■5:12b■29:4b■31:14b-**NE**-3:26b,29b-**JOB**-1:3a■15:2■27:21■38:24-**PS**-48:7■75:6(4161)■78:26■103:12b■107:3b-**IS**-2:6a■11:14a■27:8■41:2b■43:5b■46:11b-**JER**-18:17■19:2(2777)■31:40b■49:28a-**EZE**-8:16^{2}a■10:19(6931)■11:1(6931),23a■17:10■19:12■25:4a,10a■27:26■39:11(6926)■40:6,22,23,32,44■41:14■42:9,10,12,15,16■43:1,2,4,17■44:1■45:7a,7■46:1,12■47:1,8(6930),18,18(6931),18■48:1,2,3,4,5,6,7,8^2,10,16,17,21,23,24,25,26,27,32-**DA**-8:9b■11:44b-**HO**-12:1■13:15-**JOE**-2:20(6931)-**AM**-8:12b-**JON**-4:5a,8-**HAB**-1:9-**ZEC**-8:7b■14:4a,4b■N.T.-all=395-**M'T**-2:1,2,9■8:11■24:27-**LU**-13:29-**REV**-7:2■16:12■21:13

EASTER-**AC**-12:4(3957)

EASTWARD-all=4217,a=6924&marked-**GE**-2:8a■13:14a■25:6a-**EX**-27:13■38:13-**LE**-16:14a-**NU**-3:38■32:19■34:3a,11a,15a-**DE**-3:17,27■4:49-**JOS**-11:8■13:8,27,32■16:6■19:12a■20:8-**1SA**-13:5(6926)-**1KI**-7:39a■17:3a-**2KI**-10:33(4217,8121)■13:17a-**1CH**-5:9■7:28■9:18■26:14,17-**NE**-12:37-**EZE**-11:1(6921)■40:10(6921),19(6921)■45:7(6921)■47:1(6921),2(6921),3(6921)■48:18(6921)

EASY-**PR**-14:6(7043)■N.T.-**M'T**-11:30(5548)-**1CO**-14:9(2154)-**JAS**-3:17(2138)

EAT-all=398&marked-**GE**-2:16,17■3:1,2,3,5,6^2,11,12,13,14,17^2,18,19,22■9:4■18:8■19:3■24:33^2,54■25:28(6310),34■26:30■27:4,7,10,19,25^2,31■28:20■31:46,54^2■32:32■37:25■39:6■40:17,19■41:4,20■43:25,32^2■45:18■47:22-**EX**-2:20■10:5^2,12,15■12:7,8^2,9,11^2,15,16,18,20^2,43,44,45,48■13:6■16:3,8,12,15(402),25,35^2■18:12■22:31■23:11^2,15■24:11■29:32,33^2■32:6■34:15,18,28-**LE**-3:17■6:16^2,18,26,29■7:6,19,21,23,24,26■8:31^2■10:12,13,14■11:2,3,4,8,9^2,11,21,22,39(402),42■17:12^2,14■19:25,26■21:22■22:4,6,7,8,10^2,11^2,12,13^2,14,16■23:6,14■24:9■25:12,19,20,22^2■26:5,10,16,26,29^2,38-**NU**-6:3,4■9:11■11:4,5,13,18^3,19,21■15:19■18:10^2,11,13,31■23:24■24:8■25:2-**DE**-2:6,28■4:28■8:9■9:9,18■11:15■12:7,15^2,16,17,18,20^3,21,22^2,23^2,24,25,27■14:3,4,6,7,8,9^2,10,11,12,20,21^2,23,26,29■15:20,22,23■16:3^2,7,8■18:1,8■20:6(2490),14,19■23:24■26:12■27:7■28:31,33,39,51,53,55,57■32:13,38-**JOS**-5:11,12■24:13-**J'G**-9:27■13:4,7,14^2,16■14:9■19:4,6,8,21-**RU**-2:14^2-**1SA**-1:7,18■2:36■9:13^3,19,24^2■14:32,33,34■20:24,34■28:22,23,25■30:11-**2SA**-3:35(1262)■9:7,10^2,11,13■11:11,13■12:3,17(1262),20,21■13:5,6(1262),9,10(1262),11■16:2■17:29■19:28,35-**1KI**-1:25■2:7■13:8,9,15,16,17,18,19,22■14:11^2■16:4^2■17:12,15■18:19,41,42■19:5,6,7,8,21■21:4,7,23,24^2-**2KI**-4:8^2,40^2,41,42,43^2,44■6:22,28^2,29^2■7:2,8,19■9:10,34,36■18:27,31■19:29^2■23:9■25:29-**1CH**-29:22-**2CH**-28:15■30:18,22■31:10-**EZR**-2:63■6:21■9:12■10:6-**NE**-5:2■7:65■8:10,12■9:25,36-**ES**-4:16-**JOB**-1:4■3:24(3899)■31:8■42:11-**PS**-14:4■22:26,29■27:2■41:9■50:13■53:4■78:24,25,29■102:4■105:35■127:2■128:2■141:4(3898)-**PR**-1:31■4:17(3898)■9:5(3898)■13:2■18:21■23:1(3898),6(3898),7■24:13■25:16,21,27■27:18■30:17-**EC**-2:24,25■3:13■5:11,12,18,19■6:2■8:15■9:7■10:16,17-**SONG**-4:16■5:1-**IS**-1:19■3:10■4:1■5:17■7:15,22^2■9:20^2■11:7■21:5■22:13■23:18■30:24■36:12,16■37:30^2■50:9■51:8^2■55:1,2■61:6■62:9■65:4,13,21,22,25-**JER**-2:7■5:17^4■7:21■15:16■16:8■19:9^2■22:15,22(7462)■29:5,28■41:1■52:33-**LA**-2:20-**EZE**-2:8■3:1^2,2,3^2■4:9,10^2,12,13,16■5:10^2■12:18,19■16:13■22:9■24:17,22■25:4■33:25■34:3,19(7462)■39:17,18,19■42:13■44:3,29,31-**DA**-1:12,13,15■4:25(2939),32(2939),33(399)-**HO**-2:12■4:8,10■8:13■9:3,4-**JOE**-2:26-**AM**-6:4■7:4,12■9:14-**OB**-1:7-**MIC**-3:3■6:14■7:1-**NA**-3:15-**HAB**-1:8-**HAG**-1:6-**ZEC**-7:6^2■11:9,16■N.T.-all=5315,a=2068-**M'T**-6:25,31■12:1a,4^2■14:16,20■15:2a,20,27a,32,37,38a■24:49a,26:17,21a,26-**M'R**-1:6a■2:16a,26^2■3:20■5:43■6:31,36,37^2,42,44■7:2a,3a,4a,5a,28a■8:1,2,8■11:14■14:12,14,18a,22a,22-**LU**-4:2■5:30a,33a■6:1a,4^2■7:36■9:13,17■10:8a■12:19,22,29,45a■14:1,15■15:16a,23■17:8,27a,28a■22:8,11,15,16,30a■24:43-**JOH**-4:31,32,33■6:5,23,26,31^2,49,50,51,52,53,58■18:28-**AC**-2:46(3335)■9:9■10:13,41(4906)■11:3(4906),7■23:12,14(1089),21■27:35a-**RO**-14:2,21,23-**1CO**-5:11(4906)■8:7a,8^2,10a,13■9:4■10:3,7,18a,25a,27a,28a,31a■11:20,22a,24,26a,27a,28a,33,34a■15:32-**GA**-2:12(4906)-**2TH**-3:8,10a,12a-**2TI**-2:17(3542,2192)-**HEB**-13:10-**JAS**-5:3-**RE**-2:7,14,17,20■10:9(2719)■17:16■19:18

EATEN-all=398&marked-**GE**-3:11,17■6:21■14:24■27:33■31:38■41:21^2(935,413,7130)■43:2-**EX**-12:46■13:3,7■21:28■22:5(1197)■29:34-**LE**-6:16,23,26,30■7:6,15,16^2,18,19■10:17,18,19■11:13,34,41,47^2■17:13■19:6,7,23■22:30-**NU**-28:17-**DE**-6:11■8:10,12■12:22■14:19■20:6(2490)■26:14■29:6■31:20-**JOS**-5:12-**RU**-3:7-**1SA**-1:9■14:30■28:20■30:12^2-**2SA**-19:42-**1KI**-13:22,23,28-**2KI**-6:23-**NE**-5:14-**JOB**-6:6■13:28■31:17^2,39-**PS**-69:9■102:9-**PR**-23:8-**SONG**-5:1-**IS**-3:14■5:5■6:13(1197)■44:19-**JER**-10:25■24:2,3,8■29:17■31:29-**EZE**-4:14■18:2,6,11,15■34:18(7462)■45:21-**HO**-10:13-**JOE**-1:4^3■2:25■N.T.-all=5315&marked-**M'T**-14:21(2068)-**M'R**-8:9-**LU**-13:26■17:8-**JOH**-2:17(2719)■6:13(977)-**AC**-10:10(1089),14■12:23(4662)■20:11(1089)■27:38(2880)-**RE**-10:10

EATER-all=398-**J'G**-14:14-**IS**-55:10-**NA**-3:12

EATERS-**PR**-23:20(2151)

EATEST-all=398-**GE**-2:17-**1SA**-1:8-**1KI**-21:5

EATETH-all=398&marked-**EX**-12:15,19-**LE**-7:18,20,25^2,27■11:40■14:47■17:10^2,14,15■19:8-**NU**-13:32-**1SA**-14:24,28-**JOB**-5:5■21:25■40:15-**PS**-106:20-**PR**-13:25■30:20■31:27-**EC**-4:5■5:17■6:2-**IS**-28:4(1104)■29:8■44:16■59:5-**JER**-31:30■**N.T.**-all=2068&marked-**M'T**-9:11-**M'R**-2:16■14:18-**LU**-15:2(4906)-**JOH**-6:54(5176),56(5176),57(5176),58(5176)■13:18(5176)-**RO**-14:2,3^3,6^3,20,23-**1CO**-9:7^2■11:29^2

EATING-all=398&marked-**EX**-12:4(400)■16:16(400),18(400),21(400)-**J'G**-14:9-**RU**-3:3-**1SA**-14:34■30:16-**1KI**-1:41■4:20-**2KI**-4:40-**1CH**-12:39-**JOB**-1:13,18■20:23(3894)-**IS**-22:13■66:17-**AM**-7:2■**N.T.**-all=2068&marked-**M'T**-11:18,19■24:38(5176)■26:26-**LU**-7:33,34■10:7-**1CO**-8:4(1035)■11:21(5315)

EBONY-**EZR**-27:15(1894)

EDGE-all=6310&marked-**GE**-34:26-**EX**-13:20(7097)■17:13(5310)■26:4^2(8193),5(7097),10^2(8193)■36:11(8193),12(7097),17^2(7097)-**NU**-21:24■33:6(7097),37(7097)-**DE**-13:15^2■20:13-**JOS**-6:21■8:24^2■10:28,30,32,35,37,39■11:11,12,14■13:27(7097)■19:47-**J'G**-1:8,25■4:15,16■18:27■20:37,48■21:10-**1SA**-15:8■22:19^2-**2SA**-15:14-**2KI**-10:25-**JOB**-1:15,17-**PS**-89:43(6697)-**EC**-10:10(6440)-**JER**-21:7■31:29(6949),30(6949)-**EZE**-18:2(6949)■43:13(8193)■**N.T.**-**LU**-21:24(4750)-**HEB**-11:34(4750)

EDGES-**EX**-28:7(7098)■39:4(7099)-**J'G**-3:13(6366)■**N.T.**-**RE**-2:12(1366)

EDIFICATION-all=3619-**RO**-15:2-**1CO**-14:3-**2CO**-10:8■13:10

EDIFIED-all=3618-**AC**-9:31-**1CO**-14:7

EDIFIETH-all=3618-**1CO**-8:1■14:4^2

EDIFY-**RO**-14:19(3619)-**1CO**-10:23(3618)-**1TH**-5:11(3618)

EDIFYING-all=3619&marked-**1CO**-14:5,12,26-**2CO**-12:19-**EPH**-4:12,16,29-**1TI**-1:4(3618)

EFFECT-**NU**-30:8(6565)-**PS**-33:10(5106)-**IS**-32:17(5656)-**JER**-48:30(6213)-**EZE**-12:23(1697)■**N.T.**-all=2673&marked-**M'T**-15:6(208)-**M'R**-7:13(208)-**RO**-3:3■4:14■9:6(1601)-**1CO**-1:17(2758)-**GAL**-3:17■5:4

EFFECTED-**2CH**-7:11(6743)

EFFECTUAL-**1CO**-16:9(1756)-**2CO**-1:6(1754)-**EPH**-3:7(1753)■4:16(1753)-**PH'M**-6(1756)-**JAS**-5:16(1754)

EFFECTUALLY-**GA**-2:8(1754)-**1TH**-2:13(1754)

EFFEMINATE-**1CO**-6:9(3120)

EGG-**JOB**-6:6(2495)■**N.T.**-**LU**-11:12(5609)

EGGS-all=1000-**DE**-22:6^2-**JOB**-39:14-**IS**-10:14■59:5^2

EIGHT-all=8083-**GE**-5:4,7,10,13,16,17,19■17:12■21:4■22:23-**EX**-26:2,25■36:9,30-**NU**-2:24■3:28■4:48■7:8■29:29■35:7-**DE**-2:14-**JOS**-21:41-**J'G**-3:8■12:14-**1SA**-4:15■17:12-**2SA**-23:8■24:9-**1KI**-7:10-**2KI**-8:17■10:36■22:1-**1CH**-12:24,30,35■16:38■23:3■24:4■25:7-**2CH**-11:21■13:3■21:5,20■29:17■34:1■36:9-**EZR**-2:6,16,23,41■8:11-**NE**-7:11,13,15,16,21,22,26,27,44,45■11:6,8,12,14-**EC**-11:2-**JER**-41:15■52:29-**EZE**-40:9,31,34,37,41-**MIC**-5:5■**N.T.**-all=3638-**LU**-2:21■9:28-**JOH**-5:5■20:26-**AC**-9:33-**1PE**-3:20

EIGHTEEN-all=8083,6240&marked-**GE**-14:14-**J'G**-3:1414■10:8■20:25,44-**2SA**-8:13-**1KI**-7:15-**2KI**-24:8■25:17-**1CH**-12:31■18:12■26:9■29:7(7239,8083)-**2CH**-11:21-**EZR**-8:9,18-**NE**-7:11-**JER**-52:21-**EZE**-48:35■**N.T.**-all=1176,2532,3638-**LU**-13:4,11,16

EIGHTEENTH-all=8083,6240-**1KI**-15:1-**2KI**-3:1■22:3■23:23-**1CH**-24:15■25:25-**2CH**-13:1■34:8■35:19-**JER**-32:1■52:29

EIGHTH-all=8066&marked-**EX**-22:30-**LE**-9:1■12:3■14:10,23■15:14,29■22:27■23:36,39■25:22-**NU**-6:10■7:54■29:35-**1KI**-6:38■8:66■12:32,33■16:29(8083)-**2KI**-15:8(8083)■24:12(8083)-**1CH**-12:12■24:10■25:15■26:5■27:11-**2CH**-7:9■29:17■34:3(8083)-**NE**-8:18-**EZE**-43:27-**ZEC**-1:1■**N.T.**-all=3590&marked-**LU**-1:59-**AC**-7:8-**PH'P**-3:5(3637)-**2PE**-2:5-**RE**-17:11■21:20

EIGHTIETH-**1KI**-6:1(8084)

EIGHTY-all=8084-**GE**-5:25,26,28

EITHER-all=176&marked-**LE**-10:1(376)■13:49,51,53,57,58,59■25:49-**NU**-6:2(376)-**1KI**-7:15(8145)■18:27(3588)-**1CH**-21:12(518)-**2CH**-18:9(376)-**EC**-9:1(1571)■**N.T.**-all=2228&marked-**M'T**-6:24■12:33-**LU**-6:42■15:8■16:13-**JOH**-19:18(1782,2532)-**AC**-17:21-**1CO**-14:6-**PH'P**-3:12-**JAS**-3:12-**RE**-22:2(1782,2532)

ELDER-all=1419&marked-**GE**-10:21■25:23(7227)■27:42■29:16-**1SA**-18:17-**1KI**-2:22-**JOB**-32:4(2205,3117)-**EZE**-16:46,61■23:4■**N.T.**-all=4245&marked-**LU**-15:25-**RO**-9:12(3187)-**1TI**-5:1,2,19-**1PE**-5:1(4850),5-**2JO**-1-**3JO**-1

ELDERS-all=2205&marked-**GE**-50:7^2-**EX**-3:16,18■4:29■12:21■17:5,6■18:12■19:7■24:1,9,14-**LE**-4:15■9:1-**NU**-11:16^2,24,25,30■16:25■22:4,7^2-**DE**-5:23■19:12■21:2,3,4,6,19,20■22:15,16,17,18■25:7,8,9■27:1■29:10■31:9,28■32:7-**JOS**-7:6■8:10,33■9:11■20:4■23:2■24:1,31-**J'G**-2:7■8:14,16■11:5,7,8,9,10,11■21:16-**RU**-4:2,4,9,11-**1SA**-4:3■8:4■11:3■15:30■16:4■30:26-**2SA**-3:17■5:3■12:17■17:4,15■19:11-**1KI**-8:1,3■20:7,8■21:8,11-**2KI**-6:32^2■10:1,5■19:2■23:1-**1CH**-11:3■15:25■21:16-**2CH**-5:2,4■34:29-**EZR**-5:5(7868),9(7868)■6:7(7868),8(7868),14(7868)■10:8,14-**PS**-107:32-**PR**-31:23-**IS**-37:2-**JER**-26:17■29:1-**LA**-1:19■2:10■4:16■5:12,14-**EZE**-8:1■14:1■20:1,3-**JOE**-1:14■2:16■**N.T.**-all=4245&marked-**M'T**-15:2■16:21■21:23■26:3,47,57,59■27:1,3,12,20,41■28:12-**M'R**-7:3,5■8:31■11:27■14:43,53■15:1-**LU**-7:3■9:22■20:1■22:52,66(4244)-**AC**-4:5,8,23■6:12■11:30■14:23■15:2,4,6,22,23■16:4■20:17■21:18■22:5(4244)■23:14■24:1■25:15-**1TI**-5:17-**TIT**-1:5-**HEB**-11:2-**JAS**-5:14-**1PE**-5:1-**RE**-4:4,10■5:5,6,8,11,14■7:11,13■11:16■14:3■19:4

ELDEST-all=1419&marked-**GE**-24:2(2205)■27:1,15■44:12-**NU**-1:20(1060)■26:5(1060)-**1SA**-17:13,14,28-**2KI**-3:27(1060)-**2CH**-22:1(7223)-**JOB**-1:13(1060),18(1060)■**N.T.**-**JOH**-8:9(4245)

ELECT-all=972-**IS**-42:1■45:4■65:9,22■**N.T.**-all=1588-**M'T**-24:24,31-**M'R**-13:22,27-**LU**-18:7-**RO**-8:33-**COL**-3:12-**1TI**-5:21-**TIT**-1:1-**1PE**-1:2■2:6-**2JO**-1:1,13

ELECTED-**1PE**-5:13(4899)

ELECTION-all=1589-**RO**-9:11■11:5,7,28-**1TH**-1:4-**2PE**-1:10

ELECT'S-all=1588-**M'T**-24:22-**M'R**-13:20-**2TI**-2:10

ELEMENTS-all=4747-**GA**-4:3,9-**2PE**-3:10,12

ELEVEN-all=559,6240&marked-**GE**-32:22■37:9-**EX**-26:7(6249,6240),8(6249,6240)■36:14(6249,6240),15(6249,6240)-**NU**-29:20(6249,6240)-**DE**-1:2-**JOS**-15:51-**J'G**-16:5(505,3967)■17:2(505,3967),3(505,3967)-**2KI**-23:36■24:18-**2CH**-36:5,11-**JER**-52:1-**EZE**-40:49(6249,6240)■**N.T.**-all=1733-**M'T**-28:16-**M'R**-16:14-**LU**-24:9,33-**AC**-1:26■2:14

ELEVENTH-all=6249,6240-**NU**-7:72-**DE**-1:3-**1KI**-6:38(259,6240)-**2KI**-9:29(259,6240)-**1CH**-12:13■24:12■25:18■27:14-**JER**-1:3■39:2■52:5-**EZE**-26:1■30:20(259,6240)■31:1(259,6240)-**ZEC**-1:7■**N.T.**-all=1734-**M'T**-20:6,9-**RE**-21:20

ELMS-**HO**-4:13(424)

ELOQUENT-**EX**-4:10(376,1697)-**IS**-3:3(995)■**N.T.**-**AC**-18:24(3052)

ELSE-all=5750&marked-**GE**-30:1(369)■42:16(518,3808)-**EX**-8:21(3588)■10:4(3588)-**DE**-4:35,39-**JOS**-23:12(3588)-**1KI**-8:60-**1CH**-21:12(518)-**IS**-45:5,6,14,18,21,22■46:9■47:8,10-**JOE**-2:27■**N.T.**-all=1490&marked-**M'T**-9:17-**M'R**-2:21,22-**LU**-5:37■14:32-**JOH**-14:11-**AC**-17:21(2087)-**RO**-2:15(2532)-**1CO**-7:14(1893,686)■14:16(1893)■15:29(1893)-**RE**-2:5,16

EMBALM-**GE**-50:2(2590)

EMBALMED-all=2590-50:2,3,26

EMBOLDENED-**1CO**-8:10(3618)

EMBOLDENETH-**JOB**-16:3(4834)

EMBRACE-all=2263-**2KI**-4:16-**JOB**-24:8-**PR**-4:8■5:20-**EC**-3:5-**SONG**-2:6■8:3-**LA**-4:5

EMBRACED-all=2263-**GE**-29:13■33:4■48:10■**N.T.**-**AC**-20:1(782)-**HEB**-11:3(782)

EMBRACING-**EC**-3:5(2263)■**N.T.**-**AC**-20:10(4843)

EMBROIDER-**EX**-28:39(7660)

EMBROIDERER-**EX**-35:35(7551)■38:23(7551)

EMERALD-all=5036-**EX**-28:18■39:11-**EZE**-28:13■**N.T.**-**RE**-4:3(4664)■21:19(4665)

EMERALDS-**EZE**-27:16(5306)

EMERODS-all=6076&marked-**DE**-28:27-**1SA**-5:6,9,12■6:4,5,11(2914),17(2914)

EMINENT-all=1354&marked-**EZE**-16:24,31,39■17:22(8524)

EMPIRE-**ES**-1:20(4438)

EMPLOY-**DE**-20:19(935,6640)

EMPLOYED-**1CH**-9:33(5921)-**EZR**-10:15(5975)

EMPLOYMENT-allsupplied

EMPTIED-**GE**-24:20(6168)■42:35(7324)-**2CH**-24:11(6168)-**NE**-5:13(7386)-**IS**-19:6(1809)■24:3(1238)-**JER**-48:11(7324)-**NA**-2:2(1238)

EMPTIERS-**NA**-2:2(1238)

EMPTINESS-**IS**-34:11(922)

EMPTY-all=7387&marked-**GE**-31:42■37:24(7386)■41:27(7386)-**EX**-3:21■23:15■34:20-**LE**-14:36(6437)-**DE**-15:13■16:16-**J'G**-7:16(7385)-**RU**-1:21■3:17-**1SA**-6:3■20:18(6485),25(6485),27(6485)-**2SA**-1:22-**2KI**-4:3(7385)-**JOB**-22:9■26:7(8414)-**EC**-11:3(7324)-**IS**-24:1(1238)■29:8(7385)■32:6(7324)-**JER**-14:3■48:12(7324)■51:2(1238),34(7385)-**EZE**-24:11(7385)-**HO**-10:1(1238)-**NA**-2:10(950)-**HAB**-1:17(7324)-**ZEC**-4:12(7324)■**N.T.**-all=2756&marked-**M'T**-12:44(4980)-**M'R**-12:3-**LU**-1:53■20:10,11

EMULATION-**RO**-11:14(3863)

EMULATIONS-**GA**-5:20(2205)

ENABLED-**1TI**-1:12(1743)

ENCAMP-all=2583-**EX**-14:2^2-**NU**-1:50■2:17,27■3:38■10:31-**2SA**-12:28-**JOB**-19:12-**PS**-27:3-**ZEC**-9:8

ENCAMPED-all=2583-**EX**-13:20■15:27■18:5-**NU**-33:10,11,12,13,14,17,24,26,30,32,34,35,46-**JOS**-4:19■5:10■10:5,31,34-**J'G**-6:4■9:50■10:17^2■20:19-**1SA**-11:1■13:16-**2SA**-11:11-**1KI**-16:15,16-**1CH**-11:15-**2CH**-32:1

ENCAMPETH-all=2583-**PS**-34:7■53:5

ENCAMPING-**EX**-14:9(2583)

ENCHANTER-**DE**-18:10(5172)

ENCHANTERS-**JER**-27:9(6049)

ENCHANTMENT-**LE**-19:26(5172)-**NU**-23:23(5172)-**EC**-10:11(3908)

ENCHANTMENTS-all=5172&marked-**EX**-7:11(3858),22(3909)■8:7

(3909),18(3909)-NU-24:1-2KI-17:17■21:6-2CH-33:6-IS-47:9(2267),12(2267)

ENCOUNTERED-AC-17:18(4820)

ENCOURAGE-all=2388-DE-1:38■3:28-2SA-11:25-PS-64:5

ENCOURAGED-all=2388-J'G-20:22-1SA-30:6-2CH-31:4■35:2-IS-41:7

END-all=7097,a=3615,b=7093&marked-GE-6:13b■8:3,6b■23:9■27:30a■41:1b■47:21^2■49:33a-EX-8:22(4616)■12:41b■23:16(3318)■25:19^2(7098)■26:28■31:18a■34:22(8622)■36:33■37:8^2(7098)-LE-8:33(4390)■16:20a■17:5(4616)-NU-4:15a■16:31a-DE-9:11b■11:12(319)■13:7^2■14:28■15:1b■17:16(4616),20(4616)■20:9a■26:12a■28:49,64■31:10b,24a■32:20(319),45a-JOS-8:24a■9:16■10:20a■15:5,8■18:15,16,19■19:49a,51a-J'G-3:18a■6:21■11:39b■15:17a■19:9(2583)-RU-2:23a■3:7-1SA-3:12a■9:27■10:13a■13:10a■14:27,43■18:1a■24:16a-2SA-6:18a■11:19a■13:36a■14:26b■24:8-1KI-1:41a■2:39b■3:1a■7:40a■8:54a■9:10-2KI-8:3■10:21(6310),25a■18:10■21:16(6310)-1CH-16:2a-2CH-7:1a■8:1b■20:16(5490),23a■21:19b■24:10a,23(8622)■29:17a,29a-EZR-9:11(6310)■10:17a-NE-3:21(8503)■4:2a-JOB-6:11b■16:3b■18:2(7078)■26:10(8503)■28:3b■34:36(5331)-PS-7:9(1584)■9:6(8552)■19:4,6■30:12(4616)■37:37(319),38(319)■39:4b■46:9■61:2■73:17(319)■102:27(8552)■107:27(1104)■119:33(6118),96b,112(6118)-PR-5:4(319)■14:12(319),13(319)■16:25(319)■20:21(319)■23:18(319)■25:8(319)-EC-3:11(5490)■4:8b,16b■7:2(5490),8(319),14(1700)■10:13(319)■12:12b-IS-2:7^2■5:26■7:3■9:7b■13:5b■16:4(657)■23:15b,17b■33:1(5239)■38:12(7999),13(7999)■42:10■45:17(5704,5769,5703)■46:10(319)■48:20■49:6■62:11-JER-1:3(8537)■3:5(5331)■4:27a■5:10a,18a,31(319)■12:12^2■17:11(319)■25:33^2■26:8a■29:11(319)■30:11^{2}a■31:17(319)■34:14b■43:1a■44:27a■46:28^{2}a■51:13b,31,63a-LA-4:18^{2}b-EZE-3:16■7:2b,3b,6b■11:13a■20:17a,26(4616)■21:25b,29b■29:13b■31:14(4616)■35:5b■39:14■41:12(6285)■42:15a■43:23a■48:1-DA-1:5(7117),15(7117),18(7117)■4:11(5491),22(5491),29(7118),34(7118)■6:26(5491)■7:26(5491),28(5491)■8:17b,19b■9:24(2856),26^{2}b■11:6b,27b,35b,40b,45b■12:4b,6b,8(319),9b,13^{2}b-AM-3:15(5486)■7:2a■8:2b,10(319)-OB-9(4616)-NA-1:8a,9a■2:9■3:3-HAB-2:3b■N.T.-all=5056&marked-M'T-10:22■11:1(5055)■13:39(4930),40(4930),49(4930)■24:3(4930),6,13,14,31(206)■26:58■28:1(3796),20(4930)-M'R-3:26■13:7,13-LU-1:33■21:9■22:37-JOH-13:1-AC-7:19(1519)-RO-1:11(1519)■4:16(1519)■6:21,22■10:4-1CO-1:8■15:24-2CO-1:13■3:13■11:15-EPH-3:21(165,3588)-PH'P-3:19-1TH-3:13(1519)-1TI-1:5-HEB-3:6,14■6:8,11,16(4009)■7:3■9:26(4930)■13:7(1545)-JAS-5:11-1PE-1:9,13(5049)■4:7,17-2PE-2:20(2078)-RE-2:26■21:6■22:13

ENDAMAGE-EZR-4:13(5142)

ENDANGER-DA-1:10(2325)

ENDANGERED-EC-10:9(5533)

ENDEAVOUR-2PE-1:15(4704)

ENDEAVOURED-AC-16:10(2212)-1TH-2:17(4704)

ENDEAVOURING-EPH-4:4(4704)

ENDEAVOURS-PS-28:4(4611)

ENDED-all=3615&marked-GE-2:2■41:53■47:18(8552)-DE-31:30(8552)■34:8(8552)-RU-2:21-2SA-20:18(8552)-1KI-7:51(7999)-2CH-29:34-JOB-31:40(8552)-PS-72:20-IS-60:20(7999)-JER-8:20-EZE-4:8■N.T.-all=4931&marked-M'T-7:28-LU-4:2,13■7:1(4137)-JOH-13:2(1096)-AC-19:21(4137)■21:27

ENDETH-IS-24:8(2308)

ENDING-RE-1:8(5056)

ENDLESS-1TI-1:4(562)-HEB-7:16(179)

ENDOW-EX-22:16(4117)

ENDS-all=7098,a=657&marked-EX-25:18,19■28:14(4020),22(1383),23,24,25,26■37:7,8(7099)■38:5(7099)■39:15(1383),16,17,18,19-DE-33:17a-1SA-2:10a-1KI-8:8(7218)-2CH-5:9(7218)-JOB-28:24■37:3(3671)■38:13(3671)-PS-19:6■22:27a■48:10(7099)■59:13a■65:5(7099)■67:7a■72:8a■98:3a■135:7(7097)-PR-17:24(7097)■30:4a-IS-26:15(7097)■40:28■41:5,9■43:6(7097)■45:22a■52:10a-JER-10:13(7097)■16:19a■25:31(7097)■51:16(7097)-EZE-15:4-MIC-5:4a-ZEC-9:10a■N.T.-AC-13:47(2078)-RO-10:18(4009)-1CO-10:11(5056)

ENDUED-GE-30:20(2064)-2CH-2:12(3045),13(3045)■N.T.-LU-42:49(1746)-JAS-3:13(1990)

ENDURE-all=5975&marked-GE-33:14(7272)-EX-18:23-ES-8:6^2(3201)-JOB-8:15(6965)-PS-9:7(3427)■30:5(3885)■72:5(6440),17(1961)■89:36(1961)■102:12(3427),26■104:31(1961)-EZE-22:14■N.T.-all=5278&marked-M'T-24:13-M'R-4:17(2076)■13:13-2TH-1:4(430)-2TI-2:3(2553),10■4:3(430),5(2553)-HEB-12:7,20(5342)-JAS-5:11-1PE-5:19(5297)

ENDURED-PS-81:15(1961)■N.T.-all=2578&marked-RO-9:22(5342)-2TI-3:11(5297)-HEB-6:15(3114)■10:32■11:27(2594)■12:2,3

ENDURETH-all=5975&marked-PS-72:7(1097)■111:3,10■112:3,9■N.T.-all=5278&marked-M'T-10:22-JOH-6:27(3306)-1CO-13:7-JAS-1:12-1PE-1:25(3306)

ENDURING-PS-19:9(5975)■N.T.-2CO-1:6(5281)-HEB-10:34(3306)

ENEMIES-all=341,a=6862&marked-GE-14:20a■22:17■49:8-EX-1:10(8130)■23:22,27■32:25(6965)-LE-26:7,8,16,17,32,36,37,38,41,44-NU-10:9,35■14:42■23:11■24:8a,10,18■32:21-DE-1:42■6:19■12:10■20:1,3,4,14■21:10■23:9,14■25:19■28:7,25,31,48,53,55,68■30:7■32:31,41a■33:7a,29-JOS-7:8,12^2,13■10:13,19,25■21:44^2■22:8■23:1-J'G-2:14^2,18■3:28■5:31■8:34■11:36-IS-2:1■4:3■12:10,11■14:24,30,47■18:25■20:15,16■25:22,26,29■29:8■30:26-2SA-3:18■5:20■7:1,9,11■12:14■18:19,32■19:6(8130),9■22:1,4,38,41,49■24:13a-1KI-3:11■8:48-2KI-17:39■21:14^2-1CH-12:17a■14:11■17:8,10■21:12■22:9-2CH-1:11(8130)■6:28,34,36■20:27,29-NE-4:15■5:9■6:1,16■9:27^{2}a,28-ES-8:13■9:1,5,16,22-JOB-19:11a-PS-3:7■5:8(8324)■6:7(6887),10■7:6(6887)■8:2(6887)■9:3■10:5(6887)■17:9■18:t,3,37,40,48■21:8■23:5(6887)■25:2,19■27:2a,6,11(8324),12a■31:11(6887),15■35:19■37:20■38:19■41:2,5■42:10(6887)■44:5a,7a■45:5■54:5(8324),7■56:2(8324),9■59:1,10(8324)■60:12a■66:3■68:1,21,23■69:4,18■71:10■72:9■74:4(6887),23(6887)■78:53,66a■80:6■81:14■83:2■89:10,42,51■92:9^2,11(7790)■97:3a■102:8■105:24a■106:11a,42■108:13a■110:1,2■112:8a■119:98,139a,157a■127:5■132:18■136:24a■138:7■139:20(6145),22■143:9,12-PR-16:7-IS-1:24■9:11■26:11a■42:13■59:18■62:8■66:6,14-JER-12:7■15:9,14■17:4■19:7,9■20:4,5■21:7■34:20,21■44:30■48:5a■49:37-LA-1:2,5,21■2:16■3:46,52-EZE-39:23a-DA-4:19(6146)-AM-9:4-MIC-4:10■5:9■7:6-NA-1:2,8■3:13-ZEC-10:5■N.T.-all=2190-M'T-5:44■22:44-M'R-12:36-LU-1:71,74■6:27,35■19:27,43■20:43-RO-5:10■11:28-1CO-15:25-PH'P-3:18-COL-1:21-HEB-1:13■10:13-RE-11:5,12

ENEMIES'-all=341-LE-26:34,39-EZE-39:27

ENEMY-all=341&marked-EX-15:6,9■23:22(340)-LE-26:25-NU-10:9■35:23-DE-28:57■32:27,42■33:27-J'G-16:23,24-IS-2:32(6862)■18:29■19:17■24:4,19■26:8■28:16(6145)-2SA-4:8■22:18-1KI-8:33,37,44,46^2■21:20-2CH-6:24■25:8■26:13-EZR-8:22,31-ES-3:10(6887)■7:4(6862),6■8:1(6887)■9:10(6887),24(6887)-JOB-13:24■16:9(6862)■27:7■33:10-PS-7:4(6887),5■8:2■9:6■13:2,4■18:17■31:8■41:11■42:9■43:2■44:10(6862),16■55:3,12■61:3■64:1■74:3,10,18■78:42(6862)■89:22■106:10■107:2(6862)■143:3-PR-24:17■25:21(8130)■27:6(8130)-IS-59:19(6862)■63:10-JER-6:25■15:11■18:17■30:14■31:16■44:30-LA-1:5(6862),7(6862),9,16■2:3,4,5,7,17,22■4:12-EZE-36:2-HO-8:3-MIC-2:8■7:8,10-NA-3:11-ZEP-3:15■N.T-all=2190-M'T-5:43■13:25,28,39-LU-10:19-AC-13:10-RO-12:20-1CO-15:26-GAL-4:16-2TH-3:15-JAS-4:4

ENEMY'S-EX-23:4(341)-JOB-6:23(6862)-PS-78:61(6862)

ENFLAMING-IS-57:5(2552)

ENGAGED-JER-30:21(6148)

ENGINES-2CH-26:15(2810)-EZE-26:9(4239)

ENGRAFTED-JAS-1:21(1721)

ENGRAVE-EX-28:11(6605)-ZEC-3:9(6605)

ENGRAVEN-2CO-3:7(1795)

ENGRAVER-all=2796-EX-28:11■35:35■38:23

ENGRAVINGS-all=6603-EX-28:11,21,36■39:14,30

ENJOIN-PH'M-8(2004)

ENJOINED-ES-9:31(6965)-JOB-36:23(6485)■N.T.-HEB-9:20(1781)

ENJOY-all=7200&marked-LE-26:34^2(7521),43(7521)-NU-36:8(3423)-DE-28:41(1961)-JOS-1:15(3423)-EC-2:1,24■3:13■5:18-IS-65:22(1086)■N.T.-AC-24:2(5177)-1TI-6:17(619)-HEB-11:25(2192,619)

ENJOYED-2CH-36:21(7521)

ENLARGE-all=7337&marked-GE-9:27(6601)-EX-34:24-DE-12:20■19:8-1CH-4:10(7235)-PS-119:32-IS-54:2-AM-1:3-MIC-1:16■N.T.-M'T-23:5(3170)

ENLARGED-all=7337-1SA-2:1-2SA-22:37-PS-4:1■18:36■25:17-IS-5:14■57:8■60:5■N.T.-2CO-6:11(4115),13(4115)■10:15(3170)

ENLARGEMENT-ES-4:14(7305)

ENLARGETH-DE-33:20(7337)-JOB-12:23(7849)-HAB-2:5(7337)

ENLARGING-EZE-41:7(7337)

ENLIGHTEN-PS-18:28(5050)

ENLIGHTENED-all=215-1SA-14:27,29-JOB-33:30-PS-97:4■N.T.-EPH-1:18(5461)-HEB-6:4(5461)

ENLIGHTENING-PS-19:8(215)

ENMITY-all=342-GE-3:15-NU-35:21■N.T.-all=2189-LU-23:12-RO-8:7-EPH-2:15,16-JAS-4:4

ENOUGH-all=7227&marked-GE-24:25■33:9,11(3605)■34:21(3027)■45:28-EX-9:28■36:5(1767)-JOS-17:16(4672)-2SA-24:16-1KI-19:4-1CH-21:15-2CH-31:10(7644)-PR-27:27(1767)■28:19(7644)■30:15(1952),16(1962)-IS-56:11(7654)-JER-49:9(1767)-HO-4:10(7644)-OB-5(1767)-NA-2:12(1767)-HAG-1:6(7654)-MAL-3:10(1767)■N.T.-M'T-10:25(713)■25:9(714)-M'R-14:41(566)-LU-15:17(4052)■22:38(2425)-AC-27:38(2880)

ENQUIRE-all=1875,a=7592&marked-GE-24:57a■25:22-EX-18:15-DE-12:30■13:14■17:9-J'G-4:20a-1SA-9:9■17:56a■22:15a■28:7-1KI-22:5,7,8-2KI-1:2,3,6,16^2■3:11■8:8■16:15(1239)■22:13,18-1CH-10:13■18:10a■21:30-2CH-18:4,6,7■32:31■34:21,26-EZR-7:14(1240)-JOB-8:8a-PS-27:4(1239)-EC-7:10a-IS-21:12(1158)-JER-21:2■37:7-EZE-14:7■20:1,3■N.T.-M'T-10:11(1833)-LU-22:23(4802)-JOH-16:19(2212)-AC-9:11(2212)■19:39(1934)■23:15(1231),20(4441)

ENQUIRED-all=7592,a=1875&marked-DE-17:4a-J'G-6:29a■8:14■20:27-1SA-10:22■22:10,13■23:2,4■28:6■

30:8-**2SA**-2:1▪5:19,23▪11:3a▪16:23▪21:1(1245)-**1CH**-10:14a▪13:3a▪14:10,14-**PS**-78:34(7836)-**EZE**-14:3a▪20:3a,31a▪36:37a-**DA**-1:20(1245)-**ZEP**-1:6a▪**N.T.**-**M'T**-2:7(198),16(198)-**JOH**-4:52(4441)-**1PE**-1:10(1567)

ENQUIREST-**JOB**-10:6(1245)

ENQUIRY-**PR**-20:25(1239)▪**N.T.**-**AC**-10:17(1331)

ENRICH-**1SA**-17:25(6238)-**EZE**-27:33(6238)

ENRICHED-all=4148-**1CO**-1:5(4148)-**2CO**-9:11(4148)

ENRICHEST-**PS**-65:9(6238)

ENSAMPLE-**PH'P**-3:17(5179)-**2TH**-3:9(5179)-**2PE**-2:6(2562)

ENSAMPLES-all=5179-**1CO**-10:11-**1TH**-1:7-**1PE**-5:3

ENSIGN-all=5251&marked-**NU**-2:2(226)-**IS**-5:26▪11:10,12▪18:3▪30:17▪31:9-**ZEC**-9:16(5264)

ENSIGNS-**PS**-74:4(226)

ENSNARED-**JOB**-34:30(4170)

ENSUE-**1PE**-3:11(1377)

ENTANGLE-**M'T**-22:15(3802)

ENTANGLED-**EX**-14:3(943)▪**N.T.**-**GA**-5:1(1758)-**2PE**-2:20(1707)

ENTANGLETH-**2TI**-2:4(1707)

ENTER-all=935&marked-**GE**-12:11-**EX**-40:35-**NU**-4:3,23▪5:24,27▪20:24-**DE**-23:1,2^{2},3^{2},8▪29:12(5674)-**JOS**-10:19-**J'G**-18:9-**1KI**-14:12▪22:30-**2KI**-7:4▪11:5▪19:23-**2CH**-7:2▪23:19▪30:8-**NE**-2:8-**ES**-4:2-**JOB**-22:4▪34:23(1980)-**PS**-37:15▪45:15▪95:11▪100:4▪118:20▪143:2-**PR**-4:14▪18:6▪23:10-**IS**-2:10▪3:14▪26:2,20▪37:24▪57:2▪59:14-**JER**-7:2▪8:14▪14:18▪16:5▪17:20,25▪21:13▪22:2,4▪41:17▪42:15,18-**LA**-1:10▪3:13-**EZE**-7:22▪13:9▪20:38▪26:10^{2}▪37:5▪42:14▪44:2,3,9,16,17,21▪46:2,8-**DA**-11:7,17,24,40,41-**HO**-11:9-**JOE**-2:9-**AM**-5:5-**JON**-3:4-**ZEC**-5:4▪**N.T.**-all=1525&marked-**M'T**-5:20▪6:6▪7:13,21▪10:5,11▪12:29,45▪18:3,8,9▪19:17,23,24▪25:21,23▪26:41-**M'R**-1:45▪3:27▪5:12▪6:10▪9:25,43,45,47▪10:15,23,24,25▪13:15▪14:38-**LU**-7:6▪8:16(1531),32▪9:4▪10:5,8,10▪11:26▪13:24^{2}▪18:17,24,25▪21:21▪22:40,46▪24:26-**JOH**-3:4,5▪10:9-**AC**-14:22▪20:29-**HEB**-3:11,18,19▪4:3^{2},5,6,11▪10:19(1529)-**RE**-15:8▪21:27▪22:14

ENTERED-all=935&marked-**GE**-7:13▪19:3,23▪31:33▪43:30-**EX**-33:9-**JOS**-2:3▪8:19▪10:20-**J'G**-6:5▪9:46-**2SA**-10:14-**2KI**-7:8▪9:31-**1CH**-19:15-**2CH**-12:11▪15:12▪27:2▪32:1-**NE**-2:15▪10:29-**JOB**-38:16.22-**JER**-2:7▪9:21▪34:10▪37:16-**LA**-1:10▪4:12-**EZE**-2:2▪3:24▪16:8▪36:20▪41:6▪44:2-**OB**-11,13-**HAB**-3:16▪**N.T.**-all=1525&marked-**M'T**-8:5,23(1684)▪9:1(1684)▪12:4▪24:38-**M'R**-1:21,29(2064)▪2:1▪3:1▪4:1(1684)▪5:13▪6:56(1531)▪7:17,24▪8:10(1684)▪11:2(1531),11-**LU**-1:40▪4:38▪5:3(1684)▪6:6▪7:1,44▪8:30,33▪9:34,52▪10:38▪11:52▪17:12,27▪19:1▪22:3,10▪24:3-**JOH**-4:38▪6:17(1684),22(1684)▪13:27▪18:1,33▪21:3(305)-**AC**-3:2(1531),8▪5:21▪9:17▪10:24▪11:8,12▪16:40▪18:7(2064),19▪19:30▪21:8,26(1524)▪23:16▪25:23▪28:8-**RO**-5:12,20(3922)-**1CO**-2:9(305)-**HEB**-4:6,10▪6:20▪9:12,24-**JAS**-5:4-**2JO**-7-**RE**-11:11

ENTERETH-all=935&marked-**NU**-4:30,35,39,43-**2CH**-31:16-**PR**-2:10▪17:10(5181)-**EZE**-42:12▪46:9^{2}▪**N.T.**-all=1531-**M'T**-15:17-**M'R**-5:40▪7:18,19-**LU**-22:10-**JOH**-10:1(1535),2(1535)-**HEB**-6:19(1535)▪9:25(1535)

ENTERING-all=6607,a=935&marked-**EX**-35:15-**JOS**-8:29▪13:5a▪20:4-**J'G**-3:3a▪9:35,40,44▪18:16,17-**1SA**-23:7a-**2SA**-10:8▪11:23-**1KI**-6:31▪8:65a▪19:13-**2KI**-7:3▪10:8▪14:25a▪23:8,11a-**1CH**-5:9a▪13:5a-**2CH**-7:8a▪18:9▪23:4a,13(3996),15(3996)▪26:8a▪33:14a-**IS**-23:1a-**JER**-1:15▪17:27a-**EZE**-44:5(3966)-**AM**-6:14a▪**N.T.**-all=1531&marked-**M'T**-23:13(1525)-**M'R**-4:19▪7:15▪8:13(1684)▪16:5(1525)-**LU**-11:52(1525)▪19:30-**AC**-8:3▪27:2(1910)-**1TH**-1:9(1529)-**HEB**-4:1(1525)

ENTERPRISE-**JOB**-5:12(8454)

ENTERTAIN-**HEB**-13:2(5381)

ENTERTAINED-**HEB**-13:2(3579)

ENTICE-all=6601&marked-**EX**-22:16-**DE**-13:6(5496)-**J'G**-14:15▪16:5-**2CH**-18:19,20,21-**PR**-1:10

ENTICED-**JOB**-31:27(6601)-**JER**-20:10(6601)▪**N.T.**-**JAS**-1:14(1185)

ENTICETH-**PR**-16:29(6601)

ENTICING-**1CO**-2:4(3981)-**COL**-2:4(4086)

ENTIRE-**JAS**-1:4(3648)

ENTRANCE-all=3996&marked-**NU**-34:8(935)-**J'G**-1:24,25-**1KI**-18:46(935)▪22:10(6607)-**1CH**-4:39-**2CH**-12:10(6607)-**PS**-119:130(6608)-**EZE**-40:15(2978)▪**N.T.**-**1TH**-2:1(1529)-**2PE**-1:11(1529)

ENTRANCES-**MIC**-5:6(6607)

ENTREAT-**JER**-15:11(6293)▪**N.T.**-**AC**-7:6(2559)

ENTREATED-all=5195&marked-**M'T**-22:6-**LU**-18:32▪20:11(818)-**AC**-7:19(2559)▪27:3(5530)-**1TH**-2:2

ENTREATETH-allsupplied

ENTRIES-**EZE**-40:38(6607)

ENTRY-all=6607&marked-**2KI**-16:18(3996)-**1CH**-9:19(3996)-**2CH**-4:22-**PR**-8:3(6310)-**JER**-19:2▪26:10▪36:10▪38:14(3996)▪43:9-**EZE**-8:5(872)▪27:3(3996)▪40:11,40▪42:9(3996)▪46:19(3996)

ENVIED-all=7065&marked-**GE**-26:14▪30:1▪37:11-**PS**-106:16-**EC**-4:4(7068)-**EZE**-31:9

ENVIES-**1PE**-2:1(5355)

ENVIEST-**NU**-11:29(7065)

ENVIETH-**1CO**-13:4(2206)

ENVIOUS-all=7065-**PS**-37:1▪73:3-**PR**-24:1,19

ENVIRON-**JOS**-7:9(5437)

ENVY-all=7068&marked-**JOB**-5:2-**PR**-3:31(7065)▪14:30▪23:17(7065)▪27:4-**EC**-9:6-**IS**-11:13,13(7065)▪26:11-**EZE**-35:11▪**N.T.**-all=5355&marked-**M'T**-27:18-**M'R**-15:10-**AC**-7:9(2206)▪13:45(2205)▪17:5(2206)-**RO**-1:29-**PH'P**-1:15-**1TI**-6:4-**TIT**-3:3-**JAS**-4:5

ENVYING-all=2205&asmarked-**RO**-13:13-**1CO**-3:3-**GA**-5:26(5354)-**JAS**-3:14,16

ENVYINGS-**2CO**-12:20(2205)-**GA**-5:21(5355)

EPHAH-all=374-**EX**-16:36-**LE**-5:11▪6:20▪19:36-**NU**-5:15▪28:5-**J'G**-6:19-**RU**-2:17-**1SA**-1:24▪17:17-**IS**-5:10-**EZE**-45:10,11^{2},13^{2},24^{2},▪46:5^{2},7^{2},11^{2},14-**AM**-8:5-**ZEC**-5:6,7,8,9,10

EPHOD-all=646&marked-**EX**-25:7▪28:4,6,8(642),12,15,25,26,27^{2},28^{3},31▪29:5^{2}▪35:9,27▪39:2,5(642),7,8,18,19,20^{2},21^{3},22-**LE**-8:7^{2}-**J'G**-8:27▪17:5▪18:14,17,18,20-**1SA**-2:18,28▪14:3▪21:9▪22:18▪23:6,9▪30:7^{2}-**2SA**-6:14-**1CH**-15:27-**HO**-3:4

EPHPHATHA-**M'R**-7:34(2188)

EPISTLE-all=1992-**AC**-15:30▪23:33-**RO**-1:t▪16:22-**1CO**-1:t▪5:9-**2CO**-1:t▪3:2,3▪7:8-**GA**-1:t-**EPH**-1:t-**PH'P**-1:t-**COL**-1:t▪4:16-**1TH**-1:t▪5:27-**2TH**-1:▪2:15▪3:14,17**1TI**-1:t-**2TI**-1:t-**TIT**-1:t-**PH'M**-1:t-**HEB**-1:t-**JAS**-1:t-**1PE**-1:t-**2PE**-1:t▪3:1-**1JO**-1:t-**2JO**-1:t-**3JO**-1:t-**JUDE**-1:t

EPISTLES-**2CO**-3:1(1992)-**2PE**-3:16(1992)

EQUAL-all=8505&marked-**JOB**-28:17(6186),19(6186)-**PS**-17:2(4339)▪55:13(6187)-**PR**-26:7(1809)-**IS**-40:25(7737)▪46:5(7737)-**LA**-2:13(7737)-**EZE**-18:25^{2},29^{2}▪33:17^{2},20▪**N.T.**-all=2470-**M'T**-20:12-**LU**-20:36(2465)-**JOH**-5:18-**PH'P**-2:6-**COL**-4:1(2471)-**RE**-21:16

EQUALITY-**2CO**-8:14^{2}(2471)

EQUALLY-**EX**-36:22(7947)

EQUALS-**GA**-1:14(4915)

EQUITY-all=4339&marked-**PS**-98:9▪99:4-**PR**-1:3▪2:9▪17:26(3476)-**EC**-2:21(3788)-**IS**-11:4(4334)▪59:14(5229)-**MIC**-3:9(3477)-**MAL**-2:6(4334)

ERE-all=2962&marked-**EX**-1:19-**NU**-11:33▪14:11(3808)-**1SA**-3:3-**2SA**-2:26(3808)-**2KI**-6:32-**JER**-47:6(3808)-**HO**-8:5(3808)▪**N.T.**-**JOH**-4:49(4250)

ERECTED-**GE**-33:20(5324)

ERR-all=8582&marked-**2CH**-33:9-**PS**-95:10▪119:21(7686),118(7686)-**PR**-14:22▪19:27(7686)-**IS**-3:12▪9:16▪19:14▪28:7(7686)▪30:28▪35:8▪63:17-**JER**-23:13,32-**HO**-4:12-**AM**-2:4-**MIC**-3:5▪**N.T.**-all=4105-**M'T**-22:29-**M'R**-12:24,27-**HEB**-3:10-**JAS**-1:16▪5:19

ERRAND-all=1697-**GE**-24:33-**J'G**-3:19-**2KI**-9:5

ERRED-all=7683&marked-**LE**-5:18-**NU**-15:22-**1SA**-26:21-**JOB**-6:24▪19:4-**PS**-119:110(8582)-**IS**-28:7^{2}(7686)▪29:24(8582)▪**N.T.**-**1TI**-6:10(635),21(795)-**2TI**-2:18(795)

ERRETH-**PR**-10:17(8582)-**EZE**-45:20(7686)

ERROR-**2SA**-6:7(7944)-**JOB**-19:4(4879)-**EC**-5:6(7648)▪10:5(7684)-**IS**-32:6(8432)-**DA**-6:4(7960)▪**N.T.**-all=4106-**M'T**-27:64-**RO**-1:27-**JAS**-5:20-**2PE**-2:18▪3:17-**1JO**-4:6-**JUDE**-11

ERRORS-**PS**-19:12(7691)-**JER**-10:15(8595)▪51:18(8595)▪**N.T.**-**HEB**-9:7(51)

ESCAPE-all=4422,a=6412,b=6413&marked-**GE**-19:17^{2},19,20,22▪32:8b-**JOS**-8:22a-**1SA**-27:1^{2}-**2SA**-15:14b▪20:6(5337)-**1KI**-18:40-**2KI**-9:15a▪10:24▪19:31b-**EZR**-9:8b-**ES**-4:13-**JOB**-11:20(4498,6)-**PS**-55:8(4655)▪56:7(6405)▪71:2(6403)▪141:10(5674)-**PR**-19:5-**EC**-7:26-**IS**-20:6▪37:32b▪66:19a-**JER**-11:11(3318)▪25:35b▪32:4▪34:3▪38:18,23▪42:17a▪44:14^{2}a,28a▪46:6▪48:8▪50:28a,29b-**EZE**-6:8a,9a▪7:16(6403),16a▪17:15,18-**DA**-11:41,42b-**JOE**-2:3-**OB**-14a▪**N.T.**-all=1628-**M'T**-23:33(5343,575)-**LU**-21:36-**AC**-27:42(1309)-**RO**-2:3-**1CO**-10:13(1545)-**1TH**-5:3-**HEB**-2:3▪12:25(5343)

ESCAPED-all=4422,a=6412,b=6413&marked-**GE**-14:13a-**EX**-10:5b-**NU**-21:29a-**DE**-23:15(5337)-**J'G**-3:26^{2},29▪12:5(6412)▪21:17b-**1SA**-14:41(3318)▪19:10,12,17,18▪22:1,20▪23:13▪30:17-**2SA**-1:3▪4:6-**1KI**-20:20-**2KI**-19:30b,37-**1CH**-4:43b-**2CH**-16:7▪20:24b▪30:6b▪36:20(7611)-**EZR**-9:15b-**NE**-1:2b-**JOB**-1:15,16,17,19▪19:20-**PS**-124:7^{2}-**IS**-4:2b▪10:20b▪37:31b,38▪45:20a-**JER**-41:15▪51:50a-**LA**-2:22a-**EZE**-24:27a▪33:21,22▪**N.T.**-all=1295&marked-**JOH**-10:39(1831)-**AC**-27:44▪28:1,4-**2CO**-11:33(1628)-**HEB**-11:34(5343)▪12:25(5343)-**2PE**-1:4(668)▪2:18(668),20(668)

ESCAPETH-**1KI**-19:17^{2}(4422)-**IS**-15:9(6413)-**JER**-48:19(4422)-**EZE**-24:26(6412)-**AM**-9:1(6412)

ESCAPING-**EZR**-9:14(6413)

ESCHEW-**1PE**-3:11(1578)

ESCHEWED-**JOB**-1:1(5493)

ESCHEWETH-**JOB**-1:8(5493)▪2:3(5493)

ESPECIALLY-**PS**-31:11(3966)▪**N.T.**-all=3122-**AC**-26:3-**GA**-6:10-**1TI**-5:17-**2TI**-4:13

ESPIED-**GE**-42:27(7200)-**EZE**-20:6(8446)

ESPOUSALS-**SONG**-3:11(2861)-**JER**-2:2(3623)

ESPOUSED-**2SA**-3:14(781)▪**N.T.**-all=3423&marked-**M'T**-1:18-**LU**-1:27▪2:5-**2CO**-11:2(718)

ESPY-**JOS**-14:7(7270)-**JER**-48:19(6822)

ESTABLISH-all=6965,a=3559&marked-**GE**-6:18▪9:9,11▪17:7,19,21-**LE**-26:9-**NU**-30:13-**DE**-8:18▪28:9▪29:13-**1SA**-1:23-**2SA**-7:12a,25-**1KI**-9:5▪15:4(5975)-**1CH**-17:11a▪22:10a▪28:7a

-2CH-9:8(5975)-JOB-36:7(3427)-PS-7:9a■48:8a■87:5a■89:2a,4a■90:17^{2}a■99:4a-PR-15:25(5324)-IS-9:7(5582)■49:8■62:7a-JER-33:2a-EZE-16:60,62-DA-6:7(6966),8(6966)■11:14(5975)-AM-5:15(3322)■N.T.-RO-3:31(2476)■10:3(2476)-1TH-3:2(4741)-HEB-10:9(2476)

ESTABLISHED-all=3559,a=6965&marked-GE-9:17a■41:32-EX-6:4a■15:17-LE-25:30a-DE-19:15a■32:6-1SA-3:20(539)■13:13■20:31■24:20a-2SA-5:12■7:16(539),16,26-1KI-2:12,24,45,46-1CH-17:14,23(539),24(539),24-2CH-1:9(539)■12:1■20:20(539)■25:3(2388)■30:5(5975)-JOB-21:8■22:28(6965)-PS-24:2■40:2■78:5a,69(3245)■89:21,37■93:2■96:10■102:28■112:8(5564)■119:90■140:11-PR-3:19■4:26■8:28(553)■12:3,19■15:22a■16:3,12■20:18■24:3■25:5■29:14■30:4a-IS-2:2■7:9(539)■16:5■45:18■54:14-JER-10:12■30:20■51:15-DA-4:36(8627)-MIC-4:1-HAB-1:12(3245)-ZEC-5:11■N.T.-M'T-18:16(2476)-AC-16:5(4732)-RO-1:11(4741)-2CO-13:1(2476)-HEB-8:6(3549)■13:9(950)-2PE-1:12(4741)

ESTABLISHETH-NU-30:14(6965)-PR-29:4(5975)-DA-6:15(6966)

ESTABLISHMENT-2CH-32:1(571)

ESTATE-all=3653&marked-1CH-17:17(8448)-EC-3:18(1700)-DA-11:7,20,21,38■N.T.-COL-4:8(3588,4012)

ESTATES-all supplied

ESTEEM-JOB-36:19(6186)-IS-53:4(2803)■N.T.-PH'P-2:3(2233)-1TH-5:13(2233)

ESTEEMED-all=2803&marked-DE-32:15(5034)-1SA-2:30(7043)■18:23(7043)-JOB-23:12(6845)-IS-29:16,17■53:3-LA-4:2■N.T.-1CO-6:4(1848)

ESTEEMETH-JOB-41:27(2803)■N.T.-RO-14:5^2(2919),14(3049)

ESTEEMING-HEB-11:26(2233)

ESTIMATE-LE-27:14^2(6186)

ESTIMATION-all=6187-LE-5:15,18■6:6■27:2,3^2,4,5,6^2,7,8,13,15,16,17,18,19,23^2,27^2-NU-18:16

ESTIMATIONS-LE-27:25(6187)

ESTRANGED-all=2114&marked-JOB-19:13-PS-58:3■78:30-JER-19:4(5234)-EZE-14:5

ETERNAL-DE-33:27(6924)-IS-60:15(5769)■N.T.-all=166&marked-M'T-19:16■25:46-M'R-3:29■10:17,30-LU-10:25■18:18-JOH-3:15■4:36■5:39■6:54,68■10:28■12:25■17:2,3-AC-13:48-RO-1:20(126)■2:7■5:21■6:23-2CO-4:17,18■5:1-EPH-3:11(165)-1TI-1:17(165)■6:12,19-2TI-2:10-TIT-1:2■3:7-HEB-5:9■6:2■9:12,14,15-1PE-5:10-1JO-1:2■2:25■3:15■5:11,13,20-JUDE-7,21

ETERNITY-IS-57:15(5703)

EUNUCH-IS-56:3(5631)-JER-52:25(5631)■N.T.-all=2135-AC-8:27,34,36,38,39

EUNUCHS-all=5631-2KI-9:32■20:18-IS-39:7■56:4-JER-29:2■34:19■38:7■41:16-DA-1:3,7,8,9,10,11,18■N.T.-M'T-19:12^2(2135),12^3(2134)

EVANGELIST-AC-21:8(2099)-2TI-4:5(2099)

EVANGELISTS-EPH-4:11(2099)

EVEN-all=6153,a=1571,b=853&marked-GE-10:21a■14:23(5704)■19:1■20:5a■27:34a,38a-EX-10:12b■12:15(389),18^2■16:6,12,13■18:14■29:39,41■30:8■32:29(3588)-LE-5:12b■11:24,25,27,28,31,32,39,40^2■14:46■15:5,6,7,8,10^2,11,16,17,18,19,21,22,23,27■17:15■22:6■23:5,32^2■26:28(637)-NU-9:3,5,11,15,21■11:20(5704)■18:29b■19:7,8,10,19,21,22■28:4,8-DE-12:22(389),30a,31a■16:4,6■23:2a,3a,18a■28:67-JOS-2:24a■5:10■7:11^{2}a-J'G-3:9b■19:16■20:23,26■21:2-RU-2:7(227),15a,17-1SA-5:6b■20:5-2SA-1:12■3:9(3588)■11:13■15:21(3588)-1KI-1:30^2(3588)■7:51b■14:14a■21:19a■22:35-1CH-11:2a,8(5704)■23:30-2CH-18:13(3588),34■20:4a■28:10(7535)-NE-4:3a■5:8a,13(3602)-ES-2:18b■4:2(5704)-JOB-23:2a■31:6(6664)■34:17(637)■41:9a-PS-26:12(4334)■84:2a,3b■108:1(637)■139:10a-PR-14:13a,20a■16:4a,7a■17:15a,28a■20:11a,12a■22:19(637)■23:15a■28:9a-EC-2:12b,15a■11:5(3602)-IS-7:17b■8:7b■35:2(637)■43:19(637)■49:19(3588),25a■57:6a,7a-JER-6:11a■7:11a,15b■12:6^{2}a■16:5b■19:11(3602)■28:11(3602)■31:19a■39:12(3651)■41:10(853)■42:5(3651)■43:1b,6b■49:37b■51:60b-LA-4:3a-EZE-4:1b,13(3602)■5:8a■12:4,7■18:11a■21:13a■24:18■34:23b■36:12b■37:19b■44:7b-DA-2:43(1887)■7:11(5705),18(5705)-JOE-1:2(518)-AM-2:11(637)-OB-11a-ZEC-9:7a,12a■11:7(3651),10b,14b-MAL-1:10a■N.T.-all=2532,a=2531-M'T-5:46,47,48(5618)■6:29(3761)■7:12■8:16(3798),27■9:18(737)■12:8■13:12■18:33■20:8(3798),14,28(5618)■23:37(3739,5158)■25:29■26:20(3798)■27:57(3798)-M'R-1:27,32(3798,1096)■4:25,35(3798),41■6:2,47(3798)■10:45■11:6a,19(3796)■13:22,35(3796),54(2193)■15:42(3798)-LU-1:2a,15(2089)■6:33■8:18,25■9:54■10:11,17,21(3483)■12:7,41,57■18:11■19:26,32a,37(2536),42■20:37■24:24(3779)-JOH-5:21,23a■6:16(3798),57(2548)■8:25■10:15(2504)■11:22,37■12:50a■15:10a■17:14a,16,18(2504),22a■20:21(2504)■21:25(3761)-AC-5:39■11:5(891)■15:8,11(2548)■26:11■27:25(3779)-RO-1:13,26(5037),28a■3:22(1161)■4:6(2509)■5:14,18,21■6:19(3779)■8:23■9:24,30(1161)■11:5■15:3,6-1CO-1:6a■2:11■3:5■5:7■7:7,8(2504)■9:14■10:33(2504)■11:1a,5,14(3761)■12:2(5613)■13:12a■14:7(3676),12■15:22,24■16:1-2CO-1:3,8,13,14(2509)■3:10,15(2193)■7:14■10:7,13■11:12-GA-2:16■3:6a■4:3,29■5:12-EPH-2:3,5■4:4,32■5:12,23,25a,29,33(5613)-PH'P-1:7a,15■2:8(1161)■3:15,18,21■4:16-COL-3:13-1TH-2:2,14,18(3303),19■3:4,12,13■4:5,13■5:11a-2TH-2:16■3:1,10-1TI-3:11(5615)-TIT-1:15-PH'M-19-HEB-7:4■11:12,19-JAS-2:17■3:5,14(1063)-1PE-3:6(5613)-2PE-1:14■2:1^2■3:15a-1JO-2:6a,18,27a■3:3a,7a■4:3-3JO-2a,3a-JUDE-7(5613),23-RE-1:7(3483)■2:13,27(2504)■3:4,21(2504)■16:7(3483)■17:11■18:6■21:11(5613)■22:20(3483)

EVENING-all=6153&marked-GE-1:5,8,13,19,23,31■8:11■24:11■29:23■30:16-EX-12:6■16:8■18:13■27:21-LE-24:3-DE-23:11-JOS-10:26-J'G-19:9(6150)-1SA-14:24■17:16(6150)■30:17-1KI-17:6-2KI-16:15-1CH-16:40-2CH-2:4■13:11^2■31:3-EZR-3:3■9:4,5-ES-2:14-JOB-4:20-PS-55:17■59:6,14■65:8■90:6■104:23■141:2-PR-7:9-EC-11:6-JER-6:4-EZE-33:22■46:2-DA-8:26■9:21-HAB-1:8-ZEP-2:7■3:3-ZEC-14:7■N.T.-all=3798&marked-M'T-14:15,23■16:2-M'R-14:17-LU-24:29(2073)-JOH-20:19-AC-28:23(2073)

EVENINGS-JER-5:6(6160)

EVENINGTIDE-2SA-11:2(6256,6153)-IS-17:14(6256,6153)

EVENT-all=4745-EC-2:14■9:2,3

EVENTIDE-GE-24:63(6256,6153)-JOS-7:6(6153)■8:29(6256,6153)■N.T.-M'R-11:11(3798,5610)-AC-4:3(2073)

EVER-all=5769,a=5703,b=3605,3117,c=5331&marked-GE-3:22■13:15■43:9b■44:32b-EX-3:15■12:14,17,24■14:13■15:18a■19:9■21:6■27:21■28:43■29:28■30:21■31:17■32:13-LE-6:13(8548),18,22■7:34,36■10:9,15■16:29,31■17:7■23:14,21,31,41■24:3■25:23(6783)30(6783),46-NU-10:8■15:15■18:8,11,19^2,23■19:10■22:32(5750)■24:20a,24a-DE-4:40b■5:29■12:28■13:16■15:17■18:5b■19:9b■23:3,6■28:46■29:29■32:40-JOS-4:7,24b■8:28■14:9-1SA-1:22■2:30,32b,35b■3:13,14■13:13■20:15,23,42■27:12■28:2b-2SA-2:26(5331)■3:28■7:13,16^2,24,25,26,29^2-1KI-1:31■2:33^2■5:1b■8:13■9:3,5■10:9■11:39b■12:7b-2KI-5:27■21:7-1CH-15:2■16:34,36,36(5704,5769),41■17:12,14,22,23,24,27^2■22:10■23:13^2,25■28:4,7,8,9(5703)■29:10,10(5704,5769),18-2CH-2:4■5:13■6:2■7:3,6,16■9:8■10:7b■13:5■20:7,21■21:7b■30:8■33:4,7(5865)-EZR-3:11■9:12^2-NE-2:3■9:5■13:1-JOB-4:20c■14:20c■19:24a■20:7c■23:7c■36:7c■41:4-PS-5:11■9:5,5a,7,18a■10:16,16a■12:7■13:1c■19:9a■21:4,4a,6a■22:26a■23:6(753,3117)■25:15(8548)■28:9■29:10■30:12■33:11■37:18,26b,28,29a■41:12■44:8,23c■45:2,6,6a,17,17a■48:8,14a■49:8,9c,11■51:3(8548)■52:5c,8,8a,9■61:4,7,8a■66:7■68:16c■72:17,19■73:26■74:1c,10c,19c■75:9■77:7,8c■78:69■79:5c,13■81:15■83:17a■85:5■89:1,2,4,29a,36,37,46c■92:7a■93:5(753,3117)■102:12■103:9■104:5(5769,5703),31■105:8■106:1■107:1■110:4■111:3a,5,8a,8,9,10■112:3a,6,9a■117:2■118:1,2,3,4,29■119:44,44a,89,98,111,152,160■125:1,2■131:3■132:14a■135:13,136:1,2,3,4,5,6,7,8,9,10,11,12,13,14,15,16,17,18,19,20,21,22,23,24,25,26■138:8■145:1,1a,2,2a,21,21a■146:6,10■148:6a,6-PR-8:23(6924)■12:19a■27:24■29:14a-EC-1:4■2:16■3:14■9:6-SONG-6:12(3808)-IS-9:7■26:4a■28:28c■30:8a,8■32:14,17■33:20c■34:10,10c,17■40:8■47:7■51:6,8■57:16■59:21■60:21■64:9a■65:18a-JER-3:12■7:7■17:4,25■25:5■31:36b,40■32:39b■33:11■35:6,19b■49:33■50:39c■51:26,62-LA-3:31■5:19,20c-EZE-37:25^2■43:7,9-DA-2:4,20,44■3:9■4:34■5:10■6:6,21,24(3809),26(5957)■7:18(5957)■12:3,3a,7-HO-2:19-JOE-2:2■3:20-AM-1:11c-OB-10-JON-2:6-MIC-2:9■4:5,5a,7■7:18a-ZEC1:5-MAL-1:4■N.T.-165&marked-M'T-6:13■21:19■24:21(3364)-M'R-11:14■15:8(104)-LU-1:33,55■15:31(3842)-JOH-4:29(3745),39(3745)■6:51,58■8:35^2■10:8(3745)■12:34■14:16■18:20(3842)-AC-23:15(4253)-RO-1:25■9:5■11:36■16:27-2CO-9:9-GA-1:5-EPH-5:29(4218)-PH'P-4:20-1TH-4:17(3842)■5:15(3842)-1TI-1:17-2TI-3:7(3842)■4:18-PH'M-15(166)-HEB-1:8■5:6■6:20■7:17,21,24,25(3842)■10:12(1336),14(1336)■13:8,21-1PE-1:23,25■4:11■5:11-2PE-2:17■3:18(2250,165)-1JO-2:17-2JO-2-JUDE-13,25-RE-1:6■4:9,10■5:13,14■7:12■10:6■11:15■14:11■15:7■19:3■20:10■22:5

EVERLASTING-all=5769&marked-GE-9:16■17:7,8,13,19■21:33■48:4■49:26-EX-40:15-LE-16:34■24:8-NU-25:13-DE-33:27-2SA-23:5-1CH-16:17-PS-24:7,9■41:13■90:2■93:2■100:5■103:17■105:10■106:48■112:6■119:142,144■139:24■145:13-PR-8:23■10:25-IS-9:6(5703)■24:5■26:4■33:14■35:10■40:28■45:17■51:11■54:8■55:3,13■56:5■61:19,20■61:7,8■63:12,16-JER-10:10■20:11■23:40■31:3■32:40-EZE-16:60■37:26-DA-4:3(5957),34(5957)■7:14(5957),27(5957)■9:24■12:2^2-MIC-5:2-HAB-1:12(6924)■3:6(5703),6■N.T.-all=166&Marked-M'T-18:8■19:29■25:41,46-LU-16:9■18:30-JOH-3:16,36■4:14■5:24■6:27,40,47■12:50-AC-13:46-RO-6:22■16:26-GA-6:8-2TH-1:9■2:16-1TI-1:16■6:16-HEB-13:20-2PE-1:11-JUDE-6(126)-RE-14:6

EVERMORE-all=5769&marked-DE-28:29(3605,3117)-2SA-22:51-2KI-17:37(3605,3117)-1CH-17:14-PS-16:11(5331)■18:50■37:27■77:8(1755)■86:12■89:28,52■92:8■105:4(8548)■106:31■113:2■115:18■121:8■132:12(5703)■133:3-EZE-37:26,28■N.T.-all=3588,165&marked-JOH-6:34(3842)-2CO-11:31-1TH-5:16(3842)-HEB-7:28-RE-1:18

EVERY-all=3605,a=376,b=5437&marked-GE-1:21^2,25,26,28,29^2,30^3,31■2:5^2,9,16,19^2,20■3:1,14■4:14,22■6:5,17,19^2,20^2■7:2,4,8,14^4,21^2,23■8:1,17^2,

19,20^2,21■9:2,3,10^2,12,15,16■10:5a■
13:10■16:12^2■17:10,12,23■20:13■30:33,
35■34:15,22,23,24■45:1■46:34-**EX**-1:22^2■
7:12a■9:19,22,25^2■10:5,12,15■12:16,
44■13:12,13■14:7■18:22^2,26■25:2■26:2■
27:18■28:21a■30:13,14■33:7,8a■34:19■
35:10,21^2,22,23,24^2,29■36:1,2^2,8,30(259)■
38:26■39:14a-**LE**-2:13■6:18,23■7:6,10■
11:15(853,3605),21,26^2,33,34,35,41,46^2■
15:4,12,14,17,20^2,26■17:15■20:9a■27:28
-**NU**-1:2,4^{2}a,20,22■2:34a■3:15■4:19a,30,
35,39,43,47,49a■5:2,9■8:16,17■13:2a,2■
16:3,27a■17:6■18:7,9^3,10,11,13,14,15,
29,31■19:15■21:8■25:5a■26:54a■29:14
(259)■30:4,11,13■31:17^2,23■32:27,29■
35:8a,15■36:7a,8,9a-**DE**-1:22,41a■2:34■
3:6■4:4■8:3■11:24■12:2,13,31■13:16
(3632)■14:6,14,19■15:2■19:3■20:13■
21:5■23:9■26:11■28:61■30:9-**JOS**-1:3■
4:10■11:14-**J'G**-5:30(7218)■7:5^2,16,18■
8:34b■16:5a■20:16■21:11-**1SA**-2:36■
3:11,18■12:11b■14:47b■15:9■20:15a■
22:2^3,7■23:14-**2SA**-2:16a,27a■6:19^{2}a■
13:37■15:4,36■18:17a■20:1a,2a,12-**1KI**-
5:3b,4b■7:30(259),30,a,36a,38(259)■9:8■
11:15,16■14:23^2■19:18■20:20a,24a■
22:28-**2KI**-3:19^2,25■8:9■12:4■16:4■
17:10■18:31a■23:35a■25:9-**1CH**-13:1■
16:3^{2}a■22:15,18b■26:32■27:1(259)■
28:14,17,21-**2CH**-1:2■2:14■6:29a■
7:21■11:12,23■14:7b■20:23a,27■
28:4,24,25■30:17,18■31:16,19,21■32:22b
-**EZR**-2:1a■3:5■8:34■9:4-**NE**-3:28■
4:15a,17a,18a,22a,23a■5:7a■7:3a,6a■
8:16a■10:28,31■11:3a,20a■13:10a,30a
-**ES**-1:22a■3:14■4:3■6:13■8:11,13,17■
9:27-**JOB**-1:4a,10b■2:11a,12a■12:10■
18:11b■19:10b■20:22■21:33■28:10■
36:25■37:7■39:8■40:11,12■42:2,11a
-**PS**-7:11■12:2a,8b■29:9■31:13b■32:6■
39:5,11■50:10■53:3■56:5■63:11■64:6a■
69:34■71:18,21b■104:11■115:8■119:101,
104,128,160■128:1■135:18■145:2,16■
150:6-**PR**-1:19■2:9■7:12■13:16■14:15■
15:3■16:5■19:6■20:3,6a■21:2,5■27:7■
30:5-**EC**-3:1^2,11,13,17■4:4■5:19■8:6,9■
10:3■12:14^2-**SONG**-4:2■6:6■8:11-**IS**-
1:23■2:12^2,15■3:5^{2}a■4:3,5■7:22,23■9:5,
17^2■13:7,14a,15^2■14:18a■15:2,3■16:7■
19:2^{2}a,7,14,17■24:10■27:25■30:25,32■
34:15(802)■36:162a■40:4^2■41:6^2■
43:7■44:23■45:23^2■47:15a■51:13■
52:5■53:6a■54:17■55:1■56:6,11a■57:5■
58:6-**JER**-1:15a■2:20■3:6^2,13■4:29■
5:2,8a■6:3a,13^2,25b■8:6,10^2■9:4a,4^2,
5a,20(802)■10:14^2■11:8a■12:4■13:12^2■
15:10■16:12a,16■18:11a,12a,16■
19:8,9a■20:7,10b■22:7a■23:17,30a,
35^{2}a■25:5a■30:6,16■31:25,30a■32:19a■
34:10^{2}a■36:7a■43:6■47:4■48:8,37^2■49:17,
29b■50:13,16^{2}a■51:9a,17^2-**LA**-2:19■4:1
-**EZE**-1:9a,11a,12a,23^2■6:13^2■7:16a■8:10■
10:22a■12:14,22,23a■13:18b■14:7a■16:15,
24,25^2,31^2,33b,44■17:23■18:30■19:8d■
20:28,39a,47■21:7^2,10■22:6a■23:22b■24:4■
28:13,23b■29:18^2■33:20a,26a,30a■34:6,8■
36:3b■37:21b■38:20■39:4,17^2,17b■41:5b,
10b■44:5,29,30^2■45:20a■47:9^2-**DA**-3:10
(3606),29(3606)■6:12(3606),26(3606)■
11:36■12:1-**HO**-4:3■9:1-**JO**-2:7a,8(1397)
-**AM**-2:8■4:3(802)■8:3,8,10-**OB**-9a-**JON**-
1:7a■3:8a-**MIC**-4:5a-**HAB**-1:10-**ZEP**-
2:11a,15■3:19-**HAG**-2:14,22a-**ZEC**-5:3^2■
10:1a,4■11:6a,9(802)■12:4^2■13:4a■14:13a,
16,21-**MAL**-1:11■2:17■**N.T.**-all=3956,
a=1538-**M'T**-3:10■4:4■7:8,17,19,21,26■
8:33■9:35■12:25^2,36■13:47,52■15:13■
16:27a■18:16,35a■19:3,29■20:9(303),10
(303)■25:15a,29■26:22a-**M'R**-1:45(3836)■
7:14■8:25(537)■9:49^2■13:34a■15:24(5100)■
16:15,20(3837)-**LU**-2:3a,23,41(2596)■
3:5^2,9■4:4,37,40a■5:17■6:30,40,44a■8:1
(2596),4(2596)■9:6(3837),43■10:1■11:4,
10,17■16:5a,16,19(2596)■18:14■19:15
(5101),26,43(3840)-**JOH**-1:9■2:10■3:8,
20■6:7a,40,45■7:23(3650),53a■13:10
(3650)15:2^2■16:32a■18:37■19:23a■21:25
(2596)-**AC**-2:5,6a,8a,38a,43,45(5100)■3:23,
26a■4:35a■5:16(537),42(2596)■8:3(2596),
4(1330)■10:35■11:29a■13:27■14:23(2596)■
15:21(2596),21,36■16:26■17:27a,30(3837)■
18:4■20:23(2596),31a■21:26a,28(3837)■
22:19(2596)■26:11■28:2,22(3837)-**RO**-
1:16■2:6a,9,10■3:2,4,19■10:4■12:3,3a,
5(2596)■13:1■14:5,5a,11^2,12a■15:2-**1CO**-
1:2,5,12a■3:5a,8a,10a,13^{2}a■4:5a,17(3837),
17■6:18■7:2^{2}a,7a,17^{2}a,20a,24■8:7■9:25■
10:24a■11:3,4,5,21a■12:7a,11a,18a■14:26a■
15:23a,30,38a■16:2a,16-**2CO**-2:14■4:2,8
(1722,3956),5:10a■7:5■8:7(376)■9:7a,8,
11■10:5^2■13:1-**GA**-3:10,13■5:3■6:4a,5a
-**EPH**-1:21■4:7a,14,16,16(1520)a,25a■
5:24,33(2596,1520)-**PH'P**-1:3,4,18■2:4^{2}a,
9,10,11■4:6,12,21-**COL**-1:10,15,23,28^2■4:6
(1519)a-**1TH**-1:8■2:11a■4:4a■5:18-**2TH**-
1:3a■2:17■3:6,17-**1TI**-2:8(1722,3956)■
4:4■5:10-**2TI**-2:19,21■4:18-**TIT**-1:5(2596),
16■3:1-**PH'M**-6-**HEB**-2:2,9■3:4■5:1,13■
6:11a■8:3,11a,19,25(2596)■10:3(2596),11■
12:1,6■13:21-**JAS**-1:14a,17,19■3:7,16-**1PE**-
1:17a■2:13■3:15■4:10a-**1JO**-2:29■3:3,4:1,
2,3,7■5:1-**RE**-1:7■2:23a■5:8a,9,13■6:11a,
14,15■14:6■16:3,20,21■18:2^2,17■20:13a,
21:21a■22:2(2596,1520)a,12a,18

EVIDENCE-all=5612-**JER**-32:10,
11,12,14^2,16■**N.T.**-**HEB**-11:1(1650)

EVIDENCES-**JER**-32:14(5612),44
(5612)

EVIDENT-**JOB**-6:28(5921,6440)■
N.T.-**GA**-3:11(1212)-**PH'P**-1:28(1732)
-**HEB**-7:14(4271),15(2612)

EVIDENTLY-**AC**-10:3(5320)-**GA**-
3:1(4270)

EVIL-all=7451,a=7489&marked-**GE**-
2:9,17■3:5,22■6:5■8:21■19:19■37:2,20,33■
44:4,5a,34■47:9■48:16■50:15,17,20-**EX**-
5:19,22a,23a■10:10■23:2■32:12,14■33:4
-**LE**-5:4a■26:6-**NU**-13:32(1681)■14:27,35,
37■20:5■32:13-**DE**-1:35,39■4:25■7:15■
13:5■15:9a■17:7,12■19:19,20■21:21■
22:14,19,21,22,24■24:7■26:6a■28:54a,56a■
29:21■30:15■31:29^2-**JOS**-23:15■24:15a
-**J'G**-2:11,15■3:7,12^2■4:1■6:1■9:23,57■
10:6■13:1■20:13,34,41-**1SA**-2:23■6:9■
12:19■15:19■16:14,15,16,23^2■18:10■
19:9■20:7,9,13■24:11,17■25:3,17,21,26,28,
39■26:18■29:6-**2SA**-3:39■12:9,11■13:16■
15:14■17:14■19:7,35■24:16-**1KI**-5:4■9:9■
11:6■13:33■14:9a,10,22■15:26,34■16:7,19,
25,30■17:20a■21:20,21,29^2■22:8,18,23,
52-**2KI**-3:2■6:33■8:12,18,27■13:2,11■
14:24■15:9,18,24,28■17:2,13,17■21:2,9,
12,15,16,20■22:16,20■23:32,37■24:9,19
-**1CH**-2:3■4:10■7:23■21:15,17a-**2CH**-
7:22■12:14■18:7,17,22■20:9■21:6■22:4■
29:6■33:2,6,22■34:24,28■36:5,9,12-**EZR**-
9:13-**NE**-6:13■9:28■13:7,17,18,27-**ES**-
7:7■8:6-**JOB**-1:1,8■2:3,10,11■5:19■8:20a■
24:21(7462)■28:28■30:26■31:29■35:12■
42:11-**PS**-5:4■7:4■10:15■15:3■21:11■23:4■
34:13,14,16,21■35:12■36:4■37:8a,19,27■
38:20■40:14■41:5,8(1100)■49:5■50:19■
51:4■52:3■54:5■56:5■64:5■78:49■90:15■
91:10■97:10■109:5,20■112:7■119:101■121:7■
140:1,11sup,11■141:4-**PR**-1:16,33■2:12,
14■3:7,29■4:14,27■5:14■6:24■8:13^2■11:19■
12:12,20,21(205)■13:19,21■14:16,19,22■
15:3,15,28■16:4,6,17,27,30■17:11,13^2■19:23■
20:8,22,30■21:10■22:3■23:6■24:1,8a,19a,
20■27:12■28:5,10,22■29:6■31:12-**EC**-
2:21■4:3■5:1,13,14,16■6:1,2■8:3,5,11^2,12■
9:3^2,12^2■10:5■11:2,10■12:1,14-**IS**-1:16
(7455),16a■3:9■5:20■7:5,15,16■13:11■
31:2■32:7■33:15■41:23a■45:7■47:11■56:2■
57:1■59:7,15■65:12■66:4-**JER**-1:14■2:3,
19■3:5,17■4:4(7455),6,22a■5:12■6:1,19■
7:24,30■8:3■9:3■10:5a■11:8,11,15,17^2,23■
12:14■13:10,23a■15:11■16:10,12■17:17,
18■18:8^2,10,11^2,12,20■19:3,15■21:10,12
(7455)■23:2(7455),10,12,17,22,22(7455)■
24:3,3(7455),8,8(7455)■25:5,5(7455),29a,
32■26:3^2,3(7455),13,19^2■28:8■29:11,17
(7455)■32:23,30,32,42■35:15,17■36:3^2,7,
31■38:9a■39:16■40:2■41:11■42:6,10,17■
44:2,7,11,17,22(7455),23,27,29■45:5■48:2■
49:23,37■51:24,60,64■52:2-**LA**-3:38-**EZE**-
5:16,17■6:10,11■7:5■14:22■33:11■34:25■
36:31■38:10-**DA**-9:12,13,14-**JOE**-2:13
-**AM**-3:6■5:13,14,15■6:3■9:4,10-**JON**-1:7,
8■3:8,10^2■4:2-**MIC**-1:12■2:1,3^2■3:2,11■
7:3-**NA**-1:11-**HAB**-1:13■2:9^2-**ZEP**-1:12a■
3:15-**ZEC**-1:4^2■7:10■8:17-**MAL**-1:8^2■
2:17■**N.T.**-all=4190,a=2556&marked
-**M'T**-5:11(4190,4487),37,39,45■6:13,23,34
(2549)■7:11,17,18■9:4■12:34,35^2,39■
15:19■20:15■24:48a■27:23a-**M'R**-3:4(2554)■
7:21a,22,23■9:39(2551)■15:14a-**LU**-6:9
(2554),22,35,45^2■7:21■8:2■11:4,13,29,34■
16:25a■23:22a-**JOH**-3:19,20(5337)■5:29
(5337)■7:7■17:15■18:23(2560),23a-**AC**-
7:6(2559),19(2559)■9:13a■14:2(2559)■
19:12,13,15,16■23:5(2560),9a■24:20(92)
-**RO**-1:30a■2:9a■3:8a■7:19a,21a■9:11a■
12:9,17a,21^{2}a■13:3a,4^{2}a■14:20a■16:19a
-**1CO**-10:6a,30(987)■13:5a■15:33a-**2CO**-
6:8(1426)■13:7a-**GA**-1:4-**EPH**-4:31
(988)■5:16■6:13-**PH'P**-3:2a-**COL**-3:5a
-**1TH**-5:15a,22-**2TH**-3:3-**1TI**-6:4,10a
-**2TI**-2:9(2557)■3:13■4:14a,18-**TIT**-
1:12a■2:8(2337)■3:2(987)-**HEB**-
3:12■5:14a■10:22-**JAS**-1:13a■2:4■3:8a,16
(5337)■4:11^3(2635),16-**1PE**-2:1(2636)■
3:9a,10a,11a,12a,16(2635),17(2554)■4:4
(987),14(987)-**2PE**-2:2(987),10(987),
12(987)-**1JO**-3:12-**2JO**-11-**3JO**-11a,11(2554)
-**JUDE**-8(987),10(987)-**RE**-2:2a

EVILDOER-**1SA**-9:17(7489)-**1PE**-
4:15(2555)

EVILDOERS-all=7489-**PS**-37:1,9■
94:16■119:115-**IS**-1:4■14:20■31:2-**JER**-
20:13■23:14■**N.T.**-all=2555-**1PE**-2:12,
14■3:16

EVILFAVOUREDNESS-**DE**-17:1
(1697,7451)

EVILS-all=7451-**DE**-3:17^2,18,21-**PS**-
40:12-**JER**-2:13-**EZE**-6:9■20:43■**N.T.**
-**LU**-3:19(4190)

EWE-all=3535&marked-**GE**-21:28,29,
30-**LE**-14:10■22:28(7716)-**NU**-6:14
-**2SA**-12:3

EWES-**GE**-31:38(7353)■32:14(7353)
-**PS**-78:71(5763)

EXACT-all=5065&marked-**DE**-15:2,3
-**NE**-5:7(5378),10(5383),11(5383)-**PS**-89:22
(5378)-**IS**-58:3■**N.T.**-**LU**-3:13(4288)

EXACTED-**2KI**-15:20(3318)■23:35(5065)

EXACTETH-**JOB**-11:6(5382)

EXACTION-**NE**-10:31(4855)

EXACTIONS-**EZE**-45:9(1646)

EXACTORS-**IS**-60:17(5065)

EXALT-all=7311&marked-**EX**-15:2
-**1SA**-2:10-**JOB**-17:4-**PS**-34:3■37:34■
66:7■92:10■99:5,9■107:32■118:28■
140:8-**PR**-4:8(5549)-**IS**-13:2■14:13■
25:1-**EZE**-21:26(1361)■29:15(5375)■
31:14(1361)-**DA**-11:14(5375),36-**HO**-
11:7-**OB**-4(1361)■**N.T.**-**M'T**-23:12
(5312)-**2CO**-11:20(1869)-**1PE**-5:6(5312)

EXALTED-all=7311,a=5375&
marked-**NU**-24:7a-**1SA**-2:1-**2SA**-5:12a■
22:47-**1KI**-1:5a■14:7■16:2-**2KI**-19:22
-**1CH**-29:11a-**NE**-9:5-**JOB**-5:11(7682)■
24:24(7426)■36:7(1361)-**PS**-12:8■13:2■
18:46■21:13■46:10^2■47:9(5927)■57:5,
11■75:10■89:16,17,19,24■97:9(5927)■
108:5■112:9■118:16(7426)-**PR**-11:11
-**IS**-2:2a,11(7682),17(7682)■5:16(1361)■
12:4(7682)■30:18■33:5(7682),10■37:23■
40:4a■49:11■52:13-**EZE**-17:24(1361)■
19:11(1361)■31:5(1361)-**HO**-13:1a,6
-**MIC**-4:1a■**N.T.**-5312&marked-**M'T**-
11:23■23:12-**LU**-1:52■10:15■14:11■
18:14-**AC**-2:33■5:31■13:17-**2CO**-11:7■
12:7^2(5229)-**PH'P**-2:9(5251)-**JAS**-1:9(5311)

EXALTEST-**EX**-9:17(5549)

EXALTETH-all=7311&marked-**JOB**-
36:22(7682)-**PS**-148:14-**PR**-14:29,34■
17:19(1361)■**N.T.**-**LU**-14:11(5312)■18:14
(5312)-**2CO**-10:5(1869)-**2TH**-2:4(5229)

EXAMINATION-**AC**-25:26(351)

EXAMINE-**EZR**-10:16(1875)-**PS**-
26:2(974)■**N.T.**-**1CO**-9:3(350)■11:28
(1381)-**2CO**-13:5(3985)

EXAMINED-all=350&marked-**LU**-

23:14-AC-4:9▪12:19▪22:24(426),29(426)▪28:18

EXAMINING-AC-24:8(350)

EXAMPLE-all=5262&marked-M'T-1:19(3856)-JOH-13:15-1TI-4:12(5179)-HEB-4:11▪8:5-JAS-5:10-1PE-2:21(5261)-JUDE-7(1164)

EXAMPLES-1CO-10:6(5179)

EXCEED-DE-25:3^{2}(3254)▪N.T.-M'T-5:20(4052)-2CO-3:9(4052)

EXCEEDED-1SA-20:41(1431)-1KI-10:23(1431)-JOB-36:9(1396)

EXCEEDEST-2CH-9:6(3254)

EXCEEDETH-1KI-10:7(3254)

EXCEEDING-all=3966&marked-GE-15:1▪17:6▪27:34-EX-1:7▪19:16-NU-14:7-2SA-8:8▪12:2-1KI-4:29▪7:47-1CH-20:2▪22:5(4605)-2CH-11:12(7235,3966)▪14:14(7235)▪16:12(4605)▪32:27-PS-21:6(2302)▪43:4(8057)▪119:96-JER-48:29-EZE-9:9▪16:13▪23:15(5628)▪37:10▪47:10-DA-3:22(3493)▪6:23(7689)▪7:19(3493)▪8:9-JON-3:3(430)▪4:6(1419)▪N.T.-all=3029&marked-M'T-2:10(4970),16▪4:8▪8:28▪17:23(4970)▪6:22(4970),38(4036)-M'R-6:26(4036)▪9:3▪14:34(4036)-LU-23:8-AC-7:20(3588,2316)-RO-7:13(2596,5236)-2CO-4:17(1519,5263)▪7:4(5248)▪9:14(5235)-EPH-1:19(5235)▪2:7(5235)▪3:20(5228)-1TI-1:14(5250)-RE-16:21(4970)

EXCEEDINGLY-all=3966&marked-GE-7:19▪13:13▪16:10(7235)▪17:2,20▪27:33(1419)▪30:43▪47:27-1SA-26:21(7235,3966)-2SA-13:15(1419,3966)-2KI-10:4-1CH-29:25(4605)-2CH-1:1(4605)▪17:12(4605)▪26:8(4605)-NE-2:10(1419)-ES-4:4-JOB-3:22(413,1524)-PS-68:3(8057)▪119:167▪123:3(7227),4(7227)-DA-7:7(3493)-JON-1:10(1419),16(1419)▪4:1(1419)▪N.T.-M'T-19:25(4970)-M'R-4:41(5401,3173)▪15:14(4056)-AC-16:20(1613)▪26:11(4057)▪27:18(4971)-2CO-7:13(4056)-GA-1:14(4056)-1TH-3:10(5228,1537,4053)-HEB-12:21(1630)

EXCEL-GE-49:4(3498)-1CH-15:21(5329)-PS-103:20(1368)▪N.T.-1CO-14:12(4052)

EXCELLED-1KI-4:30(7227)

EXCELLENCY-all=1347&marked-GE-49:3(3499)-EX-15:7-DE-33:26(1346),29(1346)-JOB-4:21(3499)▪13:11(7613)▪20:6(7863)▪37:4▪40:10(1363)-PS-47:4▪62:4(7613)▪68:34(1346)-EC-7:12(3504)-IS-13:19▪35:2^{2}(1926)▪60:15-EZE-24:21-AM-6:8▪8:7-NA-2:2^{2}▪N.T.-1CO-2:1(5247)-2CO-4:7(5236)-PH'P-3:8(5242)

EXCELLENT-all=3493&marked-ES-1:4(1420)-JOB-37:23(7689)▪8:1(117),9(117)▪16:3(117)▪36:7(3368)▪76:4(117)▪141:5(7218)▪148:13(7682)▪150:2(7230)-PR-8:6(5057)▪12:26(8446)▪17:7(3499),27(7119)▪22:20(7991)-SONG-5:15(977)-IS-4:2(1347)▪12:5(1348)▪28:29(1431)-EZE-16:7(5716)-DA-2:31▪4:36▪5:12,14▪6:3▪N.T.-LU-1:3(2903)-AC-23:26(2903)-RO-2:18(1308)-1CO-12:31(2596,2536)-PH'P-1:10(1308)-HEB-1:4(1313)▪8:6(1313)▪11:4(4119)-2PE-1:17(3169)

EXCELLEST-PR-31:29(5927)

EXCELLETH-EC-2:13^{2}(3504) N.T.-2CO-3:10(5235)

EXCEPT-all=3588,518&marked-GE-31:42(3884)▪32:26(3588,518)▪42:15(3588,518)▪43:3(1115),5(1115),10(3884)▪44:23(518,3808),26(369)▪47:26(7535)-NU-16:13(3588)-DE-32:30(518,3808,3588)-JOS-7:12(518,3808)-1SA-25:34(3588,3884)-2SA-3:9(3588),13▪5:6-2KI-4:24-ES-2:14▪4:11(905)-PS-127:1^{2}(518,3808)-PR-4:16(518,3808)-IS-1:9(3884)-DA-2:11(3861)▪3:28(3861)▪6:5(3861)-AM-3:3(1115)▪N.T.-all=3362&marked-M'T-5:20▪12:29▪18:3▪19:9(1508)▪24:22(1508)▪26:42-M'R-3:27▪7:3,4▪13:20(1508)-LU-9:13(1509)▪13:3,5-JOH-3:2,3,5,27▪4:48▪6:44,53,65▪12:24▪15:4^{2}▪19:11(1508),20:25-AC-8:1(4133),31▪15:1▪24:21(2228)▪26:29(3923)▪27:31-RO-7:7(1508)▪9:29(1508)▪10:15-1CO-7:5(1509)▪14:5(1622,1508),6,7,9▪15:36-2CO-12:13(1508)▪13:5(1509)-2TH-2:3-2TI-2:5-RE-2:5,22

EXCEPTED-1CO-15:27(1622)

EXCESS-M'T-23:25(192)-EPH-5:18(810)-1PE-4:3(3632),4(401)

EXCHANGE-LE-27:10(8545)-JOB-28:17(8545)-EZE-48:14(4171)▪N.T.-all=465-M'T-16:26-M'R-8:37

EXCHANGERS-M'T-25:27(5133)

EXCLUDE-GA-4:17(1576)

EXCLUDED-RO-3:27(1576)

EXCUSE-LU-14:18(3868)-RO-1:20(379)-2CO-12:19(626)

EXCUSED-LU-14:18(3868)

EXCUSING-RO-2:15(626)

EXECRATION-JER-42:18(423)▪44:12(423)

EXECUTE-all=6213&marked-EX-12:12-NU-5:30▪8:11(5647)-DE-10:18-1KI-6:12-PS-119:84▪149:7,9-IS-16:3-JER-7:5▪21:12(1777)▪22:3▪23:5▪33:15-EZE-5:8,10,15▪11:9▪16:41▪25:11,17▪30:14,19▪45:9-HO-11:9-MIC-5:15▪7:9-ZEC-7:9(8199)▪8:16(8199)▪N.T.-JOH-5:27(4160)-JUDE-15(4160)

EXECUTED-all=6213&marked-NU-33:4-DE-33:31-2SA-8:15-1CH-18:14-2CH-24:24-EZR-7:26(5648)-EC-8:11-JER-23:20-EZE-11:12▪18:8,17▪20:24▪23:10▪28:22,26▪39:21▪N.T.-LU-1:8(2407)

EXECUTEDST-1SA-28:18(6213)

EXECUTEST-PS-99:4(6213)

EXECUTETH-all=6213-PS-9:16▪103:6▪146:7-JER-5:1-JOE-2:11

EXECUTING-2KI-10:30(6213)

EXECUTION-ES-9:1(6213)

EXECUTIONER-M'R-6:27(4688)

EXEMPTED-1KI-15:22(5355)

EXERCISE-PS-131:1(1980)-JER-9:24(6213)▪N.T.-M'T-20:25(2634),25(2715)-M'R-10:42(2634),42(2715)-LU-22:25(2961),25(1850)-AC-24:16(778)-1TI-4:7(1128),8(1129)

EXERCISED-EC-1:13(6031)▪3:10(6031)▪N.T.-all=1128-HEB-5:14▪12:11-2PE-2:14

EXERCISETH-RE-13:12(4160)

EXHORT-all=3870&marked-AC-2:40▪27:22(3867)-2CO-9:5-1TH-4:1▪5:14-2TH-3:12-1TI-2:1▪6:2-2TI-4:2-TIT-1:9▪2:6,15-HEB-3:13-1PE-5:1-JUDE-3

EXHORTATION-all=3874&asmarked-LU-3:18(3870)-AC-13:15▪20:2(3870)-RO-12:8-1CO-14:3-2CO-8:17-1TH-2:3-1TI-4:13-HEB-12:5▪13:22

EXHORTED-AC-11:23(3870)▪15:32(3870)

EXHORTETH-RO-12:8(3870)

EXHORTING-all=3870&marked-AC-14:22▪18:27(4389)-HEB-10:25-1PE-5:12

EXILE-2SA-15:19(1540)-IS-51:14(6808)

EXORCISTS-AC-19:13(1845)

EXPECTATION-all=8615&marked-PS-9:18▪62:5-PR-10:28▪11:7,23▪23:18▪24:14-IS-20:5(4007),6(4007)-ZEC-9:5(4007)▪N.T.-LU-3:15(4328)-AC-12:11(4329)-RO-8:19(603)-PH'P-1:20(603)

EXPECTED-JER-29:11(8615)

EXPECTING-AC-3:5(4328)-HEB-10:13(1551)

EXPEDIENT-all=4851-JOH-11:50▪16:7▪18:14-1CO-6:12▪10:23-2CO-8:10▪12:1

EXPEL-JOS-23:5(1920)-J'G-11:7(1644)

EXPELLED-JOS-13:13(3423)-J'G-1:20(3423)-2SA-14:14(5080)▪N.T.-AC-13:50(1544)

EXPENCES-EZR-6:4(5313),8(5313)

EXPERIENCE-GE-30:27(5172)-EC-1:16(7200)▪N.T.-RO-5:4(1382)

EXPERIMENT-2CO-9:13(1382)

EXPERT-all=6186&marked-1CH-12:33,35,36-SONG-3:8(3925)-JER-50:9(7919)▪N.T.-AC-26:3(1109)

EXPIRED-all=8666&marked-1SA-18:26(4390)-2SA-11:1-1CH-17:11(4390)▪20:1-2CH-36:10-ES-1:5(4390)-EZE-43:27(3615)▪N.T.-AC-7:30(4137)-RE-20:7(5055)

EXPLOITS-all supplied

EXPOUND-J'G-14:14(5046)

EXPOUNDED-J'G-14:19(5046)▪N.T-all=1620-M'R-4:34(1956)-LU-24:27(1329)-AC-11:4▪18:26▪28:23

EXPRESS-HEB-1:3(5481)

EXPRESSED-all=5344-NU-1:17-1CH-12:31▪16:41-2CH-28:15▪31:19-EZR-8:20

EXRESSLY-1SA-20:21(559)▪N.T.-1TI-4:1(4490)

EXTEND-PS-109:12(4900)-IS-66:12(5186)

EXTENDED-EZR-7:28(5186)▪9:9(5186)

EXTENDETH-all supplied

EXTINCT-JOB-17:1(2193)-IS-43:17(1846)

EXTOL-PS-30:1(7311)▪68:4(5549)▪145:1(7311)-DA-4:37(7313)

EXTOLLED-PS-66:17(7318)-IS-52:13(5375)

EXTORTION-EZE-22:12(6233)▪N.T.-M'T-23:25(724)

EXTORTIONER-PS-109:11(5383)-IS-16:4(4160)▪N.T.-1CO-5:11(727)

EXTORTIONERS-all=727-LU-18:11-1CO-5:10▪6:10

EXTREME-DE-28:22(2746)

EXTREMITY-JOB-35:15(6580)

EYE-all=5869&marked-EX-21:24,26^{2}-LE-21:20▪24:20-DE-7:16▪13:8▪15:9▪19:13,21^{2}▪25:12▪28:54,56▪32:10▪34:7-2SA-22:25-EZR-5:5(5870)-JOB-7:7,8▪10:18▪13:1▪16:20▪17:2,7▪20:9▪24:15^{2}▪28:7,10▪29:11▪42:5-PS-6:7▪17:8▪31:9▪32:8▪33:18▪35:19,21▪54:7▪88:9▪92:11▪94:9-PR-7:2▪10:10▪20:12▪22:9▪23:6▪28:22▪30:17-EC-1:8▪4:8-IS-13:18▪52:8▪64:4-JER-13:17-LA-1:16▪2:4,18▪3:48,49,51-EZE-5:11▪7:4,9▪8:18▪9:5,10▪16:5▪20:17-MIC-4:11-ZEC-2:8▪11:17^{2}▪N.T.-all=3788&marked-M'T-5:29,38▪6:22^{2},23▪7:3^{2},4^{2},5^{2}▪18:9,9(3442)▪19:24(5169)▪20:15-M'R-7:22▪9:47,47(3442)▪10:25(5168)-LU-6:41^{2},42^{4}▪11:34,34sup▪18:25(5168)-1CO-2:9▪12:16,17,21▪15:52-RE-1:7

EYEBROWS-LE-14:9(1354,5869)

EYED-GE-29:17(5869)-1SA-18:9(5770)

EYELIDS-all=6079-JOB-16:16▪41:18-PS-11:4▪132:4-PR-4:25▪6:4,25▪30:13-JER-9:18

EYE'S-EX-21:26(5869)

EYES-all=5869&marked-GE-3:5,6,7▪6:8▪13:10,14▪16:4,5▪18:2▪19:8▪20:16▪21:19▪22:4,13▪24:63,64▪27:1▪30:27,41▪31:10,12,40▪33:1,5▪34:11▪37:25▪39:7▪41:37^{2}▪42:24▪43:29▪44:21▪45:12▪46:4▪47:19▪48:10▪49:12▪50:4-EX-5:21^{2}▪8:26▪13:9,16▪14:10▪24:17-LE-4:13▪20:4▪26:16-NU-5:13▪10:31▪11:6▪15:39▪16:14▪20:8,12▪22:31▪24:2,3,4,15,16▪27:14▪33:55-DE-1:30▪3:21,27^{2}▪4:3,9,19,34▪6:8,22▪7:19▪9:17▪10:21▪11:7,12,18▪12:8▪13:18▪14:1▪16:19▪21:7▪24:1▪28:31,32,34,65,67▪29:2,3,4▪34:4-JOS-5:13▪23:13▪24:7-J'G-16:21,28▪17:6▪19:17▪21:25-RU-2:9,10-1SA-2:33▪3:2▪4:15▪6:13▪11:2▪12:3,16▪14:27,29▪20:3,29▪24:10▪25:8▪26:21,24^{2}▪27:5-2SA-6:20▪12:11▪13:34▪15:25▪18:24▪19:27▪22:28▪24:3-1KI-1:20,48▪8:29,52▪9:3▪10:7▪11:33▪14:4,8▪15:5,11▪16:25▪20:6▪22:43-2KI-4:34,35▪6:17^{2},20^{2}▪7:2,19▪10:5,30▪19:16,22▪22:20▪25:7^{2}-1CH-13:4▪17:17▪21:16,23-2CH-6:20,40▪7:15,16▪9:6▪14:2▪16:9▪20:12▪21:6▪29:6,8▪34:28-EZR-3:12(5870)▪9:8-NE-1:6▪6:16-ES-1:17▪8:5-JOB-2:12▪3:10▪4:16▪7:8▪10:4▪11:4,20▪14:3▪15:12▪16:9▪17:5▪19:27▪21:8,20▪24:23▪27:19▪28:21▪29:15▪31:1,7,16▪32:1▪34:21▪

36:7▪39:29▪40:24▪41:18-PS-10:8▪11:4▪13:3▪15:4▪17:2,11▪19:8▪25:15▪26:3▪31:22▪34:15▪36:1,2▪38:10▪50:21▪66:7▪69:3,23▪73:7▪77:4▪91:8▪101:3,6▪115:5▪116:8▪118:23▪119:18,37,82,123,136,148▪121:1▪123:1,2^{3}▪131:1▪132:4▪135:16▪139:16▪141:8▪145:15-PR-3:7,21▪4:21,25▪5:21▪6:4,13▪10:26▪12:15▪15:3,30▪16:2,30▪17:8,24▪20:8,13▪21:2,10▪22:12▪23:5,26,29,33▪25:7▪27:20▪28:27▪29:13▪30:12,13-EC-2:10,14▪5:11▪6:9▪8:16▪11:7,9-SONG-1:15▪4:1,9▪5:12▪6:5▪7:4▪8:10-IS-1:15,16▪3:8,16▪5:15,21▪6:5,10^{2}▪11:3▪13:16▪17:7▪29:10,18▪30:20▪32:3▪33:15,17,20▪35:5▪37:17,23▪38:14▪40:26▪42:7▪43:8▪44:18▪49:5,18▪51:6▪52:10▪59:10▪60:4▪65:12,16▪66:4-JER-3:2▪5:3,21▪7:11▪9:1,18▪13:20▪14:6,17▪16:9,17^{2}▪20:4▪22:17▪24:6▪29:21▪31:16▪32:4,19▪34:3▪39:6,7▪42:2▪52:2,10,11-LA-2:11▪4:17▪5:17-EZE-1:18▪6:9▪8:5^{2}▪10:12▪12:2,12▪18:6,12,15▪20:7,8,24▪21:6▪22:26▪23:16,27,40▪24:16,21,25▪33:25▪36:23▪37:20▪38:16,23▪40:4▪44:5-DA-4:34(5870)▪7:8(5870),20(5870)▪8:3,5,21▪9:18▪10:5,6-HO-13:14-JOE-1:16-AM-9:4,8-MIC-7:10-HAB-1:13-ZEP-3:20-HAG-2:3-ZEC-1:18▪2:1▪3:9▪4:10▪5:1,5,9▪6:1▪8:6^{2}▪9:1,8▪12:4▪14:12-MAL-1:5▪N.T.-all=3788&marked-M’T-9:29,30▪13:15^{2},16▪17:8▪18:9▪20:33,34sup,34▪21:42▪26:43-M’R-8:18,23(3659),25▪9:47▪12:11▪14:40-LU-2:30▪4:20▪6:20▪10:23▪16:23▪18:13▪19:42▪24:16,31-JOH-4:35▪6:5▪9:6,10,11,14,15,17,21,26,30,32▪10:21▪11:37,41▪12:40^{2}▪17:1-AC-9:8,18,40▪26:18▪28:27^{2}-RO-3:18▪11:8,10-GA-3:1▪4:15-EPH-1:18-HEB-4:13-1PE-3:12-2PE-2:14-1JO-1:1▪2:11,16-RE-1:14▪2:18▪3:18▪4:6,8▪5:6▪7:17▪19:12▪21:4

EYESALVE-RE-3:18(2854)

EYESERVICE-EPH-6:6(3787)-COL-3:22(3787)

EYESIGHT-PS-18:24(5869)

EYEWITNESSES-LU-1:2(845)-2PE-1:16(2030)

F

FABLES-all=3454&marked-1TI-1:4▪4:7-2TI-4:4-TIT-1:14-2PE-1:16

FACE-all=6440,a=639&marked-GE-1:2^{2},29▪2:6▪3:19a▪4:14^{2}▪6:1,7▪7:3,4,18,23▪8:8,9,13▪11:4,8,9▪16:6,8▪17:3,17▪19:1a,13▪24:47a▪30:33▪31:21▪32:20,30▪33:10^{2}▪35:1,7▪36:6▪38:15▪41:56▪43:3,5,31▪44:23,26▪46:28,30▪48:11,12a▪50:1,18-EX-2:15▪3:6▪10:5(5869),15(5869),28^{2},29▪14:25▪16:14▪32:12▪33:11,16,20,23▪34:29,30,33,35^{3}-LE-13:41▪17:10▪19:32▪20:3,5,6▪26:17-NU-6:25▪11:31▪12:3,14▪14:14(5869)▪16:4▪22:5(5869),11(5869),31a▪24:1-DE-1:17▪5:4▪6:15▪7:6,10^{2}▪25:9▪31:17,18▪32:20▪34:10-JOS-5:14▪7:6,10-J’G-6:22-RU-2:10-1SA-5:3,4▪17:49▪20:15,41a▪24:8a▪25:23,41a▪26:20▪28:14a-2SA-2:22▪3:13^{2}▪9:6▪14:4a,22,24^{2},28,32,33a▪18:8,28a▪19:4▪24:20a-1KI-1:23a,31a▪8:14▪13:6,34▪18:7,42▪19:13▪20:38(5869),41(5869)▪21:4-2KI-4:29,31▪8:15▪9:30(5869),32,37▪12:17▪13:14▪14:8,11▪18:24▪20:2-1CH-16:11▪21:21a-2CH-6:3,42▪7:14▪20:18a▪25:17,21▪30:9▪32:21▪35:22-EZR-9:6,7-ES-1:14▪7:8-JOB-1:11▪2:5▪4:15▪11:15▪13:24▪15:27▪16:8,16▪21:31▪22:26▪23:17▪24:15▪26:9▪30:10▪33:26▪34:29▪37:12▪38:30▪41:13,14-PS-5:8▪10:11▪13:1▪17:15▪21:12▪22:24▪24:6▪27:8^{2},9▪30:7▪31:16▪34:16▪41:12▪44:15,24▪51:9▪67:1▪69:7,17▪80:3,7,19▪84:9▪88:14▪89:14,23▪102:2▪104:15,29,30▪105:4▪119:135▪132:10▪143:7-PR-7:13,15▪8:27▪21:29▪24:31▪27:19-EC-8:1^{2}-IS-6:2▪8:17▪14:21▪16:4▪23:17▪25:7▪27:6▪28:25▪29:22▪36:9▪38:2▪49:23a▪50:6,7▪54:8▪59:2▪64:7▪65:3-JER-1:13▪2:27▪4:30(5869)▪8:2▪13:26▪16:4,17▪18:17▪21:10▪22:25▪25:26▪28:16▪32:31,33▪33:5▪44:11-LA-2:19▪3:35-EZE-1:10^{3},28▪3:8,23▪4:3,7▪6:2▪7:22▪9:8▪10:14^{4}▪11:13▪12:6,12▪13:17▪14:3,4,7,8▪15:7^{2}▪20:35,46▪21:2,16▪25:2▪28:21▪29:2▪34:6▪35:2▪38:2,18a,20▪39:14,23,24,29▪40:15^{2}▪41:14,19^{2},21,25▪43:3▪44:4-DA-2:46(600)▪8:5,17,18▪9:3,8,17▪10:6,9^{2},15▪11:17,18,19-HO-5:5,15▪7:2,10-JOE-2:6,20-AM-5:8▪9:6,8-MIC-3:4-NA-2:1▪3:5-ZEC-5:3▪N.T-all=4383&marked.-M’T-6:17▪11:10▪16:3▪17:2,6▪18:10▪26:39,67-M’R-1:2▪14:65-LU-1:76▪2:31▪5:12▪7:27▪9:51,52,53▪10:1▪12:56▪17:16▪21:35▪22:64-JOH-11:44(3799)-AC-2:25(1799)▪6:15▪7:45▪17:26▪20:25,38▪25:16-1CO-13:12▪14:25-2CO-3:7,13,18▪4:6▪11:20-GA-1:22▪2:11-COL-2:1-1TH-2:17▪3:10-JAS-1:23-1PE-3:12-2JO-12(4750)-3JO-14(4750)-RE-4:7▪6:16▪10:1▪12:14▪20:11▪22:4

FACES-all=6440&marked-GE-9:23▪18:22▪30:40▪42:6(639)-EX-19:7▪20:20▪25:20^{2}▪37:9^{2}-LE-9:24-NU-14:5▪16:22,45▪20:6-J’G-13:20▪18:23-2SA-19:5-1KI-2:15▪18:39-1CH-12:8▪21:16-2CH-3:13▪7:3(639)▪29:6-NE-8:6(639)-JOB-9:24▪40:13-PS-34:5▪83:16-IS-3:15▪13:8▪25:8▪53:3-JER-1:8,17▪5:3▪7:19▪30:6▪42:15,17▪44:12▪50:5▪51:51-LA-5:12-EZE-1:6,8,10,11,15▪3:8▪7:18▪8:16▪10:14,21,22^{2}▪14:6▪20:47▪41:18-DA-1:10▪9:7-JOE-2:6-NA-2:10-HAB-1:9-MAL-2:3▪N.T.-all=4383-M’T-6:16-LU-24:5-RE-7:11▪9:7▪11:16

FADE-all=5034-2SA-22:46-PS-18:45-IS-64:6-JER-8:13-EZE-47:12▪N.T.-JAS-1:11(3133)

FADETH-all=5034-IS-1:30▪24:4^{2}▪40:7,8▪N.T.-1PE-1:4(268)▪5:4(262)

FADING-IS-28:1(5034),4(5034)

FAIL-all=3615&marked-GE-47:16(656)-DE-28:32▪31:6(7503),8(7503)-JOS-1:5(7503)-1SA-17:32(5307)-2SA-3:29(3772)-1KI-2:4(3772)▪8:25(3772)▪9:5(3772)▪17:14(2637),16(2638)-1CH-28:20(7503)-2CH-6:16(3722)▪7:18(3722)-EZR-4:22(7960)▪6:9(7960)-ES-6:10(5307)▪9:27(5674),28(5674)-JOB-11:20▪14:11(235)▪17:5▪31:16-PS-12:1(6461)▪69:3▪77:8(1584)▪89:33(8266)▪119:82,123-PR-22:8-EC-12:5(6565)-IS-19:3(1238),5(5405)▪21:16▪31:3▪32:6(2637),10▪34:16(5737)▪38:14(1809)▪42:4(3543)▪51:14(2637)▪57:16(5484)▪58:11(3576)-JER-14:6▪15:18(3808,539)▪48:33(7673)-LA-2:11▪3:22-HO-9:2(3584)-AM-8:4(7673)-HAB-3:17(3584)▪N.T.-all=1587&marked-LU-16:9,17(4098)▪22:32-1CO-13:8(2673)-HEB-1:12▪11:32(1952)▪12:15(5302)

FAILED-all=5307&marked-GE-42:28(3318)▪47:15(8552)-JOS-3:16(8552)▪21:45▪23:14^{2}-1KI-8:56-JOB-19:14(2308)-PS-142:4(6)-SONG-5:6(3318)-JER-51:30(5405)-LA-4:17(3615)

FAILETH-all=3615&marked-GE-47:15(656)-JOB-21:10(1602)-PS-31:10(3782)▪38:10(5800)▪40:12(5800)▪71:9▪73:26▪109:24(3584)▪143:7-EC-10:3(2638)-IS-15:6▪40:26(5737)▪41:17(5405)▪44:12(369)▪59:15(5737)-EZE-12:22(6)-ZEP-3:5(5737)▪N.T-LU-12:33(413)-1CO-13:8(1601)

FAILING-DE-28:65(3631)▪N.T.-LU-21:26(674)

FAIN-JOB-27:22(1272)▪N.T.-LU-15:16(1987)

FAINT-all=5889&marked-GE-25:29,30-DE-20:3(7401),8(4549)▪25:18-JOS-2:9(4127),24(4127)-J’G-8:4,5-1SA-14:28(5774),31(5774)▪30:10(6296),21(6296)-2SA-16:2(3287)▪21:15(5774)-PR-24:10(7503)-IS-1:5(1742)▪13:7(7503)▪29:8▪40:29(3287),30(3286),31(3286)▪44:12(3286)-JER-8:18(1742)▪51:46(7401)-LA-1:13(1738),22(1742)▪2:19(5848)▪5:17(1739)-EZE-21:7(3543),15(4127)-AM-8:13(5968)▪N.T-all=1590&marked-M’T-15:32-M’R-8:3-LU-18:1(1573)-2CO-4:1(1573),16(1573)-GA-6:9(1590)-EPH-3:13(1573)-HEB-12:3,5

FAINTED-GE-45:26(6313)▪47:13(3856)-PS-107:5(5848)-IS-51:20(5968)JER-45:3(3021)-EZE-31:15(5969)-DA-8:27(1961)-JON-2:7(5848)▪4:8(5968)▪N.T-M’T-9:36(1590)-RE-2:3(2577)

FAINTEST-JOB-4:5(3811)

FAINTETH-PS-84:2(3615)▪119:81(3615)-IS-10:18(4549)▪40:28(3286)

FAINTHEARTED-DE-20:8(7390,3824)-IS-7:4(3824,7401)-JER-49:23(4127)

FAINTNESS-LE-26:36(4816)

FAIR-all=3303,a=3302&marked-GE-6:2(2896)▪12:11,14▪24:16(2896)▪26:7(2896)-1SA-17:42-2SA-13:1▪14:27-1KI-1:3,4-ES-1:11(2896)▪2:2(2896,4758),3(2896,4758),7(3303,8389)-JOB-37:22(2091)▪42:15-PR-7:21(3948)▪11:22▪26:25(2603)-SONG-1:15^{2}a,16a▪2:10a,13a▪4:1^{2}a,7a,10a▪6:10▪7:6a-IS-5:9(2896)▪54:11(6320)-JER-4:30a▪11:16▪12:6(2896)▪46:20(3304)-EZE-16:17(8597),39(8597)▪23:26(8597)▪31:3,7a,9-DA-4:12(8209),21(8209)-HO-10:11(2898)-AM-8:13-ZEC-3:5^{2}(2889)▪N.T.-M’T-16:2(2105)-AC-7:20(791)▪27:8(2568)-RO-16:18(2129)-GAL-6:12(2146)

FAIRER-J’G-15:2(2896)-PS-45:2(3302)-DA-1:15(2896)

FAIREST-all=3303-SONG-1:8▪5:9▪6:1

FAIRS-all=5801-EZE-27:12,14,16,19,22,27

FAITH-DE-32:20(529)-HAB-2:4(530)▪N.T.-all=4102&marked-M’T-6:30(3640)▪8:10,26(3640)▪9:2,22,29▪14:31(3640)▪15:28▪16:8(3640)▪17:20▪21:21▪23:23-M’R-2:5▪4:40▪5:34▪10:52▪11:22-LU-5:20▪7:9,50▪8:25,48▪12:28(3640)▪17:5,6,19▪18:8,42▪22:32-AC-3:16^{2}▪6:5,7,8▪11:24▪13:8▪14:9,22,27▪15:9▪16:5▪20:21▪24:24▪26:18-RO-1:5,8,12,17^{2}▪3:3,22,25,27,28,30^{2},31▪4:5,9,11,12,13,14,16^{2},19,20▪5:1,2▪9:30,32▪10:6,8,17▪11:20▪12:3,6▪14:1,22,23^{2}▪16:26-1CO-2:5▪12:9▪13:2,13▪15:14,17▪16:13-2CO-1:24^{2}▪4:13▪5:7▪8:7▪10:15▪13:5-GA-1:23▪2:16^{2},20▪3:2,5,7,8,9,11,12,14,22,23^{2},24,25,26▪5:5,6,22▪6:10-EPH-1:15▪2:8▪3:12,17▪4:5,13▪6:16,23-PH’P-1:25,27▪2:17▪3:9^{2}-COL-1:4,23▪2:5,7,12-1TH-1:3,8▪3:2,5,6,7,10▪5:8-2TH-1:3,4,11▪3:2-1TI-1:2,4,5,14,19^{2}▪2:7,15▪3:9,13▪4:1,6,12▪5:8,12▪6:10,11,12,21-2TI-1:5,13▪2:18,22▪3:8,10,15▪4:7-TIT-1:1,4,13▪2:2▪3:15-PH’M-5,6-HEB-4:2▪6:1,12▪10:22,23(1680),38▪11:1,3,4,5,6,7^{2},8,9,11,13,17,20,21,22,23,24,27,28,29,30,31,33,39▪12:2▪13:7-JAS-1:3,6▪2:1,5,14^{2},17,18^{3},20,22^{2},24,26▪5:15-1PE-1:5,7,9,21▪5:9-2PE-1:1,5-1JO-5:4-JUDE-3,20-RE-2:13,19▪13:10▪14:12

FAITHFUL-all=539&marked-NU-12:7-DE-7:9-1SA-2:35▪22:14-2SA-20:19-NE-7:2(571)▪9:8▪13:13-PS-12:1▪31:23▪89:37▪101:6▪119:86(530),138(530)-PR-11:13▪13:17(529)▪14:5(529)▪20:6(529)▪25:13▪27:6▪28:20(530)-IS-1:21,26▪8:2▪49:7-JER-42:5-DA-6:4(540)-HO-11:12▪N.T-all=4103-M’T-24:45▪25:21^{2},23^{2}-LU-12:42▪16:10^{2},11,12▪19:17-AC-16:15-1CO-1:9▪4:2,17▪7:25▪10:13-GA-3:9-EPH-1:1▪6:21-COL-1:2,7▪4:7,9-1TH-5:24-2TH-3:3-1TI-1:12,15▪3:11▪4:9▪6:2-2TI-2:2,11,13-TIT-1:6,9▪3:8-HEB-2:17▪3:2,2sup,5▪10:23▪11:11-1PE-4:19▪5:12-1JO-1:9-RE-1:5▪2:10,13▪3:14▪17:14▪19:11▪21:5▪22:6

FAITHFULLY-all=530&marked-2KI-12:15▪22:7-2CH-19:9▪31:12▪34:12-PR-29:14(571)-JER-23:28(571)▪N.T.-3JO-5(4103)

FAITHFULNESS-all=530&marked

-1SA-26:23-PS-5:9(3559)■26:5■40:10■88:11■89:1,2,5,8,24,33■92:2■119:75,90■143:1-IS-11:5■25:1-LA-3:23-HO-2:20

FAITHLESS-all=571-M'T-17:17-M'R-9:19-LU-9:41-JOH-20:27

FALL-all=5307,a=3782&marked-GE-2:21■43:18■45:24(7264)■49:17-EX-5:3(6293)■15:16■21:33-LE-11:32,37,38■26:7,8,36,37a-NU-11:31(5203)■14:3,29,32,43■34:2-DE-22:4,8-JOS-6:5-J'G-8:21(6293)■15:12(6293),18-RU-2:16(7997)■3:18-1SA-3:19■14:45■18:25■21:13(3381)■22:17(6293),18(6293)■26:20-2SA-1:15(6293)■14:11■24:14^{2}-1KI-1:52■2:29(6293),31(6293)■22:20-2KI-7:4■10:10■14:10■19:7-1CH-12:19■21:13^{2}-2CH-18:19■21:15(3318)■25:8a,19-ES-6:13^{2}-JOB-13:11■31:22-PS-5:10■9:3a■10:10■35:8■37:24■45:5■63:10(5064)■64:8a■72:11(7812)■78:28■82:7■91:7■118:3■140:10(4131)■141:10■145:14-PR-4:16a■10:8(3832),10(3832)■11:5,14,28■16:18(3783)■22:14■24:16a■26:27■28:10,14,18■29:16(4658)-EC-4:10■10:8■11:3-IS-3:25■8:15■10:4,34■13:15■22:25■24:18,20■28:13a■30:13,25■31:3a,3,8■34:4(5034)■37:7■40:30a■44:19(5456)■45:14(7812)■46:6(5456)■47:11■54:15-JER-3:12■6:15,21a■8:4,12■9:22■15:8■19:7■20:4■23:12,19(2342)■25:27,34■30:23(2342)■37:14■39:18■44:12■46:6,16a■48:44■49:21,26■50:30,32■51:4,44,47,49^{2}-LA-1:14a-EZE-5:12■6:7,11,12■11:10■13:11^{2},14■17:21■23:25■24:6,21■25:13■26:15(4658),18(4658)■27:27,34■29:5■30:4,5,6^{2},17,22,25■31:16(4658)■32:10(4658),12(4658),20(4658)■33:12a,27■35:8■36:15a■38:20^{2}■39:3,4,5■44:12(4383)■47:14-DA-3:5(5308),10(5308),15(5308)■11:14a,19,26,33a,34a,35a-HO-4:5^{2}a,14(3832)■5:5^{2}a■7:16■10:8■13:16■14:9(3872)-JOE-2:8-AM-3:5,14■7:17■8:14■9:9-MIC-7:8-NA-3:12■N.T-all=4098&marked-M'T-4:9■7:27(4431)■10:29■12:11(1706)■15:14,27■21:44^{2}■24:29-M'R-13:25(1601)-LU-2:34(4431)■6:39■8:13(868)■10:18■20:18^{2}■21:24■23:30-JOH-12:24-AC-27:17(1601),32(1601),34-RO-11:11,11(3900),12(3900)■14:13(4625)-1CO-10:12-1TI-3:6(1706)-HEB-4:11■6:6(3895)■10:31(1706)-JAS-1:2(4045)■5:12-2PE-1:10(4417)■3:17(1601)-RE-4:10■6:16■9:1

FALLEN-all=5307&marked-GE-4:6-LE-13:40(4803),41(4803)■25:35(4131,3027)-NU-32:19(935)-JOS-2:9■8:24-J'G-3:25■18:1■19:27-1SA-5:3,4■26:12■31:8-2SA-1:4,10,12,19,25,27■3:38■22:39-1CH-10:8-2CH-20:24■29:9-ES-7:8-JOB-1:16-PS-7:15■16:6■18:38■20:8■36:12■55:4■57:6■69:9-IS-3:8■9:10■14:12■16:9■21:9■26:18■59:14(3782)-JER-38:19■46:12■48:32■50:15■51:8-LA-2:21■5:16-EZE-13:12■31:12■32:22,23,24,27-HO-7:7■14:1(3782)-AM-5:2■9:11-ZEC-11:2■N.T-all=4098&marked-LU-14:5(1706)-AC-8:16(1968)■15:16■20:9(2702)■26:14(2667)■27:29(1601)■28:6(2667)-1CO-15:6(2837),18(2837)-GA-5:4(1601)-PH'P-1:12(2064)-RE-2:5(1601)■14:8■17:10■18:2

FALLEST-JER-37:13(5307)

FALLETH-all=5307&marked-EX-1:10(7122)-LE-11:33,35-NU-33:54(3318)-2SA-3:29,34■17:12-JOB-4:13■33:15-PR-13:17■17:20■24:16,17-EC-4:10■9:12■11:3-IS-34:4(5304)■44:15(5456),17(5456)-JER-21:9-DA-3:6(5038),11(5038)■N.T.-all=4098&marked-M'T-17:15-LU-11:17■15:12(1911)-RO-14:4-JAS-1:11(1601)-1PE-1:24(1601)

FALLING-NU-24:4(5307),16(5307)-JOB-4:4(3782)■14:18(5307)-PS-56:13(1762)■116:8(1762)-PR-25:26(4131)-IS-34:4(5034)■N.T.-LU-8:47(4363)■22:44(2597)-AC-1:8(4248,1096)■27:41(4045)-1CO-14:25(4098)-2TH-2:3(646)-JUDE-24(679)

FALLOW-DE-14:5(3180)-JER-4:3(5215)-HO-10:12(5215)

FALLOWDEER-1KI-4:23(3180)

FALSE-all=8267&marked-EX-20:16■23:1(7723),7-DE-5:20(7723)■19:16(2555),18-2KI-9:12-JOB-36:4-PS-27:12■35:11(2555)■119:104,128■120:3(7423)-PR-6:19■11:1(4820)■12:17■14:5■17:4(205)■19:5,9■20:23(4820)■21:28(3577)■25:14,18-JER-14:14■23:32■37:14-LA-2:14(7723)-EZE-21:23(7723)-ZEC-8:17■10:2(7723)-MAL-3:5■N.T-all=5578&marked-M'T-7:15■15:19(5577)■19:18(5576)■24:11,24sup,24■26:59(5580),60^{2}(5575)-M'R-10:19(5576)■13:22(5580),22■14:56(5576),57(5576)-LU-6:26■18:20(5576)■19:8(4811)-AC-6:13(5571)■13:6-RO-13:9(5576)-1CO-15:15(5575)-2CO-11:13(5570),26(5569)-GA-2:4(5569)-2TI-3:3(1228)-TIT-2:3(1228)-2PE-2:1,1(5572)-1JO-4:1-RE-16:13■19:20■20:10

FALSEHOOD-all=8267&marked-2SA-18:13-JOB-21:34(4604)-PS-7:14■119:118■144:8,11-IS-28:15■57:4■59:13-JER-10:14■13:25■51:17-HO-7:1-MIC-2:11

FALSELY-all=8267&marked-GE-21:23(8266)-LE-6:3(5921,8267),5■19:11(3584),12-DE-19:18-PS-44:17(8266)-JER-5:2,31■6:13■7:9■8:10■29:9■40:16■43:2-HO-10:4(7723)-ZEC-5:4■N.T.-M'T-5:11(5574)-1TI-6:20(5581)

FALSIFYING-AM-8:5(5791)

FAME-all=8088&marked-GE-45:16(6963)-NU-14:15-JOS-6:27(8089)■9:9(8089)-1KI-4:31(8034)■10:1,7(8052)-1CH-14:17(8034)■22:5(8034)-2CH-9:1,6(8052)-ES-9:4(8089)-JOB-28:22-IS-66:19-JER-6:24(8089)-ZEP-3:19(8034)■N.T-all=189&marked-M'T-4:24■9:26(5345),31(1310)■14:1-M'R-1:28-LU-4:14(5345),37(2279)■5:15(3056)

FAMILIAR-JOB-19:14(3045)-PS-41:9(7965)

FAMILIARS-JER-20:10(7965)

FAMILIES-all=4940&marked-GE-10:5,18,20,31,32■12:3■28:14■36:40■47:12(2945)-EX-6:14,15,17,19,24,25■12:21-LE-25:45-NU-1:2,18,20,22,24,26,28,30,32,34,36,38,40,42■2:34■3:15,18,19,20^{2},21,23,27,29,30,33,35,39■4:2,18,22,24,28,29,33,34,36,37,38,40,41,42^{2},44,45,46■11:10■26:7,12,14,15,18,20,22,23,25,26,27,28,34,35,37^{2},38,41,42^{2},43,44,47,48,50,57,58■27:1■33:54■36:1^{2},12-JOS-7:14■13:15,23,24,28,29,31■15:1,12,20■16:5,8■17:2^{2}■18:11,20,21,28■19:1,8,10,16,17,23,24,31,32,39,40,48■21:4,5,6,7,10,20,26,27,33,34,40^{2}-1SA-9:21■10:21-1CH-2:53,55■4:2,8,21,38■5:7■6:19,54,60,62,63,66■7:5-2CH-35:5(1004),5(1004,1),12(1004,1)-NE-4:13-JOB-31:34-PS-68:6(1004)■107:41-JER-1:15■2:4■10:25■25:9■31:1■33:24-EZE-20:32-AM-3:2-NA-3:4-ZE-12:14■14:17

FAMILY-all=4940-LE-20:5■25:10,41,47,49-NU-3:21,21,27^{4},33^{2}■26:5^{2},6^{2},12^{3},13^{2},15^{3},16^{2},17^{2},20^{3},21^{2},23^{2},24^{2},26^{3},29^{2},30^{2},31^{2},32^{2},35^{3},36,38^{3},39^{2},40^{2},42,44^{3},45^{2},48^{2},49^{2},57^{3},58^{5}■27:4,11■36:6,8,12-DE-29:18-JOS-7:14,17^{3}-J'G-1:25■6:15(504)■9:1■13:2■17:7■18:2,11,19■21:24-RU-2:1-1SA-9:21■10:21■18:18■20:6,29-2SA-14:7■16:5-1CH-4:27■6:61,70,71■13:14(1004)-ES-9:28-JER-3:14■8:3-AM-3:1-MIC-2:3-ZEC-12:12^{3},13^{2},14■14:18■N.T-EPH-3:15(3965)

FAMINE-all=7458&marked-GE-12:10^{2}■26:1^{2}■41:27,30^{2},31,36^{2},50,56^{2},57■42:5,19(7459),33(7459)■43:1■45:6,11■47:4,13^{2},20-RU-1:1-2SA-21:1■24:13-1KI-8:37■18:2-2KI-6:25■7:4■8:1■25:3-1CH-21:12-2CH-20:9■32:11-JOB-5:20,22(3720)■30:3(3720)-PS-33:19■37:19(7459)■105:16-IS-14:30■51:19-JER-5:12■11:22■14:12,13,15^{2},16,18■15:2■16:4■18:21■21:7,9■24:10■27:8,13■29:17,18■32:24,36■34:17■38:2■42:16,17,22■44:12^{2},13,18,27■52:6-LA-5:10-EZE-5:12,16^{2},17■6:11,12■7:15^{2}■12:16■14:13,21■36:29,30-AM-8:11^{2}■N.T.-all=3042-LU-4:25■15:14-RO-8:35-RE-18:8

FAMINES-all=3042-M'T-24:7-M'R-13:8-LU-21:11

FAMISH-PR-10:3(7456)-ZEP-2:11(7329)

FAMISHED-GE-41:55(7456)-IS-5:13(7458)

FAMOUS-all=8034&marked-NU-16:2(7148)■26:9(7121)-RU-4:11(7121,8034),14(7121)-1CH-5:24■12:30-PS-74:5(3045)■136:18(117)-EZE-23:10■32:18(117)

FAN-all=2219&marked-IS-30:24(4214)■41:16-JER-4:11■15:7,7(4214)■51:2■N.T.-3:12(4425)-LU-3:17(4425)

FANNERS-JER-51:2(2114)

FAR-all=7350,a=7368,b=4801&marked-GE-18:25^{2}(2486)■44:4a-EX-8:28a■23:7a-NU-2:2(5048)-DE-12:21a■13:7■14:24a■20:15■28:49■29:22■30:11-JOB-3:16a■8:1a■9:6,9,22-J'G-9:17(5048)■18:7,28■19:11(3966)-1SA-2:30(2486)■20:9(2486)■22:15(2486)-2SA-15:17b■20:20(2486)■23:17(2486)-1KI-8:41,46-2KI-20:14-2CH-6:32,36■26:15-EZR-6:6(7352)-NE-4:19-ES-9:20-JOB-5:4■11:14■13:21■19:13■21:16■22:18,23■30:10■34:10(2486)-PS-10:5(5048)■22:1,11a,19a■35:22a■38:21a■55:7a■71:12a■73:27(7369)■88:8a,18a■97:9(3966)■103:12^{2}■109:17a■119:150a,155-PR-4:24a■5:8a■15:29■19:7a■22:5a,15a■25:25b■27:10■30:8(7369)■31:10-EC-7:23,24-IS-5:26■6:12a■8:9b■10:3b■13:5b■17:13b■22:3■26:15a■29:13a■30:27b■33:13,17b■39:3■43:6■46:11b,12,13a■49:1,12,19a■54:14a■57:9,19■59:9a,11a■60:4,9-JER-2:5a■4:16b■5:15b■6:20b■8:19b■12:2■25:26■27:10a■48:24,47(2008)■49:30(3966)■51:64(2008)-LA-1:16a■3:17(2186)-EZE-6:12■7:20(5079)■8:6a■11:15a,16a■12:27■22:5■23:40b■43:9■44:10-DA-9:7■11:2(1419)-JOE-2:20a■3:6a,8-MIC-7:11a-HAB-1:8-ZEC-6:15■10:9b■N.T.-all=3112-M'T-15:8(4206)■16:22(2436)-M'R-6:35^{2}(4183)■7:6(4206)■8:3(3113)■12:34-LU-7:6■15:13(3117)■19:12(3117)■22:51(2193)■24:50(2193)-JOH-21:8-AC-11:19(2193),22(2193)■17:27■22:21■28:15(891)-2CO-4:17(1519,5236)■10:14(891)-EPH-1:21(5231)■2:13■4:10(5231)-PH'P-1:23(4183,3123)-HEB-7:15(4054)

FARE-1SA-17:18(7965)-JON-1:3(7939)■N.T.-AC-15:29(4517)

FARED-LU-16:19(2165)

FAREWELL-LU-9:61(657)-AC-18:21(657)■23:30(4517)-2CO-13:11(5463)

FARM-M'T-22:5(68)

FARTHER-M'T-26:39(4281)-M'R-1:19(4260)■10:1(4008)

FARTHING-M'T-5:26(2835)■10:29(787)-M'R-12:42(2835)

FARTHINGS-LU-12:6(787)

FASHION-EX-26:30(4941)-1KI-6:38(4941)-2KI-16:10(1823)-JOB-31:15(3559)-EZE-43:11(8498)■N.T.-M'R-2:12(3778)-LU-9:29(1419)-AC-7:44(5179)-1CO-7:31(4976)-PH'P-2:8(4976)-JAS-1:11(4383)

FASHIONED-all=3335&marked-EX-32:4-JOB-10:8(6213)-PS-119:73(3559)■139:16-IS-22:11-EZE-16:7(3559)■N.T.-PH'P-3:21(4832)

FASHIONETH-all=3335-PS-33:15-IS-4:12■45:9

FASHIONING-1PE-1:14(4964)

FASHIONS-EZE-42:11(4941)

FAST-all=6685,a=6684&marked-2SA-12:21a,23a-1KI-21:9,12-2CH-20:3-EZR-5:8(629)■8:21-ES-4:16^{2}a-IS-58:3,4^{2}a,5^{2},6-JER-14:12a■36:9■48:16(3966)-JOE-1:14■2:15-JON-3:5-ZEC-7:5a■8:19^{4}■N.T.-all=3522&marked-M'T-6:16^{2},

18■9:14^2,15-M'R-2:18^3,19^2,20-LU-5:33,34,35■18:12-AC-16:24(805)■27:9(3521)-1TH-5:21(2722)-TIT-1:9(472)-HEB-3:6(2722)■10:23(2722)

FASTED-all=6684-J'G-20:26-1SA-7:6■31:13-2SA-1:12■12:16,22-1KI-21:27-1CH-10:12-EZR-8:23-NE-1:14-IS-58:3-ZEC-7:5■N.T.-all=3522-M'T-4:2-AC-13:2,3

FASTEN-all=5414&marked-EX-28:14,25■39:31-IS-22:23(8628)-JER-10:4(2388)

FASTENED-all=8628&marked-EX-39:18(5414)■40:18(5414)-J'G-4:21(6795)■16:14-1SA-31:10-2SA-20:8(6775)-1KI-6:6(270)-1CH-10:10-2CH-9:18(270)-ES-1:6(270)-JOB-38:6(2883)-EC-12:11(5193)-IS-22:25■41:7(2388)-EZE-40:43(3559)■N.T.-LU-4:20(816)-AC-11:6(816)■28:3(2510)

FASTENING-AC-3:4(816)

FASTEST-M'T-6:17(2522)

FASTING-all=6685&marked-NE-9:1-ES-4:3-PS-35:13■69:10■109:24-JER-36:6-DA-6:18(2908)■9:3-JOE-2:12■N.T.-all=3521-M'T-15:32(3523)■17:21-M'R-8:3(3523)■9:29-AC-10:30(3522)■14:23■27:33(777)-1CO-7:5

FASTINGS-ES-9:31(6685)■N.T.-all=3521-LU-2:37-2CO-6:5■11:27

FAT-all=2459&marked-GE-4:4■41:4(1277),20(1277)■45:18■49:20(8082)-EX-23:18■29:13^2,22^3-LE-1:8(6309),12(6309)■3:3^2,4,9^3,10,14^2,15,16,17■4:8^3,9,19,26^2,31^2,35^2■6:12-LE-7:3^2,4,23,24^2,25,30,31,33■8:16^2,20(6309),25^3,26■9:10,19,20^2,24■10:15■16:25■17:6-NU-13:20(8082)■18:17-DE-31:20(1878)■32:14^2,15^2(8080),38-J'G-3:17(1277),22-1SA-2:15,16,29(1254)■15:22■28:24(4770)-2SA-1:22-1KI-1:9(4806),19(4806),25(4806)■4:23(1277)■8:64^2-1CH-4:40(8082)-2CH-7:7^2■29:35■35:14-NE-8:10(4924)■9:25^2(8082),35(8082)-JOB-15:27(6371)-PS-17:10■22:29(1879)■37:20(3368)■92:14(1879)■119:70(2954)-PR-11:25(1878)■13:4(1878)■15:30(1878)■28:25(1878)-IS-1:11■5:17(4220)■6:10(8082)■10:16(4924)■25:6^2(8081)■28:1(8081),4(8081)■30:23(1879)■34:6^2(1878),7(1878)■43:24■58:11(2502)-JER-5:28(8080)■50:11(6335)-EZE-34:3,14(8082),16(8082),20(1277)■39:19■44:7,15■45:15(4945)-AM-5:22(4806)-HAB-1:16(8082)-ZEC-11:16(1277)

FATFLESHED-GE-41:2(1277),18(1277)

FATHER-all=1,a=2859,b=25,c=2&marked-GE-2:24■4:20,21■9:18,22^2,23■10:21■11:28,29■17:4,5■19:31,32^2,33^2,34^2,35,36,37,38■20:12■22:7,21■26:3,15,18^2,24■27:6,9,10,12,14,18,19,22,26,30,31^2,32,34^3,38^3,39,41^2■28:2,7,8,13■29:12■31:5,6,7,9,16,18,29,35,42,53^2■32:9^2■33:19■34:4,6,11,13,19■35:18,27■36:9,24,43■37:1,2,4,10^2,11,22,32,35■38:13(2524),25(2524)■42:13,29,32^2,35,36,37■43:2,7,8,11,23,27,28■44:17,19,20^2,22,22sup,24,25,27,30,31,32^2,34^2■45:3,8,9,13,13sup,18,19,23^2,25,27■46:1,3,5,29■47:1,5,6,7,11,12■48:1,9,17,18,19■49:2,25,26,28■50:2,5^2,6,7,10,14^2,15,16,17-EX-2:18■3:1a,6■4:18a■18:1a,2a,4,5a,6a,7a,8a,12^{2}a,14a,15a,17a,24a,27a■20:12■21:15,17■22:17■40:15-LE-18:7,9,11■19:3■20:9^2■21:2,9,11■24:10(1121,376)-NU-3:4,24,30,35■6:7■10:29a■12:14■18:2■27:3,4^2,7,11■30:4^2,5^2,16■36:6,8,12-DE-5:16■21:13,18,19■22:15,16,19,29■26:5■27:16,22■32:6,7■33:9-JOS-2:13,18■6:23■15:13,18■17:1,4■19:47■21:11■24:2,3,32-J'G-1:14,16a■4:11a■6:25■8:32■9:1,17,28,56■11:36,37,39■14:2,3^2,4,5,6,9,10,16■15:1,2,6■16:31^2■17:10■18:19,29■19:3,4a,4,5,6,7a,8,9a,9-RU-2:11■4:17-1SA-2:25,27,28,30■4:19(2524),21(2524)■9:3,5■10:2,12■14:1,27,28,29,51^2■19:2,3^2,4■20:1,2^2,3,6,8,9,10,12,13^2,32,33,34■22:3,15■23:17^2■24:11-2SA-2:32■3:8■6:21■7:14■9:7■10:2^2,3■13:5■16:3,21■17:8^2,10,23■19:37■21:14-1KI-1:6■2:12,24,26^2,31,32,44■3:3,6,7,14■5:1,3,5■6:12■7:14,51■8:15,17,18,20,24,25,26■9:4,5■11:4,6,27,33,43■12:4^2,6,9,10,11^2,14^2■13:11,12■15:3^2,11,15,19,24,26■19:20■20:34^2■22:43,46,50,52,53-2KI-2:12■3:2^2,13■4:18,19■5:13■6:21■9:25■13:14,25■14:3^2,5,21■15:3,34,38■16:2■18:3■20:5■21:3,20,21^2■22:2■23:34■24:9-1CH-2:17,21,23,24,42^2,44,45,49^3,50,51^2,52,55■4:3,4^3,5,11,12,14,17,18^3,19,21^2■7:14,22,31■8:29b■9:19,35b■17:13b■19:2^{2}b,3b■22:10b■24:2b,19b■25:3b,6b■26:6b,10b■28:4^{3}b,6b,9b■29:10b,23b-2CH-1:8b,9b■2:3b,7b,14^{2}b,17b■3:1b■4:16b■5:1b■6:4b,7b,8b,10b,15b,16b■7:17b,18b■8:14b■9:31b■10:4^{2}b,6b,9b,10b,11^{2}b,14^{2}b■15:18b■16:3b■17:2b,3b,4b■20:32b■21:3b,4b,12^{2}b■22:4b■24:22b■25:3b■26:1b,4b■27:2b■28:1b■29:2b■33:22^2,23■34:2,3-ES-2:7^2-JOB-15:10■17:14■29:16■31:18■38:28■42:15-PS-27:10■68:5■89:26■103:13-PR-1:8■3:12■4:1■10:1■15:20■17:21,25■19:13,26■20:20■23:22,24,25■28:7,24■29:3■30:11,17-IS-3:6■8:4■9:6■22:21■38:5,19■43:27■45:10■51:2■58:14■63:16^2■64:8-JER-2:27■3:4,19■12:6■16:7■20:15■22:11,15■31:9■35:6,8,10,16,18-EZE-16:3,45■18:4,17,18,19,20^2■22:7■44:25-DA-5:2c,11^{3}c,13c,18c-AM-2:7c-MIC-7:6c-ZEC-13:3^{2}c-MAL-1:6^{2}c■2:10c■N.T.-all=3962&marked-M'T-2:22■3:9■4:21,22■5:16,45,48■6:1,4,6^2,8,9,14,15,18^2,26,32■7:11,21■8:21■10:20,21,29,32,33,35,37■11:25,26,27^3■12:50■13:43■15:4^2,5,6,13■16:17,27■18:10,14,19,35■19:5,19,29■20:23■21:31■23:9^2■24:36■25:34■26:39,42,53■28:19-M'R-1:20■5:40■7:10^2,11,12■8:38■9:21,24■10:7,19,29■11:10,25,26■13:12,32■14:36■15:21-LU-1:32,59,62,67,73■2:48■3:8■6:36■8:51■9:42,59■10:21^2,22^2■11:2,11,13■12:30,53^2■14:26■15:12,18^2,20^2,21,22,27,28,29■16:24,27,30■18:20■22:29,42■23:34,46■24:49-JOH-1:14,18■3:35■4:12,21,23^2,53■5:17,18,19,20,21,22,23^2,26,30,36^2,37,45■6:27,32,37,42,44,45,46^2,57^2,65■8:16,18,19^3,27,28,29,38^2,39,41^2,42,44^3,49,53,54,56■10:15^2,17,18,29,30,32,36,37,38■11:41■12:26,27,28,49,50■13:1,3■14:6,7,8,9^2,10^2,11^2,12,13,16,20,21,23,26,28^2,31^2■15:1,8,9,15,16,23,24,26^2■16:3,10,15,16,17,23,25,26,27,28^2,32■17:1,5,11,21,24,25■18:11,13(3995)■20:17^2,21-AC-1:4,7■2:33■7:2,4,14■16:1,3■28:8-RO-1:7■4:1,11,12^2,16,17,18■6:4■8:15■9:10■15:6-1CO-1:3■8:6■15:24-2CO-1:2,3^2■6:18■11:31-GA-1:1,3,4■4:2,6-EPH-1:2,3,17■2:18■3:14■4:6■5:20,31■6:2,23-PH'P-1:2■2:11,22■4:20-COL-1:2,3,12■2:2■3:17-1TH-1:1^2,3■2:11■3:11,13-1TH-1:1,2■2:16-1TI-1:2■5:1-2TI-1:2-TIT-1:4-PH'M-3-HEB-1:5■7:3(540),10■12:7,9-JAS-1:17,27■2:21■3:9-1PE-1:2,3,17-2PE-1:17-1JO-1:2,3■2:1,13,15,16,22,23,23sup,24■3:1■4:14■5:7-2JO-3^2,4,9-JUDE-1-RE-1:6■2:27■3:5,21

FATHERLESS-all=3490&marked-EX-22:22,24-DE-10:18■14:29■16:11,14■24:17,19,20,21■26:12,13■27:19-JOB-6:27■22:9■24:3,9■29:12■31:17,21-PS-10:14,18■68:5■82:3■94:6■109:9,12■146:9-PR-23:10-IS-1:17,23■9:17■10:2-JER-5:28■7:6■22:3■49:11-LA-5:3(369,1)-EZE-22:7-HO-14:3-ZEC-7:10-MAL-3:5■N.T.-JAS-1:27(3737)

FATHER'S-all=1&marked-GE-9:23■12:1■20:13■24:7,23,38,40■26:15■28:21■29:9,12■31:1^2,5,14,19,30■35:22■37:2,12■38:11^2■41:51■46:31^2■47:12■48:17■49:4,8■50:1,8,22-EX-2:16■6:20(1733)■15:2-LE-16:32■18:8^2,11,12^2,14■20:11^2,17,19■22:13^2-NU-2:2■18:1■27:7,10■30:3,16■36:11(1730)-DE-22:21^2,30^2■27:20^2-JOS-2:12,18■6:25-J'G-6:15,25,27■9:5,18■11:2,7■14:15,19■19:2,3-1SA-2:31■9:20■17:15,25,34■18:2,18■22:1,11,16,22■24:21-2SA-3:7,29■9:7■14:9■15:34■16:19,21,22■19:28■24:17-1KI-11:12,17■12:10■18:18-2KI-10:3■23:30■24:17(1730)-1CH-5:1■7:2,40■12:28■21:17■23:11-2CH-2:13■10:10■21:13■36:1-EZR-2:59-NE-1:6-ES-4:14-PS-45:10-PR-4:3■6:20■13:1■15:5■27:10-IS-7:17■22:23,24-JER-35:14-EZE-18:14■22:11■N.T.-all=3962-M'T-26:29-LU-2:49■9:26■12:32■15:17■16:27-JOH-2:16■5:43■6:39■10:25,29■14:2,24■15:10-AC-7:20-1CO-5:1-RE-14:1

FATHERS-all=1&marked-GE-15:15■31:3■46:34■47:3,9,30■48:15,16,21■49:29-EX-3:13,15,16■4:5■6:25■10:6■12:3■13:5,11■20:5■34:7-LE-25:41■26:39,40-NU-1:2,4,16,18,20,22,24,26,28,30,32,34,36,38,40,42,44,45,47■2:32,34■3:15,20■4:2,22,29,34,38,40,42,46■7:2■11:12■13:2■14:18,23■17:2^2,3■20:15^2■26:55■31:26■32:8,28■33:54■34:14^2■36:1^2,3,4,7,8-DE-1:8,11,21,35■4:1,31,37■5:3,9■6:3,10,18,23■7:8,12,13■8:1,3,16,18■9:5■10:11,15,22■11:9,21■12:1■13:6,17■19:8^2■24:16^2■26:3,7,15■27:3■28:11,36,64■29:13,25■30:5^2,9,20■31:7,16,20■32:17-JOS-1:6■4:21■5:6■14:1■18:3■19:51■21:1^2,43,44■22:14,28■24:2,6^2,14,15,17-J'G-2:1,10,12,17,19,20,22■3:4■6:13■21:22-IS-12:6,7,8^2,15-2SA-7:12-1KI-1:21■2:10■8:1,21,34,40,48,53,57,58■9:9■11:21,43■13:22■14:15,20,22,31^2■15:8,12,24^2■16:6,28■19:4■21:3,4■22:40,50^2-2KI-8:24^2■9:28■10:35■12:18,21■13:9,13■14:6^2,16,20,22,29■15:7^2,9,22,38^2■16:20^2■17:13,14,15,41■19:12■20:17,21■21:8,15,18,22■22:13,20■23:32,37■24:6-1CH-4:38■5:13,15,24^2,25■6:19■7:4,7,9,11■8:6,10,13,28■9:9,13,19,33,34■12:17,30■15:12■17:11■23:9,24^2■24:4^2,6,30,31^2■26:13,21,26,31,32■27:1■29:6,15,18,20-2CH-1:2■5:2■6:25,31,38■7:22■9:31■11:16■12:16■13:12,18■14:1,4■15:12■16:13■17:14■19:4,8■20:6,33■21:1^2,10,19■23:2■24:18,24■25:4^2,5,28■26:2,12,23^2■27:9■28:6,9,25,27■29:5,6,9■30:7^2,8,19,22■31:17■32:13,14,15,33■33:8,12,20■34:21,28,32,33■35:4,5,24■36:15-EZR-1:5■2:68■3:12■4:2,3,15(2)■5:12(2)■7:27■8:1,28,29■9:7■10:11,16-NE-7:70,71■8:13■9:2,9,16,23,32,34,36■10:34■11:13■12:12,22,23■13:18-JOB-8:8■15:18■30:1-PS-22:4■39:12■44:1■45:16■49:19■78:3,5,8,12,57■95:9■106:6,7■109:14-PR-17:6■19:14■22:28-IS-14:21■37:12■39:6■64:11■65:7-JER-2:5■3:18,24,25■6:21■7:7,14,18,22,25,26■9:14,16■11:4,5,7,10■13:14■14:20■16:3,11,12,13,15,19■17:22■19:4■23:27,39■24:10■25:5■30:3■31:29,32■32:18,22■34:5,13,14,15■44:3,9,10,17,21■47:3■50:7-LA-5:7-EZE-2:3■5:10^2■18:2■20:4,18,27,30,36,42■36:28■37:25■47:14-DA-2:23(2)■9:6,8,16■11:24,37,38-HO-9:10-JOE-1:2-AM-2:4-MIC-7:20-ZEC-1:2,4,5,6■8:14-MAL-2:10■3:7■4:6^2■N.T.-all=3962&marked-M'T-23:30,32-LU-1:17,55,72■6:23,26■11:47,48-JOH-4:20■6:31,49,58■7:22-AC-3:13,22,25■5:30■7:2,11,12,15,19,32,38,39,44,45^2,51,52■13:17,32,36■15:10■22:1,3(3971),14■24:14(3971)■26:6■28:17(3971),25-RO-9:5■15:8-1CO-4:15■10:1-GA-1:14(3967)-EPH-6:4-COL-3:21-1TI-1:9(3964)-HEB-1:1■3:9■8:9■12:9-1PE-1:18(3970)-2PE-3:4-1JO-2:13,14

FATHERS'-all=1-EX-6:14■10:6-NU-17:6■26:2■32:14-NE-2:3,5-EZE-20:24■22:10■N.T.-RO-11:28(3962)

FATHOMS-AC-27:28^2(3712)

FATLING-IS-11:6(4806)

FATLINGS-1SA-15:9(4932)-2SA-6:13(4806)-PS-66:15(4220)-EZE-39:18(4806)■N.T.-M'T-22:4(4619)

FATNESS-all=1880&marked-GE-27:28(4924),39(4924)-J'G-9:9-JOB-15:27(2459)■36:16-PS-36:8■63:5■65:11■

73:7(2459)■109:24(8081)-**IS**-17:4(4924)■34:6(2459),7(2459)■55:2-**JER**-31:14■**N.T.**-**RO**-11:17(4096)

FATS-**JOE**-2:24(3342)■3:13(3342)

FATTED-**1KI**-4:23(75)-**JER**-46:21(4770)■**N.T.**-all=4618-**LU**-15:23,27,30

FATTER-**DA**-1:15(1277)

FATTEST-**PS**-78:31(4924)-**DA**-11:24(4924)

FAULT-**EX**-5:16(2398)-**DE**-25:2(7564)-**1SA**-29:3(3972)-**2SA**-3:8(5771)-**PS**-59:4(5771)-**DA**-6:4[2](7844)■**N.T.**-all=156&marked-**M'T**-18:15(1651)-**M'R**-7:2(3201)-**LU**-23:4(158),14(158)-**JOH**-18:38■19:4,6-**RO**-9:19(3201)-**1CO**-6:7(2275)-**GA**-6:1(3900)-**HEB**-8:8(3201)-**RE**-14:5(299)

FAULTLESS-**HEB**-8:7(273)-**JUDE**-24(299)

FAULTS-**GE**-41:9(2399)■**N.T.**-**JAS**-5:16(3900)-**1PE**-2:20(264)

FAULTY-**2SA**-14:13(818)-**HO**-10:2(816)

FAVOUR-all=2580&marked-**GE**-18:3■30:27■39:21-**EX**-3:21■11:3■12:36-**NU**-11:11,15-**DE**-24:1■28:50(2603)■33:23(7522)-**JOS**-11:20(8467)-**RU**-2:13-**1SA**-2:26(2896)■16:22■20:29■25:8■29:6(2896)-**2SA**-15:25-**1KI**-11:19-**NE**-2:5(3190)-**ES**-2:15,17(2617)■5:2,8■7:3■8:5-**JOB**-10:12(2617)-**PS**-5:12(7522)■30:5(7522),7(7522)■35:27(2655)■44:3(7520)■45:12(6440)■89:17(7522)■102:13(2603),14(2603)■106:4(7522)■109:12(2603)■112:5(2603)■119:58(6440)-**PR**-3:4■8:35(7522)■11:27(7522)■12:2(7522)■13:15■14:9(7522),35(7522)■16:15(7522)■18:22(7522)■19:6(6440),12(7522)■21:10(2603)■22:1■28:23■29:26(6440)■31:30-**EC**-9:11-**SONG**-8:10(7965)-**IS**-26:10(2603)■27:11(2603)■60:10(7522)-**JER**-16:13(2594)-**DA**-1:9(2617)■**N.T.**-all=5485-**LU**-1:30■2:52-**AC**-2:47■7:10,46■25:3

FAVOURABLE-all=7520-**J'G**-21:22(2603)-**JOB**-33:26-**PS**-77:7■85:1

FAVOURED-all=4758&marked-**GE**-29:17■39:6■41:2,3,4[2],18(8389),19(8389)-**LA**-4:16(2603)-**DA**-1:4■**N.T.**-**LU**-1:28(5487)

FAVOUREST-**PS**-41:11(2654)

FAVOURETH-**2SA**-20:11(2654)

FEAR-all=3372,a=6343,b=3373,c=3374&marked-**GE**-9:2(4172)■15:1■20:11c■21:17■26:24■31:42a,53a■32:11b■35:17■42:18b■43:23■46:3■50:19,21-**EX**-9:30■14:13■15:16(367)■18:21b■20:20,20c■23:27(367)-**LE**-19:3,14,32■25:17,36,43-**NU**-14:9[2]■21:34-**DE**-1:21■2:25c■3:2,22■4:10■5:29■6:2,13,24■8:6■10:12,20■11:25a■13:4,11■14:23■17:13,19■19:20■20:3■21:21■28:58,66(6342),67a,67(6342)■31:6,8,12,13-**JOS**-4:24■8:1■10:8,25■22:24(1674)■24:14-**J'G**-4:18■6:10,23■7:10b■9:21(6440)-**RU**-3:11-**1SA**-4:20■11:7a■12:14,20,24■21:10(6440)■22:23■23:17,26(6440)-**2SA**-9:7■13:28■23:3c-**1KI**-8:40,43■17:13■18:12-**2KI**-4:1b■6:16■17:28,34b,35,36,37,38,39■25:24-**1CH**-14:17a■16:30(2342)■28:20-**2CH**-6:31,33■14:14a■17:10a■19:7a,9c■20:17,29(6343)-**EZR**-3:3(367)-**NE**-1:11■5:9c,15c■6:14,19-**ES**-8:17a■9:2a,3a-**JOB**-1:9■4:6c,14a■6:14c■9:34(367),35■11:15■15:4c■21:9a■22:4c,10a■25:2a■28:28c■31:34(6206)■37:24■39:16a,22a■41:33(2844)-**PS**-2:11c■5:7c■9:20(4172)■14:5(6342)■15:4b■19:9c■22:23b,23(1481),25b■23:4■25:14b■27:1,3■31:11a,13(4032),19b■33:8,18b■34:7b,9,9b,11c■36:1a■40:3■46:2■48:6(7461)■49:5■52:6■53:5[2]a■55:19■56:4■60:4b■61:5b■64:1a,4,9■66:16b■67:7■72:5■85:9b■86:11■90:11c■96:9(2342)■102:15■103:11b,13b,17b■105:38a■111:5b,10c■115:11b,13b■118:4b,6■119:38c■39(3025)63,74b,79b,120a■135:20b■145:19b■147:11b-**PR**-1:7c,26a,27a,29c,33a■2:5c■3:7,25a■8:13c■9:10c■10:24(4034),27c■14:26c,27c■15:16c,33c■16:6c■19:23c■20:2(367)■22:4c■23:17c■24:21■29:25(2731)-**EC**-3:14■5:7■8:12b,12■12:13-**SONG**-3:8a-**IS**-2:10a,19a,21a■7:4,25c■8:12,12(4172),13(4172)■11:2c,3c■14:3(7267)■19:16(6342)■21:4(2731)■24:17a,18a■25:3■29:13c,23(6206)■31:9(4032)■33:6c■35:4■41:10,13,14■43:1,5■44:2,8(6342),11(6342)■51:7■54:4,14■59:19■60:5(6342)■63:17c-**JER**-2:19(6345)■5:22,24■6:25(4032)■10:7■20:10(4032)■23:4■26:19b■30:5a,10■32:39,40c■33:9(6342)■35:11[2](6440)■37:11(6440)■40:9■41:9(6440)■46:5(4032),27,28■48:43a,44a■49:5a,24(7374),29(4032)■50:16(6440)■51:46-**LA**-3:47a,57-**EZE**-3:9■30:13c-**DA**-1:10b■6:26(1763)■10:12,19-**HO**-3:5(6342)■10:5(1481)-**JOE**-2:21-**AM**-3:8-**JON**-1:9b-**MIC**-7:17-**ZEP**-3:7,16-**HAG**-1:12■2:5-**ZEC**-8:13,15■9:5-**MAL**-1:6(4172)■2:5(4172)■3:5■4:2b■**N.T.**-all=5401,a=5399&marked-**M'T**-1:20a■10:26a,28[2]a,31a■14:26■21:26a■28:4,5a,8-**LU**-1:12,13a,30a,50a,65,74(870)■2:10a■5:10a,26■7:16■8:37,50a■12:5[2]a,7a,32a■18:4a■21:26■23:40a-**JOH**-7:13■12:15a■19:38■20:19-**AC**-2:43■5:5,11■9:31■13:16a■19:17■27:24a-**RO**-3:18■8:15■11:20a■13:7-**1CO**-2:3■16:10(870)-**2CO**-7:1,11,15■11:3a■12:20a-**EPH**-5:21■6:5-**PH'P**-1:14(870)■2:12-**1TI**-5:20(5401,2192)-**2TI**-1:7(1167)-**HEB**-2:15■4:1a■11:7(2125)■12:21(1630,1510),28(2124)■13:6a-**1PE**-1:17■2:17a,18■3:2,15-**1JO**-4:18[2]-**JUDE**-12(870),23-**RE**-1:17a■2:10a■11:11,18a■14:7a■15:4a■18:10,15■19:5a

FEARED-all=3372&marked-**GE**-19:30■26:7-**EX**-1:17,21■2:14■9:20(3373)■14:31-**DE**-25:18(3373)■32:17(8175),27(1481)-**JOS**-4:14[2]■10:2-**J'G**-6:27■8:20-**1SA**-3:15■12:18■14:26■15:24-**2SA**-3:11■10:19■12:18-**1KI**-1:50■3:28■18:3(3373)-**2KI**-17:7,25,32(3373),33(3373),41(3373)-**1CH**-16:25-**2CH**-20:3-**NE**-7:2-**JOB**-1:1(3373)■3:25(6342)-**PS**-76:7,8,11(4172)■78:53(6342)■89:7(6206)■96:4■130:4-**IS**-41:5■51:13(6342)■57:11-**JER**-3:8■42:16(3373)■44:10-**EZE**-11:8-**DA**-5:19(1763)-**HO**-10:3-**JON**-1:16-**MAL**-2:5■3:16[2]■**N.T.**-all=5399&marked-**M'T**-14:5■21:46■27:54-**M'R**-4:41(5399,5401)■6:20■11:18,32■12:12-**LU**-9:34,45■18:2■19:21■20:19■22:2-**JOH**-9:22-**AC**-5:26■10:2■16:38-**HEB**-5:7(2124)

FEAREST-**GE**-22:12(3373)-**IS**-57:11(3372)-**JER**-22:25(1481)

FEARETH-all=3373&marked-**1KI**-1:51(3372)-**JOB**-1:8■2:3-**PS**-25:12■112:1(3372)■128:1,4-**PR**-13:13■14:2,16■28:14(6342)■31:30-**EC**-7:18■8:13■9:2-**IS**-50:10■**N.T.**-all=5399-**AC**-10:22,35■13:26-**1JO**-4:18

FEARFUL-**EX**-15:11(3372)-**DE**-20:8(3373)■28:58(3372)-**J'G**-7:3(3373)-**IS**-35:4(4116)■**N.T.**-**M'T**-8:26(1169)-**M'R**-4:40(1169)-**LU**-21:11(5400)-**HEB**-10:27(5398),31(5398)-**RE**-21:8(1169)

FEARFULLY-**PS**-139:14(3372)

FEARFULNESS-**PS**-55:5(3374)-**IS**-21:4(6427)■33:14(7461)

FEARING-**JOS**-22:25(3372)■**N.T.**-all=5399&marked-**M'R**-5:33-**AC**-23:10(2125)■27:17,29-**GA**-2:12-**COL**-3:22-**HEB**-11:27

FEARS-**PS**-34:4(4035)-**EC**-12:5(2849)-**IS**-66:4(4035)■**N.T.**-**2CO**-7:5(5401)

FEAST-all=2282,a=4960&marked-**GE**-19:3a■21:8a■26:30a■29:22a■40:20a-**EX**-5:1(2287)■10:9■12:14,14(2287)■13:6■23:14(2287),15,16[2]■32:5■34:18,22[2],25-**LE**-23:6,34,39,41-**NU**-28:17■29:12-**DE**-16:10,13,14,15(2287),16[2]■31:10-**J'G**-14:10a,12a,17a■21:19(2282)-**1SA**-25:36[2]a-**2SA**-3:20a-**1KI**-3:15a■8:2,65■12:32[2],33-**2CH**-5:3■7:8,9■8:13[3]■30:13,21,22(4150)■35:17-**EZR**-3:4■6:22-**NE**-8:14,18-**ES**-1:3a,5a,9a■2:18[2]a■8:17a-**PS**-81:3-**PR**-15:15a-**EC**-10:19(3899)-**IS**-25:6[2]a-**LA**-2:7(4150)-**EZE**-45:21,23,25-**DA**-5:1(3900)-**HO**-2:11■9:5■12:9(4150)-**AM**-5:21-**ZEC**-14:16,18,19■**N.T.**-all=1859&marked-**M'T**-26:5■27:15-**M'R**-14:2■15:6-**LU**-2:41,42■5:29(1408)■14:13(1408)■22:1(1859)■23:17(1859)-**JOH**-2:8(755),9[2](755),23■4:45[2]■5:1■6:4■7:2,8[2],10,11,14,37■10:22(1456)■11:56■12:12,20■13:1,29-**AC**-18:21-**1CO**-5:8(1858)-**2PE**-2:13(4910)-**JUDE**-12(4910)

FEASTED-**JOB**1:4(6213,4960)

FEASTING-all=4960-**ES**-9:17,18,19,22-**JOB**-1:5-**EC**-7:2-**JER**-16:8

FEASTS-all=4150&marked-**LE**-23:2[2],4,37,44-**NU**-15:3■29:39-**1CH**-23:31-**2CH**-2:4■8:13■31:3-**EZR**-3:5-**NE**-10:33-**PS**-35:16(4580)-**IS**-5:12(4960)-**JER**-51:39(4960)-**LA**-1:4■2:6-**EZE**-36:38■45:17(2282)■46:9,11(2282)-**HO**-2:11-**AM**-8:10(2282)-**NA**-1:15(2282)-**ZEC**-8:19-**MAL**-2:3(2282)■**N.T.**-all=1173-**M'T**-23:6-**M'R**-12:39-**LU**-20:46-**JUDE**-12

FEATHERED-**PS**-78:27(3671)-**EZE**-39:17(3671)

FEATHERS-all=5133&marked-**LE**-1:16-**JOB**-39:13(2624)-**PS**-68:13(84)■91:4(84)-**EZE**-17:3,7

FED-all=7462&marked-**GE**-30:36■36:24■41:2,18■47:17(5095)■48:15-**EX**-16:32(398)-**DE**-8:3(398),16(398)-**2SA**-20:3(3557)-**1KI**-18:4(3557),13(3557)-**1CH**-27:29-**PS**-37:3■78:72■81:16(398)-**IS**-1:11(4806)-**JER**-5:8(2109)-**EZE**-16:19(398)■34:3(1277),8[2]-**DA**-4:12(2110)■5:21(2939)-**ZEC**-11:7■**N.T.**-**M'T**-25:37(5142)-**M'R**-5:14(1006)-**LU**-8:34(1006)■16:21(5526)-**1CO**-3:2(4222)

FEEBLE-all=7503&marked-**GE**-30:42(5848)-**DE**-25:18(2826)-**1SA**-2:5(535)-**2SA**-4:1-**2CH**-28:15(3782)-**NE**-4:2(537)-**JOB**-4:4(3766)-**PS**-38:8(6313)■105:37(3782)-**PR**-30:26(3808,6099)-**IS**-16:14(3808,3524)■35:3(3782)-**JER**-6:24■49:24■50:43-**EZE**-7:17■21:7-**ZEC**-12:8(3782)■**N.T.**-**1CO**-12:22(772)-**HEB**-12:12(3886)

FEEBLEMINDED-**1TH**-5:14(3642)

FEEBLENESS-**JER**-47:3(7510)

FEEBLER-**GE**-30:42(5848)

FEED-all=7462&marked-**GE**-25:30(3938)■29:7■30:31■37:12,13,16-**EX**-22:5(1197)■34:3-**1SA**-17:15-**2SA**-5:2■7:7■19:33(3557)-**1KI**-17:4(3557)■22:27(398)-**1CH**-11:2■17:6-**2CH**-18:26(398)-**JOB**-24:2-**PS**-28:9■49:14■78:71-**PR**-10:21■30:8(2963)-**SONG**-1:8■4:5■6:2-**IS**-5:17■11:7■14:30■27:10■30:23■40:11■49:9,26(398)■58:14(398)■61:5■65:25-**JER**-3:15■6:3■9:15(398)■23:2,4,15(398)■50:19-**LA**-4:5(398)-**EZE**-34:2[2],3,10,13,14[2],15,16,23[2]-**DA**-11:26(398)-**HO**-4:16■9:2-**JON**-3:7-**MIC**-5:4■7:14[2]-**ZEP**-2:7■3:13-**ZEC**-11:4,7,9,16(3557)■**N.T.**-all=4165&marked-**LU**-15:15(1006)-**JOH**-21:15(1006),16,17(1006)-**AC**-20:28-**RO**-12:20(5595)-**1CO**-13:3(5595)-**1PE**-5:2-**RE**-7:17■12:6(5142)

FEEDEST-**PS**-80:5(398)-**SONG**-1:7(7462)

FEEDETH-all=7462-**PR**-15:14-**SONG**-2:16■6:3-**IS**-44:20-**HO**-12:1■**N.T.**-**M'T**-6:26(5142)-**LU**-12:24(5142)-**1CO**-9:7(4165)

FEEDING-all=7462-**GE**-37:2-**JOB**-1:14-**EZE**-34:10■**N.T.**-all=1006&marked-**M'T**-8:30-**M'R**-5:11-**LU**-8:32■17:7(4165)-**JUDE**-12(4165)

FEEDINGPLACE-**NA**-2:11(4829)

FEEL-**GE**-27:12(4959),21(4184)-**J'G**-16:26(4184)-**JOB**-20:20(3045)-**PS**-58:9(995)-**EC**-8:5(3045)■**N.T.**-**AC**-17:27(5584)

FEELING-**EPH**-4:19(524)-**HEB**-4:15(4834)

FEET-all=7272&marked-**GE**-18:4■19:2■24:32[2]■43:24■49:10,33-**EX**-3:5■4:25■12:11■24:10■25:26■30:19,21■37:13■40:31-**LE**-8:24■11:21,23,42-**NU**-20:19

-DE-2:28■11:24■28:57■33:3-JOS-3:13,15■4:3,9,18■9:5■10:24^{2}■14:9-J'G-3:24■4:10,15,17■5:27^{2}■19:21-RU-3:4(4772),7(4772),8(4772),14(4772)-1SA-2:9■14:13■24:3■25:24,41-2SA-3:34■4:4,12■9:3,13■11:8■19:24■22:10,34,37(7166),39-1KI-2:5■5:3■14:6,12■15:23-2KI-4:27,37■6:32■9:35■13:21■19:24(6471)■21:8-1CH-28:2-2CH-3:13■16:12-NE-9:21-ES-8:3-JOB-12:5■13:27^{2}■18:8,11■29:15■30:12■33:11-PS-8:6■18:9,33,36(7166),38■22:16■25:15■31:8■40:2■47:3■56:13■58:10(6471)■66:9■73:2■74:3(6471)■105:18■115:7■116:8■119:59,101,105■122:2-PR-1:16■4:26■5:5■6:13,18,28■7:11■19:2■26:6■29:5(6471)-SONG-5:3■7:1(6471)-IS-3:16■6:2■7:20■23:7■26:6■28:3■32:20■37:25(6471)■41:3■49:23■52:7■59:7■60:13,14-JER-13:16■14:10■18:22■38:22-LA-1:13■3:34-EZE-1:7^{2}■2:1,2■3:24■16:25■24:17,23■25:6■32:2■34:18^{2},19^{2}■37:10■43:7-DA-2:33(7271),34(7271),41(7271),42(7271)■7:4(7271),7(7271),19(7271)■10:6(4772)-NA-1:3,15-HAB-3:5,19-ZEC-14:4,12-MAL-4:3■N.T.-all=4228&marked-M'T-7:6■10:14■15:30■18:8,29■28:9-M'R-5:22■6:11■7:25■9:45-LU-1:79■7:38^{3},44^{2},45,46■8:35,41■9:5■10:39■15:22■17:16■24:39,40-JOH-11:2,32■12:3^{2}■13:5,6,8,9,10,12,14^{2}■20:12-AC-3:7(939)■4:35,37■5:2,9,10■7:33,58■10:25■13:25,51■14:8,10■16:24■21:11■22:3■26:16-RO-3:15■10:15■16:20-1CO-12:21■15:25,27-EPH-1:22■6:15-1TI-5:10-HEB-2:8■12:13-RE-1:15,17■2:18■3:9■10:1■11:11■12:1■13:2■19:10■22:8

FEIGN-1KI-14:5(5234)■N.T.-LU-20:20(5271)

FEIGNED-PS-17:1(4820)■N.T.-2PE-2:3(4112)

FEIGNEDLY-JER-3:10(8267)

FEIGNEST-1KI-14:6(5234)-NE-6:8(908)

FELL-all=5307&marked-GE-4:5■14:10■15:12^{2}■17:3,17■33:4■44:14■45:14■46:29■50:1,18-EX-32:28-LE-9:24■16:9(5927),10(5927)-NU-11:9^{2}(3381)■14:5■16:4,22,45■20:6■22:27(7257),31(7812)-DE-9:18,25^{2}-JOS-5:14■6:20■7:6■8:25■11:7■16:1(3318)■17:5■22:20(1961)-J'G-4:16■5:27^{3}■7:13■8:10■12:6■13:20■16:30■19:26■20:44,46-RU-2:10-1SA-4:10,18■11:7■14:13■17:49,52■20:41■22:18(6298)■25:23,24■28:20■29:3■30:13■31:1,4,5-2SA-1:2■2:16,23^{2}■4:4■9:6■11:17■13:2■14:4,22■18:28(7812)■19:18■20:8■21:9,22-1KI-2:25(6293),32(6293),34(6293),46(6293)■18:7,38,39■20:30-2KI-1:2,13(3766)■2:13,14■3:19■4:8(1961),11(1961),18(1961),37■6:5,6■7:20(1961)■25:11-1CH-5:10,22■10:1,4,5■12:19,20■20:8■21:14,16■26:14■27:24(1961)-2CH-13:17■15:9■17:10(1961)■20:18■21:19(3318)■25:13(6584)-EZR-9:5(3766)-ES-8:3,17■9:2,3-JOB-1:15,17(6584),19,20-PS-27:2■78:64■105:38■107:12(3782)-JER-39:9■46:16■52:15-LA-1:7■5:13(3782)-EZE-1:28■3:23■8:1■9:8■11:5,13■39:23■43:3■44:4-DA-2:46(5308)■3:7(5308),23(5308)■4:31(5308)■7:20(5308)■8:17■10:7-JON-1:7■N.T.-all=4098&asmarked-M'T-2:11■7:25,27■13:4,5,7,8■17:6■18:26,29■26:39-M'R-3:11(4363)■4:4,5,7,8■5:22,33(4363)■7:25(4363)■9:20■14:35-LU-1:12(1968)■5:8(4363),12■6:49■8:5,6,7,8,14,28(4363),41■10:30(4045)■36(1706)■13:4■15:20(1968)■16:21■17:16-JOH-11:32■18:6-AC-1:26■5:5,10■9:4,18(634)■10:10(1968),25,44(1968)■11:15(1968)■12:7(1601)■13:11(1968)■16:29(4363)■19:17(1968),35(1356)■20:9,10(1968),37(1968)■22:7-RO-11:22■15:3(1968)-1CO-10:8-HEB-3:17■11:30-RE-1:17■5:8,14■6:13■7:11■8:10^{2}■11:11,13,16■16:2(1096),19,21(2597)■19:4,10■22:8

FELLED-2KI-3:25(5307)

FELLER-IS-14:8(3772)

FELLEST-2SA-3:34(5307)

FELLING-2KI-6:5(5307)

FELLOES-1KI-7:33(2839)

FELLOW-all=7453&marked-EX-2:13-J'G-7:13,14,22-1SA-14:20■29:4(376)-2SA-2:16-EC-4:10(2270)-IS-34:14-JON-1:7-ZEC-13:7(5997)

FELLOWCITIZENS-EPH-2:19(4847)

FELLOWDISCIPLES-JOH-11:16(4827)

FELLOWHEIRS-EPH-3:6(4789)

FELLOWHELPER-2CO-8:23(4904)

FELLOWHELPERS-3JO-8(4904)

FELLOWLABOURER-1TH-3:2(4904)-PH'M-1(4904)

FELLOWLABOURERS-PH'P-4:3(4904)-PH'M-24(4904)

FELLOWPRISONER-COL-4:10(4869)-PH'M-23(4869)

FELLOWPRISONERS-RO-16:7(4869)

FELLOW'S-2SA-2:16(7453)

FELLOWS-all=2270&marked-J'G-11:37(7464)■18:25(582)-PS-45:7-IS-44:11-EZE-37:19-DA-2:13(2269),18(2269)■7:20(2273)-ZEC-3:8(7453)■N.T.-M'T-11:16(2083)-AC-17:5(435)-HEB-1:9(3353)

FELLOWSERVANT-all=4889-M'T-18:29,33-COL-1:7■4:7-RE-19:10■22:9

FELLOWSERVANTS-all=4889-M'T-12:28,31■24:49-RE-6:11

FELLOWSHIP-LE-6:2(8667,3027)-PS-94:20(2266)■N.T.-all=2842&marked-AC-2:42-1CO-1:9■10:20(2844)-2CO-6:14(3352)■8:4-GA-2:9-EPH-3:9■5:11(4790)-PH'P-1:5■2:1■3:10-1JO-1:3^{2},6,7

FELLOWSOLDIER-PH'P-2:25(4961)-PH'M-2(4961)

FELLOWWORKERS-COL-4:11(4904)

FELT-GE-27:22(4959)-EX-10:21(4959)-PR-23:35(3045)■N.T.-M'R-5:29(1097)-AC-28:5(3958)

FEMALE-all=5347&marked-GE-1:27■5:2■6:19■7:2^{2}(802),3,9,16-LE-3:1,6■4:28,32■5:6■12:7■27:4,5,6,7-NU-5:3-DE-4:16■N.T.-all=2338-M'T-19:4-M'R-10:6-GA-3:28

FENCE-PS-62:3(1447)

FENCED-all=1219,a=4013&marked-NU-32:17a,36a-DE-3:5■9:1■28:52-JOS-10:20a■14:12■19:35a-1SA-6:18a-2SA-20:6(1211)■23:7(4390)-2KI-3:19a■10:2a■17:9a■18:8a,13■19:25-2CH-8:5(4692)■11:10(4694),23(4694)■12:4(4694)■14:6(4694)■17:2,19a■19:5■21:3(4694)■32:1■33:14-JOB-10:11(7753)■19:8(1443)-IS-2:15■5:2(5823)-JER-5:17a■15:20-EZE-36:35-DA-11:15a-HO-8:14-ZEP-1:16

FENS-JOB-40:21(1207)

FERRET-LE-11:30(604)

FERRY-2SA-19:18(5679)

FERVENT-AC-18:25(2204)-RO-12:11(2204)-2CO-7:7(2205)-1PE-4:8(1618)

FERVENTLY-1PE-1:22(1619)

FETCH-all=3947&marked-GE-18:5■27:9,13,45■42:16-EX-2:5-NU-20:10(3318)-DE-19:12■24:10(5670),19■30:4-J'G-11:5■20:10-1SA-4:3■6:21(5927)■16:11■20:31■26:22-2SA-14:13(7725),20(5437)-1KI-17:10,11-2KI-6:13-NE-8:15(935)-JOB-36:3(5375)-IS-56:12-JER-36:21■N.T.-AC-16:37(1806)

FETCHED-all=3947&marked-GE-18:4■27:14-J'G-18:18-1SA-7:1(5927)■10:23-2SA-4:6■9:5■11:27(622)■14:2-1KI-7:13■9:28-2KI-11:4-2CH-1:17(5927)■12:11(5375)-JER-26:23(3318)

FETCHETH-DE-19:5(5080)

FETCHT-GE-18:7(3947)

FETTERS-all=5178&marked-J'G-16:21-2SA-3:34-2KI-25:7-2CH-33:11■36:6-JOB-36:8(2131)-PS-105:18(3525)■149:8(3525)■N.T.-M'R-5:4^{2}(3976)-LU-8:29(3976)

FEVER-DE-28:22(6920)■N.T.-all=4446&marked-M'T-8:14(4445),15-M'R-1:30(4445),31-LU-4:38,39-JOH-4:52-AC-28:8

FEW-all=4592&marked-GE-27:44(259)■29:20(259)■34:30(4962)■47:9-LE-25:52■26:22(4591)-NU-9:20(4557)■13:18■26:54,56■35:8,8(4591)-DE-4:27(4962)■26:5■28:62■33:6(4557)-JOS-7:3-1SA-14:6■17:28-2KI-4:3(4591)-1CH-16:19(4962),19-2CH-29:34-NE-2:12■7:4-JOB-10:20■14:1(7116)■16:22(4557)-PS-105:12(4962),12■109:8-EC-5:2■9:14■12:3-IS-10:7,19(4557)■24:6(4213)-JER-30:19(4591)■42:2-EZE-5:3■12:16(4557)-DA-11:20(259)■N.T.-all=3641&marked-M'T-7:14■9:37■15:34■20:16■22:14■25:21,23-M'R-6:5■8:7-LU-10:2■12:48■13:23-AC-17:4,12■24:4(4935)-EPH-3:3-HEB-12:10■13:22(1024)-1PE-3:20-RE-2:14,20■3:4

FEWER-NU-33:54(4592)

FEWEST-DE-7:7(4592)

FEWNESS-LE-25:16(4591)

FIDELITY-TIT-2:10(4102)

FIELD-all=7704,a=1251,&marked-GE-2:5^{2},19,20■3:1,14,18■4:8■23:9,11,13,17^{3},19,20■24:63,65■25:9,10,27,29■27:3,5,27■29:2■30:14,16■31:4■33:19■34:5,7,28■36:35■37:7,15■39:5■41:48■47:20,24■49:29,30^{2},32■50:13^{2}-EX-1:14■9:3,19^{2},21,22,25^{3}■10:5,15■16:25■22:5^{3},6,31■23:11,16^{2},29-LE-14:7■17:5■19:9,19■23:22■25:3,4,12,34■26:4■27:16,17,18,19,20^{2},21^{2},22,24,28-NU-22:4,23■23:14-DE-5:21■7:22■14:22■20:19■21:1■22:25,27■24:19^{2}■28:3,16,38-JOS-8:24■15:18-J'G-1:14■5:4,18■9:32,42,43■13:9■19:16■20:31-RU-2:2,3^{2},8,9,17,22■4:5-IS-4:2■6:14,18■11:5■14:15■17:44■19:3■20:5,11^{2},24,35■30:11-2SA-10:8■11:23■14:6,30^{2}(2513),31(2513)■17:8■18:6■20:12■21:10-1KI-11:29■14:11■21:24-2KI-4:39■7:12■8:6■9:25,37■18:17■19:26-1CH-1:46■19:9■27:26-2CH-26:23■31:5-NE-13:10-JOB-5:23^{2}■24:6■40:20-PS-8:7■50:11■78:12,43■80:13■96:12■103:15■104:11-PR-24:27,30■27:26■31:16-EC-5:9-SONG-2:7■3:5■7:11-IS-5:8■7:3■36:2■37:27■40:6■43:20■55:12■56:9-JER-4:17■6:25■7:20■9:22■12:4,9■14:5,18■17:3■18:14■26:18■27:6■28:14■32:7,8,9,25■35:9■41:8-LA-4:9-EZE-7:15■16:5,7■17:5,24■20:46■26:6,8■29:5(776)■31:4,5,6,13,15■32:4■33:27■34:5,8,27■36:30■38:20■39:4,5,10,17-DA-2:38a■4:12a,15a,21a,23^{2}a,25a,32a-HO-2:12,18■4:3■10:4-JOE-1:10,11,12,19,20■2:22-MIC-1:6■3:12■4:10-ZEC-10:1-MAL-3:11■N.T.-all=68&marked-M'T-6:28,30■13:24,27,31,36,38,44^{2}■24:18,40■27:7,8,10-M'R-13:16-LU-2:8■12:28■15:25■17:7,31,36-AC-1:18(5564),19^{2}(5564)

FIELDS-all=7704&marked-EX-8:13-LE-14:53■25:31■27:22-NU-16:14■19:16■20:17■21:22-DE-11:15■32:13,32(7709)-JOS-21:12-J'G-9:27,44-1SA-8:14■22:7■25:15-2SA-1:21■11:11-1KI-2:26■16:4-2KI-23:4(7709)-1CH-6:56■16:32■27:25-2CH-31:19-NE-11:25,30■12:29,44-JOB-5:10(2351)-PS-107:37■132:6-PR-8:26(2351)■23:10-IS-16:8(7709)■32:12-JER-6:12■8:10■13:27■31:40(8309)■32:15,43,44■39:10(3010)■40:7,13-EZE-29:5-HO-12:11-OB-19-MIC-2:2,4-HAB-3:17(7709)■N.T.-LU-15:15(68)-JOH-4:35(5561)-JAS-5:4(5561)

FIERCE-all=2740&marked-GE-49:7(5794)-EX-32:12-NU-25:4■32:14-DE-28:50(5794)-1SA-20:34(2750)■28:18-2CH-28:11,13■29:10-EZR-10:14-JOB-4:10(7826)■10:16(7826)■28:8(7826)■

41:10(393)-IS-7:4(2750)▪13:9,13▪19:4(5794)▪33:19(3267)-JER-4:8,26▪12:13▪25:37,38▪30:24▪49:37▪51:45-LA-1:12▪2:3(2750)▪4:11-DA-8:23(5794)-JON-3:9-HAB-1:8(2300)-ZEP-2:2▪3:8▪N.T.-M'T-8:28(5467)-LU-23:5(2001)-2TI-3:3(434)-JAS-3:4(4642)

FIERCENESS-all=2740&marked-DE-13:17-JOS-7:26-2KI-23:26-2CH-30:8-JOB-39:24(7494)-PS-78:49▪85:3-JER-25:38-HO-11:9-NA-1:6▪N.T.-RE-16:19(2372)▪19:15(2372)

FIERCER-2SA-19:43(7185)

FIERY-all=5135,a=8314&marked-NU-21:6a,8a-DE-8:15a▪33:2(799)-PS-21:9(784)-IS-14:29a▪30:6a-DA-3:6,11,15,17,20,21,23,26▪7:9,10▪N.T.-EPH-6:16(4448)-HEB-10:27(4442)-1PE-4:12(4451)

FIFTEEN-all=2568,6240&marked-GE-5:10▪7:20▪25:7(7657,2568)-EX-27:14,15▪38:14,15,25(7657,2568)-LE-27:7-NU-31:37(7657,2568)-J'G-8:10-2SA-9:10▪19:17-1KI-7:3-2KI-14:17▪20:6-2CH-25:25-IS-38:5-EZE-45:12(6235,2568)-HO-3:2▪N.T.-all=1178&marked-JOH-11:18-AC-7:14(1440,4002)▪27:28-GA-1:18

FIFTEENTH-all=2568,6240-EX-16:1-LE-23:6,34,39-NU-28:17▪29:12▪33:3-1KI-12:32,33-2KI-14:23-1CH-24:14▪25:22-2CH-15:10-ES-9:18,21-EZE-32:17▪45:25▪N.T.-LU-3:1(4003)

FIFTH-all=2549&marked-GE-1:23▪30:17▪41:34(2567)▪47:24,26(2569)-LE-5:16▪6:5▪19:25▪22:14▪27:13,15,19,27,31-NU-5:7▪7:36▪29:26▪33:38-JOS-19:24-J'G-19:8-2SA-2:23(2570)▪3:4,27(2570)▪4:6(2570)▪20:10(2570)-1KI-6:31▪14:25-2KI-8:16(2568)▪25:8-1CH-2:14▪3:3▪8:2▪12:10▪24:9▪25:12▪26:3,4▪27:8-2CH-12:2-EZR-7:8,9-NE-6:5,15(2568)-JER-1:3▪28:1▪36:9▪52:12-EZE-1:1(2568),2(2568),2▪8:1(2568)▪20:1▪33:21(2568)-ZEC-7:3,5▪8:19▪N.T.-all=3391-RE-6:9▪9:1▪16:10▪21:20

FIFTIES-all=2572&marked-EX-18:21,25-DE-1:15-1SA-8:12-2KI-1:14▪N.T.-M'R-6:40(4004)-LU-9:14(4004)

FIFTIETH-all=2572-LE-25:10,11-2KI-15:23,27

FIFTY-all=2572-GE-6:15▪7:24▪8:3▪9:28,29▪18:24^{2},26,28-EX-26:5^{2},6,10^{2},11▪27:12,13,18▪30:23^{2}▪36:12^{2},13,17^{2},18▪38:12,13,26-LE-23:16▪27:3,16-NU-1:23,25,29,31,43,46▪2:6,8,13,15,16^{2},30,31,32▪4:3,23,30,35,36,39,43,47▪8:25▪16:2,17,35▪26:10,34,47▪31:30,47,52-DE-22:29-JOS-7:21-1SA-6:19-2SA-15:1▪24:24-1KI-1:5▪7:2,6▪9:23▪10:29▪18:4,13,19,22-2KI-1:9,10^{3},11,12^{2},13^{3}▪2:7,16,17▪13:7▪15:2,20,25▪21:1-1CH-5:21^{2}▪8:40▪9:9▪12:33-2CH-1:17▪2:17▪3:9▪8:10,18▪26:3▪33:1-EZR-2:7,14,15,22,29,30,31,37,60▪8:3,6,26-NE-5:17▪6:15▪7:10,12,20,33,34,40,70-ES-5:14▪7:9-IS-3:3-EZE-40:15,21,25,29,33,36▪42:2,7,8▪45:2▪48:17^{4}-HAG-2:16▪N.T.-all-4004&marked-LU-7:41▪16:6-JOH-8:57▪21:11-AC-13:20▪19:19(4002,3461)

FIG-all=8384&marked-GE-3:7-DE-8:8-J'G-9:10,11-1KI-4:25-2KI-18:31-PS-105:33-PR-27:18-SONG-2:13-IS-34:4▪36:16-JER-5:17▪8:13-HO-2:12▪9:10-JOE-1:7,12▪2:22-AM-4:9-MIC-4:4-NA-3:12-HAB-3:17-HAG-2:19-ZEC-3:10▪N.T.-all=4808-M'T-21:19^{2},20,21▪24:32-M'R-11:13,20,21▪13:28-LU-13:6,7▪21:29-JOH-1:48,50-JAS-3:12-RE-6:13

FIGHT-all=3898&marked-EX-1:10▪14:14▪17:9-DE-1:30,41,42▪2:32(4421)▪3:22▪20:4,10-JOS-9:2▪10:25▪11:5▪19:47-J'G-1:1,3,9▪8:1▪9:38▪10:9,18▪11:6,8,9,12,25,32▪12:1,3▪20:20(4421)-1SA-4:9▪8:20▪13:5▪15:18▪17:9,10,20(4634),32,33▪18:17▪23:1▪28:1▪29:8-2SA-11:20-1KI-12:21,24▪20:23,25,26(4421)▪22:31,32-2KI-3:21▪10:3▪19:9-2CH-11:1,4▪13:12▪18:30,31▪20:17▪32:2(4421),8▪35:20,22^{2}-NE-4:8,14,20-PS-35:1▪56:2▪144:1(4421)-IS-19:2▪29:7^{2}(6633),8(6633)▪30:32▪31:4(6633)-JER-1:19▪15:20▪21:4,5▪32:5,24,29▪33:5▪34:22▪37:8,10▪41:12▪51:30-DA-10:20▪11:11-ZEC-10:5▪14:3,14▪N.T.-all=75&marked-JOH-18:36-AC-5:39(2314)▪23:9(2313)-1CO-9:26(4438)-1TI-6:12,12(73)-2TI-4:7,7(73)-HEB-10:32(119)▪11:34(4171)-JAS-4:2(3164)-RE-2:16(4170)

FIGHTETH-all=3898-EX-14:25-JOS-23:10-1SA-25:28

FIGHTING-1SA-17:19(3898)-2CH-26:11(6213,4421)-PS-56:1(3898)

FIGHTINGS-2CO-7:5(3163)-JAS-4:1(3163)

FIGS-all=8384&marked-NU-13:23▪20:5-2KI-20:7-NE-13:15-SONG-2:13(6291)-IS-38:21-JER-8:13▪24:1,2^{3},3,5,8▪29:17▪N.T.-all=4810&marked-M'T-7:16-M'R-11:13-LU-6:44-JAS-3:12-RE-6:13(3653)

FIGURE-DE-4:16(5566)-IS-44:13(8403)▪N.T.-RO-5:14(5179)-1CO-4:6(3345)-HEB-9:9(3850)▪11:19(3850)-1PE-3:21(499)

FIGURES-1KI-6:29(4734)▪N.T.-AC-7:43(5179)-HEB-9:24(499)

FILE-1SA-13:21(6477,6310)

FILL-all=4390&marked-GE-1:22▪42:25▪44:1-EX-10:6▪16:32(4393)-LE-25:19(7648)-DE-23:24(7643)-1SA-16:1-1KI-18:33-JOB-8:21▪15:2▪20:23▪23:4▪38:39▪41:7-PS-81:10▪83:16▪110:6-PR-1:13▪7:18(7301)▪8:21-IS-8:8(4393)▪14:21▪27:6▪56:12(5433)-JER-13:13▪23:24▪33:5▪51:14-EZE-3:3▪7:19▪9:7▪10:2▪24:4▪30:11▪32:4(7646),5▪35:8-ZEP-1:9-HAG-2:7▪N.T.-all=4137&marked-M'T-9:16(4138)▪15:33(5526)▪23:32-JOH-2:7(1072)-RO-15:13-EPH-4:10-COL-1:24(466)-1TH-2:16(378)-RE-18:6(2767)

FILLED-all=4390,a=7646&marked-GE-6:11,13▪21:19▪24:16▪26:15-EX-1:7▪2:16▪16:12a▪28:3▪31:3▪35:31,35▪40:34,35-NU-14:21-DE-26:12a▪31:20a-JOS-9:13-1KI-7:14▪8:10,11▪18:35▪20:27-2KI-3:17,20,25▪21:16▪23:14▪24:4-2CH-5:13,14▪7:1,2▪16:14-EZR-9:11-NE-9:25a-JOB-3:15▪16:8(7059)▪22:18-PS-38:7▪71:8▪72:19▪78:29a▪80:9▪104:28a▪123:3a,4a▪126:2-PR-1:31a▪3:10▪5:10a▪12:21▪14:14a▪18:20a▪20:17▪24:4▪25:16a▪30:16a,22a-EC-1:8▪6:3a,7-SONG-5:2-IS-6:1,4▪21:3▪33:5▪34:6▪43:24(7301)▪65:20-JER-13:12^{2}▪15:17▪16:18▪19:4▪41:9▪46:12▪51:5,34-LA-3:15a,30a-EZE-8:17▪10:3,4▪11:6▪23:33▪28:16▪36:38▪39:20a▪43:5▪44:4-DA-2:35(4391)-HO-13:6^{2}a-NA-2:12-HAB-2:14,16a-ZEC-9:13,15▪N.T.-all=4130,a=4137,b=5526&marked-M'T-5:6b▪14:20b▪15:37b▪27:48-M'R-2:21(4138)▪6:42b▪7:27b▪8:8b▪15:36(1072)-LU-1:15,41,53(1705),67▪2:40a▪3:5a▪4:28▪5:7,26▪6:11,21b▪8:23(4845)▪9:17b▪14:23(1072)▪15:16(1072)-JOH-2:7(1072)▪6:12(1075),13(1072),26b▪12:3a▪16:6a▪19:29-AC-2:2a,4▪3:10▪4:8,31▪5:3a,17a,28a▪9:17▪13:9,45,52a▪19:29-RO-1:29a▪15:14a,24(1075)-2CO-7:4a-EPH-3:19a▪5:18a-PH'P-1:11a-COL-1:9a-2TI-1:4a-JAS-2:16b-RE-8:5(1072)▪15:1(5505),8(1072)▪18:6(2767)▪19:21b

FILLEDST-DE-6:11(4390)-EZE-27:33(7646)

FILLEST-PS-17:14(4390)

FILLET-JER-52:21(2339)

FILLETED-all=2836-EX-27:17▪38:17,28

FILLETH-JOB-9:18(7646)-PS-84:6(5844)▪107:9(4390)▪129:7(4390)▪147:14(7646)▪N.T.-EPH-1:23(4137)

FILLETS-all=2838-EX-27:10,11▪36:38▪38:10,11,12,17,19

FILLING-AC-14:17(1705)

FILTH-IS-4:4(6675)▪N.T.-1CO-4:13(4027)-1PE-3:21(4509)

FILTHINESS-all=2932&marked-2CH-29:5(5079)-EZR-6:21▪9:11(5079)-PR-30:12(6675)-IS-28:8(6675)-LA-1:9-EZE-16:36(5178)▪22:15▪24:11,13^{2}▪36:25▪N.T.-2CO-7:1(3436)-EPH-5:4(151)-JAS-1:21(4507)-RE-17:4(168)

FILTHY-all=444&marked-JOB-15:16▪PS-14:3▪53:3-IS-64:6(5708)-ZEP-3:1(4754)-ZEC-3:3(6674),4(6674)▪N.T.-COL-3:8(148)-TIT-1:7(150),11(150)-1PE-5:2(147)-2PE-2:7(766)-RE-22:11(4510)

FINALLY-all=3063&marked-2CO-13:11-EPH-6:10-PH'P-3:1▪4:8-2TH-3:1-1PE-3:8(5056)

FIND-all=4672&marked-GE-18:26,28,30▪19:11▪32:5,19▪33:8,15▪34:11▪38:22▪41:38▪47:25-EX-5:11▪16:25▪33:13-NU-32:23▪35:27-DE-4:29▪22:23,25,28▪24:1-J'G-9:33▪14:12▪17:8,9-RU-1:9▪2:2,13-1SA-1:18▪9:13^{2}▪10:2▪20:21,36▪23:17▪24:19▪25:8-2SA-15:25▪16:4▪17:20-1KI-18:5,12-2CH-2:14(2803)▪20:16▪32:4-EZR-4:15(7192)▪7:16(7192)-JOB-3:22▪11:7^{2}▪17:10▪23:3▪34:11▪37:23-PS-10:15▪17:3▪21:8^{2}▪132:5-PR-1:13,28▪2:5▪3:4▪4:22▪8:9,12,17▪16:20▪19:8▪20:6▪28:23▪31:10-EC-3:11▪7:14,24,26,27,28▪8:17^{3}▪11:1▪12:10-SONG-5:6,8▪8:1-IS-34:14▪41:12▪58:3-JER-2:24▪5:1▪6:16▪10:18▪29:13▪45:3-LA-1:6▪2:9-DA-6:4^{2}(7912),5^{2}(7912)-HO-2:6,7▪5:6▪12:8-AM-8:12▪N.T.-all=2147-M'T-7:7,14▪10:39▪11:29▪16:25▪17:27▪18:13▪21:2▪22:9▪24:46-M'R-11:2,13▪13:36-LU-2:12▪5:19▪6:7▪11:9▪12:37,38,43▪13:7▪15:4,8▪18:8▪19:30,48▪23:4-JOH-7:34,35,36▪10:9▪18:38▪19:4,6▪21:6-AC-7:46▪17:27▪23:9-RO-7:18,21-2CO-9:4▪12:20-2TI-1:18-HEB-4:16-RE-9:6▪18:14

FINDEST-GE-31:32(4672)-EZE-3:1(4672)

FINDETH-all=4672&marked-GE-4:14-JOB-33:10-PS-119:162-PR-3:13▪8:35▪17:20▪18:22▪21:10,21-EC-9:10-LA-1:3▪N.T.-all=2147-M'T-7:8▪10:39▪12:43,44▪26:40-M'R-14:37-LU-11:10,25-JOH-1:41,43,45▪5:14

FINDING-GE-4:15(4672)-JOB-9:10(2714)-IS-58:13(4672)▪N.T.-all=2147&marked-LU-11:24-AC-4:21▪19:1▪21:2,4(429)-RO-11:33(421)

FINE-all-2896&marked-GE-18:6(5560)-2CH-3:5,8-EZ-8:27(6668)-JOB-28:1(2212)-IS-19:9(8305)-DA-2:32▪N.T.-RE-18:13(4585)

FINER-PR-25:4(6884)

FINEST-PS-81:16(2459)▪147:14(2459)

FINGER-all=676-EX-8:19▪29:12▪31:18-LE-4:6,17,25,30,34▪8:15▪9:9▪14:16^{2},27▪16:14^{2},19-NU-19:4-IS-58:9▪N.T.-all=1147-LU-11:20▪16:24-JOH-8:6▪20:25,27

FINGERS-all=676&marked-2SA-21:20-1CH-20:6-PS-8:3▪144:1-PR-6:13▪7:3-SONG-5:5-IS-2:8▪17:8▪59:3-JER-52:21-DA-5:5(677)▪N.T.-all=1147-M'T-23:4-M'R-7:33-LU-11:46

FINING-PR-17:3(4715)▪27:21(4715)

FINISH-GE-6:16(3615)-DA-9:24(3607)-ZEC-4:9(1214)▪N.T.-all=5048&marked-LU-14:28(535),29(1615),30(1615)-JOH-4:34▪5:36-AC-20:24-RO-9:28(4931)-2CO-8:6(2005)

FINISHED-all=3615&marked-GE-2:1-EX-39:32▪40:33-DE-31:24(8552)-JOS-4:10(8552)-RU-3:18-1KI-6:9,14,22(8552),38▪7:1,22(8552)▪9:1,25(7999)-1CH-27:24▪28:20-2CH-4:11▪5:1(7999)▪7:11▪8:16▪24:14▪29:28▪31:1,7-EZR-5:16(8000)▪6:14(3635),15(3319)

-**NE**-6:15(7999)-**DA**-5:26(8000)■12:7■ **N.T.**-all=5055&marked-**M'T**-13:53■19:1■26:1-**JOH**-17:4(5048)■19:30-**AC**-21:7(1274)-**2TI**-4:7-**HEB**-4:3(1096) -**JAS**-1:15(658)-**RE**-10:7■11:7■20:5

FINISHER-**HEB**-12:2(5047)

FINS-all=5579-**LE**-11:9,10,12-**DE**-14:9,10

FIR-all=1265&marked-**2SA**-6:5-**1KI**-5:8,10■6:15,34■9:11-**2KI**-19:23-**2CH**-2:8■3:5-**PS**-104:17-**SONG**-1:17(1266) -**IS**-14:8■37:24■41:19■55:13■60:13 -**EZE**-27:5■31:8-**HO**-14:8-**NA**-2:3 -**ZEC**-11:2

FIRE-all=784&marked-**GE**-19:24■22:6,7-**EX**-3:2^{2}■9:23,24■12:8,9,10■13:21,22■14:24■19:18■22:6,6(1200)■24:17■29:14,34■32:20,24■35:3■40:38 -**LE**-1:7^{2},8,12,17,17sup■2:14■3:5,5sup■4:12■6:9,10,12,13,30■7:17,19■8:17,32■9:11,24■10:1^{2},2■13:52,55,57■16:12,13,27■19:6■20:14■21:9■23:8,27-**NU**-3:4■6:18■9:15,16■11:1,2,3■14:14■16:7,18,35,37,46■18:9■21:28■26:10,61■31:10,23^{3}-**DE**-1:33■4:11,12,15,24,33,36^{2}■5:4,5,22,23,24,25,26■7:5,25■9:3,10,15,21■10:4■12:3,31■13:16■18:10,16■32:22,22(3857)-**JOS**-6:24■7:15,25■8:8,19■11:6,9,11-**J'G**-1:8■6:21■9:15,20^{2},49,52■12:1■14:15■15:5,6,14■16:9■18:27■20:48-**1SA**-30:1,3,14-**2SA**-14:30^{2},31■22:9,13■23:7-**1KI**-9:16■16:18■18:23^{2},24,25,38■19:12^{2}-**2KI**-1:10^{2},12^{2},14■2:11■6:17■8:12■16:3■17:17,31■19:18■21:6■23:10,11■25:9-**1CH**-14:12■21:26-**2CH**-7:1,3■28:3■33:6■35:13■36:19-**NE**-1:3■2:3,13,17■9:12,19 -**JOB**-1:16■15:34■18:5■20:26■22:20■28:5■31:12■41:19-**PS**-11:6■18:8,12,13■21:9■29:7■39:3■46:9■50:3■57:4(3857)■66:12■68:2■74:7■78:14,21,63■79:5■80:16■83:14,14(3857)■89:46■97:3■104:4■105:32,39■106:18■118:12■140:10■148:8-**PR**-6:27■16:27■26:20,21■30:16 -**SONG**-8:6-**IS**-1:7■4:5■5:24■9:5,18,19■10:16,17■26:11■27:11(215)■29:6■30:14,27,30,33■31:9(217)■33:11,12,14■37:19■42:25(3857)■43:2■44:16,16(217),19■47:14,14(217)■50:11^{2}■54:16■64:2^{2},11■65:5■66:15^{2},16,24-**JER**-4:4■5:14■6:29■7:18,31■11:16■15:14■17:4,27■19:5■20:9■21:10,12,14■22:7■23:29■29:22■32:29■34:2,22■36:23^{2},32■37:8,10■38:17,18,23■39:8■43:12,13■48:45■49:2,27■50:32■51:32,58^{2}■52:13-**LA**-1:13■2:3,4■4:11-**EZE**-1:4^{2},13^{2},27^{2}■5:2(217),4^{3}■8:2^{2}■10:2,6,7■15:4,5,6,7^{2}■16:41■19:12,14■20:31,47■21:31,32■22:20,21,31■23:25,47■24:10,12■28:14,16,18■30:8,14,16■36:5■38:19,22■39:6,9^{2},10-**DA**-3:22(5135),24(5135),25(5135),26(5135),27^{2}(5135)■7:9(5135)■10:6 -**HO**-7:6■8:14-**JOE**-1:19,20■2:3,5,30 -**AM**-1:4,7,10,12,14■2:2,5■5:6■7:4-**OB**-18-**MIC**-1:4,7-**NA**-1:6■3:13,15-**HAB**-2:13-**ZEP**-1:18■3:8-**ZEC**-2:5■3:2■9:4■11:1■12:6^{2}■13:9-**MAL**-3:2■**N.T.**-all=4442&marked-**M'T**-3:10,11,12■5:22■7:19■13:40,42,50■17:15■18:8,9■25:41 -**M'R**-9:22,43,44,45,46,47,48,49■14:54(5457)-**LU**-3:9,16,17■9:54■12:49■17:29■22:55,56(5457)-**JOH**-15:6-**AC**-2:3,19■7:30■28:2(4443),3(4443),5-**RO**-12:20-**1CO**-3:13,15-**2TH**-1:8-**HEB**-1:7■11:34■12:18,29-**JAS**-3:5,6,6^{2}(5394)■5:3-**1PE**-1:7-**2PE**-3:7,12(4448)-**JUDE**-7,23-**RE**-1:14■2:18■3:18■4:5■8:5,7,8■9:17(4447),17,18■10:1■11:5■13:13■14:10,18■15:2■16:8■17:16■18:8■19:12,20■20:9,10,14,15■21:8

FIREBRAND-**J'G**-15:4(3940) -**AM**-4:11(181)

FIREBRANDS-**J'G**-15:4(3940) -**PR**-26:18(2131)-**IS**-7:4(181)

FIREPANS-all=4289&marked -**EX**-27:3■38:3-**2KI**-25:15-**JER**-52:19

FIRES-**IS**-24:15(217)

FIRKINS-**JOH**-2:6(3355)

FIRM-**JOS**-3:17(3559)■4:3(3559) -**JOB**-41:23(3332),24(3332)-**PS**-73:4(1277)-**DA**-6:7(8631)■**N.T.**-**HEB**-3:6(949)

FIRMAMENT-all=7549-**GE**-1:6,7^{3},8,14,15,17,20-**PS**-19:1■150:1-**EZE**-1:22,23,25,26■10:1-**DA**-12:3

FIRST-all=7223,a=1121,b=259&marked-**GE**-1:5b■2:11b■8:5b,13^{2}b■13:4■25:25■26:1■28:19■38:28■41:20■43:18(8462),20(8462)-**EX**-4:8■12:2,5a,15^{2},16,18■22:29(4395)■23:19(7225)■28:17sup17b■29:38a■34:1^{2},4,26(7225)■39:10b,10sup■40:2,2b,17,17b -**LE**-4:21■5:8■9:3a,15■12:6a■14:10(1323)■23:5,7,12a,18a,19a,24b,35,39,40-**NU**-1:1b,18b■2:9■6:12a,14,14(1323)■7:12,15a,17a,21a,23a,27a,29a,33a,35a,39a,41a,45a,47a,51a,53a,57a,59a,63a,65a,69a,71a,75a,77a,81a,83a,87a,88a■9:1,5■10:13,14■15:20(7225),21(7225),27(1323)■18:13(1061)■20:1■24:20(7225)■28:3a,9a,11a,16,18,19a,27a■29:1b,2a,8a,13a,17a,20a,23a,26a,29a,32a,36a■33:3^{2},38b-**DE**-1:3b■9:18■10:1,2,3,4,10■11:14(3138)■13:9■16:4■17:7■18:4(7225)■26:2(7225)■33:21(7225)-**JOS**-4:19■8:5,6■21:10-**J'G**-1:1(8462)■18:29■20:18^{2}(8462),22,32,39-**1SA**-14:14,35(2490)-**2SA**-3:13(6440)■17:9(8462)■19:20,43■21:9-**1KI**-16:23b■17:13■18:25■20:9,17-**1CH**-9:2■11:6^{2}■12:9(7218),15■15:13■16:7(7218)■23:19(7218),20(7218)■24:7,21(7218)■25:9■27:2,3■29:29-**2CH**-3:3■9:29■12:15■16:11■17:3■20:34■25:26■26:22■28:26■29:3^{2},17^{2}■35:1,27■36:22b-**EZR**-1:1b■3:6b,12■5:13(2298)■6:3(2298),19■7:9b,9b■8:31■10:16b,17b,17-**NE**-7:5■8:2b,18 -**ES**-1:14■3:7,12-**JOB**-15:7■42:14 -**PR**-18:7-**IS**-1:26■9:1■41:4,27■43:27■44:6■48:12■60:9-**JER**-4:31(1069)■7:12■16:18■24:2(1073)■25:1(7224)■33:7,11■36:28■50:17-**EZE**-10:14b■26:1b■29:17,17b■30:20■31:1b■32:1b■40:21■44:30^{2}(7225)■45:18,18b,21■46:13a-**DA**-1:21b■6:2(2298)■7:1(2298),4(6933),8(6933),24(6933)■8:1(8462),21■9:1b,2b■10:4,12■11:1b -**HO**-2:7■9:10(7225)-**JOE**-2:23-**AM**-6:7(7218)-**MIC**-4:8-**HAG**-1:1b■2:3 -**ZEC**-6:2■12:7■14:10■**N.T.**-all=4413,a=4412&marked-**M'T**-5:24a■6:33a■7:5a■8:21a■10:2■12:29a,45■13:30a■17:10a,11a,27■19:30^{2}■20:8,10,16■21:28,31,36■22:25,38■23:26a■26:17■27:64■28:1(3391)-**M'R**-3:27a■4:28a■7:27a■9:11a,12a,35■10:31^{2}■12:20,28,29,30■13:10a■14:12■16:2(3391)9,9a-**LU**-1:3(509)■2:2■6:1(1207),42a■9:59a,61a■10:5a■11:26,38a■12:1a■13:30■14:18,28a,31a■16:5■17:25a■19:16■20:29■21:9a■24:1(3391)-**JOH**-1:41■5:4■8:7■10:40a■12:16a■18:13a■19:32,39a■20:1(3391),4,8,19(3391)-**AC**-3:26a■7:12a■11:26a■12:10■13:46a■15:14a■20:7(3391),18■26:4(746),20a,23■27:43-**RO**-1:8a,16a■2:9a,10a■10:19■11:35(4272)■15:24a -**1CO**-1:t■11:18a■12:28a■14:30■15:3(1722,4413),45,46a,47■16:2(3391),subscr.-**2CO**-8:5a,12(4295)-**GA**-4:13(4386)-**EPH**-1:12(4276)■4:9a■6:2 -**PH'P**-1:5-**1TH**-1:t■4:16a,subscr.-**2TH**-2:3a-**1TI**-1:t,16■2:1a,13■3:10a■5:4a,12,subscr.-**2TI**-1:5a■2:6■4:16,subscr.-**TIT**-3:10(3391),subscr.-**HEB**-2:3(746)■4:6(4386)■5:12(746)■7:2a,27(4386)■8:7,13■9:1,2,6,8,15,18■10:9-**JAS**-3:17a -**1PE**-1:t■4:17a-**2PE**-1:20a■3:3a-**1JO**-1:t■4:19-**JUDE**-6(746)-**RE**-1:5(4416),11,17■2:4,5,8,19■4:1,7■8:7■13:12^{2}■16:2■20:5,6■21:1,19■22:13

FIRSTBEGOTTEN-**HEB**-1:6(4416)

FIRSTBORN-all=1060&marked -**GE**-10:15■19:31(1067),33(1067),34(1067),37(1067)■22:21■25:13■27:19,32■29:26(1067),35:23■36:15■38:6,7■41:51,43:33■46:8■48:14,18■49:3-**EX**-4:22,23■6:14■11:5^{4}■12:12,29^{4}■13:2,13,15^{4}■22:29■34:20-**NU**-3:2,12,13^{3},40,41,42,43,45,46,50■8:16,17^{2},18■18:15■33:4 -**DE**-21:15,16(1069),16,17,17(1062)■25:6-**JOS**-6:26■17:1^{2}-**J'G**-8:20-**1SA**-8:2■14:49(1067)■17:13-**2SA**-3:2-**1KI**-16:34-**1CH**-1:13,29■2:3,13,25,27,42,50■3:1,15■4:4■5:1^{2},3■6:28■8:1,30,39■9:5,31,36■26:2,4,10-**2CH**-21:3-**NE**-10:36 -**JOB**-18:13-**PS**-78:51■89:27■105:36■135:8■136:10-**IS**-14:30-**JER**-31:9-**MIC**-6:7-**ZEC**-12:10■**N.T.**-all=4416-**M'T**-1:25-**LU**-2:7-**RO**-8:29-**COL**-1:15,18 -**HEB**-11:28■12:23

FIRSTFRUIT-**DE**-18:4(7225)■**N.T.**-**RO**-11:16(536)

FIRSTFRUITS-all=1061,a=7225 -**EX**-23:16,19■34:22,26-**LE**-2:12a,14^{2}■23:10a,17,20-**NU**-18:12a■28:26-**DE**-26:10a-**2KI**-4:42-**2CH**-31:5a-**NE**-10:35^{2},37a■12:44a■13:31-**PR**-3:9a-**JER**-2:3a -**EZE**-20:40a■44:30■48:14a■**N.T.**-all=536-**RO**-8:23■16:5-**1CO**-15:20,23■16:15-**JAS**-1:18-**RE**-14:4

FIRSTLING-all=1060&marked -**EX**-13:12(6363),13(6363)■34:19(6363),20(6363)-**LE**-27:26,26(1069)-**NU**-18:15,17^{2}-**DE**-15:19^{3}■33:17

FIRSTLINGS-all=1062&marked -**GE**-4:4-**NU**-3:41(1060)-**DE**-12:6,17■14:23-**NE**-10:36

FIRSTRIPE-all=1063&marked-**NU**-13:20(1061)-**HO**-9:10-**MIC**-7:1 -**NA**-3:12

FISH-all=1710,a=1709&marked-**GE**-1:26,28-**EX**-7:18,21-**NU**-11:5,22a-**DE**-4:18-**2CH**-33:14a-**NE**-3:3a■12:39a■13:16a-**JOB**-41:7a-**PS**-8:8a■105:29 -**IS**-19:10(5315)■50:2-**JER**-16:16(1770) -**EZE**-29:4^{2},5■47:9,10^{2}-**JON**-1:17^{2}a■2:10a-**ZEP**-1:10a■**N.T.**-all=2486&marked-**M'T**-7:10■17:27-**LU**-11:11■24:42-**JOH**-21:9(3795),10(3795),13(3795)

FISHERMEN-**LU**-5:2(231)

FISHER'S-**JOH**-21:7(1903)

FISHERS-**IS**-19:8(1771)-**JER**-16:16(1728)-**EZE**-47:10(1728)■**N.T.**-all=231-**M'T**-4:18,19-**M'R**-1:16,17

FISHES-all=1709&marked-**GE**-9:2 -**1KI**-4:33-**JOB**-12:8-**EC**-9:12-**EZE**-38:20 -**HO**-4:3-**HAB**-1:14-**ZEP**-1:3■**N.T.**-all=2486&marked-**M'T**-14:17,19■15:34(2485),36-**M'R**-6:38,41^{2},43■8:7(2485) -**LU**-5:6,9■9:13,16-**JOH**-6:9(3795),11(3795)■21:6,8,11-**1CO**-15:39

FISHHOOKS-**AM**-4:2(5518,1729)

FISHING-**JOH**-21:3(232)

FISHPOOLS-**SONG**-7:4(1295)

FISH'S-**JON**-2:1(1710)

FIST-**EX**-21:18(106)-**IS**-58:4(106)

FISTS-**PR**-30:4(2651)

FIT-**LE**-16:21(6261)-**PR**-24:27(6257)■**N.T.**-**LU**-9:62(2111)■14:35(2111)-**AC**-22:22(2520)-**COL**-3:18(433)

FITCHES-all=7100&marked-**IS**-28:25,27^{2}-**EZE**-4:9(3698)

FITLY-**PR**-25:11(5921,655)-**SONG**-5:12(5921,4402)■**N.T.**-**EPH**-2:21(4883)■4:16(4883)

FITTED-**1KI**-6:35(3474)-**PR**-22:18(3559)■**N.T.**-**RO**-9:22(2675)

FITTETH-**IS**-44:13(6213)

FIVE-all=2568&marked-**GE**-5:6,11,15,17,21,23,30,32■11:11,12,32■12:4■14:9■18:28^{3}■43:34■45:6,11,22■47:2-**EX**-22:1■26:3^{2},9,26,27^{2},37^{2}■27:1,18■30:23,24■36:10^{2},16,31,32^{2},38^{2}■38:1^{2},18,26,28 -**LE**-26:8■27:5,6^{2}-**NU**-1:21,25,33,37,41,46■2:11,15,19,23,28,32■3:22,47,50■4:48■7:17,23,29,35,41,47,53,59,65,71,77,83■8:24■11:19■18:16■26:18,22,27,37,41,50■31:8,28,32,36,39,43,45-**JOS**-8:12■10:5,16,17,22,23,26■13:3■14:10^{2}-**J'G**-3:3■18:2,7,14,17■20:35,45,46-**1SA**-6:4,16,18■17:5,40■21:3■22:18■25:18^{2},42 -**2SA**-4:4■21:8■24:9-**1KI**-4:32■6:6,10,24^{2}■

7:3,16^{2},23,39^{2},49^{2}■9:23■22:42^{2}-2KI-6:25■7:13■13:19■14:2■15:33■18:2■19:35■21:1■23:36■25:19-1CH-2:4,6■3:20■4:32,42■7:3,7■11:23■29:7-2CH-3:11^{2},12^{2},15^{2}■4:2,6^{2},7^{2},8^{2}■6:13^{2}■13:17■15:19■20:31^{2}■25:1■26:13■27:1,8■29:1■33:1■35:9^{2}■36:5-EZR-1:11■2:5,8,20,33,34,66,67,69-NE-7:13,20,25,36,67,68,69,70-ES-9:6,12,16-JOB-1:3^{2}-IS-7:8■17:6■19:18■30:17■37:36-JER-52:22,30,31-EZE-8:16■11:1■40:1,7,13,21,25,29,30^{2},33,36,48^{2}■41:2^{2},9,11,12■42:16,17,18,19,20^{2}■45:1,2^{2},3,5,6^{2},12■48:8,9,10^{2},13^{2},15^{2},16^{4},20,21^{2},30,32,33,34-DA-12:12■N.T.-all=4002,a=4000&marked-M'T-14:17,19,21a■16:9,9a■25:2^{2}a,15a,16^{2}a,20^{4}a-M'R-6:38a,41a,44a■8:19,19a-LU-1:24■7:41(4001)■9:13,14a,16■12:6,52■14:19■16:28■19:18,19-JOH-4:18■5:2■6:9,10a,13,19-AC-4:4■20:6■24:1-1CO-14:19■15:6(4001)-2CO-11:24(3999)-RE-9:5,10■17:10

FIXED-all=3559&marked-PS-57:7^{2}■108:1■112:7■N.T.-LU-16:26(4741)

FLAG-JOB-8:11(260)

FLAGON-2SA-6:19(809)-1CH-16:3(809)

FLAGONS-SONG-2:5(809)-IS-22:24(5035)-HO-3:1(809)

FLAGS-all=5488-EX-2:3,5-IS-19:6

FLAKES-JOB-41:23(4651)

FLAME-all=3852&marked-EX-3:2(3827)-NU-21:28-J'G-13:20^{2}(3851)■20:38(4864),40(4864),40(3632)-JOB-15:30(7957)■41:21(3851)-PS-83:14■106:18-SONG-8:6(7957)-IS-5:24■10:17■29:6(3851)■30:30(3851)■43:2■47:14-JER-48:45-EZE-20:47(7957)-DA-3:22(7631)■7:9(7631),11(785)■11:33-JOE-1:19■2:3,5(3851)-OB-18■N.T.-all=5395-LU-16:24-AC-7:30-HEB-1:7-RE-1:14■2:18■19:12

FLAMES-PS-29:7(3852)-IS-13:8(3851)■66:15(3851)

FLAMING-all=3852&marked-GE-3:24(3858)-PS-104:4(3857)105:32-IS-4:5-LA-2:3-EZE-20:47-HO-7:6-NA-2:3(784)■N.T.-2TH-1:8(5395)

FLANKS-all=3689&marked-LE-3:4,10,15■4:9■7:4-JOB-15:27

FLASH-EZE-1:14(965)

FLAT-LE-21:18(2763)-JOS-6:5(8478),20(8478)

FLATTER-PS-5:9(2505)■78:36(6601)

FLATTERETH-all=2505&marked-PS-36:2-PR-2:16■7:5■20:19(6601)■28:23■29:5

FLATTERIES-DA-11:21(2519),32(2514),34(2519)

FLATTERING-JOB-32:21(3655),22(3655)-PS-12:2(2513),3(2513)-PR-7:21(2506)■26:28(2509)-EZE-12:24(2509)■N.T.-1TH-2:5(2850)

FLATTERY-JOB-17:5(2506)-PR-6:24(2513)

FLAX-all=6593&marked-EX-9:31^{2}(6594)-JOS-2:6-J'G-15:14-PR-31:13-IS-19:9■42:3(6594)-EZE-40:3-HO-2:5,9■N.T.-M'T-12:20(3043)

FLAY-all=6584&marked-LE-1:6-2CH-29:34-MIC-3:3

FLAYED-2CH-35:11(6584)

FLEA-1SA-24:14(6550)■26:20(6550)

FLED-all=5127,a=1272&marked-GE-14:10^{2}■16:6a■31:20a,21a,22a■35:7a■39:12,13,15,18-EX-2:15a■4:3■14:5a,27-NU-16:34■35:25,26,32-JOS-7:4■8:15,20■10:11,16■20:6-J'G-1:6■4:15,17■7:21,22■8:12■9:21a,40,51■11:3a■20:45,47-1SA-4:10,16,17■14:22■17:24,51■19:8,10,12a,18a■20:1a■21:10a■22:17a,20a■23:6a■27:4a■30:17■31:1,7^{2}-2SA-1:4■4:3a,4■10:13,14^{2},18■13:29,34a,37a,38a■18:17■19:8,9a■23:11a-1KI-2:7a,28,29■11:17a,23a,40a■12:2a■20:20,30^{2}-2KI-3:24■7:7^{2}■8:21■9:10,23,27^{2}■14:12,19-1CH-10:1,7^{2}■11:13■19:14,15^{2},18-2CH-10:2a■13:16■14:12■25:22,27-NE-13:10a-PS-3:ta■31:11(5074),57ta■104:7■114:3-IS-10:29■21:14(5074),15(5074)■22:3(5074),3a■33:3(5074)-JER-4:25(5074)■9:10(5074)■26:21a■39:4a■46:5,21■48:45■52:7a-LA-4:15(5132)-DA-10:7a-HO-7:13(5074)■12:12a-JON-1:10a■4:2a-ZEC-14:5■N.T.-all=5343&marked-M'T-8:33■26:56-M'R-5:14■14:50,52■16:8-LU-8:34-AC-7:29■14:6(2703)■16:27(1628)■19:16(1628)-HEB-6:18(2703)-RE-12:6■16:20■20:11

FLEDDEST-GE-35:1(1272)-PS-114:5(5127)

FLEE-all=5127,a=1272&marked-GE-16:8a■19:20■27:43a■31:27a-EX-9:20■14:25■21:13-LE-26:17,36-NU-10:35■24:11a■35:6,11,15-DE-4:42■19:3,4,5■28:7,25-JOS-8:5,6^{2},20■20:3,4,9-J'G-20:32-2SA-4:4■15:14(1227)■17:2■18:3■19:3■24:13-1KI-12:18-2KI-9:3-2CH-10:18-NE-6:11a-JOB-9:25a■20:24a■27:22a■30:10(7368)■41:28a-PS-11:1(5110)■64:8(5074)■68:1,12(5074)■139:7a■143:9(3680)-PR-28:1,17-SONG-2:17■4:6-IS-10:3■13:14■17:13■20:6■30:16,17sup,17■31:8■35:10■48:20a■51:11-JER-4:29a■6:1(5756)■25:35(4498)■46:6■48:6,9(5323)■49:8,24,30■50:16,28■51:6-AM-2:16■5:19■7:12a■9:1-JON-1:3a-NA-2:8■3:7(5074),17(5074)-ZEC-2:6■14:5^{2}■N.T.-all=5343-M'T-2:13■3:7■10:23■24:16-M'R-13:14-LU-3:7■21:21-JOH-10:5-AC-27:30-1CO-6:18■10:14-1TI-6:11-2TI-2:22-JAS-4:7-RE-9:6

FLEECE-all=1492&marked-DE-18:4(1488)-J'G-6:37^{2},38^{2},39^{2},40-JOB-31:20(1488)

FLEEING-LE-26:36(4499)-DE-4:42(5127)-JOB-30:3(6207)

FLEETH-all=5127&marked-DE-19:11-JOB-14:2(1272)-IS-24:18-JER-48:19,44(5211)-AM-9:1-NA-3:16(5775)■N.T.-JOH-10:12(5343),13(5343)

FLESH-all=1320&marked-GE-2:21,23,24■6:3,12,13,17,19■7:15,16,21■8:17■9:4,11,15^{2},16,17■17:11,13,14,23,24,25■29:14■37:27■40:19-EX-4:7■12:8,46■16:3,8,12■21:28■22:31■29:14,31,32,34■30:32-LE-4:11■6:10,27■7:15,17,18,19^{2},20,21■8:17,31,32■9:11■11:8,11■12:3■13:2^{2},3^{2},4,10,11,13,14,15^{2},16,18,24,24sup,38,39,43■14:9■15:2,3^{2},7,13,16,19■16:4^{2},24,26,27,28■17:11,14^{3},16■19:28■21:5■22:6■26:29^{2}-NU-8:7■11:4,13^{2},18^{3},21,33■12:12■16:22■18:15,18■19:5,7,8■27:16-DE-5:26■12:15,20^{3},23,27^{2}■14:8■16:4■28:53,55■32:42-J'G-6:19,20,21^{2}■8:7■9:2-1SA-2:13,15^{2}■17:44■25:11(2878)-2SA-5:1■6:19(829)■19:12,13-1KI-17:6^{2}■19:21■21:27-2KI-4:34■5:10,14■6:30■9:36-1CH-11:1■16:3(829)-2CH-32:8-NE-5:5-JOB-2:5■4:15■6:12■7:5■10:4,11■13:14■14:22■19:20,22,26■21:6■31:31■33:21,25■34:15■41:23-PS-16:9■27:2■38:3,7■50:13■56:4■63:1■65:2■73:26(7607)■78:20(7607),27(7607),39■79:2■84:2■109:24■119:120■136:25■145:21-PR-4:22■5:11■11:17(7607)■14:30■23:20-EC-4:5■5:6■11:10■12:12-IS-9:20■17:4■22:13■31:3■40:5,6■44:16,19■49:26^{2}■58:7■65:4■66:16,17,23,24-JER-7:21■11:15■12:12■17:5■19:9^{3}■25:31■32:27■45:5■51:35(7607)-LA-3:4-EZE-4:14■11:3,7,11,19^{2}■16:26■20:48■21:4,5■23:20■24:10■32:5■36:26^{2}■37:6,8■39:17,18■40:43■44:7,9-DA-1:15■2:11(1321)■4:12(1321)■7:5(1321)■10:3-HO-8:13-JOE-2:28-MIC-3:2(7607),3(7607),3-ZEP-1:17(3894)-HAG-2:12-ZEC-2:13■11:9,16■14:12■N.T.-all=4561&marked-M'T-16:17■19:5,6■24:22■26:41-M'R-10:8^{2}■13:20■14:38-LU-3:6■24:39-JOH-1:13,14■3:6,6sup■6:51,52,53,54,55,56,63■8:15■17:2-AC-2:17,26,30,31-RO-1:3■2:28■3:20■4:1■6:19■7:5,18,25■8:1,3^{3},4,5^{2},8,9,12^{2},13■9:3,5,8■11:14■13:14■14:21(2907)-1CO-1:26,29■5:5■6:16■7:28■8:13(2907)■10:18■15:39^{3},50-2CO-1:17■4:11■5:16^{2}■7:1,5■10:2,3■11:18■12:7-GA-1:16■2:16,20■3:3■4:13,14,23,29■5:13,16,17^{2},19,24■6:8,12,13-EPH-2:3^{2},11^{2},15■5:29,30,31■6:5,12-PH'P-1:22,24■3:3,4^{2}-COL-1:22,24■2:1,5,11,13,23■3:22-1TI-3:16-PH'M-16-HEB-2:14■5:7■9:13■10:20■12:9-JAS-5:3-1PE-1:24■3:18,21■4:1^{2},2,6-2PE-2:10,18-1JO-2:16■4:2,3-2JO-7-JUDE-7,8,23-RE-17:16■19:18^{4},21

FLESHHOOK-1SA-2:13(4207),14(4207)

FLESHHOOKS-all=4207&marked-EX-27:3■38:3-NU-4:14-1CH-28:17-2CH-4:16

FLESHLY-2CO-1:12(4559)■3:3(4560)-1PE-2:11(4559)

FLEW-1SA-14:32(6213)-IS-6:6(5774)

FLIES-PS-78:45(6157)■105:31(6157)■N.T.-EC-10:1(2070)

FLIETH-DE-4:17(5774)■14:19(5775)■28:49(1675)-PS-91:5(5774)

FLIGHT-LE-26:8(7291)-DE-32:30(5127)-1CH-12:15(1272)-IS-52:12(4499)-AM-2:14(4498)■N.T.-M'T-24:20(5437)-M'R-13:18(5437)

FLINT-all=2496&marked-DE-8:15-PS-114:8-IS-5:28(6864)■50:7-EZE-3:9(6864)

FLINTY-DE-32:13(2496)

FLOATS-1KI-5:9(1702)

FLOCK-all=6629,a=5739-GE-4:4■21:28■27:9■29:10■30:31,32,40■31:4,38■33:13■37:2,12■38:17-EX-2:16,17,19■3:1^{2}-LE-1:2■3:6■5:6,18■6:6■27:32-NU-15:3-DE-12:17,21■15:14,19■16:2-1SA-17:34a-2SA-12:4-2CH-35:7-EZR-10:19-JOB-21:11■30:1-PS-77:20■78:52a■80:1■107:41-SONG-1:8■4:1a,2a■6:5a,6a-IS-40:11a■63:11-JER-13:17a,20a,20■23:2,3■25:34,35,36■31:10a,12■49:20■50:45■51:23a-EZE-24:5■34:3,6,8^{4},10^{3},12a,15,17,19,22,31■36:37,38■43:23,25■45:15-AM-6:4■7:15-JON-3:7-MIC-2:12a■4:8a■7:14-HAB-3:17-ZEC-9:16■10:2,3a■11:4,7^{3},11,17-MAL-1:14a■N.T.-all=4168&marked-M'T-26:31(4167)-LU-2:8(4167)■12:32-AC-20:28,29-1CO-9:7^{2}(4167)-1PE-5:2,3

FLOCKS-all=6629,a=5739&marked-GE-13:5■24:35■26:14■29:2^{2}a,3a,8a■30:36,38^{2},39,40,40a■32:5,7■33:13■37:14■45:10■46:32■47:1,4,17■50:8-EX-10:9,24■12:32,38■34:3-LE-1:10■5:15-NU-11:22■31:9(4735),30■32:26(4735)-DE-7:13(6251)■8:13■12:6■14:23■28:4(6251),18(6251),51(6251)-J'G-5:16a-1SA-30:20-2SA-12:2-1KI-20:27(2835)-1CH-4:39,41■27:31-2CH-17:11■32:28a,29-NE-10:36-JOB-24:2a-PS-65:13■78:48(4735)-PR-27:23-SONG-1:7a-IS-17:2a■32:14a■60:7■61:5■65:10-JER-3:24■5:17■6:3a■10:21(4830)■31:24a■33:12,13■49:29■50:8-EZE-25:5■34:2■36:38-HO-5:6-JOE-1:18a-MIC-5:8a-ZEP-2:6,14a

FLOOD-all=3999,a=5104&marked-GE-6:17■7:6,7,10,17■9:11^{2},15,28■10:1,32■11:10-JOS-24:2a,3a,14a,15a-JOB-14:11a,■22:16a■28:4(5158)-PS-29:10■66:6a■74:15(5158)■90:5(2229)-IS-28:2(2230)■59:19a-JER-46:7(2975),8(2975)■47:2(5158)-DA-9:26(7858)■11:22(7858)-AM-8:8^{2}(2975)■9:5^{2}(2975)-NA-1:8(7858)■N.T.-all=2627&marked-M'T-24:38,39-LU-6:48(4132)■17:27-2PE-2:5-RE-12:15(4215),15(4216),16(4215)

FLOODS-all=5104&marked-EX-15:8(5140)-2SA-22:5(5158)-JOB-20:17■28:11-PS-18:4(5158)■24:2■32:6(7858)■69:2(7641)■78:44(5140)■93:3^{3}■98:8-SONG-8:7-IS-44:3(5140)-EZE-31:15-JON-2:3-N.T.-M'T-7:25(4215),27(4215)

FLOOR-all=1637&marked-GE-50:11-NU-5:17(7172)-DE-15:14-J'G-6:37-RU-3:3,6,14-1KI-6:15^{2}(7172),16(7172),30(7172)■7:7(7172)-2CH-34:11(7136)

-IS-21:10-HO-9:2▪13:3-MIC-4:12 -N.T.-M'T-3:12(257)-LU-3:17(257)
FLOORS-JOE-2:24(1637)
FLOTES-2CH-2:16(7513)
FLOUR-all=5560&marked-EX-29:2,40-LE-2:1,2,4,5,7▪5:11▪6:15,20▪7:12▪14:10,21▪23:13,17▪24:5-NU-6:15▪7:13,19,25,31,37,43,49,55,61,67,73,79▪8:8▪15:4,6,9▪28:5,9,12²,13,20,28▪29:3,9,14-J'G-6:19(7058)-1SA-1:24(7058)▪28:24(7058)-2SA-13:8(1217)▪17:28(7058)-1KI-4:22-2KI-7:1,16,18-1CH-9:29▪23:29-EZE-16:13,19▪46:14▪N.T.-RE-18:13(4585)
FLOURISH-all=6524&marked-PS-72:7,16(6692)▪92:7(6692),12,13▪132:18(6692)-PR-11:28▪14:11-EC-12:5(5006)-SONG-7:12-IS-17:11▪66:14-EZE-17:24
FLOURISHED-SONG-6:11(6524)▪N.T.-PH'P-4:10(330)
FLOURISHETH-PS-90:6(6692)▪103:15(6692)
FLOURISHING-PS-92:14(7488)-DA-4:4(7487)
FLOW-all=5102&marked-JOB-20:28(5064)-PS-147:18(5140)-SONG-4:16(5140)-IS-2:2▪48:21(5140)▪60:5▪64:1(2151)-JER-31:12▪51:44-JOE-3:18²(3212)-MIC-4:1(5102)▪N.T.-JOH-7:38(4482)
FLOWED-JOS-4:18(3212)-IS-64:3(2151)-LA-3:54(6687)
FLOWER-all=6731&marked-EX-25:33²(6525)▪37:19²(6525)-1SA-2:33(582)-JOB-14:2▪15:33(5328)-PS-103:15-IS-18:5(5328)▪28:1,4(6733)▪40:6,7,8-NA-1:4(6525)-N.T.-all=438-1CO-7:36(5230)-JAS-1:10,11-1PE-1:24²
FLOWERS-all=6525&marked-EX-25:31,34▪37:17,20-LE-15:24(5079),33(5079)-NU-8:4-1KI-6:18(6731),29(6731),32(6731),35(6731)▪7:26,49-2CH-4:5,21-SONG-2:12(5339)▪5:13(4026)
FLOWETH-all=2100-LE-20:24-NU-13:27▪14:8▪16:13,14-DE-6:3▪11:9▪26:9,15▪27:3▪31:20-JOS-5:6
FLOWING-all=2100&marked-EX-3:8,17▪13:5▪33:3-PR-18:4(5042)-IS-66:12(7857)-JER-11:5▪18:14(5140)▪32:22▪49:4-EZE-20:6,15
FLUTE-all=4953-DA-3:5,7,10,15
FLUTTERETH-DE-32:11(7363)
FLUX-AC-28:8(1420)
FLY-all=5774&marked-GE-1:20-1SA-15:19(5860)-2SA-22:11-JOB-5:7▪20:8▪39:26(82)-PS-18:10,10(1675)▪55:6▪90:10-PR-23:5-IS-6:2▪7:18(2070)▪11:14▪60:8-JER-48:40(1675)▪49:22(1675)-EZE-13:20²(6524)-DA-9:21(3286)-HO-9:11-HAB-1:8▪N.T.-all=4072-RE-12:14▪14:6▪19:17
FLYING-all=5774&marked-LE-11:21(5775),23(5775)-PS-148:10(3671)-PR-26:2-IS-14:29▪30:6▪31:5-ZEC-5:1,2▪N.T.-RE-4:7(4072)▪8:13(4702)
FOAL-GE-49:11(5895)-ZEC-9:9(1121)▪N.T.-M'T-21:5(5207)
FOALS-GE-32:15(5895)
FOAM-HO-10:7(7110)
FOAMETH-M'R-9:18(875)-LU-9:39(876)
FOAMING-M'R-9:20(875)-JUDE-13(1890)
FODDER-JOB-6:5(1098)
FOES-1CH-21:12(6862)-ES-9:16(8130)-PS-27:2(341)▪30:1(341)▪89:23(6862)▪N.T.-M'T-10:36(2190)-AC-2:35(2190)
FOLD-all=5116&marked-IS-13:20(7257)▪65:10-EZE-34:14²,-MIC-2:12(1699)-HAB-3:17(4356)▪N.T.-JON-10:16(833),16(4167)-HEB-1:12(1667)
FOLDEN-NA-1:10(5440)
FOLDETH-EC-4:5(2263)
FOLDING-1KI-6:34²(1550)-PR-6:10(2264)▪24:33(2264)
FOLDS-all=1448&marked-NU-32:24,36-PS-50:9(4356)-JER-23:3(5116)-ZEP-2:6
FOLK-GE-38:15(5971)-PR-30:26(5971)-JER-51:58(3816)
FOLKS-all supplied
FOLLOW-all=7291&marked-GE-24:5(3212,310),8(3212,310),39(3212,310)▪44:4-EX-11:8(7272)▪14:4,17(310)▪21:22(1961),23(1961)▪23:2(1961,310)-DE-16:20▪18:22(1961)-J'G-3:28▪8:5(7272)▪9:3(935,310)-1SA-25:27(1980,7272)▪30:21(3212,310)-2SA-17:9(310)-1KI-18:21(3212,310)▪19:20(3212,310)▪20:10(7272)-2KI-6:19(3212,310)-PS-23:6▪38:20▪45:14(310)▪94:15(310)▪119:150-IS-5:11▪51:1-JER-17:16(310)▪42:16(1692)-EZE-13:3(1980,310)-HO-2:7▪6:3▪N.T.-all=190&marked-M'T-4:19(1205,3694)▪8:19,22▪9:9▪16:24▪19:21-M'R-2:14▪5:37(4870)▪6:1▪8:34▪10:21▪14:13▪16:17(3877)-LU-5:27▪9:23,57,59,61▪17:23(1377)▪18:22▪22:10,49(2071)-JOH-1:43▪10:4,5,27▪12:26▪13:36,37▪21:19,22-AC-3:24(2517)▪12:8-RO-14:19(1377)-1CO-14:1(1377)-PH'P-3:12(1377)-1TH-5:15(1377)-2TH-3:7(3401),9(3401)-1TI-5:24(1872)▪6:11(1377)-2TI-2:22(1377)-HEB-12:14(1377)▪13:7(3401)-1PE-1:11(3326,5023)▪2:21(1872)-2PE-2:2(1811)-3JO-11(3401)-RE-14:4,13
FOLLOWED-all=310&marked-GE-24:61(3212,310)▪32:19(1980,310)-NU-14:24▪16:25(3212,310)▪32:11,12-DE-1:36▪4:3(1980,310)-JOS-6:8▪14:8,9,14-J'G-2:12(3212,310)▪9:4(3212,310),49(3212,310)-1SA-13:7▪14:22(1692)▪17:13(1890,310),14(1890,310)▪31:2(1692)-2SA-1:6(1692)▪2:10(1961,310)▪3:31(1980,310),11:8(3318,310)▪17:23(6213)▪20:2-1KI-12:20▪14:8▪16:21²,22²▪18:18(3212,310)▪20:19-2KI-3:9(7272),4:30(3112,310)▪5:21(7291)▪9:27(7291)▪13:2(3212,310)▪17:15(3212,310)-1CH-10:2(1692)-NE-4:23-EZE-10:11(3212,310)-AM-7:15▪N.T.-all=190&marked-M'T-4:20,22,25▪8:1,10,23▪9:9,19,27▪12:15▪14:13▪19:2,27,28▪20:29,34▪21:9▪26:58▪27:55,62(2076,3326)-M'R-1:18,36(2614)▪2:14,15▪3:7▪5:24▪10:28,32,52▪11:9▪14:51,54▪15:41-LU-5:11,28▪7:9▪9:11▪18:28,43▪22:39,54▪23:27,49(4870),55(2628)-JOH-1:37,40▪6:2▪11:31▪18:15-AC-12:9▪13:43▪16:17(2628)▪21:36-RO-9:30(1377),31(1377)-1CO-10:4-1TI-5:10(1872)-2PE-1:16(1811)-RE-6:8▪8:7(1096)▪14:8,9▪19:14
FOLLOWEDST-RU-3:10(3212,310)
FOLLOWERS-all=3402&marked-1CO-4:16▪11:1-EPH-5:1-PH'P-3:17(4831)-1TH-1:6▪2:14-HEB-6:12-1PE-3:13
FOLLOWETH-all=7291&marked-2KI-11:15(935,310)-2CH-23:14(935,310)-PS-63:8(1692)-PR-12:11▪15:9▪21:21▪28:19-IS-1:23-EZE-16:34(310)-HO-12:1(7291)▪N.T.-all=190-M'T-10:38-M'R-9:38²-LU-9:49-JOH-8:12
FOLLOWING-all=310&marked-GE-41:31(310,3651)-DE-7:4▪12:30-JOS-22:16,18,23,29-J'G-2:19(3212,310)-1SA-12:14,20▪14:46▪15:11▪24:1-2SA-2:19,21,22,26,27,30▪7:8-1KI-1:7▪9:6▪21:26(3212,310)-2KI-17:21▪18:6-1CH-17:7-2CH-25:27▪34:33-PS-48:13(314)▪78:71▪109:13(312)▪N.T.-all=190&marked-M'R-16:20(1872)-LU-13:33(2192)-JOH-1:38,43(1887)▪6:22(1887)▪20:6▪21:20-AC-21:1(1836),18(1966)-2PE-2:15(1811)
FOLLY-all=200,a=5039&marked-GE-34:7a-DE-22:21a-JOS-7:15a-J'G-19:23a▪20:6a,10a-1SA-25:25a-2SA-13:12a-JOB-4:18(8417)▪24:12(8604)▪42:8a-PS-49:13(3689)▪85:8(3690)-PR-5:23▪13:16▪14:8,18,24,29▪15:21▪16:22▪17:12▪18:13▪26:4,5,11-EC-1:17(5531)▪2:3(5531),12(5531),13(5531)▪7:25(3689)▪10:1(5531),6(5529)-IS-9:17a-JER-23:13(8604)▪N.T.-2CO-11:1(877)-2TI-3:9(454)
FOOD-all=3899,a=400&marked-GE-2:9(2978)▪3:6(2978)▪6:21(2978),21(402)▪41:35²a,36a,48²a▪42:7a,10a▪43:2a,4a,20a,22a▪44:1a,25a▪47:24a,24(398)-EX-21:10(7607)-LE-3:11,16▪19:23(3978)▪22:7-DE-10:18-1SA-14:24²,28-2SA-9:10-1KI-5:9,11(4361)-JOB-24:5▪38:41(6718)▪40:20(944)-PS-78:25▪104:14▪136:25▪146:7▪147:9-PR-6:8(3978)▪13:23a▪27:27²▪28:3▪30:8▪31:14-EZE-48:18▪N.T.-AC-14:17(5160)-2CO-9:10(1035)-1TI-6:8(1304)-JAS-2:15(5160)
FOOL-all=3684,a=191&marked-1SA-26:21(5528)-2SA-3:33(5036)-PS-14:1(5036)▪49:10▪53:1(5036)▪92:6-PR-7:22a▪10:8a,10a,18,23▪11:29a▪12:15a▪13:16▪14:16▪15:5a▪17:7(5036),10,12,16,21,21(5036),24,28a▪18:2▪19:1,10▪20:3a▪23:9▪24:7a▪26:1,4,5,6,8,10,11,12▪27:22a▪28:26▪29:11,20▪30:22(5030)-EC-2:14,15,16²,19(5530)▪4:5▪6:8▪7:6▪10:3²(5530),12,14(5536)-JER-17:11(5030)-HO-9:7a▪N.T.-all=876&marked-M'T-5:22(3474)-LU-12:20-1CO-3:18(3474)▪15:36-2CO-11:16²,23(3912)▪12:6,11
FOOLISH-all=3684&marked-DE-32:6(5036),21(5036)-JOB-2:10(5039)▪5:2(191),3(91)-PS-5:5(1984)▪39:8(5036)▪73:3(1984),22(1198)▪74:18(5036),22(5036)-PR-9:6(6612),13(3687)▪10:1,14(191)▪14:1(200),3(191),7▪15:7,20▪17:25▪19:13▪21:20▪29:9(191)-EC-4:13▪7:17(5530)▪10:15-IS-44:25(5528)-JER-4:22(191)▪5:4(2973),21(5530)▪10:8(3688)-LA-2:14(8602)-EZE-13:3(5036)-ZEC-11:15(196)▪N.T.-all=3474&marked-M'T-7:26▪25:2,3,8-RO-1:21(801)▪2:20(878)▪10:19(801)-1CO-1:20(3471),27-GAL-3:1(453),3(453)-EPH-5:4(3473)-1TI-6:9(453)-2TI-2:23-TIT-3:3(453),9-1PE-2:15(878)
FOOLISHLY-all=5528&marked-GE-31:28-NU-12:11(2973)-1SA-13:13(5528)-2SA-24:10-1CH-21:8-2CH-16:9-JOB-1:22(8604)-PS-75:4(1984)-PR-14:17(200)▪30:32(5034)▪N.T.-2CO-11:17(1722,877),21(1722,877)
FOOLISHNESS-all=200&marked-2SA-15:31(5528)-PS-38:5▪69:5-PR-12:23▪14:24▪15:2,14▪19:3▪22:15▪24:9▪27:22-EC-7:25(5531)▪10:13(5531)▪N.T.-all=3472-M'R-7:22(877)-1CO-1:18,21,23,25(3474)▪2:14▪3:19
FOOL'S-all=3684&marked-PR-12:16(191)▪18:6,7▪26:3▪27:3(191)-EC-5:3▪10:2
FOOLS-all=3684&marked-2SA-13:13(5036)-JOB-12:17(1984)▪30:8(5036)-PS-75:4(1984)▪94:8▪107:17(191)-PR-1:7(191),22,32▪3:35▪8:5▪10:21(191)▪12:23▪13:19,20▪14:8,9(191),24,33▪15:2,14▪16:22(191)▪19:29▪26:7,9-EC-5:1,4▪7:4,5,9▪9:17-IS-19:11(191),13(2973)▪35:8(191)▪N.T.-all=3474&marked-M'T-23:17,19-LU-11:40(878)▪24:25(453)-RO-1:22(3471)-1CO-4:10-2CO-11:19(878)-EPH-5:15(781)
FOOT-all=7272&marked-GE-8:9▪41:44-EX-12:37(7273)▪21:24▪29:20▪30:18(3653),28(3653)▪31:9(3653)▪35:16(3653)▪38:8(3653)▪39:39(3653)▪40:11(3653)-LE-8:11(3653),23▪13:12▪14:14,17,25,28-NU-22:25-DE-2:5▪8:4▪11:10▪19:21▪25:9▪28:35,56,65▪29:5▪32:35▪33:24-JOS-1:3▪5:15-J'G-5:15-2SA-2:18▪14:25▪21:20-2CH-33:8-JOB-2:7▪23:11▪28:4▪31:5▪39:15-PS-9:15▪26:12▪36:11▪38:16▪66:6▪68:23▪91:12▪94:18▪121:3-PR-1:15▪3:23,26▪4:27▪25:17,19-EC-5:1-IS-1:6▪14:25(947)▪18:7(4001)▪20:2▪26:6▪41:2▪58:13-JER-2:25▪12:10(947)-LA-1:15(5541)-EZE-1:7▪6:11▪29:11²▪32:13-DA-8:13(4823)-AM-2:15▪N.T.-all=4228&marked-M'T-4:6▪5:13(2662)▪14:13(3979)▪18:8▪22:13-M'R-9:45-LU-4:11-JOH-11:44-AC-7:5-1CO-12:15

-HEB-10:29(2662)-RE-1:13(4158)■10:2

FOOTMEN-all=7273&marked-NU-11:21-J'G-20:2(376,7273)-1SA-4:10■15:4■22:17(7323)-2SA-8:4(376,7273)■10:6-1KI-20:29-2KI-13:7-1CH-18:4(376,7273)■19:18(376,7273)-JER-12:5

FOOTSTEPS-all=6119&marked-PS-17:5(6471)■77:19■89:51-SONG-1:8

FOOTSTOOL-all=1916,7272&marked-1CH-28:2-2CH-9:18(3534)-PS-99:5■110:1■132:7-IS-66:1-LA-2:1■N.T.-all=5286,3588,4228&marked-M'T-5:35■22:24-M'R-12:36-LU-20:43-AC-2:35■7:49-HEB-1:13■10:13-JAS-2:3(5286)

FORASMUCH-all=3606,6903,1768&marked-GE-41:39(310)-NU-10:31(3588,5921,3651)-DE-12:12(3588)-JOS-17:14(5704)-J'G-11:36(310,834)-1SA-24:18(854,834)-2SA-19:30(310,834)-1KI-11:11(3282,834),13:21(3282,834)■14:7(3282,834)■16:2(3282,834)-2KI-1:16(3282,834)-EZR-7:14-IS-8:6(3282,365)■29:13(3282,365)-DA-2:40,41,45■4:18■5:12■6:4,22-AM-5:11(3282)■N.T.-LU-1:1(1895)-AC-9:38(5607)■11:17(1487)■15:24(1894)-1CO-14:12(1893)-HEB-2:14(1893)

FORBAD-DE-2:37(6680)■N.T.-all=2967-M'T-3:14(1254)-M'R-9:38-LU-9:49-2PE-2:16

FORBARE-all=2308-1SA-23:13-2CH-25:16-JER-41:8

FORBEAR-all=2308&marked-EX-23:5-DE-23:22-1KI-22:6,15-2CH-18:5,14■25:16■35:21-NE-9:30(4900)-JOB-16:6-PR-24:11(2820)-JER-40:4-EZE-2:5,7■3:11,27■24:17(1826)-ZEC-11:12■N.T.-1CO-9:6(3361)-2CO-12:6(5339)-1TH-3:1(4722),5(4722)

FORBEARANCE-RO-2:4(463)■3:25(463)

FORBEARETH-NU-9:13(2308)-EZE-3:27(2310)

FORBEARING-PR-25:15(639)-JER-20:9(3557)■N.T.-EPH-4:2(430)■6:9(477)-COL-3:13(430)

FORBID-all=2486&marked-GE-44:7,17-NU-11:28(3607)-JOS-22:29■24:16-1SA-12:23■14:45■20:2■24:6■26:11-1KI-21:3-1CH-11:19-JOB-27:5■N.T.-all=3361,1096,a=2967&marked-M'T-19:14a-M'R-9:39a■10:14a-LU-6:29a■9:50a■18:16a■20:16-AC-10:47a■24:23a-RO-3:4,6,31■6:2,15■7:7,13■9:14■11:1,11-1CO-6:15■14:39a-GA-2:17■3:21■6:14

FORBIDDEN-LE-5:17(3808)-DE-4:23(6680)■N.T.-AC-16:6(2967)

FORBIDDETH-3JO-10(2967)

FORBIDDING-all=2967&marked-LU-23:2-AC-28:31(209)-1TH-2:16-1TI-4:3

FORBORN-JER-51:30(2308)

FORCE-all=3581&marked-GE-31:31(1497)-DE-22:25(2388)■34:7(3893)-1SA-2:16(2394)-2SA-13:12(6031)-EZR-4:23(153)-ES-7:8(3533)-JOB-30:18■40:16(202)-JER-18:21(3027)■23:10(1369)■48:45-EZE-34:4(2394)■35:5(3027)-AM-2:14■N.T.-all=726&marked-M'T-11:12-JOH-6:15-AC-23:10-HEB-9:17(949)

FORCED-all=6031&marked-J'G-1:34(3905)■20:5-1SA-13:12(662)-2SA-13:14,22,32-PR-7:21(5080)

FORCES-all=2428&marked-2CH-17:2-JOB-36:19(3981)-IS-60:5,11-JER-40:7,13■41:11,13,16■42:1,8■43:4,5-DA-11:10,38(4581)-OB-11

FORCIBLE-JOB-6:25(4834)

FORCING-DE-20:19(5080)-PR-30:33(4330)

FORD-GE-32:22(4569)

FORDS-all=4569-JOS-2:7-J'G-3:28-IS-16:2

FORECAST-DA-11:24(2803),25(2803)

FOREFATHERS-JER-11:10(7223)-2TI-1:3(4269)

FOREFRONT-all=4136,6440&marked-EX-26:9■28:37-LE-8:9-1SA-14:5(8127)-2SA-11:15-2KI-16:14(6440)-2CH-20:27(7218)-EZE-40:19^2■47:1

FOREHEAD-all=4696&marked-EX-28:38^2-LE-13:41(1371),42^2(1372),43(1372)-1SA-17:49^2-2CH-26:19,20-JER-3:3-EZE-3:8,9■16:12(639)■N.T.-RE-14:9(3359)■17:5(3359)

FOREHEADS-EZE-3:8(4696)■9:4(4696)■N.T.-all=3359-RE-7:3■9:4■13:16■14:1■20:4■22:4

FOREIGNER-EX-12:45(8453)-DE-15:3(5237)

FOREIGNERS-OB-11(5237)■N.T.-EPH-2:19(3941)

FOREKNEW-RO-11:2(4267)

FOREKNOW-RO-8:29(4267)

FOREKNOWLEDGE-AC-2:23(4268)-1PE-1:2(4268)

FOREMOST-all=7223-GE-32:17■33:2-2SA-18:27

FOREORDAINED-1PE-1:20(4267)

FOREPART-all=6440-EX-28:27■39:20-1KI-6:20-EZE-42:7■N.T.-AC-27:41(4408)

FORERUNNER-HEB-6:20(4274)

FORESAW-AC-2:25(4308)

FORESEEING-GA-3:8(4275)

FORESEETH-PR-22:3(7200)■27:12(7200)

FORESHIP-AC-27:30(4408)

FORESKIN-all=6190&marked-GE-17:11,14,23,24,25-EX-4:25-LE-12:3-DE-10:16-HAB-2:16(6188)

FORESKINS-all=6190-JOS-5:3-1SA-18:25,27-2SA-3:14-JER-4:4

FOREST-all=3293&marked-1SA-22:5-1KI-7:2■10:17,21-2KI-19:23-2CH-9:16,20-NE-2:8(6508)-PS-50:10■104:20-IS-9:18■10:18,19,34■21:13■22:8■29:17■32:15,19■37:24■44:14,23■56:9-JER-5:6■10:3■12:8■21:14■26:18■46:23-EZE-15:2,6■20:46,47-HO-2:12-AM-3:4-MIC-3:12■5:8-ZEC-11:2

FORESTS-2CH-27:4(2793)-PS-29:9(3295)-EZE-39:10(3293)

FORETELL-2CO-13:2(4302)

FORETOLD-M'R-13:23(4280)-AC-3:24(4293)

FOREWARN-LU-12:5(5263)

FOREWARNED-1TH-4:6(4277)

FORFEITED-EZR-10:8(2763)

FORGAT-all=7911&marked-GE-40:23-J'G-3:7-1SA-12:9-PS-78:11■106:13,21-LA-3:17(5382)-HO-2:13

FORGAVE-PS-78:38(3722)■N.T.-all=5483-M'T-18:27(863),32(863)-LU-7:42,43-2CO-2:10^2-COL-3:13

FORGAVEST-PS-32:5(5375)■99:8(5375)

FORGED-PS-119:69(2950)

FORGERS-JOB-13:4(2950)

FORGET-all=7911&marked-GE-27:45■41:51(5382)-DE-4:9,23,31■6:12■8:11,14,19■9:7■25:19-1SA-1:11-2KI-17:38-JOB-8:13■9:27■11:16■24:20-PS-9:17(7913)■10:12■13:1■45:10■50:22■59:11■74:19,23■78:7■102:4■103:2■119:16,83,93,109,141,153,176■137:5^2-PR-3:1■4:5■31:5,7-IS-49:15^3■54:4■65:11(7913)-JER-2:32■23:27,39(5382)-LA-5:20-HO-4:6-AM-8:7■N.T.-HEB-6:10(1950)■13:16(1950)

FORGETFUL-HEB-13:2(1950)-JAS-1:25(1953)

FORGETFULNESS-PS-88:12(5388)

FORGETTEST-PS-44:24(7911)-IS-51:13(7911)

FORGETTETH-JOB-39:15(7911)-PS-9:12(7911)-PR-2:17(7913)■N.T.-JAS-1:24(1950)

FORGETTING-PH'P-3:13(1950)

FORGIVE-all=5545&marked-GE-50:17^2(5375)-EX-10:17(5375)■32:32(5375)-NU-30:5,8,12-JOS-24:19(5375)-1SA-25:28(5375)-1KI-8:30,34,36,39,50-2CH-6:21,25,27,30,39■7:14-PS-25:18(5375)■86:5(5546)-IS-2:9(5375)-JER-18:23(3722)■31:34■36:3-DA-9:19-AM-7:2■N.T.-all=863&marked-M'T-6:12,14^2,15^2■9:6■18:21,35-M'R-2:7,10■11:25^2,26^2-LU-5:21,24■6:37(630)■11:4■17:3,4■23:34-2CO-2:7(5483),10(5483)■12:13(5483)-1JO-1:9

FORGIVEN-all=5545&marked-LE-4:20,26,31,35■5:10,13,16,18■6:7■19:22-NU-14:19(5375)■15:25,26,28-DE-21:8(3722)-PS-32:1(5375)■85:2(5375)-IS-33:24(5375)■N.T.-all=863&marked-M'T-9:2,5■12:31^2,32^2-M'R-2:5,9■3:28■4:12-LU-5:20,23■6:37(630)■7:47^2,48■12:10^2-AC-8:22-RO-4:7-EPH-4:32(5483)-COL-2:13(5483)-JAS-5:15-1JO-2:12

FORGIVENESS-PS-130:4(5547)■N.T.-all=859-M'R-3:29-AC-5:31■13:38■26:18-EPH-1:7-COL-1:14

FORGIVENESSES-DA-9:9(5547)

FORGIVETH-PS-103:3(5545)■N.T.-LU-7:49(863)

FORGIVING-EX-34:7(5375)-NU-14:18(5375)■N.T.-EPH-4:32(5483)-COL-3:13(5483)

FORGOT-DE-24:19(7911)

FORGOTTEN-all=7911&marked-GE-41:30-DE-26:13■31:21■32:18-JOB-19:14■28:4-PS-9:18■10:11■31:12■42:9■44:17,20■77:9■119:61,139-EC-2:16■8:10■9:5-IS-17:10■23:15,16■44:21(5382)■49:14(7913)■65:16-JER-2:32■3:21■13:25■18:15■20:11■23:27,40■30:14■44:9■50:5,6-LA-2:6-EZE-22:12■23:35-HO-4:6■8:14■13:6■N.T.-all=1950&marked-M'T-16:5-M'R-8:14-LU-12:6-HEB-12:5(1585)-2PE-1:9(3024,2983)

FORKS-1SA-13:21(7969,7053)

FORM-all=8403&marked-GE-1:2(8414)-1SA-28:14(8389)-2SA-14:20(6440)-2CH-4:7(4941)-JOB-4:16(4758)-IS-45:7(3335)■52:14(8389)■53:2(8389)-JER-4:23(8414)-EZE-8:3,10■10:8■43:11^2(6699)-DA-2:31(7299)■3:19(6755),25(7299)■N.T.-all=3444&marked-M'R-16:12-RO-2:20(3446)■6:17(5179)-PH'P-2:6,7-2TI-1:13(5296)■3:5(3446)

FORMED-all=3335&marked-GE-2:7,8,19-DE-32:18(2342)-2KI-19:25-JOB-26:5(2342),13(2342),33:6(7169)-PS-90:2(2342)■94:9■95:5-PR-26:10(2342)-IS-27:11■37:26■43:1,7,10,21■44:2,10,21,24■45:18^2■49:5■54:17-JER-1:5■33:2-AM-7:1■N.T.-RO-9:20(4110)-GAL-4:19(3445)-1TI-2:13(4111)

FORMER-all=7223&marked-GE-40:13-NU-21:26-DE-24:4-RU-4:7(6440)-1SA-17:30-2KI-1:14■17:34,40-NE-5:15-JOB-8:8■30:3(570)-PS-79:8■89:49-EC-1:11■7:10-IS-41:22■42:9■43:9,18■46:9■48:3■61:4■65:7,16,17-JER-5:24(3138)■10:16(3335)■34:5■36:28■51:19(3335)-EZE-16:55^3(6927)-DA-11:13,29-HO-6:3(3138)-JOE-2:23^2(4175)-HAG-2:9-ZEC-1:4■7:7,12■8:11■14:8(6931)-MAL-3:4(6931)■N.T.-AC-1:1(4413)-EPH-4:22(4387)-HEB-10:32(4386)-1PE-1:14(4386)-RE-21:4(4413)

FORMETH-AM-4:13(3335)-ZEC-12:1(3335)

FORMS-EZE-43:11^2(6699)

FORNICATION-all=2181&marked-2CH-21:11-IS-23:17-EZE-16:26,29(8457)■N.T.-all=4202&marked-M'T-5:32■19:9-JOH-8:41-AC-15:20,29■21:25-RO-1:29-1CO-5:1^2■6:13,18,18(4203)■7:2■10:8(4203)-2CO-12:21-GA-5:19-EPH-5:3-COL-3:5-1TH-4:3-JUDE-7(1608)-RE-2:14(4203),20(4203),21■9:21■14:8■17:2(4203),2,4■18:3,3(4203),9(4203)■19:2

FORNICATIONS-EZE-16:15(8457)■N.T.-M'T-15:19(4202)-M'R-7:21(4202)

FORNICATOR-1CO-5:11(4205)-HEB-12:16(4205)

FORNICATORS-all=4205-**1CO**-5:9,10■6:9

FORSAKE-all=5800&marked-**DE**-4:31(7503)■12:19■14:27■31:6,8,16,17-**JOS**-1:5■24:16,20-**J'G**-9:11(2308)-**1SA**-12:22(5203)-**1KI**-6:13■8:57(5203)-**2KI**-21:14(5203)-**1CH**-28:9,20-**2CH**-7:19■15:2-**EZR**-8:22-**NE**-9:31■10:39-**JOB**-20:13-**PS**-27:9,10■37:8■38:21■71:9,18■89:30■94:14■119:8,53■138:8(7503)-**PR**-1:8(5203)■3:3■4:2,6■6:20(5203)■9:6■27:10■28:4-**IS**-1:28■41:17■42:16■55:7■65:11-**JER**-17:13■23:33(5203),39(5203)■51:9-**LA**-5:20-**EZE**-20:8-**DA**-11:30-**JON**-2:8■**N.T.**-**AC**-21:21(646,575)-**HEB**-13:5(1459)

FORSAKEN-all=5800&marked-**DE**-28:20■29:25-**J'G**-6:13(5203)■10:10,13-**1SA**-8:8■12:10-**1KI**-11:33■18:18■19:10,14-**2KI**-22:17-**2CH**-12:5■13:10,11■21:10■24:20,24■28:6■29:6■34:25-**EZR**-9:9,10-**NE**-13:11-**JOB**-18:4■20:19-**PS**-9:10■22:1■37:25■71:11-**IS**-1:4■2:6(5203)■7:16■17:2,9■27:10(7971)■32:14(5203)■49:14■54:6,7■60:15■62:4,12-**JER**-1:16■2:13,17,19■4:29■5:7,19■7:29(5203)■9:13,19■12:7■15:6(5203)■16:11^{2}■17:13■18:14(5428)■19:4■22:9■25:38■51:5(488)-**EZE**-8:12■9:9■36:4-**AM**-5:2(5203)-**ZEP**-2:4■**N.T.**-all=1459&marked-**M'T**-19:27(863),29(863)■27:46-**M'R**-15:34-**2CO**-4:9-**2TI**-4:10-**2PE**-2:15(2641)

FORSAKETH-all=5800-**JOB**-6:14-**PS**-37:28-**PR**-2:17■15:10■28:13■**N.T.**-**LU**-14:33(657)

FORSAKING-**IS**-6:12(5805)■**N.T.**-**HEB**-10:25(1459)

FORSOMUCH-**LU**-19:9(2530)

FORSOOK-all=5800&marked-**DE**-32:15(5203)-**J'G**-2:12,13■10:6-**1SA**-31:7-**1KI**-9:9■12:8,13-**2KI**-21:22-**1CH**-10:7-**2CH**-7:22■10:8,13■12:1-**PS**-78:60(5203)■119:87-**IS**-58:2-**JER**-14:5■**N.T.**-all=863&marked-**M'T**-26:56-**M'R**-1:18■14:50-**LU**-5:11-**2TI**-4:16(1459)-**HEB**-11:27(2641)

FORSOOKEST-**NE**-9:17(5800),19(5800)

FORSWEAR-**M'T**-5:33(1964)

FORT-all=1785&marked-**2SA**-5:9(4686)-**IS**-25:12(4869)-**EZE**-4:2■21:22■26:8-**DA**-11:19(4581)

FORTH-all=3318,a=7971-**GE**-1:11(1876),12,20(8317),21(8317),24■3:16(3205),18(6779),22a■8:7sup,7,9a,16,17,18,19■9:7(8317),18■10:11■11:31■12:5■14:18■15:4,5■19:10a,16,17■24:43,45,53■30:39(3209)■38:24,25,29(6556)■39:13(2351)■40:10sup,10(1310)■41:47(6213)■42:15-**EX**-3:10,11,12■4:4^{2}a,14■5:20■7:4■8:3(8317),18,20■12:31,39,46■13:8,16■14:11■16:3,32■19:1,17■29:46■32:11-**LE**-4:12,21■6:11■14:3,45■16:24,27■22:27(3205)■24:14,23■25:21(6213),38,42,55■26:10,13,45-**NU**-1:3,20,22,24,26,28,30,32,34,36,38,40,42,45■2:9(5265),16(5265)■11:20,31(5265)■17:8■19:3■20:8,8sup,16■24:8(4161)■26:4■31:13■33:1■34:4(8444),8(8444)-**DE**-1:27■2:23■4:20,45,46■6:12■8:14(4161),15(4161)■9:12,26■14:22,28■16:1,3^{2},6■17:5■21:2,10■22:15■23:4,9,12■24:9■25:11a,17■26:8■29:25■33:14sup,14(1645)-**JOS**-2:3■5:5■9:12■10:23■18:11,17■19:1-**J'G**-1:24■3:21a,23■5:25(7126),31■6:8,18,21a■9:43■11:31■14:12(2330),13(2330),14^{2},16(2330)■15:15a■19:22,25■20:21,25,33(1518)-**RU**-1:7■2:18-**1SA**-11:7■12:8■14:11,27a■17:20,55■18:30^{2}■22:3,17a■23:13■24:10a■30:21-**2SA**-■6:6a■11:1■12:30,31■13:39■15:5a,16,17■16:5,11■18:2sup,2,3,12a■19:7^{2}■20:8■22:20,49(4161)-**1KI**-2:30,36■8:16,19,51■9:9■13:4^{2}a■19:11■20:33■21:13■22:21,22^{2}-**2KI**-2:3,21,23,24■6:15■8:3■9:11,15■10:22^{2},25,26■11:7,12,15■18:7■19:3(3205),31■21:15■23:4-**1CH**-12:33,36■13:9a■14:15■16:23(1319)19:16■24:7■25:9-**2CH**-1:17■6:5,9■7:22■20:20^{2}■21:9(5674)■23:14■25:5■26:6■29:5■32:21(3329)-**EZR**-1:7^{2},8■6:5(5312)-**NE**-8:15,16■9:7,15-**ES**-4:6■5:9-**JOB**-1:11a,12a,12■2:5a,7■5:6■8:16■10:18■14:2,9(6213)■15:35(3205)■23:10■24:5■28:9a,11■38:8(1518),27(6779),32■39:1(3205),2(3205),3(6398),4-**PS**-1:3(5414)■7:14(3205)■17:2■18:19■19:6(4161)■37:6■44:9■55:20a■68:7■78:52(5265)■79:13(5608)■88:8■90:2(3205)■92:14(5107)■104:14,23■105:30(8317),37,43■108:11■125:3a■146:4-**PR**-7:15■8:24(2342),25(2342)■10:31(5107)■25:4,6(1921),8■27:1(3205)■30:27,33^{3}■31:20(6566)-**EC**-2:6(6779)■5:15■7:18-**SONG**-1:8■2:13(2590)■3:11■7:11,12(5132)■8:5^{2}(2254)-**IS**-2:3■5:2^{2}(6213),4^{2}(6213)7:3■11:1■13:10■14:29■23:4(3205)■26:18(3205)■28:19(5674),29■33:11(3205)■34:1(6631)■36:3■37:3(3205),9,32,36■41:21(5066),22(5066)■42:1,3,13■43:8,17(4161),19(6779)■45:8(6509),10(2342)■48:1,3,20■49:9,17■51:5,18(3205)■54:16(4161)■55:10(3205),11,12(2986),12sup■58:9a■59:4(3205)■61:11,11^{2}sup■62:1■65:9,23(3205)■66:7(3205)■66:8(2342),8(3205),9^{2}(3205),24-**JER**-1:5,9a■2:27(3205),37■4:4,7■6:25■7:25■10:13,20,20sup■11:4■12:2(6213)■14:18■15:1,2,19■17:22■19:2■20:3,18■22:11■23:15,19■25:32■26:23■29:16■30:23■31:4,24(5265),39■32:21■34:13■37:5,7,12■38:2,8,17,18,21,22(4163)■39:4■41:6■43:12■44:17■46:9■48:7,45■49:5(6440)■50:8,25■51:10,16,44■52:7,31-**EZE**-1:13■3:22,23■5:4■7:10■8:3a■9:7■11:7■12:4^{2},4(4161),6,7^{2},12■14:22(4163),22■16:14■17:2(2330),6(6213),6sup,8(6213),23(5375)■20:6,9,10,22,38■21:3,4,5,19■24:12■27:33■28:18■30:9■31:6(3205)■32:2(1518)■33:30■36:20■38:4,8■39:9■42:1,15■44:5(4161),19■46:2,8,9^{2},10,12^{2},21■47:3,8-**DA**-2:13(5312),14(5312)■3:26^{2}(5312),5:5(5312)■7:10(5312)■8:9■9:15,22,23,25(4161)■10:20■11:11,11(5975),44-**HO**-6:3(4161),5■9:13,16(3205)■10:1(7737)■13:13(4866)■14:5(5221)-**JOE**-2:16■3:18-**AM**-5:3■8:5(6605)-**JO**-1:5(2904),12(2904),15(2904)-**MIC**-1:3,11■4:2,10(1518),10■5:2,2(4163),3(3205)■7:9-**HAB**-1:4■3:5,13-**ZEP**-2:2(3205)-**HAG**-1:11■2:19(5375)-**ZEC**-2:3■3:8(935)■4:7■5:3,4,5^{2},6■6:5,6^{3},7■9:14■10:4■14:2,3-**MAL**-4:2■**N.T.**-all=1831,a=1614,b=4160-**M'T**-1:21(5088),23(5088),25(5088)■2:16(649)■3:8b,10b■7:17^{2}b,18^{2}b,19b■8:3a■9:9(3855),25(1544),38(1544)■10:5(649),16(649)■12:13^{2}a,20(1544),35(1544),35sup,49a■13:3,23b,24(3908),26b,31(3908),41(649),43(1584),49(3318),52(1544)■14:2(1754),14,31a■15:18(3318)■21:43b■22:3(649),4(649)■24:26,32(1631)■25:1-**M'R**-1:38,41a■2:12,13■3:3(1519,3588,3319),5,6,14(649)■4:8(5348),20(2592),28(2592),29(3860)■6:7,14(1754),17a,24■7:26(1544)■8:11■9:29■10:17(1607)■11:1a■13:28(1631)■14:13a,16■16:20-**LU**-1:1(392),31(5088),57(1080)■2:7(5088)■3:7(1607),8b,9b■5:13a,27■6:10a,43^{2}b,45^{2}(4393)■7:17■8:14(4198),22(321),27■10:2(1544),3(649)■12:16(2164),37(3928)■14:7(3004)■15:22(1627)■20:9(1554),20(649)■21:30(4261)■22:53a-**JOH**-1:43■2:10(5087),11(5319)■5:29(1607)■8:42■10:4(1544)■11:43(1854),44■12:13■15:6(1854)■16:28,30■18:1,4■19:4^{2}(1854),5(1854),13(1854),17■20:3■21:3,18a-**AC**-2:33(1632)■4:30a■5:10(1627),15(1627),19(1806),34(1854)■7:7■9:30(1821),40(1854)■11:22(1821)■12:1(1911),4(321),6(4254)■13:4(1599)16:3■17:18(2604)■21:2(321)■23:28(2609)■24:2(2564)■25:26(4254)■26:1a,25(669)-**RO**-3:25(4388)■10:21(1600)-**1CO**-4:9(584)■16:11(4311)-**GA**-3:1(4270)■4:4(1821),6(1821),27(4486)-**PH'P**-2:16(1907)■3:13(1901)-**1TI**-1:16(1731)-**HEB**-1:14(649)■6:7(5088)■13:13-**JAS**-1:15(616),15(5088)■3:11(1032)■5:18(985)-**1PE**-2:9(1804)-**3JO**-7-**JUDE**-7(4295)-**RE**-5:6(649)■6:2■12:5(5088),13(5088)■16:14(1607)

FORTHWITH-**EZR**-6:8(629)■**N.T.**-all=2112&marked-**M'T**-13:5■26:49-**M'R**-1:29,43■5:13-**JOH**-19:34(2117)-**AC**-9:18(3916)■12:10■21:30

FORTIETH-all=705-**NU**-33:38-**DE**-1:3-**1CH**-26:31-**2CH**-16:13

FORTIFIED-**2CH**-11:11(2388)■26:9(2388)-**NE**-3:8(5800)-**MIC**-7:12(4692)

FORTIFY-**J'G**-9:31(6696)-**NE**-4:2(5800)-**IS**-22:10(1219)-**JER**-51:53(1219)-**NA**-2:1(553)■3:14(2388)

FORTRESS-all=4686&marked-**2SA**-22:2-**PS**-18:2■31:3■71:3■91:2■144:2-**IS**-17:3(4013)■25:12(4013)-**JER**-6:27(4013)■10:17(4693)■16:19(4581)-**DA**-11:7(4581),10(4581)-**AM**-5:9(4013)-**MIC**-7:12(4693)

FORTRESSES-**IS**-34:13(4013)-**HO**-10:14(4013)

FORTS-all=1785&marked-**2KI**-25:1-**IS**-29:3(4694)■32:14(6076)-**JER**-52:4-**EZE**-17:17■33:27(4679)

FORTY-all=705&marked-**GE**-5:13■7:4,12,17■8:6■18:28,29■25:20■26:34■32:15■47:28■50:3-**EX**-16:35■24:18■26:19,21■34:28■36:24,26-**LE**-25:8-**NU**-1:21,25,33,41■2:11,15,19,28■13:25■14:33,34^{2}■26:7,18,41,50■32:13■35:6,7-**DE**-2:7■8:2,4■9:9,11,18,25■10:10■25:3■29:5-**JOS**-4:13■5:6■14:7,10■21:41-**J'G**-3:11■5:8,31■8:28■12:6,14■13:1-**1SA**-4:18■17:16-**2SA**-2:10■5:4■10:18■15:7-**1KI**-2:11■4:26■6:17■7:3,38■11:42■14:21■15:10■19:8-**2KI**-2:24■8:9■10:14■12:1■14:23-**1CH**-5:18■12:36■19:18■29:27-**2CH**-9:30■12:13■22:2■24:1-**EZR**-2:8,10,24,25,34,38,64(702,7239),66-**NE**-5:15■7:13,15,28,29,36,41,44,62,66(702,7239),67,68■9:21■11:13-**JOB**-42:16-**PS**-95:10-**JER**-52:30-**EZE**-4:6■29:11,12,13■41:2■46:22-**AM**-2:10■5:25-**JON**-3:4■**N.T.**-all=5062&marked-**M'T**-4:2-**M'R**-1:13-**LU**-4:2-**JOH**-2:20-**AC**-1:3■4:22■7:23(5063),30,36,42■13:18(5063),21■23:13,21-**2CO**-11:24-**HEB**-3:9,17-**RE**-7:4■11:2■13:5■14:1,3■21:17

FORTY'S-**GE**-18:29(705)

FORUM-**AC**-28:15(675)

FORWARD-all=5265&marked-**GE**-26:13(1980)-**EX**-14:15-**NU**-1:51■2:17^{2},24,34■4:5,15■10:5,17,18,21,22,25,28,35■21:10■22:1■32:19(1973)-**J'G**-9:44(6584)-**1SA**-10:3(1973)■16:13(4605)■18:9(1973)■30:25(4605)-**1CH**-23:4(5921)-**EZR**-3:8(5921),9(5921)-**JOB**-23:8(6924)■30:13(3276)-**JER**-7:24(6440)-**EZE**-1:9(6440),12(6440)■10:22(6440)■39:22(1973)■43:27(1973)■**N.T.**-**M'R**-14:35(4281)-**AC**-19:33(4261)-**2CO**-8:10(2309),17(4707)-**GA**-2:10(4704)-**3JO**-6(4311)

FORWARDNESS-**2CO**-8:8(4710)■9:2(4288)

FOUGHT-all=3898-**EX**-17:8,10-**NU**-21:1,23,26-**JOS**-10:14,29,31,34,36,38,42■23:3■24:8,11-**J'G**-1:5,8■5:19,20^{2}■9:17,39,45,52■11:20■12:4-**1SA**-4:10■12:9■14:47■19:8■23:5■31:1-**2SA**-2:28■8:10■10:17■11:17■12:26,27,29■21:15-**2KI**-8:29■9:15■12:17■13:12■14:15-**1CH**-10:1■18:10■19:17-**2CH**-20:29■22:6■27:5-**PS**-109:3-**IS**-20:1■63:10-**JER**-34:1,7-**ZEC**-14:3,12(6633)■**N.T.**-**1CO**-15:32(2341)-**2TI**-4:7(75)-**RE**-12:7^{2}(4170)

FOUL-**JOB**-16:16(2560)-**EZE**-34:18(7515)■**N.T.**-**M'T**-16:3(5494)-**M'R**-9:25(169)-**RE**-18:2(169)

FOULED-**EZE**-34:19(4833)

FOULEDST-**EZE**-32:2(7515)

FOUND-all=4672&marked-GE-2:20■6:8■8:9■11:2■16:7■18:3,29,30,31,32■19:19■26:19,32■27:20■30:14,27■31:33,34,35,37■33:10■36:24■37:15,17,32■38:20,23■39:4■44:8,9,10,12,16^2,17■47:14,29■50:4-EX-9:19■12:19■15:22■16:27■21:16■22:2,4,7,8■33:12,13,16,17■34:9■35:23,24-LE-6:3,4-NU-11:11,15■15:32,33■32:5-DE-17:2■18:10■20:11■21:1■22:3,14,17,20,22,27,28■24:1,7■32:10-JOS-2:22■10:17-J'G-1:5■6:17■14:18■15:15■21:12-RU-2:10-1SA-9:4^2,11,20■10:2,16,21■12:5■13:19,22^2■14:30■16:22■20:3,29■25:28■27:5■29:3,6,8■30:11■31:8-2SA-7:27■14:22■17:12-1KI-1:3,52■7:47(2713)■11:19,29■13:14,28■14:13■18:10■19:19■20:36,37■21:20^2-2KI-2:17■4:39■9:35■12:5,10,18■14:14■16:8■17:4■18:15■19:8■20:13■22:8,9,13■23:2,24■25:19^2-1CH-4:40,41■10:8■17:25■20:2■24:4■26:31■28:9■29:8-2CH-2:17■4:18(2713)■15:2,4,15■19:3■20:25■21:17■22:8■25:5,24■29:16■34:14,15,17,21,30■36:8-EZR-2:62■4:19(7912)■6:2(7912)■8:15■10:18-NE-5:8■7:5^2,64■8:14■13:1-ES-2:23■5:8■6:2■7:3■8:5-JOB-19:28■20:8■28:12,13■31:29■32:3,13■33:24■42:15-PS-32:6■36:2■37:36■69:20■76:5■84:3■89:20■107:4■116:3■132:6-PR-6:31■7:15■10:13■16:31■24:14■25:16-EC-7:27,28^2,29■9:15-SONG-3:1,2,3,4■5:7■8:10-IS-10:10,14■13:15■22:3■30:14■35:9■37:8■39:2■51:3■55:6■57:10■65:1,8-JER-2:5,26,34^2■5:26■11:9■14:3■15:16■23:11■29:14■31:2■41:3,8,12■48:27■50:7,20,24■52:25^{2}LA-2:16-EZE-22:30■26:21■28:15-DA-1:19,20■2:25,35(7912)■5:11(7912),12(7912),14(7912),27(7912)■6:4(7912),11(7912),22(7912),23(7912)■11:19■12:1-HO-9:10■12:4,8■14:8-JON-1:3-MIC-1:13-ZEP-3:13-ZEC-10:10-MAL-2:6■N.T.-all=2147&marked-M'T-1:18■2:8■8:10■13:44,46■18:28■20:6■21:19■22:10■26:43,60,60sup■27:32-M'R-1:37■7:30■11:4,13■14:16,40,55-LU-1:30■2:16(429),45,46■4:17■7:9,10■8:35■9:36■13:6■15:5,6,9^2,24,32■17:18■19:32■22:13,45■23:2,14,22■24:2,3,23,24,33-JOH-1:41,45■2:14■6:25■9:35■11:17■12:14-AC-5:10,22,23^2,39■7:11,46■8:40■9:2,33■10:27■11:26■12:19■13:6,22,28■17:6,23■18:2■19:19■24:5,12,18,20■25:25(2638)■27:6,28^2■28:14-RO-4:1■7:10■10:20-1CO-4:2■15:15-2CO-2:13■5:3■7:14(1096)■11:12■12:20-GAL-2:17-PH'P-2:8■3:9-2TI-1:17-HEB-11:5■12:17-1PE-1:7■2:22-2PE-3:14-2JO-4-RE-2:2■3:2■5:4■12:8■14:5■16:20■18:21,22,24■20:11,15

FOUNDATION-all=3245&marked-EX-9:18-JOS-6:26-1KI-5:17■6:37■7:9(4527),10■16:34-2CH-8:16(4143)■23:5(3247)■31:7-EZR-3:6,10,11,12■5:16(787)-JOB-4:19(3247)■22:16(3247)-PS-87:1(3248)■102:25■137:7(3247)-PR-10:25(3247)-IS-28:16(3248),16(4143)■44:28■48:13-EZE-13:14(3247)-HAB-3:13(3247)-HAG-2:18-ZEC-4:9(3248)■8:9(3248)■12:1(3248)■N.T.-all=2310,a=2602&marked-M'T-13:35a■25:34a-LU-6:48,49■11:50a■14:29-JOH-17:24a-RO-15:20-1CO-3:10,11,12-EPH-1:4a■2:20-1TI-6:19-2TI-2:19-HEB-1:10(2311)■4:3a■6:1■9:26a-1PE-1:20a-RE-13:8a■17:8a■21:19

FOUNDATIONS-all=4146&marked-DE-32:22-2SA-22:8,16-EZR-4:12(787)■6:3(787)-JOB-38:4(3245),6(134)-PS-11:3(8356)■18:7,15■82:5■104:5(4349)-PR-8:29-IS-16:7(808)■24:18■40:21■51:13(3245),16(3245)■54:11(3245)■58:12-JER-31:37■50:15(803)■51:26-LA-4:11(3247)-EZE-30:4(3247)■41:8(4328)-MIC-1:6(3247)■6:2■N.T.-all=2310-AC-16:26-HEB-11:10-RE-21:14,19

FOUNDED-all=3245-PS-24:2■89:11■104:8■119:152-PR-3:19-IS-14:32■23:13-AM-9:6■N.T.-M'T-7:25(2311)-LU-6:48(2311)

FOUNDER-all=6884-J'G-17:4-JER-6:29■10:9,14■51:17

FOUNDEST-NE-9:8(4672)

FOUNTAIN-all=4726&marked-GE-16:7^2(5869)-LE-11:36(4599)■20:18^2-DE-33:28(5869)-JOS-15:9(4599)-1SA-29:1(5869)-NE-2:14(5869)■3:15(5869)■12:37(5869)-PS-36:9■68:26■74:15(4599)■114:8(4599)-PR-5:18■13:14■14:27■25:26(4599)-EC-12:6(4002)-SONG-4:12(4599),15(4599)-JER-2:13■6:7(953)■9:1■17:13-HO-13:15(4599)-JOE-3:18(4599)-ZEC-13:1■N.T.-all=4077-M'R-5:29-JAS-3:11,12-RE-21:6

FOUNTAINS-all=4599&marked-GE-7:11■8:2-NU-33:9(5869)-DE-8:7(5869)-1KI-18:5-2CH-32:3(5869),4-PR-5:16■8:24,28(5869)-IS-41:18■N.T.-all=4077-RE-7:17■8:10■14:7■16:4

FOUR-all=702&marked-GE-2:10■11:13,15,16,17■14:9■15:13■23:15,16■32:6■33:1■47:24-EX-12:40,41■22:1■25:12^2,26^3,34■26:2,8,32^2■27:2,4^2,16^2■28:17■36:9,15,36^2■37:3^2,13^3,20■38:2,5,19^2,29■39:10-LE-11:20,21,23,27,42-NU-1:29,31,37,43■2:6,8,9,16,23,30■7:7,8,85,88■25:9■26:25,43,47,50-DE-3:11■22:12-JOS-19:7■21:18,22,24,29,31,35,37,39-J'G-9:34■11:40■19:2■20:2,17,47■21:12-1SA-4:2■22:2■25:13■27:7■30:10,17-2SA-21:20,22-1KI-6:1■7:2,19,27^2,30^2,32,34,38,42■9:28■10:26■15:33■18:19,19,22,33■22:6-2KI-7:3■14:13-1CH-3:5■5:18■7:1,7■9:24,26■12:26■20:6■21:5,20■23:4,5^2,10,12■24:18■25:31■26:17,18■27:1,2,4,5,7,8,9,10,11,12,13,14,15-2CH-1:14■4:13■8:18■9:25■13:3■18:5■25:23-EZR-1:10,11■2:7,15,31,40,67■6:17(703)-NE-6:4■7:12,23,34,43,69■11:6,18-JOB-1:19■42:16-PR-30:15,18,21,24,29-IS-11:12■17:6-JER-15:3■36:23■49:36■52:21,30-EZE-1:5,6^2,8,10^3,15,16,17,18■7:2■10:9,10,11,12,14,21^2■14:21■37:9■40:41^2,42■41:5■42:20■43:14,15^2,16,17,20■45:19■46:21,22^2,23■48:16^4,30,32,33,34-DA-1:17■3:25(703)■7:2(703),3(703),6^2(703),17(703)■8:8^2,22■10:4■11:4-AM-1:3,6,9,11,13■2:1,4,6-HAG-1:15■2:10,18,20-ZEC-1:7,18,20■2:6■6:1,5■N.T.-all=5064&marked-M'T-15:38(5070)■16:10(5070)■24:31-M'R-2:3■8:9(5070),20(5070)■13:27-LU-2:37-JOH-4:35(5072)■11:17,39(5066)■19:23-AC-5:36(6071)■7:6(6071)■10:11,30(5067)■11:5■12:4■13:20(5071)■21:9,23,38(5070)■27:29-GA-3:17(5071)-RE-4:4^2,6,8,10■5:6,8,14^2■6:1,6■7:1^3,2,4,11■9:13,14,15■11:16■14:1,3^2■15:7■19:4■20:8■21:17

FOURFOLD-2SA-12:6(706)■N.T.-LU-19:8(5073)

FOURFOOTED-all=5074-AC-10:12■11:6-RO-1:23

FOURSCORE-all=8048-GE-16:16■35:28-EX-7:7^2-NU-2:9■4:48-JOS-14:10-J'G-3:30-1SA-22:18-2SA-19:32,35-1KI-5:15■12:21-2KI-6:25■10:24■19:35-1CH-7:5■15:9■25:7-2CH-2:2,18■11:1■14:8■17:15,18■26:17-EZE-8:8-NE-7:26■11:18-ES-1:4-PS-90:10-SONG-6:8-IS-37:36-JER-41:5■N.T.-LU-2:37(3589)■16:7(3589)

FOURSQUARE-all=7251&marked-EX-27:1■28:16■30:2■37:25■38:1■39:9-1KI-7:31-EZE-40:47■48:20(7243)■N.T.-RE-21:16(5068)

FOURTEEN-all=702,6246&marked-GE-31:41(72012,6240)■46:22(702,6240)-NU-1:27(702,7657)■2:4(702,7657)■16:49(702,7657)■29:13,15,17,20,23,26,29,32-JOS-15:36■18:28-1KI-8:65-1CH-25:5-2CH-13:21-JOB-42:12-EZE-43:17^2■N.T.-all=1180-M'T-1:17^3-2CO-12:2-GA-2:1

FOURTEENTH-all=702,6240-GE-14:5-EX-12:6,18-LE-23:5-NU-9:3,5,11■28:16-JOS-5:10-2KI-18:13-1CH-24:13■25:21-2CH-30:15■35:1-EZR-6:19-ES-9:15,17,18,19,21-IS-36:1-EZE-40:1■45:21■N.T.-AC-27:27(5065),33(5065)

FOURTH-all=7243&marked-GE-1:19■2:14■15:16-EX-20:5(7256)■28:20■29:40(7253),40■34:7(7256)■39:13-LE-19:24■23:13-NU-7:30■14:18(7256)■15:4,5■23:10(7255)■28:5,7,14■29:23-DE-5:9(7256)-JOS-19:17-J'G-19:5-1SA-9:8(7253)-2SA-3:4-1KI-6:1,33,37■22:41(702)-2KI-6:25(7255)■10:30■15:12■18:9-1CH-2:14■3:2,15■8:2■12:10■23:19■24:8,23■25:11■26:2,4,11■27:7-2CH-3:2(702)■20:26-EZR-8:33-NE-9:1(702),3^2-JER-25:1■28:1■36:1■39:2■45:1■46:2■51:59■52:6-EZE-1:1■10:14-DA-2:40(7244)■3:25(7244)■7:7(7244),19(7244),23(7244)■11:2-ZEC-6:3■7:1^2(702)■8:19■N.T.-all=5067-M'T-14:25-M'R-6:48-RE-4:7■6:7^2,8■8:12■16:8■21:19

FOWL-all=5775&marked-GE-1:20,28,21,22,26,28,30■2:19,20■7:14,21,23■8:17,19,20■9:2,10-LE-7:26■11:46■17:13■20:25-DE-4:17(6833)-1KI-4:23(1257),33-JOB-28:7(5861)-PS-8:8(6833)■148:10(6833)-JER-9:10-EZE-17:23(6833)■39:17(6833)■44:31-DA-7:6(5776)

FOWLER-all=3353-PS-91:3-PR-6:5-HO-9:8

FOWLERS-PS-124:7(3369)

FOWLS-all=5775&marked-GE-6:7,20■7:3,8■15:11(5861)-LE-1:14■11:13,20■20:25-DE-14:20■28:26-1SA-17:44,46-1KI-14:11■16:4■21:24-NE-5:18(6833)-JOB-12:7■28:21■35:11-PS-50:11■78:27■79:2■104:12-IS-18:6^2(5861)-JER-7:33■15:3■16:4■19:7■34:20-EZE-29:5■31:6,13■32:4■38:20-DA-2:38(5776)■4:12(6853),14(6853),21(6853)-HO-2:18■4:3■7:12-ZEP-1:3■N.T.-all=4071&marked-M'T-6:26■13:4-M'R-4:4,32-LU-8:5■12:24■13:19-AC-10:12■11:6-RE-19:17(3732),21(3732)

FOX-NE-4:3(7776)■N.T.-LU-13:32(258)

FOXES-all=7776-J'G-15:4-PS-63:10-SONG-2:15-LA-5:18-EZE-13:4■N.T.-M'T-8:20(258)-LU-9:58(258)

FRAGMENTS-all=2801-M'T-14:20-M'R-6:43■8:19,20-LU-9:17-JOH-6:12,13

FRAIL-PS-39:4(2310)

FRAME-J'G-12:6(3559)-PS-103:14(3336)-JER-18:11(3335)-EZE-40:2(4011)-HO-5:4(5414)

FRAMED-IS-29:16(3336),16(3335)■N.T.-EPH-2:21(4883)-HEB-11:3(2675)

FRAMETH-PS-50:19(6775)■94:20(3335)

FRANKINCENSE-all=3828&marked-EX-30:34-LE-2:1,2,15,16■5:11■6:15■24:7-NU-5:15-1CH-9:29-NE-13:5,9-SONG-3:6■4:6,14■N.T.-M'T-2:11(3030)-RE-18:13(3030)

FRANKLY-LU-7:42(5435)

FRAUD-PS-10:7(8496)■N.T-JAS-5:4(650)

FRAY-all=2729-DE-28:26-JER-7:33-ZEC-1:21

FRECKLED-LE-13:39(933)

FREE-all=2670&marked-EX-21:2,5,11(2600),26,27■36:3(5071)-LE-19:20(2666)-NU-5:19(5352),28(5352)-DE-15:12,13,18■24:5(5355)-1SA-17:25-1CH-9:33(6362)-2CH-29:31(5081)-JOB-3:19■39:5-PS-51:12(5082)■88:5■105:20(6605)-IS-58:6-JER-34:9,10,11,14-AM-4:5(5071)■N.T.-all=1658&marked-M'T-17:26-JOH-8:32(1659),33,36(1659),36-RO-5:15(5486),16(5468)■6:18(1659),20,22(1659)■7:3■8:2(1659)-1CO-7:21,22■9:1,19■12:13-GA-3:28■4:26,31■5:1(1659)-EPH-6:8-COL-3:11-1PE-2:16-RE-6:15■13:16■19:18

FREED-JOS-9:23(3772)■N.T.-RO-

6:7(1344)

FREEDOM-LE-19:20(2668)■N.T.-AC-22:28(4174)

FREELY-NU-11:5(2600)PS-54:6(5071)-HO-14:4(5071)■N.T.-all=1432&marked-M'T-10:8-AC-2:29(3326,3954)■26:26(3955)-RO-3:24-2CO-11:7-RE-21:6■22:17

FREEMAN-1CO-7:22(558)

FREEWILL-all=5071&marked-LE-22:18,21,23■23:38-NU-15:3■29:39-DE-12:6,17■16:10■23:23-2CH-31:14-EZR-1:4■3:5■7:13(5069),16(5069)■8:28-PS-119:108

FREEWOMAN-all=1658-GA-4:22,23,30

FREQUENT-2CO-11:23(4056)

FRESH-NU-11:8(3955)-JOB-29:20(2319)-PS-92:10(7488)■N.T.-JAS-3:12(1099)

FRESHER-JOB-33:25(7375)

FRET-all=2734&marked-LE-13:55(6356)-1SA-1:6(7481)-PS-37:1,7,8-PR-24:19-IS-8:21(7107)

FRETTED-EZE-16:43(7264)

FRETTETH-PR-19:3(2196)

FRETTING-all=3992-LE-13:51,52■14:44

FRIED-LE-7:12(7246)-1CH-23:29(7246)

FRIEND-all=7453&marked-GE-38:12,20-EX-33:11-DE-13:6-J'G-14:20(7462)-2SA-13:3■15:37(7463)■16:16(7463),17^{2}-1KI-4:5(7463)-2CH-20:7(157)-JOB-6:14,27(7451)-PS-35:14■88:18-PR-6:1,3^{2}■17:17,18■18:24(157)■19:6■22:11■27:6(157),9,10,14,17-SONG-5:16-IS-41:8(157)-JER-6:21■19:9-HO-3:1-MIC-7:5■N.T.-all=5384&marked-M'T-11:19(5384)■20:13(2083)■12:12(2083)■26:50(2083)-LU-7:34■11:5^{2},6,8■14:10-JOH-3:29■11:11■19:12-AC-12:20(3982)-JAS-2:23■4:4

FRIENDLY-J'G-19:3(3820)-RU-2:13(3820)-PR-18:24(7489)

FRIENDS-all=7453&marked-GE-26:26(4828)-1SA-30:26-2SA-3:8(4828)■19:6(157)-1KI-16:11-ES-5:10(157),14(157)■6:13(157)-JOB-2:11■16:20■17:5■19:19(4962),21■32:3■42:7,10-PS-38:11-PR-14:20(157)■16:28(441)■17:9(441)■18:24■19:4,7(4828)-SONG-5:1-JER-20:4(157),6(157)■38:22(605,7965)-LA-1:2-ZEC-13:6(157)■N.T.-all=5384-M'R-3:21(3588,3844)■5:19(4674)-LU-7:6■12:4■14:12■15:6,9,29■16:9■21:16■23:12-JOH-15:13,14,15-AC-10:24■19:31■27:3-3JO-14^{2}

FRIENDSHIP-PR-22:24(7462)■N.T.-JAS-4:4(5373)

FRINGE-NU-15:38(6734),39(6734)

FRINGES-NU-15:38(6734)-DE-22:12(1434)

FRO-all=7751&marked-GE-8:7(7725)-2KI-4:35(259,2008)-2CH-16:9-JOB-1:7■2:2-JER-5:1■49:3-EZE-27:19(235)-DA-12:4-JOE-2:9(8264)-AM-8:12-ZEC-4:10■N.T.-EPH-4:14(2831)

FROGS-all=6854&marked-EX-8:2,3,4,5,6,7,8,9,11,12,13-PS-78:45■105:30■N.T.-RE-16:13(944)

FRONT-2SA-10:9(6440)-2CH-3:4(6440)

FRONTIERS-EZE-25:9(7097)

FRONTLETS-all=2903-EX-13:16-DE-6:8■11:18

FROST-all=7140&marked-GE-31:40-EX-16:14(3713)-JOB-37:10■38:29(3713)-PS-78:47(2602)-JER-36:30

FROWARD-all=6141&marked-DE-32:20(8419)-2SA-22:27-JOB-5:13(6617)-PS-18:26,26(6617)■101:4-PR-2:12(8419),15(3868)■3:32(3868)■4:24(6143)■6:12(6143)■8:8(6617),13(8419)■10:31(8419)■11:20■16:28(8419),30(8419)■17:20■21:8(2019)■22:5■N.T.-1PE-2:18(4646)

FROWARDLY-IS-57:17(7726)

FROWARDNESS-all=8419-PR-2:14■6:14■10:32

FROZEN-JOB-38:30(3920)

FRUIT-all=6529&marked-GE-1:11,12,29■3:2,3,6■4:3■30:2-EX-10:15■21:22(3206)-LE-19:23,24,25■23:39(8393)■25:3(8393),19,21(8393),22(8393)■26:4■27:30-NU-13:20,26,27-DE-1:25■7:13■11:17(2981)■22:9(4395),9(8393)■26:2■28:4^{2},11^{2},18,33,42,51,53■30:9^{2}-JOS-5:12(8393)-J'G-9:11(8270)-2KI-19:30-NE-9:25(3978),36■10:35,37-PS-1:3■21:10■72:16■92:14(5107)■104:13■105:35■127:3■132:11-PR-1:31■8:19■10:16(8393)■11:30■12:14■13:2■18:20,21■27:18■31:16,31-SONG-2:3■8:11,12-IS-3:10■4:2■10:12■13:18■14:29■27:6(8570),9■28:4(1061)■37:30,31■57:19(5108)■65:21-JER-2:7■6:19■7:20■11:16,19(3899)■12:2■17:8,10■21:14■29:5,28■32:19-LA-2:20-EZE-17:8,9,23■19:12,14■25:4■34:27■36:8,11(6509),30■47:12^{2},12(1061)-DA-4:12(4),14(4),21(4)-HO-9:16■10:1^{2},13■14:8-JOE-2:22-AM-2:9■6:12■9:14-MIC-6:7■7:13-HAB-3:17(2981)-HAG-1:10(2981)-ZEC-8:12-MAL-1:12(5108)■3:11(7920)■N.T.-all=2590&marked-M'T-3:10■7:17^{2},18^{2},19■12:33^{3}■13:8,23(2592),26■21:19,34■26:29(1081)-M'R-4:7,8,20(2592),28(2592),29■11:14■12:2■14:25(1081)-LU-1:42■3:9■6:43^{2},44■8:8,14(5062),15(2592)■13:6,7,9■20:10■22:18(1081)-JOH-4:36■12:24■15:2^{3},4,5,8,16^{2}-AC-2:30-RO-1:13■6:21,22■7:4(2592),5(2592)■15:28-1CO-9:7-GA-5:22-EPH-5:9-PH'P-1:22■4:17-COL-1:6(2592)-HEB-12:11■13:15-JAS-3:18■5:7,18-JUDE-12(5352),12(175)-RE-22:2

FRUITFUL-all=6509&marked-GE-1:22,28■8:17■9:1,7■17:6,20■26:22■28:3■35:11■41:52■48:4■49:22-EX-1:7-LE-26:9-PS-107:34(6529)■128:3■148:9(6529)-IS-5:1(1121,8081)■10:18(3759)■17:6■29:17^{2}(3759)■32:12,15^{2}(3759),16(3759)-JER-4:26(3759)■23:3-EZE-17:5(2233)■19:10-HO-13:15(6500)■N.T.-AC-14:17(2593)-COL-1:10(2592)

FRUITS-all=8393&marked-GE-43:11(2173)-EX-22:29(4395)■23:10-LE-25:15,16,22■26:20(6529)-DE-33:14-2KI-8:6■19:29(6529)-JOB-31:39(3581)-PS-107:37(6529)-EC-2:5(6529)-SONG-4:13(6529),16(6529)■6:11(3)-LA-4:9(8570)MAL-3:11(6529)■N.T.-all=2590&marked-M'T-3:8■7:16,20■21:34,41,43-LU-3:8■12:17,18(1081)-2CO-9:10(1801)-PH'P-1:11-2TI-2:6-JAS-3:17-RE-18:14(3703)■22:2

FRUSTRATE-EZR-4:5(656)■N.T.-GA-2:21(114)

FRUSTRATETH-IS-44:25(6565)

FRYINGPAN-LE-2:7(4802)■7:9(4802)

FUEL-all=402&marked-IS-9:5(3980),19(3980)-EZE-15:4,6■21:32

FUGITIVE-GE-4:12(5128),14(5128)

FUGITIVES-J'G-12:4(6412)-2KI-25:11(5307)-IS-15:5(1280)-EZE-17:21(4015)

FULFIL-all=4390&marked-GE-29:27-EX-5:13(3615)■23:26-1KI-2:27-1CH-22:13(6213)-2CH-36:21^{2}-PS-20:4,5■145:19(6213)■N.T.-all=4137&marked-M'T-3:15■5:17-AC-13:22(4160)-RO-2:27(5055)-GA-5:16(5055)■6:2(378)-PH'P-2:2-COL-1:25■4:17-2TH-1:11-JAS-2:8(5055)-RE-17:17(4160)

FULFILLED-all=4390&marked-GE-25:24■29:21,28■50:3^{2}-EX-5:14(3615)■7:25-LE-12:4,6-NU-6:5,13-2SA-7:12■14:22(6213)-1KI-8:15,24-2CH-6:4,15-EZR-1:1(3615)-JOB-36:17-JER-44:25-LA-2:17(1214)■4:18-EZE-5:2-DA-4:33(5487)■10:3■N.T.-all=4137&marked-M'T-1:22■2:15,17,23■4:14■5:18(1096)■8:17■12:17■13:14(378),35■21:4■24:34(1096)■26:54,56■27:9,35-M'R-1:15■13:4(4931)■14:49■15:28-LU-1:20■2:43(5048)■4:21■21:22,24,32(1096)■22:16■24:44-JOH-3:29■12:38■13:18■15:25■17:12,13■18:9,32■19:24,28(5048),36-AC-1:16■3:18■9:23■12:25■13:25,27,29(5055),33(1603)■14:26-RO-8:4■13:8-2CO-10:6-GA-5:14-JAS-2:23-RE-6:11■15:8(5055)■17:17(5055)■20:3(5055)

FULFILLING-PS-148:8(6213)■N.T-RO-13:10(4138)-EPH-2:3(4160)

FULL-all=4392,a=4390&marked-GE-15:16(8003)■25:8(7649)■35:29(7649)■41:1(3117),7,22-EX-8:21a■16:3(7648),8(7646),33(4393)■22:3(7999)-LE-2:14(3759)■16:12^{2}(4393)■19:29a■25:29(3117),30(8549)■26:5(7648)-NU-7:13,14,19,20,25,26,31,32,37,38,43,44,49,50,55,56,61,62,67,68,73,74,79,80,86■22:18(4393)■24:13(4393)-DE-6:11,11(7646)■8:10(7646),12(7646)■11:15(7646)■21:13(3117)■33:23■34:9-J'G-6:38■16:27a-RU-1:21a■2:12(8003)-1SA-2:5(7646)■18:27a■27:7(3117)-2SA-8:2(4393)■13:23(3117)■14:28(3117)■23:11-2KI-4:4,6a,39(4393)■6:17a■7:15■9:24a■10:21a■15:13(3117)-1CH-11:13■21:22,24■23:1(7646)■29:28(7646)-2CH-24:15(7646)-NE-9:25-ES-3:5a■5:9a-JOB-5:26(3624)■7:4(7646)■10:15(7646)■14:1(7646)■20:11(4390)■21:23(8537),24a■32:18a■36:16a■42:17(7646)-PS-10:7a■17:14(7646)■26:10a■33:5a■48:10a■65:9a■73:10■74:20a■75:8■78:25(7648)■88:3(7654)■104:16(7654)■24a■119:64a■127:5a■144:13-PR-17:1■27:7(7646),20(7646)■30:9(7646)-EC-1:7■4:6(4393)■9:3a■10:14(7235)■11:3a-IS-1:11(7646),15a,21■2:7^{2}a,8a■6:3(4393)■11:9a■13:21a■15:9a■22:2,7a■25:6■28:8a■30:27a■51:20-JER-4:12■5:7(7646),27^{2}■6:11,11a■23:10a■28:3(3117),11(3117)■35:5-LA-1:1(7227)■3:30(7646)-EZE-1:18■7:23^{2}a■9:9^{2}a■10:4a,12■17:3■28:12■32:6a,15(4393)■37:1■39:19(7654)■41:8(4393)-DA-3:19(4391)■8:23(8552)■10:2(3117)-JOE-2:24a■3:13a-AM-2:13-MIC-3:8a■6:12a-NA-3:1-HAB-3:3a-ZEC-8:5a■N.T.-all=4134&marked-M'T-6:22(5460)■13:48(4137)■14:20■15:37■23:25(1073),27(1073),28(3324)-M'R-4:28,37(1072)■6:43■8:19,20(4138)-LU-1:57(4130)■4:1■5:12■6:25(1705)■11:34(5460),34sup,36^{2}(5460),39(1073)-JOH-1:14■7:8(4137)■15:11(4137)■16:24(4137)■19:29(3324)■21:11(3324)-AC-2:13(3325),28(4137)■6:3,5,8■7:23(4137),55■9:36■11:24■13:10■19:28-RO-1:29(3324)■3:14(1073)■15:14(3324)-1CO-4:8(2880)-PH'P-4:12(5526),18(4137)-COL-2:2(4136)-2TI-4:5(4135)-HEB-5:14(5046)■6:11(4136)■10:22(4136)-JAS-3:8(3324),17(3324)-2PE-2:14(3324)-1JO-1:4(4137)-2JO-8,12(4137)-RE-4:6(1073),8(1073)■5:8(1073)■15:7(1073)■17:3(1073),4(1073)■21:9(1073)

FULLER-M'R-9:3(1102)

FULLER'S-all=3526-2KI-18:17-IS-7:3■36:2

FULLERS'-MAL-3:2(3526)

FULLY-all=4390&marked-NU-7:1(3615)■14:24(4392)-RU-2:11(5046)-1KI-11:6-EC-8:11-NA-1:10■N.T.-all=4135&marked-AC-2:1(4845)-RO-4:21■14:5■15:19(4137)-2TI-3:10(3877)■4:17

FULNESS-all=4393&marked-NU-18:27(4395)-DE-33:16-1CH-16:32-JOB-20:22(4390)-PS-16:11(7648)■24:1■50:12■89:11■96:11■98:7-EZE-16:49(7653)■19:7■N.T.-all=4138-JOH-1:16-RO-11:12,25■15:29-1CO-10:26,28-GA-4:4-EPH-1:10,23■3:19■4:13-COL-1:19■2:9

FURBISH-JER-46:4(4838)

FURBISHED-all=4803-EZE-21:9,10,11^{2},28

FURIOUS-all=2534&marked-PR-22:24■29:22-EZE-5:15■25:17-DA-2:12(7108)-NA-1:2(1167,2534)

FURIOUSLY-2KI-9:20(7697)-EZE-23:25(2534)

FURLONGS-all=4712-LU-24:13-JOH-6:19▪11:18-RE-14:20▪21:16

FURNACE-all=3564,a=861&marked-GE-15:17(8574)▪19:28(3536)-EX-9:8(3536),10(3536)▪19:18(3536)-DE-4:20-1KI-8:51-PS-12:6(5948)-PR-17:3▪27:21-IS-31:9(8574)▪48:10-JER-11:4-EZE-22:18,20,22-DA-3:6a,11a,15a,17a,19a,20a,21a,22a,23a,26a▪N.T.-all=2575-M'T-13:42,50-RE-1:15▪9:2

FURNACES-NE-3:11(8574)▪12:38(8574)

FURNISH-DE-15:14(6059)-PS-78:19(6186)-IS-65:11(4390)-JER-46:19(6213,3627)

FURNISHED-1KI-9:11(5375)-PR-9:2(6186)▪N.T-M'T-22:10(4130)-M'R-14:15(4766)-LU-22:12(4766)-2TI-3:17(1822)

FURNITURE-all=3627&marked-GE-31:34(3733)-EX-31:7,8^{2},9▪35:14▪39:33-NA-2:9

FURROW-JOB-39:10(8525)

FURROWS-all=8525&marked-JOB-31:38-PS-65:10(1417)▪129:3(4618)-EZE-17:7(6170),10(6170)-HO-10:4,10(5869)▪12:11

FURTHER-all=3254&marked-NU-22:26-DE-20:8-1SA-10:22(5750)-ES-9:12(5750)-JOB-38:11-PS-140:8(6329)-EC-12:12(3148)▪N.T.-all=2089&marked-M'T-26:65-M'R-5:35▪14:63-LU-22:71▪24:28(4206)-AC-4:17(1909,4118)▪21:28▪24:4(1909,4118)▪27:28(1339)-2TI-3:9(1909,4118)-HEB-7:11

FURTHERANCE-PH'P-1:12(4297),25(4297)

FURTHERED-EZR-8:36(5375)

FURTHERMORE-EX-4:6(5750)-EZE-23:40(637)▪N.T.-2CO-2:12(1611)-1TH-4:1(3063)-HEB-12:9(1534)

FURY-all=2534&marked-GE-27:44-LE-26:28-JOB-20:23(2740)-IS-27:4▪34:2▪42:25▪51:13^{2},17,20,22▪59:18▪63:3,5,6▪66:15-JER-4:4▪6:11▪7:20▪10:25▪21:5,12▪23:19▪25:15▪30:23▪32:31,37▪33:5▪36:7▪42:18^{2}▪44:6-LA-2:4▪4:11-EZE-5:13^{2},15▪6:12▪7:8▪8:18▪9:8▪13:13^{2}▪14:19▪16:38,42▪19:12▪20:8,13,21,33,34▪21:17▪22:20,22▪24:8,13▪25:14▪30:15▪36:6,18▪38:18-DA-3:13(2528),19(2528)▪8:6▪9:16▪11:44-MIC-5:15-NA-1:6-ZEC-8:2

G

GADDEST-JER-2:36(235)

GAIN-all=1214&marked-J'G-5:19-JOB-22:3-PR-1:19▪3:14(8393)▪15:27▪28:8(8636)-IS-33:15▪56:11-EZE-22:13,27-DA-2:8(2084)▪11:39(4242)-MIC-4:13▪N.T.-all=2770&marked-M'T-16:26-M'R-8:36-LU-9:25-AC-16:16(2039)▪19:24(2039)-1CO-9:19,20^{2},21,22-2CO-12:17(4122),18(4122)-PH'P-1:21(2771)▪3:7(2771)-1TI-6:5(4200),6(4200)-JAS-4:13(2770)

GAINED-JOB-27:8(1214)-EZE-22:12(1214)▪N.T.-all=2770&marked-M'T-18:15▪25:17,20,22-LU-19:15(1281),16(4333),18(4160)-AC-27:21

GAINS-AC-16:19(2039)

GAINSAY-LU-21:15(471)

GAINSAYERS-TIT-1:9(483)

GAINSAYING-AC-10:29(369)-RO-10:21(483)-JUDE-11(485)

GALBANUM-EX-30:34(2468)

GALL-all=7219&marked-DE-29:18▪32:32-JOB-16:13(4845)▪20:14(4846),25(4846)-PS-69:21-JER-8:14▪9:15▪23:15-LA-3:5,19-AM-6:12▪N.T.-M'T-27:34(5521)-AC-8:23(5521)

GALLANT-IS-33:21(117)

GALLERIES-all=862&marked-SONG-7:5(7298)-EZE-41:15,16▪42:5

GALLERY-EZE-42:3(862)

GALLEY-IS-33:21(590)

GALLOWS-all=6086-ES-5:14^{2}▪6:4▪7:9,10▪8:7▪9:13,25

GAP-EZE-22:30(6556)

GAPED-JOB-16:10(6473)-PS-22:13(6475)

GAPS-EZE-13:5(6556)

GARDEN-all=1588&marked-GE-2:8,9,10,15,16▪3:1,2,3,8^{2},10,23,24▪13:10-DE-11:10-1KI-21:2-2KI-9:27▪21:18^{2},26▪25:4-NE-3:15-ES-1:5(1594)▪7:7(1594),8(1594)-JOB-8:16(1593)-SONG-4:12,16^{2}▪5:1▪6:2,11(1594)-IS-1:30(1593)▪51:3▪58:11▪61:11(1593)-JER-31:12▪39:4▪52:7-LA-2:6-EZE-28:13▪31:8^{2},9▪36:35-JOE-2:3▪N.T.-all=2779-LU-13:19-JOH-18:1,26▪19:41

GARDENER-JOH-20:15(2780)

GARDENS-all=1593&marked-NU-24:6-EC-2:5-SONG-4:15(1588)▪6:2(1588)▪8:13(1588)-IS-1:29▪65:3▪66:17-JER-29:5,28-AM-4:9▪9:14

GARLANDS-AC-14:13(4725)

GARLICK-NU-11:5(7762)

GARMENT-all=899&marked-GE-9:23(8071)▪25:25(155)▪39:12^{2},13,15,16,18-LE-6:10(4055),27▪13:47^{2},49,51,52,53,56,57,58,59▪14:55▪15:17▪19:19-DE-22:5(8071),11(8162)-JOS-7:21(155),24(155)-J'G-8:25(8071)-2SA-13:18(3801),19(3801)▪20:8(4055)-1KI-11:29(8008),30(8008)-2KI-9:13-EZR-9:3,5-ES-8:15(8509)-JOB-13:28▪30:18(3830)▪38:9(3830),14(3830)▪41:13(3830)-PS-69:11(3830)▪73:6(7897)▪102:26▪104:2(8008),6(3830)▪109:18(4055),19-PR-20:16▪25:20▪27:13▪30:4(8071)-IS-50:9▪51:6,8▪61:3(4594)-JER-43:12-EZE-18:7,16-DA-7:9(3831)-MIC-2:8(8008)-HAG-2:12-ZEC-13:4(155)-MAL-2:16(3830)▪N.T.-all=2440&marked-M'T-9:16^{2},20,21▪14:36▪22:11(1742),12(1742)-M'R-2:21▪5:27▪6:56▪10:50▪13:16▪16:5(4749)-LU-5:36▪8:44▪22:36-AC-12:8-HEB-1:11-JUDE-23(5509)-RE-1:13(4158)

GARMENTS-all=899&marked-GE-35:2(8071)▪38:14,19▪49:11(3830)-EX-28:2,3,4^{2}▪29:5,21^{4},29▪31:10^{2}▪35:19^{2},21▪39:1,41^{2}▪40:13-LE-6:11▪8:2,30^{4}▪16:4,23,24,32▪21:10-NU-15:38▪20:26,28-JOS-9:5(8008),13(8008)-J'G-14:12,13-1SA-18:4(4055)-2SA-10:4(4063)▪13:31-1KI-10:25(8008)-2KI-5:22,23,26▪7:15▪25:29-1CH-19:4(4063)-EZR-2:69(3801)-NE-7:70(3801),72(3801)-JOB-37:17-PS-22:18▪45:8▪133:2(4060)-EC-9:8-SONG-4:11(8008)-IS-9:5(8071)▪52:1▪59:6,17▪61:10▪63:1,2,3-JER-36:24▪52:33-LA-4:14(3830)-EZE-16:16,18▪26:16▪42:14^{2}▪44:17,19^{3}-DA-3:21(3831)-JOE-2:13-ZEC-3:3,4,5▪N.T.-all=2440&marked-M'T-21:8▪23:5▪27:35^{2}-M'R-11:7,8▪15:24-LU-19:35▪24:4(2067)-JOH-13:4,12▪19:23-AC-9:39-JAS-5:2-RE-3:4▪16:15

GARNER-M'T-3:12(596)-LU-3:17(596)

GARNERS-PS-144:13(4200)-JOE-1:17(214)

GARNISH-M'T-23:29(2885)

GARNISHED-2CH-3:6(6823)-JOB-26:13(8235)▪N.T.-all=2885-M'T-12:44-LU-11:25-RE-21:19

GARRISON-all=4673&marked-1SA-10:5(5333)▪13:3(5333),4(5333),23▪14:1,4,6,11,12(4675),15-2SA-23:14-1CH-11:16(5333)▪N.T.-2CO-11:32(5432)

GARRISONS-all=5333&marked-2SA-8:6,14^{2}-1CH-18:13-2CH-17:2-EZE-26:11(4676)

GAT-all=5927&marked-EX-24:18-NU-11:30(622)▪14:40▪16:27-J'G-9:48,51▪19:28(3212)-1SA-13:15▪24:22▪26:12(3212)-2SA-4:7(3212)▪8:13(6213)▪13:29(7392)▪17:23(3212)▪19:3(935)-EC-2:8(6213)-LA-5:9(935)

GATE-all=8179&marked-GE-19:1▪22:17▪23:10,18▪24:60▪28:17▪34:20,24^{2}-EX-27:16▪32:26,27▪38:15,18,31▪39:40▪40:8,33-NU-4:26-DE-21:19▪22:15,24▪25:7-JOS-2:5,7▪7:5▪8:29▪20:4-J'G-9:35,40,44▪16:2,3▪18:16,17-RU-4:1,10,11-1SA-4:18▪9:18▪21:13-2SA-3:27▪10:8▪11:23▪15:2▪18:4,24,33▪19:8^{2}▪23:15,16-1KI-17:10(6607)▪22:10-2KI-7:1,3,17^{2},18,20▪9:31▪10:8▪11:6^{2},19▪14:13▪15:35▪23:8^{2}▪25:4-1CH-9:18▪11:17,18▪19:9(6607)▪26:13,16-2CH-8:14▪18:9▪23:5,15,20▪24:8▪25:23▪26:9▪27:3▪32:6▪33:14▪35:15-NE-2:13,14,15▪3:1,3,6,13^{2},14,15,26,28,29,31,32▪8:1,3,16^{2}▪12:31,37^{2},39^{4}-ES-2:19,21▪3:2,3▪4:2^{2},6▪5:1(6607),9,13▪6:10,12-JOB-5:4▪29:7▪31:21-PS-69:12▪118:20▪127:5-PR-17:19(6607)▪22:22▪24:7-SONG-7:4-IS-14:31▪22:7▪24:12▪28:6▪29:21-JER-7:2▪17:19▪19:2▪20:2▪26:10▪31:38,40▪36:10▪37:13▪38:7▪39:3,4▪52:7-LA-5:14-EZE-8:3,5,14▪9:2▪10:19▪11:1^{2}▪40:3,6^{2},6sup,7^{2},8,9^{2},10,11^{2},13,14,15^{2},16,19,20,21,22,23^{3},24,27^{2},28^{2},32,35,39,40^{2},41,44^{3},48▪42:15▪43:1,4▪44:1,2,3,4▪45:19▪46:1,2^{4},3,8,9^{5},12^{2},19▪47:2^{2}▪48:31^{2},32^{2},33^{2},34^{2}-DA-2:49(8651)-AM-5:10,12,15-OB-13-MIC-1:9,12▪2:13-ZEP-1:10-ZEC-14:10^{2}▪N.T.-all=4439-M'T-7:13^{2},14-LU-7:12▪13:24▪16:20(4440)-AC-3:2(2374),10▪10:17(4440)▪12:10,13(4440),14^{2}(4440)-HEB-13:12-RE-21:21(3588,4440)

GATES-all=8179,a=1817&marked-EX-20:10-DE-3:5a▪5:14▪6:9▪11:20▪12:12,15,17,18,21▪14:21,27,28,29▪15:7,22▪16:5,11,14,18▪17:2,5,8▪18:6▪23:16▪24:14▪26:12▪28:52,55,57▪31:12-JOS-6:26a-J'G-5:8,11-1SA-17:52▪23:7a-2SA-18:24-1KI-16:34a-2KI-23:8-1CH-9:19(5592),22(5592),23▪22:3-2CH-8:5a▪14:7a▪23:19▪31:2-NE-1:3▪2:3,8,13,17▪6:1▪7:3▪11:19▪12:25,30▪13:19^{2},19a,22-JOB-38:17-PS-9:13,14▪24:7,9▪87:2▪100:4▪107:16a,18▪118:19▪122:2▪147:13-PR-1:21▪8:3,34a▪14:19▪31:23,31-SONG-7:13(6607)-IS-3:26(6607)▪13:2(6607)▪26:2▪38:10▪45:1a,1,2a▪54:12▪60:11,18▪62:10-JER-1:15▪7:2▪14:2▪15:7▪17:19,20,21,24,25,27^{2}▪22:2,4,19▪49:31a▪51:58-LA-1:4▪2:9▪4:12-EZE-21:15,22▪26:2a,10▪38:11a▪40:18^{2},38▪44:11,17^{2}▪48:31^{2},32,33,34-OB-11-NA-2:6▪3:13-ZEC-8:16▪N.T.-all=4440&marked-M'T-16:18(4439)-AC-9:24(4439)▪14:13-RE-21:12^{2},13^{4},15,21,25▪22:14

GATHER-all=622,a=3950,b=6908&marked-GE-6:21▪31:46a▪34:30▪41:35b▪49:1,2b-EX-3:16▪5:7(7179),12(7179)▪9:19(5756)▪16:4a,5a,16a,26a,27a▪23:10-LE-8:3(6950)▪19:9a,10a▪23:22a▪25:3,5(1219),11(1219),20-NU-8:9a▪10:4(3259)▪11:16▪19:9▪20:8(6950)▪21:16-DE-4:10(6950)▪11:14▪13:16b▪28:30(2490),38,39(103)▪30:3b,4b▪31:12,28-RU-2:7-1SA-7:5b-2SA-3:21b▪12:28-1KI-18:19b-2KI-4:39a▪22:20-1CH-13:2b▪16:35b▪22:2(3664)-2CH-24:5b▪34:28-EZR-10:7b-NE-1:9b▪7:5b▪12:44(3664)-ES-2:3b▪4:16(3664)▪8:11(6950)-JOB-11:10(6950)▪24:6(3953)▪34:14▪39:12-PS-26:9▪39:6▪50:5▪56:6(1481)▪94:21(1413)▪104:22,28a▪106:47b-PR-28:8b-EC-2:26▪3:5(3664)-SONG-6:2a-IS-10:31(5756)▪11:12b▪34:15(1716)▪40:11b▪43:5b▪49:18b▪54:7b,15^{2}(1481)▪56:8b▪60:4b▪62:10(5619)▪66:18b-JER-4:5(4390)▪6:1(5756)▪7:18a▪9:22▪10:17▪23:3b▪29:14b▪31:8b,10b▪32:37b▪40:10▪49:5b,14b▪51:11(4390)-EZE-11:17b▪16:37^{2}b▪20:34b,41b▪22:19b,20(6910),20b,21(3664)▪24:4▪29:13b▪34:13b▪36:24b▪37:21b▪39:17-DA-3:2(3673)-HO-8:10b▪9:6b-JOE-1:14▪2:6b,16^{2}▪3:2b,11b-MIC-2:12b▪4:6b,12b▪5:1(1413)-NA-2:10b-HAB-1:9,15-ZEP-2:1^{2}(7197)▪3:8,18,19b,20b-ZEC-10:8b,10b▪14:2▪N.T.-all=4863marked-M'T-3:12▪6:26▪7:16(4816)▪13:28(4816),29(4816),30(4816),30,41

(4816)■24:31(1996)■25:26-**M'R**-13:27 (1996)-**LU**-3:17■6:44(4816),44(5166) -**JOH**-6:12■11:52■15:6-**EPH**-1:10(346) -**RE**-14:18(5166)■16:14■19:17■20:8

GATHERED-all=622,a=6950, b=6908&marked-**GE**-1:9(6960)■12:5 (7408)■25:8,17■29:3,7,8,22■35:29■41:48b, 49(6651)■47:14(3950)■49:29,33^{2} -**EX**-4:29■8:14(6651)■15:8(6192)■16:17 (3950),18^{2}sup,18(3950),21(3950),22(3950)■ 23:16■32:1a,26■35:1a-**LE**-8:4a■23:39■ 26:25-**NU**-10:7a■11:8(3950),22,24,32^{2}■ 14:35(3259)■15:32(7197)■16:3a,11 (3259),19a,42a■20:2a,10a,24,26■21:23■ 27:3(3259),13^{2}■31:2-**DE**-16:13■32:50^{2}■ 33:5-**JOS**-9:2b■10:5,6b■22:12a■24:1 -**J'G**-1:7(3950)■2:10■3:13■4:13(2199)■ 6:33,34(2199),35(2199)■7:23(6817),24 (6817)■9:6,27(1219),47b■10:17(6817)■ 11:3(3950),20■12:1(6817),4b■16:23b■ 18:22(2199)■20:1a,11,14-**1SA**-5:8,11■ 7:6b,7b■8:4b■13:5,11■14:48(6213)■ 15:4(8085)■17:1^{2},2■20:38(3950)■22:2b■ 25:1b■28:1b,4^{2}b■29:1b-**2SA**-2:25b,30b■ 6:1(3254)■10:15,17■12:29■14:14■ 17:11■20:14(7035)■21:13■23:9,11-**1KI**-10:26■11:24b■18:20b■20:1b■22:6b -**2KI**-3:21(6817)■4:39(3950)■6:24b■ 10:18b■22:4,9(5413),20■23:1-**1CH**-11:1b, 13■13:5a■15:3a■19:7,17■23:2-**2CH**-1:14■11:1a■12:5■13:7b■15:9b,10b■ 18:5b■20:4b■23:2b■24:5b,11■25:5b■ 28:24■29:4,15,20■30:3■32:4b,6b■34:9, 17(5413),28,29-**EZR**-3:1■7:28b■8:15b■ 10:9b-**NE**-5:16b■8:1,13■12:28■13:11b -**ES**-2:8b,19b■9:2a,15a,16a-**JOB**-16:10 (4390)■27:19■30:7(5596)-**PS**-35:15^{2}■ 47:9■59:3(1481)■102:22b■107:3b■ 140:2(1481)-**PR**-27:25■30:4-**EC**-2:8 (3664)-**SONG**-5:1(717)-**IS**-10:14■ 13:4■22:9b■24:22,22(626)■27:12(3950)■ 33:4■34:15b,16b■43:9b■44:11b■49:5■ 56:8b■60:7b■62:9-**JER**-3:17(6960)■8:2■ 25:33■26:9a■40:12,15b-**EZE**-28:25b■ 29:5b■38:8b,12,13a■39:27b,28(3664) -**DA**-3:3(3673),27(3673)-**HO**-1:11b■10:10 -**MIC**-1:7b■4:11■7:1-**ZEC**-12:3■14:14■ **N.T.**-all=4863&marked-**M'T**-2:4■13:2, 40(4816),47,48(4816)■18:20■22:10,34,41■ 23:37(1996)■24:28■25:32■27:17,27 -**M'R**-1:33(1996)■2:2■4:1■5:21■6:30 -**LU**-8:4(4896)■11:29(1865)■12:1(1996)■ 13:34(1996)■15:13■17:37■24:33(4867) -**JOH**-6:13■11:47-**AC**-4:6,26,27■12:12■ 14:27■15:30■17:5(3792)■20:8■28:3 (4962)-**1CO**-5:4-**RE**-14:19(5166)■ 16:16■19:19

GATHERER-**AM**-7:14(1103)

GATHEREST-**DE**-24:21(1219)

GATHERETH-all=622&marked -**NU**-19:10-**PS**-33:7(3664)■41:6(6908)■ 147:2(3664)-**PR**-6:8(103)■10:5(103)■ 13:11(6908)-**IS**-10:14■17:5,5(3950)■ 56:8(6908)-**NA**-3:18(6908)-**HAB**-2:5■ **N.T.**-all=4863&marked-**M'T**-12:30■ 23:37(1996)-**LU**-11:23-**JOH**-4:36

GATHERING-all=7197&marked -**GE**-1:10(4723)■49:10(3349)-**NU**-15:33-**1KI**-17:10,12-**2CH**-20:25(962) -**IS**-32:10(625)■33:4(625)■**N.T.** -**M'T**-25:24(4863)-**AC**-16:10(4822) -**2TH**-2:1(1997)

GATHERINGS-**1CO**-16:2(3048)

GAVE-all=5414&marked-**GE**-2:20 (7121)■3:6,12■14:20■16:3■18:7■20:14■ 21:14,27■24:32,53■25:5,6,34■27:17■ 28:4■29:24,28,29■30:4,9,35■35:4,12■ 38:18,26■39:21■40:11,21■41:45■43:24^{2}■ 45:21^{2},22^{2}■46:18,25■47:11,17,22-**EX**-2:21■11:3■12:36■31:18■32:24-**NU**-3:51■ 7:6,7,8,9■11:25■17:6■31:41,47■32:33, 38(7121),40-**DE**-2:12■3:12,13,15,16■ 9:11■10:4■22:16■29:8-**JOS**-1:14,15■ 11:23■12:6,7■13:8^{2},14,15,24,29,33■14:3, 4,13■15:13,17,19■17:4■18:7■19:49,50■ 21:3,8,9,11,12,13,21,43■22:4,7■24:3,4^{2}, 8-**J'G**-1:13,15,20■3:6■5:25■6:9■9:4■ 14:9,19■15:2■17:4■20:36■21:14-**RU**-2:18■3:17■4:7,13,17(7121)-**1SA**-1:4,5■ 9:23■18:4,27sup,27■20:40■21:6■22:10■27:6■ 30:11,12-**2SA**-12:8^{2}■24:9-**1KI**-4:29■ 5:10,11^{2},12■9:11■10:10^{2},13^{2}■11:18^{2},19■ 12:13(3289)■13:3■14:8,15■19:21-**2KI**-10:15■12:11,14■13:5■15:19■17:3(7725)■ 18:15,16■21:8■22:8■23:35■25:6(1696) -**1CH**-2:35■6:55,56,57,64,65,67■21:5, 25■25:5■28:11■29:7,8-**2CH**-9:9^{2},12■ 10:8(3289)■11:23■13:5■21:3^{2}■24:12■ 26:8■27:5■28:21■30:7,24(7311)■32:24■ 34:10,11■35:7,8,(7311),8,9(7311)■36:17 -**EZR**-2:69■3:7■5:12(3052)■7:11■10:19 -**NE**-2:1,9■7:70^{2},71,72■8:8(7760)■ 12:47-**ES**-2:9,18■3:10■4:8■8:2-**JOB**-1:21■42:10(3254),11,15-**PS**-18:13■ 68:11■69:21,21sup■78:29(935),46, 48(5462),50(5462),62(5462)■81:12 (7971)■99:7■105:32,44■106:15,41■ 135:12■136:21-**PR**-8:29(7760)-**EC**-1:13, 17■12:7-**IS**-41:2^{2}■42:24■43:3■50:6 -**JER**-7:7,14■16:15■17:4■23:39■ 24:10■30:3■32:12■36:32■39:5(1696), 10■40:5■44:30■52:9(1696)-**EZE**-16:19■20:11,12,25■36:28■39:23 -**DA**-1:2,7^{2}(7760),16,17■2:48(3052)■ 5:18(3052),19(3052)-**HO**-2:8■13:11 -**MAL**-2:5■**N.T.**-all=1325-**M'T**-8:18 (2753)■10:1■14:19■15:36^{2}■21:23■25:15, 35,35(4222),37(4222),42,42(4222)■ 26:26,27,48■27:10,34,48(4222)■28:12 -**M'R**-2:26■5:13(2010)■6:7,28^{2},41■8:6^{2}■ 11:28■13:34■14:22,23■15:23,36(4222),45 (1433)-**LU**-2:38(437)■4:20(591)■6:4■ 7:21(5483)■9:1,16■10:35■15:16■18:43■ 20:2■22:19sup,19■24:30(1929),42(1929) -**JOH**-1:12■3:16■4:5,12■6:31,32■7:22■ 10:29■12:49■13:26■14:31(1781)■18:14 (4823)■19:9,30(3860),38(2010)-**AC**-1:26■2:4■3:5(1907)■4:33(591)■7:5,8,10, 42(3860)■8:6(4337),10(4337)■9:41■10:2 (4160)■11:17■12:23,23sup■13:20,21,22 (3140)■14:3(3140),17■15:24(1291)■ 26:10(2702)■27:3(2010)-**RO**-1:24 (3860),26(3860),28(3860)-**1CO**-3:5 -**2CO**-8:5-**GA**-1:4■2:5(1502),9,20 (3860)■3:18(5483)-**EPH**-1:22■ 4:8,11■5:25(3860)-**1TH**-4:2-**1TI**-2:6-**TIT**-2:14-**HEB**-7:4,13(4337)■ 12:9(1788)-**JAS**-5:18-**1PE**-1:21-**1JO**-3:23■5:10(3140)-**JUDE**-3(4160)-**RE**-1:1■2:21■11:13■13:2,4■15:7■20:13

GAVEST-all=5414-**GE**-3:12-**1KI**-8:34,40,48-**2CH**-6:25,31,38■20:7-**NE**-9:7(7760),13,15,20^{2},22,24,27,30,35^{2},36 -**PS**-21:4■74:14■**N.T.**-all=1325-**LU**-7:44,45■15:29■19:23-**JOH**-17:4,6^{2},8,12, 22■18:9

GAY-**JAS**-2:3(2986)

GAZE-**EX**-19:21(7200)

GAZING-**AC**-1:11(1689)

GAZINGSTOCK-**NA**-3:6(7210)■ **N.T.**-**HEB**-10:33(2301)

GENDER-**LE**-19:19(7250)■**N.T.** -**2TI**-2:23(1080)

GENDERED-**JOB**-38:29(3205)

GENDERETH-**JOB**-21:10(5674)■ **N.T.**-**GA**-4:24(1080)

GENEALOGIES-all=3187-**1CH**-5:17■7:5,7■9:1-**2CH**-12:15■31:19■**N.T.** -**1TI**-1:4(1076)-**TIT**-3:9(1076)

GENEALOGY-all=3188-**1CH**-4:33■5:1,7■7:9,40■9:22-**2CH**-31:16,17, 18-**EZR**-2:62■8:1,3-**NE**-7:5^{2},64

GENERAL-**1CH**-27:34(8269)■**N.T.**-all=2526&marked-**HEB**-12:23(3831)-**JAS**-1:t-**1PE**-1:t-**2PE**-1:t-**1JO**-1:t-**JUDE**-1:t

GENERALLY-**JER**-48:38(3605)

GENERATION-all=1755&marked -**GE**-7:1■15:16-**EX**-1:6■17:16-**NU**-32:13-**DE**-1:35■2:14■23:2,3,8■29:22■ 32:5,20-**J'G**-2:10^{2}-**ES**-9:28-**PS**-12:7■ 14:5■22:30■24:6■48:13■49:19■71:18■ 73:15■78:4,6,8^{2}■95:10■102:18■109:13■ 112:2■145:4-**PR**-27:24■30:11,12,13,14 -**EC**-1:4-**IS**-13:20■34:10,17■51:8■53:8 -**JER**-2:31■7:29■50:39-**LA**-5:19-**DA**-4:3 (1859),34(1859)-**JOE**-1:3■3:20■**N.T.**-all=1074&marked-**M'T**-1:1(1078)■3:7 (1081)■11:16■12:34(1081),39,41,42,45■ 16:4■17:17■23:33(1081),36■24:34 -**M'R**-8:12^{2},38■9:19■13:30-**LU**-1:50■ 3:7(1081)■7:31■9:41■11:29,30,31,32,50, 51■16:8■17:25■21:32-**AC**-2:40■8:33■ 13:36-**HEB**-3:10-**1PE**-2:9(1085)

GENERATIONS-all=1755,a= 8435&marked-**GE**-2:4a■5:1a■6:9a^{2}■9:12■ 10:1a,32a■11:10a,27a■17:7,9,12■25:12a, 13a,19a■36:1a,9a■37:2a-**EX**-3:15■6:16a, 19a■12:14,17,42■16:32,33■27:21■29:42■ 30:8,10,21,31■31:13,16■40:15-**LE**-3:17■ 6:18■7:36■10:9■17:7■21:17■22:3■23:14, 21,31,41,43■24:3■25:30-**NU**-1:20a,22a, 24a,26a,28a,30a,32a,34a,36a,38a,40a, 42a■3:1a■10:8■15:14,15,21,23,38■18:23■ 35:29-**DE**-7:9■32:7-**JOS**-22:27,28-**J'G**-3:2-**RU**-4:18a-**1CH**-1:29a■5:7a■7:2a, 4a,9a■8:28a■9:9a,34a■16:15■26:31a -**JOB**-42:16-**PS**-33:11■45:17■49:11■ 61:6■72:5■79:13■85:5■89:1,4■90:1■ 100:5■102:12,24■105:8■106:31■119:90■ 135:13■145:13■146:10-**IS**-41:4■51:9■ 58:12■60:15■61:4-**JOE**-2:2■**N.T.**-all=1074-**M'T**-1:17^{4}-**LU**-1:48-**COL**-1:26

GENTLE-all=1933&marked-**1TH**-2:7(2261)-**2TI**-2:24(2261)-**TIT**-3:2 -**JAS**-3:17-**1PE**-2:18

GENTLENESS-**2SA**-22:36(6031) -**PS**-18:35(6038)■**N.T.**-**2CO**-10:1(1932) -**GA**-5:22(5544)

GENTLY-**2SA**-18:5(3814)

GERAHS-all=1626&marked-**EX**-30:13 -**LE**-27:25-**NU**-3:47■18:16-**EZE**-45:12

GET-all=5927,a=3212&marked-**GE**-12:1a■19:14(3318)■22:2a■31:13(3318)■ 34:4(3947)■42:2(3381)■44:17■45:17 (935)-**EX**-1:10■5:4a,11(3947)■7:15a■ 10:28a■11:8(3318)■12:31(3318)■14:17 (3513)■19:24(3381)■32:7(3381)-**LE**-14:21(5381),22(5381),30(5381)■31(5381), 32(5381)-**NU**-6:21(5381)■13:17■14:25 (5265)■16:24,45(7426)■22:13a■27:12 -**DE**-2:13(5674)■3:27■5:30(7725)■8:18 (6213)■9:12(3381)■17:8■28:43■32:49 -**JOS**-2:16a■7:10(6965)■17:15■22:4a -**J'G**-7:9(3381)■14:2(3947),3(3947)-**RU**-3:3(3381)-**1SA**-9:13■15:6(3381)■20:29 (4422)■22:5(935)■23:26a■25:5-**2SA**-20:6(4672)-**1KI**-1:13(935)■2:26a■12:18■ 14:2(1980),12a■17:3a,9a■18:41,44 (3381)-**2KI**-3:13a■7:12(935)-**2CH**-10:18 -**NE**-9:10(6213)-**PR**-4:5(7069),7^{2}(7069)■ 6:33(4672)■16:16^{2}(7069)■17:16(7069)■ 22:25(3947)-**EC**-3:6(1245)-**SONG**-4:6a -**IS**-22:15(935)-**IS**-30:22(3318)■40:9■ 47:5(935)-**JER**-5:5a■13:1(7069)■19:1 (7069)■46:4■48:9(3318)■49:30(5110), 31-**LA**-3:7(3318)-**EZE**-3:4(935),11(935)■ 22:27(1214)-**DA**-4:14(5111)-**JOE**-3:13 (3381)-**ZEP**-3:19(776)-**ZEC**-6:7a■ **N.T.**-all=5217&marked-**M'T**-4:10■ 14:22(1684)■16:23-**M'R**-6:45(1684)■ 8:33-**LU**-4:8■9:12(2147)■13:31(1831) -**AC**-7:3(1831)■10:20(2597)■22:18(1831)■ 27:43(1826)-**2CO**-2:11(4122)

GETTETH-all=7069&marked-**2SA**-5:8(5060)-**PR**-3:13(6329)■9:7(3947), 9sup■15:32■18:15■19:8-**JER**-17:11 (6213)■48:44(5927)

GETTING-**GE**-31:18(7075)-**PR**-4:7 (7069)■21:6(6467)

GHOST-all=1478&marked-**GE**-25:8, 17■35:29■49:33-**JOB**-3:11■10:18■11:20 (5315)■13:19■14:10-**JER**-15:9(5315) -**LA**-1:19■**N.T.**-all=4151&marked-**M'T**-1:18,20■3:11■12:31,32■27:50■28:19-**M'R**-1:18■3:29■12:36■13:11■15:37(1606),39 (1606)-**LU**-1:15,35,41,67■2:25,26■3:16, 22■4:1■12:10,12■23:46(1606)-**JOH**-1:33■ 7:39■14:26■19:30■20:22-**AC**-1:2,5,8,16■ 2:4,33,38■4:8,31■5:3,5(1634),10(1634), 32■6:3,5■7:51,55■8:15,17,18,19■9:17, 31■10:38,44,45,47■11:15,16,24■12:23 (1634)■13:2,4,9,52■15:8,28■16:6■19:2^{2}, 6■20:23,28■21:11■28:25-**RO**-5:5■9:1■ 14:17■15:13,16-**1CO**-2:13■6:19■12:3

-2CO-6:6■13:14-1TH-1:5,6-2TI-1:14-TIT-3:5-HEB-2:4■3:7■6:4■9:8■10:15-1PE-1:12-2PE-1:21-1JO-5:7-JUDE-20

GIANT-all=7497&marked-2SA-21:16,18,20,22-1CH-20:4,6,8-JOB-6:14(1368)

GIANTS-all=7497&marked-GE-6:4(5303)-NU-13:33(5303)■13:33(1368)-DE-2:11,20■3:11,13-JOS-12:4■13:12■15:8■17:15■18:16

GIER-LE-11:18(7360)-DE-14:17(7360)

GIFT-all=7810&marked-GE-34:12(4976)-EX-23:8^{2}-NU-18:6(4979),7(4979),11(4976)-DE-16:19-2SA-19:42(5379)-PS-45:12(4503)-PR-17:8,23■18:16(4976)■21:14(4976)■25:14(4991)-EC-3:13(4991)■5:19(4991)■7:7(4979)-EZE-46:16(4979),17(4979)■N.T.-all=1431,a=5486&marked-M'T-5:23(1435),24^{2}(1435)■8:4(1435)■15:5(1435)■23:18(1435),19^{2}(1435)-M'R-7:11(1435)-JOH-4:10-AC-2:38■8:20■10:45■11:17-RO-1:11a■5:15a■5:15,16(1434),16a,17■6:23a-1CO-1:7a■7:7a-2CO-1:11a■8:4(5485)■9:15-EPH-2:8(1435)■3:7■4:7-PH'P-4:17(1390)-1TI-4:14a-2TI-1:6a-HEB-6:4-JAS-1:17(1394)-1PE-4:10a

GIFTS-all=4979&marked-GE-25:6-EX-28:38-LE-23:38-NU-18:29-2SA-8:2(4503),6(4503)-1CH-18:2(4503),6(4503)-2CH-19:7(7810)■21:3■26:8(4503)■32:23(4503)-ES-2:18(4864)■9:22-PS-68:18■72:10(814)-PR-6:35(7810)■15:27■19:6(4976)■29:4(8641)-IS-1:23(7810)-EZE-16:33(5078),33(5083)■20:26,31,39■22:12(7810)-DA-2:6(4978),48(4978)■5:17(4978)■N.T.-all=1435&marked-M'T-2:11■7:11-LU-11:13(1390)■21:1,5(334)-RO-11:29(5486)■12:6(5486)-1CO-12:4(5486),9(5486),28(5486),30(5486),31(5486)-EPH-4:8(1390)-HEB-2:4(3311)■5:1■8:3,4■9:9■11:4-RE-11:10

GIN-JOB-18:9(6341)-IS-8:14(6341)-AM-3:5(4170)

GINS-PS-140:5(4170)■141:9(4170)

GIRD-all=2296&marked-EX-29:5(640),9-J'G-3:16-1SA-25:13-2SA-3:31-2KI-4:29■9:1-JOB-38:3(247)■40:7(247)-PS-45:3-IS-8:9^{2}(247)■15:3■32:11(2290)-JER-1:17■4:8■6:26■49:3-EZE-7:18■27:31■44:18-JOE-1:13■N.T.-LU-12:37(4024)■17:8(4024)-JOH-21:18(2224)-AC-12:8(2224)-1PE-1:13(328)

GIRDED-all=2296&marked-EX-12:11-LE-8:7^{2},13■16:4-DE-1:41-1SA-2:4(247),18■17:39■25:13^{2}-2SA-6:14■20:8■21:16■22:40(247)-1KI-18:46(8151)■20:32-NE-4:18(631)-PS-18:39(247)■30:11(247)■65:6(247)■93:1(247)■109:19-IS-45:5(247)-LA-2:10-EZE-16:10(2280)■23:15(2289)-DA-10:5-JOE-1:8■N.T.-LU-12:35(4024)-JOH-13:4(1241),5(1241)-RE-15:6(4024)

GIRDEDST-JOH-21:18(2224)

GIRDETH-1KI-20:11(2296)-JOB-12:18(631)-PS-18:32(247)-PR-31:17(2296)

GIRDING-IS-3:24(4228)■22:12(2296)

GIRDLE-all=232&marked-EX-28:4(73),8(2805),27(2805),28(2805),39(73)■29:5(2805)■39:5(2805),20(2805),21(2805),29(73)-LE-8:7(73),7(2805)■16:4(73)-1SA-18:4(2290)-2SA-18:11(2290)■20:8(2290)-1KI-2:5(2290)-2KI-1:8-JOB-12:18-PS-109:19(4206)-IS-3:24(2290)■5:27■11:5^{2}■22:21(73)-JER-13:1,2,4,6,7^{2},10,11■N.T.-all=2223-M'T-3:4-M'R-1:6-AC-21:11^{2}-RE-1:13

GIRDLES-all=73&marked-EX-28:40■29:9-LE-8:13-PR-31:24(2289)-EZE-23:15(232)■N.T.-RE-15:6(2223)

GIRL-JOE-3:3(3207)

GIRLS-ZEC-8:5(3207)

GIRT-2KI-1:8(247)■N.T.-JOH-21:7(1241)-EPH-6:14(4024)-RE-1:13(4024)

GIVE-all=5414,a=3051&marked-GE-12:7■13:15,17■14:21■15:2,7■17:8,16■23:4,9^{2},11^{3},13sup,13■24:7,41■26:3,4■27:28■28:4,13,20,22,22sup■29:19^{2},21a,26,27■30:1a,14,26,28,31^{2}■34:8,9,11,12^{2},14,16,21■35:12^{2}■38:9,16,17,18■42:25,27■43:14■45:18■47:15a,16a,16,19,24■48:4-EX-2:9■3:21■5:7,10■6:4,8^{2}■10:25■12:25■13:5,11■16:8■17:2■21:23,30,32,34(7725)■22:17,29,30■24:12■25:16,21■30:12,13,14,15^{2}sup,15■32:13■33:1-LE-5:16■6:5■7:32■14:34■15:14■20:24■22:14■23:10,38■25:2,37,38,51(7725),52(7725)■26:4,6■27:23-NU-3:9,48■5:7■6:26(7760)■7:5■10:29■11:13^{2},18sup,18,21■13:2■14:8■15:2,21■18:28■19:3■20:8,21■21:16■22:13,18■24:13■25:12■27:4,7,9,10,11■31:29,30■32:29■34:13■35:2^{2},4,6,7,8^{2},13,14^{2}■36:2^{2}-DE-1:8,20,25,35,36,39■2:5,9,19,28,31■4:38■5:31■6:10,23■7:3,13■10:11■11:9,14,21■14:21■15:10,14■16:10■18:3,4■19:8^{2}■20:16■22:14(7760),19,29■23:14■24:1,15■26:3■28:11,12,55,65■30:20■31:5,7■32:49,52■34:4-JOS-1:2,6■2:12■5:6■7:19(7760)■8:18■9:24■14:12■15:16,19^{2}■17:4■18:4a■20:4■21:2,43-J'G-1:12,15a,15■7:2■8:5,6,15,24,25■14:12,13■16:5■17:10■20:7a■21:1,7,18,22-RU-4:12-1SA-1:11^{2}■2:10,15,16,20(7760),28,32(3190)■6:5■8:6,14,15■9:8■10:4■14:41a■17:10,25,44,46,47■18:17,21■21:3,9■22:7■25:8,11■27:5■30:22-2SA-12:11■13:5(1262)■16:20a■21:6■24:23-1KI-2:17■3:5,9,25,26,27■5:6■8:32,36,39,50■11:11,13,31,35,36,38■13:7,8■14:16■15:4■17:19■18:23■21:2^{3},3,4,6^{3},7,15-2KI-4:42,43■5:22■6:28,29■8:19■10:15■11:10■14:9■15:20■22:5■23:35^{2}-1CH-16:18,28^{2}a,29a■21:23^{2}■22:9,12■29:19-2CH-1:7,10,12■2:10■21:7■25:9,18■30:12,24(7311)■31:4,15,19■32:11■35:12-EZR-4:21(7761)■9:8^{2},9^{2},12-NE-2:8■4:4■9:8^{2},15■10:30■13:25-ES-1:19,20■8:1-JOB-2:4■3:11(1478)■13:19(1478)-PS-2:8(5415)■28:4^{2}■29:1^{2}a,2a,11■37:4■49:7■51:16■60:11a■72:1■78:20■84:11■85:12■86:16■96:7^{2}a,8a■104:27■105:11■108:12a■111:6■132:4-PR-1:4■3:28■4:2,9■5:9■6:4,31■9:9■23:26■29:15,17sup,17■30:8,15a■31:3,6,31-EC-2:3(4900),26■5:1■11:2-SONG-2:13■7:12,13■8:7-IS-3:4■7:14,22(6213)■19:4(5534)■30:20,23■36:8sup,8■41:27■42:6,8,12(7760)■43:4,6,20,20sup■45:3■48:11■49:6,8,20(5066)■55:10■56:5^{2}■61:3■62:7,8-JER-3:15,19■4:12(1696),16■8:10■11:5■13:16■14:13,22■15:13■17:3,10■19:7■20:4,5■22:25■24:7,8■25:31■26:24■29:6,11■30:16■32:3,19,22,28,39■34:2,18,20,21■37:21■38:16■44:30■45:5■48:9-LA-2:18■3:65-EZE-2:8■3:3■7:21■11:17,19^{2}■15:6■16:33,36,38,39,41,61■17:15■20:28,42■21:11,27■23:31,46■25:10■29:19,21■33:15(7999),27■36:26^{2}■39:4,11■43:19■44:28,30■45:8,16(1961,413)■46:5(4991),11(4991),16,17■47:14,23-DA-1:12■2:16(5415)■5:17(3052)■6:2(3052)■8:13■11:17,21-HO-2:5,15■4:18a■9:14^{3}■11:8■13:10-JOE-2:17-MIC-1:14■5:3■6:7,14-HAG-2:9-ZEC-3:7■8:12^{3}■10:1■11:12a-MAL-2:2■N.T.-all=1325&marked-M'T-4:9■5:31,42■6:11■7:6,9(1929),10(1929),11^{2}■9:24(402)■10:8,42(4222)■12:36(591)■14:7,8,16■16:19,26■17:27■19:7,21■20:8(591),14,23,28■22:17■24:29,45■25:8,28■26:15■53(3936)-M'R-6:22,23,25,37^{2}■8:37■9:41(4222)■10:21,40,45■12:9,14,15■13:24■14:11-LU-1:32,77,79(2014)■4:6^{2}■6:30,38^{2}■8:55■9:13■10:7(3844)■19■11:3,7,8^{2},13,11^{2}(1929),13^{2},36(5461),41■12:32,33,42,51,58■14:9■15:12■16:2(591),12■17:18■19:8,24■20:10,16,22■21:15■22:5■23:2-JOH-1:22■4:7,10,14^{2},15■6:27,34,51^{2},52■7:19■9:24■10:28■11:22■13:26(1929),29,34■14:16,27^{2}■15:16■16:23■17:2-AC-3:6■5:31■6:4(4342)■7:5,38■8:19■13:34■19:40(591)■20:32,35-RO-8:32(5483)■12:19,20(4222)■14:12-1CO-7:5(4980),25■10:32(1096)■13:3(3860)■14:7,8-2CO-5:12■8:10-EPH-1:17■4:27,28(3330)-COL-4:1(3930)-2TH-3:16-1TI-4:15(2468)■5:14-2TI-1:16■2:7,25■4:8(591)-HEB-13:17(591)-JAS-2:16-1PE-4:5(591)-1JO-5:16-RE-2:7,10,17^{2},23,26,28■4:9■10:9■11:3,18■13:15■14:7■16:9,19■17:13(1239),17■18:7■19:7■21:6■22:12(591)

GIVEN-all=5414,a=3052&marked-GE-1:29■9:3■15:3,18■16:5■20:16■24:35,36■27:37■29:33■30:6,18^{2}■31:9■33:5(2603)■38:14■43:23■48:9,22-EX-5:16,18■16:15,29■21:4■31:6-LE-6:17■7:34,36■10:14,17■17:11■19:20■20:3-NU-3:9■8:16,19■16:14■18:6,7,8^{2},11,12,19,21,24,26■20:12,24■21:29■26:54,62■27:12■32:5,7,9■33:53-DE-2:5,9,19,24■3:18,19,20sup,20^{2}■8:10■9:23■12:15,21■13:12■16:17■20:14■22:17(7760)■26:9,10,11,12,13,14,15■28:31,32,52,53■29:4,26(2505)-JOS-1:3,13sup,13■2:9,14■6:2,16■8:1■14:3■15:19■17:14■18:3■22:7■23:13,15,16■24:13,33-J'G-1:15■15:6,18■18:10-1SA-1:27■15:28■18:19^{2}■22:13■25:27,44■28:17■30:23-2SA-4:10■9:9■12:8(3254)■17:7(3289)■18:11■19:42(5375)■22:36,41-1KI-1:48■2:21■3:6,12,13■5:7■8:36,56■9:7,12,13,16■12:8(3289)■13:5■18:26-2KI-5:1,17■8:29(5221)■9:15(5221)■23:11■25:30-1CH-5:1■22:18sup,18■28:5■29:3,14-2CH-2:12■6:27■7:20■22:6(5221)■25:9■32:29■34:18■36:23-EZR-1:2■4:21(7761)■6:4a,8a,9a■7:6,19a■9:13-NE-2:7■10:29■13:10-ES-2:3,9,13■3:11,14,15■4:8■5:3■7:3■8:7,13,14■9:14-JOB-3:20■9:24■10:18(1478)■15:19■24:23■37:10■38:36■39:19-PS-18:35,40■21:2■44:11■60:4■61:5■72:15■78:24■79:2■111:5■112:9■115:16■118:18■120:3■124:6-PR-19:17(1576)■23:2(1167)-EC-1:13■3:10■5:19,19sup■6:2■8:8(1167)■9:9■12:11-IS-3:11(6213)■8:18■9:6■33:16■35:2■37:10■43:28■47:6■50:4■55:4-JER-3:8■8:13■12:7■13:20■15:9(5301)■21:10■25:5■27:5,6^{2}■28:14■32:22,24,25,43■35:15■38:3,18■39:17■50:15■52:34-LA-1:11■2:7(5462)■5:6-EZE-4:15■11:15■15:6■16:17,34■17:18■18:7,8,13,16■20:15■21:11■28:25■29:5,20■33:24■35:12■37:25■47:11-DA-2:23a,37a,38a■4:16a■5:28a■7:4a,6a,11a,14a,22a,25a,27a■8:12■11:6,11-HO-2:12-JOE-2:23■3:3-AM-4:6■9:15■N.T.-all=1325&marked-M'T-7:7■9:8■10:19■12:39■13:11^{2},12■14:9,11■16:4■19:11■21:43■22:30(1547)■25:29■26:9■28:18-M'R-4:11,24(4369),25■5:43■6:2■8:12■13:11■14:5,44-LU-6:38■8:10,18■11:9,29■12:48■19:15,26■22:19-JOH-1:17■3:27,35■4:10■5:26,27,36■6:39,65■11:57■12:5■13:3,15■17:2^{2},7,8,9,11,14,22,24^{2}■18:11■19:11-AC-3:16■4:12■5:32■8:18■17:31(3930)■24:26■27:24(5483)-RO-5:5■11:8,35(4272)■12:3,6,13(1377)■15:15-1CO-1:4■2:12(5483)■3:10■11:15■12:7,8,24-2CO-1:22■5:5,18■9:9■10:8■12:7■13:10-GA-2:9■3:21,21(2227),22■4:15-EPH-3:2,7,8■4:7,19(3860)■5:2(3860)■6:19-PH'P-1:29(5483)■2:9(5483)-COL-1:25-1TH-4:8-2TH-2:16-1TI-3:3(3943),8(4337)■4:14-2TI-1:7,9-TIT-1:7(3943),7sup■2:3(1402)-PH'M-22(5483)-HEB-2:13-JAS-1:5-2PE-1:3(1433),4(1433)■3:15-1JO-3:24■4:13■5:11,20-RE-6:2,4^{2},8,11■7:2■8:2,3■9:1,3,5■10:9■11:1,2■12:14■13:5^{2},7^{2}■16:6,8■20:4

GIVER-2CO-9:7(1395)

GIVEST-all=5414&marked-DE-15:9,10,-JOB-35:7-PS-50:19(7971)■104:28■145:15-EZE-16:33,34

GIVETH-all=5414&marked-GE-49:21-EX-16:29■20:12-LE-20:2,4■27:9-NU-5:10-DE-2:29■4:1,21,40■5:16■8:18■9:6■11:17,31■12:1,9■13:1■15:4,7■16:5,18,20■17:2,14■18:9■19:1,2,10,14■21:1,23■24:3,4■25:15,19■26:1,2■27:2,3■28:8-JOS-1:11,15-J'G-21:18

-JOB-5:10▪14:10(1478)▪35:10▪36:6,31 -PS-37:21▪68:35▪127:2▪136:25▪144:10▪ 146:7▪147:9,16-PR-2:6▪3:34▪13:15▪ 21:26▪22:9,16▪23:31▪26:8▪28:27▪ 31:15-EC-2:26^2▪5:18▪8:15-IS-40:29▪42:5 -JER-5:24▪22:13▪31:35-LA-3:30-DA-2:21(3052)▪4:17(5415),25(5415),32 (5415)▪N.T.-all=1325&marked-JOH-3:34▪6:32,33,37▪10:11(5087)▪14:27▪21:13-AC-17:25-RO-12:8(3330)-1CO-15:38, 57-1TI-6:17(3930)-JAS-1:5▪4:6^2-1PE-4:11(5524)▪5:5

GIVING-all=5414&marked-DE-10:18▪21:17-RU-1:6-1KI-5:9-2CH-6:23-JOB-11:20(4646)▪N.T.-all=1325 &marked-AC-8:9(3004)▪15:8-RO-9:4 (3548)-1CO-14:7-2CO-6:3-PH'P-4:15 (1394)-1PE-3:7(632)-2PE-1:5(3923)

GLAD-all=8056,a=1523&marked -EX-4:14-J'G-18:20(3190)-1SA-11:9 -1KI-8:66(2896)-1CH-16:31-2CH-7:10 -ES-5:9(2896)▪8:15-JOB-3:22(7797)▪ 22:19-PS-9:2▪14:7▪16:9▪21:6(2302)▪ 31:7a▪32:11▪34:2▪35:27▪40:16(8055) 45:8▪46:4▪48:11a▪53:6▪64:10▪67:4▪ 68:3▪69:32▪70:4▪90:14,15▪92:4▪96:11a▪ 97:1,8▪104:15,34▪105:38▪107:30▪118:24▪ 119:74▪122:1▪126:3-PR-10:1▪12:25▪ 15:20▪17:5▪23:25▪24:17a▪27:11-SONG-1:4a-IS-25:9a▪35:1(7796)▪39:2▪65:18 (7796)▪66:10a-JER-20:15▪41:13▪50:11 -LA-1:21(7796)▪4:21-DA-6:23(2868) -HO-7:3-JOE-2:21a,23a-JON-4:6-HAB-1:15a-ZEP-3:14-ZEC-10:7▪N.T.-all= 5463&marked-M'T-5:12(21)-M'R-4:11 -LU-1:19(2097)▪8:1(2097)▪15:32▪22:5▪ 23:8-JOH-8:56▪11:15▪20:20-AC-2:26 (21)▪11:23▪13:32(2097),48-RO-10:15▪ 16:19(2097)-1CO-16:17-2CO-2:2 (2165)▪13:9-1PE-4:13-RE-19:7

GLADLY-all=2234&marked-M'R-6:20▪12:37-AC-2:41(780)▪21:17(780) -2CO-11:19▪12:9(2236),15(2236)

GLADNESS-all=8057&marked -NU-10:10-DE-28:47(2898)-2SA-6:12 -1CH-16:27(2304)▪29:22-2CH-29:30▪ 30:21,23-NE-8:17▪12:27-ES-8:16,17 (8342)▪9:17,18,19-PS-4:7▪30:11▪45:7 (8342),15▪51:8▪97:11▪100:2▪105:43 (7440)▪106:5-PR-10:28-SONG-3:11 -IS-16:10▪22:13▪30:29▪35:10▪51:3, 11-JER-7:34▪16:9▪25:10▪31:7▪33:11▪ 48:33-JOE-1:16(1524)-ZEC-8:19▪N.T.-all=5479&marked-M'R-4:16-LU-1:14 (20)-AC-2:46(20)▪12:14▪14:17(2167) -PH'P-2:29-HEB-1:9(20)

GLASS-JOB-37:18(7209)▪N.T.-all= 5193&marked-1CO-13:12(2072)-2CO-3:18(2734)-JAS-1:23(2072)-RE-4:6▪ 15:2^2▪21:18(5194),21(5194)

GLASSES-IS-3:23(1549)

GLEAN-all=3950&marked-LE-19:10(5953)-DE-24:21(5953)-RU-2:2, 7,8,15^2,16,23-JER-6:9(5953)

GLEANED-all=3950&marked -J'G-20:45(5953)-RU-2:3,17^2,18,19

GLEANING-all=5955&marked -LE-23:22(3951)-J'G-8:2-IS-17:6▪ 24:13-JER-49:9

GLEANINGS-LE-19:9(3951)

GLEDE-DE-14:13(7201)

GLISTERING-1CH-29:2(6320)▪ N.T.-LU-9:29(1823)

GLITTER-EZE-21:10(1300)

GLITTERING-all=1300&marked -DE-32:41-JOB-20:25▪39:23(3851) -EZE-21:28-NA-3:3-HAB-3:11

GLOOMINESS-JOE-2:2(653) -ZEP-1:15(653)

GLORIEST-JER-49:4(1984)

GLORIETH-JER-9:24(1984)▪N.T. -1CO-1:31(2744)-2CO-10:17(2744)

GLORIFIED-all=6286&marked -LE-10:3(3513)-IS-26:15(3513)▪44:23▪ 49:3▪55:5▪60:9,21▪61:3▪66:5(3513)-EZE-28:22(3513)▪39:13(3513)-DA-5:23(1922) -HAG-1:8(3513)▪N.T.-all=1392&marked -M'T-9:8▪15:31-M'R-2:12-LU-4:15▪ 5:26▪7:16▪13:13▪17:15▪23:47-JOH-7:39▪11:4▪12:16,23,28▪13:31^2,32▪14:13▪ 15:8▪17:4,10-AC-3:13▪4:21▪11:18▪13:48▪ 21:20-RO-1:21▪8:17(4888),30-GA-1:24 -2TH-1:10(1740),12(1740)▪3:1-HEB-5:5-1PE-4:11,14-RE-18:7

GLORIFIETH-PS-50:23(3513)

GLORIFY-all=3513&marked-PS-22:23▪50:15▪86:9,12-IS-24:15▪25:3▪ 60:7(6286)-JER-30:19▪N.T.-all=1392 -M'T-5:16-JOH-12:28^2▪13:32^2▪16:14▪ 17:1^2,5▪21:19-RO-15:6,9-1CO-6:20 -2CO-9:13-1PE-2:12▪4:16-RE-15:4

GLORIFYING-all=1392-LU-2:20▪ 5:25▪18:43

GLORIOUS-all=3519&marked -EX-15:6(142),11(142)-DE-28:58(3513) -2SA-6:20(3513)-1CH-29:13(8597) -NE-9:5-ES-1:4-PS-45:13(3520)▪66:2▪ 72:19▪76:4(215)▪87:3(3513)▪111:3 (1926)▪145:5,12-IS-4:2▪11:10▪22:23▪ 28:1(6643),4(6643)▪30:30(1935)▪33:21 (117)▪49:5(3513)▪60:13(3513)▪63:1 (1921),12(8597),14(8597)-JER-17:12 -EZE-27:25-DA-11:16(6643),41(6643),45 (6643)▪N.T.-all=1391&marked-LU-13:17(1741)-RO-8:21-2CO-3:7(1722, 1391),8(1722,1391),10(1392),11(1223, 1391),11(1722,1391)▪4:4-EPH-5:27 (1741)-PH'P-3:21-COL-1:11-1TI-1:11 -TIT-2:13

GLORIOUSLY-IS-24:23(3519)

GLORY-all=3519,a=8597,b=1984& marked-GE-31:1▪45:13-EX-8:9(6286)▪ 16:7,10▪24:16,17▪28:2,40▪29:43▪33:18, 22▪40:34,35-LE-9:6,23-NU-14:10,21, 22▪16:19,42▪20:6-DE-5:24▪33:17(1926) -JOS-7:19-1SA-2:8▪4:21,22▪6:5-1KI-8:11-2KI-14:10(3513)-1CH-16:10b,24, 27(1935),28,29,35(7623)▪22:5a▪29:11a -2CH-5:14▪7:1,2,3-ES-5:11-JOB-19:9▪ 29:20▪39:20(1935)▪40:10(1935)-PS-3:3▪ 4:2▪8:1(1935),5▪16:9▪19:1▪21:5▪24:7, 8,9,10^2▪29:1,2,3,9▪30:12▪45:3(1935)▪ 49:16,17▪57:5,8,11▪62:7▪63:2,11b▪ 64:10b▪72:19▪73:24▪78:61a▪79:9▪84:11▪ 85:9▪89:17a,44(2892)▪90:16(1926)▪ 96:3,7,8▪97:6▪102:15,16▪104:31▪105:3b▪ 106:5b,20▪108:1,5▪113:4▪115:1▪138:5▪ 145:11▪148:13(1935)▪149:5-PR-3:35▪ 4:9a▪16:31a▪17:6a▪19:11a▪20:29a▪25:2, 27▪28:12a-IS-2:10(1926),19(1926),21 (1926)▪3:8▪4:5▪5:14(1926)▪6:3▪8:7▪ 10:3,12a,16,18▪13:19(6643)▪14:18▪16:14▪ 17:3,4▪20:5a▪21:16▪22:18,24▪23:9(6643)▪ 24:16(6643)▪28:5(6643)▪35:2^2▪40:5▪ 41:16b▪42:8,12▪43:7▪45:25b▪46:13a▪ 48:11▪58:8▪59:19▪60:1,2,7a,13,19a▪ 61:6▪62:2,3a▪63:15a▪66:11,12,18,19^2 -JER-2:11▪4:2b▪9:23^{3}b,24b▪13:11a,16, 18a▪14:21▪22:18(1935)▪48:18-EZE-1:28▪3:12,23^2▪8:4▪9:3▪10:4^2,18,19▪ 11:22,23▪20:6(6643)▪24:25a▪25:9(6643)▪ 26:20(6643)▪31:18▪39:21▪43:2^2,4,5▪ 44:4-DA-2:37(3367)▪4:36(3367)▪5:18 (3367),20(3367)▪7:14(3367)▪11:20 (1925),39-HOS-4:7▪9:11▪10:5-MIC-1:15▪2:9(1926)-NA-2:9-HAB-2:14,16^2▪ 3:3(1935)-HAG-2:3,7,9-ZEC-2:5, 8▪6:13(1935)▪11:3(155)▪12:7^{2}a,-MAL-2:2▪N.T.-all=1391,a=2744&marked -M'T-4:8▪6:2(1392),13,29▪16:27▪19:28▪ 24:30▪25:31^2-M'R-8:38▪10:37▪13:26 -LU-2:9,14,32▪4:6▪9:26,31,32▪12:27▪ 17:18▪19:38▪21:27▪24:26-JOH-1:14▪ 2:11▪7:18^2▪8:50▪11:4,40▪12:41▪17:5, 22,24-AC-7:2,55▪12:23▪22:11-RO-1:23▪ 2:7,10▪3:7,23▪4:2(2745),20▪5:2,3a▪6:4▪ 8:18▪9:4,23^2▪11:36▪15:7,17(2746)▪ 16:27-1CO-1:29a,31a▪2:7,8▪3:21a▪4:7a▪ 9:16(2745)▪10:31▪11:7^2,15▪15:40^2,41^4, 43-2CO-1:20▪3:7,9^2,10(1392),10,18^2▪ 4:6,15,17▪5:12(2745),12a▪8:19,23-2CO-10:17a▪11:12a,18^{2}a,30a▪12:1a,5^{2}a,6a,9a -GA-1:5▪5:26(2755)▪6:13a,14a-EPH-1:6,12,14,17,18▪3:13,16,21-PH'P-1:11▪ 2:11▪3:19▪4:19,20-COL-1:27^2▪3:4-1TH-2:6,12,20-2TH-1:4a,9▪2:14-1TI-1:17▪ 3:16-2TI-2:10▪4:18-HEB-1:3▪2:7,9,10▪ 3:3▪9:5▪13:21-JAS-2:1▪3:14(2620)-1PE-1:7,8(1392),11,21,24▪2:20(2811)▪4:13, 14▪5:1,4,10,11-2PE-1:3,17^2▪3:18-JUDE-24,25-RE-1:6▪4:9,11▪5:12,13▪7:12▪ 11:13▪14:7▪15:8▪16:9▪18:1▪19:1▪21:11, 23,24,26

GLORYING-1CO-5:6(2745)▪9:15 (2745)-2CO-7:4(2746)▪12:11(2744)

GLUTTON-DE-21:20(2151)-PR-23:21(2151)

GLUTTONOUS-M'T-11:19(5314) -LU-7:34(5314)

GNASH-PS-112:10(2786)-LA-2:16(2786)

GNASHED-PS-35:16(2786)▪N.T. -AC-7:54(1031)

GNASHETH-JOB-16:9(2786)-PS-37:12(2786)▪N.T.-M'R-9:18(5149)

GNASHING-all=1030-M'T-8:12▪ 13:42,50▪22:13▪24:51▪25:30-LU-13:28

GNAT-M'T-23:24(2971)

GNAW-ZEP-3:3(1633)

GNAWED-RE-16:10(3145)

GO-all=3212,a=3318,b=935,c=5927, d=1980,e=7971,f=3381,g=5674,h=7725 &marked-GE-3:14▪8:16a▪9:10a▪11:3 (3051)4(3051),7(3051),7f,31▪12:5,19▪ 15:2d,15b▪16:2b,8▪18:21f▪19:2d,34b▪ 22:5▪24:4,11a,38,42d,51,55,56,58^2▪ 26:2f,16▪27:3a,9,13▪28:2,20d▪29:7,21b▪ 30:3b,25,26▪31:18b▪32:26^{2}e▪33:12^2▪ 35:1c,3c▪37:14,17,30b,35f▪38:8b,16 (3051)▪41:55▪42:15a,19,38f,38▪43:2h, 4f,5f,8,13h▪44:25h,26^{2}f,33c,34c▪45:1a, 9c,17,28▪46:3f,4f,31c▪50:5c,6c-EX-2:7, 8▪3:11,16,18,19d,20e,21^2▪4:12,18^2,19,21e, 23^{2}e,26(7503),27▪5:1e,2^{2}e,3,7,8,11,17, 18▪6:1e,11b,11e▪7:14e,16e▪8:1b,1e,2e,3c, 8e,20e,21e,25,27,28e,28,29a,29e,32e▪9:1b, 1e,2e,7e,13e,17e,28e,35e▪10:1b,3e,4e,7e, 8,8d,9^2,10e,11,20e,24^2,26,27e▪11:1^{2}e, 4a,8a,10e▪12:22a,31▪13:15e,17e,21▪ 14:5e,15(5265),16b,21▪16:4a,29a▪17:5g, 5d,9a▪18:23b▪19:10,12c,21f▪20:26c▪ 21:2a,3^{2}a,4a,5a,7a,11a,26e,27e▪23:23▪ 24:2c▪30:20b▪32:1,7,23,27g,30c,34^2▪ 33:1c,3c,14,15d▪34:9,24c-LE-6:13(3518)▪ 8:33a▪9:7(7126)▪10:7a,9b▪11:27d▪14:3a, 36^{2}b,38a,53e▪15:16a▪16:10e,18a,22e, 26e▪19:16▪21:11b,12a,23b▪25:28a,30a, 31a,33a,54a▪26:6g,13-NU-1:3a,20a,22a, 24a,26a,30a,32a,34a,36a,38a,40a,42a,45a▪ 2:24(5265),31(5265)▪4:19b,20b▪5:12 (7847),22b▪8:15b,24b▪10:5(5265),9b,30, 32▪13:17c,30c,31c▪14:40c,42c,44c▪16:30f, 46▪20:17,19c,19g,20g▪21:22▪22:12,13d, 18g,20,35▪23:3,16h▪24:13g,14d▪26:2a▪ 27:17a,17b,21a▪31:3(1961),23^{2}g▪32:6b, 9b,21g▪34:4a,9a,11f,12f-DE-1:7b,8b, 21c,22c,26c,28c,33,37b,38b,39b,41^{2}c,42c▪ 2:27▪3:25g,27g,28g▪4:1b,5b,14g,21g, 21b,22^{2}g,26g,34b▪5:27(7126),30▪6:1g, 14,18b▪8:1b▪9:1b,5b,23c▪10:11b▪11:8b, 8g,10b,28,31b▪12:10g,26b▪13:2,6,13▪ 14:25d▪15:12e,13e,16a▪16:7d▪20:5,6,7, 8▪21:13b,14e▪22:7e,13b▪23:10a,12a▪ 24:2d,5a,10b,15b,19h▪25:5b,7c▪26:2d, 3b▪27:3b▪28:14(5493),14,25a,41▪29:18▪ 30:12c,13g,18b▪31:2a,2g,3^{2}g,6d,7a,8d, 13g,16sup,16b,21(6213)▪32:47g,52b▪34:4g -JOS-1:2g,11b,16▪2:1,16,19a▪3:3d,4▪ 6:3(5362),22b▪7:2c,3^{2}c▪8:1c,3c,4(7368)▪ 9:11,12▪10:13b▪14:11a▪18:3b,4d,8▪ 22:9,12c,33c▪23:12h,12b-J'G-1:1c,2c,3d, 25e▪2:1c,6e▪4:6,8,8d,8^2,9▪5:11f▪6:14▪ 7:3(4994),4^4,7,10^{2}f,11f▪9:9d,11d,13d, 38a▪10:14▪11:8d,35h,37,38▪12:1,5g▪ 15:1^{2}b,5e▪16:17(5493),20a▪17:9d▪18:2, 5d,6^2,9c,9,10b,19▪19:5,9d,15b,25e,27▪ 20:8,14a,18c,23(5066),23c,28a,28c▪21:10, 20,21d-RU-1:8,11,12,16,18▪2:2^2,8,8g, 9^{2}d,22a▪3:4b,17b-1SA-1:17▪3:9▪5:11h▪ 6:6e,8d,20c▪8:20a,22▪9:3,6,6d,7,9,10, 13c,14c,19c,19e▪10:3(2498),8f,9▪11:14▪ 14:1g,4g,6g,9c,10c,36f,37f▪15:3,6,18, 27▪16:1,2▪17:32,33,37,39^2,55a▪18:2h▪ 19:3a,17e▪20:5e,11a,13d,19f,21,22,29e, 40,42▪23:2^2,4f,8f,13d,13a,22,23d▪24:19e▪

25:5b,19g,35c▪26:6^{2}f,11,19▪28:1a,7▪29:4h,4f,7,8b,9c▪30:10g-**2SA**-1:15 (5066)▪2:1^{3}c▪3:16,21▪5:19^{2}c,23c,24a▪7:3,5▪11:1a,8f,10f,11b▪12:23d▪13:7,13,24,25^2,26^2,27e,39a▪14:8,21,30▪15:7,9 20,20d,22▪16:9g,21b▪17:11d▪18:2a,3a,21▪19:7^{2}a,15,20f,26,34c,36g,37g,38g▪21:17a▪24:1,2(7751),12d,18c-**1KI**-1:13,53▪2:2d,6f,29,36a▪3:7a▪8:44a▪9:6d▪11:2b,10,17b,21,22,22e▪12:24c,27c,27sup,28c▪13:8b,16b,17▪14:3b,7▪15:17a▪17:12b,13b▪18:1,5,8,11,14,43c,43h,44c▪19:11a,15,20▪20:22,31a,33b,42e,42 (1961)▪21:16f,18f▪22:4,6,6c,12c,15,15c,20c,22^{2}a,25b,48,49-**2KI**-1:2,3c,3d,6,15f▪2:16,18,23c▪3:7,7c,8c▪4:3,7,23d,24,29▪5:5,5b,10d,19,24e▪6:2^2,3^2,13,22▪7:5b,9b,14▪8:1,8,10▪9:1,2b,15a,15,34(6485)▪10:13f,25b▪11:7a,9a▪12:17c▪17:27▪18:21b,25c▪19:31a▪20:5c,8c,9d,9h,10 (5186)▪22:4c,13-**1CH**-7:11a▪14:10^{2}c,14c,15a▪17:4,11▪20:1a▪21:2,10,18c,30-**2CH**-1:10a▪6:34a▪7:19d▪11:4c▪14:11b▪16:1a,3▪18:2c,3,5,5c,11c,14,14c,19c,21^{2}a,24b,29b▪20:16f,17a,27h,36,37▪23:6b,8a▪24:5a▪25:5a,7b,8b,10,13▪26:18a,20a▪34:21▪36:23c-**EZR**-1:3c,5c▪5:15 (236)▪7:9(4609),13(1946),28c▪8:31▪9:11b-**NE**-3:15f▪4:3c▪6:11^{2}b▪8:10,15a▪9:12,15b,19,23b-**ES**-1:19a▪2:12b,13b,15b▪4:8b,16,16b▪5:14b-**JOB**-4:21(5265)▪6:18c▪10:21▪15:13a,30(5493)▪16:22d▪17:16f▪21:13(5181),29g▪23:8d▪24:5a,10d▪27:6(7503)▪31:37(7126)▪37:8b▪38:35▪39:4a▪41:19d▪42:8-**PS**-22:29f▪26:4b▪28:1f▪30:3f,9f▪32:8▪38:6d▪39:13▪42:9▪43:2d,4b▪48:12(5362)▪49:19b▪55:10(5437),15f▪58:3(8582)▪59:6(5437),14(5437)▪60:10a▪63:9b▪66:13b▪71:16b▪78:52(5265)▪80:18(5472)▪84:7▪85:13d▪88:4f▪89:14(6923)▪104:8c,8f,26d▪107:7,23f,26f▪108:11a▪115:17f▪118:19b▪119:35(1869)▪122:1,4c▪129:8g,132:3c,7b▪139:7▪143:7f-**PR**-1:12f▪2:19b▪3:28▪4:13(7503),14(833)▪5:5f,23(7686)▪6:3,6,28d▪7:25(8582)▪9:6(833)▪14:7▪15:12▪18:8f▪19:7(7368)▪22:6(6310),10a,24b▪23:30b▪25:8a▪26:22f▪27:10b▪28:10(7686)▪30:27a,29(6806)-**EC**-2:1▪3:20d▪5:15,16▪6:6d▪7:2^2▪8:3▪9:7▪10:15▪12:5(5437)-**SONG**-1:8a▪3:2(5437),3 (5437),4(7503),11a▪6:6c▪7:8c,11a-**IS**-2:3d,3c,3a,19b,21b▪3:16▪5:24c▪6:8,9▪7:3a,6c▪8:6d,7d,8g▪11:15(1869)▪13:2b▪14:19f▪15:5c▪18:2▪20:2▪21:2c,6▪22:15▪23:16(5437)▪27:4(6585)▪28:13▪30:2f,8b▪31:1f▪33:21▪34:10c▪35:9c▪36:6b,10c▪37:32a▪38:5d,10,15(1718),18f,22c▪42:10f,13a▪45:2,13e,16d▪48:17,20a▪49:9a,17a▪51:23g▪52:11^{2}a,12a,12,12d▪54:9g▪55:12a▪58:6e,8d▪60:20b▪62:1a,10g▪66:24a-**JER**-1:7▪2:2d,25,37a▪3:1d,12d▪4:5b,29b▪5:10c▪6:4c,5c,25a▪7:12▪9:2▪10:5(6805)▪11:12d▪13:1d,4,6▪14:18a,18(5503)▪15:1a,2a,5(5493)▪16:5,8b▪17:19d,19a▪18:2f,11(4994)▪19:1d,2a,10d▪20:6▪21:2c,12a▪22:1f,20c,22▪25:6,32a▪27:18b▪28:13d▪29:12d▪30:16▪31:4a,6c,22(2559),24(5265),39a▪34:2d,3b,9e,10^{2}e,11e,14^{2}e▪35:2d,11b,13d,15▪36:5b,6b,19▪37:12▪38:17a,18a,21a▪39:16d▪40:1e,4,5h,5^2,5e,15▪41:10g,17▪42:14b,15b,17b,19b,22b▪43:2b,12a▪44:12b▪46:8c,11c,6h,22▪48:5c,7a▪49:3,12sup,12,28c▪50:4,6(8582),8a,21c,27f,33e▪51:9,45a,50d-**LA**-4:18-**EZE**-1:12,20^2▪3:1,4,11,22a,24b,25a▪8:6(7368),9b▪9:4g,5g,7a▪10:2b▪12:4a,4(4161),11,12a▪13:20e▪14:11(8582),17g▪15:7a▪20:10a,29b,39▪21:4a,16 (258)▪23:44b▪24:14(6544)▪26:11f,20f▪30:9a,17,18▪31:14f▪32:18f,19f,24f,25f,29f,30f▪38:11c,11b,39:9a▪40:26(5930)▪42:14a▪44:3a,19a▪46:2a,8b,8a,9^{3}a,10b,10a,12a▪47:8f,8b,15b-**DA**-11:44a▪12:9,13-**HO**-1:2▪2:5,7▪3:1▪4:15c▪5:6,14,15▪7:11d,12▪11:3(8637)-**JOE**-2:16a-**AM**-1:15d▪2:7▪4:3a▪6:2,2f▪7:12,15▪8:9b▪9:4-**JON**-1:2,3b▪3:2(3312)-**MIC**-1:8(3312)▪2:3(3312)▪3:6b▪4:2c,2a,10a,10b▪5:8g-**NA**-3:14b-**HAB**-1:4a-**HAG**-1:8c-**ZEC**-6:5a,6^{3}a,7,8a,10b▪8:21d,21^2,23▪9:14a,14d▪14:2a,3a,8a,16c,18c-**MAL**-4:2a▪**N.T.**-all=4198,a=5217,b=565&marked-**M'T**-2:8,20,22b▪5:24a,41sup,41a▪7:13(1525)▪8:4a,9,13a,21b,31b,32a▪9:6a,13▪10:5b,6,7,11(1831)▪11:4▪13:28b▪14:15b,22(4254),29(2064)▪16:21b▪17:27▪18:15a▪19:21a,24(1330)▪20:4a,7a,14a,18(305)▪21:2,28a,30b,31 (4254)▪22:9▪23:13^2(1525)▪24:26 (1831)▪25:6(1831),9,46b▪26:18(5217),32(4254),36b▪27:65a▪28:7,10b,10a,19-**M'R**-1:38(71),44a▪2:11a▪5:19a,34a▪6:36b,37b,38a,45(4254)▪7:29a▪8:26 (1525)▪9:43b▪10:21a,25(1525),33(305),52a▪11:2,6(863)▪12:38(4043)▪13:15 (2597)▪14:12b,13a,14(1525),28(4254),42(71)▪16:7a,15-**LU**-1:17(4281),76(4313)▪2:15(1330)▪5:14b,24▪7:8,22,50▪8:14,22(1330),31b,48,51(1525)▪9:5(1831),12b,13,51,53,59b,60b▪10:3,7(3327),10 (1831),37▪11:5▪13:32▪14:4(630),10,10 (4320),18(1831),19,21(1831),23(1831)▪15:4,18,28(1525)▪17:7(3928),14,19,23b▪18:25(1525),31(305)▪19:30a▪21:8▪22:8,33,68(630)▪23:22(630)-**JOH**-1:43(1831)▪4:4(1330),16a,50▪6:67a,68b▪7:3a,8(305),19(2212),33a,35^2▪8:11,14^{2}a,21^{2}a,22a▪9:7a,11a▪10:9(1525)▪11:7(71),11,15(71),16 (71),44a▪13:33a,36a▪14:2,3,4a,12,28a,28,31(71)▪15:16a▪16:5a,7^{2}b,10a,16a,17a,28▪18:8a▪19:12(630)▪20:17▪21:3a,3 (2064)-**AC**-1:11,25▪3:3(1524),13(630)▪4:15b,21(630),23(630)5:20,40(630)▪7:40 (4313)▪8:26,29(4334)▪9:6(1525),11,15▪10:20▪11:12(4905),22(1330)15:2(305),33(630),36(1994)▪16:3(1831),7,10(1831),35(630),36(630),36▪17:9(630),14▪18:6▪19:21▪20:1,22▪21:4(305),12(305)▪22:10▪23:10(2597),23,32▪24:25▪25:5(4782),9 (305),12,20▪27:3▪28:18(630),26-**RO**-15:25-**1CO**-5:10(1831)▪10:27▪16:4,6-**2CO**-9:5(4281)-**EPH**-4:26(1931)-**1TH**-4:6(5233)-**HEB**-6:1(5342)▪11:8(1831)▪13:13(1831)-**JAS**-4:13(33),13▪5:1(33)-**RE**-3:12(1831)▪10:8a▪13:10a▪16:1a,14 (1607)▪17:8a▪20:8(1831)

GOAD-**J'G**-3:31(4451)

GOADS-**1SA**-13:21(1861)-**EC**-12:11(1861)

GOAT-all=8163&marked-**GE**-15:9 (5795)-**LE**-3:12(5795)▪4:24▪7:23(5795)▪9:15▪10:16▪16:9,10,15,18,20,21^2,22^2,26,27▪17:3(5795)▪22:27-**NU**-15:27▪18:17▪28:22▪29:22,28,31,34,38-**DE**-14:4(5795),5(689)-**PR**-30:31(8495)-**EZE**-43:25-**DA**-8:5(5795),5(6842),8(6842),21(6842)

GOATS-all=5795,a=6260&marked-**GE**-27:9,16▪30:32,33,35(8495),35▪31:38▪32:14,14(8495)▪37:31-**EX**-12:5-**LE**-1:10▪4:23,28▪5:6▪9:3▪16:5,7(8163),8(8163)▪22:19▪23:19-**NU**-7:16,17a,22,23a,28,29a,34,35a,40,41a,46,47a,52,53a,58,59a,64,65a,70,71a,76,77a,82,83a,87,88a▪15:24▪28:15,30▪29:5,11,16,19,25-**DE**-32:14a-**1SA**-24:2(3277)▪25:2-**2CH**-17:11(8495)▪29:21,23(8163)-**EZR**-6:17(5796)▪8:35(6842)-**JOB**-39:1(3277)-**PS**-50:9a,13a▪66:15a▪104:18 (3277)-**PR**-27:26a-**SONG**-4:1▪6:5-**IS**-1:11a▪34:6a-**JER**-50:8a▪51:40a-**EZE**-27:21a▪34:17a▪39:18a▪43:22▪45:23-**ZEC**-10:3a▪**N.T.**-all=5131&marked-**M'T**-25:32(2056),33(2055)-**HEB**-9:12,13,19▪10:4

GOATS'-all=5795-**EX**-25:4▪26:7▪35:6,23,26▪36:14-**NU**-31:20-**1SA**-19:13,16-**PR**-27:27

GOATSKINS-**HEB**-11:37(122,1192)

GOBLET-**SONG**-7:2(101)

GODDESS-**1KI**-11:5(430),33(430)▪**N.T.**-all=2299-**AC**-19:27,35,37

GODHEAD-**AC**-17:29(2304)-**RO**-1:20(2305)-**COL**-2:9(2320)

GODLINESS-all=2150&marked-**1TI**-2:2,10(2317)▪3:16▪4:7,8▪6:3,5,6,11-**2TI**-3:5-**TIT**-1:1-**2PE**-1:3,6,7▪3:11

GODLY-all=6263&marked-**PS**-4:3▪12:1▪32:6-**MAL**-2:15(430)▪**N.T.**-all=2316&marked-**2CO**-1:12▪7:9(2596,2316),10(2596,2316),11(2596,2316)▪11:2-**1TI**-1:4-**2TI**-3:12(2153)-**TIT**-2:12 (2153)-**2PE**-2:9(2152)-**3JO**-6(516,2316)

GOD-WARD-**EX**-18:19(4136,430)▪**N.T.**-**2CO**-3:4(4314,2316)-**1TH**-1:8 (4314,2316)

GOEST-all=935,a=3212&marked-**GE**-10:19,30▪25:18▪28:15a▪32:17a-**EX**-4:21a▪33:16a▪34:12-**NU**-14:14 (1980)-**DE**-7:1▪11:10,29▪12:29▪20:1 (3318)▪21:10(3318)▪23:20▪28:6(3318),19(3318),21,63▪30:16▪32:50(5927)-**JOS**-1:7a,9a-**J'G**-14:3(1980)▪19:17a-**RU**-1:16a-**1SA**-27:8▪28:22a-**2SA**-15:19a-**1KI**-2:37(3318),42(3318)-**PS**-44:9(3318)-**PR**-4:12a▪6:22(1980)-**EC**-5:1a▪9:10 (1980)-**JER**-45:5a-**ZEC**-2:2(1980)▪**N.T.**-all=5217&marked-**M'T**-8:19 (565)-**LU**-9:57(565)▪12:58-**JOH**-11:8▪13:36▪14:5▪16:5

GOETH-all=3318,a=1980,b=935,c=5927&marked-**GE**-2:14a▪32:20a▪38:13c-**EX**-7:15▪22:26b▪28:29b,30b,35b-**LE**-11:21a,27a,42^{2}a▪14:46b▪15:32▪16:17b▪22:3(7126),4▪27:21-**NU**-5:29 (7847)▪21:15(5186)-**DE**-1:30a▪9:3 (5674)▪11:30(3996)▪19:5b▪20:4a▪23:9▪24:13b-**JOS**-10:10(4609)▪11:17c▪12:7c▪16:1c,2,3(3381)▪19:12,12c,13,27,34-**J'G**-5:31▪20:31c▪21:19c-**1SA**-6:9c▪22:14 (5493)▪30:24(3381)-**2KI**-5:18b▪11:8▪12:20(3381)-**2CH**-23:7-**EZR**-5:8(5648)-**JOB**-7:9(3381)▪9:11(5674)▪34:8(732)▪37:2▪39:21▪41:20,21-**PS**-41:6▪68:21a▪88:16(5674)▪97:3(3212)▪104:23▪126:6 (3212)▪146:4-**PR**-6:29b▪7:22a,22(925)▪20:19a▪26:9c,20(3518)▪31:18(3518)-**EC**-1:5b,6a▪3:21c,21(3381)▪12:5a-**SONG**-7:9a-**IS**-28:19(5674)▪30:29a▪55:11▪59:8(1869)▪63:14-**JER**-5:6▪6:4 (6437)▪21:9▪22:10a▪30:23▪38:2▪44:17▪49:17(5674)▪50:13(5674)-**EZE**-7:14a▪33:31a▪33:31a▪40:40c▪42:9b▪44:27b▪48:1b-**HOS**-6:4a,5-**ZEC**-5:3,5,6▪**N.T.**-all=5217&marked-**M'T**-8:9 (4198)▪12:45(4198)▪13:44▪15:11(1525),17(5562)▪17:21(1607)▪18:12(4198)▪26:24▪28:7(4254)-**M'R**-3:13(305)▪7:19 (1607)▪14:21,45(4334)▪16:7(4254)-**LU**-7:8(4198)▪11:26(4198)▪22:22(4198)-**JOH**-3:8▪7:20(2212)▪10:4(4198)▪11:31▪12:35-**AC**-8:26(2597)-**JAS**-1:24(565)-**1JO**-2:11-**RE**-14:4▪17:11▪19:15(1607)

GOING-all=3318&marked-**GE**-12:9 (1980)▪15:12(935)▪37:25(1980)-**EX**-17:12(935)▪23:4(8582)▪37:18,19,21-**LE**-11:20(1980)-**NU**-32:7(5674)▪34:4 (8444)-**DE**-16:6(935)▪33:18-**JOS**-1:4 (3996)▪6:9(1980),11(5362),13(1980)▪7:5(4174)▪10:11(4174),27(935)▪15:7 (4608)▪18:17(4608)▪23:14(1980)-**J'G**-1:36(4608)▪19:18(1980),28(3212)-**1SA**-9:11,27(3381)▪10:3(5927)▪17:20▪29:6-**2SA**-2:19(3212)▪3:25(4161)▪5:24(6807)-**1KI**-17:11(3212)▪22:36(935)-**2KI**-2:23 (5927)▪9:27(4608)▪19:27-**1CH**-14:15 (6807)▪26:16(5927)-**2CH**-11:4(3212)▪18:34(935)-**NE**-3:19(5927),31(5944),32 (5944)▪12:37(4608)-**JOB**-1:7(7751)▪2:2(7751)▪33:24(3381),28(5674)-**PS**-19:6(4161)▪50:1(3996)▪104:19(3996)▪113:3(3996)▪121:8▪144:14-**PR**-7:27 (3381)▪14:15(838)▪30:29(3212)-**IS**-13:10▪37:28-**JER**-48:5(4608),5(4174)▪50:4(1980)-**EZE**-27:19(235)▪40:31(4608),34(4608),37(4608)▪44:5(4161)▪46:12-**DA**-6:14(4606)▪9:25(4161)-**HO**-6:3 (4161)-**JON**-1:3(935)-**MAL**-1:11(3996)▪**N.T.**-**M'T**-4:21(4260)▪20:17(305)▪26:46(71)▪28:11(4108)-**M'R**-6:31(5217)▪10:32(305)-**LU**-14:31(4198)-**JOH**-4:51 (2597)▪8:59(1330)-**AC**-9:28(1607)▪20:5 (4281)-**RO**-10:3(2212)-**1TI**-5:24(4254)-**HEB**-7:18(4254)-**1PE**-2:25(4105)-**JUDE**-7(565)

GOINGS-all=8444&marked-NU-33:2^2(4161)■34:5,8,9,12-JOS-15:4,7,11■16:3,8■18:12,14-JOB-34:21(6806)-PS-17:5(838)■40:2(838)■68:24^2(1979)■140:4(6471)-PR-5:21(4570)■20:24(4703)-IS-59:8(4570)-EZE-42:11(4161)■43:11(4161)■48:30-MIC-5:2(4163)

GOLD-all=2091&marked-GE-2:11,12■13:2■24:22,35,53■41:42■44:8-EX-3:22■11:2■12:35■20:23■25:3,11^2,12,13,17,18,24^2,26,28,29,31,36,38,39■26:6,29^3,32^2,37^2■28:5,6,8,11,13,14,15,20,22,23,24,26,27,33,36■30:3^2,5■31:4■32:24,31■35:5,22^2,32■36:13,34^3,36^2,38■37:2^2,3,4,6,7,11^2,12,13,15,16,17,22,23,24,26^2,27,28■38:24^2■39:2,3,5,6,8,13,15,16,17,19,25,30■40:5-NU-7:14,20,84,86■8:4■22:18■24:13■31:22,50,52,51,54-DE-7:25■8:13■17:17■29:17-JOS-6:19,24■7:21,24■22:8-J'G-8:26-1SA-6:8,11,15-2SA-1:24■8:7,10,11■12:30■21:4-1KI-6:20,21^3,22^2,28,30,32^2,35■7:48,49^2,50^2,51■9:11,14,28■10:2,10,11,14^2,16^2,17^2,18,21^2,22,25■12:28■14:26■15:15,18,19■20:3,5,7■22:48-2KI-5:5■7:8■12:13,18■14:14■16:8■18:14■20:13■23:33,35^2■24:13■25:15-1CH-18:7,10,11■20:2■21:25■22:14,16■28:14^2,15^2,16,17,17sup,18^2■29:2,3,4^2,5,7-2CH-1:15■2:7,14■3:4,5,6,7,8,9^2,10■4:7,8,20,21,22^2■5:1■8:18■9:1,9,10,13^2,14,15^2,16^2,17,18,20^2,21,24■12:9■13:11■15:18■16:2,3■21:3■24:14■25:24■32:27■36:3-EZR-1:4,6,9,10,11■2:69■5:14(1772)■7:15(1772),16,(1722)18(1772)■8:25,26,27^2,28,30,33-NE-7:70,71,72-ES-1:6,7■8:15-JOB-3:15■22:24^2(1220)■23:10■28:1,6,15(5458),16(3800),17,17(6337),19(3800)■31:24,24(3800)■36:19(1222)■42:11-PS-19:10,10(6337)■21:3(6337)■45:9(3800),13■68:13(2742)■72:15■105:37■115:4■119:72,127,127(6337)■135:15-PR-3:14(2742)■8:10(2742),19(2742),19(6337)■11:22■16:16(2742)■17:3■20:15■22:1■25:11,12,12(3800)■27:21-EC-2:8-SONG-1:11■3:10■5:11(6337),14(6337),15(6337)-IS-2:7,20■13:12(6337),17■30:22■31:7■39:2■40:19■46:6■60:6,9,17-JER-4:30■10:4,9■52:19-LA-4:1,1(3800),2(6337)-EZE-7:19^2■16:13,17■27:22■28:4,13■38:13-DA-2:32(1722),35(1722),38(1722),45(1722)■3:1(1722)■5:4(1722),7(1722),16(1722),23(1722),29(1722)■10:5(3800)■11:8,38,43-HO-2:8■8:4-JOE-3:5-NA-2:9-HAB-2:19-ZEP-1:18-HAG-2:8-ZEC-4:2■6:11■9:3(2742)■13:9■14:14-MAL-3:3■N.T.-all=5557,a=5553&marked-M'T-2:11■10:9■23:16,17^2-AC-3:6a■17:29■20:33a-1CO-3:12-1TI-2:9-2TI-2:20(5552)-HEB-9:4a-JAS-2:2(5554)■5:3-1PE-1:7a,18a■3:3a-RE-3:18a■4:4(5552)■9:7,20(5552)■17:4■18:12,16■21:18a,21a

GOLDEN-all=2091,a=1722&marked-GE-24:22-EX-25:25■28:34■30:4■32:2,3■39:20,38■40:26-LE-8:9-NU-4:11■7:26,32,38,44,50,56,62,68,74,80,86-J'G-8:24,26-1SA-6:4,17,18-2KI-10:29-1CH-28:17-2CH-4:19■13:8-EZR-6:5a-ES-4:11■5:2■8:4-EC-12:6-IS-13:12(3800)■14:4(4062)-JER-51:7-DA-3:5a■3:7a,10a,12a,14a,18a■5:2a,3a-ZEC-4:12^2■N.T.-all=5552-HEB-9:4^2-RE-1:12,13,20■2:1■5:8■8:3^2■9:13■14:14■15:6,7■17:4■21:15

GOLDSMITH-all=6884&marked-IS-40:19■41:7■46:6

GOLDSMITH'S-NE-3:31(6885)

GOLDSMITHS-NE-3:8(6884),32(6884)

GONE-all=3318,a=1980,b=5927,c=3212,d=5674,e=3381,f=935&marked-GE-27:30■28:7c■31:30a■34:17a■42:33c■44:4■49:9b-EX-9:29■12:32c■16:14b■19:1■33:8f-NU-5:19(7847),20(7847)■7:89f■13:32d■16:46■21:28-DE-9:9b■13:13■17:3c■23:23(4161)■27:4d■32:36(235)-JOS-2:7■4:23d■23:16a-J'G-3:24■4:12b,14■18:24c■20:3b-RU-1:13,15(7725)-1SA-14:3a,17a■15:12(5437),12e,20c■20:41f■25:37-2SA-2:27b■3:7f,22c,23c,24c■6:13(6805)■13:15c■17:20d,22d■23:9b■24:8(7751)-1KI-1:25e■2:41a■9:16b■11:15b■13:24c■14:9c■18:12c■20:40(369)■21:18e■22:13a-2KI-1:4b,6b,16b■2:9d■5:2■6:15■7:12■20:4,11e-1CH-14:15■17:5(1961)-JOB-1:5(5362)■7:4(4059)■19:10c■23:12(4185)■24:24(369)■28:4(5128)-PS-14:3(5493)■19:4■38:4d,10(369)■42:4d,7d■47:5b■51:tf■53:3(5472)■73:2(5186)■77:8(656)■89:34(4161)■103:16(369)■109:23a■119:176(8582)■124:4d,5d-PR-7:19a■20:14(235)-EC-8:10a-SONG-2:11a■5:6d■6:1a,2e-IS-1:4(2114)■10:29d■15:2b,8(5362)■16:8d■22:1b■24:11(1540)■38:8^{2}e■41:3f■46:2a■51:5■53:6(8582)■57:8-JER-2:23a■3:6a■4:7■5:23c■9:10a■10:20■14:2b■15:6c,9f■23:15,19■29:16■34:21b■40:5(7725)■44:8f,14f,28f■48:11a,15b,15e,32d■50:6a-LA-1:5a,6c,18a-EZE-7:10■9:3b■13:5b■19:14■24:6■31:12e■32:21e,24e,27e,30e■36:20■37:21a-DA-2:5(230),8(230),14(5312)■10:20-HO-8:9b■9:6a-AM-8:5d-JON-1:5e-MIC-2:13-MAL-3:7(5493)■N.T.-all=1831&marked-M'T-10:23(5055)■12:43■14:34(1276)■18:12(4105),12sup■25:8(4570)■26:71-M'R-1:19(4260)■5:30■7:29,30■10:17(1607)-LU-2:15(565)■5:2(576)■8:46■11:14,24■19:7(1525)■24:28(4198)-JOH-4:8(565)■6:22(565)■7:10(305)■12:19(565)■13:31-AC-13:6(1330),42(1826)■16:6(1330),19■18:22(305)■20:2(1330),25(1330)■24:6(3985)■26:31(402)■27:28(1339)-RO-3:12(1578)-1PE-3:22(4198)-2PE-2:15(4105)-1JO-4:1-JUDE-11(4198)

GOOD-all=2896&marked-GE-1:4,10,12,18,21,25,31■2:9^2,12,17,18■3:5,6,22■15:15■18:7■19:8■21:16(7368)■24:50■25:8■26:29■27:9■30:20■31:24,29■32:12(3190)■40:16■41:5,22,24,26^2,35,37(3190)■43:28(7965)■44:4■45:18(2898),20(2898),23(2898)■46:29(5750)■49:15■50:20-EX-3:8■18:17■21:34(7999)■22:11(7999),13(7999),14(7999),15(7999)-LE-5:4(3190)■24:18(7999)■27:10^2,12,14,33-NU-10:29(2895),29■13:19■14:7■23:19(6965)■24:13-DE-1:14,25,35,39■2:4(3966)■3:25■4:15(3966),21,22■6:11(2898),18^2,24■8:7,10,16(3190)■9:6■10:13■11:17■12:28■26:11■28:12,63(3190)■30:5(3190),9^2,15■33:16(7522)-JOS-9:25■21:45■23:11(3966),13,14,15^2,16■24:20(3190)-J'G-8:32■9:11■10:15■17:13(3190)■18:9,22(7368)■19:24-RU-2:22-1SA-1:23■2:24■3:18■11:10■12:23■14:36,40■15:9■19:4^2■20:12■24:4(3190),17,19■25:3,8,15,21,30■26:16■29:6,9-2SA-3:19■4:10(1319)■10:12sup,12■13:22■14:17,32■15:3,26■16:12■17:7,14■18:27■19:18,27,35,37,38■24:22-1KI-1:42■2:38,42■3:9■8:36,56■12:7■14:13,15■21:2■22:8,13^2,18-2KI-3:19^2,25^2■8:9(2898)■10:5■20:3,19,19sup-1CH-4:40■13:2(2895)■16:34■19:13sup,13■21:23■28:8■29:28-2CH-5:13■6:27■7:3■10:7■14:2■18:7,12^2,17■19:3,11■24:16■30:18,22■31:20-EZR-3:11■5:17(2869)■7:9,18(3191)■8:18,22■9:12(2898)-NE-2:8,18^2■5:9,19■6:19■9:13,20,36(2898)■13:14(2617),31-ES-3:11■5:4(2895)■7:9■8:17■9:19,22-JOB-2:10■7:7■9:25■10:3■13:9■15:3(3276)■21:16(2898)■22:18,21■24:21(3190)■30:26■34:4■39:4(2492)-PS-4:6■14:1,3■25:8■34:8,10,12,14■35:12■36:3(3190),4■37:3,27■38:20^2■39:2■45:1■51:18(3190)■52:3,9■53:1,3■54:6■69:16■73:1,28■84:11■85:12■86:5,17■92:1■100:5■103:5■104:28■106:1,5■107:1■109:5,21■111:10■112:5■118:1,29■119:39,66(2898),68,68(2895),71,122■122:9■125:4(2895),4■128:5(2898)■133:1■135:3■136:1■143:10■145:9■147:1-PR-2:9,20■3:4,27■4:2■11:17(1580),23,27■12:2,14,25■13:2,15,21,22■14:14,19,22■15:3,23,30■16:20,29■17:13,20,22(3190)26■18:5,22■19:2,8■20:23■24:13,23,25■25:25,27■28:10,21■31:12,18-EC-2:3,24,26^2■3:12^2,13■4:8,9■5:11(3788),18^2■6:3,6,12■7:11,18,20■9:2^2,18■11:6■12:14-SONG-1:3-IS-1:19(2898)■5:20■7:15,16■38:3■39:8■40:9^2(1319)■41:23(3190),27(1319)■52:7(1319),7■55:2■61:1(1319)■65:2-JER-4:22(3190)■5:25■6:16■8:15■10:5(3190)■13:10(6743),23(3190)■14:11,19■17:6■18:4(3474),10,11(3190)20^2■21:10■24:2,3,5^2,6■26:14■29:10,32■32:39,40(3190),41(2895)42■33:9,11,14■39:16■40:4^2■42:6■44:27-LA-3:25,26,27,38-EZE-17:8■18:18■20:25■24:4■34:14^2,18■36:31-DA-4:2(8232)-HO-4:13■8:3-AM-5:14,15■9:4-MIC-1:12■2:7(3190)■3:2■6:8■7:2(2623)-NA-1:7,15(1319)-ZEP-1:12(3190)-ZEC-1:13■11:12-MAL-2:13(7522),17■N.T.-all=18,a=2570-M'T-3:10a■5:13(2480),16a,44(2573),45■7:11^2,17,17a,18,18a,19a■8:30(3112)■11:26(2107)■12:33a,34,35^2■13:8a,23a,24a,27a,37a,38a,48a■17:4a■19:10(4851),16^2,17■20:15■22:10■25:21,23■26:10,24-M'R-3:4(15)■4:8a,20a■9:5a,50a■10:17,18■14:6a,7(2095),21a-LU-1:53■2:10(2097),14(2107)■3:9a■6:9(15),27(2573),33(15),35(15),38a,43^{2}a,45^2■8:8,15a,15■9:33a■10:42■11:13■14:34a■16:25■18:18,19■19:17■23:50-JOH-1:46■2:10^{2}a■5:29■7:12■10:11a,14a,32a,33a-AC-4:9(2108)■9:36■10:22,38(2109)■11:24■14:17(15)■15:38(515)■18:18(2425)■23:1-RO-2:10■3:8,12(5544)■5:7■7:12,13^2,16a,18,18a,19,21a■8:28■9:11■10:15■11:24(2565)■12:2,9,21■13:3^2,4■14:16,21a■15:2■16:18(5542),19-1CO-5:6a■7:1a,8a,26^{2}a■15:33(5543)-2CO-5:10■6:8(2162)■9:8-GA-4:18^{2}a■6:6,10-EPH-2:10■4:28,29■6:7(2133),8-PH'P-1:6,15(2107)■4:8(2163)-COL-1:10-1TH-3:1(2106),6(2097),6■5:15,21a-2TH-2:16,17-1TI-1:5,8a,18a,19■2:3a,10■3:1a,7a,13a■4:4a,6^{2}a■5:4a,10a,10,25a■6:12^{2}a,13a,18(14),18a,19a-2TI-1:14a■2:3a,21■3:3(865),17■4:7a-TIT-1:8(5358),16■2:3(2567),5,7a,10,14a■3:1,8^{2}a,14a-PH'M-6-HEB-5:14a■6:5a■9:11■10:1,24a■13:9a,16(2140),18a,21-JAS-1:17■2:3(2573)■3:13a,17■4:17a-1PE-2:12a,18■3:10,11,13,16^2,21■4:10a-1JO-3:17(979)-3JO-11,11(15)

GOODLIER-1SA-9:2(2896)

GOODLIEST-1SA-8:16(2896)-1KI-20:3(2896)

GOODLINESS-IS-40:6(2617)

GOODLY-all=2896&marked-GE-27:15(2530)■39:6(3303,8389)■49:21(8233)-EX-2:2■39:28(6287)-LE-23:40(1926)-NU-24:5-DE-3:25■6:10■8:12-JOS-7:21-1SA-9:2■16:12-2SA-23:21(4758)-1KI-1:6-2CH-36:10(2532),19(4261)-JOB-39:13(7443)-PS-16:6(8231)■80:10(410)-JER-3:19(6643)■11:16(3303,8389)-EZE-17:8(155),23(117)-HO-10:1-JOE-3:5-ZEC-10:3(1935)■11:13(145)■N.T.-M'T-13:45(2573)-LU-21:5(2573)-JAS-2:2(2986)-RE-18:14(2986)

GOODMAN-PR-7:19(376)■N.T.-all=3611-M'T-20:11■24:43-M'R-14:14-LU-12:39■22:11

GOODNESS-all=2896,a=2617,b=2898&marked-EX-18:9■33:19b■34:6a-NU-10:32-J'G-8:35-2SA-7:28-1KI-8:66-1CH-17:26-2CH-6:41■7:10■32:32a■35:26a-NE-9:25b,35b-PS-16:2■21:3■23:6■27:13b■31:19b■33:5a■52:1a■65:4b,11■68:10■107:8a,9,15a,21a,31a■144:2a■145:7b-PR-20:6a-IS-63:7b-JER-2:7b■31:12b,14b■33:9-HO-3:5b■6:4a■10:1-ZEC-9:17b■N.T.-all=19&marked-RO-2:4(5544),4(5543)■11:22^3■15:14-GA-5:22-EPH-5:9-2TH-1:11

GOODNESS'-PS-25:7(2898)

GOODS-all=7399&marked-GE-14:11,12,16^2,21■24:10(2898)■31:18■

46:6-EX-22:8(4399),11-NU-16:32■31:9(2428)■35:3-DE-28:11(2896)-2CH-21:14-EZR-1:4,6■6:8(5232)■7:26(5232)-NE-9:25(2898)-JOB-20:10(202),21(2898)-EC-5:11(2896)-EZE-38:12(7075),13(7075)-ZEP-1:13(2428)■N.T.-all=5224&marked-M'T-12:29(4632)■24:47■25:14-M'R-3:27(4632)-LU-6:30(4674)■11:21■12:18(18),19(18)■15:12(3776)■16:1■19:8-AC-2:45(5223)-1CO-13:3-HEB-10:34-RE-3:17(4147)

GOPHER-GE-6:14(1613)

GORE-EX-21:28(5055)

GORED-EX-21:31^{2}(5055)

GORGEOUS-LU-23:11(2986)

GORGEOUSLY-EZE-23:12(4358)■N.T.-LU-7:25(1741)

GOSPEL-all=2098,a=2097&marked-M'T-1:t■4:23■9:35■11:5a■24:14■26:13-M'R-1:t■1:1,14,15■13:10■14:9■16:15-LU-1:t■4:18a■7:22a■9:6a■20:1a-JOH-1:t-AC-8:25a■14:7a,21a■15:7■16:10a■20:24-RO-1:1,9,15a,16■2:16■10:15a,16■11:28■15:16,19,20a,29■16:25-1CO-1:17a■4:15■9:12,14^{2},16^{2}a,18a,18^{2}■15:1-2CO-2:12■4:3,4■8:18■9:13■10:14,16a■11:4,7-GA-1:6,7,8a,9a,11■2:2,5,7,7sup,14■3:8(4283)■4:13a-EPH-1:13■3:6■6:15,19-PH'P-1:5,7,12,17,27^{2}■2:22■4:3,15-COL-1:5,23-1TH-1:5■2:2,4,8,9■3:2-2TH-1:8■2:14-1TI-1:11-2TI-1:8,10■2:8-PH'M-13-HEB-4:2a-1PE-1:12a,25a■4:6a,17-RE-14:6

GOSPEL'S-all=2098-M'R-8:35■10:29-1CO-9:23

GOT-all=7069&marked-GE-36:6(7408)■39:12(3318),15(3318)-PS-44:3(3423)-EC-2:7-JER-13:2,4

GOTTEN-all=6213&marked-GE-4:1(7069)■12:5■31:1,18^{2}(7408)■46:6(7408)-NU-31:50(4672)-DE-8:17-2SA-17:13(622)-JOB-28:15(5414)■31:25(4672)-EC-1:16(3254)-IS-15:7-JER-48:36-EZE-28:4^{2}■38:12-DA-9:15-■N.T.-AC-21:1(645)

GOURD-all=7021-JON-4:6^{2},7,9,10

GOURDS-2KI-4:39(6498)

GOVERN-1KI-21:7(6213)-JOB-34:17(2280)-PS-67:4(5148)

GOVERNMENT-IS-9:6(4951),7(4951)■22:21(4475)■N.T.-2PE-2:10(2963)

GOVERNMENTS-1CO-12:28(2941)

GOVERNOR-all=6346&marked-GE-42:6(7989)■45:26(4910)-1KI-18:3(5921)■22:26(8269)-2KI-23:8(8269)■25:23(6485)-1CH-29:22(5057)-2CH-1:2(5387)■18:25(8269)■28:7(5057)■34:8(8269)-EZR-5:3(6347),6(6347),14(6347)■6:6(6347),7(6347),13(6347)-NE-3:7■5:14^{2},18■12:26-PS-2:28(4910)-JER-20:1(5057)■30:21(4910)■40:5(6485),7(6485)■41:2(6485),18(6485)-HAG-1:1,14■2:2,21-ZEC-9:7(441)-MAL-1:8■N.T.-all=2232&marked-M'T-2:6(2233)■27:2,11^{2},14,15,21,23,27-LU-2:2(2230)■3:1(2230)■20:20(2230)-JOH-2:8(755),9(755)-AC-7:10(2233)■23:24,26,33,34■24:1,10■26:30-2CO-11:32(1481)-JAS-3:4(2116)

GOVERNOR'S-M'T-28:14(2232)

GOVERNORS-all=6346&marked-J'G-5:9(2710),14(2710)-1KI-10:15-1CH-24:5(8269)-2CH-9:14■23:20(4910)-EZR-8:36-NE-2:7,9■5:15-ES-3:12-DA-2:48(5461)■3:2(5461),3(5461),27(5461)■6:7(5461)-ZEC-12:5(441),6(441)■N.T.-M'T-10:18(2232)-GAL-4:2(3623)-1PE-2:14(2232)

GRACE-all=2580&marked-GE-6:8■19:19■32:5■33:8,10,15■34:11■39:4■47:25,29■50:4-EX-33:12,13^{2},16,17■34:9-NU-32:5-J'G-6:17-RU-2:2,10-1SA-1:18■20:3■27:5-2SA-14:22■16:4-EZR-9:8(8467)-ES-2:17-PS-45:2■84:11-PR-1:9■3:22,34■4:9■22:11-JER-31:2-ZEC-4:7■12:10■N.T.-all=5485&marked-LU-2:40-JOH-1:14,16,17-AC-4:33■11:23■13:43■14:3,26■15:11,40■18:27■20:24,32-RO-1:5,7■3:24■4:4,16■5:2,15:17,20,21■6:1,14,15■11:5,6^{3}■12:3,6■15:15■16:20,24-1CO-1:3,4■3:10■10:30■15:10^{3}■16:23-2CO-1:2,12■4:15■6:1■8:1,6,7,9,19■9:8,14■12:9■13:14-GA-1:3,6,15■2:9,21■5:4■6:18-EPH-1:2,6,7■2:5,7,8■3:2,7,8■4:7,29■6:24-PH'P-1:2,7■4:23-COL-1:2,6■3:16■4:6,18-1TH-1:1■5:28-2TH-1:2,12■2:16■3:18-1TI-1:2,14■6:21-2TI-1:2,9■2:1■4:22-TIT-1:4■2:11■3:7,15-PH'M-3,25-HEB-2:9■4:16^{2}■10:29■12:15,28■13:9,25-JAS-1:11(2143)■4:6^{2}-1PE-1:2,10,13■3:7■4:10■5:5,10,12-2PE-1:2■3:18-2JO-3-JUDE-4-RE-1:4■22:21

GRACIOUS-all=2587,a=2603&marked-GE-43:29a-EX-22:27■33:19a■34:6-NU-6:25a-2SA-12:22a-2KI-13:23a-2CH-30:9-NE-9:17,31-JOB-33:24a-PS-77:9(2589)■86:15■103:8■111:4■112:4■116:5■145:8-PR-11:16(2580)-EC-10:12(2580)-IS-30:18a,19a■33:2a-JER-22:23a-JOE-2:13-AM-5:15-JON-4:2-MAL-1:9a■N.T.-LU-4:22(5485)-1PE-2:3(5543)

GRACIOUSLY-all=2603&marked-GE-33:5,11-PS-119:29-HO-14:2(2896)

GRAFF-RO-11:23(1461)

GRAFFED-all=1461-RO-11:17,19,23,24^{2}

GRAIN-AM-9:9(6872)■N.T.-all=2848-M'T-13:31■17:20-M'R-4:31-LU-13:19■17:6-1CO-15:37

GRANDMOTHER-2TI-1:5(3125)

GRANT-all=5414&marked-LE-25:24-RU-1:9-1SA-1:17-1CH-21:22^{2}-2CH-12:7-EZR-3:7(7558)-NE-1:11-ES-5:8-JOB-6:8-PS-20:4■85:7■140:8■N.T.-all=1325&marked-M'T-20:21(2036)-M'R-10:37-LU-1:74-AC-4:29-RO-15:5-EPH-3:16-2TI-1:18-RE-3:21

GRANTED-all=5414&marked-1CH-4:10(935)-2CH-1:12-EZR-7:6-NE-2:8-ES-5:6■7:2■8:11■9:12,13-JOB-10:12(6213)-PR-10:24■N.T.-all=1325&marked-AC-3:14(5483)■11:18■14:3-RE-19:8

GRAPE-all=1155&marked-LE-19:10(6528)-DE-32:14(6025)-JOB-15:33(1154)-SONG-2:13(5563)■7:12(5563)-IS-18:5-JER-31:29,30

GRAPEGATHERER-JER-6:9(1219)

GRAPEGATHERERS-JER-49:9(1219)-OB-5(1219)

GRAPEGLEANINGS-MIC-7:1(5955)

GRAPES-all=6025&marked-GE-40:10,11■49:11-LE-25:5-NU-6:3^{2}■13:20,23-DE-23:24■32:32-NE-13:15-SONG-2:15(5563)-IS-5:2■5:2(891),4,4(891)-JER-8:13-EZE-18:2(1154)-HO-9:10-AM-9:13■N.T.-all=4718-M'T-7:16-LU-6:44-RE-14:18

GRASS-all=2682,a=6212&marked-GE-1:11(1877),12(1877)-NU-22:4(3418)-DE-11:15a■29:23a■32:2a-2SA-23:4(1877)-1KI-18:5-2KI-19:26a,26-JOB-5:25a■6:5(1877)■40:15-PS-37:2■72:16a■90:5■92:7a■102:4a,11a■103:15■104:14■106:20a■129:6■147:8-PR-19:12a■27:25(1877)-IS-15:6(1877)■35:7■37:27a,27■40:6,7^{2},8■44:4■51:12-JER-14:5(1758),6a■50:11(1877)-DA-4:15(1883),15(6211),23(1883),25(6211),32(6211),33(6211)■5:21(6211)-AM-7:2a-MIC-5:7a-ZEC-10:1a■N.T.-all=5528-M'T-6:30■14:19-M'R-6:39-LU-12:28-JOH-6:10-JAS-1:10,11-1PE-1:24^{3}-RE-8:7■9:4

GRASSHOPPER-LE-11:22(2284)-JOB-39:20(697)-EC-12:5(2284)

GRASSHOPPERS-all=697&marked-NU-13:33(2284)-J'G-6:5■7:12-IS-40:22(2284)-JER-46:23-AM-7:1(1462)-NA-3:17(1462)

GRATE-all=4345-EX-27:4■35:16■38:4,5,30■39:39

GRAVE-all=7585,a=6913&marked-GE-35:20^{2}(6900)■37:35■42:38■44:29,31■50:5a-EX-28:9(6605),36(6605)-NU-19:16a,18a-1SA-2:6-2SA-3:32a■19:37a-1KI-2:6,9■13:30a■14:13a-2KI-22:20a-2CH-2:7(6603),14(6605)■34:28a-JOB-3:22a■5:26a■7:9■10:19a■14:13■17:13■21:13,32a■24:19■30:24(1164)■33:22(7845)-PS-6:5■30:3■31:17■49:14^{2},15■88:3,5a,11a■89:48-PR-1:12■30:16-EC-9:10-SONG-8:6-IS-14:11,19a■38:10,18■53:9a-JER-20:17a-EZE-31:15■32:23(6900),24(6900)-HO-13:14^{2}-NA-1:14a■N.T.-all=3419&marked-JOH-11:17,31,38■12:17-1CO-15:55(86)-1TI-3:8(4586),11(4586)-TIT-2:2(4586)

GRAVECLOTHES-JOH-11:44(2750)

GRAVED-1KI-7:36(6605)-2CH-3:7(6605)

GRAVEL-PR-20:17(2687)-IS-48:19(4579)-LA-3:16(2687)

GRAVEN-all=6459,a=6456&marked-EX-20:4■32:16(2801)■39:6(6605)-LE-26:1-DE-4:16,23,25■5:8■7:5a,25a■12:3a■27:15-J'G-17:3,4■18:14,17,20,30,31-2KI-17:41a■21:7-2CH-33:19a■34:7a-JOB-19:24(2672)-PS-78:58a■97:7-IS-10:10a■21:9a■30:22a■40:19,20■42:8,17■44:9,10,15,17■45:20■48:5■49:16(2710)-JER-8:19a■10:14■17:1(2790)■50:38a■51:17,47a,52a-HO-11:2a-MIC-1:7a■5:13a-NA-1:14-HAB-2:18,18(6458)■N.T.-AC-17:29(5480)

GRAVE'S-PS-141:7(7585)

GRAVES-all=6913-EX-14:11-2KI-23:6-2CH-34:4-JOB-17:1-IS-65:4-JER-8:1■26:23-EZE-32:22,23,25,26■37:12^{2},13^{2}■39:11■N.T.-all=3419&marked-M'T-27:52,53-LU-11:44-JOH-5:28-RE-11:9(3418)

GRAVETH-IS-22:16(2710)

GRAVING-EX-32:4(2747)-2CH-2:14(6603)-ZEC-3:9(6603)

GRAVINGS-1KI-7:31(4734)

GRAVITY-1TI-3:4(4587)-TIT-2:7(4587)

GRAY-all=7872-GE-42:38■44:29,31-DE-32:25-PR-20:29-HO-7:9

GRAYHEADED-1SA-12:2(7867)-JOB-15:10(7867)-PS-71:18(7872)

GREASE-PS-119:70(2459)

GREAT-all=1419,a=7227,b=1431&marked-GE-1:16,21■6:5a■7:11a■10:12■12:2,2b,17■13:6a■15:1(7235),12,14,18■17:20■18:18,20a■19:11,13b■20:9■21:8,18■24:35b■26:13^{2}b,14a■27:34■29:2■30:8(430)■39:9■41:29■45:7■46:3■48:19b■50:9(3515),10-EX-3:3■6:6■7:4■11:3,6,8(2750)■12:30■14:31■18:22■32:10,11,21,30,31-LE-11:17(3244)-NU-11:33a■13:28■14:17b,18a■23:24(3833)■24:9(3833)■32:1(6099)■34:6,7-DE-1:7,17,19,28■2:7,10,21■3:5(3966)■4:6,7,8,32,34,36■5:22,25■6:10,22■7:19■8:15■9:1,2■10:17,21■11:7■14:16(3244)■18:16■25:13,14■26:5,8■27:2■28:59■29:3^{2},24,28■34:12-JOS-1:4^{2}■6:5,20■7:9,26■8:29■9:1■10:2,10,11,18,20,27■11:8a■14:12,15■15:12,47■17:14a,15a17a,17■19:28a■22:10■23:4,9■24:17,26-J'G-2:7■5:15,16■11:33■12:2(3966)■15:8,18■16:5,6,15,23■20:38(7235)■21:5-1SA-2:17■4:5,6,10,17■5:9^{2}■6:9,14,15,18,19■7:10■12:16,17a,22,24b■14:15(430),20,33,45■17:25■19:5,8,22■20:2■23:5■25:2■26:13a■30:2,16,19-2SA-3:22a,38■5:10■7:9^{2},19(7350),21(1420),22b,23(1420)■12:14(5006),30(3966)■18:7,9,17^{2},29■19:32■20:8■22:36(7235)■23:10,12■24:14(3966),14a-1KI-1:40■3:4,6^{2},8a,9(3515)■4:13■5:7a,17■7:9,10,12■8:42,65■10:2(3515),10(7235),11(3966),18■11:19(3966)■18:32(1004),45■19:7a,11■20:13,21,28■22:31-2KI-3:27■4:8,38■5:1,13■6:14(3515),23,25■7:6■8:4,13■10:6,11,19■16:15■17:21,36■18:17(3515),19,28■22:13■23:2,26■25:9,26-1CH-11:14■12:22■16:25■17:8,17(7350),19(1420)■21:13(3966),13a■22:8■

25:8▪26:13▪29:1,9,12b,22-**2CH**-1:8,10▪2:5^{2},9▪4:9,18(3966)▪6:32▪7:8▪9:1(3515), 9(3966),17▪13:8a,17a▪15:5a,13▪16:14▪17:12(1432)▪18:30▪20:2a,12a,15a▪21:3a,14,15a▪24:24(7230),25a▪25:10 (2750)▪26:15▪28:5^{2},13a▪30:13(7230), 21,24(7230),26▪31:15▪34:21,30▪36:18 -**EZR**-3:11▪4:10(7229)▪5:8(7229),8 (1560),11(7229)▪6:4(1560)▪9:7,13▪10:1a-**NE**-1:3,5,10▪3:27▪4:1(7235),14,19 (7235)▪5:1,7▪6:3▪7:4▪8:6,12,17▪9:17a, 18,25,26,31a,32,35a,37▪11:14▪12:31,43^{2}▪13:5,27-**ES**-1:5,20a,20▪2:18▪4:3▪8:15▪9:4▪10:3-**JOB**-1:3a,19▪2:13b▪3:19▪5:9, 25a▪9:10▪22:5a▪23:6a▪30:18a▪31:25a, 34a▪32:9a▪35:15(3966)▪36:18a,26 (7689)▪37:5,6(4306)▪38:21a▪39:11a -**PS**-14:5(6343)▪18:35(7235),50b▪19:11a, 13a▪21:5▪22:25a▪25:11a▪31:19a▪32:6a▪33:17(7230)▪35:18a▪36:6(410),6a▪40:9a,10a▪47:2▪48:1,2a▪57:10▪58:6 (4459)▪68:11a▪71:19,20(7229)▪76:1▪77:13,19a▪78:15a▪80:5(7991)▪86:10, 13▪92:5b▪95:3▪96:4▪99:2,3▪103:11 (1396)▪104:1b,25^{2}▪106:21▪107:23a▪108:4▪111:2▪115:13▪117:2(1396)▪119:156a,162a,165a▪126:2b,3b▪131:1▪135:5,10a▪136:4,7,17▪138:5▪139:17 (6105)▪144:7a▪145:3,7a,8▪147:5,5a-**PR**-13:7a▪14:29a▪15:16a▪16:8(7230)▪18:9 (1167),16▪22:1a▪25:6▪26:10a▪28:12a,16a -**EC**-1:16b,16(7235)▪2:4b,7(7235),7 (1241),9b,21a▪8:6a▪9:13,14^{2}▪10:4,6a -**IS**-5:9▪6:12a▪8:1▪9:2▪12:6▪13:4a▪16:14a▪19:20a▪23:3a▪27:1,13▪29:6▪30:25a▪32:2(3515)▪33:23(4766)▪34:6, 15(7091)▪36:2(3515),4,13▪47:9(3966)▪51:10a▪53:12a▪54:7,13a▪63:7a-**JER**-4:6▪5:5,27b▪6:1,22▪10:6,22▪11:16▪13:9a▪14:17▪16:6,10▪20:17(2030)▪21:5,6▪22:8▪25:14,32▪26:19▪27:5,7▪28:8▪30:7▪31:8▪32:17,18,19,21,37,42▪33:3▪36:7▪41:12a▪43:9▪44:7,15,26▪45:5▪48:3▪50:9,22,41▪51:54,55,55a▪52:13-**LA**-1:1a,3(7230)▪2:13▪3:23a-**EZE**-1:4,24a▪3:12,13▪8:6▪9:9▪13:11(417),13(417)▪16:7b,26(1432)▪17:3^{2},5a,7^{2},8a,9,17a▪21:14▪23:23(7991)▪24:9b,12a▪25:17▪26:10a▪27:26a▪28:5(7230)▪29:3,18▪30:16(2342)▪31:4b,6a,7a,15a▪32:13a▪36:23▪37:10▪38:4a,13,15,19,22(417)▪39:17▪41:8(679)▪47:9a,10,15,19,20▪48:28-**DA**-2:6(7690),31(7690),31(7229), 35(7229),45(7229),48(7236),48(7260)▪4:3(7260),10(7690),30a▪5:1a▪7:2a,3(7260), 7(7260),8(7260),11(7260),17(7260),20 (7260)▪8:4b,8b,8,9b,10b,21▪9:4,12,18a▪10:4,7,8▪11:3a,5a,10a,11a,13,25^{2},28,44▪12:1-**HO**-1:11▪8:12(7239)▪9:7a▪10:15 (7451)▪13:5(8514)-**JOE**-1:6(3833)▪2:2a, 11a,11,13a,20b,21b,25,31▪3:13a-**AM**-3:9a,15a▪6:2a,11▪7:4a▪8:5b-**JON**-1:2, 4,12,17▪3:2,3▪4:2a,11-**MIC**-5:4b▪7:3 -**NA**-1:3b▪3:3(3514),10,17(1462)-**HAB**-3:15a-**ZEP**-1:10,14-**ZEC**-1:14▪4:7▪7:12▪8:2^{2}▪12:11b▪14:4,13a,14(3966)-**MAL**-1:11^{2},14▪4:5▪**N.T.**-all=3173,a=4183 &marked-**M'T**-2:10,18a▪4:16,25a▪5:12a,19,35▪6:23(4214)▪7:27▪8:1a,10 (5118),18a,24,26▪12:15a▪13:2a,46(4186)▪14:14a▪15:28,30a,33(5118)▪19:2a,22a▪20:25(3171),26,29a▪21:8(4118)▪22:36, 38▪24:21,24,30a,31▪26:47a▪27:60▪28:2, 8-**M'R**-1:35(3029)▪3:7a,8a,8(3745)▪4:1a, 32,37,39▪5:11,19(3745),20(3745),42▪7:36(3123)▪8:1(3827)▪9:14a▪10:22a,42, 43,46(2425),48a▪13:2,26a▪14:43a▪16:4 -**LU**-1:15,32,49(3167),58(3170)▪2:10,36a▪4:25,38▪5:6a,15a,29,29a▪6:17a,23a,35a, 49▪7:9(5118),16▪8:37,39^{2}(3745)▪9:48▪10:2a,13(3819)▪13:19▪14:16,25a▪15:20 (3112)▪16:26▪21:11^{2},23,27a▪23:27a▪24:52-**JOH**-5:3a▪6:2a,5a,18▪7:37▪21:11 -**AC**-2:20▪4:33^{2}▪5:5,11▪6:7a,8▪7:11▪8:1, 2,8,9,10▪9:16(3745)▪10:11▪11:5,21a,28▪14:1a▪15:3▪16:26▪17:4a▪19:27,28,34,35▪21:40a▪22:6(2425),28a▪23:9,10a▪24:2a, 7a▪25:23a▪26:22▪28:6a,29a-**RO**-9:2▪15:23(1974)-**1CO**-9:11▪16:9-**2CO**-1:10 (5082)▪3:12a▪7:4^{2}a▪8:2a,22a▪11:15 -**EPH**-2:4a▪5:32-**COL**-2:1(2245)▪4:13a -**1TH**-2:17a-**1TI**-3:13a,16▪6:6-**2TI**-2:20 -**TIT**-2:13-**PH'M**-7a-**HEB**-2:3(5082)▪4:14▪7:4(4080)▪10:32a,35▪12:1(5118)▪13:20-**JAS**-3:4(5082),5(3166),5(2245) -**1PE**-3:4(4185)-**2PE**-1:4(3176)▪2:18 (5246)-**JUDE**-6,16(5246)-**RE**-1:10▪2:22▪6:4,12,15(3175),17▪7:9a,14▪8:8,10▪9:2, 14▪11:8,11,12,13,15,17,18,19▪12:1,3,9, 12,14▪13:2,5,13,16▪14:2,8,19▪15:1,3▪16:1,9,12,14,17,18^{2},19^{2},21^{2}▪17:1,5,6,18▪18:1,2,10,16,17(5118),18,19,21^{2},23(3175)▪19:1,2,5,6a,17,18▪20:1,11,12▪21:3,10^{2},12

GREATER-all=1419&marked -**GE**-1:16▪4:13▪39:9▪41:40(1431)▪48:19 (1431)-**EX**-18:11-**NU**-14:12-**DE**-1:28▪4:38▪7:1(7227)▪9:1,14(7227)▪11:23 -**JOS**-10:2-**1SA**-14:30(7235)-**2SA**-13:15, 16-**1CH**-11:9(1980),9-**2CH**-3:5-**ES**-9:4 -**JOB**-33:12(7235)-**LA**-4:6(1431)-**EZE**-8:6,13,15▪43:14-**DA**-11:13(7227)-**AM**-6:2(7227)-**HAG**-2:9▪**N.T.**-all=3187 &marked-**M'T**-11:11^{2}▪12:6,41(4119),42 (4119)▪23:14(4055),17,19-**M'R**-4:32▪12:31,40(4055)-**LU**-7:28^{2}▪11:31(4119) 32(4119)▪12:18▪20:47(4055)▪22:27 -**JOH**-1:50▪4:12▪5:20,36▪8:53▪10:29▪13:16^{2}▪14:12,28▪15:13,20▪19:11-**AC**-15:28(4119)-**1CO**-14:5▪15:6(4119) -**HEB**-6:13,16▪9:11▪11:26-**JAS**-3:1-**2PE**-2:11-**1JO**-3:20▪4:4▪5:9-**3JO**-4(3186)

GREATEST-all=1419&marked -**1CH**-12:14,29(4768)-**JOB**-1:3-**JER**-6:13▪8:10▪31:34▪42:1,8▪44:12-**JON**-3:5▪**N.T.**-all=3187&marked-**M'T**-13:32▪18:1,4▪23:11-**M'R**-9:34-**LU**-9:46▪22:24,26-**AC**-8:10(3173)-**1CO**-13:13-**HEB**-8:11(3173)

GREATLY-all=3966&marked-**GE**-7:18▪19:3▪24:35▪32:7-**EX**-19:18-**NU**-11:10▪14:39-**DE**-17:17-**JOS**-10:2-**J'G**-2:15▪6:6-**1SA**-11:6,15▪12:18▪16:21▪17:11▪28:5▪30:6-**2SA**-10:5▪12:5▪24:10 -**1KI**-2:12▪5:7▪18:3-**1CH**-4:38(7230)▪16:25▪19:5▪21:8-**2CH**-25:10▪33:12 -**JOB**-8:7-**PS**-21:1▪38:6▪47:9▪48:1▪62:2(7227)▪65:9(7227)▪78:59▪89:7 (7227)▪96:4▪105:24▪107:38▪109:30▪112:1▪116:10▪119:51▪145:3-**PR**-23:24 -**JER**-9:19▪20:11-**EZE**-20:13-**DA**-5:9 -**OB**-2-**ZEP**-1:14-**ZEC**-9:9▪**N.T.**-all=3029&marked-**M'T**-27:14,54(4970) -**M'R**-5:23(4183),38(4183)▪9:15(1568)▪12:27(4183)-**JOH**-3:29(5479)-**AC**-3:11 (1569)▪6:7(4970)-**1CO**-16:12(4183) -**PH'P**-1:8(1971)▪4:10(3171)-**1TH**-3:6(1971)-**2TI**-1:4(1971)▪4:15-**2JO**-4-**3JO**-3

GREATNESS-all=1433&marked -**EX**-15:7(7230),16(1419)-**NU**-14:19 -**DE**-3:24▪5:24▪9:26▪11:2▪32:3-**1CH**-17:19(1420),21(1420)▪29:11(1420) -**2CH**-9:6(4768)▪24:27(7230)-**NE**-13:22 (7230)-**ES**-10:2(1420)-**PS**-66:3(7230)▪71:21(1420)▪79:11▪145:3(1420),6(1420)▪150:2-**PR**-5:23(7230)-**IS**-40:26(7230)▪57:10(7230)▪63:1(7230)-**JER**-13:22 (7230)-**JER**-13:22(7230)-**EZE**-31:2,7, 18-**DA**-4:22(7238)▪7:27(7238)-**EPH**-1:19(3174)

GREAVES-**1SA**-17:6(4697)

GREEDILY-**PR**-21:36(8378)▪**N.T.**-**JUDE**-11(1632)

GREEDINESS-**EPH**-4:19(4124)

GREEDY-**PS**-17:12(3700)-**PR**-1:19 (1214)▪15:27(1214)-**IS**-56:11(5794, 5315)▪**N.T.**-**1TI**-3:3(866),8(146)

GREEN-all=7488&marked-**GE**-1:30(3418)▪9:3(3418)▪30:37(3892) -**EX**-10:15(3418)-**DE**-12:2-**J'G**-16:7 (3892),8(3892)-**1KI**-14:23-**2KI**-16:4▪17:10▪19:26(3419)-**2CH**-28:4-**ES**-1:6 (3768)-**JOB**-8:16(7373)▪15:32▪39:8 (3387)-**PS**-23:2(1877)▪37:2(3418),35▪52:8-**SONG**-1:16▪2:13(6291)-**IS**-15:6 (3418)▪37:27(3419)▪57:5-**JER**-2:20▪3:6,13▪11:16▪17:2,8-**EZE**-6:13▪17:24 (3892)▪20:47(3892)-**HO**-14:8▪**N.T.**-all=5515&marked-**M'R**-6:39-**LU**-23:31 (5200)-**RE**-8:7▪9:4

GREENISH-**LE**-13:49(3422)▪14:37(3422)

GREENESS-**JOB**-8:12(3)

GREET-**1SA**-25:5(7592,7965)▪**N.T.**-all=782-**RO**-16:3,6,8,11-**1CO**-16:20-**2CO**-13:12-**PH'P**-4:21-**COL**-4:14-**1TI**-5:26 -**TIT**-3:15-**1PE**-5:14-**2JO**-13-**3JO**-14

GREETETH-**2TI**-4:21(782)

GREETING-all=5463-**AC**-15:23▪23:36-**JAS**-1:1

GREETINGS-all=783-**M'T**-23:7 -**LU**-11:43▪20:46

GREW-all=1431&marked-**GE**-2:5 (6779)▪19:25(6780)▪21:8,20▪25:27▪26:13(1432)▪47:27(6509)-**EX**-1:12(6555)▪2:10-**J'G**-11:2▪13:24-**1SA**-2:21,26(1432)▪3:19-**2SA**-12:3-**EZE**-17:6(6779),10 (6780)-**DA**-4:11(7236),20(7236)▪**N.T.**-all=837&marked-**M'R**-4:7(305)▪5:26 (2064)-**LU**-1:80▪2:40▪13:19-**AC**-7:17▪12:24▪19:20

GREY-**PR**-20:29(7872)

GREYHEADED-**PS**-71:18(7872)

GREYHOUND-**PR**-30:31(2223,4975)

GRIEF-all=3708&marked-**GE**-26:35(4786)-**1SA**-1:16▪25:31(6330) -**2CH**-6:29(4341)-**JOB**-2:13(3511)▪6:2▪16:6(3511)-**PS**-6:7▪31:9,10(3015)▪69:26(4341)-**PR**-17:25-**EC**-1:18▪2:23 -**IS**-17:11(2470)▪53:3(2483),10(2470) -**JER**-6:7(2483)▪10:19(2483)▪45:3(3015) -**LA**-3:32(3013)-**JON**-4:6(7451)▪**N.T.** -**2CO**-2:5(3076)-**HEB**-13:17(4727) -**1PE**-2:19(3077)

GRIEFS-**IS**-53:4(2483)

GRIEVANCE-**HAB**-1:3(5999)

GRIEVE-**1SA**-2:33(109)-**1CH**-4:10 (6087)-**PS**-78:40(6087)-**LA**-3:33(3013)▪**N.T.**-**EPH**-4:30(3076)

GRIEVED-all=6087&marked -**GE**-6:6▪34:7▪45:5▪49:23(4843)-**EX**-1:12(6973)-**DE**-15:10(7489)-**J'G**-10:16 (7114)-**1SA**-1:8(7489)▪15:11(2734)▪20:3,34▪30:6(4784)-**2SA**-19:2-**NE**-2:10 (7489)▪8:11▪13:8(7489)-**ES**-4:4(2342) -**JOB**-4:2(3811)▪30:25(5701)-**PS**-73:21 (2556)▪95:10(6962)▪112:10(3707)▪119:158(6962)▪139:21(6962)-**IS**-54:6▪57:10(2470)-**JER**-5:3(2342)-**DA**-7:15 (3735)▪11:30(3512)-**AM**-6:6(2470)▪**N.T.**-all=3076&marked-**M'R**-3:5 (4818)▪10:22-**JOH**-21:17-**AC**-4:2(1278)▪16:18(1278)-**RO**-14:15-**2CO**-2:4,5 -**HEB**-3:10(4360),17(4360)

GRIEVETH-**RU**-1:13(4843)-**PR**-26:15(3811)

GRIEVING-**EZE**-28:24(3510)

GRIEVOUS-all=3515&marked-**GE**-12:10▪18:20(3513)▪21:11(7489),12(7489)▪41:31▪50:11-**EX**-8:24▪9:3,18,24▪10:14 -**1KI**-2:8(4834)▪12:4(7185),4(7186)-**2CH**-10:4(7185),4(7186)-**PS**-10:5(2342)▪31:18(6277)-**PR**-15:1(6089),10(7451) -**EC**-2:17(7451)-**IS**-15:4(3415)▪21:2 (7186)-**JER**-6:28(5493)▪10:19(2470)▪14:17 (2470)▪16:4(8463)▪23:19(2342)▪30:12 (2470)-**NA**-3:19(2470)▪**N.T.**-all=926& marked-**M'T**-23:4(1418)-**LU**-11:46(1418) -**AC**-20:29▪25:7-**PH'P**-3:1(3636)-**HEB**-12:11(3077)-**1JO**-5:3-**RE**-16:2(4190)

GRIEVOUSLY-**IS**-9:1(3513)-**JER**-23:19(2342)-**LA**-1:8(2399),20(4784) -**EZE**-14:13(4604)▪**N.T.**-**M'T**-8:6 (1171)▪15:22(2560)

GRIEVOUSNESS-**IS**-10:1(5999)▪21:15(3514)

GRIND-all=2912&marked-**J'G**-16:21-**JOB**-31:10-**IS**-3:15▪47:2-**LA**-5:13(2911)▪**N.T.**-**M'T**-21:44(3039) -**LU**-20:18(3039)

GRINDERS-**EC**-12:3(2912)

GRINDING-**EC**-12:4(1913)▪**N.T.** -**M'T**-24:41(229)-**LU**-17:35(229)

GRISLED-all=1261-**GE**-31:10,12

-ZEC-6:3,6

GROAN-JOB-24:12(5008)-JER-51:52(602)-EZE-30:24(5008)-JOE-1:18(584)■N.T.-all=4727-RO-8:23-2CO-5:2,4

GROANED-JOH-11:33(1690)

GROANETH-RO-8:22(4959)

GROANING-all=585&marked-EX-2:24(5009)■6:5(5009)-JOB-23:2-PS-6:6■38:9■102:5,20(603)■N.T.-JOH-11:38(1690)-AC-7:34(4726)

GROANINGS-J'G-2:18(5009)-EZE-30:24(5009)■N.T.-RO-8:26(4726)

GROPE-all=4959&marked-DE-28:29-JOB-5:14■12:25-IS-59:10^{2}(1659)

GROPETH-DE-28:29(4959)

GROSS-IS-60:2(6205)-JER-13:16(6205)■N.T.-M'T-13:15(3975)-AC-28:27(3975)

GROUND-all=776,a=127&marked-GE-2:5a,6a,7a,9a,19a■3:17a,19a,23a■4:2a,3a,10a,12a■5:29a■7:23a■8:8a,13a,21a■18:2■19:1,25a■33:3■38:9■44:11,14-EX-3:5a■4:3^{2}■8:21a■9:23■16:14■32:20(2912)-LE-20:25a-NU-11:8(2912)■16:31a-DE-4:18a■9:21(2192)■15:23■22:6■28:4a,11a,56-JOS-24:32(7704)-J'G-4:21■6:39,40■13:20■20:21,25-RU-2:10-1SA-3:19■5:4■8:12(2758)■14:25(7704),32,45■20:31a,41■25:23■26:7■28:14-2SA-2:22■8:2■14:4,14,22,33■17:12a,19(7383)■18:11■20:10■23:11(7704),12(2513)■24:20-1KI-1:23■7:46a-2KI-2:8,15,19■4:37■13:18-1CH-11:13(7704)■21:21■27:26a-2CH-4:17a■7:3■20:18-NE-8:6■10:35a,37a-JOB-1:20■2:13■5:6a■14:8(6083)■16:13■18:10■39:24-PS-74:7■89:39,44■105:35a■107:35a■143:3■147:6-IS-3:26■14:12■21:9■25:12■26:5■28:24a■29:4^{2}■30:23a,24a■44:3■47:1■51:23■53:2-JER-7:20a■14:2,4a■25:33a■27:5-LA-2:2,9,10^{2},21-EZE-12:6,12■13:14■19:12,13■24:7■26:11,16■28:17■38:20■41:16,20■42:6■43:14-DA-8:5,7,10,12,18■10:9,15-HO-2:18a-AM-3:14-OB-3-HAG-1:11a-ZEC-8:12-MAL-3:11a■N.T.-all=1093&marked-M'T-10:29■13:8,23■15:35-M'R-4:8,20,26■8:6■9:20■14:35-LU-8:8,15■12:16(5561)■13:7■14:18(68)■19:44(1474)■22:44-JOH-4:5(5564)■8:6,8■9:6(5476)■12:24■18:6(5476)-AC-7:33■22:7(1475)-1TI-3:15(1477)

GROUNDED-IS-30:32(4145)■N.T.-EPH-3:17(2311)-COL-1:23(2311)

GROVE-all=842&marked-GE-21:33(815)-DE-16:21-J'G-6:25,26,28,30-1KI-15:13■16:33-2KI-13:6■17:16■21:3,7■23:4,6,7,15-2CH-15:16

GROVES-all=842-EX-34:13-DE-7:5■12:3-J'G-3:7-1KI-14:15,23■18:19-2KI-17:10■18:4■23:14-2CH-14:3■17:6■19:3■24:18■31:1■33:3,19■34:3,4,7-IS-17:8■27:9-JER-17:2-MIC-5:14

GROW-all=6779&marked-GE-2:9■48:16(1711)-NU-6:5(1431)-J'G-16:22-2SA-23:5-2KI-19:29-(5599)-EZR-4:22(7680)-JOB-8:11(1342),19■14:19(5599)■31:40(3318)■39:4(7235)-PS-92:12(7685)■104:14■147:8-IS-11:1(6509)■17:11(7735)■53:2(5927)-JER-12:2(3212)■33:15-EZE-44:20(7971)■47:12(5927)-HO-14:5(6524),7(6524)-JON-4:10(1431)-ZEC-6:12-MAL-4:2(6335)■N.T.-all=837&marked-M'T-6:28■13:30(4886)■21:19(1096)-M'R-4:27(3373)-LU-12:27-AC-5:24(1096)-EPH-4:15-1PE-2:2-2PE-3:18

GROWETH-all=5599&marked-EX-10:5(6779)-LE-13:39(6524)■25:5,11-DE-29:23(5927)-J'G-19:9(2583)-JOB-38:38(3332)-PS-90:5(2498),6(2498)■129:6(8025)-IS-37:30■N.T.-M'R-4:32(305)-EPH-2:21(837)-2TH-1:3(5232)

GROWN-all=1431&marked-GE-38:11,14-EX-2:11■9:32(648)-LE-13:37(6779)-RU-1:13-2SA-10:5(6779)-1KI-12:8,10-2KI-4:18■19:26(6965)-1CH-19:5(6779)-EZR-9:6-PS-144:12-PR-24:31(5927)-IS-37:27(6965)-JER-50:11(6335)-EZE-16:7(6779)-DA-4:22^{2}(7236),33(7236)■N.T.-M'T-13:32(837)

GROWTH-AM-7:1^{2}(3954)

GRUDGE-LE-19:18(5201)-PS-59:15(3885)■N.T.-JAS-5:9(4727)

GRUDGING-1PE-4:9(1112)

GRUDGINGLY-2CO-9:7(1537,3077)

GUARD-all=2876,a=7323&marked-GE-37:36■39:1■40:3,4■41:12-2SA-23:23(4928)-1KI-14:27a,28^{2}a-2KI-10:25^{2}a■11:4a,6a,11a,13a,19^{2}a■25:8,10,11,12,15,18,20-1CH-11:25(4928)-2CH-12:10a,11^{2}a-NE-4:22(4929),23(4929)-JER-39:9,10,11,13■40:1,2,5■41:10■43:6■52:12,14,15,16,19,24,26,30-EZE-38:7(4929)-DA-2:14(2877)■N.T.-AC-28:16(4759)

GUARD'S-GE-41:10(2876)

GUEST-LU-19:7(2647)

GUESTCHAMBER-M'R-14:14(2646)-LU-22:11(2646)

GUESTS-all=7121-1KI-1:41,49-PR-9:18-ZEP-1:7■N.T.-M'T-22:10(345),11(345)

GUIDE-all=5148&marked-JOB-38:32-PS-25:9(1869)■31:3(5095)■32:8(3289)■48:14(5090)■55:13(441)■73:24■112:5(3557)-PR-2:17(441)■6:7(7101)■11:3■23:19(833)-IS-49:10(5095)■51:18(5095)■58:11-JER-3:4(441)-MIC-7:5(441)■N.T.-LU-1:79(2720)-JOH-16:13(3594)-AC-1:16(3595)■8:31(3594)-RO-2:19(3595)-1TI-5:14(3616)

GUIDED-EX-15:13(5095)-2CH-32:22(5095)-JOB-31:18(5148)-PS-78:52(5090),72(5148)

GUIDES-M'T-23:16(3595),24(3595)

GUIDING-all supplied

GUILE-EX-21:14(6195)-PS-32:2(7423)■34:13(4820)■55:11(4820)■N.T.-all=1388-JOH-1:47-2CO-12:16-1TH-2:3-1PE-2:1,22■3:10-RE-14:5

GUILT-all supplied

GUILTINESS-GE-26:10(817)

GUILTLESS-all=5352&marked-EX-20:7-NU-5:31■32:22(5355)-DE-5:11-JOS-2:19(5355)-1SA-26:9-2SA-3:28(5355)■14:9(5355)-1KI-2:9■N.T.-M'T-12:7(338)

GUILTY-all=816&marked-GE-42:21-LE-4:13,22,27■5:2,3,4,5,17■6:4-NU-5:6■35:31(7563)-J'G-21:22-EZR-10:19-PR-30:10-EZE-22:4-ZEC-11:5■N.T.-all=1777&marked-M'T-23:18(3784)■26:66-M'R-14:64-RO-3:19(5267)-1CO-11:27-JAS-2:10

GULF-LU-16:26(5490)

GUSH-JER-9:18(5140)

GUSHED-all=2100&marked-1KI-18:28(8210)-PS-78:20■105:41-IS-48:21■N.T.-AC-1:18(1632)

GUTTER-2SA-5:8(6794)

GUTTERS-GE-30:38(7298),41(7298)

H

HA-JOB-39:25(1889)

HABERGEON-EX-28:32(8473)■39:23(8473)-JOB-41:26(8302)

HABERGEONS-2CH-26:14(8302)-NE-4:16(8302)

HABITABLE-PR-8:31(8398)

HABITATION-all=5116&marked-EX-15:2(5115),13-LE-13:46(4186)-DE-12:5(7933)■26:15(4583)-1SA-2:29(4583),32(4583)-2SA-15:25-2CH-6:2(2073)■29:6(4908)-EZR-7:15(4907)-JOB-5:3,24■8:6■18:15-PS-26:8(4583)■33:14(3427)■68:5(4583)■69:25(2918)■71:3(4583)■89:14(4349)■91:9(4583)■97:2(4349)■104:12(7931)■107:7(4186),36(4186)■132:5(4908),13(4186)-PR-3:33-IS-22:16(4908),27:10■32:18■33:20■34:13■35:7■63:15(2073)-JER-9:6(3427)■10:25■25:30(4583),30■31:23■33:12■41:17(1628)■49:19■50:7,19,44,45-EZE-29:14(4351)-DA-4:21(7932)-OB-3(3427)-HAB-3:11(2073)-ZEC-2:13(4583)■N.T.-AC-1:20(1886)■17:26(2733)-EPH-2:22(2732)-JUDE-6(3613)-RE-18:2(2732)

HABITATIONS-all=4186&marked-GE-36:43■49:5(4380)-EX-12:20■35:3-LE-23:17-NU-15:2-1CH-4:33,41(4583)■7:28-PS-74:20(4999)■78:28(4908)-IS-54:2(4908)-JER-9:10(4999)■21:13(4585)■25:37(4999)■49:20(5116)-LA-2:2(4999)-EZE-6:14-AM-1:2(4999)■N.T.-LU-16:9(4638)

HAD-all=1961&marked-GE-11:3■12:16■13:5■30:43■39:4(3426),5^{3}(3426)■43:23(935)-EX-10:23■36:7-LE-21:3-NU-3:4■14:24■26:33■27:3■30:6■32:1-DE-9:21,25-JOS-5:12sup,12■17:1,3,6,8,11■19:2■21:4,10,20-J'G-8:30^{2}■10:4,4sup■12:9,14■18:27sup,27-1SA-1:2sup,2■9:2-2SA-4:2■12:2■15:2■21:15-1KI-4:24sup,24■5:15■9:19■11:3■17:7■21:1-2KI-1:17sup,17-1CH-2:22,34■4:5■6:66■7:15■11:20■14:4■18:10sup,10■23:17,22■24:2,28■29:25-2CH-1:3,12,14■8:6■9:25■10:6■14:8■17:5,13■18:1■21:6■26:10■32:27-EZR-10:44sup,44(3426),44(7760)-NE-4:6-JOB-42:12,13-PS-106:23(3884)■119:56-EC-2:7^{2}-JER-44:17■52:25-LA-1:7-EZE-10:10,10sup■19:11■29:18■35:5■41:6■44:22,25-DA-7:1(2370)-HAB-3:4■N.T.-all=2192&marked-M'T-3:4■12:10■13:5^{2},6,46sup,46■18:25^{2}■19:22(2258,2192)■21:28■22:11(1746),28■27:16-M'R-1:22■2:25■3:1,3,10sup,10■4:5^{2},6■5:3,15,25(1510),26^{2}sup,26(3844)■7:25■8:7,14sup,14■10:22(2258,2192)■12:22(2983),23,44-LU-1:7(1510)■4:33,40■6:8■7:41(1510),42■8:27,42(1510)■9:11■10:39(1510)■13:6,11■15:11■16:1,1sup■17:6■20:33■21:4-JOH-4:18■5:4(2722),5■12:6■13:29,29sup■15:22^{2}sup,22,24^{2}sup,24■17:5-AC-2:44,45■4:32(1510),35■7:5(5607)■44(1510),44^{2}sup■9:31■13:5■14:9■15:2(1096)■18:18■19:13■21:9(1510)■24:19■25:19,26(1096)■28:9,19,29sup,29-RO-6:21-1CO-7:29-2CO-1:9■2:13■7:5-GA-4:22-1TH-1:9-HEB-2:14■7:6■9:1,4^{2}■10:2■11:15sup,15,36(2983)■12:9-1JO-2:7-2JO-1:5-3JO-1:13-RE-1:16■4:4,7,8■6:2,5sup,5■8:6,9■9:8,9,10,11,14,19■10:2■13:11,14sup,14,17■14:18^{2}■16:2■17:1■18:19■19:12■21:9,12^{2},14,15,23

HADST-JER-3:3(1961)

HAFT-J'G-3:22(5325)

HAIL-all=1259&marked-EX-9:18,19,22,23^{2},24,25^{2},26,28,29,33,34■10:5,12,15-JOB-38:22-PS-18:12,13■78:47,48■105:32■148:8-IS-28:2,17■32:19(1258)-HAG-2:17■N.T.-all=5463&marked-M'T-26:49■27:29■28:9-M'R-15:18-LU-1:28-JOH-19:3-RE-8:7(5464)■11:19(5464)■16:21^{2}(5464)

HAILSTONES-all=68,417&marked-JOS-10:11(68,1259)-IS-30:30(68,1259)-EZE-13:11,13■38:22

HAIR-all=8181&marked-LE-13:3,4,10,20,25,26,30,31,32,36,37,40(4803),41(4803)■14:8,9^{2}-NU-6:5,18-J'G-16:22■20:16(8185)-1SA-14:45(8185)-2SA-14:11(8185),26-1KI-1:52(8185)-EZR-9:3-JOB-4:15(8185)-SONG-4:1■6:5■7:5(1803)-IS-3:24(4748)■7:20-JER-7:29(5145)-EZE-16:7-DA-3:27(8177)■7:9(8177)■N.T.-all=2359&marked-M'T-3:4■5:36-M'R-1:6-LU-21:18-JOH-11:2■12:3-AC-27:34-1CO-11:14(2863),15(2863),15(2864)-1TI-2:9(4117)-1PE-3:3-RE-6:12(5155)■9:8

HAIRS-LE-13:21(8181)-PS-40:12(8185)■69:4(8185)-DA-4:33(8177)■N.T.-all=2359-M'T-10:30-LU-7:38,44■12:7-RE-1:14

HAIRY-all=8181&marked-GE-25:25■27:11(8163),23(8163)-2KI-1:8(1167,8181)-PS-68:21

HALE-LU-12:58(2694)

HALF-all=2677,a=4276&marked-GE-24:22(1235)-EX-24:6^2■25:10^4,17^2,23■26:12,16■30:13^{2}a,15a,23a■36:21■37:1^3,6^2,10■38:26a-LE-6:20a-NU-12:12■15:9,10■28:14■31:29a,30a,36(4275),42a,43(4275),47a■32:33■34:13,14,15-DE-3:12,13,16(8432)■29:8-JOS-1:12■4:12■8:33^2■12:2,5,6■13:7,25,29^2,31^2■14:2,3■18:7■21:5,6,25a,27■22:1,7^2,9,10,11,13,15,21-1SA-14:14-2SA-10:4■18:3■19:40-1KI-3:25■7:31,32,35■10:7■13:8■16:9a,21^2-1CH-2:52,54■5:18,23,26■6:61,61a,70a,71■12:31,37■26:32■27:20,21-2CH-9:6-NE-3:9,12,16,17,18■4:6,16^2,21■12:32,38,40■13:24-ES-5:3,6■7:2-PS-55:23(2673)-EZE-16:51■40:42^2■43:17-DA-12:7-ZEC-14:2,4^2,8^2■N.T.-all=2255&marked-M'R-6:23-LU-10:30(2253)■19:8-RE-8:1(2256)■11:9,11■12:14

HALING-AC-8:3(4951)

HALL-all=4232&marked-M'T-27:27-M'R-15:16(833)-LU-22:55(833)-JOH-18:28^2,33■19:9-AC-23:35

HALLOW-all=6942-EX-28:38■29:1■40:9-LE-16:19■22:2,3,32■25:10-NU-6:11-1KI-8:64-JER-17:22,24,27-EZE-20:20■44:24

HALLOWED-all=6942,a=6944&marked-EX-20:11■29:21-LE-12:4a■19:8a■22:32-NU-3:13■5:10a■16:37,38■18:8a,29(4720)-DE-26:13a-1SA-21:4a,6a-1KI-9:3,7-2KI-12:18^{2}a-2CH-7:7■36:14■N.T.-M'T-6:9(37)-LU-11:2(37)

HALT-1KI-18:21(6452)-PS-38:17(6761)■N.T.-all=5560-M'T-18:8-M'R-9:45-LU-14:21-JOH-5:3

HALTED-GE-32:31(6761)-MIC-4:7(6761)

HALTETH-MIC-4:6(6761)-ZEP-3:19(6761)

HALTING-JER-20:10(6761)

HAMMER-all=6360&marked-J'G-4:21(4718)■5:26(1989),26sup-1KI-6:7(4717)-IS-41:7-JER-23:29■50:23

HAMMERS-PS-74:6(3597)-IS-44:12(4717)-JER-10:4(4717)

HAND-all=3027,a=3709,c=3225&marked-GE-3:22■4:11■8:9■9:2,5^3■13:9(8041),9c■14:15(8040),20,22■16:6,12^2■19:10,16^3■21:18,30■22:6,10,12■24:2,9,10,18,49c■25:26■27:17,41(7126)■30:35■31:29,39■32:11^2,13,16■33:10,19■35:4■37:22,27■38:18,20^2,28^2,29,30■39:3,4,6,8,12,13,22,23■40:11,11a,13,21a■41:35,42^2,44■42:37■43:9,12^2,15,21,26■44:17■46:4■47:29■48:13c,13^2(8040),13c,14c,14(8040),17^2,18c,22■49:8-EX-2:19■3:8,19,20■4:2,4^2,4a,6^3,7^2,13,17,20,21■5:21■6:1^2■7:4,5,15,17,19■8:5,6,17■9:3,15,22■10:12,21,22■12:11■13:3,9^2,14,16^2■14:8,16,21,22c,26,27,29c,30■15:6^{2}c,9,12c,20■16:3■17:5,9,11^2■18:9,10^3■19:13■21:13,16,20,24■22:4,8,11■23:1,31■24:11■25:25(2948)■29:20■32:4,11,15■33:22a,23a■34:4,29■35:29■38:21-LE-1:4■3:2,8,13■4:4,24,29,33■8:23,36■9:22■10:11■14:14,15(8042),16a,17a,17,18a,25,26(8042),27a,28a,28,29a,32■16:21■22:25■25:14,28■26:25,46-NU-4:28,33,37,45,49■5:18,25■6:21■7:8■9:23■10:13■11:15(2026),23■15:23■16:40■20:11,17c,20■21:2,26,34■22:7,23,26(3325),29,31■25:7■27:18,23■31:6■33:1,3■35:18,21,25■36:13-DE-1:27■2:7,15,24,27c,30■3:2,8,24■4:34■5:15,32c■6:8,21■7:8^2,19,24■8:17■9:26■10:3■11:2,18■12:6,7,11,17■13:9^2,17■14:25,29■15:3,7,8,9(7126),10,11■16:10■17:11c,20c■19:5,12,21■23:20,25■24:1,3■25:11^2,12a■26:4,8■28:8,12,14c,20,32■30:9■32:27,35(7138),39,40,41■33:2c,3■34:12-JOS-1:7c■2:19■4:24■5:13■6:2■7:7■8:1,7,18^3,19,26■9:25,26■10:6,8,19,30,32■11:8■14:2■17:7c■19:27(8040)■20:2,5,9■21:2,8,44■22:9,31■23:6c■24:8,10,11-J'G-1:2,4,35■2:15,16,18,23■3:4,8,10,21,28,30■4:2,7,9,14,21,24■5:26,26c■6:1,2,9^2,14a,21,36,37■7:2,6,7,8,9,14,15,16■8:6,7,15,22■9:17,29,48■10:12■11:21■12:3■13:1,5■14:6■15:12,13,15,17,18^2■16:18,23,26■17:3■18:19■20:28,48(4672)-RU-1:13■4:5,9-1SA-2:13■4:3a,8■5:6,7,9,11■6:3,5,9■7:3,8,13■9:8,16■10:18■12:3,4,5,9^3,10,11,15■13:22■14:10,12,19,26,27^2,37,43■16:16,23■17:22,37,40^2,46,49,50,57■18:10^2,17^2,21,25■19:5a,9^2■20:16■21:3^2,4,8■22:6,17^2■23:4,6,7,11,12,14,16,17,20■24:4,6,10^2,11^2,12,13,15,18,20■25:8,26,33,35,39■26:8,9,11,18,23^2■27:1^2■28:17,19^2,21a■30:23-2SA-1:14■3:8,12,18^3■4:11■5:19^2■8:1■10:2,10■11:14■12:7,25■13:5,6,10,19■14:16a,19■15:5■16:8■18:2^3,12a,12,14a,28■19:9^{2}a■20:9,10,21■21:20,22■22:1^{2}a■23:10^2,21^2■24:14^2,16^2,17-1KI-2:25,46■7:26(2947)■8:15,24,42,53,56■11:12,26,27,31,34,35■13:4^2,6^2■14:18■15:18■16:7■17:11■18:9,44a,46■20:6,13,28,42■22:3,6,12,15,34-2KI-3:10,13,15,18■4:29■5:11,18,24■6:7■7:2,17■8:8,20,22■9:1,7■10:15^2■11:8,11^2■12:15■13:3^2,5,16^2,25^2■14:5,25,27■15:19^2■16:7^{2}a■17:7,20,39■18:21a,29,30,33,34,35^2■19:10,14,19■20:6a■21:14■22:5(3207),7(3207),9(3207)-1CH-4:10■5:10,20■6:15■11:23^2■13:9,10■14:10^2,11■16:7■18:1■19:11■20:8^2■21:13^2,15,16,17■22:18■26:28■28:19■29:8,12^2,16-2CH-4:5(2947),6:15,32■10:15■12:5,7■13:8,16■16:7,8■17:5■18:5,11,14,33■20:6■21:10^2■23:7,10,18■24:11,24■25:15,20■26:11^2,13,19■28:5^2,9■30:6a,12,16■31:13■32:11a,13,14^2,15^3,17^2,22^2■33:8■34:2c,9,10,17^2■35:6■36:17-EZR-1:8■5:12(3028)■6:12(3028)■7:6,9,14(3028),25(3028),28■8:18,22,26,31,31a,33■9:2,7-NE-1:10■2:8,18■6:5■8:4c,4(8040)■9:14,27^2,28,30■11:24■12:31c-ES-2:21■3:10■5:2■6:2,9■8:7■9:2,10,15-JOB-1:11,12■2:5,6,10(854)■5:15■6:9,23^2■9:24,33■10:7■11:14■12:6,9,10■13:14a,21a■15:23,25■19:21■20:22■21:5,16■23:9(8040),9c■26:13■27:11,22■28:9■29:9a,20■30:12c,21,24■31:21,25,27■33:7(405)■34:20■35:7■37:7■40:4,14c■41:8a-PS-10:12,14■16:8c,11c■17:7c,14■18:t^{2}a,35c■20:6c■21:8,8c■26:10c■31:5,8,15^2■32:4■36:11■37:24,33■38:2■39:10■44:2,3c■45:4c,9c■48:10c■60:5c■63:8c■71:4,4a■73:23■74:11,11c■75:8■77:10c,20■78:42,54c,61■80:15c,17,17c■81:14■82:4■88:5■89:13,13c,21,25,25c,42c,48■91:7c■95:4,7■97:10■98:1c■104:28■106:10^2,26,41,42■107:2■108:6c■109:6c,27,31c■110:1c,5c■118:15c,16^{2}c■119:109a,173■121:5■123:2^2■127:4■129:7a■136:12■137:5c■138:7,7c■139:5a,10,10c■142:4c■144:7^2,8c,11,11c■145:16■149:6-PR-1:24■3:16c,16(8040),27■4:27(3227)■6:1a,3a,5^2■10:4a,4■11:21■12:24■16:5■17:16■19:24■21:1■26:6,9,15■27:16c■30:32■31:20a-EC-2:24■5:14,15■7:18■9:1,10■10:2c■11:6-SONG-2:6(8040),6c■5:4■8:3(8040),3c-IS-1:12,25■3:6■5:25^2■6:6■8:11■9:12,17,20c,20(8040),21■10:4,5,10,13,14,32■11:8,11,14,15■13:2,6(7138)■14:26,27■19:4,16■22:21■23:11■25:10■26:11■28:2,4a■31:3■34:17■36:6a,15,18,19,20^2■37:10,14,20■38:6a■40:2■41:10c,13c,20■42:6■43:13■44:5,20c■45:1c■47:6■48:13,13c■49:2,22■50:2,11■51:16,17,18,22,23■53:10■54:3c■56:2■57:10■59:1■62:3,3a,8c■63:12c■64:8■66:2,14-JER-1:9■6:9,12■11:21■12:7a■15:6,17,21,21a■16:21■18:4,6^2■20:4,5,13■21:5,7^3,10,12■22:3,24,25^4■23:23(7138)■25:15,17,28■26:14,24^2■27:3,6,8■29:3,21■31:11,32■32:3,4^2,21,24,25,28,36,43■34:2,3^2,20^2,21^3■36:14^2■37:17■38:3,5,16,18^2,19,23^2■39:17■40:4■41:5■42:11■43:3,9■44:25,30^3■46:24,26^3■50:15■51:7,25-LA-1:7,10,14■2:3c,4c,7,8■3:3■5:6,8,12-EZE-1:3■2:9■3:14,18,20,22■6:11a,14■8:1,3,11■9:1,2■10:2(2651),7,8■12:7,23(7126)■13:9,21^2,23■14:9,13■16:27,39,46(8040),46c,49■17:18■18:8,17■20:5^2,6,15,22,23,28,33,34,42■21:11,16(3221),22c,24(3079)31,■22:13(3079)■23:9^2,28^2,31■25:7,13,14,16■27:15■28:9,10■29:7a■30:10,12^2,22,24,25■31:11■33:6,8,22■34:10,27■35:3■36:7,8(7126)■37:1,17,19^2,20■38:12■39:3^2,21,23■40:1,3,5,5(2948),43(2948)■43:13(2948)■44:12■46:7■47:3,14-DA-1:2■2:38(3028)■3:17(3028)■4:35(3028)■5:5^2(3028),23(3028),24(3028)■7:25(3028)■8:4,7,25^2■9:15■10:10■11:11,16,41,42■12:7c,7(8040)-HO-2:10■7:5■12:7-JOE-1:15(7138)■3:8-AM-1:8■5:19■7:7■9:2-JON-4:11(3235),11(8040)-MIC-2:1■4:10a■5:9,12■7:16-HAB-2:16c■3:4-ZEP-1:4,7(7138)■2:13,15-ZEC-2:1,9■3:1c■4:10■8:4■11:6^3■12:6c■13:7■14:13^3-MAL-1:10,13■2:13■N.T.all=5495&marked-M'T-3:2(1448),12■4:17(1448)■5:30■8:3,15■9:18,25■10:7(1448)■12:10,13,49■14:31■18:8■22:13■26:18(1451),23,45(1448),46(1448),51-M'R-1:15(1448),31,41■3:1,3,5^2■5:41■7:32■8:23■9:27,43■14:42(1448)-LU-1:1(2021),66,71,74■3:17■5:13■6:6,8,10^2■8:54■9:62■15:22■22:21-JOH-2:13(1451)■3:35■7:2(1451)■10:28,29,39■11:44■20:25,27-AC-3:7■4:28,30■7:25,35,50■9:8(5496),12,41■11:21■12:11,17■13:11,11(5497),16■19:33■21:40■22:11(5496)■23:19■26:1■28:3,4-RO-13:12(1448)-2CO-12:15,21■16:21-GA-3:19■6:11-P'HP-4:5(1451)-COL-4:18-2TH-2:2(1764)■3:17-2TI-4:6(2186)-PH'M-19-HEB-8:9-1PE-4:7(1448)■5:6-RE-1:3(1451)■16,17■6:5■8:4■10:2,5,8,10■13:16■14:9,14■17:4■19:2■20:1■22:10(1451)

HANDBREATH-EX-37:12(2948)-2CH-4:5(2947)-PS-39:5(2947)

HANDED-2SA-17:2(3027)

HANDFUL-LE-2:2(4393,7062)■5:12(4393,7062)■6:15(7062)■9:17(4390,3709)-NU-5:26(7061)-1KI-17:12(4393,3709)-PS-72:16(6451)-EC-4:6(4393,3709)-JER-9:22(5995)

HANDFULS-GE-41:47(7062)-EX-9:8(4393,2651)-RU-2:16(6653)-1KI-20:10(8168)-EZE-13:19

HANDKERCHIEFS-AC-19:12(4676)

HANDLE-all=8610&marked-GE-4:21-J'G-5:14(4900)-1CH-12:8(6186)-2CH-25:5(270)-PS-115:7(4184)-JER-2:8■46:9^2-EZE-27:29■N.T.-LU-24:39(5584)-COL-2:21(2345)

HANDLED-EZE-21:11(8610,3709)■N.T.-M'R-12:4(821)-1JO-1:1(5584)

HANDLES-SONG-5:5(3709)

HANDLETH-PR-16:20(5921)-JER-50:16(8610)-AM-2:15(8610)

HANDLING-EZE-38:4(8610)■N.T.-2CO-4:2(1389)

HANDMAID-all=519,a=8198&marked-GE-16:1a■25:12a■29:24a,29a■30:4a■35:25a,26a-EX-23:12-J'G-19:19-RU-2:13a■3:9^2-1SA-1:11^3,16,18a■25:24^2,25,27a,28,31,41■28:21a,22a-2SA-14:6a,7a,12a,15,15a,16,17a■14:19a■20:17-1KI-1:13,17■3:20-2KI-4:2a,16a-PS-86:16■116:16-PR-30:23a-JER-34:16a■N.T.-LU-1:38(1399)

HANDMAIDEN-LU-1:48(1399)

HANDMAIDENS-GE-33:6(8198)-RU-2:13(8198)■N.T.-AC-2:18(1399)

HANDMAIDS-all=8198&marked-GE-33:1,2-2SA-6:20(519)-IS-14:2-JER-34:11^2,16-JOE-2:29

HANDS-all=3027,a=3709&marked-GE-5:29■16:9■20:5a■24:22,30,47■27:16,22,23^2■31:42a■37:21,22■39:1■43:22■48:14■49:24^2-EX-9:29a,33a■15:17■17:12^3■29:10,15,19,24a,25■30:19,21■32:19■35:25■40:31-LE-4:15■7:30■8:14,18,22,24,27^{2}a,28a■15:11■16:12(2651),21■24:14-NU-5:18a■6:19a■8:10,12■24:10a■27:23-DE-1:25■3:3■4:28■9:15,17■12:18■16:15■17:7^2■20:13■21:6,7,10■24:19■27:15■31:29■33:7,11■34:9-JOS-

2:24-J'G-2:14^{2}■6:13a■7:2,11,19,20^{2}■8:3,6a,15a,34■9:16■10:7^{2}■11:30,32■12:2,3a■13:23■14:9a■15:14■16:24■18:10■19:27-1SA-5:4■7:14■10:4■11:7■14:13,48■17:47■21:13■30:15-2SA-2:7■3:34■4:1,12■16:21■21:9■22:21,35■23:6-1KI-8:22,38,54■14:27■16:7-2KI-3:11■4:34a■5:20■9:23,35■10:24■11:12a,16■12:11■13:16■19:18■22:17-1CH-12:17a■25:2,3,6■29:5-2CH-6:4,12a,13a,29a■8:18■12:10■15:7■23:15■29:23■32:19■34:25■35:11-EZR-1:6■4:4■5:8(3028)■6:22■9:5a■10:19-NE-2:18■4:17■6:9^{2}■8:6■9:24■13:21-ES-3:6,9■9:16-JOB-1:10■4:3■5:12,18■9:30a■10:3a,8■11:13a■14:15■16:11,17a■17:3,9■20:10■22:30a■27:23a■30:2■31:7a■34:19-PS-7:3a■8:6■9:16a■18:20,24,34■22:16■24:4a■26:6a,10■28:2,4,5■44:20a■47:1a■55:20■58:2■63:4a■68:31■73:13a■76:5■78:72a■81:6a■88:9a■90:17^{2}■91:12a■92:4■95:5■98:8a■102:25■111:7■115:4,7■119:48a,73■125:3■128:2a■134:2■135:15■138:8■140:4■141:2a■143:5,6■144:1-PR-6:10,17■12:14■14:1■17:18a■21:25■22:26a■24:33■30:28■31:13a,16a,19,19a,20,31-EC-2:11■4:5,6(2651)■5:6■7:26■10:18-SONG-5:5,14■7:1-IS-1:15a,15■2:8■3:11■5:12■13:7■17:8■19:25■25:11^{2}sup,11■29:23■31:7■33:15a■35:3■37:19■45:9,11,12■49:16a■55:12a■59:3a,6a■60:21■65:2,22-JER-1:16■2:37■4:31a■6:24■10:3,9■19:7■21:4■23:14■25:6,7,14■30:6■32:30■33:13■38:4^{2}■44:8■47:3■48:37■50:43-LA-1:14,17■2:15a,19a■3:41a,64■4:2,6,10-EZE-1:8■7:17,21,27■10:7(2651),12,21■11:9■13:22■16:11■21:7,14a,17a■22:14■23:37,42,45■25:6-DA-2:34(3028),45(3028)■3:15(3028)■10:10-HO-14:3-JON-3:8a-MIC-5:13■7:3a-NA-3:19a-HAB-3:10-ZEP-3:16-HAG-1:11a■2:14,17-ZEC-4:9^{2}■8:9,13■13:6■N.T.-all=5495&marked-M'T-4:6■15:2,20■17:22■18:8,28(2902)■19:13,15■21:46(2902)■26:45,50■27:24-M'R-5:23■6:2,5■7:2,3,5■8:23,25■9:31,43■10:16■14:41,46,58(5499),58(886)■16:18-LU-4:11,40■6:1■9:44■13:13■20:19■21:12■22:53■23:46■24:7,39,40,50-JOH-7:30,44■8:20(4084)■13:3,9■19:3(4475)■20:20,25,27■21:18-AC-2:23■4:3■5:12,18■6:6■7:41,48(5499)■8:17,18,19■9:17■11:30■12:1,7■13:3■14:3■17:24(5499),25■19:6,11,26■20:34■21:11^{2},27■24:7■27:19(849)■28:8,17-RO-10:21-1CO-4:12-2CO-5:1(886)■11:33-EPH-2:11(5499)■4:28-COL-2:11(886)-1TH-4:11-1TI-2:8■4:14■5:22-2TI-1:6-HEB-1:10■2:7■6:2■9:11(5499),24(5499)■10:31■12:12-JAS-4:8-1JO-1:1-RE-7:9■9:20■20:4

HANDSTAVES-EZE-39:9(4731,3027)

HANDWRITING-COL-2:14(5498)

HANDYWORK-PS-19:1(4639,3027)

HANG-all=8518&marked-GE-40:19-EX-26:12(5628),13(1961,5628),32(5414),33(5414)■40:8(5414)-NU-25:4(3363)-DE-21:22■28:66(8511)-2SA-21:6(3363)-ES-6:4■7:9-SONG-4:4-IS-22:24-LA-2:10(3381)-EZE-15:3■N.T.-M'T-22:40(2910)-AC-28:4(2910)-HEB-2:12(3935)

HANGED-all=8518&marked-GE-40:22■41:13-DE-21:23-JOS-8:29■10:26-2SA-4:12■17:23(2614)■18:10■21:9(3363),12(8511),13,(3363)-EZR-6:11(4223)-ES-2:23■5:14■7:10■8:7■9:13,14,25-PS-137:2-LA-5:12-EZE-27:10,11■N.T.-all=2910&marked-M'T-18:6■27:5(519)-M'R-9:42(4029)-LU-17:2(4029)■23:39-AC-5:30■10:39

HANGETH-JOB-2:7(8518)■N.T.-GA-3:13(2910)

HANGING-all=4539&marked-EX-26:36,37■27:16■35:15,17■36:37■38:18■39:38,40■40:5,8,28,33-NU-3:25,31■4:25,26-JOS-10:26(8518)

HANGINGS-all=7050&marked-EX-27:9,11,12,14,15■35:17■38:9,12,14,15,16,18■39:40-NU-3:26■4:26-2KI-23:7(1004)

HAPLY-1SA-14:30(3863)■N.T.-M'R-11:13(686)-LU-14:29(3379)-AC-5:39(3379)■17:27(686)-1CO-9:4(3381)

HAPPEN-1SA-28:10(7136)-PR-12:21(579)-IS-41:22(7136)■N.T.-M'R-10:32(4819)

HAPPENED-1SA-6:9(1961)-2SA-1:6(7136)■20:1(7122)-ES-4:7(7136)-JER-44:23(7122)■N.T.-all=4819&marked-LU-24:14-AC-3:10-RO-11:25(1096)-1CO-10:11-1PE-4:12-2PE-2:22

HAPPENETH-all=7136&marked-EC-2:14,15(4745),15■8:14^{2}(5060)■9:11

HAPPIER-1CO-7:40(3107)

HAPPY-all=835&marked-GE-30:13(837)-DE-33:29-1KI-10:8-2CH-9:7-JOB-5:17-PS-127:5■128:2■137:8,9■144:15^{2}■146:5-PR-3:13,18(833)■14:21■16:20■28:14■29:18-JER-12:1(7951)-MAL-3:15(833)■N.T.-all=3107&marked-JOH-13:17-AC-26:2-RO-14:22-JAS-5:11(3106)-1PE-3:14■4:14

HARD-all=6381&marked-GE-18:14■35:16(7185),17(7185)-EX-1:14(7186)■18:26(7186)-LE-3:9(3980)-DE-1:17(7185)■15:18(7185)■17:8■26:6(7186)-J'G-9:52(5066)-1SA-14:22(1692)■31:2(1692)-2SA-1:6(1692)■3:39(7186)■13:2-1KI-10:1(2420)■21:1(681)-2KI-2:10(7185)-1CH-10:2(5221)-2CH-9:1(2420)-JOB-41:24(3332)-PS-60:3(7186)■63:8(1692)■88:7(5564)■94:4(6277)-PR-13:15(386)-IS-14:3(7186)-JER-32:17,27-EZE-3:5(3515),6(3515)-DA-5:12(280)■N.T.-all=4642&marked-M'T-25:24-M'R-10:24(1422)-JOH-6:60-AC-9:5(4642)■18:7(4927)■26:14-HEB-5:11(1421)-2PE-3:16(1425)-JUDE-15

HARDEN-all=2388&marked-EX-4:21■7:3(7185)■14:4,17-DE-15:7(553)-JOS-11:20-1SA-6:6(5513)-JOB-6:10(5339)-PS-95:8(7185)■N.T.-all=4645-HEB-3:8,15■4:7

HARDENED-all=2388&marked-EX-7:13,14(3515),22■8:15(3513),19,32(3513)■9:7(3515),12,34(3513),35■10:1(3513),20,27■11:10■14:8-DE-2:30(7185)-1SA-6:6(3513)-2KI-17:14(7185)-2CH-36:13(553)-NE-9:16(7185),17(7185),29(7185)-JOB-9:4(7185)■39:16(7188)-IS-63:17(7188)-JER-7:26(7185)■19:15(7185)-DA-5:20(8631)■N.T.-all=4456&marked-M'R-6:52■8:17-JOH-12:40-AC-19:9(4645)-HEB-3:13(4645)

HARDENETH-PR-21:29(5810)■28:14(7185)■29:1(7185)■N.T.-RO-9:18(4645)

HARDER-JER-5:3(2388)-EZE-3:9(2389)

HARDHEARTED-EZE-3:7(7186,3820)

HARDLY-GE-16:6(6031)-EX-13:15(7185)-IS-8:21(7185)■N.T.-all=1423&marked-M'T-19:23-M'R-10:23-LU-9:39(3425)■18:24-AC-27:8(3433)

HARDNESS-38:38(4165)■N.T.-all=4641&marked-M'T-19:8-M'R-3:5(4457)■10:5■16:14-RO-2:5(4643)-2TI-2:3(2553)

HARE-LE-11:6(768)-DE-14:7(768)

HARLOT-all=2181&marked-GE-34:31■38:15,21^{2}(6948),22(6948),24-LE-21:14-JOS-6:17,25-J'G-11:1■16:1-PR-7:10-IS-1:21■23:15,16-JER-2:20■3:1,6,8-EZE-16:15,16,28,31,35,41■23:5,19,44-HOS-2:5■3:3■4:15-JOE-3:3-AM-7:17-MIC-1:7^{2}-NA-3:4■N.T.-all=4204-1CO-6:15,16-HEB-11:31-JAS-2:25

HARLOT'S-JOS-2:1(2181)■6:22(2181)

HARLOTS-1KI-3:16(2181)-PR-29:3(2181)-HO-4:14(6948)4■N.T.-all=4204-M'T-21:31,32-LU-15:30-RE-17:5

HARLOTS'-JER-5:7(2181)

HARM-all=7451&marked-GE-31:52-LE-5:16(2398)-NU-35:23-IS-26:21(7489)-2SA-20:6(3415)-2KI-4:41(1697,7451)-1CH-16:22(7489)-PS-105:15(7489)-PR-3:30-JER-39:12■N.T.-AC-16:28(2556)■27:21(5196)■28:5(2556),6(824),21(4190)-1PE-3:13(2559)

HARMLESS-M'T-10:16(185)-PH'P-2:15(185)-HEB-7:26(172)

HARNESS-1KI-22:34(8302)-2CH-9:24(5402)■18:33(8302)-JER-46:4(631)

HARNESSED-EX-13:18(2571)

HARP-all=3658&marked-GE-4:21■31:27-1SA-10:5■16:16,23-1CH-25:3-JOB-21:12■30:31-PS-33:2■43:4■49:4■57:8■71:22■81:2■92:3■98:5^{2}■108:2■147:7■149:3■150:3-IS-5:12■16:11■23:16■24:8-DA-3:5,7,10,15(7030)■N.T.-1CO-14:7(2788)

HARPED-1CO-14:7(2789)

HARPERS-RE-14:2(2790)■18:22(2790)

HARPING-RE-14:2(2789)

HARPS-all=3658-2SA-6:5-1KI-10:12-1CH-13:8■15:16,21,28■16:5■25:1,6-2CH-5:12■9:11■20:28■29:25-NE-12:27-PS-137:2-IS-30:32-EZE-26:13■N.T.-all=2788-RE-5:8■14:2■15:2

HARROW-JOB-39:10(7702)

HARROWS-2SA-12:31(2757)-1CH-20:3(2757)

HART-all=354-DE-12:15,22■14:5■15:22-PS-42:1-SONG-2:9,17■8:14-IS-35:6

HARTS-1KI-4:23(354)-LA-1:6(354)

HARVEST-all=7105-GE-8:22■30:14■45:6-EX-23:16■34:21,22-LE-19:9^{2}■23:10^{2},22^{2}■25:5-DE-24:19-JOS-3:15-J'G-15:1-RU-1:22■2:21,23-1SA-6:13■8:12■12:17-2SA-21:9^{2},10■23:13-JOB-5:5-PR-6:8■10:5■20:4■25:13■26:1-IS-9:3■16:9■17:11■18:4,5■23:3-JER-5:17,24■8:20■50:16■51:33-HO-6:11-JOE-1:11■3:13-AM-4:7■N.T.-all=2326&marked-M'T-9:37,38^{2}■13:30^{2},39-M'R-4:29-LU-10:2^{3}-JOH-4:35^{2}-RE-14:15

HARVESTMAN-IS-17:5(7105)-JER-9:22(7114)

HAST-EX-13:12(1691)-DE-12:26(1961)-2KI-4:2(3426)-JOB-33:32(3426)-PR-3:28(3426)■N.T.-all=2192&marked-M'T-19:21(5224)■25:25,25sup-M'R-10:21-LU-12:19■18:22-JOH-4:11^{2},18^{2}■6:68■7:20■8:48,52■13:8-AC-8:21(2076)■23:19-RO-2:20■14:22-1CO-4:7■8:10-PH'M-5-JAS-2:18-RE-2:3sup,3,3sup,6,14,15■3:4,8,8sup,11

HASTE-all=4116,a=2363&marked-GE-19:22■24:46■43:30■45:9,13-EX-10:16■12:11(2649),33(4116)■34:8(4116)-DE-16:3(2649)■32:35a-J'G-9:48■13:10-1SA-9:12■20:38a■21:8(5169)■23:26(2648),27■25:18-2SA-4:4(2648)-2KI-7:15(2648)-2CH-35:21(926)-EZR-4:23(924)-ES-5:5■6:10-JOB-20:2a-PS-22:19a■31:22(2648)■38:22a■40:13a■70:1sup,1a,5a■71:12(2439)■116:11(2648)■119:60a■141:1a-PR-1:16■28:20(213)-SONG-8:14(1272)-IS-28:16a■49:17■52:12(2649)■59:7-JER-9:18-DA-2:25(927)■3:24(927)■6:19(927)-NA-2:5■N.T.-all=4692&marked-M'R-6:25(4710)-LU-1:39(4710)■2:16■19:5,6-AC-22:18

HASTED-all=4116&marked-GE-18:7■24:18,20-EX-5:13(213)-JOS-4:10■8:14,19■10:13(213)-J'G-20:37(2363)-1SA-17:48■25:23,34,42■28:24-2SA-19:16-1KI-20:41-2KI-9:13-2CH-26:20(1765)-ES-6:12(1765),14(926)-JOB-31:5(2363)-PS-48:5(2648)■104:7(2648)■N.T.-AC-20:16(4692)

HASTEN-all=2363&marked-1KI-22:9(4116)-2CH-24:5(4116)-PS-16:4(4116)■55:8-EC-2:25-IS-5:19■60:22-JER-1:12(8245)

HASTENED-GE-18:6(4116)■19:15(213)-2CH-24:5(4116)-ES-3:15(1765)■8:14(926)-JER-17:16(213)

HASTENETH-IS-51:14(4116)

HASTETH-all=4116&marked-JOB-9:26(2907)■40:23(2648)-PR-7:23■19:2(213)■28:22(926)-EC-1:5(7602)-JER-48:16-HAB-1:8(2363)-ZEP-1:14

HASTILY-GE-41:14(7323)-J'G-2:23(4118)■9:54(4120)-1SA-4:14(4116)-1KI-20:33(4116)-PR-20:21(926)■25:8(4118)■N.T.-JOH-11:31(5030)

HASTING-IS-16:5(4106)■N.T.-2PE-3:12(4692)

HASTY-PR-14:29(7116)■21:5(213)■29:20(213)-EC-5:2(4116)■7:9(926)■8:3(926)-IS-28:4(1061)-DA-2:15(2685)-HAB-1:6(4116)

HATCH-IS-34:15(1234)■59:5(1234)

HATCHETH-JER-17:11(3205)

HATE-all=8130&marked-GE-24:60■26:27■50:15(7852)-EX-20:5-LE-19:17■26:17-NU-10:35-DE-5:9■7:10,15■19:11■22:13■24:3■30:7■32:41■33:11-J'G-11:7■14:16-2SA-22:41-1KI-22:8-2CH-18:7■19:2-JOB-8:22-PS-9:13■18:40■21:8■25:19■34:21■35:19■38:19■41:7■44:10■55:3(7852)■68:1■69:4,14■83:2■86:17■89:23■97:10■101:3■105:25■118:7■119:104,113,128,163■129:5■139:21,22-PR-1:22■6:16■8:13^{2},36■9:8■19:7■25:7■25:17■29:10-EC-3:8-IS-61:8-JER-44:4-EZE-16:27-DA-4:19(8131)-AM-5:10,15,21■6:8-MIC-3:2-ZEC-8:17■N.T.-all=3404-M'T-5:43,44■6:24■24:10-LU-1:71■6:22,27■14:26■16:13-JOH-7:7■15:18-RO-7:15-1JO-3:13-RE-2:6,15■17:16

HATED-all=8130&marked-GE-27:41(7852)■29:31,33■37:4,5,8■49:23(7852)-DE-1:27(8135)■4:42■9:28(8135)■19:4,6■21:15^{2},15(8146),16,17-JOS-20:5-J'G-15:2-2SA-5:8■13:15^{2},22■22:18-ES-9:1,5-JOB-31:29-PS-18:17■26:5■31:6■44:7■55:12■106:10,41-PR-1:29■5:12■14:17,20-EC-2:17,18-IS-60:15■66:5-JER-12:8-EZE-16:37■35:6-HO-9:15-MAL-1:3■24:9■N.T.-all=3404-M'T-10:22-M'R-13:13-LU-19:14■21:17-JOH-15:18,18sup,24,25■17:14-RO-9:13-EPH-5:29-HEB-1:9

HATEFUL-PS-36:2(8130)■N.T.-TIT-3:3(4767)-RE-18:2(3404)

HATEFULLY-EZE-23:29(8135)

HATERS-PS-81:15(8130)■N.T.-RO-1:30(2319)

HATEST-all=8130-2SA-19:6-PS-5:5■45:7■50:17-EZE-23:28■N.T.-RE-2:6(3404)

HATETH-all=8130&marked-EX-23:5-DE-7:10■12:31■16:22■22:16-JOB-16:9(7852)■34:17-PS-11:5■120:6-PR-11:15■12:1■13:5,24■15:10,27■26:24,28■28:16■29:24-IS-1:14-MAL-2:16■N.T.-all=3404-JOH-3:20■7:7■12:25■15:19,23-1JO-2:9,11■3:15■4:20

HATH-all=1961&marked-GE-39:8sup,8(3426)■47:18(413)-LE-15:2■20:27■21:17-DE-10:9■21:16,17(4672)-1SA-28:7^{2}(1172)-2CH-25:8(3426)-JOB-5:16■38:28(3426),28sup-PR-16:22(1167)■17:8(1167)-EC-2:22(1933),22sup■10:20(1167)■N.T.-all=2192&marked-M'T-5:23■8:20■9:6■11:15,18■13:9,12^{3},21,27,43,44sup,44■21:3■25:28,29^{3}-M'R-2:10■3:22,26,29,30■4:9,25^{3}■9:17■11:3-LU-3:11^{3}■5:24■7:33■8:8,18^{2}■9:58■12:5sup,5,44(5224)■14:33(5224),35■19:24,25,26^{3},31,34■20:24■22:36^{2}■24:39-JOH-3:29,36■4:44■5:24,26■6:9,47,54■10:20■12:48■14:21,30■15:13■16:15,21■19:11-AC-9:14■15:21■23:17,18-RO-4:2■7:2(5220)■9:21-1CO-7:7,12,13,37,37sup■12:12■14:26^{3}-2CO-8:12^{2}-GA-4:27sup,27-EPH-5:5-COL-4:13-1TI-6:16,16sup-HEB-3:3sup,3■7:24■10:35■11:10-JAS-2:14,17-1JO-2:23^{2}■3:3,15,17■4:16,18■5:10,10sup,12^{2}-2JO-9^{2}-RE-2:7,11,12,17,18,29■3:1,6,7,13,22■9:11■12:6,12■13:18■16:9■17:7,9■19:16■20:6^{2}

HATING-EX-18:21(8130)■N.T.-TIT-3:3(3404)-JUDE-23(3404)

HATRED-all=8135&marked-NU-35:20-2SA-13:15-PS-25:19■109:3,5■139:22-PR-10:12,18■5:17■26:26-EC-9:1,6-EZE-25:15(342)■35:5(342),11-HO-9:7(4895),8(4895)■N.T.-GA-5:20(2189)

HATS-DA-3:21(3737)

HAUGHTILY-MIC-2:3(7317)

HAUGHTINESS-all=7312&marked-IS-2:11,17■13:11(1346)■16:6(1346)-JER-48:29

HAUGHTY-all=1361&marked-2SA-22:28(7311)-PS-131:1-PR-16:18(1363)■18:12■21:24(3093)-IS-3:16■10:33(1364)■24:4(4791)-EZE-16:50-ZEP-3:11

HAUNT-1SA-23:22(7272)■30:31(1980)-EZE-26:17(3427)

HAVE-all=1961&marked-GE-18:12■26:29sup,29■32:5■33:9(3426),11(3426)■43:7(3426)■44:19(3426),20(3426)-EX-18:16■20:3■28:7,32-LE-7:7,8,10,33■13:2,24,29,38■15:19,25■16:4■19:36■23:7,23■24:22■25:26,44■26:37-NU-5:18■9:14■15:29■18:20sup,20■25:13■28:25,26■29:1,7,12,35■32:30(270)■34:6■35:13-DE-5:7■21:15,18,18sup■23:12,13■25:13,14,15^{2}■28:65-JOS-11:20■17:17-J'G-17:13-1SA-2:15(3947)■8:19■9:8(4672)-2SA-9:10■11:9■13:9(3318)■19:28(3426)-1KI-11:32,32sup■17:12(3426)■21:2-2KI-11:15(3318)-1CH-29:3sup,3(3426)3sup-2CH-1:12^{2}sup,12■16:9(3426)■23:14(3318)■35:23(5674)-EZR-4:16(383),20(1934)-JOB-6:8(935),10,10sup■16:18-PS-16:6(5921)-PR-1:14■14:26■30:3(3045)-EC-4:9(3426)■6:3■7:12(1167)-IS-30:29■43:8(3426),8sup■50:11sup,11■56:11(3045)-JER-4:10■23:17■29:7,32■33:21■35:9■36:30■41:8(3426)■44:14(5375)-EZE-6:8■37:24■41:6■44:18^{2}■45:5,10,21■47:22(5307)-DA-2:30(383)■3:25(383)■6:2(1934)-MIC-2:5■5:12■N.T.-all=2192&marked-M'T-3:9,14■5:46■6:1,2sup,2(568),5(568),8,16(568)■8:20,20sup■12:11■14:4,17■15:32sup,32,34■17:20■18:12(1099)■19:16,21,27sup,27(2701)■21:21■26:11^{2},65,65sup■27:65-M'R-2:17,19■3:15■4:17,23,40■6:18,36,38■7:16■8:2^{2}sup,2,5,16,17^{2}■9:50sup,50,50sup■10:21,23■11:22,23(2071),24(2071),25■14:7^{2}-LU-1:14(2071)■3:8■6:32(2076),33(2076),34(2076)■7:40■8:13,18■9:3,13(2076),58,58sup,13(2076),58■10:28,28sup■11:5,6,41(1751)■12:4,17,24(2076),33(5224),50■14:10(2071),18,19sup,19,28■15:31(1699)■16:28,29■18:22,24■19:17■22:37■24:17(474),39,41-JOH-2:3■3:15,16■4:17^{2},32■5:7,26,36,38,39,40,42■6:40,53■8:6,12,26,26sup,41,49■9:41■10:10^{2},16,18^{2},18sup■12:8^{2},35,36■13:29,35■15:22■16:12,22,33^{2},33sup■17:13■18:39(2076)■19:7,10^{2},11,15■20:31■21:5-AC-3:6(5225),6■13:15(2076)■18:10(2076)■19:25(2076),38■21:23(1526),23■23:29■24:15,16,23,25(3335)■25:16,16(2983),26,26sup,26-RO-1:13sup,13■2:14■5:1,2■6:22■8:9,23■9:2(2076),9(2071)■10:2■12:4^{2}■13:3■14:22■15:4,17-1CO-2:16■4:5(1096),15sup,15■5:1■6:4,19■7:2^{2},25,28,29,40■8:1■9:4,5,6,16(2076),17■11:10,16,22^{2}■12:21^{2},23,24,30■13:1,2^{3},3■15:19(2070),31,34-2CO-1:15■2:3,4■3:4,12■4:1,1sup,7■5:1,12■8:11-GA-2:4■6:4,10-EPH-1:7■2:18■3:12■4:28-PH'P-1:7■2:20,27■3:4,17■4:18(568)-COL-1:14■2:1,1sup,23■3:13■4:1-1TH-3:6■4:12,13sup,13■5:1-2TH-3:9-1TI-3:7■5:4,16■6:2-2TI-1:3-PH'M-7-HEB-4:14,15■5:12^{2},14■6:18,18sup,19■7:5,28■8:1sup,1,3■10:2sup,2,34■11:15,15sup■12:9,28■13:5(3918),10^{2},14,18-JAS-1:4■2:1,14■3:14■4:2^{3} ■5:4,4sup-1PE-4:8-2PE-1:19■2:14-1JO-1:3sup,3,6,7,8■2:1,20,28■3:17,21■4:17,21■5:13,14,15-3JO-4-RE-1:18■2:4■2:10,14,20,24sup,24,25■3:17■9:3,4■11:6^{2}■12:17■13:9■14:11■17:13■19:10■22:14(2071)

HAVEN-GE-49:13^{2}(2348)-PS-107:30(4231)■N.T.-AC-27:12^{2}(3040)

HAVENS-AC-27:8(2568)

HAVING-NE-13:4(5414)-IS-41:15(1167)-DA-8:20(1167)■N.T.-all=2192&marked-M'T-7:29■8:9■9:36■15:30■18:8,9■22:12,24,25■26:7-M'R-6:34■8:1,18■9:43,45,47■11:13■12:6■14:3-LU-7:8■8:43(5607,1722)■11:36■15:4,8■17:7■20:28-JOH-5:2■18:10-AC-2:47■4:37(5225,846)-RO-2:14■12:6■15:23-1CO-6:1■7:37■11:4-2CO-4:13■6:10■7:1■9:8■10:6,15-EPH-2:12■5:27■6:14sup,14(1746)-PH'P-1:23,30■2:2■3:9-1TI-3:4■4:8■5:12■6:8-2TI-2:19■3:5-TIT-1:6■2:8-HEB-7:3■10:1,19-1PE-2:12■3:16-2PE-2:14-2JO-12-JUDE-19-RE-5:6,8■7:2■8:3■9:17■12:3,12■13:1■14:1,6,14,17■15:1,2,6^{2}■17:3,4■18:1■20:1■21:11

HAVOCK-AC-8:3(3075)

HAWK-all=5322&marked-LE-11:16(8464),16-DE-14:15(8464),15-JOB-39:26

HAY-PR-27:25(2682)-IS-15:6(2682)■N.T.-1CO-3:12(5528)

HAZEL-GE-30:37(3869)

HEAD-all=7218,a=7217&marked-GE-3:15■40:13,16,17,19,20■47:31■48:14^{2},17^{2},18■49:26,26(6936)-EX-12:9■26:24■29:6,7,10,15,17,19■36:29-LE-1:4,8,12,15■3:2,8,13■4:4,11,15,24,29,33■5:8■8:9,12,14,18,20,22■9:13■13:12,29,30,40,41,44,45■14:9,18,29■16:21^{2}■21:5,10^{2}■24:14-NU-1:4■5:18■6:5^{2},7,9^{2},11,18^{2}■17:3■25:15-DE-19:5(1270)■21:12■28:13,23,35(6936),44■33:16,16(6936)20(6936)-JOS-2:19^{2}■11:10■22:14-J'G-5:26■9:53■10:18■11:8,9,11■13:5■16:13,17,19,22-1SA-1:11■4:12■5:4■10:1■14:45■15:17■17:5,7(3852),38,46,51,54,57■25:39■28:2■31:9-2SA-1:2,10,16■2:16■3:8,29■4:7,8^{2},12■12:30^{2}■13:19^{2}■14:25(6936),26^{2}■15:30^{2},32■16:9■18:9■20:21,22■22:44-1KI-2:32,33^{2},37,44■8:32■19:6(4763)-2KI-2:3,5■4:19■6:5(1270),25,31,32■9:3,6,30■19:21■25:27-1CH-10:9,10(1538)■20:2^{2}■29:11-2CH-6:23-EZR-9:3,6-NE-4:4-ES-2:17■6:8,12■9:25-JOB-1:20■10:15■16:4■19:9■20:6■29:3■41:7-PS-3:3■7:16■18:43■21:3■22:7■23:5■27:6■38:4■40:12■44:14■60:7■68:21■69:4■83:2■108:8■110:7■118:22■133:2■140:7,9■141:5-PR-1:9■4:9■10:6■11:26■25:22-EC-2:14■9:8-SONG-2:6■5:2,11■7:5^{2}■8:3-IS-1:5,6■3:17(6936)■7:8^{2},9^{2},20■9:14,15■19:15■28:1,4■37:22■51:11,20■58:5■59:17-JER-2:16(6936),37■9:1■18:16■22:6■23:19■30:23■48:37,45(6936)■52:31-LA-2:15■3:54■5:16-EZE-5:1■8:3■9:10■10:1,11■13:18■16:12,25,31,43■17:19■21:19,21■29:18■33:4■42:12-DA-1:10■2:28a,32a,38a■3:27a■4:5a,10a,13a■7:1a,9a,15a,20a-HOS-1:11-JOE-3:4,7-AM-2:7■8:10■9:1-OB-15-JON-2:5■4:6,8-MIC-2:13-HAB-3:13,14-ZEC-1:21■3:5^{2}■6:11■N.T.-all=2776&marked-M'T-5:36■6:17■8:20■10:30■14:8,11■21:42■26:7■27:29,30,37-M'R-6:24,25,27,28■12:4(2775),10■14:3■15:19-LU-7:38,44,46■9:58■12:7■20:17■21:18-JOH-13:9■19:2,30■20:7,12-AC-4:11■18:18■27:34-RO-12:20-1CO-11:3^{3},4^{2},5^{2},7,10■12:21-EPH-1:22■4:15■5:23^{2}-COL-1:18■2:10,19-1PE-2:7-RE-1:14■10:1■12:1■14:14■19:12

HEADBANDS-IS-3:20(7196)

HEADLONG-LU-4:29(2630)-AC-1:18(4248)

HEADS-all=7218&marked-GE-2:10-EX-6:14,25■18:25-LE-10:6■19:27-NU-1:16■7:2■8:12■10:4■13:3■25:4■30:1-DE-1:15■5:23■33:5,21-JOS-7:6■14:1■19:51■21:1^{2}■22:21,30■23:2■24:1-J'G-7:25■8:28■9:57-1SA-29:4-1KI-8:1■20:31,32-2KI-10:6,7,8-1CH-5:24■7:2,7,9,11,40■8:6,10,13,28■9:13■12:19,32-2CH-3:16■5:2■28:12-JOB-2:12-PS-24:7,9■66:12■74:13,14■109:25■110:6-IS-15:2■35:10-JER-14:3,4-LA-2:10^{2}-EZE-1:22^{2},25,26■7:18■11:21■22:31■23:15,42■24:23■27:30■32:27■44:18,20^{2}

-**DA**-7:6(7217)-**MIC**-3:1,9,11■**N.T.**-all=2776-**M'T**-27:39-**M'R**-15:29-**LU**-21:28-**AC**-18:6■21:24-**RE**-4:4■9:7,17^{2},19■12:3^{2}■13:1^{2},3■17:3,7,9■18:19

HEADSTONE-**ZEC**-4:7(68,7222)

HEADY-**2TI**-3:4(4312)

HEAL-all=7495-**NU**-12:13-**DE**-32:39-**2KI**-20:5,8-**2CH**-7:14-**PS**-6:2■41:4■60:2-**EC**-3:3-**IS**-19:22^{2}■57:18,19-**JER**-3:22■17:14■30:17-**LA**-2:13-**HO**-5:13■6:1■14:4-**ZEC**-11:16■**N.T.**-all=2323&marked-**M'T**-8:7■10:1,8■12:10■13:15(2390)-**M'R**-3:2,15-**LU**-4:18(2390),23■5:17(2390)■6:7■7:3(1295)■9:2(2390)■10:9■14:3-**JOH**-4:47(2390)■12:40(2390)-**AC**-4:30(2392),28:27(2392)

HEALED-all=7495&marked-**GE**-20:17-**EX**-21:19-**LE**-13:18,37■14:3,48-**DE**-28:27,35-**1SA**-6:3-**2KI**-2:21,22■8:29■9:15-**2CH**-22:6■30:20-**PS**-30:2■107:20-**IS**-6:10■53:5-**JER**-6:14■8:11■15:18■17:14■51:8,9^{2}-**EZE**-30:21(5414,7499)■34:4■47:8,9,11-**HO**-7:1■11:3■**N.T.**-all=2323,a=2390&marked-**M'T**-4:24■8:8a,13a,16■12:15,22■14:14■15:30■19:2■21:14-**M'R**-1:34■3:10■5:23(4982),29a■6:5,13-**LU**-4:40■5:15■6:17a,18,19a■7:7a■8:2a,36(4982),43,47a■9:11a,42a■13:14^{2}■14:4■17:15a■22:51a-**JOH**-5:13a-**AC**-3:11a■4:14■5:16■8:7■14:9(4982)■28:8a,9-**HEB**-12:13a-**JAS**-5:16a-**1PE**-2:24a-**RE**-13:3,12

HEALER-**IS**-3:7(2280)

HEALETH-all=7495&marked-**EX**-15:26-**PS**-103:3■147:3-**IS**-30:26

HEALING-all=4832&marked-**JER**-14:19^{2}■30:13(8585)-**NA**-3:19(3545)-**MAL**-4:2■**N.T.**-all=2323&marked-**M'T**-4:23■9:35-**LU**-9:6,11(2322)-**AC**-4:22(2392)■10:38(2390)-**1CO**-12:9(2386),30(2386)-**RE**-22:2(2322)

HEALINGS-**1CO**-12:28(2386)

HEALTH-all=4832&marked-**GE**-43:28(7965)-**2SA**-20:9(7965)-**PS**-42:11(3444)■43:5(3444)-**PR**-3:8(7500)4:22■12:18■13:17■16:24(4832)-**IS**-58:8(724)-**JER**-8:15,22(724)■30:17(724)■33:6(724)■**N.T.**-**AC**-27:34(4991)-**3JO**-2(5198)

HEAP-all=1530&marked-**GE**-31:46^{2},48,51,52^{3}-**EX**-15:8(5067)-**DE**-13:16(8510)■32:23(5595)-**JOS**-3:13(5067),16(5067)■7:26■8:28(8510),29-**RU**-3:7(6194)-**2SA**-18:17-**JOB**-8:17■16:4(2266)■27:16(6651)■36:13(7760)-**PS**-33:7(5067)■78:13(5067)-**PR**-25:22(2846)-**EC**-2:26(3664)-**SONG**-7:2(6194)-**IS**-17:1(4596),11(5067)■25:2-**JER**-30:18(8510)■49:2(8510)-**EZE**-24:10(7235)-**MIC**-1:6(5856)-**HAB**-1:10(6651)■3:15(2563)-**HAG**-2:16(6194)■**N.T.**-**RO**-12:20(4987)-**2TI**-4:3(2002)

HEAPED-**ZEC**-9:3(6651)■**N.T.**-**JAS**-5:3(2343)

HEAPETH-**PS**-39:6(6651)-**HAB**-2:5(6908)

HEAPS-all=1530&marked-**EX**-8:14(2563)-**J'G**-15:16(2565)-**2KI**-10:8(6652)■19:25-**2CH**-31:6(6194),7(6194),8(6194),9(6194)-**NE**-4:2(6194)-**JOB**-15:28-**PS**-79:1(5856)-**IS**-37:26-**JER**-9:11■26:18(5856)■31:21(8564)■50:26(6194)■51:37-**HO**-12:11-**MIC**-3:12(5856)

HEAR-all=8085,a=6030&marked-**GE**-4:23■21:6■23:6,8,11,13■37:6■42:21,22■49:2-**EX**-6:12■7:16■15:14■19:9■20:19■22:23,27■32:18-**LE**-5:1-**NU**-9:8■12:6■14:13■16:8■20:10■23:18■30:4-**DE**-1:16,17^{2},43■2:25■3:26■4:6,10,28,33,36■5:1,25,27^{2}■6:3,4■9:1■12:28■13:11,12■17:13■18:16■19:20■20:3■21:21■29:4■30:12,13,17■31:12,13■32:1■33:7-**JOS**-3:9■6:5■7:9-**J'G**-5:3,16■7:11■14:13-**1SA**-2:23,24■8:18a■13:3■15:14■16:2■22:7,12■25:24■26:19-**2SA**-14:16■15:3,10,35,36■16:21■17:5■19:35■20:16,17^{2}■22:7,45-**1KI**-4:34■8:30,32,34,36,39,42,43,45,49■10:8,24■18:26a,37a■22:19-**2KI**-7:1,6■14:11■17:14■18:12,28■19:4,7,16^{2}■20:16-**1CH**-14:15■28:2-**2CH**-6:21,23,25,27,30,33,35,39■7:14■9:7,23■13:4■15:2■18:18■20:9,20■25:20■28:11■29:5-**NE**-1:6■4:4,20■8:2■9:29-**JOB**-3:18■5:27■13:6,17■15:17■21:2■22:27■27:9■30:20a■31:35■33:1■34:2,16■35:13■37:2■42:4-**PS**-4:1a,1,3■5:3■10:17(7181)■13:3a■17:1,6a,6■18:44■20:1a,6a,9a■27:7■28:2■30:10■34:2■38:15a■39:12■49:1■50:7■51:8■54:2■55:2a,17,19■59:7■60:5a■61:1■64:1■66:16,18■69:13a,16a,17a■81:8■84:8■85:8■86:1a■92:11■94:9■95:7■102:1,20■115:6■119:145a,149■130:2■135:17(238)■138:4■140:6(238)■141:6■143:1,7a,8■145:19-**PR**-1:5,8■4:1,10■5:7■8:6,33■19:20,27■22:17■23:19-**EC**-5:1■7:5^{2},21■12:13-**SONG**-2:14■8:13-**IS**-1:2,10,15■6:9,10■7:13■18:3■28:12,14,23^{2}■29:18■30:9,19,21■32:3,9■33:13■34:1^{2}■36:13■37:4,7,17^{2}■39:5■41:17a■42:18,23■43:9■44:1■47:8■48:1,14,16■50:4■51:21■55:3■59:1,2■65:12,24■66:4,5-**JER**-2:4■4:21■5:21^{2}■6:10,18,19■7:2,16■9:10,20■10:1■11:2,6,10,14■13:10,11,15,17■14:12■17:20,23■18:2■19:3,15■20:16■21:11■22:2,5,21,29■23:22■25:4■28:7,15■29:19,20■31:10■33:9■34:4■36:3,25■37:20■38:25■42:14,15■44:24,26■49:20■50:45-**LA**-1:18-**EZE**-2:5,7,8■3:10,11,17,27■6:3■8:18■12:2■13:2,19■16:35■18:25■20:47■24:26(2045)■25:3■33:7,30,31,32■34:7,9■36:1,4,15■37:4■40:4■44:5-**DA**-3:5(8086),10(8086),15(8086)■5:23(8086)■9:17,18,19-**HO**-2:21^{3}a,22^{2}a■4:1■5:1-**JOE**-1:2-**AM**-3:1,13■4:1■5:1,23■7:16■8:4-**MIC**-1:2■3:1,4a,9■6:1^{2},2,9■7:7-**NA**-3:19-**HAB**-1:2-**ZEC**-1:4■3:8■7:11,12,13^{2}■8:9■10:6a■13:9a-**MAL**-2:2(8085)■**N.T.**-all=191&marked-**M'T**-10:14,27■11:4,5,15■12:19,42■13:9^{2},13,14,15,16,17,18,43^{2}■15:10■17:5■18:15,16,17^{2}(3878)■21:33■24:6-**M'R**-4:9,12■4:18,20,23,24^{2},33■6:11■7:16,37■8:18■9:7■12:29■13:7-**LU**-5:1,15■6:17,27■7:22■8:8,12,13,18,21■9:9,35■10:24■11:28,31■14:35■15:1■16:2,29,31■18:6■19:48■21:9,38-**JOH**-5:25^{2},28,30■6:60■7:51■8:43,47■9:27^{2}■10:3,8,16,20,27■12:47■14:24■16:13-**AC**-2:8,11,22,33■3:22,23■7:37■10:22,33■13:7,44■15:7■17:21,32■19:26■21:22■22:1,14■23:35(1251)■24:4■25:22^{2}■26:3,29■28:22,26,27,28-**RO**-10:14■11:8-**1CO**-11:18■14:21(1522)-**GA**-4:21-**PH'P**-1:27,30-**2TH**-3:11-**1TI**-4:16-**2TI**-4:17-**HEB**-3:7,15■4:7-**JAS**-1:19-**1JO**-5:15-**3JO**-4-**RE**-1:3■2:7,11,17,29■3:6,13,20,22■9:20■13:9

HEARD-all=8085&marked-**GE**-3:8,10■14:14■16:11■17:20■18:10■21:17^{2},26■24:30,52■27:5,6,34■29:13,33■30:6■31:1■34:5,7■35:22■37:17,21■39:15,19■41:15■42:2■43:25■45:2,16■2:15,24■3:7■4:31■6:5■16:9,12■18:1■23:13■28:35■32:17■33:4-**LE**-10:20■24:14-**NU**-7:89■11:1,10■12:2■14:14,15,27■16:4■20:16■21:1■22:36■24:4,16■30:7^{2},8,11,12,14■30:15■33:40-**DE**-1:34■4:12,32,33■5:23,24,26,28^{2}■9:2■17:4■26:7-**JOS**-2:10,11■5:1■6:20■9:1,3,9,16■10:1■11:1■22:11,12,30■24:27-**J'G**-7:15■9:30,46■18:25■20:3-**RU**-1:6-**1SA**-1:13■2:22■4:6,14,19■7:7^{2},9(6030)■8:21■11:6■13:3,4■14:22,27■17:11,23,28,31■22:1,6■23:10,11,25■25:4,7,39■31:11-**2SA**-3:28■4:1■5:17^{2}■7:22■8:9■10:7■11:26■13:21■18:5■19:2-**1KI**-1:11,41^{2},45■2:42■3:28■4:34■5:1,7■6:7■9:3■10:1,6,7■11:21■12:2,20■13:4,26■14:6■15:21■16:16■17:22■19:13■20:12,31■21:15,16,27-**2KI**-3:21■5:8■6:30■9:30■11:13■19:1,4,6,8,9,11,20,25■20:5,12■22:11,18,19■25:23-**1CH**-10:11■14:8^{2}■17:20■18:9■19:8-**2CH**-5:13■7:12■9:1,5,6■10:2■15:8■16:5■20:29■23:12■30:27■33:13■34:19,26,27-**EZR**-3:13■4:1■9:3-**NE**-1:4■2:10,19■4:1,7,15■5:6■6:1,16■8:9■12:43■13:3-**ES**-1:18■2:8-**JOB**-2:11■4:16■13:1■15:8■16:2■19:7(6030)■20:3■26:14■28:22■29:11■33:8■37:4■42:5-**PS**-3:4(6030)■6:8,9■10:17■18:6■19:3■22:21(6030),24■28:6■31:13■34:4(6030),6■38:13■40:1■44:1■48:8■61:5■62:11■66:8,19■76:8■78:3,21,59■81:5■97:8■106:44■116:1■118:21(6030)■120:1(6030)■132:6-**PR**-21:13(6030)-**EC**-9:16,17-**SONG**-2:12-**IS**-6:8■10:30(7181)■15:4■16:6■21:10■24:16■28:22■30:30■37:1,4,6,8,9^{2},11,26■38:5■39:1■40:21,28■42:2■48:6■49:8(6030)■52:15■58:4■60:18■64:4■65:19■66:8,19-**JER**-3:21■4:19,31■6:7,24■7:13■8:6,16■9:19■18:13,22■20:1,10■23:18^{2},25■25:8,36■26:7,10,11,12,21^{2}■30:5■31:15,18■33:10■34:10■35:17■36:11,13,16,24■37:5■38:1,7■40:7,11■41:11■42:4■46:12■48:4,5,29■49:2,14,21,23■50:43,46■51:46,51-**LA**-1:21^{2}■3:56,61-**EZE**-1:24,28■2:2■3:12■10:5■19:4,9■26:13■27:30■33:5■35:12,13■43:6-**DA**-3:7(8086)■5:14(8086),16(8086)■6:14(8086)■8:13,16■10:9^{2},12■12:7,8-**HO**-7:12■14:8(6030)-**OB**-1-**JON**-2:2(6030)-**MIC**-5:15-**NA**-2:13-**HAB**-3:2,16-**ZEP**-2:8-**ZEC**-8:23-**MAL**-3:16■**N.T.**-all=191&marked-**M'T**-2:3,9,18■2:22■4:12■5:21,27,33,38,43■6:7(1522)■8:10■9:12■11:2■12:24■13:17■14:1,13^{2}■15:12■17:6■19:22,25■20:24,30■21:45■22:7,22,33,34■26:65■27:47-**M'R**-2:17■3:8,21■4:15,16■5:27,36■6:14,16,20^{2},29,55■7:25■10:41,47■11:14,18■12:28,37■14:11,58,64■15:35■16:11-**LU**-1:13(1522),41,58,66■2:18,20,47■4:23,28■7:3,9,22,29■8:14,15,50■9:7■10:24,39■12:3■14:15■15:25■16:14■18:22,23,26■19:11■20:16■22:71■23:6,8-**JOH**-1:37,40■3:32■4:1,42,47■5:37■6:45,60■7:32,40■8:9,26,40■9:32,35,40■11:4,6,20,29,41■12:12,18,29,34■14:28■15:15■18:21■19:8,13■21:7-**AC**-1:4■2:6,37■4:4,20,24■5:5,11,21,24,33■6:11,14■7:12,34,54■8:14,30■9:4,13,21,38■10:31(1522),44,46■11:1,7,18■13:48■14:9,14■15:24■16:14,25(1874),38■17:8,32■18:26■19:2,5,10,28■21:12,20■22:2,7,9,15,26■23:16■24:22,24■26:14■28:15-**RO**-10:14,18■15:21-**1CO**-2:9-**2CO**-6:2(1873)■12:4-**GA**-1:13,23-**EPH**-1:13,15■3:2■4:21-**PH'P**-2:26■4:9-**COL**-1:4,5(4257)6,9,23-**1TH**-2:13(189)-**2TI**-1:13■2:2-**HEB**-2:1,3■3:16■4:2■5:7(1522)■12:19-**JAS**-5:11-**2PE**-1:18-**1JO**-1:1,3,5■2:7,18,24^{2}■3:11■4:3-**2JO**-6-**RE**-1:10■3:3■4:1■5:11,13■6:1,3,5,6,7■7:4■8:13■9:13,16■10:4,8■11:12■12:10■14:2^{2},13■16:1,5,7■18:4,22^{2},23■19:1,6■21:3■22:8^{2}

HEARDEST-all=8085&marked-**DE**-4:36-**JOS**-14:12-**2KI**-22:19-**2CH**-34:27-**NE**-9:9,27,28-**PS**-31:22■119:26(6030)-**IS**-48:7,8-**JON**-2:2

HEARER-**JAS**-1:23(202),25(202)

HEARERS-**RO**-2:13(202)-**EPH**-4:29(191)-**2TI**-2:14(191)-**JAS**-1:22(202)

HEAREST-all=8085&marked-**RU**-2:8-**1SA**-24:9-**2SA**-5:24-**1KI**-8:30-**2CH**-6:21-**PS**-22:2(6030)■65:2■**N.T.**-all=191-**M'T**-21:16■27:13-**JOH**-3:8■11:42

HEARETH-all=8085-**EX**-16:7,8-**NU**-30:5-**DE**-29:19-**1SA**-3:9,10,11-**2SA**-17:9-**2KI**-21:12-**JOB**-34:28-**PS**-34:17■38:14■69:33-**PR**-8:34■13:1^{2},8■15:29,31,32■18:13■21:28■25:10■29:24-**IS**-41:26■42:20-**JER**-19:3-**EZE**-3:27■33:4■**N.T.**-all=191-**M'T**-7:24,26■13:19,20,22,23-**LU**-6:47,49■10:16-**JOH**-3:29■5:24■8:47■9:31^{2}■18:37-**2CO**-12:6-**1JO**-4:5,6^{2}■5:14-**RE**-22:17,18

HEARING-all=8085&marked-**DE**-31:11(241)-**2SA**-18:12(241)-**2KI**-4:31(7182)-**JOB**-33:8(241)■42:5(8088)-**PR**-20:12■28:9-**EC**-1:8-**IS**-11:3(4926)■21:3■33:15-**EZE**-9:5(241)■10:13(241)-**AM**-8:11■**N.T.**-all=191,a=189&marked

-M'T-13:13,14a,15-M'R-4:12■6:2-LU-2:46■8:10■18:36-AC-5:5■8:6■9:7■18:8■25:21(1233),23(201)■28:26a,27-RO-10:17^{2}a-1CO-12:17^{2}a-GA-3:2a,5a-PH'M-5-HEB-5:11a-2PE-2:8a

HEARKEN-all=8085,a=7181&marked-GE-4:23(238)■21:12■23:15■34:17■49:2-EX-3:18■4:1,8,9■6:30■7:4,22■11:9■15:26■18:19-LE-26:14,18,21,27-NU-23:18(238)-DE-1:45■4:1■7:12■11:13■13:3,8,18■15:5■17:12■18:15,19■21:18■23:5■26:17■27:9■28:1,2,13,15■30:10-JOS-1:17,18■24:10-J'G-2:17■3:4■9:7^2■11:17■19:25■20:13-1SA-8:7,9,22■15:1,22a■28:22■30:24-2SA-12:18■13:14,16-1KI-8:28,29,30,52■11:38■20:8■22:28-2KI-10:6■17:40■18:31,32-2CH-6:19,20,21■10:16■18:27■20:15a■33:10a-NE-13:27-JOB-13:6a■32:10■33:1(238),31,33■34:10,16(238),34■37:14(238)-PS-5:2a■34:11■45:10■58:5■81:8,11-PR-7:24■8:32■23:22■29:12a-SONG-8:13a-IS-28:23a■32:3a■34:1a■36:16■42:23a■46:3,12■48:12■49:1a■51:1,4a,7■55:2-JER-6:10a,17^{2}a■7:27■11:11■16:12■17:24,27■18:19■23:16■26:3,4,5■27:9,14,16,17■29:8,12■35:13■37:2■38:15■44:16-EZE-3:7^2■20:8,39-DA-9:19a-HO-5:1a■9:17-MIC-1:2a-ZEC-1:4a■7:11a■N.T.-all=191&marked-M'R-4:3■7:14-AC-2:14(1801)■4:19■7:2■12:13(5219)■15:13-JAS-2:5

HEARKENED-all=8085&marked-GE-3:17■16:2■23:16■30:17,22■34:24■39:10-EX-6:9,12■7:13■8:15,19■9:12■16:20■18:24-NU-14:22■21:3-DE-9:19,23■10:10■18:14■26:14■34:9-JOS-1:17■10:14-J'G-2:20■11:28■13:9-1SA-2:25■12:1■19:6■25:35■28:21,23-1KI-2:15,16,24■15:20■20:25-2KI-13:4■16:9■20:13■21:9■22:13-2CH-10:15■16:4■24:17■25:16■30:20■35:22-NE-9:16,29,34(7181)-ES-3:4-JOB-9:16(238)-PS-81:13■106:25-IS-21:7(7181)■48:18(7181)-JER-6:19(7181)■7:24,26■8:6■25:3,4,7■26:5■29:19■32:33■34:14,17■35:14,15,16■36:31■37:14■44:5-EZE-3:6-DA-9:6-MAL-3:16(7181)■N.T.-AC-27:21(3980)

HEARKENEDST-DE-28:45(8085)

HEARKENETH-PR-1:33(8085)■12:15(8085)

HEARKENING-PS-103:20(8085)

HEART-all=3820,a=3824&marked-GE-6:5,6■8:21^2■17:17■20:5a,6a■24:45■27:41■42:28■45:26-EX-4:14,21■7:3,13,14,22,23■8:15,19,32■9:7,12,14,34,35■10:1^2,20,27■11:10■14:4,5a,8■15:8■23:9(5315)■25:2■28:29,30^2■35:5,21,26,29,34,35■36:2^2-LE-19:17a■26:16(5315)-NU-15:39a■32:7,9-DE-1:28a■2:30a■4:9a,29a,39a■5:29a■6:5a,6a■7:17a■8:2a,5a,14a,17a■9:4a,5a■10:12a,16a■11:13a,16a,18a■13:3a■15:7a,9a,10a■17:17a,20a■18:21a■19:6a■20:8a■24:15(5315)■26:16a■28:28a,47a,65,67a■29:4,18a,19a,19■30:2a,6^{3}a,10a,14a,17a-JOS-5:1a■14:7a,8■22:5a■24:23a-J'G-5:9,15,16■16:15,17,18^2■18:20■19:5,6,8a,9a-RU-3:7-1SA-1:8a,13■2:1,33(5315),35a■4:13■9:19a■10:9■12:20a,24a■13:14a■14:7^{2}a■16:7a■17:28a,32■21:12a■24:5■25:31,36,37■27:1■28:5-2SA-3:21(5315)■6:16■7:3a,21,27■13:28,33■14:1■17:10■18:14■19:14a,19■24:10-1KI-2:4a,44a■3:6a,9,12■4:29■8:17a,18^{2}a,23a,38a,39a,48a,61a,66a■9:3a,4a■10:2a,24■11:2a,3,4^{3}a,9a■12:26,27,33■14:8a■15:3^{2}a,14a■18:37■21:7-2KI-5:26■6:11■9:24■10:15a,30a,31a■12:4■14:10■20:3a■22:19a■23:3,25a-1CH-12:17a,33,38,38a■15:29■16:10■17:2a,19■22:19a■28:2a,9■29:9,17^{2}a,18^{2}a,19a-2CH-1:11a■6:7a,8^{2}a,30a,38■7:10,11,16■9:1a,23■12:14■15:12a,15a,17a■16:9a■17:6■19:3a,9a■22:9a■25:2a,19■26:16■29:10a,31,34a■30:12,19a■31:21a■32:25,26,31a■34:27a,31a■36:13a-EZR-6:22■7:10a,27-NE-2:2,12■6:8■7:5■9:8a-ES-1:10■5:9■6:6■7:5-JOB-7:17■8:10■9:4a■10:13a■11:13■12:24■15:12■17:4,11a■22:22a■23:16■27:6a■29:13■31:7,9,27■33:3■34:14■36:13■37:1,24■38:36(7907)■41:24-PS-4:4a,7■7:10■9:1■10:6,11,13,17■11:2■12:2■13:2a,5■14:1■15:2a■16:9■17:3■19:8,14■20:4a■22:14,26a■24:4a■25:17a■26:2■27:3,8,14■28:7^2■31:24a■32:11■33:11,21■34:18■36:1,10■37:4,15,31■38:8,10■39:3■40:8(4578),10,12■41:6■44:18,21■45:1,5■49:3■51:10,17■53:1■55:4,21■57:7■58:2■61:2■62:8a,10■64:6■10■66:18■69:20,32a■73:1a,7a,13a,21a,26^{2}a■77:6a■78:8,18a,37,72a■84:2,5a■86:11a,12a■94:15■95:8a,10a■97:11■101:2a,4,5a■102:4a■104:15^{2}a■105:3,25■107:12■108:1■109:16a,22■111:1a■112:7,8■119:2,7a,10,11,32,34,36,58,69,70,80,111,112,145,161■131:1■138:1■139:23a■140:2■141:4■143:4■147:3-PR-2:2,10■3:1,3,5■4:4,21a,23■5:12■6:14,18,21,25a■7:3,10,25■8:5■10:8,20■11:20,29■12:8,20,23,25■13:12,14:10,13,14,30,33■15:7,13^2,14,15,28,30■16:1,5,9,21,23■17:16,20,22■18:2,12,15■19:3,21■20:5,9■21:1,4■22:11,15,17■23:7(5315),7,12,15,17,19,26,33■24:2,12(3826),17■25:3,20■26:23,25■27:9,11,19■28:14,25(5315),26■31:11-EC-1:13,16^2,17■2:1,3^2,10^2,15^2,20,22,23■3:11,17,18■5:2,20■7:2,3,4^2,7,22,25,26■8:5,9,11,16■9:1,3,3a,7■10:2^2■11:9^2,10-SONG-3:11■4:9^2(3823)■5:2■8:6-IS-1:5a■6:10,10a■7:2a■9:9a■10:7^{2}a,12a■13:7a■14:13a■15:5■19:1a,21:4a■29:13■30:29a■32:4a,6■33:18■35:4■38:3■42:25■44:19,20■47:7,8a,10■49:21a■51:7■57:1,11,15,17■59:13■60:5a■63:4,17■65:14^2■66:14-JER-3:10,15,17■4:4a,9^2,14,18,19^2■5:23,24a■7:24,31■8:18■9:8(7130),14,26■11:8,20■12:3,11■13:10,22a■14:14■15:16a■16:12■17:1,5,9,10■18:12■20:9,12■22:17■23:9,16,17,20,26^2■24:7^2■29:13a■31:21,24■31:21■32:39,41■48:29,36^2,41■49:16,22^2■51:46a-LA-1:20,22■2:18,19■3:41a,51(5315),65■5:15,17-EZE-3:10a■6:9■11:19^3,21^2■13:17,22■14:3,4,5,7■16:30(3826)■18:31■20:16■21:7,15■22:14■25:6(5315),15(5315)■27:31(5315)■28:2^2,5a,6,17■31:10a,33:31■36:5a,26^3■40:4■44:7,9-DA-1:8■2:30(3825)■4:16^2(3825)■5:20(3825),21(3825),22(3825)■6:14(1079)■7:4(3825),28(3821)■8:25(3824)■10:12■11:12a,28a-HO-4:8(5315),11■7:6,11■10:2■11:8■13:6,8-JOE-2:12a,13a-OB-3^2-NA-2:10-ZEP-1:12a■2:15a■3:14-ZEC-7:10a■10:7^2■12:5-MAL-2:2^2■4:6^2■N.T.-all=2588&marked-M'T-5:8,28■6:21■11:29■12:34,35,40■13:15^2,19■15:8,18,19■22:37■24:48-M'R-6:52■7:6,19,21■8:17■10:5(4641)■11:23■12:30,33■16:14(4641)-LU-2:19,51■6:45^3■8:15■9:47■10:27■12:34,45■24:25,32-JOH-12:40^2■13:2■14:1,27■16:6,22-AC-2:26,37,46■4:32■5:3,4■7:23,51,54■8:21,22,37■11:23■13:22■16:14■21:13■28:27^2-RO-1:21■2:5,29■6:17■9:2■10:6,8,9,10-1CO-2:9■7:37^2■14:25-2CO-2:4■3:3,15■5:12■6:11■8:16■9:7-EPH-4:18■5:19■6:5,6(5590)-PH'P-1:7-COL-3:22-1TH-2:17-1TI-1:5-2TI-2:22-HEB-3:10,12■4:12■10:22■13:9-JAS-1:26-1PE-1:22■3:4-2PE-2:14-1JO-3:20^2,21-RE-18:7

HEARTED-all=3820-EX-28:3■31:6■35:10,22,25■36:1,2,8

HEARTH-all=254-PS-102:3(4168)-IS-30:14(3344)-JER-36:22,23^2-ZEC-12:6(3595)

HEARTILY-COL-3:23(1537,5590)

HEART'S-PS-10:3(5315)■21:2(3820)■N.T.-RO-10:1(2588)

HEARTS-all=3820,a=3824&marked-GE-18:5-EX-14:17■31:6-LE-26:36a,41a-DE-20:3a■32:46a-JOS-2:11a■7:5a■11:20■23:14a-J'G-9:3■16:25■19:22-1SA-6:6a,6■7:3^{2}a■10:26-2SA-15:6,13-1KI-8:39a,58a-1CH-28:9a-2CH-6:14,30a■11:16a■20:33a-JOB-1:5a-PS-7:9(3826)■28:3a■33:15■35:25■74:8■90:12a■125:4(3826)-PR-15:11(3826)■17:3(3826)■21:2(3826)■31:6(3515)-IS-44:18(3826)-JER-31:33■32:40a■42:20(5315)■48:41-EZE-13:2■32:9-DA-11:27a-HO-7:2a-ZEC-7:12■8:17■N.T.-all=2588&marked-M'T-9:4■18:35■19:8(4641)-M'R-2:6,8■3:5■4:15-LU-1:17,51,66■2:35■3:15■5:22■8:12■16:15■21:14,26(674),34■24:38-AC-1:24(2589)■7:39■14:17■15:8(2589),9-RO-1:24■2:15■5:5■8:27■16:18-1CO-4:5-2CO-1:22■3:2■4:6■7:3-GA-4:6-EPH-3:17■6:22-PH'P-4:7-COL-2:2■3:15,16■4:8-1TH-2:4■3:13-2TH-2:17■3:5-HEB-3:8,15■4:7■8:10■10:16,22-JAS-3:14■4:8■5:5,8-1PE-3:15-2PE-1:19-1JO-3:19-RE-2:23■17:17

HEARTS'-PS-81:12(3820)

HEARTY-PR-27:9(5315)

HEAT-all=2527&marked-GE-8:22■18:1-DE-29:24(2750)■32:24(7565)-1SA-11:11-2SA-4:5-1KI-1:1(3179),2(2552)-JOB-24:19■30:30(2721)-PS-19:6(2535)-EC-4:11(2552)-IS-4:6(2721)■18:4^2■25:4(2721),5^2(2721)■49:10(8273)-JER-17:8■36:30(2721)■51:39-EZE-3:14(2534)-DA-3:19(228)■N.T.-all=2742&marked-M'T-20:12-LU-12:55-AC-28:3(2329)-JAS-1:11-2PE-3:10(2741),12(2741)-RE-7:16(2738)■16:9(2738)

HEATED-DA-3:19(228)-HO-7:4(1197)

HEATH-JER-17:6(6176)■48:6(6176)

HEATHEN-all=1471-LE-25:44■26:33,38,45-DE-4:27-2SA-22:44,50-2KI-16:3■17:8,11,15■21:2-1CH-16:24,35-2CH-20:6■28:3■33:2,9■36:14-EZR-6:21-NE-5:8,9,17■6:6,16-PS-2:1,8■9:5,15,19■10:16■18:43,49■33:10■44:2,11,14■46:6,10■47:8■59:5,8■78:55■79:1,6,10^2■80:8■94:10■96:3,10■98:2■102:15■105:44■106:35,41,47■110:6■111:6■115:2■126:2■135:15■149:7-IS-16:8-JER-9:16■10:2^2,25■18:13■49:14,15-LA-1:3,10■4:15,20-EZE-7:24■11:12,16■12:16■16:14■20:9,14■20:22,23,32,41■22:4,15,16■23:30■25:7,8■28:25■30:3■31:11,17■34:28,29■36:3,4,5,6,7,15,19,20,21,22,23^2,24,30,36■37:21,28■38:16■39:7,21^2,23,28-JOE-2:17,19■3:11,12^2-AM-9:12-OB-1,2,15,16-MIC-5:15-HAB-1:5■3:12-ZEP-2:11-HAG-2:22-ZEC-1:15■8:13■9:10■14:14,18-MAL-1:11,14■N.T.-all=1484&marked-M'T-6:7(1482)■18:17(1482)-AC-4:25-2CO-11:26-GA-1:16■2:9■3:8

HEAVE-all=8641&marked-EX-29:27,28^3-LE-7:14,32,34■10:14,15-NU-6:20■15:19,20^2,20(7311),21■18:8,11,19,24,26,27,28^2,29■31:29,41-DE-12:6,11,17

HEAVED-all=7311-EX-29:27-NU-18:30,32

HEAVEN-all=8064,a=8065&marked-GE-1:1,8,9,14,15,17,20■6:17■7:11,19,23■8:2^2■11:4■14:19,22■15:5■19:24■21:17■22:11,15,17■24:3,7■26:4■27:28,39■28:12,17■49:25-EX-9:8,10,22,23■10:21,22■16:4■17:14■20:4,11,22■24:10■31:17■32:13-LE-26:19-DE-1:10,28■2:25■3:24■4:11,19^3,26,32,36,39■5:8■7:24■9:1,14■10:14,22■11:11,17,21■17:3■25:19■26:15■28:12,23,24,62■29:20■30:4,12^2,19■31:28■32:40■33:13,26-JOS-2:11■8:20■10:11,13-J'G-5:20■13:20■20:40-1SA-2:10■5:12-2SA-18:9■21:10■22:8,14-1KI-8:22,23,27,30,32,34,35,36,39,43,45,49,54■18:45■22:19-2KI-1:10^2,12^2,14■2:1,11■7:2,19■14:27■17:16■19:15■21:3,5■23:4,5-1CH-21:16,26■29:11-2CH-2:6,12■6:13,14,18,21,23,26,27,30■7:1,13,14■18:18■20:6■28:9■30:27■32:20■33:3,5■36:23-EZR-1:2■5:11(8065),12(8065)■6:9(8065),10(8065)■7:12(8065),21(8065),23^2(8065)-NE-1:4,5,9■2:4,20■9:6^2,13,15,23,27,28-JOB-1:16■2:12■11:8■16:19■20:27■22:12,14■26:11■28:24■35:11■37:3■38:29,33,37■41:11-PS-11:4■14:2■19:6■20:6■33:13■53:2■57:3■69:34■73:25■76:8■77:18(1534)■

78:23,24,26■79:2■80:14■85:11■89:6(7834),29,37(7834)■102:19■103:11■104:12■105:40■107:26■113:6■115:15,16■119:89■121:2■124:8■134:3■135:6■136:26■139:8■146:6■147:8■148:13-PR-23:5■25:3■30:4-EC-1:13■2:3■3:1■5:2-IS-13:5,10■14:12,13■34:4,5■37:16■40:12■55:10■63:15■66:1-JER-7:18,33■8:2,7■10:2■15:3■16:4■19:7,13■23:24■31:37■32:17■33:22,25■34:20■44:17,18,19,25■49:36■51:9,15,48,53-LA-2:1■3:50■4:19-EZE-8:3■29:5■31:6,13■32:4,7,8■28:20-DA-2:18a,19a,28a,37a,38a,44a■4:11a,12a,13a,15a,20a,21a,22a,23^{2}a,25a,31a,33a,34a,35a,37a■5:21a,23a■6:27a■7:2a,13a,27a■8:8,10■9:12■11:4■12:7-HO-2:18■4:3■7:12-AM-9:2,6-JON-1:9-NA-3:16-ZEP-1:3,5-HAG-1:10-ZEC-2:6■5:9-MAL-3:10■N.T.-all=3772&marked-M'T-3:2,17■4:17■5:3,10,12,16,18,19^{2},20,34■5:45,48■6:1,9,10,20■7:11,21^{2}■8:11■10:7,32,33■11:11,12,23,25■12:50■13:11,24,31,33,44,45,47,52■14:19■16:1,17,19^{3}■18:1,3,4,10^{2},14,18^{2},19,23■19:14,21,23■20:1■21:25^{2}■22:2,30■23:9,13,22■24:29,30^{2},31,35,36■25:1■26:64■28:2,18-M'R-1:11■6:41■7:34■8:11■10:21■11:25,26,30,31■12:25■13:25^{2},27,31,32■14:62■16:19-LU-2:15■3:21,22■4:25■6:23■9:16,54■10:15,18,20,21■11:2^{2},16■15:7,18,21■16:17■17:24^{2},29■18:13,22■19:38■20:4,5■21:11,26,33■22:43■24:51-JOH-1:32,51■3:13^{3},27,31■6:31,32^{2},33,38,41,42,50,51,58■12:28■17:1-AC-1:10,11^{3}■2:2,5,19■3:21■4:12,24■7:42,49,55■9:3■10:11,16■11:5,9■14:10,15,17(3771)■17:24■22:6■26:13(3771)-RO-1:18■10:6-1CO-8:5■15:47-2CO-5:2■12:2-GA-1:8-EPH-1:10■3:15■6:9-PH'P-2:10(2032)■3:20-COL-1:5,16,20,23■4:1-1TH-1:10■4:16-2TH-1:7-HEB-9:24■10:34■12:23,25,26-JAS-5:12,18-1PE-1:4,12■3:22-2PE-1:18-1JO-5:7-RE-3:12■4:1,2■5:3,13■6:13,14■8:1,10,13(3321)■9:1■10:1,4,5,6,8■11:6,12^{2},13,15,19■12:1,3,4,7,8,10■13:6,13■14:2,6(3321),7,13,17■15:1,5■16:11,17,21■18:1,4,5,20■19:1,11,14,17(3321)■20:1,9,11■21:1^{2},2,3,10

HEAVENLY-all=2032&marked-M'T-6:14(3770),26(3770),32(3770)■15:13(3770)■18:35-LU-2:13(3770)■11:13(1537,3772)-JOH-3:12-AC-26:19(3770)-1CO-15:48^{2},49-EPH-1:3,20■2:6■3:10-2TI-4:18-HEB-3:1■6:4■8:5■9:23■11:16■12:22

HEAVEN'S-M'T-19:12(3772)

HEAVENS-all=8064&marked-GE-2:1,4^{2}-DE-10:14■32:1■33:28-J'G-5:4-2SA-22:10-1KI-8:27-1CH-16:26,31■27:23-2CH-2:6■6:18,25,33,35,39-EZR-9:6-NE-9:6-JOB-9:8■14:12■15:15■20:6■26:13■35:5-PS-2:4■8:1,3■18:9,13■19:1■33:6■36:5■50:4,6■57:5,10,11■68:4(6160),8,33■73:9■89:2,5,11■96:5,11■97:6■102:25■103:19■104:2■108:4,5■113:4■115:3,16■123:1■136:5■144:5■148:1,4^{2}-PR-3:19■8:27-IS-1:2■5:30(6183)■13:13■34:4■40:22■42:5■44:23,24■45:8,12,18■48:13■49:13■50:3■51:6^{2},13,16■55:9■64:1■65:17■66:22-JER-2:12■4:23,25,28■9:10■10:11^{2}(8065),12,13■14:22■51:16-LA-3:41,66-EZE-1:1-DA-4:26(8065)-HO-2:21-JOE-2:10,30■3:16-HAB-3:3-HAG-2:6,21-ZEC-6:5■8:12■12:1■N.T.-all=3772-M'T-3:16■24:29-M'R-1:10-LU-12:33-AC-2:34■7:56-2CO-5:1-EPH-4:10-HEB-1:10■4:14■7:26■8:1■9:23-2PE-3:5,7,10,12,13-RE-12:12

HEAVIER-all=3513-JOB-6:3■23:2-PR-27:3

HEAVILY-EX-14:25(3517)-PS-35:14(6957)-IS-47:6(3513)

HEAVINESS-all=8424&marked-EZR-9:5(8589)-JOB-9:27(6440)-PS-69:20(5136)■119:28-PR-10:1■12:25(1674)■14:13-IS-29:2(8386)■61:3(3544)■N.T.-RO-9:2(3077)-2CO-2:1(3077)-PH'P-2:26(85)-JAS-4:9(2726)-1PE-1:6(3076)

HEAVY-all=3513&marked-EX-17:12(5315)■18:18(5315)-NU-11:14(5315)-1SA-4:18■5:6,11-2SA-14:26-1KI-12:4(3515),10,11(5315),14■14:6(7186)■20:43(5620)■21:4(5620)-2CH-10:4(3515),10,11(3515),14-NE-5:18-JOB-33:7-PS-32:4■38:4(5315),4-PR-25:20(7451)■27:3(3514)■31:6(4751)-IS-6:10■24:20■30:27(3514)■58:6(4133)■59:1-LA-3:7■N.T.-all=916&marked-M'T-23:4(926)■26:37(85),43-M'R-14:33(85),40-LU-9:32

HEDGE-all=1447&marked-JOB-1:10(7535)-PR-15:9(4881)-EC-10:8-IS-5:5(4881)-EZE-13:5■22:30-HO-2:6(7753)-MIC-7:4(4534)■N.T.-M'R-12:1(5418)

HEDGED-JOB-3:23(5526)-LA-3:7(1443)■N.T.-M'T-21:33(5418,4060)

HEDGES-all=1448&marked-1CH-4:23-PS-80:12(1447)■89:40-JER-49:3-NA-3:17■N.T.-LU-14:23(5418)

HEED-all=8104&marked-GE-31:24,29-EX-10:28■19:12■34:12-NU-23:12-DE-2:4■4:9,15,23■11:16■12:13,19,30■24:8■27:9(5535)-JOS-22:5■23:11-1SA-19:2-2SA-20:10-1KI-2:4■8:25-2KI-10:31-1CH-22:13■28:10(7200)-2CH-6:16■19:6(7200),7■33:8-EZR-4:22(2095)-JOB-36:21-PS-39:1■119:9-PR-17:4(7181)-EC-7:21(5414,3820)■12:9(238)-IS-7:4■21:7(7182)-JER-9:4■17:21■18:18(7181),19(7181)-HO-4:10-MAL-2:15,16■N.T.-all=991&marked-M'T-6:1(4337)■16:6(3708)■18:10(3708)■24:4-M'R-4:24■8:15(3708)■13:5,9,23,33-LU-8:18■11:35(4648)■12:15(3708)■17:3(4337)■21:8,34(4337)-AC-3:5(1907)■5:35(4337)■8:6(4337),10(4337)■20:28(4337)■22:26(3708)-1CO-3:10■8:9■10:12-GA-5:15-COL-4:17-1TI-1:4(4337)■4:1(4337),16(1907)-TIT-1:14(4337)-HEB-2:1(4337)■3:12-2PE-1:19(433)

HEEL-all=6119&marked-GE-3:15■25:26-JOB-18:9-PSA-41:9-HO-12:3(6117)■N.T.-JOH-13:18(4418)

HEELS-GE-49:17(6119)-JOB-13:27(8328)-PS-49:5(6120)-JER-13:22(6119)

HEIFER-all=5697&marked-GE-15:9-NU-19:2(6510),5(6510),6(6510),9(6510),10(6510)-DE-21:3,4,6-J'G-14:18-1SA-16:2-IS-15:5-JER-46:20■48:34■50:11-HO-4:16(6510)■10:11-HEB-9:13(1151)

HEIFER'S-DE-21:4(5697)

HEIGHT-all=6967&marked-GE-6:15-EX-25:10,23■27:1,18■30:2■37:1,10,25■38:1,18-1SA-16:7(1364)■17:4(1363)-1KI-6:2,20,26■7:2,16^{2},23,27,32-2KI-19:23(4791)■25:17^{2}-2CH-3:4(1363)■4:1,2■33:14(1361)-EZR-6:3(7312)-JOB-22:12(1363),12(7218)-PS-102:19(4791)-PR-25:3(7312)-IS-7:11(1361)■37:24^{2}(4791)-JER-31:12(4791)■49:16(4791)■51:53(4791)■52:21,22-EZE-17:23(4791)■19:11(1363)■20:40(4791)■31:5,10,10(1363),14,14(1363)■32:5(7419)■40:5■41:8(1364)-DA-3:1(7314)■4:10(7314),11(7314),20(7314)-AM-2:9^{2}(1363)■N.T.-RO-8:39(5313)-EPH-3:18(5311)-RE-21:16(5311)

HEIGHTS-PS-148:1(4791)-IS-14:14(1116)

HEINOUS-JOB-31:11(2154)

HEIR-all=3423-GE-15:3,4^{2}■21:10-2SA-14:7-PR-30:23-JER-49:1,2-MIC-1:15■N.T.-all=2818&marked-M'T-21:38-M'R-12:7-LU-20:14-RO-4:13-GA-4:1,7,30(2816)-HEB-1:2■11:7

HEIRS-JER-49:2(3423)■N.T.-all=2818&marked-RO-4:14■8:17-GA-3:29-TIT-3:7-HEB-1:14(2816)■6:17■11:9(4789)-JAS-2:5-1PE-3:7(4789)

HELD-all=2790&marked-GE-24:21■34:5■48:17(8557)-EX-17:11(7311)■36:12(6901)-LE-10:3(1826)-NU-30:7,11,14-J'G-7:20(2388)■16:26(2388)-RU-3:15(270)-1SA-10:27-2SA-18:16(2820)-1KI-8:65(6213)-2KI-18:36-2CH-4:5(3557)-NE-4:16(2388),17(2388),21(2388)■5:8-ES-5:2(3447)■7:4■8:4(3447)-JOB-23:11(270)■29:10(2244)-PS-32:9(1102)■39:2(2814)■94:18(5582)-SONG-3:4(270)■7:5(631)-IS-36:21■57:11(2814)-JER-50:33(2388)-DA-12:7(7311)■N.T.-all=4623&marked-M'T-12:14(2983)■26:63■28:9(2902)-M'R-3:4■9:34■14:61■15:1(4160)-LU-14:4(2270)■20:26(4601)■22:63(4912)-AC-3:11(2902)■11:18(2270)■14:4(2258)■15:13(4601)-RO-7:6(2722)-RE-6:9(2192)

HELL-all=7585-DE-32:22-2SA-22:6-JOB-11:8■26:6-PS-9:17■16:10■18:5■55:15■86:13■116:3■139:8-PR-5:5■7:27■9:18■15:11,24■23:14■27:20-IS-5:14■14:9,15■28:15,18■57:9-EZE-31:16,17■32:21,27-AM-9:2-JON-2:2-HAB-2:5■N.T.-all=1067,a=86&marked-M'T-5:22,29,30■10:28■11:23a■16:18a■18:9■23:15,33-M'R-9:43,45,47-LU-10:15a,12:5■16:23a-AC-2:27a,31a-JAS-3:6-2PE-2:4(5020)-RE-1:18a■6:8a■20:13a,14a

HELM-JAS-3:4(4079)

HELMET-all=3553&marked-1SA-17:5,38(6959)-IS-59:17-EZE-23:24(6959)■27:10■38:5■N.T.-EPH-6:17(4030)-1TH-5:8(4030)

HELMETS-2CH-26:14(3553)-JER-46:4(3553)

HELP-all=5826,a=5828,b=5833,c=3467&marked-GE-2:18a,20a■49:25-EX-18:4a■23:5^{2}(5800)-DE-22:4(6965)■32:38■33:7a,26a,29a-JOS-1:14■10:4,6,33-J'G-5:23^{2}b-1SA-11:9(8668)-2SA-10:11(3447),11c,19c■14:4c-2KI-6:26c,27c-1CH-12:17,22■18:5■19:12(8668),12c,19c■22:17-2CH-14:11^{2}■19:2■20:9c■25:8■26:13■28:16,23^{2}■29:34(2388)■32:3,8-EZR-1:4(5375)■8:22-JOB-6:13b■8:20(2388)■29:12(5826)■31:21b-PS-3:2(3444)■12:1c■20:2a■22:11(5826),19b■27:9b■33:20a■35:2b■37:40■38:22b■40:13b,17b■42:5(3444)■44:26b■46:1b,5■59:4(7125)■60:11b,11(8668)■63:7b■70:1b,5a■71:12b■79:9■89:19a■94:17b■107:12■108:12b,12(8668)■109:26■115:9a,10a,11a■118:7■119:86,173,175■121:1a,2a■124:8a■146:3(8668),5a-EC-4:10(6965)-IS-10:3b■20:6b■30:5a,7■31:1b,2b■41:10,13,14■44:2■50:7,9■63:5-JER-37:7b-LA-1:7■4:17b-EZE-12:14a■32:21-DA-10:13■11:34a,45-HO-13:9a■N.T.-all=997&marked-M'T-15:25-M'R-9:22,24-LU-5:7(4815)■10:40(4878)-AC-16:9■21:28■26:22(1947)-PH'P-4:3(4815)-HEB-4:16

HELPED-all=5826&marked-EX-2:17(3467)-1SA-7:12-1KI-1:7■20:16-1CH-5:20■12:19,21■15:26-2CH-18:31■20:23■26:7,15■28:21(5833)-EZR-10:15-ES-9:3(5375)-JOB-26:2-PS-28:7■116:6(3467)■118:13-IS-41:6■49:8-ZEC-1:15■N.T.-AC-18:27(4820)-RE-12:16(997)

HELPER-all=5826-2KI-14:26-JOB-30:13-PS-10:14■30:10■54:4■72:12-JER-47:4■N.T.-RO-16:9(4904)-HEB-13:6(998)

HELPERS-all=5826&marked-1CH-12:1,18-JOB-9:13-EZE-30:8-NA-3:9(5833)■N.T.-RO-16:3(4904)-2CO-1:24(4904)

HELPETH-1CH-12:18(5826)-IS-31:3(5826)■N.T.-RO-8:26(4878)-1CO-16:16(4903)

HELPING-EZR-5:2(5582)-PS-22:1(3467)■N.T.-2CO-1:11(4943)

HELPS-AC-27:17(996)-1CO-12:28(484)

HELVE-DE-19:5(6086)

HEM-all=7757-EX-8:33^{2},34■39:25,26■N.T.-M'T-9:20(2899)■14:36(2899)

HEMLOCK-HO-10:4(7219)-AM-6:12(3939)

HEMS-EX-39:24(7757)

HEN-M'T-23:37(3733)-LU-13:34(3733)

HENCE-all=2088&marked-GE-37:17■42:15■50:25-EX-11:1^{2}■13:19■

33:1,15-DE-9:12-JOS-4:3-J'G-6:18-RU-2:8 -1KI-17:3-IS-30:22(3318)-JER-38:10-ZEC-6:7(3212)■N.T.-all=1782&marked -M'T-4:10(5217)■17:20-LU-4:9■13:31■16:26-JOH-2:16■7:3■14:31■18:36-AC-1:5(3326,5025)■22:21(1821)-JAS-4:1

HENCEFORTH-all=3254&marked -GE-4:12-NU-18:22(5750)-DE-17:16■19:20-J'G-2:21-2KI-5:17(5750)-2CH-16:9(6258)-PS-125:2(6258)■131:3(6258) -IS-9:7(6258)■52:1(6258)■59:21-MIC-4:7(6258)■N.T.-all=3568&marked -M'T-23:39(575,737)■26:29(575,737) -LU-1:48■5:10■12:52-JOH-14:7(737)■15:15(3765)-AC-4:17(3371)■18:6-RO-6:6(3371)-2CO-5:15(3371),16(575,3588,3568),16(2089)-GA-6:17(3063)-EPH-4:14(3063),17(3371)-2TI-4:8(3063) -HEB-10:13(3063)-RE-14:13(534)

HENCEFORWARD-NU-15:23 (1973)■N.T.-M'T-21:19(3371)

HERALD-DA-3:4(3744)

HERB-all=6212&marked-GE-1:11,12,29,30■2:5■3:18■9:3-EX-9:22,25■10:12,15-DE-32:2(1877)-2KI-19:26 (1877)-JOB-8:12(2682)■38:27(1877) -PS-37:2(1877)■104:14(6212)-IS-37:27 (1877)■66:14(1877)

HERBS-all=6212&marked-EX-10:15 -DE-11:10(3419)-1KI-21:2(3419)-2KI-4:39(219)-PS-105:35(6212)-PR-15:17 (3419)■27:25-IS-18:4(216)■26:19 (219)■42:15-JER-12:4■N.T.-all=3001 &marked-M'T-13:32-M'R-4:32-LU-11:42-RO-14:2-HEB-6:7(1008)

HERD-all=1241-GE-18:7-LE-1:2,3■3:1■27:32-NU-15:3-DE-12:21■15:19■16:2-1SA-11:5-2SA-12:4-JER-31:12 -JON-3:7-HAB-3:17■N.T.-all=34-M'T-8:30,31,32^{2}-M'R-5:11,13-LU-8:32,33

HERDMAN-AM-7:14(951)

HERDMEN-all=7462&marked-GE-13:7^{2},8■26:20^{2}-1SA-21:7-AM-1:1(5349)

HERDS-all=1241&marked-GE-13:5■24:35■26:14■32:7■33:13■45:10■46:32■47:1,17,18(4735)■50:8-EX-10:9,24■12:32,38■34:3-NU-11:22-DE-8:13■12:6,17■14:23-1SA-30:20-2SA-12:2 -1CH-27:29^{2}-2CH-32:29-NE-10:36 -PR-27:23(5739)-IS-65:10-JER-3:24■5:17-HOS-5:6-JOE-1:18(5739)

HERE-all=6311,a=2009&marked -GE-16:13(1988)■19:12,15(4672)■21:23 (2008)■22:5,7a,11a■27:18a■31:11a,37 (3541)■37:13a■40:15■46:2a-EX-3:4a■24:14(2088)■33:16(645)-NU-22:8,19 (2088)■23:1^{2}(2088),15(3541),29^{2}(2088)■32:6,16-DE-5:3,31■12:8■29:15^{2}-JOS-18:6,8-J'G-4:20■18:3■19:9■20:7(1988) -RU-2:8(3541)■4:1,2-1SA-1:26(2088)■3:4a,5(2005),6(2005),8(2005),16a■9:11 (2008)■14:34(2008)■16:11(8552)■21:8,9(2008)■22:12(2005)■23:3■29:3,3sup -2SA-1:7a■11:12(2008)■18:30(3541)■20:4-1KI-2:30■18:8,11,14■19:9,13■20:40(2008)■22:7-2KI-2:2,4,6■3:11^{2}■7:3,4■19:23-1CH-29:17-2CH-18:6 -JOB-38:11,35a-PS-132:14-IS-6:8(2005)■21:9(2008)■22:16^{3}■28:10 (8033),13(8033)■52:5■58:9a-EZE-8:6,9,17-HO-7:9(2236)■N.T.-all=5602&marked-M'T-12:41,42■14:8,17■16:28■17:4^{2}■20:6■24:2,23■26:36 (848),38■28:6-M'R-6:3■8:4■9:1,5■13:21■14:32,34■16:6-LU-4:23■9:12,27,33■11:31,32■17:21,32■22:38■24:6,41 (1759)-JOH-6:9■11:21,32-AC-4:10 (3936)■9:14■10:33(3918)■16:28(1759)■24:19(3918)■25:24(4840),24(1759)-COL-4:9-HEB-7:8■13:14-JAS-2:3^{2}-RE-13:10,18■14:12^{2}■17:9

HEREAFTER-IS-41:23(268)-EZE-20:39(310)-DA-2:29(311,1836),45 (311,1836)■N.T.-all=3326,5023& marked-M'T-26:64(575,737)-M'R-11:14(3370)-LU-22:69(575,3568)-JOH-1:51(575,737)■13:7■14:30(2089)-1TI -1:16(3195)-RE-1:19■4:1■9:12

HEREBY-all=2063-42:15,33-NU-16:28-JOS-3:10■N.T.-all=1722,5129& marked-1CO-4:4-1JO-2:3,5■3:16,19,24■4:2,6(1537,5124),13

HEREIN-GE-34:22(2063)-2CH-16:9(5921,2063)■N.T.-all=1722,5129 -JOH-4:37■9:30:15:8-AC-24:16-2CO-8:10-1JO-4:10,17

HEREOF-M'T-9:26(3778)-HEB-5:3(5026)

HERESIES-all=139-1CO-11:19-GA-5:20-2PE-2:1

HERESY-AC-24:14(139)

HERETICK-TIT-3:10(141)

HERETOFORE-all=8543-EX-4:10■5:7,8,14-JOS-3:4-RU-2:11-1SA-4:7(865)■N.T.-2CO-13:2(4258)

HEREUNTO-1PE-2:21(1519,5124)

HEREWITH-EZE-16:29(2063) -MAL-3:10(2063)

HERITAGE-all=5159&marked -EX-6:8(4181)-JOB-20:29■27:13-PS-16:6■61:5(3425)■94:5■111:6■119:111 (5157)■127:3■135:12^{2}■136:21,22-IS-54:17■58:14-JER-2:7■3:19■12:7,8,9,15■17:4■50:11-JOE-2:17■3:2-MIC-2:2■7:14,18-MAL-1:3■N.T.-1PE-5:3(2819)

HERITAGES-IS-49:8(5159)

HERON-LE-11:19(601)-DE-14:18(601)

HERS-all supplied

HERSELF-IS-5:14(5315)■N.T.-all=1438&marked-M'T-9:21-M'R-4:28 (844)-LU-1:24-HEB-11:11(846)-RE-2:20■18:7■19:7

HEW-all=6458&marked-EX-34:1 -DE-10:1■12:3(1438)■19:5(2404)-1KI-5:6^{2}(3772),18-1CH-22:2(2672)-2CH-2:2(2672)-JER-6:6(3772)-DA-4:14 (1414),23(1414)

HEWED-all=1496&marked-EX-34:4(6458)-DE-10:3(6458)-1SA-11:7 (5408)■15:33(8158)-1KI-5:17■6:36■7:9,11,12-2KI-12:12(4274)-IS-22:16 (2672)-JER-2:13(2672)-HO-6:5(2672)

HEWER-DE-29:11(2404)

HEWERS-all=2404&marked -JOS-9:21,23,27-1KI-5:15(2672)-2KI-12:12(2672)-1CH-22:15(2672)-2CH-2:10,18(2672)-JER-46:22

HEWETH-IS-10:15(2672)■22:16 (2672)■44:14(3772)

HEWN-all=1496&marked-EX-20:25-2KI-22:6(4274)-2CH-34:11(4274) -PR-9:1(2672)-IS-9:10■10:33(1438)■33:9(7060)■51:1(2672)-LA-3:9-EZE-40:42-AM-5:11■N.T.-all=1581& marked-M'T-3:10■7:19■27:60(2998) -M'R-15:46(2998)-LU-3:9■23:53(2991)

HID-all=5641,a=2244,b=2934,c=5956&marked-GE-3:8a,10a■4:14■35:4b -EX-2:2(6845),12b■3:6-LE-4:13c■5:3c,4c-NU-5:13c-DE-33:19b-JOS-2:4(6845),6b■6:17a,25a■7:21b,22b■10:16a,17a,27a-J'G-9:5a-1SA-3:18(3582)■10:22a■14:11a,22a■20:24-2SA-17:9a■18:13(3582)-1KI-10:3c■18:4a,13a-2KI-4:27c■6:29a■7:8^{2}b■11:2,3a-1CH-21:20a -2CH-9:2c■22:9a,11,12a-JOB-3:10,21 (4301),23■5:21a■6:16c■10:13(6845)■15:18(3582)■17:4(6845)■20:26a■28:11 (8587),21c■29:8a■38:30a-PS-9:15b■17:14(6845)■19:6■22:24■32:5(3680)■35:7b,8b■38:9■40:10(3680)■55:12■69:5 (3582)■119:11(6845)■139:15(3582)■140:5b-PR-2:4(4301)-IS-28:15■29:14■40:27■42:22a■49:2a,2■50:6■53:3■54:8■57:17■59:2■64:7■65:16-JER-13:5b,7b■16:17,17(6845)■18:22b■33:5■36:26■43:10b-EZE-22:26c■39:23,24-HO-5:3 (3582)■13:12(6845),14-AM-9:3-NA-3:11c-ZEP-2:3■N.T.-all=2928&marked -M'T-5:14■10:26(2927)■11:25(613)■13:33(1470),44■25:18(613),25-M'R-4:22(2927)■7:24(2990)-LU-1:24(4032)■8:17(614),47(2990)■9:45(3871)■10:21 (613)■12:2(2927)■13:21(1470)■18:34■19:42-JOH-8:59-2CO-4:3(2572)-EPH-3:9(613)-COL-1:26(613)■2:3(614)■3:3 -1TI-5:25-HEB-11:23-RE-6:15

HIDDEN-all=6845&marked-LE-5:2(5956)-DE-30:11(6381)-JOB-3:16 (2934)■15:20■24:1-PS-51:6(5640)■83:3 -PR-28:12(2664)-IS-45:3(4301)■48:6 (5341)-OB-6(4710)■N.T.-all=2927& marked-AC-26:26(2990)-1CO-2:7(613)■4:5-2CO-4:2-1PE-3:4-RE-2:17(2928)

HIDE-all=5641&marked-GE-18:17 (3680)■47:18(3582)-EX-2:3(6845)-LE-8:17(5785)■9:11(5785)■20:4(5956)-DE-7:20■22:1(5956),3(5956),4(5956)■31:17,18■32:20-JOS-2:16(2247)■7:19(3582) -J'G-6:11(5127)-1SA-3:17^{2}(3582),■13:6 (2244)■19:2(2244)■20:2,5,19■23:19■26:1-2SA-14:18(3582)-1KI-17:3■22:25(2247)-2KI-7:12(2247) -2CH-18:24(2244)-JOB-13:20■14:13 (6845)■20:12(3582)■24:4(2244)■33:17 (3680)■34:22■40:13(2934)-PS-13:1■17:8■27:5(6845),5,9■30:7■31:20■51:9■54:t■55:1(5956)■56:6(6845)■64:2■69:17■78:4(3582)■89:46■102:2■119:19■143:7,9(3680)-PR-2:1(6845)■28:28-IS-1:15 (5956)■2:10(2934)■3:9(3582)■16:3■26:20(2247)■29:15■58:7(5956)-JER-13:4(2934),6(2934)■23:24■36:19■38:14 (3582),25(3582)■43:9(2934)■49:10(2247) -LA-3:56(5956)-EZE-28:3(6004)■31:8 (6004)■39:29-DA-10:7(2244)-AM-9:3 (2244)-MIC-3:4■N.T.-JOH-12:36 (2928)-JAS-5:20(2572)-RE-6:16(2928)

HIDEST-all=5641&marked-JOB-13:24-PS-10:1(5956)■44:24■88:14■104:29-IS-45:15

HIDETH-all=5641&marked-1SA-23:23(2244)-JOB-23:9(5848)■34:29■42:3(5956)-PS-10:11■139:12(2821)-PR-10:18(3680)■19:24(2934)■22:3■26:15 (2934)■27:12,16(6845)■28:27(5956) -IS-8:17■N.T.-M'T-13:44(2928)

HIDING-all=5643&marked-JOB-31:33(2934)-PS-32:7■119:114-IS-28:17■32:2(4224)-HAB-3:4(2253)

HIGGAION-PS-9:16(1902)

HIGH-all=1116,a=5945,b=4791,c=7311,d=1364,e=1419&marked-GE-7:19d■14:18a,19a,20a,22a■29:7e-EX-14:8c■25:20(4605)■37:9(4605)■39:31 (4605)-LE-21:10e■26:30-NU-20:19 (4546),28■22:41■23:3(8205)■24:16a■33:3c,52■35:25e,28^{2}e-DE-2:27(1870)■3:5d■12:2c■26:19a■28:1a,43(4605),52d■32:8a,13,27c■33:29-JOS-20:6e-J'G-5:18 (4791)-1SA-9:12,13,14,19,25■10:5,13■13:6(6877)-2SA-1:19,25■22:3(4869),14a,34,49c■23:1(5920)-1KI-3:2,3,4■6:10 (6967),23(6967)■7:15(6967),35(6967)■9:8a■11:7■12:31,32■13:2,32,33^{2}■14:23^{2}d■15:14■21:9(7218),12(7218)■22:43^{2}-2KI-12:3^{2},10e■14:4^{2}■15:4^{2},35^{2}■16:4■17:9,10d,11,29,32^{2}■18:4,22■19:22(4791)■21:3■22:4e,8e■23:4e,5,8^{2},9,13,15^{3},19,20-1CH-14:2(4605)■16:39■17:17(4608)■21:29 -2CH-1:3,13■3:15(753)■6:13(6967)■7:21a■11:15■14:3,5■15:17■17:6■20:19(4605),33■21:11■23:20a■24:11(7218)■27:3a■28:4,25■31:1■32:12■33:3,17,19■34:3,4 (4605),9e-NE-3:1e,20e,25a■13:28e-ES-5:14d■7:9d-JOB-5:11(4791)■11:8(1363)■16:19(4719)■21:22c■22:12c■25:2(4791)■31:2(4791)■38:15c■39:18(4791),27c■41:34d-PS-7:7(4791),17a■9:2a■18:2 (4869),27c,33■21:7a■46:4a■47:2a■49:2(376)■50:14a■56:2(4791)■57:2a■62:9(376)■68:15(1386),16(1386),18(4791)■69:29(7682)■71:19(4791)■73:11a■75:5 (4791)■77:10a■78:17a,35a,56a,58,69c■82:6a■83:18a■89:13c■91:1a,9a,14(7682)■92:1a,8(4791)■93:4(4791)■97:9a■99:2c■101:5(1362)■103:11(1361)■104:18d■107:11a,41(7682)■113:4c,5(1361)■131:1 (6381)■138:6c■139:6(7682)■144:2(4869)■149:6(7319)■150:5(8643)-PR-8:2(4791)■9:14(4791)■18:11(7682)■21:4(7312)■24:7c-EC-12:5d-IS-2:13c,14c,15d■6:1c■10:12(7312),33(7312)■13:2(8192)■14:14a■15:2■16:12■22:16(4791)■24:18(4791),

21(4791)▪25:12(4869)▪26:5(4791)▪30:13(7682),25d,26(4791)▪32:15(4791)▪33:5(4791),16(4791)▪36:7(1111)▪37:23(4796)▪40:9d,26(4791)▪41:18(8203)▪49:9(8203)▪52:13(1361)▪57:7(5375),15c,15(4791)▪58:4(4791),14-**JER**-2:20d▪3:2(8205),6d,21(8205)▪4:11(8205)▪7:29,31▪12:12(8205)▪14:6(8205)▪17:2d,3,12b▪19:5▪20:2a▪25:30b▪26:18▪31:21(8564)▪32:35▪48:35▪49:16(1361)▪51:58d-**LA**-3:35a,38a-**EZE**-1:18(1362)▪6:3,6,13c▪16:16,24(7413),25(7413),31(7413),39(7413)▪17:22c,22d,24d▪20:28c,29▪21:26d▪31:3(1362),4c▪34:6c,14b▪36:2▪40:2d,42(1363)▪41:22d▪43:7-**DA**-3:26(5943)▪4:2(5943),17(5943),24(5943),32(5943),34(5943)▪5:18(5943),21(5943)▪7:18(5946),22(5946),25(5943),25(5946),27(5946)▪8:3d-**HO**-7:16(5920)▪10:8▪11:7(5920)-**AM**-4:13▪7:9-**OB**-3b-**MIC**-1:3,5▪3:12▪6:6(4791)-**HAB**-2:9(4719)▪3:10(7315),19-**ZEP**-1:16d-**HAG**-1:1e,12e,14e▪2:2e,4e-**ZEC**-3:1e,8e▪6:11e▪**N.T.**-all=749&marked-**M'T**-4:8(5308)▪17:1(5308)▪26:3,51,57,58,62,63,65-**M'R**-2:26▪5:7(5310)▪9:2(5308)▪14:47,53,54,60,61,63,66-**LU**-1:78(5311)▪3:2▪4:5(5308)▪8:28(5310)▪22:50,54▪24:49(5311)-**JOH**-11:49,51▪18:10,13,15^{2},16,19,22,24,26▪19:31(3173)-**AC**-4:6^{2}▪5:17,21,24(2409),27▪7:1,48(5310)▪9:1▪13:17(5308)▪16:17(5310)▪22:5▪23:2,4,5▪24:1▪25:2-**RO**-12:16(5308)-**2CO**-10:5(5313)-**EPH**-4:8(5311)▪6:12(2032)-**PH'P**-3:14(507)-**HEB**-1:3(5308)▪2:17▪3:1▪4:14,15▪5:1,5,10▪6:20▪7:1(5310),26,27,28▪8:1,3▪9:7,11,25▪10:21(3173)▪13:11-**RE**-21:10(5308),12(5308)

HIGHER-all=1364&marked-**NU**-24:7(7311)-**1SA**-9:2▪10:23(1361)-**2KI**-15:35(5945)-**NE**-4:13(6706)-**JOB**-35:5(1361)-**PS**-61:2(7311)▪89:27(5945)-**EC**-5:8^{2}-**IS**-55:9^{2}(1361)-**JER**-36:10(5945)-**EZE**-9:2(5945)▪42:5(3201)▪43:13(1354)-**DA**-8:3^{2}▪**N.T.**-**LU**-14:10(511)-**RO**-13:1(5242)-**HEB**-7:26(5308)

HIGHEST-all=5945&marked-**PS**-18:13▪87:5-**PR**-8:26(7218)▪9:3(4791)-**EC**-5:8(1364)-**EZE**-17:3(6788),22(6788)▪41:7▪**N.T.**-all=5310&marked-**M'T**-21:9-**M'R**-11:10-**LU**-1:32,35,76▪2:14▪6:35▪14:8(4411)▪19:38▪20:46(4410)

HIGHLY-**LU**-16:15(5308)-**AC**-12:20(2371)-**RO**-12:3(5252)-**PH'P**-2:9(5251)-**1TH**-5:13(1537,4053)

HIGHMINDED-**RO**-11:20(5309)-**1TI**-6:17(5309)-**2TI**-3:4(5187)

HIGHNESS-**JOB**-31:23(7613)-**IS**-13:3(1346)

HIGHWAY-all=4546&marked-**J'G**-21:19-**1SA**-6:12-**2SA**-20:12^{2},13-**2KI**-18:17-**PR**-16:17-**IS**-7:3▪11:16▪19:23▪35:8(4547)▪36:2▪40:3▪62:10-**JER**-31:21▪**N.T.**-**M'R**-10:46(3598)

HIGHWAYS-all=4546&marked-**J'G**-5:6(734)▪20:31,32,45-**IS**-33:8▪49:11-**AM**-5:16(2351)▪**N.T.**-**M'T**-22:9(1327,3598),10(3598)-**LU**-14:23(3598)

HILL-all=2022,a=1389&marked-**EX**-17:9a,10a▪24:4-**NU**-14:44,45-**DE**-1:41,43-**JOS**-5:3a▪13:6▪15:9▪17:16▪18:13,14▪21:11▪24:30,33a-**J'G**-2:9▪7:1a▪16:3-**1SA**-7:1a▪9:11(4608)▪10:5a,10a▪23:19a▪25:20▪26:1a,3a,13-**2SA**-2:24a,25a▪13:34▪21:9-**1KI**-11:7▪14:23a▪16:24^{3}-**2KI**-1:9▪4:27▪17:10a-**PS**-2:6▪3:4▪15:1▪24:3▪42:6▪43:3▪68:15^{2},16▪99:9-**SONG**-4:6a-**IS**-5:1(7161)▪10:32a▪30:17a,25a▪31:4a▪40:4a-**JER**-2:20a▪16:16a▪31:39a▪49:16a▪50:6a-**EZE**-6:13a▪20:28a▪34:6a,26a▪**N.T.**-all=3735&marked-**M'T**-5:14-**LU**-1:39(3714),65(3714)▪3:5(1015)▪4:29▪9:37-**AC**-17:22(697)

HILL'S-**2SA**-16:13(2202)

HILLS-all=1389,a=2022&marked-**GE**-7:19a▪49:26-**NU**-23:9-**DE**-1:7a▪8:7a,9(2042)▪11:11a▪12:2▪33:15-**JOS**-9:1a▪10:40a▪11:16a-**1KI**-20:23a,28a▪22:17a-**2KI**-16:4-**2CH**-28:4-**JOB**-15:7-**PS**-18:7a▪50:10(2042)▪65:12a▪68:16▪72:3▪80:10a▪95:4a▪97:5a▪98:8a▪104:10a,13a,18a,32a▪114:4,6▪121:1a▪148:9-**PR**-8:25-**SONG**-2:8-**IS**-2:2,14▪5:25a▪7:25a▪40:12▪41:15▪42:15▪54:10▪55:12▪65:7-**JER**-3:23▪4:24▪13:27▪17:2-**EZE**-6:3▪35:8▪36:4,6-**HO**-4:13▪10:8-**JOE**-3:18-**AM**-9:13-**MIC**-4:1▪6:1-**NA**-1:5-**HAB**-3:6-**ZEP**-1:10▪**N.T.**-**LU**-23:30(1015)

HIMSELF-all=1931&marked-**GE**-32:21-**EX**-21:3^{2}(1610),4(1610)-**LE**-25:26(3027),49(3027)-**NU**-19:12,12sup▪35:19-**J'G**-3:19-**1SA**-10:19,22-**1KI**-11:29▪19:4▪4(5315)-**2CH**-13:9(3027)▪20:3(6440)▪26:20▪32:9-**EZR**-10:8-**JOB**-18:4(5315)▪32:2(5315)-**PS**-50:6▪87:5-**PR**-11:25▪16:4(4617)▪21:13▪28:10-**IS**-7:14▪38:15▪45:18-**JER**-51:14(5315)-**HO**-7:8▪13:1-**AM**-2:14(5315),15^{2}(5315)▪6:8(5315)▪**N.T.**-all=1438,a=846-**M'T**-6:4a▪8:17a,26,45^{2}▪13:21▪16:24▪18:4▪23:12^{2}▪27:42,57a-**M'R**-3:26▪5:5,30▪6:17a▪8:34▪12:33,36a,37a▪15:31-**LU**-3:23a▪6:3a▪7:39▪9:23,25▪10:1a,29▪11:18,26▪12:17,21▪14:11^{2}▪15:17▪16:3▪18:4,11,14^{2}▪19:12▪20:42a▪23:2,7a,35,51a▪24:12,15a,27,36a-**JOH**-2:24▪4:2a,12a,44a,53a▪5:18,19,20a,26^{2},37a▪6:6a,15a,61▪7:4a,18▪8:22▪9:21(848)▪11:38,51▪13:4,32▪16:13,27a▪19:7,12(848)▪21:1,7-**AC**-1:3▪2:34a▪5:36▪8:9,13a,34▪10:17▪12:11▪14:17▪16:27▪18:19a▪19:22a,31▪20:13a▪25:4,25(848)▪28:16-**RO**-14:7,12,22▪15:3-**1CO**-2:15a▪3:15a,18▪11:28,29▪14:4,28▪15:28a-**2CO**-5:18,19▪10:7^{2},18▪11:14a-**GA**-1:4▪2:12,20▪6:3sup,3,4-**EPH**-1:5(848),9(848)▪2:15,20(848)▪5:2,25,27,28,33-**PH'P**-2:7,8▪3:21-**COL**1:20(848)-**1TH**-3:11a▪4:16a-**2TH**-2:4^{2},16a▪3:16a-**1TI**-2:6-**2TI**-2:13,21-**TIT**-2:14^{2}▪3:11(843)-**HEB**-1:3▪2:14a,18a▪5:2a,3,4,5▪6:13▪7:27▪9:7,14,25,26(848)▪12:3(848)-**JAS**-1:24,27-**1JO**-2:6a▪3:3▪5:10,18-**3JO**-10a-**RE**-21:3a

HIN-all=1969-**EX**-29:40^{2}▪30:24-**LE**-19:36▪23:13-**NU**-15:4,5,6,7,9,10▪28:5,7,14^{3}-**EZE**-4:11▪45:24▪46:5,7,11,14

HIND-**GE**-49:21(355)-**PR**-5:19(365)-**JER**-14:5(365)

HINDER-all=268&marked-**GE**-24:56(309)-**NU**-22:16(4513)-**2SA**-2:23(310)-**1KI**-7:25-**2CH**-4:4-**NE**-4:8(6213,8442)-**JOB**-9:12(7725)▪11:10(7725)-**PS**-78:66(268)-**JOE**-2:20(5490)-**ZEC**-14:8(314)▪**N.T.**-**M'R**-4:38(4403)-**AC**-8:36(2967)▪27:41(4403)-**1CO**-9:12(5100,1461,1325)-**GA**-5:7(343)

HINDERED-**EZR**-6:8(989)▪**N.T.**-**LU**-11:52(2967)-**RO**-15:22(1465)-**1TH**-2:18(1465)-**1PE**-3:7(1581)

HINDERETH-**IS**-14:6(2820)

HINDERMOST-**GE**-33:2(314)-**JER**-50:12(319)

HINDMOST-**NU**-2:31(314)-**DE**-25:18(2179)-**JOS**-10:19(2179)

HINDS-all=355&marked-**JOB**-39:1-**PS**-29:9-**SONG**-2:7▪3:5

HINDS'-all=355&marked-**2SA**-22:34-**PS**-18:33-**HAB**-3:19

HINGES-**1KI**-7:50(6596)-**PR**-26:14(6735)

HIP-**J'G**-15:8(7785)

HIRE-all=7939&marked-**GE**-30:18,32,33▪31:8-**EX**-22:15-**DE**-23:18(868)▪24:15-**1KI**-5:6-**1CH**-19:6(7936)-**IS**-23:17(868),18(868)▪46:6(7936)-**EZE**-16:31(868),41(868)-**MIC**-1:7^{2}(868)▪3:11(4242)-**ZEC**-8:10▪**N.T.**-all=3408&marked-**M'T**-20:1(3409),8-**LU**-10:7-**JAS**-5:4

HIRED-all=7936,a=7916&marked-**GE**-30:16-**EX**-12:45a▪22:15a-**LE**-9:13a▪22:10a▪25:6a,40a,50a,53a-**DE**-15:18a▪23:4▪24:14a-**J'G**-9:4▪18:4-**1SA**-2:5-**2SA**-10:6-**2KI**-7:6-**1CH**-19:7-**2CH**-24:12▪25:6-**EZR**-4:5-**NE**-6:12,13▪13:2-**IS**-7:20(7917)-**JER**-46:21a-**HO**-8:9(8566),10(8566)▪**N.T.**-**M'T**-20:7(3409)-**M'R**-1:20(3411)-**LU**-15:17(3407),19(3407)-**AC**-28:30(3410)

HIRELING-all=7916-**JOB**-7:1,2▪14:6-**IS**-16:14▪21:16-**MAL**-3:5▪**N.T.**-**JOH**-10:12(3411),13^{2}(3411)

HIRES-**MIC**-1:7(868)

HIREST-**EZE**-16:33(7806)

HISS-all=8319-**1KI**-9:8-**JOB**-27:23-**IS**-5:26▪7:18-**JER**-19:8▪49:17▪50:13-**LA**-2:15,16-**EZE**-27:36-**ZEP**-2:15-**ZEC**-10:8

HISSING-all=8322&marked-**2CH**-29:8-**JER**-18:16(8292)▪19:8▪25:9,18▪29:18▪51:37-**MIC**-6:16

HIT-**1SA**-31:3(4672)-**1CH**-10:3(4672)

HITHER-all=5066&marked-**GE**-15:16(2008)-**EX**-3:5(1988)-**JOS**-3:9-**J'G**-18:3(1988)-**RU**-2:14(1988)-13:9▪14:8,34,36(1988),38(1988),38(1988)▪15:32▪16:11(6311)▪23:9▪30:7-**2KI**-8:7(2008)-**PS**-73:10(1988)-**PR**-25:7(2008)▪**N.T.**-all=5602&marked-**M'T**-8:29▪14:18▪17:17▪22:12-**M'R**-11:3-**LU**-9:41▪14:21▪19:27-**JOH**-4:15(1759),16(1759)▪6:25▪20:27^{2}-**AC**-9:21▪10:32(3333)▪17:6(1759)▪25:17(1759)-**RE**-4:1▪11:12▪17:1(1204)▪21:9(1204)

HITHERTO-all=5704,2008&marked-**EX**-7:16(5704,3541)-**JOS**-17:14(5704,3541)-**J'G**-16:13-**1SA**-1:16▪7:12-**2SA**-7:18(1988)▪15:34(227)-**1CH**-9:18▪12:29▪17:16(1988)-**JOB**-38:11(5704,6311)-**PS**-71:17-**IS**-18:2(1973),7(1973)-**DA**-7:28(5705,3542)▪**N.T.**-**JOH**-5:17(2193,737)▪16:24(2193,737)-**RO**-1:13(891,1204)-**1CO**-3:2(3768)

HO-**IS**-55:1(1945)-**ZEC**-2:6(1945)

HOAR-all=7872&marked-**EX**-16:14(3713)-**1KI**-2:6,9-**IS**-46:4

HOARFROST-**PS**-147:16(3713)

HOARY-all=7872&marked-**LE**-19:32-**JOB**-38:29(3713)▪41:32-**PR**-16:31

HOISED-**AC**-27:40(1869)

HOLD-all=2388,a=2790,b=270&marked-**GE**-19:16▪21:18▪25:26b-**EX**-9:2▪14:14a▪15:14b,15b▪26:5(6901)-**NU**-30:4a,14a-**DE**-21:19(8610)▪22:28(8610)▪32:41b-**J'G**-9:46(6877),49^{2}(6877)▪16:29(3943)▪18:19a▪19:29-**RU**-3:15b-**1SA**-15:27▪22:4(4686),5(4686)▪24:22(4686)-**2SA**-1:11▪2:21b,22(5375)▪4:10b▪5:7(4686),17(4686)▪6:6b▪13:11,20a▪18:9▪23:14(4686)▪24:7(4013)-**1KI**-1:50,51b▪2:28▪9:9▪13:4(8610)-**2KI**-2:3(2814),5(2814),12▪6:32(3905)▪7:9(2814)-**1CH**-11:16(4686)▪12:8(4679),16(4679)▪13:9b-**2CH**-7:22-**NE**-8:11(2013)-**ES**-4:11(3447)-**JOB**-6:24a▪8:15▪11:3a▪13:5a,13a,19a▪17:9b▪21:6b▪27:6,20(5381)▪30:16b▪33:31a,33a▪36:17(8551)▪38:13b▪41:26(6965)-**PS**-17:5(8551)▪35:2▪39:12a▪40:12(5381)▪48:6b▪69:24(5381)▪83:1a▪109:1a▪116:3(4672)▪119:53b,117(5582),143(4672)▪139:10b-**PR**-2:19(5381)▪3:18▪4:13▪5:5(8551)▪30:28(8610)▪31:19(8551)-**EC**-2:3b▪7:18b-**SONG**-3:8b▪7:8b-**IS**-3:6(8610)▪4:1▪5:29b▪13:8a▪21:3b▪27:5▪31:9(5553)▪41:13▪42:6▪56:2,4,6▪62:1(2814),6(2814)▪64:7,12(2814)-**JER**-2:13(3557)▪4:19a▪6:23,24▪8:5,21▪50:42,43-**EZE**-29:7(8610)▪30:21(8610)▪41:6^{2}b-**AM**-6:10(2013)-**MIC**-4:8(6076)▪6:14(5253)-**NA**-1:7(4581)-**HAB**-1:10(4013)-**ZEC**-1:6(5381)▪8:23^{2}▪9:3(4692),12(1225)▪11:5(816)▪14:13▪**N.T.**-all=2902&marked-**M'T**-6:24(472)▪12:11▪14:3▪20:31(4623)▪21:26(2192)▪26:48,55,57-**M'R**-1:25(5392)▪3:21▪6:17▪7:4,8▪10:48(4623)▪12:12▪14:51-**LU**-4:35(5392)▪16:13(472)▪18:39(4623)▪19:40(4623)▪20:20(1949),26(1949)▪23:26(1949)-**AC**-4:3(5084)▪12:17(4061)▪18:9(4623)-**RO**-1:18(2722)-**1CO**-14:30(4601)-**PH'P**-2:29(2192)-**1TH**-5:21(2722)-**2TH**-2:15-**1TI**-6:12

(1949),19(1949)-**2TI**-1:13(2192)-**HEB**-3:6(2722),14(2722)■4:14■6:18■10:23(2722)-**RE**-2:14,15,25■3:3(5083),11■18:2(5438)■20:2

HOLDEN-**2KI**-23:22(6213),23(6213)-**JOB**-36:8(3920)-**PS**-18:35(5582)■71:6(5564)■73:23(270)-**PR**-5:22(8551)-**IS**-42:14(2814)■45:1(2388)■**N.T.**-**LU**-24:16(2902)-**AC**-2:24(2902)-**RO**-14:4(2476)

HOLDEST-**ES**-4:14(2790)-**JOB**-13:24(2803)-**PS**-77:4(270)-**JER**-49:16(8610)-**HAB**-1:13(2790)-**RE**-2:13(2902)

HOLDETH-**JOB**-2:3(2388)■26:9(270)-**PS**-66:9(7760)-**PR**-11:12(2790)■17:28(2790)-**DA**-10:21(2388)-**AM**-1:5(8551),8(8551)■**N.T.**-**RE**-2:1(2902)

HOLDING-**IS**-33:15(8551)-**JER**-6:11(3557)■**N.T.**-all=2902&marked-**M'R**-7:3-**PH'P**-2:16(1907)-**COL**-2:19-**1TI**-1:19(2192)■3:9(2192)-**TIT**-1:9(472)-**RE**-7:1

HOLDS-all=4013&marked-**NU**-13:19-**J'G**-6:2(4679)-**1SA**-23:14(4679),19(4679),29(4679)-**2KI**-8:12-**2CH**-11:11(4694)-**PS**-89:40-**IS**-23:11(4581)-**JER**-48:18,41(4679)■51:30(4679)-**LA**-2:2,5-**EZE**-19:9(4686)-**DA**-11:24,39-**MIC**-5:11-**NA**-3:12,14■**N.T.**-**2CO**-10:4(3794)

HOLE-all=6310&marked-**EX**-28:32^{3}■39:23^{3}-**2KI**-12:9(2356)-**SONG**-5:4(2356)-**IS**-11:8(2356)■51:1(4718)-**JER**-13:4(5357)-**EZE**-8:7(2356)

HOLE'S-**JER**-48:28(6354)

HOLES-all=2356&marked-**1SA**-14:11-**IS**-2:19(4631)■7:19(5357)■42:22-**JER**-16:16(5357)-**MIC**-7:17(4526)-**NA**-2:12-**HAG**-1:6(5344)-**ZEC**-14:12■**N.T.**-**M'T**-8:20(5454)-**LU**-9:58(5454)

HOLIER-**IS**-65:5(6942)

HOLIEST-all=39-**HEB**-9:3,8■10:19

HOLILY-**1TH**-2:10(3743)

HOLINESS-all=6944-**EX**-15:11■28:36■39:30-**1CH**-16:29-**2CH**-20:21■31:18-**PS**-29:2■30:4■47:8■48:1■60:6■89:35■93:5■96:9■97:12■108:7■110:3-**IS**-23:18■35:8■62:9■63:15,18-**JER**-2:3■23:9■31:23-**AM**-4:2-**OB**-17-**ZEC**-14:20,21-**MAL**-2:11■**N.T.**-all=38&marked-**LU**-1:75(3742)-**AC**-3:12(2150)-**RO**-1:4(42)■6:19,22-**2CO**-7:1(42)-**EPH**-4:24(3742)-**1TH**-3:13(42)■4:7-**1TI**-2:15-**TIT**-2:3(2412)-**HEB**-12:10(41),14

HOLLOW-all=3709&marked-**GE**-32:25^{2},32^{2}-**EX**-27:8(5014)■38:7(5014)-**LE**-14:37(8258)-**J'G**-15:19(4388)-**IS**-40:12(8168)-**JER**-52:21(5014)

HOLPEN-all=5826&marked-**PS**-83:8(2220)■86:17-**IS**-31:3-**DA**-11:34■**N.T.**-**LU**-1:54(482)

HOLY-all=6944,a=6918&marked-**EX**-3:5■12:16^{2}■15:13■16:23■19:6a■20:8(6942)■22:31■26:33,34■28:2,4,29,35,38^{2},43■29:6,29,30,31a,33,34,37^{2}■30:10,25^{2},29,29(6942),31,32,35,36,37■31:10,11,14,15■35:2,19^{2},21■37:29■38:24■39:1^{2},30,41^{2}■40:9,10,13-**LE**-2:3,10■5:15,16■6:16a,17,18(6942),25,26a,27(6942),27a,29,30■7:1,6a,6■8:9■10:10,12,13a,17^{2},18^{2}■11:44a,45a■14:13^{2}■16:2,3,4^{2},16,17,20,23,24a,27,32,33■19:2^{2}a,24■20:3,7a,26a■21:6a,6,7a,8^{2}a,22■22:2^{2},3,4,6,7,10^{2},12,14^{2},15,16,32■23:2,3,4,7,8,20,21,24,27,35,36,37■24:9a,9■25:12■27:9,10,14,21,23,28,30,32,33-**NU**-4:4,15,19,20■5:9,17a■6:5a,8a,20■15:40a■16:3a,5a,7a■18:9^{2},10^{2},17,19,32■28:7,18,25,26■29:1,7,12■31:6■35:25-**DE**-7:6a■12:26■14:2a,21a■23:14a■26:15,19a■28:9a■33:8(2623)-**JOS**-5:15■24:19a-**1SA**-2:2a■6:20a■21:5-**1KI**-6:16■7:50■8:4,6,8,10-**2KI**-4:9a■19:22a-**1CH**-6:49■16:10,35■22:19■23:13,28,32■29:3,16-**2CH**-3:8,10■4:22■5:5,7,11■8:11■23:6■29:5,7■30:27■31:6,14■35:3a,3,5,13-**EZR**-2:63■8:28^{2}■9:2,8-**NE**-7:65■8:9a,10a,11a■9:14■10:31,33■11:1,18-**JOB**-6:10a-**PS**-2:6■3:4■5:7■11:4■15:1■16:10(2623)■20:6■22:3a■24:3■28:2■33:21■43:3■46:4a■51:11■65:4a■68:5,17,35(4720)■71:22a■78:41a■79:1■86:2(2623)■87:1■89:18a,19(2623),20■98:1■99:3a,5a,9,9a■103:1■105:3,42■106:47■111:9a■138:2■145:17(2623),21-**PR**-9:10a■20:25■30:3a-**EC**-8:10a-**IS**-1:4a■4:3a■5:16a,19a,24a■6:3a,13■10:17a,20a■11:9■12:6a■17:7a■27:13■29:19a,23a■30:11a,12a,15a,29(6942)■31:1a■37:23a■40:25a■41:14a,16a,20a■43:3a,14a,15a■45:11a■47:4a■48:2,17a■49:7^{2}a■52:1,10■54:5a■55:5a■56:7■57:13,15^{2}a■58:13,13a■60:9a,14a■62:12■63:10,11■64:10,11■65:11,25■66:20-**JER**-11:15■25:30■31:40■50:29■51:5a-**EZE**-7:24(6942)■20:39,40,40sup■21:2(4720)■22:8,26^{2}■28:14■36:20,21,22,38■39:7^{2},7a,25■41:4■42:13^{3},13a,14,14sup■43:7,8,12■44:8,13^{2},19,23■45:1^{2},3,4,4(4720),6,7^{2}■46:19■48:10,12,14,18^{2},20,21^{2}-**DA**-4:8(6922),9(6922),13(6922),17(6922),18(6922),23(6922)■5:11(6922)■8:24a■9:16,20,24^{2}■11:28,30^{2},45■12:7-**HO**-11:9a-**JOE**-2:1■3:17^{2}-**AM**-2:7-**OB**-16-**JON**-2:4,7-**MIC**-1:2-**HAB**-1:12a■2:20■3:3a-**ZEP**-3:11-**HAG**-2:12,12(6942)-**ZEC**-2:12,13■8:3■**N.T.**-all=40&marked-**M'T**-1:18,20■3:11■4:5■7:6■12:32■24:15■25:31■27:53■28:19-**M'R**-1:8,24■3:29■6:20■8:38■12:36■13:11-**LU**-1:15,35^{2},41,49,67,70,72■2:23,25,26■3:16,22■4:1,34■9:26■11:13■12:10,12-**JOH**-1:33■7:39■14:26■17:11■20:22-**AC**-1:2,5,8,16■2:4,7(3741),33,38■3:14,21■4:8,27,30,31■5:3,32■6:3,5,13■7:33,51,55■8:15,17,18,19■9:17,31■10:22,38,44,45,47■11:15,16,24■13:2,4,9,35(3741),52■15:8,28■16:6■19:2^{2},6■20:23,28■21:11,28■28:25-**RO**-1:2■5:5■7:12■9:1■11:16^{3}■12:1■14:17■15:13,16■16:16-**1CO**-2:13■3:17■6:19■7:14,34■9:13(2413)■12:3■16:20-**2CO**-6:6■13:12,14-**EPH**-1:4,13■2:21■3:5■4:30■5:27-**COL**-1:22■3:12-**1TH**-1:5,6■4:8■5:26,27-**1TI**-2:8(3741)-**2TI**-1:9,14■3:15(2413)-**TIT**-1:8(3741)■3:5-**HEB**-2:4■3:1,7■6:4■7:26(3741)■9:8,12(39),24(39),25(39)■10:15-**1PE**-1:12,15,16■2:5,9■3:5-**2PE**-1:18,21^{2}■2:21■3:2,11-**1JO**-2:20■5:7-**JUDE**-20^{2}-**RE**-3:7■4:8■6:10■11:2■14:10■15:4(3741)■18:20■20:6■21:2,10■22:6,11,11(37),19

HOLYDAY-**PS**-42:4(2287)■**N.T.**-**COL**-2:16(1859)

HOME-all=1004&marked-**GE**-39:16■43:16,26-**EX**-9:19-**LE**-18:9-**DE**-21:12(8432)■24:5-**JOS**-2:18-**J'G**-11:9(7725)■19:9(168)-**RU**-1:21(7725)-**1SA**-2:20(4725)■6:7,10■10:26■18:2(7725)■24:22-**2SA**-13:7■14:13(7725)■17:23-**1KI**-5:14■13:7,15-**2KI**-14:10-**2CH**-25:10^{2}(4725),19-**ES**-5:10-**JOB**-39:12(7725)-**PS**-68:12-**PR**-7:19,20-**EC**-12:5-**JER**-39:14-**LA**-1:20-**HAB**-2:5(5115)-**HAG**-1:9■**N.T.**-**M'T**-8:6(3614)-**M'R**-5:19(3624)-**LU**-15:6(3624)-**JOH**-20:10(1438)-**AC**-21:6(2398)-**1CO**-11:34(3624),14:35(3624)-**2CO**-5:6(1736)-**1TI**-5:4(2398)-**TIT**-2:5(3626)

HOMEBORN-**EX**-12:49(249)-**JER**-2:14(1004)

HOMER-all=2563&marked-**LE**-27:16-**IS**-5:10-**EZE**-45:11^{3},13^{2},14^{2}-**HO**-3:2,2(3963)

HOMERS-**NU**-11:32(2563)

HONEST-all=2570&marked-**LU**-8:15-**RO**-12:17-**2CO**-8:21■13:7-**PH'P**-4:8(4586)-**1PE**-2:12

HONESTLY-**RO**-13:13(2156)-**1TH**-4:12(2156)-**HEB**-13:18(2573)

HONESTY-**1TI**-2:2(4587)

HONEY-all=1706-**GE**-43:11-**EX**-3:8,17■13:5■16:31■33:3-**LE**-2:11■20:24-**NU**-13:27■14:8■16:13,14-**DE**-6:3■8:8■11:9■26:9,15■27:3■31:20■32:13-**JOS**-5:6-**J'G**-14:8,9,18-**1SA**-14:25,26,29,43-**2SA**-17:29-**1KI**-14:3-**2KI**-18:32-**2CH**-31:5-**JOB**-20:17-**PS**-19:10■81:16■119:103-**PR**-24:13■25:16,27-**SONG**-4:11■5:1-**IS**-7:15,22-**JER**-11:5■32:22■41:8-**EZE**-3:3■16:13,19■20:6,15■27:17■**N.T.**-all=3192-**M'T**-3:4-**M'R**-1:6-**RE**-10:9,10

HONEYCOMB-all=5317&marked-**1SA**-14:27(3295,1706)-**PS**-19:10(5317,6688)-**PR**-5:3■16:24(6688,1706)■24:13■27:7-**SONG**-4:11■5:1(3293)■**N.T.**-**LU**-24:42(3193,2781)

HONOUR-all=3519,a=3513,b=3366&marked-**GE**-49:6-**EX**-14:17a,18a■20:12a-**LE**-19:15(1921),32(1921)-**NU**-22:17a,37a■24:11a,11■27:20(1935)-**DE**-5:16a■26:19(8597)-**J'G**-4:9(8597)■9:9a■13:17a-**1SA**-2:30a■15:30a-**2SA**-6:22a■10:3a-**1KI**-3:13-**1CH**-16:27(1926)■17:18■19:3a■29:12,28-**2CH**-1:11,12■17:5■18:1■26:18■32:27,33-**ES**-1:4b,20b■6:3b,6^{2}b,7b,9^{2}b,11b■8:16b-**JOB**-14:21a-**PS**-7:5■8:5(1926)■21:5(1935)■26:8■49:12b,20b■66:2■71:8(8597)■91:15(3515)■96:6(1935)■104:1(1935)■112:9■145:5(1926)■149:9(1926)-**PR**-3:9a,16■4:8a■5:9(1935)■8:18■11:16■14:28(1927)■15:33■18:12■20:3■21:21■22:4■25:5■26:1,8■29:23■31:25(1926)-**EC**-6:2■10:1-**IS**-29:13a■43:20a■58:13a-**JER**-33:9(8597)-**DA**-2:6(3367)■4:30(3367)■36(1923),37(1922)■5:18(1923)■11:21(1935),38^{2}a-**MAL**-1:6■**N.T.**-all=5092,a=5091&marked-**M'T**-13:57(820)■15:4a,6a■19:19a-**M'R**-6:4(820)■7:10a■10:19a-**LU**-18:20a-**JOH**-4:44■5:23^{2}a,41(1391),44^{2}(1391)■8:49a,54(1392),54(1391)■12:26a-**RO**-2:7,10■9:21■12:10■13:7-**1CO**-12:23,24-**2CO**-6:8(1391)-**EPH**-6:2a-**COL**-2:23-**1TH**-4:4-**1TI**-1:17■5:3a,17■6:1,16-**2TI**-2:20,21-**HEB**-2:7,9■3:3■5:4-**1PE**-1:7■2:17^{2}a■3:7-**2PE**-1:17-**RE**-4:9,11■5:12,13■7:12■19:1,7(1391)■21:24,26

HONOURABLE-all=3513&marked-**GE**-34:19-**NU**-22:15-**1SA**-9:6■22:14-**2SA**-23:19,23-**2KI**-5:1(5375,6440)-**1CH**-4:9■11:21,25-**JOB**-22:8(5375,6440)-**PS**-45:9(3368)■111:3(1935)-**IS**-3:3(5375,6440),5(3519)■5:13(3519)■9:15(5375,6440)■23:8(1935),9■42:21(142)■43:4■58:13-**NA**-3:10■**N.T.**-all=2158&marked-**M'R**-15:43-**LU**-14:8(1784)-**AC**-13:50■17:12-**1CO**-4:10(1741)■12:23(820)-**HEB**-13:4(5093)

HONOURED-all=3513&marked-**EX**-14:4-**PR**-13:18■27:18-**IS**-43:23-**LA**-1:8■5:12(1921)-**DA**-4:34(1922)■**N.T.**-**AC**-28:10(5092)-**1CO**-12:26(1392)

HONOUREST-**1SA**-2:29(3513)

HONOURETH-all=3513-**PS**-15:4-**PR**-12:9■14:31-**MAL**-1:6■**N.T.**-all=5091&marked-**M'T**-15:8-**M'R**-7:6-**JOH**-5:23■8:54(1392)

HONOURS-**AC**-28:10(5091)

HOODS-**IS**-3:23(6797)

HOOF-all=6541-**EX**-10:26-**LE**-11:3,4^{2},5,6,7,26-**DE**-14:6,7^{2},8

HOOFS-all=6541&marked-**PS**-69:31(6536)-**IS**-5:28-**JER**-47:3-**EZE**-26:11■32:13-**MIC**-4:13

HOOK-**2KI**-19:28(2397)-**JOB**-41:1(100),2(2443)-**IS**-37:29(2397)■**N.T.**-**M'T**-17:27(44)

HOOKS-all=2053&marked-**EX**-26:32,37■27:10,11,17■36:36,38■38:10,11,12,17,19,28-**EZE**-29:4(2397)■38:4(2397)■40:43(8240)-**AM**-4:2(6793)

HOPE-all=8615,a=3176&marked-**RU**-1:12-**EZR**-10:2(4723)-**JOB**-4:6■5:16■6:11a■7:6■8:13,14(3689)■11:18,20■14:7,19■17:15^{2}■19:10■27:8■31:24(3689)■41:9(8431)-**PS**-16:9(983)■22:9(982)■31:24a■33:18a,22a■38:15a■39:7(8431)■42:5a,11a■43:5a■71:5(8615),14a■78:7(3689)■119:49a,81a,114a,116(7664)■130:5a,7a■131:3a■146:5(7664)■147:11a-**PR**-10:28(8431)■11:7(8431)■13:12(8431)■14:32(2620)■19:18■26:12■29:20-**EC**-9:4(986)-**IS**-38:18(7663)■57:10(2976)-**JER**-2:25(2976)■14:8(4723)■17:7

(4009),13(4723),17(4268)▪18:12(2976)▪31:17▪50:7(4723)-LA-3:18(8431),21a,24a,26(2342),29-EZE-13:6a▪19:5▪37:11-HO-2:15-JOE-3:16(4268)-ZEC-9:12▪N.T.-all=1680&marked-LU-6:34(1679)-AC-2:26▪16:19▪23:6▪24:15▪26:6,7(1679)▪27:20▪28:20-RO-4:18▪5:2,4,5▪8:20,24^{2},24(1679),25(1679)▪12:12▪15:4,13^{2}-1CO-9:10^{3}▪13:13▪15:19(1679)-2CO-1:7▪3:12▪10:15-GA-5:5-EPH-1:18▪2:12▪4:4-PH'P-1:20▪2:23(1679)-COL-1:5,23,27-1TH-1:3▪2:19-4:13▪5:8-2TH-2:16-1TI-1:1-TIT-1:2▪2:13▪3:7-HEB-3:6▪6:11,18▪7:19-1PE-1:3,13(1679),21▪3:15-1JO-3:3

HOPED-all=3176&marked-ES-9:1(7663)-JOB-6:20(982)-PS-119:43,74,147,166(7663)▪N.T.-all=1679-LU-23:8-AC-24:26-2CO-8:5-HEB-11:1

HOPE'S-AC-26:7(1679)

HOPETH-1CO-13:7(1679)

HOPING-LU-6:35(560)-1TI-3:14(1679)

HORN-all=7161&marked-JOS-6:5-1SA-2:1,10▪16:1,13-2SA-22:3-1KI-1:39-1CH-25:5-JOB-16:15-PS-18:2▪75:4,5▪89:17,24▪92:10,10sup▪112:9▪132:17▪148:14-JER-48:25-LA-2:3,17-EZE-29:21-DA-7:8^{2}(7162),11(7162),20(7162),21(7162)▪8:5,8,9,21-MIC-4:13-ZEC-1:21▪N.T.-LU-1:69(2768)

HORNET-DE-7:20(6880)-JOS-24:12(6880)

HORNETS-EX-23:28(6880)

HORNS-all=7161&marked-GE-22:13-EX-27:2^{2}▪29:12▪30:2,3,10▪37:25,26▪38:2^{2}-LE-4:7,18,25,30,34▪8:15▪9:9▪16:18-DE-33:17-JOS-6:4(3104),6(3104),13(3104)-1KI-1:50,51▪2:28▪22:11-2CH-18:10-PS-22:21▪69:31(7160)▪75:10^{2}▪118:27-JER-17:1-EZE-27:15▪34:21▪43:15,20-DA-7:7(7162),8^{2}(7162),20(7162),24(7162)▪8:3^{2},6,7,20-AM-3:14▪6:13-HAB-3:4-ZEC-1:18,19,21^{2}▪N.T.-all=2768-RE-5:6▪9:13▪12:3▪13:1^{2},11▪17:3,7,12,16

HORRIBLE-all=8186&marked-PS-11:6(2152)▪40:2(7588)-JER-5:30▪18:13▪23:14-HO-6:10

HORRIBLY-JER-2:12(8175)-EZE-32:10(8178)

HORROR-GE-15:12(367)-PS-55:5(6427)▪119:53(2152)-EZE-7:18(6427)

HORSE-all=5483-GE-49:17-EX-15:1,19,21-1KI-10:29▪20:20,25-2CH-1:17▪23:15-NE-3:28-ES-6:8,9,10,11-JOB-39:18,19-PS-32:9▪33:17▪76:6▪147:10-PR-21:31▪26:3-IS-43:17▪63:13-JER-8:6▪31:40▪51:21-AM-2:15-ZEC-1:8▪9:10▪10:3▪12:4^{2}▪14:15▪N.T.-all=2462-RE-6:2,4,5,8▪14:20▪19:11,19,21

HORSEBACK-2KI-9:18(7392,5483),19(7392,5483)-ES-6:9(7392),11(7392)▪8:10(5483)

HORSEHOOFS-J'G-5:22(6119,5483)

HORSELEACH-PR-30:15(5936)

HORSEMAN-2KI-9:17(7395)-NA-3:3(6571)

HORSEMEN-all=6571-GE-50:9-EX-14:9,17,18,23,26,28▪15:19-JOS-24:6-1SA-8:11▪13:5-2SA-1:6(1167,6571)▪8:4▪10:18-1KI-1:5▪4:26▪9:19,22▪10:26^{2}▪20:20-2KI-2:12▪13:7,14▪18:24-1CH-18:4▪19:6-2CH-1:14^{2}▪8:6,9▪9:25▪12:3▪16:8-EZR-8:22-NE-2:9-IS-21:7,9▪22:6,7▪28:28▪31:1▪36:9-JER-4:29▪46:4-EZE-23:6,12▪26:7,10▪27:14▪38:4-DA-11:40-HO-1:7-JOE-2:4-HAB-1:8^{2}▪N.T.-AC-23:23(2460),32(2460)-RE-9:16(2461)

HORSES-all=5483&marked-GE-47:17-EX-9:3▪14:9,23-DE-11:4▪17:16^{2}▪20:1-JOS-11:4,6,9-2SA-15:1-1K1-4:26,28▪10:25,28▪18:5▪20:1,21▪22:4-2KI-2:11▪3:7▪5:9▪6:14,15,17▪7:6,7,10,13,14▪9:33▪10:2▪11:16▪14:20▪18:23▪23:11-2CH-1:16,17▪9:24,25,28▪25:28-EZR-2:66-NE-7:68-PS-20:7-EC-10:7-SONG-1:9(5484)-IS-2:7▪30:16▪31:1,3▪36:8▪66:20-JER-4:13▪5:8▪6:23▪8:16▪12:5▪17:25▪22:4▪46:4,9▪50:37,42▪51:27-EZE-17:15▪23:6,12,20,23▪26:7,10,11▪27:14▪38:4,15▪39:20-HO-1:7▪14:3-JOE-2:4-AM-4:10▪6:12-MIC-5:10-NA-3:2-HAB-1:8▪3:8,15-HAG-2:22-ZEC-1:8▪6:2^{2},3^{2},6▪10:5▪14:20▪N.T.-all=2462-RE-9:7,9,17^{2}▪18:13▪19:14,18

HORSES'-IS-5:28(5483)▪N.T.-JAS-3:3(2462)

HOSANNA-all=5614-M'T-21:9^{2},15-M'R-11:19,10-JOH-12:13

HOSEN-DA-3:21(6361)

HOSPITALITY-all=5382&marked-RO-12:13(5381)-1TI-3:2-TIT-1:8-1PE-4:9

HOST-all=6635,a=4264,b=2428&marked-GE-2:1▪21:22,32▪32:2a-EX-14:4b,17b,24^{2}a,28b▪15:4b▪16:3a-NU-2:4,6,8,11,13,15,19,21,23,26,28,30▪4:3▪10:15,16,18,19,20,22,23,24,25,26,27▪31:14b,48-DE-2:14a,15a▪4:19▪17:3▪23:9a-JOS-1:11a▪3:2a▪5:14,15▪8:13a▪18:9a-J'G-4:2,15a,16^{2}a▪7:1a,8a,9a,10a,11^{2}a,13a,14a,15^{2}a,21a,22^{2}a▪8:11a,12a-1SA-11:11a▪12:9▪14:15a,19a,48b,50▪17:20b,46a,55▪26:5▪28:5a,19a▪29:6a-2SA-2:8▪3:23▪5:24a▪8:9b,16▪10:7,16,18▪17:25▪19:13▪20:23▪23:16a▪24:2b,4^{2}b-1KI-1:19,25▪2:32^{2},35▪4:4▪11:15,21▪16:16▪20:1b▪22:19,34a,36b-2KI-3:9a▪4:13▪5:1▪6:14b,15b▪7:4a,6a,6b,14a▪9:5b▪11:15b▪17:16▪18:17(2426)▪21:3,5▪23:4,5▪25:1b,19-1CH-9:19a▪11:15a,18a▪12:14,21,22a▪14:15a,16a▪18:9b,15▪19:8,16,18▪25:1▪26:26▪27:3,5-2CH-14:9b,13a▪16:7b,8b▪18:18,33▪23:14b▪24:23b,24b▪26:11b,14▪28:9▪33:3,5,11-NE-9:6^{2}-PS-27:3a▪33:6,16b▪136:15b-IS-13:4▪24:21▪34:4^{2}▪40:26▪45:12-JER-8:2▪19:13▪33:22▪51:3▪52:25-EZE-1:24a-DA-8:10^{2},11,12,13-OB-20(2426)-ZEP-1:5▪N.T.-LU-2:13(4756)▪10:35(3830)-AC-7:42(4756)-RO-16:23(3581)

HOSTAGES-2KI-14:14(1121,8594)-2CH-25:24(1121,8594)

HOSTS-all=6635&marked-EX-12:41-NU-1:52▪2:32▪10:25-JOS-10:5(4264)▪11:4(4264)-J'G-8:10^{2}(4264)-1SA-1:3,11▪4:4▪15:2▪17:45-2SA-5:10▪6:2,18▪7:8,26,27-1KI-2:5▪15:20(2428)▪18:15▪19:10,14-2KI-3:14-1CH-11:9▪17:7,24-PS-24:10▪46:7,11▪48:8▪59:5▪69:6▪80:4,7,14,19▪84:1,3,8,12▪89:8▪103:21▪108:11▪148:2-IS-1:9,24▪2:12▪3:1,15▪5:7,9,16,24▪6:3,5▪8:13,18▪9:7,13,19▪10:16,23,24,26,33▪13:4,13▪14:22,23,24,27▪17:3▪18:7^{2}▪19:4,12,16,17,18,20,25▪21:10▪22:5,12,14^{2},15,25▪23:9▪24:23▪25:6▪28:5,22,29▪29:6▪31:4,5▪37:16,32▪39:5▪44:6▪45:13▪47:4▪48:2▪51:15▪54:5-JER-2:19▪3:19▪5:14▪6:6,9▪7:3,21▪8:3▪9:7,15,17▪10:16▪11:17,20,22▪15:16▪16:9▪19:3,11,15▪20:12▪23:15,16,36▪25:8,27,28,29,32▪26:18▪27:4,18,19,21▪28:2,14▪29:4,8,17,21,25▪30:8▪31:23,35▪32:14,15,18▪33:11,12▪35:13,17,18,19▪38:17▪39:16▪42:15,18▪43:10▪44:2,7,11,25▪46:10^{2},18,25▪48:1,15▪49:5,7,26,35▪50:18,25,31,33,34▪51:5,14,19,33,57,58-HO-12:5-AM-3:13▪4:13▪5:14,15,16,27▪6:8,14▪9:5-MIC-4:4-NA-2:13▪3:5-HAB-2:13-ZEP-2:9,10-HAG-1:2,5,7,9,14▪2:4,6,7,8,9^{2},11,23^{2}-ZEC-1:3^{3},4,6,12,14,16,17▪2:8,9,11▪3:7,9,10▪4:6,9▪5:4▪6:12,15▪7:3,4,9,12^{2},13▪8:1,2,3,4,6^{2},7,9^{2},11,14^{2},18,19,20,21,22,23▪9:15▪10:3▪12:5▪13:2,7▪14:16,17,21^{2}-MAL-1:4,6,8,9,10,11,13,14▪2:2,4,7,8,12,16▪3:1,5,7,10,11,12,14,17▪4:1,3

HOT-all=2734&marked-EX-16:21(2552)▪22:24▪32:10,11,19,22-LE-13:24(784)-DE-9:19(2534)▪19:6(3179)-JOS-9:12(2525)-J'G-2:14,20▪3:8▪6:39▪10:7-1SA-11:9(2527)▪21:6(2527)-NE-7:3(2527)-JOB-6:17(2527)-PS-6:1(2534)▪38:1(2534)▪39:3(2552)▪78:48(7565)-EZE-24:11(3179)-DA-3:22(228)-HO-7:7(2552)▪N.T.-1TI-4:2(2743)-RE-3:15^{2}(2200),16(2200)

HOTLY-GE-31:36(1814)

HOTTEST-2SA-11:15(2389)

HOUGH-JOS-11:6(6131)

HOUGHED-all=6131-JOS-11:9-2SA-8:4-1CH-18:4

HOUR-all=8160-DA-3:6,15▪4:19:33▪5:5▪N.T.-all=5610&marked-M'T-8:13▪9:22▪10:19▪15:28▪17:18▪20:3,5,6,9,12▪24:36,42,44,50▪25:13▪26:40,45,55▪27:45^{2},46-M'R-13:11,32▪14:35,37,41▪15:25,33^{2},34-LU-7:21▪10:21▪12:12,39,40,46▪20:19▪22:14,53,59▪23:44^{2}▪24:33-JOH-1:39▪2:4▪4:6,21,23,52^{2},53▪5:25,28▪7:30▪8:20▪12:23,27^{2}▪13:1▪16:21,32▪17:1▪19:14,27-AC-2:15▪3:1^{2}▪10:3,9,30^{2}▪16:18,33▪22:13▪23:23-1CO-4:11▪8:7(734)▪15:30-GA-2:5-RE-3:3,10▪8:1(2256)▪9:15▪11:13▪14:7▪17:12▪18:10,17,19

HOURS-all=5610-JOH-11:9-AC-5:7▪19:34

HOUSE-all=1004,a=1005&marked-GE-7:1▪12:1,15,17▪14:14▪15:2,3▪17:2,13,23^{2},27▪19:2,3,4,10,11▪20:13,18▪24:2,7,23,27,28,31,23,38,40▪2▪27:15▪28:2,17,21,22▪29:13▪30:30▪31:14,30,41▪33:17▪34:19,26,29,30▪36:6▪38:11^{2}▪39:2,4,5^{3},8,9,11^{2},14▪40:3,7,14▪41:10,40,51▪42:19▪43:16,17,18,19^{2},24,26▪44:1,8,14▪45:2,8,16▪46:27,31^{2}▪47:14▪50:4,7,8^{2},22-EX-2:1▪3:22▪7:23▪8:3^{2},24▪12:3^{2},4,22,30,46^{2}▪13:3,14▪16:31▪19:3▪20:2,17▪22:7,8▪23:19▪34:26▪40:38-LE-10:6▪14:34,35^{2},36^{3},37,38^{2},39,41,42,43^{2},44^{2},45^{2},46,47^{2},48^{3},49,51,52,53,55▪16:6,11,17:3,8,10▪22:11,13,18▪25:29,30,33▪27:14,15-NU-1:2,4,18,20,22,24,26,28,30,32,34,36,38▪40,42,44,45▪2:2,32,34▪3:15,20,24,30,35▪4:2,29,34,38,40,42,46▪7:2▪12:7▪17:2^{2},3,8▪18:1,11,13▪20:29▪22:18▪24:13,25:14,15▪26:2▪30:3,10,16▪34:14^{2}-DE-5:6,21▪6:7,9,12▪7:8,26▪8:14▪11:19,20▪13:5,10▪15:16▪20:5^{2},6,7,8▪21:12,13▪22:2,8^{2},21^{2}▪23:18▪24:1,2,3,10▪25:9,10,14▪26,11,13▪28:30-JOS-2:1,3,12,15,19^{2}▪6:17,22,24▪9:23▪17:17▪18:5▪20:6▪21:45▪22:14^{2}▪24:15,17-J'G-1:22,23,35▪4:17▪6:8,15▪8:27,29,35▪9:1,4,5,6,16,18,19,20^{2},27,46▪10:9▪11:2,7,31,34▪12:1▪14:15,19▪16:21,25,26,27,29,30,31▪17:4,5,8,12▪18:2,3,13,15^{2},18,19,22^{2},26,31▪19:2,3,15,18^{2},21,22^{3},23^{2},26,27^{2},29▪20:5,8,18(1008)▪26(1008),31(1008)▪21:2(1008)-RU-1:8,9▪2:7▪4:11^{2},12-1SA-1:7,19,21,24▪2:11,27^{2},28,30,31^{2},32,33,35,36▪3:12,13,14^{2},15▪5:2,5▪7:1,2,3,17▪9:18,20,25,26▪10:25▪15:34▪17:25▪18:2,10▪19:9,11▪20:15,16▪21:15▪22:1,11,14,15,16,22▪23:18▪24:21▪25:1,3,6,28,35,36▪28:24▪31:9,10-2SA-1:12▪2:4,7,10,11▪3:1^{2},6^{2},8,10,19,29^{2}▪4:5,6,7,11▪5:8,11▪6:3,4,5,10,11,12^{2},15,19,21▪7:1,2,5,6,7,11,13,16,18,19,25,26,27,29^{2}▪9:1,2,3,4,5,9,12▪11:2,4,8^{2},9^{2},10^{2},11,13,27▪12:8^{2},10,11,15,17,20^{2}▪13:7,8,20▪14:8,9,24^{2},31▪15:16,35▪16:3,5,8,21,22▪17:18,20,23▪19:5,11^{2},17,20,28,30▪20:3^{2}▪21:1,4▪23:5▪24:17-1KI-1:53▪2:24,27,31,33,34,36▪3:1^{2},2,17^{2},18▪5:3,5^{2},17,18▪6:1,2,3^{3},4,5^{2},6^{2},7^{2},8,9^{2},10^{2},12,14,15^{3},16,17,18,19,21,22^{2},27^{2},29,30,37,38▪7:1^{2},2,8^{2},12^{2},39^{3},40,45,48,50^{2},51^{2}▪8:6,10,11,13,16,17,18,19^{2},20,27,29,31,33,38,42,43,44,48,63,64▪9:1^{2},3,7,8^{2},10,15,24,25▪10:4,5,12^{2},17,21▪11:18,20,28,38▪12:16,19,20,21^{2},23,24,26,27,31▪13:2,8,18,19,34▪14:4,8,10^{2},12,13,14,26^{2},27,28▪15:15,18^{2},27,29▪16:3^{2},7^{2},9^{2},11,12,18^{2},32▪17:15,17,23▪18:3,18▪20:6,31,43▪21:2,4,22^{2},29▪22:17,39-2KI-4:2^{2},32,35▪5:9,18^{3},24▪6:32▪7:11▪8:3,5,18,27^{3}▪9:6,7,8,9^{2},27▪10:3,5,10,11,12,14,21^{2},23,25,26,27,30▪11:3,4^{2},5,6,7,15,16,18^{2},19^{2},20▪12:4^{2},5,6,7^{2},8,9^{2},10,11^{2},12^{2},13^{2},14,16,18^{2},20▪13:6▪14:14^{2}▪15:5^{2},25,35▪16:8^{2},14^{2},18^{2}▪17:21▪18:15^{2}▪19:1,14,30,37▪

20:1,5,8,13^{3},15^{2},17■21:4,5,7^{2},13,18,23
-22:3,4,5^{3},6,8,9^{2}■23:2^{2},6,7,11,12,24,27■
24:13^{2}■25:9^{2},13^{2},16-**1CH**-2:54(5854),55■
4:21^{2},38■5:13,15,24^{2}■6:31,32,48■7:2,
4,7,9,23,40■9:9,11,13^{2},19,23^{2},26,27■10:6,
10■12:28,29,30■13:7,13,14^{2}■14:1■15:25■
16:43^{2}■17:1^{2},4,5,6,10,12,14,16,17,23,
24,25,27■21:17■22:1,2,5,6,7,8,10,11,14,
19■23:4,11,24^{2},28^{2},32■24:4^{2},19,30■
25:6^{2}■26:6,12,13,15,20,22,27■28:2,3,4^{2},
6,10,12^{2},13^{2},20,21■29:2,3^{3},7,8,16-**2CH**-
2:1^{2},3,4,5,6^{2},9,12^{2}■3:1,3,4,5,6,7,8^{2},10,11,
12,15■4:11,16,19,22^{2}■5:1^{2},7,13,14■6:2,
5,7,8,9^{2},10,18,20,22,24,29,32,33,34,38■
7:1,2^{2},3,5,7,11^{2},12,16,20,21^{2}■8:1,11^{2},
16^{2}■9:3,4,11,16,20■10:16,19■11:1,4■
12:9^{2},10,11■15:18■16:2,10■17:14■
18:16■19:1,11■20:5,9^{2},28■21:6,7,13^{2},
17■22:3,4,7,8,9,10,12■23:3,5^{2},6,7,9,12,
14,15,17,18^{2},19,20^{2}■24:4,5,7^{2},8,12^{3},13,
14^{2},16,18,21,27■25:24^{2}■26:19,21^{3}■27:3■
28:7,21^{2},24^{3}■29:3,5,15,16^{2},17,18,20,
25,31,35■30:1,15■31:10^{2},11,13,16,17,
21■32:21■33:4,5,7^{2},15^{2},20,24■34:8^{2},9,
10^{3},14,15,17,30^{2}■35:2,3,8,21■36:7,10,
14,17,18^{2},19,23-**EZR**-1:2,3,4,5,7^{2}■2:36,
59,68^{2}■3:8^{2},9,11,12^{2}■4:3,24a■5:2a,3a,
8a,9a,11a,12a,13a,14a,15a,16a,17^{2}a,22■
6:1a,3^{2}a,4a,5^{2}a,7^{2}a,8a,11^{2}a,12a,15a,16a,
17a,22■7:16a,17a,19a,20^{2}a,23a,24a,27■
8:17,25,29,30,33,36■9:9■10:1,6,9,16-**NE**-
1:6■2:8^{2}■3:10,16,20,21^{2},23^{2},24,25,28,
29■4:16■5:13■6:10^{2}■7:3,39,61■8:16sup,16■
10:32,33,34,35,36^{2},37,38^{2},39■11:11,
12,16,22■12:29,37,40■13:4,7,9,11,14
-**ES**-1:8,9,22■2:3,8,9^{2},11,13^{2},14,16■4:13,
14■5:1^{4}■6:4,12■7:8,9■8:1,2,7■9:4-**JOB**-
1:10,13,18,19■7:10■8:15■17:13■19:15■
20:19,28■21:21,28■27:18■30:23■38:20■
39:6■42:11-**PS**-5:7■23:6■26:8■27:4
30:t■31:2■36:8■42:4■45:10■49:16■
50:9■52:t,8■55:14■59:t■65:4■66:13■
69:9■84:3,4,10■92:13■93:5■98:3■101:2,
7■102:7■104:17■105:21■112:3■113:9■
114:1■115:10,12^{2}■116:19■118:3,26■
119:54■122:1,5,9■127:1■128:3■132:3■
134:1■135:2^{2},19^{2},20-**PR**-2:18■3:33■5:8,
10■6:31■7:6,8,11,27■9:1,14■11:29■12:7■
14:1,11■15:6,25,27■17:1,13■19:14■21:9,
12■24:3,27■25:17,24■27:10-**EC**-2:7■
5:1■7:2^{2},4^{2}■10:18■12:3-**SONG**-1:17■
2:4■3:4■8:2,7-**IS**-2:2,3,5,6■3:6,7■5:7,
8■6:4■7:2,13,17■8:17■10:20■14:1,2,17,
18■22:8,15,18,21,22,23,24■23:1■24:10■
29:22■31:2■36:3■37:1,14,31,38■38:1,
20,22■39:2^{3},4^{2},6■42:7■44:13■46:3^{2}■
48:1■56:5,7^{2}■58:1,7■60:7■63:7■64:11■
66:1,20-**JER**-2:4^{2},26■3:18^{2},20■5:11,15,
20■7:2,10,11,14,30■9:26■10:1■11:10,15,
17■12:6,7,14■13:11^{2}■16:5,8■17:26■18:2,
3,6^{2}■19:14■20:1,2,6■21:11,12■22:1,4,5,
6,13,14■23:8,11,34■26:2^{2},6,7,9^{2},10,10sup,
12,18■27:16,18^{2},21^{2}■28:1,3,5,6■29:26■
31:27^{2},31^{2},33■32:2,34■33:11,14,17■34:13,
15■35:2^{2},3,4,5,7,18■36:3,5,6,8,10^{2},12■
37:15,17,20■38:7,8,11,14,17,22,26■39:8■
41:5■43:9■48:13■51:51■52:13,17^{2},20
-**LA**-2:7-**EZE**-2:5,8■3:1,4,5,7^{2},9,17,24,
26,27■4:3,4,5,6■5:4■6:11■8:1,6,10,11,
12,14,16,17■9:3,6,7,9■10:4^{2},18,19■11:1,
5,15■12:2^{2},3,6,9,10,24,25,27■13:5,9■
14:4,5,6,7,11■17:2,12■18:6,15,25,29^{2},
30,31■20:5,13,27,30,31,39,40,44■22:18■
23:39■24:3,21■25:3,8,12■27:14■
28:24,25■29:6,16,21■33:7,10,11,20■
34:30■35:15■36:10,17,21,22^{2},32,37■
37:11,16■38:6■39:12,22,23,25,29■
40:4,5,45,47,48■41:5^{2},6^{2},7^{3},8,10,13,
14,17,19,26■42:15■43:4,5,6,7,10,
11,12^{2},21■44:4^{2},5^{2},6^{2},7,11^{2},12,14,22,30■
45:5,6,8,17^{2},19,20■46:24■47:1^{4}■48:21
-**DA**-1:2^{3}■2:17a■4:4a,30a■5:3a,10a,23a■
6:10a-**HO**-1:4^{2},6,7■5:1^{2},12,14■6:10■
8:1■9:4,8,15■11:12-**JOE**-1:9,13,14,16■
3:18-**AM**-1:4,5■2:8■3:13,15■5:1,3,4,6,
19,25■6:1,9,10^{2},11^{2},14■7:9,10,16■9:8,9
-**OB**-17,18^{4}-**MIC**-1:5,10(1035)■2:2,7■
3:1,9^{2},12■4:1,2■6:4,10,16■7:6-**NA**-1:14
-**HAB**-2:9,10■3:13-**ZEP**-2:7-**HAG**-1:2,
4,8,9^{2},14■2:3,7,9-**ZEC**-1:16■3:7■4:9■
5:4^{3},11■6:10■7:2(1008),3■8:9,13,15,19■
9:8■10:3,6^{2}■11:13■12:4,7,8,10,12^{2},13■
13:1■6:1■14:20,21-**MAL**-3:10■**N.T.**-
all=3624,a=3614&marked-**M'T**-2:11a■
5:15a■7:24a,25a,26a,27a■8:14a■9:6,7,
10a,23a,28a■10:6,12a,13a,14a,25(3617)■
12:4,25a,29^{2}a,44■13:1a,36a,57a■15:24■
17:25a■20:11(3617)■21:13■23:38■24:17a,
43(3617),43a■26:6a-**M'R**-1:29a■2:1,11,
15a,26■3:19,25^{2}a,27^{2}a■5:38■6:4a,10■
7:17,24a,30■8:26■9:28,33a■10:10a,29a■
11:17^{2}■13:15a^{2},34a,35a■14:3a,14(3617)
-**LU**-1:23,27,33,40,56,69■2:4■4:38a■5:24,
25,29a■6:4,48^{2}a,49^{2}a■7:6a,10,36a,37a,44a■
8:27a,39,41,51a■9:4a,61■10:5a,5,7^{2}a,38■
11:17,24■12:39(3617),39,52■13:25(3617),
35■14:1,21(3617),23■15:8a,25a■16:27■
17:31a■18:14,29a■19:5,9,46■22:10a,11a,
54-**JOH**-2:16,17■4:53a■7:53■8:35a■
11:20,31a■12:3a■14:2a-**AC**-2:2,36,46■
5:42■7:10,20,42,47,49■8:3■9:11a,17a■
10:2,6a,17a,22,30,32a■11:11a,12,13,14■
12:12a■16:15,31,32a,34,34(3832)■17:5a■
18:7^{2}a,8■19:16■20:20■21:8-**RO**-16:5
-**1CO**-16:15a,19-**2CO**-5:1^{2}a,2(3613)
-**COL**-4:15-**1TI**-3:4,5,15■5:8(3609),
13a,14(3616)-**2TI**-1:16■2:20a-**PH'M**-2
-**HEB**-3:2,3^{2},4,5,6^{2}■8:8,10■10:21■11:7
-**1PE**-2:5■4:17-**2JO**-10a

HOUSEHOLD-all=1004&marked
-**GE**-18:19■31:37■38:2■45:11■
47:12-**EX**-1:1■12:4-**LE**-16:17-**DE**-6:22■
14:26■15:20-**JOS**-2:18■6:25■7:14,18
-**J'G**-6:27■18:25-**1SA**-25:17■27:3-**2SA**-2:3■
6:11,20■15:16■16:2■17:23■19:18,41
-**1KI**-4:6,7■5:9,11■11:20-**2KI**-7:9■8:1,
2■18:18,37■19:2-**1CH**-24:6-**NE**-13:8
-**JOB**-1:3(5657)-**PR**-27:27■31:5,21^{2},27
-**IS**-36:22■37:2■**N.T.**-all=3624&
marked-**M'T**-10:25(3615),36(3615)■
24:45(2322)-**LU**-12:42(2322)-**AC**-10:7
(3610)■16:15-**1CO**-1:16-**GA**-6:10(3609)
-**EPH**-2:19(3609)-**PH'P**-4:22(3614)
-**2TI**-4:19

HOUSEHOLDER-all=3617&
marked-**M'T**-13:27,52■20:1■21:33

HOUSEHOLDS-all=1004&
marked-**GE**-42:33■45:18■47:24-**NU**-
18:31-**DE**-11:6■12:7-**JOS**-7:14

HOUSES-all=1004&marked-**GE**-
42:19-**EX**-1:21■6:14■8:9,11,13,21^{2},24■
9:20■10:6^{3}■12:7,13,15,19,23,27^{2}-**LE**-
25:31,32,33-**NU**-4:22■16:32■17:6■
32:18-**DE**-6:11■8:12■19:1-**JOS**-9:12
-**J'G**-18:14,22-**1KI**-9:10■13:32■20:6
-**2KI**-17:29,32■23:7,19■25:9-**1CH**-
15:1■28:11■29:4-**2CH**-25:5■34:11■
35:4-**NE**-4:14■5:3,11■7:4■9:25■10:34
-**JOB**-1:4■3:15■4:19■15:28■21:9■22:18■
24:16-**PS**-49:11■83:12(4999)-**PR**-1:13■
30:26-**EC**-2:4-**IS**-3:14■5:9■6:11■
8:14■13:16,21,22(490)■22:10^{2}■32:13■
42:22■65:21-**JER**-5:7,27■6:12■17:22■
18:22■19:13^{2}■29:5,28■32:15,29■33:4^{2}■
35:9■39:8■43:12,13■52:13^{2}-**LA**-5:2
-**EZE**-7:24■11:3■16:41■23:47■26:12■
28:26■33:30■45:4-**DA**-2:5(1005)■3:29
(1005)-**HO**-11:11-**JOE**-2:9-**AM**-3:15^{2}■
5:11-**MIC**-1:14■2:2,9-**ZEP**-1:9,13^{2}■2:7
-**HAG**-1:4-**ZEC**-14:2■**N.T.**-all=3614&
marked-**M'T**-11:8(3624)■19:29■23:14
-**M'R**-8:3(3624)■10:30■12:40-**LU**-16:4
(3624)■20:47-**AC**-4:34-**1CO**-11:22-**1TI**-
3:12(3624)-2TI-3:6-TIT-1:11(3624)

HOUSETOP-**PR**-21:9(1406)■25:24
(1406)■**N.T.**-all=1430-**M'T**-24:17-**M'R**-
13:15-**LU**-5:19■17:31-**AC**-10:9

HOUSETOPS-all=1406&marked
-**PS**-129:6-**IS**-22:1■37:27-**JER**-48:38
-**ZEP**-1:5■**N.T.**-**M'T**-10:27(1430)-**LU**-
12:3(1430)

HOW-all=349,a=4100,b=5704,c=
834,d=637,e=3588&marked-**GE**-26:9■
27:20a■28:17a■30:29^{2}(854)c■38:29a■
39:9■44:8,16a,34■47:8a,18(3588,518)
-**EX**-2:18(4069)■6:30■10:3b,7(4970)■16:2
8b-**NU**-14:11^{2}b,27b■23:8^{2}a■24:5a-**DE**-
1:12■7:17■9:7c■11:4c,6c■12:30■18:21■
25:18c■29:16^{2}c■31:27d■32:30-**JOS**-2:10c■
9:7■10:1^{2}e■14:12e■18:3b-**J'G**-13:12a■
16:15■20:3■21:7a,16a-**RU**-3:18b
-**1SA**-1:14b■2:22c■10:27a■12:24c■
14:29e,30d■15:2c■16:1b,2■23:3d■24:10c
-**2SA**-1:4a,5,14,19,25,27■2:22,26b■4:11d■
6:9,20a■12:18■16:11d■19:34a-**1KI**-
8:27d■12:6■14:19c■18:21b■19:1c■20:7e■
21:29e■22:16b,45c-**2KI**-5:7e,13d■6:15,
32e■8:5c■10:4■14:15c,28c■17:28■18:24■
20:3c,20c-**1CH**-13:12(1963)■18:9e
-**2CH**-6:18d■18:15b■32:15d-**NE**-
2:6b,17c-**ES**-5:11c■8:6^{2}(346)-**JOB**-
4:19d■6:25a■7:19b■8:2b,2sup■9:2a,
14d■13:23a■15:16d■18:2b■19:2b■21:17a,
17sup,34■22:12e,13a■25:4^{2}a,6d■26:2a,
2sup,3a,3sup,14a■34:19c■37:17c-**PS**-3:1a■
4:2b,2sup■6:3b■8:1a,9a■11:1■13:1^{2}b,2b^{2}■
21:1a■31:19a■35:17a■36:7a■39:4a■
62:3b■66:3a■73:11,19■74:9b,10b■78:40
(4101),43c■79:5b■80:4b■82:2b■84:1a■
89:46b,47a■90:13b■92:5a■94:3b■
104:24a■119:84a,97a,103a,159e■132:2c■
133:1a■137:4■139:17^{2}a-**PR**-1:22b■
5:12■6:9b■15:11d,23a■16:16a■19:7d■
20:24a■21:27d■30:13a-**EC**-2:16■4:11■
10:15c-**SONG**-4:10^{2}a■5:3^{2}■7:1a,6a
-**IS**-1:21■6:11b■14:4,12■19:11■20:6■
36:9■38:3c■48:11■52:7a-**JER**-2:21,
23■3:19■4:14b,21b■5:7(335)■8:8■9:7,
19■12:4b,5^{2},5sup■22:23a■23:26b■
31:22b■36:17■47:5b,6b,7■48:14,17,
39^{2}■49:25■50:23^{2}■51:41,41sup,41-**LA**-
1:1,1sup^{2}■2:1■4:1,2-**EZE**-14:21d■
15:5d■16:30a■26:17■33:10-**DA**-4:3^{2}
(4101)■8:13b■10:17(1963)■12:6b-**HO**-
8:5■11:8,8sup,8,8sup-**JOE**-1:18a
-**OB**-5,6,6sup-**MIC**-2:4-**HAB**-1:2b■
2:6b-**ZEP**-2:15-**HAG**-2:3a-**ZEC**-
1:12b■9:17^{2}a■**N.T.**-all=4459,a=4214,
b=3745,c=5101,d=5613&marked
-**M'T**-6:23a,28■7:4,11sup,11a■10:19,
25a■12:4,12a,14(3704),29^{2},34■15:34a■
16:9a,10a,11■17:17(2193),17(4219)■
18:12c,21(4212)■21:20■22:12,15(3704),
43,45■23:33■26:54■27:13a-**M'R**-
2:16c,26■3:6(3704),23■4:13,27d,40■
5:16,19b,20b■6:38a■8:5a,19a,20a,
21■9:12,19^{2}(2193),21a■10:23,
24■11:18■12:26d,35,41■14:1,11■15:4a
-**LU**-1:34,58(3754),62c■2:49c■
:4d,2■7:22(3754)■8:18,39^{2}b,47d■
9:41(2193)■10:26■11:13a,18(4559)■
12:11(4559),24a,27,28a,50,56■13:34
(4212)■14:7■15:17a■16:2c,5a,7a■
18:24■19:15c■20:41,44■21:5(3754)■
22:2,4,61d■23:55d■24:6d,20(3704),
35d-**JOH**-3:4,9,12■4:1(3754),9■5:44,
47■6:42,52■7:15■8:33■9:10,15,16,19,
26■10:24(2193)■11:36■12:19(3754),34■
14:5,9,22c,28(3754)-**AC**-2:8■4:21■
5:9c■8:31■9:13b,16b,27^{2}■10:28d,38d■
11:13,16d■12:17■15:14(2531),36■
20:20d,35(3754)■21:20a-**RO**-3:6■
4:10■6:2■8:32■10:14^{3},15d■11:2d,12a,
24a,33d-**1CO**-3:10■6:3(3386)■7:16c,32,
33,34■14:7,9,16,26c■15:12,35-**2CO**-
3:8■7:15d-**GA**-4:9,13(3754)■6:11(4080)
-**EPH**-6:21c-**PH'P**-1:8d■2:23(4012)
-**COL**-4:6-**1TH**-1:9■2:10d,11d■4:1
-**TH**-3:7-**1TI**-3:5,15-**2TI**-1:18b-**PH'M**-
16a,19(3754)-**HEB**-2:3■7:4(4080)■
8:6b■9:14a■10:29a■12:17(3754)-**JAS**-
2:22(3754)■3:5(2245)-**1JO**-3:17■4:20
-**RE**-2:2(3754)■3:3■6:10(2193)■18:7b

HOWBEIT-**J'G**-18:29(199)-**1SA**-
8:9(389)-**2SA**-12:14(657)-**1KI**-11:13
(7535)-**2CH**-32:31(3561)■**N.T.**-all=
235&marked-**JOH**-6:23(1161)■7:13
(3305),27-**AC**-7:48-**1CO**-8:7■14:20■
15:46-**GA**-4:8-**TI**-1:16-**HEB**-3:16

HOWL-all=3213-**IS**-13:6■14:31■
15:2,3■16:7■23:1,6,14■52:5■65:14-**JER**-
4:8■25:34■47:2■48:20,31,39■49:3■51:8
-**EZE**-21:12■30:2-**JOE**-1:5,11,13-**MIC**-
1:8-**ZEP**-1:11-**ZEC**-11:2^{2}■**N.T.**-**JAS**-

5:1(3649)
HOWLED-HO-7:14(3213)
HOWLING-all=3213&marked-DE-32:10(3214)-IS-15:8^2-JER-25:36-ZEP-1:10-ZEC-11:3
HOWLINGS-AM-8:3(3213)
HOWSOEVER-J'G-19:20(7535)-2SA-18:22(1961,4101)-ZEP-3:7(3605,834)
HUGE-2CH-16:8(7230)
HUMBLE-all=6041&marked-EX-10:3(6031)-DE-8:2(6031),16(6031)-J'G-19:24(6031)-2CH-7:14(3665)■34:27(3665)-JOB-22:29(7807,5869)-PS-9:12■10:12,17■34:2■69:32-PR-6:3(7511)■16:19(8213)■29:23(8217)-IS-57:15^2(8217)-JER-13:18(8213)■N.T.-all=5013&marked-M'T-18:4■23:12-2CO-12:21-JAS-4:6(5011),10-1PE-5:5(5011),6
HUMBLED-all=3665&marked-LE-26:41-DE-8:3(6031)■21:14(6031)■22:24(6031),29(6031)-2KI-22:19-2CH-12:6,7^2,12■30:11■32:26■33:12,19,23^2■36:12-PS-35:13(6031)-IS-2:11(8213)■5:15^2(8213)■10:33(8213)-JER-44:10(1792)-LA-3:20(7743)-EZE-22:10(6031),11(6031)-DA-5:22(8214)■N.T.-PH'P-2:8(5013)
HUMBLEDST-2CH-34:27(3665)
HUMBLENESS-COL-3:12(5012)
HUMBLETH-1KI-21:29^2(3665)-PS-10:10(7817)■113:6(8213-)IS-2:9(8213)■N.T.-LU-14:11(5013)■18:14(5013)
HUMBLY-2SA-16:4(7812)-MIC-6:8(6800)
HUMILIATION-AC-8:33(5014)
HUMILITY-all=6038-PR-15:33■18:12■22:4■N.T.-all=5012-AC-20:19-COL-2:18,23-1PE-5:5
HUNDRED-all=3967&marked-GE-5:3,4,5,6,7,8,10,11,13,14,16,17,18,19,20,22,23,25,26,27,28,30,31,32■6:3,15■7:6,24■8:3■9:28,29■11:10,11,13,15,17,19,21,23,25,32■14:14■15:13■17:17■21:5■23:1,15,16■25:7,17■32:6,14^2■33:1,19■35:28■45:22■47:9,28■50:22,26-EX-6:16,18,20■12:37,40,41■14:7■27:9,11,18■30:23^3,24■38:9,11,24,25^2,26^2,27^2,28,29-LE-26:8^2-NU-1:21,23,25,27,29,31,33,35,37,39,41,43,46^2■2:4,6,8,9^2,11,13,15,16^2,19,21,23,24^2,26,28,30,31^2,32^2■3:22,28,34,43,46,50■4:36,40,44,48■7:13,19,25,31,37,43,49,55,61,67,73,79,85,86■11:21■16:2,17,35,49■26:7,10,14,18,22,25,27,34,37,41,43,47,50,51^2■31:28,32,36^2,37,39,43^2,45,52■33:39-DE-22:19■31:2■34:7-JOS-7:21■24:29,32-J'G-2:8■3:31■4:3,13■7:6,7,8,16,19,22■8:4,10,26■11:26■15:4■16:5■17:2,3,4■18:11,16,17■20:2,10^2,15,16,17,35,47■21:12-1SA-11:8■13:15■14:2■15:4■17:7■18:25,27■22:2■23:13■25:13^2,18^3■27:2■30:9,10^2,17,21-2SA-2:31■3:14■8:4^2■10:18■14:26■15:11,18■16:1^3■21:16■23:8,18■24:9^2-1KI-4:23■5:16■6:1■7:2,20,42■8:63■9:23,28■10:10,14,16^2,17,26,29^2■11:3^2■12:21■18:4,13,19^2,22■20:15,29■22:6-2KI-3:4^2,26■4:43■14:13■18:14■19:35■23:33-1CH-4:42■5:18,21^2■7:2,9,11■8:40■9:6,9,13,22■11:11,20■12:14,24,25,26,27,30,32,35,37■15:5,6,7,8,10■18:4■21:3,5^2,25■22:14■25:7■26:30,32■29:7-2CH-1:14,17^2■2:2,17^2,18■3:4,8,16■4:8,13■5:12■7:5■8:10,18■9:9,13,15^2,16^2■11:1■12:3■13:3^2,17■14:8^2,9■15:11■17:11^2,14,15,16,17,18■18:5■24:15■25:5,6^2,9,23■26:12,13^2■27:5■28:6,8■29:32,33■35:8^2,9■36:3-EZR-1:10,11■2:3,4,5,6,7,8,9,10,11,12,13,15,17,18,19,21,23,25,26,27,28,30,31,32,33,34,35,36,38,41,42,58,60,64,65^2,66^2,67^2,69■6:17(3969)■7:22^4(3969)■8:3,4,5,9,10,12,20,26^3-NE-5:17■7:8,9,10,11,12,13,14,15,16,17,18,20,22,23,24,26,27,29,31,32,34,35,36,37,38,39,41,44,45,60,62,66,67^2,68^2,69^2,70,71■11:6,8,12,13,14,18,19-ES-1:1,4■8:9■9:6,12,15,30-JOB-1:3■42:16-PR-17:10-EC-6:3■8:12-SONG-8:12-IS-37:36■65:20^2-JER-52:23,29,30^2-EZE-4:5,9■40:19,23,27,47■41:13^2,14,15■42:2,8,16(520),17,18,19,20■45:2^2,15■48:16^4,17^4,30,32,33,34-DA-6:1(3969)■8:14■12:11,12-AM-5:3^2■N.T.-all=1540&marked-M'T-18:12,28-M'R-4:8,20■6:37(1250)■14:5(5145)-LU-7:41(4001)■15:4■16:6,7-JOH-6:7(1250)■12:5(5145)■19:39■21:8(1250),11-AC-1:15■5:36(5071)■7:6(5071)■13:20(5071)■23:23^2(1250)■27:37(1250)-RO-4:19(1541)-1CO-15:6(4001)-GA-3:17(5071)-RE-7:4■9:16(3461)■11:3(1250)■12:6(1250)■13:18(5516)■14:1,3,20(5516)■21:17
HUNDREDFOLD-GE-26:12(3967,8180)-2SA-24:3(3967,6471)■N.T.-all=1542&marked-M'T-13:8(1540),23(1540)■19:29-M'R-10:30-LU-8:8
HUNDREDS-all=3967-EX-18:21,25-NU-31:14,48,52,54-DE-1:15-1SA-22:7■29:2-2SA-18:1,4-2KI-11:4,9,10,15,19-1CH-13:1■26:26■27:1■28:1■29:6-2CH-1:2■23:1,9,14,20■25:5■N.T.-M'R-6:40(1540)
HUNDREDTH-all=3967&marked-GE-7:11■8:13-NE-5:11
HUNGER-all=7457&marked-EX-16:3-DE-8:3(7456)■28:48■32:24-NE-9:15-PS-34:10(7456)-PR-19:15(7456)-IS-49:10(7456)-JER-38:9■42:14(7456)-LA-2:19■4:9-EZE-34:29■N.T.-all=3983&marked-M'T-5:6-LU-6:21,25■15:17(3042)-JOH-6:35-RO-12:20-1CO-4:11■11:34-2CO-11:27(3042)-RE-6:8(3042)■7:16
HUNGERBITTEN-JOB-18:12(7457)
HUNGERED-M'T-21:18(3983)-LU-4:2(3983)
HUNGRED-all=3983-M'T-4:2■12:1,3■25:35,37,42,44-M'R-2:25-LU-6:3
HUNGRY-all=7456-1SA-2:5-2SA-17:29-2KI-7:12-JOB-5:5■22:7■24:10-PS-50:12■107:5,9,36■146:7-PR-6:30■25:21■27:7-IS-8:21^2■9:20■29:8■32:6■44:12■58:7,10■65:13-EZE-18:7,16■N.T.-all=3983&marked-M'R-11:12-LU-1:53-AC-10:10(4361)-1CO-11:21-PH'P-4:12
HUNT-all=6679&marked-GE-27:5-1SA-26:20(7291)-JOB-38:39-PS-140:11-PR-6:26-JER-16:16-LA-4:18-EZE-13:18^2,20^2,-MIC-7:2
HUNTED-EZE-13:21(4686)
HUNTER-all=6718&marked-GE-10:9^2■25:27-PR-6:5
HUNTERS-JER-16:16(6719)
HUNTEST-1SA-24:11(6658)-JOB-10:16(6679)
HUNTETH-LE-17:13(6679)
HUNTING-GE-27:30(6718)-PR-12:27(6718)
HURL-NU-35:20(7993)
HURLETH-JOB-27:21(8175)
HURLING-all supplied
HURT-all=7451&marked-GE-4:23(2250)■26:29■31:7(7489),29-EX-21:22(5062),35(5062)■22:10(7665),14(7665)-NU-16:15(7489)-JOS-24:20(7489)-1SA-20:21(1697)■24:9■25:7(3637),15(3637)-2SA-18:32-2KI-14:10-2CH-25:19-EZR-4:22(5142)-ES-9:2-PS-15:4(7489)■35:4,26■38:12■41:7■70:2■71:13,24■105:18(6031)-EC-5:13■8:9■10:9(6087)-IS-11:9(7489)■27:3(6485)■65:25(7489)-JER-6:14(7667)■7:6■8:11(7667),21(7667),21(7665)■10:19(7667)■24:9■25:6(7489),7■38:4-DA-3:25(2257)■6:22(2255),22(2248),23(2257)■N.T.-all=91&marked-M'R-16:18(984)-LU-4:35(984)■10:19-AC-18:10(2559)■27:10(5196)-RE-2:11■6:6■7:2,3■9:4,10,19■11:5^2
HURTFUL-EZR-4:15(5142)-PS-144:10(7451)■N.T.-1TI-6:9(983)
HURTING-1SA-25:34(7489)
HUSBAND-all=376&marked-GE-3:6,16■16:3■29:32,34■30:15,18,20-EX-4:25(2860),26(2860)■21:22(1167)-LE-19:20■21:3,7-NU-5:13,19,20^2,27,29■30:6,7,8,11,12^2,13^2,14-DE-21:13(1167)■22:22(1167),23■24:3^2,4(1167)■25:11■28:56-J'G-13:6,9,10■14:15■19:3■20:4-RU-1:3,5,9,12^2■2:11-1SA-1:8,22,23■2:19■4:19,21■25:19-2SA-3:15,16■11:26,26(1167)■14:5,7-2KI-4:1,9,14,22,26-PR-12:4(1167)■31:11(1167),23(1167),28(1167)-IS-54:5(1167)-JER-3:20(1167)■6:11■31:32(1167)-EZE-16:32,45■44:25-HO-2:2,7-JOE-1:8(1167)■N.T.-all=435-M'T-1:16,19-M'R-10:12-LU-2:36■16:18-JOH-4:16,17^2,18-AC-5:9,10-RO-7:2(5220),2^3,3^2-1CO-7:2,3^2,4^2,10,11^2,13,14^2,16,34,39^2-2CO-11:2-GA-4:27-EPH-5:23,33-1TI-3:2-TIT-1:6-RE-21:2
HUSBANDMAN-GE-9:20(376,127)-JER-51:23(406)-AM-5:16(406)-ZEC-13:5(5647)■N.T.-all=1092-JOH-15:1-2TI-2:6-JAS-5:7
HUSBANDMEN-all=406&marked-2KI-25:12(1461)-2CH-26:10-JER-31:24■52:16(3009)-JOE-1:11■N.T.-all=1092-M'T-21:33,34,35,38,40,41-M'R-12:1,2^2,7,9-LU-20:9,10^2,14,16
HUSBANDRY-2CH-26:10(127)■N.T.-1CO-3:9(1091)
HUSBAND'S-NU-30:10(376)-DE-25:5(2993),5(2992),7(2993),7(2992)-RU-2:1(376)
HUSBANDS-all=582&marked-RU-1:11,13(376)-ES-1:17(1167),20(1167)-JER-29:6-EZE-16:45■N.T.-all=435&marked-JOH-4:18-1CO-14:35-EPH-5:22,24,25-COL-3:18,19-1TI-3:12-TIT-2:4(5362),5-1PE-3:1,5,7
HUSK-NU-6:4(2085)-2KI-4:42(6861)
HUSKS-LU-15:16(2769)
HYMN-M'T-26:30(5214)
HYMNS-EPH-5:19(5215)-COL-3:16(5215)
HYPOCRISIES-1PE-2:1(5272)
HYPOCRISY-IS-32:6(2612)■N.T.-all=5272&marked-M'T-23:28-M'R-12:15-LU-12:1-1TI-4:2-JAS-3:17(505)
HYPOCRITE-all=2611&marked-JOB-13:16■17:8■20:5■27:8■34:30(120,2611)-PR-11:9-IS-9:17■N.T.-all=5273-M'T-7:5-LU-6:42■13:15
HYPOCRITE'S-JOB-8:13(2611)
HYPOCRITES-JOB-15:34(2611)■36:13(2611)-IS-33:14(120,2611)■N.T.-all=5273-M'T-6:2,5,16■15:7■16:3■22:18■23:13,14,15,23,25,27,29■24:51-M'R-7:6-LU-11:44■12:56
HYPOCRITICAL-PS-35:16(2611)-IS-10:6(2611)
HYSSOP-all=231-EX-12:22-LE-14:4,6,49,51,52-NU-19:6,18-1KI-4:33-PS-51:7■N.T.-JOH-19:29(5301)-HEB-9:19(5301)

I

ICE-all=7140-JOB-6:16■38:29-PS-147:17
IDLE-EX-5:8(7504),17(7504)-PR-19:15(7423)■N.T.-all=692&marked-M'T-12:36■20:3,6^2-LU-24:11(3026)-1TI-5:13^2
IDLENESS-PR-31:27(6104)-EC-10:18(8220)-EZE-16:49(8252)
IDOL-all=4656&marked-1KI-15:13^2-2CH-15:16^2■33:7(5566),15(5566)-IS-48:5(6090)■66:3(205)-JER-22:28(6089)-ZEC-11:17(457)■N.T.-all=1497&marked-AC-7:41-1CO-8:4,7,7(1494)■10:19
IDOLATER-1CO-5:11(1496)-EPH-5:5(1496)
IDOLATERS-all=1496-1CO-5:10■6:9■10:7-RE-21:8■22:15
IDOLATRIES-1PE-4:3(1495)
IDOLATROUS-2KI-23:5(3649)
IDOLATRY-1SA-15:23(8655)■N.T.-all=1495&marked-AC-7:16(2712)-1CO-10:14-GA-5:20-COL-3:5
IDOL'S-1CO-8:10(1493)
IDOLS-all=1544,a=457,b=6091&

marked-LE-19:4a■26:1a,30-DE-29:17
-1SA-31:9b-1KI-15:12■21:26-2KI-17:12■
21:11,21■23:24-1CH-10:9b■16:26a-2CH-
15:8(8251)■24:18b■34:7(2553)-PS-96:5a■
97:7a■106:36b,38b■115:4b■135:15b
-IS-2:8a,18a,20^{2}a■10:10a,11^{2}a■19:1a,
3a■31:7^{2}a■45:16(6736)■46:1b■57:5
(410)-JER-50:2b,38(367)-EZE-6:4,5,6,
9,13^{2}■8:10■14:3,4^{2},5,6,7■16:36■18:6,
12,15■20:7,8,16,18,24,31,39^{2}■22:3,4■
23:7,30,37,39,49■30:13■33:25■36:18,25■
37:23■44:10,12-HO-4:17b■8:4b■13:2■
14:8-MIC-1:7-HAB-2:18a-ZEC-10:2
(8655)■13:2b■N.T.-all=1494&marked
-AC-15:20(1497),29■21:25-RO-2:22
(1497)-1CO-8:1,4,10■10:19,28■12:2
(1497)-2CO-6:16(1497)-1TH-1:9(1497)
-1JO-5:21(1497)-RE-2:14,20■9:20(1497)

IF-all=518,a=3588,b=834&marked
-GE-4:7^{2},24a■13:9^{2},16■15:5■18:3,21,26,
28,30■20:7■24:41,42,49^{2}■25:22■27:46■
28:20■30:27,31■31:8^{2},50^{2}■32:8■33:10,
13■34:15,17,22■37:26a■42:19■43:4,5,9
11,14b■44:26,29,32■47:6,16,29■50:4
-EX-1:16^{2}■4:8,9■8:21■9:2■10:4■12:4■
13:13■15:26■18:23■19:5■20:25■21:2a,
3^{2},4,5,7a,8,9,10,11,13b,14a,18a,19,20a,
21,22,23,26a,27,28a,29,30,32,33,35a■
22:1a,2,3^{2},4,5,6a,7a,7,8,10a,12,13a,14a,
15^{2},16a,17,23,25,26■23:4a,5a,22■29:34■
32:32^{2}■33:13,15■34:9,20■40:37-LE-
1:2a,3,10,14■2:4,5,7,14■3:1^{2},6,7,12■4:2a,
3,13,27,28(176),32■5:1a,1,2b,2sup,3a,4a,7,
11,15a,17a■6:2a,28■7:12,16,18■
11:37a,38a,39a■12:2a,5,8■13:4,7,12,
16a,21^{2},22,23,24a,27,28,29a,30a,31a,
35a,37,42a,51a,53,57■14:21,43,48■
15:8a,16a,19a,23,24,25^{2}a,28■17:16■
19:5a,7,33a■20:4,12b,13b,14b,15b,
16b,17b,18b,20b,21b■21:9a■
22:9a,11a,12a,13a,14a■24:19a■25:14a,
20a,25a,25sup,26a,28,29a,30,33b,
35a,39a,47a,51,52,54■26:3,14,15,
15sup,18,21,23,27,41(176)■27:4,5,
6,7^{2},8,9,10,11,13,15,16,17,18,19,20^{2},
22,27^{2},31,33-NU-5:8,12a,19^{2},20^{2}a,
27,28■6:9a■9:10a,14a■10:4,9a,32a■
11:15^{2}■12:6■14:8■15:14a,22a,24,27■
16:29,29sup,30■20:19■21:2,9■22:18,20,
34■24:13■27:8a,9,10,11■30:2a,5,6,8,10,
12,14,15■32:5,20,23,29,30■33:55■35:16,
17,18,20,22,26-DE-4:29a■5:25■6:25a■
7:12(6112),17a■8:19■11:13,22,27b,28■
12:21a■13:1a,6a,12a■14:24^{2}a■15:5,7a,
12a,16a,21,21sup■17:2a,8a■18:6a,
21a■19:8,9a,11a,16a■20:11,12■21:1a,
14,15a,15sup,18a,22a■22:2,2sup,6a,
8a,13a,20,22a,23a,25,28a■23:10a,
22a■24:3sup,3a,7a,12■25:1a,2,5a,7■
28:1,2a,9a,13a,15,58■30:4,10^{2}a,17■32:41
-JOS-2:14,19,20■14:12(194)■17:15,
15a■20:5a■22:19,22,23^{2},24■24:15,20
-J'G-4:8^{2}■6:17,31,36,37■7:10■8:19
(3863)■9:15^{2},16^{2},19,20■11:9,10,30■
13:16,23(3863)■14:12,13,18(3883)■
16:7,11,13,17■21:21-RU-1:12a■1:17a■
3:13^{2}■4:4^{2}-1SA-1:11■2:16sup,16,25^{2}■
3:9,17■6:3,9^{2}■7:3■11:3■12:14,15,
25■14:9,10,30(3863)■17:9^{2}■19:11■
20:6,7^{2},8,9,10(176),13a,21,22,29■
21:4,9■23:3a,23■24:19a■25:22■26:19^{2}■
27:5-2SA-3:35■7:14b■10:11^{2}■11:20■
12:8■13:26(3808)■14:32■15:8,26,33,
34■17:6,13■18:3^{2},25■19:6(3863),7a,13
-1KI-1:52^{2}■2:4,23a■3:14■6:12■8:37^{3}a,
44a,46a■9:4,6■11:38■12:7,27■13:8■
18:21^{2}■20:39■21:2,6■22:28-2KI-1:10,
12■2:10■4:29^{2}a■6:31■7:4^{4}■9:15■10:6■
18:21b,22a,23■20:19■21:8-1CH-12:17^{2}■
13:2■19:12^{2}■22:13■28:7,9^{2}-2CH-6:22,
24,28^{3}a,34a,36a■7:13^{2}(2005),13,17,19■
10:7■15:2^{2}■18:27■20:9■25:8■30:9
-EZR-4:13(2006),16(2006)■5:17(2006)
-NE-2:5■4:3■13:21-ES-1:19■3:9■4:14,
16b■5:4,8^{2}■6:13■7:3^{2},4(432)■8:5■9:13
-JOB-6:28■8:4,5,6,18■9:3,16,19^{2},20,23,
24,27,30■10:14,15^{2}■11:10,13,14■13:10,
19a■14:14■16:4(3863)■17:13■19:5■21:4,
15a■22:23■24:17a,25■27:14■31:5,5sup,
7,7sup,9,9sup,13,16,19,20,20sup,21,24,
25,26,29,31,33,38,39■33:5,23,32,33■
34:14,14sup,16,32■35:6,6sup,7■36:8,
11,12■37:20■38:5a,18-PS-7:3^{2},4,12■
11:3a■41:6■44:20■50:12■59:15■66:18■
73:15■81:8■89:30,31■90:10■95:7■124:1,
2(3884)■130:3■132:12■137:5,6^{2}■139:8,
8sup,24-PR-1:10,11■2:1,3,4■3:30■
6:1,1sup,30■9:12,12sup■19:19■
22:18a,27■23:2,15■24:12a■25:21^{2}■
30:4a,32^{2}-EC-4:10,11,12■5:8■6:3■
10:10■11:3,3sup-SONG-1:8■8:7,9,
9sup-IS-1:19,20■7:9■8:20■21:12■
36:8■47:12^{2}(194)■58:13-JER-4:1,
1sup■5:1^{2}■7:5^{2}■12:5a,5sup,16,17■
13:17,22a■14:18^{2}■15:2a,19^{2}■17:24,
27■21:2(194)■22:4,5■26:3(194),
4,15■27:18■31:36,37■33:20,25,
25sup■38:15^{2},17,18,25a■40:4^{2}■
42:5,10,13,15■49:9^{2}■51:8(194)
-LA-1:12■3:29(194)-EZE-3:19a,21a■
10:10b■14:9a,15(3863)■18:5a■20:39■
21:13■33:6a,6sup,9a,9sup,10a■43:11■
46:16a,17a-DA-2:5(2006),6(2006),
9(2006)■3:15^{2}(2006),17(2006)■4:27
(2006)■5:16(2006)-HO-8:7(194)-JOE-
3:4-AM-3:4■5:19b■6:9-OB-5^{3}-JON-1:6
(194)-MIC-2:11(3863)■5:8-NA-3:12
-HAG-2:12(2005),13-ZEC-3:7^{2}■8:6a■
11:12^{2}-MAL-1:6^{2},8^{2}a■2:2■N.T.-all=
1487,a=1437&marked-M'T-4:3,6,9a■
5:13a,29,46a,47a■6:14a,15a,22a,23^{2},30■
7:9a,10a,11■8:2a,31■9:21a■10:13^{2}a,25■
11:14,21,23■12:7,11a,26,27,28■14:28■
15:14a■16:24,26a■17:4,20a■18:8,9,12a,
13a,15^{2}a,16a,17^{2}a,19a,35a■19:10,17,21■
21:3a,21a,21(2579),24a,25a,26a■22:24a,
45■23:30■24:23a,24,26a,43,48a■26:24,
39,42■27:40,42,43■28:14a-M'R-1:40a■
3:24a,25a,26■4:26■5:28(2579)■6:56
(2579)■7:11a,16■8:3a,23,36a■9:23,35,
43a,45a,47a,50a■10:12a■11:3a,13,25,26,
31a,32a■12:19a■13:21a,22■14:21,31a,
35■15:44■16:18(2579)-LU-4:3,7a,9■
5:12a,36(1490)■6:32(1487),33a,34a■7:39■
9:23■10:6a,6(1490),13■11:12a,13,18
(1499),19,20,36■12:26,28,38a,39,45a,
49■13:9(2579),9■14:26,34a,■15:8a■
16:11,12,30a,31■17:3,3a,4a,6■19:8,31a,
40a,42■20:5a,6a,28a■22:42,67a,68a■
23:31,35,37,39-JOH-1:25■3:12,12a■
4:10■5:31a,43a,47■6:51a,62a■7:4,17a,
23,37a■8:16a,19,24a,31a,36a,39,42,46,
51a,52a,54a,55a■9:22a,31a,33,41■10:9a,
24,35,37,38■11:9a,10a,12,21,32,40a,48a,
57a■12:24a,26^{2}a,32a,47a■13:8a,14,17,17a,
32,35a■14:2(1490),3a,7,14a,15a,23a,28■
15:6a,7a,10a,14a,18,19,20^{2},22,24■16:7^{2}a■
18:8,23^{2},30,36■19:12a■20:15■21:22a,
23a,25a-AC-4:9■5:38a,39■8:22,37■9:2a■
13:15■16:15■17:27■18:14,15■19:38,39■
20:16■23:9■24:19,20■25:5a,11^{2}■26:5a,
32■27:12(1513),39-RO-1:10(1513)■
2:25^{2}a,26■3:3,5,7■4:2,14■5:10(1477),15
(1477),17(1477)■6:5(1477),8(1477)■7:2a,
3^{2}a,16,20■8:9(1512),9,10,11a,13a,13,17,
17(1512),25,31■9:22■10:9a■11:6^{2},12,14
(1513),15,16^{2},17,18,21,22a,23a,24■
12:18,20^{2}a■13:4a,9■14:15,23a■15:24a,
27-1CO-3:12,14,15,17,18■4:7(1499),
7sup,19a■5:11a■6:2,4a■7:8a,9,11a,12,
15,21(1499),28^{2}a,36,36a,39a,40a■
8:2,3,8^{2}a,10a,13■9:2,11^{2},12,16a,17^{2}■
10:27,28a,30■11:6^{2},14a,15a,16,31,34■
12:15a,16a,17^{2},19■14:6a,8a,11a,14a,
23a,24a,27(1535),28a,30a,35,37,38■
15:2,12,13,14,15(1512),16,17,19,29,
32^{2}■16:4a,7a,10a,22-2CO-2:2,5,10■
3:7,9,11■4:3(1499)■5:1a,3(1489),14,
17■7:14■8:12■9:4a■10:7■11:4,4sup,
15(1499),16(1490),20^{3},30■13:2a,2sup
-GA-1:9,10■2:14,17,18,21■3:4(1489),
18,21,29■4:7,15■5:2a,11,15,18,25■
6:1a,3-EPH-3:2(1489)■4:21(1489)
-PH'P-1:22■2:1^{4},17■3:4,11(1513),12
(1499),15■4:8^{2}-COL-1:23(1489)■2:20■
3:1,13a■4:10a-1TH-3:8a■4:14-2TH-
3:10,14-1TI-1:8a,10■2:15a■3:1,5,15a■
5:4,8,10^{5},16■6:3-2TI-2:5a,11,12^{2},13,21a,
25(3379)-TIT-1:6-PH'M-17,18-HEB-
2:2■3:6a,7a,14a,15a■4:3,5,7a,8■6:3a■
7:11■8:4,7■9:13■10:38a■11:15■12:7,8,
25,25sup■13:23a-JAS-1:5,23,26■
2:2a,8,9,11,11sup,15a,17a■3:2,14■
4:11,15a■5:19a-1PE-1:6,17■2:3(1512),
19,20^{2}■3:1,13a,17■4:11^{2},14,16,17,18
-2PE-2:4,20-1JO-1:6a,7a,8a,9a,10a■
2:1a,3a,15a,19,24a,29a■3:13,20a,21a■
4:11,12a,20a■5:9,14a,15a,16a-2JO-
10-3JO-10a-RE-3:3a,20a■11:5^{2}■
13:9■14:9■22:18a,19a

IGNOMINY-PR-18:3(7036)

IGNORANCE-all=7684&marked
-LE-4:2,13(7686),22,27■5:15,18-NU-
15:24,25^{2},26,27,28,29■N.T.-all=52&
marked-AC-3:17■17:30-EPH-4:18
-1PE-1:14■2:15(56)

IGNORANT-all=3808,3045-PS-
73:22-IS-56:10■63:16■N.T.-all=50
&marked-AC-4:13(2399)-RO-1:13■
10:3■11:25-1CO-10:1■12:1■14:38-2CO-
1:8■2:11-1TH-4:13-HEB-5:2-2PE-
3:5(2990),8(2990)

IGNORANTLY-NU-15:28(7683)
-DE-19:4(1097,1847)■N.T.-AC-17:23
(50)-1TI-1:13(50)

ILL-all=7451&marked-GE-41:3,4,19,
20,21,27■43:6(7489)-DE-15:21-JOB-
20:26(3415)-PS-106:32(3415)-IS-3:11
-JER-40:4(7489)-JOE-2:20(6709)
-MIC-3:4(7489)■N.T.-RO-13:10(2556)

ILLUMINATED-HEB-10:32(5461)

IMAGE-all=6755&marked-GE-1:26
(6754),27^{2}(6754)■5:3(6754)■9:6(6754)-LE-
26:1sup,1(6676),1(4906)-DE-16:22(4676)
-1SA-19:13(8655),16(8655)-2KI-
3:2(4676)■10:27(4676)-2CH-3:10(6816)
-JOB-4:16(8544)-PS-73:20(6754)-JER-
10:14(6459),14sup■51:17(6459)-EZE-
8:3(5566),5(5566)-DA-2:31^{2},34,35■3:1,2,
3^{2},5,7,10,12,14,15,18-HO-3:4■N.T.-
all=1504&marked-M'T-22:20-M'R-
12:16-LU-20:24-RO-1:23■8:29-1CO-
11:7■15:49,49sup-2CO-3:18■4:4-COL-
1:15■3:10-HEB-1:3(5481)■10:1-RE-
13:14,15^{3}■14:9,11■15:2■16:2■19:20■20:4

IMAGERY-EZE-8:12(4906)

IMAGE'S-DA-2:32(6755)

IMAGES-all=4676&marked-
GE-31:19(8655),34(8655),35(8655)
-EX-23:24■34:13-LE-26:30(2553)
-DE-7:5,5sup-1SA-6:5^{2}(6754),11(6754)
-2SA-5:21(6091)-1KI-14:23-2KI-
10:26■11:18(6754)■17:10■18:4■
23:14,24(8655)-2CH-14:3■23:17(6754)■
31:1■34:4(2553),4sup7(6456)-PS-
78:58(6456)-IS-17:8(2553)■27:9
(2553)-JER-43:13■50:2(1544)-EZE-6:4
(2553),6(2553)■7:20(6754)■16:17(6754)■
21:21(8655)■23:14(6754)■30:13(457)
-HO-10:1,2-AM-5:26(6754)-MIC-
5:13,13sup

IMAGINATION-all=8307&marked
-GE-6:5(3336)■8:21(3336)-DE-
29:19■31:21(3336)-1CH-29:18(3336)
-JER-3:17■7:24■9:14■11:8■13:10■16:12■
18:12■23:17■N.T.-LU-1:51(1271)

IMAGINATIONS-all=4284&
marked-1CH-28:9(3336)-PR-6:18-LA-
3:60,61■N.T.-RO-1:21(1261)-2CO-
10:5(3053)

IMAGINE-all=2803&marked
-JOB-6:26■21:27(2554)-PS-2:1(1897)■
38:12(1897)■62:3(2050)■140:2-PR-
12:20(2790)-HO-7:15-NA-1:9-ZEC-
7:10■N.T.-AC-4:25(3191)

IMAGINED-GE-11:6(2161)-PS-
10:2(2803)■21:11(2803)

IMAGINETH-NA-1:11(2803)

IMMEDIATELY-all=2112,a=3916
&marked-M'T-4:22■8:3■14:31■
20:34■24:29■26:74-M'R-1:12(2117),28
(2117),31,42■2:8,12■4:5,15,16,17,29■
5:2,30■6:27,50■10:52■14:43-LU-1:64a■
4:39a■5:13,25a■6:49■8:44a,47a■12:36■

13:13a■18:43a■19:11a■22:60a-JOH-5:9■6:21■13:30■18:27■21:3(2117)-AC-3:7a■9:18,34■10:33(1824)■11:11(1824)■12:23a■13:11a■16:10,26a■17:10,14■21:32(1824)-GA-1:16-RE-4:2

IMMORTAL-1TI-1:17(862)

IMMORTALITY-all=110&marked-RO-2:7(861)-1CO-15:53,54-1TI-6:16-2TI-1:10(861)

IMMUTABILITY-HEB-6:17(276)

IMMUTABLE-HEB-6:18(276)

IMPART-LU-3:11(3330)-RO-1:11(3330)

IMPARTED-JOB-39:17(2505)■N.T.-1TH-2:8(3330)

IMPEDIMENT-M'R-7:32(3424)

IMPENITENT-RO-2:5(279)

IMPERIOUS-EZE-16:30(7986)

IMPLACABLE-RO-1:31(786)

IMPLEAD-AC-19:38(1458)

IMPORTUNITY-LU-11:8(335)

IMPOSE-EZR-7:24(7412)

IMPOSED-HEB-9:10(1945)

IMPOSSIBLE-all=102&marked-M'T-17:20(101)■19:26-M'R-10:27-LU-1:37(101)■17:1(418)■18:27-HEB-6:4,18■11:6

IMPOTENT-JOH-5:3(770),7(770)-AC-4:9(772)■14:8(102)

IMPOVERISH-JER-5:17(7567)

IMPOVERISHED-J'G-6:6(1809)-IS-40:20(5533)-MAL-1:4(7567)

IMPRISONED-AC-22:19(5439)

IMPRISONMENT-EZR-7:26(613)■N.T.-HEB-11:36(5438)

IMPRISONMENTS-2CO-6:5(5438)

IMPUDENT-PR-7:13(5810)-EZE-2:4(7186,6440)■3:7(2389,4696)

IMPUTE-1SA-22:15(7760)-2SA-19:19(2803)■N.T.-RO-4:8(3049)

IMPUTED-LE-7:18(2803)■17:4(2803)■N.T.-all=3049&marked-RO-4:11,22,23,24■5:13(1677)-JAS-2:23

IMPUTETH-PS-32:2(2803)■N.T.-RO-4:6(3049)

IMPUTING-2CO-5:19(3049)

INASMUCH-DE-19:6(3588)-RU-3:10(1115)■N.T.-all=1909,3745&marked-M'T-25:40,45-RO-11:13-PH'P-1:7-HEB-3:3(2596,3745)■7:20(2596,3745)-1PE-4:13(2526)

INCENSE-all=7004,a=6999&marked-EX-25:6■30:1,7,7sup,8a,8,9,27■31:8,11■35:8,15^2,28■37:25,29■39:38■40:5,27-LE-4:7■10:1■16:12,13^2-NU-4:16■7:14,20,26,32,38,44,50,56,62,68,74,80,86■16:7,17,18,35,40,46,47-DE-33:10-1SA-2:28-1KI-3:3a■9:25a■11:8a■12:33a■13:1a,2a■22:43a-2KI-12:3a■14:4a■15:4a,35a■16:4a■17:11a■18:4a■22:17a■23:5^{2}a,8a-1CH-6:49■23:13a■28:18-2CH-2:4■13:11■25:14a■26:16a,16,18^{2}a,19a,19■28:3a,4a,25a■29:7,11a■30:14a■32:12a■34:25a-PS-66:15■141:2-IS-1:13■43:23(3828)■60:6(3828)■65:3a,7a■66:3(3828)-JER-1:16a■6:20(3828)■7:9a■11:12a,13a,17a■17:26(3828)■18:15a■19:4a,13a■32:29a■41:5(3828)■44:3a,5a,8a,15a,17a,18a,19a,21(7002),23a,25a■48:35a-EZE-8:11■16:18■23:41-HO-2:13a■4:13a■11:2a-HAB-1:16a-MAL-1:11a■N.T.-all=2368&marked-LU-1:9(2370),10,11-RE-8:3,4

INCENSED-IS-41:11(2734)■45:24(2734)

INCLINE-all=5186&marked-JOS-24:23-1KI-8:58-PS-17:6■45:10■49:4■71:2■78:1■88:2■102:2■119:36■141:4-PR-2:2(7181)■4:20-IS-37:17■55:3-DA-9:18

INCLINED-all=5186-J'G-9:3-PS-40:1■116:2■119:112-PR-5:13-JER-7:24,26■11:8■17:23■25:4■34:14■35:15■44:5

INCLINETH-PR-2:18(7743)

INCLOSE-SONG-8:9(6696)

INCLOSED-EX-39:6(4142),13(4142)-J'G-20:43(3803)-PS-17:10(5462)■22:16(5362)-SONG-4:12(5274)-LA-3:9(1443)■N.T.-LU-5:6(4788)

INCLOSINGS-EX-28:20(4396)■39:13(4396)

INCONTINENCY-1CO-7:5(192)

INCONTINENT-2TI-3:3(193)

INCORRUPTIBLE-all=862-1CO-9:25■15:52-1PE-1:4,23

INCORRUPTION-all=861-1CO-15:42,50,53,54

INCREASE-all=8393,a=7235,b=2981&marked-GE-47:24-LE-19:25■25:7,12,16a,20,36(8635),37(4768)■26:4b,20b-NU-18:30^2■32:14(8635)-DE-6:3a■7:13(7698),22a■14:22,28■16:15■26:12■28:4(7698),18(7698),51(7698)■32:13(8570),22b-J'G-6:4b■9:29(7239)-1SA-2:33(4768)-1CH-27:23a-2CH-31:5■32:28-EZR-10:10(3254)-NE-9:37-JOB-8:7(7685)■20:28b■31:12-PS-44:12a■62:10(5107)■67:6b■71:21a■73:12(7685)■78:46b■85:12b■107:37■115:14(3254)-PR-1:5(3254)■3:9■9:9(3254)■13:11a■14:4■18:20■22:16a■28:28a-EC-5:10,11a■6:11a-IS-9:7(4768)■29:19(3254)■30:23■57:9a-JER-2:3■23:3a-EZE-5:16(3254)■18:8(8635),13(8635),17(8635)■22:12(8635)■34:27b■36:11a,29a,30(8570),37a■48:18-DA-11:39a-HO-4:10(6555)-ZEC-8:12b■10:8a■N.T.-all=837&marked-LU-17:5(4369)-JOH-3:30-1CO-3:6,7-2CO-9:10-EPH-4:16(838)-COL-2:19(838)-1TH-3:12(4121)■4:10(4052)-2TI-2:16(4298)

INCREASED-all=7235&marked-GE-7:17,18■30:30(6555),43(6555)-EX-1:7(8317)■23:30(6509)-1SA-14:19(7227)-2SA-15:12(7227)-1KI-22:35(5927)-1CH-4:38(6555)■5:23-2CH-18:34(5927)-EZR-9:6-JOB-1:10(6555)-PS-3:1(7231)■4:7(7231)■49:16■105:24(6509)-PR-9:11(3254)-EC-2:9(3254)■5:11(7231)-IS-9:3(1431)■26:15^2(3254)■51:2-JER-3:16(6509)■5:6(6105)■15:8(6105)■29:6■30:14(6105),15(6105)-LA-2:5-EZE-16:7,26■23:14(3254)■28:5■41:7(5927)-DA-12:4-HO-4:7(7230)■10:1-AM-4:9-ZEC-10:8■N.T.-all=837&marked-M'R-4:8-LU-2:52(4298)-AC-6:7■9:22(1743)■16:5(4052)-2CO-10:15-RE-3:17(4147)

INCREASEST-JOB-10:17(7235)

INCREASETH-all=7235&marked-JOB-10:16(1342)■12:23(7679)-PS-74:23(5927)-PR-11:24(3254)■16:21(3254)■23:28(3254)■24:5(553)■28:8■29:16-EC-1:18(3254)-IS-40:29-HO-12:1-HAB-2:6■N.T.-COL-2:19(837)

INCREASING-COL-1:10(837)

INCREDIBLE-AC-26:8(571)

INCURABLE-all=605&marked-2CH-21:18(369,4832)-JOB-34:6-JER-15:18■30:12,15-MIC-1:9

INDEBTED-LU-11:4(3784)

INDEED-all=552&marked-GE-17:19(61)■20:12(546)-NU-21:2(389)■22:37-DE-2:15(1571)-JOS-7:20(546)-2SA-14:5(61)-2KI-8:27-JOB-19:4(551),5(551)-PS-58:1■N.T.-all=3303&marked-M'T-3:11■13:32■20:23■23:27■26:41-M'R-1:8■9:13(2532)■10:39■11:32(3689)■14:21-LU-3:16■11:48■23:41■24:34(3689)-JOH-1:47(230)■4:42(230)■6:55^2(230)■7:26(230)■8:31(230),36(3689)-AC-4:16■11:16■22:9-RO-6:11■8:7(1063)■14:20-1CO-11:7-2CO-8:17■11:1(235)-PH'P-1:15■2:27(2532)■3:1-COL-2:23-1TH-4:10(1063)-1TI-5:3(3689),5(3689),16(3689)-1PE-2:4

INDIGNATION-all=2195&marked-DE-29:28(7110)-2KI-3:27(7110)-NE-4:1(3707)-ES-5:9(2534)-JOB-10:17(3708)-PS-69:24■78:49■102:10-IS-10:5,25■13:5■26:20■30:27,30(2197)■34:2(7110)■66:14(2194)-JER-10:10■15:17■50:25-LA-2:6-EZE-21:31■22:24,31-DA-8:19■11:30(2194),36-MIC-7:9(2197)-NA-1:6-HAB-3:12-ZEP-3:8-ZEC-1:12(2194)-MAL-1:4(2194)■N.T.-all=23&marked-M'T-20:24■26:8-M'R-14:4-LU-13:14-AC-5:17(2205)-RO-2:8(2372)-2CO-7:11(24)-HEB-10:27(2205)-RE-14:10(3709)

INDITING-PS-45:1(7370)

INDUSTRIOUS-1KI-11:28(6213,4399)

INEXCUSABLE-RO-2:1(379)

INFALLIBLE-all supplied

INFAMOUS-EZE-22:5(2931,8034)

INFAMY-PR-25:10(1681)-EZE-36:3(1681)

INFANT-1SA-15:3(5768)-IS-65:20(5764)

INFANTS-JOB-3:16(5768)-HO-13:16(5768)■N.T.-LU-18:15(1025)

INFERIOR-JOB-12:3(5307)■13:2(5307)-DA-2:39(772)■N.T.-2CO-12:13(2274)

INFIDEL-2CO-6:15(571)-1TI-5:8(571)

INFINITE-JOB-22:5(369,7093)-PS-147:5(369,4557)-NA-3:9(369,7097)

INFIRMITIES-all=769&marked-M'T-8:17-LU-5:15■7:21(3554)■8:2-RO-8:26■15:1(771)-2CO-11:30■12:5,9,10-1TI-5:23-HEB-4:15

INFIRMITY-LE-12:2(1738)-PS-77:10(2470)-PR-18:14(4245)■N.T.-all=769-LU-13:11,12-JOH-5:5-RO-6:19-GA-4:13-HEB-5:2■7:28

INFLAME-IS-5:11(1814)

INFLAMMATION-LE-13:28(6867)-DE-28:22(1816)

INFLICTED-supplied

INFLUENCES-JOB-38:31(4575)

INFOLDING-EZE-1:4(3947)

INFORM-DE-17:10(3384)

INFORMED-DA-9:22(995)■N.T.-all=1718&marked-AC-21:21(2727),24(2727)■24:1■25:2,15

INGATHERING-EX-23:16(614)■34:22(614)

INHABIT-all=3427&marked-NU-35:34-PR-10:30(7931)-IS-42:11■65:21,22-JER-17:6(7931)■48:18-EZE-33:24-AM-9:14-ZEP-1:13

INHABITANT-all=3427&marked-JOB-28:4(1481)-IS-5:9■6:11■9:9■12:6■20:6■24:17■33:24(7934)-JER-2:15■4:7■9:11■10:17■21:13■22:23■26:9■33:10■34:22■44:22■46:19■48:19,43■51:29,35,37-AM-1:5,8-MIC-1:11^2,12,13,15-ZEP-2:5■3:6

INHABITANTS-all=3427&marked-GE-19:25■34:30■50:11-EX-15:14,15■23:31■34:12,15-LE-18:25■25:10-NU-13:32■14:14■32:17■33:52■55-DE-13:13,15-JOS-2:9,24■7:9■8:24,26■9:3,11,24■10:1■11:19■13:6■15:15,63■17:7,11^4-J'G-1:11,19sup,19,27sup,27^3,30^2,31^2,32,33^4■2:2■5:23■10:18■11:8,21■20:15■21:9,10,12-RU-4:4-1SA-6:21■23:5■27:8■31:11-2SA-5:6-1KI-17:1(8453)■21:11-2KI-19:26■22:16,19■23:2-1CH-8:6,13^2■9:2■11:4,5■22:18-2CH-15:5■20:7,15,18,20,23^2■21:11,13■22:1■32:22,26,33■33:9■34:24,27,28,30,32■35:18-EZR-4:6-NE-3:13■7:3■9:24-JOB-26:5(7934)-PS-33:8,14■49:1■75:3■83:7-IS-5:3■8:14■10:13,31■18:3■21:14■22:21■23:2,6■24:1,5,6■26:9,18,21■37:27■38:11■40:22■42:10,11■49:19-JER-1:14■4:4■6:12■8:1■10:18■11:2,9,12■13:13^2■17:20,25■18:11■19:3,12■21:6■23:14■25:2,9,29,30■26:15■32:32■35:13,17■36:31■42:18■46:8■47:2■49:8,20,30■50:21,34,35■51:12,24,35-LA-4:12-EZE-11:15■12:19■15:6■26:17■27:8,35■29:6-DA-4:35^2(1753)■9:7-HO-4:1■10:5(7934)-JOE-1:2,14■2:1-MIC-6:12,16-ZEP-1:4,11■2:5-ZEC-8:20,21■11:6■12:5,7,8,10■13:1■N.T.-RE-17:2(2730)

INHABITED-all=3427&marked-GE-36:20-EX-16:35-LE-16:22(1509)-J'G-1:17,21-1CH-5:9-IS-13:20■44:26■45:18■54:5-JER-6:8■17:6■22:6■46:26(7931)■50:13,39-EZE-12:20■26:17,19,20■29:11■34:13(4186)■36:10,35■38:12

-ZEC-2:4■7:7^{2}■9:5■12:6■14:10,11

INHABITERS-RE-8:13(2730)■12:12(2730)

INHABITEST-PS-22:3(3427)

INHABITETH-JOB-15:28(3427)-IS-57:15(7931)

INHABITING-PS-74:14(6728)

INHERIT-all=5157,a=3423&marked-GE-15:7a,8a■28:4a-EX-23:30■32:13-LE-20:24a■25:46a-NU-18:24(5159)■26:55■32:19■33:54■34:13-DE-1:38■2:31a■3:28■12:10■16:20a■19:3,14■21:16■31:7-JOS-17:14(5159)-J'G-11:2-1SA-2:8-2CH-20:11a-PS-25:13a■37:9a,11a,22a,29a,34a■69:36■82:8-PR-3:35■8:21■11:29■14:18-IS-49:8■54:3a■57:13a■60:21a■65:9a-JER-8:10a■12:14■49:1a-EZE-47:13,14a-ZEC-2:12■N.T.-all=2816-M'T-5:5■19:29■25:34-M'R-10:17-LU-10:25■18:18-1CO-6:9,10■15:50^{2}-GA-5:21-HEB-6:12-1PE-3:9-RE-21:7

INHERITANCE-all=5159,a=5157,&marked-GE-31:14■48:6-EX-15:17■34:9a-LE-25:46a-NU-16:14■18:20a,20,21,23,24,26■26:53,54^{3},62■27:7^{2},8,9,10,11■32:18,19,32■33:54a,54^{2},54sup■34:2,14,15,18a,29a■35:2,8■36:2^{2},3^{3},4^{2},7^{2},8^{2},9^{2},12-DE-4:20,21,38■9:26,29■10:9^{2}■12:9,12■14:27,29■15:4■18:1^{2},2^{2}■19:10,14■20:16■21:23■24:4■25:19■26:1■29:8■32:8a,9■33:4(4181)-JOS-1:6a■11:23■13:6,7,8,14^{2},15,23,24,28,32a,33^{2}■14:1a,2,3^{2},9,13,14■15:20■16:4a,5,8,9■17:4^{2},6a■18:2,4,7^{2},20,28■19:1,2,8,9,9a,9,10,16,23,31,39,41,48,49a,49,51a■21:3■23:4■24:28,30,32-J'G-2:6,9■18:1^{2}■20:6■21:17(3425),23,24-RU-4:5,6,10-1SA-10:1■26:19-2SA-14:16■20:1,19■21:3-1KI-8:36,51,53■12:16■21:3,4-2KI-21:14-1CH-16:18■28:8a-2CH-6:27■10:16-EZR-9:12(3423)-NE-11:20-JOB-31:2■42:15-PS-2:8■16:5(2506)■28:9■33:12■37:18■47:4■68:9■74:2■78:55,62,71■79:1■94:14■105:11■106:5,40-PR-13:22a■17:2■19:14■20:21-EC-7:11-IS-19:25■47:6■63:17-JER-3:18a■10:16■12:14■16:18■32:8(3425)■51:19-LA-5:2-EZE-22:16(2490)■33:24(4181)■35:15■36:12■44:28■45:1■46:16^{2},17^{2},18,18a■47:14,22^{2},23■48:29■N.T.-2817&marked-M'T-21:38-M'R-12:7-LU-12:13■20:14-AC-7:5■20:32■26:18(2819)-GA-3:18-EPH-1:11(2820),14,18■5:5-COL-1:12(2819)■3:24-HEB-1:4(2820)■9:15■11:8-1PE-1:4

INHERITANCES-JOS-19:51(5159)

INHERITED-all=5157&marked-NU-32:18-JOS-14:1-PS-105:44(3423)-JER-16:19-EZE-33:24(3423)■N.T.-HEB-12:17(2816)

INHERITETH-NU-35:8(5157)

INHERITOR-IS-65:9(3423)

INIQUITIES-all=5771&marked-LE-16:21,22■26:39-NU-14:34-EZR-9:6,7,13-NE-9:2-JOB-13:23,26■22:5-PS-38:4■40:12■51:9■64:6(5766)■65:3(1647,5771)■79:8■90:8■103:3,10■107:17■130:3,8-PR-5:22-IS-43:24■50:1■53:5,11■59:2,12■64:6,7■65:7-JER-5:25■11:10■14:7■33:8-LA-4:13■5:7-EZE-24:23■28:18■32:27■36:31,33■43:10-DA-4:27(5758)■9:13,16-AM-3:2-MIC-7:19■N.T.-all=458&marked-AC-3:26(4198)-RO-4:7-HEB-8:12■10:17-RE-18:5(92)

INIQUITY-all=5771,a=205,b=5766&marked-GE-15:16■19:15■44:16-EX-20:5■28:38,43■34:7^{2},9-LE-5:1,17■7:18■10:17■17:16■18:25■19:8■20:17,19■22:16■26:39,40■41:43-NU-5:15,31^{2}■14:18^{2},19■15:31■18:1^{2},23■23:21a■30:15-DE-5:9■19:15■32:4b-JOS-22:17,20-1SA-3:13,14■15:23a■20:1,8■25:24-2SA-7:14(5753)■14:9,32■19:19■22:24■24:10-1CH-21:8-2CH-19:7b-NE-4:5-JOB-4:8a■5:16b■6:29b,30b■7:21■10:6,14■11:6,14a■14:17,15:5,16b■20:27■21:19a■22:23b■31:3a,11,28,33■33:9■34:8a,10b,22a,32b■36:10a,21a,23b-PS-5:5a■6:8a■7:3b,14a■14:4a■18:23■25:11■28:3a■31:10■32:2,5^{2}■36:2,3a,12a■37:1b■38:18■39:11■41:6a■49:5■51:2,5■53:1b,4a■55:3a■56:7a■59:2a■64:2a■66:18a■69:27■78:38■85:2■89:32■92:7a,9a■94:4a,16a,20(1942),23a■106:6(5753),43■107:42b■109:14■119:3b,133a■125:3b,5a■141:4a,9a-PR-10:29a■16:6■19:28a■21:15a■22:8b-EC-3:16(7562)-IS-1:4,13a■5:18■6:7■13:11■14:21■22:14■26:21■27:9■29:20a■30:13■31:2a■32:6a■33:24■40:2■53:6■57:17■59:3,4a,6a,7a■64:9-JER-2:5b,22■3:13■9:5(5753)■13:22■14:10,20■16:10,17,18■18:23■25:12■30:14,15■31:30,34■32:18■33:8■36:3,31■50:20■51:6-LA-2:14■4:6,22^{2}-EZE-3:18,19,20b■4:4^{2},5^{2},6,17■7:13,16,19■9:9■14:3,4,7,10■16:49■18:8b,17,18,19,20^{2},24b,26^{2}b,30■21:23,24,25,29■28:15b,18b■29:16■33:6,8,13^{2}b,15b,18b■35:5■39:23■44:10,12^{2}-DA-9:5(5753),24-HO-4:8■5:5■6:8a■7:1■8:13■9:7,9■10:9(5932),13b■12:8,11a■13:12■14:1,2-MIC-2:1a■3:10b■7:18-HAB-1:3a,13(5999)■2:12b-ZEP-3:5b,13b-ZEC-3:4,9-MAL-2:6b,6■N.T.-all=458&marked-M'T-7:23■13:41■23:28■24:12-LU-13:27(93)-AC-1:18(93)■8:2393)-RO-6:19-1CO-13:6(93)-2TH-2:7-2TI-2:19(93)-TIT-2:14-HEB-1:9-JAS-3:6(93)-2PE-2:16(3892)

INJURED-GA-4:12(91)

INJURIOUS-1TI-1:13(5197)

INJUSTICE-JOB-16:17(2555)

INK-JER-36:18(1773)■N.T.-all=3188-2CO-3:3-2JO-12-3JO-13

INKHORN-all=7083-EZE-9:2,3,11

INN-all=4411-GE-42:27■43:21-EX-4:24■N.T.-LU-2:7(2646)■10:34(3829)

INNER-all=6442&marked-1KI-6:27■6:36■7:12,50■20:30(2315)■22:25(2315)-2KI-9:2(2315)-1CH-28:11-2CH-4:22■18:24(2315)■29:16(6441)-ES-4:11■5:1-EZE-8:3,16■10:3■40:15,19,23,27,28,32,44^{2}■41:15,17■42:3,15■43:5■44:17^{2},21,27■45:19■46:1■N.T.-AC-16:24(2802)-EPH-3:16(2080)

INNERMOST-PR-18:8(2315)■26:22(2315)

INNOCENCY-all=5356&marked-GE-20:5-PS-26:6■73:13-DA-6:22(2136)-HO-8:5(5356)

INNOCENT-all=5355&marked-EX-23:7-DE-19:10,13■21:8,9■27:25-1SA-19:5-1KI-2:31(2600)-2KI-21:16■24:4^{2}-JOB-4:7■9:23,28(5352)■17:8■22:19,30■27:17■33:9(2643)-PS-10:8■15:5■19:13(5352)■94:21■106:38-PR-1:11■6:17,29(5352)■28:20(5352)-IS-59:7-JER-2:35(5352)■7:6■22:3,17■26:15-JOE-3:19-JON-1:14■N.T.-M'T-27:4(121),24(121)

INNOCENTS-JER-2:34(5355)■19:4(5355)

INNUMERABLE-all=369,4557&marked-JOB-21:33-PS-40:12■104:25-JER-46:23■N.T.-LU-12:1(3461)-HEB-11:12(382)■12:22(3461)

INORDINATE-EZE-23:11(5691)■N.T.-COL-3:5(3806)

INQUISITION-DE-19:18(1875)-ES-2:23(1254)-PS-9:12(1875)

INSCRIPTION-AC-17:23(1924)

INSIDE-1KI-6:15(1004)

INSOMUCH-all=5620&marked-M'T-8:24■12:22■13:54■15:31■24:24■27:14-M'R-1:27,45■2:2,12■3:10■9:26-LU-12:1-AC-1:19■5:15-2CO-1:8■8:6(1519)-GA-2:13

INSPIRATION-JOB-32:8(5397)■N.T.-2TI-3:16(2315)

INSTANT-IS-29:5(6621)■30:13(6621)-JER-18:7(7821),9(7821)■N.T.-LU-2:38(5610)■23:23(1945)-RO-12:12(4842)-2TI-4:2(2186)

INSTANTLY-LU-7:4(4705)-AC-26:7(1722,1616)

INSTEAD-all=8478&marked-GE-2:21■4:25■44:33-NU-3:12,41^{2},45^{2}■5:19,20,29■8:16,16sup■10:31-J'G-15:2-2SA-17:25-1KI-3:7-2KI-14:21■17:24-1CH-29:23-2CH-12:10-ES-2:4,17-JOB-31:40-PS-45:16-IS-3:24^{5}■55:13^{2}-JER-22:11■37:1-EZE-16:32

INSTRUCT-all=3256&marked-DE-4:36-NE-9:20(7919)-JOB-40:2(3250)-PS-16:17■32:8(7919)-SONG-8:2(3925)-IS-28:26-DA-11:33(995)■N.T.-1CO-2:16(4822)

INSTRUCTED-all=3256&marked-DE-32:10(995)-2KI-12:2(3384)-1CH-15:22■25:7(3925)-2CH-3:3(3245)-JOB-4:3-PS-2:10-PR-5:13(3925)■21:11(7919)-IS-8:11■40:14(995)-JER-6:8■31:19(3045)■N.T.-all=2727&marked-M'T-13:52(3100)■14:8(4264)-LU-1:4-AC-18:25-RO-2:18-PH'P-4:12(3453)

INSTRUCTER-GE-4:22(3913)

INSTRUCTERS-1CO-4:15(3807)

INSTRUCTING-2TI-2:25(3811)

INSTRUCTION-all=4148&marked-JOB-33:16(4561)-PS-50:17-PR-1:2,3,7,8■4:1,13■5:12,23■6:23■8:10,33■10:17■12:1■13:1,18■15:5,32,33■16:22■19:20,27■23:12,23■24:32-JER-17:23■32:33■35:13-EZE-5:15-ZEP-3:7■N.T.-2TI-3:16(3809)

INSTRUCTOR-RO-2:20(3810)

INSTRUMENT-NU-35:16(3627)-IS-54:16(3627)

INSTRUMENTS-all=3627&marked-GE-49:5-EX-25:9-NU-3:8■4:12,26,32^{2}■7:1■31:6-1SA-8:12■18:6(7991)-2SA-24:22sup,22-1KI-19:21-1CH-9:29■12:33,37■15:16■16:42■23:5■28:14^{3}-2CH-4:16■5:1,13■7:6■23:13■29:26,27■30:21■34:12-NE-12:36-PS-7:13■150:4(4482)-IS-32:7-EZE-40:42-DA-6:18(1761)-AM-6:5-ZEC-11:15■N.T.-RO-6:13^{2}(3696)

INSURRECTION-EZR-4:19(5376)-PS-64:2(7285)■N.T.-M'R-15:7(4955),7(4714)-AC-18:12(2721)

INTEGRITY-all=8537&marked-GE-20:5,6-1KI-9:4-JOB-2:3(8538),9(8538)■27:5(8538)■31:6(8538)-PS-7:8■25:21■26:1,11■41:12■78:72-PR-11:3(8538)■19:1■20:7

INTELLIGENCE-DA-11:30(995)

INTEND-JOS-22:33(559)-2CH-28:13(559)■N.T.-AC-5:28(1014),35(3195)

INTENDED-PS-21:11(5186)

INTENDEST-EX-2:14(559)

INTENDING-LU-14:28(2309)-AC-12:4(1011)■20:13(3195)

INTENT-2SA-17:14(5668)-2KI-10:19(4616)-EZE-40:4(4616)-DA-4:17(1701)■N.T.-JOH-11:15(2443)-AC-10:29(3056)-EPH-3:10(2443)

INTENTS-JER-30:24(4209)■N.T.-HEB-4:12(1771)

INTERCESSION-all=6293-IS-53:12-JER-7:16■27:18■36:25■N.T.-all=1793&marked-RO-8:26(5241),27,34■11:2-HEB-7:25

INTERCESSIONS-1TI-2:1(1783)

INTERCESSOR-IS-59:16(6293)

INTERMEDDLE-PR-14:10(6148)

INTERMEDDLETH-PR-18:1(1566)

INTERMISSION-LA-3:49(2014)

INTERPRET-all=6622-GE-41:8,12,15^{2}■N.T.-all=1329-1CO-12:30■14:5,13,27

INTERPRETATION-all=6591&marked-GE-40:5(6623),12(6623),16(6623),18(6623)■41:11(6623)-J'G-7:15(7667)-PR-1:6(4426)-EC-8:1(6592)-DA-2:4,5,6^{2},7,9,16,24,25,26,30,36,45■4:6,7,9,18^{2},19^{2},24■5:7,8,12,15^{2},16,17,26■7:16■N.T.-all=2059&marked-JOH-1:42■9:7-AC-9:36(1329)■13:8(3177)-1CO-12:10(2058)■14:26(2058)-HEB-7:2-2PE-1:20(1955)

INTERPRETATIONS-GE-40:8(6623)-DA-5:16(6591)

INTERPRETED-all=6622&marked-GE-40:22■41:12,13-EZR-4:7(8638)■N.T.-all=3177&marked-M'T-1:23-M'R-5:41■15:22,34-JOH-1:38(2059),41-AC-4:36

INTERPRETER-GE-40:8(6622)■42:23(3887)-JOB-33:23(3887)■N.T.-1CO-14:28(1328)

INTERPRETING-DA-5:12(6591)

INTO-all=413,a=5921&marked-GE-6:18,19■7:1,7,9,13,15■8:9^{2}■12:11(935)■19:2,3■21:32■22:2■24:20■28:15■36:6■37:22,36■39:20■40:3,11,11a,21a■42:17,25,37a■49:33-EX-4:7^{2}■7:23■9:20■13:5,11■15:22,25■16:3■18:5,27■23:20■24:13,15,18,18sup■25:16■29:3a,30■30:20■33:11■40:20,21,32,35-LE-6:30■9:23■10:9■12:4■14:7a,8,15a,26a,34,40,41,45,46,53■16:2,3,23^{2},26,28■19:23■23:10■25:2-NU-5:17■7:89■11:30■14:8,16,24,30,40■15:2,18■16:47■17:8■19:6,7,14■20:4,12,24,27■22:13■25:8■27:12■31:27,54■32:7,9■33:38,51■34:2■35:28-DE-1:31(5704)■2:29■6:10■7:1,26■8:7■9:21,28■11:5(5704)■13:16■17:8■18:9■19:11■23:11(8432)■24:10■26:9■29:28■30:5■31:20,21,23■32:49-JOS-4:5■10:19,20,27■22:13■24:8,8sup-J'G-7:15,15sup■9:46■11:19(5704)■19:11,12,22,23,29-RU-4:11-1SA-2:36■4:3,5,6,7■6:14■7:1■9:14(8432),14sup■14:26■21:15■27:1■29:11-2SA-4:6(5704)■5:8■6:10a■11:11■17:13,13(5704)■18:17-1KI-3:1■6:8a,8■8:6■13:18■14:28,28sup■16:18■17:19,21a,22■20:30^{2},30sup,33a■21:4■22:35-2KI-4:4a,11,39^{2},41■6:5■7:8^{2},12■10:15,24a■12:4sup,4a,4sup,11a,15a■19:32,33■22:5a,7a,9a,20■23:12-1CH-11:15■13:13■19:2■21:27-2CH-5:7■7:2,11a■12:11sup,11■26:16■27:2■34:17a-EZR-10:6-NE-2:8a■6:11■7:5■8:1■9:23-ES-1:22^{2}■2:14,16■3:9,13■4:2,11■7:7,8-JOB-10:9■16:11■37:8(1119)■38:16(5704),22■40:23-PS-16:4a■35:13a■60:9(5704),9sup■73:17■79:12■95:11■108:10sup,10(5704)■132:3sup,3a-EC-1:7-SONG-3:4^{2}■6:11■8:2-IS-13:14■22:18■24:18■37:33,34■40:9a■65:6a,7a,17a-JER-2:7■4:5■6:9a■7:31a■8:14■14:18^{2}sup,18■16:13a,15a■19:5a■21:4■22:7a,26a,28a■26:22sup,22,23■27:6■28:6■29:14■32:18,35a■35:2sup,2,4,11■36:12sup,12a,23■37:16^{2}■38:6,9,11,14■41:7^{2}■42:17(935),18(935)■44:21a■47:6■48:44■51:50a,51a,63-LA-1:3(1473)■2:12-EZE-3:22,23■5:4^{2}■8:16■10:7■14:19■20:6,10,15,28,32a,35,38,42^{2}■22:19,20■23:39■29:14sup,14a■32:9,24■36:24■37:12,21■38:8,10a■40:2,17,32■42:1^{2},14■43:4,5■44:9,16,19^{2},21,27■46:19,20,21■47:8a,8sup-DA-11:9sup,9-HO-11:5-JO-2:20■3:2-AM-7:12-JON-1:4,5^{2},12,15■2:7-MIC-3:5a-NA-3:12a-HAG-1:6-ZEC-5:4^{2},8■6:6■10:10-MAL-3:10■N.T.-all=1519,a=1909&marked-M'T-1:17^{2}(3350)■2:11,12,13,14,20,21,22■3:10,12■4:1,5,8,12sup,12,18■5:1,20,25,29,30■6:6,13,26,30■7:19,21■8:5,12,14,23,28,31,32^{2},33■9:1^{2},17^{2},23,26,28,38■10:5^{2},11,12,23■11:7■12:4,9,11,29,44■13:2,8a,20a,23a,30,36,42,47,48,50,54■14:13,15,22,23,32,34,35■15:11,14,17^{2},21,29,39■16:13■17:1,15^{2},22,25■18:3,8^{2},9^{2},12a,30■19:1,17,23,24■20:1,2,4,7■21:2,10,12,17,18,21,23,31■22:9a,10,13■24:16a,38■25:21,23,30,41,46^{2}■26:18,30,32,41,45,52,71■27:6,27,53■28:7,10,11,16^{2}-M'R-1:12,14,16(1722),21^{2},29,35,38,45■2:1,11,22^{2},26■3:1,13,19,27■4:1,26a,37■5:1,12^{2},13^{2},18■6:1,10,31,32,36^{2},45,46,51,53a,56■7:15,17,18,19^{2},24^{2},33■8:10^{2},13,26,27■9:2,22^{2},25,28,31,42,43^{3},45^{3},47^{2}■10:1,17,23,24,25■11:2^{2},11^{2},15■12:41,43■13:15■14:13,16,26,28,38,41,54,68■15:16(2080)■16:5,7,12,15,19-LU-1:9,39^{2},40,79■2:3,4,15,27,39■3:3,9,17■4:1,5,14,16,37,38,42■5:3,4,16(1722),19,24,37,38■6:4,6,12,38,39■7:1,11,24,36,44■8:22,29,30,31,32,33^{2},37,41,51■9:4,10,12,28,34,44^{2},52■10:1,2,5,8,10^{2},38^{2}■11:4■12:5,28,58■13:19■14:1,5,21,23■15:13,15■16:4,9,16,22,28■17:2,12,27■18:10,24,25■19:4a,12,23a,30,45■21:1,24■22:3,10^{2},33,40,46,54,66■23:19,25,42(1722),46■24:7,26,51-JOH-1:9,43■3:4,5,17,19,22,24,35(1722)■4:3,14,28,38,43,45,46,47,54■5:4(1722),7,24■6:3,14,15,17,21,22■7:3,14■8:2■9:39■10:1,36,40■11:7,27,30,54■12:24,46■13:2,3,5,27■15:6■16:13,20,21,28■17:18^{2}■18:1,11,15,28,33,37■19:9,17■20:6,11,25^{2},27■21:3,7-AC-1:11^{3},13■20:20^{2},34■3:1,2,3,8■5:15(2596),21■7:3,4,9,15,16,23a,34,39,45(1722),55■8:3(1531),38■9:6,8,11a,17,39■10:10a,16,22,24■11:8,10,12■12:17■13:14■14:1,20,22,25■16:7(2596),9,10,15,19,23,24,34,37,40■17:10■18:7,18,19,27■19:8,22,29,31■20:1,2,3,4(891),18■21:3,8,11,26,28,29,34,37,38■22:4,10,11,23,24■23:10,16,20,28■25:23■27:1,6,17,30,38,39,41■28:5,17,23-RO-1:23(1722),25(1722),26■5:2,12■6:3^{2},4■8:21■10:6,7,18■11:24■15:24,28-1CO-2:9a■11:20a■12:13^{2}■14:9,23a-2CO-1:16■2:13■7:5■8:16(1722)■11:13,14■12:4-GA-1:6(1722),17,21■3:27■4:6-EPH-4:9,15-COL-1:13-2TH-3:5^{2}-1TI-1:3,12,15■3:6,7,16(1722)■6:7,9^{2}-2TI-3:6-HEB-1:6■3:11,18■4:1,3^{2},5,10,11■6:19■8:10■9:6,7,12,24^{2},25■10:5,16a,31■11:8■13:11-JAS-1:25■4:13■5:4,12(5259)-1PE-1:12■2:9■3:22-2PE-1:11-1JO-4:1,9-2JO-7,10-JUDE-4-RE-2:10,22^{2}■5:6■8:5,8■11:11a■12:6,9,14^{2}■13:10sup,10■14:10(1722),19^{2}■15:8■16:16,17,19■17:3,8,11■18:21■19:20■20:3,10,14,15■21:24,26,27■22:14

INTREAT-all=6279&marked-GE-23:8(6293)-EX-8:8,9,28,29■9:28■10:17-RU-1:16(6293)-1SA-2:25(6419)-1KI-13:6(2470)-PS-45:12(2470)-PR-19:6(2740)■N.T.-1CO-4:13(3870)-PH'P-4:3(2065)-1TI-5:1(3870)

INTREATED-all=6279&marked-GE-25:21^{2}-EX-8:30■10:18-J'G-13:8-2SA-21:14■24:25-1CH-5:20-2CH-33:13,19-EZR-8:23-JOB-19:16(2603),17(2589)-PS-119:58(2470)-IS-19:22■N.T.-LU-15:28(3870)-HEB-12:19(3868)-JAS-3:17(2138)

INTREATIES-PR-18:23(8469)

INTREATY-2CO-8:4(3874)

INTRUDING-COL-2:18(1687)

INVADE-2CH-20:10(935)-HAB-3:16(1464)

INVADED-all=6584&marked-1SA-23:27■27:8■30:1-2KI-13:20(935)-2CH-28:18

INVASION-1SA-30:14(6584)

INVENT-AM-6:5(2803)

INVENTED-2CH-26:15(2803)

INVENTIONS-PS-99:8(5949)■106:29(4611),39(4611)-PR-8:12(4209)-EC-7:29(2810)

INVENTORS-RO-1:30(2182)

INVISIBLE-all=517-RO-1:20-COL-1:15,16-1TI-1:17-HEB-11:27

INVITED-all=7121-1SA-9:24-2SA-13:23-ES-5:12

INWARD-all=1004&marked-EX-28:26■39:19-2SA-5:9-1KI-7:25-2CH-3:13■4:4-JOB-19:19(5475)■38:36(2910)-PS-5:9(7130)■49:11(7130)■51:6(2910)■64:6(7130)-PR-20:27(2315),30(2315)-IS-16:11(7130)-JER-31:33(7130)-EZE-40:9,16(6441)■41:3(6441)■42:4(6442)■N.T.-LU-11:39(2081)-RO-7:22(2080)-2CO-4:16(2081)■7:15(4698)

INWARDLY-PS-62:4(7130)■N.T.-M'T-7:15(2081)-RO-2:29(1722,2927)

INWARDS-all=7130-EX-29:13,17,22-LE-1:9,13■3:3^{2},9^{2},14^{2}■4:8^{2},11■7:3■8:16,21,25■9:14

IRON-all=1270,a=6523&marked-GE-4:22-LE-26:19-NU-31:22■35:16-DE-3:11■4:20■8:9■27:5■28:23,48■33:25-JOS-6:19,24■8:31■17:16,18■22:8-J'G-1:19■4:3,13-1SA-17:7-2SA-12:31^{2}■23:7-1KI-6:7■8:51■22:11-2KI-6:6-1CH-20:3■22:3,14,16■29:2,7-2CH-2:7,14■18:10■24:12-JOB-19:24■20:24■28:2■40:18■41:27-PS-2:9■105:18■107:10,16■149:8-PR-27:17-EC-10:10-IS-10:34■45:2■48:4■60:17^{2}-JER-1:18■6:28■11:4■15:12■17:1■28:13,14-EZE-4:3^{2}■22:18,20■27:12,19-DA-2:33a,34a,35a,40^{3}a,41^{3}a,42a,43^{2}a,45a■4:15a,23a■5:4a,23a■7:7a,19a-AM-1:3-MIC-4:13■N.T.-all=4603&marked-AC-12:10-RE-2:27■9:9■12:5■18:12(4604)■19:15

IRONS-JOB-41:7(7905)

ISLAND-JOB-22:30(336)-IS-34:14(338)■N.T.-all=3520&marked-AC-27:16(3519),26■28:1,7,9-RE-6:14■16:20

ISLANDS-all=339&marked-IS-11:11■13:22(338)■41:1■42:12,15■59:18-JER-50:39

ISLE-all=339-IS-20:6■23:2,6■N.T.-all=3520-AC-13:6■28:11-RE-1:9

ISLES-all=339-GE-10:5-ES-10:1-PS-72:10■97:1-IS-24:15■40:15■41:5■42:4,10■49:1■51:5■60:9■66:19-JER-2:10■25:22■31:10-EZE-26:15,18^{2}■27:3,6,7,15,35■39:6-DA-11:18-ZEP-2:11

ISSUE-all=2100,a=2101&marked-GE-48:6(4138)-LE-12:7(4726)■15:2,2a,3^{3}a,4,6,7,8,9,11,12,13,13a,15a,19,19a,25,25a,26a,28a,30a,32,33■22:4-NU-5:2-2SA-3:29-2KI-20:18(3318)-IS-22:24(6849)■39:7(3318)-EZE-23:20(2231)■47:8(3318)■N.T.-all=4511&marked-M'T-9:20(131)■22:25(4690)-M'R-5:25-LU-8:43,44

ISSUED-all=3318&marked-JOS-8:22-JOB-38:8-EZE-47:1,12-DA-7:10(5047)■N.T.-RE-9:17(1607),18(1607)

ISSUES-PS-68:20(8444)-PR-4:23(8444)

ITCH-DE-28:27(2775)

ITCHING-2TI-4:3(2833)

ITS-supplied

ITSELF-PS-68:8(2088)■N.T.-all=1438&marked-M'T-6:34■12:25^{2}-M'R-3:24,25-LU-11:17-JOH-15:4■20:7(5565)■21:25(846)-RO-8:16(846),21(846)■26(846)■14:14-1CO-11:14(846)-EPH-4:16-HEB-9:24(846)-3JO-12(846)

IVORY-all=8127&marked-1KI-10:18,22(8143)■22:39-2CH-9:17,21(8143)-PS-45:8-SONG-5:14■7:4-EZE-27:6,15-AM-3:15■6:4-RE-18:12(1661)

J

JACINTH-RE-9:17(5191)■21:20(5192)

JAILOR-AC-16:23(1200)

JANGLING-1TI-1:6(3150)

JASPER-all=3471-EX-28:20■39:13-EZE-28:13■N.T.-all=2393-RE-4:3■21:11,18,19

JAVELIN-all=2595&marked-NU-25:7(7420)-1SA-18:10,11■19:9,10^{2}■20:33

JAW-all=3895&marked-J'G-15:16,19-JOB-41:2-PR-30:14(4973)

JAWBONE-all=3895-J'G-15:15,16,17

JAWS-all=3895&marked-JOB-29:17(4973)-PS-22:15(4455)-IS-30:28-EZE-29:4■38:4-HO-11:4

JEALOUS-all=7065&marked-EX-20:5(7067)■34:14(7067)-NU-5:14^{2},30-DE-4:24(7067)■5:9(7067)■6:15(7067)-JOS-24:19(7072)-1KI-19:10,14-EZE-39:25-JOE-2:18-NA-1:2(7072)-ZEC-1:14■8:2^{2}■N.T.-2CO-11:2(2206)

JEALOUSIES-NU-5:29(7068)

JEALOUSY-all=7068&marked-NU-5:14^{2},15,18,25,30■25:11-DE-29:20■32:16(7065),21^{2}(7065)-1KI-14:22(7065)-PS-78:58(7065)■79:5-PR-6:34-SONG-8:6-IS-42:13-EZE-8:3,3(7069),5■16:38,42■23:25■36:5,6■38:19-ZEP-1:18■3:8-ZEC-1:14■8:2■N.T.

-**2CO**-11:2(2205)

JEOPARDED-**J'G**-5:18(2778)

JEOPARDY-**LU**-8:23(2793)-**1CO**-15:30(2793)

JESTING-**EPH**-5:4(2160)

JEWEL-**PR**-11:22(5141)■20:15(3627)-**EZE**-16:12(5141)

JEWELS-all=3627&marked-**GE**-24:53^{2}-**EX**-3:22^{2}■11:2■12:35^{2}■35:22-**NU**-31:50,51-**1SA**-6:8,15-**2CH**-20:25■32:27-**JOB**-28:17-**SONG**-7:1(2484)-**IS**-3:21(5141)■61:10-**EZE**-16:17,39■23:26-**HO**-2:13(2484)-**MAL**-3:17(5459)

JOD-all supplied

JOIN-**EX**-1:10(3254)-**2CH**-20:35(2266)-**EZR**-9:14(5859)-**IS**-5:8(5060)9:11(5526)■56:6(3867)-**JER**-50:5(3867)-**EZE**-37:17(7126)-**DA**-11:6(2266)■**N.T.**-all=2853-**AC**-5:13■8:29■9:26

JOINED-all=2266&marked-**GE**-14:3,8(6186)■29:34(3867)-**EX**-28:7^{2}-**NU**-18:2(3867),4(3867)■25:3(6775),5(6775)-**1SA**-4:2(5203)-**1KI**-20:29(7126)-**2CH**-18:1(2859)■20:36,37-**EZR**-4:12(2338)-**NE**-4:6(7194)-**ES**-9:27(3867)-**JOB**-3:6(2302)■41:17(1692),23(1692)-**PS**-83:8(3867)■106:28(6775)-**EC**-9:4(977)-**IS**-13:15(5595)■14:1(3867),20(3161)■56:3(3867)-**EZE**-1:9,11■46:22(7000)-**HO**-4:17-**ZEC**-2:11(3867)■**N.T.**-all=2853&marked-**M'T**-19:6(4801)-**M'R**-10:9(4801)-**LU**-15:15-**AC**-5:36(4347)■18:7(4927)-**1CO**-1:10(2675)■6:16,17-**EPH**-4:16(4883)■5:31(4347)

JOINING-**2CH**-3:12(1692)

JOININGS-**1CH**-22:3(4226)

JOINT-**GE**-32:25(3363)-**PS**-22:14(6504)-**PR**-25:19(4154)■**N.T.**-**EPH**-4:16(860)

JOINT-HEIRS-**RO**-8:17(4789)

JOINTS-**1KI**-22:34(1694)-**2CH**-18:33(1694)-**SONG**-7:1(2542)-**DA**-5:6(7001)■**N.T.**-**COL**-2:19(860-)**HEB**-4:12(719)

JOT-**M'T**-5:18(2503)

JOURNEY-all=1870&marked-**GE**-24:21■29:1(5575,7272)■30:36■31:23■33:12(5265)■46:1(5265)-**EX**-3:18■5:3■8:27■13:20(5265)■16:1(5265)-**NU**-9:10,13■10:6(5265),13(5265),33^{2}■11:31^{2}■33:8,12(5265)-**DE**-1:7(5265),40(5265)■2:1(5265),24(5265)■10:6(5265),11(4550)-**JOS**-9:11,13-**J'G**-4:9-**1SA**-15:18-**2SA**-11:10-**1KI**-18:27■19:4,7-**2KI**-3:9-**NE**-2:6(4109)-**PR**-7:19-**JON**-3:3(4109),4(4109)■**N.T.**-all=3598&marked-**M'T**-10:10■25:15(589)-**M'R**-6:8■13:34(590)-**LU**-2:44■9:3■11:6■15:13(589)-**JOH**-4:6(3597)-**AC**-1:12■10:9(3596)■22:6(4198)-**RO**-1:10(2137)■15:24(4198),24(1279)

JOURNEYED-all=5265&marked-**GE**-11:2■12:9■13:11■20:1■33:17■35:5,16,21-**EX**-12:37■17:1■40:37-**NU**-9:17,18,19,20,21^{2},22^{2},23■11:35■12:15■20:22■21:4,11■33:22-**DE**-10:7-**JOS**-9:17-**J'G**-17:8(6213,1870)■**N.T.**-**LU**-10:33(3593)-**AC**-9:3(4198),7(4922)■26:13(4198)

JOURNEYING-**NU**-10:2(4550),29(5265)■**N.T.**-**LU**-13:22(4197,4160)

JOURNEYINGS-**NU**-10:28(4550)-**2CO**-11:26(3597)

JOURNEYS-all=4550-**GE**-13:3-**EX**-17:1■40:36,38-**NU**-10:6,12■33:1,2^{2}

JOY-all=8057,a=8342,b=4885&marked-**1SA**-18:6-**1KI**-1:40-**1CH**-12:40■15:16,25■29:9,17-**2CH**-20:27■30:26-**EZR**-3:12,13■6:16(2305),22-**NE**-8:10(2304)■12:43^{2}-**ES**-8:16a,17■9:22^{2}-**JOB**-8:19b■20:5■29:13(7442)■33:26(8643)-**PS**-16:11■21:1(8055)■27:6(8643)■30:5(7440)■42:4(7440)■43:4(1524)■48:2b■51:8a,12a■105:43a■126:5(7440)■132:9(7442),16(7442)■137:6-**PR**-12:20■14:10■15:21,23■17:21(8056)■21:15■23:24(8056)-**EC**-2:10,26■5:20■9:7-**IS**-9:3,3^{2}(8055),17(8055)■12:3a■16:10(1524)■22:13a■24:8b,11■29:19■32:13b,14b■35:2(1525),10^{2}■51:3a,11^{2}■55:12■60:15b■61:3a,7■65:14(2898),18b,19(7796)■66:5,10b-**JER**-15:16a■31:13a■33:9a,11a■48:33■49:25b-**LA**-2:15b■5:15b-**EZE**-24:25b■36:5-**HO**-9:1(1524)-**JOE**-1:12a,16-**HAB**-3:18(1523)-**ZEP**-3:17,17(1523)-**ZEC**-8:19a■**N.T.**-all=5479&marked-**M'T**-2:10■13:20,44■25:21,23■28:8-**LU**-1:14,44(20)■2:10■8:13■10:17■15:7,10■24:41,52-**JOH**-3:29■15:11^{2}■16:20,21,22,24■17:13-**AC**-2:28(2167)■8:8■13:52■15:3■20:24-**RO**-5:11(2744)■14:17■15:13,32-**2CO**-1:24■2:3,3sup■7:13■8:2-**GA**-5:22-**PH'P**-1:4,25■2:2,17(5463),18(5463)■4:1-**1TH**-1:6■2:19,20■3:9,9(5463)-**2TI**-1:4-**PH'M**-7(5485),20(3685)-**HEB**-12:2■13:17-**JAS**-1:2■4:9-**1PE**-1:8■4:13(21)-**1JO**-1:4-**2JO**-12-**3JO**-4-**JUDE**-24(20)

JOYED-**2CO**-7:13(5463)

JOYFUL-all=8056&marked-**1KI**-8:66-**EZR**-6:22(8055)-**ES**-5:9-**JOB**-3:7(7445)-**PS**-5:11(5970)■35:9(1523)■63:5(7445)■89:15(8643)■96:12(5937)■98:8(7442)■113:9■149:2(1523),5(5937)-**EC**-7:14(2896)-**IS**-49:13(1523)■56:7(8055)■61:10(1523)■**N.T.**-**2CO**-7:4(5479)

JOYFULLY-**EC**-9:9(2416)■**N.T.**-**LU**-19:6(5463)-**HEB**-10:34(3326,5479)

JOYFULNESS-**DE**-28:47(8057)■**N.T.**-**COL**-1:11(5479)

JOYING-**COL**-2:5(5463)

JOYOUS-all=5947-**IS**-22:2■23:7■32:13■**N.T.**-**HEB**-12:11(5479)

JUBILE-all=3104&marked-**LE**-25:9(8643),10,11,12,13,15,28^{2},30,31,33,40,50,52,54■27:17,18^{2},21,23,24-**NU**-36:4

JUDGE-all=8199,a=1777&marked-**GE**-15:14a■16:5■18:25■19:9■31:37(3198),53■49:16a-**EX**-2:14■5:21■18:13,16,22^{2}-**LE**-19:15-**NU**-35:24-**DE**-1:16■16:18■17:9,12■25:1,2■32:36a-**J'G**-2:18^{2},19■11:27-**1SA**-2:10a,25(430),25(6419)■3:13■8:5,6,20■24:12,15(1784),15-**2SA**-15:4-**1KI**-3:9^{2}■7:7■8:32-**1CH**-16:33-**2CH**-1:10,11■6:23■19:6■20:12-**EZR**-7:25(934,1778)-**JOB**-9:15■22:13■23:7■31:28(6416)-**PS**-7:8a,8■9:8■10:18■26:1■35:24■43:1■50:4a,6■54:1a■58:1■67:4■68:5(1781)■72:2a,4■75:2,7■82:2,8■94:2■96:10a,13^{2}■98:9^{2}■110:6a■135:14a-**PR**-31:9-**EC**-3:17-**IS**-1:17,23■2:4■3:2,13a■5:3■11:3,4■33:22■51:5-**JER**-5:28a,28-**LA**-3:59-**EZE**-7:3,8,27■11:10,11■16:38■18:30■20:4^{2}■21:30■22:2^{2}■23:24,36,45■24:14■33:20■34:17,20,22■44:24-**JOE**-3:12-**AM**-2:3-**OB**-21-**MIC**-3:11■4:3■5:1■7:3-**ZEC**-3:7a■**N.T.**-all=2919,a=2923&marked-**M'T**-5:25^{2}a■7:1,2-**LU**-6:37■12:14(1348),57,58^{2}a■18:2a,6a■19:22-**JOH**-5:30■7:24^{2},51■8:15,16,26■12:47^{2},48■18:31-**AC**-4:19■7:7,27(1348),35(1348)■10:42a■13:46■17:31■18:15a■23:3■24:10a-**RO**-2:16,27■3:6■14:3,10,13^{2}-**1CO**-4:3(350),5■5:12^{2}■6:2,2(2922),3,5(1252)■10:15■11:13,31(1252)■14:29(1252)-**2CO**-5:14-**COL**-2:16-**2TI**-4:1,8a-**HEB**-10:30■12:23a■13:4-**JAS**-4:11,11a■5:9a-**1PE**-4:5-**RE**-6:10■19:11

JUDGED-all=8199&marked-**GE**-30:6(1777)-**EX**-18:26^{2}-**J'G**-3:10■4:4■10:2,3■12:7,8,9,11^{2},13,14■15:20■16:31-**1SA**-4:18■7:6,15,16,17-**1KI**-3:28-**2KI**-23:22-**PS**-9:19■37:33■109:7-**JER**-22:16(1777)-**EZE**-16:38(4941),52(6419)■28:23(5307)■35:11■36:19-**DA**-9:12■**N.T.**-all=2919&marked-**M'T**-7:1,2-**LU**-6:37■7:43-**JOH**-16:11-**AC**-16:15■24:6■25:9,10,20■26:6-**RO**-2:12■3:4,7-**1CO**-2:15(350)■4:3(350)■5:3■6:2■10:29■11:31,32■14:24(350)-**HEB**-11:11(2233)-**JAS**-2:12-**1PE**-4:6-**RE**-11:18■16:5■19:2■20:12,13

JUDGES-all=8199&marked-**EX**-21:6(430),22(6414)■22:8(430),9^{2}(430)**NU**-25:5-**DE**-1:16■16:18■19:17,18■21:2■25:1■32:31(6414)-**JOS**-8:33■23:2■24:1-**J'G**-1:t■2:16,17,18-**RU**-1:1-**1SA**-8:1,2-**2SA**-7:11-**2KI**-23:22-**1CH**-17:6,10■23:4■26:29-**2CH**-1:2■19:5,6-**EZR**-7:25(1782)■10:14-**JOB**-9:24■12:17■31:11(6414)-**PS**-2:10■141:6■148:11-**PR**-8:16-**IS**-1:26■40:23-**DA**-3:2(148),3(148)■9:12-**HOS**-7:7■13:10-**ZEP**-3:3■**N.T.**-all=2923-**M'T**-12:27-**LU**-11:19-**AC**-13:20-**JAS**-2:4

JUDGEST-**PS**-51:4(8199)-**JER**-11:20(8199)■**N.T.**-all=2919-**RO**-2:1^{3},3■14:4-**JAS**-4:12

JUDGETH-all=8199&marked-**JOB**-21:22■36:31(1777)-**PS**-7:11■58:11■82:1-**PR**-29:14■**N.T.**-all=2919&marked-**JOH**-5:22■8:50■12:48-**1CO**-2:15(350)■4:4(350)■5:13-**JAS**-4:11^{2}-**1PE**-1:17■2:23-**RE**-18:8

JUDGING-all=8199-**2KI**-15:5-**2CH**-26:21-**PS**-9:4-**IS**-16:5■**N.T.**-**M'T**-19:28(2919)-**LU**-22:30(2919)

JUDGMENT-all=4941&marked-**GE**-18:19-**EX**-12:12(8201)■21:31■23:6■28:15,29,30^{2}-**LE**-19:15,35-**NU**-27:11,21■35:12,29-**DE**-1:17^{2}■10:18■16:18,19■17:8,9,11■24:17■25:1■27:19■32:4,41-**JOS**-20:6-**J'G**-4:5■5:10(4055)-**1SA**-8:3-**2SA**-8:15■15:2,6-**1KI**-3:11,28^{2}■7:7■10:9■20:40-**2KI**-25:6-**1CH**-18:14-**2CH**-9:8■19:6(1697,4941),8■20:9(8196)■22:8(8199)■24:24(8201)-**EZR**-7:26(1780)-**ES**-1:13(1779)-**JOB**-8:3■9:19,32■14:3■19:7,29(1779)■22:4■27:2■29:14■32:9■34:4,5,12,23■35:14(1779)■36:17^{2}(1779)■37:23■40:8-**PS**-1:5■7:6■9:7,8(1777),16■25:9■33:5■35:23■37:6,28,30■72:2■76:8(1779),9■89:14■94:15■97:2■99:4^{2}■101:1■103:6■106:3,30(6419)■111:7■119:66(2940),84,121,149■122:5■143:2■146:7■149:9-**PR**-1:3■2:8,9■8:20■13:23■16:10■17:23■18:5■19:28■20:8(1779)■21:3,7,15■24:23■28:5■29:4,26■31:5(1779)-**EC**-3:16■5:8■8:5,6■11:9■12:14-**IS**-1:17,21,27■3:14■4:4■5:7,16■9:7■10:2(1779)■16:3(6415),5■28:6,7(6417),17■30:18■32:1,16■33:5■34:5■40:14,27■41:1■42:1,3,4■49:4■51:4■53:8■54:17■56:1■59:8,9,11,14,15■61:8-**JER**-4:2■5:1,4,5■7:5■8:7■9:24■10:24■21:12■22:3,15■23:5■33:15■39:5■48:21,47■49:12■51:9,47(6485),52(6485)■52:9-**EZE**-18:8■23:10(8196),24■34:16■39:21■44:24(8199)■45:9-**DA**-4:37(1780)■7:10(1780),22(1780),26(1780)-**HO**-2:19■5:1,11■10:4■12:6-**AM**-5:7,15,24■6:12-**MIC**-3:1,8,9■7:9-**HAB**-1:4^{2},7,12-**ZEP**-2:3■3:5-**ZEC**-7:9■8:16-**MAL**-2:17■3:5■**N.T.**-all=2920&marked-**M'T**-5:21,22■7:2(2917)■10:15■11:22,24■12:18,20,36,41,42■23:23■27:19(968)-**M'R**-6:11-**LU**-10:14■11:31,32,42-**JOH**-5:22,27,30■7:24■8:16■9:39(2917)■12:31■16:8,11■18:28^{2}(4232),33(4232)■19:9(4232),13(968)-**AC**-8:33■18:12(968),16(968),17(968)■23:35(4232)■24:25(2197)■25:6(968),10(968),15(1349),17(968)-**RO**-1:32(1345)■2:2(2917),3(2917),5(1341)■5:16(2917)■14:10(968)-**1CO**-1:10(1106)■4:3(2250)■7:25(1106),40(1106)-**2CO**-5:10(968)-**GA**-5:10(2917)-**PH'P**-1:9(144)-**2TH**-1:5-**1TI**-5:24-**HEB**-6:2(2917)■9:27■10:27-**JAS**-2:6(2922),13^{2}-**1PE**-4:17(2917)-**2PE**-2:3(2917),4,9■3:7-**1JO**-4:17-**JUDE**-6,15-**RE**-14:7■17:1(2917)■18:10■20:4(2917)

JUDGMENTS-all=4941&marked-**EX**-6:6(8201)■7:4(8201)■21:1■24:3-**LE**-18:4,5,26■19:37■20:22■25:18■26:15,43,46-**NU**-33:4(8201)■35:24■36:13-**DE**-4:1,5,8,14,45■5:1,31■6:1,20■7:11,12■8:11■11:1,32■12:1■26:16,17■30:16■33:10,21-**2SA**-22:23-**1KI**-2:3■6:12■8:58■9:4■11:33-**1CH**-16:12,14■22:13■28:7-**2CH**-7:17■19:10-**EZR**-7:10-**NE**-1:7■9:13,29■10:29-**PS**-10:5■18:22■19:9■36:6■48:11■72:1■89:30■97:8■105:5,7■119:7,13,20,30,39,43,52,62,75,102,106,108,120,137,156,160,164,167,175■

147:19,20-PR-19:29(8201)-IS-26:8,9-JER-1:16■12:1-EZE-5:6^{2},7^{2},8,10(8201),15(8201)■11:9(8201),12■14:21(8201)■16:41(8201)■18:9,17■20:11,13,16,18,19,21,24,25■23:24■25:11(8201)■28:22(8201),26(8201)■30:14(8201),19(8201)■36:27■37:24■44:24-DA-9:5-HO-6:5-ZEP-3:15-MAL-4:4■N.T.-RO-11:33(2917)-1CO-6:4(2922)-RE-15:4(1345)■16:7(2920)■19:2(2920)

JUICE-SONG-8:2(6071)

JUMPING-NA-3:2(7540)

JUNIPER-all=7574-1KI-19:4,5-JOB-30:4-PS-120:4

JURISDICTION-LU-23:7(1849)

JUST-all=6662&marked-GE-6:9-LE-19:36^{2}(6664)-DE-16:18(6664),20(6664)■25:15^{2}(6664)■32:4-2SA-23:3-NE-9:33-JOB-4:17(6663)■9:2(6663)■12:4■27:17■33:12(6663)■34:17-PS-7:9■37:12-PR-3:33■4:18■9:9■10:6,7,20,31■11:1(8003),9■12:13,21■13:22■16:11(4941)■17:15,26■18:17■20:7■21:15■24:16■29:10(3477),27-EC-7:15,20■8:14-IS-26:7^{2}■29:21■45:21-LA-4:13-EZE-18:5,9■45:10^{2}(6664)-HO-14:9-AM-5:12-HAB-2:4-ZEP-3:5-ZEC-9:9■N.T.-all=1342&marked-M'T-1:19■5:45■13:49■27:19,24-M'R-6:20-LU-1:17■2:25■14:14■15:7■20:20■23:50-JOH-5:30-AC-3:14■7:52■10:22■22:14■24:15-RO-1:17■2:13■3:8(1738),26■7:12-GA-3:11-PH'P-4:8-COL-4:1-TIT-1:8-HEB-2:2(1738)■10:38■12:23-JAS-5:6-1PE-3:18-2PE-2:7-1JO-1:9-RE-15:3

JUSTICE-all=6666,a=6664&marked-GE-18:19-DE-33:21-2SA-8:15■15:4(6663)-1KI-10:9-1CH-18:14-2CH-9:8-JOB-8:3a■36:17(4941)■37:23-PS-82:3(6663)■89:14a■119:121a-PR-1:3a■8:15a■21:3-EC-5:8a-IS-9:7■56:1■58:2a■59:4a,9,14-JER-22:15■23:5■31:23a■50:7a-EZE-45:9

JUSTIFICATION-RO-4:25(1347)■5:16(1345),18(1347)

JUSTIFIED-all=6663-JOB-11:2■13:18■25:4■32:2-PS-51:4■143:2-IS-43:9,26■45:25-JER-3:11-EZE-16:51,52■N.T.-all=1344-M'T-11:19■12:37-LU-7:29,35■18:14-AC-13:39^{2}-RO-2:13■3:4,20,24,28■4:2■5:1,9■8:30^{2}-1CO-4:4■6:11-GA-2:16^{3},17■3:11,24■5:4-1TI-3:16-TIT-3:7-JAS-2:21,24,25

JUSTIFIER-RO-3:26(1344)

JUSTIFIETH-PR-17:15(6663)-IS-50:8(6663)■N.T.-RO-4:5(1344)■8:33(1344)

JUSTIFY-all=6663-EX-23:7-DE-25:1-JOB-9:20■27:5■33:32-IS-5:23■53:11■N.T.-all=1344-LU-10:29■16:15-RO-3:30-GA-3:8

JUSTIFYING-1KI-8:32(6663)-2CH-6:23(6663)

JUSTLE-NA-2:4(8264)

JUSTLY-MIC-6:8(4941)■N.T.-LU-23:41(1346)-1TH-2:10(1346)

K

KEEP-all=8104,a=6213,b=5341&marked-GE-2:15■3:24■6:19,20■17:9,10■18:19■28:15,20■30:31■33:9(1961)■41:35-EX-12:6(4931),14^{2}(2287),25,47a,48^{2}a■13:5(5647),10■15:26■16:28■19:5■20:6,8(6942)■22:7,10■23:7(7368),14(2287),15,20■31:13,14,16■34:18-LE-6:4(6485)■8:35■18:4,5,26,30■19:3,19,30■20:8,22■22:9,31■23:39(2287),41(2287)■25:18■26:2,3-NU-1:53■3:7,8,32■6:24■8:26■9:2a,3^{2}a,4a,6a,10a,11a,12a,13a,14a■18:3,4,5,7■29:12(2287),31:30■36:7(1692),9(1692)-DE-4:2,6,9,40■5:1,10,12,15a,29■6:2,17■7:8,9,11,12^{2}■8:2,6■10:13■11:1,8,22■13:4,18■16:1a,10a,15(2287)■17:19■19:9■23:9,23■26:16,17,18■27:1■28:9,45■29:9■30:10,16-JOS-6:18■10:18■22:5■23:6-J'G-2:22,22sup-RU-2:21(1692)-1SA-2:9■7:1-2SA-15:16■16:21■20:3-1KI-2:3^{2}■3:14■6:12■8:25,58,61■9:4,6■11:38■20:39-2KI-11:6,7■17:13■23:3,21a-1CH-4:10a■12:33(5737),38(5737)■22:12■23:32■28:8■29:18,19-2CH-6:16■13:11■22:9(6113)■23:6■28:10(3533)■30:1a,2a,3a,5a,13a,23a■34:31■35:16a,18a-EZR-8:29-NE-1:9■12:27a■13:22-ES-3:8a■9:21a,27a-JOB-20:13(4513)-PS-12:7■17:8■19:13(2820)■25:10b,20■34:13b■37:34■39:1■78:7b■89:28,31■91:11■103:9(5201),18■105:45b■106:3■119:2b,4,5,8,17,33b,34b,44,57,60,63,69b,88,100b,101,106,115b,129b,134,136,145b,146■127:1■132:12■140:4■141:3b,9-PR-2:11b,20■3:1b,21b,26■4:4,6b,13b,21,23b■5:2b■6:20b,22,24■7:1,2,5■8:32■22:5,18■28:4-EC-3:6■5:1■8:2■12:13-SONG-8:12(5201)-IS-26:3b■27:3^{2}b■42:6b■43:6(3607)■56:1,4-JER-3:5,12(5201)■31:10■42:4(4513)-EZE-11:20■18:21■20:19■36:27■43:11■44:16,24-DA-9:4-HO-12:6-MIC-7:5-NA-1:15(2287)■2:1b-ZEC-3:7^{2}■13:5(7069)■14:16(2287),18(2287),19(2287)-MAL-2:7(2287)■N.T.-all=5083,a=5442&marked-M'T-19:17■26:18(4160)-M'R-7:9-LU-4:10(1314)■8:15(2722)■11:28(5442)■19:43(4912)-JOH-8:51,52,55■12:25a■14:15,23■15:10,20■17:11,15-AC-5:3(3557)■10:28(2853)■12:4a■15:5,24,29(1301)■16:4a,23■18:21(4160)■21:25a■24:23-RO-2:25(4238),26a-1CO-5:8(1858),11(4874),7:37■9:27(5299)■11:2(2722)■14:28(4601),34(4601)■15:2(2722)-2CO-11:9-GA-6:13a-EPH-4:3-PH'P-4:7(5432)-2TH-3:3a-1TI-5:22■6:14,20a-2TI-1:12a,14a-JAS-1:27■2:10-1JO-2:3■3:22■5:2,3,21a-JUDE-21,24a-RE-1:3■3:10■12:17■14:12■22:9

KEEPER-all=8104&marked-GE-4:2(7462),9■39:21(8269),22(8269),23(8269)-1SA-17:20,22■28:2-2KI-22:14-2CH-34:22-NE-2:8■3:29-ES-2:3,8,15-JOB-27:18(5341)-PS-121:5-SONG-1:6(5201)-JER-35:4■N.T.-AC-16:27(1200),36(1200)

KEEPERS-all=8104&marked-2KI-11:5■22:4■23:4■25:18-1CH-9:19^{2}-ES-6:2-EC-12:3-SONG-5:7■8:11(5201)-JER-4:17■52:24-EZE-40:45,46■44:8,14■N.T.-all=5441&marked-M'T-28:4(5083)-AC-5:23■12:6,19-TIT-2:5(3626)

KEEPEST-all=8104&marked-1KI-8:23-2CH-6:14-NE-9:32■N.T.-AC-21:24(5442)

KEEPETH-all=8104&marked-EX-21:18(5307)-DE-7:9-1SA-16:11(7462)-NE-1:5-JOB-33:18(2820)-PS-34:20■121:3,4■146:6-PR-2:8(5341)■10:17■13:3(5341),3,6(5341)■16:17(5341)■19:8,16■21:23^{2}■24:12(5341)■27:18(5341)■28:7(5341)■29:11(7623),18-EC-8:5-IS-26:2■56:2^{2},6-JER-48:10(4513)■N.T.-all=5083&marked-LU-11:21(5442)-JOH-7:19(4160)■9:16■14:21,24-1JO-2:4,5■3:24■5:18-RE-2:26■16:15■22:7

KEEPING-all=8104&marked-EX-34:7(5341)-NU-3:28,38-DE-8:11-1SA-25:16(7462)-NE-12:25-PS-19:11-EZE-17:14-DA-9:4■N.T.-LU-2:8(5442)-1CO-7:19(5084)

KEPT-all=8104,a=6213&marked-GE-26:5■29:9(7462)■39:9(2820)■42:16(631)-EX-3:1(7462)■16:23(4931),32(4931),33(4931),34(4931)■21:29,36-NU-5:13(5641)■9:5a,7(1639),19,23■17:10(4931)■19:9(4931)■24:11(4513)■31:47-DE-32:10(5341)■33:9(5341)-JOS-5:10a■22:2,3-RU-2:23(1692)-1SA-9:24■13:13,14■17:34(7462)■21:4,6(6113)■25:21,33(3607),34(4513),39(2820)■26:15,16-2SA-22:22,24,44-1KI-2:43■3:6■8:24■11:10,11,34■13:21■14:8,27-2KI-9:14■12:9■17:19■18:6-1CH-10:13■12:1(6113),29-2CH-6:15■7:8a,9a■12:10■30:21a,23a■34:9,21■35:1a,17a,18^{2}a,19a■36:21(7673)-EZR-3:4a■6:16(5648),19a,22a-NE-1:7■8:18a■9:34a■11:19■12:45-ES-2:14,21■9:28a-JOB-23:11■28:21(5641)-PS-17:4■18:21,23■32:3(2790)■42:4(2287)■50:21(2790)■78:10,56■99:7■119:22(5341),55,56(5341),67,158,167,168-EC-2:10(680)■5:13-SONG-1:6(5201)-IS-30:29(6942)-JER-16:11■35:18-EZE-5:7a■18:9,19■20:21■44:8,15■48:11-DA-7:28(5202)-HO-12:12-AM-1:11■2:4-MIC-6:16-MAL-2:9■3:7,14■N.T.-all=5083&marked-M'T-8:33(1006)■14:6(71)■19:20(5442)-M'R-4:22(1096)■9:10(2902)-LU-2:19(4933),51(1301)■8:29(5442)■9:36(4601)■18:21(5442)■19:20(2192)-JOH-2:10■12:7■15:10,20■17:6,12,12(5442)■18:16(2377),17(2377)-AC-5:2(3557)■7:53(5442)■9:33(2621)■12:5,6■15:12(4601)■20:20(5288)■22:2(3930),20(5442)■23:35(5442)■25:4,21■27:43(2967)■28:16(5442)-2CO-11:9,32(5432)-GA-3:23(5432)-2TI-4:7-HEB-11:28(4160)-JAS-5:4(650)-1PE-1:5(5432)-2PE-3:7(2343)-JUDE-6-RE-3:8,10

KERCHIEFS-EZE-13:18(4556),21(4556)

KERNELS-NU-6:4(2785)

KETTLE-1SA-2:14(1731)

KEY-J'G-3:25(4668)-IS-22:22(4668)■N.T.-all=2807-LU-11:52-RE-3:7■9:1■20:1

KEYS-M'T-16:19(2807)-RE-1:18(2807)

KICK-1SA-2:29(1163)■N.T.-AC-9:5(2979)■26:14(2979)

KICKED-DE-32:15(1163)

KID-all=8163&marked-GE-37:31■38:17(1423),20(1423),23(1423)-EX-23:19(1423)■34:26(1423)-LE-4:23,28(8166)■5:6(8166)■9:3■23:19-NU-7:16,22,28,34,40,46,52,58,64,70,76,82■15:11(5795),24■28:15,30■29:5,11,16,19,25-DE-14:21(1423)-J'G-6:19(1423,5795)■13:15(1423,5795),19(1423,5795)■14:6(1423)■15:1(1423,5795)-1SA-16:20(1423,5795)-IS-11:6(1423)-EZE-43:22■45:23■N.T.-LU-15:29(2056)

KIDNEYS-all=3629-EX-29:13,22-LE-3:4^{2},10^{2},15^{2}■4:9^{2}■7:4^{2}■8:16,25■9:10,19-DE-32:14-IS-34:6

KIDS-all=1423&marked-GE-27:9,16-LE-16:5(8163)-NU-7:87(8163)-1SA-10:3-1KI-20:27(5795)-2CH-35:7(1121,5795)-SONG-1:8

KILL-all=4191,a=7819,b=2026&marked-GE-4:15(5221)■12:12b■26:7b■27:42b■37:21(5221)-EX-1:16■2:14b■4:24■12:6a,21a■16:3■17:3■20:13(7523)■22:1(2873),24b■29:11a,20a-LE-1:5a,11a■3:2a,8a,13a■4:4a,24^{2}a,33a■7:2^{2}a■14:13a,19a,25a,50a■16:11a,15a■20:4,16b■22:28a-NU-11:15b■14:15■16:13■22:29b■31:17^{2}b■35:27(7523)-DE-4:42(7523)■5:17(7523)■12:15(2076),21(2076)■13:9b,32:39-J'G-13:23■15:13■16:2b■20:31(2491),39(2491)-1SA-16:2b■17:9^{2}(5221)■19:1,2,17■24:10b■30:15-2SA-13:28■14:7,32■21:4-1KI-11:40,12:27b-2KI-5:7■7:4■11:15-2CH-35:6a-ES-3:13b-PS-59:t-EC-3:3b-IS-14:30■29:1(5362)-EZE-34:3(2076)■N.T.-all=615&marked-M'T-5:21^{2}(5407)■10:28^{2}■17:23■21:38■23:34■24:9■26:4-M'R-3:4■9:31■10:19(5407),34■12:7-LU-12:4■13:31■15:23(2380)■18:20(5407)■20:14■22:2(337)-JOH-5:18■7:1,19,20,25■8:22,37,40■10:10(2380)-AC-7:28(337)■9:23(337),24(337)■10:13(2380)■21:31■23:15(337)■25:3(337)■26:21(1315)■27:42-RO-13:9(5407)-JAS-2:11^{2}(5407)■4:2(5407)-RE-2:23■6:4(4969),8■9:5■11:7

KILLED-all=7819&marked-GE-37:31-EX-21:29(4191)-LE-4:15■6:25^{2}■8:19■14:5,6-NU-16:41(4191)■31:19(2026)-1SA-24:11(2026)■25:11(2873)■28:24(2076)-2SA-12:9(5221)■21:17(4191)-1KI-16:7(5221),10(4191)■21:19(7523)-2KI-15:25(4191)-1CH-19:18(4191)-2CH-18:2(3076)■25:3(5221)■

29:22^{3},24■30:15■35:1,11-EZR-6:20-PS-44:22(2026)-PR-9:2(2873)-LA-2:21(2873)■N.T.-all=615&marked-M’T-16:21■21:35■22:4(2380)■23:31(5407)-M’R-6:19■8:31■9:31■12:5,8■14:12(2380)-LU-11:47,48■12:5■15:27(2380),30(2380)■20:15■22:7(2380)-AC-3:15■12:2(337)■16:27(337)■23:12,21(337),27-RO-8:36(2289)■11:3-2CO-6:9(2289)-1TH-2:15-JAS-5:6(5407)-RE-6:11■9:18,20■11:5■13:10,15

KILLEDST-EX-2:14(2026)-1SA-24:18(2026)

KILLEST-M’T-23:37(615)-LU-13:34(615)

KILLETH-all=5221&marked-LE-17:3^{2}(7819)■24:17,18,21^{2}-NU-35:11,15,30-DE-19:4-JOS-20:3,9-1SA-2:6(4191)■17:25,26,27-JOB-5:2(2026)■24:14(6991)-PR-21:25(4191)-IS-66:3(7819)■N.T.-all=615-JOH-16:2-2CO-3:6-RE-13:10

KILLING-J’G-9:24(2026)-2CH-30:17(7821)-IS-22:13(7819)-HOS-4:2(7523)■N.T.-M’R-12:5(615)

KIN-LE-18:6(1320)■20:19(7607)■21:2(7607)■25:25(7138),49(1320)■N.T.-M’R-6:4(4773)

KIND-all=4327&marked-GE-1:11,12^{2},21^{2},24^{2},25^{3}■6:20^{3}■7:14^{4}-LE-11:14,15,16,19,22^{4},29-DE-14:13,14,15,18-2CH-10:7(2896)■N.T.-all=1085&marked-M’T-13:47■17:21-M’R-9:29-LU-6:35(5543)-1CO-13:4(5541)-EPH-4:32(5543)-JAS-1:18(5100)■3:7(5449)

KINDLE-all=3341&marked-EX-35:3(1197)-PR-26:21(2787)-IS-9:18■10:16(3344)■30:33(1197)■43:2(1197)■50:11(6919)-JER-7:18(1197)■17:27■21:14■33:18(6999)■43:12■49:27■50:32-EZE-20:47■24:10(1814)-AM-1:14-OB-18(1814)-MAL-1:10(215)

KINDLED-all=2734&marked-GE-30:2■39:19-EX-4:14■22:6(1197)-LE-10:6(8313)-NU-11:1,10■11:33■12:9■22:22,27■24:10■25:3■32:10-DE-6:15■7:4■11:17■29:27■31:17■32:22(6919)-JOS-7:1■23:16-J’G-9:30■14:19-1SA-11:6■17:28■20:30-2SA-6:7■12:5■22:9(1197),13(1197)■24:1-2KI-13:3■22:13(3341),17(3341)■23:26-1CH-13:10-2CH-25:10,15-JOB-19:11■32:2^{2},3,5■42:7-PS-2:12(1197)■18:8(1197)■78:21(5400)■106:18(1197),40■124:3-IS-5:25■50:11(1197)-JER-11:16(3341)■15:14(6919)■17:4(6919)■44:6(1197)-LA-4:11(3341)-EZE-20:48(1197)-HO-8:5■11:8(3648)-ZEC-10:3■N.T.-LU-12:49(381)■22:55(681)-AC-28:2(381)

KINDLETH-JOB-41:21(3857)-IS-44:15(5400)■N.T.-JAS-3:5(381)

KINDLY-all=2617&marked-GE-24:49■34:3(5921,3820)■47:29■50:21(5921,3820)-JOS-2:14-RU-1:8-1SA-20:8-2KI-25:28(2896)-JER-52:32(2896)■N.T.-RO-12:10(5387)

KINDNESS-all=2617&marked-GE-20:13■21:23■24:12,14■40:14-JOS-2:12^{2}-J’G-8:35-RU-2:20■3:10-1SA-15:6■20:14,15-2SA-2:5,6,6(2896)■3:8■9:1,3,7■10:2^{2}■16:17-1KI-2:7■3:6-1CH-19:2^{2}-2CH-24:22-NE-9:17-ES-2:9-PS-31:21■117:2■119:76■141:5-PR-19:22■31:26-IS-54:8,10-JER-2:2-JOE-2:13-JON-4:2■N.T.-all=5544&marked-AC-28:2(5368)-2CO-6:6-EPH-2:7-COL-3:12-TIT-3:4-2PE-1:7^{2}(5360)

KINDRED-all=4138&marked-GE-12:1■24:4,7,38(4940),40(4940),41(4940)■31:3,13■32:9■43:7-NU-10:30-JOS-6:23(4940)-RU-2:3(4940)■3:2(4130)-1CH-12:29(250)-ES-2:10,20■8:6-JOB-32:2(4940)-EZE-11:15(1353)■N.T.-all=4772&marked-LU-1:61-AC-4:6(1085)■7:3,13(1085),14,19(1085)-RE-5:9(5443)■14:6(5443)

KINDREDS-all=4940-1CH-16:28-PS-22:27■96:7■N.T.-ll=5443&marked-AC-3:25(3965)-RE-1:7■7:9■11:9■13:7

KINDS-all=2177&marked-GE-8:19(4940)-2CH-16:14-JER-15:3(4940)-EZE-47:10(4327)-DA-3:5,7,10,15■N.T.-1CO-12:10(1085)■14:10(1085)

KINE-all=6510&marked-GE-32:15■41:2,3^{2},4^{2},18,19,20^{2},26,27-DE-7:13(504)■28:4(504),18(504),51(504)■32:14(1241)-1SA-6:7^{2},10,12,14-2SA-17:29(1241)-AM-4:1

KING-all=4428,a=4427,b=4430-GE-14:1^{2},2^{4},8^{3},9^{3},17,18,21,22■20:2■26:1,8■36:31■40:1^{2},5■41:46-EX-1:8,15,17,18■2:23■3:18,19■5:4■6:11,13,27,29■14:5,8-NU-20:14■21:1,21,26^{2},29,33,34■22:4,10■23:7,21■24:7■32:33^{2}■33:40-DE-1:4^{2}■2:24,26,30■3:1,2,3,6,11■4:46,47■7:8■11:3■17:14,15^{2}■28:36■29:7^{2}■33:5-JOS-2:2,3■6:2■8:1,2^{2},14,23,29■9:10^{2}■10:1^{3},3^{5},5^{3},23^{3},28^{3},30^{3},33,37,39^{3}■11:1^{4},10■12:2,4,5,9^{2},10^{2},11^{2},12^{2},13^{2},14^{2},15^{2},16^{2},17^{2},18^{2},19^{2},20^{2},21^{2},22^{2},23^{2},24■13:10,21,27,30■24:9-J’G-3:8,10,12,14,15,17,19■4:2,17,23,24^{2}■8:18■9:6,8,15,16a,18a■11:12,13,14,17^{3},19,25,28■17:6■18:1■19:1■21:25-1SA-2:10■8:5,6,9,10,11,18,19,20,22■10:19,24■11:15a■12:1,2,9,12^{3},13^{2},14,17,19,25■15:1,8,11,17,20,23,26,32,35a■16:1■17:25,55,56■18:6,18,22,25,27■19:4■20:5,24,25■21:2,10,11,12■22:3,4,11^{2},14,15,16,17^{2},18■23:17a,20■24:8,14,20a■25:36■26:14,15^{2},17,19,20■27:2■28:13■29:3,8-2SA-2:4,7,9a,11■3:3,17,21,23,24,31,32,33,36,37,38,39■4:8^{2}■5:2,3^{3},6,11,12,17■6:12,16,20■7:1,2,3,18■8:3,5,8,9,10,11,12■9:2,3^{2},4^{2},5,9,11^{3}■10:1,5,6■11:8,19■12:7■13:6^{2},13,21,24^{2},25,26,31,33,35,36,37,39■14:3,4^{2},5,8,9^{3},10,11,12,13^{2},15^{2},16,17^{2},18^{2},19^{3},21,22^{3},24,29,32,33^{4}■15:2,3,6,7,9,15^{2},16^{2},17,18,19^{2},21^{3},23,25,27,34■16:2,3^{2},4^{2},5,6,9^{2},10,14,16■17:2,16,17,21■18:2,4^{2},5^{2},12,13,19,21,25,26,27,28^{3},29,30,31,32^{2},33■19:1,2,4^{2},5,8^{3},9,10,11^{3},12,14,15^{2},16,17,18,19^{3},20,22,23^{2},24^{2},25^{2},26^{2},27^{2},28^{2},29,30^{2},31,32,33,34^{2},35,36^{2},37,38,39^{2},40^{2},41^{3},42,43^{2}■20:2,3,4,21,22■21:2,5,6,7,8,14■22:51■24:2,3^{2},4,9,20^{2},21,22,23^{2},24-1KI-1:1,2^{3},3,4^{2},5a,13^{2},14,15^{3},16^{2},18,19,20^{2},21,22,23^{3},24,25,27^{2},28^{2},29,31^{2},32^{2},33,34^{2},35a,36^{2},37^{2},38,39,43,43a,44,45,47^{2},48,51^{2},53^{2}■2:17,18,19^{2},20,22,23,25,26,29,30^{2},31,35^{2},36,38^{2},39,42,44,45,46■3:1,4,7a,16,22,23,24^{2},25,26,27,28^{2}■4:1,7,19^{2},27^{2}■5:1^{2},13,17■6:2■7:13,14,40,45,46,51■8:1,2,5,14,62,63,64,66■9:11^{2},14,15,16,26,28■10:3,6,9,10^{2},12,13,16,17,18,21,22,23,26,27■11:1,18,23,26,27,37,40■12:1a,2,6,12,13,15,16^{2},18^{2},20a,23,27^{2},28■13:4,6,7,8,11■14:2,14,25^{2},27,28■15:1,9,16,17^{2},18^{2},19,20,22^{2},25,28,32,33■16:8,10,15,16,16a,21a,23,29,31■19:15,16■20:1,2,4^{2},7,9,11,13,20,21,22^{2},23,28,31,32,38,39^{2},40,41,43■21:1,10,13,18■22:2,3^{2},4,5,6^{2},8^{2},9,10^{2},13,15^{2},16,18,26,27,29^{2},30^{2},31^{2},32,33,34,35,37^{2},41,44,47,51-2KI-1:3,6,9sup,9,11,15,17■3:1,4^{2},5^{2},6,7^{2},9^{2},10,11,12^{2},13^{2},14,26^{2}■4:13■5:1,5^{2},6,7,8^{2}■6:8,9,10,11^{2},12^{2},21,24,26^{2},28,30■7:2,6,12,14,15,17^{2},18■8:3,4,5^{3},6^{2},7,8,9,13,16^{3},20,25^{2},26,28,29^{2}■9:3,6,12,13a,14,15^{2},16,18,19,21,27■10:5a,13^{2}■11:2,7,8^{2},10,11,12,12a,14^{2},17^{2},19■12:6,7,17,18^{2}■13:1,3,4,7,10,12,14,16,18,22,24■14:1^{2},5,8,9^{2},11^{2},13^{2},15,17^{2},21a,22,23^{2}■15:1^{2},5,8,13,17,19,20^{2},23,27,29^{2},32^{2},37■16:1,5^{2},6,7^{3},8,9^{2},10^{3},11^{2},12^{3},15,16,17,18■17:1,3,4^{4},5,6,7,21a,24,26,27■18:1^{2},7,9^{3},10,11,13^{2},14^{3},16^{2},17^{2},18,19,21,23,28,29,30,31,33■19:1,4,5,6,8,9,10^{2},13^{2},20,32,36■20:6,12,14,18■21:3,11,23,24,24a■22:3^{2},9^{2},10^{2},11,12,16,18,20■23:1,2,3,4,12,13^{2},21,23,25,29^{3},30a,34a■24:1,7^{3},10,11,12^{3},13,16,17,17a,20■25:1,2,5,6^{2},8^{2},11,20,21,22,23,24,27^{3},30-1CH-1:43■3:2■4:23,41■5:6,17^{2},26^{2}■11:2,3^{2},10a■12:31a,38^{2}a■14:1,2,8■15:29■17:16■18:3,5,9^{2},10,11,17■19:1,5,7■20:2■21:3,23,24■23:1a■24:6,31■25:2■26:26,30,32^{2}■27:1,24,31■28:1^{2},2,4,4a■29:1,9,20,22,23,24^{2},25,29-2CH-1:9a,11a,14,15■2:3,11,11a,12■4:11,16,17■5:3,6■6:3■7:4,5^{2},6■8:10,11,15,18■9:5,8^{2},9^{2},11,12^{2},15,16,17,20,22,25,27■10:1a,2,6,12,13^{2},15,16^{2},18^{2}■11:3,22a■12:2^{2},6,9,10,11,13■13:1■15:16■16:1^{2},2,3,4,6,7^{3}■17:19^{2}■18:3^{2},4,5,7^{2},8,9^{2},11,12,14,15,17,19,25,26,28^{2},29^{2},30^{2},31,32,33,34■19:1,2■20:15,35^{2}■21:2,8,12■22:1a,1,5^{2},6^{2},11^{2}■23:3,7^{2},9,10,11a,11,12,13^{2},16,20^{2}■24:6,12,14,17^{2},21,22,23■25:3,7,17^{2},18^{2},21^{2},23^{2},25^{2}■26:1a,2,13,18,21■27:5■28:5^{2},7,16,19,20,21^{2},22■29:15,18,19,20,23,24,27,29,30■30:2,4,6^{2},12,24,26■31:13■32:1,7,8,9^{2},10,11,20,21,22,23■33:11,25,25a■34:16^{2},18^{2},19,20,22,24,26,28,29,30,31■35:3,4,16,20,21,23,23■36:1a,3,4,4a,6,10,10a,13,17,18,22^{2},23-EZR-1:1,2,7,8■2:1■3:7,10■4:2,3,5^{2},7,8b,11b,12b,13b,14b,16b,17b,23b,24b■5:6b,7b,8b,11b,12b,13^{2}b,14b,17^{3}b■6:1b,3^{2}b,10b,13b,14b,15b,22■7:1,6,7,8,11,12b,14b,15b,21b,23b,26b,28■8:1,22^{2},25-NE-2:1^{2},2,3,4,5,6^{2},7,8,9,19■5:14■6:6,7^{2}■7:6■9:22^{2}■13:6^{3},26^{3}-ES-1:2,5,7,8,9,10^{2},11,12,13,15,16^{3},17,19^{3},21^{2}■2:1,2,3,4^{2},6^{2},12,13,14^{2},15,16,17,18^{2},21,22,23■3:1,2,7,8,9,10,11,12,15■4:8,11^{3},16■5:1,2^{2},3,4^{2},5^{2},6,8^{4},11^{2},12^{2},14^{2}■6:1^{2},2,3,4^{2},5,6^{3},7^{2},8^{2},9^{2},10,11■7:1,2,3^{2},5,6,7^{2},8^{2},9^{3}■8:1^{2},2,3,4^{2},5^{2},7,10,11,12,15■9:2,3,11,12,13,14,20,25■10:1,2,3-JOB-15:24■18:14■29:25■34:18■41:34-PS-2:6■5:2■10:16■18:50■20:9■21:1,7■24:7,8,9,10^{2}■29:10■33:16■44:4■45:1,11,14■47:2,6,7■48:2■63:11■68:24■72:1■74:12■84:3■89:18■95:3■98:6■105:20■135:11■136:19,20■145:1■149:2-PR-1:1■16:10,14■20:2,8,26,28■22:11■24:21■25:1,5,6■29:4,14■30:27,31■31:1-EC-1:1,12■2:12■4:13■5:9■8:4■9:14■10:16,17,20-SONG-1:4,12■3:9,11■7:5-IS-6:1,5■7:1^{3},6,17,20■8:4,7,21■10:12■14:4,28■19:4■20:1,4,6■23:15■30:33■32:1■33:17,22■36:1^{2},2^{2},4,6,8,13,14,15,16,18■37:1,4,5,6,8,9,10^{2},13^{2},21,33,37■38:6,9■39:1,3,7■41:21■43:15■44:6■57:9-JER-1:2,3^{2}■3:6■4:9■8:19■10:7,10■13:18■15:4■20:4■21:1,2,4,7^{2},10,11■22:1,2,11,18,24,25■23:5■24:1^{2},8■25:1^{2},3,9,11,12,19,26■26:1,18,19,21^{2},22,23■27:1,3^{6},6,8^{2},9,11,12^{2},13,14,17,18,20^{2},21■28:1,2,3,4^{2},11,14■29:2,3^{2},16,21,22■30:9■32:1,2^{2},3^{2},4^{2},28,36■34:1,2^{2},3,4,6,7,8,21^{2}■35:1,11■36:1,9,16,20^{2},21^{3},22,24,25,26,27,28,29^{2},30,32■37:1^{3},3,7,17^{3},18,19,20,21■38:3,4,5^{2},7,8,9,10,11,14^{2},16,17,18,19,22^{2},23,25^{2},26,27■39:1^{2},3^{2},4,5,6^{2},11,13■40:5,7,9,11,14■41:1,2,9^{2},18■42:11■43:10■44:30^{3}■45:1■46:2^{3},13,17,18,26■48:15■49:1,3,28,30,34,38■50:17^{2},18^{2},43■51:31,34,57,59■52:3,4,5,8,9^{2},10,11,12^{2},15,20,26,27,31^{3},34-LA-2:6,9-EZE-1:2■7:27■17:12^{2},16,16a■19:9■21:19,21■24:2■26:7■28:12■29:2,3,18,19■30:10,21,22,24,25^{2}■31:2■32:2,11■37:22,24-DA-1:1^{2},2,3,5^{2},10^{2},18,19^{2},20,21■2:2^{3},3,4,4b,5b,7b,8b,10^{2}b,11^{2},12b,15b,16^{2}b,24^{3}b,25^{2}b,26b,27^{3}b,28b,29b,30b,31b,36b,37b,45b,46b,47b,48,49^{2}■3:1b,2^{2}b,3b,5b,7b,9^{2}b,10b,12b,13b,16b,17b,18b,24^{2}b,30b■4:1b,18b,19b,22b,23b,24b^{2},27b,28b,30b,31b,37b■5:1b,2b,3b,5b,7^{2}b,8b,9b,10^{2}b,11^{2}b,12b,13^{3}b,17^{2}b,18b,30b■6:2b,3b,6^{2}b,7b,8b,9b,12^{3}b,13^{2}b,14b,15^{3}b,16^{2}b,17b,18b,19b,20b,21b,22b,23b,24b,25b■7:1b■8:1,21^{2},23■9:1a■10:1■11:3,5,6,7,8,9,11^{2},13,14,15,25,^{2},36,40^{2}-HO-1:1■3:4,5■5:1,13■7:3,5■8:10■10:3^{2},6,7,15■11:5■13:10^{2},11-AM-1:1^{2},15■2:1■7:10-JON-3:6,7-MIC-2:13■4:9■6:5-NA-3:18-ZEP-1:1■3:15-HAG-1:1,15-ZEC-7:1■9:5,9■11:6■14:5,9,16,17-MAL-1:14■N.T.-all=935-M’T-1:6^{2}■2:1,2,3,9■5:35■14:9■18:23■21:5■22:2,7,11,13■25:34,40■27:11,29,37,42-M’R-6:14,22,25,26,27■15:2,9,12,18,26,32-LU-1:5■14:3,1^{2}■19:38■23:2,3,37,38-JON-1:49■6:15■12:13,15■18:22,37^{2},39■19:3,12,14,15^{2},19,21^{2}-AC-7:10,18■12:1■13:21,22■17:7■25:13,14,24,26■26:2,7,13,19,

26,27,30-2CO-11:32-1TI-1:17■6:15-HEB-7:1,2^{2}■11:27-1PE-2:13,17-RE-9:11■15:3■17:14■19:16

KINGDOM-all=4467,a=4438,b=4437,c=4410&marked-GE-10:10■20:9-EX-19:6-NU-24:7a■32:33^{2}-DE-3:4,10,13■17:18,20-JOS-13:12(4468),21(4468),27(4468),30(4468),31(4468)-1SA-10:16c■25c■11:14c■13:13,14■14:47c■15:28(4468)■18:8c■20:31a■24:20■28:17-2SA-3:10,28■5:12■7:12,13,16■16:3(4468),8c-1KI-1:46c■2:12a,15^{2}c,22c,46■9:5■10:20■11:11,13,31,34,35c■12:21c,26■14:8■18:10^{2}■21:7c-2KI-14:5■15:19-1CH-10:14c■11:10a■12:23a■14:2a■16:20■17:11a,14a■22:10a■28:5a,7a■29:11-2CH-1:1a■2:1a■7:18a■9:19■11:1,17a■12:1a■13:5,8■14:5■17:5■21:3,4■22:9■23:20■25:3■29:21■32:15■33:13a■36:20a,22a-EZR-1:1a-NE-9:35a-ES-1:2a,4a,14a■2:3a■3:6a,8a■4:14a■5:3a,6a■7:2a■9:30a-PS-22:28c■45:6a■103:19a■105:13■145:11a,12a,13a-EC-4:14a-IS-9:7■17:3■19:2■34:12c■60:12-JER-18:7,9■27:8-LA-2:2-EZE-16:13c■17:14■29:14-DA-2:37b,39^{2}b,40b,41b,42b,44^{2}b■4:3b,17b,18b,25b,26,29b,30b,31b,32b,34b,36^{2}b■5:7b,11b,16b,18b,21b,26b,28b,29b,31b■6:1^{2}b,4b,7b,26^{2}b■7:14^{2}b,18^{2}b,22b,23b,24b,27^{3}b■8:23a■10:13a■11:4^{2}a,9a,17a,20a,21^{2}a-HO-1:4(4468)-AM-9:8-OB-21c-MIC-4:8■N.T.-all=932-M'T-3:2■4:17,23■5:3,10,19^{2},20■6:10,13,33■7:21■8:11,12■9:35■10:7■11:11,12■12:25,26,28■13:11,19,24,31,33,38,41,43,44,45,47,52■16:19,28■18:1,3,4,23■19:12,14,23,24■20:1,21■21:31,43■22:2■23:13■24:7,14■25:1,14,34■26:29-M'R-1:14,15■3:24^{2}■4:11,26,30■6:23■9:1,47■10:14,15,23,24,25■11:10■12:34■13:8■14:25■15:43-LU-1:33■4:43■6:20■7:28■8:1,10■9:2,11,27,60,62■10:9,11■11:2,17,18,20■12:31,32■13:18,20,28,29■14:15■16:16■17:20^{2},21■18:16,17,24,25,29■19:11,12,15■21:10,31■22:16,18,29,30■23:42,51-JOH-3:3,5■18:36^{3}-AC-1:3,6■8:12■14:22■19:8■20:25■28:23,31-RO-14:17-1CO-4:20■6:9,10■15:24,50-GA-5:21-EPH-5:5-COL-1:13■4:11-1TH-2:12-2TH-1:5-2TI-4:1,18-HEB-1:8■12:28-JAS-2:5-2PE-1:11-RE-1:9■12:10■16:10■17:12,17

KINGDOMS-all=4467&marked-DE-3:21■28:25-JOS-11:10-1SA-10:18-1KI-4:21-2KI-19:15,19-1CH-29:30-2CH-12:8■17:10■20:6,29■36:23-EZR-1:2-NE-9:22-PS-46:6■68:32■79:6■102:22■135:11-IS-10:10■13:4,19■14:16■23:11,17■37:16,20■47:5-JER-1:10,15■10:7■15:4■24:9■25:26■28:8■29:18■34:1,17■49:28■51:20,27-EZE-29:15■37:22-DA-2:44(4437)■7:23(4437)■8:22(4438)-AM-6:2-NA-3:5-ZEP-3:8-HAG-2:22^{2}■N.T.-all=932-M'T-4:8-LU-4:5-HEB-11:33-RE-11:15^{2}

KINGLY-DA-5:20(4437)

KING'S-all=4428,a=4430-GE-14:17■39:20-NU-20:17■21:22-1SA-18:22,23,25,26,27■20:29■21:8■22:14■23:20■26:16,22-1SA-9:11,13■11:2,8,9,20,24■12:30■13:4,18,23,27,29,30,32,33,35,36■14:1,24,26,28,32■15:15,35■16:2■18:12,18,20,29■19:18,42■24:4-1KI-1:9^{2},25,28,44,47■2:19■4:5■9:1,10■10:12,28■11:14■13:6■14:26,27■15:18■16:18^{2},18■22:12,26-2KI-7:9,11■9:34■10:6,7,8■11:2,4,5,12,16,19,20■12:10,18■13:16■14:14■15:5,25■16:8,15,18■18:15,36■22:12■24:13,15■25:4,9,19-1CH-9:18■21:4,6■25:5,6■27:25,32,33^{2},34■29:6-2CH-1:16■7:11■9:11,21■12:9,10■16:2■18:5,25■19:11■21:17■22:11■23:3,5,11,15,20■24:8,11^{2}■25:16,24■26:11,21■28:7■29:25■31:3■34:20■35:7,10,15-EZR-4:14a■5:17a■6:4a,8a■7:20a,27,28■8:36,36-NE-1:11■2:8,9,14,18■3:15,25■5:4■11:23,24-ES-1:5,12,13,14,18,20,22■2:2,3,8^{2},9,13,14,15,19,21^{2}■3:2,3^{2},8^{2},9,12^{3},13,15■4:2^{2},3,5,6,7,11^{2},13■5:1^{2},9,13■6:2,3,4,5,9,10,12,14■7:4,8,10■8:5,8^{4},9,10,14,17■9:1,4,12,16-PS-45:5,13,15■61:6■72:1■99:4-PR-14:28,35■16:15■19:12■21:1-EC-8:2-IS-36:21-JER-22:6■26:10■36:12■38:7,8■39:4,8■41:10■43:6■52:7,13,25-EZE-17:13(4410)-DA-1:3(4410),4,5,8,13,15■2:10a,14a,15a,23a■3:22a,27a,28a■4:31a■5:5a,6a,8a■6:12a■8:27■11:6-AM-7:1,13,13(4467)-ZEP-1:8-ZEC-14:10■N.T.-AC-12:20(935),20(937)-HEB-11:28(935)

KINGS-all=4428,a=4430&marked-GE-14:5,9,10,17■17:6,16■35:11■36:31-NU-31:8,8-DE-3:8,21■4:47■7:24■31:4-JOS-2:10■5:1^{2}■9:1,10■10:5,6,16,17,22,23,24^{2},40,42■11:2,5,12^{2},17,18■12:1,7,24■24:12-J'G-1:7■5:3,19^{2}■8:5,12,26-1SA-14:47■27:6-2SA-10:19■11:1-1KI-1:t■3:13■4:24,34■10:15,23,29^{2}■14:19,29■15:7,23,31■16:5,14,20,27,33■20:1,12,16^{2},24,31^{2}■22:39,45-2KI-1:t,18■3:10,13,21,23■7:6^{2}■8:18,23■10:4,34■11:19■12:18,19■13:8,12,13■14:15,16,18,28,29■15:6,11,15,21,26,31,36■16:3,19■17:2,8■18:5■19:11,17■20:20■21:17,25■23:5,11,12,19,22^{2},28■24:5■25:28-1CH-1:43■9:1■16:21■19:9■20:1-2CH-1:12,17^{2}■9:14,22,23,26■16:11■20:34■21:6,13,20■24:16,25,27■25:26■26:23■27:7■28:2,16,23,26,27■30:6■32:4,32■33:18■34:11■35:18,27■36:8-EZR-4:13a,15a,19a,20a,22a■6:12a■7:12■9:7^{2},9-NE-9:24,32^{2},34,37-ES-10:2-JOB-3:14■12:18■36:7-PS-2:2,10■48:4■68:12,14,29■72:10^{2},11■76:12■89:27■102:15■105:14,30■110:5■119:46■135:10■136:17,18■138:4■144:10■148:11■149:8-PR-8:15■16:12,13■22:29■25:2,3■31:3,4^{2}-EC-2:8-IS-1:1■7:16■10:8■14:9,18■19:11■24:21■37:11,18■41:2■45:1■49:7,23■52:15■60:3,10,11,16■62:2-JER-1:18■2:26■8:1■13:13■17:19,20,25■19:3,4,13■20:5■22:4■25:14,18,20^{2},22^{2},24^{2},25^{2},26■27:7■32:32■33:4■34:5■44:9,17,21■46:25■50:41■51:11,28■52:32-LA-4:12-EZE-26:7■27:33,35■28:17■32:10,29■43:7^{2},9-DA-2:21a,37a,44a,47a■7:17a,24^{2}a■8:20■9:6,8■10:13■11:2-HO-1:1■7:7■8:4-MIC-1:1,14-HAB-1:10■N.T.-all=935&marked-M'T-10:18■17:25-M'R-13:9LU-0:24■21:12■22:25-AC-4:26■9:15-1TI-2:2■6:15(936)-HEB-7:1-RE-1:5,6■5:10■6:15■10:11■16:12,14■17:2,10,12^{2},14,18■18:3,9■19:16,18,19■21:24

KINGS'-all=4428&marked-PS-45:9-PR-30:28-DA-11:27■N.T.-M'T-11:8(935)-LU-7:25(933)

KINSFOLK-JOB-19:14(7138)■N.T.-LU-2:44(4773)

KINSFOLKS-1KI-16:11(1350)-2KI-10:11(3045)■N.T.-LU-21:16(4773)

KINSMAN-all=1350&marked-NU-5:8■27:11(7607)-RU-2:1(3045)■3:9,12^{2},13^{3}■4:1,3,6,8,■N.T.-JOH-18:26(4773)-RO-16:11(4773)

KINSMAN'S-RU-3:13(1350)

KINSMEN-RU-2:20(1350)-PS-8:11(7138)■N.T.-all=4773-LU-14:12-AC-10:24-RO-9:3■16:7,21

KINSWOMAN-LE-18:12(7067),13(7067)-PR-7:4(4129)

KINSWOMEN-LE-18:17(7608)

KISS-all=5401-GE-27:26■31:28-2SA-20:9-1KI-19:20-PS-2:12-PR-24:26-SONG-1:2■8:1-HO-13:2■N.T.-all=5370&marked-M'T-26:48(5368)-M'R-14:44(5368)-LU-7:45,45(2705)■22:47(5368),48-RO-16:16-1CO-16:20-2CO-13:12-1TH-5:26-1PE-5:14

KISSED-all=5401-GE-27:27■29:11,13■31:55■33:4■45:15■48:10■50:1-EX-4:27■18:7-RU-1:9,14-1SA-10:1■20:41-2SA-14:33■15:5■19:39-1KI-19:18-JOB-31:27-PS-85:10-PR-7:13■N.T.-all=2705-M'T-26:49-M'R-14:45-LU-7:38■15:20-AC-20:37

KISSES-PR-27:6(5390)-SONG-1:2(5390)

KITE-LE-11:14(344)-DE-14:13(344)

KNEAD-GE-18:6(3888)-JER-7:18(3888)

KNEADED-all=3888-1SA-28:24-2SA-13:8-HO-7:4

KNEADINGTROUGHS-EX-8:3(4863)■12:34(4863)

KNEE-IS-45:23(1290)■N.T.-all=1119-RO-11:4■14:11-PH'P-2:10

KNEEL-GE-24:11(1288)-PS-95:6(1288)

KNEELED-2CH-6:13(1288)-DA-6:10(1289)■N.T.-all=5087,1119&marked-M'R-10:17(1120)-LU-22:41-AC-7:60■9:40■20:36■21:5

KNEELING-1KI-8:54(3766)■N.T.-M'T-17:14(1120)-M'R-1:40(1120)

KNEES-all=1290&marked-GE-30:3■48:12■50:33-DE-28:35-J'G-7:5,6■16:19-1KI-8:54■18:42■19:18-2KI-1:13■4:20-2CH-6:13-EZR-9:5-JOB-3:12■4:4-PS-109:24-IS-35:3■66:12-EZE-7:17■21:7■47:4-DA-5:6(755)■6:10(1291)■10:10-NA-2:10■N.T.-all=1119-M'R-15:19-LU-5:8-EPH-3:14-HEB-12:12

KNEW-all=3045,a=5234&marked-GE-3:7■4:1,17,25■8:11■9:24■28:16■31:32■37:33a■38:9,16,26■39:6■42:7a,8a,23-EX-1:8-NU-22:34■24:16-DE-8:16■9:24■29:26■32:17■33:9■34:10-J'G-2:10■3:2■11:39■13:16,21■14:4■18:3a■19:25■20:34-1SA-1:19■2:12■3:20■10:11■14:3■18:28■20:9,33,39^{2}■22:15,17,22■23:9■26:12,17a-2SA-3:26■11:16,20■15:11■18:29■22:44-1KI-1:4■18:7a-2KI-4:39-2CH-33:13-NE-2:16-ES-1:13^{2}a-JOB-2:12a■23:3■29:16■42:3-PS-35:11,15-PR-24:12-IS-42:16,25■48:4(1847),7,8■55:5-JER-1:5■2:8■11:19■32:8■41:4■44:3,15-EZE-10:20■19:7-DA-5:21(3046)■6:10(3046)■11:38-HO-8:4■11:3-JON-1:10■4:2-ZEC-7:14■11:11■N.T.-all=1097,a=1492,b=1921&marked-M'T-1:25■7:23■12:15,25a■17:12b■24:39■25:24■27:18a-M'R-1:34a■6:33b,38,54b■8:17■12:12■15:10,45-LU-2:43■6:8a■7:37b■9:11■12:47,48■18:34■23:7b■24:31b-JOH-1:10,31a,33a■2:9^{2}a,24,25■4:1,53■5:6■6:6a,61a,64a■11:42a,57■12:9■13:1a,11a,28■16:19■18:2a■20:9a,14a■21:4a-AC-3:10b■7:18a■9:30b■12:14b■13:27(50)■16:3a■19:32a,34b■22:29a■26:5(4267)■27:39b■28:1b-RO-1:21-1CO-1:21■2:8-2CO-5:21■12:2a,3a-GA-4:8a-COL-1:6b■2:1a-1JO-3:1-JUDE-5a-RE-19:12a

KNEWEST-all=3045&marked-DE-8:3-RU-2:11-NE-9:10-PS-142:3-IS-48:8-DA-5:22(3046)■N.T.-all=1492&marked-M'T-25:26-LU-19:22,44(1097)-JOH-4:10

KNIFE-all=3979&marked-GE-22:6,10-J'G-19:29-PR-23:2(7915)-EZE-5:1(2719),2(2719)

KNIT-J'G-20:11(2270)-1SA-18:1(7194)-1CH-12:17(3162)■N.T.-AC-10:11(1210)COL-2:2(4822),19(4822)

KNIVES-all=2719&marked-JOS-5:2,3-1KI-18:28-EZR-1:9(4252)-PR-30:14(3979)

KNOCK-all=2925-M'T-7:7-LU-11:9■13:25-RE-3:20

KNOCKED-AC-12:13(2925)

KNOCKETH-SONG-5:2(1849)■N.T.-all=2925-M'T-7:8-LU-11:10■12:36

KNOCKING-AC-12:16(2925)

KNOP-all=3730-EX-25:33^{2},35^{3}■37:19^{2},21^{3}

KNOPS-all=3730&marked-EX-25:31,34,36■37:17,20,22-KI-6:18(6497)■7:24^{2}(6497)

KNOW-all=3045,a=3046&marked-GE-3:5,22■4:9■12:11■15:8,13■18:19,21■19:5■20:6,7■22:12■24:14■27:2■29:5^{2}■31:6■37:32(5234)■42:33,34■43:7■44:27■48:19-EX-3:7■4:14■5:2■6:7■7:5,17■8:10,22■9:14,29,30■10:2,26■11:7■14:4,18■16:6,12■18:11,16■23:9■29:46■31:13■33:5,12^{2},13,17■36:1-LE-23:43-NU-14:31,34■16:28■22:19-DE-3:19■4:35,39■7:9■8:2,3^{2}■11:2■13:3■18:21■22:2■29:6,16■31:21,27,29-JOS-2:9■3:4,

7,10■4:22,24■22:22■23:13,14-J'G-3:2,4■6:37■17:13■18:5,14■19:22-RU-3:11,14(5234),18■4:4-1SA-3:7■6:9■14:38■17:28,46,47■20:3,30■21:2■22:3■23:22■24:11,20■25:11,17■28:1,2■29:9-2SA-3:25^2,38■7:21■14:20■19:20,22■24:2-1KI-2:37,42■3:7■8:38,43^2,60■17:24■18:12,37■20:13,28■22:3-2KI-2:3,5■5:8,15■7:12■8:12■9:11■10:10■17:26^2■19:19,27-1CH-12:32■21:2■28:9■29:17-2CH-2:8■6:29,33^2■12:8■13:5■20:12■25:16■32:13,31-EZR-4:15a■7:25^{2}a-NE-4:11-ES-2:11■4:5,11-JOB-5:24,25,27■7:10(5234)■8:9■9:2,5,21,28■10:13■11:6,8■13:2(1847),2,18,23■15:9■19:6,25,29■21:19,27,29(5234)■22:13■23:5■24:1(2534),13(2534),16,17(2534)■30:23■31:6■32:22■34:4■36:26■37:7,15,16■38:12,20(995)■42:2-PS-4:3■9:10,20■20:6■36:10■39:4^2■41:11■46:10■50:11■51:6■56:9■59:13■71:15■73:11,16■78:6■82:5■83:18■87:4■89:15■100:3■101:4■103:16(5234)■109:27■119:75,125■135:5■139:23^2■140:12■142:4(5234)■143:8-PR-1:2■4:1,19■5:6■10:32■22:21■24:12■27:23■29:7(1847)■30:18-EC-1:17^2■3:12,14■7:25^2■8:12,16,17■9:5^2■11:9-SONG-1:8-IS-1:3■5:19■7:15,16■9:9■19:12,21■37:20,28■41:20,22,23,26■43:10,19■44:8,9■45:3,6■47:8,11^2■48:6■49:23,26■50:4,7■51:7■52:6,6sup■58:2(1847)■59:8^2,12■60:16-JER-2:19,23■5:1,4■6:18,27■7:9■8:7■9:3,6■10:23,25■11:18■13:12■14:18■15:15■16:13,21^2■17:9■22:16(1847),28■24:7■26:15■29:11,23■31:34■36:19■38:24■40:14,15■42:19,22■44:28,29■48:17,30-EZE-2:5■5:13■6:7,10,13,14■7:4,9,27■11:5,10,12■12:15,16,20■13:9,14,21,23■14:8,23■15:7■16:2,62■17:12,21,24■20:4,12,20,26,38,42,44■21:5■22:16,22■23:49■24:24,27■25:5,7,11,14,17■26:6■28:19,22,23,24,26■29:6,9,16,21■30:8,19,25,26■32:15■33:29,33■34:27,30■35:4,9,12,15■36:11,23,36,38■37:6,13,14,28■38:14,16,23■39:6,7,22,23,28-DA-2:3,8a,9a,21a,30a■4:9a,17a,25a,32a■5:23a■6:15a■7:16a,19a■8:19■9:25■11:32-HO-2:8,20■5:3■6:3^2■8:2■9:7■13:4,5■14:9-JOE-2:27■3:17-AM-3:10■5:12-JON-1:7,12-MIC-3:1■4:12■6:5-ZEC-2:9,11■4:9■6:15-MAL-2:4■N.T.-all=1492,a=1097&marked-M'T-6:3a■7:11,16(1921),20(1921)■9:6,30a■13:11a■20:22,25■22:16■24:32a,33a,42,43a■25:12,13■26:2,70,72,74■28:5-M'R-1:24■2:10■4:11a,13,13a■5:43a■7:24a■9:30a■10:38,42■12:14,24■13:28a,29a,33,35■14:68,71-LU-1:4(1921),18a,34a■4:34■5:24■8:10a■9:55■11:13■12:39a■13:25,27■19:15a■20:21■21:20a,30a,31a■22:57,60■23:34■24:16(1921)-JOH-1:26■3:2,11■4:22^2,25,32,42■5:32,42a■6:42■7:17a,26a,27,28^2,29,51a■8:14,19,28a,32a,37a,52,55^3■9:12,20,21^2,24,25^2,29^2,30,31■10:4,5,14a,15a,27a,38a■11:22,24,49■12:50■13:7a,12a,17,18,35a■14:4^2,5,7a,17,20a,31a■15:18a,21■17:3a,23a■18:21■19:4a■20:2,13■21:24-AC-1:7a■2:22,36a■3:16■10:28(1987),37■12:11■15:7(1987)■17:19a,20a■19:15,15(1987),25(1987)■20:18(1987),25,29,34a■21:24a,34a■22:14a,19(1987),24(1921)■24:10(1987),22(1231)■26:4(2467),27■28:22(1110)-RO-3:19■6:3(50),16■7:1(50),1a,14,18■8:22,26,28■10:19a■14:14-1CO-1:16■2:2,12,14a■3:16■4:4(4892) 19a■5:6■6:2,3,9,15,16,19■8:1,2a,4■9:13,24■11:3■12:2■13:9a,12a,12(1921)■14:11■15:58■16:15-2CO-2:4a,9a■5:1,16,16a■8:9a■9:2■13:5(1921),6a-GA-3:7a■4:13-EPH-1:18■3:19a■5:5a■6:21,22a-PH'P-1:19,25■2:19a,22a■3:10■4:12^2,15-COL-4:6,8a-1TH-1:5■2:1,2,5,11■3:3,4,5a■4:2,4,5■5:2,12-2TH-1:8■2:6■3:7-1TI-1:8■3:5,15■4:3(1921)-2TI-1:12■3:1a-TIT-1:16-HEB-8:11a,11■10:30■12:17(2467)■13:23a-JAS-2:20a■4:4,14(1987)■5:20a-1PE-1:18-2PE-1:12■3:17(4267)-1JO-2:3a,4a,5a,18a,20,21^2,29,29a■3:2,5,14,15,19a,24a■4:2a,6a,13a■5:2a,13,15^2,18,19,20,20a-3JO-12-JUDE-10,10(1987)-RE-2:2,9,13,19,23a■3:1,3a,8,9a,15

KNOWEST-all=3045&marked-GE-30:26,29■47:6-EX-10:7■32:22-NU-10:31■11:16■20:14-DE-7:15■9:2■20:20■28:33-JOS-14:6-J'G-15:11-1SA-28:9-2SA-1:5■2:26■3:25■7:20■17:8-1KI-1:18■2:5,9,15,44■5:3,6■8:39^2-2KI-2:3,5■4:1-1CH-17:18-2CH-6:30-JOB-10:7(1847)■15:9■20:4■34:33■38:5,18,21,33■39:1,2-PS-40:9■69:5■139:2,4-PR-27:1-EC-11:2,5^2,6-IS-55:5-JER-5:15■12:3■15:14,15■17:4,16■18:23■33:3-EZE-37:3-DA-10:20-ZEC-4:5,13■N.T.-all=1492&marked-M'T-15:12-M'R-10:19-LU-18:20■22:34-JOH-1:48(1097)■3:10(1097)■13:7■16:30■19:10■21:15,16,17,17(1097)-AC-1:24(2589)■25:10(1921)-RO-2:18(1097)-1CO-7:16^2-2TI-1:15,18(1097)-RE-3:17■7:14

KNOWETH-all=3045&marked-GE-33:13-LE-5:3,4-DE-2:7■34:6-JOS-22:22-1SA-3:13■20:3■23:17-2SA-14:22■17:10-1KI-1:11-ES-4:14-JOB-11:11■12:3(854),9■14:21■15:23■18:21■23:10■28:7,13,23■34:25(5234)■35:15-PS-1:6■37:18■39:6■44:21■74:9■90:11■92:6■94:11■103:14■104:19■138:6■139:14-PR-7:23■9:13,18■14:10■24:22-EC-2:19■3:21■6:8,12■7:22■8:1,7■9:1,12■10:15-IS-1:3■29:15-JER-8:7■9:24-DA-2:22(3046)-HO-7:9^2-JOE-2:14-NA-1:7-ZEP-3:5■N.T.-all=1097,a=1492&marked-M'T-6:8a,32a■11:27^2(1921)■24:36a-M'R-4:27a■13:32a-LU-10:22■12:30a■16:15-JOH-7:15a,27,49■10:15■12:35a■14:17■15:15a■19:35a-AC-15:8(2589)■19:35■26:26(1987)-RO-8:27a-1CO-2:11^{2}a■3:20■8:2a,2■11:11a,31a■12:2,3a-2TI-2:19-JAS-4:17a-2PE-2:9a-1JO-2:11a■3:1,20■4:6,7,8-RE-2:17■12:12a

KNOWING-GE-3:5(3045)-1KI-2:32(3045)■N.T.-all=1492&marked-M'T-9:4■22:29-M'R-5:30(1921),33■6:20■12:15-LU-8:53■9:33■11:17-JOH-13:3■18:4■19:28■21:12-AC-2:30■5:7■18:25(1987)■20:22-RO-1:32(1921)■2:4(50)■5:3■6:6(1097),9■13:11-2CO-1:7■4:14■5:6,11-GA-2:16-EPH-6:8,9-PH'P-1:17-COL-3:24■4:1-1TH-1:4-1TI-1:9■6:4(1987)-2TI-2:23■3:14-TIT-3:11-PH'M-21-HEB-10:34(1097)■11:8(1987)-JAS-1:3(1097)■3:1-1PE-3:9■5:9-2PE-1:14,20(1097)■3:3(1097)

KNOWLEDGE-all=1847,a=3045&marked-GE-2:9,17-EX-31:3■35:31-LE-4:23a,28a-NU-15:24(5869)■24:16-DE-1:39a-RU-2:10(5234),19(5234)-1SA-2:3(1844)■23:23a-1KI-9:27a-2CH-1:10(4093),11(4093),12(4093)■8:18a■30:22(7922)-NE-10:28a-JOB-15:2■21:14,22■33:3■34:2a,35■35:16■36:3(1843),4(1844),12■37:16(1843)■38:2■42:3-PS-14:4a■19:2■53:4a■73:11(1844)■94:10■119:66■139:6■144:3a-PR-1:4,7,22,29■2:3(998),5,6,10■3:20■5:2■8:9,10,12■9:10■10:14■11:9■12:1,23■13:16■14:6,7,18■15:2,7,14■17:27■18:15^2■19:2,25,27■20:15■21:11■22:12,17,20■23:12■24:4,5,14a■28:2a■30:3-EC-1:16,18■2:21,26■7:12■9:10■12:9-IS-5:13■8:4a■11:2,9(1844)■28:9(1844)■32:4■33:6■40:14■44:19,25■45:20a■47:10■53:11■58:3a-JER-3:15(1844)■4:22a■10:14■11:18a■51:17-DA-1:4,17(4093)■2:21(998)■5:12(998)■12:4-HO-4:1,6^2■6:6-HAB-2:14a-MAL-2:7■N.T.-all=1108,a=1922&marked-M'T-14:35(1921)-LU-1:77■11:52-AC-4:13(1921)■17:13(1097)■24:8(1921),22(1492)-RO-1:28a■2:20■3:20a■10:2a■11:33■15:14-1CO-1:5■8:1^2,7,10,11■12:8■13:2,8■14:6■15:34(56)-2CO-2:14■4:6■6:6■8:7■10:5■11:6-EPH-1:17a■3:4(4097),19■4:13a-PH'P-1:9a■3:8-COL-1:9a,10■2:3■3:10a-1TI-2:4a-2TI-3:7a-HEB-10:26a-JAS-3:13(1990)-1PE-3:7-2PE-1:2,3a,5,6,8a■2:20a■3:18

KNOWN-all=3045,a=3046&marked-GE-19:8■24:16■41:21,31■45:1-EX-2:14■6:3■21:36■33:16-LE-4:14■5:1-NU-12:6■31:17,18,35-DE-1:13,15■11:2,28■13:2,6,13■21:1■28:36,64■31:13-JOS-24:31-J'G-3:1■16:9■21:12-RU-3:3,14-1SA-6:3■28:15-2SA-17:19-1KI-14:2■18:36-1CH-16:8■17:19-EZR-4:12a,13a■5:8a-NE-4:15■9:14-ES-2:22-PS-9:16■18:43■31:7■48:3■67:2■69:19■76:1■77:19■78:3,5■79:6,10■88:12■89:1■91:14■95:10■98:2■103:7■105:1■106:8■119:79,152■139,1■145:12■147:20-PR-1:23■10:9■12:16■14:33■20:11(5234)■22:19■31:23-EC-6:5,10-IS-12:5■19:21■38:19■40:21,28■42:16■44:18■45:4,5■61:9■64:2■66:17-JER-4:22■5:5■9:16■19:4■28:9-LA-4:8(5234)-EZE-20:5,9■32:9■35:11■36:32■38:23■39:7-DA-2:5a,9a,15a,17a,23^{2}a,25a,26a,28a,29a,30a,45a■3:18a■4:6a,7a,18a,26a■5:8a,15a,16a,17a-HO-5:4,9-AM-3:2-NA-3:17-HAB-3:2-ZEC-14:7■N.T-all=1097,a=1107&marked-M'T-10:26■12:7,16(5318),33■24:43(1492)-M'R-3:12(5318)-LU-2:15a,17(1232)■6:44■7:39■8:17■12:2,39(1492)■19:42■24:18,35-JOH-8:19^2(1942),55■10:14■14:7,9■15:15a■16:3■17:7,8,25^3■18:15(1110),16(1110)-AC-1:19(1110)■2:14(1110),28a■4:10(1110)■7:13(319),13(5318)■9:24,42(1110)■13:38(1110)■15:18(1110)■19:17(1110)■22:30■23:28■28:28(1110)-RO-1:19(1110)■3:17■7:7,7(1492)■9:22a,23a■11:34■16:26a-1CO-2:8,16■8:3■13:12(1921)■14:7,9-2CO-3:2■5:16■6:9(1921)-GA-4:9^2-EPH-1:9a■3:3a,5a,10a■6:19a,21a-PH'P-4:5,6a-COL-1:27a■4:9a-2TI-3:10(3877),15(1492)■4:17(4135)-HEB-3:10-2PE-1:16a■2:21^2(1921)-1JO-2:13^2,14■3:6■4:16-2JO-1-RE-2:24

L

LABOUR-all=5999,a=3018&marked-GE-31:42a■35:16(3205),17(3205)-EX-5:9(6213)■20:9(5647)-DE-5:13(5647)■26:7-JOS-7:3(3021)■24:13(3021)-NE-4:22(4399)-JOB-9:29(3021)■39:11a,16a-PS-78:46a■90:10■104:23(5656)■105:44■107:12■109:11a■127:1(5998)■128:2a■144:14(5445)-PR-10:16(6468)■13:11(3027)■14:23(6089)■21:25(6213)■23:4(3021)-EC-1:3,8(3023)■2:10^2,11,18,19,20,21,22,24■3:13■4:8,8(6001),9■5:15,18,19■6:7■8:15,17(5998)■9:9■10:15-IS-22:4(213)■45:14a■55:2a■65:23(3021)-JER-3:24a■20:18■51:58(3021)-LA-5:5(3021)-EZE-23:29a■29:20(6468)-MIC-4:10(1518)-HAB-2:13(3021)■3:17(4639)-HAG-1:11(3018)■N.T.-all=2872&marked-M'T-11:28-JOH-4:38■6:27(2038)-RO-16:6,12-1CO-3:8(2873)■4:12■15:58(2873)-2CO-5:9(5389)-GA-4:11-EPH-4:28-PH'P-1:22(2041)■2:25(4904)-COL-1:29-1TH-1:3(2873)■2:9(2873)■3:5(2873)■5:12-2TH-3:8(2873)-1TI-4:10■5:17-HEB-4:11(4704)■6:10(2873)-RE-2:2(2873)

LABOURED-all=5998&marked-NE-4:21(6213)-JOB-20:18(3022)-EC-2:11,19,21,22(6001)■5:16-IS-47:12(3021),15(3021)■49:4(3021)■62:8(3021)-DA-6:14(7712)-JON-4:10■N.T.-all=2872&marked-JOH-4:38-RO-16:12-1CO-15:10-PH'P-2:16■4:3(4866)-RE-2:3

LABOURER-LU-10:7(2040)-1TI-5:18(2040)

LABOURERS-all=2040&marked-M'T-9:37,38■20:1,2,8-LU-10:2^2-1CO-3:9(4904)-JAS-5:4

LABOURETH-PR-16:26(6001),26(5998)-EC-3:9(6001)■N.T.-1CO-16:16(2872)-2TI-2:6(2872)

LABOURING-EC-5:12(5647)■N.T.-AC-29:35(2872)-COL-4:12(75)-1TH-2:9(2873)

LABOURS-all=3018&marked-EX-23:16^{2}(4639),16(4639)-DE-28:33-PR-5:10(6089)-IS-58:3(6092)-JER-20:5-HO-12:8-HAG-2:17(4639)■N.T.-all=2873-JOH-4:38-2CO-6:5■10:15■11:23-RE-14:13

LACE-all=6616-EX-28:28,37■39:21,31

LACK-all=2637&marked-GE-18:28-EX-16:18-DE-8:9-JOB-4:11(1097)■38:41(1097)-PS-34:10(7326)-PR-28:27(4270)-EC-9:8(2637)-HO-4:6(1097)■N.T.-M'T-19:20(5302)-2CO-8:15(1641)-PH'P-2:30(5303)-1TH-4:12(5332)-JAS-1:5(3007)

LACKED-DE-2:7(2637)-2SA-2:30(6485)■17:22(5737)-1KI-4:27(5737)■11:22(2638)-NE-9:21(2637)■N.T.-LU-8:6(3361,2192)■22:35(5302)-AC-4:34(1729)-1CO-12:24(5302)-PH'P-4:10(170)

LACKEST-M'R-10:21(5302)-LU-18:22(3007)

LACKETH-all=2638&marked-NU-31:49(6485)-2SA-3:29-PR-6:32■12:9-2PE-1:9(3361,3918)

LACKING-LE-2:13(7673)■22:23(7038)-J'G-21:3(6485)-1SA-30:19(5737)-JER-23:4(6485)■N.T.-all=5303-1CO-16:17-2CO-11:9-1TH-3:10

LAD-all=5288-GE-21:12,17^{2},18,19,20■22:5,12■37:2■43:8■44:22,30,31,32,33^{2},34-J'G-16:26-1SA-20:21^{2},35,36^{2},37^{2},38^{2},39,40,41-2SA-17:18-2KI-4:19■N.T.-JOH-6:9(3808)

LADDER-GE-28:12(5551)

LADE-GE-45:17(2943)-1KI-12:11(6006)■N.T.-LU-11:46(5412)

LADED-GE-42:26(5375)■44:13(6006)-NE-4:17(6006)■N.T.-AC-28:10(2007)

LADEN-GE-45:23^{2}(5375)-IS-1:4(3515)■N.T.-M'T-11:28(5412)-2TI-3:6(4987)

LADETH-HAB-2:6(3515)

LADIES-J'G-5:29(8282)-ES-1:18(8282)

LADING-NE-13:15(6006)■N.T.-AC-27:10(5414)

LAD'S-GE-44:30(5288)

LADS-GE-48:16(5288)

LADY-IS-47:5(1404),7(1404)■N.T.-2JO-1(2959,5(2959)

LAID-all=7760,a=7901,b=5414&marked-GE-9:23■15:10b■22:6,9sup,9■38:19(5493)■39:16(3241)■41:48^{2}b■48:14(7896),17(7896)-EX-2:3■5:9(3515)■16:24(3241),34(3241)■19:7■21:30(7896),30(7896)■24:11(7971)-LE-8:14(5564),18(5564),22(5564)-NU-16:18■17:7(3241)■27:23(5564)-DE-26:6b■29:22(2470)■32:34(3647)■34:9(5564)-JOS-2:8a■4:8(3241)■7:23(3332)■10:27-J'G-9:24,48-RU-3:7a,15(7896)■4:16(7896)-1SA-3:2a,3a■6:11■10:25(3241)■15:2■19:13■21:12■25:18-2SA-13:8a,19■18:17(5324)-1KI-3:20^{2}a■8:31(5375)■13:29(3241),30(3241)■17:19a■18:33■19:6a■21:4a-2KI-4:21a,31,32a■5:23b■9:25(5375)■11:16■12:11(3318),12(3318)■20:7-2CH-6:22(5375)■16:14a■23:15■29:23(5564)■31:6b-EZR-5:8,16(3052)■6:1(5182),3(5446)-NE-13:5b-ES-8:7(7971)■9:10(7971),15(7971),16(7971)■10:1-JOB-6:2(5375)■29:9■38:5,6(3384)-PS-3:5a■21:5(7737)■31:4(2934),19(6845)■49:14(8371)■62:9(5927)■79:1■88:6(7896)■89:19(7737)■104:18(935)■119:30(7737),110b■139:5(7896)■141:9(3369)■142:3(2934)-PR-13:22(6845)-SONG-7:13(6845)-IS-6:7(5060)■10:28(6485)■14:8a■15:7(6486)■23:18(2630)■42:25■51:23■53:6(6293)■57:11-JER-36:20(6485)-EZE-4:5b■11:7■32:19a,27b,29b,32a■33:29b■39:21■40:42(3240)-DA-6:17-HO-11:4(5186)-JOE-1:7-OB-7,13(7971)-JON-3:6(5674)-MIC-5:1-HAB-2:19(8610)-HAG-2:15-ZEC-3:9b■7:14-MAL-1:3■N.T.-all=5087,a=2007&marked-M'T-3:10(2749)■8:14(906)■19:15a■26:50(1911)■27:60-M'R-6:5a,29,56■7:30(906)■14:46(1911)■15:46(2698),47■16:6-LU-1:66■2:7(347)■3:9(2749)■4:40a■6:48■12:19(2749)■13:13a■14:29■16:20(906)■19:20(606),22■23:26sup,26a,53,53(2749),55■24:12(2749)-JOH-7:30(1911),44(1911)■11:34,41(2749)■13:4■19:41,42■20:2,13,15■21:9(1945)-AC-3:2■4:3(1911),35,37■5:2,15,18(1911)■6:6a■7:16,58(659)■8:17a■9:37■13:3a,29,36(4639)■16:23a■19:6a■20:3(1096)■21:27(1911)■23:29(1462),30(2071)■25:7(5242),16(1462)■28:3a,8a-RO-16:4(5294)-1CO-3:10,11■9:16(1945)-COL-1:5(606)-2TI-4:8(606),16(3049)-1JO-3:16-RE-1:17a

LAIDST-PS-66:11(7760)

LAIN-NU-5:19(7901),20(5414,7903)-J'G-21:11(3045,4904)-JOB-3:13(7901)■N.T.-JOH-20:12(2749)

LAKE-all=3041-LU-5:1,2■8:22,23,33-RE-19:20■20:10,14,15■21:8

LAMA-M'T-27:46(2982)-M'R-15:34(2982)

LAMB-all=3532,a=7716&marked-GE-22:7a,8a-EX-12:3^{2}a,4^{2}a,5a,21(6629)■13:13a■29:39^{2},40,41■34:20a-LE-3:7(3775)■4:32,35(3775)■5:6(3776),7(7716)■9:3■12:6,8(7716)■14:10(3535),12,13,21,24,25■17:3(3775)■22:23(7716)■23:12-NU-6:12,14,14(3535)■7:15,21,27,33,39,45,51,57,63,69,75,81■15:5,11a■28:4^{2},7,8,13,14,21,29■29:4,10,15-1SA-7:9(2924)■17:34a-2SA-12:3(3535),4(3535),6(3535)-IS-11:6■16:1(3733)■53:7a■65:25(2924)■66:3-JER-11:19-EZE-45:15a■46:13,15-HO-4:16■N.T.-all=721&marked-JOH-1:29(286)-AC-8:32(286)-1PE-1:19(286)-RE-5:6,8,12,13■6:1,16■7:9,10,14,17■12:11■13:8,11■14:1,4^{2},10■15:3■17:14^{2}■19:7,9■21:14,22,23■22:1,3

LAMB'S-RE-21:9(721),27(721)

LAMBS-all=3532&marked-GE-21:28(3535)■21:29(3535),30(3535)■30:40(3775)-EX-29:38-LE-14:10■23:18,19,20-NU-7:17,23,29,35,41,47,53,59,65,71,77,83,87,88■28:3,9,11,19,21,27,29■29:2,4,8,10,13,15,17,18,20,21,23,24,26,27,29,30,32,33,36,37-DE-32:14(3733)-1SA-15:9(3733)-2KI-3:4(3733)-1CH-29:21-2CH-29:21,22,32■35:7-EZR-6:9(563),17(563)■7:17■8:35-PS-37:20(3733)■114:4(1121,6629),6(1121,6629)-PR-27:26-IS-1:11■5:17■34:6(3733)■40:11(2922)-JER-51:40(3733)-EZE-27:21(3733)■39:18(3733)■46:4,5,6,7,11-AM-6:4(3733)■N.T.-LU-10:3(704)-JOH-21:15(721)

LAME-all=6455&marked-LE-21:18-DE-15:21-2SA-4:4(5223),4(6452)■5:6,8^{2}■9:3(5223)■19:26-JOB-29:15-PR-26:7-IS-33:23■35:6-JER-31:8-MAL-1:8,13■N.T.-all=5560-M'T-11:5■15:30,31■21:14-LU-7:22■14:13-AC-3:2,11■8:7-HEB-12:13

LAMENT-all=5594&marked-J'G-11:40(8567)-IS-3:26(578)■19:8(56)■32:12-JER-4:8■16:5,6■22:18^{2}■34:5■49:3-LA-2:8(56)-EZE-27:32(6969)■32:16^{3}(6969)-JOE-1:8(421),13-MIC-2:4(5091)■N.T.-JOH-16:20(2354)-RE-18:9(2875)

LAMENTABLE-DA-6:20(6088)

LAMENTATION-all=7015&marked-GE-50:10(4553)-2SA-1:17-PS-78:64(1058)-JER-6:26(4553)■7:29■9:10,20■31:15(5092)■48:38(4553)-LA-2:5(592)-EZE-19:1,14■26:17■27:2,32■28:12■32:2,16-AM-5:1,16(5092)■8:10-MIC-2:4(5092)■N.T.-M'T-2:18(2355)-AC-8:2(2870)

LAMENTATIONS-all=7015-2CH-35:25^{2}-EZE-2:10

LAMENTED-all=5594&marked-1SA-6:19(56)■7:2(5091)■25:1■28:3-2SA-1:17(6969)■3:33(6969)-2CH-35:25(6969)-JER-16:4■25:33■N.T.-M'T-11:17(2875)-LU-23:27(2354)

LAMP-all=5216&marked-GE-15:17(3940)-EX-27:20-1SA-3:3-2SA-22:29-1KI-15:4-JOB-12:5(3940)-PS-19:1105■132:17-PR-6:23■13:9■20:20-IS-62:1(3940)■N.T.-RE-8:10(2985)

LAMPS-all=5216&marked-EX-25:37^{2}■30:7,8■35:14■37:23■39:37^{2}■40:4,25-LE-24:2,4-NU-4:9■8:2^{2},3-J'G-7:16(3940),20(3940)-1KI-7:49-1CH-28:15^{3}-2CH-4:20,21■13:11■29:7-JOB-41:19(3940)-EZE-1:13(3940)-DA-10:6(3940)-ZEC-4:2^{2}■N.T.-all=2895-M'T-25:1,3,4,7,8-RE-4:5

LANCE-JER-50:42(3591)

LANCETS-1KI-18:28(7420)

LAND-all=776,a=127&marked-GE-2:11,12,13■4:16■10:10,11■11:2,28,31■12:1,5^{2},6^{2},7,10^{2}■13:6,7,9,10,12,15,17■15:7,13,18■16:3■17:8^{2}■19:28■20:15■21:21,23,32,34■22:2■23:2,7,12,13,15,19■24:5^{2},7^{2},37■26:1,2,3,12,22■27:46■28:4,13,15a■29:1■31:3,13^{2},18■32:3■33:18■34:1,10,21^{2},30■35:6,12^{2},22■36:5,6,7,16,17,20,21,30,31,34,43■37:1^{2}■40:15■41:19,29,30^{2},31,33,34^{2},36^{2},41,43,44,45,46,48,52,53,54,55,56■42:5,6^{2},7,9,12,13,29,30,32,34■43:1,11■44:8■45:6,8,10,17,18^{2},19,20,25,26■46:6,12,20,28,31,34■47:1^{2},4^{3},6^{3},11^{2},13^{3},14^{2},15^{2},19^{4}a,20a,20,22a,23^{2}a,26^{2}a,27,28■48:3,4,5,7,21■49:15,30■50:5,7,8,11,13,24^{2}-EX-1:7,10■2:15,22■3:8^{2},17^{2}■4:20■5:5,12■6:1,4^{2},8,11,13,26,28■7:2,3,4,19,21■8:5,6,7,14,16^{2},17^{2},22,24^{2},25■9:5,9^{2},22^{2},23,24,25,26■10:12^{3},13^{2},14,15^{3},21,22■11:3,5,6,9,10■12:1,12^{2},13,17,19,25,29,33,41,42,48,51■13:5^{2},11,15,17,18■14:3■16:1,3,6,32,35^{2}■18:3,27■19:1■20:2,12a■22:21■23:9,10,19a,26,29,30,31,33■29:46■32:1,4,7,8,11,13,23■33:1^{2},3■34:12,15,24,26a-LE-11:45■14:34^{2}■16:22■18:3^{2},25^{2},27^{2},28■19:9,23,29^{2},33,34,36■20:2,4,22,24a,24■22:24,33■23:10,22,39,43■24:16(249)■25:2^{2},4,5,6,7,9,10,18,19,23^{2},24^{2},38^{2},42,45,55■26:1,4,5,6^{3},13,20^{2},32,33,34^{3},38,41,42,43,44,45■27:24,30^{2}-NU-1:1■3:13■8:17■9:1,14■10:9,30■11:12a■13:2,16,17,18,19,20^{2},21,25,26,27,28,29,32^{3}■14:2,3,6,7^{2},8^{2},9,14,16,23,24,30,31,34,36^{2},37,38■15:2,18,19,30(249)41■16:13,14■18:13,20■20:12,23,24■21:4,22,24,26,31,34,35■22:5,6,13■26:4,19,53,55■27:12■32:1^{2},4,5,7,8,9^{2},11a,17,22^{2},29^{2},30,32,33■33:1,37,38,40,51,52,53^{2},54,55^{2}■34:2^{3},12,13,17,18,29■35:10,14,28,32,33^{3},34■36:2-DE-1:5,7,8^{2},21,22,25^{2},27,35,36■2:5,9,12,19,20,24,27,29,31^{2},37■3:2,8,12,13,18,20,25,28■4:1,5,14,21,22^{2},25,26,38,46,47■5:6,15,16a,31,33■6:1,3,10,12,18,23■7:1,13^{2}a■8:1,7,8^{2},9^{2},10,14■9:4,5,6,7,23,28^{2}■10:7,11,19■11:3,8,9a,9,10^{2},11^{2},12,14,17a,17,21a,25,29,30,31■12:1,10,29■13:5,10■15:4,7,11^{2},15■16:3^{2},20■17:14■18:9■19:1,2,3,8,10,14■20:1■21:1a,23a■23:7,20■24:4,14,22■25:15a,19■26:1,2,9^{2},10a,15a,15■27:2,3^{2}■28:8,11a,12,18a,21a,24,33a,42a,51a,52^{2},63a■29:1,2^{2},8,16,22^{2},23,24,25,27,28a,28■30:5,9a,16,18a,20a■31:4,7,13a,16,20a,21,23■32:10,43a,47a,49^{2},52^{2}■33:13,28■34:1,2^{2},4,5,6,11^{2}-JOS-1:2,4,6,11,13,14,15^{2}■2:1,9^{2},14,18,24■5:6^{2},11,12^{2}■7:9■8:1■9:24^{2}■10:42■11:3,16^{2},22,23^{2}■12:1^{2}■13:1,2,4,5,7,25■14:1,4,5,7,9,15■15:19■17:5,6,8,12,15,16■18:1,3,4,6,8^{2},9,10■19:49■21:2,43■22:4,9^{2},10,11,13,15,19^{2},32^{2},33■23:5,13a,15a,16■24:3,8^{2},13,15,17,18-J'G-1:2,15,26,27,32,33■2:1,2,6,12■3:11,30■5:31■6:5,9,10■9:37■10:4,8■11:3,5,12,13,15^{2},17,18^{2},19,21■12:15■18:2^{2},7,9^{2},10,17,30■19:30■20:1■21:12,21-RU-1:1,7■2:11■4:3(7704)-1SA-6:5^{2}■9:4^{3},5,16■12:6■13:3,7,17,19■14:14(7704),25,29■21:11■22:5■23:23,27■27:1,8^{2},9■28:3,9■29:11■30:16^{2}■31:9-2SA-3:12■5:6■7:23■9:7(7704),10a■10:2■

15:4■17:26■19:9,29(7704)■21:14■24:6,8,13^{2},25-1KI-4:10,19,21■6:1■8:9,21,34a,36,37^{2},40a,46,47^{2},48^{2}■9:7a,8,9,11,13,18,19,21,26■10:6■11:18■12:28■14:15a,24■15:12,20■17:7■18:5,6■20:7■22:46-2KI-3:27■4:38■5:2,4■6:23■8:1,2,3,3(7704),5(7704),6■10:33■11:3,14,18,19,20■13:20■15:5,19,20,29■16:15■17:5,7,23a,26^{2},27,36■18:25,32^{4},33■19:7^{2},37■21:8a,24^{2}■23:24,30,33^{2},35^{2}■24:7,14,15■25:3,12,19^{2},21,21a,22,24-1CH-1:43,45■2:22■4:40■5:9,11,23,25■6:55■7:21■10:9■11:4■13:2■16:18■19:2,3■21:12■22:2,18^{2}■28:8-2CH-2:17■6:5,25a,27,28^{2},31a,36,37^{2},38^{2}■7:13,14,20a,21,22■8:6,8,17■9:5,11,12,26■14:1,6,7■15:8■17:2■19:3,5■20:7,10■22:12■23:13,20,21■26:21■30:9,25■32:4,21,31■33:8a,25^{2}■34:7,8■36:1,3,21-EZR-4:4■6:21■9:11^{2},12■10:2,11-NE-4:4■5:14,16(7704)■9:8,10,15,22^{3},23,24^{3},25a,35,36■10:30,31-ES-8:17■10:1-JOB-1:1,10■10:21,22■28:13■31:38a■37:13■42:15-PS-10:16■27:13■35:20■37:3,29,34■42:6■44:3■52:5■63:1■66:6■74:8■78:12■80:9■81:5,10■85:1,9,12■88:12■101:6,8■105:11,16,23,27,30,32,35,36■106:22,24,38■107:34■116:9■135:12■136:21,137:4a■142:5■143:6,10-PR-2:21■12:11a■28:2,19a■29:4■31:23-EC-10:16,17-SONG-2:12-IS-1:7a,19■2:7^{2},8■5:30■6:11a,12■7:16a,18,22,24■8:8■9:1^{2},2,19■10:23■11:16■13:5,9,14■14:1a,2a,20,21,25■15:9a■16:1,4■18:1,2,7■19:17a,18,19,20,24■21:1,14■23:1,10,13■24:3,11,13■26:1,10■27:13^{2}■30:6■32:2,13a■33:17■34:6,7,9■36:10^{2},17^{2},18,20■37:7^{2},38■38:11■41:18■49:12,19■53:8■57:13■60:18,21■61:7■62:4^{3}-JER-1:1,14,18^{2}■2:2,6^{4},7,15,31■3:1,2,9,16,18^{2},19■4:5,7,20,27■5:19^{2},30■6:8,12■7:7,22,25,34■8:16^{2}■9:12,19■10:17,18■11:4,5,7,19■12:4,5,11,12^{2},14a,15■13:13■14:8,15,18■15:7,14■16:3,6,13^{2},14,15,15a,18■17:4,6,26■18:16■22:12,27,28■23:7,8a,10^{2},15■24:5,6,8^{2},10a■25:5a,9,11,12,13,20^{2},38■26:17,20■27:7,10a,11a■30:3,10■31:16,23,32■32:15,20,21,22^{2},41,43,44■33:11,13,15■34:13,19■35:7a,11,15a■36:29■37:1,2,7,12,19■39:5,10■40:4,6,7^{2},9,12■41:2,18■42:10,12a,13,14,16■43:4,5,7,11,12,13■44:1,8,9,12^{2},13,14^{2},15,21,22,24,26^{2},27,28^{2}■45:4■46:12,13,16,27■47:2^{2}■48:24,33■50:1,3,8,16,18,21,22,25,28,34,38,45■51:2,4,5,27,28,29^{2},43^{2},46^{2},47,52,54■52:6,9,16,25^{2},27^{2}a-LA-4:21-EZE-1:3■6:14■7:2a,2,7,23,28■8:17■9:9■11:15,17a■12:13,19a,19^{2},20,22a■13:9a■14:13,15,16,17^{2},19■15:8■16:3,29■17:4,5,13■18:2a■19:4,7■20:5,6,8,9,10,15,28,36,38a,40,42a■21:2a,3a,19,30,32■22:24,29,30■23:15,19,27,48■25:3a,6a■26:20■27:17,29■28:25a■29:9,10,14^{2},19,20■30:5,11^{2},12^{2},13^{2},25■31:12■32:4,6,8,15,23,24,25,26,27,32■33:2^{2},3,24a,24^{2},25,26,28,29■34:13a,25,27a,28,29■36:5,6a,17a,18,20,24a,28,34,35■37:12a,14a,21a,22,25■38:2,8,9,11,12,16^{2},18a,19a■39:12,13,14,15,16,26,28■40:2■45:1^{2},4,8^{2},16,22■46:3,9■47:13,14,15,18,21■48:12,14,29-DA-1:2■9:6,15■11:9a,16,19,28^{2},39a,41,42-HO-1:2,11■2:3,15■4:1^{2},3■7:16■9:3■10:1■11:5,11■12:9■13:4,5-JO-1:2,6,10a,14■2:1,3,18,20,21a■3:2,19-AM-2:10^{2}■3:1,9,11■5:2a■7:2,10,11a,12,17^{3}a■8:4,8,11■9:5,7,15^{2}a-JON-1:13(3004)-MIC-5:5,6^{3},11■6:4■7:13,15-NA-3:13-HAB-1:6■2:8,17■3:7,12-ZEP-1:2a,3a,18^{2}■2:5■3:19-HAG-1:11■2:4-ZEC-1:21■2:6,12a■3:9■5:11■7:5,14^{2}■9:1,16a■10:10^{2}■11:6^{2},16■12:12■13:2^{2},8■14:10-MAL-3:12■**N.T.**-all=1093,&marked-M'T-2:6,20,21■4:15^{2}■9:26■10:15■11:24■14:34■23:15(3584)■27:45-M'R-1:5(5561)■4:1■6:47,53■15:33-LU-4:25■5:3,11■8:27■14:35■15:14(5561)■21:23-JOH-3:22■6:21■21:8,9,11-AC-4:37(68)■5:3(5564),8(5564)■7:3,4^{2},6,11,29,36,40■10:39(5561)■13:17,19^{2}■27:39,43,44-HEB-8:9■11:9-JUDE-5

LANDED-AC-18:22(2718)■21:3(2609)

LANDING-AC-28:12(2609)

LANDMARK-all=1366-DE-19:14■27:17-PR-22:28■23:10

LANDMARKS-JOB-24:2(1367)

LANDS-all=776&marked-GE-10:5,31■41:54,57■47:18(127),22(127)-LE-26:36,39-2KI-19:11,17-1CH-14:17-2CH-9:28■13:9■17:10■32:13^{3},17-EZR-9:1,2,7,11-NE-5:3(7704),4(7704),5(7704),11(7704)■9:30■10:28-PS-49:11(127)■66:1■100:1■105:44■106:27■107:3-IS-36:20■37:11-JER-16:15■27:6-EZE-20:6,15■39:27■**N.T.**-all=68&marked-M'T-19:29-M'R-10:29,30-AC-4:34(5564)

LANES-LU-14:21(4505)

LANGUAGE-all=3956&marked-GE-11:1(8193),6(8193),7(8193),9(8193)-NE-13:24sup,24-ES-1:22^{2}■3:12■8:9^{2}-PS-19:3(1697)■81:5(8193)■114:1(3937)-IS-19:18(8193)-JER-5:15-EZE-3:5,6-DA-3:29(3961)-ZEP-3:9(8193)■**N.T.**-AC-2:6(1258)

LANGUAGES-all=3691&marked-DA-3:4,7■4:1■5:19■6:25■7:14-ZEC-8:23(3956)

LANGUISH-all=535-IS-16:8■19:8■24:4-JER-14:2-HOS-4:3

LANGUISHED-LA-2:8(535)

LANGUISHETH-all=535-IS-24:4,7■33:9-JER-15:9-JOE-1:10,12-NA-1:4^{2}

LANGUISHING-PS-41:3(1741)

LANTERNS-JOH-18:3(5322)

LAP-2KI-4:39(899)-NE-5:13(2684)-PR-16:33(2436)

LAPPED-J'G-7:6(3952),7(3952)

LAPPETH-J'G-7:5^{2}(3952)

LAPWING-LE-11:19(1744)-DE-14:18(1744)

LARGE-all=7342&marked-GE-34:21-EX-3:8-J'G-18:10(7342,3027)-2SA-22:20(4800)-NE-4:19■7:4(7342,3027)■9:35-PS-18:19(4800)■31:8(4800)■118:5(4800)-IS-22:18(7342,3027)■30:23(7337),33(7337)-JER-22:14(7304)-EZE-23:32-HOS-4:16(4800)■**N.T.**-M'T-28:12(2425)-M'R-14:15(3173)-LU-22:12(3173)-GA-6:11(4080)-RE-21:16(5118)

LARGENESS-1KI-4:29(7341)

LASCIVIOUSNESS-all=766-M'R-7:22-2CO-12:21-GA-5:19-EPH-4:19-1PE-4:3-JUDE-4

LAST-all=314,a=319&marked-GE-49:1a,19(6119)-NU-23:10a-2SA-19:11,12■23:1-1CH-23:27■29:29-2CH-9:29■12:15■16:11■20:34■25:26■26:22■28:26■35:27-EZR-8:13-NE-8:18-PR-5:11a■23:32a-IS-2:2a■41:4■44:6■48:12-JER-12:4a■50:17-LA-1:9a-DA-4:8(318)■8:3,19a-AM-9:1a-MIC-4:1a■**N.T.**-all=2078-M'T-12:45■19:30^{2}■20:8,12,14,16■21:37(5305)■22:27(5305)■26:60(5305)■27:64-M'R-9:35■10:31■12:6,22-LU-11:26■12:59■13:30^{2}■20:32(5305)-JOH-6:39,40,44,54■7:37■8:9■11:24■12:48-AC-2:17-1CO-4:9■15:8,26,45,52-PH'P-4:10(4218)-2TI-3:1-HEB-1:2-JAS-5:3-1PE-1:5,20-2PE-3:3-1JO-2:18^{2}-JUDE-18-RE-1:11,17■2:8,19■15:1■21:9■22:13

LASTED-J'G-14:17(1961)

LASTING-DE-33:15(5769)

LATCHET-IS-5:27(8288)■**N.T.**-all=2438-M'R-1:7-LU-3:16-JOH-1:27

LATE-PS-127:2(309)-MIC-2:8(865)■**N.T.**-JOH-11:8(3568)

LATELY-AC-18:2(4373)

LATIN-LU-23:38(4513)-JOH-19:20(4513)

LATTER-all=319&marked-EX-4:8(314)-NU-24:14,20-DE-4:30■8:16■11:14(4456)■24:3^{2}(314)■31:29■32:29-RU-3:10(314)-2SA-2:26(314)-JOB-8:7■19:25(314)■29:23(4456)■42:12-PR-16:15(4456)■19:20-IS-41:22■47:7-JER-3:3(4456)■5:24(4456)■23:20■30:24■48:47■49:39-EZE-38:8,16-DA-2:28(320)■8:23■10:14■11:29-HO-3:5■6:3(4456)-JOE-2:23(4456)-AM-7:1^{2}(3954)-HAG-2:9(314)-ZEC-10:1(4456)■**N.T.**-1TI-4:1(5305)-JAS-5:7(3797)-2PE-2:20(2078)

LATTICE-J'G-5:28(822)-2KI-1:2(7639)-SONG-2:9(2762)

LAUD-RO-15:11(1867)

LAUGH-all=7832&marked-GE-18:13(6711),15(6711)■21:6(6712),6(6711)-JOB-5:22■9:23(3932)■22:19(3932)-PS-2:4■22:7(3932)■37:13■52:6■59:8■80:6(3932)-PR-1:26■29:9-EC-3:4■**N.T.**-LU-6:21(1070),25(1070)

LAUGHED-all=6711&marked-GE-17:17■18:12,15-2KI-19:21(3932)-2CH-30:10(7832)-NE-2:19(3932)-JOB-12:4(7832)■29:24(7832)-IS-37:22(3932)-EZE-23:32(6712)■**N.T.**-all=2606-M'T-9:24-M'R-5:40-LU-8:53

LAUGHETH-JOB-41:29(7832)

LAUGHING-JOB-8:21(7814)

LAUGHTER-all=7814-PS-126:2-PR-14:13-EC-2:2■7:3,6■10:19■**N.T.**-JAS-4:9(1071)

LAUNCH-LU-5:4(1877)

LAUNCHED-all=321-LU-8:22-AC-21:1■27:2,4

LAVER-all=3595-EX-30:18,28■31:9■35:16■38:8■39:39■40:7,11,30-LE-8:11-1KI-7:30,38^{3}-2KI-16:17

LAVERS-all=3595-1KI-7:38,40,43-2CH-4:6,14

LAVISH-IS-46:6(2107)

LAW-all=8451,a=2859&marked-GE-11:31(3618)■19:12a,14^{2}a■38:11(3618),13(2524),16(3618),24(3618),25(2524)■47:26(2706)-EX-3:1a■4:18a■12:49■13:9■16:4■18:1a,2a,5a,6a,7a,8a,12^{2}a,14a,15a,17a,24a,27a■24:12-LE-6:9,14,25■7:1,7,11,37■11:46■12:7■13:59■14:2,32,54,57■15:32■18:15(3618)■20:12(3618)■24:22(4941)-NU-5:29,30■6:13,21^{2}■10:29a■15:16,29■19:2,14■31:21-DE-1:5■4:8,44■17:11,18,19■27:3,8,23a,26■28:58,61■29:21,29■30:10■31:9,11,12,24,26■32:46■33:2(1881),4,10-JOS-1:7,8■8:31,32,34^{2}■22:5■23:6■24:26-J'G-1:16a■4:11a■15:6a■19:4a,5a,7a,9a-RU-1:6(3618),7(3618),8(3618),14(2545),15^{2}(2994),22(3618)■2:11(2545),18(2545),19^{2}(2545),20(3618),22(3618),23(2545)■3:1(2545),6(2545),16(2545),17(2545)■4:15(3618)-1SA-4:19(3618),19(2524),21(2524)■18:18a,21(2860),22(2860),23(2860),26(2860),27(2860)■22:14a-1KI-2:3-2KI-8:27a■10:31■14:6■17:13,34,37■21:8■22:8,11■23:24,25-1CH-2:4(3618)■16:17(2706),40■22:12-2CH-6:16■12:1■14:4■15:3■17:9■19:10■23:18■25:4■30:16■31:3,4,21■33:8■34:14,15,19■35:26-EZR-3:2■7:6,10,12(1882),14(1882),21(1882),26^{2}(1882)■10:3-NE-6:18a■8:1,2,3,7,8,9,13,14,18■9:3,26,29,34■10:28,29,34,36■12:44■13:3,28a-ES-1:8(1881),13(1881),15(1881)■4:11(1881),16(1881)-JOB-22:22-PS-1:2^{2}■19:7■37:31■40:8,78:1,5,10■81:4(4941)■89:30■94:12,20(2706)■105:10(2706)■119:1,18,29,34,44,51,53,55,61,70,72,77,85,92,97,109,113,126,136,142,150,153,163,165,174-PR-1:8■3:1■4:2■6:20,23■7:2■13:14■28:4^{2},7,9■29:18■31:5(2710),26-IS-1:10■2:3■5:24■8:16,20■30:9■42:4,21,24■51:4,7-JER-2:8■6:19■8:8■9:13■16:11■18:18■26:4■31:33■32:11(4687),23■44:10,23-LA-2:9-EZE-7:26■22:11(3618),26■43:12^{2}-DA-6:5(1882),8(1882),12(1882),15(1882)■9:11^{2},13-HO-4:6■8:1,12-AM-2:4-MIC-4:2■7:6(3618),6(2545)-HAB-1:4-ZEP-3:4-HAG-2:11-ZEC-7:12-MAL-2:6,7,8,9■4:4■**N.T.**-all=3551&marked-M'T-5:17,18■7:12■10:35(3565),35(3994)■11:13■12:5■22:36,

40■23:23-LU-2:22,23,24,27,39■5:17(3547)■10:26■12:53(3994),53(3565),53(3994)■16:16,17■24:44-JOH-1:17,45■7:19^2,23,49,51■8:5,17■10:34■12:34■15:25■18:13(3995),31■19:7-AC-5:34(3547)■6:13■7:53■13:15,39■15:5,24■18:13,15■19:38(60)■21:20,24,28■22:3,12■23:3,3(3891),29■24:6,14■25:8■28:23-RO-2:12^2(460),12^2,13^2,14^3,15,17,18,20,23^2,25^2,26,27^2■3:19^2,20^2,21^2,27^2,28,31^2■4:13,14,15^2,16■5:13^2,20■6:14,15■7:1^2,2^2,3,4,5,6,7^3,8,9,12,14,16,21,22,23^3,25^2■8:2^2,3,4,7■9:4(3548),31^2,32■10:4,5■13:8,10-1CO-6:1(2919),6(2919),7(2917)■7:39■9:8,9,20^2,21^3(459),21(1772)■14:21,34■15:56-GA-2:16^3,19,21■3:2,5,10^2,11,12,13,17,18,19,21^3,23,24■4:4,5,21■5:3,4,14,18,23■6:2,13-EPH-2:15-PH'P-3:5,6,9-1TI-1:7(3547),8,9-TIT-3:9(3544)-HEB-7:5,11(3549),12,16,19,28^2■8:4■9:19,22■10:1,8,28-JAS-1:25■2:8,9,10,11,12■4:11^3-1JO-3:4(4160,458),4(458)

LAWFUL-all=4941&marked-EZR-7:24(7990)-IS-49:24(6662)-EZE-18:5,19,21,27■33:14,16,19■N.T.-all=1833,a=1832&marked-M'T-12:2a,4a,10a,12a■14:4a■19:3a-M'T-20:15■22:17■27:6-M'R-2:24,26■3:4■6:18■10:2■12:14-LU-6:2,4,9■14:3■20:22-JOH-5:10■18:31-AC-16:21■19:39(1772)■22:25a-1CO-6:12^{2}a■10:23^{2}a-2CO-12:4a

LAWFULLY-1TI-1:8(3545)-2TI-2:5(3545)

LAWGIVER-all=2710-GE-49:10-NU-21:18-DE-33:21-PS-60:7■108:8-IS-33:22■N.T.-JAS-4:12(3550)

LAWLESS-1TI-1:9(459)

LAWS-all=8451&marked-GE-26:5-EX-16:28■18:16,20-LE-26:46-EZR-7:25(1882)-NE-9:13,14-ES-1:19(1881)■3:8^2(1881)-PS-105:45-IS-24:5-EZE-43:11■44:5,24-DA-7:25(1882)■9:10■N.T.-HEB-8:10(3551)■10:16(3551)

LAWYER-all=3544-M'T-22:35-LU-10:25-TIT-3:13

LAWYERS-all=3544-LU-7:30■11:45,46,52■14:3

LAY-all=7901,a=7760,b=5414,c=5564,d=3241&marked-GE-19:4,33^2,34,35^2■22:12(7971)■28:11■30:16■34:2■35:22■37:22(7971)■41:35(6651)-EX-5:8(7760)■7:4b■16:13(7902),14(7902),14sup,23d,33d■21:22(7896)■22:25a-LE-2:15a■3:2c,8c,13c■4:4c,15c,24c,29c,33c■16:21c■24:14c-NU-8:12c■12:11(7896)■17:4d■19:9d■24:9■27:18c-DE-7:15b■11:18a,25b■14:28d■21:8b■22:22,25,29-JOS-8:2a-J'G-4:22(5307)■5:27■6:20d■7:12(5307),13(5307)■16:3■18:19a-RU-3:4,8,14-1SA-2:22■3:5,9,15■6:8b■11:2a■19:24(5307)■26:5^2,7^2-2SA-4:5,7■11:4■12:3,16,24■13:5,6,14,31■19:32(7871)-1KI-13:31d■18:23^{2}a■19:5■21:27-2KI-4:11,29a,34■9:16■10:8a-NE-13:21(7971)-ES-2:21(7971)■3:6(7971)■4:3(3331)■6:2(7971)■9:2(7971)-JOB-9:33(7896)■17:3a■21:5a■22:22a,24(7896)■29:19(3885)■34:23a■40:4a■41:8a-PS-4:8■7:5(7931)■84:3(7896)■104:22(7257)-PR-7:1(6845)■10:14(6845)-EC-7:2b-IS-5:8(7126)■11:14(7971)■22:22b■28:17a■30:32(5117)■34:15(4422)■35:7(7258)■47:7a■54:11(7257)-JER-6:21b-EZE-3:20b■4:1b,2b,4a■6:5b■19:2(7257)■23:8■25:14b,17b■26:12a,16(5493)■28:17b■32:5b■33:28b■35:4a■36:29b■37:6b■42:13d,14d■44:19d-AM-2:8(5186)-JON-1:5,14b-MIC-1:7a■7:16a-MAL-2:2^{2}a■N.T.-all=5087&marked-M'T-8:20(2827)■9:18(2007)■23:4(2007)■28:6(2749)-M'R-1:30(2621)■2:4(2621)■5:23(2007)■16:18(2007)-LU-5:18,25(2621)■9:58(2827)■19:44(1474)■20:19(1911)■21:12(1911)-JOH-5:3(2621)■10:15,17,18^2■11:38(1945)■13:37,38■15:13-AC-7:60(2476)■8:19(2007)■15:28(2007)■27:20(1945)■28:8(2621)-RO-8:33(1458)■9:33-1CO-3:11■16:2-2CO-12:14(2343)-1TI-5:22(2007)■6:12(1949),19(1949)-HEB-12:1(659)-JAS-1:21(659)-1PE-2:6-1JO-3:16

LAYEDST-LU-19:21(5087)

LAYEST-NU-11:11(7760)

LAYETH-all=7760&marked-JOB-21:19(6845)■24:12■41:26(5381)-PS-33:7(5414)■104:3-PR-2:7(6845)■26:24(7896)■31:19(7971)-IS-57:1-JER-9:8■12:11■N.T.-LU-15:5(2007)

LAYING-PS-64:5(2934)■N.T.-all=1936&marked-M'R-7:8(863)-LU-11:54(1748)-AC-8:18■9:24(1917)■25:3(4160)-1TI-4:14■6:19(597)-HEB-6:1(2598),2-1PE-2:1(659)

LEAD-all=5148&marked-GE-33:14(5095)-EX-13:21■15:10(5777)■32:34-NU-27:17(3318)■31:22(5777)-DE-4:27(5090)■20:9(7218)■28:37(5090)■32:12-1SA-30:22(5090)-NE-9:19-JOB-19:24(5777)-PS-5:8■25:5(1869)■27:11■31:3■43:3■60:9■61:2■108:10■125:5(3212)■139:10,24■143:10-PR-6:22■8:20(1980)-SONG-8:2(5090)-IS-3:12(833)■11:6(5090)■20:4(5090)■40:11(5095)■42:16(1869)■49:10(5090)■57:18(5148)■63:14(5090)-JER-6:29(5777)■31:9(2986)■32:5(3212)-EZE-22:18(5777),20(5777)■27:12(5777)-NA-2:7(5090)-ZEC-5:7(5777),8(5777)■N.T.-all=3594&marked-M'T-6:13(1533)■15:14-M'R-13:11(71)■14:44(520)-LU-6:39■11:4(1533)■13:15(520)-AC-13:11(5497)-1CO-9:5(4013)-1TI-2:2(1236)-2TI-3:6(162)-HEB-8:9(1806)-RE-7:17

LEADER-all=5057&marked-1CH-12:27■13:1-IS-55:4

LEADERS-2CH-32:21(5057)-IS-9:16(833)■N.T.-M'T-15:14(3595)

LEADEST-PS-80:1(5090)

LEADETH-all=3212&marked-JOB-12:17,19-PS-23:2(5095),3(5090)-PR-16:29-IS-48:17(1869)■N.T.-M'T-7:13(520),14(520)-M'R-9:2(399)-JOH-10:3(1806)-AC-12:10(5342)-RO-2:4(71)■-RE-13:10(4863)

LEAF-all=5929-GE-8:11-LE-26:36-JOB-13:25-PS-1:3-IS-1:30■34:4■64:6-JER-8:13■17:8-EZE-47:12^2

LEAGUE-all=1285&marked-JOS-9:6,7,11,15,16-J'G-2:2-1SA-22:8(3772)-2SA-3:12,13,21■5:3-1KI-5:12■15:19^2-2CH-16:3^2-JOB-5:23-EZE-30:5-DA-11:23(2266)

LEAN-all=8172&marked-GE-41:20(7534)-NU-13:20(7330)-J'G-16:26-2SA-13:4(1800)-2KI-18:21(5564)-JOB-8:15-PR-3:5-IS-17:4(7329)■36:6(5564)-EZE-34:20(7330)-MIC-3:11

LEANED-all=8172&marked-2SA-1:6-2KI-7:2,17-EZE-29:7-AM-5:19(5564)■N.T.-JOH-21:20(377)

LEANETH-2SA-3:29(2388)-2KI-5:18(8127)

LEANFLESHED-GE-41:3(1851,1320),4(1851,1320),19(7534)

LEANING-SONG-8:5(7514)■N.T.-JOH-13:23(345)

LEANNESS-JOB-16:8(3585)-PS-106:15(7332)-IS-10:16(7332)■24:16(7334)

LEANNOTH-PS-88t

LEAP-GE-31:12(5927)-LE-11:21(5425)-DE-33:22(2178)-JOB-41:19(4422)-PS-68:16(7520)-IS-35:6(1801)-JOE-2:5(7540)-ZEP-1:9(1801)■N.T.-LU-6:23(4640)

LEAPED-GE-31:10(5927)-2SA-22:30(1801)-1KI-18:26(6452)-PS-18:29(1801)■N.T.-LU-1:41(4640),44(4640)-AC-14:10(242)■19:16(2177)

LEAPING-2SA-6:16(6339)-SONG-2:8(1801)■N.T.-AC-3:8(1814),8(242)

LEARN-all=3925&marked-DE-4:10■5:1■14:23■17:19■18:9■31:12,13-PS-119:71,73-PR-22:25(502)-IS-1:17■2:4■26:9,10■29:24-JER-10:2■12:16-MIC-4:3■N.T.-all=3129&marked-M'T-9:13■11:29■24:32-M'R-13:28-1CO-4:6■14:31,35-GA-3:2-1TI-1:20(3811)■2:11■5:4,13-TIT-3:14-RE-14:3

LEARNED-all=3925&marked-GE-30:27(5172)-PS-106:35■119:7-PR-30:3-IS-29:11(3045,5612),12^2(3045,5612)■50:4^2(3928)-EZE-19:3,6■N.T.-all=3129&marked-JOH-6:45■7:15-AC-7:22(3811)-RO-16:17-EPH-4:20-PH'P-4:9,11-COL-1:7-2TI-3:14^2-HEB-5:8

LEARNING-all=3948&marked-PR-1:5■9:9■16:21,23-DA-1:4(5612),17(5612)■N.T.-AC-26:24(1121)-RO-15:4(1319)-2TI-3:7(3129)

LEASING-PS-4:2(3577)■5:6(3577)

LEAST-all=6996&marked-GE-24:55(176)■32:10(6994)-NU-11:32(4591)-J'G-3:2(7535)■6:15(6810)-1SA-9:21(6810)■21:4(389)-2KI-18:24-1CH-12:14-IS-36:9-JER-6:13■8:10■31:34■42:1,8■44:12■49:20(6810)■50:45(6810)-JON-3:5■N.T.-all=1646&marked-M'T-2:6■5:19^2■11:11(3398)■13:32(3398)■25:40,45-LU-7:28(3398)■9:48(3398)■12:26■16:10^2■19:42(2534)-AC-5:15(2579)■8:10(3398)-1CO-6:4(1848)■15:9-EPH-3:8(1647)-HEB-8:11(3398)

LEATHER-2KI-1:8(5785)

LEATHERN-M'T-3:4(1193)

LEAVE-all=5800,a=3241,b=7604&marked-GE-2:24■28:15■33:15(3322)■42:33a■44:22^2-EX-16:19(3498)■23:11(3499)-LE-7:15a■16:23a■19:10■22:30(3498)■23:22-NU-9:12b■10:31■22:13(5414)■32:15a-DE-28:51b,54(3498)-JOS-4:3a-J'G-9:9(2308),13(2308)-RU-1:16■2:16-1SA-9:5(2308)■14:36b■25:22b-2SA-14:7b-1KI-8:57-2KI-2:2,4,6■4:30,43(3498)■13:7b-1CH-28:8(5157)-EZR-9:8b-NE-5:10■6:3(7503)■10:31(5203)■13:6(7592)-JOB-9:27■10:1■39:11-PS-16:10■17:14a■27:9(5203)■37:33■49:10■119:121a■141:8(6168)-PR-2:13■17:14(5203)-EC-2:18a,21(5414)■10:4a-IS-10:3■65:15a-JER-9:2■14:9a■17:11■18:14■44:7(3498)■48:28■49:9b,11-EZE-6:8(3498)■12:16(3498)■16:39a■22:20a■23:29■29:5(5203)■32:4(5203)■39:2(8338)-DA-4:15(7662),23(7662),26(7662)-HO-12:14(5203)-JOE-2:14b-AM-5:3^{2}b,7a-OB-5b-ZEP-3:12b-MAL-4:1■N.T.-all=863&marked-M'T-5:24■18:12■19:5(2641)■23:23(863)-M'R-5:13(2010)■10:7(2641)■12:19(2641),19-LU-11:42■15:4(2641)■19:44-JOH-14:18,27■16:28,32■19:38(2010)-AC-2:27(1459)■6:2(2641)■18:18(657)■21:6(782)-1CO-7:13-2CO-2:13(657)-EPH-5:31(2641)-HEB-13:5(447)-RE-11:2(1544)

LEAVED-IS-45:1(1817)

LEAVEN-all=2557&marked-EX-12:15(7603),19(7603)■13:7(7603)■34:25-LE-2:11,11(7603)■6:17■10:12(4682)■23:17-AM-4:5■N.T.-all=2219-M'T-13:33■16:6,11,12-M'R-8:15^2-LU-12:1■13:21-1CO-5:6,7,8^2-GA-5:9

LEAVENED-all=2557&marked-EX-12:15,19,20,34,39■13:3,7■23:18-LE-7:13-DE-16:3,4(7603)-HO-7:4■N.T.-M'T-13:33(2220)-LU-13:21(2220)

LEAVENETH-1CO-5:6(2220)-GA-5:9(2220)

LEAVES-all=1817&marked-GE-3:7(5929)-1KI-6:34(6763),34(7050)-JER-36:23-EZE-17:19(2964)■41:24,24sup-DA-4:12(6074),14(6074),21(6074)■N.T.-all=5444-M'T-21:19■24:32-M'R-11:13^2■13:28-RE-22:2

LEAVETH-JOB-39:14(5800)-ZEC-11:17(5800)■N.T.-M'T-4:11(863)-JOH-10:12(863)

LEAVING-all=863-M'T-4:13(2641)-LU-10:30-RO-1:27-HEB-6:1-1PE-2:21(5277)

LED-all=3212&marked-GE-24:27

(5148),48(5148)-EX-3:1(5090)■13:17 (5148),18(5437)■15:13(5148)-DE-8:2, 15■29:5■32:10(5437)-JOS-24:3-2KI-6:19-1CH-20:1(5090)-2CH-25:11 (5090)-PS-78:14(5148),53(5148)■106:9■107:7(1869)■136:16-PR-4:11(1869) -IS-9:16(833)■48:21■55:12(2986)■63:12,13-JER-2:6,17■23:8(935)-LA-3:2(5090)-EZE-17:12(935)■47:2(5437) -AM-2:10■N.T.-all=71&marked-M'T-4:1(321)■26:57(520)■27:2(520),31(520) -M'R-8:23(1806)■14:53(520)■15:16(520), 20(1806)-LU-4:1,29■21:24(163)■22:54, 66(321)■23:1,26(520),32■24:50(1806) -JOH-18:13(520),28■19:16(520)-AC-8:32■9:8(5496)■21:37(1521)■22:11 (5496)-RO-8:14-1CO-12:2-GA-5:18 -EPH-4:8(162)-2TI-3:6-2PE-3:17(4879)

LEDDEST-2SA-5:2(3318)-1CH-11:2(3318)-NE-9:12(5148)-PS-77:20 (5148)■N.T.-AC-21:38(1806)

LEDGES-all=7948&marked-1KI-7:28,29^{2},35(3027),36(3027)

LEEKS-NU-11:5(2682)

LEES-all=8105-IS-25:6^{2}-JER-48:11 -ZEP-1:12

LEFT-all=7604,a=8040,b=3498,c=5800&marked-GE-11:8(2308)■13:9a,9 (8041)■14:15a■17:22(3615)■18:33 (3615)■24:27c,49a■29:35(5975)■30:9 (5975)■32:8,24b■39:6c,12c,13c,15c,18c■41:49(2308)■42:38■44:12(3615),20b■47:18■48:13^{2}a,14a■50:8c-EX-2:20c■9:21c■10:12,15b,26■14:22a,29a■16:20b■34:25(3885)-LE-2:10b■10:12b,16b■14:15(8042),16(8042),26(8042),27(8042)■26:36(7604),39(7604),43c-NU-20:17a■21:35■22:26a■26:65b-DE-2:27a,34■3:3■4:27■5:32a■7:20■17:11a,20a■28:14a, 55,62■32:36c-JOS-1:7a■6:23(3241)■8:17,17b■10:33,37,39,40■11:8,11b,14, 15(5493),22b■19:27a■22:3c■23:6a-J'G-2:21c,23(3241)■3:1(3241),21a■4:16■6:4■7:20a■8:10b■9:5b■16:29a-RU-1:3,5,18 (2308)■2:11c,14b,20c■4:14(7673)-1SA-2:36b■5:4■6:12a■9:24■10:2(5203)■11:11■17:20(5203),22(5203),28(5203)■25:34b■30:9b,13c-2SA-2:19a,21a■5:21c■9:1b■13:30b■14:7,19(8041)■15:16c■16:6a, 21(3240)■17:12b■20:3(3240)-1KI-7:21 (8042),39a,47(3240),49a■9:20b,21b■14:10c■15:18b,21(2308),29■16:11■17:17b■19:3(3240),10b,14b,18,20c■20:30b■21:21c■22:19a-2KI-3:25■4:44b■7:7c,13^{2}■8:6c■10:11,14,21■11:11(8042)■14:26c■17:16c,18■19:4(4672)■20:17b■22:2a■23:8a■25:11,12,22-1CH-6:44a, 61b■12:2a■13:2■14:12c■16:37c-2CH-3:17a,17(8042)■4:6a,7a,8a■8:7b,8b■11:14c■12:5c■16:5(2308)■18:18a■21:17■23:10(8042)■24:18c,25c■28:14c■31:10^{2}b■32:31c■34:2a,21-NE-1:2,3■6:1b■8:4a -JOB-20:21(8300),26(8300)■23:9a■32:15 (6275)-PS-36:3(2308)■106:11b-PR-3:16a■4:27a■29:15(7971)-EC-10:2a -SONG-2:6a■8:3a-IS-1:8b,9b■4:3■7:22b■9:20a■10:14c■11:11,16■17:6,9c■18:6c■24:6,12■27:10c■30:17b,21(8041)■32:14c■37:4(4672)■39:6b■49:21■54:3a -JER-12:7(5203)■21:7■27:18b■31:2 (8300)■34:7b■38:22,27(2790)■39:10■40:6,11(5414)■42:2■43:6(3240)■44:18 (2308)■49:25c■50:26(7611)■52:16 -EZE-1:10a■4:4(8042)■9:8■14:22b■16:46a■21:16(8041)■23:8c■24:21c■31:12^{2} (5203)■36:36■39:3a,28b■41:9(3240),11^{2} (3240)■48:15b-DA-2:44(7662)■10:8,17■12:7a-HO-4:10c-JOE-1:4^{3}(3499)-JON-4:11a-HAG-2:3-ZEC-4:3a,11a■12:6a■13:8b■14:16b■N.T.-all=863,a=2641,b =2176&marked-M'T-4:20,22■6:3(710)■8:15■15:37(4052)■16:4a■20:21b,23b■21:17a■22:22,25■23:38■24:2,40,41■25:33b,41b■26:44■27:38b-M'R-1:20, 31■8:8(4051),13■10:28,29,37b,40b■12:12,20,21,22■13:2,34■14:52a■15:27b-LU-4:39■5:4(3973),28a■10:40a■13:35■17:34,35,36■18:28,29■20:31a■21:6■23:33(710)-JOH-4:3,28■52■8:9a, 29-AC-2:31a■14:17■18:19a■21:3a,3b, 32(3973)■23:32(1439)■24:27a■25:14a -RO-9:29(1459)■11:3(5275)-2CO-6:7 (710)-1TH-3:1a-2TI-4:13(620),20(620) -TIT-1:5a-HEB-2:8■4:1a-JUDE-6 (620)-RE-2:4■10:2b

LEFTEST-NE-9:28(5800)

LEFTHANDED-J'G-3:15(334, 3027,3225)■20:16(334,3027,3225)

LEG-IS-47:2(7640)

LEGION-all=3003-M'R-5:9,15-LU-8:30

LEGIONS-M'T-26:53(3003)

LEGS-all=3767&marked-EX-12:9■29:17-LE-1:9,13■4:11■8:21■9:14■11:21 -DE-28:35(7785)-1SA-17:6(7272)-PS-147:10(7785)-PR-26:7(7785)-SONG-5:15(7785)-IS-3:20(6807)-DA-2:33 (8243)-AM-3:12(3767)■N.T.-all=4628-JOH-19:31,32,33

LEISURE-M'R-6:31(2119)

LEND-all=5391&marked-EX-22:25 (3867)-LE-25:37(5414)-DE-15:6(5670), 8(5670)■23:19,20^{2}■24:10(5383),11(5383)■28:12(3867),44(3867)■N.T.-all=1155&marked-LU-6:34^{2},35■11:5(5531)

LENDER-PR-22:7(3867)-IS-24:2 (3867)

LENDETH-all=3867&marked-DE-15:2(5383)-PS-37:26■112:5-PR-19:17

LENGTH-all=753&marked-GE-6:15■13:17-EX-25:10,17,23■26:2,8,13, 16■27:11,18■28:16■30:2■36:9,15,21■37:1,6,10,25■38:1,18■39:9-DE-3:11■30:20-J'G-3:16-1KI-6:2,3,20■7:2,6,27 -2CH-3:3,4,8■4:1-JOB-12:12-PS-21:4 -PR-3:2,16■29:21(319)-EZE-31:7■40:11,18,20,21,25,36,49■41:2,4,12,15, 22^{2}■42:2,7,8■45:1,3,5,7■48:8,9,10^{2},13^{2}, 18-ZEC-2:2■5:2■N.T.-all=3372&marked-RO-1:10(4218)-EPH-3:18 -RE-21:16^{2}

LENGTHEN-1KI-3:14(748)-IS-54:2(748)

LENGTHENED-DE-25:15(748)

LENGTHENING-DA-4:27(754)

LENT-all=7592&marked-EX-12:36 -DE-23:19(5391)-1SA-1:28^{2}■2:20-JER-15:10^{2}(5383)

LENTILES-all=5742-GE-25:34 -2SA-17:28■23:11-EZE-4:9

LEOPARD-all=5246&marked -IS-11:6-JER-5:6■13:23-DA-7:6(5245) -HO-13:7■N.T.-RE-13:2(3197)

LEOPARDS-SONG-4:8(5246) -HAB-1:8(5246)

LEPER-all=6879-LE-13:45■14:2,3■22:4-NU-5:2-2SA-3:29-2KI-5:1,11,27■15:5-2CH-26:21^{2},23■N.T.-all=3015 -M'T-8:2■26:6-M'R-1:40■14:3

LEPERS-2KI-7:8■N.T.-all=3015 -M'T-10:8,11:5-LU-4:27■7:22■17:12

LEPROSY-all=6883-LE-13:2,3,8,9, 11,12^{2},13,15,20,25^{2},27,30,42,43,47,49,51, 52,59■14:3,7,32,34,44,54,55,57-DE-24:8-2KI-5:3,6,7,27-2CH-26:19■N.T. -all=3014-M'T-8:3-M'R-1:42-LU-5:12,13

LEPROUS-all=6879-EX-4:6-LE-13:44-NU-12:10^{2}-2KI-7:3-2CH-26:20

LESS-all=4591&marked-EX-16:17■30:15-NU-22:18(6996)■26:54■33:54 -1SA-22:15(6996)■25:36(6996)-EZR-9:13(4295)-IS-40:17(657)■N.T.-M'R-4:31(3398)■15:40(3398)-1CO-12:23 (820)-2CO-12:15(2276)-EPH-3:8(1647) -PH'P-2:28(253)-HEB-7:7(1640)

LESSER-GE-1:16(6996)-IS-7:25 (7716)-EZE-43:14(6996)

LEST-all=6435&marked-GE-3:3,22■4:15(1115)■11:4(6435)■14:23(3808)■19:15,17,19■26:7,9■32:11■38:9(1115), 11,23■42:4■44:34■45:11-EX-1:10■5:3■13:17■19:21,22,24■20:19■23:29, 33■33:3■34:12^{2},15-LE-10:6(3808),7,9 (3808)■19:29(3808)■22:9(3808)-NU-16:26,34■18:32(3808)-DE-1:42(3808)■4:9^{2},16,19,23■6:12,15■7:22,25■8:12■9:28■19:6■20:5,6,7,8■22:9■24:15(3808)■25:3■29:18^{2}■32:27^{2}-JOS-2:16■6:18■9:20 (3808)■24:27-J'G-7:2■14:15■18:25-RU-4:6-1SA-9:5■13:19■15:6■20:3■27:11■29:4(3808)■31:4-2SA-1:20^{2}■12:28■13:25(3808)■15:14■17:16■20:6-2KI-2:16-1CH-10:4-JOB-32:13■36:18■42:8(1115)-PS-2:12■7:2■13:3,4■28:1■32:9(1077)■38:16■50:22■59:11■91:12■125:3(4616,3808)-PR-5:6,9,10■9:8■20:13■22:25■24:18■25:8,10,16,17■26:4, 5■30:6,9^{2},10■31:5-EC-7:21(634,3808) -IS-6:10■27:3■28:22■36:18■48:5,7 -JER-1:17■4:4■6:8^{2}■10:24■21:12■37:20 (3808)■38:19■51:46-HO-2:3-AM-5:6 -MAL-4:6■N.T.-all=2443,3361,a=3379, b=3361-M'T-4:6a■5:25a■7:6a■13:15a, 29a■15:32a■17:27■25:9a■26:5■27:64a -M'R-3:9■4:12a■13:5b,36b■14:2a,38 -LU-4:11a■8:12■12:58a■14:8a,12a,29, 16:28■18:5■21:34a■22:46-JOH-3:20■5:14■12:35,42■18:28-AC-5:26,39a■13:40b■23:10b■27:17b,29(3381),42b■28:27a-RO-11:21(3381),25■15:20-1CO-1:15,17■8:9(3381),13■9:12,27(3381)■10:12b-2CO-2:3,7(3381),11■4:4(1519, 3588,3361)■9:3(3588,3361),4(3381)■11:3(3381)■12:6b,7^{2},20^{2}(3381),21b■13:10-GA-2:2(3381)■4:11(3381)■6:1b 12-EPH-2:9-PH'P-2:27-COL-2:4,8b■3:21-1TH-3:5(3381)-1TI-3:6,7-HEB-2:1a■3:12a,13■4:1a,11■11:28■12:3,13, 15^{2}-JAS-5:9,12-2PE-3:17-RE-16:15

LET-all=3381&marked-GE-24:14 (5186),18,46-EX-3:19(5414)■5:4(6544)■17:11(5117)-JOS-2:15,18-1SA-19:12 -2SA-16:11(3240)-2KI-13:21(3212)■23:18(3240)-2CH-16:1(5414)-SONG-8:11(5414)-IS-43:13(7725)-JER-38:6 (7971),11(7971)-EZE-1:24(7503),25 (7503)-HO-4:17(3240)N.T.-all=863&marked-M'T-7:4■8:22■13:30■15:14■21:33(1554),41(1554)■27:49-M'R-1:24 (1439)■2:4(5465)■7:27■11:6■12:1(1554)■14:6■15:36-LU-4:34(1439)■5:4(5465), 5(5465),19(2524)■6:42■9:60,61(2010)■13:8■20:9(1554)■22:68(630)-JOH-11:44,48■12:7■18:8■19:12(630)-AC-2:29(1832)■3:13(630)■5:38(1439)■40 (630)■9:25(5465,2524)■10:11(2524)■11:5(2524)■15:33(630)■16:35(630),36 (630)■17:9(630)■23:22(630)■27:15 (1929),30(5465),32(1439)■28:18(630) -RO-1:13(2967)-2CO-11:33(5465) -2TH-2:7(2722)

LETTER-all=5612&marked-2SA-11:14,15-2KI-5:5,6^{2},7■10:2,6,7■19:14 -EZR-4:7(5406),8(104),11(104),18(5407), 23(5407)■5:5(5407),6(104),7(6600)■7:11(5406)-NE-2:8(107)■6:5(107)-ES-9:26(107),29(107)-IS-37:14-JER-29:1,29■N.T.-all=1121&marked-AC-23:25(1992) -RO-2:27,29■7:6-2CO-3:6^{2}■7:8(1992)-GA-6:11-2TH-2:2(1992)-HEB-13:22(1989)

LETTERS-all=5612&marked-1KI-21:8^{2},9,11-2KI-10:1■20:12-2CH-30:1 (107),6(107)■32:17-NE-2:7(107),9(107)■6:17(107),17sup,19(107)-ES-1:22■3:13■8:5,10■9:20,25,30-IS-39:1-JER-29:25■N.T.-all=1992&marked-LU-23:38 (1121)-JOH-7:15(1121)-AC-9:2■22:5■28:21(1121)-1CO-16:3-2CO-10:9,10,11

LETTEST-JOB-41:1(8257)■N.T. -LU-2:29(630)

LETTETH-PR-17:14(6362)■N.T. -2TH-2:7(2722)

LETTING-all supplied

LEVIATHAN-all=3882&marked -JOB-41:1-PS-74:14■104:26-IS-27:1^{2}

LEVITICAL-HEB-7:11(3020)

LEVY-all=4522&marked-NU-31:28 (7311)-1KI-5:13^{2},14■9:15,21(5927)

LEWD-EZE-16:27(2154)■23:44 (2154)■N.T.-AC-17:5(4190)

LEWDLY-EZE-22:11(2154)

LEWDNESS-all=2154&marked -J'G-20:6-JER-11:15(4029)■13:27 -EZE-16:43,58■22:9■23:21,27,29,35,

48^2,49■24:13-HO-2:10(5040)■6:9■N.T.-AC-18:14(4467)

LIAR-JOB-24:25(3576)-PR-17:4(8267)■19:22(376,3576)■30:6(3576)-JER-15:18(391)■N.T.-all=5583&marked-JOH-8:44,55-RO-3:4-1JO-1:10■2:4■2:22■4:20■5:10

LIARS-DE-33:29(3584)-PS-116:11(3576)-IS-44:25(907)-JER-50:36(907)■N.T.-1TI-1:10(5583)-TIT-1:12(5583)-RE-2:2(5571)■21:8(5571)

LIBERAL-all=5081&marked-PR-11:25(1293)-IS-32:5,8^2■N.T.-2CO-9:13(572)

LIBERALITY-1CO-16:3(5485)-2CO-8:2(572)

LIBERALLY-DE-15:14(6059)-JAS-1:5(574)

LIBERTY-all=1865&marked-LE-25:10-PS-119:45(7342)-IS-61:1-JER-34:8,15,16(2670),17^2-EZE-46:17■N.T.-all=1657&marked-LU-4:18(859)-AC-24:23(425)■26:32(630)■27:3(2010)-RO-8:21-1CO-7:39(1658)■8:9(1849)■10:29-2CO-3:17-GA-2:4■5:1,13^2-HEB-13:23(630)-JAS-1:25■2:12-1PE-2:16-2PE-2:19

LICE-all=3654-EX-8:16,17^2,18^2-PS-105:31

LICENCE-AC-21:40(2010)■25:16(5117)

LICK-all=3897&marked-NU-22:4-1KI-21:19(3952)-PS-72:9-IS-49:23-MIC-7:17

LICKED-1KI-18:38(3897)■21:19(3952)■22:38(3952)■N.T.-LU-16:21(621)

LICKETH-NU-22:4(3897)

LID-2KI-12:9(1817)

LIE-all=7901,a=3576,b=7257&marked-GE-19:32,34■30:15■39:7,10,12,14■47:30-EX-21:13(6658)■22:16■23:11(5203)-LE-6:2(3584)■15:18,24■18:20(5414,7903),22,23(5414,7903),23(7250)■19:11(8266)■20:12,13,15(5414,7903),16(7250),18,20■26:6-NU-5:13■10:5(2583),6(2583)■23:19a,24-DE-19:11(693)■22:23,25,28■25:2(5307)■28:30(7693)■29:20b-JOS-8:4(693)-RU-3:4,7,13-1SA-3:5,6,9■15:29(8266)-2SA-11:11,13■12:11■13:11-1KI-1:2-2KI-4:16a-JOB-6:28a■7:4■11:19b■20:11■21:26■27:19■34:6a-PS-23:2b■57:4■62:9a■88:5■89:35a■119:69a-PR-3:24■14:5a-EC-4:11-SONG-1:13(3885)-IS-11:6b,7b■13:21b■14:18,30b■17:2b■27:10b■43:17■44:20a■50:11■51:20■63:8(8266)■65:10(7258)-JER-3:25■27:10(8267),14(8267),15(8267),16(8267)■28:15(8267)■29:21(8267),31(8267)■33:12b-LA-2:21-EZE-4:4^2,6,9■21:29a■31:18■32:21,27,28,29,30■34:14b,15b-HO-2:18-JOE-1:13(3885)-AM-6:4-MIC-1:14(391)■2:11a-HAB-2:3a-ZEP-2:7b,14b,15(4769)■3:13b-ZEC-10:2(8267)■N.T.-all=5574&marked-JOH-5:6(2621)■8:44(5579)■20:6(2749)-AC-5:3-RO-1:25(5579)■3:7(5582)■9:1-2CO-11:31-GA-1:20-EPH-4:14(3180)-COL-3:9-2TH-2:11(5579)-1TI-2:7-TIT-1:2(893)-HEB-6:18-JAS-3:14-1JO-1:6■2:21(5579),27(5579)-RE-3:9■21:27(5579)■22:15(5579)

LIED-1KI-13:18(3584)-PS-78:36(3576)-IS-57:11(3576)■N.T.-AC-5:4(5574)

LIEN-GE-26:10(7901)-PS-68:13(7901)-JER-3:2(7693)

LIERS-all supplied

LIES-all=3576,a=8267&marked-J'G-16:10,13-JOB-11:3(907)■13:4a-PS-40:4■58:3■62:4■63:11a■101:7a-PR-6:19■14:5,25■19:5,9■29:12(1697,8267)■30:8(1697,3576)-IS-9:15a■16:6(907)■28:15,17■59:3a,4(7723)-JER-9:3a,5a■14:14a■16:19a■20:6a■23:14a,25a,26a,32a■48:30(907)-EZE-13:8,9,19,22■22:28■24:12(8383)-DA-11:27-HO-7:3(3585),13■10:13(3585)■11:12(3585)■12:1-AM-2:4-MIC-6:12a-NA-3:1(3585)-HAB-2:18a-ZEP-3:13-ZEC-13:3a■N.T.-1TI-4:2(5573)

LIEST-all=7901&marked-GE-28:13-DE-6:7■11:19-JOS-7:10(5307)-PR-3:24

LIETH-all=7901&marked-GE-4:7(7257)■49:25(7257)-EX-22:19-LE-6:3(3584)■14:47■15:4,20,24,26,33■19:20■20:11,13(4904)-NU-21:15(8172)-DE-27:20,21,22,23-RU-3:4-NE-3:25(3318),26(3318),27(3318)-JOB-14:12■40:21-PS-41:8■88:7(5564)-PR-23:34^2-EZE-29:3(6437)-MIC-7:5■N.T.-M'T-8:6(906)-M'R-5:23(2192)-AC-27:12(991)-1JO-5:19(2749)-RE-21:16(2749)

LIEUTENANTS-all=323&marked-EZR-8:36-ES-3:12■8:9■9:3

LIFE-all=2416,a=5315&marked-GE-1:20,30■2:7,9■3:14,17,22,24■6:17■7:11,15,22■9:4a,5a■18:10,14■19:17a,19a■23:1■25:7,17■27:46^2■32:30a■42:15,16■44:30a■47:9^2-EX-4:19a■6:16,18,20■21:23a,30a-LE-17:11a,14^{3}a■18:18-NU-35:31a-DE-4:9■6:2■12:23^{2}a■16:3■17:19■19:21a■24:6a■28:66^2■30:15,19^2,20■32:47-JOS-1:5■2:14a■4:14-J'G-9:17a,12:3a■16:30■18:25a-RU-4:15a-1SA-1:11■7:15■18:18■19:5a,11a■20:1a■22:23a■23:15a■25:29■26:24^{2}a■28:9a,21a-2SA-1:9a■4:8a■14:7a■15:21■16:11a■18:13a■19:5a-1KI-1:12^{2}a■2:23a■3:11(3117),11a■4:21■11:34■15:5,6■19:2a,3a,4a,10a,14a■20:31a,39a,42a-2KI-1:13a,14a■4:16,17■7:7a■8:1(2421),5^3(2421)■10:24a■25:29,30-2CH-1:11a,11(3117)-EZR-6:10(2417)-NE-6:11(2425)-ES-7:3a,7a■8:11a-JOB-2:4a,6a■3:20■6:11a■7:7,15(6106)■9:21■10:1,12■13:14a■24:22■31:39a■33:4(2421),18,20,22,28■36:6(2421),14-PS-7:5■16:11■17:14■21:4■23:6■26:9■27:1,4■30:5■31:10,13a■34:12■36:9■38:12a■42:8■61:6(3117,5921)■63:3■64:1■66:9■78:50■88:3■91:16(3117)■103:4■128:5■133:3■143:3-PR-1:19a,2:19■3:2,18,22■4:10,13,22,23■5:6■6:23,26a■7:23a■8:35■9:11■10:11,16,17■11:19,30■12:10a,28■13:3a,8a,12,14■14:27,30■15:4,24,31■16:15,22■18:21■19:23■21:21■22:4■31:12-EC-2:3,17■3:12■5:18,20■6:12^2■7:12(2421)■8:15■9:9^2-IS-15:4a■38:12,16,20■43:4a■57:10-JER-4:30a■8:3■11:21a■21:7a,8,9a■22:25a■34:20a,21a■38:2a,16a■39:18a■44:30^{2}a■45:5a■49:37a■52:33,34-LA-2:19a■3:53-EZE-3:18(2421)■7:13■13:22(2421)■32:10a■33:15-DA-12:2-JON-1:14a■2:6■4:3a-MAL-2:5■N.T.-all=2222,a=5590&marked-M'T-2:20a■6:25^{2}a■7:14■10:39^{2}a■16:25^{2}a■18:8,9■19:16,17,29■20:28a■25:46-M'R-3:4a■8:35^{2}a■9:43,45■10:17,30,45a-LU-1:75■6:9a■8:14(979)■9:24^{2}a■10:25■12:15,22a,23a■14:26a■17:33^{2}a■18:18,30■21:34(982)-JOH-1:4■3:15,16,36^2■4:14,36■5:24^2,26^2,29,39,40■6:27,33,35,40,47,48,51,53,54,63,68■8:12■10:10,11a,15a,17a,28■11:25■12:25^{2}a,25,50■13:37a,38a■14:6■15:13a■17:2,3■20:31-AC-2:28■3:15■5:20■8:33■11:18■13:46,48■17:25■20:10a,24a■26:4(981)■27:22a-RO-2:7■5:10,17,18,21■6:4,22,23■7:10■8:2,6,10,38■11:3a,15■16:4a-1CO-3:22■6:3(982),4(982)■14:7(895)■15:19-2CO-1:8(2198)■2:16■3:6(2227)■4:10,11,12■5:4-GA-3:21(2227)■6:8-EPH-4:18-PH'P-1:20■2:16,30a■4:3-COL-3:3,4-1TI-1:16■2:2(979)■4:8■6:12,19-2TI-1:1,10■2:4(979)■3:10(72)-TIT-1:2■3:7-HEB-7:3,16-JAS-1:12■4:14-1PE-3:7,10■4:3(979)-2PE-1:3-1JO-1:1,2^2■2:16(979),25■3:14,15,16a■5:11^2,12^2,13,16,20-JUDE-21-RE-2:7,10■3:5■8:9a■11:11■13:8,15(4151)■17:8■20:12,15■21:6,27■22:1,2,14,17,19

LIFETIME-2SA-18:18(2416)■N.T.-LU-16:25(2222)-HEB-2:15(2198)

LIFT-all=5375,a=7311&marked-GE-7:17a■13:14■14:22a■18:2■21:16,18■31:12■40:13,19■41:44a-EX-14:16a■20:25(5130)-NU-6:26■16:3■23:24-DE-3:27■4:19■22:4(6965)■27:5(5130)■32:40-JOS-8:31(5130)-2KI-19:4■25:27-1CH-25:5a-EZR-9:6a-JOB-10:15■11:15■22:26■38:34a-PS-4:6■7:6■10:12■24:7^2,9^2■25:1■28:2,9■63:4■74:3a■75:4a,5a■86:4■93:3■94:2■110:7a■119:48■121:1■123:1■134:2■143:8-EC-4:10(6965)-IS-2:4■5:26■10:15^{2}a,24,26,30(6670)■13:2■24:14■33:10■37:4■40:9^{2}a,26■42:2,11■49:18,22■51:6■52:8■58:1a■59:19(5127)■60:4■62:10a-JER-3:2■7:16■11:14■13:20■22:20(5414)■51:14(6030)-LA-2:19■3:41-EZE-8:5■11:22■17:14■21:22a■23:27■26:8(6965)■33:25-MIC-4:3-ZEC-1:21■5:5■N.T.-all=1869&marked-M'T-12:11(1458)-LU-13:11(352)■16:23■18:13■21:28-JOH-4:35-HEB-12:12(461)-JAS-4:10(5312)

LIFTED-all=5375,a=7311&marked-GE-13:10■22:4,13■24:63,64■27:38■29:11■31:10■33:1,5■37:25,28(5927)■39:15a,18a■40:20■43:29-EX-7:20a■14:10-LE-9:22-NU-14:1■20:11a■24:2-DE-8:14a■17:20a-JOS-4:18(5423)■5:13-J'G-2:4■8:28■9:7■19:17■21:2-RU-1:9,14-1SA-6:13■11:4■24:16■30:4-2SA-3:32■13:34,36■18:24,28■20:21■22:49a■23:18(5782)-1KI-11:26a,27a-2KI-9:32■14:10■19:22-1CH-11:11(5782)■14:2■21:16-2CH-5:13a■17:6(1361)■26:16(1361)■32:25(1361)-JOB-2:12^2■31:21(5130),29(5782)-PS-24:4■27:6a■30:1(1802)■41:9(1431)■74:5(935)■83:2■93:3^2■102:10■106:26-PR-30:13-IS-2:12,13,14■6:1■26:11a■37:23-JER-51:9■52:31-EZE-1:19^2,20,21^2■3:14■8:3,5■10:15(7426),16,17a,17(7426),19■11:1■18:6,12,15■20:5^2,6,15,23,28,42■28:2(1361),5(1361),17(1361)■31:10(1361),10a■36:7■44:12■47:14-DA-4:34(5191)■5:20(7313),23(7313)■7:4(5191)■8:3■10:5■11:12a-MIC-5:9a-HAB-2:4(6075)■3:10-ZEC-1:18,21■2:1■5:1,9^2■6:1■9:16(5264)■14:10(7213)■N.T.-all=1869&marked-M'T-17:8-M'R-1:31(1453)■9:27(1453)-LU-6:20■11:27■17:13(142)■24:50-JOH-3:14^2(5312)■6:5■8:7(352),10(352),28(5312)■11:41(142)■12:32(5312),34(5312)■13:18■17:1-AC-2:14■3:7(1453)■4:24(142)■9:41(450)■14:11■22:22-1TI-3:6(5188)-RE-10:5(142)

LIFTER-PS-3:3(7311)

LIFTEST-JOB-30:22(5375)-PS-9:13(7311)■18:48(7311)-PR-2:3(5414)

LIFTETH-all=7311&marked-1SA-2:7,8-2CH-25:19(5375)-JOB-39:18(4754)-PS-107:25■113:7■147:6(5749)-IS-18:3(5375)-JER-51:3(5927)-NA-3:3(5927)

LIFTING-1CH-11:20(5782)■15:16(7311)-NE-8:6(4607)-JOB-22:29(1466)-PS-141:2(4864)-PR-30:32(5375)-IS-9:18(1348)■33:3(7427)■N.T.-1TI-2:8(1869)

LIGHT-all=216,a=3974&marked-GE-1:3,4^2,5,15,16^{2}a,17,18■44:3-EX-10:23■13:21■14:20■25:6a,37(5927),37■27:20a■35:8a,14^{2}a,28a■39:37a■40:4(5927)-LE-24:2a-NU-4:9a,16a■8:2■21:5(7052)-DE-27:16(7034)-J'G-9:4(6348)■19:26-RU-2:3(7136)-1SA-14:36■18:23(7043)■25:22,34,36■29:10-2SA-2:18(7031)■17:12(5117),22■21:17(5216)■23:4-1KI-7:4(4237),5(4237)■11:36(5216)■16:31(7043)-2KI-3:18(7043)■7:9■8:19(5216)■20:10(7043)-2CH-21:7(5216)-NE-9:12,19-ES-8:16(219)-JOB-3:4(5105),9,16,20■10:22(3313)■12:22,25■17:12■18:5,6,18■22:28■24:13,14,16■25:3■28:11■29:3,24■30:26■33:28,30■36:30,32■37:15,21■38:15,19,24■41:18-PS-4:6■18:28(215)■27:1■36:9■37:6■38:10■43:3■44:3■49:19■56:13■74:16a■78:14■89:15■90:8a■97:11■104:2■105:39■112:4■118:27■119:105,130■139:11,12(219)■148:3-PR-4:18■6:23■13:9■15:30a■16:15-EC-2:13■11:7■12:2-IS-2:5■5:20,30■8:20(7837)■9:2^2■10:17■13:10^2■30:26^4■42:6,16■45:7■49:6(7043),6■50:10(5051),11(217)■51:4■58:8,10■59:9■60:1,3,19^3,20-JER-4:23■13:16■

25:10■31:35[2]-LA-3:2-EZE-8:17(7043)■22:7(7043)■32:7-DA-2:22(5094)■5:11,14-HO-6:5-AM-5:18,20-MIC-2:1■7:8,9-HAB-3:4,11-ZEP-3:4(6348),5-ZEC-14:6,7■N.T.-all=5457&marked-M'T-4:16[2]■5:14,15(2545),15(2989),16■6:22(5460),22(3088),23■10:27■11:30(1645)■17:2■22:5(272)■24:29(5338)-M'R-13:24(5338)-LU-1:79(2014)■2:32■8:16■11:33(5338),34(3088),34(5460),35,36[2](5460),36(5461)■12:3■15:8(681)■16:8-JOH-1:4,5,7,8[2],9■3:19[2],20[2],21■5:35(3088),35■8:12[2]■9:5■11:9,10,12:35[2],36[2],46-AC-9:3■12:7■13:47■16:29■22:6,9,11■26:13,18,23-RO-2:19■13:12-1CO-4:5(5461)-2CO-4:4(5462),6,6(5462),17(1645)■6:14■11:14-EPH-5:8[2],13[2],14(2017)-COL-1:12-1TH-5:5-1TI-6:16-2TI-1:10(5461)-1PE-2:9-2PE-1:19(3088)-1JO-1:5,7■2:8,9,10-RE-7:16(4098)■18:23■21:11(5458),23(3088),24■22:5,5(5461)

LIGHTED-all=5307&marked-GE-24:64■28:11(6293)-EX-40:25(5927)-NU-8:3(5927)-JOS-15:18(6795)-J'G-1:14(6795)■4:15(3381)-1SA-25:23(3381)-2KI-5:21(5307)■10:15(4672)-IS-9:8(5307)■N.T.-LU-8:16(681)■11:33(681)

LIGHTEN-1SA-6:5(7043)-2SA-22:29(5050)-EZR-9:8(215)-PS-13:3(215)-JON-1:5(7043)■N.T.-LU-2:32(602)-RE-21:23(5461)

LIGHTENED-PS-34:5(5102)■77:18(215)■N.T.-AC-27:18(1546,4160),38(2893)-RE-18:1(5461)

LIGHTENETH-PR-29:13(215)■N.T.-LU-17:24(797)

LIGHTER-all=7043-1KI-12:4,9,10-2CH-10:10

LIGHTEST-NU-8:2(5927)

LIGHTETH-EX-30:8(5927)-DE-19:5(4672)■N.T.-JOH-1:9(5461)

LIGHTING-IS-30:30(5183)■N.T.-M'T-3:16(2064)

LIGHTLY-all=7043&marked-GE-26:10(4592)-DE-32:15(5034)-1SA-2:30■18:23(7034)-IS-9:1-JER-4:24■N.T.-M'R-9:39(5035)

LIGHTNESS-JER-3:9(6963)■23:32(6350)■N.T.-2CO-1:17(1644)

LIGHTNING-all=1300&marked-2SA-22:15-JOB-28:26(2385)■37:3(216)■38:25(2385)-PS-144:6-EZE-1:13,14(965)-DA-10:6-ZEC-9:14■N.T.-all=796-M'T-24:27■28:3-LU-10:18■17:24

LIGHTNINGS-all=1300&marked-EX-19:16■20:18(3940)-JOB-38:35-PS-18:14■77:18■97:4■135:7-JER-10:13■51:16-NA-2:4■N.T.-all=796-RE-4:5■8:5■11:19■16:18

LIGHTS-all=3974&marked-GE-1:14,15,16-1KI-6:4(8261)-PS-136:7(216)-EZE-32:8■N.T.-LU-12:35(3088)-AC-20:8(2985)-PH'P-2:15(5458)-JAS-1:17(5457)

LIGN-supplied

LIGURE-EX-28:19(3958)■39:12(3958)

LIKE-all=3644,a=1819&marked-EX-7:11(3651)■9:14,24■11:6■15:11[2]■23:11(3651)■30:32,33,38-NU-23:10-DE-4:32■7:26■18:15,18■22:3(3651)■25:7(2654),8(2654)■33:29-J'G-11:17(1571)-1SA-10:24■19:24(1571)■26:15-2SA-7:22■22:34(7737)-1KI-3:12[2],13■8:23■10:20(3651)-2KI-18:5■23:25[2]-1CH-17:20-2CH-1:12(3651)■6:14■9:19(3651)■30:26(2063)■35:18-NE-6:5(2088)■13:26-JOB-1:8■2:3■13:12(4911)■14:9■30:19(4911)■36:22■40:9sup,9,17■41:33(4915)-PS-17:12(1825)■28:1(5973)■29:6■35:10■49:12(4911),20(4911)■58:4(1823),4■71:19■73:5(5973)■88:5■89:8■102:6a,6sup,26a■115:8■135:18■140:3■143:7(4911)■144:4a-PR-26:4(7737)-SONG-2:9a,17a■7:1,7a■8:14a-IS-1:9a,18a■13:4(1823)■14:10(4911),14a■26:17■46:5a,9■51:6[2]sup-JER-10:6,7■23:29(3541)■30:7■36:32(1922)■48:6(2421)■49:19,19sup■50:44sup,44-LA-1:21-EZE-5:9■18:10(251)■31:2a,8[3]a,18a■32:2a-DA-3:25(1821)■5:21(5974)■7:5(1821)-JOE-2:2-JON-1:4(2803)-MIC-7:18■N.T.-all=3664&marked-M'T-3:16(5616)■6:8(3666),29(5613)■11:16■12:13(5613)■13:31,33,44,45,47,52■20:1■21:24(2504)■22:2(3666),39■23:27(3945)■28:3(5613)-M'R-1:10(5616)■4:31(5613)■7:8(3946),13(3946)■12:31■13:29(2532)-LU-3:22(5616)■6:23(5024),47,48,49■7:31,32■12:27(5613),36■13:18,19,21■20:31(5615)-JOH-1:32(5616)■7:46(3779)■8:55■9:9-AC-1:11(3779)■2:3(5616)■3:22(3945)■7:37(5613)■8:32(5613)■11:17(2470)■14:15(3663)■17:29■19:25(5108)-RO-1:23(3667),28(1381)■6:4(5618)■9:29(3666)-1CO-16:13(407)-GA-5:21-PH'P-3:21(4832)-1TH-2:14(5024)-1TI-2:9(5615)-HEB-2:17(3666)■4:15(2596,3665)■7:3(871)-JAS-1:6(1503),23(1503)■5:17(3663)-1PE-3:21(499)-2PE-1:1(2472)-1JO-3:2-JUDE-7-RE-1:13,14(5616),15■2:18(5613),18■4:3[2],6,7[3]■9:7[2],10,19■11:1■13:2,4,11■14:14■16:13■18:18,21(5613)■21:11,11(5613),18

LIKED-1CH-28:4(7521)

LIKEMINDED-RO-15:5(3588,846,5426)-PH'P-2:2(3588,846,5426),20(2473)

LIKEN-all=1819-IS-40:18:25■46:5-LA-2:13■N.T.-all=3666-M'T-7:24■11:16-M'R-4:30-LU-7:31■13:20

LIKENED-PS-89:6(1819)-JER-6:2(1819)■N.T.-all=3666-M'T-7:26■13:24■18:23■25:1

LIKENESS-all=1823&marked-GE-1:26■5:1,3-EX-20:4(8544)-DE-4:16(8403),17[2](8403),18[2](8403),23(8544),25(8544)■5:8(8544)-PS-17:15(8544)-IS-40:18-EZE-1:5[2],10,13,16,22,26[3],28■8:2■10:1,10,21,22■N.T.-all=3667&marked-AC-14:11(3666)-RO-6:5,5sup■8:3-PH'P-2:7

LIKETH-DE-23:16(2896)-ES-8:8(2896)-AM-4:5(157)

LIKEWISE-all=1571,a=3651&marked-EX-22:30a■26:4a■27:11a■36:11a-LE-7:1(2063)-DE-12:30a■15:17a■22:3a-J'G-1:3■7:17a■8:8(2063)■9:49-1SA-19:21■31:5-2SA-1:11■17:5-1KI-11:8a-1CH-10:5■19:15■23:30a■24:31■29:24-NE-4:22■5:10■4:16a-JOB-31:38(3162)-PS-52:5-EC-7:22-JER-40:11-EZE-40:16a-NA-1:12a■N.T.-all=3668,a=2532,b=5615&marked-M'T-17:12(3779)■18:35a■20:5b,10a■21:30b,36b■22:26■24:33a■25:17b■26:35■27:41-M'R-4:16■12:21b■14:31b■15:31-LU-2:38(437)■3:11,14a■5:33■6:31■10:32,37■13:3b,5■14:33(3779)■15:7(3779),10(3779)■16:25■17:10a,28,31■19:19a■21:31a■22:20b,36-JOH-5:19■6:11■21:13-AC-3:24a-RO-1:27■6:11(3779)■8:26b■16:5a-1CO-7:3,4,22■14:9a-GA-2:13a-COL-4:16a-1TI-3:8b■5:25b-TIT-2:3b,6b-HEB-2:14(3898)■9:21-JAS-2:25-1PE-3:1,7(36)■4:1a■5:5-JUDE-8-RE-8:12

LIKING-JOB-39:4(2492)

LILIES-all=7799-1KI-7:26-2CH-4:5-SONG-2:16■4:5■5:13■6:2,3■7:2■N.T.-M'T-6:28(2918)-LU-12:27(2918)

LILY-all=7799-1KI-7:19,22-SONG-2:1,2-HO-14:5

LIME-IS-33:12(7875)-AM-2:1(7875)

LIMIT-EZE-43:12(1366)

LIMITED-PS-78:41(8428)

LIMITETH-HEB-4:7(3724)

LINE-all=6957&marked-JOS-2:18(8615),21(8615)-2SA-8:2[2](2256)-1KI-7:15(2339),23-2KI-21:13-2CH-4:2-JOB-38:5-PS-19:4■78:55(2256)-IS-28:10,13,17■34:11,17■44:13(8279)-JER-31:39-LA-2:8-EZE-40:3(6616)■47:3-AM-7:17(2256)-ZEC-1:16■2:1(2256)■N.T.-2CO-10:16(2583)

LINEAGE-LU-2:4(3965)

LINEN-all=8336,a=906&marked-GE-41:42-EX-25:4■26:1,31,36■27:9,16,18■28:5,6,8,15,39[2],42a■35:6,23,25,35■36:8,35,37■38:9,16,18,23■39:2,3,5,8,27,28,28a,28,29-LE-6:10[2]a■13:47(6593),48(6593),52(6593),59(6593)■16:4[4]a,23,32■19:19(8162)-DE-22:11(6593)-1SA-2:18a■22:18a-2SA-6:14a-1KI-10:28[2](4723)-1CH-4:21(948)■15:27(948),27a-2CH-1:16[2](4723)■2:14(948)■3:14(948)■5:12(948)-ES-1:6(948)■8:15(948)-PR-7:16(948)■31:24(5466)-IS-3:23(5466)-JER-13:1(6593)-EZE-9:2a,3a,11a■10:2a,6a,7a■16:10,13■27:7,16(948)■44:17(6593),18[2](6593)-DA-10:5a■12:6a,7a■N.T.-all=4616&marked-M'T-27:59-M'R-14:51,52■15:46[2]-LU-16:19(1040)■23:53■24:12(3608)-JOH-19:40(3608)■20:5(3608),6(3608),7(3608)-RE-15:6(3043)■18:12(1040),16(1039)■19:8[2](1039),14(1039)

LINES-2SA-8:2(2256)-PS-16:6(2256)

LINGERED-GE-19:16(4102)■43:10(4102)

LINGERETH-2PE-2:3(691)

LINTEL-EX-12:22(4947),23(4947)-1KI-6:31(352)-AM-9:1(3730)

LINTELS-ZEP-2:14(3730)

LION-all=738,a=3715&marked-GE-49:9,9(3833)-NU-23:24(3833),24■24:9,9(3833)-DE-33:20(3833)-J'G-14:5,8[2],9,18-1SA-17:34,36■37-2SA-17:10■23:20-1KI-13:24[2],25,26,28[2]■20:36[2]-1CH-11:22-JOB-4:10,10(7826),11(3918)■10:16(7826),28:8(7826)■38:39(3833)-PS-7:2■10:9■17:12,12a■22:13■91:13(7826),13a-PR-19:12a■20:2a■22:13■26:13[2]■28:1a,15(739)■30:30(3918)-EC-9:4-IS-5:29(3833)■11:6a,7■21:8■30:6(3918)■31:4,4a■35:9■38:13■65:25-JER-2:30■4:7■5:6■12:8■25:38a■49:19■50:44-LA-3:10-EZE-1:10■10:14■19:3a,5a,6a■22:25■32:2a■41:19-DA-7:4-HO-5:14(7826),14a■11:10■13:7(7826),8(3833)-JOE-1:6,6(3833)-AM-3:4,4a,8,12■5:19-MIC-5:8,8a-NA-2:11(739),11(3833),12■N.T.-all=3023-2TI-4:17-1PE-5:8-RE-4:7■5:5■10:3■13:2

LIONESS-EZE-19:2(3833)

LIONESSES-NA-2:12(3833)

LIONLIKE-2SA-23:20(739)-1CH-11:22(739)

LION'S-all=738&marked-GE-49:9-DE-33:22-JOB-4:11(3833)■28:8(7830)-PS-22:21-NA-2:11

LIONS-all=738,a=3715&marked-2SA-1:23-1KI-7:29[2],36■10:19,20-2KI-17:25,26-1CH-12:8-2CH-9:18,19-JOB-4:10a■38:39a-PS-34:10a■35:17a■57:4(3833)■58:6a■104:21a-IS-5:29a■15:9-JER-2:15a■50:17■51:38a-EZE-19:2,2a,6■38:13a-DA-6:7(744),12(744),16(744),19(744),20(744),24[2](744),27(744)-NA-2:11,11a,13a-ZEP-3:3-ZEC-11:3a■N.T.-all=3023-HEB-11:33-RE-9:8,17

LIONS'-SONG-4:8(738)-JER-51:38(738)-DA-6:22(744)

LIP-LE-13:45(822)-PS-22:7(8193)-PR-12:19

LIPS-all=8193&marked-EX-6:12,30-LE-5:4-NU-30:6,8,12-DE-23:23-1SA-1:13-2KI-19:28-JOB-2:10■8:21■11:5■13:6■15:6■16:5■23:12■27:4■32:20■33:3 PS 12:2,3,4■16:4■17:1,4■21:2■31:18■34:13■40:9■45:2■51:15■59:7,12■63:3,5■66:14■71:23■89:34■106:33■119:13,171■120:2■140:3,9■141:3-PR-4:24■5:2,3■7:21■8:6,7■10:13,18,19,21,32■12:13,22■13:3■14:3,7,23■15:7■16:10,13,21,23,27,30■17:4,7,28■18:6■7,20■19:1■20:15,19■22:11,18■23:16■24:2,26,28■26:23,24■27:2-EC-10:12-SONG-4:3,11■5:13■7:9-IS-6:5[2],7■11:4■28:11■29:13■30:27■37:29■57:19■59:3-JER-17:16-LA-3:62-EZE-24:17(8222),22

(8222)■36:3-**DA**-10:16-**HO**-14:2-**MIC**-3:7(8222)-**HAB**-3:16-**MAL**-2:6,7■**N.T.**-all=5491-**M'T**-15:8-**M'R**-7:6-**RO**-3:13-**1CO**-14:21-**HEB**-13:15-**1PE**-3:10

LIQUOR-**NU**-6:3(4952)-**SONG**-7:2(4197)

LIQUORS-**EX**-22:29(1831)

LISTED-**M'T**-17:12(2309)-**M'R**-9:13(2309)

LISTEN-**IS**-49:1(8085)

LISTETH-**JOH**-3:8(2309)-**JAS**-3:4(3730,1014)

LITTERS-**IS**-66:20(6632)

LITTLE-all=4592,a=2945,b=6996&marked-**GE**-18:4■19:20^{2}(4705)■24:17,43■30:30■34:29a■35:16(3530)■43:2,8a,11■44:20b,25■45:19a■46:5a■47:24a■48:7(3530)■50:8a,21a-**EX**-10:10a,24a■12:4(4591)■16:18(4591)■23:30-**LE**-11:17(3563)-**NU**-14:31a■16:27a■31:9a,17a■32:16a,17a,24a,26a-**DE**-1:39a■2:34a■3:19a■7:22■14:16(3563)■20:14a■28:38■29:11a-**JOS**-1:14a■8:35a■22:17-**J'G**-4:19■18:21a-**RU**-2:7-**1SA**-2:19b■14:29,43■15:17b■20:35b-**2SA**-12:3b,8■15:22a■16:1■19:36-**1KI**-3:7b■8:64b■11:17b■12:10b■17:10,12,13b■18:44b■20:27(2835)-**2KI**-2:23b■4:10b■5:2b,14(6995),19(3530)■10:18-**2CH**-10:10b■20:13a■31:18a-**EZR**-8:21a■9:8^{2}-**NE**-9:32(4591)-**ES**-3:13a■8:11a-**JOB**-4:12(8102)■10:20■21:11(5759)■24:24■26:14(8102)■36:2(2191)-**PS**-2:12■8:5■37:10,16■68:27(6810)■137:9(5768)-**PR**-6:10^{2}■10:20■15:16■16:8■24:33^{2}■30:24b-**EC**-5:12■9:14b■10:1-**SONG**-2:15b■3:4■8:8b-**IS**-10:25■11:6(6995)■26:20■28:10(2191),13(2191)■29:17■40:15(1851)■54:8(8241)■60:22b■63:18(4705)-**JER**-14:3(6810)■48:4(6810)■51:33-**EZE**-9:6a■11:16■16:47■31:4(8585)-**DA**-7:8(2192)■8:9(4704)■11:34-**HO**-1:4■8:10-**AM**-6:11b-**MIC**-5:2(6810)-**HAG**-1:6,9■2:6-**ZEC**-1:15■13:7(6819)■**N.T.**-all=3398,a=3397,b=3813&marked-**M'T**-6:30(3640)■8:26(3640)■10:42■14:31(3640)■15:35(2485)■16:8(3640)■18:2b,3b,4b,5b,6,10,14■19:13b,14b■26:39a-**M'R**-1:19(3641)■4:36(4142)■5:23(2365)■9:42■10:14b,15b■14:35a,70a-**LU**-5:3(3641)■7:47^{2}(3641)■12:28(3640),32■17:2■18:16b,17b■19:3,17(1646)■22:58(1024)-**JOH**-6:7(1024)■7:33■12:35■13:33(5040),33a■14:19a■16:16^{2}a,17^{2}a,18,19^{2}■21:8(4142)-**AC**-5:34(1024)■20:12(3357)■27:28(1024)■28:2(5177)-**1CO**-5:6-**2CO**-8:15(3641)■11:1a,16a-**GA**-4:19(5040)■5:9-**1TI**-4:8(3641)■5:23(3641)-**HEB**-2:7(1024),9(1024)■10:37a-**JAS**-3:5,5(3641)■4:14(3641)-**1JO**-2:1(5040),12(5040),13b,18b,28(5040)■3:7(5040),18(5040)■4:4(5040)■5:21(5040)-**RE**-3:8■6:11■10:2(974),8(974),9(974),10(974)■20:3

LIVE-all=2421,a=2416,b=2425&marked-**GE**-3:22b■12:13■17:18■19:20■20:7■27:40■31:32■42:2,18■43:8■45:3a■47:19-**EX**-1:16b■19:13■21:35a■22:18■33:20b-**LE**-16:20a,21a■18:5b■25:35a,36a-**NU**-4:19■14:21a,28a■21:8b■24:23-**DE**-4:1,10a,33,42b■5:33■8:1,3^{2}■12:1a■16:20■19:4b,5b■30:6a,16,19■31:13a■32:40a■33:6-**JOS**-6:17■9:15,20,21-**1SA**-20:14a-**2SA**-1:10■12:22a■19:34a-**1KI**-1:31■8:40a■20:32-**2KI**-4:7■7:4■10:19■18:32■20:1-**2CH**-6:31a-**NE**-2:3■5:2■9:29-**ES**-4:11-**JOB**-7:16■14:14■21:7■27:6(3117)-**PS**-22:26■49:9■63:4a■69:32■72:15■104:33a■116:2(3117)■118:17■119:17,77,116,144,175■146:2a-**PR**-4:4■7:2■9:6■15:27-**EC**-6:3,6■9:3a,9a■11:8-**IS**-6:6(7531)■26:14,19■38:1,16^{2}■49:18a■55:3-**JER**-21:9■22:24a■27:12,17■35:7■38:2,2b,17^{2},20■46:18a-**LA**-4:20-**EZE**-3:21■5:11a■13:19■14:16a,18a,20a■16:6^{2},48a■17:16a,19a■18:3a,9,13b,13,17,19,21,22,23,24b,28,32■20:3a,11b,13b,21b,25,31a■33:10,11a,11,12,13,15,16,19,27a■34:8a■35:6a,11a■37:3,5,6,9,14■47:9,9b-**DA**-2:4(2418)■3:9(2418)■5:10(2414)■6:6(2414),21(2414)-**HO**-6:2-**AM**-5:4,6,14-**JON**-4:3a,8a-**HAB**-2:4-**ZEP**-2:9a-**ZEC**-1:5■10:9■13:3■**N.T.**-all=2198&marked-**M'T**-4:4■9:18-**M'R**-5:23-**LU**-4:4■7:25(5225)■10:28■20:38-**JOH**-5:25■6:51,57^{2},58■11:25■14:19-**AC**-7:19(2225)■17:28■22:22■25:24■28:4-**RO**-1:17■6:2,8(4800)■8:12,13^{2}■10:5■12:18(1514)■14:8^{2},11-**1CO**-9:13(2068),14-**2CO**-4:11■5:15^{2}■6:9■7:3(4800)■13:4,11(1514)-**GA**-2:14,19,20^{3}■3:11,12■5:25-**EPH**-6:3(2071,3118)-**PH'P**-1:21,22-**1TH**-3:8■5:10-**2TI**-2:11(4800)■3:12-**TIT**-2:12-**HEB**-10:38■12:9■13:18(390)-**JAS**-4:15-**1PE**-2:24■4:2(980),6(2198)-**2PE**-2:18(390)-**1JO**-4:9-**RE**-13:14

LIVED-all=2421&marked-**GE**-5:3,5(2425),6,7,9,10,12,13,15,16,18,19,21,25,26,28,30■9:28■11:11,12(2425),13,14(2425),15,16,17,18,19,20,21,22,23,24,25,26■25:6(2416)■25:7(2425)■47:28■50:22-**NU**-14:38■21:9(2425)-**DE**-5:26-**2SA**-19:6(2416)-**1KI**-12:6(2416)-**2KI**-14:17-**2CH**-10:6(2416)■25:25-**JOB**-42:16-**PS**-49:18(2416)-**EZE**-37:10■**N.T.**-all=2198&marked-**LU**-2:36-**AC**-23:1(4176)■26:5-**COL**-3:7-**JAS**-5:5(5171)-**RE**-20:4,5(326)

LIVELY-**EX**-1:19(2422)-**PS**-38:19(2416)■**N.T.**-all=2198-**AC**-7:38-**1PE**-1:3■2:5

LIVER-all=3516-**EX**-29:13,22-**LE**-3:4,10,15■4:9■7:4■8:16,25■9:10,19-**PR**-7:23-**LA**-2:11-**EZE**-21:21

LIVES-all=5315&marked-**GE**-9:5■45:7(2421)■47:25(2421)-**EX**-1:14(2416)-**JOS**-2:13■9:24-**J'G**-5:18■18:25-**2SA**-1:23(2416)■19:5^{2}■23:17-**1CH**-11:19^{2}-**ES**-9:16-**PR**-1:18-**JER**-19:7,9■46:26■48:6-**LA**-5:9-**DA**-7:12(2417)■**N.T.**-all=5590-**LU**-9:56-**AC**-15:26■27:10-**1JO**-3:16-**RE**-12:11

LIVEST-**DE**-12:19(3117)-**2SA**-11:11(2416)■**N.T.**-**GA**-2:14(2198)-**RE**-3:1(2198)

LIVETH-all=2416&marked-**GE**-9:3-**DE**-5:24(2425)**J'G**-8:19-**RU**-3:13-**1SA**-1:26,28(3117)■14:39,45■17:55■19:6■20:3,21,31(2425)■25:6,26,34■26:10,16■28:10■29:6-**2SA**-2:27■4:9■11:11■12:5■14:11,19■15:21^{2}■22:47-**1KI**-1:29■2:24■3:23■17:1,12,23■18:10,15■22:14-**2KI**-2:2,4,6■3:14■4:30■5:16,20-**2CH**-18:13-**JOB**-19:25■27:2-**PS**-18:46■89:48(2421)-**JER**-4:2■5:2■12:16■16:14,15■23:7,8■38:16■44:26-**EZE**-47:9-**DA**-4:34■12:7-**HO**-4:15-**AM**-8:14^{2}■**N.T.**-all=2198-**JOH**-4:50,51,53■11:26-**RO**-6:10■7:1,2,3■14:7-**1CO**-7:39-**2CO**-13:4-**GA**-2:20-**1TI**-5:6-**HEB**-7:8,25■9:17-**1PE**-1:23-**RE**-1:18■4:9,10■5:14■10:6■15:7

LIVING-all=2416&marked-**GE**-1:21,24,28■2:7,19■3:20■6:19■8:1,17,21■9:10,12,15,16-**LE**-11:10,46■14:6^{2},7,51,52,53-**NU**-16:48-**DE**-5:26-**JOS**-3:10-**RU**-2:20-**1SA**-17:26,36-**2SA**-20:3(2424)-**1KI**-3:22,22,23,25,26^{2},27-**2KI**-19:4,16-**JOB**-12:10■28:13,21■30:23■33:30-**PS**-27:13■42:2■52:5■56:13■58:9■69:28■84:2■116:9■142:5■143:2■145:16-**EC**-4:2,15■6:8■7:2■9:4^{2},5-**SONG**-4:15-**IS**-4:3■8:19■37:4,17■38:11,19■53:8-**JER**-2:13■10:10■11:19■17:13■23:36-**LA**-3:39-**EZE**-1:5,13^{2},14,15^{2},19^{2},20,21,22■3:13■10:15,17,20■26:20■32:23,24,25,26,27,32-**DA**-2:30(2417)■4:17(2417)■6:20(2417),26(2417)-**HO**-1:10-**ZEC**-14:8■**N.T.**-all=2198&marked-**M'T**-16:16■22:32■26:63-**M'R**-12:27,44(979)-**LU**-8:43(979)■15:12(979),13,30(979)■20:38■21:4(979)■24:5-**JOH**-4:10,11■6:51,57,69■7:38-**AC**-14:15-**RO**-9:26■12:1■14:9-**1CO**-15:45-**2CO**-3:3■6:16-**COL**-2:20-**1TH**-1:9■3:15■4:10■6:17-**TIT**-3:3(1236)-**HEB**-3:12■9:14■10:20,31■12:22-**1PE**-2:4-**RE**-7:2,17■16:3

LIZARD-**LE**-11:30(3911)

LO-all=2009,a=2005&marked-**GE**-8:11■15:3,12■18:2,10■19:28■29:2,7a■37:7■42:28■47:23(1883)■48:11■50:5-**EX**-7:15■8:20,26a■19:9-**NU**-14:40■22:38■23:6,9a■24:11-**DE**-22:17-**JOS**-14:10-**J'G**-7:13■13:5-**1SA**-4:13■10:2■14:43(2114)■21:14-**2SA**-1:6■15:24■24:17-**1KI**-1:22,51■3:12-**2KI**-7:6,15-**1CH**-17:1■21:23(7200)-**2CH**-16:11■25:19■27:7a■29:9-**NE**-5:5■6:12-**JOB**-3:7■5:27■9:11a,19■13:1a■21:16a■26:14a■33:29a■40:16-**PS**-11:2■37:36■40:7,9■48:4■52:7■55:7■59:3■68:33a■73:27a■83:2■92:9^{2}■127:3■132:6■139:4a-**PR**-24:31-**EC**-1:16■7:29(7200)-**SONG**-2:11-**IS**-6:7■25:9■36:6■49:12■50:9a-**JER**-1:15■4:23,24,25,26■5:15■8:8,9■25:29■30:3,10■36:12■49:15■50:9-**EZE**-2:9■4:15(7200)■8:2,17■13:10,12■17:18■18:14,18■23:39,40■30:9,21■33:32,33■37:2,8■40:17■42:8-**DA**-3:25(1888)■7:6(718)■10:13,20-**HO**-9:6-**AM**-4:2,13■7:1■9:9-**HAB**-1:6-**HAG**-1:9-■**N.T.**-all=2400&marked-**M'T**-2:9■3:16,17■24:23■25:25(2396)■26:47■28:7,20-**M'R**-10:28■13:21■14:42-**LU**-1:44■2:9■9:39■13:16■15:29■17:21^{2}■18:28■23:15-**JOH**-7:26(2396)■16:29(2396)-**AC**-13:46■27:24-**HEB**-10:7,9-**RE**-5:6■6:5,12■7:9■14:1

LOADEN-**IS**-46:1(6006)

LOADETH-**PS**-68:19(6006)

LOAF-**EX**-29:23(3603)-**1CH**-16:3(3603)■**N.T.**-**M'R**-8:14(740)

LOAN-**1SA**-2:20(7596)

LOATHE-**JOB**-7:16(3988)

LOATHETH-**NU**-21:5(6973)-**PR**-27:7(947)

LOATHESOME-**NU**-11:20(2214)-**JOB**-7:5(3988)-**PS**-38:7(7033)-**PR**-13:5(887)

LOAVES-all=3899&marked-**LE**-23:17-**J'G**-8:5(3603)-**1SA**-10:3(3603)■17:17■25:18-**1KI**-14:3-**2KI**-4:42■**N.T.**-all=740-**M'T**-14:17,19^{2}■15:34,36■16:9,10-**M'R**-6:38,41^{2},44,52■8:5,6,19-**LU**-9:13,16■11:5-**JOH**-6:9,11,13,26

LOCK-**SONG**-5:5(4514)-**EZE**-8:3(6734)

LOCKED-**J'G**-3:23(5274),24(5274)

LOCKS-all=4514&marked-**NU**-6:5(6545)-**J'G**-16:13(4253),19(4253)-**NE**-3:3,6,13,14,15-**SONG**-4:1(6777),3(6777)■5:2(6977),11(6977)■6:7(6777)-**IS**-47:2(6777)-**EZE**-44:20(6545)

LOCUST-all=697&marked-**EX**-10:19-**LE**-11:22,22(5556)-**DE**-28:38,42(6767)-**1KI**-8:37-**PS**-78:46■109:23-**JOE**-1:4^{2}■2:25

LOCUSTS-all=697&marked-**EX**-10:4,12,13,14^{2},19-**2CH**-6:28■7:13(2284)-**PS**-105:34-**PR**-30:27-**IS**-33:4(1357)-**NA**-3:15,17■**N.T.**-all=200-**M'T**-3:4-**M'R**-1:6-**RE**-9:3,7

LODGE-all=3885&marked-**GE**-24:23,25-**NU**-22:8-**JOS**-4:3-**J'G**-19:9,11,13,15,20■20:4-**RU**-1:16-**2SA**-17:8,16-**NE**-4:22■13:21-**JOB**-24:7■31:32-**SONG**-7:11-**IS**-1:8(4412)■21:13■65:4-**JER**-4:14-**ZEP**-2:14■**N.T.**-**M'T**-13:32(2681)-**M'R**-4:32(2681)-**LU**-9:12(2647)-**AC**-21:16(3579)

LODGED-all=3885&marked-**GE**-32:13,21-**JOS**-2:1(7901)■3:1■4:8(4411)■6:11■8:9-**J'G**-18:2■19:4,7-**1KI**-19:9-**1CH**-9:27-**NE**-13:20-**IS**-1:21■**N.T.**-all=3579&marked-**M'T**-21:17(835)-**LU**-13:19(2681)-**AC**-10:18,23,32■28:7-**1TI**-5:10(3580)

LODGEST-**RU**-1:16(3885)

LODGETH-**AC**-10:6(3579)

LODGING-all=4411&marked-**JOS**-4:3-**J'G**-19:15(3885)-**IS**-10:29-**JER**-9:2■**N.T.**-**AC**-28:23(3578)-**PH'M**-22(3578)

LODGINGS-**2KI**-19:23(4411)

LOFT-1KI-17:19(5944)■**N.T.**-AC-20:9(5152)

LOFTILY-PS-73:8(4791)

LOFTINESS-IS-2:17(1365)-JER-48:29(1363)

LOFTY-all=7311&marked-PS-131:1-PR-30:13-IS-2:11(1365),12■5:15(1364)■26:5(7682)■57:7(1364),15(5375)

LOG-all=3849-LE-14:10,12,15,21,24

LOINS-all=4975&marked-GE-35:11(2504)■37:34■46:26(3409)-EX-1:5(3409)■12:11■28:42-DE-33:11-2SA-20:8-1KI-2:5■8:19(2504)■12:10■18:46■20:31,32-2KI-1:8■4:29■9:1-2CH-6:9(2504)■10:10-JOB-12:18■31:20(2504)■38:3(2504)■40:7(2504),16-PS-38:7(3689)■66:11■69:23-PR-31:17-IS-5:27■(2504)■11:5■20:2■21:3■32:11(2504)■45:1-JER-1:17■13:1,2,4,11■30:6(2504)■48:37-EZE-1:27^{2}■8:2^{2}■21:6■23:15■29:7■44:18■47:4-DA-5:6(2783)■10:5-AM-8:10-NA-2:1,10■**N.T.**-all=3751-M'T-3:4-M'R-1:6-LU-12:35-AC-2:30-EPH-6:14-HEB-7:5,10-1PE-1:13

LONG-all=5704,a=753,b=3117&marked-GE-26:8(748)■48:15(5750)-EX-10:3(4970),7■16:28■19:13(4900)■20:12(748)■27:1(753),9(753),11(753)-LE-26:34b,35b-NU-9:18b■14:11^{2},27■20:15(7227)-DE-1:6(7227)■2:3(7227)■12:19b■14:24(7235)■19:6(7235)■20:19(7227)■31:13b-JOS-6:5(4900)■9:13(7230)■11:18(7227)■18:3■23:1(7227)■24:7(7227)-J'G-5:28(954)-1SA-1:14,28b■7:2(7235)■16:1■20:31b■25:15b■29:8b-2SA-2:26■3:1(752)■14:2(7227)■19:34b-1KI-3:11(7227)■18:21-2KI-9:22■19:25(7350)-2CH-1:11(7227)■3:11a■6:13a■31b■15:3(7227)■26:5b■30:5(7230)■36:21b-NE-2:6-ES-5:13(6256)-JOB-3:21(2442)■6:8(8615)■7:19(4101)■8:2,2sup■18:2■19:2■27:6b-PS-4:2,2sup■6:3■13:1^{2},2^{2}■35:17■62:3■72:5(5973),7■17(6440)■74:9,10■80:4■82:2■89:46■90:13■91:16a■94:3^{2},4■104:33■116:2b■120:6(7227)■129:3(748)■143:3(5769)-PR-1:22■3:2a■6:9■7:19(7350)■25:15a-EC-12:5(5769)-IS-6:11■22:11(7350)■37:26(7350)■42:14(5769)-JER-4:14,21■12:4■23:26■29:28(752)■31:22■47:5,6-LA-5:20a-EZE-31:5(748)■40:7a,29a,30a,33a,42a,47a■41:13^{2}a■42:11a,20a■43:16,17■45:6a■46:22a-DA-8:13■10:1(1419)■12:6-HO-8:5-HAB-1:2■2:6-ZEC-1:12■**N.T.**-all=2193&marked-M'T-9:15(1909)■11:21(3819)■17:17^{2}■23:14(3117)■25:19(4183)-M'R-2:19(5550)■9:19^{2},21(4214)■12:40(3117)-LU-8:27(2425)■9:41■18:7(3114)■20:9(2425)■47(3117)■23:8(2425)-JOH-5:6(4183)■9:5(3752)■10:24■14:9(5118)-AC-8:11(2425)■14:3(2425),28(3756,3641)■20:9(1909,4119),11(2425)■27:14(4183),21(4183)-RO-1:11(1971)■7:1(5550)-1CO-7:39(5550)■11:14(2863),15(2863)■13:4(3114)-2CO-9:14(1971)-GA-4:1(5550)-EPH-6:3(2118)-PH'P-1:8(1971)-HEB-4:7(5118)-JAS-5:7(3114)-RE-6:10

LONGED-2SA-13:29(3615)■23:15(183)-1CH-11:17(183)-PS-119:40(8373),131(2968),174(8373)■**N.T.**-PH'P-2:26(1971)■4:1(1973)

LONGEDST-GE-31:30(3700)

LONGER-all=5750&marked-EX-2:3■9:28(3254)-J'G-2:14-2KI-6:33-JOB-11:9(752)-JER-44:22■**N.T.**-all=3370&marked-LU-16:2(2089)-AC-18:20(4119)■25:24-RO-6:2(2089)-GA-3:25(2089)-1TH-3:1,5-1TI-5:23-1PE-4:2-RE-10:6(2089)

LONGETH-GE-34:8(2836)-DE-12:20(183)-PS-63:1(3642)■84:2(3700)

LONGING-PS-107:9(8264)■119:20(8375)

LONGSUFFERING-all=750,639-EX-34:6-NU-14:18-PS-86:15-JER-15:15■**N.T.**-all=3115&marked-RO-2:4■9:22-2CO-6:6-GA-5:22-EPH-4:2-COL-1:11■3:12-1TI-1:16-2TI-3:10■4:2-1PE-3:20-2PE-3:9(3114)■3:15

LONGWINGED-EZE-17:3(750,83)

LOOK-all=7200,a=5027,b=6437&marked-GE-9:16■12:11(4758)■13:14■15:5a■19:17a■24:16(4758)■26:7(4758)■40:7(6440)■41:33■42:1-EX-3:6a■5:21■10:10■25:40■39:43-LE-13:3^{2},5,6,21,25,26,27,31,32,34,36,39,43,50,51,53,55,56■14:3,37,39,44,48-NU-15:39-DE-9:27b■26:15(8259)■28:32-J'G-7:17-1SA-1:11■16:7a,12(7210)■17:18(6485)-2SA-9:8b■11:2(4758)■16:12-1KI-18:43a-2KI-3:14a■6:32■9:2■10:3,23■14:8-1CH-12:17-2CH-24:22-ES-1:11(4758)-JOB-3:9(6960)■6:28b■20:21(2342)■35:5a■40:12-PS-5:3(6822)■22:17a■25:18■35:17■40:12■80:14a■84:9a■85:11(8259)■101:5(5869)■119:132b-PR-4:25a■6:17(5869)■21:4(5869)■23:31■27:23(7896)-EC-12:3-SONG-1:6■4:8(7789)■6:13(2372)-IS-5:30a■8:17(6960),21b,22a■14:16(7688)■17:7(8159)■8(8159)■22:4(8159),8a■31:1(8159)■33:20(2372)■42:18a■45:22b■51:1a,2a,6a■56:11b■59:11(6960)■63:15a■66:2a,24-JER-13:16(6960)■39:12(7760)■40:4(7760)■46:5b■47:3b-LA-3:50(8259)-EZE-23:15(4758)■29:16b■43:17b-DA-7:20(2376)-HO-3:1b-JON-2:4a-MIC-4:11(2372)■7:7(6822)-NA-2:8b■3:7-HAB-1:13a■2:15-ZEC-12:10■**N.T.**-all=991&marked-M'T-11:3(4328)-M'R-8:25(308)-LU-7:19(4328),20(4328)■9:38(1914)■21:28(352)-JOH-4:35(2300)■7:52(1492)■19:37(3700)-AC-3:4,12(816)■6:3(1980)■18:15(3700)-1CO-16:11(1551)-2CO-3:13(816)■4:18(4648)■10:7-PH'P-2:4(4648)■3:20(553)-HEB-9:28(558)-1PE-1:12(3879)-2PE-3:13(4328),14(4328)-2JO-8-RE-4:3(3706)■5:3,4

LOOKED-all=7200,a=6437,b=8259,c=5027&marked-GE-6:12■8:13■16:13:18:2,16b■19:26c,28b■22:13■26:8b■29:2,32■33:1■37:25■39:23■40:6-EX-2:11,12a,25■3:2■4:31■14:24b■16:10a■33:8c-NU-12:10a■16:42a■17:9■24:20,21-DE-9:16■26:7-JOS-5:13■8:20a-J'G-5:28b■6:14a■9:43■13:19,20■20:40a-1SA-6:19■9:16■14:16■16:6■17:42c■24:8c-2SA-1:7a■2:20a■6:16b■13:34■18:24■22:42(8159)■24:20b-1KI-18:43c■19:6c-2KI-2:24■6:30■9:30b,32b■11:14■14:11-1CH-21:21c-2CH-13:14a■20:24a■23:13■26:20a-NE-4:14a-ES-2:15a-JOB-6:19c■30:26(6960)-PS-14:2b■34:5c■53:2b■69:20(6960)■102:19b■109:25■142:4c-PR-7:6b-24:32-EC-2:11a-SONG-1:6(7805)-IS-5:2(6960),4(6960),7(6960)■22:11c■63:5c■64:3(6960)-JER-8:15(6960)■14:19(6960)-LA-2:16(6960)-EZE-1:4■2:9■8:7■10:1,9,11a■16:8■21:21■40:20(6440)■44:4■46:19a-DA-1:13■10:5■12:5-OB-12,13-HAG-1:9a-ZEC-2:1■4:2■5:1,9■6:1■**N.T.**-all=1492&marked-M'R-3:5(4017),34(4017)■5:32(4017)■6:41(308)■8:24(308),33■9:8(4017)■10:23(4017)■11:11(4017)■14:67(1689)■16:4(308)-LU-1:25(1896)■2:38(4327)■10:32■19:5(308)■21:1(308)■22:56(816),61(1689)-JOH-13:22(991)-AC-1:10(816)■7:55(816)■10:4(816)■22:13(308)■28:6^{2}(4328)-HEB-11:10(1551)-1JO-1:1(2300)-RE-4:1■6:8■14:1,14■15:5

LOOKEST-JOB-13:27(8104)-HAB-1:13(5027)

LOOKETH-all=6437&marked-LE-13:12(4758,5869)-NU-21:8(7200),20(8259)■23:28(8259)-JOS-15:2-1SA-13:18(8259)■16:7^{2}(7200)-JOB-7:2(6960)■28:24(5027)■33:27(7789)-PS-33:13(5027),14(7688)■104:32(5027)-PR-14:15(995)■31:27(6822)-SONG-2:9(7688)■6:10(8259)■7:4(6822)-IS-28:4(7200)-EZE-8:3■11:1■40:6(6440),22(6440)■43:1■44:1■46:1,12■47:2■**N.T.**-M'T-5:28(991)■24:50(4328)-LU-12:46(4328)-JAS-1:25(3879)

LOOKING-all=6437&marked-JOS-15:7-1KI-7:25^{4}-1CH-15:29(8259)-2CH-4:4^{4}-JOB-37:18(7209)■**N.T.**-all=4327&marked-M'T-14:19(308)-M'R-7:34(308)■10:27(1689)■15:40(2334)-LU-6:10(4017)■9:16(308),62(991)■21:26(4329)-JOH-1:36(1689)-AC-6:15(816)■23:21-TIT-2:13-HEB-10:27(1561)■12:2(872),15(1983)-2PE-3:12(4328)-JUDE-21

LOOKINGGLASSES-EX-38:8(4759)

LOOKS-all=5869&marked-PS-18:27-IS-2:11■10:12-EZE-2:6(6440)■3:9(6440)

LOOPS-all=3924-EX-26:4,5^{3},10^{2},11■36:11,12^{3},17^{2}

LOOSE-all=6605&marked-GE-49:21(7971)-LE-14:7(7971)-DE-25:9(2502)-JOS-5:15(5394)-JOB-6:9(5425)■30:11(7971)■38:31-PS-102:20-IS-20:2■45:1■52:2■58:6-JER-40:4-DA-3:25(8271)■**N.T.**-all=8089-M'T-16:19■18:18■21:2-M'R-11:2,4-LU-13:15■19:30,31,33-JOH-11:44-AC-13:25■24:26-RE-5:2,5■9:14

LOOSED-all=6605&marked-EX-28:28(2118)■39:21(2118)-DE-25:10(2502)-J'G-15:14(4549)-JOB-30:11■39:5-PS-105:20(5425)■116:16-EC-12:6(7368)-IS-5:27■33:23(5203)■51:14-DA-5:6(8271)■**N.T.**-all=3089&marked-M'T-16:19■18:18,27(630)-M'R-7:35-LU-13:12(630),16-AC-2:24■13:13(321)■16:26(447)■22:30■27:21(321),40(447)-RO-7:2(2673)-1CO-7:27,27(3080)-RE-9:15-20:3,7

LOOSETH-JOB-12:18(6605)-PS-146:7(5425)

LOOSING-M'R-11:5(3089)-LU-19:33(3089)-AC-16:11(321)■27:13(142)

LOP-IS-10:33(5586)

LORDLY-J'G-5:25(117)

LORDS-all=5633&marked-GE-19:2(113)-NU-21:28(1167)-DE-10:17(113)-JOS-13:3-J'G-3:3■16:5,8,18^{2},23,27,30-1SA-5:8,11■6:4^{2},12,16,18■7:7■29:2,6,7-1CH-12:19-EZR-8:25(8269)-PS-136:3(113)-IS-16:8(1167)■26:13(113)-JER-2:31(7300)-EZE-23:23(7991)-DA-4:36(7261)■5:1(7261),9(7261),10(7261),23(7261)■6:17(7261)■**N.T.**-all=2962&marked-M'R-6:21(3175)-1CO-8:5-1TI-6:15(2961)-1PE-5:3(2634)-RE-17:14■19:16

LORDSHIP-M'R-10:42(2634)-LU-22:25(2961)

LOSE-J'G-18:25(622)-1KI-18:5(3772)-JOB-31:39(5307)-PR-23:8(7843)-EC-3:6(6)■**N.T.**-all=622&marked-M'T-10:39,42■16:25^{2},26(2210)-M'R-8:35^{2},36(2210)■9:41-LU-9:24^{2},25■15:4,8■17:33^{2}-JOH-6:39■12:25-2JO-8

LOSETH-M'T-10:39(622)

LOSS-GE-31:39(2398)-EX-21:19(7674)-IS-47:8(7921),9(7921)■**N.T.**-all=2209&marked-AC-27:21,22(580)-1CO-3:15-PH'P-3:7,8,8(2210)

LOST-all=6&marked-EX-22:9(9)-LE-6:3(9),4(9)-NU-6:12(5307)-DE-22:3(9),3-1SA-9:3,20-1KI-20:25(5307)-PS-119:176-IS-49:20(7923),21(7908)-JER-50:6-EZE-19:5■34:4,16■37:11■**N.T.**-all=622&marked-M'T-5:13(3471)■10:6■15:24■18:11-M'R-9:50(358,1096)-LU-14:34(3471)■15:4,6,9,24,32■19:10-JOH-6:12■17:12■18:9-2CO-4:3

LOT-all=1486&marked-LE-16:8^{2},9,10-NU-26:55,56■33:54^{2}■34:13■36:2,3-DE-32:9(2256)-JOS-14:2■15:1■16:1■17:1,14,17■18:11,18■19:1,10,17,24,32,40,51■21:4^{2},5,6,8,10,20,40-J'G-1:3^{3}■20:9-1CH-6:54,61,63,65■16:18(2256)■24:5,7■25:9■26:14^{2}-ES-3:7■9:24-PS-16:5■105:11(2256)■125:3-PR-1:14■

16:33■18:18-IS-17:14■34:17■57:6-JER-13:25-EZE-24:6-DA-12:13-JON-1:7-MIC-2:5■N.T.-LU-1:9(2975)-AC-1:26(2819)■8:21(2819)■13:19(2624)

LOTHE-all=6962&marked-EX-7:18(3811)-EZE-6:9■20:43■36:31

LOTHED-JER-14:19(1602)-EZE-16:45(1602)-ZEC-11:8(7114)

LOTHETH-EZE-16:45(1602)

LOTHING-EZE-16:5(1604)

LOTS-all=1486&marked-LE-16:8-JOS-18:6,8,10-1CH-24:31■25:8■26:13,14-NE-10:34■11:1-PS-22:18-JOE-3:3-OB-11-JON-1:7^2-NA-3:10■N.T.-all=2819&marked-M'T-27:35^2■M'R-15:24-LU-23:34-JOH-19:24,24(2975)-AC-1:26

LOUD-all=1419&marked-GE-39:14-EX-19:16(2389)-DE-27:14(7311)-1SA-28:12-2SA-15:23■19:4-1KI-8:55-2KI-18:28-2CH-15:14■20:19■30:21(5797)■32:18-EZR-3:12,13■10:12-NE-9:4■12:42(8085)-ES-4:1-PS-150:5(8085)-PR-7:11(1993)■27:14-IS-36:13-EZE-8:18■9:1■11:13■N.T.-all=3173-M'T-27:46,50-M'R-1:26■5:7■15:34,37-LU-1:42■4:33■8:28■17:15■19:37■23:23,46-JOH-11:43-AC-7:57,60■8:7■14:10■16:28■26:24-RE-5:2,12■6:10■7:2,10■8:13■10:3■12:10■14:7,9,15,18■19:17

LOUDER-EX-19:19(3966)

LOVE-all=157,a=160&marked-GE-27:4■29:20a,32-EX-20:6■21:5-LE-19:18,34-DE-5:10■6:5■7:7(2836),9,13■10:12,15,19■11:1,13,22■13:3■19:9■30:6,16,20-JOS-22:5■23:11-J'G-5:31■16:15-1SA-18:22-2SA-1:26^{2}a■13:4,15a-1KI-11:2a-2CH-19:2-NE-1:5-PS-4:2■5:11■18:1(7355)■31:23■40:16■69:36■70:4■91:14(2836)■97:10■109:4a,5a■116:1■119:97,113,119,127,132,159,163,165,167■122:6■145:20-PR-1:22■4:6■5:19a■7:18(1730)■8:17,21,36■9:8■10:12a■15:17a■16:13■17:9a■18:21■20:13a■27:5-EC-3:8■9:1a,6a-SONG-1:2(1730),3,4(1730),4,9(7474),15(7474)■2:2(7474),4a,5a,7a,10(7474),13(7474)■3:5a,10a■4:1(7474),7(7474),10^2(1730)■5:2(7474),8a■6:4(7474)■7:6a■8:4a,6a,7^{2}a-IS-38:17(2836)■56:6■61:8■63:9a■66:10-JER-2:2a,33a■5:31■31:3a-EZE-16:8(1730)■23:11(5691),17(1730)■33:31(5690)-DA-9:4-HO-3:1,1a,1■4:18a■9:15a■11:4a■14:4-AM-5:15-MIC-3:2■6:8a-ZEP-3:17a-ZEC-8:17,19■N.T.-all=26,a=25&marked-M'T-5:43a,44a,46a■6:5(5368),24a■19:19a■22:37a,39a■23:6(5368)■24:12-M'R-12:30a,31a,33^{2}a,38(2309),38sup-LU-6:27a,32^{2}a,35a■7:42a■10:27a■11:42,43a■16:13a■20:46(5368)-JOH-5:42■8:42a■10:17a■13:34^{2}a,35■14:15a,21a,23^{2}a,31a■15:9,10^2,12a,13,17a,19(5368)■17:26■21:15(5368),16(5368),17(5368)-RO-5:5,8■8:28a,35,39■12:9,10(5360)■13:8a,9a,10^2■15:30-1CO-2:9a■4:21■8:3a■16:22(5368),24-2CO-2:4,8■5:14■6:6■8:7,8,24■11:11a■12:15a■13:11,14-GA-5:6,13,14a,22-EPH-1:4,15■2:4■3:17,19■4:2,15,16■5:2,25a,28a,33a■6:23■24a-PH'P-1:9,17■2:1,2-COL-1:4,8■2:2■3:19a-1TH-1:3■3:12■4:9(5360),9a■5:8,13-2TH-2:10■3:5-1TI-1:14■6:10(5365),11-2TI-1:7,13■4:8a-TIT-2:4(5362),4(5388)■3:4(5363),15(5368)-PH'M-5,7-HEB-6:10■10:24■13:1(5360)-JAS-1:12a■2:5a,8a-1PE-1:8,22(5360),22a■2:17a■3:8(5361),10a-1JO-2:5,15^{2}a,15■3:1,11a,14a,16,17,18a,23a■4:7a,7,8,9,10,11a,12,12a,16^3,17,18^3,19a,20^{2}a,21a■5:2^{2}a,3-2JO-1a,3,5a,6-3JO-1a-JUDE-2,21-RE-2:4■3:19(5368)

LOVED-all=157&marked-GE-24:67■25:28^2■27:14■29:18,30■34:3■37:3,4-DE-4:37■7:8(160)■23:5■33:3(2245)-J'G-16:4-1SA-1:5■16:21■18:1,3(160),16,20■28■20:17(160),17,17(160)-2SA-12:24■13:1,15-1KI-3:3■10:9(160)■11:1-2CH-2:11(160)■9:8(160)■11:21■26:10-ES-2:17-JOB-19:19-PS-26:8■47:4■78:68■109:17■119:47,48-IS-43:4■48:14-JER-2:25■8:2■14:10■31:3-EZE-16:37-HO-9:1,10■11:1-MAL-1:2^3■2:11■N.T.-all=25&marked-M'R-10:21-LU-7:47-JOH-3:16,19■11:5,36(5368)■12:43■13:1^2,23,34■14:21,28■15:9^2,12■16:27(5368)■17:23,26■19:26■20:2(5368)■21:7,20-RO-8:37■9:13-2CO-12:15-GA-2:20-EPH-2:4■5:2(26),25-2TH-2:16-2TI-4:10-HEB-1:9-2PE-2:15-1JO-4:10^2,11,19-RE-1:5■3:9■12:11

LOVEDST-IS-57:8(157)■N.T.-JOH-17:24(25)

LOVELY-2SA-1:23(157)-SONG-5:16(4261)-EZE-33:32(5690)■N.T.-PH'P-4:8(4375)

LOVER-1KI-5:1(157)-PS-88:18(157)■N.T.-TIT-1:8(5382),8(5358)

LOVERS-all=157&marked-PS-38:11-JER-3:1(7453)■4:30(5689)■22:20,22■30:14-LA-1:2,19-EZE-16:33,36,37■23:5,9,22-HO-2:5,7,10,12,13■8:9(158)■N.T.-2TI-3:2(5367),4(5369),4(5377)

LOVE'S-PH'M-9(26)

LOVES-PS-45:t(3039)-PR-7:18(159)-SONG-7:12(1730)

LOVEST-all=157-GE-22:2-J'G-14:16-2SA-19:6-PS-45:7■52:3,4-EC-9:9■N.T.-all=5368&marked-JOH-11:3■21:15(25),16(25),17^2

LOVETH-all=157-GE-27:9■44:20-DE-10:18■15:16-RU-4:15-PS-11:5,7■33:5■34:12■37:28■87:2■99:4■119:140■146:8-PR-3:12■12:1■13:24■15:9,12■17:17,19■19:8■21:17^2■22:11■29:3-EC-5:10^2-SONG-1:7■3:1,2,3,4-IS-1:23-HO-10:11■12:7■N.T.-all=25&marked-M'T-10:37^2(5368)-LU-7:5,47-JOH-3:35■5:20(5368)■12:25(5368)■14:21^2,24■16:27(5368)-RO-13:8-2CO-9:7-EPH-5:28-HEB-12:6-1JO-2:10■3:10,14■4:7,8,20,21■5:1^2-3JO-9(5383)-RE-22:15(5368)

LOVING-PR-5:19(158)■22:1(2896)-IS-56:10(157)

LOVINGKINDNESS-all=2617-PS-17:7■26:3■36:7,10■40:10,11■42:8■48:9■51:1■63:3■69:16■88:11■89:33■92:2■103:4■107:43■119:88,149,159■138:2■143:8-JER-9:24■16:5■31:3■32:18-HO-2:19

LOVINGKINDNESSES-all=2617-PS-25:6■89:49-IS-63:7^2

LOW-all=8213&marked-DE-28:43(4295)-J'G-11:35(3766)-1SA-2:7-1CH-27:28(8219)-2CH-9:27■26:10■28:18,19(3665)-JOB-5:11(8217)■14:21(6819)■24:24(4355)■40:12(3665)-PS-49:2(120)■79:8(1809)■106:43(4355)■107:39(7817)■116:6(1809)■136:23■142:6(1809)-PR-29:23(8213)-EC-10:6(8216)■12:4(8217),4(7817)-IS-2:12,17■13:11■25:5(6030),12■26:5^2■29:4(7817)■32:19,19(8219)■40:4-LA-3:55(8482)-EZE-17:6(8217),24(8217)■21:26(8217)■26:20(8482)■N.T.-all=5011&marked-LU-1:48((5014),52■3:5(5013)-RO-12:16-JAS-1:9,10(5014)

LOWER-all=8481&marked-GE-6:16(8482)-LE-13:20(8217),21(8217),26(8217)■14:37(8217)-NE-4:13(8482)-PS-8:5(2637)■63:9(8482)-PR-25:7(8213)-IS-22:9■44:23(8482)-EZE-40:18,19■42:5■43:14■N.T.-EPH-4:9(2737)-HEB-2:7(1642),9(1642)

LOWEST-all=8482&marked-DE-32:22-1KI-12:31(7098)■13:33(7098)-2KI-17:32(7098)-PS-86:13■88:6■139:15-EZE-41:7(8481)■42:6(8481)■N.T.-LU-14:9(2078),10(2078)

LOWETH-JOB-6:5(1600)

LOWING-1SA-6:12(1600)■15:14(6963)

LOWLINESS-EPH-4:2(5012)-PH'P-2:3(5012)

LOWLY-all=6041&marked-PS-138:6(8217)-PR-3:34■11:2(6800)■16:19-ZEC-9:9-M'T-11:29(5011)

LOWRING-M'T-16:3(4768)

LUCRE-1SA-8:3(1215)■N.T.-1TI-3:3(866),8(146)-TIT-1:7(146)-1PE-5:2(147)

LUCRE'S-TIT-1:11(2771)

LUKEWARM-RE-3:16(5513)

LUMP-2KI-20:7(1690)-IS-38:21(1690)■N.T.-all=5445-RO-9:21■11:16-1CO-5:6,7-GA-5:9

LUNATICK-M'T-4:24(4583),17:15(4583)

LURK-PR-1:11(6845),18(6845)

LURKING-1SA-23:23(4224)-PS-10:8(3993)■17:12(3427)

LUST-EX-15:9(5315)-PS-78:18(5315),30(8378)■81:12(8307)-PR-6:25(2530)■N.T.-all=1939&marked-M'T-5:28(1937)-RO-1:27(3715)■7:7-1CO-10:6(1511,1938)-GA-5:16-1TH-4:5(3806)-JAS-1:14,15■4:2(1937)-1PE-1:4■2:10-1JO-2:16,17

LUSTED-NU-11:34(183)-PS-106:14(183)■N.T.-1CO-10:6(1937)-RE-18:14(1937)

LUSTETH-all=183-DE-12:15,20,21■14:26■N.T.-GA-5:17(1937)-JAS-4:5(1971)

LUSTING-NU-11:4(8378)

LUSTS-all=1939&marked-M'R-4:19-JOH-8:44-RO-1:24■6:12■13:14-GA-5:24-EPH-2:3■4:22-1TI-6:9-2TI-2:22■3:6■4:3-TIT-2:12■3:3-JAS-4:1(2237),3(2237)-1PE-1:14■2:11■4:2,3-2PE-2:18■3:3-JUDE-16,18

LUSTY-J'G-3:29(8082)

LYING-all=8267&marked-GE-29:2(7257)■34:7(7901)-EX-23:5(7257)-NU-31:17(4904),18(4904),35(4904)-DE-21:1(5307)■22:22(7901)-J'G-21:12(4904)-1KI-22:22,23-2CH-18:21,22-PS-31:6(7723),18■52:3■59:12(3585)■109:2■119:29,163■120:2■139:3(7252)-PR-6:17■10:18■12:19,22■13:5■17:7■21:6■26:28-IS-30:9(3586)■32:7■56:10(7901)■59:13(3584)-JER-7:4,8■29:23-LA-3:10-EZE-13:6(3577),7(3577),19(3576)-DA-2:9(3538)-HO-4:2(3584)-JON-2:8(7723)■N.T.-all=2749&marked-M'T-9:2(906)-M'R-5:40(345)-LU-2:12,16-JOH-13:25(1968)■20:5,7-EPH-4:25(5579)-2TH-2:9(5579)

M

MAD-all=1984&marked-DE-28:34(7696)-1SA-21:13,14(7696),15^2(7696)-2KI-9:11(7696)-PS-102:8-PR-26:18(3856)-EC-2:2■7:7-IS-44:25-JER-25:16■29:26(7696)■50:38■51:7-HOS-9:7(7696)■N.T.-all=3105&marked-JOH-10:20-AC-12:15■26:11(1693),24(1519,3130),25-1CO-14:23

MADE-all=6213,a=5414,b=3772,c=7760&marked-GE-1:7,16,16sup,25,31■2:2^2,3,4,22(1129)■3:1,7■5:1■6:6,7■7:4■8:6■9:6■13:4■14:2■15:18b■17:5a■19:3■21:8,27b,32b■24:21(6743)■26:30■27:14,31,37c■29:22■31:46■33:17■37:3■40:20■41:43sup,43a■45:8c,9c■47:26c■50:10-EX-1:21■2:14c■4:11c■7:1a■14:21c■15:17(6466)■15:25sup,25c■18:25a■20:11■24:8b■25:31■26:31■31:17■32:4,8,20,20sup,31,35■34:27b■35:29,29sup■36:4,8^2,11^2,12^2,13,14^2,17^2,18,19,20,23,24,25,27,28,31,33,34,35^2,36,37■37:1,2,4,6,7^2,8,10,11,12^2,15,16,17^2,23,24,25,26,27,28,29■38:1,2,3^2,4,6,7,8,9,22,28,30■39:1^2,2,4,8,9,15,16,19,20,22,24,25,27,30,42-LE-2:7,8,11,11sup■6:21■13:48(4399),51■26:46a-NU-4:26■6:4■8:4■11:8■21:9■31:20(3627)-DE-1:15a■5:2b,3b■9:9b,12,16,21■10:3,5,22c■26:19■29:1b,25b■31:16b■32:6,15-JOS-5:3■8:28c■9:15^2,16b,27a■11:18■22:25a,28■24:25b-J'G-3:16■6:2,19■8:27,33c■9:27■11:11c■13:15■14:10■17:4,5■18:24,27,31■21:15-1SA-2:19■8:1c■9:22a■14:14(5221)■18:3b,13c■

20:16b▪22:8b▪23:18b▪30:25c-**2SA**-3:20▪5:3b▪6:8(6555)▪7:9▪13:8(3835),10▪15:4c▪17:25c▪22:5c,12(7896)▪23:5c-**1KI**-2:24▪3:15▪5:12b▪6:4,5,6a,23,31,33▪7:6,7,8,16,18,23,27,29,37,38,40^3,45,48,51▪8:9b,21b▪9:26▪10:9c,12,16,18,20,27^{2}a▪12:28,31^2,32^2,33▪13:33▪14:7a,9,15,26,27▪15:12,13▪16:2a,2sup▪16:33▪18:26,32▪20:34c,34b▪22:11,39(1129),48(6235)-**2KI**-3:2▪10:27c▪11:4b,17b▪12:13▪13:7c▪12:13▪15:15(7194)▪16:11▪17:8,15b,16^2,19,29^2,30^3,31,32,35b,38b▪18:4▪19:15▪20:20▪21:3,7▪23:3b,12^2,15sup,15,19▪24:13▪25:16-**1CH**-5:10,19▪9:30(7543),31(4639)▪11:3b▪12:18a▪15:1▪16:16b,26▪17:8▪18:8▪21:29▪22:8▪23:5▪26:10c-**2CH**-1:3,5,15^{2}a▪2:11a,12▪3:8,10,14,15,16^2▪4:1,2,6,7,8^2,9,11,14,18,19▪5:1,10b▪6:11b,13▪7:6,7,9▪9:8a,11,15,17,19,27^{2}a▪11:15▪12:9,10▪13:8,9▪15:16▪16:14(3738)▪18:10▪20:36▪21:7b,11,19▪23:3b,16b▪24:8,9a,14▪25:16a▪26:13,15▪28:2,24,25▪32:5,27▪33:3,7,22▪34:31b▪35:25a-**EZR**-4:19^{2}sup,19(5648)▪5:13(7761),14(7761),17sup,17(7761)▪6:1(7761),3(7761),11(7761),11(5648),12(7761)-**NE**-3:16▪4:7(5927,752)▪8:4,16,17▪9:6,18▪10:32(5975)▪13:26a-**ES**-1:3,5,9▪2:18^2▪5:14^2▪7:9▪9:17,18,19-**JOB**-1:17c▪10:8(6087),9▪15:7(2342)▪17:6(3322),13(7502)▪28:26▪31:1b,15,24c▪33:4▪38:9c▪39:6c▪40:15,19▪41:33-**PS**-7:15(3738),15(6466)▪9:15▪18:11(7896),43c▪21:6(7896),6sup▪33:6▪39:5a▪45:1(4639)▪46:8c▪50:5b▪52:7c▪69:11a▪74:17(3335)▪86:9▪88:8(7896)▪89:3b▪91:9c▪95:5▪96:5▪100:3▪104:24,26(3335)▪105:9b,21c▪106:19,46a▪111:4▪115:15▪118:24▪119:73▪121:2▪124:8▪134:3▪136:5,7▪139:15▪146:6▪148:6a▪149:2-**PR**-8:26▪16:4(6466)▪20:12-**EC**-2:5,6▪3:11▪7:29▪10:19-**SONG**-1:6c▪3:9,10▪6:12c-**IS**-2:8▪5:2(2672)▪14:17c▪17:8▪22:11▪25:2c▪27:11▪28:15b,15c▪29:16▪31:7▪37:16▪43:7▪44:2▪45:12,18▪46:4▪49:2^{2}c▪51:10c,12a▪53:9a▪57:8b,16▪66:2-**JER**-1:18a▪2:7c,15(7896),28▪8:8▪10:11(5648),12▪11:10b▪12:10a,11c▪14:22▪18:4^2▪19:11(7495)▪20:8(1961)▪27:5▪29:26a▪31:32b▪32:17,20▪34:8b,13b,15b,18b▪37:15▪38:16▪41:9▪51:15,34(3322)▪52:20-**LA**-1:13a▪2:7a▪3:11c,45c-**EZE**-3:8a,9a,17▪7:20▪13:5(1443)▪16:24▪17:13b▪19:5c▪20:28c▪22:4,4a,13▪27:5(1129),6^2,11▪29:3,9▪40:14,17▪41:18,19,20,25^2▪46:23-**DA**-2:5(7761),48(7236)▪3:1(5648),10(7761),15(5648),29(7739)▪4:6(7761)▪5:1(5648),21(7737)▪7:21(5648)-**HO**-8:4sup,4,6▪13:2-**AM**-5:26-**OB**-2a-**JON**-1:9▪4:5-**ZEC**-7:12c▪9:13c▪10:3c▪11:10b-**MAL**-2:9a▪**N.T.**-all=1096,a=4160,b=5319-**M'T**-4:3▪9:16,22^2(4982)▪11:1(5055)▪14:36(1295)▪15:6(208),28(2390)▪18:25(591)▪19:4^{2}a,12^2(2134)▪20:12a▪21:13a▪22:2a,5(272)▪23:15▪24:45(2525)▪25:6,16a▪26:19(2090)▪27:24,64(805),66(805)-**M'R**-2:21,27▪5:34(4982)▪6:21a,56(4982)▪8:25a▪10:6a,52(4982)▪11:17a▪14:4,16(2090),58(5499),58(886)▪15:7(4955)-**LU**-1:62(1770)▪2:2,15(1107)▪17(1232)▪3:5^2(1519),4:3▪5:29a▪8:17,48(4982),50(4982)▪9:15(347)▪11:40a▪12:14(2525)▪13:13(461)▪14:12,16a▪17:19(4982)▪19:6(4692),46a▪22:13(2090)▪23:12,19▪24:22(1839),28(4364)-**JOH**-1:3^2,10,14,31▪2:9▪15a▪3:21b▪4:1a,46a▪5:4,6,9,11a,14,15a▪7:23a▪8:33▪9:6a,11a,14a,39▪12:2a▪15:15(1107)▪17:23(5048)▪18:18a▪19:7a,23a-**AC**-1:1a▪2:28(1107),36a▪3:12a,16(4732),25(1303)▪4:9(4982),24a,35(1239)▪7:10(2525),13(319),13,27(2525),35(2525),41(3447),43a,48(5499),50a▪8:2a▪9:39a▪10:10(3903),17(1239)▪12:5,20(3982),21(1215)▪13:32▪14:2(2559),5,15a▪15:7(1586)▪16:13(1511),24(805)▪17:24a,24(5499),26a▪18:12(2721)▪19:24a,26,33(626)▪20:28(5087)▪21:40▪22:6(4198)▪23:13a▪26:6▪27:40(2722)-**RO**-1:3,20(4161)▪2:25▪4:14(2758),14(2673),17(5087)▪5:19^2(2525)▪16:18(1659),22(1659)▪7:13▪8:2(1659),20(5293)▪9:20a,29(3666)▪10:10(3670),20▪11:9▪14:21(770)▪15:27(2841)▪16:26b,26(1107)-**1CO**-1:17(2758),20(3471),30▪3:13▪4:9,13▪7:21▪9:19(1402),22▪11:19▪12:13(4222)▪14:25▪15:22(2227),45,45sup-**2CO**-2:2(3076)▪3:6(2427),10(1392)▪4:10b,11b▪5:1(886),11^{2}b,21a,21▪7:8^2(3076),9^2(3076)▪10:16(2092)▪11:6b▪12:9(5048)-**GA**-3:3(2005),13,16(4483),19(1861)▪4:4▪5:1(1659)-**EPH**-1:6(5487),9(1107)▪2:6(4776),11(5499),13,14a▪3:3(1107),5(1107),7▪5:13b-**PH'P**-2:7^2▪3:10(4832)▪4:6(1107)-**COL**-1:12(2427),20(1517),23,25,26b▪2:11,15(1165)-**1TI**-1:9(2749),19(3489)▪2:1a-**2TI**-1:10b-**TIT**-3:7-**HEB**-1:2a,4▪2:9(1642),17(3666)▪3:14▪5:5,9(5048)▪6:4,13(1861),20▪7:3(871),12,16,19(5048),21,22,26▪8:9a,13(3822)▪9:2(2680),8b,11(5499),24(5499)▪10:13(5087),33(2301)▪11:3,22(3421),34(1743),40(5048)▪12:23(5048),27a-**JAS**-1:10(5014)▪2:22(5048)▪3:9-**1PE**-2:7▪3:22(5293)-**2PE**-1:16(1107)▪2:12(1080)-**1JO**-2:19b▪4:17(5048),18(5048)▪5:10a-**RE**-1:6a▪5:10a▪7:14(3021)▪8:11(4087)▪14:7a,8(4222)▪15:4b▪17:2(3182)▪18:15(4147),19(4147),19(2049)▪19:7(2090)

MADEST-**NE**-9:8(3772),14(3045)-**EZE**-16:17(6213)▪**N.T.**-**AC**-21:38(387)-**HEB**-2:7(1642)

MADNESS-all=1947&marked-**DE**-28:28(7697)-**EC**-1:17▪2:12▪7:25▪9:3▪10:13(1948)-**ZEC**-12:4(7697)▪**N.T.**-**LU**-6:11(454)-**2PE**-2:16(3913)

MAGICIAN-**DA**-2:10(2749)

MAGICIANS-all=2748&marked-**GE**-41:8,24-**EX**-7:11,22▪8:7,18,19▪9:11^2-**DA**-1:20▪2:2,27(2749)▪4:7(2749),9(2749)▪5:11(2749)

MAGISTRATE-**J'G**-18:7(3423,6114)-**LU**-12:58(758)

MAGISTRATES-**EZR**-7:25(8200)▪**N.T.**-all=4755&marked-**LU**-12:11(746)-**AC**-16:20,22,35,36,38-**TIT**-3:1(3980)

MAGNIFICAL-**1CH**-22:5(1431)

MAGNIFICENCE-**AC**-19:27(3163)

MAGNIFIED-all=1431&marked-**GE**-19:19-**JOS**-4:14-**2SA**-7:26-**1CH**-17:24▪29:25-**2CH**-1:1▪32:23(5375)-**PS**-35:27▪40:16▪70:4▪138:2-**JER**-48:26,42-**LA**-1:9-**DA**-8:11-**ZEP**-2:8,10-**MAL**-1:5▪**N.T.**-all=3170-**AC**-5:13▪19:17-**PH'P**-1:20

MAGNIFY-all=1431&marked-**JOS**-3:7-**JOB**-7:17▪19:5▪36:24(7679)-**PS**-34:3▪35:26▪38:16▪55:12▪69:30-**IS**-10:15▪42:21-**EZE**-38:23-**DA**-8:25▪11:36,37-**ZEC**-12:7▪**N.T.**-**LU**-1:46(3170)-**AC**-10:46(3170)-**RO**-11:13(1392)

MAID-all=8198&marked-**GE**-16:2,3,5,6,8▪29:24,29▪30:3(519),7,9,10,12-**EX**-2:5(519),8(5959)▪21:20(519),26(519)▪22:16(1330)-**LE**-12:5(5347)▪25:6(519)-**DE**-22:14(1331),17(1331)-**2KI**-5:2(5291),4(5291)-**ES**-2:7(5291)-**JOB**-31:1(1330)-**PR**-30:19(5959)-**IS**-24:2-**JER**-2:32(1330)▪51:22(1330)-**AM**-2:7(5921)▪**N.T.**-**M'T**-9:24(2877),25(2877)-**M'R**-14:69(3814)-**LU**-8:54(3816)▪22:56(3814)

MAIDEN-all=5291&marked-**GE**-30:18(8198)-**J'G**-19:24(1330)-**2CH**-36:17(1330)-**ES**-2:4,9,13-**PS**-123:2(8198)▪**N.T.**-**LU**-8:51(3816)

MAIDENS-all=5291&marked-**EX**-2:5-**RU**-2:8,22,23▪3:2-**1SA**-9:11-**ES**-2:8,9▪4:16-**JOB**-41:5-**PS**-78:63(1330)▪148:12(1330)-**PR**-9:3▪27:27▪31:15-**EC**-2:7(8198)-**EZE**-44:22(1330)▪**N.T.**-**LU**-12:45

MAID'S-**ES**-2:12(5291)

MAIDS-all=519&marked-**EZR**-2:65-**ES**-2:9(5291)▪4:4-**JOB**-19:15-**LA**-5:11(1330)-**EZE**-9:6(1330)-**NA**-2:7-**ZEC**-9:17(1330)▪**N.T.**-**M'R**-14:66(3814)

MAIDSERVANT-all=519&marked-**EX**-11:5(8198)▪20:10,17▪21:7,32-**DE**-5:14^2,21▪12:18▪15:17▪16:11,14-**J'G**-9:18-**JOB**-31:13-**JER**-34:9(8198),10(8198)

MAIDSERVANT'S-**EX**-21:27(519)

MAIDSERVANTS-all=8198&marked-**GE**-12:16▪20:17(519)▪24:35▪30:43-**DE**-12:12(519)-**1SA**-8:16-**2SA**-6:22(519)-**2KI**-5:26-**NE**-7:67(519)

MAIDSERVANTS'-**GE**-31:33(519)

MAIL-**1SA**-17:5(7193)

MAIMED-**LE**-22:22(2782)▪**N.T.**-all=2948&marked-**M'T**-15:30,31▪18:8-**M'R**-9:43-**LU**-14:13(376),21(376)

MAINSAIL-**AC**-27:40(736)

MAINTAIN-all=6213&marked-**1KI**-8:45,49,59-**1CH**-26:27(2388)-**2CH**-6:35,39-**JOB**-13:15-**PS**-140:12▪**N.T.**-**TIT**-3:8(4291),14(4291)

MAINTAINED-**PS**-9:4(6213)

MAINTAINEST-**PS**-16:5(8551)

MAINTENANCE-**EZR**-4:14(4415)-**PR**-27:27(2416)

MAJESTY-all=1926&marked-**1CH**-29:11(1935),25(1935)-**ES**-1:4(1420)-**JOB**-37:22(1935)▪40:10(1347)-**PS**-21:5▪29:4▪45:3,4▪93:1(1348)▪96:6▪104:1▪145:5(1935),12-**IS**-2:10(1347),19(1347),21(1347)▪24:14(1347)▪26:10(1348)-**EZE**-7:20(1347)-**DA**-4:30(1923),36(7238)▪5:18(7238),19(7238)-**MIC**-5:4(1347)▪**N.T.**-all=3172&marked-**HEB**-1:3▪8:1-**2PE**-1:16(3168)-**JUDE**-25(3172)

MAKE-all=6213,a=5414,b=3772,c=7760&marked-**GE**-1:26▪2:18▪3:21▪6:14^2,15,16^2▪9:12a▪11:4▪12:2,2sup▪13:16c▪17:2a,6sup,6a,20sup,20a▪18:6sup,6▪21:13c,18c▪26:28b▪31:44b▪32:12c▪35:1,3▪46:3▪47:6sup,6c▪48:4sup,4a,20-**EX**-5:8,16▪18:16a▪20:4,23^2,24,25▪23:27a,32b▪25:8,9,10,11,13,17,18^2,19^2,23,24,25^2,26,28,29^2,31,37,39,40▪26:1^2,4^2,5^2,6,7^2,10,11,14,15,17,18,19,22,23,26,29,31,36,37▪27:1,2,3^2,4^2,6,8^2,9▪28:2,3,4^2,6,11,13,14,15^3,22,23,26,27,31,33,36,39^2,40^3,42▪29:2▪30:1^2,3,4^2,5,18,25,32,35,37^2,38▪31:6▪32:1,10,23▪34:10b,12b,15b,17▪35:10,33▪36:3,5,6,7,22-**LE**-19:4,28a▪22:22a,24▪26:1,19a,31a-**NU**-5:21^{2}a▪10:2^2▪14:4a,12▪15:3^2,38▪16:30(1254)▪21:8▪31:23^2(5674)-**DE**-1:13c▪4:16,23,25▪5:8▪7:2b▪9:14▪10:1▪14:1c▪15:1▪16:18a,21▪21:14(6014)▪22:8,12▪26:19▪28:13a,24a,59(6381)▪29:1b,14b-**JOS**-5:2▪6:18sup,18c▪7:19a▪9:6b,7b,11b-**J'G**-2:2b▪17:3-**RU**-4:11a-**1SA**-6:5,7▪8:5c,12▪11:1b,2b▪12:22▪13:19▪17:25▪22:7c▪25:28▪28:2c▪-**2SA**-3:12b,13b,21b▪7:11,23c▪13:6(3823)-**1KI**-9:22a▪16:3a▪17:13^2▪19:2c▪20:34c▪21:22a-**2KI**-3:16▪4:10▪6:2▪7:2,19▪9:9a▪18:31-**1CH**-7:21c,22a-**2CH**-4:11,16▪7:11,20a▪8:9a▪20:36▪29:10b-**EZR**-5:3(3635),4(1124),9(3635)▪6:8(7761)▪7:13(7761),21(7761)▪10:3b,11a-**NE**-8:12,15▪9:38b-**ES**-1:20▪9:22-**JOB**-18:2c▪24:25^{2}c▪28:25▪31:15▪41:4b-**PS**-21:9(7896)▪39:8c▪41:3(2015)▪66:2c▪83:11(7896),13(7896)▪84:6▪89:27a,29c▪110:1(7896)▪115:8▪135:18▪139:8(3331)-**PR**-20:18▪23:5▪30:26c-**SONG**-1:11-**IS**-3:7c▪10:23▪14:23c▪16:3(7896)▪19:10▪25:6▪27:5^2▪36:16▪41:15^{2}c,18c▪42:15^{2}c,16c▪43:19c▪44:9(3335),19▪45:7▪49:11c▪50:2c,3c▪51:3c▪53:10c▪54:12c▪55:3b▪60:13c,15c,17c▪61:8b▪62:7c▪63:12,14▪66:22-**JER**-4:7c,27▪5:10,14a,18▪6:8c,26▪7:18▪9:11^{2}a▪10:22c▪13:16(7896)▪15:20a▪16:20▪18:4,16c▪19:8c,12a▪20:4a▪22:6(7896)▪25:9c,12c,18a▪26:6^{2}a▪27:2▪28:13▪29:17a,22c▪30:11^2▪31:21c,31b,33b▪32:40b▪34:17a,22a▪44:19▪46:28^2▪49:15a▪50:3(7896)▪51:25a,

29c,39(7896),39sup-EZE-4:9■5:14a■6:14a■7:23■11:13■13:18■14:8(8074)■15:8a■17:17■18:31■20:17■22:30(1443)■24:17■25:4a,5a,13a■26:4a,8a,12a,12sup,19a,21a■27:5■29:10a,12a■32:15a■34:25b,26a■35:3a,7a,9a,14■37:19,22,26b■43:18,27-DA-3:29(7761)■6:26(7761)■11:6-HO-2:3c,6(1443),12c,18b,18sup■11:8a■12:1b-JOE-2:19a-AM-8:10c■9:14-MIC-1:6c,8■4:7c,13^{2}c■6:16a-NA-1:8,9,14c-HAB-2:18■3:19c,19sup-ZEP-1:18■2:13c■3:20a-HAG-2:23c-ZEC-6:11■10:1■12:2c,3c,6c-MAL-2:15■3:17■N.T.-all=4160&marked-M'T-1:19(3856)■3:3■4:19■5:36■8:2(2511)■12:16,33^2■17:4■22:4(5087)■23:5(4115),14(4336),15^2,25(2511)■24:47(2525)■25:21(2525),23(2525)■27:65(805)-M'R-1:3,17,40(2511)■3:12■5:39(2350)■6:39(347)■9:5■12:36(5087),40(4336),42(1510)■14:15(2090)-LU-1:17(2090)■3:4■5:12(2511),33,34■9:14(2625),33,52(2090)■11:39(2511),40■12:37(347),42(2525),44(2525)■14:18(3868),31(4820)■15:19,29(2165),32(2165)■16:9■17:8(2090)■19:5(4692)■20:43(5087),47(4336)■22:12(2090)-JOH-1:23(2116)■2:16■6:10,15■8:32(1659),36(1659)■10:24(142)■14:23-AC-2:28(4137),35(5087)■7:40,44■9:34(4766)■22:18(4692)■23:23(2090)■26:16(4400),24(4062)-RO-1:9■3:3(2673),31(2673)■9:21,22(1107),23(1107),28,13:14■14:4(2476),19(3753)■15:18(1519),26-1CO-4:5(5319)■6:15■8:13^2(4624)■9:15(2758),18(5087)■10:13-2CO-2:2(3076)■9:5(4294),8(4052)■12:17(4122),18(4122)-GA-2:18(4921)■3:17(2673)■6:12(2146)-EPH-2:15(2936)■3:9(5461)■5:13(5319)■6:19(1107),21(1107)-COL-1:27(1107)■4:4(5319),9(1107)-1TH-3:12(4121)-2TH-3:9(1325)-2TI-3:15(4679)■4:5(4135)-HEB-1:13(5087)■2:10(5055),17(2433)■7:25(1793)■8:5(2005),5,8(4931),10(1303)■9:9(5055)■10:1(5055),16(1303)■12:13■13:21(2675)-JAS-3:18-1PE-5:10(2675)-2PE-1:8(2525),10■2:3(1710)-1JO-1:10-RE-3:9(1325),9,12■10:9(4087)■11:7,10(2165)■12:17■13:4(4170),7,14■17:14(4170),16■19:11(4170),19■21:5

MAKER-all=6213&marked-JOB-4:17■32:22■35:10■36:3(6466)-PS-95:6-PR-14:31■17:5■22:2-IS-1:31(6467)■17:7■22:11■45:9(3335),11(3335)■51:13■54:5-JER-33:2-HOS-8:14-HAB-2:18^2(3335)■N.T.-HEB-11:10(1217)

MAKERS-IS-45:16(2796)

MAKEST-all=6213&marked-J'G-18:3-PS-44:13,14■80:6(7760)■104:20(7896)-IS-45:9-EZE-16:31-HAB-1:14■N.T.-all=4160&marked-LU-14:12,13-JOH-8:53■10:33-RO-2:17(2744),23(2744)

MAKETH-all=6213&marked-EX-4:11(7760)-DE-20:20■27:15■29:12(3772)-2SA-22:34(7737)-JOB-9:9■15:47■25:2■27:18■41:31sup,31(7760)-PS-18:32(5414),33(7737)■40:4(7760)■104:3(7760),4■107:41■135:7■147:14(7760)■31:22,24-EC-3:11■11:5-IS-27:9(7760)■40:23■43:16(5414)■44:13,15(6466),15,17,24■46:6-JER-10:13■51:16-EZE-22:3-AM-4:13■5:8■N.T.-all=4160&marked-M'T-5:45(393)-M'R-7:37-LU-5:36(4977)-JOH-19:12-AC-9:34(2390)-RO-5:5(2617)■8:26(5241),27(1793),34(1793)■11:2(1793)-1CO-4:7(1252)-2CO-2:2(2165),14(5319)-GA-2:6(1308)-EPH-4:16-HEB-1:7(4160)■7:28(2525)-RE-13:13■22:15

MAKING-EC-12:12(6123)-EZE-27:16(4639),18(4639)-HO-10:4(3772)■N.T.-all=4160&marked-M'T-9:23(2350)-M'R-7:13(208)-JOH-5:18-RO-1:10(1189)-2CO-6:10(4148)-EPH-1:16■2:15■5:19(5567)-PH'P-1:4-1TH-1:2-PH'M-4-2PE-2:6-JUDE-22(1252)

MALE-all=2145&marked-GE-1:27■5:2■6:19■7:2^2(376),3,9,16■17:23■34:15,22,24-EX-12:5■34:19(2142)-LE-1:3,10■3:1,6■4:23■7:6■12:7■22:19■27:3,5,6,7-NU-1:2,20,22■3:15■5:3■18:10■31:17-DE-4:16■20:13(2138)-JOS-17:2-J'G-21:11,12-1KI-11:15,16-MAL-1:14■N.T.-all=730-M'T-19:4-M'R-10:6-LU-2:23-GA-3:28

MALFACTOR-JOH-18:30(2555)

MALEFACTORS-all=2557-LU-23:32,33,39

MALES-all=2145&marked-GE-34:25-EX-12:48■13:12,15■23:17(2138)-LE-6:18,29-NU-3:22,28,34,39,40,43■26:62■31:7-DE-15:19■16:16(2138)-JOS-5:4-2CH-31:16,19-EZR-8:3,4,5,6,7,8,9,10,11,12,13,14

MALICE-all=2549-1CO-5:8■14:20-EPH-4:31-COL-3:8-TIT-3:3-1PE-2:1

MALICIOUS-3JO-10(4190)

MALICIOUSNESS-RO-1:29(2549)-1PE-2:16(2549)

MALIGNITY-RO-1:29(2550)

MALLOWS-JOB-30:4(4408)

MAMMON-all=3126-M'T-6:24-LU-16:9,11,13

MAN-all=376,a=120,b=1397,c=582&marked-GE-1:26a,27a■2:5a,7^{2}a,8a,15a,16a,18a,22^{2}a,23,24,25a■3:12a,22a,24a■4:1,23■5:1a■6:3a,5a,6a,7^{2}a,9■7:21a,23a■9:5^{2}a,6^{2}a■13:16■16:12sup,12a■17:10(2145)■12(2145),14(2145)■19:8,9,31■20:7■24:16,21,22,26,29,30^2,32,58,61,65■25:27^2■26:11,13■27:11■29:19,30:43■31:50■32:24■34:25■37:15^2,17■38:25■39:2■40:5^2■41:11,12^2,33,38,44■42:13,30,33■43:3,5,6,7,11,13,14,17^2,24■44:11^2,13,15,17,20■45:1^2,22■47:20■49:6-EX-1:1■2:1,12,20,21■7:12■8:17a,18a■9:9a,10a,19a,22a,25a■11:2,3,7■12:3,4,12a,16(5315)■13:2a,13a,15a■15:3■16:16,16(1538),16,18,19,21,29■19:13■21:7,12,14,16,20,26,28,29,33^2■22:1,5,7,10,14,16■24:14(1167)■25:2■30:12■32:1,23,27^4,29■33:4,8,10,11,11sup■20a■34:3^2,24■35:22,23,24,29■36:1,2,4,6■38:26(1538)-LE-1:2a■5:3a,3sup,4a■6:3a■7:21a■12:2(2145)■13:2a,9a,29,38,40,44■14:11■15:2,18,24,33(2145)■16:17a,21■17:3,4^2,8,9,10,13■18:5a■19:3■20:3,4,5,10,11,12,13,14,15,17,18,20,21,27■21:4(1167),18^2,19,21■22:4^2,5a,14■24:10,17(5315,120),19,20a,21a■25:10^2,13,26,27,29■27:2,14,16,20,26,28,28a,31-NU-1:4,52^2■2:2,17■3:13a■5:6,8,10,13,15,19,20,31■6:2■7:5■8:17a■9:6a,7a,10,13^2■11:10■12:3■13:2■14:15■15:32,35■16:7,17^2,18,22■17:9■18:15a■19:9,11a,13a,14a,16a,20■21:9■23:19,19a■24:3b,15b■25:8^2■26:64,65■27:8,16,18■30:2,16■31:17(376,2145),18(376,2145),26a,35(2145)47a,49,50,53■32:18■36:8-DE-1:16,17,31,41■3:11,20■4:32a■5:24a■7:24(375)■8:3^{2}a,5■11:25■12:8■16:17■17:2,5^2,12^2■19:11,15,16■20:5^2,6^2,7^2,8■21:3,15,18,22■22:5^{2}b,13,16,18,22^2,23,24,25^3,26,28,29,30■23:10■24:1,5,7,11,12,16■25:7,9■27:15■28:30,54■29:18,20■32:25sup,25■33:1■34:6-JOS-1:5■2:11■3:12■4:2,4,5■5:13■6:5,20,21,26■7:14b,17b,18b■8:17■10:8,14■11:14a■14:6,15a■17:1■21:44■22:20■23:9,10■24:28-J'G-1:24,25,26■2:6■3:15,17,28,29■4:20^2,22■5:30b■6:16■7:7,8,13,14,21,24,25■9:9,13,49,55■10:1,18■11:39■13:2,6,8,10,11^2■16:7a,11a,17a,19■17:1,5,6,8,11■18:7a,19,28a,■19:6,7,9,10,15,16,17^2,18,20,22^2,23^2,24,25,28^2■20:1,8,11■21:11(2145),12,21,22,24^2,25-RU-1:1,2■2:1,20■3:3,8,16,18■4:7-1SA-1:1,3,11c,21■2:9,13,15,16,25^2,27,33■4:10,12,13,14,16,18■8:22■9:1^2,6^2,7^2,8,9,10,16,17■10:6,22,25■11:13■13:2,14,20■14:24,28,34^2,36,52,52(1121)■15:3,29a■16:7^{2}a,16,17,18sup,18■17:8,10,12sup,12,24,25^2,26,27,33,41■18:23■20:22(5958)■21:1,2,7,14■24:19■25:2^2,3^2,10,13^2,25,29a■26:15,23■27:3,9,11■28:14■30:6,17,22-2SA-1:2■2:3■3:34(1121)■7:19a■12:4,4sup,4,5^2,7■13:3,9,29■14:16■15:2,4,5,30■16:5,7,8,23■17:3,8■18:10,11,12,12sup,24,26^2,27■19:8,14,22,32■20:1^2,2,12,21,22■21:4,5,20■22:49■23:1b,7,20,21■24:14a-1KI-1:42,49,52(1121)■2:2,4,9■4:25,27,28■7:14■8:25,31,38a,38,39,46a■9:5■10:25■11:28,28sup■12:22,24■13:1,4,5,6^2,7,8,11,12,14^2,21,26,29,31■17:18,24■20:20,24,28,35^2,37^2,39^3,42■22:8,17,34,36-2KI-1:6,7,8,9,10,11,12,13■3:25■4:7,9,16,21,22,25^2,27^2,29,40,42^2■5:1^2,7sup,7,8,14,15,20,26■6:2,6,9,10,15,19,32■7:2,5,10,10a,17,18,19■8:2,4,7,8,11■9:11,13■10:21■11:8,9,11■12:4(5315),5■13:19,21^3■14:6,12■15:20■18:21,31■22:15■23:10,16,17,18-1CH-11:22,23■16:3,21,43■17:17a■20:6■21:13a■22:9■23:3b,14■27:32■28:3■29:1a-2CH-2:7,13,14■6:5,16,22,29a,30a,36a■7:18■8:14■9:24■10:16■11:2,4■14:11c■15:13■18:7,16,33,33sup■19:6a■20:27■23:7,8,10■25:4,7,9^2,22■30:16■31:1,2■32:19a■34:23-EZR-3:1,2■8:18-NE-1:11■2:10a,12a■5:13■6:11■7:2■8:1■9:29a■12:24,36-ES-1:22■4:11■6:6,7,9^2,11■9:2,4-JOB-1:1^2,3,8■2:3,4■3:3b,23b■4:17c,17(1396)■5:7a,17c■7:1c,17c■9:2c,32■10:4c,5c■11:2,12,12a■12:14■13:9c■14:1a,10b■10a,12,14b,19c■15:7a,14c,16■16:21b,21a■20:4a,29a■21:4a,33a■22:2b,8■25:4c,6c,6a■27:13a■28:13c,28a■32:8c,13,21a■33:12c,17a,17b,23a,26c,29b■34:7b,9b,11a,11,15a,21,23,29a,34b■35:8,8a■36:25a,25c,28a■37:7a,20■38:3b,26,26a■40:7b■42:11-PS-1:1■5:6■8:4c,4a■9:19c■10:18c■18:25b,48■■22:6■25:12■31:20■32:2a■34:8b,12■36:6a■37:7,23b,37sup,37■38:14■39:5a,6,11,11a■40:4b■43:1■49:12a,20a■52:7b■55:13c■56:1c,11a■58:11a■60:11a■62:3,12■76:10a■78:25■80:17,17a■84:5a,12a■87:5■88:4b■89:48b■90:t,3c■92:6■94:10a,11a,12b■103:15c■104:14a,15c,23a■105:14a,17■108:12a■109:16■112:1,5■118:6a,8a■119:134a■127:5b■128:4b■135:8a■140:1a,1,4,11■144:3a,3c,4a■146:3a■147:10-PR-2:12sup,12■3:4a,13^{2}a,30a■5:21■6:11,12,27,34b■8:4a,34a■10:23■11:7a,12,17■12:2,3a,8,14,23a,25,27sup,27a■13:2■14:7,12,14,17■15:18,20a,21,23■16:1a,2,14,25,27,28,29■17:12,18a,27■18:12,14,24■19:3a,11a,22a■20:3,5^2,6,17,24a,25a,27a■21:2,8,16a,17,20a,28,29■22:24(1167),24,29■23:2(1167)■24:5b,5,12a,29,30a,34■25:18■26:12,19,21■27:8,17,19a,20a,21■28:2a,3b,11,12a,14a,17a,20a,21b,23a■29:5b,6,9,13,20,22,22(1167),25a,27■30:1b,2,2a,19b-EC-1:3a,8,13a■2:12a,18,21^{2}a,22a,24a,26a■3:11a,13a,19a,21(1121,120)a,22a■4:4■5:19a■6:2,3,7a,10a,11a,12^{2}a■7:5,14a,20a,28a,29a■8:6a,8a,9a,15a,17^{2}a,17sup,■9:1a,12a,15,15a,15■10:14a■11:8a■12:5a,13a-SONG-3:8■8:7-IS-2:9(1201),9,11a,17a,20a,22a■3:2sup,2,6■4:1■5:15a,15■6:5,11a■7:21■9:19,20■13:12c,12a,14sup,14■14:16■17:7a■24:10(935)■29:21a■31:7,8,8a■32:2■33:8sup,8c■36:6■38:11a■41:28■42:13^2■44:13,13a,15a■45:12a■46:11■47:3a■49:7(5315)■50:2■51:12c,12a■52:14■53:3■55:7■56:2c,2a■57:1■58:5a■59:16■66:3,7(2145)-JER-2:6,6a■3:1■4:25a,29■5:1■7:5,20a■8:6■9:12■10:14a,23a,23sup■11:3■12:11,15^2■13:11■14:9^2■15:10^2■16:20a,17:5b,5a,7b,10■20:15,15(2145),16■21:6a■22:8,28,30,30b,30■23:9,9b,27,34■26:3,11,16,20■27:5a■29:26,32■30:6(2145),6b■31:22b,27a,30a,34^2■32:43a■33:10^{2}a,12a,17,18■34:9^2,14,15,16^2,17■35:4,15,19■36:3,19,29a■37:10■38:4^2,24■40:15■41:4■44:7,26■49:5,18,18a,33,33a■50:3a,40,40a,42■51:6,17a,22,22sup,43,43a,45,62a-LA-

3:1b,27b,36a,39a,39b-EZE-1:5a,8a,10a,26a■2:1a,3a,6a,8a■3:1a,3a,4a,10a,17a,25a■4:1a,12a,16a■5:1a■6:2a■7:2a■8:5a,6a,8a,11,12a,12,15a,17a■9:1,2^{2},3,6,11■10:2,3,6,14a,21a■11:2a,4a,15a■12:2a,3a,9a,18a,22a,27a■13:2a,17a■14:3a,4,8,13^{2}a,17a,19a,21a■15:2a,16:2a■17:2a■18:5,8■20:3a,4a,7,8,11a,13a,21a,27a,46a■21:2a,6a,9a,12a,14a,19a,28a■22:2a,18a,24a,30■23:2a,36a■24:2a,16a,25a■25:2a,13a■26:2a■27:2a■28:2^{2}a,9a,12a,21a■29:2a,8a,11a,18a■30:2a,21a■31:2a■32:2a,10,13a,18a■33:2a,2,7a,10a,12a,24a,30a■34:2a■35:2a■36:1a,11a,17a■37:3a,9a,11a,16a■38:2a,14a■39:1a,17a■40:3,4,4a■41:19a■43:6,7a,10a,18■44:2,5a■46:18■47:3,6a-DA-2:10(606),25(1400)■3:10(606)■5:11(1400)■6:7(606),12^{2}(606)■7:4(606),8(606),13(606)■8:15b,17a■9:21■10:5,11,18a,19■12:6,7-HO-3:3■4:4■6:9■9:7,12a■11:4a,9-AM-2:7■4:13a■5:19-JON-3:7a,8a-MIC-2:2b,2,11■4:4■5:7■6:8a■7:2sup,2-HAB-2:5b-ZEP-1:3^{2}a■3:6-HAG-1:9-ZEC-1:8,10,21■2:1■4:1■6:12■7:9■8:4,10a,16■9:1a■12:1a■13:5a,7b-MAL-2:10,12■3:8a,17■N.T.-all=444,a=3367,b=3762,c=435,d=5100&marked-M'T-4:4■6:24b■7:9,24c,26c■8:4a,9,9sup,20,28d■9:6,9,16b,30a,32■10:23,35■11:8,19^{2},27b■12:8,10,11,12,13,32,35^{2},40,43,45■13:24,31,37,41,44,45,52■15:11^{2},18,20^{2}■16:13,20a,26^{2},27,27sup,28■17:8b,9a,9,12,14,22■18:7,11,12■19:3,5,6,10,20(3495),22(3495),28■20:1,7b,18,28■21:28■22:11,16b,24d,46b,46sup■24:4d,27,30^{2},36b,37,39,44■25:13,14,24,31■26:2,24^{4},45,64,72,74■27:32,57-M'R-1:23,44a■2:10,21b,22b,27^{2},28■3:1,3,5,27b,27(2478)■4:26■5:2,3b,8,37b,43a■6:20c■7:11,15^{2},18,20,23,24b,36a■8:4d,30a,31,36,37,38■9:8b,9a,9,12,31,39■10:2c,7,9,29b,29b,33,45■11:2,14a■12:1,14,34b■13:26,32b,34■14:13,21^{4},41,51(3495),62,71■15:39■16:5(3495),8b-LU-1:27c,34c■2:25^{2},52■3:14a■4:4,33■5:8c,12c,14a,18,20,24,36b,37b,39b■6:5,6,8,10,45^{2},48,49■7:8,14(3495),25,34^{2}■8:16b,27c,29,33,35,38c,41c,51b,56a■9:21a,22,25,26,36b,38c,44,56,58,62b■10:4a,22b,30■11:24,26,30,33b■12:8,10,14,16,40■13:19■14:2,16,30■15:4,11,16b■16:1,19■17:22,24,26,30■18:2,4,8,29b,31■19:2c,7c,10,21,22,30■20:9■21:27,36■22:10,22^{2},48,58,60,69■23:4,6,14^{2},47,50c,53b■24:7-JON-1:6,9,13c,18b,30c,51■2:10,25^{2}■3:1,2b,3d,4,5d,13b,13,14,27,32b■4:27b,29■50■5:5,7sup,7,9,12,15,22b,27,34■6:27,44b,50d,53,62,65b■7:4b,13b,22,23^{2},27sup,27b,30b,44b,46^{2},51■8:10b,11b,15b,20b,28,40,51d,52d■9:1,4b,11,16^{2},24^{2},30■10:18b,29b,33■11:10d,47,50■12:23,34^{2}■13:28b,31■14:6b,23d■15:6d,13b,13d■16:21,22b■18:14,29,31b■19:5,41b-AC-2:6(1520),8(1520),22c■3:2c■4:9,14,17,22■5:1c,13b,23b■6:5c,13■7:56■8:9c,27c■9:7a,8b,12c,13c,33■10:1c,22c,26,28c,28,30c,47d■11:24c,29(1538)■12:22■13:7c,21c,22c,41d■14:8c■16:9c■17:31c■18:10b,24c■19:16,35■20:9(3494)■21:11c,28,39■22:3c,12c,25,26■23:9,17(3494),18(3494),22(3494),22a,27c,30c■24:5c■25:5c,11b,14c,16,17c,22■26:31,32■28:4-RO-1:23■2:1,3,9,10(3956)■3:4,5,28■4:6,8c■5:12■6:6■7:1,3^{2}c,22,24■8:24d■9:20■10:5■12:17a■13:8a■14:7b,20-1CO-2:9,11^{3},11b,14,15b,14■3:11b,18a,18sup,21a■4:1,2d■6:18■7:1,16c,26■8:7(3956)■9:8■10:13(442),24a■11:3^{2}c,4c,7^{2}c,8^{2}c,9^{2}c,11^{2}c,12^{2}c,14c,28■12:3^{2}b,7(1538),11(1538)■13:11c■14:2b■15:21^{2},45,47^{2}■16:11d-2CO-4:16■5:16b■7:2^{3}b■8:12d,20d■11:9b,16d,20^{3}d■12:2,3,4-GA-1:1,11,12■2:16■3:11b,12,15b■5:3■6:1,3d,7,17a-EPH-2:15■3:16■4:13c,22,24■5:6a,29b,31-PH'P-2:8,20b-COL-1:28^{3}■2:16d,18a■3:9■4:6(1520)-1TH-3:3a■4:8-2TH-2:3d,3-1TI-1:8d■2:5,12c■3:1d,5d■4:12a■5:9c,22a■6:11,16sup,16-2TI-2:4b,5d,21d■3:17■4:16b-TIT-2:15a■3:2a,10-HEB-2:6^{2}■5:4d■7:13b■8:2■12:14b■13:6-JAS-1:7,8c,12c,13a,13b,19,20c,23c■2:2c,2sup,14d,18d,20,24■3:2sup,2c,8■5:17-1PE-1:24■2:13(442),19d■3:4-2PE-1:21■2:19d-1JO-3:7a■4:12b-RE-1:13■2:17b■3:7^{2}b,8b,11a■4:7■5:3b,4b■7:9b■9:5■12:5(730),13(730)■13:17d,18■14:3b,14■15:8b■18:11b■19:12b■21:17■22:18(3956)

MANDRAKES-all=1736-GE-30:14^{2},15^{2},16-SONG-7:13

MANEH-EZE-45:12(4488)

MANGER-all=5336-LU-2:7,12,16

MANIFEST-EC-3:18(1305)■N.T.-all=5319&marked-LU-8:17(5318)-JOH-1:31■3:21■9:3■14:21(1718),22-AC-4:16-RO-1:19■10:20(1717)■16:26-1CO-3:13(5318)■4:5■11:19(5318)■14:25■15:27(1212)-2CO-2:14■4:10,11■5:11^{2}■11:6-GA-5:19(5318)-EPH-5:13^{2}-PH'P-1:13(5318)-COL-1:26■4:4-1TI-3:16■5:25(4271)-2TI-1:10■3:9(1552)-HEB-4:13(852)■9:8-1PE-1:20-1JO-2:19■3:10(5318)-RE-15:4

MANIFESTATION-RO-8:19(602)-1CO-12:7(5321)-2CO-4:2(5321)

MANIFESTED-all=5319-M'R-4:22-JOH-2:11■17:6-RO-3:21-TIT-1:3-1JO-1:2^{2}■3:5,8■4:9

MANIFESTLY-2CO-3:3(5319)

MANIFOLD-all=7227&marked-NE-9:19,27-PS-104:24(7231)-AM-5:12■N.T.-LU-18:30(4179)-EPH-3:10(4182)-1PE-1:6(4164)■4:10(4164)

MANKIND-LE-18:22(2145)■20:13(2145)-JOB-12:10(1320,376)■N.T.-1CO-6:9(733)-1TI-1:10(733)-JAS-3:7(5449,442)

MANNA-all=4478-EX-16:15,31,33,35^{2}-NU-11:6,7,9-DE-8:3,16-JOS-5:12^{2}-NE-9:20-PS-78:24■N.T.-all=3131-JOH-6:31,49,58-HEB-9:4-RE-2:17

MANNER-all=4941,a=1697&marked-GE-18:11(734),25a■19:31(1870)■32:19a■39:19a■40:13-EX-7:11(3651)■21:9■22:9a,9sup■23:11(3651)■35:35(3605)-LE-5:10■9:16■24:22-NU-9:14■15:13(3541),16,24■29:6,18,21,24,27,30,33,37-DE-15:2a■22:3(3651)-JOS-6:15-J'G-18:7-1SA-8:9,11■10:25■17:27a,30^{2}a■18:24a■19:24(1571)■21:5(1870)■27:11(3541)-2SA-7:19(8452)■14:3a■15:6a■17:6-1KI-18:28■22:20^{2}(3541)-2KI-1:7■11:14■17:26^{2},27,33,40-1CH-24:19-2CH-4:20■18:19(3541)■30:16-NE-6:4a,5a■8:18-ES-1:13a■2:12(1881)-PS-144:13(2177)-IS-5:17(1699)■10:24(1870),26(1870)■51:6(3654)-JER-13:9(3541)■22:21(1870)■30:18-EZE-20:30(1870)■23:15(1823),45^{2}-AM-4:10(1870)■8:14(1870)■N.T.-all=4217&marked-M'T-6:9(3779)■8:27-M'R-4:41(686)■13:1,29(3779)-LU-1:29,66(686)■7:39■8:25(686)■9:55(3634)■20:31(5615)-JOH-19:40(1485)-AC-1:11(5158)■10:12(1485)■15:1(1485)23(3592)■17:2(1486)■20:18(4458)■22:3(195)■23:25(5179)■25:16(1485),20(4012)■26:4(981)-RO-6:19(442)-1CO-7:7(3779)■11:25(5615)-GA-2:14(1483)-1TH-1:5(3634),9(3697)-2TI-3:10(72)-HEB-10:25(1485)-JAS-1:24(3697)-1PE-1:11(4169)■3:5(3779)-2PE-3:11-1JO-3:1-JUDE-7(5158)-RE-11:5(3779)

MANNERS-LE-20:23(2708)-2KI-17:34(4941)-EZE-11:12(4941)■N.T.-AC-13:18(5159)-1CO-15:33(2239)-HEB-1:1(4187)

MAN'S-all=376,a=120&marked-GE-8:21^{2}a■9:5a,6a■20:3(1167)■42:11,25,35■43:21■44:1,26-EX-4:11a■12:44■21:35■22:5(312),7■30:32a-LE-7:8■15:16■20:10-NU-5:10,12■17:2,5-DE-20:19a■24:2-J'G-7:22■19:26-RU-2:19-1SA-12:4■14:20■17:32a-2SA-12:4■17:18,25-1KI-18:44-2KI-12:4■23:8-ES-1:8-JOB-10:5(1397)■32:21-PS-104:15(582)-PR-12:14a■13:8■16:7,9a■18:4,16a■18:20■19:21■20:24(1397)■29:23a,26-EC-8:1a-IS-8:1(582)■13:7(582)-JER-3:1■23:36-EZE-4:15a■10:8a■38:21■39:15a-DA-4:16(606)■5:5(606)■7:4(606)■8:16a-JON-1:14-MIC-7:6■N.T.-all=444-M'T-10:36-M'R-12:19(5100)-LU-6:22■12:15(5100)■16:12(245)■20:28(5100)-JOH-18:17-AC-5:28■7:58(3494)■11:12(435)■17:29■20:33(3762)-RO-5:19■14:4(245)■15:20(245)-1CO-2:4(442),13(442)■4:3(442)-2CO-4:2■10:16(245)-GA-2:6■3:15-2PE-2:16

MANSERVANT-all=5650-EX-20:10,17■21:32-DE-5:14^{7},21■12:18■16:11,14-JOB-31:13-JER-34:9,10

MANSERVANT'S-EX-21:27(5650)

MANSERVANTS-NE-7:67(5650)

MANSIONS-JOH-14:2(3438)

MANSLAYER-NU-35:6(7523),12(7523)

MANSLAYERS-1TI-1:9(409)

MANTLE-all=4598&marked-J'G-4:18(8063)-1SA-15:27■28:14-1KI-19:13(155),19(155)-2KI-2:8(155),13(155),14(155)-EZR-9:3,5-JOB-1:20■2:12-PS-109:29

MANTLES-IS-3:22(4595)

MANY-all=7227,a=7235&marked-GE-17:4(1995),5(1995)■21:34■37:34-EX-5:5■19:21■23:2-LE-15:25■25:51-NU-9:19■10:36(7233)■13:18■22:3■24:7■26:54,56■35:8,8a-DE-1:46■2:1,10,21■3:5■7:1■15:6^{2}■25:3■28:12■31:17,21-JOS-11:4■22:3-J'G-7:2,4■8:30■9:40■16:24a-1SA-2:5■14:6■25:10(7231)-2SA-1:4a■12:2a■22:17■23:20-1KI-2:38■4:20■7:47(7230)■11:1■18:1,25-2KI-9:22■1CH-4:27■5:22■7:4a,22■8:40a■11:22■23:11a,17a-28:5-2CH-11:23(1995)■14:11■16:8a■26:10■30:17,18■32:23-EZR-3:12^{2}■5:11(7690)■10:13,13a-NE-5:2■6:17a,18■7:2■9:28,30■13:26-ES-1:4■2:8■4:3■8:17-JOB-4:3■11:19■16:2■23:14■41:3a-PS-3:1,2■4:6■18:16■22:12■25:19(7231)■29:3■31:13■32:10■34:19■37:16■40:3,5■55:18■56:2■71:7■78:38a■93:4■106:43■110:6■119:157■129:1,2-PR-4:10a■6:35a■7:26,26(3605)■10:21■14:20■19:4,6,21■28:2,27■29:26■31:29-EC-5:7(7230)■6:3^{2},11a■7:29■11:1(7230),8^{2}a■12:9a,12a-SONG-8:7-IS-1:15a■2:3,4■5:9■8:7,15■17:12,13■22:9(7231)■23:16a■24:22(7230)■31:1■42:20■52:14,15■53:11,12■66:16(7231)-JER-3:1■5:6(7231)■11:15■12:10■13:6■14:7(7231)■16:16^{2}■20:10■22:8■25:14■27:7■28:8■32:14■35:7■36:32■37:16■42:2a■46:11a,16a■50:41■51:13-LA-1:22-EZE-3:6■12:27■16:41■17:7,9,17■19:10■22:25a■26:3■27:3,15,33■32:3,9,10■33:24■37:2■38:6,8^{2},9,15,22,23■39:27■43:2■47:7,10-DA-2:48(7690)■8:25,26■9:27■11:14,18,26,33,33sup,34,39,40,41,44■12:2,3,4,10-HO-3:3,4■8:11a-AM-8:3-MIC-4:2,3,11,13■5:7,8-NA-1:12■3:15^{2}(3513)-HAB-2:8,10-ZEC-2:11■8:20,22-MAL-2:6,8■N.T.-all=4183,a=3745&marked-M'T-3:7■7:13,22^{2}■8:11,16,30■9:10■10:31■13:3,17,58■14:36a■15:30,34(4214)■16:9(4214),10(4214),21■19:30■20:16,28■22:9a,10a,14■24:5^{2},10,11^{2},12■25:21,23■26:28,60■27:13(4214),19,52,53,55-M'R-1:34^{2}■2:2,15^{2}■3:10,10a■4:2,33■5:9,26■6:2,13^{2},20,31,33,34,38(4214),56a■7:4,8,13■8:5(4214),19(4214),20(4214),31■9:12,26■10:31,45,48■11:8■12:5,41■13:6^{2}■14:24,56■15:3,4(4214),41-LU-1:1,14,16■2:34,35■3:18■4:25,27,41■7:11(2425),21^{2},47■8:3,30,32(2425)■9:22■10:24,41■11:8a,53(4119)■12:7,19,47■13:24■14:16■15:13,17(4214),29(5118)■17:25■21:8■22:65■23:8,9(2425)-JOH-1:12a■2:12,23■4:39,41■6:9(5118),60,66■7:31,40■8:26,30■10:20,32,41,42■

11:19,45,47,55■12:11,37(5118),42■14:2■16:12■19:20■20:30■21:11(5118),25-AC-1:3,5■2:39a,40(4119),43■3:24a■4:4,6a,34a■5:12,36a,37a■8:7^2,25■9:13,23(2425),42,43(2425)■10:27,45a■12:12(2425)■13:31(4119),43,48a■14:21(2425)■15:32,35■16:18,23■17:12■18:8■19:18,19(2425)■20:8(2425),19■21:10(4119),20(4214)■24:10,17(4119)■25:7,14(4119)■26:9,10■27:7(2425),20(4119)■28:10,23(4119)-RO-2:12^{2}a■4:17,18■5:15^2,16,19^2■6:3a■8:14a,29■12:4,5■15:23■16:2-1CO-1:26^2■4:15■8:5■10:5(4119),17,33■11:30,30(2425)■12:12^2,14,20■14:10(5118)■16:9-2CO-1:11^2■2:4,6(4119),17■4:15(4119)■6:10■8:22■9:2(4119),12■11:18■12:21-GA-1:14■3:4(5118),10a,16,27a■4:27■6:12a,16a-PH'P-1:14(4119)■3:15a,18-COL-2:1a-1TI-6:1a,9,10,12-2TI-1:18a■2:2-TIT-1:10-HEB-2:10■5:11■7:23(4119)■9:28■12:15-JAS-3:1,2-2PE-2:2-1JO-2:18■4:1-2JO-7,12-3JO-13-RE-1:15■2:24a■3:19a■5:11■8:11■9:9■10:11■13:15a■14:2■17:1■18:17a■19:6,12

MAR-all=7843&marked-LE-19:27-RU-4:6-1SA-6:5-2KI-3:19(3510)-JOB-30:13(5420)-JER-13:19

MARANATHA-1CO-16:22(3134)

MARBLE-all=8336&marked-1CH-29:2(7893)-ES-1:6^2-SONG-5:15■N.T.-RE-18:12(3139)

MARCH-PS-68:7(6805)-JER-46:22(3212)-JOE-2:7(3212)-HAB-1:6(1980)■3:12(6805)

MARCHED-EX-14:10(5265)

MARCHEDST-J'G-5:4(6805)

MARINERS-all=4419&marked-EZE-27:8(7751),9,27,29-JON-1:5

MARISHES-EZE-47:11(1360)

MARK-all=8104&marked-GE-4:15(226)-RU-3:4(3045)-1SA-20:20(4307)-2SA-13:28(7200)-1KI-20:7(3045),22(3045)-JOB-7:20(4645)■16:12(4307)■18:2(995)■21:5(6437)■33:31(7181)■39:1-PS-37:37■48:13(7896)■56:6■130:3-LA-3:12(4307)-EZE-9:4(8420),6(8420)■44:5^2(7760)■N.T.-all=5480&marked-RO-16:17(4648)-PH'P-3:14(4649),17(4648)-RE-13:16,17■14:9,11■15:2■16:2■19:20■20:4

MARKED-1SA-1:12(8104)-JOB-22:15(8104)■24:16(2856)-JER-2:22(3799)■23:18(7181)■N.T.-LU-14:7(1907)

MARKEST-JOB-10:14(8104)

MARKET-all=4627-EZE-27:13,17,19,25■N.T.-M'R-7:4(58)-AC-17:17(58)

MARKETH-JOB-33:11(8104)-IS-44:13^2(8388)

MARKETPLACE-all=58-M'T-20:3-LU-7:32-AC-16:19

MARKETPLACES-M'R-12:38(58)

MARKETS-all=58-M'T-11:16■23:7-LU-11:43■20:46

MARKS-LE-19:28(7085)■N.T.-GA-6:17(4742)

MARRED-all=7843&marked-IS-52:14(4893)-JER-13:7■18:4-NA-2:2■N.T.-M'R-2:22(622)

MARRIAGE-EX-21:10(5772)-PS-78:63(1984)■N.T.-all=1062&marked-M'T-22:2,4,9,30(1548)■24:38(1547)■25:10-M'R-12:25(1061)-LU-17:27(1548)■20:34(1548),35(1548)-JOH-2:1,2-1CO-7:38^2(1447)-HEB-13:4-RE-19:7,9

MARRIAGES-all=2859-GE-34:9-DE-7:3-JOS-23:12

MARRIED-all=1166&marked-GE-19:14(3947)-EX-21:3(1166,802)-NU-12:1^2(3947)■36:3(802),11(802),12(802)-DE-22:22■24:1-1CH-2:21(3947)-2CH-13:21(5375)-NE-13:23(3427)-PR-30:23-IS-54:1■62:4-JER-3:14-MAL-2:11■N.T.-all=1060&marked-M'T-22:25-M'R-6:17■10:12-LU-14:20■17:27-RO-7:3^2(1096),4(1096)-1CO-7:10,33,34,39

MARRIETH-IS-62:5(1166)■N.T.-all=1060-M'T-19:9-LU-16:18^2

MARROW-JOB-21:24(4221)-PS-63:5(2459)-PR-3:8(8250)-IS-25:6(4229)■N.T.-HEB-4:12

MARRY-GE-38:8(2992)-NU-36:6^2(802)-DE-25:5(1961,376)-IS-62:5(1166)■N.T.-all=1060&marked-M'T-5:32■19:9,10■22:24,(1918),30-M'R-10:11■12:25-LU-20:34,35-1CO-7:9^2,28^2,36-1TI-4:3■5:11,14

MARRYING-NE-13:27(3427)■N.T.-M'T-24:38(1060)

MART-IS-23:3(5505)

MARTYR-AC-22:20(3144)-RE-2:13(3144)

MARTYRS-RE-17:6(3144)

MARVEL-EC-5:8(8539)■N.T.-all=2296&marked-M'R-5:20-JOH-3:7■5:20,28■7:21-AC-3:12-2CO-11:14(2298)-GA-1:6-1JO-3:13-RE-17:7

MARVELLED-GE-43:33(8539)-PS-48:5(8539)■N.T.-all=2296-M'T-8:10,27■9:8,33■21:20■22:22■27:14-M'R-6:6■12:17■15:5,44-LU-1:21,63■2:33■7:9■11:38■20:26-JOH-4:27■7:15-AC-2:7■4:13

MARVELLOUS-all=6381&marked-1CH-16:12,24-JOB-5:9■10:16-PS-9:1■17:7(6395)■31:21■78:12(6382)■98:1■105:5■118:23■139:14-IS-29:14^2-DA-11:36-MIC-7:15-ZEC-8:6^2■N.T.-all=2298-M'T-21:42-M'R-12:11-JOH-9:30-1PE-2:9-RE-15:1,3

MARVELLOUSLY-2CH-26:15(6381)-JOB-37:5(6381)-HAB-1:5(8539)

MARVELS-EX-34:10(6381)

MASONS-all=2672&marked-2SA-5:11(2796,68)-2KI-12:12(1443)■22:6(1443)-1CH-14:1(2796,7023)■22:2-2CH-24:12-EZR-3:7

MAST-PR-23:34(2260)-IS-33:23(8650)

MASTER-all=113marked-GE-24:9,10^2,12^2,14,27^2,35,36,37,39,42,48,49,54,56,65■39:2,3,8,19,20-EX-21:4,5,6^2,8,32■22:8(1167)-DE-23:15^2-J'G-19:11,12,22(1167),23(1167)-1SA-20:38■24:6■25:10,14,17■26:16■29:4■30:13,15-2SA-2:7-1KI-22:17-2KI-2:3,5,16■5:1,18,20,22,25■6:5,15,22,23■8:14■9:7,31■10:9■18:27■19:4,6-1CH-12:19■15:27(8269)-2CH-18:16-JOB-3:19-PR-27:18■30:10-IS-24:2■36:8,12■37:4,6-DA-1:3(7227)■4:9(729)■5:11(729)-MAL-1:6^2■2:12(5782)■N.T.-all=1320&marked-M'T-8:19■9:11■10:24,25^2■12:38■17:24■19:16■22:16,24,36■23:8(2519),10(2519)■26:18,25(4461),49(4461)-M'R-4:38■5:35■9:5(4461),17,38■10:17,20,35■11:21(4461)■12:14,19,32■13:1,35(2962)■14:14,45(4461)-LU-3:12■5:5(1988)■6:40^2■7:40■8:24(1988),45(1988),49■9:33(1988),38,49(1988)■10:25■11:45■12:13■13:25■14:21■17:13(1988)■18:18■19:39■20:21,28,39■21:7■22:11-JOH-1:38■3:10■4:31(4461)■8:4■9:2(4461)■11:8(4461),28■13:13,14■20:16-AC-27:11(2942)-RO-14:4(2962)-EPH-6:9(2962)-COL-4:1(2962)

MASTERBUILDER-1CO-3:10(753)

MASTER'S-all=113&marked-GE-24:27,36,44,48■24:51■39:7,8-EX-21:4-1SA-29:10-2SA-9:9,10^2■12:8^2■16:3-2KI-6:32■10:2,3^2,6■18:24-IS-1:3(1167)■36:9■N.T.-2TI-2:21(1203)

MASTERS-all=113&marked-PS-123:2-PR-25:13-EC-12:11(1167)-JER-27:4^2-AM-4:1■N.T.-all=2962&marked-M'T-6:24■23:10(2519)-LU-16:13-AC-16:16,19-EPH-6:5,9-COL-3:22■4:1-1TI-6:1(1203),2(1203)-TIT-2:9(1203)-JAS-3:1(1320)-1PE-2:18(1203)

MASTERS'-ZEP-1:9(113)■N.T.-M'T-15:27(2962)

MASTERIES-all supplied

MASTERY-EX-32:18(1369)-DA-6:24(6981)

MASTS-EZE-27:5(8650)

MATE-IS-34:15(7468),16(7468)

MATRIX-all=7358-EX-13:12,15■34:19-NU-3:12■18:15

MATTER-all=1697&marked-GE-24:9■30:16-EX-18:22^2,26■23:7-NU-16:49■25:18■31:16-DE-3:26■17:8■19:15■22:26-RU-3:18-1SA-10:16■20:23,39■30:24-2SA-1:4■18:13■19:42■20:21-1KI-8:59■15:5-1CH-26:32■27:1-2CH-8:15■24:5-EZR-5:5(2941),17(1836)■10:4,9,14,16-ES-2:23■9:26(3602)-JOB-19:28■32:18(4405)-PS-45:1■64:5-PR-11:13■16:20■17:9■18:13■25:2-EC-5:8(2659)■10:20■12:13-JER-38:27-EZE-9:11-DA-1:14■2:10(4406),23(4406)■3:16(6600)■4:17(6600)■7:28^2(4406)■9:23■N.T.-all=3056&marked-M'R-1:45-AC-8:21■15:6■19:38■24:22(2596)-1CO-6:1(4229)-2CO-7:11(4229)-GAL-2:6(1308)-1TH-4:6(4229)-JAS-3:5(5208)

MATTERS-all=1697&marked-EX-24:14-DE-17:8-1SA-16:18-2SA-11:19■15:3■19:29-2CH-19:11-2CH-19:11^2-NE-11:24-ES-3:4■9:31,32-JOB-33:13-PS-35:20■131:1(1419)-DA-1:20■7:1(4406)

MATTOCK-1SA-13:20(4281)-IS-7:25(4576)

MATTOCKS-1SA-13:21(4281)-2CH-34:6(2719)

MAUL-PR-25:18(4650)

MAW-DE-18:3(6896)

MAY-GE-16:2(194)■44:26(3201)-DE-21:16(3201)■22:19(3201),29(3201)■24:4(3201)-JOS-9:19(3201)-J'G-21:18(3201)-1KI-13:16(3201)■20:9(3201)-2KI-19:4(194)-JOB-1:5-EC-6:10(3201)-JER-13:23(3201)-ZEP-2:3(194)■N.T.-M'T-26:42(1410)-M'R-4:32(1410)■14:7(1410)■20:13(2481)-AC-17:19(1410)■19:40(1410)■21:37(1832)■25:11(1410)-1CO-14:31(1410)-EPH-3:4(1410)

MAYEST-all=3201-DE-7:22■12:17■16:5■17:15■22:3■N.T.-LU-16:2(1410)-AC-8:37(1832)-1CO-7:21■(1410)

MEADOW-GE-41:2(260),18(260)

MEADOWS-J'G-20:33(4629)

MEAL-all=7058&marked-GE-18:6(7058,5560)-NU-5:15-1KI-4:22■17:12,14,16-2KI-4:41-1CH-12:40-IS-47:2-HO-8:7■N.T.-M'T-13:33(224)-LU-13:21(224)

MEALTIME-RU-2:14(6256,400)

MEAN-all=120&marked-1KI-18:45(5704,3541)-PR-22:29(2823)-IS-2:9■5:15■N.T.-M'R-9:10(2076)-JOH-4:31(3342)-AC-10:17(1498)■17:20(2309,1511)■21:13(4160),39(767)-RO-2:15(3342)

MEANEST- all supplied

MEANETH-IS-10:7(1819)■N.T.-M'T-9:13(2076)■12:7(2076)-AC-2:12(2309,1511)

MEANING-DA-8:15(998)■N.T.-AC-27:2(3195)-1CO-14:11(1411)

MEANS-all=3027&marked-2SA-14:14(4284)-1KI-10:29-2CH-1:17-EZR-4:16(6903)-PR-6:26(1157)-JER-5:31-MAL-1:9■N.T.-all=4458&marked-M'T-5:26(3361)-LU-8:36(4459)■10:19(3364)-JOH-9:21(4459)-AC-18:21(3843)■27:12-RO-1:10■11:14-1CO-8:9■9:22(3843),27-2CO-11:3-GA-2:2-PH'P-3:11-1TH-3:5-2TH-2:3(5158)■3:16(5158)-HEB-9:15(1096)

MEANT-GE-50:20(2803)N.T.-LU-15:26(1498)■18:36(1498)

MEASURE-all=4060&marked-EX-26:2,8-LE-19:35(4884)-NU-35:5(4058)-DE-21:2(4058)■25:15(374)-JOS-3:4-1KI-6:25■7:37-2KI-7:1(5429),16(5429),18(5429)-1CH-23:29(4884)-2CH-3:3-JOB-11:9(4055)■28:25-PS-39:4■80:5(7991)-IS-5:14(2706)■27:8(5432)■40:12(7991)■65:7(4058)-JER-30:11(4941)■46:28(4941)■51:13(520)-EZE-4:11(4884),16(4884)■40:10^2,21,22■41:17■43:10(4058)■45:3,3(4058),11(8506),11(4971)■

46:22■47:18(4058)-MIC-6:10(374)-ZEC-2:2(4058)■N.T.-all=3358&marked-M'T-7:2■23:32-M'R-4:24■6:51(4053)■7:37(5249)■10:26(4057)-LU-6:38^2-JOH-3:34-RO-12:3-2CO-1:8(5236)■10:13(280),13^2,15(280)■11:23(5234)-GA-1:13(5236)-EPH-4:7,13,16-RE-6:6(5518)■11:1(3354),2(3354)■21:15(3354),17

MEASURED-all=4058&marked-RU-3:15-2SA-8:2^2-IS-40:12-JER-31:37■33:22-EZE-40:5,6,8,9,11,13,19,20,23,24,27,28,32,35,47,48■41:1,2,3,4,5,13,15■42:15,16,17,18,19,20■47:3,4^2,5-HO-1:10-HAB-3:6(4128)■N.T.-all=3354&marked-M'T-7:2(488)-M'R-4:24-LU-6:38(488)-RE-21:16,17

MEASURES-all=4060&marked-GE-18:6(5429)-DE-25:14(374)-1SA-25:18(5429)-1KI-4:22^2(3734)■5:11^2(3734)■7:9,11■18:32(5429)-2KI-7:1(5429),16(5429),18(5429)-2CH-2:10^2(3734)■27:5(3734)-EZR-7:22-JOB-38:5(4461)-PR-20:10(374)-JER-13:25(4055)-EZE-40:24,28,29,32,33,35■43:13■48:16,30,33■N.T.-M'T-13:33(4568)-LU-13:21(4658)■16:6(943),7(2884)-RE-6:6(5518)

MEASURING-all=4060-JER-31:39-EZE-40:3,5■42:15,16^2,17,18,19-ZEC-2:1■N.T.-2CO-10:12(3354)

MEAT-all=3978,a=400,b=3899&marked-GE-1:29(402),30(402)■9:3(402)■45:23(4202)-LE-11:34a■22:11b,13b■25:6(402),7(398)-NU-28:24b-DE-2:6a,28a■20:20■28:26-J'G-14:14-1SA-20:5(398),24b,27b,34b-2SA-3:35b■12:3(6595)■13:5b,5(1279),7(1279),10(1279)-1KI-10:5■19:8(396)-1CH-12:40-2CH-9:4-EZR-3:7-JOB-6:7b■12:11a■20:14b,21a■30:4b■33:20■34:3(398)■36:31a■38:41a-PS-42:3b■44:11■59:15(398)■69:21(1267)■74:14■78:18a,25(6720),30a■79:2■104:21a,27a■107:18a■111:5(2964)■145:15a-PR-6:8b■23:3b■30:22b,25b■31:15(2964)-IS-62:8■65:25b-JER-7:33■16:4■19:7■34:20-LA-1:11a,19a■4:10(1262)-EZE-4:10■16:19b■29:5(402)■34:5(402),8(402),10(402)■47:12^2-DA-1:5(6598),8(6598),10,13(6598),15(6598),16(6598)■4:12(4203),21(4203)■11:26(6598)-HO-11:4(398)-JO-1:16a-HAB-1:16■3:17a-HAG-2:12-MAL-1:12a■3:10(2964)■N.T.-all=5160&marked-M'T-3:4■6:25■10:10■24:45■25:35(5315),42(5315)-LU-3:11(1033)■8:55(5315)■9:13(1033)■12:23,42(4620)■24:41(1034)-JOH-4:8,32(1035),34(1033)■6:27^2(1035),55(1035)■21:5(4371)-AC-2:46■9:19■16:34(5132)■27:33,34,36-RO-14:15^2(1033),17(1035),20(1033)-1CO-3:2(1033)■8:8(1033),13(1033)■10:3(1033)-COL-2:16(1035)-HEB-5:12,14■12:16(1035)

MEATS-all=1033-M'R-7:19-1CO-6:13^2-1TI-4:3-HEB-9:10■13:9

MEDDLE-all=1624&marked-DE-2:5,19-2KI-14:10-2CH-25:19-PR-20:19(6148)■24:21(6148)

MEDDLED-PR-17:14(1566)

MEDDLETH-PR-26:17(5674)

MEDDLING-PR-20:3(1566)

MEDIATOR-all=3316-GA-3:19,20,20sup-1TI-2:5-HEB-:6■9:15■12:24

MEDICINE-PR-17:22(1456)-EZE-47:12(8644)

MEDICINES-JER-30:13(7499)■46:11(7499)

MEDITATE-all=1897&marked-JOS-1:8-PS-1:2■63:6■77:12■119:15(7878),23(7878),48(7878),78(7878),■148(7878)■143:5-IS-33:18■N.T.-LU-21:14(4304)-1TI-4:15(3191)

MEDITATION-PS-5:1(1901)■19:14(1902)■49:3(1900)■104:34(7879)■119:97(7881),99(7881)

MEEK-all=6035-NU-12:3-PS-22:26■25:9^2■37:11■76:9■147:6■149:4-IS-11:4■29:19■61:1-AM-2:7-ZEP-2:3■N.T.-all=4239&marked-M'T-5:5■11:29(4235)■21:5-1PE-3:4

MEEKNESS-PS-45:4(6037)-ZEP-2:3(6038)■N.T.-all=4236&marked-1CO-4:21-2CO-10:1-GA-5:23■6:1-EPH-4:2-COL-3:12-1TI-6:11-2TI-2:25-TIT-3:2-JAS-1:21(4240)■3:13(4240)-1PE-3:15(4240)

MEET-all=7125&marked-GE-2:18(5828),20(5828)■14:17■18:2■19:1■24:17,65■29:13■30:16■32:6■33:4■46:29-EX-4:14,27■8:26(3559)■18:7■19:17■23:4(6293)■25:22(3259)■29:42(3259),43(3259)■30:6(3259),36(3259)-NU-17:4(3259)■22:36■23:3,15(7136)■31:13-DE-3:18(1121)-JOS-2:16(6293)■9:11-J'G-4:18,22■6:35■11:31,34■19:3-RU-2:22(6293)-1SA-10:3(4672),5(6293)■13:10■15:12■17:48^2■18:6■25:32,34■30:21^2-2SA-6:20■10:5■15:32■19:15,16,20,24,25-1KI-2:8,19■18:16^2■21:18-2KI-1:3,6,7■2:15■4:26,29(4672),31■5:21,26■8:8,9■9:17,18■10:15■16:10-1CH-12:17(6440)■19:5-2CH-15:2(6440)■19:2(6440)-EZR-4:14(749)-NE-6:2(3259),10(3259)-ES-2:9(7200)-JOB-5:14(6298)■39:21-PR-7:15■11:24(3476)■17:12(6298)■22:2(6298)■29:13(6298)-IS-7:3■14:9■34:14(6298)■47:3(6293)-JER-26:14(3477)■27:5(3474)■41:6■51:31^2-EZE-15:4(6743),5^2(6213)-HO-13:8(6298)-AM-4:12-ZEC-2:3■N.T.-all=514&marked-M'T-3:8■8:34(4877)■15:26(2570)■25:1(529),6(529)-M'R-7:27(2570)■14:13(528)-LU-14:31(528)■15:32(1163)■22:10(4876)-JOH-12:13(5222)-AC-26:20■28:15(529)-RO-1:27(1163)-1CO-15:9(2425)■16:4-PH'P-1:7(1342)-COL-1:12(2427)-1TH-4:17(529)-2TH-1:3-2TI-2:21(2173)-HEB-6:7(2111)-2PE-1:13(1342)

MEETEST-2KI-10:3(3477)-IS-64:5(6293)

MEETETH-GE-32:17(6298)-NU-35:19(6293),21(6293)

MEETING-1SA-21:1(7125)-IS-1:13(6116)

MELODY-IS-23:16(5059)■51:3(2172)-AM-5:23-EPH-5:19(5567)

MELONS-NU-11:5(20)

MELT-all=4549&marked-EX-15:15(4127)-JOS-2:11■14:8(4529)-2SA-17:10-PS-58:7(3988)■112:10-IS-13:7■19:1-JER-9:7(6884)-EZE-21:7■22:20^2(5413)-AM-9:5(4127),13(4127)-NA-1:5(4127)■N.T.-2PE-3:10(3089),12(5080)

MELTED-all=4549&marked-EX-16:21-JOS-5:1■7:5-J'G-5:5(5140)-1SA-14:16(4127)-PS-22:14■46:6(4127)■97:5■107:26(4127)-IS-34:3-EZE-22:21(5413),22(2046),22(5413)

MELTETH-PS-58:8(8557)■68:2(4549)■119:28(1811)■147:18(4529)-IS-40:19(5258)-JER-6:29(6884)-NA-2:10(4549)

MELTING-IS-64:2(2003)

MEMBER-all=3196-1CO-12:14,19,26^2-JAS-3:5

MEMBERS-JOB-17:7(3338)■N.T.-all=3196-M'T-5:29,30-RO-6:13^2,19^2■7:5,23^2■12:4^2,5-1CO-6:15^3■12:12^2,18,20,22,25,26^2,27-EPH-4:25■5:30-COL-3:5-JAS-3:6■4:1

MEMORIAL-all=2146&marked-EX-3:15(2143)■12:14■13:9■17:14■28:12^2,29■30:16■39:7-LE-2:2(234),9(234),16(234)■5:12(234)■6:15(234)■23:24■24:7(234)-NU-5:15,18,26(234)■10:10■16:40■31:54-JOS-4:7-NE-2:20-ES-9:28(2143)-PS-9:6(2143)■135:13(2143)-HO-12:5(2143)-ZEC-6:14■N.T.-all=3422-M'T-26:13-M'R-14:9-AC-10:4

MEMORY-all=2143-PS-109:15■145:7-PR-10:7-EC-9:5-IS-26:14

MEN-all=582,a=376,b=120,c=1167,d=1400,e=4962,f=606&marked-GE-6:1b,2b,4^{2}b,4■11:5b■12:20■13:13■14:24sup,24■17:23,27■18:2,16,22■19:4,5,8,10,11,12,16■20:8■24:13,54,59■26:7^2■29:22■32:6a,28■33:1a■34:7,20,21,22■38:21,22■39:11,14■43:15,16^2,17,18,24,33■44:3,4■46:32■47:2,6-EX-2:13■4:19■5:9■10:7,11(1397)■12:37(1397)■17:9■18:21^2,25■21:18,22■22:31■32:28a■35:22-LE-18:27■27:29b-NU-1:5,17,44a■5:6b■9:6,7■11:16a,24a,26■12:3b■13:2,3,16,31,32■14:22,36,37,38■16:2,14,26,29sup,29^{2}b,30,32b,35a■18:15b■22:9,20,35■25:5■26:10a■31:11b,21,28,32,42,49,53■32:11,14■34:17,19-DE-1:13,15,22,23,35■2:14,16,34e■3:6e■4:3a■13:13■19:17■21:21■22:21■25:1,11■27:14a■29:10a■31:12■32:26■33:6e-JOS-2:1,2,3,4^2,5^2,7,9,14,17,23■3:12a■4:2,4a■5:4,6■6:3,22■7:2^2,3a,4a,4,5,5a■8:3a,12a,14,20,21,25a,25■9:6a,7a,14■10:2,6,18,24sup,24a■18:4,8,9■24:11(1167)-J'G-1:4a■3:29^{2}a,31a■4:6a,10a,14a■6:27^2,28,30■7:6a,7a,8a,16a,19a,23a,24a■8:1a,4a,5,8^2,9,10sup.10a,14,14a,15^2,16,17,18,22a■9:2c,3c,6c,7c,18c,20^{2}c,23^{2}c,24c,25c,26c,28,36,39c,46c,47c,49,49a,51,55a,57■11:3■12:1a,4^2,5■14:18,19a■15:10a,11a,15,16■16:27,27a■18:2^2(582,1121),7,11a,14,16a,17,17a,22■19:16,22,25■20:5c,10,11a,12,13,15^{2}a,16a,17^{3}a,20^{2}a,21a,22a,25a,31a,33a,34a,35a,36a,38a,39^{2}a,41^{2}a,42a,44a,44,45^{2}a,46a,46,47a,48a,48(4974)■21:1a,10a-RU-4:2-1SA-2:17sup,17,26■4:2a,9^2■5:7,9,12■6:10,15,19^{2}a,20■7:1,11■8:22■10:2,3■11:1,5,8a,9a,9,10,12,15■8:9■13:6a,15a■14:2a,8,12,14a,22a,24a■15:4a■17:2a,12,19a,24a,25a,26,28,52■18:5,27,27a■22:2a,6,19a■23:3,5,8,11c,12c,12,13,24,25,26^3■24:2a,2,3,4,6,22■25:11,13,13a,15,20■26:2a,19b■27:2a,3,8■28:1,8■29:2,4,11■30:1,3,9a,10a,17a,21,22sup,22a,31■31:1,6,7^2,12a-2SA-1:11■2:3,4^2,5,17,29,30a,31,31a,32■3:20^2,34(1121),39■4:2,11■5:6,21■6:19a■7:14,14b■8:5a■10:5,6^{2}a,12(2388)■11:16,17,23■12:1■13:9a■15:1a,6,11a,13a,18a,22■16:13,15a,18a■17:1a,8,8sup,10(1121),12,14a,24a■18:28■19:14a,16a,17a,28,41^{2}a,41,42a,43^{3}a■20:2a,4a,7,7sup,11a■21:6,12c,17■23:3b,9,9a,17,17sup■24:9^{3}a,15a-1KI-1:5a,9■2:32■4:31b■5:13a■8:2a,39b■9:22■10:8■11:18,24■13:25■18:13a,22a■20:17,30a,33■21:10,11,13^2■22:6a-2KI-2:7a,16(582,1121),17a,19■3:26a■4:40,43a■5:24■7:3■10:6,6sup,14a,24a,24■11:9■12:15■15:25a■17:30^3■18:27■20:14■23:2a,14b,17■24:16■25:4,19^2,19a,23^2,24,25-1CH-4:12,22,42■5:18sup,18,21(5315,120),24^2,■7:21,40sup,40■8:40■9:9,13(1368)■10:1a,7a,12a■11:19■12:8,38■18:5a■19:5^2■21:5^{2}a,14a■24:4(1397)■26:7(1121),8a,9(1121),12(1397),30(1121),32(1121)-2CH-2:2a■5:3a■6:18b,30b■8:9■9:7■13:3sup,3^{2}a,3sup,7,15^{2}a,17a■17:13■18:5a■23:8■24:24■26:17(1121)■28:6(1121),15■31:19■34:12,30a-EZR-1:4■2:2,22,23,27,28■4:11f,21d■5:4d,10d■6:8d■8:16d■10:1,9,17-NE-1:2■2:12■3:2,7,22■4:23■5:5■7:7,26,27,28,29,30,31,32,33■8:2a,3■11:2,6-ES-9:6a,12a,15a-JOB-1:3(1121)■4:13■7:20b■11:3e,11e■22:15e■24:12e■28:4■31:31e■32:1,5■33:15,16,27■34:8,10,34,36■36:24■37:7,24-PS-4:2a■9:20■11:4b■12:1b,8b■14:2b■17:4b,14^{2}e■21:10b■22:6b■26:9■31:19b■33:13b■36:7b■45:2b■53:2b■55:23■57:4b■58:1b■59:2■62:9(1121)b,9a■64:9b■66:5b,12■68:18b■73:5,5b■76:5■78:60b■82:7b■89:47(1121)b■90:3b■105:12e■107:8sup,8b,15sup,15b,21sup,21b,31sup,31b■115:16b■116:11b■124:2b■139:19■141:4a■145:12b-PR-8:4a,31b■15:11b■20:6b■23:28b■24:1,9b■25:1■28:5,28b■29:8■30:14b-EC-2:3b,8sup,8b■3:10b,18b,19b■6:1b■7:2b■8:11b■9:3b,12b,14■

12:3-IS-2:11,17▪3:25e▪5:3a,7a,13e,22▪6:12b▪7:13▪21:9a▪22:6b▪24:6▪28:14▪29:13,19b▪31:3b▪36:12▪39:3▪41:14e▪43:4b▪44:11b▪45:14▪46:8a▪51:7▪52:14b▪53:3a▪57:1▪66:24-JER-4:3a,4a▪5:26sup,26▪6:23a▪9:22b▪11:2a,9a,21,23▪17:25a▪18:11a,21▪19:10▪26:22^{2}▪32:19b,20b,32a▪33:5b▪34:18▪35:13a▪36:31a▪37:10▪38:4,9,10,11,16▪39:4,17▪40:7^{2},8,9▪41:1,2,3,5a,7,8,9,12,15,16▪42:17▪43:2,6(1397),9▪44:15,19,20(1397),27a▪47:2b▪48:14,31,36▪49:15b,26sup,26,28(1121)▪50:30sup,30▪51:14b,32▪52:7,25^{2},25a-LA-3:33a-EZE-8:11a,16a▪9:2,4,6▪11:1a,2,15▪12:16▪14:3,14,16,18▪16:17(2145)▪19:3b,6b▪21:31▪22:9▪23:7(1121),14,40,42,45▪24:17,22▪25:4(1121),10(1121)▪27:10,11(1121),13b,15(1121),27▪30:5(1121)▪31:14b▪34:31b▪36:10b,12b,12sup,13b,14b,37b,38b▪38:20b▪39:14,20sup,20a-DA-2:38f,43f▪3:12d,13d,20d,21d,22d,23d,24d,25d,27d▪4:17^{2}f,25^{2}f,32^{2}f,33f▪5:21^{2}f▪6:5d,11d,15d,24d▪9:7a▪10:7,16b-HO-6:7b▪13:2b-JOE-1:12b▪2:7sup,7▪3:9^{2}-AM-6:9-OB-7^{2}-JON-1:10^{2},13,16-MIC-2:12b▪5:5b,7b▪7:2b,6-NA-2:3sup,3-HAB-1:14b-ZEP-1:12,17b,17sup-HAG-1:11b-ZEC-2:4b▪3:8▪7:2▪8:10b,23▪11:6b▪N.T.-all=444,a=435&marked-M'T-4:19▪5:13,16,19▪6:1,2,5,14,15,16,18▪7:12▪8:27▪9:8▪10:17,32,33▪12:31^{2},36,41a▪13:25▪14:21a,35a▪15:9,38a▪16:13,23▪17:22▪19:12,26▪21:25,26▪22:16▪23:5,7,13,28-M'R-1:17a▪3:28▪6:44a▪7:7,8,21▪8:24,27,33▪9:31▪10:27▪11:30,32,32sup▪12:14▪14:51(3495)-LU-1:25▪2:14▪5:10,18a▪6:22,26,31▪7:20a,31▪9:14a,30,32a,44▪11:31,32a,44,46▪12:8,9,36▪13:4▪14:24a▪16:15^{2}▪17:12a▪18:10,11,27▪20:4,6▪22:63a▪23:11(4753)▪24:4a,7-JOH-1:4▪3:19▪4:28▪5:41▪6:10,10a,14▪8:17▪12:43▪17:6-AC-1:10a,11a,16▪2:5a,14a,17(3495),22a,29a,37a▪3:12a▪4:4,12,13,16▪5:4,10(3495),14a,25a,29,35a,35,36a,38^{2}▪6:3a,11a▪7:2a▪8:2a,3a,12a▪9:2a,7a,38a▪10:5a,17a,19a,21a▪11:3a,11a,13a,20a▪13:15a,16a,26a,38a▪14:11,15▪15:7a,13a,17,22^{2}a,25a,26▪16:17,20,35▪17:12a,22a,26,30,34a▪18:13▪19:7a,35a,37a▪20:30a▪21:23a,26a,28a,28sup,38a▪22:1,4,15▪23:1a,6a,21a▪24:16▪25:23a,24a▪28:17a-RO-1:18,27^{2}(730)▪2:16,29▪5:12,18^{2}▪6:19(442)▪11:4a▪12:17,18▪14:18-1CO-1:25^{2}▪2:5▪3:3,21▪4:9▪7:7,23▪13:1▪14:2,3,20(5046)▪15:19,32,39▪16:13(407)-2CO-3:2▪5:11▪8:21-GA-1:1,10^{3}▪3:15-EPH-3:5▪4:8,14▪5:28a▪6:7-PH'P-2:7▪4:5-COL-2:8,22▪3:23-1TH-2:4,6,13,15-2TH-3:2,2sup-1TI-2:1,4,5,8a▪4:10▪5:24▪6:5,9-2TI-2:2▪3:2,8,13-TIT-1:14▪2:11▪3:2,8-HEB-5:1^{2}▪6:16▪7:8▪9:27-JAS-3:9-1PE-2:4,15▪4:2,6-2PE-1:21▪3:7-1JO-2:13(3495),14(3495)▪5:9-JUDE-4-RE-8:11▪9:4,6,7,10,15,18,20▪11:13▪13:13▪14:4▪16:2,8,9,18,21^{2}▪18:13▪21:3

MENCHILDREN-EX-34:23(2138)

MEND-2CH-24:12(2388)

MENDING-M'T-4:21(2675)-M'R-1:19(2675)

MENE-DA-5:25(4484),26(4484)

MENPLEASERS-EPH-6:6(441)-COL-3:22(441)

MEN'S-all=120&marked-GE-24:32(582)▪44:1(582)-DE-4:28-1SA-24:9-1KI-13:2-2KI-19:18▪23:20-PS-115:4▪135:15-IS-37:19-HAB-2:8,17▪N.T.-all=444&marked-M'T-23:4-LU-9:56▪21:26-AC-17:25-JUDE-16(4283)

MENSERVANTS-all=5650-GE-12:16▪20:14▪24:35▪30:43▪32:5-EX-21:7-DE-12:12-1SA-8:16-2KI-5:26▪N.T.-LU-12:45(3816)

MENSTEALERS-1TI-1:10(405)

MENSTRUOUS-IS-30:22(1739)-LA-1:17(5079)-EZE-18:6(5079)

MENTION-all=2142-GE-40:14-EX-23:13-JOS-23:7-1SA-4:18-JOB-28:18-PS-71:16▪87:4-IS-12:4▪19:17▪26:13▪48:1▪49:1▪62:6▪63:7-JER-4:16▪20:9▪23:36-AM-6:10▪N.T.-all=3417&marked-RO-1:9-EPH-1:16-1TH-1:2-PH'M-4-HEB-11:22(3421)

MENTIONED-all=2142&marked-JOS-21:9(7121)-1CH-4:38(935)-2CH-20:34(5927)-EZE-16:56(8052)▪18:22,24▪33:16

MERCHANDISE-all=4627&marked-DE-21:14(6014)▪24:7(6014)-PR-3:14(5504),14(5505)▪31:18(5504)-IS-23:18^{2}(5504)▪45:14(5505)-EZE-26:12(7404)▪27:9,15(5506),24(4819),27^{2},33,34▪28:16(7404)▪N.T.-M'T-22:5(1711)-JOH-2:16(1712)-RE-18:11(1117),12(1117)

MERCHANT-all=5503&marked-PR-31:24-SONG-3:6(7402)-IS-23:11(3667)-EZE-27:3(7402),12,16,18,20(7402)-HO-12:7(3667)-ZEP-1:11(3667)▪N.T.-M'T-13:45(1713)

MERCHANTMEN-GE-37:28(5503)-1KI-10:15(8446)

MERCHANTS-all=7402&marked-1KI-10:15,28(5503)-2CH-1:16(5503)▪9:14(5503)-NE-3:31,32▪13:20-JOB-41:6(3669)-IS-23:2(5503),8(5503)▪47:15(5503)-EZE-17:4▪27:13,15,17,21(5503),22^{2},23^{2},24,36(5503)▪38:13(5503)-NA-3:16▪N.T.-all=1713-RE-18:3,11,15,23

MERCHANTS'-PR-31:14(5503)

MERCIES-all=7356&marked-GE-32:10(2617)-2SA-24:14-1CH-21:13-2CH-6:42(2617)-NE-9:19,27,28-PS-25:6▪40:11▪51:1▪69:16▪77:9▪79:8▪89:1(2617)▪103:4▪106:7(2617),45(2617)▪119:41(2617),77,156▪145:9-PR-12:10-IS-54:7▪55:3(2617)▪63:7,15-JER-16:5▪42:12-LA-3:22(2617),32(2617)-DA-2:18(7359)▪9:9,18-HO-2:19-ZEC-1:16▪N.T.-all=3628&marked-AC-13:34(3741)-RO-12:1-2CO-1:3-PH'P-2:1-COL-3:12

MERCIES'-all=2617&marked-NE-9:31(7356)-PS-6:4▪31:16▪44:26

MERCIFUL-all=2603&marked-GE-19:16(2551)-EX-34:6(7349)-DE-4:31(7349)▪21:8(3722)▪32:43-2SA-22:26(2623),26(2616)-1KI-20:31(2617)-2CH-30:9(7349)-NE-9:17(7349),31(7349)-PS-18:25(2623),25(2616)▪26:11▪37:26▪41:4,10▪56:1▪57:1▪59:5▪67:1▪86:3▪103:8(7349)▪116:5(7355)▪117:2(2617)▪119:58,76(2617),132-PR-11:17(2617)-IS-57:1(2617)-JER-3:12(2623)-JOE-2:13(7349)-JON-4:2(7349)▪N.T.-M'T-5:7(1655)-LU-6:36(3629)▪18:13(2433)-HEB-2:17(1655)▪8:12(2436)

MERCY-all=2617,a=7355,b=3727,c=2603&marked-GE-19:19▪24:27▪39:21▪43:14(7356)-EX-15:13▪20:6▪25:17b,18b,19b,20^{2}b,21b,22b▪26:34b▪30:6b▪31:7b▪33:19a▪34:7▪35:12b▪37:6b,7b,8b,9^{2}b▪39:35b▪40:20b-LE-16:2^{2}b,13b,14^{2}b,15^{2}b-NU-7:89b▪14:18,19-DE-5:10▪7:2c,9,12▪13:17(7356)-J'G-1:24-2SA-7:15▪15:20▪22:51-1KI-3:6▪8:23-1CH-16:34,41▪17:13▪28:11b-2CH-1:8▪5:13▪6:14▪7:3,6▪20:21-EZR-3:11▪7:28▪9:9-NE-1:5,11(7356)▪9:32▪13:22-JOB-37:13-PS-4:1c▪5:7▪6:2c▪9:13c▪13:5▪18:50▪21:7▪23:6▪25:7,10,16c▪27:7c▪30:10c▪31:7,9c▪32:10▪33:18,22▪36:5▪37:21c▪51:1c▪52:8▪57:3,10▪59:10,16,17▪61:7▪62:12▪66:20▪69:13▪77:8▪85:7,10▪86:5,13,15,16c▪89:2,14,24,28▪90:14▪94:18▪98:3▪100:5▪101:1▪102:13(7355)▪103:8,11,17▪106:1▪107:1▪108:4▪109:12,16,21,26▪115:1▪118:1,2,3,4,29▪119:64,124▪123:2c,3c▪130:7▪136:1,2,3,4,5,6,7,8,9,10,11,12,13,14,15,16,17,18,19,20,21,22,23,24,25,26▪138:8▪143:12▪145:8▪147:11-PR-3:3▪14:21c,22,31c▪16:6▪20:28^{2}▪21:21▪28:13a-IS-9:17a▪14:1a▪16:5▪27:11a▪30:18a▪47:6(7356)▪49:10a,13a▪54:8a,10a▪55:7a▪60:10a-JER-6:23a▪13:14a▪21:7a▪30:18a▪31:20a▪33:11,26a▪42:12a▪50:42a-EZE-39:25a-DA-4:27(2604)▪9:4-HO-1:6a,7a▪2:4a,23^{2}a▪4:1▪6:6▪10:12▪12:6▪14:3a-JON-2:8-MIC-6:8▪7:18,20-HAB-3:2a-ZEC-1:12a▪7:9▪10:6a▪N.T.-ll=1656,a=1653&marked-M'T-5:7a▪9:13,27a▪12:7▪15:22a▪17:15a▪20:30a,31a▪23:23-M'R-10:47a,48a-LU-1:50,54,58,72,78▪10:37▪16:24a▪17:13a▪18:38a,39a-RO-9:15a,16a,18a,18sup,23▪11:30a,31,31a,32a▪12:8a▪15:9-1CO-7:25a-2CO-4:1a-GA-6:16-EPH-2:4-PH'P-2:27a-1TI-1:2,13a,16a-2TI-1:2,16,18-TIT-1:4▪3:5-HEB-4:16▪10:28(3628)-JAS-2:13(448),13^{2}▪3:17▪5:11(3629)-1PE-1:3▪2:10^{2}a-2JO-3,-JUDE-2,21

MERCYSEAT-HEB-9:5(2435)

MERRILY-ES-5:14(8056)

MERRY-all=2896&marked-GE-43:34(7937)-J'G-9:27(1974)▪16:25▪19:6(3190),9(3190),22(3190)-RU-3:7(3190)-1SA-25:36-2SA-13:28-1KI-4:20(8056)▪21:7(3190)-2CH-7:10-ES-1:10-PR-15:13(8056),15▪17:22(8056)-EC-8:15(8055)▪9:7▪10:19(8055)-JER-30:19(7832)▪31:4(7832)▪N.T.-all=2165&marked-LU-12:19▪15:23,24,29,32-JAS-5:13(2114)-RE-11:10

MERRYHEARTED-IS-24:7(8056,3820)

MESS-GE-43:34(4864)-2SA-11:8(4864)

MESSAGE-all=1697&marked-J'G-3:20-1KI-20:12-PR-26:6-HAG-1:13(4400)▪N.T.-LU-19:14(4242)-1JO-1:5(1860)▪3:11(31)

MESSENGER-all=4397&marked-GE-50:16(6680)-1SA-4:17(1319)▪23:27-2SA-11:19,22,23,25▪15:13(5046)-1KI-19:2▪22:13-2KI-5:10▪6:32^{2},33▪9:18▪10:8-2CH-18:12-JOB-1:14▪33:23-PR-13:17▪17:11▪25:13(6735)-IS-42:19-JER-51:31(5046)-EZE-23:40-HAG-1:13-MAL-2:7▪3:1^{2}▪N.T.-all=32&marked-M'T-11:10-M'R-1:2-LU-7:27-2CO-12:7-PH'P-2:25(652)

MESSENGERS-all=4397&marked-GE-32:3,6-NU-20:14▪21:21▪22:5▪24:12-DE-2:26-JOS-6:17,25▪7:22-J'G-6:35^{2}▪7:24▪9:31▪11:12,13,14,17,19-1SA-6:21▪11:3,4,7,9^{2}▪16:19▪19:11,14,15,16,20^{2},21^{2}▪25:14,42-2SA-2:5▪3:12,14,26▪5:11▪11:4▪12:27-1KI-20:2,5,9^{2}-2KI-1:2,3,5,16▪7:15▪14:8▪16:7▪17:4▪19:9,14,23-1CH-14:1▪19:2,16-2CH-36:15,16-NE-6:3-PR-16:14-IS-14:32▪18:2▪37:9,14▪44:26▪57:9(6735)-JER-27:3-EZE-23:16▪30:9-NA-2:13▪N.T.-all=32&marked-LU-7:24▪9:52-2CO-8:23(652)-JAS-2:25

MESSES-GE-43:34(4864)

MET-all=6298&marked-GE-32:1(6293)▪33:8-EX-3:18(7136)▪4:24,27▪5:3(7122),20(6293)-NU-23:4(7136),16(7136)-DE-23:4(6923)▪25:18(7136)-JOS-11:5(3259)▪17:10(6293)-1SA-10:10(7125)▪25:20-2SA-2:13▪16:1(7135)▪18:9(7122)-1KI-13:24(4672)▪18:7(7125)-2KI-9:21(4672)▪10:13(4672)-NE-13:2(6923)-PS-85:10-PR-7:10(7125)-JER-41:6-AM-5:19(6293)▪N.T.-all=5221&marked-M'T-8:28▪28:9(528)-M'R-5:2(528)▪11:4(296)-LU-8:27▪9:37(4876)▪17:12(528)-JOH-4:51(528)▪11:20,30▪12:18-AC-10:25▪(4876)▪16:16(528)▪17:17(3909)▪20:14(4820)-HEB-7:1(4876),10(4876)

METE-all=4058-EX-16:18-PS-60:6▪108:7▪N.T.-all=3354-M'T-7:2-M'R-4:24-LU-6:38

METED-IS-18:2(6978),7(6978)▪40:12(8505)

METEYARD-LE-19:35(4060)
MICE-all=5909-1SA-6:4,5,11,18
MIDDAY-1KI-18:29(6672)-NE-8:3(4276,3117)■N.T.-AC-6:13(2250,3319)
MIDDLE-all=8484&marked-EX-26:28(8432)■36:33-JOS-12:2(8432)-J'G-7:19(8484)■9:37(2872)■16:29(8432)-1SA-25:29(8432)-2SA-10:4(2677)-1KI-6:6,8^{3}■8:64(8432)-2KI-20:4-2CH-7:7-JER-39:3-EZE-1:16(8432)■N.T.-EPH-2:14(3320)
MIDDLEMOST-EZE-42:5(8484),6(8484)
MIDNIGHT-all=2676,3915&marked-EX-11:4■12:29(2677,3915)-J'G-16:3(2677,3915)-RU-3:8(2677,3915)-1KI-3:20(8432,3915)-JOB-34:20-PS-119:62■N.T.-all=3317&marked-M'T-25:6(3319,3571)-M'R-13:35-LU-11:5-AC-16:25■20:7■27:27(3319,3571)
MIDST-all=8432,a=7130&marked-GE-1:6■2:9■3:3■15:10■19:29■48:16a-EX-3:2,4,20a■8:22a■11:4■14:16,22,23,27,29■15:19■23:25a■24:16,18■26:28■27:5(2677)■28:32■33:3a,5a■34:12a■38:4(2677)■39:23-LE-16:16-NU-2:17■5:3■16:47■19:6■33:8■35:5-DE-4:11(3820),12,15■33,34a,36■5:4,22,23,24,26■9:10■10:4■11:3,6a■13:5a,16■17:20a■18:15a■19:2■23:14a■32:51-JOS-3:17■4:3,5,8,9,10,18■7:13a,21,23■8:13,22■10:13(2677)■13:9,16-J'G-15:4■18:20a■20:42-1SA-11:11■16:13a■18:10■-2SA-1:25■4:6■6:17■18:14(3820)■20:12■23:12,20■24:5-1KI-3:8■6:27■8:51■20:39a■22:35(2436)-2KI-6:20-1CH-11:14■16:1■19:4(2677)-2CH-6:13■20:14■32:4-NE-4:11■9:11-ES-4:1-JOB-21:21(2686)-PS-22:14,22■46:2(3820),5a■48:9a■55:10a,11a■57:6■74:4a,12a■78:28a■102:24(2677)■110:2a■116:19■135:9■136:14■137:2■138:7a-PR-4:21■5:14■8:20■14:33a■23:34(3820)■30:19(3820)-SONG-3:10-IS-4:4a■5:2,8a,25a■6:5,12a■7:6■10:23a■12:6a■16:3■19:1a,3a,14a,19,24a■24:13a,18■25:11a■29:23a■30:28(2673)■41:18■52:11■58:9■66:17-JER-6:1a,6a■9:6■12:16■14:9a■17:11(2677)■21:4■29:8a■30:21a■37:12■41:7^{2}■46:21a■50:8,37■51:1(3820),6,45,47,63■52:25-LA-1:15a■3:45a■4:13a-EZE-1:4^{2},5■5:2,4,5,8,10,12■6:7■7:4,9■8:11■9:4^{3}■10:10■11:7^{2},9,11,23■12:2■13:14■14:8,9■15:4■16:53■17:16■20:8■21:32■22:3,7,9,13,18,19,20,21,22^{2},25^{2},27a■23:39■24:7■26:5,12,15■27:4(3820),25(3820),26(3820),27,27(3820),32,34■28:2(3820),8(3820),14,16^{2},18,22,23■29:3,4,12,21■30:7^{2}■31:14,17,18■32:20,21,25^{2},28,32■36:23■37:1,26,28■38:12(2872)■39:7■41:7(8484)■43:7,9■46:10■48:8,10,15,21,22-DA-3:6(1459),11(1459),15(1459),21(1459),23(1459),24(1459),25(1459),26(1459)■4:10(1459)■7:15(1459)■9:27(2677)-HO-5:4a■11:9a-JOE-2:27a-AM-2:3a■3:9a,9■6:4■7:8a,10a-JON-2:3(3824)-MIC-2:12■5:7a,8a,10a,13a,14a■6:14a■7:14-NA-3:13a-HAB-2:19a■3:2^{2}a-ZEP-2:14■3:5a,11a,12a,15a,17a-ZEC-2:5,10,11■5:4,7,8■8:3,8■14:1a,4(2677)■N.T.-all=3319&marked-M'T-10:16■14:24■18:2,20-M'R-6:47■7:31■9:36■14:60-LU-2:46■4:30,35■5:19■6:8■17:11■21:21■22:55■23:45■24:36-JOH-7:14(3322)■8:3,9,59■19:18■20:19,26-AC-1:15,18■2:22■4:7■17:22■27:21-PH'P-2:15-HEB-2:12-RE-1:13■2:1,7■4:6■5:6^{2}■6:6■7:17■8:13(3321)■14:6(3321)■19:17(3321)■22:2
MIDWIFE-all=3205-GE-35:17■38:28-EX-1:16
MIDWIVES-all=3205-EX-1:15,17,18,19^{2},20,21
MIGHT-all=1369&marked-GE-43:32(3201)■49:3(3581)-NU-14:13(3581)-DE-3:24■6:5(3966)■8:17(6108)■28:32(410)-J'G-5:31■6:14(3581)■16:30(3581)-2SA-6:14(5797)■17:17(3201)-1KI-15:23■16:5,27■22:45-2KI-10:34■13:8,12■14:15,28■20:20■23:25(3966)■24:16(2428)-1CH-7:2(2428),5(2428)■12:8(2428)■13:8(5797)■29:2(3581),12,30-2CH-20:6,12(3581)-ES-10:2-PS-76:5(2428)■145:6(5807)-EC-9:10(3581)-IS-11:2■33:13■40:26(202),29(202)-JER-9:23■10:6■16:21■49:35■51:30-EZE-32:29,30-DA-2:20(1370),23(1370)■4:30(8632)-MIC-3:8■7:16-ZEC-4:6(2428)■N.T.-all=1410&marked-M'T-8:28(2480)■26:9-M'R-14:5-AC-26:32■27:12-EPH-1:21(1411)■3:16(1411)■6:10(2479)-COL-1:11(1411)-1TH-2:6-2PE-2:11(1411)-RE-7:12(2479)■13:17
MIGHTEST-allsupplied
MIGHTIER-all=6099&marked-GE-26:16(6105)-EX-1:9-NU-14:12-DE-4:38■7:1■9:1,14■11:23-PS-93:4(117)-EC-6:10(8623)■N.T.-all=2478-M'T-3:11-M'R-1:7-LU-3:16
MIGHTIES-1CH-11:12(1368),24(1368)
MIGHTIEST-1CH-11:19(1368)
MIGHTILY-DE-6:3(3966)-J'G-4:3(2393)-JON-3:8(2393)-NA-2:1(3966)■N.T.-AC-18:28(2159)■19:20(2596,2904)-COL-1:29(1722,1411)-RE-18:2(1722,2479)
MIGHTY-all=1368,a=2389&marked-GE-6:4■10:8,9^{2}■18:18(6090)■23:6(430)■49:24(46)-EX-1:7(6105),20■3:19a■9:28(430)■10:19(3966)■15:10(117),15(352)■32:11a-LE-19:15(1419)-NU-22:6(6099)-DE-3:24a■4:34a,37(1419)■5:15a■6:21a■7:8a,19a,21(1419),23(1419)■9:26a,29(1419)■10:17■11:2a■26:5(6099),8a■34:12a-JOS-1:14■4:24a■6:2■8:3■10:2,7-J'G-5:13,22(47),23■6:12■11:1-RU-2:1-1SA-2:4■4:8(117)■9:1■16:18-2SA-1:19,21,22,25,27■10:7■16:6■17:8,10■20:7■23:8,9,16,17,22-1KI-1:8,10■11:28-2KI-5:1■15:20■24:14,15(193)-1CH-1:10■5:24■7:7,9,11,40■8:40■11:10,11■12:1,4,21,25,28,30■19:8■26:6,31■27:6■28:1■29:24-2CH-6:32a■13:3,21(2388)■14:8■17:13,14,16,17■25:6■26:12,13(2428)■27:6(2388)■28:7■32:3,21-EZR-4:20(8624)■7:28-NE-3:16■9:11(5794),32■11:14-JOB-5:15a■6:23(6184)■9:4(533)■12:19(386),21(650)■21:7(1396)■22:8(2220)■24:22(47)■34:20(47),24(3524)■35:9(7227)■36:5^{2}(3524)■41:25(410)-PS-24:8■29:1(1121,410)■33:16■45:3■50:1(410)■52:1■59:3(5794)■68:33(5797)■69:4(6105)■74:15(386)■78:65■82:1(410)■89:6,13(1369),19,50(7227)■93:4(117)■106:2(1369),8(1369)■112:2■120:4■127:4■132:2(46),5(46)■135:10(6099)■145:4(1369),12(1369)■150:2(1369)-PR-16:32■18:18(6099)■21:22■23:11a-EC-7:19(7989)-SONG-4:4-IS-1:24(46)■3:2,25(1369)■5:15(376),22■9:6■10:21,34(117)■11:15(5868)■13:3■17:12(3524)■21:17■22:17(1397)■28:2a,2(3524)■30:29(6697)■31:8(376)■42:13■43:16(5794)■49:24,25,26(46)■60:16(46)■63:1(7227)-JER-5:15(386),16■9:23■14:9■20:11■26:21■32:18,19(7227)■33:3(1219)■41:16(1397)■46:5,6,9,12■48:14,41■49:22■50:9,36■51:30,56,57-LA-1:15(47)-EZE-17:13(352),17(1419)■20:33a,34a■31:11(410)■32:12,21,27^{2}■38:15(7227)■39:18,20-DA-3:20(1401)■4:3(8624)■8:24(6105),24(6099)■9:15a■11:3■25(6099)-HO-10:13-JOE-2:7■3:9,11-AM-2:14,16■5:12(6099),24(386)-OB-9-JON-1:4(1419)-NA-2:3-HAB-1:12(6697)-ZEP-1:14■3:17-ZEC-9:13■10:5,7■11:2(117)■N.T.-all=1411&marked-M'T-11:20,21,23■13:54,58■14:2-M'R-6:2,5,14-LU-1:49(1415),52(1413)■9:43(3168)■10:13■15:14(2478)■19:37■24:19(1415)-AC-2:2(972)■7:22(1415)■18:24(1415)-RO-15:19-1CO-1:26(1415),27(2478)-2CO-10:4(1415)■12:12■13:3(1414)-GA-2:8(1754)EPH-1:19(2479)-2TH-1:7-1PE-5:6(2900)-RE-6:13(3173),15(1415)■10:1(2478)■16:18(5082)■18:10(2478),21(2478)■19:6(2478),18(2478)
MILCH-GE-32:15(3243)-1SA-6:7(5763),10(5763)
MILDEW-all=3420-DE-28:22-1KI-8:37-2CH-6:28-AM-4:9-HAG-2:17
MILE-M'T-5:41(3400)
MILK-all=2461&marked-GE-18:8■49:12-EX-3:8,17■13:5■23:19■33:3■34:26-LE-20:24-NU-13:27■14:8■16:13,14-DE-6:3■11:9■14:21■26:9,15■27:3■31:20■32:14-JOS-5:6-J'G-4:19■5:25-JOB-10:10■21:24-PR-27:27■30:33-SONG-4:11■5:1,12-IS-7:22■28:9■55:1■60:16■66:11(4711)-JER-11:5■32:22-LA-4:7-EZE-20:6,15■25:4-JOE-3:18■N.T.-all=1051-1CO-3:2■9:7-HEB-5:12,13-1PE-2:2
MILL-EX-11:5(7347)■N.T.-M'T-24:41(3459)
MILLET-EZE-4:9(1764)
MILLIONS-GE-24:60(7233)
MILLS-NU-11:8(7347)
MILLSTONE-DE-24:6(7347)-J'G-9:53(7393)-2SA-11:21(7393)■N.T.-M'T-18:6(3458,3684)-M'R-9:42(3037,3457)-LU-17:2(3458,3684)-RE-18:21(3458),22(3458)
MILLSTONES-IS-47:2(7347)-JER-25:10(7347)
MINCING-IS-3:16(2952)
MIND-all=3820,a=5315&marked-GE-23:8a■26:35(7307)-LE-24:12(6310)-NU-16:28■24:13-DE-18:6a■28:65a■30:1(3824)-1SA-2:35a■9:20-1CH-22:7(3824)■28:9a-NE-4:6-JOB-34:33(5973)-PS-31:12-PR-29:11(7307)-IS-26:3(3336)■46:8■65:17-JER-3:16■15:1a■19:5■32:35■44:21■51:50(3824)-LA-3:21-EZE-11:5(7307)■20:32(7307)■23:17a,18^{2}a,22a,28a■38:10(3824)-DA-5:20(7307)-HAB-1:11(7307)■N.T.-all=3563&marked-M'T-22:37(1271)-M'R-5:15(4993)■12:30(1271)■14:72(363)-LU-8:35(4993)■10:27(1271)-AC-17:11(4288)-RO-1:28■7:23,25■8:5(5426),7(5427),27(5427)■11:34■12:2,16^{2}(5426)■14:5■15:6(3661),15(1878)-1CO-1:10■2:16^{2}-2CO-8:12(4288),19(4288)■9:2(4288)■13:11(5426)-EPH-2:3(1271)■4:17,23-PH'P-1:27(5590)■2:2(5426),3(5012),5(5426)■3:16(5426),19(5426)■4:2(5426)-COL-1:21(1271)■2:18-2TH-2:2-2TI-1:7(4995)-TIT-1:15■3:1(5279)-PH'M-14(1106)-HEB-8:10(1271)-1PE-1:13■3:8(3675)■4:1(1771)■5:2(4290)-RE-17:9,13(1106)
MINDED-2CH-24:4(5973,3820)■N.T.-all=1014&marked-M'T-1:19-AC-27:39-RO-8:6^{2}(5427)-2CO-1:15,17(1011)-GAL-5:10(5426)-PH'P-3:15^{2}-(5426)-TIT-2:6(4993)-JAS-1:8(1374)■4:8(1374)
MINDFUL-all=2142&marked-1CH-16:15-NE-9:17-PS-8:4■111:5■115:12-IS-17:10■N.T.-all=3403&marked-2TI-1:4-HEB-2:6■11:15(3421)-2PE-3:2
MINDING-AC-20:13(3195)
MINDS-all=3515-2SA-17:8-2KI-9:15-EZE-24:25■36:5■N.T.-all=3540&marked-AC-14:2(5590)-2CO-3:14■4:4■11:3-PH'P-4:7-1TI-6:5(3563)-2TI-3:8(3563)-HEB-10:16(1271)■12:3(5590)-2PE-3:1(1271)
MINE-2SA-14:30(3027)-PS-50:11(5978)-PR-23:15(589)■N.T.-all=3450,1699&marked-M'T-7:24,26■20:15a,23a■25:27-M'R-9:24-LU-1:44■2:30■9:38(3427)■11:6■18:3■19:23(846),27-JOH-2:4■5:30(1683),30a■6:38a■7:16a■8:50■9:11,15,30■10:14a■14:24a■16:14a,15^{2}a■17:10a-AC-13:22■21:13■26:4-RO-11:13■12:19(1698)■16:13(1700),23-1CO-1:15a■4:3(1683)■9:2a,3a■10:33(1683)■16:21a-2CO-11:30■12:5-GA-

1:14■6:11a-PH'P-1:4■3:9a-2TH-3:17a-PH'M-12a,18a-RE-22:16

MINGLE-IS-5:22(4537)-DA-2:43(6151)

MINGLED-all=1101&marked-EX-9:24(3947)■29:40-LE-2:4,5■7:10,12^2■9:4■14:10,21■19:19^2(3610)■23:13-NU-6:15■7:13,19,25,31,37,43,49,55,61,67,73,79■8:8■15:4,6,9■28:5,9,12^2,13,20,28■29:3,9,14-EZR-9:2(6148)-PS-102:9(4537)■106:35(6148)-PR-9:2(4537),5(4537)-IS-19:14(4537)-JER-25:20(6154),24(6154)■50:37-EZR-30:5(6154)■N.T.-all=3396-M'T-27:34-LU-13:1-RE-8:7■15:2

MINISH-EX-5:19(1639)

MINISHED-PS-107:39(4591)

MINISTER-all=8334&marked-EX-24:13■28:35,43■29:30■30:20■35:19■39:26,41-NU-1:50■3:6,31■4:9,12,14■8:26■16:9■18:2-DE-10:8■17:12■18:5,7■21:5-JOS-1:1-1SA-2:11-1KI-8:11-1CH-15:2■16:4,37■23:13■26:12-2CH-5:14■8:14■13:10■23:6■24:14(8335)■29:11■31:2-NE-10:36,39-PS-9:8(1777)-IS-60:7,10-JER-33:22-EZE-40:46■42:14■43:19■44:11,15,16,17,27■45:4■N.T.-all=1249&marked-M'T-20:26,28(1247)■25:44(1247)-M'R-10:43,45(1247)-LU-4:20(5257)-AC-13:5(5257)■24:23(5256)■26:16(5257)-RO-13:4^2■15:8,16(3011),25(1247),27(3008)-1CO-9:13(2038)-2CO-9:10(5524)-GA-2:17-EPH-3:7■4:29(1325)■6:21-COL-1:7,23,25■4:7-1TH-3:2-1TI-1:4(3930)■4:6-HEB-1:14(1248)■6:10(1247)■8:2(3011)-1PE-1:12(1247)■4:10(1247),11(1247)

MINISTERED-all=8334&marked-1SA-2:18■3:1-2SA-13:17-1KI-1:4,15■19:21-2KI-25:14-1CH-6:32■28:1-2CH-22:8-ES-2:2■6:3-JER-52:18-EZE-44:12,19-DA-7:10(8120)■N.T.-all=1247&marked-M'T-4:11■8:15■20:28-M'R-1:13,31■10:45■15:41-LU-4:39■8:3-AC-13:2(3008)■19:22■20:34(5256)-2CO-3:3-PH'P-2:25(3011)-COL-2:19(2023)-2TI-1:18-PH'M-13-HEB-6:10-2PE-1:11(2023)

MINISTERETH-2CO-9:10(2023)-GA-3:5(2023)

MINISTERING-1CH-9:28(5656)-EZE-44:11(8334)■N.T.-all=1248&marked-M'T-27:55(1247)-RO-12:7■15:16(2418)-2CO-8:4■9:1-HEB-1:14(3010)■10:11(3008)

MINISTERS-all=8334&marked-1KI-10:5-2CH-9:4-EZR-7:24(6399)■8:17-PS-103:21■104:4-IS-61:6-JER-33:21-EZE-44:11■45:4,5■46:24-JOE-1:9,13^2■2:17■N.T.-all=1249&marked-LU-1:2(5257)-RO-13:6(3011)-1CO-3:5■4:1(5257)-2CO-3:6■6:4■11:15^2,23-HEB-1:7(3011)

MINISTRATION.-all=1248&marked-LU-1:23(3009)-AC-6:1-2CO-3:7,8,9^2■9:13

MINISTRY-NU-4:12(8335),47(5656)-2CH-7:6(3027)-HO-12:10(3027)■N.T.-all=1248&marked-AC-1:17,25■6:4■12:25■20:24■21:19-RO-12:7-1CO-16:15-2CO-4:1■5:18■6:3-EPH-4:12-COL-4:17-1TI-1:12-2TI-4:5,11-HEB-8:6(3009)■9:21(3009)

MINSTREL-2KI-3:15^2(5059)

MINSTRELS-M'T-9:23(834)

MINT-M'T-23:23(2238)-LU-11:42(2238)

MIRACLE-EX-7:9(4159)■N.T.-all=4392&marked-M'R-9:39(1411)-LU-23:8-JOH-4:54■6:14■10:41■12:18-AC-4:16,22

MIRACLES-NU-14:22(226)-DE-11:3(226)■29:3(4159)-J'G-6:13(6381)■N.T.-all=4592&marked-JOH-2:11,23■3:2■6:2,26■7:31■9:16■11:47■12:37-AC-2:22(1411)■6:8■8:6,13(1411)■15:12■19:11(1411)-1CO-12:10,28,29-GA-3:5-HEB-2:4-RE-13:14■16:14■19:20

MIRE-all=2916&marked-2SA-22:43-JOB-8:11(1207)■30:19(2563)■41:30-PS-69:2(3121),14-IS-10:6(2563)■57:20(7516)-JER-38:6^2,22(1206)-MIC-7:10-ZEC-9:3■10:5■N.T.-2PE-2:22(1004)

MIRTH-all=8057&marked-GE-31:27-NE-8:12-PS-137:3-PR-14:13-EC-2:1,2■7:4■8:15-IS-24:8(4885),11(4885)-JER-7:34(8342)■16:9■25:10-EZE-21:10(7797)-HO-2:11(4885)

MIRY-PS-40:2(3121)-EZE-47:11(1207)-DA-2:41(2917),43(2917)

MISCARRYING-HO-9:14(7921)

MISCHIEF-all=7451&marked-GE-42:4(611),38(611)■44:29(611)-EX-21:22(611),23(611)■32:12,22-1SA-23:9-2SA-16:8-1KI-11:25■20:7-2KI-7:9(5771)-NE-6:2-ES-8:3-JOB-15:35(5999)-PS-7:14(5999),16(5999)■10:7(5999),14(5999)■26:10(2154)■28:3■36:4(205)■52:1■55:10(205)■62:3(205)■94:20(5999)■119:150(2154)■140:9(5999)-PR-4:16(7489)■6:14,18■10:23(2154)■11:27■12:21■13:17■17:20■24:2(5999),16■28:14-IS-47:11(1943)■59:4(5999)-EZE-7:26(1943)■11:2(205)-DA-11:27(4827)-HO-7:15■N.T.-AC-13:10(4468)

MISCHIEFS-DE-32:23(7451)-PS-52:2(1942)■140:2(7451)

MISCHIEVOUS-PS-21:11(4209)■38:12(1942)-PR-24:8(4209)-EC-10:13(7451)-MIC-7:3(1942)

MISERABLE-JOB-16:2(5999)■N.T.-1CO-15:19(1652)-RE-3:17(1652)

MISERABLY-M'T-21:41(2560)

MISERIES-LA-1:7(4788)■N.T.-JAS-5:1(5004)

MISERY-all=5999&marked-J'G-10:16-JOB-3:20(6001)■11:16-PR-31:7-EC-8:6(7451)-LA-3:19(4788)■N.T.-RO-3:16(5004)

MISS-J'G-20:16(2398)-1SA-20:6(6485)

MISSED-all=6485&marked-1SA-20:18■25:15,21

MISSING-1SA-25:7(6485)-1KI-20:39(6485)

MIST-GE-2:6(108)■N.T.-AC-13:11(887)-2PE-2:17(2217)

MISTRESS-all=1404&marked-GE-16:4,8,9-1KI-17:17(1172)-2KI-5:3-PS-123:2-PR-30:23-IS-24:2-NA-3:4(1172)

MISUSED-2CH-36:16(8591)

MITE-LU-12:59(3016)

MITES-M'R-12:42(3016)-LU-21:2(3016)

MITRE-all=4701&marked-EX-28:4,37^2,39■29:6^2■39:28,31-LE-8:9^2■16:4-ZEC-3:5^2(6797)

MIXED-EX-12:38(6154)-NE-13:3(6154)-PR-23:30(4469)-IS-1:22(4107)-DA-2:41(6151),43^2(6151)-HO-7:8(1101)-HEB-4:2(4786)

MIXT-supplied

MIXTURE-PS-75:8(4538)■N.T.-JOH-19:39(3395)-RE-14:10(194)

MOCK-GE-39:14(6711),17(6711)-JOB-13:9(2048)■21:3(3932)-PR-1:26(3932)■14:9(3887)-JER-38:19(5953)-LA-1:7(7832)-EZE-22:5(7046)■N.T.-all=1702-M'T-20:19-M'R-10:34-LU-14:29

MOCKED-all=2048&marked-GE-19:14(6711)-NU-22:29(5953)-J'G-16:10,13,15-1KI-18:27-2KI-2:23(7046)-2CH-30:10(3932)■36:16(3931)-NE-4:1(3932)-JOB-12:4(7832)■N.T.-all=1702&marked-M'T-2:16■27:29,31-M'R-15:20-LU-18:32■22:63■23:11,36-AC-17:32(5512)-GA-6:7(3456)

MOCKER-PR-20:1(3887)

MOCKERS-JOB-17:2(2049)-PS-35:16(3934)-IS-28:22(3887)-JER-15:17(7832)-JUDE-18(1703)

MOCKEST-JOB-11:3(3932)

MOCKETH-all=3932&marked-JOB-13:9(2048)■39:22(7832)-PR-17:5■30:17-JER-20:7

MOCKING-GE-21:9(6711)-EZE-22:4(7048)■N.T.-M'T-27:41(1702)-M'R-15:31(1702)-AC-2:13(5512)

MOCKINGS-HEB-11:36(1701)

MODERATELY-JOE-2:23(6666)

MODERATION-PH'P-4:5(1933)

MODEST-1TI-2:9(2887)

MOIST-NU-6:3(3892)

MOISTENED-JOB-21:24(8248)

MOISTURE-PS-32:4(3955)■N.T.-LU-8:6(2429)

MOLE-LE-11:30(8580)

MOLES-IS-2:20(2661)

MOLLIFIED-IS-1:6(7401)

MOLTEN-all=4541&marked-EX-32:4,8■34:17-LE-19:4-NU-33:52-DE-9:12,16■27:15-J'G-17:3,4■18:14,17,18-1KI-7:16(3332),23(3332),30(3332),33(3332)■14:9-2KI-17:16-2CH-4:2(3332)■28:2■34:3,4-NE-9:18-JOB-28:2(6694)■37:18(3332)-PS-106:19-IS-30:22■41:29(5262)■42:17■44:10(5258)■48:5(5262)-JER-10:14(5262)■51:17(5262)-EZE-24:11(5413)-HO-13:2-MIC-1:4(4549)-NA-1:14-HAB-2:18

MOMENT-all=7281-EX-33:5-NU-16:21,45-JOB-7:18■20:5■21:13■34:20-PS-30:5■73:19-PR-12:19-IS-26:20■27:3■47:9■54:7,8-JER-4:20-LA-4:6-EZE-26:16■32:10■N.T.-LU-4:5(4743)-1CO-15:52(823)-2CO-4:17(3901)

MONEY-all=3701&marked-GE-17:12,13,23,27■23:9,13■31:15■33:19(7192)■42:25,27,28,35^2■43:12^2,15,18,21^2,22^2,23■44:1,2,8■47:14^2,15^2,16,18-EX-12:44■21:11,21,34,35■22:7,17,25■30:16-LE-22:11■25:37,51■27:15,18,19-NU-3:48,49,50,51■18:16-DE-2:6^2,28^2■14:25^2,26■21:14■23:19-J'G-5:19■16:18■17:4-1KI-21:2,6,15-2KI-5:26■12:4^4,7,8,9,10^2,11,13,15,16 ■15:20■22:7,9■23:35-2CH-24:5,11^2,14■34:9,14,17-EZR-3:7■7:17(3702)-NE-5:4,10,11-ES-4:7-JOB-31:39■42:11(7192)-PS-15:5-PR-7:20-EC-7:12■10:19-IS-43:24■52:3■55:1^2,2-JER-32:9,10,25,44-LA-5:4-MIC-3:11■N.T.-all=694&marked-M'T-17:27(4715)■22:19(3546)■25:18,27■28:12,15-M'R-6:8(5475)■12:41(5745)■14:11-LU-9:3■19:15,23■22:5-JOH-2:14(2773),15(2772)-AC-4:37(5536)■7:16■8:18(5536),20,20(5536)■24:26(5536)-1TI-6:10(5365)

MONEYCHANGERS-M'T-21:12(2855)-M'R-11:15(2855)

MONSTERS-LA-4:3(8577)

MONTH-all=2320&marked-GE-7:11■8:4^2,5,5sup,5,13sup,13,14^2■29:14-EX-12:2^2,3,6,18sup,18^2■13:4,5■16:1■19:1■23:15■34:18^2■40:2,17^2-LE-16:29■23:5,6,24,27,32,34,39,41■25:9■27:6-NU-1:1,18■3:15,22,28,34,39,40,43■9:1,3,5,11,22■10:11■11:20,21■18:16■20:1■26:62■28:14,16,17■29:1^2,6,7,12■33:3^2,38-DE-1:3■16:1^2■21:13(3391)-JOS-4:19■5:10-1SA-20:27,34-1KI-4:7,27■5:14^2■6:1,37(3391),38(3391),38■8:2(3391),2■12:32^2,33^2-2KI-15:13(3391)■25:1,3,8,25,27^2-1CH-12:15■27:1,2,3,4,5,7,8,9,10,11,12,13,14,15-2CH-3:2■5:3■7:10■15:10■29:3,17^3■30:2,13,15■31:7^2■35:1-EZR-3:1,6,8■6:15(3393),19■7:8,9^2■8:31■10:9^2,16,17-NE-1:1■2:1■7:73■8:2,14■9:1-ES-2:16■3:7^3,12,13■8:9,12■9:1,15,17,19,21,22-JER-1:3■2:24■28:1,17■36:9,22■39:1,2■41:1■52:4,6,12,31^2-EZE-1:1sup,1,2■8:1sup,1■20:1sup,1■24:1^2■26:1■29:1sup,1,17sup,17■30:20^2■31:1sup,1■32:1^2,17■33:21sup,21■40:1■45:18sup,18,20,21sup,21,25sup,25-DA-10:4-HO-5:7-HAG-1:1,15■2:1sup,1,20-ZEC-1:1,7^2■7:1,3■11:8(3391)■N.T.-all=3376-LU-1:26,36-RE-9:15■22:2

MONTHLY-IS-47:13(2320)

MONTHS-all=2320&marked-GE-38:24-EX-2:2(3391)■12:2-NU-10:10■28:11,14-J'G-11:37,38,39■19:2■20:47-1SA-6:1■27:7-2SA-2:11■5:5■6:11■24:8,13-1KI-5:14■11:16-2KI-15:8■23:31■24:8-1CH-3:4■13:14■21:12■27:1-2CH-

36:2,9-ES-2:12^{3}-JOB-3:6(3391)■7:3(3391)■7:3(3391)■14:5■21:21■29:2(3391)■39:3(3391)-EZE-39:12,14■47:12-DA-4:29(3393)-AM-4:7■N.T.-all=3376&marked-LU-1:24,56■4:25-JOH-4:35(5072)-AC-7:20■18:11■19:8■20:3■28:11-GA-4:10-HEB-11:23(5150)-JAS-5:17-RE-9:5,10■11:2■13:5

MONUMENTS-IS-65:4(5341)

MOON-all=3394&marked-GE-37:9-DE-4:19■17:3■33:14(3391)-JOS-10:12,13-1SA-20:5(2320),18(2320),24(2320)-2KI-4:23(2320)■23:5-JOB-25:5■31:26-PS-8:3■72:5,7■81:3(2320)■89:37■104:19■121:6■136:9■148:3-EC-12:2-SONG-6:10(3842)-IS-13:10■24:23(3842)■30:26(3842)■60:19,20(3391)■66:23(2320)-JER-8:2■31:35-EZE-32:7■46:1,6(2320)-JOE-2:10,31■3:15-AM-8:5(2320)-HAB-3:11■N.T.-all=4582&marked-M'T-24:29-M'R-13:24-LU-21:25-AC-2:20-1CO-15:41-COL-2:16(3561)-RE-6:12■8:12■12:1■21:23

MOONS-all=2320&marked-1CH-23:31-2CH-2:4■8:13■31:3-EZR-3:5-NE-10:33-IS-1:13,14-EZE-45:17■46:3-HO-2:11

MORE-all=5750,a=3254,b=7227&marked-GE-8:12,21^{2}■9:11^{2},15■17:5■32:28■34:19(3513)■35:10■36:7b■37:5a,8a,9■38:26sup,26■44:23a-EX-1:9b,12^{2}(3651)■5:7a■8:29a■9:29,34a■10:28a,29■11:6a■14:13■16:17b■30:15(7235)■36:5(7235),6-LE-6:5a■11:42(7235)■13:5(8145),33(8145),54(8145)■17:7■26:18a,21a■27:20-NU-3:46(5736)■8:25■18:5■22:15b,15sup,18(1490),19a■26:54(7235)■33:54b,54(7235)-DE-1:11a■3:26■5:22a,25a■7:7(7230),17b■10:16■13:11a■17:13,16■18:16■19:9,20■20:1b■28:68■31:2-JOS-2:11■5:1,12■7:12a■10:11b■23:13a-J'G-8:28a■10:13a■13:21a■16:30b■18:24-RU-1:17a-1SA-1:18■2:3(7235)■3:17a■7:13a(5750)■14:30(637),44a■15:35a■18:8,29a■20:13a■22:15(1490)■25:22a,36(1490)■26:21■27:1,4a-2SA-2:28,28a(5750)■3:9a,35a■5:13■7:10,10a,20■10:19■14:10a(5750),11(7235)■18:8(7235)■19:13a,28,29,35■21:17-1KI-2:23a■10:5,10■16:33a■19:2a■20:10a-2KI-2:12,21■4:6■6:16b,23a(5750),31a■9:35(3588,518)■21:8a■24:7-1CH-14:3^{2}■17:9,9a,18a,(5750)■19:19■21:3a■24:4b-2CH-9:4■10:11a■25:9(7235)■28:22a■32:7b■33:23(7235)-EZR-7:20(7608)-NE-2:17■13:18a-ES-2:14■6:6(3148)-JOB-7:7(7725),10^{2}■20:9a,9■24:20■32:15,16■34:19(6440),23■35:2a■41:8a-PS-10:18a(5750)■40:5(6105),12(6105)■41:8a■69:4(7231)■71:14a■73:7(5674)■74:9■77:7a(5750)■78:17■83:4■88:5■103:16■104:35■139:18(7235)-PR-4:18(1980)■31:7-EC-2:15(3148),16(5973),25(2351)■4:2(4480),13■5:1(7138)■6:8(3148)■9:5,6-IS-1:5,5sup,13■2:4■5:4■10:20■15:9a■23:10,12a(5750)■26:21■30:19(1058),20■32:5■47:1a,5a■51:22a■52:1a(5750)■54:1b,4,9■56:12(3499)■60:18,19,20■62:4^{2},8■65:19,20-JER-2:31■3:16^{2},17■7:32■10:20■11:19■16:14■19:6■20:9■22:10,11,12,30■23:4,7,36■30:8■31:12a,29,34^{2},40■33:24■34:10■38:9■42:18■44:26■46:23(7231)■48:2■49:7■50:39■51:44-LA-4:15a,16a,22a-EZE-5:6^{2}(4480),7(4480),9■12:23,24,25,28■13:21,23■14:11^{2},21■16:41,42,63■18:3■19:9■20:39■21:5■23:27■24:13,27■26:13,14■28:24■29:15,15sup,16■30:13■32:13■33:22■34:10,22,28,29^{2}■36:12,14^{2},15^{3},30■37:22^{2},23■39:7,28,29■43:7■45:8-DA-2:30(4481)■3:19(5922)■7:20-HO-1:6■2:16,17■9:15a■14:3,8-JOE-2:2a,19■3:17-AM-5:2■7:8,13■8:2■9:15-JON-4:11b-MIC-4:3■5:13-NA-1:12,14,15a(5750)■2:13-ZEP-3:11a(5750),15-ZEC-9:8■11:6■13:2■14:11,21-MAL-2:13■N.T.-all=3123,a=2089,b=4119,c=3765,d=4056&marked-M'T-5:37(4053),47(4053)■6:25b,30■7:11■10:15(414),25,31(1308),37^{2}(5228)■11:9(4055),22(414),24(414)■18:13,16a■19:6c■20:10b,31(3185)■21:36b■22:46c■25:20(243)■26:53b■27:23(4057)-M'R-1:45(3370)■4:24(4369)■6:11(414)■7:12c,36(3745),36■8:14(1508)■9:8c,25(3370)■10:8c,48■12:33b,43b■14:5(1833),25c,31■15:14(4056)-LU-3:13b■5:15■7:26(4055)■9:13b■10:12(414),14(414),35(4325)■11:13■12:4(4055),7(1308),23b,24,28,48(4055)■15:19c,21c■18:30(4179),39■20:36a■21:3b■22:16c,44(1617)■23:5(2001)-JOH-4:1b,41b■5:14(3370),18■6:66c■7:31b■8:11(2001)■11:54a■12:43■14:19a■15:2b,4(3761)■16:10a,21a,25a■17:11a■19:8■21:15b-AC-4:19■5:14■8:39c■9:22■13:34(2001)■18:26(197)■19:32b■20:25c,35(3122),38c■22:2■23:13b,15(197),20(197),21b■24:10(2115),22(197)■25:6b■27:11,12b-RO-1:25(3844)■5:9,10,15,17■6:9a,9c■7:17a,20a■8:37(5245)■11:6a^{4},12,24■12:3(3844)■14:13(2001)■15:15(5112),23(2001)-1CO-6:3(1065)■9:19b■12:22,23^{2}(4055),24(4055),31(2596,5236)■14:18■15:10(4055)-2CO-1:12d■2:4d■3:9,11■4:17(1519,5236)■5:16a■7:7,13,15d■8:17(4707),22(4707)■10:8(4055)■11:23(5228),23^{2}d■12:15d-GA-1:14d■3:18a■4:7a,27-EPH-2:19c■4:14(2001),28(2001)-PH'P-1:9,14d,24(316)■2:12■3:4-1TH-2:17d■4:1,10-2TI-2:16b■3:4-PH'M-16,21(5228)-HEB-2:1d■3:3^{2}b■6:17(4054)■7:15(4055)■8:12a■9:14■10:2a,17,18a,25,26a■11:32a■12:19(4369),25-JAS-4:6(3187)-RE-2:19b■3:12a■7:16a■9:12a■12:8a■18:11c,14c,21a,22a■18:22^{3}a,23^{2}a■20:3a■21:1a,4^{2}a■22:3a

MOREOVER-all=1571&marked-GE-32:20-EX-3:15(5750)■11:3-LE-25:45-NU-13:28■16:14(637)-DE-1:28■7:20-RU-4:10-1SA-12:23■20:3(5750)■28:19-2SA-12:8(3254)■17:13(518)-1KI-1:47■2:5■8:41-2KI-21:16■23:15,24-1CH-11:2■12:40■29:3(5750)-2CH-6:32■17:6(5750)■19:8■21:11■36:14-NE-5:14■6:17-ES-5:12(637)-PS-19:11-EC-3:16(5750)■6:5■12:9(3148)-EZE-20:12■23:38(5750)■N.T.-all=1161&marked-M'T-6:16■18:15-LU-16:21(235,2532)-AC-2:26(2089)■11:12■19:26(2532)-RO-5:20■8:30-1CO-4:2(3739,1161,3063)■10:1■15:1-2CO-1:23■8:1-1TI-3:7-HEB-9:21■11:36-2PE-1:15(1161,2532)

MORNING-all=1242&marked-GE-1:5,8,13,19,23,31■19:15(7837),27■20:8■21:14■22:3■24:54■26:31■28:18■29:25■31:55■40:6■41:8■44:3■49:27-EX-7:15■8:20■9:13■10:13■12:10^{2},22■14:24,27■16:7,8,12,13,19,20,21,23,24■18:13,14■19:16■23:18■24:4■27:21■29:34,39,41■30:7■34:2^{2},4,25■36:3-LE-6:9,12,20■7:15■9:17■19:13■24:3-NU-9:12,15,21^{2}■14:40■22:13,21■28:4,8,23-DE-16:4,7■28:67^{2}-JOS-3:1■6:12■7:14,16■8:10-J'G-6:28,31■9:33■16:2■19:5,8,25,27■20:19-RU-2:7■3:13^{2},14-1SA-1:19■3:15■5:4■11:11■14:36■15:12■17:16(7925),20■19:2,11■20:35■25:22,34,36,37■29:10^{2},11-2SA-2:27■11:14■17:22■23:4^{2}■24:11,15-1KI-3:21^{2}■17:6■18:26-2KI-3:20,22■7:9■10:8,9■16:15■19:35-1CH-9:27■16:40■23:30-2CH-2:4■13:11■20:20■31:3-EZR-3:3-NE-4:21(7837)■8:3(216)-JOB-1:5■4:20■7:18,21(7836)■11:17■24:17■38:7,12■41:18(7837)-PS-5:3^{2}■30:5■49:14■55:17■59:16■65:8■73:14■88:13■90:5,6■92:2■110:3(4891)■130:6^{2}■139:9(7837)■143:8-PR-7:18■27:14-EC-10:16■11:6-SONG-6:10(7837)-IS-5:11■14:12(7837)■17:11,14■21:12■28:19■33:2■37:36■38:13■50:4■58:8(7837)-JER-5:8(7904)■20:16■21:12-LA-3:23-EZE-7:7(6843),10(6843)■12:8■24:18^{2}■33:22■46:13,14,15-DA-6:19(5053)■8:26-HO-6:3(7837),4■7:6■10:15(7837)■13:3-JOE-2:2(7837)-AM-4:4,13(7837)■5:8-JON-4:7(7837)-MIC-2:1-ZEP-3:5■N.T.-all=4404&marked-M'T-16:3■21:18(4405)■27:1(4405)-M'R-1:35■11:20■13:35■15:1-JOH-21:4(4405)-AC-28:23-RE-2:28(4407)■22:16(3720)

MORROW-all=4279,a=4283&marked-GE-19:34a-EX-8:10,23,29■9:5,6a,18■10:4■16:23■17:9■18:13a■19:10■32:5,6a,30a-LE-7:16a■19:6a■22:30(1242)■23:11a,15,16-NU-11:18■14:25■16:5(1242),7,16,41a■17:8a■22:41(1242)■33:3a-JOS-3:5■5:11a,12a■7:13■11:6■22:18-J'G-6:38a■9:42a■19:9■20:28■21:4-1SA-5:3a,4a■9:16,19(1242)■11:9,10,11a,18:10a■19:11■20:5,12,18,27a■28:19■31:8a-2SA-11:12,12a-1KI-19:2■20:6-2KI-6:28■7:1,18■8:15a■10:6-1CH-10:8a■29:21a-2CH-20:16,17-ES-2:14(1242)■5:8,12,14(1242)■9:13-PR-3:28■27:1-IS-22:13■56:12-JER-20:3a-ZEP-3:3(1242)■N.T.-all=839&marked-M'T-6:30,34^{2}-M'R-11:12(1887)-LU-10:35■12:28■13:32,33-AC-4:5■10:9(1887),23(1887),24(1887)■20:7(1887)■22:30(1887)■23:15,20,32(1887)■25:17(1836),22,23(1887)-1CO-15:32-JAS-4:13,14

MORSEL-all=6595&marked-GE-18:5-J'G-19:5-RU-2:14-1SA-2:36(3603)■28:22-1KI-17:11-JOB-31:17-PR-17:1■23:8-HEB-12:16(1035)

MORSELS-PS-147:17(6595)

MORTAL-JOB-4:17(582)■N.T.-all=2349-RO-6:12■8:11-1CO-15:53,54-2CO-4:11

MORTALITY-2CO-5:4(2349)

MORTALLY-DE-19:11(5315)

MORTAR-NU-11:8(4085)-PR-27:22(4388)

MORTER-all=2563&marked-GE-11:3-EX-1:14-LE-14:42(6083),45(6083)-IS-41:25-NA-3:14

MORTGAGED-NE-5:3(6148)

MORTIFY-RO-8:13(2289)-COL-3:5(3499)

MOST-all=6944,a=5945&marked-GE-14:18a,19a,20a,22a-EX-26:33,34■29:37■30:10,29,36■40:10-LE-2:3,10■6:17,25,29■7:1,6■10:12,17■14:13■21:22■24:9■27:28-NU-4:4,19■18:9^{2},10■24:16-DE-32:8-2SA-22:14-1KI-6:16■7:50■8:6-1CH-6:49■23:13-2CH-3:8,10■4:22■5:7■31:14-NE-7:65-ES-6:9(6579)-JOB-34:17(3524)-PS-7:17a■9:2a■21:7a■46:4a■47:2a■50:14a■56:2(4791)■57:2a■73:11a■77:10■78:17,56■82:6a■83:18■91:1,9■92:1■107:11a-PR-20:6(7230)-SONG-5:11(3800)-IS-14:14a-LA-3:35a,38a■4:1(2896)■35:7(8077)■41:4■42:13^{2}■43:12■44:13■45:3■48:12-DA-3:20(2429),26(5943)■4:17(5943),24(5943),25(5943),32(5943),34(5943)■5:18(5943),21(5943)■7:18(5946),22(5946),25(5943),25(5946),27a■9:24■11:39(4581)-HO-7:16(5920)■11:7(5920)■12:14(8563)■N.T.-all=5310&marked-M'T-11:20(4118)-M'R-5:7-LU-1:3(2903)■7:42(4119),43(4119)■8:28-AC-7:48■16:17■20:38(3122)■23:26(2903)■24:3(2903)■26:25(2903)-1CO-14:27(4119)-2CO-12:9(2236)-HEB-7:1-JUDE-20(40)

MOTE-all=2595-M'T-7:3,4,5-LU-6:41,42^{2}

MOTH-all=6211-JOB-4:19■13:28■27:18-PS-39:11-IS-50:9■51:8-HO-5:12■N.T.-all=4597-M'T-6:19,20-LU-12:33

MOTHEATEN-JAS-5:2(4598)

MOTHER-all=517,a=2545&marked-GE-2:24■3:20■20:12■21:21■24:53,55,67■27:11,13,14^{2}■28:5,7■30:14■32:11■37:10■44:20-EX-2:8■20:12■21:15,17-LE-18:7^{2},9■19:3■20:9^{2},14■21:2,11-NU-6:7-DE-5:16■

13:6■21:13,18,19■22:15■27:16,22,23(2859)■33:9-**JOS**-2:13,18■6:23-**J'G**-5:7,28■8:19■14:2,3,4,5,6,9,16■17:2^2,3^2,4^2-**RU**-1:14a■2:11a,11,18a,19^{2}a,23a■3:1a,6a,16a,17a-**1SA**-2:19■15:33■22:3-**2SA**-17:25■19:37■20:19-**1KI**-1:11■2:13,19,20,22■3:27■15:13■17:23■19:20■22:52-**2KI**-3:2,13■4:19,20,30■9:22■11:1■24:12,15-**1CH**-2:26■4:9-**2CH**-15:16■22:3,10-**ES**-2:7^2-**JOB**-17:14-**PS**-27:10■35:14■51:5■109:14■113:9■131:2-**PR**-1:8■4:3■6:20■10:1■15:20■19:26■20:20■23:22,25■28:24■29:15■30:11,17■31:1-**SONG**-3:11■6:9■8:1,5-**IS**-8:4■49:1■50:1■66:13-**JER**-15:8,10■16:7■20:14,17■22:26■50:12-**EZE**-16:3,44,45■19:2,10■22:7■23:2■44:25-**HO**-2:2,5■4:5■10:14-**MIC**-7:6,6a-**ZEC**-13:3^2■N.T.-all=3384&marked-**M'T**-1:18■2:11,13,14,20,21■8:14(3994)■10:35,35(3994),37■12:46,47,48,49,50■13:55■14:8,11■15:4^2,5,6■19:5,19,29■20:20■27:56^2-**M'R**-1:30(3994)■3:31,32,33,34,35■5:40■6:24,28■7:10^2,11,12■10:7,19,29■15:40-**LU**-1:43,60■2:33,34,43,48,51■4:38(3994)■7:12,15■8:19,20,21,51■12:53^2,53^2(3994)■14:26■18:20-**JOH**-2:1,3,5,12■6:42■19:25,26^2,27-**AC**-1:14■12:12-**RO**-16:13-**GA**-4:26-**EPH**-5:31■6:2-**2TI**-1:5-**HEB**-7:3(282)-**RE**-17:5

MOTHER'S-all=517-**GE**-24:28,67■27:29■28:2^2■29:10^3■43:29-**EX**-23:19■34:26-**LE**-18:13^2■20:17,19■24:11-**NU**-12:12-**DE**-14:21-**J'G**-9:1^2,3■16:17-**RU**-1:8-**1SA**-20:30-**1KI**-11:26■14:21,31■15:2,10■22:42-**2KI**-8:26■12:1■14:2■15:2,33■18:2■21:1,19■22:1■23:31,36■24:8,18-**2CH**-12:13■13:2■20:31■22:2■24:1■25:1■26:3■27:1■29:1-**JOB**-1:21■31:18-**PS**-22:9,10■50:20■69:8■71:6■139:13-**EC**-5:15-**SONG**-1:6■3:4■8:2-**IS**-50:1-**JER**-52:1-**EZE**-16:45■N.T.-all=3384-**M'T**-19:12-**LU**-1:15-**JOH**-3:4■19:25-**AC**-3:2■14:8-**GA**-1:15

MOTHERS-all=517-**JER**-16:3-**LA**-2:12■5:3■N.T.-**M'R**-10:30(3384)-**1TI**-1:9(3389)■5:2(3384)

MOTHERS'-**LA**-2:12(517)

MOTIONS-**RO**-7:5(3804)

MOULDY-**JOS**-9:5(5350),12(5350)

MOUNT-all=2022&marked-**GE**-10:30■14:6■(2042)■22:14■31:21,23,25^2,54^2■36:8,9-**EX**-4:27■18:5■19:2,11,12^2,13,14,16,17,18^2,20^3,23^2■24:12,13,15^2,16,17,18^2■25:40■26:30■27:8■31:18■32:1,15,19■33:6■34:2^2,3^2,4,29^2,32-**LE**-7:38■25:1■26:46■27:34-**NU**-3:1■10:33■20:22,23,25,27,28^2■21:4■27:12■28:6■33:23,24,37,38,39,41■34:7,8-**DE**-1:2,6,7■2:1,5■3:8,12■4:48■5:4,5,22■9:9^2,10,15^2,21■10:1,3,4,5,10■11:29^2■27:4,12,13■32:49,50^2■33:2-**JOS**-8:30,33^2■11:17^2■12:1,5,7■13:5,11,19■15:9,10^2,11■16:1■17:15■19:50■20:7^2■21:21■24:4,30,33-**J'G**-1:35■2:9■3:3^2,27■4:5,6,12,14■7:3,24■9:7,48■10:1■12:15■17:1,8■18:2,13■19:1,16,18-**1SA**-1:1■9:4■13:2■14:22■31:1,8-**2SA**-1:6■20:21-**1KI**-4:8■12:25■18:19,20■19:8,11-**2KI**-2:25■4:25■5:22■19:31■23:13,16-**1CH**-4:42■5:23■6:67■10:1,8-**2CH**-3:1■13:4^2■15:8■19:4■20:10,22,23■33:15-**NE**-8:15■9:13-**JOB**-20:6(5927)■39:27(1361)-**PS**-48:2,11■74:2■78:68■107:26(5927)■125:1-**SONG**-4:1-**IS**-4:5■8:18■9:18(55)■10:12,32■14:13■16:1■18:7■24:23■27:13■28:21■29:3(4674),8■31:4■37:32■40:31(5927)-**JER**-4:15■6:6(5550)■31:6■50:19■51:53(5927)-**EZE**-4:2(5550)■10:16(7311)■21:22(5550)■26:8(5550)■35:2,3,7,15-**DA**-11:15(5550)-**JOE**-2:32-**OB**-8,9,17,19,21^2-**MIC**-4:7-**HAB**-3:3-**ZEC**-14:4^2■N.T.-all=3735-**M'T**-21:1■24:3■26:30-**M'R**-11:1■13:3■14:26-**LU**-19:29,29sup,37■21:37■22:39-**JOH**-8:1-**AC**-1:12■7:30,38-**GA**-4:24,25-**HEB**-8:5■12:18,22-**2PE**-1:18-**RE**-14:1

MOUNTAIN-all=2022&marked-**GE**-12:8■14:10■19:17,19,30-**EX**-3:1,12■15:17■19:3■20:18-**NU**-13:17■14:40-**DE**-1:19,20,24,44■2:3■3:25■4:11^2■5:23■32:49■33:19■34:1-**JOS**-2:16,22,23■11:16■14:12■15:8■17:18■18:16■20:7-**J'G**-1:9,19,34■3:27-**1SA**-17:3^2■23:14,26^2-**2KI**-2:16■6:17-**2CH**-2:2,18-**JOB**-14:18-**PS**-11:1■30:7(2042)■48:1■78:54-**SONG**-4:6-**IS**-2:2,3■11:9■13:2■25:6,7,10■30:17,25,29■40:4,9■56:7■57:7,13■65:11,25■66:20-**JER**-3:6■16:16■17:3(2042)■26:18■31:23■50:6■51:25^2-**LA**-5:18-**EZE**-11:23■17:22,23■20:40^2■28:14,16■40:2■43:12-**DA**-2:35(2906),45(2906)■9:16,20■11:45-**JOE**-2:1■3:17-**AM**-4:1■6:1-**OB**-16-**MIC**-3:12■4:1,2■7:12-**ZEP**-3:11-**HAG**-1:8-**ZEC**-4:7■8:3■14:4■N.T.-all=3735-**M'T**-4:8■5:1■8:1■14:23■15:29■17:1,9,20■21:21■28:16-**M'R**-3:13■6:46■9:2,9■11:23-**LU**-3:5■4:5■6:12■8:32■9:28-**JOH**-4:20,21■6:3,15-**HEB**-12:20-**RE**-6:14■8:8■21:10

MOUNTAINS-all=2022-**GE**-7:20■8:4,5■22:2-**EX**-32:12-**NU**-13:29■23:7(2042)■33:47,48-**DE**-2:37■12:2■32:22■33:15(2042)-**JOS**-10:6■11:2,3,21^3■12:8■15:48■18:12-**J'G**-5:5■6:2■9:25,36^2■11:37,38-**1SA**-26:20-**2SA**-1:21-**1KI**-5:15■19:11-**2KI**-19:23-**1CH**-12:8-**2CH**-18:16■21:11■26:10■27:4-**JOB**-9:5■24:8■28:9■39:8■40:20-**PS**-36:6(2042)■46:2,3■50:11■65:6■72:3,16■76:4(2042)■83:14■87:1(2042)■90:2■104:6,8■114:4,6■125:2■133:3(2042)■144:5■147:8■148:9-**PR**-8:25■27:25-**SONG**-2:8,17■4:8(2042)■8:14-**IS**-2:2,14■13:4■14:25■17:13■18:3,6■22:5■34:3■37:24■40:12■41:15■42:11,15■44:23■49:11,13■52:7■54:10■55:12■64:1,3■65:7,9-**JER**-3:23■4:24■9:10■13:16■17:26■31:5■32:44■33:13■46:18■50:6-**LA**-4:19-**EZE**-6:2,3^2,13■7:7,16■18:6,11,15■19:9■22:9■31:12■32:5,6■33:28■34:6,13,14^2■35:8,12■36:1^2,4^2,6,8■37:22■38:8,20,21■39:2,4,17-**HO**-4:13■10:8-**JOE**-2:2,5■3:18-**AM**-3:9■4:13■9:13-**JON**-2:6-**MIC**-1:4■4:1■6:1,2-**NA**-1:5,15■3:18-**HAB**-3:6(2042),10-**HAG**-1:11-**ZEC**-6:1^2■14:5^2-**MAL**-1:3■N.T.-all=3735-**M'T**-18:12■24:16-**M'R**-5:5,11■13:14-**LU**-21:21■23:30-**1CO**-13:2-**HEB**-11:38-**RE**-6:15,16■16:20■17:9

MOUNTED-**EZE**-10:19(7426)

MOUNTING-**IS**-15:5(4608)

MOUNTS-all=5550-**JER**-32:24■33:4-**EZE**-17:17

MOURN-all=56&marked-**GE**-23:2(5594)-**1SA**-16:1-**2SA**-3:31(5594)-**1KI**-13:29(5594)■14:13(5594)-**NE**-8:9-**JOB**-2:11(5110)■5:11(6937)■14:22-**PS**-55:2(7300)-**PR**-5:11(5098)■29:2(584)-**EC**-3:4(5594)-**IS**-3:26■16:7(1897)■19:8(578)■38:14(1897)■59:11(1897)■61:2(57),3(57)■66:10-**JER**-4:28■12:4■48:31(1897)-**LA**-1:4(57)-**EZE**-7:12,27■24:16(5594),23(5594),23(5098)■31:15(6937)-**HO**-4:3■10:5-**JOE**-1:9-**AM**-1:2■8:8■9:5-**ZEC**-12:10(5594),12(5594)■N.T.-all=3996&marked-**M'T**-5:4■9:15■24:30(2875)-**LU**-6:25-**JAS**-4:9-**RE**-18:11

MOURNED-all=56&marked-**GE**-37:34■50:3(1058),10(5594)-**EX**-33:4-**NU**-14:39■20:29(1058)-**1SA**-15:35-**2SA**-1:12(5594)■11:26(5594)■13:37■14:2-**1KI**-13:30(5594)■14:18(5594)-**1CH**-7:22-**2CH**-35:24-**EZR**-10:6-**NE**-1:4-**ZEC**-7:5(5594)■N.T.-**M'T**-11:17(2354)-**M'R**-16:10(3996)-**LU**-7:32(2354)-**1CO**-5:2(3996)

MOURNER-**2SA**-14:2(56)

MOURNERS-**JOB**-29:25(57)-**EC**-12:5(5594)-**IS**-57:18(57)-**HOS**-9:4(205)

MOURNETH-all=56&marked-**2SA**-19:1-**PS**-35:14(57)■88:9(1669)-**IS**-24:4,7■33:9-**JER**-12:11■14:2■23:10-**JOE**-1:10-**ZEC**-12:10(5594)

MOURNFULLY-**MAL**-3:14(6941)

MOURNING-all=60&marked-**GE**-27:41■37:35(57)■50:4(1086),10,11^2-**DE**-26:14(205)■34:8-**2SA**-11:27■14:2■19:2-**ES**-4:3■6:12(57)■9:22-**JOB**-3:8(3882)■30:28(6937),31-**PS**-30:11(4553)■38:6(6937)■42:9(6937)■43:2(6937)-**EC**-7:2,4-**IS**-22:12(4553)■51:11(585)■60:20■61:3-**JER**-6:26■9:17(6969)■16:5(4798),7■31:13-**LA**-2:5(8386)■5:15-**EZE**-2:10(1899)■7:16(1993)■24:17■31:15(56)-**DA**-10:2(56)-**JOE**-2:12(4553)-**AM**-5:16■8:10^2-**MIC**-1:8,11(4553)-**ZEC**-12:11^2■N.T.-**M'T**-2:18(3602)-**2CO**-7:7(3602)-**JAS**-4:9(3997)-**RE**-18:8(3997)

MOUSE-**LE**-11:29(5909)-**IS**-66:17(5909)

MOUTH-all=6310&marked-**GE**-4:11■8:11■24:57■29:2,3^2,8,10■42:27■43:12,21■44:1,2■45:12-**EX**-4:11,12,15^2,16■13:9■23:13-**NU**-12:8■16:30,32■22:28,38■23:5,12,16■26:10■30:2■32:24■35:30-**DE**-8:3■11:6■17:6^2■18:18■19:15^2■23:23■30:14■32:1-**JOS**-1:8■6:10■9:14■10:18,22,27-**J'G**-7:6■9:38■11:35,36^2■18:19-**1SA**-1:12■2:1,3■14:26,27■17:35-**2SA**-1:16■14:3,19■17:19■18:25■22:9-**1KI**-7:31^3■8:15,24■13:21■17:24■19:18■22:13,22,23-**2KI**-4:34-**1CH**-16:12-**2CH**-6:4,15■18:21,22■35:22■36:12,21,22-**EZR**-1:1-**NE**-9:20-**ES**-7:8-**JOB**-3:1■5:15,16■7:11■8:2,21■9:20■12:11(2441)■15:5,6,13,30■16:5,10■19:16■20:12,13(2441)■21:5■22:22■23:4,12■29:9,10(2441),23■31:27,30(2441)■32:5■33:2,2(2441)■34:3■35:16■37:2■40:4,23■41:19,21-**PS**-5:9■8:2■10:7■17:3,10■18:8■19:14■22:21■32:9(5716)■33:6■34:1■35:21■36:3■37:30■38:13,14■39:1,9■40:3■49:3■50:16,19■51:15■54:2■55:21■58:6■59:7,12■62:4■63:5,11■66:14,17■69:15■71:8,15■73:9■78:1,2,36■81:10■89:1■103:5(5716)■105:5■107:42■109:2^2,30■119:13,43,72,88,103,108,131■126:2■137:6(2441)■138:4■141:3,7■144:8,11■145:21■149:6(1627)-**PR**-2:6■4:5,24■5:3(2441),7■6:2^2,12■7:24■8:7(2441),8,13■10:6,11^2,14,31,32■11:9,11■12:6,14■13:2,3■14:3■15:2,14,23,28■16:10,23,26■18:4,6,7,20■19:24,28■20:17■21:23■22:14■24:7■26:7,9,15,28■27:2■30:20,32■31:8,9,26-**EC**-5:2,6■6:7■10:12,13-**SONG**-1:2■5:16(2441)■7:9(2441)-**IS**-1:20■5:14■6:7■9:12,17■10:14■11:4■19:7■29:13■30:2■34:16■40:5■45:23■48:3■49:2■51:16■53:7^2,9■55:11■57:4■58:14■59:21^4■62:2-**JER**-1,9^2■5:14■7:28■9:8,12,20■12:2■15:19■23:16■32:4■34:3■36:4,6,17,18,27,32■44:17,26■45:1■48:28■51:44-**LA**-2:16■3:29,38■4:4(2441)-**EZE**-2:8■3:2,3,17,26(2441),27■4:14■16:56,63■21:22■24:27■29:21■33:7,22^2,31■34:10■35:13-**DA**-3:26(8651)■4:31(6433)■6:17(6433)■7:5(6433),8(6433),20(6433)■10:3,16-**HO**-2:17■6:5■8:1(2441)-**JOE**-1:5-**AM**-3:12-**MIC**-4:4■6:12■7:5,16-**NA**-3:12-**ZEP**-3:13-**ZEC**-5:8■8:9■9:7■14:12-**MAL**-2:6,7■N.T.-all=4750&marked-**M'T**-4:4■5:2■12:34■13:35■15:8,11^2,17,18■17:27■18:16■21:16-**LU**-1:64,70■4:22■6:45■11:54■19:22■21:15■22:71-**JOH**-19:29-**AC**-1:16■3:18,21■4:25■8:32,35■10:34■11:8■15:7,27(3056)■18:14■22:14■23:2-**RO**-3:14,19■10:8,9,10■15:6-**2CO**-6:11■13:1-**EPH**-4:29■6:19-**COL**-3:8-**2TH**-2:8-**2TI**-4:17-**JAS**-3:10-**1PE**-2:22-**JUDE**-16-**RE**-1:16■2:16■3:16■9:19■10:9,10■11:5■12:15,16^2■13:2,5,6■14:5■16:13^3■19:15,21

MOUTHS-all=6310&marked-**GE**-44:8-**DE**-31:19,21-**PS**-22:13■78:30■115:5■135:16,17-**IS**-52:15-**JER**-44:25-**LA**-3:46-**DA**-6:22(6433)-**MIC**-3:5■N.T.-all=4750&marked-**TIT**-1:11(1993)-**HEB**-11:33-**JAS**-3:3-**RE**-9:17,18

MOVE-**EX**-11:7(2782)-**LE**-11:10(8318)-**DE**-23:35(5130)-**J'G**-13:25

(6470)-**2SA**-7:10(7264)-**2KI**-21:8(5110)▪23:18(5128)-**JER**-10:4(6328)-**MIC**-7:17(7264)▪**N.T.**-**M'T**-23:4(2795)-**AC**-17:28(2795)▪20:24(3056,4160)

MOVEABLE-**PR**-5:6(5128)

MOVED-all=4131&marked-**GE**-1:2(7363)▪7:21(7430)-**JOS**-10:21(2782)▪15:18(5496)-**J'G**-1:14(5496)-**RU**-1:19(1949)-**1SA**-1:13(5128)-**2SA**-18:33(7264)▪22:8(7264)▪24:1(5496)-**1CH**-16:30▪17:9(7264)-**2CH**-18:31(5496)-**EZR**-4:15(5648)-**ES**-5:9(2111)-**JOB**-37:1(5425)▪41:23-**PS**-10:6▪13:4▪15:5▪16:8▪18:7(7264)▪21:7▪30:6▪46:5,6▪55:22▪62:2,6▪66:9(4132)▪93:1▪96:10▪99:1(5120)▪112:6▪121:3(4132)-**PR**-12:3-**SONG**-5:4(1993)-**IS**-6:4(5128)▪7:2^{2}(5128)▪10:14(5074)▪14:9(7264)▪19:1(5128)▪24:19(4132)▪40:20▪41:7-**JER**-4:24(7043)▪25:16(1607)▪46:7(1607),8(1607)▪49:21(7493)▪50:46(7493)▪**N.T.**-all=4697&marked-**M'T**-9:36▪14:14▪18:27▪20:24(23)▪21:10(4579)▪21:10-**M'R**-1:41▪6:34▪15:11(383)-**AC**-2:25(4531)▪7:9(2206)▪17:5(2206)▪21:30(2795)-**COL**-1:23(3334)-**1TH**-3:3(4525)-**HEB**-11:7(2125)▪12:28(761)-**2PE**-1:21(5342)-**RE**-6:14(2795)

MOVEDST-**JOB**-2:3(5496)

MOVER-**AC**-24:5(2795)

MOVETH-all=7430&marked-**GE**-1:21,28▪9:2-**LE**-11:46-**JOB**-40:17(2654)-**PS**-69:34(7430)-**PR**-23:31(1980)-**EZE**-47:9

MOVING-**GE**-1:20(8318)▪9:3(7430)-**JOB**-16:5(5205)-**PR**-16:30(7169)▪**N.T.**-**JOH**-5:3(2796)

MOWER-**PS**-129:7(7114)

MOWINGS-**AM**-7:1(1488)

MOWN-**PS**-72:6(1488)

MUCH-all=7227,a=7235,b=637&marked-**GE**-26:16(3966)▪30:43▪34:12(3966,7235)▪41:49a▪43:34a▪44:1(834)▪50:20-**EX**-12:38(3515)▪14:28(5704)▪16:5(834),18a▪30:23(4276)▪36:5a,7(3498)-**LE**-13:7(6581),22(6581),27(6581),35(6581)-**NU**-16:3,7▪20:20(3515)▪21:4(7114),6-**DE**-2:5(5704)▪3:19▪28:38-**JOS**-11:4▪13:1a▪19:9▪22:8^{2},8a-**RU**-1:13(3966)-**1SA**-14:30b,14sup▪18:30(3966)▪19:2(3966)▪20:13(3254)▪23:3b▪26:24^{2}(1431)-**2SA**-4:11b▪8:8a▪13:34▪14:25(3966)▪16:11b▪17:12(1571)-**1KI**-4:29(7235)▪8:27b▪10:2▪12:28-**2KI**-5:13(637,3588)▪10:18a▪12:10(7225)▪21:6a,16a-**1CH**-18:8▪20:2a▪22:4(7230),8-**2CH**-2:16(3605)▪6:18b▪14:13a,14a▪17:13▪20:25▪24:11▪25:9a,13▪26:10▪27:3(7230),5(1931)▪28:8▪30:13▪32:4^{2},15(637,3588),27a,29▪33:6a▪36:14-**NE**-4:10a▪6:16(3966)▪9:37a▪-**ES**-1:18(1767)-**JOB**-4:19b▪9:14b(3588)▪15:10(3524)▪25:6b▪31:25(3524)▪42:10(634)-**PS**-19:10▪33:16(7230)▪35:18(6079)▪119:107(3966)-**PR**-7:21(7230)▪11:31b▪13:23(7230)▪14:4(7230)▪15:6,11b▪17:7b▪19:7b,10b,24(1571)▪21:27b▪25:16(1767),27a-**EC**-1:18(7230)▪5:12a,17a,20a▪7:16a,17a▪9:18a▪12:12a-**IS**-21:7▪30:33a▪56:12(3966)-**JER**-2:22a,36(3966)▪40:12(7335)-**EZE**-14:21b▪15:5b(3588)▪17:15▪22:5▪23:32(4767)▪26:7-**DA**-4:12(7690),21(7690)▪7:5(7690),28(7690)-**JON**-4:11-**NA**-2:10(2479)-**HAG**-1:6a,9a▪**N.T.**-all=4183,a=4214&marked-**M'T**-6:7(4180),26(3123),30▪7:11a▪10:25a▪12:12a▪13:5▪15:33(5118)▪26:9-**M'R**-1:45▪2:2(3366)▪3:20(3383)▪4:5▪5:10,21,24,34▪7:36(3123)▪10:14(23),41(23)▪12:41-**LU**-5:15(3123)▪6:3(3761)▪34(2470)▪7:11,12(2425),26(4055),47▪8:4▪9:37▪10:40▪11:13a▪12:19,24a,28a,48^{3}▪16:5a,7a,10^{2}▪18:13(3761),39▪24:4(1280)-**JOH**-3:23▪6:10,11(3745)▪7:12▪12:9,12,24▪14:30▪15:5,8-**AC**-5:8(5118),8(5118),37(2425)▪9:13(3745)▪10:2▪11:24(2425),26(2425)▪14:22▪15:7▪16:16▪18:10,27▪19:2(3761),26(2425)▪20:2▪26:24▪27:9(2425),10,16(3433)-**RO**-1:15(3588)▪3:2▪5:9,10,15,17,20(5248)▪9:22▪11:12(4124),24(4124)▪12:18(3588)▪15:22(5248)▪16:6,12-**1CO**-2:3▪5:1(3761)▪6:3(3386)▪12:22▪16:19-**2CO**-2:4▪3:9,11▪6:4▪8:4,15,22-**PH'P**-1:14(4056)▪2:12-**1TH**-1:5,6,2:2-**1TI**-3:8-**2TI**-4:14-**TIT**-2:3-**PH'M**-8,16a-**HEB**-1:4(5118)▪7:22(5118)▪8:6(3745)▪9:14a▪10:25(5118),29a▪12:9,20(2579),25-**JAS**-5:16-**1PE**-1:7-**RE**-5:4▪8:3▪18:7(3745),7(5118)▪19:1

MUFFLERS-**IS**-3:19(7479)

MULBERRY-all=1057-**2SA**-5:23,24-**1CH**-14:14,15

MULE-all=6505&marked-**2SA**-13:29▪18:9^{3}-**1KI**-1:33(6506),38(6506),44(6506)-**PS**-32:9-**ZEC**-14:15

MULES-all=6505&marked-**GE**-36:24(3222)-**1KI**-10:25▪18:5-**1CH**-12:40-**2CH**-9:24-**EZR**-2:66-**NE**-7:68-**ES**-8:10(7409),14(7409)-**IS**-66:20-**EZE**-27:14

MULES'-**2KI**-5:17(6505)

MULTIPLIED-all=7235&marked-**GE**-47:27-**EX**-1:7,12,20▪11:9-**DE**-1:10▪8:13^{2}▪11:21-**JOS**-24:3-**1CH**-5:9-**JOB**-27:14▪35:6(7231)-**PS**-16:4▪38:19(7231)▪107:38-**PR**-9:11▪29:16-**IS**-9:3▪59:12(7231)-**JER**-3:16-**EZE**-5:7(1995)▪11:6▪16:25,29,51▪21:15▪23:19▪31:5▪35:13(6280)-**DA**-4:1(7680)▪6:25(7680)-**HO**-2:8▪8:14▪12:10-**NA**-3:16▪**N.T.**-all=4129-**AC**-6:1,7▪7:17▪9:31▪12:24-**1PE**-1:2-**2PE**-1:2-**JUDE**-2

MULTIPLIEDST-**NE**-9:23(7235)

MULTIPLIETH-**JOB**-9:17(7235)▪34:37(7235)▪35:16(3527)

MULTIPLY-all=7235&marked-**GE**-1:22^{2},28▪3:16▪6:1(7231)▪8:17▪9:1,7^{2}▪16:10▪17:2,20▪22:17▪26:4,24▪28:3▪35:11▪48:4-**EX**-1:10▪7:3▪23:29(7227)▪32:13-**LE**-26:9-**DE**-7:13▪8:1,13▪13:17▪17:16^{2},17^{2}▪28:63▪30:5,16-**1CH**-4:27-**JOB**-29:18-**JER**-30:19▪33:22-**EZE**-16:7(7233)▪36:10,11,30▪37:26-**AM**-4:4▪**N.T.**-**2CO**-9:10(4129)-**HEB**-6:14(4129)

MULTIPLYING-**GE**-22:17(7235)▪**N.T.**-**HEB**-6:14(4129)

MULTITUDE-all=7230,a=1995&marked-**GE**-16:10▪28:3(6951)▪30:30▪32:12▪48:4(6951),16,19(4393)-**EX**-12:38(7227)▪23:2(7227)-**LE**-25:16-**NU**-11:4(628)▪32:1(7227)-**DE**-1:10▪10:22▪28:62-**JOS**-11:4-**J'G**-4:7a▪6:5▪7:12^{2}-**1SA**-13:5▪14:16a-**2SA**-6:19a▪17:11-**1KI**-3:8▪4:20▪8:5▪20:13a-**2KI**-7:13^{2}a▪19:23(7393)▪25:11a-**2CH**-1:9(7227)▪5:6▪13:8a▪14:11a▪20:2a,15a,24a▪30:18(4768)▪32:7a-**NE**-13:3(6154)-**ES**-5:11▪10:3-**JOB**-11:2▪31:34a▪32:7▪33:19(7379)▪35:9▪39:7a-**PS**-5:7,10▪33:16▪42:4(5519),4a▪49:6▪51:1▪68:30(5712)▪69:13,16▪74:19(2416)▪94:19▪97:1(7227)▪106:7,45▪109:30(7227)-**PR**-10:19▪11:14▪14:28▪15:22▪20:15▪24:6-**EC**-5:3^{2},7-**IS**-1:11▪5:13a,14a▪13:4a▪16:14a▪17:12a▪29:5^{2}a,7a,8a▪31:4(4393)▪32:14a▪37:24▪47:9,12,13▪60:6(8229)▪63:7-**JER**-3:23a▪10:13a▪12:6(4392)▪30:14,15▪44:15(6951)▪46:25(582)▪49:32(527)▪51:16(527),42(527)▪52:15(527)-**LA**-1:5▪3:32-**EZE**-7:11a,12a,13a,14a▪14:4▪19:11▪23:42a▪27:12,16,18^{2},33▪28:16,18▪29:19a▪30:4a,10a,15a▪31:2a,5(7227),9,18a▪32:12^{2}a,16a,18a,24a,25a,26a,31a,32a▪39:11a-**DA**-10:6a▪11:10a,11^{2}a,12a,13a-**HO**-9:7▪10:1,13-**NA**-3:3,4-**ZEC**-2:4▪**N.T.**-all=3793,a=4128&marked-**M'T**-13:2,34,36▪14:5,14,15,19^{2}▪15:10,31,32,33,35,36,39▪17:14▪20:29,31▪21:8,11,46▪22:33▪23:1▪26:47▪27:20,24-**M'R**-2:13▪3:7a,8a,9,20,32▪4:1^{2},36▪5:31▪7:33▪8:1,2▪9:14,17▪14:43▪15:8-**LU**-1:10a▪2:13a▪3:7▪5:6a,19▪6:17a,19▪8:37a,45▪9:12,16▪12:1(3461)▪18:36▪19:37a,39▪22:6,47▪23:1a-**JOH**-5:3a13▪6:2▪21:6a-**AC**-2:6a▪4:32a▪5:16a▪6:2a,5a▪14:1a,4a▪15:12a,30a▪16:22▪17:4a▪19:9a,33(2793)▪21:22a,34,36a▪23:7a▪24:18▪25:24a-**HEB**-11:12a-**JAS**-5:20a-**1PE**-4:8a-**RE**-7:9▪19:6

MULTITUDES-**EZE**-32:20(1995)-**JOE**-3:14(1995)▪**N.T.**-all=3793&marked-**M'T**-4:25▪5:1▪8:1,18▪9:8,33,36▪11:7▪12:15▪13:2▪14:22,23▪15:30▪19:2▪21:9▪26:55-**LU**-5:15▪14:25-**AC**-5:14(4128)▪13:45-**RE**-17:15

MUNITION-**IS**-29:7(4685)-**NA**-2:1(4694)

MUNITIONS-**IS**-33:16(4679)

MURDER-all=7523&marked-**PS**-10:8(2026)▪94:6-**JER**-7:9-**HO**-6:9▪**N.T.**-all=5408&marked-**M'T**-19:18(5407)-**M'R**-15:7-**LU**-23:19,25-**RO**-1:29

MURDERER-all=7523&marked-**NU**-35:16^{2},17^{2},18^{2},19,21^{2},30,31-**2KI**-6:32-**JOB**-24:14-**HO**-9:13(2026)▪**N.T.**-all=5406&marked-**JOH**-8:44(443)-**AC**-3:14▪28:4-**1PE**-4:15-**1JO**-3:15^{2}(443)

MURDERERS-**2KI**-14:6(5221)-**IS**-1:21(7523)-**JER**-4:31(2026)▪**N.T.**-all=5406&marked-**M'T**-22:7-**AC**-7:52▪21:38(4607)-**1TI**-1:9(3964),9(3389)-**RE**-21:8▪22:15

MURDERS-all=5408-**M'T**-15:19-**M'R**-7:21-**GA**-5:21-**RE**-9:21

MURMUR-all=3885-**EX**-16:7,8-**NU**-14:27^{2},36▪16:11▪17:5▪**N.T.**-**JOH**-6:43(1111)-**1CO**-10:10(1111)

MURMURED-all=3885&marked-**EX**-15:24▪16:2▪17:3-**NU**-14:2,29▪16:41-**DE**-1:27(7279)-**JOS**-9:18-**PS**-106:25(7279)-**IS**-29:24▪**N.T.**-all=1111&marked-**M'T**-20:11-**M'R**-14:5(1690)-**LU**-5:30▪15:2(1234)▪19:7(1234)-**JOH**-6:41,61▪7:32-**1CO**-10:10

MURMURERS-**JUDE**-16(1113)

MURMURING-**JOH**-7:12(1112)-**AC**-6:1(1112)

MURMURINGS-all=8519&marked-**EX**-16:7,8^{2},9,12-**NU**-14:27▪17:5,10-**PH'P**-2:14(1112)

MURRAIN-**EX**-9:3(1698)

MUSE-**PS**-143:5(7878)

MUSED-**LU**-3:15(1260)

MUSICAL-**1CH**-16:42(7892)-**NE**-12:36(7892)-**EC**-2:8(7705)

MUSICIAN-all=5329-**PS**-4:t▪5:t▪6:t▪8:t▪9:t▪11:t▪12:t▪13:t▪14:t▪18:t▪19:t▪20:t▪21:t▪22:t▪31:t▪36:t▪39:t▪40:t▪41:t▪42:t▪44:t▪45:t▪46:t▪47:t▪49:t▪51:t▪52:t▪53:t▪54:t▪55:t▪56:t▪57:t▪58:t▪59:t▪60:t▪61:t▪62:t▪64:t▪65:t▪66:t▪67:t▪68:t▪69:t▪70:t▪75:t▪76:t▪77:t▪80:t▪81:t▪84:t▪85:t▪88:t▪109:t▪139:t▪140:t

MUSICIANS-**RE**-18:22(3451)

MUSICK-all=7892&marked-**1CH**-15:16-**2CH**-5:13▪7:6▪23:13▪34:12-**EC**-12:4-**LA**-3:63(4485)▪5:14(5058)-**DA**-3:5(2170),7(2170),10(2170),15(2170)-**AM**-6:5▪**N.T.**-**LU**-15:25(4858)

MUSING-**PS**-39:3(1901)

MUST-**EZR**-10:12(5921)▪**N.T.**-all=1163&marked-**M'T**-16:21▪17:10▪18:7(318)▪24:6▪26:54-**M'R**-8:31▪9:11▪13:7,10▪14:49(2443)-**LU**-2:49▪4:43▪9:22▪13:33▪14:18(2192)▪17:25▪19:5▪21:9▪22:7,37▪24:7,44-**JOH**-3:7,14,30▪4:24▪9:4▪10:16▪12:34▪20:9-**AC**-1:16,22▪3:21▪4:12▪9:6,16▪14:22▪16:30▪17:3▪18:21▪19:21▪21:22▪23:11▪27:24,26-**1CO**-5:10(3784)▪11:19▪15:25,53-**2CO**-5:10▪11:30-**1TI**-3:2,7-**2TI**-2:6,24-**TIT**-1:7,11-**HEB**-9:26▪11:6-**RE**-1:1▪4:1▪10:11▪11:5▪13:10▪17:10▪20:3▪22:6

MUSTARD-all=4615-**M'T**-13:31▪17:20-**M'R**-4:31-**M'R**-4:31-**LU**-13:19▪17:6

MUSTERED-**2KI**-25:19(6633)-**JER**-52:25(6633)

MUSTERETH-**IS**-13:4(6485)

MUTTER-**IS**-8:19(1897)

MUTTERED-**IS**-59:3(1897)

MUTUAL-**RO**-1:12(1722,240)

MUZZLE-**DE**-25:4(2629)▪**N.T.**-**1CO**-9:9(5392)-**1TI**-5:18(5392)

MYRRH-all=4753&marked-**GE**-37:25(3910)▪43:11(3910)-**EX**-30:23-**EC**-

2:12-PS-45:8-PR-7:17-SONG-1:13■3:6■4:6,14■5:1,5^{2},13■N.T.-M'T-2:11(4666)-M'R-15:23(4669)-JOH-19:39(4666)

MYRTLE-all=1918-NE-8:15-IS-41:19■55:13-ZEC-1:8,10,11

MYSELF-&marked-2SA-18:2(589)-PS-131:2(5315)-EC-2:14(589)-JER-21:5(589)■N.T.-all=1683&marked-LU-7:7-JOH-5:31■7:17,28■8:14,18,28,42,54■10:18■12:49■14:3,10,21■17:19-AC-20:24■24:10■26:2,2sup,9-RO-9:3(846)■11:4■16:2(846)-1CO-4:4,6■7:7■9:19-2CO-2:1■11:7,9^{2}■12:5-GA-2:18-PH'M-17(1691)

MYSTERIES-all=3466-M'T-13:11-LU-8:10-1CO-4:1■13:2■14:2

MYSTERY-all=3466-M'R-4:11-RO-11:25■16:25-1CO-2:7■15:51-EPH-1:9■3:3,4,9■5:32■6:19-COL-1:26,27■2:2■4:3-2TH-2:7-1TI-3:9,16-RE-1:20■10:7■17:5,7

N

NAIL-all=3489-J'G-4:21^{2},22■5:26-EZR-9:8-IS-22:23,25-ZEC-10:4

NAILING-COL-2:14(4338)

NAILS-all=4548&marked-DE-21:12(6856)-1CH-22:3-2CH-3:9-EC-12:11(4930)-IS-41:7-JER-10:4-DA-4:33(2953)■7:19(2953)■N.T.-JOH-20:25^{2}(2247)

NAKED-all=6174&marked-GE-2:25■3:7(5903),10(5903),11(5903)-EX-32:25^{2}(6544)-1SA-19:24-2CH-28:15(4636),19(6544)-JOB-1:21^{2}■22:6■24:7,10■26:6-EC-5:15-IS-20:2,3,4■58:7-LA-4:21(6168)-EZE-16:7(5903),22(5903),39(5903)■18:7(5903),16(5903)■23:29(5903)-HO-2:3-AM-2:16-MIC-1:8,11(6181)-HAB-3:9(5783)■N.T.-all=1131&marked-M'T-25:36,38,43,44-M'R-14:51,52-JOH-21:7-AC-19:16-1CO-4:11(1130)-2CO-5:3-HEB-4:13-JAS-2:15-RE-3:17■16:15■17:16

NAKEDNESS-all=6172&marked-GE-9:22,23^{2}■42:9,12-EX-20:26■28:42-LE-18:6,7^{2},8^{2},9^{2},10^{3},11^{2},12,13,14,15^{2},16^{2},17^{2},18,19■20:11,17^{2},18,19,20,21-DE-28:48(5903)-1SA-20:30-IS-47:3-LA-1:8-EZE-16:8,36,37^{2}■22:10■23:10,18,29-HO-2:9-NA-3:5(4626)-HAB-2:15(4589)■N.T.-all=1132-RO-8:35-2CO-11:27-RE-3:18

NAME-all=8034&marked-GE-2:11,13,14,19■3:20■4:17,19^{2},21,25,26^{2}■5:2,3,29■10:25^{2}■11:4,9,29^{2}■12:2,8■13:4■16:1,11,13,15■17:5^{2},15^{2},19■19:22,37,38■21:3,33■22:14,24■24:29■25:1,25,26,30■26:20,21,22,25,33■28:19^{2}■29:16^{2},32,33,34,35■30:6,8,11,13,18,20,21,24■31:48■32:2,27,28,29^{2},30■33:17■35:8,10^{4},15,18■36:32,35,39^{2}■38:1,2,3,4,5,6,29,30■41:45,51,52■48:6,16^{2}■50:11-EX-1:15^{2}■2:10,22■3:13,15■5:23■6:3sup,3■9:16■15:3,23■16:31■17:7,15■18:3,4■20:7^{2},24■23:13,21■28:21■31:2■33:12,17,19■34:5,14■35:30■39:14-LE-18:21■19:12^{2}■20:3■21:6■22:2,32■24:11^{2},16^{2}-NU-4:32■6:27■11:3,26^{2},34■17:2,3■21:3■25:14,15■26:46,59■27:4■32:42-DE-3:14■5:11^{2},6:13■7:24■9:14■10:8,20■12:5,11,21■14:23,24■16:2,6,11■18:5,7,19,20^{2},22■21:5■22:14,19■25:6^{2},7,10■26:2,19■28:10,58■29:20■32:3-JOS-5:9■7:9^{2},26■9:9■14:15■15:15■19:47■21:9■23:7-J'G-1:10,11,17,23,26^{2}■2:5■8:31■13:2,6,17,18,24■15:19■16:4■17:1■18:29^{3}-RU-1:2^{3},4^{2}■2:1,19■4:5,10,14,17^{2}-1SA-1:1,2^{2},20■7:12■8:2^{2}■9:1,2■14:4^{2},49^{2},50^{2}■16:3(559)■17:12,23,45■18:30■20:42■21:7■24:21■25:3^{2},5,9,25^{2}■28:8(559)-2SA-3:7■4:2^{2},4■5:20■6:2,18■7:9^{2},13,23,26■8:13■9:2,12■12:24,25,28■13:1,3■14:7,27■16:5■17:25■18:18^{2}■20:1,21■22:50■23:18,22-1KI-1:47^{2}■3:2■5:3,5^{2}■7:21^{2}■8:16,17,18,19,20,29,33,35,42,43^{2},44,48■9:3,7■10:1■11:26,36■13:2■14:21^{2},31■15:2,10■16:24^{2}■18:24^{2},25,26,31,32■21:8■22:16,42-2KI-2:24■5:11■8:26■12:1■14:2,7,27■15:2,33■18:2■21:1,4,7,19■22:1■23:27,31,34,36■24:8,17,18-1CH-1:19^{2},43,46,50^{2}■2:26,29,34■4:3,9,41■7:15^{2},16^{2},23■8:29■9:35■11:20,24■12:31■13:6■14:11■16:2,8,10,29,35,41■17:8,21,24■21:19■22:7,8,9,10,19■23:13■28:3■29:13,16-2CH-2:1,4■3:17^{2}■6:5,6,7,8,9,10,20,24,26,33^{2},34,38■7:14,16,20■12:13^{2}■13:2■14:11■18:15■20:8,9,26,31■22:2■24:1■25:1■26:3,8,15■27:1■28:9,15■29:1■31:19■33:4,7,18■36:4-EZR-2:61■5:1(8036),14(8036)■6:12(8036)■8:20-NE-1:9,11■7:63■9:5,7,10-ES-2:5,14,22■3:12■8:8^{2},10■9:26-JOB-1:1,21■18:17■42:14^{3}-PS-5:11■7:17■8:1,9■9:2,5,10■18:49■20:1,5,7■22:22■29:2■33:21■34:3■41:5■44:5,8,20■45:17■48:10■52:9■54:1,6■61:5,8■63:4■66:2,4■68:4^{2}■69:30,36■72:17^{2},19■74:7,10,18,21■75:1■76:1■79:6,9■80:18■83:4,16,18■86:9,11,12■89:12,16,24■91:14■92:1■96:2,8■99:3,6■100:4■102:15,21■103:1■105:1,3■106:47■109:13■111:9■113:1,2,3■115:1■116:4,13,17■118:10,11,12,26■119:55,132■122:4■124:8■129:8■135:1,3,13■138:2^{2}■140:13■142:7■145:1,2,21■148:5,13^{2}■149:3-PR-10:7■18:10■21:24■22:1■30:4,9-EC-6:4■7:1-SONG-1:3-IS-4:1■7:14■8:3■9:6■12:4^{2}■14:22■18:7■24:15■25:1■26:8,13■29:23■30:27■41:25■42:8■43:1,7■44:5^{2}■45:3,4■47:4■48:1^{2},2,19■49:1■50:10■51:15■52:5,6■54:5■55:13■56:5^{2},6■57:15■59:19■60:9■62:2^{2}■63:12,14,16,19■64:2,7■65:1,15^{2}■66:22-JER-3:17■7:10,11,12,14,30■10:6,16,25■11:16,19,21■12:16■13:11■14:9,14,15■15:16■16:21■20:3,9■23:6,25,27^{2}■25:29■26:9,16,20■27:15■29:9,21,23,25■31:35■32:18,20,34■33:2,9■34:15,16■37:13■44:16,26^{2}■46:18■48:15,17■50:34■51:19,57■52:1-LA-3:55-EZE-20:29,39■24:2■36:20,21,23■39:7^{2},16,25■43:7,8■48:35-DA-1:7■2:20(8036),26(8036)■4:8^{2}(8036),19(8036)■9:6,18,19■10:1-HO-1:4,6,9■2:17-JO-2:26,32-AM-2:7■4:13■5:8,27■6:10■9:6,12-MIC-4:5^{2}■5:4■6:9-NA-1:14-ZEP-1:4■3:9,12,20-ZEC-5:4■6:12■10:12■13:3,9■14:9-MAL-1:6^{2},11^{3},14■2:2,5■3:16■4:2■N.T.-all=3686&marked-M'T-1:21,23,25■6:9■7:22^{3}■10:41^{2},42■12:21■18:5,20■21:9■23:39■24:5■27:32■28:19-M'R-5:9^{2},22■6:14■9:37,38,39,41■11:9,10■13:6■16:17-LU-1:5,13,27^{2},31,49,59,61,63■2:21,25■6:22■8:30■9:48,49■10:17■11:2■13:35■19:38■21:8■24:18,47-JON-1:6,12■2:23■3:18■5:43^{2}■10:3,25■12:13,28■14:13,14,26■15:16■16:23,24,26■17:6,11,12,26■18:10■20:31-AC-2:21,38■3:6,16■4:7,10,12,17,18,30■5:28,40,41■7:58(2564)■8:12,16■9:14,15,21,27,29■10:43,48■13:6,8■15:14,17,26■16:18■19:5,13,17■21:13■22:16■26:9■28:7-RO-1:5■2:24■9:17■10:13■15:9-1CO-1:2,10,13,15■5:4■6:11-EPH-1:21■5:20-PH'P-2:9,10-COL-3:17-2TH-1:12■3:6-1TI-6:1-2TI-2:19-HEB-1:4■2:12■6:10■13:15-JAS-2:7■5:10,14-1PE-4:14-1JO-3:23■5:13^{2}-3JO-14-RE-2:13,17■3:1,5^{2},8,12^{2}■6:8■8:11■9:11^{2}■11:18■13:1,6,17^{2}■14:1,11■15:2,4■16:9■17:5■19:12,13,16■22:4

NAMED-all=7121&marked-GE-23:16(1696)■27:36(7121,8034)■48:16-JOS-2:1(8034)-1SA-4:21■17:4(8034)■22:20(8034)-2KI-17:34(8034)-1CH-23:14-EC-6:10(8034,7121)-IS-61:6-JER-44:26-DA-5:12(8036)-AM-6:1(5344)-MIC-2:7(559)■N.T.-all=3686&marked-M'T-9:9(3004)■27:57-M'R-14:32■15:7(3004)-LU-1:5,26■2:21(2564)■5:27■6:13(3687),14(3687)■8:41■10:38■16:20■19:2(2564)■23:50-JOH-3:1-AC-5:1,34■9:10,12,33,36■11:28■12:13■16:1,14■17:34■18:2,7,24■19:24■20:9■21:10■27:1-RO-15:20(3687)-1CO-5:1(3687)-EPH-1:21(3687)■3:15(3687)■5:3(3687)

NAMELY-RO-13:9(1722)

NAME'S-all=8034-1SA-12:22-1KI-8:41-2CH-6:32-PS-23:3■25:11■31:3■79:9■106:8■109:21■143:11-IS-48:9■66:5-JER-14:7,21-EZE-20:9,14,22,44■36:22■N.T.-all=3686-M'T-10:22■19:29■24:9-M'R-13:13-LU-21:12,17-JOH-15:21-AC-9:16-1JO-2:12-3JO-7-RE-2:3

NAMES-all=8034-GE-2:20■25:13^{2},16■26:18■36:10,40^{2}■46:8-EX-1:1■6:16■28:9,10^{2},11,12,21^{2},29■39:6,14^{2}-NU-1:2,5,17,18,20,22,24,26,28,30,32,34,36,38,40,42■3:2,3,17,18,40,43■13:4,16■26:33,53,55■27:1■32:38^{2}■34:17,19-DE-12:3-JOS-17:3-1SA-14:49■17:13-2SA-5:14■23:8-1KI-4:8-1CH-4:38■6:17,65■8:38■9:44■14:4■23:24-EZR-5:4,10^{2}■8:13■10:16-PS-16:4■49:11■147:4-IS-40:26-EZE-23:4^{2}■48:1,31-DA-1:7-HO-2:17-ZEC-13:2■N.T.-all=3686-M'T-10:2-LU-10:20-AC-1:15■18:15-PH'P-4:3-RE-3:4■13:8■17:3,8■21:12^{2},14

NAMETH-2TI-2:19(3687)

NAPKIN-all=4676-LU-19:20-JOH-11:44■20:7

NARROW-all=331&marked-NU-22:26(6862)-JOS-17:15(213)-1KI-6:4-PR-23:27(6862)-IS-49:19(3334)-EZE-40:16■41:16,26■N.T.-M'T-7:14(2346)

NARROWED-1KI-6:6(4052)

NARROWER-IS-28:20(6887)

NARROWLY-JOB-13:27(8104)

NATION-all=1471&marked-GE-12:2■15:14■17:20■18:18■20:4■21:13,18■35:11■46:3-EX-9:24■19:6■21:8(5971)■32:10■33:13■34:10-LE-18:26(249)■20:23-NU-14:12-DE-4:6,7,8,34■9:14■26:5■28:33(5971),36,49^{2},50■32:21,28-2SA-7:23-1KI-18:10^{2}-2KI-17:29^{2}-1CH-16:20■17:21-2CH-15:6■32:15-JOB-34:29-PS-33:12■43:1■83:4■105:13■106:5■147:20-PR-14:34-IS-1:4■2:4■9:3■10:6■14:32■18:2^{2},7■26:2,15^{2}■49:7■51:4(3816)■55:5■58:2■60:12,22■65:1■66:8-JER-2:11■5:9,15^{3},29■6:22■7:28■9:9■12:17■18:7,8,9■25:12,32■27:8^{2},13■31:36■33:24■48:2■49:31,36■50:3,41-LA-4:17-EZE-2:3■37:22-DA-3:29(524)■8:22■12:1-JOE-1:6-AM-6:14-MIC-4:3,7-HAB-1:6-ZEP-2:1,5-HAG-2:14-MAL-3:9■N.T.-all=1484&marked-M'T-21:43■24:7-M'R-7:26(1085)■13:8-LU-7:5■21:10■23:2-JOH-11:48,50,51,52■18:35-AC-2:5■7:7■10:22,28(246)35■24:2,10,17■26:4■28:19-RO-10:19-GAL-1:14(1985)-PH'P-2:15(1074)-1PE-2:9-RE-5:9■14:6

NATIONS-all=1471&marked-GE-10:5,20,31,32^{2}■14:1,9■17:4,5,6,16■18:18■22:18■25:16(523),23■26:4■27:29(3816)■35:11■48:19-EX-34:24-LE-18:24,28-NU-14:15■23:9■24:8,20-DE-2:25(5971)■4:6(5971),19(5971),27(5971),38■7:1^{2},17,22■8:20■9:1,4,5■11:23^{2}■12:2,29,30■14:2(5971)■15:6^{2}■17:14■18:9,14■19:1■20:15■26:19■28:1,12,37(5971),65■29:16,18,24■30:1,3(5971)■31:3■32:8,43-JOS-12:23■23:3,4^{2},7,9,12,13-J'G-2:21,23■3:1-1SA-8:5,20-2SA-7:23■8:11-1KI-4:31■11:2■14:24-2KI-17:26,33,41■18:33■19:12,17■21:9-1CH-14:17■16:24(5971),31■17:21■18:11-2CH-7:20(5971)■13:9(5971)■32:13,14,17,23-EZR-4:10(524)-NE-1:8(5971)■9:22(5971)■13:26-JOB-12:23^{2}-PS-9:17,20■22:27,28■47:3(3816)■57:9(3816)■66:7■67:2,4^{2}(3816)■72:11,17■82:8■86:9■96:5(5971)■106:27,34(5971)■108:3(3816)■113:4■117:1■118:10■135:10-PR-24:24(3816)-IS-2:2,4■5:26■9:1■10:7■11:12■13:4■14:6,9,12,18,26■17:12(3816),13(3816)■23:3■25:3,7■29:7,8■30:28■33:3■34:1,2■36:18■37:12,18(776)■40:15,17■41:2■43:9■45:1,20■52:10,15■55:5■60:12■61:11■64:2■66:18,19,20-JER-1:5,10■3:17,19■4:2,16■6:18■9:26■10:7^{2},10■22:8■25:9,11,13,14,15,17,31■26:6■27:7^{2},11■28:11,14■29:14,18■30:11■31:7,10■33:9■36:2■43:5■44:8■46:12,28■50:2,9,12,23,46■51:7^{2},20,27^{2},28,41,44-LA-1:1

-EZE-5:5,6,7^2,8,14,15■6:8,9■12:15■19:4, 8■25:10■26:3,5■28:7■29:12,15^2■30:11, 23,26■31:6,12,16■32:2,9,12,16,18■ 35:10■36:13,14,15■37:22■38:8,12,23■ 39:27-DA-3:4(524),7(524)■4:1(524)■ 5:19(524)■6:25(524)■7:14(524)-HO- 8:10■9:17-JOE-3:2^2-AM-6:1■9:9-MIC- 4:2,3,11■7:16-NA-3:4,5-HAB-1:17■2:5, 8■3:6-ZEP-2:14■3:6,8-HAG-2:7^2-ZEC- 2:8,11■7:14■8:22,23■12:9■14:2,3, 16,19-MAL-3:12■N.T.-all=1484 -M'T-24:9,14■25:32■28:19-M'R-11:17■ 13:10-LU-12:30■21:24,25■24:47-AC- 13:19■14:16■17:26-RO-1:5■4:17,18■ 16:26-GA-3:8-RE-2:26■7:9■10:11■11:9, 18■12:5■13:7■14:8■15:4■16:19■17:15■ 18:3,23■19:15■20:3,8■21:24,26■22:2

NATIVE-JER-22:10(4138)

NATIVITY-all=4138&marked-GE-11:28-RU-2:11-JER-46:16-EZE-16:3, 4■21:30(4351)■23:15

NATURAL-DE-34:7(3893)■N.T.-all=5591&marked-RO-1:26(5446),27 (5446)■11:21(2596,5449),24(2596,5449) -1CO-2:14■15:44^2,46-JAS-1:23(1083) -2PE-2:12(5446)

NATURALLY-PH'P-2:20(1103) -JUDE-10(5447)

NATURE-all=5449&marked-RO-1:26■2:14,27■11:24^2-1CO-11:14-GA-2:15■ 4:8-EPH-2:3-JAS-3:6(1078)-2PE-1:4

NAUGHT-2KI-2:19(7451)-PR-20:14(7451)

NAUGHTINESS-1SA-17:28(7455) -PR-11:6(1942)■N.T.-JAS-1:21(2549)

NAUGHTY-PR-6:12(1100)■17:4 (1942)-JER-24:2(7451)

NAVEL-JOB-40:16(8306)-PR-3:8 (8270)-SONG-7:2(8326)-EZE-16:4(8270)

NAVES-1KI-7:33(1354)

NAVY-all=590-1KI-9:26,27■10:11,22^2

NAY-all=3808&marked-GE-18:15■ 19:2■23:11■33:10(408)■42:10,12-NU-22:30-JOS-5:14■24:21-J'G-12:5■19:23 (408),23sup-RU-1:13(408)-1SA-2:24 (408)■8:19■12:12-2SA-13:12(408),25 (408)■16:18■24:24-1KI-2:20(6440), 20sup■2:30■3:22,23-2KI-3:13(408)■ 4:16(408)■20:10-1CH-21:24-JER-6:15(1571)■8:12(1571)■N.T.-all= 3756&marked-M'T-5:37■13:29-LU-12:51(3780)■13:3(3780),5(3780)■ 16:30(3780)-JOH-7:12-AC-16:37 -RO-3:27(3780)■7:7(235)■8:37(235)■ 9:20(3304)-1CO-6:8(235)■12:22(235) -2CO-1:17,18,19-JAS-5:12

NEAR-all=5066,a=7126,b=7138& marked-GE-12:11a■18:23■19:9,20b■ 20:4a■27:21,22,25^2,26,27■29:10■33:3,6,7^2■ 37:18a■43:19■44:18■45:4^2,10b■48:10, 13-EX-12:48a■13:17b■14:20a■16:9a■ 19:22■20:21■24:2■28:43■30:20■40:32a -LE-9:5a■10:4a,5a■18:6(7607),12(7607), 13(7607),17(7608)■20:19(7607)■21:2b -NU-3:6b■5:16b■16:5^{2}a,9b,10b,40a■ 17:13b■31:48■32:16■36:1-DE-1:22a■ 4:11a■5:23a,27a■16:21(681)■21:5■25:11a -JOS-3:4a■10:24^{2}a■15:46(3027)■17:4a■ 18:13(5921)■21:1-J'G-18:22(5973)■ 19:13a■20:24a,34(5060)-RU-2:20b -1SA-7:10■9:18■10:20a,21a■14:36a,38■ 17:16,40,41a■30:21-2SA-1:15■14:30 (413)■18:25a■19:42b■20:16a,17a -1KI-8:46b■18:30^2,36■21:2b■22:24 -2KI-4:27■5:13-2CH-6:36b■18:23■ 21:16(3027)■29:31-ES-5:2a■9:1(5060) -JOB-31:37a■33:22a■41:16-PS-22:11b■ 32:9a■73:28(7132)■75:1b■107:18 (5060)■119:151b,169a■148:14b-PR-7:8(681)■10:14b■27:10b-IS-13:22b■ 26:17a■29:13■33:13b■34:1a■41:1, 1a,5a■45:20,21■46:13a■48:16a■ 50:8b,8■51:5b■54:14a■55:6b■56:1b■ 57:3a,19b■65:5-JER-12:2b■25:26b■ 30:21a■42:1■46:3■48:16b,24b■52:25 (7200)-LA-3:57a■4:18a-EZE-6:12b■ 7:7b,12(5060)■9:1a,6■11:3b■18:6a■ 22:4a,5b■30:3^{2}b■40:46(7131)■44:13^2, 15a,16a■45:4(7131)-DA-3:8(7127), 26(7127)■6:12(7127)■7:13(7127),16 (7127)■8:17(681)■9:7b-JOE-3:9,14b -AM-6:3-OB-15b-ZEP-1:14b■3:2a -MAL-3:5a■N.T.-all=1448&marked -M'T-21:34■24:33(1451)-M'R-13:28 (1451)-LU-15:1■18:40■19:41■21:8■ 22:47■24:15-JOH-3:23(1451)■4:5(4139)■ 11:54(1451)-AC-7:31(4334)■8:29 (4334)■9:3■10:24(316)■21:33■23:15■ 27:27(4317)-HEB-10:22(4334)

NEARER-RU-3:12(7138)■N.T.-RO-13:11(1452)

NECESSARY-JOB-23:12(2706)■ N.T.-all=316&marked-AC-13:46■15:28 (1876)■28:10(4314,3588,5532)-1CO-12:22-2CO-9:5-PH'P-2:25-TIT-3:14 -HEB-9:23(318)

NECESSITIES-AC-20:34(5532) -2CO-6:4(318)■12:10(318)

NECESSITY-all=318&marked-LU-23:17(2192,318)-RO-12:13(5532)-1CO-7:37■9:16-2CO-9:7-PH'P-4:16(5532) -PH'M-14-HEB-7:12■8:3(316)■9:16

NECK-all=6677,a=6203&marked -GE-27:16,40■33:4■41:42■45:14^2■46:29■ 49:8a-EX-13:13a■34:20a-LE-5:8a-DE-21:4a■28:48■31:27a-1SA-4:18(4665) -2KI-17:14a-2CH-36:13a-NE-9:29a -JOB-15:26■16:12a■39:19■41:22-PS-75:5-PR-1:9(1621)■3:3(1621),22(1621)■ 6:21(1621)■29:1a-SONG-1:10■4:4,9■ 7:4-IS-8:8■10:27■30:28■48:4a■52:2■ 66:3(6202)-JER-7:26(6202)■17:23 (6202)■27:2,8,11■28:10,11,12,14■30:8 -LA-1:14-EZE-16:11(1627)-DA-5:7 (6676),7(6676),16(6676),29(6676)-HOS-10:11(6676)-HAB-3:13(6676)■N.T.-all=5137-M'T-18:6-M'R-9:42-LU-15:20■17:2-AC-15:10■20:37

NECKS-all=6677&marked-JOS-10:24^2-J'G-5:30■8:21,26-2SA-22:41 (6203)-2KI-17:14(6203)-NE-3:5■9:16 (6203),17(6203)-PS-18:40(6203)-IS-3:16(1627)-JER-19:15(6203)■27:12 -LA-5:5-EZE-21:29-MIC-2:3■N.T. -RO-16:4(5137)

NECROMANCER-DE-18:11 (1875,4191)

NEED-DE-15:8(4270)-1SA-21:15 (2638)-2CH-2:16(6878)-EZR-6:9(2818) -PR-31:11(2637)■N.T.-all=5532& marked-M'T-3:14■6:8,32(5535)■9:12 (2192,5532)■14:16(2192,5532)■21:3■ 26:65-M'R-2:17,25■11:3■14:63(2192, 5532)-LU-5:31■9:11■12:30(5535)■15:7 (2192,5532)■19:31,34■22:71-JOH-13:29-AC-2:45■4:35-RO-16:2(5535) -1CO-7:36(3784)■12:21^2,24-2CO-3:1 (5535)-PH'P-4:19-1TH-1:8(2192,5532)■ 4:9■5:1-HEB-4:16(2121)■5:12^2■7:11■ 10:36-1PE-1:6(1163)-1JO-2:27 (2192,5532)■3:17-RE-3:17■21:23■22:5

NEEDED-JOH-2:25(2192,5532) -AC-17:25(4326)

NEEDEST-JOH-16:30(2192,5532)

NEEDETH-LU-11:8(5535)-JOH-13:10(2192,5532)-EPH-4:28(5532) -2TI-2:15(422)-HEB-7:27(2192,318)

NEEDFUL-EZR-7:20(2819)■ N.T.-LU-10:42(5532)-AC-15:5(1163) -PH'P-1:24(316)-JAS-2:16(2006) -JUDE-3(318)

NEEDLE-M'T-19:24(4476)-M'R-10:25(4476)

NEEDLE'S-LU-18:25(4476)

NEEDLEWORK-all=7551&marked -EX-26:36(4639,7551)■27:16■28:39■ 36:37■38:18■39:29-J'G-5:30^2(7553) -PS-45:14(7553)

NEEDS-all=318&marked-M'T-18:7 -LU-14:18-AC-21:2(3843)-RO-13:5

NEEDY-all=34&marked-DE-15:11■ 24:14-JOB-24:4,14-PS-9:18■12:5■35:10■ 37:14■40:17■70:5■72:4,12,13^2■74:21■ 82:3(7326),4■86:1■109:16,22■113:7 -PR-30:14■31:9,20-IS-10:2(1800), 14:30■25:4■26:6(1800)■32:7■41:17 -JER-5:28■22:16-EZE-16:49■18:12■ 22:29-AM-4:1■8:4,6

NEESINGS-JOB-41:18(5846)

NEGLECT-M'T-18:17^2(3878)-1TI-4:14(272)-HEB-2:3(272)

NEGLECTED-AC-6:1(3865)

NEGLECTING-COL-2:23(857)

NEGLIGENT-2CH-29:11(7952)■ N.T.-2PE-1:12(272)

NEIGHBOUR-all=7453,&marked -EX-3:22(7934)■11:2,2(7468)■12:4(7934)■ 20:16■21:14■22:7,9,10,14■32:27(7138) -LE-6:2^2(5997)■19:13,15(5997),16,17 (5997),18■24:19(5997)■25:14(5997),15 (5997)-DE-4:42■5:20■15:2^2■19:4,5^2, 11■22:26■23:25■27:24-JOS-20:5-RU-4:7-1SA-15:28■28:17-2SA-12:11-1KI-8:31■20:35-2CH-6:22-JOB-12:4■ 16:21-PS-12:2■15:3,3(7138)■101:5-PR-3:28,29■11:9,12■12:26■14:20,21■16:29■ 18:17■19:4■21:10■24:28■25:8,9,18■ 26:19■27:10(7934)■29:5-EC-4:4 -IS-3:5■19:2■41:6-JER-6:21(7934)■ 7:5■9:4^2,5,8,20(7468)■22:8■23:27,30, 35■31:34■34:15,17■49:18(7934)■50:40 (7934)-HAB-2:15-ZEC-3:10■8:10,16, 17■14:13^2■N.T.-all=4139-M'T-5:43■ 19:19■22:39-M'R-12:31,33-LU-10:27, 29,36-AC-7:27-RO-13:9,10■15:2-GAL-5:14-EPH-4:25-HEB-8:11-JAS-2:8

NEIGHBOUR'S-all=7453&marked -EX-20:17^3■22:8,11,26-LE-18:20(5997)■ 20:10■25:14(5997)-DE-5:21^3■19:14■ 22:24■23:24,25■27:17-JOB-31:9-PR-6:29■25:17-JER-5:8■22:13-EZE-18:6, 11,15■22:11■33:26-ZEC-11:6

NEIGHBOURS-all=7934&marked -JOS-9:16(7138)-RU-4:17-2KI-4:3-PS-28:3(7453)■31:11■44:13■79:4, 12■80:6■89:41-JER-12:14■49:10 -EZE-16:26■22:12(7453)■23:5(7138),12 (7138)■N.T.-all=1069&marked-LU-1:58(4040)■14:12■15:6,9-JOH-9:8

NEIGHBOURS'-JER-29:23(7453)

NEIGHED-JER-5:8(6670)

NEIGHING-JER-8:16(4684)

NEIGHINGS-JER-13:27(4684)

NEITHER-all=3808,a=408,b=369 &marked-GE-3:3■8:21■9:11^2■17:5■ 19:17a■21:26^2■22:12a■24:16■29:7■39:9■ 45:6b-EX-4:8,9,10(1571)■5:2(1571, 3808),23■7:22,23■8:32■9:29,35■10:6, 14,23■12:39(1571,3808),46■13:7■16:24■ 20:23,26■22:21,25,31■23:2^2,13,18■24:2■ 30:9,32■32:18b■34:3^2,24,25,28■36:6a -LE-2:13■3:17■5:11■7:18■10:6■11:43, 44■17:12■18:3,17,18,21,23^2■19:10,11^2, 13,16,19,26,27,31a■21:5,7,11,12,15■ 22:24,25,32■23:14,22■25:4,5,11■26:1^2, 6,20,44■27:33-NU-1:49■5:13■6:3■ 11:19■14:9a,23■16:15■18:3(3808,1571), 20,22,32■20:5b,17■21:5b■23:21,23,25■ 35:23■36:9-DE-1:21a,29,42■2:9a,27■ 4:2,28,31■5:18,19,20,21^2■7:3,16,26■ 8:3,4■9:9,18■13:8^3■16:4,19,22■17:17^2■ 18:16■20:3a■21:4,7■22:5■24:5,15,16■ 26:13,14■28:36,39,64,65■29:6,14■30:11, 13■31:8^2■32:28b,39b■33:9-JOS-1:9a■ 2:11■5:1,12■6:10■7:12■8:1a■11:14■ 23:7^2-J'G-1:27,29,30,31,33■2:23■8:23, 35■11:34b■13:6,7a,14a,23■20:8-RU-2:8(1571,3808)-1SA-1:15■2:2b■4:20■ 5:5■12:4■13:22■16:8(1571,3808),9(1571, 3808)■20:27(1571)■21:8(1571,3808)■ 24:11b■25:7,15■26:12b■27:9(3608),11 (3608)■28:6(1571),15(1571)■30:15(518)■ 19^2(4480)-2SA-1:21a■2:28■7:10,22b■ 12:17■13:22■14:7(1115),14■18:3 (518)19:6b■19a,24■20:1■21:4b,10■ 24:24-1KI-3:11,12,26(1571,3808)■5:4b■ 6:7■7:47■11:2■12:16■13:8,16■17:14, 16■18:29b■22:31-2KI-3:17■4:23,31b■ 5:17■6:19■7:10b■10:14■12:8(1115)■ 13:7,23■17:34b,38■18:30a■21:8■23:25 -1CH-4:27■17:9,20b■19:19■27:24 -2CH-1:11,12■6:5■9:9■13:20■20:12■ 25:4■26:18■30:3■32:15a■33:8■34:2,28■ 35:18-EZR-9:12a■10:13-NE-2:12,12b,

16■4:11,23b■5:5b,16■8:10a,11a■9:17,34,35-**ES**-2:7b■3:8b■4:16a-**JOB**-3:4a,9a,26^2■5:4b,6,21,22a■7:10■8:20■9:33■15:29^2■18:19■20:9■21:9■23:12■28:13,15,19■31:30■32:14,21■33:7,9■34:12■35:13■36:26■39:7,17,22,24-**PS**-5:4■6:1■16:10■18:37■22:24■26:4■27:9a■33:17■37:1a■38:3b■44:3,6,17■55:12■69:15a■73:5■74:9■75:6■78:37■81:9■82:5■86:8b■91:10■92:6■94:7,14■103:9■109:12a■115:7,17■121:4(3804)■129:8■131:1■135:17b-**PR**-3:11a■4:5a■6:25a,35■15:12■22:22■23:6a■24:1a,19a■27:10a■30:3,8a-**EC**-1:11■4:8(1571)b,8sup■5:6a■6:10■7:16a,17a■8:8b,8,13,16(1571)b■9:5b,6b,11-**SONG**-8:7-**IS**-1:6,23■2:4,7^2■3:7b■5:12,27■7:4a,7,12■8:12■9:13,17■10:7■11:3■13:20^3■16:10■17:8■19:15■22:11■23:4■26:18(1077)■28:27(1077)■29:22■31:1■33:20(1077),21■36:15a■40:28■42:24■43:2,10,18a,23,24■44:8a,19■47:7,8■49:10■50:5■51:7a,18b■53:9■54:4a,10■55:8■56:3^{2}a■57:16■59:1,6,9■60:19,20■62:4■64:4,9a■66:19,24-**JER**-2:6■3:16^4,17■4:28■5:12^2,15,24■6:15(1571,3808)■7:6,16^{2}a,31■8:12■9:10,13,16,23a■10:5(1571)b■11:14a■14:13,14^2■15:10■16:2,4,5,6,7^2,17■17:8,16,22^2,23■18:23a■19:4,5■21:7■22:3a,10a■23:4■25:33■29:8a,32■30:10a■32:23,35■33:18,22■34:14■35:7,9■37:2■38:16(518)■42:13(1115)■44:10■48:11■49:18,31■50:39,40■51:43,62(1115)-**EZE**-2:6a■3:9■4:14■5:7^2,11(1571),11■7:4,9,11,13,19■8:18■9:5a,10■11:12■13:9^2,15b■14:11,16(518),18,20(518)■16:4,16,49,51■17:17■18:6^3,8,15,16^2,20■20:8,17,18a,21■22:26■23:8■24:14,16^2■29:11,15■31:14^2■32:13■33:12■34:4^4,8,10,28,29■36:14,15^3■37:22,23■38:11b■39:10,29■44:20,21,22■47:12■48:14-**DA**-3:27(3809)■6:4(3809),18(3809)■8:4b■9:6,10■10:3^2,17■11:6,15^{2}b,17,20,37-**HO**-2:2■4:15a■9:4■14:3-**JO**-2:2,8-**AM**-2:14,15^2■5:22■7:14-**OB**-12^{2}a,14^{2}a-**JON**-3:7b■4:10-**MIC**-2:3■4:3,12-**HAB**-2:5■3:17b-**ZEP**-1:12,18■3:13-**ZEC**-8:10b■11:16■13:4-**MAL**-1:10^2■3:11■**N.T.**-all=3761,a=3777,b=3366,c=3756,d=2532,e=3383-**M'T**-5:15,34e,35e,36e■6:15,20a,26,28■7:6b,18■9:17■10:9(3361),10b■11:18e,27■12:4,19,32^{2}a■13:13■16:9,10■21:27■22:16d,c,30a,46■23:10b,13,13c■24:18(3361),20b■25:13e-**M'R**-4:22■5:4,d(3762)■8:14d(3762),17,26b■11:26,33■12:21,24b,25a■13:11b,15b,19c(3361),32■14:40d,c,59,68■16:8d(3762),13-**LU**-1:15c(3361)■3:14b■6:43■7:7,33e■8:17,27d,c,43c■9:3^{3}e■10:4(3361)■11:33■12:22b,24^{2}c,29(3361),33,47b■14:12b,35a■15:29(3763)■16:26b,31■17:21■18:2b,34d,c■20:8,21d,c,35a,36a-**JOH**-3:20d,c■4:15b,21a■5:37a■6:24■7:5■8:11,19a,42■9:3a■10:28d,c■13:16■14:17,27b■17:20b-**AC**-2:27,31■4:12d,c,32,34■8:21c■9:9c■15:10a■16:21■17:25■19:37a■20:24■21:21b■23:8b,12e,21e■24:12a,12^2(2228),13(2228),18c■25:8^{2}a■27:20e■28:21^{2}a-**RO**-1:21(2228)■2:28■6:13b■8:7,38a■9:7,11b■14:21(3361)-**1CO**-2:9d,c,14d,c■3:2(235)a,7^{2}a■5:8b■6:9a■8:8^{2}a■10:7b,8b,9b,10b■11:9(2542)c,11^{2}a,16■15:50-**GA**-1:1,12,12a,17■2:3■3:28^{3}c■5:6a■6:13,15a-**EPH**-4:27e■5:4d,c■6:9d,c-**PH'P**-2:16-**COL**-3:11c-**1TH**-2:5a,6a-**2TH**-2:2e■3:8,10b-**1TI**-1:4b,7e■5:22b-**HEB**-4:13d,c■7:3e■9:12,18,10:8-**JAS**-1:13(2582,3762),17(2228)■5:12^{2}e-**1PE**-2:22■3:14b■5:3b-**2PE**-1:8c-**1JO**-2:15b■3:6,18b-**2JO**-10b-**3JO**-10a-**RE**-3:15a,16a■5:3^2,4a■7:3e,16^2■9:20a,21d,c■12:8a■20:4a,4d,c■21:4a,23

NEPHEW-**JOB**-18:19(5220)-**IS**-14:22(5220)

NEPHEWS-**J'G**-12:14(1121)-**1TI**-5:4(1549)

NEST-all=7064&marked-**NU**-24:21-**DE**-22:6■32:11-**JOB**-29:18■39:27-**PS**-84:3-**PR**-27:8-**IS**-10:14■16:2■34:15(7077)-**JER**-22:23(7077)■48:28(7077)49:16-**OB**-4-**HAB**-2:9

NESTS-**PS**-104:17(7077)-**EZE**-31:6(7077)■**N.T.**-**M'T**-8:20(2682)-**LU**-9:58(2682)

NET-all=7568&marked-**EX**-27:4,5-**JOB**-18:8■19:6(4685)-**PS**-9:15■10:9■25:15■31:4■35:7,8■57:6■66:11(4685)■140:5-**PR**-1:17■12:12(4686)■29:5-**EC**-9:12(4686)-**IS**-51:20(4364)-**LA**-1:13-**EZE**-12:13■17:20■19:8■32:3,3(2674)-**HO**-5:1■7:12-**MIC**-7:2(2764)-**HAB**-1:15(2764),16(2764),17(2764)■**N.T.**-all=1350&marked-**M'T**-4:18(293)■13:47(4522)-**M'R**-1:16(293)-**LU**-5:5,6-**JOH**-21:6,8,11^2

NETHER-all=8482&marked-**EX**-19:17-**DE**-24:6(7347)-**JOS**-15:19■16:3(8481)■18:13(8481)-**J'G**-1:15-**1KI**-9:17(8481)-**1CH**-7:24(8481)-**2CH**-8:5(8481)-**JOB**-41:24-**EZE**-81:14,16,18■32:18,24

NETHERMOST-**1KI**-6:6(8481)

NETS-all=2764&marked-**1KI**-7:17(7638)-**PS**-141:10(4365)-**EC**-7:26-**IS**-19:8(4364)-**EZE**-26:5,14■47:10■**N.T.**-all=1350-**M'T**-4:20,21-**M'R**-1:18,19-**LU**-5:2,4

NETTLES-all=2738&marked-**JOB**-30:7-**PR**-24:31-**IS**-34:13(7057)-**HO**-9:6(7057)-**ZEP**-2:9

NETWORK-all=7639&marked-**EX**-27:4(4639,7568)■38:4(4639,7568)-**1KI**-7:18,20,42-**JER**-52:22,23

NETWORKS-**1KI**-7:41(7639),42(7639)-**IS**-19:9(2355)

NEVER-all=3808&marked-**GE**-41:19-**LE**-6:13-**NU**-19:2-**DE**-15:11-**J'G**-2:1(3808,5769)■14:3(369)■16:7,11-**2SA**-12:10(3808,5704,5769)-**2CH**-18:7(369)■21:17-**JOB**-3:16■9:30(1253)■21:25-**PS**-10:6(1755),11(1074,5331)■15:5(3808,5769)■30:6(3808,5769)■31:1(408,3808)■49:19(5704,5331,3808)■55:22(3808,5769)■71:1(408,5769)■119:93(5769,3808)-**PR**-10:30(5769,1077)■27:20^2■30:15-**IS**-13:20(3808,5331)■14:20(3808,5769)■25:2(5769,3808)■56:11■62:6■63:19(5769,3808)-**JER**-33:17(3808)-**EZE**-16:63■26:21(3808,3769)■27:36(5704,5769)■28:19(5704,5769)-**DA**-2:44(5957,3809)■12:1-**JOE**-2:26(3808,5769),27(3808,5769)-**AM**-8:7(518,5331),14-**HAB**-1:4(3808,5331)■**N.T.**-all=3763&marked-**M'T**-7:23■9:33■21:16,42■26:33■27:14(3761,1520)-**M'R**-2:12,25■3:29(3756,1519,3588,165)■9:43(3756),45(3756)■11:2(3762,4455)■14:21(3756)-**LU**-15:29■19:30(3762)■23:29^2(3756),53(3764)-**JOH**-4:14(3364,1519,3588,165)■6:35(165),35(3364,4455)■7:15(3361),46■8:33(3762,4455),51(3364,1519,3588,165),52(3364,1519,3588,165)■10:28(3364,1519,3588,165)■11:26(3364,1519,3588,165)■13:8(3364,1519,3588,165)■19:41(3764)-**AC**-10:14■14:8-**1CO**-13:8-**2TI**-3:7(3368)-**HEB**-10:1,11■13:5(3364)-**2PE**-1:10(3364,4219)

NEVERTHELESS-all=389&marked-**LE**-11:4,36-**NU**-13:28(657)■18:15■24:22(3588,518)■31:23-**DE**-14:7-**1SA**-15:35(3588)-**1KI**-8:19(7535)■15:4(3588),14(7535),23(7535)■22:43-**2KI**-3:3(7535)■13:6■23:9-**2CH**-12:8(3588)■15:17(7535)■19:3(61)■30:11■33:17(61)-**NE**-13:26(1571)-**PS**-31:22(403)-**IS**-9:1(3588)-**JER**-5:18(1571)■26:24■28:7■36:25(1571)-**DA**-4:15(1297)■**N.T.**-all=1161&marked-**M'T**-26:39(4133),64(4133)-**M'R**-14:36(235)-**LU**-5:5■13:33(4133)■18:8(4133)■22:42(4133)-**JOH**-11:15(235)■12:42(3676,3305)■16:7(235)-**AC**-14:17(2544)■27:11-**RO**-5:14(235)-15:15-**1CO**-7:2,28,37■19:12(235)■11:11(4133)-**2CO**-3:16■7:6(235)■12:16(235)-**GA**-2:20■4:30(235)-**EPH**-5:33(4133)-**PH'P**-1:24■3:16(4133)-**2TI**-1:12(235)■2:19(3305)-**HEB**-12:11-**2PE**-3:13-**RE**-2:4(235)

NEW-all=2319,a=2320&marked-**EX**-1:8-**LE**-23:16■26:10-**NU**-16:30(1278)■28:26-**DE**-20:5■22:8■24:5■32:1=7-**JOS**-9:13-**J'G**-5:8■15:13,15(2961)■16:11,12-**1SA**-6:7■20:5a,18a,24a-**2SA**-6:3^2■21:16-**1KI**-11:29,30-**2KI**-2:20■4:23a-**1CH**-13:7■23:31-**2CH**-2:4a■8:13a■20:5■31:3a-**EZR**-3:5a■6:4(2323)-**NE**-10:33a,39(8492)■13:5(8492),12(8492)-**JOB**-32:19-**PS**-33:3■40:3■81:3a■96:1■98:1■144:9■149:1-**PR**-3:10(8492)-**EC**-1:9,10-**SONG**-7:13-**IS**-1:13a,14a■24:7(8492)■41:15■42:9,10■43:19■48:6■62:2■65:8(8492),17■66:22,23a-**JER**-26:10■31:22,31■36:10-**LA**-3:23-**EZE**-11:19■18:31■36:26^2■45:17a■46:1a,3a,6a■47:12(1069)-**HO**-2:11a■4:11(8492)■9:2(8492)-**JOE**-1:10(8492)-**AM**-8:5a-**HAG**-1:11(8492)-**ZEC**-9:17(8492)■**N.T.**-all=2537,a=3501&marked-**M'T**-9:16(46),17^{2}a,17■13:52■26:28,29■27:60-**M'R**-1:27■2:21(46),21,22^{3}a,22■14:24,25■16:17-**LU**-5:36^3,37^{2}a,38a,38,39■22:20-**JOH**-13:34■19:41-**AC**-2:13(1098)■17:19,21-**1CO**-5:7a■11:25-**2CO**-3:6■5:17^2-**GA**-6:15-**EPH**-2:15■4:24-**COL**-2:16(3561)■3:10a-**HEB**-8:8,13■9:15■10:20(4372)■12:24a-**2PE**-3:13-**1JO**-2:7,8-**2JO**-5-**RE**-2:17■3:12^2■5:9■14:3■21:1,2,5

NEWBORN-**1PE**-2:2(738)

NEWLY-**DE**-32:17(7138)-**J'G**-7:19(6965)

NEWNESS-**RO**-6:4(2538)■7:6(2538)

NEWS-**PR**-25:25(8052)

NEXT-all=5921,3027&marked-**GE**-17:21(312)-**EX**-12:4(7138)-**NU**-11:32(4283)■27:11(7138)-**DE**-21:3(7138),6(7138)-**1SA**-17:13(4932)■23:17(4932)■30:17(4283)-**2KI**-6:29(312)-**1CH**-5:12(4932)■16:5(4932)-**2CH**-17:15,16,18■28:7(4932)■31:12(4932),15-**NE**-3:2^2,4^3,5,7,8^2,9,10^2,12,17,19■13:13-**ES**-1:14(7138)■10:3(4932)-**JON**-4:7(4283)■**N.T.**-all=1887&marked-**M'T**-27:62-**M'R**-1:38(2192)-**LU**-9:37(1836)-**JOH**-1:29,35■12:12-**AC**-4:3(839)■7:26(1966)■13:42(3342),44(2064)■14:20■16:11(1966)■20:15(1966),15(2087),15(2192)■21:8,26(2192)■25:6■27:3(2087),18(1836)■28:13(1206)

NIGH-all=7126,a=5066&marked-**GE**-47:29-**EX**-3:5■14:10■24:2a■32:19■34:30a,32a-**LE**-10:3(7138)■21:3(7138),21^{2}a,23a■25:49(7607)-**NU**-1:51■3:10,38■8:19a■18:3,4,7,22■24:17-**DE**-1:7(7934)■2:19■4:7■13:7■20:2,10■22:2■30:14-**JOS**-8:11a-**1SA**-17:48-**2SA**-10:13a■11:21a■15:5-**1KI**-2:1■8:59-**1CH**-12:40■19:14a-**ES**-9:20-**PS**-32:6(5060)■34:18■69:18■73:2(4952)■85:9(7138)■88:3(5060)■91:7a,10■119:150■145:18(7138)-**PR**-5:8-**EC**-12:1(5060)-**IS**-5:19-**JOE**-2:1■**N.T.**-all=1448,a=1451&marked-**M'T**-15:8,29(3844)■21:1■24:32a-**M'R**-5:11(4314),21(3844)■13:29a-**LU**-7:12■10:9,11■15:25■18:35■19:11a,29,37■21:20,28,30a,31a■22:1■24:28-**JOH**-6:4a,19a,23a■11:18a,55a■19:20a,42a-**AC**-7:17■9:38a■10:9■22:6■27:8a-**RO**-10:8a-**EPH**-2:13a,17a-**PH'P**-2:27(3897),30-**HEB**-6:8a■7:19-**JAS**-4:8■5:8

NIGHT-all=3915&marked-**GE**-1:5,14,16,18■8:22■14:15■19:5,33,34,35■20:3■26:24■30:15,16■31:24,39,40■32:13,21,22■40:5■41:11■46:2■49:27(6153)-**EX**-10:13■12:8,12,30,31,42^2■13:21^2,22■14:20^2,21■40:38-**LE**-6:9,20(6153)■8:35■11:16(8464)-**NU**-9:16,21■11:9,32■14:1,14■22:8,19,20-**DE**-1:33■14:15(8464)■16:1■23:10■28:66-**JOS**-1:8■2:2■4:3■8:3,9,13■10:9-**J'G**-6:25,27,40■7:9■9:32,34■16:2^2■19:25■20:5-**RU**-1:12■3:2,13-**1SA**-14:34,36■15:11,16■19:10,11,24■25:16■26:7■28:8,20,25■31:12

-2SA-2:29,32■4:7■7:4■17:1,16■19:7■21:10-1KI-3:5,19■8:29,59-2KI-6:14■7:12■8:21■19:35■25:4-1CH-9:33■17:3-2CH-1:7■6:20■7:12■21:9■35:14-NE-1:6■2:12,13,15■4:9,22■6:10■9:12,19-ES-4:16■6:1-JOB-3:3,6,7■4:13■5:14■7:4(6153)■17:12■20:8■24:14■26:10(2822)■27:20■30:17■33:15■34:25■35:10■36:20-PS-1:2■6:6■16:7■17:3■19:2■22:2■30:5(6153)■32:4■42:3,8■55:10■74:16■77:2,6■78:14■88:1■90:4■91:5■92:2■104:20■105:39■119:55■121:6■134:1■136:9■139:11,12-PR-7:9■31:15,18-EC-2:23■8:16-SONG-3:1,8■5:2-IS-4:5■5:11(5399)■15:1^{2}■16:3■21:4(5399),11^{2},12■26:9■27:3■28:19■29:7■30:29■34:10■38:12,13■59:10(5399)■60:11■62:6-JER-6:5■9:1■14:17■16:13■31:35■33:20^{2},25■36:30■39:4■49:9■52:7-LA-1:2■2:18,19-DA-2:19(3916)5:30(3916)■6:18(956)■7:2(3916),7(3916),13(3916)-HO-4:5■7:6-AM-5:8-OB-5-JON-4:10-MIC-3:6-ZEC-1:8■14:7■N.T.-all=3571&marked-M'T-2:14■14:25■26:31,34■27:64■28:13-M'R-4:27■5:5■6:48■14:27,30-LU-2:8,37■5:5■6:12(1273)■12:20■17:34■18:7■21:37-JOH-3:2■7:50■9:4■11:10■13:30■19:39■21:3-AC-5:19■9:24,25■12:6■16:9,33■17:10■18:9■20:31■23:11,23,31■26:7■27:23,27-RO-13:12-1CO-11:23-2CO-11:25(3574)-1TH-2:9■3:10■5:2,5,7^{2}-2TH-3:8-1TI-5:5-2TI-1:3-2PE-3:10-RE-4:8■7:15■8:12■12:10■14:11■20:10■21:25■22:5

NIGHTS-all=3515-GE-7:4,12-EX-24:18■34:28-DE-9:9,11,18,25■10:10-1SA-30:12-1KI-19:8-JOB-2:13■7:3-IS-21:8-JON-1:17■N.T.-all=3571-M'T-4:2,12:40^{2}

NINE-all=8672-GE-5:5,8,11,14,20,27■9:29■11:19,24■17:1,24-EX-38:24-LE-25:8-NU-1:23■2:13■29:26■34:13-DE-3:11-JOS-13:7■14:2■15:32,44,54■21:16-J'G-4:3,13-2SA-24:8-2KI-14:2■15:13,17■17:1■18:2-1CH-3:8■9:9-2CH-25:1■29:1-EZR-1:9■2:8,36,42-NE-7:38,39■11:1,8■N.T.-all=1768&marked-M'T-18:12,13-LU-15:4,7■17:17(1767)

NINETEEN-all=8672,6240-GE-11:25-JOS-19:38-2SA-2:30

NINETEENTH-all=8672,6240-2KI-25:8-1CH-24:16■25:26-JER-52:12

NINETY-all=8673-GE-5:9,17,30■17:1,17,24-1SA-4:15-1CH-9:6-EZR-2:16,20,58■8:35-NE-7:21,25,60-JER-52:23-EZE-4:5,9■41:12-DA-12:11■N.T.-all=1768-M'T-18:12,13-LU-15:4,7

NINTH-all=8671&marked-LE-23:32(8672)■25:22-NU-7:60-2KI-17:6■18:10(8672)■25:1,3(8672)-1CH-12:12■24:11■25:16■27:12-2CH-16:12(8672)-EZR-10:9-JER-36:9,22■39:1,2(8672)■52:4,6(8672)-EZE-24:1-HAG-2:10,18-ZEC-7:1■N.T.-all=1766-M'T-20:5■27:45,46-M'R-15:33,34-LU-23:44-AC-3:1■10:3,30-RE-21:20

NITRE-PR-25:20(5427)-JER-2:22(5427)

NO-all=3808,a=369,b=408&marked-GE-8:9■9:15■11:30a■13:8b■15:3■16:1■26:29■30:1a■31:50■32:28■37:22^{2},24,32■38:21,22,26■40:8a■41:44■42:11,31,34■44:23■45:1■47:4a,13a-EX-2:12a■3:19■5:7,16a,18■8:22(1115)■9:26,28^{2}■10:14,28,29■12:16,19,43,48■13:3,7■14:11a,13■15:22■16:4,18,19b,29b■17:1a■20:3■21:8,22■22:2a,10a■23:8,13,32■30:9,12■33:4,20■34:3,7,14,17■35:3-LE-2:11^{2}■5:11■6:30■7:23,24,26■11:12a■12:4■13:21a,26^{2}a,31a,32■16:17,29■17:7,12,14■19:15,35■20:14■21:3■22:10,13a,13,21■23:3,7,8,21,25,28,31,35,36■25:31a,36b■26:1,37■27:26,28-NU-1:53■3:4■5:8a,13a,15,19■6:3,5,6■8:19,25,26■14:8■16:40■18:5,20,23,24,32■19:2a,15a■20:2,5■21:5a■22:26a■23:23■26:33,62■27:3,4a,8a,9a,10a,11a,17a■28:18,25(3605,3803),26(3605,3803)■29:1(3605,3803),12(3605,3803),35(3605,3803)■33:14■35:31,32-DE-1:39■3:26b■4:12a,15■5:22■7:2,16,24■8:2,15a■10:9,16■11:17,25■12:12a■13:11,14:27a,29a■15:4,19■16:3,4,8■17:13,16■18:1,2■19:20■20:12■21:14■22:26a■23:14,17,22■24:1,6■25:5a■28:26a,29a,32a,65,68,68a■31:2■32:12a,20,39a■34:6-JOS-8:20,31■10:14■11:20(1115)■14:4■17:3■18:7■22:25a,27a■23:9,13-J'G-2:2■4:20a■5:19■6:4■8:28■10:13■11:39■13:5,7b,21■15:13■17:6a■18:1a,7^{2}a,10a,28^{2}a■19:1a,15a,18a,19a,30■21:12,25a-1SA-1:2a,11,15,18■2:3b,9,24■3:1a■6:7■7:13■10:14a,27■11:3a■13:19■14:6a,26a■15:35■17:32b,50a■18:2■20:21a,34■21:1a,2b,4a,6,9a■25:31■26:12a,21■27:4■28:10(518),15,20^{2}■29:3■30:4a,12-2SA-1:21b■2:28■6:23■7:10■12:6■13:12,16b■24:25■15:3a,26■18:13,18a,20,22a■20:1a,10■21:4a,17-1KI-1:1■3:2,18a,22,26b,27■6:18a■8:16,23a,35,46a■9:22■10:5,10,12■13:9,17,22b■17:7,17■18:10(518),23^{2},25,26a■21:4,5a■22:17,18,47a-2KI-1:16a,17■2:12■3:9■4:14a,41■5:15a,25■6:23■7:5a,10a■9:35■10:31■12:7b,8(1115)■17:4■19:18■22:7■23:10(1115),18b,25■25:3-1CH-2:34■12:17■16:21,22b■17:9■22:16a■23:22,26a■24:2,28-2CH-6:5,14a,26,36a■7:13■8:9■9:4■13:9■14:6a,11a■15:5a,19■17:10■18:16a,16■19:7a■20:12a■21:19■22:9a■32:15■35:18■36:16a,17-EZR-4:16(3809)■9:14a■10:6-NE-2:14a,17,20a■6:1,8■13:19,21,26-ES-1:19■2:14■5:12■8:8a■9:2-JOB-3:7b■4:18■5:19■7:7,8,9,10■9:25■10:18■11:3a■12:2(551),14,24■13:4(457)■14:12(1115)■15:3,15,19,28■16:18b■18:17■19:7,16■20:9,21■23:6■24:7a,15,20,22■26:2,3,6a■28:7,18■30:13,17■32:3,5a,15,16,19■34:22a,32■36:16,19■38:11,26^{2}■40:5■41:8b,16■42:2,15-PS-3:2a■5:9a■6:5a■10:18(1077)■14:1a,4■19:3a■22:6■23:4■32:2a,9a■33:16a■34:9a■36:1a■38:3a,7a,14a■39:13a■40:17b■41:8■50:9■53:1a,4,5■55:19a■63:1(1097)■69:2a■70:5b■72:12a■73:4a■74:9a■77:7■78:64■81:9■83:4■84:11■88:4a,5■91:10■92:15■101:3■102:27■103:16■104:35a■105:14,15b■107:4,40■119:3■142:4^{2}a■143:2■144:14^{2}a■146:3a-PR-1:24a■3:30■6:7a■8:24^{2}a■10:22,25a■11:14a■12:21,28b■14:4a■17:16a,20,21■18:2■21:10,30a■22:24b■24:20■25:28a■26:20(657),20a■28:1a,3a,17b,24a■29:9a,18a■30:20,27a,31(510)■31:7,11-EC-1:9a,11a■2:11a,16a■3:11(1097),12a,19a■4:1^{2}a,8a,13,16a■5:4a■6:3,6■7:21(808)■8:5,8^{2}a,15a■9:1a,8b,10a,15■10:11a,20b■12:1a,12a-SONG-4:7a■5:6■8:8a-IS-1:6,13,30a■5:8(675)■13(1097)■8:20a■9:7a,17,19■10:15,20■13:14a,18■14:8■15:6■16:10^{2}■19:7a■23:10a,12^{2}■26:21■27:11^{2}■28:8(1097)■29:16■30:7(7385),16,19■32:5■33:8,21(1077)■34:16■35:9■37:19■38:11■40:20,28a,29a■41:28^{2}■43:10,11a,12a,24■44:6a,8a,12■45:5a,9a,14(657)20,21a■47:1a,1,5,6■48:22a■50:2^{3}a,10a■51:22■52:1,11b■53:2^{2},9■54:17■55:1a■57:1a,21a■58:3■59:8a,10a,15a,16^{2}a■60:15a,18,19,20■62:4,7b,8(518)■65:19,20-JER-2:6^{2},11,13,25sup,25,30,31■3:3,16■4:22,23a,25a■5:7■6:10,14a,23■7:32,32a■8:6a,11a,13a,15a,22^{2}a■10:14■11:1923■12:11a,12a■14:3,4,5,6a,19^{2}a■16:14,19a,20■17:21b,24^{2}(1115)■19:6,11a■22:3b,10,12,28(363),30■23:4,7,17,36■25:6,27,35(4480)■30:8,13a,17a■31:29,34^{2}■35:6^{2},8(1115)■36:19b■38:6a,9a,24b■39:12b■40:15■41:4■42:14^{2},18■44:2a,5(1115),17,22,26(518)■45:3■48:2a,8,33,38a■49:1a,7a,18,33,36■50:14b,39,40■51:17,43■52:6-LA-1:3,6,9a■2:9a,9,18b■4:4a,6,15,16,22■5:5-EZE-12:23,24,25■13:10a,15a,16a,21,23■14:11,15(1097)■15:5■16:34,41,42■18:32■19:9,14■20:39■21:13,27,32■22:26■24:6,17,27■26:13,14,21a■28:3,9,24■29:11,15,16,18■30:13■33:11(518),22■34:5(1097),8a,22,28,29■36:12,14,29,30■37:8a,22■39:10■43:7■44:2,9,17,25^{2},28■45:8-DA-1:4a■2:10(3609,3809),35(3609,3809)■3:25(3809),27(3809),29(3809)■4:9(3609,3809)■6:2(3809),15(3609,3809),22(3809),23(3609,3809)■8:4,7■10:3,8^{2},16,17-HO-1:6■2:16,17■4:1a,4b■8:7^{2}a,8a■9:15,16(1077)■10:3a■13:4,4a-JOE-1:18a■2:19■3:17-AM-3:4a,5a■5:2,20■6:10(657)■7:14■9:15-MIC-3:7a■4:9a■5:12,13■7:1a-NA-1:12,14,15■2:13■3:18a,19a-HAB-1:14■2:19a■3:17^{2}-ZEP-2:5a■3:5,6(1097),11-HAG-2:12-ZEC-1:21■4:5,13■8:10,17■9:8,11■10:2(639)■11:6■13:2,5■14:11,17,18,21-MAL-1:10(639)■N.T.-all=3762,a=3756,b=3361,c=3367,d=3765,e=3364,f=3370&marked-M'T-5:18e,20e,26e■6:1a,24,25b,31b,34b■8:4c,10(3761),28b■9:16,30,36b,10:19b,42e■11:27■12:39a■13:5b,6b■16:4a,7a,8a,20■17:8,9■19:6d,18a■20:7,13a■21:19f■22:23b,24b,25b,46■23:9b■24:4b,22a(3956),36,36(3761)■25:3a,42^{2}a■26:55a-M'R-1:45f■2:2f,2sup,17a,21,22■3:27■4:5b,6b,7a,17a,40a■5:3,3(3777),37,43c■6:5,8b,31(3761)■7:12d,24,36c■8:12(1487),16a,17a,30c■9:3a,8,9c,25f,39■10:8d,29■11:14c■12:14,18b,19b,20a,22a,34■13:11b,20a(3956),32,32sup■14:25d-LU-1:7a,33a■2:7a■3:13c,14c■4:24■5:14c,36,37,39■7:9(3761),44a,45a■8:13a,14a,16,27a,51,56c■9:13a,21c,36,62■10:4c,22,11:20(686),29a,33,36(3365,5100)■12:4(3365,5100),11b,17a,22b,33a,13:11b■15:7a,16,19d,21d■16:2a,13■18:17e,29■20:22a,31a■22:36b,53a■23:4,14,15(235),22-JOH-1:18,21a,47a■2:3a■3:2,13,32■4:9a,17^{2}a,27,38a,44a■5:7a,14f,22■6:37e,44,53a,65,66d■7:4,13,18a,27,30,44,52a■8:10,11,11f,15,20,37a,44a■9:4,41a■10:18,29,41■11:10a,54d■13:8a,28■14:6,19d■15:4(3761),13,22a■16:10d,21d,22,25d,29■17:11d■18:38■19:4,6a,9a,11a,15a■21:5a-AC-1:20b■4:17b,17c■5:13,23■7:5sup,5a,11a■8:39d■9:7c,8■10:34a■12:18a■13:28c,34f,37a,41e■15:2a,9,24a,28c■16:28c■18:10,15a■19:23a,24a,26a,40c■20:25d,33,38d■21:25c,39a■23:8b,9,22c■25:10,11,26a■27:20a,22■28:2a,5,6c,18c,31(209)-RO-2:11a■3:9a,9(3843),18a,20a(3956),22a■4:15a,15(3761)■5:13b■6:9^{2}d■7:3b,17d,18a,20d■8:1■10:12a,19a■11:6^{4}d,12:17c■13:1a,8c,10a■14:7,13b■15:23f-1CO-1:7c,10b,29b(3956)■2:11,15■3:11,18c,21c■4:6b,11(790)■7:25a,37b■8:13e■9:10(1063)■10:13a,24c,25c,27c■11:16a■12:3^{2},21^{2}a,24a,25b■13:5a■14:2,28b■15:12a,13a■16:2b,11b-2CO-2:13a■3:10(3761)■5:16,16d■21b,6:3c■7:2^{3},5■8:15a,20b■11:9,10a(3762),14,15,16c■13:7b,c-GA-2:6,6a,16a(3956)■3:11,15,18d,25d■4:7d,8b■5:4(2673),23a,6:17c-EPH-2:12b,19d■4:14f,28f,29b■5:5(3956)a,6c,11b,29-PH'P-2:7(5013),20■3:3a■4:15-COL-2:16b,18c■3:25a-1TH-3:1f,3c,5f■4:6b,13b■5:1a-2TH-2:3b■3:14b-1TI-1:3b■3:3b■4:12c■5:22c,23f■6:16^{2}-2TI-2:4,14■3:9a■4:16-TIT-1:7b■2:8c,15c■3:2c,2(269)-HEB-5:4a■6:13■7:13■8:7a,12e■9:17b,22a■10:2c,6a,17b,18d,26d,38a■12:11(3956)a,14,17a■13:10a,14a-JAS-1:13c,17a■2:11a,13b■3:8,12-1PE-2:22a■3:10b■4:2f-2PE-1:20(3956)a-1JO-1:5a,8a■2:7a,21(3956)a,27a■3:5a,7c,15(3956)a■4:12,18a-3JO-4a-RE-2:17■3:7^{2},8,11c,12e■5:3,4■7:9,16a■10:6a■13:17b■14:3,5a,11a■15:8■17:12(3768)■18:7a,7e,11,14e,21e,22^{2}e,22(3956)e,23^{2}e■19:12■20:3b,6a,11a■21:1a,4a,22a,23a,25a,27e■22:3a,5^{2}a

NOBLE-EZR-4:10(3358)-ES-6:9(6579)■N.T.-AC-17:11(2104)■24:3(2908)■26:25(2908)-1CO-1:26(2104)

NOBLEMAN-LU-19:12(2104,444)-JOH-4:46(937),49(937)

NOBLES-all=2715&marked-EX-24:11(678)-NU-21:18(5081)-J'G-5:13(117)-1KI-21:8,11-2CH-23:20(117)-NE-2:16■3:5(117)■4:14,19■5:7■6:17■7:5■10:29(117)■13:17-ES-1:3(6579)-JOB-29:10(5057)-PS-83:11(5081)■149:8(3513)-PR-8:16(5081)-EC-10:17-IS-13:2(5081)■34:12■43:14(1281)-JER-14:3(117)■27:20■30:21(117)■39:6-JON-3:7(1419)-NA-3:18(117)

NOISE-all=6963&marked-EX-20:18■32:17^{2},18-JOS-6:10(8085)-J'G-5:11-1SA-4:6^{2},14^{2}■14:19(1995)-1KI-1:41,45-2KI-7:6^{2}■11:13-1CH-15:28(8085)-2CH-23:12-EZR-3:13^{3}-JOB-36:29(8663),33(7452)■37:2(7267)-PS-33:3(8643)■42:7■55:2(1949)■59:6(1993),14(1993)■65:7^{2}(7588)■93:4■98:4sup,4(6476)-IS-13:4^{2}■14:11(1998)■17:12(1993)■24:8(7588),18■25:5(7588)■29:6■31:4(1995)■33:3■66:6(7588)-JER-4:19(1993),29■10:22■11:16■25:31(7588)■46:17(7588)■47:3■49:21^{2}■50:46■51:55(7588)-LA-2:7-EZE-1:24^{3}■3:13^{3}■19:7■26:10,13(1995)■37:7■43:2-JOE-2:5^{2}-AM-5:23(1995)-MIC-2:12(1949)-NA-3:2-ZEP-1:10-ZEC-9:15■N.T.-M'T-9:23(2350)-2PE-3:10(4500)-RE-6:1(5456)

NOISED-M'T-2:1(191)-LU-1:65(1255)-AC-2:6(1096,5408)

NOISESOME-PS-91:3(1942)-EZE-14:15(7451),21(7451)-RE-16:2(2556)

NONE-all=3808,a=369&marked-GE-23:6(376,3808)■28:17a■39:9a,11a■41:8a,15a,24a,39a-EX-8:10a■9:14a,24■11:6■12:22■15:26■16:26,27■23:15■34:20-LE-18:6(376,3808)■21:1■22:30■25:26■26:6a,17a,36a,37a■27:29(3606,3808)-NU-7:9■9:12■21:35(1115)■30:8(6565)-DE-2:34■3:3(1115)■4:35a,39a■7:15■22:27a■28:31a,66■32:36(657)■33:26a-JOS-6:1a■8:22(1115)■9:23■10:21,28,30,33(1115),37,39,40■11:8(1115),13,22■13:14■14:3-J'G-19:28a■21:8(3808,376),9a(376)-RU-4:4a-1SA-2:2^{2}a■3:19■10:24a■14:24■21:9a■22:8sup,8a-2SA-7:22a■14:6a,19(376),25(3808,376)■22:42a-1KI-3:12■8:60a■10:21a■12:20■15:22a■21:25-2KI-6:12■9:10a,15(408)■10:11(1115),19(376,408),25(408)■17:18■18:5■24:14-1CH-15:2■17:20a■23:17■29:15a-2CH-1:12■9:11,20a■10:16■16:1(1115)■20:6a,24a■23:6(408),19-EZR-8:15-NE-4:23a-ES-1:8a■4:2a-JOB-1:8a■2:3a,13a■3:9a■10:7a■11:19a■18:15(1097)■20:21a■29:12■32:12a■35:10,12■41:10-PS-7:2a■10:15(1077)■14:1a,3a■18:41a■22:11a,29■25:3■33:10(5106)■34:22■37:31■49:7(376,3808)■50:22a■53:1a,3a■69:20a,20,25(408)■71:11a■73:25■76:5■79:3a■81:11■86:8a■107:12a■109:12(408)■139:16(3808,259)-PR-1:25,30■2:19■3:31(408)-SONG-4:2a-IS-1:31a■5:27a,27,29a■10:14■14:6(1097),31a■17:2a■22:22^{2}a■34:10a,12a,16(802,3808)■41:17a,26^{3}a■42:22^{2}a■43:13a■44:19■45:5a,6(657),6a,14a,18a,21a,22a■46:9a,9(657)■47:8(657),10a,10(657),15a■50:2a■51:18a■57:1a■59:4a,11a■63:3a(376),5^{2}a■64:7a■66:4a-JER-4:4a,22■7:33a■9:10(1097,376),12(1997),22a■10:6a,7a,20a■13:19a■14:16a■21:12a■23:14(1115)■30:7a,10a,13a■34:9(1115),10(1115)■35:14■36:30■42:17■44:7(1115),14^{2}■46:27a■48:33■49:5a■50:3,9,20a,29(408),32a■51:62(1115)-LA-1:2a,4(1997),7a,17a,21a■2:22■5:8a-EZE-7:11,14a,25a■12:28■16:5,34■18:7■22:30■31:14■33:16,28a■34:6a,28a■39:26a,28-DA-1:19■2:11(3809)■4:35(3809)■6:4(3809)■8:7,27a■10:21a■11:16a,45a■12:10-HO-2:10■5:14a■7:7a■11:7■12:8-JOE-2:27a-AM-5:2a,6a-OB-7a-MIC-2:5■3:11■4:4a■5:8a■7:2a-NA-2:8a,9a,11a■3:3a-ZEP-2:15(657)■3:6(1097),6a,13a-HAG-1:6a-ZEC-7:10(408)■8:17(408)-MAL-2:15(408)■N.T.-all=3762,a=3756&marked-M'T-12:43a■15:6(208)■19:17■26:60^{2}a-M'R-7:13(208)■10:18■12:31a,32a■14:55a-LU-1:61■3:11(3361)■4:26,27■11:24(3361)■13:6a,7a■14:24■18:19,34-JOH-6:22a■7:19■8:10(3367)■15:24■16:5■17:12■18:9■21:12-AC-3:6a■4:12(3777)■7:5a■8:16,24(3367)■11:19(3367)■18:17■20:24■24:23(3367)■25:11,18■26:22,26(5100,3762)a-RO-3:10a,11^{2}a,12a■4:14(2673)■8:9a■9:6(1601)■14:7-1CO-1:14,17(1758)■2:8■7:29(3361)■8:4■9:15■10:32(677)■14:10-2CO-1:13a-GA-1:19a■3:17(208)■5:10-1TH-5:15(3361,5100)-1TI-5:14(3361)-1PE-4:15(3387)-1JO-2:10a-RE-2:10(3367),24(3367)

NOON-all=6672-GE-43:16,25-2SA-4:5-1KI-18:26,27■20:16-2KI-4:20-PS-55:17-SONG-1:7-IS-58:10■59:10-JER-6:4-AM-8:9-ZEP-2:4■N.T.-AC-22:6(3314)

NOONDAY-all=6672-DE-28:29-JOB-5:14■11:17-PS-37:6■91:6-IS-16:3-JER-15:8

NOONTIDE-JER-20:16(6256,6672)

NOR-all=3808,a=408,b=369&marked-GE-45:5a-EX-4:1,10(1571)■10:6■11:6■20:5■22:21,28■23:24■34:3a,28■36:6a-LE-11:26b■12:4■17:16■19:4,14,15,18,20,26,28■21:5,10,11,12,23■22:22■25:4,11,20,37■27:10-NU-5:15■6:3■9:12■11:19^{2}■23:25-DE-1:45■2:19a■4:28,31■5:9■7:2,3,7■9:9,18,23■10:17■12:32■13:8■14:1,8■15:7,19■17:16■18:22■21:4■22:30■23:17■24:17sup,17■26:14■28:39,50■29:23■31:6a,6■33:9■34:7-JOS-1:5■6:10■10:25a■13:13a■22:19a,26,28■23:7^{2}■24:12-J'G-2:10(1571)■11:34(176)■13:14a,23(3908)■14:16(3908)■19:30(3908)-1SA-12:4,21■15:29■20:27(1571)■21:8(1571)■26:12b■28:6(1571),15(1571),18■30:12,15(518),19^{2}(5703)-2SA-3:34■19:24-1KI-3:11■5:4b■8:5,57a■10:12■12:24■13:8,9^{2},16sup,16,17^{2},28■18:26b,29b■20:8-2KI-3:14(518)■4:23,31b■6:10■14:6,26b■17:35^{2}■18:12■19:32^{2},32sup-1CH-22:13a■28:20a,20-2CH-5:6■11:4■20:15a,17a■29:7■32:7a,7sup,15a-EZR-9:12■10:6-NE-8:9a■9:31,34^{2}■10:30■13:25(518)-ES-3:2■4:16a■5:9■9:28-JOB-1:22■7:19■14:12■18:19^{2}■24:13■27:4(518)■28:8■34:19,22b■36:19-PS-1:1^{2}■15:3^{2},5■16:4(1077)■19:3b■22:24■24:4■37:33■40:4■49:7■59:3■89:22,33,34■103:10■121:4■131:1■144:14(369)-PR-5:13■21:30b■31:4a-EC-1:8■3:14b■6:5■9:11^{3}-SONG-2:7(518)■3:5(518)-IS-3:7b■5:6,27^{3}■8:12■11:9■22:2■23:4,4sup,18■28:28sup,28■30:5^{2}■31:4■32:5■35:9(1077)■37:33^{3}■40:16b■42:2^{2},4■43:23■44:9(1077),19,20■45:13,17■46:7■48:1,19■49:10^{2}■51:14■52:12■53:2■57:11■59:4b■64:4■65:17,23,25-JER-4:11■6:20,25a■7:16a,22,24,26,28■8:2,13b■11:8■13:14■15:10■16:5,6^{2}■17:23(1115)■19:5■20:9■21:7■23:4,32■25:4,33■31:40■35:7^{2},9(1115),15■36:24■42:14^{2}■44:5,10,23,23^{2}sup■46:6a■49:31,33-EZE-2:6a■3:18■7:11,12a■13:23■14:16a,20(518)■16:4■20:18a■22:24■23:27■24:16,22,23■29:5,11■32:13■44:20■48:14-DA-3:12(3809),14(3809),18(3809),27^{2}(3809),28(3809)■5:10a,23(3809)■6:4(3809)■10:3■11:4,20,37-HO-1:10■4:1^{2}b,4a,15a■5:13■7:10-AM-5:5■8:11-OB-13a-JON-3:7sup,7a-MIC-5:7-ZEP-1:6,18(1571)■3:13-ZEC-1:4■4:6■8:10b■11:16^{2}■14:7■N.T.-all=3777,a=3761,b=3366&marked-M'T-5:35(3383)■6:20,20a,25b,26a■10:9b,10(3361),10b,14b,24a■11:18(3383)■12:19a■22:29b,30■24:21(3364a)■25:13a-M'R-6:11b■8:26b■12:25-LU-1:15(2532)■6:44a■7:33(3383)■9:3(3383)■10:4(3361)■12:24^{2}a■14:12^{2}(3364),35■17:23(3364)■18:4(3756)■20:35■21:15a■22:68(2228)■23:15a-JOH-1:13^{2}a,25■4:21■5:37■8:19■9:3■11:50a■12:40(2532)■16:3a-AC-4:18b■8:21a■9:9a■13:27(2532)■15:10■19:37■23:8(3383)■24:12,18a■25:8■27:20(3383)-RO-8:38^{3},39■9:16a■14:21^{2}b-1CO-2:6a,9(2532,3756)■6:9^{2},10,10^{2}(3756)■10:32(2532)■12:21(2228)-2CO-4:2b■7:12a-GA-3:28^{3}a■4:14a■5:6■6:15-EPH-5:4(2532),4(2228),5(2228)-COL-3:11^{2}(2532),11sup-1TH-2:3a,3,5,6^{2}■5:5a-2TH-2:2(3383)-1TI-1:7(3383)■2:12a■6:16a,17b-2TI-1:8b-HEB-7:3(3383)■9:25a■12:5b,18(2532)■13:5a(3364)-2PE-1:8a-RE-3:15,16■5:3a■7:1(3383),3(3383),16a■9:20,21^{3}■14:11(2532)■21:4

NORTH-all=6828&marked-GE-28:14-EX-26:20,35■27:11■36:25■38:11-NU-2:25■34:7,9■35:5-JOS-8:11,13■11:2■15:5,6,10■16:6■17:9,10■18:5,12^{2},16,17,19■19:14,27■24:30-J'G-2:9■7:1■21:19-1KI-7:25-2KI-16:14-1CH-9:24-2CH-4:4-JOB-26:7■37:9(4215),22-PS-48:2■89:12■107:3-PR-25:23-EC-1:6■11:3-SONG-4:16-IS-14:13,31■41:25■43:6■49:12-JER-1:13,14,15■3:12,18■4:6■6:1,22■10:22■13:20■16:15■23:8■25:9,26■31:8■46:6,10,20,24■47:2■50:3,9,41■51:48-EZE-1:4■8:3,5^{2},14■9:2■20:47■21:4■26:7■32:30■38:6,15■39:2■40:20,23,35,40,44^{2},46■41:11■42:1^{2},2,4,11,13,17■44:4■46:9^{2},19■47:15,17^{2}■48:1,10,16,17,30-DA-11:6,7,8,11,13,15,40,44-AM-8:12-ZEP-2:13-ZEC-2:6■6:6,8^{2}■14:4■N.T.-LU-13:29(1005)-AC-27:12(5566)-RE-21:13(1005)

NORTHERN-JER-15:12(6828)-JOE-2:20(6830)

NORTHWARD-all=6828-GE-13:14-EX-40:22-LE-1:11-NU-3:35-DE-2:3■3:27-JOS-13:3■15:7,8,11■17:10■18:18,19-J'G-12:1-1SA-14:5-1CH-26:14,17-EZE-8:5■40:19■47:2,17■48:1,31-DA-8:4

NOSE-all=639-LE-21:18(2763)-2KI-19:28-JOB-40:24■41:2-PR-30:33-SONG-7:4,8-IS-3:21■37:29■65:5-EZE-8:17■23:25

NOSES-PS-115:6(639)

NOSTRILS-all=639&marked-GE-2:7■7:22-EX-15:8-NU-11:20-2SA-22:9,16-JOB-4:9■27:3■39:20(5170)■41:20(5156)-PS-18:8,15-IS-2:22-LA-4:20-AM-4:10

NOTABLE-DA-8:5(2380),8(2380)■N.T.-M'T-37:16(1978)-AC-2:20(2016)■4:16(1110)

NOTE-IS-30:8(2710)■N.T.-RO-16:7(1978)-2TH-3:14(4593)

NOTED-DA-10:21(7559)

NOTHING-all=3808,a=369,b=3808,1697&marked-GE-11:6(3808,3605)■19:8b■26:29(7535)■40:15(3808,3972)-EX-9:4■12:10,20■16:18■21:2(2600)■22:3a■23:26-NU-6:4■11:6a(3605)■16:26(408,3605)■22:16(408)-DE-2:7■20:16(3808,3605)■22:26b■28:55(3605)-JOS-11:15b-J'G-3:2■7:14a■14:6(3972)a-1SA-3:18■20:2b■22:15b■25:21(3808,3972),36b■27:1a■30:19-2SA-12:3a(3605)■24:24(2600)-1KI-4:27b■8:9a■10:21(3808,3972)■11:22■18:43(3808,3972)■22:16-2KI-10:10■20:13b,15(1697),17b-2CH-5:10a■9:2b■14:11a■18:15-EZR-4:3-NE-2:2a■5:8,12■8:10■9:21-ES-2:15b■5:13a■6:3b,10(1697)-JOB-6:18(8414),21■8:9■24:25(408)■26:7(1099)■34:9-PS-17:3(1077)■19:6a■39:5a■49:17(3808,3605)■119:165a-PR-8:8a■9:13(1077,4100)■10:2■13:4a,7(3808,3605)■20:4a■22:27a-EC-2:24a■3:14a,22a■5:14(3808,3972),15(3808,3972)■6:2a■7:14(3808,3972)-IS-34:12(657)■39:2b,4b,6b■40:17a,17(657,8414),23a■41:11a,12a,24a,29(657)■44:10(1115)-JER-10:24(4591)■13:7(3808,3605),10(3808,3605)■32:17b,23■38:14(408,1697)■39:10(3808,3972)■42:4b■50:26(408)-LA-1:12-EZE-13:3(1115)-DA-4:35(3809)-JOE-2:3-AM-3:4(1115),5,7b-HAG-2:3a■N.T.-ll=3762,a=3367&

marked-M'T-5:13■10:26■15:32(3756, 5100)■17:20■21:19■23:16,18■26:62■27:12,19a,24-M'R-1:44a■4:22(3756, 5100)■5:26a■6:8a,36(3756,5100)■7:15■8:1(3385),2(3756,5100)■9:29■11:13■14:60,61■15:3(3756,3762),4,5-LU-1:37 (3756,3956,4487)■4:2■5:5■6:35a■7:42 (3361)■8:17(3756)■9:3a■10:19■11:6 (3756,3739)■12:2■22:35■23:9,15,41 -JOH-3:27■4:11(3777)■5:19,30(3756, 3762)■6:12(3361,5100),39(3361,848),63■7:26■8:28,54■9:33■11:49(3756)■12:19■14:30■15:5■16:23,24■18:20■21:3-AC-4:14,21a■10:20a■11:8(3956,2763),12a■17:21■19:36a■20:20■21:24■23:14a,29a■25:25a■26:31■27:33a■28:17-RO-14:14 -1CO-1:19(114)■4:4,5(3385)■7:19^{2}■8:2, 4■9:16(3756)■13:2,3-2CO-6:10a■7:9a■8:15(3756)■12:11^{2}■13:8(3756,5100) -GA-2:6■4:1■5:2■6:3a-PH'P-1:20,28a■2:3a■4:6a-1TH-4:12a-1TI-4:4■5:21a■6:4a,7,7(3761,5100)-TIT-1:15■3:13a -PH'M-14-HEB-2:8■7:14,19-JAS-1:4a, 6a-3JO-7a-RE-3:17

NOTICE-2SA-3:36(5234)-2CO-9:5(4293)

NOTWITHSTANDING-all=389 &marked-EX-21:21-LE-27:28-DE-12:15(7535)-JOS-22:19-J'G-4:9(657)-1SA-29:9-1KI-11:12-2KI-23:26-2CH-6:9 (7535)■N.T.-all=4133&marked-LU-10:11,20-PH'P-1:18■4:14-RE-2:20(235)

NOUGHT-all=2600&marked-GE-29:15-DE-13:17(408,3972)■15:9(3808)■28:63(8045)-NE-4:15(6565)-JOB-1:9■8:22(369)■14:18(5034)■22:6-PS-33:10 (6331)■44:12(3808,1952)-PR-1:25(6544) -IS-8:10(6565)■29:20(656),21(8414)■41:12(657),24(659)■49:4(8414)■52:3, 5-JER-14:14(434)-AM-5:5(205)■6:13 (3808,1697)-MAL-1:10sup,10■N.T.-all=1848&marked-M'R-9:12(1847)-LU-23:11-AC-4:11■5:36(3762),38(2647)■19:27(557)-RO-14:10-1CO-1:28(2673)■2:6(2673)-2TH-3:8(1432)-RE-18:17(2049)

NOURISH-GE-45:11(3557)■50:21 (3557)-IS-7:21(2421)■23:4(1431)■44:14(1431)

NOURISHED-GE-47:12(3557) -2SA-12:3(2421)-IS-1:2(1431)-EZE-19:2(7235)■N.T.-all=5142&marked -AC-7:20(397),21(397)■12:20-1TI-4:6 (1789)-JAS-5:5-RE-12:14

NOURISHER-RU-4:15(3557)

NOURISHETH-EPH-5:29(1625)

NOURISHING-DA-1:5(1431)

NOURISHMENT-COL-2:19(2023)

NOVICE-1TI-3:6(3504)

NOW-all=6258,a=4994&marked-GE-2:23(6471)■3:22■4:11■11:6■12:11a,19■15:5a■16:2a■18:3a,21a,27a,31a■19:2a, 8a,9(6288),19a,20a■20:7■21:23■22:12■24:42a,49■26:22,28a,29■27:26a,36,37 (645),43■29:32,34(6471,6258),35■30:20 (6471),30sup,30■31:12a,13,16,28,30,42, 44■32:4,10■33:10a,15a■37:20,32a■43:10,11(645)■44:10,30,33■45:5,8■46:30(6471),34■47:4■48:5■50:4a,5,17^{2}a, 21-EX-3:3a,9,10,18■4:6a,12■5:5,18■6:1■9:15,18,19■10:11a,17■11:2a■18:11, 19■19:5■32:10,30,32,34■33:5,13,13a■34:9a-NU-11:6,23■12:6a,13a■14:17,19 (2008),22(2088),41(2088)■20:10a■22:4,6,11,19,29,33,34,38■24:11,14,17■31:17-DE-2:13■4:1,32a■5:25■10:12, 22■26:10■31:19,21(3117)■32:39-JOS-1:2■2:12■3:12■5:5(3588),14■7:19a■9:6,11,12,19,23,25■13:7■14:10^{2},11, 12■22:4^{2},26a,31(227)■24:14,23-J'G-6:13,17a,39a■7:3(6288)■8:2(6288), 6,15■9:16,32,38,38(645)■11:7,8,13,23, 25■12:6a■13:3a,4a,7,12■14:2,12a■15:3(6471),18■16:10■17:3,13■18:14■19:9a,24a■20:9,13-RU-2:2a,7■3:2,11, 12-1SA-2:16(3588,6258),30■6:7■8:5,9■9:3a,6,6a,9(3117),12,13■10:19■12:2,7, 10,13,16■13:12,13,14■14:17a,30■15:1,3, 25,30■16:15a,16a,17■17:17a,29■18:22■19:2■20:29,31,36a■22:7a,12a■23:20■24:20,21■25:7,7sup,17,26^{2},27■26:8, 11,16,19,20■27:1,5a■28:22■29:7,10 -2SA-2:6,7,14a■3:18■4:11■7:2a,8,25, 28,29■12:10,23,28■13:7a,13,17a,20, 24a,25a,28sup,28a,33■14:2a,15, 15a,17a,18a,21a,32■15:34■16:11■17:1a, 5a,9,16■18:3^{2},19a■19:7^{2},9,10■20:6■24:2a, 10,13,14a,16-1KI-1:12,18,18sup■2:9,16, 24■3:7■5:4,6■8:25,26■12:4,11,16,26■13:6a■14:14■17:24■18:11,14,19,43a■19:4■20:31a■21:7■22:13a,23-2KI-1:5 (2088),14■2:16a■3:15,23■4:9a,13a,26■5:6,8a,15a,15,22■6:1a■7:4,9,12a■8:6■9:12a,26,34a■10:2,10(645),19■12:7■13:19■18:19a,20,21,23,25■19:19,25■20:3a-1CH-17:7,23,26,27■21:8,12,13a, 15■22:5a,11,19■28:8,10■29:13,17,20a -2CH-1:9,10■2:7,13,15■6:16,17,40,41■7:15,16■10:4,16■13:8■18:22■19:7■20:10■25:19■28:10,11■29:5,10,11,31■30:8■32:15■35:3-EZR-4:13(3705),14, 21,23(116)■5:16(3705),17(3705)■6:6 (3705)■9:8,10,12■10:2,3,11,14a-NE-1:6a,6(3117),11a■5:5■6:6,7,9■9:32 -JOB-1:11a■2:5a■3:13■4:5■5:1a■6:3, 21,28■7:21■8:6■12:7a■13:6a,18a,19■14:16■16:7,19■17:3a,10a,15(645)■19:6 (645),23(645)■22:21a■24:25(645)■30:1, 9,16■33:2a■35:15■37:21■38:3a■40:7a, 10a,15a,16a■42:5,8-PS-2:10■12:5■17:11■20:6■27:6■39:7■50:22a■74:6■115:2a■116:14a,18a■118:2,3a,4a,25^{2}a■119:67■122:8a■124:1a■129:1a-PR-5:7■6:3(645)■7:12(6471),24■8:32-EC-2:1a, 16(3528)■3:15(3528)■9:6(3528),7(3528) -SONG-3:2a■7:8a-IS-1:18a,21■5:1a, 3,5■7:3a,13a■16:14■19:12a■22:1(645)■28:22■29:22■30:8■33:10^{3}■36:4a,5,8, 10■37:20,26■38:3a■43:1,19■44:1■47:8,12a,13a■48:7,16■49:5,19■51:21a■52:5■64:8-JER-2:18■4:12,31a■5:1a,21a, 24a■7:12a,13a■14:10a■17:15a■18:11, 11a,13a■25:5a■26:13■27:6,16,18a■28:7a,15a■29:27■30:6a■32:36■34:15 (3117)■35:15a■36:15a,17a■37:3a,20■38:12a,25a■40:4■42:15,22■44:7■45:3a -EZE-4:14■7:3,8■8:5a,8a■17:12a■18:25a■19:13■23:43■26:18■39:25■43:9■46:12(3588)-DA-2:23^{2}(3705)■3:15 (3705)■4:37(3705)■5:12(3705),15(3705), 16(3705)■6:8(3705),10(1768),16(116)■9:15,17,22■10:11,20■11:2-HO-2:7,10■4:16■5:7■8:10,13■10:2,3■13:2-JOE-2:12-AM-6:7■7:16-JON-4:3-MIC-4:9, 10,11■5:1,4■6:1a,5a■7:4,10-NA-1:13 -HAG-1:5■2:2a,3,4,11a,15a,18a-ZEC-1:4a■3:8a■5:5a■8:11■9:8-MAL-1:8a, 9■2:1■3:10a,15■N.T.-all=1161,a=3568, b=2236,c=737,d=3767,e=3570& marked-M'T-1:18,22■2:1■3:10b,15c■4:12■8:18■9:18c■10:2■11:2,12c■14:15b, 24b■15:32b■21:18■22:25■24:32■26:6, 17,20,45(3063),48,53c,65a,69■27:15,42a, 43a,45,54,62■28:11-M'R-1:14■4:37 (2235)■5:11■6:35^{2}b■8:2b,14(2532)■10:30a■11:11b■12:20d■13:12,28■14:41 (3063)■15:6,32a,42b■16:9-LU-1:57■2:15(1211),29a,41(2532)■3:1,9b,21■4:40■5:4■6:21^{2}a,25a■7:1,6b,12,39■8:11,22 (2532),38■9:7■10:36d,38■11:7b,39a■14:17b■15:25■16:25a■18:22■19:37b, 42a■20:37■21:30^{2}b■22:1,36a■23:47■24:1(2532)-JOH-1:44■2:8a,10c,23■4:6, 18a,23a,42(3765),43,51b■5:2,6b,25a■6:10(1160),17b■7:2,14b■8:5,40a,52a■9:19c,21a,25c,31,41a■11:1,5,18,22a,30, 57■12:27a,31^{2}a■13:1,2b,7c,19c,23,28, 31a,33c,36a,37c■14:29a■15:3b,22a,24a■16:5a,12c,19d,22a,29a,30a,31c,32a■17:5a,7a,11(3765),13a■18:14,24d,36a,40■19:23,25,28b,29d,41■21:4b,6(3765),7d, 10a,14b-AC-1:18d■2:6,33a,37■3:1,17a■4:3b,13,29a■5:24,38a■7:4a,11,34a,52a■8:14■9:36■10:5a,17,33a■11:19d■12:1,11a, 18■13:1,11a,13,43■15:10a■16:6,36a, 37a■17:1,16,30a■18:14■20:22a,25a,32a■21:3■22:1a■16a■23:15a,21a■24:13a,17■25:1d■26:6a,17a■27:9,9^{2}(2235),22a-RO-1:10b,13■3:19,21a■4:4,19b,23■5:9a,11a■6:8,19a,21a,22e■7:6e,17e,20■8:1a,9,22a■11:12,30a,31a■13:11b,11a■14:15(3765)■15:5,8(1160),13,23e,25e,30,33■16:17,25, 26a-1CO-1:10,12■2:12■3:2a,8,12■4:7 (2532),8b,18■5:11e■6:7b,13■7:1,14a, 25■8:1■9:25d■10:6,11■11:2,17■12:1,4, 18e,20a,27■13:12^{2}c,13e■14:6e■15:12, 20e,50■16:1,5,7c,10-2CO-1:21■2:14■3:17■5:5,16a,20d■6:2^{2}a,13■7:9a■8:11e, 14a,22e■9:10■10:1■13:2a,7-GA-1:9c, 10c,20b,23a■2:20a■3:3a,16,20■4:1b,9a,20c, 25a,28,29a■5:19-EPH-2:2a,13e,19d■3:5a, 10a,20■4:9■5:8a-PH'P-1:5a,20a,30a■2:12a■3:18a■4:10b,15,20-COL-1:21e, 24a,26e■3:8e-1TH-3:6c,8a,11■5:14-2TH-2:1,6a,7c,16■3:6,12,16-1TI-1:5,17■4:1,8a■5:5-2TI-1:10a■3:8■4:6b-PH'M-9e,11e, 16(3765)-HEB-2:8a■7:4■8:1,6e,13■9:5a, 6,24a,26a■10:18,38■11:1,16e■12:11, 26a■13:20-JAS-2:11■4:13a,16a■5:1a-1PE-1:6c,8c,12a■2:10^{2}a,25a■3:21a-2PE-3:1b, 7a,18a-1JO-2:8b,9c,18a,28a■3:2a■4:3a -2JO-5a-JUDE-24,25a-RE-12:10c

NUMBER-all=4557,a=6485& marked-GE-13:16(4487)■15:5(5608)■34:30■41:49-EX-12:4(4373)■16:16■23:26■30:12a-LE-15:13(5608),28(5608)■23:16(5608)■25:8(5608),15^{2},16,50-NU-1:2,3a,18,20,22,24,26,28,30,32,34,36, 38,40,42,49a■3:15^{2}a,22,28,34,40,40a,43, 48(5736)■4:23a,29a,30a,37a,41a■14:29, 34■15:12^{2}■23:10■26:53■29:18,21,24,27, 30,33,37■31:36-DE-4:27■16:9^{2}(5608)■25:2■32:8-JOS-4:5,8-J'G-6:5■7:6,12■21:23-1SA-6:4,18■14:17a-2SA-2:15■21:20■24:1(4487),2a,2,4a,9(4662)-1KI-18:31■20:25(4487)-1CH-7:2,9(3187),40 (4557,3187)■11:11■21:1(4487),2(5608),2, 5(4662)■22:16■23:3,24,31■25:1, 7■27:1,23,24(4487)24-2CH-12:3■26:11, 12■29:32■35:7-EZR-1:9■2:2■3:4■6:17 (4510)■8:34-NE-7:7-EZR-9:11-JOB-1:5■3:6■5:9■9:10■14:5■15:20■21:21■25:3■31:37■34:24(2714)■36:26■38:21, 37(5608)■39:2(5608)-PS-90:12(4487)■105:12,34■147:4-SONG-6:8-IS-21:17■40:26■65:11(4507),12(4487)-JER-2:28, 32■11:13^{2}■44:28-EZE-4:4,5,9■5:3-DA-9:2-HO-1:10-JOE-1:6■N.T.-all=706 &marked-M'R-10:46(3793)-LU-22:3 -JOH-6:10-AC-1:15(3793)■4:4■5:36■6:7■11:21■16:5-RO-9:27-2CO-10:12(1469) -1TI-5:9(2639)-RE-5:11■7:4,9■9:16 (705),16■13:17,18^{3}■15:2■20:8

NUMBERED-all=6485&marked -GE-13:16(4487)■16:10(5608)■32:12 (5608)-EX-30:13,14■38:25,26-NU-1:19, 21,22,23,25,27,29,31,33,35,37,39,41,43, 44^{2},45,46,47■2:4,6,8,9,11,13,15,16,19,21, 23,24,26,28,30,31,32^{2},33■3:16,22^{2},34, 39^{2},42,43■4:34,36,37,38,40,41,42,44,45^{2}, 46^{2},48,49^{2}■7:2■14:29■26:7,18,22,25,27, 34,37,41,43,47,50,51,54,57,62^{2},63^{2},64^{2} -JOS-8:10-J'G-20:15^{2},17■21:9-1SA-11:8■13:15■14:17■15:4-2SA-18:1■24:10 (5608)-1KI-3:8(4487)■8:5(4487)■20:15^{2}, 26,27-2KI-3:6-1CH-21:17(4487)■23:3 (5608),27(4557)-2CH-2:17^{2}(5608)■5:6 (4487)■25:5-EZR-1:8(5608)-PS-40:5 (5608)-EC-1:15(4487)-IS-22:10(5608)■53:12(4487)-JER-33:22(5608)-DA-5:26 (4483)-HO-1:10(5608)■N.T.-M'T-10:30(705)-M'R-15:28(3049)-LU-12:7(705)-AC-1:17(2674),26(4785)

NUMBEREST-EX-30:12^{2}(6485) -JOB-14:16(5608)

NUMBERING-GE-41:49(5608) -2CH-2:17(5610)

NUMBERS-1CH-12:23(4557) -2CH-17:14(6486)-PS-71:15(5615)

NURSE-all=3243&marked-GE-24:59■35:8-EX-2:7^{2},9-RU-4:16(539) -2SA-4:4(539)-2KI-11:2-2CH-22:11■N.T.-1TH-2:7(5162)

NURSED-EX-2:9(5134)-IS-60:4 (539)

NURSING-NU-11:12(539)-IS-49:23(539),23(3243)

NURTURE-EPH-6:4(3809)

NUTS-GE-43:11(992)■N.T.-SONG-6:11(93)

O

OAK-all=424&marked-GE-35:4,8(437)-JOS-24:26(427)-J'G-6:11,19-2SA-18:9^2,10,14-1KI-13:14-1CH-10:12-IS-1:30■6:13(437)■44:14(437)-EZE-6:13

OAKS-all=437&marked-IS-1:29(352)■2:13-EZE-27:6-HO-4:13-AM-2:9-ZEC-11:2

OAR-EZE-27:29(4880)

OARS-IS-33:21(7885)-EZE-27:6(4880)

OATH-all=7621,a=423&marked-GE-24:8,41^{2}a■26:3,28a■50:25(7650)-EX-22:11-LE-5:4-NU-5:19(7650),21^2■30:2,10,13-DE-7:8■29:12a,14a-JOS-2:17,20■9:20-J'G-21:5-1SA-14:26,27(7650),28(7650)-2SA-21:7-1KI-2:43■8:31^{2}a■18:10(7650)-2KI-11:4(7650)-1CH-16:16-2CH-6:22^{2}a■15:15-NE-5:12(7650)■10:29-PS-105:9-EC-8:2■9:2-JER-11:5-EZE-16:59a■17:13a,16a,18a,19a-DA-9:11-ZEC-8:17■N.T.-all=3727&marked-M'T-14:7■26:72-LU-1:73-AC-2:30■23:21(332)-HEB-6:16,17■7:20(3728),21^2(3728),28(3728)-JAS-5:12

OATH'S-M'T-14:9(3727)-M'R-6:26(3727)

OATHS-EZE-21:23(7621)-HAB-3:9(7621)■N.T.-M'T-5:33(3727)

OBEDIENCE-all=5218&marked-RO-1:5■5:19■6:16■16:19,26-1CO-14:34(5293)-2CO-7:15■10:5,6-PH'M-21-HEB-5:8-1PE-1:2

OBEDIENT-all=8085&marked-EX-24:7-NU-27:20-DE-4:30■8:20-2SA-22:45-PR-25:12-IS-1:19■42:24■N.T.-AC-6:7(5219)-RO-15:18(5218)-2CO-2:9(5255)-EPH-6:5(5219)-PH'P-2:8(5255)-TIT-2:5(5293),9(5293)-1PE-1:14(5218)

OBEISANCE-all=7812-GE-37:7,9■43:28-EX-18:7-2SA-1:2■14:4■15:5-1KI-1:16-2CH-24:17

OBEY-all=8085&marked-GE-27:8,13,43-EX-5:2■19:5■23:21,22-DE-11:27,28■13:4■21:18,20■27:10■28:62■30:2,8,20-JOS-24:24-1SA-8:19■12:14,15■15:19,22-NE-9:17-JOB-36:11,12-PS-18:44-PR-30:17(3349)-IS-11:14(4928)-JER-7:23■11:4,7■12:17■18:10■26:13■35:14■38:20■42:6^2,13-DA-7:27(8086)■9:11-ZEC-6:15■N.T.-all=5219&marked-M'T-8:27-M'R-1:27■4:41-LU-8:25■17:6-AC-5:29(3980),32(3980)■7:39(5255,1036)-RO-2:8(544),8(3982)■6:12,16(5218),16-GA-3:1(3982)■5:7(3982)-EPH-6:1-COL-3:20,22-2TH-1:8■3:14-TIT-3:1(3980)-HEB-5:9■13:17(3982)-JAS-3:3(3982)-1PE-3:1(544)■4:17(544)

OBEYED-all=8085-GE-22:18■26:5■28:7-JOS-5:6■22:2-J'G-2:2■6:10-1SA-15:20,24■28:21-1KI-20:36-2KI-18:12-1CH-29:23-2CH-11:4-PR-5:13-JER-3:13,25■9:13■11:8■17:23■32:23■34:10■35:8,10,18■40:3■42:21■43:4,7■44:23-DA-9:10,14-ZEP-3:2-HAG-1:12■N.T.-all=5219&marked-AC-5:36(3982),37(3982)-RO-6:17■10:16-PH'P-2:12-HEB-11:8-1PE-3:6

OBEYEDST-1SA-28:18(8085)-JER-22:21(8085)

OBEYETH-all=8085-1SA-50:10-JER-7:28■11:3

OBEYING-J'G-2:17(8085)-1SA-15:22(8085)■N.T.-1PE-1:22(5218)

OBJECT-AC-24:19(2723)

OBLATION-all=8641,a=7133&marked-LE-2:4a,5a,7a,12a,13a■3:1a■7:14a,29a■22:18a-NU-18:9a■31:50a-IS-19:21(4503)■40:20■66:30(4503)-JER-14:12(4503)-EZE-44:30■45:1,6,7^2,13,16■48:9,10,12(8642),18,20^2,21^3-DA-2:46(4541)■9:21(4503),27(4503)

OBLATIONS-LE-7:38(7133)-2CH-31:14(8614)-IS-1:13(4503)-IS-1:13(4503)-EZE-20:40(4864)■44:30(8641)

OBSCURE-PR-20:20(380)

OBSCURITY-IS-29:18(652)■58:10(2822)■59:9(2822)

OBSERVATION-LU-17:20(3907)

OBSERVE-all=8104&marked-EX-12:17^2,24■31:16(6213)■34:11,22(6213)-LE-19:26(6049),37-NU-28:2-DE-5:32■6:3,25■8:1■11:32■12:1,28,32■15:5■16:1,12,13(6213)■17:10■24:8^2■28:1,13,15,28■31:12■32:46-JOS-1:7,8-J'G-13:14-1KI-20:33(5172)-2KI-17:37■21:8-2CH-7:17-NE-1:5■10:29-PS-105:45■107:43■119:34-PR-23:26(5341)-JER-8:7-EZE-20:18■37:24-HO-13:7(7789)-JON-2:8■N.T.-all=5083&marked-M'T-23:3^2■28:20-AC-16:21(4160)■21:25-GA-4:10(3906)-1TI-5:21(5442)

OBSERVED-all=8104&marked-GE-37:11-EX-12:42^2(8107)-NU-15:22(6213)-DE-33:9-2SA-11:16-2KI-21:6(6049)-2CH-33:6(6049)-HO-14:8(7789)■N.T.-M'R-6:20(4933)■10:20(5442)

OBSERVER-DE-18:10(6049)

OBSERVERS-DE-18:14(6049)

OBSERVEST-IS-42:20(8104)

OBSERVETH-EC-11:4(8104)

OBSTINATE-DE-2:30(553)-IS-48:4(7186)

OBTAIN-GE-16:2(1129)-PR-8:35(6329)-IS-35:10(5381)■51:11(5381)-DA-11:21(2388)■N.T.-all=5177&marked-M'T-5:7(1653)-LU-20:35-RO-11:31(1653)-1CO-9:24(2638),25(2983)-1TH-5:9(4047)-2TI-2:10-HEB-4:16(2983)■11:35-JAS-4:2(2013)

OBTAINED-all=5375&marked-NE-13:6(7592)-ES-2:9,15,17■5:2-HO-2:23■N.T.-all=1653&marked-AC-1:17(2975)■22:28(2932)■26:22(5177)■27:13(2902)-RO-11:7^2(2013),30-1CO-7:25-EPH-1:11(2820)-1TI-1:13,16-HEB-1:4(2816)■6:15(2013)■8:6(5177)■9:12(2147)■11:2(3140),4(3140),33(2013),39(3140)-1PE-2:10^2-2PE-1:1(2975)

OBTAINETH-PR-12:2(6329)■18:22(6329)

OBTAINING-2TH-2:14(4047)

OCCASION-all=5931&marked-GE-43:18(1556)-J'G-9:33(4672)■14:4(8385)-1SA-10:7(4672)-EZR-7:20(5308)-JER-2:24(8385)-DA-6:4^2,5■N.T.-all=874&marked-RO-7:8,11■14:13(4625)-2CO-5:12■8:8(1223)■11:12-GA-5:13-1TI-5:14-1JO-2:10(4625)

OCCASIONED-1SA-22:22(5437)

OCCASIONS-DE-22:14(5949),17(5949)-JOB-33:10(8569)

OCCUPATION-GE-46:33(4639)■47:3(4639)-JON-1:8(4399)■N.T.-AC-18:3(5078)

OCCUPIED-all=5414&marked-EX-38:24(6213)-J'G-16:11(6213,4399)-EZE-27:16,19,21(5503),22■N.T.-HEB-13:9(4043)

OCCUPIERS-EZE-27:27(6148)

OCCUPIETH-1CO-14:16(378)

OCCUPY-EZE-27:9(6148)■N.T.-LU-19:13(4231)

OCCURRENT-1KI-5:4(6294)

ODD-NU-3:48(5736)

ODIOUS-1CH-19:6(887)-PR-30:23(8130)

ODOUR-JOH-12:3(3744)-PH'P-4:18(3744)

ODOURS-LE-26:31(5207)-2CH-16:14(1314)-ES-2:12(1314)-DA-2:46(5208)■N.T.-RE-5:8(2368)■18:13(2368)

OFF-all=5921-GE-7:4■8:3,7,8,11sup,11,13■24:64■27:40■38:14■40:19^2-LE-8:28■16:12-NU-7:89■10:11■12:10■16:46-DE-4:26■6:15■11:17■21:13■25:9■28:21,63-JOS-5:9,15■10:27■15:18■23:13,15,16-J'G-1:14■4:15■13:20■15:14■16:12-1SA-4:18■6:5^3■17:39■25:23-2SA-11:2,24■12:30-2KI-16:17^2-1CH-20:2-IS-6:6■10:27^2■14:25^2■20:2,2sup■25:8^2-JER-24:10■28:10,12,16■30:8-EZE-10:18-HO-11:4-AM-9:8-MIC-3:2sup,2,3-NA-1:13-ZEP-1:2(5921,6440),3(5921,6440)■N.T.-all=609&marked-M'T-5:30(1581)■8:30(575)■10:14(1621)■18:8(1581)■26:51(851),58(575)■27:31(1562),55(575)-M'R-5:6(575)■6:11(1621)■9:43,45■11:8(1537)■14:47,54(575)■15:20,40(575)-LU-9:5(660)■10:11(631)■15:20(568)■16:23(575)■22:50(851)-JOH-11:18(575)■18:10,26-AC-7:33(3089)■12:7(1601)■13:51(1621)■16:22(4048)■22:23(4496)■27:32,32(1601)■28:5(660)-RO-11:17(1575),19(1575),20(1575),22(1581)■13:12(659)-2CO-11:12(1581)-GA-5:12-EPH-2:13(3112)■4:22(659)-COL-2:11(554)■3:8(659),9(554)-1TI-5:12(114)-2PE-1:14(595)-RE-18:10(575),15(575),17(575)

OFFENCE-1SA-25:31(4383)-IS-8:14(4383)-HO-5:15(816)■N.T.-all=3900&marked-M'T-16:23(4625)■18:7(4625)-AC-24:16(677)-RO-5:15^2,17,18,20■9:33(4625)■14:20(4348)-1CO-10:32(677)-2CO-6:3(4349)■11:7(266)-GA-5:11(4625)-PH'P-1:10(677)-1PE-2:8(4625)

OFFENCES-EC-10:4(2399)■N.T.-all=4625&marked-M'T-18:7^2-LU-17:1-RO-4:25(3900)■5:16(3900)■16:17

OFFEND-all=816&marked-JOB-34:31(2254)-PS-73:15(898)■119:165(4383)-JER-2:3■50:7-HO-4:15-HAB-1:11■N.T.-all=4624&marked-M'T-5:29,30■13:41(4625)■17:27■18:6,8,9-M'R-9:42,43,45,47-LU-17:2-JOH-6:61-1CO-8:13^2-JAS-2:10(4417)■3:2^2(4417)

OFFENDED-all=2398&marked-GE-20:9■40:1-2KI-18:14-2CH-28:13(819)-PR-18:19(6586)-JER-37:18-EZE-25:12(816)-HO-13:1(816)■N.T.-all=4624&marked-M'T-11:6■13:21,57■15:12■24:10■26:31,33^2-M'R-4:17■6:3■14:27,29-LU-7:23-JOH-16:1-AC-25:8(264)-RO-14:21-2CO-11:29

OFFENDER-IS-29:21(2398)■N.T.-AC-25:11(91)

OFFENDERS-1KI-1:21(2400)

OFFER-all=6213,a=7126,b=5927&marked-GE-22:2b-EX-23:18(2076)■29:36,38,39^2,41■30:9b■34:25(7819)■35:24(7311)-LE-1:3^{2}a■2:1a,12a,13a,14^{2}a■3:1^{2}a,3a,6a,7^{2}a,9a,12a,14a■4:14a■5:8a,10■6:14a,20a,21a,22■7:3a,11a,12^{2}a,13a,14a,25a,38a■9:2a,7^2■12:7a■14:12a,19,20b,30■15:15,30■16:6a,9,24■17:4a,5^2(2076),7(2076),9■19:5^2(2076),6(2077)■21:6a,17a,21^{2}a■22:15(7311),18^{2}a,20a,22a,23,24a,25a,29^2(2076)■23:8a,12,16a,18a,25a,27a,36^{2}a,37a■27:11a-NU-5:25a■6:11,14a,16,17^2■7:11a,18a■8:11(5130),12,13(5130),15(5130)■9:7a■15:7a,14,19(7311),20(7311),24■18:12(5414),19(7311),24(7311),26(7311),28(7311),29(7311)■28:2a,3a,4^2,8^2,11a,19a,20,21,23,24,27a,31■29:2,8a,13a,36a-DE-12:13b,14b,27■18:3(2076)■27:6b,7(2076)■33:19(2076)-JOS-22:23b,23-J'G-3:18a■6:26b■11:31b■13:16,16b■16:23(2076)-1SA-1:21(2076)■2:19(2076),28b■10:8b-2SA-24:12(5190),22b,24b-1KI-3:4b■9:25b■13:2(2076)-2KI-5:17■10:24-1CH-16:40b■21:10(5186),24b■23:31b-2CH-23:18b■24:14b■29:21b,27b■35:12a,16b-EZR-3:2b,6b■6:10(7127)■7:17(7127)-JOB-42:8b-PS-4:5(2076)■16:4(5258)■27:6(2076)■50:14(2076)■51:19b■66:15b,15■72:10a■116:17(2076)-IS-57:7(2076)-JER-14:12b■33:18b-EZE-6:13(5414)■20:31(5375)■43:18b,22a,23a,24a,24b■44:7a,15a,27a■45:1(7311),13(7311)■46:4a■48:8(7311),9(7311),20(7311)-DA-2:46(5260)-HO-9:4(5258)-AM-4:5(6999)■5:22b-HAG-2:14a-MAL-1:7(5066),8^2(5066),8a■3:3(5066)■N.T.-all=4374&marked-M'T-

5:24■8:4-M'R-1:44-LU-2:24(1325)■5:14■6:29(3930)■11:12(1929)-HEB-5:1,3■7:27(399)■8:3^{2},4■9:25■13:15(399)-1PE-2:5(399)-RE-8:3(1325)

OFFERED-all=5927,a=7126,b=2076&marked-GE-8:20■22:13■31:54b■46:1a-EX-24:5■32:6■35:22(5130)■40:29-LE-7:8a,15(7133)■9:15(2398),16(6213)■10:1a,19a■16:1a-NU-3:4a■7:2a,10^{2},12a,19a■8:21(5130)■16:35a,38a,39a■22:40b■23:2,4,14,30■26:61a■28:15(6213),24(6213)■31:52(7311)-JOS-8:31-J'G-6:28■13:19■20:26■21:4-1SA-1:4b■2:13b■6:14,15■7:9■13:9,12-2SA-6:17■15:12b■24:25-1KI-3:15,15(6213)■8:62b,63^{2}b,64(6213)■12:32,33^{2}■22:43b-2KI-3:20,27■16:12-1CH-6:49(6999)■15:26b■16:1a■21:26■29:21-2CH-1:6■4:6(4639)■7:4b,5b,7(6213)■8:12■15:11b■24:14■29:7-EZR-3:3,5sup,5(5068)■6:3(1684),17(7127)■7:15(5069)■8:25(7311),35a-NE-12:43b-JOB-1:5-IS-57:6■66:3-JER-32:29(6999)-EZE-20:28b■48:12(8641)-AM-5:25(5066)-JON-1:16b-MAL-1:11(5066)■N.T.-all=4374&marked-AC-7:41(321),42■8:18■15:29(1494)■21:25(1494),26-1CO-8:1(1494),4(1494),7(1494),10(1494)■10:19(1494),28(1494)-PH'P-2:17(4689)-2.TI-4:6(4689)-HEB-5:7■9:7,14,28■10:1,2,8,12■11:4,17^{2}-JAS-2:21(399)

OFFERETH-all=7126&marked-LE-6:26(2398)■7:8,9,16,18,29,33■17:8(5926)■21:8■22:21-NU-15:4-PS-50:23(2076)-IS-66:3(5927)-JER-48:35(5927)-MAL-2:12(5066)

OFFERING-all=4503,a=8641,b=7133&marked-GE-4:3,4,5-EX-25:2^{2}a,3a■29:27sup,27a,28^{3}a,41,41^{2}sup■30:9,9sup,13a,14a,15a■35:5^{2}a,21a,24^{2}a■36:3a,6a■38:24(8573),29(8573)■40:29^{2}sup,29-LE-1:2^{2}b,3b,10b,14^{2}b■2:1^{2}b,3,4,5,6,7,8,9,9sup,10,11,13^{2},14^{2},15■3:2b,6b,6sup,7b,8b,12b,14b■4:23b,28b,32b■5:6(817),11b,11^{2}sup,13■6:14,15^{2},20b,20,21,23■7:9,10,13b,14a,16b,32a,37sup,37,37sup■8:18(5930)■9:4,7^{2}sup,7b,15b,17,22(6213)■10:12■14:20sup,20,21,31^{2}sup,31■17:4b■22:12a■23:13,13^{2}sup,14b,16,18sup,18,18sup,37^{2}sup,37■27:9b-NU-4:16■5:9a,15b,15^{2},18^{2},25^{2},26■6:14b,15,17,21b■7:3b,10b,11b,12,13b,13,17b,19b,19,23b,25b,25,29b,31b,31,35b,37b,37,41b,43b,43,47b,49b,49,53b,55b,55,59b,61b,61,65b,67b,67,71b,73b,73,77b,79b,79,83b,87sup,87,87sup■8:8,8sup,11(8573),13(8573),15(8573),21(8573)■9:7b,13b■15:4b,4,6,9,13(7126),19a,20^{2}a,21a,24sup,24,24^{2}sup,25b■16:15■18:9,9^{2}sup,11a,24a,26a,27a,28^{2}a,29a■28:2b,5,8,8sup,9,9sup,12^{2},13,13sup,20,26,28,31sup,31■29:3,6,6sup,6,9,11^{3}sup,11,14,16^{2},16,16sup,18,19^{2}sup,19,21,22^{2}sup,22,22sup,24,25^{2}sup,25,25sup,27,28^{2}sup,28,28sup,30,31^{2}sup,31,31sup,33,34^{2}sup,34,34sup,37,38^{2}sup,38,38sup■31:29a,41a,52a-DE-12:11a,17a-JOS-22:23sup,23-J'G-13:19,23sup,23-1SA-2:17,29■3:14■7:10(5927),10sup■13:10(5927),10sup■26:19-2SA-6:18(5927)-1KI-18:29(5927),36(5927)-2KI-3:20■10:25(6213)■16:13sup,13,13sup,15^{3}-1CH-16:2(5927),29■21:23■23:29-2CH-8:13(5927)■29:29(5927)■30:22(2076)■35:14(5927)-EZR-8:25(8614)-NE-10:33,33sup,34b,39(8614)■13:9,31b-PS-40:6,6^{2}sup■96:8-IS-43:23■57:6sup,6■66:20^{2}-EZE-20:28b■40:43b■42:13,13^{2}sup■44:29,29^{2}sup■45:15,15sup,17sup,17,17sup,24,25^{2}sup,25■46:5^{2},7,11,14^{2},15sup,15,20sup,20■48:8a-JOE-1:9,13■2:14-ZEP-3:10-MAL-1:10,11,13■2:12,13■3:3,4■N.T.-all=4376-LU-23:36(4374)-AC-21:26-RO-15:16-EPH-5:2-HEB-10:5,8,10,11(4374),14,18

OFFERINGS-all=4503&marked-EX-24:5sup,5(2077)-LE-2:13(7133)■17:5(2077)-NU-18:8(8641),19(8641)■29:39^{2}sup,39-JOS-22:23(2077),29sup,29-1SA-2:29-2SA-1:21(8641)-1KI-8:64sup,64,64^{2},64,64sup-2CH-7:7^{3}sup,7■30:22(2077)■31:10(8641),12(8641),14(8641)■33:16(2077),16sup-EZR-7:17-NE-10:37(8641)■12:44(8641)■13:5^{2}-PS-20:3-JER-7:18(5262)■17:26sup,26■33:18■41:5-EZE-20:40(8641)■45:17sup,17,17^{2}sup-HO-8:13(1890)-AM-5:22sup,22,22sup,25-MAL-3:8(8641)■N.T.-M'R-12:33(3646)-LU-21:4(1435)-AC-24:17(4376)-HEB-10:6(3646),8(3646),8sup

OFFICE-all=6486&marked-GE-41:13(3653)-NU-4:16-1CH-6:32(5656)■23:28(4612)-2CH-24:11-PS-109:8■N.T.-LU-1:8(2407),9(2405)-RO-11:13(1248)■12:4(4234)-1TI-3:1(1984),10(1247),13(1247)-HEB-7:5(2405)

OFFICER-all=5631&marked-GE-37:36■39:1-J'G-9:28(6496)-1KI-4:5(5324),19(5333)■22:9-2KI-8:6■25:19-2CH-24:11(6496)■N.T.-M'T-5:25(5257)-LU-12:58^{2}(4233)

OFFICERS-all=7860&marked-GE-40:2(5631),7(5631)■41:34(6496)-EX-5:6,10,14,15,19-NU-11:16■31:14(6485),48(6485)-DE-1:15■16:18■20:5,8,9■29:10■31:28-JOS-1:10■3:2■8:33■23:2■24:1-1SA-8:15(5631)-1KI-4:5(5324),7(5324),27(5324)■5:16(5324)■9:23(5324)-2KI-11:15(6485),18(6486)■24:12(5631),15(5631)-1CH-23:4■26:29,30(6486)■27:1■28:1(5631)-2CH-8:10(5324)■18:8(5631)■19:11■34:13-ES-1:8(7227)■2:3(6496)■9:3(6213)-IS-60:17(6486)-JER-29:26(6496)■N.T.-all=5257-JOH-7:32,45,46■18:3,12,18,22■19:6-AC-5:22,26

OFFICES-1CH-24:3(6486)-2CH-7:6(4931)■23:18(6486)-NE-13:14(4929)

OFFSCOURING-LA-3:45(5501)■N.T.-1CO-4:13(4067)

OFFSPRING-all=6631-JOB-5:25■21:8■27:14■31:8-IS-22:24■44:3■48:19■61:9■65:23■N.T.-all=1085-AC-17:28,29-RE-22:16

OFT-2KI-4:8(1767)■N.T.-all=4178&marked-M'T-9:14(4183)■17:15■18:21(4212)-M'R-7:3(4435)-AC-26:11-1CO-11:25(3740)-2CO-11:23-2TI-1:16-HEB-6:7

OFTEN-all=3740&marked-M'T-23:37(4212)-M'R-5:4(4178)-LU-5:33(4437)■13:34(4212)-1CO-11:26-2CO-11:26,27^{2}-PH'P-3:18-1TI-5:23(4437)-HEB-9:25(4178),26(4178)-RE-11:6

OFTENER-AC-24:26(4437)

OFTENTIMES-JOB-33:29(6471,7969)-EC-7:22(6471,7227)■N.T.-all=4178&marked-LU-8:29(4183,5550)-RO-1:13-2CO-8:22-HEB-10:11

OFTIMES-all=4178-M'T-17:15-M'R-9:22-JOH-18:2

OH-all=4994&marked-GE-18:30,32■19:18,20■44:18(944)-EX-32:31(577)-J'G-6:13(944),15(944)-1SA-1:26(994)-1CH-4:10(518)-JOB-6:2(3863)-PS-7:9■81:13(3863)-IS-64:1(3863)-JER-44:4

OIL-all=8081a=3323&marked-GE-28:18■35:14-EX-25:6^{2}■27:20■29:2^{2},7,21,40■30:24,25^{2},31■31:11■35:8^{2},14,15,28^{2}■37:29■39:37,38■40:9-LE-2:1,2,4^{2},5,6,7,15,16■5:11■6:15,21■7:10,12^{3}■8:2,10,12,30■9:4■10:7■14:10,12,15,16^{2},17,18,21^{2},24,26,27,28,29■21:10,12■23:13■24:2-NU-4:9,16^{2}■5:15■6:15^{2}■7:13,19,25,31,37,43,49,55,61,67,73,79■8:8■11:8■15:4,6,9■18:12■28:5,9,12^{2},13,20,28■29:3,9,14■35:25-DE-7:13a■8:8■11:14a■12:17a■14:23a■18:4a■28:40,51a■32:13■33:24-1SA-10:1■16:1,13-2SA-1:21■14:2-1KI-1:39■5:11■7:12,14,16-2KI-4:2,6,7■9:1,3,6■18:32a-1CH-9:29■12:40■27:28-2CH-2:10,15■11:11■31:5a■32:28a-EZR-3:7■6:9(4887)■7:22(4887)-NE-5:11a■10:37a,39a■13:5a,12a-ES-2:12-JOB-24:11(6671)■29:6-PS-23:5■45:7■55:21■89:20■92:10■104:15■109:18■141:5-PR-5:3■21:17,20-IS-41:19■61:3-JER-31:12a■40:10■41:8-EZE-16:9,13,18,19■23:41■27:17■32:14■45:14,24,25■46:5,7,11,14,15-HO-2:5,8a,22a■12:1-JOE-1:10a■2:19a,24a-MIC-6:7,15-HAG-1:11a■2:12■N.T.-all=1637-M'T-25:3,4,8-M'R-6:13-LU-7:46■10:34■16:6-HEB-1:9-JAS-5:14-RE-6:6■18:13

OILED-EX-28:23(8081)-LE-8:26(8081)

OINTMENT-all=8081&marked-EX-30:25(4888),25(7545)-2KI-20:13-1CH-9:30(4842)-JOB-41:31(4841)-PS-133:2-PR-27:9,16-EC-7:1■9:8■10:1-SONG-1:3-IS-1:6■39:2■57:9■N.T.-all=3464-M'T-26:7,9,12-M'R-14:3,4-LU-7:37,38,46-JOH-11:2■12:3^{2},5

OINTMENTS-all=8081-SONG-1:3■4:10-AM-6:6■N.T.-LU-23:56(3464)-RE-18:13(3464)

OLD-all=1121,a=2204,b=2205,c=6924,d=5769&marked-GE-5:32■6:4■7:6■11:10■12:4■15:9^{3}(8027),15(7872)■16:16■17:1,12,17,17(1323),24,25■18:11b,12(1086),12a,13a■19:4b,31a■21:2(2208),4,5,7(2208)■23:1(2416)■24:1a,36(2209)■25:8(7872),8b,20,26■26:34■27:1a,2a■35:29b■37:2,3(2208)■41:46■43:27b■44:20b,20(2208)■47:8(3117,8140)■49:9(3833)■50:26-EX-7:7^{2}■10:9b■30:14■38:26-LE-13:11(3462)■19:32b■25:22^{2}(3465)■26:10(3462),10(3465)■27:3,5,6,7-NU-1:3,18,20,22,24,26,28,30,32,34,36,38,40,42,45■3:15,22,28,34,39,40,43■4:3^{2},23^{2},30^{2},35^{2},39^{2},43^{2},47^{2}■8:24■14:29■18:16■26:2,4,62■32:11■33:39-DE-2:20(6440)■8:4(1086)■19:14(7223)■28:50b■29:5^{2}(1086)■31:2■32:7d■34:7-JOS-5:11(5669),12(5669)■6:21(5288)■9:4^{2}(1087),5^{2}(1087),13(1086)■13:1^{2}a■14:7,10■23:1a,2a■24:2d,29-J'G-2:8■8:32(7872)■19:16b,17b,20b,22b-RU-1:12a■4:15(7872)-1SA-2:22a,31b,32b■4:15,18a■8:1a,5a■12:2a■17:12a■27:8d■28:14b-2SA-2:10■4:4■5:4■19:32,35■20:18(7223)-1KI-1:1a,15a■11:4(2209)■12:6b■12:8b,13b■13:11b,25b,29b■14:21■15:23(2209)■22:42-2KI-4:14a■8:17,26■11:21■14:2,21■15:2,33■16:2■18:2■21:1,19■22:1■23:31,36■24:8,18-1CH-2:21■4:40(6440)■23:1a,27■27:23■29:28(7872)-2CH-10:6b,8b,13b■12:13■20:31■21:5,20■22:2■24:1,15a,15■25:1,5■26:1,3■27:1,8■28:1■29:1■31:16,17■33:1,21■34:1■36:2,5,9,11,17b-EZR-3:8■4:15(5957),19(5957)-NE-3:6(3465)■9:21(1086)■12:39(3465),46c-ES-3:13b-JOB-14:8a■20:4(5703)■21:7(6275)■22:15d■32:6(3453)■42:17b-PS-6:7(6275)■25:6d■32:3(1086)■37:25a■44:1c■55:19c■68:33c■71:9(2209),18(2209)■74:2c,12c■77:5c,11c■78:2c■92:14(7872)■93:2(227)■102:25(6440),26(1086)■119:52d,152c■143:5c■148:12b-PR-8:22(227)■17:6b■20:29■22:6a■23:10d,22a-EC-1:10d■4:13b-SONG-7:13(3465)-IS-15:5(7992)■20:4b■22:11(3465)■25:1(7350)■30:6(3918),33(865)■43:18(6931)■46:4(2209),9d■50:9(1086)■51:6(1086),9d■57:11d■58:12d■61:4d■63:9d,11d■65:20b,20^{2}-JER-2:20d■6:16d■28:8d■31:3(7350),13b■38:11(1094),12(1094)■46:26c■48:34(7992)■51:22b■52:1-LA-1:7c■2:17c,21b■3:4(1086),6d■5:21c-EZE-9:6b■23:43(1087)■25:15d■26:20^{2}d■36:11(6927)■38:17(6931)-DA-5:31(1247)-JOE-1:2b■2:28b-AM-9:11d-MIC-5:2c■6:6■7:14d,20c-NA-2:8(3117)-ZEC-8:4b-MAL-3:4d■N.T.-all=3820&marked-M'T-2:16(1332)■5:21(744),27(744),33(744)■9:16,17■13:52-M'R-2:21^{2},22-LU-1:18(4246),36(1094)■5:36^{2},37,39^{2}■9:8(744),19(744)■12:33(3822)-JOH-3:4(1088)■21:18(1095)-AC-2:17(4245)■7:23(5550)■15:21(744)■21:16(744)-RO-4:19(1541)■6:6-1CO-5:7,8-2CO-3:14■5:17(744)-EPH-4:22-COL-

3:9-1TI-4:7(1126)-HEB-1:11(3822)■8:13(3822),13(1095)-1PE-3:5(4218) -2PE-1:9(3819),21(4218)■2:5(744)■3:5 (1597)-1JO-2:7^2-JUDE-4(3819)-RE-12:9(744)■20:2(744)

OLDNESS-RO-7:6(3821)

OLIVE-all=2132&marked-GE-8:11-EX-27:20■30:24-LE-24:2-DE-6:11■8:8■24:20■28:40^2-J'G-9:8,9-1KI-6:23(8081),31(8081),32(8081),33(8081) -2KI-18:32-1CH-27:28-NE-8:15-JOB-15:33-PS-52:8,24■128:3-IS-17:6■24:13 -JER-11:16-HOS-14:6-AM-4:9-HAB-3:17-HAG-2:19-ZEC-4:3,11,12■N.T.-all=1636&marked-RO-11:17(65), 17,24(65),24(2565),24-JAS-3:12-RE-11:4

OLIVES-all=2132-J'G-15:5-MIC-6:15-ZEC-14:4^2■N.T.-all=1636-M'T-21:1■24:3■26:30-M'R-11:1■13:3■14:26 -LU-19:29,37■21:37■22:39-JOH-8:1

OLIVEYARD-EX-23:11(2132)

OLIVEYARDS-all=2132&marked -JOS-24:13-1SA-8:14-2KI-5:26-NE-5:11■9:25

OMER-all=6016-EX-16:16,18,32,33,36

OMERS-EX-16:22(6016)

OMITTED-M'T-23:23(863)

OMNIPOTENT-RE-19:6(3841)

ON-all=5921,a=413&marked-GE-6:1■8:9■17:3■20:9■21:14■22:9■24:45■33:4■37:23■40:16,19■46:29-EX-2:6■12:7^2,23, 29■16:14■17:9■19:4,20a■21:30■24:6,8■25:26■26:10,35^2■28:9,10^2,23,24a,25,27, 37■34:33■36:11■38:2,7■39:7,17,18,19, 19a,20■40:20,24-LE-1:8,11,12■2:12a■3:4,5sup,5■4:12■6:10sup,10■7:4■8:26■9:24■11:2,27,34■15:6,23■16:10-NU-3:29,35■4:12■14:5-DE-7:25■9:10■10:2,4■21:22■22:6■28:1,2■30:7■32:11,13-JOS-5:14a■6:7sup,7a,8a, 13^{2}a■8:29■10:26■13:16■17:7a,8a■22:20 -J'G-6:37,40■8:26■9:48■10:4■12:14■13:5,20sup,20■15:18a■16:29-RU-2:10■3:15-1SA-2:34a■5:5■6:7,15a■11:7■13:5■16:7a■17:3^{2}a■21:13■23:24a■25:18,20,23■26:13■27:11-2SA-1:10■2:13^2,25■3:29,29a■4:7■8:7a■9:6■12:30■13:5,19^3,19sup■14:4,9,22a, 26,33■17:12■21:10-1KI-1:20,46,48■2:4,15,19,24■3:6■4:29■7:9(5704),29, 35,36^2,39^2,39sup,41,43■8:20,23,25, 27,54■9:26■10:9,19sup,19a■11:30■14:23■16:11,24(853)■18:7,23^2,33^2,39, 46a■20:20■22:10,19,24-2KI-1:9,13■2:15■3:11■4:20,21■5:18■6:31■7:2,17■8:15sup,15■9:3,6a,13a,17,32(854),33a■10:3,15(854),30■11:19■13:21■14:20■15:12■16:4,14■18:14,20,21^2,24, 26,27■20:7■23:8,12-1CH-6:39,44,49, 78,78sup■10:5■15:20,21■18:7■29:15, 23,25-2CH-3:7,13,15,16■4:12^2■6:10,18■8:12■9:8■14:11■16:7^2,8■18:9■20:29■24:25■26:15■28:4■29:21■32:18■36:15 -EZR-6:15(5705)-NE-2:14a■8:4,4sup -ES-1:2■2:23■6:4■7:10■9:25-JOB-4:13■16:16■29:24a■38:26^2-PS-22:8a-PR-9:14-SONG-3:1-IS-9:20^2■11:8^2■15:3■16:12■26:5(4791)■28:4■30:17■31:1,4■36:5,6,9,11■47:1■51:5a■60:7-JER-7:29■13:2,27■18:3■30:6■36:23a,23■48:11a-LA-1:2-EZE-1:8, 10a,10sup■3:23■4:6■7:16a■16:11,12■23:5a■40:40a■41:25a,26sup,26a■43:20,20a-DA-6:14■8:18■10:9-HO-4:8a■10:5,8^2■11:4-JOE-2:5-AM-5:19-JON-4:10-HAB-1:13a■2:15, 16-ZEP-1:9,12-ZEC-12:6■N.T.-all=1909,a=1722,b=1519,c=1537,d=1746 &marked-M'T-1:18(3799),20(1760)■4:5■5:14(1886),15,39,45sup,45,45sup■6:25(1746)■9:2,6,36(4012)■10:29,34■13:2■14:13(3979),19,25,26,28,29■15:32, 35■16:19^2■17:6■18:18^2,19■19:13(2007), 15(2007)■20:21^{2}c,23c■21:7(1883),19c, 44^2■22:11d,40a,44c■23:4■24:17,20a■25:33^{2}c,34c,41c■26:5a,7,12,39,50,64c■27:19,25,28(4060),30b,31d,38^{2}c, 48(4060)-M'R-2:10,21,23a,24a■3:9(4342)■4:1,5,8b,16,20,21,38■5:23 (2007)■6:9d,47■8:2,6,23b■9:3,20,22,40■10:37^{2}c,40^{2}c■11:7(1911)■12:36c■13:15■14:2a,3(2596),6a,35,46,62c,65(1716)■15:20d,27^{2}c,36(4060)■16:5a,18,19c-LU-1:11c,25(1896),59a,65■2:14■4:9,16a,31a, 40(2007)■5:12,17a■6:1a,2a,6a,7a,20b, 29,48■7:13■8:8b,13,15a,16,22a,23b,32a■9:37a■10:19(1883)34,35,37(3326)■11:33■12:22d,49b,51a■13:7a,10a,13(2007)■14:5a■15:5,20,22(1746),22b■17:16■18:8, 32(1716)■19:43(3840)■20:1a,18,19,42c■21:12,26(1904),35^2■22:21,30,69c■23:26 (2007),30,33^{2}c,54(2020)-JOH-1:12b,33■2:11b■3:18b,36b,36■4:6,39b■5:9a,16a■6:2,19,29b,35b,40b,47b■7:22a,23^{2}a,30, 31b,38b,39b,44,48b■8:6b,8b,30b■9:6(5476), 35b,36b■10:42b■11:45b,48b■12:11b,15, 37b,42b,44^{2}b,46b■13:22b,23a,25■14:12b■16:8b■17:4,20b■19:2(2007),2(4016),18 (1782),19,31a,37b■20:22(1720)■21:4b, 6b,20-AC-2:18^2,21(1941),25c,30,34c■3:4b,12■4:5,22■5:5,15,18,30■6:6(2007), 15b■7:54,55c,56c■8:17,18(1936),19(2007), 36(2596)■9:12(2007),17,21(1941)■10:7 (4342),19(4012),39,44,45■11:15,17■12:8 (5265)■13:3(2007),9b,11■14:10,23b■16:31■17:26■18:10(2007)■19:4^{2}b,6,16,17■20:10 (1968),37■21:5^2,23,27,40■22:16(1941), 19■23:24(1913)■25:6,17^2■27:20(1945),44^2■28:3,3(2510),4c,8(2007)-RO-4:5,24■9:23,33■10:11,14(1941)■11:22■12:7^{2}a, 8a,20■13:12d,14d■15:3■16:6b,19-1CO-1:4(4012)■11:10■14:25■15:53^{2}d,54^{2}d -2CO-1:11(5228)■4:8a■5:12(5228)■7:5a■8:1a,24(5228)■10:7(991)■11:20b-GA-3:13, 14b,27d■6:16-EPH-1:10■4:8(5311), 24d■6:3,11d,14d-PH'P-1:29b-COL-3:1a,2sup,2,6,10d,12d-1TH-5:8d-1TI-1:16,18■4:14(1936)■5:22(2007)■6:12 (1949),19(1949)-2TI-1:6(1936)■2:22 (1941)-TIT-3:6-PH'M-18(1677)-HEB-1:3^{2}a,13c■2:16^2(1949)■6:2(1936)■8:1a, 4■10:12a■11:13■12:25-JAS-5:5,17-1PE-1:17(1941)■2:6,24■3:3(1745),22a■4:14^2 (2596),16a-1JO-5:10b,13^{2}b-RE-1:10a■3:3■4:2,4,9,10■5:1^2,10,13a■6:2,5,8 (1883),10,16^2■7:1^4,11,15,16■9:7,17■10:2■11:10,16■13:13(1519),14^2■14:1,6,14,15, 16^2■15:2■17:8,9■18:19,20c■19:4,12, 16,18,19■20:6,9,11■21:13^4(575)■22:2

ONCE-all=259&marked-GE-18:32 (6471)-EX-10:17(6471)■30:10^2-LE-16:34 -DE-7:22(4118)-JOS-6:3,11,14-J'G-6:39^2 (6471)■16:18(6471),28(6471),28sup-1SA-26:8(6471,259)-1KI-10:22-2KI-6:10-2CH-9:21-NE-5:18(996)■13:20(6471)-JOB-33:14■40:5-PS-62:11■76:7(227)■89:35-PR-28:18-IS-42:14(3162)■66:8(6471)-JER-10:18(6471)■13:27(5750)■16:21(6471)-HAG-2:6■N.T.-all=530&marked-LU-23:18 (3826)-RO-6:10(2178)■7:9(4218)-1CO-15:6 (2178)-2CO-11:25-GA-1:23(4218)-EPH-5:3 (3366)-PH'P-4:16-1TH-2:18-HEB-6:4■7:27(2178)■9:7,12(2178),26,27,28■10:2,10 (2178)■12:26,27-1PE-3:18,20-JUDE-3,5

ONE-all=259,a=376&marked -GE-16a■42:5,8-PS-2:10■12:5■17:11■20:6■27:6■39:7■50:22a■74:6■115:2a■116:14a,18a■118:2,3a,4a,25^{2}a■119:67■122:8a■124:1a■129:1a-PR-5:7■6:3(645)■7:12(6471),24■8:32-EC-2:1a, 16(3528)■3:15(3528)■9:6(3528),7(3528) -SONG-3:2a■7:8a-IS-1:18a,21■5:1a, 3,5■7:3a,13a■16:14■19:12a■22:1(645)■28:22■29:22■30:8■33:10^3■36:4a,5,8, 10■37:20,26■38:3a■43:1,19■44:1■47:8,12a,13a■48:7,16■49:5,19■51:21a■52:5■64:8-JER-2:18■4:12,31a■5:1a,21a, 24a■7:12a,13a■14:10a■17:15a■18:11, 11a,13a■25:5a■26:13■27:6,16,18a■28:7a,15a■29:27■30:6a■32:36■34:15 (3117)■35:15a■36:15a,17a■37:3a,20■38:12a,25a■40:4■42:15,22■44:7■45:3a -EZE-4:14■7:3,8■8:5a,8a■17:12a■18:25a■19:13■23:43■26:18■39:25■43:9■46:12(3588)-DA-2:23^2(3705)■3:15 (3705)■4:37(3705)■5:12(3705),15(3705), 16(3705)■6:8(3705),10(1768),16(116)■9:15,17,22■10:11,20■11:2-HO-2:7,10■4:16■5:7■8:10,13■10:2,3■13:2-JOE-2:12-AM-6:7■7:16-JON-4:3-MIC-4:9, 10,11■5:1,4■6:1a,5a■7:4,10-NA-1:13 -HAG-1:5■2:2a,3,4,11a,15a,18a-ZEC-1:4a■3:8a■5:5a■8:11■9:8-MAL-1:8a, 9■2:1■3:10a,15■N.T.-all=1161,a=3568, 1:9■2:21,24■3:22■4:19■10:5a,25■11:1, 3a,6^2,7a■13:11a■19:9■21:15■22:2■26:10,31a■27:38,45■30:33(3605)■31:49a■32:8■33:13■34:14a,16,22■37:19a■40:5■41:5,11,22,25,26■42:11,13^2,16,19, 21a,27,28a,32,33■43:33a■44:28■48:22■49:16,28a-EX-1:15■8:31■9:6,7■10:19, 23a■11:1■12:18,46,49■14:20(2088), 28■16:15a,22■17:12(2088)■18:3,16 a■23:29■24:3■25:12,19(2088),32,33, 36■26:2^3,3^2(802),4,5,5(802),6,8,8sup, 8,10,11,16,17,17(802),19,21,24,25,26■27:9■28:10,21a■29:1,3,15,23^2,39,40■36:9,9sup,9,10^2,11,12^2,13^2,15^3,18,22^2, 24,26,29,31■37:3,8,9a,19,22■39:14a -LE-4:27(5315)■5:4,5,7,13■7:7,10a, 14■8:26^2■12:8■13:2■14:5,10^2,12,21^2, 22,30,31,50■15:15,30■16:5,8■19:11a■20:9a■22:28■23:18,19■24:5,22■25:14a, 17a,46a,48■26:26,37a-NU-1:4a,41, 44■2:16,28,34a■4:19a,49a■6:11,14^3, 19^2■7:13^2,14,15,16,19^2,20,21,22,25^2,26, 27,28,31^2,33^2,34,37^2,38,39,40,43,44,45, 46,49^2,50,51,52,55^2,56,57,58,61^2,62,63, 64,67^2,68,69,70,73^2,74,75,76,79^2,80,81, 82■8:12■9:14■10:4■11:19,26■13:23■14:4a,15■15:5,11,12,15,16,24^2,29■16:15^2, 22■17:3,6sup,6■25:5a,6a■26:54a■28:4,7,11,12^2,13,15,19,22,27,28^2,29,30■29:2,4^2,5,8,9,10,11,16,19,22,25,28,31, 34,36,38■31:28,30,34,39,47■34:18■35:8a,30■36:7a,8,9a,-DE-1:23,35a■4:42■6:4■12:14■13:12■15:7■17:6■19:5,11,15■21:15■23:16■24:5■25:5, 11^2■28:7,25■32:30-JOS-9:2■10:2, 42■12:9^2,10^2,11,12^2,13^2,14^2,15^2,16^2, 17^2,18^2,19^2,20^2,21^2,22^2,23^2,24^2■17:14^2, 17■20:4■22:14a■23:10,14^2-J'G-6:16,29a■8:18■9:2,5,18■10:18a■16:5a,29■17:5,11■18:19■19:13■20:1,8,11,31■21:3,6,8-RU-1:4■2:13■4:1(492)-1SA-1:2,24■2:34,36sup,36■6:4,17^2■9:3■10:3,11a, 12a■11:7■13:17■14:4(2088),4,5,40■16:18■17:3(2088),36■20:15a,41^{2}a■22:2^{3}a,20■25:14■26:15,22■27:1 -2SA-1:15■2:13(2088),16a,21,25,27a■3:13■4:2■6:19a^2,20■7:23■9:11■11:25 (2088)■12:1^2,3■13:13,30■14:6,27■15:2■17:12,13(1571),22■18:17a■19:7,14■20:11a■23:8■24:12-1KI-2:16,20■3:17^2, 23(2063),25■4:22■6:24,24sup, 25,26,27,27sup,27(3671),34■7:16, 17,18,27,34,36a,37,38^2,42,44■8:56■10:14,16,17,20(2088)■11:13,32,36■12:29,30■14:21■15:10■18:6,23,25, 40a■19:2■20:20a,29■22:8,13^2-2KI-3:11,23a■4:22,39■6:3,5,12■7:3a,6a,8,9a, 13■8:26■9:1■12:9a■14:23■17:27,28■18:24,31a■22:1a■23:35a■24:18■25:16, 17-1CH-1:19■11:11■12:14,38■16:3^{2}a■17:21■21:10■23:11■24:5(428),6sup, 6,6sup,17■25:28-2CH-3:11,11sup,17■4:15■5:13^2■9:13,15,16■12:13■16:13■18:7,8,12^2■22:2■28:6■30:12■32:12■34:1■36:11-EZR-2:1a,26■3:1■10:13 -NE-1:2■3:28a■4:15a,17sup,17,18a,22a, 23a■5:7a,18■7:3a,6a,30,37■8:1,16a■11:1,3a,20a■13:10a,30a-ES-1:7(3627)■3:13■4:11■6:9a■7:9■8:12■9:19a,22a -JOB-1:4a■2:10,11a,12a■9:3,22■14:4■23:13■31:15■33:23■41:16,17a■42:11a -PS-12:2a■14:3■27:4■34:20■49:16a■53:3sup,3■64:6a■82:7■106:11-PR-1:14■6:28a■20:6a-EC-2:14■3:19^2(2088), 19,20■4:8,9,10,11,12■6:6■7:14(2088), 27,28■9:2,3,18■12:11-SONG-4:9^2■6:6^2,9^3■8:11a-IS-3:5^{2}a■4:1■5:10■6:2,6■9:14■10:17sup,17■13:8a■14:18a■19:2^{2}a, 18■23:15■27:12■30:17^2■34:16■36:9,16^{3}a■40:26a■41:6^{2}a■47:9,15a■

53:6a▪56:11a▪66:8,13a,17-JER-
1:15a▪3:14▪5:8a▪6:3a▪9:4a,5a▪
11:8a▪13:14a▪16:12a▪18:11a,12a▪19:9a▪
22:7a▪23:30a,35^{2}a▪24:2▪25:5a,26a▪
31:30a▪32:19a,39▪34:10a,10a,17a▪35:2▪
36:16a▪38:7a▪46:16a▪50:16^{2}a▪51:9a▪
52:1,20,21,22-EZE-1:6^2,9(802),9a,11a,
12a,15,16,23(802),23^{2}a▪3:13(802)▪4:9,
17a▪7:16▪9:2▪10:9,10sup,10,14,21^2,
22a▪11:19▪14:7a▪18:10,30a▪19:3▪
20:39a▪21:19▪22:6a▪23:2,13▪24:23a▪
33:20a,24,26a,30(2297),30a▪34:23▪
37:16,17^2,19^2,22^2,24▪40:5^2,6^2,7^3,8,10^2,
12sup,12,26,42,44,49▪41:11,24▪42:4▪
43:14,14sup▪45:7sup,7,11,15,20a▪
46:17,22▪47:14a▪48:8,31^2,32^2,33^2,34^2
-DA-2:9(2298),43(1836)▪3:19(2298)▪4:19
(2298)▪5:6(1668)▪7:3(1668),5(2298),16
(2298)▪8:3,9,13▪9:27▪10:13^2▪11:27▪
12:5-HO-1:11-JO-2:7a,8a,8(1397)-AM-
4:7^2,8▪6:9-OB-9a,11-JON-1:7a▪3:8a
-MIC-4:5a-HAB-1:2(6918)▪3:3(6918)
-ZEP-2:11a▪3:9-HAG-2:1,22a-ZEC-
3:9^2▪4:3▪8:10a,21▪10:1a▪11:6a,7,8,9
(802)▪13:4a▪14:7,9,13a-MAL-2:10^2,
15^2▪3:16a▪N.T.-all=1520,a=3391,b=240,
c=5100-M'T-5:18,18a,19a,29,30,36a▪
6:24^2,27,29▪10:29,42▪12:11,29c,47c▪
13:46▪16:14▪17:4^{2}a▪18:5,6,9(3442),10,
12,14,16,24,28▪19:5a,6a,16,17▪20:12a,
13,21▪21:24,35(3739)▪22:5(3538,
3303),35▪23:8,9,10,15▪24:10^{2}b,40,41▪
25:15(3739,3303),15,18,24,32b,40,45▪
26:14,21,40a,47,51▪27:38,48-M'R-
4:41b▪5:22▪6:15▪8:14,28▪9:5a,17,37,
38c,42,47(3442),50b▪10:8a,8sup▪10:17,
18,21,37▪11:29▪12:6,28,29,32▪14:10,
18,19,20,37a,43,47,66a▪15:6,21c,
27,36-LU-2:15b▪4:40▪5:3▪6:9c,
11b▪7:8(5129),32b,36c,41▪8:25b,
49c▪9:8,19c,33^{2}a,43(3956),49c▪
10:42▪11:1c,45c,46▪12:1b,6,13c,25,
27,52▪13:10a,23c▪14:1c,15c,18a▪15:4,7,
8a,10,19,26▪16:5,13^2,17a,30c,31c▪17:2,
15,22a,34a,34,35a,36▪18:10,19,22▪20:1a,
3▪22:47,50,59a▪23:17,26c,33(3739,
3303),39▪24:17b,18,32b-JOH-1:40▪4:33b,
37(243)▪5:44b▪6:8,22,70,71▪7:21,50▪
8:9,41▪9:25▪10:16a,16,30▪11:49,50,52▪
12:2,4▪13:14b,21,22b,23,34^{2}b,35b▪
15:12b,17b▪17:11,21^2,22,23▪18:14,22,
26,39▪19:34▪20:12,24▪21:25-AC-1:14
(3661),22▪2:1(3661),1(3858,848),7b,12
(243),46(3661)▪4:24(3661),32sup,32a▪
5:12(3661),25c,34c▪7:24c,26(1515),26b,57
(3661)▪8:6(3661)▪9:43c▪10:6c▪11:28▪
12:10a,20(3661)▪15:25(3661),39b▪17:26,
27▪18:12(3361)▪19:9c,29(3661),32
(3303),34a,38b▪20:31▪21:6b,7a,16c,26▪
22:12▪23:6,17▪24:21a▪25:19c▪28:13a,
25-RO-1:27b▪2:15b▪3:10,12,30▪5:7c,
12,15^2,16^2,17^3,18^2,19^2▪9:10▪10:4(3956)▪
12:4,5^2,5b,10^{2}b,16▪13:8▪14:2(3739),
5,5sup(3739,3303),13b,19b▪15:5b,
6(3661),6,7b,14b▪16:16-1CO-3:4c,
8▪4:6▪5:1c▪6:7(1438),16,16a,17▪
7:5b,7(3739,3303)▪8:4,6^2▪9:24▪
10:8a,17^2▪11:5,20(3588,846),21sup,21
(3739,3303),33b▪12:8(3739,3303),11,
12^3,13^3,14,18,19,20,25b,26^2▪14:23(3588,
846),24c,24sup,27,31(2596,1520),31▪
15:39(243),40(2087),41(243)▪16:20b
-2CO-2:16(3303)▪5:14▪11:2,24a▪
13:11(3588,846),12b-GA-3:16,20,28▪
4:22,24a▪5:13b,14,15^{2}b,17b,26▪6:2b
-EPH-2:14,15,16,18▪4:2b,4,4a,5,5a,
6,7,25b,32b,32(1438)▪5:21b,31a-PH'P-
1:16(3303),27,27a▪2:2(4861),2(3888,
1520)▪3:13-COL-3:9b,13b,13(1438),
15,16(1438)-1TH-2:11▪3:12b▪4:9b,
18b▪5:11-2TH-:3-1TI-2:5▪3:2a,
12a▪5:9-TIT-1:6a,12c▪3:3b-HEB-2:6c,
11▪3:13(1438)▪10:12a,14a,24b▪11:12▪
12:16a-JAS-2:10,16c,19▪4:11b,
12▪5:9b,16^{2}b,19c-1PE-1:22b▪3:8
(3675)▪4:9b,10(1438)▪5:5b,14b
-2PE-3:8,8^{2}a-1JO-1:7a▪3:11b,23b▪4:7b,
7sup,11b,12▪5:7,8-2JO-5b-RE-5:5▪6:1a,
1,4b▪7:13▪9:12a▪11:10b▪13:3a▪15:7▪
17:1,10,12a,13a▪18:8a,10a,17a▪21:9,21

ONE'S-supplied

ONES-JER-48:45(1121)

ONIONS-NU-11:5(1211)

ONLY-all=7535,a=905,b=389&
marked-GE-6:5▪7:23b▪14:24▪19:8▪
22:2(3173),12(3162),16(3173)▪24:8▪
27:13b▪34:22b,23b▪41:40▪47:22,26a▪
50:8-EX-8:9,11,28▪9:26▪10:17b,17,24▪
12:16a▪21:19▪22:20a,27a-LE-21:23b▪
27:26b-NU-1:49b▪12:2▪14:9b▪18:3b▪
20:19▪31:22b▪36:6b-DE-2:28,35,37▪
3:11▪4:9,12(2108)▪8:3a▪10:15▪12:16,
23,26▪15:5,23▪20:20▪22:25a▪28:13,
29b,33b▪29:14a-JOS-1:7,17,18▪6:15,
17,24▪8:2,27▪11:13a,22▪13:6,14-J'G-
3:2▪6:37a,39a,40a▪10:15b▪11:34(3173)▪
16:28b▪19:20-1SA-1:13,23b▪5:4▪7:3a,
4a▪12:24b▪18:17b▪20:39b-2SA-13:32a,
33a▪17:2a▪20:21a▪23:10b-1KI-3:2,3▪
4:19(259)▪8:39a▪12:20a▪14:8,13a▪15:5▪
18:22a▪19:10a,14a▪22:31a-2KI-10:23a▪
17:18a▪19:19a▪21:8-2CH-6:30a▪
18:30a▪33:17-EZR-10:15b-ES-1:16a
-JOB-1:12(3535),15,16,17,19▪13:20b▪
34:29(3162)-PS-4:8(910)▪51:4a▪62:2b,
4b,5b,6b▪71:16a▪72:18a▪91:8-PR-4:3
(3173)▪5:17a▪11:23b▪13:10▪14:23b▪
17:11b▪21:5^{2}b-EC-7:29a-IS-4:1▪
26:13a▪28:19▪37:20a-JER-3:13b▪6:26
(3173)▪32:30^{2}b-EZE-7:5(259)▪14:16a,
18a▪44:20(3697)-AM-3:2▪8:10(3173)
-ZEC-12:10(3173)▪N.T.-all=3440,a=
3441&marked-M'T-4:10a▪5:47▪8:8▪
10:42▪12:4a▪14:36▪17:8a▪21:19,21▪
24:36a-M'R-2:7(1520)▪5:36▪6:8▪9:8a
-LU-4:8a▪7:12(3439)▪8:42(3439),50▪9:38
(3439)▪24:18a-JOH-1:14(3439),18
(3439)▪3:16(3439),18(3439)▪5:18,44a▪
11:52▪12:9▪13:9▪17:3a-AC-8:16▪
11:19▪18:25▪19:27▪21:13▪26:29▪27:10
-RO-1:32▪3:29▪4:12,16▪5:3,11▪8:23▪
9:10,24▪13:5▪16:4a,27a-1CO-7:39▪
9:6a▪14:36a▪15:19-2CO-7:7▪8:10,19,
21▪9:12-GA-1:23▪2:10▪3:2▪4:8▪5:13▪
6:12-EPH-1:21-PH'P-1:27,29▪2:12,27▪
4:15a-COL-4:11a-1TH-1:5,8▪2:8
-2TH-2:7-1TI-1:17a▪5:13▪6:15a,16a
-2TI-2:20▪4:8,11a-HEB-9:10▪11:17
(3439)▪12:26-JAS-1:22▪2:24-1PE-2:18
-1JO-2:2▪4:9(3439)▪5:6-2JO-1:1a
-JUDE-4a,25a-RE-9:4a▪15:4a

ONWARD-all supplied

ONYCHA-EX-30:34(7827)

ONYX-all=7718-GE-2:12-EX-25:7▪
28:9,20▪35:9,27▪39:6,13-1CH-29:2
-JOB-28:16-EZE-28:13

OPEN-all=6605,a=6440&marked
-GE-1:20a▪38:14(5869)-EX-21:33-LE-
14:7a,53a▪17:5a-NU-8:16(6363)▪16:30
(6475)▪19:15,16a▪24:3(8365),4(1540),
15(8365),16(1540)-DE-15:8,11▪20:11▪
28:12-JOS-8:17▪10:22-1SA-3:1(6555)
-2SA-11:11a-1KI-6:18(6358),29(6358),32
(6358),35(6358)▪8:29,52-2KI-6:17(6491),
20(6491)▪9:3▪13:17▪19:16(6491)-2CH-
6:20,40▪7:15-NE-1:6▪6:5-JOB-11:5▪
14:3(6491)▪32:20▪34:26(4725)▪35:16
(6475)▪41:14-PS-5:9▪49:4▪51:15▪78:2▪
118:19▪119:18(1540)-PR-13:16(6566)▪
20:13(6491)▪27:5(1540)▪31:8,9-SONG-
5:2,5-IS-9:12(3605)▪22:22^2▪24:18▪26:2▪
28:24▪37:17(6491)▪41:18▪42:7(6491)▪
45:1,8▪60:11-JER-5:16▪9:22a▪13:19▪
32:11(1540),14(1540),19(6491)▪50:26
-EZE-2:8(6475)▪3:27▪16:5a,63(6610)▪
21:22▪25:9a▪29:5▪32:4a▪33:27a▪37:2a,
12▪39:5a▪46:12(6605)-DA-6:10(6606)▪
9:18(6491)-NA-3:13-ZEC-11:1▪12:4
(6491)-MAL-3:10▪N.T.-all=455&
marked-M'T-13:35▪25:11-LU-12:36▪
13:25-JOH-1:51▪10:21-AC-16:27▪
18:14▪19:38(71)▪26:18-RO-3:13-2CO-
3:18(343)▪6:11-EPH-6:19(1722,457)
-COL-4:3-1TI-5:24(4271)-HEB-6:6
(3856)-RE-3:8,20▪5:2,3,4,5,9▪10:2,8

OPENED-all=6605&marked-GE-
3:5(6491),7(6491)▪4:11(6475)▪7:11▪8:6▪
21:19(6491)▪29:31▪30:22▪41:56▪42:27▪
43:21▪44:11-EX-2:6-NU-16:32▪22:28,
31(1540)▪26:10-DE-11:6(6475)-J'G-
3:25^2▪4:19▪11:35(6475),36(6475)▪19:27
-1SA-3:15-2KI-4:35(6491)▪6:17(6491),
20(6491)▪9:10▪13:17▪15:16-2CH-29:3
-NE-7:3▪8:5^2▪13:19-JOB-3:1▪29:23
(6473)▪31:32▪33:2▪38:17(1540)-PS-
39:9▪40:6(3738)▪78:23▪105:41▪106:17▪
109:2▪119:131(6473)-SONG-5:6-IS-
5:14(6473)▪10:14(6475)▪14:17▪35:5
(6491)▪48:8▪50:5▪53:7-JER-20:12
(1540)▪50:25-LA-2:16(6475)▪3:46
(6475)-EZE-1:1▪3:2▪16:25(6589)▪
24:27▪33:22^2▪37:13▪44:2▪46:1^2-DA-
7:10(6606)▪10:16-NA-2:6-ZEC-13:1▪
N.T.-all=455&marked-M'T-2:11▪3:16▪
5:2▪7:7,8▪9:30▪17:27▪20:33▪27:52
-M'R-1:10(4977)▪7:34(1272),35(1272)
-LU-1:64▪3:21▪4:17(380)▪11:9,10▪
24:31(1272),32(1272),45(1272)-JOH-
9:10,14,17,21,26,30,32▪11:37-AC-5:19,
23▪7:56▪8:32,35▪9:8,40▪10:11,34▪
12:10,14,16▪14:27▪16:14(1272),26
-1CO-16:9-2CO-2:12-HEB-4:13(5136)
-RE-4:1▪6:1,3,5,7,9,12▪8:1▪9:2▪11:19▪
12:16▪13:6▪15:5▪19:11▪20:12^2

OPENEST-PS-104:28(6605)▪
145:16(6605)

OPENETH-all=6363&marked
-EX-13:2,12,15▪34:19-NU-3:12▪18:15
-JOB-27:19(6491)▪33:16(1540)▪36:10
(1540),15(1540)-PS-38:13(6605)▪146:8
(6491)-PR-13:3(6589)▪24:7(6605)▪31:26
(6605)-IS-53:7(6605)-EZE-20:26▪
N.T.-LU-2:23(1272)-JOH-10:3(455)
-RE-3:7^2(455)

OPENING-1CH-9:27(4668)-JOB-
12:14(6605)-PR-8:6(4669)-IS-42:20
(6491)▪61:1(6495)-EZE-69:21(6610)▪
N.T.-AC-17:3(1272)

OPENINGS-PR-1:21(6607)

OPENLY-GE-38:21(5879)▪N.T.-
all=1722,3588,5318&marked-M'T-6:4,
6,18-M'R-1:45(5320)▪8:32(3954)-JOH-
7:4(1722,3954),10(5320),13(3954)▪11:54
(3954)▪18:20(3954)-AC-10:40(1717),
16:37(1219)-COL-2:15(1722,3954)

OPERATION-PS-28:5(4639)-IS-
5:12(4639)▪N.T.-COL-2:12(1753)

OPERATIONS-1CO-12:6(1755)

OPINION-all=1843-JOB-32:6,10,17

OPINIONS-1KI-18:21(5587)

OPPORTUNITY-M'T-26:16(2120)
-LU-22:6(2120)-GA-6:10(2540)-PH'P-
4:10(170)-HEB-11:15(2540)

OPPOSE-2TI-2:25(475)

OPPOSED-AC-18:6(498)

OPPOSEST-JOB-30:21(7852)

OPPOSETH-2TH-2:4(480)

OPPOSITIONS-1TI-6:20(477)

OPPRESS-all=6231&marked-EX-
33:9(3905)▪22:21(3905)▪23:9(3905)-LE-
25:14(3238),17(3238)-DE-23:16(3238)▪
24:14-J'G-10:12(3905)-JOB-10:3-PS-
10:18(6206)▪17:9(7703)▪119:122-PR-
22:22(1792)-IS-49:26(3238)-JER-7:6▪
30:20(3905)-EZE-45:8(3238)-HO-12:7
-AM-4:1-MIC-2:2-ZEC-7:10-MAL-
3:5▪N.T.-JAS-2:6(2616)

OPPRESSED-all=6231&marked
-DE-28:29,33-J'G-2:18(3905)▪4:3(3905)▪
6:9(3905)▪10:8(7533)-1SA-10:18(3905)▪
12:3(7533),4(7533)-2KI-13:4(3905),22
(3905)-2CH-16:10(7533)-JOB-20:19
(7533)-PS-9:9(1790)▪10:18(1790)▪74:21
(1790)▪103:6▪106:42(3905)▪146:7-EC-
4:1-IS-1:17(2541)▪3:5(5065)▪23:12▪38:14
(6234)▪52:4▪53:7(5065)▪58:6(7533)
-JER-50:33-EZE-18:7(3238),12(3238),
16(3238),18▪22:29-HO-5:11-AM-3:9
(6217)▪N.T.-AC-7:24(2669)▪10:38(2616)

OPPRESSETH-all=6231&marked
-NU-10:9(6887)-PS-56:1(3905)
-PR-14:31▪22:16▪28:3

OPPRESSING-all=3238&marked
-JER-46:16▪50:16-ZEP-3:1

OPPRESSION-all=6233&marked-**EX**-3:9(3906)-**DE**-26:7(3906)-**2KI**-13:4(3906)-**JOB**-36:15(3906)-**PS**-12:5(7701)■42:9(3906)■43:2(3906)■44:24(3906)■55:3(6125)■62:10■73:8■107:39(6115)■119:134-**EC**-5:8■7:7-**IS**-5:7(4939)■30:12■54:14■59:13-**JER**-6:6■22:17-**EZE**-22:7,29■46:18(3238)

OPPRESSIONS-**JOB**-35:9(6217)-**EC**-4:1(6217)-**IS**-33:15(4642)

OPPRESSOR-all=5065&marked-**JOB**-3:18■15:20(6184)-**PS**-72:4(6231)-**PR**-3:31(376,2555)■28:16(4642)-**IS**-9:4■14:4■51:13^{2}(6693)-**JER**-21:12(6231)■22:3(6216)■25:38(3238)-**ZEC**-9:8■10:4

OPPRESSORS-**JOB**-27:13(6184)-**PS**-54:3(6184)■119:121(6231)-**EC**-4:1(6231)-**IS**-3:12(5065)■14:2(5065)■16:4(7429)■19:20(3905)

OR-all=176&marked-**GE**-24:49,50■31:24(5704),29(5704),43■44:8,19-**EX**-4:11^{2}■5:3■11:7(5704)■19:13sup,13■21:4,6,18,20,21,26,27,28,29,31,32,33^{2},36■22:1,4(5704),5,6,7,10^{2},14■23:4■28:43■30:20-**LE**-1:10,14■3:6■4:23,28■5:1,2^{3},3,4^{2},6,7,11■6:2^{3},3,4^{3},5■7:16,21■11:32,42(5704)■12:6sup,6,7,8■13:2^{2},16,19,24^{2},29^{2},30,38,42^{2},43,47,48^{2},49^{2},51,51sup,52,53,56^{2},57,58,59^{3}■14:22,30,37■15:3,14,23,25,29■17:3^{2},8,13■18:9^{2},10■20:17,27■21:18^{2},19^{2},20^{3}■22:4^{2},5^{2},21,22^{2},27,28■25:14,49^{2}■27:10,26-**NU**-5:6,14,30■6:2,10■9:10,22■11:8■15:3^{4},5,6,8^{2},11,14■16:29■18:15,17■19:18■22:18■24:13■30:2,6,10■35:18,20,21,22,23-**DE**-4:16,32,34■13:1^{2},3,5,6^{2},7■14:21■15:12,21■17:3,5^{2},6,12■22:1,4,6^{3}■24:3■27:22■29:18-**JOS**-7:3-**J'G**-18:19■19:13■21:22-**1SA**-2:14■13:19■14:6■20:2,10■21:3,8■22:15■26:10■29:3-**2SA**-2:21■3:35■17:9■19:35(854)-**1KI**-8:46■20:39■21:2-**2KI**-2:16■4:13■6:27■13:19-**2CH**-6:36■15:13^{2}(5704)■18:30(854)-**EZR**-7:26^{2}(2008)-**JOB**-3:15,16■12:8■13:22■16:3■22:11■35:7■38:5,6,28,31,36-**EC**-2:19■11:6■12:6(5704)-**SONG**-2:9,17■8:14-**IS**-7:11■27:5■50:1-**JER**-23:33■40:5-**EZE**-14:17,19-**AM**-3:12-**MAL**-1:8■2:17■**N.T.**-all=2228,a=1535&marked-**M'T**-5:17,18,36■6:24,31^{2}■7:4,9,10(2532),16■9:5■10:11,14,19,37^{2}■11:3■12:5,25,29,33■13:21■15:4,5,6■16:14,26■17:25^{2}■18:8^{3},16^{2},20■19:29^{4}■21:25■22:17■23:17,19■24:23■25:37,38,39^{2},44^{2}■27:17-**M'R**-2:9■3:4^{2},33■4:17,21,30■6:15,56■7:10,11,12■8:37■10:29^{4}■11:30■12:14,15■13:21,35^{3}-**LU**-2:24■5:23■6:9^{2}■7:19,20■8:16■9:25■11:12(2228,2532)■12:11^{2},14,29,38(2532),41■13:14,15■14:5,12,31,32(1161)■16:13■17:1,21,23■18:11,29^{2}■20:2,4,22■22:27-**JOH**-2:6■4:27■6:19■7:17,48■9:2,21■13:29■14:11(1161)■18:34-**AC**-1:7■3:12^{2}■4:7,34■5:38■7:49■8:34■9:2(2532)■10:14,28^{2}■11:8■17:21(2532),29■18:14■19:12■20:33■23:9,15(4253),29■24:20,23■25:11(2532)■26:31■28:6,17,21-**RO**-2:4,15■3:1■4:9,10,13■6:16■8:35^{2}■9:11■10:7■11:34,35■12:7^{2}a,8■14:4,8(5037),10,13,21^{2}-**1CO**-1:13■2:1■3:22^{3}a■4:3,21■5:10^{3},11^{3}■7:11,15,16■8:5a■9:6,7,8,10■10:19,31a■11:4,5,6,22■12:13^{2}a,26a■13:1■14:6^{2},7a,7,23,24,27,29,36,37■15:11a,37-**2CO**-1:6a,13,17■3:1(2228,3361),1■5:9a,10a,13a■6:15■8:23a■9:7■10:12■11:4^{2}■12:2a,3a,6■13:1(2532)-**GA**-1:8,10^{2}■2:2■3:2,5,15■4:9(1161)-**EPH**-3:20■5:3,27■6:8a-**PH'P**-1:18a,20a,27a■2:3-**COL**-1:16^{2}a,20a■2:16^{3}■3:17-**1TH**-2:19■5:10a-**2TH**-2:2(3383),4,15a-**1TI**-2:9■5:4,16,19-**TIT**-1:6■3:12-**PH'M**-18-**HEB**-2:6■10:28■12:16,20-**JAS**-2:3,15■4:13,15-**1PE**-1:11■2:14a■3:3,9■4:15^{2}-**RE**-2:5(1161),16(1161)■3:15■13:16,17^{3}■14:9■20:4(2532)■21:27(2532)

ORACLE-all=1687&marked-**2SA**-16:23(1697)-**1KI**-6:5,16,19,20,21,22,23,31■7:49■8:6,8-**2CH**-3:16■4:20■5:7,9-**PS**-28:2

ORACLES-all=3051-**AC**-7:38-**RO**-3:2-**HEB**-5:12-**1PE**-4:11

ORATION-**AC**-12:21(1215)

ORATOR-**IS**-3:3(3908)■**N.T.**-**AC**-24:1(4489)

ORCHARD-**SONG**-4:13(6508)

ORCHARDS-**EC**-2:5(6508)

ORDAIN-**1CH**-9:22(3245)■17:9(7760)-**IS**-26:12(8239)■**N.T.**-**1CO**-7:17(1299)-**TIT**-1:5(2525)

ORDAINED-all=6213&marked-**NU**-28:6-**1KI**-12:32,33-**2KI**-23:5(5414)-**2CH**-11:15(5975)-**ES**-9:27(6965)-**PS**-8:2(3245),3(3559)■81:5(7760)■132:17(6186)-**IS**-30:33(6186)-**JER**-1:5(5141)-**DA**-2:24(4483)-**HAB**-1:12(7760)■**N.T.**-all=5500&marked-**M'R**-3:14(4160)-**JOH**-15:16(5087)-**AC**-1:22(1096)■10:42(3724)■13:48(5021)■14:23■16:4(2919)■17:31(3724)-**RO**-13:1(5021)-**1CO**-2:7(4304)■9:14(1299)-**GA**-3:19(1299)-**EPH**-2:10(4282)-**1TI**-2:7(5087)-**2TI**-subscr.-**TIT**-subscr.-**HEB**-5:1(2525)■8:3(2525)■9:6(2680)-**JUDE**-4(4270)

ORDAINETH-**PS**-7:13(6466)

ORDER-all=6186&marked-**GE**-22:9-**EX**-26:17(7947)■27:21■39:37(4634)■40:4,4(6187),23-**LE**-1:7,8,12■6:12■24:3,4,8-**JOS**-2:6-**J'G**-13:12(4941)-**2SA**-17:23(6680)-**1KI**-18:33■20:14(631)-**2KI**-20:1(6680)-**1CH**-6:32(4941)■15:13(4941)■23:31(4941)■25:2(3027),6(3027)-**2CH**-8:14(4941)■29:35(3559)-**JOB**-10:22(5468)■23:4■33:5■37:19-**PS**-40:5■50:21■110:4(1700)■119:133(3559)-**EC**-12:9(8626)-**IS**-9:7(3559)■38:1(6680)■44:7-**JER**-46:3-**EZE**-41:6(6471)■**N.T.**-all=5010&marked-**LU**-1:1(1299),3(2517),8-**AC**-11:4(2517)■18:23(2517)-**1CO**-11:34(1299)■14:40■15:23(5001)■16:1(1299)-**COL**-2:5-**TIT**-1:5(1930)-**HEB**-5:6,10■6:20■7:11^{2},17,21

ORDERED-**J'G**-6:26(4634)-**2SA**-23:5(6186)-**JOB**-13:18(6186)-**PS**-37:23(3559)

ORDERETH-**PS**-50:23(7760)

ORDERINGS-**1CH**-24:19(6486)

ORDERLY-**AC**-21:24(4740)

ORDINANCE-all=2708&marked-**EX**-12:14,17,24(2706),43■13:10■15:25(4941)-**LE**-18:30(4931)■22:9(4931)-**NU**-9:14^{2}■10:8■15:15^{2}■18:8(2706)■19:2■31:21-**JOS**-24:25(4941)-**1SA**-30:25(4941)-**2CH**-35:13(4941),25(2706)-**EZR**-3:10(3027)-**PS**-99:7(2706)-**IS**-24:5(2706)■58:2(4941)-**EZE**-45:14(2706)■46:14-**MAL**-3:14(4931)■**N.T.**-**RO**-13:2(1296)-**1PE**-2:13(2937)

ORDINANCES-all=2708&marked-**EX**-18:20(2706)-**LE**-18:3,4-**NU**-9:12-**2KI**-17:34(4941),37(4941)-**2CH**-33:8(4941)-**NE**-10:32(4687)-**JOB**-38:33-**PS**-119:91(4941)-**IS**-58:2(4941)-**JER**-31:35,36(2706)■33:25-**EZE**-11:20(4941)■43:11^{2},18■44:5-**MAL**-3:7(2706)■**N.T.**-all=1345&marked-**LU**-1:6-**1CO**-11:2(3862)-**EPH**-2:15(1378)-**COL**-2:14(1378),20(1379)-**HEB**-9:1,10

ORDINARY-**EZE**-16:27(2706)

ORGAN-all=5748-**GE**-4:21-**JOB**-21:12■30:31

ORGANS-**PS**-150:4(5748)

ORNAMENT-**PR**-1:9(3880)■4:9(3880)■25:12(2481)-**IS**-30:22(642)■49:18(5716)-**EZE**-7:20(5716)

ORNAMENTS-all=5716&marked-**EX**-33:4,5,6-**J'G**-8:21(7720),26(7720)-**2SA**-1:24-**IS**-3:18(5914),20(6807)■61:10(6287)-**JER**-2:32■4:30-**EZE**-16:7,11■23:40

ORPHANS-**LA**-5:3(3490)

OSPRAY-**LE**-11:13(5822)-**DE**-14:12(5822)

OSSIFRAGE-**LE**-11:13(6538)-**DE**-14:12(6538)

OSTRICH-**JOB**-39:13(5133)

OSTRICHES-**LA**-4:3(3283)

OTHER-all=312,a=8145,b=5676,c=2088,d=259&marked-**GE**-4:19a■8:10,12■13:11(251)■29:27,30■41:3,19■43:14,22-**EX**-1:15a■14:20c■17:12d,12c■18:4d,7(7453)■20:3■23:13■25:12a,19d,19c,32a,33d■26:13c,27a■27:15a■29:19a,39a,41a■32:15c■34:14■36:25a,32a,33a■37:3a,18a■38:15a-**LE**-5:7d■6:11■8:22a■12:8d■14:22d,31d,42^{2}■15:15d,30d■16:8d-**NU**-6:11d■8:12d■11:26a,31(3541)■21:13b■28:4a,8a■36:3d-**DE**-5:7■6:14■7:4■8:19■11:16,28,30b■13:2,6,13■17:3■18:20■28:14,36,64sup,64■29:26■30:17■31:18,20-**JOS**-2:10b■7:7b■8:22(428)■12:1b■13:27b,32b■14:3b■17:5b■20:8b■22:4b■23:16■24:2b,2,3b,8b,14b,15b,16-**J'G**-2:12,17,19■7:25b■10:8b,13■11:18b■16:29d■20:31sup,31d-**RU**-1:4a■2:22-**1SA**-1:2a■8:8■14:1b,4c,4d,5d,40d■17:3c■19:21■21:9■26:13b,19■28:8■31:7^{2}b-**2SA**-2:13(428),13c■4:2a■12:1d■13:16■14:6d-**1KI**-3:22,23(2063),25d,26(2063)■6:24a,24(3671),25a,26a,27a,34a■7:16a,17a,18a,20a■9:6,9■10:20c■11:4,10■12:29d■14:9■18:23d■20:29(428)-**2KI**-3:22(5048)■5:17■17:7,35,37,38■22:17-**1CH**-6:78b■12:37b■23:17-**2CH**-3:11^{2},12d,12^{2},17d■7:19,22■9:19c■28:25■30:23,23sup■34:25-**EZR**-1:10■2:31-**NE**-3:11a,20a■4:17d■5:5■7:33,34■12:38a-**ES**-9:16(7605)-**EC**-3:19c■6:5c■7:14c-**JER**-1:6■7:6,9,18■11:10■13:10■16:11,13■19:4,13■22:9■24:2d■25:6■32:29■35:15■36:16(7453)■44:3,5,8,15-**EZE**-1:23(269)■40:6d,40■41:1(6311),2(6311),15(6311),19(6311),24,26(6311)■42:14■44:19■45:7c■47:7c■48:21c-**DA**-2:11(321),44(321)■3:29(321)■7:20(317)■8:3a■12:5,5d-**HO**-3:1-**OB**-11(5048)-**ZEC**-4:3d■11:7d,14a■**N.T.**-all=243,a=2087&marked-**M'T**-4:21■5:39■6:24^{2}a■8:18(4008),28(4008)■12:13,45a■13:8■14:22(4008)■16:5(4008)■20:21(1520)■21:36,41■22:4■23:23(2548)■24:31(1565),40(1520),41(1520)■25:11(3062),16,17,20,22■27:61■28:1-**M'R**-3:5■4:8,19(3026),35(4008),36■5:1(4008),21(4008)■6:45(4008)■7:4,8■8:13(4008)■10:37(1520)■12:31,32■15:27(1520),41-**LU**-3:18a■4:43a■5:7a■6:10,29■7:41a■8:8a,22(4008)■10:1a,31(492),32(492)■11:26a,42(2548)■14:32(846)■16:13^{2}a■17:34a,35a,36a■18:10a,11(3062),14(1565)■22:65a■23:32a,33(3739),40a■24:10(3062)-**JON**-4:38■6:22(4008),22,23,25(4008)■10:1(237),16■15:24■18:16■19:18,32■20:2,3,4,8,12(1520),25,30■21:2,8,25-**AC**-2:4a,40a■4:12,12a■8:34a■15:2,39(240)■17:9(3062)■19:39a■23:6a■26:22(1622)■27:1a-**RO**-1:13(3062)■8:39a■13:9a-**1CO**-1:16■3:11■7:5(240)■8:4a■9:5(3062)■10:29a■14:17a,21(2084),21a,29■15:37(3062)-**2CO**-1:13■2:16(3739)■8:13■10:15(245)■11:8■12:13(3062)■13:2(3062)-**GA**-1:19a■2:13(3062)■4:22(1520)■5:17(240)-**EPH**-3:5a■4:17(3062)-**PH'P**-1:13(3062)■2:3(240)■3:4■4:3(3062)-**2TH**-1:3(240)-**1TI**-1:3(2085),10a■5:22(245)-**JAS**-5:12-**1PE**-4:15(244)-**2PE**-3:16(3062)-**RE**-2:24■8:13(3062)■17:10

OTHERS-all=312&marked-**JOB**-8:19■31:10■34:24-**PS**-49:10-**PR**-5:9-**EC**-7:22-**JER**-6:12■8:10-**EZE**-9:5(428)-**DA**-11:4■**N.T.**-all=243,a=2087&marked-**M'T**-15:30a■16:14a■20:3,6■21:8■26:67(3588)■27:42-**M'R**-6:15^{2}■8:28■11:8■12:5,9■15:31-**LU**-5:29■8:3a,10(3062)■9:8,19■11:16a■18:9(3062)■20:16■23:35-**JOH**-7:12,41■9:9,16■10:21■12:29■18:34-**AC**-2:13a■15:35a■17:32(3588),34a■28:9(3062)-**1CO**-9:2,12,27■14:19-**2CO**-8:8a-**EPH**-2:3(3062)-**PH'P**-2:4a-**1TH**-2:6■4:13(3062)■5:6(3062)-**1TI**-5:20(3062)-**2TI**-2:2a-**HEB**-9:25(245)■11:35,36a-**JUDE**-23(3739)

OTHERWISE-**2SA**-18:13(176)-**2CH**-30:18(3808)■**N.T.**-all=1893&

marked-M’T-6:1(1490)-LU-5:36(1490)-RO-11:6^{2},22-2CO-11:16(1490)-GA-5:10(243)-PH’P-3:15(2088)-1TI-5:25(247)■6:3(2085)-HEB-9:17

OUCHES-all=4865&marked-EX-28:11,13,14,25■39:6,13,16,18

OUGHT-all=3972&marked-GE-39:6-EX-5:11(1697)-LE-25:14(4465)-JOS-21:45(1697)-1SA-12:4,5■25:7-2SA-3:35■N.T.-all=1163,a=3784&marked-M’T-5:23(5100)■21:3(5100)■23:23-M’R-7:12(3762)■8:23(5100)■11:25(5100)■13:14-LU-11:42■12:12■13:14,16■18:1■24:26-JOH-4:20■13:14a■19:7a-AC-4:32(5100)■5:29■17:29a■19:36■20:35■24:19,19(5100)■25:10,24■26:9■28:19(5100)-RO-8:26■12:3■15:1a-1CO-8:2■11:7a,10a-2CO-2:3■12:11a,14a-EPH-5:28a■6:20-COL-4:4,6-1TH-4:1-2TH-3:7-1TI-5:13-TIT-1:11-PH’M-18(5100)-HEB-2:1■5:3a,12a-JAS-3:10(5534)-2PE-3:11-1JO-2:6a■3:16a■4:11a-3JO-8a

OUGHTEST-all=1163-M’T-25:27-AC-10:6-1TI-3:15

OURS-all=2257&marked-M’R-12:7-LU-20:14-1CO-1:2-2CO-1:14-TIT-3:14(2251)-1JO-2:2(2251)

OURSELVES-all=587-NU-32:17-EZR-4:3-PS-100:3■N.T.-all=1438&marked-AC-23:14-RO-8:23^{2}sup,23■15:1-1CO-11:31-2CO-1:9^{2}■3:1,5^{2}■4:2,5^{2}■5:12■6:4■7:1■10:12^{2},14-2TH-1:4(846)■3:9-TIT-3:3(2249)-HEB-10:25-1JO-1:8

OUTCAST-JER-30:17(5080)

OUTCASTS-all=5080&marked-PS-147:2(1760)-IS-11:12(1760)■16:3,4■27:13■56:8(1760)-JER-49:36

OUTER-EZE-10:5(2435)■N.T.-all=1857-M’T-8:12■22:13■25:30

OUTGOINGS-all=8444&marked-JOS-17:9,18■18:19■19:14,22,29,33-PS-65:8(4161)

OUTLANDISH-NE-13:26(5237)

OUTLIVED-J’G-2:7(748,3117,310)

OUTMOST-EX-26:10(7020)-NU-34:3(7097)-DE-30:4(7097)

OUTRAGEOUS-PR-27:4(7858)

OUTRUN-JOH-20:4(4370,5032)

OUTSIDE-all=7097&marked-J’G-7:11,17,19-1KI-7:9(2351)-EZE-40:5(2351)■N.T.-M’T-23:25(1855),26(1623)-LU-11:39(1855)

OUTSTRETCHED-all=5186-DE-26:8-JER-21:5■27:5

OUTWARD-all=2435&marked-NU-35:4-1SA-16:7(5869)-1CH-26:29-NE-11:16-ES-6:4-EZE-40:17,20,34■44:1■N.T.-M’T-23:27(1855)-RO-2:28(1722,3588,5318)-2CO-4:16(1854)■10:7(4383)-1PE-3:3(1855)

OUTWARDLY-M’T-23:28(1855)-RO-2:28(1722,5318)

OUTWENT-M’R-6:33(4281)

OVEN-all=8574-LE-2:4■7:9■11:35■26:26-PS-21:9-LA-5:10-HO-7:4,6,7-MAL-4:1■N.T.-M’T-6:30(2823)-LU-12:28(2823)

OVENS-EX-8:3(8574)

OVER-all=5921,a=5674,b=5048,c=5980&marked-GE-8:1■9:14■21:16b^{2}■31:21a,52^{2}a,■32:10a,16a,21a,22a,23a,31a■33:3a,14a■37:8■39:4,5■41:33,34,40,41,43,45,56■42:6■47:6,20,26■49:22-EX-1:8,11■2:14■5:14■8:5^{2},6,9■10:12,13,14,21■12:13,23,27■14:2(6440),7,16,21,26,27■15:16^{2}a■16:18(5736),23(5736)■18:21,25■25:27c,37(5921,5676)■26:12,13,35(5227)■28:27c■30:6■36:14■37:9c,14c■39:20c■40:19,24(5227),36-LE-14:5,6,50■16:21-NU-1:50^{3}■3:49(5736)■4:6(4605)■7:2(5975)■8:2(5922,6440),3(5922,6440)■10:10,10sup,14,15,16,18,19,20,22,23,24,25,26,27■14:14■16:13■27:16■32:5a,7a,21a,27a,29a,30a,32a■33:51a■35:10a-DE-1:1(4136),15■2:13^{2}a,14a,18a,19(4136),24a,29a■3:18a,25a,27a,28a,29(4136)■4:14a,21a,22^{2}a,26a,46(4136)■9:1a,3a■11:30(4136),31a■12:10a■17:14,15^{3}■21:6■27:2a,3a,4a,12a■28:23,36,63^{2}■30:9^{2},13a,18a■31:2a,3^{2}a,13a,15■32:11,47a,49(5921,6440)■34:1(5921,6440),4a,6(4136)-JOS-1:2a,11a■2:23a■3:1a,6a,11a,14a,16a,17a^{2}■4:1a,3a,5a,7a,8a,10a,11^{2}a,12a,13a,18,22a,23^{2}a■5:1a,13b■7:7a,26■8:31,33(413),33(413,4136)■9:1(413,4136)■18:13a,17(5227),18(4136)■22:11(413,4136),19a■24:11a-J’G-3:28a■6:33a■8:4a■9:8^{2},9,10,11,12,13,14,15,18,22,26a■10:9a■11:11,29^{3}a,32a■12:1a,3a,5a■19:10(5227),12a■20:43(5227)-RU-2:5,6■3:9-1SA-2:1■8:7,9,19■9:16■10:1,19■11:12■12:1,12,13,14■13:1,7a,14■14:1a,4a,5^{2}(4136),6a,8a,23a,47■15:1,1sup,7(5921,6440),17,26,35■16:1■17:50(4480)■18:5■19:20■22:2,9■23:17■26:13a,22a■27:2a■30:10a-2SA-1:17,24(413)■2:4,7,8a,9(413),9(1591),9,10,11,15a,29a■3:10,17,33(413),34■4:12■5:2^{2},3,5^{2},12,17,23(4136)■6:21^{2}■7:8,11,26■8:15,16■10:17a■12:7■15:22^{2}a,23^{3}a■16:9a,13c■17:16a,19,20a,21a,22^{2}a,24a■18:1,8,24(413),33■19:10,15a,17(6743),18^{3}a,22,31^{2}a,33a,36a,37a,38a,39^{2}a,41a■20:21(1157),23(413),23^{2},24■23:23(413)■24:5a-1KI-1:34,35■2:11,35,37a■4:1,4,5,6^{2},7■5:7,14,16,16sup■6:1■7:20c,39(4136)■8:7(413),16■9:23,23sup■11:25,37,42■12:17,18,20■13:30■14:2,7,14■15:1,9,25^{2},33■16:2,8,16,18,23,29^{2}■19:15,16■20:29(5227)■22:41,51^{2}-2KI-2:8a,9a,14a■3:1■5:11(413)■8:13,20,21a■9:3,6^{2}(413),12(413),29■10:5^{2},22,36■11:3,18■13:1,10,14■15:5,8,17,23,27■17:1■18:18,37■19:2■21:13■25:19,22-1CH-5:11b■6:31■8:32b■9:19^{2},20,26,31,32,38b■11:2,3,25■12:4,15a,38■14:2,8,14(4136)■17:7,10■18:14,15,17■19:17a■21:16■22:10■23:1■24:31^{2}c■26:20,20sup,22,26,26sup,29,32■27:2,4,16,25^{2},26,27^{2},28^{2},29^{2},30^{2},31■28:4^{2},5■29:3,12(4605),26,27,30a,30-2CH-1:9,11,13■2:11■4:10(4136)■5:8■6:5,6,36(6440)■9:8,30■10:17,18■13:1,5■19:11■20:31■22:12■26:21■31:12,14■32:6■34:13■36:4,10-EZR-4:10(1541),20(5922),20sup■9:6(4605)-NE-2:7a■3:10b,16b,19b,23b,25b,26b,27b,28b,29b,30b,31b■5:15■7:2,3b■9:37^{3}■11:9,21,22b■12:8,9b,24^{2}c,37b,38(4136),44■13:13,26-ES-3:12■5:1^{2}(5227)■8:2-JOB-6:5■7:12■14:16■16:11■26:7■41:34■42:11-PS-13:2■38:4a■41:11■42:7■47:2,8■60:8■65:13(5848)■68:34■78:50(5462),62(5462)■83:18■88:16a■103:16a■104:9a■108:9■109:6■110:6■118:18(5414)■124:4a,5a■145:9-PR-19:11■20:26■24:31(5927)■28:15-EC-1:12■7:14c,16(7235),16(3148),17(7235)-SONG-2:4,11(2498)-IS-8:7^{2},8a■10:29a■11:15,15(1869)■15:2■16:8a■19:4(5534),16■22:15■23:2a,6a,11,12a■25:7^{2}■28:19a■31:9a■35:8a■36:3,22■37:2■40:27a■45:14^{2}a■47:2a■51:10a,23^{2}a■54:9a■62:5^{2}-JER-1:10^{2}■2:10a■5:6,22a■6:17■13:21■15:3■23:4■31:28^{2},39b■32:41■33:26(413)■40:11■41:10a■43:10■44:27■48:32a,40(413)■49:19(413),22■50:44(413)-LA-2:17■3:54-EZE-1:20c,21c,22,25,26■3:13c■10:1,2,4,18,19■11:22■16:8,27■19:8■27:32■29:15■32:3,8,31■34:23■37:24■40:18c,23b■41:6(413),15(413,6440),16b■42:1b,3^{2}b,7c,10(413,6440),10sup■45:6c,7c■46:9(5226)■47:5^{2}a,20(5227)■48:13c,15(5922,6440),18^{2}c,21^{2}(5922,6440),21c-DA-1:11■2:48^{2}(5922),49(5922)■3:12■4:16(5922),17(5922),23(5922),25(5922),32(5922)■5:5(6903),21(5922)■6:1,1sup(5922),2(5924),3(5922)■9:1■11:40a-HO-10:5,11a■12:4(413)-JON-2:3a■4:6^{2}-MIC-3:6^{2}■4:7-NA-3:19-HAB-1:11a-ZEP-3:17^{2}-HAG-1:10-ZEC-1:21(413)■5:3■9:14■14:9■N.T.-all=1909-M’T-2:9(1883)■9:1(1276)■10:23(5055)■14:34(1276)■21:2(561)■24:45,47■25:21^{2},23^{2}■27:37(1883),45,61(561)-M’R-4:35(1330)■5:21(1276),53(1276)■11:2(2713)■12:41(2713)■13:3(2713)■15:26(1924),33,39(1537,1727)-LU-1:33■2:8■4:10(4012),39(1883)■6:38(5240)■8:22(1330),26(495)■9:1■10:19■11:42(3928),44(1883)■12:14,42,44■15:7^{2},10■19:14,17(1883),19(1883),27,30(2713),41■23:38,44-JOH-6:1(4008),13(4052),17(4008)■18:1(4008)-AC-6:3■7:10,11,16(3346),27■8:2■16:9(1224)■18:23(1330)■19:13■20:2(1330),15(481),28(1722)■21:2(1276)■27:5(1277),7^{2}(2596)-RO-1:28(3860)■5:14■9:5-1CO-7:37(4012)-2CO-3:13■8:15(4121)-EPH-1:22(5228)■4:19(3860)-1TH-3:7■5:12(4291)-HEB-2:7■3:6■9:5(5231)■10:21-JAS-5:14-1PE-3:12■5:3(2634)-JUDE-7(1608)-RE-2:26■6:8■9:11■11:6,10■13:7■14:8■15:2^{3}(1537)■16:9■17:18■18:11,20

OVERCAME-AC-19:16(2634)-RE-3:21(3528)■12:11(3528)

OVERCHARGE-2CO-2:5(1912)

OVERCHARGED-LU-21:34(925)

OVERCOME-GE-49:19^{2}(1464)-EX-32:18(2476)-NU-13:30(3201)■22:11(3898)-2KI-16:5-SONG-6:5(7292)-IS-28:1(1986)-JER-23:9(5674)■N.T.-all=3528&marked-LU-11:22-JOH-16:33-RO-3:4■12:21^{2}-2PE-2:19(2274),20(2274)-1JO-2:13,14■4:4-RE-11:7■13:7■17:14

OVERCOMETH-all=3528-1JO-5:4^{2},5-RE-2:7,11,17,26■3:5,12,21■21:7

OVERDRIVE-GE-33:13(1849)

OVERFLOW-all=7857&marked-DE-11:4(6687)-PS-69:2,15-IS-8:8■10:22■28:17■4:2-JER-47:2-DA-11:10,26,40-JOE-2:24(7783)■3:13(7783)

OVERFLOWED-PS-78:20(7857)-2PE-3:6(2626)

OVERFLOWETH-JOS-3:15(4390)

OVERFLOWING-all=7857&marked-JOB-28:11(1065)■38:25(7858)-IS-28:2,15,18■30:28-JER-47:2-EZE-13:11,13■38:22-HAB-3:10(2230)

OVERFLOWN-1CH-12:15(4390)-JOB-22:16(3332)-DA-11:22(7857)

OVERLAID-all=6823&marked-EX-26:32■36:34^{2},36,38■37:2,4,11,15,26,28■39:2,6,28-1KI-3:19(7901)■6:20,21^{2},22^{2},28,30,32■10:18-2KI-18:16-2CH-3:4,5(2645),7(2645),8(2645),9(2645),10■4:9■9:17-SONG-5:14(5968)■N.T.-HEB-9:4(4028)

OVERLAY-all=6823&marked-EX-25:11^{2},13,24,28■26:29^{2},37■27:2,6■30:3,5-1CH-29:4(2902)

OVERLAYING-EX-38:17(6826),19(6826)

OVERLIVED-JOS-24:31(748,3117,310)

OVERMUCH-2CO-2:7(4055)

OVERPASS-JER-5:28(5674)

OVERPAST-PS-57:1(5674)-IS-26:20(5674)

OVERPLUS-LE-25:27(5736)

OVERRAN-2SA-18:23(5674)

OVERRUNNING-NA-1:8(5674)

OVERSEE-2CH-2:2(5329)

OVERSEER-all=6496&marked-GE-39:4(6485),5(6485)-NE-11:9,14,22■12:42-PR-6:7(7860)

OVERSEERS-2CH-2:18(5329)■31:13(6496)■34:12(6485),13(5329),17(6485)■N.T.-AC-20:28(1985)

OVERSHADOW-LU-1:35(1982)-AC-5:15(1982)

OVERSHADOWED-all=1982-M’T-17:5-M’R-9:7-LU-9:34

OVERSIGHT-all=6485&marked-GE-43:12(4870)-NU-3:32(6486)■4:16(6486)-2KI-12:11■22:5,9-1CH-9:23(5921)-2CH-34:10-NE-11:16(5921)■13:4(5414)■N.T.-1PE-5:2(1983)

OVERSPREAD-GE-9:19(5310)

OVERSPREADING-DA-9:27(3671)

OVERTAKE-all=5381&marked-GE-44:4-EX-15:9-DE-19:6■28:2,15,45

-JOS-2:5-1SA-30:8^{2}-2SA-15:14-IS-59:9-JER-42:16-HO-2:7■10:9-AM-9:10(5066),13(5066)■N.T.-1TH-5:4(2638)

OVERTAKEN-PS-18:37(5381)■N.T.-GA-6:1(4301)

OVERTAKETH-1CH-21:12(5381)

OVERTHREW-all=2015&marked-GE-19:25,29-EX-14:27(5287)-DE-29:23-PS-136:15(5286)-IS-13:19(4114)-JER-20:16(2015)■50:40(4114)-AM-4:11(4114)■N.T.-M'T-21:12(2690)-M'R-11:15(2690)-JOH-2:15(390)

OVERTHROW-all=2015&marked-GE-19:21,29(2018)-EX-23:24(2040)-DE-12:3(5422)■29:23(4114)-2SA-10:3■11:25(2040)-1CH-19:3-PS-106:26(5307),27(5307)■140:4(1760),11(4073)-PR-18:5(5186)-JER-49:18(4114)-HAG-2:22^{2}■N.T.-AC-5:39(2647)-2TI-2:18(396)-2PE-2:6(2692)

OVERTHROWETH-all=5557&marked-JOB-12:19-PR-13:6■21:12■22:12■29:4(2040)

OVERTHROWN-all=5307&marked-EX-15:7(2040)-J'G-9:40-2SA-17:9-2CH-14:13-JOB-19:6(5791)-PS-141:6(8058)-PR-11:11(2040)■12:7(2015)■14:11(8045)-IS-1:7(4114)-JER-18:23(3782)-LA-4:6(2015)-DA-11:41(3782)-AM-4:11(2015)-JON-3:4(2015)■N.T.-1CO-10:5(2693)

OVERTOOK-all=5381&marked-GE-31:23(1692),25■44:6-EX-14:9-J'G-18:22(1692)■20:42(1692)-2KI-25:5-JER-39:5■52:8-LA-1:3

OVERTURN-JOB-12:15(2015)-EZE-21:27(5754)

OVERTURNED-J'G-7:13(2015)

OVERTURNETH-all=2015-JOB-9:5■28:9■34:25

OVERWHELM-JOB-6:27(5307)

OVERWHELMED-all=5848&marked-PS-55:5(3680)■61:2■77:3■78:53(3680)■102:t■124:4(7857)■142:3■143:4

OWE-RO-13:8(3784)

OWED-M'T-18:24(3781),28(3784)-LU-7:41(3784)

OWEST-all=3784&marked-M'T-18:28-LU-16:5,7-PH'M-19(4359)

OWETH-PH'M-18(3784)

OWL-all=3244&marked-LE-11:16(1323,3284),17(3563),17-DE-14:15(1323,3284),16(3563),16-PS-102:6(3563)-IS-34:11,14(3917),15(7091)

OWLS-all=1323,3284&marked-JOB-30:29-IS-13:21■34:13■43:20-JER-50:39-MIC-1:8

OWN-LE-14:15(3548),26(3548)■16:29(249)■17:15(249)■18:26(249)■24:22(249)-1CH-29:14(3027)-PR-14:10(5315)-DA-11:16(7522)■N.T.-all=2398,a=1438,b=848-M'T-9:1■25:14-M'R-15:20-LU-2:3■6:41,44■10:34■14:26a■22:71a-JOH-4:44■5:43■7:18■8:44■10:3,4,12■13:1■15:19■16:32■17:5(4572)■19:27■20:10a-AC-1:7,25■2:6,8■3:12■4:23,32■7:21a■12:10b,36■14:16b■17:28(2596)■20:28■21:11b■25:19■27:19(849)■28:30-RO-4:19a■8:3a,32■10:3■11:24,25a■12:16a■14:4,5■16:4a,18a-1CO-3:8^{2}■4:3(1683),12■6:14b,18,19a■7:2a,2,4^{2},35(846),37■9:7■10:24a,29,33(1683)■11:21■13:5a■15:23■16:21(1699)-2CO-8:17(830)-GA-6:4a,5-EPH-1:11b,20b■5:22,24,28a,29a-PH'P-2:4a,12a■3:9(1699)-COL-3:18-1TH-2:8a,14,15■4:11^{2}-2TH-3:12a-1TI-1:2(1103)■3:4,5,12■5:8^{2}■6:1-2TI-1:9■4:3-TIT-1:4(1103),12■2:5,9-PH'M-19sup,19(4572)-HEB-3:6b■4:10b■7:27■9:12■12:10b■13:12-JAS-1:14,26b-1PE-2:24b■3:1,5-2PE-2:12b,13b,22■3:3,16,17-JUDE-6,13a,16b,18a-RE-1:5b

OWNER-all=1167&marked-EX-21:28,29^{2},34^{2},36■22:11,12,14,15-1KI-16:24(113)-IS-1:3(7069)■N.T.-AC-27:11(3490)

OWNERS-all=1167&marked-JOB-31:39-PR-1:19-EC-5:11,13■N.T.-LU-19:33(2962)

OWNETH-AC-21:11(2076)

OX-all=7794&marked-EX-20:17■21:28^{3},29^{2},32^{2},33,35^{2},35sup,36^{2}■22:1^{2},4,9,10■23:4,12■34:19-LE-7:23■17:3■27:26-NU-7:3■22:4-DE-5:14,21■14:4,5(8377)■18:3■22:1,4,10■25:4■28:31-JOS-6:21-J'G-3:31(1241)■6:4-1SA-12:3■14:34^{2}■15:3-NE-5:18-JOB-6:5■24:3■40:15(1241)-PS-69:31■106:20-PR-7:22■14:4■15:17-IS-1:3■11:7(1241)■32:20■66:3-JER-11:19(441)-EZE-1:10■N.T.-all=1016-LU-13:15■14:5-1CO-9:9-1TI-5:18

OXEN-all=1241&marked-GE-12:16■20:14■21:27■32:5(7794)■34:28-EX-9:3■20:24■22:1,30(7794)■24:5(6499)-NU-7:3,6,7,8,17,23,29,35,41,47,53,59,65,71,77,83,87,88■22:40■23:1(6499)-DE-14:26-JOS-7:24(7794)-1SA-11:7^{2}■14:32■15:9,14,15,21■22:19(7794)■27:9-2SA-6:6,13(7794)■24:22^{2},24-1KI-1:9,19(7794),25(7794)■4:23■7:25,29^{2},44■8:5,63■19:20,21^{2}-2KI-5:26■16:17-1CH-12:40^{2}■13:9■21:23-2CH-4:3^{2},4,15■5:6■7:5■15:11■18:2■29:33■31:6■35:8,9,12-JOB-1:3,14■42:12-PS-8:7(504)■144:14(441)-PR-14:4(5091)-IS-7:25(7794)■22:13■30:24(504)-DA-4:25(8450),32(8450),33(8450)■5:21(8450)-AM-6:12■N.T.-all=1016&marked-M'T-22:4(5022)-LU-14:19-JOH-2:14,15-AC-14:13(5022)-1CO-9:9

P

PACES-2SA-6:13(6806)

PACIFIED-ES-7:10(7918)-EZE-16:63(3722)

PACIFIETH-PR-21:14(3711)-EC-10:4(3240)

PACIFY-PR-16:14(3722)

PADDLE-DE-23:13(3489)

PAID-EZR-4:20(3052)-JON-1:3(5414)■N.T.-M'T-5:26(591)-LU-12:59(591)

PAIN-all=2342&marked-JOB-14:22(3510)■33:19(4341)19sup-PS-25:18(5999)■48:6(2427)-IS-13:8■21:3(2479)■26:17,18■66:7(2256)-JER-6:24(2427)■12:13(2470)■15:18(3511)■22:23(2427)■30:23■51:8(4341)-EZE-30:4(2479),9(2479,)16-MIC-4:10-NA-2:10(2479)■N.T.-RE-16:10(4192)■21:4(4192)

PAINED-all=2342&marked-PS-55:4-IS-23:5-JER-4:19(3176)-JOE-2:6■N.T.-RE-12:2(928)

PAINFUL-PS-73:16(5999)

PAINFULNESS-2CO-11:27(3449)

PAINS-1SA-4:19(6735)-PS-116:3(4712)■N.T.-AC-2:24(5604)-RE-16:11(4192)

PAINTED-2KI-9:30(7760,6320)-JER-22:14(4886)

PAINTEDST-EZE-23:40(3583)

PAINTING-JER-4:30(6320)

PAIR-LU-2:24(2201)-RE-6:5(2218)

PALACE-all=1002&marked-1KI-16:18(759)■21:1(1964)-2KI-15:25(759)■20:18(1964)-1CH-29:1,19-2CH-9:11(1004)-EZR-4:14(1964)■6:2-NE-1:1■2:8■7:2-ES-1:2,5,5(1055)■2:3,5,8■3:15■7:7(1055),8(1055)■8:14■9:6,11,12-PS-45:15(1964)■144:12(1964)-SONG-8:9(2918)-IS-25:2(759)■39:7(1964)-JER-30:18(759)-DA-1:4(1964)■4:4(1965),29(1965)■5:5(1965)■6:18(1965)■8:2■11:45(643)-AM-4:3(2038)-NA-2:6(1964)■N.T.-all=833&marked-M'T-26:3,58,69-M'R-14:54,66-LU-11:21-JOH-18:15-PH'P-1:13(4232)

PALACES-all=759&marked-2CH-36:19-PS-45:8(1964)■48:3,13■122:7-PR-30:28(1964)-IS-13:22(1964)■23:13■32:14■34:13-JER-6:5■9:21■17:27■49:27-LA-2:5,7-EZE-25:4(2918)-HO-8:14-AM-1:4,7,10,12,14■2:2,5■3:9^{2},10,11■6:8-MIC-5:5

PALE-IS-29:22(2357)■N.T.-RE-6:8(5515)

PALENESS-JER-30:6(3420)

PALM-all=8561,a=8558&marked-EX-15:27a-LE-14:15(3709),26(3709)■23:40a-NU-33:9a-DE-34:3a-J'G-1:16a■3:13a■4:5(8560)-1KI-6:29,32^{2},35■7:36-2CH-3:5■28:15a-NE-8:15a-PS-92:12a-SONG-7:7a,8a-JER-10:5(8560)-EZE-40:16,22,26,31,34,37■41:18^{2},19^{2},20,25,26-JOE-1:12a■N.T.-JOH-12:13(5404)■18:22(4475)

PALMERWORM-all=1501-JOE-1:4■2:25-AM-4:9

PALMS-all=3709-1SA-5:4-2KI-9:35-IS-49:16-DA-10:10■N.T.-M'T-26:67(4474)-M'R-14:65(4475)-RE-7:9(5404)

PALSIES-AC-8:7(3886)

PALSY-all=3885&marked-M'T-4:24■8:6■9:2^{2},6-M'R-2:3,4,5,9,10-LU-5:18(3886)■5:24(3886)-AC-9:33(3886)

PAN-all=4227&marked-LE-2:5■6:21■7:9-1SA-2:14(3595)-2SA-13:9(4958)-1CH-23:29-EZE-4:3

PANGS-all=6735&marked-IS-13:8■21:3^{2}■26:17(2256)-JER-22:23(2256)■48:41(6887)■49:22(6887)■50:43(2427)-MIC-4:9(2427)

PANS-EX-27:3(5518)-NU-11:8(6517)-1CH-9:31(2281)-2CH-35:13(6745)

PANT-AM-2:7(7602)

PANTED-PS-119:131(7602)-IS-21:4(8582)

PANTETH-PS-38:10(5503)■42:1^{2}(6165)

PAPER-1SA-19:7(6169)■N.T.-2JO-12(5489)

PAPS-EZE-23:21(7699)■N.T.-all=3149-LU-11:27■23:29-RE-1:13

PARABLE-all=4912-NU-23:7,18■24:3,15,20,21,23-JOB-27:1■29:1-PS-49:4■78:2-PR-26:7,9-EZE-17:2■24:3-MIC-2:4-HAB-2:6■N.T.-all=3850&marked-M'T-13:18,24,31,33,34,36■15:15■21:33■24:32-M'R-4:10,13,34■7:17■12:12■13:28-LU-5:36■6:39■8:4,9,11■12:16,41■13:6■14:7■15:3■18:1,9■19:11■20:9,19■21:29-JOH-10:6(3942)

PARABLES-EZE-20:49(4912)■N.T.-all=3850-M'T-13:3,10,13,34,35,53■21:45■22:1-M'R-3:23■4:2,11,13,33■12:1-LU-8:10

PARADISE-all=3857-LU-23:43-2CO-12:4-RE-2:7

PARAMOURS-EZE-23:20(6370)

PARCEL-all=2513-GE-33:19-JOS-24:32-RU-4:3-1CH-11:13,14■N.T.-JOH-4:5(5564)

PARCHED-all=7039&marked-LE-23:14-RU-2:14-IS-17:17■25:18-2SA-17:28^{2}-IS-35:7(8273)-JER-17:6(2788)

PARCHMENTS-2TI-4:13(3200)

PARDON-all=5545&marked-EX-23:21(5375)■34:9-NU-14:19-IS-15:25(5375)-2KI-5:18^{2}■24:4-2CH-30:18(3722)-NE-9:17(5547)-JOB-7:21(5375)-PS-25:11-IS-55:7-JER-5:1,7■33:8■50:20

PARDONED-NU-14:20(5545)-IS-40:2(7521)-LA-3:42(5545)

PARDONETH-MIC-7:18(5375)

PARE-DE-21:12(6213)

PARENTS-all=1118&marked-M'T-10:21-M'R-13:12-LU-2:27,41■8:56■18:29■21:16-JOH-9:2,3,18,20,22,23-RO-1:30-2CO-12:14^{2}-EPH-6:1-COL-3:20-1TI-5:4(4269)-2TI-3:2-HEB-11:23(3962)

PARLOUR-all=5944&marked-J'G-3:20,23,24,25-1SA-9:22(3957)

PARLOURS-1CH-28:11(2315)

PART-all=2506&marked-EX-29:26(4490)-LE-2:6(6626)■7:33(4940)■8:29(4940)-NU-18:20^{2}-DE-10:9■12:12■14:27,29■18:1-JOS-14:4■15:13■18:7■19:9■22:25,27-RU-1:17(6504)■2:3(2513)-1SA-30:24^{2},24(2505)-2SA-14:6(5337)■20:1-NE-3:9(6418),12(6418),14(6418),15(6418),16(6418),17(6418),18(6418)-JOB-32:17■41:6(2673)-PS-22:18(2505)-PR-17:2(2505)-IS-44:16^{2}(2677),19(2677)-DA-1:2(7117)■2:33(4481),41

(4481),42^{2}■5:5(6447),24(6447)-AM-7:4■ N.T.-all=3313&marked-LU-10:42 (3310)■11:36-JOH-13:8■19:23-AC-1:17(2819),25(2819)■5:2sup,2■8:21 (3310)■16:12(3310)■23:6,9■27:41 (4403)-RO-11:25-1CO-13:9,10,12■15:6 (4119)-2CO-1:14■2:5■6:15(3310) -EPH-4:16-HEB-2:14(3348)■7:2 (3307)-RE-20:6■21:8■22:19

PARTAKER-PS-50:18(2506)■N.T. -1CO-9:10(3348),23(4791)■10:30(3348) -1TI-5:22(2841)-2TI-1:8(4777)■2:6 (3335-)1PE-5:1(2844)-2JO-11(2841)

PARTAKERS-all=3353&marked -M'T-23:30(2844)-RO-15:27(2841) -1CO-9:12(3348),13(4829)■10:17(3348), 18(2844),21(3348)-2CO-1:7(2844) -EPH-3:6(4830)■5:7(4830)-PH'P-1:7 (4791)-COL-1:12(3310)-1TI-6:2(482) -HEB-2:14(2841)■3:1,14■6:4■12:8,10 (3335)-1PE-4:13(2841)-2PE-1:4(2844) -RE-18:4(4790)

PARTAKEST-RO-11:17(1096,4791)

PARTED-GE-2:10(6504)-2KI-2:11 (6504),14(2673)-JOB-38:24(2505) -JOE-3:2(2505)■N.T.-all=1266& marked-M'T-27:35^{2}-M'R-15:24-LU-23:34■24:51(1339)-JOH-19:24-AC-2:45

PARTETH-LE-11:3(6536)-DE-14:6 (6536)-PR-18:18(6504)

PARTIAL-MAL-2:9(5375,6440)■ N.T.-JAS-2:4(1252)

PARTIALITY-1TI-5:21(4346)-JAS-3:17(87)

PARTICULAR-1CO-12:27(3313) -EPH-5:33(3588,1520)

PARTICULARLY-AC-21:19(1520, 1538,2593)■N.T.-HEB-9:5(2596,3313)

PARTIES-supplied

PARTING-EZE-21:21(517)

PARTITION-1KI-6:21(5674)■ N.T.-EPH-2:14(5418)

PARTLY-DA-2:42(7118)■N.T. -1CO-11:18(3313,5100)-HEB-10:33 (5124,3303,)33(5124,1161)

PARTNER-PR-29:24(2505)■N.T. -2CO-8:23(2844)-PH'M-17(2844)

PARTNERS-LU-5:7(3353),10(2844)

PARTRIDGE-1SA-26:20(7124)-JER-17:11(7124)

PARTS-all=2506&marked-GE-47:24 (3027)-LE-1:8(5409)-JOS-18:5,6,9-1KI-6:38(1697)■16:21(2677)-2KI-11:7 (3027)-NE-11:1(3027)-JOB-26:14 (7098)■41:12(905)-PS-136:13(1506) -JER-34:18(1335),19(1335)■38:15 (3411)■39:2(3411)■48:8-ZEC-13:8 (6310)■N.T.-all=3313&marked -M'R-8:10-JOH-19:23-AC-2:10■20:2 -RO-15:23(2825)-EPH-4:9-RE-16:19

PASS-all=5674&marked-GE-8:1, ■18:3,5■30:32■31:52^{2}■32:16■33:14■ 41:32(6213)■50:20(6213)-EX-12:12,13 (6452)■23,23(6452)■15:16^{2}(5674)■ 33:19,22sup,22-LE-18:21-NU-20:17^{2}, 18■21:22,23■27:7,8■32:27,29,30,32■ 34:4^{2}-DE-2:4,18,24,27,28,29,30■3:18■ 9:1■11:31■18:10■27:2-JOS-1:11^{2},14■ 3:6,14^{2}■4:5■6:7^{2}■21:45(935)■22:19-J'G-3:28■11:17,19,20■13:12(935),17(935)■ 19:12-1SA-9:27■14:8■16:8,9,10-2SA-12:31■15:22■17:16,21sup,21-1KI-18:6 -2KI-6:9■16:3■17:17■21:6■23:10-2CH-33:6-NE-2:14-JOB-6:15■11:16■14:5■ 19:8■34:20-PS-37:5(6213),7(6213)■ 58:8(1980)■78:13■80:12■89:41■104:9■ 136:14■148:6-PR-4:15^{2}■8:29■16:30 (3615)■19:11■22:3■27:12-IS-8:8(2498), 21,21sup■21:1(2498)■23:2,6,10■ 23:12■28:15,18,19,21■30:32(4569)■ 31:9■33:21■34:10■35:8■47:2■51:10 -JER-2:10■5:22^{2}■8:13■9:10■15:14■ 22:8■32:35■33:13■51:43-LA-1:12■ 2:15■3:44■4:21-EZE-5:1,14,17■12:25 (6213)■14:15^{2}■16:21■20:26,31,37■23:37■ 29:11^{2}(5964)■33:28■37:2■39:15■46:21■ 47:5-DA-4:16(2499),23(2499),25(2499), 32(2499)■7:14(5709)■11:10,40-JOE-3:17 -AM-5:5,17■6:2■7:8■8:2-MIC-1:11■ 2:8,13-NA-1:12,15-HAB-1:11-ZEP-2:2-ZEC-3:4■9:8■10:11■13:2sup,2■ N.T.-all=3928&marked-M'T-:18^{2}■ 8:28■24:34,35^{2}■26:39,42-M'R-4:35 (1330)■13:30,31^{2}■14:35-LU-11:42■ 16:17,26(1224),26(1276)■18:36(1279)■ 19:4(1330)■21:32,33^{2}-AC-9:32(1330)■ 18:27(1330)-1CO-7:36(5230)■16:5^{2} (1330)-2CO-1:16(1330)-JAS-1:10-1PE-1:17(390)-2PE-3:10

PASSAGE-NU-20:21(5674)-JOS-22:11 (1552)-1SA-13:23(4569)-IS-10:29(4569)

PASSAGES-all=4569&marked-J'G-12:5,6-1SA-14:4-JER-22:20(5676)■51:32

PASSED-all=5674&marked-GE-12:6■ 15:17■31:21■32:10,22,31■33:3■37:28 -EX-12:27(6452)■34:6-NU-14:7■ 20:17■33:8,51-DE-2:8^{2}■27:3■29:16 -JOS-2:23■3:1,4,16,17^{2}■4:1,7,10,11^{2},12, 13,23■5:1■6:8■10:29,31,34■15:3^{2},4,6,7, 10^{2},11■16:6■18:9,18,19■24:17-J'G-3:26■ 8:4■10:9■11:29^{3},32■12:3■18:13■19:14 -1SA-9:4^{4},27■14:23■15:12■27:2■29:2^{2} -2SA-2:29■10:17■15:18^{2},22,23^{3}■17:22, 24■24:5-1KI-13:25■19:11,19■20:39 -2KI-4:8^{2},31■6:30■14:9-1CH-19:17 -2CH-9:22(1431)■25:18■30:10-JOB-4:15(2498)■9:26(2498)■15:19■28:8 (5710)-PS-18:12■37:36■48:4■90:9(6437) -SONG-3:4-IS-10:28■40:27■41:3-JER-2:6■11:15■34:18,19■46:17-EZE-16:6, 8,15,25■36:34■47:5-DA-3:27(5709)-HO-10:11-JON-2:3-MIC-2:13-NA-3:19 -HAB-3:10-ZEC-7:14■N.T.-all=1330 &marked-M'T-9:1(1276),9(3855)■ 20:30(3855)■27:39(3899)-M'R-2:14 (3855)■5:21(1276)■6:48(3928),53 (1276)■9:30(3899)■11:20(3899)■15:21 (3855),29(3899)-LU-10:31(492),32 (492)■17:11■19:1-JOH-5:24(3327)■ 8:59(3855)■9:1(3855)-AC-9:32■12:10 (4281)■14:24■15:3■17:1(1353),23■ 19:1,21-RO-5:12-1CO-10:1-2CO-5:17(3928)-HEB-4:14■11:29(1224)-1JO-3:14(3327)-RE-21:1(3928),4(565)

PASSEDST-J'G-12:1(5674)

PASSENGERS-all=5674&marked -PR-9:15(5674,1870)-EZE-39:11^{2},14,15

PASSEST-all=5674-DE-3:21■30:18 -2SA-15:33-1KI-2:37-IS-43:2

PASSETH-all=5674&marked-EX-30:13,14■33:22-LE-27:32-JOS-3:11■ 16:2■19:13-1KI-9:8-2KI-4:9■12:4 -2CH-7:21-JOB-9:11(2498)■14:20 (1980)■30:15■37:21-PS-8:8■78:39 (1980)■103:16■144:4-PR-10:25■26:17 -EC-1:4(1980)-IS-29:5-JER-9:12■ 13:24■18:16■19:8-EZE-35:7-HO-13:3 (1980)-MIC-7:18-ZEP-2:15■3:6-ZEC-9:8■N.T.-LU-18:37(3928)-1CO-7:31 (3855)-EPH-3:19(5235)-PH'P-4:7 (5242)-1JO-2:17(3855)

PASSING-all=5674&marked-J'G-19:18-2SA-15:24-2KI-6:26-PS-84:6 -PR-7:8-IS-31:5-EZE-39:14■N.T. -LU-4:30(1330)-AC-5:15(2064)■8:40 (1330)■16:8(3928)■27:8(3881)

PASSION-AC-1:3(3958)

PASSIONS-AC-14:15(3663)-JAS-5:17(3663)

PASSOVER-all=6453-EX-12:11, 21,27,43,48■34:25-LE-23:5-NU-9:2, 4,5,6,10,12,13,14^{2}■28:16■33:3-DE-16:1, 2,5,6-JOS-5:10,11-2KI-23:21,22,23 -2CH-30:1,2,5,15,18■35:1^{2},6,7,8,9,11, 13,16,17,18^{2},19-EZR-6:19,20-EZE-45:21■N.T.-all=3957-M'T-26:2,17,18, 19-M'R-14:1,12^{2},14,16-LU-2:41■22:1, 7,8,11,13,15-JOH-2:13,23■6:4■11:55^{2}■ 12:1■13:1■18:28,39■19:14-1CO-5:7 -HEB-11:28

PASSOVERS-2CH-30:17(6453)

PAST-all=8032&marked-GE-50:4 (5674)-EX-21:29,36-NU-21:22(5674) -DE-4:32(7223),42■19:4,6-1SA-15:32 (5493)■19:7-2SA-3:17■5:2■11:27 (5493)■16:1(5674)-1KI-18:29(5674) -1CH-11:2-JOB-9:10(369)■14:13(7725)■ 17:11(5674)■29:2(6924)-PS-90:4(5674) -EC-3:15(7291)-SONG-2:11(5674) -JER-8:20(5674)■N.T.-all=3928& marked-M'T-14:15-M'R-16:1(1230) -LU-9:36(1096)-AC-12:10(1330)■14:16 (3944)■27:9-RO-3:25(4266)■11:33 (421)-GA-5:21(4302)-EPH-4:19(524) -2TI-2:18(1096)-HEB-1:1(3819)■11:11 (3844)-1PE-4:3-1JO-2:8(3855)-RE-9:12 (565)■11:14(565)

PASTOR-JER-17:16(7462)

PASTORS-all=7462-JER-2:8■3:15■ 10:21■12:10■22:22■23:1,2■N.T.-EPH-4:11(4166)

PASTURE-all=4829&marked-GE-47:4-1CH-4:39,40,41-JOB-39:8-PS-74:1(4830)■79:13(4830)■95:7(4830)■ 100:3(4830)-IS-32:14-JER-23:1 (4830)■25:36(4830)-LA-1:6-EZE-34:14^{2},18,31(4830)-HO-13:6(4830) -JOE-1:18■N.T.-JOH-10:9(3542)

PASTURES-all=4999&marked-1KI-4:23(7471)-PS-23:2■65:12,13(3733)-IS-30:23(3733)■49:9(4830)-EZE-34:18 (4829)■45:15(4945)-JOE-1:19,20■2:22

PATE-PS-7:16(6936)

PATH-all=734&marked-GE-49:17 -NU-22:24(4934)-JOB-28:7(5410)■ 30:13(5410)■41:32(5410)-PS-16:11■ 27:11■77:19(7635)■119:35(5410),105 (5410)■139:3■142:3(5410)-PR-1:15 (5410)■2:9(4570)■4:14,18,26(4570)■ 5:6-IS-26:7(4570)■30:11■40:14■43:16 (5410)-JOE-2:8(4546)

PATHS-all=734,a=5410&marked -JOB-6:18■8:13■13:27■19:8a■24:13a■ 33:11■38:20a-PS-8:8■17:4,5(4570)■ 23:3(4570)■25:4,10■65:11(4570)-PR-2:8,13,15(4570),18(4570),19,20■3:6,17a■ 4:11(4570)■7:25a■8:2a,20a-IS-2:3■ 3:12■42:16a■58:12a■59:7(4546),8a -JER-6:16a■18:15(7635),15a-LA-3:9a -HO-2:6a-MIC-4:2■N.T.-all=5147& marked-M'T-3:3-M'R-1:3-LU-3:4 -HEB-12:13(5163)

PATHWAY-PR-12:28(1870,5410)

PATIENCE-all=5281&marked -M'T-18:26(3144),29(3144)-LU-8:15■ 21:19-RO-5:3,4■8:25■15:4,5-2CO-6:4■ 12:12-COL-1:11-1TH-1:3-2TH-1:4 -1TI-6:11-2TI-3:10-TIT-2:2-HEB-6:12(3115)■10:36■12:1-JAS-1:3,4■5:7 (3114),10(3115),11-2PE-1:6-RE-1:9■ 2:2,3,19■3:10■13:10■14:12

PATIENT-EC-7:8(750)■N.T.-all= 3114&marked-RO-2:7(5281)■12:12 (5278)-1TH-5:14-2TH-3:5(5281)-1TI-3:3(1933)-2TI-2:24(420)-JAS-5:7,8

PATIENTLY-PS-37:7(2342)■40:1 (6960)■N.T.-AC-26:3(3116)-HEB-6:15 (3114)-1PE-2:20^{2}(5278)

PATRIARCH-AC-2:29(3966)-HEB-7:4(3966)

PATRIARCHS-AC-7:8(3966),9(3966)

PATRIMONY-DE-18:8(5921,1)

PATTERN-all=8403&marked-EX-25:9^{2},40-NU-8:4(4758)-JOS-22:28-2KI-16:10-1CH-28:11,12,18,19-EZE-43:10 (8508)■N.T.-1TI-1:16(5296)-TIT-2:7 (5179)-HEB-8:5(5179)

PATTERNS-HEB-9:23(5262)

PAVED-EX-24:10(3840)-SONG-3:10(7528)

PAVEMENT-all=7531&marked -2KI-16:17(4837)-2CH-7:3-ES-1:6-EZE-40:17^{2},18^{2}■42:3■N.T.-JOH-19:13(3038)

PAVILION-PS-18:11(5521)■27:5 (5520)■31:20(5521)-JER-43:10(8237)

PAVILIONS-all=5521-2SA-22:12 -1KI-20:12,16

PAW-1SA-17:37^{2}(3027)

PAWETH-JOB-39:21(2658)

PAWS-LE-11:27(3709)

PAY-all=7999&marked-EX-21:19 (5414),22(5414),36■22:7,9,17(8254) -NU-20:19(5414,4377)-DE-23:21-2SA-15:7-1KI-20:39(8254)-2KI-4:7-2CH-

8:8(5427)■27:5(7725)-EZR-4:13(5415)-ES-3:9(8254)■4:7(8254)-JOB-22:27-PS-22:25■50:14■66:13■76:11■116:14,18-PR-19:17■22:27-EC-5:4^{2},5-JON-2:9■N.T.-all=591&marked-M'T-17:24(5055)■18:25,26,28,29,30,34■23:23(586)-LU-7:42-RO-13:6(5055)

PAYED-PR-7:14(7999)■N.T.-HEB-7:9(1183)

PAYETH-PS-37:21(7999)

PAYMENT-M'T-18:25(591)

PE-supplied

PEACE-all=7965,a=8002&marked-GE-15:15■24:21(2790)■26:29,31■28:21■34:5(2790)■41:16■43:23■44:17-EX-4:18■14:14(2790)■18:23(7965)■20:24a■24:5a■29:28a■32:6a-LE-3:1a,3a,6a,9a■4:10a,26a,31a,35a■6:12a■7:11a,13a,14a,15a,18a,20a,21a,29^{2}a,32a,33a,34a,37a■9:4a,18a,22a■10:3(1826),14a■17:5a■19:5a■22:21a■23:19a■26:6-NU-6:14a,17a,18a,26■7:17a,23a,29a,35a,41a,47a,53a,59a,65a,71a,77a,83a,88a■10:10a■15:8a■25:12■29:39a■30:4(2790),7(2790),11(2790),14^{2}(2790)-DE-2:26■20:10,11,12(7999)■23:6■27:7a■29:19-JOS-8:31a■9:15■10:1(7999),4(7999),21■11:19(7999)■22:23a,27a-J'G-4:17■6:23■8:9■11:31■18:6,19(2790)■19:20■20:26a■21:4a-1SA-1:17■7:14■10:8a,27(2790)■11:15a■13:9a■20:7,13,21,42■25:6^{3},35■29:7-2SA-3:21,22,23■6:17a,18a■10:19(7999)■13:20(2790)■15:9,27■17:3■19:24,30■24:25a-1KI-2:5,6,33■3:15a■4:24■5:12■8:63a,64^{2}a■9:25a■20:18■22:17,27,28,44(7999)-2KI-2:3(2814),5(2814)■5:19■7:9(2814)■9:17,18^{2},19^{2},22^{2},31■16:13a■18:36(2790)■20:19■22:20-1CH-12:18^{2}■16:1a,2a■19:19(7999)■21:26a■22:9-2CH-7:7a■15:5■18:16,26,27■19:1■29:35a■30:22a■31:2a■33:16a■34:28-EZR-4:17(8001)■5:7(8001)■9:12-NE-5:8(2790)■8:11(2013)-ES-4:14(2790)■9:30■10:3-JOB-5:23(7999),24■11:3(2790)■13:5(2790),13(2790)■22:21(7999)■25:2■29:10(6963)■33:31(2790),33(2790)-PS-4:8■7:4(7999)■28:3■29:11■34:14■35:20■37:11,37■39:2(2814),12(2790)■55:18,20■72:3,7■83:1(2790)■85:8,10■109:1■119:165■120:6,7■122:6,7,8■125:5■128:6■147:14-PR-3:2,17■7:14a■11:12(2790)■12:20■16:7(7999)■17:28(2790)-EC-3:8-IS-9:6,7■26:3,12■27:5^{2}■32:17■33:7■36:21(2790)■38:17■39:8■42:14(2814)■45:7■48:18,22■52:7■53:5■54:10,13■55:12■57:2,11(2814)■57:19,21■59:8^{2}■60:17■62:1(2814),6(2814)■64:12(2814)■66:12-JER-4:10,19(2790)■6:14■8:11,15■12:5,12■14:13,19■16:5■23:17■28:9■29:7^{2},11■30:5■33:6■34:5■43:12-LA-3:17-EZE-7:25■13:10,16^{2}■34:25■37:26■43:27a■45:15a,17a■46:2a,12^{2}a-DA-4:1(8001)■6:25(8001)■8:25(7962)■10:19-AM-5:22a-OB-7-MIC-3:5■5:5-NA-1:15-ZEP-1:7(2013)-HAG-2:9-ZEC-6:13■8:10,16,19■9:10-MAL-2:5,6■N.T.-all=1515-M'T-10:13^{2},34^{2}■20:31(4623)■26:63(4623)-M'R-1:25(5392)■3:4(4623)■4:39(4623)■5:34■9:34(4623),50(1518)■10:48(4623)■14:61(4623)-LU-1:79■2:14,29■4:35(5392)■7:50■8:48■10:5,6^{2}■11:21■12:51■14:4(2270),32■18:39(4623)■19:38,40(4623),42■20:26(4601)■24:36-JOH-14:27■16:33■20:19,21,26-AC-10:36■11:18(2270)■12:17(4601),20■15:13(4601),33■16:36■18:9(4623)-RO-1:7■2:10■3:17■5:1■8:6■10:15■14:17,19■15:13,33■16:20-1CO-1:3■7:15■14:30(4601),33■16:11-2CO-1:2■13:11(1518),11-GA-1:3■5:22■6:16-EPH-1:2■2:14,15,17■4:3■6:15,23-PH'P-1:2■4:7,9-COL-1:2,20(1517)■3:15-1TH-1:1■5:3,13(1518),23-2TH-1:2■3:16-1TI-1:2-2TI-1:2■2:22-TIT-1:4-PH'M-3-HEB-7:2■11:31■12:14■13:20-JAS-2:16■3:18-1PE-1:2■3:11■5:14-2PE-1:2■3:14-2JO-3-3JO-14-JUDE-2-RE-1:4■6:4

PEACEABLE-GE-34:21(8003)-2SA-20:19(7999)-1CH-4:40(7961)-IS-32:18(7965)-JER-25:37(7965)■N.T.-1TI-2:2(2272)-HEB-2:11(1516)-JAS-3:17(1516)

PEACEABLY-all=7965&marked-GE-37:4-J'G-11:13■21:13-1SA-16:4,5-1KI-2:13^{2}-1CH-12:17-JER-9:8-DA-11:21(7962),24(7962)■N.T.-RO-12:18(1518)

PEACEMAKERS-M'T-5:9(1518)

PEACOCKS-1KI-10:22(8500)-2CH-9:21(8500)-JOB-39:13(7443)

PEARL-M'T-13:46(3135)-RE-21:21(3135)

PEARLS-JOB-28:18(1378)■N.T.-all=3135-M'T-7:6■13:45-1TI-2:9-RE-17:4■18:12,16■21:21

PECULIAR-all=5459-EX-19:5-DE-14:2■26:18-PS-135:4-EC-2:8■N.T.-TIT-2:14(4041)-1PE-2:9(1519,4047)

PEDIGREES-NU-1:18(3205)

PEELED-IS-18:2(4178),7(4178)-EZE-29:18(4803)

PEEP-IS-8:19(6850)

PEEPED-IS-10:14(6850)

PELICAN-all=6893-LE-11:18-DE-14:17-PS-102:6

PEN-all=5842&marked-J'G-5:14(7626)-JOB-19:24-PS-45:1-IS-8:1(2747)-JER-8:8■17:1■N.T.-3JO-13(2563)

PENCE-all=1220-M'T-18:28-M'R-14:5-LU-7:41■10:35-JOH-12:5

PENKNIFE-JER-36:23(8593)

PENNY-all=1220-M'T-20:2,9,10,13■22:19-M'R-12:15-LU-20:24-RE-6:6^{2}

PENNYWORTH-M'R-6:37(1220)-JOH-6:7(1220)

PENTECOST-all=4005-AC-2:1■20:16-1CO-16:8

PENURY-PR-14:23(2470)■N.T.-LU-21:4(5303)

PEOPLE-all=5971,a=3816&marked-GE-11:6■14:16■17:14,16■19:4■23:7,11,12,13■25:8,17,23^{3}a,23■26:10,11■27:29■28:3■29:1(1121)■32:7■34:16,22■35:6,29■41:40,55■42:6■47:21,23■48:4,19■49:10,16,29,33■50:20-EX-1:9^{2},20,22■3:7,10,12,21■4:16,21,30,31■5:1,4,5,6,7,10^{2},12,16,22,23^{2}■6:7■7:4,14,16■8:1,3,4,8^{2},9,11,20,21^{2},22,23,29^{2},31,32■9:1,7,13,14,15,17,27■10:3,4■11:2,3^{2},8■12:27,31,33,34,36■13:3,17^{2},18,22■14:5^{2},6,13,31■15:13,14,16^{2},24■16:4,27,30■7:1,2,3^{2},4,5,6,13■18:1,10,13^{2},14^{3},15,18,19,21,22,23,25,26■19:5,7,8^{2},9^{2},10,11,12,14^{2},15,16,17,21,23,24,25■20:18^{2},20,21■22:25,28■23:11,27■24:2,3^{2},7,8■30:33,38■31:14■32:1^{2},3,6,7,9^{2},11,12,14,17,21,22,25,28,30,31,34,35■33:1,3,4,5,8,10^{2}12,13,16^{3}■34:9,10^{2}■36:5,6-LE-4:3,27■7:20,21,25,27■9:7^{2},15,18,22,23^{2},24■10:3,6(5712)■16:15,24^{2},33■17:4,9,10■18:29■19:8,16,18■20:2,3,4,5,6,17,18,24,26■21:1,4,14,15■23:29,30■26:12-NU-5:21,27■9:13■11:1,2,8,10,11,12,13,14,16,17,18,21,24^{2},29,32,33^{2},34,35■12:15,16■13:18,28,30,31,32■14:1,9,11,13,14,15,16,19^{2},39■15:26,30■16:41,47^{2}■20:1,3,20,24,26■21:2,4,5,6^{3},7^{2},16,18,23,29,33,34,35■22:3,5^{2},6,11,12,17,41■23:9,24■24:14^{3}■25:1,2^{2},4,15(523)■27:13■31:2,3■32:15■33:14-DE-1:28■2:4,10,16,21,32,33■3:1,2,3,28■4:6,10,20,33■5:28■6:14■7:6^{3},7^{2},14,16,19■9:2,6,12,13^{2},26,27,29■10:11,15■13:7,9■14:2^{2},21■16:18■17:7,13,16■18:3■20:1,2,5,8,9^{2},11,16■21:8^{2}■26:15,18,19■27:1,9,11,12,15,16,17,18,19,20,21,22,23,24,25,26■28:9,10,32,64■29:13■31:7,12,16■32:6,8,9,21,36,43^{2},44,50^{2}■33:3,5,7,17,19,21,29-JOS-1:2,6,10,11■3:3,5,6^{2},14^{2},16,17(1471)■4:1(1471),2,10^{2},11^{2},19,24■5:4,5^{2},6(1471),8(1471)■6:5^{2},7,8,10,16,20^{4}■7:3^{2},4,5,7,13■8:1^{2},3,5,9,10^{2},11^{2},13,14,16,20,33■10:7,13(1471),21,33■11:4,7■14:8■17:14,15,17■24:2,16,17,18,19,21,22,24,25,27,28-J'G-1:16■2:4,6,7,12,20(1471)■3:18■4:13■5:2,9,11,13,14,18■7:1,2,3^{2},4,5,6,7,8■8:5■9:29,32,33,34,35,36^{2},37,38,42,43^{2},45,48^{2},49■10:18■11:11,20,21,23■12:2■14:3,16,17■16:24,30■18:7,10,20,27■20:2^{2},8,10,16,22,26,31^{2}■21:2,4,9,15-RU-1:6,10,15,16■2:11■3:11■4:4,9,11-1SA-2:13,23,24,29■4:3,4,17■5:10,11■6:19^{3}■8:7,10,19,21■9:2,12,13,16^{3},17,24■10:11,17,23^{2},24^{3},25^{2}■11:4^{2},5,7,11,12,14,15■12:6,18,19,20,22^{2}■13:2,4,5,6^{2},7,8,11,14,15,16,22■14:2,3,15,17,20,24^{2},26^{2},27,28^{3},30,31,32^{2},33,34^{2},38,39,40,41,45^{2}■15:1,4,8,9,15,21,24,30■17:27,30■18:5,13■23:8■26:5,7^{2},14,15■27:12■30:4,6^{2},21^{2}■31:9-2SA-1:4^{2},12■2:26,27,28,30■3:18,31,32,34,35,36^{2},37■5:2,12■6:2,18,19^{2},21■7:7,8,10,11,23^{3},24^{2}■8:15■10:10,12,13■11:7,17■12:28,29,31^{2}■13:34■14:13,15■15:12,17,23^{2},24,30■16:6,14,15,18■17:2,3^{2},8,9,16,22,29^{2}■18:1,2^{2},3,4,5,6,7,8,16^{2}■19:2^{2},3^{2},8^{2},9,39,40^{2}■20:12,13(376)15,22■22:28,44^{2},48■23:10,11■24:2^{2},3,4,9,10,15,16,17,21-1KI-1:39,40^{2}■3:2,8^{2},9^{2}■4:34■5:7,16■6:13■8:16^{2},30,33,34,36^{2},38,41,43^{2},44,50,51,52,53,56,59,60,66^{2}■9:7,20,23■12:5,6,7,9,10,12,13,15,16,23,27^{2},30,31■13:33■14:2,7^{2}■16:2^{2},15,16,21^{2},22^{2}■18:21^{2},22,24,30^{2},37,39■19:21■20:8,10,15,42■21:9,12,13■22:4,28,43-2KI-3:7■4:13,41,42,43■6:18(1471),30■7:16,17,20■8:21■9:6■10:9,18■11:13^{2},14,17^{3},18,19,20■12:3,8■13:7■14:4,21■15:4,5,10,35■16:15■18:26,36■20:5■21:24^{2}■22:4,13■23:2,3,6,21,30,35■24:14■25:3,11,19^{2},22,26-1CH-5:25■10:9■11:2^{2},13■13:4■14:2■16:2,8,20,26,28,36,43■17:6,7,9,10,21^{3},22^{2}■18:14■19:7,11,13,14■20:3^{2}■21:2,3,5,17^{2},22■22:18■23:25■28:2,21■29:9,14,17,18-2CH-1:9,10^{2},11■2:11,18■6:5^{2},6,21,24,25,27^{2},29,32,33^{2},34,39■7:4,5,10^{2},13,14■8:7,10■10:5,6,7,9,10,12,15,16■12:3■13:17■14:13■16:10■17:9■18:2,3,27■19:4■20:7,21,25,33■21:14,19■23:5,6,10,12^{2},13,16^{2},17,20^{2},21■24:10,20,23^{2}■25:11,15^{2}■26:1,21■27:2■29:36^{2}■30:3,13,18,20,27■31:4,8,10■32:4,6,8,13,14,15,17^{2},18,19■33:10,17,25^{2}■34:30■35:3,5,7,8,12(1121,5971),13(1121,5971)■36:1,14,15,16,23-EZR-1:3■2:2,70■3:1,3,11,13^{3}■4:4^{2}■5:12(5972)■6:12(5972)■7:13(5972),16(5972),25(5972)■8:15,36■9:1^{2},2,11,14■10:1,2,9,11,13-NE-1:10■4:6,13,14,19,22■5:1,13,15^{2},18,19■7:4,5,7,72,73■8:1,3,5^{3},6,7^{2},9^{3},11,12,13,16■9:10,24,30,32■10:14,28^{2},30,31,34■11:1^{2},2,24■12:30,38■13:1,24-ES-1:5,11,16,22^{2}■2:10,20■3:6^{2},8^{3},11,12^{2},14■4:8,11■7:3,4■8:6,9,11,13,17■9:2■10:3-JOB-12:2,24■17:6■18:19■34:20,30■36:20,31-PS-2:1a■3:6,8■7:7a,8■9:8a,11■14:4,7■18:27,43^{2},47■22:6,31■28:9■29:11^{2}■33:10,12■35:18■44:2a,12,14a■45:5,10,12,17■47:1,3,9^{2}■49:1■50:4,7■53:4,6■56:7■57:9■59:11■60:3■62:8■65:7a■66:8■67:3^{2},4,5^{2}■68:7,30^{2},35■72:2,3,4■73:10■74:14,18■77:14,15,20■78:1,20,52,62,71■79:13■80:4■81:8,11,13■83:3■85:2,6,8■87:6■89:15,19,50■94:5,8,14■95:7,10■96:3,7,10,13■97:6■98:9■99:1,2■100:3■102:18,22■105:1,13,20,24,25,43,44a■106:4,40,48■107:32■108:3■110:3■111:6,9■113:8■114:1■116:14,18■117:1(523)■125:2■135:12,14■136:16■144:2,15^{2}■148:11a,14^{2}■149:4,7a-PR-11:14,26a■14:28,28a,34a■24:24■28:15■29:2^{2},18■30:25-EC-4:16■12:9-IS-1:3,4,10■2:3,4,6■3:5,7,12^{2},13,14,15■5:13,25■6:5,9,10■7:2,8,17■8:6,9,11,12,19■9:2,9,13,16,19■10:2,6,13,14,22,24■11:10,11,16■12:4■13:4,14■14:2,6,20,32■17:12■18:2,7^{2}■19:25■22:4■23:13■24:2,4,13■25:3,6,7,8■26:11,20■27:11■28:5,11,14■29:13,14■30:5,6,9,19,26,28■32:13,18■33:3,12,19^{2},24■34:1a,5■36:11■40:1,7■41:1a■42:5,6,22■43:4a,8,9a,20,21■44:7■47:6■49:1a,8,13,22■51:4^{2},5,7,16,22■52:4,5,6,9■53:8■55:4^{2}a■56:3,7■57:14■58:1■60:2a,21■61:9■62:10^{2},12■63:3,6,8,11,14,18■64:9■65:2,3,10,18,19,22-JER-1:18■2:11,13,31,32■4:10,11^{2},22■5:14,21,23,26,

31■6:14,19,21,22,26,27■7:12,16,23,33■8:5,7,11,19,21,22■9:1,2,7,15■10:3■11:4,14■12:14,16^{3}■13:10,11■14:10,11,16,17■15:1,7,20■16:5,10■17:19■18:15■19:1,11,14■21:7,8■22:2,4■23:2,13,22,27,32^{2},33,34■24:7■25:1,2,19■26:7,8^{2},9,11,12,16,17,18,23,24■27:12,13,16■28:1,5,7,11,15■29:1,16,25,32^{2}■30:3,22■31:1,2,7,14,33■32:21,38,42■33:24^{2}■34:1,8,10,19■35:16■36:6,7,9^{2},10,13,14■37:2,4,12,18■38:1,4^{2}■39:8,9^{2},10,14■40:5,6■41:10^{2},13,14,16■42:1,8■43:1,4■44:15,20^{2},21,24■46:16,24■48:42,46■49:1■50:6,16,41■51:45,58■52:6,15^{2},25^{2},28-**LA**-1:1,7,11,18■2:11■3:14,45,48■4:3,6,10-**EZE**-3:5,6,11■7:27■11:1,17,20■12:19■13:9,10,17,18,19^{2},21,23■14:8,9,11■17:9,15■18:18■20:34,35,41■21:12^{2}■22:29■23:24■24:18,19■25:7,14■26:2,7,11,20■27:3,33,36■28:19,25■29:13■30:11■31:12■32:3,9,10■33:2^{2},3,6,12,17,30,31^{2}■34:13,30■36:3,8,12,15,20,28■37:12,13,18,23,27■38:6,8,9,12,14,15,16,22■39:4,7,13,27■42:14■44:11,19^{2},23■45:8,9,16,22■46:3,9,18,20,24-**DA**-2:44(5972)■3:4(5972),7^{2}(5972),29(5972)■4:1(5972)■5:19(5972)■6:25(5972)■7:14(5972),27(5972)■8:24■9:6,15,16,19,20,24,26■10:14■11:14,23(1471),32,33■12:1^{2},7-**HO**-1:9,10■2:23^{2}■4:4,6,8,9,12,14■6:11■7:8■9:1■10:5,10,14■11:7-**JO**-2:2,5,6,16,17^{2},18,19,26,27■3:2,3,8(1471),16-**AM**-1:5■3:6■7:8,15■8:2■9:10,14-**OB**-13-**JON**-1:8■3:5(582)-**MIC**-1:2,9■2:4,8,9,11■3:3,5■4:1,3,5,13■5:7,8■6:2,3,5,16■7:14-**NA**-3:13,18-**HAB**-2:8,10,13,13a■3:13,16-**ZEP**-1:11■2:8,9■22:8,9,9(1471),10■3:9,12,20-**HAG**-1:2,12^{2},13,14■2:2,4,14-**ZEC**-2:11■7:5■8:6,7,8,11,12,20,22■9:16■10:9■11:10■12:2,3,3(1471),4,6,3■13:9■14:2,12-**MAL**-1:4■2:9■**N.T.**all=2992,a=3793&marked-**M'T**-1:21■2:4,6■4:16,23■7:28a■9:23a,25a,35■12:23a,46a■14:13a■15:8■21:23,26a■26:3,5,47■27:1,15a,25,64-**M'R**-5:21a,24a■6:33a,34a,45a■7:6,14a,17a■8:6^{2}a,34■9:15a,25a■10:1a,46a■11:18a,32■12:12a,37a,41a■14:2■15:11a,15a-**LU**-1:10,17,21,68,77■2:10,31,32■3:10a,15,18,21■4:42a■5:1a,3a■6:17■7:1,9a,11a,12a,16,24a,29■8:4a,40a,42a,47■9:11a,13,18a,37a■11:14a,29a■12:1a,54a■13:14a,17a■18:43■19:47,48■20:1,6,9,19,26,45■21:23,38■22:2,66■23:4a,5,13,14,27,35,48a■24:19-**JON**-6:22a,24a■7:12^{2}a,20a,31a,32a,40a,43a,49a■8:2■11:42a,50■12:9a,12a,17a,18a,29a,34a■18:14-**AC**-2:47■3:9,11,12,23■4:1,2,8,10,17,21,25,27■5:12,13,20,25,26,34,37■6:8,12■7:17,34■8:6a,9(1484)■10:2,41,42■11:24a,26a■12:4,11,22(1218)■13:15,17^{2},24,31■14:11a,13a,14a,18a,19a■15:14■17:5(1218),8a,13a■18:10■19:4,26a,30(1218),33(1218),35a■21:27a,28,30,35a,36,39,40■23:5■24:12a■26:17,23■28:17,26,27-**RO**-9:25^{2},26■10:19(1484),21■11:1,2■15:10,11-**1CO**-10:7■14:21-**2CO**-6:16-**TIT**-2:14-**HEB**-2:17■4:9■5:3■7:5,11■8:10■9:7,19^{2}■10:30■11:25■13:12-**1PE**-2:9,10^{2}-**2PE**-2:1-**JUDE**-5-**RE**-5:9■7:9■11:9■14:6■18:4■19:1a■21:3

PEOPLE'S-LE-9:15(5971)-EZE-46:18(5971)■N.T.-M'T-13:15(2992)-HEB-7:27(2992)

PEOPLES-RE-10:11(2992)■17:15(2992)

PERADVENTURE-all=194&marked-GE-18:24,28,29,30,31,32■24:5,39■27:12■31:31(6435)■32:20■43:12■50:15(3863)-EX-32:30-NU-22:6,11■23:3,27-JOS-9:7-1SA-6:5■9:6-1KI-18:5,27■20:31-2KI-2:16-JER-20:10■N.T.-RO-5:7(5029)-2TI-2:25(3379)

PERCEIVE-all=3045&marked-DE-29:4-JOS-22:31-1SA-12:17-2SA-19:6-2KI-4:9-JOB-9:11(995)■23:8(995)-EC-3:22(7200)-IS-6:9■33:19(8085)■N.T.-all=2334&marked-M'T-13:14(1492)-M'R-4:12(1492)■7:18(3539)■8:17(3539)-LU-8:46(1097)-JOH-4:19■12:19-AC-8:23(3708)■10:34(2638)■17:22■27:10■28:26(1492)-2CO-7:8(991)-1JO-3:16(1097)

PERCEIVED-all=3045&marked-GE-19:33,35-J'G-6:22(7200)-1SA-3:8(995)■28:14-2SA-5:12■12:19(995)■14:1-1KI-22:33(7200)-1CH-14:2-2CH-18:32(7200)-NE-6:12(5234),16■13:10-ES-4:1-JOB-38:18(995)-EC-1:17■2:14-IS-64:4(238)-JER-23:18(7200)■38:27(8085)■N.T.-all=1097&marked-M'T-16:8■21:45■22:18-M'R-2:8(1921)-LU-1:22(1921)■5:22(1921)■9:45(143)■20:19,23(2657)-JOH-6:15-AC-4:13(2638)■23:6,29(2147)-GA-2:9

PERCEIVEST-PR-14:7(3045)■N.T.-LU-6:41(2657)

PERCEIVETH-JOB-14:21(995)■33:14(7789)-PR-31:18(2938)

PERCEIVING-all=1492-M'R-12:28-LU-9:47-AC-14:9

PERDITION-all=684-JOH-17:12-PH'P-1:28-2TH-2:3-1TI-6:9-HEB-10:39-2PE-3:7-RE-17:8,11

PERES-DA-5:28(6537)

PERFECT-all=8549,a=8003,b=8535&marked-GE-6:9■17:1-LE-22:21-DE-18:13■25:15^{2}a■32:4-1SA-14:41-2SA-22:31,33-1KI-8:61a■11:4a■15:3a,14a-2KI-20:3a-1CH-12:38a■28:9a■29:9a,19a-2CH-4:21(4357)■15:17a■16:9a■19:9a■25:2a-EZR-7:12(1585)-JOB-1:1b,8b■2:3b■8:20b■9:20b,21b,22b■22:3(8552)■36:4■37:16-PS-18:30,32■19:7■37:37b■64:4b■101:2,2(8537),6■138:8(1584)■139:22(8503)-PR-2:21■4:18(3559)■11:5-IS-18:5(8552)■38:3a■42:19(7999)-EZE-16:14(3632)■27:3(3632),11(3634)■28:12(3632),15■N.T.-all=5046,a=5048&marked-M'T-5:48^{2}■19:21-LU-1:3(199)■6:40(2675)-JOH-17:23a-AC-3:16(3647)■22:3(195)■24:22(197)-RO-12:2-1CO-2:6■13:10-2CO-12:9a■13:11(2675)-GA-3:3(2005)-EPH-4:13-PH'P-3:12a,15-COL-1:28■4:12-1TH-3:10(2675)-2TI-3:17(739)-HEB-2:10a■5:9a■7:19a■9:9a,11■10:1a■11:40a■12:23a■13:21(2675)-JAS-1:4^{2},17,25■2:22a■3:2-1PE-5:10(2675)-1JO-4:17a,18,18a-RE-3:2(4137)

PERFECTED-2CH-8:16(8003)■24:13(5927,724)-EZE-27:4(3634)■N.T.-all=5048&marked-M'T-21:16(2675)-LU-13:32-HEB-10:14-1JO-2:5■4:12

PERFECTING-2CO-7:1(2005)-EPH-4:12(2677)

PERFECTION-JOB-11:7(8503)■15:29(4512)■28:3(8503)-PS-50:2(4359)■119:96(8502)-IS-47:9(8537)-LA-2:15(3632)■N.T.-LU-8:14(5052)-2CO-13:9(2676)-HEB-6:1(5051)■7:11(5050)

PERFECTLY-JER-23:20(998)■N.T.-all=197&marked-M'T-14:36(1295)-AC-18:26■23:15,20-1CO-1:10(2675)-1TH-5:2(199)

PERFECTNESS-COL-3:14(5047)

PERFORM-all=6965,a=6213&marked-GE-26:3-EX-18:18a-NU-4:23(6633)-DE-4:13a■9:5■23:23a-1SA-3:12-2SA-14:15a-1KI-6:12■12:15-2KI-23:3,24-2CH-10:15■34:31a-ES-5:8a-PS-61:8(7999)■119:106,112a-IS-9:7a■19:21(7999)■44:28(7999)-JER-1:12a■11:5■28:6■29:10■33:14■44:25^{2}a-EZE-12:25a-MIC-7:20(5414)-NA-1:15(7999)■N.T.-M'T-5:33(591)-LU-1:72(4160)-RO-4:21(4160)■7:18(2716)-2CO-8:11(2005)-PH'P-1:6(2005)

PERFORMANCE-LU-1:45(5050)-2CO-8:11(2005)

PERFORMED-all=6965&marked-1SA-15:11,13-2SA-21:14(6213)-1KI-8:20-2CH-6:10-NE-9:8-ES-1:15(6213)■5:6(6213)■7:2(6213)-PS-65:1(7999)-IS-10:12(1214)-JER-23:20■30:24■34:18■35:14,16■51:29-EZE-37:14(6213)■N.T.-LU-1:20(1096)■2:39(5055)-RO-15:28(2005)

PERFORMETH-NE-5:13(6965)-JOB-23:14(7999)-PS-57:2(1548)-IS-44:26(7999)

PERFORMING-NU-15:3(6381),8(6381)

PERFUME-all=7004-EX-30:35,37-PR-27:9

PERFUMED-PR-7:17(5130)-SONG-3:6(6999)

PERFUMES-IS-57:9(7547)

PERHAPS-AC-8:22(686)-2CO-2:7(3381)-PH'M-15(5029)

PERIL-RO-8:35(2794)

PERILOUS-2TI-3:1(5467)

PERILS-2CO-11:26^{6}(2794)

PERISH-all=6&marked-GE-41:36(3772)-EX-19:21(5307)■21:26(7843)-LE-26:38-NU-17:12■24:20(8),24(8)-DE-4:26■8:19,20■11:17■26:5■28:20,22■30:18-JOS-23:13,16-J'G-5:31-1SA-26:10(5595)■27:1(5595)-2KI-9:8-ES-3:13■4:16■7:4■8:11■9:28(5486)-JOB-3:3■4:9,20■6:18■8:13■18:17■20:7■29:13■31:19■34:15(1478)■36:12(5674)-PS-1:6■2:12■9:3,18■37:20■41:5■49:10,12(1820),20(1820)■68:2■73:27■80:16■83:17■92:9■102:26■112:10■146:4-PR-10:28■11:7,10■19:9■21:28■28:28■29:18(6544)■31:6-EC-5:14-IS-26:14■27:13■29:14■41:11■60:12-JER-4:9■6:21■10:11,15■18:18■27:10,15■40:15■48:8■51:18-EZE-7:26■25:7-DA-2:18(7)-AM-1:8■2:14■3:15-JON-1:6,14■3:9-ZEC-9:5■N.T.-all=622&marked-M'T-5:29,30■8:25■9:17■18:14■26:52-M'R-4:38-LU-5:37■8:24■13:3,5,33■15:17■21:18-JOH-3:15,16■10:28■11:50-AC-8:20(1510,1519,684)■13:41(853)-RO-2:12-1CO-1:18■8:11-2CO-2:15■4:16(1311)-COL-2:22(5356)-2TH-2:10-HEB-1:11-2PE-2:12(2704)■3:9

PERISHED-all=6&marked-NU-16:33■21:30-JOS-22:20(1478)-2SA-1:27-JOB-4:7■30:2-PS-9:6■10:16■83:10(8045)■119:92-EC-9:6-JER-7:28■48:36■49:7-LA-3:18-JOE-1:11-JON-4:10-MIC-4:9■7:2■N.T.-all=622&marked-M'T-8:32(599)-LU-11:51-AC-5:37-1CO-15:18-HEB-11:31(4881)-2PE-3:6-JUDE-11

PERISHETH-all=6-JOB-4:11-PR-11:7-EC-7:15-IS-57:1-JER-9:12■48:46■N.T.-all=622-JOH-6:27-JAS-1:11-1PE-1:7

PERISHING-JOB-33:18(5674)

PERJURED-1TI-1:10(1965)

PERMISSION-1CO-7:6(4774)

PERMIT-1CO-16:7(2010)-HEB-6:3(2010)

PERMITTED-AC-26:1(2010)-1CO-14:34(2010)

PERNICIOUS-2PE-2:2(684)

PERPETUAL-all=5769&marked-GE-9:12-EX-29:9■30:8(8548)■31:16-LE-3:17■6:20(8548)■24:9■25:34-NU-19:21-PS-9:6(5331)■74:3(5331)■78:66-JER-5:22■8:5(5331)■15:18(5331)■18:16■23:40■25:9,12■49:13■50:5■51:39,57-EZE-35:5,9■46:14-HAB-3:6-ZEP-2:9

PERPETUALLY-1KI-9:3(3605,3117)-2CH-7:16(3605,3117)-AM-1:11(5703)

PERPLEXED-ES-3:15(943)-JOE-1:18(943)■N.T.-LU-9:7(1280)■24:4(1280)-2CO-4:8(639)

PERPLEXITY-IS-22:5(3998)-MIC-7:4(3998)■N.T.-LU-21:25(640)

PERSECUTE-all=7291&marked-JOB-19:22,28-PS-7:1,5■10:2(1841)■31:15■35:3,6■69:26■71:11■83:15■119:84,86-JER-17:18■29:18(7291,310)-LA-3:66■N.T.-all=1377&marked-M'T-5:11,44■10:23■23:34-LU-11:49(1559)■21:12-JOH-5:16■15:20-RO-12:14

PERSECUTED-all=7291&marked-DE-30:7-PS-109:16■119:161■143:3-IS-14:6(4783)-LA-3:43■N.T.-all=1377&marked-M'T-5:10,12-JOH-15:20-AC-7:52■22:4■26:11-1CO-4:12■15:9-2CO-4:9

-GA-1:13,23▪4:29-1TH-2:15(1559)-RE-12:13

PERSECUTEST-all=1377-AC-9:4, 5▪22:7,8▪26:14,15

PERSECUTING-PH'P-3:6(1377)

PERSECUTION-LA-5:5(7291)▪ **N.T.**-all=1375&marked-M'T-13:21-M'R-4:17-AC-8:1▪11:19(2347)▪13:50-RO-8:35 -GA-5:11(1377)▪6:12(1377)-2TI-3:12(1377)

PERSECUTIONS-all=1375-M'R-10:30-2CO-12:10-2TH-1:4-2TI-3:11^2

PERSECUTOR-1TI-1:13(1376)

PERSECUTORS-all=7291&marked -NE-9:11-PS-7:13(1814)▪119:157▪ 142:6-JER-15:15▪20:11-LA-1:3▪4:19

PERSEVERANCE-EPH-6:18(4343)

PERSON-all=5315,a=6440&marked -LE-19:15^{2}a-NU-5:6▪19:18(376,120)▪ 31:19▪38:11,15,30^2-DE-27:25▪28:50a -JOS-20:3,9-1SA-9:2(376)▪16:18(376)▪ 25:35a-2SA-4:11(376)▪14:14▪17:11a -JOB-13:8a▪32:21a-PR-6:12(120)▪ 18:5a▪24:8(1167)▪28:17-JER-43:6▪ 52:25a-EZE-16:5▪33:6▪44:25(120) -MAL-1:8a▪**N.T.**-all=4383&marked -M'T-22:16-M'R-12:14-LU-20:21 -2CO-2:10-GA-2:6-HEB-1:3(5287)

PERSONS-all=5315,a=6440& marked-GE-14:21▪36:6-EX-16:16-LE-27:2-NU-19:18▪31:28(120),30(120),35 (5315,120),40^2(5315,120),46(5315, 120)-DE-1:17a▪10:17a,22▪16:19a-J'G-9:2(376),4(582),5(376),18(376)▪20:39 (376)-1SA-9:22(376)▪22:18(376),22-2KI-10:6(376),7(376)-2CH-19:7a-JOB-13:10a▪34:19a-PS-26:4(4962)▪82:2a -PR-24:23a▪28:21a-JER-52:29,30^2 -LA-4:16a-EZE-17:17▪27:13-JON-4:11(120)-ZEP-3:4(582)-MAL-1:9a▪ **N.T.**-all=4382&marked-AC-10:34 (4381)-RO-2:11-2CO-1:11(4383)-EPH-6:9-COL-3:25-1TI-1:10(678)-JAS-2:1,9 (4380)-1PE-1:17(678)-JUDE-16(4383)

PERSUADE-all=6601&marked -1KI-22:20,21,22-2CH-32:11(5496),15 (5496)-IS-36:18(5496)▪**N.T.**-all= 3982-M'T-28:14-2CO-5:11-GA-1:10

PERSUADED-2CH-18:2(5496) -PR-25:15(6601)▪**N.T.**-all=3982&marked -M'T-27:20-LU-16:31▪20:6-AC-13:43▪ 14:19▪18:4▪19:26▪21:14▪26:26-RO-4:21 (4135)▪8:38(3982)▪14:5(4135),14▪15:14 -2TI-1:5,12-HEB-6:9▪11:13

PERSUADEST-AC-26:28(3982)

PERSUADETH-2KI-18:32(5496)▪ **N.T.**-AC-18:13(374)

PERSUADING-AC-19:8(3982)▪ 28:23(3982)

PERSUASION-GA-5:8(3988)

PERTAIN-all =supplied

PERTAINED-2SA-9:9(1961)

PERTAINETH-DE-22:5(3627) -1SA-27:6(1961)▪**N.T.**-HEB-7:13(3348)

PERTAINING-AC-1:3(4012)

PERVERSE-all=6141&marked -NU-22:32(3399)-DE-32:5-1SA-20:30 (5753)-JOB-6:30(1942)▪9:20(6140) -PR-4:24(3891)▪8:8▪12:8(5753)▪14:2 (3868)▪17:20(2015)▪19:1▪23:33(8419)▪ 28:6,18(6140)-IS-19:14(5773)▪**N.T.**-all=1294&marked-M'T-17:17-LU-9:41 -AC-20:30-PH'P-2:15-1TI-6:5(3859)

PERVERSELY-2SA-19:19(5753) -1KI-8:47(5753)-PS-119:78(5791)

PERVERSENESS-NU-23:21(5999) -PR-11:3(5558)▪15:4(5558)-IS-30:12 (3868)▪59:3(5766)-EZE-9:9(4297)

PERVERT-all=5791&marked-DE-16:19(5557)▪24:17(5186)-JOB-8:3^2▪ 34:12-PR-17:23(5186)▪31:5(8138) -MIC-3:9(6140)▪**N.T.**-AC-13:10(1294) -GA-1:7(3344)

PERVERTED-1SA-8:3(5186)-JOB-33:27(5753)-IS-47:10(7725)-JER-3:21 (5753)▪23:36(2015)

PERVERTETH-EX-23:8(5557) -DE-27:19(5186)-PR-10:9(6140)▪ 19:3(5557)▪**N.T.**-LU-23:14(654)

PERVERTING-LU-23:2(1294)

PESTILENCE-all=1698-EX-5:3▪9:15-LE-26:25-NU-14:12-DE-28:21-2SA-24:13,15-1KI-8:37-1CH-21:12,14-2CH-6:28▪7:13▪20:9-PS-78:50▪91:3,6-JER-14:12▪21:6,7,9▪24:10▪ 27:8,13▪28:8▪29:17,18▪32:24,36▪34:17▪ 38:2▪42:17,22▪44:13-EZE-5:12,17▪6:11, 12▪7:15^2▪12:16▪14:19,21▪28:23▪33:27▪ 38:22-AM-4:10-HAB-3:5

PESTILENCES-M'T-24:7(3061) -LU-21:11(3061)

PESTILENT-AC-24:5(3061)

PESTLE-PR-27:22(5940)

PETITION-all=7596&marked -1SA-1:17,27-1KI-2:16,20-ES-5:6,7,8▪ 7:2,3▪9:12-DA-6:7(1159),13(1159)

PETITIONS-PS-20:5(4862)-1JO-5:15(155)

PHARISEE-all=5330-M'T-23:26 -LU-7:39▪11:37,38▪18:10,11-AC-5:34▪ 23:6^2▪26:5-PH'P-3:5

PHARISEE'S-LU-7:36(5330),37 (5330)

PHARISEES-all=5330-M'T-3:7▪ 5:20▪9:11,14,34▪12:2,14,24,38▪15:1,12▪ 16:1,6,11,12▪19:3▪21:45▪22:15,34,41▪ 23:2,13,14,15,23,25,27,29▪27:62-M'R-2:16,18,18,24▪3:6▪7:1,3,5▪8:11,15▪ 10:2▪12:13-LU-5:17,21,30,33▪6:2,7▪ 7:30,36▪11:39,42,43,44,53▪12:1▪13:31▪ 14:1,3▪15:2▪16:14▪17:20▪19:39-JOH-1:24▪3:1▪4:1▪7:32^2,45,47,48▪8:3,13▪ 9:13,15,16,40▪11:46,47,57▪12:19,42▪18:3 -AC-15:5▪23:6,7,8

PHARISEES'-AC-23:9(5330)'

PHILOSOPHERS-AC-17:18(5386)

PHILOSOPHY-COL-2:8(5385)

PHYLACTERIES-M'T-23:5(5440)

PHYSICIAN-JER-8:22(7495)▪ **N.T.**-all=2395-M'T-9:12-M'R-2:17 -LU-4:23▪5:31-COL-4:14

PHYSICIANS-all=7495-GE-50:2^2 -2CH-16:12-JOB-13:4▪**N.T.**-M'R-5:26 (2395)-LU-8:43(2395)

PICK-PR-30:17(5365)

PICTURES-NU-33:52(4906)-PR-25:11(4906)-IS-2:16(7914)

PIECE-all=4060&marked-GE-15:10 (1335)-EX-37:7(4749)-J'G-9:53(6400) -1SA-2:36(95),36(6595)▪30:12(6400) -2SA-6:19(829)▪11:21(6400)▪23:11 (2513)-2KI-3:19(2513),25(2513)-1CH-16:3(829)-NE-3:11,19,20,21,24,27,30 -JOB-41:42(6400)-PR-6:26(3603)▪28:21 (6595)-SONG-4:3(6400)▪6:7(6400)-JER-37:21(3603)-EZE-24:4(5409),6(5409) -AM-3:12(915)▪**N.T.**-all=1915&marked -M'T-9:16-M'R-2:21,21(4138)-LU-5:36^2▪ 15:8(1406),9(1406)▪24:42(3313)

PIECES-all=5409&marked-GE-15:17(1506)-EX-29:17^2-LE-1:6,12▪2:6 (6595)▪6:21(6595)▪8:20^2▪9:13-J'G-19:29-1KI-11:30(7168),31(7168)-2KI-2:12(7168)-PS-68:30(7518)-EZE-13:19 (6595)▪24:4-DA-2:5(1917)▪3:29(1917)▪ **N.T.**-LU-15:6(1406)-AC-23:10(1288)

PIERCE-NU-24:8(4272)-2KI-18:21 (5344)-IS-36:6(5344)▪**N.T.**-LU-2:35(1330)

PIERCED-J'G-5:26(4272)-JOB-30:17(5365)-PS-22:16(738)-ZEC-12:10 (1856)▪**N.T.**-JOH-19:34(3572),37 (1574)-1TI-6:10(4044)-RE-1:7(1574)

PIERCETH-JOB-40:24(5344)

PIERCING-IS-27:1(1281)▪**N.T.** -HEB-4:12(1338)

PIERCINGS-PR-12:18(4094)

PIETY-1TI-5:4(2151)

PIGEON-GE-15:9(1469)-LE-12:6(3123)

PIGEONS-all=3123-LE-1:14▪5:7, 11▪12:8▪14:22,30▪15:14,29-NU-6:10▪ **N.T.**-LU-2:24(4058)

PILE-IS-30:33(4071)-EZE-24:9(4071)

PILGRIMAGE-all=4033-GE-47:9^2 -EX-6:4-PS-119:54

PILGRIMS-HEB-11:13(3927)-1PE-2:11(3927)

PILLAR-all=5982,a=4676&marked -GE-19:26(5333)▪28:18a,22a▪31:13a,45a, 51a,52^{2}a▪35:14a,14(4678),20a,20(4678) -EX-13:21^2,22^2▪14:19,24▪33:9,10-NU-12:5▪14:14^2-DE-31:15^2-J'G-9:6(5324)▪ 20:40-2SA-18:18^2(4678),-1KI-7:21^2-2KI-11:14▪23:3▪25:17^2-2CH-23:13-NE-9:12^2, 19^2-PS-99:7-IS-19:19a-JER-1:18▪52:21, 22▪**N.T.**-1TI-3:15(4769)-RE-3:12(4769)

PILLARS-all=5982&marked-EX-24:4(4676)▪26:32,37▪27:10^2,11^2,12,14, 15,16,17▪35:11,17▪36:36,38▪37:10^2,11^2, 12^2,14,15,17^3,19,28▪39:33,40▪40:18 -NU-3:36,37▪4:31,32-DE-12:3(4676) -J'G-16:25,26,29-1SA-2:8(4690)-1KI-7:2^2,3,6^2,15,16,17,18,19,20,21,22^2,41^3, 42▪10:12(4552)-2KI-18:16(547)▪25:13, 16-1CH-18:8-2CH-3:15,16,17▪4:12^3, 13-ES-1:6-JOB-9:6▪26:11-PS-75:3-PR-9:1-SONG-3:6(8490),10▪5:15-JER-27:19▪52:17,20,21-EZE-40:49▪42:6 -JOE-2:30(8490)▪**N.T.**-GA-2:9(4769) -RE-10:1(4769)

PILLED-GE-30:37(6478),38(6478)

PILLOW-1SA-19:13(3523),16(3523)▪ **N.T.**-M'R-4:38(4344)

PILLOWS-GE-28:11(4763),18(4763) -EZE-13:18(3704),20(3704)

PILOTS-all=2259-EZE-27:8,27,28,29

PIN-all=3489-J'G-16:14^2-EZE-15:3

PINE-all=4743&marked-LE-26:39^2 -NE-8:15(6086,8081)-IS-41:19(8410)▪ 60:13(8410)-LA-4:9(2100)-EZE-24:23▪33:10

PINETH-M'R-9:18(3583)

PINNING-IS-38:12(1803)

PINNACLE-M'T-4:5(4419)-LU-4:9(4419)

PINS-all=3489-EX-27:19^2▪35:18^2▪ 38:20,31^2▪39:40-NU-3:37▪4:32

PIPE-all=2485-1SA-10:5-IS-5:12▪ 30:29▪**N.T.**-1CO-14:7(836)

PIPED-1KI-1:40(2490)▪**N.T.**-all= 832-M'T-11:17-LU-7:32-1CO-14:7

PIPERS-RE-18:22(834)

PIPES-all=2485&marked-1KI-1:40 -JER-48:36^2-EZE-28:13(2345)-ZEC-4:2(4166),12(6804)

PISS-2KI-18:27(7890)-IS-36:12(7890)

PISSETH-all=8366-1SA-25:22,34 -1KI-14:10▪16:11▪21:21-2KI-9:8

PIT-all=953,a=7845&marked-GE-37:20,22,24^2,28,29^2-EX-21:33^2,34-LE-11:36-NU-16:30(7585),33(7585)-2SA-17:9(6354)▪18:17(6354)▪23:20-2KI-10:14-1CH-11:22-JOB-17:16(7585)▪ 33:18a,24a,28a,30a-PS-7:15▪9:15a▪ 28:1▪30:3,9a▪35:7a▪40:2▪55:23(875)▪ 57:6(7882)▪69:15(875)▪88:4,6▪94:13a▪ 143:7-PR-1:12▪22:14(7745)▪23:27(875)▪ 26:27a▪28:10(7816),17-EC-10:8(1475) -IS-14:15,19▪24:17(6354),18^2(6354),22▪ 30:14(1360)▪38:17a,18▪51:1,14a-JER-18:20(7745),22(7743,7882)▪41:7,9▪48:43 (6354),44^2(6354)-EZE-19:4a,8a▪26:20^2▪ 28:8a▪31:14,16▪32:18,23,24,25,29,30 -ZEC-9:11▪**N.T.**-all=5421&marked -M'T-12:11(999)-LU-14:5-RE-9:1,2^3

PITCH-all=2583&marked-GE-6:14 (3722),14(3724)-EX-2:3(2203)-NU-1:52,53▪2:2^2,3,5,12▪3:23,29,35-DE-1:33-JOS-4:20(6965)-IS-13:20(167)▪ 34:9^2(2203)-JER-6:3(8628)

PITCHED-all=2583&marked-GE-12:8(5186)▪13:12(167)▪26:17,25(5186)▪ 31:25^2(8628)▪33:18-EX-17:1▪19:2▪ 33:7(5186)-NU-1:51▪2:34▪9:17,18▪ 12:16▪21:10,11,12,13▪22:1▪33:5,6,7,8,9, 15,16,18,19,20,21,22,23,25,27,28,29,31, 33,36,37,41,42,43,44,45,47,48,49-JOS-8:11▪11:5-J'G-4:11(5186)▪6:33▪7:1▪ 11:18,20▪15:9▪18:12-1SA-4:1^2▪13:5▪ 17:1,2▪26:3,5^2▪28:4^2▪29:1-2SA-6:17 (5186)▪17:26▪23:13▪24:5-1KI-20:27,29 -2KI-25:1-1CH-15:1(5186)▪16:1(5186)▪ 19:7-2CH-1:4(5186)-JER-52:4▪**N.T.** -HEB-8:2(4078)

PITCHER-all=3537-GE-24:14,15, 16,17,18,20,43,45,46-EC-12:6▪**N.T.** -M'R-14:13(2765)-LU-22:10(2765)

PITCHERS-all=3537&marked

-J'G-7:16^{2},19,20-LA-4:2(5035)

PITIED-all=2550&marked-PS-106:46(7356)-LA-2:2,17,21■3:43-EZE-16:5(2347)

PITIETH-PS-103:13^{2}(7355)-EZE-24:21(4263)

PITIFUL-LA-4:10(7362)■N.T.-JAS-5:11(4184)-1PE-3:8(2155)

PITS-1SA-13:6(953)-PS-119:85(7882)-JER-2:6(7745)■14:3(1356)-LA-4:20(7825)

PITY-all=2550&marked-DE-7:16(2347)■13:8(2347)■19:13(2347),21(2347)■25:12(2347)-2SA-12:6-JOB-6:14(2617)■19:21(2603)-PS-69:20(5110)-PR-19:17(2603)■28:8(2603)-IS-13:18(7355)■63:9(2551)-JER-13:14■15:5■21:7-EZE-5:11■7:4,9■8:18■9:5,10■36:21-JOE-2:18-AM-1:11(7356)-JON-4:10(2347)-ZEC-11:5,6■N.T.-M'T-18:33(1653)

PLACE-all=4725,a=8478&marked-GE-1:9■12:6■13:3,4,14■18:24,26,33■19:12,13,14,27■20:11,13■21:31■22:3,4,9,14■26:7^{2}■28:11^{3},16,17,19■29:3,22■30:25■31:55■32:2,30■33:17■35:7,13,14,15■38:14(6607),21,21sup,22,22sup■39:20■40:3,13(3653)-EX-3:5,8■10:23a■15:17(4349)■16:29a,29■17:7■18:21(7760),23■21:13■23:20■29:31■33:21-LE-1:16■4:12,24,29,33■6:11,16,25,26,27■7:2,6■10:13,14,17■13:19,28a■14:13^{2},28,40,41,42a,45■16:24■24:9-NU-2:17(3027)■9:17■10:29■11:3,34■13:24■14:40■18:31■19:9■20:5^{2}■21:3■22:26■23:13,27■24:11,25■32:1,17-DE-1:31,33■2:37(3027)■9:7■11:5,24■12:3,5,11,13,14,18,21,26■14:23,23(7931),24,25■15:20■16:2,2(7931),6(4724),6(7931),7,11,11(7931),15,16■17:8,10■18:6■21:19■23:12,16■26:2,2(7931),9■29:7■31:11-JOS-1:3■3:3■4:18■5:9,15■7:26■8:19■9:27■20:4-J'G-2:5■6:26(4634)■7:7,21a■9:55■11:19■15:17■18:10,12■19:16,28■20:22,33,36-RU-1:7■3:4■4:10-1SA-3:2,9■5:3,11■6:2■9:22■12:8■14:9a,46■15:12(3027)■20:19,25,27,37■21:2■23:22,28■26:5^{2},25■27:5■29:4-2SA-2:16,23a,23■5:20■6:8,17■7:10,10a■11:16■15:17(1004),19,21■17:9,12■18:18(3027)■19:39■23:7(7675)-1KI-4:28■5:9■8:6,6sup,7,21,29^{2},30^{2},35,39,43,49■10:19■13:8,16,22■20:24■21:19■22:10-2KI-5:11■6:1,2,6,8,9,10■18:25■22:16,17,19,20-1CH-13:11■14:11■15:1,3■16:27■17:9,9a■21:22,25■28:11(1004)-2CH-3:1■5:7,8■6:2(4349),20^{2},21^{2},26,30(4349),33(4349),39(4349),40■7:12,15■9:18■20:26■24:11■30:16(5977)■34:24,25,27,28,31(5977)■35:10(5977),15(4612)-EZR-1:4^{2}■2:68(4349)■5:15(870)■6:3(870),5(870),5(5182),7(870)■8:17^{2}■9:8-NE-1:9■2:3(1004),14■3:31(1004)■4:20■8:7(5977)■9:3(5977)■13:11(5977)-ES-4:14■7:8(1004)-JOB-2:11■6:17■7:10■8:17(1004),18■9:6■14:18■16:18■18:4,21■20:9■26:7(8414)■27:21,23■28:1,6,12,20,23■36:20a■37:1■38:12,19■40:12a-PS-18:19(4800)■24:3■26:8■33:14(4349)■37:10■44:19■103:16■104:8■132:5-PR-15:3■25:6■27:8-EC-1:5,7■3:16^{2},20■6:6■8:10■10:4■11:3-IS-5:8■7:23■13:13■14:2■18:7■22:23,25■26:21■28:8,25(1367)■33:21■45:19■46:7a,7,13(5414)■49:20^{2}■54:2■56:5(3027)■60:13^{2}■66:1-JER-4:7■6:3(3027)■7:3,6,7,12,14,20,32■13:7■14:13■16:2,3,9■17:12■19:3,4^{2},6,7,11,12,13■22:3,11,12■24:5■27:22■28:3^{2},4,6■29:10,14■32:37■33:10,12■38:9a■40:2■42:18,22■44:29■51:62-EZE-3:12■6:13■10:11■12:3■17:16■21:19(3027),30■37:14(3241),26(5414)■38:15■39:11■41:9(1004),11,11sup■42:13,13sup,13(4725)■43:7^{2}■45:4,4sup■46:19,20-DA-2:35(870)■8:11(4349)■11:31(5414)-HO-1:10■5:15■11:11(3427)-JO-3:7-AM-8:3-MIC-1:3-NA-1:8■3:17-ZEP-1:4■2:11-HAG-2:9-ZEC-6:12a■10:6(3427)■12:6a■14:10a,10-MAL-1:11■N.T.-all=5117&marked-M'T-9:24(402)■12:6(5602)■14:13,15,35■24:15■26:36(5564),52■27:33^{2}■28:6-M'R-1:35■6:10(3699),10(1564),31,32,35■14:32(5564)■15:22^{2}■16:6-LU-4:17,37,42■9:10,12■10:1,32■11:1■14:9■16:28■19:5■22:40■23:5(5602),33-JON-4:20■5:13■6:10,23■8:37(5562)■10:40■11:6,30,48■14:2,3■18:2■19:13,17sup,17,20,41■20:7-AC-1:25■4:31■6:13,14■7:7,33,49■8:32(4042)■12:17■21:12(1786),28^{2}■25:23(201)■27:8,41-RO-9:26■12:19■15:23-1CO-1:2-2CO-2:14-GA-2:5(1502)-EPH-4:27-1TH-1:8-HEB-8:7■11:8■12:17-JAS-3:11(3692)-2PE-1:19-RE-2:5■12:6,8,14■16:16■20:11

PLACED-all=3427&marked-GE-3:24(7931)■47:11-1KI-12:32(5975)-2KI-17:6,24,26-2CH-1:14(3240)■4:8(3240)■17:2(5414)-JOB-20:4(7760)-PS-78:60(7931)-IS-5:8-JER-5:22(776)-EZE-17:5(3947)

PLACES-all=4725&marked-GE-36:40-EX-20:24■25:27(1004)■26:29(1004)■30:4(1004)■36:34(1004)■37:14(1004),27(1004)■38:5(1004)-DE-12:2-JOS-5:8(8478)-J'G-19:13■20:33-1SA-7:16■30:31-2KI-23:14-2CH-33:19,19sup-NE-4:12,13,13sup■12:27-JOB-3:14(2723)■21:28(168)■37:8(4585)-PS-103:22■141:6(3027)-PR-8:2sup,2(1004)-JER-8:3■17:26(5439)■24:9■29:14■40:12■45:5-EZE-34:12■46:24(1004)-AM-4:6-N.T.-all=5117-M'T-12:43■24:7-M'R-1:45■13:8-LU-11:24■21:11-AC-24:3(3837)-RE-6:14

PLAGUE-all=5061,a=4046&marked EX-11:1■12:13(5063)■30:12(5063)-LE-13:2,3^{4},4,5^{2},6^{2},9,12,13,17^{2},20,22,25,27,29,30,31^{2},32,44,45,46,47,49^{2},50^{2},51^{3},52,53,54,55^{3},56,57sup,57,58,59■14:3,32,34,35,36,37^{2},39,40,43,44,48^{2},54-NU-8:19(5063)■11:33(4347)■14:37a■16:46(5063),47(5063),48a,49a,50a■25:8a,9a,18a■26:1a■31:16a-DE-24:8■28:61(4347)-JOS-22:17(5063)-1SA-6:4a-2SA-24:21a,25a-1KI-8:37,38-1CH-21:22a-2CH-21:14a-PS-89:23(5063)■91:10■106:29a,30a-ZEC-14:12a,15^{2}a,18a■N.T.-M'R-5:29(3148),34(3148)-RE-16:21^{2}(4127)

PLAGUED-all=5060&marked-GE-12:17-EX-32:35(5062)-JOS-24:5(5062)-1CH-21:17(4046)-PS-73:5,14

PLAGUES-all=4347&marked-GE-12:17(5061)-EX-9:14(4046)-LE-26:21-DE-28:59^{2}■29:22-1SA-4:8-JER-19:8■49:17■50:13-HO-13:14(1698)■N.T.-all=4127&marked-M'R-3:10(3148)-LU-7:21(3148)-RE-9:20■11:6■15:1,6,8■16:9■18:4,8■21:9■22:18

PLAIN-all=6160,a=4334,b=3603&marked-GE-11:2(1237)■12:6(436)■13:10b,11b,12b,18(436)■14:13(436)■17:17b,25b,28b,29b■25:27(8535)-DE-1:1,7■2:8■3:10a,17^{2}■4:43a,49^{2}■34:3b-JOS-3:16■8:14■11:16■12:1,3^{2}■13:9a,16a,17a,21a■20:8a-J'G-4:11(436)■9:6(436),37(436)■11:33(58)-1SA-10:3(436)■23:24-2SA-2:29■4:7■15:28■18:23b-1KI-7:46b■20:23a,25a-2KI-14:25■25:4-2CH-4:17b■3:22b■6:2(1237)■12:28b-PS-27:11a-PR-8:9(5228)■15:19(5549)-IS-28:25(7737)■40:4(1237)-JER-17:26(8219)■21:13a■39:4■48:8a,21a■52:7-EZE-3:22(1237),23(1237)■8:4(1237)-DA-3:1(1236)-AM-1:5(1237)-OB-19(8219)-HAB-2:2(874)-ZEC-4:7a■7:7(8219)■14:10■N.T.-M'R-7:35(3723)-LU-6:17(5117,3977)

PLAINLY-EX-21:5(559)-DE-27:8(874)-1SA-2:27(1540)■10:16(5046)-EZR-4:18(6568)-IS-32:4(6703)■N.T.-all=3954&marked-JOH-10:24■11:14■16:25,29-HEB-11:14(1718)

PLAINNESS-2CO-3:12(3954)

PLAINS-all=6160&marked-GE-18:1(436)-NU-22:1■26:3,63■31:12■33:48,49,50■35:1■36:13-DE-11:30(436)■34:1,8-JOS-4:13■5:10■11:2■12:8■13:32-2SA-17:16-2KI-25:5-1CH-27:28(8219)-2CH-9:27(8219)■26:10(4334)-JER-39:5■52:8

PLAISTER-LE-14:42(2902)-DE-27:2(7874),2(7875),4(7874),4(7875)-IS-38:21(4799)-DA-5:5(1528)

PLAISTERED-LE-14:43(2902),48(2902)

PLAITING-1PE-3:3(1708)

PLANES-IS-44:13(4741)

PLANETS-2KI-23:5(4208)

PLANKS-1KI-6:15(6763)-EZE-41:25(6086),26(5646)

PLANT-all=5193&marked-GE-2:5(7880)-EX-15:17-DE-16:21■28:30,39-2SA-7:10-2KI-19:29-1CH-17:9-JOB-14:9(5194)-PS-107:37-EC-3:2-IS-5:7(5194)■17:10,11(5194)■37:30■41:19(5414)■51:16■65:21,22-JER-1:10■18:9■24:6■29:5,28■31:5^{2},28■32:41■35:7■42:10-EZE-17:22(8362),23(8362)■28:26■34:29(4302)■36:36-DA-11:45-AM-9:14,15-ZEP-1:13■N.T.-M'T-15:13(5451)

PLANTATION-EZE-17:7(4302)

PLANTED-all=5193&marked-GE-2:8■9:20■21:33-LE-19:23-NU-24:6-DE-20:6-JOS-24:13-PS-1:3(8362)■80:8,15■92:13(8362)■94:9■104:16-EC-2:4,5■3:2-IS-5:2■40:24-JER-2:21■11:17■12:2■17:8(8362)■45:4-EZE-17:8(8362),10(8362)■19:10(8362),13(8362)-HO-9:13(8362)-AM-5:11■N.T.-all=5452&marked-M'T-15:13■21:33-M'R-12:1-LU-13:6■17:6,28■20:9-RO-6:5(4854)-1CO-3:6(5452)

PLANTEDST-DE-6:11(5193)-PS-44:2(5193)

PLANTERS-JER-31:5(5193)

PLANTETH-PR-31:16(5192)-IS-44:14(5192)■N.T.-all=5452-1CO-3:7,8■9:7

PLANTING-IS-60:21(4302)■61:3(4302)

PLANTINGS-MIC-1:6(4302)

PLANTS-1CH-4:23(4194)-PS-128:3(8363)■144:12(5195)-SONG-4:13(7973)-IS-16:8(8291)■17:10(5194)-JER-48:32(5189)-EZE-31:4(4302)

PLAT-2KI-9:26^{2}(2513)

PLATE-all=6731-EX-28:36■39:30-LE-8:9

PLATES-EX-39:3(6341)-NU-16:38(6341)-1KI-7:30(5633),36(3871)

PLATTED-all=4120-M'T-27:29-M'R-15:17-JOH-19:2

PLATTER-M'T-23:25(3953),26(3953)-LU-11:39(4094)

PLAY-all=7832&marked-EX-32:6(6711)-1SA-16:16(5059),17(5059)-2SA-2:14■6:21-JOB-40:20■41:5-PS-33:3(5059)■104:26-IS-11:8(8173)-EZE-33:32(5059)■N.T.-1CO-10:7(3815)

PLAYED-all=5059&marked-1SA-16:23■18:7(7832),10■19:9-2SA-6:5(7832)-2KI-3:15-1CH-13:8(7832)

PLAYEDST-all supplied

PLAYER-1SA-16:16(5059)

PLAYERS-PS-68:25(5059)■87:7(2490)

PLAYETH-supplied

PLAYING-1SA-16:18(5059)-1CH-15:29(7832)-ZEC-8:5(7832)

PLEA-DE-17:8(1779)

PLEAD-all=7378&marked-J'G-6:31^{3},32-1SA-24:15-JOB-9:19■13:19■16:21(3198)■19:5(3198)■23:6-PS-35:1-PR-43:1■74:22■119:154■22:23■23:11■31:9(1777)-IS-1:17■3:13■43:26(8199)■66:16(8199)-JER-2:9^{2},29,35(8199)■12:1■25:31(8199)■30:13(1777)■50:34■51:36-EZE-17:20(8199)■20:35(8199),36(8199)■38:22(8199)-HO-2:2-JOE-3:2(8199)-MIC-6:2(3198)■7:9

PLEADED-1SA-25:39(7378)-LA-3:58(7378)-EZE-20:36(8199)

PLEADETH-1SA-51:22(7378)■59:4(8199)

PLEADINGS-JOB-13:6(7379)

PLEASANT-all=2532&marked-GE-2:9(2530)■3:6(8378)■49:15(5276) 2SA-1:23(5273),26(5276)-1KI-20:6(4261)-2KI-2:19(2896)-2CH-32:27-PS-16:6(5273)■81:2(5273)■106:24■133:1(5273)■135:3(5273)■147:1(5273)-PR-2:10(5276)■5:19(5280)■9:17(5276)■15:26(5278)■16:24(5278)■22:18(5273)■24:4(5273)-EC-11:7(2896)-SONG-1:16(5273)■4:13(4022),16(4022)■7:6(5276),13(4022)-IS-2:16■5:7(8191)■13:22(6027)■17:10■32:12(2531)■54:12(2656)■64:11(4261)-JER-3:19■12:10■23:10(4999)■25:34■31:20(8191)-LA-1:7(4262),10(4621),11(4622)■2:4(4622)-EZE-26:12■33:32(3303)-DA-8:9(6643)■10:3(2530)■11:38(2530)-HO-9:6(4261),13(5116)■13:15-JOE-3:5(4261)-AM-5:11(2531)-MIC-2:9(8588)-NA-2:9-ZEC-7:14-MAL-3:4(6148)

PLEASANTNESS-PR-3:17(5278)

PLEASE-all=2895&marked-EX-21:8(7451,5869)-NU-23:27(3477,5869)-1SA-20:13(3190)-2SA-7:29(2974)-1KI-21:6(2655)-1CH-17:27(2974)-2CH-10:7(7521)-NE-2:5,7-ES-1:19■3:9■5:8■7:3■8:5(2896)■9:13(2896)-JOB-6:9(2974)■20:10(7521)-PS-69:31(3190)-PR-16:7(7521)-SONG-2:7(2654)■3:5(2654)■8:4(2654)-IS-2:6(5606)■55:11(2654)■56:4(2654)■N.T.-all=700&marked-JOH-8:29(701)-RO-8:8■15:1,2-1CO-7:32,33,34■10:33-GA-1:10-1TH-2:15■4:1-2TI-2:4-TIT-2:9(2001,1511)-HEB-11:6(2100)

PLEASED-all=3190,5869&marked-GE-28:8(7451,5869)■33:10(7521)■34:18■45:16-NU-24:1(2895)-DE-1:23-JOS-22:30,33-J'G-13:23(2654)■14:7(3477,5869)-1SA-12:22(2974)■18:20(3477,5869),26(3477,5869)-2SA-3:36,36(2896,5869)■17:4(3477,5869)■19:6(3477,5869)-1KI-3:10■9:1(2654),12(3477,5869)-2CH-30:4(3477,5869)-NE-2:6(3190)-ES-1:21■2:4,9■5:14(3190)-PS-40:13(7521)■51:19(2654)■115:3(2654)■135:6(2654)-IS-42:21(2654)■53:10(2654)-DA-6:1(8232)-JON-1:14(2654)-MIC-6:7(7521)-MAL-1:8(7521)■N.T.-all=2106&marked-M'T-3:17■12:18■14:6(700)■17:5-M'R-1:11■6:22(700)-LU-3:22-AC-6:5(700)■12:3(701)■15:22(1380),34(1380)-RO-15:3(700),26,27-1CO-1:21■7:12(4909),13(4909)■10:5■12:18(2309)■15:38(2309)-GAL-1:10(700),15-COL-1:19-HEB-11:5(2100)■13:16(2100)-2PE-1:17

PLEASETH-GE-16:6(2896,5869)■20:15(2896,5869)-J'G-14:3(3477,5869)-ES-2:4(3190,5869)-EC-7:26(2896,6440)■8:3(2654)

PLEASING-ES-8:5(2896)-HO-9:4(6148)■N.T.-COL-1:10(699)-1TH-2:4(700)-1JO-3:22(701)

PLEASURE-all=2656&marked-GE-18:12(5730)-DE-23:24(5315)-1CH-29:17(7521)-EZR-5:17(7470)■10:11(7522)-NE-9:37(7522)-ES-1:8(7522)-JOB-21:21,25(2896)■22:3-PS-5:4(2655)■35:27(2655)■51:18(7522)■102:14(7521)■103:21(7522)■105:22(5315)■111:2■147:10(7521),11(7521)■149:4(7521)-PR-21:17(8057)-EC-2:1(2896)■5:4■12:1-IS-21:4(2837)■44:28■46:10■48:14■53:10■58:3,13^{2}-JER-2:24(185,5315)■22:28■34:16(5315)■48:38-EZE-16:37(6148)■18:23(2654),32(2654)■33:11(2654)-HO-8:8-HAG-1:8(7521)-MAL-1:10■N.T.-all=2106&marked-LU-12:32-AC-24:27(5485)■25:9(5485)-RO-1:32(4909)-2CO-12:10-EPH-1:5(2107),9(2107)-PH'P-2:13(2107)-2TH-1:11(2107)■2:12-1TI-5:6(4684)-HEB-10:6,8,38■12:10(3588,1380)-JAS-5:5(5171)-2PE-2:13(2237)-RE-4:11(2307)

PLEASURES-JOB-36:11(5273)-PS-16:11(5273)■36:8(5730)-IS-47:8(5719)■N.T.-LU-8:14(2237)-2TI-3:4(5569)-TIT-3:3(2237)

PLEDGE-all=2254&marked-GE-38:17(6162),18(6162),20(6162)-EX-22:26-DE-24:6^{2},10(5667),11(5667),12(5667),13(5667),17-1SA-17:18(6161)-JOB-22:6■24:3,9-PR-20:16■27:13-EZE-18:7(2258),12(2258),16(2258)■33:15(2258)-AM-2:8

PLEDGES-2KI-18:23(6148)-IS-36:8(6148)

PLENTEOUS-all=7227&marked-GE-41:34(7647),47-DE-28:11(3498)■30:9(3498)-PS-86:5,15■103:8■130:7(7235)-IS-30:23(8082)-HAB-1:16(1277)■N.T.-M'T-9:37(4188)

PLENTEOUSNESS-GE-41:53(7647)-PR-21:5(4195)

PLENTIFUL-all=3759&marked-PS-68:9(5071)-IS-16:10-JER-2:7■48:33

PLENTIFULLY-JOB-26:3(7230)-PS-31:32(3499)■N.T.-LU-12:16(2164)

PLENTY-all=7647&marked-GE-27:28(7230)■41:29,30,31-LE-11:36(4723)-1KI-10:11(7235)-2CH-31:10(7230)-JOB-22:25(8443)■37:23(7230)-PR-3:10■28:19(7646)-JER-44:17(7646)-JOE-2:26(398)

PLOTTETH-PS-37:12(2161)

PLOUGH-LU-9:62(723)

PLOW-all=2790-DE-22:10-JOB-4:8-PR-20:4-IS-28:24-HO-10:11-AM-6:12■N.T.-1CO-9:10(722)

PLOWED-all=2790-J'G-14:18-PS-129:3-JER-26:18-HO-10:13-MIC-3:12

PLOWERS-PS-129:3(2790)

PLOWETH-1CO-9:10(722)

PLOWING-1KI-19:19(2790)-JOB-1:14(2790)-PR-21:4(2515)■N.T.-LU-17:7(722)

PLOWMAN-IS-28:24(2790)-AM-9:13(2790)

PLOWMEN-IS-61:5(406)-JER-14:4(406)

PLOWSHARES-all=855-IS-2:4-JOE-3:10-MIC-4:3

PLUCK-all=5428&marked-LE-1:16(5493)-NU-33:52(8045)-DE-23:52(6998)-2CH-7:20-JOB-24:9(1497)-PS-25:15(3318)■52:5(5255)■74:11(3615)■80:12(717)-EC-3:2(6131)-JER-12:14^{2},17■18:7■22:24(5423)■24:6■31:28■42:10■45:4-EZE-17:9(5375)■23:34(5423)-MIC-3:2(1497)■5:14■N.T.-M'T-5:29(1808)■12:1(5089)■18:9(1807)-M'R-2:23(5089)■9:47(1544)-JOH-10:28(726),29(726)

PLUCKED-all=5428&marked-EX-4:7(3318)-DE-28:63(5255)-RU-4:7(8025)-2SA-23:21(1497)-1CH-11:23(1497)-EZR-9:3(4803)-NE-13:25(4803)-JOB-29:17(7993)-IS-50:6(4803)-JER-6:29(5423)■12:15■31:40-EZE-19:12-DA-7:4(4804),8(6132)■11:4-AM-4:11(5337)-ZEC-3:2(5337)■N.T.-M'R-5:4(1288)-LU-6:1(5089)■17:6(1610)-GA-4:15(1846)-JUDE-12(1610)

PLUCKETH-PR-14:1(2040)

PLUCKT-GE-8:11(2965)

PLUMBLINE-AM-7:7(594),8^{2}(594)

PLUMMET-2KI-21:13(4949)-IS-28:17(4949)-ZEC-4:10(68,913)

PLUNGE-JOB-9:31(2881)

POETS-AC-17:28(4163)

POINT-GE-25:32(1980)-NU-34:7(8376),8(8376),10(184)-JER-17:1(6856)-EZ-21:15(19)■N.T.-M'R-5:23(2079)-JOH-4:47(3795)

POINTED-JOB-41:30(2742)

POINTS-EC-5:16(5980)

POISON-all=2534&marked-DE-32:24,33-JOB-6:4■20:16(7219)-PS-58:4■140:3■N.T.-RO-3:13(2447)-JAS-3:8(2447)

POLE-NU-21:8(5251),9(5251)

POLICY-DA-8:25(7922)

POLISHED-PS-144:12(2404)-IS-49:2(1305)-DA-10:6(7044)

POLISHING-LA-4:7(1508)

POLL-NU-3:47(1538)-EZE-44:20(3697)-MIC-1:16(1494)

POLLED-2SA-14:26^{3}(1548)

POLLS-all=1538&marked-NU-1:2,18,20,22-1CH-23:3,24

POLLUTE-all=2490&marked-NU-18:32■35:33(2610)-JER-7:30(2930)-EZE-7:21,22■13:19■20:31(2930),39■39:7■44:7-DA-11:31

POLLUTED-all=2490,a=2930&marked-EX-20:25-2KI-23:16a-2CH-36:14a-EZR-2:62(1351)-NE-7:64(1351)-PS-106:38(2610)-IS-47:6■48:11-JER-2:23a■3:1(2610),2(2610)■34:16-LA-2:2■4:14(1351)-EZE-4:14a■14:11a■16:6(947),22(947)■20:9,13,14,16,21,22,24,26a,30a■23:17a,30a■36:18a-HO-6:8(6121)■9:4a-AM-7:17(2931)-MIC-2:10a-ZEP-3:1(1351),4-MAL-1:7^{2}(1351),12(1351)■N.T.-AC-21:28(2840)

POLLUTING-IS-56:2(2490),6(2490)

POLLUTION-EZE-22:10(2931)

POLLUTIONS-AC-15:20(234)-2PE-2:20(3393)

POMEGRANATE-all=7416-EX-28:34■39:26-1SA-14:2-SONG-4:3■6:7■8:2-JOE-1:12-HAG-2:19

POMEGRANATES-all=7416-EX-28:33■39:24,25^{2}-NU-13:23■20:5-DE-8:8-1KI-7:18,20sup,20,42^{2}-2KI-25:17-2CH-3:16■4:13^{2}-SONG-4:13■6:11■7:12-JER-52:22^{2},23^{2}

POMMELS-2CH-4:12^{2}(1543),13(1543)

POMP-all=1347&marked-IS-5:14(7588)■14:11-EZE-7:24■30:18■32:12■33:28■N.T.-AC-25:23(5325)

PONDER-PR-4:26(6424)■5:6(6424)

PONDERED-LU-2:19(4820)

PONDERETH-PR-5:21(6424)■21:2(8505)■24:12(8505)

PONDS-EX-7:19(98)■8:5(98)-IS-19:10(99)

POOL-all=1295&marked-2SA-2:13^{3}■4:12-1KI-22:38-2KI-18:17■20:20-NE-2:14■3:15,16-IS-7:3■22:9,11■35:7(98)■36:2(1295)■41:18(98)-NA-2:8(1295)■N.T.-all=2861-JOH-5:2,4,7■9:7,11

POOLS-EX-7:19(4723)-PS-84:6(1293)-EC-2:6(1295)-IS-14:23(98)■42:15(98)

POOR-all=6041,a=1800,b=34,c=7326&marked-GE-41:19a-EX-22:25■23:3a,6b,11b■30:15a-LE-14:21a■19:10,15a■23:22■25:25(4134),35(4134),39(4134),47(4134)-DE-15:4b,7^{2}b,9b,11b,11■24:12,14,15-J'G-6:15a-RU-3:10a-1SA-2:7(3423),8a■18:23c-2SA-12:1c,3c,4c-2KI-25:12(1803)-ES-9:22b-JOB-5:15b,16a■20:10a,19a■24:4(6035),9,14■29:12,16b■30:25b■31:16a,19b■34:19a,28a■36:6,15-PS-9:18■10:2,8(2489),9^{2},10(2489),14(2489)■12:5■14:6■34:6■35:10^{2}■37:14■40:17■41:1a■49:2b■68:10■69:29,33b■70:5■72:2,4,12,13a■74:19,21■82:3a,4a■86:1■107:41b■109:16,22,31■112:9b■113:7a■132:5b■140:12b-PR-10:4c,15a■13:7c,8c,23c■14:20c,21(6035,6041),31a,31b■17:5c■18:23c■19:1c,4a,7c,17a,22c■21:13a,17(4270)■22:2c,7c,9a,16a,22a■28:3c,3a,6a,8a,11a,15a,27c■29:7a,13c,14a■30:9(3423),14(6041)■31:9(6041),20(6041)-EC-4:13(4542),14c■5:8(7326)■6:8■9:15^{2}(4542),16(4542)-IS-3:14,15■10:2,30■11:4a■14:30a,32■25:4a■26:6■29:19b■32:7(6035,6041)■41:17■58:7■66:2-JER-2:34b■5:4a■20:13b■22:16■39:10a■40:7(1803)■52:15(1803),16(1803)-EZE-16:49■18:12,17■22:29-DA-4:27(6033)-AM-2:6b,7a■4:1a■5:11a,12b■8:4(6035,6041),6a-HAB-3:14-ZEP-3:12a-ZEC-7:10■11:7,11■N.T.-all=4434&marked-M'T-5:3■11:5■19:21■26:9,11-M'R-10:21■12:42,43■14:5,7-LU-4:18■6:20■7:22■14:13,21■18:22■19:8■21:2(3998),3-JOH-12:5,6,8■13:29-RO-15:26-2CO-6:10■8:9(4433)■9:9(3993)-GA-2:10-JAS-2:2,3,5,6-RE-3:17■13:16

POORER-LE-27:8(4134)

POOREST-2KI-24:14(1803)

POPLAR-GE-30:37(3839)

POPLARS-HO-4:13(3839)

POPULOUS-DE-26:5(7227)-NA-3:8(527)

PORCH-all=197&marked-J'G-3:23(4528)-1KI-6:3▪7:6^2,7^2,8^2,12,19,21-1CH-28:11-2CH-3:4▪8:12▪15:8▪29:7,17-EZE-8:16▪40:7,8,9^2,15,39,40,48,49▪41:25,26▪44:3▪46:2,8-JOE-2:17▪N.T.-all=4745&marked-M'T-26:71(4440)-M'R-14:68(4259)-JOH-10:23-AC-3:11▪5:12

PORCHES-EZE-41:15(197)▪N.T.-JOH-5:2(4745)

PORT-NE-2:13(8179)

PORTER-all=7778-2SA-18:26-2KI-7:10-1CH-9:21-2CH-31:14▪N.T.-M'R-13:34(2377)-JOH-10:3(2377)

PORTERS-all=7778&marked-2KI-7:11-1CH-9:17,18,22,24,26▪15:18▪16:38,42(8179)▪23:5▪26:1,12,19-2CH-8:14▪23:4,19▪34:13▪35:15-EZR-2:42,70▪7:7,24(8652)▪10:24-NE-7:1,45,73▪10:28,39▪11:19▪12:25,45,47▪13:5

PORTION-all=2506&marked-GE-14:24^2▪31:4▪47:22^2(2706)▪48:22(7926)-LE-6:17(2506)-NU-31:30(270),36,47(270)-DE-21:17(6310)▪32:9▪33:21(2513)-JOS-17:14(2256)▪19:9(2256)-1SA-1:5(4490)▪9:23(4490)-1KI-12:16-2KI-2:9(6310)▪9:10,21(2513),25(2513),36,37-2CH-10:16▪28:21(2505)▪31:3(4521),4(4521),16(1697)-EZR-4:16(2508)-NE-2:20▪12:47(1697)-JOB-20:29▪24:18(2513)▪26:14(1697)▪27:13▪31:2-PS-11:6(4521)▪16:5(4490)▪17:14▪63:10(4521)▪73:26▪119:57▪142:5-PR-31:15(2706)-EC-2:10,21▪3:22▪5:18,19▪9:6,9▪11:2-IS-17:14▪57:6▪61:7-JER-10:16▪12:10^2(2513)▪13:25(4490)▪51:19▪52:34(1697)-LA-3:24-DA-1:8(6598),13(6598),15(6598),16(6598)▪4:15(2508),23(2508)▪11:26(6598)-MIC-2:4-HAB-1:16-ZEC-2:12▪N.T.-M'T-24:51(3313)-LU-12:42(4620),46(3313)▪15:12(3313)

PORTIONS-all=4490&marked-DE-18:8(2506)-JOS-17:5(2256)-1SA-1:4-2CH-31:19-NE-8:10,12▪12:44(4521),47(4521)▪13:10(4521)-ES-9:19,22-EZE-45:7(2506)▪47:13(2256)▪48:21(2506),29(4256)-HO-5:7(2506)

POSSESS-all=3423&marked-GE-22:17▪24:60-LE-20:24-NU-13:30▪14:24▪27:11▪33:53-DE-1:8,21,39▪2:24,31▪3:18,20▪4:1,5,14,22,26▪5:31,33▪6:1,18▪7:1▪8:1▪9:1,4,5,6,23▪10:11▪11:8^2,10,11,23,29,31^2▪12:1,2,29▪15:4▪17:14▪19:2,14▪21:1▪23:20▪25:19▪28:21,63▪30:5,16,18▪31:3,13▪32:47▪33:23-JOS-1:11^2▪18:3▪23:5▪24:4,8-J'G-2:6▪11:23,24^3▪18:9-1KI-21:18-1CH-28:8-EZR-9:11-NE-9:15,23-JOB-7:3(5157)▪13:26-IS-14:2(5157),21▪34:11,17▪57:13(5157)▪61:7-JER-30:3-EZE-7:24▪33:25,26▪35:10▪36:12-DA-7:18(2631)-HO-9:6-AM-2:10▪9:12-OB-17,19^2,19sup,20(423)-HAB-1:6(423)-ZEP-2:9(5157)-ZEC-8:12(5157)▪N.T-all=2932-LU-18:12▪21:19-1TH-4:4

POSSESSED-all=3423&marked-NU-21:24,35-DE-3:12▪4:47▪30:5-JOS-1:15▪12:1▪13:1▪19:47▪21:43▪22:9(270)-J'G-3:13▪11:21,22-2KI-17:24-NE-9:22,24,25-PS-139:13(7069)-PR-8:22(7069)-IS-63:18-JER-32:15(7069),23-DA-7:22(2631)▪N.T.-all=1139&marked-M'T-4:24▪8:16,28,33▪9:32▪12:22-M'R-1:32▪5:15,16,18-LU-8:36-AC-4:32(5224)▪8:7(2192)▪16:16(2192)-1CO-7:30(2722)

POSSESSEST-DE-26:1(3423)

POSSESSETH-NU-36:8(3423)▪N.T.-LU-12:15(5224)

POSSESSING-2CO-6:10(2722)

POSSESSION-all=272&marked-GE-17:8▪23:4,9,18(4736),20▪26:14(4735)▪36:43▪47:11▪48:4▪49:30▪50:13-LE-14:34^2▪25:10,13,24,25,27,28,32,33^2,34,41,45,46▪27:16,21,22,24,28-NU-24:18^2(3424)▪26:56(5159)▪27:4,7▪32:5,22,29,32▪35:2,8,28-DE-2:5(3425),9^2(3425),12(3425),19^2(3425)▪3:20(3425)▪11:6(7272)▪32:49-JOS-1:15(3425)▪12:6(3425),7(3425)▪21:12,41▪22:4,9,19^2,19(270)-1KI-21:15(3423),16(3423),19(3423)-1CH-28:1(4735)-2CH-11:14▪20:11(3425)▪31:1-NE-11:3-PS-2:8▪44:3(3423)▪69:35(3423)▪83:12(3423)-PR-28:10(5157)-IS-14:23(4180)-EZE-11:15(4181)▪25:4(4181),10(4181)▪36:2(4181),3(4181),5(4181)▪44:28▪45:5,6,7^2,8▪46:16,18^3▪48:20,21,22^2▪N.T.-AC-5:1(2933)▪7:5(2697),45(2697)-EPH-1:14(4047)

POSSESSIONS-all=270&marked-GE-34:10▪47:27-NU-32:30-1SA-25:2(4639)-1CH-7:28(272)▪9:2(272)-2CH-32:29(4735)-EC-2:7(4735)-OB-17(4180)▪N.T.-all=2933&marked-M'T-19:22-M'R-10:22-AC-2:45▪28:7(5564)

POSSESSOR-GE-14:19(7069),22(7069)

POSSESSORS-ZEC-11:5(7069)▪N.T.-AC-4:34(2935)

POSSIBLE-all=1415&marked-M'T-19:26▪24:24▪26:39-M'R-9:23▪10:27▪13:22▪14:35,36-LU-18:27-AC-2:24▪20:16▪27:39(1410)-RO-12:18-GA-4:15-HEB-10:4(102)

POST-all=352&marked-EX-12:7(4947)▪21:6(4201)-1SA-1:9(4201)-JOB-9:25(7323)-JER-51:31(7323)-EZE-40:14,16,48▪41:3▪43:8(4201)▪46:2(4201)

POSTERITY-all=310&marked-GE-45:7(7611)-NU-9:10(1755)-1KI-16:3^2▪21:21-PS-49:13▪109:13(319)-DA-11:4(319)-AM-4:2(319)

POSTS-all=352,a=4201,&marked-EX-12:7a,22a,23a-DE-6:9a▪11:20a-J'G-16:3a-1KI-6:31a,33a▪7:5a-2CH-3:7(5592)▪30:6(7323),10(7323)-ES-3:13(7323),15(7323)▪8:10(7323),14(7323)-PR-8:34a-IS-6:4(520)▪57:8a-EZE-40:9,10,14,16,21,24,26,29,31,33,34,36,37^2,38,49▪41:1,16(5592),21a▪43:8a▪45:19^{2}a-AM-9:1(5592)

POT-all=5518&marked-EX-16:33(6803)-LE-6:28(3627)-J'G-6:19(6517)-1SA-2:14(6517)-2KI-4:2(610),38,39,40,41^2-JOB-41:20(1731),31-PR-17:3(4715)▪27:21(4715)-EC-7:6-JER-1:13-EZE-24:3,6-MIC-3:3-ZEC-14:21▪N.T.-HEB-9:4(4713)

POTENTATE-1TI-6:15(1413)

POTS-all=5518&marked-EX-16:3▪38:3-1KI-7:45-2KI-25:14-2CH-4:11,16▪35:13-PS-58:9▪68:13(8240)▪81:6(1731)-JER-35:5(1375)-ZEC-14:20▪N.T.-M'R-7:4(3582),8(3582)

POTSHERD-all=2789-JOB-2:8-PS-22:15-PR-26:23-IS-45:9

POTSHERDS-IS-45:9(2789)

POTTAGE-all=5138-GE-25:29▪25:34-2KI-4:38,39,40-HAG-2:12

POTTER-all=3335-IS-41:25▪64:8-JER-18:4^2,6-LA-4:2-ZEC-11:13^2▪N.T.-RO-9:21(2763)-RE-2:27(2764)

POTTER'S-all=3335&marked-PS-2:9-IS-29:16-JER-18:2,3,6▪19:1,11-DA-2:41(6353)▪N.T.-M'T-27:7(2763),10(2763)

POTTERS-1CH-4:23(3335)

POTTERS'-IS-30:14(3335)

POUND-all=4488-1KI-10:17-EZR-2:69-NE-7:71,72▪N.T.-all=3414&marked-LU-19:16,18,20,24-JOH-12:3(3046)▪19:39(3046)

POUNDS-all=3414-LU-19:13,16,18,24,25

POUR-all=8210,a=3332&marked-EX-4:9▪29:7a,12▪30:9(5258)-LE-2:1a,6a▪4:7,18,25,30,34▪14:15(3332),18(5414),26(3332),41▪17:13-NU-5:15a▪24:7(5140)-DE-12:16,24▪15:23-J'G-6:20-1KI-18:33a-2KI-4:4a,41a▪9:3a-JOB-36:27(2212)-PS-42:4▪62:8▪69:24▪79:6-PR-1:23(5042)-IS-44:3^{2}a▪45:8(5140)-JER-6:11▪7:18(5258)▪10:25▪14:16▪18:21(5064)▪44:17(5258),18(5258),19(5258),25(5258)-LA-2:19-EZE-7:8▪14:19▪20:8,13,21▪21:31▪24:3a▪30:15-HO-5:10-JOE-2:28,29-MIC-1:6(5064)-ZEP-3:8-ZEC-12:10-MAL-3:10(7324)▪N.T.-all=1632-AC-2:17,18-RE-16:1

POURED-all=8210,a=3332,b=5413&marked-GE-28:18a▪35:14(5258),14a-EX-9:33b▪30:32(3251)-LE-4:12^2(8211)▪8:12a,15a▪9:9a▪21:10a-NU-28:7(5258)-DE-12:27-1SA-1:15▪7:6▪10:1a-2SA-13:9a▪23:16(5258)-1KI-13:3,5-2KI-3:11a▪4:5a,40a▪9:6a▪16:13(5258)-1CH-11:18(5258)-2CH-12:7b▪34:21b,25b-JOB-3:24b▪10:10b▪29:6(6694)▪30:16-PS-22:14▪45:2a▪77:17(2229)▪142:2-SONG-1:3(7324)-IS-26:16(6694)▪29:10(5258)▪32:15(6168)▪42:25▪53:12(6168)▪57:6-JER-7:20(5413)▪19:13(5258)▪32:29(5258)▪42:18^{2}b▪44:6b,19(5258)-LA-2:4,11,12▪4:1,11-EZE-16:36▪20:28(5258),33,34▪22:22,31▪23:8▪24:7▪36:18▪39:29-DA-9:11b,27b-MIC-1:4(5064)-NA-1:6b-ZEP-1:17▪N.T.-all=1632&marked-M'T-26:7(2708),12(906)-M'R-14:3(2708)-JOH-2:15-AC-10:45-RE-14:10(2467)▪16:2,3,4,8,10,12,17

POUREDST-EZE-16:15(8210)

POURETH-all=8210&marked-JOB-12:21▪16:13,20(1811)-PS-75:8(5064)▪102:t▪107:40-PR-15:2(5042)▪28(5042)-AM-5:8▪9:6▪N.T.-JOH-13:5(906)

POURING-EZE-9:8(8210)

POURTRAY-EZE-4:1(2710)

POURTRAYED-EZE-8:10(2707)▪23:14(2707),14(2710)

POVERTY-all=7389&marked-GE-45:11(3423)-PR-6:11▪10:15▪11:24(4270)▪13:18▪20:13(3423)▪23:21(3423)▪24:34▪28:19,22(2639)▪30:8▪31:7▪N.T.-all=4432-2CO-8:2,9-RE-2:9

POWDER-EX-32:20(1854)-DE-28:24(80)-2KI-23:6^2(6083),15(6083)-2CH-34:7(1854)▪N.T.-M'T-21:44(3039)-LU-20:18(3039)

POWDERS-SONG-3:6(81)

POWER-all=3581,a=5797,b=3027&marked-GE-31:6,29(410)▪32:28(8280)▪49:3(5794)-EX-9:16▪15:6▪21:8(4910)▪32:11-LE-26:19(5797),37(8617)-NU-14:17▪22:38(3201)-DE-4:37▪8:17,18▪9:29▪32:36b-JOS-8:20b▪17:17-1SA-9:1(2428)▪30:4-2SA-22:33(2428)-2KI-17:36▪19:26b-1CH-20:1(2428)▪29:11(1369),12-2CH-14:11▪20:6▪22:9▪25:8▪26:13▪32:9(4475)-EZR-4:23(2429)▪8:22a-NE-1:10▪5:5b-ES-1:3(2428)▪8:11(2428)▪9:1(7980)▪10:2(8633)-JOB-1:12b▪5:20b▪21:7(2428)▪23:6▪24:22▪26:2,12,14(1369)▪36:22▪37:23▪41:12(1369)-PS-21:13(1369)▪22:20b▪37:35(6184)▪49:15b▪59:11(2428),16a▪62:11a▪63:2a▪65:6(1369)▪66:3a,7(1369)▪68:35(8592)▪71:18(1369)▪78:26a▪79:11(2220)▪90:11a▪106:8(1369)▪110:3(2428)▪111:6▪145:11(1369)▪147:5▪150:1a-PR-3:27(410)▪18:21b-EC-4:1▪5:19(7980)▪6:2(7980)▪8:4(7983),8(7989),8(7983)-IS-37:27b▪40:26,29▪43:17(5808)▪47:14b▪50:2-JER-10:12▪27:5▪32:17▪51:15-EZE-17:9(2220)▪22:6(2220)▪30:6a-DA-2:37(3632)▪3:27(7981)▪4:30(2632)▪6:27(3028)▪8:6,7,22,24^2▪11:6,25,43(4910)▪12:7b-HO-12:3(8280),4(7786)▪13:14b-MIC-2:1(410)▪3:8-NA-1:3▪2:1-HAB-1:11▪2:9(3709)▪3:4(5797)-ZEC-4:6▪9:4(2428)▪N.T.-all=1411,a=1849&marked-M'T-6:13▪9:6a,8a▪10:1a▪22:29▪24:30▪26:64▪28:18a-M'R-2:10a▪3:15a▪6:7a▪9:1▪12:24▪13:26▪14:62-LU-1:17,35▪4:6a,14,32a,36▪5:17,24a▪9:1,43(3168)▪10:19a,19▪12:5a▪20:20(746)▪21:27▪22:53a,69▪24:49-JOH-1:12a▪10:18^{2}a▪17:2a▪19:10^{2}a,11a-AC-1:7,8▪3:12▪4:7,33▪5:4a▪6:8▪8:10,19a▪10:38▪26:18a-RO-1:4,16,20▪9:17,21a,22(1415)▪13:1a,2a,3a▪15:13,19▪16:25(1410)-1CO-1:18,24▪2:4,5▪4:19,20▪5:4▪6:12(1850),14▪7:4^2(1850),37a▪9:4a,5a,6a,

12^{2}a,18a■11:10a■15:24,43-2CO-4:7■6:7■8:3^{2}■12:9■13:4^{2},10a-EPH-1:19,19(2904),21■2:2a■3:7,20■6:10(2904)-PH’P-3:10-COL-1:11(2904),13a■2:10a-1TH-1:5-2TH-1:9(2479)11■2:9■3:9a-1TI-6:16(2904)-2TI-1:7,8■3:5-HEB-1:3■2:14(2904)■7:16-1PE-1:5-2PE-1:3,16■2:11(2479)-JUDE-25a-RE-2:26a■4:11■5:12,13(2904)■6:8a■7:12■9:3^{2}a,10a,19a■11:6^{2}a,17■12:10a■13:2,4a,5a,7a,12a,14(1325),15(1325)■14:18a■15:8■16:9a■17:12a,13■18:1a■19:1■20:6a

POWERFUL-PS-29:4(3581)■N.T.-2CO-10:10(2478)-HEB-4:12(1756)

POWERS-all=1849&marked-M’T-24:29(1411)-M’R-13:25(1411)-LU-2:11■21:26(1411)-RO-8:38(1411)■13:1^{2}-EPH-3:10■6:12-COL-1:16■2:15-TI-3:1-HEB-6:5(1411)-1PE-3:22(1411)

PRACTICES-all supplied

PRACTISE-all=6213&marked-PS-141:4(5953)-IS-32:6-DA-8:24-MIC-2:1

PRACTISED-1SA-23:9(2790)-DA-8:12(6213)

PRAETORIUM-M’R-15:16(4232)

PRAISE-all=1984,a=3034,b=8416&marked-GE-29:35a■49:8a-LE-19:24(1974)-DE-10:21b,26:19b-J’G-5:2(1288)-1CH-16:4,35b■23:5,30■25:3■29:13-2CH-7:6a■8:14■20:19,21,21a,22b■23:13■29:30■31:2-EZR-3:10-NE-9:5b■12:24,46b-PS-7:17a■9:1a,14b■21:13(2167)■22:22,23,25b,26■28:7a■30:9a■33:1b,2a■34:1b■35:18,28b■40:3b■42:4(8426),5a,11a■43:4a,5a■44:8a■45:17a 48:10b■49:18a■50:23(8426)■51:15b■52:9a■54:6a■56:4,10^{2}■57:7(2167),9a■63:3(7623),5■65:1b■66:2b,8b■67:3^{2}a,5^{2}a■69:30,34■71:6b,8b,14b,22a■74:21■76:10a■79:13b■86:12a■88:10a■89:5a■99:3a■100:t(8426),4b■102:18,21b■104:35■105:45■106:1,2b,12b,47b,48■107:8a,15a,21a,31a,32■108:1(2167),3a■109:1b,30a,30■111:1,1a,10b■112:1■113:1^{2},9■115:17,18■116:19■117:1,1(7623),2■118:19a,21a,28a■119:7a,164,171b,175■135:1^{2},3,21■138:1a,1(2167),2a,4a■139:14a■142:7a■145:tb,2,4(7623),10a,21b■146:1,2,10■147:1,1b,12(7623),12,20■148:1^{2},2^{2},3^{2},4,5,7,13,14b,14■149:1,1b,3,9■150:1^{3},2^{2},3^{2},4^{2},5^{2},6^{2}-PR-27:2,21(4110)■28:4■31:31-IS-12:1a,4a■25:1a■38:18a,19a■42:8b,10b,12b■43:21b■48:9b■60:18b■61:3b,11b■62:7b,9-JER-13:11b■17:14b,26(8426)■20:13■31:7■33:9b,11a,11(8426)■48:2b■49:25b■51:41b-DA-2:23(7624)■4:37(7624)-JOE-2:26-HAB-3:3b-ZEP-3:19b,20b-N.T.-all=1868&marked-M’T-21:16(136)-LU-18:43(136)■19:37(134)-JOH-9:24(1391)■12:43^{2}(1391) RO-2:29■13:3■15:11(134)-1CO-4:5■11:2(1867),17(1867),22(1867)-2CO-8:18-EPH-1:6,12,14-PH’P-1:11■4:8-HEB-2:12(5214)■13:15(133)-1PE-1:7■2:14■4:11(1391)-RE-19:5(134)

PRAISED-all=1984&marked-J’G-16:24-2SA-14:25■22:4-1CH-16:25,36■23:5-2CH-5:13■7:3(3034),6■30:21-EZR-3:11-NE-5:13-PS-18:3■48:1■72:15(1288)■96:4■113:3■145:3-PR-31:30-EC-4:2(7623)-SONG-6:9-IS-64:11-DA-4:34(7624)■5:4(7624),23(7624)■N.T.-LU-1:64(2127)

PRAISES-all=8416&marked-EX-15:11-2CH-29:30(1984)-PS-22:3■56:12(8426)■78:4-IS-60:6■63:7■N.T.-1PE-2:9(703)

PRAISETH-PR-31:28(1984)

PRAISING-all=1984-1CH-5:13■23:12-EZR-3:11-PS-84:4■N.T.-all=134-LU-2:13,20■24:53-AC-2:47■3:8,9

PRANSING-NA-3:2(1725)

PRANSINGS-J’G-5:22^{2}(1726)

PRATING-PR-10:4(8193),10(8193)■N.T.-3JO-10(5396)

PRAY-all=4994,a=6419&marked-GE-12:13■13:8,9■16:2■18:3,4■19:2,7,8■20:7a■23:13(3863)■24:2,12,14,17,23,43,45■25:30■27:3,19,21■30:14,27■32:11,29■33:10,11,14■34:8■37:6,14,16■38:16,25■40:8,14,16■44:18,33■45:4■47:4,29^{2}■48:9■50:4,5,17(577),17-EX-4:13,18■5:3■10:17■32:32■33:13■34:9-NU-10:31■11:15■16:8,26■20:17■21:7a■22:6,16,17,19■23:13,27-DE-3:25-JOS-2:12■7:19-J’G-1:24■4:19■6:18,39■8:5■9:2,38■10:15■11:17,19■13:4,15■15:2■16:10,28^{2}■18:5■19:6,8,9,11,23-RU-2:7-1SA-2:36■3:17■7:5a■9:18■10:15■12:19a,23a■14:29■15:25,30■16:22■19:2■20:29^{2}■22:3■23:22■25:8,24,25,28■26:8,11,19■28:8,22■30:7-2SA-1:4,9■7:27a■13:5,6,13,26■14:2,11,12,18■15:7,31■16:9■18:22■19:37■20:16■24:17-1KI-1:12■2:17■8:26,30a,33a,35a,42a,44a,48a■13:6a■14:2■17:10,11,21■19:20■20:7,31,32,35,37■22:5,13-2KI-1:13■2:2,4,6,9,16,19■4:10,22,26■5:7,15,17,22■6:2,3,17,18■7:13■8:4■18:23,26-1CH-17:25a■21:17-2CH-6:24a,26a,32a,37(2603),38a■7:14a■18:4,12-EZR-6:10(6739)-NE-1:6a,11■5:10,11-JOB-4:7■6:29■8:8■21:15■22:22■32:21■33:1,26(6279)■42:8a-PS-5:2a■32:6a■55:17(7878)■119:76■122:6(7592)-IS-5:3■16:12a■29:11,12■36:8,11■45:20a-JER-7:16a■11:14a■14:11a■21:2■29:7a,12a■32:8■37:3a,20^{2}■42:2a,4a,20a-LA-1:18-EZE-33:30-JON-1:8■4:2(577)-MIC-3:1,9-HAG-2:15-ZEC-7:2(2470)■8:21(2470),22(2470)-MAL-1:9■N.T.-all=4336&marked-M’T-5:44■6:5,6,7,9■9:38(1189)■14:23■19:13■24:20■26:36,41,53(3870)-M’R-5:17(3870)■6:46■11:24■13:18,33■14:32,38-LU-6:12,28■9:28■10:2(1189)■11:1,2■14:18(2065),19(2065)■16:27(2065)■18:1,10■21:36(1189)■22:40,46-JOH-14:16(2065)■16:26(2065)■17:9(2065),15(2065),20(2065)-AC-8:22(1189),24(1189),34(1189)■10:9■24:4(3870)■27:34(3870)-RO-8:26-1CO-11:13■14:13,14,15^{2}-2CO-5:20(1189)■13:7(2172)-PH’P-1:9-COL-1:9-1TH-5:17,25-2TH-1:11■3:1-1TI-2:8-HEB-13:18-JAS-5:13,14,16(2172)-1JO-5:16(2065)

PRAYED-all=6419&marked-GE-20:17-NU-11:2■21:7-DE-9:20,26-1SA-1:10,27■2:1■8:6-2KI-4:33■6:17,18■19:15,20■20:2-2CH-30:18■32:20,24■33:13-EZR-10:1-NE-1:4■2:4-JOB-42:10-IS-37:15,21■38:2-JER-32:16-DA-6:10(6739)■9:4-JON-2:1■4:2■N.T.-all=4336&marked-M’T-26:39,42,44-M’R-1:35■5:18(3870)■14:35,39-LU-5:3(2065),16■9:29■18:11■22:32(1189),41,44-JOH-4:31(2065)-AC-1:24■4:31(1189)■6:6■8:15■9:40■10:2(1189),30,48(2065)■13:3■14:23■16:9(3870),25■20:36■21:5■22:17■23:18(2065)■28:8-JAS-5:17,18

PRAYER-all=8605&marked-2SA-7:27-2KI-8:28^{2},29,38,45,49,54■9:3-2KI-19:4■20:5-2CH-6:19^{2},20,29,35,39,40■7:12,15■30:27■33:18,19-NE-1:6,11^{2}■4:9(6419)■11:17-JOB-15:4(7878)■16:17■22:27(6279)-PS-4:1■6:9■17:t,1■35:13■39:12■42:8■54:2■55:1■61:1■64:1(7879)■65:2■66:19,20■69:13■72:15(6419)■80:4■84:8■86:t,6■88:2,13■90:t■102:t,1,17^{2}■109:4,7■141:2,5■142:t■143:1-PR-15:8,29■28:9-IS-26:16(3908)■37:4■38:5■56:7^{2}-JER-7:16■11:14-LA-3:8,44-DA-9:3,13(2470),17,21-JON-2:7-HAB-3:1■N.T.-all=4335&marked-M’T-17:21■21:13,22■23:14(4336)-M’R-9:29■11:17-LU-1:13(1162)■6:12■19:46■22:45-AC-1:14■3:1■6:4■10:31■12:5■16:13,16-RO-10:1(1162)■12:12-1CO-7:5-2CO-1:11(1162)■9:14(1162)-EPH-6:18-PH’P-1:4(1162),19(1162)■4:6-COL-4:2-1TI-4:5(1783)-JAS-5:15(2171),16(1162)-1PE-4:7

PRAYERS-PS-72:20(8605)-IS-1:15(8605)■N.T.-all=4335&marked-M’T-12:40(4336)-LU-2:37(1162)■5:33(1162)■20:47(4336)-AC-2:42■10:4-RO-1:9■15:30-EPH-1:16-COL-4:12-1TH-1:2-1TI-2:1■5:5-2TI-1:3(1162)-PH’M-4,22-HEB-5:7(1162)-1PE-3:7,12(1162)-RE-5:8■8:3,4

PRAYEST-M’T-6:5(4336),6(4336)

PRAYETH-all=6419-1KI-8:28-2CH-6:19,20-IS-44:17■N.T.-all=4336-AC-9:11-1CO-11:5■14:14

PRAYING-all=6419&marked-1SA-1:12,26-1KI-8:54-2CH-7:1-DA-6:11(1156)■9:20■N.T.-all=4336&marked-M’R-11:25-LU-1:10■3:21■9:18■11:1-AC-11:5■12:12-1CO-11:4-2CO-8:4(1189)-EPH-6:18-COL-1:3■4:3-1TH-3:10(1189)-JUDE-20

PREACH-NE-6:7(7121)-IS-61:1(1319)-JON-3:2(7121)■N.T.-all=2784,a=2097&marked-M’T-4:17■10:7,27■11:1-M’R-1:4,38■3:14■16:15-LU-4:18a,18,19,43a■9:2,60(1229)-AC-5:24a■10:42■14:15a■15:21■16:6(2980),10a■17:3(2605)-RO-1:15a■10:8,15,15a■15:20a-1CO-1:17a,23■9:14(2605),16^{2}a,18a■15:11-2CO-4:5■10:16a-GA-1:8a,9a,16a■2:2■5:11-EPH-3:8a-PH’P-1:15,16(2605)-COL-1:28(2605)-2TI-4:2-RE-14:6a

PREACHED-PS-40:9(1319)■N.T.-all=2097,a=2784&marked-M’T-11:5■24:14a■26:13a-M’R-1:7a,39a■2:2(2980)■6:12a■14:9a■16:20a-LU-3:18■4:44a■7:22■16:16■20:1■24:47a-AC-3:20(4296)■4:2(2605)■8:5a,25(2980),25,35,40■9:20a,27(3954)■10:37a■13:5(2605),24(4296),38(2605),42(2980)■14:7,21,25(2980)■15:36(2605)■17:13(2605),18■20:7(1256)-RO-15:19(4137)-1CO-9:27a■15:1,2,12a-2CO-1:19a■11:4a,7-GA-1:8,11■3:8(4283)■4:13-EPH-2:17-PH’P-1:18(2605)-COL-1:23a-1TH-2:9a-1TI-3:16a-HEB-4:2,2(189),6-1PE-1:12,25■3:19a■4:6

PREACHER-all=6953-EC-1:1,2,12■7:27■12:8,9,10■N.T.-all=2783&marked-RO-10:14(2784)-1TI-2:7-2TI-1:11-2PE-2:5

PREACHEST-RO-2:21(2784)

PREACHETH-AC-19:13(2784)-2CO-11:4(2784)-GA-1:23(2097)

PREACHING-JON-3:2(7150)■N.T.-all=2784&marked-M’T-3:1■4:23■9:35■12:41(2782)-M’R-1:14-LU-3:3■8:1■9:6(2097)■11:32(2782)-AC-8:4(2097),12(2097)■10:36(2097)■11:19(2980),20(2907)■15:35(2097)■20:9(1256),25■28:31-RO-16:25(2782)-1CO-1:18(3056),21(2782)■2:4(2782)■15:14(2782)-2TI-4:17(2782)-TIT-1:3(2782)

PRECEPT-IS-28:10(6673),13(6673)-29:13(4687)■N.T.-M’R-10:5(1785)-HEB-9:19(1785)

PRECEPTS-all=6490&marked-NE-9:14(4687)-PS-119:4,15,27,40,45,56,63,69,78,87,93,94,100,104,110,128,134,141,159,168,173-JER-35:18(4687)-DA-9:5(4687)

PRECIOUS-all=3368&marked-GE-24:53(4030)-DE-33:13(4022),14^{2}(4022),15(4022),16(4022)-1SA-3:1■26:21(3365)-2SA-12:30-1KI-10:2,10,11-2KI-1:13(3365),14(3365)■20:13(5238),13(2898)-1CH-20:2■29:2-2CH-3:6■9:1,9,10■20:25(2530)■21:3(4030)■3:27-EZR-1:6(4030)■8:27(2530)-JOB-28:10(3366),16-PS-49:8(3365)■72:14(3365)■116:15■126:6(4901)■133:2(2896)■139:17(3365)-PR-1:13■3:15■6:26■12:27■17:8(2580)■20:15(3366)■24:4-EC-7:1(2896)-IS-13:12(3365)■28:16■39:2(5238),2(2896)■43:4(3365)-JER-15:19■20:5(3366)-LA-4:2-EZE-22:25(3366)■27:20(2667),22■28:13-DA-11:8(2532),38,43(2530)■N.T.-all=5093&marked-M’T-26:7(927)-M’R-14:3(4185)-1CO-3:12-JAS-5:7-1PE-1:7,19■2:4(1784),6(1784),7(5092)-2PE-1:1(2472),4-RE-17:4■18:12^{2},16■21:11,19

PREDESTINATE-RO-8:29(4309),30(4309)

PREDESTINATED-EPH-1:5(4309),11(4309)

PREEMINENCE-EC-3:19(4195)■N.T.-COL-1:18(4409)-3JO-9(5383)

PREFER-PS-137:6(5927)

PREFERRED-ES-2:9(8138)-DA-6:3(5330)■N.T.-all=1096-JOH-1:15,27,30

PREFERRING-RO-12:10(4285)-1TI-5:21(4299)

PREMEDITATE-M'R-13:11(3191)

PREPARATION-1CH-22:5(3559)-NA-2:3(3559)■N.T.-all=3904&marked-M'T-27:62-M'R-15:42-LU-23:54-JOH-19:14,31,42-EPH-6:15(2091)

PREPARATIONS-PR-16:1(4633)

PREPARE-all=3559&marked-EX-16:5-NU-15:5(6213),6(6213),12(6213)■23:1,29-DE-19:3-JOS-1:11■22:26(6213)-1SA-7:3■23:22-1KI-18:44(631)-1CH-9:32■29:18-2CH-2:9■31:11■35:4,6-ES-5:8(6213)-JOB-8:8■11:13■27:16,17-PS-10:17■59:4■61:7(4487)■107:36-PR-24:27■30:25-IS-14:21■21:5(6186)■40:3(6437),20■57:14(6437)■62:10(6437)■65:11(6186)-JER-6:4(6942)■12:3(6942)■22:7(6942)■46:14■51:12,27(6942),28(6942)-EZE-4:15(6213)■12:3(6213)■35:6(6213)■38:7■43:25(6213),25■45:17,22,23,24■46:2,7,12^2,13^2,14,15-JOE-3:9(6942)-AM-4:12-MIC-3:5(6942)-MAL-3:1(6437)■N.T.-all=2090&marked-M'T-3:3■11:10(2680)■26:17-M'R-1:2(2680),3■14:12-LU-1:76■3:4■7:27(2680)■22:8,9-JOH-14:2,3-1CO-14:8(3903)-PH'M-22

PREPARED-all=3559,a=6213&marked-GE-24:31(6437)■27:17a-EX-12:39a■23:20-NU-21:27■23:4(6186)-JOS-4:4,13(2502)-2SA-15:1a-1KI-1:5a■5:18■6:19-2KI-6:23(3739)-1CH-12:39■15:1,3,12■22:3,5,14^2■29:2,3,16-2CH-1:4■3:1■8:16■12:14■16:14(7543)■17:18(3502)■19:3■20:33■26:14■27:6■29:19,36■31:11■35:10,14,15,16,20-EZR-7:10-NE-5:18^{2}a■8:10■13:5a-ES-5:4a,5a,12a■6:4,14a■7:10-JOB-28:27■29:7-PS-7:13■9:7■57:6■68:10■74:16■103:19-PR-8:27■19:29■21:31-IS-30:33■64:4a-EZE-23:41(6186)■28:13■38:7-DA-2:9(2164)-HO-2:8a■6:3-JON-1:17(4487)■4:6(4487),7(4487),8(4487)-NA-2:5-ZEP-1:7■N.T.-all=2090&marked-M'T-20:23■22:4■25:34,41-M'R-10:40■14:15-LU-1:17(2680)■2:31■12:47■23:56■24:1-RO-9:23(4282)-1CO-2:9-2TI-2:21-HEB-10:5(2675)■11:7(2680),16-RE-8:6■9:7,15■12:6■16:12■21:2

PREPAREDST-PS-80:9(6437)

PREPAREST-NU-15:8(6213)-PS-23:5(6186)■65:9(3559)

PREPARETH-all=3559-2CH-30:19-JOB-15:35-PS-147:8

PREPARING-NE-13:7(6213)■N.T.-1PE-3:20(2680)

PRESBYTERY-1TI-4:14(4244)

PRESCRIBED-IS-10:1(3789)

PRESCRIBING-EZR-7:22(3792)

PRESENCE-all=6440&marked-GE-3:8■4:16■16:12■23:11(5869),18(5869)■25:18■27:30■41:46■45:3■47:15(5048)-EX-10:11(5869)■33:14,15■35:20-LE-22:3-NU-20:6-DE-25:9(5869)-JOS-4:11■8:32-1SA-18:11■19:7,10■21:15(5921)-2SA-16:19^3■24:4-1KI-1:28■8:22(5048)■12:2■21:13(5048)-2KI-3:14■5:27■13:23■24:20■25:19-1CH-16:27,33■24:31-2CH-6:12(5048)■9:23■10:2■20:9■34:4-NE-2:1-ES-1:10■8:15-JOB-1:12■2:7■23:15-PS-9:3■16:11■17:2■23:5(5048)■31:20■51:11■68:2,8^2■95:2■97:5^2■100:2■114:7^2■116:14(5048),18(5048)■139:7■140:13-PR-14:7(5048)■17:18■25:6,7-IS-1:7(5048)■19:1■63:9■64:1,2,3-JER-4:26■5:22■23:39■28:1(5869),5^2(5869),11(5869)■32:12(5869)■52:3-EZE-38:20-DA-2:27(6925)-JON-1:3^2,10-NA-1:5-ZEP-1:7■N.T.-all=1799&marked-LU-1:19■13:26■14:10■15:10-JOH-20:30-AC-3:13(4383),16(561),19(4383)■5:41(4383)■27:35-1CO-1:29-2CO-10:1(4383),10(3952)-PH'P-2:12(3952)-1TH-2:17(4383),19(1715)-2TH-1:9(4383)-HEB-9:24(4383)-JUDE-24(2714)-RE-14:10^2

PRESENT-all=4503,a=4672&marked-GE-32:13,18,20,21■33:10■43:11,15,25,26-EX-34:2(5324)-LE-14:11(5975)■16:7(5975)■27:8(5975),11(5975)-NU-3:6(5975)-DE-31:14(3320)-J'G-3:15,17,18^2■6:18-1SA-9:7(8670)■10:19(3320)■13:15a,16a■21:3a■30:26(1293)-2SA-20:4(5975)-1KI-9:16(7964)■10:25■15:19(7810)■20:27(3557)-2KI-8:8,9■16:8(7810)■17:4■18:31(1293)■20:12-1CH-29:17(4672)-2CH-5:11a■9:24■29:29a■30:21a■31:1a■34:32a,33a■35:7a,17a,18a-EZR-8:25a-ES-1:5a■4:16a-JOB-1:6(3320)■2:1^2(3320)-PS-46:1a-IS-18:7(7862)■36:16(1293)■39:1-JER-36:7(5307)■42:9(5307)-EZE-27:15(814)-DA-9:18(5307)-HO-10:6■N.T.-all=3918&marked-LU-2:22(3936)■13:1-JOH-14:25(3306)-AC-10:33■21:18(3854)■25:24(4840)■28:2(2186)-RO-7:18(3873),21(3873)■8:18(3568),38(1764)■11:5(3568)■12:1(3936)-1CO-3:22(1764)■4:11(737)■5:3^2■7:26(1764)■15:6(737)-2CO-4:14(3936)■5:8(1736),9(1736)■10:2,11■11:2(3936),9■13:2,10-GA-1:4(1764)■4:18,20-EPH-5:27(3936)-COL-1:22(3936),28(3936)-2TI-4:10(3568)-TIT-2:12(3568)-HEB-9:9(1764)■12:11-2PE-1:12-JUDE-24(2476)

PRESENTED-all=3320&marked-GE-46:29(7200)■47:2(3322)-LE-2:8(7126)■7:35(7126)■9:12(4672),13(4672),18(4672)■16:10(5975)-DE-31:14-JOS-24:1-J'G-6:19(5066)■20:2-1SA-17:16-JER-38:26(5307)-EZE-20:28(5414)■N.T.-M'T-2:11(4374)-AC-9:41(3936)■23:33(3936)

PRESENTING-DA-9:20(5307)

PRESENTLY-1SA-2:16(3117)-PR-12:6(3117)■N.T.-M'T-21:19(3916)■26:53(3936)-PH'P-2:23(1824)

PRESENTS-all=4503&marked-1SA-10:27-1KI-4:21-2KI-17:3-2CH-17:5,11■32:23(4030)-PS-68:29(7862)■72:10■76:11(7862)-MIC-1:14(7964)

PRESERVE-all=5341,a=8104&marked-GE-19:32(2421),34(2421)■45:5(4241),7(7760)-DE-6:24(2421)-PS-12:7■16:1a■25:21■32:7■40:11■41:2a■61:7■64:1■79:11(3498)■86:2a■121:7^{2}a,8a■140:1,4-PR-2:11a■4:6a■14:3a■20:28■22:12-IS-31:5(4422)■49:8-JER-49:11(2421)■N.T.-LU-17:33(2225)-2TI-4:18(4982)

PRESERVED-all=8104&marked-GE-32:30(5337)-JOS-24:17-1SA-30:23-2SA-8:6(3467,)14(3467)-1CH-18:6,13-JOB-10:12■29:2-PS-37:28-IS-49:6(5336)-HO-12:13■N.T.-M'T-9:17(4933)-LU-5:38(4933)-1TH-5:23(5083)-JUDE-1(5083)

PRESERVER-JOB-7:20(5341)

PRESERVEST-NE-9:6(2421)-PS-36:6(3467)

PRESERVETH-all=8104&marked-JOB-36:6(2421)-PS-31:23(5341)■97:10■116:6■145:20■146:9-PR-2:8■16:17

PRESIDENTS-all=5632-DA-6:2,3,4,6,7

PRESS-JOE-3:13(1660)-HAG-2:16(6333)■N.T.-all=2793&marked-M'R-2:4■5:27,30-LU-8:19,45(598)■19:3-PH'P-3:14(1377)

PRESSED-GE-19:3(6484),9(6484)■40:11(7818)-J'G-16:16(6693)-2SA-13:25(6555),27(6555)-ES-8:14(1765)-EZ-23:3(4600)-AM-2:13(5781),13(5781)■N.T.-M'R-3:10(1968)-LU-5:1(1945)■6:38(4085)-AC-18:5(4912)-2CO-1:8(916)

PRESSES-NE-13:15(1660)-PR-3:10(3342)-IS-16:10(3342)

PRESSETH-PS-38:2(5181)■N.T.-LU-16:16(971)

PRESSFAT -HAG-2:16(3342)

PRESUME-DE-18:20(2102)-ES-7:5(4390)

PRESUMED-NU-14:44(6075)

PRESUMPTUOUS-PS-19:13(2086)■N.T.-2PE-2:10(5113)

PRESUMPTUOUSLY-all=2102&marked-EX-21:14-NU-15:30(3027)-DE-1:43■17:12(2087),13■18:22(2087)

PRETENCE-all=4392-M'T-23:14-M'R-12:40-PH'P-1:18

PREVAIL-all=3201&marked-GE-7:20(1396)-NU-22:6-J'G-16:5-1SA-2:9(1396)■17:9■26:25-1KI-22:22-2CH-14:11(6113)■18:21-ES-6:13-JOB-15:24(8630)■18:9(2388)-PS-9:19(5810)■12:4(1396)■65:3(1396)-EC-4:12(8630)-1SA-7:1(3898)■16:12■42:13(1396)■47:12(6206)-JER-1:19■5:22■15:20■20:10,11-DA-11:7(2388)■N.T.-M'T-16:18(2729)■27:24(5623)-JOH-12:19(5623)

PREVAILED-all=1396,a=3201&marked-GE-7:18,19,24■30:8a■32:25a,28a■47:20(2388)■49:26-EX-17:11^2-J'G-1:35(3513)■3:10(5810)■4:24(7186)■6:2(5810)-1SA-17:50(2388)-2SA-11:23■24:4(2388)-1KI-16:22(2388)-2KI-25:3(2388)-1CH-5:2■21:4(2388)-2CH-8:3(2388)■13:18(553)■27:5(2388)-PS-13:4a■129:2a-JER-20:7a■38:22a-LA-1:16-DA-7:21(3202)-HO-12:4a-OB-7a■N.T.-all=2480&marked-LU-23:23(2729)-AC-19:16,20-RE-5:5(3528)■12:8

PREVAILEST-JOB-14:20(8630)

PREVAILETH-LA-1:13(7287)

PREVENT-all=6923-JOB-3:12-PS-59:10■79:8■88:13■119:148-AM-9:10■N.T.-1TH-4:15(5348)

PREVENTED-all=6923-2SA-22:6,19-JOB-30:27■41:11-PS-18:5,18■119:147-IS-21:14■N.T.-M'T-17:25(4399)

PREVENTEST-PS-21:3(6923)

PREY-all=2964,a=957&marked-GE-49:9,27(5706)-NU-14:3a,31a■23:24■31:11(4455),12(4455),26(4455),27(4455),32a-DE-1:39a■2:35(962)■3:7(962)-JOS-8:2(962),27(962)■11:14(962)-J'G-5:30^3(7998)■8:24(7998),25(7998)-2KI-21:14a-NE-4:4(961)-ES-3:13(962)■8:11(962)■9:15(961),16(961)-JOB-4:11■9:26(400)■24:5■38:39■39:29(400)-PS-17:12(2963)■76:4■104:21■124:6-PR-23:28(2863)-IS-5:29■10:2(7998),6a■31:4■33:23(5706),23a■42:22a■49:24(4455),25(4455)■59:15(7997)-JER-21:9(7998)■30:16(962)■38:2(7998)■39:18(7998)■45:5(7998)-EZE-7:21a■19:3,6■22:25,27■26:12(962)■29:19a■34:8a,22a,28a■36:4a,5a■38:12a,13a-DA-11:24(961)-AM-3:4-NA-2:12,13■3:1-ZEP-3:8(5706)

PRICE-all=4242&marked-LE-25:16^2(4736),50(3701)-DE-23:18-2SA-24:24-1KI-10:28-1CH-21:22(3701),24(3701)-2CH-1:16-JOB-28:13(6187),15,18(4901)-PS-44:12-PR-17:16■27:26■31:10(4377)-IS-45:13■55:1-JER-15:13-ZEC-11:12^2(7939),13(3365)■N.T.-all=5092&marked-M'T-13:46(4186)■27:6,9-AC-5:2,3■19:19-ICO-6:20■7:23-1PE-3:4(4185)

PRICES-AC-4:34(5092)

PRICKED-PS-73:21(8150)■N.T.-AC-2:37(2669)

PRICKING-EZE-28:24(3992)

PRICKS-NU-33:55(7899)■N.T.-AC-9:5(2759)■26:14(2759)

PRIDE-all=1347&marked-LE-26:19-1SA-17:28(2087)-2CH-32:26(1363)-JOB-33:17(1466)■35:12■41:15(1346),34(7830)-PS-10:2(1346),4(1363)■31:20(7407)■36:11(1346)■59:12■73:6(1346)-PR-8:13(1344)■11:2(2087)■13:10(2087)■14:3(1346)■16:18■29:23(1346)-IS-9:9(1346)■16:6^2■23:9■25:11(1346)■28:1(1348),3(1348)-JER-13:9^2,17(1466)■48:29^2■49:16(2087)-EZE-7:10(2087)■16:49,56■30:6-DA-4:37(1466)■5:20

(2103)-HO-5:5■7:10-OB-3(2087)-ZEP-2:10■3:11(1346)-ZEC-9:6■10:11■11:3■N.T.-M'R-7:22(5243)-1TI-3:6(5187)-1JO-2:16(212)

PRIEST-all=3548&marked-GE-14:18■41:45,50■46:20-EX-2:16■3:1■18:1■29:30■31:10■35:19■38:21■39:41-LE-1:7,9,12,13,15,17■2:2,8,9,16■3:11,16■4:3,5,6,7,10,16,17,20,25,26,30,31,34,35^{2}■5:6,8,10,12^{2},13,16^{2},18^{2}■6:6,7,10,12,22,23,26■7:5,7,8^{2},31,32,34■12:6,8■13:2,3^{2},4,5^{2},6^{2},7^{2},8^{2},9,10,11,12,13,15,16,17^{2},19,20^{2},21^{2},22,23,25^{2},26^{2},27^{2},28,30^{2},31^{2},32,33,34^{2},36^{2},37,39,43,44,49,50,53,54,55,56■14:2,3^{2},4,5,11,12,14^{2},15,16,17,18,19,20^{2},23,24^{2},25,26,27,28,31,35,36^{3},38,39,40,44,48^{2}■15:14,15^{2},29,30^{2}■16:32■17:5,6■19:22■21:9,10,21■22:10,11,14■23:10,11,20^{2}■27:8^{3},11,12^{2},14^{2},18,23-NU-3:6,32■4:16,28,33■5:8,9,10,15,16,17^{2},18^{2},19,21^{2},23,25,26,30■6:10,11,16,17,19,20^{2}■7:8■15:25,28■16:37,39■18:28■19:3,4,6,7^{2}■25:7,11■26:1,3,63,64■27:2,19,21,22■31:6,12,13,21,26,29,31,41,51,54■32:2,28■33:38■34:17■35:25,28^{2},32-DE-17:12■18:3■20:2■26:3,4-JOS-14:1■17:4■19:51■20:6■21:1,4,13■22:13,30,31,32-J'G-17:5,10,12,13■18:4,6,17,18,19^{3},24,27-1SA-1:9■2:11,14,15,28,35■14:3,19^{2},36■21:1,2,4,5,6,9■22:11■23:9■30:7-2SA-15:27-1KI-1:7,8,19,25,26,32,34,38,9,42,44,45■2:22,26,27,35■4:2-2KI-11:9^{2},10,15^{2},18^{2}■12:2,7,9,10■16:10,11^{2},15,16■22:4,8,10,12,14■23:4,24■25:18^{2}-1CH-16:39■24:6■27:5■29:22-2CH-13:9■15:3■19:11■22:11■23:8^{2},9,14^{2},17■24:2,20,25■26:17,20■31:10■34:9,14,18-EZR-2:63■7:5,11,12(3549),21■8:33■10:10,16-NE-3:1,20■7:65■8:2,9■10:38■12:26■13:4,13,28-PS-110:4-IS-8:2■24:2■28:7-JER-6:13■8:10■14:18■18:18■20:1■21:1■23:11,33,34■29:25,26^{2},29■37:3■52:24^{2}-LA-2:6,20-EZE-1:3■7:26■44:13(3547),21,22,30■45:19-HO-4:4,6(3547),9-AM-7:10-HAG-1:1,12,14■2:2,4-ZEC-3:1,8■6:11,13■N.T.-all=749,a=2409&marked-M'T-8:4a■26:3,57,62,63,65-M'R-1:44a■2:26■14:47,53,54,60,61,63,66-LU-1:5a■5:14a■10:31a■22:50-JOH-11:49,51■18:13,15^{2},16,19,22,24,26-AC-4:6,6(748)■5:17,21,24,27■7:1■9:1■14:13(2409)■22:5■23:2,4,5■24:1■25:2-HEB-2:17■3:1■4:14,15■5:1,5,6a,10■6:20■7:1a,3(2409),11a,15a,17a,21a,26■8:1,3,4a■9:7,11,25■10:11a,21a■13:11

PRIESTHOOD-all=3550-EX-40:15-NU-16:10■18:1■25:13-JOS-18:7-EZR-2:62-NE-7:64■13:29^{2}■N.T.-all=2420&marked-HEB-7:5(2405),11,12,14,24-1PE-2:5(2406),9(2406)

PRIEST'S-all=3547,a=3548&marked-EX-28:1,3,4,41■29:1,9(3550),44■30:30■31:10■35:19■39:41■40:13,15-LE-5:13a■7:9a,14a,35■14:13a,18a,29a■16:32■22:12a,13a■27:21a-NU-3:3,4,10(3550)■18:7^{2}(3550)-DE-10:6■18:3a-J'G-18:20a-1SA-2:13^{2}a,15a,36(3550)-1CH-6:10■24:2-2CH-11:14■24:11a-EZE-44:30a-MAL-2:7a■N.T.-all=749&marked-M'T-26:51,58-LU-1:8(2407),9(2405)■22:54-JOH-18:10

PRIESTS-all=3548&marked-GE-47:22^{2},26-EX-19:6,22,24-LE-1:5,8,11■2:2■3:2■6:29■7:6■13:2■16:33■21:1-NU-3:3■10:8-DE-17:9,18■18:1■19:17■21:5■24:8■27:9■31:9-JOS-3:3,6,8,13,14,15,17■4:9,10,11,16,17,18■6:4^{2},6^{2},8,9^{2},12,13sup,13,16,20■8:33■21:19-J'G-18:30-1SA-1:3■5:5■6:2■22:11,17^{2},18^{2},19,21-2SA-8:17■15:35^{2}■17:15■19:11■20:25-1KI-4:4■8:3,4,6,10,11■12:31,32■13:2,33^{2}-2KI-10:11,19■12:4,5,6,7,8,9■17:27,28,32■19:2■23:2,4,8^{2},9,20-1CH-9:2,10,30■13:2■15:11,14,24■16:6,39■18:16■23:2■24:6,31■28:13,21-2CH-4:6,9■5:5,7,11^{2},12,14■6:41■7:2,6^{2}■8:14^{2},15■11:13,15■13:9^{2},10,12,14■17:8■19:8■23:4,6,18■24:5■26:17,18,19^{2},20■29:4,16,21,22,24,26,34^{3}■30:3,15,16,21,24,25,27■31:2^{2},4,9,15,17,19^{2}■34:5,30■35:2,8^{2},10,11,14^{3},18■36:14-EZR-1:5■2:36,61,70■3:2,8,10,12■6:9(3549),16(3549),18(3549),20^{2}■7:7,13(3549)■16(3549),24(3549)■8:15,24,29,30■9:1,7■10:5,18-NE-2:16■3:1,22,28■5:12■7:39,63,73■8:13■9:32,34,38■10:8,28,34,36,37,39■11:3,10,20■12:1,7,12,22,30,41,44^{2}■13:5,30-PS-78:64■99:6■132:9,16-IS-37:2■61:6■66:21-JER-1:1,18■2:8,26■4:9■5:31■8:1■13:13■19:1■26:7,8,11,16■27:16■28:1,5■29:1,25■31:14■32:32■33:18,21■34:19■48:7■49:3-LA-1:4,19■4:13,16-EZE-22:26■40:45,46■42:13,14■43:19,24,27■44:15,31■45:4■46:2,19,20■48:10,11,13-HO-5:1■6:9■10:5(3649)-JO-1:9,13■2:17-MIC-3:11-ZEP-1:4■3:4-HAG-2:11,12,13-ZEC-7:3,5-MAL-1:6■2:1■N.T.-all=749&marked-M'T-2:4■12:4(2409),5(2409)■16:21■20:18■21:15,23,45■26:3,14,47,59■27:1,3,6,12,20,41,62■28:11-M'R-2:26(2409)■8:31■10:33■11:18,27■14:1,10,43,53,55■15:1,3,10,11,31-LU-3:2■6:4(2409)■9:22■17:14(2409)■19:47■20:1,19■22:2,4,52,66■23:4,10,13,23■24:20-JOH-1:19(2409)■7:32,45■11:47,57■12:10■18:3,35■19:6,15,21-AC-4:1(2409),23■5:24■6:7(2409)■9:14,21■19:14■22:30■23:14■25:15■26:10,12-HEB-7:21(2409),23(2409),27,28■8:4(2409)■9:6(2409)-RE-1:6(2409)■5:10(2409)■20:6(2409)

PRIESTS'-all=3548-JOS-4:3,18-1KI-12:16-EZR-2:69-NE-7:20,72■12:35

PRINCE-all=5387,a=8269&marked-GE-23:6■34:2-EX-2:14a-NU-7:11,18,24,30,36,42,48,54,60,66,72,78■16:13(8323)■17:6■25:14,18■34:18,22,23,24,25,26,27,28-JOS-22:14-2SA-3:38a-1KI-11:34■14:7(5057)■16:2(5057)-1CH-2:10■5:6-EZR-1:8-JOB-21:28(5081)■31:37(5057)-PR-14:28(7333)■17:7(5081)■19:6(5081)■25:7(5081),15(7101)■28:16(5057)-IS-9:6a-JER-51:59a-EZE-7:27■12:10,12■21:25■28:2(5057)■30:13■34:24■37:25■38:2,3■39:1■44:3■45:7,16,22■46:2,4,8,10,12,16,17,18■48:21^{2},22-DA-1:7a,8a,9a,10a,11a,18a■8:11a,25a■9:25(5057),26(5057)■10:13a,20^{2}a,21a■11:18(7101),22(5057)■12:1a-HO-3:4a-MIC-7:3a■N.T.-all=758&marked-M'T-9:34■12:24-M'R-3:22-JOH-12:31■14:30■16:11-AC-3:15(747)■5:31(747)-EPH-2:2-RE-1:5

PRINCE'S-SONG-7:1(5081)-EZE-45:17(5387)■48:22(5387)

PRINCES-all=8269,a=5387&marked-GE-12:15(8269)■17:20a■25:16a-NU-1:16a,44a■7:2^{2}a,3a,10^{2}a,84a■10:4a■16:2a■17:2a,6a■21:18■22:8,13,14,15,21,35,40■23:6,17■27:2a■31:13a■32:2a■36:1a-JOS-9:15a,18^{2}a,19a,21^{2}a■13:21a■17:4a■22:14a,30a,32a-J'G-5:3(7336),15■7:25■8:3,6,14■10:18-1SA-2:8(5081)■18:30■29:3^{2},4^{2},9-2SA-10:3■19:6-1KI-4:2■9:22■20:14,15,17,19-2KI-11:14■24:12,14-1CH-4:38a■7:40a■19:3■22:17■23:2■24:6■27:22■28:1^{2},21■29:6,24-2CH-12:5,6■17:7■21:4,9■22:8■23:13■24:10,17,23■28:14,21■29:30■30:2,6,12,24■31:8■32:3,31■35:8■36:18-EZR-7:28■8:20■9:1,2■10:8-NE-9:32,34,38■12:31,32-ES-1:3^{2},11,14,16^{2},18,21■2:18■3:1■5:11■6:9-JOB-3:15■12:19(3548),21(5081)■29:9■34:18(5081),19-PS-45:16■47:9(5081)■68:27^{2},31(2831)■76:12(5057)■82:7■83:11(5257)■105:22■107:40(5081)■113:8^{2}(5081)■118:9(5081)■119:23,161■146:3(5081)■148:11-PR-8:15(7336),16■17:26(5081)■19:10■28:2■31:4(7336)-EC-10:7,16,17-IS-1:23■3:4,14■10:8■19:11,13^{2}■21:5■23:8■30:4■31:9■32:1■34:12■40:23(7336)■41:25(5461)■43:28■49:7-JER-1:18■2:26■4:9■8:1■17:25^{2}■24:1,8■25:18,19■26:10,11,12,16,21■29:2■32:32■34:10,19,21■35:4■36:12^{2},14,19,21■37:14,15■38:4,17,18,22^{2},25,27■39:3^{2},13(7227)■41:1(7227)■44:17,21■48:7■49:3,38■50:35■51:57■52:10-LA-1:6■2:2,9■5:12-EZE-11:1■17:12■19:1a■21:12a■22:6a,27■23:15(7991)■26:16a■27:21a■32:29a,30(5257)■39:18a■45:8a,9a-DA-1:3(6579)■3:2(324),3(324),27(324)■5:2(7261),3(7261)■6:1(324),2(324),3(324),4(324),6(324),7(324)■8:25■9:6,8■10:13■11:5,8(5257)-HO-5:10■7:3,5,16■8:4,10■9:15■13:10-AM-1:15■2:3-MIC-3:1(7101),9(7101)-HAB-1:10(7336)-ZEP-1:8■3:3■N.T.-all=758&marked-M'T-2:6(2232)■20:25-1CO-2:6,8

PRINCESS-LA-1:1(8282)

PRINCESSES-1KI-11:3(8282)

PRINCIPAL-all=7218&marked-EX-30:23-LE-6:5-NU-5:7-1KI-4:5(3548)-2KI-25:19(8269)-1CH-24:6(1),31-NE-11:17-PR-4:7(7225)-IS-16:8(8291)■28:25(7795)-JER-25:34(117),35(117),36(117)■52:25(8269)-MIC-5:5(5257)■N.T.-AC-25:23(3588,2596,1851,5607)

PRINCIPALITIES-JER-13:18(4761)■N.T.-all=746-RO-8:38-EPH-3:10■6:12-COL-1:16■2:15-TIT-3:1

PRINCIPALITY-EPH-1:21(746)-COL-2:10(746)

PRINCIPLES-HEB-5:12(4747)■6:1(746)

PRINT-LE-19:28(5414)-JOB-13:27(2707)■N.T.-JOH-20:25^{2}(5179)

PRINTED-JOB-19:23(2710)

PRISED-ZEC-11:13(3365)

PRISON-all=4307&marked-GE-39:20^{2}(1004,5470),21(1004,5470),22^{2}(1004,5470),23(1004,5470)■40:3(1004,5470),5(1004,5470)■42:19(4929)-J'G-16:21(631),25(631)-1KI-22:27(1004,3608)-2KI-17:4(1004,3608)■25:27(1004,3608),29(3608)-2CH-16:10(4115),18:26(1004,3608)-NE-3:25■12:39-PS-142:7(4525)-EC-4:14(1004,612)-IS-24:22(4525)■42:7(4525),7(3608),22(3608)■53:8(6115)■61:1(6495)-JER-29:26(4115)■32:2,8,12■33:1■37:4(1004,3608),15(1004,612),15(1004,3608),18(1004,3608),21^{2}■38:6,13,28■39:14,15■52:11(1004,6468),31(1004,3608),(3608)■N.T.-all=5438&marked-M'T-4:12(3860)■5:25(5438)■11:2(1201)■14:3,10■18:30■25:36,39,43,44-M'R-1:14(3860)■6:17,27-LU-3:20■12:58■22:33■23:19,25-JOH-3:24-AC-5:18(5084),19,21(1201),22,23(1201),25■8:3■12:4,5,6,7(3612),17■16:23,24,26(1201),27(1200),27,36(1200),37,40■26:10-1PE-3:19-RE-2:10■20:7

PRISONER-PS-79:11(616)■102:20(615)■N.T.-all=1198-M'T-27:15,16-M'R-15:6-AC-23:18■25:27■28:17-EPH-3:1■4:1-2TI-1:8-PH'M-1,9

PRISONERS-all=615&marked-GE-39:20,22-NU-21:1(7628)-JOB-3:18-PS-69:33■146:7(631)-IS-10:4(616)■14:17■20:4(7628)■24:22(616)■42:7(616)■49:9(631)-LA-3:34-ZEC-9:11,12■N.T.-all=1198&marked-AC-16:25,27■27:1(1202),42(1202)■28:16

PRISONS-LU-21:12(5438)-AC-22:4(5438)-2CO-11:23(5438)

PRIVATE-2PE-1:20(2398)

PRIVATELY-all=2596,2398-M'T-24:3-M'R-6:32■9:28■13:3-LU-9:10■10:23-AC-23:19-GAL-2:2

PRIVILY-all=2934&marked-J'G-9:31(8649)-1SA-24:4(3909)-PS-10:8(6845)■11:2(652)■31:4■64:5■101:5■(5643)■142:3■N.T.-all=2977-M'T-1:19■2:7-AC-16:37-GAL-2:4(3922)-2PE-2:1(3918)

PRIVY-DE-23:1(8212)-1KI-2:44(3045)-EZE-21:14(2314)■N.T.-AC-5:2(4894)

PRIZE-1CO-9:24(1017)-PH'P-3:14(1017)

PROCEED-all=3318&marked-EX-25:35-JOS-6:10-2SA-7:12-JOB-

40:5(3254)-**IS**-29:14(3524)▪51:4-**JER**-9:3▪30:19,21-**HAB**-1:7▪**N.T.**-all=1607&marked-**M'T**-15:18,19(1831)-**M'R**-7:21-**EPH**-4:29-**2TI**-3:9(4298)

PROCEEDED-**NU**-30:12(4161)▪32:24(3318)-**J'G**-11:36(3318)-**JOB**-36:1(3254)▪**N.T.**-all=1607&marked-**LU**-4:22-**JOH**-8:42(1831)-**AC**-12:3(4369)-**RE**-4:5▪19:21

PROCEEDETH-all=3318&marked-**GE**-24:50-**NU**-30:2-**DE**-8:3(4161)-**1SA**-24:13-**EC**-10:5-**LA**-3:38-**HAB**-1:4▪**N.T.**-all=1607&marked-**M'T**-4:4-**JOH**-15:26-**JAS**-3:10(1831)-**RE**-11:5

PROCEEDING-**RE**-22:1(1607)

PROCESS-**GE**-4:3(7093)▪38:12(7235)-**EX**-2:23(7227)

PROCLAIM-all=7121&marked-**EX**-33:19-**LE**-23:2,4,21,37▪25:10-**DE**-20:10-**J'G**-7:3-**1KI**-21:9-**2KI**-10:20(6942)-**NE**-8:15(5676)-**ES**-6:9-**PR**-20:6-**IS**-61:1,2-**JER**-3:12▪7:2▪11:6▪19:2▪34:8,17-**JOE**-3:9-**AM**-4:5

PROCLAIMED-all=7121&marked-**EX**-34:5,6▪36:6(5674)-**1KI**-21:12-**2KI**-10:20▪23:16,17-**2CH**-20:3-**EZR**-8:21-**ES**-6:11-**IS**-62:11(8085)-**JER**-36:9-**JON**-3:5,7(2199)▪**N.T.**-**LU**-12:3(2784)

PROCLAIMETH-**PR**-12:23(7121)

PROCLAIMING-**JER**-34:15(7121),17(7121)▪**N.T.**-**RE**-5:2(2784)

PROCLAMATION-all=5674,6963&marked-**EX**-32:5(7121)-**1KI**-15:22(8085)▪22:36(7440)-**2CH**-24:9(6963)▪30:5▪36:22-**EZR**-1:1▪10:7-**DA**-5:29(3745)

PROCURE-**JER**-26:19(6213)▪33:9(6213)

PROCURED-**JER**-2:17(6213)▪4:18(6213)

PROCURETH-**PR**-11:27(1245)

PRODUCE-**IS**-41:21(7126)

PROFANE-all=2490&marked-**LE**-18:21▪19:12▪20:3▪21:4,6,7(2491),9,12,14(2491),15,23▪22:2,9,15,32-**NE**-13:17-**JER**-23:11(2610)-**EZE**-21:25(2491)▪22:26(2455)▪23:39▪24:21▪28:16▪42:20(2455)▪44:23(2455)▪48:15(2455)-**AM**-2:7▪**N.T.**-all=952&marked-**M'T**-12:5(953)-**AC**-24:6(953)-**1TI**-1:9▪4:7▪6:20-**2TI**-2:16-**HEB**-12:16

PROFANED-all=2490-**LE**-19:8-**PS**-89:39-**IS**-43:28-**EZE**-22:8,26^{2}▪23:38▪25:3▪36:20,21,22,23^{2}-**MAL**-1:12▪2:11

PROFANENESS-**JER**-23:15(6213)

PROFANETH-**LE**-21:9(2490)

PROFANING-**NE**-13:18(2490)-**MAL**-2:10(2490)

PROFESS-**DE**-26:3(5046)▪**N.T.**-**M'T**-7:23(3670)-**TIT**-1:16(3670)

PROFESSED-**2CO**-9:13(3671)-**1TI**-6:12(3670)

PROFESSING-**RO**-1:22(5335)-**1TI**-2:10(1861)▪6:21(1861)

PROFESSION-all=3671-**1TI**-6:12-**HEB**-3:1▪4:14▪10:23

PROFIT-all=3276&marked-**GE**-37:26(1215)-**1SA**-12:21-**ES**-3:8(7737)-**JOB**-21:15▪35:3-**PS**-30:9(1215)-**PR**-10:2▪11:4▪14:23(4195)-**EC**-1:3(3504)▪2:11(3504)▪3:9(3504)▪5:9(3504),16(3504)▪7:11(3148)-**IS**-30:5^{2},6▪44:9▪47:12▪48:17▪57:12-**JER**-2:8,11▪7:8▪12:13▪16:19▪23:32-**MAL**-3:14(1215)▪**N.T.**-all=4815&marked-**M'R**-8:36(5623)-**RO**-3:1(5622)-**1CO**-7:35▪10:33^{2}▪12:7▪14:6(5623)-**GA**-5:2(5623)-**2TI**-2:14(5539)-**HEB**-4:2(5623)▪12:10(4851)-**JAS**-2:14(3786),16(3786)

PROFITABLE-**JOB**-2:22^{2}(5532)-**EC**-10:10(3504)-**IS**-44:10(3276)-**JER**-13:7(6743)▪**N.T.**-all=4851&marked-**M'T**-5:29,30-**AC**-20:20-**1TI**-4:8(5624)-**2TI**-3:16(5624)-**2TI**-4:11(2173)-**TIT**-3:8(5624)-**PH'M**-11(2173)

PROFITED-**JOB**-33:27(7737)▪**N.T.**-all=5623&marked-**M'T**-15:5▪16:26-**M'R**-7:11-**GA**-1:14(4298)-**HEB**-13:9

PROFITETH-**JOB**-34:9(5532)-**HAB**-2:18(3276)▪**N.T.**-all=5623&marked-**JOH**-6:63-**RO**-2:25-**1CO**-13:3-**1TI**-4:8(5624,2076)

PROFITING-**1TI**-4:15(4297)

PROFOUND-**HO**-5:2(6009)

PROGENITORS-**GE**-49:26(2029)

PROGNOSTICATORS-**IS**-47:13(3045)

PROLONG-all=748&marked-**DE**-4:26,40▪5:33▪11:9▪17:20▪22:7▪30:18▪32:47-**JOB**-6:11▪15:29(5186)-**PS**-61:6(3254)-**PR**-28:16-**EC**-8:13-**IS**-53:10

PROLONGED-all=748&marked-**DE**-5:16▪6:2-**PR**-28:2-**EC**-8:12-**IS**-13:22(4900)-**EZE**-12:22,25(4900),28(4900)-**DA**-7:12(754,3052)

PROLONGETH-**PR**-10:27(3254)-**EC**-7:15(748)

PROMISE-all=1697&marked-**1KI**-8:56-**2CH**-1:9-**NE**-5:12,13^{2}-**PS**-77:8(562)▪105:42▪**N.T.**-all=1860&marked-**LU**-24:49-**AC**-1:4▪2:33,39▪7:17▪13:23,32▪23:21▪26:6-**RO**-4:13,14,16,20▪9:8,9-**GA**-3:14,17,18^{2},19(1861),22,29▪4:23,28-**EPH**-1:13▪2:12▪3:6▪6:2-**1TI**-4:8-**2TI**-1:1-**HEB**-4:1▪6:13(1861),15,17▪9:15▪10:36▪11:9^{2},39-**2PE**-2:19(1861)▪3:4,9,13(1862)-**1JO**-2:25

PROMISED-all=1696&marked-**EX**-12:25-**NU**-14:40(559)-**DE**-1:11▪6:3▪9:28▪10:9▪12:20▪15:6▪19:8▪23:23▪26:18▪27:3-**JOS**-9:21▪22:4▪23:5,10,15-**2SA**-7:28-**1KI**-2:24▪5:12▪8:20,56^{2}▪9:5-**2KI**-8:19(559)-**1CH**-17:26-**2CH**-6:10,15,16▪21:7(559)-**NE**-9:23(559)-**ES**-4:7(559)-**JER**-32:42▪33:14▪**N.T.**-all=1861&marked-**M'T**-14:7(3670)-**M'R**-14:11-**LU**-22:6(1843)-**AC**-7:5-**RO**-1:2(4279)▪4:21-**TIT**-1:2-**HEB**-10:23▪11:11▪12:26-**JAS**-1:12▪2:5-**1JO**-2:25

PROMISEDST-**1KI**-8:24(1696),25(1696)-**NE**-9:15(559)

PROMISES-all=1860&marked-**RO**-9:4▪15:8-**2CO**-1:20▪7:1-**GAL**-3:16,21-**HEB**-6:12▪7:6▪8:6▪11:13,17,33-**2PE**-1:4(1862)

PROMISING-**EZE**-13:22(2421)

PROMOTE-all=3513&marked-**NU**-22:17,37▪24:11-**ES**-3:1(1431)-**PR**-4:8(7311)

PROMOTED-all=5128&marked-**J'G**-9:9,11,13-**ES**-5:11(1431)-**DA**-3:30(6744)

PROMOTION-**PS**-75:6(7311)-**PR**-3:35(7311)

PRONOUNCE-**LE**-5:4(981)-**J'G**-12:6(1696)

PRONOUNCED-all=1696&marked-**NE**-6:12-**JER**-11:17▪16:10▪18:8▪19:15▪25:13▪26:13,19▪34:5▪35:17▪36:7,18(7126),31(1691)▪40:2(1691)

PRONOUNCING-**LE**-5:4(981)

PROOF-all=1382&marked-**2CO**-2:9▪8:24(1732)▪13:3-**PH'P**-2:22-**2TI**-4:5(4135)

PROOFS-**AC**-1:3(5039)

PROPER-**1CH**-29:3(5459)▪**N.T.**-**AC**-1:19(2398)-**1CO**-7:7(2398)-**HEB**-11:23(791)

PROPHECIES-**1CO**-13:8(4394)-**1TI**-1:18(4394)

PROPHECY-all=5016&marked-**2CH**-9:29▪15:8-**NE**-6:12-**PR**-30:1(4853)▪31:1(4853)-**DA**-9:24(5030)▪**N.T.**-all=4394&marked-**M'T**-13:14-**RO**-12:6-**1CO**-12:10▪13:2-**1TI**-4:14-**2PE**-1:19(4397),20,21-**RE**-1:3▪11:6▪19:10▪22:7,10,18,19

PROPHESIED-all=5012&marked-**NU**-11:25,26-**1SA**-10:10,11▪18:10▪19:20,21^{2},23,24-**1KI**-18:29▪22:10,12-**1CH**-25:2,3-**2CH**-18:7,9,11▪20:37-**EZR**-5:1(5013)-**JER**-2:8▪20:1,6▪23:13,21▪25:13▪26:9,11,18,20^{2}▪28:6,8▪29:31▪37:19-**EZE**-11:13▪37:7^{2},10▪38:17-**ZEC**-13:4▪**N.T.**-all=4395-**M'T**-7:22▪11:13-**M'R**-7:6-**LU**-1:67-**JOH**-11:51-**AC**-19:6-**1CO**-14:5-**1PE**-1:10-**JUDE**-14

PROPHESIETH-all=5012-**JER**-28:9-**EZE**-12:27-**ZEC**-13:3▪**N.T.**-all=4395-**1CO**-11:5▪14:3,4,5

PROPHESY-all=5012&marked-**NU**-11:27-**1SA**-10:5,6-**1KI**-22:8,18-**1CH**-25:1-**2CH**-18:17-**IS**-30:10^{2}(2372)-**JER**-5:31▪11:21▪14:14^{2},15,16▪19:14▪23:16,25,26,32▪25:30▪26:12▪27:10,14,15^{2},16^{2}▪29:9,21▪32:3-**EZE**-4:7▪6:2▪11:4▪13:2^{3},16,17^{2}▪20:46▪21:2,9,14,28▪25:2▪28:21▪29:2▪30:2▪34:2^{2}▪35:2▪36:1,3,6▪37:4,9,12▪38:2,14▪39:1-**JOE**-2:28-**AM**-2:12▪3:8▪7:12,13,15,16-**MIC**-2:6^{3}(5197),11(5197)-**ZEC**-13:3(5197)▪**N.T.**-all=4395-**M'T**-15:7▪26:68-**M'R**-14:65-**LU**-22:64-**AC**-2:17,18▪21:9-**1CO**-13:9▪14:1,24,31,39-**RE**-10:11▪11:3

PROPHESYING-**1SA**-10:13(5012)▪19:20(5012)-**EZE**-6:14(5017)▪**N.T.**-**1CO**-11:4(4395)▪14:6(4394),22(4394)

PROPHESYINGS-**1TH**-5:20(4394)

PROPHET-all=5030&marked-**GE**-20:7-**EX**-7:1-**NU**-12:6-**DE**-13:1,3,5▪18:15,18,20^{2},22^{2}▪34:10-**J'G**-6:8-**1SA**-3:20▪9:9▪22:5-**2SA**-7:2▪12:25▪24:11-**1KI**-1:8,10,22,23,32,34,38,44,45▪11:29▪13:11,18,20,23,25,26,29^{2}▪14:2,18▪16:7,12▪18:22,36▪19:16▪20:13,22,38▪22:7-**2KI**-3:11▪5:3,8,13▪6:12▪9:1,4▪14:25▪19:2▪20:1,11,14▪23:18-**1CH**-17:1▪29:29-**2CH**-9:29▪12:5,15▪13:22▪15:8▪18:6▪21:12▪25:15,16▪26:22▪28:9▪29:25▪32:20,32▪35:18▪36:12-**EZR**-5:1(5029)▪6:14(5029)-**PS**-51:t▪74:9-**IS**-3:2▪9:15▪28:7▪37:2▪38:1▪39:3-**JER**-1:5▪6:13▪8:10▪14:18▪18:18▪20:2▪23:11,28,33,34,37▪25:2▪28:1,5,6,9^{3},10^{2},11,12^{2},15,17▪29:1,26(5012),27(5012),29▪32:2▪34:6▪36:8,26▪37:2,3,6,13▪38:9,10,14▪42:2,4▪43:6▪45:1▪46:1,13▪47:1▪49:34▪50:1▪51:59-**LA**-2:20-**EZE**-2:5▪7:26▪14:4,7,9^{2},10▪33:33-**DA**-9:2-**HO**-4:5▪9:7,8▪12:13^{2}-**AM**-7:14-**MIC**-2:11(5197)-**HAB**-1:1▪3:1-**HAG**-1:1,3,12▪2:1,10-**ZEC**-1:1,7▪13:5-**MAL**-4:5▪**N.T.**-all=4396&marked-**M'T**-1:22▪2:5,15,17▪3:3▪4:14▪8:17▪10:41▪11:9^{2}▪12:17,39▪13:35,57▪14:5▪16:4▪21:4,11,26,46▪24:15▪27:9,35-**M'R**-6:4,15▪11:32▪13:14-**LU**-1:76▪3:4▪4:17,24,27▪7:16,26^{2},28,39▪11:29▪13:33▪20:6▪24:19-**JOH**-1:21,23,25▪4:19,44▪6:14▪7:40,52▪9:17▪12:38-**AC**-2:16,30▪3:22,23▪7:37,48▪8:28,30,34▪13:6(5578),20▪21:10▪28:25-**1CO**-14:37-**TIT**-1:12-**2PE**-2:16-**RE**-16:13(5578)▪19:20(5578)▪20:10(5578)

PROPHETESS-all=5031-**EX**-15:20-**J'G**-4:4-**2KI**-22:14-**2CH**-34:22-**NE**-6:14-**IS**-8:3▪**N.T.**-**LU**-2:36(4398)-**RE**-2:20(4398)

PROPHET'S-**AM**-7:14(5030)▪**N.T.**-**M'T**-10:41(4396)

PROPHETS-all=5030&marked-**NU**-11:29-**1SA**-10:5,10,11^{2},12▪19:20,24▪28:6,15-**1KI**-18:4^{2},13^{2},19^{2},20,22,25,40▪19:1,10,14▪20:35,41▪22:6,10,12,13,22,23-**2KI**-2:3,5,7,15▪3:13^{2}▪4:1,38^{2}▪5:22▪6:1▪9:1,7▪10:19▪7:13^{2},23▪21:10▪23:2▪24:2-**1CH**-16:22-**2CH**-18:5,9,11,12,21,22▪20:20▪24:19▪29:25▪36:16-**EZR**-5:1(5029)2(5029)▪9:11-**NEH**-6:7,14▪9:26,30,32-**PS**-105:15-**IS**-29:10▪30:10(2374)-**JER**-2:8,26,30▪4:9▪5:13,31▪7:25▪8:1▪13:13▪14:13,14,15^{2}▪23:9,13,14,15^{2},16,21,25,26^{2},30,31▪25:4▪26:5,7,8,11,16▪27:9,14,15,16,18▪28:8▪29:1,8,15,19▪32:32▪35:15▪37:19▪44:4-**LA**-2:9,14▪4:13-**EZE**-13:2,3,4,9,16▪22:25,28▪38:17-**DA**-9:6,10-**HO**-6:5▪12:10^{2}-**AM**-2:11,12▪3:7-**MIC**-3:5,6,11-**ZEP**-3:4-**ZEC**-1:4,5,6▪7:3,7,12▪8:9▪13:2,4▪**N.T.**-all=4396&marked-**M'T**-2:23▪5:12,17▪7:12,15(5578)▪11:13▪13:17▪16:14▪22:40▪23:29,30,31,34,37▪24:11(5578),24(5578)▪26:56-**M'R**-1:2▪6:15▪8:28▪13:22(5578)-**LU**-1:70▪6:23,26(5578)▪9:8,19▪10:24▪11:47,49,50▪13:28,34▪16:16,29,31▪18:31▪24:25,27,44-**JOH**-1:45▪6:45▪8:52,53-**AC**-3:18,21,24,25▪7:42,52▪

10:43▪11:27▪13:1,15,27,40▪15:15,32▪24:14▪26:22,27▪28:23-RO-1:2▪3:21▪11:3▪16:26(4397)-1CO-12:28,29▪14:29,32-EPH-2:20▪3:5▪4:11-1TH-2:15-HEB-1:1▪11:32-JAS-5:10-1PE-1:10-2PE-2:1(5578)▪3:2-1JO-4:1(5578)-RE-10:7▪11:10,18▪16:6▪18:20,24▪22:6,9

PROPITIATION-RO-3:25(2435) 1JO-2:2(2434)▪4:10(2434)

PROPORTION-1KI-7:36(4626) -JOB-41:12(6187)▪N.T.-RO-12:6(356)

PROSELYTE-M'T-23:15(4339) -AC-6:5(4339)

PROSELYTES-AC-2:10(4339)▪13:43(4339)

PROSPECT-all=6440-EZE-40:44^{2},45,46▪42:15▪43:4

PROSPER-all=6743&marked -GE-24:40,42▪39:3,23-NU-14:41 -DE-28:29▪29:9(7919)-JOS-1:7(7919) -1KI-2:3(7919)▪22:12,15-1CH-22:11,13 -2CH-13:12▪18:11,14▪20:20▪24:20▪26:5-NE-1:11▪2:20-JOB-12:6(7951) -PS-1:3▪73:12(7951)▪122:6(7951)-PR-28:13-EC-11:6(3787)-IS-53:10▪54:17▪55:11-JER-2:37▪5:28▪10:21 (7919)▪12:1▪20:11(7919)▪22:30^{2}▪23:5 (7919)▪32:5-LA-1:5(7951)-EZE-16:13▪17:9,10,15-DA-8:24,25▪11:27,36▪N.T. -3JO-2(2137)

PROSPERED-all=6743&marked -GE-24:56-J'G-4:24(1980)-2SA-11:7 (7965)-2KI-18:7(7919)-1CH-29:23 -2CH-14:7▪31:21▪32:30-EZR-6:14 (6744)-JOB-9:4(7999)-DA-6:28(6744)▪8:12▪N.T.-1CO-16:2(2137)

PROSPERETH-EZR-5:8(6744) -PS-37:7(6743)-PR-17:8(7919)▪N.T. -3JO-2(2137)

PROSPERITY-all=2896&marked -DE-23:6-1KI-10:7-JOB-15:21(7965)▪36:11-PS-30:6(7961)▪35:27(7965)▪73:3 (7965)▪118:25(6743)▪122:7(7962)-PR-1:32(7962)-EC-7:14-JER-22:21(7962)▪33:9(7965)-LA-3:17-ZEC-1:17▪7:7(7961)

PROSPEROUS-all=6743&marked -GE-24:21▪39:2-JOS-1:8-J'G-18:5-JOB-8:6(7999)-IS-48:15-ZEC-8:12(7965)▪N.T.-RO-1:10(2137)

PROSPEROUSLY-2CH-7:11 (6743)-PS-45:4(6743)

PROSTITUTE-LE-19:29(2490)

PROTECTION-DE-32:38(5643)

PROTEST-GE-43:3(5749)-1SA-8:9 (5749)▪N.T.-1CO-15:31(3513)

PROTESTED-all=5749-1KI-2:42 -JER-11:7-ZEC-3:6

PROTESTING-JER-11:7(5749)

PROUD-all=2086&marked-JOB-9:13 (7293)▪26:12(7293)▪38:11(1347)▪40:11 (1343),12(1343)-PS-12:3(1419)▪31:23 (1346)▪40:4(7295)▪86:14▪94:2(1343)▪101:5(7342)▪119:21,51,69,78,85,122▪123:4(1349)▪124:5(2121)▪138:6(1364)▪140:5(1343)-PR-6:17(7311)▪15:25(1343)▪16:5(1362),19(1343)▪21:4(7342),24,24 (2087)▪28:25(7342)-EC-7:8(1362) -IS-2:12(1343)▪13:11▪16:6(1341)-JER-13:15(1341)▪43:2▪48:29(1343)▪50:29 (2102),31(2087),32(2087)-HAB-2:5 (3093)-MAL-3:15▪4:1▪N.T.-all=5244&marked-LU-1:51-RO-1:30-1TI-6:4(5187)-2TI-3:2-JAS-4:6-1PE-5:5

PROUDLY-all=2102&marked-EX-18:11-1SA-2:3(1364)-NE-9:10,16,29 -PS-17:10(1348)▪31:18(1346)-IS-3:5 (7292)-OB-12(1431)

PROVE-all=5254&marked-EX-16:4▪20:20-DE-8:2,16▪33:8-J'G-2:22▪3:1,4▪6:39-1KI-10:1-2CH-9:1-PS-26:2-EC-2:1-DA-1:12-MAL-3:10(974)▪N.T.-all=1381&marked-LU-14:19-JOH-6:6 (3985)-AC-24:13(3936)▪25:7(584)-RO-12:2-2CO-8:8▪13:5-GA-6:4-1TH-5:21

PROVED-all=974&marked-GE-42:15,16-EX-15:25(5254)-1SA-17:39^{2} (5254)-PS-17:3▪66:10▪81:7▪95:9-EC-7:23(5254)-DA-1:14(5254)▪N.T.-all=1381&marked-RO-3:9(4256)-2CO-8:22 -1TI-3:10-HEB-3:9

PROVENDER-all=4554&marked -GE-24:25,32▪42:27▪43:24-J'G-19:19, 21(1101)-IS-30:24(1098)

PROVERB-all=4912&marked-DE-28:37-1SA-10:12▪24:13-1KI-9:7-2CH-7:20-PS-69:11-PR-1:t,6-IS-14:4-JER-24:9-EZE-12:22,23,23(4911)▪14:8▪16:44(4911)▪18:2(4911),3(4911)-HAB-2:6(2426)▪N.T.-LU-4:23(3850)-JOH-16:29(3943)-2PE-2:22(3942)

PROVERBS-all=4912&marked -NU-21:27(4911)-1KI-4:32-PR-1:t,1▪10:1▪25:1-EC-12:9-EZE-16:44(4911)▪N.T.-JOH-16:25^{2}(3942)

PROVETH-DE-13:3(5254)

PROVIDE-GE-22:8(7200)▪30:30 (6213)-EX-18:21(2372)-1SA-16:17 (7200)-2CH-2:7(3559)-PS-78:20(3559)▪N.T.-M'T-10:9(2532)-LU-12:33 (4160)-AC-23:24(3936)-RO-12:17(4306) -1TI-5:8(4306)

PROVIDED-DE-33:21(7200)-1SA-16:1(7200)-2CH-32:29(6213)-PS-65:9 (3559)▪N.T.-LU-12:20(2090)-HEB-11:40(4265)

PROVIDENCE-AC-24:2(4307)

PROVIDETH-JOB-38:41(3559) -PR-6:8(3559)

PROVIDING-2CO-8:21(4306)

PROVINCE-all=4082&marked -EZR-2:1▪5:8(4083)▪6:2▪7:16-NE-1:3▪7:6▪11:3-ES-1:22▪3:12^{2},14▪4:3▪8:9,11, 13,17▪9:28-EC-5:8-DA-2:48(4083),49 (4083)▪3:1(4083),12(4083),30▪8:2▪11:24▪N.T.-AC-23:24(1885)▪25:1(1885)

PROVINCES-all=4082&marked -1KI-20:14,15,17,19-EZR-4:15(4083) -ES-1:1,3,16,22▪2:3,18▪3:8,13▪4:11▪8:5, 9^{2},12▪9:2,3,4,12,16,20,30-EC-2:8-LA-1:1-EZE-19:8-DA-3:2,3

PROVING-AC-9:22(4822)-EPH-5:10(1381)

PROVISION-GE-42:25(6720)▪45:21(6720)-JOS-9:5(6718),12(6679) -1KI-4:7(3557),22(3899)-2KI-6:23(3740) -1CH-29:19(3559)-PS-132:15(6718) -DA-1:5(1697)▪N.T.-RO-13:14(4307)

PROVOCATION-all=3708&marked -1KI-15:30▪21:22-JOB-17:2(4784)-PS-95:8(4808)-JER-32:31(5921)-EZE-20:28▪N.T.-HEB-3:8(3894),15(3894)

PROVOCATIONS-2KI-23:26(3708) -NE-9:18(5007),26(5007)

PROVOKE-EX-23:21(4843)-NU-14:11(5006)-DE-31:20(5006)-JOB-12:6 (7264)-PS-78:40(4784)-IS-3:8(4784)▪N.T.-all=3863&marked-LU-11:53 (653)-RO-10:19▪11:11,14-1CO-10:22 -EPH-6:4(3949)-COL-3:21(2042) -HEB-3:16(3893)▪10:24(3948)

PROVOKED-all=3707&marked -NU-14:23(5006)▪16:30(5006)-DE-32:16,16sup-1SA-1:6,7-2KI-23:26 -1CH-21:1(5496)-EZR-5:12(7265) -PS-78:56(4784)▪106:7(4784),33 (4784),43(4784)-IS-1:4(5006)▪N.T. -1CO-13:5(3947)-2CO-9:2(2042)

PROVOKEDST-all supplied

PROVOKETH-PR-20:2(5674)

PROVOKING-DE-32:19(3707) -PS-78:17(4784)▪N.T.-GA-5:26(4292)

PRUDENCE-2CH-2:12(7922) -PR-8:12(6195)▪N.T.-EPH-1:8(5428)

PRUDENT-all=6175&marked -1SA-16:18(995)-PR-12:16,23▪13:16▪14:8,15,18▪15:5(6191)▪16:21(995)▪18:15(995)▪19:14(7919)▪22:3▪27:12 -IS-3:2(7080)▪5:21(995)▪10:13(995)▪29:14(995)-JER-49:7(995)-HO-14:9 (995)-AM-5:13(7919)▪N.T.-all=4908 -M'T-11:25-LU-10:21-AC-13:7-1CO-1:19

PRUDENTLY-IS-52:13(7919)

PRUNE-LE-25:3(2168),4(2168)

PRUNED-IS-5:6(2167)

PRUNING-IS-18:5(4211)

PRUNINGHOOKS-all=4211-IS-2:4-JOE-3:10-MIC-4:3

PSALM-all=4210&marked-PS-1:t▪3:t▪4:t▪5:t▪6:t▪8:t▪9:t▪11:t▪12:t▪13:t▪15:t▪18:t▪19:t▪20:t▪21:t▪22:t▪23:t▪24:t▪29:t▪30:t▪31:t▪38:t▪39:t▪40:t▪41:t▪47:t▪48:t▪49:t▪50:t▪51:t▪62:t▪63:t▪64:t▪65:t▪66:t▪67:t▪68:t▪72:t▪73:t▪75:t▪76:t▪77:t▪79:t▪80:t▪81:2 (2172)▪82:t▪83:t▪84:t▪85:t▪87:t▪88:t▪92:t▪98:5(2172)▪100:t▪101:t▪108:t▪109:t▪110:t▪139:t▪140:t▪141:t▪143:t▪N.T.-AC-13:33(5568)-1CO-14:26(5568)

PSALMIST-2SA-23:1(2158)

PSALMS-1CH-16:9(2167)-PS-1:t▪95:2(2158)▪105:2(2167)▪N.T.-all=5568&marked-LU-20:42▪24:44-AC-1:20 -EPH-5:19-COL-3:16-JAS-5:13(5567)

PSALTERIES-all=5035&marked -2SA-6:5-1KI-10:12-1CH-13:8▪15:16,20, 28▪16:5(3627)▪25:1,6-2CH-5:12▪9:11▪20:28▪29:25-NE-12:27

PSALTERY-all=5035&marked -1SA-10:5-PS-33:2▪57:8▪71:22(3627)▪81:2▪92:3▪108:2▪144:9▪150:3-DA-3:5(6460),7(6460),10(6460),15(6460)

PUBLICAN-all=5057-M'T-10:3▪18:17-LU-5:27▪18:10,11,13

PUBLICANS-all=5057&marked -M'T-5:46,47▪9:10,11▪11:19▪21:31,32 -M'R-2:15,16^{2}-LU-3:12▪5:29,30▪7:29, 34▪15:1▪19:2(754)

PUBLICK-M'T-1:19(3856)

PUBLICKLY-AC-18:28(1219)▪20:20(1219)

PUBLISH-all=8085&marked-DE-32:3(7121)-1SA-31:9(1319)-2SA-1:20 (1319)-NE-8:15-PS-26:7-JER-4:5,16▪5:20▪31:7▪46:14^{2}▪50:2^{2}-AM-3:9▪4:5▪N.T.-M'R-1:45(2784)▪5:20(2784)

PUBLISHED-ES-1:20(8085),22 (1696)▪3:14(1540)▪8:13(1540)-PS-68:11 (1319)-JON-3:7(559)▪N.T.-all=2784&marked-M'R-7:36▪13:10-LU-8:39-AC-10:37(1096)▪13:49(1308)

PUBLISHETH-all=8085-IS-52:7^{2} -JER-4:15-NA-1:15

PUFFED-all=5448-1CO-4:6,18,19▪5:2▪13:4-COL-2:18

PUFFETH-PS-10:5(6315)▪12:5 (6315)▪N.T.-1CO-8:1(5448)

PULL-all=2040&marked-1KI-13:4 (7725)-PS-31:4(3318)-IS-22:19-JER-1:10(5422)▪12:3(5423)▪18:7(5422)▪24:6▪42:10-EZE-17:9(5423)-MIC-2:8(6584)▪N.T.-M'T-7:4(1544)-LU-6:42^{2}(1544)▪12:18(2507)▪14:5(385)

PULLED-GE-8:9(4026)▪19:10 (935)-EZR-6:11(5256)-LA-3:11(6582) -AM-9:15(5428)-ZEC-7:11(5414)▪N.T. -AC-23:10(1288)

PULLING-2CO-10:4(2506)-JUDE-23(726)

PULPIT-NE-8:4(4026)

PULSE-DA-1:12(2235),16(2235)

PUNISH-all=6485&marked-LE-26:18(3256),24(5221)-PR-17:26(6064) -IS-10:12▪13:11▪24:21▪26:21▪27:1 -JER-9:25▪11:22▪13:21▪21:14▪23:34▪25:12▪27:8▪29:32▪30:20▪36:31▪44:13, 29▪46:25▪50:18▪51:44-HO-4:9,14▪12:2-AM-3:2-ZEP-1:8,9,12-ZEC-8:14 (7489)▪N.T.-AC-4:21(2849)

PUNISHED-all=6485&marked -EX-21:20(5358),21(5358),22(6064) -EZR-9:13(2820)-PR-21:11(6064)▪22:3 (6064)▪27:12(6064)-JER-44:13▪50:18 -ZEP-3:7-ZEC-10:3▪N.T.-AC-22:5 (5097)▪26:11(5097)-2TH-1:9(1349,5099) -2PE-2:9(2849)

PUNISHMENT-all=5771&marked -GE-4:13-LE-26:41,43-1SA-28:10-PR-19:19(6066)-LA-3:39(2399)▪4:6,6(2403), 22-EZE-4:10^{3}-ZEC-14:19^{2}(2403)▪N.T.-M'T-25:46(2851)-2CO-2:6(2009) -HEB-10:29(5098)-1PE-2:14(1557)

PUNISHMENTS-JOB-19:29 (5771)-PS-149:7(5771)

PUR-all=6332-ES-3:7▪9:24,26

PURCHASE-all=4736&marked-GE-49:32(4735)-LE-25:33(1350)-JER-32:11,12^{2},14,16■N.T.-1TI-3:13(4046)

PURCHASED-all=7069-GE-25:10-EX-15:16-RU-4:10-PS-74:2■78:54■N.T.-AC-1:18(2932)■8:20(2932)■20:28(4046)-EPH-1:14(4047)

PURE-all=2889&marked-EX-25:11,17,24,29,31,36,38,39■27:20(2134)■28:14,22,36■30:3,23(1865),34(2134),35■31:8■37:2,6,11,16,17,22,23,24,26,29■39:15,25,30,37-LE-24:2(2134),4(2888),6(2888),7(2134)-DE-32:14(2561)-2SA-22:27(1305)-1KI-5:11(3795)■6:20(5462),21(5462)■7:49(5462),50(5462)■10:21(5462)-1CH-28:17-2CH-3:4■4:20(5462),22(5462)■9:17,20(5462)■13:11-EZR-6:20-JOB-4:17(2891)■8:6(2134)■11:4(2134)■16:17(2134)■25:5(2141)■28:19-PS-12:6■18:26(1305)■19:8(1249)■21:3(6337)■24:4(1249)■119:140(6884)-PR-15:26■20:9(2891),11(2134)■21:8(2134)■30:5(6884),12-DA-7:9(5343)-MIC-6:11(2135)-ZEP-3:9(1305)-MAL-1:11■N.T.-all=2513&marked-M'T-5:8-AC-20:26-RO-14:20-PH'P-4:8(53)-1TI-1:5■3:9■5:22(53)-2TI-1:3■2:22-TIT-1:15^{2}-HEB-10:22-JAS-1:27■3:17(53)-1PE-1:22-2PE-3:1(1506)-1JO-3:3(53)-RE-15:6■21:18,21■22:1

PURELY-IS-1:25(1252)

PURENESS-JOB-22:30(1252)-PR-22:11(2890)■N.T.-2CO-6:6(54)

PURER-LA-4:7(2141)-HAB-1:13(2889)

PURGE-all=3722&marked-2CH-34:3(2891)-PS-51:7(2398)■65:3■79:9-IS-1:25(6884)-EZE-20:38(1305)■43:20,26-DA-11:35(1305)-MAL-3:3(2212)■N.T.-M'T-3:12(1245)-LU-3:17(1345)-1CO-5:7(1571)-2TI-2:21(1571)-HEB-9:14(2511)

PURGED-all=3722&marked-1SA-3:14-2CH-34:8(2891)-PR-16:6-IS-4:4(1740)■6:7■22:14■27:9-EZE-24:13(2891),13(2891)■N.T.-HEB-1:3(4160,2512)■9:22(2511)■10:2(2508)-2PE-1:9(2512)

PURGETH-JOH-15:2(2508)

PURGING-M'R-7:19(2511)

PURIFICATION-NU-19:9(2403),17(2403)-2CH-30:19(2893)-NE-12:45(2893)-ES-2:3(8562),9(8562)■N.T.-LU-2:22(2512)-AC-21:26(49)

PURIFICATIONS-ES-2:12(4795)

PURIFIED-all=2398&marked-LE-8:15-NU-8:21■31:23-2SA-11:4(6942)-2SA-6:20(2891)-NE-6:20(2891)-NE-12:30^{2}(2891)-PS-12:6(2212)-DA-12:10(1305)■N.T.-AC-24:18(48)-HEB-9:23(2511)-1PE-1:22(48)

PURIFIER-MAL-3:3(2891)

PURIFIETH-NU-19:13(2398)■N.T.-1JO-3:3(48)

PURIFY-all=2398&marked-NU-19:12^{2},19,20■31:19,20-JOB-41:25-IS-66:17(2891)-EZE-43:26(2891)-MAL-3:3(2891)■N.T.-all=48&marked-JOH-11:55-AC-21:24-TIT-2:14(2511)-JAS-4:8

PURIFYING-all=2893&marked-LE-12:4,4(2892),5,6(2892)-NU-8:7(2403)-1CH-23:28-ES-2:12(8562)■N.T.-JOH-2:6(2152)■3:25(2512)-AC-15:9(2511)■21:6(48)-HEB-9:13(2514)

PURIM-all=6332-ES-9:26,28,29,31,32

PURITY-1TI-4:12(47)■5:2(47)

PURLOINING-TIT-2:10(3557)

PURPLE-all=713&marked-EX-25:4■26:1,31,36■27:16■28:5,6,8,15,33■35:6,23,35■36:8,35,37■38:18,23■39:1,2,3,5,8,24,29-NU-4:13-J'G-8:26-2CH-2:7(710),14■3:14-ES-1:6■8:15-PR-31:22-SONG-3:10■7:5-JER-10:9-EZE-27:7,16■N.T.-all=4209&marked-M'R-15:17,20-LU-16:19-JOH-19:2(4210),5(4210)-AC-16:14(4211)-RE-17:4■8:12,16(4210)

PURPOSE-all=2656&marked-RU-2:16(7997)-1KI-5:5(559)-2CH-28:10(559)-EZR-4:5(6098)-NE-8:4(1697)-JOB-33:17(4639)-PR-20:18(4284)-EC-3:1,17■8:6-IS-14:26(6098)■30:7(7385)-JER-26:3(2803)■36:3(2803)■49:30(4284)■51:29(4284)-DA-6:17(6640)■N.T.-all=4286&marked-AC-11:23■27:13,43(1013)-RO-8:28■9:11-2CO-1:17^{2}(1011)-EPH-1:11■3:11-2TI-1:9■3:10

PURPOSED-all=3289&marked-2CH-32:2(6440)-PS-17:3(2161)■140:4(2803)-IS-14:24,26,27■19:12■23:9■46:11(3335)-JER-4:28(2161)■49:20(2803)■50:45(2803)-LA-2:8(2803)-DA-1:8(7760)■N.T.-AC-19:21(5087)■20:3(1096,1106)-RO-1:13(4388)-EPH-1:9(4388)■3:11(4160)

PURPOSES-all=4284&marked-JOB-17:11(2154)-PR-15:22-IS-19:10(8356)-JER-49:20■50:45

PURPOSETH-2CO-9:7(4255)

PURPOSING-all supplied

PURSE-PR-1:14(3599)■N.T.-all=905&marked-M'R-6:8(2223)-LU-10:4■22:35,36

PURSES-M'T-10:9(2223)

PURSUE-all=7291&marked-GE-35:5-EX-15:9-DE-19:6■28:22,45-JOS-2:5■8:16■10:19■20:5-1SA-24:14■25:29■26:18■30:8^{2}-2SA-17:1■20:6,7,13■24:13-JOB-13:25■30:15-PS-34:14-IS-30:16-JER-48:2(3212)-EZE-35:6^{2}-HO-8:3-AM-1:11-NA-1:8

PURSUED-all=7291&marked-GE-14:14,15■31:23,36(1814)-EX-14:8,9,23-DE-11:4-JOS-2:7^{2}■8:16,17■24:6-J'G-1:6■4:16,22■7:23,25■8:12■20:45(1692)-1SA-7:11■17:52■23:25■30:10-2SA-2:19,24,28■20:10■22:38-1KI-20:20-2KI-25:5-2CH-13:19■14:13-PS-18:37-IS-41:3-JER-39:5■52:8-LA-4:19(1814)

PURSUER-LA-1:6(7291)

PURSUERS-all=7291-JOS-2:16^{2},22^{2}■8:20

PURSUETH-all=7291-LE-26:17,36,37-PR-11:19,19sup■13:21■19:7■28:1

PURSUING-all=7291&marked-J'G-8:4,5-IS-23:38-2SA-18:16-1KI-18:27(7873)■22:33(310)-2CH-18:32(310)

PURTENANCE-EX-12:9(7130)

PUSH-all=5055&marked-EX-21:29(5056),32,36(5056)-DE-33:17-1KI-22:11-2CH-18:10-JOB-30:12(7971)-PS-44:5-DA-11:40

PUSHED-EZE-34:21(5055)

PUSHING-DA-8:4(5055)

PUT-all=5414,a=7760,b=7971,c=3847-GE-2:8a,15(3240)■3:15(7896),22b■8:9b■19:10b■24:2a,9a,47a■27:15c,16c■28:11a,18a,20c■29:3(7725)■30:40^{2}(7896),42a■31:34a■32:16a■33:2a■35:2(5493)■37:34a■38:14(5493),19c,28■39:4,20■40:3,15a■41:10,42,42a■42:17(622)■43:22a■44:1a,2a■46:4(7896)■47:29a■48:18a■50:26(3455)-EX-2:3a■3:5(5394),22a■4:4^{2}b,6^{2}(935),7^{2}(7725),15a,21a■5:21■8:23a■12:15(7673)■15:26a■16:33■17:12a,14(4229)■22:5b,8b,11b■23:1(7896)■24:6a■25:12,14(935),16,21^{2},26■26:11(935),34,35■27:5,7(935)■28:12a,23,24,25,26a,27,30,37a,41c■29:3,5c,6a,6,8c,9(2280),10(5564),12,15(5564),17,19(5564),20,24a,30c■30:6,18^{2},36■31:6■32:27a■33:4(7896),5(3381),22a■34:33,35(7725)■35:34■36:1,2■37:5(935),13■38:7(935)■39:7a,16,17,18,19a,20,25■40:3a,5a,7,13c,18,19a,20^{2}(5114),22,24a,26a,29a,30-LE-1:4(5564),7■2:1,15■4:7,18,25,30,34■5:11a,11■6:10^{2}c,10a,11(6584),11c,12(3518)■8:7^{2},8a,8,9^{2}a,13c,13(2280),15,23,24,26a,27■9:9,20a,10:1,1a■11:32(935),38■14:14,17,25,28,29,34,42(935)■15:19(5079)■16:4^{2}c,13,18,23(6584),23c,24c,32c■18:19(5079)■19:14■21:7(1644),10c■22:14(3254)■24:7,12(3240)-NU-4:6,6a,7,8a,10^{2},11(7725),12^{2},14,14a■5:2b,3^{2}b,4b,15,17,18■6:18,19,27a■8:10(5564)■11:17a,29■15:34(3240),38■16:7,7a,14(5365),17,18,46,46a,47■19:17■20:26(3847),28(3847)■21:9a■23:5a,12a,16a■27:20■36:3(3254),4(3254)-DE-2:25■7:15a,22(5394)■10:2a,5a■11:29■12:5a,7(4916),21a■13:5sup,5(1197)■17:7(1197),12(1197)■18:18■19:13(1197),19(1197)■21:9(1197),13(5493),21(1197)■22:5c,19b,21(1197),22(1197),24(1197),29b■23:24■24:7(1197)■25:6(4229)■26:2a■28:14■30:7■31:19a,26a■33:10a,14(1645)-JOS-6:24■7:6(5927),11a■10:24^{2}a■17:13■24:7a,14(5943),23(5943)-J'G-1:28a■3:21b■5:26b■6:19^{2}a,21b,37(3322)■7:16■8:27(3322)■9:49a■10:16(5493)■12:3a■14:12(2330),13(2330),16(2330)■15:4a,15b■16:3a,21(5365)■18:7(3637),21a■20:13(1197)-RU-3:3a-1SA-1:14(5493)■2:36(5596)■6:8a,15a■7:3(5493),4(5493)■8:16(6213)■11:11a■14:26(5381),27b,27(7725),38,39(5493),40a,49b,54a■19:5a,13a■21:6a■22:17b■24:10b■28:3(5493),8c,21a■31:10a-2SA-1:24(5927)■3:34(5056)■6:6b■7:15(5493)■8:6a,14^{2}a■12:13(5674),31a■13:17b,19(3947)■14:2c,3a,19a■15:5b■18:12b■20:3,8(3830)-1KI-2:5,35^{2}■5:3■7:39,51■8:9(3240)■9:3a■10:17,24■11:36a■12:4,9,29■13:4^{2}b■14:21a■18:23^{2}a,25,33(6186),42a■20:6a,24a,31a■21:27a■22:10c,23,27a,30c-2KI-2:20a■3:2(5493),21(2296)■4:34a■6:7b■9:13a■10:7a■11:12■12:9■10(6695)■13:16(7392),16^{2}a■14:6^{3}(4191)■16:14,17■17:29(3240)■18:11(5148)■19:28a■21:4a,7a■23:5(7673),24(1197)■25:7(5786)-1CH-10:10a■12:15a■13:9b,10b■18:6a,13a■21:27(7725)■27:24(5927)-2CH-1:5a■2:14■3:16^{2}■4:6■5:1,10■6:11a,20a■9:16,23■10:4,9,11(6006),11(3254)■11:11■12:13a■15:8(5674)■16:10■17:19■18:22,26a,29c■22:11■23:11■29:7(3518)■33:7a,14a■34:10■35:3,24(7392)■36:3(5493),7-EZR-1:7■6:12(7972)■7:27■10:3(3318)■19(3318)-NE-2:12■3:5(935)■4:23(6584),23(7973)■7:5-ES-4:1c■5:1c■8:3(5674)-JOB-1:11b,12b■2:5b■13:14a■18:5(1846),6(1846)■21:17(1846)■23:6a■27:17c■29:14c■38:36(7896)■41:2a-PS-4:7■8:6(7896)■9:5(4229),20(7896)■18:22(5493)■27:9(5186)■30:11(6605)■40:3■55:20b■56:8■73:28(7896)■78:66■88:8(7368),18■125:3b-PR-4:24(5493),24(7368)■8:1■13:9(1846)■20:20(1846)■23:2a■24:20(1846)■25:6(1921)-EC-3:14(3254)■10:10(1396)■11:10(5674)-SONG-5:3(6584),3c,4b-IS-1:16(5493)■5:20^{2}a■10:13(3381)■11:8(1911)■20:2(2502)■37:29a■42:1■47:11(3722)■50:1^{2}b■51:9c,16a,23a■52:1^{2}c■59:17^{2}c,21a■63:11a-JER-1:9b,9■3:1b,8b,19(7896)■4:1(5493)■7:21(5595)■13:1^{2}a,2a■18:21(2026)■20:2■27:2,8■28:14■29:26■31:33■32:14,40■37:4,15,18■38:7,12a■39:7(5876)■40:10a■46:4c■47:6(622)■52:11(5786),11(5411)-EZE-3:25■4:9■8:3b,17b■10:7■11:19■14:3■16:11,12,14a■17:2(2330)■19:9■23:42■24:17a■26:16(6584)■29:4■30:13,21a,24,25■32:7(3518),25■36:26,27■37:6,14,19■38:4■42:14c■43:9(7368),20■44:19(6584),19c,22(1644)■45:19-DA-5:19(8214)-HO-2:2(5493)-JOE-3:13b-JON-3:5c-MIC-2:12a■N.T.-all=1746,a=5087,b=906,c=630-M'T-1:19c■5:15a,31c,32c■6:25(1749)■8:3(1614),17^{2}b,25(1544)■10:21(2289)■12:18a■13:24(3908),31(3908)■14:3a,5(615)■19:3c,6(5562),7c,8c,9^{2}c,13(2007)■21:7(2007)■25:27b■26:52(654),59(2289)■27:1(2289),6b,28(4060),29(2007),31,48(4060)-M'R-1:14(3860),41(1614)■2:22b■4:21a■5:40(1544)■6:9■7:32(2007),33b■8:23(2007),25(2007)■10:2c,4c,9(5562),11c,12c,16a■13:12(2289)■14:1(615),55(2289)■15:17(4060),20,36(4060)-LU-1:52(2507)■5:13(1614),38b■8:54(1544)■9:62(1911)■12:22■14:7(3004)■15:22,22(1325)■16:4(3179),18c■18:33(615)■21:16(2289)■23:32(337)-JOH-5:7b■9:15(2007)■11:53(615)■12:6b,10(615),42(1096)■13:2b■16:2(4160)■18:11b,31(615)■19:2(2007),

2(4016),19a,29(4060),29(4374)■20:25b-AC-1:7a■4:3a■5:18a,25a,34(4160)■7:33(3089)■9:40(1544)■12:4a,19(520)■13:46(683)■15:9(1252),10(2007)■26:10(337)■27:6(1688)-RO-13:12,14■14:13a-1CO-5:13(1808)■7:11(863),12(863)■13:11(2673)■15:24(2673),25a,27^{3}(5293),28(5293),53^{2},54^{2}-2CO-3:13a■8:16(1325)-GA-3:27-EPH-1:22(5293)■4:22(659),24■31(142)■6:11-COL-3:8(659),9(554),10,12-1TH-2:4(4160)-1TI-1:19(683)■4:6(5294)-2TI-1:6(363)■2:14(5279)-TIT-3:1(5279)-PH'M-18(1677)-HEB-2:5(5293),8^{2}(5293),8(506),8(5293),13(3982)■6:6(3856)■8:10(1325)■9:26(115)■10:16(1325)-JAS-3:3b-1PE-2:15(5392)■3:18(2289)-2PE-1:12(5279),14(595)-JUDE-5(5279)-RE-2:24b■11:9a■17:17(1325)

PUTRIFYING-IS-1:6(2961)

PUTTEST-NU-24:21(7760)-DE-12:18(4916)■15:10(4916)-2KI-18:14(5414)-JOB-13:27(7760)-PS-119:119(7673)-HAB-2:15(5596)

PUTTETH-all=5414&marked-EX-30:33-NU-22:38(7760)-DE-25:11(7971)■27:15(7760)-1KI-20:11(6605)-JOB-28:9(7971)■33:11(7760)-PS-15:5■75:7(8213)-SONG-2:13(2590)-JER-43:12(5844)-LA-3:29-EZE-14:4(7760),7(7760)-MIC-3:5■N.T.-M'T-9:16(1911)■24:32(1631)-M'R-2:22(906)■4:29(649)■13:28(1631)-LU-5:36(1911),37(906)■8:16(5087)■11:33(5087)■16:18(630)-JOH-10:4(1544)

PUTTING-GE-21:14(7760)-LE-16:21(5414)-IS-58:9(7971)-MAL-2:16(7971)■N.T.-AC-9:12(2007),17(2007)■19:33(4261)-RO-15:15(1878)-EPH-4:25(659)-COL-2:11(555)-1TH-5:8(1746)-1TI-1:12(5087)-2TI-1:6(1936)-1PE-3:3(1745),21(595)-2PE-1:13(5279)

Q

QUAILS-all=7958-EX-16:13-NU-11:31,32-PS-105:40

QUAKE-JOE-2:10(7264)-NA-1:5(7493)■N.T.-M'T-27:51(4579)-HEB-12:21(1790)

QUAKED-EX-19:18(2729)-2SA-14:15(7264)

QUAKING-EZ-12:18(7494)-DA-10:7(2731)

QUANTITY-all supplied

QUARREL-LE-26:25(5359)-2KI-5:7(579)■N.T.-M'R-6:19(1758)-COL-3:13(3437)

QUARRIES-J'G-3:19(6456),26(6456)

QUARTER-all=6285&marked-GE-19:4(7098)-NU-34:3-JOS-15:5■18:14,15-IS-47:16(5676)■56:11(7098)■N.T.-M'R-1:45(3836)

QUARTERS-EX-13:7(1366)-DE-22:12(3671)-1CH-9:24(7307)-JER-49:36(7098)-EZE-38:6(3411)■N.T.-AC-16:3(5117)■28:7(5117)-RE-20:8(1137)

QUATERNIONS-AC-12:4(5069)

QUEEN-all=4436&marked-1KI-10:1,4,10,13■11:19(1377)■15:13(1377)-2KI-10:13(1377)-2CH-9:1,3,9,12■15:16(1377) NE 2:6(7694) ES 1:9,11,12,15,16,17^{2},18■2:4(4427),17(4427),22■4:4■5:2,3,12■7:1,2,3,5,6,7,8■8:1,7■9:12,29,31-PS-45:9(7694)-JER-7:18(4446)■13:18(1377)■29:2(1377)■44:17(4446),18(4446),19(4446),25(4446)-DA-5:10^{2}(4433)■N.T.-all=938-M'T-12:42-LU-11:31-AC-8:27-RE-18:7

QUEENS-SONG-6:8(4436),9(4436)-IS-49:23(8282)

QUENCH-all=3158-2SA-14:7■21:17-PS-104:11(7665)-SONG-8:7-IS-1:31■42:3-JER-4:4■21:12-AM-5:6■N.T.-all=4570-M'T-12:20-EPH-6:16-1TH-5:19

QUENCHED-all=3518&marked-NU-11:2(8257)-2KI-22:17-2CH-34:25-PS-118:12(1846)-IS-34:10■43:17■66:24-JER-7:20■17:27-EZE-20:47,48■N.T.-all=4570&marked-M'R-9:43(762),44,45(762),46,48-HEB-11:34

QUESTION-M'R-8:11(4802)■9:16(4802)■11:29(3056)-JOH-3:25(2214)-AC-15:12(2213)■18:15(2213)■19:40(1458)■23:6(2919)■24:21(2919)

QUESTIONED-2CH-31:9(1875)■N.T.-M'R-1:27(4802)-LU-23:9(1905)

QUESTIONING-M'R-9:10(4802),14(4802)

QUESTIONS-1KI-10:1(2420),3(1697)-2CH-9:1(2420),2(1697)■N.T.-all=2214&marked-LU-2:46(1905)-AC-23:29(2213)■25:19(2213),20■26:3(2213)-1TI-1:4■6:4-2TI-2:23-TIT-3:9

QUICK-all=2416&marked-LE-13:10(4241),24(4241)-NU-16:30-PS-55:15■124:3■N.T.-all=2198-AC-10:42-2TI-4:1-HEB-4:12-1PE-4:5

QUICKEN-all=2421-PS-71:20■80:18■119:25,37,40,88,107,149,154,156,159■143:11■N.T.-RO-8:11(2227)

QUICKENED-PS-119:50(2421),93(2421)■N.T.-1CO-15:36(2227)-EPH-2:5(4806)-COL-2:13(4806)-1PE-3:18(2227)

QUICKENETH-all=2227-JOH-5:21^{2}■6:63-RO-4:17-1TI-6:13

QUICKENING-1CO-15:45(2227)

QUICKLY-all=4120&marked-GE-18:6(4116)■27:20(4116)-EX-32:8(4118)-NU-16:46-DE-9:3(4118),12^{2}(4118),16(4116)■11:17■28:20(4118)-JOS-2:5(4118)■8:19■10:6■23:16-J'G-2:17(4118)-1SA-20:19(3966)-2SA-17:16,18,21-2KI-1:11-2CH-18:8(4116)-EC-4:12■N.T.-all=5035&marked-M'T-5:25■28:7,8-M'R-16:8-LU-14:21(5030)■16:6(5030)-JOH-11:29■13:27(5032)-AC-12:7(1722,5034)■22:18(1722,5034)-RE-2:5,16■3:11■11:14■22:7,12,20

QUICKSANDS-AC-27:17(4950)

QUIET-all=8252&marked-J'G-16:2(2790)■18:7,27-2KI-11:20-1CH-4:40-2CH-14:1,5■20:30■23:21-JOB-3:13,26(5117)■21:23(7961)-PS-35:20(7282)■107:30(8367)-PR-1:33(7599)-EC-9:17(5183)-IS-7:4■14:7■32:18(7600)■33:20(7600)-JER-30:10(7599)■47:6,7■49:23■51:59(4496)-EZE-16:42-NA-1:12(8003)■N.T.-AC-19:36(2687)-1TH-4:11(2270)-1TI-2:2(2263)-1PE-3:4(2272)

QUIETED-PS-131:2(1826)-ZEC-6:8(5117)

QUIETETH-JOB-37:17(8252)

QUIETLY-2SA-3:27(7987)

QUIETNESS-all=8252&marked-J'G-8:28-1CH-22:9(8253)-JOB-20:20(7961)■34:29-PR-17:1(7962)-EC-4:6(5183)-IS-30:15■32:17■N.T.-AC-24:2(1515)-2TH-3:12(2271)

QUIT-EX-21:19(5352),28(5355)-JOS-2:20(5355)-1SA-4:9(1961)■N.T.-1CO-16:13(407)

QUITE-NU-17:10(3615)-JOB-6:13(5080)-HAB-3:9(6181)

QUIVER-all=827&marked-GE-27:3(8522)-JOB-39:23-PS-127:5-IS-22:6■49:2-JER-5:16-LA-3:13

QUIVERED-HAB-3:16(6750)

R

RABBI-all=4461-M'T-23:7,8-JOH-1:38,49■3:2,26■6:25

RACA-M'T-5:22(4469)

RACE-PS-19:5(734)-EC-9:11(4793)■N.T.-1CO-9:24(4712)-HEB-12:1(73)

RAFTERS-SONG-1:17(7351)

RAGE-all=7264&marked-2KI-5:12(2534)■19:27,28-2CH-16:10(2197)■28:9(2197)-JOB-39:24(7267)■40:11(5678)-PS-2:1(7283)■7:6(5678)-PR-6:34(2534)■29:9-IS-37:28,29-JER-46:9(1984)-DA-3:13(7266)-HO-7:16(2195)-NA-2:4(1984)■N.T.-AC-4:25(5433)

RAGED-PS-46:6(1993)

RAGETH-PR-14:16(5674)

RAGGED-all supplied

RAGING-PS-89:9(1348)-PR-20:1(1993)-JON-1:15(2197)■N.T.-LU-8:24(2830)-JUDE-13(66)

RAGS-PR-23:21(7168)-IS-64:6(899)-JER-38:11(4418),12(4418)

RAIL-2CH-32:17(2778)

RAILED-1SA-25:14(5860)■N.T.-M'R-15:29(987)-LU-23:39(987)

RAILER-1CO-5:11(3060)

RAILING-1PE-3:9(3059)-2PE-2:11(989)-JUDE-9(988)

RAILINGS-1TI-6:4(988)

RAIMENT-all=899,a=8071&marked-GE-24:53■27:15,27■28:20■41:14a■45:22^{2}a-EX-3:22a■12:35a■21:10(3682)■22:9(8008),26(8008),27a-LE-11:32-NU-31:20-DE-8:4a■10:18a■21:13a■22:3a■24:13(8008),17-JOS-22:8(8008)-J'G-3:16(4055)■8:26-RU3:3a-1SA-28:8-2KI-5:5■7:8-2CH-9:24(8008)-ES-4:4-JOB-27:16(4403)-PS-45:14(7553)-IS-14:19(3830)■63:3(4403)-EZE-16:13(4403)-ZEC-3:4(4254)■N.T.-all=2440&marked-M'T-3:4(1742)■6:25(1742),28(1742)■11:8■17:2■27:31■28:3(1742)-M'R-9:3-LU-7:25■9:29(2441)■12:23(1742)■23:34-JOH-19:24-AC-18:6■22:20-1TI-6:8(4629)-JAS-2:2(2066)-RE-3:5,18■4:4

RAIN-all=4306,a=1653,b=4305,&marked-GE-2:5b■7:4b,12a■8:2a-EX-9:18b,33,34■16:4b-LE-26:4a-DE-11:11,14,14(4456),14(3138),17■28:12,24■32:2,2(8164)-1SA-12:17,18-2SA-1:21■23:4-1KI-8:35,36■17:1,7a,14a■18:1b,41a,44a,45a-2KI-3:17a-2CH-6:26,27■7:13-EZR-10:9a,13a-JOB-5:10■20:23b■28:26■29:23,23(4456)■36:27■37:6a■38:26b,28-PS-11:6b■68:9a■72:6■84:6(4175)■105:32a■135:7■147:8-PR-16:15(4456)■25:14a,23a■26:1■28:3-EC-11:3a■12:2a-SONG-2:11a-IS-4:6■5:6b,6■30:23■44:14a■55:10a-JER-3:3(4456)■5:24a■10:13■14:4a,22a■51:16-EZE-1:28a■38:22b,22a-HO-6:3a,3(3384)■10:12(3384)-JOE-2:23(4175),23a,23(4175),23(4456)-AM-4:7a,7^{2}b-ZEC-10:1,1(4456),1■14:17■N.T.-all=5205&marked-M'T-5:45(1026)■7:25(1028),27(1028)-AC-14:17■28:2-HEB-6:7-JAS-5:7,17(1026),18-RE-11:6(1026,5205)

RAINBOW-RE-4:3(2463)■10:1(2463)

RAINED-all=4305&marked-GE-19:24-EX-9:23-PS-78:24,27-EZE-22:24(1656)-AM-4:7^{2}■N.T.-LU-7:29(1026)-JAS-5:17(1026)

RAINY-PR-27:15(5464)

RAISE-all=6965&marked-GE-38:8-EX-23:1(5375)-DE-18:15,18■½5:7-JOS-8:29-RU-4:5,10-1SA-2:35-2SA-12:11,17-1KI-14:14-1CH-17:11-JOB-3:8(5782)■19:12(5549)■30:12(5549)-PS-41:10-IS-15:5(5782)■29:3■44:26■49:6■58:12■61:4-JER-23:5■30:9■50:9(5782),32■51:1(5782)-EZE-23:22(5782)■34:29-HO-6:2-JOE-3:7(5782)-AM-5:2■6:14■9:11^{2}-MIC-5:5-HAB-1:3(5375),6-ZEC-11:16■N.T.-all=450&marked-M'T-3:9(1453)■10:8(1453)■22:24-M'R-12:19(1817)-LU-3:8(1453)■20:28(1817)-JOH-2:19(1453)■6:39,40,44,54-AC-2:30■3:22■7:37■26:8(1453)-1CO-6:14(1825)-2CO-4:14(1453)-HEB-11:19(1453)-JAS-5:15(1453)

RAISED-all=5782,a=6965&marked-EX-9:16(5975)-JOS-5:7a■7:26a-J'G-2:16a,18a■3:9a,15a-2SA-23:1a-1KI-5:13(5927)■9:15(5927)-2CH-32:5(5927)■33:14(1361)-EZR-1:5-JOB-14:12-SONG-8:5-IS-14:9a■23:13a(6209)■41:2,25■45:13-JER-6:22■25:32■29:15a■50:41■51:11-DA-7:5(6966)-AM-2:11a-ZEC-2:13■N.T.-all=1453&marked-M'T-1:24(1326)■11:5■16:21■17:23-LU-1:69■7:22■9:22■20:37-JOH-12:1,9,17-AC-2:24(450),32(450)■3:15,26(450)■4:10■5:30■10:40■12:7■13:22,23,30,33(450),34(450),37,50(1892)■17:31(450)-RO-4:24,25■6:4,9■7:4■8:11^{2}■9:17(1825)■10:9-1CO-6:14■15:15^{2},16,17,35,

42,43^{2},44,52-2CO-4:14-GA-1:1-EPH-1:20■2:6(4891)-COL-2:12-1TH-1:10-2TI-2:8-HEB-11:35(386)-1PE-1:21
RAISER-DA-11:20(5674)
RAISETH-1SA-2:8(6965)-JOB-41:25(7613)-PS-107:25(5975)■113:7(6965)■145:14(2210)■146:8(2210)■N.T.-JOH-5:21(1453)-2CO-1:9(1453)
RAISING-HO-7:4(5872)■N.T.-AC-24:12(4160,1999)
RAISINS-all=6778-1SA-25:18■30:12-2SA-16:1-1CH-12:40
RAM-all=352-GE-15:9■22:13^{2}-EX-29:15^{2},16,17,18,19^{2},20,22^{2},26,27,31,32-LE-5:15,16,18■6:6■8:18^{2},20,21,22^{2},29■9:2,4,18,19■16:3,5■19:21,22-NU-5:8■6:14,17,19■7:15,21,27,33,39,45,51,57,63,69,75,81■15:6,11■23:2,4,14,30■28:11,12,14,19,20,27,28■29:2,3,8,9,14,36,37-EZR-10:19-EZE-43:23,25■45:24■46:4,5,6,7,11-DA-8:3,4,6,7^{4},20
RAMPART-LA-2:8(2426)-NA-3:8(2426)
RAM'S-JOS-6:5(3104)
RAMS-all=352&marked-GE-31:10(6260),12(6260),38■32:14-EX-29:1,3■35:23-LE-8:2■23:18-NU-7:17,23,29,35,41,47,53,59,65,71,77,83,87,88■23:1,29■29:13,14,17,18,20,21,23,24,26,27,29,30,32,33-DE-32:14-1SA-15:22-2KI-3:4-1CH-15:26■29:21-2CH-13:9■17:11■29:21,22,32-EZR-6:9(1798),17(1798)■7:17(1798)■8:35-JOB-42:8-PS-66:15■114:4,6-IS-1:11■34:6■60:7-JER-51:40-EZE-4:2(3733)■21:22(3733)■27:21■34:17■39:18■45:23-MIC-6:7
RAMS'-all=352&marked-EX-25:5■26:14■35:7■36:19■39:34-JOS-6:4(3104),6(3104),8(3104),13(3104)
RAN-all=7323&marked-GE-18:2,7■24:17,20,28,29■29:12,13■33:4-EX-9:23(1980)-NU-11:27■16:47-JOS-7:22■8:19-J'G-7:21■9:21(5127),44(6584)■13:10-1SA-3:5■4:12■10:23■17:22,48,51■20:36-2SA-18:21,23-1KI-2:39(1272)■18:35,46■19:20■22:35(3332)-2CH-32:4(7857)-PS-77:2(5064)■105:41(1980)■133:2(3331)-JER-23:21-EZE-1:14(7519)■47:2(6379)-DA-8:6■N.T.-all=5143&marked-M'T-8:32(3729)■27:48-M'R-5:6,13(3729)■6:33(4936),55(4063)■15:36-LU-8:33(3729)■15:20■19:4(4390)■24:12-JOH-20:4-AC-3:11(4936)■7:57(3729)■8:30(4370)■12:14(1532)■14:14(1530)■21:30(4980),32(2701)■27:41(2027)-JUDE-11(1632)
RANG-1SA-4:5(1949)-1KI-1:45(1949)
RANGE-JOB-39:8(3941)
RANGES-all=7713&marked-LE-11:35(3600)-2KI-11:8,15-2CH-23:14
RANGING-PR-28:15(8264)
RANK-GE-41:5(1277),7(1277)-1CH-12:33(5737),38(4634)
RANKS-1KI-7:4,5(6471)-JOE-2:7(734)■N.T.-M'R-6:40(4237)
RANSOM-all=3724&marked-EX-21:30(6306)■30:12-JOB-33:24■36:18-PS-49:7-PR-6:35■13:8■21:18-IS-43:3-HO-13:14(6299)■N.T.-M'T-20:28(3083)-M'R-10:45(3083)-1TI-2:6(487)
RANSOMED-IS-35:10(6299)■51:10(1350)-JER-31:11(1350)
RARE-DA-2:11(3358)
RASE-PS-137:7(6168)
RASH-EC-5:2(926)-IS-32:4(4116)
RASHLY-AC-19:36(4312)
RASOR-all=4177&marked-NU-6:5(8593)-J'G-13:5■16:17-1SA-1:11-PS-52:2(8593)-IS-7:20(8593)-EZE-5:1(8593)
RATE-all=1697-EX-16:4-1KI-10:25-2KI-25:30-2CH-8:13■9:24
RATHER-PS-84:10(977)-PR-8:10(408)■17:12(408)■N.T.-all=3128&marked-M'T-10:6,28■18:8(2228),9(2228)■25:9■27:24-M'R-5:26■15:11-LU-10:20■11:28(3304),41(4133)■12:31(4133),51(2228)-JOH-3:19-AC-5:29-RO-8:34■14:13-1CO-5:2■6:7^{2}■7:21■9:12■14:1,5,19(2309)-2CO-2:7■3:8■5:8■12:9-GA-4:9-EPH-4:28■5:4,11-PH'P-1:12-1TI-1:4■6:2-PH'M-9-HEB-11:25■12:9,13■13:19(4056)-2PE-1:10
RATTLETH-JOB-39:23(7439)
RATTLING-NA-3:2(7494)
RAVEN-all=6158-GE-8:7-LE-11:15-DE-14:14-JOB-38:41-SONG-5:11-IS-34:11
RAVENS-all=6158-1KI-17:4,6-PS-147:9-PR-30:17■N.T.-LU-12:24(2876)
RAVENING-all=2963-PS-22:13-EZE-22:25,27■N.T.-M'T-7:15(727)-LU-11:39(724)
RAVENOUS-IS-35:9(6530)■46:11(5861)-EZE-39:4(5861)
RAVIN-GE-49:27(2963)-NA-2:12(2966)
RAVISHED-PR-5:19(7686),20(7686)-SONG-4:9^{2}(3823)-IS-13:16(7693)-LA-5:11(6031)-ZEC-14:2(7693)
RAW-all=2416&marked-EX-12:9(4995)-LE-13:10,14,15^{2},16-1SA-2:15
REACH-all=5060&marked-EX-26:28(1272)■28:42(1961)-LE-26:5^{2}(5381)-NU-34:11(4229)-JOB-20:6-IS-8:8■30:28(2673)-JER-48:32-ZEC-14:5■N.T.-JOH-20:27^{2}(5342)-2CO-10:13(2185)
REACHED-GE-28:12(5060)-JOS-19:11^{2}(6293)-RU-2:14(6642)-DA-4:11(4291),20(4291)■N.T.-2CO-10:14(2185)-RE-18:5(190)
REACHETH-all=6293&marked-JOS-19:22,26,27,34^{2}-2CH-28:9(5060)-PR-31:20(7971)-JER-4:10(5060),18(5060)■51:9(5060)-DA-4:22(4921)
REACHING-2CH-3:11^{2}a(5060),12(5060)■N.T.-PH'P-3:13(1901)
READ-all=7121&marked-EX-24:7-DE-17:19■31:11-JOS-8:34,35-2KI-5:7■19:14■22:8,10,16■23:2-2CH-34:18,24,30-EZR-4:18(7123),23(7123)-NE-8:3,8,18■9:3■13:1-ES-6:1-IS-29:11,12■34:16■37:14-JER-29:29■36:6^{2},10,13,14,15^{2},21,23■51:61-DA-5:7(7123),8(7123),15(7123),16(7123),17(7123)■N.T.-all=314-M'T-12:3,5■19:4■21:16,42■22:31-M'R-2:25■12:10,26-LU-4:16■6:3-JOH-19:20-AC-8:28,30,32■13:27■15:21,31■23:34-2CO-1:13■3:2,15-EPH-3:4-COL-4:16^{3}-1TH-5:27-RE-5:4
READEST-LU-10:26(314)-AC-8:30(314)
READETH-HAB-2:2(7121)■N.T.-all=314-M'T-24:15-M'R-13:14-RE-1:3
READINESS-AC-17:11(4288)-2CO-8:11(4288)■10:6(2092)
READING-NE-8:8(4744)-JER-36:8(7121)■51:63(7121)■N.T.-all=320-AC-13:15-2CO-3:14-1TI-4:13
READY-all=3559&marked-GE-18:6(4116)■43:16,25■46:29(631)-EX-14:6(631)■17:4(5750)■19:11,15■34:2-NU-32:17(2363)-DE-1:41(1951)-JOS-8:4-2SA-18:22(4672)-1KI-6:7(8003)-2KI-9:21^{2}(631)-1CH-28:2-2CH-35:14-EZR-7:6(4106)-ES-3:14(6264)■8:13(6264)-JOB-3:8(6264)■12:5■15:23,24(6264),28(6257)■18:12-PS-7:12■11:2■21:12■38:17■45:1(4106)-PR-24:11(4131)-EC-5:1(7138)-IS-32:4(4116)■41:7(2896)■51:13-EZE-7:14-DA-3:15(6263)-HO-7:6(7126)■N.T.-all=2092,a=2090&marked-M'T-22:4,8■24:44■25:10■26:19a-M'R-14:15a,16a,38(4289)-LU-1:17a■7:2(3195)■9:52a■12:40■14:17■17:8a■22:12a,13a,33-JOH-7:6-AC-10:10(3903)■20:7(3195)■21:13(2093)■23:15,21,23a-RO-1:15(4289)-2CO-8:19(4288)■9:2(3903),3(3903),5■10:16■12:14(2093)-1TI-6:18(2130)-2TI-4:6(4689)-TIT-3:1-HEB-8:13(1451)-1PE-1:5■3:15■4:5(2093)■5:2(4289)-RE-3:2(3195)■12:4(3195)■19:7a
REALM-all=4438&marked-2CH-20:30-EZR-7:13(4437),23(4437)-DA-1:20■6:3(4437)■9:1■11:2
REAP-all=7114-LE-19:9,9sup■23:10,22■25:5,11-RU-2:9-1SA-8:12-2KI-19:29-JOB-4:8■24:6-PS-126:5-PR-22:8-EC-11:4-IS-37:30-JER-12:13-HO-8:7■10:12-MIC-6:15■N.T.-all=2325-M'T-6:26■25:26-LU-12:24-JOH-4:38-1CO-9:11-2CO-9:6^{2}-GA-6:7,8^{2},9-RE-14:15^{2}
REAPED-HO-10:13(7114)■N.T.-JAS-5:4(270),4(2325)-RE-14:16(2325)
REAPER-AM-9:13(7114)
REAPERS-all=7114-RU-2:3,4,5,6,7,14-2KI-4:18■N.T.-M'T-13:30(2327),39(2327)
REAPEST-LE-23:22(7114)■N.T.-LU-19:21(2325)
REAPETH-IS-17:5(7114)■N.T.-JOH-4:36^{2}(2325),37(2325)
REAPING-1SA-6:13(7114)■N.T.-M'T-25:24(2325)-LU-19:22(2325)
REAR-all=6965-EX-26:30-LE-26:1-2SA-24:18■N.T.-JOH-2:20(1453)
REARED-all=6965&marked-EX-40:17,18^{2},33-NU-9:15-2SA-18:18(5324)-1KI-16:32-2KI-21:3-2CH-3:17■33:3
REASON-all=6440&marked-GE-41:31■47:13-EX-2:23^{2}(4480)■3:7■8:24-NU-18:32(5921)-DE-5:5-1SA-12:7(8198)-1KI-9:15(1697)-2CH-5:14■20:15■21:15(4480),19(5973)-JOB-6:16(4480)■13:3(3198)■15:3(3198)■37:19-PS-44:16■88:9-PR-26:16(2940)-EC-7:25(2808)-IS-1:18(3198)-EZE-21:12(413)■28:17(5921)-DA-4:36(4486)■5:10(6903)■N.T.-all=1260&marked-M'T-16:8-M'R-2:8■8:17-LU-5:21,22-JOH-12:11(1223)-AC-6:2(701)■18:14(3056)-RO-8:20(1223)-2CO-3:10(1752)-HEB-5:3(1223),14(1223)-1PE-3:15(3056)-2PE-2:2(1223)-RE-8:13(1537)■9:2(1537)■18:19(1537)
REASONABLE-RO-12:1(3050)
REASONED-all=1260&marked-M'T-16:7■21:25-M'R-2:8■8:16■11:31(3049)-LU-20:5(4817),14■24:15(4802)-AC-17:2(1256)■18:4(1256),19(1256)■24:25(1256)
REASONING-JOB-13:6(8433)■N.T.-M'R-2:6(1260)■12:28(4802)-LU-9:46(1261)-AC-28:29(4803)
REASONS-JOB-32:11(8394)
REBEL-all=4775-NU-14:9-JOS-1:18(4784)■22:16,18,19^{2},29-1SA-2:14(4784),15(4784)-NE-2:19■6:6-JOB-24:13-ISA-1:20(4784)-HO-7:14(5493)
REBELLED-all=4784,a=4775&marked-GE-14:4a-NU-20:24■27:14-DE-1:26,43■9:23-1KI-12:19(6586)-2KI-1:1(6586)■3:5(6586),7(6586)■18:7a■24:1a,20a-2CH-10:19(6856),13:6a■36:13a-NE-9:26a-PS-5:10■105:28■107:11-IS-1:2(6586)■63:10-JER-52:3a-LA-1:18,20■3:42-EZE-2:3a■17:15a■20:8,13,21-DA-9:5a,9a-HO-13:16
REBELLEST-2KI-18:20(4775)-IS-36:5(4775)
REBELLION-all=4805&marked-DE-31:27-JOS-22:22(4777)-1SA-15:23-EZE-4:19(4776)-NE-9:17-JOB-34:37(6588)-PR-17:11-JER-28:16(5627)■29:32(5627)
REBELLIOUS-all=4805,a=4784&marked-DE-9:7a,24a■21:18a,20a■31:27a-1SA-20:30(4780)-EZR-4:12(4779),15(4779)-PS-66:7(5637)■68:6(5637),18(5637)■78:8a-IS-1:23(5637)■30:1(5637),9(4805)■50:5a■65:2(5637)-JER-4:17a■5:23a-EZE-2:3(4775),5,6,7,8■3:9,26,27■12:2^{2},3,9,25■17:12■24:3■44:6
REBELS-NU-17:10(4805)■20:10(4784)-EZE-20:38(4775)
REBUKE-all=1606&marked-LE-19:17(3198)-DE-28:20(4045)-RU-2:16(1605)-2KI-19:3(8433)-1CH-12:17(3198)-PS-6:1(3198)■18:15■38:1(3198)■68:30(1605)■76:6■80:16■104:7-PR-9:8(3198)■13:1,8■24:25(3198)■27:5(8433)-EC-7:5-IS-2:4(3198)■17:13(1605)■25:8(2781)■30:17^{2}■37:3(8433)■50:2■51:20■54:9(1605)■66:15-JER-15:15(2781)-HO-5:9(8433)-MIC-4:3(3198)

-ZEC-3:2^{2}(1605)-MAL-3:11(1605)■N.T.-all=2008&marked-M'T-16:22-M'R-8:32-LU-17:3■19:39-PH'P-2:15(298)-1TI-5:1(1969),20(1651)-2TI-4:2-TIT-1:13(1651)■2:15(1651)-JUDE-9-RE-3:19(1651)

REBUKED-all=1605&marked-GE-31:42(3198)■37:10-NE-5:7(7378)-PS-9:5■106:9■119:21■N.T.-all=2008&marked-M'T-8:26■17:18■19:13■20:31-M'R-1:25■4:39■8:33■9:25■10:13-LU-4:35,39■8:24■9:42,55■18:15,39■23:40-HEB-12:5(1651)-2PE-2:16(2192,1649)

REBUKER-HO-5:2(4148)

REBUKES-all=8433-PS-39:11-EZE-5:15■25:17

REBUKETH-all=3198&marked-PR-9:7■28:23-AM-5:10-NA-1:4(1605)

REBUKING-2SA-22:16(1606)■N.T.-LU-4:41(2008)

RECALL-LA-3:21(7725)

RECEIPT-all=5058-M'T-9:9-M'R-2:14-LU-5:27

RECEIVE-all=3947&marked-GE-4:11■33:10■38:20-EX-27:3(1878)■29:25-NU-18:28-DE-9:9■33:3(5375)-1SA-10:4-2SA-18:12(8254)-1KI-5:9(5375)■8:64(3557)-2KI-5:16,26■12:7,8-2CH-7:7(3557)-JOB-2:10^{2}(6901)■22:22■27:13-PS-6:9■24:5(5375)■49:15■73:24■75:2-PR-1:3■2:1■4:10■8:10■10:8■19:20-IS-57:6(5162)-JER-5:3■9:20■17:23■32:33■35:13-EZE-3:10■16:61■36:30-DA-2:6(6902)-HO-10:6■14:2-MIC-1:11-ZEP-3:7■N.T.-all=2983,a=1209&marked-M'T-10:14(1209),41^{2}■11:5(308),14a■18:5a■19:11(5562),12(5562),29■20:7■21:22,34■23:14-M'R-2:2(5562)■4:16,20(3858)■6:11a■9:37^{2}a■10:15a,30,51(308)■11:24■12:2,40-LU-6:34^{2}(618)■8:13a■9:5a,48^{2}a,53a■10:8a,10a■16:4a,9a■18:17a,30(618),41(308),42(308)■19:12■20:47■23:41(618)-JOH-3:11,27■5:37,41,43^{2},44■7:33,39■14:3(3880),17■16:14,24■20:22-AC-1:8■2:38■3:5,21a■7:59a■8:15,19■9:12(308),17(308)■10:43■16:21(3858)■18:27(588)■20:35■22:13(308),18(3858)■26:18-RO-5:17■13:2■14:1(4355)■15:7(4355)■16:2(4327)-1CO-3:8,14■4:7^{2}■14:5-2CO-5:10(2865)■6:1a,17(1523)■7:2(5562),9(2210)■8:4a■11:4,16a-GA-3:14■4:5(618)-EPH-6:8(2865)-PH'P-2:29(4327)-COL-3:24(618),25(2865)■4:10a-1TI-5:19(3858)-PH'M-12(4355),15(568),17(4355)-HEB-7:5,8■9:15■10:36(2865)■11:8-JAS-1:7,12,21a■3:1■4:3■5:7-1PE-5:4(2865)-2PE-2:13(2865)-1JO-3:22■5:9-2JO-8(618),10-3JO-8(618),10(1926)-RE-4:11■5:12■13:16(1325)■14:9■17:12■18:4

RECEIVED-all=3947&marked-GE-26:12(4672)-EX-32:4■36:3-NU-12:14(622)■23:20■34:14^{2},15■36:3(1961),4(1961)-JOS-13:8■18:2(2505),7-J'G-13:23-1SA-12:3■25:35-1KI-10:28-2KI-19:14-1CH-12:18(6901)-2CH-1:16■4:5(2388)■29:22(6901)-ES-4:4(6901)-JOB-4:12-PS-68:18-PR-24:32-IS-37:14■40:2-JER-2:30-EZE-18:17-ZEP-3:2■N.T.-all=2983,a=3880&marked-M'T-10:8■13:19(4687),20(4687),22(4687),23(4687)■17:24■20:9,10^{2},11,34(308)■25:16,18,20,22,24,27(2865)-M'R-7:4a■10:52(308)■15:23■16:19(353)-LU-6:24(568)■8:40(588)■9:11(1209),51(354)■10:38(5264)■15:27(618)■18:43(308)■19:6(5264),15-JOH-1:11a,12,16■3:33■4:45(1209)■6:21■9:11(308)■15(308),18^{2}(308)■10:18■13:30■17:8■18:3■19:30-AC-1:9(5274)■2:33,41(588)■3:7(4732)■7:38(1209),53■8:14(1209),17■9:18(308),19■10:16(353),47■11:1(1209)■15:4(588)■16:24■17:7(5264),11(1209)■19:2■20:24■21:17(1209)■22:5(1209)■26:10■28:2(4355),7(324),21(1209),30(588)-RO-1:5■4:11■5:11■8:15^{2}■14:3(4355)■15:7(4355)-1CO-2:12■4:7■11:23a■15:1a,3a-2CO-4:1(1653)■7:15(1209)■11:4,24-GA-1:9a,12a■3:2■4:14(1209)-PH'P-4:9a,18(1209)-COL-2:6a■4:10,17a-1TH-1:6(1209)■2:13a,13(1209)■4:1a-2TH-2:10(1209)■3:6a-1TI-3:16(353)■4:3(3336),4-HEB-2:2■7:6(1183),11(3549)■10:26■11:11,13,17(324),19(2865),31(1209),35,39(2865)-JAS-2:25(5264)-1PE-1:18■4:10-2PE-1:17-1JO-2:27-2JO-4-RE-2:27■3:3■17:12■19:20■20:4

RECEIVEDST-LU-16:25(618)

RECEIVER-IS-33:18(8254)

RECEIVETH-all=3947&marked-J'G-19:18(622)-JOB-35:7-PR-21:11-JER-7:28-MAL-2:13■N.T.-all=2983&marked-M'T-7:8■10:40^{2}(1209),41^{2}■13:20■18:5(1209)-M'R-9:37^{2}(1209)-LU-9:48^{2}(1209)■11:10■15:2(4327)-JOH-3:32■4:36■12:48■13:20^{2}-1CO-2:14(1209)■9:24-HEB-6:7(3335)■7:9■12:6(3858)-3JO-9(1926)-RE-2:17■14:11

RECEIVING-2KI-5:20(3947)■N.T.-AC-17:15(2983)-RO-1:27(618)■11:15(4356)-PH'P-4:15(3028)-HEB-12:28(3880)-1PE-1:9(2865)

RECKON-all=2803&marked-LE-25:50■27:18,23-NU-4:32(6485)-EZE-44:26(5608)■N.T.-M'T-18:24(4868)-RO-6:11(3049)■8:18(3049)

RECKONED-all=3187&marked-NU-18:27(2803)■23:9(2803)-2SA-4:2(2803)-2KI-12:15(2803)-1CH-5:1,7,17■7:5,7■9:1,22-2CH-31:19-EZR-2:62■8:3-NE-7:5,64-IS-38:13(7737)■N.T.-all=3049-LU-22:37-RO-4:4,9,10

RECKONETH-M'T-25:19(4868,3056)

RECKONING-2KI-22:7(2803)-1CH-23:11(6486)

RECOMMENDED-AC-14:26(3860)■15:40(3860)

RECOMPENCE-all=1576&marked-DE-32:35(8005)-JOB-15:31(8545)-PR-12:4-IS-35:4■59:18^{2}■65:6-JER-51:6-LA-3:64-HOS-9:7(7966)-JOE-3:4^{2}■N.T.-all=3405&marked-LU-14:12(468)-RO-1:27(489)■11:9(468)-2CO-6:13(489)-HEB-2:2■10:35■11:26

RECOMPENCES-IS-34:8(7966)-JER-51:56(1578)

RECOMPENSE-all=5414&marked-NU-5:7(7725),8(7725)-RU-2:12(7999)-2SA-19:36(1580)-JOB-34:33(7999)-PR-20:22(7999)-IS-5:6(7999)-JER-16:18(7999)■25:14(7999)■50:29(7999)-EZE-7:3,4,8,9■9:10■11:21■16:43■17:19■23:49-HO-12:2(7725)-JOE-3:4(1580)■N.T.-all=467&marked-LU-14:14-RO-12:17(591)-2TH-1:6-HEB-10:30

RECOMPENSED-all=7725&marked-NU-5:8-2SA-22:21,25-PS-18:20,24-PR-11:31(7999)-JER-18:20(7999)-EZE-22:31(5414)■N.T.-LU-14:14(467)-RO-11:35(467)

RECOMPENSEST-JER-32:18(7999)

RECOMPENSING-2CH-6:23(5414)

RECONCILE-LE-6:30(3722)-1SA-29:4(7521)-EZE-45:20(3722)■N.T.-EPH-2:16(604)-COL-1:20(604)

RECONCILED-all=2644&marked-M'T-5:24(1259)-RO-5:10^{2}-1CO-7:11-2CO-5:18,20-COL-1:21(604)

RECONCILIATION-all=3722&marked-LE-8:15-2CH-29:24(2398)-EZE-45:15,17-DA-9:24■N.T.-2CO-5:18(2643),19(2643)-HEB-2:17(2433)

RECONCILING-LE-16:20(3722)■N.T.-RO-11:15(2643)-2CO-5:19(2644)

RECORD-EX-20:24(2142)-DE-30:19(5749)■31:28(5749)-1CH-16:4(2142)-EZR-6:2(1799)-JOB-16:19(7717)-IS-8:2(5749)■N.T.-all=3140&marked-JOH-1:19(3141),32,34■8:13,13(3141)14,14(3141)■12:17■19:35,35(3141)-AC-20:26(3143)-RO-10:2-2CO-1:23(3144)■8:3-GA-4:15-PH'P-1:8(3144)-COL-4:13-1JO-5:7,10(3141),11(3141),12-3JO-12,12(3141)-RE-1:2

RECORDED-NE-12:22(3789)

RECORDER-all=2142-2SA-8:16■20:24-1KI-4:3-2KI-18:18,37-1CH-18:15-2CH-34:8-IS-36:3,22

RECORDS-EZR-4:15^{2}(1799)-ES-6:1(2146)

RECOUNT-NA-2:5(2142)

RECOVER-all=2421&marked-J'G-11:26(5337)-1SA-30:8(5337)-2SA-8:3(7725)-1KI-1:2■5:3(622),6(622),7(622),11(622)■8:8,9,10,14-2CH-13:20(6113)■14:13(4241)PS-39:13(1082)-IS-11:11(7069)■38:16(2492),21-HO-2:9(5337)■N.T.-M'R-6:18(2192,2573)-2TI-2:26(366)

RECOVERED-all=7725&marked-1SA-30:18(5337),19,22(5337)-2KI-13:25■14:28■16:6■20:7(2421)-IS-38:9(2421)■39:1(2388)-JER-8:22(5927)■41:16

RECOVERING-LU-4:18(309)

RED-all=119&marked-GE-25:25(132),30(122)■49:12(2447)-EX-25:5■26:14■35:7,23■36:19■39:34-NU-19:2(122)-2KI-3:22(122)-ES-1:6(923)-PS-75:8(2560)-PR-23:31-IS-1:18■27:2(2561)■63:2(122)-NA-2:3-ZEC-1:8^{2}(122)■6:2(122)■N.T.-M'T-16:2(4449),3(4449)-RE-6:4(4450)■12:3(4450)

REDDISH-all=125-LE-13:19,24,42,43,49■14:37

REDEEM-all=1350,a=6299&marked-EX-6:6■13:13^{3}a,15a■34:20^{2}a-LE-25:25^{2},26,26(1353),29^{2}(1353),32(1353),48,49^{2},49(1353)■27:13,15,19,20,27(6299),31-NU-18:15^{2}a,16a,17a-RU-4:4^{4},6^{3}-2SA-7:23a-1CH-17:21a-JOB-5:20a■6:23a-PS-25:22a■26:11a■44:26a■49:7a,15a■69:18■72:14■130:8a-IS-50:2(6304)-JER-15:21a-HO-13:14-MIC-4:10■N.T.-GA-4:5(1805)-TIT-2:14(3804)

REDEEMED-all=1350,a=6299&marked-GE-48:16-EX-15:13■21:8a-LE-19:20a■25:30,31(1353),48(1353),54■27:20,27,28,29(6299),33-NU-3:46(6302),48(6302),49(6306),51(6306)■18:16a-DE-7:8a■9:26a■13:5a■15:15a■21:8a■24:18a-2SA-4:9a-1KI-1:29a-1CH-17:21a-NE-1:10a■5:8(7069)-PS-31:5a■71:23a■74:2■77:15■106:10■107:2^{2}■136:24(6561)-IS-1:27a■29:22a■35:9■43:1■44:22,23■48:20■51:11(6299)■52:3,9■62:12■63:4,9-JER-31:11a-LA-3:58-HO-7:13a-MIC-6:4a-ZEC-10:8a■N.T.-all=59&marked-LU-1:68(4160,3085)■24:21(3084)-GA-3:13(1805)-1PE-1:18(3084)-RE-5:9■14:3,4

REDEEMEDST-2SA-7:23(6299)

REDEEMER-all=1350-JOB-19:25-PS-19:14■78:35-PR-23:11-IS-41:14■43:14■44:6,24■47:4■48:17■49:7,26■54:5,8■59:20■60:16■63:16-JER-50:34

REDEEMETH-PS-34:22(6299)■103:4(1350)

REDEEMING-RU-4:7(1353)■N.T.-EPH-5:16(1805)-COL-4:5(1805)

REDEMPTION-all=1353&marked-LE-25:24,51,52-NU-3:49(6306)-PS-49:8(6306)■111:9(6304)■130:7(6304)-JER-32:7,8■N.T.-all=629&marked-LU-2:38(3085)■21:28-RO-3:24■8:23-1CO-1:30-EPH-1:7,14■4:30-COL-1:14-HEB-9:12(3085),15(629)

REDNESS-PR-23:29(2498)

REDOUND-2CO-4:15(4052)

REED-all=7070-1KI-14:15-2KI-18:21-JOB-40:21-IS-36:6■42:3-EZE-29:6■40:3,5^{3},6^{2},7^{2},8■41:8■42:16^{2},17,18,19■N.T.-all=2563-M'T-11:7■12:20■27:29,30,48-M'R-15:19,36-LU-7:24-RE-11:1■21:15,16

REEDS-all=7070&marked-IS-19:6■35:7-JER-51:32(98)-EZE-42:16,17,18,19

REEL-PS-107:27(2287)-IS-24:20(5128)

REFINE-ZEC-13:9(6884)

REFINED-all=2212&marked-1CH-28:18■29:4-IS-25:6■48:10(6884)-ZEC-13:9(6884)

REFINER-MAL-3:3(6884)

REFINER'S-MAL-3:2(6884)

REFORMATION-HEB-9:10(1357)

REFORMED-LE-26:23(3256)

REFRAIN-GE-45:1(662)-JOB-7:11(2820)-PR-1:15(4513)-EC-3:5(7368)-IS-48:9(2413)■64:12(662)-JER-31:16(4513)■N.T.-AC-5:38(868)-1PE-3:10(3973)

REFRAINED-all=622&marked-GE-43:31-ES-5:10-JOB-29:9(6113)-PS-40:9(3607)-PS-119:101(3601)-IS-42:14-JER-14:10(2820)

REFRAINETH-PR-10:19(2820)

REFRESH-1KI-13:7(5582)-AC-27:3(1958,5177)-PH'M-20(375)

REFRESHED-all=5314&marked-EX-23:12■31:17-1SA-16:23(7304)-2SA-16:14-JOB-32:20(7304)■N.T.-all=373&marked-RO-15:32(4875)-1CO-16:18-2CO-7:13-2TI-1:16(404)-PH'M-7

REFRESHETH-PR-25:13(7725)

REFRESHING-IS-8:12(4774)■N.T.-AC-3:19(403)

REFUGE-all=4733,a=4268&marked-NU-35:6,11,12,13,14,15,25,26,27,28,32-DE-33:27(4585)-JOS-20:2,3■21:13,21,27,32,38-2SA-22:3(4498)-1CH-6:57,67-PS-9:9^{2}(4869)■14:6a■46:1a,7(4869),11(4869)■48:3(4869)■57:1(2620)■59:16(4498)■62:7a,8a■71:7a■91:2a,9a■94:22a■104:18a■142:4(4498),5a-PR-14:26a-IS-4:6a■25:4a■28:15a,17a-JER-16:19(4498)■N.T.-HEB-6:18(2703)

REFUSE-all=3985&marked-EX-4:23■8:2(3986)■9:2(3986)■10:3,4(3986)■16:28■22:17-1SA-15:9(4549)-JOB-34:33(3988)-PR-8:33(6544)■21:7,25-IS-1:20■7:15(3988),16(3988)-JER-8:5■9:6■13:10(3987)■25:28■38:21(3986)-LA-3:45(3973)-AM-8:6(4651)■N.T.-all=3868-AC-25:11-1TI-4:7■5:11-HEB-12:25

REFUSED-all=3985&marked-GE-37:35■39:8■48:19-NU-20:21-1SA-8:19■16:7(3988)■28:23-2SA-2:23■13:9-1KI-20:35■21:15-2KI-5:16-NE-9:17-ES-1:12-JOB-6:7-PS-77:2■78:10,67(3988)■118:22(3988)-PR-1:24-IS-54:6(3988)-JER-5:3^{2}■11:10■31:15■50:33-EZE-5:6(3988)-HO-11:5-ZEC-7:11■N.T.-AC-7:35(720)-1TI-4:4(579)-HEB-11:24(720)■12:25(3868)

REFUSEDST-JER-3:3(3985)

REFUSETH-all=3985&marked-EX-7:14-NU-22:13,14-DE-25:7-PR-10:17(5800)■13:18(6544)■15:32(6544)-IS-8:6(3988)-JER-15:18

REGARD-all=3820&marked-GE-45:20(5869,2347,5921)-EX-5:9(8159)-LE-19:31(6437)-DE-28:50(5375)-1SA-4:20■25:25-2SA-13:20-2KI-3:14(5375)-JOB-3:4(1875)■35:13(7789)■36:21(6437)-PS-28:5(995)■31:6(8104)■66:18(7200)■94:7(995)■102:17(6437)-PR-5:2(8104)■6:35(5375,6440)-EC-8:2(5921,1700)-IS-5:12(5027)■13:17(2803)-LA-4:16(5027)-DA-11:37^{2}(995)-AM-5:22(5027)-HAB-1:5(5027)-MAL-1:9(5375)■N.T.-LU-18:4(1788)-AC-8:11(4337)-RO-14:6(5426)

REGARDED-EX-9:21(3820)-1KI-18:29(7182)-1CH-17:17(7200)-PS-106:44(7200)-PR-1:24(7181)-DA-3:12(7761,2942)■N.T.-LU-1:48(1914)■18:2(1788)-HEB-8:9(272)

REGARDEST-JOB-30:20(995)■N.T.-M'T-22:16(991)-M'R-12:14(991)

REGARDETH-all=8104&marked-DE-10:17(5375)-JOB-34:19(5234)■39:7(8085)-PR-12:10(3045)■13:18■15:5■29:7(995)-EC-5:8■11:4(7200)-IS-33:8(2803)-DA-6:13(7761,2942)-MAL-2:13(6437)■N.T.-RO-14:6^{2}(5426)

REGARDING-JOB-4:20(7760)■N.T.-PH'P-2:30(3851)

REGENERATION-M'T-19:28(3824)-TIT-3:5(3824)

REGION-all=2256&marked-DE-3:4,13-1KI-4:11(5299),13■N.T.-all=4066&marked-M'T-3:5■4:16(5561)-M'R-1:28■6:55-LU-3:1(5561)■4:14■7:17-AC-13:49(5561)■14:6■16:6(5561)

REGIONS-AC-8:1(5561)-2CO-11:10(2825)-GA-1:21(2825)

REGISTER-EZR-2:62(3791)-NE-7:5(5612),64(3791)

REHEARSE-EX-17:14(7760)-J'G-5:11(5867)

REHEARSED-1SA-8:21(1696)■17:31(5046)■N.T.-AC-11:4(756)■14:27(312)

REIGN-all=4427,a=4438&marked-GE-37:8-EX-15:18-LE-26:17(7287)-DE-15:6^{2}(4910)-J'G-9:2^{2}(4910),8,10,12,14-1SA-8:7,9,11■9:17(6113)■11:12■12:12-2SA-2:10■3:21■5:4-1KI-1:11,13^{2},17,24,30■2:15■6:1■11:37■14:21■15:25,33■16:8,11,15,23,29■22:41,42,51-2KI-3:1■8:16,17,25,26■9:29■11:3,21■12:1■13:1,10■14:2,23■15:1,2,8,13,17,23,27,32,33■16:1,2■17:1■18:1,2■21:1,19■22:1■23:31,33,36■24:8,12,18■25:1,27-1CH-4:31■26:31a■29:30a-2CH-1:8■3:2a■12:13■13:1■15:10a,19a■16:1a,12a,13■17:7■20:31■21:5,20■22:2■23:3■24:1■25:1■26:3■27:1,8■28:1■29:1,3,19a■33:1,21■34:1,3,8■35:19a■36:2,5,9,11,20-EZR-4:5a,6^{2}a,24(4437)■6:15(4437)■7:1a■8:1a-NE-12:22a-ES-1:3■2:16a-JOB-34:30-PS-146:10-PR-8:15-EC-4:14-1SA-24:23■32:1-JER-1:2■22:15■23:5■26:1(4468)■27:1(4467)■28:1(4467)■33:21■49:34a■51:59■52:1,4,31a-DA-1:1a■2:1a■6:28^{2}(4437),8:1a■9:2-MIC-4:7-N.T.-all=936&marked-M'T-2:22-LU-1:33■3:1(2231)■19:14,27-RO-5:17,21■6:12■15:12(757)-1CO-4:8,8(4821)■15:25-TI-2:12(4821)-RE-5:10■11:15■20:6■22:5

REIGNED-all=4427&marked-GE-36:31,32,33,34,35,36,37,38,39-JOS-12:5(4910)■13:10,12,21-J'G-4:2■9:22(7786)-1SA-13:1^{2}-2SA-2:10■5:4,5^{2}■8:15■10:1■16:8-1KI-2:11^{2}■4:21(4910)■11:24,25,42,43■12:17■14:19,20^{2}21^{2},31■15:1,2,8,9,10,24,25,28,29■16:6,10,22,23,28,29■22:40,42,50,51-2KI-1:17■3:1,27■8:15,17,24■10:35,36■12:1,21■13:9,24■14:1,2,16,29■15:2,7,10,13,14,22,25,30,33,38■16:2,20■18:2■19:37■20:21■21:1,18,19,26■22:1■23:31,36■24:6,8,18-1CH-1:43^{2},44,45,46,47,48,49,50■3:4^{2}■18:14■19:1■29:26,27^{3},28-2CH-1:13■9:26(4910),30,31■10:17■12:13^{2},16■13:2■14:1■17:1■20:31^{2}■21:1,5,20■22:1,2,12■24:1,27■25:1■26:3,23■27:1,8,9■28:1,27■29:1■32:33■33:1,20,21■34:1■36:2,5,8,9,11-ES-1:1-1SA-37:38-JER-22:11■37:1■52:1■N.T.-all=936&marked-RO-5:14,17,21-1CO-4:8-RE-11:17■20:4

REIGNEST-1CH-29:12(4910)

REIGNETH-all=4427-1SA-12:14-2SA-15:10-1KI-1:18-1CH-16:31-PS-47:8■93:1■96:10■97:1■99:1-PR-30:22-IS-52:7■N.T.-RE-17:18(2192,932)■19:6(936)

REIGNING-1SA-16:1(4427)

REINS-all=3629&marked-JOB-16:13■19:27-PS-7:9■16:7■26:2■73:21■139:13-PR-23:16-IS-11:5(2504)-JER-11:20■12:2■17:10■20:12-LA-3:13■N.T.-RE-2:23(3510)

REJECT-HO-4:6(3988)■N.T.-M'R-6:26(114)■7:9(114)-TIT-3:10(3868)

REJECTED-all=3988&marked-1SA-8:7^{2}■10:19■15:23^{2},26^{2}■16:1-2KI-17:15,20-IS-53:3(2310)-JER-2:37■6:19,30■7:29■8:9■14:19-LA-5:22-HO-4:6■N.T.-all=593&marked-M'T-21:42-M'R-8:31■12:10-LU-7:30(114)■9:22■17:25■20:17-GA-4:14(1609)-HEB-6:8(96)■12:17

REJECTETH-JOH-12:48(114)

REJOICE-all=8055,a=1523,b=7797&marked-LE-23:40-DE-12:7,12,18■14:26■16:11,14,15■26:11(8056)■27:7■28:63b■30:9b■32:43(7442)■33:18-J'G-9:19^{2}■16:23(8057)-1SA-2:1■19:5-2SA-1:20-1CH-16:10,31(1523),32(5970)-2CH-6:41■20:27-NE-12:43-JOB-3:22■20:18(5965)■21:12-PS-2:11(1523)■5:11■9:2(5970),14a■13:4a,5a■14:7a■20:5(7442)■21:1a■30:1■31:7■32:11(1524)■33:1(7442),21■35:9(7997),19,24,26■38:16(8056)■40:16b■48:11■51:8a■53:6a■58:10■60:6(5937)■63:7(7442),11■65:8(7442),12(1524)■66:6■68:3(5970),3b,4(5937)■70:4b■71:23(7442)■85:6■86:4■89:12(7442),16(1523),42■90:14(7442)■96:11(8056),12(7442)■97:1a,12■98:4(7442)■104:31■105:3■106:5■107:42■108:7(5937)■109:28■118:24a■119:162b■149:2-PR-2:14(8056)■5:18■23:15,16(5937),24(1523),25(1523)■24:17■27:9■28:12(5970)■29:2,6■31:25(7832)-EC-3:12,22■4:16■5:19■11:8,9-SONG-1:4-1SA-8:6(4885)■9:3a■13:3(5947)■14:8,29■23:12(5937)■24:8(5947)■25:9■29:19a■35:1a,2a■41:16a■61:7(7442),10b■62:5b■65:13,18a,19a■66:10,10b,14b-JER-31:13^{2}(8057)■32:41b■51:39(5937)-LA-2:17■4:21b-EZE-7:12■35:15(8057)-HO-9:1-JOE-2:21,23-AM-6:13-MIC-7:8(8056)-HAB-1:15■3:18(5937)-ZEP-3:11(5947),14(5937),17b-ZEC-2:10■4:10■9:9a■10:7,7(1523)■N.T.-all=5463&marked-M'T-5:12-LU-1:14■6:23■10:20^{2}■15:6(4796),9(4796)■19:37-JOH-4:36■5:35(21)■14:28■16:20,22-AC-2:26(2165)-RO-5:2(2744)■12:15■15:10(2165)-1CO-7:30■12:26(4796)-2CO-2:3■7:9,16-GA-4:27(2165)-PH'P-1:18■2:16(2745),17(4796),18(4796),28■3:1,3(2744)■4:4^{2}-COL-1:24-1TH-5:16-JAS-1:9(2744)■4:16(2744)-1PE-1:6(21),8(21)■4:13-RE-11:10■12:12(2165)■18:20(2165)■19:7(21)

REJOICED-all=8055&marked-EX-18:9(2302)-DE-28:63(7797)■30:9(7797)-J'G-19:3-1SA-6:13■11:15-1KI-1:40(8056)■5:7-2KI-11:14(8056),20-1CH-29:9^{2}-2CH-15:15■23:13(8056),21■24:10■29:36■30:25-NE-12:43^{2},44(8057)-ES-8:15(6670)-JOB-31:25,29-PS-35:15■97:8(1523)■119:14(7797)-EC-2:10-JER-15:17(5937)■50:11(5937)-EZE-25:6-HO-10:5(1523)-OB-12■N.T.-all=5463&marked-M'T-2:10-LU-1:47(21),58(4796)■10:21(21)■13:17-JOH-8:56(21)-AC-7:41(2165)■15:31■16:34(21)-1CO-7:30-2CO-7:7-PH'P-4:10-2JO-4-3JO-3

REJOICEST-JER-11:15(5937)

REJOICETH-all=8055&marked-1SA-2:1(5970)-JOB-39:21(7797)-PS-16:9(1523)■19:5(7797)■28:7(5937)-PR-11:10(5970)■13:9■15:30■29:3-IS-5:14(5938)■62:5(4885)■64:5(7797)-EZE-35:14■N.T.-all=5463&marked-M'T-18:13-JOH-3:29-1CO-13:6,6(4796)-JAS-2:13(2620)

REJOICING-all=7440&marked-1KI-1:45(8056)-2CH-23:18(8057)-JOB-8:21(8643)-PS-19:8(8055)■45:15(1524)■107:22■118:15■119:111(8342)■126:6-PR-8:30(7832),31(7832)-IS-65:18(1525)-JER-15:16(8057)-HAB-3:14(5951)-ZEP-2:15(5947)■N.T.-all=5463&marked-LU-15:5-AC-5:41■8:39-RO-12:12-1CO-15:31(2746)-2CO-1:12(2746),14(2745)■6:10-GA-6:4(2745)-PH'P-1:26(2745)-1TH-2:19(2746)-HEB-3:6(2745)-JAS-4:16(2746)

RELEASE-all=8059&marked-DE-15:1,2,2(8058),2,3(8058),9■31:10-ES-2:18(2010)■N.T.-all=630-M'T-27:15,17,21-M'R-15:9,11-LU-23:16,17,18,20-JOH-18:39^{2}■19:10,12

RELEASED-all=630-M'T-27:26-M'R-15:6,15-LU-23:25

RELIED-2CH-13:18(8172)■16:7^{2}(8172)

RELIEF-AC-11:29(1248)

RELIEVE-all=7729&marked-LE-25:35(2388)-IS-1:17(833)-LA-1:11,16,19■N.T.-1TI-5:16^{2}(1884)

RELIEVED-1TI-5:10(1884)

RELIEVETH-PS-146:9(5749)

RELIGION-all=2356&marked-AC-26:5-GA-1:3(2454),14(2454)-JAS-1:26,27

RELIGIOUS-AC-13:43(4576)-JAS-

1:26(2357)

RELY-2CH-16:8(8172)

REMAIN-all=7604,a=3498,b=3427 &marked-GE-38:11b-EX-8:9,11■12:10a■23:18(3885)■29:34a-LE-19:6a■25:28 (1961),52■27:18a-NU-33:55a-DE-2:34 (8300)■16:4(3885)■19:20■21:13b,23 (3885)-JOS-1:14b■2:11(6965)■8:22 (8300)■10:28(8300),30(8300)■23:4,7,12 -J'G-5:17(1481)■21:7a,16a-1SA-20:19b -1KI-11:16b■18:22a-2KI-7:13-EZR-9:15-JOB-21:32(8245)■27:15(8300)■37:8(7931)-PS-55:7(3885)-PR-2:21a■21:16(5117)-IS-10:3(5975)■32:16b■44:13b■65:4b■66:22^{2}(5975)-JER-8:3^{2}■17:25b■24:8■27:11(3241),19a,21a■30:18b■38:4■42:17(8300)■44:7(7611), 14(8300)■51:62(3427)-EZE-17:21■31:13 (7931)■32:4(7931)■39:14a-AM-6:9a -OB-14(8300)-ZEC-5:4(3885)■12:14■ **N.T.**-all=3306&marked-LU-10:7 -JOH-6:12(4052)■15:11,16■19:31-1CO-7:11■15:6-1TH-4:15(4035),17(4035) -HEB-12:27-1JO-2:24-RE-3:2(3062)

REMAINDER-all=3498&marked -EX-29:34-LE-6:16■7:16,17-2SA-14:7 (7611)-PS-76:10(7611)

REMAINED-all=7604,a=3427& marked-GE-7:23■14:10-EX-8:31■10:15 (3498),19■14:28-NU-11:26■35:28a■36:12(1961)-DE-3:11■4:25(3462)-JOS-10:20(8277)■11:22■13:12■18:2(3498)■21:20(3498),26(3498)-J'G-7:3-1SA-11:11■23:14a■24:3a-2SA-13:20a-1KI-22:46 -2KI-10:11,17■13:6(5975)■24:14■25:22 -1CH-13:14a-EC-2:9(5975)-JER-34:7■37:10,16a,21a■38:13a■39:9^{2}■41:10■48:11 (5975)■51:30a■52:15-LA-2:22(8300) -EZE-3:15-DA-10:8,13(3498),17(5975)■ **N.T.**-all=4052&marked-M'T-11:23 (3306)■14:20-LU-1:22(1265)■9:17 -JOH-6:13-AC-5:4(3306)■27:41(3306)

REMAINEST-LA-5:19(3427)■ **N.T.**-HEB-1:11(1265)

REMAINETH-all=3498&marked -GE-8:22(3117)-EX-10:5(7604)■12:10■16:23(2736)■26:12^{2}(5736),13(5736) -LE-8:32■10:12■16:16(7931)-NU-24:19(8300)-JOS-13:1(7604),2(7604) -J'G-5:13(8300)-1SA-16:11(7604) -EZR-1:4(7604)-JOB-19:4(3885)■21:34(7604)■41:22(3885)-IS-4:3-JER-38:2(3427)■47:4(8300)-EZE-6:12 (7604)-HAG-2:5(5975)-ZEC-9:7 (7604)■**N.T.**-all=3306&marked-JOH-9:41-1CO-7:29(3588,3063)-2CO-3:11,14■9:9-HEB-4:6(620),9(620)■10:26(620)-1JO-3:9

REMAINING-all=8300&marked -NU-9:22(7931)-DE-3:3-JOS-10:33, 37,39,40■11:8■21:40(3498)-2SA-21:5 (3320)-2KI-10:11-JOB-18:19-OB-18■ **N.T.**-JOH-1:33(3306)

REMEDY-all=4832-2CH-36:16 -PR-6:15■29:1

REMEMBER-all-2142-GE-9:15, 16■40:23■41:9-EX-13:3■20:8■32:13 -LE-26:42^{3},45-NU-11:5■15:39,40-DE-5:15■7:18■8:2,18■9:7,27■15:15■16:3, 12■24:9,18,22■25:17■32:7-JOS-1:13-J'G-9:2■16:28-1SA-1:11■15:2(6485)■25:31 -2SA-14:11■19:19-1KI-9:25■20:3-1CH-16:12-2CH-6:42-NE-1:8■4:14■13:14, 22,29,31-JOB-4:7■7:7■10:9■11:16■14:13■21:6■36:24■41:8-PS-20:3,7■22:27■25:6,7^{2}■42:4,6■63:6■74:2,18,22■77:10,11^{2}■79:8■89:47,50■103:18■105:5■106:4■119:49■132:1■137:6,7■143:5-PR-31:7-EC-5:20■11:8■12:1 -SONG-1:4-IS-38:3■43:18,25■44:21■46:8,9■47:7■54:4■64:5,9-JER-2:2■3:16■14:10,21■15:15■17:2■18:20■31:20,34■44:21■51:50-LA-5:1-EZE-6:9■16:60, 61,63■20:43■23:27■36:31-HO-7:2■8:13■9:9-MIC-6:5-HAB-3:2-ZEC-10:9 -MAL-4:4■**N.T.**-all=3421&marked -M'T-16:9■27:63(3415)-M'R-8:18-LU-1:72(3415)■16:25(3415)■17:32■23:42 (3415)■24:6(3415)-JOH-15:20■16:4 -AC-20:31,35-1CO-11:2(3415)-GA-2:10-EPH-2:11-COL-4:18-1TH-2:9 -2TH-2:5-2TI-2:8-HEB-8:12(3415)■10:17(3415)■13:3(3403),7-3JO-10 (5279)-JUDE-17(3415)-RE-2:5■3:3

REMEMBERED-all=2142&marked -GE-8:1■19:29■30:22■42:9-EX-2:24■6:5-NU-10:9-J'G-8:34-1SA-1:19-2CH-24:22-ES-2:1■9:28-JOB-24:20-PS-45:17■77:3■78:35,39,42■98:3■105:8,42■106:7, 45■109:14,16■111:4(2143)■119:52,55■136:23■137:1-EC-9:15-IS-23:16■57:11■63:11■65:17-JER-11:19-LA-1:7■2:1-EZE-3:20■16:22,43■21:24,32■25:10■33:13 -HO-2:17-AM-1:9-JON-2:7-ZEC-13:2■ **N.T.**-all=3415&marked-M'T-26:75 -LU-22:61(5279)■24:8-JOH-2:17,22■12:16-AC-11:16-RE-18:5(3421)

REMEMBEREST-PS-88:5(2142)■ **N.T.**-M'T-5:23(3415)

REMEMBERETH-all=2142-PS-9:12■103:14-LA-1:9■**N.T.**-JOH-16:21 (3421)-2CO-7:15(363)

REMEMBERING-LA-3:19(2142)■ **N.T.**-1TH-1:3(3421)

REMEMBRANCE-all=2142,a=2143&marked-EX-17:14a-NU-5:15 -DE-25:19a■32:26a-2SA-18:18-1KI-17:18-JOB-18:17a-PS-6:5a■30:4a■34:16a■38:t■70:t■77:6■83:4■97:12a■102:12a■112:6a-EC-1:11^{2}(2146)■2:16 (2146)-IS-26:8a■43:26■57:8(2146) -LA-3:20-EZE-21:23,24■23:19,21 (6485)■29:16-MAL-3:16(2146)■ **N.T.**-all=364&marked-M'R-11:21 -LU-1:54(3415)■22:19-JOH-14:26 (5279)-AC-10:31(3415)-1CO-4:17 (363)■11:24,25-PH'P-1:3(3417)-1TH-3:6(3417)-1TI-4:6(5294)-2TI-1:3(3417),5(5280),6(363)■2:14(5279) -HEB-10:3,32(363)-2PE-1:12(5179),13 (5280),15(3418)■3:1(5280)-JUDE-5 (5179)-RE-16:19(3415)

REMEMBRANCES-JOB-13:12(2146)

REMISSION-all=859&marked -M'T-26:28-M'R-1:4-LU-1:77■3:3■24:47-AC-2:38■10:43-RO-3:25(3929) -HEB-9:22■10:18

REMIT-JOH-20:23(863)

REMITTED-JOH-20:23(863)

REMNANT-all=7611,a=3499,b=7605&marked-EX-26:12(5629)-LE-2:3(3498)■14:18(3498)-DE-3:11a■28:54a-JOS-12:4a■13:12a■23:12a-2SA-21:2a-1KI-12:23a■14:10(310)■22:46a -2KI-19:4,30(7604),31■21:14■25:11a -1CH-6:70(3498)-2CH-30:6(7604)■34:9 -EZR-3:8(7605)■9:14-NE-1:3(7604) -JOB-22:20a-IS-1:9(8300)■10:20b,21b, 22b■11:11b,16b■14:22b,30■15:9■16:14b■17:3b■37:4,31(7604),32■46:3 -JER-6:9■11:23■15:11(8293)■23:3■25:20■31:7■39:9a■40:11,15■41:16■42:2, 15,19■43:5■44:12,14,28■47:4,5-EZE-5:10■6:8(3498)■11:13■14:22(6413)■23:25(319)■25:16-JOE-2:32(8300) -AM-1:8■5:15■9:12-MIC-2:12■4:7■5:3a,7,8■7:18-HAB-2:8a-ZEP-1:4■2:7, 9a■3:13-HAG-1:12,14-ZEC-8:6,12■**N.T.**-all=3062&marked-M'T-22:6-RO-9:27 (2640)■11:5(3005)-RE-11:13■12:17■19:21

REMOVE-all=5493&marked-GE-48:17-NU-36:7(5437),9(5437)-DE-19:14 (5453)-JOS-3:3(5265)-J'G-9:29-2SA-6:10-2KI-23:27■24:3-2CH-33:8-JOB-24:2(5472)■27:5-PS-36:11(5110)■39:10■119:22(1556),29-PR-4:27■5:8(7368)■22:28(5253)■23:10(5253)■30:8(7368) -EC-11:10-IS-13:13(7493)■46:7(4185) -JER-4:1(5110)■27:10(7368)■32:31■50:3(5110),8(5110)-EZE-12:3^{2}(1540), 11(1473)■21:26■45:9-HO-5:10(5253) -JOE-2:20(7368)■3:6(7368)-MIC-2:3 (4185)-ZEC-3:9(4185)■14:4(4185)■ **N.T.**-M'T-17:20^{2}(3327)-LU-22:42 (3911)-1CO-13:2(3179)-RE-2:5(2795)

REMOVED-all=5265,a=5493& marked-GE-8:13a■12:8(6275)■13:18 (167)■26:22(6275)■30:35a■47:21(5674) -EX-8:31a■14:19■20:18(5128)-NU-12:16■21:12,13■33:5,7,9,10,11,14,16,21,24,25, 26,28,32,34,36,37,46,47-DE-28:25 (2189)-JOS-3:1,14-1SA-6:3a■18:13a -2SA-20:12(5437),13(3014)-1KI-15:12a, 13a,14a-2KI-15:4a,35a■16:17a■17:18a, 23a,26(1540)■18:4a■23:27a-1CH-8:6 (1540),7(1540)-2CH-15:16a■35:12a -JOB-14:18(6275)■18:4(6275)■19:10■36:16(5496)-PS-46:2(4171)■91:6a■103:12(7368)■104:5(4131)■125:1(4131) -PR-10:30(4131)-IS-6:12(7368)■10:13a, 31(5074)■22:25(4185)■24:20(5110)■26:15(7368)■29:13(7368)■30:20(3670)■33:20■38:12(1556)■54:10^{2}(4131)-JER-15:4(2189)■24:9(2189)■29:18(2189)■34:17(2189)-LA-1:8(5206)■3:17(2186) -EZE-7:19(5079)■23:46(2189)■36:17 (5079)-AM-6:7a-MIC-2:4(4185)■**N.T.** -M'T-21:21(142)-M'R-11:23(142)-AC-7:4(3351)■13:22(3179)-GA-1:6(3346)

REMOVETH-DE-27:17(5253) -JOB-9:5(6275)■12:20(5493)-EC-10:9 (5265)-DA-2:21(5709)

REMOVING-GE-30:32(5493) -IS-49:21(5493)-EZE-12:3(1473),4 (1473)■**N.T.**-HEB-12:27(3331)

REND-all=7167&marked-LE-10:6 (6533)■13:56■21:10(6533)-2SA-3:31 -1KI-11:11,12,13,31-2CH-34:27-EC-3:7 -IS-64:1-EZE-13:11(1234),13(1234)■29:7(1234)-HO-13:8-JOE-2:13■**N.T.** -M'T-7:6(4486)-JOH-19:24(4977)

RENDER-all=7725&marked-NU-18:9-DE-32:41,43-J'G-9:57-1SA-26:23 -2CH-6:30(5415)-JOB-33:26■34:11 (7999)-PS-28:4■38:20(7999)■56:12 (7999)■79:12■94:2■116:12-PR-24:12, 29■26:16-IS-66:15-JER-51:6(7999), 24(7999)-LA-3:64-HO-14:2(7999)-JOE-3:4(7999)-ZEC-9:12■**N.T.**-all=591& marked-M'T-21:41■22:21-M'R-12:17 -LU-20:25-RO-2:6■13:7-1CO-7:3 -1TH-3:9(467)■5:15

RENDERED-all=7725-J'G-9:56 -2KI-3:4-2CH-32:25-PR-12:14

RENDEREST-PS-62:12(7999)

RENDERETH-IS-66:6(7999)

RENDERING-1PE-3:9(591)

RENDING-PS-7:2(6561)

RENEW-all=2318&marked-1SA-11:14-PS-51:10-IS-40:31(2498)■41:1 (2498)-LA-5:21■**N.T.**-HEB-6:6(340)

RENEWED-2CH-15:8(2318) -JOB-29:20(2498)-PS-103:5(2318)■ **N.T.**-2CO-4:16(341)-EPH-4:23(365) -COL-3:10(341)

RENEWEST-JOB-10:17(2318) -PS-104:30(2318)

RENEWING-RO-12:2(342)-TIT-3:5(342)

RENOUNCED-2CO-4:2(550)

RENOWN-all=8034-GE-6:4-NU-16:2-EZE-16:14,15■34:29■39:13-DA-9:15

RENOWNED-all=7121&marked -NU-1:16-IS-14:20-EZE-23:23■26:17(1984)

RENT-all=7167&marked-GE-37:29, 33(2963),34■44:13-EX-28:32-LE-13:45 (6533)-NU-14:6-JOS-7:6■9:4(1234),13 (1234)-J'G-11:35■14:6^{2}(8156)-1SA-4:12■15:27,28■28:17-2SA-1:2,11■13:19,31■15:32-1KI-1:40(1234),11:30■13:3,5■14:8■19:11(6561)■21:27-2KI-2:12■5:7, 8^{2}■6:30■11:14■17:21■18:37■19:1■22:11,19-2CH-23:13■34:19-EZR-9:3,5 -ES-4:1-JOB-1:20■2:12■26:8(1234) -IS-3:24(5364)■36:22■37:1-JER-36:24■41:5-EZE-30:16(1234)■**N.T.**-all=4977&marked-M'T-9:16(4978)■26:65 (1284)■27:51^{2}-M'R-2:21(4978)■9:26 (4682)■14:63(1284)■15:38-LU-5:36■23:45-AC-14:14(1284)■16:22(4048)

RENTEST-JER-4:30(7167)

REPAIR-all=2388&marked-2KI-12:5,7,8,12,12(2393)■22:5,6-2CH-24:4 (2318),5,12(2318)■34:8,10(918)-EZR-

9:9(5975)-IS-61:4(2318)

REPAIRED-all=2388&marked-J'G-21:23(1129)-1KI-11:27(5462)■18:30(7495)-2KI-12:6,14-1CH-11:8(2421)-2CH-29:3■32:5■33:16(1129)-NE-3:4^{3},5,6,7,8^{2},9,10^{2},11,12,13,14,15,16,17^{2},18,19,20,21,22,23^{2},24,27,28,29^{2},30^{2},31,32

REPAIRER-IS-58:12(1443)

REPAIRING-2CH-24:27(3247)

REPAY-all=7999&marked-DE-7:10-JOB-21:31■41:11-IS-59:18^{2}■N.T.-LU-10:35(591)-RO-12:19(467)-PH'M-19(661)

REPAYED-PR-13:21(7999)

REPAYETH-DE-7:10(7999)

REPEATETH-PR-17:9(8138)

REPENT-all=5162&marked-EX-13:17■32:12-NU-23:19-DE-32:36-1SA-15:29^{2}-1KI-8:47(7725)-JOB-42:6-PS-90:13■110:4■135:14-JER-4:28■18:8,10■26:3,13■42:10-EZE-14:6(7725)■18:30(7725)■24:14-JOE-2:14-JON-3:9■N.T.-all=3340&marked-M'T-3:2■4:17-M'R-1:15■6:12-LU-13:3,5■16:30■17:3,4-AC-2:38■3:19■8:22■17:30-2CO-7:8(3338)-HEB-7:21(3338)-RE-2:5^{2},16,21,22■3:3,19

REPENTANCE-HO-13:14(5164)■N.T.-all=3341&marked-M'T-3:8,11■9:13-M'R-1:4■2:17-LU-3:3,8■5:32■15:7■24:47-AC-5:31■11:18■13:24■19:4■20:21■26:20-RO-2:4■11:29(278)-2CO-7:9,10-2TI-2:25-HEB-6:1,6■12:17-2PE-3:9

REPENTED-all=5162&marked-GE-6:6-EX-32:14-J'G-2:18■21:6,15-1SA-15:35-2SA-24:16-1CH-21:15-PS-106:45-JER-8:6■20:16■26:19■31:19-AM-7:3,6-JON-3:10-ZEC-8:14■N.T.-all=3340&marked-M'T-11:20,21■12:41■21:29(3338),32(3338)■27:3(3338)-LU-10:13■11:32-2CO-7:10(278)■12:21-RE-2:21■9:20,21■16:9,11

REPENTEST-JON-4:2(5162)

REPENTETH-all=5162&marked-GE-6:7-IS-15:11-JOE-2:13■N.T.-LU-15:7(3340),10(3340)

REPENTING-JER-15:6(5162)

REPENTINGS-HO-11:8(5150)

REPETITIONS-M'T-6:7(945)

REPLENISH-GE-1:28(4390)■9:1(4390)

REPLENISHED-all=4390-IS-2:6■23:2-JER-31:25-EZE-26:2■27:25

REPLIEST-RO-9:20(470)

REPORT-all=8088&marked-GE-37:2(1681)-EX-23:1-NU-13:32(1681)■14:37(1681)-DE-2:25-1SA-2:24(8052)-1KI-10:6(1697)-2CH-9:5(1697)-NE-6:13(8034)-PR-15:30(8052)-IS-23:5^{2}■28:19(8052)■53:1(8052)-JER-20:10(5046)■50:43■N.T.-all=3140-JOH-12:38(189)-AC-6:3■10:22■22:12-RO-10:16(189)-1CO-14:25(518)-2CO-6:8(1426),8(2162)-PH'P-4:8(2163)-1TI-3:7(3141)-HEB-11:2,39-3JO-12

REPORTED-NE-6:6(8085),7(8085),19(559)-ES-1:17(559)-EZE-9:11(7725)■N.T.-M'T-28:15(1310)-AC-4:23(518)■16:2(3140)-RO-3:8(987)-1CO-5:1(191)-1TI-5:10(3140)-1PE-1:12(312)

REPROACH-all=2781&marked-GE-30:23■34:14-JOS-5:9-RU-2:15(3637)-1SA-11:2■17:26■25:39-2KI-19:4(2778),16(2778)-NE-1:3■2:17■4:4■5:9■6:13(2778)-JOB-19:5■20:3(3639)■27:6(2778)-PS-15:3■22:6■31:11■39:8■42:10(2778)■44:13■57:3(2778)■69:7,10,19,20■71:13■74:10(2778)■78:66■79:4,12■89:41,50,50sup■102:8(2778)■109:25■119:22,39-PR-6:33■14:34(2617)■18:3■19:26(2659)■22:10(7036)-IS-4:1■30:5■37:4(2778),17(2778)■51:7■54:4-JER-6:10■20:8■23:40■24:9■29:18■31:19■42:18■44:8,12■49:13■51:51-LA-3:30,61■5:1-EZE-5:14,15■16:57■21:28■22:4■36:15,30-DA-9:16■11:18^{2}-HO-12:14-JOE-2:17,19-MIC-6:16-ZEP-2:8■3:18■N.T.-all=3680&marked-LU-1:25(3681)■6:22(3679)-2CO-11:21(819)-1TI-3:7■4:10(3679)-HEB-11:26■13:13

REPROACHED-all=2778&marked-2KI-19:22,23-JOB-19:3(3637)-PS-55:12■69:9■74:18■79:12■89:51^{2}-IS-37:23,24-ZEP-2:8,10■N.T.-RO-15:3(3679)-1PE-4:14(3679)

REPROACHES-PS-69:9(2781)-IS-43:28(1421)-RO-15:3(3679)2CO-12:10(5196)-HEB-10:33(3680)

REPROACHEST-LU-11:45(5195)

REPROACHETH-all=2778&marked-NU-15:30(1442)-PS-44:16■74:22(2781)■119:42-PR-14:31■17:5■27:11

REPROACHFULLY-JOB-16:10(2781)-1TI-5:14(5484,3059)

REPROBATE-JER-6:30(3988)■N.T.-all=96-RO-1:28-2TI-3:8-TIT-1:16

REPROBATES-all=96-2CO-13:5,6,7

REPROOF-all=8433&marked-JOB-26:11(1606)-PR-1:23,25,30■5:12■10:17■12:1■13:18■15:5,10,31,32■17:10(1606)■29:15(8433)■N.T.-2TI-3:16(1650)

REPROOFS-PS-38:14(8433)-PR-6:23(8433)

REPROVE-all=3198-2KI-19:4-JOB-6:25,26■13:10■22:4-PS-50:8,21■141:5-PR-9:8■19:25■30:6-IS-11:3,4■37:4-JER-2:19-HO-4:4■N.T.-all=1651-JOH-16:8-EPH-5:11-2TI-4:2

REPROVED-all=3198&marked-GE-20:16■21:25-1CH-16:21-PS-105:14-PR-29:1(8433)-JER-29:27(1605)-HAB-2:1(8433)■N.T.-all=1651-LU-3:19-JOH-3:20-EPH-5:13

REPROVER-PR-25:12(3198)-EZE-3:26(3198)

REPROVETH-all=3198&marked-JOB-40:2-PR-9:7(3256)■15:12-IS-29:21

REPUTATION-EC-10:1(3368)■N.T.-AC-5:34(5093)-GA-2:2(1380)-PH'P-2:7(2758),29(1784)

REPUTED-DA-4:35(2804)

REQUEST-all=1246&marked-J'G-8:24(7596)-2SA-14:15(1697),22(1697)-EZR-7:6-NE-2:4(1245)-ES-4:8(1245)■5:3,6,7,8■7:2,3,7(1245)■9:12-JOB-6:8(7596)-PS-21:2(782)■106:15(7596)■N.T.-RO-1:10(1189)-PH'P-1:4(1162)

REQUESTED-all=7592&marked-J'G-8:26-1KI-19:4-1CH-4:10-DA-1:8(1245)■2:49(1156)

REQUESTS-PH'P-4:6(155)

REQUIRE-all=1875&marked-GE-9:5^{3}■31:39(1245)■43:9(1245)-DE-10:12(7592)■18:19■23:21-JOS-22:23(1245)-1SA-20:16(1245)-2SA-3:13(7592)■4:11(1245)■19:38(977)-1KI-8:59(3117)-1CH-21:3(1245)-2CH-24:22-EZR-7:21(7593)■8:22(7592)-NE-5:12(1245)-PS-10:13-EZE-3:18(1245),20(1245)■20:40■33:6,8(1245)■34:10-MIC-6:8■N.T.-1CO-1:22(154)■7:36(1096)

REQUIRED-all=7592&marked-GE-42:22(1875)-1SA-21:8(1961)-2SA-12:20-1CH-16:37(3117)-2CH-8:14(3117)■24:6(1875)-EZR-3:4(3117)-NE-5:18(1245)-ES-2:15(1245)-PS-40:6■137:3,3sup-PR-30:7-IS-1:12(1245)■N.T.-LU-11:50(1567),51(1567)■12:20(523),48(2212)■19:23(4238)■23:24(155)-1CO-4:2(2212)

REQUIREST-RU-3:11(559)

REQUIRETH-EC-3:15(1245)-DA-2:11(7593)

REQUIRING-LU-23:23(154)

REQUITE-all=7999&marked-GE-50:15(7725)-DE-32:6(1580)-2SA-2:6(6213)■16:12(7725)-2KI-9:26-PS-10:14(5414)■41:10-JER-51:56■N.T.-1TI-5:4(287,591)

REQUITED-J'G-1:7(7999)-1SA-25:21(7725)

REQUITING-2CH-6:23(7725)

REREWARD-all=622&marked-NU-10:25-JOS-6:9,13-1SA-29:2(314)-IS-52:12■58:8

RESCUE-DE-28:31(3467)-PS-35:17(7725)-HO-5:14(5337)

RESCUED-1SA-14:45(6299)■30:18(5337)■N.T.-AC-23:27(1807)

RESCUETH-DA-6:27(5338)

RESEMBLANCE-ZEC-5:6(5869)

RESEMBLE-LU-13:18(3666)

RESEMBLED-J'G-8:18(8389)

RESERVE-JER-3:5(5201)■50:20(7604)■N.T.-2PE-2:9(5083)

RESERVED-all=3498&marked-GE-27:36(680)-J'G-21:22(3947)-RU-2:18-2SA-8:4-1CH-18:4-JOB-21:30(2820)■38:23(2820)■N.T.-all=5083&marked-AC-25:21-RO-11:4(2641)-1PE-1:4-2PE-2:4,17■3:7-JUDE-6,13

RESERVETH-JER-5:24(8104)-NA-1:2(5201)

RESIDUE-all=7611&marked-EX-10:5(3499)-NE-11:20(7605)-IS-21:17(7605)■28:5(7605)■38:10(3499)■44:17,19(3499)-JER-8:3■15:9■24:8■27:19(3499)■29:1(3499)■39:3■41:10■52:15(3499)-EZE-9:8■23:25(319)■34:18(3499),18(3498)■36:3,4,5■48:18(3498),21(3498)-DA-7:7(7606),19(7606)-ZEP-2:9-HAG-2:2-ZEC-8:11■14:2(3499)-MAL-2:15(7605)■N.T.-M'R-16:13(3062)-AC-15:17(2645)

RESIST-ZEC-3:1(7853)■N.T.-all=436&marked-M'T-5:39-LU-21:15-AC-6:10■7:51(496)-RO-13:2-2TI-3:8-JAS-4:7■5:6(498)-1PE-5:9

RESISTED-RO-9:16(436)-HEB-12:4(478)

RESISTETH-all=498&marked-RO-13:2,2(436)-JAS-4:6-1PE-5:5

RESOLVED-LU-16:4(1097)

RESORT-NE-4:20(6908)-PS-71:3(935)■N.T.-M'R-10:1(4848)-JOH-18:20(4905)

RESORTED-2CH-11:13(3320)■N.T.-M'R-2:13(2064)-JOH-10:41(2064)■18:2(4863)-AC-16:13(4905)

RESPECT-all=6437&marked-GE-4:4(8159),5(8159)-EX-2:25(3045)-LE-19:15(5375)■26:9-NU-16:15-DE-1:17(5234)■16:19(5234)-2SA-14:14(5375)-1KI-8:28-2KI-13:23-2CH-6:19■19:7(4856)-PS-74:20(5027)■119:6(5027),15(5027),117(8159)■138:6(7200)-PR-24:23(5234)■28:21(5234)-IS-17:7(7200),8(7200)■22:11(7200)■N.T.-all=4382&marked-RO-2:11-2CO-3:10(3313)-EPH-6:9-PH'P-4:11(2596)-COL-2:16(3313)■3:25-HEB-11:26(578)-JAS-2:1,3(1914),9(4380)-1PE-1:17(678)

RESPECTED-LA-4:16(5375)

RESPECTER-AC-10:34(4381)

RESPECTETH-JOB-37:34(7200)-PS-40:4(6437)

RESPITE-EX-8:15(7309)-1SA-11:3(7503)

REST-all=3499,a=5117,&marked-GE-8:9(4494)■18:4(8172)■30:36(3498)■49:15(4496)-EX-5:5(7673)■16:23(7677)■23:11(8058),12(7673),12a■28:10(3498)■31:15(7677)■33:14a■34:21^{2}(7673)■35:2(7677)-LE-5:9(7604)■14:17,29(3498)■16:31(7677)■23:3(7677),32(7677)■25:4(7677),5(7677)■26:34(7673),35^{2}(7673)-NU-31:32-DE-3:13,20a■5:14a■12:9(4496),10a■25:19a■28:65(4494)-JOS-1:13a,15a■3:13a■10:20(8300)■13:27■14:15(8252)■17:2(3498),6(3498)■21:5(3498),34(3498),44a■22:4a■23:1a-J'G-3:11(8252),30(8252)■5:31(8252)■7:6-RU-1:9(4496)■3:1(4494),18(8252)-1SA-13:2■15:15(3498)-2SA-3:29(2342)■7:1a,11a■10:10■12:28■21:10a-1KI-5:4a■8:56(4496)■11:41■14:19,29■15:7,23,31■16:5,14,20,27■20:30(3498)■22:39,45-2KI-1:18■2:15a■4:7(3498)■8:23■10:34■12:19■13:8,12■14:15,18,28■15:6,11,15,21,26,31,36■16:19■20:20■21:17,25■23:28■24:5■25:11-1CH-4:43(7611)■6:31(4494),77(3498)■11:8(7605)■12:38(7611)■16:41(7605)■19:11■22:9(4496),9a,18a■23:25a■24:20(3498)■28:2(4496)-2CH-9:29(7605)■13:22■14:6(8252),6a,7a,11(8172)■15:15a■20:30a,34■24:14(7605)■25:26■26:22■27:7■28:26■32:32■

33:18■35:26■36:8-EZR-4:3(7605),7(7605),9(7606),10^{2}(7606),17^{2}(7606)■6:16(7606)■7:18(7606)-NE-2:16■4:14,19■6:1,11■7:72(7611)■9:28a■10:28(7605)■11:1(7605)-ES-9:12(7605),16(5118)-JOB-3:13a,17a,18(7599),26(8252)■11:18(7901)■14:6(2308)■17:16(5183)■30:17(7901)PS-16:9(7931)■17:14■37:7(1826)■38:3(7965)■55:6(7931)■94:13(8252)■95:11(4496)■116:7(4496)■125:3a■132:8(4496),14(4496)-PR-29:9(5183),17a-EC-6:5(5183)-SONG-1:7(7257)-IS-7:19a■10:19(7605)■11:2a,10(3499)■14:3a,7a■18:4(8252)■23:12a■25:10a■28:12(4496)12a■30:15(5183)■34:14(7280),14(4494)■51:4(7280)■57:2a,20(8252)■62:1(8252),7(1824)■63:14a■66:1(4496)-JER-6:16(4771)■30:10(8252)■31:2(7280)■39:9■45:3(4496)■46:27(8252)■47:6(7280)■50:34■52:15-LA-1:3(4494)■2:18(6314)■5:5a-EZE-5:13■16:42■21:17■24:13■38:11(8252)■44:30a■48:23-DA-2:18(7606)■4:4(7954)■7:12(7606)■12:13a-MIC-2:10(4496)-HAB-3:16a-ZEP-3:17(2790)-ZEC-1:11(8252)■9:1(4496)■11:9(7604)■N.T.-all=3062&marked-M'T-11:28(373),29(372)■12:43(372)■26:45(373)■27:49-M'R-6:31(373)■14:41(373)-LU-10:6(1879)■11:24(372)■12:26■24:9-JOH-11:13(2838)-AC-2:26(2681),37■5:13■7:49(2663)■9:31(1515)■27:44-RO-11:7-1CO-7:12■11:34-2CO-2:13(425)■7:5(425)■12:9(1981)-2TH-1:7(425)-HEB-3:11(2663),18(2663)■4:1(2663),3^{2}(2663),4(2664),5(2663),8(2664),9(4520),10(2663),11(2663)-1PE-4:2(1954)-RE-2:24■4:8(2192,372)■6:11(373)■9:20■14:11(372),13(373)■20:5

RESTED-all=5117&marked-GE-2:2(7673),3(7673)■8:4-EX-10:14■16:30(7673)■20:11■31:17(7673)-NU-9:18(2583),23(2583)■10:12(7931),36■11:25,26-JOS-11:23(8252)-1KI-6:10(270)-2CH-32:8(5564)-ES-9:17(5118),18(5118),22-JOB-30:27(1826)■N.T.-LU-23:56(2270)

RESTEST-RO-2:17(1879)

RESTETH-JOB-24:23(8172)-PR-14:33(5117)-EC-7:9(5117)■N.T.-1PE-4:14(378)

RESTING-NU-10:33(4496)-2CH-6:41(5118)-PR-24:15(7258)-IS-32:18(4496)

RESTINGPLACE-JER-50:6(7258)

RESTITUTION-all=7999&marked-EX-22:3,5,6,12-JOB-20:18(8545)■N.T.-AC-3:21(605)

RESTORE-all=7725&marked-GE-20:7^{2}■40:13■42:25-EX-22:1(7999),4(7999)-LE-6:4,5(7999)■24:21(7999)■25:27,28-NU-35:25-DE-22:2-J'G-11:13■17:3-1SA-12:3-2SA-9:7■12:6(7999)■16:3-1KI-20:34-2KI-8:6-NE-5:11,12-JOB-20:10,18-PS-51:12-PR-6:31(7999)-IS-1:26■42:22■49:6■57:18(7999)-JER-27:22■30:17(5927)-EZE-33:15-DA-9:25-JOE-2:25(7999)■N.T.-M'T-17:11(600)-LU-19:8(591)-AC-1:6(600)-GA-6:1(2675)

RESTORED-all=7725&marked-GE-20:14■40:21■41:13■42:28-DE-28:31-J'G-17:3,4-1SA-7:14-1KI-13:6^{2}-2KI-8:1(2421),5^{3}(2421)■14:22,25-2CH-8:2(5414)■26:2-EZR-6:5(8421)-PS-69:4-EZE-18:7,12■N.T.-all=600-M'T-12:13-M'R-3:5■8:25-LU-6:10-HEB-13:19

RESTORER-RU-4:15(7725)-IS-58:12(7725)

RESTORETH-PS-23:3(7725)■N.T.-M'R-9:12(600)

RESTRAIN-JOB-15:8(1639)-PS-76:10(2296)

RESTRAINED-GE-8:2(3607)■11:6(1219)■16:2(6113)-EX-36:6(3607)-IS-3:13(3543)-IS-63:15(662)-EZE-31:15(4513)■N.T.-AC-14:18(2664)

RESTRAINEST-JOB-15:4(1639)

RESTRAINT-1SA-14:6(4622)

RESTS-all supplied

RESURRECTION-all=386&marked-M'T-22:23,28,30,31■27:53(1454)-M'R-12:18,23-LU-14:14■20:27,33,35,36-JOH-5:29^{2}■11:24,25-AC-1:22■2:31■4:2,33■17:18,32■23:6,8■24:15,21-RO-1:4■6:5-1CO-15:12,13,21,42-PH'P-3:10,11(1815)-2TI-2:18-HEB-6:2■11:35-1PE-1:3■3:21-RE-20:5,6

RETAIN-JOB-2:9(2388)-PR-4:4(8551)■11:16(8551)-EC-8:8(3607)-DA-11:6(6113)■N.T.-JOH-20:23(2902)-RO-1:28(2192)

RETAINED-J'G-7:8(2388)■19:4(2388)-DA-10:8(6113),16(6113)■N.T.-JOH-20:33(2902)-PH'M-13(2722)

RETAINETH-PR-3:18(8551)■11:16(8551)-MIC-7:18(2388)

RETIRE-2SA-11:15(7725)-JER-4:6(5756)

RETIRED-J'G-20:39(2015)-2SA-20:22(6327)

RETURN-all=7725&marked-GE-3:19^{2}■14:17■16:9■18:10,14■31:3,13■32:9-EX-4:18,19,21■13:17-LE-25:10^{2},13,27,28,41^{2}■27:24-NU-10:36■14:3,4■23:5■32:18,22■35:28-DE-3:20■17:16^{2}■20:5,6,7,8■30:2,3,8-JOS-1:15■20:6■22:4(6437),8-J'G-7:3■11:31-RU-1:6,7,8,10,15,16-1SA-6:3,4,8■7:3,17(8666)■9:5■15:26■26:21■29:4,7,11-2SA-2:26■3:16■10:5■12:23■15:19,20,27,34■19:14■24:13-1KI-2:32,33,44■8:48■12:24,26■13:16■19:15■20:22(8666),26(8666)■22:17,28-2KI-18:14■19:7,33■20:10-1CH-19:5-2CH-6:24,38■10:6,9■11:4■18:16,26,27■30:6,9-NE-2:6■4:12■9:17-ES-4:15■9:25-JOB-1:21■6:29^{2}■7:10■10:21■15:22■16:22■17:10■22:23■33:25■36:10■39:4-PS-6:4,10■7:7,16■59:6,14■73:10■74:21■80:14■90:3,13■94:15■104:29■116:7-PR-2:19■26:27-EC-1:7■5:15■12:2,7^{2}-SONG-6:13^{2}-IS-6:13■10:21,22■19:22■21:12■35:10■37:7,34■44:22■45:23■51:11■55:7,11■63:17-JER-3:1^{7},12,22■4:1^{2}■5:3■8:4■15:7,19^{3}■18:11■22:10,11,27^{2}■23:14,20■24:7■29:10■30:3,10,24■31:8■32:44■33:7,11,26■34:11,16,22■35:15■36:3,7■37:7,20■38:26■42:12■44:14^{3},28■46:27■50:9-EZE-7:13^{2}■13:22■16:55^{3}■18:23■21:5,30■29:14■35:9(3427)■46:9,17■47:6-DA-10:20■11:9,10,13,28^{2},29,30^{2}-HO-2:7,9■3:5■5:15■6:1■7:10,16■8:13■9:3■11:5^{2},9■12:14■14:1,7-JOE-2:14■3:4,7-OB-15-MIC-1:7■5:3-MAL-1:4■3:7^{2},18■N.T.-all=1994&marked-M'T-2:12(844)■10:13■12:44■24:18-LU-8:39(5290)■11:24(5290)■12:36(360)■17:31■19:12(5290)-AC-13:34(5290)■15:16(390)■18:21(344)■20:3(5290)

RETURNED-all=7725&marked-GE-8:3,9,12■14:7■18:33■21:32■22:19■31:55■32:6■33:16■37:29,30■38:22■42:24■43:10,18■44:13■50:14-EX-4:18,20■5:22■14:27,28■19:8■32:31■34:31-LE-22:13-NU-13:25■14:36■16:50■23:6■24:25-DE-1:45-JOS-2:16,22,23■4:18■6:14■7:3■8:24■10:15,21,38,43■22:9,32-J'G-2:19■5:29■7:3,15■8:13■11:39■14:8■21:23-RU-1:22^{2}-1SA-1:19■6:16,17■17:15,53,57■18:6■23:28■24:1■25:39■26:25■27:9-2SA-1:1,22■2:30■3:16,27■6:20■8:13■10:14■11:4■12:31■14:24(5437)■16:8■17:3,20■18:16■19:15,39■20:22■23:10-1KI-12:24■13:10,33■19:21-2KI-2:25■3:27■4:35■5:15■7:15■8:3■9:15■14:14■19:8,36■23:20-1CH-16:43(5437)■20:3-2CH-10:2■11:4■14:15■19:1,8■20:27■22:6■25:10,24■28:15■31:1■32:21■34:7,9-EZR-5:5(8421),11(8421)-NE-2:15■4:15■9:28-ES-2:14■7:8-PS-35:13■60:t■78:34-EC-4:1,7■9:11-IS-37:8,37■38:8-JER-3:7■14:3■40:12■41:14■43:5-EZE-1:14■8:17■47:7-DA-4:34,36^{2}-HO-6:11-AM-4:6,8,9,10,11-ZEC-1:6,16■7:14■8:3■N.T.-all=5290&marked-M'T-21:18(1877)-M'R-14:40-LU-1:56■2:20(1994),39,43■4:1,14■8:37,40■9:10■10:17■17:18■19:15(1880)■23:48,56■24:9,33,52-AC-1:12■5:22(390)■8:25■12:25■13:13■14:21■21:6■23:32-GA-1:17-HEB-11:15(344)-1PE-2:25(1994)

RETURNETH-all=7725&marked-PS-146:4-PR-26:11,11(8138)-EC-1:6-IS-55:10-EZE-35:7-EZE-9:8

RETURNING-IS-30:15(7729)■N.T.-all=5290-LU-7:10-AC-8:28-HEB-7:1

REVEAL-JOB-20:27(1540)-JER-33:6(1540)-DA-2:47(1541)■N.T.-all=601-M'T-11:27-LU-10:22-GA-1:16-PH'P-3:15

REVEALED-all=1540&marked-DE-29:29-1SA-3:7,21-2SA-7:27-IS-22:14■23:1■40:5■53:1■56:1-JER-11:20-DA-2:19(1541),30(1541)■10:1■N.T.-all=601&marked-M'T-10:26■11:25■16:17-LU-2:26(5537),35■10:21■12:2■17:30-JOH-12:38-RO-1:17,18■8:18-1CO-2:10■2:13■14:30-GA-3:23-EPH-3:5-2TH-1:7(602)■2:3,6,8-1PE-1:5,12■4:13(602)■5:1

REVEALER-DA-2:47(1541)

REVEALETH-all=1540&marked-PR-11:13■20:19-DA-2:22(1541),28(1541),29(1541)-AM-3:7

REVELATION-all=602-RO-2:5■16:25-1CO-14:6,26-GA-1:12■2:2-EPH-1:17■3:3-1PE-1:13-RE-1:t,1

REVELATIONS-2CO-12:1(602),7(602)

REVELLINGS-GA-5:21(2970)-1PE-4:3(2970)

REVENGE-JER-15:15(5358)■20:10(5360)-EZE-25:15(5360)■N.T.-2CO-7:11(1557)■10:6(1556)

REVENGED-EZE-25:12(5358)

REVENGER-all=1350-NU-35:19,21,24,25,27^{2}■N.T.-RO-13:4(1558)

REVENGERS-2SA-14:11(1350)

REVENGES-DE-32:42(6546)

REVENGETH-NA-1:2^{2}(5358)

REVENGING-PS-79:10(5360)

REVENUE-EZE-4:13(674)-PR-8:19(8393)-IS-23:3(8393)

REVENUES-all=8393-PR-15:6■16:8-JER-12:13

REVERENCE-all=7812&marked-LE-19:30(3372)■26:2(3372)-2SA-9:6-1KI-1:31-ES-3:2,5-PS-89:7(3372)■N.T.-all=1788&marked-M'T-21:37-M'R-12:6-LU-20:13-EPH-5:33(5399)-HEB-12:9,28(127)

REVERENCED-ES-3:2(7812)

REVEREND-PS-111:9(3372)

REVERSE-all=7725&marked-NU-23:20-ES-8:5,8

REVILE-EX-22:28(7043)■N.T.-M'T-5:11(3679)

REVILED-all=3058&marked-M'T-27:39(987)-M'R-15:32(3679)-JOH-9:28-1CO-4:12-1PE-2:23,23(486)

REVILERS-1CO-6:10(3060)

REVILEST-AC-23:4(3058)

REVILINGS-IS-51:7(1421)-ZEP-2:8(1421)

REVIVE-all=2421&marked-NE-4:2-PS-85:6■138:7-IS-57:15^{2}-HO-6:2■14:7-HAB-3:2

REVIVED-all=2421-GE-45:27-J'G-15:19-1KI-17:22-2KI-13:21■N.T.-RO-7:9(326)■14:9(326)

REVIVING-EZR-9:8(4241),9(4241)

REVOLT-2CH-21:10(6586)-IS-1:5(5627)■59:13(5627)

REVOLTED-all=6586&marked-2KI-8:20,22^{2}-2CH-21:8,10-IS-31:6(5627)-JER-5:23(5493)

REVOLTERS-JER-6:28(5637)-HO-5:2(7846)■9:15(5637)

REVOLTING-JER-5:23(5637)

REWARD-all=7939&marked-GE-

15:1-NU-18:31-DE-10:17(7810)■27:25 (7810)■32:41(7999)-RU-2:12(4909) -1SA-24:19(7999)-2SA-3:39(7999)■4:10 (1309)■19:36(1578)-1KI-13:7(4991) -2CH-20:11(1580)-JOB-6:22(7809) -PS-15:5(7810)■19:11(6118)■40:15 (6118)■54:5(7725)■58:11(6529)■70:3 (6118)■91:8(8011)■94:2(1576)■109:20 (6468)■127:3-PR-11:18(7938)■21:14 (7810)■24:14(319),20(319)■25:22(7999)-EC-4:9■9:5-IS-3:11(1576)■5:23 (7810)■40:10■45:13(7810)■62:11 -JER-0:5(4864)-EZE-16:34^{2}(868)-HO-4:9(7725)■9:1(868)-OB-15(1576)-MIC-3:11(7810)■7:3(7966)■N.T.-all=3408 &marked-M'T-5:12,46■6:1,2,4(591), 5,6(591),16,18(591)■10:41^{2},42■16:27 (591)-M'R-9:41-LU-6:23,35■23:41 (514)-AC-1:18-RO-4:4-1CO-3:8,14■ 9:17,18-COL-2:18(2603)■3:24(469) -1TI-5:18-2TI-4:14(591)-HEB-2:2 (3405)■10:35(3405)■11:26(3405)-2PE-2:13-2JO-8-JUDE-11-RE-11:18■18:6 (591)■22:12

REWARDED-all=1580&marked -GE-44:4(7999)-1SA-24:17^{2}-2SA-22:21 -2CH-15:7(7939)-PS-7:4■18:20■35:12 (7999)■103:10■109:5(7760)-PR-13:13 (7999)-IS-3:9-JER-31:16(7939)■ N.T.-RE-18:6(591)

REWARDER-HEB-11:6(3406)

REWARDETH-all=7999&marked -JOB-21:19-PS-31:32■137:8-PR-17:13 (7725)■26:10^{2}(7936)

REWARDS-IS-1:23(8021)-DA-2:6(5023)■5:17(5023)-HO-2:12(866)

RIB-GE-2:22(6763)

RIBBAND-NU-15:38(6616)

RIBS-GE-2:21(6763)-DA-7:5(5967)

RICH-all=6223,a=6238&marked -GE-13:2(3513)■14:23(6238)-EX-30:15 -LE-25:47(5381)-RU-3:10-1SA-2:7a -2SA-12:1,2,4-JOB-15:29a■27:19■34:19 (7771)-PS-45:12■49:2,16a-PR-10:4a, 15,22a■13:7a■14:20■18:11,23■21:17a■ 22:2,7,16■23:4a■28:6,11,20a,22(1952) -EC-5:12■10:6,20-IS-53:9-JER-5:27a■ 9:23-HO-12:8a-MIC-6:12-ZEC-11:5a■ N.T.-all=4145&marked-M'T-9:23,24■ 27:57-M'R-10:25■12:41-LU-1:53(4147)■ 6:24■12:16,21(4147)■14:12■16:1,19, 21,22■18:23,25■19:2■21:1-RO-10:12 (4147)-1CO-4:8(4147)-2CO-6:10 (4148)■8:9,9(4147)-EPH-2:4-1TI-6:9 (4147),17,18(4147)-JAS-1:10,11■ 2:5,6■5:1-RE-2:9■3:17,18(4147)■6:15■ 13:16■18:3(4147),15(4147),19(4147)

RICHER-DA-11:2(6238)

RICHES-all=6239,a=2428&marked -GE-31:16■36:7(7399)-JOS-22:8(5233) -1SA-17:25-1KI-3:11,13■10:23-1CH-29:12,28-2CH-1:11,12■9:22■17:5■18:1■ 20:25(7399)■32:27-ES-1:4■5:11-JOB-20:15a■36:19(7769)-PS-37:16(1995)■ 49:6■52:7■62:10a■73:12a■104:24(7075)■ 112:3■119:14(1952)-PR-3:16■8:18,18 (1952)■11:4(1952),16,28■13:7(1952), 8■14:24■19:14(1952)■22:1,4■24:4(1952)■ 27:24(2633)■30:8-EC-4:8■5:13,14■5:19■ 6:2■9:11-IS-8:4a■10:14a■30:6a■45:3 (4301)■61:6a-JER-9:23■17:11■48:36 (3502)-EZE-26:12a■27:12(1952),18 (1952),27(1952),33(1952)■28:4a,5^{2}a -DA-11:2,13(7399),24(7399),28(7399)■ N.T.-all=4149&marked-M'T-13:22 -M'R-4:19■10:23(5536),24(5536)-LU-8:14■18:24(5536)-RO-2:4■9:23■11:12^{2}, 33-2CO-8:2-EPH-1:7,18■2:7■3:8,16 -PH'P-4:19-COL-1:27■2:2-1TI-6:17 -HEB-11:26-JAS-5:2-RE-5:12■18:17

RICHLY-COL-3:16(4146)-1TI-6:17(4146)

RID-all=5337&marked-GE-37:22 -EX-6:6-LE-26:6(7673)-PS-82:4■144:7 (6475),11(6475)

RIDDANCE-LE-23:22(3615)-ZEP-1:18(3617)

RIDDEN-NU-22:30(7392)

RIDDLE-all=2420-J'G-14:12,13,14, 15,16,17,18,19-EZE-17:2

RIDE-all=7392-GE-41:43-DE-32:13 -J'G-5:10-2SA-16:2■19:26-1KI-1:33,38, 44-2KI-10:16-JOB-30:22-PS-45:4■66:12 -IS-30:16■58:14-JER-6:23■50:42-HO-10:11■14:3-HAB-3:8-HAG-2:22

RIDER-all=7392-GE-49:17-EX-15:1,21-JOB-39:18-JER-51:21^{2}-ZEC-12:4

RIDERS-all=7392-2KI-18:23-ES-8:10-IS-36:8-HAG-2:22-ZEC-10:5

RIDETH-all=7392-LE-15:9-DE-33:26-ES-6:8-PS-68:4,33-IS-19:1-AM-2:15

RIDGES-PS-65:10(8525)

RIDING-all=7392-NU-22:22-2KI-4:24-JER-17:25■22:4-EZE-23:6,12,23■ 38:15-ZEC-1:8■9:9

RIE-EX-9:32(3698)-IS-28:25(3698)

RIFLED-ZEC-14:2(8155)

RIGHT-all=3225,a=3233,b=3477& marked-GE-13:9(3231),9■18:25(4941)■ 24:48(571),49■48:13^{2},14,17,18-EX-14:22,29■15:6^{2},12,26b■29:20^{3}a,22a-LE-7:32,33■8:23^{3}a,24^{3}a,25,26■9:21■14:14^{3}a, 16a,17^{3}a,25^{3}a,27a,28^{3}a-NU-18:18■20:17■ 22:26■27:7(3651)-DE-2:27■5:32■6:18b■ 12:8b,25b,28b■13:18b■17:11,20■21:9b, 17(4941)■28:14■32:4b■33:2-JOS-1:7■ 9:25b■17:7■23:6-J'G-3:16,21■5:26■ 7:20■12:6(3651)■16:29■17:6b■21:25b -RU-4:6(1353)-1SA-6:12■11:2■12:23b -2SA-2:19,21■14:19(3231)■15:3(5228)■ 16:6■19:28(6666),43■20:9■24:5-1KI-2:19■6:8a■7:21a,39,39a,49■11:33b,38b■ 14:8b■15:5b,11b■22:19,43b-2KI-10:15b, 30b■11:11a■12:2b,9■14:3b■15:3b,34b■ 16:2b■17:9(3651)■18:3b■22:2b,2■23:13 -1CH-6:39■12:2(3231)■13:4b-2CH-3:17,17(3227)■4:6,7,8,10a■14:2b■18:18■ 20:32b■23:10a■24:2b■25:2b■26:4b■ 27:2b■28:1b■29:2b■31:20b■34:2b,2 -EZR-8:21b-NE-2:20(6666)■8:4■9:13b, 33(571)■12:31-ES-8:5(3787)-JOB-6:25 (3476)■23:9■30:12■33:27b■34:6(4941), 17(4941),35:2(4941)■36:6(4941)■40:14■ 42:7(3559),8(3559)-PS-9:4(4941),4(6664)■ 16:8,11■17:1(6664),7■18:35■19:8b■ 20:6■21:8■26:10■33:4b■44:3■45:4,6 (4334),9■46:5(6437)■48:10■51:10(3559)■ 60:5■63:8■73:23■74:11■77:10■78:37 (3559),54■80:15,17■89:13,25,42■91:7■ 98:1■107:7b■108:6■109:6,31■110:1,5■ 118:15,16^{2}■119:75(6664),128(3474)■ 121:5■137:5■138:7■139:10,14(3966)■ 140:12(4941)■142:4■144:8,11-PR-3:16■ 4:11(3476),25(5227),27■8:6(4339),9b■ 9:15(3474)■12:5(4941),15b■14:12b■ 16:8(4941),13b,25b■20:11b■21:2b,8b■ 23:16(4339)■24:6(5228)■27:16-EC-4:4 (3788)■10:2-SONG-2:6■8:3-IS-9:20■ 10:2(4941)■3:10(5229),21(541)■32:7 (4941)■41:10,13■44:20■45:1,19(4339)■ 48:13■54:3■62:8■63:12-JER-2:21(571)■ 5:28(4941)■17:11(4941),16(5227)■22:24■ 32:7(4941),8(4941)■34:15b■49:5(6440) -LA-2:3,4■3:35(4941)-EZE-1:10■4:6 (3227)■10:3■16:46■18:5(6666),19(6666), 21(6666),27(6666)■21:16(3231),22,27 (4941)■33:14(6666),16(6666),19(6666)■ 39:3■47:1(3233),2(3233)-DA-12:7-HO-14:9b-AM-3:10(5229)-JON-4:11 -HAB-2:16-ZEC-3:1■4:3,11■11:17^{2}■ 12:6■N.T.-all=1188&marked-M'T-5:29,30,39■6:3■20:4(1342),7(1342),21, 23■22:44■25:33,34■26:64■27:29,38-M'R-5:15(4993)■10:37,40■12:36■14:62■15:27■ 16:5,19-LU-1:11■6:6■8:35(4993)■10:28 (3723)■12:57(1342)■20:42■22:50,69■ 23:33-JOH-18:10■21:6-AC-2:25,33,34■ 3:7■4:19(1342)■5:31■7:55,56■8:21(2117)■ 13:10(2117)-RO-8:34-2CO-6:7-GA-2:9 -EPH-1:20■6:1(1342)-COL-3:1-HEB-1:3,13■8:1■10:12■12:2■13:10(1849) -1PE-3:22-2PE-2:15(2117)-RE-1:16,17, 20■2:1■5:1,7■10:2■13:16■22:14(1849)

RIGHTEOUS-all=6662,a=6663 marked-GE-7:1■18:23,24^{2},25^{2},26,28■ 20:4■38:26a-EX-9:27■23:7,8-NU-23:10 (3477)-DE-4:8■16:19■25:1-J'G-5:11^{2} (6666)-1SA-12:7(6666)■24:17-2SA-4:11 -1KI-2:32■8:32-2KI-10:9-2CH-6:23■ 12:6-EZR-9:15-NE-9:8-JOB-4:7■9:15a■ 10:15a■15:14a■17:9■22:3a,19■23:7 (3477)■32:1■34:5a■35:7a■36:7■40:8a -PS-1:5,6■5:12■7:9,11■11:3,5,7■14:5■ 19:9a■31:18■32:11■33:1■34:15,19,21■ 35:27(6664)■37:16,17,21,25,29,30,32,39■ 52:6■55:22■58:10,11■64:10■68:3■69:28■ 72:7■75:10■92:12■94:21■97:11,12■ 107:42(3477)■112:4,6■116:5■118:15, 20■119:7(6664),62(6664),106(6664), 137,138(6664),160(6664),164(6664)■ 125:3^{2}■129:4■140:13■141:5■142:7■ 145:17■146:8-PR-2:7(3477),20■3:32 (3477)■10:3,11,16,21,24,25,28,30,32■ 11:8,10,21,23,28,30,31■12:3,5,7,10,12, 26■13:5,9,21,25■14:9(3477),19,32■15:6, 19(3477),28,29■16:13(6664)■18:5,10■ 21:12,18,26■23:24■24:15,24■25:26■ 28:1,10(3477),12,28■29:2,6,7,16-EC-3:17■7:16■8:14■9:1,2-IS-3:10■5:23■ 24:16■26:2■41:2(6664),26■53:11■57:1^{2}■ 60:21-JER-12:1■20:12■23:5-LA-1:18 -EZE-3:20,21^{2}■13:22■16:52a■18:20, 24,26■21:3,4■23:45■33:12^{2},13,18-DA-9:14-AM-2:6-HAB-1:4,13-MAL-3:18■ N.T.-all=1342&marked-M'T-9:13■ 10:41^{2}■13:17,43■23:28,29,35^{2}■25:37,46 -M'R-2:17-LU-1:6■5:32■18:9■23:47 -JOH-7:24■17:25-RO-2:5(1341)■3:10■ 5:7,19-2TH-1:5,6-1TI-1:9-2TI-4:8-HEB-11:4-JAS-5:16-1PE-3:12■4:18-2PE-2:8^{2} -1JO-2:1,29■3:7,12-RE-16:5,7■19:2■ 2:11,11(1344)

RIGHTEOUSLY-all=6664&marked -DE-1:16-PS-67:4(4334)■96:10(4339) -PR-31:9-IS-33:15(6666)-JER-11:20■ N.T.-TIT-2:12(1346)-1PE-2:23(1346)

RIGHTEOUSNESS-all=6666, a=6664&marked-GE-15:6■30:33-LE-19:15a-DE-6:25■9:4,5,6■24:13■33:19a -1SA-26:23-2SA-22:21.25-1KI-3:6■8:32 -2CH-6:23-JOB-6:29a■8:6■27:6■ 29:14a■33:26■35:2a,8■36:3a-PS-4:1a, 5a■5:8■7:8a,17a■9:8a■11:7■15:2a■ 17:15a■18:20a,24a■22:31■23:3a■ 24:5■31:1■33:5■35:24a,28a■36:6,10■ 37:6a■40:9a,10■45:4a,7a■48:10a■50:6a■ 51:14,19a■52:3a■58:1a■65:5a■69:27■ 71:2,15,16,19,24■72:1,2a,3■85:10a,11a, 13a■88:12■89:16■94:15a■96:13a■ 97:2a,6a■98:2,9a■99:4■103:6,17■106:3, 31■111:3■112:3,9■118:19a■119:40,123a, 142,142a,144,172a■132:9a■143:1■145:7 -PR-2:9a■8:8a,18,20■10:2■11:4,5,6,18, 19■12:17a,28■13:6■14:34■15:9■16:8,12, 31■21:21^{2}■25:5a-EC-3:16a■7:15a-IS-1:21a,26a,27■5:7,16,23■10:22■11:4a, 5a■16:5a■26:9a,10a■28:17■32:1a,16, 17^{2}■33:5■41:10a■42:6a■45:8a,8,13a,19a, 23,24■46:12,13■48:1,18■51:1a,5a,6,7a, 8■54:14,17■56:1■57:12■58:2,8a■59:16, 17■60:17■61:3a,10,11■62:1a,2a■63:1■ 64:5a-JER-4:2■9:24■22:3■23:6a■33:15^{2}, 16a■51:10-EZE-3:20a,20■14:14,20■ 18:20,22,24^{2},26■33:12,13,18-DA-4:27 (6665)■9:7,16,24a■12:3(6663)-HO-2:19a■10:12,12a-AM-5:7,24■6:12-MIC-6:5■7:9-ZEP-2:3a-ZEC-8:8-MAL-3:3■4:2■N.T.-all=1343&marked-M'T-3:15■5:6,20^{2}■6:33■21:32-LU-1:75-JOH-16:8,10-AC-10:35■13:10■17:31■24:25 -RO-1:17■2:26(1345)■3:5,21,22,25,26■ 4:3,5,6,9,11^{2},13,22■5:17,18(1345),21■ 6:13,16,18,19,20■8:4(1345),10■9:28,30^{2}, 31^{2}■10:3^{3},4,5,6,10■14:17-1CO-1:30■ 15:34(1346)-2CO-3:9■5:21■6:7,14■ 9:9,10■11:15-GA-2:21■3:6,21■5:5-EPH-4:24■5:9■6:14-PH'P-1:11■3:6,9^{2}-1TI-6:11-2TI-2:22■3:16■4:8-TIT-3:5-HEB-1:8(2118),9■5:13■7:2■11:7,33■12:11 -JAS-1:20■2:23■3:18-1PE-2:24-2PE-1:1■2:5,21■3:13-1JO-2:29■3:7,10-RE-19:8(1345),11

RIGHTEOUSNESS'-PS-143:11 (6666)-IS-42:21(6664)■N.T.-M'T-5:10

(1343)-**1PE**-3:14(1343)

RIGHTEOUSNESSES-all=6666-**IS**-64:6-**EZE**-33:13-**DA**-9:18

RIGHTLY-**GE**-27:36(3588)■**N.T.**-**LU**-7:43(3723)■20:21(3723)

RIGOUR-all=6531-**EX**-1:13,14-**LE**-25:43,46,53

RING-all=2885-**GE**-41:42-**EX**-26:24■36:29-**ES**-3:10,12■8:2,8^{2},10■**N.T.**-**LU**-15:22(1146)-**JAS**-2:2(5554)

RINGLEADER-**AC**-24:5(4414)

RINGS-all=2885&marked-**EX**-25:12^{3},14,15,26^{2},27■26:29■27:4,7■28:23^{2},24,26,27,28^{2}■30:4■35:22■36:34■37:3^{3},5,13^{2},14,27■38:5,7■39:16^{2},17,19,20,21^{2}-**NU**-31:50-**ES**-1:6(1550)-**SONG**-5:14(1550)-**IS**-3:21-**EZE**-1:18^{2}(1354)

RINGSTRAKED-all=6124-**GE**-30:35,39,40■31:8^{2},10,12

RINSED-all=7857-**LE**-6:28■15:11,12

RIOT-**TIT**-1:6(810)-**1PE**-4:4(810)-**2PE**-2:13(5172)

RIOTING-**RO**-13:13(2970)

RIOTOUS-**PR**-23:20(2151)■28:7(2151)■**N.T.**-**LU**-15:13(811)

RIP-**2KI**-8:12(1234)

RIPE-**GE**-40:10(1310)-**NU**-18:13(1001)-**JOE**-3:13(1310)■**N.T.**-**RE**-14:15(3583),18(187)

RIPENING-**IS**-18:5(1580)

RIPPED-all=1234-**2KI**-15:16-**HO**-13:16-**AM**-1:13

RISE-all=6965&marked-**GE**-19:2(7952)■31:35-**EX**-8:20(7925)■9:13(7925)■12:31■21:19-**LE**-19:32-**NU**-10:35■22:20■23:18,24■24:17-**DE**-2:13,24■19:11,15,16■28:7■29:22■31:16■32:38■33:11^{2}-**JOS**-8:7■18:4-**J'G**-8:21■9:33(7925)■20:38(5927)-**1SA**-22:13■24:7■29:10(7925)-**2SA**-12:21■18:32-**2KI**-16:7-**NE**-2:18-**JOB**-20:27■30:12-**PS**-3:1■17:7■18:38,48■27:3■35:11■36:12■41:8■44:5■59:1■74:23■92:11■94:16■119:62■127:2■139:21(8618)■140:10-**PR**-24:22■28:12,28-**EC**-10:4(5927)■12:4-**SONG**-2:10■3:2-**IS**-5:11(7925)■14:21,22■24:20■26:14■28:21■32:9■33:10■43:17■54:17■58:10(2224)-**JER**-25:27■37:10■47:2(5927)■49:14■51:1,64-**LA**-1:14-**DA**-7:24(6966)-**AM**-5:2■7:9■8:8(5927),14■9:5(5927)-**OB**-1-**NA**-1:9-**HAB**-2:7-**ZEP**-3:8-**ZEC**-14:13■**N.T.**-all=1453,a=450&marked-**M'T**-5:45(393)■10:21(1881)■12:41a,42■20:19a■24:7,11■26:46■27:63-**M'R**-3:26a■4:27■8:31a■9:31a■10:34a,49■12:23a,25a,26■13:8,12(1881),22■14:42-**LU**-5:23■6:8■11:7a,8,8a,31,32a■12:54(393)■18:33a■21:10■22:46a■24:7a,46a-**JOH**-5:8■11:23a,24a■20:9a-**AC**-3:6■10:13a■26:16a,23(386)-**RO**-15:12a-**1CO**-15:15,16,29,32-**1TH**-4:16a-**HEB**-7:11a-**RE**-11:1■13:1(305)

RISEN-all=6965&marked-**GE**-19:23(3318)-**EX**-22:3(2224)-**NU**-32:14-**J'G**-9:18-**RU**-2:15-**1SA**-25:29-**2SA**-14:7-**1KI**-8:20-**2KI**-6:15-**2CH**-6:10■13:6■21:4-**PS**-20:8■27:12■54:3■86:14-**IS**-60:1(2224)-**EZE**-7:11■47:5(1342)-**MIC**-2:8■**N.T.**-all=1453&marked-**M'T**-11:11■14:2■17:9(450)■26:32■27:64■28:6,7-**M'R**-6:14,16■9:9(450)■14:28■16:6,9(450),14-**LU**-7:16■9:7,8(450),19(450)■13:25■24:6,34-**JOH**-2:22■21:14-**AC**-17:3(450)-**RO**-8:34-**1CO**-15:13,14,20-**COL**-2:12(4891)■3:1(4891)-**JAS**-1:11(393)

RISEST-**DE**-6:7(6965)■11:19(6965)

RISETH-all=6965&marked-**DE**-22:26-**JOS**-6:26-**2SA**-23:4(2224)-**JOB**-9:7(2224)■14:12■24:22■27:7■31:14-**PR**-24:16■31:15-**IS**-47:11(7873)-**JER**-46:8(5927)-**MIC**-7:6■**N.T.**-**JOH**-13:4(1453)

RISING-all=7925&marked-**LE**-13:2(7613),10^{2}(7613),19(7613),28(7613),43(7613)■14:56(7613)-**NU**-2:3(4217)-**JOS**-12:1(4217)-**2CH**-36:15-**NE**-4:21(5927)-**JOB**-16:8(6965)■24:5(7836),14(6965)-**PS**-50:1(4217)■113:3(4217)-**PR**-27:14■30:31(510)-**IS**-41:25(4217)■45:6(4217)■59:19(4217)■60:3(2225)-**JER**-7:13,25■11:7■25:3,4■26:5■29:19■32:33■35:14,15■44:4-**LA**-3:63(7012)-**MAL**-1:11(4217)■**N.T.**-**M'R**-1:35(450)■9:10(305)■16:2(393)-**LU**-2:34(386)

RITES-**NU**-9:3(2708)

RIVER-all=5104,a=5158,b=2975,c=5103&marked-**GE**-2:10,13,14^{2}■15:18^{2}■31:21■36:37■41:1b,2b,3^{2}b,17b,18b-**EX**-1:22b■2:5b■4:9^{2}b■7:17b,18^{3}b,20^{2}b,21^{3}b,24^{2}b,25b■8:3b,9b,11b■17:5b■23:31-**NU**-22:5■34:5a-**DE**-1:7■2:24a,36^{2}a,37a■3:8a,12a,16^{2}a■4:48a■11:24-**JOS**-1:4■12:1a,2^{3}a■13:9^{2}a,16^{2}a■15:4a,7a,47a■16:8a■17:9^{2}a■19:11a-**J'G**-4:7a,13a■5:21^{2}a-**2SA**-8:3■10:16■17:13a■24:5a-**1KI**-4:21,24^{2}■8:65a■14:15-**2KI**-10:33a■17:6■18:11■23:29■24:7^{2}a-**1CH**-1:48■5:9,26■18:3■19:16-**2CH**-7:8a■9:26-**EZR**-4:10c,11c,16c,17c,20c■5:3c,6^{2}c■6:6^{2}c,8c,13c■7:21c,25c■8:15,21,31,36-**NE**-2:7,9■3:7-**JOB**-40:23-**PS**-36:8a■46:4■65:9(6388)■72:8■80:11■105:41-**IS**-7:20■8:7■11:15■19:5■23:3b,10b■27:12■48:18■66:12-**JER**-2:18■17:8(3105)■46:2,6,10-**LA**-2:18a-**EZE**-1:1,3■3:15,23■10:15,20,22■29:3b,9b■43:3■47:5^{2}a,6a,7a,9a,12a,19a■48:28a-**DA**-8:2(180),3(180),6(180)■10:4■12:5^{2}b,6b,7b-**AM**-6:14a-**MIC**-7:12-**ZEC**-9:10■10:11b■**N.T.**-all=4215-**M'R**-1:5-**AC**-16:13-**RE**-9:14■16:12■22:1,2

RIVER'S-all=2975&marked-**EX**-2:3,5■7:15-**NU**-24:6

RIVERS-all=2975,a=5104&marked-**EX**-7:19■8:5-**LE**-11:9(5158),10(5158)-**DE**-10:7(5158)-**2KI**-5:12a■19:24-**JOB**-20:17(6390)■28:10■29:6(6388)-**PS**-1:3(6388)■74:15a■78:16a,44■89:25a■107:33a■119:136(6388)■137:1a-**PR**-5:16(6388)■21:1(6388)-**EC**-1:7^{2}(5158)-**SONG**-5:12(650)-**IS**-7:18■18:1a,2a,7a■19:6a■30:25(6388)■32:2(6388)■33:21(5103)■37:25■41:18(5103)■42:15(5103)■43:2(5103),19(5103),20(5103)■44:27(5103)■47:2(5103)■50:2(5103)-**JER**-31:9(5158)■46:7a,8a-**LA**-3:48(6388)-**EZE**-6:3(650)■29:3,4^{3},5,10■30:12■31:4a,4(8585),12(650)■32:2^{2}a,6(650),14a■34:13(650)■35:8(650)■36:4(650),6(650)■47:9(5158)-**JOE**-1:20(650)■3:18(650)-**MIC**-6:7(5158)-**NA**-1:4a■2:6a■3:8-**HAB**-3:8^{2}a,9a-**ZEP**-3:10a■**N.T.**-**JOH**-7:38(4215)-**RE**-8:10(4215)■16:4(4215)

ROAD-**1SA**-27:10(6584)

ROAR-all=7580&marked-**1CH**-16:32(7481)-**PS**-46:3(1993)■74:4■96:11(7481)■98:7(7481)■104:21-**IS**-5:29^{2}(5098),30■42:13(6873)■59:11(1993)-**JER**-5:22(1993)■25:30^{2}■31:35(1993)■50:42(1993)■51:38,55(1993)-**HO**-11:10^{2}-**JOE**-3:16-**AM**-1:2■3:4

ROARED-all=7580&marked-**J'G**-14:5-**PS**-38:8-**IS**-51:15(1993)-**JER**-2:15-**AM**-3:8

ROARETH-**JOB**-37:4(7580)-**JER**-6:23(1993)■**N.T.**-**RE**-10:3(3455)

ROARING-all=7581&marked-**JOB**-4:10-**PS**-22:1,13(7580)■32:3-**PR**-19:12(5099)■20:2(5099)■28:15(5098)-**IS**-5:29,30(5100)■31:4(1897)-**EZE**-19:7■22:25(7580)-**ZEP**-3:3-**ZEC**-11:3(7581)■**N.T.**-**LU**-21:25(2278)-**1PE**-5:8(5612)

ROARINGS-**JOB**-3:24(7581)

ROAST-all=6748&marked-**EX**-12:8,9-**DE**-16:7(1310)-**1SA**-2:15(6740)-**IS**-44:16

ROASTED-**2CH**-32:13(1310)-**IS**-44:19(6740)-**JER**-29:22(7033)

ROASTETH-**PR**-12:27(2760)-**IS**-44:16(6740)

ROB-all=962&marked-**LE**-19:13(1497)■26:22(7921)-**1SA**-23:1(8154)-**PR**-22:22(1497)-**IS**-10:2■17:14-**EZE**-39:10-**MAL**-3:8(6906)

ROBBED-all=6906&marked-**J'G**-9:2(1497)-**2SA**-17:8(7909)-**PS**-119:61(5749)-**PR**-17:12(7909)-**IS**-10:13(8154)■42:22(962)-**JER**-50:37(962)-**EZE**-33:15(1500)■39:10(962)-**MAL**-3:8^{2},9■**N.T.**-**2CO**-11:8(4813)

ROBBER-**JOB**-5:5(6782)■18:9(6782)-**EZE**-18:10(6530)■**N.T.**-**JOH**-10:1(3027)■18:40(3027)

ROBBERS-all=6530&marked-**JOB**-12:6(7703)-**IS**-42:24(962)-**JER**-7:11-**EZE**-7:22-**DA**-11:14-**OB**-5(7703)■**N.T.**-**JOH**-10:8(3027)-**AC**-19:37(2417)-**2CO**-11:26(3027)

ROBBERY-all=1498&marked-**PS**-62:10-**PR**-21:7(7701)-**IS**-61:8-**EZE**-22:29-**AM**-3:10(7701)-**NA**-3:1(6563)■**N.T.**-**PH'P**-2:6(725)

ROBBETH-**PR**-28:24(1497)

ROBE-all=4598&marked-**EX**-28:4,31,34■29:5■39:22,23,24,25,26-**LE**-8:7-**IS**-18:4■24:4,11^{2}-**1CH**-15:27-**JOB**-29:14-**IS**-22:21(3801)■61:10-**JON**-3:6(155)-**MIC**-2:8(145)■**N.T.**-**M'T**-27:28(5511),31(5511)-**LU**-15:22(4749)■23:11(2066)-**JOH**-19:2(2440),5(2440)

ROBES-all=899&marked-**2SA**-13:18(4598)-**1KI**-22:10,30-**2CH**-18:9,29-**EZE**-26:16(4598)■**N.T.**-all=4749-**LU**-20:46-**RE**-6:11■7:9,13,14

ROCK-all=6697,a=5553&marked-**EX**-17:6^{2}■33:21,22-**NU**-20:8^{2}a,10^{2}a,11a■24:21a-**DE**-8:15■32:4,13a,13,15,18,30,31,37-**J'G**-1:36a■6:20a,21,26(4581)■7:25■13:19■15:8a,11a,13a■20:45a,47^{2}a■21:13a-**1SA**-2:2■14:4^{2}a■23:25a-**2SA**-21:10■22:2a,3,32,47^{2}■23:3-**1CH**-11:15-**2CH**-25:12^{2}a-**NE**-9:15a-**JOB**-14:18■18:4■19:24■24:8■28:9(2496)■29:6■39:1a,28^{2}a-**PS**-18:2a,31,46■27:5■28:1■31:2,3a■40:2a■42:9a■61:2■62:2,6,7■71:3a■78:16a,20,35■81:16■89:26■92:15■94:22■95:1■105:41■114:8-**PR**-30:19-**SONG**-2:14a-**IS**-2:10■8:14■10:26■17:10■22:16a■32:2a■42:11a■48:21^{2}■51:1-**JER**-5:3a■13:4a■18:14■21:13■23:29a■48:28a■49:16a-**EZE**-24:7a,8a■26:4a,14a-**AM**-6:12a-**OB**-3a■**N.T.**-all=4073-**M'T**-7:24,25■16:18■27:60-**M'R**-15:46-**LU**-6:48^{2}■8:6,13-**RO**-9:33-**1CO**-10:4^{2}-**1PE**-2:8

ROCKS-all=5553&marked-**NU**-23:9(6697)-**1SA**-13:6■24:2(6697)-**1KI**-19:11-**JOB**-28:10(6697)■30:6(3710)-**PS**-78:15(6697)■104:18-**PR**-30:26-**IS**-2:19(6697),21(6697),21■7:19■33:16■57:5-**JER**-4:29(3710)■16:16■51:25-**NA**-1:6(6697)■**N.T.**-all=4073&marked-**M'T**-27:51-**AC**-27:29(5138,5117)-**RE**-6:15,16

ROD-all=4294,a=7626&marked-**EX**-4:2,4,17,20■7:9,10,12^{2},15,17,19,20■8:5,16,17■9:23■10:13■14:16■17:5,9■21:20a-**LE**-27:32a-**NU**-17:2^{2},3^{2},5,6^{2},8,9,10■20:8,9,11-**1SA**-14:27,43-**2SA**-7:14a-**JOB**-9:34a■21:9a-**PS**-2:9a■23:4a■74:2a■89:32a■110:2■125:3a-**PR**-10:13a■13:24a■14:3(2415)■22:8a,15a■23:13a,14a■26:3a■29:15a-**IS**-9:4a■10:5a,15a,24a,26■11:1(2415),4a■14:29a■28:27a■30:31a-**JER**-1:11(4731)■10:16a■48:17(4731)■51:19a-**LA**-3:1a-**EZE**-7:10,11■19:14^{2}■20:37a■21:10a,13a-**MIC**-5:1a■6:9■7:14a■**N.T.**-all=4464-**1CO**-4:21-**HEB**-9:4-**RE**-2:27■11:1■12:5■19:15

RODE-all=7392-**GE**-24:61-**J'G**-10:4■12:14-**1SA**-25:20,42■30:17-**2SA**-18:9■22:11-**1KI**-13:13■18:45-**2KI**-9:16,25-**NE**-2:12-**ES**-8:14-**PS**-18:10

RODS-all=4294&marked-**GE**-30:37^{2}(4731),38(4731),39(4731),41^{2}(4731)-**EX**-7:12-**NU**-17:2,6^{2},7,9-**EZE**-19:11,12■**N.T.**-**2CO**-11:25(4463)

ROE-all=6643&marked-**2SA**-2:18-**PR**-5:19(3280)■6:5-**SONG**-2:9,17■8:14-**IS**-13:14

ROEBUCK-all=6643-**DE**-12:15,22■14:5■15:22

ROEBUCKS-**1KI**-4:23(6643)

ROES-all=6643&marked-**1CH**-12:8-**SONG**-2:7■3:5■4:5(6646)■7:3(6646)

ROLL-all=4039&marked-**GE**-29:8(1556)-**JOS**-10:18(1556)-**1SA**-14:33(1556)-**EZE**-6:2(4040)-**IS**-8:1(1549)-**JER**-36:2,4,6,14^2,20,21,23,25,27,28^2,29,32■51:25(1556)-**EZE**-2:9(4040)■3:1(4040),2(4040),3(4040)-**MIC**-1:10(6428)-**ZEC**-5:1(4040),2(4040)■**N.T.**-**M'R**-16:3(617)

ROLLED-all=1556-**GE**-29:3,10-**JOS**-5:9-**JOB**-30:14-**IS**-9:5■34:4■**N.T.**-all=617&marked-**M'T**-27:60(4351)■28:2-**M'R**-15:46(4351)■16:4-**LU**-24:2-**RE**-6:14(1507)

ROLLER-**EZE**-30:21(2848)

ROLLETH-**PR**-26:27(1556)

ROLLING-**IS**-17:13(1534)

ROLLS-**EZR**-6:1(5609)

ROOF-all=1406-**GE**-19:8(6982)-**DE**-22:8-**JOS**-2:6^2,8-**J'G**-16:27-**2SA**-11:2^2■18:24-**NE**-8:16-**JOB**-29:10(2441)-**PS**-137:6(2441)-**SONG**-7:9(2441)-**LA**-4:4(2441)-**EZE**-3:26(2441)■40:13■**N.T.**-all=4721-**M'T**-8:8-**M'R**-2:4-**LU**-7:6

ROOFS-**JER**-19:13(1406)■32:29(1406)

ROOM-all=8478&marked-**GE**-24:23(4725),25(4725),31(4725)■26:22(7337)-**2SA**-19:13-**1KI**-2:35^2■5:1,5■8:20■19:16-**2KI**-15:25■23:34-**2CH**-6:10■26:1-**PS**-31:8(4800)-**PR**-18:16(7337)■**N.T.**-all=5117&marked-**M'T**-2:22(473)-**M'R**-2:2(5362)■14:15(508)-**LU**-2:7■14:8(4411),9,10,22-**AC**-1:13(5253)■24:27(1240)-**1CO**-14:16

ROOMS-**GE**-6:14(7064)-**1KI**-20:24(8478)-**1CH**-4:41(8478)■**N.T.**-all=4411-**M'T**-23:6-**M'R**-12:39-**LU**-14:7■20:46

ROOT-all=8328&marked-**DE**-29:18-**J'G**-5:14-**1KI**-14:15(5428)-**2KI**-19:30-**JOB**-5:3(8327)■14:8■19:28■29:19■31:12(8327)-**PS**-52:5(8327)■80:9(8327)-**PR**-12:3,12-**IS**-5:24■11:10■14:29,30■27:6(8327)■37:31■40:24(8327)■53:2-**JER**-1:10(5428)■12:2(8327)-**EZE**-31:7-**HO**-9:16-**MAL**-4:1■**N.T.**-all=4991&marked-**M'T**-3:10■13:6,21,29(1610)-**M'R**-4:6,17-**LU**-3:9■8:13■17:6(1610)-**RO**-11:16,17,18■15:12-**1TI**-6:10-**HEB**-12:15-**RE**-5:5■22:16

ROOTED-**DE**-29:28(5428)-**JOB**-18:14(5423)■31:8(8327)-**PR**-2:22(5255)-**ZEP**-2:4(6131)■**N.T.**-**M'T**-15:13(1610)-**EPH**-3:17(4492)-**COL**-2:7(4492)

ROOTS-all=8328&marked-**2CH**-7:20(5428)-**JOB**-8:17■18:16■28:9■30:4-**IS**-11:1-**JER**-17:8-**EZE**-17:6,7,9^2-**DA**-4:15(8330),23(8330),26(8330)■7:8(6132)■11:7-**HO**-14:5-**AM**-2:9■**N.T.**-**M'R**-11:20(4491)-**JUDE**-12(1610)

ROPE-**IS**-5:18(5688)

ROPES-all=5688&marked-**J'G**-16:11,12-**2SA**-17:13(2256)-**1KI**-20:31,32■**N.T.**-**AC**-27:32(4979)

ROSE-all=6965,a=7925&marked-**GE**-4:8■18:16■19:1■20:8a■21:14a,32■22:3a,3,19■24:54■25:34■26:31a■28:18a■31:17,21,55a■32:22,31(2224)■37:35■43:15■46:5-**EX**-10:23■12:30■15:7■24:4a,13■32:6a,6■33:8,10■34:4a-**NU**-14:40a■16:2,25■22:13,14,21■24:25■25:7-**DE**-33:2(2224)-**JOS**-3:1a,16■6:12a,15a■7:16a■8:10a,14a-**J'G**-6:21(5927),38a■7:1a■9:34,35,43■19:5,7,9,10,27,28■20:5,19,33■21:4a-**RU**-3:14-**1SA**-1:9,19a■15:12a■16:13■17:20a■24:7■28:25■29:11a-**2SA**-15:2a■18:31■22:40,49-**1KI**-1:49■2:19■3:21■21:16-**2KI**-3:22a,24■7:5■8:21-**2CH**-20:20a■21:9■26:19(2224)■28:15■29:20a-**EZR**-1:5■5:2■10:6-**NE**-3:1■4:14-**JOB**-1:5a-**PS**-18:39■124:2-**SONG**-2:1(2261)■5:5-**IS**-35:1(2261)-**JER**-26:17-**LA**-3:62-**DA**-3:24■8:27-**JON**-1:3■4:7(5927)-**ZEP**-3:7a■**N.T.**-all=450&marked-**M'R**-10:50-**LU**-4:29■5:25,28■16:31■22:45■24:33-**JOH**-11:31-**AC**-5:17,36,37■10:41■14:20■15:5(1817),7■16:22(4911)■26:30-**RO**-14:9-**1CO**-10:7■15:4(1453),12(1453)-**2CO**-5:15(1453)-**1TH**-4:14-**RE**-19:3(305)

ROT-all=5307&marked-**NU**-5:21,22,27-**PR**-10:7(7537)-**IS**-40:20(7537)

ROTTEN-**JOB**-13:28(7538)■41:27(7539)-**JER**-38:11(4418),12(4418)-**JOE**-1:17(5685)

ROTTENNESS-all=7538&marked-**PR**-12:4■14:30-**IS**-5:24(4716)-**HO**-5:12-**HAB**-3:16

ROUGH-**DE**-21:4(386)-**IS**-27:8(7186)■40:4(7406)-**JER**-51:27(5569)-**DA**-8:21(8163)-**ZEC**-13:4(8181)■**N.T.**-**LU**-3:5(5138)

ROUGHLY-all=7186&marked-**GE**-42:7,30-**1SA**-20:10-**1KI**-12:13-**2CH**-10:13-**PR**-18:23(5794)

ROUND-all=5439&marked-**GE**-19:4(5921)■23:17■35:5■37:7(5437)■41:48-**EX**-7:24■16:13,14(2636)■19:12■25:11,24,25^2■27:17■28:32,33^2,34■29:16,20■30:3^2■37:2,11,12^2,26^2■38:16,20,31^2■39:23,25,26■40:8,33-**LE**-1:5,11■3:2,8,13■7:2■8:15,19,24■9:12,18■14:41■16:18■19:27(5362)■25:31,44-**NU**-1:50,53■3:26,37■4:26,32■11:24,31,32■16:34■22:4■32:33■34:12■35:2,4-**DE**-6:14■12:10■13:7■21:2■25:19-**JOS**-6:3(5362)■7:9(5921)■15:12■18:20■19:8■21:11,42,44■23:1-**J'G**-2:12,14■7:21■19:22(5437)■20:5(5437),29,43(3803)-**1SA**-14:21■26:5,7■31:9-**2SA**-5:9■7:1■22:12-**1KI**-3:1■4:24,31■6:5^3,6,29(4524)■7:12,18,20,23(5696),23,24^2,31^2(5696),35(5696),36■10:19(5696)■18:35-**2KI**-6:17■11:8,11■17:15■23:5(4524)■25:1,4,10,17-**1CH**-4:33■6:55■9:27■10:9■11:8■22:9■28:12-**2CH**-4:2(5696),2,3^2■14:14■15:15■17:10■20:30■23:7,10■34:6-**NE**-12:28,29-**JOB**-10:8■16:13(5437)■19:12■22:10■37:12(4524)■41:14-**PS**-3:6■18:11■22:12(3803)■27:6■34:7■44:13■48:12(5362)■50:3■59:6(5437),14(5437)■76:11■78:28■79:3,4■88:17(5437)■89:8■97:2,3■125:2^2■128:3-**SONG**-7:2(5469)-**IS**-3:18(7720)■15:8(5362)■29:3(1754)■42:25■49:18■60:4-**JER**-1:15■4:17■6:3■12:9■21:14■25:9■46:5,14■50:14,15,29,32■51:2■52:4,7,14,22,23-**LA**-1:17■2:3,22-**EZE**-1:18,27^2,28■4:2■5:5,6,7^2,12,14,15■6:5,13■8:10■10:12■11:12■16:37,57^2■23:24■27:11^2■28:24,26■31:4■32:23,24,25,26■34:26■36:4,36■37:2■40:5,14,16^2,17,25,29,30,33,36,43■41:5,6,7,8,10,11,12,16^2,17,19■42:15,16,17,20■43:12,13,20■45:1,2^2■46:23^3■48:35-**JOE**-3:11,12-**AM**-3:11-**JON**-2:5(5437)-**NA**-3:8-**ZEC**-2:5■7:7■12:2,6■14:14■**N.T.**-all=2943&marked-**M'T**-3:5(4066)■14:35(4066)-**M'R**-1:28(4066)■3:5(4017),34■5:32(4017)■6:6,36,55(4066)■9:8(4017)■10:23(4017)■11:11(4017)-**LU**-1:65(4039)■2:9(4034)■4:14(4066),37(4066)■7:17(4066)■8:37(4066)■9:12■19:43(4033)-**JOH**-10:24(2944)-**AC**-5:16(4038)■9:3(4015)■14:6(4066),20(2944)■22:6(4015)■25:7(4026)■26:13(4034)-**RO**-15:19-**HEB**-9:4(3840)-**RE**-4:3,4,6■5:11■7:11

ROUSE-**GE**-49:9(6965)

ROVERS-all supplied

ROW-all=2905&marked-**EX**-28:17^2,18,19,20■39:10^2,11,12,13-**LE**-24:6(4635),7(4635)-**1KI**-6:36■7:3,12-**EZR**-6:4(5073)-**EZE**-46:23(2905)

ROWED-**JON**-1:13(2864)■**N.T.**-**JOH**-6:19(1643)

ROWERS-**EZE**-27:26(7751)

ROWING-**M'R**-6:48(1643)

ROWS-all=2905&marked-**EX**-28:17■39:10-**LE**-24:6(4634)-**1KI**-6:36■7:2,4,12,18,20,24,42-**2CH**-4:3,13-**EZE**-6:4(5073)-**SONG**-1:10(8447)-**EZE**-46:23(2918)

ROYAL-all=4438&marked-**GE**-49:20(4428)-**JOS**-10:2(4467)-**1SA**-27:5(4467)-**2SA**-12:26(4410)-**1KI**-10:13(4428)-**2KI**-11:1(4467)■25:25(4410)-**1CH**-29:25-**2CH**-22:10(4467)-**ES**-1:7,9,11,19^2■2:16,17■5:1^2■6:8^2■8:15-**IS**-62:3(4410)-**JER**-41:1(4410)■43:10(8237)-**DA**-6:7(4430)■**N.T.**-**AC**-12:21(937)-**JAS**-2:8(937)-**1PE**-2:9(934)

RUBBING-**LU**-6:1(5597)

RUBBISH-**NE**-4:2(6083),10(6083)

RUBIES-all=6443-**JOB**-28:18-**PR**-3:15■8:11■20:11■31:10-**LA**-4:7

RUDDER-**AC**-27:40(4079)

RUDDY-**1SA**-16:12(132)■17:42(132)-**SONG**-5:10(122)-**LA**-4:7(119)

RUDE-**2CO**-11:6(2399)

RUDIMENTS-**COL**-2:8(4747),20(4747)

RUE-**LU**-11:42(4076)

RUIN-**2CH**-28:23(3782)-**PS**-89:40(4288)-**PR**-24:22(6365)■26:28(4072)-**IS**-3:6(4384)■23:13(4654)■25:2(4654)-**EZE**-18:30(4383)■27:27(4658)■31:13(4658)■**N.T.**-**LU**-6:49(4485)

RUINED-**IS**-3:8(3782)-**EZE**-36:35(2040),36(2040)

RUINOUS-**2KI**-19:25(5327)-**IS**-17:1(4654)■37:26(5327)

RUINS-**EZE**-21:15(4383)-**AM**-9:11(2034)■**N.T.**-**AC**-15:16(2679)

RULE-all=4910,a=7287&marked-**GE**-1:16^2(4475),18■3:16■4:7-**LE**-5:43a,46a,53a-**JG**-8:22,23^3-**1KI**-9:23a-**2CH**-8:10a-**NE**-5:15(7980)-**ES**-1:22(8323)■9:1(7980)-**PS**-110:2a■136:8(4475),9(4475)-**PR**-8:16(8323)■12:24■17:2■19:10■25:28(4623)■29:2-**EC**-2:19(7980)-**IS**-3:4,12■14:2a■19:4■28:14■32:1(8323)■40:10■41:2a■44:13(6957)■52:5■63:19-**JER**-5:31a-**EZE**-19:11,14■20:33(4427)■29:15a-**DA**-2:39(7981)■4:26(7990)■11:3,39-**JOE**-2:17-**ZEC**-6:13■**N.T.**-all=4165&marked-**M'T**-2:6-**M'R**-10:42(757)-**1CO**-15:24(746)-**2CO**-10:13(2583),15(2583)-**GA**-6:16(2583)-**PH'P**-3:16(2583)-**COL**-3:15(1018)-**1TI**-3:5(4291)■5:17(4291)-**HEB**-13:7(2233),17(2233),24(2233)-**RE**-2:27■12:5■19:15

RULED-all=4910&marked-**GE**-24:2■41:40(5401)-**JOS**-12:2-**RU**-1:1(8199)-**1KI**-5:16(7287)-**1CH**-26:6(4474)-**EZR**-4:20(7990)-**PS**-106:41-**IS**-14:6(7287)-**LA**-5:8-**EZE**-34:4(7287)-**DA**-5:21(7990)■11:4

RULER-all=5057,a=4910,b=8269&marked-**GE**-43:16(834,5921)■45:8a**EX**-22:28(5387)-**LE**-4:22(5387)-**NU**-13:2(5387)-**J'G**-9:30b-**1SA**-25:30-**2SA**-6:21■7:8-**1KI**-1:35■11:28(6485)-**2KI**-25:22(6485)-**1CH**-5:2■9:11,20■11:2■17:7■26:24■27:4,16■28:4-**2CH**-6:5■7:18a■11:22■19:11■26:11(7860)■31:12,13-**NE**-3:9b,12b,14b,15b,16b,17b,18b,19b■7:2b■11:11-**PS**-68:27(7287)■105:20a,21a-**PR**-6:7a■23:1a■28:15a■29:12a-**EC**-10:4a,5(7989)-**IS**-3:6(7101),7(7101)■16:1a-**JER**-51:46a-**DA**-2:10(7990),38(7981),48(7981)■5:7(7981),16(7981),29(7990)-**MIC**-5:2a-**HAB**-1:14a■**N.T.**-all=758&marked-**M'T**-9:18■24:45(2525),47(2525)■25:21(2525),23(2525)-**M'R**-5:35(752),36(752),38(752)-**LU**-8:41,49(752)■12:42(2525),44(2525)■13:14(752)■18:18-**JOH**-2:9(755)■3:1-**AC**-7:27,35^2■18:8(752),17(752)■23:5

RULER'S-**PR**-29:26(4910)■**N.T.**-**M'T**-9:23(758)

RULERS-all=8269,a=5461&marked-**GE**-47:6-**EX**-16:22(5387)■18:21^2,25^2■34:31(5387)■35:27(5387)-**DE**-1:13(7281)-**J'G**-15:11(4910)-**1KI**-9:22-**2KI**-10:1■11:4,19-**1CH**-21:2■26:32(6485)■27:31■29:6-**2CH**-29:20■35:8(5057)-**EZR**-9:2(5461)■10:14-**NE**-2:16^{2}a■4:14a,16,19a■5:7a,17a■7:5a■11:1■12:40a■13:11a-**ES**-3:12■8:9■9:3-**PS**-2:2(7336)-**IS**-1:10(7101)■14:5(4910)■22:3(7101)■29:10(7218)■49:7(4910)-**JER**-33:26(4910)■51:23a,28a,57a-**EZE**-23:6a,12a,23a-**DA**-3:2(7984),3(7984)-**HO**-4:18(4043)■**N.T.**-all=758&marked-**M'R**-5:22(752)■13:9(2232)-**LU**-21:12(2232)■23:13,35■24:20

-JOH-7:26,48■12:42-AC-3:17■4:5,8,26■13:15(752),27■14:5■16:19■17:6(4178),8(4178)-RO-13:3-EPH-6:12(2888)

RULEST-2CH-20:6(4910)-PS-89:9(4910)

RULETH-all=4910&marked-2SA-23:3-PS-59:13■66:7■103:19-PR-16:32■22:7-EC-8:9(7980)■9:17-DA-4:17(7980),25(7980),32(7980)-HO-11:12(7300)RO-12:8(4291)-1TI-3:4(4291)

RULING-2SA-23:3(4910)-JER-22:30(4910)■N.T.-2TI-3:12(4291)

RUMBLING-JER-47:3(1995)

RUMOUR-all=8052&marked-2KI-19:7-IS-37:7-JER-49:14■51:46^{3}-EZE-7:26-OB-1■N.T.-LU-7:17(3056)

RUMOURS-M'T-24:6(189)-M'R-13:7(189)

RUMP-all=451-EX-29:22-LE-3:9■7:3■8:25■9:19

RUN-all=7323&marked-GE-49:22(6805)-LE-15:3(7325),25(2100)-J'G-18:25(6293)-1SA-8:11■17:17■20:6,36-2SA-15:1■18:19,22^{2},23^{2}■22:30-1KI-1:5-2KI-4:22,26■5:20-2CH-16:9(7751)-PS-18:29■19:5■58:7(1980)■59:4■78:16(3381)■104:10(1980)■119:32,136(3381)-PR-1:16-EC-1:7(1980)-SONG-1:4-IS-33:4(8264)■40:31■55:5■59:7-JER-5:1(7751)■9:18(3381)■12:5■13:17(3381)■14:17(3381)■49:3(7751),19■50:44■51:31-LA-2:18(3381)-EZE-24:16(935)■32:14(3212)-DA-12:4(7751)-JOE-2:4,7,9(8264),9-AM-5:24(1556)■6:12■8:12(7751)-NA-2:4-HAB-2:2-HAG-1:9-ZEC-2:4■4:10(7751)■N.T.-all=5143&marked-M'T-28:8-1CO-9:24^{2},26-GA-2:2■5:7-PH'P-2:16-HEB-12:1-1PE-4:4(4936)

RUNNEST-PR-4:12(7323)

RUNNETH-all=7323&marked-EZE-8:15(935)-JOB-15:26■16:14-PS-23:5(7310)■147:15-PR-18:10-LA-1:16(3381)■3:48(3381)■N.T.-M'T-9:17(1632)-JOH-20:2(5143)-RO-9:16(5143)

RUNNING-all=2416&marked-LE-14:5,6,50,51,52■15:2(2100),13■22:4(2100)-NU-19:17(2416)-2SA-18:24(7323),26^{2}(7323),27^{2}(4794)-2KI-5:21(7323)-2CH-23:12(7323)-PR-5:15(5140)■6:18(7323)-IS-33:4(4944)-EZE-31:4(1980)■N.T.-M'R-9:15(4370),25(1998)■10:17(4370)-LU-6:38(5240)-AC-27:16(5295)-RE-9:9(5143)

RUSH-JOB-8:11(1573)-IS-9:14(100)■17:13(7582)■19:15(100)

RUSHED-J'G-9:44(6584)■20:37(6584)■N.T.-AC-19:29(3729)

RUSHES-IS-35:7(1573)

RUSHETH-JER-8:6(7857)

RUSHING-all=7588&marked-IS-17:12,12(7582),12,13-JER-47:3(7494)-EZE-3:12(7494),13(7494)■N.T.-AC-2:2(5342)

RUST-M'T-6:19(1035),20(1035)-JAS-5:3(2447)

S

S.[for ST.or SAINT]-all=40-M'T-1:t-M'R-1:t-LU-1:t-JOH-1:t-RE-1:t

SABACHTHANI-M'T-27:46(4518)-M'R-15:34(4518)

SABBATH-all=7676&marked-EX-16:23,25,26,29■20:8,10,11■31:14,15^{2},16■35:2,3-LE-16:31■23:3^{2},11,15,16,24(7677),32^{2},39^{2}(7677)■24:8■25:2,4^{2},6-NU-15:32■28:9,10-DE-5:12,14,15-2KI-4:23■11:5,7,9^{2}■16:18-1CH-9:32-2CH-23:4,8^{2}■36:21(7673)-NE-9:14■10:31^{2}■13:15^{2},16,17,18,19^{3},21,22-PS-92:t-IS-56:2,6■58:13^{2}■66:23-JER-17:21,22^{2},24^{2},27^{2}-EZE-46:1,4,12-AM-8:5■N.T.-all=4521&marked-M'T-12:1,2,5^{2},8,10,11,12■24:20■28:1-M'R-1:21■2:23,24,27^{2},28■3:2,4■6:2■15:42(4315)■16:1-LU-4:16,31■6:1,2,5,6,7,9■13:10,14^{2},15,16■14:1,3,5■23:54,56-JOH-5:9,10,16,18■7:22,23^{2}■9:14,16■19:31^{2}-AC-1:12■13:14,27,42,44■15:21■16:13■17:2■18:4-COL-2:16

SABBATHS-all=7676&marked-EX-31:13-LE-19:3,30■23:15,38■25:8^{2}■26:2,34^{2},35,43-1CH-23:31-2CH-2:4■8:13■31:3■36:21-NE-10:33-IS-1:13■56:4-LA-1:7(4868)■2:6-EZE-20:12,13,16,20,21,24■22:8,26■23:38■44:24 45:17■46:3-HO-2:11

SACK-all=572&marked-GE-42:25(8242),27(8242),28,35(8242)■43:21■44:11^{2},12-LE-11:32(8242)

SACKBUT-all=5443-DA-3:5,7,10,15

SACKCLOTH-all=8242-GE-37:34-2SA-3:31■21:10-1KI-20:31,32■21:27^{2}-2KI-6:30■19:1,2-1CH-21:16-ES-4:1,2,3,4-JOB-16:15-PS-30:11■35:13■69:11-IS-3:24■15:3■20:2■22:12■37:1,2■50:3■58:5-JER-4:8■6:26■48:37■49:3-LA-2:10-EZE-7:18■27:31-DA-9:3-JOE-1:8,13-AM-8:10-JON-3:5,6,8■N.T.-all=4526-M'T-11:21-LU-10:13-RE-6:12■11:3

SACKCLOTHES-NE-9:1(8242)

SACK'S-all=572-GE-42:27■44:1,2

SACKS-all=572&marked-GE-42:25(3672),35(8242)■43:12,18,21,22,23■44:1-JOS-9:4(8242)

SACKS'-GE-44:8(572)

SACRIFICE-all=2077,a=2076&marked-GE-31:54-EX-3:18a■5:3a,8a,17a■8:8a,25a,26^{2}a,27a,28a,29a■10:25■12:27■13:15a■20:24a■23:18,18(2282)■29:28■34:15a,15,25^{2}-LE-3:1,3,6,9■4:10,26,31,35■7:11,12,13,15,16^{2},17,18,20,21,29^{2},37■9:4a,18■17:8■19:5■22:21,29■23:19(6213),19,37■27:11(7133)-NU-6:17,18■7:17,23,29,35,41,47,53,59,65,71,77,83,88■15:3,5,8-DE-15:21a■16:2a,5a,6a■17:1a■18:3-JOS-22:26-J'G-16:23-1SA-1:3a,21■2:13,19,29■3:14■9:12,13■10:8a■15:15a,21a,22■16:2a,3,5a,5^{2}■20:6,29-1KI-3:4a■8:62,63■12:27■18:29(4503),36(4503)-2KI-5:17■10:19■14:4a■16:15sup,15■17:35a,36-2CH-7:5,12■11:16a■28:23a■33:17a-EZR-4:2a■9:4(4503),5(4503)-NE-4:2a-PS-40:6■50:5■51:16■54:6a■107:22■116:17■118:27(2282)■141:2(4503)-PR-15:8■21:3,27-EC-5:1-IS-19:21■34:6■57:7-JER-33:18■46:10-EZE-39:17,17a,17,19a■40:42■44:11■46:24-DA-9:27-HO-3:4■4:13a,14a■6:6■8:13a■12:11a■13:2a-JON-1:16■2:9a-HAB-1:16a-ZEP-1:7,8-ZEC-14:21a-MAL-1:8a■N.T.-all=2378&marked-M'T-9:13■12:7-M'R-9:49-LU-2:24-AC-7:41■14:13(2380),18(2380)-RO-12:1-1CO-8:4(1494)■10:19(1494),20^{2}(2380),28(1494)-EPH-5:2-PH'P-2:17■4:18-HEB-7:27■9:26■10:5,8,12,26■11:4■13:15

SACRIFICED-all=2076&marked-EX-24:5■32:8-DE-32:17-JOS-8:31-J'G-2:5-1SA-2:15■6:15■11:15-2SA-6:13-1KI-3:2,3■11:8-2KI-12:3■15:4,35■16:4■17:32(6213)-1CH-21:28■29:21-2CH-5:6■28:4,23■33:16,22■34:4-PS-106:37,38-EZE-16:20■39:19-HO-11:2■N.T.-1CO-5:7(2380)-RE-2:14(1494),20(1494)

SACRIFICEDST-DE-16:4(2076)

SACRIFICES-all=2077&marked-GE-46:1-EX-10:25■18:12-LE-7:32,34■10:14■17:5,7-NU-10:10■25:2-DE-12:6,11,27■32:38■33:19-JOS-22:27,28,29-1SA-6:15■10:8■11:15■15:22-2SA-15:12-2KI-10:24-1CH-29:21^{2}-2CH-7:1,4■29:31^{2}-EZR-6:3(1685)-NE-12:43-PS-4:5■27:6■50:8■51:17,19■106:28,107:22-PR-17:1-IS-1:11■29:1(2282)■43:23,24■56:7-JER-6:20■7:21,22■17:26,26sup-EZE-20:28-HO-4:19■8:13■9:4-AM-4:4■5:25■N.T.-all=2378-M'R-12:33-LU-13:1-AC-7:42-1CO-10:18-HEB-5:1■8:3■9:9,23■10:1,11■13:16-1PE-2:5

SACRIFICETH-all=2076&marked-EX-22:20-EC-9:2-IS-65:3■66:3-MAL-1:14

SACRIFICING-1KI-8:5(2076)■12:32(2076)

SACRILEGE-RO-2:22(2416)

SAD-GE-40:6(2196)-1KI-21:5(5620)-NE-2:1(7451),2(7451)-EZE-13:22(3512),22(3510)■N.T.-M'T-6:16(4659)-M'R-10:22(4768)-LU-24:17(4659)

SADDLE-all=2280&marked-LE-15:9(4817)-2SA-19:26-1KI-13:13,27

SADDLED-all=2280-GE-22:3-NU-22:21-J'G-19:10-2SA-16:1■17:23-1KI-2:40■13:13,23,27-2KI-4:24

SADLY-GE-40:7(7451)

SADNESS-EC-7:3(7455)

SAFE-all=7965&marked-1SA-12:11(983)-2SA-18:29,32-JOB-21:9-PS-119:117(3467)-PR-18:10(7682)■29:25(7682)-IS-5:29(6403)-EZE-34:27(983)■N.T.-LU-15:27(5198)-AC-23:24(1295)■27:44(1295)-PH'P-3:1(809)

SAFEGUARD-1SA-22:23(4931)

SAFELY-all=983&marked-LE-26:5-1KI-4:25-PS-78:53-PR-1:33■3:23-IS-41:3(7965)-JER-23:6■32:37■33:16-EZE-28:26■34:25,28■33:8,11,14■39:26-HO-2:18-ZEC-14:11■N.T.-M'R-14:44(806)-AC-16:23(806)

SAFETY-all=983&marked-LE-25:18,19-DE-12:10■33:12,28-JOB-3:26(7951)■5:4(3468),11(3468)■11:18■24:23-PS-4:8■12:5(3468)■33:17(8668)-PR-11:14(8668)■21:31(8668)■24:6(8668)-IS-14:30■N.T.-AC-5:23(803)-1TH-5:3(803)

SAFFRON-SONG-4:14(3750)

SAID-all=559,a=1696,b=560&marked-GE-1:3,6,9,11,14,20,24,26,28,29■2:18,23■3:1^{2},2,3,4,9,10,11,12,13^{2},14,16,17,22■4:1,6,9^{2},10,13,15,23■6:3,7,13■7:1■8:21■9:1,12,17,25,26■10:9■11:3,4,6■12:1,7,11,18■13:8,14■14:19,21,22■15:2,3,5^{2},7,8,9,13■16:2,5,6,8^{2},9,10,11,13■17:1,9,15,17,18,19,23a■18:3,5a,6,9^{2},10,13,15,17,20,23,26,27,28,29^{2},30^{2},31^{2},32^{2}■19:2^{2},5,7,9,12,14,17,18,21,31,34■20:2,3,4,5^{2},6,9,10,11,13,15,16■21:1,6,7(4448),10,12^{2},16,17,24,26,29,30■22:1^{2},2,5,7^{3},8,11,12,14,16■24:2,5,6,12,17,18,19,23,24,25,27,31,33^{2},34,39,40,42,45,46,47^{2},50■24:54,55,56,57,58^{2},60,65^{2}■25:22,23,30,31,32,33■26:2,7^{2},9^{2},10,16,22,24,27,28^{2},32■27:1^{2},2,11,13,18^{2},19,20^{2},21,22,24^{2},25,26,27,31,32^{2},33,34,35,36^{2},37,38,39,41,42,46■28:1,13,16,17■29:4^{2},5^{2},6^{2},7,8,14,15,18,19,21,25,26,32,33,34,35■30:1,2,3,6,8,11,13,14,15^{2},16,18,20,23,24,25,27,28,29,31^{2},34■31:3,5,8^{2},11,12,14,16,24,26,31^{2},35,36,43,46,48,49,51■32:2,8,9,16,20,26^{2},27^{2},28,29^{2}■33:5^{2},8^{2},9,10,12,13,15^{2}■34:11,13a,14,30,31■35:1,2,10,11,17■37:6,8,9,10,13^{2},14,16,17,19,21,22,26,30,32,33,35■38:8,11^{2},16^{2},17^{2},18^{2},21,22^{2},23,24,25,26,29■39:7,8■40:8^{2},9,12,16,18■41:15,17a,25,38,39,41,44,54,55■42:1,2,4,7^{2},9,10,12,13,14,18,21,28,31,33,36,38■43:2,5,6,7,8,11,16,18,20,23,27,29^{2},31■44:4,7,10,15,16,17,18,20,22,25,26,27,28■45:3,4^{2},17,24,27(1697),28■46:2,3,30,31■47:1,3^{2},4,8,9,15,16,18,23,25,29,30(1697),30,31■48:2,3,4,8,9^{2},11,15,18,19,21■49:1,29■50:6,11,15,18,19,24-EX-1:9,16,18,19■2:6,7,8,9,10,13,14^{2},18,19,20,22■3:3,4,5,6,7,11,12,13,14^{2},15,17■4:1,2^{2},3,4,6,7,10,11,13,14,18^{2},19,21,25,26,27■5:2,3,4,5,17,19,21,22■6:1,2,26,30■7:1,13a,14,22a■8:8,9,10^{2},15a,16,19^{2}a,20,25,26,28,29■9:1,8,13,22,27,29■10:1,3,7,8,9,10,12,16,21,24,25,28,29■11:1,4,9■12:21,31,31a,32a,33,43■13:3,17■14:5,11,13,15,25,26■15:9,26■16:3,4,6,8,15^{2},19,23,23a,25,28,32,33■17:2^{2},3,5,9,10,14,16■18:3,6,10,14,15,17,24■19:8,9,10,15,21,23,24■20:19,20,22■23:13■24:1,3,3a,7,7a,8,12,14■30:34■32:1,2,4,5,7a,8,9,11,17,18,21,22,23,24,26,27,29,30,31,33■33:1a,5,12^{2},14,15,17,18,19,20,21■34:1,9,10,27■35:1,30-LE-8:5,31■9:2,6,7■10:3,4,5a,6,19a■16:2■17:12,14■20:24■21:1-NU-3:40■7:11■9:7,8■10:29^{2},30,31,35,36■11:4,11,16,21^{2},23,27,28,29■12:2,6,11,14■13:17,

27,30,31■14:2,4,11,13,20,31,35a,41■
15:35■16:3,8,12,15,16,22,28,34,40a,46■
17:10■18:1,24■20:10,18,19,20■21:2,7,8,
14,34■22:4,8,9,10,12,13,14,16,18,20,28,
29,30^2,32,34,35,37,38■23:1,3,4,5,7,11,
12,13,15,16,17,18,19,23,25,26,27,29,30■
24:3,3^2(5002),4(5002),10,12,15,15^2(5002),
16(5002),20,21,23■25:4,5■26:65■27:12,
18■31:15,21,49■32:5,6,16,20,29,31a■
36:2,5a-**DE**-1:14,20,21a,22,25,27,29,39,
41,42■2:9,31■3:2,26■4:10■5:1,24,28■
9:3a,12,25,26■10:1,11■11:25a■17:16■
18:2a,17■29:2,13a■31:2^2,3a,7,14,16,23■
32:20,26,46■33:2,7,8,9,12,13,18,20,22,
23,24■34:4-**JOS**-1:3a■2:4,9,16,17,21,
24■3:5,7,9,10■4:5■5:2,9,13,14^2,15■
6:2,6,7,16,22■7:3,7,10,19,20,25■8:1,18■
9:6,7,8^2,9,19,21,24■10:8,12,18,22,24,
25■11:6,23a■13:1,14a,33a■14:6,6a,10a,
12a■15:16,18■17:16■18:3■22:2,21a,26,
28,31■23:2■24:2,16,19,21,22^2,24,27
-**J'G**-1:2,3,7,12,14,15,20a,24■2:1^2,3,15a,
20■3:19^2,20,24,28■4:6,8,9,14,18,19,20,
22■5:23■6:8,10,12,13,14,15,16,17,18,20,
22,23,25,27a,29^2,30,31,36,36a,37a,39■
7:2,4,5,7,9,13,14,15,17■8:1,2,3a,5,6,7,
15,18,19,20,21,22,23,24■9:3,7,8,9,10,11,
12,13,14,15,28,29,36^2,37,38,48,54■10:11,
15,18■11:2,6,7,8,9,10,15,19,30,35,36,37,
38■12:1,2,4,5^3,6^2■13:3,7,8,10,11^2,12,13^2,
15,16,17,18,22,23■14:2,3^2,12,13,14,15,
16^2,18^2■15:1,2,3,6,7,10,11^2,12^2,16,18■
16:5,6,7,9,10,11,12,13^2,14,15,17,20^2,23,
24,25,26,28,30■17:2^2,3,9^2,10,13■18:2,3,
4,5,6,8,9,14,18,19,23,24,25■19:5,6,8,9,
11,12,13,17,18,20,23,28,30■20:3,4,18^2,
23,28,32^2,39■21:3,5,6,8,16,17,19-**RU**-
1:8,10,11,15,16,19,20■2:2^2,4,5,6,7,8,10,
11,13,14,19^2,20^2,21,22■3:1,5,9,10,14,
15,16,17^2,18■4:1,2,3,4,5,6,8,9,11,14
-**1SA**-1:8,11,14,15,17,18,22,23,26■2:1,15,
16,20,23,27,30■3:5^2,6,8,9,11,16,17,17^{2}a,
18■4:3,6,7^2,14,16^2,17,20a,22■5:7,8,11■
6:3,4,20■7:5,6,8■8:5,6,7,11,19,22^2■9:3,
5,6,7,8,10a,11,12,17(6030)18,19,21,23^2,
24^2,27■10:1,11,12,14^2,15^2,16,18,19,24^2,
27■11:1,3,5,9,10,12^2,13,14■12:1^2,4,5,6,
10,12,19,20■13:9,11^2,12,13,19■14:1,6,7,
8,11,12^2,17,18,19,28,29,33,34,36^3,38,
40^2,41,42,43^2,45■15:1,6,13,14,15,16,16a,16,
17,18,20,22,24,26,28,30,32^2,33■16:1,2^2,
4,5,6,7,8,9,10,11^3,12,15,17,18,19■17:8,
10,17,25,28,29,32,33,34,37^2,39,43,44,
45,55^2,56,58■18:7,8,11,17^2,18,21^2,23,25■
19:4,14,17^2,22^2■20:1,2,3,4,5,9,10,11,12,
18,27,29,30,32,36,37,40,42■21:1,2^2,4,5,
8,9^2,11,14■22:3,5,7,9,12,13,14,16,17,18,
22■23:2,3,4,7,9,10,11,12^2,17,21■24:4^2,
6,9,10,16,17■25:5,10,13,19,21,24,32,35,
39,41■26:6^2,8,9,10,14,15,17^2,18,21,22,
25■27:1,5,10^2■28:1,2^2,7^2,8,9,11^2,13^2,
14^2,15,16,21,23■29:3^2,4,6,8,9^2■30:7,13^2,
15^2,20,22,23■31:4-**2SA**-1:3^2,4,5,6,8,9,13,
14,15,16■2:1^3,5,14^2,20,21,22,26,27■3:7,
8,13,16,21,24,28,31,33,38■4:8,9■5
:2,8^2,19,20,23■6:9,20,21■7:2,3,18,
25a■9:1,2^2,3^2,4^2,6,7,8,9,11■10:2,3,5,11■
11:3,5,8,10,11,12,23,25■12:1,5,7,13^2,18,
19^2,21,22^2,27■13:4^2,5,6,9,10,11,15,16,17,
20,24,25,26^2,32,35,35a■14:2,4,5,7,8,9,
10,11^2,12^2,13,15,17,18^2,19^2,21,22,24,30,
31■15:2^2,3,4,7,9,14,15,19,21,22,25,27,31,
33■16:2^2,3^3,4^2,7,9,10^2,11,16,17,18,20,21■
17:1,5,7,8,14,15,20^2,21,29■18:2,4,10,11,
12,14,18,19,20,21,22^2,23sup,23,25,26^2,27^2,
28^2,29,30,31,32,33■19:5,19,21,22,23,25,26,
29^2,30,33,34,41,43■20:1,4,6,9,11,17^2,20,
21■21:2,3,4^2,6■22:2■23:1^2(5002),3,15,
17■24:2,3,10,13,14,16,17,18,21^2,22,23,
24-**1KI**-1:2,16,17,24^2,28,29,31,32,33,36,
39,41,42,43,48,52,53■2:4,13^2,14^2,15,16,
17,18,20^2,21,22,26,30^2,30a,31,31a,36,38,
38a,42,44■3:5,6,11,17,22^2,23,24,25,26^2,
27■5:7■8:12,15,18,23,29■9:3,13■10:6■
11:2,11,21,22,31■12:5,6,9,26,28■13:2,6,
7a,8,12a,13,14^2,15,16,17(1697),18,26■
14:2,5,6■17:1,10,11,12,13^2,18,19,20,
21,23,24■18:5,7,9,10,15,17,21,22,24,25,
27,30,33,34^2,36,39,40,41,43^3,44^2■19:4,5,
7,9,10,11,13,14,15,20^2■20:2,4,5,7,8,9,10,
11,12,14^2,18,22,23,28sup,28,31,32^2,33^2,
34,35,36,37,39^2,40,42■21:3,4,5a,6a,6,7,
15,20■22:3,4^2,5,6^2,7,8^2,9,11,14,15,16,17^2,
18,19,20^3,21,22^3,24,25,26,28^2,30,32,34,49
-**2KI**-1:2,3a,5,6^2,7a,8,9a,10a,11a,11,12a,13a,
15a,16a■2:2^2,3^2,4^2,5,6^2,9^2,10,14,15,16^2,
17,18,19,20,21,23■3:7,8,10,11^2,12,13^2,14,
16,23■4:2^2,3,6^2,7,9,12,13,14,15,16^2,17a,
19^2,22,23^2,24,25,27,28,29,30,36^2,38,40,41^2,
42,43^2■5:3,4a,5,7,11,13,15,16,17,19,20,
21,22,23,25^2,26■6:1,3,5,6,7,11,12,13,15,
17,18,19,20,21,27,28^2,29,31,32,33■7:1,
2^2,3,6,9,12,13,17a,19^2■8:5,8,9,10,12,13,
14■9:1,5^3,6,11^2,12^2,15,17^2,18^2,19,21,22,
23,25,27,31,32,33,34,36■10:4,8,9,13,14,
15,16,18,20,22,23,24,25,30■11:12,15^2■
12:4,7■13:14,15,16,17^3,18^2,19■14:27a■
17:12,23a■18:19,22,25,26,27■19:3,6,
15,23■20:1,7,8,9,14^2,15,16,19^2■
21:4,7■22:8,9,15■23:17,18,27^2■
24:13a■25:24-**1CH**-10:4■11:2,
5,6,17,19■12:17,18,13:2,4■14:10,
11,14■15:2,12■16:36■17:1,2,16,23a■
19:2,3,5,12■21:2,8,11,13,15,17,22^2,24■
22:1,5,7,11a■23:25■27:23■28:2,3,6,20■
29:1,10,20-**2CH**-1:7,8,11■2:12■6:1^2,4,
8,14,20■7:12■8:11■9:5■10:5,9■12:5,6■
13:4■14:7,11■15:2■16:7■18:3,4,5^2,6,7^2,
8,10,13,14^2,15,16^2,17,18,19,20^2,21^2,23,
24,25,27^2,29,31,33■19:2,6■20:6,15,20■
22:9■23:3,3a,11,13,14^2■24:5,6,20,22■
25:9,15,16^2■26:18,23■28:9,13,23■29:5,
18,31■33:4,7■34:15■35:3,23-**EZR**-2:63■
4:2,3■5:3b,4b,9b,15b■8:28■9:6■10:2,10,
12,12a-**NE**-1:3,5■2:2,3,4,5,6,7,17,18,19,
20■4:2,3,10,11,12,14,19,22■5:2,3,4,7,8,
9,12,13^2■6:10,11■7:3,65■8:9,10■9:5,
18■13:11,17,21-**ES**-1:13■2:2■3:3,8,11■
5:3,5,5a,6,7,8a,12,14■6:3^2,4,5^2,6,10,10a,
13■7:2,3,5,6,8,9^2■8:5,7■9:12,13-**JOB**-
1:5,7^2,8,9,12,14,16,17,18,21■2:2^2,3,4,6,
9,10■3:2,3■4:1■6:1■8:1■9:1,22■11:1,4■
12:1■15:1■16:1■17:14(7121)■18:1■
19:1■20:1■21:1■22:1,17■23:1■25:1■
26:1■27:1■28:28■29:1,18■31:24,31■
32:6,7,10■34:1,5,9,31■35:1■36:1■38:1,
11■40:1,3,6■42:1,7-**PS**-2:7■10:6,11,13■
12:4■14:1■16:2■18:t■27:8■30:6■31:14,
22■32:5■35:21■38:16■39:1■40:7■41:4■
52:t■53:1■54:t■55:6■68:22■74:8■75:4■
77:10■78:19■82:6■83:4,12■87:5■89:2■
94:18■95:10■102:24■106:23■110:1
(5002)■116:11■119:57■122:1■126:2■
137:7■140:6■142:5-**PR**-4:4■7:13■25:7
-**EC**-1:10■2:1,2,15,15a■3:17,18■7:23■
8:14■9:16-**SONG**-2:10■7:8-**IS**-6:3,5,
7,8,9,11■7:3,12,13■8:1,3■14:13■18:4■
20:3■21:6,9,12,16■22:4■23:12■24:16■
25:9■28:12,15■29:13■30:16■32:5■36:4,
7,10,11,12,13■37:3,6,24■38:1,3,10,11,21,
22■39:3^2,4,5,8^2■40:6■41:6,9■45:19■
47:10^2■49:3,4,6,14■51:23■63:8■65:1■66:5
-**JER**-1:6,7,9,11,12,13,14■2:6,8■3:6,7,11,
19^2■4:10,11,27■5:4,12■6:6,16,17■10:19■
11:5,6,9■12:4■13:6■14:11,13,14■15:1,
11■16:14■17:19■18:10,12,18■19:14■
20:3,9■21:3■23:17a,25■24:3^2■25:5■
26:16■28:5,6,15■29:15■32:6,8,25■35:5,
6,11,18■36:15,16,19■37:14,17^3,18■38:4,
5,12,14,15,17,19,20,24,25^{2}a■40:2,3a,14■
41:6,8■42:2,4,5,9,19a■44:20,24■46:16■
50:7■51:61-**LA**-3:18,54■4:15,20-**EZE**-
2:1,3■3:1,3,4,10,22,24■4:13,14,15,16■
6:10a■8:5,6,8,9,12,13,15,17■9:4,5,7,8,9■
10:2■11:2,5^2,13,15■12:9■13:12■16:6^2■
20:7,8,13,18,21,29,49■21:17a■23:36,43■
24:19■26:2■27:3■28:2■29:3,9■35:10■
36:2,20■37:3,4,9,11■40:4a,45a■41:4,
22a■42:13■43:7,18■44:2,5■46:20,24■
47:6,8-**DA**-1:10,11,18■2:3,5b,7b,8b,10b,
15b,20b,24b,25b,26b,27b,47b■3:9b,14b,
16b,24b^2,25b,26b,28b■4:14b,19b^2,30b■
5:7b,10b,13b,17b■6:5b,6b,12b,13b,15b,
16b,20b,21(4449)■7:2b,5b,23b■8:13,14,
16,17,19■9:4,22■10:11,12,16,19^2,20■
12:6,8,9-**HO**-1:2,4,6,9,10^2■2:5,12■3:1,
3■12:8-**JOE**-2:32-**AM**-1:2■7:2:5,8^3,12,
14,15■8:2^3■9:1-**JON**-1:6,7,8,9,10,11,12,
14■2:2,4■3:4,10a■4:2,4,8,9^2,10-**MIC**-
3:1■7:10-**HAB**-2:2-**ZEP**-2:15■3:7,16
-**HAG**-2:12,13^2,14-**ZEC**-1:6,9^2,10,11,12,
14,19,21■2:2^2,4■3:2,4,5■4:2^2,5^2,11,12,
13^2,14■5:2,3,5,6^2,8,10,11■6:4,5,7■
11:9,12,13,15-**MAL**-1:13■3:7,14■**N.T.**-
all=2036,a=3004,b=2046,c=5346,d=
4483&marked-**M'T**-2:5,8■3:7,15■4:3,
4,7c■5:21b,27b,31b,33b,38b,43b■8:8c,
10d,13d,19d,21d,22d,32d■9:2d,3d,4d,
11d,12d,15d,21a,22,24a,28a,34a■11:3,
4,25■12:2,3,11,23a,24,25,39,47,48,49■
13:10,11(2063),27(2063),28(2063),28c,
29c,37,52,54a,57■14:2,4a,8c,16,18,28,29,
31a■15:3,10,12,13,15,16,24,26,27,28,32,
34■16:2,6,8,14,16,17,23,24■17:4,5a,7,
11,17,19,20,22,24■18:3,21,32a■19:4,5,
11,14,16,17,18,21c,23,26,27,28■20:4,13,
17,21,22,25,32■21:11a,13a,16,19a,
21,23a,24,27,27c,28,29,30^2,38■22:1a,13,
18,24,29,37,44■24:2,4■25:8,12,21c,22,
23c,24,26■26:1,5a,10,15,18,21,23,25,
25a,25,26,33,34c,35a,35,49,50,52a,55,61,
61c,62,63,64,66,71a,73,75b■27:4,6,11c,13a,
17,21^2,23c,25,41a,43,47a,49a,63,65c■28:5,
6,10a-**M'R**-1:17,37a,38a■2:5,8,14a,16a,
19,24a,25a,27a■3:21a,22a,23a,30a,32,
34a■4:2a,9a,11a,13a,21a,24a,26a,30a,39,
40,41a■5:7,8a,28a,30a,31a,34,35a,41a■
6:4a,10a,14a,15^{2}a,16,18a,22(846),22,24^2,
31,35a,37■7:6,9a,10,14a,20a,27,28a,29■
8:5,20,21a,24a,34■9:1a,5a,17,21,23,24a,
26a,29,31a,36,39■10:3,4,5,14,18,20,21,
29,36,37,38,39^2,51a,51,52■11:5a,6,14,
29,33a■12:7,15,16,17,24,32^2,34,35a,36^2,
38a■13:2■14:2a,4a,6,12a,16,18,20,22,24,
29c,31a,36a,48,61a,62,67a,70a,72■15:2,
12,14a,31a,35a,39■16:3a,7,8,15-**LU**-
1:13,18,19,28,30,34,35,38,42,46,60,61■
2:10,15,24b,28,34,48,49■3:7a,12,13,14,
22a■4:3,6,8,9,12,12b,22a,23,24,43■5:4,5,
10,20,22,24,27,31,33,34■6:2,3,5a,8,9,
10,20a■7:9,13,14,20,22,31,40,43^2,44c,48,
50■8:8a,10,20a,21,22,25,28,30,45^2,46,
48,52■9:3,7a,9,12,13^2,14,19,20^2,23a,33,
33a,41,43,48,49,50,54,55,57,58,59^2,60,
61,62■10:2a,18,21,23,26,27,28,29,30,
35,37^2,40,41■11:1,2,5,15,17,27,28,39,
45a,46,49,53a■12:13,14,15,18,20,22,41,
42,54a■13:2,7,8a,12,14a,15,17a,18a,20,
23^2,32■14:12a,15,16,18,19,20,21,22,23,
25■15:11,12,17,21,22,27,29,31■16:1a,2,3,
5a,6^2,7^2,7a,15,24,25,27,30,31■17:1,5,6,
13a,14,17,19,20,22,37a,37■18:4,6,16,19,
21,22,24,26,27,28,29,31,41,42■19:5,8,9,
12,13,17,19,24,25,32,33,34,39,40■20:3,
8,13,16,17,23,24,25,34,39^2,41,42,45■
21:3,5,8,10a■22:9,10,13b,15,17,25,31,33,
34a,35^2,36,38^2,40,46,48,49,51,52,56,58c,
58,60,61,67,70c,70,71■23:3c,4,14,22,28,
34a,42a,43,46^2■24:5,17,18,19^2,23a,24,
25,32,38,41,44,46-**JOH**-1:22,23c,23,
25,30,33,38,42,46,48,50^2■2:16,18,19,20,
22a,22■3:2,3,7,9,10,26,27,28■4:10,13,
17,17a,17,27,32,33a,42a,48,52,53■5:10a,
11,12,14,18a,19■6:6a,10,12a,14a,25,26,
28,29,30,32,34,35,36,41,42a,43,53,59,
60,61,65a,65b,67■7:3,6a,9,11a,12^{2}a,16,
20,21,25a,31a,33,35,36,38,40a,41^{2}a,42,
45,52■8:6a,7,10,11^2,13,14,19a,21,22a,23,
24,25a,25(2980),28,31a,39,41,42,48,
52,57,58■9:7,8a,9a,9sup,9a,10,11^2,12,12a,
15,16^{2}a,17,20,23,24,25,26,28,30,34,35,36,
37,38c,39,40,41■10:7,20a,21a,24a,26,34,
36,41a■11:4,11,12,14,16,21,25,28,34,34a,
36a,37,39a,40,41,42,47a,49■12:6,7,19,
29^{2}a,30,33a,35,39,41,44,50b■13:7,11,12,
21^2,27a,29a,31a,33,36a,37a■14:23,26,28^2■
15:20■16:4,6(2980),15,17,18a,19^2,29a■17:1■
18:4,6,7,11,20(2980),21(2980),21,25^2,29,
30,31^2,33,37,38■19:3a,21a,21,24,30■
20:14,20,21,22,25a,25,26,28■21:6,17^2,20,
23-**AC**-1:7,11,15,24■2:13a,14(669),34,37,
38c■3:4,6,22■4:8,19,23,24,25,32a■5:3,8,
9,19,29,35■6:2,11a,13a■7:1,2c,3,7,33,37,
56,60■8:20,24,29,30,31,34,36c,37^2■9:5^2,

6^2,10^2,15,17,21a,34,40■10:4^2,14,19,21,
22,28c,30c,31c,34■11:8,13,16a■12:8,11,
15,15a,17■13:2,10,16,22,25a,34c,46■
14:10■15:7,36■16:18,30c,31,37c■17:18a,
22c,28b,32■18:6,14■19:2^2,3^2,4,15,25,35c■
20:10,18,35■21:4a,11a,20a,37a,37c,39■
22:8,10^2,13,14,19,21,22a,25,27,27c,28c■
23:1,3,4,5c,7(2980),11,14,17c,18c,20,35c■
24:22■25:5c,9,10,22^{2}c,24c■26:1c,15^2,24c,
25c,28c,29,32c■27:10a,21,31■28:4a,6a,
17a,21,29-RO-7:7a■9:12d,26d,29(4280)
-2CO-11:24-2CO-6:16■7:3(4280)9:3a■
12:9b-GA-1:9(4280)■2:14-TIT-1:12
-HEB-1:5,13b■3:10,15a■4:3b,7b■5:5
(2980)■7:21a■10:7,8a,9b,15(4280),30■
11:8(2980)■12:21■13:5b-JAS-2:11^2
-JUDE-9-RE-4:1a■5:14a■6:11d,16a■
7:14b,14■10:8a,9^{2}a,11a■17:7■19:3b,10a■
21:5,5a,6■22:6
SAIDST-all=559&marked-GE-12:19■
26:9■32:9,12■44:21,23-EX-32:13
(1696)-J'G-9:38-1KI-2:42-JOB-35:2,3
-PS-27:8■89:19-IS-47:7■57:10-JER-
2:20,25■22:21-LA-3:57-EZE-25:3
-HO-13:10■N.T.-JOH-4:18■(2046)
SAIL-IS-33:23(5251)-EZE-27:7(5251)■
N.T.-AC-20:3(321),16(3896)■27:1(636),
2(4126)■27:17(4632),24(4126)
SAILED-all=636&marked-LU-8:23
(4126)-AC-13:4■14:26■15:39(1602)■
18:18(1602),21(321)■20:6(1602),13(321),
15■21:3(4126)■27:4(5284),5(1277),7
(1020),7(5284),13(3881)
SAILING-AC-21:2(1276)■27:6
(4126),9(4144)
SAILORS-RE-18:17(3492)
SAINT-all=6918-PS-106:16-DA-
8:13^2■N.T.-PH'P-4:21(40)
SAINTS-all=2623&marked-DE-
33:2(6944),3(6918)-1SA-2:9-2CH-6:41
-JOB-5:1(6918)■15:15(6918)-PS-16:3■
30:4■31:23■34:9(6918)■37:28■50:5■52:9■
79:2■85:8■89:5(6918),7(6918)■97:10■
116:15■132:9,16■145:10■148:14■149:1,
5,9-PR-2:8-DA-7:18(6922),21(6922),
22^2(6922),25(6922),27(6922)-HO-11:12
(6918)-ZEC-14:5(6918)■N.T.-all=40
-M'T-27:52-AC-9:13,32,41■26:10-RO-
1:7■8:27■12:13■15:25,26,31■16:2,15
-1CO-1:2■6:1,2■14:33■16:1,15-2CO-1:1■
8:4■9:1,12■13:13-EPH-1:1,15,18■2:19■
3:8,18■4:12■5:3■6:18-PH'P-1:1■4:22
-COL-1:2,4,12,26-1TH-3:13-2TH-1:10
-PH'M-5,7-HEB-6:10■13:24-JUDE-
3,14-RE-5:8■8:3,4■11:18■13:7,10■
14:12■15:3■16:6■17:6■18:24■19:8■20:9
SAINTS'-1TI-5:10(40)
SAITH-all=559,a=5002,b=5001-GE-
22:16a■32:4■41:55■44:7(1696)■45:9
-EX-4:22■5:1,10■7:17■8:1,20■9:1,13■
10:3■11:4■32:27-NU-14:28■20:14■
22:16■24:13(1696)■32:27(1696)-JOS-
5:14(1696)■7:13■22:16■24:2-J'G-6:8■
11:15-1SA-2:27,30^{2}a■9:6(1696)■10:18■
15:2■20:3■24:13-2SA-7:5,8■12:7,11■
14:10(1696)■17:5(6310)■24:12(1696)
-1KI-2:30■3:23^2■11:31■12:24■13:2,21■
14:7■17:14■20:2,13,14,28,32,42■21:19^2■
22:11,14,27-2KI-1:4,6,16■2:21■3:16,17■
4:43■5:13■7:1■9:3,6,12,18,19,26,26a■
18:19,29,31■19:3,6,20,32,33a■20:1,5,
17■21:12■22:15,16,18,19a-1CH-17:4,7■
21:10,11-2CH-11:4■12:5■18:10,13,26■
20:15■21:12■24:20■32:10■34:23,24,26,
27a■36:23-EZR-1:2-NE-6:6-JOB-28:14^2■
33:24■35:10■37:6■39:25-PS-12:5■
36:1a■50:16-PR-9:4,16■20:14■22:13■
23:7■24:24■26:13,19■28:24■30:16,20
-EC-1:2■7:27■10:3■12:8-IS-1:11,18,24a■
3:15a,16■7:7■10:8,13,24■14:22^{2}a,23a■
17:3a,6a■19:4a■22:14,15,25a■28:16■
29:11,12,22■30:1a,12,15■31:9a■33:10■
36:4,14,16■37:3,6,21,33,34a■38:1,5■
39:6■40:1,25■41:14a,21^2■42:5,22■43:1,
10a,12a,14,16■44:2,6,16,17,24,26,27,28■
45:1,10,11,13,14,18■48:17,22■49:5,7,8,
18a,22,25■50:1■51:22■52:3,4,5^{2}a,7■54:1,
6,8,10,17a■55:8a■56:1,4,8a■57:15,19,21■
59:20a,21^2■65:7,8^2,13,25■66:1,2a,9^2,12,
17a,20,21,22a,23-JER-1:8a,15a,19a■
2:2,3a,5,9a,12a,19a,22a,29a■3:1a,10a,
12^{2}a,13a,14a,16a,20a■4:1a,3,9a,17a■5:9a,
11a,14,15a,18a,22a,29a■6:9,12a,15,16,21,
22■7:3,11a,13a,19a,20,21,30a,32a■8:1a,
3a,4,12,13a,17a■9:3a,6a,7,9a,13,15,17,
22a,23,24a,25a■10:2,18■11:3,11,21,22■
12:14,17a■13:1,9,11a,12,13,14a,25a■
14:10,15■15:2,3a,6a,9a,19,20a■16:3,5,
5a,9,11a,14a,16a■17:5,21,24a■18:6a,11,
13■19:1,3,6a,11,12a,15■20:4■21:4,7a,8,
10a,12,13a,14a■22:1,3,5a,6,11,14,16a,
18,24a,30■23:1a,2,2a,4a,5a,7a,11a,12a,15,
16,23a,24^{2}a,28a,29a,30a,31^{2}a,32^{2}a,33a,
38■24:5,8■25:7a,8,9a,12a,15,27,28,29a,
31a,32■26:2,4,18■27:2,4,8a,11a,15a,16,
19,21,22a■28:4a,11,13,14,16■29:4,8,9a,
10,11a,14^{2}a,16,17,19^{2}a,21,23a,31,32,
32a■30:3a,3,5,8a,10a,11a,12a,18,21a■
31:1a,2,7,14a,15,16,16a,17a,20a,23,27a,
28a,31a,32a,33a,34a,35,36a,37,37a,38a■
32:3,5a,14,15,28,30a,36,42,44a■33:2,4,
10,11,12,13,14a,17,20,25■34:2^2,4,5a,
13,17,17a,22a■35:13,13a,17,18,19■36:29,
30■37:7,9■38:2,3,17■39:16,17a,18a■
42:9,11a,15,18■43:10■44:2,7,11,25,26,
29a,30■45:2,4,5a■46:5a,8,18a,23a,25,
26a,28a■47:2■48:1,12a,15a,25a,30a,35a,
38a,40,43a,44a,47a■49:1,2,2a,5a,6a,7,
12,13a,16a,18,26a,28,30a,31a,32a,35,
37a,38a,39a■50:4a,10a,18,20a,21a,
30a,31a,33,35a,40a■51:1,24a,25a,26a,33,
36,39a,48a,52a,53a,57a,58-LA-3:24,37
-EZE-2:4■3:11,27■5:5,7,8,11a■6:3,11■
7:2,5■11:5,7,8a,16,17,21a■12:10,19,23,
25a,28,28a■13:3,6a,7a,8,8a,13,16a,18,
20■14:4,6,11a,14a,16a,18a,20a,21,23a■
15:6,8a■16:3,8a,14a,19a,23a,30a,36,43a,
48a,58a,59,63a■17:3,9,16a,19,22■18:3a,
9a,23a,29,30a,32a■20:3,3a,5,27,30,31a,
33a,36a,39,40a,44a,47■21:3,7a,9,13a,24,
26,28■22:3,12a,19,28,31a■23:22,28,32,
34,35,46■24:3,6,9,14a,21■25:3,6,8,12,
13,14a,15,16■26:3,5a,7,14a,15,19,21b,
27:3■28:2,6,10a,12,22,25■29:3,8,13,19,
20a■30:2,6,6a,10,13,22■31:10,15,18a■
32:3,8a,11,14a,16a,31a,32a■33:11a,25,27■
34:2,8,10,11,15a,17,20,30a,31a■35:3,6a,
11a,14■36:2,3,4,5,6,7,13,14a,15a,22,
23a,32a,33,37■37:5,9,12,14a,19,21■38:3,
10,14,17,18a,21a■39:1,5a,8a,10a,13a,17,
20a,25,29a■43:18,19a,27a■44:6,9,12a,
15a,27a■45:9a,9,15a,18■46:1,16■47:13,
23a■48:29a-HO-2:13a,16a,21a■11:11a
-JOE-2:12a-AM-1:3,5,6,8,9,11,13,15■
2:1,3,4,6,11a,16a■3:10a,11,12,13b,15b■
4:3b,5b,6b,8b,9b,10b,11b■5:3,4,16,17,27■
6:8a,14a■7:3,6,11,17■8:3a,9a,11a■9:7a,
8a,12a,13a,15-OB-1,3,4a,8a-MIC-2:3■
3:5■4:6a■5:10■6:1-NA-1:12■2:13a■
3:5a-HAB-2:19-ZEP-1:2a,3a,10a■2:9a■
3:8a,20-HAG-1:5,7,8,9a,13a■2:4^{3}a,6,7,
8a,9a,9,11,14a,17a,23^{3}a-ZEC-1:3,3a,3,4,
4a,14a,16,16a,17■2:5a,6^{2}a,8,10a■3:7,9a,
10a■4:6■5:4a■7:13■8:2,3,4,6,6a,7,9,11a,
14^2,17a,19,20,23■10:12a■11:4,6a■12:1a,
4a■13:2a,7a,8a-MAL-1:2a,2,4^2,6,8,9,10,
11,13^2,14■2:2,4,8,16^2■3:1,5,7,10,11,12,
13,17■4:1,3■N.T.-all=3004&marked
-M'T-4:6,9,10,19■7:21■8:4,7,20,26■
9:6,9,28,37■12:13,44■13:14,51■15:34■
16:15■17:25,26,26(5346)■18:22■19:8,
18,20■20:6,7,8,21,23■21:16,31,42■22:8,
12,20,21,43■26:18,31,36,38,40,45,64■
27:22-M'R-1:41,44■2:10,17■3:3,4,5■
4:35■5:19,36,39■6:38,50■7:18,34■8:1,
12,17,29^2■9:19,35■10:11,23,24,27,42■
11:2,21,22,23^2,33■12:16,43■13:1■14:13,
14,27,30,32,34,37,41,45,63■15:28■16:6
-LU-3:11■5:39■7:40(5346)■11:24■16:29■
18:6■19:22■20:42■22:11■24:36-JOH-
1:21,29,36,38,39,41,43,45,46,47,48,49,
51■2:3,4,5^2,7,8,10■3:4■4:7,9,10,11,15,16,
19,21,25,26,28,34,49,50■5:6,8■6:5,8,20,
42■7:50■8:22,25,39■11:7,11,23,24,27,
39,40,44■12:4■13:6,8,9,10,25■14:5,6,8,
9,22■16:17,18,18(2980)■18:5,17^2,26,38^2■
19:4,5,6,9,10,14,15,24,26,27,28,35,37■
20:2,13,15^2,16^2,17,19,22,27,29■21:3,5,7,
10,12,15^3,16^3,17^2,19,21,22-AC-2:17,34■
7:48,49■12:8■13:35■15:17■21:11■22:2
(5346)-RO-3:19,19(2980)■4:3■9:15,17,
25■10:8,11,16,19,20,21■11:2,4,9■12:19■
14:11■15:10,12-1CO-1:12■3:4■6:16
(5346)■9:8,10■14:21,34■15:27(2036)
-2CO-6:2,17,18-GA-3:16■4:30-EPH-
4:8■5:14-1TI-5:18-HEB-1:6,7■3:7■5:6■
8:5(5346),8^2,9,10,13■10:5,16,30-JAS-
2:23■4:5,6-1JO-2:4,6,9-RE-1:8■2:1,7,8,
11,12,17,18,29■3:1,6,7,13,14,22■5:5■
14:13■17:15■18:7■19:9^2■22:9,10,20
SAKE-all=4616,a=5668&marked
-GE-3:17a■8:21a■12:13a,16a■18:29a,31a,
32a■20:11(1697)■26:24a■30:27(1558)■
39:5(1558)-EX-18:18(182)■21:26(8478),
27(8478)-NU-25:11(7068),18(1697)
-1SA-12:22a■23:10a-2SA-5:12a■7:21a■
9:1a,7a-1KI-8:41■11:12,13^2,32^2,34■15:4
-2KI-8:19■19:34^2■20:6^2-1CH-17:19a
-2CH-6:32-PS-6:4■23:3■25:7,11■31:3■
44:26■69:7(5921)■79:9■106:8■109:21■
132:10a-IS-37:35■42:21■43:14,25■
45:4■48:9,11■54:15(5921)■62:1■63:17■
66:5-JER-14:7,21-EZE-20:9,14,22,44
-DA-9:17,19-JON-1:12(7945)-MIC-3:12
(1558)■N.T.-all=1752&marked-M'T-
5:10,11■10:18,39■16:25■19:29-M'R-
8:35■10:29■13:9-LU-6:22■9:24■18:29■
21:12-RO-8:36-EPH-4:32(1722)
SAKES-all=6616&marked-GE-18:26
(5668)-DE-1:37(1558)■3:26(6616)■4:21
(1697)-1CH-16:21(5921)-PS-7:7(5921)■
105:14(5921)■106:32(5668)■122:8-IS-
65:8-EZE-36:22,32-DA-2:30(1701)
SALE-all=4465-LE-25:27,50-DE-18:8
SALT-all=4417&marked-GE-14:3■
19:26-LE-2:13^3-NU-18:19■34:3,12
-DE-3:17■29:23-JOS-3:16■12:3■15:2,
5,62(5898)■18:19-J'G-9:45-2SA-8:13
-2KI-2:20,21■14:7-1CH-18:12-2CH-
13:5■25:11-EZR-6:9(4416)■7:22(4416)
-JOB-6:6-PS-60:0-JER-17:6(4420)-EZE-
43:24■47:11■N.T.-all=217&marked
-M'T-5:13^2-M'R-9:49(251),50^2-LU-
14:34-COL-4:6-JAS-3:12(252)
SALTED-EZE-16:4(4414)■N.T.-
all=233-M'T-5:13-M'R-9:49^2
SALTNESS-M'R-9:50(1096,358)
SALTPITS-ZEP-2:9(4417)
SALUTATION-all=783-LU-1:29,
41,44-1CO-16:21-COL-4:18-2TH-3:17
SALUTATIONS-M'R-12:38(783)
SALUTE-all=782&marked-1SA-
10:4(7965)■13:10(1288)■25:14(1288)
-2SA-8:10(7592,7965)-2KI-4:29^2(1288)■
10:13(7965)■N.T.-all=782-M'T-5:47■
10:12-M'R-15:18-LU-10:4-AC-25:13
-RO-16:5,7,9,10^2,11,12^2,13,14,15,16^2,21,
22-1CO-16:19^2-2CO-13:13-PH'P-4:21,
22-COL-4:15-2TI-4:19-TIT-3:15
-PH'M-23-HEB-13:24^2-3JO-14
SALUTED-all=7592,7965&marked
-J'G-18:15-1SA-17:22■30:21-2KI-10:15
(1288)■N.T.-all=782-M'R-9:15-LU-
1:40-AC-18:22■21:7,19
SALUTETH-all=782-RO-16:23^2
-COL-4:10,12-1PE-5:13
SALVATION-all=3444,a=3468,b=
8668&marked-GE-49:18-EX-14:13■
15:2-DE-32:15-1SA-2:1■11:13b■14:45■
19:5b-2SA-22:3a,36a,47a,51■23:5a
-1CH-16:23,35a-2CH-6:41b■20:17
-JOB-13:16-PS-3:8■9:14■13:5■14:7■
18:2a,35a,46a■20:5■21:1,5■24:5a■25:5a■
27:1a,9a■35:3,9■37:39b■38:22b■40:10b,
16b■50:23a■51:12a,14b■53:6■62:1,2,6,
7a■65:5a■68:19,20(4190)■69:13a,29■
70:4■71:15b■74:12■78:22■79:9a■85:4a,
7a,9a■88:1■89:26■91:16■95:1a■96:2■
98:2,3■106:4■116:13■118:14,15,21■
119:41b,81b,123,155,166,174■132:16a■
140:7■144:10b■149:4-IS-12:2^2,3■
17:10a■25:9■26:1■33:2,6■45:8a,17b■
46:13^{2}b■49:6,8■51:5a,6,8■52:7,10■
56:1■59:11,16(3467),17■60:18■61:10a■

62:1,11a▪63:5(3467)-JER-3:23b-LA-3:26b-JON-2:9-MIC-7:7a-HAB-3:8,13^{2}a,18a-ZEC-9:9(3467)▪N.T.-all=4991&marked-LU-1:69,77▪2:30(4992)▪3:6(4992)▪19:9-JOH-4:22-AC-4:12▪13:26,47▪16:17▪28:28(4992)-RO-1:16▪10:10▪11:11▪13:11-2CO-1:6^{2}▪6:2^{2}▪7:10-EPH-1:13▪6:17(4992)-PH'P-1:19,28▪2:12-1TH-5:8,9-2TH-2:13-2TI-2:10▪3:15-TIT-2:11(4992)-HEB-1:14▪2:3,10▪5:9▪6:9▪9:28-1PE-1:5,9,10-2PE-3:15-JUDE-3-RE-7:10▪12:10▪19:1

SAME-all=1931&marked-GE-2:13▪6:4(1992)▪7:11(2088)▪10:12▪14:8▪15:8▪19:37,38▪23:2,19▪25:30(2088)▪26:12,24▪32:13▪48:7-EX-5:6▪12:6(2088)▪19:1(2088)-LE-22:30▪23:6(2088),28(6106),29(6106),30^{2}(6106)-NU-4:8(853)▪6:11▪9:13▪15:30▪32:10-DE-9:20▪14:28▪27:11▪31:22-JOS-6:15(2088)▪11:16(2088)▪15:8-J'G-6:25▪7:4^{2},9-1SA-4:12▪6:15,16▪9:17(2088)▪17:23(428),30(2088)▪31:6-2SA-2:23(8478)▪5:7▪23:8-1KI-8:64▪13:3-2KI-3:6▪8:22-1CH-1:27▪17:3-2CH-7:8▪15:11▪16:10▪18:7▪20:26▪21:10▪27:5▪32:12,30▪34:28▪35:16-EZR-4:15(1459)▪5:16(1791)▪10:23(1933)-NE-4:22▪6:4(2088)▪10:37(1992)-PS-75:8(2088)▪102:27-PR-28:24-EC-9:15-IS-7:20-JER-28:1,17▪31:1▪39:10-EZE-3:18▪10:16(1992),22(1992)▪21:26(2063)▪23:38,39▪24:2^{2}(6106)▪38:10,18-DA-7:21(1797)▪12:1-ZEP-1:9▪ZEC-6:10▪N.T.-all=846,a=3778,b=1565&marked-M'T-3:4▪5:19a,46▪10:19b▪12:50▪13:1b,20a▪15:22b▪18:1b,4a,28b▪21:42a▪22:23b▪24:13a▪25:16▪26:23a,44,48,55b▪27:44-M'R-3:35a▪4:35b▪8:35a▪10:10▪13:13a▪14:39,44-LU-2:8,25a▪6:33,38▪7:21▪9:24a,48a▪10:7,10▪12:12▪13:31▪16:1a▪20:17a,19,47a▪23:12,40,51a▪24:13,33-JOH-1:2a,7a,33b,33a▪3:2a,26a▪4:53b▪5:9b,11b,36▪7:18a▪8:25(3748)▪10:1b▪11:49b▪12:21a,48b▪15:5a▪18:13b▪20:19b-AC-1:11a▪2:36(5126),41b▪7:19a,35(5126)▪8:35(5026)▪12:6b▪13:33(5026)▪14:9a▪15:27▪16:17a,18,33b▪18:3(3673)▪19:23b▪21:9(5129)▪22:13▪24:20a▪28:7b-RO-1:32▪2:1,3▪9:17,21▪10:12▪12:4,16▪13:3-1CO-1:10^{2}▪7:20(5026)▪8:3a▪9:8(5023)▪10:3,4▪11:23,25(5615)▪12:4,5,6,8,9^{2},25▪15:39-2CO-1:6▪2:3▪3:14,18▪4:13▪6:13▪7:8b▪8:6,16,19a▪9:4(5026),5(5026)▪12:18^{2}-GA-2:8(2532),10(846,5124)▪3:7a-EPH-3:6(4954)▪6:8a,9,22-PH'P-1:30▪2:18▪3:1,16^{2}▪4:2-COL-4:2,8-2TI-2:2(5023)-HEB-1:12▪2:14▪4:11▪6:11▪10:11▪13:8-JAS-3:2a,10,11-1PE-2:7a▪4:1,4,10▪5:9-2PE-2:19a▪3:7-1JO-2:23(3761),27-RE-3:5a▪11:13b▪14:10

SANCTIFICATION-all=38-1CO-1:30-1TH-4:3,4-2TH-2:13-1PE-1:2

SANCTIFIED-all=6942-GE-2:3-EX-19:14▪29:43-LE-8:10,15,30▪10:3▪27:15,19-NU-7:1^{2}▪8:17▪20:13-DE-32:51-1SA-7:1▪16:5▪21:5-1CH-15:14-2CH-5:11▪7:16,20▪29:15,17,19,34▪30:3,8,15,17,24▪31:18-NE-3:1^{2}▪12:47^{2}-JOB-1:5-IS-5:16▪13:3-JER-1:5-EZE-20:41▪28:22,25▪36:23▪38:16▪39:27▪48:11▪N.T.-all=37-JOH-10:36▪17:19-AC-20:32▪26:18-RO-15:16-1CO-1:2▪6:11▪7:14^{2}-1TI-4:5-2TI-2:21-HEB-2:11▪10:10,14,29-JUDE-1

SANCTIFIETH-all=37-M'T-23:17,19-HEB-2:11▪9:13

SANCTIFY-all=6942-EX-13:2▪19:10,22,23▪28:41▪29:27,33,36,37,44^{2}▪30:29▪31:13▪40:10,11,13-LE-8:11,12▪11:44▪20:7,8▪21:8^{2},15,23▪22:9,16▪27:14,16,17,18,22,26-NU-11:18▪20:12▪27:14-DE-5:12▪15:19-JOS-3:5▪7:13^{2}-1SA-16:5-1CH-15:12▪23:13-2CH-29:5^{2},17,34▪30:17▪35:6-NE-13:22-IS-8:13▪29:23^{2}▪66:17-EZE-20:12▪36:23▪37:28▪38:23▪44:19▪46:20-JOE-1:14▪2:15,16▪N.T.-all=37-JOH-17:17,19-EPH-5:26-1TH-5:23-HEB-13:12-1PE-3:15

SANCTUARIES-all=4720-LE-21:23▪26:31-JER-51:51-EZE-28:18-AM-7:9

SANCTUARY-all=6944,a=4720&marked-EX-15:17a▪25:8a▪30:13,24▪36:1,3,4,6▪38:24,25,26,27-LE-4:6▪5:15▪10:4▪12:4a▪16:33a▪19:30a▪20:3a▪21:12^{2}a▪26:2▪27:3,25-NU-3:28,31,32,38a,47,50▪4:12,15^{2},16▪7:9,13,19,25,31,37,43,49,55,61,67,73,79,85,86▪8:19▪10:21a▪18:1a,3,5,16▪19:20a-JOS-24:26a-1CH-9:29▪22:19a▪24:5▪28:10a-2CH-20:8a▪26:18a▪29:21a▪30:8a,19▪36:17a-NE-10:39a-PS-20:2▪63:2▪68:24▪73:17a▪74:3,7a▪77:13▪78:54,69a▪96:6a▪102:19▪114:2▪134:2▪150:1-IS-8:14a▪16:12a▪43:28▪60:13a▪63:18a-JER-17:12a-LA-1:10a▪2:7a,20a▪4:1-EZE-5:11a▪8:6a▪9:6a▪11:16a,38a▪23:39a▪24:21a▪25:3a▪37:26a,28a▪41:21,23▪42:20▪43:21a▪44:1a,5a,7sup,7a,8a,9a,11a,15a.16a,27^{2}▪45:2,3a,4^{2}a,18a▪47:12a▪48:8a,10a,21a-DA-8:11a,13,14▪9:17a,26▪11:31a-ZEP-3:4▪N.T.-all=39-HEB-8:2▪9:1,2▪13:11▪

SAND-all=2344-GE-22:17▪32:12▪41:49-EX-2:12-DE-33:19-JOS-11:4-J'G-7:12-1SA-13:5-2SA-17:11-1KI-4:20,29-JOB-6:3▪29:18-PS-78:27▪139:18-PR-27:3-IS-10:22▪48:19-JER-5:22▪15:8▪33:22-HO-1:10-HAB-1:9▪N.T.-all=285-M'T-7:26-RO-9:27-HEB-11:12-RE-13:1▪20:8

SANDALS-M'R-6:9(4547)-AC-12:8(4547)

SANG-all=7891&marked-EX-15:1-NU-21:17-J'G-5:1-1SA-29:5(6030)-2CH-29:28-EZR-3:11(6030)-NE-12:42-JOB-38:7(7442)-PS-7:0▪106:12▪N.T.-AC-16:25(5214)

SANK-EX-15:5(3381),10(6749)

SAP-supplied

SAPPHIRE-all=5601-EX-24:10▪28:18▪39:11-JOB-28:16-LA-4:7-EZE-1:26▪10:1▪28:13▪N.T.-RE-21:19(4552)

SAPPHIRES-all=5601-JOB-28:6-SONG-5:14-IS-54:11

SARDINE-RE-4:3(4555)

SARDIUS-all=124-EX-28:17▪39:10-EZE-28:13▪N.T.-RE-21:20(4556)

SARDONYX-RE-21:20(4557)

SAT-all=3427&marked-GE-18:1▪19:1▪21:16^{2}▪31:34▪37:25▪38:14▪43:33▪48:2-EX-2:15▪12:29▪16:3▪17:12▪18:13▪32:6-LE-15:6,22-DE-33:3(8497)-J'G-6:11▪13:9▪19:6,15▪20:26-RU-2:14▪4:1^{2},2-1SA-1:9▪4:13▪19:9▪20:24,25^{2}▪28:23-2SA-2:13▪7:1,18▪18:24▪19:8▪23:8-1KI-2:12,19^{2}▪13:20▪16:11▪19:4▪21:13▪22:10-2KI-1:9▪4:20▪6:32^{2}▪11:19▪13:13-1CH-17:1,16▪29:23-2CH-18:9^{2}-EZR-9:3,4▪10:9,16-NE-1:4▪8:17-ES-1:2,14▪2:19,21▪3:15▪5:1-JOB-2:8,13▪29:25-PS-26:4▪137:1-SONG-2:3-JER-3:2▪15:17^{2}▪26:10▪32:12▪36:12,22▪39:3-EZE-3:15▪8:1^{2},14▪14:1▪20:1-JON-3:6▪4:5▪N.T.-all=2521,a=2523&marked-M'T-4:16^{2}▪9:10(345),10(4873)▪13:1,2,48a▪14:9(4873)▪15:29▪24:3▪26:7(345),20(345),55(2516),58,69▪28:2-M'R-2:15(2621),15(4873)▪3:32,34▪4:1▪6:22(4873),26(4873),40(377)▪9:35a▪10:46▪11:2a,7a▪12:41a▪13:3▪14:3(2621),18(345),54(4775)▪16:14(345),19a-LU-4:20a▪5:3,29(2621)▪7:15(339),36(347),37(345)49(4873)▪10:39(3869)▪11:37(377)▪14:15(4873)▪18:35▪19:30a▪22:14(377),55,56▪24:30(2625)-JOH-4:6(2516)▪6:3,10(377)▪8:2a▪9:8▪11:20(2516)▪12:2(4873),14a▪19:13a-AC-2:3a▪3:10▪6:15(2516)▪9:40(339)▪12:21a▪13:14a▪14:8▪16:13a▪20:9▪25:17a▪26:30(4775)-1CO-10:7a-HEB-1:3a▪10:12a-RE-4:2,3,9,10▪5:1,7▪6:2,4,5,8▪9:17▪11:16▪14:14,15,16▪19:4,11,19,21▪20:4a,11▪21:5

SATAN-all=7854-1CH-21:1-JOB-1:6,7^{2},8,9,12^{2}▪2:1,2^{2},3,4,6,7-PS-109:6-ZEC-3:1,2^{2}▪N.T.-all=4567-M'T-4:10▪12:26▪16:23-M'R-1:13▪3:23,26▪4:15▪8:33-LU-4:8▪10:18▪11:18▪13:16▪22:3,31-JOH-13:27-AC-5:3▪26:18-RO-16:20-1CO-5:5▪7:5-2CO-2:11▪11:14▪12:7-1TH-2:18-2TH-2:9-1TI-1:20▪5:15-RE-2:9,13,24▪3:9▪12:9▪20:2,7

SATAN'S-RE-2:13(4567)

SATEST-PS-9:4(3427)-EZE-23:41(3427)

SATIATE-JER-31:14(7301)▪46:10(7646)

SATIATED-JER-31:25(7301)

SATISFACTION-NU-35:31(3724),32(3724)

SATISFIED-all=7646&marked-EX-15:9(4390)-LE-26:26-DE-14:29▪33:23(7649)-JOB-19:22▪27:14▪31:31-PS-17:15▪22:26▪36:8(7301)▪37:19▪59:15▪63:5▪65:4▪81:16(7649)▪104:13▪105:40(7649)-PR-12:11,14▪18:20▪19:23(7649)▪20:13▪27:20▪30:15-EC-1:8▪4:8▪5:10-IS-9:20▪44:16▪53:11▪66:11-JER-31:14▪50:10,19-LA-5:6-EZE-16:28,29-JOE-2:19,26-AM-4:8-MIC-6:14-HAB-2:5

SATISFIEST-PS-145:16(7646)

SATISFIETH-PS-103:5(7646)▪107:9(7646)-IS-55:2(7654)

SATISFY-all=7646&marked-JOB-38:27-PS-90:14▪91:16▪132:15-PR-5:19(7301)▪6:30(4390)-IS-58:10,11-EZE-7:19▪N.T.-M'R-8:4(5526)

SATISFYING-PR-13:25(7648)▪N.T.-COL-2:23(4140)

SATYR-IS-34:14(8163)

SATYRS-IS-13:21(8163)

SAVE-all=3467,a=2421,b=3588,518&marked-GE-12:12a▪14:24(1107)▪39:6b▪45:7a▪50:20a-EX-1:22a▪12:16(389)▪22:20(1115)-NU-14:30b▪26:65b▪32:12b-DE-1:36(2108)▪15:4(657)▪20:4,16a▪22:27▪28:29-JOS-2:13a▪10:6▪11:13(2108),19(1115)▪14:4b▪22:22-J'G-6:14,15,31,36,37▪7:7,14(1115,518)-1SA-4:3▪7:8▪9:16▪10:24a,27▪11:3▪14:6▪19:11(4422)▪21:9(2108)▪23:2▪30:17b,22b-2SA-3:18▪12:3b▪16:16a▪22:28,32^{2}(1107),42-1KI-1:12(4422),25a,34a,39a▪3:18(2108)▪8:9(7535)▪18:5a▪20:31a▪22:31b-2KI-4:2b▪7:4a▪11:12a▪15:4(7535)▪16:7▪19:19,34▪24:14(2108)-1CH-16:35-2CH-2:6(518)▪5:10(7535)▪18:30b▪21:17▪23:6b,11a-NE-2:12b▪6:11(2425)-JOB-2:6(8104)▪20:20(4422)▪22:29▪40:14-PS-3:7▪6:4▪7:1▪18:27,31(1107),31(2108),41▪20:9▪22:21▪28:9▪31:2,16▪37:40▪44:3,6▪54:1▪55:16▪57:3▪59:2▪60:5▪69:1,35▪71:2,3▪72:4,13▪76:9▪80:2(3444)▪86:2,16▪106:47▪108:6▪109:26,31▪118:25▪119:94,146▪138:7▪145:19-PR-20:22-IS-25:9▪33:22▪35:4▪37:20,35▪38:20▪45:20▪46:7▪47:13,15▪49:25▪59:1▪63:1-JER-2:27,28▪11:12▪14:9▪15:20▪17:14▪30:10,11▪31:7▪42:11▪46:27▪48:6(4422)-LA-4:17-EZE-3:18a▪13:18a,19a▪18:27a▪34:22▪36:29▪37:23-DA-6:7(3861),12(3861)-HO-1:7^{2}▪13:10▪14:3-HAB-1:2-ZEP-3:17,19-ZEC-8:7,13▪9:16▪10:6▪12:7▪N.T.-all=4982,a=1508&marked-M'T-1:21▪8:25▪11:27a▪13:57a▪14:30▪16:25▪17:8a▪18:11▪19:11(235)▪27:40,42,49-M'R-3:4▪5:37a▪6:5a,8a▪8:35^{2}▪9:8(235)▪15:30,31-LU-4:26a▪6:9▪8:51a▪9:24^{2},56▪17:18a,33▪18:19a▪19:10▪23:35,37,39-JOH-6:22a,46a▪12:27,47▪13:10(2228)-AC-2:40▪20:23(4133)▪21:25a▪27:43(1295)-RO-11:14-1CO-1:21▪2:2a,11a▪7:16^{2}▪9:22-2CO-11:24(3844)-GA-1:19a▪6:14a-1TI-1:15▪4:16-HEB-5:7▪7:25-JAS-1:21▪2:14▪4:12▪5:15,20-1PE-3:21-JUDE-23-RE-13:17a

SAVED-all=3467&marked-EX-1:17(2421),18(2421)▪14:30-NU-10:9▪22:33(2421)▪31:15(2421)-DE-33:29-JOS-6:25(2421)-J'G-7:2▪8:19(2421)▪21:14(2421)-1SA-10:19▪14:23▪23:5▪27:11

(2421)-2SA-19:5(4422),9(5337)■22:4-2KI-6:10(8104)■14:27-1CH-11:14-2CH-32:22-NE-9:27-PS-18:3■33:16■34:6■44:7■80:3,7,19■106:8,10■107:13-PR-28:18-IS-30:15■43:12■45:17,22■63:9■64:5-JER-4:14■8:20■17:14■23:6■30:7■33:16■N.T.-all=4982&marked-M'T-10:22■19:25■24:13,22■27:42-M'R-10:26■13:13,20■15:31■16:16-LU-1:71(4991)■7:50■8:12■13:23■18:26,42■23:35-JOH-3:17■5:34■10:9-AC-2:21,47■4:12■11:14■15:1,11■16:30,31■27:20,31-RO-5:9,10■8:24■9:27■10:1(4991),9,13■11:26-1CO-1:18■3:15■5:5■10:33■15:2-2CO-2:15-EPH-2:5,8-1TH-2:16-2TH-2:10-1TI-2:4,15-2TI-1:9-TIT-3:5-1PE-3:20(1295)■4:18-2PE-2:5(5442)-JUDE-5-RE-21:24(4982)

SAVEST-all=3467-2SA-22:3-JOB-26:2-PS-17:7

SAVETH-all=3467-1SA-14:39■17:47-JOB-5:15-PS-7:10■20:6■34:18■107:19

SAVING-GE-19:19(2421)-PS-20:6(3468)■28:8(3444)■67:2(3444)-EC-5:11(518)-AM-9:8(657)■N.T.-M'T-5:32(3924)-LU-4:27(1508)-HEB-10:39(4047)■11:7(4991)-RE-2:17(1508)

SAVIOUR-all=3467-2SA-22:3-2KI-13:5-PS-106:21-IS-19:20■43:3,11■45:15,21■49:26■60:16■63:8-JER-14:8-HO-13:4■N.T.-all=4990-LU-1:47■2:11-JOH-4:42-AC-5:31■13:23-EPH-5:23-PH'P-3:20-1TI-1:1■2:3■4:10-2TI-1:10-TIT-1:3,4■2:10,13■3:4,6-2PE-1:1,11■2:20■3:2,18-1JO-4:14-JUDE-25

SAVIOURS-NE-9:27(3467)-OB-21(3467)

SAVOUR-all=7381&marked-GE-8:21-EX-5:21■29:18,25,41-LE-1:9,13,17■2:2,9,12■3:5,16■4:31■6:15,21■8:21,28■17:6■23:13,18■26:31-NU-15:3,7,10,13,14,24■18:17■28:2,6,8,13,24,27■29:2,6,8,13,36-EC-10:1-SONG-1:3-EZE-6:13■16:19■20:28,41-JOE-2:20(6709)■N.T.-all=3744&marked-M'T-5:13(3471)-LU-14:34(3471)-2CO-2:14,15(2175),16^{2}-EPH-5:2

SAVOUREST-M'T-16:23(5426)-M'R-8:33(5426)

SAVOURS-EZR-6:10(5208)

SAVOURY-all=4303-GE-27:4,7,9,14,17,31

SAW-all=7200&marked-GE-1:4,10,12,18,21,25,31■3:6■6:2,5■9:22,23■12:5■16:4,5■18:2■21:9,19■22:4■24:30,63,64■26:8,28■28:6■29:10,31■30:1,9■31:10■32:2,25■33:5■34:2■37:4,18■38:2,14,15■39:3,13■40:16■41:19,22■42:1,7,21,35■43:16,29■44:28■45:27■48:17■49:15■50:11,15,23-EX-2:2,5,6,12■3:4■8:15■9:34■10:23■14:30,31■16:15■18:14■20:18^{2}■24:10,11(2372)■32:1,5,19,25■33:10■34:30,35-LE-9:24■13:28,32,33■20:29■22:2,23,25,27,31,33■24:1,2,4(2372),16(2372)■25:7■32:1,9-DE-1:19■4:12,15■7:19■32:19-JOS-7:21■8:14,20,21-J'G-1:24■3:24■9:36,55■11:35■12:3■14:1,11■16:1,18,24■18:7,26■19:3,17,30■20:36,41-RU-1:18■2:18-1SA-5:7■6:13■9:17■10:11,14■12:12■13:6,11■14:52■17:24,42,51,55■18:15,28■19:20■22:9■23:15■25:23,25■26:3,12■28:5,12,13,21■31:5,7-2SA-1:7■6:16■10:6,9,14,15,19■11:2■12:19■14:24,28■17:18,23■18:10^{2},26,29■20:12^{2}■24:17,20-1KI-3:28■12:16■13:25■16:18■18:17,39■19:3■22:17,19,32-2KI-2:12^{2},15■3:22,26■4:25■5:21■6:17,20,21■9:22,27■11:1■12:10■13:4■14:26■16:10,12-1CH-10:5,7■15:29■19:6,10,15,16,19■21:16,20,21,28-2CH-7:3■10:16■12:7■15:9■18:18,31■22:10■24:11■25:21■31:8■32:2-NE-6:16■13:15,23-ES-1:14■3:5■5:2,9■7:7-JOB-2:13■3:16■20:9(7805)■29:8,11■31:21■32:5■42:16-PS-48:5■73:3■77:16■95:9■97:4■114:3-PR-24:32(2372)-EC-2:13,24■3:16■4:7■8:10■9:11-SONG-3:3■6:9-IS-1:1(2372)■2:1(2372)■6:1■10:15(4883)■21:7■41:5■59:15,16-JER-3:7,8■39:4■41:13■44:17-LA-1:7-EZE-1:1,27^{2},28■3:23■8:4,10■10:15,20,22■11:1■16:6,50■19:5■20:28■23:11,13,14■41:8■43:3^{3}-DA-3:27(2370)■4:5(2370),10(2370),13(2370),23(2370)■5:5(2370)■7:2(2370),7(2370),13(2370)■8:2^{3},3,4,7■10:7^{2},8-HO-5:13,13sup■9:10,13-AM-1:1(2372)■9:1-JON-3:10-MIC-1:1(2372)-HAB-3:7,10-HAG-2:3-ZEC-1:8,18■N.T.-all=1492-M'T-2:9,10,11(2147),16■3:7,16■4:16,18,21■8:14,18,34■9:8,9,11,22,23,36■12:2,22(991)■14:14,26,30(991)■15:31(991)■17:8■18:31■20:3■21:15,19,20,38■22:11■25:37,38,39,44■26:8,71■27:3,24,54■28:17-M'R-1:10,16,19■2:5,12,14,16■3:11(2334)■5:6,16,22■6:33,34,48,49,50■7:2■8:23(991),25(1689)■9:8,14,20,25,38■10:14■11:20■12:34■14:67,69■15:39■16:4(2334),5-LU-1:12,29■2:48■5:2,8,20,27(2300)■7:13,39■8:28,34,36,47■9:32,49,54■10:31,33■11:38■13:12■15:20■17:14,15■18:15,24,43■19:5,7■20:14■21:1,2■22:49,58■23:8,47■24:24-JOH-1:32(2300),34(3708),38(2300),39,47,48,50■2:23(2334)■5:6■6:2(3708),5(2300),22,24,26■8:10(2300),56■9:1■11:31,32,33■12:41■19:6,26,33,35(3708)■20:5(991),8,14(2334),20■21:9(991)-AC-3:9,12■4:13(2334)■6:15■7:31,55■8:18(2300),39■9:8(991),35,40■10:3,11(2334)■11:5,6■12:3,9(991),16■13:12,36,37,45■14:11■16:19■17:16(2334)■21:27(2300),32■22:9(2300),18■26:13■28:4,6(2334),15-GA-1:19■2:7,14-PH'P-1:30-HEB-3:9■11:23-RE-1:2,12,17■4:4■5:1,2■6:1,2,9■7:1,2■8:2■9:1,17■10:1,5■11:11(2334)■12:13■13:1,2,3■14:6■15:1,2■16:13■17:3,6^{2}■18:1,18(3708)■19:11,17,19■20:1,4,4sup,11,12■21:1,2,22■22:8(991)

SAWED-1KI-7:9(1641)

SAWEST-all=2370&marked-GE-20:10(7200)-1SA-19:5(7200)■28:13(7200)-2SA-18:11(7200)-PS-50:18-IS-57:8(2372)-DA-2:31,34,41^{2},43,45■4:20■8:20(7200)■N.T.-all=1492-RE-1:20^{2}■17:8,12,15,16,18

SAWN-HEB-11:37(4249)

SAWS-all=4050-2SA-12:31-1KI-7:9-1CH-20:3

SAY-all=559,a=1696&marked-GE-12:12,13■14:23■20:13■24:14^{2},43,44■26:7■32:18,20■34:11,12■37:17,20■41:15■43:7■44:4,16■45:9,17■46:31,33,34■50:17-EX-3:13^{3},14,15,16,18■4:1,12a,22,23■5:16,17■6:6,29a■7:9,16,19■8:1,5,16,20■9:13■12:26,27■13:14■14:3■16:9■19:3■20:22■21:5■32:12■33:5-LE-1:2■15:2■17:2,8■18:2■19:2■20:2■21:1■22:3,18■23:2,10■25:2,20■27:2-NU-5:12,19,21,22■6:2■8:2■11:12,18■14:28■15:2,18■18:26,30■21:27■22:19a,20a,38a■23:16a■25:12■28:2,3■33:51■34:2■35:10-DE-1:42■4:6■5:27,30■6:21■7:17■8:17■9:28■12:20■15:16■17:14■18:21■20:3,8■21:7,20■22:14,16■25:7,8,9■26:3,5,13■27:14,15,16,17,18,19,20,21,22,23,24,25,26■28:67^{2}■29:22,24,25■30:12,13■31:17■32:27,37,40■33:27-JOS-7:8,13■8:6■9:11■22:11,27,28^{2}-J'G-4:20^{2}■7:4^{2},11a,18■9:54■12:6■16:15■18:8,24■21:22-RU-1:12-1SA-2:36■3:9■8:7■10:2■11:9■13:4■14:9,10,34■15:16a■16:2■18:22,25■19:24■20:6,7,21,22■25:6-2SA-7:8,20a■11:20,21,25■13:5,28■14:12a,32■15:10,26,34■16:10■17:9■19:2,13■20:16■21:4■24:1,12-1KI-1:13,25,34,36■2:14(1697),14a,16a,17(7725),20^{2}(7725)■9:8(7725)■12:10a■13:22a■14:5a■16:16■18:44■22:8,27-2KI-1:3a,6a■2:18■4:13,26,28■7:4■8:10■9:3,17,37■18:22■19:6,9■22:18-1CH-5:3■16:31,35■17:7■21:18-2CH-7:21■10:10■18:7,15,26■20:21■34:26-EZR-8:17a■9:10-ES-1:18-JOB-6:22■7:4,13■9:12,27■10:2■19:28■20:7■21:14,28■22:29■23:5■28:22■32:11(4405),13■33:27,32(4405)■34:18■36:23■37:19■38:35-PS-3:2■4:6■11:1■13:4■35:3,10,25^{2},27■40:15,16■42:3,9,10■58:11■64:5■66:3■70:3,4■73:11,15■79:10■91:2■94:7■96:10■106:48■107:2■115:2■118:2,3,4■122:8a■124:1■129:1,8■139:11-PR-1:11■3:28■5:12■7:4■20:9,22■24:29■30:9,15-EC-5:6■6:3■7:10■8:4■12:1-IS-2:3■3:10■5:19■7:4■8:12^{2},19■9:9■12:1,4■14:4,10■19:11■20:6■22:15■29:15,16^{2}■30:10,22■33:24■35:4■36:4,5,7■37:6,9■38:5,15a■40:9■41:26■42:17■43:6,9■44:5,19,20■45:9,24■48:5,7,20■49:9,20,21■51:16■56:3■57:14■58:9■62:11■65:5-JER-1:7■2:23,27,31■3:1,12,16■4:5^{2}■5:2,15a,19,24■7:2,10,28■8:4,8■10:11(560)■11:3■13:12,13,18,21,22■14:13,15,17■15:2■16:10,11,19■17:15,20■19:3,11■21:3,8,13■22:2,8■23:7,17^{2},33,34,35,37,38^{3}■25:27,28,30■26:4■27:4^{2}■31:7,10,29■32:3,36,43■33:10,11■36:29■37:7■38:22,25,26■39:12a■42:13,20■43:2,10■45:3,4■46:14■48:14,17,19■50:2■51:35^{2},62,64-LA-2:12,16-EZE-2:4,8a■3:18,27■6:3,11■8:12■9:9■11:3,16,17■12:10,11,19,23a,25a,27,28■13:2,7,11,15,18■14:4,6,17■16:3■17:3,9,12■18:19,25■19:2■20:3,5,27,30,32,47,49■21:3,7,9^{2},28^{2}■22:3,24■24:3■25:3,8■26:17■27:3■28:2,9,12,22■29:3■30:2■32:2■33:2,8,11,12,13,14,17,20,25,27■34:2■35:3■36:1,3,6,13,22,35■37:4,9,11,12,19a,21a■38:3,11,13,14■39:1■44:5a,6-DA-4:35(560)-HO-2:1,7,23^{2}■10:3,8■13:2■14:2,3-JOE-2:17^{2},19■3:10-AM-3:9■4:1■5:16■6:10^{3},13■8:14■9:10-MIC-2:4■3:11■4:2,11-NA-3:7-HAB-2:1a,6-ZEP-1:12-HAG-1:2-ZEC-1:3■11:5■12:5■13:3,5,6,9^{2}-MAL-1:2,5,6,7^{2},12■2:14,17^{2}■3:8,13■N.T.-all=3004,a=2036,b=2046&marked-M'T-3:9^{2}■4:17■5:11a,18,20,22,22^{2}a,26,28,32,34,39,44■6:2,5,16,25,29■7:4b,22b■8:9,10,11■9:5^{2}a■10:15,23,42■11:7,9,11,18,19,22,24■12:6,31,36■13:17,30b,51■14:17■15:5,5a,33■16:2,13,15,18,28■17:10,12,20,20b■18:3,10,13,18,19,22■19:7,9,10,23,24,28■20:7,22,33■21:3a,3b,16,21,21a,25a,25b,26a,31^{2},41,43■22:21,23,42■23:3,16,30,36,39,39a■24:2,23a,26a,34,47,48a■25:12,34b,40b,40,41b,45■26:13,18a,21,22,29,34(5346),64■27:22,33,64a■28:13a-M'R-1:44a■2:9^{2}a,11,18■3:28■4:38■5:41■6:11,37,38■7:2,11,11a■8:12,19,27,29■9:1,6(2980),11,13,41■10:15,28,29,47■11:3^{2}a,23,23a,24,28,31a,31b,32a■12:14,18,35,43■13:5,21a,30,37■14:9,14a,18,19,25,30,58,65,69-LU-3:8^{2}■4:21,23b,24■5:23^{2}a,24■6:27,42,46■7:7a,8,9,14,26,28,33,34,40^{2}a,47,49■9:18,19a,20■10:5,9,10a,12■11:2,5a,7a,8,9,18,29,51■12:1,4,5,8,11a,12a,19b,22,27,37,44,45a,54,55■13:24,25b,26,27b,35,35a■14:9b,10a,17a,24■15:7,10,18b■16:9■17:6,7b,8b,10,21b,23b■18:17,29■19:26,31b■20:5a,5b,6a,41a■21:3,32■22:11b,16,18,37,70■23:29b,30,43-JOH-1:38,51■3:3,5,11■4:20,35^{2}■5:19,24,25,34■6:26,32,47,53■7:26■8:4,26(2980),34,46,48,51,54,55,58■9:17,19,41■10:1,7,36■11:8■12:24,27a,49a■13:13,16,20,21,33,38■14:12■16:12,20,23,26■20:13,16,17a■21:3,18-AC-3:22(2980)■4:14(471)■5:38■6:14■13:15■17:18■21:23■23:8,18(2980),30■24:20a■26:22(2980)■28:26a-RO-3:5b,8■4:1b,9■6:1b■7:7b■8:31b■9:1,14b,19b,20b,30b■10:6a,18,19■11:1b,11b,19b■12:3■15:8-1CO-1:12,15a■7:8,29(5346)■9:8(2980)■10:15(5346),19(5346),28a,29■11:22a■12:3a,15a,16a,21a■14:16b,23b■15:12,35b,50(5346)-2CO-9:4■10:10(5346)■11:16■12:6b-GA-1:9■3:17■4:1■5:2,16-EPH-4:17-PH'P-4:4b-COL-2:4■4:17a-1TH-4:15■5:3-1TI-1:7-2TI-2:7-TIT-2:8-PH'M-19,21-HEB-5:11(3056)■7:9(2031)a■11:14,32■13:6-JAS-1:13■2:3^{2}a,14,16a,18b■4:13,15-1JO-1:6a,8a,10a■4:20a■5:16-RE-2:2(5335),9,24■3:9■6:3,5,6,7■16:5,7■22:17,17a

SAYEST-all=559-EX-33:12-NU-22:17-RU-3:5-1KI-18:11,14-2KI-18:20-2CH-25:19-NE-5:12■6:8-JOB-22:13■

35:14-**PS**-90:3-**PR**-24:12-**IS**-40:27■47:8-**JER**-2:35^{2}-**AM**-7:16■**N.T.**-all=3004&marked-**M'T**-26:70■27:11-**M'R**-5:31■14:68■15:2-**LU**-8:45(2036)■20:21■22:60■23:3-**JOH**-1:22■8:5,33,52■9:17■12:34■14:9■18:34■37-**RO**-2:22-**1CO**-14:16-**RE**-3:17

SAYING-all=559,a=1697&marked-**GE**-1:22■2:16■3:17■5:29■8:15■9:8■15:1,4,18■17:3■18:12,13,15■19:15■21:22■22:20■23:3,5,8,10,13,14■24:7,30,37■26:11,20■27:6^{2}■28:6,20■31:1,29■32:4,6,17^{2},19■34:4,8,20■37:11a,15■38:13,21,24,25,28■39:12,14,17,19■40:7■41:9,16■42:14,22,28,29,37■43:3^{2},7■44:1,19,32■45:16,26■47:5■48:20^{2}■50:4^{2},5,16^{2},25-**EX**-1:22■3:16■5:6,8,10,13,15■6:10,12,29■7:8,9,16■9:5■11:8■12:1,3■13:1,8,14,19■14:1,12■15:1,24■16:11,12■17:4,7■19:3,12,23■20:1■25:1■30:11,17,22,31■31:1,12,13■33:1■35:4^{2}■36:5,6■40:1-**LE**-1:1■4:1,2■5:14■6:1,8,9,19,24,25■7:22,23,28,29■8:1,31■9:3■10:3,8,16■11:1,2■12:1,2■13:1■14:1,33,35■15:1■17:1,2■18:1■19:1■20:1■21:16,17■22:1,17,26■23:1,9,23,24,26,33,34■24:1,13,15■25:1■27:1-**NU**-1:1,48■2:1■3:5,11,14,44■4:1,17,21■5:1,5,11■6:1,22,23^{2}■7:4■8:1,5,23■9:1,9,10■10:1■11:13,18,20■12:13■13:1,32■14:7,15,17,26,40■15:1,17,37■16:5,20,23,24,26,36,41,44■17:1,12■18:25■19:1,2■20:3,7,23■21:21■22:5■23:26■24:12■25:10,16■26:1,3,52■27:2,6,8,15■28:1■30:1■31:1,3,25■32:2,10,25,31■33:50■34:1,13,16■35:1,9■36:5,6-**DE**-1:5,6,9,16,23a,28,34,37■2:2,4,17,26■3:18,21,23■5:5■6:20■9:4,13,23■12:30■13:2,6,12,13■15:9■11■18:16■19:7■20:5■22:17■27:1,9,11■29:19■31:10,25■32:48■34:4-**JOS**-1:1,10,11,12,13,16■2:1,2,3■3:3,6,8■4:1,3,6,15,17,21^{2},22■6:10,26■7:2■8:4■9:11,22^{2}■10:3,6,17■14:9■17:4,14,17■18:8■20:1,2■21:2■22:8,15,24^{2}-**J'G**-1:1■5:1■6:13,32■7:2,3,24■8:9,15■9:1,31■10:10■11:12,17■13:6■15:13■16:2^{2},18■19:22■20:8,12,23,28■21:1,5,10,18,20-**RU**-2:15■4:4,17-**1SA**-4:21■5:10■6:2,21■7:3,12■9:15,26■10:2■11:7■13:3■14:24,28,33■15:10,12■16:22■17:26,27■18:8a,24■19:2,11,15,19■20:42■21:11■23:1,2,19,27■24:1,8,9■25:14,40■26:1,6,14,19■27:11^{2},12■28:10,12■29:5■30:8,26-**2SA**-1:16■2:1,4■3:12^{2},14,17,18,23,35■4:10■5:1,6,19■6:12■7:4,7,26,27■11:6,10,15,19■13:7,28,30■14:32■15:8,10,13,31■17:4a,6,6a,16■18:5,12■19:8,9,11^{2}■20:18^{2}■21:17■24:11,19a-**1KI**-1:5,6,11,13,23,30,47,51^{2}■2:1,4,8,23,29,30,38a,39,42■5:2,5,8■6:11■8:15,25,47,55■9:5■12:3,7,9,10^{2},12,14,15a,16,22,23■13:3,4a,4,9,18,21,27,31,32a■15:18,29a■16:1■17:2,8,15a■18:1,26,31■19:2■20:4a,5^{2},13,17■21:2,9,10,14,17,19^{2},23,28■22:12,13,31,36-**2KI**-2:22a■3:7■4:1,31■5:4,6,8,10,14a,22■6:8,9,13,26■7:10,12,14,18■8:1,2a,4,6,7,8,9■9:12,13,18,20,36■10:1,5,6,8,17a■11:5■14:6,8,9^{2}■15:12■16:7,15■17:13,26,27,35■18:14,28,30,32,36■19:9,10^{2},20■20:2,4■21:10■22:3,10,12■23:21-**1CH**-4:9,10■11:1■12:19■13:12■14:10■16:18■17:3,6,24■21:9,10,19a■22:8-**2CH**-2:3■6:4,16,37■7:18■10:3,6,7,9,10^{2},12,14,16■11:2,3■12:7■16:2■18:11,12,19^{2},30■19:9■20:2,8,37■21:12■25:4,7,17,18^{2}■30:6,18■32:4,6,9,11,12,17■34:16,18,20■35:21■36:22-**EZR**-1:1■5:11(560)■8:22■9:1,11-**NE**-1:8■6:2,3,7,8,9■8:11,15-**ES**-1:21a-**JOB**-24:15-**PS**-49:4(2420)■71:11■105:11■119:82-**EC**-1:16-**IS**-3:7■4:1■6:8■7:2,5,10■8:5,11■14:24■16:14■19:25■20:2■23:4■29:11,12■30:21■36:15,18,21■37:9,10^{2},15,21■38:4■41:7,13■44:28■46:10■56:3-**JER**-1:4,11,13■2:1,2,27■4:10■5:20■6:14■7:1,4,23■8:6,11■11:1,4,6,7,21■13:3,8■18:1,5,11■20:15■21:1■23:25,33,38■24:4■25:2■26:1,8,9,11,12,17,18■27:1,9,12,14,16^{2}■28:1,2,11,12,13■29:3,22,24,25^{2},28,30,31■30:1,2■31:34■32:3,6,7,13,16,26■33:1,19,23,24■34:1,12,13■35:1,6,12,15■36:1,5,14,17,27,29^{2}■37:3,6,9,13,19■38:1,8,10,16■39:11,15,16■40:9,15■42:14,20■43:2,8■44:1,4,15,20,25^{2},26■45:1■49:34-**EZE**-3:16■6:1■7:1■9:1,11■10:6■11:14■12:1,8,17,21,22,26■13:1,6,10■14:2,12■15:1■16:1,44■17:1,11■18:1,2■20:2,5,45■21:1,8,18■22:1,17,23,28■23:1■24:1,15,20■25:1■26:1■27:1■28:1,11,20■29:1,17■30:1,20■31:1■32:1,17■33:1,10,21,23,24,30■34:1■35:1,12■36:16■37:15,18■38:1-**DA**-4:23(560)-**AM**-2:12■3:1■7:10■8:5-**JON**-1:1■3:1,7■4:2a-**HAG**-1:1,2,3,13■2:1,2,10,11,20,21-**ZEC**-1:4,7,14,17,21■2:4■3:4,6■4:4,6^{2},8■6:8,9,12^{2}■7:3,4,5,8,9■8:1,18,21,23■**N.T.**-all=3004,a=3056,b=2036&marked-**M'T**-1:20,22■2:2,13,15,17,20■3:2,3,14,17■4:14■5:2■6:31■8:2,3,6,17,25,27,29,31■9:14,18,27,29,30,33■10:5■11:17■12:10,17,38■13:3,24,31,35,36■14:15,26,27,30,33■15:1,4,7,12a,22,23,25■16:7,13,22■17:9,10,14,25■18:1,26,28,29■19:3,11a,22a,25■20:12,30,31■21:2,4,9,10,15,20,25,37■22:4,16,24,31,35,42,43■23:2■24:3,5■25:9,11,20,37,44,45■26:8,17,27,39,42,44b,48,65,68,69,70■27:4,9,11,19,23,24,29,40,46,54,63■28:9,13,15a,18-**M'R**-1:7,15,24,25,27,40■2:12■3:11,33■5:9,12,23■6:2,25■7:29a,37■8:15,16,26,27,32a,33■9:7,10a,11,25,32(4487),38■10:22a,26,35,49■11:9,17,31■12:6,18,26■13:6■14:44,57,60,68■15:4,9,29,34,36-**LU**-1:24,29a,63,66,67■2:13,17(4487),50(4487)■3:4,10,14,16■4:4,34,35,36,41■5:8,12,13b,21,26,30■7:4,6,16,19,20,32,39■8:9,24,25,30,38,49,50,54■9:18,22b,35,38,45^{2}(4487)■10:17,25■11:45■12:16,17■13:25,31■14:3,5b,7,30■15:2,3,6,9■17:4■18:2,3,13,18,34(4487),38,41■19:7,14,16,18,20,30b,38,42,46■20:2,5,14,21,28■21:7,8■22:8b,19,20,42,57,59,64,66■23:2^{2},3,5,18,21,35,37,39,40,47■24:7,23,29,34-**JOH**-1:15,26,32■4:31,37a,39a,42(2981),51■6:52,60a■7:15,28,36a,37,40a■8:12,51a,52a,55a■9:2,19■10:33■11:3,28b,31,32■12:21,23,38a■15:20a■18:9a,22b,32a,40■19:6,8a,12,13a■21:23a-**AC**-1:6■2:7,12,40■3:25■4:16■5:23,25,28■6:5a■7:26b,27b,29a,35b,40b,59(3007)■8:10(3007),19(3007),26(3007)■9:4(3007)■10:3b,26■11:3,4,7,18■12:7■13:15■14:11,15■15:5,13,24■16:9,15,17,20b,28,35,36a■17:7,19■18:13,21b■19:4,13,21b,26,28■20:23■21:14b,21,40■22:7,18,26■23:9,12,23b■24:2,9(5335)■25:14■26:14,22,31■27:24,33■28:26-**RO**-11:2■13:9a-**1CO**-11:25■15:54a-**1TI**-1:15a■3:1a■4:9a-**2TI**-2:11a,18-**TIT**-3:8a-**HEB**-2:6,12■4:7■6:14■8:11■9:20■12:26-**2PE**-3:4-**JUDE**-14-**RE**-1:11,17■4:8,10■5:9,12,13■6:1,10■7:3,10,12,13■8:13■9:14■10:4■11:1,12,15,17■12:10■13:4,14■14:7,8,9,13,18■15:3■16:1,17■17:1■18:2,4,10,16,18,19,21■19:1,4,5,6,17■21:3,9

SAYINGS-all=1697&marked-**NU**-14:39-**J'G**-13:17-**1SA**-25:12-**2CH**-13:22■33:19-**PS**-49:13(6310)■78:2(2420)-**PR**-1:6(2420)■4:10(561),20(561)■**N.T.**-all=3056&marked-**M'T**-7:24,26,28■19:1■26:1-**LU**-1:65(4487)■2:51(4487)■6:47■7:1(4487)■9:28,44-**JOH**-10:19■14:24-**AC**-14:18(3004)-**RO**-3:4-**RE**-19:9■22:6,7,9,10

SCAB-all=4556&marked-**LE**-13:2(5597),6,7,8■14:56(5597)-**DE**-28:27(1618)-**IS**-3:17(5596)

SCABBARD-**JER**-47:6(8593)

SCABBED-**LE**-21:20(3217)■22:22(3217)

SCAFFOLD-**2CH**-6:13(3595)

SCALES-all=7193&marked-**LE**-11:9,10,12-**DE**-14:9,10-**JOB**-41:15(650,4043)-**IS**-40:12(6425)-**EZE**-29:4^{2}■**N.T.**-**AC**-9:18(3013)

SCALETH-**PR**-21:22(5927)

SCALL-all=5424-**LE**-13:30,31^{2},32^{2},33^{2},34^{2},35,36,37^{2}■14:54

SCALP-**PS**-68:21(6936)

SCANT-**MIC**-6:10(7332)

SCAPEGOAT-all=5799-**LE**-16:8,10^{2},26

SCARCE-**AC**-14:18(3433)■27:7(3433)

SCARCELY-**RO**-5:7(3433)-**1PE**-4:18(3433)

SCARCENESS-**DE**-8:9(4544)

SCAREST-**JOB**-7:14(2865)

SCARLET-all=8144,8438&marked-**GE**-38:28(8144),30(8144)-**EX**-25:4■26:1,31,36■27:16■28:5,6,8,15,33■35:6,23,25,35■36:8,35,37■38:18,23■39:1,2,3,5,8,24,29-**LE**-14:4,6,49,51,52-**NU**-4:8■19:6-**JOS**-2:18(8144),21(8144)-**2SA**-1:24(8144)-**PR**-31:21(8144)-**SONG**-4:3(8144)-**IS**-1:18(8144)-**LA**-4:5(8144)-**DA**-5:7(711),16(711),29(711)-**NA**-2:3(8529)■**N.T.**-all=2847-**M'T**-27:28-**HEB**-9:19-**RE**-17:3,4■18:12,16

SCATTER-all=6327&marked-**GE**-11:9■49:7-**LE**-26:33(2210)-**NU**-16:37(2219)-**DE**-4:27■28:64■32:26(6284)-**1KI**-14:15(2219)-**NE**-1:8-**PS**-59:11(5128)■68:30(967)■106:27(2219)■144:6-**IS**-28:25(2236)■41:16-**JER**-9:16■13:24■18:17■23:1■49:32(2219),36(2219)-**EZE**-5:2(2219),10(2219),12(2219)■6:5(2219)■10:2(2236)■12:14(2219),15■20:23■22:15■29:12■30:23,26-**DA**-4:14(921)■11:24(967)■12:7(5310)-**HAB**-3:14-**ZEC**-1:21(2219)

SCATTERED-all=6327&marked-**GE**-11:4,8-**EX**-5:12-**NU**-10:35-**DE**-30:3-**1SA**-11:11■13:8,11(5310)-**2SA**-18:8■22:15-**1KI**-22:17-**2KI**-25:5-**2CH**-18:16-**ES**-3:8(6340)-**JOB**-4:11(6504)■18:15(2219)-**PS**-18:14■44:11(2219)■53:5(6340)■60:1(6555)■68:1,14(6566)■89:10(6340)■92:9(6504)■141:7(6340)-**IS**-18:2(4900),7(4900)■33:3(5310)-**JER**-3:13(6340)■10:21■23:2■30:11■31:10(2219)■40:15■50:17(6340)■52:8-**EZE**-6:8(2219)■11:16,17■17:21(6566)■20:34,41■28:25■29:13■34:5^{2},6,12(6566),12,21■36:19-**JOE**-3:2-**NA**-3:18(6340)-**HAB**-3:6-**ZEC**-1:19(2219),21(2219)■13:7■**N.T.**-all=1287&marked-**M'T**-9:36(4496)■26:31-**M'R**-14:27-**LU**-1:51-**JOH**-11:52■16:32(4650)-**AC**-5:36(1262)■8:1(1289),4(1289)■11:19(1289)-**JAS**-1:1(1290)-**1PE**-1:1(1290)

SCATTERETH-all=6327&marked-**JOB**-37:11■38:24-**PS**-147:16(6340)-**PR**-11:24(6340)■20:8(2219),26(2219)-**IS**-24:1■**N.T.**-all=4650-**M'T**-12:30-**LU**-11:23-**JOH**-10:12

SCATTERING-**IS**-30:30(5311)

SCENT-**JOB**-14:9(7381)-**JER**-48:11(7381)-**HO**-14:7(2143)

SCEPTRE-all=7626&marked-**GE**-49:10-**NU**-24:17-**ES**-4:11(8275)■5:2^{2}(8275)■8:4(8275)-**PS**-45:6^{2}-**IS**-14:5-**EZE**-19:14-**AM**-1:5,8-**ZEC**-10:11■**N.T.**-**HEB**-1:8(4464)

SCEPTRES-**EZE**-19:11(7626)

SCHISM-**1CO**-12:25(4978)

SCHOLAR-**1CH**-25:8(8527)-**MAL**-2:12(6030)

SCHOOL-**AC**-19:9(4981)

SCHOOLMASTER-**GA**-3:24(3807),25(3807)

SCIENCE-**DA**-1:4(4093)■**N.T.**-**1TI**-6:20(1108)

SCOFF-**HAB**-1:10(7046)

SCOFFERS-**2PE**-3:3(1703)

SCORCH-**RE**-16:8(2739)

SCORCHED-all=2739-**M'T**-13:6-**M'R**-4:6-**RE**-16:9

SCORN-**ES**-3:6(959)-**JOB**-16:20(3887)-**PS**-44:13(3933)■79:4(3933)-**HAB**-1:10(4890)■**N.T.**-all=2606-**M'T**-9:24-**M'R**-5:40-**LU**-8:53

SCORNER-all=3887-**PR**-9:7,8■13:1■14:6■15:12■19:25■21:11,24■22:10■24:9-**IS**-29:20

SCORNERS-all=3887&marked-**PR**-1:22■3:24■19:29-**HO**-7:5(3945)

SCORNEST-**PR**-9:12(3887)-**EZE**-

16:31(7046)

SCORNETH-**JOB**-39:7(7832),18(7832)-**PR**-3:34(3887)■19:28(3887)

SCORNFUL-**PS**-1:1(3887)-**PR**-29:8(3944)-**IS**-28:14(3944)

SCORNING-**JOB**-34:7(3933)-**PS**-123:4(3933)-**PR**-1:22(3944)

SCORPION-**LU**-11:12(4651)-**RE**-9:5(4651)

SCORPIONS-all=6137&marked-**DE**-8:15-**1KI**-12:11,14-**2CH**-10:11,14-**EZE**-2:6■**N.T.**-all=4651-**LU**-10:19-**RE**-9:3,10

SCOURED-**LE**-6:28(4838)

SCOURGE-all=7752&marked-**JOB**-5:21■9:23-**IS**-10:26■28:15(7885),18■**N.T.**-all=3164&marked-**M'T**-10:17■20:19■23:34-**M'R**-10:34-**LU**-18:33-**JOH**-2:15(5416)-**AC**-22:25(3147)

SCOURGED-**LE**-19:20(1244)■**N.T.**-**M'T**-27:26(5417)-**M'T**-15:15(5417)-**JOH**-19:1(3146)

SCOURGES-**JOS**-23:13(7850)

SCOURGETH-**HEB**-12:6(3146)

SCOURGING-**AC**-22:24(3148)

SCOURGINGS-**HEB**-11:36(3148)

SCRABBLED-**1SA**-21:13(8427)

SCRAPE-**LE**-14:41(7096)-**JOB**-2:8(1623)-**EZE**-26:4(5500)

SCRAPED-**LE**-14:41(7106),43(7096)

SCREECH-**IS**-34:14(3917)

SCRIBE-all=5608&marked-**2SA**-8:17■20:25-**2KI**-12:10■18:18,37■19:2■22:3,8,9,10,12■25:19-**1CH**-18:16■24:6■27:32-**2CH**-24:11■26:11■34:15,18,20-**EZR**-4:8(5613),9(5613),17(5613),23(5613)■7:6,11^{2},12(5613),21(5613)-**NE**-8:1,4,9,13■12:26,36■13:13-**IS**-33:18■36:3,22■37:2-**JER**-36:10,12,20,26,32■37:15,20■52:25■**N.T.**-all=1122-**M'T**-8:19■13:52-**M'R**-12:32-**1CO**-1:20

SCRIBE'S-**JER**-36:12(5608),21(5608)

SCRIBES-all=5608-**1KI**-4:3-**1CH**-2:55-**2CH**-34:13-**ES**-3:12■8:9-**JER**-8:8■**N.T.**-all=1122-**M'T**-2:4■5:20■7:29■9:3■12:38■15:1■16:21■17:10■20:18■21:15■23:2,13,14,15,23,25,27,29,34■26:3,57■27:41-**M'R**-1:22■2:6,16■3:22■7:1,5■8:31■9:11,14,16■10:33■11:18,27■12:28,35,38■14:1,43,53■15:1,31-**LU**-5:21,30■6:7■9:22■11:44,53■15:2■19:47■20:1,19,39,46■22:2,66■23:10-**JOH**-8:3-**AC**-4:5■6:12■23:9

SCRIP-**1SA**-17:40(3219)■**N.T.**-all=4082-**M'T**-10:10-**M'R**-6:8-**LU**-9:3■10:4■22:35,36

SCRIPTURE-**DA**-10:21(3791)■**N.T.**-all=1124-**M'R**-12:10■15:28-**LU**-4:21-**JOH**-2:22■7:38,42■10:35■13:18■17:12■19:24,28,36,37■20:9-**AC**-1:16■8:32,35-**RO**-4:3■9:17■10:11■11:2-**GA**-3:8,22■4:30-**1TI**-5:18-**2TI**-3:16-**JAS**-2:8,23■4:5-**1PE**-2:6-**2PE**-1:20

SCRIPTURES.-all=1124&marked-**M'T**-21:42■22:29■26:54,56-**M'R**-12:24■14:49-**LU**-24:27,32,45-**JOH**-5:39-**AC**-17:2,11■18:24,28-**RO**-1:2■15:4■16:26-**1CO**-15:3,4-**2TI**-3:15(1121)-**2PE**-3:16

SCROLL-**IS**-34:4(5612)■**N.T.**-**RE**-6:14(975)

SCUM-all=2457-**EZE**-24:6^{2},11,12^{2}

SCURVY-**LE**-21:20(1618)■22:22(1618)

SEA-all=3220&marked-**GE**-1:26,28■9:2■14:3■22:17■32:12■41:49■49:13-**EX**-10:19■13:18■14:2^{2},9,16^{2},21^{3},22,23,26,27^{3},28,29,30■15:1,4^{2},8,10,19^{3},21,22■20:11■23:31^{2}-**NU**-11:22,31■13:29■14:25■21:4■33:8,10,11■34:3,5,6,7,11,12-**DE**-1:7,40■2:1■3:17■4:49■11:4,24■30:13^{2}■34:2-**JOS**-1:4■2:10■3:16■4:23■5:1■9:1■11:4■12:3^{3}■13:27■15:2,4,5^{2},11,12,46,47■16:3,6,8■17:9,10■18:14,19■19:11,29■23:4■24:6^{2},7-**J'G**-5:17■7:12■11:16-**1SA**-13:5-**2SA**-17:11■22:16-**1KI**-4:20,29■5:9^{2}■7:23,24,25,39,44■9:26,27■10:22■18:43,44-**2KI**-14:25■16:17■25:13,16-**1CH**-16:32■18:8-**2CH**-2:16■4:2,3,4,6,10,15■8:17,18■20:2-**EZR**-3:7-**NE**-9:9,11^{2}-**ES**-10:1-**JOB**-6:3■7:12■9:8■11:9■12:8■14:11■26:12■28:14■36:30■38:8,16■41:31-**PS**-8:8■33:7■46:2■65:5■66:6■68:22■72:8■74:13■77:19■78:13,27,53■80:11■89:9,25■93:4■95:5■96:11■98:7■104:25■106:7,9,22■107:23■114:3,5■136:13,15■139:9■146:6-**PR**-8:29■23:34■30:19-**EC**-1:7-**IS**-5:30■9:1■10:22,26■11:9,11,15■16:8■18:2■19:5■21:1■23:2,4^{2},11■24:14,15■27:1■42:10■43:16■48:18■50:2■51:10^{2},15■57:20■60:5■63:11-**JER**-5:22■6:23■25:22■27:19■31:35■33:22■46:18■47:7■48:32^{2}■49:21,23■50:42■51:36,42■52:17,20-**LA**-2:13-**EZE**-25:16■26:3,5,16,17,18■27:3,9,29,32■38:20■39:11■47:8^{2},10,15,17,18,19,20■48:28-**DA**-7:2(3221),3(3221)-**HO**-1:10■4:3-**JOE**-2:20^{2}-**AM**-5:8■8:12■9:3,6-**JON**-1:4^{2},5,9,11^{2},12^{2},13,15^{2}-**MIC**-7:12,19-**NA**-1:4■3:8^{2}-**HAB**-1:14■2:14■3:8,15-**ZEP**-1:3■2:5,6-**HAG**-2:6-**ZEC**-9:4,10■10:11^{2}■14:8^{2}■**N.T.**-all=2281&marked-**M'T**-4:13(3864),15,18^{2}■8:24,26,27,32■13:1,47■14:24,25,26■15:29■17:27■18:6■21:21■23:15-**M'R**-1:16^{2}■2:13■3:7■4:1^{3},39,41■5:1,13^{2},21■6:47,48,49■7:31■9:42■11:23-**LU**-6:17(3882)■17:2,6■21:25-**JOH**-6:1^{2},16,17,18,19,22,25■21:1,7-**AC**-4:24■7:36■10:6,32■14:15■17:14■27:5(3989),30,38,40■28:4-**RO**-9:27-**1CO**-10:1,2-**2CO**-11:26-**HEB**-11:12,29-**JAS**-1:6■3:7(1724)-**JUDE**-13-**RE**-4:6■5:13■7:1,2,3■8:8^{2},9■10:2,5,6,8■12:12■13:1^{2}■14:7■15:2^{2}■16:3^{2}■18:7,19,21■20:8,13■21:1

SEAFARING-**EZE**-26:17(3220)

SEAL-all=2856&marked-**1KI**-21:8(2368)-**NE**-9:38-**ES**-8:8-**JOB**-38:14(2368)■41:15(2368)-**SONG**-8:6^{2}(2368)-**IS**-8:16-**JER**-32:44-**DA**-9:24■12:4■**N.T.**-all=4973&marked-**JOH**-3:33(4972)-**RO**-4:11-**1CO**-9:2-**2TI**-2:19-**RE**-6:3,5,7,9,12■7:2■8:1■9:4■10:4(4972)■20:3(4972)■22:10(4972)

SEALED-all=2856&marked-**DE**-32:34-**1KI**-21:8-**NE**-10:1-**ES**-3:12■8:8,10-**JOB**-14:17-**SONG**-4:12-**IS**-29:11^{2}-**JER**-32:10,11,14-**DA**-6:17(2857)■12:9■**N.T.**-all=4972&marked-**JOH**-6:27-**RO**-15:28-**2CO**-1:22-**EPH**-1:13■4:30-**RE**-5:1(2696)■7:3,4^{2},5^{3},6^{3},7^{3},8^{3}

SEALEST-**EZE**-28:12(2856)

SEALETH-all=2856-**JOB**-9:7■33:16■37:7

SEALING-**M'T**-27:66(4972)

SEALS-all=4973-**RE**-5:1,2,5,9■6:1

SEAM-**JOH**-19:23(729)

SEARCH-all=2713&marked-**LE**-27:33(1239)-**NU**-10:33(8446)■13:2(8446),32(8446)■14:7(8446),36(8446),38(8446)-**DE**-1:22(2658),33(8446)■13:14-**JOS**-2:2(2658),3(2658)-**J'G**-18:2^{2}-**1SA**-23:23(2664)-**2SA**-10:3-**1KI**-20:6(2664)-**2KI**-10:23(2664)-**1CH**-19:3-**EZR**-4:15(1240),19(1240)■5:17(1240)■6:1(1240)-**JOB**-8:8(2714)■13:9■38:16(2714)-**PS**-44:21■64:6(2664),6(2665)■77:6(2664)■139:23-**PR**-25:2,27(2714)-**EC**-1:13(8446)■7:25-**JER**-2:34(4290)■17:10■29:13(1875)-**LA**-3:40(2664)-**EZE**-34:6(1875),8(1875),11(1875)■39:14-**AM**-9:3(2664)-**ZEP**-1:12(2664)■**N.T.**-**M'T**-2:8(1833)-**JOH**-5:39(2045)■7:52(2045)

SEARCHED-all=2713&marked-**GE**-31:34(4959),35(2664),37(4959)■44:12(2664)-**NU**-13:21(8446),32(8446)■14:6(8446),34(8446)-**DE**-1:24(7270)-**JOB**-5:27■28:27■29:16■32:11■36:26(2714)-**PS**-139:1-**JER**-31:37■46:23-**OB**-6(2664)■**N.T.**-**AC**-17:11(350)-**1PE**-1:10(1830)

SEARCHEST-**JOB**-10:6(1875)-**PR**-2:4(2664)

SEARCHETH-all=2713&marked-**1CH**-28:9(1875)-**JOB**-28:3■39:8(1875)-**PR**-18:17■28:11■**N.T.**-all=2045-**RO**-8:27-**1CO**-2:10-**RE**-2:23

SEARCHING-**NU**-13:25(8446)-**JOB**-11:7(2714)-**PR**-20:27(2664)-**IS**-40:28(2714)■**N.T.**-**1PE**-1:11(2045)

SEARCHINGS-**J'G**-5:16(2714)

SEARED-**1TI**-4:2(2743)

SEAS-all=3220-**GE**-1:10,22-**LE**-11:9,10-**DE**-33:19-**NE**-9:6-**PS**-8:8■24:2■65:7■69:34■135:6-**IS**-17:12-**JER**-15:8-**EZE**-27:4,25,26,27,33,34■28:2,8■32:2-**DA**-11:45-**JON**-2:3■**N.T.**-**AC**-27:41(1337)

SEASON-all=6256,a=4150&marked-**GE**-40:4(3117)-**EX**-13:10a-**LE**-2:13(4414)■26:4-**NU**-9:2a,3a,7a,13a■28:2a-**DE**-11:14■16:6a■28:12-**JOS**-24:7(3117)-**2KI**-4:16a,17a-**1CH**-21:29-**2CH**-15:3(3117)-**JOB**-5:26■38:32-**PS**-1:3■104:27■145:15-**PR**-15:23-**EC**-3:1(2165)■10:17-**JER**-5:24■33:20-**EZE**-34:26-**DA**-7:12(2166)-**HO**-2:9a■**N.T.**-all=2540&marked-**M'T**-24:45-**M'R**-9:50(741)■12:2-**LU**-1:20■4:13■12:42■13:1■20:10-**JOH**-5:4,35(5610)-**AC**-13:11■19:22(5550)■24:25-**2CO**-7:8(5610)-**GA**-6:9-**2TI**-4:2(2121),2(171)-**PH'M**-15(5610)-**HEB**-11:25(4340)-**1PE**-1:6(3641)-**RE**-6:11(5550)■20:3(5550)

SEASONED-**LU**-14:34(741)-**COL**-4:6(741)

SEASONS-all=4150&marked-**GE**-1:14-**EX**-18:22(6256),26(6256)-**LE**-23:4-**PS**-104:19-**DA**-2:21(2166)■**N.T.**-all=2540&marked-**M'T**-21:41-**AC**-1:7■14:17■20:18(5550)-**1TH**-5:1(2540)

SEAT-all=3678&marked-**J'G**-3:20-**1SA**-1:9■4:13,18■20:18(4186),25^{2}(4186)-**2SA**-23:8(7674)-**1KI**-2:19■10:19(7675)-**ES**-3:1-**JOB**-23:3(8499)■29:7(4186)-**PS**-1:1(4186)-**PR**-9:14-**EZE**-8:3(4186)■28:2(4186)-**AM**-6:3(7675)■**N.T.**-all=968&marked-**M'T**-23:2(2515)■27:19-**JOH**-19:13-**AC**-18:12,16,17■25:6,10,17-**RO**-14:10-**2CO**-5:10-**RE**-2:13(2332)■13:2(2332)■16:10(2332)

SEATED-**DE**-33:21(5603)

SEATS-all=4410&marked-**M'T**-21:12(2515)■23:6-**M'R**-11:15(2515)■12:39-**LU**-1:52(2362)■11:43■20:46-**RE**-4:4^{2}(2362)■11:16(2362)

SEATWARD-supplied

SECOND-all=8145,a=4932,b=8147&marked-**GE**-1:8■2:13■6:16■7:11■8:14■22:15■30:7,12■32:19■41:5,43a,52■47:18-**EX**-2:13■16:1■26:4,5,10,20■28:18■36:11,12,17■39:11■40:17-**LE**-5:10■13:58-**NU**-1:1^{2},18■2:16■7:18■9:1,11■10:6,11^{2}■29:17-**JOS**-5:2■6:14■10:32■19:1-**J'G**-6:25,26,28■20:24,25-**1SA**-8:2a■20:27,34■26:8(8138)-**2SA**-3:3a■14:29-**1KI**-6:1■9:2■15:25b■18:34^{2}(8138)■19:7-**2KI**-1:17b■9:19■10:6■14:1b■15:32b■19:29■23:4a■25:17,18a-**1CH**-2:13■3:1,15■7:15■8:1,39■12:9■15:18a■23:11,19,20■24:7,23■25:9■26:2,4,11■27:4■29:22-**2CH**-3:2■27:5■30:2,13,15■35:24a-**EZR**-1:10a■3:8^{2}■4:24(8648)-**NE**-8:13■11:9a,17a-**ES**-2:14,19■7:2■9:29-**JOB**-42:14-**EC**-4:8,15-**IS**-11:11■37:30-**JER**-1:13■13:3■33:1■41:4■52:22,24a-**EZE**-10:14■43:22-**DA**-2:1b■7:5(8578)-**JON**-3:1-**ZEP**-1:10a-**HAG**-1:1b,15b■2:10b-**ZEC**-1:1,7■6:2■**N.T.**-all=1208&marked-**M'T**-21:30■22:26,39■26:42■**M'R**-12:21,31■14:72-**LU**-6:1(1207)■12:38■19:18■20:30-**JOH**-3:4■4:54■21:16-**AC**-7:13■10:15■12:10■13:33-**1CO**-15:47-**2CO**-1:t■1:15■13:2,subscr-**2TH**-1:t,subscr-**2TI**-1:t,subscr^{2}-**TIT**-3:10-**HEB**-8:7■9:3,7,28■10:9-**2PE**-1:t■3:1-**2JO**-1:t-**RE**-2:11■4:7■6:3^{2}■8:8■11:14■16:3■20:6,14■21:8,19

SECONDARILY-**1CO**-12:28(1208)

SECRET-all=5643&marked-**GE**-49:6(5475)-**DE**-27:15■29:29(5641)-**J'G**-3:19■13:18(6383)-**1SA**-5:9(8368)■19:2-**JOB**-14:13(5641)■15:8(5475),11(328)■20:26(6845)■29:4(5475)■40:13(2934)-**PS**-10:8(4565)■17:12(4565)■18:11■19:12(5641)■25:14(5475)■27:5■31:20■64:2

(5475),4(4565)■81:7■90:8(5956)■91:1■139:15-**PR**-3:32(5475)■9:17■21:14■25:9(5475)■27:5(5641)-**EC**-12:14(5956)-**SONG**-2:14-**IS**-3:17(6596)■45:3(4565),19■48:16-**JER**-13:17(4565)■23:24(4565)■49:10(4565)-**LA**-3:10(4565)-**EZE**-7:22(6845)■28:3(5640)-**DA**-2:18(7328),19(7328),22(5642),27(7328),30(7328),47(7328)■4:9(7328)-**AM**-3:7(5475)■**N.T.**-all=2927&marked-**M'T**-6:4²,6²,18²■13:35(2928)■24:26(5009)-**M'R**-4:22(614)-**LU**-8:17■11:33(2926)-**JOH**-7:4,10■18:20-**RO**-16:25(4601)-**EPH**-5:12(2931)

SECRETLY-all=5643&marked-**GE**-31:27(2244)-**DE**-13:6■27:24■28:57-**JOS**-2:1(2791)-**1SA**-18:22(3909)■23:9(2790)-**2SA**-12:12-**2KI**-17:9(2644)-**JOB**-4:12(1589)■13:10■31:27-**PS**-10:9(4565)■31:20(6845)-**JER**-37:17■38:16■40:15-**HAB**-3:14(4565)■**N.T.**-**JOH**-11:28(2977)■19:38(2928)

SECRETS-all=7328&marked-**DE**-25:11(4016)-**JOB**-11:6(8587)-**PS**-44:21(8587)-**PR**-11:13(5475)■20:19(5475)-**DA**-2:28,29,47■**N.T.**-**RO**-2:16(2927)-**1CO**-14:25(2927)

SECT-all=139-**AC**-5:17■15:5■24:5■26:5■28:22

SECURE-all=982&marked-**J'G**-8:11(983)■18:7,10,27-**JOB**-11:18■12:6(987)■**N.T.**-**M'T**-28:14(4160,275)

SECURELY-**PR**-3:29(983)-**MIC**-2:8(983)

SECURITY-**AC**-17:9(2425)

SEDITION-**EZR**-4:15(849),19(849)■**N.T.**-all=4714-**LU**-23:19,25-**AC**-24:5

SEDITIONS-**GA**-5:20(1370)

SEDUCE-**M'R**-13:22(635)-**1JO**-2:26(4105)-**RE**-2:20(4105)

SEDUCED-**2KI**-21:9(8582)-**IS**-19:13(8582)-**EZE**-13:10(2937)

SEDUCERS-**2TI**-3:13(1114)

SEDUCETH-**PR**-12:26(8582)

SEDUCING-**1TI**-4:1(4108)

SEE-all=7200,a=2372&marked-**GE**-2:19■8:8■11:5■12:12■18:21■19:21(2009)■21:16■27:1,27■31:5,12,50■32:20■34:1■37:14,20■39:14■41:41■42:9,12■43:3,5■44:23,26,34■45:12,28■48:10,11-**EX**-1:16■3:3,4■4:18,21■5:19■6:1■7:1■10:5,28,29■12:13■13:17■14:13²■16:7,29,32■23:5■31:2■33:12,20²,23■34:10■35:30-**LE**-13:8,10,15,17,30■14:36²■20:17-**NU**-4:20■11:15,23■13:18■14:23²■22:41■23:9,13³■24:17■27:12■32:8,11-**DE**-1:35,36■3:25,28■4:28■18:16■22:1,4■23:14■28:10,34,67,68■29:4,22■30:15■32:20,39,52■34:4-**JOS**-3:3■6:2■8:1,8■22:10(4758)-**J'G**-9:37(2009)■14:8■16:5■21:21-**1SA**-2:32(5027)■3:2■4:15■6:9,13■10:24■12:16,17■14:17,29,38■15:35■17:28■19:3,15■20:29■21:14■23:22,23■24:11²,15■25:35■26:16-**2SA**-3:13²■7:2■13:5²,6■14:24,30,32■15:3,28■24:3,13-**2KI**-9:12■12:16■14:4■17:23■20:7,22■22:25-**2KI**-2:10■3:14,17■6:17,20,32■7:2,13,14,19■8:29■9:16,17■10:16■19:16■22:20■23:17-**2CH**-10:16■18:16,24■20:17■22:6■25:17■29:8■30:7■34:28-**EZR**-4:14(2370)-**NE**-2:17■4:11■9:9-**ES**-3:4■5:13■8:6²-**JOB**-3:9■6:21■7:7,8(7789)■9:11,25■10:15■17:15(7789)■9:26a,27a■20:17■21:20■22:11,19■23:9■24:1a,15(7789)■28:27■31:4■33:26,28■34:32a■35:5,14(7789)■36:25a■37:21-**PS**-10:11■14:2■16:10■22:7■27:13■31:11■34:8,12■36:9■37:34■40:3■41:6■49:9,19■52:6■53:2■58:8a■59:10■63:2■64:5,8■66:5■69:23,32■74:9■86:17■89:48■91:8■92:11(5027)■94:7,9(5027)■97:6■106:5■107:24,42■112:8,10■115:5■118:7■119:74■128:5,6■135:16■139:16,24-**PR**-24:18■29:16-**EC**-1:10■2:3■3:18,22■7:11■8:16-**SONG**-2:14■6:11²,13a■7:12-**IS**-5:19■6:9,10■13:1a■14:16■18:3■26:11²a■29:18■30:10,20■32:3■33:17a,19,20■35:2■37:17■38:11■40:5■41:20■42:18■44:9,18■48:6a■49:7■52:8,10,15■53:2,10,11■60:4,5■61:9■62:2■64:9(5027)■66:14,18-**JER**-1:10,11,13■2:10²,19,23,31■3:2■4:21■5:1,12,21■6:16■7:12■11:20■12:4■14:13■17:6,8■20:12,18■22:10,12■23:24■30:6²■42:14,18■51:61-**LA**-1:11,12-**EZE**-8:6,13,15■12:2,6,12,13■13:9(2374),16(2374),23a■14:22,23■16:37■20:48■21:29a■32:31■33:6■39:21-**DA**-1:10■2:8(2370)■3:25(2370)■5:23(2370)-**JOE**-2:28-**AM**-6:2-**JON**-4:5-**MIC**-6:9■7:10,16-**HAB**-1:1a■2:1-**ZEP**-3:15-**HAG**-2:3-**ZEC**-2:2■4:10■5:2,5■9:5,5sup■10:7-**MAL**-1:5■**N.T.**-all=1492,a=991,b=3700,c=2334,d=3708&marked-**M'T**-5:8b,16■7:5(1227)■8:4d■9:30d■11:4a,7(2300),8,9■12:38■13:13a,14a.15,16a,17,17a■15:31a■16:28■22:11(2300)■23:39■24:2a,6d,15,30b,33■26:58,64b■27:4b,24b,49■28:1c,6,7b,10b-**M'R**-1:44d■4:12a■5:14,15c,32■6:38■8:18a,24a■12:15■13:1(2396),14,26b,29■14:62b■15:32,36■16:7b-**LU**-2:15,26■3:6b■6:42(1227)■7:22(308),24(2300),25,26■8:10a,16a,20,35■9:9,27■10:23a,24,24a■11:33a■12:54■13:28b,35■14:18■17:22,22b,23²(2400)■19:3,4■20:13■21:20,27b,30a,31■23:8■24:39,39c-**JOH**-1:33,39,46,50b,51b■3:3,36b■4:29,48■6:19c,30,62c■7:3c■8:51c,56■9:15a,19a,25a,39²a,41a■11:34,40b■12:9,21,40■14:19c■16:10c,16c,16b,17c,17b,19c,19b,22b■18:26■20:25-**AC**-2:17(3070),27,31,33a■3:16c■7:56c■8:36(2400)■13:35■19:21,26c■20:25b,38(2234)■22:11(1689),14■25:24c■28:20,26a,27-**RO**-1:11■7:23a■8:25a■11:8a,10a■15:21b,24(2300)-**1CO**-1:26a■8:10■13:12a■16:7,10a-**GA**-1:18(2477)■6:11-**EPH**-3:9(5461)■5:15a-**PH'P**-1:27■2:23(542),28-**1TH**-2:17■3:6,6sup,10■5:15d-**1TI**-6:16-**2TI**-1:4-**HEB**-2:8d,9a■3:19a■8:5d■10:25a■11:5■12:14b,25a■13:23b-**JAS**-2:24d-**1PE**-1:8d■3:10-**2PE**-1:9(3467)-**1JO**-3:2b■5:16-**3JO**-14-**RE**-1:7b,12a■3:18a■6:1a,3a,5a,7a■9:20a■11:9a■16:15a■18:7,9a■19:10b■22:4d,9d

SEED-all=2233&marked-**GE**-1:11²,12²,29²■3:15■4:25■7:3■9:9■12:7■13:15,16²■15:3,5,13,18■16:10■17:7²,8,9,10,12,19■19:32,34■21:12,13■22:17²,18■24:7,60■26:3,4³,24■28:4,13,14²■32:12■35:12■38:8,9²■46:6,7■47:19,23,24■48:4,11,19-**EX**-16:31■28:43■30:21■32:13²■33:1-**LE**-11:37,38■12:2■15:16,17,18,32■18:21■20:2,3,4■21:15,17,21■22:3,4,4(7902,2233)■26:16■27:16²,30-**NU**-5:28■11:7■14:24■16:40■18:19■20:5■24:7■25:13-**DE**-1:8■4:37■10:15■11:9,10■14:22■22:9■28:38,46,59■30:6,19■31:21■34:4-**JOS**-24:3-**RU**-4:12-**1SA**-2:20■8:15■20:42■24:21-**2SA**-4:8■7:12■22:51-**1KI**-2:33²■11:14,39■18:32-**2KI**-5:27■11:1■17:20■25:25-**1CH**-16:13■17:11-**2CH**-20:7■22:10-**EZR**-2:59■9:2-**NE**-7:61■9:2,8-**ES**-6:13■9:27,28,31■10:3-**JOB**-5:25■21:8■39:12-**PS**-18:50■21:10■22:23²,30■25:13■37:25■26,28■69:36■89:4,29,36■102:28■105:6■106:27■112:2■126:6-**PR**-11:21-**EC**-11:6-**IS**-1:4■5:10■6:13■14:20■17:11■23:3■30:23■41:8■43:5■44:3■45:19,25■48:19■53:10■54:3■55:10■57:3,4■59:21²■61:9²■65:9,23■66:22-**JER**-2:21■7:15■22:28,30■23:8■29:32■30:10■31:27,36,37■33:22,26³■35:7,9■36:31■41:1■46:27■49:10-**EZE**-17:5,13■20:5■43:19■44:22-**DA**-1:3■2:43(2234)■9:1-**JOE**-1:17(6507)-**AM**-9:13-**HAG**-2:19-**ZEC**-8:12-**MAL**-2:3,15■**N.T.**-all=4690&marked-**M'T**-13:19(4687),20(4687),22(4687),23(4687),24,27,37,38■22:24-**M'R**-4:26(4703),27(4703),31■12:19,20,21,22-**LU**-1:55■8:5(4703),11(4703)■20:28-**JOH**-7:42■8:33,37-**AC**-3:25■7:5,6■13:23-**RO**-1:3■4:13,16,18■9:7²,8,29■11:1-**1CO**-15:38-**2CO**-9:10,10(4703)■11:22-**GA**-3:16²,19,29-**2TI**-2:8-**HEB**-2:16■11:11,18-**1PE**-1:23(4701)-**1JO**-3:9-**RE**-12:17

SEED'S-**IS**-59:21(2233)

SEEDS-all=4690-**M'T**-13:32-**M'R**-4:31-**GA**-3:16

SEEDTIME-**GE**-8:22(2233)

SEEING-all=7200&marked-**GE**-19:1■28:8-**EX**-4:11(6493)■22:10■23:9(3588)-**LE**-10:17(5388)-**NU**-15:26(5388)■16:3(5388)■35:23-**J'G**-17:13(5388)■19:23(310)■21:16(5388)-**1SA**-17:36(5388)-**1KI**-1:48■11:28-**EZR**-9:13(5388)-**JOB**-14:5(518)-**PR**-20:12-**EC**-1:8■6:11(5388)-**IS**-21:3■33:15■42:20-**EZE**-21:4(3282)-**DA**-2:47(1768)■**N.T.**-1492&marked-**M'T**-5:1■9:2■13:13(991),14(991)-**M'R**-4:12(991)■11:13-**LU**-1:34(1893)■5:12■8:10(991)■23:40(3754)-**JOH**-9:7(991)■21:21-**AC**-2:15(1063),31(4275)■3:3■7:24■8:6(991)■9:7(2334)■13:11(991),46(1894)■16:27■28:26(991)-**RO**-3:30(1897)-**1CO**-14:16(1894)-**2CO**-11:18(1893)-**2TH**-1:6(1512)-**HEB**-4:6(1893)■5:11(1893)■11:27(3708)-**2PE**-2:8(990)

SEEK-all=1245,a=1875&marked-**GE**-37:16■43:18(1556)-**LE**-13:36(1239)■19:31-**NU**-15:39(8446)■16:10■24:1(7125)-**DE**-4:29,29a■12:5a■22:2a■23:6a-**RU**-3:1-**1SA**-9:3■10:2,14■16:16■23:15,25■24:2■25:26,29■26:2,20■27:1■28:7-**2SA**-5:17-**1KI**-2:40■18:10■19:10,14-**2KI**-2:16■6:19-**1CH**-4:39■14:8■16:10,11a,11■22:19a■28:8a,9a-**2CH**-7:14■11:16■12:14a■14:4a■15:2a,12a,13a■19:3a■20:3a,4■30:19a■31:21a■34:3a-**EZR**-4:2a■6:21a■7:10a■8:21,22■9:12a-**NE**-2:10-**JOB**-5:8a■7:21(7836)■8:5(7836)-**PS**-4:2■9:10a■10:4a,15a■14:2a■22:26a■24:6a,6■27:4,8²■34:10a,14■35:4■38:12,12a■40:14,16■53:2a■54:3■63:1(7836),9■69:6,32a■70:2,4■71:13,24■83:16■104:21■105:3,4a,4■109:10a■119:2a,45a,155a,176■122:9-**PR**-1:28(7836)■7:15(7836)■8:17(7836)■21:6■23:30(2713),35■28:5■29:10,26-**EC**-1:13a■7:25■8:17-**SONG**-3:2■6:1-**IS**-1:17a■8:19²a■9:13a■11:10a■19:3a■26:9(7836)■31:1a■34:16a■41:12,17■45:19■51:1■55:6a■58:2a-**JER**-2:24,33■4:30■5:1■11:21■19:7,9■21:7■22:25■29:7a,13■30:14a■34:20,21■38:16■44:30■45:5■46:26■49:37■50:4-**LA**-1:11-**EZE**-7:25,26■34:6,11(1239),12(1239),16-**DA**-9:3-**HO**-2:7■3:5■5:6,15,15(7836)■7:10■10:12a-**AM**-5:4a,5a,6a,14a■8:12-**NA**-3:7,11-**ZEP**-2:3²-**ZEC**-8:21,22■11:16■12:9-**MAL**-2:7,15■3:1■**N.T.**-all=2212&marked-**M'T**-2:13■6:32(1934),33■7:7■28:5-**M'R**-1:37■3:32■8:12(1934)■16:6-**LU**-11:9,29(1934)■12:29,30(1934),31■13:24■15:8■17:33■19:10■24:5-**JOH**-1:38■5:30,44■6:26■7:25,34,36■8:21,37,40,50■13:33■18:4,7,8-**AC**-10:19,21■11:25(327)■15:17(1567)■17:27-**RO**-2:7■11:3-**1CO**-1:22■7:27²■10:24■14:12-**2CO**-12:14■13:3-**GA**-1:10■2:17-**PH'P**-2:21-**COL**-3:1-**HEB**-11:6(1567),14(1934)■13:14(1934)-**1PE**-3:11-**RE**-9:6

SEEKEST-all=1245-**GE**-37:15-**J'G**-4:22-**2SA**-17:3■20:19-**1KI**-11:22-**PR**-2:4-**JER**-45:5■**N.T.**-**JOH**-4:27(2212)■20:15(2212)

SEEKETH-all=1245&marked-**1SA**-19:2■20:1■22:23■23:10■24:9-**2SA**-16:11-**1KI**-20:7-**2KI**-5:7(579)-**JOB**-39:29(2658)-**PS**-37:32-**PR**-11:27(7836),27(1875)■14:6■15:14■17:9,11,19■18:1,15■31:13(1875)-**EC**-7:28-**IS**-40:20-**JER**-5:1■30:17(1875)■38:4(1875)-**LA**-3:25(1875)-**EZE**-14:10(1875)■34:12(1243)■**N.T.**-all=2212&marked-**M'T**-7:8■12:39(1934)■16:4(1934)■18:12-**LU**-11:10-**JOH**-4:23■7:4,18²■8:50-**RO**-3:11(1567)■11:7(1934)-**1CO**-13:5

SEEKING-**ES**-10:3(1875)-**IS**-16:5(1875)■**N.T.**-all=2212-**M'T**-12:43■13:45-**M'R**-8:11-**LU**-2:45■11:24,54■13:7-**JOH**-6:24-**AC**-13:8,11-**1CO**-10:33-**1PE**-5:8

SEEM-all=1961,5869&marked-GE-27:12-DE-15:18(7185)■25:3(7034)-JOS-24:15-1SA-24:4-2SA-19:37,38-1KI-21:2-EZR-7:18(3191)-NE-9:32(4591)-JER-40:4²(5869)-NA-2:4(4758)■N.T.-all=1380-1CO-11:16■12:22-2CO-10:9-HEB-4:1-JAS-1:26

SEEMED-all=5869&marked-GE-19:14(1961,5869)■29:20(1961,5869)-2SA-3:19²-JER-18:4■27:5■N.T.-all=1380&marked-M'T-11:26(1096,2107)-LU-1:3■10:21(1096,2107)■24:11(5316)-AC-15:25,28-GA-2:6²,9

SEEMETH-all=5869&marked-LE-14:35(7200)-JOS-9:25-J'G-10:15■19:24-1SA-1:23■3:18■11:10■14:36,40■18:23-2SA-10:12■15:26■18:4■24:22-ES-3:11-PR-14:12(6440)■16:25(6440)-JER-26:14■40:4,5■N.T.-all=1380-LU-8:18-AC-17:18■25:27-1CO-3:18-HEB-12:11

SEEMLY-PR-19:10(5000)■26:1(5000)

SEEN-all=7200&marked-GE-7:1■8:5■9:14■22:14■31:12,42■32:30■33:10²■45:13■46:30-EX-3:7,9■10:6■13:7²■14:13■19:4■20:22■32:9■33:23■34:3-LE-5:1■13:7²-NU-14:14,22■23:21■27:13-DE-1:28,31■3:21■4:3,9■5:24■9:13■10:21■11:2,7■16:4■21:7■29:2,3,17■33:9-JOS-23:3■24:7-J'G-2:7■5:8■6:22■9:48■13:22■14:2■18:9■19:30-1SA-6:16■16:18■17:25■23:22■24:10-2SA-17:17■18:21■22:11-1KI-6:18■8:8²■10:4,7,12■13:12■20:13-2KI-9:26■20:5,15²■23:29-1CH-29:17-2CH-5:9²■9:3,6,11-EZR-3:12-ES-9:26-JOB-4:8■5:3■7:8(7210)■8:18■10:18■13:1■15:17(2372)■20:7■27:12(2372)■28:7(7805)■31:19■33:21(7210),21■38:17,22-PS-10:14■18:15■35:21,22■37:25,35■48:8■54:7■55:9■63:2(2372)■68:24■90:15■98:3■119:96-PR-25:7-EC-1:14■3:10■4:3■5:13,18■6:1,5,6■7:15■8:9■9:13■10:5,7-IS-6:5■9:2■16:12■22:9■38:5■39:4²■44:16■47:3■57:18■60:2■64:4■66:8,19-JER-1:12■3:6■7:11■12:3■13:27■23:13,14■44:2■46:5-LA-1:8,10■2:14²(2372),16■3:1,59,60-EZE-8:12,15,17■11:24■13:3,6(2372),7(2372),8(2372)■47:6-DA-2:26(2370)■4:9(2370),18(2370)■8:6,15■9:21-HO-6:10-ZEC-9:8,14■10:2(2372)■N.T.-all=1492,a=3708&marked-M'T-2:2■6:1(2300),5(5316)■9:33(5316)■13:17■21:32■23:5(2300)■9:1,9■16:11(2300),14(2300)-LU-1:22a■2:17,20,26,30■5:26■7:22■9:36a■10:24■19:37■23:8■24:23a,37(2334)-JOH-1:18a■3:11a,32a■4:45a■5:37a■6:14,36a,46²a■8:38²a,57a■9:8(2334),37a■11:45(2300)■14:7a,9a■15:24a■20:18a,25a,29a,29-AC-1:3(3700),11(2300)■4:20■7:34²,44a■9:12,27■10:17■11:13,23■13:31(3700)■16:10,40■21:29(4308)■22:15a■26:16-RO-1:20(2529)■8:24(991)-1CO-2:9■9:1a■15:5(3700),6(3700),7(3700),8(3700)-2CO-4:18⁴(991)-PH'P-4:9-COL-2:1a,18a-1TI-3:16(3700)■6:16-HEB-11:1(991),3(991),7(991),13-JAS-5:11-1PE-1:8-1JO-1:1a,2a,3a■3:6a■4:12(2300),14(2300),20²a-3JO-11(3780)-RE-1:19■11:19(3700)■22:8(991)

SEER-all=2374,a=7200&marked-1SA-9:9²a,11a,19a-2SA-15:27a■24:11-1CH-9:22a■21:9■25:5■26:28a■29:29a,29-2CH-9:29■12:15■16:7a,10a■19:2■29:25,30■35:15-AM-7:12

SEER'S-1SA-9:18(7200)

SEERS-all=2374&marked-2KI-17:13-2CH-33:18,19-IS-29:10■30:10(7200)-MIC-3:7

SEEST-all=7200&marked-GE-13:15■16:13(7210)■31:43-EX-10:28-DE-4:19■12:13■20:1■21:11-J'G-9:36-1KI-21:29-JOB-10:4-PR-2:29(2372)■26:12■29:20(2372)-EC-5:8-IS-58:3,7-JER-1:11,13■7:17■20:12■24:3■32:24-EZE-8:6■40:4-DA-1:13-AM-7:8■8:2-ZEC-4:2■5:2■N.T.-all=991&marked-M'R-5:31■13:2-LU-7:44-AC-21:20(2334)-JAS-2:22-RE-1:11

SEETH-all=7200&marked-GE-16:13(7210)■44:31-EX-4:14■12:23-LE-13:20-DE-32:36-1SA-16:7sup,7-2KI-2:19-JOB-8:17(2372)■10:4■11:11■22:14■28:10,24■34:21■42:5-PS-37:13■49:10■58:10(2372)-EC-8:16-IS-21:6■28:4■29:15,23■47:10-EZE-8:12■9:9■12:27(2372)■18:14■33:3■39:15■N.T.-all=2334&marked-M'T-6:4(991),6(991),18(991)-M'R-5:38-LU-16:23(3708)-JOH-1:29(991)■5:19(991)■6:40■9:21(991)■10:12■11:9(991)■12:45■14:17,19■20:1(991),6,12■21:20(991)-RO-8:24(991)-2CO-12:6(991)-1JO-3:17

SEETHE-all=1310-EX-16:23■23:19■29:31■34:26-DE-14:21-2KI-4:38-EZE-24:5-ZEC-14:21

SEETHING-1SA-2:13(1310)-JOB-41:20(5301)-JER-1:13(5301)

SEIZE-JOS-8:7(3423)-JOB-3:6(3947)-PS-55:15(3451)■N.T.-M'T-21:38(2722)

SEIZED-JER-49:24(2388)

SELAH-all=5542-PS-3:2,4,8■4:2,4■7:5■9:16,20■20:3■21:2■24:6,10■32:4,5,7■39:5,11■44:8■46:3,7,11■47:4■48:8■49:13,15■50:6■52:3,5■54:3■55:7,19■57:3,6■59:5,13■60:4■61:4■62:4,8■66:4,7,15■67:1,4■68:7,19,32■75:3■76:3,9■77:3,9,15■81:7■82:2■83:8■84:4,8■85:2■87:3,6■88:7,10■89:4,37,45,48■140:3,5,8■143:6-HAB-3:3,9,13

SELF-JOH-5:30(1683)■17:5(4572)-1CO-4:3(1683)-PH'M-19(4572)-1PE-2:24(846)

SELFSAME-all=2088,6106-GE-7:13■17:23,26-EX-12:17,41,51-LE-23:14,21-DE-32:48-JOS-5:11-EZE-40:1■N.T.-M'T-8:13(1565)-1CO-12:11(846)-2CO-5:5(846,5124)■7:11(846)

SELFWILL-GE-49:6(7522)

SELFWILLED-TIT-1:7(829)-2PE-2:10(829)

SELL-all=4376&marked-GE-25:31■37:27-EX-21:7,8,35■22:1-LE-25:14,15,16,29,47-DE-2:28(7666)■14:21■21:14-J'G-4:9-1KI-21:25-2KI-4:7-NE-5:8■10:31-PR-23:23-EZE-30:12■48:14-JOE-3:8²-AM-8:5(7666),6(7666)-ZEC-11:5■N.T.-all=4453&marked-M'T-19:21■25:9-M'R-10:21-LU-12:33■18:22■22:36-JAS-4:13(1710)-RE-13:17(4453)

SELLER-all=4376-IS-24:2-EZE-7:12,13■N.T.-AC-16:14(4211)

SELLERS-NE-13:20(4376)

SELLEST-PS-44:12(4376)

SELLETH-all=4376&marked-EX-21:16-DE-24:7-RU-4:3-PR-11:26(7666)■31:24-NA-3:4■N.T.-M'T-13:44(4453)

SELVEDGE-EX-26:4(7098)■36:11(7098)

SELVES-LE-11:43-(5315)-JOS-23:11(5315)■N.T.-all=1438&marked-LU-21:30-AC-20:30(846)-2CO-8:5■13:5²-2TI-3:2(5367)-JAS-1:22(846)

SENATE-AC-5:21(1087)

SENATORS-PS-105:22(2205)

SEND-all=7971&marked-GE-24:7,12(7136),40,54,56■27:45■30:25■37:13■38:17²■42:16■43:4,5,8,14■45:5-EX-3:10■4:13²■7:2■8:21■9:14,19■12:33■23:20,27,28■33:2,12-LE-16:21■26:22,25,36(935)-NU-13:2²■22:37■31:4-DE-1:22■7:20■11:15(5414)■19:12■24:1■28:20,48■32:24-JOS-18:4-J'G-13:8-1SA-5:11■6:2,3²,8■9:16,26■11:3■12:17(5414)■16:1,11,19■20:12■20:13,21,31■21:2■25:25-2SA-11:6■14:32■15:36■17:16-1KI-8:44■18:1(5414),19■20:6,9,34-2KI-2:16,17■4:22■5:5,7■6:13■7:13■9:17■15:37■19:7(5414)-1CH-13:2-2CH-2:3,7,8,15■6:27(5414),34■7:13■28:16■32:9-EZR-5:17(7972)-NE-2:5,6■8:10,12-JOB-21:11■38:35-PS-20:2■43:3■57:3²■68:9(5130),33(5414)■110:2■144:7-PR-10:26■22:21■25:13-EC-10:1(5042)-IS-6:8²■10:6,16■16:1■19:20■32:20■37:7■57:9■66:19-JER-1:7■2:10■8:17■9:16,17■9:16,17■16:16²■24:10■25:9,15,16,27■27:3■29:17,31■42:5,6■43:10■48:12■49:37■51:2-EZE-2:3,4■5:16²,17■7:3■14:13,19,21■28:23■39:6-HO-8:14-JOE-2:19-AM-1:4,7,10,12■2:2,5■8:11-MAL-2:2■3:1■4:5■N.T.-all=649,a=3992&marked-M'T-9:38(1544)■10:16,34²(906)■11:10■12:20(1544)■13:41■14:15(630)■15:23(630),32(630)■21:3■23:34■24:31-M'R-1:2■3:14■5:10,12a■6:7,36(630)■8:3(630)■11:3■12:13■13:27-LU-7:27■9:12(630)■10:2(1544),3■11:49■12:49(906)■16:24a,27a■20:13a■24:49-JOH-13:20a■14:26a■15:26a■16:7a■17:8■20:21a-AC-3:20■7:34,35■10:5a,22(3343),32a■11:13,29a■15:22a,25a■22:21(1821)■25:3(3343),21a,25a,27a■26:17-1CO-16:3a-PH'P-2:19a,23a,25a-2TH-2:11a-TIT-3:12a-JAS-3:11(1032)-RE-1:11a■11:10a

SENDEST-all=7971-DE-15:13,18-JOS-1:16-2KI-1:6-JOB-14:20-PS-104:30

SENDETH-all=7971&marked-DE-24:3-1KI-17:14(5414)-JOB-5:10■12:15-PS-104:10■147:15,18-PR-26:6-SONG-1:12(5414)-IS-18:2■N.T.-all=649-M'T-5:45(1026)-M'R-11:1■14:13-LU-14:32

SENDING-all=7971&marked-2SA-13:16-2CH-36:15-ES-9:19(4916),22(4916)-PS-78:49(4917)-IS-7:25(4916)-JER-7:25■25:4■26:5■29:19■35:15■44:4-EZE-17:15■N.T.-RO-8:3(3992)

SENSE-NE-8:8(7922)

SENSES-HEB-5:14(145)

SENSUAL-JAS-3:15(5591)-JUDE-19(5591)

SENT-all=7971,a=7972&marked-GE-3:23■8:7,8,10,12■12:20■19:13,29■20:2■21:14■24:59■25:6■26:27,29,31■27:42■28:5,6■31:4,27,42■32:3,5,18,23²(5674)■37:14,32■38:20,23,25■41:8,14■42:4■43:34■44:3■45:7,8,23,24,27■46:5,28-EX-2:5■3:12,13,14,15■4:28■5:22■7:16■9:7,23(5414),27■18:2(7964)■24:5-NU-13:3,16,17■14:36■16:12,28,29■20:14,16■21:6,21,32■22:5,10,15,40■31:6■32:8-DE-2:26■9:23■24:4■34:11-JOS-2:1,3,21■6:17,25■7:2,22■8:3,9■10:3,6■11:1■14:7,11■22:6,7,13■24:5,9,12-J'G-3:15,18■4:6■5:15■6:8,14,35²■7:8,24■9:23,31■11:12,14,17²,19,28,38■12:9■16:18■18:2■19:29■20:6,12■21:10,13-1SA-4:4■5:8,10,11■6:21■10:25■11:7■12:8,11,18(5414)■13:2■15:1,18,20■16:12,19,20,22■17:31(3497)■18:5■19:11,14,15,17,20,21²■20:22■22:11■25:5,14,32,39,40■26:4■30:26■31:9-2SA-2:5■3:12,14,15,21,22,23,24,26■5:11■8:10■9:5■10:2,3²,4,5,6,7,16■11:1,3,4,5,6²,14,18,22,27■12:1,25,27■13:7■14:2,29²,32■15:10,12■18:2,29■19:11,14■22:15,17■24:13,15(5414)-1KI-1:44,53■2:25,29,36,42■5:1,2,8,14■7:13■8:66■9:14,27■12:3,18,20■14:6■15:18,19,20■18:10,20■19:2■20:2,5,7,10,17,34■21:8,11²,14-2KI-1:2,6,9,11,13,16■2:2,4,6,17■3:7■5:6,8,10,22■6:9,10,14,23,32²■7:14■8:9■9:19■10:1,5,7,21■11:4■12:18■14:8,9²,19■16:7,8,10,11■17:4,13,25,26■18:14,17,27,27sup■19:2,4,9,16,20■20:12■22:3,15,18■23:1,16■24:2²-1CH-8:8■10:9■12:19■14:1■18:10■19:2,3,4,5,6,8,16■21:12,14(5414),15-2CH-2:3,11,13■7:10■8:18■10:3,18■16:2,3,4■17:7■24:19,23■25:13(7725),15,17,18²,27■30:1■32:21,31■34:8,23,26,29■35:21■36:10,15-EZR-4:11a,14a,17a,18a■5:6a,7a■6:13a■7:14a■8:16,17(6680)-NE-2:9■6:2,3,4,5,8,12,17(1980),19-ES-1:22■3:13■4:4■5:10■8:10■9:20,30-JOB-1:4,5■22:9■39:5-PS-18:14,16■59:t■77:17(5414)■78:25,45■80:11■105:17,20,26,28■106:15■107:20■111:9■135:9-PR-9:3■17:11-IS-9:8■20:1■36:2,12,12sup■37:2,4,9,17,21■39:1■42:19■43:14■48:16■55:11■61:1-JER-7:25■14:3,

14,15■19:14■21:1■23:21,32,38■24:5■25:4,17■26:5,12,15,22■27:15■28:9,15■29:1,3,9,19,20,25,28,31■35:15■36:14,21■37:3,7,17■38:14■39:13,14■40:14■42:9,20,21■43:1,2■44:4■49:14-**LA**-1:13-**EZE**-2:9■3:5,6■13:6■23:16,40^2■31:4-**DA**-3:2a,28a■5:24a■6:22a■10:11-**HO**-5:13-**JOE**-2:25-**AM**-4:10■7:10-**OB**-1-**JON**-1:4(2904)-**MIC**-6:4-**HAG**-1:12-**ZEC**-1:10■2:8,9,11■4:9■6:15■7:2,12■9:11-**MAL**-2:4■**N.T.**-all=649,a=3992&marked-**M'T**-2:8a,16■10:5,40■11:2a■13:36(863)■14:10a,22(630),23(630),35■15:24,39(630)■20:2■21:1,34,36,37■22:3,4,7a,16■23:37■27:19-**M'R**-1:43(1544)■3:31■4:36(863)■6:17,27,45(628),46(657)■8:9(630),26■9:37■12:2,3,4^2,5,6-**LU**-1:19,26,53(1821)■4:18,26a,43■7:3,6a,10a,20■8:38(630)■9:2,48,52■10:1,16■13:34■14:17■15:15a■19:14,29,32■20:10(640),10(1821),11a,11(1821),12a,20■22:8,35■23:7(375),11(375),15(375)-**JOH**-1:6,19,22a,24,33a■3:17,28,34■4:34a,38■5:23a,24a,30a,33,36,37a,38■6:29,38a,39a,40a,44a,57■7:16a,18a,28a,29,32,33a■8:16a,18a,26a,29a,42■9:4a,7■10:36■11:3,42■12:44a,45a,49a■13:16(652),20a■14:24a■15:21a■16:5a■17:3,18^2,21,23,25■18:24■20:21-**AC**-3:26■5:21■7:12(1821),14■8:14■9:17,30(1821),38■10:8,17,20,21,29^2(3343),33a,36■11:11,22(1821),30■12:11(1821)■13:3(630),4(1599),15,26■15:27■16:35,36■17:10(1599),14(1821)■19:22,31a■20:17a■23:30a■24:24(3343),26(3343)■28:28-**RO**-10:15-**1CO**-1:17-**2CO**-8:18(4842),22(4842)■9:3a■12:17,18(4882)-**GA**-4:4(1821),6(1821)-**EPH**-6:22a■2:28a■4:16a-**COL**-4:8a-**1TH**-3:2a,5(375)-**2TI**-4:12-**PH'M**-12(628)-**HEB**-1:14-**JAS**-2:25(1524)-**1PE**-1:12■2:14a-**1JO**-4:9,10,14-**RE**-1:1■5:6■22:6,16a

SENTENCE-all=1697&marked-**DE**-17:9,10,11(6310),11-**PS**-17:2(4941)-**PR**-16:10(7081)-**EC**-8:11(6599)-**JER**-4:12(4941)■**N.T.**-**LU**-23:24(1948)-**AC**-15:19(2919)-**2CO**-1:9(610)

SENTENCES-**DA**-5:12(280)■8:23(2420)

SENTEST-all=7971-**EX**-15:7-**NU**-13:27■24:12-**1KI**-5:8

SEPARATE-all=914&marked-**GE**-13:9(6504)■30:40(6504)■49:26(5139)-**LE**-15:31(5144)■22:2(5144)-**NU**-6:2(6381),2(5144),3(5144)■8:14■16:21-**DE**-19:2,7,2■29:21-**JOS**-16:9(3995)-**1KI**-8:53-**EZR**-10:11-**JER**-37:12(2505)-**EZE**-41:12(1508),13(1508),14(1508),15(1508)■42:1(1508),10(1508),13(1508)■**N.T.**-all=873&marked-**M'T**-25:32-**LU**-6:22-**AC**-13:2-**RO**-8:35(5562),39(5562)-**2CO**-6:17-**HEB**-7:26(5562)-**JUDE**-19(592)

SEPARATED-all=914&marked-**GE**-13:11(6504),14(6504)■25:23(6504)-**EX**-33:16(6395)-**LE**-20:24,25-**NU**-16:9-**DE**-10:8■32:8(6504)■33:16(5139)-**1CH**-12:8■23:13■25:1-**2CH**-25:10-**EZR**-6:21(6395)■8:24■9:1■10:8,16-**NE**-4:19(6504)■9:2■10:28■13:3-**PR**-18:1(6504)■19:4(6504)-**IS**-56:3■59:2-**HOS**-4:14(6504)■9:10(5144)■**N.T.**-all=873-**AC**-19:9-**RO**-1:1-**GA**-1:15■2:12

SEPARATETH-all=5144&marked-**NU**-6:5,6-**PR**-16:28(6504)■17:9(6504)-**EZE**-14:7

SEPARATING-**ZEC**-7:3(5144)

SEPARATION-all=5079,a=5145&marked-**LE**-12:2,5■15:20,25^3,26^2-**NU**-6:4a,5a,8a,12^{2}a,13,18^2,19,21^{2}a■9:9,13,20,21^2■31:23-**EZE**-42:20(914)

SEPULCHRE-all=6913&marked-**GE**-23:6-**DE**-34:6(6900)-**J'G**-8:32-**1SA**-10:2(6900)-**2SA**-2:32■4:12■17:23■21:14-**1KI**-13:22,31-**2KI**-9:28(6900)■13:21■21:26(6900)■23:17,30(6900)-**PS**-5:9-**IS**-22:16^2-**JER**-5:16■**N.T.**-all=3419&marked-**M'T**-27:60,61(5028),64(5028),66(5028)■28:1(5028),8-**M'R**-15:46^2■16:2,3,5,8-**LU**-23:53(3418),55■24:1(3418),2,9,12,22,24-**JOH**-19:41,42■20:1^2,2,3,4,6,8,11^2-**AC**-2:29(3418)■7:16(3418)■13:29-**RO**-3:13(5028)

SEPULCHRES-all=6913-**GE**-23:6-**2KI**-23:16^2-**2CH**-16:14■21:20■24:25■28:27■32:33■35:24-**NE**-2:3,5■3:16■**N.T.**-all=3419&marked-**M'T**-23:27(5028),29-**LU**-11:47,48

SERAPHIMS-**IS**-6:2(8314),6(8314)

SERJEANTS-**AC**-16:35(4465),38(4465)

SERPENT-all=5175&marked-**GE**-3:1,2,4,13,14■49:17-**EX**-4:3■7:9(8577),10(8577),15-**NU**-21:8(8314),9^3-**2KI**-18:4-**JOB**-26:13-**PS**-58:4■140:3-**PR**-23:32■30:19-**EC**-10:8,11-**IS**-14:29(8314)■27:1^2■30:6(8314)-**JER**-46:22-**AM**-5:19■9:3-**MIC**-7:17■**N.T.**-all=3789-**M'T**-7:10-**LU**-11:11-**JOH**-3:14-**2CO**-11:3-**RE**-12:9,14,15■20:2

SERPENT'S-**IS**-14:29(5175)■65:25(5175)

SERPENTS-all=5175&marked-**EX**-7:12(8577)-**NU**-21:6,7-**DE**-8:15■32:24(2119)-**JER**-8:17■**N.T.**-all=3789&marked-**M'T**-10:16■23:33-**M'R**-16:18-**LU**-10:19-**1CO**-10:9-**JAS**-3:7(2062)-**RE**-9:19

SERVANT-all=5650,a=5288marked-**GE**-9:25,26,27■18:3,5■19:19■24:2,5,9,10,14,17,34,52,53,59,61,65^2,66■26:24■32:4,10,18,20■33:5,14■39:17,19■41:12■43:28■44:10,17,18^2,24,27,30,31,32,33■49:15(5647)-**EX**-4:10■12:44,45(7916)■14:31■21:2,5,20,26■33:11(8334)-**LE**-22:10(7916)■25:6,6(7916),40(7916),50(7916),53(7916)-**NU**-11:11,28(8334)■12:7,8■14:24-**DE**-3:24■5:15■15:17,18(7916)■23:15■24:14(7916)■34:5-**JOS**-1:1,2,7,13,15■5:14■8:31,33■9:24■11:12,15■12:6^2■13:8■14:7■18:7■22:2,4,5■24:29-**J'G**-2:8■7:10a,11a■15:18■19:3a,9a,11a,13a-**RU**-2:5a,6a-**1SA**-2:13a,15a■3:9,10■9:5a,7a,8a,10a,22a,27a■10:14a■17:32,34,36,58■19:4■20:7,8^2■22:8,15^2■23:10,11^2■25:39,41■26:18,19■27:5,12■28:2■29:3,8■30:13-**2SA**-3:18■7:5,8,20,21,25,26,27^2,28,29^2■9:2^2,6,8,9a,11■11:21,24■13:17a,18(8334),24^2,35■14:19,20,22^2■15:2,8,21,34^3■16:1a■18:29■19:17a,19,20,26^3,27,28,35^2,36,37^2■24:10,21-**1KI**-1:19,26^2,27,51■2:38■3:6,7,8,9■8:24,25,26,28^2,29,30,52,53,56,59,66■11:11,26,32,36,38■12:7■14:8,18■15:29■16:9■18:9,12,36,43a■19:3a■20:9,32,39,40-**2KI**-4:1^2,12a,24a,25a,38a■5:6,15,17^2,18^2,20a,25■6:15(8334),15a■8:4a,13■9:36■10:10■14:25■16:7■17:3■18:12■19:34■20:6■21:8■22:12■24:1■25:8-**1CH**-2:34,35■6:49■16:13■17:4,7,18^2,23,24,25^2,26,27■21:8-**2CH**-1:3■6:15,16,17,19^2,20,21,42■13:6■24:6,9■32:16■34:20-**NE**-1:6,7,8,11^2■2:5,10,19■4:22a■6:5a■9:14■10:29-**JOB**-1:8■2:3■3:19■7:2■19:16■41:4■42:7,8^3-**PS**-18:t■19:11,13■27:9■31:16■35:27■36:t■69:17■78:70■86:2,4,16■89:3,20,39■105:6,17,26,42■109:28■116:16^2■119:17,23,38,49,65,76,84,122,124,125,135,140,176■132:10■136:22■143:2,12■144:10-**PR**-11:29■12:9■14:35■17:2■19:10■22:7■29:19,21■30:10,22-**EC**-7:21-**IS**-20:3■22:20■24:2■37:35■41:8,9■42:1,19^2■43:10■44:1,2,21^2,26■48:20■49:3,5,6,7■50:10■52:13■53:11-**JER**-2:14■25:9■27:6■30:10■33:21,22,26■34:16■43:10■46:27,28-**EZE**-28:25■34:23,24■37:24,25^2-**DA**-6:20(5649)■9:11,17■10:17-**HAG**-2:23-**ZEC**-3:8-**MAL**-1:6■4:4■**N.T.**-1401&marked-**M'T**-8:6(3816)■8(3816),9,13(3816)■10:24,25■12:18(3816)■18:26,27,28,32■20:27■23:11(1249)■24:45,46,48,50■25:21,23,26,30■26:51-**M'R**-9:35(1249)■10:44■12:2,4■14:47-**LU**-1:54(3816),69(3816)■2:29■7:2,3,7(3816),8,10■12:43,45,46,47■14:17,21^2,22,23■16:13(3610)■17:7,9■19:17,22■20:10,11■22:50-**JOH**-8:34,35■12:26(1249)■13:16■15:15,20■18:10-**AC**-4:25(3816)-**RO**-1:1■14:4(3610)■16:1(1249),subscr.(1249)-**1CO**-7:21,22^2■9:19(1402)-**GA**-1:10■4:1,7-**PH'P**-2:7-**COl**-4:12-**2TI**-2:24-**TIT**-1:1-**PH'M**-16,subscr.(3610)-**HEB**-3:5(2324)-**JAS**-1:1-**2PE**-1:1-**JUDE**-1-**RE**-1:1■15:3

SERVANT'S-all=5650-**GE**-19:2-**2SA**-7:19-**1KI**-11:13,34-**2KI**-8:19-**1CH**-17:17,19-**IS**-45:4■**N.T.**-**JOH**-18:10(1401)

SERVANTS-all=5650,a=5288&marked-**GE**-9:25■14:15■20:8■21:25■26:14(5657),15,19,25,32■27:37■32:16^2■40:20^2■41:10,37,38■42:10,11,13■44:7,9,16^2,19,21,23,31■45:16■47:3,4^2,19,25■50:2,7,17,18-**EX**-5:15,16^2,21■7:10,20■8:3,4,9,11,21,29,31■9:14,20^2,21,30,34■10:1,6,7■11:3,8■12:30■14:5■32:13-**LE**-25:42,55^2-**NU**-22:18,22a■31:49■32:4,5,25,27,31-**DE**-9:27■29:2■32:36,43■34:11-**JOS**-9:8,9,11,24■10:6-**J'G**-3:24■6:27■19:19-**1SA**-4:9(5647)■8:14,15,17■9:3■12:19■16:15,16,17,18a■17:8,9^2■18:5,22^2,23,24,26,30■19:1■21:2a,7,11,14■22:6,7,9,14,17■24:7(582)■25:8,10^2,19a,40,41■28:7^2,23,25■29:10-**2SA**-2:12,13,15,17,30,31■3:22,38■6:20■8:2,6,7,14■9:10^2,12■10:2^2,3,4,19■11:1,9,11,13,17,24^2■12:18,19^2,21■13:24,28a,29a,31,36■14:30^2,31■15:14,15^2,18■16:6,11■17:20■18:7,9■19:5,6,7,14,17■20:6■21:15,22■24:20-**1KI**-1:2,9,33,47■2:39^2,40^2■3:15■5:1,6^2,9■8:23^2,36■9:22,27^2■10:5,8,13■11:17■12:7■15:18■20:6^2,12,23,31■22:3,49-**2KI**-1:13■2:16■3:11■5:13,23a■6:3,8,11,12■7:12,13■9:7^2,11,28■10:5,19(5647),23■12:20,21■14:5■17:13,23■18:24,26■19:5,6a■21:10,23■22:9■23:30■24:2,10,11,12■25:24-**1CH**-18:2,6,7,13■19:2,3,4,19,19(5647)■20:8■21:3-**2CH**-2:8^2,10,15■6:14,23,27■8:9,18^3■9:4,7,10^2,12,21■10:7■12:8■24:25■25:3■32:9,16■33:24■34:16■35:23,24■36:20-**EZR**-2:55,58,65■4:11(5649)■5:11(5649)■9:11-**NE**-1:6,10,11■2:20■4:16a,23a■5:5,10a,15a,16a■7:57,60■9:10,36^2■11:3■13:19a-**ES**-1:3■2:2a,18■3:2,3■4:11■5:11■6:3a,5a-**JOB**-1:15a,16a,17a■4:18-**PS**-34:22■69:36■79:2,10■89:50■90:13,16■102:14,28■105:25■113:1■119:91■123:2■134:1■135:1,9,14-**PR**-29:12(8334)-**EC**-2:7,7sup■10:7^2-**IS**-14:2■36:9,11■37:5,6a,24■54:17■56:6■65:9,13^3,14,15■66:14-**JER**-7:25■21:7■22:2,4■25:4,19■26:5■29:19■34:11^2,16■35:15■36:24,31■37:2,18■44:4■46:26-**LA**-5:8-**EZE**-38:17■46:17-**DA**-1:12,13■2:4(5649),7(5649)■3:26(5649),28(5649)■9:6,10-**JOE**-2:29-**AM**-3:7-**MIC**-6:4-**ZEC**-1:6■2:9(5647)■**N.T.**-all=1401&marked-**M'T**-13:27,28■14:2(3816)■18:23■21:34,35,36■22:3,4,6,8,10,13(1249)■25:14,19■26:58(5257)-**M'R**-1:20(3411)■13:34■14:54(5257),65(5257)-**LU**-12:37,38■15:17(3407),19(3407),22,26(3816)■17:10■19:13,15-**JOH**-2:5(1249),9(1249)■4:51■15:15■18:18,26,36(5257)-**AC**-2:18■4:29■16:17-**RO**-6:16^2,17,18(1402)19^2,20,22(1402)-**1CO**-7:23-**2CO**-4:5-**EPH**-6:5,6-**PH'P**-1:1-**COL**-3:22■4:1-**1TI**-6:1-**TIT**-2:9-**1PE**-2:16,18(3610)-**2PE**-2:19-**RE**-1:1■2:20■7:3■10:7■11:18■19:2,5■22:3,6

SERVANTS'-all=5650-**GE**-46:34-**EX**-8:24-**IS**-63:17■65:8

SERVE-all=5647&marked-**GE**-15:13,14■25:23■27:29,40■29:15,18,25,27-**EX**-1:13,14■3:12■4:23■7:16■8:1,20■9:1■10:3,8,11,24,26^2■12:31■14:12^2■20:5■21:2,6■23:24,25,33-**LE**-25:39(5656),40-**NU**-4:24,26■8:25■18:7,21-**DE**-4:19,28■5:9■6:13■7:4,16■8:19■10:12,20■11:13,16■12:30■13:2,4,6,13■15:12■20:11■28:14,36,48,64■29:18■30:17■31:20-**JOS**-16:10■22:5■23:7■24:14^2,15^3,16,18,19,20,21,22,24-**J'G**-2:19■9:28^3,38-**1SA**-7:3■10:7■11:1■12:10,14,20,24■17:9■26:19-**2SA**-15:8■16:19^2■22:44-**1KI**-9:6■12:4,7-**2KI**-10:18■17:35■25:24

-1CH-28:9-2CH-7:19■10:4■29:11(8334)■30:8■33:16■34:33^{2}■35:3-JOB-21:15■36:11■39:9-PS-2:11■18:43■22:30■72:11■97:7■100:2■101:6(8334)■102:22-IS-14:3■19:23■43:23,24■56:6(8334)■60:12-JER-5:19■11:10■13:10■16:13■17:4■25:6,11,14■27:6,7^{2},8,9,11,12,13,14,17■28:14^{2}■30:8,9■34:9,10■35:15■40:9^{2},10(5975,6440)■44:3-EZE-20:32(8334),39,40■29:18■48:18,19^{2}-DA-3:12(6399),14(6399),17(6399),18(6399),28(6399)■7:14(6399),27(6399)-ZEP-3:9-MAL-3:14■N.T.-all=3000,a=1398&marked-M'T-4:10■6:24^{2}a-LU-1:74■4:8■10:40(1247)■12:37(1247)■15:29a■16:13^{2}■17:8(1247)■22:26(1247)-JOH-12:26^{2}(1247)-AC-6:2(1247)■7:7■27:23-RO-1:9■6:6a■7:6a,25a■9:12a■16:18a-GA-5:13a-COL-3:24a-1TH-1:9a-2TI-1:3-HEB-8:5■9:14■12:28■13:10-RE-7:15■22:3

SERVED-all=5647&marked-GE-14:4■29:20,30■30:26,29■31:6,41■39:4(8334)■40:4(8334)-DE-12:2■17:3■29:26-JOS-23:16■24:2,14,15,31-J'G-2:7,11,13■3:6,7,8,14■8:1(6213)■10:6^{2},10,13,16-1SA-7:4■8:8■12:10-2SA-10:19■16:19-1KI-4:21■9:9■16:31■22:53-2KI-10:18■17:12,16,33,41■18:7■21:3,21-1CH-19:5(5921)■27:1(8334)-2CH-7:22■24:18■33:3,22-NE-9:35-ES-1:10(8334)-PS-106:36■137:8(1580)-EC-5:9-JER-5:19■8:2■16:11■22:9■34:14■52:12(5975,6440)-EZE-29:18,20■34:27-HO-12:12■N.T.-LU-2:37(3000)-JOH-12:2(1247)-AC-13:36(5256)-RO-1:25(3000)-PH'P-2:22(1398)

SERVEDST-DE-28:47(5647)

SERVEST-DA-6:16(6399),20(6399)

SERVETH-NU-3:36(5656)-MAL-3:17(5647),18(5647)■N.T.-LU-22:27^{2}(1247)-RO-14:18(1398)

SERVICE-all=5656&marked-GE-29:27■30:26-EX-1:14^{2}■12:25,26■13:5■27:19■30:16■31:10(8278)■35:19(8287),19(8334),21,24■36:1,3,5■38:21■39:1(8278),1(8334),40,41(8278),41(8334)-NU-3:7,8,26,31■4:4,19,23,24,26,27^{2},28,30(6635),31,32,33^{2},35(6635),37(5647),39(6635),41(5647),43(6635),47^{2},49■7:5^{2},7,8,9■8:11,15(5647),19,22,24,25,26■16:9■18:4,6,7,21^{2},23,31-JOS-22:27-1KI-12:4-1CH-6:31(3027),48■9:13,19■23:24,26,28^{2},32■24:3,19■25:1^{2},6■26:8,30■28:13^{2},14^{2},20,21^{2}■29:5(3027),7-2CH-8:14■12:8^{2}■24:12■29:35■31:2,16,21■34:13■35:2,10,15,16-EZR-6:18(5673)■7:19(6402)■8:20-NE-10:32-PS-104:14-JER-22:13(5647)-EZE-29:18^{2}■44:14■N.T.-all=2999&marked-JOH-16:2-RO-9:4■12:1■15:31(1248)-2CO-9:12(3009)■11:8(1248)-GA-4:8(1398)-EPH-6:7(1398)-PH'P-2:17(3009),30(3009)-1TI-6:2(1398)-HEB-9:1,6,9(3000)-RE-2:19(1248)

SERVILE-all=5656-LE-23:7,8,21,25,35,36-NU-28:18,25,26■29:1,12,35

SERVING-EX-14:5(5647)-DE-15:18(5647)■N.T.-all=1398&marked-LU-10:40(1248)-AC-20:19■26:7(3000)-RO-12:11-TIT-3:3

SERVITOR-2KI-4:43(8334)

SERVITUDE-2CH-10:4(5656)-LA-1:3(5656)

SET-all=7760,a=5414,b=5975,c=7896,d=6965,e=5324,f=5265,g=4150&marked-GE-1:17a■4:15■6:16■9:13a■17:21g■18:8a■19:16(3240)■21:2g,28e,29e■24:33■28:11(935),12e,18,22■30:36,38(3322),40a■31:17(5375),21,37,45(7311)■35:14e,20e■41:33c,41a■43:9(3322),31,32■44:21■47:7b■48:20-EX-1:11■4:20(7392)■5:14■7:23c■9:5g■21:1■23:31c■25:7(4394),30a■26:17(7947),35■28:11(4142),17(4390),20(7660)■31:5(4390)■35:9(4394),27(4394),33(4390)■39:10(4390)■40:2d,5a,6a,7a,8,18,20,21,23(6186);28,30,33a-LE-17:10a■20:3a,5,6a■24:6■26:1a,11a,17a-NU-1:51d■2:9f,16f,17^{2}f,34f■4:15f■5:16b,18b,30b■7:1d■8:13b■10:17f,18f,21f,21d,22f,25f,28f,35f■11:24b■21:8,10f■22:1f■24:1c■27:16(6485),19b,22b■29:39g-DE-1:8a,21a■4:8a,44■11:26a,32a■14:24■16:22d■17:14,15^{2},15a■19:14(1379)■26:4(3240),10(3240)■27:2d,4d■28:1a,36d,56(3322)■30:1a,15a,19a■32:8e,46-JOS-4:9d■6:26e■8:8(3341),12,13■10:18(6485)■18:1(7931)■24:25,26d-J'G-1:8(7971)■6:18(3240)■7:5(3322),19d,22■9:25,33(6584)■16:25b,18:30d,31■20:29,36,48(7971)-RU-2:5e,6e-1SA-2:8(3427),8c■5:2(3322),3(7725)■6:18(3240)■7:12■9:20,23,24^{2}■10:19■12:13a■13:8g■15:11(4427),12e■18:5,30(3335)■22:9e■26:24^{2}(1431)■28:22-2SA-3:10d■6:3(7392),17(3322)■7:12d■11:15(3051)■12:20■15:24(3332)■18:1,13(3320)■19:28c■20:5g■23:23-1KI-2:15,19,24(3427)■5:5a■6:19a,27a■7:16a,21^{3}d,39a■8:21■9:6a■10:9a■12:29■14:4d■15:4d■16:34e■20:12^{2}■21:9(3427),10(3427),12(3427)-2KI-4:4f,10,38(8239),43a,44a■6:22■8:12(7971)■10:3■12:4(6817),9a,17■17:10e■18:23a■21:7■25:19(6496),28a-1CH-6:31b■9:22(530),26(530),31(530)■11:14(3320),25■16:1(3322)■21:18b■22:2b,19a■23:4(5329),31g■29:2(4394)-2CH-2:18(6213)■3:5(5927)■4:7a,10a■6:10(3427),13a■7:19a■9:8a■11:16a■13:3(631)■17:2a■19:5b,8b■20:3a,17(3320),22a■23:10b,14(6485),19b,20(3427)■24:8a,13b■25:14b■29:25b,35(3559)■31:3g,15(530),18(530)■32:6a■33:7,19b■34:12(5329)■35:2b-EZR-2:68b■3:3(3559),5g,8(5329),9(5329),10b■4:10(3488),12(3635),13(3635),16(3635)■5:11(3635)■6:11(2211),18(6966)■7:25(4483)■9:9(7311)-NE-1:9(7931)■2:6a■3:1b,3b,6b,13b,14b,15b■4:9b,13^{2}b■5:7a■6:1b■7:1b■9:37a■10:33g■13:11b,19b-ES-2:17■3:1■6:8a■8:2-JOB-5:11■7:17c,20■9:19(3259)■14:13(2706)■16:12d■19:8■30:1c■34:14,24(5975)■36:16(5183)■38:10,33-PS-2:2(3320),6(5258)■3:6c■4:3(6395)■8:1a■10:8(6845)■12:5c■16:8(7737)■17:11c■19:4■27:5(7311)■31:8b■40:2d■54:3■62:10c■73:9(8371),18c■74:4,17e■78:7,8(3559)■85:13■86:14■89:25,42(7311)■90:8c■101:3c■104:9■109:6(6485)■113:8(3427)■122:5(3427)■132:11c■140:5c■141:2(3559),3c-PR-8:23(5258),27(2710)■22:28(6213)■23:5(5774)-EC-3:11a■7:14(6213)■10:6a-SONG-5:12(3427),14(4390),15(3245)■7:2(5473)■8:6-IS-9:11(7682)■11:12(5375)■14:1(3240)■17:10(2232)■19:2(5526)■21:6b,8(5324)■22:7c■23:13d■27:4a,■36:8a■41:19■42:4,25■45:20(5375)■46:7(3240)■49:22(7311)■50:7■57:7,8■62:6(6485)■66:19-JER-1:10(6485),15a■4:6(5375)■5:26(5324)■6:1(5375),17d,27a■7:12(7931),30■9:13a■10:20d■11:13■21:8a,10■23:4d■24:1(3259),6■26:4a■31:21(5324),21c■32:20,34■34:16(7971)■35:5a■38:22(5496)■40:11(6485)■42:15,17■43:10■44:10a,11,12■49:38■50:2(5375)■51:12(5375),12d,27(5375)■52:32a-LA-2:17(7311)■3:6(3427),12(5324)-EZE-2:2(5975)■3:24(5975)■4:2a,2,3a,3(3559),7(3559)■5:5■6:2■7:20,20a■9:4(8427)■12:6a■13:17■14:3(5927),8a■15:7a,7■16:18a,19a■17:4,5,22a■19:8a■20:46■21:2,15a,16(3259)■22:10(5079)■23:24,24a,25a,41■24:2(5564),3(8239),7,8a,11b,25(4853)■25:2,4(3427)■26:9a,20(3427),20a■27:10a■28:2a,6a,14a,21■29:2■30:8a,14a,16a■31:4(7311)■32:8a,23a,25a■33:2a,7a■34:23d■35:2■37:1(5117),26a■38:2■39:9(1197),15(1129),21a■40:2(5117),4■44:8-DA-1:11(4487)■2:44(6966),49(4483)■3:1(6966),2(6966),3^{2}(6966),5(6966),7(6966),12(4483),12(6966),14(6966),18(6966)■5:19(7313)■6:1(3966),3(3966),14(7761)■7:10(3488)■8:18b■9:3a,10a■10:10(5128),12a,15a■11:11b,13b,17■12:11a-HO-2:3(3322),3c■4:8(5375)■6:11c■11:8(7761)-AM-7:8■8:5(6605)■9:4-OB-4-NA-3:6-HAB-2:1(3320),9-ZEC-3:5^{2}■5:11(3240)■6:11■8:10(7971)-MAL-3:15(1129)■N.T.-all=2476&marked-M'T-5:1(2523),14(2749)■10:35(1369)■18:2■21:7(1940)■25:33■27:19(2521),37(2007)-M'R-1:32(1416)■4:21(2007)■6:41(3908)■8:6^{2}(3908),7(3908)■9:12(1847),36■12:1(4060)-LU-1:1(392)■2:34(2749)■4:9,18(649)■7:8(5021)■9:16(3908),47,51(4741)■10:8(3908),34(1913)■11:6(3908)■19:35(1913)■22:55(4776)■23:11(1848)-JOH-2:6(2749),10(5087)■3:33(4972)■6:11(345)■8:3■13:12(377)■19:29(2749)-AC-4:7,11(1848)■5:27■6:6,13■7:5(968),26(4900)■12:21(5002)■13:9(816),47(5087)■15:16(461)■16:34(3908)■17:5(2350)■18:10(2007)■19:27(2064)■21:2(321)■22:30■23:24(1913)■26:32(630)-RO-3:25(4388)■14:10(1848)-1CO-4:9(584)■6:4(2523)■10:27(3908)■11:34(1299)■12:18(5087),28(5087)-GA-3:1(4270)-EPH-1:20(2523)-PH'P-1:17(2749)-COL-3:2(5426)■1:5(1930)-HEB-2:7(2525)■6:18(4295)■8:1(2523)■12:1(4295),2(4295),2(2523)■13:23(630)-JAS-3:6(5394)-JUDE-7(4295)-RE-3:8(1325),21(2523)■4:2(2749)■10:2(5087)■20:3(4972)

SETTER-AC-17:18(2604)

SETTEST-all=4916&marked-DE-23:20■28:8,20-JOB-7:12(7760)-PS-21:3(7896)■41:12(5324)

SETTETH-NU-1:51(5265)■4:5(5265)-DE-24:15(5375)■27:16(7034)-2SA-22:34(5975)-JOB-28:3(7760)-PS-18:33(5975)■36:4(3320)■65:6(3559)■68:6(3427)■75:7(7311)■83:14(3857)-JER-5:26(7918)■43:3(5496)-EZE-14:4(5927),7(5927)-DA-2:21(6966)■4:17(6966)■N.T.-M'T-4:5(2476)-LU-8:16(2007)-JAS-3:6(5394)

SETTING-EZE-43:8(5414)■N.T.-M'T-27:66(3326)-LU-4:40(1416)

SETTINGS-EX-28:17(4396)

SETTLE-all=5835&marked-1CH-17:14(5975)-EZE-36:11(3427)■43:14^{3},17,20■45:19■N.T.-LU-21:14(5087)-1PE-5:10(2311)

SETTLED-1KI-8:13(4349)-2KI-8:11(5975)-PS-119:89(5324)-PR-8:25(2883)-JER-48:11(8252)-ZEP-1:12(7087)■N.T.-COL-1:23(1476)

SETTLEST-PS-65:10(5181)

SEVEN-all=7651&marked-GE-5:7,25,26,31^{2}■7:4,10■8:10,12^{2},14■11:21■21:28,29,30■23:1■25:17■29:18,20,27,30■31:23■33:3■41:2,3,4,5,6,7,18,19,20,22,23,24,26^{2},27^{4},29,30,34,36,47,48,53,54■46:25■47:28■50:10-EX-2:16■6:16,20■7:25■12:15,19■13:6,7■22:30■23:15■25:37■29:30,35,37■34:18■37:23■38:24,25,28-LE-4:6,17■8:11,33^{2},35■12:2■13:4,5,21,26,31,33,50,54■14:7,8,16,27,38,51■15:13,19,24,28■16:14,19■22:27■23:6,8,15,18,34,36,39,40,41,42■25:8^{3}■26:18,21,24,28-NU-1:31,39■2:8,26,31■3:22■4:36■8:2■12:14^{2},15■13:22■16:49■19:4,11,14,16■23:1^{2},4,14,29^{2}■26:7,34,51■28:11,17,19,21,24,27,29■29:2,4,8,10,12,32,36■31:19,36,43,52-DE-7:1■15:1■16:3,4,9^{2},13,15■28:7,25■31:10-JOS-6:4^{3},6,8,13,15^{2}■18:2,5,6,9-J'G-6:1,25■8:26■12:9■14:12,17■16:7,8,13,19■20:15,16-RU-4:15-1SA-2:5■6:1■10:8■11:3■13:8■16:10■31:13-2SA-2:11■5:5■8:4■10:18■21:6,9■23:39■24:13-1KI-2:11■6:6,38■7:17■8:65■11:3■16:15■18:43■19:18■20:15,29,30-2KI-3:9,26■4:35■5:10,14■8:1,2,3■11:21■24:16■25:27^{2}-1CH-3:4,24■5:13,18■7:5■9:13,25■10:12■12:25,27,34■15:26■18:4■19:18■26:30,32■29:4,27-2CH-7:8,9^{2}■13:9■15:11■17:11^{2}■24:1■26:13■29:21^{2}■30:21,22,23^{2},24■35:17-EZR-2:5,9,25,33,38,65^{2},66,67■6:22■7:14(7655)■8:35-NE-7:14,18,19,29,37,41,67^{2},68,69,72■8:18-ES-1:1,5,10,14■2:9■8:9■9:30-JOB-1:2,3■2:13■5:19■42:13(7658)-PS-12:6(7659)■119:164

-PR-6:16■9:1■24:16,25-EC-11:2-IS-4:1■11:15■30:26-JER-15:9■34:14■52:25,30,31-EZE-3:15,16■29:17■39:9,12,14■40:22,26■41:3■43:25,26■44:26■45:21,23[3],25-DA-3:19(7655)■4:16(7655),23(7655),25(7655),32(7655)■9:25-AM-5:8(3598)-MIC-5:5-ZEC-3:9■4:2[3],10■N.T.-all=2033&marked-M'T-12:45■15:34,36,37■16:10■18:21(2034),22(2034),22■22:25,28-M'R-8:5,6,8,20[2]■12:20,22,23■16:9-LU-2:36■8:2■11:26■17:4[2](2034)■20:29,31,33-AC-6:3■13:9■19:14■20:6■21:4,8,27■28:14-RO-11:4(2035)-HEB-11:30-RE-1:4[2],11,12,13,16,20[5]■2:1[2]■3:1■4:5[2]■5:1,5,6[2]■8:2[2],6■10:3,4[2]■11:13■12:3[2]■13:1■15:1,6[2],7,8■16:1■17:1,3,7,9,10,11■21:9[2]

SEVENFOLD-all=7659-GE-4:15,24[2]-PS-79:12-PR-6:31-IS-30:26

SEVENS-GE-7:2(7651),3(7651)

SEVENTEEN-all=7651,6240&marked-GE-37:2■47:28-J'G-8:14(7657,7651)-1KI-14:21-2KI-13:1-1CH-7:11-2CH-12:13-EZR-2:39-NE-7:42-JER-32:9

SEVENTEENTH-all=7651,6240-GE-7:11■8:4-1KI-22:51-2KI-16:1-1CH-24:15■25:24

SEVENTH-all=7637,a=7651&marked-GE-2:2[2],3■8:4-EX-12:15,16■13:6■16:26,27,29,30■20:10,11■21:2■23:11,12■24:16■31:15,17■34:21■35:2-LE-13:5,6,27,32,34,51■14:9,39■16:29■23:3,8,16,24,27,34,39,41■25:4,9,20-NU-6:9■7:48■19:12[2],19[2]■28:25■29:1,7,12,32■31:19,24-DE-5:14■15:9,12■16:8-JOS-6:4,15,16■19:40-J'G-14:15,17,18-2SA-12:18-1KI-8:2■16:10a,15a■18:44■20:29-2KI-11:4■121a■13:10a■15:1a■18:9a■25:8a,25-1CH-2:15■12:11■24:10■25:14■26:3,5■27:10-2CH-5:3■7:10■23:1■31:7-EZR-3:1,6■7:7a,8-NE-7:73■8:2,14■10:31-ES-1:10■2:16a-JER-28:17■41:1■52:28a-EZE-20:1■30:20a■45:20a,25a-HAG-2:1-ZEC-7:5■8:19■N.T.-all=1442&marked-M'T-22:26(2035)-JOH-4:52-HEB-4:4[2]-JUDE-14-RE-8:1■10:7■11:15■16:17■21:20

SEVENTY-all=7657-GE-4:24■5:12,31■11:26■12:4-EX-1:5■24:1,9■38:28,29-NU-7:13,19,25,31,37,43,49,55,61,67,73,79,85■11:16,24,25■31:32-J'G-9:56-2SA-24:15-2KI-10:1,6,7-1CH-21:14-EZR-2:3,4,5,36,40■8:7,14,35-NE-7:8,9,39,43■11:19-ES-9:16-IS-23:15[2],17-JER-25:11,12■29:10-EZE-8:11■41:12-DA-9:2,24-ZEC-7:5■N.T.-M'T-18:22(1441)-LU-10:1(1440),17(1440)

SEVER-EX-8:22(6395)■9:4(6395)-EZE-39:14(914)■N.T.-M'T-13:49(873)

SEVERAL-2KI-15:5(2669)-2CH-26:21(2669)■N.T.-M'T-25:15(2398)-RE-21:21(308,1520)

SEVERALLY-1CO-12:11(2398)

SEVERED-LE-20:26(914)-DE-4:41(914)-J'G-4:11(6504)

SEVERITY-RO-11:22[2](663)

SEW-EC-3:7(8609)-EZE-13:1 8(8609)

SEWED-GE-3:7(8609)-JOB-16:15(8609)

SEWEST-JOB-14:17(2950)

SEWETH-M'R-2:21(1976)

SHADE-PS-121:5(6738)

SHADOW-all=6738,a=6757&marked-GE-19:8-J'G-9:15,36-2KI-20:9,10[2],11-1CH-29:15-JOB-3:5a■7:2■8:9■10:21a,22a■12:22a■14:2■16:16a■17:7■24:17[2]a■28:3a■34:22a■38:17a■40:22(6752)-PS-17:8■23:4a■36:7■44:19a■57:1■63:7■80:10■91:1■102:11■107:10a,14a■109:23■144:4-EC-6:12■8:13-SONG-2:3-IS-4:6■9:2a■16:3■25:4,5■30:2,3■32:2■34:15■38:8■49:2■51:16-JER-2:6a■13:16a■48:45-LA-4:20-EZE-17:23■31:6,12,17-DA-4:12(2927)-HO-4:13■14:7-AM-5:8a-JON-4:5,6■N.T.-all=4639&marked-M'T-4:16-M'R-4:32-LU-1:79-AC-5:15-COL-2:17-HEB-8:5■10:1-JAS-1:17(644)

SHADOWING-IS-18:1(6767)-EZE-31:3(6751)■N.T.-HEB-9:5(2683)

SHADOWS-all=6752-SONG-2:17■4:6-JER-6:4

SHADY-JOB-40:21(6628),22(6628)

SHAFT-all=3409&marked-EX-25:31■37:17-NU-8:4-IS-49:2(2671)

SHAKE-all=7493&marked-J'G-16:20(5287)-NE-5:13(5287)-JOB-4:14(6342)■15:33(2554)■16:4(5128)-PS-22:7(5128)■46:3■69:23(4571)■72:16-IS-2:19(6206),21(6206)■10:15(5130),32(5130)■11:15(5130)■13:2(5130),13(7264)■14:16■24:18■33:9(5287)■52:2(5287)-JER-23:9(7363)-EZE-26:10,15■27:28■31:16■38:20-DA-4:14(5426)-JOE-3:16-AM-9:1-HAG-2:6,7,21-ZEC-2:9(5130)■N.T.-M'T-10:14(1621)■28:4(4579)-M'R-6:11(1621)-LU-6:48(4531)■9:5(660)-HEB-12:26(4579)

SHAKED-PS-109:25(5128)

SHAKEN-all=5128&marked-LE-26:36(5086)-1KI-14:15(5110)-2KI-19:21-NE-5:13(5287)-JOB-16:12(6327)■38:13(5287)-PS-18:7(1607)-IS-37:22-NA-2:3(7477)■3:12■N.T.-all=4531&marked-M'T-11:7■24:29-M'R-13:25-LU-6:38■7:24■21:26-AC-4:31■16:26-2TH-2:2-HEB-12:27[2]-RE-6:13(4579)

SHAKETH-JOB-9:6(7264)-PS-29:8[2](2342)■60:2(4131)-IS-10:15(5130)■19:16(5130)■33:15(5287)

SHAKING-all=7494&marked-JOB-41:29-PS-44:14(4493)-IS-17:6(5363)■19:16(8573)■24:13(5363)■30:32(8573)-EZE-37:7(7494)■38:19(7494)

SHAMBLES-1CO-10:25(3111)

SHAME-all=3639,a=1322,b=7036&marked-EX-32:25(8103)-J'G-18:7(3637)-1SA-20:34(3637)-2SA-13:13(2781)-2CH-32:21a-JOB-8:22a-PS-4:2■35:4(3637),26a■40:14(3637),15a■44:7(954),9(3637),15a■53:5(954)■69:7,19a■70:3a■71:24(2659)■83:16b,17(2659)■89:45(955)■109:29■119:31(954)■132:18a-PR-3:35b■9:7b■10:5(954)■11:2b■12:16b■13:5(2659),18b■14:35(954)■17:2(954)■18:13■19:26(954)■25:8(3637),10(2616)■29:15(954)-IS-20:4(6172)■22:18b■30:3a,5a■47:3(2781)■50:6■54:4(2659),4a■61:7a-JER-3:24a,25a■13:26b■20:18a■23:40(3640)■46:12b■48:39(954)■51:51-EZE-7:18(955)■16:52[2],54,63■32:24,25,30■34:29■36:6,7,15■39:26■44:13-DA-12:2(2781)-HO-4:7b,18b■9:10a■10:6(1317)-OB-10(955)MIC-1:11a■2:6■7:10(955)-NA-3:5b-HAB-2:10a,16b-ZEP-3:5a,19a■N.T.-all=152&marked-LU-14:9-AC-5:41(818)-1CO-4:14(1788)■6:5(1791)■11:6(149),14(819),22(2617)■14:35(149)■15:34(1791)-EPH-5:12(149)-PH'P-3:19-HEB-6:6(3856)■12:2-JUDE-13-RE-3:18■16:15(808)

SHAMED-GE-38:23(937)-2SA-19:5(3001)-PS-14:6(954)

SHAMEFACEDNESS-1TI-2:9(127)

SHAMEFUL-JER-11:13(1322)-HAB-2:16(7022)

SHAMEFULLY-HO-2:5(3001)■N.T.-M'R-12:4(821)-LU-20:11(818)-1TH-2:2(5195)

SHAMELESSLY-2SA-6:20(1540)

SHAMETH-PR-28:7(3637)

SHAPE-LU-3:22(1491)-JOH-5:37(1491)

SHAPEN-PS-51:5(2342)

SHAPES-RE-9:7(3667)

SHARE-1SA-13:20(4282)

SHARP-all=8150&marked-EX-4:25(6864)-JOS-5:2(6697),3(6697)-1SA-14:4[2](8127)-JOB-41:30(2303),30(2742)-PS-45:5■52:2(3913)■57:4(2299)■120:4-PR-5:4(2299)■25:18-IS-5:28■41:15(2742)■49:2(2299)-EZE-5:1(2299)■N.T.-all=3691-RE-1:16■2:12■14:14,17,18[2]■19:15

SHARPEN-1SA-13:20(3913),21(5324)

SHARPENED-all=2300&marked-PS-140:3(8150)-EZE-21:9,10,11

SHARPENETH-JOB-16:9(3913)-PR-27:17(2300)

SHARPER-HEB-4:12(5114)

SHARPLY-J'G-8:1(2394)■N.T.-TIT-1:13(664)

SHARPNESS-2CO-13:10(664)

SHAVE-all=1548&marked-LE-13:33■14:8,9[2]■21:5-NU-6:9[2],18■8:7(5674,8593)-DE-21:12-J'G-16:19-IS-7:20-EZE-44:20■N.T.-AC-21:24(3587)

SHAVED-all=1548&marked-GE-41:14-2SA-10:4-1CH-19:4-JOB-1:20(1494)

SHAVEN-all=1548-LE-13:33-NU-6:19-J'G-16:17,22-JER-41:5■N.T.-1CO-11:5(3587),6(3587)

SHEAF-all=6016&marked-GE-37:7[2](485)-LE-23:10,11,12,15-DE-24:19-JOB-24:10-ZEC-12:6(5995)

SHEAR-all=1494-GE-31:19■38:13-DE-15:19-1SA-25:4

SHEARER-AC-8:32(2751)

SHEARERS-all=1494-1SA-25:7,11-IS-53:7

SHEARING-1SA-25:2(1494)-2KI-10:12(1044,7462),14(1044)

SHEATH-all=8593&marked-1SA-17:51-2SA-20:8-1CH-21:27(5084)-EZE-21:3,4,5,30■N.T.-JOH-18:11(2336)

SHEAVES-all=485&marked-GE-37:7[2]-RU-2:7(6016),15(6016)-NE-13:15(6194)-PS-126:6-AM-2:13(5995)-MIC-4:12(5995)

SHED-all=8210&marked-GE-9:6■37:22-LE-17:4-NU-35:33[2]-DE-19:10■21:7-1SA-25:31-2SA-20:10-1KI-2:5(7760),31-2KI-21:16■24:4-1CH-22:8[2]■28:3-PS-79:3,10■106:38-PR-1:16■6:17-IS-59:7-JER-7:6■22:3,17-LA-4:13-EZE-16:38■22:4,6,9,12,27■23:45■33:25■35:5(5064)■36:18-JOE-3:19■N.T.-all=1632-M'T-23:35■26:28-M'R-14:24-LU-11:50■22:20-AC-2:33■22:20-RO-3:15■5:5-TIT-3:6-RE-16:6

SHEDDER-EZE-18:10(8210)

SHEDDETH-GE-9:6(8210)-EZE-22:3(8210)

SHEDDING-HEB-9:22(130)

SHEEP-all=6629,a=7716&marked-GE-4:2■12:16■20:14■21:27■29:2,3,6,7,8,9,10■30:32(3775),33(3775),35(3775)■31:19■34:28■38:13-EX-9:3■12:5(3532)■20:24■22:1a,1,1a,4a,9a,10a,30■34:19a-LE-1:10(3775)■7:23(3775)■22:19(3775),21,27(3775)■27:26a-NU-18:17(3775)■22:40■27:17■31:28,32,36,37,43■32:24(6792),36-DE-7:13■14:4(3775),26■15:19■17:1a■18:3a,4■22:1a■28:4,18,31,51■32:14-JOS-6:21a■7:24-J'G-6:4a-1SA-8:17■14:32,34a■15:3a,9,14,15,21■16:11,19■17:15,20,28,34■22:19a■25:2[2],4,16,18■27:9-2SA-7:8■17:29■24:17-1KI-1:9,19,25■4:23■8:5,63■22:17-2KI-5:26-1CH-5:21■12:40■17:7■21:17-2CH-5:6■7:5■14:15■15:11■18:2,16■29:33■30:24[2]■31:6-NE-3:1,32■5:18■12:39-JOB-1:3,16■31:20(3532)■42:12-PS-8:7(6792)■44:11,22■49:14■74:1■78:52■79:13■95:7■100:3■119:176a■144:13-SONG-6:6(7353)-IS-7:21■13:14■22:13■53:6,7(7353)-JER-12:3■23:1■50:6,17a-EZE-34:6,11,12[2]-JOE-1:18-MIC-2:12■5:8-ZEC-13:7■N.T.-all=4263&marked-M'T-9:36■10:6,16■12:11,12■15:24■18:12■25:32,33■26:31-M'R-6:34■14:27-LU-15:4,6-JOH-2:14,15■5:2(4262)■10:2,3[2],4[2],7,8,11,12[3],13,15,16,26,27■21:16,17-AC-8:32-RO-8:36-HEB-13:20-1PE-2:25-RE-18:13

SHEEPCOTE-2SA-7:8(5116)-1CH-17:7(5116)

SHEEPCOTES-1SA-24:3(1448,6629)

SHEEPFOLD-JOH-10:1(833,4263)

SHEEPFOLDS-NU-32:16(1488,6629)-J'G-5:16(4942)-PS-78:70(4356,6629)

SHEEPMASTER-2KI-3:4(5349)

SHEEP'S-M'T-7:15(4263)

SHEEPSHEARERS-GE-38:12(1494,6629)-2SA-13:23(1494),24(1494)

SHEEPSKINS-HEB-11:37(3374)
SHEET-AC-10:11(3607)■11:5(3607)
SHEETS-J'G-14:12(5466),13(5466)
SHEKEL-all=8255&marked-GE-24:22(1235)-EX-30:13^{3},15,24■38:24,25,26^{2}-LE-5:15■27:3,25^{2}-NU-3:47^{2},50■7:13,19,25,31,37,43,49,55,61,67,73,79,85,86■18:16-1SA-9:8-2KI-7:1^{2},16^{2},18^{2}-NE-10:32-EZE-45:12-AM-8:5
SHEKELS-all=8255-GE-23:15,16-EX-21:32■38:24,25,29-LE-5:15■27:3,4,5^{2},6^{2},7^{2},16-NU-3:47■7:13,19,25sup,25,31sup,31,37sup,37,43sup,43,49sup,49,55sup,55,61sup,61,67sup,67,73sup,73,79sup,79■18:16■31:52-JOS-7:21^{2}-1SA-17:5,7-2SA-14:26■24:24-2KI-15:20-1CH-21:25-2CH-3:9-NE-5:15-JER-32:9-EZE-4:10■45:12^{2}
SHELTER-JOB-24:8(4268)-PS-61:3(4268)
SHEPHERD-all=7462&marked-GE-46:34(7462,6629)■49:24-NU-27:17-1KI-22:17-2CH-18:16-PS-23:1■80:1-EC-12:11-IS-40:11■44:28■63:11-JER-31:10■43:12■49:19■50:44■51:23-EZE-34:5,8,12,23^{2}■37:24-AM-3:12-ZEC-10:2■11:15,16,17(7473)■13:7^{2}(7462)■N.T.-all=4166&marked-M'T-9:36■25:32■26:31-M'R-6:34■14:27-JOH-10:2,11,12,14,16-HEB-13:20-1PE-2:25■5:4(750)
SHEPHERD'S-1SA-17:40(7462)-IS-38:12(7473)
SHEPHERDS-all=7462-GE-46:32(7462,6629)■47:3(7462,6629)-EX-2:17,19-1SA-25:7-IS-13:20■31:4■56:11-JER-6:3■23:4■25:34,35,36■33:12■50:6-EZE-34:2^{4},7,8^{2},9,10^{2}-AM-1:2-MIC-5:5-NA-3:18-ZEP-2:6-ZEC-10:3■11:3,5,8■N.T.-all=4166-LU-2:8,15,18,20
SHEPHERDS'-SONG-1:8(7462)
SHERD-IS-30:14(2789)
SHERDS-EZE-23:34(2789)
SHERIFFS-DA-3:2,3(8614)
SHEW-all=5046,a=7200,b=6213,c=2324,d=3045,&marked-GE-12:1a■20:13b■24:12b■40:14b■46:31-EX-7:9(5414)■9:16a■10:1(7896)■13:8■14:13b■18:20d■25:9a■33:13d,18a-NU-16:5d-DE-1:33a■3:24a■5:5■13:17(5414)■17:9,10,11■32:7-JOS-2:12b■5:6a-J'G-1:24a,24b■4:22a■6:17b-1SA-3:15■8:9■9:6,27(8085)■10:8d■14:12d■16:3d■20:2(1540),12(1540),13(1540),14b■22:17(1540)■25:8-2SA-2:6b■3:8b■9:1b,3b,7b■10:2b■15:25a-1KI-2:7b■18:1a,2a,15a-2KI-6:11■7:12-1CH-16:23(1319)■19:2b-EZR-2:59-NE-7:61-ES-1:11a■2:10■4:8a-JOB-10:2d■11:6■15:17(2331)■32:6(2331),10(2331),17(2331)■33:23■36:2(2331)-PS-4:6a■9:1(5608),14(5608)■16:11d■25:4d,14d■39:6(6754)■50:23a■51:15■71:15(5608)■79:13(5608)■85:7a■86:17b■88:10b■91:16a■92:2,15■94:1(3313)■96:2(1319)■106:2(8085)■109:16b-IS-3:9(1971)■30:30a■41:22^{2},23■43:9(8085),21(5608)■44:7■47:6(7760)■49:9(1540)■58:1■60:6(1319)-JER-16:10,13(5414)■18:17a■33:3■42:3,12(5414)■51:31■22:2d-EZE-22:2(3645)■33:31b■37:18■40:4^{2}a■43:10,11d-DA-2:2,4c,6^{2}c,7c,9c,10c,11c,16c,24c,27c■4:2c■5:7c,12c,15c■9:23■10:21■11:2-JOE-2:30(5414)-MIC-7:15a-NA-3:5a-HAB-1:3a-ZEC-1:9a■7:9b■N.T.-all=1166&marked-M'T-8:4■11:4(518)■12:18(518)■14:2(1754)■16:1(1925),21■22:19(1925)■24:1(1925),24(1325)-M'R-1:44■6:14(1754)■13:22(1325)■14:15-LU-1:19(2097)■5:14■6:47(5263)■8:39(1334)■17:14(1925)■20:24(1925),47(4392)■22:12-JOH-5:20■7:4(5319)■11:57(3377)■14:8,9■16:13(312),14(312),15(312),25(312)-AC-1:24(322)■2:19(1325)■7:3■9:16(5263)■12:17(518)■16:17(2605)■24:27(2698)■26:23(2605)-RO-2:15(1731)■9:17(1731),22(1731)-1CO-11:26(2605)■12:31■15:51(3004)-2CO-8:24(1731)-GA-6:12(2146)-EPH-2:7(1731)-COL-2:15(1165),23(3056)-1TH-1:9(518)-1TI-1:16(1731)■5:4(2151)■6:15-2TI-2:15(3936)-HEB-6:11(1731),17(1925)-JAS-2:18^{2}■3:13-1PE-2:9(1804)-1JO-1:2(518)-RE-1:1■4:1■17:1■21:9■22:6
SHEWBREAD-all=3899,6440&marked-EX-25:30■35:13■39:36-NU-4:7(6440)-1SA-21:6-1KI-7:48-1CH-9:32(3899,4635)■23:29(3899,4635)■28:16(4635)-2CH-2:4(4635)■4:19■13:11(3899,4635)■29:18(4635)-NE-10:33(3899,4635)■N.T.-all=740,4286-M'T-12:4-M'R-2:26-LU-6:4-HEB-9:2
SHEWED-all-7200,a=6213,b=5046&marked-GE-19:19a■24:14a■32:10a■39:21(5186)■41:25b,39(3045)■48:11-EX-15:25(3384)■25:40■26:30■27:8-LE-13:19,49■24:12(6567)-NU-8:4■13:26■14:11a-DE-4:35,36■5:24■6:22(5414)■34:1,12a-JOS-2:12a-J'G-1:25■4:12b■8:35^{2}a■13:10b,23■16:18b-RU-2:11b,19b■3:10(3190)-1SA-11:9b■15:6a■19:7b■22:21b■24:18b-2SA-2:5a■10:2a■11:22b-1KI-1:27(3045)■3:6a■16:27a■22:45a-2KI-6:6■8:10,13■11:4■20:13^{2},15■22:10-1CH-19:2a-2CH-1:8a■7:10a-ES-1:4■2:10b,20b■3:6b-PS-71:18b,20■78:11■98:2(1540)■105:27(7760)■111:6b■118:27■142:2b-PR-26:26(1540)-IS-39:2^{2},4■40:14(3045)■43:12(8085)■48:3(8085),5(8085),6(8085)-JER-24:1■38:21-EZE-11:25■20:11(3045)■22:26(3045)-AM-7:1,4,7■8:1-MIC-6:8b-ZEC-1:20■3:1■N.T.-all=1166&marked-M'T-28:11(518)-LU-1:51(4160),58(3170)■4:5■7:18(518)■10:37(4160)■14:21(518)■20:37(3377)■24:40(1925)-JOH-10:32■20:20■21:1^{2}(5319),14(5319)-AC-1:3(3936)■3:18(4293)■4:22(1096)■7:26(3700),36(4160),52(4293)■10:28,40(1325,1717,1096)■11:13(518)■19:18(312)■20:20(312),35(5263)■23:22(1718)■26:20(518)■28:2(3930),21(518)-RO-1:19(5319)-1CO-10:28(3377)-HEB-6:10(1731)■8:5-JAS-2:13(4160)-2PE-1:14(1213)-RE-21:10■22:1,8
SHEWEDST-NE-9:10(5414)-JER-11:18(7200)
SHEWEST-JER-32:18(6213)■N.T.-JOH-2:18(1166)■6:30(4160)
SHEWETH-all=5046&marked-GE-41:28(7200)-NU-23:3(7200)-1SA-22:8^{2}(1540,241)-2SA-22:51(6213)-JOB-36:9,33-PS-18:50(6213)■19:1,2(2331)■147:19-PR-12:17■27:25(7200)-IS-41:26■N.T.-M'T-4:8(1166)-JOH-5:20(1166)-RO-9:16(1653)■12:8(1653)
SHEWING-EX-20:6(6213)-DE-5:10(6213)-PS-78:4(5608)-SONG-2:9(6692)-DA-5:12(263)■N.T.-LU-1:80(323)-AC-9:39(1925)■18:28(1925)-TH-2:4(584)-TIT-2:7(3930),10(1731)■3:2(1731)
SHIBBOLETH-J'G-12:6(7641)
SHIELD-all=4043&marked-GE-15:1-DE-33:29-J'G-5:8-1SA-17:7(6793),41(6793),45(3591)-2SA-1:21^{2}■22:3,36-1KI-10:17-2KI-19:32-1CH-12:8(6793),24(6793),34(6793)-2CH-9:16■17:17■25:5(6793)-JOB-39:23(3591)-PS-3:3■5:12(6793)■18:35■28:7■33:20■35:2■59:11■76:3■84:9,11■91:4(6793)■115:9,10,11■119:114■144:2-PR-30:5-IS-21:5■22:6-JER-46:3(6793),9-EZE-23:24■27:10■38:5-NA-2:3■N.T.-EPH-6:16(2375)
SHIELDS-all=4043&marked-2SA-8:7(7982)-1KI-10:17■14:26,27-2KI-11:10(7982)-1CH-18:7(7982)-2CH-9:16■11:12(6793)■12:9,10■14:8■23:9(7982)■26:14■32:5,27-NE-4:16-PS-47:9-SONG-4:4(7982)-IS-37:33-JER-51:11(7982)-EZE-27:11(7982)■38:4■39:9
SHINE-all=215&marked-NU-6:25-JOB-3:4(3313)■10:3(3313)■11:17(5774)■18:5(5050)■22:28(5050)■37:15(3313)■41:18(1984),32-PS-31:16■67:1■80:1(3313),3,7,19■104:15(6670)■119:135-EC-8:1-IS-13:10(5050)■60:1-JER-5:28(6245)-DA-9:17■12:3(2094)■N.T.-all=5316&marked-M'T-5:16(2989)■13:43(1584)■17:2(2989)-2CO-4:4(826),6(2989)-PH'P-2:15-RE-18:23■21:23
SHINED-DE-33:2(3313)-JOB-29:3(1984)■31:26(1984)-PS-50:2(3313)-IS-9:2(5050)-EZE-43:2(215)■N.T.-AC-9:3(4015)■12:7(2989)-2CO-4:6(2989)
SHINETH-JOB-25:5(166)-PS-139:12(215)-PR-4:18(215)■N.T.-all=5316&marked-M'T-24:27-LU-17:24(2989)-JOH-1:5-2PE-1:19-1JO-2:8-RE-1:16
SHINING-all=5051-2SA-23:4-PR-4:18-IS-4:5-JOE-2:10■3:15-HAB-3:11■N.T.-M'R-9:3(4744)-LU-11:36(796)■24:4(797)-JOH-5:35(5316)-AC-26:13(4034)
SHIP-all=591&marked-PR-30:19-IS-33:21(6716)-JON-1:3,4,5,5(5600)■N.T.-all=4143&marked-M'T-4:21,22■8:23,24■9:1■13:2■14:13,22,24,29,32,33■15:39-M'R-1:19,20■3:9(4142)■4:1,36,37■5:2,18,21■6:32,45,47,51,54■8:10,13,14-LU-5:3,7■8:22,37-JOH-6:17,19,21^{2}■21:3,6,8(4142)-AC-20:13,38■21:2,3,6■27:2,6,10,11(3490),15,17,19,22,30,31,37,38,39,41(3491),44■28:11
SHIPMASTER-JON-1:6(7227,2259)-RE-18:17(2942)
SHIPMEN-1KI-9:27(582,591)■N.T.-AC-27:27(3492),30(3492)
SHIPPING-JOH-6:24(4143)
SHIPS-all=591&marked-GE-49:13-NU-24:24(6716)-DE-28:68-J'G-5:17-1KI-22:48^{2},49-2CH-8:18■9:21^{2}■20:36^{2},37-JOB-9:26-PS-48:7■104:26■107:23-PR-31:14-IS-2:16■23:1,14■43:14■60:9-EZE-27:9,25,29■30:9(6716)-DA-11:30(6716),40■N.T.-all=4143&marked-M'R-4:36(4142)-LU-5:2,3,7,11-JAS-3:4-RE-8:9■18:17,19
SHIPWRECK-2CO-11:25(3489)-1TI-1:19(3489)
SHITTAH-IS-41:19(7848)
SHITTIM-all=7848-EX-25:5,10,13,23,28■26:15,26,32,37■27:1,6■30:1,5■35:7,24■36:20,31,36■37:1,4,10,15,25,28■38:1,6-DE-10:3
SHIVERS-RE-2:27(4937)
SHOCK-JOB-5:26(1430)
SHOCKS-J'G-15:5(1430)
SHOD-2CH-28:15(5274)-EZE-16:10(5274)■N.T.-M'R-6:9(5265)-EPH-6:15(5265)
SHOE-all=5275-DE-25:9,10■29:5-JOS-5:15-RU-4:7,8-PS-60:8■108:9-IS-20:2
SHOELATCHET-GE-14:23(8288,5275)
SHOE'S-JOH-1:27(5266)
SHOES-all=5275&marked-EX-3:5■12:11-DE-33:25(4515)-JOS-9:5,13-1KI-2:5-SONG-7:1-IS-5:27-EZE-24:17,23-AM-2:6■8:6■N.T.-all=5266-M'T-3:11■10:10-M'R-1:7-LU-3:16■10:4■15:22■22:35-AC-7:33■13:25
SHONE-all=7160&marked-EX-34:29,30,35-2KI-3:22(2224)■N.T.-LU-2:9(4034)-AC-22:6(4015)-RE-8:12(5316)
SHOOK-all=1607&marked-2SA-6:6(8058)■22:8^{2}-NE-5:13(5287)-PS-18:7■68:8(7493)■77:18(7493)-IS-23:11(7264)■N.T.-AC-13:51(1621)■18:6(1621)■28:5(660)-HEB-12:26(4531)
SHOOT-all=3384&marked-EX-36:33(1272)-1SA-20:20,36-2SA-11:20-2KI-13:17■19:32-1CH-5:18(1869)-2CH-26:15-PS-11:2■22:7(6362)■64:4^{2},7■144:6(7971)-JER-50:14(3034)-EZE-31:14(5414)■36:8(5414)■N.T.-LU-21:30(4261)
SHOOTERS-2SA-11:24(3384)
SHOOTETH-JOB-8:16(3318)-IS-27:8(7971)■N.T.-M'R-4:32(4160)
SHOOTING-AM-7:1(5927)
SHORE-all=8193&marked-GE-22:17-EX-14:30-JOS-11:4■15:2(7097)-J'G-5:17(2348)-1SA-13:5-1KI-4:29■9:26-JER-47:7(2348)■N.T.-all=123&marked-M'T-13:2,48-M'R-6:53(4358)-JOH-21:4-AC-21:5■27:39,40-HEB-11:12(5491)
SHORN-SONG-4:2(7094)■N.T.all=

2751-**AC**-18:18-**1CO**-11:6[2]

SHORT-NU-11:23(7114)-**JOB**-17:12 (7138)■20:5(7138)-**PS**-89:47(2465)■ **N.T.**-**RO**-3:23(5302)■9:28[2](4932)-**1CO**-7:29(4958)-**1TH**-2:17(5610)-**HEB**-4:1 (5302)-**RE**-12:12(3641)■17:10(3641)

SHORTENED-all=7114-**PS**-89:45■ 102:23-**PR**-10:27-**IS**-50:2■59:1■**N.T.** -all=2856-**M'T**-24:22[2]-**M'R**-13:20[2]

SHORTER-**IS**-28:20(7114)-**EZE**-42:5(7114)

SHORTLY-**GE**-41:32(4116)-**JER**-27:16(4120)-**EZE**-7:8(7138)■**N.T.**-all= 5030&marked-**AC**-25:4(1722,5034) -**RO**-16:20(1722,5034)-**1CO**-4:19 -**PH'P**-2:19,24-**1TI**-3:14(5032)-**2TI**-4:9-**HEB**-13:23(5032)-**2PE**-1:14(5031) -**3JO**-14(2112)-**RE**-1:1(1722,5034)■ 22:6(1722,5034)

SHOT-all=3384&marked-**GE**-40:10 (5927)■49:23(7232)-**EX**-19:13-**NU**-21:30-**1SA**-20:20(7971),36,37-**2SA**-11:24 -**2KI**-13:17-**2CH**-35:23-**PS**-18:14(7232) -**JER**-9:8(7819)-**EZE**-17:6(7971),7 (7971)■31:5(7971),10(7971)

SHOULD-all=3195&marked-**M'T**-26:35(1163)-**M'R**-10:32■14:31(1163)-**LU**-9:31■19:11■22:23■24:21-**JOH**-6:71■7:39■ 11:51■12:4,33■18:32-**AC**-11:28■19:27■ 20:38■22:29■23:27■26:22,23■27:21 (1163)■28:6-**1CO**-9:10(3784)-**GA**-3:23 -**1TH**-3:4-**1TI**-1:16-**HEB**-11:8-**2PE**-2:6 -**RE**-6:11sup,11,11sup

SHOULDER-all=7785,a=7926& marked-**GE**-21:14a■24:15a,45a■49:15a -**EX**-29:22,27-**LE**-7:32,33,34■8:25,26■ 9:21■10:14,15-**NU**-6:19(2220),20■18:18 -**DE**-18:3(2220)-**JOS**-4:5a-**J'G**-9:48a-**1SA**-9:24-**NE**-9:29(3802)-**JOB**-31:22(7929), 36a-**PS**-81:6a-**IS**-9:4a,6a■10:27a■22:22a■ 46:7(3802)-**EZE**-12:7(3802),12(3802)■ 24:4(3802)■29:7(3802),18(3802)■34:21 (3802)-**ZEC**-7:11(3802)

SHOULDERPIECES-all=3802 -**EX**-28:7,25■39:4,18

SHOULDERS-all=3802&marked -**GE**-9:23(7926)-**EX**-12:34(7926)■28:12[2]■ 39:7-**NU**-7:9-**DE**-33:12-**J'G**-16:3-**1SA**-9:2(7926)■10:23(7926)■17:6-**1CH**-15:15 -**2CH**-35:3-**IS**-11:14■14:25(7926)■30:6■ 49:22-**EZE**-12:6■**N.T.**-**M'T**-23:4(5606) -**LU**-15:5(5606)

SHOULDEST-all supplied

SHOUT-all=7321,a=8643&marked -**EX**-32:18(6030)-**NU**-23:21a-**JOS**-6:5,5 (8643),10[2],16,20a-**1SA**-4:5a,6[2]a-**2CH**-13:15-**EZR**-3:11a,13[2]a-**PS**-5:11(7442)■ 32:11(7442)■35:27(7442)■47:1,5a■ 65:13■132:9(7442),16(7442)-**IS**-12:6■ 42:11(6681)■44:23-**JER**-25:30(6030, 1959)■31:7(6670)■50:15■51:14(1959) -**LA**-3:8(7768)-**ZEP**-3:14-**ZEC**-9:9■ **N.T.**-**AC**-12:22(2019)-**1TH**-4:16(2752)

SHOUTED-all=7321&marked -**EX**-32:17(7452)-**LE**-9:24(7442)-**JOS**-6:20[2]-**J'G**-15:14-**1SA**-4:5■10:24■17:20, 52-**2CH**-13:15-**EZR**-3:11,12(8643),13 -**JOB**-38:7

SHOUTETH-**PS**-78:65(7442)

SHOUTING-all=8643&marked -**2SA**-6:15-**1CH**-15:28-**2CH**-15:14-**JOB**-39:25-**PR**-11:10(7440)-**IS**-16:9(1959), 10(7321),10(1959)-**JER**-20:16■48:33[2] (1959)-**EZE**-21:22-**AM**-1:14■2:2

SHOUTINGS-**ZEC**-4:7(8663)

SHOVEL-**IS**-30:24(7371)

SHOVELS-all=3257-**EX**-27:3■ 38:3-**NU**-4:14-**1KI**-7:40,45-**2KI**-25:14 -**2CH**-4:11,16-**JER**-52:18

SHOWER-all=1653-**EZE**-13:11,13■ 34:26■**N.T.**-**LU**-12:54(3655)

SHOWERS-all=7241&marked -**DE**-32:2-**JOB**-24:8(2230)-**PS**-65:10■ 72:6-**JER**-3:3■14:22-**EZE**-34:26(1653) -**MIC**-5:7(7241)-**ZEC**-10:1(1653)

SHRANK-**GE**-32:32[2](5384)

SHRED-**2KI**-4:39(6398)

SHRINES-**AC**-19:24(3485)

SHROUD-**EZE**-31:3(2793)

SHRUBS-**GE**-21:15(7880)

SHUN-**2TI**-2:16(4026)

SHUNNED-**AC**-20:27(5288)

SHUT-all=5462,a=6113&marked -**GE**-7:16■19:6,10-**EX**-14:3-**LE**-13:4,5, 11,21,26,31,33,50,54■14:38,46-**NU**-12:14,15-**DE**-11:17a■15:7(7092)■ 32:30,36a-**JOS**-2:7■6:1-**J'G**-3:23■9:51 -**1SA**-1:5,6■6:10(3607)■23:7-**2SA**-20:3 (6887)-**1KI**-8:35a■14:10a■21:21a-**2KI**-4:4,5,21,33■6:32■9:8a■14:26a■17:4a -**2CH**-6:26a■7:13a■28:24■29:7-**NE**-6:10a,10■7:3(1479)■13:19-**JOB**-3:10■ 11:10■38:8(5526)■41:15-**PS**-31:8■69:15 (332)■77:9(7092)■88:8(3607)-**EC**-12:4 -**SONG**-4:12(5274)-**IS**-6:10(8173)■ 22:22[2]■24:10,22■26:20■44:18(2902)■ 45:1■52:15(7092)■60:11■66:9a-**JER**-13:19■20:9a■32:2(3607),3(3607)■33:1a■ 36:5a■39:15a-**EZE**-3:24■44:1,2[2]■46:1, 2,12-**DA**-6:22(5463)■8:26(5640)■12:4 (5640)-**MAL**-1:10■**N.T.**-all=2808& marked-**M'T**-6:6■23:13■25:10-**LU**-3:20 (2623)■4:25■11:7■13:25(608)-**JOH**-20:19, 26-**AC**-5:23■21:30■26:10(2623)-**GA**-3:23(4788)-**RE**-3:8■11:6■20:3■21:25

SHUTTETH-**JOB**-12:14(5462) -**PR**-16:30(6095)■17:28(331)-**IS**-33:15 (6105)-**LA**-3:8(5640)■**N.T.**-all=2808 -**1JO**-3:17-**RE**-3:7[2]

SHUTTING-**JOS**-2:5(5462)

SHUTTLE-**JOB**-7:6(708)

SICK-all=2470&marked-**GE**-48:1 -**LE**-15:33(1739)-**1SA**-19:14■30:13-**2SA**-12:15(605)■13:2,5,6-**1KI**-14:1,5■17:17 -**2KI**-1:2■8:7,29■13:14■20:1,12-**2CH**-22:6■32:24-**NE**-2:2-**PS**-35:13-**PR**-13:12■ 23:35-**SONG**-2:5■5:8-**IS**-1:5(2483)■ 33:24■38:1,9■39:1-**JER**-14:18(8463) -**EZE**-34:4,16-**DA**-8:27-**HO**-7:5-**MIC**-6:13-**MAL**-1:8,13■**N.T.**-all=770,a= 3885&marked-**M'T**-4:24(2192,2560)■ 8:6a,14(4445),16(2192,2560)■9:2[2]a,6a, 12(2192,2560)■10:8■14:14(732)■25:36, 39(772),43(772),44(772)-**M'R**-1:30 (4445),34(2192,2560)■2:3a,4a,5a,9a,10a, 17(2192,2560)■6:5(732),13(732),55(2192, 2560),56■16:18(732)-**LU**-4:40■5:24a,31 (2192,2560)■7:2(2192,2560),10■9:2■ 10:9(772)-**JOH**-4:46■11:1,2,3,6-**AC**-5:15(772),16(772)■9:33a,37■19:12-**PH'P**-2:26,27-**2TI**-4:20-**JAS**-5:14,15(2577)

SICKLE-**DE**-16:9(2770)■23:25(2770) -**JER**-50:16(4038)-**JOE**-3:13(4038)■ **N.T.**-all=1407-**M'R**-4:29-**RE**-14:14,15, 16,17,18[2],19

SICKLY-**1CO**-11:30(732)

SICKNESS-all=2483&marked-**EX**-23:25(4245)-**LE**-20:18(1739)-**DE**-7:15■ 28:61-**1KI**-8:37(4245)■17:17-**2KI**-13:14 -**2CH**-6:28(4245)■21:15[2],19-**PS**-41:3 -**EC**-5:17-**IS**-38:9-**HO**-5:13■**N.T.**-all=3554&marked-**M'T**-4:23■9:35■ 10:1-**JOH**-11:4(769)

SICKNESSES-**DE**-28:59(2483)■ 29:22(8463)■**N.T.**-**M'T**-8:17(3554) -**M'R**-3:15(3554)

SIDE-all=6285,a=6763,b=6654,c= 5439,d=5676,e=3802,&marked-**GE**-6:16b-**EX**-2:5(3027)■25:12[2]a,32[2]b■ 26:18,20a,20,26a,27[2]a,35[2]a■27:9[2],11, 12,13,14e,15e■28:26d■32:27(3409)■ 36:11(8193),23,25a,31a,32a■37:3[2]a, 18[2]b■38:9,11,12,13,14e,15e■39:19d■ 40:22(3409),24(3409)-**LE**-1:11(3409), 15(7023)■5:9(7023)-**NU**-2:3(6924)■3:29 (3409),35(3409)■11:31[2](3541)■16:27c■ 21:13d■22:1d■32:19[2]d,32d■34:11(6924), 11e,15d■35:5[4],14d-**DE**-1:1d,5d,7(2348)■ 3:8d■4:32(7097),41d,46d,47d,49d■ 11:30d■31:26b-**JOS**-1:14d,15d■2:10d■ 5:1d■7:7d■9:1d■12:1d,7d■13:27d,32d■ 14:3d■15:8e,10e,11e■17:5d■18:12,12e, 13e,16e,18e,19e,20■19:27■20:8d■22:4d, 7d■24:2d,3d,8d,14d,15d-**J'G**-7:12(8193), 18c,25d■8:34c■10:8d■11:18sup,18d■ 19:1(3411),18(3411)-**1SA**-4:18(3027)■ 6:8b■12:11c■14:1d,4[2]d,40[2]d,47c■20:20b, 25b■23:26[2]b■26:13d■31:7[2]d-**2SA**-2:16b■ 13:34b■16:13a■18:4(3027)■24:5(3225) -**1KI**-4:24[2]d■5:4c■6:8e■7:30d,39[3]e-**2KI**-3:22(5048)■12:9(3225)■16:14(3409) -**1CH**-4:39(4217)■6:78d,78(4217)■ 12:37d■22:18c■26:30d-**2CH**-4:10e■ 8:17(8193)■14:7c■23:10[2]e■32:22c-**EZR**-4:10(5675),11(5675),16(5675)■5:3(5675), 6[2](5675)■6:13(5675)■8:36d-**NE**-3:7d■ 4:18(4975)-**JOB**-1:10c■18:11c,12a■ 19:10c-**PS**-12:8c■31:13c■65:12(2296)■ 71:21(5437)■91:7b-**EC**-4:1(3027)-**IS**-60:4b-**JER**-6:25c■20:10c■49:29c■ 52:23(7307)-**EZE**-1:10(3225),10(8040)■ 4:4b,6b,8b,9b■9:2(4975),3(4975),11 (4975)■10:3(3225)■11:23(6924)■16:33c■ 19:8c■23:22c■25:9e■28:23c■34:21b■ 36:3c■37:21c■39:17c■40:10(6311),18e, 40[2]e,41[2]e,44[2]e■41:1(6311),5a,5c,6[2]a,7a, 8a,9[2]a,10c,11a,26[2]sup,26a■42:9(6921),16 (7307),17(7307),18(7307),19(7307)■ 45:7[2]sup,7[2]■47:2e,15,17,18[2],19[2],20[2]■48:2[2], 3,4,5,6,7,8[2],16[4],21,23,24,25,26,27,28,30, 32,33,34-**DA**-7:5(7859)■10:4(3027)-**OB**-11 (5048)-**JON**-4:5(6924)■**N.T.**-all=3844, a=4008&marked-**M'T**-8:18a,28a■13:1, 4,19■14:22a■16:5a■20:30-**M'R**-2:13■ 4:1,4,15,35a■5:1a,21a■6:45a■8:13a■10:1a, 46■16:5(1188)-**LU**-1:11(1188)■8:5,12, 22a■10:31(492),32(492)■18:35■19:43 (3840)-**JOH**-6:22a,25a■19:18(1782),34 (4125)■20:20(4125),25(4125),27(4125)■ 21:6(3313)-**AC**-10:6,32■12:7(4125)■ 16:13-**RE**-22:2(1782)

SIDES-all=3411&marked-**EX**-25:14 (6763),32(6654)■26:13(6654),22,23,27■ 27:7(6763)■28:27(3802)■30:3(7023),4 (6654)■32:15(5676)■36:27,28,32■37:5 (6763),18(6654),26(7023),27(6654)■38:7 (6763)■39:20(3802)-**NU**-33:55(6654) -**JOS**-23:13(6654)-**J'G**-2:3(6654)-**1SA**-24:3-**1KI**-4:24(5676)■6:16-**2KI**-19:23 -**PS**-48:2■128:3-**IS**-14:13,15■37:24■ 66:12(6654)-**JER**-6:22■48:28(5676)■ 49:32(5676)-**EZE**-1:8(7253),17(7253)■ 10:11(7253)■32:23■41:2(3802),26(3802)■ 42:20(7307)■46:19■48:1(6285)-**AM**-6:10-**JON**-1:5

SIEGE-all=4692&marked-**DE**-20:19■28:53,55,57-**1KI**-15:27(6696) -**2CH**-32:10(4692)-**IS**-29:3(6696)-**JER**-19:9-**EZE**-4:2,3(6696),7,8■5:2-**MIC**-5:1-**NA**-3:14-**ZEC**-12:2

SIEVE-**IS**-30:28(5299)-**AM**-9:9(3531)

SIFT-**IS**-30:28(5130)-**AM**-9:9(5128)■ **N.T.**-**LU**-22:31(4617)

SIFTED-**AM**-9:9(5128)

SIGH-all=584-**IS**-24:7-**LA**-1:4,11,21 -**EZE**-9:4■21:6[2]

SIGHED-**EX**-2:23(584)■**N.T.**-**M'R**-7:34(4727)■8:12(389)

SIGHEST-**EZE**-21:7

SIGHETH-**LA**-1:8(584)

SIGHING-**JOB**-3:24(585)-**PS**-12:5 (603)■31:10(585)■79:11(603)-**IS**-21:2 (585)■35:10(585)-**JER**-45:3(585)

SIGHS-**LA**-1:22(585)

SIGHT-all=5869,a=6440,b=4758& marked-**GE**-2:9b■18:3■19:19■21:11,12■ 23:4a,8a■32:5■33:8,10,15■38:7■39:4,21■ 47:18a,25,29-**EX**-3:3b,21■4:30■7:20[2]■ 9:8■11:3[3]■12:36■15:26■17:6■19:11■ 24:17b■33:12,13[2],16,17■34:9■40:38 -**LE**-10:19■13:3b,4b,5,25b,30b,31b,32b, 34b,37■14:37b■20:17■25:53■26:45 -**NU**-3:4a■11:11,15■13:33[2]■19:5■20:27■ 25:6[2]■27:19■32:5,13■33:3-**DE**-4:6,25, 37a■6:18■9:18■12:25,28■17:2■21:9■ 28:34b,67b■31:7,29■34:12-**JOS**-3:7■ 4:14■10:12■23:5a■24:17-**J'G**-2:11■3:7, 12[2]■4:1■6:1,17,21■10:6■13:1-**RU**-2:2, 13-**1SA**-1:18■12:17■15:17,19■16:22■ 18:5[2]■29:6,9-**2SA**-6:22■7:9a,19■12:9,11■ 13:5,6,8■14:22■16:4,22■22:25-**1KI**-8:25a■9:7a■11:6,19,38■14:22■15:26,34■ 16:7,19,30■21:20,25■22:52-**2KI**-1:13, 14■3:2,18■8:18,27■12:2■13:2,11■14:3,

24■15:3,9,18,24,28,34■16:2■17:2,17,18a,20a,23a■18:3■20:3■21:2,6,15,16,20■22:2■23:27a,32,37■24:3a,9,19-1CH-2:3■19:13■22:8a■28:8■29:25-2CH-6:16a■7:20a■20:32■22:4■24:2■25:2■26:4■27:2■28:1■29:2■32:23■33:2,6,22■34:2■36:5,9,12-EZR-9:9a-NE-1:11a■2:5a■8:5-ES-2:15,17a■5:2,8■7:3■8:5-JOB-15:15■18:3■19:15■21:8a■25:5■34:26(7200)■41:9b-PS-5:5■9:19a■10:5(5048)■19:14a■51:4■72:14■76:7a■78:12(5048)■79:10■90:4■98:2■101:7■116:5■1143:2a-PR-1:17■3:4■4:3a-EC-2:26a■6:9b■8:3a■11:9b-IS-5:21a■11:3b■26:17a■38:3■43:4-JER-4:1a■7:15a,30■15:1a■18:10,23a■19:10■32:12■34:15■43:9■51:24-EZE-4:12■5:8,14■10:2,19■12:3^2,4^2,5,6,7■16:41■20:9,14,22^2,43a■21:23■22:16■28:18,25■36:31a,34■39:27■43:11-DA-4:11(2379),20(2379)HO-2:2a,10■6:2a-AM-9:3-JON-2:4-MAL-2:17■N.T.-all=1799,a=308&marked-M'T-11:5a,26(1715)■20:34a-M'R-10:51a,52a-LU-1:15■4:18(309)■7:21(991)■10:21(1715)■15:21■16:15■18:41a,42a,43a■23:48(2335)-JOH-9:11a,15a,18^{2}a-AC-1:9(3788)■4:19■7:10(1726),31(3705)■8:21■9:9(991),12a,17a,18a■10:31■22:13a-RO-3:20■12:17-2CO-2:17(2714)■4:2■5:7(1491)■7:12■8:21^2-GA-3:11(3844)-COL-1:22(2714)-1TH-1:3(1715)-1TI-2:3■6:13-HEB-4:13■12:21(5324)■13:21-JAS-4:10-1PE-3:4-1JO-3:22-RE-4:3(3706)■13:13,14

SIGHTS-LU-21:11(5400)

SIGN-all=226&marked-EX-4:8^2■8:23■13:9■31:13,17-NU-16:38■26:10(5251)-DE-6:8■11:18■13:1,2■28:46-JOS-4:6-J'G-6:17-1SA-2:34■14:10-1KI-13:3^2(4159),5(4159)-2KI-19:29■20:8,9-2CH-32:24(4159)-IS-7:11,14■19:20■20:3■37:30■38:7,22■55:13■66:19-JER-6:1(4864)■44:29-EZE-4:3■12:6(4159),11(4159)■14:8■20:12,20■24:24(4159),27(4159)■39:15(6725)-DA-6:8(7560)■N.T.-all=4592&marked-M'T-12:38,39^3■16:1,4^3■24:3,30■26:48-M'R-8:11,12^2■13:4-LU-2:12,34■11:16,29^3,30■21:7-JOH-2:18■6:30-AC-28:11(3902)-RO-4:11-1CO-1:22■14:22-RE-15:1

SIGNED-all=7560-DA-6:9,10,12,13

SIGNET-all=2368&marked-GE-38:18,25(2858)-EX-28:11,21,36■39:14,30-JER-22:24-DA-6:17^2(5824)-HAG-2:23(2268)

SIGNETS-EX-39:6(2368)

SIGNIFICATION-1CO-14:10(880)

SIGNIFIED-AC-11:28(4591)-RE-1:1(4591)

SIGNIFIETH-HEB-12:27(1213)

SIGNIFY-AC-21:26(1229)■23:15(1718)■25:27(4591)-1PE-1:11(1213)

SIGNIFYING-all=4591&marked-JOH-12:33■18:32■21:19-HEB-9:8(1213)

SIGNS-all=226&marked-GE-1:14-EX-4:9,17,28,30■7:3■10:1,2-NU-14:11-DE-4:34■6:22■7:19■26:8■29:3■34:11-JOS-24:17-1SA-10:7,9-NE-9:10-PS-74:4,9■78:43■105:27(1697,226)-IS-8:18-JER-10:2■32:20,21-DA-4:2(852),3(852)■6:27(852)■N.T.-all=4591&marked-M'T-16:3(4592)■24:24(4592)-M'R-13:22(4592)■16:17(4592),20(4592)-LU-1:62(1770)■21:11,25-JOH-4:48■20:30-AC-2:19,22,43■4:30■5:12■7:36■8:13■14:3-RO-15:19-2CO-12:12^2-2TH-2:9-HEB-2:4

SILENCE-all=1826&marked-J'G-3:19(2013)-JOB-4:16(1827)■29:21■31:34-PS-31:18(481)■32:3(2790)■35:22(2790)■39:2(1747)■50:3(2790),21(2790)■83:1(1824)■94:17(1745)■115:17(1745)-EC-3:7(2814)-IS-15:1(1820)■41:1(2790)■62:6(1824)■65:6(2814)-JER-8:14-LA-2:10■3:28-AM-5:13■8:3(2013)-HAB-2:20(2013)■N.T.-all=4601&marked-M'T-22:34(5392)-AC-15:12■21:40(4602)■22:2(2271)-1CO-14:28,34-1TI-2:11(2271),12(2271)-1PE-2:15(5392)-RE-8:1(4602)

SILENT-all=1826&marked-1SA-2:9-PS-22:2(1747)■28:1^2(2790)■30:12■31:17-IS-47:5(1748)-JER-8:14-ZEC-2:13(2013)

SILK-PR-31:22(8336)-EZE-16:10(4897),13(4897)■N.T.-RE-18:12(2596)

SILLY-JOB-5:2(6601)-HO-7:11(6601)■N.T.-2TI-3:6(1133)

SILVER-all=3701,a=3702&marked-GE-13:2■20:16■23:15,16^2■24:35,53■37:28■44:2,8■45:22-EX-3:22■11:2■12:35■20:23■21:32■25:3■26:19,21,25,32■27:10,11,17^2■31:4■35:5,24,32■36:24,26,30,36■38:10,11,12,17^3,19^2,25,27-LE-5:15■27:3,6^2,16-NU-7:13^2,19^2,25^2,31^2,37^2,43^2,49^2,55^2,61^2,67^2,73^2,79^2,84,85^2■10:2■22:18■24:13■31:22-DE-7:25■8:13■17:17■22:19,29■29:17-JOS-6:19,24■7:21^2,22,24■22:8■24:32(7192)-J'G-9:4■16:5■17:2^2,3^2,4,10-1SA-2:36■9:8-2SA-8:10,11■18:11,12■21:4■24:24-1KI-7:51■10:21,22,25,27,29■15:15,18,19■16:24■20:3,5,7,39-2KI-5:5,22,23■6:25^2■7:8■12:13^2■14:14■15:19,20■16:8■18:14,15■20:13■22:4■23:33,35^2■25:15-1CH-18:10,11■19:6■22:14,16■28:14,15,16,17sup,17■29:2,3,4,5,7-2CH-1:15,17■2:7,14■5:1■9:14,20,21,24,27■15:18■16:2,3■17:11■21:3■24:14■25:6,24■27:5■32:27■36:3-EZR-1:4,6,9,10,11■2:69■5:14a■6:5a■7:15a,16a,18a,22a■8:25,26^2,28,30,33-NE-5:15■7:71,72-ES-1:6^2■3:9,11-JOB-3:15■22:25■27:16,17■28:1,15-PS-12:6■66:10■68:13,30■105:37■115:4■119:72■135:15-PR-2:4■3:14■8:10,19■10:20■16:16■17:3■22:1■25:4,11■26:23■27:21-EC-2:8■5:10^2■12:6-SONG-1:11■3:10■8:9,11-IS-1:22■2:7,20■13:17■30:22■31:7■39:2■40:19■46:6■48:10■60:9,17-JER-6:30■10:4,9■32:9■52:19-EZE-7:19^2■16:13,17■22:18,20,22■27:12■28:4■38:13-DA-2:32a,35a,45a■5:2a,4a,23a■11:8,38,43-HO-2:8■3:2■8:4■9:6■13:2-JOE-3:5-AM-2:6■8:6-NA-2:9-HAB-2:19-ZEP-1:11,18-HAG-2:8-ZEC-6:11■9:3■11:12,13■13:9■14:14-MAL-3:3^2■N.T.-all=694&marked-M'T-10:9(696)■26:15■27:3,5,6,9-LU-15:8(1406)-AC-3:6■17:29(696)■19:19,24(693)■20:33-1CO-3:12(696)-2TI-2:20(693)-JAS-5:3(696)-1PE-1:18-RE-9:20(693)■18:12(696)

SILVERLINGS-IS-7:23(3701)

SILVERSMITH-AC-19:24(695)

SIMILITUDE-all=8544&marked-NU-12:8-DE-4:12,15,16-2CH-4:3(1823)-PS-106:20(8403)■144:12(8403)-DA-10:16(1823)■N.T.-RO-5:14(3667)-HEB-7:15(3665)-JAS-3:9(3669)

SIMILITUDES-HO-12:10(1819)

SIMPLE-all=6612&marked-PS-19:7■116:6■119:130-PR-1:4,22,32■7:7■8:5■9:4,13(6615),16■14:15,18■19:25■21:11■22:3■27:12-EZE-45:20■N.T.-RO-16:18(172),19(185)

SIMPLICITY-2SA-15:11(8537)-PR-1:22(6612)■N.T.-all=572-RO-12:8-2CO-1:12■11:3

SIN-all=2403,a=2398,b=2399&marked-GE-4:7■18:20■20:9(2401)■31:36■39:9a■42:22a■50:17-EX-10:17■20:20a■23:33a■29:14,36■30:10■32:21(2401),30(2401),30,31(2401),32,34■34:7(2402),9-LE-4:2a,3a,3(819),3^2,8,13(7686),14^2,20,21,23,24,25,26,27a,28^2,29^2,32,33^2,34,35■5:1a,6^3,7,8,9^2,10,11^2,12,13,15a,17a■6:2a,17,25^2,26a,30■7:7,37■8:2,14^2■9:2,3,7,8,10,15^2,22■10:16,17,19^2■12:6,8■14:13^2,19,22,31■15:15,30■16:3,5,6,9,11^2,15,25,27^2■19:17b,22^2■20:20b■22:9b■23:19■24:15b-NU-5:6,7■6:11,14,16■7:16,22,28,34,40,46,52,58,64,70,76,82,87■8:8,12■9:13b■12:11■15:24,25,27a,27■16:22a■18:9,22b,32b■19:9,17■27:3b■28:15,22■29:5,11^2,16,19,22,25,28,31,34,38■32:23-DE-9:21,27■15:9b■19:15,15b■20:18a■21:22b■22:26b■23:21b,22b■24:4a,15b,16b-1SA-2:17,25^{2}a,12:23a■14:33a,34a,38■15:23,25■19:4a,5a■20:1-2SA-12:13-1KI-8:34,35,36,46a■12:30■13:34■14:16^{2}a■15:26,26a,30a,34,34a■16:2a,13a,19,19a,26,26a■17:18(5771)■21:22a■22:52a-2KI-3:3a■10:29a,31a■13:2a,6a,11a■14:6b,24a■15:9a,18a,24a,28a■17:21(2401)■21:11a,16,16a,17■23:15a-2CH-6:22a,25,26,27,36a■7:14■25:4b■29:21,23,24-EZR-6:17(2409)■8:35-NE-4:5■6:13a■10:33■13:26^{2}a-JOB-2:10a■5:24a■10:6,14a■13:23■14:16■31:30a■34:37■35:3-PS-4:4a■32:1(2401),5^2■38:3,18■39:1a■40:6(2401)■51:2,3,5b■59:3,12■85:2■109:7(2401),14■119:11a-PR-10:16,19(6588)■14:9(817),34■20:9■21:4■24:9-EC-5:6a-IS-3:9■5:18(2402)■6:7■27:9■30:1■31:7b■53:10(817),12b-JER-16:10,18■17:1,3■18:23■31:34■32:35a■36:3■51:5(817)-EZE-3:20,21^{2}a■18:24■33:14■40:39■42:13■43:19,21,22,25■44:27,29■45:17,19,22,23,25■46:20-DA-9:20-HO-4:8■8:11^{2}a■10:8■12:8b■13:2a,12-AM-8:14(819)-MIC-1:13■3:8■6:7-ZEC-13:1■N.T.-all=266,a=264&marked-M'T-12:31■18:21a-JOH-1:29■5:14a■8:7(361),11a,34,46■9:2a,41^2■15:22^2,24■16:8,9■19:11-AC-7:60-RO-3:9,20■4:8■5:12^2,13^2,20,21■6:1,2,6^2,7,10,11,12,13,14,15a,16,17,18,20,22,23■7:7^2,8^2,9,11,13^2,14,17,20,23,25■8:2,3^2,10■14:23-1CO-6:18(265)■8:12^{2}a■15:34a,56^2-2CO-5:21-GA-2:17■3:22-EPH-4:26a-2TH-2:3-1TI-5:20a-HEB-3:13■4:15■9:26,28■10:6,8,18,26a■11:25■12:1,4■13:11-JAS-1:15■2:9■4:17-1PE-2:22■4:1-2PE-2:14-1JO-1:7,8■2:1^{2}a■3:4^2,5,8,9,9a■5:16a,16,16a,16,17^2

SINCE-all=4480&marked-GE-44:28(2008)■46:30(310)-EX-4:10(227)■5:23■9:18,24(227)■10:6-NU-22:30(5750)-DE-4:32■34:10(5750)-JOS-2:12(3588)■14:10(227)-RU-2:11(310)-2SA-7:11-1KI-8:16-2KI-21:15-1CH-17:5-2CH-6:5-EZR-5:16(4481)-JOB-20:4-IS-14:8(227)-JER-7:25■20:8(1767)■23:38(518)■31:20(1767)■44:18(4480,227)■48:27(1767)■N.T.-all=575&marked-M'T-24:21-M'R-9:21(5613)-LU-1:70■7:45■16:16■24:21-JOH-9:32(1537)-AC-3:21■24:11(575,3739)-1CO-15:21(1894)-2CO-13:3(1893)-COL-1:6,9-HEB-7:28(3326)■9:26-2PE-3:4(575,3739)-RE-16:18(575,3739)

SINCERE-PH'P-1:10(1506)-1PE-2:2(97)

SINCERELY-J'G-9:16(8549),19(8549)■N.T.-PH'P-1:16(55)

SINCERITY-JOS-24:14(8549)■N.T.-all=1505&marked-1CO-5:8-2CO-1:12■2:17■8:8(1103)-EPH-6:24(861)-TIT-2:7(861)

SINEW-all=1517-GE-32:32^2-IS-48:4

SINEWS-all=1517&marked-JOB-10:11■30:17(6207)■40:17-EZE-37:6,8

SINFUL-NU-32:14(2400)-IS-1:4(2398)-AM-9:8(2401)■N.T.-all=268&marked-M'R-8:38-LU-5:8■24:7-RO-7:13■8:3(266)

SING-all=2167,a=7891,b=7442&marked-EX-15:1a,21a■32:18(6031)-NU-21:17(6030)-J'G-5:3a,3-1SA-21:11(6030)-2SA-22:50-1CH-16:9a,23a,33b-2CH-20:22(7440)■23:13(1984)■29:30(1984)-JOB-29:13b-PS-13:6a■21:13a■27:6a,6■30:4,12■33:2,3a■47:6^2,7■51:14b■57:7a,9■59:16a,16b,17■61:8■65:13a■66:2,4^2■67:4b■68:4a,4,32a,32■71:22,23■81:1b■89:1a■92:1■95:1b■96:1^{2}a,2a■98:1a,4,5■101:1a,1■104:12(5414,6963),33a,33■105:2a,2■108:1a,3■135:3■137:3a,4a■138:1,5a■144:9a,9■145:7b■146:2■147:1,7(6030),7■149:1a,3,5b-PR-29:6b-IS-5:1a■12:5■23:15(7892)■24:14b■26:19b■27:2(6031)■35:6b■42:10a,11b■44:23b■49:13b■52:8b,9b■54:1b■65:14b-JER-20:13a■31:7b,12b■51:48b-EZE-27:25(7788)-HO-2:15(6030)-ZEP-2:14a■3:14b-ZEC-2:10b■N.T.-all=5567&marked-RO-15:9-1CO-14:15^2-HEB-2:12(5214)

-JAS-5:13-RE-15:3(103)

SINGED-DA-3:27(2761)

SINGER-1CH-6:33(7891)-HAB-3:19(5329)

SINGERS-all=7891&marked-1KI-10:12-1CH-9:33■15:16,19,27^{2}-2CH-5:12,13■9:11■20:21■23:13■29:28(7892)■35:15-EZR-2:41,70■7:7,24(2171)■10:24-NE-7:1,44,73■10:28,39■11:22,23■12:28,29,42,45,46,47■13:5,10-PS-68:25■87:7-EC-2:8-EZE-40:44

SINGETH-PR-25:20(7891)

SINGING-all=7440&marked-1SA-18:6(7891)-2SA-19:35(7891)-1CH-6:32(7892)■13:8(7892)-2CH-23:18(7892)■35:25(7891)-EZR-2:65(7891)-NE-7:67(7891)■12:27(7892)-PS-100:2(7445)■126:2-SONG-2:12(2158)-IS-14:7■16:10(7442)■35:2(7442)■44:23■48:20■49:13■51:11■54:1■55:12-ZEP-3:17■N.T.-EPH-5:19(103)-COL-3:16(103)

SINGLE-M'T-6:22(573)-LU-11:34(573)

SINGLENESS-AC-2:46(858)-EPH-6:5(572)-COL-3:22(572)

SINGULAR-LE-27:2(6381)

SINK-PS-69:2(2883),14(2883)-JER-51:64(8257)■N.T.-M'T-14:30(2670)-LU-5:7(1036)■9:44(5087)

SINNED-all=2398-EX-9:27,34■10:16■32:30,31,33-LE-4:3,14,22,23,28^{2}■5:5,6,10,11,13■6:4-NU-6:11■12:11■14:40■21:7■22:34■32:23-DE-1:41■9:16,18-JOS-7:11,20-J'G-10:10,15■11:27-1SA-7:6■12:10■15:24,30■19:4■24:11■26:21-2SA-12:13■19:20■24:10,17-1KI-8:33,35,47,50■15:30■16:13,19■18:9-2KI-17:7■21:17-1CH-21:8,17-2CH-6:24,26,37,39-NE-1:6^{2}■9:29-JOB-1:5,22■7:20■8:4■24:19■33:27-PS-41:4■51:4■78:17,32■106:6-IS-42:24■43:27■64:5-JER-2:35■3:25■8:14■14:7,20■33:8^{2}■40:3■44:23■50:7,14-LA-1:8■5:7,16-EZE-18:24■28:16■37:23-DA-9:5,8,11,15-HO-4:7■10:9-MIC-7:9-HAB-2:10-ZEP-1:17■N.T.-all=264&marked-M'T-27:4-LU-15:18,21-JOH-9:3-RO-2:12^{2}■3:23■5:12,14,16-1CO-7:28^{2}-2CO-12:21(4258)■13:2(4258)-HEB-3:17-2PE-2:4-1JO-1:10

SINNER-all=2398&marked-PR-11:31■13:6(2403),22-EC-2:26■7:26■8:12■9:2,18-IS-65:20■N.T.-all=268-LU-7:37,39■15:7,10■18:13■19:7-JOH-9:16,24,25-RO-3:7-JAS-5:20-1PE-4:18

SINNERS-all=2400-GE-13:13-NU-16:38-1SA-15:18-PS-1:1,5■25:8■26:9■51:13■104:35-PR-1:10■13:21■23:17-IS-1:28■13:9■33:14-AM-9:10■N.T.-all=268&marked-M'T-9:10,11,13■11:19■26:45-M'R-2:15,16^{2},17■14:41-LU-5:30,32■6:32,33,34■7:34■13:2,4(3781)■15:1,2-JOH-9:31-RO-5:8,19-GA-2:15,17-1TI-1:9,15-HEB-7:26■12:3-JAS-4:8-JUDE-15

SINNEST-JOB-35:6(2398)

SINNETH-all=2398&marked-NU-15:28(7683),28,29(6213)-DE-19:15-1KI-8:46-2CH-6:36-PR-8:36■14:21■19:2■20:2-EC-7:20-EZE-14:13■18:4,20■33:12■N.T.-all=264-1CO-6:18■7:36-TIT-3:11-1JO-3:6^{2},8■5:18

SINNING-GE-20:6(2398)-LE-6:3(2398)

SINS-all=2403&marked-LE-16:16,21,30,34■26:18,21,24,28-NU-16:26-DE-9:18-JOS-24:19-1SA-12:19-1KI-14:16,22■15:3,30■16:2,13^{2},19,31-2KI-3:3■10:29(2399),31■13:2,6,11■14:24■15:9,18,24,28■17:22■24:3-2CH-28:10(819),13■33:19-NE-1:6■9:2,37-JOB-13:23-PS-25:7,18■51:9(2399)■69:5(819)■79:9■103:10(2399)-PR-5:22■10:12(6588)■28:13(6588)-IS-1:18(2399)■38:17(2399)■40:2■43:24,25■44:22■58:1■59:2,12-JER-5:25■14:10■15:13■30:14,15■50:20-LA-3:39(2399)■4:13,22-EZE-16:51,52■18:14,21■21:24■23:49(2399)■33:10,16-DA-4:27(2408)■9:16(2399),24-HO-8:13■9:9-AM-5:12-MIC-1:5■6:13■7:19■N.T.-all=266&marked-M'T-1:21■3:6■9:2,5,6■26:28-M'R-1:4,5■2:5,7,9,10■3:28(265)■4:12(265)-LU-1:77■3:3■5:20,21,23,24■7:47,48,49■11:4■24:47-JOH-8:21,24^{2}■9:34■20:23,23sup-AC-2:38■3:19■5:31■10:43■13:38■22:16■26:18-RO-3:25(265)■4:7■7:5■11:27-1CO-15:3,17-GA-1:4-EPH-1:7(3900)■2:1,5(3900)-COL-1:14■2:11,13(3900)-1TH-2:16-1TI-5:22,24-2TI-3:6-HEB-1:3■2:17■5:1,3■7:27■8:12■9:28■10:2,3,4,11,12,17,26-JAS-5:15,20-1PE-2:24^{2}■3:18■4:8-2PE-1:9-1JO-1:9^{2}■2:2,2sup,12■3:5■4:10-RE-1:5■18:4,5

SIR-GE-43:20(113)■N.T.-all=2962-M'T-13:27■21:30■27:63-JOH-4:11,15,19,49■5:7■12:21■20:15-RE-7:14

SIRS-all=435&marked-AC-7:26■14:15■16:30(2962)■19:25■27:10,21,25

SISTER-all=269&marked-GE-4:22■12:13,19■20:2,5,12■24:30,59,60■25:20■26:7,9■28:9■30:1,8■34:13,14,27,31■36:3,22■46:17-EX-2:4,7■6:20(1733),23■15:20-LE-18:9,11,12,13,18■20:17,19^{2}■21:3-NU-6:7■25:18■26:59-DE-27:22-J'G-15:2-RU-1:15^{2}(2994)-2SA-13:1,2,4,5,6,11,20,22,32■17:25-1KI-11:19^{2},20-2KI-11:2-1CH-1:39■3:9,19■4:3,19■7:15,18,30,32-2CH-22:11-JOB-17:14-PR-7:4-SONG-4:9,10,12■5:1,2■8:8,8-JER-3:7,8,10■22:18-EZE-16:45,46^{2},48,49,56■22:11■23:4,11^{2},18,31,33■44:25■N.T.-all=79-M'T-12:50-M'R-3:35-LU-10:39,40-JOH-11:1,5,28,39■19:25-RO-16:1,15-1CO-7:15■9:5-JAS-2:15-2JO-13

SISTER'S-all=269-GE-24:30■29:13-LE-20:17-1CH-7:15-EZE-23:32■N.T.-AC-23:16(79)-COL-4:10(431)

SISTERS-all=269-JOS-2:13-1CH-2:16-JOB-1:4■42:11-EZE-16:45,51,52^{2},55,61-HO-2:1■N.T.-all=79-M'T-13:56■19:29-M'R-6:3■10:29,30-LU-14:26-JOH-11:3-1TI-5:2

SIT-all=3427&marked-GE-27:19-NU-32:6-J'G-5:10-RU-3:18■4:1,2-1SA-9:22(5414)■16:11(5437)■20:5-2SA-19:8-1KI-1:13,17,20,24,27,30,35,48■3:6■8:20,25-2KI-7:3,4■10:30■15:12■18:27-1CH-28:5-2CH-6:16-PS-26:5■69:12■107:10■110:1■119:23■127:2■132:12-EC-10:6-IS-3:26■14:13■16:5■30:7(7674)■36:12■42:7■47:1^{2},5,8,14■52:2-JER-8:14■13:13,18■16:8■33:17■36:15,30■48:18-LA-1:1■2:10-EZE-26:16■28:2■33:31■44:3-DA-7:9(3488),26(3488)-JOE-3:12-MIC-4:4■7:8-ZEC-3:8■6:13-MAL-3:3■N.T.-all=2523,a=2521&marked-M'T-8:11(347)■14:19(347)■15:35(377)■19:28^{2}■20:21,23■22:44a■23:2■25:31■26:36-M'R-6:39(347)■8:6(377)■10:37,40■12:36a■14:32-LU-1:79a■9:14(2625),15(347)■12:37(347)■13:29(347)■14:8(2625),10(377),10(4873)■16:6■17:7(377)■20:42a■22:30,69a-JOH-6:10(377)-AC-2:30,34a■8:31-1CO-8:10(2621)-EPH-2:6(4776)-HEB-1:13a-JAS-2:3^{2}a-RE-3:21■17:3a■18:7a■19:18a

SITH-EZE-35:6(518)

SITTEST-all=3427-EX-18:14-DE-6:7■11:19-PS-50:20-PR-23:1-JER-22:2■N.T.-AC-23:3(2521)

SITTETH-all=3427&marked-EX-11:5-LE-15:4,6,20,23,26-DE-17:18-1KI-1:46-ES-6:10-PS-1:1■2:4■10:8■29:10^{2}■47:8■99:1-PR-9:14■20:8■31:23-IS-28:6■40:22-JER-17:11(1716)■29:16-LA-3:28-ZEC-1:11■5:7■N.T.-all=2521&marked-M'T-23:22-LU-14:28(2523),31(2523)■22:27^{2}(345)-1CO-14:30-COL-3:1-2TH-2:4(2523)-RE-5:13■6:16■7:10,15■17:1,9,15

SITTING-all=3427&marked-DE-22:6(7257)-J'G-3:20-1KI-10:5(4186)■13:14■22:19-2KI-4:38■9:5-2CH-9:4(4186),18■18:18-NE-2:6-ES-5:13-IS-6:1-JER-17:25■22:4,30■38:7-LA-3:63■N.T.-all=2521&marked-M'T-9:9■11:16■20:30■21:5(1910)■26:64■27:36,61-M'R-2:6,14■5:15■14:62■16:5-LU-2:46(2516)■5:17,27■7:32■8:35■10:13-JOH-2:14■12:15■20:12(2516)-AC-2:2■8:28■25:6(2523)-RE-4:4

SITUATE-1SA-14:5(4690)-EZE-27:3(3427)-NA-3:8(3427)

SITUATION-2KI-2:19(4186)-PS-48:2(5131)

SIX-all=8337&marked-GE-7:6,11■8:13■16:16■30:20■31:41■46:26-EX-12:37■14:7■16:26■20:9,11■21:2■23:10,12■24:16■25:32,33,35■26:9,22■28:10^{2}■31:15,17■34:21■35:2■36:16,27■37:18,19,21■38:26-LE-12:5■23:3■24:6■25:3^{2}-NU-1:21,25,27,46■2:4,9,11,15,31,32■3:28,34■4:40■7:3■11:21■26:41,51■31:32,37,38,44■35:6,13,15-DE-5:13■15:12,18■16:8-JOS-6:3,14■7:5■15:59,62-J'G-3:31■12:7■18:11,16,17■20:15,47-RU-3:15,17-1SA-13:5,15■14:2■17:4,7■23:13■27:2■30:9-2SA-2:11■5:5■6:13■15:18■21:20^{2}-1KI-6:6■10:14^{2},16,19,20,29■11:16■16:23-2KI-5:5■11:3■13:19■15:8-1CH-3:4^{2},22■4:27■7:2,4,40■8:38■9:6,9,44■12:24,26,35■20:6■21:25■23:4■25:3■26:17-2CH-1:17■2:2,17,18■3:8■9:13^{2},15,18,19■16:1■22:12■26:12■29:33■35:8-EZR-2:10,11,13,14,22,26,30,35,60,66,67■8:26,35-NE-5:18■7:10,15,16,18,20,30,62,68,69-ES-2:12^{2}-JOB-5:19■42:12-PR-6:16-IS-6:2-JER-34:14■52:23,30-EZE-9:2■40:5,12■41:1^{2},3,5,8■46:1,4,6-DA-3:1(8353)■N.T.-all=1803&marked-M'T-17:1-M'R-9:2-LU-4:25■13:14-JOH-2:6,20■12:1-AC-11:12■18:11-JAS-5:17-RE-4:8■13:18(5516)■14:20(1812)

SIXSCORE-1KI-9:14(3967,6242)-JON-4:11(8147,6240,7239)

SIXTEEN-all=8337,6240-GE-46:18-EX-26:25■36:30-NU-26:22■31:40,46,52-JOS-15:41■19:22-2KI-13:10■14:21■15:2,33■16:2-1CH-4:27■24:4-2CH-13:21■26:1,3■27:1,8■28:1■N.T.-AC-27:37(1440,1803)

SIXTEENTH-all=8337,6240-1CH-24:14■25:23-2CH-29:17

SIXTH-all=8345&marked-GE-1:31■30:19-EX-16:5,22,29■26:9-LE-25:21-NU-7:42■29:29-JOS-19:32-2SA-3:5-1KI-16:8(8337)-2KI-18:10(8337)-1CH-2:15■3:3■12:11■24:9■25:13■26:3,5■27:9-EZR-6:15(8353)-NE-3:30-EZE-4:11■8:1■39:2(8338)■45:13,13(8341)■46:14-HAG-1:1,15■N.T.-all=1623-M'T-20:5■27:45-M'R-15:33-LU-1:26,36■23:44-JOH-4:6■19:14-AC-10:9-RE-6:12■9:13,14■16:12■21:20

SIXTY-all=8346-GE-5:15,18,20,21,23,27-LE-27:3,7-NU-7:88^{2}-EZR-2:13■N.T.-all=1835-M'T-13:23-M'R-4:8,20

SIXTYFOLD-M'T-13:8(1835)

SIZE-all=4060&marked-EX-36:9,15-1KI-6:25(7095)■7:37(7095)-1CH-23:29

SKIES-all=7834-2SA-22:12-PS-18:11■77:17-IS-45:8-JER-51:9

SKILFUL-1CH-5:18(3925)■15:22(995)■28:21(2451)-2CH-2:14(3045)-EZE-21:31(2796)-DA-1:4(7919)-AM-5:16(3045)

SKILFULLY-PS-33:3(3190)

SKILFULNESS-PS-78:72(8394)

SKILL-all=3045&marked-1KI-5:6-2CH-2:7,8■34:12(995)-EC-9:11-DA-1:17(7919)■9:22(7919)

SKIN-all=5785&marked-EX-22:27■29:14■34:29,30,35-LE-4:11■7:8■11:32■13:2^{2},3^{2},4^{2},5,6,7,8,10,11,12^{2},18,20,21,22,24,25,26,27,28,30,31,32,34^{2},35,36,38,39^{2},43,48,49^{2},51^{2},52,53,56,57,58■15:17-NU-19:5-JOB-2:4■7:5■10:11■16:15(1539)■18:13■19:20^{2},26■30:30■41:7-PS-102:5(1320)-JER-13:23-LA-3:4■4:8■5:10-EZE-16:10■37:6,8-MIC-3:2,3■N.T.-M'R-1:6(1193)

SKINS-all=5785-**GE**-3:21■27:16-**EX**-25:5■26:14^2■35:7,23■36:19^2■39:34^2-**LE**-13:59■16:27-**NU**-4:6,8,10,11,12,14■31:20

SKIP-**PS**-29:6(7540)

SKIPPED-**PS**-114:4(7540),6(7540)

SKIPPEDST-**JER**-48:27(5110)

SKIPPING-**SONG**-2:8(7092)

SKIRT-all=3671-**DE**-22:30■27:20-**RU**-3:9-**1SA**-15:27■24:4,5,11^2-**EZE**-16:8-**HAG**-2:12^2-**ZEC**-8:23

SKIRTS-all=7757&marked-**PS**-133:2(6310)-**JER**-2:34(3671)■13:22,26-**LA**-1:9-**EZE**-5:3(3671)-**NA**-3:5

SKULL-**J'G**-9:53(1538)-**2KI**-9:35(1538)■**N.T.**-all=2898-**M'T**-27:33-**M'R**-15:22-**JOH**-19:17

SKY-**DE**-33:26(7834)-**JOB**-37:18(7834)■**N.T.**-all=3772-**M'T**-16:2,3^2-**LU**-12:56-**HEB**-11:12

SLACK-all=7503&marked-**DE**-7:10(309)■23:21(309)-**JOS**-10:6■18:3-**2KI**-4:24(6113)-**PR**-10:4(7423)-**ZEP**-3:16■**N.T.**-**2PE**-3:9(1019)

SLACKED-**HAB**-1:4(6313)

SLACKNESS-**2PE**-3:9(1022)

SLAIN-all=2491,a=2026,b=4191,c=5221&marked-**GE**-4:23a■34:27-**LE**-14:51(7819)■26:17(5062)-**NU**-11:22(7819)■14:16(7819)■19:16,18■22:33a■23:24■25:14^{2}c,15c,18c■31:8,19-**DE**-1:4c■21:1^2,2,3,6■28:31(2873)■32:42-**JOS**-11:6■13:22-**J'G**-9:18a■15:16c■20:4(7523),5a-**1SA**-4:11b■18:7c■19:6b,11b■20:32b■21:11c■22:21a■31:1,8-**2SA**-1:16b,19,22,25■3:30b■4:11a■12:9a■13:30c,32b■18:7(5062)■21:12c,16c-**1KI**-1:19(2076),25(2076)■9:16a■11:15■13:26b■16:16c■19:1a,10a,14a-**2KI**-3:23(2717)■11:2^{2}b,8b,15b,16b■14:5c-**1CH**-5:22■10:1,8■11:11-**2CH**-13:17■21:13a■22:1a,9b,11b■23:14b,21b■28:9a-**ES**-7:4a■9:11a,12a-**JOB**-1:15c,17c■39:30-**PS**-62:3(7523)■88:5■89:10-**PR**-7:26a■22:13(7523)■24:11(2027)-**IS**-10:4a■14:19a,20a■22:2■26:21a■27:7^{2}a■34:3■66:16-**JER**-9:1■14:18■18:21c■25:33■33:5c■41:4b,9c,9,16c,18c■51:4,47,49^2-**LA**-2:20a,21a■3:43a■4:9^2-**EZE**-6:4,7,13■9:7■11:6^2,7■16:21(7819)■21:14^2,29■23:39(7819)■26:6a■28:8■30:4,11■31:17,18■32:20,21,22,23,24,25^3,26(2490),28,29,30^2,31,32■35:8^2■37:9a-**DA**-2:13^2(6992)■5:30(6992)■7:11(6992)■11:26-**HO**-6:5a-**AM**-4:10a-**NA**-3:3-**ZEP**-2:12■**N.T.**-all=615&marked-**LU**-9:22-**AC**-2:23(337)■5:36(337)■7:42(4968),52■13:28(337)■23:14-**EPH**-2:16-**HEB**-11:37(1722,5408,599)-**RE**-2:13■5:6(4969),9(4969),12(4969)■6:9(4969)■11:13■13:8(4969)■18:24(4969)■19:21

SLANDER-all=1681-**NU**-14:36-**PS**-31:13-**PR**-10:18

SLANDERED-**2SA**-19:27(7270)

SLANDEREST-**PS**-50:20(5414,1848)

SLANDERETH-**PS**-101:5(3960)

SLANDEROUSLY-**RO**-3:8(987)

SLANDERS-**JER**-6:28(7400)■9:4(7400)

SLANDERERS-**1TI**-3:11(1228)

SLANG-**1SA**-17:49(7049)

SLAUGHTER-all=4347&marked-**GE**-14:17(5221)-**JOS**-10:10,20-**J'G**-11:33■15:8-**1SA**-4:10,17(4046)■6:19■14:14,30■17:57(5221)■18:6(5221)■19:8■23:5-**2SA**-1:1(5221)■17:9(4046)■18:7(4046)-**1KI**-20:21-**2CH**-13:17■25:14(5221)■28:5-**ES**-9:5(2027)-**PS**-44:22(2878)-**PR**-7:22(2875)-**IS**-10:26■14:21(4293)■27:7(2027)■30:25(2027)■34:2(2875),6(2875)■53:7(2875)■65:12(2875)-**JER**-7:32(2028)■11:19(2873)■12:3(2873),3(2028)■19:6(2028)■25:34(2873)■48:15(2875)■50:27(2875)■51:40(2873)-**EZE**-9:2(4660)■21:10(2873),15(2875),22(7524),28(2875)■26:15(2027)-**HO**-5:2(7819)-**OB**-9(6993)-**ZEC**-11:4(2028),7(2028)■**N.T.**-all=4967&marked-**AC**-8:32■9:1(5408)-**RO**-8:36-**HEB**-7:1(2871)-**JAS**-5:5

SLAVE-supplied

SLAVES-**RE**-18:13(4983)

SLAY-all=4191,a=2026,b=5221&marked-**GE**-4:14a■18:25■20:4a,11a■22:10(7819)■27:41a■34:30b■37:18,20a,26a■42:37■43:16(2875)-**EX**-2:15a■4:23a■5:21a■21:14a■23:7a■29:16(7819)■32:12a,27a-**LE**-4:29(7819),33(7819)■14:13(7819)■20:15a-**NU**-19:3(7819)■25:5a■35:19^2,21-**DE**-9:28■19:6b■27:25b-**JOS**-13:22a-**J'G**-8:19a,20a■9:54-**1SA**-2:25■5:10,11■14:34(7819)■15:3■19:5,11,15■20:8,33■22:17-**2SA**-1:9■3:37■21:2b-**1KI**-1:51■3:26,27■15:28■17:18■18:9,12a.14a■19:17^2■20:36b-**2KI**-8:12a■10:25b■17:26-**2CH**-20:23(2763)■23:14-**NE**-4:11a■6:10^{2}a-**ES**-8:11a-**JOB**-9:23■13:15(6991)■20:16a-**PS**-34:21■37:14(2873),32■59:11a■94:6a■109:16■139:19(6991)-**PR**-1:32a-**IS**-11:4■14:30a■27:1a■65:15-**JER**-5:6b■15:3a■18:23(1194)■20:4b■29:21b■40:14(5221,5315),15^{2}b■41:8■50:27(2717)-**EZE**-9:6a■13:19■23:47■26:8,11■40:39(7819)■44:11(7819)-**DA**-2:14(6992)-**HO**-2:3■9:16-**AM**-2:3a■9:1a,4a-**HAB**-1:17a-**ZEC**-11:5a■**N.T.**-all=615&marked-**LU**-11:49■19:27(2695)-**JOH**-5:16-**AC**-5:33(337)■9:29(337)■11:7(2380)-**RE**-9:15

SLAYER-all=7523&marked-**NU**-35:11,24(5221),25,26,27,28-**DE**-4:42■19:3,4,6-**JOS**-20:3,5,6■21:13,21,27,32,38-**EZE**-21:11(2026)

SLAYETH-**GE**-4:15(2026)-**DE**-22:26(7523,5315)-**JOB**-5:2(4191)-**EZE**-28:9(2026),9(2490)

SLAYING-all=2026&marked-**JOS**-8:24■10:20(5221)-**J'G**-9:56-**1KI**-17:20(4191)-**IS**-22:13■57:5(7819)-**EZE**-9:8(5221)

SLEEP-all=8142,a=3462,b=7901&marked-**GE**-2:21a■15:12(8639)■28:11b,16■31:40-**EX**-22:27b-**DE**-24:12b,13b■31:16b-**J'G**-16:14,19a,20-**1SA**-26:12(8639)-**2SA**-7:12b-**1KI**-1:21b-**ES**-6:1-**JOB**-4:13(8639)■7:21b■14:12-**PS**-4:8a■13:3a■76:5,6(7290)■78:65(3463)■90:5■121:4a■127:2■132:4-**PR**-3:24■4:16a,16■6:4,9b,9,10,10b■19:15a■20:13■24:33,33b-**EC**-5:12,12a■8:16-**SONG**-5:2(3463)-**IS**-5:27(3463)■29:10(8639)-**JER**-31:26■51:39a,39,57a,57-**EZE**-34:25a-**DA**-2:1■6:18(8139)■8:18(7290)■10:9(7290)■12:2(3463)-**ZEC**-4:1■**N.T.**-all=2518&marked-**M'T**-1:24(5258)■26:45-**M'R**-4:27■14:41-**LU**-9:32(5258)■22:46-**JOH**-11:11(1852),12(2837),13(5258)-**AC**-13:36(2837)■16:27(1853)■20:9^2(5258)-**RO**-13:11(5258)-**1CO**-11:30(2837)■15:51(2837)-**1TH**-4:14(2837)■5:6,7,10

SLEEPER-**JON**-1:6(7290)

SLEEPEST-**PS**-44:23(3462)-**PR**-6:22(7901)■**N.T.**-**M'R**-14:37(2518)-**EPH**-5:14(2518)

SLEEPETH-**1KI**-18:27(3463)-**PR**-10:5(7290)-**HO**-7:6(3463)■**N.T.**-all=2518&marked-**M'T**-9:24-**M'R**-5:39-**LU**-8:52-**JOH**-11:11(2837)

SLEEPING-**1SA**-26:7(3463)-**IS**-56:10(1957)■**N.T.**-**M'R**-13:36(2518)■14:37(2518)-**LU**-22:45(2837)-**AC**-12:6(2837)

SLEIGHT-**EPH**-4:14(2940)

SLEPT-all=7901&marked-**GE**-2:21(3462)■41:5(3462)-**2SA**-11:9-**1KI**-2:10■3:20(3463)■11:21,43■14:20,31■15:8,24■16:6,28■19:5(3462)■22:40,50-**2KI**-8:24■10:35■13:9,13■14:16,22,29■15:7,22,38■16:20■20:21■21:18■24:6-**2CH**-9:31■12:16■14:1■16:13■21:1■26:2,23■27:9■28:27■32:33■33:20-**JOB**-3:13(3462)-**PS**-3:5(3462)■76:5(5123)■**N.T.**-all=2837&marked-**M'T**-13:25(2518)■25:5(2518)■27:52■28:13-**1CO**-15:20

SLEW-all=2026,a=5221,b=4191,c=7819&marked-**GE**-4:8,25■34:25,26■38:7b,10b■49:6-**EX**-2:12a■13:15-**LE**-8:15c,23c■9:8c,12c,15c,18c-**NU**-31:7,8^2-**JOS**-8:21a■9:26■10:10a,11,26b■11:17b-**J'G**-1:4a,5a,10a,17a■3:29a,31a■7:25^2■8:17,18,21■9:5,24,44a,45,54■12:6c■14:19a■15:15a■16:24(2491),30^{2}b■20:45a-**1SA**-1:25c■4:2a■11:11a■14:13b,32c,34c■17:35b,36a,50b,51b■18:27a■19:5a,8a■22:18b■29:5a■30:2b■31:2a-**2SA**-1:10b■3:30■4:7b,10,12■8:5a■10:18(2126)■14:6b,7■18:15b■21:1b,18a,19a,21a■23:8(2491),12a,18(2491),20^{2}a,21,21a-**1KI**-1:9(2076)■2:5,32,34b■11:24■13:24b■16:11a■18:13,40c■19:21(2076)■20:20a,21a,29a,36a-**2KI**-9:31■10:7c,9,9a,11a,14c,17a■11:18,20b■12:20a■14:5a,6b,7a,19b■15:10b,14b,30b■16:9b■17:25■21:23b,24a■23:20(2076),29b■25:7c,21b-**1CH**-2:3b■7:21■10:2a,14b■11:14a,20(2490),22^{2}a,23a,23■18:5a,12a■19:18■20:4a,5a,7a-**2CH**-13:17a■21:4■22:8,11b■23:15b,17■24:22,25■25:3,4b,27b■28:6,7■32:21(5307)■33:24b,25a■36:17-**NE**-9:26-**ES**-9:6,10,15,16-**PS**-78:31,34■105:29b■135:10■136:18-**IS**-66:3a-**JER**-20:17b■26:23a■39:6^{2}c■41:2b,3a,7c,8b■52:10^{2}c-**LA**-2:4-**EZE**-9:7a■40:41c,42c-**DA**-3:22(6992)■5:19(6992)■**N.T.**-all=615&marked-**M'T**-2:16(337)■21:39■22:6■23:35(5407)-**LU**-13:4-**AC**-5:30(1315)■10:39(337)■22:20(337)-**RO**-7:11-**1JO**-3:12^2(4969)

SLEWEST-**1SA**-21:9(5221)

SLIDDEN-**JER**-8:5(7725)

SLIDE-**DE**-32:35(4131)-**PS**-26:1(4571)■37:31(4571)

SLIDETH-**HO**-4:16(5637)

SLIGHTLY-**JER**-6:14(7043)■8:11(7043)

SLIME-**GE**-11:3(2564)-**EX**-2:3(2564)

SLIMEPITS-**GE**-14:10(2564)

SLING-all=7050&marked-**J'G**-20:16(7049)-**1SA**-17:40,50■25:29(7049),29-**PR**-26:8(4773)-**JER**-10:18(7049)-**ZEC**-9:15

SLINGERS-**2KI**-3:25(7051)

SLINGS-**2CH**-26:14(7050)

SLINGSTONES-**JOB**-41:28(68,7050)

SLIP-all=4571&marked-**2SA**-22:37-**JOB**-12:5-**PS**-17:5(4131)■18:36■**N.T.**-**HEB**-2:1(3901)

SLIPPED-**1SA**-19:10(6362)-**PS**-73:2(8210)

SLIPPERY-**PS**-35:6(2519)■73:18(2513)-**JER**-23:12(2519)

SLIPPETH-**DE**-19:5(5394)-**PS**-38:16(4131)■94:18(4131)

SLIPS-**IS**-17:10(2156)

SLOTHFUL-all=6102&marked-**J'G**-18:9(6101)-**PR**-12:24(7423),27(7423)■15:19■18:9(7503)■19:24■21:25■22:13■24:30■26:13,14,15■**N.T.**-**M'T**-25:26(3636)-**RO**-12:11(3636)-**HEB**-6:12(3576)

SLOTHFULNESS-**PR**-19:15(6103)-**EC**-10:18(6103)

SLOW-all=750&marked-**EX**-4:10(3515)-**NE**-9:17-**PS**-103:8■145:8-**PR**-14:29■15:18■16:32-**JOE**-2:13-**JON**-4:2-**NA**-1:3■**N.T.**-**LU**-24:25(1021)-**TIT**-1:12(692)-**JAS**-1:19(1021)

SLOWLY-**AC**-27:7(1020)

SLUGGARD-all=6102-**PR**-6:6,9■10:26■13:4■20:4■26:16

SLUICES-**IS**-19:10(7938)

SLUMBER-all=5123&marked-**PS**-121:3,4■132:4(8572)-**PR**-6:4(8572),10(8572)■24:33(8572)-**IS**-5:27■56:10-**NA**-3:18■**N.T.**-**RO**-11:8(2659)

SLUMBERED-**M'T**-25:5(3573)

SLUMBERETH-**2PE**-2:3(3573)

SLUMBERINGS-**JOB**-33:15(8572)

SMALL-all=6996&marked-**GE**-19:11■30:15(4592)-**EX**-16:14^2(1851)■18:22,26■30:36(1854)-**LE**-16:12(1851)-**NU**-16:9(4592),13(4592)-**DE**-1:17■9:21(3190),21(1854)■25:13,14-**1SA**-5:9■20:2■30:2,19-**2SA**-7:19(6994)■17:13(1571)-**1KI**-2:20■19:12(1851)■22:31-**2KI**-19:26(7116)■23:2,6(1854),15(1854)■25:26-**1CH**-17:17(6994)■25:8■26:13-**2CH**-15:13■18:30■24:24(4705)■31:15■34:30■36:18-**ES**-1:5,20-**JOB**-3:19■8:7(4705)■15:11(4592)■

36:27(1639)-**PS**-104:25▪115:13▪119:141 (6810)-**PR**-24:10(6862)-**IS**-1:9(4592)▪7:13(4592)▪16:14(4213)▪22:24▪29:5 (1851)▪37:27(7116)▪41:15(1854)▪54:7▪60:22(6810)-**JER**-16:6▪30:19(6819)▪44:28(4962)▪49:15-**EZE**-16:20(4592)▪34:18(4592)-**DA**-11:23(4592)-**AM**-7:2,5▪8:5(6694)-**OB**-2(6696)-**ZEC**-4:10(6696)▪**N.T.**-all=3641&marked-**M'R**-3:9(4142)▪8:7(2485)-**JOH**-2:15(4979)▪6:9(3795) -**AC**-12:18▪15:2▪19:23,24▪26:22(3398)▪27:20-**1CO**-4:3(1646)-**JAS**-3:4(1646) -**RE**-11:18(3398)▪13:16(3398)▪19:5 (3398),18(3398)▪20:12(3398)

SMALLEST-**1SA**-9:21(6996)-**1CO**-6:2(1646)

SMART-**PR**-11:15(7321,7451)

SMELL-all=7381&marked-**GE**-27:27^{2} -**EX**-30:38(7306)-**LE**-26:31(7306)-**DE**-4:28(7306)-**PS**-115:6(7306)-**SONG**-1:12▪2:13▪4:10,11^{2}▪7:8,13-**IS**-3:24(1314)-**DA**-3:27(7382)-**HO**-14:6-**AM**-5:21(7306)▪**N.T.**-**PH'P**-4:18(2175)

SMELLED-**GE**-8:21(7306)▪27:27 (7306)

SMELLETH-**JOB**-39:25(7306)

SMELLING-**SONG**-5:5(5674), 13(5674)▪**N.T.**-**1CO**-12:17(3750)

SMITE-all=5221&marked-**GE**-8:21▪32:8,11-**EX**-3:20▪7:17▪8:2(5062),16▪9:15▪12:12,13,23^{2}(5062)▪17:6▪21:18, 20,26,27(5307)-**NU**-14:12▪22:6▪24:17 (4272)▪25:17▪35:16,17,18,21-**DE**-7:2▪13:15▪19:11▪20:13▪28:22,27,28,35▪33:11(4272)-**JOS**-7:3(6221)▪10:4(6221)▪12:6▪13:12-**J'G**-6:16▪20:31,39▪21:10 -**1SA**-15:3▪17:46▪18:11▪19:10▪20:33▪23:2^{2}▪26:8,8sup,10(5062)-**2SA**-2:22▪5:24▪13:28▪15:14▪17:2▪18:11-**1KI**-14:15▪20:35^{2},37-**2KI**-3:19▪6:18,21,22^{2}▪9:7, 27▪13:17,18,19-**1CH**-14:15-**2CH**-21:14(5062)-**PS**-121:6▪141:5(1986) -**PR**-19:25-**IS**-3:17(5596)▪10:24▪11:4, 15▪19:22^{2}(5062)▪49:10▪58:4-**JER**-18:18▪21:6,7▪43:11▪46:13▪49:28-**EZE**-5:2▪6:11▪9:5▪21:12(5606),14,17▪32:15▪39:3 -**AM**-3:15▪6:11▪9:1-**MIC**-5:1-**NA**-2:10 (6375)-**ZEC**-9:4▪10:11▪11:6(3807)▪12:4^{2}▪13:7▪14:12(5062),18(5062)-**MAL**-4:6▪**N.T.**-all=3960&marked-**M'T**-5:39 (4474)▪24:49(5180)▪26:31-**M'R**-14:27 -**LU**-22:49-**AC**-23:2(5180),3(5180) -**2CO**-11:20(1194)-**RE**-11:6▪19:15

SMITERS-**IS**-50:6(5221)

SMITEST-**EX**-2:13(5221)▪**N.T.** -**JOH**-18:23(1194)

SMITETH-all=5221&marked-**EX**-21:12,15-**DE**-25:11▪27:24-**JOS**-15:16 -**J'G**-1:12-**2SA**-5:8-**1CH**-11:6-**JOB**-26:12(4272)-**IS**-9:13-**LA**-3:30-**EZE**-7:9▪**N.T.**-**LU**-6:29(5180)

SMITH-**1SA**-13:19(2796)-**IS**-44:12 (2796,1720)-**IS**-54:16(2796)

SMITHS-all=4525-**2KI**-24:14,16 **JER**-24:1▪29:2

SMITING-all=5221-**EX**-2:11-**2SA**-8:13-**1KI**-20:37-**2KI**-3:24-**MIC**-6:13

SMITTEN-all=5221,a=5062&marked-**EX**-7:25▪9:31,32▪22:2-**NU**-14:42a▪22:28,32▪33:4-**DE**-1:42a▪28:7a,25a-**J'G**-1:8▪20:32a,36a,39a-**1SA**-4:2a,3a,10a▪5:12▪6:19▪7:10a▪13:4▪30:1 -**2SA**-2:31▪8:9,10▪10:15a,19a▪11:15 -**1KI**-8:33a▪11:15-**2KI**-2:14▪3:23▪13:19^{2}▪14:10-**1CH**-18:9,10-**2CH**-20:22a▪25:16, 19▪26:20(5060)▪28:17-**JOB**-16:10 -**PS**-3:7▪69:26▪102:4▪143:3(1792)-**IS**-5:25▪24:12(3807)▪27:7▪53:4-**JER**-2:30▪14:19▪37:10-**EZE**-22:13▪33:21▪40:1-**HO**-6:1▪9:16-**AM**-4:9▪**N.T.**-**AC**-23:3(5180)-**RE**-8:12(4141)

SMOKE-all=6227&marked-**GE**-19:28^{2}(7008)-**EX**-19:18(6225),18^{2}-**DE**-29:20(6225)-**JOS**-8:20,21-**J'G**-20:38,40 -**2SA**-22:9-**JOB**-41:20-**PS**-18:8▪37:20▪68:2▪74:1(6225)▪102:3▪104:32(6225)▪119:83(7008)▪144:5(6225)-**PR**-10:26 -**SONG**-3:6-**IS**-4:5▪6:4▪9:18▪14:31▪34:10▪51:6▪65:5-**HO**-13:3-**JOE**-2:30 -**NA**-2:13▪**N.T.**-all=2586-**AC**-2:19 -**RE**-8:4▪9:2^{3},3,17,18▪14:11▪15:8▪18:9, 18▪19:3

SMOKING-**GE**-15:17(6227)-**EX**-20:18(6226)-**IS**-7:4(6226)▪42:3 (3544)▪**N.T.**-**M'T**-12:20(5187)

SMOOTH-**GE**-27:11(2509),16 (2513)-**1SA**-17:40(2512)-**IS**-30:10 (2513)▪57:6(2511)▪**N.T.**-**LU**-3:5(3006)

SMOOTHER-**PS**-55:21(2505)-**PR**-5:3(2513)

SMOOTHETH-**IS**-41:7(2505)

SMOTE-all=5221&marked-**GE**-14:5, 7,15▪19:11▪36:35-**EX**-7:20▪8:17▪9:25^{2}▪12:27(5062),29▪21:19-**NU**-3:13▪8:17▪11:33▪14:45▪20:11▪21:24,35▪22:23, 25,27▪24:10(5606)▪32:4▪35:21-**DE**-2:33▪3:3▪4:46▪25:18▪29:7-**JOS**-7:5^{2}▪8:22,24▪9:18▪10:10,26,28,30,32,33,35, 37,39,40,41▪11:8^{2},10,11,12,14,17▪12:1, 7▪13:21▪19:47▪20:5-**J'G**-1:25▪3:13▪4:21(8628)▪5:26(1986),26(4277)▪7:13▪8:11▪9:43▪11:21,33▪12:4▪15:8▪18:27▪20:35(5062),37,48-**1SA**-4:8▪5:6,9▪6:9 (5060),19▪7:11▪13:3▪14:31,48▪15:7▪17:35^{2},49,50▪19:10▪22:19▪23:5▪24:5▪25:38(5062)▪27:9▪30:17-**2SA**-1:15▪2:23▪3:27▪4:6,7▪5:20,25▪6:7▪8:1,2,3▪10:18▪11:21▪14:6,7▪18:15▪20:10▪21:17▪23:10▪24:10,17-**1KI**-15:20,27, 29▪16:10▪20:21,37▪22:24,34-**2KI**-2:8, 14▪3:24,25▪6:18▪8:21▪9:24▪10:25, 32▪12:21▪13:18▪15:5,10,14,16^{2},25,30▪18:8▪19:35,37▪25:21,25-**1CH**-1:46▪4:41,43▪13:10▪14:11,16▪18:1,2,3▪20:1▪21:7-**2CH**-13:15(5062)▪14:12(5062),14, 15▪16:4▪18:23,33▪21:9,18(5062)▪22:5▪25:11,13▪28:5^{2},23-**NE**-13:25-**ES**-9:5 -**JOB**-1:19(5060)▪2:7-**PS**-60:t▪78:20,31 (3766),51,66▪105:33,36▪135:8,10▪136:10, 17-**SONG**-5:7-**IS**-10:20▪14:6,29▪27:7(4347),7▪30:31▪37:36,38▪41:7 (1986)▪57:17▪60:10-**JER**-20:2▪31:19 (5606)▪37:15▪41:2▪46:2▪47:1▪52:27 -**DA**-2:34(4223),35(4223)▪5:6(5368)▪8:7-**JON**-4:7-**HAG**-2:17▪**N.T.**-all=3960&marked-**M'T**-26:51(851),67(4474),68 (3817)▪27:30(5180)-**M'R**-14:47(3817)▪15:19(5180)-**LU**-18:13(5180)▪22:50,63 (1194),64(3817)▪23:48(5180)-**JOH**-18:10(3817)▪19:3(1325,4475)-**AC**-7:24▪12:7,23

SMOTEST-**EX**-17:5(5221)

SNAIL-**LE**-11:30(2546)-**PS**-58:8(7642)

SNARE-all=4170,a=6341&marked -**EX**-10:7▪23:33▪34:12-**DE**-7:16-**J'G**-2:3▪8:27-**1SA**-18:21▪28:9(5367) -**JOB**-18:8(7639),10(2256)-**PS**-69:22a▪91:3a▪106:36▪119:110a▪124:7^{2}a▪140:5a▪142:3a-**PR**-7:23a▪18:7▪20:25▪22:25▪29:6,8(6315),25-**EC**-9:12a-**IS**-8:14▪24:17a,18a▪29:21(6983)-**JER**-48:43a, 44a▪50:24(3369)-**LA**-3:47(6354)-**EZE**-12:13(4686)▪17:20(4686)-**HO**-5:1a▪9:8a-**AM**-3:5^{2}a▪**N.T.**-all=3803&marked -**LU**-21:35-**RO**-11:9-**1CO**-7:35(1029) -**1TI**-3:7▪6:9-**2TI**-2:26

SNARED-all=3369&marked-**DE**-7:25▪12:30(5367)-**PS**-9:16(5367)-**PR**-6:2▪12:13(4170)-**EC**-9:12-**IS**-8:15▪28:13▪42:22(6351)

SNARES-all=6341&marked-**JOS**-23:13-**2SA**-22:6(4170)-**JOB**-22:10▪40:24 (4170)-**PS**-11:6▪18:5(4170)▪38:12 (5367)▪64:5(4170)▪141:9-**PR**-13:14 (4170)▪14:27(4170)▪22:5-**EC**-7:26 (4685)-**JER**-5:26(3353)▪18:22

SNATCH-**IS**-9:20(1504)

SNEEZED-**2KI**-4:35(2237)

SNORTING-**JER**-8:16(5170)

SNOUT-**PR**-11:22(639)

SNOW-all=7950&marked-**EX**-4:6 -**NU**-12:10-**2SA**-23:20-**2KI**-5:27-**JOB**-6:16▪9:30▪24:19▪37:6▪38:22-**PS**-51:7▪68:14(7949)▪147:16▪148:8-**PR**-25:13▪26:1▪31:21-**IS**-1:18▪55:10-**JER**-18:14 -**LA**-4:7-**DA**-7:9(8517)▪**N.T.**-all=5510 -**M'T**-28:3-**M'R**-9:3-**RE**-1:14

SNOWY-**1CH**-11:22(7950)

SNUFFDISHES-all=4289-**EX**-25:38▪37:23-**NU**-4:9

SNUFFED-**JER**-14:6(7602)-**MAL**-1:13(5301)

SNUFFERS-all=4212&marked-**EX**-37:23(4457)-**1KI**-7:50-**2KI**-12:13▪25:14 -**2CH**-4:22-**JER**-52:18

SNUFFETH-**JER**-2:24(7602)

SO-all=3651&marked-**GE**-1:7,9,11,15, 24,30▪6:22▪13:16(834)▪15:5(3541)▪18:5▪25:22▪29:26,28▪32:19(1571)▪41:13▪42:20▪43:11▪44:5(834),17 (2063)▪45:21▪48:18▪50:3,17(3541)-**EX**-6:9▪7:6,10,20,22▪8:7,17,18,18sup,24,26▪10:10,11▪12:28,50▪14:4,28(5704)▪17:6▪25:9,33▪27:8▪37:19▪39:32,42,43▪40:16 -**LE**-4:20▪8:35▪10:13▪16:16▪24:19,20▪27:12,14-**NU**-1:54▪2:17,34^{2}▪5:4^{2}▪6:21▪8:4,20,22▪9:5,14,16▪12:7▪14:28▪15:12 (3602),14,20▪17:11sup,11▪32:23,31▪36:10 -**DE**-3:21▪4:5▪7:19▪8:20▪12:4,22,30,31▪18:14▪22:3,5(428),26▪25:9(3602)▪28:63 -**JOS**-1:17▪2:21▪4:8▪5:15▪6:14(3541)▪8:22(5704)▪9:26▪10:1,23,39▪11:15^{2}▪14:5▪23:15-**J'G**-1:7▪2:17▪3:22(3588)▪5:31▪6:20,38,40▪7:17▪8:18(1992)▪11:10▪14:10▪15:11▪19:24(2063)▪21:14,23 -**RU**-1:17(3541)-**1SA**-1:7^{2}▪2:5(5704),14 (3602)▪3:17(3541)▪5:7▪6:10▪8:8▪9:21 (1697)▪11:7(3541)▪14:44(3541)▪15:33▪17:27(3541)▪19:17(3602)▪20:13(3541)▪25:22(3541),25▪26:24▪27:11(3541)▪30:23-**2SA**-3:9(3541),9,35(3541)▪5:25▪7:17▪9:11▪13:35▪14:17▪16:10(3588), 10,19,23▪17:12(1571)▪19:13(3541)▪20:18,21▪23:5-**1KI**-1:6(3602),30,36,37▪2:7,23(3541),38▪6:26,33▪7:18▪8:25 (7535)▪12:32▪13:9▪14:4▪17:17(3966)▪19:2(3541)▪20:10(3541),25,40▪21:5 (2088)▪22:8,12,22-**2KI**-2:10▪6:31(3541)▪7:20▪15:12▪16:11▪18:21-**1CH**-13:4▪17:15▪20:3▪21:3(1992)-**2CH**-6:31(3605)▪8:14▪18:7,11,21▪27:5(2063)▪32:17▪35:12-**EZR**-6:13(3660)▪10:12,16-**NE**-5:12,13(3602),15▪6:13▪8:17-**ES**-1:8, 13▪2:4,12▪3:2▪4:16▪5:13(6256)▪6:10▪7:5▪9:14-**JOB**-5:27▪7:3,9▪8:13▪9:2,35▪27:6(3605)-**PS**-1:4▪42:1▪48:5,8,10▪61:8▪63:2▪65:9▪72:7(5704)▪83:15▪90:12▪103:15(3652)▪123:2▪127:2,4▪147:20-**PR**-1:19▪6:29▪15:7▪23:7▪24:14,29▪26:1, 2,8,19▪27:8,19-**EC**-3:19▪5:16▪7:6▪8:10▪9:12(1992)▪11:5(3602)-**SONG**-2:2,3▪5:9(3602)-**IS**-10:7^{2},11▪14:24,24 (3652)▪16:6▪18:4(3541)▪20:2,4▪26:17▪29:8(3652)▪31:4,5(3652)▪36:6▪38:13,14▪47:7(5704)▪52:15▪54:9▪55:9,11▪61:11▪63:14▪65:8▪66:13,22-**JER**-2:26▪3:20▪5:19,27,31▪6:7▪11:5(543)▪13:11▪18:6▪19:11(3602)▪24:5,8sup,8▪28:6,11(3602)▪31:28▪32:42▪33:22▪34:5▪38:12▪42:18,20▪48:30^{2}-**EZE**-1:28▪12:7,11▪15:6▪20:36▪22:20,22▪23:44▪34:12▪35:15▪36:38▪45:20-**HO**-3:3(1571)▪4:7▪10:15(3602)▪11:2(3602)-**JO**-2:4-**AM**-3:12▪5:14-**HAG**-2:14^{2}-**ZEC**-1:6▪7:13▪8:15▪11:11▪14:15▪**N.T.**-all=3779,a=5620,b=2532,c=5118, d=3767,e=1161&marked-**M'T**-1:17d▪5:12,16,19,47▪6:30▪7:12,17▪8:10c,28a, 31e▪9:33▪11:26^{2}▪12:40,45▪13:2a,27e,32a, 40,49▪15:33^{2}c▪18:13(1437),14,31e,35▪19:8,10,12▪20:8e,16,26,34e▪22:10b▪23:28▪24:27,33,37,39,46▪25:20b▪27:64b, 66e▪28:15e-**M'R**-2:2(3366),8▪3:20a,20 (3383)▪4:1a,26,32a,37a,40▪6:31(3761)▪7:18▪8:8e▪9:3(3634)▪10:8a,43▪13:29b▪14:59▪15:5a,39▪16:19(3303)-**LU**-5:7a, 10(3668)▪6:3(3761),10,26(2596,5623)▪7:9c▪9:15▪10:21(3483),21▪11:2b,30▪12:21,28,38,43,54▪14:21b,33d▪16:5b, 26(3704)▪17:10,24,26▪18:13(3761),39 (3123)▪20:15b,20(1519)▪21:31▪22:26▪24:24-**JOH**-3:8,14,16▪4:40d,46d,53d▪5:21,26▪6:9c,10d,19d,57b▪7:43d▪8:7e, 59▪11:28(5023)▪12:37c,50▪13:12d,33b▪14:9c,31▪15:8b,9(2504)▪18:22▪20:4e,

20(5124)■21:11c,15d-AC-1:11■3:18■4:21e■5:8^{2}c■7:1,8,15e■51b■8:32■10:14(3365)■11:8(3365)■12:8,15■13:4d,8,47■14:1■15:30d,39a,39(5037)■16:5d,26a■17:11,33■19:2(3761),10a,12a,14(5124),16a,20■20:11,13,24(5613),35■21:11,35(4819)■22:24■23:7(5124),11,18d,22d■24:9,14■27:17,44■28:9d,14-RO-1:15,20(1519)■4:18■5:12,15,18,19,21■6:3(3745),4,19■7:3(686),25(686)■9:16(686)■10:17(686)■11:5,16b,26,31■12:5,20(5124)■14:12(686)■15:19a,20-1CO-1:7a■2:11■3:7a,15■4:1■5:1(3761),3■6:5■7:17^{2},26,36,37(5124),38a,40■8:12■9:14,15,24,26^{2}■11:12,28■12:12■13:2a■14:9,10c,12,25■15:11,15(686),22,42,45,54e■16:1-2CO-1:5,7,10(5082)■2:7a■3:7a■4:12a■7:7a,14■8:6,11■10:7■11:3,22^{3}(2504)-GA-1:6,9b■3:3,4c,9a■4:3,29,31(686)■5:17(2443)■6:2-EPH-4:20,21■5:24,28,33-PH’P-1:13a■2:23(5613)■3:17■4:1-COL-3:13-1TH-1:7a,8a■2:4,8,14,17■5:2-2TH-1:4a■2:4a■3:17-1TI-3:11(5615)-2TI-3:8-HEB-1:4c■2:3(5082)■3:11(5613),19b■4:7c■5:3,5■6:15■7:9(5613),22c■9:28■10:25c,33■11:3(1519)■12:1c,21■13:6a-JAS-1:11■2:12,17,26■3:4(5082),5,6,10.12-1PE-1:15b■2:15-2PE-1:11-1JO-2:6■4:11,17b-RE-1:7(3483)■2:15■3:16■8:12(2443)■13:13(2443)■16:7(3483),18(5082),18■17:3b■18:7c,17c■22:20(3483)

SOAKED-IS-34:7(7301)

SOBER-all=3525&marked-2CO-5:13(4993)-1TH-5:6,8-1TI-3:2(4998),11(3524)-TIT-1:8(4998)■2:2(3524),4(4994),6(4993)-1PE-1:13■4:7(4993)■5:8

SOBERLY-RO-12:3(1519,4993)-TIT-2:12(4996)

SOBERNESS-AC-26:25(4997)

SOBRIETY-1TI-2:9(4997),15(4997)

SOCKET-EX-38:27(134)

SOCKETS-all=134-EX-26:19^{3},21^{3},25^{3},32,37■27:10,11,12,14,15,16,17,18■35:11,17■36:24^{3},26^{3},30^{2},36,38■38:10,11,12,14,15,17,19,27^{3},30,31^{2}■39:33,40■40:18-NU-3:36,37■4:31,32-SONG-5:15

SOD-GE-25:29(2102)-2CH-35:13(1310)

SODDEN-all=1310&marked-EX-12:9-LE-6:28^{2}-NU-6:19(1311)-1SA-2:15-LA-4:10

SODERING-IS-41:7(1694)

SOEVER-all=834-LE-15:9-DE-12:32-2SA-15:35-1KI-8:38-2CH-6:29■N.T.-all=302&marked-M’R-3:28(3745,302)■6:10(1437)■11:24(3745,302)-JOH-5:19■20:23^{2}-RO-3:19(1437)

SOFT-all=7390&marked-JOB-23:16(7401)■41:3-PS-65:10(4127)-PR-15:1■25:15■N.T.-all=3120-M’T-11:8^{2}-LU-7:25

SOFTER-PS-55:21(7401)

SOFTLY-all=328&marked-GE-33:14-J’G-4:21(3814)-RU-3:7(3909)-1KI-21:27-IS-8:6■N.T.-AC-27:13(5285)

SOIL-EZE-17:8(7704)

SOJOURN-all=1481&marked-GE-12:10■19:9■26:3■47:4-EX-12:48-LE-17:8,10,13■19:33■20:2■25:45-NU-9:14■15:14-J’G-17:8,9-RU-1:1-1KI-17:20-2KI-8:1-PS-120:5-IS-23:7■52:4-JER-42:15,17,22■43:2■44:12,14,28-LA-4:15-EZE-20:38(4033)■47:22■N.T.-AC-7:6(1510,3941)

SOJOURNED-all=1481-GE-20:1■21:23,34■32:4■35:27-DE-18:6■26:5-J’G-17:7■19:16-2KI-8:2-PS-105:23■N.T.-HEB-11:9(3939)

SOJOURNER-all=8453&marked-GE-23:4-LE-22:10■25:35,40,47(1616),47-NU-35:15-PS-39:12

SOJOURNERS-LE-25:23(8453)-2SA-4:3(1481)-1CH-29:15(8453)

SOJOURNETH-all=1481-EX-3:22■12:49-LE-16:29■17:12■18:26■25:6-NU-15:15,16,26,29■19:10-JOS-20:9-EZR-1:4-EZE-14:7■47:23

SOJOURNING-EX-12:40(4186)-J’G-19:1(1481)■N.T.-1PE-1:17(3940)

SOLACE-PR-7:18(5965)

SOLD-all=4376&marked-GE-25:33■31:15■37:28,36■41:56(7666)■42:6(7666)■45:4,5■47:20,22-EX-22:3-LE-25:23,25,25(4465),27,28(4465),29(4465),33(4465),34,39,42,48,50■27:20,27,28-DE-15:12■28:68■32:30-J’G-2:14■3:8■4:2■10:7-1SA-12:9-1KI-21:20-2KI-17:17-NE-5:8^{2}■13:15,16-ES-7:4^{2}-PS-105:17-IS-50:1^{2}■52:3-JER-34:14-LA-5:4(935,4242)-EZE-7:13(4465)-JOE-3:3,6,7-AM-2:6■N.T.-all=4453&marked-M’T-10:29■13:46(4097)■18:25(4097)■21:12^{2}■26:9(4097)-M’R-11:15^{2}■14:5(4097)-LU-12:6■17:28■19:45-JOH-2:14,16■12:5(4097)-AC-2:45(4097)■4:34(4453),34(4097),37■5:1,4(4097),8(591)■7:9(591)-RO-7:14(4097)-1CO-10:25-HEB-12:16(591)

SOLDIER-all=4757&marked-JOH-19:23-AC-10:7■28:16-2TI-2:3,4(4758)

SOLDIERS-1CH-7:4(6635)-2CH-25:13(1121)-EZR-8:22(2428)-IS-15:4(2502)■N.T.-all=4757&marked-M’T-8:9■27:27,27sup■28:12-M’R-15:16-LU-3:14(4754)■7:8■23:36-JOH-19:2,23,24,32,34-AC-12:4,6,18■21:32^{2},35■23:10(4753),23,31■27:31,32

SOLDIERS’-AC-27:42(4757)

SOLE-all=3709-GE-8:9-DE-28:35,56,65-JOS-1:3-2SA-14:25-2KI-19:24-JOB-2:7-IS-1:6■37:25-EZE-1:7

SOLEMN-all=4150,a=6116&marked-LE-23:36a-NU-10:10■15:3■29:35a-DE-16:8a,15(2287)-2KI-10:20a-2CH-2:4■7:9a■8:13-NE-8:18a-PS-81:3(2282)-IS-1:13a-LA-1:4■2:6,7,22-EZE-36:38■46:9-HO-2:11■9:5■12:9-JOE-1:14a■2:15a-AM-5:21a-NA-1:15(2282)-ZEP-3:18-MAL-2:3(2282)

SOLEMNITIES-all=4150-IS-33:20-EZE-45:17■46:11

SOLEMNITY-DE-31:10(4150)-IS-30:29(2282)

SOLEMNLY-GE-43:3(5749)-1SA-8:9(5749)

SOLES-all=3709-DE-11:24-JOS-3:13■4:18-1KI-5:3-IS-60:14-EZE-43:7-MAL-4:3

SOLITARILY-MIC-7:14(910)

SOLITARY-JOB-3:7(1565)■30:3(1565)-PS-68:6(3173)■107:4(3452)-IS-35:1(6723)-LA-1:1(910)■N.T.-M’R-1:35(2048)

SOME-all=259&marked-GE-37:20■47:2(7097)-EX-16:20(582)-NU-31:3(582)-DE-24:1(1697)-JOS-8:22(428)-1SA-27:5-2SA-17:9^{2},12-2KI-2:16^{2}-2CH-12:7(4592)-NE-2:12(4592)■7:70(7097)■12:44(582)-PS-20:7(428)-DA-12:2^{2}(428)■N.T.-all=5100,a=3588,b=3303-M’T-13:4a,b,5a(243),7a(243),8a,b,8a(1161),23a,b,24a(1161)■16:14^{2}a,b,28■27:47■28:11,17a-M’R-4:4a,b,5(243),7(243),8^{2}(1520),20^{2}(1520)■7:2■8:28(243)■9:1■12:5a,b,5a■14:4,65■15:35-LU-8:5a,b,6(2087),7(2087)■9:7,8,19(243),27■11:15■13:1■19:39■21:5■23:8-JOH-6:64■7:12a,b,25,41(243),44■9:9(243),16■11:37,46■13:29-AC-5:15■8:9,31,34■11:20■15:36■17:4,18,18a,21,32a,b■18:23■19:32(243)■21:34(243)■27:27,44a,b,44(1161)■28:24a,b,24a-RO-1:11,13■3:3,8■5:7■11:14,17■15:15(575,3313)-1CO-4:18■6:11■8:7■9:22■10:7,8,9,10■12:28a,b■15:6,12,34,35,37-2CO-3:1■10:2,12-GA-1:7-EPH-4:11a,b,11^{2}a-PH’P-1:15^{2}-COL-3:7(4218)-1TH-3:5(3381)-2TH-3:11-1TI-1:3,6,19■4:1■5:15,24^{2}■6:10,21-2TI-2:18,20a,b,20a-HEB-3:4,16■4:6■10:25■11:40■13:2-2PE-3:9,16-JUDE-22a,b

SOMEBODY-LU-8:46(5100)-AC-5:36(5100)

SOMETHING-1SA-20:26(4745)■N.T.-all=5100-LU-11:54-JOH-13:29-AC-3:5■23:18-GA-6:3

SOMETIME-COL-1:21(4218)-1PE-3:20(4218)

SOMETIMES-all=4218-EPH-2:13■5:8-TIT-3:3

SOMEWHAT-all=3544&marked-LE-13:6,21,26,28,56-2KI-5:20(3972)■N.T.-all=5100&marked-LU-7:40-AC-23:20■25:26-RO-15:24(3313)-2CO-10:8-GA-2:6-HEB-8:3

SON-all=1121marked-GE-4:17,25,26■5:28■9:24■11:31■12:5■14:12■16:11,15■17:16,19,23,25,26■18:10,14■19:12,37,38■21:2,3,4,5,7,9,10^{2},10sup,11,13,23(5220)■22:2,3,6,7,8,9,10,12,13,16,16sup■23:8■24:3,4,5,6,7,8,15,24,36,37,38,40,44,47,48■25:6,9,11,12,19■27:1^{2},5,6,8,13,15^{2},17,18,20^{2},21^{2},24,26,27,32,37,42^{2},43■28:5,9■29:5,12,13,32,33,33sup34,35■30:5,6,7,10,12,17,19,23,24■34:2,8,18,20,24,26■35:17■36:10^{2},12,17,32,33,35,38,39■37:3,34,35■38:3,4,5,11,26■42:38■43:29^{2}■5:9,28■46:10■47:29■48:2,19■49:9■50:23-EX-1:16,22■2:2,10,22■4:22,23^{2},25■6:15,25■10:2■13:8,14■20:10■21:9,31■23:12■29:30■31:2,6■32:29■33:11■35:30,34■38:21,22,23-LE-12:6■21:2■24:10^{2},11■25:49-NU-1:5,6,7,8,9,10^{2},11,12,13,14,15■2:3,5,7,10,12,14,18,20,22,25,27,29■3:24,30,32,35■4:16,28,33■7:8,12,17,18,23,24,29,30,35,36,41,42,47,48,53,54,59,60,65,66,71,72,77,78,83■10:14,15,16,18,19,20,22,23,24,25,26,27,29■11:28■13:4,5,6,7,8,9,10,11,12,13,14,15,16■14:6^{2},30^{2},38^{2}■16:1^{3},37■20:25,26,28■22:2,4,5,10,16■23:18,19■24:3,15■25:7^{2},11^{2},14■26:1,33,65^{2}■27:1^{4},4,8,18■31:6,8■32:12^{2},28,33,39,40,41■34:17,19,20,21,22,23,24,25,26,27,28■36:1,12-DE-1:31,36,38■3:14■5:14■6:2,20,21■7:3^{2},4■8:5■10:6■11:6■12:18■13:6■16:11,14■18:10■21:15,16^{2},17,18,20■23:4■28:56■31:23■32:44■34:9-JOS-1:1■2:1,23■6:6■7:1^{2},18^{2},19,24■13:22,31■14:1,6,13,14■15:6,8,13,17■17:2,3^{3},4■18:16,17■19:49,51■21:1,12■22:13,20,31,32■24:9^{2},29,33^{2}-J’G-1:13■2:8■3:9,11,15,31■4:6,12■5:1,6,12■6:11,29,30■7:14■8:13,22,23,29,31,32■9:1,5,18,26,28^{2},30,31,35,57■10:1■11:1,2,25,34■12:13,15■13:3,5,7,24■15:6(2860)■17:2,3■18:30^{2}■19:5(2860)■20:28^{2}-RU-4:13,17-1SA-1:1^{3},20,23■3:6,16■4:16,20■7:1■9:1^{2},2,3■10:2,11,21■13:16,22■14:1,3^{3},39,40,42,50,51■16:18,19,20■17:12,17,55,56,58^{2}■18:18(2860),21(2859),22(2859),23(2859),26(2859),27(2859)■19:1,2■20:27^{2},30^{2},31■22:7,8^{3},9^{2},11,12,13,14(2860),20■23:6,16■24:16■25:8,10,17,44■26:5,6,14,17,21,25■27:2■30:7-2SA-1:4,5,12,13,17■2:8^{2},10,12^{2},13,15■3:3,4^{2},14,15,23,25,28,37■4:1,2,4,8■7:14■8:3,10,12,16^{2},17^{2},18■9:3,4,5,6^{2},9,10^{2},12■10:1,2■11:21,27■12:24■13:1^{2},3,4,25,32,37^{2}■14:1,11^{2},16■15:27^{2}■16:3,5,8,9,11,19■17:25,27^{2}■18:2,12,18,19,20,22^{2},27,33^{2}■19:2,4^{2},16,18,21,24■20:1^{2},2,6,7,10,13,21,22,23,24■21:7^{3},8,12,13,14,17,19,21■23:1,9,11,18,20^{2},22,24,26,29^{2},33,34^{3},36,37-1KI-1:5,7,8,11,12,13,17,21,26,30,32,33,36,38,42,44■2:1,5^{3},8,13,22,25,29,32^{2},34,35,39,46■3:6,20,21,22^{2},23^{2},26■4:2,3,4,5^{2},6,8(1133),9(1128),10(1136),11(1125),12,13(1127),13,14,16,17,18,19■5:5,7■7:14■8:19■11:12,13,20,23,26,36,43■12:2,15,16,21,23■14:1,5,20,21,31■15:1,4,8,18^{2},24,25,27,33■16:1,3,6,7,8,13,21,22,26,28,29^{2},30,31,34sup,34■17:12,13,17,18,19,20,23■19:16^{2},19■21:22^{2}■22:8,9,11,24,26,40,41,49,50,51,52-2KI-1:17^{2}■3:1,3,11,27■4:6,16,17,28,36,37■6:28^{2},29^{3},31,32■8:1,5^{2},9,16^{2},24,25^{2},27(2860),28,29^{2}■9:2^{2},9^{2},14^{2},20,29■10:15,23,29,35■11:1,2,4,12■12:21^{3}■13:1^{2},2,3,9,10,11,24,25^{2}■14:1^{2},8^{2},9,13,16,17^{2},23^{2},24,25,27,29■15:1,5,7,8,9,10,13,14^{2},17,18,22,23,24,25,27,28,30^{3},32^{2},37,38■16:1^{2},3,5,7,20■17:1,21■18:1^{2},9,18^{2},26,37^{2}■19:2,20,37■20:1,12,21■21:6,7,18,24,26■22:3^{2},12^{2},14^{2}■23:10,15,30,34■24:6■25:22^{2},23^{4},25^{2}-1CH-1:43,44,46,49■2:18,45,50■3:2^{2},10^{3},11^{2},12^{2},13^{2},14,16,17■4:2,8,15,21,25^{2},26^{2},34,

35^{2},37^{3}■5:1,4^{2},5^{2},6,8^{2},14^{4},15■6:20^{2},21^{2},22^{2},23^{2},24^{2},26,27^{2},29^{2},30^{2},33^{2},34^{2},35^{2},36^{2},37^{2},38^{2},39^{2},40^{2},41^{2},42^{2},43^{2},44^{2},45^{2},46^{2},47^{2},50^{2},51^{2},52^{2},53,56■7:16,17^{2},20^{3},21,23,25^{2},26^{2},27,29■8:30,34,37^{2}■9:4^{4},7^{2},8^{4},11^{4},12^{5},14^{3},15^{2},16^{4},19^{2},20,21,36,40,43^{2}■10:14■11:6,12,22^{2},24,26,28,30,31,34,35^{2},37,38,39,41,42,43,45■12:1,18■15:17^{3}■16:38■17:13■18:10,12,15^{2},16^{2},17■19:1,2■20:5,6(3025),7■22:5,6,7,9,10,11,17■23:1■24:6^{2},29■26:1,6,14,24^{2},25^{3},28^{3}■27:2,5,6,7,9,16^{2},17,18,19^{2},20^{2},21^{2},22,24,25^{2},26,29,32,34■28:5,6^{2},9,11,20■29:1,19,22,26,28-**2CH**-1:1,5■2:12,14■6:9■9:29,31■10:2,15,16■11:3,17,18^{2},22■12:16■13:6^{2},7■14:1■15:1■17:1,16■18:7,8,10,23,25■19:2,11■20:14^{3},34,37■21:1,17■22:1^{2},5,6^{2},7,9,10,11■23:1^{5},3,11■24:20,22,26^{2},27■25:17^{2},18,23^{2},25^{2}■26:21,22,23■27:9■28:3,6,7,12^{4},27■29:12^{6}■30:26■31:14■32:20,32,33■33:6,7,20,25■34:8^{2},20^{2},22^{2}■35:3,4■36:1,8-**EZR**-3:2^{2},8^{2}■5:1(1247),2^{2}(1247)■6:14(1247)■7:1^{2},2^{2},3^{2},4^{2},5^{2}■8:4,5,6,7,8,9,10,11,12,18,33^{4}■10:2,6,15^{2},18-**NE**-1:1■3:2,4^{4},6^{2},8^{2},9,10^{2},11^{2},12,14,15,16,17,18,19,20,21,23^{2},24,25^{2},29^{2},30^{3},31■6:10^{2},18(2860),18^{3}■8:17■10:1,9,38■11:4^{4},5^{5},7^{4},9^{2},10,11^{4},12^{4},13^{3},14,15^{3},17^{4},22^{3},24^{2}■12:1,23,24,26^{2},35^{4},45■13:13^{2},28,28(2860)-**ES**-2:5^{2}■3:1,10■8:5■9:10,24-**JOB**-18:19(5209)■25:6■32:2,6■35:8-**PS**-2:7,12(1248)■3:t■8:4■50:20■72:1,20■80:17■86:16■89:22■116:16■144:3■146:3-**PR**-1:1,8,10,15■2:1■3:1,11,12,21■4:3,10,20■5:1,20■6:1,3,20■7:1■10:1^{2},5^{2}■13:1,24■15:20■17:2,25■19:13,18,26,27■23:15,19,26■24:13,21■27:11■28:7■29:17,21(4497)■30:1■31:2^{2}(1248)-**EC**-1:1■5:14■10:17■12:12-**IS**-1:1■2:1■7:1^{3},3,4,5,6,9,14■8:2,3,6■9:6■13:1■14:12,22(5209)■19:11^{2}■20:2■22:20■36:3^{2},22^{2}■37:2,21,38■38:1■39:1■49:15■51:12■56:2,3-**JER**-1:1,2,3^{2}■6:26(3173)■7:31,32■15:4■19:2,6■20:1■21:1^{2}■22:11,18,24■24:1■25:1,3■26:1,20,22,24■27:1,7,20■28:1,4■29:3^{2},21^{2},25■31:20■32:7,8,9,12^{2},12sup,16,35■33:21■35:1,3^{2},4^{2},6,8,14,16,19■36:1,4,8,9,10,11^{2},12^{4},14^{3},26^{3},32■37:1^{2},3^{2},13^{2}■38:1^{4},6■39:14^{2}■40:5^{2},6,7,8^{3},9^{2},11^{2},13,14^{2},15^{2},16^{2}■41:1^{3},2^{3},6^{2},7,9,10^{2},11^{2},12,13,14,15,16^{3},18^{2}■42:1^{2},8■43:2^{2},3,4,5,6^{3}■45:1^{2}■46:2■49:18,33■50:40■51:43,59^{2}-**EZE**-1:3■2:1,3,6,8■3:1,3,4,10,17,25■4:1,16■5:1■6:2■7:2■8:5,6,8,11,12,15,17■11:1^{2},2,4,13,15■12:2,3,9,18,22,27■13:2,17■14:3,13,20■15:2■16:2■17:2■18:4,10,14,19^{2},20^{2}■20:3,4,27,46■21:2,6,9,10,12,14,19,28■22:2,18,24■23:2,36■24:2,16,25■25:2■26:2■27:2■28:2,12,21■29:2,18■30:2,21■31:2■32:2,18■33:2,7,10,12,24,30■34:2■35:2■36:1,17■37:3,9,11,16■38:2,14■39:1,17■40:4■43:7,10,18■44:5,25■47:6-**DA**-3:25(1247)■5:22(1247)■7:13(1247)■8:17■9:1-**HO**-1:1^{2},3,8■11:1■13:13-**JO**-1:1-**AM**-1:1■7:14-**JON**-1:1-**MIC**-6:5■7:6-**ZEP**-1:1^{4}-**HAG**-1:1^{2},12^{2},14^{2}■2:2^{2},4,23-**ZEC**-1:1^{2},7^{2}■6:10,11,14-**MAL**-1:6■3:17■**N.T.**-all=5207&marked-**M'T**-1:1^{2},20,21,23,25■2:15■3:17■4:3,6■7:9■8:20,29■9:2(5048),6,27■10:23,37■11:19,27^{3}■12:8,23,32,40■13:37,41,55■14:33■15:22■16:13,16,27,28■17:5,9,12,15,22■18:11■19:28■20:18,28,30,31■21:9,15,28(5043),37^{2},38■22:2,42,42sup,45■23:35■24:27,30^{2},37,39,44■25:13,31■26:2,24^{2},45,63,64■27:40,43,54■28:19-**M'R**-1:1,11■2:5(5043),10,28■3:11■5:7■6:3■8:31,38■9:7,9,12,17,31■10:33,45,46,47,48■12:6^{2},35,37■13:12(5043),26,32■14:21^{2},41,61,62■15:39-**LU**-1:13,31,32,35,36,57■2:7,48(5043)■3:2,22,23■4:3,9,22,41■5:24■6:5,22■7:12,34■8:28■9:22,26,35,38,41,44,56,58■10:6,22^{3}■11:11,30■12:8,10,40,53^{2}■15:13,19,21^{2},24,25,30,31(5043)■16:25(5043)■17:22,24,26,30■18:8,31,38,39■19:9,10■20:13,41,44■21:27,36■22:22,48,69,70■24:7-**JOH**-1:18,34,42,45,49,51■3:13,14,16,17,18,35,36^{2}■4:5,46,47,50,51(3816),53■5:19^{2},20,21,22,23^{2},25,26,27■6:27,40,42,53,62,69■8:28,35,36■9:19,20,35■10:36■11:4,27■12:23,34^{2}■13:31■14:13■17:1^{2},12■19:7,26■20:31-**AC**-3:13(3816),26(3816)■4:36■7:21,56■8:37■9:20■13:21,33■16:1■23:6,16-**RO**-1:3,4,9■5:10■8:3,29,32■9:9-**1CO**-1:9■4:17(5043)■15:28-**2CO**-1:19-**GA**-1:16■2:20■4:4,6,7^{2},30^{3}-**EPH**-4:13-**PHIL**-2:22(5043)-**COL**-1:13■4:10(431)-**1TH**-1:10-**2TH**-2:3-**1TI**-1:2(5043),18(5043)-**2TI**-1:2(5043)■2:1(5043)-**TIT**-1:4(5043)-**PH'M**-10(5043)-**HEB**-1:2,5^{2},8■2:6■3:6■4:14■5:5,8■6:6■7:3,28■10:29■11:24■12:5,6,7-**JAS**-2:21-**1PE**-5:13-**2PE**-1:17-**1JO**-1:3,7■2:22,23,23sup,24■3:8,23■4:9,10,14,15■5:5,9,10^{2},11,12^{2},13^{2},20^{2}-**2JO**-3,9-**RE**-1:13■2:18■14:14■21:7

SONG-all=7892&marked-**EX**-15:1,2(2176)-**NU**-21:17-**DE**-31:19^{2},21,22,30■32:44-**J'G**-5:12-**2SA**-22:1-**1CH**-6:31■15:22^{2}(4853),27(4853)■25:6-**2CH**-29:27-**JOB**-30:9(5058)-**PS**-18:t■28:7■30:t■33:3■40:3■42:8■45:t■46:t■48:t■65:t■66:t■67:t■68:t■69:12(5058),30■75:t■76:t■77:6(5058)■83:t■87:t■88:t■92:t■96:1■98:1■108:1■118:14(2176)■120:t■121:t■122:t■123:t■124:t■125:t■126:t■127:t■128:t■129:t■130:t■131:t■132:t■133:t■134:t■137:3(1697,7892),4■144:9■149:1-**EC**-7:5-**SONG**-1:t,1-**IS**-5:1■12:2(2176)■24:9■26:1■30:29■42:10-**LA**-3:14-**EZE**-33:32■**N.T.**-all=5603-**RE**-5:9■14:3^{2}■15:3^{2}

SONGS-all=7892&marked-**GE**-31:27-**1KI**-4:32-**1CH**-25:7-**NE**-12:46-**JOB**-35:10(2158)-**PS**-32:7(7438)■119:54(2158)■137:3-**PR**-25:20-**SONG**-1:1-**IS**-23:16■24:16(2158)■35:10(7440)■38:20(5058)-**EZE**-26:13-**AM**-5:23■8:3,10■**N.T.**-**EPH**-5:19(5603)-**COL**-3:16(5603)

SON'S-all=1121&marked-**GE**-11:31■16:15■21:23(5220)■24:51■27:25,31■30:14,15^{2},16■37:32,33-**EX**-10:2-**LE**-18:10,15,17-**DE**-6:2-**J'G**-8:22-**1KI**-11:35■21:29-**PR**-30:4-**JER**-27:7

SONS-all=1121&marked-**GE**-5:4,7,10,13,16,19,22,26,30■6:2,4,10,18■7:7,13^{2}■8:16,18■9:1,8,18,19■10:1^{2},2,3,4,6,7^{2},20,25,29,31,32■11:11,13,15,17,19,21,23,25■19:12,14^{2}(2860)■23:3,11,16,20■25:3,4,6,9,10,13,16■27:29■29:34■30:20,35■31:1,17,28,55■32:22(3206)■34:5,7,13,25,27■35:5,22,23,24,25,26^{2},29■36:5,6,10,11,12,13^{2},14,15^{2},16,17^{2},18,19,20■37:2^{2},35■41:50■42:1,5,11,13,32,37■46:5,7,8,9,10,11,12^{2},13,14,15^{2},16,17^{2},18,19,21,22,23,24,25,27■48:1,5,8,9■49:1,2,33■50:12,13-**EX**-3:22■4:20■6:14,15,16,17,18,19,21,22,24■10:9■12:24■18:3,5,6■21:4■22:29■27:21■28:1^{2},4,40,41,43■29:4,8,9^{2},10,15,19,20,21^{3},24,27,32,35,44■30:19,30■31:10■32:2,26■34:16^{2},20■35:19■39:27■40:12,14,31-**LE**-1:5,7,8,11■2:2■3:2,5,8,13■6:9,14,16,20,22,25■7:10,33,34,35■8:2,6,13,14,18,22,24,30^{2},31^{2},36■9:1,9,12,18■10:1,4,6,9,12,14,16■13:2■16:1■17:2■21:1,24■22:2,18■26:29-**NU**-2:14,18,22■3:2,3,9,10,17,18,19,20,25,29,36,38,48,51■4:2^{2},4,5,15^{3},19,22,27^{2},28,29,33,34,38,41,42,45■6:23■7:7,8,9■8:13,19,22■10:8,17■13:33■16:1^{2},7,8,10,12,27■18:1^{2},2,7,8,9,11,19■21:29,35■26:8,9,12,19,20,21,23,26,28,29,30,33,35,36,37^{2},38,40,41,42,45,47,48■27:3■36:1,3,5,11,12-**DE**-1:28■2:33■4:9■11:6■12:12,31■18:5■21:5,16■23:17■28:32,41,53■31:9■32:8,19-**JOS**-7:24■15:14■17:3,6^{2}■24:32-**J'G**-1:20■3:6■8:19,30■9:2,5,18,24■10:4■11:2^{2}■12:9^{2},14■17:5,11■18:30■19:22-**RU**-1:1,2,3,5(3206),11,12■4:15-**1SA**-1:3,4,8■2:12,21,22,24,29,34■3:13■4:4,11,17■8:1,3,5,11■12:2■14:49■16:1,5,10■17:12,13^{2}■22:20■28:19■30:3,6,19■31:2^{2},6,7,8,12-**2SA**-2:18■3:2,39■4:2,5■5:13■6:3■8:18■9:10^{2},11■13:23,27,29,30,32,33,35,36■14:6,27■15:27,36■16:10■19:5,17,22■21:6,8^{2},16(3211),18(3211)■23:32-**1KI**-1:9,19,25■2:7■4:3,31■11:20■12:31■13:11,12,13,27,31■18:31■20:35■21:10-**2KI**-2:3,5,7,15■4:1,1(3206)4,5,38^{2}■5:22■6:1■9:26■10:1,2,3,6^{2},7,8■11:2■15:12■17:17■19:37■20:18■25:7-**1CH**-1:5,6,7,8,9^{2},17,19,23,28,31,32^{2},33^{2},34,35,36,37,38,39,40^{2},41^{2},42^{2}■2:1,3,4,5,6,7,8,9,16,18,23,25,27,28^{2},30,31^{2},32,33^{2},34,42^{2},43,47,50,52,54■3:1,9^{2},15,16,17,19^{2},21^{3},22^{2},23,24■4:1,4,6,7,13^{2},15^{2},16,17,18,19,20^{2},21,24,26,27,42^{2}■5:1^{2},3,4,18■6:1,2,3,16,17,18,19,22,25,26,28,29,33,44,49,50,54,57,61,62,63,66,70,71■7:1,2,3^{2},4,7,8^{2},10^{2},11,12,13^{2},14,16,17^{2},19,20,30,31,33,34,35,36,38,39■8:3,6,10,12,16,18,21,25,27,35,38^{2},39,40^{3}■9:5,6,7,30,32,41,44^{2}■10:2^{2},6,7,8,12■11:34,44,46■12:3^{2},7,14■14:3■15:5,6,7,8,9,10,17■16:42■17:11■18:17■21:20■23:6,8,9,10^{2},11,12,13^{2},14,15,16,17^{3},18,19,20,21^{2},22^{2},23,24,28,32■24:1^{2},3^{2},4^{4},5^{2},20^{3},21,22,23,24^{2},25,26^{2},27,28,30^{2},31■25:1,2^{2},3,4,5^{2},9,10,11,12,13,14,15,16,17,18,19,20,21,22,23,24,25,26,27,28,29,30,31■26:1,2,4,6,7,8^{2},9,10,11,15,19^{2},21^{2},22,29■27:32■28:1,4,5^{2}■29:24-**2CH**-5:12■11:14,21■13:5,8,9,10,21■20:14■21:2^{2},7,17^{2}■22:8,11■23:3,11■24:3,7,25,27■26:18■28:8■29:9,11,12^{2},13^{2},14^{2},21■31:18,19■32:33■34:12^{2}■35:14^{2},15■36:20-**EZR**-3:9^{3},10■6:10(1123)■7:23(1123)■8:2^{3},3^{2},4,5,6,7,8,9,10,11,12,13,14,15,18^{2},19^{2}■9:2,12^{2}■10:2,18^{2},20,21,22,25,26,27,28,29,30,31,33,34,43-**NE**-3:3■4:14■5:2,5■10:9,28,30,36■11:6,7,22■12:23,28,35■13:25^{2},28-**ES**-9:10,12,13,14,25-**JOB**-1:2,4,5,6,13,18■2:1■14:21■38:7,32■42:13,16-**PS**-4:2■31:19■33:13■42:t■44:t■45:t■46:t■47:t■48:t■49:t■57:4■58:1■77:15■84:t■85:t■87:t■88:t■89:6■106:37,38■144:12■145:12-**PR**-8:4,31-**EC**-1:13■2:3,8■3:10,18,19■8:11■9:3,12-**SONG**-2:3-**IS**-37:38■39:7■43:6■45:11■49:22■51:18^{2},20■52:14■56:5,6■57:3■60:4,9,10,14■61:5■62:5,8-**JER**-3:24■5:17■6:21■7:31■11:22■13:14■14:16■16:2,3■19:5,9■29:6^{3}■32:19,35■35:3,4,5,6,8,14,16■39:6■40:8^{2}■48:46■49:1■52:10-**LA**-4:2-**EZE**-5:10^{2}■14:16,18,22■16:20■20:31■23:4,10,25,37,47■24:21,25■40:46^{2}■44:15■46:16,18■48:11-**DA**-5:21(1123)■10:16■11:10-**HO**-1:10-**JOE**-1:12■2:28■3:8-**AM**-2:11■7:17-**MIC**-5:7-**ZEC**-9:13^{2}-**MAL**-3:3,6■**N.T.**-all=5207marked-**M'T**-20:20,21■21:28(5043)■26:37-**M'R**-3:17,28■10:35-**LU**-5:10■11:19■15:11-**JON**-1:12(5043)-**AC**-2:17■7:16,29■19:14-**RO**-8:14,19-**1CO**-4:14(5043)-**2CO**-6:18-**GA**-4:5(5206),6,22-**EPH**-3:5-**PH'P**-2:15(5043)-**HEB**-2:10■7:5■11:21■12:7,8-**1JO**-3:1(5043),2(5043)

SONS'-all=1121-**GE**-6:18■7:7■8:16,18■46:7^{2},26-**EX**-29:21,28,29■39:41-**LE**-2:3,10■7:31■8:27,30^{2}■10:13,14,15■24:9-**DE**-4:9-**1CH**-8:40-**JOB**-42:16-**EZE**-46:16,17

SOON-all=834&marked-**GE**-18:33■27:30-**EX**-2:18(4116)■32:19-**DE**-4:26(4116)-**JOS**-2:7-**J'G**-8:33-**2KI**-14:5-**JOB**-32:22(4592)-**PS**-37:2(4120)■68:31(7323)■81:14(4592)■90:10(2440)■106:13(4116)-**PR**-14:17(7116)-**IS**-66:8(1571)-**EZE**-23:16(4758)■**N.T.**-**M'T**-21:20(3916)-**M'R**-5:36(2112)■11:2(2112)-**LU**-15:30(3753)-**JOH**-16:21(3752)-**AC**-12:18(1096)-**GA**-1:6(5030)-**2TH**-2:2(5030)-**TIT**-1:7(3711)-**RE**-10:10(3753)■12:4(3752)

SOONER-**HEB**-13:19(5032)

SOOTHSAYER-**JOS**-13:22(7030)

SOOTHSAYERS-all=1505&marked-**IS**-2:6(6049)-**DA**-2:27■4:7■5:7,11-**MIC**-5:12(6049)

SOOTHSAYING-**AC**-16:16(3132)

SOP-all=5596-**JOH**-13:26^{2},27,30

SOPE-**JER**-2:22(1287)-**MAL**-3:2(1287)

SORCERER-**AC**-13:6(3097),8(3097)

SORCERERS-all=3784&marked-EX-7:11-JER-27:9(3786)-DA-2:2-MAL-3:5▪N.T.-RE-21:8(5332)▪22:15(5333)

SORCERESS-IS-57:3(6049)

SORCERIES-IS-47:9(3785),12(3785)▪N.T.-AC-8:11(3095)-RE-9:21(5331)▪18:23(5331)

SORCERY-AC-8:9(3096)

SORE-all=3966&marked-GE-19:9▪20:8▪34:25(3510)▪41:56(2388),57(2388)▪43:1(3515)▪47:4(3515),13(3515)▪50:10(3515)-EX-14:10-LE-13:42(5061),43(5061)-NU-22:3-DE-6:22(7451)▪28:35(7451),59(7451)-JOS-9:24-J'G-10:9▪15:18▪20:34(3513)▪21:2(1065,1419)-1SA-1:6(3708)▪5:7(7185)▪14:52(2389)▪17:24▪21:12▪28:15,20,21▪31:3(3513),3,4-2SA-2:17(7188)▪13:36(1419)-1KI-17:17(2389)▪18:2(2389)-2KI-3:26(2388)▪20:3(1419)-1CH-10:3(3513),4-2CH-6:28(5061),29(5061)▪21:19(7451)▪35:23-NE-2:2(7235)▪13:8-JOB-2:7(7451)▪5:18(3510)-PS-6:3,10▪38:8(5704,3966),11(5061)▪71:20(7451)▪77:2(3027)-EC-1:13(7451)▪4:8(7451)▪5:13(2470),16(2470)-IS-27:1(7186)▪38:3(1419)▪64:9,12-JER-50:12▪52:6(2388)-EZE-14:21(7451)▪27:35(8178)-DA-6:14(7690)-MIC-2:10(4834)▪N.T.-M'T-17:6(4970),15(2560)▪21:15(23)-M'R-6:51(3029)▪9:6(1630),26(4183)▪14:33(1568)-LU-2:9(3173)-AC-20:37(2425)-RE-16:2(1668)

SORELY-GE-49:23(4843)

SORER-HEB-10:29(5501)

SORES-IS-1:6(4347)-LU-16:20(1669),21(1668)-RE-16:11(1668)

SORROW-all=3015&marked-GE-3:16(6093),16(6089),17(6093)▪42:38▪44:29(7451),31-EX-15:14(2427)-LE-26:16(1727)-DE-28:65(1671)-1CH-4:9(6090)-NE-2:2(7455)-ES-9:22-JOB-3:10(5999)▪6:10(2427)▪17:7(3708)▪41:22(1670)-PS-13:2▪38:17(4341)▪39:2(3511)▪55:10(5999)▪90:10(205)▪107:39▪116:3-PR-10:10(6094),22(6089)▪15:13(6094)▪17:21(8424)▪23:29(17)-EC-1:18(4341)▪5:17(3708)▪7:3(3708)▪11:10(3708)-IS-5:30(6862)▪14:3(6090)▪17:11(3511)▪29:2(592)▪35:10▪50:11(4620)▪51:11▪65:14(3511)-JER-8:18▪20:18▪30:15(4341)▪31:12(1669),13▪45:3(4341)▪49:23(1674)▪51:29(2342)-LA-1:12(4341),18(4341)▪3:65(4044)-EZE-23:33-HO-8:10(2490)▪N.T.-all=3077&marked-LU-22:45-JOH-16:6,20,21,22-RO-9:2(3601)-2CO-2:3,7▪7:10^{2}-PH'P-2:27-1TH-4:13(3076)-RE-18:7^{2}(3997)▪21:4(3997)

SORROWED-2CO-7:9(3076),11(3076)

SORROWETH-1SA-10:2(1672)

SORROWFUL-1SA-1:15(7186)-JOB-6:7(1741)-PS-69:29(3510)-PR-14:13(3510)-JER-31:25(1669)-ZEP-3:18(3013)-ZEC-9:5(2342)▪N.T.-all=3076&marked-M'T-19:22▪26:22,37,38(4036)-M'R-14:19,34(4036)-LU-18:23(4036),24(4036)-JOH-16:20-2CO-6:10-PH'P-2:28(253)

SORROWING-LU-2:48(3600)-AC-20:38(3600)

SORROWS-all=2256&marked-EX-3:7(4341)-2SA-22:6-JOB-9:28(6094)▪21:17▪39:3-PS-16:4(6094)▪18:4,5▪32:10(4341)▪116:3▪127:2(6089)-EC-2:23(4341)-IS-13:8▪53:3(4341),4(4341)-JER-13:21▪49:24-DA-10:16(6735)-HO-13:13▪N.T.-M'T-24:8(5604)-M'R-13:8(5604)-1TI-6:10(3601)

SORRY-1SA-22:8(2470)-NE-8:10(6087)-PS-38:18(1672)-IS-51:19(5110)▪N.T.-all=3076&marked-M'T-14:9▪17:23▪18:31-M'R-6:26(4036)-2CO-2:2^{2}▪7:8^{2},9^{2}

SORT-GE-7:14(3671)-EZR-4:8(3660)-NE-6:4(1697)-EZE-39:4(3671)-DA-1:10(1524)▪N.T.-RO-15:15(3313)-1CO-3:13(3697)-3JO-6(516)

SORTS-EZE-27:24(4360)▪38:4(4358)

SOTTISH-JER-4:22(5530)

SOUGHT-all=1245,a=1875&marked-GE-43:30-EX-2:15▪4:19,24▪33:7-LE-10:16a-NU-35:23-DE-13:10-JOS-2:22-J'G-14:4▪18:1-1SA-10:21▪13:14▪14:4▪19:10▪23:14▪27:4-2SA-3:17▪4:8▪17:20▪21:2-1KI-1:2,3▪10:24▪11:40-2KI-2:17-1CH-15:13a▪26:31a-2CH-1:5a▪9:23▪14:7^{2}a▪15:4,15▪16:12a▪17:3a,4a▪22:9,9a▪25:15a,20a▪26:5^{2}a-EZR-2:62-NE-7:64▪12:27-ES-2:2,21▪3:6▪6:2▪9:2-PS-34:4a▪37:36▪77:2a▪78:34a▪86:14▪111:2a▪119:10a,94a-EC-2:3(8446)▪7:29▪12:9(2713),10-SONG-3:1^{2}▪5:6-IS-62:12a▪65:1a,1,10a-JER-8:2a▪10:21a▪26:21▪44:30▪50:20-LA-1:19-EZE-22:30▪26:21▪34:4-DA-2:13(1158)▪4:36(1158)▪6:4(1158)▪8:15-OB-6(1156)-ZEP-1:6-ZEC-6:7▪N.T.-all=2212&marked-M'T-2:20▪21:46▪26:16▪26:59-M'R-11:18▪12:12▪14:1,11,55-LU-2:44(327),48,49▪4:42▪5:18▪6:19▪11:16▪13:6▪19:3,47▪20:19▪22:2,6-JOH-5:16,18▪7:1,11,30▪10:39▪11:8,56▪19:12-AC-12:19(1934)▪17:5-RO-9:32▪10:20-1TH-2:6-2TI-1:17-HEB-8:7▪12:17(1567)

SOUL-all=5315&marked-GE-2:7▪12:13▪17:14▪19:20▪27:4,19,25,31▪34:3,8▪35:18▪42:21▪49:6-EX-12:15,19▪30:12▪31:14-LE-4:2▪5:1,2,4,15,17▪6:2▪7:18,20^{2},21^{2},25,27^{2}▪17:10,11,12,15▪19:8▪20:6^{2}▪22:3,6,11▪23:29,30^{2}▪26:11,15,30,43-NU-9:13▪11:6▪15:27,28,30^{2},31▪19:13,20,22▪21:4,5▪30:2,4^{2},5,6,7,8,10,11,12,13▪31:28-DE-4:9,29▪6:5▪10:12▪11:13,18▪12:15,20^{2},21▪13:3,6▪14:26^{2}▪26:16▪30:2,6,10-JOS-22:5-J'G-5:21▪10:16▪16:16-1SA-1:10,15,26▪2:16▪17:55▪18:1^{3},3▪20:3,4,17▪23:20▪24:11▪25:26,29^{2}▪26:21▪30:6-2SA-4:9▪5:8▪11:11▪14:19-1KI-1:29▪2:4▪8:48▪11:37▪17:21,22-2KI-2:2,4,6▪4:27,30▪23:3,25-1CH-22:19-2CH-6:38▪15:12▪34:31-JOB-3:20▪6:7▪7:11,15▪9:21▪10:1^{2}▪12:10▪14:22▪16:4▪19:2▪21:25▪23:13▪24:12▪27:2,8▪30:15(5082),16,25▪31:30▪33:18,20,22,28,30-PS-3:2▪6:3,4▪7:2,5▪11:1,5▪13:2▪16:10▪17:13▪19:7▪22:20,29▪23:3▪24:4▪25:1,13,20▪26:9▪30:3▪31:7,9▪33:19,20▪34:2,22▪35:3,4,7,9,12,13,17▪40:14▪41:4▪42:1,2,4,5,6,11▪43:5▪44:25▪49:8,15,18▪54:3,4▪55:18▪56:6,13▪57:1,4,6▪59:3▪62:1,5▪63:1,5,8,9▪66:9,16▪69:1,10,18▪70:2▪71:10,13,23▪72:14▪74:19▪77:2▪78:50▪84:2▪86:2.4^{2},13,14▪88:3,14▪89:48▪94:17,19,21▪103:1,2,22▪104:1,35▪106:15▪107:5,9^{2},18,26▪109:20,31▪116:4,7,8▪119:20,25,28,81,109,129,167,175▪120:2,6▪121:7▪123:4▪124:4,5,7▪130:5,6▪131:2▪138:3▪139:14▪141:8▪142:4,7▪143:3,6,8,11,12▪146:1-PR-2:10▪3:22▪6:30,32▪8:36▪10:3▪11:17,25▪13:2,4^{2},19,25▪15:32▪16:17,24▪18:7▪19:2,8,15,16,18▪20:2▪21:10,23▪22:5,23,25▪23:14▪24:12,14▪25:13,25▪27:7^{2}▪29:10,17,24-EC-2:24▪4:8▪6:2,3▪7:28-SONG-1:7▪3:1,2,3,4▪5:6▪6:12-IS-1:14▪3:9▪10:18▪26:8,9▪29:8^{2}▪32:6▪38:15,17▪42:1▪44:20▪51:23▪53:10,11,12▪55:2,3▪58:3,5,10^{2},11▪61:10▪66:3-JER-4:10,19,31▪5:9,29▪6:8▪9:9▪12:7▪13:17▪14:19▪18:20▪20:13▪31:12,14,25^{2}▪32:41▪38:16,17,20▪50:19▪51:6,45-LA-1:11,16▪2:12▪3:17,20,24,25,58-EZE-3:19,21▪4:14▪18:4^{3},20,27▪24:21▪33:5,9-HO-9:4-JON-2:5,7-MIC-6:7▪7:1-HAB-2:4,10-ZEC-11:8^{2}▪N.T.-all=5590-M'T-10:28^{2}▪12:18▪16:26^{2}▪22:37▪26:38-M'R-8:36,37▪12:30,33▪14:34-LU-1:46▪2:35▪10:27▪12:19,20-JOH-12:27-AC-2:27,31,43▪3:23▪4:32-RO-2:9▪13:1-1CO-15:45-2CO-1:23-1TH-5:23-HEB-4:12▪6:19▪10:38,39-JAS-5:20-1PE-2:11-2PE-2:8-3JO-2-RE-16:3▪18:14

SOUL'S-JOB-16:4(5315)

SOULS-all=5315&marked-GE-12:5▪46:15,18,22,25,26^{2},27^{2}-EX-1:5^{2}▪12:4▪30:15,16-LE-16:29,31▪17:11▪18:29▪20:25▪23:27,32-NU-16:38▪29:7▪30:9▪31:50-JOS-10:28,30,32,35,37^{2},39▪11:11▪23:14-1SA-25:29-PS-72:13▪97:10-PR-11:30▪14:25-IS-57:16(5397)-JER-2:34▪6:16▪26:19▪44:7-LA-1:19-EZE-7:19▪13:18^{3},19^{2},20^{3}▪14:14,20▪18:4▪22:25,27▪N.T.-all=5590-M'T-11:29-LU-21:19-AC-2:41▪7:14▪14:22▪15:24▪27:37-1TH-2:8-HEB-13:17-JAS-1:21-1PE-1:9,22▪2:25▪3:20▪4:19-2PE-2:14-RE-6:9▪18:13▪20:4

SOUND-all=6963&marked-EX-28:35-LE-25:9^{2}(5674)▪26:36-NU-10:7(7321)-JOS-6:5,20-2SA-5:24▪6:15▪15:10-1KI-1:40,41▪14:6▪18:41-2KI-6:32-1CH-14:15▪15:19(8085),28▪16:5(8085),42(8085)-2CH-5:13-NE-4:20-JOB-15:21▪21:12▪37:2(1899)▪39:24-PS-47:5▪77:17▪89:15(8643)▪92:3(1902)▪98:6▪119:80(8549)▪150:3(8629)-PR-2:7(8454)▪3:21(8454)▪8:14(8454)▪14:30(4832)-EC-12:4-IS-16:11(1993)-JER-4:19,21▪6:17▪8:16▪25:10▪42:14▪48:36^{2}(1993)▪50:22▪51:54-EZE-10:5▪26:13,15▪27:28▪31:16▪33:4,5-DA-3:5(7032),7(7032),10(7032),15(7032)-JOE-2:1(7321)-AM-2:2▪6:5(6310)▪N.T.-all=5456&marked-M'T-6:2(4537)▪24:31-LU-15:27(5198)-JOH-3:8-AC-2:2(2279)-RO-10:18(5353)-1CO-14:7,8▪15:52(4537)-1TI-1:10(5198)-2TI-1:7(4995),13(5198)▪4:3(5198)-TIT-1:9(5198),13(5198)▪2:1(5198),2(5198),8(5199)-HEB-12:19(2279)-RE-1:15▪8:6(4537),13(4537)▪9:9^{2}▪10:7(4537)▪18:22

SOUNDED-all=2690&marked-EX-19:19(1961)-1SA-20:12(2713)-2CH-7:6▪13:14▪23:13(8628)▪29:28-NE-4:18(8628)▪N.T.-all=4537&marked-LU-1:44(1096)-AC-27:28^{2}(1001)-1TH-1:8(1837)-RE-8:7,8,10,12▪9:1,13▪11:15

SOUNDETH-supplied

SOUNDING-1CH-15:16(8085)-2CH-5:12(2690)▪13:12(8643)-PS-150:5(8643)-IS-63:15(1995)-EZE-7:7(1906)▪N.T.-1CO-13:1(2278)

SOUNDNESS-all=4974-PS-38:3,7-IS-1:6▪N.T.-AC-3:16(3647)

SOUNDS-1CO-14:7(5353)

SOUR-all=1155&marked-IS-18:5-JER-31:29,30-EZE-18:2-HO-4:18(5493)

SOUTH-all=5045,a=8486,b=1864&marked-GE-12:9▪13:1,3▪20:1▪24:62▪28:14-EX-26:18,35a▪27:9▪36:23▪38:9-NU-2:10a▪10:6a▪13:22,29▪21:1▪33:40▪34:3^{2},4^{2}▪35:5-DE-1:7▪33:23b▪34:3-JOS-10:40▪11:2,16▪12:3a,8▪13:4a▪15:1,2,3^{2},4,7,8,19▪18:5,13,15,16,19^{2}▪19:8,34-J'G-1:9,15,16▪21:19-1SA-20:41▪23:19(3225),24(3225)▪27:10^{3}▪30:1,14^{2},27-2SA-24:7-1KI-7:25,39-1CH-9:24-2CH-4:4,10▪28:18-JOB-9:9a▪37:9(2315),17b▪39:26a-PS-75:6(4057)▪78:26a▪89:12(3225)▪107:3(3220)▪126:4-EC-1:6b▪11:3b-SONG-4:16a-IS-21:1▪30:6▪43:6a-JER-13:19▪17:26▪32:44▪33:13-EZE-20:46a,46b,46,47^{2}▪21:4▪40:2,24^{2}b,27^{2}b,28^{2}b,44b,45b▪41:11b▪42:12b,13b,18b▪46:9^{2}▪47:1,19,19a▪48:10,16,17,28,33-DA-8:9▪11:5,6,9,11,14,15,25^{2},29,40-OB-19,20-ZEC-6:6a▪7:7▪9:14a▪14:4,10▪N.T.-all=3558&marked-M'T-12:42-LU-11:31▪12:55▪13:29-AC-8:26(3314)▪27:12(3047),13▪28:13-RE-21:13

SOUTHWARD-all=5045&marked-GE-13:14-EX-26:18(8486)▪27:9(8486)▪36:23(8486)▪38:9(8486)▪40:24-NU-3:29(8486)▪13:17-DE-3:27(8486)-JOS-15:1(8486),2,21▪17:9,10▪18:13,14^{2}-1SA-14:5-1CH-26:15,17-EZE-47:19^{2}▪48:28-DA-8:4

SOW-all=2232-GE-47:23-EX-23:10-LE-19:19▪25:3,4,11,20,22▪26:16-DE-22:9-2KI-19:29-JOB-4:8▪31:8-PS-107:37▪126:5-EC-11:4,6-IS-28:24▪30:23▪32:20▪

37:30-JER-4:3■31:27■35:7-HO-2:23■10:12-MIC-6:15-ZEC-10:9■N.T.-all=4687&marked-M'T-6:26■13:3,27-M'R-4:3-LU-8:5■12:24■19:21,22-2PE-2:22(5300)

SOWED-GE-26:12(2232)-J'G-9:45(2232)■N.T.-all=4687-M'T-13:4,24,25,39■25:26-M'R-4:4-LU-8:5

SOWEDST-DE-11:10(2232)

SOWER-IS-55:10(2232)-JER-50:16(2232)■N.T.-all=4687-M'T-13:3,18-M'R-4:3,14-LU-8:5-2CO-9:10

SOWEST-all=4687-1CO-15:36,37^{2}

SOWETH-all=7971&marked-PR-6:14,19■11:18(2232)■16:28■22:8(2232)-AM-9:13(4900)■N.T.-all=4687-M'T-13:37-M'R-4:14-JOH-4:36,37-2CO-9:6^{2}-GA-6:7,8^{2}

SOWING-LE-11:37(2221)■26:5(2233)

SOWN-all=2232&marked-EX-23:16-LE-11:37-DE-21:4■22:9■29:23-J'G-6:3-PS-97:11-IS-19:7(4218)■40:24■61:11(2221)-JER-2:2■12:13-EZE-36:9-HO-8:7-NA-1:14-HAG-1:6■N.T.-all=4687-M'T-13:19■25:24-M'R-4:15^{2},16,18,20,31,32-1CO-9:11■15:42,43^{2},44-JAS-3:18

SPACE-all=3117&marked-GE-29:14■32:16(7305)-LE-25:8,30(4390)-DE-2:14-JOS-3:4(7350)-1SA-26:13(4725)-EZR-9:8(7281)-JER-28:11(5750)-EZE-40:12^{2}(1366)■N.T.-all=1909&marked-LU-22:59(1339)-AC-5:7(1292),34(1024)■15:33(5550)■19:8,10,34■20:31(4158)-RE-2:21(5550)■14:20(575)

SPAKE-all=1696,a=559,b=6032&marked-GE-8:15■9:8a■16:13■18:29■19:14■21:22a■22:7a■23:3,13■24:7,30■27:5,6a■29:9■31:11a,29a■34:3,4a■35:15■39:10,14a,17,19■41:9■42:7,14,22a,30,37a■43:3a,27a,29a■44:6■46:2a■47:5a■49:28■50:4,17,21-EX-1:15a■4:30■5:10a■6:2,9,10,12,13,27,28,29■7:7,8a,19a■8:1a,5a■12:1a■13:1■14:1■15:1a■16:9a,10,11■19:19,25a■20:1■25:1■30:11,17,22■31:1,12a■33:11■34:34■35:4a■36:5a■40:1-LE-1:1■4:1■5:14■6:1,8,19,24■7:22,28■8:1■10:3,8,12■11:1■12:1■13:1■14:1,33■15:1■16:1■17:1■18:1■19:1■20:1■21:16■22:1,17,26■23:1,9,23,26,33■24:1,13,23■25:1■27:1-NU-1:1■2:1■3:1,5,11,14,44■4:1,17,21■5:1,4,5,11■6:1,22■7:4a,89■8:1,5,23■9:1,4,9■10:1■11:25■12:1,4a■13:1■14:7a,26■15:1,17,37a■16:5,20,23,26,36,44■17:1,6,12a■18:8,20a,25■19:1■20:3a,7,12a,23a■21:5,16a■22:7■24:12■25:10,16■26:1a,3,52■27:6a,15■28:1■30:1■31:1,3,25a■32:2a,25a■33:50■34:1,16■35:1,9■36:1-DE-1:1,3,6,9a,43■2:1,2a,17■4:12,15,45■5:22,28■9:10,13a■10:4■13:2■27:9■28:68a■31:1,30■32:44,48-JOS-1:1a,12a■3:6a■4:1a,8,12,15a,21a■7:2a■9:11a,22■10:12■14:10,12■17:14,17a■20:1,2■21:2■22:8a,15,30■23:14■24:27-J'G-2:4■8:8,9a■9:3,37■15:13a■19:22a-RU-4:1-1SA-1:13■7:3a■9:9a,17a■10:16a■16:4■17:23,26a,28,30a,31■18:23,24■19:1,4■20:26■25:9,40■28:12a,17■30:6a-2SA-3:19■5:1a,6a■7:7■12:18■13:22■14:4a■17:6a■20:18a■22:1■23:2,3■24:17a-1KI-1:11a,42■2:4,27■3:22,26a■4:32,33^{2}■5:5■6:12■8:12a,15,20■12:3,7,10^{2},14,15■13:18,26,27,31a■14:18■15:29■16:12,34■17:16■20:28a■21:2,6,23■22:13,38-2KI-1:9■2:22■5:13■7:17■8:1■9:12a,36■10:10^{2},17■14:25■15:12■17:26a■18:28■21:10■22:19■24:2■25:28-1CH-15:16a■17:6■21:9,19-2CH-1:2a■6:4■10:3,7,10^{2},15■18:12,19a■30:22■32:6,16,19,24a■33:10,18■34:22■35:25a-NE-4:2a■8:1a■13:24-ES-3:4a■4:10a■8:3-JOB-2:13■3:2(6030)■19:18■32:16■35:1(6030)-PS-18:t■33:9a■39:3■78:19■99:7■105:31a,34a■106:33(981)-PR-30:1(5002)-SONG-2:10(6030)■5:6-IS-7:10■8:5,11a■20:2■65:12■66:4-JER-7:13,22■8:6■14:14■19:5■20:8■22:21■25:2■26:11a,12a,17a,18a■27:12,16■28:1a,11a■30:4■31:20■34:6■36:2■37:2■38:8■40:15a■43:2a■45:1■46:13■50:1■51:12■52:32-EZE-1:28■2:2^{2}■3:24■10:2a■11:25■24:18-DA-1:3a■2:4■3:9b,14b,19b,24b,26b,28b■4:19b,30b■5:7b,10b,13b■6:12(560),16b,20b■7:2b,11(4449),20(4449)■8:13■9:6,12■10:16-HO-12:4■13:1-JON-2:10a-HAG-1:13a-ZEC-1:21a■3:4a■4:4a,6a■6:8-MAL-3:16■N.T.-all=2980,a=2036,b=3004&marked-M'T-9:18,33■12:22■13:3,33,34^{2}■14:27■16:11a■17:5,13a■21:45b■22:1a■23:1■26:47■28:18-M'R-3:9a■4:33,34■5:35■7:35■8:32■9:18a■12:26a■14:31b,39a,43-LU-1:42(400),55,64,70■2:38,50■4:36(4814)■5:36b■6:39a■7:39a■8:4a,49■9:11,31b,34b■11:14,27b,37■12:16a■13:6b■14:3a■15:3a■18:1b,9a■19:11a■20:2a■21:5b,29a■22:47,60,65b■23:20(4377)■24:6,36,44-JOH-1:15a■2:21b■6:71b■7:13,39a,46■8:12,20,27b,30■9:22a,29■10:6a,6,41a■11:13(2046),51a,56b■12:29,36,38a,41■13:22b,24b,28a■17:1■18:9a,16a,20,32a■21:19a-AC-1:16(4277)■2:31■4:1,31■6:10■7:6,38■8:6b,26■9:29■10:7,44■11:20■13:45(483)■14:1■16:13,32■18:9a,25■19:6,9(2551)■20:38(2046)■21:40(4377)■22:2(4377),9■26:24(626)■28:19(483),21,25-1CO-13:11■14:5-2CO-7:14-HEB-1:1■4:4(2046)■7:14■12:25(5537)-2PE-1:21-RE-1:12■10:8■13:11

SPAKEST-all=1696&marked-J'G-13:11■17:2(559)-1SA-28:21-1KI-8:24,26,53-2CH-6:15-NE-9:13-PS-89:19-JER-48:27(1697)

SPAN-all=2239&marked-EX-28:16^{2}■39:9^{2}-1SA-17:4-IS-40:12-LA-2:20(2949)-EZE-43:13

SPANNED-IS-48:13(2946)

SPARE-all=2347,a=2550&marked-GE-18:24(5375),26(5375)-DE-13:8a■29:20(5545)-1SA-15:3a-NE-13:22-JOB-6:10a■16:13a■20:13a■27:22a■30:10(2820)-PS-39:13(8159)■72:13-PR-6:34a■19:18(5375)-IS-9:19a■13:18■30:14a■54:2(2820)■58:1(2820)-JER-13:14■21:7■50:14a■51:3a-EZE-5:11■7:4,9■8:18■9:5,10■24:14-JOE-2:17-JON-4:11-HAB-1:17a-MAL-3:17a■N.T.-all=5339&marked-LU-15:17(4052)-RO-11:21-1CO-7:28-2CO-1:23■13:2

SPARED-all=2550&marked-1SA-15:9,15■24:10(2347)-2SA-12:4■21:7-2KI-5:20(2820)-PS-78:50(2820)-EZE-20:17(2347)■N.T.-all=5339-RO-8:32■11:21-2PE-2:4,5

SPARETH-all=2820&marked-PR-13:24■17:27■21:26-MAL-3:17(2550)

SPARING-AC-20:29(5339)

SPARINGLY-2CO-9:6(5340)

SPARK-JOB-18:5(7632)-IS-1:31(5213)

SPARKLED-EZE-1:7(5340)

SPARKS-JOB-5:7(1121,7565)■41:19(3590)-IS-50:11^{2}(2131)

SPARROW-PS-84:3(6833)■102:7(6833)

SPARROWS-all=4765-M'T-10:29,31-LU-12:6,7

SPAT-JOH-9:6(4429)

SPEAK-all=1696,a=559&marked-GE-18:27,30,31,32■24:33,50■27:6■31:24,29■32:4a,19■37:4■44:16,18■50:4-EX-4:14,15■5:23■6:11,29■7:2^{2},9■11:2■12:3■14:2,15■16:12■19:6,9■20:19^{2}■23:2(6030),22■25:2■28:3■29:42■30:31■31:13■32:12a■34:34,35-LE-1:2■4:2■6:25■7:23,29■9:3■11:2■12:2■15:2■16:2■17:2■18:2■19:2■21:1a,17■22:2,18■23:2,10,24,34■24:15■25:2■27:2-NU-5:6,12■6:2,23■7:89■8:2■9:10■12:6,8^{2}■14:15a■15:2,18,38■16:24,37a■17:2■18:26■19:2■20:8■22:8,35,38■23:5,12■24:13■27:7,8■33:51■35:10-DE-3:26■5:1,27^{2},31■9:4a■18:18,19,20^{2}■20:2,5,8■25:8■26:5(6030)■27:14(6030)■31:28■32:1-JOS-4:10■20:2■22:24a-J'G-5:10(7878)■6:39■9:2■19:3,30■21:13-1SA-3:9,10■25:17,24-2SA-3:19,27■7:17■13:13■14:3,12,13,15^{2},18■17:6■19:7,10(2790),11■20:16,18-1KI-2:17a,18,19■12:7,10a,23a■21:19^{2}■22:13,14,24-2KI-18:19a,26,27■19:10a-1CH-17:15-2CH-10:7■11:3a■18:12,13,23■32:17a-NE-13:24-ES-5:14a■6:4a-JOB-7:11■8:2(4448)■9:35■10:1■11:5■12:8(7878)■13:3,7,13,22■16:4,6■18:2■21:3■27:4■32:7,20■33:31,32■34:33■36:2(4405)■37:20,20a■41:3■42:4-PS-2:5■5:6■12:2^{2}■17:10■28:3■29:9a■31:18■35:20,28(1897)■38:12■40:5■41:5a■45:1a■49:3■50:7■52:3■58:1■59:12(5608)■63:11■69:12(7878)■71:10a■73:8^{2},15(5608)■75:5■77:4■85:8^{2}■94:4■109:20■115:5,7(1897)■119:23,46,172(6030)■120:7■127:5■135:16■139:20a■145:5(7878),6a,11a,21-PR-8:6,7(1897)■23:9,16-EC-3:7-SONG-7:9(1680)-IS-8:10,20a■14:10(6030)■19:18■28:11■29:4■30:10■32:4,6■36:11^{2},12■37:10a■40:2■41:1■45:19■50:4(5790)■52:6■56:3a■59:4■63:1-JER-1:6,7,17■5:5,14■6:10■7:27■9:5^{2},22■10:5■11:2■12:6■13:12a■18:7,9,11a,20■20:9■22:1■23:16,28■26:2^{2},8,15■27:9a,14a■28:7■29:24a■32:4■34:2a,3■35:2■38:20■39:16a-EZE-2:1,7■3:1,4,10,11,27■11:5a■12:25^{2}■14:4■17:2(4911)■20:3,27,49(4911)■24:21a,27■29:3■31:2a■32:21■33:2,8,10^{2}a,24a,30■37:18a■39:17a-DA-2:9(560)■3:29(560)■7:25(4449)■10:11,19■11:27,36-HO-2:14-HAB-2:3(6315)■3:13-HAG-2:2a,21a-ZEC-2:4■6:12a■7:3a,5a■8:16■9:10■N.T.-all=2980,a=3004marked-M'T-8:8(2036)■10:19^{2},20,27(2036)■12:34,36,46,47■13:13■15:31-M'R-1:34■2:7■7:37■9:39(2551)■12:1a■13:11^{3}■14:71a■16:17-LU-1:19,20,22■4:41■6:26(2036)■7:15,24a■11:53(658)■12:10(2046),13(2036)■20:9a-JOH-1:37■3:11■4:26■6:63■7:17■8:26a,28,38■9:21■12:49,50^{2}■13:18a■14:10^{2}■16:13^{2},25■17:13-AC-2:4,6,7,11,29(2036)■4:17,18(5350),20,29■5:20,40■6:11,13■10:32,46■11:15■14:9■18:9■21:37(2036),37(1097),39■23:5(2046)■24:10a■26:1a,25(669),26■28:20(4354)-RO-3:5a■6:19a■7:1■11:13a■15:18-1CO-1:10a■2:6,7,13■3:1■6:5a■7:6a,12a,35a■10:15a■12:30■13:1■14:6,9,18,19,21,23,27,28,29,34,35,39■15:34a-2CO-2:17■4:13■6:13a■7:3a■8:8a■11:17,21^{2}a,23■12:19-GA-3:15a-EPH-4:25■5:12a,32a■6:20sup,20-PH'P-1:14■4:11a-COL-4:3,4-1TH-1:8■2:2,4,16-1TI-2:7a-TIT-2:1,15■3:2(987)-HEB-2:5■6:9■9:5a-JAS-1:19■2:12■4:11(2635)-1PE-2:12(2635)■3:10,16(2635)■4:11^{2}-2PE-2:10(987),12(987),18(5350)-1JO-4:5-2JO-12-3JO-14-JUDE-8(987),10(987)-RE-2:24a■13:15

SPEAKER-PS-140:11(376,3956)■N.T.-AC-14:12(3056)

SPEAKEST-all=1696-1SA-9:21-2SA-19:29-2KI-6:12-JOB-2:10-PS-50:20■51:4-IS-40:27-JER-40:16■43:2-EZE-3:18-ZEC-13:3■N.T.-all=2980&marked-M'T-13:10-LU-12:41(3004)-JOH-16:29,29(3004)■19:10-AC-17:19

SPEAKETH-all=1696&marked-GE-45:12-EX-33:11-NU-23:26-DE-18:22-1KI-20:5(559)-JOB-2:10■17:5(5046)■33:14-PS-12:3■15:2■37:30(1897)■41:6■144:8,11-PR-2:12■6:13(4448),19(6315)■12:17(6315),18(981)■14:25(6315)■16:13■19:5(6315),9(6315)■21:28■26:25(6963)-IS-9:17■32:7■33:15-JER-9:8^{2}■10:1■28:2(559)■29:25(559)■30:2(559)-EZE-10:5-AM-5:10-HAG-1:2(559)-ZEC-6:12(559)■7:9(559)■N.T.-all=2980&marked-M'T-10:20■12:32^{2}(2036),34-LU-5:21■6:45-JOH-3:31,34■7:18,26■8:44■19:12(483)-AC-2:25(3004)■8:34(3004)-RO-10:6(3004)-1CO-14:2^{3},3,4,5,11^{2},13-1TI-4:1(3004)-HEB-11:4■12:5(1256),24,25^{2}-JAS-4:11^{2}(2635)-JUDE-16

SPEAKING-all=1696&marked-GE-24:15,45-EX-34:33-NU-7:89■16:31-DE-4:33■5:26■11:19■20:9■32:45-J'G-15:17-RU-1:18-1SA-18:1■

24:16-**2SA**-13:36-**ES**-10:3-**JOB**-1:16, 17,18■4:2(4405)■32:15(4405)-**PS**-34:13■ 58:3-**IS**-58:9,13■59:13■65:24-**JER**-7:13■25:3■26:7,8■35:14■38:4,27(2790)■ 43:1-**EZE**-43:6-**DA**-7:8(4449)■8:13,18■ 9:20,21■**N.T.**-all=2980&marked-**M'T**-6:7(4180)-**LU**-5:4-**AC**-1:3(3004)■7:44■ 13:43(4354)■20:30■26:14-**1CO**-12:3■ 14:6-**2CO**-13:3-**EPH**-4:15(226),31(988)■ 5:19-**1TI**-4:2(5573)■5:13-**1PE**-4:4(987) -**2PE**-2:16(5350)■3:16-**RE**-13:5

SPEAKINGS-**1PE**-2:1(2636)

SPEAR-all=2595&marked-**JOS**-8:18^{2} (3591),26(3591)-**J'G**-5:8(7420)-**1SA**-13:22■17:7,45,47■21:8■22:6■26:7,8,11, 12,16,22-**2SA**-1:6■2:23^{2}■21:16(7013), 19■23:7,18,21^{3}-**1CH**-11:11,20,23^{3}■ 12:24(7420),34■20:5-**2CH**-25:5(7420) -**JOB**-39:23■41:26,29(3591)-**PS**-35:3■ 46:9-**JER**-6:23(3591)-**NA**-3:3-**HAB**-3:11■**N.T.**-**JOH**-19:34(3057)

SPEARMEN-**PS**-68:30(7070)■**N.T.** -**AC**-23:23(1187)

SPEAR'S-**1SA**-17:7(2595)

SPEARS-all=7420&marked-**1SA**-13:19(2595)-**2KI**-11:10(2595)-**2CH**-11:12■14:8■23:9(2595)■26:14-**NE**-4:13,16,21-**JOB**-41:7(6767)-**PS**-57:4 (2595)-**IS**-2:4(2595)-**JER**-46:4-**EZE**-39:9-**JOE**-3:10-**MIC**-4:3(2595)

SPECIAL-**DE**-7:6-(5459)■**N.T.** -**AC**-19:11(3756,3858,5177)

SPECIALLY-all=3122-**AC**-25:26 -**1TI**-4:10■5:8-**TIT**-1:10-**PH'M**-16

SPECKLED-all=5348&marked-**GE**-30:32^{2},33,35,39■31:8^{2},10,12-**JER**-12:9 (6641)-**ZEC**-1:8(8320)

SPECTACLE-**1CO**-4:9(2302)

SPED-**J'G**-5:30(4672)

SPEECH-all=565&marked-**GE**-4:23■11:1(1697),7(8193)-**EX**-4:10(6310) -**DE**-22:14(1697),17(1697)■32:2-**2SA**-14:20(1697)■19:11(1697)-**1KI**-3:10 (1697)-**2CH**-32:18(3066)-**NE**-13:24 (3066)-**JOB**-12:20(8193)■13:17(4405)■ 21:2(4405)■24:25(4405)■29:22(4405) -**PS**-17:6■19:2(562),3(562)-**PR**-7:21 (3948)■17:7(8193)-**SONG**-4:3(4057) -**IS**-28:23■29:4^{2}■32:9■33:19(8193) -**JER**-31:23(1697)-**EZE**-1:24(1999)■3:5 (8193),6(8193)-**HAB**-3:2(8088)■**N.T.**-all=3056&marked-**M'T**-26:73(2981) -**M'R**-7:32(3424)■14:70(2981)-**JOH**-8:43(2981)-**AC**-14:11(3072)■20:7-**1CO**-2:1,4■4:19-**2CO**-10:10■11:6-**COL**-4:6 -**TIT**-2:8

SPEECHES-**NU**-12:8(2420)-**JOB**-6:26(561)■15:3(4405)■32:14(561)■33:1 (4405)■**N.T.**-**RO**-16:18(2129)

SPEECHLESS-**M'T**-22:12(5392) -**LU**-1:22(2974)-**AC**-9:7(1769)

SPEED-**GE**-24:12(7136)-**1SA**-20:38 (4120)-**2SA**-15:14(4116)-**1KI**-12:18(553) -**2CH**-10:18(553)-**EZR**-6:12(629)-**IS**-5:19(4116),26(4120)■**N.T.**-**AC**-17:15 (5613,5033)-**2JO**-10(5463),11(5463)

SPEEDILY-all=4118&marked-**GE**-44:11(4116)-**1SA**-27:1(4422)-**2SA**-17:16 (5674)-**EZR**-6:13(629)■7:17(629),21 (629),26(629)-**ES**-2:9(926)-**PS**-31:2 (4120)■69:17■79:8■102:2■143:7-**EC**-8:11(4120)-**IS**-58:8(4120)-**JOE**-3:4 (4120)-**ZEC**-8:21(1980)■**N.T.**-**LU**-18:8(1722,5034)

SPEEDY-**ZEP**-1:18(926)

SPEND-all=3615&marked-**DE**-32:23-**JOB**-21:13(1086,3615)■36:11 -**PS**-90:9-**IS**-55:2(8254)■**N.T.**-**AC**-20:16 (5551)-**2CO**-12:15(1159)

SPENDEST-**LU**-10:35(4325)

SPENDETH-**PR**-21:20(1104)■29:3 (6)-**EC**-6:12(6213)

SPENT-all=3615&marked-**GE**-21:15■ 47:18(8552)-**LE**-26:20(8552)-**J'G**-19:11 (7286)-**1SA**-9:7(235)-**JOB**-7:6-**PS**-31:10 -**IS**-49:4-**JER**-37:21(8552)■**N.T.** -**M'R**-5:26(1159)-**LU**-8:43(4321)■15:14 (1159)■24:29(2827)-**AC**-17:21(2119)■ 18:23(4160)■27:9(1230)-**RO**-13:12 (4298)-**2CO**-12:15(1550)

SPEWING-**HAB**-2:16(7022)

SPICE-**EX**-35:28(1314)-**1KI**-10:15 (7402)-**2CH**-9:9(1314)-**SONG**-5:1(1313) -**EZE**-24:10(7543)

SPICED-**SONG**-8:2(7544)

SPICERY-**GE**-37:25(5219)

SPICES-all=1314&marked-**GE**-43:11 (5219)-**EX**-25:6■30:23,34^{2}(5561)■35:8■ 37:29(5561)-**1KI**-10:2,10^{2},25-**2KI**-20:13 -**1CH**-9:29,30-**2CH**-9:1,9,24■32:27 -**SONG**-4:10,14,16■5:13■6:2■8:14 -**IS**-39:2-**EZE**-27:22■**N.T.**-all=759 -**M'R**-16:1-**LU**-23:56■24:1-**JOH**-19:40

SPIDER-**PR**-30:28(8079)

SPIDER'S-**JOB**-8:14(5908)-**IS**-59:5(5908)

SPIED-all=7200&marked-**EX**-2:11 -**JOS**-6:22(7270)-**2KI**-9:17■13:21■ 23:16,24

SPIES-all=7270&marked-**GE**-42:9, 11,14,16,30,31,34-**NU**-21:1(871)-**JOS**-6:23 -**J'G**-1:24(8104)-**1SA**-26:4-**2SA**-15:10■ **N.T.**-**LU**-20:20(1455)-**HEB**-11:31(2685)

SPIKENARD-all=5373-**SONG**-1:12■4:13,14■**N.T.**-**M'R**-14:3(3487, 4101)-**JOH**-12:3(3487,4101)

SPILLED-**GE**-38:9(7843)■**N.T.** -**M'R**-2:22(1632)-**LU**-5:37(1632)

SPILT-**2SA**-14:14(5064)

SPIN-**EX**-35:25(2901)■**N.T.**-**M'T**-6:28(3514)-**LU**-12:27(3514)

SPINDLE-**PR**-31:19(3601)

SPIRIT-all=7307&marked-**GE**-1:2■ 6:3■41:8,38■45:27-**EX**-6:9■28:3■31:3■ 35:21,31-**LE**-20:27(178)-**NU**-5:14^{2},30■ 11:17,25^{2},26,29■14:24■24:2■27:18-**DE**-2:30■34:9-**JOS**-5:1-**J'G**-3:10■6:34■ 9:23■11:29■13:25■14:6,19■15:14,19 -**1SA**-1:15■10:6,10■11:6■16:13,14^{2},15, 16,23^{2}■18:10■19:9,20,23■28:7^{2}(178), 8(178)■30:12-**2SA**-23:2-**1KI**-10:5■ 18:12■21:5■22:21,22,23,24-**2KI**-2:9, 15,16-**1CH**-5:26^{2}■10:13(178)■12:18■ 28:12-**2CH**-9:4■15:1■18:20,21,22,23■ 20:14■21:16■24:20■33:6(178)■36:22 -**EZR**-1:1,5-**NE**-9:20,30-**JOB**-4:15■ 6:4■7:11■10:12■15:13■20:3■21:4■26:4 (5397),13■27:3■32:8,18■33:4■34:14 -**PS**-31:5■32:2■34:18■51:10,11,12,17■ 76:12■77:3,6■78:8■104:30■106:33■139:7■ 142:3■143:4,7,10-**PR**-1:23■11:13■14:29■ 15:4,13■16:18,19,32■17:22,27■18:14^{2}■ 20:27(5397)■25:28■29:23-**EC**-1:14,17■ 2:11,17,26■3:21^{2}■4:4,6,16■6:9■7:8^{2},9■ 8:8■10:4■11:5■12:7-**IS**-4:4^{2}■11:2^{4}■ 19:3,14■26:9■28:6■29:4(178),10,24■ 30:1■31:3■32:15■34:16■38:16■40:7, 13■42:1,5■44:3■48:16■54:6■57:15^{2}, 16■59:19,21■61:1,3■63:10,11,14■65:14■ 66:2-**JER**-51:11-**EZE**-1:12■1:20^{3},21■ 2:2■3:12,14^{2},24■8:3■10:17■11:1,5,19, 24^{2}■13:3■18:31■21:7■36:26,27■37:1, 14■39:29■43:5-**DA**-2:1,3■4:8(7308),9 (7308),18(7308)■5:11(7308),12(7308), 14(7308)■6:3(7308)■7:15(7308)-**HO**-4:12■5:4-**JOE**-2:28,29-**MIC**-2:7,11■3:8 -**HAG**-1:14^{3}■2:5-**ZEC**-4:6■6:8■7:12■12:1, 10■13:2-**MAL**-2:15^{2},16■**N.T.**-all=4151 &marked-**M'T**-3:16■4:1■5:3■10:20■ 12:18,28,43■14:26(5326)■22:43■26:41 -**M'R**-1:10,12,23,26■2:8■3:30■5:2,8■6:49 (5326)■7:25■8:12■9:17,20,25^{2}■14:38 -**LU**-1:17,47,80■2:27,40■4:1,14,18,33■ 8:29,55■9:39,42,55■10:21■11:13,24■13:11■ 23:46■24:37,39-**JOH**-1:32,33■3:5,6,8,34■ 4:23,24^{2}■6:63^{2}■7:39■11:33■13:21■14:17■ 15:26■16:13-**AC**-2:4,17,18■5:9■6:10■ 7:59■8:29,39■10:19■11:12,28■16:7,16, 18■17:16■18:5,25■19:15,16,21■20:22■ 21:4■23:8,9-**RO**-1:4,9■2:29■7:6■8:1,2,4, 5,9^{3},10,11^{2},13,14,15^{2},16^{2},23,26^{2},27■11:8■ 12:11■15:19,30-**1CO**-2:4,10^{2},11^{2},12^{2},14■ 3:16■4:21■5:3,4,5■6:11,17,20■7:34,40■ 12:3,4,7,8^{2},9^{2},11,13^{2}■14:2,14,15^{2},16■ 15:45■16:18-**2CO**-1:22■2:13■3:3,6^{2},8, 17^{2},18■4:13■5:5■7:1,13■11:4■12:18 -**GA**-3:2,3,5,14■4:6,29■5:5,16,17^{2},18,22, 25^{2}■6:1,8,18-**EPH**-1:13,17■2:2,18, 22■3:5,16■4:3,4,23,30■5:9,18■6:17,18 -**PH'P**-1:19,27■2:1■3:3-**COL**-1:8■2:5 -**1TH**-4:8■5:19,23-**2TH**-2:2,8,13-**1TI**-3:16■4:1,12-**2TI**-1:7■4:22-**PH'M**-25 -**HEB**-4:12■9:14■10:29-**JAS**-2:26■4:5 -**1PE**-1:2,11,22■3:4,18■4:6,14-**1JO**-3:24■ 4:1,2^{2},3,3sup,6^{2},13■5:6^{2},8-**JUDE**-19-**RE**-1:10■2:7,11,17,29■3:6,13,22■4:2■11:11■ 14:13■17:3■18:2■19:10■21:10■22:17

SPIRITS-all=178&marked-**LE**-19:31■20:6-**NU**-16:22(7307)■27:16(7307) -**DE**-18:11-**1SA**-28:3,9-**2KI**-21:6■23:24 -**PS**-104:4(7307)-**PR**-16:2(7307)-**IS**-8:19■ 19:3-**ZEC**-6:5(7307)■**N.T.**-all=4151 -**M'T**-8:16■10:1■12:45-**M'R**-1:27■3:11■ 5:13■6:7-**LU**-4:36■6:18■7:21■8:2■ 10:20■11:26-**AC**-5:16■8:7■19:12,13 -**1CO**-12:10■14:32-**1TI**-4:1-**HEB**-1:7, 14■12:9,23-**1PE**-3:19-**1JO**-4:1-**RE**-1:4■ 3:1■4:5■5:6■16:13,14

SPIRITUAL-**HO**-9:7(7307)■**N.T.**-all=4152&marked-**RO**-1:11■7:14■15:27 -**1CO**-2:13,15■3:1■9:11■10:3,4^{2}■12:1■14:1, 12(4151),37■15:44^{2},46^{2}-**GA**-6:1-**EPH**-1:3■5:19■6:12-**COL**-1:9■3:16-**1PE**-2:5^{2}

SPIRITUALLY-**RO**-8:6(3588,4151) -**1CO**-2:14(4153)-**RE**-11:8(4153)

SPIT-**LE**-15:8(7556)-**NU**-12:14(3417) -**DE**-25:9(3417)-**JOB**-30:10(7536)■**N.T.**-all=1716&marked-**M'T**-26:67■27:30 -**M'R**-7:33(4429)■8:23(4429)■10:34■ 14:65■15:19

SPITE-**PS**-10:14(3708)

SPITEFULLY-**M'T**-22:6(5195)-**LU**-18:32(5195)

SPITTED-**LU**-18:32(1716)

SPITTING-**IS**-50:6(7536)

SPITTLE-**1SA**-21:13(7388)-**JOB**-7:19(7536)■**N.T.**-**JOH**-9:6(4427)

SPOIL-all=7998&marked-**GE**-49:27 -**EX**-3:22(5337)■15:9-**NU**-31:9(962),11, 12,53(962)-**DE**-2:35■3:7■13:16^{2}■20:14^{2} -**JOS**-8:2,27■11:14■22:8-**J'G**-5:30■14:19 (2488)-**1SA**-14:30,32,36(962)■15:19, 21■30:16,19,20,22,26^{2}-**2SA**-3:22■8:12■ 12:30■23:10(6584)-**2KI**-3:23■21:14 (4933)-**1CH**-20:2-**2CH**-14:13,14(961)■ 15:11■20:25^{2}■24:23■25:13(961)-**2CH**-28:8^{2},14(961),15-**EZR**-9:7(961)-**ES**-3:13■8:11■9:10(961)-**JOB**-29:17(2964) -**PS**-44:10(8154)■68:12■89:41(8155)■ 109:11(962)■119:162-**PR**-1:13■16:19■ 22:23(6906)■24:15(7703)■31:11-**SONG**-2:15(2254)-**IS**-3:14(1500)■8:4■9:3■ 10:6■11:14(962)■17:14(8154)■33:1 (7703),4,23■42:22(4933),24(4882)■53:12 -**JER**-5:6(7703)■6:7(7701)■15:13(957)■ 17:3(957)■20:5(962),8(7701)■30:16(7701), 16(4933)■47:4^{2}(7703)■49:28(7703),32■ 50:10^{2}-**EZE**-7:21■14:15(7921)■25:7 (957)■26:5(957),12(7997)■29:19(7997)■ 32:12(7703)■38:12,13^{2}■39:10(7997)■ 45:9(7701)-**DA**-11:24,33(961)-**HO**-10:2 (7703)■13:15(8154)-**NA**-2:9(962)-**HAB**-2:8(7997),17(7701)-**ZEP**-2:9(962)-**ZEC**-2:9■14:1■**N.T.**-all=1283&marked-**M'T**-12:29^{2}-**M'R**-3:27^{2}-**COL**-2:8(4812)

SPOILED-all=7703&marked-**GE**-34:27(962),29(962)-**EX**-12:36(5337) -**DE**-28:29(1497)-**J'G**-2:14(8155),16 (8154)-**1SA**-14:48(8154)■17:53(8155) -**2KI**-7:16(962)-**2CH**-14:14(962)-**JOB**-12:17(7758),19(7758)-**PS**-76:5(7997) -**PR**-22:23(6906)-**IS**-13:16(8155)■18:2 (958),7(958)■24:3(962)■33:1^{2}■42:22 (8154)-**JER**-2:14(957)■4:13,20^{2},30■9:19■ 10:20■21:12(1497)■22:3(1497)■25:36■ 48:1,15,20■49:3,10■51:55-**EZE**-18:7 (1497),12(1497),18(1497)■23:46(957)■ 39:10(7997)-**HO**-10:14,14(7701)-**AM**-3:11(962)■5:9^{2}(7701)-**MIC**-2:4-**HAB**-2:8(7997)-**ZEC**-2:8(7997)■11:2,3^{2}■ **N.T.**-**COL**-2:15(554)

SPOILER-all=7703&marked-**IS**-16:4,4(7701)■21:2-**JER**-6:26■15:8■48:8, 18,32■51:56

SPOILERS-all=7703&marked-J'G-2:14(8154)-1SA-13:17(7843)■14:15(7843)-2KI-17:20(8154)-JER-12:12■51:48,53

SPOILEST-IS-33:1(7703)

SPOILETH-PS-35:10(1497)-IS-21:2(7703)-HO-7:1(6584)-NA-3:16(6584)

SPOILING-all=7701&marked-PS-35:12(7908)-IS-22:4-JER-48:3-HAB-1:3■N.T.-HEB-10:34(724)

SPOILS-JOS-7:21(7998)-1CH-26:27(7998)-IS-25:11(698)■N.T.-LU-11:22(4661)-HEB-7:4(205)

SPOKEN-all=1696,a=559&marked-GE-12:4■18:19■19:21■21:1,2■24:51■28:15■41:28■44:2-EX-4:10,30■9:12,35■10:29■19:8■32:13a,34■33:17■34:32-LE-10:11-NU-1:48■10:29■12:2^{2}■14:7,28■15:22■21:7■23:2,17,19-DE-1:14■5:28^{2}■6:19■13:5■18:17sup,17,21,22^{2}■26:19-JOS-6:8a■21:45-RU-2:13-1SA-1:16■3:12■20:23■25:30-2SA-2:27■3:18a■6:22a■7:19,25,29■14:19■17:6-1KI-2:23■12:9■13:3,11■14:11■18:24(1697)■21:4■22:23,28-2KI-1:17■4:13■7:18■19:21■20:9,19-1CH-17:17,23-2CH-2:15a■6:10,17■10:9■18:22,27-EZR-8:22a-NE-2:18a-ES-6:10■7:9-JOB-21:3■32:4(1697)■33:2,8a■34:35■40:5■42:7^{2},8-PS-50:1■60:6■62:11■66:14■87:3■108:7■109:2■116:10-PR-25:11-EC-7:21-SONG-8:8-IS-1:2,20■16:13,14■21:17■22:25■23:4a■24:3■25:8■31:4a■37:22■38:7,15a■39:8■40:5■45:19■46:11■48:15,16■58:14■59:3-JER-3:5■4:28■9:12■13:15■23:21,35,37■25:3■26:16■27:13■29:23■30:2■32:24■33:24■35:14,17■36:2,4■38:1■44:16,25■48:8a■51:62-EZE-5:13,15,17■12:28■13:7,7a,8■14:9■17:21,24■21:32■22:14,28■23:34■24:14■26:5,14■28:10■30:12■34:24■35:12a■36:5,6,36■37:14■38:17,19■39:5,8-DA-4:31(560)■10:11,15,19-HO-7:13■10:4■12:10-JOE-3:8-AM-3:1,8■5:14a-OB-12(6310),18-MIC-4:4■6:12-ZEC-10:2-MAL-3:13■N.T.-all=2980,a=4483,b=2036-M'T-1:22a■2:15a,17a,23a■3:3a■4:14a■8:17a■12:17a■13:35a■21:4a■22:31a■24:15a■26:65(987)■27:9a,35a-M'R-1:42b■5:36■12:12b■13:14a■14:9■16:19-LU-2:33,34(483)■12:3b,3■18:34(3004)■19:28b■20:19b■24:25,40b-JOH-4:50b■9:6b■11:13(3004),43b■12:48,49■14:25■15:3,11,22■16:1,25,33■18:1b,22b,23■20:18b■21:19b-AC-1:9b■2:16(2046)■3:21,24■8:24(2046)■9:27■13:40(2046),45(3004),46■16:14■19:36(369),41b■20:36b■23:9■26:30b■27:11(3004),35b■28:22(483),24(3004),25b-RO-1:8(2605)■4:18(2046)■14:16(987)■15:21(312)-1CO-10:30(987)■14:9-2CO-4:13-HEB-1:2■2:2,3■3:5■4:8■7:13(3004)■8:1(3004)■9:19■12:19(4369)■13:7-JAS-5:10-1PE-4:14(987)-2PE-2:2(987)■3:2(4280)-JUDE-15,17(4280)

SPOKES-1KI-7:33(2840)

SPOKESMAN-EX-4:16(1696)

SPOON-all=3709-NU-7:14,20,26,32,38,44,50,56,62,68,74,80

SPOONS-all=3709-EX-25:29■37:16-NU-4:7■7:84,86^{2}-1KI-7:50-2KI-25:14-2CH-4:22■24:14-JER-52:18,19

SPORT-all=7832&marked-J'G-16:25,25(6711),27-PR-10:23(7814)■26:19-IS-57:4(6026)

SPORTING-GE-26:8(6711)■N.T.-2PE-2:13(1792)

SPOT-all=934&marked-LE-13:2,4,19,23,24,25,26,28,39(933)■14:56-NU-19:2(8549)■28:3(8549),9(8549),11(8549)■29:17(8549),26(8549)-DE-32:5(3971)-JOB-11:15(3971)-SONG-4:7(3971)■N.T.-all=784&marked-EPH-5:27(4696)-1TI-6:14-HEB-9:14(299)-1PE-1:19-2PE-3:14

SPOTS-LE-13:38(934),39(934)-JER-13:23(2272)■N.T.-2PE-2:13(4696)-JUDE-12(4694)

SPOTTED-all=2921-GE-30:32^{2},33,35^{2},39■N.T.-JUDE-23(4695)

SPOUSE-all=3618-SONG-4:8,9,10,11,12■5:1

SPOUSES-HO-4:13(3618),14(3618)

SPRANG-M'R-4:5(1816),8(305)-LU-8:7(4855),8(5453)-AC-16:29(1530)-HEB-7:14(393)■11:12(1080)

SPREAD-all=6566,a=6581&marked-GE-10:18(6327)■28:14(6555)■33:19(5186)■35:21(5186)-EX-9:29,33■37:9■40:19-LE-13:5a,6a,7a,22a,23a,27a,28a,32a,34a,35a,36a,51a,53a,55a■14:39a,44a,48a-NU-4:6,7,8,11,13,14■11:32(7849)■24:6(5186)-DE-22:17-J'G-8:25■15:9(5203)-RU-3:9-1SA-30:16(5203)-2SA-5:18(5203),22(5203)■16:22(5186)■17:19,19(7849)■21:10(5186)■22:43(7554)-1KI-6:32(7286)■8:7,22,38,54-2KI-8:15■19:14-1CH-14:9(6584),13(6584)■28:18-2CH-3:13■5:8■6:12,13,29■26:8(3212),15(3318)-EZR-9:5-JOB-29:19(6605)■37:18(7554)-PS-105:39■140:5-PR-1:17(2219)-IS-1:15■14:11(3331)■19:8■25:7(5259),11■33:23■37:14■42:5(7554)■58:5(3331)■65:2-JER-8:2(7849)■10:9(7554)■43:10(5186)■48:40■49:22-LA-1:10,13-EZE-2:10■12:13■16:8■17:20■19:8■26:14(4894)■32:3■47:10(4894)-HO-5:1■7:12■14:6(3212)-JOE-2:2-HAB-1:8(6335)-ZEC-1:17(6327)■2:6-MAL-2:3(2219)■N.T.-M'T-9:31(1310)■21:8(4766)-M'R-1:28(1831)■6:14(5318)■11:8(4766)-LU-19:36(5291)-AC-4:17(1268)-1TH-1:18(1831)

SPREADEST-EZE-27:7(4666)

SPREADETH-all=6566&marked-LE-13:8(6581)-DE-32:11-JOB-9:8(5186)■26:9(6576)■36:30■41:30(7502)-PR-29:5-IS-25:11■40:19(7554),22(4969)■44:24(7554)-JER-4:31■17:8(7971)-LA-1:17

SPREADING-LE-13:57(6524)-PS-37:35(6168)-EZE-17:6(5628)■26:5(4894)

SPREADINGS-JOB-36:29(4666)

SPRIGS-IS-18:5(2150)-EZE-17:6(6288)

SPRING-all=6779&marked-NU-21:17(5927)-DE-8:7(3318)-J'G-19:25(5927)-1SA-9:26(5927)-2KI-2:21(4161)-JOB-5:6■38:27-PS-85:11■92:7(6524)-PR-25:26(4726)-SONG-4:12(1530)-IS-42:9■43:19■44:4■45:8■58:8,11(4161)■61:11^{2}-EZE-17:9(6780)-HO-13:15(4726)-JOE-2:22(1876)■N.T.-M'R-4:27(985)

SPRINGETH-1KI-4:33(3318)-2KI-19:29(7823)-IS-37:30(7823)-HO-10:4(6524)

SPRINGING-GE-26:19(2416)-PS-65:10(6780)■N.T.-JOH-4:14(242)-HEB-12:15(5453)

SPRINGS-all=1543&marked-DE-4:49(794)-JOS-10:40(794)■12:8(794)■15:19^{2}-J'G-1:15^{2}-JOB-38:16(5033)-PS-87:7(4599)■104:10(4599)-IS-35:7(4002)■41:18(4161)■49:10(4002)-JER-51:36(4726)

SPRINKLE-all=5137,a=2236-EX-9:8a■29:16a,20a,21-LE-1:5a,11a■3:2a,8a,13a■4:6,17■5:9■7:2a■14:7,16,27,51■16:14^{2},15,19■17:6a-NU-8:7■18:17a■19:4,18,19-2KI-16:15a-IS-52:15-EZE-36:25a■43:18a

SPRINKLED-all=2236&marked-EX-9:10■24:6,8-LE-6:27^{2}(5137)■8:11(5137),19,24,30(5137)■9:12,18-NU-19:13,20-2KI-9:33(5137)■16:13-2CH-29:22^{3}■30:16■35:11-JOB-2:12-IS-63:3(5137)■N.T.-all=4472-HEB-9:19,21■10:22

SPRINKLETH-LE-7:14(2236)-NU-19:21(4137)

SPRINKLING-HEB-9:13(4472)■11:28(4378)■12:24(4473)-1PE-1:2(4473)

SPROUT-JOB-14:7(2498)

SPRUNG-GE-41:6(6779),23(6779)-LE-13:42(6524)■N.T.-M'T-4:16(393)■13:5(1816),7(305),26(985)-LU-8:6(5453)

SPUE-LE-18:28(6958)■20:22(6958)-JER-25:27(7006)■N.T.-RE-3:16(1692)

SPUED-LE-18:28(6958)

SPUN-EX-35:25(4299),26(2901)

SPUNGE-all=4699-M'T-27:48-M'R-15:36-JOH-19:29

SPY-all=7270&marked-NU-13:16(8446),17(8446)■21:32-JOS-2:1■6:25-J'G-18:2,14,17-2SA-10:3-2KI-6:13(7200)-1CH-19:3(7200)■N.T.-GA-2:4(2684)

SQUARE-all=7251-1KI-7:5-EZE-43:16■45:2

SQUARED-EZE-41:21(7251)

SQUARES-EZE-43:16(7253),17(7253)

STABILITY-IS-33:6(530)

STABLE-1CH-16:30(3559)-EZE-25:5(5116)

STABLISH-all=6965&marked-2SA-7:13(3559)-1CH-17:12(3559)■18:3(5324)-2CH-7:18-ES-9:21-PS-119:38■N.T.-all=4741-RO-16:25-1TH-3:13-2TH-2:17■3:3-JAS-5:8-1PE-5:10

STABLISHED-2CH-17:5(3559)-PS-93:1(3559)■148:6(5975)■N.T.-COL-2:7(950)

STABLISHETH-HAB-2:12(3559)■N.T.-2CO-1:21(950)

STACKS-EX-22:6(1430)

STACTE-EX-30:34(5198)

STAFF-all=4294,a=4938&marked-GE-32:10(4731)■38:18,25-EX-12:11(4731)■21:19a-LE-26:26-NU-13:23(4132)■22:27(4731)-J'G-6:21a-1SA-17:7(2671),40(4731)-2SA-3:29(6418)■21:19(6086)■23:7(6086),21(7626)-2KI-4:29^{2}a,31a■18:21a-1CH-11:23(7626)■20:5(6086)-PS-23:4a■105:16-IS-3:1a■9:4■10:5,15,24■14:5■28:27■30:32■36:6a-JER-48:17-EZE-4:16■5:16■14:13■29:6a-HO-4:12(4731)-ZEC-8:4a■11:10(4731),14(4731)■N.T.-M'R-6:8(4464)-HEB-11:21(4464)

STAGGER-JOB-12:25(8582)-PS-107:27(5128)-IS-29:9(5128)

STAGGERED-RO-4:20(1252)

STAGGERETH-IS-19:14(8582)

STAIN-JOB-3:5(1350)-IS-23:9(2490)■63:3(1351)

STAIRS-all=4609&marked-1KI-6:8(3883)-2KI-9:13-NE-3:15■9:4(4608)■12:37-SONG-2:14(4095)-EZE-40:6■43:17■N.T.-AC-21:35(304),40(304)

STAKES-IS-33:20(3489)■54:2(3489)

STALK-GE-41:5(7070),22(7070)-HO-8:7(7054)

STALKS-JOS-2:6(6086)

STALL-AM-6:4(4770)-MAL-4:2(4770)■N.T.-LU-13:15(5336)

STALLED-PR-15:17(75)

STALLS-all=723&marked-1KI-4:26-2CH-9:25■32:28-HAB-3:17(7517)

STAMMERERS-IS-32:4(5926)

STAMMERING-IS-28:11(3934)■33:19(3932)

STAMP-2SA-22:43(1854)-EZE-6:11(7554)

STAMPED-all=1854&marked-DE-9:21(3807)-2KI-23:6,15-2CH-15:16-EZE-25:6(7554)-DA-7:7(7512),19(7512)■8:7(7429),10(7429)

STAMPING-JER-47:3(8161)

STANCHED-LU-8:44(2476)

STAND-all=5975,a=6965,b=3320&marked-GE-19:9(5066)■24:13(5324),43(5324)-EX-7:15(5324)■8:20b■9:11,13b■14:13b■17:6,9(5324)■18:14(5324)■33:10,21(5324)-LE-18:23■19:16■26:37(8617)■27:14a,17a-NU-1:5■9:8■11:16b■16:9■23:3b,15b■27:21■30:4^{2}a,5a,7^{2}a,9a,11^{2}a,12a■35:12-DE-5:31■7:24b■9:2b■10:8■11:25b■18:5,7■19:17■24:11■25:8■27:12,13■29:10(5324)-JOS-1:5b■3:8,13■7:12a,13a■10:8,12(1826)■20:4,6■23:9-J'G-2:14■4:20-1SA-6:20■9:27■12:7b,16b■14:9■16:22■19:3-2SA-1:9■18:30b-1KI-1:2■8:11■10:8■17:1■18:15■19:11-2KI-3:14■5:11,16■6:31■10:4-1CH-21:16■23:30-2CH-5:14■9:7■20:9,17■29:11■34:32■35:5-EZR-9:15■10:13,14-NE-7:3■9:5a-ES-3:4■8:11-JOB-8:15■19:25a■30:20■33:5b■37:14■38:14b■41:10b-PS-1:5a■5:5b■20:8(5749)■

24:3a■30:7■33:8(1481)■35:2a■38:11^{2}■45:9(5324)■73:7(3318)■76:7■78:13(5324)■89:28(539),43a■94:16b■109:6,31■111:8(5564)■122:2■130:3■134:1■135:2■147:17-PR-12:7■19:21a■22:29^{2}b■25:6■27:4-EC-4:15■8:3-IS-7:7a■8:10a■11:10■14:24a■21:8■27:9a■28:18a■32:8a■40:8a■44:11■46:10a■47:12,13■48:13■50:8■51:17a■61:5■65:5(7126)-JER-6:16■7:2,10■14:6■15:19■17:19■26:2■35:19■44:28a,29a■46:4b,14b,21■48:19■49:19■50:44■51:50-EZE-2:1■13:5■17:14■22:30■27:29■29:7(5976)■31:14■33:26■44:11,15,24■46:2■47:10-DA-1:4,5■2:44(6966)■7:4(6966)■8:4,7,22,23,25■10:11■11:2,3,4,6,7,14,16^{2},17,20,21,25,31■12:1,13-AM-2:15-MIC-5:4-NA-1:6■2:8-HAB-2:1-ZEC-3:7■4:14■14:4,12-MAL-3:2■N.T.-2476&marked-M'T-12:25,26,47■20:6■24:15-M'R-3:3(1453),24,25,26■9:1■11:25(4739)-LU-1:19(3936)■6:8■8:20■11:18■13:25■21:36-JOH-11:42(4026)-AC-1:11■4:10(3936)■5:20■8:38■10:26(450)■14:10(450)■25:10■26:6,16-RO-5:2■9:11(3306)■14:4,10(3936)-1CO-2:5(1510)■15:1■16:13(4739)-2CO-1:24-GA-4:20(639)■5:1(4739)-EPH-6:11,13,14-PH'P-1:27(4739)■4:1(4739)-COL-4:12-1TH-3:8(4739)-2TH-2:15(4739)-JAS-2:3-1PE-5:12-RE-3:20■6:17■10:5■15:2■18:15■20:12

STANDARD-all=1714&marked-NU-1:52■2:2,3,10,18,25■10:14,18,22,25-IS-49:22(5251)■59:19(5127)■62:10(5251)-JER-4:6(5251),21(4251)■50:2(5251)■51:12(5251),27(5251)

STANDARDBEARER-IS-10:18(5264)

STANDARDS-all=1714-NU-2:17,31,34

STANDEST-all=5975-GE-24:31-EX-3:5-JOS-5:15-PS-10:1■N.T.-AC-7:33(2476)-RO-11:20(2476)

STANDETH-all=5975&marked-NU-14:14-DE-1:38■17:12■29:15-J'G-16:26(3559)-ES-6:5■7:9-PS-1:1■26:12■33:11■82:1(5324)-PR-8:2(5324)-SONG-2:9-IS-3:13(5324),13■46:7■59:14-DA-12:1-ZEC-11:16(5324)■N.T.-all=2476&marked-JOH-1:26■3:29-RO-14:4(4739)-1CO-7:37■10:12-2TI-2:19-HEB-10:11-JAS-5:9-RE-10:8

STANDING-all=5975&marked-EX-22:6(7054)■26:15■36:20-LE-26:1(4676)-NU-22:23(5324),31(5324)-DE-23:25^{2}(7054)-J'G-15:5^{2}(7504)-1SA-19:20■22:6(5324)-1KI-13:25,28■22:19-2CH-9:18■18:18-ES-5:2-PS-69:2(4613)■107:35(98)■114:8(98)-DA-8:6-AM-9:1(5324)-MIC-1:11(5979)■5:13(4676)-ZEC-3:1^{2}■6:5(3320)■N.T.-all=2476&marked-M'T-6:5■16:28■20:3,6-M'R-3:31■13:14-LU-1:11■5:2■9:27■18:13-JOH-8:9■19:26(3936)■20:14-AC-2:14■4:14■5:23,25■7:55,56■22:20(2186)■24:21-HEB-9:8(2192,4714)-2PE-3:5(4921)-RE-7:1■11:4■18:10■19:17

STANK-all=887-EX-7:21■8:14■16:20-2SA-10:6

STAR-NU-24:17(3556)-AM-5:26(3556)■N.T.-all=792&marked-M'T-2:2,7,9,10-AC-7:43(798)-1CO-15:41^{2}-2PE-1:19(5459)-RE-2:28■8:10,11■9:1■22:16

STARE-PS-22:17(7200)

STARGAZERS-IS-47:13(2374,3556)

STARS-all=3556&marked-GE-1:16■15:5■22:17■26:4■37:9-EX-32:13-DE-1:10■4:19■10:22■28:62-J'G-5:20-1CH-27:23■4:21■9:23-JOB-3:9■9:7■22:12■25:5■38:7-PS-8:3■136:9■147:4■148:3-EC-12:2-IS-13:10■14:13-JER-31:35-EZE-32:7-DA-8:10■12:3-JOE-2:10■3:15-AM-5:8(3598)-OB-4-NA-3:16■N.T.-all=792&marked-M'T-24:29-M'R-13:25-LU-21:25(798)-AC-27:20(798)-1CO-15:41-HEB-11:12(798)-JUDE-13-RE-1:16,20^{2}■2:1■3:1■6:13■8:12■12:1,4

STATE-2CH-24:13(4971)-ES-1:7(3027)■2:18(3027)-PS-39:5(5324)-PR-27:23(6440)■28:2(3651)-IS-22:19(4612)■N.T.-PH'P-2:19(3588,4012),20(3588,4012)-COL-4:7(3588,2596)

STATELY-EZE-23:41(3520)

STATION-IS-22:19(4673)

STATURE-all=6967&marked-NU-13:32(4060)-1SA-16:7-2SA-21:20(4055)-1CH-11:23(4060)■20:6(4060)-SONG-7:7-IS-10:33■45:14(4060)-EZE-13:18■17:6■19:11■31:3■N.T.-all=2244-M'T-6:27-LU-2:52■12:25■19:3-EPH-4:13

STATUTE-all=2708,a=2706&marked-EX-15:25a■27:21■28:43■29:9,28a■30:21a-LE-3:17■6:18a,22a■7:34a,36■10:9,15a■16:29,31,34■17:7■23:14,21,31,41■24:3,9a-NU-18:11a,19a,23■19:10,21■27:11■35:29-JOS-24:25a-1SA-30:25a-PS-81:4a-DA-6:7(7010),15(7010)

STATUTES-all=2706,a=2708&marked-GE-26:5a-EX-15:26■18:16-LE-10:11■18:5a,26a■19:19a,37a■20:8a,22a■25:18a■26:3a,15a,43a,46a-NU-30:16-DE-4:1,5,6,8,14,40,45■5:1,31■6:1,2a,17,20,24■7:11■8:11a■10:13a■11:1a,32■12:1■16:12■17:19■26:16,17■27:10■28:15a,45a■30:10a,16a-2SA-22:23a-1KI-2:3a■3:3a,14■6:12a■8:58,61■9:4,6a■11:11a,33a,34a,38a-2KI-17:8a,13a,15,19a,34a,37■23:3a-1CH-22:13■29:19-2CH-7:17,19a■19:10■33:8■34:31-EZR-7:10,11-NE-1:7■9:13,14■10:29-PS-18:22a■19:8(6490)■50:16■89:31a■105:45■119:5,8,12,16a,23,26,33,48,54,64,68,71,80,83,112,117,118,124,135,145,155,171■147:19-JER-44:10a,23a-EZE-5:6^{2}a,7a■11:12,20a■18:9a,17a,19a,21a■20:11a,13a,16a,18,19a,21a,24a,25■33:15a■36:27■37:24a■44:24a-MIC-6:16a-ZEC-1:6-MAL-4:4

STAVES-all=905&marked-EX-25:13,14,15,27,28■27:6^{2},7^{2}■30:4,5■35:12,13,15,16■37:4,5,14,15,27,28■38:5,6,7■39:35,39■40:20-NU-4:6,8,11,14■21:18(4938) 1SA 17:43(4731) 1KI 8:7,8^{2} 1CH 15:15(4133)-2CH-5:8,9^{2}-HAB-3:14(4294)-ZEC-11:7(4731)■N.T.-all=3586&marked-M'T-10:10(4464)■26:47,55-M'R-14:43,48-LU-9:3(4464)■22:52

STAY-all=5975&marked-GE-19:17-EX-9:28-LE-13:5,23,28,37-JOS-10:19-RU-1:13(5702)-1SA-15:16(7503)■20:38-2SA-22:19(4937)■24:16(7503)-1CH-21:15(7503)-JOB-37:4(6117)■38:37(7901)-PS-18:18(4937)-PR-28:17(8551)-SONG-2:5(5564)-IS-3:1(4937),1(8172),1(4937)■10:20(4937),20(8172)■19:13(6438)■29:9(4102)■30:12(8172)■31:1(8172)■48:2(5564)■50:10(8172)-JER-4:6-DA-4:35(4223)-HO-13:13

STAYED-all=5975&marked-GE-8:10(2342),12(3176)■32:4(309)-EX-10:24(3322)■17:12(8551)-NU-16:48(6113),50(6113)■25:8(6113)-DE-10:10-JOS-10:13-1SA-24:7(8156)■30:9-2SA-17:17■24:21(6113),25(6113)-1KI-22:35-2KI-4:6■13:18■15:20-1CH-21:22(6113)-2CH-18:34-JOB-38:11(7896)-PS-106:30(6113)-IS-26:3(5564)-LA-4:6(2342)-EZE-31:15(3607)-HAG-1:10^{2}(3607)■N.T.-LU-4:42(2722)-AC-19:22(1907)

STAYETH-IS-27:8(1898)

STAYS-all=3027&marked-1KI-10:19^{2}-2CH-9:18^{2}

STEAD-all=8478-GE-22:13■30:2■36:33,34,35,36,37,38,39-EX-29:30-LE-6:22■16:32-NU-32:14-DE-2:12,22,23■10:6-JOS-5:7-2SA-10:1■16:8-1KI-1:30,35■11:43■14:20,27,31■15:8,24,28■16:6■28,10■22:40,50-2KI-1:17■3:27■8:15,24■10:35■12:21■13:9,24■14:16,29■15:7,10,14,22,30,38■16:20■19:37■20:21■21:18,24,26■23:30■24:6,17-1CH-1:44,45,46,47,48,49,50■19:1■29:28-2CH-1:8■12:16■14:1■17:1■21:1■22:1■24:27■26:23■27:9■28:27■32:33■33:20,25■36:1,8-JOB-16:4■34:24-PR-11:8-EC-4:15-IS-37:38-JER-29:26■N.T.-2CO-5:20(5228)-PH'M-13(5228)

STEADS-1CH-5:22(8478)

STEADY-EX-17:12(530)

STEAL-all=1589-GE-31:27■44:8-EX-20:15■22:1-LE-19:11-DE-5:19-2SA-19:3-PR-6:30■30:9-JER-7:9■23:30■N.T.-all=2813-M'T-6:19,20■19:18■27:64-M'R-10:19-LU-18:20-JOH-10:10-RO-2:21■13:9-EPH-4:28

STEALETH-all=1589-EX-21:16-JOB-27:20-ZEC-5:3

STEALING-DE-24:7(1589)-HO-4:2(1589)

STEALTH-2SA-19:3(1589)

STEDFAST-JOB-11:15(3332)-PS-78:8(539),37(539)-DA-6:26(7011)■N.T.-all=949&marked-1CO-7:37(1476)■15:58(1476)-2CO-1:7-HEB-2:2■3:14■6:19-1PE-5:9(4731)

STEDFASTLY-RU-1:18(553)-2KI-8:11(7760)■N.T.-all=816&marked-LU-9:51(4741)-AC-1:10■2:42(4342)■6:15■7:55■14:9-2CO-3:7,13

STEDFASTNESS-COL-2:5(4733)-2PE-3:17(4740)

STEEL-all=5154&marked-2SA-22:35-JOB-20:24-PS-18:34-JER-15:12(5178)

STEEP-EZE-38:20(4095)-MIC-1:4(4174)■N.T.-all=2911-M'T-8:32-M'R-5:13-LU-8:33

STEM-IS-11:1(1503)

STEP-1SA-20:3(6587)-JOB-31:7(838)

STEPPED-JOH-5:4(1684)

STEPPETH-JOH-5:7(2597)

STEPS-all=6806,a=4609&marked-EX-20:26a-2SA-22:37-1KI-10:19a,20a-2CH-9:18a,19a-JOB-14:16■18:7■23:11(838)■29:6(1978)■31:4,37-PS-17:11(838)■18:36■37:23(4703),31(838)■44:18(838)■56:6(6119)■57:6(6471)■73:2(838)■85:13(6471)■119:133(6471)-PR-4:12■5:5■16:9-IS-26:6(6471)-JER-10:23-LA-4:18-EZE-40:22a,26a,31a,34a,37a,49a-DA-11:43(4703)■N.T.-all=2487-RO-4:12-2CO-12:18-1PE-2:21

STERN-AC-27:29(4403)

STEWARD-all=834,5921&marked-GE-15:2(1121,4943)■43:19(376,834,5921)■44:1,4-1KI-16:9■N.T.-all=3622&marked-M'T-20:8(2012)-LU-8:3(2012)■12:42(3623)■16:1(3623),2(3621),3,8-TIT-1:7

STEWARDS-1CH-28:1(8269)■N.T.-all=3623&marked-1CO-4:1,2-1PE-4:10

STEWARDSHIP-all=3622-LU-16:2,3,4

STICK-all=6086&marked-2KI-6:6-JOB-33:21(8205)■41:17(3920)-PS-38:2(5181)-LA-4:8-EZE-29:4^{2}(1692)■37:16^{3},17,19^{3}

STICKETH-PR-18:24(1695)

STICKS-all=6086-NU-15:32,33-1KI-17:10,12-EZE-37:20■N.T.-AC-28:3(5434)

STIFF-DE-31:27(7186)-PS-75:5(6277)-JER-17:23(7185)

STIFFENED-2CH-36:13(7185)

STIFFHEARTED-EZE-2:4(2389,3820)

STIFFNECKED-all=7186,6203&marked-EX-32:9■33:3,5■34:9-DE-9:6,13■10:16(7185,6203)-2CH-30:8(7185,6203)■N.T.-AC-7:51(4644)

STILL-all=5750&marked-GE-12:9(5265)-EX-15:16(1826)-LE-13:57-JOS-10:12(1826)13(1826),13sup-J'G-18:9(2814)-2SA-14:32-1KI-19:12(1827)-2KI-12:3■15:4,35-2CH-33:17-JOB-2:3,9■32:16(5975)■37:14(5975)-PS-4:4(1826)■8:2(7673)■23:2(4496)■46:10(7503)■49:9■76:8■78:32■83:1(8252)■84:4■92:14■107:29(2814)■139:18-EC-12:9-IS-5:25■9:12,17,21■10:4■23:2(1826)■30:7(7673)■42:14(2790)-JER-31:20■47:6(1826)■51:50(5975)■N.T.-all=2476&marked-M'T-20:32-M'R-4:39(5392)■10:49-LU-7:14-AC-8:38-1TI-1:3(4357)

-RE-22:11^{4}(2089)

STILLED-NU-13:30(2013)-NE-8:11(2814)

STILLEST-PS-89:9(7623)

STILLETH-PS-65:7(7623)

STING-1CO-15:55(2759),56(2759)

STINGETH-PR-23:32(6567)

STINGS-RE-9:10(2759)

STINK-all=887&marked-GE-34:30-EX-7:18▪16:24-PS-38:5-IS-3:24(4716)▪34:3(889)-JOE-2:20(889)-AM-4:10(889)

STINKETH-IS-50:2(887)▪N.T.-JOH-11:39(3605)

STINKING-EC-10:1(887)

STIR-all=5782&marked-NU-24:9(6965)-JOB-17:8▪41:10-PS-35:23▪78:38▪80:2-PR-15:1(5927)-SONG-2:7▪3:5▪8:4-IS-10:26▪13:17▪42:13-DA-11:2,25▪N.T.-AC-12:18(5017)▪19:23(5017)-2TI-1:6(329)-2PE-1:13(1326)▪3:1(1326)

STIRRED-all=5782&marked-EX-35:21(5375),26(5375)▪36:2(5375)-1SA-22:8(6965)▪26:19(5496)-1KI-11:14(6965),23(6965)▪21:25(5496)-1CH-5:26-2CH-21:16▪36:22-EZR-1:1-PS-39:2(5916)-DA-11:10^{2}(1624),25(1624)-HAG-1:14▪N.T.-AC-6:12(4787)▪13:50(3951)▪14:2(1892)▪17:13(4531),16(3947)▪21:27(4797)

STIRRETH-all=5782&marked-DE-32:11-PR-10:12▪15:18(1624)▪28:25(1624)▪29:22(1624)-IS-14:9▪64:7▪N.T.-LU-23:5(383)

STIRS-IS-22:2(8663)

STOCK-LE-25:47(6133)-JOB-14:8(1503)-IS-40:24(1503)▪44:19(944)-JER-2:27(6086)▪10:8(6086)▪N.T.-AC-13:26(1085)-PH'P-3:5(1085)

STOCKS-JOB-13:27(5465)▪33:11(5465)-PR-7:22(5914)-JER-3:9(6086)▪20:2(4115),3(4115)▪29:26(6729)-HO-4:12(6086)▪N.T.-AC-16:24(3586)

STOLE-all=1589-GE-31:20-2SA-15:6-2KI-11:2-2CH-22:11▪N.T.-M'T-28:13(2813)-EPH-4:28(2813)

STOLEN-all=1589-GE-30:33▪31:19,26,30,32,39▪40:15-EX-22:7,12-JOS-7:11-2SA-19:41▪21:12-PR-9:17-OB-5

STOMACHER-IS-3:24(6614)

STOMACH'S-1TI-5:23(4751)

STONE-all=68,a=7275&marked-GE-2:12▪11:3▪28:18,22▪29:2,3^{2},8,10▪31:45▪35:14▪49:24-EX-4:25(6697)▪7:19▪8:26(5619)▪15:5,16▪17:4(5619),12▪20:25▪21:18▪24:12▪28:10^{2},11▪31:18▪34:1,4^{2}-LE-20:2a,27a▪24:14a,16a,23a▪26:1-NU-14:10a▪15:35a▪35:17,23-DE-4:13,28▪5:22▪9:9,10,11▪10:1,3▪13:10(5619)▪17:5(5619)▪21:21a▪22:21(5619),24(5619)▪28:36,64▪29:17-JOS-4:5▪15:6▪18:17▪24:26,27-J'G-9:5,18-1SA-6:14,15▪7:12▪14:33▪17:49^{2},50▪20:19▪25:37-2SA-17:13(6872)▪20:8-1KI-1:9▪6:7,18,36(1496)▪8:9▪21:10(5619)-2KI-3:25▪12:12^{2}▪19:18▪22:6-1CH-22:14,15-2CH-2:14▪34:11-NE-4:3▪9:11-JOB-28:2▪38:6,30▪41:24-PS-91:12▪118:22,22sup-PR-17:8▪24:31▪26:8,27▪27:3-IS-8:14▪28:16,16sup▪37:19-JER-2:27▪51:26^{2},63-LA-3:9(1496),53-EZE-1:26▪10:1,9▪16:40a▪20:32▪23:47a▪28:13▪40:42-DA-2:34(69),35(69),45(69)▪5:4(69),23(69)▪6:17(69)-AM-5:11(1496)-HAB-2:11,19-HAG-2:15-ZEC-3:9^{2}▪7:12(8068)▪12:3▪N.T.-all 3037&marked-M'T-4:6▪7:9▪21:42,44▪24:2▪27:60,66▪28:2-M'R-12:10▪13:2▪15:46▪16:3,4-LU-4:3,11▪11:11▪19:44▪20:6(2642),17,18▪21:6▪23:53(2991)▪24:2-JOH-1:42(4074)▪2:6(3035)▪8:7▪10:31(3034),32(3034),33(3034)▪11:8(3034),38,39,41▪20:1-AC-4:11▪14:5(3036)▪17:29-2CO-3:3(3035)-1PE-2:4,6,7,8-RE-2:17^{2}(5586)▪4:3▪9:20(3035)▪18:21▪21:11^{2}

STONED-all=5619&marked-EX-19:13▪21:28,29,32-NU-15:36(7275)-JOS-7:25,25(7275)-1KI-12:18(7275)▪21:13,14,15-2CH-10:18(7275)▪24:21(7275)▪N.T.-all=3036&marked-M'T-21:35-JOH-8:5-AC-5:26(3034)▪7:58,59▪14:19(3034)-2CO-11:25(3034)-HEB-11:37(3034)▪12:20

STONE'S-LU-22:41(3037)

STONES-all=68&marked-GE-28:11▪31:46^{2}-EX-25:7▪28:9,11,12^{2},17^{2},21▪31:5▪35:9,27^{2},33▪39:6,7,10,14-LE-14:40,42^{2},43,45▪20:2,27▪21:20(810)▪24:23-NU-14:10▪15:35,36-DE-8:9▪13:10▪17:5▪21:21▪22:21,24▪27:2,4,5,6,8-JOS-4:3,6,7,8,9,20,21▪7:25^{2},26▪8:29,31,32▪10:11,18,27-J'G-20:16-1SA-17:40-2SA-12:30▪16:6,13▪18:17-1KI-5:17^{2},18▪7:9,9(1496),10^{2},11,11(1496),12(1496)▪10:2,10,11,27▪12:18▪15:22▪18:31,32,38▪21:13-2KI-3:19,25▪16:17-1CH-12:2▪20:2▪22:2▪29:2,2^{2},8-2CH-1:15▪3:6▪9:1,9,10,27▪10:18▪16:6▪24:21▪26:14,15▪32:27-EZR-5:8(69)▪6:4(69)-NE-4:2-JOB-5:23▪6:12▪8:17▪14:19▪22:24(6697)▪28:3,6▪40:17(6344)▪41:30(2789)-PS-102:14▪137:9(5553)▪144:12(2106)-EC-3:5^{2}▪10:9-IS-5:2(5619)▪9:10(1496)▪14:19▪27:9▪34:11▪54:11,12▪60:17▪62:10-JER-3:9▪43:9,10-LA-3:16(2687)▪4:1-EZE-16:40▪23:47▪26:12▪27:22▪28:14,16-DA-11:38-MIC-1:6-ZEC-5:4▪9:15,16▪N.T.-all=3037&marked-M'T-3:9▪4:3-M'R-5:5▪12:4(3036)▪13:1-LU-3:8▪19:40▪21:5-JOH-8:59▪10:31-1CO-3:12-2CO-3:7-1PE-2:5-RE-17:4▪18:12,16▪21:19

STONESQUARERS-1KI-5:18(1382)

STONEST-M'T-23:37(3036)-LU-13:34(3036)

STONING-1SA-30:6(5619)

STONY-PS-141:6(5553)-EZE-11:19(68)▪36:26(68)▪N.T.-all=4075-M'T-13:5,20-M'R-4:5,16

STOOD-all=5975,a=5324,b=6965&marked-GE-18:2a,8,22▪19:27▪23:3b,7b▪24:30▪28:13a▪37:7a,7sup▪41:1,3,17,46▪43:15▪45:1a,1-EX-2:4(3320),17b▪5:20a▪9:10▪14:19▪15:8a▪18:13▪19:17(3320)▪20:18,21▪32:26▪33:8a,9▪34:5(3320)-LE-9:5-NU-11:32b▪12:5▪16:18,27a,48▪22:22(3320),24,26▪23:6a,17a▪27:2-DE-4:11▪5:5▪31:15-JOS-3:16,17▪4:3(4673),9(4673),10▪5:13▪8:33▪10:13(1826),13▪11:13▪20:9▪21:24-J'G-3:19▪6:31▪7:21▪9:7,35,44▪16:29(3559)▪18:16a,17a▪20:28-1SA-1:26a▪3:10(3320)▪4:20a▪6:14▪10:23(3320)▪16:21▪17:3^{2},8,26,51▪22:7a,17a▪26:13-2SA-1:10▪2:23,25,28▪13:31a▪18:4,30▪20:11,12^{2},15▪23:12(3320)-1KI-1:28▪3:15,16▪7:25▪8:14,22,55▪10:19,20▪12:6,8▪13:1,24^{2}▪19:13▪22:21-2KI-2:7^{2},13▪3:21▪4:12,15▪5:9,15,25▪8:9▪9:17▪10:4,9▪11:11,14▪13:21b▪18:17,28▪23:3^{2}-1CH-6:39▪21:1,15▪28:2b-2CH-3:13▪4:4▪5:12▪6:3,12,13▪7:6▪9:19▪10:6,8▪13:4b▪18:20▪20:5,13,19b,20,23▪23:13▪24:20▪28:12b▪29:26▪30:16▪34:31▪35:10-EZR-2:63▪3:2b,9▪10:10b-NE-7:65▪8:4^{2},5▪9:2,3b,4b▪12:39,40-ES-5:1,9b▪7:7▪8:4▪9:16-JOB-4:15(5568),16▪29:8▪30:28b▪32:16-PS-33:9▪104:6▪106:23,30-IS-6:2▪36:2,13-JER-15:1▪18:20▪19:14▪23:18,22▪28:5▪36:21▪44:15▪46:15▪48:45-LA-2:4a-EZE-1:21,24,25▪3:23▪8:11^{2}▪9:2▪10:3,6,17,18,19▪11:23▪21:21▪37:10▪40:3▪43:6-DA-1:19▪2:2,31(6966)▪3:3(6966)▪7:10(6966),16(6966)▪8:3,15,17(5977),22▪10:11,16▪11:1▪12:5-HO-10:9-AM-7:7a-OB-14-HAB-3:6,11-ZEC-1:8,10,11▪3:3,4,5▪N.T.-all=2476,a=3936&marked-M'T-2:9▪12:46▪13:2▪20:32▪26:73▪27:11,47-M'R-10:49▪11:5▪14:47a,60(450),69a,70a▪15:35a,39a-LU-4:16(450),39(2186)▪5:1▪6:8,17▪7:14,38▪9:32(4921)▪10:25(450)▪17:12▪18:11,40▪19:8,24a▪23:10,35,49▪24:4(2186),36-JOH-1:35▪6:22▪7:37▪11:56▪12:29▪18:5,16,18^{2},22a,25▪19:25▪20:11,19,26▪21:4-AC-1:10a,15(450)▪3:8▪4:26a▪5:34(450)▪9:7,39a▪10:17(2186),30▪11:13,28(450)▪12:14▪13:16(450)▪14:20(2944)▪16:9▪17:22▪21:40▪22:13(2186),25▪23:2a,4a,11(2186)▪24:20▪25:7(4026),18▪27:21,23a-2TI-4:16(4836),17-RE-5:6▪7:9,11▪8:2,3▪11:1,11▪12:4▪13:1▪14:1▪18:17

STOODEST-NU-22:34(5324)-DE-4:10(5975)-OB-11(5975)

STOOL-2KI-4:10(3678)

STOOLS-EX-1:16(70)

STOOP-JOB-9:13(7817)-PR-12:25(7812)-IS-46:2(7164)▪N.T.-M'R-1:7(2955)

STOOPED-GE-49:9(3766)-1SA-24:8(6915)▪28:14(6915)-2CH-36:17(3486)▪N.T.-JOH-8:6(2955),8(2955)▪20:11(3879)

STOOPETH-IS-46:1(7164)

STOOPING-LU-24:12(3879)-JOH-20:5(3879)

STOP-1KI-18:44(6113)-2KI-3:19(5640)-2CH-32:3(5640)-PS-35:3(5462)▪107:42(7092)-EZE-39:11(2629)▪N.T.-2CO-11:10(5420)

STOPPED-all=5640&marked-GE-8:2(5534)▪26:15,18-LE-15:3(2856)-KI-3:25-2CH-32:4,30-NE-4:7-PS-63:11(5534)-JER-51:32(8610)-ZEC-7:11(3513)▪N.T.-AC-7:57(4912)-RO-3:19(5420)-TIT-1:11(1993)-HAB-11:33(5420)

STOPPETH-all=331&marked-JOB-5:16(7092)-PS-58:4-PR-21:13-IS-33:15

STORE-all=4543&marked-GE-41:36(6487)-LE-26:10(3462)-DE-28:5(4863),17(4863)-1KI-9:19-2KI-20:17(686)-1CH-29:16(1995)-2CH-8:4,6▪11:11(214)▪16:4▪17:12▪31:10(1995)-NE-5:18(7235)-IS-39:6(686)-AM-3:10(686)-NA-2:9(8498)▪N.T.-1CO-16:2(2343)-1TI-6:19(597)-2PE-3:7(2343)

STOREHOUSE-MAL-3:10(214)▪N.T.-LU-12:24(5009)

STOREHOUSES-GE-41:56(834)-DE-28:8(618)-1CH-27:25(214)-2CH-32:28(4543)-PS-33:7(214)-JER-50:26(3965)

STORIES-AM-9:6(4609)

STORK-all=2624-LE-11:19-DE-14:18-PS-104:17-JER-8:7-ZEC-5:9

STORM-all=5492&marked-JOB-21:18-PS-55:8(5584)▪83:15▪107:29(5591)-IS-4:6(2230)▪25:4^{2}(2230)▪28:2(8178)▪29:6-EZE-38:9(7722)-NA-1:3(8183)▪N.T.-M'R-4:37(2978)-LU-8:23(2978)

STORMY-all=5591-PS-107:25▪148:8-EZE-13:11,13

STORY-2CH-13:22(4097)▪24:27(4097)

STOUT-IS-10:12(1433)-DA-7:20(7229)-MAL-3:13(2388)

STOUTHEARTED-PS-76:5(47,3820)-IS-46:12(47,3820)

STOUTNESS-IS-9:9(1433)

STRAIGHT-all=3474&marked-1SA-6:12-2CH-32:30-PS-5:8-PR-4:25-EC-1:15(8626)▪7:13(8626)-IS-40:3,4(4334)▪42:16(4334)▪45:2-JER-31:9-EZE-1:7,9(5676),12(5676),23▪10:22(5676)▪N.T.-all=2117&marked-M'T-3:3-M'R-1:3-LU-3:4,5▪13:13(461)-JOH-1:23(2116)-AC-9:11▪16:11(2113)▪21:1(2113)-HEB-12:13(3717)

STRAIGHTWAY-1SA-9:13(3651)▪28:20(4116)-PR-7:22(6597)-DA-10:17(6258)▪N.T.-all=2112&marked-M'T-3:16(2117)▪4:20▪14:22,27▪21:2,3▪25:15▪27:48-M'R-1:10,18,20,21▪2:2▪3:6▪5:29,42▪6:25,45,54▪7:35▪8:10▪9:15,20,24▪11:3▪14:45▪15:1-LU-5:39▪8:55(3916)▪12:54▪14:5-JOH-13:32(2117)-AC-5:10(3916)▪9:20▪16:33(3916)▪22:29▪23:30(1824)-JAS-1:24

STRAIN-M'T-23:24(1368)

STRAIT-all=6887&marked-1SA-13:6-2SA-24:14-2KI-6:1(6862)-1CH-21:13-JOB-36:16(6862)-IS-49:20(6862)▪N.T.-all=4728&marked-M'T-7:13,14-LU-13:24-PH'P-1:23(4912)

STRAITEN-JER-19:9(6693)

STRAITENED-JOB-18:7(3334)▪37:10(4164)-PR-4:12(3334)-EZR-42:6(680)-MIC-2:7(7114)▪N.T.-LU-12:50(4912)-2CO-6:12^2(4729)

STRAITENETH-JOB-12:23(5148)

STRAITEST-AC-26:5(196)

STRAITLY-M'R-3:12(4183)▪5:43(4183)-AC-4:17(547)

STRAITNESS-all=4689&marked-DE-28:53,55,57-JOB-36:16(4164)-JER-19:9

STRAITS-JOB-20:22(3334)-LA-1:3(4712)

STRAKE-AC-27:17(5465)

STRAKES-GE-30:37(6479)-LE-14:37(8258)

STRANGE-all=2114,a=5237,b=5236&marked-GE-35:2b,4b▪42:7(5234)-EX-2:22a▪18:3a▪21:8a▪30:9-LE-10:1-NU-3:4▪26:61-DE-32:12b,16-JOS-24:20b,23b-J'G-10:16b▪11:2(312)-1SA-7:3b-1KI-11:1a,8a-2KI-19:24-2CH-14:3b▪33:15b-EZR-10:2a,10a,11a,14a,17a,18a,44a-NE-13:27a-JOB-19:3(1970),17▪31:3(5235)-PS-44:20▪81:9,9b▪114:1(3937)▪137:4b▪144:7b,11b-PR-2:16▪5:3,20▪6:24a▪7:5▪20:16a▪21:8▪22:14▪23:27a,33▪27:13a-IS-17:10▪28:21,21a▪43:12-JER-2:21a▪5:19b▪8:19b-EZE-3:5(6012),6(6012)-DA-11:39b-HO-5:7▪8:12-ZEP-1:8a-MAL-2:11b▪N.T.-all=3579&marked-LU-5:26(3861)-AC-7:6(245)▪17:18(3581),20▪26:11(1854)-HEB-11:9(245)▪13:9(3581)-1PE-4:4,12,12(3581)-JUDE-7(2087)

STRANGELY-DE-32:27(5234)

STRANGER-all=1616,a=2114,b=5237&marked-GE-15:13▪17:8(4033),12(1121,5235),27(1121,5235)▪23:4▪28:4(4033)▪37:1(4033)-EX-2:22▪12:19,43(1121,5235),48,49▪20:10▪22:21▪23:9^2,12▪29:33a▪30:33a-LE-16:29▪17:12,15▪18:26▪19:10,33,34▪22:10a,12(376)a,13a▪23:22▪24:16,22▪25:6(8453),35,47(8453),47-NU-1:51a▪3:10a,38a▪9:14^2▪15:14,15^2,16,26,29,30▪16:40(376)a▪18:4a,7a▪19:10▪35:15-DE-1:16▪5:14▪10:18,19▪14:21,29▪16:11,14▪17:15(376)b▪23:7,20b▪24:17,19,20,21▪25:5(376)a▪26:11,12,13▪27:19▪28:43▪29:11,22b▪31:12-JOS-8:33▪20:9-J'G-19:12b-RU-2:10b-2SA-1:13(376,1616)▪15:19b-1KI-3:18a▪8:41b,43b-2CH-6:32b,33b-JOB-15:19a▪19:15a▪31:32-PS-39:12▪69:8a▪94:6▪119:19-PR-2:16b▪5:10b,20b▪6:1a▪7:5b▪11:15a▪14:10a▪20:16a▪27:2b,13a-EC-6:2(376)b-IS-56:3(5236),6(5236)▪62:8(5236)-JER-7:6▪14:8▪22:3-EZE-14:7▪22:7,29▪44:9^2(1121,5236)▪47:23-OB-12(5235)-ZEC-7:10▪3:5▪N.T.-all=3581&marked-M'T-25:35,38,43,44-LU-17:18(241)▪24:18(3939)-JOH-10:5(245)-AC-7:29(3941)

STRANGER'S-LE-22:25(1121,5236)▪25:47(1616)

STRANGERS-all=2114,a=1616&marked-GE-31:15(5237)▪36:7(4033)-EX-6:4(1481)▪22:21a▪23:9a-LE-17:8a,10a,13a▪19:34a▪20:2a▪22:18a▪25:23a,45(8453)-DE-10:19a▪24:14a▪31:16(5236)-JOS-8:35a-2SA-22:45(1121,5236),46(1121,5236)-1CH-16:19(1481)▪22:2a▪29:15a-2CH-2:17(582)a▪15:9(1481)▪30:25a-NE-9:2(1121,5236)▪13:30(5236)-PS-18:44(1121,5236),45(1121,5236)▪54:3▪105:12(1481)▪109:11▪146:9a-PR-5:10-IS-1:7^2▪2:6(5237)▪5:17(1481)▪14:1a▪25:2,5▪29:5▪60:10(5236)▪61:5-JER-2:25▪3:13▪5:19▪30:8▪35:7(1481)▪51:51-LA-5:2-EZE-7:21▪11:9▪16:32▪28:7,10▪30:12▪31:12▪44:7(1121,5236)▪47:22a-HOS-7:9▪8:7-JOE-3:17-OB-11▪N.T.-all=3581&marked-M'T-17:25(245),26(245)▪27:7-JOH-10:5(245)-AC-2:10(1927)▪13:17(1722,3940)▪17:21-EPH-2:12,19-1TI-5:10(3580)-HEB-11:13▪13:2(5381)-1PE-1:1(3927)▪2:11(3941)-3JO-5

STRANGERS'-PR-5:17(2114)

STRANGLED-NA-2:12(2614)▪N.T.-all=4156-AC-15:20,29▪21:25

STRANGLING-JOB-7:15(4267)

STRAW-all=8401&marked-GE-24:25,32-EX-5:7^2,10,11,12,13,16,18-J'G-19:19-1KI-4:28-JOB-41:27-IS-11:7▪25:10(4963)▪65:25

STRAWED-EX-32:20(2219)▪N.T.-M'T-21:8(4766)▪25:24(1287),26(1287)-M'R-11:8(4766)

STREAM-all=5158&marked-NU-21:15(793)-JOB-6:15(650)-PS-124:4-IS-27:12▪30:28,33▪57:6▪66:12-DA-7:10(5103)-AM-5:24▪N.T.-LU-6:48(4215),49(4215)

STREAMS-all=5158&marked-EX-7:19(5104)▪8:5(5104)-PS-46:4(6388)▪78:16(5140),20▪126:4(650)-SONG-4:15(5140)-IS-11:15▪30:25(2988)▪33:21(2975)▪34:9▪35:6

STREET-all=7339&marked-GE-19:2-DE-13:16-JOS-2:19(2351)-J'G-19:15,17,20-2SA-21:12▪22:43(2351)-2CH-29:4▪32:6-EZR-10:9-NE-8:1,3,16^2-ES-4:6▪6:9,11-JOB-18:17(2351,6440)▪29:7▪31:32(2351)-PR-7:8(7784)-IS-42:2(2351)▪51:23(2351)▪59:14-JER-37:21(2351)-LA-2:19(2351)▪4:1(2351)-EZE-16:24,31-DA-9:25▪N.T.-all=4113&marked-AC-9:11(4505)▪12:10(4505)-RE-11:8▪21:21▪22:2

STREETS-all=2351,a=7339&marked-2SA-1:20-1KI-20:34-PS-18:42▪55:11a▪144:13,14a-PR-1:20a▪5:16a▪7:12a▪22:13a▪26:13a-EC-12:4(7784),5(7784)-SONG-3:2(7784)-IS-5:25▪10:6▪15:3,3a▪24:11▪51:20-JER-5:1▪7:17,34▪9:21a▪11:6,13▪14:16▪33:10▪44:6,9,17,21▪48:38a▪49:26a▪50:30a▪51:4-LA-2:11a,12a,21▪4:5,8,14,18a-EZE-7:19▪11:6▪26:11▪28:23-AM-5:16a-MIC-7:10-NA-2:4▪3:10-ZEP-3:6-ZEC-8:4a,5^{2}a▪9:3▪10:5▪N.T.-all=4113&marked-M'T-6:2(4505),5▪12:19-M'R-6:56(58)-LU-10:10▪13:26▪14:21-AC-5:15

STRENGTH-all=5797,a=3581,b=4581,c=1369&marked-GE-4:12a▪49:3(202),24(386)-EX-13:3(2392),14(2392),16(2392)▪14:27(386)▪15:2,13-LE-26:20a-NU-23:22(8443)▪24:8(8443)-DE-21:17(202)▪33:25(1679)-JOS-11:13(8510)▪14:11a-J'G-5:21▪8:21c▪16:5a,6a,9a,15a,17a,19a-1SA-2:4(2428),9a,10▪15:29(5331)▪28:20a,22a-2SA-22:33b,40(2428)-1KI-19:8a-2KI-9:24(3027)▪18:20c▪19:3a-1CH-16:11,27,28▪26:8a▪29:12(2388)-2CH-6:41▪13:20a-NE-4:10a▪8:10b-JOB-6:11a,12a▪9:4a,19a▪12:13c,16,21(4206)▪18:7(202),12(202),13^2(905)▪21:23(6106)▪26:2▪30:2a▪36:5a,19a▪37:6▪39:11a,19c,21a▪40:16a▪41:22-PS-8:2▪18:1(2391),2(6697),32(2428),39(2428)▪19:14(6697)▪20:6c▪21:1,13▪22:15a,19(360)▪27:1b▪28:7,8,8b▪29:1,11▪31:4b,10a▪33:16a,17(2428)▪37:39b▪38:10a▪39:13(1082)▪43:2b▪46:1▪52:7b▪54:1c▪59:9,17▪60:7b▪62:7▪65:6a▪68:28,34^2,35▪71:9a,16c,18(2220)▪73:4(193),26(6697)▪74:13▪77:14▪78:4(5807),51(202),61▪80:2c▪81:1▪84:5,7(2428)▪86:16▪88:4(353)▪89:17▪90:10c,10(7296)▪93:1▪95:4(8443)▪96:6,7▪99:4▪102:23a▪103:20a▪105:4,36(202)▪108:8b▪110:2▪118:14▪132:8▪138:3▪140:7▪144:1(6697)▪147:10c-PR-8:14c▪10:29b▪14:4a▪20:29a▪21:22▪24:5a,10a▪31:3(2428),17,25-EC-9:16c▪10:10(2428),17c-IS-5:22(2428)▪10:13a▪12:2▪17:10b▪23:4b,10(4206),14b▪25:4^{2}b▪26:4(6697)▪27:5b▪28:6c▪30:2b,3b,7(7293),15c▪33:6(2633)▪36:5c▪37:3a▪40:9a,29(6109),31a▪41:1a▪42:25(5807)▪44:12^{2}a▪45:24▪49:4a,5▪51:9▪52:1▪62:8▪63:1a,6(5332),15c-JER-16:19▪20:5(2633)▪51:53-LA-1:6a,14a▪3:18(5331)-EZE-24:21,25b▪30:15b,18▪33:28-DA-2:37(8632),41(5326)▪10:8^{2}a,16a,17a▪11:2(2394),15a,17(8633),31b-HO-7:9a▪12:3(202)-JOE-2:22(2428)▪3:16b-AM-3:11▪6:13(2392)-MIC-5:4-NA-3:9(6109),11b-HAB-3:19(2428)-HAG-2:22(2392)-ZEC-12:5(556)▪N.T.-all=1411&marked-M'R-12:30(2479),33(2479)-LU-1:51(2904)▪10:27(2479)-AC-3:7(4732)▪9:22(1743)-RO-5:6(772)-1CO-15:56-2CO-1:8▪12:9-HEB-9:17(2480)▪11:11-RE-1:16▪3:8▪5:12(2479)▪12:10▪17:13(1849)

STRENGTHEN-all=2388&marked-DE-3:28(553)-J'G-16:28-1KI-20:22-EZR-6:22-NE-6:9-JOB-16:5(553)-PS-20:2(5582)▪27:14(553)▪31:24(553)▪41:3(5582)▪68:28(5810)▪89:21(553)▪119:28(6965)-IS-22:21▪30:2(5810)▪33:23▪35:3▪41:10(553)▪54:2-JER-23:14-EZE-7:13▪16:49▪30:24,25▪34:16-DA-11:1(4581)-AM-2:14(553)-ZEC-10:6(1396),12(1396)▪N.T.-LU-22:32(4741)-1PE-5:10(4599)-RE-3:2(4741)

STRENGTHENED-all=2388&marked-GE-48:2-J'G-3:12▪7:11-1SA-23:16-2SA-2:7-1CH-11:10-2CH-1:1▪11:17▪12:1(2394),13▪13:7(553)▪17:1▪21:4▪23:1▪24:13(553)▪25:11▪26:8▪28:20▪32:5-EZR-1:6▪7:28-NE-2:18-JOB-4:3,4(553)-PS-52:7(5810)▪147:13-PR-8:28(5810)-EZE-13:22▪34:4-DA-10:18,19^2▪11:6,12(5810)-HO-7:15▪N.T.-AC-9:19(1765)-EPH-3:16(2901)-COL-1:11(1412)-2TI-4:17(1743)

STRENGTHENEDST-PS-138:3(7292)

STRENGTHENETH-JOB-15:25(1396)-PS-104:15(5582)-PR-31:17(553)-EC-7:19(5810)-IS-44:14(553)-AM-5:9(1082)▪N.T.-PH'P-4:13(1743)

STRENGTHENING-LU-22:43(1765)-AC-18:23(1991)

STRETCH-all=5186,a=7971&marked-EX-3:20a▪7:5,19▪8:5,16▪9:15a,22▪10:12,21▪14:16,26▪25:20(6566)-JOS-8:18-1SA-24:6a▪26:9a,11a,23a-2SA-1:14a-2KI-21:13-JOB-11:13(6566)▪30:24a▪39:26(6566)-PS-68:31(7323)▪138:7a▪143:6(6566)-IS-28:20(8311)▪31:3▪34:11▪54:2-JER-6:12▪10:20▪15:6▪51:25-EZE-6:14▪14:9,13▪25:7,13,16▪30:25▪35:3-DA-11:42a-AM-6:4(5628)-ZEP-1:4▪2:13▪N.T.-all=1614&marked-M'T-12:13-M'R-3:5-LU-6:10-JOH-21:18-2CO-10:14(5239)

STRETCHED-all=5186&marked-GE-22:10(7971)▪48:14(7971)-EX-6:6▪8:6,17▪9:23▪10:13,22▪14:21,27-DE-4:34▪5:15▪7:19▪9:29▪11:2-JOS-8:18,19,26-2SA-24:16(7971)-1KI-6:27(6566)▪8:42▪17:21(4058)-2KI-4:34(1457),35(1457)▪17:36-1CH-21:16-2CH-6:32-JOB-38:5-PS-44:20(6566)▪88:9(7849)▪136:6(7554),12-PR-1:24-IS-3:16▪5:25^2▪9:12,17,21▪10:4▪14:26,27▪16:8(5203)▪23:11▪42:5▪45:12▪51:13-JER-6:4▪10:12▪32:17,21▪51:15-LA-2:8-EZE-1:11(6504),22▪10:7(7971)▪16:27▪20:33,34-HO-7:5(4900)-AM-6:7(5628)-ZEC-1:16▪N.T.-all=1614&marked-M'T-12:13,49▪14:31▪26:51-M'R-3:5-LU-22:53-AC-12:1(1911)▪26:1-RO-10:21(1600)

STRETCHEDST-EX-15:12(5186)

STRETCHEST-PS-104:2(5186)

STRETCHETH-all=5186&marked-JOB-15:25▪26:7-PR-31:20(6566)-IS-40:22▪44:13,24-ZEC-12:1

STRETCHING-IS-8:8(4298)▪N.T.-AC-4:30(1614)

STRICKEN-all=935&marked-GE-18:11▪24:1-JOS-13:1^2▪23:1,2-J'G-5:26(2498)-1KI-1:1-PR-6:1(8628)▪23:35(5221)-IS-1:5(5221)▪16:7(5218)▪53:4(5060),8(5061)-JER-5:3(5221)-LA-4:9(1856)▪N.T.-LU-1:7(4260),18(4260)

STRIFE-all=7379&marked-GE-13:7,8(4808)-NU-27:14(4808)-DE-

1:12-J'G-12:2-2SA-19:9(1777)-PS-31:20▪55:9▪80:6(4066)▪106:32(4808)-PR-15:18(4066),18▪16:28(4066)▪17:1,14(4066),19(4683)▪20:3▪22:10(1779)▪26:17,20(4066),21▪28:25(4066)▪29:22(4066)▪30:33-IS-58:4-JER-15:10-EZE-47:19(4808)▪48:28(4808)-HAB-1:3▪N.T.-all=2052&marked-LU-22:24(5379)-RO-13:13(2054)-1CO-3:3(2054)-GA-5:20-PH'P-1:15(2054)▪2:3-1TI-6:4(2054)-HEB-6:16(485)-JAS-3:14,16

STRIFES-PR-10:12(4090)▪N.T.-2CO-12:20(2052)-1TI-6:4(3055)-2TI-2:23(3163)

STRIKE-EX-12:7(5414),22(5060)-2KI-5:11(5130)-JOB-17:3(8628)▪20:24(2498)-PS-110:5(4272)-PR-7:23(6398)▪17:26(5221)▪22:26(8628)-HAB-3:14(5344)▪N.T.-M'R-14:65(906)

STRIKER-1TI-3:3(4131)-TIT-1:7(4131)

STRIKETH-JOB-34:26(5606)-PR-17:18(8628)▪N.T.-RE-9:5(3817)

STRING-PS-11:2(3499)▪N.T.-M'R-7:35(1199)

STRINGED-PS-150:4(4482)-IS-38:20(5058)-HAB-3:19(5058)

STRINGS-PS-21:12(4340)

STRIP-all=6584-NU-20:26-1SA-31:8-1CH-10:8-IS-32:11-EZE-16:39▪23:26-HO-2:3

STRIPE-EX-21:25(2250)

STRIPES-DE-25:3(5521),3(4347)-2SA-7:14(5061)-PS-89:32(5061)-PR-17:10(5221)▪19:29(4112)▪20:30(4347)-IS-53:5(2250)▪N.T.-all=4127&marked-LU-12:48^{2}-AC-16:23,33-2CO-6:5▪11:23-1PE-2:24(3468)

STRIPLING-1SA-17:56(5958)

STRIPPED-all=6584&marked-EX-33:6(5337)-NU-20:28-1SA-18:4▪19:24▪31:9-1CH-10:9-2CH-20:25(5337)-JOB-19:9▪22:6-MIC-1:8(7758)▪N.T.-M'T-27:28(1562)-LU-10:30(1562)

STRIPT-GE-37:23(6584)

STRIVE-all=7378&marked-GE-6:3(1777)▪26:20-EX-21:18,22(5327)-DE-25:11(5327)▪33:8-J'G-11:25-JOB-33:13-PS-35:1(3401)-PR-3:30▪25:8-IS-41:11(7379)-HO-4:4^{2}▪N.T.-M'T-12:19(2051)-LU-13:24(75)-RO-15:30(4865)-2TI-2:5^{2}(118),14(3054),24(3164)

STRIVED-RO-15:20(5389)

STRIVEN-JER-50:24(1624)

STRIVETH-IS-45:9(7378)▪N.T.-1CO-9:25(75)

STRIVING-PH'P-1:27(4866)-COL-1:29(75)-HEB-12:4(464)

STRIVINGS-2SA-22:44(7379)-PS-18:43(7379)▪N.T.-TIT-3:9(3163)

STROKE-all=5061&marked-DE-17:8▪21:5-ES-9:5(4347)-JOB-23:2(3027)▪36:18(5607)-PS-39:10-IS-14:6(4347)▪30:26(4273)-EZE-24:16(4046)

STROKES-PR-18:6(4112)

STRONG-all=2388,a=2389,b=5794,c=5797,d=6099,e=4013&marked-GE-49:14(1634),24(6339)-EX-6:1^{2}a▪10:19a▪13:9a▪14:21b-NU-13:18a,19e,28b▪20:20a▪21:24b▪24:21(386)-DE-2:36(7682)▪11:8▪31:6,7,23-JOS-1:6,7,9,18▪10:25▪14:11a▪17:13,18a▪19:29e▪23:9d-J'G-1:28▪6:2(4679)▪9:51c▪14:14b▪18:26a-1SA-4:9▪14:52(1368)▪23:14(4679),19(4679),29(4679)-2SA-3:6▪5:7(4686)▪10:11^{2}▪11:25▪15:12(533)▪16:21▪22:18b,18(553)▪24:7e-1KI-2:2▪8:42a▪19:11a-2KI-2:16(2428)▪8:12e▪24:16(1368)-1CH-19:12^{2}▪22:13▪26:7(2428),9(2428)▪28:10,20-2CH-11:11(4694),12,17(559)▪15:7▪16:9▪25:8▪26:15,16(2394)▪32:7-EZR-9:12-NE-1:10a▪9:25(1219)-JOB-8:2(3524)▪9:19(533)▪30:21(6108)▪33:19(386)▪37:18a▪39:28(4686)▪40:18(650)-PS-10:10d▪18:17b,17(553)▪19:5(1368)▪22:12(47)▪24:8(5808)▪30:7c▪31:2(4581),21(4692)▪35:10a▪38:19(6105)▪60:9(4692)▪61:3c▪71:3(6697),7c▪80:15(553),17(553)▪89:8(2626),10c,13(5810),40e▪108:10e▪136:12a-PR-7:26d▪10:15c▪11:16(6184)▪14:26c▪18:10c,11c,19c▪21:14b▪24:5c▪30:25b-EC-9:11(1368)▪12:3(2428)-SONG-8:6b-IS-1:31(2634)▪8:7d,11(2393)▪17:9(4581)▪23:11(4581)▪25:3b▪26:1c▪27:1a▪28:2(533),22▪31:1(6105),9(5553)▪35:4▪40:10a,26(533)▪41:21(6110)▪53:12d▪60:22d-JER-8:16(47)▪21:5a▪32:21▪47:3(47)▪48:14(2428),17c,18e,41(4679)▪49:19(386)▪50:34a,44(386)▪51:12-LA-2:2e,5e-EZE-3:8^{2}a,14▪7:24b▪19:11c,12c,14c▪22:14▪26:11c,17a▪30:21,22a▪32:21(410)▪34:16a-DA-2:40(8624),42(8624)▪4:11(8631),20(8631),22(8631)▪7:7(8624)▪8:8(6105)▪10:19▪11:5^{2},23(6105),24e,32,39(4581)-JOE-1:6d▪2:2d,5d,11d▪3:10(1368)-AM-2:9(2634),14a▪5:9b-MIC-2:11(7941)▪4:3d,7d,8(6076)▪5:11e▪6:2(386)-NA-1:7(4581)▪2:1▪3:12e,14e,14-HAB-1:10e-HAG-2:4^{3}-ZEC-8:9,13,22d▪9:3(4692),12(1225)▪N.T.-all=2478&marked-M'T-12:29^{2}-M'R-3:27^{2}-LU-1:15(4608),80(2901)▪2:40(2901)▪11:21-AC-3:16(4732)-RO-4:20(1743)▪15:1(1415)-1CO-4:10▪16:13(2901)-2CO-10:4(3794)▪12:10(1415)▪13:9(1415)-EPH-6:10(1743)-2TH-2:11(1753)-2TI-2:1(1743)-HEB-5:7,12(4731),14(4731)▪6:18▪11:34(1743)-1JO-2:14-RE-5:2▪18:2(3173),8

STRONGER-all=2388&marked-GE-25:23(553)▪30:41(7194),42(7194)-NU-13:31(2389)-J'G-14:18(5794)-2SA-1:23(1396)▪3:1(2390),1sup▪13:14-1KI-20:23^{2},25-JOB-17:9(555),9sup-PS-105:24▪142:6(553)-JER-20:7▪31:11▪N.T.-all=2478-LU-11:22-1CO-1:25▪10:22

STRONGEST-PR-30:30(1368)

STRONGLY-supplied

STROVE-all=5327&marked-GE-26:20(6229),21(7378),22(7378)-EX-2:13-LE-24:10-NU-20:13(7378)▪26:9^{2}-2SA-14:6-PS-60:t-DA-7:2(1519)▪N.T.-JOH-6:52(3164)-AC-7:26(3164)▪23:9(1264)

STROWED-2CH-34:4(2236)

STRUCK-1SA-2:14(5221)-2SA-12:15(5062)▪20:10(8138)-2CH-13:20(5062)▪N.T.-M'T-26:51(3960)-LU-22:64(5180)-JOH-18:22(1325,4475)

STRUGGLED-GE-25:22(7533)

STUBBLE-all=7179&marked-EX-5:12▪15:7-JOB-13:25▪21:18(8401)▪41:28,29-PS-83:13-IS-5:24▪33:11▪40:24▪41:2▪47:14-JER-13:24-JOE-2:5-OB-18-NA-1:10-MAL-4:1▪N.T.-1CO-3:12(2562)

STUBBORN-all=5637&marked-DE-21:18,20-J'G-2:19(7186)-PS-78:8-PR-7:11

STUBBORNNESS-DE-9:27(7190)-1SA-15:23(6484)

STUCK-1SA-26:7(4600)-PS-119:31(1692)▪N.T.-AC-27:41(2043)

STUDS-SONG-1:11(5351)

STUDIETH-PR-15:28(1897)▪24:2(1897)

STUDY-EC-12:12(3854)▪N.T.-1TH-4:11(5389)-2TI-2:15(4704)

STUFF-all=3627&marked-GE-31:37^{2}▪45:20-EX-22:7▪36:7(4399)-JOS-7:11-1SA-10:22▪25:13▪30:24-NE-13:8-EZE-12:3,4^{2},7^{2}▪N.T.-LU-17:31(4632)

STUMBLE-all=3782&marked-PR-3:23(5062)▪4:12,19-IS-5:27▪8:15▪28:7(6328)▪59:10▪63:13-JER-13:16(5062)▪18:15▪20:11▪31:9▪46:6▪50:32-DA-11:19-NA-2:5▪3:3-MAL-2:8-N.T.-1PE-2:8(4350)

STUMBLED-all=3782&marked-1SA-2:4-1CH-13:9(8058)-PS-27:2-JER-46:12▪N.T.-RO-9:32(4350)▪11:11(4417)

STUMBLETH-PR-24:17(3782)▪N.T.-all=4350-JOH-11:9,10-RO-14:21

STUMBLING-IS-8:14(5063)▪57:14(4383)▪N.T.-1PE-2:8(4348)-1JO-2:10(4625)

STUMBLINGBLOCK-all=4383&marked-LE-19:14-IS-57:14-EZE-3:20▪7:19▪14:3,4,7▪N.T.-ROM-11:9(4625)▪14:13(4348)-1CO-1:23(4625)▪8:9(4348)-RE-2:14(4625)

STUMBLINGBLOCKS-JER-6:21(4383)-ZEP-1:3(4384)

STUMBLINGSTONE-RO-9:32(3037,4348),33(3037,4348)

STUMP-all=6136-DA-4:15,23,26

SUBDUE-all=3533&marked-GE-1:28-1CH-17:10(3665)-PS-47:3(1696)-IS-45:1(7286)-DA-7:24(8214)-MIC-7:19-ZEC-9:15▪N.T.-PH'P-3:21(5293)

SUBDUED-all=3665&marked-NU-32:22(3533),29(3533)-DE-20:20(3381)-JOS-18:1(3533)-J'G-3:30▪4:23▪8:28▪11:33-1SA-7:13-2SA-8:1,11(3533)▪22:40(3766)-1CH-18:1▪20:4▪22:18(3533)-PS-18:39(3766)▪81:14▪N.T.-1CO-15:28(5293)-HEB-11:33(2610)

SUBDUEDST-NE-9:24(3665)

SUBDUETH-PS-18:47(1696)▪144:2(7286)-DA-2:40(2827)

SUBJECT-all=5293&marked-LU-2:51▪10:17,20-RO-8:7,20▪13:1,5-1CO-14:32▪15:28-EPH-5:24-COL-2:20(1379)-TIT-3:1-HEB-2:15(1777)-JAS-5:17(3663)-1PE-2:18▪3:22▪5:5

SUBJECTED-RO-8:20(5293)

SUBJECTION-PS-106:42(3665)-JER-34:11(3533),16(3533)▪N.T.-all=5293&marked-1CO-9:27(1396)-2CO-9:13(5292)-GA-2:5(5292)-1TI-2:11(5292)▪3:4(5292)-HEB-2:5,8^{2}▪12:9-1PE-3:1,5

SUBMIT-all=3584&marked-GE-16:9(6031)-2SA-22:45-PS-18:44▪66:3▪68:30(7511)▪N.T.-all=5293&marked-1CO-16:16-EPH-5:22-COL-3:18-HEB-13:17(5226)-JAS-4:7-1PE-2:13▪5:5

SUBMITTED-1CH-29:24(5414,3027)-PS-81:15(3584)▪N.T.-RO-10:3(5293)

SUBMITTING-EPH-5:21(5293)

SUBORNED-AC-6:11(5260)

SUBSCRIBE-IS-44:5(3789)-JER-32:44(3789)

SUBSCRIBED-JER-32:10(3789),12(3789)

SUBSTANCE-all=7399&marked-GE-7:4(3351),23(3351)▪12:5▪13:6▪15:14▪34:23(7075)▪36:6(7075)-DE-11:6(3351)▪33:11(2428)-JOS-14:4(7075)-1CH-27:31▪28:1-2CH-21:17▪31:3▪32:29▪35:7-EZR-8:21▪10:8-JOB-1:3(4735),10(4735)▪5:5(2428)▪6:22(3581)▪15:29(2428)▪20:18(2428)▪22:20(7009)▪30:22(7738)-PS-105:21(7075)▪139:15(6108),16(1564)-PR-1:13(1952)▪3:9(1952)▪6:31(1952)▪8:21(3426)▪10:3(1942)▪12:27(1952)▪28:8(1952)▪29:3(1952)-SONG-8:7(1952)-IS-6:13^{2}(4678)-JER-15:13(2428)▪17:3(2428)-HOS-12:8(202)-OB-13(2428)-MIC-4:13(2428)▪N.T.-LU-8:3(5224)▪15:13(3776)-HEB-10:34(5223)▪11:1(5287)

SUBTIL-GE-3:1(6175)-2SA-13:3(2450)-PR-7:10(5341)

SUBTILLY-1SA-23:22(6191)-PS-105:25(5230)▪N.T.-AC-7:19(2686)

SUBTILITY-GE-27:35(4820)-2KI-10:19(6122)-PR-1:4(6195)▪N.T.-M'T-26:4(1388)-AC-13:10(1388)-2CO-11:3(3834)

SUBURBS-all=4054&marked-LE-25:34-NU-35:2,3,4,5,7-JOS-14:4▪21:2,3,8,11,13^{2},14^{2},15^{2},16^{3},17^{2},18^{2},19,21^{2},22^{2},23^{2},24^{2},25^{2},26,27^{2},28^{2},29^{2},30^{2},31^{2},32^{3},33,34^{2},35^{2},38^{2},39^{2},41,42-2KI-23:11(6503)-1CH-5:16▪6:55,57^{2},58^{2},59^{2},60^{3},64,67^{2},68^{2},69^{2},70^{2},71^{2},72^{2},73^{2},74^{2},75^{2},76^{3},77^{2},78^{2},79^{2},80^{2},81^{2}▪13:2-2CH-11:14▪31:19-EZE-27:28▪45:2▪48:15,17

SUBVERT-LA-3:36(5791)■N.T.-TIT-1:11(396)

SUBVERTED-TIT-3:11(1612)

SUBVERTING-AC-15:24(384)-2TI-2:14(2692)

SUCCEED-DE-25:6(6965)

SUCCEEDED-all=3423-DE-2:12,21,22

SUCCEEDEST-DE-12:29(3423)■19:1(3423)

SUCCESS-JOS-1:8(7919)

SUCCOUR-2SA-8:5(5826)■18:3(5826)■N.T.-HEB-2:18(997)

SUCCOURED-2SA-21:17(5826)■N.T.-2CO-6:2(997)

SUCCOURER-RO-16:2(4368)

SUCH-all=428&marked-GE-41:19(2007)-EX-9:18(834),24(834)■10:14(3651)■11:6(834)-LE-10:19-DE-5:29(2888)■13:14(2063)■17:4(2063)■25:16-J'G-19:30(2063)-RU-4:1(6423)-1SA-2:23■4:7(2063)■21:2(492)-2SA-12:8(2007)■13:12(3651),18(3651)■14:13(2063)■19:36(2063)-1KI-10:10(1931),12(3651)-2KI-6:8(6423),8(492),9(2088)■7:19(2088)■23:22(2088)-2CH-1:12(834)■9:9(1932),11(1992)-EZR-4:10(3706),11(3706),17(3706)■7:12(3706)-NE-6:8,11(3644)-ES-4:11(834)-JOB-12:3(3644)■14:3(2088)■16:2■18:21■23:14(2007)-PS-144:15(3602)-PR-30:20(3651)-IS-20:6(3541)■58:5(2088)■66:8(2063),8-JER-2:10(2063)■5:9(834),29(834)■9:9(834)■18:13■38:4-EZE-17:15■18:14(2007)■2:10(1836)■10:15■12:1(834)■N.T.-all=5108&marked-M'T-9:8■18:5■19:14■24:21(3634)■26:18(1170)-M'R-4:18(3778),20(3748),33■6:2■7:8,13■9:37■10:14■13:19(3634)-LU-9:9(3634)■13:2■18:16-JOH-4:23■7:32(5023)■8:5■9:16-AC-16:24■18:15(5130)■21:25■22:22■26:29-RO-1:32■2:2,3■16:18-1CO-5:1,5,11■6:11(5023)■7:15,28■11:16■15:48^{2}■16:16,18-2CO-2:6,7■3:4,12■10:11(3634),11^{2}■11:13■12:2,3,5,20^{2}(3634)-GA-5:21(5125),21,23■6:1-EPH-5:27-PH'P-2:29-1TH-4:6(5130)-2TH-3:12-1TI-6:5-2TI-3:5(5128)-TIT-3:11-PH'M-9-HEB-7:26■8:1■11:14■12:3■13:5(3588),16-JAS-4:13(3592),16-2PE-1:17(5107)■3:14(5023)-3JO-8-RE-16:18(3634)■20:6(5130)

SUCK-all=3243&marked-GE-21:7-DE-32:13■33:19-1SA-1:23-1KI-3:21-JOB-3:12■20:16■39:30(5966)-IS-60:16^{2}■66:11,12-LA-4:3-EZE-23:34(4680)-JOE-2:16■N.T.-all=2337-M'T-24:19-M'R-13:17-LU-21:23■23:29

SUCKED-SONG-8:1(3243)■N.T.-LU-11:27(2337)

SUCKING-all=3243&marked-NU-11:12-1SA-7:9(2461)-IS-11:8■49:15(5764)-LA-4:4

SUCKLING-all=3243-DE-32:25-1SA-15:3-JER-44:7

SUCKLINGS-all=3243&marked-1SA-22:19-PS-8:2-LA-2:11■N.T.-M'T-21:16(2337)

SUDDEN-JOB-22:10(6597)-PR-3:25(6597)■N.T.-1TH-5:3(160)

SUDDENLY-all=6597&marked-NU-6:9■12:4■35:22(6621)-DE-7:4(4118)-JOS-10:9■11:7-2SA-15:14(4116)-2CH-29:36-JOB-5:3■9:23-PS-6:10(7281)■64:4,7-PR-6:15,15(6621)■24:22■29:1(6621)-EC-9:12-IS-29:5■30:13■47:11■48:3-JER-4:20■6:26■15:8■18:22■49:19(7820)■50:44(7820)■51:8-HAB-2:7(6621)-MAL-3:1■N.T.-all=1810&marked-M'R-9:8(1819)■13:36-LU-2:13■9:39-AC-2:2(869)■9:3■16:26(869)■22:6■28:6(869)-1TI-5:22(5030)

SUE-M'T-5:40(2919)

SUFFER-all=5414&marked-EX-12:23-LE-19:17(5375)■22:16(5375)-NU-21:23-JOS-10:19-J'G-1:34■15:1■16:26(3240)-1KI-15:17-ES-3:8(3240)-JOB-9:18■21:3(5375)-36:2(3803)-PS-16:10■55:22■88:15(5375)■101:5(3201)■121:3-PR-19:19(5375)-EC-5:6,12(3240)■N.T.-all=3958&marked-M'T-3:15(863)■8:21(2010),31(2010)■16:21■17:12,17(430)■19:14(863)■23:13(863)-M'R-7:12(863)■8:31■9:12,19(430)■10:14(863)■11:16(863)-LU-8:32(2010)■9:22,41(430),59(2010)■17:25■18:16(863)■22:15,51(1439)■24:46-AC-2:27(1325)■3:18■5:41(818)■9:16■13:35(1325)■21:39(2010)■26:23(3805)-RO-8:17(4841)-1CO-3:15(2210)■4:12(430)■9:12(4722)■10:13(1439)■12:26,26(4841)-2CO-1:6■11:19(430),20(430)-GA-5:11(1377)■6:12(1377)-PH'P-1:29■4:12(5302)-1TI-2:12(2010)-2TI-1:12■2:9(2553),12(5278)■3:12(1377)-HEB-11:25(4778)■13:3(2558),22(430)-1PE-2:20■3:14,17■4:15,19-RE-2:10■11:9(863)

SUFFERED-all=5414&marked-GE-20:6■31:7,28(5203)-DE-18:14-J'G-3:28-1SA-24:7-2SA-21:10-1CH-16:21(3240)-JOB-31:30-PS-105:14(3240)-JER-15:15(5375)■N.T.-all=3958&marked-M'T-3:15(863)■19:8(2010)■24:43(1439)■27:19-M'R-1:34(863)■5:19(863),26,37(863)■10:4(2010)-LU-4:41(1439)■8:32(2010),51(863)■12:39(863)■13:2■24:26-AC-13:18(5159)■14:16(1439)■16:7(1439)■17:3■19:30(1439)■28:16(2010)-GA-3:4-PH'P-3:8(2210)-1TH-2:2(4310),14-HEB-2:18■5:8■7:23(2967)■9:26■13:12-1PE-2:21,23■3:18■4:1^{2}■5:10

SUFFEREST-RE-2:20(1439)

SUFFERETH-PS-66:9(5414)■N.T.-M'T-11:12(971)-AC-28:4(1439)-1CO-13:4(3114)

SUFFERING-AC-27:7(4330)-HEB-2:9(3804)-JAS-5:10(2552)-1PE-2:19(3958)-JUDE-7(5254)

SUFFERINGS-all=3804-RO-8:18(3804)-2CO-1:5,6,7-PH'P-3:10-COL-1:24-HEB-2:10-1PE-1:11■4:13■5:1

SUFFICE-all=7227&marked-NU-11:22^{2}(4672)-DE-3:26-1KI-20:10(5606)-EZE-44:6■45:9■N.T.-1PE-4:3(713)

SUFFICED-J'G-21:14(4672)-RU-2:14(7646),18(7648)

SUFFICETH-JOH-14:8(714)

SUFFICIENCY-JOB-20:22(5607)■N.T.-2CO-3:5(2426)■9:8(841)

SUFFICIENT-all=1767&marked-EX-36:7-DE-15:8■33:7(7227)-PR-25:16-IS-40:16^{2}■N.T.-all=2425&marked-M'T-6:34(713)-JOH-6:7(714)-2CO-2:6,16■3:5■12:9(714)

SUFFICIENTLY-2CH-30:3(4078)-IS-23:18(7654)

SUIT-J'G-17:10(6187)-2SA-15:4(7379)-JOB-11:19(2470)

SUITS-supplied

SUM-all=7218&marked-EX-21:30(3724)■30:12■38:21(6485)-NU-1:2,49■4:2,22■26:2■31:26,49-2SA-24:9(4557)-2KI-22:4(8552)-1CH-21:5(4557)-ES-4:7(6575)-PS-139:17-EZE-28:12(8508)-DA-7:1(7217)■N.T.-AC-7:16(5092)■22:28(2774)-HEB-8:1(2774)

SUMMER-all=7019&marked-GE-8:22-J'G-3:20(4747),24(4747)-2SA-16:1,2-PS-32:4-PS-74:17-PR-6:8■10:5■26:1■30:25-IS-16:9■18:6(6972)■28:4-JER-8:20■40:10,12■48:32-DA-2:35(7007)-AM-3:15■8:1,2-MIC-7:1-ZEC-14:8■N.T.-all=2330-M'T-24:32-M'R-13:28-LU-21:30

SUMPTUOUSLY-LU-16:19(2988)

SUN-all=8121&marked-GE-15:12,17■19:23■28:11■32:31■37:9-EX-16:21■17:12■22:3,26-LE-22:7-NU-25:4-DE-4:19■11:30■16:6■17:3■23:11■24:13,15■33:14-JOS-1:4■8:29■10:12,13^{2},27■12:1-J'G-5:31■8:13(2775)■9:33■14:18(2775)■19:14-1SA-11:9-2SA-2:24■3:35■12:11,12■23:4-1KI-22:36-2KI-3:22■23:5,11^{2}-2CH-18:34-NE-7:3-JOB-8:16■9:7(2775)■30:28(2535)■31:26(216)-PS-19:4■50:1■58:8■72:5,17■74:16■84:11■89:36■104:19,22■113:3■121:6■136:8■148:3-EC-1:3,5,9,14■2:11,17,18,19,20,22■3:16■4:1,3,7,15■5:13,18■6:1,5,12■7:11■8:9,15^{2},17■9:3,6,9^{2},11,13■10:5■11:7■12:2-SONG-1:6■6:10(2535)-IS-13:10■24:23(2535)■30:26(2535),26■38:8^{2}■41:25■45:6■49:10■59:19■60:19,20-JER-8:2■15:9■31:35-EZE-8:16■32:7-DA-6:14(8122)-JOE-2:10,31■3:15-AM-8:9-JON-4:8^{2}-MIC-3:6-NA-3:17-HAB-3:11-MAL-1:11■4:2■N.T.-all=2246-M'T-5:45■13:6,43■17:2■24:29-M'R-1:32■4:6■13:24■16:2-LU-4:40■21:25■23:45-AC-2:20■13:11■26:13■27:20-1CO-15:41-EPH-4:26-JAS-1:11-RE-1:16■6:12■7:16■8:12■9:2■10:1■12:1■16:8■19:17■21:23■22:5

SUNDER-all supplied

SUNDERED-JOB-41:17(6504)

SUNDRY-HEB-1:1(4181)

SUNG-IS-26:1(7891)■N.T.-M'T-26:30(5214)-M'R-14:26(5214)-RE-5:9(103)■14:3(103)

SUNK-all=2883&marked-1SA-17:49-2KI-9:24(3766)-PS-9:15-JER-38:6,22-LA-2:9■N.T.-AC-20:9(2702)

SUNRISING-all=4217,8121&marked-NU-21:11■34:15(4217)-DE-4:41,47-JOS-1:15■13:5■19:12,27,34-J'G-20:43

SUP-HAB-1:9(4041)■N.T.-LU-17:8(1172)-RE-3:20(1172)

SUPERFLUITY-JAS-1:21(4050)

SUPERFLUOUS-LE-21:18(8311)■22:23(8311)■N.T.-2CO-9:1(4053)

SUPERSCRIPTION-all=1923-M'T-22:20-M'R-12:16■15:26-LU-20:24■23:38

SUPERSTITION-AC-25:19(1175)

SUPERSTITIOUS-AC-17:22(1174)

SUPPED-1CO-11:25(1172)

SUPPER-all=1173&marked-M'R-6:21-LU-14:12,16,17,24■22:20(1172)-JOH-12:2■13:2,4■21:20-1CO-11:20,21-RE-19:9,17

SUPPLANT-JER-9:4(6117)

SUPPLANTED-GE-27:36(6117)

SUPPLE-EZE-16:4(4935)

SUPPLIANTS-ZEP-3:10(6282)

SUPPLICATION-all=8467&marked-1SA-13:12(2470)-1KI-8:28,30,33(2603),38,45,47(2603),49,52^{2},54,59(2603)■9:3-2CH-6:19,24(2603),29,35■33:13-ES-4:8(2603)-JOB-8:5(2603)■9:15(2603)-PS-6:9■30:8(2603)■55:1■119:170■142:1(2603)-IS-45:14(6419)-JER-36:7■37:20■38:26■42:2,9-DA-6:11(2604)■9:20-HO-12:4(2603)■N.T.-all=1162-AC-1:14-EPH-6:18^{2}-PH'P-4:6

SUPPLICATIONS-all=8469&marked-2CH-6:21,39(8467)-JOB-41:3-PS-28:2,6■31:22■86:6■116:1■130:2■140:6■143:1-JER-3:21■31:9-DA-9:3,17,18,23-ZEC-12:10■N.T.-1TI-2:1(1162)■5:5(1162)-HEB-5:7(2428)

SUPPLIED-1CO-16:17(378)-2CO-11:9(4322)

SUPPLIETH-2CO-9:12(4322)-EPH-4:16(2024)

SUPPLY-PH'P-1:19(2024)■2:30(378)■4:19(4137)

SUPPORT-AC-20:35(482)-1TH-5:14(472)

SUPPOSE-2SA-13:32(559)■N.T.-all=1380&marked-LU-7:43(5274)■12:51■13:2-JOH-21:25(3633)-AC-2:15(5274)-1CO-7:26(3543)-2CO-11:5(3049)-HEB-10:29-1PE-5:12(3049)

SUPPOSED-all=3543&marked-M'T-20:10-M'R-6:49(1380)-LU-3:23■24:37(1380)-AC-7:25■21:29■25:18(5282)-PH'P-2:25(2233)

SUPPOSING-all=3543&marked-LU-2:44-JOH-20:15(1380)-AC-14:19■16:27■27:13(1380)-PH'P-1:16(3633)-1TI-6:5

SUPREME-1PE-2:13(5242)

SURE-all=539&marked-GE-23:17(6965),20(6965)-EX-3:19(3045)-NU-32:23(3045)-DE-12:23(2388)-1SA-2:35■

20:7(3045)■25:28-**2SA**-1:10(3045)■23:5(8104)-**1KI**-11:38-**NE**-9:38(548)-**JOB**-24:22-**PS**-19:7■93:5■111:7-**PR**-6:3(7292)■11:15(982),18(571)-**IS**-22:23,25■28:16(3245)■32:18(4009)■33:16■55:3-**DA**-2:45(546)■4:26(7011)■**N.T.**-all=1492&marked-**M'T**-27:64(805),65(805),66(805)-**LU**-10:11(1097)-**JOH**-6:69(1097)■16:30-**AC**-13:34(4103)-**RO**-2:2■4:16(949)■15:29-**2TI**-2:19(4731)-**HEB**-6:19(804)-**2PE**-1:10(949),19(949)

SURELY-all=3588,a=518,3808,b=389,c=518&marked-**GE**-9:5b■20:7,11(7535)■28:16(403)■29:14b,32■31:42■43:10■44:28b-**EX**-2:14(403)■4:25■19:13■23:33-**NU**-14:23c,35c■22:33■32:11c-**DE**-1:35c■8:19■13:9■16:15b■30:18-**JOS**-14:9c-**J'G**-3:24b■6:16■20:39b-**RU**-1:10-**1SA**-14:39■15:32(403)■16:6b■17:25■20:26■25:21b,34(3588,518)■28:2(3651)-**2SA**-2:27■9:7■11:23■15:21■24:24(3588,518)-**1KI**-8:13(403)■11:2(403)■13:32■18:15■20:23c,25c■22:32b-**2KI**-1:4,6,16■3:14■23:22■24:3b-**ES**-6:13-**JOB**-8:6■13:3(199)■14:18(199)■18:21b■20:20■28:1■31:36a■33:8b■34:12(551)■34:31■35:13b■37:20■40:20-**PS**-23:6b■32:6(7535)■39:6^{2}b,11b■62:9b■73:18b■76:10■85:9b■91:3■112:6■131:2a■132:3c■139:11b,19c-**PR**-1:17■3:34c■10:9(983)■22:16b■30:2,33-**EC**-4:16■7:7■8:12■10:11c-**IS**-7:9■14:24a■16:7b■19:11b■22:14c■29:16c■40:7(403)■45:14b,24b■49:4(403),18■53:4(403)■60:9■62:8c■63:8b-**JER**-2:35b■3:20(403)■4:10(403)■5:2(403),4b■16:19b■22:6a,22■24:8■26:15■31:19■34:3■46:18■49:12,20^{2}a■50:45^{2}a■51:14(3588,518)-**LA**-3:3b-**EZE**-3:6a■5:11a■17:16a,19a■20:33a,27a■34:8a■36:5a,7a■38:19a-**HO**-5:9(539)■12:11b-**AM**-3:7-**ZEP**-2:9■**N.T**-all=230&marked-**M'T**-26:73-**M'R**-14:70-**LU**-1:1(4135)■4:23(3843)-**JOH**-17:8-**HEB**-6:14(2229)■22:20(3483)

SURETIES-**PR**-22:26(6148)

SURETISHIP-**PR**-11:15(8628)

SURETY-all=6148&marked-**GE**-15:13(3045)■18:13(552)■26:9(389)■43:9■44:32-**JOB**-17:3-**PS**-119:122-**PR**-6:1■11:15■17:18(6161)■20:16■27:13■**N.T.**-**AC**-12:11(230)-**HEB**-7:22(1450)

SURFEITING-**LU**-21:34(2897)

SURMISINGS-**1TI**-6:4(5283)

SURNAME-**IS**-44:5(3655)■**N.T.**-all=1941&marked-**M'T**-10:3-**AC**-10:5,32■11:13■12:12,25■15:37(2564)

SURNAMED-**IS**-45:4(3655)■**N.T.**-all=1941&marked-**M'R**-3:16(2007,3686),17(2007,3686)-**LU**-22:3-**AC**-1:23■4:36■10:18■15:22

SURPRISED-**IS**-33:14(270)-**JER**-48:41(8610)■51:41(8610)

SUSTAIN-all=3557-**1KI**-17:9-**NE**-9:21-**PS**-55:22-**PR**-18:14

SUSTAINED-all=5564-**GE**-27:37-**PS**-3:5-**IS**-59:16

SUSTENANCE-**J'G**-6:4(4241)-**2SA**-19:32(3557)■**N.T.**-**AC**-7:11(5527)

SWADDLED-**LA**-2:22(2946)-**EZE**-16:4(2853)

SWADDLING-**LU**-2:7(4683),12(4683)

SWADDLINGBAND-**JOB**-38:9(2854)

SWALLOW-all=1104&marked-**NU**-16:30,34-**2SA**-20:19,20-**JOB**-7:19■20:18-**PS**-21:9■56:1(7602),2(7602)■57:3(7602)■69:15■84:3(1866)-**PR**-1:12■26:2(1866)-**EC**-10:12-**IS**-25:8■38:14(5693)-**JER**-8:7(5693)-**HO**-8:7-**AM**-8:4(7602)-**OB**-16(3886)-**JON**-1:17■**N.T.**-**M'T**-23:24(2666)

SWALLOWED-all=1104&marked-**EX**-7:12■15:12-**NU**-16:32■26:10-**DE**-11:6-**2SA**-17:16-**JOB**-6:3(3886)■20:15■37:20-**PS**-35:25■106:17■124:3-**IS**-28:7■49:19-**JER**-51:34,44(1105)-**LA**-2:2,5^2,16-**EZE**-36:3(7602)-**HO**-8:8■**N.T.**-all=2666-**1CO**-15:54-**2CO**-2:7■5:4-**RE**-12:16

SWALLOWETH-**JOB**-5:5(7602)■39:24(1572)

SWAN-**LE**-11:18(8580)-**DE**-14:16(8580)

SWARE-all=7650&marked-**GE**-21:31■24:7,9■25:33■26:3,31■31:53■47:31■50:24-**EX**-13:5,11■33:1-**NU**-14:16,23,30(5375)■32:10,11-**DE**-1:8,34,35■2:14■4:21,31■6:10,18,23■7:12,13■8:1,18■9:5■10:11■11:9,21■26:3■28:11■30:20■31:20,21,23■34:4-**JOS**-1:6■5:6^2■6:22■9:15,20■14:9■21:43,44-**J'G**-2:1-**1SA**-19:6■20:3■24:22■28:10-**2SA**-3:35■19:23■21:17-**1KI**-1:29,30■2:8-**2KI**-25:24-**2CH**-15:14-**EZR**-10:5-**PS**-95:11■132:2-**JER**-38:16■40:9-**EZE**-16:8-**DA**-12:7■**N.T.**-all=3660-**M'R**-6:23-**LU**-1:73-**HEB**-3:11,18■6:13■7:21-**RE**-10:6

SWAREST-all=7650-**EX**-32:13-**NU**-11:12-**DE**-26:15-**1KI**-1:17-**PS**-89:49

SWARM-**EX**-8:24^2(6157)-**J'G**-14:8(5712)

SWARMS-all=6157-**EX**-8:21^2,22,29,31

SWEAR-all=7650&marked-**GE**-21:23,24■24:3,37■25:33■47:31■50:5,6-**EX**-6:8(5375)-**LE**-5:4■19:12-**NU**-30:2-**DE**-6:13■10:20-**JOS**-2:12,17,20■23:7-**J'G**-15:12-**1SA**-20:17■24:21■30:15-**2SA**-19:7-**1KI**-1:13,51■2:42■8:31(422)-**2CH**-6:22(422)■36:13-**EZR**-10:5-**NE**-13:25-**IS**-3:7(5375)■19:18■45:23■48:1■65:16-**JER**-4:2■5:2■7:9■12:16^2■22:5■32:22-**HOS**-4:15-**AM**-8:14-**ZEP**-1:5^2■**N.T.**-all=3660-**M'T**-5:34,36■23:16^2,18,20,21,22■26:74-**M'R**-14:71-**HEB**-6:13,16-**JAS**-5:12

SWEARERS-**MAL**-3:5(7650)

SWEARETH-all=7650-**LE**-6:3-**PS**-15:4■63:11-**EC**-9:2-**IS**-65:16-**ZEC**-5:3,4■**N.T.**-all=3660-**M'T**-23:18,20,21,22

SWEARING-**LE**-5:1(423)-**JER**-23:10(423)-**HO**-4:2(422)■10:4(422)

SWEAT-**GE**-3:19(2188)-**EZE**-44:18(3154)■**N.T.**-**LU**-22:44(2402)

SWEEP-**IS**-14:23(2894)■28:17(3261)■**N.T.**-**LU**-15:8(4563)

SWEEPING-**PR**-28:3(5502)

SWEET-all=5207,a=5561&marked-**GE**-8:21-**EX**-15:25(4985)■25:6a■29:18,25,41■30:7a,23^2(1314),34^{2}a■31:11a■35:8a,15a,28a■37:29a■39:38a■40:27a-**LE**-1:9,13,17■2:2,9,12■3:5,16■4:7a,31■6:15,21■8:21,28■16:12a■17:6■23:13,18■26:31-**NU**-4:16a■15:3,7,10,13,14,24■18:17■28:2,6,8,13,24,27■29:2,6,8,13,36-**2SA**-23:1(5273)-**2CH**-2:4a■13:11a■16:14(1314)-**EZR**-6:10(5208)-**NE**-8:10(4477)-**ES**-2:12(1314)-**JOB**-20:12(4985)■21:33(4985)■38:31(4575)-**PS**-55:14(4985)■104:34(6148)■119:103(4452)■141:6(5276)-**PR**-3:24(6148)■9:17(4985)■13:19(6148)■16:24(4966)■20:17(6149)■23:8(5273)■24:13(4966)■27:7(4966)-**EC**-5:12(4966)■11:7(4966)-**SONG**-2:3(4966),14(6149)■5:5(5674),13(4840),13(5674),16(4477)-**IS**-3:24(1314)■5:20(4966)■23:16(3190)■49:26(6071)-**JER**-6:20(2896),20(6148)■31:26(6148)-**EZE**-6:13■16:19■20:28,41-**DA**-2:46(5208)-**AM**-9:13(6071)-**MIC**-6:15(8492)■**N.T.**-all=1099&marked-**2CO**-2:15(2175)-**PH'P**-4:18(2175)-**JAS**-3:11-**RE**-10:9,10

SWEETER-**J'G**-14:18(4966)-**PS**-19:10(4966)

SWEETLY-**JOB**-24:20(4988)-**SONG**-7:9(4339)

SWEETNESS-**J'G**-9:11(4987)■14:14(4966)-**PR**-16:21(4986)■27:9(4986)-**EZE**-3:3(4966)

SWEETSMELLING-**EPH**-5:2(2175)

SWELL-**NU**-5:21(6639),22(6638)■5:27(6638)-**DE**-8:4(1216)

SWELLED-**NE**-9:21(1216)

SWELLING-all=1347&marked-**PS**-46:3(1346)-**IS**-30:13(1158)-**JER**-12:5■49:19■50:44■**N.T.**-**2PE**-2:18(5246)-**JUDE**-16(5246)

SWELLINGS-**2CO**-12:20(5450)

SWEPT-**J'G**-5:21(1640)-**JER**-46:15(5502)■**N.T.**-**M'T**-12:44(4563)-**LU**-11:25(4563)

SWERVED-**1TI**-1:6(795)

SWIFT-all=7031&marked-**1CH**-12:8(4116)-**JOB**-9:26(16)■24:18-**PR**-6:18(4116)-**EC**-9:11-**IS**-18:2■19:1■30:16,16(7043)■66:20(3753)-**JER**-2:23■46:6-**AM**-2:14,15-**MIC**-1:13(7409)-**MAL**-3:5(4116)■**N.T.**-**RO**-3:15(3691)-**JAS**-1:19(5036)-**2PE**-2:1(5031)

SWIFTER-all=7043&marked-**2SA**-1:23-**JOB**-7:6■9:25-**JER**-4:13-**LA**-4:19(7031)-**HAB**-1:8

SWIFTLY-**PS**-147:15(4120)-**IS**-5:26(7031)-**DA**-9:21(3288)-**JOE**-3:4(7031)

SWIM-**2KI**-6:6(6687)-**PS**-6:6(7811)-**IS**-25:11(7811)-**EZE**-47:5(7813)■**N.T.**-**AC**-27:42(1579),43(2860)

SWIMMEST-**EZE**-32:6(6824)

SWIMMETH-**IS**-25:11(7811)

SWINE-**LE**-11:7(2386)-**DE**-14:8(2386)■**N.T.**-all=5519-**M'T**-7:6■8:30,31,32^2-**M'R**-5:11,12,13,14,16-**LU**-8:32,33■15:15,16

SWINE'S-all=2386-**PR**-11:22-**IS**-65:4■66:3,17

SWOLLEN-**AC**-28:6(4092)

SWOON-**LA**-2:11(5848)

SWOONED-**LA**-2:12(5848)

SWORD-all=2719&marked-**GE**-3:24■27:40■31:26■34:25,26■48:22-**EX**-5:3,21■15:9■17:13■18:4■22:24■32:27-**LE**-26:6,7,8,25,33,36,37-**NU**-14:3,43■19:16■20:18■21:24■22:23,29,31■31:8-**DE**-13:15^2■20:13■28:22■32:25,41,42■33:29-**JOS**-5:13■6:21■8:24^2■10:11,28,30,32,35,37,39■11:10,11,12,14■13:22■19:47■24:12-**J'G**-1:8,25■4:15,16■7:14,20,22■8:10,20■9:54■18:27■20:2,15,17,25,35,37,46,48■21:10-**1SA**-13:22■14:20■15:8,33■17:39,45,47,50,51■18:4■21:8^2,9■22:10,13,19^2■25:13^3■31:4^2,5-**2SA**-1:12,22■2:16,26■3:29■11:25■12:9^2,10■15:14■18:8■20:8,10■23:10■24:9-**1KI**-1:51■2:8,32■3:24^2■19:1,10,14,17^2-**2KI**-6:22■8:12■10:25■11:15,20■19:7,37-**1CH**-5:18■10:4^2,5■21:5^2,12^2,16,27,30-**2CH**-20:9■21:4■23:14,21■29:9■32:21■36:17,20-**EZR**-9:7-**NE**-4:18-**ES**-9:5-**JOB**-1:15,17■5:15,20■15:22■19:29^2■20:25(1300)■27:14■33:18(7973)■36:12(7973)■39:22■40:19■41:26-**PS**-7:12■17:13■22:20■37:14,15■42:10(7524)■44:3,6■45:3■57:4■63:10■64:3■76:3■78:62,64■89:43■144:10■149:6-**PR**-5:4■12:18■25:18-**SONG**-3:8-**IS**-1:20■2:4■3:25■13:15■14:19■21:15■22:2■27:1■31:8^3■34:5,6■37:7,38■41:2■49:2■51:19■65:12■66:16-**JER**-2:30■4:10■5:12,17■6:25■9:16■11:22■12:12■14:12,13,15^2,16,18■15:2,3,9■16:4■18:21^2■19:7■20:4^2■21:7^2,9■24:10■25:16,27,29,31■26:23■27:8,13■29:17,18■31:2■32:24,36■33:4■34:4,17■38:2■39:18■41:2■42:16,17,22■43:11■44:12^2,13,18,27,28■46:10,14,16■47:6■48:2,10■49:37■50:16,35,36^2,37^2■51:50-**LA**-1:20■2:21■4:9■5:9-**EZE**-5:2,12^2,17■6:3,8,11,12■7:15^2■11:8^2,10■12:14,16■14:17^2,21■17:21■21:3,4,5,9,11,12,14^3,15,19,20,28■23:10,25■24:21■25:13■26:6,8,11■28:23■29:8■30:4,5,6,17,21,22,24,25■31:17,18■32:10,11,20^2,21,22,23,24,25,26,28,29,30,31,32■33:2,3,4,6^2,26,27■35:5,8■38:8,21^2■39:23-**DA**-11:33-**HO**-1:7■2:18■7:16■11:6■13:16-**JOE**-2:8(7973)-**AM**-1:11■4:10■7:9,11,17■9:1,4,10-**MIC**-4:3■5:6■6:14-**NA**-2:13■3:3,15-**ZEP**-2:12-**HAG**-2:22-**ZEC**-9:13■11:17■13:7■**N.T.**-all=3162&marked-**M'T**-10:34■26:51,52^3-**M'R**-14:47-**LU**-2:35(4501)■21:24■22:36,49-**JOH**-18:10,11-**AC**-12:2■16:27-**RO**-8:35■13:4-**EPH**-6:17-**HEB**-4:12■11:34,37-**RE**-1:16(4501)■2:12(4501),16(4501)■6:4,8(4501)■13:10^2,14■19:15(4501),21

(4501),21sup

SWORDS-all=2719&marked-1SA-13:19-2KI-3:26-NE-4:13-PS-55:21(6609)■59:7-PR-30:14-SONG-3:8-IS-2:4■21:15-EZE-16:40■23:47■28:7■30:11■32:12,27■38:4-JOE-3:10-MIC-4:3■N.T.-all=3162-M'T-26:47,55-M'R-14:43,48-LU-22:38,52

SWORN-all=7650&marked-GE-22:16-EX-13:19■17:16(3027,5920,3676)-LE-6:5-DE-7:8■13:17■19:8■28:9■29:13■31:7-JOS-9:18,19-J'G-2:15■21:1,7,18-1SA-3:14■20:42-2SA-3:9■21:2-2CH-15:15-NE-6:18(1167,7621)■9:15(5375)-PS-24:4■89:3,35■102:8■110:4■119:106■132:11-IS-14:24■45:23■54:9^{2}■62:8-JER-5:7■11:5■44:26■49:13■51:14-EZE-21:23-AM-4:2■6:8■8:7-MIC-7:20■N.T.-all=3660-AC-2:30■7:17-HEB-4:3

SYCAMINE-LU-17:6(4807)

SYCOMORE-all=8256-1KI-10:27-1CH-27:28-2CH-1:15■9:27-PS-78:47-AM-7:14■N.T.-LU-19:4(4809)

SYCOMORES-IS-9:10(8256)

SYNAGOGUE-all=4864&marked-M'T-12:9■13:54-M'R-1:21,23,29■3:1■5:22(752),36(752),38(752)■6:2-LU-4:16,20,28,33,38■6:6■7:5■8:41■13:14(752)-JOH-6:59■9:22(656)■12:42(656)■18:20-AC-6:9^{2}■13:14,15(752),42■14:1■17:1,10,17■18:4,7,8(752),17,19,26■19:8■22:19■26:11-RE-2:9■3:9

SYNAGOGUE'S-M'R-5:35(752)-LU-8:49(752)

SYNAGOGUES-PS-74:8(4150)■N.T.-all=4864&marked-M'T-4:23■6:2,5■9:35■10:17■23:6,34-M'R-1:39■12:39■13:9-LU-4:15,44■11:43■12:11■13:10■20:46■21:12-JOH-16:2(656)-AC-9:2,20■13:5■15:21■24:12

T

TABERING-NA-2:7(8608)

TABERNACLE-all=168,a=4908&marked-EX-25:9a■26:1a,6a,7a,9,12a,13a,15a,17a,18a,20a,22a,23a,26a,27^{2}a,30a,35a■27:9a,19a,21■28:43■29:4,10,11,30,32,42,44■30:16,18,20,26,36■31:7^{2}■33:7^{3},8^{2},9^{2},10,11■35:11a,15a,18a,21■36:8a,13a,14a,20a,22a,23a,25a,27a,28a,31a,32^{2}a,37■38:8,20a,21^{2}a,30,31a■39:32a,33a,38,40a■40:2a,5a,6a,9a,12,17a,18a,19a,21a,22a,24a,28a,29a,33a,34a,35a,36a,38a-LE-1:1,3,5■3:2,8,13■4:4,5,7^{2},14,16,18^{2}■6:16,26,30■8:3,4,10a,31,33,35■9:5,23■10:7,9■12:6■14:11,23■15:14,29,31a■16:7,16,17,20,23,33■17:4,4a,5,6,9■19:21■24:3■26:11a-NU-1:1,50^{3}a■1:51^{2}a,53^{2}a■2:2,17■3:7,7a,8,8a,23a,25,25a,25,26a,29a,35a,36a,38a,38■4:3,4,15,16a,23,25a,25^{2},26a,28,30,31,31a,33,35,37,39,41,43,47■5:17a■6:10,13,18■7:1a,3a,5,89■8:9,15,19,22,24,26■9:15^{3}a,17,18a,19a,20a,22a■10:3,11a,17^{2}a,21■11:16,24,26■12:4,5,10■14:10■16:9a,18,19,24a,27a,42,43,50■17:4,7,8,13a■18:2,3,4^{2},6,21,22,23,31■19:4,13a■20:6■25:6■27:2■31:30a,47a,54-DE-31:14^{2},15^{2}-JOS-18:1■19:51■22:19a,29a-1SA-2:22-2SA-6:17■7:6a-1KI-1:39■2:28,29,30■8:4^{2}-1CH-6:32,48a■9:19,21,23■16:39a■17:5a■21:29a■23:26a,32-2CH-1:3,5a,6,13■5:5^{2}■24:6-JOB-5:24■18:6,14,15■19:12■20:26■29:4■31:31■36:29(5521)-PS-15:1■19:4■27:5,6■61:4■76:2(5520)■78:60a,67■132:3-PR-14:11-IS-4:6(5521)■16:5■33:20-JER-10:20-LA-2:4,6(7900)-EZE-37:27a■41:1-AM-5:26(5522)■9:11(5521)■N.T.-all=4633&marked-AC-7:43,44,46(4638)■15:16-2CO-5:1(4636),4(4636)-HEB-8:2,5■9:2,3,6,8,11,21■13:10-2PE-1:13(4638),14(4638)-RE-13:6■15:5■21:3

TABERNACLES-all=168&marked-LE-23:34(5521)-NU-24:5(4908)-DE-16:13(5521),16(5521)■31:10(5521)-2CH-8:13(5521)-EZR-3:4(5521)-JOB-11:14■12:6■15:34■22:23-PS-43:3(4908)■46:4(4908)■78:51■83:6■84:1(4908)■118:15■132:7(4908)-DA-11:45(168)-HO-9:6■12:9(168)-ZEC-14:16(5521),18(5521),19(5521)-MAL-2:12(168)■N.T.-all=4633&marked-M'T-17:4-M'R-9:5-LU-9:33-JOH-7:2(4634)-HEB-11:9

TABLE-all=7979&marked-EX-25:23,27,28,30■26:35^{3}■30:27■31:8■35:13■37:10,14,15,16■39:36■40:4,22,24-LE-24:6-NU-3:31■4:7-J'G-1:7-1SA-20:29,34-2SA-9:7,10,11,13■19:28-1KI-2:7■4:27■7:48■10:5■13:20■18:19-2KI-4:10-1CH-28:16-2CH-9:4■13:11■29:18-NE-5:17-JOB-36:16-PS-23:5■69:22■78:19■128:3-PR-3:3(3871)■7:3(3871)■9:2-SONG-1:12(4524)-IS-21:5■30:8(3871)■65:11-JER-17:1(3871)-EZE-23:41■39:20■41:22■44:16-DA-11:27-MAL-1:7,12■N.T.-all=5132&marked-M'T-15:27-M'R-7:28-LU-1:63(4093)■16:21■22:21,30-JOH-13:28(345)-RO-11:9-1CO-10:21^{2}-HEB-9:2

TABLES-all=3871,a=7979&marked-EX-24:12■31:18■32:15^{2},16^{2},19■34:1^{3},4^{2},28,29-DE-4:13■5:22■9:9^{2},10,11^{2},15,17■10:1,2^{2},3^{2},4,5-1KI-8:9-1CH-28:16^{2}a-2CH-4:8a,19■5:10-IS-28:8-EZE-40:39^{2}a,40^{2}a,41^{3}a,42a,43a-HAB-2:2■N.T.-all=5132&marked-M'T-21:12-M'R-7:4(2825)■11:15-JOH-2:15-AC-6:2-2CO-3:3^{2}(4109)-HEB-9:4(4109)

TABLETS-EX-35:22(3558)-NU-31:50(3558)-IS-3:20(1004,5315)

TABRET-all=8596&marked-GE-31:27-1SA-10:5-JOB-17:6(8611)-IS-5:12

TABRETS-all=8596-1SA-18:6-IS-24:8■30:32-JER-31:4-EZE-28:13

TACHES-all=7165-EX-26:6^{2},11^{2},33■35:11■36:13^{2},18■39:33

TACKLING-AC-27:19(4631)

TACKLINGS-IS-33:23(2256)

TAIL-all=2180-EX-4:4-DE-28:13,44-J'G-15:4-JOB-40:17-IS-9:14,15■19:15■N.T.-RE-12:4(3769)

TAILS-J'G-15:4(2180)-IS-7:4(2180)■N.T.-all=3769-RE-9:10^{2},19^{2}

TAKE-all=3947,a=5375,b=5493,c=3920,d=270&marked-GE-3:22■6:21■7:2■12:19■14:21,23^{2},24■15:9■19:15,19(1692)■21:30■22:2■23:13■24:3,4,7,37,38,40,48,51■27:3a,3(6679),46■28:1,2,6^{2}■30:15■31:31(1497),32,50■33:11■34:9,16,17,21■38:23■42:33,36■43:11,12,13,18■44:29■45:18,19-EX-2:9(3212)■4:4d,9,17■6:7■7:9,15,19■8:8b■9:8■10:17b,26■12:3,4,5,7,21,22,32■15:14d,15d■16:16,33■17:5^{2}■20:7a■21:10,14■22:26(2254)■23:8,25b■25:2,3■26:5(6901)■28:1(7126),5,9■29:1,5,7,12,13,15,16,19,20,21,22,26,31■30:16,23,34■33:23b■34:16■35:5■40:9-LE-2:2(7061),9(7311)■3:4b,9b,10b,15b■4:5,8(3318),9b,19(7311),25,30,31b,34,35b■5:12(7061)■6:10(7311),15(7311)■7:4b■8:2■9:2,3■10:12■14:4,6,10,12,14,15,21,24,25,40(2502),42^{2},49,51■15:14,29■16:5,7,12,14,18■18:7,18■20:14,17,21■21:7^{2},13,14^{2}■23:40■24:5■25:36-NU-1:2a,49a,51(3381)■3:40a,41,45,47^{2}■4:2a,5(3381),9,12,22a■5:17^{2},25,26(7061)■6:18,19■7:5■8:6,8^{2}■11:17(680)■16:6,17,37(7311),46■17:2,10(3615)■18:26■19:4,6,17,18■20:8,25■21:7b■25:4■26:2a■27:18■31:26a,29,30■34:18■35:31,32-DE-1:13(3051)■4:34■5:11a■7:3,15b,25■12:26a■15:17■16:19■20:7,14(962),19(8610)■21:3■22:6,7,13,15,18,30■24:4,6(2254),17(2254)■25:5,7,8■26:2,4■27:9(5535)■31:26■32:41d-JOS-3:6a,12■4:2,3a,5(7311)■6:6a,18■7:13b,14^{2}c■8:1,29(3381)■9:11■10:42c■11:12c■20:4(622)■22:19d-J'G-4:6■6:20,25,26■7:24c■14:3,8,15(3423)■15:2(1961)■20:10-1SA-2:16^{2}■6:7,8■8:11,13,14,16■9:3■16:2■17:17,18,46b■19:14,20■20:21■21:9■23:26(8610)■24:11■25:11,39,40■26:11-2SA-2:21■4:11(1197)■5:6b■12:4,11,28^{2}c■13:33(7760)■16:9b■19:19(7760),30■20:6■24:10(5674),22-1KI-1:33■2:31b■11:31,34,35,37■14:3,10(1197)■16:3(1197)■18:40(8610)■19:4,10,14■20:6,18^{2}(8610),24b■21:15(3423),16(3423),21(1197)■22:3,26-2KI-2:1(5927),3,5■4:1,29,36a■5:15,16,20,23■6:2,7(7311),32b■7:13■8:8■9:1,3,17,25a,26a■10:6,14(8610)■12:5■13:15,18■18:32■20:7,18-1CH-7:21■17:13b■21:23,24a■28:10(7200)-2CH-18:25■19:6(7200)■20:25(962)■32:18c-EZR-4:22(2095)■5:14(5312),15(5376)■9:12a-NE-5:2■10:30■13:25a-ES-4:4b■6:10-JOB-7:21(5674)■9:34b■11:18(7901)■13:14a■18:9d■21:12a■23:10(5978)■24:2(1497),3(2254),9(2254),10a■27:20(5381)■30:17(7901)■31:36a■32:22a■36:17(8551),18(5496)■38:13d,20■41:4■42:8-PS-7:5(5381)■13:2(7896)■16:4a■27:10(622)■31:13■35:2(2388)■50:9,16a■51:11■52:5(2846)■58:9(8175)■69:24(5381)■71:11(8610)■81:2a■89:33(6331)■102:24(5927)■109:8■116:13a■119:43(5337)■139:9a,20a-PR-2:19(5381)■4:13(2388)■5:5(8551),22c■6:25,27(2846)■20:16,16(2254)■22:27■25:4(1898),5(1898)■27:13,13(2254)■30:9(8610)-EC-5:15a,19a■7:18d,21(5414)-SONG-2:15d■7:8d-IS-1:25b■3:1b,6(8610),18b■4:1(2388),1(622)■5:5b,23b■8:1■10:2(1497),6(7997),6(962)■13:8d■14:2,2sup,4a■16:3(935)■18:5b■23:16■25:8b■27:5(2388),6(2388),9b■28:19■30:1(6213),14(2846),14(2834)■33:23(962)■36:17■38:21a■39:7■40:24,24a■44:15■47:2,3■56:4(2388)■57:13,14(7311)■58:9b■64:7(2388)■66:21-JER-3:14■4:4b■5:10b■7:29a■9:10a,18a■13:4,6,21d■15:15,19(3318)■16:2■18:22c■20:5,10■25:9,10(6),15,28■29:6^{2}■32:3c,14,24c,25(5749),28c,44(5749)■33:26■34:22c■36:2,14,26,28■37:8c■38:3c,10^{2}■39:12■43:9,10■44:12■46:11■49:29,29a■51:8,26-EZE-4:1,3,9■5:1^{3},2,3,4■10:6■11:18b,19b■14:5(8610)■15:3■16:6,39■17:22■19:1a■21:26(7311)■23:25b,25,26,29■24:5,16,25■26:17a■27:2a,32a■28:12a■29:19a,19(962),19(7997)■30:4■32:2a■33:2,4,6■36:24,26b■37:16^{2},19,21■38:12(7997),12(962),13(7997),13(962),13^{2}■39:10a■43:20,21■44:22^{2}■45:9(7311),18,19■46:18-DA-6:23(5267)■7:18(6902),26(5709)■11:15c,18c,31b-HO-1:2,6a■2:9,17b■4:11■5:14a■11:4(7311)■14:2,2a-AM-3:5(5927)■4:2a■5:1a,11,12,23b■6:10a■9:2,3-JON-1:12a■4:3-MIC-2:2^{2}a,4,6(5253)■6:14(5253)-NA-2:9^{2}(962)-HAB-1:10c,15(5927)■2:6a-ZEP-3:11b-HAG-2:23-ZEC-1:6(5381)■3:4b■6:10,11■8:23^{2}(2388)■9:7b■11:15■14:21-MAL-2:3a■N.T.-all=142,a=2983-M'T-1:20(3880)■2:13(3880),20(3880)■5:40a■9:6■11:12(726),29■15:26a■16:5a,24■17:25a,27,27a■18:16(3880),23(4868)■20:14■22:13■24:17,18■25:28■26:4(2902),26a,52a,55(4815)-M'R-2:9,11■6:8■7:27a■8:14a,34■10:21■12:19a■13:15,16■14:1(2902),22a,36(3911),44(2902),48(4815)■15:24,36(2507)■16:18-LU-1:25(851)■5:24■6:4a■9:3,23■11:35(4648)■14:9(2722)■16:6(1209),7(1209)■17:31■19:24■20:20(1949),26(1949),28a■22:17a,36-JOH-2:16■5:8,11,12■6:7a,15(726)■7:30(4084),32(4084)■10:17a,18a,39(4084)■11:39,48,57(4084)■16:15a■17:15■18:31a■19:6a,38■20:15-AC-1:20a,25a■12:3(4815)■15:14a,37(4838),38(4838)■20:13(353)■21:24(3880)■23:10(726)■27:33(3335),34(4355)-RO-11:27(851)-1CO-6:15■11:24a-2CO-11:20a-EPH-6:13(353),17(1209)-2TI-4:11(353)-HEB-10:4(851),11(4014)-JAS-5:10a-1JO-3:5-RE-3:11a■5:9a■6:4a■10:8a,9a■22:17(2902),19^{2}(851)

TAKEN-all=3947,a=3920,b=5493,c=5375,d=8610&marked-GE-2:22,23■3:19,23■12:15,19■18:27(2974),31(2974)■20:3■21:25(1497)■27:33(6679),35,36■

30:15,23(622)■31:1,9(5337),16(5337),34-**EX**-14:11■25:15b■40:36(5927),37^{2}(5927)-**LE**-4:10(7311),31(7311),35(7311)■6:2(1497)■7:34■14:43(2502)-**NU**-3:12■5:13d■8:16,18■9:17(5927),21^{2}(5927),22(5927)■10:11(5927),17(3381)■16:15c■18:6■21:26■31:26(7628),49c■36:3^{2}(1639),4(1639)-**DE**-4:20■20:7■24:1,5^{2}■26:14(1197)■28:31(1497)-**JOS**-7:11,15a,16a,17a,18a■8:8d,21a■10:1a-**J'G**-1:8a■11:36(6213)■14:9(7287)■15:6■17:2■18:24-**1SA**-4:11,17,19,21,22■7:14■10:20a,21^{2}a■12:3^{2},4■14:41a,42a■21:6b,6■30:16,19-**2SA**-12:9,10,27a■18:9(5414),18■23:6-**1KI**-7:8■9:9(2388),16a■16:18a■22:43b-**2KI**-2:9,10,16c■4:20c■12:3b■13:25■14:4b■18:10a,22b■24:7-**1CH**-24:6^{2}(270)-**2CH**-15:8a,17b■17:2a■19:3(1197)■20:33b■28:18a■32:12b-**EZR**-9:2c■10:2(3427),10(3427),14(3427),17(3427),18(3427),44c-**NE**-5:15■6:18-**ES**-2:15,16■8:2(5674)-**JOB**-1:21■16:12(247)■19:9b■20:19(1497)■22:6(2254)■24:24(7092)■27:2b■28:2■30:16(270)■34:5b,20b-**PS**-9:15a■10:2d■40:12(5381)■59:12a■85:3c■119:53(270),143(4672)-**PR**-3:26(3921)■4:16(1497)■6:2a■7:20■11:6a-**EC**-2:18(6001)■3:14(1639)■7:26a■9:12(270)-**IS**-6:6,7b■8:4c,15a■10:27b,29(3885)■16:10(622)■17:1b■21:3(270)■24:18a■28:13a■33:20(6813)■36:7b■41:9(2388)■49:24,25■51:22■52:5■53:8■57:1^{2}(622)■64:6c-**JER**-6:11a,24(2388)■8:21(2388)■16:5(622)■29:22■34:3d■38:23d,28^{2}a■39:5■40:1,10d■48:1a,7a,33(622),41a,44a,46■49:20(3289),24(270)■50:2a,9a,24a,45(3289)■51:31a,41a,56a-**LA**-4:20a-**EZE**-12:13d■15:3■16:17,20■17:12,13^{2},13(935),20d■18:8,13,17(7725)■19:4d,8d■21:23d,24d■22:12^{2},25■27:5■33:6■36:3(5927)-**DA**-5:2(5312),3(5312)■6:23(5267)■7:12(5709)■8:11(7311)■11:12c■12·11b-**HO**-4:3(622)-**JOE**-3:5-**AM**-3:4a,5,12(5337)■4:10(7628)■6:13-**MIC**-2:9■4:9(2388)-**ZEP**-3:15(5493)-**ZEC**-14:2■**N.T.**-all=142,a=2983&marked-**M'T**-4:24(4912)■9:15(522)■13:12■16:7a■21:43■24:40(3880),41(3880)■25:29■27:59a■28:12a-**M'R**-2:20(522)■4:25■6:41a■9:36(1723)-**LU**-1:1(2021)■4:38(4912)■5:5a,9(4815),35(522)■8:18,37(4912)■9:17■10:42(851)■11:52■17:34(3880),35(3880),36(3880)■19:26-**JOH**-7:44(4084)■8:3(2638),4(2638)■13:12a■19:31■20:1,2,13-**AC**-1:2(353),9(1869),11(353),22(353)■2:23a,33^{2}■17:9a■20:9■21:6(782)■23:27(4815)■27:17,20(4014),33(4355),40(4014)-**1CO**-5:2(1808)■10:13a-**2CO**-3:16(4014)-**1TH**-2:17(642)-**2TH**-2:7(1096)-**1TI**-5:9(2639)-**2TI**-2:26(2221)-**HEB**-5:1a-**2PE**-2:12(259)-**RE**-5:8a■11:17a■19:20(4084)

TAKER-supplied

TAKEST-**EX**-4:9(3947)■30:12(5375)-**J'G**-4:9(1980)-**1CH**-22:13(8104)-**PS**-104:29(622)-**EC**-9:9(6001)■**N.T.**-**LU**-19:21(142)

TAKETH-all=3947&marked-**EX**-20:7(5375)-**DE**-5:11(5375)■10:17■24:6(2254)■25:11(2388)■27:25■32:11-**JOS**-7:14(3920)■15:16(3920)-**J'G**-1:12(3920)-**1SA**-17:26(5943)-**1KI**-14:10(1197)-**JOB**-5:5,13(3920)■9:12(2862)■12:20,24(5493)■21:6(270)■27:8(7953)■40:24-**PS**-15:3(5375),5■137:9(270)-**PR**-1:19■16:32(3920)■17:23■25:20(5710)■26:17(2388)■30:28(8610)-**EC**-1:3(5998)■5:18(5998)-**IS**-13:14(6908)■40:15(5190)■44:14■51:18(2388)■56:6(2388)-**EZE**-16:32-**AM**-3:12(5337)■**N.T.**-all=142&marked-**M'T**-4:5(3880),8(3880)■9:16■10:38(2983)■12:45(3880)■17:1(3880)-**M'R**-2:21■4:15■5:40(3880)■9:2(3880),18(2638)■14:33(3880)-**LU**-6:29,30■8:12■9:39(2983)■11:22,26(3880)■16:3(851)-**JOH**-1:29■10:18■15:2■16:22■21:13(2983)-**RO**-3:5(2018)-**1CO**-3:19(1405)■11:21(4301)-**HEB**-5:4(2983)■10:9(337)

TAKING-**2CH**-19:7(4727)-**JER**-50:46(8610)-**HO**-11:3(3947)■**N.T.**-all=2983&marked-**LU**-4:5(321)■19:22(142)-**RO**-7:8,11-**2CO**-11:8-**EPH**-6:16(353)-**2TH**-1:8(1325)-**3JO**-7

TALE-**EX**-5:8(4971),18(8506)-**1CH**-9:28(4557)-**PS**-90:9(1899)

TALEBEARER-all=5372&marked-**LE**-19:16(7400)-**PR**-11:13(1980,7400)■18:8■20:19(7400)■26:20,22

TALENT-all=3603-**EX**-25:39■37:24■38:27-**2SA**-12:30-**1KI**-20:39-**2KI**-5:22■23:33-**1CH**-20:2-**2CH**-36:3-**ZEC**-5:7■**N.T.**-all=5007&marked-**M'T**-25:24,25,28-**RE**-16:21(5006)

TALENTS-all=3603&marked-**EX**-38:24,25,27^{2},29-**1KI**-9:14,28■10:10,14■16:24-**2KI**-5:5,23^{2}■15:19■18:14^{2}■23:33-**1CH**-19:6■22:14^{2}■29:4^{2},7^{4}-**2CH**-3:8■8:18■9:9,13■25:6,9■27:5■36:3-**EZR**-7:22(3604)■8:26^{3}-**ES**-3:9■**N.T.**-all=5007-**M'T**-18:24■25:15,16^{2},20^{4},22^{3},28

TALES-**EZE**-22:9(7400)■**N.T.**-**LU**-24:11(3026)

TALK-all=1696&marked-**NU**-11:17-**DE**-5:24■6:7-**1SA**-2:3-**2KI**-18:26-**1CH**-16:9(7878)-**JOB**-11:2(8193)■13:7■15:3(1697)-**PS**-69:26(5608)■71:24(1897)■77:12(7878)■105:2(7878)■119:27(7878)■145:11-**PR**-6:22(7878)■14:23(1697)■24:2-**EC**-10:13(6310)-**JER**-12:1-**EZE**-3:22-**DA**-10:17■**N.T.**-**M'T**-22:15(3056)-**JOH**-14:30(2980)

TALKED-all=1696&marked-**GE**-4:8(559)■17:3■35:13,14■45:15-**EX**-20:22■33:9■34:29,31-**DE**-5:4-**J'G**-14:7-**1SA**-14:19■17:23-**1KI**-1:22-**2KI**-2:11■6:33■8:4-**2CH**-25:16-**JER**-38:25-**DA**-9:22-**ZEC**-1:9,13,19■2:3■4:1,4,5■5:5,10■6:4■**N.T.**-all=2980&marked-**M'T**-12:46-**M'R**-6:50-**LU**-9:30(4814)■24:14(3656),32-**JOH**-4:27-**AC**-10:27(4926)■20:11(3656)■26:31-**RE**-17:1■21:9,15

TALKERS-**EZE**-36:3(3956)■**N.T.**-**TIT**-1:10(3151)

TALKEST-**J'G**-6:17(1696)-**1KI**-1:14(1696)■**N.T.**-**JOH**-4:27(2980)

TALKETH-**PS**-37:30(1696)■**N.T.**-**JOH**-9:37(2980)

TALKING-all=1696&marked-**GE**-17:22-**1KI**-18:27(7879)-**ES**-6:14-**JOB**-29:9(4405)-**EZE**-33:30■**N.T.**-**M'T**-17:3(4814)-**M'R**-9:4(4814)-**EPH**-5:4(3473)-**RE**-4:1(2980)

TALL-all=7311&marked-**DE**-2:10,21■9:2-**2KI**-19:23(6967)-**IS**-37:24(6967)

TALLER-**DE**-1:28(7311)

TAME-**M'R**-5:4(1150)-**JAS**-3:8(1150)

TAMED-**JAS**-3:7^{2}(1150)

TANNER-all=1033-**AC**-9:43■10:6,32

TAPESTRY-all supplied

TARE-**2SA**-13:31(7167)-**2KI**-2:24(1234)■**N.T.**-**M'R**-9:20(4682)-**LU**-9:42(4952)

TARES-all=2215-**M'T**-13:25,26,27,29,30,36,38,40

TARGET-**1SA**-17:6(3591)-**1KI**-10:16(6793)-**2CH**-9:15(6793)

TARGETS-all=6793-**1KI**-10:16-**2CH**-9:15■14:8

TARRIED-all=3427&marked-**GE**-24:54(3885)■28:11(3885)■31:54(3885)-**NU**-9:19(748),22(748)-**J'G**-3:25(2342),26(4102)■19:8(4102)-**RU**-2:7-**1SA**-13:8(3176)■14:2-**2SA**-11:1■15:17(5975),29■20:5(3186)-**2KI**-2:18-**1CH**-20:1-**PS**-68:12(5116)■**N.T.**-all=1961&marked-**M'T**-25:5(5549)-**LU**-1:21(5549)■2:43(5278)-**JOH**-3:22(1304)-**AC**-9:43(3306)■15:33(4160)■18:18(4357)■20:5(3306),15(3306)■21:4,10■25:6(1304)■27:33(4328)■28:12

TARRIEST-**AC**-22:16(3195)

TARRIETH-**1SA**-30:24(3427)-**MIC**-5:7(6960)

TARRY-all=3427&marked-**GE**-19:2(3885)■27:44■45:9(5975)-**EX**-12:39(4102)■24:14-**LE**-14:8-**NU**-22:19-**J'G**-5:28(309)■6:18■19:6(3885),9(3885),10(3885)-**RU**-1:13(7663)■3:13(3885)-**1SA**-1:23■10:8(3176)■14:9(1826)-**2SA**-10:5■11:12■15:28(4102)■18:14(3176)■19:7(3885)-**2KI**-2:2,4,6■7:9(2442)■9:3(2442)■14:10-**1CH**-19:5-**PS**-101:7(3559)-**PR**-23:30(309)-**IS**-46:13(309)-**JER**-14:8(3885)-**HAB**-2:3(4102),3(309)■**N.T.**-all=3306&marked-**M'T**-26:38-**M'R**-14:34-**LU**-24:29,49(2523)-**JOH**-4:40■21:22,23-**AC**-10:48(1961)■18:20■28:14(1961)-**1CO**-11:33(1551)■16:7(1961),8(1961)-**1TI**-3:15(1019)-**HEB**-10:37(5549)

TARRYING-**PS**-40:17(309)■70:5(309)

TASK-**EX**-5:14(2706),19(1697)

TASKMASTERS-all=5065&marked-**EX**-1:11(8269,4522)■3:7■5:6,10,13,14

TASKS-**EX**-5:13(1697)

TASTE-all=2938&marked-**EX**-16:31(2940)-**NU**-11:8(2940)-**1SA**-14:43-**2SA**-3:35■19:35-**JOB**-6:6(2940),30(2441)■12:11-**PS**-34:8■119:103(2441)-**PR**-24:13-**SONG**-2:3-**JER**-48:11(2940)-**JON**-3:7■**N.T.**-all=1089-**M'T**-16:28-**M'R**-9:1-**LU**-9:27■14:24-**JOH**-8:52-**COL**-2:21-**HEB**-2:9

TASTED-**1SA**-14:24(2938),29(2938)-**DA**-5:2(2942)■**N.T.**-all=1089-**M'T**-27:34-**JOH**-2:9-**HEB**-6:4,5-**1PE**-2:3

TASTETH-**JOB**-34:3(2938)

TATTLERS-**1TI**-5:13(5397)

TAUGHT-all=3925&marked-**DE**-4:5■31:22-**J'G**-8:16(3045)-**2KI**-17:28(3384)-**2CH**-6:27(3384)■17:9^{2}■23:13(3045)■30:22(7919)■35:3(4000)-**NE**-8:9(995)-**PS**-71:17■119:102(3384),171-**PR**-4:4(3384),11(3384)■31:1(3256)-**EC**-12:9-**IS**-29:13■40:13(3045),14^{2}■54:13(3928)-**JER**-2:33■9:5,14■12:16■13:21■28:16(1696)■29:32(1696)■32:33-**EZE**-23:48(3256)-**HO**-10:11■11:3(8637)■**N.T.**-all=1321&marked-**M'T**-5:2■7:29(2258,1321)■13:54■28:15-**M'R**-1:21,22(2258,1321)■2:13■4:2■6:30■9:31■10:1■11:17■12:35-**LU**-4:15,31(2258,1321)■5:3■6:6■11:1■13:26■19:47(2258,1321)■20:1-**JOH**-6:45(1318),59■7:14,28■8:2,20,28■18:20-**AC**-4:2■5:21■11:26■14:21(3100)■15:1■18:25■20:20■22:3(3811)-**GA**-1:12■6:6(2727)-**EPH**-4:21-**COL**-2:7-**1TH**-4:9(2312)-**2TH**-2:15-**TIT**-1:9(1322)-**1JO**-2:27-**RE**-2:14

TAUNT-**JER**-24:9(8148)-**EZE**-5:15(1422)

TAUNTING-**HAB**-2:6(4426)

TAVERNS-**AC**-28:15(4999)

TAXATION-**2KI**-23:35(6187)

TAXED-**2KI**-23:35(6186)■**N.T.**-all=582-**LU**-2:1,3,5

TAXES-**DA**-11:20(5065)

TAXING-**LU**-2:2(583)-**AC**-5:37(583)

TEACH-all=3384,a=3925&marked-**EX**-4:12,15■18:20(2094)■24:12■35:34-**LE**-10:11■14:57-**DE**-4:1a,9(3045),10a,14a■5:31a■6:1a,7(8150)■11:19a■17:11■20:18a■24:8■31:19a■33:10-**J'G**-3:2a■13:8-**1SA**-12:23-**2SA**-1:18a-**1KI**-8:36-**2KI**-17:27-**2CH**-17:7a-**EZR**-7:10a,25(3046)-**JOB**-6:24■8:10■12:7,8■21:22a■27:11■32:7(3045)■33:33(502)■34:32■37:19(3045)-**PS**-25:4a,5a,8,9a,12■27:11■32:8■34:11a■45:4■51:13a■60:t■86:11■90:12(3045)■119:12a,26a,33,64a,66a,68a,108a,124a,135a■132:12a■143:10a-**PR**-9:9(3045)-**IS**-2:3■28:9,26-**JER**-9:20a■31:34a-**EZE**-44:23-**DA**-1:4a-**MIC**-3:11■4:2-**HAB**-2:19■**N.T.**-all=1321&marked-**M'T**-5:19^{2}■11:1■28:19(3100)-**M'R**-4:1■6:2,34■8:31-**LU**-11:1■12:12-**JOH**-7:35■9:34■14:26-**AC**-1:1■4:18■5:28,42■16:21(2605)-**1CO**-4:17■11:14■14:19(2727)-**1TI**-1:3(2085)■2:12■3:2(1317)■4:11■6:2,3(2085)-**2TI**-2:2,24(1317)-**TIT**-2:4(4994)-**HEB**-5:12■8:11-**1JO**-2:27-**RE**-2:20

TEACHER-1CH-25:8(995)-HAB-2:18(3384)■N.T.-all=1320-JOH-3:2-RO-2:20-1TI-2:7-2TI-1:11

TEACHERS-all=3384&marked-PS-119:99(3925)-PR-5:13-IS-30:20[2]■43:27(3887)■N.T.-all=1320&marked-AC-13:1-1CO-12:28,29-EPH-4:11-1TI-1:7(3547)-2TI-4:3-TIT-2:3(2567)-HEB-5:12-2PE-2:1(5572)

TEACHEST-PS-94:12(3925)■N.T.-all=1321-M'T-22:16-M'R-12:14-LU-20:21[2]-AC-21:21-RO-2:21[2]

TEACHETH-all=3925&marked-2SA-22:35-JOB-35:11(502)■36:22(3384)-PS-18:34■94:10■144:1-PR-6:13(3384)■16:23(7919)-IS-9:15(3384)■48:17■N.T.-all=1321&marked-AC-21:28-RO-12:7-1CO-2:13[2](1318)-GAL-6:6(2727)-1JO-2:27

TEACHING-2CH-15:3(3384)-JER-32:33(3925)■N.T.-all=1321&marked-M'T-4:23■9:35■15:9■21:23■26:55■28:20-M'R-6:6■7:7■14:49-LU-5:17■13:10,22■21:37■23:5-AC-5:25■15:35■18:11■28:31-RO-12:7(1319)-COL-1:28■3:16-TIT-1:11■2:12(3811)

TEAR-all=2963&marked-J'G-8:7(1758)-PS-7:2■35:15(7167)■50:22-JER-15:3(5498)■16:7(6536)-EZE-13:20(7167),21(7167)-HO-5:14■13:8(1234)-AM-1:11-NA-2:12-ZEC-11:16(6561)

TEARETH-all=2963-DE-33:20-JOB-16:9■18:4-MIC-5:8■N.T.-M'R-9:18(4486)-LU-9:39(4682)

TEARS-all=1832&marked-2KI-20:5-ES-8:3(1058)-PS-6:6■39:12■42:3■56:8■80:5[2]■116:8■126:5-EC-4:1-IS-16:9■25:8■38:5-JER-9:1,18■13:17■14:17■31:16-LA-1:2■2:11,18-EZE-24:16-MAL-2:13■N.T.-all=1144-M'R-9:24-LU-7:38,44-AC-20:19,31-2CO-2:4-2TI-1:4-HEB-5:7■12:17-RE-7:17■21:4

TEATS-IS-32:12(7699)-EZE-23:3(1717),21(1717)

TEDIOUS-AC-24:4(1465)

TEETH-all=8127&marked-GE-49:12-NU-11:33-DE-32:24-1SA-2:13-JOB-4:10■13:14■16:9■19:20■29:17■41:14-PS-3:7■35:16■37:12■57:4■58:6,6(4973)■112:10■124:6-PR-10:26■30:14,14(4973)-SONG-4:2■6:6-IS-41:15(6374)-JER-31:29,30-LA-2:16■3:16-EZE-18:2-DA-7:5(8128),7(8128)19(8128)-JOE-1:6,6(4973)-AM-4:6-MIC-3:5-ZEC-9:7■N.T.-all=3599&marked-M'T-8:12■13:42,50■22:13■24:51■25:30■27:44(3679)-M'R-9:18-LU-13:28-AC-7:54-RE-9:8

TEIL-IS-6:13(424)

TEKEL-DA-5:25(8625),27(8625)

TELL-all=5046,a=559,b=5608&marked-GE-12:18■15:5b■21:26■22:2a■24:23,49[2]■26:2a■29:15■31:27■32:5,29■37:16■40:8b■43:6,22(3045)■45:13■49:1-EX-9:1(1696)■10:2b■14:12(1696)■19:3-LE-14:35-NU-14:14a■23:3-DE-17:11a■32:7a-JOS-7:19-J'G-14:16■16:6,10,13■20:3(1696)-RU-3:4■4:4-1SA-6:2(3045)■9:8,18,19■10:15■14:43■15:16■17:55(3045)■19:3■20:9,10■22:22■23:11■27:11-2SA-1:4,20■7:5a■12:18,18a,22(3045)■13:4■15:35■17:16■18:21-1KI-1:20■14:3,7a■18:8a,11a,12,14a■20:9a,11(1696)■22:16(1696),18a-2KI-4:2■7:9■8:4b■9:12,15■20:5a■22:15a-1CH-17:4a,10■21:10(1696)-2CH-18:17a■34:23a-JOB-1:15,16,17,19■8:10a■12:7■34:34a-PS-22:17b■26:7b■48:12b,13b■50:12a-PR-30:4(3045)-EC-6:12■8:7■10:14[2],20-SONG-1:7■5:8-IS-5:5(3045)■6:9a■19:12■42:9(8085)■45:21■48:20(8085)-JER-15:2a■19:2(1696)■23:27b,28b,32b■28:13a■34:2a■35:13a■36:16,17■48:20-EZE-3:11a■12:23■17:12a■24:19-DA-2:4(560),7(560),9(560),36(560)■4:9(560)-JOE-1:3b-JON-1:8■3:9(3045)■N.T.-all=2036,a=3004&marked-M'T-8:4■10:27a■16:20■17:9■18:15(1650),17■21:5,24,24(2046),27(1492),27a■22:4,17■24:3■26:63■28:7,9(518),10(518)-M'R-1:30a■5:19(312)■7:36■8:26,30a■9:9(1334)■10:32a■11:29(2046),33(1492),33a■13:4■16:7-LU-4:25a■5:14■7:22(518),42■8:56■9:21,27a■10:24a■12:51a,59a,59a■13:3a,5a,27a,32■17:34a■18:8a,14a■19:40a■20:2,7(1492),8a■22:34a,67[2]-JOH-3:8(1492),12■4:25(312)■8:14(1492),45a■10:24■12:22a■13:19a■16:7a,18(1492)■18:34■20:15-AC-5:8■10:6(2980)■11:14(2980)■15:27(518)■17:21a■22:27a■23:17(518),19(518),22(1583)-2CO-12:2[2](1492),3(1492)-GA-4:16(226),21a■5:21(4302)-PH'P-3:18a-HEB-11:32(1334)-RE-17:7(2046)

TELLEST-PS-56:8(5608)

TELLETH-2SA-7:11(5046)-2KI-6:12(5046)-PS-41:6(1696)■101:7(1696)■147:4(4487)-JER-33:13(4487)■N.T.-JOH-12:22(3004)

TELLING-J'G-7:15(4557)-2SA-11:19(1696)-2KI-8:5(5608)

TEMPER-EZE-46:14(7450)

TEMPERANCE-all=1466-AC-24:25-GA-5:23-2PE-1:6[2]

TEMPERATE-1CO-9:25(1467)-TIT-1:8(1468)■2:2(4998)

TEMPERED-EX-29:2(1101)■30:35(4414)■N.T.-1CO-12:24(4786)

TEMPEST-all=5591&marked-JOB-9:17(8183)■27:20(5492)-PS-11:6(7307)■55:8■83:15-IS-28:2(2230)■29:6■30:30(2230)■32:2(2230)■54:11(5590)-AM-1:14-JON-1:4,12■N.T.-M'T-8:24(4578)-AC-27:18(5492),20(5494)-HEB-12:18(2366)-2PE-2:17(2978)

TEMPESTUOUS-PS-50:3(8175)-JON-1:11(5490),13(5490)■N.T.-AC-27:14(5189)

TEMPLE-all=1964,a=1004&marked-1SA-1:9■3:3-2SA-22:7-1KI-6:3,5,17,33■7:21,50-2KI-11:10a,11[3]a,13a■18:16■23:4■24:13-1CH-6:10a■10:10a-2CH-3:17■4:7,8,22■23:10[3]a■26:16■27:2■29:16■35:20a■36:7-EZR-3:6,10■4:1■5:14[3](1965),15(1965)■6:5[2](1965)-NE-6:10[2],11-PS-5:7■11:4■18:6■27:4■29:9■48:9■65:4■68:29■79:1■138:2-IS-6:1■44:28■66:6-JER-7:4[2]■24:1■50:28■51:11-EZE-8:16[2]■41:1,4,15,20,21,23,25■42:8-DA-5:2(1965),3(1965)-AM-8:3-JON-2:4,7-MIC-1:2-HAB-2:20-HAG-2:15,18-ZEC-6:12,13,14,15■8:9-MAL-3:1■N.T.-all=2411,a=3485&marked-M'T-4:5■12:5,6■21:12[2],14,15,23■23:16[2]a,17a,21a,35a■24:1[2]■26:55,61a■27:5a,40a,51a-M'R-11:11,15[2],16,27■12:35■13:1,3■14:49,58a■15:29a,38a-LU-1:9a,21a,22a■2:27,37,46■4:9■11:51(3624)■18:10■19:45,47■20:1■21:5,37,38■22:52,53■23:45a■24:53-JOH-2:14,15,19a,20a,21a■5:14■7:14,28■8:2,20,59■10:23■11:56■18:20-AC-2:46■3:1,2[2],3,8,10■4:1■5:20,21,24,25,42■19:27■21:26,27,28,29,30■22:17■24:6,12,18■25:8■26:21-1CO-3:16a,17[2]a,17sup■6:19a■9:13-2CO-6:16[2]a-EPH-2:21a-2TH-2:4-RE-3:12■7:15■11:1,2,19[2]■14:15,17■15:5,6,8[2]■16:1,17■21:22[2]

TEMPLES-all=7541&marked-J'G-4:21,22■5:26-SONG-4:3■6:7-HO-8:14(1964)-JOE-3:5(1964)■N.T.-AC-7:48(3485)■17:24(3485)

TEMPORAL-2CO-4:18(4340)

TEMPT-all=5254&marked-GE-22:1-EX-17:2-DE-6:16-IS-7:12-MAL-3:15(974)■N.T.-all=3985&marked-M'T-4:7(1598)■22:18-M'R-12:15-LU-4:12(1598)■20:23-AC-5:9■15:10-1CO-7:5■10:9(1598)

TEMPTATION-PS-95:8(4531)■N.T.-all=3986-M'T-6:13■26:41-M'R-14:38-LU-4:13■8:13■11:4■22:40,46-1CO-10:13[2]-GA-4:14-1TI-6:9-HEB-3:8-JAS-1:12-RE-3:10

TEMPTATIONS-all=4531-DE-4:34■7:19■29:3■N.T.-all=3986-LU-22:28-AC-20:19-JAS-1:2-1PE-1:6-2PE-2:9

TEMPTED-all=5254-EX-17:7-NU-14:22-DE-6:16-PS-78:18,41,56■95:9■106:14■N.T.-all=3985&marked-M'T-4:1-M'R-1:13-LU-4:2■10:25(1598)-1CO-10:9,13-GA-6:1-1TH-3:5-HEB-2:18[2]■3:9■4:15■11:37-JAS-1:13,13(551),14

TEMPTER-M'T-4:3(3985)-1TH-3:5(3985)

TEMPTETH-JAS-1:13(3985)

TEMPTING-all=3985-M'T-16:1■19:3■22:35-M'R-8:11■10:2-LU-11:16-JOH-8:6

TEN-all=6235,a=7233&marked-GE-5:14■16:3■18:32■24:10,22,55(6218)■31:7,41■32:15[2]■42:3■45:23[2]■50:22,26-EX-26:1,16■27:12■34:28■36:8,21■38:12-LE-26:8a,26■27:5,7-NU-7:14,20,26,32,38,44,50,56,62,68,74,80,86■11:19,32■14:22■29:23-DE-4:13■10:4,22■32:30a■33:2a,17a-JOS-15:57■17:5■21:5,26■22:14■24:29-J'G-1:4■2:8■3:29■4:6,10,14■6:27■7:3■12:11■17:10■20:10,10a,34-RU-1:4■4:2-1SA-1:8■15:4■17:17,18■18:7a,8a■21:11a■25:5,38■29:5a-2SA-15:16■18:3,11,15■19:43■20:3-1KI-4:23■5:14■6:3,23,24,25,26■7:10,23,24,27,37,38[2],43■11:31[2],35■14:3-2KI-5:5[2]■13:7[2]■14:7■15:17■20:9[2],10[2],11■24:14■25:25-1CH-6:61■29:7(7239),7-2CH-4:1,2,3,6,7,8■14:1■25:11,12■27:5[2]■30:24■36:9-EZR-1:10■8:12,24-NE-4:12■5:18■11:1-ES-3:9■9:10,12,13,14-JOB-19:3-PS-3:6a■33:2(6218)■91:7a■92:3(6218)■144:9(6218),13(7231)-EC-7:19-SONG-5:10a-IS-5:10■38:8[2]-JER-41:1,2,8■42:7-EZE-40:11■41:2■42:4■45:1,3,5,14[2]■48:9,10[2],13[2],18[2]-DA-1:12,14,15,20■7:7(6236),10(7240),20(6236),24[2](6236)■11:12(7239)-AM-5:3■6:9-MIC-6:7a-HAG-2:16-ZEC-5:2■8:23■N.T.-all=1176&marked-M'T-18:24(3463)■20:24■25:1,28-M'R-10:41-LU-14:31■15:8■17:12,17■19:13[2],16,17,24,25-AC-25:6-1CO-4:15(3463)■14:19(3463)-JUDE-14(3461)-RE-2:10■5:11(3461)■12:3■13:1[2]■17:3,7,12,16

TEND-supplied

TENDER-all=7390&marked-GE-18:7■29:17■33:13-DE-28:54,56-2KI-22:19(7401)-1CH-22:5■29:1-2CH-34:27(7401)-JOB-14:7(3127)-PR-4:3-IS-47:1■53:2(3126)-EZE-17:22■N.T.-M'T-24:32(527)-M'R-13:28(527)-LU-1:78(4698)-JAS-5:11(3629)

TENDERHEARTED-2CH-13:7(7390,3824)■N.T.-EPH-4:32(2155)

TENDERNESS-DE-28:56(7391)

TENDETH-all supplied

TENONS-all=3027-EX-26:17,19[2]■36:22,24[2]

TENOR-GE-43:7(6310)-EX-34:27(6310)

TEN'S-GE-18:32(6235)

TENS-all=6235-EX-18:21,25-DE-1:15

TENT-all=168&marked-GE-9:21■12:8■13:3,12(167),18(167)■18:1,2,6,9,10■24:67■26:25■31:25,33[3],34■33:19■35:21-EX-18:7■26:11,12,13,14,36■33:8,10■35:11■36:14,18,19■39:32,33,40■40:2,6,7,19[2],22,24,26,29,30,32,34,35-LE-14:8-NU-3:25■9:15■11:10■19:14[2],18■25:8(6898)-JOS-7:21,22[2],23,24-J'G-4:11,17,18,20,21■5:24■7:8,13[2]■20:8-1SA-4:10■13:2■17:54-2SA-7:6■16:22■18:17■19:8■20:22-2KI-7:8[2]-1CH-15:1■16:1■17:5-2CH-1:4■25:22-PS-78:60-IS-13:20(167)■38:12■40:22■54:2-JER-10:20■37:10

TENTH-all=6224,a=6241,b=6218&marked-GE-8:5[2]■28:22(6237)-EX-12:3b■16:36■29:40a-LE-5:11■6:20■14:10a,21a■16:29b■23:13a,17a,27b■24:5a■25:9b■27:32-NU-5:15■7:66■15:4a,6a,9a■18:21(4643),26(4643)■28:5,9a,12[2]a,13a,20[2]a,21a,28[2]a,29a■29:3[2]a,4a,7b,9[2]a,10a,14[2]a,15a-DE-23:2,3-JOS-4:19b-1SA-8:15(6237),17(6237)-2KI-

25:1^{2}b-**1CH**-12:13■24:11■25:17■27:13 -**EZR**-10:16-**ES**-2:16-**IS**-6:13-**JER**-32:1■39:1■52:4,4b,12b-**EZE**-20:1b■24:1,1b■29:1■33:21■40:1b■45:11(4643), 11,14(4643)-**ZEC**-8:19■**N.T.**-all=1182 &marked-**JOH**-1:39-**HEB**-7:2(1181), 4(1181)-**RE**-11:13■21:20

TENTMAKERS-**AC**-18:3(4635)

TENTS-all=168&marked-**GE**-4:20■9:27■13:5■25:27■31:33-**EX**-16:16-**NU**-13:19(4264)■16:26,27■24:5-**DE**-1:27■5:30■11:6■16:7■33:18-**JOS**-3:14■22:4, 6,7,8-**J'G**-6:5■8:11-**1SA**-17:53(4264) -**2SA**-11:11(5521)■20:1-**1KI**-8:66■12:16^2 -**2KI**-7:7,10,16(4264)■8:21■13:5■14:12 -**1CH**-4:41■5:10-**2CH**-7:10■10:16^2■14:15■31:2(4264)-**EZR**-8:15(2583)-**PS**-69:25■78:55■84:10■106:25■120:5-**SONG**-1:5,8(4908)-**JER**-4:20■6:3■30:18■35:7,10■49:29-**HAB**-3:7-**ZEC**-12:7■14:15(4264)

TERAPHIM-all=8655-**J'G**-17:5■18:14,17,18,20-**HOS**-3:4

TERMED-**IS**-62:4^2(559)

TERRACES-**2CH**-9:11(4546)

TERRESTRIAL-**1CO**-15:40^2(1919)

TERRIBLE-all=3372,a=6184&marked-**EX**-34:10-**DE**-1:19■7:21■8:15■10:17,21-**J'G**-13:6-**2SA**-7:23-**NE**-1:5■4:14■9:32-**JOB**-37:22■39:20(367)■41:14(367)-**PS**-45:4■47:2■65:5■66:3, 5■68:35■76:12■99:3■106:22■145:6 -**SONG**-6:4(366),10(366)-**IS**-13:11a■18:2,7■21:1■25:3a,4a,5a■29:5a,20a■49:25a■64:3-**JER**-15:21a■20:11a-**LA**-5:10(2152)-**EZE**-1:22■28:7a■30:11a■31:12a■32:12a-**DA**-2:31(1763)■7:7 (574)-**JOE**-2:11,31-**HAB**-1:7(366) -**ZEP**-2:11■**N.T.**-**HEB**-12:21(5398)

TERRIBLENESS-**DE**-26:8(4172) -**1CH**-17:21(3372)-**JER**-49:16(8606)

TERRIBLY-**IS**-2:19(6206),21(6206)

TERRIFIED-**DE**-20:3(6206)■**N.T.**-**LU**-21:9(4422)■24:37(4422) -**PH'P**-1:28(4426)

TERRIFIEST-**JOB**-7:14(1204)

TERRIFY-**JOB**-3:5(1204)■9:34(1204)■31:34(2865)■**N.T.**-**2CO**-10:9(1629)

TERROR-all=2851&marked-**GE**-35:5(2847)-**LE**-26:16(928)-**DE**-32:25 (367)■34:12(4172)-**JOS**-2:9(367)-**JOB**-31:23(6343)■33:7(367)-**PS**-91:5(6343) -**IS**-10:33(4637)■19:17(2283)■33:18 (367)■54:14(4288)-**JER**-17:17(4288)■20:4(4032)■32:21(4172)-**EZE**-26:17,21 (1091)■27:36(1091)■28:19(1091)■32:23,24,25,26,27,30,32■**N.T.**-all=5401 -**RO**-13:3-**2CO**-5:11-**1PE**-3:14

TERRORS-all=1091&marked-**DE**-4:34(4172)-**JOB**-6:4(1161)■18:11,14■20:25 (367)■24:17■27:20■30:15-**PS**-55:4(367)■73:19■88:15(367),16(1161)-**JER**-15:8 (928)-**LA**-2:22(4032)-**EZE**-21:12(4048)

TESTAMENT-all=1242-**M'T**-26:28-**M'R**-14:24-**LU**-22:20-**1CO**-11:25-**2CO**-3:6,14-**HEB**-7:22■9:15^2, 16,17,20-**RE**-11:19

TESTATOR-**HEB**-9:16(1303), 17(1303)

TESTIFIED=5749&marked-**EX**-21:29-**DE**-19:18(6030)-**RU**-1:21(6030) -**2SA**-1:16(6030)-**2KI**-17:13,15-**2CH**-24:19-**NE**-9:26■13:15,21■**N.T.**-all=1263&marked-**JOH**-4:39(3140),44 (3140)■13:21(3140)-**AC**-8:25■18:5■23:11■28:23-**1CO**-15:15(3140)-**1TH**-4:6-**1TI**-2:6(3142)-**HEB**-2:6-**1PE**-1:11 (4303)-**1JO**-5:9(3140)-**3JO**-3(3140)

TESTIFIEDST-**NE**-9:29(5749), 30(5749)

TESTIFIETH-**HO**-7:10(6030)■**N.T.**-all=3140-**JOH**-3:32■21:24 -**HEB**-7:17-**RE**-22:20

TESTIFY-all=6030&marked-**NU**-35:30-**DE**-8:19(5749)■19:16■31:21■32:46(5749)-**NE**-9:34(5749)-**JOB**-15:6 -**PS**-50:7(5749)■81:8(5749)-**IS**-59:12 -**JER**-14:7-**HO**-5:5-**AM**-3:13(5749) -**MIC**-6:3■**N.T.**-all=3140&marked -**LU**-16:28(1263)-**JOH**-2:25■3:11■5:39■7:7■15:26-**AC**-2:40(1263)■10:42 (1263)■20:24(1263)■26:5-**GA**-5:3(3143) -**EPH**-4:17(3143)-**1JO**-4:14-**RE**-22:16, 18(4828)

TESTIFYING-**AC**-20:21(1263) -**HEB**-11:4(3140)-**1PE**-5:12(1957)

TESTIMONIES-all=5713,a=5715 -**DE**-4:45■6:17,20-**1KI**-2:3a-**2KI**-17:15a■23:3a-**1CH**-29:19a-**2CH**-34:31a -**NE**-9:34a-**PS**-25:10■78:56■93:5■99:7■119:2,14a,22,24,31a,36a,46,59, 79,95,99a,111a,119,125,129a,138,144a, 146,152,157a,167,168-**JER**-44:23a

TESTIMONY-all=5715&marked -**EX**-16:34■25:16,21,22■26:33,34■27:21■30:6^2,26,36■31:7,18■32:15■34:29■38:21■39:35■40:3,5,20,21-**LE**-16:13■24:3-**NU**-1:50,53^2■4:5■7:89■9:15■10:11■17:4, 10-**JOS**-4:16-**RU**-4:7(8584)-**2KI**-11:12 -**2CH**-23:11-**PS**-19:7■78:5■81:5■119:88■122:4■132:12(5713)-**IS**-8:16(8584),20 (8584)■**N.T.**-all=3142,a=3141&marked -**M'T**-8:4■10:18-**M'R**-1:44■6:11■13:9 -**LU**-5:14■9:5■21:13-**JOH**-3:32a,33a■5:34a■8:17a■21:24a-**AC**-13:22(3140)■14:3(3140)■22:18a-**1CO**-1:6■2:1-**2CO**-1:12-**2TH**-1:10-**2TI**-1:8-**HEB**-3:5■11:5(3140)-**RE**-1:2a,9a■6:9a■11:7a■12:11a,17a■15:5■19:10^{2}a

TETRARCH-**M'T**-14:1(5076)-**LU**-3:1^3 (5075),19(5076)■9:7(5076)-**AC**-13:1(5076)

THAN-all=4480&marked-**LE**-13:21, 25,26,30,31,32,34■14:37-**NU**-3:46 (5921)-**JOS**-10:2-**RU**-3:10-**1SA**-27:1 (3588)-**2SA**-18:8(834)■20:5,6■23:23 -**2KI**-9:35(3588,518)■21:9-**1CH**-24:4 -**2CH**-20:25(369)■33:9-**JOB**-9:25■11:9^2■23:2(5921)■30:8■34:19(6440) -**EC**-1:16(5921)■2:16(5973)■4:2■5:8^2 (5921)■6:8■8:15(3588,518)■9:4-**EZE**-5:6^2,7-**DA**-1:10,15,20(5921)■2:30(4481)■3:19(1768)■7:20(4481)■8:3■11:13-**AM**-6:2■**N.T.**-all=2228,a=3844&marked -**M'T**-10:15,37^2(5228)■11:22,24■18:8,9, 13■19:24■26:53-**M'R**-6:11■8:14(1508)■9:43,45,47■10:25■14:5(1883)-**LU**-3:13a■10:12,14■15:7■16:8(5228),17■17:2■18:14,25-**JOH**-3:19■4:1■12:43(2260) -**AC**-4:19■5:29■15:28(4133)■25:6■27:11-**RO**-1:25a■8:37(5245)■13:11 -**1CO**-3:11a■7:9■9:15■14:5,19-**2CO**-1:13-**GA**-1:8a,9a■4:27-**1TI**-1:4-**2TI**-3:4-**PH'M**-21(5228)-**HEB**-1:4a■2:7a, 9a■3:3a■4:12(5228)■9:23a■11:4a,25■12:24a-**1PE**-3:17-**2PE**-2:21-**1JO**-4:4

THANK-all=3034&marked-**1CH**-16:4,7■23:30■29:13-**2CH**-29:31^2(8426)■33:16(8426)-**DA**-2:23(3029)■**N.T.**-all=2168&marked-**M'T**-11:25(1843)-**LU**-6:32(5485),33(5485),34(5485)■10:21 (1843)■17:9(2192,5485)■18:11-**JOH**-11:41-**RO**-1:8■7:25-**1CO**-1:4,14■14:18 -**PH'P**-1:3-**1TH**-2:13-**2TH**-1:3-**1TI**-1:12(2192,5485)-**2TI**-1:3(2192,5485) -**PH'M**-4

THANKED-**2SA**-14:22(1288)■**N.T.**-**AC**-28:15(2168)-**RO**-6:17(5485)

THANKFUL-**PS**-100:4(3034)■**N.T.**-**RO**-1:21(2168)-**COL**-3:15(2170)

THANKFULNESS-**AC**-24:3(2169)

THANKING-**2CH**-5:13(3034)

THANKS-all=3034&marked-**2SA**-22:50-**1CH**-16:8,34,35,41■25:3-**2CH**-31:2-**EZR**-3:11-**NE**-12:24,31(8426),38 (8426),40(8426)-**PS**-6:5■18:49■30:4,12■35:18■75:1^2■79:13■92:1■97:12■105:1■106:1,47■107:1■118:1,29■119:62■122:4■136:1,2,3,26■140:13-**DA**-6:10(3029)■**N.T.**-all=2168&marked-**M'T**-15:36■26:27-**M'R**-8:6■14:23-**LU**-2:38(437)■17:16■22:17,19-**JOH**-6:11,23-**AC**-27:35-**RO**-14:6^2■16:4-**1CO**-10:30■11:24■14:16(2169),17■15:57(5485) -**2CO**-1:11■2:14(5485)■8:16(5485)■9:15 (5485)-**EPH**-1:16■5:4(2169),20-**COL**-1:3,12■3:17-**1TH**-1:2■3:9(2169)■5:18 -**2TH**-2:13-**1TI**-2:1(2169)-**HEB**-13:15 (3670)-**RE**-4:9(2169)■11:17

THANKSGIVING-all=8426&marked-**LE**-7:12^2,13,15■22:29-**NE**-11:17(3034)■12:8(1960),46(3034)-**PS**-26:7■50:14■69:30■95:2■100:4■107:22■116:17■147:7-**IS**-51:3-**JER**-30:19-**AM**-4:5-**JON**-2:9■**N.T.**-all=2169-**2CO**-4:15■9:11-**PH'P**-4:6-**COL**-2:7■4:2 -**1TI**-4:3,4-**RE**-7:12

THANKSGIVINGS-**NE**-12:27 (8426)■**N.T.**-**2CO**-9:12(2169)

THANKWORTHY-**1PE**-2:19(5485)

THEATRE-**AC**-19:29(2302),31(2302)

THEE-WARD-supplied

THEFT-**EX**-22:3(1591),4(1591)

THEFTS-**M'T**-15:19(2829)-**M'R**-7:22(2829)-**RE**-9:21(2809)

THEIRS-all=1992&marked-**GE**-15:13-**EX**-29:9-**LE**-18:10(2007)-**NU**-16:26-**JOS**-21:10-**1CH**-6:54-**2CH**-18:12 -**JER**-44:28-**EZE**-7:11■44:29■**N.T.** -**M'T**-5:3(846),10(846)-**2TI**-3:9(3588,1565)

THEMSELVES-all=1992,a=905 &marked-**GE**-3:7■30:40a■32:16a■43:32^{2}a-**EX**-5:7■12:39■18:26■26:9^{2}a■36:16^{2}a-**NU**-8:7■11:32-**JOS**-8:27■11:14-**1SA**-3:13-**2SA**-10:8a-**1KI**-18:23 -**2KI**-8:20-**1CH**-19:9a-**2CH**-14:13■21:8■35:14^2-**EZR**-6:20■9:2-**NE**-4:2■8:16 -**ES**-9:31(5315)-**EC**-3:18-**IS**-3:9■46:2 (5315)■47:14(5315)-**JER**-11:17■49:29 -**EZE**-6:9(6440)■10:22■34:10(853)■43:26(3027)■45:5-**HOS**-1:11■4:14-**AM**-6:5■**N.T.**-all=1438,a=846,b=240& marked-**M'T**-9:3■14:15■16:7■19:12■21:25,38-**M'R**-1:27(848)■2:8■4:17■6:36, 51■8:16b■9:2(3441),8,10,34b■10:26■11:31■12:7■14:4■15:31b■16:3-**LU**-4:36b■7:30,49■18:9■20:5,14,20■22:23■23:12■24:12(3441)-**JOH**-6:52b■7:35■11:55 56b■12:19■16:17b■17:13(848)■18:28a■19:24b-**AC**-4:15b■15:32a■16:37a■23:12, 21■24:15a■26:31b■28:4a,25a,29-**RO**-1:24,27■2:14■13:2-**1CO**-16:15-**2CO**-5:15■8:3(830)■10:12^3-**GA**-6:13a-**EPH**-4:19-**PH'P**-2:3-**1TH**-1:9a-**1TI**-2:9■3:13■6:10,19-**2TI**-4:3-**TIT**-1:12a-**HEB**-6:6■9:23a-**1PE**-1:12■3:5-**2PE**-2:1,19a -**JUDE**-12,19-**RE**-6:15■8:6

THEN-all=227,a=116&marked-**GE**-4:26■12:6■13:7■24:41■49:4-**EX**-4:26■12:44,48■15:1,15-**LE**-26:34^2,41^2-**NU**-21:17-**DE**-4:41■29:20-**JOS**-1:8^2■8:30■10:12,33■14:11■20:6■22:1-**J'G**-5:8,13, 19,22■8:3■13:21-**1SA**-6:3■20:12■22:15 (3117)■23:3(3588)-**2SA**-5:24^2■19:6■21:17,18■23:14-**1KI**-3:16■8:1,12■9:11, 24■16:21■22:49-**2KI**-8:22■12:17■13:19■14:8■15:16■16:5-**1CH**-11:16^2■14:15■15:2■16:7,33■22:13-**2CH**-5:2■6:1■8:12,17-**EZR**-4:9a,24a■5:2a,4a,5a, 9a,16a■6:1a,13a-**JOB**-3:13■11:15■13:20■22:26■28:27■33:16■38:21-**PS**-2:5■19:13■40:7■51:19^2■56:9■69:4■89:19■96:12■119:6,92■124:3(233),4(233),5 (233)■126:2^2-**PR**-1:28■2:5,9■3:23■20:14-**EC**-2:15-**SONG**-8:10-**IS**-33:23■35:5,6■41:1■58:8,9,14■60:5-**JER**-8:22 (3588)■11:15,18■22:15,16,22■32:2■33:26(1571)-**EZE**-21:10(176)■32:14 -**DA**-2:14a,15a,17a,19^{2}a,25a,35a,46a,48a■3:3a,13^{2}a,19a,21a,24a,26^{2}a,30a■4:7a, 19a■5:3a,6a,8a,9a,13a,17a,24a,29a■6:3a,4a,5a,6a,11a,12a,13a,14a,15a,16a, 18a,19a,21a,23a,25a■7:1a,11a,19a -**HO**-2:7-**MIC**-3:4-**HAB**-1:11-**ZEP**-3:9,11■**N.T.**-all=3767,a=5119,b=1161, c=2532,d=686,e=1534&marked-**M'T**-1:19b,24b■2:7a,16a,17a■3:5a,13a,15a■4:1a,5a,10a,11a■5:24a■7:5a,11,23a■8:26a■9:6a,14a,15a,29a,37a■11:20a■12:12,13a,14b,22a,26,28d,29a,38a,44a, 45a,47a■13:26a,27,28,36a,43a,52b,56■14:33b■15:1a,12a,15b,21c,25b,28a, 32b■16:6b,12a,20a,22c,24a,27a■17:4b,10, 13a,17b,19a,26d■18:21a,27b,32a■19:7, 13a,23b,25d,27a■20:20a■21:1a,25■

22:8a,13a,15a,21a▪22:35c,43,45▪23:1a,32c▪24:9a,10a,14a,16a,21a,23a,30^{2}a,40a,45d▪25:1a,7a,16b,24b,31a,34a,37a,41a,44a,45a▪26:3a,14a,25b,31a,36a,38a,45a,50a,52a,54,56a,65a,67a,74a▪27:3a,9a,13a,16a,22,25c,26a,27a,38a,58a▪28:10a,16b-**M'R**-2:20a▪3:27a,31▪4:28e▪7:1c,5(1899)▪10:21b,28c▪11:31▪12:18c▪13:14a,21a,26a,27a▪14:63b▪15:12,14b▪16:19-**LU**-1:34b▪2:28c▪3:7,10,12b▪5:35a▪6:9,42a▪7:6b,22c,31▪18:12e,19b,24b,33b,35b,37c▪9:1b,12b,16b,46b▪10:37▪11:13,26a,45b▪12:20b,26,28b,41b,42d▪13:7b,15,18b,23b,26a▪14:10a,12b,16b,21a▪15:1b▪16:3b,7(1899),27b▪17:1b▪18:26c,28b,31b▪19:15(1532),16b,23c▪20:5,9b,13b,17,27b,39b,44c,45b▪21:10a,20a,21a,27a▪22:3b,7b,36,52b,54b,70b,70▪23:4b,9b,30a,34b▪24:12b,25b,45a-**JOH**-1:21,22,25,38b▪2:10a,18,20▪3:25▪4:5,9,11,28,30,45,48,52▪5:4,12,19▪6:5,14,21,28,30,32,34,41,42,53,67,68▪7:6,10a,11,25,28,30,33,33sup,35,45,47▪8:12,19,21,22,25,28a,28,31,31sup,41,48,52,57,59▪9:12,15,19,24,26b,28▪10:7,24,31▪11:7(1899),12,14,16,17,20,21,31,32,36,41,45,47,53,56▪12:1,3,4,7,16a,28,35▪13:6,14,22,25b,27,30▪16:17▪18:3,6,7,10,11,12,16,17,19,27,28,29,31,33,37(3766),40▪19:1a,5,10,16a,20,21,23,27e,32,40▪20:2,6,8a,10,19,20,21,27e▪21:5,9,13,20b,23-**AC**-1:12a▪2:38b,41▪3:6b▪4:8a▪5:9b,10b,17b,25b,26a,29b,34b▪6:2b,9b,11a▪7:1b,4a,14b,29b,32b,33b,42b,57b▪8:5b,13b,17a,24b,29b,35b▪9:13b,19b,25b,31,39b▪10:21b,23,34b,46a,48a▪11:16b,17,18d,22b,25b,29b▪12:3b,15b▪13:9b,12a,16b,46b▪14:13b▪15:12b,22a▪16:1b,29b▪17:14a,18b,22b,29▪18:9b,17b▪19:3,4b,13b,36▪21:13b,26a,33a▪22:27b,29▪23:3a,5(5037),17b,19b,31▪24:10b▪25:2b,10b,12a,22b▪26:1b,1a,28b,32b▪27:20(3063),29(5037),32a,36b▪28:1a-**RO**-3:1,9,27,31▪4:1,9,10▪5:9▪6:1,15,18b,21a(3767)▪7:3d,7,13,16b,17b,21d,25d▪8:8b,17(2535),31▪9:14,16d,19,30▪10:14,17d▪11:1,5,7,11,19▪12:6b▪13:3b▪14:12d,16▪15:1b-**1CO**-3:5▪4:5a▪5:10d▪6:4,15▪7:38c▪9:18▪10:19▪12:28c▪13:10a,12^{2}a▪14:15,26▪15:5e,7e,13(3761),14d,16(3761),18d,24e,28a,54a-**2CO**-2:2c▪3:12▪4:12(3303)▪5:14d▪6:1▪12:10a,b,c-**GA**-1:18(1899)▪2:1(1899),21d▪3:19,21,29d▪4:7c,8a,15,29a,31d▪5:11d,16b▪6:4a-**EPH**-5:15-**PH'P**-1:18(1063)-**COL**-3:1,4a-**1TH**-4:1,17(1899)▪5:3a-**2TH**-2:8a-**1TI**-2:13e▪3:2,10e-**HEB**-2:14▪4:14▪7:27(1899)▪9:1,9(3588)▪10:7a,9a▪12:8d,26a-**JAS**-1:15e▪2:4c,24(5106)▪3:17(1899)▪4:14(1899)-**1PE**-4:1-**2PE**-3:6a,11-**1JO**-1:5c-**RE**-22:9c

THENCE-all=8033&marked-**GE**-2:10▪11:8,9▪12:8▪18:16,22▪20:1▪24:7▪26:17,22,23▪27:9,45▪28:2,6▪30:32▪42:2,26▪49:24-**NU**-13:23,24▪21:12,13,16▪22:41▪23:13,27-**DE**-4:29▪5:15▪6:23▪10:7▪19:12▪24:18▪30:4^2-**JOS**-6:22▪15:14,15▪18:13▪19:13,34-**J'G**-1:11,20▪8:8▪18:11,13▪19:18▪21:24^2-**1SA**-4:4▪10:3,23▪17:49▪22:1,3▪23:29-**2SA**-6:2▪14:2▪16:5▪21:13-**1KI**-1:45▪2:36▪9:28▪12:25▪19:19-**2KI**-2:21,23,25^2▪6:2▪7:8^2▪10:15▪17:27,33▪23:12▪24:13-**1CH**-13:6-**2CH**-8:18▪26:20-**EZR**-6:6(8536)-**NE**-1:9-**JOB**-39:29-**IS**-52:11▪65:20-**JER**-5:6(2007)▪13:6▪22:24▪37:12▪38:11▪43:12▪49:16,38▪50:9-**HO**-2:15-**AM**-6:2▪9:2^2,3^2,4-**OB**-4▪**N.T.**-all=1564&marked-**M'T**-4:21▪5:26▪9:9,27▪11:1▪12:9,15▪13:53▪14:13▪15:21,29▪19:15-**M'R**-1:19▪6:1,11▪7:24▪9:30▪10:1-**LU**-9:4▪12:59▪16:26-**JOH**-4:43▪11:54-**AC**-7:4▪13:4▪14:26▪16:12▪18:7▪20:15▪21:1▪27:4,12▪28:13(3606),15

THENCEFORTH-**LE**-22:27(1973)-**2CH**-32:23(310,3651)▪**N.T.**-**M'T**-5:13(2089)-**JOH**-19:12(1537,5127)

THERE-all=8033&marked-**GE**-2:8,12▪11:2,7,9,31▪12:7,8,10▪13:4,18▪14:10▪18:28,30^2,31,32▪21:31,33▪22:2,9▪23:13▪25:10▪26:8,17,19,25^3▪28:11▪29:2▪31:46▪32:13,29▪33:20▪35:1^2,3,7^2▪38:2▪39:11,20,22▪41:12▪43:25,30▪44:14▪45:11▪46:3▪48:7▪49:31^3▪50:5,10-**EX**-8:22▪15:25^2,27▪17:3,6▪19:2▪24:12▪29:42,43▪34:2,5,28▪40:30-**LE**-8:31▪16:23-**NU**-9:17▪11:16,17,34▪13:33▪14:35,43▪19:18▪20:1,4,26,28▪21:32▪32:26▪33:9,38-**DE**-1:28▪4:28▪10:5,6▪12:5,7,11sup,11,14^2,21▪14:23,24,26▪16:2,6,11▪17:12▪18:7▪21:4▪26:2,5^2▪27:5,7▪28:36,64,65,68▪31:26▪33:19,21▪34:5-**JOS**-2:1,16,22▪3:1▪4:8,9▪8:32▪14:12▪17:15▪18:1,10▪22:10▪24:26-**J'G**-1:7▪2:5▪5:27▪6:24▪7:4▪9:21▪14:10▪16:1,27▪17:7▪18:2▪19:2,4,7▪20:26,27▪21:2,4,9sup,9-**RU**-1:2,4,17▪4:1-**1SA**-1:3,22,28▪4:4▪6:14▪7:6,17^3▪11:14,15^3▪14:34▪20:6▪21:6▪22:22▪23:22▪27:5▪31:12-**2SA**-1:21^{2}sup,21▪2:4,18sup,18,23▪3:27▪4:3▪5:20,21▪6:7^2▪10:18▪13:38▪14:30,32▪15:21,29,35,36▪16:14▪17:13▪18:7sup,7,8,11▪20:1sup,1▪23:9▪24:25-**1KI**-1:14,34▪2:36▪3:4▪5:9▪6:19▪8:8,9,21,29,64▪9:3^2▪10:20▪11:16,36▪13:17▪14:2,21▪17:4,9^{2}10▪18:40▪19:3,9▪20:40(2008)-**2KI**-2:21,21sup▪4:10,11▪5:18▪6:2,10▪7:4,5sup,5,10sup,10▪9:2,16,27▪11:16▪14:19▪15:20▪16:6▪17:11,25,27▪19:32▪23:16,20,27,34-**1CH**-3:4▪4:23,40,41,41sup,41,43▪11:13▪12:39▪13:10▪14:11,12▪16:37▪21:26,28-**2CH**-1:3▪5:9▪6:5,6,20▪7:7,16^2▪8:2▪9:19,19sup▪12:13▪20:26▪23:15▪25:27▪28:9,18▪32:21-**EZR**-5:17sup,17(8536)▪6:12(8536)▪8:15^2,21,32-**NE**-1:3,9sup,9▪2:11-**JOB**-3:17^2,19▪23:7▪35:12▪39:30-**PS**-14:5▪36:12▪48:6▪53:5▪66:6▪68:27▪76:3▪87:4,6▪104:26▪107:36▪122:5▪132:17▪133:3▪137:1,3▪139:8,10-**PR**-8:27▪9:18-**EC**-3:16^2,17sup,17▪11:3-**IS**-13:20^2,21^3▪22:18^2▪23:12▪27:10^2▪28:10,13▪33:21▪34:12,14,15^2▪35:8,9^2,9sup▪37:33▪48:16▪52:4▪65:9-**JER**-3:6▪7:2▪8:14,22▪13:4,6▪16:13▪18:2▪19:2▪20:6^2▪22:1,26▪27:22▪29:6▪32:5▪36:12▪37:13,16,20▪38:26▪41:1,3▪42:14,15,16^3,17▪43:2▪44:12,14^2,28▪46:17▪47:7▪49:18,33sup,33▪50:40-**EZE**-1:3▪3:15,22^2,23▪8:1,4,14▪12:13▪13:20▪17:20▪20:28^4,35,40^3,43▪23:3^2▪29:14▪30:18▪32:22,24,26,29,30▪34:14▪35:10▪39:11^2,28▪42:13,14▪46:19▪47:23▪48:35-**DA**-10:13-**HO**-2:15▪6:7,10▪9:15▪10:9▪12:4▪13:8-**JOE**-3:2,12-**AM**-7:12-**JON**-4:5-**MIC**-4:10-**NA**-3:15-**HAB**-3:4-**ZEP**-1:14-**HAG**-2:14-**ZEC**-5:11▪**N.T.**-all=1563&marked-**M'T**-2:13,15▪5:23,24▪6:21▪8:12▪10:11▪12:45▪13:42,50,58▪14:23▪15:29▪18:20▪19:2▪21:17▪22:11,13▪24:23(5602),28,51▪25:30▪26:71▪27:36,47,55,61▪28:7,10-**M'R**-1:13,35,38▪2:6▪3:1▪5:11sup,11▪6:5,10▪11:5▪13:21▪14:15▪16:7-**LU**-2:6▪6:6▪8:32sup,32▪9:4▪10:6▪11:26▪12:18,34▪13:28▪15:13▪17:21,23▪22:12▪23:33▪24:18(1722,846)-**JOH**-2:1sup,1,6sup,6,12▪3:22,23sup,23▪4:6,40▪5:5▪6:3,22sup,22,24▪10:40,42▪11:15,31,54▪12:2,9,26▪19:42-**AC**-9:33,38(1722,846)▪10:18(1759)▪14:7,28▪15:34(847)▪16:1▪17:14,21(1927)▪18:19(847)▪19:21▪20:13(1564),22(1722,846)▪21:3(1566),4(847)▪22:5(1566),10▪25:9,14,20▪27:6-**RO**-9:26-**2CO**-3:17-**TIT**-3:12-**HEB**-7:8-**JAS**-2:3▪3:16▪4:13-**RE**-2:14▪12:6▪21:25sup,25▪22:5sup,5

THEREABOUT-**LU**-24:4(4012,5127)

THEREAT-**M'T**-7:13(1223,846)

THEREBY-**JER**-18:16(5921)▪19:8(5921)▪51:43(2004)▪**N.T.**-**JOH**-11:4(1223,846)-**EPH**-2:16(1722,846)-**HEB**-12:11(1223,846),15(1223,5026)▪13:2(1223,5026)-**1PE**-2:2(1722,846)

THEREFORE-all=3651,a=5921,3651&marked-**GE**-2:24a▪4:15▪11:9a▪18:5a▪19:8a,22a▪20:6a▪25:30a▪26:33a▪29:32(3588),33(1571),34a,35a▪30:6a,15▪31:48a▪32:32a▪33:10a,17a▪42:21a,22(1571)-**EX**-5:8a,17a▪13:15a▪15:23a▪16:29a-**LE**-17:12a-**NU**-18:24a▪20:12-**DE**-5:15a▪15:11a,15a▪24:18a,22a-**1SA**-5:5a▪10:12a▪12:16(1571)▪20:29a▪23:28a▪28:18a-**2SA**-5:20a▪22:50a-**1KI**-9:9a▪20:23a▪22:19-**2KI**-1:4,6▪19:32▪21:12▪22:20-**1CH**-11:7a▪14:11a▪17:25a-**2CH**-7:22a▪16:7a▪18:18▪19:2(2063)▪20:26a-**EZR**-4:14(5921,1836)-**ES**-9:19a,26a-**JOB**-6:3a▪7:11(1571)▪9:22a▪17:4a▪20:2,21a▪22:10a▪23:15a▪32:10▪34:10,25▪37:24▪42:3-**PS**-1:5a▪16:9▪18:49a▪25:8a▪42:6a▪45:2a,7a,17a▪46:2a▪73:10▪78:21▪110:7a▪116:10(3588)▪119:104a,119,127a,128a,129a-**PR**-6:15a▪7:15a-**EC**-5:2a▪8:11a-**SONG**-1:3a-**IS**-1:24▪5:13,14,24,25a▪7:14▪8:7▪9:17a▪10:16,24▪13:7a,13a▪15:4a,7a▪16:7,9a▪17:10a▪21:3a▪22:4a▪24:6^{2}a▪25:3a▪26:14▪27:9,11a▪28:16▪29:14,22▪30:7,13,16^{2}a,18^2▪37:33▪50:7^{2}a▪51:21▪52:6^2▪53:12▪57:10a▪59:9a▪61:7▪65:13-**JER**-2:33▪5:27a▪6:15,18,21▪7:20,32▪8:10,12▪9:7,15▪10:21a▪11:11,21,22▪12:8a▪14:15▪15:19▪16:14,21▪18:13,21▪19:6▪20:11a▪22:18▪23:2,7,15,30,38,39▪25:8▪28:16▪29:28a,32▪30:16▪31:3a,20a▪32:28a,36▪34:17▪35:17,19▪36:30▪42:15▪44:11,23(5921,3652),26▪48:11a,12,31a,36a▪49:2,20,26▪50:18,30,39,45▪51:7a,36,47-**LA**-1:8a▪3:21a,24a-**EZE**-5:7,8,10▪7:20a▪11:4,7,16,17▪12:23,28▪13:8^2,13,23▪14:4,6▪15:6▪16:37▪17:19▪18:30▪20:27▪21:24▪22:4,19^2▪23:22,35▪24:9▪25:4,7,9,13,16▪26:3▪28:6,7▪29:8,10,19▪30:22▪31:5a,10▪34:7,9,20▪35:6,11▪36:3,4,5,6,7,14,22▪37:12▪38:14▪39:25▪41:7a▪42:6a▪44:12a-**DA**-2:6(2006),9(2006),10(3606,6903,1768),24(3606,6903,1768)▪3:7(3606,6903,1836),22(3606,6903,1836)-**HO**-2:6,9,14▪4:3a,13a▪6:5a▪13:3,6a-**JOE**-2:12(1571)-**AM**-3:2a,11▪4:12▪5:11,13,16▪6:7▪7:17-**JON**-4:2a-**MIC**-1:14▪2:3,5▪3:6,12▪5:3-**HAB**-1:4^{2}a,15a,16a,17-**ZEP**-2:9▪3:8-**HAG**-1:10a-**ZEC**-1:16▪10:2a▪**N.T.**-all=3767,a=1223,5124&marked-**M'T**-3:8,10▪5:19,23,48▪6:2,8,9,22,23,25a,31,34▪7:12,24▪9:38▪10:16,26,31,32▪12:27a▪13:13a,18,40,52a▪14:2a▪18:4,23a,26▪19:6,27(686)▪21:40,43a▪22:9,17,21,28▪23:3,14a,20▪24:15,42,44a▪25:13,27,28▪27:17,64▪28:19-**M'R**-1:38(1519,5124)▪2:28(5620)▪6:14a▪8:38(1063)▪10:9(3767)▪11:24a▪12:6,9,23,24a,27,37▪13:35-**LU**-1:35(1352)▪3:8,9▪4:7,43(1519,5124)▪6:36▪7:42▪8:18▪10:2,40▪11:19a,34,35,36▪12:3(473,5607),7,22a,40▪13:14▪14:20(1222,5124)▪15:28▪16:11,27▪19:12▪20:15,25(5106),29,33▪21:8,14,36▪23:16,20,22-**JOH**-1:31a▪2:22▪3:29▪4:1,6,33▪5:10,16a,18a▪6:13,15,24,30,43,45,52,60,65a▪7:3,22a,40▪8:13,24,36,47a▪9:7,8,10,16,23a,41▪10:17a,19,39▪11:3,6,33,38,54▪12:9,17,19,21,29,39a,50▪13:11a,24,31▪15:19a▪16:15a,18,22▪18:4,8,25,31,37,39▪19:1,4,6,8,11a,13,16,24^2,26,30,31,38,42▪20:3,25▪21:6,7-**AC**-1:6▪2:26a,30,33,36▪3:19▪8:4,22▪10:20(235),29(1352),29,32,33^2▪12:5▪13:38,40▪14:3▪15:2,10,27▪16:11,36▪17:12,17,20,23▪19:32▪20:11,31(1352)▪21:22,23▪23:15▪25:5,17▪26:22▪28:20,28-**RO**-2:1(1352),21,26▪3:20(1360),28▪4:16(1233,5124),22(1352)▪5:1,18(686,3767)▪6:4,12▪8:1(686),12(686,3767)▪9:18(686,3767)▪11:22▪12:1,20▪13:2(5620),7,10,12▪14:8,13,19(686,3767)▪15:17,28▪16:19-**1CO**-3:21(5620)▪4:5(5620)▪5:7,8(5628)▪6:7,20(1211)▪7:8(1160),26▪8:4▪9:26(5106)▪10:31▪11:20▪12:15(3756,3844,5124),16(3756,3844,5124)▪14:11,23▪15:11,58(5620)▪16:11,18-**2CO**-1:17▪4:1a,13^2(1352)▪5:6,11,17(5620)▪7:1,13a▪8:7(235),11(2532)▪9:5▪

11:15■12:9,10(1352)■13:10a-**GA**-2:17 (686)■3:5,7(686)■4:16(5620)■5:1■6:10 (685,3767)-**EPH**-2:19(686)■4:1,17■5:1, 7,24(235)■6:14-**PH'P**-2:1,23,28,29■3:15■ 4:1(5620)-**COL**-2:6,16■3:5,12-**1TH**-3:7a■4:8(5105)■5:6(686,3767)-**2TH**-2:15(686,3767)-**1TI**-2:1,8■4:10(1519, 5124)■5:14-**2TI**-1:8■2:1,3,21■4:1 -**PH'M**-15a,17-**HEB**-1:9a■2:1a■4:1,6,9 (686),11,16■7:11■9:23■10:19,35■11:12 (1352)■13:13(5106),15-**JAS**-4:4,7,17■ 5:7-**1PE**-2:7■4:7■5:6-**2PE**-3:17-**1JO**-2:24■3:1a■4:5a-**3JO**-8-**RE**-2:5■3:3^{2},19■ 7:15a■12:12a■18:8(5124)

THEREFROM-all supplied

THEREIN-all=8033&marked-**GE**-18:24(7130)-**EX**-16:33■21:33■30:18■ 40:3,7-**LE**-6:3(2007)■10:1(2004)■25:19 (5921)-**NU**-13:18(5921)■16:7(2004), 46(5921)-**J'G**-8:25■18:7(7130)-**1KI**-8:16-**2KI**-2:20■12:9-**EZR**-6:2(1459) -**NE**-9:6(5921)-**PS**-37:29(5921)-**PR**-22:14 -**IS**-5:2(8432)■34:1(4393)■42:10(4393) -**JER**-4:29(2004)■36:2(413),29(5921), 32(5921)■47:2(4393)■48:9(2004)-**EZE**-2:10(413)■12:19(4393)■24:5(8432)■ 28:26(5921)■30:12(4393)-**AM**-6:8 (4393)-**MIC**-1:2(4393)-**HAB**-2:18 (5921)-**ZEC**-2:4(8432)■**N.T.**-all=1722, 846&marked-**M'R**-10:15(1519,846)-**LU**-10:9■18:17(1519,846)■19:45-**AC**-1:20■ 14:15■17:24-**RO**-1:17■6:2-**1CO**-7:24 (1722,1519)-**EPH**-6:20-**PH'P**-1:18(1722, 5129)-**COL**-2:7-**HEB**-4:6(1519,846)■ 13:9(1722,3639)-**2PE**-2:20(5125)■3:10 -**RE**-1:3■10:6^{3}■11:1■13:12■21:22

THEREINTO-**LU**-21:21(1519,846)

THEREOF-**1KI**-17:13(8033)**N.T.**-all=846&marked-**M'T**-2:16■6:34■12:36 (4012,846)■13:32,44■21:43-**LU**-21:20■ 22:16(1538,846)-**JOH**-3:8■4:12(1538, 846)■6:50(1538,846)■7:7(3012,846)-**AC**-15:16-**RO**-6:12-**1CO**-9:7,23■10:26,28 -**2TI**-3:5-**HEB**-7:18-**JAS**-1:11-**1PE**-1:24-**1JO**-2:17-**RE**-5:2,5,9■16:12,21■ 21:15,17,23

THEREON-all=5921-**GE**-35:14^{2} -**EX**-17:12■20:24,26■30:7,9^{2}■40:27, 35-**LE**-2:1,6,15■5:11■6:12■10:1■11:38 -**NU**-4:6,7^{2},13■5:15■9:22■16:18-**DE**-27:6-**JOS**-8:29,31■22:23^{2}-**2SA**-17:19■ 19:26-**1KI**-13:13-**2KI**-16:12-**1CH**-15:15 -**2CH**-3:5,14■33:16-**EZR**-3:2,3■6:11 -**ES**-5:14■7:9-**IS**-30:12-**EZE**-15:3■ 40:39■43:18^{2}-**ZEC**-4:2■**N.T.**-all=1883, 846&marked-**M'T**-21:7,19(1722,846)■ 23:20,22-**M'R**-11:13(1722,846)■14:72 (1911)-**LU**-13:6(1722,846)■19:35 (1913)-**JOH**-12:14(1909,846)■21:9 (1945)-**1CO**-3:10(2026)-**RE**-5:3(846), 4(846)■6:4(1909,846)■21:12(1924)

THEREOUT-**LE**-2:2(8033)

THERETO-all=5921-**LE**-5:16■ 6:5■27:27,31-**NU**-19:17-**DE**-12:32-**1CH**-22:14-**2CH**-10:14■**N.T.**-**GA**-3:15(1928)

THEREUNTO-**EPH**-6:18(1519, 846,5124)-**1TH**-3:3(1519,5124)-**HEB**-10:1(4334)-**1PE**-3:9(1519,5124)

THEREUPON-**1CO**-3:10(2026), 14(2026)

THEREWITH-**DE**-16:3(5921) -**EZE**-4:15(5921)-**JOE**-2:19(854)■ **N.T.**-**1TI**-6:8(5125)-**JAS**-3:9^{2}(1722, 846)-**3JO**-10(1909,5125)

THESE-all=428,a=2088,b=1992, c=2063,d=479&marked-**GE**-2:4■6:9■ 9:19■10:1,5,20,29,31,32^{2}■11:10,27■14:3, 13b■15:1,10■19:8■20:8■22:1,20,23■ 24:28■25:4,7,12,13,16^{2},17,19■26:3(411), 4(411)■27:36a,46■29:13■31:43■32:17■ 34:21■35:26■36:1,5,9,10,12,13^{2},14,15, 16^{2},17^{3},18^{2},19^{2},20,21,23,24,25,26,27, 28,29,30,31,40,43■37:2■38:25^{2}■39:7,17■ 40:1■43:7■44:6(411),7■45:6a■46:8,15, 18^{2},22,25^{2}■48:1,8■49:28-**EX**-1:1■4:9■ 6:14^{2},15,16,19,24,25,26(1931),27b,27 (1931)■10:1■11:8,10■19:6,7■20:1■ 21:1,11■24:8■25:39■28:4■32:4,8■34:27^{2}■ 35:1-**LE**-2:8■5:4,5,13■11:2c,4a,9a,13,21a, 22,24,29a,31a■16:4b■18:24^{2},26,27(411), 29■20:23■21:14■22:22,25■23:2,4,37■ 25:54■26:14,23,46■27:34-**NU**-1:5,16,17, 44■2:32■3:1,2,3,17,18,20,21,27,33■4:15 37,41,45■5:23■13:4,16■14:22a,39■15:13, 22■16:14b,26,28,29,31,38■21:25■22:9, 28a,32a,33a■24:10a■26:7,14,18,22,25, 27,30,34,35,36,37^{2},41,42^{2},47,50,51,53,57, 58,63,64■27:1■28:23■29:39■30:16■31:16 (2007)■33:1,2■34:17,19,29■35:15,24,29■ 36:13-**DE**-1:1,35■2:7a■3:5,21■4:6,30, 42(411),45■5:22■6:1c,6,24,25c■7:12, 17■8:2a,4a■9:4,5■10:21■11:18,22c,23■ 12:1,28,30■14:4c,7a,9a,12a■15:5c■16:12■ 17:19■18:12^{2},14■19:9c,11(411)■20:15 (428,2007),16■22:17■26:16■27:4,12,13■ 28:2,15,45,65b■29:1,18b■30:1,7■31:1,3, 17,28■32:45-**JOS**-4:6,7,21■9:13^{2}■ 10:16,24,42■11:5,14■12:1,7■13:32■ 14:1,10a■17:2,3,9■19:8,16,31,48,51■ 20:9■21:3,8,9,42^{2}■22:3■23:3,4,7^{2}, 12^{2},13■24:26,29-**J'G**-2:4■3:1■9:3■ 13:23,23c■16:15a■18:14,18■20:17a, 25,35,44,46-**RU**-3:17■4:18-**1SA**-4:8^{2}■6:17■10:7■14:6■16:10■17:17a, 18,39■18:26■21:12■23:2■24:16■25:37■ 29:3,3a,4b■31:4-**2SA**-3:5,39■5:14■7:17, 21c■13:21■14:19■16:2■21:22■23:1,8, 17,22■24:17-**1KI**-4:2,8■7:9,45■8:59■9:13, 23■10:8,10(1931)■11:2b■17:1,17■18:36■ 20:19■21:1■22:11,17,23-**2KI**-1:7,13■ 2:21■3:10,13■6:20■7:8■10:9■17:41■ 18:27■20:14■21:11■23:16,17■25:16,17 -**1CH**-1:23,29,31(428)b,33,43,54■2:1,18, 23,33c,50,55b■3:1,5■4:2,3,4,6,12,18,23b, 31,33c,38,41■5:14,24■6:17,19,33,50,54■ 7:8,11,17,29,33,40■8:6,6(428)b,10,28^{2}, 32b,38^{2},40■9:9,22sup,22b,26b,33,34^{2},44^{2}■ 10:4■11:10,19^{2},19sup,24■12:1,14,15 (428)b,23,38■14:4■17:15■20:8(411)■ 21:17■23:9,10,24■24:19,30,31b■25:5,6■ 26:8,12,19■27:22,31■29:17-**2CH**-3:3,13■ 4:18■8:10■9:7■14:7,8■15:8■17:14,19■ 18:10,16,22■21:2■24:26■29:32■32:1■ 35:7-**EZR**-2:1,59,62■4:21d■5:9(1836), 11(1836),15(412)■6:8^{2}d■7:1■8:1,13■9:1, 14■10:44-**NE**-1:4,10b■5:6■6:6,7,14■ 7:6,61,64■10:8■11:3,7■12:1,7,26■13:26 -**ES**-1:5■2:1■3:1■4:11a■9:20,26,27,28^{2}, 31,32-**JOB**-8:2■10:13■12:3,9■19:3a■ 26:14■32:1■33:29■42:7-**PS**-15:5■42:4■ 50:21■73:12■107:24b,43-**PR**-6:16(2007)■ 24:23■25:1-**EC**-7:10■11:9■12:12b-**IS**-7:4■34:16(2007)■36:12,20■38:16(5291)■ 39:3■40:26■42:16■44:21■45:7■47:7,9■ 48:14■49:12^{3},21,21(2004),21■51:19(2007)■ 57:6■60:8■64:12■65:5-**JER**-2:34■3:7, 12■4:18■5:4b,5b,9,19,25,29■7:2,4b,10, 13,27■9:9,24■10:11(429)■11:6■13:22■ 14:22■16:10■17:20■20:1■22:2,5■24:5■ 25:9,11,30■26:7,10,15■27:6,12■28:14■ 29:1■30:4,15■31:21■32:14■34:6,7 (2007)■36:16,17,18,24■38:9,16,24,27■ 43:1,10■45:1■51:60,61■52:20,22-**LA**-1:16■4:9b■5:17-**EZE**-8:15■11:2■14:3, 14,16,18■16:5,30,43■17:12,18■18:10,13■ 23:10b,30■24:19■27:24b■30:17(2007)■ 36:20■37:3,4,5,9,11,18■40:24,28,29,32, 33,35,46b■42:5(2007),9■43:13,18■46:24■ 47:8,9■48:1,1sup,16,29,30-**DA**-1:6b,17■ 2:28(1836),40(459),44(581),44(459)■ 3:12d,13d,21d,23d,27d■6:2(4481),5d,6, (459),11d,15d■7:17(459)■10:21■11:41■ 12:7,8-**HO**-2:12b■14:9-**AM**-6:2-**MIC**-2:7 -**HAB**-2:6-**HAG**-2:13-**ZEC**-1:9^{2},10,12a, 19^{2},21^{3}■3:7■4:4,5,11,13,14■5:10b■6:4,5■ 7:3a■8:6b,9,10b,12,15,16,17■13:6■14:15b■ **N.T.**-all=5023,a=3778,b=5130,c=5128, d=5125,e=5025&marked-**M'T**-1:20■3:9b■ 4:3a,9■5:19b,37b■6:29b,32,32b,33■7:24c, 26c,28c■9:18■10:2,5c,42b■11:25■13:34, 51,53e,54(3588),56■15:20■18:6b,10b, 14b■19:1c,20■20:12a,21a■21:16a,23, 24,27■22:40e■23:23,36■24:2,3,8,33,34■ 25:40b,45b,46a■26:1c,62a-**M'R**-2:8■ 4:11(3588),15a,16a,18a,20a■6:2■7:23■ 8:4c■9:42(3588)■10:20■11:28^{2},29,33■ 12:31b,40a■13:2e,4^{2},8,29,30■14:60a■ 16:17-**LU**-1:19,20,65■2:19,51■3:8b■ 4:28■5:27■7:9,18b■8:8,13a,21a■9:28c, 44c■10:1,21,36b■11:27,42,53■12:27b, 30,30b,31■13:2a,17■14:6,15,21■15:26, 29(5118)■16:14■17:2b■18:21,22,34b■ 19:11,15c,40a■20:2,8,16c■21:4a,6,7^{2},9, 12b,22a,28b,31,36■23:31,49■24:9,10,14b, 17a,18e,21,26,44a,48b-**JOH**-1:28,50b■ 2:16,18■3:2,9,10,22■5:3e,16,19,20b,34■ 6:1,5a,59■7:1,4,9,31b■8:20,28,30■9:22, 40■10:19c,21■11:11■12:16^{3},36,41■ 13:17■14:12b,25■15:11,17,21■16:1,3,4^{2}, 6,25,33■17:1,11a,13,20b,25a■18:1,8c■ 19:24,36■20:18,31■21:1,15b,24b,24-**AC**-1:9, 14a,21b,24b■2:7a,15a,22c■3:24e■4:16d■ 5:5c,5,11,24c,32b,35d,36b,38b■7:1, 50,54■10:44,47c■11:12a,18,22(846),27d■ 12:17■13:42■14:15b,15,18■15:17,28b■ 16:17a,20a,38■17:6a,7a,8,11a,20■18:1■ 19:21,36b,37c■20:5a,34a■21:12,38b■ 23:22■24:8b,9,20a■24:22■25:9b,11,11a, 20b■26:21b,26^{2}b,29b■27:31a■28:29-**RO**-2:14a■8:31,37d■9:8■11:24a,31a■14:18d■ 15:23d-**1CO**-4:6,14■9:8,15b,15■10:6, 11■12:2(3588),11,23d■13:13,13b-**2CO**-2:16■7:1e■13:10-**GA**-4:24a■5:17-**EPH**-5:6-**PH'P**-4:8-**COL**-3:8(3588),14d■4:11a -**1TH**-3:3e■4:18d-**2TH**-2:5-**1TI**-3:10a, 14■4:6,11,15■5:7,21■6:2,11-**2TI**-1:12■ 2:14,21b■3:8a-**TIT**-2:15■3:8b,8-**HEB**-1:2b■7:13■9:6b,23d,23e■10:18b■11:13a, 39a-**JAS**-3:10-**1PE**-1:20(3588)-**2PE**-1:4b, 8,9,10,12b,15b■2:12a,17a■3:11b,16b-**1JO**-1:4■2:1,26■5:7a,8a,13-**JUDE**-8a,10a, 12a,14d,16a,19a-**RE**-2:1(3592),8(3592), 12(3592),18(3592)■3:1(3592),7(3592),14 (3592)■7:1,13a,14a■9:18b,20e■11:4a,6a,10a■ 14:4^{3}a■16:9e■17:13a,14a,16a■18:1,15b■ 19:1,9a,20(3588)■21:5a■22:6a,8^{2},16,18,20

THICK-all=5688&marked-**EX**-10:22 (653)■19:9(5645),16(3515)-**LE**-23:40 (5687)-**DE**-32:15(5666)-**1KI**-7:26(5672) -**NE**-8:15(5687)-**JOB**-15:26(5672) -**PS**-74:5(5441)-**EZE**-6:13(5687)■8:11 (6282)■19:11■20:28(5687)■31:3,10,14■ 41:12(7341),25(5645)

THICKER-**1KI**-12:10(5666)-**2CH**-10:10(5666)

THICKET-**GE**-22:13(5442)-**JER**-4:7(5441)

THICKETS-**1SA**-13:6(2337)-**IS**-9:18(5442)■10:34(5442)-**JER**-4:29(5645)

THICKNESS-**2CH**-4:5(5672)-**JER**-52:21(5672)-**EZE**-41:9(7341)■42:10(7341)

THIEF-all=1590-**EX**-22:2,7,8-**DE**-24:7-**JOB**-24:14■30:5-**PS**-50:18-**PR**-6:30■29:24-**JER**-2:26-**HO**-7:1-**JOE**-2:9-**ZEC**-5:4■**N.T.**-all=2812&marked -**M'T**-24:43■26:55(3027)-**M'R**-14:48 (3027)-**LU**-12:33,39■22:52(3027)-**JOH**-10:1,10■12:6-**1TH**-5:2,4-**1PE**-4:15 -**2PE**-3:10-**RE**-3:3■16:15

THIEVES-all=1590-**IS**-1:23-**JER**-48:27■49:9-**OB**-5■**N.T.**-all=3027& marked-**M'T**-6:19(2812),20(2812)■ 21:13■27:38,44-**M'R**-11:17■15:27-**LU**-10:30,36■19:46-**JOH**-10:8(2812)-**1CO**-6:10(2812)

THIGH-all=3409&marked-**GE**-24:2, 9■32:25^{2},31,32^{2}■47:29-**NU**-5:21,22,27 -**J'G**-3:16,21■15:8-**PS**-45:3-**SONG**-3:8 -**IS**-47:2(7785)-**JER**-31:19-**EZE**-21:12■ 24:4■**N.T.**-**RE**-19:16(3382)

THIGHS-**EX**-28:42(3409)-**SONG**-7:1(3409)-**DA**-2:32(3410)

THIN-all=1851&marked-**GE**-41:6,7, 23,24,27(7534)-**LE**-13:30-**1KI**-7:29 (4174)-**IS**-17:4(1809)

THINE-**1KI**-21:19(859)■**N.T.**-all=4675,a=4674&marked-**M'T**-5:25, 33,43■6:4,13,17,22,23■7:3a,4^{2},5■9:6■ 12:13■18:9■20:14a,15■22:44■25:25a -**M'R**-2:11■3:5■9:47■12:36-**LU**-4:7■ 5:24,33a■6:41(2398),42^{3}■7:44■8:39■ 11:34■12:58■13:12■15:31a■19:22,42,43■ 20:43■22:42a-**JOH**-2:17■8:10■9:10,17, 26■17:5(4572),6(4671),9(4671),10a,10

(3588,4674),11■18:35a-AC-2:27■4:30■5:3,4(4671),4(3588,4674),4■8:22(4671),37(3588)■10:4(3588),31■13:35■23:35-RO-10:6,9■11:3■12:20-1CO-10:29(1438)-1TI-5:23-PH'M-19(4572)-HEB-1:10,13-RE-3:18

THING-all=1697,a=3627&marked-GE-18:14■19:21■20:10■21:11,26■22:16■24:50■30:31^2■34:7(3651),14,19■39:9(3972),23(3972)■41:28,32,37■44:7-EX-1:18■2:14,15■9:5,6■12:24■16:16,32■18:11,14,17,18,23■29:1■33:17■35:4-LE-4:13■5:2■8:5■9:6■11:10(5315)■13:48(4399),49a,52a,53a,57a,58a,59a■15:4a,6a,22a,23a■17:2■23:37-NU-18:7■20:19■22:38(3972)■30:1■31:23■32:20■35:22a■36:6-DE-1:14,32■4:32■12:32■13:14■15:10,15■17:4,5■18:22^2■22:20■23:9,14,19■24:10(4859),18,22■32:47^2-JOS-4:10■9:24■14:6■21:45■22:24,33■23:14^2-J'G-6:29^2■11:37■18:7,10■19:19,24■20:9■21:11-RU-3:18-1SA-3:11,17^2■8:6■12:16■14:12■15:9(4399)■18:20■20:2■21:2■22:15■24:6■26:16■28:10,18-2SA-2:6■3:13■11:11,25,27■12:6,12,21■13:12(3651),20,33■14:13,15,18,20,21■15:11,35,36■17:19■24:3-1KI-1:27■3:10,11■10:3■11:10■12:24,30■13:33,34■14:5,13■20:9,24-2KI-5:13,18^2■6:11■7:2,19■8:13■11:5■17:12-1CH-13:4■17:23■21:7,8-2CH-11:4■23:4,19■29:36■30:4-EZR-9:3■10:13-NE-2:19■13:17-ES-2:4,22■5:14■8:5-JOB-4:12■15:11■22:28(562)-PS-101:3■141:4-PR-25:2-EC-1:10■5:2■7:8■8:1,3,5-IS-38:7-JER-7:23■22:4■32:27■33:14■38:5,14■40:3,16■42:3,4■44:4,17-EZE-14:9■47:9(5315)-DA-2:5(4406),8(4406),11(4406),15(4406),17(4406)■4:33(4406)■5:15(4406),26(4406)■6:12(4406)■10:1^3-AM-6:13■N.T.-M'T-18:19(4229)■21:24(3056)-LU-2:15(4487)■20:3(3056)-AC-5:4(4229)-RO-9:20(4110)-2CO-10:5(5313)-PH'P-3:13(1520)

THINGS-all=1697&marked-GE-15:1■20:8■22:1,20■24:28,66■29:13■39:7■40:1■48:1-LE-8:36-DE-1:18■4:9,30■30:1-JOS-23:14,15^2■24:29-1SA-2:23■19:7■25:37-2SA-11:18■13:21-1KI-17:17■18:36■21:1-2KI-17:9,11■23:17-1CH-4:22-2CH-12:12■19:3■32:1-EZR-7:1-NE-6:8-ES-2:1■3:1■9:20-EC-1:8■6:11-IS-42:16-JER-20:1■26:10■42:5-EZE-11:25■38:10-DA-7:16(4406)■N.T.-all=4229&marked-LU-1:1,4(3056)■2:19(4487)-JOH-11:11(5023)-AC-5:24(3056),32(4487)■20:24(3056)-RO-10:15(18)-HEB-7:13■10:1sup,1■11:1-1PE-1:12(846)

THINGS'-supplied

THINK-all=2803&marked-GE-40:14(2142)-NU-36:6(5869)-2SA-13:33(559)-2CH-13:8(559)-NE-5:19(2142)■6:6,14(2142)-ES-4:13(1819)-JOB-31:1(995)■41:32-EC-8:17(559)-IS-10:7-JER-23:27■29:11-EZE-38:10-DA-7:25(5452)-JON-1:6(6245)-ZEC-11:12(5869)■N.T.-all=1380&marked-M'T-3:9■5:17(3543)■6:7■9:4(1760)■10:34(3543)■18:12■21:28■22:42■24:44■26:66-M'R-14:64(5316)-LU-12:40■13:4-JOH-5:39,45■11:56■16:2-AC-13:25(5282)■17:29(3543)■26:2(2233)-RO-12:3(5252),3^2(5426)-1CO-4:6(5426),9■7:36(3543),40■8:2■12:23■14:37-2CO-3:5(3049)■10:2^2(3049),7(3049),11(3049)■11:16■12:6(3049),19-GA-6:3-EPH-3:20(3539)-PH'P-1:7(5426)■4:8(3049)-JAS-1:7(3633)■4:5-2PE-1:13(2233)

THINKEST-2SA-10:3(5869)-1CH-19:3(5869)-JOB-35:2(2803)■N.T.-all=1380&marked-M'T-17:25■22:17■26:53-LU-10:36-AC-28:22(5426)-RO-2:3(3049)

THINKETH-2SA-18:27(7200)-PS-40:17(2803)-PR-23:7(8176)■N.T.-1CO-10:12(1380)■13:5(3049)-PH'P-3:4(1380)

THINKING-2SA-4:10(1931,1961)■5:6(559)

THIRD-all=7992&marked-GE-1:13■2:14■6:16■22:4■31:22■32:19■34:25■40:20■42:18■50:23(8029)-EX-19:1,11^2,15(7969),16■20:5(8029)■28:19■34:7(8029)■39:12-LE-7:17,18■19:6,7-NU-2:24■7:24■14:18(8029)■15:6,7■19:12^2,19■28:14■29:20■31:19-DE-5:9(8029)■23:8■26:12-JOS-9:17■19:10-J'G-20:30-1SA-3:8■17:13■19:21■20:5,12■30:1-2SA-1:2■3:3■18:2^3-1KI-3:18■6:6,8■12:12^2■15:28(7969),33(7969)■18:1,34^2(8027)■22:2-2KI-1:13^2■11:5,6^2■18:1(7969)■19:29■20:5,8-1CH-2:13■3:2,15■8:1,39■12:9■23:19■24:8,23■25:10■26:2,4,11■27:5^2-2CH-10:12^2■15:10■17:7(7969)■23:4,5^2■27:5■31:7-EZR-6:15(8531)-NE-10:32-ES-1:3(7969)■5:1■8:9-JOB-42:14-IS-19:24■37:30-JER-38:14-EZE-5:2^3,12^3■10:14■21:14■31:1■46:14-DA-1:1(7969)■2:39(8523)■5:7(8523),16(8531),29(8531)■8:1(7969)■10:1(7969)-HO-6:2-ZEC-6:3■13:8,9■N.T.-all=5154&marked-M'T-16:21■17:23■20:3,19■22:26■26:44■27:64-M'R-9:31■10:34■12:21■14:41■15:25-LU-9:22■12:38■13:32■18:33■20:12,31■23:22■24:7,21,46-JOH-2:1■21:14,17^2-AC-2:15■10:40■20:9(5152)■23:23■27:19-1CO-15:4-2CO-12:2,14■13:1-3JO-t-RE-4:7■6:5^2■8:7,8,9^2,10^2,11,12^5■9:15,18■11:14■12:4■14:9■16:4■21:19

THIRDLY-1CO-12:28(5154)

THIRST-all=6772&marked-EX-17:3-DE-28:48■29:19(6771)-J'G-15:18-2CH-32:11-NE-9:15,20-JOB-24:11(6770)-PS-69:21■104:11-IS-5:13■41:17■49:10(6770)■50:2-JER-2:25(6773)■48:18-LA-4:4-HO-2:3-AM-8:11,13■N.T.-all=1372&marked-M'T-5:6-JOH-4:13,14,15■6:35■7:37■19:28-RO-12:20-1CO-4:11-2CO-11:27(1373)-RE-7:16

THIRSTED-EX-17:3(6770)-IS-48:21(6770)

THIRSTETH-PS-42:2(6770)■63:1(6770)-IS-55:1(6771)

THIRSTY-all=6771&marked-J'G-4:19(6770)-2SA-17:29-PS-107:5-PR-25:21-IS-21:14■29:8■32:6■35:7(6774)■44:3■65:13(6770)-EZE-19:13(6772)■N.T.-all=1372-M'T-25:35,37,42

THIRTEEN-all=7969,6240&marked-GE-17:25-NU-3:43(7969),46(7969)■29:13,14-JOS-19:6■21:4,6,19,33-1KI-7:1-1CH-6:60,62■26:11-EZE-40:11

THIRTEENTH-all=7969,6240-GE-14:4-1CH-24:13■25:20-ES-3:12,13■8:12■9:1,17,18-JER-1:2■25:3

THIRTIETH-all=7970-2KI-15:13,17■25:27-2CH-15:19■16:1-NE-5:14■13:6-JER-52:31-EZE-1:1

THIRTY-all=7970&marked-GE-5:3,5,16■6:15■11:12,14,16,17,18,20,22■18:30^2■25:17■32:15■41:46■46:15■47:9-EX-6:16,18,20■12:40,41■21:32■26:8■36:15■38:24-LE-12:4■27:4-NU-1:35,37■2:21,23■4:3,23,30,35,39,40,43,47■7:13,19,25,31,37,43,49,55,61,67,73,79,85■20:29■26:7,37,51■31:35,36,38,39,40,43,44,45-DE-2:14■34:8-JOS-7:5■8:3■12:24-J'G-10:4^2■12:9^2,14■14:11,12,13,19■20:31,39-1SA-4:10■9:22■11:8■13:5-2SA-5:4,5■6:1■23:13,23,24,39-1KI-2:11■4:22■5:13■6:2■7:2,6,23■16:23,29■20:1,15,16■22:31,42-2KI-8:17■13:10■15:8■18:14■22:1-1CH-3:4■7:4,7■11:15,25,42■12:4,34■15:7■19:7■23:3^2■27:6■29:27-2CH-3:15■4:2■16:12■20:31■21:5,20■24:15■34:1■35:7-EZR-1:9,10■2:35,42,65,66,67-NE-7:38,45,67,68,69,70-ES-4:11-JER-38:10■52:29-EZE-40:17■41:6,22-DA-6:7(8533),12(8533)■12:12-ZEC-11:12,13■N.T.-all=5144-M'T-13:23■26:15■27:3,9-M'R-4:8-LU-3:23-JOH-5:5■6:19-GA-3:17

THIRTYFOLD-M'T-13:8(5144)-M'R-4:20(5144)

THIS-all=2088,a=2063,b=1931,c=1836,d=3651,e=1791,f=6311&marked-GE-2:23a■3:13a,14a■5:1,29■6:15■7:1■9:12a■11:6■12:7a,12a,18a■15:2b,4,7a,18a■17:10a,21■18:25,32(6471)■19:13,14,14sup,20a,21,21sup■20:5a,6a,10,11,13■21:10^{2}a,26■24:58,65(1976)■25:32■26:3a,10a,11,33■28:15a,16,17^3,20,22a■29:25a,27a,33■30:31■31:1,13a,38,48,48sup,51,51sup,52,52sup,52,52a■32:2,10,19,32■33:8■34:4a,14,15a■35:17■36:24b■37:6,10,19(1976),22,32a■38:21,22,23,28■39:9,9a,11,19(428)■40:12,14,18■41:28b,38,39a■42:18a,21a,28a■43:10,11a,29■44:5,7,15,29■45:17a,19a,23a■47:26■48:4a,9,15,18■49:28a■50:11,20,24a-EX-1:18■2:6,9,12(3541),15■3:3,12,15^2,21■4:17■5:22,23■7:17a,23a■8:19b,23,32a■9:5,14a,16a■10:6,7,17sup,17■12:2,3,12,14,17,24,26a,42■13:3^2,5,10a,14a■14:5a,12■15:1a■16:3^2,15b,16,23b,32■17:3,4,14a■18:14,18,18sup,23^2■21:31■25:3a■26:13■29:1,38■30:13,31■32:1,9,13a,21,23,31■33:12,17■35:4■37:8■38:15,21(428)-LE-6:9a,14a,20,25a■7:1a,11a,35a,37a■8:5,34■9:6■10:3b■11:46a■12:7a■13:59a■14:2a,32a,54a,57a■15:3a,32a■16:34a■17:2a,7a■23:27,34■25:13a■26:16a,18(428),27a-NU-4:4a,24a,28a,31a,33a■5:29a,30a,31b■6:13a,20b,21a,23(3541)■7:17,23,29,35,41,47,53,59,65,71,77,83,84a,88a■8:4,24a■9:3■11:11,12,13,14,31(3541)■13:17,27■14:2,3a,8a,11,13,14a,14,15,16,19^2,27a,29,32,35a,35■16:6a,21a,45a■18:9,11■19:2a,14a■20:4,5,10,12,13(1992)■21:2,17■22:6,17,24,30■24:14■26:9b■27:12■28:3,14a,17,24(428)■29:7■30:1■31:21a■32:5a,15,20,22a■34:2a,6,7,9,12a,13a■35:5■36:6-DE-1:5sup,5a,6,31,32,35■2:3,7,22,25,30■3:12a,14,18a,26,27,28■4:6b,6,8a,8sup,,20,22,32,38,44a■5:3a,3sup,24,25a,28■6:24■8:17,18■9:4,6a,7,13,27■10:8,15■11:4,5■13:11■15:2,10,15■17:18a,19a■18:3,16a■19:4■21:7,20■22:14a,16,20,26■24:18,22■26:9,9a,16■27:3a,8a,9,26a■28:58a,58^2,61a■29:4,7,9a,14a,19a,20,21,24a,24,27b,27,28,29a■30:10,11a,11sup■31:2sup,2,7,9a,11a,12a,16,19^{2}a,21a,22a,24a,26,30a■32:27a,29a,34b,44a,46^{2}a,47,49■33:1a,7a■34:4a,6-JOS-1:2sup,2,4,6,8,11,13a■2:14,17,18,20■3:7■4:6a,9a,22■5:4,9sup,9■6:25,26a■7:7,25,26^2■8:20(2007),22,28,29,33■9:12,20a,24,27■10:13b,27■11:6a■13:2a,7a,13,23a,28a■14:10,10sup,12,14■15:4,12,20a,63■16:8a,10■18:14a,19,20a,28a■19:8a,16a,23a,31a,39a,48a■22:3,16,16^{2}sup,17,22,24a,31sup,31■23:8,9,13a,15a■24:27a-J'G-1:21,26■2:2^{2}a,20■4:14■6:13a,14,20(1975),24,26,29^2■7:4^2,14a■9:19,29,38■10:4,15■11:37■12:3■15:6a,7a,11a,18a,19a■16:28■18:3(6311),12,24■19:11a,23,23a,24,30■20:3a,9a,12a,16■21:3a,11a-RU-1:19a■2:5a■4:7^{2}a,12a-1SA-1:3b,27■2:20a,23(428),34■4:6a,14■5:5■6:9a,18,20■8:8,11■9:6a,17■10:11,27■11:2a,13■12:2,5,8,16,20a■14:10,29,38,45^2■15:14■16:8,9,12■17:10,17,25,26(1975),26,27,32,33,36,37,46^2,47,55■18:24(428)■20:2,3a,21(2007)■21:11,15^2■22:8,13,15a■23:26■24:6,16,19■25:21,25,27a,31a,32,33■26:16,17,21,24■27:6■28:10,18■29:3^2,5,6,8■30:8,15^2,20,24,25-2SA-1:17a■2:1d,5,6^2■3:38■4:3,8■6:8■7:6,17,19^{2}a,27a,28■8:1d■10:1d■11:3a,11,25■12:5a,6,11a,12,14,21■13:1d,12a,16a,17a,20a■14:3,13,15,19a,20sup,20,21■15:1d,6■16:9,12,17,18■17:6,7a■18:18,20^2■19:21a,42■21:18d■22:1a■23:17a,17sup■24:3-1KI-1:27,30,45b■2:23,26■3:6^2,9,10,11,17a,18a,19a,22a,23a■5:7sup,7■6:12■7:8,28,37a■8:8,24,27,29^2,30,31,33,35,38,42,43,54a,61■9:3,8,8a,9a,13,15,21■10:12■11:10,11a,27,39a■12:6,7,9,10,19,24,27^2,30■13:3,8,16,33,34■14:2,15a■17:21,24■18:36,37■20:7,9,12,13^2,24,28,39■22:20(3541),27-2KI-1:2■2:19,22■3:16,18a,23■4:9b,

12a,13a,16,36a,43■5:6,7,18^2,20■6:11,
18,19sup,19(2090),24d,28a,33a■7:2,9b■
8:5a,5,8,9,13,22■9:1,11,25,26a,34a,36b,
37a■10:2,27■11:5■14:7■15:12b■16:6■
17:12,23,34,41■18:19,21,22,25,25a,
30a■19:3,21,29,29sup,31a,32a,33a,
34a■20:6^{2}a,9,17■21:7,15■22:13^2,16,17,
19,20■23:3a,3,21,23,27a-1CH-4:41,43■
5:26■11:11(428),19a■13:11■17:5,15,
17a,19a,26a■18:1d■19:1d■20:4d■
21:3a,7,8■22:1^2■27:6b■28:7■29:14a,
16,18a-2CH-1:10^2,11a■2:4a■5:9■6:15,
18,20^2,21,22,24,26,29,32,33,34a,40■
7:12,15,16,20,21,21a,21,22a■8:8■10:6,
7,9,19■11:4■14:11■16:10a■18:19
(3602),26■19:10(3541)■20:1d,7a,9^2,12,
15,17a,26,35d■21:10,18a■23:4■24:4d,
18a■25:9,16a■28:22b■29:9■30:9a■
31:1a,10■32:9,15a,20a,30b■33:7,14d■
34:21,24,25,27,28,31■35:19,20a-EZR-
1:9(428)■3:12■4:8(3660),11c,11sup,13e,
15^{2}e,16e,16c,16sup,19e,21e,22c■5:3sup,
3^{2}c,4(3660),4c,5c,8e,9c,12c,13c,17e,17c■
6:7^{2}e,8e,11^{2}c,12e,15c,16c,17c■7:6b,11,17c,
24c,27a■8:1(428),23a■9:2,3,7^2,10a,13a,
15^{2}a■10:2a,5,13sup,13,14,15a-NE-1:11sup,
11■2:2,19■5:10,12,13^2,16a,18^2,19■6:4,16a■
9:1,10,18,32,38a■13:4,6,14,17,18,18a,22a,
27a-ES-1:1b,18■4:14^{2}a■5:13■6:3■7:6■
9:26(3602),29a-JOB-1:3b,22a■2:10a,11a■
3:1d■5:27a■8:19b■9:22b■10:13a■12:9a■
17:8a■18:21■19:26a■20:4a,29■21:2a■
27:13■31:11b,28b■33:12a■34:16a■35:2a■
36:21■37:1a,14a■38:2■42:16a-PS-7:3a■
12:7(2098)■18:ta■24:6,8,10■27:3a■32:6a
■34:6■41:11a■44:17a,21a■48:14■49:1a,
13■50:22a■56:9■62:11(2098)■73:16a■
74:2,18a■77:10b■78:32a,54■80:14a■
81:4b■87:4,6■92:6a■102:18■104:25■
109:20a,27a■118:20,23a,24■119:50a,56a■
132:14a■149:9b-PR-6:3a-EC-1:10,13b,
17■2:1b,10,15,19,21,23(2088)b,24,26■
4:4b,4,8,16■5:10,16(2090),19(2090)■
6:2,5,9■7:6,10,18^2,23(2090),27,29■
8:9,10,14■9:1^2,3,13(2090)■11:6■12:13
-SONG-3:6a■5:16■7:7a■8:5a-IS-
1:12a■3:6a■5:25a■6:7,9,10■8:6,11,
12,20■9:7a,12a,16,17a,21a■10:4a■
12:5a■14:4,16,26^{2}a,28■16:13■17:14■20:6■
22:14,15■23:7a,8a,13■24:3■25:6,7,9^2,10■
26:1■27:9a,9■28:11,12^{2}a,14,29■29:11,12,
13,(2068)14■30:7a,9b,12,13,21■36:4,6,7,10^{2}a,
15a■37:3,22,30,30sup,32a,33a,34a,35a■
38:6^{2}a,7^2■39:6■41:20a■42:22b,23a■43:9a,
21(2098)■45:21a■46:8a■47:8a■48:1a,16a,
20a■50:11a■51:21a■54:9a,17a■56:2a,
12■58:5,6■59:21a■63:1^2■66:2-JER-1:10■
2:12a,17a■3:10a,25■4:8a,10,11,18a,28a■
5:7a,9,14^2,20a,21a,23,29(2068)■6:6b,19,
21■7:2,3,6,7,10,11,16,20,23,25,28,33■
8:3a,5■9:9,12a,15,24a■10:18a,19■11:2,
3,5,6,7,8,14■13:10^2,12,25■14:10,11,13,
15a,17■15:1,20■16:2,3^2,5,6a,9,10,10a,13a,
21a■17:24a,25a,25■18:6■19:3,4^2,6,7,8a,
11,11a,12,12a,15a■20:5a■21:4a,6a,7a,8,
9a,10a■22:1,3,4^2,5,8^{2}a,11,12a,16b,21,28,
30■23:6,32,33,38■24:5,6a,8a■25:3,9a,
11a,13,15a,18■26:1,6,6a,9,9a,11,11a,12,
12a,15a,16,20a■27:1,16,17a,19a,22■28:3^2,
4,6,7,15■29:10,16a,28b,32■30:17b,21b
(2088)■31:23,26a,33a■32:3a,8b,14^2,15a,
20^2,22a,23a,28a,29^{2}a,31a,31,35a,36a,37,
41a,42a,42,43a■33:4a,5a,10,12,16,24■
34:2a,22a■35:14,16■36:1,2,7,29^{2}a■37:8a,
10a,18,19a■38:2a,3a,4,4a,4^2,16a,17a,18a,
21,23a■39:16a■40:2a,2,3,16■42:2a,10a,
13a,18■44:2,4,6,10,22,23a,23,29a,29■45:4b■
46:7,10b■50:17,25b■51:6b,62,63■52:28
-LA-2:15,16,20(3541)■3:21a■5:17-EZE-
1:5,23(2007),28b■2:3■3:1a,3a■4:3b■
5:5a■6:10a■8:5■10:15b,20b■11:2a,3b,
6a,7b,11b,15b■12:10,23■16:49■17:7a■
18:2,3■19:14b■20:27a,29■21:11b,26a■
23:38a■24:2^2■31:18b■32:16b■36:35
(1977),37a■39:8b■40:10^{2}f,12sup,12f,
21f,26f,34f,37f,39f,41f,45(2090),48^{2}f,49f■
41:4,22■43:12^{2}a,13■44:2■45:1b,2,3a,13a,
16a■46:3b,20■47:12,13,14a,15,20a,21a■
48:29a-DA-1:14■2:12c,18c,30c,31(1797),32b,
36c,38b,47c■3:16c,29c■4:18c,24c,24b,30
(1668)■5:7c,15c,22c,24c,25c,26c■6:3c,5c,
28c■7:6c,7c,16c,8(1668),16c■8:16(1975)■
9:7,13a■10:11,17^2■12:5(2008)-HO-
5:1a■7:10a,16(2097)-JOE-1:2^{2}a■3:9a
-AM-3:1■4:1,5d,12a■5:1■7:3a,6a,6b■
8:4a,8a■9:12a-OB-20-JON-1:7a,8a,10a,
14■4:2-MIC-1:5a■2:3a,3b,10a,11■3:9a■
5:5-HAB-1:11(2098)-ZEP-1:4,37a■
2:10a,15a-HAG-1:2,4■2:3,7,9^2,14,15,18,
19-ZEC-2:4(1975)■3:2■4:6,9■5:3a,3,5a,
6^{2}a,7a,8a■8:6,11,12■14:12a,15a,19a-MAL-
1:9a■2:1a,4a■N.T.-all=5124,a=3778,
b=5026,c=5127,d=3588,e=5129,f=5126
,g=4594,h=3779&marked-M'T-1:18h,22■
3:3a,17a■6:9h,11g■7:12a■8:9e,9,27a■9:3a,
28■10:23b■11:10a,14(846),16b,23g■12:6
(5602),23a,24a,32e,41b,42b,45b■13:15c,
19a,22c,28,40c,54a,55a,56e■14:2a,15d■
15:8a,11,12d,15b■16:18b,22■17:5a,20e,
21■18:4■19:5c,11f,26■20:14e■21:4,10a,
11a,21d,21e,23b,38a,42a,44f■22:20a,38a■
23:36b■24:14,21(3568),34a,43(1565)■
26:8a,9,12,13,13^{2}a,26,28,29c,31b,34b,
39,42,56,61a,71a■27:8g,19g,24c,37a,47a,
54a■28:14,15a,15g-M'R-1:27a,27■2:7a,
12h■4:13b,19d,41a■5:32■6:2e,2d,3a■
35d■7:6a,29f■8:12a,12b,38b■9:7a,21,29■
10:5b,7c,30e■11:3,23e,28b■12:7a,10b,
11a,16a,30a,31a,43a■13:19(3568),30a■
14:4a,9,9sup,22,24,27b,30g,30b,36,58f,
69a,71f■15:39a-LU-1:18,29a,34,36a,43,
61e,66■2:2a,11g,12,15,17c,34a■3:20■
4:3e,6b,21g,21a,22a,23b,36a■5:6,21a■
6:3■7:4,8,17a,27a■31b,39a,39d,44b,45a,
46a,49a■8:9a,11a,14d,25a■9:9a,13f,35a,
45c,48■10:5e,11,20e,28■11:29a,30b,31b,
32b,50b,51b■12:18,20b,39,41b,56f■
13:6b,7b,8,16b,16c■14:9e,30a■15:2a,3b,
24a,30a,32a■16:2,8c,24b,26(5125),28f■
17:6b,18a,25b■18:1d,5b,9b,11a,14a,23
(5023),30e,34■19:9g,9e,14f,42b■20:2b,
9b,14a,17,19b,34f■21:3a,23e,32a■22:15,
17,19^2,20,23,34g,37,42,53a,56a,59a■
23:2f,4e,5(5602),14e,14f,18f,38a,41a,47a,
52a■24:21(5125)-JOH-1:15a,19a,30a,
34a■2:11b,12,19f,20a,22■3:19a,29a■
4:13c,15,20e,21e,27e,29a,42a,54■5:1
(5023),28■6:6,14a,29,34f,39,40,42a,50a,
51c,52a,58a,58f,60sup,60a,61■7:8^{2}b,
15a,25a,26a,27f,31a,36a,39,40d,40a,41a,
46a,49a■8:4a,6,23^{2}c,40■9:2a,3a,8a,9a,
16a,19a,20a,24a,29f,33a,39f■10:16b,18b,
41c■11:4a,9c,26,37^{2}a,39(2235),47a,51■
12:5,6,7(846),18^2,25e,27,27b,27,30a,31^{2}c,
33,34a■13:1c,28,35e■14:30(3127)■
15:12a,13b■16:11c,17,18,30e■17:3a■
18:17c,29c,34,36^{2}c,37^2,38,40f■19:12f,20f,
28,38(5023)■20:22,30e■21:1h,14,19^2,21a,
23a,24a-AC-1:6e,11a,16b,17b,18a,25b■
2:6b,12,14,16,29b,32f,33,40b■3:12e,12
(846),16b,16f■4:7,9g,10a,11a,17e,22■
5:4,20b,24,28e,28c,37f,38■6:3b,13c,13a,
14f,14a■7:4b,6h,7e,29e,35f,37a,38a,40a,
60b,60■8:10a,19b,21e,22b,29e,32a,34■
9:2d,13c,21a,21,22a,36a■10:16,17d,30b■
11:10■13:17c,23c,26b,33g,34h,38c■15:2c,
6c,15e,16(5023),23(3592)■16:18,36(5128)■
17:3a,18a,19a,23(3739),30d,32c■18:10b,
13a,21d,25a■19:10,17,25b,26a,27,40g,
40b■20:26g,29■21:11a,23,28a,28f,28c■
22:3b,3g,4b,22c,26a,28b■23:1b,9e,13b,
17f,18f,25f,27f■24:2e,5f,10e,14,21b,21g,
25(3568)■25:5(846),24f■26:2g,16,22b,
26,29g,31a,32a■27:10d,21b,23b,33g,34■
28:4a,9c,20^{2}b,22b,26f,27c-RO-1:26■
2:3■3:26d(3568),4:9a■5:2b■6:6■7:24c■
8:18d■9:9a,9f,17■10:6h■11:5d,8g,25,27a■
12:2e■13:6^2,9d,9e■14:9,13■15:9,28,28f■
16:22d-1CO-1:12,20^{2}c■2:6^{2}c,8c■3:12f,18e,
19c■4:11d,13(737),17■5:2,3,10c■7:6,7h,26,
29,31c,31e,35■8:7(737),9a■9:3a,12d,12b,17,
23,10:28■11:10,17,22e,24^2,25^2,26f,26,27^{2}f,
30■14:21e■15:19f,50,53^2,54^2■16:12(3568)
-2CO-1:12a,15b■2:1,3,6a,9■3:10e,14g,
15g■4:1b,4c,7f■5:1d,2e,4d■7:11,11d■8:7,
10,14d(3568),19,20,20b■9:3e,4d,6,12b,
13b■10:7,11■11:10a,17b■12:8c,13b■
13:1,9-GA-1:4d■3:2,17■4:25d■5:8d,
14d■6:16e-EPH-1:21d■2:2c■3:1c,8a,
14c■4:17■5:5,31c,32■6:1,12c-PH'P-
1:6,7,9,19,22,25■2:5■3:15-COL-1:9,
27c■2:4■3:20■4:16d-1TH-2:13■3:5■
4:3,15■5:18,27d-2TH-1:11d■2:11■3:10,
14d-1TI-1:9,15d,16,18b■2:3■3:1d■
4:9d,16■6:7d,14d,17d(3568)-2TI-1:15■
2:19b■3:1,6(5130)■4:10d-TIT-1:5c,
13a■2:12d■3:8d-HEB-1:5g■3:3a■4:4h,
5e■5:4d■6:3■7:1a,4a,24d,27■8:3f,10a■
9:8,11b,15,20,27■10:12a,16a■12:27d■
13:19-JAS-1:25a,26c,27a■2:5c■3:15a■
4:15-1PE-1:25■2:19,20■3:5h■4:6,16e■
5:12b-2PE-1:5,13e,14d,17a,18b,20■3:1b,
3,5,8-1JO-1:5a■2:25a■3:3b,8,10e,11a,
17d,23a■4:3,9e,17e,21b■5:2e,3a,4a,6a,
9a,11^{2}a,14a,20a-2JO-6^{2}a,7a,10b-JUDE-
4,5-RE-1:3d■2:6,24b■4:1(5023)■7:9
(5023)■11:5h,15b■20:5a,14a■22:7c,9c,
10c,18c,18e,19e,19b

THISTLE-all=2336&marked-2KI-
14:9^2-2CH-25:18^2-HO-10:8(1863)

THISTLES-GE-3:18(1863)-JOB-
31:40(2336)■N.T.-M'T-7:16(5146)

THITHER-all=8033&marked
-GE-19:20,22^2■24:6■29:3■39:1■42:2
-EX-10:26■26:33-NU-35:6,11,15-DE-
1:37,38,39■4:42■12:5,6,11■19:3,4■
32:52-34:4-JOS-7:3,4■20:3,9-J'G-8:27■
9:51■18:3,17■19:15■21:10-1SA-2:14■
9:6■10:5,10,22(1988)■19:23■22:1-2SA-
2:2-1KI-19:9-2KI-2:8(2008),14(2008)■
4:8,10,11■6:6,9,14■9:2■17:27-2CH-1:6
-EZR-10:6-NE-4:20■5:16■13:9-JOB-
1:21■6:20(5704)-EC-1:7-IS-7:24,25■
55:10■57:7-JER-22:11,27■31:8(2008)■
40:4-EZE-1:20■11:18■40:1,3■47:9-JOE-
3:11■N.T.-all=1563&marked-M'T-
2:22-M'R-6:33-LU-17:37■21:2-JOH-
11:8■18:2,3-AC-8:30(4370)■14:19
(1904)■17:10(3854),13

THITHERWARD-J'G-18:15
(8033)-JER-50:5(2008)■N.T.-RO-
15:24(1563)

THONGS-AC-22:25(2438)

THORN-JOB-41:2(2336)-PR-26:9
(2336)-IS-55:13(5285)-EZE-28:24
(6975)-HO-10:8(6975)-MIC-7:4(4534)■
N.T.-2CO-12:7(4647)

THORNS-all=6975&marked-GE-
3:18-EX-22:6-NU-33:55(6796)-JOS-
23:13(6796)-J'G-8:7,16-2SA-23:6-2CH-
33:11(2336)-JOB-5:5(6791)-PS-58:9
(329)■118:12-PR-15:19(2312)■22:5
(6791)■24:31(7063)-EC-7:6(5518)
-SONG-2:2(2336)-IS-5:6(7898)■7:19
(5285),23(7898),24(7898),25(7898)■9:18
(7898)■10:17(7898)■27:4(7898)■32:13■
33:12■34:13(5518)-JER-4:3■12:13
-EZE-2:6(5544)-HO-2:6(5518)■9:6
(2336)-NA-1:10(5518)■N.T.-all=173&
marked-M'T-7:16■13:7^2,22■27:29
-M'R-4:7^2,18■15:17(174)-LU-6:44■8:7^2,
14-JOH-19:2,5(174)-HEB-6:8

THOROUGHLY-EX-21:19(7495)
-2KI-11:18(3190)

THOSE-all=428,a=1992&marked
-GE-6:4a■15:17■19:25(411)■33:5■41:35
-EX-2:11a-LE-11:27a-NU-9:7a■14:22
(582),37(582)-DE-7:22(411)■17:9a■
18:9a■19:5,17a■26:3a■29:3a-JOS-4:20■
10:22,23,24■11:10,12,18■17:12■20:4,6a■
21:16■24:17-J'G-2:23■17:6a■18:1^{2}a■
19:1a■20:27a,28a■21:25a-1SA-3:1a■
7:16■10:9■11:6■17:11,28(2007)■18:23■
19:7■25:9,12■27:8(2007)■28:1a,3a■
30:20(1931)-2SA-16:23a-1KI-3:2a■
4:27■21:27-2KI-4:4■10:32a■15:37a■
18:4a■20:1a-2CH-14:6■15:5a■32:14,
24a-EZR-5:9(479),14(1994)-NE-6:17a■
13:15a,23a-ES-1:2a■2:21a-EC-5:14
(1931)■7:28-IS-38:1a■64:5sup,5a■66:2^2,
19a-JER-3:16a,18a■4:12■5:18a■14:15a■
31:29a,33a,36■33:15a,16a■38:22(2007)■
49:36■50:4a,20a-EZE-18:11■33:24■
38:17a■40:25-DA-3:22(479)■4:37(1768)■

6:24(479)■10:2a■11:4,14a-**JOE**-2:29a■3:1a-**ZEC**-4:10■7:5(2088)■8:23a■14:3a■N.T.-all=3588,a=1565&marked-**M’T**-3:1a■4:24■15:18■16:23■21:40a,41(846)■22:7a,10a■24:19a,22^{2}a,29a■25:7a,19a■27:54-**M’R**-1:9a■2:20a■6:55■7:15a■8:1a■10:13■12:7a■13:17a,19a,20,24-**LU**-1:1,24(5025),39(5025),45■2:1a,33■4:2a■5:35a■6:12(5025),32■8:12■9:36a■12:37a,38a■13:4a■14:7,24a■17:10■19:27a■20:1a■21:23a,26-**JOH**-2:14■6:14■8:10a,26(5023),29,31■10:32(846)■17:11(846),12(846)-**AC**-1:15(5025)■2:18a■3:24■6:1(5025)■7:41a■8:6■9:37a■13:45■16:3a,35a■17:11,11(5023)■18:17(5130)■20:2a■21:5,15(5025)■27:11■28:31-**RO**-1:28■4:17■6:21sup,21a■10:5(846)■15:17-**1CO**-8:4,10■12:22-**2CO**-7:6■11:28-**EPH**-5:12-**PH’P**-3:7(5023),13^{2}■4:3(846),9(5023)-**COL**-3:1-**1TI**-5:8-**2TI**-2:25-**HEB**-3:5■5:14■6:4■7:21,27■8:10a■10:1(3588,846),3(846),16a■12:27^{2}■13:11(5130)-**JAS**-2:16-**2PE**-2:6,18-**1JO**-3:22-**2JO**-8-**JUDE**-10(3745),10(5125)-**RE**-1:3■2:10,13■4:9■9:4,6a■13:14■20:12

THOUGH-all=3588,a=518&marked-**DE**-29:19-**JOS**-17:18^{2}-**J’G**-13:16a■15:3,7a-**1SA**-14:39(3588)a■21:5-**2SA**-18:12(3863)-**NE**-1:9a■6:1(1571)-**JOB**-9:15a■14:8a■16:6a■20:12a■27:8,16a■30:24a-**PS**-23:4■27:3^{2}a■37:24■44:19■49:18■68:13a■138:6,7a-**PR**-6:35■27:22a-**EC**-8:17(834),17a-**IS**-1:18^{2}a■10:22a■12:1■63:16-**JER**-2:22a■4:30^{3}■5:2a■12:6■14:7a■15:1a■22:24a■30:11■32:5■37:10a■46:23■49:16■51:5,53^{2}-**LA**-3:32a-**EZE**-2:6^{2}■12:3(3518)■32:25,26,27-**DA**-5:22(3606,6903,1768)■9:9-**HO**-4:15a■8:10■9:12(3588)a,16■13:15-**AM**-5:22(3588)a■9:2^{2}a,3^{2}a,4-**OB**-4^{3}a-**NA**-1:12a-**HAB**-1:5■2:3a-**ZEC**-9:2■10:6(834)■N.T.-all=1437,a=1499&marked-**M’T**-26:33a,35(2579)-**LU**-11:8a■16:31■18:4a,7(2532)-**JOH**-4:2(2544)■8:14(2579)■10:38(2579)■11:25(2579)-**AC**-13:41■17:27(2544)-**RO**-4:11(1223)■9:6(3754),27-**1CO**-4:15■8:5(1512)■9:16■13:1,2^{2},3^{2}-**2CO**-4:16a■5:16a■7:8^{3}a,12a■10:8■11:6a,21(3754)■12:6,11a,15a■13:4(1487)-**GA**-1:8■3:15(3676)-**PH’P**-3:4(2539),12(3754)-**COL**-2:5a-**HEB**-5:8(2539)■6:9a■7:5(2539)■12:17(2539)-**JAS**-2:14-**2PE**-1:12(2539)

THOUGHT-all=2803&marked-**GE**-20:11(559)■38:15■48:11(6419)■50:20-**EX**-32:14(1696)-**NU**-24:11(559)■33:56(1819)-**DE**-15:9(1697)■19:19(2161)-**J’G**-15:2(559)■20:5(1819)-**RU**-4:4(559)-**1SA**-1:13■9:5(1672)■18:25■20:26(559)-**2SA**-13:2(5869)■14:13■19:18(5869)■21:16(559)-**2KI**-5:11(559)-**2CH**-32:1(559)-**NE**-6:2-**ES**-3:6(5869)■6:6(559)-**JOB**-12:5(6248)■42:2(4209)-**PS**-48:9(1819)■73:16■119:59■139:2(7454)-**PR**-24:9(2154)■30:32(2161)-**EC**-10:20(4093)-**IS**-14:24(1819)-**JER**-18:8-**EZE**-38:10(4284)-**DA**-4:2(8232,6925)■6:3(6246)-**AM**-4:13(7807)-**ZEC**-1:6(2161)■8:14(2161),15(2161)-**MAL**-3:16■N.T.-all=3309&marked-**M’T**-1:20(1760)■6:25,27,28,31,34^{2}■10:19-**M’R**-13:11(4305)■14:72(1911)-**LU**-9:47(1261)■12:11,17(1260),22,25,26■19:11(1380)-**JOH**-11:13(1380)■13:29(1380)-**AC**-8:20(3543),22(1963)■10:19(1760)■12:9(1380)■26:8(2919),9(1380)-**1CO**-13:11(3049)-**2CO**-9:5(2233)■10:5(3540)-**PH’P**-2:6(2233)-**1TH**-3:1(2106)

THOUGHTEST-**PS**-50:21(1819)

THOUGHTS-all=4284&marked-**GE**-6:5-**J’G**-5:15(2711)-**1CH**-28:9■29:18-**JOB**-4:13(5587)■17:11(4180)■20:2(5587)■21:27-**PS**-10:4(4209)■33:11■40:5■56:5■92:5■94:11,19(8312)■119:113(5588)■139:17(7454),23(8312)■146:4(6250)-**PR**-12:5■15:26■16:3■21:5-**IS**-55:7,8,9■59:7■65:2■66:18-**JER**-4:14■6:19■23:20(4209)■29:11^{2}-**DA**-2:29(7476),30(7476)■4:5(2031),19(7476)■5:6(7476),10(7476)-**MIC**-4:12■N.T.-all=1261&marked-**M’T**-9:4(1761)■12:25(1761)■15:19-**M’R**-7:21-**LU**-2:35■5:22■6:8■11:17(1270)■24:38-**RO**-2:15(3053)-**1CO**-3:20-**HEB**-4:12(1761)-**JAS**-2:4

THOUSAND-all=505&marked-**GE**-20:16-**EX**-12:37■32:28■38:25,26,28,29-**LE**-26:8(7233)-**NU**-1:21,23,25,27,29,31,33,35,37,39,41,43,46^{2}■2:4,6,8,9^{2},11,13,15,16^{2},19,21,23,24,26,28,30,31^{2},32^{2}■3:22,28,34,39,43,50■4:36,40,44,48■7:85■11:21■16:49■25:9■26:7,14,18,22,25,27,34,37,41,43,47,50,51^{2},62■31:4,5^{2},6,32^{2},33,34,35,36^{2},38,39,40,43^{2},44,45,46,52■35:4,5^{4}-**DE**-1:11■7:9■32:30^{2}-**JOS**-3:4■4:13■7:3,4■8:3,12,25■23:10-**J’G**-1:4■3:29■4:6,10,14■5:8■7:3^{2}■8:10^{2},26■9:49■12:6■15:11,15,16■16:27■20:2,10^{2},10(7233),15,17,21,25,34,35,44,45^{2},46■21:10-**1SA**-4:2,10■6:19■11:8^{2}■13:2^{3},5^{2}■15:4^{2}■17:5,18■18:13■24:2■25:2■26:2-**2SA**-6:1■8:4^{2},5,13■10:6^{3},18■17:1■18:3,7,12■19:17■24:9^{2},15-**1KI**-3:4■4:26^{2},32^{2}■5:11,13,14,15^{2},16■7:26■8:63^{2}■10:26^{2}■12:21■19:18■20:15,29,30-**2KI**-3:4^{2}■5:5■13:7■14:7■15:19■18:23■19:35■24:14,16^{2}-**1CH**-5:18,21^{4}■7:2,4,5,7,9,11,40■9:13■12:14,24,25,26,27,29,30,31,33,34^{2},35,36,37■16:15■18:4^{3},5,12■19:6,7,18^{2}■21:5^{3},14■22:14^{2}■23:3,4^{2},5^{2}■26:30,32■27:1,2,4,5,7,8,9,10,11,12,13,14,15■29:4^{2},7,7(7239),7,7(7239,505)7,21^{2}-**2CH**-1:6,14^{2}■2:2^{3},10^{4},17^{2},18^{3}■4:5■7:5^{2}■9:25^{2}■11:1■12:3■13:3^{2},17■14:8^{2},9■15:11■17:11^{2},14,15,16,17,18■25:5,6,11,12,13■26:12,13^{2}■27:5^{2}■28:6,8■29:33■30:24^{2}■35:7^{2},8,9-**EZR**-1:9,10,11■2:3,6,7,12,14,31,35,37,38,39,64,65,67,69^{2}■8:27-**NE**-3:13■7:8,11,12,17,19,34,38,40,41,42,66,67,69,70,71(7239),71,72,72(7239)-**ES**-3:9■9:16-**JOB**-1:3^{2}■9:3■33:23■42:12^{4}-**PS**-50:10■60:t■68:17(7239)■84:10■90:4■91:7,7(7233)■105:8-**EC**-6:6■7:28-**SONG**-4:4■5:10(7233)■8:11,12-**IS**-7:23■30:17■36:8■37:36■60:22-**JER**-52:28,30-**EZE**-45:1^{2},3^{2},5^{2},6^{2}■47:3,4^{2},5■48:8,9^{2},10^{4},13^{4},15^{2},16^{4},18^{2},20,21^{2},30,32,33,34,35-**DA**-5:1^{2}(506)■7:10(506),10(7240)■8:14■12:11,12-**AM**-5:3-**JON**-4:11(7239)■N.T.-all=5505,a=5507&marked-**M’T**-14:21(4000)■15:38(5070)■16:9(4000),10(5070)■18:24(3463)-**M’R**-5:13(1367)■6:44(4000)■8:9(5070),19(4000),20(5070)-**LU**-9:14(4000)■14:31^{2}-**JOH**-6:10(4000)-**AC**-2:41(5153)■4:4■19:19(3461)■21:38(5070)-**RO**-11:4(2035)-**1CO**-4:15(3463)■10:8■14:19(3463)-**2PE**-3:8^{2}a-**RE**-5:11(3461)■7:4,5^{3},6^{3},7^{3},8^{3}■9:16(3461)■11:3a,13■12:6a■14:1,3,20a■20:2a,3a,4a,5a,6a,7a■21:16

THOUSANDS-all=505&marked-**GE**-24:60-**EX**-18:21,25■20:6■34:7-**NU**-1:16■10:4,36■31:5,14,48^{2},52,54-**DE**-1:15■5:10■33:2(7233),17(7233),17-**JOS**-22:14,21,30-**1SA**-8:12■10:10■18:7^{2},8(7233),8■21:11,11(7233)■22:7■23:23■29:2,5,5(7233)-**2SA**-18:1,4-**1CH**-12:20■13:1■15:25■26:26■27:1■28:1■29:6-**2CH**-1:2■17:14■25:5-**PS**-3:6(7233)■68:17■119:72■144:13(503),13(7232)-**JER**-32:18-**DA**-7:10(506)■11:12(7239)-**MIC**-5:2■6:7,7(7233)■N.T.-**AC**-21:20(3461)-**JUDE**-14(3461)-**RE**-5:11(5505)

THREAD-all=2339&marked-**GE**-14:23-**JOS**-2:18-**J’G**-16:9(6616),12-**SONG**-4:3

THREATEN-**AC**-4:17(546)

THREATENED-**AC**-4:21(4324)-**1PE**-2:23(546)

THREATENING-**EPH**-6:9(547)

THREATENINGS-**AC**-4:29(547)■9:1(547)

THREE-all=7969,a=8532&marked-**GE**-5:22,23■6:10,15■7:13■9:19,28■11:13,15■14:14■15:9^{3}(8027)■18:2,6■29:2,34■30:36■38:24■40:10,12,13,16,18,19■42:17■45:22■46:15-**EX**-2:2■3:18■5:3■6:18■7:7■8:27■10:22,23■15:22■21:11■23:14,17■25:32^{2},33^{2}■27:1,14,15■32:28■37:18^{2},19^{2}■38:1,14,15,26-**LE**-12:4■14:10■19:23■25:21■27:6-**NU**-1:23,43,46■2:13,30,32■3:50■4:44■10:33^{2}■12:4^{2}■15:9■22:28,32,33■24:10■26:7,25,47,62■28:12,20,28■29:3,9,14■31:36,43■33:8,39■35:14^{2}-**DE**-4:41■14:28■16:16■17:6■19:2,3(8027),7,9,15-**JOS**-1:11■2:16,22■3:2■7:3,4■9:16■15:14■17:11■18:4■21:32-**J’G**-1:20■7:6,7,8,16,20,22■8:4■9:22,43■10:2■11:26■14:14■15:4,11■16:15,27■19:4-**1SA**-1:24■2:13,21■9:20■10:3^{3}■11:8,11■13:2,17■17:13^{2},14■20:19(8027),20,41■21:5(8032)■24:2■25:2■26:2■30:12,13■31:6,8-**2SA**-2:18,31■5:5■6:11■13:38■14:27■18:14■20:4■21:1,16■23:9,13(7991),16,17,18(7992),18^{2},19^{2},22,23■24:12,13^{2}-**1KI**-2:11,39■4:32■5:16■6:36■7:4^{2},5,12,25^{4},27■9:25■10:17^{2},22■11:3■12:5■15:2■17:21■22:1-**2KI**-2:17■3:10,13■9:32■12:6■13:1,25■17:5■18:10,14■23:31^{2}■24:1,8■25:17,18-**1CH**-2:3,16,22■3:4,23■7:6■10:6■11:11,12,15,18,19,20^{3},21^{2},24,25■12:27,29,39■13:14■21:10,12^{3}■23:8,9,23■24:18■25:5,30■29:4,27-**2CH**-2:2,17,18■4:4^{4},5■6:13■7:10■8:13■9:16^{2},21■10:5■11:17^{2}■13:2■14:8,9■17:14■20:25■25:5,13■26:13■29:33■31:16■35:7,8■36:2^{2},9-**EZR**-2:4,11,17,19,21,25,28,32,34,35,36,58,64,65■6:4a■8:5,15,32■10:8,9-**NE**-2:11■7:9,17,22,23,29,32,35,36,38,39,60,66,67-**ES**-4:16■8:9■9:15-**JOB**-1:2,3,4,17■2:11■32:1,3,5■42:13-**PR**-30:15,18,21,29-**IS**-15:5(7992)■16:14■17:6■20:3-**JER**-25:3■36:23■48:34(7992)■52:24,28,30-**EZE**-4:5,9■14:14,16,18■40:10^{2},21,48^{2}■41:6,16,22■42:3(7992),6(8027)■48:31,32,33,34-**DA**-1:5■3:23a,24a■6:2a,10a,13a■7:5a,8a,20a,24a■8:14■10:2,3■11:2■12:12-**AM**-1:3,6,9,11,13■2:1,4,6■4:4,7,8-**JON**-1:17■3:3-**ZEC**-11:8■N.T.-all=5140&marked-**M’T**-12:40^{2}■13:33■15:32■17:4■18:16,20■26:61■27:40,63-**M’R**-8:2,31■9:5■14:5(5145),58■15:29-**LU**-1:56■2:46■4:25■9:33■10:36■11:5■12:52■13:7,21-**JOH**-2:6,19,20■12:5(5145)■21:11-**AC**-2:41(5153)■5:7■7:20■9:9■10:19■11:10(5151),11■17:2■19:8■20:3,31(5148)■25:1■28:7,11,12,15,17-**1CO**-10:8■13:13■14:27,29-**2CO**-13:1-**GA**-1:18-**1TI**-5:19-**HEB**-10:28■11:23(5150)-**JAS**-5:17-**1JO**-5:7^{2},8^{2}-**RE**-6:6■8:13■9:18■11:9,11■16:13,19■21:13^{4}

THREEFOLD-**EC**-4:12(8027)

THREESCORE-all=8346,a=7657&marked-**GE**-25:7a,26■46:26,27a■50:3a-**EX**-15:27a■38:25a-**LE**-12:5-**NU**-1:27a,39■2:4a,26■3:43a,46a,50■26:22a,25,27,43■31:33a,34,37a,38a,39■33:9a-**DE**-3:4■10:22a-**JOS**-13:30-**J’G**-1:7a,8:14a,30a■9:2a,4a,5a,18a,24a■12:14a-**1SA**-6:19a-**2SA**-2:31-**1KI**-4:13,22■5:15a■6:2■10:14-**2KI**-25:19-**1CH**-2:21,23■5:18■9:13■16:38■21:5a■26:8-**2CH**-2:2a,18a■3:3■9:13■11:21^{2}■12:3■29:32a■36:21a-**EZR**-2:9,64,69(7239)■6:3^{2}(8361)■8:10,13-**NE**-7:14,18,19,66,72■11:6-**PS**-90:10a-**SONG**-3:7a■6:8a-**IS**-7:8a-**JER**-52:25a-**EZE**-40:14a-**DA**-3:1(8361)■5:31(8361)■9:25,26-**ZEC**-1:12a■N.T.-all=1835&marked-**LU**-24:13-**AC**-7:14(1440)■23:23(1440)■27:37(1440)-**1TI**-5:9-**RE**-11:3■12:6■13:18(5516)

THRESH-all=1758&marked-**IS**-41:15-**JER**-51:33(1869)-**MIC**-4:13-**HAB**-3:12

THRESHED-**J’G**-6:11(2251)-**IS**-28:27(1758)-**AM**-1:3(1758)

THRESHETH-**1CO**-9:10(248)

THRESHING-all=1758&marked-**LE**-26:5(1786)-**2SA**-24:22(4173)-**2KI**-13:7-**1CH**-21:20,23(4173)-**IS**-21:10(4098)■28:27(2742),28■41:15(4173)-**AM**-1:3(2742)

THRESHINGFLOOR-all=1637-**GE**-50:10-**NU**-15:20■18:27,30-**RU**-

3:2-2SA-6:6▪24:18,21,24-1CH-13:9▪21:15,18,21,22,28-2CH-3:1-JER-51:33
THRESHINGFLOORS-1SA-23:1(1637)-DA-2:35(147)
THRESHINGPLACE-2SA-24:16(1637)
THRESHOLD-all=4670&marked-J'G-19:27(5592)-1SA-5:4,5-1KI-14:17(5592)-EZE-9:3▪10:4,18▪40:6²(5592),7(5592)▪43:8(5592)▪46:2▪47:1-ZEP-1:9
THRESHOLDS-NE-12:25(624)-EZE-43:8(5592)-ZEP-2:14(5592)
THREW-2SA-16:13(5619)-2KI-9:33(8058)-2CH-31:1(5422)▪N.T.-M'R-12:42(906)-LU-9:42(4952)-AC-22:23(906)
THREWEST-NE-9:11(7993)
THRICE-all=7969,6471-EX-34:23,24-2KI-13:18,19▪N.T.-all=5151-M'T-26:34,75-M'R-14:30,72-LU-22:34,61-JOH-13:38-AC-10:16-2CO-11:25²▪12:8
THROAT-all=1627&marked-PS-5:9▪69:3▪115:7-PR-23:2(3930)-JER-2:25▪N.T.-M'T-18:28(4155)-RO-3:13(2995)
THRONE-all=3678&marked-GE-41:40-EX-11:5▪12:29-DE-17:18-1SA-2:8-2SA-3:10▪7:13,16▪14:9-1KI-1:13,17,20,24,27,30,35,37²,46,47,48▪2:4,12,19,24,33,45▪3:6▪5:5▪7:7▪8:20,25▪9:5²▪10:9,18,19²▪16:11▪22:10,19-2KI-10:3,30▪11:19▪13:13▪15:12▪25:28-1CH-17:12,14▪22:10▪28:5▪29:23-2CH-6:10,16▪7:18▪9:8,17,18²▪18:9,18▪23:20-NE-3:7-ES-1:2▪5:1-JOB-26:9▪36:7-PS-9:4,7▪11:4▪45:6▪47:8▪89:4,14,29,36,44▪93:2▪94:20▪97:2▪103:19▪132:11,12-PR-16:12▪20:8,28▪25:5▪29:14-IS-6:1▪9:7▪14:13▪16:5▪22:23▪47:1▪66:1-JER-1:15▪3:17▪13:13▪14:21▪17:12,25▪22:2,4,30▪29:16▪33:17,21▪36:30▪43:10▪49:38▪52:32-LA-5:19-EZE-1:26²▪10:1▪43:7-DA-5:20(3764)▪7:9(3764)-JON-3:6-HAG-2:22-ZEC-6:13²▪N.T.-all=2362&marked-M'T-5:34▪19:28▪23:22▪25:31-LU-1:32-AC-2:30▪7:49▪12:21(968)-HEB-1:8▪4:16▪8:1▪12:2-RE-1:4▪3:21²▪4:2²,3,4,5²,6³,9,10²▪5:1,6,7,11,13▪6:16▪7:9,10,11²,15²,17▪8:3▪12:5▪14:3,5▪16:17▪19:4,5▪20:11▪21:5▪22:1,3
THRONES-all=3678&marked-PS-122:5²-IS-14:9-EZE-26:16-DA-7:9(3764)▪N.T.-all=2362-M'T-19:28-LU-22:30-COL-1:16-RE-20:4
THRONG-M'R-3:9(2346)-LU-8:45(4912)
THRONGED-M'R-5:24(4918)-LU-8:42(4846)
THRONGING-M'R-5:31(4918)
THROUGH-all=5674&marked-GE-6:13(6440)-EX-14:16(8432)▪36:33(8432)-NU-20:19,20▪25:8sup,8(413)▪33:8(8432)-DE-29:16(7130)-JOS-1:11(7130)▪2:15(1157)▪3:2(7130)▪24:17(7130)-J'G-5:28(1157)-1SA-19:12(1157)-2SA-4:7(1870)▪6:16(1157)▪23:16(1234)▪24:2(7751)-2KI-1:2(1157)▪3:26(1234)▪24:20(5921)-1CH-11:18(1234)-2CH-23:20(8432)▪32:4(8432)-NE-9:11(8432)-JOB-24:16(2864)▪29:7(5921)-PS-81:5(5921)▪136:14(8432)-EC-10:18(1811)-SONG-2:9(4480)-IS-13:15(1856)▪14:19(2944)▪28:7³sup,7(4480)▪43:2²sup,2(1119)▪60:15▪62:10-JER-51:4(1856)▪52:3(5921)-EZE-9:4▪41:19(413)▪47:3,4²-DA-8:25(5921)-AM-5:17(7130)-MIC-5:8-ZEC-4:12(3027)▪N.T.-all=1223,a=1722&marked-M'T-6:19(1358),20(1358)▪9:34a▪12:1,43▪19:24-M'R-2:23▪6:55(4063)▪7:31(303)▪9:30▪10:25▪11:16-LU-1:78▪2:35(1330)▪4:14(2596),30▪5:19▪6:1▪9:6(2596)▪10:17a▪11:15a,18a,24▪12:39(1358)▪13:22(2596)▪17:1,11▪18:25▪19:1(1330)-JOH-1:7▪3:17▪4:4▪8:59▪15:3▪17:11a,17a,19a,20▪20:31a-AC-1:2▪3:16(1909),17(2596)▪4:2a▪8:18,40▪10:43▪13:6(1330),38▪14:22▪15:3(1330),11,41(1350)▪16:4(1279)▪17:1(1653)▪18:27▪19:1(1330),21(1330)▪20:3▪21:4-RO-1:8,24a▪2:23,24▪3:7a,24,25,25a,30,31▪4:13²▪5:1,9,11,21▪6:11a,23a▪7:25▪8:3,37▪11:36▪12:3▪15:4,13a,17a,19a▪16:27-1CO-1:1▪4:15▪8:11(1909)▪10:1▪13:12▪15:57▪16:5²(1330)-2CO-3:4▪4:15▪9:11▪11:3a,33▪13:4(1537)-GA-2:19▪3:8(1537),14a,14▪4:7,13▪5:10a-EPH-1:7▪2:7a,8,18,22a▪4:6,18-PH'P-1:19▪2:3(2596)▪3:9▪4:7a,13a-CO-1:14,20,22▪2:8,12-2TH-2:13a,16a-1TI-6:10(4044)-2TI-1:10▪3:15-TIT-1:3a▪3:6-PH'M-22-HEB-2:10,14▪6:12▪9:14▪10:10,20▪11:29(1224),33,39▪12:20(2700)▪13:20a,21-1PE-1:2a,5,6a,22▪4:11-2PE-1:1a,2a,3,4a▪2:3a,18a,18sup,20a-1JO-4:9-RE-8:13a▪18:3(1537)
THROUGHLY-PS-51:2(7235)▪N.T.-M'T-3:12(1245)-LU-3:17(1245)-2CO-11:6(1722,3956)-2TI-3:17(1822)
THROUGHOUT-all=5921-1CH-5:10(5921)-2CH-20:3(5921)▪N.T.-all=2596&marked-M'T-4:24(1519)-M'R-1:28(1519),39(1519)▪14:9(1519)-LU-1:65(1722)▪4:25(1909)▪7:17²(1722)▪8:1,39▪23:5-JOH-19:23(1223,3650)-AC-8:1▪9:31,32(1223),42▪10:37▪11:28(1909)▪13:49(1223)▪14:24(1330)▪16:6▪24:5▪26:20(1519)-RO-1:8(1722)▪9:17(1722)-2CO-8:18(1223)-EPH-3:21(1519)
THROW-all=2040&marked-J'G-2:2(5422)▪6:25-2SA-20:15(5307)-2KI-9:33(8058)-JER-1:10▪31:28-EZE-16:39-MIC-5:11-MAL-1:4
THROWING-NU-35:17(3027)
THROWN-all=2040&marked-EX-15:1(7411),21(7411)-J'G-6:32(5422)-2SA-20:21(7993)-1KI-19:10,14-JER-31:40▪33:4(5422)▪50:15-LE-2:2,17-EZE-38:20-NA-1:6(5422)▪N.T.-all=2647&marked-M'T-24:2-M'R-13:2-LU-4:35(4496)▪21:6-RE-18:21(906)
THRUST-all=1856&marked-EX-11:1(1644)▪12:39(1644)-NU-22:25(3905)▪25:8▪35:20(1920),22(1920)-DE-13:5(5080),10(5080)▪15:17(5414)▪33:27(1644)-J'G-3:21(8628)▪6:38(2115)▪9:41(1644),54▪11:2(1644)-1SA-11:2(5365)▪31:4²-2SA-18:14(8628)▪23:6(5074)-1KI-2:27(1644)-2KI-4:27(1920)-1CH-10:4-2CH-26:20(926)-PS-118:13(1760)-IS-13:15▪14:19(2944)-JER-51:4-EZE-16:40(1333)▪34:21(1920)▪46:18(3238)-JOE-2:8(1766)-ZEC-13:3▪N.T.-all=906&marked-LU-4:29(1544)▪5:3(1877)▪10:15(2601)▪13:28(1544)-JOH-20:25,27-AC-7:27(683),39(683)▪16:24,37(1544)▪27:39(1856)-HEB-12:20(2700)-RE-14:15(3992),16,18(3992),19
THRUSTETH-JOB-32:13(5086)
THUMB-all=931-EX-29:20-LE-8:23▪14:14,17,25,28
THUMBS-LE-8:24(931)-J'G-1:6(931,3027),7(931,3027)
THUMMIM-all=8550-EX-28:30-LE-8:8-DE-33:8-EZR-2:63-NE-7:65
THUNDER-all=6963&marked-EX-9:23,29-1SA-2:10(7481)▪7:10▪12:17,18-JOB-26:14(7482)▪28:26▪38:25▪39:19(7483),25(7482)▪40:9(7481)-PS-77:18(7482)▪81:7(7482)▪104:7(7482)-IS-29:6(7482)▪N.T.-all=1027-M'R-3:17-RE-6:1▪14:2
THUNDERBOLTS-PS-78:48(7565)
THUNDERED-all=7481-1SA-7:10-2SA-22:14-PS-18:13▪N.T.-JOH-12:29(1027,1096)
THUNDERETH-all=7481-JOB-37:4,5-PS-29:3
THUNDERINGS-EX-9:28(6963)▪20:18(6963)▪N.T.-all=1027-RE-4:5▪8:5▪11:19▪19:6
THUNDERS-all=6963-EX-9:33,34▪19:16▪N.T.-all=1027-RE-10:3,4²▪16:18
THUS-all=3541,a=3651,b=3602,c=2063&marked-GE-24:30▪25:22(2088)▪31:8²,41(2088)▪32:4²▪42:25a▪45:9-EX-3:14▪4:22▪5:1,10,15▪7:17▪8:1,20▪9:1,13▪10:3▪11:4▪12:11b▪14:11c▪19:3▪20:22▪26:17a,24a▪32:27▪36:22a,29a-LE-16:3c-NU-8:7,26b▪10:28(428)▪11:15b▪15:11b▪18:28a▪20:14▪22:16▪23:5,16▪32:8-DE-7:5▪20:15a▪29:24(3662)▪32:6c-JOS-2:4a▪6:3▪7:10(2088),13,20c▪10:25b▪21:42a▪22:16▪24:2-J'G-6:8▪8:1(1697,2007)▪11:15▪13:18(2088)▪18:4(2090),4(2088)-1SA-2:27▪9:9▪10:18▪11:9▪14:9,10▪15:2▪18:25▪20:7,22▪25:6▪26:18(2088)-2SA-6:22c▪7:5,8▪11:25▪12:7,11,31a▪15:26▪16:7▪17:15²c,21b▪18:14a,33▪24:12-1KI-1:48b▪2:30²▪5:11▪9:8b▪11:31▪12:10²,24▪13:2,21▪14:5(2090),5(2088),7▪17:14▪20:2,5,13,14,28,42▪21:19²▪22:11,27-2KI-1:4,6,11,16▪2:21▪3:16,17▪4:43▪5:4c▪7:1▪9:3,6,12c,12,18,19▪10:28▪18:19,29,31▪19:3,6²,10,20,32▪20:1,5▪21:12▪22:15,16,18²-1CH-17:4,7²▪21:10,11-2CH-7:21b▪10:10²▪11:4▪12:5▪18:10,26▪19:9▪20:15▪21:12▪24:11,20▪31:20c▪32:10▪34:23,24,26▪36:23-EZR-1:2▪5:3(3652),7(1836),9(3660),11(3660)▪6:2(3652)-NE-5:13b▪13:18-ES-2:13(2088)▪6:9b,11b-JOB-1:5b▪27:12(2088)-PS-63:4a▪73:15(3644),21(3588)▪128:4a-IS-7:7▪8:11▪10:24▪21:6,16▪22:15▪24:13▪28:16▪29:22▪30:12,15▪31:4▪36:4,14,16▪37:3,6²,10,21,33▪38:1,5▪42:5▪43:1,14,16▪44:2,6,24▪45:1,11,14,18▪47:15a▪48:17▪49:7,8,22,25▪50:1▪51:22▪52:3,4▪56:1,4▪57:15▪65:8,13▪66:1,12-JER-2:2,5▪4:3,27▪5:13,14▪6:6,9,16,21,22▪7:3,20,21▪8:4▪9:7,15,17,22,23▪10:2,11(1836),18▪11:3,11,21,22▪12:14▪13:1,9,12,13▪14:10,10a,15▪15:19▪16:3,5,9▪17:5,19,21▪18:11,13▪19:1,3,11,12a,15▪20:4▪21:3,4,8,12▪22:1,3,6,8b,11,18,30▪23:2,15,16,35,37,38▪24:5,8▪25:8,15,27,28,32▪26:2,4,18▪27:2,4²,16,19,21▪28:2,11b,13,14,16▪29:4,8,10,16,17,21,25,31,32▪30:2,5,12,18▪31:2,7,15,16,23,35,37▪32:3,14,15,28,36,42▪33:2,4,10,12,17,20,25▪34:2²,4,13,17▪35:13,17,18,19▪36:29,30▪37:7²,9▪38:2,3,4(5921)a,17▪39:16▪42:9,15,18▪43:10▪44:2,7,11,25,30▪45:2,4²▪47:2▪48:1,40,47(2008)▪49:1,7,12,28,35▪50:18,33▪51:1,33,36,58,64b,64(2008)-EZE-2:4▪3:11,27▪4:13b▪5:5,7,8▪6:3,11▪7:2,5▪11:5,5a,7,16,17▪12:10,19,23,28▪13:3,8,13,18,20▪14:4,6,21▪15:6▪16:3,36,59▪17:3,9,19,22▪20:3,5,27,30,39,47▪21:3,9,24,26,28▪22:3,19,28▪23:22,28,32,35,39,46▪24:3,6,9,21▪25:3,6,8,12,13,15,16▪26:3,7,15,19▪27:3▪28:2,6,12,22,25▪29:3,8,13,19▪30:2,6,10,13,22▪31:10,18b▪32:3,11▪33:10a,25,27²▪34:2,10,11,17,20▪35:3,14▪36:2,3,4,5,6,7,13,22,33,37▪37:5,9,12,19,21▪38:3,10,14,17▪39:1,17,25▪43:18▪44:6,9▪45:9,18▪46:1,16▪47:13-DA-2:24(3652),25(3652)▪4:14(3652)▪6:6(3652)▪7:5(3652),23(3652)-AM-1:3,6,9,11,13▪2:1,4,6,11c▪3:11,12▪4:12▪5:3,4,16▪7:1,4,7,11,17▪8:1-OB-1-MIC-2:3▪3:5-NA-1:12,12a-HAG-1:2,5,7▪2:6,11-ZEC-1:3,4,14,16,17▪2:8▪3:7▪6:12▪7:9▪8:2,3,4,6,7,9,14,19,20,23▪11:4-MAL-1:4,13▪N.T.-all=5023,a=3779&marked-M'T-2:5a▪3:15a▪15:6(2532)▪26:54a-M'R-2:7a-LU-1:25a▪2:48a▪9:34▪11:45▪17:30(2596,5023)▪18:11▪19:28,31a▪22:51(5127)▪23:46▪24:36,40(5124),46²a-JOH-4:6a▪9:6▪11:43,48a▪13:21▪18:22▪20:14-AC-19:41▪20:36▪21:11(3592)▪26:24,30▪27:35-RO-9:20a-1CO-14:25a-2CO-1:17(5124)▪5:14(5124)-PH'P-3:15(5124)-HEB-6:9a▪9:6a-RE-9:17a▪16:5▪18:21a
THYINE-RE-18:12(2367)
THYSELF-all=859&marked-EX-18:14-1SA-20:8-2SA-18:13,13sup-ES-4:13(5315)-JOB-15:8(413)-EC-7:22▪N.T.-all=4572&marked-M'T-4:6▪8:4▪19:19▪22:39▪27:40-M'R-1:44▪12:31▪

15:30-LU-4:9,23■5:14■6:42(846)■10:27■23:37,39-JOH-1:22■7:4■8:13,53■10:33■14:22■18:34(1438)■21:18-AC-16:28■21:24sup,24(846)■24:8(846)■26:1-RO-2:1,5,19,21■13:9(1438)■14:22-GA-5:14(1438)■6:1-1TI-4:7,16^{2}■5:22-2TI-2:15-TIT-2:7-JAS-2:8

TIDINGS-all=1319&marked-GE-29:13(8088)-EX-33:4(1697)-1SA-4:19(8052)■11:4(1697),5(1697),6(1697)-2SA-4:4(8052),10,10(1309)■13:30(8052)■18:19,20(1309),20^{2},22(1309),25(1309),26,27(1309),31-1KI-1:42■2:28(8052)-2KI-7:9(1309)-1CH-10:9-PS-112:7(8052)-IS-40:9^{2}■41:27■52:7^{2}■61:1-JER-20:15■37:5(8088)■49:23(8052)-EZE-21:7(8052)-DA-11:44(8052)-NA-1:15■N.T.-all=2097&marked-LU-1:19■2:10■8:1-AC-11:22(3056)■13:32■21:31(5334)-RO-10:15-1TH-3:6

TIE-1SA-6:7(631)-PR-6:21(6029)

TIED-all=631&marked-EX-39:31(5414)-1SA-6:10-2KI-7:10■N.T.-all=1210-M'T-21:2-M'R-11:2,4-LU-19:30

TILE-EZE-4:1(3843)

TILING-LU-5:19(2766)

TILL-all=5704&marked-GE-2:5(5647)■3:19,23(5647)■19:22■38:11,17-EX-15:16^{2}■16:19,24■40:37-NU-12:15-DE-28:45-JOS-5:6,8■8:6■10:20-J'G-3:25■6:4■11:33■16:3■19:26■21:2-RU-1:13-1SA-10:8■16:11■22:3-2SA-3:35(6440)■9:10(5647)-1KI-14:10■18:28-2KI-2:17■4:20■7:9■10:17■13:17,19■21:16-2CH-26:15(5704,3588)■29:34■36:16-EZR-2:63■5:5(5705)■9:14-NE-2:7■4:11,21■7:65■13:19-JOB-7:19■8:21■14:6,12,14■27:5-PS-18:37-PR-7:23-EC-2:3-SONG-2:7■3:5-IS-5:8■22:14■38:13■42:4■62:7^{2}-JER-9:16■23:20■24:10■27:11(5647)■49:37■52:3,11-LA-3:50-EZE-4:8,14■24:13■28:15■34:21■39:15■47:20-DA-2:9,34■4:23,25,33■5:21■6:14■7:4,9,11■10:3■11:36■12:9-HO-5:15■10:12-JON-4:5■N.T.-all=2193&marked-M'T-1:25■2:9■5:18^{2},26■10:11,23■12:20■13:33■16:28■18:21,30,34■22:44■23:39■24:34-M'R-6:10■9:1,9(1508,3752)■12:36■13:30(3360)-LU-1:80■9:27■12:50,59■13:8,21■15:8■17:8■19:13■20:43■21:32-JOH-13:38■21:22,23-AC-7:18(891,3757)■8:40■20:11(891)■21:5■23:12,21■25:21■28:23-1CO-11:26(891,3757)■15:25(891,3757)-GA-3:19(891,3757)-EPH-4:13(3360)-PH'P-1:10(1519)-1TI-4:13-HEB-10:13-RE-2:25(891)■7:3(891)■15:8(891)■20:3(891)

TILLAGE-1CH-27:26(5656)-NE-10:37(5656)-PR-13:23(5215)

TILLED-EZE-36:9(5647),34(5647)

TILLER-GE-4:2(5647)

TILLEST-GE-4:12(5647)

TILLETH-PR-12:11(5647)■28:19(5647)

TIMBER-all=6086&marked-EX-31:5-LE-14:45-1KI-5:6,8^{2},18■6:10■15:22-2KI-12:12■22:6-1CH-14:1■22:14,15-2CH-2:8,9,10,14■16:6■34:11-EZR-5:8(636)■6:4(636),11(636)-NE-2:8-EZE-26:12-HAB-2:11-ZEC-5:4

TIMBREL-all=8596-EX-15:20-JOB-21:12-PS-81:2■149:3■150:4

TIMBRELS-all=8596&marked-EX-15:20-J'G-11:34-2SA-6:5-1CH-13:8-PS-68:25(8608)

TIME-all=6256,a=3117,b=6471&marked-GE-4:3a■18:10,14sup,14■21:22■22:15■24:11^{2}■26:8a■29:7,34■30:33a■31:10■38:1,12a,27■39:11a■43:10b,18(8462),20(8462)■47:29a-EX-2:23a■8:32b■9:14b,18,27b■13:14(4279)■21:19(7674),29(8543,8032),36(8543,8032)■34:18(4150)-LE-15:25^{2}-NU-13:20a■20:15a■22:4■23:23■32:10a-DE-1:9,16■2:34■3:4,8,12,18,21,23■4:14■5:5■6:20(4279)■9:19b,20■10:1,8,10a,10b■19:4(8543,8032),6(8543,8032)■20:19a■32:35-JOS-3:15a■4:6(4279),21(4279)■5:2■6:16b,26■10:27,42b■11:6,10,18a,21■22:24(4279),27(4279),28(4279)■23:1a■24:2(5769)-J'G-3:29■4:4■10:14■11:4a,26■12:6■13:23■14:4,8a■15:1a■18:31a■20:15a■21:14,22,24-RU-4:7(6440)-1SA-1:4a,20a■3:2a■4:20■7:2a■9:13a,16,24(4150)■14:18a,21(8032)■18:19■20:12■27:7(4557)a-2SA-2:11(4557)a■5:2(865,8543)■7:6a,11a■11:1■14:2a■17:7b■23:8b■23:20a■24:15-1KI-1:6a■2:26a■8:65■11:29,42a■14:1■15:23■19:2■20:6-2KI-3:6a■4:16,17■5:26■7:1,18■8:22■10:6sup,6,36a■16:6■18:16■20:12■24:10-1CH-9:20(6440),25■11:2(8543),11b■12:22■17:10a■20:1,4(227)■21:28■29:27a-2CH-7:8■13:18■15:11a■16:7,10■18:34■21:10,19a■24:11■25:27■28:16,22■30:3,26a■35:17-EZR-4:15(3118),19(3118)■5:3(2166),16(116)■8:34■10:13-NE-2:6(2165)■4:16a,22■5:14a■6:1,5b■9:27,32a■12:44a■13:21-ES-4:14^{2}■8:9■9:27(2165)-JOB-6:17■7:1(6635)■14:14(6635)■15:32a■22:16■30:3(570)■38:23■39:1,2,18-PS-4:7■21:9■27:5a■32:6■37:19,39■41:1a■56:3a■69:13■71:9■81:15■102:13■105:19■115:18(6258)■119:126■129:1(7227),2(7227)-PR-25:13a,19a■31:25a-EC-3:1,2^{2},3^{2},4^{2},5^{3},6^{2},7^{2},8^{2},11,17■7:17■8:5,6,9■9:11,12^{2}-SONG-2:12-IS-11:11■13:22■16:13(227)■18:7■20:2■28:19(1767)■30:8a■33:2■39:1■42:23(268)■44:8(227)■45:21(227)■48:6(6258),8(227),16■49:8■60:22-JER-2:27,28■3:4(6258),17■4:11■6:15■8:1,7,12,15■10:15■11:12,14■14:8,19■15:11■18:23■27:7■30:7■31:1■33:15■39:10a■46:21■49:8■50:4,16,20,27,31■51:6,18,33^{2}-LA-5:20a-EZE-4:10,11■7:7,12■16:8,57■22:3■27:34■30:3■35:5^{2}■38:10a,17a,18a-DA-2:8(5732),9(5732),16(2166)■3:5(5732),7(2166),8(2166),15(5732)■4:36(2166)■7:12(5732),22(2166),25^{2}(5732)■8:17■9:21■11:24,35,35sup,40■12:1^{4},4,7(4150),9,11-HO-2:9■9:10(7225)■10:12-JOE-3:1-AM-5:13^{2}-MIC-2:3■3:4■5:3-NA-1:9b-ZEP-1:12■3:19,20^{2}-HAG-1:2^{2},4-ZEC-10:1■14:7■N.T.-all=2540,a=5550,b=5610,c=4218&marked-M'T-1:11(1909)■2:7a,16a■4:6(3379),17(5119)■5:21(744),25(3379),27(744),33(744)■8:29■11:25■12:1■13:15(3379),30■14:1,15b■16:21(5119)■18:1b■21:34■24:21■25:19a■26:16(5119),18-M'R-1:15■4:12(3379),17(4340)■6:35b■10:30■11:13■13:19(3568),33-LU-1:10b,57a■4:5a,11(3379),27(1909)■8:13,27a■9:51(2250)■12:56■14:17b■16:16(5119)■18:30■19:44■20:9a■21:8,34(3379),37(2250)■23:7(2250)-JOH-1:18(4455)■3:4(1208)■5:6a,37(4455)■7:6^{2},8■11:39(2235)■14:9a■16:2b,4b,25b-AC-1:6a,21a■7:17a,20■8:1(2250),11a■12:1■13:18a■14:3a,28a■15:21(1074)■17:21(2119)■18:20a,23a■19:23■20:16(5551)■24:25(3568)■27:9a-RO-3:26■5:6■8:18■9:9■11:5■13:11,11b-1CO-4:5■7:5,29■9:7c■16:12(3598),12(2119)-2CO-6:2^{2}■8:14-GA-1:13c■4:2(4287),4a-EPH-2:2c,11c,12■5:16-COL-3:7c■4:5-1TH-2:5c,17-2TH-2:6■1TI-2:6■6:19(3195)-2TI-4:3,6-PH'M-11c-HEB-1:1(3819),5c,13c■2:1c■4:7a,16(2121)■5:12a■9:9,10■11:32a-1PE-1:5,11,17a■2:10c■3:5c■4:2a,3a,17■5:6-2PE-1:21c■2:3(1597)-1JO-2:18^{2}b■4:12(4455)-JUDE-18a-RE-1:3■10:6a■11:18■12:12,14^{2}■14:15b■22:10

TIMES-all=6471,a=6256&marked-GE-27:36■31:7(4489),41(4489)■33:3■43:34(3027)-EX-23:17-LE-4:6,17■8:11■14:7,16,27,51■16:2a,14,19■25:8-NU-24:1-DE-1:11■4:42(8543)■16:16-JOS-6:4,15^{2}-J'G-16:15,20■20:30,31-1SA-3:10■18:10(3117)■19:7(865,8543)■20:25,41-2SA-3:17(8543)-1KI-8:59(3117)■9:25■17:21■18:43■22:16-2KI-4:35■5:10,14■13:19,25■19:25(3117)-1CH-21:3-2CH-8:13■18:15-EZR-10:14a-NE-4:12■6:4■9:28a■10:34a■13:31a-ES-1:13a■9:31(2165)-JOB-19:3■24:1a-PS-9:9a■10:1a■31:15a■34:1a■44:1(3117)■62:8a■106:3a,43■119:20a-PR-5:19a■17:17a-IS-14:31(4151)■33:6a■37:26(3117)-JER-8:7a-EZE-12:27a-DA-2:21(5732)■4:16(5732),23(5732),25(5732),32(5732)■6:10(2166),13(2166)■7:25(2166),25(5732)■9:25a■11:6a,14a■12:7(4150)■N.T.-all=5550&marked-M'T-16:3(2540)■18:21(2034),22(2034),22(1441)-LU-17:4^{2}(2034)■21:24(2540)-AC-1:7■3:19(2540),21■11:10(5151)■14:16(1074)■17:26(2540),30-RO-11:30(4218)-2CO-11:24(3999)-GA-1:23(4218)■4:10(2540)-EPH-1:10(2540)■2:3(4218)-1TH-5:1(2540)-1TI-4:1■6:15-2TI-3:1-TIT-1:3-1PE-1:20-RE-12:14(2540)

TIN-all=913-NU-31:22-IS-1:25-EZE-22:18,20■27:12

TINGLE-all=6750-1SA-3:11-2KI-21:12-JER-19:3

TINKLING-IS-3:16(5913)■N.T.-1CO-13:1(214)

TIP-all=8571-EX-29:20^{2}-LE-8:23,24■14:14,17,25,28■N.T.-LU-16:24(206)

TIRE-EZE-24:17(6287)

TIRED-2KI-9:30(3190)

TIRES-IS-3:18(7720)-EZE-24:23(6287)

TITHE-all=4643&marked-LE-27:30,32-NU-18:26-DE-12:17■14:22(6237),23,28-2CH-31:5,6^{2}-NE-10:38■13:12■N.T.-M'T-23:23(586)-LU-11:42(586)

TITHES-all=4643&marked-GE-14:20-LE-27:31-NU-18:24,26,28-DE-12:6,11■26:12-2CH-31:12-NE-10:37,37(6237),38(6237),38■12:44■13:5-AM-4:4-MAL-3:8,10■N.T.-LU-18:12(586)-HEB-7:5(586),6(1183),8(1181),9(1183)

TITHING-DE-26:12(6237),12(4643)

TITLE-2KI-23:17(6725)■N.T.-JOH-19:19(5102),20(5102)

TITLES-all supplied

TITTLE-M'T-5:18(2762)-LU-16:17(2762)

TOE-all=931-EX-29:20-LE-8:23■14:14,17,25,28

TOES-LE-8:24(931)-J'G-1:6(931,7272),7(931,7272)-2SA-21:20(676)-1CH-20:6(676)-DA-2:41(677),42(677)

TOGETHER-all=3162&marked-GE-13:6^{2}■22:6,8,19■36:7-EX-19:8■26:24sup,24■36:29-DE-22:10,11■25:5,11■33:5,17-JOS-9:2■11:5^{2}-J'G-6:33■19:6-1SA-11:11■17:2,10■23:8■31:6-2SA-2:13,16■10:15■12:3■14:16■21:9-1KI-3:18-2KI-9:25(6776)-1CH-10:6-EZR-2:64(259)■3:9(259)■4:3■6:20(259)-NE-4:8■6:2,7■7:66(259)-JOB-2:11■3:18■6:2■9:32■10:8■16:10■17:16■19:12■24:4■34:15■38:7■40:13-PS-2:2■14:3■31:13■34:3■35:26■37:38■40:14■41:7■47:9■48:4■49:2■55:14■71:10■74:8■83:5■88:17■98:8■102:22■122:3■133:1-IS-1:28,31■9:21■11:6,7,14■18:6■22:3^{2}■27:4■31:3■40:5■41:1,19,20,23■43:9,17,26■44:11sup,11■45:8,16,20,21■46:2■48:13■50:8■52:8,9■60:13■65:7,25(259)■66:17-JER-3:18■6:11,12,21■13:14■31:8,13,24■41:1■46:12,21■48:7■49:3■50:4,33■51:38-LA-2:8-DA-2:35(2298)-HO-1:11■11:8-AM-1:15■3:3-MIC-2:12-ZEC-10:4■N.T.-all=4863,a=4905&marked-M'T-1:18a■2:4■13:2,30(4886),30(4816)■18:20■19:6(4801)■22:10,34(1909,3588,864),41■23:37(1996)■24:28,31(1996)■26:3■27:17,62-M'R-1:33(1996)■2:2,15(4873)■3:20a■6:30,33a■7:1■9:25(1998)■10:9(4801)■12:28(4802)■13:27(1996)■15:16(4779)-LU-5:15a■8:4(4896)■9:1(4779)■11:29(1865)■12:1(1996)■13:11(4794),34(1996)■15:6(4779),9(4779),13■17:35(1909,3588,846),37■22:55(4776),66■23:12(3326,240),13(4779),48■24:14(4314,240),33(4867)-JOH-4:36(3674)■

6:13■11:52,53(4853)■20:4(3674),7(1794)■21:2(3674)-**AC**-1:4(4811),6a,15(1909,3588,846)■2:6a,44(1909,3588,846)■3:1(1909,3588,846),11(4936,1909,846)■4:6,26(1909,3588,846),27,31■5:9(4856),21(4779)■10:24(4779),27a■12:12(4867)■13:44■14:1(2596,3588,846),27■15:6,30■16:22(4911)■19:19(4851),25(4867),32(4897)■20:7,8■21:22a,30(4890)■23:12(4966)■28:17(4779),17a-**RO**-1:12(4837)■3:12(260)■6:5(4854)■8:17(4888),22(4944),28(4903)■15:30(4865)-**1CO**-1:10(2675)■3:9(4904)■5:4■7:5(1909,3588,846)■11:17a,18a,20a,33a,34a■12:24(4786)■14:23a,26a-**2CO**-1:11(4943)■6:1(4903),14(2086)-**EPH**-1:10(346)■2:5(4806),6(4891),6(4776),21(4883),22(4925)■4:16(4883)-**PH'P**-1:27(4866)■3:17(4831)-**COL**-2:2(4822),13(4806),19(4822)-**1TH**-4:17(260)■5:10(260),11(240)-**2TH**-2:1(1997)-**HEB**-10:25(1997)-**1PE**-3:7(4789)■5:13(4899)-**RE**-16:16■19:17,19■20:8

TOIL-**GE**-5:29(6093)■41:51(5999)■**N.T.**-**M'T**-6:28(2872)-**LU**-12:27(2872)

TOILED-**LU**-5:5(2872)

TOILING-**M'R**-6:48(928)

TOKEN-all=226-**GE**-9:12,13,17■17:11-**EX**-3:12■12:13■13:16-**NU**-17:10-**JOS**-2:12-**PS**-86:17■**N.T.**-**M'R**-14:44(4953)-**PH'P**-1:28(1732)-**2TH**-1:5(1730)■3:17(4592)

TOKENS-all=226-**JOB**-21:29-**PS**-65:8■135:9-**IS**-44:25

TOLD-all=5046,a=5608,b=559,c=1696&marked-**GE**-3:11■9:22■14:13■20:8c■22:3b,9b,20■24:28,33c,66a■26:32■27:42■29:12^{2},13a■31:20,22■37:5,9a,10a■38:13,24■40:9a■41:8a,12a,24b■42:29■43:7■44:24■45:26,27c■47:1■48:1b,2-**EX**-4:28■5:1b■14:5■16:22■18:8a■19:9■24:3a-**LE**-21:24c-**NU**-11:24c,27■13:27a■14:39c■23:26c■29:40b-**DE**-17:4-**JOS**-2:2b,23a■9:24■10:17-**J'G**-6:13a■7:13a■9:7,25,42,47■13:6b,6,23(8085)■14:2,6,9,16^{2},17^{2}■16:10c,13c,15,17,18-**RU**-3:16-**1SA**-3:13,18■4:13,14■8:10b■9:15(1540)■10:16^{2},25c■11:4c,5a■14:1,33,43■15:12■18:20,24,26■19:2,11,18,19,21■23:1,7,13,22b,25■24:1■25:12,14,19,36,37■27:4-**2SA**-1:5,6,13■2:4■3:23■4:10■6:12■10:5,17■11:5,10,18■14:33■15:31■17:17^{2},18,21■18:10,11,25■19:1,8■21:11■24:13-**1KI**-1:23,51■2:29,39,41■8:5a■10:3^{2},7■13:11^{2}a,25c■14:2c■18:13,16■19:1■20:17-**2KI**-1:7c■4:7,27,31■5:4■6:10b,13■7:10,11,15■8:6a,7,14b■9:18,20,36■10:8■12:10(4487),11(8505)■18:37■23:17b-**1CH**-17:25(1540)■19:5,17-**2CH**-2:2a■5:6a■9:2^{2},6■20:2■34:18-**EZR**-8:17(7760,6310)-**NE**-2:12,16,18-**ES**-2:22■3:4^{2}■4:4,7,9,12■5:11a■6:2,13a■8:1-**JOB**-15:18■37:20a-**PS**-44:1a■52:t■78:3a-**IS**-7:2■36:22■40:21■44:8(8085)■45:21■52:15a-**JER**-36:20■38:27-**DA**-4:7(560),8(560)■7:1(560),16(560)■8:26(560)-**JON**-1:10-**HAB**-1:5a-**ZEC**-10:2c■**N.T.**-all=518,a=2036&marked-**M'T**-8:33■12:48a■14:12■18:31(1285)■24:25(4280)■26:13(2980)■28:7a-**M'R**-5:14(312),16(1334),33a■6:30■9:12a■16:10,13-**LU**-1:45(2980)■2:17(2980),18(2980),20(2980)■8:20,34,36■9:10(1334),36■13:1■18:37■24:9,10(3004),35(1834)-**JOH**-3:12a■4:29a,39a,51■5:15(312)■8:40(2980)■9:27a■10:25a■11:46a■14:2a,29(2046)■16:4(2980),4a■18:8a■20:18-**AC**-5:22,25■9:6(2980)■12:14■16:36,38(312)■22:10(2980),26■23:16,30(3377)■27:25(2980)-**2CO**-7:7(312)■13:2(4280)-**GA**-5:21(4277)-**PH'P**-3:18(3004)-**1TH**-3:4(4302)-**2TH**-2:5(3004)-**JUDE**-18(3004)

TOLERABLE-all=414&marked-**M'T**-10:15■11:22,24-**M'R**-6:11-**LU**-10:12,14

TOLL-all=4061-**EZR**-4:13,20■7:24

TOMB-**JOB**-21:32(1430)■**N.T.**-**M'T**-27:60(3419)-**M'R**-6:29(3419)

TOMBS-all=3419&marked-**M'T**-8:28■23:29(5028)-**M'R**-5:2,3,5(3418)-**LU**-8:27(3418)

TONGS-all=4457&marked-**EX**-25:38-**NU**-4:9-**1KI**-7:49-**2CH**-4:21-**IS**-6:6■44:12(4621)

TONGUE-all=3956&marked-**GE**-10:5-**EX**-4:10■11:7-**DE**-28:49-**JOS**-10:21-**J'G**-7:5-**2SA**-23:2-**EZR**-4:7^{2}(762)-**ES**-7:4(2790)-**JOB**-5:21■6:24(2790),30■13:19(2790)■15:5■20:12,16■27:4■29:10■33:2■41:1-**PS**-5:9■10:7■12:3,4■15:3■22:15■34:13■35:28■37:30■39:1,3■45:1■50:19■51:14■52:2,4■57:4■64:3,8■66:17■68:23■71:24■73:9■109:2■119:172■120:2,3■126:2■137:6■139:4-**PR**-6:17,24■10:20,31■12:18,19■15:2,4■16:1■17:4,20■18:21■21:6,23■25:15,23■26:28■28:23■31:26-**SONG**-4:11-**IS**-3:8■11:15■28:11■30:27■32:4■33:19■35:6■41:17■45:23■50:4■54:17■57:4■59:3-**JER**-9:5,8■18:18-**LA**-4:4-**EZE**-3:26-**DA**-1:4-**HO**-7:16-**AM**-6:10(2013)-**MIC**-6:12-**HAB**-1:13(2790)-**ZEP**-3:13-**ZEC**-14:12■**N.T.**-all=1100&marked-**M'R**-7:33,35-**LU**-1:64■16:24-**JOH**-5:2(1447)-**AC**-1:19(1258)■2:8(1258),26■21:40(1258)■22:2(1258)■26:14(1258)-**RO**-14:11-**1CO**-4:2,4,9,13,14,19,26,27-**PH'P**-2:11-**JAS**-1:26■3:5,6^{2},8-**1PE**-3:10-**1JO**-3:18-**RE**-5:9■9:11(1447),11sup■14:6■16:16(1447)

TONGUES-all=3956-**GE**-10:20,31-**PS**-31:20■55:9■78:36■140:3-**IS**-66:18-**JER**-9:3■23:31■**N.T.**-all=1100&marked-**M'R**-16:17-**AC**-2:3,4,11■10:46■19:6-**RO**-3:13-**1CO**-12:10^{2},28,30■13:1,8■14:5^{2},6,18,21(2084),22,23,39-**RE**-7:9■10:11■11:9■13:7■16:10■17:15

TOO-**EX**-36:7(3498)-**DE**-12:21(7368)-**ES**-1:18(1767)■**N.T.**-**AC**-17:22(1174)

TOOK-all=3947,a=5375,b=3920,c=8610,d=5493&marked-**GE**-2:15,21■3:6■4:19■5:24■6:2■8:9,20■9:23■11:29,31■12:5■14:11,12■15:10■16:3■17:23■18:8■20:2,14■21:14,21,27■22:3,6^{2},10,13■24:7,10,22,61,65,67■25:1,20■26:34■27:15,36■28:9,11,18■29:23■30:9,37■31:23,45,46■32:13,22,23■33:11■34:2,25,26,28■36:2,6■37:24,31■38:2,6,28■39:20■40:11■41:42d■42:24,30(5414)■43:15^{2},34a■44:11(3381)■46:6■47:2■48:1,13,22-**EX**-2:1,3,9■4:6(3318),20^{2},25■6:20,23,25■9:10■10:19a■12:34a■13:19,22(4185)■14:6,7,25d■15:20■17:12■18:2,12■24:6,7,8■32:20■33:7■34:4,34d■40:20-**LE**-8:10,15,16,23,25,26,28,29,30■9:15■10:1-**NU**-1:17■3:49,50■7:6■11:25(680)■16:1,18,39,47■17:9■20:9■21:25,32b■22:41■23:7a,11,18a■24:3a,15a,20a,21a,23a■25:7■27:22■31:11,27c,47,51,54■32:39b,41b,42b■33:12(5265)-**DE**-1:15,23,25■2:1(5265),34b,35sup,35b■3:4b,4,8,14■9:17c,21■22:14■24:3■29:8-**JOS**-2:4■3:6a■4:8a,20■6:12a,20b■7:1,17b,21,23,24■8:12,19b,23c■9:4,14■10:27(3381),28b,32b,35b,37b,39b■11:10b,16,17b,19,23■15:17b■19:47■24:3,26-**J'G**-1:13b,18b■3:6,21,25,28b■4:21,21(7760)■5:19■6:27■7:8,24b,25b■8:12b,16,21■9:43,45b,48,48a,50b■11:13,15■12:5b,6(270),9(935)■13:19■14:9(7287),19■15:4,15■16:3(270),12,21(270),31a■17:2,4■18:17,20,27■19:1,15(622),25(2388),28,29■20:6(270)■21:23a-**RU**-1:4a■2:18a■4:2,13,16-**1SA**-1:24(5927)■2:14■5:1,2,3■6:10,15(3381)■7:9,12■8:3■9:22,24(7311)■10:1■11:7■14:32,47b,52(622)■15:8c,21■16:13,20,23■17:20a,34a,40,49,51,54,57■18:2■19:13■24:2■25:18,43■26:12■27:9■28:24■30:20■31:4,12,13-**2SA**-1:10■2:8,32a■3:15,36(5384)■4:4a,7,12■5:7b,13■7:8,15d■8:1,4b,7,8■10:4■11:4■12:4,26b,29b,30■13:8,9,10■15:5(2388)■17:19■18:14,17■20:3,9(270)■21:8,10,12■22:17■23:16a-**1KI**-1:39■3:1,20■4:15■8:3a■11:18■13:29a■14:26^{3}■15:12(5674),18,22a■16:31■17:19,23■18:4,26,31,40c■19:21■20:34■22:46(1197)-**2KI**-2:8,13(7311)14■3:26,27■4:37a■5:5,24■6:7■7:14■8:9,15■9:13■10:7,14c,15(5927)■11:2,9,19■12:9,17b,18■13:15,18,25■14:7c,13c,14,21■15:29■16:8,9c,17(3381)■17:6b■18:10b,13c■20:7■23:11(7673),16,19d,30,34■24:12■25:6c,14,15,18,19,20-**1CH**-2:19,23■4:18■7:15■10:4,9a,12a■11:5b,18a■14:3■17:7,13d■18:1,4b,7■19:4■20:2■23:22a■27:23a-**2CH**-5:4a■8:18■11:18,20,21a■12:4b,9^{2}■13:19b■14:3d,5d■16:6■22:11■23:1,8,20■24:3a,11a■25:23c■26:1■28:15(2388)■29:16(6901)■33:11b■35:24(5674)■36:1,4-**EZR**-2:61■5:14(5312)■6:5(5312)■8:30(6901)-**NE**-2:1a■7:63■9:25b-**ES**-2:7■3:10d■6:11■8:2d■9:27(6901)-**JOB**-1:15■2:8-**PS**-18:16■22:9(1518)■56:t(270)■69:4(1497)■71:6(1491)■78:70-**SONG**-5:7a-**IS**-20:1b■36:1c-**JER**-13:7■25:17■26:8c■27:20■28:3,10■31:32(2388)■32:11■35:3■36:14,21,32■37:13c,14c,17■38:6,11^{2},13(5927),14■39:14■40:2■41:12,16■43:5■52:9c,18,19,24,25,26-**LA**-5:13a-**EZE**-3:12a,14■8:3■10:7a,7■11:24a■16:50d■17:3,5■19:5■23:10■29:7c■43:5a-**DA**-1:16a■3:22(5267)■5:20(5709),31(6902)-**HO**-1:3■13:11-**AM**-7:15-**JON**-1:15a-**ZEC**-11:7,10,13■**N.T.**-all=2983,a=142,b=3880,c=2902,d=1949&marked-**M'T**-1:24b■2:14b,21b■8:17■9:25c■13:31,33■14:12a,19,20a■15:36,37a,39(1684,1519)■16:9,10,22(4355)■18:28c■20:17b■21:35,46(2192)■22:6c,15■24:39a■25:1,3,4,15(589),35(4863),38(4863),43(4863)■26:26,27,37b,50c■27:1,6,7,9,24,27b,30,31(1562),48■28:15-**M'R**-1:31c■2:12a■3:6(4160)■4:36b■5:41c■6:29a,43a■7:33(618)■8:6,8a,19a,20a,23(1949),32(4355)■9:27c,36■10:16(1723),32b■12:8,20,21■14:22,23,46c,49c■15:20(1562),46(2507)-**LU**-2:28(1209)■5:25a■8:54c■9:10b,16,28b,47(1949)■10:34(1959),35(1544)■13:19,21■14:4(1949)■15:13(589)■18:31(3830)■20:29,30,31■22:17(1209),19,54(4815)■23:53(2507)■24:30,43-**JOH**-5:9a■6:11,24(1684,1519)■8:59a■10:31(941)■11:41a,53(4823)■12:3,13■13:4■18:12(4815)■19:1,16b,23,27,38a,40-**AC**-1:16(4815)■3:7(4084)■4:13(1921)■5:33(1011)■7:21(337),43(353)■9:23(4823),25,27(1949)■10:26(1453)■12:25(4838)■13:29(2507)■15:39b■16:3,33b■17:5(4355),19(1949)■18:17(1949),18(657),26(4355)■19:13(2021)■20:14(353)■21:6(1910,1519),11a,15(643),26b,30(1949),32b,33(1949)■23:18b,19(1949),31(353)■24:6c,7(520)■27:35,36(4355)■28:15-**1CO**-11:23-**GA**-2:1(4838)-**PH'P**-2:7-**COL**-2:14a-**HEB**-2:14(3348),16^{2}(1949)■8:9(1949)■9:19■10:34(4327)-**RE**-5:7■8:5■10:10■18:21a

TOOKEST-**EZE**-16:18(3947)

TOOL-**EX**-20:25(2719)-**1KI**-6:7(3627)

TOOTH-all=8127-**EX**-21:24,27^{2}-**LE**-24:20-**DE**-19:21-**PR**-25:19■**N.T.**-**M'T**-5:38(3599)

TOOTH'S-**EX**-21:27(8127)

TOP-all=7218&marked-**GE**-11:4■28:12,18-**EX**-17:9,10■19:20^{2}■24:17■28:32■30:3(1406)■34:2■37:26(1406)-**NU**-14:40,44■20:28■21:20■23:9,14,28-**DE**-3:27■28:35(6936)■33:16(6936)■34:1-**JOS**-15:8,9-**J'G**-6:26■9:7,25,36,51(1406)■15:8(5585),11(5585)■16:3-**1SA**-9:25(1406),26(1406)■26:13-**2SA**-2:25■15:32■16:1,22(1406)-**1KI**-7:17,18,19,22,35^{2},41^{2}■10:19■18:42-**2KI**-1:9■9:13(1634)■23:12(1406)-**2CH**-3:15■4:12^{2}■25:12^{2}-**ES**-5:2-**PS**-72:16■102:7(1406)-**PR**-8:2■23:34-**SONG**-4:8^{2}-**IS**-2:2■17:6■30:17■42:11-**LA**-2:19■4:1-**EZE**-17:4,22■24:7(6706),8(6706)■26:4(6706),14(6706)■31:3(6788),10(6788),14(6788)■43:12-**AM**-1:2■9:3-**MIC**-4:1-**NA**-3:10-**ZEC**-4:2^{2}■**N.T.**-all=509&marked-**M'T**-27:51-**M'R**-15:38-**JOH**-

19:23-HEB-11:21(206)

TOPAZ-all=6357-EX-28:17■39:10-JOB-28:19-EZE-28:13■N.T.-RE-21:20(5116)

TOPS-all=7218&marked-GE-8:5-2SA-5:24-1KI-7:16-2KI-19:26(1406)-1CH-14:15-JOB-24:24-IS-2:21(5585)■15:3(1406)-EZE-6:13-HO-4:13-JOE-2:5

TORCH-ZEC-12:6(3940)

TORCHES-NA-2:2(6393),4(3940)■N.T.-JOH-18:3(2985)

TORMENT-all=929&marked-M'T-8:29(928)-M'R-5:7(928)-LU-8:28(928)■16:28(931)-1JO-4:18(2851)-RE-9:5■14:11■18:7,10,15

TORMENTED-all=928&marked-M'T-8:6-LU-16:24(3600),25(3600)-HEB-11:37(2558)-RE-9:5■11:10■14:10■20:10

TORMENTORS-M'T-18:34(930)

TORMENTS-M'T-4:24(931)-LU-16:23(931)

TORN-all=2966&marked-GE-31:39■44:28(2963)-EX-22:13(2963),13,31-LE-7:24■17:15■22:8-1KI-13:26(7665),28(7665)-IS-5:25(5478)-JER-5:6(2963)-EZE-4:14■44:31-HO-6:1(2963)-MAL-1:13(1497)■N.T.-M'R-1:26(4682)

TORTOISE-LE-11:29(6632)

TORTURED-HEB-11:25(5178)

TOSS-IS-22:18(6802)-JER-5:22(1607)

TOSSED-PS-109:23(5287)-PR-21:6(5086)■N.T.-M'T-14:24(928)-AC-27:18(5492)-EPH-4:14(2831)-JAS-1:6(4495)

TOSSINGS-JOB-7:4(5076)

TOTTERING-PS-62:3(1760)

TOUCH-all=5060-GE-3:3■20:6-EX-19:12,13-LE-5:2,3■6:27■7:21■11:8,31■12:4-NU-4:15■16:26-DE-14:8-JOS-9:19-RU-2:9-2SA-14:10■23:7-1CH-16:22-JOB-1:11■2:5■5:19■6:7-PS-105:15■144:5-IS-52:11-JER-12:14-LA-4:14,15-HAG-2:12,13■N.T.-all=680&marked-M'T-9:21■14:36-M'R-3:10■5:28■6:56■8:22■10:13-LU-6:19■11:46(4379)■18:15-JOH-20:17-1CO-7:1-2CO-6:17-COL-2:21-HEB-11:28(2345)■12:20(2345)

TOUCHED-all=5060&marked-GE-26:29■32:25,32-LE-22:6-NU-19:18■31:19-J'G-6:21-1SA-10:26-1KI-6:27^{3}■19:5,7-2KI-13:21-ES-5:2-JOB-19:21-IS-6:7-JER-1:9-EZE-3:13(5401)-DA-8:5,18■9:21■10:10,16,18■N.T.-all=680&marked-M'T-8:3,15■9:20,29■14:36■17:7■20:34-M'R-1:41■5:27,30,31■6:56■7:33-LU-5:13■7:14■8:44,45^{2},46,47■22:51-AC-27:3(2609)-HEB-4:15(4834)■12:18(5584)

TOUCHETH-all=5060&marked-GE-26:11-EX-19:12■29:37■30:29-LE-6:18■7:19■11:24,26,27,36,39■15:5,7,10,11,12,19,21,22,23,27■22:4,5-NU-19:11,13,16,21,22^{2}-J'G-16:9(7306)-JOB-4:5-PS-104:32-PR-6:29-EZE-17:10-HO-4:2-AM-9:5-ZEC-2:8■N.T.-LU-7:39(680)-1JO-5:18(680)

TOUCHING-LE-5:13(5921)-JER-1:16(5921)■22:11(413)-EZE-7:13(413)■N.T.-all=4012&marked-M'T-18:19■22:31-M'R-12:26-AC-5:35(1909)■21:25■24:21■26:2-RO-11:28(2596)-1CO-8:1■16:12-2CO-9:1-PH'P-3:5(2596),6(2596)-COL-4:10-1TH-4:9-2TH-3:4(1909)

TOW-J'G-16:9(5296)-IS-1:31(5296)■43:17(6594)

TOWARD-all=413,a=1870&marked-GE-13:12(5704)■18:16(5921,6440)■19:28^{2}(5921,6440)■30:40-EX-9:22(5921),23(5921)■10:21(5921),22(5921)■16:10■28:27(4136)■39:20(4136)-LE-9:22-NU-16:42■21:20(5921,6440)■23:28(5921,6440)■24:1■32:14-JOS-3:16(5921)■8:18^{2}■15:7sup,7^{2},21■18:17,18-J'G-19:18(5704)-1SA-17:30(413,4136)■20:12,41(681)-2SA-14:1(5921)■15:23(5921,6440)■24:5,20(5921)-1KI-7:9(5704)■8:29^{3},30,35,38,42,44a,44sup,48a■14:13■18:43a-2KI-3:14■25:4a-2CH-6:20,21,26,34a,38a■16:9■20:24(5921)■24:16(5973)-EZR-3:11(5921)-ES-1:13(6440)-JOB-11:13-PS-5:7■25:15■28:2■66:5(5921)■85:4(5973)■86:13(5921)■103:11(5921)■116:12(5921)■117:2(5921)■138:2-EC-1:6-SONG-7:10(5921)-IS-29:13(854)■38:2■63:15■66:14^{2}(854)-JER-1:13(6440)■12:3(854)■15:1■29:10(5921),11(5921)-LA-2:19(5921)-EZE-1:23■4:7■6:2■8:14(5921),16■17:6,7^{2}(5921)■20:46a,46■21:2^{2}■24:23■33:25■40:6a,20a,22a,24^{2}a,27^{2}a,31,32a,44^{2}a,45a,46a■41:11^{3}a,12a,19^{2}■42:1a,1,7a,10a,11a,12^{2}a,15^{2}a■43:1a,4a■48:21(5704),21(5921),28(5921)-DA-4:2(5974)■6:10(5049)■8:9^{2}-HO-3:1(854)-JOE-2:20^{2}-JON-2:4-ZEC-6:6,8■14:8^{2}■N.T.-all=1519,a=4314&marked-M'T-12:49(1909)■14:14(1909)■28:1-M'R-6:34(1909)-LU-2:14(1722)■12:21■13:22■24:29a-JOH-6:17-AC-1:10■8:26(2596)■20:21^{2}■24:15,16a■27:12(2596),40■28:14-RO-1:27■5:8■11:22(1909)■12:16■15:5(1722)-1CO-7:36(1909)-2CO-1:16,18a■2:8■7:4a,7(5228),15■9:8■10:1■13:4-GAL-2:8-EPH-1:8■2:7(1909)-PH'P-2:30■3:14(2596)-COL-4:5a-1TH-3:12^{2}■4:10,12a■5:14a-2TH-1:3-TIT-3:4a-PH'M-5a,5-HEB-6:1(1909),10-1PE-3:21-1JO-3:21a■4:9(1722)

TOWEL-JOH-13:4(3012),5(3012)

TOWER-all=4026&marked-GE-11:4,5■35:21-J'G-8:9,17■9:46,47,49,51^{2},52^{2}-2SA-22:3(4869),51(1431)-2KI-5:24(6076)■9:17■17:9■18:8-NE-3:1^{2},11,25,26,27■12:38,39^{2}-PS-18:2(4869)■61:3■144:2(4869)-PR-18:10-SONG-4:4■7:4^{2}-IS-2:15■5:2-JER-6:27(969)■31:38-EZE-29:10(4024)■30:6(4024)-MIC-4:8-HAB-2:1(4692)-ZEC-14:10■N.T.-all=4444-M'T-21:33-M'R-12:1-LU-13:4■14:28

TOWERS-all=4026&marked-2CH-14:7■26:9,10,15■27:4■32:5-PS-48:12-SONG-8:10-IS-23:13(971)■30:25■32:14(975)■33:18-EZE-26:4,9■27:11-ZEP-1:16(6438)■3:6(6438)

TOWN-all=5892&marked-JOS-2:15(7023)-1SA-16:4(7023)■23:7■27:5-HAB-2:12■N.T.-all=2968-M'T-10:11-M'R-8:23,26^{2}-LU-5:17-JOH-7:42■11:1,30

TOWNCLERK-AC-19:35(1122)

TOWNS-all=1323&marked-GE-25:16(2691)-NU-32:41(2333)-DE-3:5(5892)-JOS-13:30(2333)■15:45,47^{2}■17:11^{6},16-J'G-1:27^{5}■11:26^{2}-1KI-4:13(2333)-1CH-2:23(2333),23■5:16■7:28^{4}■8:12■18:1-2CH-13:19^{3}-ES-9:19(5892)-JER-19:15(5892)-ZEC-2:4(6519)■N.T.-all=2968&marked-M'R-1:38(2969)■8:27-LU-9:6,12

TRADE-GE-34:10(5503),21(5503)■46:32(582),34(582)■N.T.-RE-18:17(2038)

TRADED-all=5414-EZE-12,13,14,17■N.T.-M'T-25:16(2038)

TRADING-LU-19:15(1281)

TRADITION-all=3862-M'T-15:2,3,6-M'R-7:3,5,8,9,13-COL-2:8-2TH-3:6

TRADITIONS-GA-1:14(3862)-2TH-2:15(3862)

TRAFFICK-GE-42:34(5503)-1KI-10:15(4536)-EZE-17:4(3667)■28:5(7404),18(7404)

TRAFFICKERS-IS-23:8(3669)

TRAIN-1KI-10:2(2428)-PR-22:6(2596)-IS-6:1(7757)

TRAINED-GE-14:14(2593)

TRAITOR-LU-6:16(4273)

TRAITORS-2TI-3:4(4273)

TRAMPLE-PS-91:13(7429)-IS-63:3(7429)■N.T.-M'T-7:6(2662)

TRANCE-all=1611-AC-10:10■11:5■22:17

TRANQUILLITY-DA-4:27(7963)

TRANSFERRED-1CO-4:6(3345)

TRANSFIGURED-M'T-17:2(3339)-M'R-9:2(3339)

TRANSFORMED-RO-12:2(3339)-2CO-11:14(3345),15(3345)

TRANSFORMING-2CO-11:13(3345)

TRANSGRESS-all=5674&marked-NU-14:41-1SA-2:24-2CH-24:20-NE-1:8(4603)■13:27(4603)-PS-17:3■25:3(898)-PR-28:21(6586)-JER-2:20(5647)-EZE-20:38(6586)-AM-4:4(6586)■N.T.-M'T-15:2(3845),3(3845)-RO-2:27(3848)

TRANSGRESSED-all=6586,a=5674&marked-DE-26:13a-JOS-7:11a,15a■23:16a-J'G-2:20a-1SA-14:33(898)■15:24a-1KI-8:50-2KI-18:12a-1CH-2:7(4603)■5:25(4603)-2CH-12:2(4603)■26:16(4603)■28:19(4603)■36:14(4603)-EZR-10:10,13-IS-24:5a■43:27■66:24-JER-2:8,29■3:13■33:8■34:18a-LA-3:42-EZE-2:3■18:31-DA-9:11a-HO-6:7a■7:13■8:1a-ZEP-3:11■N.T.-LU-15:29(3928)

TRANSGRESSEST-ES-3:3(5674)

TRANSGRESSETH-PR-16:10(4603)-HAB-2:5(898)■N.T.-1JO-3:4(458,4160)-2JO-9(3845)

TRANSGRESSING-DE-17:2(5674)-IS-59:13(6586)

TRANSGRESSION-all=6588&marked-EX-34:7-NU-14:18-JOS-22:22(4604)-1SA-24:11-1CH-9:1(4604)■10:13(4604)-2CH-29:19(4604)-EZR-9:4(4604)■10:6(4604)-JOB-7:21■8:4■13:23■14:17■33:9■34:6-PS-19:13■32:1■36:1■59:3■89:32■107:17-PR-12:13■17:9,19■19:11■28:2,24■29:6,16,22-IS-24:20■53:8■57:4■58:1■59:20-EZE-33:12-DA-8:12,13■9:24-AM-4:4(6586)-MIC-1:5^{2}■3:8■6:7■7:18■N.T.-all=3847&marked-AC-1:25(3845)-RO-4:15■5:14-1TI-2:14-HEB-2:2-1JO-3:4(458)

TRANSGRESSIONS-all=6588-EX-23:21-LE-16:16,21-JOS-24:19-1KI-8:50-JOB-31:33■35:6■36:9-PS-5:10■25:7■32:5■39:8■51:1,3■65:3■103:12-IS-43:25■44:22■50:1■53:5■59:12^{2}-JER-5:6-LA-1:5,14,22-EZE-14:11■18:22,28,30,31■21:24■33:10■37:23■39:24-AM-1:3,6,9,11,13■2:1,4,6■3:14■5:12-MIC-1:13■N.T.-GA-3:19(3847)-HEB-9:15(3847)

TRANSGRESSOR-PR-21:18(898)■22:12(898)-IS-48:8(6586)■N.T.-GA-2:18(3848)-JAS-2:11(3848)

TRANSGRESSORS-all=6586&marked-PS-37:38■51:13■59:5(898)■119:158(898)-PR-2:22(898)■11:3(898),6(898)■13:2(898),15(898)■23:28(898)■26:10(5674)-IS-1:28■46:8■53:12^{2}-DA-8:23-HO-14:9■N.T.-M'R-15:28(459)-LU-22:37(459)-JAS-2:9(3848)

TRANSLATE-2SA-3:10(5674)

TRANSLATED-COL-1:13(3179)-HEB-11:5^{2}(3346)

TRANSLATION-HEB-11:5(3331)

TRANSPARENT-RE-21:21(1307)

TRAP-JOB-18:10(4434)-PS-69:22(4170)-JER-5:26(4889)■N.T.-RO-11:9(2339)

TRAPS-JOS-23:13(4170)

TRAVAIL-all=3205&marked-GE-38:27-EX-18:8(8513)-NU-20:14(8513)-LA-3:5(8513)-PS-48:6-EC-1:13(6045)■2:23(6045),26(6045)■3:10(6045)■4:4(5999),6(5999),8(6045)■5:14(6045)-IS-23:4(2342)■53:11(5999)■54:1(2342)-JER-4:31(2470)■6:24■13:21■22:23■30:6^{2}■49:24■50:43-MIC-4:9,10■N.T.-JOH-16:21(5088)-GA-4:19(5605)-1TH-2:9(3449)■5:3(5604)-2TH-3:8(3449)

TRAVAILED-all=3205&marked-GE-35:16■38:28-1SA-4:19-IS-66:7(2342),8(2342)

TRAVAILEST-GA-4:27(5605)

TRAVAILETH-all=3205&marked-JOB-15:20(2342)-PS-7:14(2254)-IS-13:8■21:3-JER-31:8-MIC-5:3■N.T.-RO-8:22(4944)

TRAVAILING-IS-42:14(3205)-HO-13:13(3205)■N.T.-RE-12:2(5605)

TRAVEL-NU-20:14(8513)-LA-3:5(8513)■N.T.-AC-19:29(4898)-2CO-8:19(4898)

TRAVELLED-AC-11:19(1330)

TRAVELLER-2SA-12:4(1982)-JOB-31:32(734)

TRAVELLERS-J'G-5:6(1980,5410)

TRAVELLETH-PR-6:11(1980)■24:34(1980)

TRAVELLING-IS-21:13(736)■63:1(6808)■N.T.-M'T-25:14(589)

TRAVERSING-JER-2:23(8308)

TREACHEROUS-all=898&marked-IS-21:2■24:16^{2}-JER-3:7(901),8■10(901),11■9:2-ZEP-3:4(900)

TREACHEROUSLY-all=898&marked-J'G-9:23-IS-21:2■24:16^{2}■33:1^{4}■48:8-JER-3:20^{2}■5:11■12:1,6-LA-1:2-HO-5:7■6:7-HAB-1:13-MAL-2:10,11,14,15,16

TREACHERY-2KI-9:23(4820)

TREAD-all=1869&marked-DE-11:24,25■33:29-JOS-1:3-1SA-5:5-JOB-24:11■40:12(1915)-PS-7:5(7429)■44:5(947)■60:12(947)■91:13■108:13(947)-IS-1:12(7429)■10:6(7760,4823)■14:25(947)■16:10■26:6(7429)■63:3,6(947)-JER-25:30■48:33-EZE-26:11(7429)■34:18(7429)-DA-7:23(1759)-HO-10:11(1758)-MIC-1:3■5:5■6:15-NA-3:14(7429)-ZEC-10:5(947)-MAL-4:3(6072)■N.T.-LU-10:19(3961)-RE-11:2(3961)

TREADER-AM-9:13(1869)

TREADERS-IS-16:10(1869)

TREADETH-all=1869&marked-DE-25:4(1758)-JOB-9:8-IS-41:25(7429)■63:2-AM-4:13-MIC-5:6,8(7429)■N.T.-1CO-9:9(248)-1TI-5:18(248)-RE-19:15(3961)

TREADING-NE-13:15(1869)-IS-7:25(4823)■22:5(4001)-AM-5:11(1318)

TREASON-all=7195-1KI-16:20-2KI-11:14-2CH-23:13

TREASURE-all=214&marked-GE-43:23(4301)-EX-1:11(4543)-DE-28:12-1CH-29:8-EZR-2:69■5:17(1596)■7:20(1596)-NE-7:70,71■10:38-PR-15:6(2633),16■21:20-IS-33:6-EZE-22:25(2633)-DA-1:2-HO-13:15■N.T.-all=2344&marked-M'T-6:21■12:35^{2}■13:44,52■19:21-M'R-10:21-LU-6:45^{2}■12:21(2343),33,34■18:22-AC-8:27(1047)-2CO-4:7-JAS-5:3(2343)

TREASURED-IS-23:18(686)

TREASURER-EZR-1:8(1489)-IS-22:15(5532)

TREASURERS-EZR-7:21(1490)-NE-13:13(686)-DA-3:2(1411),3(1411)

TREASURES-all=214&marked-DE-32:34■33:19(8226)-1KI-7:51■14:26^{2}■15:18^{2}-2KI-12:18■14:14■16:8■18:15■20:13,15■24:13^{2}-1CH-26:20^{2},22,24,26■27:25-2CH-5:1■8:15■12:9^{2}■16:2■25:24■36:18^{2}-EZR-6:1(1596)-NE-12:44-JOB-3:21(4301)■38:22^{2}-PR-2:4(4301)■8:21■10:2■21:6-IS-2:7■10:13(6259)■30:6■39:2,4■45:3-JER-10:13■15:13■17:3■20:5■41:8(4301)■48:7■49:4■50:37■51:13,16-EZE-28:4-DA-11:43(4362)-MIC-6:10■N.T.-all=2344-M'T-2:11■6:19,20-COL-2:3-HEB-11:26

TREASUREST-RO-2:5(2343)

TREASURIES-all=214&marked-1CH-9:26■28:11(1597),12^{2}-2CH-32:27-NE-13:12,13-ES-3:9(1595)■4:7-PS-135:7

TREASURY-all=214-JOS-6:19,24-JER-38:11■N.T.-all=1049&marked-M'T-27:6(2878)-M'R-12:41^{2},43-LU-21:1-JOH-8:20

TREATISE-AC-1:1(3056)

TREE-all=6086&marked-GE-1:11,12,29^{2}■2:9^{3},16,17■3:1,3,6^{2},11,12,17,22,24■18:4,8■40:19-EX-9:25■10:5■15:25-LE-27:30-DE-12:2■19:5■20:19■21:22,23■22:6-JOS-8:29^{2}-J'G-9:10,11-1SA-22:6(815)■31:13(815)-1KI-4:33■6:23,31,32,33,34■14:23-2KI-3:19■16:4■17:10-2CH-3:5■28:4-ES-2:23-JOB-14:7■19:10■24:20-PS-1:3-PR-3:18■11:30■13:12■15:4-EC-11:3^{2}-SONG-2:3-IS-40:20■41:19^{2},19^{2}sup■44:19,23■56:3■57:5■65:22-JER-2:20■3:6,13■10:3■11:19■17:8-EZE-6:13■15:2,6■17:24^{4}■20:47■21:10■31:8■34:27■36:30-DA-4:10(363),11(363),14(363),20(363),23(363),26(363)-JOE-2:22-HAG-2:19sup,19■N.T.-all=1186,a=4808&marked-M'T-3:10■7:17^{2},18^{2},19■12:33^{3}■13:32■21:19^{2}a,20a,21a■24:32a-M'R-11:13a,20a,21a■13:28a-LU-3:9■6:43^{2},44■13:6a,7a,19■19:4(4809)■21:29a■23:31(3586)-JOH-1:48a,50a-AC-5:30(3586)■10:39(3586)■13:29(3586)-RO-11:17(65),17sup,24(65),24(2565),24sup-GA-3:13(3586)-JAS-3:12a-1PE-2:24(3586)-RE-2:7(3586)■6:13a■7:1■9:4■2:2^{2}(3586),14(3586)

TREES-all=6086&marked-GE-3:2,8■23:17-EX-10:15^{2}-LE-19:23■23:40,40sup,40■26:4,20-DE-16:21■20:19,20^{2}■28:42-JOS-10:26^{2},27-J'G-9:8,9,10,11,12,13,14,15,48-2SA-5:11-1KI-4:33■5:10^{2}■9:11^{2}■10:11,12^{2}-2KI-3:25-1CH-16:33■22:4-2CH-9:10,11-EZR-3:7-NE-8:15■9:25■10:35,37-PS-74:5■96:12■104:16■105:33■148:9-EC-2:5,6-SONG-2:3■4:14-IS-7:2■10:19■44:14■55:12■61:3(352)-JER-6:6(6097)■7:20■17:2-EZE-15:2,6■17:24■20:28■31:4,5,9,14,14(352),15,16,18^{2}■47:7,12-JOE-1:12,19■N.T.-all=1186-M'T-3:10■21:8-M'R-8:24■11:8-LU-3:9■21:29-JUDE-12-RE-7:3■8:7

TREMBLE-all=7264&marked-DE-2:25■20:3(2648)-EZR-10:3(2730)-JOB-9:6(6426)■26:11(7322)-PS-60:2(7493)■99:1(7264)■114:7(2342)-EC-12:3(2111)-IS-5:25■14:16■32:11(2729)■64:2■66:5(2730)-JER-5:22(2342)■10:10(7493)■33:9■51:29(7493)-EZE-26:16(2729),18(2729)■32:10(2729)-DA-6:26(2112)-HO-11:10(2729),11(2729)-JOE-2:1,10(7493)-AM-8:8-HAB-3:7■N.T.-JAS-2:19(5425)

TREMBLED-all=2729&marked-GE-27:33-EX-19:16-J'G-5:4(7493)-1SA-4:13(2730)■14:15■16:4■28:5-2SA-22:8(7493)-EZR-9:4(2730)-PS-18:7(7493)■77:18(7264)■97:4(2342)-JER-4:24(7493)■8:16(7493)-DA-5:19(2112)-HAB-3:10(2342),16^{2}(7264)■N.T.-M'R-16:8(2192,5156)-AC-7:32(1790,1096)■24:25(1719,1096)

TREMBLETH-JOB-37:1(2729)-PS-104:32(7460)■119:120(5568)-IS-66:2(2730)

TREMBLING-all=7460&marked-EX-15:15-DE-28:65(7268)-1SA-13:7(2729)■14:15^{2}(2731)-EZR-10:9-JOB-4:14■21:6(6427)-PS-2:11■55:5-IS-51:17(8653),22(8653)-JER-30:5(2731)-EZE-12:18(7269)■26:16(2731)-DA-10:11-HO-13:1(7578)-ZEC-12:2(7478)■N.T.-all=5156&marked-M'R-5:33(5141)-LU-8:47(5141)-AC-9:6(5141)■16:29(1096,1790)-1CO-2:3-2CO-7:15-EPH-6:5-PH'P-2:12

TRENCH-all=4570&marked-1SA-17:20■26:5,7-2SA-20:15(2426)-1KI-18:32(8585),35(8585),38(8585)■N.T.-LU-19:43(5482)

TRESPASS-all=817,a=4604&marked-GE-31:36(6588)■50:17^{2}(6588)-EX-22:9(6588)-LE-5:6,7,15a,15^{2},16,18,19■6:2a,5(819),6^{2},17■7:1,2,5,7,37■14:12,13,14,17,21,24,25^{2},28■19:21^{2},22■22:16(819)■26:40a-NU-5:6a,7,8^{2},12a,27a■6:12■18:9■31:16a-JOS-7:1a■22:16a,20a,31a-1SA-6:3,4,8,17■25:28(6588)-1KI-8:31(2398)-2KI-12:16-1CH-21:3(819)-2CH-19:10^{2}(816)■24:18(819)■28:13^{2}(819),22(4603)■33:19a■33:19a-EZR-9:2a,6(819),7(819),13(819)■10:10(819),19(819)-EZE-15:8a■17:20a■18:24a■20:27a■40:39■42:13■44:29■46:20-DA-9:7a■N.T.-all=264-M'T-18:15-LU-17:3,4

TRESPASSED-all=4603&marked-LE-5:19(816)■26:40(4604)-NU-5:7(816)-DE-32:51-2CH-26:18■29:6■30:7■33:23(819)-EZR-10:2-EZE-17:20(4604)■18:24(4604)■39:23,26-DA-9:7

TRESPASSES-EZR-9:15(819)-PS-68:21(817)-EZE-39:26(4604)■N.T.-all=3900-M'T-6:14,15^{2}■18:35-M'R-11:25,26-2CO-5:19-EPH-2:1-COL-2:13

TRESPASSING-LE-6:7(819)-EZE-14:13(4603)

TRIAL-JOB-9:23(4531)-EZE-21:13(974)■N.T.-2CO-8:2(1382)-HEB-11:36(3984)-1PE-1:7(1383)

TRIBE-all=4294,a=7626-EX-31:2,6■35:30,34■38:22,23-LE-24:11-NU-1:4,21,23,25,27,29,31,33,35,37,39,41,43,47,49■2:5,7,12,14,20,22,27,29■3:6■4:18a■7:12■10:15,16,19,20,23,24,26,27■13:2,4,5,6,7,8,9,10,11^{2},12,13,14,15■18:2,2a■31:4,5,6■32:33a■34:13,14^{3},15,18,19,20,21,22,23,24,25,26,27,28■36:3:4^{2},5,6,7^{2},8^{2},9,12-DE-1:23a■3:13a■10:8a■18:1a■29:8a,18a-JOS-1:12a■3:12a■4:2a,4a,12a■7:1,14a,16a,18■12:6a■13:7a,14a,15,24,29a,29,33a■14:2,3■15:1,20,21■16:8■17:1■18:4a,7a,11,21■19:1,8,23,24,31,39,40,48■20:8^{3}■21:4^{3},5^{3},6^{4},7^{3},9^{2},17,20,23,25,27,28,30,32,34,38■22:1,7a,9a,10a,11a,13a,15a,21a-J'G-18:1a,19a,30a■20:12a■21:3a,6a,17a,24a-1SA-9:21a■10:20a,21a-1KI-7:14■11:13a,32a,36a■12:20a,21a-2KI-17:18a-1CH-5:18a,23a,26a■6:60,61^{3},62^{4},63^{3},65^{3},66,70,71,72,74,76,77,78,80■12:31,37a■23:14a■26:32a■27:20a-PS-78:67a,68-EZE-47:23a■N.T.-all=5443-LU-2:36-AC-13:21-RO-11:1-PH'P-3:5-HEB-7:13,14-RE-5:5■7:5^{3},6^{3},7^{3},8^{3}

TRIBES-all=7626,a=4294&marked-GE-49:16,28-EX-24:4■28:21■39:14-NU-1:16a■7:2a■24:2■26:55a■30:1a■31:4a■32:28a■33:54a■34:13a,15a■36:3,9a-DE-1:13,15^{2}■5:23■12:5,14■16:18■18:5■29:10,21■31:28■33:5-JOS-3:12■4:5,8■7:14,16■11:23■12:7■13:7■14:1a,2a,3a,4a■18:2■19:51a■21:1a,16■22:14a■23:4■24:1-J'G-18:1■20:2,10,12■21:5,8,15-1SA-2:28■9:21■10:19,20■15:17-2SA-5:1■7:7■15:2,10■19:9■20:14■24:2-1KI-8:1a,16■11:31,32,35■14:21■18:31-2KI-21:7-1CH-27:16,22■28:1■29:6-2CH-5:2a■6:5■11:16■12:13■33:7-EZR-6:17(7625)-PS-78:55■105:37■122:4-IS-19:13■49:6■63:17-EZE-37:19■45:8■47:13,21,22■48:1,19,23,29,31-HO-5:9-HAB-3:9a-ZEC-9:1■N.T.-all=5443&marked-M'T-19:28■24:30-LU-22:30-AC-26:7(1429)-JAS-1:1-RE-7:4■21:12

TRIBULATION-DE-4:30(6862)-J'G-10:14(6869)-1SA-26:24■N.T.-all=2347&marked-M'T-13:21■24:21,29-M'R-13:24-JOH-16:33-AC-14:22-RO-2:9■5:3■8:35■12:12-2CO-1:4■7:4-1TH-3:4(2346)-2TH-1:6-RE-1:9■2:9,10,22■7:14

TRIBULATIONS-1SA-10:19(6869)■N.T.-all=2347-RO-5:3-EPH-3:13-2TH-1:4

TRIBUTARIES-all=4522-DE-20:11-J'G-1:30,33,35

TRIBUTARY-LA-1:1(4522)

TRIBUTE-all=4522&marked-GE-49:15-NU-31:28(4371),37(4371)38(4371),39(4371),40(4371),41(4371)-DE-16:10(4530)-JOS-16:10■17:13-J'G-1:28-2SA-20:24-1KI-4:6■9:21■12:18-2KI-23:33(6066)-2CH-8:8■10:18■17:11(4853)-EZR-4:13(1093),20(1093)■6:8(4061)■7:24(1093)-NE-5:4(4060)-ES-10:1-PR-12:24■N.T.-all=2778&marked-M'T-17:24^{2}(1323),25■22:17,19-M'R-12:14-LU-20:22(5411)■23:2(5411)-RO-13:6(5411),7(5411)

TRICKLETH-LA-3:49(5064)

TRIED-all=6884&marked-2SA-22:31-JOB-23:10(974),34:36(974)-PS-12:6■17:3■18:30■66:10■105:19-IS-

28:16(976)-**JER**-12:3(974)-**DA**-12:10 -**ZEC**-13:9(974)▪**N.T.**-all=3985&marked-**HEB**-11:17-**JAS**-1:12(1384) -**1PE**-1:7(1381)-**RE**-2:2,10▪3:18(4448)

TRIEST-all=974-**1CH**-29:17-**JER**-11:20▪20:12

TRIETH-all=974-**JOB**-34:3-**PS**-7:9▪11:5-**PR**-17:3▪**N.T.**-**1TH**-2:4(1381)

TRIMMED-**2SA**-19:24(6213)▪**N.T.**-**M'T**-25:7(2885)

TRIMMEST-**JER**-2:33(3190)

TRIUMPH-**2SA**-1:20(5937)-**PS**-25:2(5970)▪41:11(7321)▪47:1(7440)▪60:8(7321)▪92:4(7442)▪94:3(5937)▪106:47(7623)▪108:9(7321)▪**N.T.**-**2CO**-2:14(2358)

TRIUMPHED-**EX**-15:1(1342),21(1342)

TRIUMPHING-**JOB**-20:5(7445)▪**N.T.**-**COL**-2:15(2358)

TRODDEN-all=1869&marked-**DE**-1:36-**JOS**-14:9-**J'G**-5:21-**JOB**-22:15▪28:8-**PS**-119:118(5541)-**IS**-5:5(4823)▪14:19(947)▪18:2(4001),7(4001)▪25:10^{2}(1758)▪28:3(7429),18(4823)▪63:3,18(947)-**JER**-12:10(947)-**LA**-1:15(5541),15-**EZE**-34:19(7429)-**DA**-8:13(4823)-**MIC**-7:10(4823)▪**N.T.**-all=2662&marked-**M'T**-5:13-**LU**-8:5▪21:24(3961)-**HEB**-10:29-**RE**-14:20(3961)

TRODE-all=7429&marked-**J'G**-9:27(1869)▪20:43(1869)-**2KI**-7:17,20▪9:33▪14:9-**2CH**-25:18(7429)▪**N.T.**-**LU**-12:1(2662)

TROOP-all=1416&marked-**GE**-30:11(1409)▪49:19-**1SA**-30:8-**2SA**-2:25(92)▪3:22▪22:30▪23:11(2416),13(2416)-**PS**-18:29-**IS**-65:11(1409)-**JER**-18:22-**HOS**-7:1-**AM**-9:6(92)

TROOPS-all=1416&marked-**JOB**-6:19(734)▪19:12-**HOS**-6:9-**MIC**-5:1(1413),1

TROUBLE-all=6869,a=6862&marked-**JOS**-6:18(5916)▪7:25(5916)-**J'G**-11:35(5916)-**2KI**-19:3-**1CH**-22:14(6040)-**2CH**-15:4a▪29:8(2189)▪32:18(926)-**NE**-9:27,32(8513)-**JOB**-3:26(7267)▪5:6(5999),7(5999)▪14:1(7267)▪15:24a▪27:9▪30:25(7186,3117)▪34:29(7561)▪38:23a-**PS**-3:1a▪9:9,13(6040)▪10:1▪13:4a▪20:1▪22:11▪27:5(7451)▪31:7(6040),9(6887)▪32:7a▪37:39▪41:1(7451)▪46:1▪50:15▪54:7▪59:16a▪60:11a▪66:14a▪69:17(6887)▪73:5(5999)▪77:2▪78:33(928),49▪81:7▪86:7▪91:15▪102:2a▪107:6a,13a,19a,26(7451),28a▪108:12▪116:3▪119:143a▪138:7▪142:2▪143:11-**PR**-11:8▪12:13▪15:6(5916),16(4103)▪25:19-**IS**-1:14(2960)▪8:22▪17:14(1091)▪22:5(4103)▪26:16a▪30:6▪33:2▪37:3▪46:7▪65:23(928)-**JER**-2:27(7451),28(7451)▪8:15(1205)▪11:12(7451),14(7451)▪14:8,19(1205)▪30:7▪51:2(7451)-**LA**-1:21(7451)-**EZE**-7:7(4103)▪32:13(4103),13(1804)-**DA**-4:19(927)▪5:10(927)▪11:44(926)▪12:1-**NA**-1:7-**HAB**-3:16-**ZEP**-1:15▪**N.T.**-all=2347&marked-**M'T**-26:10(2873,3930)-**M'R**-14:6(3930)-**LU**-7:6(4660)▪8:49(4660)▪11:7(2873)-**AC**-15:19(3926)▪16:20(1613)▪20:10(2350)-**1CO**-7:28-**2CO**-1:4,8-**GA**-1:7(5015)▪5:12(387)▪6:17(2873,3930)-**TH**-1:6(2346)-**2TI**-2:9(2558)-**HEB**-12:15(1776)

TROUBLED-all=926&marked-**GE**-34:30(5916)▪41:8(6470)▪45:3-**EX**-14:24(2000)-**JOS**-7:25(5916)-**1SA**-14:29(5916)▪16:14(1204)▪28:21-**2SA**-4:1-**1KI**-18:18(5916)-**2KI**-6:11(5590)-**EZR**-4:4(1089)-**JOB**-4:5▪21:4(7114)▪23:15▪34:20(1607)-**PS**-30:7▪38:6(5753)▪46:3(2560)▪48:5▪77:3(1993),4(6470),16(7264)▪83:17▪90:7▪104:29-**PR**-25:26(7515)-**IS**-32:10(7264),11(7264)▪57:20(1644)-**JER**-31:20(1993)-**LA**-1:20(2560)▪2:11(2560)-**EZE**-7:27▪26:18▪27:35(7481)-**DA**-2:1(6470),3(6470)▪4:5(927),19(927)▪5:6(927),9(927)▪7:15(927),28(927)-**ZEC**-10:2(6031)▪**N.T.**-all=5015&marked-**M'T**-2:3▪14:26▪24:6(2360)-**M'R**-6:50▪13:7(2360)-**LU**-1:12,29(1298)▪10:41(5182)▪24:38-**JOH**-5:4,7▪11:33(5015,1438)▪12:27▪13:21▪14:1,27-**AC**-15:24▪17:8-**2CO**-4:8(2346)▪7:5(2346)-**2TH**-1:7(2346)▪2:2(2360)-**1PE**-3:14

TROUBLEDST-**EZE**-32:2(1804)

TROUBLER-**1CH**-2:7(5916)

TROUBLES-all=6869&marked-**DE**-31:17,21-**JOB**-5:19-**PS**-25:17,22▪34:6,17▪71:20▪88:3(7451)-**PR**-21:23-**IS**-65:16▪**N.T.**-**M'R**-13:8(5016)

TROUBLEST-**M'R**-5:35(4660)

TROUBLETH-all=5916&marked-**1SA**-16:15(1204)-**1KI**-18:17-**JOB**-22:10(926)▪23:16(926)-**PR**-11:17,29▪15:27-**DA**-4:9(598)▪**N.T.**-**LU**-18:5(3930,2873)-**GA**-5:10(5015)

TROUBLING-**JOB**-3:17(7267)▪**N.T.**-**JOH**-5:4(5015)

TROUBLOUS-**DA**-9:25(5916)

TROUGH-**GE**-24:20(8628)

TROUGHS-**GE**-30:38(8268)-**EX**-2:16(7298)

TROW-**LU**-17:9(1380)

TRUCEBREAKERS-**2TI**-3:3(786)

TRUE-all=571&marked-**GE**-42:11(3651),19(3651),31(3651),33(3651),34(3651)-**DE**-17:4▪22:20-**JOS**-2:12-**RU**-3:12(551)-**2SA**-7:28-**1KI**-10:6▪22:16-**2CH**-9:5▪15:3-**NE**-9:13-**PS**-19:9▪119:160-**PR**-14:25-**JER**-10:10▪42:5-**EZE**-18:8-**DA**-3:14(6656),24(3330)▪6:12(3330)▪8:26▪10:1-**ZEC**-7:9▪**N.T.**-all=228,a=227&marked-**M'T**-22:16a-**M'R**-12:14a-**LU**-16:11-**JOH**-1:9▪3:33a▪4:23,37▪5:31a,32a▪6:32▪7:18a,28▪8:13a,14a,16a,17a,26a▪10:41a▪15:1▪17:3▪19:35,35a▪21:24a-**AC**-12:9a-**RO**-3:4a-**2CO**-1:18(4103)▪6:8a-**EPH**-4:24(3588,225)-**PH'P**-4:3(1103),8a-**1TH**-1:9-**1TI**-3:1(4103)-**TIT**-1:13a-**HEB**-8:2▪9:24▪10:22-**1PE**-5:12a-**2PE**-2:22a-**1JO**-2:8a,8▪5:20^{3}-**3JO**-12a-**RE**-3:7,14▪6:10▪15:3▪16:7▪19:2,9,11▪21:5▪22:6

TRULY-all=571&marked-**GE**-24:49▪47:29▪48:19(199)-**NU**-14:21(199)-**JOS**-2:14,24(3588)-**J'G**-9:16,19(199)-**1SA**-20:3(199)-**JOB**-36:4(551)-**PS**-62:1(389)▪73:1(389)▪116:16(577)-**PR**-12:22(530)-**JER**-3:23(403),23^{2}(403)▪10:19(389)▪28:9-**EZE**-18:9-**MIC**-3:8(199)▪**N.T.**-all=3303&marked-**M'T**-9:37▪17:11▪27:54(230)-**M'R**-14:38▪15:39(230)-**LU**-10:2▪11:48(686)▪20:21(1909,225)▪22:22-**JOH**-4:18(227)▪20:30-**AC**-1:5▪3:22▪5:23-**2CO**-12:12-**HEB**-7:23▪11:15-**1JO**-1:3(1161)

TRUMP-**1CO**-15:52(5536)-**1TH**-4:16(4536)

TRUMPET-all=7782&marked-**EX**-19:13(3104),16,19▪20:18-**LE**-25:9^{2}-**JOS**-6:5,20-**J'G**-3:27▪6:34▪7:16,18-**1SA**-13:3-**2SA**-2:28▪6:15▪15:10▪18:16▪20:1,22-**1KI**-1:34,39,41-**NE**-4:18,20-**JOB**-39:24-**PS**-47:5▪81:3▪150:3-**IS**-18:3▪27:13▪58:1-**JER**-4:5,19,21▪6:1,17▪42:14▪51:27-**EZE**-7:14(8628)▪33:3,4,5,6-**HO**-5:8(2689)▪8:1-**JOE**-2:1,15-**AM**-2:2▪3:6-**ZEP**-1:16-**ZEC**-9:14▪**N.T.**-all=4536&marked-**M'T**-6:2(4537)▪24:31-**1CO**-14:8-**HEB**-12:19-**RE**-1:10▪4:1▪8:13▪9:14

TRUMPETERS-**2KI**-11:14(2689)-**2CH**-5:13(2689)▪29:28(2690)▪**N.T.**-**RE**-18:22(4538)

TRUMPETS-all=2689,a=7782&marked-**NU**-10:2,8,9,10▪31:6-**JOS**-6:4^{2}a,6a,8a^{2},9^{2}a,13^{3}a,16a,20a-**J'G**-7:8a,18a,19a,20^{2}a,22a-**2KI**-9:13a▪12:13-**1CH**-13:8▪15:24,28▪16:6,42-**2CH**-5:12▪13:12,14▪15:14▪20:28▪23:13^{2}▪29:26,27-**EZR**-3:10-**NE**-12:35,41-**JOB**-39:25a-**PS**-98:6▪**N.T.**-**RE**-8:2(4536),6(4536)

TRUST-all=982,a=2620&marked-**J'G**-9:15a-**RU**-2:12a-**2SA**-22:3a,31a-**2KI**-18:20,21,22,24,30-**1CH**-5:20-**2CH**-32:10(982)-**JOB**-4:18(539)▪8:14(4009)▪13:15(3176)▪15:15(539),31(539)▪35:14(2342)▪39:11-**PS**-2:12a▪4:5▪5:11a▪7:1a▪9:10▪11:1a▪16:1a▪17:7a▪18:2a,30a▪25:2▪25:20a▪31:1a,6,19a▪34:22a▪36:7a▪37:3,5,40a▪40:3,4(4009)▪44:6▪49:6▪52:8▪55:23▪56:3,4,11▪61:4a▪62:8,10▪64:10a▪71:1a,5(4009)▪73:28(4268)▪91:2,4a▪115:9,10,11▪118:8a,9a▪119:42▪125:1▪141:8a▪143:8▪144:2a▪146:3-**PR**-3:5▪22:19(4009)▪28:25▪29:25▪30:5a▪31:11-**IS**-12:2▪14:32a▪26:4▪30:2a,3(2622),12▪31:1▪36:5,6,7,9,15▪42:17▪50:10▪51:5(3176)▪57:13a▪59:4-**JER**-7:4,8,14▪9:4▪28:15▪29:31▪39:18▪46:25▪49:11-**EZE**-16:15▪33:13-**HO**-10:13-**AM**-6:1-**MIC**-7:5(539)-**NA**-1:7a-**ZEP**-3:12a▪**N.T.**-all=1679&marked-**M'T**-12:21-**M'R**-10:24(3982)-**LU**-16:11(4100)-**JOH**-5:45-**RO**-15:12,24-**1CO**-16:7-**2CO**-1:9(3982),10,13▪3:4(4006)▪5:11▪10:7(3982)▪13:6-**PH'P**-2:19,24(3982)▪3:4(3982)-**1TH**-2:4(4100)-**1TI**-1:11(4100)▪4:10▪6:17-**PH'M**-22-**HEB**-2:13(3982)▪13:18(3982)-**2JO**-12-**3JO**-14

TRUSTED-all=982&marked-**DE**-32:37(2620)-**J'G**-11:20(539)▪20:36-**2KI**-18:5-**PS**-13:5▪22:4,5,8(1556)▪26:1▪28:7▪31:14▪33:21▪41:9▪52:7▪78:22-**IS**-47:10-**JER**-13:25▪48:7▪49:4-**DA**-3:28(7365)-**ZEP**-3:2▪**N.T.**-all=3982&marked-**M'T**-27:43-**LU**-11:22▪18:9▪24:21(1679)-**EPH**-1:12(4276)-**1PE**-3:5(1679)

TRUSTEDST-all=982-**DE**-28:52-**JER**-5:17▪12:5

TRUSTEST-all=982-**2KI**-18:19,21▪19:10-**IS**-36:4,6▪37:10

TRUSTETH-all=982&marked-**JOB**-40:23-**PS**-21:7▪32:10▪34:8(2620)▪57:1(2620)▪84:12▪86:2▪115:8▪135:18-**PR**-11:28▪16:20-**PR**-28:26-**IS**-26:3-**JER**-17:5,7-**HAB**-2:18▪**N.T.**-**1TI**-5:5(1679)

TRUSTING-**PS**-112:7(982)

TRUSTY-**JOB**-12:20(539)

TRUTH-all=571,a=530&marked-**GE**-24:27▪32:10▪42:16-**EX**-18:21▪34:6-**DE**-13:14▪32:4a-**JOS**-24:14-**J'G**-9:15-**1SA**-12:24▪21:5(3588,518)-**2SA**-2:6▪15:20-**1KI**-2:4▪3:6▪17:24-**2KI**-19:17(551)▪20:3,19-**2CH**-18:15▪31:20-**ES**-9:30-**JOB**-9:2(551)-**PS**-15:2▪25:5,10▪26:3▪30:9▪31:5▪33:4a▪40:10,11▪43:3▪45:4▪51:6▪54:5▪57:3,10▪60:4(7189)▪61:7▪69:13▪71:22▪85:10,11▪86:11,15▪89:14,49a▪91:4▪96:13a▪98:3a▪100:5a▪108:4▪111:8▪117:2▪119:30a,43,142,151▪132:11▪138:2▪145:18▪146:6-**PR**-3:3▪8:7▪12:17a,19▪14:22▪16:6▪20:28▪22:21^{2}▪23:23-**EC**-12:10-**IS**-5:9(518,3808)▪10:20▪16:5▪25:1(544)▪26:2(529)▪37:18(551)▪38:3,18,19▪39:8▪42:3▪43:9▪48:1▪59:4a,14,15▪61:8▪65:16^{2}(548)-**JER**-4:2▪5:1a,3a▪7:28a▪9:3a,5▪26:15▪33:6-**DA**-2:47(7187)▪4:37(7187)▪7:16(3330),19(3321)▪8:12▪9:13▪10:21▪11:2-**HO**-4:1-**MIC**-7:20-**ZEC**-8:3,8,16^{2},19-**MAL**-2:6▪**N.T.**-all=225&marked-**M'T**-14:33(230)▪15:27(3483)▪22:16-**M'R**-5:33▪12:14,32-**LU**-4:25▪9:27(230)▪12:44(230)▪21:3(230)▪22:59-**JOH**-1:14,17▪3:21▪4:23,24▪5:33▪6:14(230)▪7:40(230)▪8:32^{2},40,44^{2},45,46▪14:6,17▪15:26▪16:7,13^{2}▪17:17^{2},19▪18:37^{2},38-**AC**-4:27▪10:34▪26:25-**RO**-1:18,25▪2:2,8,20▪3:7▪9:1▪15:8-**1CO**-5:8▪13:6▪14:25(3689)-**2CO**-4:2▪6:7▪7:14^{2}▪11:10▪12:6▪13:8-**GA**-2:5,14▪3:1▪4:16(226)▪5:7-**EPH**-1:13▪4:15(226),21,25(226)▪5:9(226)▪6:14(226)-**PH'P**-1:18(226)-**COL**-1:5(226),6(226)-**1TH**-2:13(230)-**2TH**-2:10,12,13-**1TI**-2:4,7▪3:15▪4:3▪6:5-**2TI**-2:15,18,25▪3:7,8▪4:4-**TIT**-1:1,14-**HEB**-10:26-**JAS**-1:18▪3:14▪5:19-**1PE**-1:22-**2PE**-1:12▪2:2-**1JO**-1:6,8▪2:4,21^{2},27(227)▪3:18,19▪4:6▪5:6-**2JO**-1^{2},3,4-**3JO**-

1,3^{2},4,8,12

TRUTH'S-PS-115:1(571)-2JO-2(225)

TRY-all=974&marked-J'G-7:4(6884)-2CH-32:31(5254)-JOB-7:18▪12:11-PS-11:4▪26:2(6884)▪139:23-JER-6:27▪9:7▪17:10-LA-3:40(2713)-DA-11:35(6884)-ZEC-13:9▪N.T.-1CO-3:13(1381)-1PE-4:12(4314,3986)-1JO-4:1(1381)-RE-3:10(3985)

TRYING-JAS-1:3(1383)

TUMBLED-J'G-7:13(2015)

TUMULT-all=1995&marked-1SA-4:14-2SA-18:29-2KI-19:28(7600)-PS-65:7▪74:23(7588)▪83:2(1993)-IS-33:3▪37:29(7600)-JER-11:16(1999)-HO-10:14(7588)-AM-2:2(7588)-ZEC-14:13(4103)▪N.T.-all=2351-M'T-27:24-M'R-5:38-AC-21:34▪24:18

TUMULTS-AM-3:9(4103)▪N.T.-2CO-6:5(181)▪12:20(181)

TUMULTUOUS-IS-13:4(7588)▪22:2(1993)-JER-48:45(1121,7588)

TURN-all=7725,a=5493,b=6437,c=5186,d=5437-GE-19:2a▪24:49b▪27:44,45-EX-3:3a▪14:2▪32:12-LE-13:16▪19:4b-NU-14:25b▪20:17c▪21:22c▪22:23c,26c▪32:15▪34:4d-DE-1:7b,40b▪2:3b,27a▪4:30▪5:32a▪7:4a▪11:16a,28a▪13:5(5627),17▪14:25(5414)▪16:7b▪17:17a,20a▪23:13,14▪30:3,10,17b▪31:20b,29a-JOS-1:7a▪22:16,18,23,29▪23:6a▪24:20-J'G-4:18a▪11:8▪19:11a,12a▪20:8a-RU-1:11,12▪4:1a-1SA-12:20a,21a▪14:7c▪15:25,30▪22:17d,18d-2SA-2:21c,21a,22a,23a▪14:24d▪18:30d▪19:37-1KI-8:33,35▪9:6▪11:2c▪12:27▪13:9,17▪17:3b▪22:34(2015)-2KI-1:6▪4:10a▪9:18d,19d▪17:13▪18:24▪19:28▪20:5-1CH-12:23d▪14:4d-2CH-6:26,37,42▪7:14,19▪15:4▪18:33(2015)▪25:27a▪29:10▪30:6,8,9,9a▪35:22d-NE-1:9▪4:4▪9:26-ES-2:12(8447),15(8447)-JOB-5:1b▪14:6(8159)▪23:13▪24:4c▪34:15-PS-7:12▪18:37▪22:27▪25:16b▪40:4(7750)▪44:10▪56:9▪60:1▪69:16b▪80:3,7,19▪85:4,8▪86:16b▪101:3(7750)▪104:9▪106:23▪119:37(5674),39(5674),79▪125:5c▪126:4▪132:10,11-PR-1:23▪4:15(7847),27c▪9:4a,16a▪24:18▪25:10▪29:8-EC-3:20-SONG-2:17d▪6:5d-IS-1:25▪10:2c▪13:14b▪14:27▪19:6(2186)▪22:18(6801)▪23:17▪28:6▪29:21c▪30:11c▪31:6▪36:9▪37:29▪58:13▪59:20-JER-2:24,35▪3:7,14,19▪4:28▪6:9▪8:4▪13:16(7760)▪18:8,20▪21:4d▪25:5▪26:3▪29:14▪31:13(2015),18,21▪32:40▪44:5▪49:8b▪50:16-LA-2:14▪3:35c,40▪5:21-EZE-3:19,20▪4:8(2015)▪7:22d▪8:6,13,15▪14:6^{2}▪18:21,30,32▪33:9^{2},11^{2},14,19▪36:9b▪38:4,12▪39:2-DA-9:13▪11:18^{2},19-HO-5:4▪12:6▪14:2-JOE-2:12,13-AM-1:3,6,8,9,11,13▪2:1,4,6,7c▪5:7(2015),12c▪8:10(2015)-JON-3:8,9^{2}-MIC-7:19-ZEP-2:7▪3:9(2015),20-ZEP-1:3^{2},4▪9:12▪10:9▪13:7-MAL-2:6▪3:5c▪4:6▪N.T.-all=1994-M'T-5:39(4762),42(654)▪7:6(4762)-M'R-13:16-LU-1:16,17▪10:6(344)▪17:4▪21:13(576)-AC-13:8(1294),46(4762)▪14:15▪26:18,20-RO-11:26(654)-2CO-3:16-GA-4:9-PH'P-1:19(576)-2TI-3:5(665)▪4:4(654)-TIT-1:14(654)-HEB-12:25-JAS-3:3(3329)-2PE-2:21-RE-11:6(4762)

TURNED-all=7725,a=2015,b=6437,c=5493,d=5437,e=5186,f=5472&marked-GE-3:24a▪18:22b▪19:3c▪38:1e,16e▪42:24d-EX-3:4c▪4:7▪7:15a,17,20a,23b▪10:6b,19a▪14:5a▪32:8c,15b▪33:11-LE-13:3a,4a,10a,13a,17a,20a,25a-NU-14:43▪20:21e▪21:33b▪22:23e,33^{2}e▪25:4,11▪33:7-DE-1:24b▪2:1b,8b▪3:1b▪9:12c,15b,16c▪10:5b▪23:5a▪31:18b-JOS-7:12b,26▪8:20a,21▪11:10▪19:12-J'G-2:17c▪3:19▪4:18c▪8:33▪14:8c▪15:4b▪18:3c,15c,21b,23d,26b▪19:15c▪20:41a,42b,45b,47b,48-RU-3:8(3943)▪4:1c-1SA-6:12c▪8:3e▪10:6a,9b▪13:17b,18^{2}b▪14:47b▪15:11,27d,31▪17:30d▪22:18d▪25:12a-2SA-1:22(7734)▪2:19e▪18:30d▪22:38-1KI-2:15d,28^{2}e▪8:14d▪10:13b▪11:3e,4e,9e▪15:5c▪18:37d▪20:39c▪21:4d▪22:32c,33,43c-2KI-1:5^{2}▪2:24b▪4:8c,11c▪5:12b,26a▪9:23a▪15:20▪16:18d▪20:2d▪22:2c▪23:16b,25,26,34d▪24:1-1CH-10:14d▪21:20-2CH-6:3d▪9:12a▪12:12▪18:32▪20:10c▪29:6d,6(5414)▪36:4d-EZR-6:22d▪10:14-NE-2:15▪9:35▪13:2a-ES-9:1a,22a-JOB-6:18(3943)▪16:11(3399)▪19:19a▪20:14a▪28:5a▪30:15a▪31:7e▪34:27c▪37:12a▪38:14a▪41:22(1750),28a▪42:10-PS-9:3,17▪30:11a▪32:4a▪35:4f▪44:18f▪66:6a,20c▪70:2f,3▪78:9a,38,41,44a,57f,57a▪81:14▪85:3▪89:43▪105:25a,29a▪114:8a▪119:59▪126:1▪129:5f-EC-2:12b-SONG-6:1b-IS-5:25▪9:12,17,21▪10:4▪12:1▪21:4(7760)▪28:27d▪29:17▪34:9a▪38:2d▪42:17f▪44:20e▪50:5f▪53:6b▪59:14(5253)▪63:10a-JER-2:21a,27b▪3:10▪4:8▪5:25e▪6:12d▪8:6▪11:10▪23:22▪30:6a▪31:18,19▪32:33b▪34:11,15,16▪38:22f▪46:5f,21b▪48:39b▪50:6-LA-1:13,20a▪3:3,11c▪5:2a,15a,21-EZE-1:9d,12d,17d▪10:11^{2}d,16d▪17:6b▪26:2d▪42:19d-DA-9:16▪10:8a,16a-HO-7:8a▪11:8a▪14:4-JOE-2:31a-AM-6:12a-JON-3:10-NA-2:2-HAB-2:16d-ZEP-1:6f-ZEC-5:1▪6:1▪14:10d▪N.T.-all=4762,a=1994&marked-M'T-2:22(402)▪9:22a▪16:23(4672)-M'R-5:30a▪8:33a-LU-2:45(5290)▪7:9,44▪9:55▪10:23▪14:25▪17:15(5290)▪22:61-JOH-1:38▪16:20(1096)▪20:14,16-AC-2:20▪7:39,42▪9:35a▪11:21a▪15:19a▪16:18a▪17:6(387)▪19:26(3179)-1TH-1:9a-1TI-1:6(1824)▪5:15(1824)-2TI-1:15(654)▪4:4(654)-HEB-11:34(2827)▪12:13(1624)-JAS-3:4(3329)▪4:9(3344)-2PE-2:22a-RE-1:12^{2}a

TURNEST-1KI-2:3(6437)-JOB-15:13(7725)-PS-90:3(7725)

TURNETH-all=7725&marked-LE-20:6(6437)-DE-29:18(6437)-JOS-7:8(2015)▪19:27,29^{2},34-JOB-39:22-PS-107:33(7760),35(7760)▪146:9(5791)-PR-15:1▪17:8(6437)▪21:1(5186)▪26:14(5437)▪28:9(5493)▪30:30-EC-1:6(5437)-SONG-1:7(5844)-IS-9:13▪24:1(5753)▪44:25-JER-14:8(5186)▪49:24(6437)-LA-1:8▪3:3-EZE-18:24,26,27,28▪33:12,18-AM-5:8(2015)

TURNING-all=4740&marked-2KI-21:13(2015)-2CH-26:9▪36:13(7257)-NE-3:19,20,24,25-PR-1:32(4878)-IS-29:16(2017)-EZE-41:24(4142)-MIC-2:4(7725)▪N.T.-LU-23:28(4762)-JOH-21:20(1994)-AC-3:26(654)-AC-9:40(1994)-JAS-1:17(5157)-2PE-2:6(5077)-JUDE-4(3346)

TURTLE-SONG-2:12(8449)-JER-8:7(8449)

TURTLEDOVE-all=8449-GE-15:9-LE-12:6-PS-74:19

TURTLEDOVES-all=8449-LE-1:14▪5:7,11▪14:22,30▪15:14▪N.T.-LU-2:24(5167)

TURTLES-all=8449-LE-12:8▪15:29-NU-6:10

TUTORS-GA-4:2(2012)

TWAIN-all=8147-1SA-18:21-2KI-4:33-IS-6:2^{3}-JER-34:18-EZE-21:19▪N.T.-all=1417-M'T-5:41▪19:5,6▪21:31▪27:21,51-M'R-10:8^{2}▪15:38-EPH-2:15

TWELFTH-all=8147,6240-NU-7:78-1KI-19:19-2KI-8:25▪17:1▪25:27-1CH-24:12▪25:19▪27:15-2CH-34:3-EZR-8:31-ES-3:7^{2},13▪8:12▪9:1-JER-52:31-EZE-29:1▪32:1^{2},17▪33:21▪N.T.-RE-21:20(1428)

TWELVE-all=8147,6240&marked-GE-5:8▪14:4▪17:20▪25:16▪35:22▪42:13,32▪49:28-EX-15:27▪24:4^{2}▪28:21^{2}▪39:14^{2}-LE-24:5-NU-1:44▪7:3,84^{2},86,87^{3}▪17:2,6▪29:17▪31:5,33(8147),38(8147)▪33:9-DE-1:23-JOS-3:12▪4:2,3,4,8,9,20▪8:25▪18:24▪19:15▪21:7,40-J'G-19:29▪21:10-2SA-2:15^{2}▪10:6▪17:1-1KI-4:7,26▪7:15,25,44▪10:20,26▪11:30▪16:23▪18:31▪19:19-2KI-3:1▪21:1-1CH-6:63▪9:22▪15:10▪25:9,10,11,12,13,14,15,16,17,18,19,20,21,22,23,24,25,26,27,28,29,30,31-2CH-1:14▪4:4,15▪9:19,25▪12:3(505)▪33:1-EZR-2:6,18▪6:17(8648,6236)▪8:24,35^{2}-NE-5:14▪7:24-ES-2:12-PS-60:t-JER-52:20,21-EZE-43:16^{2}▪47:13-DA-4:29(8648,6236)▪N.T.-all=1427&marked-M'T-9:20▪10:1,2,5▪11:1▪14:20▪19:28^{2}▪20:17▪26:14,20,47,53-M'R-3:14▪4:10▪5:25,42▪6:7,43▪8:19▪9:35▪10:32▪11:11▪14:10,17,20,43-LU-2:42▪6:13▪8:1,42,43▪9:1,12,17▪18:31▪22:3,14,30,47-JOH-6:13,67,70,71▪11:9▪20:24-AC-6:2▪7:8▪19:7(1177)▪24:11(1177)▪26:7(1429)-1CO-15:5-JAS-1:1-RE-7:5^{3},6^{3},7^{3},8^{3}▪12:1▪21:12^{3},14^{2},16,21▪22:2

TWENTIETH-all=6242-GE-8:14-EX-12:18-NU-10:11-1KI-15:9-2KI-12:6▪13:1▪15:30▪25:27-1CH-24:16,17^{2},18^{2}▪25:27,28,29,30,31-2CH-7:10-EZR-10:9-NE-1:1▪2:1▪5:14-ES-8:9-JER-25:3▪52:30,31-EZE-29:17▪40:1-DA-10:4-HAG-1:15▪2:1,10,18,20-ZEC-1:7

TWENTY-all=6242&marked-GE-6:3▪11:24▪18:31▪23:1▪31:38,41▪32:14^{2},15▪37:28-EX-26:2,18,19,20▪27:10^{2}▪11,16▪30:13,14▪36:9,23,24,25▪38:10^{2},11^{2},18,24,26-LE-27:3,5^{2},25-NU-1:3,18,20,22,24,26,28,30,32,34,36,38,40,42,45▪3:39,43,47▪7:86,88▪8:24▪11:19▪14:29▪18:16▪25:9▪26:2,4,14,62▪32:11▪33:39-DE-31:2▪34:7-JOS-15:32▪19:30-J'G-4:3▪7:3▪8:10▪10:2,3▪11:33▪15:20▪16:31▪20:15,21,35,46-1SA-7:2▪14:14-2SA-3:20▪8:4,5▪9:10▪10:6▪18:7▪19:17▪21:20▪24:8-1KI-4:23▪5:11^{2}▪6:2,3,16,20^{3}▪8:63^{2}▪9:10,11,28▪10:10▪14:20▪15:33▪16:8,10,15,29▪20:30▪22:42-2KI-4:42▪8:26▪10:36▪14:2^{2}▪15:1,27,33▪16:2▪18:2^{2}▪21:19▪23:31,36▪24:18-1CH-2:22▪7:2,7,9,40▪12:28,30,35,37▪15:5,6▪18:4,5▪20:6▪23:4,24,27▪27:1,2,4,5,7,8,9,10,11,12,13,14,15,23-2CH-2:10^{4}▪3:3,4^{2},8^{2},11,13▪4:1^{2}▪5:12▪7:5^{2}▪8:1▪9:9▪11:21▪13:21▪20:31▪25:1^{2},5▪27:1,8▪28:1,6▪29:1^{2}▪31:17▪33:21▪36:2,5,11-EZR-1:9▪2:11,12,17,19,21,23,26,27,28,32,33,41,67▪3:8▪8:11,19,20,27-NE-6:15▪7:16,17,22,23,27,30,31,32,35,37,69,71(7239),72(7239)▪9:1▪11:8,12,14-ES-1:1▪8:9▪9:30-PS-68:17(7239)-JER-52:1,28-EZE-4:10▪8:16▪11:1▪40:13,21,25,29,30,33,36,49▪41:2,4^{2},10▪42:3▪45:1,3,5^{2},6,12^{2}▪48:8,9,10^{2},13^{2},15,20^{2},21^{2}-DA-6:1(6243)▪10:13-HAG-2:16^{2}-ZEC-5:2▪N.T.-all=1501-LU-14:31-JOH-6:19-AC-1:15▪27:28-1CO-10:8-RE-4:4^{2},10▪5:8,14▪11:16▪19:4

TWENTY'S-GE-18:31(6242)

TWICE-all=8147&marked-GE-41:32(6471)-EX-16:5(4932),22(4932)-NU-20:11(6471)-1SA-18:11(6471)-1KI-11:9(6471)-2KI-6:10-NE-13:20-JOB-33:14▪40:5▪42:10(4932)-PS-62:11-EC-6:6(6471)▪N.T.-all=1364-M'R-14:30,72-LU-18:12-JUDE-12

TWIGS-EZE-17:4(3242),22(3127)

TWILIGHT-all=5399&marked-1SA-30:17-2KI-7:5,7-JOB-3:9▪24:15-PR-7:9-EZE-12:6(5939)▪12:7(5939),12(5939)

TWINED-all=7806-EX-26:1,31,36▪27:9,16,18▪28:6,8,15▪36:8,35,37▪38:9,16,18▪39:2,5,8,24,28,29

TWINKLING-1CO-15:52(4493)

TWINS-all=8380&marked-GE-25:24▪38:27-SONG-4:2(8382),5▪6:6(8382)▪7:3

TWO-all=8147&marked-GE-1:16▪4:19▪5:18,20,26,28▪6:19,20▪7:2,9,15▪9:22▪10:25▪11:20▪19:1,8,15,16,30^{2}▪22:3▪24:22▪25:23^{2}▪27:9,36(6471)▪29:16▪31:33,41▪32:7,10,22^{2}▪33:1▪34:25▪40:2▪41:50▪42:37▪44:27▪46:27▪48:1,5-EX-2:13▪4:9▪12:7,22,23▪16:22▪18:3,6▪25:12^{2},18^{2},19,22,35^{3}▪26:17,19^{4},

21[2],23,23sup,24,25[2]■27:7■28:7[2],9,11,12[2],14,23[2],24[2],25[2],26[2],27[2]■29:1,3,13,22,38■30:4[3]■31:18■32:15■34:1,4[2],29■36:22,24[4],26[2],28,28sup,30■37:3[2],7[2],8,21[3],27[3]■39:4,16[2],17[2],18[2],19[2],20[2]-**LE**-3:4,10,15■4:9■5:7,11■7:4■8:2,16,25■12:8■14:4,10,22,49■15:14,29■16:1,5,7,8■23:13,17,18,19,20■24:5,6-**NU**-1:35,35sup,39■2:21,21sup,26■3:39,43,43sup■6:10■7:3,7,17,23,29,35,41,47,53,59,65,71,77,83,89■10:2■11:26■13:23■15:6■22:22■26:14,14sup,34,37■28:3,9[2],11,12,19,20,27,28■29:3,9,13,14[2],17,20,23,26,29,32■31:27,35,40■34:15■35:6-**DE**-3:8,21■4:13,47■5:22■9:10,11,15[2],17[2]■10:1,3[2]■14:6■17:6■19:15■21:15■32:30-**JOS**-2:1,4,10,23■6:22■9:10■14:3,4■15:60■19:30■21:16,25,27■24:12-**J'G**-3:16■7:3,25■8:12■9:44■10:3■11:37,38,39■12:6■15:4,13■16:3,28,29■19:10(6771)■20:21-**RU**-1:1,2,3,5,7,8,19■4:11-**1SA**-1:2,3■2:21,34■4:4,11,17■6:7,10■10:2,4■11:11■13:1■14:49■23:18■25:18,18sup■27:3■28:8■30:5,12,18-**2SA**-1:1■2:2,10■4:2■8:2,5■12:1■14:6[2]■15:27,36■18:24■21:8■23:20-**1KI**-2:5,32,39■3:16,18,25■5:12,14■6:23,32,34[3]■7:15,16,18,20,20sup,24,41,41sup,41,42[3]■8:9,63■9:10■10:19■11:29■12:28■14:20■15:25■16:21(2677),29■17:12■18:21,23■20:1,15sup,15,16,27■21:10,13■22:31-**2KI**-1:14■2:6,7,8,12,24[2]■4:1:22[2],23sup,23[3]■7:14■8:17,26■9:32■10:4,8,14■11:7■15:2,27■17:16■21:5,19[2]■23:12■25:16-**1CH**-1:19■4:5■7:2,7■11:21,22■12:28■18:5■19:7■24:17■25:29■26:8,17,18-**2CH**-3:10,15■4:3,12,12sup,12,13[3]■5:10■7:5■9:18■13:21■21:5,19,20■22:2■24:3■26:3■33:5-**EZR**-2:3sup,3,10,12sup,12,24,27,29,37,58,60■8:27■10:13-**NE**-5:14■6:15■7:8,9,10,17[2],28,31,33,40,60,62■11:12,13sup,13,19■12:31,40■13:6-**ES**-2:21■6:2■9:27-**JOB**-13:20■42:7-**PR**-30:7,15-**EC**-4:9,11,12-**SONG**-4:5■7:3-**IS**-7:4,21■17:6■47:9■51:19-**JER**-2:13■3:14■24:1■33:24■52:20,29-**EZE**-1:11[2],23[2]■21:19,21■23:2■35:10[2]■37:22[2]■40:9,39,40[2]■41:3,18,22,23,24[4]■43:14-**DA**-5:31(8648)■8:7■9:25,26■12:5-**HO**-10:10-**AM**-3:3,12■4:8-**ZEC**-4:3,11,12[2],14■5:9■6:1■11:7■13:8■<u>**N.T.**</u>-<u>all=1417&marked</u>-**M'T**-2:16(1332)■4:18,21■6:24■8:28■9:27■10:10,29■11:2■14:17,19■18:8,9,16[2],19,20■20:21,24,30■21:1,28■22:40■24:40,41■25:15,17[2],22[3]■26:2,37,60■27:38-**M'R**-5:13(1367)■6:7,9,37(1250),38,41[2]■9:43,45,47■11:1,4(296)■12:42■14:1,13■15:27■16:12-**LU**-2:24■3:11■5:2■7:19,41■9:3,13,16,30,32■10:1sup,1,35■12:6,52■15:11■16:13■17:34,35,36■18:10■19:29■21:2■22:38■23:32■24:4,13-**JOH**-1:35,37,40■2:6■4:40,43■6:7(1250),9■8:17■11:6■19:18■20:12■21:2,8(1250)-**AC**-1:10,23,24■7:29■9:38■10:7■12:6[2]■19:10,22,34■21:33■23:23■23[2](1250)■24:27(1333)■27:37(1250),41(1337)■28:30(1333)-**1CO**-6:16■14:27,29-**2CO**-13:1-**GA**-4:22,24-**EPH**-5:31-**PH'P**-1:23-**1TI**-5:19-**HEB**-6:18■10:28-**RE**-2:12(1366)■9:12,16■11:2,3,3(1250),4[2],10■12:6,14■13:5,11

<u>**TWOEDGED**</u>-**PS**-149:6(6374)-**PR**-5:4(6310)■<u>**N.T.**</u>-**HEB**-4:12(1366)-**RE**-1:16(1366)

<u>**TWOFOLD**</u>-**M'T**-23:15(1366)

U

<u>**UNACCUSTOMED**</u>-**JER**-31:18(3808,3925)

<u>**UNADVISEDLY**</u>-**PS**-106:33(981)

<u>**UNAWARES**</u>-<u>all=7684&marked</u>-**GE**-31:20(3820,3824),26(3820,3824)-**NU**-35:11,15-**DE**-4:42(1097,1847)-**JOS**-20:3,9-**PS**-35:8(3045)■<u>**N.T.**</u>-**LU**-21:34(160)-**GA**-2:4(3920)-**HEB**-13:2(2990)-**JUDE**-4(3921)

<u>**UNBELIEF**</u>-<u>all=570&marked</u>-**M'T**-13:58■17:20-**M'R**-6:6■9:24■16:14-**RO**-3:3■4:20■11:20,23,30(543),32(543)-**1TI**-1:13-**HEB**-3:12,19■4:6(543),11(543)

<u>**UNBELIEVERS**</u>-<u>all=571</u>-**LU**-12:46-**1CO**-6:6■14:23-**2CO**-6:14

<u>**UNBELIEVING**</u>-<u>all=571&marked</u>-**AC**-14:2(544)-**1CO**-7:14[2],15-**TIT**-1:15-**RE**-21:8

<u>**UNBLAMEABLE**</u>-**COL**-1:22(299)-**1TH**-3:13(299)

<u>**UNBLAMEABLY**</u>-**1TH**-2:10(274)

<u>**UNCERTAIN**</u>-**1CO**-14:8(82)-**1TI**-6:17(83)

<u>**UNCERTAINLY**</u>-**1CO**-9:26(82)

<u>**UNCHANGEABLE**</u>-**HEB**-7:24(531)

<u>**UNCIRCUMCISED**</u>-<u>all=6189&marked</u>-**GE**-17:14■34:14(6190)-**EX**-6:12,30■12:48-**LE**-19:23[2]■26:41-**JOS**-5:7-**J'G**-14:3■15:18-**1SA**-14:6■17:26,36■31:4-**2SA**-1:20-**1CH**-10:4-**IS**-52:1-**JER**-6:10■9:25(6190),26[2]-**EZE**-28:10■31:18■32:19,21,24,25,26,27,28,29,30,32■44:7,9■<u>**N.T.**</u>-**AC**-7:51(564)■11:3(203,2192)-**RO**-4:11(1722,3588,203),12(1722,3588,203)-**1CO**-7:18(1986)

<u>**UNCIRCUMCISION**</u>-<u>all=203</u>-**RO**-2:25,26[2],27■3:30■4:9,10[2]-**1CO**-7:18,19-**GA**-2:7■5:6■6:15-**EPH**-2:11-**COL**-2:13■3:11

<u>**UNCLE**</u>-<u>all=1730</u>-**LE**-10:4■25:49-**1SA**-10:14,15,16■14:50-**1CH**-27:32-**ES**-2:15-**JER**-32.7-**AM**-6:10

<u>**UNCLEAN**</u>-<u>all=2931,a=2930&marked</u>-**LE**-5:2[5]■7:19,21(2932),21[2]■10:10■11:4,5,6,7,8,24[2]a,25a,26,26a,27,27a,28a,28,29,31,31a,32[2]a,33a,34[2]a,35a,35,36a,38,39a,40[2]a,43a,47■12:2[2]a,5a■13:3a,8a,11a,11,14a,15a,15,20a,22a,25a,27a,30a,36,44,44a,45,46,51,55,59a■14:36a,40,41,44,45,46a,57■15:2,4[2]a,5a,6a,7a,8a,9a,10[2]a,11a,16a,17a,18a,19a,20[2]a,21a,22a,24[2]a,25,26,27[2]a,33■17:15a■20:21(5079),25[2],25a■22:4,5a,6a■27:11,27-**NU**-6:7a■9:10■18:15■19:7a,8a,10a,11a,13,14a,15,16a,17,19,20a,20,21a,22,22[2]a-**DE**-12:15,22■14:7,8,10,19■15:22■23:14(6172)■26:14-**JOS**-22:19-**J'G**-13:4,7(2932),14(2932)-**2CH**-23:19-**EZR**-9:11(5079)-**JOB**-14:4■36:14(6945)-**EC**-9:2-**IS**-6:5[2]■35:8■52:1,11■64:6-**LA**-4:15-**EZE**-22:26■44:23-**HO**-9:3-**HAG**-2:13,13[2]a,14-**ZEC**-13:2(2932)■<u>**N.T.**</u>-<u>all=169&marked</u>-**M'T**-10:1■12:43-**M'R**-1:23,26,27■3:11,30■5:2,8,13■6:7■7:25-**LU**-4:33,36■6:18■8:29■9:42■11:24-**AC**-5:16■8:7■10:14,28■11:8-**RO**-14:14[2](2839)-**1CO**-7:14-**2CO**-6:17-**EPH**-5:5-**HEB**-9:13(2840)-**RE**-16:13■18:2

<u>**UNCLEANNESS**</u>-<u>all=2932&marked</u>-**LE**-5:3[2]■7:20,21■14:19■15:3[2],25,26,30,31[2]■16:16[2],19■18:19■22:3,5(2930),5-**NU**-5:19■19:13-**DE**-23:10(7137)■24:1(6172)-**2SA**-11:4-**2CH**-29:16-**EZR**-9:11-**EZE**-36:17■39:24-**ZEC**-13:1(5079)■<u>**N.T.**</u>-<u>all=167&marked</u>-**M'T**-23:27-**RO**-1:24■6:19-**2CO**-12:21-**GA**-5:19-**EPH**-4:19■5:3-**COL**-3:5-**1TH**-2:3■4:7-**2PE**-2:10(3394)

<u>**UNCLEANNESSES**</u>-**EZE**-36:29(2932)

<u>**UNCLE'S**</u>-<u>all=1733&marked</u>-**LE**-20:20,20(1730)■25:49-**ES**-2:7-**JER**-32:8,9,12

<u>**UNCLOTHED**</u>-**2CO**-5:4(1562)

<u>**UNCOMELY**</u>-**1CO**-7:36(807)■12:23(809)

<u>**UNCONDEMNED**</u>-**AC**-16:37(178)■22:25(178)

<u>**UNCORRUPTIBLE**</u>-**RO**-1:23(862)

<u>**UNCORRUPTNESS**</u>-**TIT**-2:7(90)

<u>**UNCOVER**</u>-<u>all=1540&marked</u>-**LE**-10:6(6544)■18:6,7[2],8,9,10,11,12,13,14,15[2],16,17[2],18,19■20:18,19■21:10(6544)-**NU**-5:18(6544)-**RU**-3:4-**IS**-47:2[2]-**ZEP**-2:14(6168)

<u>**UNCOVERED**</u>-<u>all=1540&marked</u>-**GE**-9:21-**LE**-20:11,17,18,20,21-**RU**-3:7-**2SA**-6:20-**IS**-20:4(2834)■22:6(6168)■47:3-**JER**-49:10-**EZE**-4:7(2834)■<u>**N.T.**</u>-**M'R**-2:4(648)-**1CO**-11:5(177),13(177)

<u>**UNCOVERETH**</u>-**LE**-20:19(6168)-**DE**-27:20(1540)-**2SA**-6:20(1540)

<u>**UNCTION**</u>-**1JO**-2:20(5545)

<u>**UNDEFILED**</u>-**PS**-119:1(8549)-**SONG**-5:2(8535)■6:9(8535)■<u>**N.T.**</u>-<u>all=283</u>-**HEB**-7:26■13:4-**JAS**-1:27-**1PE**-1:4

<u>**UNDER**</u>-<u>all=8478&marked</u>-**GE**-1:7,9■6:17■7:19■16:9■18:4,8■21:15■24:2,9■35:4,8■41:35■47:29■49:25-**EX**-6:6,7■17:12,14■18:10■20:4■21:20■23:5■24:4,10■25:25,35[3]■26:19[3],21[2],25[2],33■27:5■30:4■36:24[3],26[2],30■37:21[3],27■38:4-**LE**-15:10■22:27■27:32-**NU**-6:18■16:31■22:27-**DE**-2:25■3:17■4:11,19,49■7:24■9:14■12:2■25:19■28:23■29:20-**JOS**-7:21,22■11:3,17■12:3■13:5■24:26-**J'G**-1:7■3:16,30■4:5■6:11,19-**RU**-2:12-**1SA**-7:11■14:2■21:3,4,8■22:6■31:13-**2SA**-2:23(413)■4:6(413)■18:9[2]■22:10,37,39,40,48-**1KI**-4:25■5:3■7:24,30,32,44■8:6■13:14■14:23■19:4,5-**2KI**-8:20,22■9:13■13:5■14:27■16:4,17■17:7,10-**1CH**-10:12■17:1■25:2(5921),3(5921),6(5921)■26:28(5921)■27:23(4295)-**2CH**-4:3,15■5:7■21:8,10[2]■26:11(5921),13(5921)■28:4-**NE**-2:14-**JOB**-9:13■20:12■26:5,8(5921)■28:5,24■30:7■37:3■40:21■41:11,30-**PS**-8:6■10:7■18:9,36,38,39,47■45:5■47:3[2]■91:4■106:42■140:3■144:2-**PR**-22:27-**EC**-1:3,9,13,14■2:3,11,17,18,19,20,22■3:1,16■4:1,3,7,15■5:13,18■6:1,12■7:6■8:9,15[2],17■9:3,6,9[2],11,13■10:5-**SONG**-2:6■4:11■8:3,5-**IS**-3:6■10:4[2],16■14:11■24:5■25:10■57:5[2]-**JER**-2:20■3:6(413,8478),13■10:11(8460)■33:13(5921)■38:11(413,8478),12■52:20-**LA**-3:34,66■5:5(5921)-**EZE**-1:8,23■6:13[2]■10:2,8,20,21■17:6,23■20:37■24:5■31:6,6sup■32:27■42:9■46:23■47:1[2]-**DA**-4:12(8460),14,21(8460)■7:27(8460)■9:12-**HO**-4:12,13-**JOE**-1:17-**AM**-2:13-**OB**-7-**JON**-4:5-**MIC**-1:4■4:4-**ZEC**-3:10-**MAL**-4:3■<u>**N.T.**</u>-<u>all=5259&marked</u>-**M'T**-2:16(2736)■5:13(2662),15■7:6(1722)■8:8,9[2]■23:37-**M'R**-4:21,32■6:11(5270)■7:28(5270)-**LU**-7:6,8[2],■8:16(5270)■11:33■13:34■17:24[2]-**JOH**-1:48,50(5278)-**AC**-2:5■4:12■23:12(332),14(332)■27:4(5248),7(5248),16(5295)-**RO**-3:9,13,19(1722)■6:14,15■7:14■16:20-**1CO**-6:12■9:20[2],21(1772),27(5299)■10:1■14:34(5293)■15:25,27[2],27(5293),28(5293)-**GA**-3:10,22,23,25■4:2,3,4,5,21■5:18-**EPH**-1:22-**PH'P**-2:10(2709)-**COL**-1:23-**1TI**-5:9(1640)■6:1-**HEB**-2:8(5270),8sup,8(506),8(5293)■7:11(1909)■9:15(1909)■10:28(1909),29(2662)-**JAS**-2:3-**1PE**-5:6-**JUDE**-6-**RE**-5:3(5270),13(5270)■6:9(5270)■12:1(5270)

<u>**UNDERGIRDING**</u>-**AC**-27:17(5269)

<u>**UNDERNEATH**</u>-**EX**-28:27(4295)■39:20(4295)-**DE**-33:27(8478)

<u>**UNDERSETTERS**</u>-<u>all=3802</u>-**1KI**-7:30[2],34[2],

<u>**UNDERSTAND**</u>-<u>all=995&marked</u>-**GE**-11:7(8085)■41:15(8085)-**NU**-16:30(3045)-**DE**-9:3(3045),6(3045)■28:49(8085)-**2KI**-18:26(8085)-**1CH**-28:19(7919)-**NE**-8:3,7,8,13(7919)-**JOB**-6:24■23:5■26:14■32:9■36:29-**PS**-14:2(7919)■19:12■53:2(7919)■82:5■92:6■94:8■107:43■119:27,100-**PR**-1:6■2:5,9■8:5■14:8■19:25■20:24■28:5[2]■29:19-**IS**-6:9,10■28:9,19■32:4■33:19(998)■36:11(8085)■41:20(7919)■43:10■44:18(7919)■56:11-**JER**-9:12-**EZE**-3:6(8085)-**DA**-8:16,17■9:13(7919),23,25(7919)■10:11,12,14■11:33(7919)■12:10[2]-**HO**-4:14■14:9-**MIC**-4:12■<u>**N.T.**</u>-<u>all=4920&marked</u>-**M'T**-13:13,14,15■15:10,17(3539)■16:9(3539),11(3539)■24:15(3539)-**M'R**-4:12■7:14■8:17,21■13:14(3539)■14:68(1987)-**LU**-8:10■24:45

-JOH-8:43(1097)■12:40(3539)-AC-24:11(1097)■28:26,27-RO-15:21-1CO-12:3(1107)■13:2(1492)-EPH-3:4(3539)-PH'P-1:12(1097)-HEB-11:3(3539)-2PE-2:12(50)

UNDERSTANDEST-JOB-15:9(995)-PS-139:2(995)-JER-5:15(8085)■N.T.-AC-8:30(1097)

UNDERSTANDETH-all=995&marked-1CH-28:9-JOB-28:23-PS-49:20-PR-8:9■14:6-JER-9:24(7919)■N.T.-all=4920&marked-M'T-13:19,23-RO-3:11-1CO-14:2(191),16(1492)

UNDERSTANDING-all=8394,a=995,b=998&marked-EX-31:3■35:31■36:1-DE-1:13a■4:6b,6a■32:28-1SA-25:3(7922)-1KI-3:9(8085),11a,12a■4:29■7:14-1CH-12:32b■22:12b-2CH-2:12b,13b■26:5a-EZR-8:16a,18(7922)-NE-8:2a■10:28a-JOB-12:3(3824),12,13,20(2940)■17:4(7922)■20:3b■26:12■28:12b,20b,28b■32:8a■34:10(3824),16b,34(3824)■38:4b,36b■39:17b-PS-32:9a■47:7(7919)■49:3■111:10(7922)■119:34a,73a,99(7919),104a,125a,130a,144a,169a■147:5-PR-1:2b,5a■2:2,3,6,11■3:4(7922),5b,13,19■4:1b,5b,7b■5:1■6:32(3820)■7:4b,7(3820)■8:1,5a,14b■9:4(3820),6b,10b,16(3820)■10:13a,13(3820),23■11:12■12:11(3820)■13:15(7922)■14:29,33a■15:14a,21,32(3820)■16:16b,22(7922)■17:18(3820),24a,27,28a■18:2■19:8,25a■20:5■21:16(7919),30■23:23b■24:3,30(3820)■28:2a,11a,16■30:2b-EC-9:11a-IS-11:2b,3(7306)■27:11b■29:14b,16a,24b■40:14,28■44:19-JER-3:15(7919)■4:22a■5:21(3820)■51:15-EZE-28:4-DA-1:4a,17a,20b■2:21(999)■4:34(4486)■5:11(7924),12(7924),14(7924)■8:23a■9:22b■10:1b■11:35(7919)-HO-13:2-OB-7,8■N.T.-all=3563&marked-M'T-15:16(801)-M'R-7:18(801)■12:33(4907)-LU-1:3(3877)■2:47(4907)■24:45-RO-1:31(801)-1CO-1:19(4907)■14:14,15^2,19,20^2(5424)-EPH-1:18(1271)■4:18(1271)■5:17(4920)-PH'P-4:7-COL-1:9(4907)■2:2(4907)-1TI-1:7(4920)-2TI-2:7(4907)-1JO-5:20(1271)-RE-13:18

UNDERSTOOD-all=995&marked-GE-42:23(8085)-DE-32:29(7919)-1SA-4:6(3045)■26:4(3045)-2SA-3:37(3045)-NE-8:12■13:7-JOB-13:1■42:3-PS-73:17■81:5(3045)■106:7(7919)-IS-40:21■44:18-DA-8:27■9:2■10:1■12:8■N.T.-all=4920&marked-M'T-13:51■16:12■17:13■26:10(1097)-M'R-9:32(50)-LU-2:50■9:45(50)■18:34-JOH-8:27(1097)■10:6(1097)■12:16(1097)-AC-7:25^2■23:27(3129),34(4441)-RO-1:20(3539)-1CO-13:11(5426)■14:9(2154)-2PE-3:16(1425)

UNDERTAKE-IS-38:14(6148)

UNDERTOOK-ES-9:23(6901)

UNDO-IS-58:6(5425)-ZEP-3:19(6213)

UNDONE-NU-21:29(6)-JOS-11:15(5493)-IS-6:5(1820)

UNDRESSED-LE-25:5(5139),11(5139)

UNEQUAL-EZE-18:25(3808,8505),29(3808,8505)

UNEQUALLY-2CO-6:14(2086)

UNFAITHFUL-PR-25:19(898)

UNFAITHFULLY-PS-78:57(898)

UNFEIGNED-all=505-2CO-6:6-1TI-1:5-2TI-1:5-1PE-1:22

UNFRUITFUL-all=175-M'T-13:22-M'R-4:19-1CO-14:14-EPH-5:11-TIT-3:14-2PE-1:8

UNGIRDED-GE-24:32(6605)

UNGODLINESS-all=763-RO-1:18■11:26-2TI-2:16-TIT-2:12

UNGODLY-all=7563&marked-2SA-22:5(1100)-2CH-19:2-JOB-16:11(5760)■34:18-PS-1:1,4,5,6■3:7■18:4(1100)■43:1(3808,2623)■73:12-PR-16:27(1100)■19:28(1100)■N.T.-all=765&marked-RO-4:5■5:6-1TI-1:9-1PE-4:18-2PE-2:5,6(764)■3:7-JUDE-4,15^2(763),15(764),15,18(763)

UNHOLY-LE-10:10(2455)■N.T.-1TI-1:9(462)-2TI-3:2(462)-HEB-10:29(2839)

UNICORN-all=7214-NU-23:22■24:8-JOB-39:9,10-PS-29:6■92:10

UNICORNS-all=7214-DE-33:17-PS-22:21-IS-34:7

UNITE-PS-86:11(3161)

UNITED-GE-49:6(3161)

UNITY-PS-133:1(3162)■N.T.-EPH-4:3(1775),13(1775)

UNJUST-PS-43:1(5766)-PR-11:7(205)■28:8(8636)■29:27(5766)-ZEP-3:5(5767)■N.T.-all=94&marked-M'T-5:45-LU-16:8(93),10■18:6(93),11-AC-24:15-1CO-6:1-1PE-3:18-2PE-2:9-RE-22:11(91)

UNJUSTLY-PS-82:2(5766)-IS-26:10(5765)

UNKNOWN-AC-17:23(57)-2CO-6:9(50)-GAL-1:22(50)

UNLADE-AC-21:3(670)

UNLAWFUL-AC-10:28(111)-2PE-2:8(459)

UNLEARNED-all=2399&marked-AC-4:13(62)-1CO-14:16,23,24-2TI-2:23(521)-2PE-3:16(261)

UNLEAVENED-all=4682-GE-19:3-EX-12:8,15,17,18,20,39■13:6,7■23:15^2■29:2^2,23■34:18^2-LE-2:4^2,5■6:16■7:12^2■8:2,26^2■23:6^2-NU-6:15,17,19^2■9:11■28:17-DE-16:3,8,16-JOS-5:11-J'G-6:19,20,21^2-1SA-28:24-2KI-23:9-1CH-23:29-2CH-8:13■30:13,21■35:17-EZR-6:22-EZE-45:21■N.T.-all=106-M'T-26:17-M'R-14:1,12-LU-22:1,7-AC-12:3■20:6-1CO-5:7,8

UNLESS-all=3884&marked-LE-22:6(3588,518)-NU-22:33(194)-2SA-2:27(3588,3884)-PS-27:13■94:17■119:92-PR-4:16(518,3808)■N.T.-1CO-15:2(1622,1508)

UNLOOSE-all=3089-M'R-1:7-LU-3:16-JOH-1:27

UNMARRIED-all=22-1CO-7:8,11,32,34

UNMERCIFUL-RO-1:31(415)

UNMINDFUL-DE-32:18(7876)

UNMOVEABLE-AC-27:41(761)-1CO-15:58(277)

UNOCCUPIED-J'G-5:6(2308)

UNPERFECT-supplied

UNPREPARED-2CO-9:4(532)

UNPROFITABLE-JOB-15:3(5532)■N.T.-M'T-25:30(888)-LU-17:10(888)-RO-3:12(889)-TIT-3:9(512)-PH'M-11(890-)HEB-13:17(255)

UNPROFITABLENESS-HEB-7:18(512)

UNPUNISHED-all=5352-PR-11:21■16:5■17:5■19:5,9-JER-25:29^2■30:11■46:28■49:12^2

UNQUENCHABLE-M'T-3:12(762)-LU-3:17(762)

UNREASONABLE-AC-25:27(249)-2TH-3:2(824)

UNREBUKEABLE-1TI-6:14(423)

UNREPROVEABLE-COL-1:22(410)

UNRIGHTEOUS-EX-23:1(2555)-JOB-27:7(5767)-PS-71:4(5765)-IS-10:1(205)■55:7(205)■N.T.-all=94-LU-16:11-RO-3:5-1CO-6:9-HEB-6:10

UNRIGHTEOUSNESS-all=5766&marked-LE-19:15,35-PS-92:15-JER-22:13(3808,6664)■N.T.-all=93&marked-LU-16:9-JOH-7:18-RO-1:18^2,29■2:8■3:5■6:13■9:14-2CO-6:14(458)-2TH-2:10,12-HEB-8:12-2PE-2:13,15-1JO-1:9■5:17

UNRIGHTEOUSLY-DE-25:16(5766)

UNRIPE-JOB-15:33(1154)

UNRULY-1TH-5:14(813)-TIT-1:6(506),10(506)-JAS-3:8(183)

UNSATIABLE-EZE-16:28(1115,7654)

UNSAVOURY-2SA-22:27(6617)-JOB-6:6(8602)

UNSEARCHABLE-all=369,2714-JOB-5:9-PS-145:3-PR-25:3■N.T.-RO-11:3(419)-EPH-3:8(421)

UNSEEMLY-RO-1:27(808)

UNSHOD-JER-2:25(3182)

UNSKILFUL-HEB-5:13(552)

UNSPEAKABLE-2CO-9:15(411)■12:4(731)-2PE-1:8(412)

UNSPOTTED-JAS-1:27(784)

UNSTABLE-GE-49:4(6349)■N.T.-JAS-1:8(182)-2PE-2:14(798)■3:16(798)

UNSTOPPED-IS-35:5(6605)

UNTAKEN-2CO-3:14(3361,348)

UNTEMPERED-all=8602-EZE-13:10,11,14,15■22:28

UNTHANKFUL-LU-6:35(884)-2TI-3:2(884)

UNTIL-all=5704&marked-GE-8:5,7■24:19(5704,515),33(5704,515)■26:13■27:44(5704,834),45■28:15(5704,834)■29:8■32:4,24■33:3,14■34:5■39:16■41:49■46:34■49:10(5704,3588)-EX-9:18■10:26■12:6,10^2,15,18,22■16:20,23,35^2■17:12■23:18,30■24:14■33:8■34:34,35-LE-7:15■8:33■11:24,25,27,28,31,32,39,40^2■12:4■14:46■15:5,6,7,10^2,16,17,18,19,21,22,23,27■16:17■17:15■19:6,13■22:4,6,30■23:14■25:22^2,28-NU-4:3,23■6:5■9:15■11:20■14:19,33■19:7,8,10,21,22■20:17■21:22,35■23:24■24:22■32:13,17,18,21■35:12,28,32-DE-1:31■2:14^2,15,29■3:3,20■7:20,23,24■9:7,21■11:5■20:20■22:2■28:20^2,21,22,24,48,51^2,52,61■31:24,30-JOS-1:15■2:16,22■3:17■4:10,23^2■5:1■6:10■7:6,13■8:24,26,29■10:13,26,27,33■11:8,14■13:13■20:6^2,9■22:17■23:13,15-J'G-4:24■5:7■6:18■13:15■18:30■19:8,25■20:23,26-RU-1:19■2:7,17,21(5704,518)■3:3,13,14,18(5704,834),18(3588,518)-1SA-1:22,23^2■3:15■7:11■9:13■11:11■14:9,24,36■15:18,35■17:52■19:2,23■20:41■25:36■30:4(5704,834)-2SA-1:12■4:3■5:25■10:5■15:24,28■17:13(5704,834)■19:7,24■21:10■22:38■23:10(5704,3588)-1KI-3:1,2■5:3■6:22■10:7■11:16,40■15:29■17:14■18:26,29■22:11,27-2KI-6:25■7:3■8:6,11■10:8,11■17:20,23■18:32■24:20-1CH-5:22■6:32■12:22■19:5■28:20-2CH-8:8,16■9:6■16:12■18:10,26,34■21:15■24:10■29:28,34■31:1■35:14■36:16,20,21-EZR-4:5,21■5:16■8:29■9:4■10:14-NE-7:3■8:3■12:23-JOB-14:13■26:10-PS-57:1■71:18■73:17■94:13■104:23■105:19■110:1■112:8■123:2■132:5-PR-7:18-SONG-2:17■3:11■4:6■8:4-IS-6:11■26:20■32:15■36:17■39:6■62:1-JER-23:20■27:7,8,22■30:24^2■32:5■36:23■37:21■38:28■44:27■52:34-EZE-21:27■33:22■46:2-DA-4:32■7:22,25■9:27-HO-7:4-MIC-5:3■7:9■N.T.-all=2193,a=891&marked-M'T1:17■2:13,15■11:12,13,23(3360)■13:30(3360)■17:9■18:22^2■24:38a,39■26:29■27:64■28:15(3360)-M'R-14:25■15:33-LU-1:20a■13:35■15:4■16:16■17:27a■21:24a■22:16,18■23:44■24:49-JOH-2:10■9:18-AC-1:2a■2:35■3:21a■10:30(3360)■13:20■20:7(3360)■21:26■23:1a,14-RO-5:13a■8:22a■11:25a-1CO-4:5■16:8-2CO-3:14a-GA-44:2a,19a-EPH-1:14(1519)-PH'P-1:5a,6a-2TH-2:7-1TI-6:14(3360)-HEB-1:13■9:10(3360)-JAS-5:7-2PE-1:19-1JO-2:9-RE-6:11■17:17a■20:5

UNTIMELY-all=5309-JOB-3:16-PS-58:8-EC-6:3■N.T.-RE-6:13(3653)

UNTOWARD-AC-2:40(4646)

UNWALLED-DE-3:5(6521)-ES-9:19(6519)

UNWASHEN-all=449-M'T-15:20-M'R-7:2,5

UNWEIGHED-supplied

UNWISE-DE-32:6(3808,2450)-HO-13:13(3808,2450)■N.T.-RO-1:14(453)-EPH-5:17(878)

UNWITTINGLY-LE-22:14(7684)-JOS-20:3(1097,1847),5(1097,1847)

UNWORTHILY-1CO-11:27(371),29(371)

UNWORTHY-AC-13:46(3756,514)-1CO-6:2(370)

UPBRAID-J’G-8:15(2778)▪N.T.-M’T-11:20(3679)

UPBRAIDED-M’R-16:14(3679)

UPBRAIDETH-JAS-1:5(3679)

UPHARSIN-DA-5:25(6237)

UPHELD-IS-63:5(5564)

UPHOLD-all=5564&marked-PS-51:12▪54:4▪119:116-PR-29:23(8551)-IS-41:10(8551)▪42:1(8551)▪63:5-EZE-30:6

UPHOLDEN-JOB-4:4(6965)-PR-20:28(5582)

UPHOLDEST-PS-41:12(8551)

UPHOLDETH-all=5564&marked-PS-37:17,24▪63:8(8551)▪145:14

UPHOLDING-HEB-1:3(5342)

UPPER-all=5945&marked-EX-12:7(5947)-LE-13:45(8222)-DE-24:6(7393)-JOS-15:19(5942)▪16:5-J’G-1:15(5942)-2KI-1:2(5944)▪18:17▪23:12(5944)-1CH-7:24▪28:11(5944)-2CH-3:9(5944)▪8:5▪32:30-IS-7:3▪36:2-EZE-42:5-ZEP-2:14(3730)▪N.T.-all=5253&marked-M’R-14:15(508)-LU-22:12(508)-AC-1:13▪9:37,39▪19:1(510)▪20:8(5250)

UPPERMOST-GE-40:17(5945)▪N.T.-M’T-23:6(4411)-M’R-12:39(4411)-LU-11:43(4410)

UPRIGHT-all=3477&marked-LE-26:13(6968)-1SA-29:6-2SA-22:24(8549),26(8549),26(8552)-2CH-29:34-JOB-1:1,8▪2:3▪8:6▪12:4(8549)▪17:8-PS-7:10▪11:2,7▪18:23(8549),25(8549),25(8549,8552)▪19:13(8552)▪25:8▪32:11▪33:1▪36:10▪37:14,18(8549),37▪49:14▪64:10▪92:15▪94:15▪97:11▪111:1▪112:2,4▪119:137▪125:4▪140:13-PR-2:21▪10:29(8537)▪11:3,6,11,20(8549)▪12:6▪13:6(8537)▪14:11▪15:8▪16:17▪21:18,29▪28:10(8549)▪29:10(8535),27-EC-7:29▪12:10(3476)-SONG-1:4(4339)-IS-26:7-JER-10:5(4749)-DA-8:18(5977)▪10:11(5977)▪11:17-MIC-7:2,4-HAB-2:4(3474)▪N.T.-AC-14:10(3717)

UPRIGHTLY-all=8549&marked-PS-15:2▪58:1(4339)▪75:2(4339)▪84:11-PR-2:7(8537)▪10:9(8537)▪15:21(3474)▪28:18-IS-33:15(4339)-AM-5:10-MIC-2:7(3477)▪N.T.-GA-2:14(3716)

UPRIGHTNESS-all=3476&marked-DE-9:5-1KI-3:6(3483)▪9:4-1CH-29:17,17(4339)-JOB-4:6(8537)▪33:3,23-PS-9:8(4339)▪25:21▪111:8(3477)▪119:7▪143:10(4334)-PR-2:13▪14:2▪28:6(8537)-IS-26:7(4339),10(5229)▪57:2(5228)

UPRISING-PS-139:2(6965)

UPROAR-1KI-1:41(1993)▪N.T.-all=2351&marked-M’T-26:5-M’R-14:2-AC-17:5(2350)▪19:40(4714)▪20:1▪21:31(4797),38(387)

UPSIDE-2KI-21:13(5921,6440)-IS-24:1(5921,6440)▪N.T.-AC-17:6(389)

UPWARD-all=4605&marked-GE-7:20-EX-38:26-NU-1:3,18,20,22,24,26,28,30,32,34,36,38,40,42,45▪3:15,22,28,34,39,40,43▪4:3,23,30,35,39,43,47▪8:24▪14:29▪26:2,4,62▪32:11-J’G-1:36-1SA-9:2▪10:23-2KI-3:21▪19:30-1CH-23:3,24-2CH-31:16,17-EZR-3:8-JOB-5:7(1361)-EC-3:21-IS-8:21▪37:31▪38:14(4791)-EZE-1:11,27▪8:2▪41:7^{3}▪43:15-HAG-2:15,18

URGE-LU-11:53(1758)

URGED-all=6484&marked-GE-33:11-J’G-16:16(509)▪19:7-2KI-2:17▪5:16,23(6555)

URGENT-EX-12:33(2388)-DA-3:22(2685)

URIM-all=224&marked-EX-28:30-LE-8:8-NU-27:21-DE-33:8-1SA-28:6-EZR-2:63-NE-7:65

USE-all=4911&marked-LE-7:24(4399)▪19:26(5172)-1CH-12:2(3231)▪28:15(5656)-JER-23:31(3947)▪31:23(559)-EZE-12:23(4912)-EZE-12:23(4912)▪16:44▪18:2,3▪21:21(7080)▪N.T.-all=5530&marked-M’T-5:44(1908)-LU-6:28(1908)-AC-14:5(5195)-RO-1:26(5540),27(5540)-1CO-7:21,31-2CO-1:17▪3:12▪13:10-EPH-4:29(5532)-1TI-1:8▪5:23-HEB-5:14(1838)-1PE-4:9(5382)

USED-all=&marked-LE-7:24(6213)-JER-2:24(3928)-EZE-35:11(6213)▪N.T.-all=5530&marked-M’R-2:18(1510)-AC-8:9(3096)▪19:19(4238)▪27:17-RO-3:13(1387)-1CO-9:12,15-1TH-2:5(1096,1722)-1TI-3:13(1247)-HEB-10:33(390)

USES-TIT-3:14(5532)

USEST-PS-119:132(4941)

USETH-PR-18:23(1696)▪N.T.-HEB-5:13(3348)

USING-COL-2:22(671)-1PE-2:16(2192)

USURER-EX-22:25(5383)

USURP-1TI-2:12(831)

USURY-all=5392&marked-EX-22:25-LE-25:36,37-DE-23:19(5391),19^{2},19(5391)20^{2}(5391)-NE-5:7(5383),10(5383)-PS-15:5-PR-28:8-IS-24:2(5383),2(5378)-JER-15:10^{2}(5383)-EZE-8:8,13,17▪22:12▪N.T.-M’T-25:27(5110)-LU-19:23(5110)

US-WARD-PS-40:5(413)▪N.T.-EPH-1:19(1519,2248)-2PE-3:9(1519,2248)

UTMOST-all=7097&marked-NU-22:36,41▪23:13-DE-34:2(314)-JER-9:26(7112)▪25:23(7112)▪49:32(7112)▪50:26(7093)-JOE-2:20(314)▪N.T.-LU-11:31(4009)

UTTER-all=2435&marked-LE-5:1(5046)-JOS-2:14(5046),20(5046)-J’G-5:12(1696)-JOB-8:10(3318)▪15:2(6030)▪27:4(1897)▪33:3(4448)-PS-78:2(5042)▪94:4(5042)▪106:2(4448)▪119:171(5042)▪145:7(5042)-PR-14:5(6315)▪23:33(1696)-EC-1:8(1696)▪5:2(3318)-IS-32:6(1696)▪48:20(3318)-JER-1:16(1696)▪25:30(5414)-EZE-24:3(4911)▪40:31,37▪42:1,3,7,8,9,14▪44:19^{2}▪46:20,21▪47:2(2531)-JOE-2:11(5414)▪3:16(5414)-AM-1:2(5414)-NA-1:8(3617),9(3617)▪N.T.-M’T-13:35(2044)-1CO-14:9(1325)-2CO-12:4(2980)

UTTERANCE-all=3056&marked-AC-2:4(669)-1CO-1:5-2CO-8:7-EPH-6:19-COL-4:3

UTTERED-all=5414&marked-NU-30:6(4008),8(4008)-J’G-11:11(1696)-2SA-22:14-NE-6:19(3318)-JOB-26:4(5046)▪42:3(5046)-PS-46:6▪66:14(4475)-JER-48:34▪51:55-HAB-3:10▪N.T.-RO-8:26(215)-HEB-5:11(3004)-RE-10:3(2980),4^{2}(2980)

UTTERETH-all=5414&marked-JOB-15:5(502)-PS-19:2(5042)-PR-1:20,21(559)▪10:18(3318)▪29:11(3318)-JER-10:13▪51:16-MIC-7:3(1696)

UTTERING-IS-59:13(1897)

UTTERLY-LE-26:44(3615)-PS-119:8(3966),43(3966)-IS-2:18(3632)-MIC-2:4(7703)-NA-1:15(3605)▪N.T.-1CO-6:7(3654)-2PE-2:12(2704)-RE-18:8(2618)

UTTERMOST-all=7097&marked-EX-26:4(7020)▪36:11(7020),17(7020)-NU-11:1▪20:16-DE-11:24(314)-JOS-15:1,5,21-1SA-14:2-1KI-6:24^{2}(7098)-2KI-7:5,8-NE-1:9-PS-2:8(657)▪65:8(7098)▪139:9(319)-IS-7:18▪24:16(3671)▪N.T.-M’T-5:26(2078)▪12:42(4009)-M’R-13:27^{2}(206)-AC-1:8(2078)▪24:22(1231)-1TH-2:16(5056)-HEB-7:25(3838)

V

VAU-supplied

VAGABOND-GE-4:12(5110),14(5110)▪N.T.-AC-19:13(4022)

VAGABONDS-PS-109:10(5128)

VAIL-all=6532&marked-GE-24:65(6809)▪38:14(6809),19(6809)-EX-26:31,33^{3},35▪27:21▪30:6▪34:33(4533),34(4533),35(4533)▪35:12▪36:35▪38:27▪39:34▪40:3,21,22,26-LE-4:6,17▪16:2,12,15▪21:23▪24:3-NU-4:5▪18:7-RU-3:15(4304)-2CH-3:14-IS-25:7(4541)▪N.T.-all=2571-2CO-3:13,14,15,16

VAILS-IS-3:23(7289)

VAIN-all=7723&marked-EX-5:9(8267)▪20:7^{2}-LE-26:16(7385),20(7385)-DE-5:11^{2}▪32:47(7386)-J’G-9:4(7386)▪11:3(7386)-1SA-12:21^{2}(8414)▪25:21(8267)-2SA-6:20(7386)-2KI-17:15(1891)▪18:20(8193)-2CH-13:7(7386)-JOB-9:29(1892)▪11:11,12(5014)▪15:2(7307)▪16:3(7307)▪21:34(1892)▪27:12(1891)▪35:16(1892)▪39:16(7385)▪41:9(3576)-PS-2:1(7385)▪26:4▪33:17(8267)▪39:6sup,6(1892)▪60:11▪62:10(1891)▪73:13(7385)▪89:47▪108:12▪127:1^{2},2▪139:20-PR-1:17(2600)▪12:11(7386)▪28:19(386)▪31:30(1892)-EC-6:12(1892)-IS-1:13▪30:7(1892)▪36:5(8193)▪45:18(8414),19(8414)▪49:4(7385),4(1892)▪65:23(7385)-JER-2:5(1891),30▪3:23(8267)▪4:14(205),30▪6:29▪8:8^{2}(8267)▪10:3(1892)▪23:16(1891)▪46:11▪50:9(7387)▪51:58(7385)-LA-2:14▪4:17(1892)-EZE-6:10(2600)▪12:24▪13:7-ZEC-10:2(1892)-MAL-3:14▪N.T.-all=2756&marked-M’T-15:9(3155)-M’R-7:7(3155)-AC-4:25-RO-1:21(3154)▪13:4(1500)-1CO-3:20(3152)▪15:2(1500),10,14^{2},17(3152),58-2CO-6:1▪9:3(2761)-GA-2:2,21(1432)▪3:4(1500)▪4:11(1500)▪5:26(2755)-EPH-5:6-PH’P-2:16-COL-2:8-1TH-2:1▪3:5-1TI-1:6(3150)▪6:20(2757)-2TI-2:16(5757)-TIT-1:10(3151)▪3:9(3152)-JAS-1:26(3152)▪2:20▪4:5(2761)-1PE-1:18(3152)

VAINGLORY-PH’P-2:3(2754)

VAINLY-COL-2:18(1500)

VALE-all=8219&marked-GE-14:3(6010),8(6010),10(6010)▪37:14(6010)-DE-1:7-JOS-10:40-1KI-10:27-2CH-1:15-JER-33:13

VALIANT-all=2428&marked-1SA-14:52▪16:18▪18:17(1121,2428)▪31:12-2SA-2:7(1121,2428)▪11:16▪13:28(1121,2428)▪17:10^{2}(1121,2428)▪23:20▪24:9-1KI-1:42-1CH-5:18▪7:2(1368),5(1368)▪10:12▪11:22,26(1368)▪28:1-2CH-13:3(1368)▪26:17▪28:6-NE-11:6-SONG-3:7^{2}(1368)-IS-10:13(3524)▪33:7(691)-JER-9:3(1396)▪46:15(47)-NA-2:3▪N.T.-HEB-11:34(2478)

VALIANTEST-J’G-21:10(1121,2428)

VALIANTLY-all=2428&marked-NU-24:18-1CH-19:13(2388)-PS-60:12▪108:13▪118:15,16

VALLEY-all=6010,a=1516,b=5158&marked-GE-14:17▪26:17b,19b-NU-14:25▪21:12b,20a▪32:9b-DE-1:24b▪3:16b,29a▪4:46a▪21:4^{2}b,6b▪34:3(1237),6a-JOS-7:24,26▪8:11a,13▪10:12▪11:2(8219),8(1237),16^{2}(8219),17(1237)▪12:7(1237)▪13:19,27▪15:7,8^{2}a,8,33(8219)▪17:16^{2}▪18:16^{2}a,16,21▪19:14a,27a-J’G-1:9(8219),19,34▪5:15▪6:33▪7:1,8,12▪16:4b▪18:28-1SA-6:13▪13:18a▪15:5b▪17:2,3a,19,52a▪21:9▪31:7-2SA-5:18,22▪8:13a▪23:13-2KI-2:16a▪3:16b,17b▪14:7a▪23:10a-1CH-4:14a,39a▪10:7▪11:15▪14:9,13▪18:12a-2CH-14:10a▪20:26^{2}▪25:11a▪26:9a▪28:3a▪33:6a,14b▪35:22(1237)-NE-2:13a,15a▪3:13a▪11:30a,35a-JOB-21:33b▪39:21-PS-23:4a▪60:ta,6▪84:6▪108:7-PR-30:17b-SONG-6:11b-IS-17:5▪22:1a,5a▪28:4a,21▪40:4a▪63:14(1237)▪65:10-JER-2:23a▪7:31a,32^{2}a▪19:2a,6^{2}a▪21:13▪31:40▪32:35a,44(8219)▪47:5▪48:8▪49:4-EZE-37:1(1237),2(1237)▪39:11^{2}a,15a-HO-1:5▪2:15-JOE-3:2,12,14^{2},18b-MIC-1:6a-ZEC-12:11(1237)▪14:4a,5^{2}a▪N.T.-LU-3:5(5327)

VALLEYS-all=6010&marked-NU-24:6(5158)-DE-8:7(1237)▪11:11(1237)-JOS-9:1(8219)▪12:8(8219)-1KI-20:28-1CH-12:15▪27:29-JOB-30:6(5158)▪39:10-PS-65:13▪104:8(1237),10(5158)-SONG-2:1-IS-7:19(5158)▪22:7▪28:1(1516)▪41:18(1237)▪57:5(5158)-JER-49:4-EZE-6:3(1516)▪7:16(1516)▪31:12(1516)▪32:5(1516)▪35:8(1516)▪36:4

(1516),6(1516)-**MIC**-1:4

VALOUR-all=2428-**JOS**-1:14■6:2■8:3■10:7-**J'G**-3:29■6:12■11:1■18:2■20:44,46-**1KI**-11:28-**2KI**-5:1■24:14-**1CH**-5:24■7:7,9,11,40■8:40■12:21,25,28,30■26:6,30,31,32-**2CH**-13:3■14:8■17:13,14,16,17■25:6■26:12■32:21-**NE**-11:14

VALUE-**LE**-27:8^{2}(6186),12(6186)-**JOB**-13:4(457)■**N.T.**-**M'T**-10:31(1308)■27:9(5091)-**LU**-12:7(1308)

VALUED-**JOB**-28:16(5541),19(5541)■**N.T.**-**M'T**-27:9(5091)

VALUEST-**LE**-27:12(6187)

VANISH-**JOB**-6:17(6789)-**IS**-51:6(4414)■**N.T.**-**1CO**-13:8(2673)-**HEB**-8:13(854)

VANISHED-**JER**-49:7(5628)■**N.T.**-**LU**-24:31(1096,855)

VANISHETH-**JOB**-7:9(3212)■**N.T.**-**JAS**-4:14(858)

VANITIES-all=1892-**DE**-32:21-**1KI**-16:13,26-**PS**-31:6-**EC**-1:2^{2}■5:7■12:8-**JER**-8:19■10:8■14:22-**JON**-2:8■**N.T.**-**AC**-14:15(3152)

VANITY-all=1892,a=7723&marked-**2KI**-17:15-**JOB**-7:3a,16■15:31^{2}a,35(205)■31:5a■35:13a-**PS**-4:2(7385)■10:7(205)■12:2a■24:4a■39:5,11■41:6a■62:9^{2}■78:33■94:11■119:37a■144:4,8a,11a-**PR**-13:11■21:6■22:8(205)■30:8a-**EC**-1:2^{3},14■2:1,11,15,17,19,21,23,26■3:19■4:4,7,8,16■5:10■6:2,4,9,11■7:6,15■8:10,14^{2}■9:9^{2}■11:8,10■12:8^{2}-**IS**-5:18a■30:28a■40:17(8414),23(8414)■41:29(205)■44:9(8414)■57:13■58:9(205)■59:4(8414)-**JER**-2:5■10:15■16:19■18:15a■51:18-**EZE**-13:6a,8a,9a,23a■21:29a■22:28a-**HO**-12:11a-**HAB**-2:13(7385)-**ZEC**-10:2(205)■**N.T.**-all=3152-**RO**-8:20-**EPH**-4:17-**2PE**-2:18

VAPOUR-**JOB**-36:27(108),33(5927)■**N.T.**-**AC**-2:19(822)-**JAS**-4:14(822)

VAPOURS-all=5387&marked-**PS**-135:7■148:8(7008)-**JER**-10:13■51:16

VARIABLENESS-**JAS**-1:17(3883)

VARIANCE-**M'T**-10:35(1369)-**GA**-5:20(2054)

VAUNT-**J'G**-7:2(6286)

VAUNTETH-**1CO**-13:4(4068)

VEHEMENT-**SONG**-8:6(3050)-**JON**-4:8(2759)■**N.T.**-**2CO**-7:11(1972)

VEHEMENTLY-**M'R**-14:31(1722,4053)-**LU**-6:48(4366),49(4366)■11:53(1171)■23:10(2159)

VEIL-**SONG**-5:7(7289)■**N.T.**-all=2665-**M'T**-27:51-**M'R**-15:38-**LU**-23:45-**HEB**-6:19■9:3■10:20

VEIN-**JOB**-28:1(4161)

VENGEANCE-all=5360,a=5359&marked-**GE**-4:15(5358)-**DE**-32:35a,41a,43a-**J'G**-11:36-**PS**-58:10a■94:1^{2}■99:8(5358)■149:7-**PR**-6:34a-**IS**-34:8a■35:4a■47:3a■59:17a■61:2a■63:4a-**JER**-11:20■20:12■46:10■50:15,15(5358),28^{2}■51:6,11,36-**LA**-3:60-**EZE**-24:8a■25:12a,14^{2},15a,17^{2}-**MIC**-5:15a-**NA**-1:2(5358)■**N.T.**-all=1557&marked-**LA**-21:22-**AC**-28:4(1349)-**RO**-3:5(3709)■12:19-**2TH**-1:8-**HEB**-10:30-**JUDE**-7(1349)

VENISON-all=6718&marked-**GE**-25:28■27:3(6720),5,7,19,25,31,33

VENOM-**DE**-32:33(7219)

VENOMOUS-all supplied

VENT-**JOB**-32:19(6605)

VENTURE-**1KI**-22:34(8537)-**2CH**-18:33(8537)

VERIFIED-all=539-**GE**-42:20-**1KI**-8:26-**2CH**-6:17

VERILY-all=389&marked-**GE**-42:21(61)-**EX**-31:13-**J'G**-15:2(559)-**1KI**-1:43(61)-**2KI**-4:14(61)-**1CH**-21:24(7069)-**JOB**-19:13-**PS**-37:3(530)■39:5■58:11^{2}■66:19(403)■73:13-**IS**-45:15(403)-**JER**-15:11(518,3808),11■**N.T.**-all=281,a=3303&marked-**M'T**-5:18,26■6:2,5,16■8:10■10:15,23,42■11:11■13:17■16:28■17:20■18:3,13,18■19:23,28■21:21,31■23:36■24:2,34,47■25:12,40,45■26:13,21,34-**M'R**-3:28■6:11■8:12■9:1,12a,41■10:15,29■11:23■12:43■13:30■14:9,18,25,30-**LU**-4:24■11:51(3483)■12:37■13:35■18:17,29■21:32■23:43-**JOH**-1:51■3:3,5,11■5:19,24,25■6:26,32,47,53■8:34,51,58■10:1,7■12:24■13:16,20,21,38■14:12■16:20,23■21:18-**AC**-16:37(1063)■19:4a■22:3a■26:9(3303,3767)-**RO**-2:25a■10:18(3304)■15:27(1063)-**1CO**-5:3a■14:17a-**GA**-3:21(3689)-**1TH**-3:4(2532)-**HEB**-2:16(1222)■3:5a■6:16a■7:5a,18a■9:1a■12:10a-**1PE**-1:20a-**1JO**-2:5(230)

VERITY-**PS**-111:7(571)■**N.T.**-**1TI**-2:7(225)

VERMILION-**JER**-22:14(8350)-**EZE**-23:14(8350)

VERY-all=3966&marked-**GE**-1:31■4:5■12:14■13:2■18:20■21:11■24:16■26:13■27:21(2088),24(2088),33(1419)■34:7■41:19,31,49■47:13■50:9,10-**EX**-1:20■9:3,16(199),18,24■10:14■11:3■12:38■30:36(1854)-**NU**-6:9(6621)■11:33■12:3■13:28■16:15■22:17■32:1-**DE**-9:20,21(3190)■20:15■27:8(3190)■28:43(4605),43(4295),54■30:14-**JOS**-1:7■3:16■8:4■9:9,13,22■10:20,27(6106)■11:4■13:1■22:8^{2}■23:6-**J'G**-3:17■11:33■13:6■18:9-**RU**-1:20-**1SA**-2:17,22■4:10■5:9,11■14:15(430),20,31■18:8,15■19:4■25:2,15,34(199),36(5704,3966)■26:4(3559)-**2SA**-1:26■2:17■3:8■11:2■13:3,21,36■18:17■19:32^{2}■24:10-**1KI**-1:4,6,15■10:2^{2},10■21:26-**2KI**-14:26■17:18■21:16-**1CH**-18:8■21:8,13■23:17(4605)-**2CH**-6:18(552)■7:8■9:1■14:13■16:8,14■24:24■30:13■32:29■33:14-**EZR**-10:1-**NE**-2:2■4:7■5:6■8:17-**ES**-1:12-**JOB**-1:3■2:13■15:10(3453)■32:6(3453)-**PS**-5:9(1942)■46:1■50:3■71:19(5704)■73:13(389)■79:8■92:5■93:5■104:1■119:107(5704,3966),138,140■142:6■147:15(5704)-**PR**-27:15(5464)-**IS**-1:9(4592)■10:25(4213)■16:6,14(4213)■24:16(899)■29:17(4213)■31:1■33:17(4801)■40:15(1851)■47:6■48:8(898)■52:13■64:9,12-**JER**-2:12■4:19(7023)■12:1(889)■14:17■18:13■24:2^{2},3^{2}■40:12■46:20(3304)-**LA**-5:22(5704,3966)-**EZE**-2:3(6106)■16:47(6985)■27:25■33:32(5690)■37:2^{2}■40:2■47:7,9-**DA**-2:12(7690)■7:20(7260)■8:8(5704,3960)■11:25(5704,3960)-**JOE**-2:11^{2}(3960)-**AM**-5:20(651)-**HAB**-2:13^{2}(1767)-**ZEC**-8:4(7230)■9:2,5■14:4■**N.T.**-all=2532&marked-**M'T**-10:30■15:28(1565)■17:18(1565)■18:31(4970)■21:8(4118)■24:24■26:7(927),37(85)-**M'R**-8:1(3827)■14:3(4185),33(85)■16:2(3029),4(4970)-**LU**-9:5■12:7■18:23^{2}(4970),24(4036)■19:17(1646),48(1582)-**JOH**-7:26(230)■8:4(1888)■12:3(4186)-**AC**-9:22(846)■10:10(4361)■24:2(2735)■25:10(2566)-**RO**-10:20(662)■13:6(846)-**1CO**-4:3(1646)-**2CO**-9:2(4119)■11:5(5228)■12:11(3029),15(2236)-**PH'P**-1:6(846)-**1TH**-5:13(5228),23(846)-**2TI**-1:17(4708),18(957)-**HEB**-10:1(846)-**JAS**-3:4(1646)■5:11(4184)

VESSEL-all=3627&marked-**LE**-6:28■11:32^{2},33,34■14:5,50■15:12^{2}-**NU**-5:17■19:15,17-**DE**-23:24-**1SA**-21:5-**1KI**-17:10-**2KI**-4:6^{2}-**PS**-2:9■31:12-**PR**-25:4-**IS**-30:14(5035)■66:20-**JER**-18:4^{2}■19:11■22:28■25:34■32:14■48:11,38■51:34-**EZE**-4:9■15:3-**HO**-8:8■**N.T.**-all=4632-**M'R**-11:16-**LU**-8:16-**JOH**-19:29-**AC**-9:15■10:11,16■11:5-**RO**-9:21-**1TH**-4:4-**2TI**-2:21-**1PE**-3:7

VESSELS-all=3627&marked-**GE**-43:11-**EX**-25:39■27:3,19■30:27^{2},28■35:13,16■37:16,24■38:3^{2},30■39:36,37,39,40■40:9,10-**LE**-8:11-**NU**-1:50^{2}■3:31,36■4:9,10,14^{2},15,16■7:1,85■18:3■19:18-**JOS**-6:19,24-**RU**-2:9-**1SA**-9:7■21:5-**2SA**-8:10^{2}■17:28-**1KI**-7:45,47,48,51■8:4■10:21^{2},25■15:15-**2KI**-4:3^{2},4,6■7:15■12:13■14:14■23:4■24:13■25:14,16-**1CH**-9:28,29■18:8,10■22:19■23:26■28:13-**2CH**-4:18,19■5:5■9:20^{2},24■15:18■24:14^{3}■25:24■28:24^{2}■29:18^{2},19■36:7,10,18,19-**EZR**-1:6,7,10,11■5:14(3984),15(3984)■6:5(3984)■7:19(3984)■8:25,26,27,28,30,33-**NE**-10:39■13:5,9-**ES**-1:7^{2}-**IS**-18:2■22:24^{2}■52:11■65:4-**JER**-14:3■27:16,18,19,21■28:3,6■40:10■48:12■49:29■52:18,20-**EZE**-27:13-**DA**-1:2^{2}■5:2(3984),3(3984),23(3984)■11:8-**HO**-13:15■**N.T.**-all=4632&marked-**M'T**-13:48(80)■25:4(80)-**RO**-9:22,23-**2CO**-4:7-**2TI**-2:20-**HEB**-9:21-**RE**-2:27■18:12^{2}

VESTMENTS-**2KI**-10:22(3830),22(4403)

VESTRY-**2KI**-10:22(4458)

VESTURE-**DE**-22:12(3682)-**PS**-22:18(3830)■102:26(3830)■**N.T.**-**M'T**-27:35(2441)-**JOH**-19:24(2441)-**HEB**-1:12(4018)-**RE**-19:13(2440),16(2440)

VESTURES-**GE**-41:42(899)

VEX-all=6887&marked-**EX**-22:21(3238)-**LE**-18:18■19:33(3238)-**NU**-25:17,18■33:55-**2SA**-12:18(6213,7451)-**2CH**-15:6(2000)-**JOB**-19:2(3013)-**PS**-2:5(926)-**IS**-7:6(6973)■11:13-**EZE**-32:9(3707)-**HAB**-2:7(2111)■**N.T.**-**AC**-12:1(2559)

VEXATION-all=7469&marked-**DE**-28:20(4103)-**EC**-1:14,17(7475)■2:11,17,22(7475),26■4:4,6,16(7475)■6:9-**IS**-9:1(4164)■28:19(2113)■65:14(7667)

VEXATIONS-**2CH**-15:5(4103)

VEXED-all=926&marked-**NU**-20:15(7489)-**J'G**-2:18(1766)■10:8(7492)■16:16(7114)-**1SA**-14:47(7561)-**2SA**-13:2(3334)-**2KI**-4:27(4843)-**NE**-9:27(6887)-**JOB**-27:2(4843)-**PS**-6:2,3,10-**IS**-63:10(6087)-**EZE**-22:5(4103),7(3238),29(3238)■**N.T.**-**M'T**-15:22(1139)■17:15(3958)-**LU**-6:18(3791)-**AC**-5:16(3791)-**2PE**-2:7(2669),8(928)

VIAL-**1SA**-10:1(6378)■**N.T.**-all=5357-**RE**-16:2,3,4,8,10,12,17

VIALS-all=5357-**RE**-5:8■15:7■16:1■17:1■21:9

VICTORY-all=8668&marked-**2SA**-19:2■23:10,12-**1CH**-29:11(5331)-**PS**-98:1(3467)-**IS**-25:8(5331)■**N.T.**-all=3534&marked-**M'T**-12:20-**1CO**-15:54,55,57-**1JO**-5:4(3529)-**RE**-15:2(3528)

VICTUAL-**EX**-12:39(6720)-**J'G**-20:10(6720)-**1KI**-4:27(3557)-**2CH**-11:11(3978),23(4202)

VICTUALS-all=6720&marked-**GE**-14:11(400)-**LE**-25:37(400)-**DE**-23:19(400)-**JOS**-1:11■9:11,14(6718)-**J'G**-7:8(6720)■17:10(4241)-**2SA**-22:10-**1KI**-4:7(3557)■11:18(3899)-**NE**-10:31(7668)■13:15(6718)-**JER**-40:5(737)■44:17(3899)■**N.T.**-**M'T**-14:15(1033)-**LU**-9:12(1979)

VIEW-**JOS**-2:1(7200)■7:2(7270)-**2KI**-2:7(5048),15(5048)

VIEWED-**JOS**-7:2(7270)-**EZR**-8:15(995)-**NE**-2:13(7663),15(7663)

VIGILANT-**1TI**-3:2(3524)-**1PE**-5:8(1127)

VILE-all=7043&marked-**DE**-25:3(7034)-**J'G**-19:24(5039)-**1SA**-3:13■15:9(5240)-**2SA**-6:22-**JOB**-18:3(2933)■40:4-**PS**-15:4(959)-**IS**-32:5(5036),6(5036)-**JER**-15:19(2151)■29:17(8182)-**LA**-1:11(2151)-**DA**-11:21(959)-**NA**-1:14■3:6(5034)■**N.T.**-**RO**-1:26(819)-**PH'P**-3:21(5014)-**JAS**-2:2(4508)

VILELY-**2SA**-1:21(1602)

VILER-**JOB**-30:8(5217)

VILEST-**PS**-12:8(2149)

VILLAGE-all=2968-**M'T**-21:2-**M'R**-11:2-**LU**-8:1■9:52,56■10:38■17:12■19:30■24:13,28

VILLAGES-all=2691&marked-**EX**-8:13-**LE**-25:31-**NU**-21:25(1323),32(1323)■32:42(1323)-**JOS**-13:23,28■15:32,36,41,44,45,46,47^{2},51,54,57,59,60,62■16:9■18:24,28■19:6,7,8,15,16,22,23,30,31,38,39,48■21:12-**J'G**-5:7(6520),11(6520)-**1SA**-6:18(3724)-**1CH**-4:32,33■

6:56▪9:16,22,25▪27:25(3723)-**2CH**-28:18^{3}(1323)-**NE**-6:2(3715)▪11:25^{2},25^{2}(1323),27(1323),28(1323),30,30(1323),31(1323)▪12:28,29-**ES**-9:19(6521)-**PS**-10:8-**SONG**-7:11(3723)-**IS**-42:11-**EZE**-38:11(6519)-**HAB**-3:14(6518)▪**N.T.**-all=2968-**M'T**-9:35▪14:15-**M'R**-6:6,36,56-**LU**-13:22-**AC**-8:25

VILLANY-**IS**-32:6(5039)-**JER**-29:23(5039)

VINE-all=1612&marked-**GE**-40:9,10▪49:11,11(8321)-**LE**-25:5(5139),11(5139)-**NU**-6:4(3196)-**DE**-32:32-**J'G**-9:12,13▪13:14-**1KI**-4:25-**2KI**-4:39▪18:31-**2CH**-26:10(3755)-**JOB**-15:33-**PS**-80:8,14▪128:3-**SONG**-6:11▪7:8,12-**IS**-5:2(8321)▪16:8,9▪24:7▪32:12▪34:4▪36:16-**JER**-2:21(8321),21▪6:9▪8:13▪48:32-**EZE**-15:2,6▪17:6^{2},7,8▪19:10-**HO**-10:1▪14:7-**JOE**-1:7,12▪2:22-**MIC**-4:4-**NA**-2:2(2156)-**HAG**-2:19-**ZEC**-3:10▪8:12-**MAL**-3:11▪**N.T.**-all=288-**M'T**-26:29-**M'R**-14:25-**LU**-22:18-**JOH**-15:1,4,5-**JAS**-3:12-**RE**-14:18,19

VINEDRESSERS-all=3755-**2KI**-25:12-**IS**-61:5-**JER**-52:16-**JOE**-1:11

VINEGAR-all=2558-**NU**-6:3-**RU**-2:14-**PS**-69:21-**PR**-10:26▪25:20▪**N.T.**-all=3690-**M'T**-27:34,48-**M'R**-15:36-**LU**-23:36-**JOH**-19:29^{2},30

VINES-all=1612&marked-**NU**-20:5-**DE**-8:8-**PS**-78:47▪105:33-**SONG**-2:13,15^{2}(3754)-**1SA**-7:23-**JER**-5:17▪31:5(3754)-**HO**-2:12-**HAB**-3:17

VINEYARD-all=3754&marked-**GE**-9:20-**EX**-22:5^{2}▪23:11-**LE**-19:10^{2}▪25:3,4-**DE**-20:6▪22:9^{2}▪23:24▪24:21▪28:30-**1KI**-21:1,2^{2},6^{3},7,15,16,18-**PS**-80:15(3657)-**PR**-24:30▪31:16-**SONG**-1:6▪8:11^{2},12-**IS**-1:8▪3:14▪5:1^{2},3,4,5,7,10▪27:2-**JER**-12:10▪35:7,9-**MIC**-1:6▪**N.T.**-all=290&marked-**M'T**-20:1,2,4,7,8▪21:28,33,39,40,41-**M'R**-12:1,2,8,9^{2}-**LU**-13:6,7(289)▪20:9,10,13,15^{2},16-**1CO**-9:7

VINEYARDS-all=3754-**NU**-16:14▪20:17▪21:22▪22:24-**DE**-6:11▪28:39-**JOS**-24:13-**J'G**-9:27▪11:33▪14:5▪15:5▪21:20,21-**1SA**-8:14,15▪22:7-**2KI**-5:26▪18:32▪19:29-**1CH**-27:27^{2}-**NE**-5:3,4,5,11▪9:25-**JOB**-24:18-**PS**-107:37-**EC**-2:4-**SONG**-1:6,14▪7:12-**IS**-16:10▪36:17▪37:30▪65:21-**JER**-32:15▪39:10-**EZE**-28:26-**HO**-2:15-**AM**-4:9▪5:11,17▪9:14-**ZEP**-1:13

VINTAGE-all=1210&marked-**LE**-26:5^{2}-**J'G**-8:2-**JOB**-24:6(3754)-**IS**-24:13▪32:10-**JER**-48:32-**MIC**-7:1-**ZEC**-11:2(1208)

VIOL-**IS**-5:12(5035)-**AM**-6:5(5035)

VIOLATED-**EZE**-22:26(2554)

VIOLENCE-all=2555&marked-**GE**-6:11,13-**LE**-6:2(1498)-**2SA**-22:3-**PS**-11:5▪55:9▪58:2▪72:14▪73:6-**PR**-4:17▪10:6,11▪13:2▪28:17(6231)-**IS**-53:9▪59:6▪60:18-**JER**-6:7▪20:8▪22:3(2554),17(4835)▪51:35,46-**EZE**-7:11,23▪8:17▪12:19▪18:7(1500),12(1500),16(1500),18(1499)▪28:16▪45:9-**JOE**-3:19-**AM**-3:10▪6:3-**OB**-10-**JON**-3:8-**MIC**-2:2(1497)▪6:12-**HAB**-1:2,3,9▪2:8,17^{2}-**ZEP**-1:9▪3:4(2554)-**MAL**-2:16▪**N.T.**-all=970&marked-**M'T**-11:12(971)-**LU**-3:14(1286)-**AC**-5:26▪21:35▪24:7▪27:41-**HEB**-11:34(1411)-**RE**-18:21(3731)

VIOLENT-all=255&marked-**2SA**-22:49-**PS**-7:16▪18:48▪86:14(6184)▪140:1,4-**PR**-16:29-**EC**-5:8(1499)▪**N.T.**-**M'T**-11:12(973)

VIOLENTLY-all=1497&marked-**GE**-21:25-**LE**-6:4(1500)-**DE**-28:31-**JOB**-20:19▪24:2-**LA**-2:6(2554)

VIOLS-**IS**-14:11(5035)-**AM**-5:23(5035)

VIPER-**IS**-30:6(660)▪59:5(660)▪**N.T.**-**AC**-28:3(2191)

VIPER'S-**JOB**-20:16(660)

VIPERS-all=2191-**M'T**-3:7▪12:34▪23:33-**LU**-3:7

VIRGIN-all=1330&marked-**GE**-24:16,43(5959)-**LE**-21:3,14-**DE**-22:19,23,28▪32:25-**2SA**-13:2-**1KI**-1:2-**2KI**-19:21-**IS**-7:14(5959)▪23:12▪37:22▪47:1▪62:5-**JER**-14:17▪18:13▪31:4,13,21▪46:11-**LA**-1:15▪2:13-**JOE**-1:8-**AM**-5:2▪**N.T.**-all=3933-**M'T**-1:23-**LU**-1:27-**1CO**-7:28,34,36,37-**2CO**-11:2

VIRGINITY-all=1331-**LE**-21:13-**DE**-22:15,17,20-**J'G**-11:37,38-**EZE**-23:3,8▪**N.T.**-**LU**-2:36(3932)

VIRGIN'S-**LU**-1:27(3933)

VIRGINS-all=1330&marked-**EX**-22:17-**J'G**-21:12-**2SA**-13:18-**ES**-2:2,3,17,19-**PS**-45:14-**SONG**-1:3(5959)▪6:8(5959)-**IS**-23:4-**LA**-1:4,18▪2:10,21-**AM**-8:13▪**N.T.**-all=3933-**M'T**-25:1,7,11-**AC**-21:9-**1CO**-7:25-**RE**-14:4

VIRTUE-all=703&marked-**M'R**-5:30(1411)-**LU**-6:19(1411)▪8:46(1411)-**PH'P**-4:8-**2PE**-1:3,5^{2}

VIRTUOUS-all=2428-**RU**-3:11-**PR**-12:4▪31:10

VIRTUOUSLY-**PR**-31:29(2428)

VISAGE-**IS**-52:14(4758)-**LA**-4:8(8389)-**DA**-3:19(600)

VISIBLE-**COL**-1:16(3707)

VISION-all=2377,a=4758&marked-**GE**-15:1(4236)-**NU**-12:6a▪24:4(4236),16(4236)-**1SA**-3:1,15a-**2SA**-7:17(2384)-**1CH**-17:15-**2CH**-32:32-**JOB**-20:8(2384)▪33:15(2384)-**PS**-89:19-**PR**-29:18-**IS**-1:1▪21:2(2380)▪22:1(2384),5(2384)▪28:7(7203)▪29:7,11(2380)-**JER**-14:14▪23:16-**LA**-2:9-**EZE**-7:13,26▪8:4a▪11:24^{2}a▪12:22,23,24,27▪13:7(4236)▪43:3^{3}a-**DA**-2:19(2376)▪7:2(2376)▪8:1,2^{2},13,15,16a,17a,26a,26,27a▪9:21,23,24▪10:1a,7^{2}(4759),8(4759),14,16a▪11:14-**OB**-1-**MIC**-3:6-**NA**-1:1-**HAB**-2:2,3-**ZEC**-13:4(2384)▪**N.T.**-all=3705&marked-**M'T**-17:9-**LU**-1:22(3701)▪24:23(3701)-**AC**-9:10,12▪10:3,17,19▪11:5▪12:9▪16:9,10▪18:9▪26:19-**RE**-9:17(3706)

VISIONS-all=2376&marked-**GE**-46:2(4759)-**2CH**-9:29(2378)▪26:5(7200)-**JOB**-4:13(2384)▪7:14(2384)-**EZE**-1:1(4759)▪8:3(4759)▪13:16(2377)▪40:2(4759)▪43:3(4759)-**DA**-1:17(2377)▪2:28▪4:5,9,10,13▪7:1,7,13,15-**HO**-12:10(2377)-**JOE**-2:28(2384)▪**N.T.**-**AC**-2:17(3706)-**2CO**-12:1(3701)

VISIT-all=6485-**GE**-50:24,25-**EX**-13:19▪32:34-**LE**-18:25-**JOB**-5:24▪7:18-**PS**-59:5▪80:14▪89:32▪106:4-**IS**-23:17-**JER**-3:16▪5:9,29▪6:15▪9:9▪14:10▪15:15▪23:2▪27:22▪29:10▪32:5▪49:8▪50:31-**LA**-4:22-**HO**-2:13▪8:13▪9:9-**AM**-3:14^{2}-**ZEP**-2:7-**ZEC**-11:16▪**N.T.**-all=1980-**AC**-7:23▪15:14,36-**JAS**-1:27

VISITATION-all=6486-**NU**-16:29-**JOB**-10:12-**IS**-10:3-**JER**-8:12▪10:15▪11:23▪23:12▪46:21▪48:44▪50:27▪51:18-**HO**-9:7-**MIC**-7:4▪**N.T.**-**LU**-19:44(1984)-**1PE**-2:12(1984)

VISITED-all=6485-**GE**-21:1-**EX**-3:16▪4:31-**NU**-16:29-**J'G**-15:1-**RU**-1:6-**1SA**-2:21-**JOB**-35:15-**PS**-17:3-**PR**-19:23-**IS**-24:22▪26:14,16▪29:6-**JER**-6:6▪23:2-**EZE**-38:8-**ZEC**-10:3▪**N.T.**-all=1980-**M'T**-25:36,43-**LU**-1:68,78▪7:16

VISITEST-**PS**-8:4(6485)▪65:9(6485)▪**N.T.**-**HEB**-2:6(1980)

VISITETH-**JOB**-31:14(6485)

VISITING-all=6485-**EX**-20:5▪34:7-**NU**-14:18-**DE**-5:9

VOCATION-**EPH**-4:1(2821)

VOICE-all=6963&marked-**GE**-3:8,10,17▪4:10,23▪16:2▪21:12,16,17^{2}▪22:18▪26:5▪27:8,13,22,38,43▪29:11▪30:6▪39:14,15,18-**EX**-3:18▪4:1,8^{2},9▪5:2▪15:26▪18:19,24▪19:5,16,19^{2}▪23:21,22▪24:3▪32:18^{2}-**LE**-5:1-**NU**-7:89▪14:1,22▪20:16▪21:3-**DE**-1:34,45▪4:12^{2},30,33,36▪5:22,23,24,25,26,28^{2}▪8:20▪9:23▪13:4,18▪15:5▪18:16▪21:18^{2},20▪26:7,14,17▪27:10,14▪28:1,2,15,45,62▪30:2,8,10,20▪33:7-**JOS**-5:6▪6:10▪10:14▪22:2▪24:24-**J'G**-2:2,4,20▪6:10▪9:7▪13:9▪18:3,25▪20:13-**RU**-1:9,14-**1SA**-1:13▪2:25▪8:7,9,19,22▪12:1,14,15▪15:1,19,20,22,24▪19:6▪24:16^{2}▪25:35▪26:17^{3}▪28:12,18,21,22,23▪30:4-**2SA**-3:32▪12:18▪13:14,36▪15:23▪19:4,35▪22:7,14-**1KI**-8:55▪17:22▪18:26,29▪19:12,13▪20:25,36-**2KI**-4:31▪7:10▪10:6▪18:12,28▪19:22-**1CH**-15:16-**2CH**-5:13▪15:14▪20:19▪30:27▪32:18-**EZR**-3:12▪10:12-**NE**-9:4-**JOB**-2:12▪3:18▪4:10,16▪9:16▪30:31▪33:8▪34:16▪37:2,4^{3},5▪38:34▪40:9-**PS**-3:4▪5:2,3▪6:8▪18:6,13▪19:3▪26:7▪27:7▪28:2,6▪29:3,4^{2},5,7,8,9▪31:22▪42:4▪44:16▪46:6▪47:1▪55:3,17▪58:5▪64:1▪66:8,19▪68:33^{2}▪74:23▪77:1^{2},18▪81:11▪86:6▪93:3▪95:7▪98:5▪102:5▪103:20▪104:7▪106:25▪116:1▪118:15▪119:149▪130:2^{2}▪141:1▪142:1^{2}-**PR**-1:20▪2:3▪5:13▪8:1,4▪27:14-**EC**-5:3,6▪10:20▪12:4▪2:8,12,14▪5:2▪8:13-**IS**-6:4,8▪10:30▪13:2▪15:4▪24:14▪28:23▪29:4▪30:19,30,31▪31:4▪32:9▪36:13▪37:23▪40:3,6,9▪42:2▪48:20▪50:10▪51:3▪52:8^{2}▪58:1,4▪65:19^{2}▪66:6^{3}-**JER**-3:13,21,25▪4:15,16,31^{2}▪6:23▪7:23,28,34^{3}▪8:19▪9:10,13,19▪10:13▪11:4,7▪16:9^{3}▪18:10,19▪22:20,21▪25:10^{3},30,36▪26:13▪30:5,19▪31:15,16▪32:23▪33:11^{4}▪35:8▪38:20▪40:3▪42:6^{2},13,21▪43:4,7▪44:23▪46:22▪48:3,34▪50:28,42▪51:16,55^{2}-**LA**-3:56-**EZE**-1:24^{2},25,28▪3:12▪8:18▪9:1▪10:5▪11:13▪19:9▪21:22▪23:42▪27:30▪33:32▪43:2-**DA**-4:31(7032)▪6:20(7032)▪7:11(7032)▪8:16▪9:10,11,14▪10:6^{2},9^{2}-**JOE**-2:11▪3:16-**AM**-1:2-**JON**-2:2,9-**MIC**-6:1,9-**NA**-2:7,13-**HAB**-3:10,16-**ZEP**-1:14▪2:14▪3:2-**HAG**-1:12-**ZEC**-6:15▪11:3^{2}▪**N.T.**-all=5456&marked-**M'T**-2:18▪3:3,17▪12:19▪17:5▪27:46,50-**M'R**-1:3,11,26▪5:7▪9:7▪15:34,37-**LU**-1:42,44▪3:4,22▪4:33▪8:28▪9:35,36▪11:27▪17:15▪19:37▪23:46-**JOH**-1:23▪3:29▪5:25,28,37▪10:3,4,5,16,27▪11:43▪12:28,30▪18:37-**AC**-2:14▪4:24▪7:31,57,60▪8:7▪9:4,7▪10:13,15▪11:7,9▪12:14,22▪14:10▪16:28▪19:34▪22:7,9,14▪24:21▪26:10(5586),14,24-**1CO**-14:11-**GA**-4:20-**1TH**-4:16-**HEB**-3:7,15▪4:7▪12:19,26-**2PE**-1:17,18▪2:16-**RE**-1:10,12,15▪3:20▪4:1▪5:2,11,12▪6:6,7,10▪7:2,10▪8:13▪9:13▪10:3,4,7,8▪11:12▪12:10▪14:2^{4},7,9,13,15▪16:1,17▪18:2,4,22,23▪19:1,5,6^{3},17▪21:3

VOICES-**J'G**-21:2(6963)-**1SA**-11:4(6963)▪**N.T.**-all=5456-**LU**-17:13▪23:23^{2}-**AC**-13:27▪14:11▪22:22-**1CO**-14:10-**RE**-4:5▪8:5,13▪10:3,4▪11:15▪11:19▪16:18

VOID-all=2638&marked-**GE**-1:2(922)-**NU**-30:12^{2}(6565),13(6565),15(6565)-**DE**-32:28(6)-**1KI**-22:10(1637)-**2CH**-18:9(1637)-**PS**-89:39(5010)▪119:126(6565)-**PR**-7:7▪10:13▪11:12▪12:11▪17:18▪24:30-**IS**-55:11(7387)-**JER**-4:23(922)▪19:7(1238)-**NA**-2:10(4003)▪**N.T.**-**AC**-24:16(677)-**RO**-3:31(2673)▪4:14(2758)-**1CO**-9:15(2758)

VOLUME-**PS**-40:7(4039)▪**N.T.**-**HEB**-10:7(2777)

VOLUNTARILY-**EZE**-46:12(5071)

VOLUNTARY-**LE**-1:3(7522)▪7:16(5071)-**EZE**-46:12(5071)▪**N.T.**-**COL**-2:18(2309)

VOMIT-all=6892&marked-**JOB**-20:15(6958)-**PR**-23:8(6958)▪25:16(6958)▪26:11-**IS**-19:14▪28:8-**JER**-48:26▪**N.T.**-**2PE**-2:22(1829)

VOMITED-**JON**-2:10(6958)

VOMITETH-**LE**-18:25(6958)

VOW-all=5088&marked-**GE**-28:20▪31:13-**LE**-7:16▪22:21,23▪27:2-**NU**-6:2(5087),2,5,21▪15:3,8▪21:2▪30:2(5087),2,3(5087),3,4,8,9,13-**DE**-12:11(5087)▪23:18,21(5087),21,22-**J'G**-11:30,39-**1SA**-1:11,21-**2SA**-15:7,8-**PS**-65:1▪76:11(5087)-**EC**-5:4,5^{2}(5087)-**IS**-19:21(5087),21▪**N.T.**-**AC**-18:18(2171)▪21:23(2171)

VOWED-all=5087&marked-**GE**-28:20-**LE**-27:8-**NU**-6:21^{2}▪21:2▪30:6(5088),8(5088),10-**DE**-23:23-**J'G**-11:30,

39-**1SA**-1:11-**2SA**-15:7,8-**PS**-132:2-**EC**-5:4-**JER**-44:25-**JON**-2:9

VOWEDST-**GE**-31:13(5087)

VOWEST-**DE**-12:17(5087)-**EC**-5:4(5087)

VOWETH-**MAL**-1:14(5087)

VOWS-all=5088-**LE**-22:18■23:38-**NU**-29:39■30:4,5,7,11,12,14-**DE**-12:6,11,17,26-**JOB**-22:27-**PS**-22:25■50:14■56:12■61:5,8■66:13■116:14,18-**PR**-7:14■20:25■31:2-**JER**-44:25^3-**JON**-1:16-**NA**-1:15

VOYAGE-**AC**-27:10(4144)

VULTURE-**LE**-11:14(1676)-**DE**-14:13(1772)

VULTURE'S-**JOB**-28:7(344)

VULTURES-**IS**-34:15(1772)

W

WAFER-all=7550-**EX**-29:23-**LE**-8:26-**NU**-6:19

WAFERS-all=7550&marked-**EX**-16:31(6838)■29:2-**LE**-2:4■7:12-**NU**-6:15

WAG-**JER**-18:16(5110)-**LA**-2:15(5128)-**ZEP**-2:15(5128)

WAGES-all=7939&marked-**GE**-29:15(4909)■30:28■31:7(4909),8,41(4909)-**EX**-2:9-**LE**-19:13(6468)-**JER**-22:13(2600)-**EZE**-29:18,19-**HAG**-1:6^2(7936)-**MAL**-3:5■**N.T.**-all=3800&marked-**LU**-3:14-**JOH**-4:36(3408)-**RO**-6:23-**2CO**-11:8-**2PE**-2:15(3408)

WAGGING-**M'T**-27:39(2795)-**M'R**-15:29(2795)

WAGON-**NU**-7:3(5699)

WAGONS-all=5699&marked-**GE**-45:19,21,27■46:5-**NU**-7:3,6,7,8-**EZE**-23:24(7393)

WAIL-**EZE**-32:18(5091)-**MIC**-1:8(5594)■**N.T.**-**RE**-1:7(2875)

WAILED-**M'R**-5:38(214)

WAILING-all=4553&marked-**ES**-4:3-**JER**-9:10(5092),18(5092),19(5092),20(5092)-**EZE**-7:11(5089)■27:31,32(5204)-**AM**-5:16^2,17-**MIC**-1:8■**N.T.**-**M'T**-13:42(2805),50(2805)-**RE**-18:15(3996),19(3996)

WAIT-all=693,a=6960&marked-**EX**-21:13(6658)-**NU**-3:10(8104)■8:24(6633)■35:20(6660),22(6660)-**DE**-19:11-**JOS**-8:4,13(6119)-**J'G**-9:25,32,34,35(3993),43■16:2,9,12■20:29,33,36,37^2,38■21:20-**1SA**-15:5■22:8,13-**2KI**-6:33(3176)-**1CH**-23:28(3027)-**2CH**-5:11(8104)-**EZR**-8:31-**JOB**-14:14(3176)■17:13a■31:9■38:40(695)-**PS**-10:9^2■25:3a,5a,21a■27:14^{2}a■37:7(2342),9a,34a■39:7a■52:9a■56:6a■59:3,9(8104)■62:5(1826)■69:3(3176),6a■71:10(8104)■104:27(7663)■130:5a■145:15(7663)-**PR**-1:11,18■7:12■12:6■20:22a■23:28■24:15-**IS**-8:17(2442)■30:18^2(2442)■40:31a■42:4(3176)■49:23a■51:5a■59:9a■60:9a-**JER**-5:26(7789)■9:8(696)■14:22a-**LA**-3:10,25a,26(1748)■4:19-**HO**-6:9(2442)■7:6■12:6a-**MIC**-7:2,7(3176)-**HAB**-2:3(2442)-**ZEP**-3:8(2442)■**N.T.**-**M'R**-3:9(4342)-**LU**-11:54(1748)■12:36(4327)-**AC**-1:4(4037)■20:3(1096,1917),19(1917)■23:16(1747),21(1748),30(1917)■25:3(4160,1747)-**RO**-8:25(553)-**1CO**-9:13(4332)-**GAL**-5:5(553)-**EPH**-4:14(3180)-**1TH**-1:10(362)

WAITED-all=6960&marked-**GE**-49:18-**1KI**-20:38(5975)-**2KI**-5:2(1961,6440)-**1CH**-6:32(5975),33(5975)-**2CH**-7:6(5975)■17:19(8334)-**NE**-12:44(5975)-**JOB**-6:19■15:22(6822)■29:21(3176),23(3176)■30:26(3176)■32:4(2442),11(3176),16(3176)-**PS**-40:1■106:13(2442)■119:95-**IS**-25:9^2■26:8■33:2-**EZE**-19:5(3176)-**MIC**-1:12(2342)-**ZEC**-11:11(8104)■**N.T.**-**M'R**-15:43(4327)-**LU**-1:21(4328)■23:51(4327)-**AC**-10:7(4342),24(4328)■17:16(1551)-**1PE**-3:20(1551)

WAITETH-all=2442&marked-**JOB**-24:15(8104)-**PS**-33:20■62:1(1747)■65:1(1747)-**PR**-27:18(8104)-**IS**-64:4-**DA**-12:12-**MIC**-5:7(3176)■**N.T.**-**RO**-8:19(553)-**JAS**-5:7(1551)

WAITING-**NU**-8:25(6635)-**PR**-8:34(8104)■**N.T.**-**LU**-2:25(4327)■8:40(4328)-**JOH**-5:3(1551)-**RO**-8:23(553)-**1CO**-1:7(553)

WAKE-**JER**-51:39(6974),57(6974)-**JOE**-3:9(5782)■**N.T.**-**1TH**-5:10(1127)

WAKED-**ZEC**-4:1(5782)

WAKENED-**JOE**-3:12(5782)-**ZEC**-4:1(5782)

WAKENETH-**IS**-50:4^2(5782)

WAKETH-**PS**-127:1(8245)-**SONG**-5:2(5782)

WAKING-**PS**-77:4(8109)

WALK-all=3212,a=1980&marked-**GE**-13:17a■17:1a■24:40a■48:15a-**EX**-16:4■18:20■21:19a-**LE**-18:3,4■20:23■26:3,12a,21,23a,24a,27a,28a-**DE**-5:33■8:6,19a■10:12■11:22■13:4,5■19:9■26:17■28:9a■29:19■30:16-**JOS**-18:8a■22:5-**J'G**-2:22■5:10a-**1SA**-2:30a,35a■8:5a-**1KI**-2:3,4■3:14,14a■6:12^2■8:23a,25,36,58,61■9:4■11:38a■16:31-**2KI**-10:31■23:3-**2CH**-6:14a,16,27,31■7:17■34:31-**NE**-5:9■10:29-**PS**-12:8a■23:4■26:11■48:12(5437)■56:13a■78:10■82:5a■84:11a■86:11a■89:15a,30■101:2a■115:7a■116:9a■119:1a,3a,45a■138:7■143:8-**PR**-1:15■2:7a,13,20■3:23-**EC**-4:15a■6:8a■11:9a-**IS**-2:3,5■3:16■8:11■30:2a,21■35:9a■40:31■42:5a,24a■50:11■59:9a-**JER**-3:17,18■6:16^2,25,■7:6,9a,23a■9:4a■13:10^{2}a■16:12a■18:12a,15a■23:14a■26:4a■31:9a■42:3a-**LA**-5:18a-**EZE**-11:20■20:18,19■33:15a■36:12,27■37:24■42:4(4109)-**DA**-4:37(1981)■9:10-**HO**-11:10■14:9-**JOE**-2:8-**AM**-3:3-**MIC**-4:2■4:5^2■6:8,16-**NA**-2:5(1979)-**HAB**-3:15(1869),19(1869)-**ZEP**-1:17a-**ZEC**-1:10a■3:7,7(4108)■6:7^{2}a■10:12a■**N.T.**-all=4043&marked-**M'T**-9:5■11:5■15:31-**M'R**-2:9■7:5-**LU**-5:23■7:22■11:44■13:33(4198)■20:46■24:17-**JOH**-5:8,11,12■7:1■8:12■11:9,10■12:35-**AC**-3:6,12■14:16(4198)■21:21-**RO**-4:12(4748)■6:4■8:1,4■13:13-**1CO**-3:3■7:17-**2CO**-5:7■6:16(1704)■10:3-**GA**-5:16,25(4748)■6:16(4748)-**EPH**-2:10■4:1,17■5:2,8,15-**PH'P**-3:16(4748),17,18-**COL**-1:10■2:6■4:5-**1TH**-2:12■4:1,12-**2TH**-3:11-**2PE**-2:10(4198)-**1JO**-1:6,7■2:6-**2JO**-6^2-**3JO**-4-**JUDE**-18(4198)-**RE**-3:4■9:20■16:15■21:24

WALKED-all=1980,a=3212&marked-**GE**-5:22,24■6:9-**EX**-2:5■14:29-**LE**-26:40,41a-**JOS**-5:6-**J'G**-2:17■5:6a■11:16a-**1SA**-8:3■12:2-**2SA**-2:29■7:6,7■11:2-**1KI**-3:6■8:25■9:4■11:33■15:3a,26a,34a■16:2a,26a■22:43a,52a-**2KI**-4:35a■8:18a,27a■13:6,11■16:3a■17:8a,19a,22a■20:3■21:21a,21,22■22:2a-**1CH**-17:6-**2CH**-6:16a■7:17■11:17■17:3,4■20:32a■21:6a,12,13a■22:3,5■28:2a■34:2a-**ES**-2:11-**JOB**-29:3a■31:5,7■38:16-**PS**-26:1,3■55:14■81:12a,13■142:3-**IS**-9:2■20:3■38:3-**JER**-2:5a,8■7:24a■8:2■9:13,14a■11:8a■16:11a■32:23■44:10,23-**EZE**-5:6,7■11:12■16:47■18:9,17■20:13,16,21■23:31■28:14-**DA**-4:29(1981)-**HO**-5:11-**AM**-2:4-**NA**-2:11-**ZEC**-1:11■6:7-**MAL**-2:6■3:14■**N.T.**-all=4043&marked-**M'T**-14:29-**M'R**-1:16■5:42■16:12-**JOH**-1:36■5:9■6:66■7:1■10:23■11:54-**AC**-3:8■14:8,10-**2CO**-10:2■12:18^2-**GA**-2:14(3716)-**EPH**-2:2-**COL**-3:7-**1PE**-4:3(4198)-**1JO**-2:6

WALKEDST-**JOH**-21:18(4043)

WALKEST-all=3212&marked-**DE**-6:7■11:19-**1KI**-2:42(1980)-**IS**-43:2■**N.T.**-**AC**-21:24(4748)-**RO**-4:15(4043)-**3JO**-3(4043)

WALKETH-all=1980&marked-**GE**-24:65-**DE**-23:14-**1SA**-12:2-**JOB**-18:8■22:14■34:8(3212)-**PS**-1:1■15:2■39:6■73:9■91:6■101:6■104:3■128:1-**PR**-6:12■10:9(3212)■13:20■14:2■15:21■19:1■20:7■28:6,18,26-**EC**-2:14■10:3-**IS**-33:15■50:10■65:2-**JER**-10:23■23:17-**EZE**-11:21-**MIC**-2:7■**N.T.**-all=4043&marked-**M'T**-12:43(1330)-**LU**-11:24(1330)-**JOH**-12:35-**2TH**-3:6-**1PE**-5:8-**1JO**-2:11-**RE**-2:1

WALKING-all=1980&marked-**GE**-3:8-**DE**-2:7(3212)-**1KI**-3:3(3212)■16:19(3212)-**JOB**-1:7■2:2■31:26-**EC**-10:7-**IS**-3:16■20:2■57:2-**JER**-6:28-**DA**-3:25(1981)-**MIC**-2:11■**N.T.**-all=4043&marked-**M'T**-4:18■14:25,26-**M'R**-6:48,49■8:24■11:27-**LU**-1:6(4198)-**JOH**-6:19-**AC**-3:8,9■9:31(4198)-**2CO**-4:2-**PE**-3:3(4198)-**2JO**-4-**JUDE**-16(4198)

WALL-all=2346,a=7023&marked-**GE**-49:6(7794),22(7791)-**EX**-14:22,29-**LE**-14:37a■25:31-**NU**-22:24^2(1447),25^{2}a■35:4a-**JOS**-2:15^2■6:5,20-**1SA**-18:11a■19:10^{2}a■20:25a■25:16,22a,34a■31:10,12-**2SA**-11:20,21^2,24■18:24■20:15,21■22:30(7791)-**1KI**-3:1■4:33a■6:5a,27^{2}a■9:15■14:10a■16:11a■20:30■21:21a,23(2426)-**2KI**-3:27■4:10a■6:26,30■9:8a,33a■14:13■18:26,27■20:2a-**2CH**-3:11a,12a■25:23■26:6^2■27:3■32:5^2,18■33:14■36:19-**EZR**-5:3(846)■9:9(1447)-**NE**-1:3■2:8,15,17■3:8,13,15,27■4:1,3,6^2,10,13,15,19■5:16■6:1,6,15■7:1■12:27,30,31^2,37,38^2■13:21-**PS**-18:29(7791)■62:3a-**PR**-18:11■24:31(1444)-**SONG**-2:9(3796)■8:9,10-**IS**-2:15■5:5(1447)■2:10■25:4a■30:13■36:11,12■38:2a■59:10a-**JER**-15:20■49:27■51:44-**LA**-2:8^2,18-**EZE**-4:3a■8:7a,8^{2}a,10a■12:5a,7a,12a■13:10(2434),12a,14a,15^{2}a■23:14a■38:20■40:5■41:5a,6^{2}a,9a,12a,17a,20a■42:7(1447),10(1444)12(1448),20■43:8a-**DA**-5:5(3797)■9:25(2742)-**HO**-2:6(1447)-**JOE**-2:7,9-**AM**-1:7,10,14■5:19a■7:7-**NA**-2:5■3:8-**HAB**-2:11a-**ZEC**-2:5■**N.T.**-all=5038&marked-**AC**-9:25■23:3(5109)-**2CO**-11:33-**RE**-21:12,14,15,17,18,19

WALLED-**LE**-25:29(2346),30(2346)-**NU**-13:28(1219)-**DE**-1:28(1219)

WALLOW-all=6428&marked-**JER**-6:26■25:34■48:26(5606)-**EZE**-27:30

WALLOWED-**2SA**-20:12(1556)■**N.T.**-**M'R**-9:20(2947)

WALLOWING-**2PE**-2:22(2946)

WALLS-all=2346,a=7023&marked-**LE**-14:37a,39a-**DE**-3:5■28:52-**1KI**-4:13■6:5a,6a,15^{2}a,16a,29a-**2KI**-25:4,10-**1CH**-29:4a-**2CH**-3:7^{2}a■8:5■14:7-**EZR**-4:12(7791),13(7791),16(7791)■5:8(3797),9(846)-**NE**-2:13■4:7-**JOB**-24:11(7791)-**PS**-51:18■55:10■122:7(2426)-**PR**-25:28-**SONG**-5:7-**IS**-22:5a,11■25:12■26:1■49:16■56:5■60:10,18■62:6-**JER**-1:15,18■5:10(8284)■21:4■39:4,8■50:15■51:12,58■52:7,14-**LA**-2:7-**EZE**-26:4,9,10,12■27:11^{2}a■33:30a■38:11■41:13a,22a,25a-**MIC**-7:11(1447)■**N.T.**-**HEB**-11:30(5038)

WANDER-all=8582&marked-**GE**-20:13-**NU**-14:33(7462)■32:13(5128)-**DE**-27:18(7686)-**JOB**-12:24■38:41-**PS**-55:7(5074)■59:15(5128)■107:40■119:10(7686)-**IS**-47:15-**JER**-14:10(5128)■48:12(6808)-**AM**-8:12(5128)

WANDERED-all=8582&marked-**GE**-21:14-**JOS**-14:10(1980)-**PS**-107:4-**IS**-16:8-**LA**-4:14(5182),15(5182)-**EZE**-34:6(7686)-**AM**-4:8(5128)■**N.T.**-**HEB**-11:37(4022),38(4105)

WANDERERS-**JER**-48:12(6808)-**HO**-9:17(5074)

WANDEREST-**JER**-2:20(6808)

WANDERETH-all=5704&marked-**JOB**-15:23■21:16(8582)■27:8^2-**IS**-16:3-**JER**-49:5

WANDERING-**GE**-37:15(8582)-**PR**-26:2(5110)-**EC**-6:9(1981)-**IS**-16:2(5074)■**N.T.**-**1TI**-5:13(4022)-**JUDE**-13(4107)

WANDERINGS-**PS**-56:8(5112)

WANT-all=4270&marked-**DE**-28:48(2640),57(2640)-**J'G**-18:10■19:19-**JOB**-24:8(1097)■30:3(2639)■31:19(1097)■23:1(2637)■34:9,10(2637)-**PR**-6:11■

10:21(2638)■13:23(3808),25(2637)■14:28(657)■21:5■22:16■24:34-IS-34:16(6485)-JER-33:17(3772),18(3772)■35:19(3772)-EZE-4:17(2637)-AM-4:6(2640)■N.T.-all=5303&marked-M'R-12:44(5304)-LU-15:14(5302)-2CO-8:14^{2}■9:12-PH'P-4:11(5304)

WANTED-JER-44:18(2637)■N.T.-JOH-2:3(5302)-2CO-11:9(5302)

WANTETH-all=2638&marked-DE-15:8(2637)-PR-9:4,16■10:19(2308)■28:16-EC-6:2-SONG-7:2(2637)

WANTING-2KI-10:19^{2}(6485)-PR-19:7(3808)-EC-1:15(2642)-DA-5:27(2627)■N.T.-all=3007-TIT-1:5■3:13-JAS-1:4

WANTON-IS-3:16(8265)■N.T.-1TI-5:11(2691)-JAS-5:5(4684)

WANTONNESS-RO-13:13(766)-2PE-2:18(766)

WANTS-J'G-19:20(4270)■N.T.-PH'P-2:25(5532)

WAR-all=4421,a=6635&marked-GE-14:2-EX-1:10■13:17■15:3■17:16■32:17-NU-1:3a,20a,22a,24a,26a,28a,30a,32a,34a,36a,38a,40a,42a,45a■10:9■26:2a■31:3a,4a,5a,6^{2}a,21a,27,28,32a,36a,49,53a■32:6,20,27a-DE-1:41■2:14,16■3:18(2428)■4:34■20:12,19(3898),20■21:10■24:5a-JOS-4:13a■5:4,6■6:3■8:1,3,11■10:5(3898),7,24■11:7,18,23■14:11,15■17:1■22:12a-J'G-3:2,10■5:8(3901)■11:4(3898),5(3898),27(3898)■18:11,16,17■20:17■21:22-1SA-8:12■14:52■16:18■17:33■18:5■19:8■23:8■28:15(3898)-2SA-1:27■3:1,6■11:7,18,19■17:8■21:15■22:35-1KI-2:5^{2}■9:22■14:30■15:6,7,16,32■20:18■22:1-2KI-8:28■13:25■14:7■16:5■18:20■24:16■25:4,19-1CH-5:10,18,18a,19,22■7:4,11a,40a■12:1,8a,23a,24a,25a,33^{2},35,36,37a,38■18:10■20:4,5,6■28:3-2CH-6:34■8:9■13:2,3■14:6■15:19■17:10(3898),13,18a■18:3■22:5■25:5a■26:11a,13■28:12a■32:6■33:14(2428)■35:21-JOB-5:20■10:17a■38:23-PS-18:34■27:3■55:21(7128)■68:30(7128)■120:7■140:2■144:1(4421,7128)-PR-20:18■24:6-EC-3:8■8:8■9:18(7128)-SONG-3:8-IS-2:4■3:2,25■7:1■21:15■36:5■37:9(3898)■41:12■42:13-JER-4:19■6:4,23■21:2(3898),4■28:8■38:4■39:4■41:3,16■42:14■48:14■49:2,26■50:30■51:20,32■52:7,25-EZE-17:17■26:9(6904)■27:10,27■32:27■39:20-DA-7:21(7129)■9:26-JOE-2:7■3:9^{2}-MIC-2:8■3:5■4:3■N.T.-all=4171&marked-LU-14:31■23:11(4753)-2CO-10:3(4754)-1TI-1:18(4754)-JAS-4:1(4754),2(4170)-1PE-2:11(4754)-RE-11:7■12:7,17■13:4(4170),7■17:14(4170)■19:11(4170),19

WARD-all=4929&marked-GE-40:3,4,7■41:10■42:17-LE-24:12-NU-15:34-2SA-20:3(4931)-1CH-12:29(4931)■25:8(4931)■26:16-NE-12:24,25,45^{2}(4931)-IS-21:8(4931)-JER-37:13(6488)-EZE-19:9(5474)■N.T.-AC-12:10(5438)

WARDROBE-2KI-22:14(899)-2CH-34:22(899)

WARDS-all=4931-1CH-9:23■26:12-NE-13:30

WARE-NE-10:31(4728)■13:16(4377),20(4465)■N.T.-LU-8:27(1737)-AC-14:6(4894)-2TI-4:15(5442)

WARES-JER-10:17(3666)-EZE-27:16(4639),18(4639),33(5801)-JON-1:5(3627)

WARFARE-1SA-28:1(6635)-IS-40:2(6635)■N.T.-1CO-9:7(4754)-2CO-10:4(4752)-1TI-1:18(4752)

WARM-all=2552&marked-2KI-4:34-JOB-6:17(2215)■37:17(2525)-EC-4:11(3179)-IS-44:15,16■47:14-HAG-1:6(2527)

WARMED-JOB-31:20(2552)■N.T.-all=2328-M'R-14:54-JOH-18:18^{2},25-JAS-2:16

WARMETH-JOB-39:14(2552)-IS-44:16(2552)

WARMING-M'R-14:67(2328)

WARN-all=2094-2CH-19:10-EZE-3:18,19,21■33:3,7,8,9■N.T.-all=3560-AC-20:31-1CO-4:14-1TH-5:14

WARNED-all=2094-2KI-6:10-PS-19:11-EZE-3:21■33:6■N.T.-all=5537&marked-M'T-2:12,22■3:7(5263)-LU-3:7(5263)-AC-10:22-HEB-11:7

WARNING-all=2094&marked-JER-6:10(5749)-EZE-3:17,18,20■33:4,5^{2}■N.T.-COL-1:28(3560)

WARP-all=8359-LE-13:48,49,51,52,53,56,57,58,59

WARRED-all=3898&marked-NU-31:7(6633),42(6633)-JOS-24:9-1KI-14:19■20:1■22:45-2KI-6:8■14:28-2CH-26:6

WARRETH-2TI-2:4(4754)

WARRING-2KI-19:8(3898)-IS-37:8(3898)■N.T.-RO-7:23(497)

WARRIOR-IS-9:5(5431)

WARRIORS-1KI-2:21(6213,4421)-2CH-11:1(6213,4421)

WARS-all=4421-NU-21:14-J'G-3:1-2SA-8:10-1KI-5:3-1CH-22:8-2CH-12:15■16:9■27:7-PS-46:9■N.T.-all=4171-M'T-24:6-M'R-13:7-LU-21:9-JAS-4:1

WASH-all=7364,a=3526&marked-GE-18:4■19:2■24:32-EX-2:5■19:10a■29:4,17■30:18,19,20,21■40:12,30-LE-1:9,13■6:27a■9:14■11:25a,28a,40^{2}a■13:6a,34a,54a,58a■14:8a,8,9a,9,47^{2}a■15:5a,6a,7a,8a,10a,11a,13a,16,21a,22a,27a■16:4,24,26a,28a■17:15a,16a■22:6-NU-8:7a■19:7a,8a,10a,19a,21a■31:24a-DE-21:6■23:11-RU-3:3-1SA-25:41-2SA-11:8-2KI-5:10,12,13-2CH-4:6^{2}-JOB-9:30-PS-26:6■51:2a,7a■58:10-IS-1:16-JER-2:22a■4:14a-EZE-23:40■N.T.-all=3538&marked-M'T-6:17■15:2-M'R-7:3,4(907)-LU-7:38(1026)-JOH-9:7,11■13:5,6,8^{2},10,14-AC-22:16(623)

WASHED-all=7364&marked-GE-43:24,31■49:11(3526)-EX-19:14(3526)■40:31,32-LE-8:6,21■13:55(3526),58(3526)■15:17(3526)-NU-8:21(3526)-J'G-19:21-2SA-12:20■19:24(3526)-1KI-22:38(7857),38-2CH-4:6(1740)-JOB-29:6-PS-73:13-PR-30:12-SONG-5:3,12-IS-4:4-EZE-16:4,9,9(7857)■40:38(1740)■N.T.-all=3068&marked-M'T-27:24(633)-LU-7:44(1026)■11:38(907)-JOH-9:7(3538),11(3538),15(3538)■13:10,12(3538),14(3538)-AC-9:37■16:33-1CO-6:11(628)-1TI-5:10(3538)-HEB-10:22-2PE-2:22-RE-1:5■7:14(4150)

WASHEST-JOB-14:19(7857)

WASHING-LE-13:56(3526)-2SA-11:2(7364)-NE-4:23(4325)-SONG-4:2(7367)■6:6(7367)■N.T.-M'R-7:4(909),8(909)-LU-5:2(637)-EPH-5:26(3067)-TIT-3:5(3067)

WASHINGS-HEB-9:10(909)

WASHPOT-PS-60:8(5518,7366)■108:9(5518,7366)

WAST-all=1961-GE-40:13-DE-5:15■15:15■16:12■23:7■24:18,22-RU-3:2(1961)-2SA-5:2-JOB-38:4-PS-99:8-EZE-16:22^{2}■28:14■N.T.-all=2258&marked-M'T-26:29-M'R-14:67-JOH-1:48(5607)■21:18-RE-11:17■16:5

WASTE-all=2723,a=2717&marked-LE-26:31,33-NU-21:30(8074)-DE-32:10(8414)-1KI-17:14(3615)-2KI-19:25(7582)-1CH-17:9(1086)-NE-2:3(2720),17(2720)-JOB-30:3(4875)■38:27(4875)-PS-79:7(8074)■80:13(3765)-IS-5:6(1326),17■15:1^{2}(7703)■23:1(7703),14(7703)■24:1(1110)■33:8(8074)■34:10a■37:18a,26(7582)■42:15a■49:17a,19■51:3■52:9■58:12■61:4(2721)■64:11-JER-2:15(8047)■4:7(5327)■27:17■46:19(8047)■49:13(2721)■50:21a-EZE-5:14■6:6^{2}a■12:20a■19:7a■26:2a■29:9,10,12a■30:12(8074)■35:4■36:35(2720),38(2720)■38:8-JOE-1:7(8047)-AM-7:9a■9:14(8074)-MIC-5:6(7489)-NA-2:10(1110)■3:7(7703)-ZEP-3:6a-HAG-1:4(2720),9(2720)-MAL-1:3(8077)■N.T.-M'T-26:8(684)-M'R-14:4(684)

WASTED-all=2717&marked-NU-14:33(8552)■24:22(1197)-DE-2:14(8552)-1KI-17:16(3615)-1CH-20:1(7843)-PS-137:3(8437)-IS-6:11(7582)■19:5■60:12-JER-44:6(2723)-EZE-30:7-JOE-1:10^{2}(7703)■N.T.-LU-15:13(1287)■16:1(1287)-GA-1:13(4199)

WASTENESS-ZEP-1:15(7722)

WASTER-PR-18:9(7843)-IS-54:16(7843)

WASTES-all=2723-IS-61:4-JER-49:13-EZE-33:24,27■36:4,10,33

WASTETH-JOB-14:10(2522)-PS-91:6(7736)-PR-19:26(7703)

WASTING-IS-59:7(7701)■60:18(7701)

WATCH-all=8245&marked-GE-31:49(6822)-EX-14:24(821)-J'G-7:19(821),19(8104)-1SA-11:11(821)■19:11(8104)-2SA-13:34(6822)-2KI-11:5(4931),6(4931),7(4931)-2CH-20:24(4707)■23:6(4931)-EZR-8:29-NE-4:9(4929)■7:3(4929)-JOB-7:12(4929)■14:16(8104)-PS-90:4(821)■102:7■130:6^{2}(8104)■141:3(8108)-IS-21:5(6822)■29:20-JER-5:6■31:28■44:27■51:12(4929)-NA-2:1(6822)-HAB-2:1(4931),1(6822)■N.T.-all=1127&marked-M'T-14:25(5438)■24:42,43(5438)■25:13■26:38,40,41■27:65(2892),66(2892)■28:11(2892)-M'R-6:48(5438)■13:33(69),34,35,37■14:34,37,38-LU-2:8(5438)■12:38^{2}(5438)■21:36(69)-AC-20:31-1CO-16:13-COL-4:2-1TH-5:6-2TI-4:5(3525)-HEB-13:17(69)-1PE-4:7(3525)-RE-3:3

WATCHED-PS-59:t(8104)-JER-20:10(8104)■31:28(8245)-LA-4:17(6822)-DA-9:14(8245)■N.T.-all=3906&marked-M'T-24:43(1127)■27:36(5083)-M'R-3:2-LU-6:7■12:39(1127)■14:1■20:20-AC-9:24

WATCHER-DA-4:13(5894),23(5894)

WATCHERS-JER-4:16(5341)-DA-4:17(5894)

WATCHES-all=821&marked-NE-7:3(4931)■12:9(4931)-PS-63:6■119:148-LA-2:19

WATCHETH-PS-37:32(6822)-EZE-7:6(6974)-RE-16:15(1127)

WATCHFUL-RE-3:2(1127)

WATCHING-1SA-4:13(6822)-PR-8:34(8245)-LA-4:17(6822)■N.T.-M'T-27:54(5083)-LU-12:37(1127)-EPH-6:18(69)

WATCHINGS-2CO-6:5(70)■11:27(70)

WATCHMAN-all=6822&marked-2SA-18:24,25,26^{2},27-2KI-9:17,18,20-PS-127:1(8104)-IS-21:6,11^{2}(8104),12(8104)-EZE-3:17■33:2,6,7-HO-9:8

WATCHMAN'S-EZE-33:6(6822)

WATCHMEN-all=6822&marked-1SA-14:16-2KI-17:9(5341)■18:8(5341)-SONG-3:3(8104)■5:7(8104)-IS-52:8■56:10■62:6(8104)-JER-6:17■31:6(5341)■51:12(8104)-MIC-7:4

WATCHTOWER-IS-21:5(6844),8(4707)

WATER-all=4325&marked-GE-2:10(8248)■16:7■18:4■21:14,15,19^{2},25■24:11,13^{2},17,32,43^{2}■26:18,19,20,32■29:7(8248),8(8248)■37:24■43:24■49:4-EX-2:10,16sup,16(8248)■4:9^{2}■7:15,18,19,21,24^{2}■8:20■12:9■15:22,27■17:1,2,3,6■20:4■23:25■29:4■30:18,20■32:20■34:28■40:7,12,30-LE-1:9,13■6:28■8:6,21■11:32,34,36,38■14:5,6,8,9,50,51,52■15:5,6,7,8,10,11^{2},12,13,16,17,18,21,22,27■16:4,24,26,28■17:15■22:6-NU-5:17^{2},18,19,22,23,24^{2},26,27^{2}■8:7■19:7,8^{2},9,13,17,18,19,20,21^{2}■20:2,5,8^{2},10,11,13,17,19,24■21:5,16■24:7■27:14^{2}■31:23^{2}■33:9,14-DE-2:6,28■8:7,15^{2}■9:9,18■11:4,11■12:16,24■15:23■23:4,11■29:11-JOS-2:10■3:8,15■7:5■9:21,23,27■15:9,19■16:1-J'G-1:15■4:19■5:4,25■6:38■7:4,5^{2},6■15:19-1SA-7:6■9:11■25:11■26:11,12,16■30:11,12-2SA-14:14■17:20,21■21:10■23:15,16-1KI-13:8,9,16,17,18,19,22^{2}■14:15■17:10■18:4,5,13,33,35^{2},38■19:6■22:27-2KI-2:19■3:9,11,17,19,20^{2},22^{2},25■6:5,22■8:15■20:20-1CH-11:17,18-2CH-18:26■32:4-EZR-10:6-NE-

3:26■8:1,3,16■9:15,20■12:37■13:2-JOB-8:11■9:30(1119)■14:9■15:16■22:7■34:7■36:27-PS-1:3■6:6(4529)■22:14■42:1■63:1■65:9■66:12■72:6(2222)■77:17■79:3■88:17■107:35■109:18■114:8-PR-8:24■17:14■20:5■21:1■25:21■27:19■30:16-EC-2:6,6(8248)-IS-1:22,30■3:1■12:3■14:23■16:9(7301)■21:14■22:11■27:3(8248)■30:14,20■32:2■35:7■37:25■41:17,18^{2}■44:3,4,12■49:10■50:2■58:11■63:12-JER-2:13■8:14■9:15■13:1■14:3■23:15■38:6-LA-1:16■2:19■3:48■5:4-EZE-4:11,16,17■7:17■12:18,19■16:4,9■17:7(8248)■21:7■24:3■26:12■31:14,16■32:6(8248)■36:25-DA-1:12-HO-2:5■5:10■10:7-JOE-3:18(8248)-AM-4:8■8:11-JON-3:7-NA-2:8-HAB-3:10-ZEC-9:11■N.T.-all=5204&marked-M'T-3:11,16■14:28,29■17:15■27:24-M'R-1:8,10■9:41■14:13-LU-3:16■7:44■8:24,25■16:24■22:10-JOH-1:26,31,33■2:7,9^{2}■3:5,23■4:7,10,11,13,14^{3},15,46■5:3,4^{2},7■7:38■13:5■19:34-AC-1:5■8:36^{2},38,39■10:47■11:16-EPH-5:26-1TI-5:23(5202)-HEB-9:19■10:22-JAS-3:12-1PE-3:20-2PE-2:17(504)■3:5,6-1JO-5:6^{2},8-JUDE-12(504)-RE-2:15■16:12■21:6■22:1,17

WATERCOURSE-2CH-32:30(4161,4325)-JOB-38:25(8585)

WATERED-all=8248&marked-GE-2:6■13:10(4945)■29:2,3,10-EX-2:17,19-PR-11:25-IS-58:11(7302)-JER-31:12(7302)■N.T.-1CO-3:6(4222)

WATEREDST-DE-11:10(8248)

WATEREST-PS-65:9(7783),10(7301)

WATERETH-PS-104:13(8248)-PR-11:25(7301)-IS-55:10(7301)■N.T.-1CO-3:7(4222),8(4222)

WATERFLOOD-PS-69:15(7641,4325)

WATERING-GE-30:38(4325)-JOB-37:11(7377)■N.T.-LU-13:15(4222)

WATERPOT-JOH-4:28(5201)

WATERPOTS-JOH-2:6(5201),7(5201)

WATERS-all=4325-GE-1:2,6^{2},7^{2},9,10,20,21,22■6:17■7:6,7,10,17,18^{2},19,20,24■8:1,3^{2},5,7,8,9,11,13■9:11,15-EX-7:17,19,20^{2}■8:6■14:21,22,26,28,29■15:8,10,19,23,25^{2},27-LE-11:9^{2},10^{2},12,46-NU-21:22■24:6,7-DE-4:18■5:8■10:7■14:9■32:51■33:8-JOS-3:13^{3},16■4:7^{2},18,23■5:1■11:5,7■15:7■18:15-J'G-5:19■7:24^{2}-2SA-5:20■12:27■22:12,17-2KI-2:8,14^{2},21^{2},22■5:12■18:31■19:24-1CH-14:11-2CH-32:3-NE-9:11-JOB-3:24■5:10■11:16■12:15■14:11,19■22:11■24:18,19■26:5,8,10■27:20■28:25■29:19■37:10■38:30,34-PS-18:11,15,16■23:2■29:3^{2}■32:6■33:7■46:3■58:7■69:1,2,14■73:10■74:13■77:16,19■78:13,16,20■81:7■93:4■104:3,6■105:29,41■106:11,32■107:23■114:8■119:136■124:4,5■136:6■144:7■147:18■148:4-PR-5:15,15sup,16■8:29■9:17■18:4■25:25■30:4-EC-11:1-SONG-4:15■5:12■8:7-IS-8:6,7■11:9■15:6,9■17:12,13■18:2■19:5,8■22:9■23:3■28:2,17■30:25■32:20■33:16■35:6■36:16■40:12■43:2,16,20■48:1:21^{2}■51:10■54:9^{2}■55:1■57:20■58:11■64:2-JER-2:13,18^{2}■6:7■9:1,18■10:13■14:3■15:18■17:8,13■18:14■31:9■41:12■46:7,8■47:2■48:34■50:38■51:13,16,55-LA-3:54-EZE-1:24■17:5,8■19:10^{2}■26:19■27:26,34■31:4,5,7,14,15■32:2,13,14■34:18■43:2■47:1^{2},2,3^{2},4^{3},5,8^{2},9,12,19■48:28-DA-12:6,7-JOE-1:20■3:18-AM-5:8,24■9:6-JON-2:5-MIC-1:4-NA-3:3,14-HAB-2:14■3:15-ZEC-14:8■N.T.-all=5204&marked-M'T-8:32-M'R-9:22-2CO-11:26(4215)-RE-1:15■7:17■8:10,11^{2}■11:6■14:2,7■16:4,5■17:1,15■19:6

WATERSPOUTS-PS-42:7(6794)

WATERSPRINGS-PS-107:33(4161,4325),35(4161,4325)

WAVE-all=8573,a=5130-EX-29:24a,24,26a,26,27-LE-7:30,34■8:27,29■9:21■10:14,15,15a,15■14:12a,12,24a,24■28:11^{2}a,12a,15,17,20a,20-NU-5:25a■6:20a,20^{2}■18:11,18■N.T.-JAS-1:6(2830)

WAVED-all=5130&marked-EX-29:27-LE-7:30■8:27,29■9:21■14:21(8573)

WAVERETH-JAS-1:6(1252)

WAVERING-HEB-10:23(186)-JAS-1:6(1252)

WAVES-all=1530&marked-2SA-22:5(4867)-JOB-9:8(1116)■38:11-PS-42:7(4867)■65:7■88:7(4867)■89:9■93:3(1796),4(4867)■107:25,29-IS-48:18■51:15-JER-5:22■31:35■51:42,55-EZE-26:3-JON-2:3-ZEC-10:11■N.T.-all=2949&marked-M'T-8:24■14:24-M'R-4:37-LU-21:25(4535)-AC-27:41-JUDE-13

WAX-all=1749-PS-22:14■68:2■97:5-MIC-1:4■N.T.-M'T-24:12(5594)-LU-12:33(3822)-1TI-5:11(2691)-2TI-3:13(4298)-HEB-1:11(3822)

WAXED-all=1980-2SA-3:1^{2}-1CH-11:9-2CH-17:12-ES-9:4■N.T.-M'T-13:15(3975)-LU-1:80(2901)■2:40(2901)■13:19(1096)-AC-13:46(3955)■28:27(3975)-HEB-11:34(1096)-RE-18:3(4147)

WAXEN-all supplied

WAXETH-HEB-8:13(1096)

WAXING-PH'P-1:14(3982)

WAY-all=1870,a=734&marked-GE-14:11(3212)■16:7■18:16(7971),19,33(3212)■24:27,40,42,48,56,61(3212),62(935)■25:34(3212)■28:20■32:1■33:16■35:3,16(776),19■38:14,16,21■42:25,38■45:21,23,24■48:7,7(776),7■49:17-EX-2:12(3541)■4:24■5:20(7125)■13:17,18,21■18:8,20■23:20■32:8■33:3,13-NU-14:25■20:17■21:1,4^{2},22,33■22:22,23^{3},26,31,32,34■24:25-DE-1:2,19,22,31,33^{2},40■2:1,8^{2},27■3:1■6:7■8:2■9:12,16■11:19,28,30■13:5■14:24■17:16■19:3,6■22:4,6■23:4■24:9■25:17,18■27:18■28:7,25,68■31:29-JOS-1:8■2:7,16,22■3:4^{2}■5:4,5,7■8:15,20(2008)■10:10■12:3■23:14■24:17-J'G-2:17,19,22■5:10■8:11■9:25■18:5,6,26■19:9,14(3212),27■20:42-RU-1:7-1SA-1:18■6:9,12^{2}■9:6,8■12:23■13:17,18^{2}■15:2,20■17:52■20:22(3212)■24:3,7■25:12■26:3,25■28:22■30:2-2SA-2:24■13:30,34■15:2,23■16:13■18:23■22:31,33-1KI-1:49■2:2,4■8:25,32,36■11:29■13:9,10^{2},12^{2},17,24^{2},25,26,28,33■15:26,34■16:2,19,26■18:6^{2},7■19:15■20:38■22:24(2088),52^{3}-2KI-2:23■3:8^{2},20■5:19(776)■6:19■7:15■8:18,27■9:27■10:12■11:16,19■16:3■19:28,33■21:21,22■22:2■25:4^{2}-2CH-6:16,23,27,34■11:17■18:23■20:32■21:6,13-EZR-8:21,22,31-NE-9:12,19^{2}-JOB-3:23■6:18■8:19■12:24■16:22a■17:9■18:10(5410)■19:8a,12■21:29,31■22:15a■23:10,11■24:4,18,24■28:23,26■29:25■31:7■36:23■38:19,24,25-PS-1:1,6^{2}■2:12■5:8■18:30,32■25:8,9,12■27:11■32:8■35:6■36:4■37:5,7,23,34■44:18a■49:13■67:2■77:13,19■78:50(5410)■80:12■85:13■86:11■89:41■101:2,6■102:23■107:4,7,40■110:7■119:1,9a,14,27,29,30,32,33,37,101a,104a,128a■139:24^{2}■142:3a■143:8■146:9-PR-1:15,31■2:8,12,20■3:23■4:11,14,19■5:8■6:23■7:8,27■8:2,13,20a,22■9:6■10:17a,29■11:5,20■12:15,26,28a■13:6,15■14:8,12■15:9,10a,19,19a,24a■16:9,17,25,29,31■19:3■20:24■21:2,8,16,29■22:5,6■23:19■26:13■28:10■29:27■30:19^{4},20-EC-10:3■11:5■12:5-IS-3:12■8:11■9:1■15:5■26:7a,8a■28:7^{2}(8582)■30:11,21■35:8^{2}■37:29,34■40:3,14,27■41:3a■42:16■43:16,19■48:15,17■49:11■51:10■53:6■55:7■56:11■57:10,14^{2},17■59:8■62:10■65:2-JER-2:17,18^{2},23,33,36■3:21■4:7(5265),18■5:4,5■6:16,25,27■10:2,23■12:1■18:11,15■21:8■23:12,22■25:5,35(4498)■26:3■28:11■31:9,21■32:39■35:15■36:3,7■39:4^{2}■42:3■48:19■50:5■52:7^{2}-EZE-3:18,19■7:27■8:5^{2}■9:2,10■11:21■13:22■14:22■16:25,27,31,43■18:25^{2},29■21:19,20,21■22:31■23:13,31■33:8,9^{2},11,17^{2},20■36:17^{2},19■42:1,4,11,12^{2}■43:2,4■44:1,3^{2},4■46:2,8^{2},9^{5}■47:2^{3},15■48:1-HO-2:6■6:9■10:13■13:7-AM-2:7-JON-3:8,10-NA-1:3■2:1-MAL-2:8■3:1■N.T.-all=3598&marked-M'T-2:12■3:3■4:15■5:25■7:13,14■8:28,30(3112)■10:5■11:10■13:4,19■15:32■20:17,30■21:8^{2},19,32■22:16-M'R-1:2,3■4:4,15■8:3,27■9:33,34■10:17,32,52■11:8^{2}■12:14-LU-1:79■3:4■7:27■8:5,12■9:57■10:4,31■12:58■14:32(4206)■15:20(3112)■18:35■19:36■20:21■24:32,35-JOH-1:23■14:4,5,6-AC-8:26,36,39■9:2,17sup,17,27■15:3(4311)■16:17■18:25,26■19:9,23■21:5^{2}(4311)■22:4■24:14,22■25:3■26:13-RO-3:2(5158),17■15:24(4311)-1CO-10:13(1545)■12:31■16:7(3938)-2CO-1:16(4311)-PH'P-1:18(5158)-COL-2:14(3319)-1TH-3:11-2TH-2:7(3319)-HEB-5:2(4105)■9:8■10:20■12:13(1624)-JAS-2:25■5:20-2PE-2:2,15^{2},21■3:1(1722)-JUDE-11-RE-16:12

WAYFARING-all=732&marked-J'G-19:7-2SA-12:4-IS-33:8(5674,734)■35:8(1980,1870)-JER-9:2■14:8

WAYMARKS-JER-31:21(6725)

WAYS-all=1870&marked-GE-19:2-LE-26:22-DE-5:33■8:6■10:12■11:22■19:9■26:17■28:7,9,25,29■30:16■32:4-JOS-22:5-1SA-8:3,5■18:14-2SA-22:22-1KI-2:3■3:14■8:39,58■11:33,38■22:43-2KI-17:13-2CH-6:30,31■7:14■13:22■17:3,6■21:12^{2}■22:3■27:6,7■28:2,26■34:2-JOB-4:6■13:15■21:14■22:3,28■24:13,23■26:14■30:12(734)■31:4■34:11(734),21,27■40:19-PS-10:5■18:21■25:4■39:1■51:13■81:13■84:5(4546)■91:11■95:10■103:7■119:3,5,15(734),26,59,168■128:1■138:5■139:3■145:17-PR-1:19(734)■2:13,15(734)■3:6,17,31■4:26■5:6(4570),21■6:6■7:25■8:32■9:15(734)■10:9■14:2,12,14■16:2,7,25■17:23(734)■19:16■22:25(734)■23:26■28:6,18■31:3,27(1979)-EC-11:9-SONG-3:2(7339)-IS-2:3■42:24■45:13■49:9■55:8,9■57:18■58:2,13■63:17■64:5■66:3-JER-2:23,33■3:2,13■6:16■7:3,5,23■12:16■15:7■16:17■17:10■18:11,15■26:13■32:19^{2}-LA-1:4■3:9,11,40-EZE-7:3,4,8,9■14:23■16:47^{2},61■18:23,25,29^{2},30■20:43,44■21:19,21■24:14■28:15■33:11,20■36:31,32-DA-4:37(735)■5:23(735)-HOS-4:9■9:8■12:2■14:9-JO-2:7-MIC-4:2-HAB-3:6(1979)-HAG-1:5,7-ZEC-1:4,6■3:7-MAL-2:9■N.T.-all=3598&marked-M'R-11:4(296)-LU-1:76■3:5-AC-2:28■13:10■14:16-RO-3:16■11:33-1CO-4:17-HEB-3:10-JAS-1:8,11(4197)-2PE-2:2(684)-RE-15:3

WAYSIDE-1SA-4:13(3197,1870)-PS-140:5(3027,4570)

WEAK-all=7504&marked-NU-13:18-J'G-16:7(2470),11(2470),17(2470)-2SA-3:39(7390)■17:2-2CH-15:7(7503)-JOB-4:3-PS-6:2(536)■109:24(3782)-IS-14:10(2740)■35:3-EZE-7:17(3212)■16:30(535)■21:7(3212)-JOE-3:10(2523)■N.T.-all=770&marked-M'T-26:41(772)-M'R-14:38(772)-AC-20:35-RO-4:19■8:3■14:1,2,21■15:1(102)-1CO-1:27(772)■4:10(772)■8:7(772),9,10(772),11,12■9:22^{2}■11:30-2CO-10:10■11:21,29■12:10■13:3,4,9-GA-4:9(772)-1TH-5:14(772)

WEAKEN-IS-14:12(2522)

WEAKENED-EZR-4:4(7503)-NE-6:9(7503)-PS-102:23(6031)

WEAKENETH-JOB-12:21(7503)-JER-38:4(7503)

WEAKER-2SA-3:1(1800)■N.T.-1PE-3:7(772)

WEAKNESS-all=769&marked-1CO-1:25(772)■2:3■15:43-2CO-12:9■13:4-HEB-7:18(772)■11:34

WEALTH-all=2428&marked-GE-34:29-DE-8:17,18-RU-2:1-2KI-15:20-2CH-1:11(5233),12(5233)-EZR-9:12(2896)-ES-10:3(2896)-JOB-21:13

(2896)■31:25-PS-49:6,10■112:3(1952)-PR-5:10(3581)■10:15(1952)■13:11(1952),22■18:11(1952)■19:4(1952)-EC-5:19(5233)■6:2(5233)-ZEC-14:14■N.T.-AC-19:25(2142)

WEALTHY-PS-66:12(7310)-JER-49:31(7961)

WEANED-all=1580-GE-21:8^{2}-1SA-1:22,23^{2},24-1KI-11:20-PS-131,2^{2}-IS-11:8■28:9-HO-1:8

WEAPON-all=3627&marked-NU-35:18-DE-23:13(240)-2CH-23:10(7973)-NE-4:17(7973)-JOB-20:24(5402)-IS-54:17-EZE-9:1,2

WEAPONS-all=3627&marked-GE-27:3-DE-1:41-J'G-18:11,16,17-1SA-21:8-2SA-1:27-2KI-11:8,11-2CH-23:7-EC-9:18-IS-13:5-JER-21:4■22:7■50:25■51:20-EZE-32:27■39:9(5402),10(5402)■N.T.-JOH-18:3(3696)-2CO-10:4(3696)

WEAR-all=3847&marked-EX-18:18(5034)-DE-22:5(1961),11-1SA-2:28(5375)■22:18(5375)-ES-6:8-JOB-14:19(7833)-IS-4:1-DA-7:25(1080)-ZEC-13:4■N.T.-M'T-11:8(5409)-LU-9:12(2827)

WEARETH-JAS-2:3(5409)

WEARIED-all=3811&marked-GE-19:11-IS-43:23(3021),24(3021)■47:13■57:10(3021)-JER-4:31(5888)■12:5-EZE-24:12-MIC-6:3-MAL-2:17^{2}(3021)■N.T.-JOH-4:6(2872)-HEB-12:3(2577)

WEARIETH-JOB-37:11(2959)-EC-10:15(3021)

WEARINESS-EC-12:12(3024)-MAL-1:13(4972)■N.T.-2CO-11:27(2873)

WEARING-1SA-14:3(5375)■N.T.-JOH-19:5(5409)-1PE-3:3(4025)

WEARISOME-JOB-7:3(5999)

WEARY-all=3811&marked-GE-27:46(6973)-DE-25:18(3023)-J'G-4:21(5774)■8:15(3286)-2SA-16:14(5889)■17:2(3023),29(5889)■23:10(3021)-JOB-3:17(3019)■10:1(5354)■16:7■22:7(5889)-PS-6:6(3021)■68:9■69:3(3021)-PR-3:11(6973)■25:17(7646)-IS-1:14■5:27(5889)■7:13^{2}■16:12■28:12(5889)■32:2(5889)■40:28(3021),30(3021),31(3021)■43:22(3021)■46:1(5889)■50:4(3287)-JER-2:24(3286)■6:11■9:5■15:6■20:9■31:25(5889)■51:58(3286),64(3286)-HAB-2:13(3286)■N.T.-LU-18:5(5299)-GA-6:9(1573)-2TH-3:13(1573)

WEASEL-LE-11:29(2467)

WEATHER-JOB-37:22(2091)-PR-25:20(3117)■N.T.-M'T-16:2(5105),3(5494)

WEAVE-IS-19:9(707)■59:5(707)

WEAVER-EX-35:35(707)-IS-38:12(707)

WEAVER'S-all=707-1SA-17:7-2SA-21:19-1CH-11:23■20:5

WEAVEST-J'G-16:13(707)

WEB-J'G-16:13(4545),14(4545)-JOB-8:14(1004)-IS-59:5(6980)

WEBS-IS-59:6(6980)

WEDDING-all=1062-M'T-22:3,8,10,11,12-LU-12:36■14:8

WEDGE-JOS-7:21(3956),24(3956)

WEDLOCK-EZE-16:38(5003)

WEEDS-JON-2:5(5488)

WEEK-all=7620-GE-29:27,28-DA-9:27^{2}■N.T.-all=4521-M'T-28:1-M'R-16:2,9-LU-18:12■24:1-JOH-20:1,19-AC-20:7-1CO-16:2

WEEKS-all=7620-EX-34:22-LE-12:5-NU-28:26-DE-16:9^{2},10,16-2CH-8:13-JER-5:24-DA-9:24,25^{2},26■10:2,3

WEEP-all=1058&marked-GE-23:2■43:30-NU-11:10,13-1SA-11:5■30:4-2SA-1:24■12:21-2CH-34:27-NE-8:9-JOB-27:15■30:25,31-EC-3:4-IS-15:2(1065)■22:4(1065)■30:19■33:7-JER-9:1■13:17,17(1830)■22:10^{2}■48:32-LA-1:16-EZE-24:16,23■27:31-JOE-1:5■2:17-MIC-1:10-ZEC-7:3■N.T.-all=2799-M'R-5:39-LU-6:21,25■7:13■8:52■23:28^{2}-JOH-11:31■16:20-AC-21:13-RO-12:15-1CO-7:30-JAS-4:9■5:1-RE-5:5■18:11

WEEPEST-1SA-1:8(1058)■N.T.-JOH-20:13(2799),15(2799)

WEEPETH-all=1058-2SA-19:1-2KI-8:12-PS-126:6-LA-1:2

WEEPING-all=1065&marked-NU-25:6(1058)-DE-34:8-2SA-3:16(1058)■15:30(1058)-EZR-3:13■10:1(1058)-ES-4:3-JOB-16:16-PS-6:8■30:5■102:9-IS-15:3,5■16:9■22:12■65:19-JER-3:21■9:10■31:9,15,15(1058),16■41:6(1058)■48:5,32■50:4(1058)-EZE-8:14(1058)-JOE-2:12-MAL-2:13■N.T.-all=2799&marked-M'T-2:18(2805),18■8:12(2805)■22:13(2805)■24:51(2805)■25:30(2805)-LU-7:38■13:28(2805)-JOH-11:33^{2}■20:11-AC-9:39-PH'P-3:18-RE-18:15,19

WEIGH-1CH-20:2(4948)-EZR-8:29(8254)-PS-58:2(6424)-IS-26:7(6424)■46:6(8254)-EZE-5:1(4948)

WEIGHED-all=8254&marked-GE-23:16-1SA-2:3(8505)-2SA-14:26-EZR-8:25,26,33-JOB-6:2■28:15■31:6-IS-40:12-JER-32:9,10-DA-5:27(8625)-ZEC-11:12

WEIGHETH-JOB-28:25(8505)-PR-16:2(8505)

WEIGHING-all supplied

WEIGHT-all=4948&marked-GE-24:22^{2}■43:21-LE-19:35■26:26-NU-7:31,37,43,49,55,61,67,73,79-DE-25:15(68)-JOS-7:21-J'G-8:26-1SA-17:5-2SA-12:30■14:26(68)■21:16^{2}-1KI-7:47■10:14-2KI-25:16-1CH-21:25■22:3,14■28:14^{2},15^{3},16,17^{2},18-2CH-3:9■4:18■9:13-EZR-8:30,34^{2}-JOB-28:25-PR-11:1(68)■16:11(6425)-JER-52:20-EZE-4:10(4946),16-ZEC-5:8(68)■N.T.-2CO-4:17(922)-HEB-12:1(3591)-RE-16:21(5006)

WEIGHTIER-M'T-23:23(926)

WEIGHTS-all=68-LE-19:36-DE-25:13-PR-16:11■20:10,23-MIC-6:11

WEIGHTY-PR-27:3(5192)■N.T.-2CO-10:10(926)

WELFARE-all=7965&marked-GE-43:27-EX-18:7-1CH-18:10-NE-2:10(2896)-JOB-30:15(3444)-PS-69:22-JER-38:4

WELL-all=3190,a=875,b=7965&marked-GE-4:7^{2}■12:13,16■16:14a■21:19a,25a,30a■24:11a,13(5869),16(5869),20a,29(5869),30(5869),42(5869),43(5869),45(5869)■25:11(883)■26:19a,20a,21a,22a,25a,32a■29:2^{2}a,6^{2}b,17(3303)■32:9■37:14^{2}b■39:6(3303)■40:14■41:2(3303),4(3303),18(3303)■43:27b■49:22(5869)-EX-1:20■2:15a■10:29(3651)-NU-11:18(2895)■21:16a,17a,18a,22a■36:5(3651)-DE-4:40■5:16,28,29,33(2895)■6:3,18■12:25,28■15:16(2895)■18:17■19:13(2895)■22:7-JOS-18:15(4599)-J'G-7:1(5878)■9:16(2895)-RU-3:1,13(2896)-1SA-9:10(2896)■16:16(2895),17,23(2895)■19:22(953)■20:7(2896)■24:18(2896),19(2896)■25:31-2SA-3:13(2896),26(953)■11:25(2090)■17:18(375),21(375)■18:28b■23:15(953),16(953)-1KI-2:18(2896)■8:18■18:24(2896)-2KI-4:23b,26^{4}b■5:21b,22b■7:9(3651)■9:11(7965)■10:30(2895)■25:24-1CH-11:17(953),18(953)-2CH-6:8(2895)■12:12(2896)-NE-2:13(5869)-JOB-12:3(71)■33:31(7181)-PS-49:18■73:2(369)■78:29(3966)■84:6(4599)■119:65(2896)■128:2(2896)-PR-5:15a■10:11(4726)■11:10(2898)■14:15(995)■30:29■31:27(6822)-EC-8:12(2896),13(2896)-SONG-4:15a-IS-1:17■3:10(2896),24(4639)■33:23(3651)■42:21(2654)-JER-1:12■7:23■15:11(2896),11sup■22:15(2896),16(2896)■38:20■40:9■42:6(2896)■44:17(2896)-EZE-24:5(7571)-DA-1:4(2896)-JON-4:4,9^{2}-ZEC-8:15■N.T.-all=2573&marked-M'T-3:17(2106)■12:12,18(2106)■15:7■17:5(2106)■25:21(2095),23(2095)-M'R-1:11(2106)■7:6,9,37■12:28,32-LU-1:7(4260),18(4260)■3:22(2106)■6:26■19:17(2095)■20:39(2573)-JOH-2:10(3184)■4:6^{2}(4077),11(5421),12(5421),14(4077),17(2573)■8:48(2573)■11:12(4982)■13:13■18:23-AC-10:33,47(2532)■15:29(2095)■16:2(3140)■25:10■28:25-RO-2:7(18)■11:20-1CO-7:37,38■9:5(2532)■10:5(2106)■14:17-2CO-6:9(1921)■11:4-GAL-4:17■5:7■6:9(2570)-EPH-6:3(2095)-PH'P-4:14-COL-3:20(2101)-2TH-3:13(2569)-1TI-3:4,12,13■5:10(3140),17-2TI-1:18(957)-TIT-2:9(1510,2101)-HEB-4:2(2509)■13:16(2100)-JAS-2:8,19-1PE-2:14(17),15(15),20(15)■3:6(15),17(15)■4:19(16)-2PE-1:17(2106),19-3JO-6

WELLBELOVED-SONG-1:13(1730)-IS-5:1^{2}(3039)■N.T.-all=27-M'R-12:6-RO-16:5-3JO-1

WELLFAVOURED-NA-3:4(2896,2580)

WELLPLEASING-PH'P-4:18(2101)-HEB-13:21(2101)

WELL'S-all=875-GE-29:2,3^{2},8,10-2SA-17:19

WELLS-all=4599&marked-GE-26:15(875),18(875)-EX-15:27(5869)-NU-20:17(875)-DE-6:11(953)-2KI-3:19,25-2CH-26:10(953)-NE-9:25(953)-IS-12:3■N.T.-2PE-2:17(4077)

WELLSPRING-PR-16:22(4726)■18:4(4726)

WEN-LE-22:22(2990)

WENCH-2SA-17:17(8198)

WENT-all=3212,a=5927,b=3318,c=935,d=1980,e=3381,f=5674,g=5265&marked-GE-2:6a,10b■4:16b■7:7c,9c,15c,16c,18■8:7b,18b,19b■9:18b,23■10:11b■11:31b■12:4,5b,10e■13:1a,3,5d■14:8b,11■17b,24d■15:17c■16:4c■17:22a■18:16d,22,33■19:6b,14b,28a,30a,33c■21:16,19■22:3,6,8,13,19■23:10c,18c■24:10,16e,45e,61,63b■25:22,34■26:1,13,23a,26d■27:5,14,22(5066)■28:5,9,10b,10■29:1(5375,7272),10(5066),23c,30c■30:4c,14,16b■31:19d,33c,33b■32:1d,21f■34:1b,6b,24^{2}b,26b■35:3d,13a,22■36:6■37:12,17■38:1e,2c,9c,11,12a,19■39:11c■41:45b,46b,46f■42:3e■43:15e,31b■44:28b■45:25a■46:29a■47:10b■49:4a■50:7^{2}a,9a,14a,18-EX-2:1,8,11b,13b■4:18,27,29■5:1c,10b■7:10c,23c■8:12b,30b■9:33b■10:6b,14a,18b■11:8b■12:28,38a,41b■13:18a,21d■14:8b,19d,19,19g,22c,23c■15:19c,19d,20b,22b,22■16:27b■17:10a■18:7b,27■19:3a,14e,20a,25e■24:9a,13a,15a,18c■32:15e■33:7b,8b■34:4a,34c,35c■38:26f■40:32c,36g-LE-9:8(7121),23c■10:2b,5(7126)■16:23c■24:10b-NU-8:22c■10:14g,33g,34g■11:8(7751),24b,26b,31g■13:21a,26,31a■14:24c,38d■16:25,33e■17:8c■20:6c,15e,27a■21:23b,33a,33b■22:14c,21,22d,23,26f,32b,35,36b,39■23:3■24:1d,25,25d■25:8c■26:4b■31:13b,21c,27b,28b,36b■32:9a,39,41d,42d■33:1b,3b,8,23g,29g,33g,38a-DE-1:19,24a,31d,33d,43a■2:13f■3:1a■5:5a■10:3a,22e■26:5e■29:26■31:1,14■34:1a-JOS-2:1,5b,5d,22■3:2(5974),6■5:13■6:1b,9d,13^{2}d,20a,23c■7:2a,4a■8:9,10a,11a,13,14b,17b■9:4,6■10:5a,9a,24d,36a■11:4b■14:8a■15:3b,3a,4b,6^{2}a,7a,8^{2}a,9b,10e,11^{2}b,15a■16:6b,6(5437),7e,7b,8■17:7d■18:8,8d,9,12^{2}a,13f,15^{2}b,17^{2}b,18e■19:11a,47b,47a■22:6■24:4e,11f,17d-J'G-1:3,4a,9e,10,11,16a,16,17,22a,26■2:6,15b■3:10b,13,19b,22c,23b,27e,28e■4:9,10^{2}a,14e,18b,21c■6:19c,33f■7:11e■8:8a,11a,29■9:1,5c,6,7,8d,21,26f,27b,27c,35b,39b,42b,50,52(5066)■11:3b,5,11,18,38,40■12:1f■13:11,20a■14:1e,5e,7e,9,10e,18c,19e,19a■15:4,8e,9a,11e■16:1,1c,3g,14g,19(5493)■17:10■18:11g,12a,14d,17d,17a,18c,20c,26,26(7725)■19:2,3,14,14c,15c,18,23b,27b■20:1b,18a,20b,23a,25b,26a,30a,31b■21:23,24b-RU-1:1,7b,7,19,21d■2:3,18c■3:6e,7c,15c■4:1a,13c-1SA-1:3a,7a,18,21a,22a■2:11,20d■3:3(3518),5,6,8,9■4:1b■5:12a■6:12^{3}d■7:7a,11b,16d■9:9,10,11a,14a,26b■10:14d,26d,26■11:15■13:7f,10b,20e,23b■14:16,19,21a,46a,46d■

15:34,34a■16:13■17:4b,7d,12c,13,13d, 15d,20,35b■18:5b,13b,16b,27,30^{2}b■19:8b, 12,18,22,23^2■20:11b,35b,42c■21:10c■ 22:1e,3■23:5,13d,16,18d,24,25,26,28,29a■ 24:2,3c,7,8b,22■25:1e,12(7725),13a,42d, 42■26:2e,13f,25■27:8a■28:8,25■29:11a■ 30:2,9,21b,22^{2}d■31:12-2SA-1:4(1961)■ 2:2a,12b,13b,15f,24c,29,32■3:16,19,21■ 4:5■5:6,10,17e■6:2,4d,12■7:18c,23d■ 8:3,6d,14d■11:9e,10e,13b,13e,17b,21 (5066),22■12:16c,24c,29■13:8,9b,19, 37,38■14:23■15:9,11^{2}d,16b,17b,24a, 30^{2}a,30d,30^{2}a■16:13,13^{2}d,22c■17:17 (980),17,18,18e,21,25c■18:6b,9c, 9f,24,33a,33■19:17(6743),18f,19b, 31f,39f,40^{2}f■20:2a,3c,5,7^{2}b,8c,8b, 13f,14f,14c,22c■21:12,15e■22:9a■ 23:13e,17d,20e,21e■24:4b,7b,19a, 20b-1KI-1:15c,38e,49,50■2:8,19c,34a, 40^2,46b■3:4■6:8a■8:66■10:5a,13,16a, 17a,29b■11:5,24,29b■12:1,25b,30■ 13:10,12^{2}d,14,19(7725),28■14:4,28c■ 15:17a■16:10c,17a,18c,31■17:5^2,10,15■ 18:2,6^{2}d,16^2,42^{2}a,43a,45■19:3,4d,8,13b,21■ 20:1a,16b,17b,21b,26a,27,39b,43■21:27d■ 22:24^{2}f,29a,30c,36f,48d-2KI-1:9a,13a, 15e■2:1,2e,6,7d,8f,11d,11a,13(7725),14f, 21b,23a,25■3:6b,7,9,12e,24(5221),25 (5437)■4:5,18b,21a,21b,25,31(7725),33c, 34a,35a,37c,37b,39b■5:4c,11,12,14e, 25c,25d,26d,27b■6:4,23,24a■7:8c,8,15, 16b■8:2,3b,9,21f,28,29(7725),29e■9:4, 6c,16,18,21^{2}b,24b,35■10:9b,23c,24c, 25■11:16c,18c■12:17a,18a■13:5b■ 14:11a■15:14a■16:9a,10■17:5a,15■ 18:7b,17a■19:1c,14a,35b,36■22:14■ 23:2a,29a,29■24:12b■25:4-1CH-2:21c■ 4:39,42d■5:18b■6:15d■7:23c,23(1961)■ 11:4,6a,15e,22e,23e■12:15f,17b,20,33b, 36b■13:6a■14:8a,8b,17b■15:25d■16:20d■ 17:21d■18:3,6d,13d■19:5■21:4d,19a, 21b■27:1b■29:30f-2CH-1:3,6a■8:3,17d, 18c■9:4a,12,15a,16a,21d■10:1,16■12:12 (1961)■14:10b■15:2b,5b■17:9(5437)■ 18:2e,12d,23f,28a,29c■19:2b,4b■ 20:20^{2}b,21b■21:9f■22:5,6e,7b■23:2 (5437),17c■25:11,21a■26:6b,11b,16c,17c■ 28:9b■29:16c,18c,20a■30:6■31:1b■ 34:22,30a■35:20b-EZR-2:1a,59a■4:23 (236)■5:8(236)■7:6a,7a■8:1a■10:6-NE-2:13b,14f,15a,16d■7:6a,61a■8:12,16b■ 9:11f,24c■12:1a,31d,32,37a,38d-ES-2:14c■3:15b■4:1b,6b,17f■5:9b■7:8b■ 8:14b,15b■9:4d-JOB-1:4d,12b■2:7b■ 18:20(6923)■29:7b■30:28d■31:34b■ 42:9-PS-18:8a■42:4(1718)■66:6f,12c■ 68:25(6923)■73:17c■77:17d■81:5b■ 105:13d■114:1b■119:67(7683)■133:2e -PR-7:8(6805)■24:30f-EC-2:20(5437) -SONG-5:7(5437)■6:11e-IS-7:1a■8:3 (7126)■37:1c,14a,36b,37■48:3b■51:23f■ 52:4e■57:17■60:15f-JER-3:8■7:24 (1961)■11:10d■13:5,7■18:3e■22:11b■ 26:21c■28:4c,11■31:2d■36:12e,20c■ 37:4b,12b■38:8b,11c■39:4^{2}b■40:6c■ 41:6b,6d,12,14,15■44:3■51:59■52:7b,7 -EZE-1:9^2,12^3,13d,13b,17^2,19,20,21,24■ 3:14,23b■8:10c,11a■9:2c,7b■10:2c,3c,4 (7311),6c,7b,11^3,16,19b,22■11:23a,24a■ 16:14b■19:6d■20:16d■23:44^{2}c■24:12b■ 27:33b■31:15e,17e■36:20c,21c,22c■ 40:6a,22a,49a■41:3c■44:10^2(8582),15 (8582)■47:3b■48:11^3(8582)-DA-2:13 (5312),16(5954),17(236),24(5954),24 (236)■6:10(5954),18(236),18(5075),19 (236)-HO-1:3■2:13■5:13■9:10c■11:2d -AM-5:3^{2}b,19c-JON-1:3^{2}e■2:6e■3:3■ 4:5b-NA-3:10d-HAB-3:5,5b,11d-ZEC-2:3^{2}b■5:5b■6:7b■8:10b■10:2g■N.T.-all=1831,a=565,b=4198,c=305,d=1525,e=2597,f=2064&marked-M'T-2:9 (4254)■3:5(1607),16c■4:23(4013),24a■ 5:1c■8:32a,33a■9:25d,26,32,35(4013)■ 11:7,8,9■12:1b,9f,14■13:1,2(1684),3,25a, 36f,46a■14:12f,14,23c,25a■15:21,29c■ 18:13(4105),28,30a■19:22a■20:1(1821), 3(1821),4a,5,6■21:6b,9(4254),12d,17,29a, 30a,33(589)■22:5a,10,15b,22a■24:1■ 25:1,10a,10d,16b,18a,25a■26:14b,30,39 (4281),42a,44a,58d,75■27:5a,53d,58 (4344),66b■28:9b,16b-M'R-1:5(1607), 20a,21(1531),35,45■2:12,13,23(3899),23 (3598,4160),26d■3:6,19f,21■4:3■5:13, 14,24a■6:1,6(4013),12,24,27a,51c■7:24a■ 8:27■10:22a■32(4254),46(1607)■11:4a,9 (4254),11,15d,19(1607)■12:1(589),12a■ 13:1(1607)■14:10a,16,26,35(4281),39a, 68■15:43d■16:8,10b,12b,13a,20-LU-1:9d,39b■2:1,3b,4c,41b,42c,44f, 51e■4:14,16d,30b,37(1607),42b■5:15 (1330),19c,27■6:1(1279),4d,12,19■7:6b, 11b,11(4848),17,24,25,26,36d■8:1(1353), 2,5,22(1684),27,33,34a,35,37(1681),39a, 42(5217)■9:6(1330),10(5298),28c,52b, 56b,57b■10:30e,34(4334),38b■11:37d■ 13:22(1279)■14:1f,25(4848)■15:15b■ 16:30b■17:11b,14(5217),29■18:10c,14e, 39(4254)■19:12b,28b,32a,36b,45d■ 20:9(589)■21:37■22:4a,13a,39b,47 (4281),62■23:52(4344)■24:13b,15 (4848),24a,28b,29d-JON-2:12e,13c■ 4:28a,30,43a,45f,47a,50b■5:1c,4e■6:1a, 3(424),16e,17f,21(5217),22(4897),66a■ 7:10c,14c,53b■8:1b,9,59■9:7a,11a■ 10:40a■11:20(5221),28a,31,46a,54a, 55c■12:11(5217),13■13:3(5217),30■ 18:1,4,6a,15(4897),16,28d,29,38■ 19:4,9d,17■20:3,5d,6d,8d,10a■21:3,11c, 23-AC-1:10b,13c,21d(1831)■3:1c■ 4:23f■5:26a■7:15e■8:4(1330),5(2718), 27b,36b,38e,39b■9:1(4334),17a, 29(2021),39(4905)■10:9(3596),9c,21e, 23,27d,38(1330)■12:9,10,17b,19(2718)■ 13:11(4013),14d■14:1d,25e■15:24, 38(4905),41(1330)■16:4(1279),13,16b, 40■17:2d,10(549)■18:22e,23(1330)■ 19:8d,12■20:10e,13(4281)■21:2(1910), 5b,15c,16(4905),18(1524),31(2212)■ 22:5b,26(4334)■23:16(3854),19(402)■ 24:11c■25:6e■26:12b,21(3987)■ 28:14f-RO-10:18-2CO-2:13■8:17-GA-1:17(424),17a,18(424)■2:1c,2c-1TI-1:3b,18(4254)-HEB-9:6(1524)■11:8, 8f-1PE-3:19b-1JO-2:19,19sup-3JO-7-RE-1:16(1607)■6:2,4■10:9a■12:17a■ 16:2a■20:9c

WENTEST-all=1980&marked-GE-49:4(5927)-J'G-5:4(3318)■8:1-1SA-10:2 -2SA-7:9■16:17■19:25-PS-68:7(3318)-IS-57:7(5927),9(7788)-JER-2:2(3212)■31:21 -HAB-3:13(3318)■N.T.-AC-11:3(1525)

WEPT-all=1058&marked-GE-21:16■ 27:38■29:11■33:4■37:35■42:24■43:30■ 45:2(5414,853,6963,1065),14^2,15■46:29■ 50:1,17-EX-2:6-NU-11:4,18,20■14:1 -DE-1:45■34:8-J'G-2:4■14:16,17■ 20:23,26■21:2-RU-1:9,14-1SA-1:7,10■ 11:4■20:41■24:16■30:4-2SA-1:12■3:32^2, 34■12:22■13:36^2■15:23,30■18:33-2KI-8:11■13:14■20:3■22:19-EZR-3:12■ 10:1-NE-1:4■8:9-JOB-2:12-PS-69:10■ 137:1-IS-38:3-HO-12:4■N.T.-all=2799&marked-M'T-26:75-M'R-5:38■ 14:72■16:10-LU-7:32■8:52■19:41■ 22:62-JOH-11:35(1145)■20:11-AC-20:37(1096,2805)-1CO-7:30-RE-5:4

WERT-RE-3:15(1498)

WEST-all=3220,a=4628&marked-GE-12:8■28:14-EX-10:19■27:12■38:12 -NU-2:18■34:6■35:5-DE-33:23-JOS-8:9,12,13■11:2,3■12:7■15:12■18:14, 15■19:34-1KI-7:25-1CH-9:24■12:15a -2CH-4:4■32:30a■33:14a-PS-75:6a■ 103:12a■107:3a-IS-11:14■43:5a■45:6a■ 49:12■59:19a-EZE-41:12■42:19■45:7^2■ 47:20^2■48:1,2,3,4,5,6,7,8^2,10,16,17,21,23, 24,25,26,27,34-DA-8:5(4628)-HO-11:10 -ZEC-8:7(3996,8121)■14:4■N.T.-all=1424&marked-M'T-8:11■24:27-LU-12:54■13:29-AC-27:12(3047),12(5566) -RE-21:13

WESTERN-NU-34:6(3220)

WESTWARD-all=3220&marked -GE-13:14-EX-26:22,27■36:27,32-NU-3:23-DE-3:27-JOS-5:1■15:8,10■16:3,8■ 18:12■19:26,34■22:7■23:4(3996,8121) -1CH-7:28(4628)■26:16(4628),18(4628), 30(4628)-EZE-45:7■46:19■48:18,21 -DA-8:4

WET-all=6647&marked-JOB-24:8 (7372)-DA-4:15,23,25,33■5:21

WHALE-JOB-7:12(8577)-EZE-32:2(8565)

WHALE'S-M'T-12:40(2785)

WHALES-GE-1:21(8577)

WHAT-all=4100,a=853,834,b=834, c=4310&marked-GE-2:19■3:13■4:10■ 9:24a■12:18■15:2■20:9^2,10■21:17■ 24:65c■25:32■26:10■27:37,46■29:15, 25■30:31■31:26,36,43■32:27■33:8c,15■ 34:11b■37:10,15,20,26■38:16,18b■39:8■ 41:25a,28b,55b■42:28■44:15,16^2■46:33■ 47:3-EX-3:13^2■4:2,12b,15a■10:2a,26■ 12:26■13:14■15:24■16:7,8,15■17:4■ 18:14■19:4b■32:1,21,23■33:5-LE-15:9b■ 17:3(376)■22:4(376)■25:20-NU-9:8■ 10:32b■13:18,19^2,20■15:34■16:11■21:14 (853)■22:9c,19,28■23:11,17,23■24:13b, 14b■31:50b-DE-1:22b,22(853),33b■ 3:24c■4:3a,7c,8c■6:20■7:18a■8:2a■ 10:12■11:4b,5b,6b■12:32(853)■20:5c,6c, 7c,8c■24:9a■25:17a■29:24■32:20-JOS-2:10b■4:6,21■5:14■7:8,9,19■9:3a■ 15:18■22:16,24a■24:7a-J'G-1:14■7:11■ 8:2,3,18(375)■9:48■10:18c■11:12■13:8, 17c■14:6a,18^2■15:11■16:5■18:3^2,8,14, 18,23,24^3■20:12■21:8c-RU-2:18a■3:4a -1SA-3:17■4:6,14,16■5:8■6:2,4■9:7^2■ 10:2,8a,11,15■11:5■13:11■14:43■15:14, 16a■16:3a■17:26,29■18:18c■19:3■20:1^3, 10,32■21:2b,3■22:3■25:17■26:18^2■28:2a, 9a,13,14,15■29:3,8^2-2SA-3:24■7:18c, 20,23c■9:8■12:21■14:5■15:2c,21b,35 (3605)■16:2,10,20■17:5■18:4b,21b,29■ 19:22,28,35^{2}a,37a■21:3,4,11a■24:13,17 -1KI-1:16■2:5a,5b,9a■3:5■8:38(3605)■ 9:13■11:22■12:9,16■13:12(335,2088), 12b■14:3,14■16:5b■17:18■18:9,13a■ 19:9,13,20■20:22a■22:14a-2KI-1:7■2:9■ 3:13■4:2^2,13,14,43■6:28,33■7:12a■8:13, 14■9:18,19,22■18:19■19:11a■20:8,14, 15■22:19b-1CH-12:32■17:16c,18,21c■ 21:12■29:14c-2CH-1:7■6:29b■10:6(349) 9,16■18:13a■19:6,10(3602)■20:12■25:9■ 32:13■35:21-EZR-5:4(4479)■6:8(3964, 1768)■8:17(1697)■9:10-NE-2:4,12,16, 19■4:2,20b■13:17-ES-1:15■2:1^{2}a,11, 15a■4:5■5:3^2,6^2■6:3,6■7:2^2■8:1■9:5, 12^3-JOB-2:10(1571)■6:11^2,25■7:17,20■ 9:12■11:8^2■13:13■15:9,9sup,12,14■16:3, 6■21:15^2,21■22:17■23:5■27:8■31:2,2sup, 14^2■34:4,7c,33■35:3^2,6^2,7^2■37:19■38:24 (335,2088)■40:4-PS-8:4■11:3■25:12c■ 30:9■34:12c■39:4c,7■46:8b■50:16■56:4, 11■66:16b■85:8■89:48c■114:5■116:12■ 118:6■120:3^2■144:3-PR-4:19■23:1a■ 25:8■27:1■30:4■31:2^3-EC-1:3■2:2, 3(335),12,22■3:9,22■5:11,16■6:8^2,11,12^2■ 7:10■8:4■10:14^2■11:2,5-SONG-5:9^2■ 6:13■8:8-IS-1:11■3:15■5:4,5a■10:3■ 14:32■19:12■21:6b,11^2■22:1,16■33:13b■ 36:4■37:11b■38:15,22■39:3,4■40:6,18■ 41:22a,22■45:9,10^2■52:5-JER-1:11,13■ 2:5,18^2,23■4:30■5:15,31■6:18a,20■7:12a, 17■8:6,9■9:12■11:15■13:21■16:10■ 23:25a,28,33^2,35^2,37^2■24:3■32:24b■ 33:24■37:18■38:25^2■48:19-LA-2:13^3■ 5:1-EZE-2:8a■8:6,12b■12:9,22■15:2■ 17:12■18:2■19:2■20:29■21:13■24:19■ 27:32■33:30■37:18■47:23b-DA-2:22 (4101),23(1768),28(4101),29^2(4101),45 (4101)■3:5(1768),15(1768)■4:35(4101)■ 8:19a■10:14a■12:8■20:29-HO-6:4^2■ 9:5,14■10:3■14:8-JO-3:4-AM-4:13■ 5:18■7:8-JON-1:6,8^2,8(335,2088),11■ 4:5-MIC-1:5^{2}c■6:1b,3,5^2,8^2-NA-1:9 -HAB-2:1^2,18-ZEC-1:9^2,19,21■2:2^2■ 4:2,4,5,11,12,13■5:2,5,6■6:4■13:6-MAL-3:13,14■N.T.-all=5101,a=3739,b=3588,c=4169&marked-M'T-2:7b■5:46, 47■6:3,8a,25^2,31^2■7:2,a,9■8:27(4217),29, 33b■9:13■10:19^2,27^{2}a■11:7,8,9■12:3,7, 11■16:26^2■17:25■18:31b■19:6a,16,20, 27■20:15a,21,22,32■21:16,23c,24c,27c, 28,40■22:17,42■24:3,42c,43c■26:8,15,

40(3779),62,65,66,70■27:4,22,23-**M'R**-1:24,27^{2}■2:25■3:8(3745)■4:24a,30c,41 (5101,686)■5:7,9,14,33a■6:2,10(3699), 24,30(3745)■8:36,37■9:6,9a,10,16,33■10:3,9a,17,32b,36,38,51■11:5,24(3745), 28c,29c,33c■12:9■13:1^{2}(4217),4,11,37a■14:8a,36,40,60,63,64,68■15:12,14,24 -**LU**-1:29(4217),66(5101,686)■3:10,12, 14■4:34,36■5:19c,22■6:3a,11,32c,33c, 34c■7:22a,24,25,26,31,39(4217)■8:9,25 (5101,686),28,30,34b,35b,36(4459),47a, 56b■9:25,33a,55(3634)■10:25,26■12:11^{2},12a,17,22^{2},29^{2},39c,49,57b■13:18■14:31■15:4,8,26■16:3,4■18:6,18,36, 41■19:48■20:2c,8c,13,15,17■21:7■22:49b,60a,71■23:22,31,34,47b■24:17, 19c,35b-**JOH**-1:21,22,38■2:4,18,25■3:32a■4:22^{2}a,27■5:12a,19^{2}(5100)■6:6,9, 28,30^{2}■7:36,51■8:5■9:17,21(4459)26■10:6■11:46a,47,56■12:6b,27,33c,49■13:7a,12,28■15:7a,15■16:17,18^{2}■18:21^{2}, 29,32c,35,38■19:22a■21:19c,21,22,23 -**AC**-2:12,37■4:7c,9,16■5:7b,35■7:40,49c, 49■8:30a,36■9:6^{2}■10:4,6,15a,17,21, 29■11:9a,17■12:18(5101,686)■13:12b■14:11a■15:12(3745)■16:30■17:18,19,20■19:3,35■20:18(4459)■21:13,19a,22,33■22:10,15a,26■23:19,30b,34c■28:22a -**RO**-3:1^{2},3,5,9,19(3745),27c■4:1,3,21a■6:1,15,21■7:7,15^{2}a■8:3b,26,27,31■9:14, 30■10:8■11:2,4,7,15■12:2-**1CO**-2:11■3:13(3697)■4:7,21■5:12■6:16(2228),19 (2228)■7:16,36a■9:18■10:15a,19■11:22 (1063),22■14:6,7b,9b,15,16,36(2228)■15:2,10a,29,32,35c-**2CO**-1:13a■6:14^{2}, 15^{2},16■7:11(4214),11^{4}sup■11:12a■12:13 -**GA**-4:30-**EPH**-1:18^{2},19■3:9,18■4:9■5:10,17-**PH'P**-1:18,22■3:7(3748)-**COL**-1:27■2:1(2245)-**1TH**-1:5(3634),9(3697)■2:19■3:9■4:2-**2TH**-2:6b-**1TI**-1:7a -**2TI**-2:7a■3:11(3634)-**HEB**-2:6■7:11■11:32■12:7■13:6-**JAS**-1:24(3697)■2:14, 16■4:14b,14c-**1PE**-1:11(1519,5101),11c■2:20c■4:17-**2PE**-3:11(4217)-**1JO**-3:1 (4217),2-**JUDE**-10(3745)-**RE**-1:11a■2:7,11,17,29■3:3c,6,13,22■7:13■18:18

WHATSOEVER-all=3605,a=3605,834&marked-**GE**-2:19a■8:19■19:12a■31:16a■39:22a-**EX**-13:2■21:30a■29:37■30:29-**LE**-5:3,4a■6:27■7:27■11:3,9,12,27,32^{2},33,42^{3}■13:58■15:26 (3605,3627)■17:8(376,834),10(376,834), 13(376,834)■21:18■22:5,18(376,834),20■23:29,30■27:32-**NU**-5:10■18:13a■19:22■22:17a■23:3(1697,4100)■30:12 -**DE**-2:37■12:8,15,20,21■14:10a,26^{2}a -**J'G**-10:15■11:31(834)-**1SA**-14:36■20:4 (4100)■25:8(853,834)-**2SA**-3:36a■15:15a■19:38a-**1KI**-8:37■10:13(834)■20:6-**2CH**-6:28■9:12-**EZR**-7:18(1401, 1768),21(3605,3627),23(3605,3627)-**ES**-2:13(853,3605,834)-**JOB**-37:12(3605, 834)-**PS**-1:3a■115:3a■135:6a-**EC**-2:10a■3:14a■8:3a■9:10a-**JER**-1:7a■42:4■44:17 (853,3605)■**N.T.**-all=3956&marked -**M'T**-5:37(3588)■7:12(3745,302)■10:11 (3739,302)■14:7(3739,1437)■15:5(3739, 1437),17■16:19(3739,1487),19(1487)■17:12(3745)■18:18^{2}(3745,1437)■20:4 (3739,1437),7(3739,1437)■21:22(3745, 302)■23:3(3745,302)■28:20(3745) -**M'R**-6:22(3739,1437),23(3739,1437)■7:11 (1437),18■9:13(3745)■10:21(3745),35 (3739,1437)■11:23(3739,302)■13:11(3739, 1437)-**LU**-4:23(3745)■9:4(3739, 302)■10:5(3739,302),8(3739,302),10 (3739,302),35(3748,302)■12:3(3745) -**JOH**-2:5(3748,302)■5:4(1221)■11:22 (3748,302)■12:50(3739)■14:13(3748, 302),26(3739)■15:14(3745),16(3748, 302)■16:13(3745,302),23(3748,302)■17:7(3745)-**AC**-3:22(3748,302)■4:28 (3745)-**RO**-14:23■15:4(3745)■16:2(3739, 302)-**1CO**-10:25,27,31(5100)-**GA**-2:6(3697, 4219)■6:7(3739,1437)-**EPH**-5:13■6:8(3739,1437,5100)-**PH'P**-4:8^{6}(3745), 11(3588,3739)-**COL**-3:17(3956,3754, 5100),23(3956,3754,1437)-**1JO**-3:22 (3739,1437)■5:4,15(3739,302)-**3JO**-5 (3739,1437)-**RE**-18:22

WHEAT-all=2406&marked-**GE**-30:14-**EX**-9:32■34:22-**NU**-18:12(1715) -**DE**-8:8■32:14-**J'G**-6:11■15:1-**RU**-2:23 -**1SA**-6:13■12:17-**2SA**-4:6■17:28-**1KI**-5:11-**1CH**-21:20,23-**2CH**-2:10,15■27:5 -**EZR**-6:9(2591)■7:22(2591)-**JOB**-31:40 -**PS**-81:16■147:14-**PR**-27:22(7383) -**SONG**-7:2-**IS**-28:25-**JER**-12:13■23:28(1250)■31:12(1715)■41:8-**EZE**-4:9■27:17■45:13-**JOE**-1:11■2:24(1250) -**AM**-5:11(1250)■8:5(1250),6(1250)■**N.T.**-all=4621-**M'T**-3:12■13:25,29,30 -**LU**-3:17■16:7■22:31-**JOH**-12:24-**AC**-27:38-**1CO**-15:37-**RE**-6:6■18:13

WHEATEN-**EX**-29:2(2406)

WHEEL-all=212&marked-**1KI**-7:32, 33-**PS**-83:13(1534)-**PR**-20:26-**EC**-12:6 (1534)-**IS**-28:27,28(1536)-**EZE**-1:15,16■10:9^{2},10,13(1534)

WHEELS-all=212&marked-**EX**-14:25-**J'G**-5:28(6471)-**1KI**-7:30,32^{2},33 -**IS**-5:28(1534)-**JER**-18:3(70)■47:3 (1534)-**EZE**-1:16,19^{2},20^{2},21^{2}■3:13■10:2(1534),6(1534),6,9^{2},12^{2},13,16^{2},19■11:22■23:24(1534)■26:10(1534)-**DA**-7:9 (1535)-**NA**-3:2

WHELP-all=1482-**GE**-49:9-**DE**-33:22-**NA**-2:11

WHELPS-all=1482&marked-**JOB**-4:11(1121)■28:8(1121)-**JER**-51:38(1484) -**EZE**-19:2,3,5-**NA**-2:12(1484)

WHEN-all=3588,a=834,b=518,c=4970&marked-**GE**-4:12■6:1,4a■12:11a, 12■14:14■15:12(1961),17(1961)■17:1 (1961)■19:15(3644)■20:13a■24:36(310)■26:8■27:40a■29:10a■30:25a,30c,33,38■31:49■32:2a,17■37:23a■38:9b■40:13a, 14a■43:2a,21■44:24■46:33■48:7sup,7 (5750)-**EX**-1:10■5:13a■7:9■8:9c■12:25, 26,48■13:5,11,14,15■17:11^{2}a■18:16■19:19 (1961)■22:27■29:30a■30:12-**LE**-4:22a■5:5■6:27a■13:2,9,14(3117)■14:34,57^{2} (3117)■15:2,13■19:23■22:29■23:10■25:2■27:2,14-**NU**-5:6,29a,30a■6:2■9:17 (6310),20a,21a■12:12a■15:2,8■18:26■19:14■26:64a■33:51■34:2■35:10■36:4b -**DE**-2:16a,22a■4:25■6:10,20■7:1■11:29■12:20,25,28,29■13:18■14:24■15:4,13■17:14■18:9,22a■19:1,5a■20:1, 10,19■21:9,10,16(3117)■22:8■23:9,21, 24,25■24:1,5,10,19,20,21■25:11■26:1, 12■27:2a■30:1■31:20,21■32:36-**JOS**-4:1a,6,11a,21a■5:8a■7:8(6310)■8:5■17:13■22:7,28-**J'G**-2:18■3:18a■4:20b■6:3b,7■8:1■11:5a,7a■13:17■16:2(5704) ,16,25■21:22-**1SA**-1:7(1767),24a■6:6a■8:1a,6a■10:7■12:8a■15:17b■17:48■20:12■22:17,22■24:1a■25:30■26:20a■28:22-**2SA**-4:11■6:13■7:1,12■12:21a■16:16a■19:25■21:12(3117)■22:5-**1KI**-8:9a,30a,35■11:4(6256)■14:28(1767)■22:25a-**2KI**-5:13,26■7:12■18:32-**1CH**-17:11-**2CH**-5:10a■6:26,27,29a■12:11 (1767)■18:24a■20:22(6256)■25:3a■29:27 (6256)■35:20a-**EZR**-4:23(4481,1768) -**NE**-2:3a,6c■4:1a,7a,12a,15a■5:6a■6:1a, 16a■7:1a■9:18■13:19a-**ES**-2:20a■9:1a -**JOB**-1:5■3:22■5:21■7:4^{2}c,13■16:22■17:16b■21:6b■22:29■27:8,9■29:5(5750), 11,11sup■30:26,26sup■31:14^{2},21, 26,29■36:13■37:4■38:40,41-**PS**-2:12■8:3■9:12■13:4■27:10■32:3■41:5c■42:2c■49:16^{2},17,18■50:18b■56:6a■58:10■63:6b■71:18(5704),23■75:2■78:34b,42a■90:4■94:8c,18b■95:9a■101:2c■102:t,16■119:32,82c,84c,171■120:7■138:4■139:15a-**PR**-2:10■3:24b, 25■4:8,12b■6:3,9c,30■21:27■22:6■23:1, 22,31^{2},35c■24:14b■26:25■30:22^{2},23 -**EC**-5:1a,4a■8:7(3588)a,16a■12:1a-**IS**-1:12,15sup,15■3:6■4:4b■6:13a■8:19,21■9:1(6256)■10:12■16:12■24:13,13b,23■25:4■26:9a■28:15,18,25b■29:8^{2},23■30:21^{2}■31:4a■43:2^{2}■53:10b■54:6■57:20■58:7■59:19-**JER**-2:17(6256),20,26■3:8,16■5:19■6:15■8:12■11:15■12:1■13:21■14:12^{2}■16:10■17:6,8■18:22■23:33■29:13■37:16■38:28a■39:4a■42:6, 20■44:19-**LAM**-3:8■4:15-**EZE**-2:2a■14:9,13,21■15:5sup,5■21:7,25(6256),29 (6256)■25:3^{3}■33:2■35:11a■37:18■38:18 (3117)-**DA**-3:7(1768)■5:20(1768)■6:10 (1768),14(1768)-**HO**-4:14^{2}■7:12a,14■11:1,10-**JO**-3:1a-**AM**-7:2b■8:5c-**JON**-4:2(5704)-**MIC**-5:5^{2},6^{2}■7:8-**HAB**-2:1 (5921)-**ZEC**-7:5,6■9:1,13■13:3■14:3 (3117)-**MAL**-3:17a■**N.T.**-all=3752, a=3753,b=1722,3588,c=5613d=4218&marked-**M'T**-2:8(1875)■5:11■6:2,5,6,6sup, 16■7:28a■9:15,25a■10:19,23■11:1a■12:3a, 43■13:4b,26a,32,48a,53a■15:2■17:25a■19:1a,28■21:1a,34a,40■23:15■24:3d, 15,32,33■25:31,37d,38d,39d,44d■26:1a, 29■27:12b-**M'R**-1:32a■2:20,25a■3:11■4:10a,15,16,29,31,32■7:17a■8:19a,20a,38■11:1a,19a,25■12:23,25■13:4d,4,7,11,14,28, 29,33d,35d■14:12a■15:20a,41a-**LU**-1:41c■2:21a,22a,27b,39c,42a■3:21b■4:25a,25c■5:4c,12b,35■6:3(3698),13a,22^{2},26■7:1 (1893),12c■8:13,40b■9:26,36b,51b■10:35sup,35b■11:1c,2,21,22(1875),24, 34(1875),34,36■12:11,36d,54,55a,58c■13:28,35a■14:8,10^{2},12,13■16:4,9■17:10, 20,sup,20d,22a■19:5c,15b,29c,41c■20:37c■21:7d,7,9,20,30,31■22:7(1722,3739),14 (a,3588),32d,35a■23:33a,42-**JOH**-1:19a■2:9c,10,22a,23c■4:1c,21a,23a,25,40c,45a, 52(1722,3739)■5:7,25a■6:12c,16c,24a,25d, 25sup■7:10c,27,31■8:7c,28,44■9:4a,14a■10:4■11:6c,32c,33c■12:16a,17a,41a■13:19,26sup,26a,31a■14:29■15:26■16:4,13,21,25a■19:6a,8a,13a,23a,30a,33c■20:24a■21:15a,18a,18-**AC**-1:13a■2:1b■3:19(3704)■5:24c■7:4(3326),17(2531), 23c■8:12a,39a■10:7c■11:2a■12:6a■13:17b,29c■14:5c■16:15c■17:13c■18:5c■19:9c■20:14c,18c■21:5a,12c,27c,35a■22:11c,20a■23:35■24:22sup,22■25:14c■27:1c,27c,39a■28:4c,16a-**RO**-2:14,16a■3:4(1723,3588)■6:20a■7:5a■11:27■13:11a-**1CO**-11:25(3326),34c■13:10,11^{2}a■14:16(1437),26■15:24^{2},27,28,54■16:2,3,5, 12-**2CO**-3:15(2259),16(2259)■10:6■12:10■13:9-**GA**-1:15a■2:11a,12a,14a■4:3a,4a, 18b-**PH'P**-4:15a-**COL**-3:4,7a■4:16 -**1TH**-3:4a■5:3-**2TH**-1:7(1722,3739), 10■3:10a-**1TI**-5:11-**2TI**-subscr.■4:3a -**TIT**-3:12-**HEB**-1:6■3:9(3756)■7:10a -**JAS**-1:2-**1PE**-3:20a■4:13b-**1JO**-2:28■3:2(1437)■5:2-**JUDE**-9a-**RE**-1:17a■4:9■5:8a■6:1a,3a,5a,7a,9a,12a■8:1a■9:5■10:3sup,3a,4a,7■11:7■12:13a■17:10■18:9■20:7■22:8a

WHENCE-all=370&marked-**GE**-3:23(834,8033)■16:8(335,2088)■29:4■42:7-**NU**-11:13■23:13(834,8033)■24:5(834,8033)-**DE**-9:28(834,8033)■11:10(834,8033)-**JOS**-2:4■9:8■20:6 (834,8033)■24:5(834,8033)-**J'G**-13:6 (335,2088)■17:9■19:17-**1SA**-25:11(834, 2088)■30:13(335,2088)-**2SA**-1:3(335, 2088),13(335,2088)-**2KI**-5:25■6:27■20:14-**NE**-4:12(834)-**JOB**-1:7■2:2 (335,2088)■28:20-**PS**-121:1-**IS**-30:6 (1992)■39:3-**JER**-29:14(834,8033) -**JON**-1:8-**NA**-3:7■**N.T.**-all=4159&marked-**M'T**-12:44(3606)■13:27,54,56■15:33■21:25-**M'R**-6:2■8:4■12:37-**LU**-1:43■11:24(3606)■13:25,27■20:7-**JOH**-1:48■2:9■3:8■4:11■6:5■7:27^{2},28■8:14^{2}■9:29,30■19:9-**AC**-14:26(3606)-**PH'P**-3:20(3739)-**HEB**-11:15(3739),19(3606) -**JAS**-4:1-**RE**-2:5■7:13

WHENSOEVER-**GE**-30:41(3605)■**N.T.**-**M'R**-14:7(3752)-**RO**-15:24(5613,1437)

WHERE-all=834,a=834,8033,b=346,c=8033,d=335&marked-**GE**-2:11a■3:9d■4:9d■13:3■18:9b■19:5b,27■21:17■27:33(645)■31:13^{2}■33:19■35:13,15, 27■37:16(375)■38:21b■39:20■40:3-**EX**-2:20b■5:11■9:26a■12:13,30■15:27c■18:5a■20:21a,24■29:42a■30:6a,36a-**LE**-4:12(413),12(5921),24,33■6:25■7:2■14:13-**NU**-9:17a■13:22c■17:4a■22:26■

33:14c,54(413,834,c)-DE-1:31■8:15■11:10■18:6a■32:37d-JOS-4:3,8(413)-J'G-5:27■6:13b■9:38b■17:8,9■18:10■19:26a■20:22a-RU-1:7a,16,17■2:19(645),19(375)■3:4a-1SA-3:3a■6:14c■9:10a,18(d,2088)■10:5a,14(370)■14:11a■19:3,22(375)■20:19a■23:22,23a■24:3c■26:5^{2}a,16d■30:31a-2SA-2:23a■9:4(375)■11:16■15:32a■16:3b■17:12a,20b■18:7c■21:12a■23:11c-1KI-4:28a■7:7a,8a■13:25■17:19a■21:19-2KI-2:14b■4:8c■6:1a,2c,6(575),13(351)■18:34^{2}b■19:13b■23:7a,8a-1CH-11:4c-2CH-3:1■25:4-EZR-1:4a■6:1(8536),3(1768)-NE-10:39c■13:5c-ES-7:5d-JOB-4:7(375)■9:24(645)■14:10b■15:23b■17:15(b,645)■20:7d■21:28^{2}b■28:12(370),12(d,2088),20d■34:22c■35:10d■38:4(375),19^{2}d■39:30■40:20c-PS-42:3b,10b■79:10b■84:3■89:49b■104:17a■115:2b-PR-15:17c■26:20(657)-EC-1:5c■8:4,10-SONG-1:7(349)-IS-7:23■10:3(575)■19:12d,12(645)■33:18^{2}b■36:19^{2}b■37:13b■49:21(375)■50:1d■51:13b■57:8(3027)■63:11^{2}b,15b■64:11■66:1^{2}d-JER-2:6b,6c,8b,28b■3:2(375)■6:16d■7:12a■13:7a,20b■16:13■17:15b■22:26a■35:7a■36:19(375)■37:19b■38:9(8478)■42:14-LA-2:12b-EZE-3:15c■6:13a■8:3a■11:16a,17■13:12b■17:10(5921)■21:30■34:12a■40:38■42:13a■43:7a■46:20a,20,24a-HO-1:10■13:10(645)-JOE-2:17b-MIC-7:10b-NA-2:11b,11a■3:17d-ZEC-1:5b-MAL-1:6^{2}b■2:17b■N.T.-all=3699,a=4226,b=3757&marked-M'T-2:2a,4a,9b■6:19^{2},20^{2},21■8:20a■13:5■18:20b■25:24,24(3606),26,26(3606)■26:17a,57■28:6,16b-M'R-2:4■4:5,15■5:40■6:55■9:44,46,48■11:4(296)■13:14■14:12a,14a,14■15:47a■16:6,20(3837)-LU-4:16b,17b■8:25a■9:6(3837),58a■10:33(2596)■12:17a,33,34■17:17a,37a■22:9a,10b,11a,11-JOH-1:28,38a,39a■3:8■4:20,46■6:23,62■7:11a,34,36,42■8:10a,19a■9:12a■10:40■11:30,32,34a,41b,57a■12:1,26■14:3■17:24■18:1■19:18,20,41■20:2a,12,13a,15a,19-AC-1:13b■2:2b■4:31(1722,3739)■7:29b,33(1722,3739)■8:4(1330)■11:11(1722,3739)■12:12b■15:36(1722,3739)■17:1,30(3837)■20:6b,8b■21:28(3837)■25:10b■27:41(1337)■28:14b,22(3837)-RO-3:27a■4:15b■5:20b■9:26b■15:20-1CO-1:20^{2}a■4:17(3837)■12:17^{2}a,19a■15:55^{2}a-2CO-3:17b-GA-4:15(5101)-PH'P-4:12(1722,3956)-COL-3:1b,11-1TI-2:8(1722,5117)-HEB-9:16■10:18-JAS-3:16-1PE-4:18a-2PE-3:4a-RE-2:13a,13^{2}■11:18■12:6,14■17:15b■20:10

WHEREABOUT-1SA-21:2(834)

WHEREAS-all=3588&marked-GE-31:37-DE-28:62(834)-2SA-7:6-1KI-8:18(3282,834)-2KI-13:19(6258)-2CH-10:11(6258)■28:13-JOB-22:20(518)-EC-4:14-IS-37:21(834)■60:15(8478)-EZE-36:34(8478,834)-DA-2:41(1768),43(1768)■4:23(1768),26(1768)-MAL-1:4■N.T.-1CO-3:3(3699)-JAS-4:14(3748)-1PE-2:12(1722,3759)■3:16(1722,3759)-2PE-2:11(3699)

WHEREBY-all=834&marked-GE-15:8(4100)-LE-22:5-NU-5:8■17:5-DE-7:19■28:20-PS-45:8(4482)-JER-3:8■17:19■23:6■33:8^{3}-EZE-18:31■39:26■40:49■46:9■47:13-ZEP-2:8■N.T.-all=1722,3739&marked-LU-1:18(2596,5101),78-AC-4:12■11:14■19:40(4012,3757)-RO-8:15■14:21-EPH-3:4(4314,3739)■4:14(4314),30-PH'P-3:21(3588)-HEB-12:28(1223,3739)-2PE-1:4(1223,3739)■3:6(1223,3739)-1JO-2:18(3606)

WHEREFORE-all=4100,a=4069,b=3651,c=5921,3651&marked-GE-10:9c■16:14c■18:13■21:31■24:31■26:27a■29:25(4100,2063)■31:27,30■32:29■40:7a■43:6■44:4,7■47:19,22c■50:11c-EX-2:13■5:4,14a,15,22■6:6b■14:11(4100,2063),15■17:2sup,2,3■20:11c■32:12-LE-10:17a-NU-9:7■11:11^{2}■12:8a■14:3,41■16:3a■20:5■21:5,14c,27c■22:32,37■25:12b■32:7-DE-10:9c■19:7c■29:24(5921,4100)-JOS-7:7,10,26c■9:22-J'G-10:13b■12:1a,3■15:19c■18:12c-1SA-2:29,30b■4:3■6:6■9:21■15:19■19:5,24c■20:27a,32■21:14■24:9■26:15,18■27:6b■28:9,16-2SA-2:22■3:7a■7:22c■11:20a■12:9a,23■14:13,31,32■15:19■16:10a■18:22(4100,2088)■19:12,25,35,42■24:21a-1KI-1:41a-2KI-4:23a■5:7(3588,389),8■9:11a-ES-9:26c-JOB-3:20■10:2(5921,4100),18■13:14(5921,4100),24■18:3a■21:7a■32:6c■33:1(199)■42:6c-PS-10:13(5921,4100)■44:24■49:5■79:10■89:47(5921,4100)■115:2-PR-17:16(4100,2088)-EC-5:6-IS-5:4a■16:11c■24:15c■28:14b■30:12b■50:2a■55:2■58:3,3sup■63:2a-JER-2:9b,29,31a■5:6c,14b,19(8478,4100)■12:1a,1sup■13:22a■16:10(5921,4100)■20:18■22:8(5921,4100),28a■23:12b■27:17■30:6a■32:3a■40:15■44:7■46:5a■49:4■51:52b-LA-3:39■5:20-EZE-5:11b■13:20b■16:35b■20:30b■21:7(5981,4100)■23:9b■24:6b■33:25b-DA-3:8(3605,6903,1836)■4:27(3861)■6:9(3605,6903,1836)■10:20-JOE-2:17-HAB-1:13-MAL-2:14(5921,4100),15■N.T.-all=1352a=5620&marked-M'T-6:30(1161)■7:20(686,1065)■9:4(2443,5101)■12:12a,31(1223,5124)■14:31(1519,5101)■18:8(1161)■19:6a■23:31a,34(1223,5124)■24:26(3767)■26:50(1909,3739)■27:8-LU-7:7,47(3739,5484)■19:23(1302)-JOH-9:27(5101)-AC-1:21(3767)■6:3(3767)■10:21(1223,3739)■13:35■15:19■19:32(5101,1752),38(3303,3767)■20:26■22:24(1223,3739),30(5101)■23:28(1223,3739)■24:26■25:26■26:3■27:25,34-RO-1:24■5:12(1223,5124)■7:4a,12a■9:32(1302)■13:5■15:7-1CO-4:16(3767)■8:13(1355)■10:12a,14(1355)■11:27a,33a■12:3■14:13(1355),22a,39a■-2CO-2:8■5:9,16a■6:17■7:12(686)■8:24(3767)■11:11(1302)-GA-3:19(5101),24a■4:7a-EPH-1:15(1223,5124)■2:11■3:13■4:8,25■5:14,17(1223,5124)■6:13(1223,5124)-PH'P-2:9,12a-COL-2:20(3767)-1TH-2:18■3:1■4:18a■5:11-2TH-1:11(1519,3739)-2TI-1:6(1223,3739)-TIT-1:13(1223,3739)-PH'M-8-HEB-2:17(3606)■3:1(3606),7,10■7:25(3606)■8:3(3606)■10:5■11:16■12:1(5105),12,28■13:12-JAS-1:19a,21■4:6-1PE-1:13■2:1(3767),6■4:19a-2PE-1:10,12■3:14-1JO-3:12(5484,5101)-3JO-10(1223,3739)-RE-17:7(1302)

WHEREIN-all=834,a=4100&marked-GE-1:30■6:17■7:15■21:23-EX-1:14■6:4■12:7■18:11■22:27a■33:16a-LE-4:23■5:18■6:28■11:32■13:46,52,54,57■18:3-NU-12:11^{2}■19:2■33:55■35:33,34(834,8432)-DE-8:9■12:2(834,8033),7■17:1■28:52(834,2004)-JOS-8:24■10:27(834,8033)■22:19(834,8033),33■24:17-J'G-16:5a,6a,15a■18:6-1SA-6:15■14:38a-2SA-7:7-1KI-2:26■8:21(834,8033),36,50■13:31-2KI-12:2■14:6■17:29(834,8033)■18:19-2CH-6:11(834,8033),27■8:1■33:19-EZR-5:7(1459)-NE-9:12,19-ES-5:11■8:11■9:22-JOB-6:24a-PS-104:25(8033)■142:3(2098)■143:8(2098)-EC-3:9■8:9-IS-2:22a■14:3■36:4■47:12■65:12-JER-5:17(834,2004)■7:14■20:14^{2}■36:14■41:9■42:3■51:43-EZE-20:34,43■23:19■37:23,25■42:14■44:19-HO-2:13-MIC-6:3a-ZEP-3:11-MAL-1:2a,6a,7a■2:17a■3:7a,8a■N.T.-all=1722,3757&marked-M'T-11:20(1722,3739)■25:13(1722,3739)-M'R-2:4(1909,3739)-LU-1:4(4012,3739),25(3739)■11:22(1909,3739)■23:53(3757)-JOH-19:41-AC-2:8■7:4(1519,3757)■10:12-RO-2:1■5:2■7:6-1CO-7:20,24■15:1-2CO-11:12■12:13(3757)-EPH-1:6,8(3757)■2:2■5:18-PH'P-4:10(1909,3757)-COL-2:12-2TI-2:9-HEB-6:17■9:2,4-1PE-1:6■3:20(1519,3757)■4:4■5:12(1519,3757)2PE-3:12(1223,3757),13-RE-2:13■18:19

WHEREINSOEVER-2CO-11:21(1722,3739,302)

WHEREINTO-LE-11:33(834,413,8432)-NU-14:24(824,8432)■N.T.-JOH-6:22(1519,3739)

WHEREOF-all=834-GE-3:11-LE-6:30■27:9-NU-5:3■21:16-DE-13:2■28:27,68-JOS-14:12■20:2■22:9-1SA-10:16-2KI-13:14■17:12-2CH-6:20■33:4-JOB-6:4-JER-32:36,43■42:16-EZE-39:8-DA-9:2-HO-2:12■N.T.-all=3739&marked-AC-2:32■3:15■24:8,13(4012,3739)■25:11■26:2-RO-6:21(1909,3739)-1CO-7:1(4012,3739)-EPH-3:7-COL-1:5,23,25-1TI-1:7(4012,5101)■6:4(1537,3739)-HEB-2:5(4012,3739)■12:8■13:10(1537,3739)-1JO-4:3

WHEREON-all=834,5921&marked-GE-28:13-EX-3:5■8:21-LE-6:27■15:4,6,17,23,24,26-DE-11:24(834)-JOS-5:15■14:9(834)-1SA-6:18-2CH-4:19(5921)■32:10(5921,4100)-ES-7:8-SONG-4:4(5921)-IS-36:6-EZE-37:20■N.T.-all=1909,3739&marked-M'R-11:2-LU-4:29■5:25■19:30-JOH-4:38(3739)

WHERESOEVER-LE-13:12(3605)-2KI-8:1(834),12:5(834,8033)-1CH-17:6(3605,834)-JER-40:5(413,3605)-DA-2:38(3606,1768)■N.T.-all=3699,1437&marked-M'T-24:28■26:13-M'R-9:18(3699,302)■14:9(3699,302),14-LU-17:37(3699)

WHERETO-JOB-30:2(4100)-IS-55:11(834)■N.T.-PH'P-3:16(1519,3739)

WHEREUNTO-all=834&marked-NU-36:4-DE-4:26-2CH-8:11-ES-10:2-JER-22:27-EZE-5:9■20:29(834,8033)■N.T.-all=3739&marked-M'T-11:16(5101)-M'R-4:30(5101)-LU-7:31(5101)■13:18(5101),20(5101)-AC-5:24(5101)■13:2■27:8-GA-4:9-COL-1:29(1519,3739)-2TH-2:14(1519,3739)-1TI-2:7(1519,3739)■4:6■6:12(1519,3739)-2TI-1:11(1519,3739)-1PE-2:8(1519,3739)■3:21-2PE-1:19

WHEREUPON-all=834,5921&marked-LE-11:35-J'G-16:26-1KI-7:48-JOB-38:6(5921,4100)-EZE-9:3■23:41(5921)■40:41(413),42(413)-AM-4:7■N.T.-all=3606&marked-M'T-14:7-AC-24:18(1722,3739)■26:12(1722,3739),19-HEB-9:18

WHEREWITH-all=834,a=4100&marked-GE-27:41-EX-3:9■4:17■16:32■17:5■29:33-NU-3:31■4:9,12,14■16:39■25:18■30:4^{2},5,6,7,8,9,11■35:17,18,23-DE-9:19■15:14■22:12■28:53,55,57,67■33:1-JOS-8:26-J'G-6:15a■9:9,38■16:6a,10a,13a-1SA-6:2a■29:4a-2SA-13:15^{2}■21:3a-1KI-8:59■15:22,26,30,34■16:26■21:22■22:22a-2KI-13:12■21:16■23:26■25:14-2CH-2:17■16:6■18:20a-NE-9:34-PS-79:12■89:51^{2}■119:42(1697)-IS-37:6-JER-18:10■19:9■21:4■33:16■52:18-LA-1:12-EZE-13:12,20■29:20■40:42-MIC-6:6a-ZEC-14:12,18■N.T.-all=3739&marked-M'T-5:13(1722,5101)-M'R-3:28(3745)■9:50(1722,5101)-LU-14:34(1722,5101)■17:8(5101)-JOH-13:5■17:26-2CO-1:4■7:7■10:2-GA-5:1-EPH-2:4■4:1■6:16(1722,3739)-1TH-3:9-HEB-10:29(1722,3739)

WHEREWITHAL-PS-119:9(4100)■N.T.-M'T-6:31(5101)

WHET-DE-32:41(8150)-PS-7:12(3913)■64:3(8150)-EC-10:10(7043)

WHETHER-all=518&marked-GE-43:6(5750)-EX-4:18(5750)■19:13■21:31(176)■22:4(5704),8(518,3808)-LE-3:1(518)■5:1(176),2(176)■13:48^{2}(176),52(176)■27:12(996),14(996),26,33(996)-NU-9:21(176),22(176)■15:30(4480)-DE-18:3-JOS-24:15-J'G-9:2(4100)-RU-3:10-2SA-15:21-1KI-20:18^{2}-2KI-1:2-CH-14:11(996)■15:13(4480)-EZR-2:59■5:17(2006)■7:26(2006)-NE-7:61-ES-4:14-JOB-34:33(3588)■37:13-PR-20:11-EC-5:12■11:6(335),6■12:14-JER-30:6■42:6-EZE-2:5,7■3:11■44:31(4480)■N.T.-all=1535,a=1487&marked-M'T-

9:5(5101)■21:31(5101)■23:17(5101),19
(5101)■26:63a■27:21(5101),49a-**M'R**-
2:9(5101)■3:2a■15:36a,44a-**LU**-3:15
(3379)■5:23(5101)■6:7a■14:28a,31a■
22:27(5101)■23:6a-**JOH**-7:17(4220)■
9:25a-**AC**-1:24(3739,1520)■4:19a■5:8a■
9:2(5037)■10:18a■17:11a■19:2a■25:20a
-**RO**-6:16(2273)■12:6■14:8^{3}(1437,5037)
-**1CO**-1:16a■3:22■7:16^{2}a■8:5■10:31■
12:13^{2},26■13:8^{3}■14:7■15:11-**2CO**-1:6^{2}■
2:9a■5:9,10,13^{2}■8:23■12:2^{2},3■13:5a-**EPH**-
6:8-**PH'P**-1:18,20,27-**COL**-1:16,20-**1TH**-
5:10-**2TH**-2:15-**1PE**-2:13-**1JO**-4:1a

WHICH-all=834,a=1931,b=1958,c=
1768&marked-**GE**-1:7^{2},21,29^{2}■2:2^{2},3,22■
3:1,3,17■4:11■5:29■6:2,4,15■7:23■8:6■
9:12,15,17■11:5,6(3605,834)■13:4,15■
14:2a,3a,6,15,17a,20,24^{2}■16:15■17:10,
12,21■18:8,10a,13(589),17,19,27(595)■
19:5,8,19,21,29(834,2004)■20:3,13■21:2,
9,25,29■22:2,9,17■23:9,16,17^{3}■24:7^{2},
24,48■25:7,9■26:2,3,15,18^{2},32■27:8,17,
27,45,46■28:4,15,22■29:27■30:26,30,
37,38■31:1,16,18^{2},43,51■32:10,12,32sup,
32■33:5,8,18■34:1,7(3651),28^{2}■35:3,4^{3},
6,12,19b,26,27■36:5,6■37:6■38:10,14■
39:1,6,17,19,23■40:5■41:28,36,43,48^{2},
50■42:9,38■43:2,26■44:5,8■45:6,27^{2}■
46:5,6,15,20,22,25,27,27sup,31■47:14,
22■48:6,22■49:1,30^{2}■50:5,10,11,13,15,
24-**EX**-1:8,15■3:7,16(853),20■4:9,18,21,
28,30■5:8,14■6:8■7:15,17■8:12,22■9:3,
19■10:2,6,15■12:16,25,39■13:3,5,12■
14:13,31■15:13(2098),16(2098),26■16:1,
5,8,15,16^{2},23^{2},23sup,32■18:3,9■19:6,7■
20:2,12■21:1■22:9■23:16,16sup,20■24:3,
8,12■25:3,16,22^{2},40■26:30■27:21■28:4,
8,26,38■29:27^{3},35,38■30:37■32:1,2,3,4,
7,8^{2},11,14,20,23,32,34,35■33:1^{2},7sup,7■
34:1,10,11,34■35:1,4,29■36:3,4,5,12■
37:16■38:8■39:19-**LE**-1:8,12■2:11■
3:4,5,10,15■4:2,3,7^{2},9,13,14,18^{2},22,27,
28^{2}■5:6,7,8,10,17■6:4^{4},5,10,15,20■
7:4,8,11,21,25,36,38■8:5,30,36■9:5,6,8,
15,18,18sup■10:1,6,11■11:2,10,21,23,
26,34^{2},37,39■13:58■14:34,40■15:12■
16:2,6,9,10,11^{2},23■17:2,5,8,13■18:5,
27,30■19:22,22sup,36■20:23,24,25■
21:3■22:2,3,6,15,18■23:2,4,10,37,
38■25:2,31,38,42,44■26:13,40,46■27:11,
22sup,22,26,29,34-**NU**-1:17,44■3:26,
39■4:26,37■5:7,9,18b■6:5,18,21■
10:29■11:5,12,17,20■12:3■13:2,16,24,
32^{2}■14:7,8,11,15,16,22,27^{2},29,30,31sup,
31,34,36,40■15:2,22,39,41■16:40■18:9,
12,13,15,16b,19,21,24,26,28■19:2^{2},15■
20:12,24■21:11,13,30,34■22:5,20,30,36^{2}■
23:12■24:4,12■27:12,17^{5}■28:3,23■30:1,
8,8sup,14,16■31:12,21sup,21,32,42,48,
49■32:4,7,9,11,38,39■33:1,4,6,7,36b,40a,
55■34:13^{2},17■35:4,6,7,8^{2},13,25,31,34■
36:6,13-**DE**-1:1,4^{2},8,14,18,19,20,25,35,
39^{2}■2:11(1992),12,14,29^{2}sup,29,35,36■
3:2,4,12sup,12,13a,19,20^{2},28■4:1,2^{2},6,
8,9,13,19,21,23^{2},28,31,32,40^{2},42,44,45,
47,48,48a■5:1,6,16,28,31^{2},33^{2}■6:1,2,6,
10^{2},11^{3},12,14,17,18^{2},20,23■7:8,9,11,12,
13,15,16,19■8:1^{2},2,3,10,11,16,18,20■9:5,
9,10,12,16,18,21,23,26^{2},28,29■10:2,4,5,
11,13,17,21■11:2,3,7,8,9,12,13,17,21,22,
27,28^{2},31,32■12:1^{2},2,5,9,10,11^{2},14,15,17,
18,21^{2},26^{2},28,28sup,31■13:2,5,6^{2},7,12,
13,18,18sup■14:4,12,23,24,25,29^{2}■15:3,
4,5,7,8,20■16:2,4,5,6,7,10,11,15,16,17,
18,20,20sup,21,22■17:2,3,5,8,10^{2},11^{3},14,
15■18:6,9,14,17,19,20,20sup,21,22■
19:2,3,4,8,9,10,14^{2},17■20:1,14,15sup,
15,16,18,20■21:1,2,3sup,3^{2},4,16,16sup,
23■22:3,9,28■23:15,16,23,23sup■24:3,4
^{2},5■25:15,19■26:1,2^{2},3,10,11,13,15,19■
27:1,2,3,4,10■28:1,8,11,13,14,15,33,34,
36,36sup,45,48,50,51,52,53,54,56,57,
60,61,64,67■29:1,3,12,16,17,22,23,25■
30:1,5,7,8,11,20■31:5,7,11,13,18,20,
21^{2},23,25,29■32:38,46^{2},49^{2},52■34:4,11,
12-**JOS**-1:2,6,7,11,13,14,15^{2}■2:3,7,17,
18,20■3:4■4:20,23■5:1^{2},6sup,6■6:25■
7:2,11,14^{3}■8:27,31,32,35■9:1,10,13,20,
27■10:11■12:1,2,2sup,7,7sup,9■13:3,
3sup,8,10,12,21,21sup,30,32■14:1,1sup■
15:7,8,9b,10,13b,25b,49b,54b,60b■
17:5■18:2,3,7,13b,14b,16,17,28b■19:50,
51■20:7b■21:9,11b,43,45■22:4,5,9,
17,28,30■23:13,14,15^{2},16^{2}■24:5,13^{3},
14,15,17,23,27,30,31,32^{2},33-**J'G**-1:16,
26a■2:1,10,17,20,21■3:1,4,20■4:11
sup,11,14■6:2,11,13,26■8:35(835)■9:24^{2},
56■10:4sup,4,8,14■11:24,28,36,39■13:8■
15:19■16:8,24,29,29sup,30^{2}■18:5,16,24,
27^{2},31■19:10b,14■20:9,13,18(4310),31,
36,42,46■21:12,14,19-**RU**-2:9,11■4:3,11,
12,14,15,15(834)a-**1SA**-1:27■2:20,29,32,
35■3:11,12,13■6:4,7,8,17■7:14■8:8,18■
9:23^{2}■10:2■12:7,16,17,21■13:5,13,14■
14:2,4,14,14sup,21,30■15:2,14,20■16:4,
19■17:1,31,40■20:23,36,37■22:9a■23:19■
24:4■25:7,27,32,33,34,35,44■26:1,3■
28:21■29:1,3,4■30:10,14,17,21,23,27^{3},
28^{3},29^{3},30^{3}-**2SA**-2:16,32■3:8,14■4:8■6:4,
21,22■7:12,23■8:11sup,11■12:3■13:10,
23■14:7,14■15:4,7,18■16:1121,23■
17:10■18:18,28■19:16,19■20:5,8■21:12,
16,18■23:15■24:2-**1KI**-1:8,9,48■2:4,8a,
24,27,31,44■3:8,13,21,28■4:2,13^{2},19,
20,34■5:3,7,8,16,16sup■6:1a,2,12^{2},38a■
7:17,20,41,45■8:1b,2a,9,15,21,26,28,29^{2},
34,36,38,40,43,44,48^{4},51,56,58,63■9:1,
3,6,7^{2},12,13,15,19,20,24,25,26■10:3,5,7,
9,10,13,24■11:2,10,11,13,23,32,37■12:4,
8^{2},9,15,28,31,32,33^{2}■13:3,4^{2},5,11,12,21,
22,26sup,26,32^{2}■14:2a,15,18,20,21,22,
24,26■15:3,20,23,27,29,30^{2}■16:12,13^{2},
15,19^{2},24,27,32,34■17:9,16■18:3,26■
19:3,18^{2}■20:19,34■21:1,4,11,15,18,25■
22:24(335,2088),38,39-**2KI**-1:4,6,7,16,
17,18■2:15,22■3:3,8(355,2088),11■
5:20■6:10,11(4310)■7:13,15■8:29■9:5
(4310),15,27,36■10:10^{2},17,31,33■13:25■
14:11,15,21a,25^{2}■15:12,15■16:14,19■
17:8,13^{2},15,19,22,26,29,32(1961),34,37■
18:6,9b,14,16,17,18,21,37■19:2,4,
6^{2},12^{2},16,20,28■20:11,17,18,19■21:2,
3,4,7^{2},8,11,25■22:4sup,4,5,16,18sup,
18,20■23:8,10,11,12^{2},13^{2},15,16,17,19,
27^{2}■24:2,13■25:4,8b,16,19,19sup
-**1CH**-2:42a■3:1■4:10,11a,18■6:65■
10:13^{2}■11:4b,5b■12:31■13:6■14:4■
15:3■16:15,16,40■17:11■20:4(227)■
21:19,24,29■22:13■23:4(428),5■26:26a,
26■27:31■29:19-**2CH**-1:3■2:5,9,14,15■
4:12sup,12,13■5:2b,3a,6,10■6:4,15,16,
17,18,19,20,21,25,27,31,32,33,34^{2},36,38^{3},
39■7:6,7,14,19,20^{2},21,22■8:2,4,7,12■9:2,
4,5,8,10,12■10:8,9,15■11:10,15■12:4,
9,13■13:4,8■15:8■16:14^{2}■17:2■18:23
(355,2088)■20:2b,11■22:6■23:9■24:22■
25:9,13,15sup,15,21■26:23■28:11,15■
29:19,32■30:7,8■32:3■33:3,7^{3},8,22sup,
22■34:9,11,24,26■35:3sup,3■36:8,8sup,
14,23-**EZR**-1:2,3^{2},5,7■2:2,61,68■4:12c,
15(1836),18c,24c■5:2c,6c,8a,14c,16c,
17c■6:5^{2}c,6c,9sup,9c,12c,13c,15c,18c■
7:6,8b,13c,14c,15c,16c,17c,20c,21c,25c,
27^{2}■9:11^{3}-**NE**-1:2,6^{2},7■2:8,13,18■4:2
(1992),3,23■5:18■6:6(3651)■7:63,72■
8:1,4,9a,14■9:15,23,26,29,35■10:29-**ES**-
1:2,18,20■2:4,6■3:3,13a■4:6,16■6:8^{2}■
7:9■8:2,5^{2},8,9,11,12a■9:13,22,25,26^{2}(4100)
-**JOB**-3:25sup,25■5:1(4310)■9:5sup,5■
15:9a,18,28sup,28■22:15,16■27:11■36:24,
28■37:21a■38:23■39:14(3588)■40:15
-**PS**-1:4■7:t■8:3■9:15(2098)■31:19■
32:8(2098)■58:5■66:14,20■68:28(2098)■
69:4■71:20,23■78:3,5,68■80:15■104:8
(2088),16■105:9■119:39,47,48,49,85■
140:2■147:9-**PR**-6:7■22:28■25:1-**EC**-
1:10■2:3,12■3:10,15sup,15,15sup■4:2
sup,2,3■5:4,18^{2}■7:13,19,24(4100),28■
8:7(4100),12,14,15■9:9-**SONG**-1:1-**IS**-
1:1,29■2:8,20■11:10,11,16■13:1,17■
17:8,9■18:1■19:16,17■21:10■22:15■
28:1,4^{2},14■29:11■30:10,24,32■31:7■
36:3■37:4,12^{2},17,22,29■38:8■39:6,7,
8■48:14(4310)■50:1(4310)■51:17,23■
52:15^{2}■55:11■59:21■62:2,8■63:7■
65:7,18■66:4,22-**JER**-2:11^{2}(1992)■3:6■
5:22■7:10,11,12,14^{2},30,31^{2}■8:17■
9:13,14■10:1■11:4^{2},5,8,10^{2},11,17■
12:14■13:4,6,10^{2}sup,10■15:4,■17:4,
19■18:1■19:2,3,5■20:2,16■21:1■
22:11sup,11,28■23:7,8,27sup,27,40■
24:2,8■25:2,13^{2},22,26,27,29■26:3,4,19■
27:8,9,20■28:1,6,9■29:8,19,22,23■
31:32■32:1b,2,8,20,22,32,34,35^{2}■33:9,
10,14,24■34:1,5,8,10,14,15,18^{2}■35:1,4^{2},
15,16■36:3,4,6,27,28,32■37:2,19■38:7a,
20■39:10■40:4,7,10■41:9,13,17■42:5,8,
16,21■43:1,9■44:3,9,14sup,14,22■45:4^{2}■
46:1,2^{2}■49:28■50:3a■51:12,59■52:7,12b,
19^{2},20,25^{2}-**LA**-1:12■2:17-**EZE**-1:2b■
3:20,23■4:10■5:9,16^{2}■6:9,9sup,9■8:14,
17■9:2,3,6,11■10:22■11:23■12:2,28■
15:2,6■16:14,17,19,36,45,51,52,59■17:3■
18:14,18■20:6b,11,13,15,15b,21,28,42■
22:4,13^{2}■26:6,17^{2}■27:27■32:9,23,24^{2},27,
29,30■33:29■35:11,12■36:4,5,21,22,23
sup,23■37:1b,19■38:8■39:19■40:6,6^{2}
sup,40,44■41:6,9,15■42:1,3^{2},11,13,14■
43:3■44:10,13■45:14(4480)■46:19■47:9,
14,16^{2},22■48:8,11^{2},22,29-**DA**-1:10■2:14c,
26c,27c,39c,44c■3:2c,12c,14c,15c,18c,
29c■4:20c,24c■5:2^{2}c,3c,13c,23c■6:8c,
12c,13c,15c,24c,26c■7:6c,11c,14^{2}c,17c,
17sup,19c,19sup,20c,23c■8:2,6,20,26■
9:1,6,10,12,14,18■10:4a■11:4,24■12:6,7
-**HO**-1:10-**JO**-2:25-**AM**-1:1■2:4■3:1■5:1,
26■9:12,15-**OB**-20-**JON**-1:9■4:10
-**MIC**-1:1■2:3■6:14■7:20-**HAB**-1:1
-**ZEP**-1:1■2:3-**HAG**-1:11■2:14-**ZEC**-
1:6,7a,12,19,21,21sup■4:12■6:6,10■7:3,
7,12■8:9■11:10■13:6■14:4,7a-**MAL**-1:14
(3426)■2:11■4:4■**N.T.**-all=3739,a=3588,
b=3748,c=5101&marked-**M'T**-1:22a,
23■2:9,15a,16,17a,20a,23a■4:13a,14a,
16^{2}a■5:6a,12a,16a,44a,45a,46a,48a■6:1a,
4a,6^{2}a,9a,18^{2}a,27c■7:6a,11a,13a,14a,15b,
21a,24b,26b■8:17a■9:8a■10:20a,28^{2}a,
32a,33a■11:4,10,14a,21a,23^{2}a■12:2,4,17a,
50a■13:14a,17^{2},19^{2}a,23,31,32,33,35a,
35sup,44,48,52sup,52b■15:1a,13,18a,
20a,27a■16:17,28b■18:6a,10a,11a,12a,
13a,14a,19a,23,28■19:4a,9a,12^{3}b,
18(4169),28a■20:1b,12a■21:4a,24,
33b,41b,42■22:2b,23a,31a,36(4169)■
23:9a,16a,24a,26a,27b■25:1b■26:25a,
28a,75a■27:3a,9a,17a,22a,35a,44a,
52a,55b,56,60■28:5a-**M'R**-1:2,44■
2:24,26■3:17,19(2076),22a,34a■4:22,25,
31■5:41■6:26a■7:4,13■9:1b,39■11:21,
23,25a,26a■12:10,18b,25a,28(4169),38a,
40,42(2076)■13:19,32a■14:18a,24a■
15:22,28a,34,39a,41a,43(3739,846),46■
16:6a-**LU**-1:2a,20b,70a,73■2:4b,10b,11,
15^{2}a,17a,18a,21a,31,37,50■3:19■4:22a■
5:3,7a,9,10,17,18,21■6:2,3,8,16,17,27sup,
27a,46,48,49■7:27,37b,39a,42c,47a■8:2,
3b,13^{2},15b,18,21a,26b,27,43b■9:27,30b,
31,36,43,46c■10:11a,13,15a,23a,24^{2},30,
36c,42b■11:2a,5c,27,33a,35a,40a,40sup,
44a,50a,51a■12:1b,3,20,24,25c,47a■13:14,
19,21,30^{2},34a■14:5c,24a,28c■15:6a,7b,9,
30a■16:1,15a,19(2532),20,21a■17:7c,10
sup,10,12,31■18:7a,9a■19:2(2532,846),
20,26a,27a,30■20:17,27a,46a,47■21:6^{2},15,
22a■22:19a,20a,23c,24c■23:27,29^{2},33a,
55b■24:1,10,19,23,44,44a-**JOH**-1:9,13,
18a,24a,29a,30,38,40a,41,42■2:9a,22,
23■3:13a,29a■4:12,25a,29,53■5:2a,12a,
15a,23a,28,30,32,36■6:2,9,13,22a,27^{2}a,
27,33a,39a,39sup,40a,41a,44a,46a,50a,
51a,51,58a■7:31,39■8:26,31a,38^{2},40,46c,
53b■9:7,40a■10:6,16,29,32(4169)■
11:2a,16a,27a,31a,37a,42a,45a,45■
12:1a,4a,38,49a■13:1a■14:24,24a■
15:3,24,26■17:4,5,6,8,9,22,24■18:1,
2a,5a,9^{2},11,13,14a,16,32■19:17,24a,32a,
39a■20:8a,16,30■21:10,20,20c,24a,
25(3745),25b-**AC**-1:2,4,7,11,11a,12,
16,16a,25■2:7a,22,33■3:2a,10a,10
sup,18,21,23(b,302),25■4:11^{2}a,20,24a,36■
5:17a■6:9a,10,14■7:3,17,18,20,34a,35
(3558),37(3558),38(3558),40,43,45,52c,
52(3558)■8:1(3558),14(3558),24,26(3778)■
9:7a,11a,21a,22a,32a,36^{2},39(3745)■10:7a,

17,17a,18a,21a,36,37sup,37,39,42a,47b■
11:6,20b,22a,28b,30■12:9a,10b■13:7,22,
27a,39■14:3a,13a,15,26■15:10,16a,19a,
23a,29■16:2,3a,4a,12b,16b,17b,21■
17:12a,21a,31,34■19:26a■20:19a,24,28^2,
32a,38■21:20a■22:10,29a■23:13a,21b■
24:14,14a,15■25:7sup,7a,24a■26:4a,7^2,
10,16^2,22■27:17,39■28:9a-**RO**-1:2,3a,27
sup,27■2:14a,15b,21a■3:30■4:11a■5:5a,
15a■6:17■7:5a,10a,15,16,19,23a■8:39a■
9:6a,23,30^{2}a■10:5a,5sup,8■11:2,7■14:22■
15:18,22(1352),26a,31■16:1sup,1a,11a,
12b,17sup,17-**1CO**-1:2a,4a,24a,28sup,
28a■2:7,8,9,11a,12a,13,13^{2}sup■3:10a,11,
14,17b■4:6,17a■6:19sup,19,20b■7:13b■
8:10a,10^{2}sup■10:16^2,20,30■11:23^2,24a■
12:6a,23■15:1^2,2,3,10sup,10a,31,36,37,
57a-**2CO**-1:1^{2}a,6^{2}a,8a,9a■2:4,6a■3:7a,
14b■4:11a,16(1352),17a■5:2a■7:14a■
8:16a,19a,20a,22a■9:2,11b■10:2a,8,13■
11:4,17,28a,31a■12:4,6,21a,21■13:3,10
-**GA**-1:7,8,11a,20,22a,23sup,23■2:2,2
sup,4,10,18,20■3:10a,16,21a■4:24b,24
sup,24b,25a,26sup,26b■5:19b,21,21sup■
6:1a-**EPH**-1:1a,9,10a,14,20,23b■2:10,
11a,17a■3:2a,5,9a,11,13b■4:15,22a,24a,
29(1536)■5:4a■6:2b,17,20-**PH'P**-1:1a,
11a,28b,30(3634)■2:5,9a,13a■3:3a,6a,9^{2}a,
12■4:3b,7a,9,13a-**COL**-1:4a,5a,6a,12a,
23sup,23a,24sup,24,25a,26a,27,29a■2:10,
14,17,18,19,22,23b■3:5a,5b,6,7,10a,14b,
15,25■4:3,9a,11a,11b,17-**1TH**-1:10a■2:13
sup,13,14a■4:5a,10a,13sup,13a,15^{2}a,17a■
5:12a,15a,21a-**2TH**-1:5sup,5■2:15,16a■
3:4,6,17-**1TI**-1:1a,4b,4a,6,11,14a,19■
2:10■3:13a,15b■4:3,3sup,14■5:13a■6:9b,
10,15,16,21,subscr.b-**2TI**-1:1a,5b,6,9a,
12,12sup,13,13a,14sup,14a■2:10a■3:11
(3634),14,15^{2}a■4:8-**TIT**-1:1a,2,3,11■2:1■
3:5,6-**PH'M**-5,6a,11a-**HEB**-1:5c,13c■
2:3b,11,13■4:3(3583)■5:8,12c■6:7a,10,
18,19,19sup■7:2,13,14,19,28sup,28a■
8:2,6b■9:2b,3a,5,9b,9,20■10:1,8b,10,11b,
20,32,35b■11:3a,4,7,8,12a,29■12:5b,14,
19■13:9-**JAS**-1:1,12,21a■2:5(3735),7a,
23a■3:9a-**1PE**-1:3a,10,11a,12^2,25a■2:7a,
7sup,8,10^{2}a,11b■3:4sup,4,19■4:11-**2PE**-
3:1,10,16^2-**1JO**-1:1^3,2b,3,5■2:7^2,8,24^2,27■
3:24■5:9-**2JO**-2a,5,8-**3JO**-6,10-**JUDE**-
10(3745),15^2,17a-**RE**-1:1^2,4^{2}a,4,7b,8a,11a,
19^3,20^2■2:6,7,8,9a,10,15,17,20a,23,24b■
3:4,9a,10a,11,12^{2}a■4:1,1sup,1,5,8a■5:6,
8,13■6:9■7:9,10a,13a,17a■8:2,3a,6a,9a,
13a■9:4b,13a,14,14a,15a,18a,20^2■10:4,
5,8,8^{2}a■11:2a,8b,16a,17a■12:4a,9a,10a,13b,
16,17a■13:2,4,14^2■14:3a,4,4a,10a,13a,
17a■16:2a,5a,9a■17:1a,7a,9a,9(3699,846),
12,12b,15,16,18,18a■18:6,14a,15a■19:2b,
14a,20,21a■20:2,4b,8a,12,12sup,13^{2}a■
21:8^2,9a,12■22:6,8a

WHILE-all=5704&marked-**GE**-8:22
(5750)■46:29(5750)-**EX**-33:22^2-**DE**-19:6
(3588)-**JOS**-14:10(834)-**J'G**-3:26-**1SA**-
7:2(3117)■9:27(3117)■14:19■20:14
(518)■22:4(3117)■25:7(3117),16(3117)■
27:11(3117)-**2SA**-7:19(7350)■18:14
(5750)-**1KI**-17:7(3117)■18:45(3541)
-**NE**-7:3-**JOB**-27:3(5750)-**PS**-39:1(5750)■
104:33(5750)■146:2sup,2(5750)-**PR**-
19:18(3588)-**EC**-12:1,2-**SONG**-1:12-**IS**-
63:18(4705)-**LA**-1:19(3588)-**DA**-4:31
(5751)-**NA**-1:10■**N.T.**-all=1722,3588
&marked-**M'T**-13:21(4340),25■14:22
(2193)■26:36(2193),73(3397)-**M'R**-2:19
(1722,3789)■6:31(3641),45(2193)■14:32
(2193)■15:44(3819)-**LU**-1:8■5:34(1722,
3739)■8:13(2540)■18:4(5550)■24:15,
32^2(5613)51-**JOH**-5:7(1722,3739)■7:33
(5550)■9:4(2193)■12:35(5550),35(2193),
36(2193)■17:12(3153)-**AC**-1:10(5613)■
10:17(5613)■15:7(2250)■18:18(2250)■
19:1■27:33(891,3739)-**1CO**-3:4(3752)■
16:7(5550,5099)-**HEB**-3:13(891,3739),15■
9:17(3753)■10:37(3397)-**1PE**-5:10(3641)

WHILES-**DA**-9:20(5750),21(5750)■
N.T.-**M'T**-5:25(2193,3755)

WHILST-all=5704&marked-**J'G**-6:31
-**NE**-6:3(834)-**JOB**-32:11-**PS**-141:10

WHIP-**PR**-26:3(7752)-**NA**-3:2(7752)

WHIPS-all=7752-**1KI**-12:11,14-**2CH**-
10:11,14

WHIRLETH-**EC**-1:6(1980)

WHIRLWIND-all=5591,a=5492&
marked-**2KI**-2:1,11-**JOB**-37:9a■38:1■
40:6-**PS**-58:9(8175)-**PR**-1:27a■10:25a
-**IS**-5:28a■17:13a■40:24■41:16■
66:15a-**JER**-4:13a■23:19^2■25:32■30:23^2
-**EZE**-1:4(7307,5591)-**DA**-11:40(8175)
-**HO**-8:7a■13:3(5590)-**AM**-1:14a-**NA**-
1:3a-**HAB**-3:14(5590)-**ZEC**-7:14(5590)

WHIRLWINDS-**IS**-21:1(5492)-**ZEC**-
9:14(5591)

WHISPER-**PS**-41:7(3907)-**IS**-29:4(6850)

WHISPERED-**2SA**-12:19(3907)

WHISPERER-**PR**-16:28(5372)

WHISPERERS-**RO**-1:29(5588)

WHISPERINGS-**2CO**-12:20(5587)

WHIT-**DE**-13:16(3632)-**1SA**-3:18
(1697)■**N.T.**-**JOH**-7:23(3650)■13:10
(3650)-**2CO**-11:5(3367)

WHITE-all=3836&marked-**GE**-
30:35,37^2■40:16(2751)■49:12-**EX**-16:31
-**LE**-13:3,4^2,10^2,13,16,17,19^2,20,21,24^2,
25,26,38,39,42,43-**J'G**-5:10(6715)-**ES**-1:6
(2353),6(1858)■8:15(2353)-**JOB**-6:6
(7388)-**EC**-9:8-**SONG**-5:10(6703)-**IS**-
1:18(3835)-**EZE**-27:18(6713)-**DA**-11:35
(3835)■12:10(3835)-**JOE**-1:7(3835)-**ZEC**-
1:8■6:3,6■**N.T.**-all=3022&marked-**M'T**-
5:36■17:2■28:3-**M'R**-9:3,3(3021)■16:5
-**LU**-9:29-**JOH**-4:35■20:12-**AC**-1:10
-**RE**-1:14^2■2:17■3:4,5,18■4:4■6:2,11■
7:9,13,14(3021)■14:14■15:6(2986)■19:8
(2986),11,14^2■20:11

WHITED-**M'T**-23:27(2867)-**AC**-
23:3(2867)

WHITER-**PS**-51:7(3835)-**LA**-4:7(6705)

WHITHER-all=834,8033,a=575&
marked-**GE**-16:8a■20:13■28:15■32:17a■
37:30a-**EX**-21:13■34:12(5921)-**LE**-18:3
(8033)■20:22(8033)-**NU**-13:27(834)■
15:18■35:25,26-**DE**-1:28a■3:21■4:5,
14,27■6:1■7:1■11:8,10,11,29■12:29■
23:12(8033),20■28:21,37,63■30:1,3,
16,18■31:13,16■32:47,50-**JOS**-2:5a
-**J'G**-19:17a-**RU**-1:16(413,834)-**1SA**-
10:14a■27:10(413)-**2SA**-2:1a■13:13a■
15:20(5921,834)■17:18(8033)-**1KI**-
2:36a,42a■8:47■18:10,12(5921,834)■
21:18-**2KI**-5:25a-**2CH**-6:37,38(834)■
10:2(834)-**NE**-2:16a-**PS**-122:4(8033)■
139:7^{2}a-**EC**-9:10-**SONG**-6:1^{2}a-**IS**-20:6
-**JER**-8:3■15:2a■16:15(834)■19:14
(834)■22:12■23:3,8■24:9■29:7,14,18■
30:11■32:37■40:4(413),12■42:22■43:5■
44:8■45:5■46:28■49:36-**EZE**-1:12■
4:13■6:9■10:11(834)■12:16■29:13■36:20,
21,22■37:21■47:9(413,834,8033)-**DA**-
9:7-**JOE**-3:7-**ZEC**-2:2a■5:10a■**N.T.**-
all=4226&marked-**LU**-10:1(3757)■
24:28(3757)-**JOH**-3:8■6:21(1519,
3739)■7:35■8:14^2,21(3699),22(3699)■
12:35■13:33(3699),36,36(3699)■14:4
(3699),5■16:5■18:20(3699)■21:18^2(3699)
-**HEB**-6:20(3699)■11:8-**1JO**-2:11

WHITHERSOEVER-all=3605,
834&marked-**JOS**-1:7,9,16-**J'G**-2:15
-**1SA**-14:47■18:5■23:13(834)-**2SA**-7:9■
8:6,14-**1KI**-2:3(3605,834,8033)■8:44
(1870,834)-**2KI**-18:7-**1CH**-17:8■18:6,
13-**ES**-4:3(4725,834)■8:17(834)-**PR**-
17:8(413,3605,834)■21:1(5921,3605,834)
-**EZE**-1:20(5921,834,8033)■21:16(575)■
47:9(413,3605,834,8033)■**N.T.**-**M'T**-
8:19(3699,1437)-**M'R**-6:56(3699,302)
-**LU**-9:57(3699,302)-**1CO**-16:6(3757,1437)
-**JAS**-3:4(3699,302)-**RE**-14:4(3699,302)

WHO-all=4310,a=834,b=1931&marked
-**GE**-3:11■14:12b■21:7,26■24:15a■
27:18,32,33■30:2a■33:5■36:1b■43:22■
48:8,14b■49:9-**EX**-2:14■3:11■4:11^2,
28a■5:2■6:12(589)■10:8■12:27a,40a■
15:11^2■18:10^{2}a■21:8a■32:26-**NU**-
6:21a■7:2(1992)■9:6a■11:4,18■12:7b■
16:5(853,834),5(853)■21:26b■23:10■
24:9,23■25:6(1992)■26:9a,63a-**DE**-
2:25a■4:7a,46a■5:3(428),26■9:2■21:1■
30:12,13■33:29,29a-**JOS**-9:8■13:12b■
17:16^{2}a-**J'G**-1:1■2:7a■6:29■7:1b■
9:28^2,38■15:6■17:7b■18:3,29a■21:5-**RU**-
2:3a,20a■3:9,16-**1SA**-2:25■4:8■6:20■
10:12,19a■11:12■14:17,45a■17:25a,
26■18:18■20:10■22:14■23:22■25:10■
26:6,9,14,15■30:24-**2SA**-1:8■4:5b,9a,
10a■6:20a■7:18■12:22■16:10■22:32
-**1KI**-1:20,27■2:24a,32a■3:9■8:24a■9:9a■
12:2b,9a,18a■13:26a■14:8^{2}a,14a,16a■
19:19b■20:14■21:11a■22:20,52a-**2KI**-
4:5(1992)■7:17a■9:32■10:9,13,29a■
13:6a,11a■14:24a■15:9a,18a,24a,28a■
17:36a■18:35■23:15a,16a-**1CH**-2:7a■
4:22a■5:8b■7:31b■8:12b,13^2(1992)■
9:31b■11:12b■16:41a■17:16■22:9b■
25:9b■29:5,14-**2CH**-1:10■2:6^2,12a■8:8a■
10:2b■18:19■20:34a,35b■22:9a■26:1b■
32:14■35:21a■36:13a,23-**EZR**-1:3■
5:3(4479),9(4479)-**NE**-3:3(1992)■
6:10b,11■9:7a-**ES**-2:6a,15a■4:11a,14■
6:2a,4■7:5,9a-**JOB**-4:2,7■9:4,12^2,19,
24■11:10■12:3,9■13:19■14:4■17:3,15■
21:31^2■23:13■24:25■26:14■34:13^2,29^2■
36:22,23^2■38:2,5^2,6,25,28,29,36^2,37^2,41■
39:5^2■41:10,11,13^2,14■42:3-**PS**-4:6■6:5■
8:1a■12:4a,4■15:1^2■16:7a■18:ta,31^2■
19:12■24:3^2,4a,8,10■35:10■39:6■59:7■
60:9^2■64:3a,5■71:19a,19■76:7■77:13■
83:12a■89:6,6sup,8■90:11■94:16^2■
106:2,2sup■108:10^2■113:5,5sup■
119:38a■130:3■140:4a■147:17-**PR**-
18:14■20:6,9■23:29^4■24:22■27:4■30:4^4,
9■31:10-**EC**-2:19,25■3:21,22■4:3a,13a■
6:12■7:13,24■8:1^2,4■10:14■11:5a■12:7a
-**SONG**-3:6■6:10■8:5-**IS**-1:12■6:8■
14:27^2■23:8■27:4■29:15,22a■33:14^2■
36:20■37:2a■40:12,13,26■41:2,4,26■
42:19^2,23,23sup,24■43:9,13■44:7,10■
45:21,21sup■49:21■50:8^2,9,10■51:12,
19■53:1,8■60:8■63:1■65:16a■66:8,8a-**JER**-
2:24■9:12,12sup■10:7■15:5^2,5sup■17:9■
18:13■20:1b,15a■21:13^2■23:18^2■30:21■
46:7■49:4,19^3■50:44^3-**LA**-2:13■3:37-**DA**-
1:10a■2:23(1768)■3:15(4479),28(1768)■
6:27(1768)-**HO**-3:1(1992)■14:9-**JOE**-2:11,
14-**AM**-1:1a■3:8^2-**OB**-3-**JON**-3:9-**MIC**-
3:3a■5:8a■6:9■7:18-**NA**-1:6^2■3:7-**HAB**-
2:5a-**HAG**-2:3-**ZEC**-4:7,10-**MAL**-1:10■
3:2^2■**N.T.**-all=5101,a=3588,b=3739,
c=3748&marked-**M'T**-1:16a■3:7■10:2a,
4a,11■12:48^2■13:9a,43a,46b■18:1■19:25■
21:10,23■24:45■26:3a,68■27:57b-**M'R**-
1:19(841),24■2:7■3:33■4:16b■5:3b,30,
31■9:34■10:26■11:28■15:7c,41b■16:3
-**LU**-1:36a■3:7■4:34■5:12(2532),21^2■7:2b,
39,49■8:45^2■9:9,31b■10:22^2,29■12:14,
42■16:11,12■18:26,30b■19:3■20:2■
22:64■23:19c,51b-**JOH**-1:19,22,27a■
4:10■5:13■6:60,64^2■7:20,49a■8:25■9:2,
19b,21,36■12:34,38■13:11a,24,25■21:12
-**AC**-1:23b■3:3b■4:25a,36a■5:36b■7:27,
35,38b,46b,53c■8:15c,27b,33■9:5■
10:32b,38b,41c■11:14b,23b■13:7(3778),
9b,31c,43c■14:8b,9b,16b,19(2532)■
15:17a,27(846),38a■16:24b■17:10c■
18:27b■19:15■21:4c,32b,33,37a■22:8■
23:33c■24:1c,6b,19b■26:15■28:7b,10b,
18c-**RO**-1:18a,25c,25b,32c■2:6b,27a■
3:5a■4:12^{2}a,16b,17a,18b,25b■5:14b■
7:24■8:31,33,34,34^{2}b,35■9:4c,5a,19,20■
10:6,7,16■11:4c,34^2,35■14:2a,4,20a■
16:4c,5b,6c,7c,7b,12a,22a-**1CO**-1:8b,30b■
2:16■3:5■4:5b,7,17^{2}b■9:7^3(5100)■10:13b■
14:8-**2CO**-1:4a,19a,22a■2:2,16■3:6b■
4:4b,6a■5:5a,18a■8:10c■10:1b■11:29^2
-**GA**-1:1a,4a,15a■2:3a,4c,9a,20a■3:1■5:7
-**EPH**-1:3a,12a,19a■2:11a,13b,14b■3:9a■
4:6a,19c■5:5b-**PH'P**-2:20c■3:19a-**COL**-
1:7b,8a,13b,15b,18b■2:12a■4:9b,11a,12a
-**1TH**-2:12a,15a■5:10a,24b-**2TH**-1:9c■
2:4a,12a■3:3b-**1TI**-1:12a,13a■2:4b,6a■
4:10b■6:13^{2}a,15a,16a,17a-**2TI**-1:9a■2:2c,
18c■4:1a-**TIT**-1:11c■2:14b-**HEB**-1:7b■
2:9b,15(3745)■5:7b■6:18a■7:1a,5a,9a,
16b,27b■8:1b,5c■9:14b■10:29a■11:33b■
12:2b,16b■13:7c-**JAS**-3:13■4:12a,12■

5:4a,10b-**1PE**-1:5a,10a,17a,21a■2:22b,23b,24b■3:5a,13,22b■4:5b■5:1a,10a-**2PE**-2:1c,15b-**1JO**-2:22■5:5-**2JO**-7a-**3JO**-9a-**JUDE**-4a-**RE**-1:2b,9a■2:1a,13b,14b,18a■4:9a■5:2■6:17■12:5b■13:4^2■14:11a■15:4,7a■18:8a,9a

WHOLE-all=3605,a=854,3605&marked-**GE**-2:6a,11a,13a■7:19■8:9■9:19■11:1,4■13:9-**EX**-10:15■12:6■16:2,3a,10■19:18■29:18a-**LE**-3:9(8549)■4:12a,13■7:14■8:21a■10:6■25:29(8552)-**NU**-3:7■8:9a■10:2(4749)■11:20(3117),21(3117)■14:2,29■20:1,22-**DE**-2:25■4:19■27:6(8003)■29:23■33:10(3632)-**JOS**-5:8(2421)■8:31(8003)■10:13(8549)■11:23a■18:1■22:12,16,18-**J'G**-19:2(3117)■21:13-**2SA**-1:9■3:19■6:19■14:7-**1KI**-6:22^2■11:34a-**2KI**-9:8-**2CH**-6:3a■15:15■16:9■26:12■30:23■33:8-**EZR**-2:64-**NE**-7:66-**ES**-3:6-**JOB**-5:18(7495)■28:24■34:13■37:3■41:11-**PS**-9:1■48:2■51:19(3632)■72:19a■97:5■105:16■111:1■119:2,10,34,58,69■138:1-**PR**-1:12(8549)■16:33-**EC**-12:13^2-**IS**-1:5■3:1^2■6:3■10:12a■13:5■14:7,26,29,31■21:8■28:22■54:5-**JER**-1:18■3:10■4:20,27,29■7:15■8:16■12:11■13:11^2■15:10■19:11(7495)■24:7■25:11■31:40■32:41■35:3■37:10■45:4■50:23■51:41,47-**LA**-2:15-**EZE**-5:10■7:13■10:12■15:5(8549)■32:4■35:14■37:11■39:25■43:11,12■45:6-**DA**-2:35(3606),48(3606)■6:1(3606),3(3606)■7:23(3606),27(3606)■8:5■9:12■10:3(3117)■11:17-**AM**-1:6(8003),9(8003)■3:1-**MIC**-4:13-**ZEP**-1:18-**ZEC**-4:10,14■5:3-**MAL**-3:9■**N.T.**-all=3650,a=5199&marked-**M'T**-5:29,30■6:22,23■8:32(3956),34(3956)■9:12(2480),21(4982),22^2(4982)■12:13a■13:2(3956),33■14:36(1295)■15:28(3390),31a■16:26■26:13■27:27-**M'R**-2:17(2480)■3:5a■4:1(3956)■5:28(4982),34(4982),34a■6:55,56(4982)■8:36■10:52(4982)■12:33(3646)■14:9■15:1,16,33-**LU**-1:10(3956)■5:31(5198)■6:10a,19(3956)■7:10(5198)■8:37(537),39,48(4982),50(4982)■9:25■11:34,36^2■13:21■17:19(4982)■19:37(537)■21:35(3956)■23:1(537)-**JOH**-4:53■5:4a,6a,9a,11a,14a,15a■7:23a■11:50-**AC**-4:9(4982),10a■6:5(3956)■9:34(2390)■11:26■13:44(3956)■15:22■19:29■28:30-**RO**-1:8■8:22(3956)■16:23-**1CO**-5:6■12:17^2■14:23-**GA**-5:3,9-**EPH**-3:15(3958)■4:16(3958)-**1TH**-5:23(3648)-**TIT**-1:11-**JAS**-2:10■3:2,3,6-**1JO**-2:2■5:19-**RE**-12:9■16:14

WHOLESOME-**PR**-15:4(4832)■**N.T.**-**1TI**-6:3(5198)

WHOLLY-all=3605&marked-**LE**-6:22(3632),23(3632)■19:9(3615)-**NU**-4:6(3632)■32:11(4390),12(4390)-**DE**-1:36(4390)-**JOS**-14:8(4390),9(4390),14(4390)-**J'G**-17:3(6942)-**1SA**-7:9(3632)-**1CH**-28:21-**JOB**-21:23-**IS**-22:1-**JER**-2:21■6:6■13:19(7965)■42:15(7760)■46:28(5352)■50:13-**EZE**-11:15-**AM**-8:8■9:5■**N.T.**-**1TH**-5:23(3651)-**1TI**-4:15(1510,1722)

WHOM-all=834,a=4310,b=1768&marked-**GE**-2:8■3:12■4:25(3588)■6:7■10:14■15:14■21:3■22:2■24:3,14,40,44,47■25:12■30:26■41:38■43:27,29■44:10,16■45:4■46:18■48:9,15-**EX**-6:5,26■14:13■18:9■22:9■23:27■28:3■32:13■33:12,19^2■35:21,23,24■36:1(834,1992)-**LE**-6:5■13:45■14:32■15:18■16:32^2■17:7(834,1992)■22:5■25:27,55(834,853)■26:45(834,853)■27:24(834,853),24-**NU**-3:3■4:41,45,46■5:7■11:16,21■12:1■16:5,7■17:5■22:6^2■26:59(834,853)■27:18■34:29-**DE**-4:46■7:19(834,6440)■9:2^2■17:15■19:17(834,1992)■21:8■24:11■28:55■29:26^2■31:4(834,853)■33:8,8sup■34:10-**JOS**-2:10(834,853)■4:4■5:6(834,1992)■10:11,25(834,853)■13:8(5973),21■24:15a,17-**J'G**-4:22■7:4■8:15,18■14:20■21:23-**RU**-2:19^2(834,5973)■4:1,1sup,12-**1SA**-6:20a■9:17,20a■10:24■12:3a,13^{2}a■16:3■17:28a,45■21:9■24:14^{2}a■25:11,25■28:8(853,834),11(853)a■29:5■30:13a-**2SA**-7:7,15,23■14:7■16:18,19a■17:3■19:10■20:3■21:8,8sup■23:8-**1KI**-5:5■7:8■11:34■13:23■17:1,20■18:15,31■20:14a■21:25,26-**2KI**-3:14■5:16■6:19,22■8:5■10:24■16:3■17:8,11,15,27,28,33,34■18:20a■19:4,10,22(853)a,22a■21:2,9■23:5■25:22-**1CH**-1:12■5:6,25■6:31■7:14■9:22(834,1992)■11:10,11■17:6,21^2■29:8-**2CH**-1:11(834,5921)■2:7■8:8■17:19■20:10■22:7■23:18■28:3■33:2,9-**EZR**-2:1,65(428)■4:10b■5:14b-**NE**-1:10■7:6,67(428)■9:37-**ES**-2:6■4:5,11■6:7a,9^2,11,13-**JOB**-9:15■15:19(1992)■19:27■25:3■26:4■30:2(5921)-**PS**-27:1^{2}a■41:9■47:4■69:26■73:25a■86:9■88:5■89:21■94:12■95:11■105:26■106:34,38■107:2-**PR**-3:12(853,834)■25:7■30:31(5973)-**EC**-4:8a■5:19■6:2■8:14(834,413),14(413)■9:9-**SONG**-3:3sup,3(853)-**IS**-6:8(853)a■8:12,18■10:3a■19:25■22:16a■28:9(853)a,9(834,413)■31:6■36:5a■37:4,10,23(853)a,23a■40:14a,18a,25a■41:8,9■42:24(2098)■43:10■46:5■47:15■49:3■50:1^2■51:19a■53:1a■57:4^{2}a,11a■66:13-**JER**-1:12■6:10a■7:9■8:2^2,2sup■9:12,16■11:12(834,1992)■14:16(834,1992)■18:8■19:4■20:6(834,1992)■24:5■25:15(834,413),17(834,413)■26:5■27:5■29:1,3,4,20,22■30:9■33:5■34:11,16■37:1■38:9(853,834)■39:17(834,6440)■40:5■41:2,9,10,16^2,18■42:9(834,413),11(834,6440)■44:3■50:20■52:28-**LA**-1:10■2:20a■4:20-**EZE**-9:6■11:7,15■16:20,37■20:9■23:7,9,22(834,1992),28^2,37,40(834,413),40■24:21■28:25■31:2(413)a,18a■32:19a■38:17-**DA**-1:4(834,1992),7(1992),11■2:24b■3:12(3487),17b■4:8b■5:11b,11sup,12b,13b,19^{3}b,19sup■6:2b(2006),16b,20b■7:20(4479)■9:21■11:21(5921),38,39-**HO**-13:10-**JO**-2:32■3:2-**AM**-6:1(1992)■7:2a,5a-**NA**-3:19a-**ZEP**-3:18(5921)-**ZEC**-1:4(834,413),10■7:14■12:10(854,834)-**MAL**-1:4■2:14■3:1^2■**N.T.**-all=3739,a=5101&marked-**M'T**-1:16■3:17■7:9■11:10■12:18^2,27a■16:13a,15a■17:5(3939),25a■18:7■19:11■20:23■23:35■24:45,46■26:24■27:9,15,17a-**M'R**-1:11■3:13■6:16■8:27a,29a■10:40■13:20■14:21,71■15:12,40■16:9-**LU**-6:13,14,34,47a■7:4,27,43,47■8:2,35,38■9:9,18a,20a■10:22■11:19a■12:5a,37,42,43,48■13:4,16■17:1■19:15■22:22■23:25-**JOH**-1:15,26,30,33,45,47■3:26,34■4:18■5:21,38,45■6:29,68a■7:25,28■8:53a,54■10:35,36■11:3■12:1,9,38a■13:18,22a,23,24,26■14:17,26■15:26■17:3,11,24■18:4a,7a■19:26,37■20:2,15a■21:7,20-**AC**-1:2,3■2:24,36■3:2,13,15,16,21■4:10^2,22,27■5:25,30,32,36■6:3,6■7:7,35,39,45,52■8:10,34a■9:5■10:21,39■13:22,25a,37■14:23■15:17,24■17:3,7,23,31■18:26(846)■19:13,16,25,27■20:25■21:16,29■22:5,8■23:29■24:6,8■25:15,16,18,19,24,26■26:15,17,26■27:23■28:4,8,15,23-**RO**-1:5,6,9■3:25■4:6,8,17,24■5:2,11■6:16^2■8:29,30^3■9:4,5,15^2,18^2,24■10:14^2■11:36(846)■13:7^2(3588),9^2(3588)■14:15■15:21■16:4-**1CO**-1:9■3:5■7:39■8:6^2,11■10:11■15:6,15-**2CO**-1:10■2:3,10^2■4:4■8:22■10:18■11:4■12:17-**GA**-1:5■2:5■3:19■4:19■6:14-**EPH**-1:7,11,13^2■2:3,21,22■3:12,15■4:16■6:22-**PH'P**-2:15■3:8,18-**COL**-1:14,27,28■2:3,11■4:8,10-**1TI**-1:10-**2TH**-2:8-**1TI**-1:15,20^2■6:16^2-**2TI**-1:3,12,15■2:17■3:14a■4:15,18-**PH'M**-10,12,13-**HEB**-1:2^2■2:10^2■3:17a,18a■4:13■5:11■6:7■7:2,4,13■11:18,38■12:6^2,7■13:21,23-**JAS**-1:17-**1PE**-1:8,8sup,12■2:4■4:11■5:8a,9-**2PE**-1:17■2:2,17,19-**1JO**-4:20^2-**2JO**-1-**3JO**-1,6-**JUDE**-13-**RE**-7:2■17:2■20:8

WHOMSOEVER-all=834&marked-**GE**-31:32■44:9-**LE**-15:11(3605,834)-**J'G**-7:4■11:24-**DA**-4:17(4479),25(4479),32(4479)■5:21(4479,1768)■**N.T.**-all=3739,302&marked-**M'T**-11:27(3739,1437)■21:44■26:48-**M'R**-14:44■15:6(3746)-**LU**-4:6(3739,1437)■12:48(3956,3739)■20:18-**JOH**-13:20(1437,5100)-**AC**-8:19-**1CO**-16:3(3739,1437)

WHORE-all=2181&marked-**LE**-19:29■21:7,9-**DE**-22:21■23:17(6948),18-**J'G**-19:2-**PR**-23:27-**IS**-57:3-**EZE**-16:28■**N.T.**-all=4024-**RE**-17:1,15,16■19:2

WHOREDOM-all=2181&marked-**GE**-38:24(2183)-**LE**-19:29■20:5-**NU**-25:1-**JER**-3:9(2184)■13:27(2184)-**EZE**-16:17,33(8457)■20:30■23:8(8457),17(8457),27(2184)■43:7(2184),9(2184)-**HO**-1:2■4:10,11(2184),13,14,18■5:3■6:10(2184)

WHOREDOMS-all=8457,a=2183&marked-**NU**-14:33(2184)-**2KI**-9:22a-**2CH**-21:13(2181)-**JER**-3:2(2184)-**EZE**-16:20,22,25,26,34,34(2181),36■23:7,8,11,11a,14,18,19,29a,29,35,43-**HO**-1:2a■2:2a,4a■4:12a■5:4a-**NA**-3:4^{2}a

WHOREMONGER-**EPH**-5:5(4205)

WHOREMONGERS-all=4205-**1TI**-1:10-**HEB**-13:4-**RE**-21:8■22:15

WHORE'S-**JER**-3:3(2181)

WHORES-**EZE**-16:33(2181)-**HO**-4:14(2181)

WHORING-all=2181-**EX**-34:15,16^2-**LE**-17:7■20:5,6-**NU**-15:39-**DE**-31:16-**J'G**-2:17■8:27,33-**1CH**-5:25-**2CH**-21:13-**PS**-73:27■106:39-**EZE**-6:9■23:30-**HO**-4:12■9:1

WHORISH-all=2181-**PR**-6:26-**EZE**-6:9■16:30

WHOSE-all=834,a=4310&marked-**GE**-1:11,12■7:22■17:14■24:23a,37■32:17^{2}a■38:25^2-**EX**-35:21,26,29■36:2^2-**LE**-13:40(3588)■14:32■15:32■16:27■21:10■22:4-**DE**-8:9,9sup■19:1■28:49■29:18-**JOS**-24:15-**J'G**-6:10■8:31(853)-**RU**-2:2,5a,12■3:2-**1SA**-10:26■12:3^{3}a■17:55a,56a,58a-**2SA**-3:12a■6:2■16:8■17:10-**1KI**-3:26■8:39-**2KI**-7:2,17■8:1,5■12:15■18:22(834,853),22(853)-**1CH**-13:6-**2CH**-6:30(834,853)-**EZR**-1:5(853)■7:15(1768)-**JOB**-3:23■4:19■5:5■8:14■12:6,10■26:4a■30:1■38:29a■39:6-**PS**-26:10■33:12■144:8,11-**PR**-2:15-**EC**-7:26(834,1931)-**IS**-2:22■5:28■6:13■18:2,7■23:8,8sup■30:13■31:9■36:7(834,853),7(853)■45:1■58:11-**JER**-19:13■32:29■33:5■44:28a■49:12-**EZE**-3:6■17:16(834,853),16(853)■20:9(853),14,22■21:25,27,29■24:6■32:23■40:45,46■42:15■43:4-**DA**-2:11(1768),26(1768)■3:1(1768),27(1768)■4:8(1768),19(1768),34(1768),37(1768)■5:23(1768),23sup■7:19(1768)■10:1-**AM**-2:9-**JON**-1:7a■8(834)a-**NA**-3:8-**ZEC**-11:5■**N.T.**-all=3739&marked-**M'T**-3:11,12■10:3(3588)■22:20(5101),28(5101),42(5101)-**M'R**-1:7■7:25■12:16(5101),23(5101)-**LU**-1:27■2:25■3:16,17■6:6(2532,846)■12:20(5101)■13:1■20:24(5100),33(5100)■24:18-**JOH**-1:6(846),27■4:46■6:42■10:12■11:2■18:26■19:24(5101)■20:23^2(5100)-**AC**-10:5,6,32■11:13(3588)■12:12(3588),25(3588)■13:6,25■15:37(3588)■16:14■18:7■27:23-**RO**-2:29■3:8,14■4:7^2■9:5-**2CO**-8:18■11:15-**GA**-3:1-**PH'P**-3:19,19(3588)■4:3-**2TH**-2:9-**TIT**-1:11-**HEB**-3:6,17■6:8■11:10■12:26■13:7,11-**1PE**-2:24■3:3,6-**2PE**-2:3-**RE**-9:11(846)■13:8,12■17:8■20:11

WHOSO-**LE**-11:27(3605)-**NU**-35:30(3605)-**DE**-19:4(834)-**PS**-107:43(4310)-**PR**-9:4(4310),16(4310)■25:14(376,834)-**DA**-3:6(4479,1768),11(4479,1768)-**ZEC**-14:17(834)■**N.T.**-all=3588&marked-**M'T**-18:5(3739,302),6(3739,302)■19:9■23:20,21■24:15-**M'R**-7:10-**JOH**-6:54-**JAS**-1:25-**1JO**-2:5(3739,302)■3:17(3739,302)

WHOSOEVER-all=3605a=834,b=376&marked-**GE**-4:15-**EX**-12:15■19:12■22:19■30:33b,33a,38a■31:15■32:24(4310),33(4310)a■35:2,5-**LE**-7:25■11:24,25,31■15:5b,a,10,19,21,22,27■

17:14■18:29(3605)a■19:20b,a■20:2b■21:17b,a■22:3b,a,5b,a,21b,a■24:15b,a-**NU**-5:2■15:14a■17:13■19:13,16(3605)a■31:19^{2}-**DE**-18:19b,a-**JOS**-1:18b,a■2:19^{2}(3605)a■20:9-**J'G**-7:3(4310)-**1SA**-11:7a-**2KI**-10:19(3605)a■21:12-**1CH**-11:6■26:28-**2CH**-13:9■15:13-**EZR**-1:4■6:11■7:26■10:8-**ES**-4:11a-**PR**-6:29■20:1-**IS**-54:15(4310)■59:8-**JER**-19:3-**DA**-5:7■6:7-**JOE**-2:32a■**N.T.**-all=3739,302,a=3739,1437,b=3956,3588&marked-**M'T**-5:19a,19,21,22b,22^{2},28b,31,32,32a,39(3748),41(3748)■7:24(3956,3748)■10:14a,32(3956,3748),33(3748,302),42a■11:6a■12:32^{2},50(3748,302)■13:12^{2}(3748)■15:5■16:25^{2}■18:4(3748)■19:9■20:26a,27a■21:44(3588)■23:12(3748),16^{2},18a,18-**M'R**-3:35■6:11(3745,302)■8:34(3748),35^{2}(3736,302),38(3736,302)■9:37^{2}a,41,42■10:11a,15a,43a,44■11:23-**LU**-6:47b■7:23a■8:18^{2}■9:5(3745,302),24^{2},26,48^{2}a■12:8(3956,3739,302),10(3956,3739)■14:11b,27(3748),33(3956)■16:18^{2}b■17:33^{2}a■18:17a■20:18b-**JOH**-3:15b,16b■4:13b,14■5:4(3588)■8:34b■11:26b■12:46b■16:2b■19:12b-**AC**-2:21(3956,3739)■10:43(3588)■13:26(3588)-**RO**-2:1b■9:33b■10:11b,13(3956,3739,302)■13:2(3588)-**1CO**-11:27-**GA**-5:4(3748),10(3748,302)-**JAS**-2:10(3748)■4:4-**1JO**-2:23b■3:4b,6^{2}b,9b,10b,15b■4:15■5:1b,18b-**2JO**-9b-**RE**-14:11(1536)■20:15(1536)■22:15b,17(3588)

WHY-all=4100,a=4069&marked-**GE**-4:6^{2}■12:18,19■25:22■27:45■42:1■47:15-**EX**-1:18a■2:20■3:3a■5:22■14:5■17:2■18:14a■32:11-**NU**-11:20■20:4■27:4-**DE**-5:25-**JOS**-7:25■17:14a-**J'G**-2:2■5:16,17,28^{2}a■6:13■8:1■9:28■11:7a,26a■13:18■15:10■21:3-**RU**-1:11,21■2:10a-**1SA**-1:8^{2}■2:23■6:3■17:8,28■19:17^{2}■20:2(4060),8■21:1a■22:13■27:5■28:12,15-**2SA**-3:24■7:7■11:10a,21■13:4a,26■16:9,17■18:11a■19:10,11,29,36,41a,43a■20:19■24:3-**1KI**-1:6a,13a■2:22,43■9:8(5921,4100)■14:6■21:5-**2KI**-1:5■7:3■8:12a■12:7a■14:10-**1CH**-17:6■21:3,3sup-**2CH**-7:21■24:6a,20■25:15,16,19■32:4-**EZR**-4:22(4101)■7:23(4101)-**NE**-2:2a,3a■6:3■13:11a,21a-**ES**-3:3a■4:5-**JOB**-3:11,11sup,12^{2}a■7:20,21■9:29■15:12■19:22,28■21:4a■24:1a■27:12■31:1■33:13a-**PS**-2:1■10:1,1sup■22:1■42:9^{2},11^{2}■43:2^{2},5^{2}■44:23■52:1■68:16■74:1,1sup,11■80:12■88:14,14sup-**PR**-5:20■22:27-**EC**-2:15■7:16,17-**SONG**-1:7-**IS**-1:5■40:27■63:17-**JER**-2:14a,33,36■8:5a,14(5921,4100),19a,22a■14:8,9,19a■15:18■26:9a■27:13■29:27■30:15■36:29a■46:15a■49:1a-**EZE**-18:19a,31■33:11-**DA**-1:10■2:15(5922,4101)-**JON**-1:10-**MIC**-4:9-**HAB**-1:3-**HAG**-1:9(3282,4100)-**MAL**-2:10a■**N.T.**-all=5101,a=1302&marked-**M'T**-6:28■7:3■8:26■9:11a,14a■13:10a■15:2a,3a■16:8■17:10,19a■19:7,17■20:6■21:25a■22:18■26:10■27:23(1063),46(2444)-**M'R**-2:7,8,18a,24■4:40■5:35,39■7:5a■8:12,17■9:11(3754),28(3754)■10:18■11:3,31a■12:15■14:4(1519,5101),6■15:14(1063),34(1519,5101)-**LU**-2:48■5:30a,33a■6:2,41,46■12:26,57■13:7(2444)■18:19■19:31a,33■20:5a,23■22:46■23:22(1063)■24:5,38,38a-**JOH**-1:25■4:27■7:19,45a■8:43,46■9:30(1063)■10:20■12:5a■13:37a■18:21,23■20:13,15-**AC**-1:11■3:12■4:25(2444)■5:3a,4■7:26(2444)■9:4■14:15■15:10■22:7,16■26:8,14-**RO**-3:7■8:24■9:19,20■14:10^{2}-**1CO**-4:7■6:7^{2}a■10:29(2444,5101),30■15:29,30-**GA**-2:14■5:11-**COL**-2:20

WICKED-all=7563,a=7451&marked-**GE**-13:13a■18:23,25^{2}■38:7a-**EX**-9:27■23:1,7-**LE**-20:17(2617)-**NU**-16:26-**DE**-15:9(1100)■17:5a■23:9a■25:1,2-**1SA**-2:9■24:13■30:22a-**2SA**-3:34(5766)■4:11-**1KI**-8:32-**2KI**-17:11a-**2CH**-6:23■7:14a■24:7(4849)-**NE**-9:35a-**ES**-7:6a■9:25a-**JOB**-3:17■8:22■9:22,24,29(7561)■10:3,7(7561),15(7561)■11:20■15:20■16:11■18:5,21(5767)■20:5,22(6001),29■21:7,16,17,28,30a■22:15(205),18■24:6■27:7,13■29:17(5767)■31:3(5767)■34:8(7562),18(1100),26,36(205)■36:6,17■38:13,15■40:12-**PS**-7:9■9:5,16,17■10:2,3,4,13,15■11:2,5,6■12:8■17:9,13■22:16(7489)■26:5■27:2(7489)■28:3■31:17■32:10■34:21■36:1,11■37:7(4209),10,12,14,16,17,20,21,28,32,34,35,38,40■39:1■50:16■55:3■58:3,10■59:5(205)■64:2(7489)■68:2■71:4■73:3■75:4,8,10■82:2,4■91:8■92:7,11(7489)■94:3^{2},13■97:10■101:3(1100),4a,8,8(205)■104:35■106:18■109:2,6■112:10^{2}■119:53,61,95,110,119,155■125:3(7562)■129:4■139:19,24(6090)■140:4,8,8(2162)■141:4(7562),10■145:20■146:9■147:6-**PR**-2:14a,22■3:25,33■4:14,19■5:22■6:12(205),18(205)■9:7■10:3,6,7,11,16,20,24,25,27,28,30,32■11:5,7,8,10,11,18,21a,23,31■12:2(4209),5,6,7,10,12,13a,21,26■13:5,9,17,25■14:11,17(4209),19,32■15:6,8,9,26a,28,29■16:4■17:4(7489),15,23■18:3,5■19:28■20:26■21:4,7,10,12^{2},18,27,27(2154),29■24:15,16,19,20,24■25:5,26■26:23a■28:1,4,12,15,28■29:2,7,12,16,27-**EC**-3:17■7:15,17(7561)■8:10,13,14^{2}■9:2-**IS**-3:11■5:23■11:4■13:11■14:5■26:10■32:7(2154)■48:22■53:9■55:7■57:20,21-**JER**-2:33a■5:26,28a■6:29a■12:1■15:21a■17:9(605)■23:19■25:31■30:23-**EZE**-3:18^{3},19^{2}■7:21■8:9a■11:2a■13:22a,22■18:20,21,23,24,27■20:44a■21:3,4,25,29■30:12a■33:8^{3},9,11^{2},12,14,15,19-**DA**-12:10^{2}-**MIC**-6:10,11(7562)-**NA**-1:11(1100),15(1100)-**HAB**-1:4,13■3:13-**ZEP**-1:3-**MAL**-3:18■4:3■**N.T.**-all=4190&marked-**M'T**-12:45(4191),45■13:19,38,49■16:4■18:32■21:41(2556)■25:26-**LU**-11:26(4191)■19:22-**AC**-2:23(459)■18:14-**1CO**-5:13-**EPH**-6:16-**COL**-1:21-**2TH**-2:8(459)■3:2-**2PE**-2:7(113)■3:17(113)-**1JO**-2:13,14■3:12■5:18

WICKEDLY-all=7561&marked-**GE**-19:7(7489)-**DE**-9:18(7451)-**J'G**-19:23(7489)-**1SA**-12:25(7489)-**2SA**-22:22■24:17(5753)-**2KI**-21:11(7489)-**2CH**-6:37■20:35■22:3-**NE**-9:33-**JOB**-13:7(5766)■34:12-**PS**-18:21■73:8(7451)■74:3(7489)■106:6■139:20(4209)-**DA**-9:5,15■11:32■12:10-**MAL**-4:1(7564)

WICKEDNESS-all=7451,a=7562,b=7564&marked-**GE**-6:5■39:9-**LE**-18:17(2154)■19:29(2154)■20:14^{2}(2154)-**DE**-9:4b,5b,27a■13:11■17:2■28:20(7455)-**J'G**-9:56■20:3,12-**1SA**-12:17,20■24:13a■25:39-**2SA**-3:39■7:10(5766)-**1KI**-1:52■2:44^{2}■8:47(7561)■21:25-**2KI**-21:6-**1CH**-17:9(5766)-**JOB**-4:8(5999)■11:11(205),14(5766)■20:12■22:5■24:20(5766)■27:4(5766)■34:10a■35:8a-**PS**-5:4a,9(1942)■7:9■10:15a■28:4(7455)■45:7a■52:7(1942)■55:11(1942),15■58:2(5766)■84:10a■89:22(5766)■94:23■107:34-**PR**-4:17a■8:7a■10:2a■11:5b■12:3a■13:6b■14:32■16:12a■21:12■26:26■30:20(205)-**EC**-3:16a■7:15,25a■8:8a-**IS**-9:18b■47:10■58:4a,6a-**JER**-1:16■2:19■3:2■4:14,18■6:7■7:12■8:6■12:4■14:16,20a■22:22■23:11,14■33:5■44:3,5,9^{5}-**LA**-1:22-**EZE**-3:19a■5:6b■7:11a■16:23,57■18:20b,27b■31:11a■33:12b,12a,19b-**HO**-7:1,2,3■9:15,15(7455)■10:13a,15-**JOE**-3:13-**JON**-1:2-**MIC**-6:10a-**NA**-3:19-**ZEC**-5:8b-**MAL**-1:4b■3:15b■**N.T.**-all=4189&marked-**M'T**-22:18-**M'R**-7:22-**LU**-11:39-**AC**-8:22(2549)■25:5(5129,824)-**RO**-1:29-**1CO**-5:8-**EPH**-6:12-**1JO**-5:19(4190)

WIDE-all=6605&marked-**DE**-15:8,11-**1CH**-4:40(7342,3027)-**JOB**-30:14(7342)-**PS**-35:21(7337)■81:10(7337)■104:25(7342,3027)-**PR**-21:9(2267)■25:24(2267)-**IS**-57:4(7337)-**JER**-22:14(4060)-**NA**-3:13■**N.T.**-**M'T**-7:13(4116)

WIDENESS-**EZE**-41:10(7341)

WIDOW-all=490-**GE**-38:11-**EX**-22:22-**LE**-21:14■22:13-**NU**-30:9-**DE**-10:18■14:29■16:11,14■24:19,20,21■26:12,13■27:19-**2SA**-14:5-**1KI**-11:26■17:9,10,20-**JOB**-24:21■31:16-**PS**-94:6■109:9■146:9-**PR**-15:25-**IS**-1:17,23■47:8-**JER**-7:6■22:3-**LA**-1:1-**EZE**-22:7■44:22^{2}-**ZEC**-7:10-**MAL**-3:5■**N.T.**-all=5503-**M'R**-12:42,43-**LU**-2:37■4:26■7:12■18:3,5■21:2,3-**1TI**-5:4,5,9-**RE**-18:7

WIDOWHOOD-all=491&marked-**GE**-38:19-**2SA**-20:3-**IS**-47:9(489)■54:4

WIDOW'S-all=490&marked-**GE**-38:14(491)-**DE**-24:17-**1KI**-7:14-**JOB**-24:3■29:13

WIDOWS-all=490-**EX**-22:24-**JOB**-22:9■27:15-**PS**-68:5■78:64-**IS**-9:17■10:2-**JER**-15:8■18:21■49:11-**LA**-5:3-**EZE**-22:25■**N.T.**-all=5503-**LU**-4:25-**AC**-6:1■9:39,41-**1CO**-7:8-**1TI**-5:3,11,16^{2}-**JAS**-1:27

WIDOWS'-all=5503-**M'T**-23:14-**M'R**-12:40-**LU**-20:47

WIFE-all=802&marked-**GE**-2:24,25■3:8,17,21■4:1,17,25■6:18■7:7,13■8:16,18■11:29^{2},31■12:5,11,12,17,18,19^{2},20■13:1■16:1,3^{2}■17:15,19■18:9,10■19:15,16,26■20:2,3(1166),7,12,14,17,18■21:21■23:19■24:3,4,7,15,36,37,38,40,51,67■25:1,10,20,21^{2}■26:7^{2},8,9,10,11,34■27:46■28:1,2,6^{2},9■29:21,28■30:4,9■34:4,8,12■36:10^{2},12,13,14,17,18^{2}■38:6,8,9,12,14■39:7,8,9,19■41:45■44:27■46:19■49:31^{2}-**EX**-4:20■6:20,23,25■18:2,5,6■20:17■21:3,4^{2},5■22:16-**LE**-18:8,14,15,16,18,20■20:10^{2},11,14,20(1753),21■21:7,13,14-**NU**-5:12,14^{2},15,29,30■26:59■30:16■36:8-**DE**-5:21■13:6■20:7■21:11,13■22:13,16,19,24,29,30■24:1,3,4,5^{2}■25:5^{2},7^{2}(2994),9(2994),11■27:20■28:30,54-**JOS**-15:16,17-**J'G**-1:12,13■4:4,17,21■5:24■11:2■13:2,11,19,20,21,22,23■14:2,3,15,16,20■15:1^{2},6■21:1,18,21,22-**RU**-1:1,2■4:5,10^{2},13-**1SA**-1:4,19■2:20■4:19■14:50■18:17,19,27■19:11■25:3,14,37,39,40,42,44■27:3■30:5,22-**2SA**-2:2■3:3,5,14■11:3,11,26,27■12:9,10^{2},15,24-**1KI**-2:17,21■4:11,15■9:16■11:19■14:2^{2},4,5,6,17■16:31■21:5,7,25-**2KI**-5:2■8:18■14:9■22:14-**1CH**-2:18,24,26,29,35■3:3■4:18,19■7:15,16,23■8:9-**2CH**-8:11■11:18■21:6■22:11■25:18■34:22-**EZR**-2:61-**NE**-7:63-**ES**-5:10,14■6:13^{2}-**JOB**-2:9■19:17■31:10-**PS**-109:9■128:3-**PR**-5:18■6:29■18:22■19:13,14-**EC**-9:9-**IS**-54:6-**JER**-3:1,20■5:8■6:11■16:2-**EZE**-16:32■18:6,11,15■22:11■24:18■33:26-**HO**-1:2■2:2■12:12^{2}-**AM**-7:17-**MAL**-2:14^{2},15■**N.T.**-all=1135&marked-**M'T**-1:20,24■5:31,32■14:3■18:25■19:3,5,9,10,29■22:24,24sup,25,28■27:19-**M'R**-6:17,18■10:2,7,11,29■12:19^{2},20,23^{2}-**LU**-1:5,13,18,24■2:5■3:19■8:3■14:20,26■16:18■17:32■18:29■20:28^{2},29,30,33^{2}-**AC**-5:1,2,7■18:2■24:24-**1CO**-5:1■7:2,3^{2},4^{2},10,11,12,14^{2},16^{2},27^{2},33,34,39■9:5-**EPH**-5:23,28,31,33^{2}-**1TI**-3:2,12■5:9-**TIT**-1:6-**1PE**-3:7(1134)-**RE**-19:7■21:9

WIFE'S-all=802-**GE**-3:20■20:11■36:39-**LE**-18:11-**J'G**-11:2-**1CH**-1:50■8:29■9:35■**N.T.**-all=3994-**M'T**-8:14-**M'R**-1:30-**LU**-4:38

WILD-all=7704&marked-**GE**-16:12(6501)-**LE**-26:22-**DE**-14:5(689),5(8377)-**1SA**-17:46(2416)■24:2(3277)-**2SA**-2:18-**2KI**-4:39^{2}■14:9-**2CH**-25:18-**JOB**-6:5(6501)■11:12(6501)■24:5(6501)■39:1(3277),5(6501),5(6171),15-**PS**-50:11(2123)■80:13(2123)■104:11(6501),18(3277)-**IS**-5:2(891),4(891)■13:21(6728),22(338)■32:14(6501)■34:14(6728),14(338)■51:20(8377)-**JER**-2:24(6501)■14:6(6501)■50:39(6728),39(338)-**DA**-5:21(6167)-**HOS**-8:9(6501)■13:8■**N.T.**-all=2342&marked-**M'T**-3:4(66)-**M'R**-1:6(66),13-**AC**-10:12■11:6-**RO**-11:17(65),24(65)

WILDERNESS-all=4057&marked-GE-14:6■16:7■21:14,20,21■36:24■37:22-EX-3:18■4:27■5:1■7:16■8:27,28■13:18,20■14:3,11,12■15:22^2■16:1,2,3,10,14,32■17:1■18:5■19:1,2-LE-7:38■16:10,21,22-NU-1:1,19■3:4,14■9:1,5■10:12^2,31■12:16■13:3,21,26■14:2,16,22,25,29,32,33^2,35■15:32■16:13■20:4■21:5,11,13,18,23■24:1■26:64,65■27:3,14■32:13,15■33:6,8^2,11,12,15,36■34:3-DE-1:1,19,31,40■2:1,7,8,26■4:43■8:2,15,16■9:7,28■11:5,24■29:5■32:10(3452),51-JOS-1:4■5:4,5,6■8:15,20,24■12:8■14:10■15:1,61■16:1■18:12■20:8■24:7-J'G-1:16■8:7,16■11:16,18,22■20:42,45,47-1SA-4:8■13:18■17:28■23:14^2,15,24,25^2■24:1■25:1,4,14,21■26:2^2,3^2-2SA-2:24■15:23,28■16:2■17:16,29-1KI-2:34■9:18■19:4,15-2KI-3:8-1CH-5:9■6:78■12:8■21:29-2CH-1:3■8:4■20:16,20,24■24:9-NE-9:19,21-JOB-1:19■12:24(8414)■24:5(6160)■30:3(6723)■38:26■39:6(6160)-PS-29:8^2■55:7■63:t■65:12■68:7(3452)■72:9(6728)■74:14(6728)■78:15,17(6723),19,40,52■95:8■102:6■106:9,14,26■107:4,33,35,40(8414)■136:16-PR-21:19-SONG-3:6■8:5-IS-14:17■16:1,8■23:13(6728)■27:10■32:15,16■33:9(6160)■35:1,6■40:3■41:18,19■42:11■43:19,20■50:2■51:3■63:13■64:10^2-JER-2:2,6,24,31■3:2■4:11,26■9:2,10,12,26■12:10,12■13:24■17:6■22:6■23:10■31:2■48:6■50:12■51:43(6160)-LA-4:3,19■5:9-EZE-6:14■19:13■20:10,13^2,15,17,18,21,23,35,36■23:42■29:5■34:25-HOS-2:3,14■9:10■13:5,15-JOE-1:19,20■2:3,22■3:19-AM-2:10■5:25■6:14(6166)-ZEP-2:13-MAL-1:3■N.T.-all=2048&marked-M'T-3:1,3■4:1■11:7■15:33(2047)-M'R-1:3,4,12,13■8:4(2047)-LU-3:2,4■4:1■5:16■7:24■8:29■15:4-JOH-1:23■3:14■6:49■11:54-AC-7:30,36,38,42,44■13:18■21:38-1CO-10:5-2CO-11:26(2047)-HEB-3:8,17-RE-12:6,14■17:3

WILES-NU-25:18(5231)■N.T.-EPH-6:11(3180)

WILFULLY-HEB-10:26(1596)

WILILY-JOS-9:4(6195)

WILL-all=7522&marked-LE-1:3■19:5■22:19,29sup,29■26:21(14),21sup-DE-21:14(5315)■25:7(14)■33:16-RU-3:13sup,13(2654),13sup-EZR-7:18(7470)-PS-27:12(5315)■40:8■41:2sup,2(5315)■143:10-PR-21:1(2654)-EC-4:13(3045)-IS-30:9(14)-EZE-3:7^2(14)■16:27(5314)-DA-4:17(6634),25(6634),32(6634),35(6634)■5:21(6634)■8:4■11:3,16,36-HO-13:10(165),14^{2}sup,14^2(165)-MAL-2:13■N.T.-all=2309,a=2307&marked-M'T-2:13(3195)■5:40■6:10a■7:21a■8:3■9:13■11:14,27(1014)■12:7,50a■15:32■16:24,25■18:14a■20:14,15,26,27,32■21:29,31a■23:4■26:15,15sup,39,42a■27:17,21,43-M'R-1:41■3:35a■6:25■8:34,35■10:43,44■14:7,36■15:9,12-LU-2:14(2107)■4:6sup,6■5:13■9:23,24■10:22(1014)■11:2a■12:47^{2}a,49■13:31■19:14■22:42a■23:25a-JOH-1:13a■4:34a■5:21,30^{2}a,40■6:38^{2}a,39a,40a,67■7:17,17a,35^2(3195)■8:44■9:27,31a■15:7■17:24■18:39(1014)■21:22,23-AC-13:22a,36(1012)■17:18,31(3195)■18:15(1014),21sup,21■21:14a■22:14a■27:10(3195)-RO-1:10a■2:18a■7:18■9:18^2,19(1013)■12:2a■15:32a-1CO-1:1a■4:19sup,19,19sup,21■7:36,37a,37sup,39■9:17(210)■12:11(1014)■14:35■16:7,12a,12sup-2CO-1:1a■8:5a,11-GA-1:4a-EPH-1:1a,5a,9a,11a■5:17a■6:6a,7(2133)-PH'P-1:15(2107)■2:13-COL-1:1a,9a■2:23(1479)■4:12a-1TH-4:3a■5:18a-1TI-2:4,8(1014)■5:11,14(1014)■6:9(1014)-2TI-1:1a■2:26a■3:12-TIT-3:8(1014)-HEB-2:4(2308)■10:7a,9a,10a,36a■13:21a-JAS-1:18(1014)■4:4(1014),15-1PE-2:15a■3:10,17a■4:2a,3a,19a-2PE-1:21a-1JO-2:17a■5:14a-3JO-13-JUDE-5(1014)-RE-3:16(3195)■11:5^2,6■17:17(1106)■22:17

WILLETH-RO-9:16(2309)

WILLING-all=14&marked-GE-24:5,8-EX-35:5(5081),21(5068),22(5081),29(5071),29(5068)-1CH-28:9(2655),21(5081)■29:5(5068)-JOB-39:9-PS-110:3(5071)-IS-1:19■N.T.-all=2309&marked-M'T-1:19■26:41(4289)-M'R-15:15(1014)-LU-10:29■22:42(1014)■23:20-JOH-5:35-AC-24:27■25:9■27:43(1014)-RO-9:22(2309)-2CO-5:8(2106)■8:3(830),12(4288)-1TH-2:8(2106)-1TI-6:18(2843)-HEB-6:17(1014)■13:18-2PE-3:9(1014)

WILLINGLY-all=5068&marked-EX-25:2-J'G-5:2,9■8:25(5414)-1CH-29:6,9^2,14,17^2-2CH-17:16■35:8(5071)-EZR-1:6■3:5■7:16-PR-31:13(2656)-LA-3:33(3820)-HO-5:11(2974)■N.T.-JOH-6:21(2309)-RO-8:20(1635)-1CO-9:17(1635)-PH'M-14(2596,1595)-1PE-5:2(1596)-2PE-3:5(2309)

WILLOW-EZE-17:5(6851)

WILLOWS-all=6155-LE-23:40-JOB-40:22-PS-137:2-IS-15:7■44:4

WILT-all=2309-M'T-8:2■13:28■15:28■17:4■19:17,21■20:21■26:17-M'R-1:40■6:22■10:51■14:12,36-LU-5:12■9:54■18:41■22:9-JOH-5:6-AC-7:28■9:6-RO-13:3-JAS-2:20

WIMPLES-IS-3:22(4304)

WIN-2CH-32:1(1234)■N.T.-PH'P-3:8(2770)

WIND-all=7307&marked-GE-8:1-EX-10:13^2,19■14:21■15:10-NU-11:31-2SA-22:11-1KI-18:45■19:11^3-2KI-3:17-JOB-1:19■6:26■7:7■8:2■15:2■21:18■30:15,22■37:21-PS-1:4■18:10,42■35:5■48:7■78:39■83:13■103:16■104:3■107:25■135:7■147:18■148:8-PR-11:29■25:14,23■27:16■30:4-EC-1:6^2■5:16■11:4-IS-7:2■11:15■17:13■26:18■27:8,8sup■32:2■41:16,29■57:13■64:6-JER-2:24■4:11,12■5:13■10:13■13:24■14:6■18:17■22:22■51:1,16-EZE-5:2■12:14■13:11,13■17:10■19:12■27:26■37:9^2-DA-2:35(7308)-HO-4:19■8:7■12:1,1sup■13:15sup,15-AM-4:13-JON-1:4■4:8-ZEC-5:9■N.T.-all=417&marked-M'T-11:7■14:24,30,32-M'R-4:37,39^2,41■6:48,51-LU-7:24■8:23,24-JOH-3:8(4151)■6:18-AC-2:2(4157)■27:7,14,15,40(4154)-EPH-4:14-JAS-1:6(416)-RE-6:13■7:1

WINDING-1KI-6:8(3583)-EZE-41:7(5437),7(4141)

WINDOW-all=2474&marked-GE-6:16(6672)■8:6■26:8-JOS-2:15,18,21-J'G-5:28-1SA-19:12-2SA-6:16-2KI-9:30,32■13:17-1CH-15:29-PR-7:6■N.T.-AC-20:9(2376)-2CO-11:33(2376)

WINDOWS-all=2474&marked-GE-7:11(699)■8:2(699)-1KI-6:4■7:4(8261),5(8260)-2KI-7:2(699),19(699)-EC-12:3(699)-SONG-2:9-IS-24:18(699)■54:12(8121)■60:8(699)-JER-9:21■22:14-EZE-40:16^2,22,25^2,29,33,36■41:16^3,26-DA-6:10(3551)-JOE-2:9-ZEP-2:14-MAL-3:10(699)

WINDS-all=7307&marked-JOB-28:25-JER-49:32,36^2-EZE-5:10,12■17:21■37:9-DA-7:2(7308)■8:8■11:4-ZEC-2:6■N.T.-all=417-M'T-7:25,27■8:26,27■24:31-M'R-13:27-LU-8:25-AC-27:4-JAS-3:4-JUDE-12-RE-7:1

WINDY-PS-55:8(7307)

WINE-all=3196,a=8492&marked-GE-9:21,24■14:18■19:32,33,34,35■27:25,28a,37a■49:11,12-EX-29:40-LE-10:9■23:13-NU-6:3^2,20■15:5,7,10■18:12a■28:7(7491),14-DE-7:13a■11:14a■12:17a■14:23a,26■16:13(3342)■18:4a■28:39,51a■29:6■32:33,38■33:28a-JOS-9:4,13-J'G-9:13a■13:4,7,14■19:19-1SA-1:14,15,24■10:3■16:20■25:18,37-2SA-13:28■16:1,2-2KI-18:32a-1CH-9:29■12:40■27:27-2CH-2:10,15■11:11■31:5a■32:28a-EZR-6:9(2562)■7:22(2562)-NE-2:1^2■5:11a,15,18■10:37a,39a■13:5a,12a,15(1660),15-ES-1:7,10■5:6■7:2,7,8-JOB-1:13,18■32:19-PS-4:7a■60:3■75:8■78:65■104:15-PR-3:10a■4:17■9:2,5■20:1■21:17■23:30,30(4469),31■31:4,6-EC-2:3■9:7■10:19-SONG-1:2,4■4:10■5:1■7:9■8:2-IS-1:22(5435)■5:11,12,22■16:10■22:13■24:7a,9,11■27:2(2561)■28:1,7^2■29:9■36:17a■49:26(6071)■51:21■55:1■56:12■62:8a■65:8a-JER-13:12^2■23:9■25:15■31:12a■35:2,5^2,6^2,8,14■40:10,12■48:33■51:7-LA-2:12-EZE-27:18■44:21-DA-1:5,8,16■5:1(2562),2(2562),4(2562),23(2562)■10:3-HO-2:8a,9a,22a■3:1(6025)■4:11,11a■7:5,14a■9:2a,4a■14:7a-JOE-1:5,5(6071),10a■2:19a,24a■3:3,18(6071)-AM-2:8,12■5:11■6:6■9:13(6071),14-MIC-2:11■6:15a,15-HAB-2:5-ZEP-1:13-HAG-1:11a■2:12-ZEC-9:15,17a■10:7■N.T.-all=3631&marked-M'T-9:17^3-M'R-2:22^4■15:23-LU-1:15■5:37^2,38■7:33■10:34-JOH-2:3^2,9,10^2■4:46-AC-2:13(1098)-RO-14:21-EPH-5:18-1TI-3:3(3943)■3:8■5:23-TIT-1:7(3943)■2:3-1PE-4:3(3632)-RE-6:6■14:8,10■16:19■17:2■18:3,13

WINEBIBBER-M'T-11:19(3630)-LU-7:34(3630)

WINEBIBBERS-PR-23:20(5433,3196)

WINEFAT-IS-63:2(1660)■N.T.-M'R-12:1(5276)

WINEPRESS-all=3342&marked-NU-18:27,30-DE-15:14-J'G-6:11(1660)■7:25-2KI-6:27-IS-5:2■63:3(6333)-LA-1:15(1660)-HO-9:2■N.T.-all=3025&marked-M'T-21:33-RE-14:19,20^2■19:15(3025,3631)

WINEPRESSES-all=3342-JOB-24:11-JER-48:33-ZEC-14:10

WINES-IS-25:6^2(8105)

WING-all=3671-1KI-6:24^3,27^2-2CH-3:11^3,12^3-IS-10:14-EZE-17:23

WINGED-GE-1:21(3671)-DE-4:17(3671)

WINGS-all=3671&marked-EX-19:4■25:20^2■37:9^2-LE-1:17-DE-32:11,11(84)-RU-2:12-2SA-22:11-1KI-6:27^2■8:6,7-2CH-3:11,13■5:7,8-JOB-39:13,13(84),26-PS-17:8■18:10■36:7■55:6(83)■57:1■61:4■63:7■68:13■91:4■104:3■139:9-PR-23:5-EC-10:20-IS-6:2■8:8■18:1■40:31(83)-JER-48:9(6731),40■49:22-EZE-1:6,8^2,9,11,11sup,23,24^2,25■3:13■10:5,8,12,16,19,21^2■11:22■17:3,7-DA-7:4^2(1611),6(1611)-HO-4:19-ZEC-5:9^2-MAL-4:2■N.T.-all=4420-M'T-23:37-LU-13:34-RE-4:8■9:8■12:14

WINK-JOB-15:12(7335)-PS-35:19(7169)

WINKED-AC-17:30(5237)

WINKETH-PR-6:13(7169)■10:10(7169)

WINNETH-PR-11:30(3947)

WINNOWED-IS-30:24(2219)

WINNOWETH-RU-3:2(2219)

WINTER-all=2779&marked-GE-8:22-PS-74:17-SONG-2:11(5638)-IS-18:6(2778)-AM-3:15-ZEC-14:8(2778)■N.T.-all=5494&marked-M'T-24:20-MR-13:18-JOH-10:22-AC-27:12(3915),12(3914)-1CO-16:6(3914)-2TI-4:21-TIT-3:12(3914)

WINTERED-AC-28:11(3916)

WINTERHOUSE-JER-36:22(2779)

WIPE-all=4229-2KI-21:13-NE-13:14 IS 25:8■N.T. LU 7:38(1591)■10:11(631)-JOH-13:5(1591)-RE-7:17(1813)■21:4(1813)

WIPED-PR-6:33(4229)■N.T.-all=1591-LU-7:44-JOH-11:2■12:3

WIPETH-2KI-21:13(4229)-PR-30:20(4229)

WIPING-2KI-21:13(4229)

WIRES-EX-39:3(6616)

WISDOM-all=2451&marked-EX-28:3■31:3,6■35:26,31,35■36:1,2-DE-4:6■34:9-2SA-14:20■20:22-1KI-2:6■3:28■4:29,30^2,34^2■5:12■7:14■10:4,6,7,8,23,24■11:41-1CH-22:12(7922)-2CH-1:10,11,

12■9:3,5,6,7,22,23-EZR-7:25(2452)-JOB-4:21■6:13(8454)■11:6■12:2,12,13,16(8454)■13:5■15:8■26:3■28:12,18,20,28■32:7,13■33:33■34:35(7919)■36:5(3820)■38:36,37■39:17,26(998)-PS-37:30■49:3(2454)■51:6■90:12■104:24■105:22(2449)■111:10■136:5(8394)-PR-1:2,3(7919),7,20(2454)■2:2,6,7(8454),10■3:13,19,21(8454)■4:5,7^2,11■5:1■7:4■8:1,5(6195),11,12,14(8454)■9:1(2454),10■10:13,21(3820),23,31■11:2,12(3820)■12:8(7922)■13:10■14:6,8,33■15:21(3820),33■16:16■17:16,24■18:1(8454),4■19:8(3820)■21:30■23:4(998),9(7922),23■24:3,7(2454),14■29:3,15■30:3■31:26-EC-1:13,16^2,17,18■2:3,9,12,13,21,26■7:11,12^2,19,23,25■8:1,16■9:10,13,15,16^2,18■10:1,3(3820),10-IS-10:13■11:2■29:14■33:6■47:10-JER-8:9■9:23■10:12■49:7^2■51:15-EZE-28:4,5,7,12,17-DA-1:4,17,20■2:14(2942),20(2452),21(2452),23(2452),30(2452)■5:11^2(2452),14(2452)-MIC-6:9(8454)■N.T.-all=4678&marked-M'T-11:19■12:42■13:54-M'R-6:2-LU-1:17(5428)■2:40,52■7:35■11:31,49■21:15-AC-6:3,10■7:10,22-RO-11:33-1CO-1:17,19,20,21^2,22,24,30■2:1,4,5,6^2,7,7sup,,13■3:19■12:8-2CO-1:12-EPH-1:8,17■3:10-COL-1:9,28■2:3,23■3:16■4:5-JAS-1:5■3:13,15,17-2PE-3:15-RE-5:12■7:12■13:18■17:9

WISE-all=2450,a=2449,b=2445&marked-GE-3:6(7919)■41:8,33,39-EX-7:11■22:23(6031)■23:8(6493)■28:3■31:6■35:10,25■36:1,2,4,8-LE-19:17(3198)-DE-1:13,15■4:6■16:19■32:29a-J'G-5:29-2SA-14:2,20■20:16-1KI-2:9■3:12■5:7-1CH-26:14(7922)■27:32(995)-2CH-2:12-ES-1:13■6:13-JOB-5:13■9:4■11:12(3823)■15:2,18■17:10■22:2(7919)■32:9a■34:2,34■37:24-PS-2:10(7919)■19:7a■36:3(7919)■49:10■94:8(7919)■107:43-PR-1:5,5sup,6■3:7,35■6:6a■8:33a■9:8,9,12a■10:1,5(7919),8,14,19(7919)■11:29,30■12:15,18■13:1,14,20,20a■14:1(2454),3,16,24,35(7919)■15:2,7,12,20,24(7919),31■16:14,21,23■17:2(7919),10(995),28■18:15■19:20a■20:1a,26■21:11a,11,20,22■22:17■23:15a,19a,24■24:5,23■25:12■26:5,12■27:11a■28:7(995),11■29:8,9,11■30:24-EC-2:14,15a,16^2,19,19a■4:13■6:8■7:4,5,7,16a,19,23a■8:1,5,17■9:1,11,15,17■10:2,12■12:9,11-IS-5:21■19:11^2,12■29:14■31:2■44:25-JER-4:22■8:8,9■9:12,23■10:7■18:18■50:35■51:57-EZE-27:8,9-DA-2:12b,13b,14b,18b,21b,24^{2}b,27b,48b■4:6b,18b■5:7b,8b,15b■12:3(7919),10(7919)-HO-14:9-OB-8-ZEC-9:2a■N.T.-all=4680,a=5429&marked-M'T-1:18(3779)■2:1(3097),7(3097),16^2(3097)■7:24a■10:16a■11:25■23:34■24:45a■25:2a,4a,8a,9a-LU-10:21■12:42a■13:11(3588,3838)-JOH-21:1(3779)-AC-7:6(3779)■13:34(3779)-RO-1:14,22■3:9(3843)■10:6(3779)■11:25a■12:16a■16:19,27-1CO-1:19,20,26,27■3:10,18^2,19,20■4:10a■6:5■10:15a-2CO-10:12(4920)■11:19a-EPH-5:15-1TI-1:17-2TI-3:15(4679)-HEB-4:4(3779)-JAS-3:13-JUDE-25

WISELY-all=7919&marked-EX-1:10(2449)-1SA-18:5,14,15,30-2CH-11:23(995)-PS-58:5(2449)■64:9■101:2-PR-16:20■21:12■28:26(2451)-EC-7:10(2451)■N.T.-LU-16:8(5430)

WISER-all=2449&marked-1KI-4:31-JOB-35:11-PS-119:98-PR-9:9■26:16(2450)-EZE-28:3(2450)■N.T.-LU-16:8(5429)-1CO-1:25(4680)

WISH-JOB-33:6(6310)-PS-40:14(2655)■73:7(4906)■N.T.-all=2172-RO-9:3-2CO-13:9-3JO-2

WISHED-JON-4:8(7592)■N.T.-AC-27:29(2172)

WISHING-JOB-31:30(7592)

WIST-all=3045-EX-16:15■34:29-LE-5:17,18-JOS-2:4■8:14-J'G-16:20■N.T.-all=1492-M'R-9:6■14:40-LU-2:49-JOH-5:13-AC-12:9■23:5

WIT-GE-24:21(3045)-EX-2:4(3045)■N.T.-2CO-5:19(5613)■8:1(1107)

WITCH-EX-22:18(3784)-DE-18:10(3784)

WITCHCRAFT-1SA-15:23(7081)-2CH-33:6(3784)■N.T.-GA-5:20(5331)

WITCHCRAFTS-all=3785-2KI-9:22-MIC-5:12-NA-3:4^2

WITHAL-all=2004&marked-EX-25:29■30:4(1992)■37:16-LE-11:21-1SA-16:12(5973)-1KI-19:1(843,3605)-PS-141:10(3162)-PR-22:18(3162)■N.T.-all=260-COL-4:3-1TI-5:13-PH'M-22

WITHDRAW-all=622&marked-1SA-14:19-JOB-9:13(7725)■13:21(7368)■33:17(5493)-PR-25:17(3365)-EC-7:18(3240)-IS-60:20-JOE-2:10■3:15■N.T.-2TH-3:6(4724)-1TI-6:5(868)

WITHDRAWEST-PS-74:11(7725)

WITHDRAWETH-JOB-36:7(1639)

WITHDRAWN-DE-13:13(5080)-SONG-5:6(2559)-LA-2:8(7725)-EZE-18:8(7725)-HO-5:6(2502)■N.T.-LU-22:41(645)

WITHDREW-NE-9:29(5414,5437)-EZE-20:22(7725)■N.T.-M'T-12:15(402)-M'R-3:7(402)-LU-5:16(5298)-GA-2:12(5288)

WITHER-all=3001&marked-PS-1:3(5034)■37:2(5034)-IS-19:6(7060),7■40:24-JER-12:4-EZE-17:9^2,10^2-AM-1:2

WITHERED-all=3001&marked-GE-41:23(6798)-PS-102:4-IS-15:6■27:11-LA-4:8-EZE-19:12-JOE-1:12^2,17-AM-4:7-JON-4:7■N.T.-all=3583&marked-M'T-12:10(3584)■13:6■21:19,20-M'R-3:1,3■4:6■11:21-LU-6:6(3584),8(3584)■8:6-JOH-5:3(3584)■15:6

WITHERETH-all=3001-JOB-8:12-PS-90:6■129:6-IS-40:7,8■N.T.-JAS-1:11(3583)-1PE-1:24(3583)-JUDE-12(5352)

WITHHELD-all=2820&marked-GE-20:6■22:12,16■30:2(4513)-JOB-31:16(4513)-EC-2:10(4513)

WITHHELDEST-NE-9:20(4513)

WITHHOLD-all=4513&marked-GE-23:6(3607)-2SA-13:13-JOB-4:2(6113)-PS-40:11(3607)■84:11-PR-3:27■23:13-EC-11:6(3240)-JER-2:25

WITHHOLDEN-all=4513&marked-1SA-25:26-JOB-22:7■38:15■42:2(1219)-PS-21:2-JER-3:3■5:25-EZE-18:16(2254)-JOE-1:13-AM-4:7

WITHHOLDETH-JOB-12:15(6113)-PR-11:24(2820),26(4513)■N.T.-2TH-2:6(2722)

WITHIN-all=1004,a=8432,b=7130&marked-GE-6:14■9:21a■18:12b,24a,26a■25:22b■39:11-EX-25:11■26:33■37:2-LE-10:18(6441)■13:55(7146)■14:41■16:2,12,15■25:29(5704),29(8537),30(5704)■26:25(413)-NU-4:10(413)■18:7-DE-23:10a■28:43b■32:25(2315)-JOS-1:11(5750)■19:1a,9a■21:41a-J'G-7:16a■9:51a-1SA-25:36(5921),37b-2SA-7:2a-1KI-6:15,16,18(6441),19(6441),21(6441),27a,29(6441),30(6441)■7:8,9,31-2KI-6:30■7:11(6441)-2CH-3:4(6441)-EZR-4:15(4481)-NE-4:22a■6:10a-JOB-6:4(5978)■14:22(5921)■19:27(2436)■20:13a,14b■24:11(996)■32:18(990)-PS-36:1b■39:3b■40:8a,10a■42:6(5921),11(5921)■43:5(5921)■45:13(6441)■51:10b■55:4b■94:19b■101:2b,7b■103:1b■109:22b■142:3(5921)■143:4(5921),4a■147:13b-PR-22:18(990)■26:24b-SONG-4:1(1157),3(1157)■6:7(1157)-IS-21:16(5750)■26:9b■63:11b-JER-4:14b■23:9b■28:3(5750),11(5750)-LA-1:20b-EZE-1:27■2:10(6440)■3:24a■7:15■11:19b■12:24a■36:26b,27b■40:7,8,16(6441),43■41:9,17(6442)■44:17-DA-6:12(5705)-JON-2:7(5921)-MIC-3:3a-ZEP-3:3b-ZEC-12:1b■N.T.-all=1722&marked-M'T-3:9■9:3,21■23:25(2081),26(1787),27(2081),28(2081)-M'R-2:8■7:21(2081),23(2081)■14:4(4314),58(1223)-LU-3:8■7:39,49■11:7(2081),40(2081)■12:17■16:3■17:21(1737)■18:4■19:44■24:32-JOH-20:26(2080)-AC-5:23(2080)-RO-8:23-1CO-5:12(2080)-2CO-7:5(2081)-HEB-6:19(2082)-RE-4:8(2081)■5:1(2081)

WITHOUT-all=2351,a=8549,b=369,c=3808,d=1097,e=2600&marked-GE-1:2(8414)■6:14■9:22■19:16■24:11,31■37:33(2963)■41:44(1107),49b-EX-12:5a■21:11b■25:11■26:35■27:21■29:1a,14■33:7^2■37:2■40:22-LE-1:3a,10a■3:1a,6a■4:3a,12,21,23a,28a,32a■5:15a,18a■8:6a,11■8:17■9:2a,3a,11■10:12(4682)■13:46,55(1372)■14:10^{2}a,40,41■16:27■22:19a■23:12a,18a■24:3,14-NU-5:3,4■6:14^{3}a■15:35,36■19:2a,3,9■20:19b■28:3a,9a,11a,19a,31a■29:2a,8a,13a,17a,20a,23a,26a,29a,32a,36a■31:13,19■35:5,22^{2}c,27-DE-8:9c■23:12■25:5■32:4b,25-JOS-6:23-J'G-2:23(1115)■6:5b■7:12b-1SA-19:5e-2SA-23:4c-1KI-6:6,29(2435),30(2435)■7:9■8:8■22:1b-2KI-10:24■11:15(413,1004)■16:18(2435)■18:25(1107)■23:4,6■25:16c-1CH-2:30c,32c■21:24e■22:14b-2CH-5:9■12:3b■15:3^{2}c■21:20c■24:8■32:3,5■33:14(2435)-EZR-7:22(3809)■10:13-NE-13:20-JOB-2:3e■4:21c■5:9(5704)b■6:6d■7:6(657)■8:11c,11d■9:10(5704)b,17e■10:22c■12:25c■24:7d,10d■26:2c■30:28c■31:19b,39d■33:9d■34:6d,20c,24c,35^{2}c■35:16d■36:12d■38:2d■39:16d■41:33d■42:3d-PS-7:4(7387)■25:3(7387)■31:11■35:7^{2}e,19e■59:4d■69:4d■105:34b■109:3e■119:78(8267),161e-PR-1:11e,20■3:30e■5:23b■6:15b■7:12■11:22(5493)■15:22b■16:8c■19:2c■22:13■23:29e■24:27,28e■25:14b,28b■29:1b-EC-10:11c-SONG-6:8b■8:1-IS-5:9b,14d■6:11^{2}b■10:4(1115)■33:7■36:10(1107)■45:17(5769,5703)■52:3c,4(657)■55:1c-JER-2:15d,32b■4:7b,23(8414)■5:21b■9:11d,21■15:13c■21:4■22:13e■26:9b■32:43b■33:10^{3}b,12b(5704)■34:22b■44:19(1107),22b■46:19b■48:9b■51:29b,37b■52:20c-LA-1:6c■3:49b,52e-EZE-2:10(268)■7:15■14:23e■17:9c■33:15(1115)■38:11b■40:19,40,44■41:9,17,17(2435),25■42:7■43:21,22a,23^{2}a,25a■45:18a,23a■46:2,4^{2}a,6^{2}a,13a■47:2-DA-2:34(1768,3809),45(1768,3809)■8:25(657)■11:18(1115)-HO-3:4^{2}b,4sup■7:1,11b-JOE-1:6b■N.T.-all=5565,a=1854&marked-M'T-5:22(1500)■10:29(427)■12:46a,47a■13:34,57(820)■15:16(801)■26:69a-M'R-1:45a■3:31a,32a■4:11a,34■6:4(820)■7:15(1855),18(801),18(1855)■11:4a■14:58(886)-LU-1:10a,74(870)■6:49■8:20a■11:40(1855)■13:25a■20:28(815),29(815)■22:35(817)-JOH-1:3■8:7(361)■15:5,25(1432)■18:16a■19:23(729)■20:11a-AC-5:23a,26(3756,3326)■9:9(3361)■10:29(369)■12:5(1618)■14:17(267)■25:17(3367,4160)-RO-1:9(89),20(379),31(801),31(794)■2:12^2(460)■3:3(2673),21,28■4:6■5:6(772)■7:8,9■10:14■11:29(278)■12:9(505)-1CO-4:8■5:12a,13a■6:18(1622)■7:32(275),35(563)■9:18(77)■21^3(459)■11:11^2■14:7(895),10(880)■16:10(870)-2CO-7:5(1855)■10:13(280),15(280)■11:28(3924)-EPH-1:4(299)■2:12,12(112)■5:27(299)-PH'P-1:10(677),14(870)■2:14,15(298)-COL-2:11(886)■4:5a-1TH-1:3(89)■2:13(89)■4:12a■5:17(89)-1TI-2:8■3:7(1855),16(3672)■5:21■6:14(784)-2TI-1:3(88)■3:3(794)-PH'M-14-HEB-4:15■7:3(282),3(35),7,20,21■9:7,14(299),18,22,28■10:23(186),28■11:6,40■12:8,14■13:5(866),11a,12a,13a-JAS-2:13(448),18,20,26^2■3:17(505)-1PE-1:17(678),19(784)■3:1(427)■4:9(427)-2PE-2:17(504)■3:14(784)-JUDE-12(870),12(504),12(175)-RE-11:2(1855)■14:5(299),10(194),20a■22:15a

WITHS-all=3499-J'G-16,7,8,9

WITHSTAND-all=5975&marked-NU-22:32(7854)-2CH-13:7(2388),8(2388)■20:6(3320)-ES-9:2-EC-4:12-DA-11:15^{2}■N.T.-AC-11:17(2967)-EPH-6:13(436)

WITHSTOOD-2CH-26:18(5975)-DA-10:13(5975)■N.T.-all=436-AC-13:8-GA-2:11-2TI-3:8■4:15

WITNESS-all=5707&marked-GE-21:30(5713)■31:44,48,50,52,52(5711)-EX-20:16■22:13■23:1-LE-5:1-NU-5:13■17:7(5715),8(5715)■18:2(5715)■35:30-DE-4:26(5749)■5:20■17:6■19:15,16,18■31:19,21,26-JOS-22:27,28,34■24:27^{2}(5713)-J'G-11:10(8085)-1SA-12:3(6030),5^{3}-1KI-21:10(5749)-2CH-24:6(5715)-JOB-16:8,8(6030),19■29:11(5749)-PS-89:37-PR-6:19■12:17■14:5^{2},25■19:5,9,28■21:28■24:28■25:18-IS-3:9■19:20■55:4-JER-29:23■42:5-LA-2:13(5749)-MIC-1:2-MAL-2:14(5749)■3:5■N.T.-all=3140,a=3141&marked-M'T-15:19(5577)■19:18(5576)■24:14(3142)■26:59(5577),62(2649)■27:13(2649)-M'R-10:19(5576)■14:55a,56(5576),56a,57(5576),59a,60(2649)■15:4(2649)-LU-4:22■11:48■18:20(5576)■22:71a-JOH-1:7a,7,8,15■3:11a,26,28■5:31,31a,32,32a,33,36a,36,37■8:18^{2}■10:25■15:27■18:23,37-AC-1:22(3144)■4:33(3142)■7:44(3142)■10:43■14:17(267)■15:8■22:5,15(3144)■23:11■26:16(3144)-RO-1:9(3144)■2:15(4828)■8:16(4828)■9:1(4828)■13:9(5576)-1TH-2:5(3144)-TIT-1:13a-HEB-2:4(4901)■10:15■11:4-JAS-5:3(3142)-1PE-5:1(3144)-1JO-1:2■5:6,8,9^{3}a,10a-3JO-6-RE-1:5(3144)■3:14(3144)■20:4a

WITNESSED-1KI-21:13(5749)■N.T.-all=3140-RO-3:21-1TI-6:13-HEB-7:8

WITNESSES-all=5707-NU-35:30-DE-17:6^{2},7■19:15^{2}-JOS-24:22^{2}-RU-4:9,10,11-JOB-10:17-PS-27:12■35:11-IS-8:2■43:9,10,12■44:8,9-JER-32:10,12,25,44■N.T.-all=3144&marked-M'T-18:16■23:31(3140)■26:60^{2}(5575),65-M'R-14:63-LU-24:48-AC-1:8■2:32■3:15■5:32■6:13■7:58■10:39,41■13:31-1CO-15:15(5575)-2CO-13:1-1TH-2:10-1TI-5:19■6:12-2TI-2:2-HEB-10:28■12:1-RE-11:3

WITNESSETH-JOH-5:32(3140)-AC-20:23(1263)

WITNESSING-AC-26:22(3140)

WIT'S-PS-107:27(2451)

WITTINGLY-GE-48:14(7919)

WITTY-all supplied

WIVES-all=802&marked-GE-4:19,23^{2}■6:2,18■7:7,13■8:16,18■11:29■28:9■30:26■31:17,50■32:22■34:21,29■36:2,6■37:2■45:19■46:5,26-EX-19:15■22:24■32:2-NU-14:3■16:27■32:26-DE-3:19■17:17■21:15■29:11-JOS-1:14-J'G-3:6■8:30■21:7^{2},14,16,18,23-RU-1:4-1SA-1:2■25:43■27:3■30:3,5,18-2SA-2:2■5:13■12:8,11^{2}■19:5-1KI-11:3^{2},4,8■20:3,5,7-2KI-4:1■24:15-1CH-4:5■7:4■8:8■14:3-2CH-11:21^{2},23■13:21■20:13■21:14,17■24:3■29:9■31:18-EZR-10:2,3,10,11,14,17,18,19,44^{2}-NE-4:14■5:1■10:28■12:43■13:23,27-ES-1:20-IS-13:16-JER-6:12■8:10■14:16■18:21■29:6^{2},23■35:8■38:23■44:9^{2},15,25-EZE-44:22-DA-5:2(7965),3(7965),23(7965)■6:24(5389)-ZEC-12:12^{2},13^{2},14■N.T.-all=1135-M'T-19:8-AC-21:5-1CO-7:29-EPH-5:22,24,25,28-COL-3:18,19-1TI-3:11-1PE-3:1^{2}

WIVES'-1TI-4:7(1126)

WIZARD-LE-20:27(3049)-DE-18:11(3049)

WIZARDS-all=3049-LE-19:31■20:6-1SA-28:3,9-2KI-21:6■23:24-2CH-33:6-IS-8:19■19:3

WOE-all=1945,a=188&marked-NU-21:29a-1SA-4:7a,8a-JOB-10:15(480)-PS-120:5(190)-PR-23:29a-EC-4:10(337)■10:16(337)-IS-3:9a,11a■5:8■11,18,20,21,22■6:5a■10:1■17:12■18:1■24:16a■28:1■29:1,15■30:1■31:1■33:1■45:9,10-JER-4:13a,31a■6:4a■10:19a■13:27a■15:10a■22:13■23:1■45:3a■48:1,46a■50:27-LA-5:16a-EZE-2:10(1958)■13:3,18■16:23a■24:6a,9a■30:2(1929)■34:2-HO-7:13a■9:12a-AM-5:18■6:1-MIC-2:1■7:1(480)-NA-3:1-HAB-2:6,9,12,15,19-ZEP-2:5■3:1-ZEC-11:17■N.T.-all=3759-M'T-11:21^{2}■18:7^{2}■23:13,14,15,16,23,25,27,29■24:19■26:24-M'R-13:17■14:21-LU-6:24,25^{2},26■10:13^{2}■11:42,43,44,46,47,52■17:1■21:23■22:22-1CO-9:16-JUDE-11-RE-8:13■9:12■11:14^{2}■12:12

WOEFUL-JER-17:16(605)

WOES-RE-9:12(3759)

WOLF-all=2061-GE-49:27-IS-11:6■65:25-JER-5:6■N.T.-JOH-10:12^{2}(3074)

WOLVES-all=2061-EZE-22:27-HAB-1:8-ZEP-3:3■N.T.-all=3074-M'T-7:15■10:16-LU-10:3-AC-20:29

WOMAN-all=802&marked-GE-2:22,23■3:1,2,4,6,12,13^{2},15,16■12:11,14,15■20:3■24:5,8,39,44-EX-2:2,9■3:22■11:2■21:22,28,29■35:29■36:6-LE-12:2■13:29,38■15:18,19,25,33(5347)■18:17,19,23■19:20■20:13,16^{2},18,27■21:7■24:10,10sup-NU-5:6,18,19,21^{2},22,24,26,27,28,30,31■6:2■12:1^{2}■25:8,15■30:3■31:17-DE-17:2,5^{2}■21:11■22:5,14,22^{3}■29:18-JOS-2:4■6:21,22-J'G-4:9■9:53,54■11:2■13:3,6,9,10,11,13,24■14:1,2,3,7,10■16:4■19:26,27■20:4■21:11-RU-1:5■3:8,11,14■4:11,12(5291)-1SA-1:15,18,23,26■2:20■15:3■25:3■27:9,11■28:7^{2},8,9,11^{2},12,13,21,23,24-2SA-3:8■11:2^{2},3,5,21■14:2^{2},4,5,8,9,12,13,18^{2},19,27■17:19,20^{2}■20:16,17,21,22-1KI-3:17^{2},18,22,26■11:26■17:9,10,17,24-2KI-4:1,8,17■6:26,28,30■8:1,2,3,5^{2},6-1CH-16:3-2CH-2:14■15:13-ES-4:11-JOB-14:1■15:14■25:4■31:9-PS-58:8-PR-2:16■6:24,26,32■7:5,10■9:13■11:16,22■12:4■14:1■21:9,19■25:24■27:15■30:20■31:10,30-EC-7:26,28-IS-45:10■49:15■54:6-JER-13:21■31:22(5347)■44:7■48:41■49:22■51:22-EZE-16:30■18:6■23:44^{2}-HO-3:1-ZEC-5:7■N.T.-all=1135&marked-M'T-5:28■9:20,22■13:33■15:22,28■22:27■26:7,10-M'R-5:25,33■7:25,26■10:12■12:22■14:3-LU-4:26■7:37,39,44,50■8:43,47■10:38■11:27■13:11,12,21■15:8■20:32■22:57-JOH-2:4■4:7,9^{2},11,15,17,19,21,25,27,28,39,42■8:3,4,9,10^{2}■16:21■19:26■20:13,15-AC-16:1,14■17:34-RO-1:27(2338)■7:2-1CO-7:1,13,34■11:3,5,6^{2},7,8^{2},9^{2},10,11^{2},12^{2},13,15-GA-4:4-1TI-2:11,12,14-RE-2:20■12:1,4,6,13,14,15,16,17■17:3,4,6,7,9,18

WOMANKIND-LE-18:22(802)

WOMAN'S-all=802-GE-38:20-EX-21:22-LE-24:11-NU-5:18,25-DE-22:5-1KI-3:19

WOMB-all=990,a=7358&marked-GE-25:23,24■29:31a■30:2,22a■38:27■49:25(7356)-EX-13:2a-NUM-8:16a■12:12a-DE-7:13-J'G-13:5,7■16:17-RU-1:11(4578)-1SA-1:5a,6a-JOB-1:21■3:10,11a■10:18a,19■24:20a■31:15,15a,18■38:8a,29-PS-22:9,10a■58:3a■71:6■110:3a■127:3■139:13-PR-30:16(7356)■31:2-EC-5:15■11:5-IS-13:18■44:2,24■46:3(7356)■48:8■49:1,5,15-JER-1:5a■20:17^{2}a,18a-EZE-20:26(7356)-HO-9:11,14a,16■12:3■N.T.-all=2836&marked-M'T-19:12-LU-1:15,31(1064),41,42,44■2:21,23(2388)■11:27-JOH-3:4-AC-3:2■14:8-RO-4:19(3388)-GA-1:15

WOMBS-GE-20:18(7358)■N.T.-LU-23:29(2836)

WOMEN-all=802&marked-GE-14:16■18:11■31:35■33:5-EX-1:19■15:20■35:22,25,26-LE-26:26-NU-31:9,15(5347),18,35-DE-2:34■3:6■20:14■31:12-JOS-8:25,35-J'G-5:24^{2}■9:49,51■16:27^{2}■21:10,14,16-RU-1:4■4:14-1SA-2:22■15:33^{2}■18:6,7■21:4,5■22:19■30:2-2SA-1:26■6:19■15:16■20:3-1KI-3:16■11:1,1sup-2KI-23:7-2CH-28:8-EZR-10:1-NE-8:2,3■13:26-ES-1:9,17■2:3^{2},8,9,12^{2},13,14,15,17■3:13■8:11-JOB-42:15-PR-31:3-SONG-1:8■5:9■6:1-IS-3:12■4:1■19:16■27:11■32:9-JER-7:18■9:20■38:22,22sup■40:7■41:16■43:6■44:15,20,24■50:37■51:30-LA-2:20■4:10■5:11-EZE-8:14■9:6■16:34,41■23:2,10,44,48-DA-11:17,37-MIC-2:9-NA-3:13-ZEC-5:9■14:2■N.T.-all=1135&marked-M'T-11:11■14:21■15:38■27:55■28:5-M'R-15:40-LU-1:28,42■7:28■8:2■23:27,49,55■24:22,24-AC-1:14■5:14■8:3,12■9:2■13:50■16:13■17:4,12■22:4-RO-1:26(2338)-1CO-14:34,35-1TI-2:9,10-2TI-3:6(1133)-TIT-2:3(4247)-HEB-11:35-1PE-3:5-RE-9:8■14:4

WOMEN'S-ES-2:11(802)

WOMENSERVANTS-all=8198-GE-20:14■32:5,22

WON-1PE-3:1(2770)

WONDER-all=4159&marked-DE-13:1,2■28:46-2CH-32:31-PS-71:7-IS-20:3■29:9(8539),14(6382)-JER-4:9(8539)-HAB-1:5(8539)■N.T.-AC-3:10(2285)■13:41(2296)-RE-12:1(4592),3(4592)■17:8(2296)

WONDERED-IS-59:16(8074)■63:5(8074)-ZEC-3:8(4159)■N.T.-all=2296&marked-M'T-15:31-M'R-6:51-LU-2:18■4:22■8:25■9:43■11:14■24:41-AC-7:31■8:13(1839)-RE-13:3■17:6

WONDERFUL-all=6381&marked-DE-28:59-2SA-1:26-2CH-2:9-JOB-42:3-PS-40:5■78:4■107,8,15,21,31■111:4■119:129(6382)■139:6(6383)-PR-30:18-IS-9:6(6382)■25:1(6382)■28:29-JER-5:30(8047)■N.T.-M'T-7:22(1411)■21:15(2297)-AC-2:11(3167)

WONDERFULLY-IS-6:6(5953)-PS-139:14(6395)-LA-1:9(6382)-DA-8:24(6381)

WONDERING-GE-24:21(7583)■N.T.-LU-24:12(2296)-AC-3:11(1569)

WONDEROUSLY-J'G-13:19(6381)

WONDERS-all=4159&marked-EX-3:20(6381)■4:21■7:3■11:9,10■15:11(6382)-DE-4:34■6:22■7:19■26:8■34:11-JOS-3:5(6381)-1CH-16:12-NE-9:10,17(6381)-JOB-9:10(6381)-PS-77:11(6382),14(6382)■78:11(6381),43■88:10(6382),12(6382)■89:5(6382)■96:3(6381)■105:5,27■106:7(6381)■107:24(6381)■135:9■136:4(6381)-IS-8:18-JER-32:20,21-DA-4:2(8540),3(8540)■6:27(8540)■12:6(6382)-JOE-2:30■N.T.-all=5059&marked-M'T-24:24-M'R-13:22-JOH-4:48-AC-2:19,22,43■4:30■5:12■6:8■7:36■14:3■15:12-RO-15:19-2CO-12:12-2TH-2:9-HEB-2:4-RE-13:13(4592)

WONDROUS-all=6381&marked-1CH-16:9-JOB-37:14,16(4652)-PS-26:7■71:17■72:18■75:1■78:32■86:10■105:2■106:22■119:18,27■145:5-JER-21:2

WONDROUSLY-JOE-2:26(6381)

WONT-EX-21:29(5056)-NU-22:30(5532)-IS-30:31(1980)-2SA-20:18(1696)-DA-3:19(2370)■N.T.-M'T-27:15(1486)-M'R-10:1(1486)-LU-22:39(2596,1485)-AC-16:13(3543)

WOOD-all=6086,a=3293&marked-GE-6:14■22:3,6,7,9^{2}-EX-7:19■25:5,10,13,23,28■26:15,26■27:1,6■30:1,5■35:7,24,33■36:20,31■37:1,4,10,15,25,28■38:1,6-LE-1:7,8,12,17■3:5■4:12■6:12■11:32■14:4,6,49,51,52■15:12-NU-13:20■19:6■31:20■35:18-DE-4:28■10:1,3■19:5a,5■28:36,64■29:11,17-JOS-9:21,23,27■17:15a,18a-J'G-6:26-1SA-6:14■14:25a,26a■23:15(2793),16(2793),18(2793),19(2793)-2SA-6:5■18:6a,8a,17a■24:22-1KI-6:15■18:23^{2},33^{3},38-2KI-2:24a■6:4■19:18-1CH-16:33a■21:23■22:4■29:2-2CH-2:16-NE-8:4■10:34■

13:31-JOB-41:27-PS-80:13a■83:14a■96:12a■132:6a-PR-26:20,21-EC-2:6a■10:9-SONG-2:3a■3:9-IS-7:2a■10:15■30:33■37:19■45:20■60:17-JER-5:14■7:18■28:13■46:22-LA-5:4,13-EZE-15:3■20:32■24:10■39:10■41:16,22^{2}-DA-5:4(636),23(636)-MIC-7:14a-HAB-2:19-HAG-1:8-ZEC-12:6■N.T.-all=3586&marked-1CO-3:12-2TI-2:20(3585)-RE-9:20(3585)■18:12^{2}

WOODS-EZE-34:25(3264)

WOOF-all=6154-LE-13:48,49,51,52,53,56,57,58,59

WOOL-all=6785&marked-J'G-6:37-2KI-3:4-PS-147:16-PR-31:13-IS-1:18■51:8-EZE-27:18■34:3■44:17-DA-7:9(6015)-HO-2:5,9■N.T.-HEB-9:19(2053)-RE-1:14(5053)

WOOLEN-all=6785&marked-LE-13:47,48,52,59■19:19(8162)-DA-22:11

WORD-all=1697,a=565,b=6310 marked-GE-15:1,4■30:34■37:14■41:40b■44:2,18-EX-8:10,13,31■9:20,21■12:35■14:12■32:28-LE-10:7-NU-3:16b,51b■4:45b■11:23■13:26■14:20■15:31■20:24b■22:8,18b,20,35,38■23:5,16■27:21^{2}b■30:2■36:5b-DE-1:22,25■4:2■5:5■9:5■18:20,21■21:5b■30:14■33:9a■34:5b-JOS-1:13■6:10■8:27,35■14:7,10■19:50b■22:9b,32-1SA-1:23■3:1,7,21■4:1■9:27■15:10,23,26-2SA-3:11■7:4,7,25■14:12,17■15:28■22:31a■23:2(4405)■24:4,11-1KI-2:4,23,27,30,42■6:11,12■8:20,26,56■12:22,24^{2}■13:1,2,5,9,17,18,20,26b,26,32■14:18■16:1,7,12,34■17:1,2,5,8,16,24■18:1,21,31,36■19:9■20:9,35■21:4,17,28■22:5,13^{2},19,38-2KI-1:16,17■3:12■4:44■6:18■7:1,16■9:26,36■10:10■14:25■15:12■18:28,36■19:21■20:4,16,19■22:9,20■23:16■24:2-1CH-10:13■11:3,10■12:23b■15:15■16:15■17:3,6■21:4,6,12■22:8-2CH-6:10,17■10:15■11:2■12:7■18:4,12,18■30:12■34:16,21,28■35:6■36:21,22-EZR-1:1■6:11(6600)■10:5-NE-1:8-ES-1:21■7:8-JOB-2:13-PS-17:4■18:30a■33:4,6■56:4,10^{2}■68:11(562)■103:20■105:8,19,19a,28■106:24■107:20■119:9,11a,16,17,25,28,38a,41a,42,43,49,50a,58a,65,67a,74,76a,81,82a,89,101,105,107,114,116a,123a,133a,140a,147,148a,154a,158a,160,161,162a,169,170a,172a■130:5■138:2a■139:4(4405)■147:15,18,19■148:8-PR-12:25■13:13■14:15■15:23■25:11■30:5a-EC-8:4-IS-1:10■2:1,3■5:24a■8:10,20■9:8■16:13■24:3■28:13,14■29:21■30:12,21■36:21■37:22■38:4■39:5,8■40:8■41:28■44:26■45:23■50:4■55:11■66:2,5^{2}-JER-1:2,4,11,12,13■2:1,4,31■5:13(1699),14■6:10■7:1,2^{2}■8:9■9:20^{2}■10:1■11:1■13:2,3,8,12■14:1,17■15:16■16:1■17:15,20■18:1,5,18■19:3■20:8■21:1,11■22:1,2,29■23:18^{2},28^{2},29,36,38■24:4■25:1,3■26:1,2■27:1,18■28:7,9,12■29:10,20,30■30:1■31:10■32:1,6,8^{2},26■33:1,19,23■34:1,4,5,8,12■35:1,12■36:1,27■37:6,17■38:21■39:15■40:1■42:7,15■43:8■44:1,16,24,26■45:1■46:1,13■47:1■49:34■50:1■51:59-LA-2:17a-EZE-1:3■3:16,17■6:1,3■7:1■11:14■12:1,8,17,21,25^{2},26,28■13:1,2,6■14:2,12■15:1■16:1,35■17:1,11■18:1■20:2,45,47■21:1,8,18■22:1,17,23■23:1■24:1,15,20■25:1,3■26:1■27:1■28:1,11,20■29:1,17■30:1,20■31:1■32:1,17■33:1,7,23,30■34:1,7,9■35:1■36:1,4,16■37:4,15■38:1-DA-3:28(4406)■4:17(3983),31(4406)■9:2■10:11-HO-1:1,2(1699)■4:1-JOE-1:1■2:11-AM-3:1■4:1■5:1■7:16,16sup■8:12-JON-1:1■3:1,3,6-MIC-1:1■4:2-HAB-3:9(562)-ZEP-1:1■2:5-HAG-1:1,3■2:1,5,10,20-ZEC-1:1,7■4:6,8■6:9■7:1,4,8■8:1,18■9:1■11:11■12:1-MAL-1:1■N.T.-all=3056,a=4487&marked-M'T-2:8(518),13(2036)■4:4a■8:8,16■12:32,36a■13:19,20,21,22^{2},23■15:23■18:16a■22:46■26:75a■27:14a■28:8(518)-M'R-2:2■4:14,15^{2},16,18,19,20,33■5:36■7:13■14:72a■16:20-LU-1:2,38a■2:29a■3:2a■4:4a,32,36■5:1,5a■7:7■8:11,12,13,15,21■10:39■11:28■12:10■22:61■24:19-JOH-1:1^{3},14■2:22■4:41,50■5:24,38■8:31,37,43■10:35■12:48■14:24■15:3,20,25■17:6,14,17,20-AC-2:41■4:4,29,31■6:2,4,7■8:4,14,25■10:36,37a,44■11:1,16a,19■12:24■13:5,7,15,26,44,46,48,49■14:3,25■15:7,35,36■16:6,32■17:11,13■18:11■19:10,20■20:32■22:22■28:25a-RO-9:6,9■10:8^{2}a,17a■15:18-1CO-4:20■12:8^{2}■14:36-2CO-1:18■2:17■4:2■5:19■6:7■10:11■13:1a-GA-5:14a■6:6a-EPH-1:13a■5:26a■6:17a-PH'P-1:14■2:16-COL-1:5,25■3:16,17-1TH-1:5,6,8■2:13^{3}■4:15-2TH-2:2,15,17■3:1,14-1TI-4:5,12■5:17-2TI-2:9,15,17■4:2-TIT-1:3,9■2:5-HEB-1:3a■2:2■4:2,12■5:13■6:5a■7:28■11:3a■12:19■13:7,22-JAS-1:18,21,22,23■3:2-1PE-1:23,25^{2}a■2:2(3050),8■3:1^{2}-2PE-1:19■3:5,7-1JO-1:1,10■2:5,7,14■3:18■5:7-RE-1:2,9■3:8,10■6:9■12:11■19:13■20:4

WORD'S-2SA-7:21(1697)■N.T.-M'R-4:17(3056)

WORDS-all=1697,a=561,b=4405&marked-GE-24:30,52■27:34,42■31:1■34:18■37:8■39:17,19■42:16,20■43:7■44:6,7,10■44:24■45:27■49:21a-EX-4:15,28,30■5:9■19:6,7,8,9■20:1■23:8■24:3^{2},4,8■34:1,27^{2},28■35:1-NU-11:24■12:6■16:31■22:7■24:4a,16a-DE-1:1,34■2:26■4:10,12,36■5:22,28^{2}■6:6■9:10■10:2■11:18■12:28■13:3■16:19■17:19■18:18,19■27:3,8,26■28:14,58■29:1,9,19,29■31:1,12,24,28,30■32:1a,44,45,46^{2}■33:3(1703)-JOS-1:18■2:21■3:9■8:34■22:30■24:26,27a-J'G-2:4■9:3,30■11:10,11,28■13:12■16:16-1SA-3:19■8:10,21■15:1,24■17:11,23,31■18:23,26■21:12■24:7,9,16■25:9,24■26:19■28:20,21-2SA-3:8■7:17,28■14:3,19■19:43^{2}■20:17■22:1■23:1-1KI-1:14■3:12■5:7■8:59■10:7■12:7■13:11■21:27■22:13-2KI-1:7■6:12,30■18:20,27,37■19:4^{2},6,16■22:11,13^{2},16,18■23:2,3,16,24-1CH-17:15■23:27■25:5-2CH-9:6■10:7■11:4■15:8■18:12■29:15,30■32:8■33:18■34:19,21,26,27,30,31■35:22■36:16-EZR-7:11■9:4-NE-1:4■2:18■5:6■6:7,19■8:9,12,13■9:8-ES-4:9,12■9:26,30-JOB-4:4b■6:3,10a,25a,26b■8:2a,10b■9:14■11:2■12:11b■15:13b■16:3,4b■18:2b■19:2b,23b■22:22a■23:5b,12a■26:4b■29:22■31:40■32:11,12a,14b■33:1,3a,8b■34:2b,3b,16b,35,37a■35:16b■36:4b■38:2b■42:7-PS-5:1a■7:t■12:6(565)■18:t■19:4b,14a■22:1■36:3■50:17■52:4■54:2a■55:21sup,21■56:5■59:12■64:3■78:1a■106:12■107:11a■109:3■119:57,103(565),130,139■138:4a■141:6a-PR-1:2a,6,21a,23■2:1a,16a■4:4,5a,20■5:7a■6:2^{2}a■7:1a,5a,24a■8:8a■10:19■12:6■15:1■16:24a■17:27a■18:4,8■19:7a,27a■22:12,17,21^{2}a■23:8,9b,12a■26:22■29:19,20■30:1,6■31:1-EC-1:1■5:2,3,7■7:21■9:16,17■10:12,13,14■12:10^{2},11-IS-29:11,18■31:2■32:7a■36:5,12,13,22■37:4^{2},6,17■41:26a■51:16■58:13■59:13,21-JER-1:1,9■3:12■5:14■6:19■7:4,8,27■11:2,3,6^{2},8,10■13:10■15:16■16:10■18:2,18■19:2,15■22:5■23:9,16,22,30,36■25:8,13,30■26:2,5,7,12,15,20,21■27:12,14,16■28:6■29:1,19,23■30:2,4■34:6,18■35:13,14■36:2,4,6,8,10,11,13,16^{2},17,18,20,24,27,28,32^{2}■37:2■38:1,4,24,27■39:16■42:4■43:1^{2}■44:28,29■45:1■51:60,61,64-EZE-2:6^{2},7■3:4,6,10■12:28■33:31,32■35:13-DA-2:9(4406)■5:10(4406)■6:14(4406)■7:11(4406),25(4406)■9:12■10:6,9^{2},11,12^{2},15■12:4,9-HO-6:5a■10:4■14:2-AM-1:1■7:10■8:11-MIC-2:7-HAG-1:12-ZEC-1:6,13■7:7,12■8:9-MAL-2:17■3:13■N.T.-all=3056,a=4487&marked-M'T-10:14■12:37^{2}■24:35■26:44-M'R-8:38■10:24■12:13■13:31■14:39-LU-1:20■3:4■4:22■9:26■20:20,26a■21:33■23:9■24:8a,11a,44-JOH-3:34a■5:47a■6:63a,68a■8:20a,47a■10:21a■12:47a,48a■14:10a,23■15:7a■17:8a-AC-2:14a,22,40■5:5,20a■6:11a,13a■7:22■10:22a,44a■11:14a■13:42a■15:15,24,32■16:38a■18:15■20:35,38■26:25a-RO-10:18a■16:18(5542)-1CO-1:17■2:4,13■14:9,19^{2}-2CO-12:4a-EPH-5:6-COL-2:4(4086)-1TH-2:5■4:18-1TI-4:6■6:3,4(3055)-2TI-1:13■2:14(3054)■4:15-HEB-12:19a-2PE-2:3■3:2a-3JO-10-JUDE-17a-RE-1:3■17:17a■21:5■22:18,19

WORK-all=4399,a=4639,b=6213,c=6467&marked-GE-2:2^{2},3■5:29a-EX-5:9(5656),11(5656),18(5647)■12:16■14:31(3027)■18:20(4640)■20:9,10■23:12a■24:10a■25:18(4749),31(4749),36(4749)■26:1a,31a■28:6,a,8a,11a,14a,15^{2}a,22a,32a■31:4b,5b,14,15^{2}■32:16a■34:10a,21(5627)■35:2^{2},21,24,29,32b,33,35b,35,35^{2}sup■36:1b,1,2,3,4^{2},5,6,7,8,8a,35a■37:17(4749),22(4749),29a■38:24^{2}■39:3b,3a,5a,8^{2}a,15a,22a,27a,32(5656),42(5656),43■40:33-LE-11:32■13:51■16:29■23:3^{2},7,8,21,25,28,30,31,35,36-NU-4:3,23(5656),30(5656),35(5656),39(5656),43(5656)■8:4a,8sup■28:18,25,26■29:1,7,12,35■31:20a-DE-4:28a■5:13,14■14:29a■15:19(5647)■16:8■24:19a■27:15a■28:12a■30:9a■31:29a■32:4c■33:11c-JOS-9:4b-J'G-19:16a-RU-2:12c-1SA-8:16■14:6b-1KI-5:16^{2}■7:8(4649),14b,14,17^{2}a,19a,22a,22,28a,29a,31a,33^{2}a,40,51■9:23^{2}■16:7a■21:20b,25b-2KI-12:11■19:18a■22:5^{2},9■25:17^{2}(7639)-1CH-4:23■6:49■9:13,19,33■16:37(1697)■22:15■23:4,24,28a■27:26■28:13,20■29:1,5,6-2CH-2:7b,14b,18(5647)■3:10a■4:5a,11■5:1■8:9,16■15:7(6468)■16:5■24:12,13■29:34■31:21a■32:19a■34:12,13-EZR-2:69■3:8■4:24(5673)■5:8(5673)■6:7(5673),22■10:13-NE-2:16■3:5(5656)■4:6b,11,15,16,17,19,21■5:16^{2}■6:3^{2},9,16■7:70,71■10:33■11:12■13:10-JOB-1:10a■7:2c■10:3(3018)■14:15a■23:9b■24:5c■34:11c,19a■36:9c,24c■37:7a-PS-8:3a■9:16c■28:4a■44:1c■58:2(6466)■62:12a■64:9c■74:6(6603)■77:12c■90:16c,17^{2}a■92:4c■95:9c■101:3b■102:25a■104:23c■111:3c■115:4a■119:126b■135:15a■141:4(5950)■143:5a-PR-11:18(6468)■16:11a■18:9■20:11c■21:8c■24:27,29c-EC-2:17a■3:11a,17a■4:3a,4a■5:6a■7:13a■8:9a,11a,14^{2}a,17^{2}a■9:10a■12:14a-SONG-7:1a-IS-2:8a■5:12c,19a■10:12a■17:8a■19:9(5647),14a,15a,25a■28:21a■29:14^{2}(6381),16a,23a■31:2b■32:6b,17a■37:19a■40:10(6468)■41:24c■43:13(6466)■45:9c,11c■49:4(6468)■54:16a■60:21a■61:8(6468)■62:11(6468)■64:8a■65:7(6468),22a-JER-10:3a,9^{2}a,15a■17:22,24■18:3■22:13c■31:16(6468)■32:19(5950),30a■48:10■50:25,29c■51:10a,18a-LA-3:64a■4:2a-EZE-1:16^{2}a■15:3,4,5,5^{2}■16:10(7553),13(7553),30a■27:7(7553),16(7553),24(7553)■33:26b-DA-11:23b-HO-6:8(6466)■13:2a■14:3a-MIC-2:1(6466)■5:13a-HAB-1:5(6466),5c■2:18(3336)■3:2c-ZEP-2:14(731)-HAG-1:14■2:4b,14a-MAL-3:15b■N.T.-all=2041&marked-M'T-7:23(2038)■21:28(2038)■26:10-M'R-6:5(1411)■13:34■14:6-LU-13:14(2038)-JOH-4:34■5:17(2038)■6:28(2038),29,30(2038)■7:21■9:4^{2}(2038)■10:33■17:4-AC-5:38■13:2,41(2040),41■14:26■15:38■27:16(3433,2480)-RO-2:15■7:5(1754)■8:28(4903)■9:28^{2}(3056)■11:6■14:20-1CO-3:13^{2},14,15■9:1■15:58■16:10-2CO-9:8-GA-6:4-EPH-4:12,19(2039)-PH'P-1:6■2:12(2716),30-COL-1:10-1TH-1:3■4:11(2088)-2TH-1:11■2:7(1754)■2:17■3:10(2038),12(2038)-1TI-3:1■5:10-2TI-2:21■4:5,18-TIT-1:16■3:1-HEB-6:10■13:21-JAS-1:4,25■3:16(4229)-1PE-1:17-RE-22:12

WORKER-1KI-7:14(2790)

WORKERS-all=6466&marked-**1CH**-22:15(2796)-**JOB**-31:3■34:8,22-**PS**-5:5■6:8■14:4■28:3■36:12■37:1(6213)■53:4■59:2■64:2■92:7,9■94:4,16■125:5■141:9-**PR**-10:29■21:15■**N.T.**-all=2040&marked-**LU**-13:27-**1CO**-12:29(1411)-**2CO**-6:1(4903)■11:13-**PH'P**-3:2

WORKETH-all=6213&marked-**JOB**-33:29(6466)-**PS**-15:2(6466)■101:7-**PR**-11:18■26:28■31:13-**EC**-3:9-**IS**-44:12^{2}(6466)■64:5-**DA**-6:27(5648)■**N.T.**-all=1754&marked-**JOH**-5:17(2038)-**AC**-10:35(2038)-**RO**-2:10(2038)■4:4(2038),5(2038),15(2716)■5:3(2716)■13:10(2038)-**1CO**-12:6,11■16:10(2038)-**2CO**-4:12,17(2716)■7:10^{2}(2716)-**GA**-3:5■5:6-**EPH**-1:11■2:2■3:20-**PH'P**-2:13-**COL**-1:29-**1TH**-2:13-**JAS**-1:3(2716),20(2716)-**RE**-21:27(4160)

WORKFELLOW-**RO**-16:21(4904)

WORKING-**PS**-52:2(6213)■74:12(6466)-**IS**-28:29(8454)-**EZE**-46:1(4639)■**N.T.**-all=1753&marked-**M'R**-16:20(4903)-**RO**-1:27(2716)■7:13(2716)-**1CO**-4:12(2038)■9:6(2038)■12:10(1755)-**EPH**-1:19■3:7■4:16,28(2038)-**PH'P**-3:21-**COL**-1:29-**2TH**-2:9■3:11(2038)-**HEB**-13:21(4160)-**RE**-16:14(4160)

WORKMAN-all=2796&marked-**EX**-35:35(2803)■38:23(2803)-**SONG**-7:1(542)-**IS**-40:19,20-**JER**-10:3,9-**HO**-8:6■**N.T.**-**M'T**-10:10(2040)-**2TI**-2:15(2040)

WORKMANSHIP-all=4339&marked-**EX**-31:3,5■35:31-**2KI**-16:10(4639)-**1CH**-28:21-**EZE**-28:13■**N.T.**-**EPH**-2:10(4161)

WORKMEN-all=6213,4399&marked-**2KI**-12:14,15-**1CH**-22:15■25:1(582,4399)-**2CH**-24:13■34:10^{2},17-**EZR**-3:9-**IS**-44:11(2796)■**N.T.**-**AC**-19:25(2040)

WORKMEN'S-**J'G**-5:26(6001)

WORK'S-**1TH**-5:13(2041)

WORKS-all=4639&marked-**EX**-5:4,13■23:24-**NU**-16:28-**DE**-2:7■3:24■15:10■16:15-**JOS**-24:31-**J'G**-2:7,10-**1SA**-8:8■19:4-**1KI**-7:14(4399)■13:11-**2KI**-22:17-**1CH**-28:19(4399)-**2CH**-20:37■32:30■34:25-**NE**-6:14■9:35(4611)-**JOB**-34:25(4566)-**PS**-8:6■14:1(5949)■17:4(6468)■28:5(6468)■33:4(4640),15(4640)■46:8(4659)■66:3,5(4659)■73:28(4399)■77:11(4611)■78:7(4611),11(5949)■86:8sup,8■92:4,5■103:22■104:13,24,31■106:13,35,39■107:22,24■111:2,6,7■118:17■138:8■139:14■141:4(5949)■143:5(6467)■145:4,5(1697),9,10,17-**PR**-8:22(4659)■16:3■24:12(6467)■31:31-**EC**-1:14■2:4,11■3:22■9:1(5652),7■11:5-**IS**-26:12■29:15■41:29■57:12■59:6^{2}■66:18-**JER**-1:16■7:13■25:6,7,14■44:8■48:7-**EZE**-6:6-**DA**-4:37(4567)■9:14-**AM**-8:7-**JON**-3:10■**MIC**-6:16■**N.T.**-all=2041&marked-**M'T**-5:16■11:2■16:27(4234)■23:3,5-**JOH**-5:20,36^{2}■6:28■7:3,7■8:39■9:3,4■10:25,32^{2},37,38■14:10,12^{2}■15:24-**AC**-7:41■9:36■15:18■26:20-**RO**-3:27■4:2,6■9:11,32■11:6^{2}■13:3,12-**2CO**-11:15-**GA**-2:16^{3}■3:2,5,10■5:19-**EPH**-2:9,10■5:11-**COL**-1:21-**1TI**-2:10■5:10,25■6:18-**2TI**-1:9■3:17■4:14-**TIT**-1:16■2:7,14■3:5,8,14-**HEB**-1:10■2:7■3:9■4:3,4,10■6:1■9:14■10:24-**JAS**-2:14,17,18^{3},20,21,22^{2},24,25,26■3:13-**1PE**-2:12-**2PE**-3:10-**1JO**-3:8,12-**RE**-2:2,5,9,13,19^{2},23,26■3:1,2,8,15■9:20■14:13■15:3■18:6■20:12,13

WORKS'-**JOH**-14:11(2041)

WORLD-all=8398&marked-**1SA**-2:8-**2SA**-22:16-**1CH**-16:30-**JOB**-18:18■34:13■37:12-**PS**-9:8■17:14(2465)■18:15■19:4■22:27(776)■24:1■33:8■49:1(2465)■50:12■73:12(5769)■77:18■89:11■90:2■93:1■96:10,13■97:4■98:7,9-**PR**-8:26-**EC**-3:11(5769)-**IS**-13:11■14:17,21■18:3■23:17(776)■24:4■26:9,18■27:6■34:1■38:11(2309)■45:17(5769)■62:11(776)■64:4(5769)-**JER**-10:12■25:26(776)■51:15-**LA**-4:12-**NA**-1:5■**N.T.**-all=2889,a=165&marked-**M'T**-4:8■5:14■12:32a■13:22a,35,38,39a,40a,49a■16:26■18:7■24:3a,14(3625),21■25:34■26:13■28:20a-**M'R**-4:19a■8:36■10:30a■14:9■16:15-**LU**-1:70a■2:1(3625)■4:5(3625)■9:25■11:50■12:30■16:8a■18:30a■20:34a,35a-**JOH**-1:9,10^{3},29■3:16,17^{2},19■4:42■6:14,33,51■7:4,7■8:12,23^{2},26■9:5^{2},32a,39■10:36■11:9,27■12:19,25,31^{2},46,47■13:1^{2}■14:17,19,22,27,30,31■15:18,19^{4}■16:8,11,20,21,28^{2},33^{2}■17:5,6,9,11^{2},12,13,14^{3},15,16^{2},18^{2},21,23,24,25■18:20,36^{2},37■21:25-**AC**-3:21a■11:28(3625)■15:18a■17:6(3625),24,31(3625)■19:27(3625)■24:5(3625)-**RO**-1:8,20■3:6,19■4:13■5:12,13■10:18(3625)■11:12,15■12:2a■16:25(166)-**1CO**-1:20a,20,21,27^{2},28■2:6^{2}a,7a,8a,12■3:18a,19,22■4:9,13■5:10^{2}■6:2^{2}■7:31^{2},33,34■8:4,13a■10:11a■11:32■14:10-**2CO**-1:12■4:4a■5:19■7:10-**GA**-1:4a■4:3■6:14^{2}-**EPH**-1:4,21a■2:2,12■3:9a,21a■6:12a-**PH'P**-2:15-**COL**-1:6■2:8,20^{2}-**1TI**-1:15■3:16■6:7,17a-**2TI**-1:9(166)■4:10a-**TIT**-1:2(166)■2:12a-**HEB**-1:6(3625)■2:5(3625)■4:3■6:5a■9:26,26a■10:5■11:7,38-**JAS**-1:27■2:5■3:6■4:4^{2}-**1PE**-1:20■5:9-**2PE**-1:4■2:5^{2},20■3:6-**1JO**-2:2,15^{3},16^{2},17■3:1,13■4:1,3,4,5^{3},9,14,17■5:4^{2},5,19-**2JO**-7-**RE**-3:10(3625)■11:15■12:9(3625)■13:3(1093),8■16:14(3625)■17:8

WORDLY-**TIT**-2:12(2886)-**HEB**-9:1(2886)

WORLD'S-**1JO**-3:17(2889)

WORLDS-**HEB**-1:2(165)■11:3(165)

WORM-all=7415&marked-**EX**-16:24-**JOB**-17:14■24:20■25:6,6(8438)-**PS**-22:6(8438)-**IS**-14:11■41:14(8438)■51:8(5580)■66:24(8438)-**JON**-4:7(8438)■**N.T.**-all=4668-**M'R**-9:44,46,48

WORMS-all=8438&marked-**EX**-16:20-**DE**-28:39-**JOB**-7:5(7415)■21:26(7415)-**IS**-14:11-**MIC**-7:17(2119)■**N.T.**-**AC**-12:23(4662)

WORMWOOD-all=3939-**DE**-29:18-**PR**-5:4-**JER**-9:15■23:15-**LA**-3:15,19-**AM**-5:7■**N.T.**-**RE**-8:11^{2}(894)

WORSE-all=7489&marked-**GE**-19:9-**2SA**-19:7-**1KI**-16:25-**2KI**-14:12(5062)-**1CH**-19:16(5062),19(5062)-**2CH**-6:24(5062)■25:22(5062)■33:9(7451)-**JER**-7:26■16:12-**DA**-1:10(2196)■**N.T.**-all=5501&marked-**M'T**-9:16■12:45■27:64-**M'R**-2:21■5:26-**LU**-11:26-**JOH**-2:10(1640)■5:14-**1CO**-8:8(5302)■11:17(2276)-**1TI**-5:8-**2TI**-3:13-**2PE**-2:20

WORSHIP-all=7812&marked-**GE**-22:5-**EX**-24:1■34:14-**DE**-4:19■8:19■11:16■26:10■30:17-**JOS**-5:14-**1SA**-1:3■15:25,30-**1KI**-9:6-**2KI**-5:18■17:36■18:22-**1CH**-16:29-**2CH**-7:19■32:12-**PS**-5:7■22:27,29■29:2■45:11■66:4■81:9■86:9■95:6■96:9■97:7■99:5,9■132:7■138:2-**IS**-2:8,20■27:13■36:7■46:6■49:7■66:23-**JER**-7:2■13:10■25:6■26:2■44:19(6087)-**EZE**-46:2,3,9-**DA**-3:5(5457),10(5457),12(5457),14(5457),15^{2}(5457),18(5457),28(5457)-**MIC**-5:13-**ZEP**-1:5^{2}■2:11-**ZEC**-14:16,17■**N.T.**-all=4352&marked-**M'T**-2:2,8■4:9,10■15:9(4576)-**M'R**-7:7(4576)-**LU**-4:7(4352,1799),8■14:10(1391)-**JOH**-4:20,21,22^{2},23^{2},24^{2}■12:20-**AC**-7:42(3000),43■8:27■17:23(2151)■18:13(4576)■24:11,14(3000)-**1CO**-14:25-**PH'P**-3:3(3000)-**COL**-2:23(1479)-**HEB**-1:6-**RE**-3:9■4:10■9:20■11:1■13:8,12,15■14:7,9,11■15:4■19:10^{2}■22:8,9

WORSHIPPED-all=7812&marked-**GE**-24:26,48,52-**EX**-4:31■12:27■32:8■33:10■34:8-**DE**-17:3■29:26-**J'G**-7:15-**1SA**-1:19,28■15:31-**2SA**-12:20■15:32-**1KI**-9:9■11:33■16:31■22:53-**2KI**-17:16■21:3,21-**1CH**-29:20-**2CH**-7:3,22■29:28,29,30■33:3-**NE**-8:6■9:3-**JOB**-1:20-**PS**-106:19-**JER**-1:16■8:2■16:11■22:9-**EZE**-8:16-**DA**-2:46(5457)■3:7(5457)■**N.T.**-all=4352&marked-**M'T**-2:11■8:2■9:18■14:33■15:25■18:26■28:9,17-**M'R**-5:6■15:19-**LU**-24:52-**JOH**-4:20■9:38-**AC**-10:25■16:14(4576)■17:25(2323)■18:7(4576)-**RO**-1:25(4573)-**2TH**-2:4(4574)-**HEB**-11:21-**RE**-5:14■7:11■11:16■13:4^{2}■16:2■19:4,20■20:4

WORSHIPPER-**JOH**-9:31(2318)-**AC**-19:35(3511)

WORSHIPPERS-all=5647-**2KI**-10:19,21,22,23^{2}■**N.T.**-**JOH**-4:23(4353)-**HEB**-10:2(3000)

WORSHIPPETH-all=7812&marked-**NE**-9:6-**IS**-44:15,17-**DA**-3:6(5457),11(5457)■**N.T.**-**AC**-19:27(4576)

WORSHIPPING-all=7812-**2KI**-19:37-**2CH**-20:18-**IS**-37:38■**N.T.**-**M'T**-20:20(4352)-**COL**-2:18(2356)

WORST-**EZE**-7:24(7451)

WORTH-**GE**-23:9(4392)-**LE**-27:23(4373)-**DE**-15:18(7939)-**2SA**-18:3(3644)-**1KI**-21:2(4242)

WORTHIES-**NA**-2:5(117)

WORTHILY-**RU**-4:11(2428)

WORTHY-**GE**-32:10(6994)-**DE**-25:2(1121)-**1SA**-1:5(639)■26:16(1121)-**1KI**-1:52(2428)■2:26(376)■**N.T.**-all=514&marked-**M'T**-3:11(2425)■8:8(2425)■10:10,11,13^{2},37^{2},38■22:8-**M'R**-1:7(2425)-**LU**-3:8,16(2425)■7:4,6(2425),7(515)■10:7■12:48■15:19,21■20:35(2661)■21:36(2661)■23:15-**JOH**-1:27-**AC**-5:41(2661)■13:25■23:29■24:2(2735)■25:11,25■26:31-**RO**-1:32■8:18-**EPH**-4:1(516)-**COL**-1:10(516)-**1TH**-2:12(516)-**2TH**-1:5(2661),11(515)-**1TI**-1:15■4:9■5:17(515),18■6:1-**HEB**-3:3(515)■10:29(515)■11:38-**JAS**-2:7(2570)-**RE**-3:4■4:11■5:2,4,9,12■16:6

WOT-all=3045-**GE**-21:26■44:15-**EX**-32:1,23-**NU**-22:6-**JOS**-2:5■**N.T.**-all=1492&marked-**AC**-3:17■7:40-**RO**-11:2-**PH'P**-1:22(1107)

WOTTETH-**GE**-39:8(3045)

WOULD-all=14&marked-**GE**-30:34(3863)-**EX**-10:27■16:3(4310,5414)-**NU**-11:29(4310,5414)■14:2^{2}(3863)■20:3(3863)■22:29(3863)-**DE**-1:26■2:30■10:10■23:5■28:67^{2}(4310,5414)-**JOS**-7:7(3863)■17:12(2974)■24:10-**J'G**-1:27(2974),35(2974)■9:29(4310,5414)■11:17sup,17■19:10,25■20:13-**1SA**-2:25(2654)■15:9■22:17■26:23■31:4-**2SA**-2:21■6:10■12:17■13:14,16,25■14:29^{2}■18:33(4310,5414)■23:16,17-**1KI**-13:33(2655)■22:49-**2KI**-5:3(305)■8:19■13:23■24:4-**1CH**-10:4■11:18,19■19:19-**2CH**-21:7-**PS**-35:25(5315)■81:11sup,11-**PR**-1:25,30-**IS**-28:12■30:15■42:24-**EZE**-20:8-**DA**-5:19^{4}(6634)■7:19(6634)■**N.T.**-all=2309&marked-**M'T**-2:18■5:42■7:12■12:38■14:5■18:23,30■22:3■23:37^{2}■27:15,34-**M'R**-3:13■6:19,26,48■7:24■9:30■10:35,36-**LU**-1:62■6:31■10:1(3195)■13:34^{2}■15:28■16:26■18:4,13■19:27-**JOH**-1:43■6:6(3195),11,15(3195)■7:1,44■9:27■12:21-**AC**-7:39■10:10■12:6(3195)■14:13■16:3,27(3195)■19:33■20:16(1096)■23:15(3195),20(3195)■24:6■25:4(3195)■26:5,29(2172)■27:30(3195)-**RO**-1:13■7:15,16,19^{2},20,21■11:25■16:19-**1CO**-4:8(3785)■7:7,32■10:1,20■11:3■12:1■14:5-**2CO**-1:8■5:4■11:1(3785)■12:20^{2}-**GA**-1:7■3:2■4:17■5:12(3785),17-**COL**-1:27■2:1-**1TH**-2:18■4:13-**2TH**-3:10-**PH'M**-14-**HEB**-12:17-**2JO**-12(1014)-**3JO**-10(1014)-**RE**-3:15(3785)

WOULDEST-**2KI**-4:13(3426)■**N.T.**-all=2309-**JOH**-21:18^{2}-**HEB**-10:5,8

WOUND-all=4347&marked-**EX**-21:25(6482)-**DE**-32:39(4272)-**1KI**-22:35-**JOB**-34:6(2671)-**PS**-68:21(4272)■110:6(4272)-**PR**-6:33(5061)■20:30(6482)-**IS**-30:26-**JER**-10:19■15:18■30:12,14-**HO**-5:13^{2}(4205)-**OB**-7(4204)-**MIC**-1:9-**NA**-3:19■**N.T.**-all=4127&marked-**JOH**-19:40(1210)-**AC**-5:6(4958)-**1CO**-8:12(5180)-**RE**-13:3,12,14

WOUNDED-all=2491&marked-DE-23:1(1795)-J’G-9:40-1SA-17:52■31:3(2342)-2SA-22:39(4272)-1KI-20:37(6481)■22:34(2470)-2KI-8:28(5221)-1CH-10:3(2342)-2CH-18:33(2470)■35:23(2470)-JOB-24:12-PS-18:38(4272)■64:7(4347)■69:26■109:22(2490)-PR-7:26■18:14(5218)-SONG-5:7(6481)-IS-51:9(2490)■53:5(2490)-JER-30:14(5221)■37:10(1856)■51:52-LA-2:12-EZE-26:15■28:23■30:24-JOE-2:8(1214)-ZEC-13:6(5221)■N.T.-LU-10:30(4127,2007)■20:12(5135)-AC-19:16(5135)-RE-13:3(4969)

WOUNDEDST-HAB-3:13(4272)

WOUNDETH-JOB-5:18(4272)

WOUNDING-GE-4:23(6482)

WOUNDS-all=4347&marked-2KI-8:29■9:15-2CH-22:6-JOB-9:17(6482)-PS-38:5(2250)■147:3(6094)-PR-18:8(3859)■23:29(6482)■26:22(3859)■27:6(6482)-IS-1:6(6482)-JER-6:7■30:17-ZEC-13:6■N.T.-LU-10:34(5134)

WOVE-2KI-23:7(707)

WOVEN-all=707-EX-28:32■39:22,27■N.T.-JOH-19:23(5307)

WRAP-IS-28:20(3664)-MIC-7:3(5686)

WRAPPED-GE-38:14(5968)-1SA-21:9(3874)-1KI-19:13(3874)-2KI-2:8(1563)-JOB-8:17(5440)■40:17(8276)-EZE-21:15(4593)-JON-2:5(2280)■N.T.-all=1794&marked-M’T-27:59-M’R-15:46(1750)-LU-2:7(4683),12(4683)■23:53-JOH-20:7

WRATH-all=639,a=5678,b=2534,c=7110&marked-GE-39:19■49:7a-EX-15:7(2740)■22:24■32:10,11,12-LE-10:6(7107)-NU-1:53c■11:33■16:46c■18:5c■25:11b-DE-9:7(7107),8(7107),22(7107)■11:17■29:23b,28b■32:27(3708)-JOS-9:20c■22:20c-1SA-28:18-2SA-11:20b-2KI-22:13b,17b■23:26-1CH-27:24c-2CH-12:7b,12■19:2c,10c■24:18c■28:11,13■29:8c,10■30:8■32:25c,26c■34:21b,25b■36:16b-EZR-5:12(7265)■7:23(7109)■8:22■10:14-NE-13:18(2740)-ES-1:18c■2:1b■3:5b■7:7b,10b-JOB-5:2(3708)■14:13■16:9■19:11,29b■20:23,28■21:20b,30a■32:2^{2},3,5■36:13,18b■40:11■42:7-PS-2:5,12■21:9■37:8b■38:1c■55:3■58:9(2740)■59:13b■76:10^{2}b■78:31,38b,49a■79:6b■85:3a■88:7b,16(2740)■89:46b■90:7b,9a,11a■95:11■102:10c■106:23b,40■110:5■124:3■138:7-PR-11:4a,23a■12:16(3708)■14:29,35a■15:1b■16:14b■19:12(2179),19b■21:14b,24a■24:18■27:3(3708),4b■29:8■30:33-EC-5:17c-IS-9:19a■10:6a■13:9a,13a■14:6a■16:6a■54:8c■60:10c-JER-7:29a■10:10c■18:20b■21:5c■32:37c■44:8(3707)■48:30a■50:13c-LA-2:2a■3:1a-EZE-7:12(2740),14(2740),19a■13:15b■21:31a■22:21a,31a■38:19a-HO-5:10a■13:11a-AM-1:11a-HAB-3:2(7267),8a-ZEP-1:15a,18a-ZEC-7:12c■8:14(7107)■N.T.-all=3709,a=2372&marked-M’T-3:7-LU-3:7■4:28a■21:23-JOH-3:36-AC-19:28a-RO-1:18■2:5^{2},8■4:15■5:9■9:22^{2}■12:19■13:4,5-GA-5:20a-EPH-2:3■4:26(3950),31a■5:6■6:4(3949)-COL-3:6,8a-1TH-1:10■2:16■5:9-1TI-2:8-HEB-3:11■4:3■11:27a-JAS-1:19,20-RE-6:16,17■11:18■12:12a■14:8a,10a,19a■15:1a,7a■16:1a,19■18:3a■19:15

WRATHFUL-PS-69:24(2740)-PR-15:18(2534)

WRATHS-2CO-12:20(2372)

WREATH-2CH-4:13(7639)

WREATHED-LA-1:14(8276)

WREATHEN-all=5688&marked-EX-28:14^{2},22,24,25■39:15,17,18-2KI-25:17^{2}(7639)

WREATHS-1KI-7:17(1434)-2CH-4:12(7639),13(7639)

WREST-all=5186&marked-EX-23:2,6-DE-16:19-PS-56:5(6087)■N.T.-2PE-3:16(4761)

WRESTLE-EPH-6:12(2076,3823)

WRESTLED-GE-30:8(6617)■32:24(79),25(79)

WRESTLINGS-GE-30:8(5319)

WRETCHED-RO-7:24(5005)-RE-3:17(5005)

WRETCHEDNESS-NU-11:15(7451)

WRING-LE-1:15(4454)■5:8(4454)-PS-75:8(4680)

WRINGED-J’G-6:38(4680)

WRINGING-PR-30:33(4330)

WRINKLE-EPH-5:27(4512)

WRINKLES-JOB-16:8(7059)

WRITE-all=3789&marked-EX-17:14■34:1,27-NU-5:23■17:2,3-DE-6:9■10:2■11:20■17:18■24:1,3■27:3,8■31:19-2CH-26:22-EZR-5:10(3790)-NE-9:38-ES-8:8-PR-3:3■7:3-IS-8:1■10:1,19■30:8-JER-22:30■30:2■31:33■36:2,17,28-EZE-24:2■37:16^{2}■43:11-HAB-2:2■N.T.-all=1125&marked-M’R-10:4-LU-1:3■16:6,7-JOH-1:45■19:21-AC-15:20(1989)■25:26^{2}-1CO-4:14■14:37-2CO-1:13■2:9■9:1■13:2,10-GA-1:20-PH’P-3:1-1TH-4:9■5:1-2TH-3:17-1TI-3:14-HEB-8:10(1924)■10:16(1924)-2PE-3:1-1JO-1:4■2:1,7,8,12,13^{3}-2JO-12,12sup-3JO-13^{2}-JUDE-3^{2}-RE-1:11,19■2:1,8,12,18■3:1,7,12,12sup,14■10:4^{2}■14:13■19:9■21:5

WRITER-J’G-5:14(5608)-PS-45:1(5608)

WRITER’S-EZE-9:2(5608),3(5608)

WRITEST-JOB-13:26(3789)-EZE-37:20(3789)

WRITETH-PS-87:6(3789)

WRITING-all=3791,a=3792&marked-EX-32:16(4385)■39:30(4385)-DE-10:4(4385)■31:24(3789)-1CH-28:19-2CH-2:11■21:12(4385)■35:4,4(4385)■36:22(4385)-EZR-1:1(4385)■4:7-ES-1:22■3:12,14■4:8■8:8,9^{2},13■9:27-IS-38:9(4385)-EZR-13:9-DA-5:7a,8a,15a,16a,17a,24a,25a■6:8a,9a,10a■N.T.-M’T-19:7(975)-LU-1:63(4093)-JOH-19:19(1125)

WRITINGS-JOH-5:47(1121)

WRITTEN-all=3789&marked-EX-24:12■31:18■32:15^{2},32-NU-11:26-DE-9:10,10sup■28:58,61■29:20,21,27■30:10-JOS-1:8■8:31,34■10:13■23:6-2SA-1:18-1KI-2:3■11:41■14:19,29■15:7,23,31■16:5,14,20,27■21:11■22:39,45-2KI-1:18■8:23■10:34■12:19■13:8,12■14:6,15,18,28■15:6,11,15,21,26,31,36■16:19■20:20■21:17,25■22:13■23:3,21,24,28■24:5-1CH-4:41■9:1■16:40■29:29-2CH-9:29■12:15■13:22■16:11■20:34■23:18■24:27■25:4,26■27:7■28:26■30:5,18■31:3■32:32■33:19■34:21,24,31■35:12,25,26,27■36:8-EZR-3:2,4■4:7■5:7(3790)■6:2(3790),18(3792)■8:34-NE-6:6■7:5■8:14,15■10:34,36■12:23■13:1-ES-1:19■2:23■3:9,12^{2}■6:2■8:5,8,9■9:23,32■10:2-JOB-19:23■31:35-PS-40:7■69:28■102:18■139:16■149:9-PR-22:20-EC-12:10-IS-4:3■65:6-JER-17:1,13■25:13■36:6,29■45:1■51:60-EZE-2:10^{2}■13:9-DA-5:24(7560),25(7560)■9:11,13■12:1-HO-8:12-MAL-3:16■N.T.-all=1125&marked-M’T-2:5■4:4,6,7,10■11:10■21:13■26:24,31■27:37-M’R-1:2■7:6■9:12■9:13■11:17■14:21,27■15:26(1924)-LU-2:23■3:4■4:4,8,10,17■7:27■10:20,26■18:31■19:46■20:17■21:22■22:37■23:38■24:44,46-JOH-2:17■6:31,45■8:17■10:34■12:14,16■15:25■19:20,22■20:30,31■21:25^{2}-AC-1:20■7:42■13:29,33■15:15■21:25(1989)■23:5■24:14-RO-1:17■2:15(1123),24■3:4,10■4:17,23■8:36■9:13,33■10:15■11:8,26■12:19■14:11■15:3,4^{2}(4270),9,15,21,subscr.-1CO-1:19,31■2:9■3:19■4:6■5:11■9:9,10,15■10:7,11■14:21■15:45,54,subscr.-2CO-3:2(1449),3(1449),7(1722,1121)■4:13■8:15■9:9,subscr.-GA-3:10^{2},13■4:22,27■6:11,subscr.-EPH-subscr.-PH’P-subscr.-COL-subscr.-1TH-subscr.-2TH-subscr.-1TI-subscr.-2TI-subscr.-TIT-subscr.-PH’M-19,subscr.-HEB-10:7■12:23(583)■13:22(1989)subscr.-1PE-1:16■5:12-2PE-3:15-1JO-2:14^{2},21,26■5:13-RE-1:3■2:17■5:1■13:8■14:1■17:5,8■19:12,16■20:12,15■21:12(1924),27■22:18,19

WRONG-all=2555&marked-GE-16:5-EX-2:13(7563)-DE-19:16(5627)-J’G-11:27(7451)-1CH-12:17■16:21(6231)-ES-1:16(5753)-JOB-19:7-PS-105:14(6231)-JER-22:3(3238),13(3808,4941)-LA-3:59(5792)-HAB-1:4(6127)■N.T.-all=91&marked-M’T-20:13-AC-7:24,26,27■18:14(92)■25:10-1CO-6:7,8-2CO-7:12^{2}■12:13(98)-COL-3:25^{2}

WRONGED-2CO-7:2(91)-PH’M-18(91)

WRONGETH-PR-8:36(2554)

WRONGFULLY-all=8267&marked-JOB-21:27(2554)-PS-35:19■38:19■69:4■119:86-EZE-22:29(3808,4941)■N.T.-1PE-2:19(95)

WROTE-all=3789&marked-EX-24:4■34:28■39:30-NU-33:2-DE-4:13■5:22■10:4■31:9,22-JOS-8:32^{2}■24:26-1SA-10:25-2SA-11:14,15-1KI-21:8,9-2KI-10:1,6■17:37-1CH-24:6-2CH-30:1■32:17-EZR-4:6,7,8(3790)-ES-8:5,10■9:20,29-JER-36:4,18,27,32■51:60-DA-5:5^{2}(3790)■6:25(3790)■7:1(3790)■N.T.-all=1125&marked-M’R-10:5■12:19-LU-1:63■20:28-JOH-5:46■8:6,8■19:19■21:24-AC-15:23■18:27■23:25-RO-16:22-1CO-5:9■7:1-2CO-2:3,4■7:12-EPH-3:3(4270)-PH’M-21-2JO-5-3JO-9

WROTH-all=7107,a=2734&marked-GE-4:5a,6a■31:36a■34:7a■40:2■41:10-EX-16:20-NU-16:15a,22■31:14-DE-1:34■3:26(5674)■9:19-JOS-22:18-1SA-18:8a■20:7a■29:4-2SA-3:8a■13:21a■22:8a-2KI-5:11■13:19-2CH-16:10(3707)■26:19^{2}(2196)■28:9(2534)-NE-4:1a,7a-ES-1:12■2:21-PS-18:7a■78:21(5674),59(5674),62(5674)■89:38(5674)-IS-28:21(7264)■47:6■54:9■57:16,17^{2}■64:5,9-JER-37:15-LA-5:22■N.T.-all=3710&marked-M’T-2:16(2373)■18:34■22:7-RE-12:17

WROUGHT-all=6213&marked-GE-34:7-EX-10:2(5953)■26:36(4639)■36:1,4,8■39:6-LE-20:12-NU-23:23(6466)■31:51(4639)-DE-13:14■17:2,4■21:3(5647)■22:21■31:18-JOS-7:15-J’G-20:10-RU-2:19^{2}-1SA-6:6(5953)■11:13■14:45^{2}■19:5-2SA-18:13■23:10,12-1KI-5:16■7:14,26(4639)■9:23■16:20(7194),25-2KI-3:2■12:11■17:11■21:6-1CH-4:21(5656)■22:2(1496)-2CH-3:14(5927)■21:6■24:12(2790),13■31:20■33:6■34:10,13-NE-4:16,17■6:16■9:18,26-JOB-12:9■36:23(6466)-PS-31:19(6466)■45:13(4865)■68:28(6466)■78:43(7760)■139:15(7551)-EC-2:11,17-IS-26:12(6466),18■41:4(6466)-JER-11:15■18:3-EZE-20:9,14,22,44■29:20-DA-4:2(5648)-JON-1:11(1980),13(1980)-ZEP-2:3(6466)■N.T.-all=2038&marked-M’T-20:12(4160)■26:10-M’R-6:2(1096)■14:6-JOH-3:21-AC-5:12(1096)■15:12(4160)■18:3■19:11(4160)■21:19(4160)-RO-7:8(2716)■15:18(2716)-2CO-5:5(2716)■7:11(2716)■12:12(2716)-GA-2:8(1754)-EPH-1:20(1754)-2TH-3:8-HEB-11:33-JAS-2:22(4903)-1PE-4:3(2716)-2JO-8-RE-19:20(4160)

WROUGHTEST-RU-2:19(6213)

WRUNG-all=4680-LE-1:15■5:9-PS-73:10-IS-51:17

Y

YARN-all=4723-1KI-10:28^{2}-2CH-1:16^{2}

YEA-all=1571,a=637&marked-GE-3:1a(3588)■20:6■27:33-DE-33:3a-J’G-5:29a-1SA-15:20(834)■21:5a■24:11a-2SA-19:30a-2KI-2:3,5■16:3-NE-5:15,16■9:18a-JOB-6:27a■15:4a■18:5■19:18■21:7■28:27■30:2,8■34:12a-PS-8:7■16:6a■18:48a■23:4■25:3■41:9■44:22(3588)■58:2a■68:16a,18a■84:2,3■85:12■102:13(3588)■118:11■137:1■139:12-PR-2:3

(3588)■16:4-EC-2:23■4:8,8sup■6:6(432)■7:18■8:17■9:3■10:3-SONG-1:16a■8:1-IS-1:15■5:10(3588)■14:8■26:8a,9a,11a■30:33■32:13(3588)■40:24[3]a■41:10a,23a,26[3]a■42:13a■43:7a,13■44:12,15[2]a,16a,19a■45:21a■46:6a,7a,11a■47:3■48:8[2],15a■49:15■66:3-JER-2:37■5:28■8:7■12:2[2],6■14:5(3588,1571),18(3588,1571)■23:11■27:21(3588)■31:19■51:44-LA-1:8-EZE-16:52-DA-11:22-HO-4:3■7:9■8:10■9:12(3588),16■12:11-JO-1:18■2:3■3:4-OB-13-HAB-2:5a-MAL-2:2■3:15[2]■N.T.-all=3483,a=235&marked-M'T-5:37■9:28■11:9■13:51■21:16■26:60(2532)-LU-2:35(1161)■7:26■11:28(3304)■12:5■14:26(2089)■24:22a-JOH-11:27■16:2a,32(2532)■21:15,16-AC-3:16(2532),24(1161)■5:8■7:43(2532)■20:34(1161)■22:27-RO-3:4(1161),31a■8:34(1161)■14:4a■15:20a-1CO-2:10(2532)■4:3a■9:16(1161)■15:15(1161)■16:6(2228)-2CO-1:17,18,19,20■5:16(1167)■7:11[4]a-GA-4:17a-PH'P-1:18a■2:17a■3:8a-2TI-3:12(1161)-PH'M-20-HEB-11:36(1161)-JAS-2:18a■5:12-1PE-5:5(1161)-2PE-1:13(1161)-3JO-12(1161)-RE-14:13

YEAR-all=8141&marked-GE-7:11■8:13■14:4,5■17:21■26:12■47:17,18[2]-EX-12:2,5■13:10(3117)■23:14,16,17,29■29:38■30:10[2]■34:23,24■40:17-LE-9:3■12:6■14:10■16:34■19:24,25■23:12,18,19,41■25:4,5,10,11,13,20,21,22[2],28,29,29(3117),30,40,50[2],52,54■27:17,18,23,24-NU-1:1■6:12,14[2]■7:15,17,21,23,27,29,33,35,39,41,45,47,51,53,57,59,63,65,69,71,75,77,81,83,87,88■9:1,22(3117)■10:11■14:34■15:27■28:3,9,11,14,19,27■29:2,8,13,17,20,23,26,29,32,36■33:38-DE-1:3■11:12[2]■14:22,28■15:9,12,20■16:16■24:5■26:12[2]■31:10-JOS-5:12-J'G-10:8■11:40■17:10(3117)-1SA-1:7■2:19(3117)■7:16■13:1-2SA-11:1■21:1-1KI-4:7■5:11■6:1[2],37,38■9:25■10:14,25■14:25■15:1,9,25,28,33■16:8,10,15,23,29■18:1■20:22,26■22:2,41,51-2KI-1:17■3:1■8:16,25,26■9:29■11:4■12:1,6■13:1,10,20■14:1,23■15:1,8,13,17,23,27,30,32■16:1■17:1,4,6■18:1,9[2],10[2],13■19:29[3]■22:3■23:23■24:12■25:1,2,8,27[2]-1CH-20:1■26:31■27:1-2CH-3:2■8:13■9:13,24■12:2■13:1■15:10,19■16:1,12,13■17:7■22:2■23:1■24:5,23■27:5[2]■29:3■34:3[2],8■35:19■36:10,22-EZR-1:1■3:8■4:24(8140)■5:13(8140)■6:3(8140),15(8140)■7:7,8-NE-1:1■2:1■5:14[2]■10:31,34,35■13:6-ES-1:3■2:16■3:7■9:27-JOB-3:6-PS-65:11-IS-6:1■14:28■20:1■21:16■29:1■34:8■36:1■37:30[3]■61:2■63:4-JER-1:2,3■11:23■17:8■23:12■25:1[2],3[2]■28:1[2],16,17■32:1[2]■36:1,9■39:1,2■45:1■46:2■48:44■51:46[2],59■52:4,5,12,28,29,30,31[2]-EZE-1:1,2■4:6■8:1■20:1■24:1■26:1■29:1,17■30:20■31:1■32:1,17■33:21■40:1[3]■46:13,17-DA-1:1,21■2:1■7:1(8140)■8:1■9:1,2■10:1■11:1-MIC-6:6-HAG-1:1,15■2:10-ZEC-1:1,7■7:1■14:16■N.T.-all=1763&marked-LU-2:41(2094)■3:1(2094)■4:19■13:8(2094)-JOH-11:49,51■18:13-AC-11:26■18:11-2CO-8:10(4070)■9:2(4070)-HEB-9:7,25■10:1,3-JAS-4:13-RE-9:15

YEARLY-all=3117&marked-LE-25:53(8141)-J'G-11:40■21:19-1SA-1:3,21■2:19■20:6-NE-10:32(8141)-ES-9:21(8141)

YEARN-GE-43:30(3648)

YEARNED-1KI-3:26(3648)

YEAR'S-EX-34:22(8141)-2SA-14:26(3117)

YEARS-all=8141&marked-GE-1:14■5:3,4,5,6,7,8,9,10,11,12,13,14,15,16,17,18,19,20,21,22,23,25,26,27,28,30,31,32■6:3■7:6■9:28,29■11:10[2],11,12,13,14,15,16,17,18,19,20,21,22,23,24,25,26,32■12:4■14:4■15:9[3](8027),13■16:3,16■17:1,17[2],24,25■21:5■23:1[2]■25:7[2],17[2],20,26■26:34■29:18,20,27,30■31:38,41[3]■35:28■37:2■41:1,26[2],27[2],29,30,34,35,36,46,47,48,50,53,54■45:6[2],11■47:9[4],28[2]■50:22,26-EX-6:16[2],18[2],20[2]■7:7[2]■12:40,41■16:35■21:2■23:10■30:14■38:26-LE-19:23■25:3[2],8[4],15[2],16[3],21,27,50,51,52[2],54■27:3,5,6,7,18-NU-1:3,18,20,22,24,26,28,30,32,34,36,38,40,42,45■4:3,23,30,35,39,43,47■8:24,25■13:22■14:29,33,34■26:2,4■32:11,13■33:29-DE-2:7,14■8:2,4■14:28■15:1,12,18■29:5■31:2,10■32:7■34:7-JOS-5:6■13:1[2]■14:7,10[2]■24:29-J'G-2:8■3:8,11,14,30■4:3■5:31■6:1,25■8:28■9:22■10:2,3,8■11:26■12:7,9,11,14■13:1■15:20■16:31-RU-1:4-1SA-4:15,18■7:3■13:1■29:3-2SA-2:10[2],11■4:4■5:4[2],5[2]■13:23,38■14:28■15:7■19:32,35■21:1■24:13-1KI-1:1(3117)■2:11[3],39■6:38■7:1■9:10■10:22■11:42■14:20,21[2]■15:2,10,25,33■16:8,23[2],29■17:1■22:1,42[2],51-2KI-3:1■8:1,2,17[2],26■10:36■11:3,21■12:1■13:1,10■14:2[2],17,21,23■15:2[2],17,23,27,33[2]■16:2[2]■17:1,5■18:2[2],10■20:6■21:1[2],19[2]■22:1[2]■23:31,36[2]■24:1,8,18[2]-1CH-2:21■3:4[2]■23:3,24,27■27:23■29:27[3]-2CH-8:1■9:21,30■11:17[2]■12:13[2]■13:2■14:1,6■18:2■20:31[2]■21:5[2],19(3117),20sup,20■22:2,12■24:1[2],15■25:1[2],5,25■26:1,3[2]■27:1[2],8[2]■28:1[2]■29:1[2]■31:16,17■33:1[2],21[2]■34:1[2]■36:2,5[2],9,11[2],21-EZR-3:8■5:11(8140)-NE-5:14■9:21,30-JOB-10:5■15:20■16:22■32:7■36:11,26■42:16-PS-31:10■61:6■77:5,10■78:33■90:4,9,10[2],15■95:10■102:24,27-PR-4:10■5:9■9:11■10:27-EC-6:3[2],6■11:8■12:1-IS-7:8■15:5■16:14■20:3■21:16■23:15[2],17■32:10■38:5,10,15■65:20[2]-JER-25:11,12■28:3,11■29:10■34:14[2]■52:1[2]-EZE-4:5■22:4■29:11,12,13■38:8,17■39:9-DA-1:5■5:31(8140)■9:2[2]■11:6,8,13-JOE-2:2,25-AM-1:1■2:10■4:4(3117)■5:25-HAB-3:2[2]-ZEC-1:12■7:3,5-MAL-3:4■N.T.-all=2094&marked-M'T-2:16(1332)■9:20-M'R-5:25,42-LU-1:7(2250),18(2250)■2:36,37,42■3:23■4:25■8:42,43■12:19■13:7,11,16■15:29-JOH-2:20■5:5■8:57-AC-4:22■7:6,23(5063),30,36,42■9:33■13:18(5063),20,21■19:10■20:31(5148)■24:10,17,27(1333)■28:30(1333)-RO-4:19(1541)■15:23-2CO-12:2-GA-1:18■2:1■3:17■4:10(1763)-1TI-5:9-HEB-1:12■3:9,17■11:24(1096,3173)-JAS-5:17(1763)-2PE-3:8[2]-RE-20:2,3,4,5,6,7

YEARS'-2KI-8:3(8141)-1CH-21:12(8141)

YELL-JER-51:38(5286)

YELLED-JER-2:15(5141,6963)

YELLOW-all=6669&marked-LE-13:30,32,36-PS-68:13(3422)

YES-all=3483&marked-M'T-17:25-M'R-7:28-RO-3:29■10:18(3304)

YESTERDAY-all=8543&marked-EX-5:14-1SA-20:27-2SA-15:20-2KI-9:26(570)-JOB-8:9-PS-90:4(865)■N.T.-all=5504-JOH-4:52-AC-7:28-HEB-13:8

YESTERNIGHT-all=570-GE-19:34■31:29,42

YET-all=5750,a=389,b=3588,c=1571&marked-GE-7:4■15:16(5704,2008)■18:22,29,32a■20:12c■21:26c■27:30a■29:7,9,27,30■31:14■37:5,8,9■38:5■40:13,19■43:6,27,28■44:14■45:3,6,11,26,28■46:30■48:7-EX-4:18■5:11b■9:17,30(2962)■10:7(2962)■11:1■36:3-LE-11:21a■25:51■26:18(5704),44(637)-NU-11:33■19:13■22:15,20a■32:14,15-DE-12:9(5704,6258)■31:27■32:52b-JOS-3:4■14:11-J'G-2:10c,17c■6:24■7:4■8:20■15:7b(518)■19:19c■20:28-RU-1:11-1SA-3:6,7[2](2962)■8:9b■10:22■12:20■13:7■16:11■20:14■23:4-2SA-1:9■3:35■5:13,22■6:22■7:19■9:1,3[2]■12:22■18:22■19:35■21:15,20■23:5b-1KI-1:14,22,42■12:2,5■20:6b,32b■22:8b,43b-2KI-6:33■13:23(5704,6258)■14:3(7535),4-1CH-12:1■14:13■20:6-2CH-1:11c■6:16(7535)■14:7■16:12c■18:7■20:33■27:2■30:18b■32:16■34:3-NE-2:16(5704,3651)-ES-6:14-JOB-5:7b■6:10■8:12■9:31(227)■29:5■36:2-PS-37:10■42:5,11■43:5■78:17,30■129:2c■141:5-PR-8:26(5704)■9:9■11:24■19:19■31:15-EC-4:2(5728),3(5728)■6:7c■7:28■8:12b■9:11[3]c-IS-6:13■10:25,32■14:1,15a■28:4■29:17■56:8■65:24-JER-2:9■9:20b■12:1a■15:9■22:24b■30:11a■31:5,23,39■33:1■34:4a■40:5■51:33-LA-4:17-EZE-7:13■8:6,13,15■16:29c■20:27■28:9(559)■29:13b■36:37-DA-4:23(1297)■5:17(1297)■10:14■11:2,27,35-HO-1:4■3:1■4:4a■11:12■12:8a,9-AM-4:7-JON-2:4a■3:4■4:2(5704)-MIC-1:15■6:10-NA-3:10c-HAB-2:3-HAG-2:6,19,19(5704)-ZEC-1:17[4]■8:4,20■11:15■13:3■N.T.-all=2089,a=1161,b=3768,c=235&marked-12:46■13:21a■15:16(188),17b,27(1063)■16:9b■17:5■19:20■24:6b,32(2236)■26:35(3364),47■27:63-M'R-5:35■7:28(1063)■8:17b,17■12:6■13:7b,28(2236)■14:29c,43■15:5(3765)-LU-3:20(2596)■8:49■9:42■11:8(1065)■14:22,32■15:20■18:5(1065),22■22:37,47,60■24:6,41,44-JOH-2:4b■3:24b■4:27(3305),35■7:6b,8[2]b,30b,33,39b,39(3764)■8:20b,57(2532)■11:30b■12:35■13:33■14:19■16:12■19:41(3764)■20:1,5(3305),9(3764),17b■21:23(2532)-AC-7:5■8:16b■9:1■10:44■18:18-RO-3:7■5:6,7(1063),8■9:11(3380),19■16:19a-1CO-2:6a,15a■3:2,3,15a■4:4c,15c■5:10(2532)■7:25a■8:2(3764)■9:2c■12:20a,31■14:19c■15:10a,17-2CO-1:10,23(3765)■4:8c,16c■5:16c■6:10a.10■9:3a■11:6c,16(2579)■12:5a■13:4c-GA-1:10■2:20(3765)■3:4(2596)■5:11[2]-PH'P-1:9,22(2532)■2:25(1161)-COL-1:21a■2:5c-2TH-2:5■3:15(2532)-HEB-2:8b■7:10,15■9:8[2]■10:37■11:4,7(3369)■12:4b,26,27-JAS-2:11a■4:2a-1PE-1:8a■4:16a-1JO-3:2b-JUDE-9a-RE-6:11■8:13(3195)■17:8(2589),10b,12b

YIELD-all=5414&marked-GE-4:12■49:20-LE-19:25(3254)■25:19■26:4[2],20[2]-DE-11:17-2CH-30:8(5414,3027)-PS-67:6■85:12■107:37(6213)-PR-7:21(5186)-IS-5:10[2](6213)-EZE-34:27[2]■36:8(5375)-HO-8:7[2](6213)-JOE-2:22-HAB-3:17(6213)■N.T.-all=3936&marked-M'R-4:8(1325)-AC-23:21(3982)-RO-6:13[2],16,19-JAS-3:12(4160)

YIELDED-GE-49:33(1478)-NU-17:8(1580)-DA-3:28(3052)■N.T.-M'T-27:50(863)-M'R-4:7(1325)-AC-5:10(1634)-RO-6:19(3936)-RE-22:2(591)

YIELDETH-NE-9:37(7235)-PR-12:12(5414)■N.T.-HEB-12:11(591)

YIELDING-all=2232&marked-GE-1:11,11(6213),12,12(6213),29-EC-10:4(4832)-JER-17:8(6213)

YOKE-all=5923&marked-GE-27:40-LE-26:13-NU-19:2-DE-21:3■28:48-1SA-6:7■11:7(6776)■14:14(6776)-1KI-12:4[2],9,10,11[2],14[2]■19:19(6776),(6776)-2CH-10:4[2],9,10,11[2],14-JOB-1:3(6776)■42:12(6776)-IS-9:4■10:27[2]■14:25■47:6■58:6(4133),9(4133)-JER-2:20■5:5■27:8,11,12■28:2,4,10(4133),11,12(4133),14■30:8■51:23(6776)-LA-1:14■3:27-EZE-34:27-HO-11:4-NA-1:13(4132)■N.T.-all=2218&marked-M'T-11:29,30-LU-14:19(2201)-AC-15:10-GA-5:1-1TI-6:1

YOKED-2CO-6:14(2086)

YOKEFELLOW-PH'P-4:3(4805)

YOKES-all=4133-JER-27:2■28:13[2]-EZE-30:18

YONDER-GE-22:5(5704,3541)-NU-16:37(1973)■23:15(3541)■32:19(5676)■N.T.-M'T-17:20(1563)■26:36(1563)

YOUNG-all=5288,a=970,b=3715,c=1241,d=1121&marked-GE-4:23(3206)■14:24■15:9(1469)■18:7■19:4■22:3,5,19■33:13(5763)■34:19■41:12-EX-10:9■24:5■29:1d,c■33:11-LE-1:14d■4:3d,c,14d,c■5:7d,11d■9:2d,c■12:6d,8d■14:22d,30d■15:14d,29d■16:3d,c■22:28d■

23:18d,c-NU-6:10d■7:15d,c,21d,c,27d,c,33d,c,39d,c,45d,c,51d,c,57d,c,63d,c,69d,c,75d,c,81d,c■8:8^{2}d,c■11:27,28(979)■15:24d,c■28:11d,c,19d,c,27d,c■29:2d,c,8d,c,13d,c,17d,c-DE-22:6^2(667),6d,7d■28:50,57(7988)■32:11(1469),25a-JOS-6:21,23-J'G-6:25(6499)■8:14■9:54^2■14:5b,10a■17:7,11,12■18:3,15■19:19■21:12(5291)-RU-2:9^2,15,21■3:10a■4:12(5291)-1SA-1:24■2:17■8:16a■9:2a,11(5291)■14:1,6■17:58■20:22(5958)■21:4,5■25:5^2,8^2,9,12,14,25,27■26:22■30:13,17-2SA-1:5,6,13,15■2:14,21■4:12■9:12(6996)■13:32,34■14:21■16:2■18:5,12,15,29,32^2-1KI-1:2(5291)■11:28■12:8(3206),10(3206),14(3206)■20:14,15,17,19-2KI-4:22■5:22■6:17■8:12a■9:4^2-1CH-12:28■22:5■29:1-2CH-10:8(3206),10(3206),14(3206)■13:7,9d,c■34:3■36:17^{2}a-EZR-6:9(1123)-ES-2:2(5291),3(5291)■3:13■8:10d-JOB-1:19■4:10b■29:8■32:6(6810,3117)■38:39b,41(3206)■39:3(3206),4d,16d,30(667)-PS-7:12b■29:6d■34:10b■37:25■58:6b■78:63a,71(5763)■84:3(667)■91:13b■104:21b■119:9■147:9d■148:12a-PR-1:4■7:7■20:29a■30:17d-EC-11:9a-SONG-2:9(6082),17(6082)■4:5(6082)■7:3(6082)■8:14(6082)-IS-5:29b■7:21c■9:17a■11:6b,7(3206)■13:18■20:4■23:4a■30:6(3833)■31:4b,8a■40:11(5763),30(5288)a■62:5a-JER-2:15b■6:11a■9:21a■11:22a■15:8a■18:21a■31:12d,13a■48:15a■49:26a■50:30a■51:3a,22,22a-LA-1:15a,18a■2:21,21a■4:3(1482)■5:13a,14a-EZE-9:6a■17:4(3242),22(3127)■19:2b,3b,5b,6b■23:6a,12a,23a■30:17a■32:2b■38:13b■41:19b■43:19d,c,23d,c,25d,c■45:18d,c■46:6d,c-HO-5:14b-JOE-2:28a-AM-2:11a■3:4b■4:10a■8:13a-MIC-5:8b-NA-2:11b,13b-ZEC-2:4■9:17a■11:3b,16■N.T.-all=3495,a=3813&marked-M'T-2:8a,9a,11a,13^{2}a,14a,20^{2}a,21a■19:20,22-M'R-7:25(2365)■10:13a■14:51^2■16:5-LU-2:24(3502)■7:14-JOH-12:14(3678)■21:18(3501)-AC-2:17■5:6(3501),10■7:19(1025),58(3494)■20:9(3494),12(3816)■23:17(3494),18(3494),22(3494)-TIT-2:4(3501),6(2501)-1JO-2:13,14

YOUNGER-all=6996&marked-GE-9:24■19:31(6810),34(6810),35(6810),38(6810)■25:23(6810)■27:15,42■29:16,18,26(6810)■43:29■48:14(6810),19-J'G-1:13■3:9■15:2-1SA-14:49-1CH-24:31-JOB-30:1(6810,3117)-EZE-16:46,61■N.T.-all=3501&marked-LU-15:12,13■22:26-RO-9:12(1640)-1TI-5:1,2,11,14-1PE-5:5

YOUNGEST-all=6996&marked-GE-42:13,15,20,32,34■43:33(6810)■44:2,12,23,26^2-JOS-6:26(6810)-J'G-9:5-1SA-16:11■17:14-1KI-16:34(6810)-2CH-21:17■22:1

YOUR-LE-11:43(5315)■N.T.-all=5216,a=3588&marked-M'T-5:12,15,16^2,20,37,44,45,47,48■6:1^2,8,14,15,21^2,25^2,26,32■7:6,11^2■9:4,11,29■10:9,13^2,14^2,20,29,30■11:29■12:27^2■13:16^2■15:3,6■17:20,24■18:14,35■19:8^2■20:26,27■23:8,9^2,10,11,32,34,38■24:20,42■25:8-M'R-2:8■6:11■7:9,13■8:17■10:5,43■11:25^2,26^2■13:18-LU-3:14■4:21■5:4,22■6:22,23,24,27,35^2,36,38■8:25■9:3a,5,44■10:6,11,20■11:13,13a,19^2,39,46,47,48■12:7,22,30,32,34^2,35,35a■13:35■16:11(5213),12(5212),15■21:14,15(5213),18,19,28^2,30(1438),34■22:53■23:28■24:38-JOH-4:35■6:49,58■7:6(5212)■8:17(5212),21,24^2,38,41,42,44,54,56■9:19,41■10:34■11:15(5209)■12:30(5209)■13:14a,14■14:1,26(5209),27■15:11,16■16:6,20,22^2,24■18:31■19:14,8,15■20:17^2-AC-2:17^3,39■3:17,19,22^2■5:28■7:37^2,43,51,52■13:41■15:24■17:23,28(2596,5209)■18:6(546),15(2596,5209)■19:37■20:30■24:22(2596,5209)■27:34(5212)-RO-1:8■6:12,13^2,19^3,22■8:11■11:25(3844,1438),28(5209),31(5212)■12:1,2,16■14:16■15:24,30a■16:19,19(5213),20-1CO-1:4,26■2:5■4:6(5209)■5:6■6:5(5213),15,19(1438),19,20^2■7:5,14,35■9:11■14:34■15:14,17^2,31(5212),34(5213),58■16:3,14,17-2CO-1:6^2,14,24^2■2:10(5209)■4:5,15(5209)■5:11,13(5213)■6:12■7:7^2,13(5213)■8:7(5209),8(5212),9,14^2,19,24^2■9:2^2,5,10^2,10sup,13,13a■10:6,8,15■11:3■12:19■13:5^2(1438),9-GA-4:6,15,16■6:13(5212),18(5212)-EPH-1:13,15(5209),18■3:17■4:4,23,26,29■5:19,22a,25(1438)■6:1,4,5sup,5,9,14,15a,22-PH'P-1:5,9,19,25,26,27sup,27,28a■2:12(1438),17,19,20,25,30■4:5,6,7,10a,17,19-COL-1:4,8,21a■2:5^2,13^2■3:3,5,8,15,16,18(2398),19a,20a,21,22a■4:1a,6,8^2-1TH-1:3(5209),4,5(5209),8■2:14(2398),17■3:2,5,6,7,9(5209),10^2,13■4:3,11^2(2398)■5:23a-2TH-1:3,4^2■2:17■3:5-PH'M-22,25-HEB-3:8,9,15■4:7■6:10■9:14■10:34,35■12:3,13■13:5a,17-JAS-1:3,21,22(1438)■2:2■3:14■4:1,3,9,9a,14,16■5:1,2^2,3^2,4,5,8,12,12a,16a-1PE-1:7,9,13,14,17,18^2,21,22■2:12,12a,16a,18a,25■3:1a,2,7,15,16■4:14(5209)■5:7,8,9-2PE-1:5,10,19■3:1,17a-1JO-1:4■2:12a-JUDE-12,20-RE-1:9■2:23

YOURS-all=5216&marked-LU-6:20(5212)-JOH-15:20(5212)-1CO-3:21,22■8:9■16:18-2CO-12:14

YOURSELVES-all=5315&marked-GE-45:5(5869)-EX-32:29(3027)-LE-11:43,44^2-NU-31:3(853)-DE-4:15-JOS-23:11-J'G-15:12(859)-2CH-29:31(3027)■30:8(3027)-JER-17:21■37:9■N.T.-all=1438&marked-M'T-3:9■6:19(5213),20(5213)■16:8■23:15(5216),31■25:9-M'R-6:31(5210,846)■9:33,50■13:9-LU-3:8■11:46(846),52(846)■12:33,57■16:9,15■17:3,14■21:34■22:17■23:28-JOH-3:28(5210,846)■6:43(240)■16:19(240)-AC-2:22(846)■5:35■13:46■15:29■20:28,34(846)■6:11,13,16■12:19-1CO-5:13(5216,846)■11:13(5213,846)-2CO-7:11■13:5-EPH-2:8(5216)■5:19-1TH-2:1(846)■3:3(846)■4:9(846)■5:2(846),11(240)■5:13,15-2TH-3:7(846)-HEB-10:34■13:3(846),17(5216)-JAS-2:4-1PE-4:8-1JO-5:21-2JO-8-JUDE-20,21

YOUTH-all=5271&marked-GE-8:21■43:33(6812)■46:34-LE-22:13-NU-30:3,16-J'G-8:20^2(5288)-1SA-17:33(5288),33,42(5288),55(5288)-2SA-19:7-1KI-18:12-JOB-13:26■20:11(5934)■29:4(2779)■30:12(6526)■31:18■33:25(5934)■36:14(5290)-PS-25:7■71:5,17■88:15(5290)■89:45(5934)■103:5■110:3(3208)■127:4■129:1,2■144:12-PR-2:17■5:18-EC-11:9(3208),9(979),10(7839)■12:1(979)-IS-47:12,15■54:4(5934),6-JER-2:2■3:4,24,25■22:21■31:19■32:30■48:11-LA-3:27-EZE-4:14■16:22,43,60■23:3,8,19,21^2-HO-2:15-JOE-1:8-ZEC-13:5-MAL-2:14,15■N.T.-all=3503-M'T-19:20-M'R-10:20-LU-18:21-AC-26:4-1TI-4:12

YOUTHFUL-2TI-2:22(3512)

YOUTHS-PR-7:7(1121)-IS-40:30(5288)

YOU-WARD-2CO-1:12(4314,5209)■13:3(1519,5209)-EPH-3:2(1519,5209)

Z

ZAIN-supplied-PS-119:49t

ZEAL-all=7068&marked-2SA-21:2(7065)-2KI-10:16■19:31-PS-69:9■119:139-IS-9:7■37:32■59:17■63:15-EZE-5:13■N.T.-all=2205-JOH-2:17-RO-10:2-2CO-7:11■9:2-PH'P-3:6-COL-4:13

ZEALOUS-NU-25:11(7605),13(7605)■N.T.-all=2207&marked-AC-21:20■22:3-1CO-14:12-GA-1:14-TIT-2:14-RE-3:19(2206)

ZEALOUSLY-GA-4:17(2206),18(2206)

NOTES

APPENDIX TO THE MAIN CONCORDANCE

Giving the occurances of the persons, places and races as well as the 49 words which are seldom looked up

A

A-all supplied

AARON-all=175-EX-4:14,27,28,29,30■5:1,4,20■6:13,20,23,26,27■7:1,2,6,7,8,9,10^{2},19,20■8:5,6,8,12,16,17,25■9:8,27■10:3,8,16■11:10■12:1,28,31,43,50■15:20■16:2,6,9,10,33,34■17:10,12■18:12■19:24■24:1,9,14■27:21■28:1^{2},2,4,12,29,30,35,38,41,43■29:4,5,9^{2},10,15,19,20,21,24,27,29,32,35,44■30:7,8,10,19,30■31:10■32:1,2,3,5^{2},21,22,25,35■34:30,31■35:19■38:21■39:1,27,41■40:12,13,31-LE-1:7■3:13■6:9,14,16,18,20,25■7:10,33,34,35■8:2,6,14,18,22,30^{2},31^{2},36■9:1,2,7,8,9,21,22,23■10:1,3^{2},4,6,8,12,16,19■11:1■13:1,2■14:33■15:1■16:1,2,3,6,8,9,11,21,23■17:2■21:1,17,21,24■22:2,4,18■24:3-NU-1:3,17,44■2:1■3:1,2,3,4,6,9,10,32,38,39,48,51■4:1,5,15,16,17,19,27,28,33,34,37,41,45,46■6:23■7:8■8:2,3,11,13,19,20,21^{2},22■9:6■10:8■12:1,4,5,10,11■13:26■14:2,5,26■15:33■16:3,11,16,17,18,20,37,40,41,42,43,46,47,50■17:6,8■18:1,8,20,28■19:1■20:2,6,8,10,12,23,24,25,26^{2},28^{2},29^{2}■25:7,11■26:1,9,59,60,64■27:13■33:1,38,39-DE-9:20^{2}■10:6■32:50-JOS-21:4,10,13,19■24:5,33-J'G-20:28-1SA-12:6,8-1CH-6:3^{2},49,50,54,57■15:4■23:13,28,32■24:1^{2},19,31-2CH-13:9,10■26:18■29:21■31:19■35:14^{2}-EZR-7:5-NE-10:38■12:47-PS-77:20■99:6■105:26■106:16■115:10,12■118:3■135:19-MIC-6:4■N.T.-all=2-LU-1:5-AC-7:40-HEB-5:4■7:11

AARONITES-1CH-12:27(175)■27:17(175)

AARON'S-all=175-EX-6:25■7:12■28:1,3,30,38,40■29:26,28-LE-1:5,8,11■2:2,3,10■3:2,5,8■7:31■8:12,13,23,24,27■9:12,18■24:9-NU-17:3,10-PS-133:2■N.T.-HEB-9:4^{2}

ABADDON-RE-9:11(3)

ABAGTHA-ES-1:10(5)

ABANA-2KI-5:12(71)

ABARIM-all=5682-NU-27:12■33:47,48-DE-32:49

ABBA-all=5-M'R-14:36-RO-8:15-GA-4:6

ABDA-1KI-4:6(5653)-RE-11:17(5653)

ABDEEL-JER-36:26(5655)

ABDI-all=5660-1CH-6:44-2CH-29:12-EZR-10:26

ABDIEL-1CH-5:15(5661)

ABDON-all=5658-JOS-21:30-J'G-12:13,15-1CH-6:74■8:23,30■9:36-2CH-34:20

ABEDNEGO-all=5665&marked-DA-1:7(5664)■2:49■3:12,13,14,16,19,20,22,23,26^{2},28,29,30

ABEL-all=1893&marked-GE-4:2,4^{2},8^{2},9,25■1SA-6:18(59)-2SA-20:14(62),15(62),18(59)■N.T.-all=6-M'T-23:35-LU-11:51-HEB-11:4■12:24

ABEL-BETH-MAACHAH-1KI-15:20(62)-2KI-15:29(62)

ABEL-MAIM-2CH-16:4(66)

ABEL-MEHOLAH-all=65-J'G-7:22-1KI-4:12■19:16

ABEL-MIZRAIM-GE-50:11(67)

ABEL-SHITTIM-NU-33:49(63)

ABEZ-JOS-19:20(77)

ABI-2KI-18:2(21)

ABIA-1CH-3:10(29)■N.T.-M'T-1:7(7)-LU-1:5(7)

ABIAH-all=29-1SA-8:2-1CH-2:24■6:28■7:8

ABI-ALBON-2SA-23:31(45)

ABIASAPH-EX-6:24(23)

ABIATHAR-all=54-1SA-22:20,21,22■23:6,9■30:7^{2}-2SA-8:17■15:24,27,29,35^{2}■17:15■19:11■20:25-1KI-1:7,19,25,42■2:22,26,27,35■4:4-1CH-15:11■18:16■24:6■27:34■N.T.-M'R-2:26(8)

ABIATHAR'S-2SA-15:36(54)

ABIB-all=24-EX-13:4■23:15■34:18^{2}-DE-16:1^{2}

ABIDA-1CH-1:33(28)

ABIDAH-GE-25:4(28)

ABIDAN-all=27-NU-1:11■2:22■7:60,65■10:24

ABIEL-all=22-1SA-9:1■14:51-1CH-11:32

ABIEZER-all=44-JOS-17:2-J'G-6:34■8:2-2SA-23:27-1CH-7:18■11:28■27:12

ABI-EZRITE-J'G-6:11(33)

ABI-EZRITES-all=33-J'G-6:24■8:32

ABIGAIL-all=26-1SA-25:3,14,18,23,32,36,39,40,42■27:3■30:5-2SA-2:2■3:3■17:25-1CH-2:16,17■3:1

ABIHAIL-all=32-NU-3:35-1CH-2:29■5:14-2CH-11:18-ES-2:15■9:29

ABIHU-all=30-EX-6:23■24:1,9■28:1-LE-10:1-NU-3:2,4■26:60,61-1CH-6:3■24:1,2

ABIHUD-1CH-8:3(31)

ABIJAH-all=29-1KI-14:1-1CH-24:10-2CH-11:20,22■12:16■13:1,2,3,4,15,17,19,20,21,22■14:1■29:1-NE-10:7■12:4,17

ABIJAM-all=38-1KI-14:31■15:1,7^{2},8

ABILENE-LU-3:1(9)

ABIMAEL-GE-10:28(39)-1CH-1:22(39)

ABIMELECH-all=40-GE-20:2,3,4,8,9,10,14,15,17,18■21:22,25,26,27,29,32■26:1,8,9,10,11,16,26-J'G-8:31■9:1,3,4,6,16,18,19,20^{2},21,22,23^{2},24,25,27,28,29^{2},31,34,35,38,39,40,41,42,44,45,47,48^{2},49,50,52,55,56■10:1-2SA-11:21-1CH-18:16-PS-34:t

ABIMELECH'S-GE-21:25(40)-J'G-9:53(40)

ABINADAB-all=41-1SA-7:1■16:8■17:13■31:2-2SA-6:3^{2},4-1KI-4:11-1CH-2:13■8:33■9:39■10:2■13:7

ABINOAM-all=42-J'G-4:6,12■5:1,12

ABIRAM-all=48-NU-16:1,12,24,25,27^{2}■26:9^{2}-DE-11:6-1KI-16:34-PS-106:17

ABISHAG-all=49-1KI-1:3,15■2:17,21,22

ABISHAI-all=52-1SA-26:6^{2},7,8,9-2SA-2:18,24■3:30■10:10,14■16:9,11■18:2,5,12■19:21■20:6,10■21:17■23:18-1CH-2:16■11:20■18:12■19:11,15

ABISHALOM-1KI-15:2(53),10(53)

ABISHUA-all=50-1CH-6:4,5,50■8:4-EZR-7:5

ABISHUR-1CH-2:28(51),29(51)

ABITAL-all=37-2SA-3:4(37)-1CH-3:3(37)

ABITUB-1CH-8:11(36)

ABIUD-M'T-1:13(10)

ABNER-all=74-1SA-14:50,51■17:55^{3},57■20:25■26:5,7,14^{3},15-2SA-2:8,12,14,17,19^{2},20,21,22,23,24,25,26,29,30■3:6,7,8,9,11,12,16,17,19^{2},20^{2},21^{2},22,23,24,25,26,27,28,30,31,32^{2},33^{2},37■4:1,12-1KI-2:5,32-1CH-26:28■27:21

ABNER'S-2SA-2:31(74)

ABRAHAM-all=85-GE-17:5,9,15,17,18,22,23,24,26■18:6,7,11,13,16,17,18,19,22,23,27,33^{2}■19:27,29■20:1,2,9,10,11,14,17■21:2,3,4,5,7,8,9,10,12,14,22,24,25,27,28,29,33,34■22:1^{2},3,4,5,6,7,8,9,10,11,13^{2},14,15,19^{2},20■23:2,3,5,7,10,12,14,16^{2},18,19,20■24:1^{2},2,6,9,12^{2},27,42,48■25:1,5,6,8,10^{2},11,12,19■26:1,3,5,15,18^{2},24■28:4^{2},13■31:42,53■32:9■35:12,27■48:15,16■49:30,31■50:13,24-EX-2:24■3:6,15,16■4:5■6:3,8■32:13■33:1-LE-26:42-NU-32:11-DE-1:8■6:10■9:5,27■29:13■30:20■34:4-JOS-24:2,3-1KI-18:36-2KI-13:23-1CH-1:27,28,34■16:16■29:18-2CH-20:7■30:6-NE-9:7-PS-47:9■105:6,9,42-IS-29:22■41:8■51:2■63:16-JER-33:26-EZE-33:24-MIC-7:20■N.T.-all=11-M'T-1:1,2,17■3:9^{2}■8:11■22:32-M'R-12:26-LU-1:55,73■3:8^{2},34■13:16,28■16:23,24,25,29,30■19:9■20:37-JOH-8:39^{2},40,52,53,56,57,58-AC-3:13,25■7:2,8,16,17,32■13:26-RO-4:1,2,3,9,12,13,16■9:7■11:1-2CO-11:22-GA-3:6,7,8,9,14,16,18■4:22-HEB-2:16■6:13■7:1,2,4,5,6,9■11:8,17-JAS-2:21,23-1PE-3:6

ABRAHAM'S-all=85-GE-17:23■20:18■21:11■22:23■24:15,34,52,59■25:7,12,19■26:24■28:9-1CH-1:32■N.T.-all=11-LU-16:22-JOH-8:33,37,39-GA-3:29

ABRAM-all=87-GE-11:26,27,29,31■12:1,4^{2},5,6,7,9,10,14,16,18■13:1,2,4,5,8,12,14,18■14:13^{2},14,19,21,22,23■15:1^{2},2,3,11,12,13,18■16:2^{2},3^{2},5,6,15,16^{2}■17:1^{2},3,5-1CH-1:27-NE-9:7

ABRAM'S-all=87-GE-11:29,31■12:17■13:7■14:12■16:1,3

ABSALOM-all=53-2SA-3:3■13:1,20,22^{2},23^{2},24,25,26,27,28,29^{2},30,32,34,37,38,39■14:1,21,23,24,25,27,28,29,31,32,33^{2}■15:1,2^{2},3,4,6^{2},7,10^{2},11,12^{2},13,14,31,34,37■16:8,15,16^{2},17,18,20,21,22^{2},23■17:1,4,5,6,7,9,14^{2},15,18,24,25,26■18:5^{2},9^{2},10,12,14,15,17,18,29,32,33^{2}■19:1,4^{2},6,9,10■20:6-1KI-1:6■2:7,28-1CH-3:2-2CH-11:20,21-PS-3:t

ABSALOM'S-all=53-2SA-13:4,20■14:30■17:20■18:18

ACCAD-GE-10:10(390)

ACCHO-J'G-1:31(5910)

ACELDAMA-AC-1:19(184)

ACHAIA-all=882-AC-18:12,27■19:21-RO-15:26■16:5-1CO-16:15-2CO-1:1■9:2■11:10-1TH-1:7,8

ACHAICUS-1CO-16:17(883)

ACHAN-all=5912-JOS-7:1,18,19,20,24■22:20

ACHAR-1CH-2:7(5917)

ACHAZ-M'T-1:9^{2}(881)

ACHBOR-all=5907-GE-36:38,39-2KI-22:12,14-1CH-1:49-JER-26:22■36:12

ACHIM-M'T-1:14^{2}(885)

ACHISH-all=397-1SA-21:10,11,12,14■27:2,3,5,6,9,10,12■28:1:2^{2}■29:2,3,6,8,9-1KI-2:39,40

ACHMETHA-EZR-6:2(307)

ACHOR-all=5911-JOS-7:24,26■15:7-IS-65:10-HO-2:15

ACHSA-all=5915-1CH-2:49(5915)

ACHSAH-all=5915-JOS-15:16,17-J'G-1:12,13

ACHSHAPH-all=407-JOS-11:1■12:20■19:25

ACHZIB-all=392-JOS-15:44■19:29-J'G-1:31-MIC-1:14

ADADAH-JOS-15:22(5735)

ADAH-all=5711-GE-4:19,20,23■36:2,4,10,12,16

ADAIAH-all=5718-2KI-22:1-1CH-6:41■8:21■9:12-2CH-23:1-EZR-10:29,39-RE-11:5,12

ADALIA-ES-9:8(118)

ADAM-all=120,a=121-GE-2:19^{2},20^{2},21a,23■3:8,9,17a,20,21■4:1,25■5:1a,2,3a,4a,5a-DE-3:28-JOS-3:16a-1CH-1:1a-JOB-31:33a■N.T.-all=76-LU-3:38-RO-5:14-1CO-15:22,45^{2}-1TI-2:13,14-JUDE-14

ADAMAH-JOS-19:36(128)

ADAMI-JOS-19:33(129)

ADAM'S-RO-5:14(76)

ADAR-all=143&marked-JOS-15:3(146)-EZR-6:15(144)-ES-3:7,13■8:12■9:1,15,17,19,21

ADBEEL-GE-25:13(110)-1CH-1:29(110)

ADDAN-EZR-2:59(135)

ADDAR-1CH-8:3(146)

ADDI-LU-3:28(78)

ADDON-RE-7:61(114)

ADER-1CH-8:15(5738)

ADIEL-all=5717-1CH-4:36■9:12■27:25

ADIN-all=5720-EZR-2:15■8:6-NE-7:20■10:16

ADINA-1CH-11:42(5721)

ADINO-2SA-23:8(5722)

ADITHAIM-JOS-15:36(5723)

ADLAI-1CH-27:29(5724)

ADMAH-all=126-GE-10:19■14:2,8-DE-29:23-HO-11:8

ADMATHA-ES-1:14(133)

ADNA-EZR-10:30(5733)-NE-12:15(5733)

ADNAH-1CH-12:20(5734)-2CH-17:14(5734)

ADONI-BEZEK-all=137-J'G-1:5,6,7

ADONIJAH-all=138-2SA-3:4-1KI-1:5,7,8,9,11,13,18,24,41,42,43,49,50,51■2:13,19,21,22,23,24,28-1CH-3:2-2CH-17:8-NE-10:16

ADONIKAM-all=140-EZR-2:13■

8:13-RE-7:18

ADONIRAM-1KI-4:6(141)■5:14(141)

ADONI-ZEDEK-JOS-10:1(139),3(139)

ADORAIM-2CH-11:9(115)

ADORAM-2SA-20:24(151)-1KI-12:18(151)

ADRAMMELECH-all=152-2KI-17:31■19:37-IS-37:38

ADRAMYTTIUM-AC-27:2(98)

ADRIA-AC-27:27(99)

ADRIEL-1SA-18:19(5741)-2SA-21:8(5741)

ADULLAM-all=5725-JOS-12:15■15:35-1SA-22:1-2SA-23:13-1CH-11:15-2CH-11:7-NE-11:30-MIC-1:15

ADULLAMITE-all=5726-GE-38:1,12,20

ADUMMIM-JOS-15:7(131)■18:17(131)

AENEAS-AC-9:33(132),34(132)

AENON-JOH-3:23(137)

AGABUS-AC-11:28(13)■21:10(13)

AGAG-all=90-NU-24:7-1SA-15:8,9,20,32^3,33

AGAGITE-all=91-ES-3:1,10■8:3,5■9:24

AGAR-GA-4:24(28),25(28)

AGEE-2SA-23:11(89)

AGRIPPA-all=67-AC-25:13,22,23,24,26■26:1,2,7,19,27,28,32

AGUR-PR-30:1(94)

AHAB-all=256-1KI-16:28,29^2,30,33■17:1■18:1,2,3,5,6,9,12,16^2,17^2,20,41,42,44,45,46■19:1■20:2,13,14■21:1,2,3,4,15,16^2,18,20,21,24,25,27,29■22:20,39,40,41,49,51-2KI-1:1■3:1,5■8:16,18^2,25,27^3,28,29■9:7,8^2,9,25,29■10:1,10,11,17,18,30■21:3,13-2CH-18:1,2^2,3,19■21:6^2,13■22:3,4,5,6,7,8-JER-29:21,22-MIC-6:16

AHAB'S-all=256-1KI-21:8(256)-2KI-10:1(256)

AHARAH-1CH-8:1(315)

AHARHEL-1CH-4:8(316)

AHASAI-NE-11:13(273)

AHASBAI-2SA-23:34(308)

AHASUERUS-all=325-EZR-4:6-ES-1:1^2,2,9,10,15,16,17,19■2:1,12,16,21■3:1,6,7,8,12■6:2■7:5■8:1,7,12■9:2,20,30■10:1,3-DA-9:1

AHASUERUS'-ES-8:10(325)

AHAVA-all=163-EZR-8:15,21,31

AHAZ-all=271-2KI-15:38■16:1,2,5,7,8,10^2,11^2,15,16,17,19,20■17:1■18:1■20:11■23:12-1CH-3:13■8:35,36■9:42-2CH-27:9■28:1,16,19,21,22,24,27■29:19-1SA-1:1■7:1,3,10,12■14:28■38:8-HO-1:1-MIC-1:1

AHAZIAH-all=274-1KI-22:40,49,51-2KI-1:2,18■8:24,25,26,29■9:16,21,23^2,27,29■10:13^2■11:1,2^2■12:18■13:1■14:13-1CH-3:11-2CH-20:35,37■22:1^2,2,7,8^2,9^2,10,11^2

AHBAN-1CH-2:29(257)

AHER-1CH-7:12(313)

AHI-1CH-5:15(277)■7:34(277)

AHIAH-all=281-1SA-14:3,18-1KI-4:3-1CH-8:7

AHIAM-2SA-23:33(279)-1CH-11:35(279)

AHIAN-1CH-7:19(291)

AHIEZER-all=295-NU-1:12■2:25■7:66,71■10:25-1CH-12:3

AHIHUD-NU-34:27(282)-1CH-8:7(284)

AHIJAH-all=281-1KI-11:29,30■12:15■14:2,4^2,5,6,18■15:27,29,33■21:22-1KI-9:9-1CH-2:25■11:36■26:20-2CH-9:29■10:15-NE-10:26

AHIKAM-all=296-2KI-22:12,14■25:22-2CH-34:20-JER-26:24■39:14■40:5,6,7,9,11,14,16■41:1,2,6,10,16,18■43:6

AHILUD-all=286-2SA-8:16■20:24-1KI-4:3,12-1CH-18:15

AHIMAAZ-all=290-1SA-14:50-2SA-15:27,36■17:17,20■18:19,22,23,27,28,29-1KI-4:15-1CH-6:8,9,53

AHIMAN-all=289-NU-13:22-JOS-15:14-J'G-1:10-1CH-9:17

AHIMELECH-all=288-1SA-21:1^2,2,8■22:9,11,14,16,20■23:6■26:6-2SA-8:17-1CH-24:3,6,31-PS-52:t

AHIMELECH'S-1SA-30:7(288)

AHIMOTH-1CH-6:25(287)

AHINADAB-1KI-4:14(292)

AHINOAM-all=293-1SA-14:50■25:43■27:3■30:5-2SA-2:2■3:2-1CH-3:1

AHIO-all=283-2SA-6:3,4-1CH-8:14,31■9:37■13:7

AHIRA-all=299-NU-1:15■2:29■7:78,83■10:27

AHIRAM-NU-26:38(297)

AHIRAMITES-NU-26:38(298)

AHISAMACH-all=294-EX-31:6■35:34■38:23

AHISHAHAR-1CH-7:10(300)

AHISHAR-1KI-4:6(301)

AHITHOPHEL-all=302-2SA-15:12,31^2,34■16:15,20,21,23^2■17:1,6,7,14^2,15,21,23■23:24-1CH-27:33,34

AHITUB all−285 1SA 14:3■22:9,11,12,20-2SA-8:17-1CH-6:7,8,11,12,52■9:11■18:16-EZR-7:2-NE-11:11

AHLAB-J'G-1:31(303)

AHLAI-1CH-2:31(304)■11:41(304)

AHOAH-1CH-8:4(265)

AHOHITE-all=1121,266-2SA-23:9,28-2CH-11:12,29■27:4

AHOLAH-all=170-EZE-3:4^2,5,36,44

AHOLIAB-all=171-DE-31:6■35:34■36:1,2■38:23

AHOLIBAH-all=172-EZE-23:4^2,11,22,36,44

AHOLIBAMAH-all=173-GE-36:2,5,14,18^2,25,41-1CH-1:52

AHUMAI-1CH-4:2(267)

AHUZAM-1CH-4:6(275)

AHUZZATH-GE-26:26(276)

AI-all=5857&marked-JOS-7:2^2,3,4,5■8:1^2,2,3,9^2,10,11^2,12,14,16(5892),17,18,20,21,23,24^2,25,26,28,29■9:3■10:1^2,2■12:9-EZR-2:28-NE-7:32-JER-49:3

AIAH-all=345-2SA-3:7■21:8,10,11-1CH-1:40

AIATH-1SA-10:28(5857)

AIJA-NE-11:31(5857)

AIJALON-all=357-JOS-21:24-J'G-1:35■12:12-1SA-14:31-1CH-6:69■8:13-2CH-11:10

AIJELETH-PS-22:t(365)

AIN-all=5871-NU-34:11-JOS-15:32■19:7■21:16-1CH-4:32

AJAH-GE-36:24(345)

AJALON-all=357-JOS-10:12■19:42-2CH-28:18

AKAN-GE-36:27(6130)

AKKUB-all=6126-1CH-3:24■9:17-EZR-2:42,45-NE-7:45■8:7■11:19■12:25

AKRABBIM-NU-34:4(6137)-J'G-1:36(6137)

ALAMETH-1CH-7:8(5964)

ALAMMELECH-JOS-19:26(487)

ALAMOTH-1CH-15:20(5961)-PS-46:t(5961)

ALEMETH-all=5964-1CH-6:60■8:36■9:42

ALEXANDER-all=223-M'R-15:21-AC-4:6■19:33^2-1TI-1:20-2TI-4:14

ALEXANDRIA-all=221-AC-18:24■27:6■28:11

ALEXANDRIANS-AC-6:9(221)

ALIAH-1CH-1:51(5933)

ALIAN-1CH-1:40(5935)

ALL-all=3605not listed,a=3885,b=3606,o=supplied-GE-19:2^{2}a■24:54a■28:11a■31:54a■35:4(3605),4o■41:45o■42:17(622)■47:13(3605),13o■48:15o-EX-3:15o■5:23o■12:9o■22:23o,26o■26:8o■28:31(3632)■39:22(3632),-LE-7:18o■11:20(3605),20o,21o,27(3605),27o,42o,42(3605)■15:24o,24(3605)■19:7o,13o,20o■25:10o,10(3605)■26:18o,27o,44(1571)■27:10o,13o,31o,33o-NU-12:3o■14:15o■22:38o■23:25^{2}o■30:6o■31:9o,9^3(3605)-DE-8:19o■16:4a■21:14o,23a■27:26o-JOS-7:7o■10:6o-J'G-9:53o■16:3(5973),30o,30(3605)■19:6a,9a,13a-1SA-16:11(8522)■20:6o,6(3605)■25:28o■28:20(4393)■30:8o-2SA-12:16a■18:28o■19:42(3605),42o■21:9o-1KI-7:23o■8:59o■9:6o■14:10(8552)■18:5o■20:27o■22:28o-2KI-5:21o,22o■9:11o■18:33o-2CH-5:1(3605),1o,1(3605)■31:1^3,1o,1(3605)-EZR-4:20b■5:7b■6:12b,17b■7:13b,16^{2}b,21b,25^{2}b-NE-5:18(5973)-JOB-4:14(7230)■29:19a-PS-14:3(3605),3o■33:11o■49:11o■57:2o■72:5o■79:13o■85:5■89:1o■90:1o■100:5o■102:12o,24o■106:31o■119:90o■135:13o■144:13o■145:13o■146:10o-EC-2:3(4557),8o■5:18(4557)■6:12(4557)-SONG-1:13a-IS-34:1(4393)■42:10(4393)■50:2o-JER-6:15o■8:12,16(4393)■11:12o■23:32o■26:19o■31:12o■41:6o■46:25o■47:2(4393-EZE-12:19(4393)■14:3o■16:4^{2}o■18:23o■20:32o■23:7o■30:12(4393)■37:22(3605),22o-DA-2:12b,38b,39b,40^{2}b,44b,48b■3:2b,3b,5b,7^{2}b,10b,15b■4:1^{2}b,6b,11b,12^{2}b,18b,20b,21b,28b,35b,37b■5:8b,19b,22b,23b■6:7b,24b,25^{2}b■7:7b,14b,16b,19b,23b,27b■10:3o-HO-11:7(3162)-JO-1:13a-AM-1:11o■3:5o■6:8(4393)-MIC-1:2(4393),10o■5:9o-NA-1:3o-ZEC-7:5(3605),5o■14:17o■**N.T.**-all=3956not listed,a=3650,b=537,o=supplied-M'T-1:22a■4:23a,24a■5:34(3654)■6:32b■9:26a,31a■14:35a■20:6a■21:4a,37o■22:37^{3}a,40a■24:14a,39b■26:56a,59a■28:9o,11b-M'R-1:28a,33a,39a■5:40b■11:32b■12:30^{4}a,33^{4}a,44(3956),44a■14:55a■16:15b-LU-2:39b■3:16b,21b■4:6b,14a■5:5a,11b,26b,28b■6:12(1273)■7:16b,(3956),17a■9:10(3745),15b■10:27^{4}a■11:22(3833)■12:1o■15:13b■17:27b,29b■19:7b,48b■20:40o■21:4^{2}b,12b■23:5a,18(3829),44a-JOH-10:49(3762)■18:38o■19:11(3762)■21:11o-AC-2:1b,2a,4b,14b,44b,47a■4:18(2527),23(3745),31b,32b■5:11a,12b■6:15b■7:10a,11a■8:37a■9:31a,42a■10:8b,22a,37a■11:10b,28a■13:29b,49a■14:27(3745)■15:4(3745)■16:3b,28b,34(3832)■17:5o,15(5613,5033)■18:8a,21(3843),23o■19:27a■20:38(3122)■21:30a,31a■22:30a■24:3(3837)■25:8o■27:33b-RO-8:36a■10:21a-1CO-11:5o,18o■14:21(3779)■15:3o,29(3654),39(4561)■16:12(3843)2CO-1:1a,3a,4a,20(3745)-GA-4:12(3762)-EPH-6:13b-PH'P-1:13a-1TH-4:10(3956),10a-2TH-3:11(3367)-HEB-3:2a,5a■9:3o,8o,17(4219)■10:10(2178)-JAS-3:2b-1JO-1:5(3762)-RE-1:2(3745)■3:10a■13:3a■18:14(3364),21(3364),22^2(3364),23(3956),23^2(3364)■21:25(3364)

ALLON-JOS-19:33(438)-1CH-4:37(438)

ALLON-BACHUTH-GE-35:8(439)

ALMODAD-GE-10:26(486)-1CH-1:20(486)

ALMON-JOS-21:18(5960)

ALMON-DIBLATHAIM-NU-33:46(5963),47(5963)

ALOTH-1KI-4:16(1175)

ALPHA-all=1-RE-1:8,11■21:6■22:13

ALPHAEUS-all=256-M'T-10:3-M'R-2:14■3:18-LU-6:15-AC-1:13

AL-TASCHITH-all=516-PS-57:t■58:t■59:t■75:t

ALUSH-NU-33:13(442),14(442)

ALVAH-GE-36:40(5933)

ALVAN-GE-36:23(5935)

AMAD-JOS-19:26(6008)

AMAL-1CH-7:35(6000)

AMALEK-all=6002-GE-36:12,16-EX-17:8,9,10,11,13,14,16-NU-24:20^2-DE-25:17,19-J'G-3:13■5:14-1SA-15:2,3,5,20■28:18-2SA-8:12-1CH-1:36■18:11-PS-83:7

AMALEKITE-all=6003-1SA-30:13-2SA-1:8,13

AMALEKITES-all=6003-GE-14:7-NU-13:29■14:25,43,45-J'G-6:3,33■7:12■10:12■12:15-1SA-14:48■15:6^2,7,8,15,18,20,32■27:8■30:1,18-2SA-1:1-1CH-4:43

AMAM-JOS-15:26(538)

AMANA-SONG-4:8(549)

AMARIAH-all=568-1CH-6:7^2,11^2,52■23:19■24:23-2CH-19:11■31:15-EZR-7:3■10:42-NE-10:3■11:4■12:2,13-ZEP-1:1

AMASA-all=6021-1SA-17:25^2-2SA-19:13■20:4,5,8,9^2,10,12^2-1KI-2:5,32-1CH-2:17^2-2CH-28:12

AMASAI-all=6022-1CH-6:25,35■12:18■15:24-2CH-29:12

AMASHAI-NE-11:13(6023)

AMASIAH-2CH-17:16(6007)

AMAZIAH-all=558-2KI-12:21■

13:12■14:1,8,9,11^2,13,15,17,18,21,23■15:1,3-1CH-3:12■4:34■6:45-2CH-24:27■25:1,5,9,10,11,13,14,15,17,18,20,21,23,25,26,27■26:1,4-AM-7:10,12,14

AMI-EZR-2:57(532)

AMINADAB-M'T-1:4^2(284)-LU-3:33(284)

AMITTAI-2KI-14:25(573)-JON-1:1(573)

AMMAH-2SA-2:24(522)

AMMI-HO-2:1(5971)

AMMIEL-all=5988-NU-13:12-SA-9:4,5■17:27-1CH-3:5■26:5

AMMIHUB-all=5989-NU-1:10■2:18■7:48,53■10:22■34:20,28-2SA-13:37-1CH-7:26■9:4

AMMINADAB-all=5992-EX-6:23-NU-1:7■2:3■7:12,17■10:14-RU-4:19,20-1CH-2:10^2■6:22■15:10,11

AMMINADIB-SONG-6:12(5993)

AMMISHADDAI-all=5996-NU-1:12■2:25■7:66,71■10:25

AMMIZABAD-1CH-27:6(5990)

AMMON-all=5983-GE-19:38-NU-21:24^2-DE-2:19^2,37■3:11,16-JOS-12:2■13:10,25-J'G-3:13■10:6,7,9,11,17,18■11:4,5,6,8,9,12,13,14,15,27,28,29,30,31,32,33,36■12:1,2,3-1SA-12:12■14:47-2SA-8:12■10:1,2,3,6^2,8,10,11,14^2,19■11:1■12:9,26,31■17:27-1KI-11:7,33-2KI-23:13■24:2-1CH-18:11■19:1,2,3,6^2,7,9,11,12,15,19■20:1,3-2CH-20:1,10,22,23■27:5^2-NE-13:23-PS-83:7-IS-11:14-JER-9:26■25:21■49:6-DA-11:41-AM-1:13-ZEP-2:8,9

AMMONITE-all=5984-DE-23:3-1SA-11:1,2-2SA-23:37-1CH-11:39-NE-2:10,19■4:3■13:1

AMMONITES-all=5984-DE-2:20-2SA-11:11-1KI-11:1,5-2CH-20:1■26:8■27:5-EZR-9:1-NE-4:7-JER-27:3■40:11,14■41:10,15■49:1,2-EZE-21:20,28■25:2,3,5,10^2

AMMONITESS-all=5984-1KI-14:21,31-2CH-12:13■24:26

AMNON-all=550-2SA-3:2■13:1,2^2,3,4,6^2,9,10^2,15^2,20,22^2,26,27,28,29,32,33,39-1CH-3:1■4:20

AMNON'S-all=550-2SA-13:7,8,28

AMOK-NE-12:7 (5987),20(5987)

AMON-all=526-1KI-22:26-2KI-21:18,19,23,24,25-1CH-3:14-2CH-18:25■33:20,21,22,23,25-NE-7:59-JER-1:2■25:3-ZEP-1:1■N.T.-M'T-1:10^2(300)

AMORITE-all=567-GE-10:16■14:13■48:22-EX-33:2■34:11-NU-32:39-DE-2:24-JOS-9:1■11:3-1CH-1:14-EZE-16:3,45-AM-2:9,10

AMORITES-all=567-GE-14:7■15:16,21-EX-3:8,17■13:5■23:23-NU-13:29■21:13^2,21,25,26,29,31,32,34■22:2■32:33-DE-1:4,7,19,20,27,44■3:2,8,9■4:46,47■7:1■20:17■31:4-JOS-2:10■3:10■5:1■7:7■9:10■10:5,6,12■12:2,8■13:4,10,21■24:8,11,12,15,18-J'G-1:34,35,36■3:5■6:10■10:8,11■11:19,21,22,23-1SA-7:14-2SA-21:2-1KI-4:19■9:20■21:26-2KI-21:11-2CH-8:7-EZR-9:1-NE-9:8-PS-135:11■136:19

AMOS-all=5986-AM-1:t,1■7:8,10,11,12,14■8:2■N.T.-LU-3:25(301)

AMOZ-all=531-2KI-19:2,20■20:1-2CH-26:22■32:20,32-IS-1:1■2:1■13:1■20:2■37:2,21■38:1

AMPHIPOLIS-AC-17:1(295)

AMPLIAS-RO-16:8(291)

AMRAM-all=6019&marked-EX-6:18,20^2-NU-3:19■26:58,59-1CH-1:41(2566)■6:2,3,18■23:12,13■24:20-EZR-10:34

AMRAMITES-all=6020-NU-3:27(6020)-1CH-26:23(6020)

AMRAM'S-NU-26:59(6019)

AMRAPHEL-GE-14:1(569),9(569)

AMZI-1CH-6:46(557)-NE-1:12(557)

AN-all supplied

ANAB-JOS-11:21(6024)■15:50(6024)

ANAH-all=6034-GE-36:2,14,18,20,24^2,25^2,29-1CH-1:38,40,41

ANAHARATH-JOS-19:19(588)

ANAIAH-NE-8:4(6043)■10:22(6043)

ANAK-all=6061-NU-13:22,28,33-DE-9:2-JOS-15:13,14^2■21:11-J'G-1:20

ANAKIMS-all=6062-DE-1:28■2:10,11,21■9:2-JOS-11:21,22■14:12,15

ANAMIM-GE-10:13(6047)-1CH-1:11(6047)

ANAMMELECH-2KI-17:31(6048)

ANAN-NE-10:26(6052)

ANANI-1CH-3:24(6054)

ANANIAH-NE-3:23(6055)■11:32(6055)

ANANIAS-all=367-AC-5:1,3,5■9:10^2,12,13,17■22:12■23:2■24:1

ANATH-J'G-3:31(6067)■5:6(6067)

ANATHOTH-all=6068-JOS-21:18-1KI-2:26-1CH-6:60■7:8-EZR-2:23-NE-7:27■10:19■11:32-IS-10:30-JER-1:1■11:21,23■29:27■32:7,8,9

AND-O.T.supplied■N.T.-all=1722

ANDREW-all=406-M'T-4:18■10:2-M'R-1:16,29■3:18■13:3-LU-6:14-JO-1:40,44■6:8■12:22^2-AC-1:13

ANDRONICUS-RO-16:7(408)

ANEM-1CH-6:73(6046)

ANER-all=6063-GE-14:13,24-1CH-6:70

ANETHOTHITE-2SA-23:27(6069)

ANETOTHITE-1CH-7:12(6069)

ANIAM-1CH-7:19(593)

ANIM-JOS-15:50(6044)

ANNA-LU-2:36(451)

ANNAS-all=452-LU-3:2-JOH-18:13,24-AC-4:6

ANTIOCH-all=490&marked-AC-6:5(491)■11:19,20,22,26^2,27■13:1,14■14:19,21,26■15:22,23,30,35■18:22-GA-2:11-2TI-3:11

ANTIPAS-RE-2:13(493)

ANTIPATRIS-AC-23:31(494)

ANTOTHIJAH-1CH-8:24(6070)

ANTOTHITE-1CH-11:28(6069)■12:3(6069)

ANUB-1CH-4:8(6036)

APELLES-RO-16:10(559)

APHARSACHITES-EZR-5:6(671)■6:6(671)

APHARSATHCHITES-EZR-4:9(671)

APHARSITES-EZR-4:9(670)

APHEK-all=663-JOS-12:18■13:4■19:30-1SA-4:1■29:1-1KI-20:26,30-2KI-13:17

APHEKAH-JOS-15:53(664)

APHIAH-2SA-9:1(647)

APHIK-J'G-1:31(663)

APHRAH-MIC-1:10(1036)

APHSES-1CH-24:15(6483)

APOLLONIA-AC-17:1(624)

APOLLOS-all=625-AC-18:24■19:1-1CO-1:12■3:4,5,6,22■4:6■16:12-TIT-3:13

APOLLYON-RE-9:11(623)

APPAIM-1CH-2:30(649),31(649)

APPHIA-PH'M-2(682)

APPII-AC-28:15(675)

AQUILA-all=207-AC-18:2,18,26-RO-16:3-1CO-16:19-2TI-4:19

AR-all=6144-NU-21:15,28-DE-2:9,18,29-IS-15:1

ARA-1CH-7:38(690)

ARAB-JOS-15:52(694)

ARABAH-JOS-18:18^2(6160)

ARABIA-all=6152-1KI-10:15-2CH-9:14-IS-21:13^2-JER-25:24-EZE-27:21■N.T.-GA-1:17(688)■4:25(688)

ARABIAN-all=6163-NE-2:19■6:1-IS-13:20-JER-3:2

ARABIANS-all=6163-2CH-17:11■21:16■22:1■26:7-NE-4:7■N.T.-AC-2:11(690)

ARAD-all=6166-NU-21:1■33:40-JOS-12:14-J'G-1:16-1CH-8:15

ARAH-all=733-1CH-7:39-EZR-2:5-NE-6:18■7:10

ARAM-all=758-GE-10:22,23■22:21-NU-23:7-1CH-1:17■2:23■7:34■N.T.-all=689-M'T-1:3,4-LU-3:33

ARAMITESS-1CH-7:14(761)

ARAM-NAHARAIM-PS-60:t(763)

ARAM-ZOBAH-PS-60:t(760)

ARAN-GE-36:28(765)-1CH-1:42(765)

ARARAT-GE-8:4(780)-JER-51:27(780)

ARAUNAH-all=728-2SA-24:16,18,20^2,21,22,23^2,24

ARBA-all=704-JOS-14:15■15:13■21:11

ARBAH-GE-35:27(704)

ARBATHITE-2SA-23:31(6164)-1CH-11:32(6164)

ARBITE-2SA-23:35(701)

ARCHELAUS-M'T-2:22(745)

ARCHEVITES-EZR-4:9(756)

ARCHI-JOS-16:2(757)

ARCHIPPUS-COL-4:17(751)-PH'M-2:2(751)

ARCHITE-all=757-2SA-15:32■16:16■17:5,14-1CH-27:33

ARCTURUS-JOB-9:9(5906)■38:32(5906)

ARD-GE-46:21(714)-NU-26:40^2(714)

ARDITES-NU-26:40(716)

ARDON-1CH-2:18(715)

ARE-O.T.supplied■N.T.-all=1526

ARELI-GE-46:16(692)-NU-26:17(692)

ARELITES-NU-26:17(692)

AREOPAGITE-AC-17:34(698)

AREOPAGUS-AC-17:19(697)

ARETAS-2CO-11:32(702)

ARGOB-all=709-DE-3:4,13,14-1KI-4:13-2KI-15:25

ARIDAI-ES-9:9(742)

ARIDATHA-ES-9:8(743)

ARIEH-2KI-15:25(745)

ARIEL-all=740-EZR-8:16-IS-29:1,2^2,7

ARIMATHAEA-all=707-M'T-27:57-M'R-15:43-LU-23:51-JOH-19:38

ARIOCH-all=746-GE-14:1,9-DA-2:14,15^2,24,25

ARISAI-ES-9:9(747)

ARISTARCHUS-all=708-AC-19:29■20:4■27:2-COL-4:10-PH'M-24

ARISTOBULUS'-RO-16:10(711)

ARKITE-GE-10:17(6208)-1CH-1:15(6208)

ARMAGEDDON-RE-16:16(717)

ARMENIA-2KI-19:37(780)-IS-37:38(780)

ARMONI-2SA-21:8(764)

ARNAN-1CH-3:21(770)

ARNON-all=769-NU-21:13^2,14,24,26,28■22:36-DE-2:24,36■3:8,12,16■4:48-JOS-12:1,2■13:9,16-J'G-11:13,18^2,22,26-2KI-10:33-IS-16:2-JER-48:20

AROD-NU-26:17(720)

ARODI-GE-46:16(722)

ARODITES-NU-26:17(722)

AROER-all=6177-NU-32:34-DE-2:36■3:12■4:48-JOS-12:2■13:9,16,25-J'G-11:26,33-2SA-30:28-2SA-24:5-2KI-10:33-1CH-5:8-IS-17:2-JER-48:19

AROERITE-1CH-11:44(6200)

ARPAD-all=774-2KI-18:34■19:13-IS-10:9-JER-49:23

ARPHAD-IS-36:19(774)■37:13(774)

ARPHAXAD-all=775-GE-10:22,24■11:10,11,12,13-1CH-1:17,18,24■N.T.-LU-3:36(742)

ARTAXERXES-all=783-EZR-4:7^2,8,11■6:14■7:1,7,11,12,21■8:1-NE-2:1■5:14■13:6

ARTAXERXES'-EZR-4:23(783)

ARTEMAS-TIT-3:12(734)

ARUBOTH-1KI-4:10(700)

ARUMAH-J'G-9:41(725)

ARVAD-EZE-27:8(719),11(719)

ARVADITE-GE-10:18(721)-1CH-1:16(721)

ARZA-1KI-16:9(777)

AS-O.T.supplied■N.T.-all=1722

ASA-all=609-1KI-15:8,9,11,13,16,17,18^2,20,22^2,23,24,25,28,32,33■16:8,10,15,23,29■22:41,43,46-1CH-3:10■9:16-2CH-14:1,2,8,10,11,12,13■15:2^2,8,10,16^2,17,19■16:1^2,2,4,6,7,10^2,11,12,13■17:2■20:32■21:12-JER-41:9■N.T.-M'T-1:7(760),8(760)

ASAHEL-all=6214-2SA-2:18^2,19,20,21,22,23,30,32■3:27,30■23:24-1CH-2:16■11:26■27:7-2CH-17:8■31:13-EZR-10:15

ASAHIAH-2KI-22:12(6222),14(6222)

ASAIAH-all=6222-1CH-4:36■6:30■9:5■15:6,11-2CH-34:20

ASAPH-all=623-2KI-18:18,37-1CH-6:39^2■9:15■15:17,19■16:5^2,7,37■25:1,2^3,6,9■26:1-2CH-5:12■20:14■29:13,30■35:15^2-EZR-2:41■3:10-NE-2:8■7:44■11:17,22■12:35,46-PS-50:t■73:t■74:t■75:t■76:t■77:t■78:t■79:t■80:t■81:t■82:t■83:t-IS-36:22

ASAPH'S-IS-36:3(623)
ASAREEL-1CH-4:16(840)
ASARELAH-1CH-25:2(841)
ASA'S-1KI-15:14(609)
ASENATH-all=621-GE-41:45,50■46:20
ASER-LU-2:36(768)-RE-7:6(768)
ASHAN-all=6228-JOS-15:42■19:7 -1CH-4:32■6:59
ASHBEA-1CH-4:21(791)
ASHBEL-all=788-GE-46:21-NU-26:38-1CH-8:1
ASHBELITES-NU-26:38(789)
ASHCHENAZ-1CH-1:6(813)-JER-51:27(813)
ASHDOD-all=795-JOS-11:22■15:46, 47-2SA-5:1,3,5,6^2,7■6:17-2CH-26:6-NE-13:23,24-IS-20:1^2-JER-25:20-AM-1:8■ 3:9-ZEP-2:4-ZEC-9:6
ASHDODITES-NE-4:7(796)
ASHDOTHITES-JOS-13:3(796)
ASHDOTH-PISGAH-all=798, 6449-DE-3:17-JOS-12:3■13:20
ASHER-all=836-GE-30:13■35:26■ 46:17■49:20-EX-1:4-NU-1:13,40,41■ 2:27^2■7:72■10:26■13:13■26:44,46,47■ 34:27-DE-27:13■33:24-JOS-17:7,10,11■ 19:24,31,34■21:6,30-J'G-1:31■ 5:17■6:35■7:23-1KI-4:16-1CH-2:2■ 6:62,74■7:30,40■12:36-2CH-30:11 -EZE-48:2,3,34
ASHERITES-J'G-1:32(843)
ASHIMA-2KI-17:30(807)
ASHKELON-all=831-J'G-14:19-JER-25:20■47:5,7-AM-1:8-ZEP-2:4,7-ZEC-9:5^2
ASHKENAZ-GE-10:3(813)
ASHNAH-JOS-15:33(823),43(823)
ASHPENAZ-DA-1:3(828)
ASHRIEL-1CH-7:14(845)
ASHTAROTH-all=6252-JOS-9:10■12:4■13:12,31-J'G-2:13■10:6-1SA-7:3,4■12:10■31:10-1CH-6:71
ASHERATHITE-1CH-11:44(6254)
ASHEROTH-GE-14:5(6255)
ASHTORETH-all=6252-1KI-11:5, 33-2KI-23:13
ASHUR-all=804-1CH-2:24(804)■4:5(804)
ASHURITES-2SA-2:9(843)-EZE-27:6(843)
ASHVATH-1CH-7:33(6220)
ASIA-all=773&marked-AC-2:9■6:9■ 16:6■19:10,22,26,27,31(775)■20:4^2,16, 18■21:27■24:18■27:2-1CO-16:19-2CO-1:8-2TI-1:15-1PE-1:1-RE-1:4,11
ASIEL-1CH-4:35(6221)
ASKELON-all=831-J'G-1:18-1SA-6:17-2SA-1:20
ASNAH-EZR-2:50(619)
ASNAPPER-EZR-4:10(620)
ASPATHA-ES-9:7(630)
ASRIEL-NU-26:31(844)-JOS-17:2(844)
ASRIELITES-NU-26:31(845)
ASSHUR-all=804-GE-10:11,22-NU-24:22,24-1CH-1:17-EZE-27:23■32:22 -HO-14:3
ASSHURIM-GE-25:3(805)
ASSIR-all=617-EX-6:24-1CH-3:17■ 6:22,23,37
ASSOS-AC-20:13(789),14(789)
ASSUR-EZR-4:2(804)-PS-83:8(804)
ASSYRIA-all=804-GE-2:14■25:18 -2KI-15:19,20^2,29^2■16:7,8,9^2,10,18■17:3, 4^3,5,6^2,23,24,26,27■18:7,9,11^2,13,14^2,16, 17,19,23,28,30,31,33■19:4,6,8,10,11,17, 20,32,36■20:6■23:29-1CH-5:6,26^2-2CH-28:16,20,21■30:6■32:1,4,7,9,10,11,21,22■ 33:11-EZR-6:22-NE-9:32-IS-7:17,18, 20■8:4,7■10:12■11:11,16■19:23^2,24,25■ 20:1,4,6■27:13■36:1,2,4,8,13,15,16,18■ 37:4,6,8,10,11,18,21,33,37■38:6-JER-2:18,36■50:17,18-EZE-23:7-HO-7:11■ 8:9■9:3■10:6■11:11-MIC-5:6■7:12-NA-3:18-ZEP-2:13-ZEC-10:10,11
ASSYRIAN-all=804-IS-10:5,24■ 14:25■19:23■23:13■30:31■31:8■52:4 -EZE-31:3-HO-5:13■11:5-MIC-5:5,6
ASSYRIANS-all=804&marked -2KI-19:35-IS-19:23■37:36-LA-5:6 -EZE-16:28(1121,804)■23:5,9(1121, 804),12(1121,804),23-HO-12:1
ASTAROTH-DE-1:4(6252)
ASUPPIM-1CH-26:15(624),17(624)
ASYNCRITUS-RO-6:14(799)
ATAD-GE-50:10(329),11(329)
ATARAH-1CH-2:26(5851)
ATAROTH-all=5852-NU-32:3,34 -JOS-16:2,7-1CH-2:54
ATAROTH-ADAR-JOS-18:13(5853)
ATAROTH-ADDAR-JOS-16:5(5853)
ATER-all=333-EZR-2:16,42-NE-7:21,45■10:17
ATHACH-1SA-30:30(6269)
ATHAIAH-NE-11:4(6265)
ATHALIAH-all=6271-2KI-8:26■ 11:1,2,3,13,14,20-1CH-8:26-2CH-22:2, 10,11,12■23:12,13,21■24:7-EZR-8:7
ATHENIANS-AC-17:21(117)
ATHENS-all-116&marked-AC-17:15, 16,22(117)■18:1-1TH-3:1■subscr-2TH-subscr
ATHLAI-EZR-10:28(6270)
ATROTH-NU-32:35(5855)
ATTAI-all=6262-1CH-2:35,36■ 12:11-2CH-11:20
ATTALIA-AC-14:25(825)
AUGUSTUS-all=828-LU-2:1-AC-25:21,25
AUGUSTUS'-AC-27:1(828)
AVA-2KI-17:24(5755)
AVEN-all=206-EZE-30:17-HO-10:8-AM-1:5
AVIM-JOS-18:23(5761)
AVIMS-DE-2:23(5757)
AVITES-JOS-13:3(5757)-2KI-17:31(5757)
AVITH-GE-36:35(5762)-1CH-1:46(5762)
AZAL-ZEC-14:5(682)
AZALIAH-2KI-22:3(683)-2CH-34:8(683)
AZANIAH-NE-10:9(245)
AZARAEL-NE-12:36(5832)
AZAREEL-all=5832-1CH-12:6■ 25:18■27:22-EZR-10:41-NE-11:13
AZARIAH-all=5838&marked-1KI-4:2,5-2KI-14:21■15:1,6,7,8,17,23,27 -1CH-2:8,38,39■3:12■6:9^2,10,11,13,14, 36■9:11-2CH-15:1■21:2^2■22:6■23:1^2■ 26:17,20■28:12■29:12^2■31:10,13-EZR-7:1,3-NE-3:23,24■7:7■8:7■10:2■12:33 -JER-43:2-DA-1:6,7,11,19■2:17(5839)
AZAZ-1CH-5:8(5811)
AZAZIAH-all=5812-1CH-15:21■ 27:20-2CH-31:13
AZBUK-NE-3:16(5802)
AZEKAH-all=5825-JOS-10:10,11■ 15:35-1SA-17:1-2CH-11:9-NE-11:30 -JER-34:7
AZEL-all=682-1CH-8:37,38^2■9:43,44^2
AZEM-JOS-15:29(6107)■19:3(6107)
AZGAD-all=5803-EZR-2:12■8:12 -NE-7:17■10:15
AZIEL-1CH-15:20(8515)
AZIZA-EZR-10:27(5819)
AZMAVETH-all=5820-2SA-23:31 -1CH-8:36■9:42■11:33■12:3■27:25-EZR-2:24-NE-12:29
AZMON-all=6111-NU-34:4,5 -JOS-15:4
AZNOTHTABOR-JOS-19:34(243)
AZOR-M'T-1:13(107),14(107)
AZOTUS-AC-8:40(108)
AZRIEL-all=5837-1CH-5:24■27:19 -JER-36:26
AZRIKAM-all=5839-1CH-3:23■ 8:38■9:14,44■2CH-28:7-NE-11:15
AZUBAH-all=5806-1KI-22:42-1CH-2:18,19-2CH-20:31
AZUR-JER-28:1(5809)-EZE-11:11(5809)
AZZAH-all=5804-DE-2:23-1KI-4:24-JER-25:20
AZZAN-NU-34:26(5821)
AZZUR-NE-10:17(5809)

B

BAAL-all=1168&marked-NU-22:41 -J'G-2:13■6:25,28,30,31,32-1KI-16:31,32^2■ 18:19,21,25,26^2,40■19:18■22:53-2KI-3:2■10:18,19^3,20,21^3,22,23^3,25,26,27^2, 28■11:18^2■17:16■21:3■23:4,5-1CH-4:33■ 5:5■8:30■9:36-2CH-23:17^2-JER-2:8■ 7:9■11:13,17■12:16■19:5^2■23:13,27■32:29, 35-HO-2:8■13:1-ZEP-1:4■N.T.-RO-11:4(896)
BAALAH-all=1173-JOS-15:9,10,11, 29-1CH-13:6
BAALATH-all=1191-JOS-19:44-1KI-9:18-2CH-8:6
BAALATH-BEER-JOS-19:8(1192)
BAAL-BERITH-all=1170-J'G-8:33■9:4
BAALE-2SA-6:2(1184)
BAAL-GAD-all=1171-JOS-11:17■12:7■13:5
BAAL-HAMON-SONG-8:11(1174)
BAAL-HANAN-all=1177-GE-36:38, 39-1CH-1:49,50■27:28
BAAL-HAZOR-2SA-13:23(1178)
BAAL-HERMON-all=1179-J'G-3:3-1CH-5:23
BAALI-HO-2:16(1180)
BAALIM-all=1168-J'G-2:11■3:7■ 8:33■10:6,10-1SA-7:4■12:10-1KI-18:18 -2CH-17:3■24:7■28:2■33:3■34:4-JER-2:23■9:14-HO-2:13,17■11:2
BAALIS-JER-40:14(1185)
BAAL-MEON-all=1186-NU-32:38 -1CH-5:8-EZE-25:9
BAAL-PEOR-all=1187-NU-25:3,5 -DE-4:3^2-PS-106:28-HO-9:10
BAAL-PERAZIM-all=1188-2SA-5:20^2-1CH-14:11^2
BAAL'S-1KI-18:22(1168)
BAAL-SHALISHA-2KI-4:42(1190)
BAAL-TAMAR-J'G-20:33(1193)
BAAL-ZEBUB-all=1176-2KI-1:2, 3,6,16
BAAL-ZEPHON-all=1189-EX-14:2,9-NU-33:7
BAANA-all=1195-1KI-4:12-NE-3:4
BAANAH-all=1195-2SA-4:2,5,6,9■ 23:29-1KI-4:16-1CH-11:30-EZR-2:2 -NE-7:7■10:27
BAARA-1CH-8:8(1199)
BAASEIAH-1CH-6:40(1202)
BAASHA-all=1201-1KI-15:16,17,19, 21,22,27^2,28,32,33■16:1,3,4,5,6,7,8,11, 12^2,13■21:22-2KI-9:9-2CH-16:1,3,5,6 -JER-41:9
BABEL-GE-10:10(894)■11:9(894)
BABYLON-all=894,a=895-2KI-17:24, 30■20:12,14,17,18■24:1,7,10,11,12^2,15^2, 16,17,20■25:1,6,7,8^2,11,13,20,21,22,23,24, 27,28-1CH-9:1-2CH-32:31■33:11■36:6^2, 7^2,10,18,20-EZR-1:11■2:1■5:12^{2}a,13a, 14^{2}a,17a■6:1a,5a■7:6,9,16a■8:1-NE-7:6■ 13:6-ES-2:6-PS-87:4■137:1,8-IS-13:1, 19■14:4,22■21:9■39:1,3,6,7■43:14■47:1■ 48:14,20-JER-20:4^2,5,6■21:2,4,7,10■ 22:25■24:1^2■25:1,9,11,12■27:6,8^2,9,11,12, 13,14,16,17,18,20^2,22■28:2,3^2,4^2,6,11,14■ 29:1,3^2,4,10,15,20,21,22^2,28■32:3,4,5,28, 36■34:1,2,3^2■35:11■36:29■7:1,17,19■38:23■ 39:1,3^2,5,6^2,7,9,11■40:1,4^2,5,7^2,9,11■41:2, 18■42:11■43:3,10■44:30■46:2,13,26■49:28, 30■50:1,2,8,9,13,14,16,17,18,23,24,28,29, 34,35,42,43,45,46■51:1,2,6,7,8,9,11,12^2, 24,29^2,30,31,33,34,35,37,41,42,44^2,47,48, 49^2,53,54,55,56,58,59,60^2,61,64■52:3,4,9, 10,11^2,12^2,15,17,26,27,31,32,34-EZE-12:13■17:12^2,16,20■19:9■21:19,21■24:2■ 26:7■29:18,19■30:10,24,25^2■32:11 -DA-1:1■2:12a,14a,18a,24^{2}a,48^{2}a, 49a■3:1a,12a,30a■4:6a,29a,30a■5:7a■ 7:1a-MIC-4:10-ZEC-2:7■6:10■ N.T.-all=897-M'T-1:11,12,17^2-AC-7:43-1PE-5:13-RE-14:8■16:19■ 17:5■18:2,10,21
BABYLONIANS-all=1121,894& marked-EZR-4:9(896)-EZE-23:15■ 23:17,23
BABYLON'S-all=894-JER-32:2■ 34:7,21■38:3,17,18,22■39:13
BACA-PS-84:6(1056)
BACHRITES-NU-26:35(1076)
BAHARUMITE-1CH-11:33(978)
BAHURIM-all=980-2SA-3:16■16:5■ 17:18■19:16 -1KI-2:8
BAJITH-IS-15:2(1006)
BAKBAKKAR-1CH-9:15(1230)
BAKBUK-all=1227-EZR-2:51-NE-7:53
BAKBUKIAH-all=1229-NE-1:17■ 12:9,25
BALAAM-all=1109-NU-22:5,7,8,9,10,12, 13,14,16,18,20,21,23,27,28,29,30,31,34,35^2, 36,37,38,39,40,41■23:1,2^2,3,4,11,16,25,26, 27,28,29,30■24:1,2,3,10^2,12,15,25■31:8, 16-DE-23:4,5-JOS-13:22■24:9,10-NE -13:2-MIC-6:5■N.T.-all=903-2PE-2:15-JUDE-11-RE-2:14

BALAAM'S-all=1109-NU-22:25, 27■23:5

BALAC-RE-2:14(904)

BALADAN-2KI-20:12(1081)-IS-39:1(1081)

BALAH-JOS-19:3(1088)

BALAK-all=1111-NU-22:2,4,7,10,13, 14,15,16,18^2,35,36,37,38,39,40,41■23:1, 2^2,3,5,7,11,13,15,16,17,18,25,26,27,28, 29,30■24:10,12,13,25-JOS-24:9-J'G-11:25-MIC-6:5

BALAK'S-NU-24:10(1111)

BAMAH-EZE-20:29(1117)

BAMOTH-NU-21:19(1120),20(1120)

BAMOTH-BAAL-JOS-13:17(1120)

BANI-all=1137-2SA-23:36-1CH-6:46■9:4-EZR-2:10■10:29,34,38-NE-3:17■8:7■9:4^2,5■10:13,14■11:22

BAPTIST-all=910&marked-M'T-3:1■11:11,12■14:2■16:4■17:13-M'R-6:14(907),24,25■8:28-LU-7:20,28,33■9:19

BAPTIST'S-M'T-14:8(910)

BARABBAS-all=912-M'T-27:16, 17,20,21,26-M'R-15:7,11,15-LU-23:18-JO-18:40^2

BARACHEL-JOB-32:2(1292), 6(1292)

BARACHIAS-M'T-23:35(914)

BARAK-all=1301-J'G-4:6,8,9,10,12, 14^2,15,16,22■5:1,12,15-HEB-11:32

BARHUMITE-2SA-23:31(1273)

BARIAH-1CH-3:22(1282)

BAR-JESUS-AC-13:6(919)

BAR-JONA-M'T-16:17(920)

BARKOS-EZR-2:53(1302)-NE-7:55(1302)

BARNABAS-all=921-AC-4:36■9:27■11:22,25,30■12:25■13:1,2,7,43,46, 50■14:12,14,20■15:2^2,12,22,25,35,36, 37,39-1CO-9:6-GA-2:1,9,13-COL-4:10

BARSABAS-AC-1:23(923)■15:22(923)

BARTHOLOMEW-all=918-M'T-10:3-M'R-3:18-LU-6:14-AC-1:13

BARTIMAEUS-M'R-10:46(924)

BARUCH-all=1263-NE-3:20■10:6■11:5-JER-32:12,13,16■36:4^2,5,8,10,13,14^2, 15,16,17,18,19,26,27,32■43:3,6■45:1,2

BARZILLAI-all=1271-2SA-17:27■19:31,32,33,34,39■21:8-1KI-2:7-EZR-2:61^2-NE-7:63^2

BASHAN-all=1316-NU-21:33^2■32:33-DE-1:4■3:1^2,3,4,10^2,11,13^2■4:43,47■29:7■32:14■33:22-JOS-9:10■12:4,5■13:11,12,30^3,31■17:1,5■20:8■21:6,27■22:7-1KI-4:13,19-2KI-10:33-1CH-5:11,12,16,23■6:62,71-NE-9:22-PS-22:12■68:15^2,22■135:11■136:20-IS-2:13■33:9-JER-22:20■50:19-EZE-27:6■39:18-AM-4:1-MIC-7:14-NA-1:4-ZEC-11:2

BASHAN-HAVOTH-JAIR-DE-3:14(1316,2334)

BASHEMATH-all=1315-GE-26:34■36:3,4,10,13,17

BASMATH-1KI-4:15(1315)

BATH-RABBIM-SONG-7:4(1337)

BATHSHEBA-all=1339-2SA-11:3■12:24-1KI-1:11,15,16,28,31■2:13,18,19-PS-51:t

BATHSHUA-1CH-3:5(1340)

BAVAI-NE-3:18(942)

BAZLITH-NE-7:54(1213)

BAZLUTH-EZR-2:52(1213)

BE-all=19613■N.T.-all=1510

BEALIAH-1CH-12:5(1183)

BEALOTH-JOS-15:24(1175)

BEBAI-all=893-EZR-2:11■8:11^2■10:28-NE-7:16■10:15

BECHER-all=1071-GE-46:21-NU-26:35-1CH-7:6,8^2

BECHORATH-2SA-9:1(1064)

BEDAD-GE-36:35(911)-1CH-1:46(911)

BEDAN-all=917-2SA-12:11-1CH-7:17

BEDEIAH-EZR-10:35(912)

BEELIADA-1CH-14:7(1182)

BEELZEBUB-all=954-M'T-10:25■12:24,27-M'R-3:22-LU-11:15,18,19

BEER-NU-21:16(876)-J'G-9:21(876)

BEERA-1CH-7:37(878)

BEERAH-1CH-5:6(880)

BEER-ELIM-IS-15:8(879)

BEERI-GE-26:34(882)-HO-1:1(882)

BEER-LAHAI-ROI-GE-16:14(883)

BEEROTH-all=881-DE-10:6-JOS-9:17■18:25-2SA-4:2-EZE-2:25-NE-7:29

BEEROTHITE-all=886-2SA-4:2, 5,9■23:37

BEEROTHITES-2SA-4:3(886)

BEERSHEBA-all=884-GE-21:14, 31,32,33■22:19^2■26:23,33■28:10■46:1,5-JOS-15:28■19:2-J'G-20:1-1SA-3:20■8:2-2SA-3:10■17:11■24:2,7,15-1KI-4:25■19:3-2KI-12:1■23:8-1CH-4:28■21:2-2CH-19:4■24:1■30:5-NE-11:27,30-AM-5:5■8:14

BEESH-TERAH-JOS-21:27(1200)

BEL-all=1078-IS-46:1-JER-50:2■51:44

BELA-all=1106-GE-14:2,8■36:32,33-NU-26:38,40-1CH-1:43,44■5:8■7:6,7■8:1,3

BELAH-GE-46:21(1106)

BELAITES-NU-26:38(1108)

BELIAL-all=1100-DE-13:13-J'G-19:22■20:13-1SA-1:16■2:12■10:27■25:17, 25■30:22-2SA-16:7■20:1■23:6-1KI-21:10, 13^2-2CH-13:7■N.T.-2CO-6:15(955)

BELSHAZZAR-all=1113-DA-5:1, 2,9,22,29,30■7:1■8:1

BELTESHAZZAR-all=1096&marked-DA-1:7(1095)■2:26■4:8,9,18, 19^3■5:12■10:1(1095)

BEN-1CH-15:18(1122)

BEN-AMMI-GE-19:38(1151)

BENAIAH-all=1141-2SA-8:18■20:23■23:20,22,30-1KI-1:8,10,26,32,36, 38,44■2:25,29,30^2,34,35,46■4:4-1CH-4:36■11:22,24,31■15:18,20,24■16:5,6■18:17■27:5,6,14,34-2CH-20:14■31:13-EZR-10:25,30,35,43-EZE-11:1,13

BENE-BERAK-JOS-19:45(1138)

BENE-JAAKAN-NU-33:31(1142), 32(1142)

BEN-HADAD-all=1130,a=1131-1KI-15:18a,20a■20:1a,2a,5a,9a,10a,16,17, 20,26,30,32,33^2,34-2KI-6:24■8:7,9■13:3, 24,25-2CH-16:2,4-JER-49:27-AM-1:4

BEN-HAIL-2CH-17:7(1134)

BEN-HANAN-1CH-4:20(1135)

BENINU-NE-10:13(1148)

BENJAMIN-all=1144-GE-35:18, 24■42:4,36■43:14,15,16,29■45:12,14, 22■46:19:21■49:27-EX-1:3-NU-1:11, 36,37■2:22^2■7:60■10:24■13:9■26:38,41■34:21-DE-27:12■34:12-JOS-18:11,20, 21,28■21:4,17-J'G-1:21^2■5:14■10:9■19:14■20:3,4,10,12,13,14,15,17,18,20,21, 23,24,25,28,30,31,32,35,36,39,41,44,46, 48■21:1,6,13,14,15,16,17,18,20,21,23-1SA-4:12■9:1,16,21■10:2,20,21■13:2, 15,16■14:16-2SA-2:9,15,25,31■3:19^2■4:2^2■19:17■21:14■23:29-1KI-4:18■12:21,23■15:22-1CH-2:2■6:60,65■7:6, 10■8:1,40■9:3,7■11:31■12:2,16,29■21:6■27:21-2CH-11:1,3,10,12,23■14:8■15:2, 8,9■17:17■25:5■31:1■34:9,32-EZR-1:5■4:1■10:9,32-NE-3:23■11:4,7,31, 36■12:34-PS-68:27■80:2-JER-1:1■6:1■17:26■20:2■32:8,44■33:13■37:12,13■38:7-EZE-48:22,23,24,32-HO-5:8-OB-19■N.T.-all=958-AC-13:21-RO-11:1-PH'M-3:5-RE-7:8

BENJAMIN'S-all=1144-GE-43:34■44:12■45:14-ZEC-14:10

BENJAMITE-all=1145-J'G-3:15-1SA-9:1,21-2SA-16:11■19:16■20:1-1KI-2:8-ES-2:5-PS-7:t

BENJAMITES-all=1145-J'G-19:16■20:35,36,40,43-1SA-9:4■22:7-1CH-27:12

BENO-1CH-24:26(1121),27(1121)

BEN-ONI-GE-35:18(1126)

BEN-ZOHETH-1CH-4:20(1132)

BEON-NU-32:3(1194)

BEOR-all=1160-GE-36:32-NU-22:5■24:3,15■31:8-DE-23:4-JOS-13:22■24:9-1CH-1:43-MIC-6:5

BERA-GE-14:2(1298)

BERACHAH-all=1294-1CH-12:3-2CH-20:26^2

BERACHIAH-1CH-6:39(1296)

BERAIAH-1CH-8:21(1256)

BEREA-all=960-AC-17:10,13■20:4

BERECHIAH-all=1296-1CH-3:20■9:16■15:17,23-2CH-28:12-NE-3:4,30■6:18-ZEC-1:1,7

BERED-GE-16:14(1260)-1CH-7:20(1260)

BERI-1CH-7:36(1275)

BERIAH-all=1283-GE-46:17^2-NU-26:44, 45-1CH-7:23,30,31■8:13,16■23:10,11

BERIITES-NU-26:44(1284)

BERITES-2SA-20:14(1276)

BERITH-J'G-9:46(1286)

BERNICE-all=959-AC-25:13,23■26:30

BERODACH-BALADAN-2KI-20:12(1255)

BEROTHAH-EZE-47:16(1268)

BEROTHAI-2SA-8:8(1268)

BEROTHITE-1CH-11:39(1307)

BESAI-EZR-2:49(1153)-NE-7:52(1153)

BESODEIAH-NE-3:6(1152)

BESOR-all 1308-1SA-30:9,10,21

BETAH-2SA-8:8(984)

BETEN-JOS-19:25(991)

BETHABARA-JOH-1:28(962)

BETH-ANATH-all=1043-JOS-19:38-J'G-1:33^2

BETH-ANOTH-JOS-15:59(1042)

BETHANY-all=963-M'T-21:17■26:6-M'R-11:1,11,12■14:3-LU-19:29■24:50-JOH-11:1,18■12:1

BETH-ARABAH-all=1026-JOS-15:6,61■18:22

BETH-ARAM-JOS-13:27(1027)

BETH-ARBEL-HO-10:14(1009)

BETH-AVEN-all=1007-JOS-7:2■18:12-1SA-13:5■14:23-HO-4:15■5:8■10:5

BETH-AZMAVETH-NE-7:28(1041)

BETH-BAAL-MEON-JOS-13:17(1010)

BETH-BARAH-J'G-7:24^2(1012)

BETH-BIREI-1CH-4:31(1011)

BETH-CAR-1SA-7:11(1033)

BETH-DAGON-JOS-5:41(1016)■19:27(1016)

BETH-DIBLATHAIM-JER-48:22(1015)

BETH-EL-all=1008-GE-12:8^2■13:3^2■28:19■31:13■35:1,3,6,8,15,16-JOS-7:2■8:9,12,17■12:9,16■16:1,2■18:13,22-J'G-1:22,23■4:5■21:19^2-1SA-7:16■10:3■13:2■30:27-1KI-12:29,32^2,33■13:1,4,10, 11^2,32-2KI-2:2^2,3,23■10:29■17:28■23:4, 15,17,19-1CH-7:28-2CH-13:19-EZR-2:28-NE-7:32■11:31-JER-48:13-HO-10:15■12:4-AM-3:14■4:4■5:5^2,6■7:10,13

BETH-ELITE-1KI-16:34(1017)

BETH-EMEK-JOS-19:27(1025)

BETHER-SONG-2:17(1336)

BETHESDA-JOH-5:2(964)

BETH-EZEL-MIC-1:11(1018)

BETH-GADER-1CH-2:51(1013)

BETH-GAMUL-JER-48:23(1014)

BETH-HACCEREM-all=1021-NE-3:14-JER-6:1

BETH-HARAN-NU-32:36(1028)

BETH-HOGLA-JOS-15:6(1031)

BETH-HOGLAH-JOS-8:19(1031), 21(1031)

BETH-HORON-all=1032-JOS-10:10, 11■16:3,5■18:13,14■21:22-1SA-13:18-1KI-9:17-1CH-6:68■7:24-2CH-8:5^2■25:13

BETH-JESIMOTH-NU-33:49(1020)

BETH-JESHIMOTH-all=1020-JOS-12:3■13:20-EZE-25:9

BETH-LEBAOTH-JOS-19:6(1034)

BETHLEHEM-all=1035-GE-35:19■48:7-JOS-19:15-J'G-12:8,10-RU-1:19^2,22■2:4■4:11-1SA-16:4■17:15■20:6, 28-2SA-2:32■23:14,15,16,24-1CH-2:51, 54■4:4■11:16,17,18,26-2CH-11:6-EZR-2:21-NE-7:26-JER-41:17-MIC-5:2■N.T.-all=965-M'T-2:1,5,6,8,16-LU-2:4,15-JO-7:42

BETHLEHEMITE-all=1022-2SA-16:1,18■17:58-2SA-21:19

BETHLEHEM-JUDAH-all=1035-J'G-17:7,8,9■19:1,2,18^2-RU-1:1,2-1SA-17:12

BETH-MAACHAH-2SA-20:14(1038),15(1038)

BETH-MARCABOTH-JOS-19:5(1024)-1CH-4:31(1024)

BETH-MEON-JER-48:23(1010)

BETH-NIMRAH-NU-32:36(1036)-JOS-13:27(1039)

BETH-PALET-JOS-15:27(1046)

BETH-PAZZEZ-JOS-19:21(1048)
BETH-PEOR-all=1047-DE-3:29■4:46■34:6-JOS-13:20
BETHPHAGE-all=967-M'T-21:1-M'R-11:1-LU-19:29
BETH-PHELET-NE-11:26(1046)
BETH-RAPHA-1CH-4:12(1051)
BETH-REHOB-J'G-18:28(1050)-2SA-10:6(1050)
BETHSAIDA-all=966-M'T-11:21-M'R-6:45■8:22-LU-9:10■10:13-JOH-1:44■12:21
BETH-SHAN-all=1052-1SA-31:10,12-2SA-21:12
BETH-SHEAN-all=1052-JOS-17:11,16-J'G-1:27-1KI-4:12^2-1CH-7:29
BETH-SHEMESH-all=1053-JOS-15:10■19:22,38■21:16-J'G-1:33^2-1SA-6:9,12^2,13,15,19,20-1KI-4:9-2KI-14:11,13-1CH-6:59-2CH-25:21,23■28:18-JER-43:13
BETH-SHEMITE-1SA-6:14(1030),18(1030)
BETH-SHITTAH-J'G-7:22(1029)
BETH-TAPPUAH-JOS-15:53(1054)
BETHUEL-all=1328-GE-22:22,23■24:15,24,47,50■25:20■28:2,5-1CH-4:30
BETHUL-JOS-19:4(1329)
BETH-ZUR-all=1049-JOS-15:58-1CH-2:45-2CH-11:7-NE-3:16
BETONIM-JOS-13:26(993)
BEULAH-IS-62:4(1166)
BEZAI-all=1209-EZR-2:17-NE-7:23■10:18
BEZALEEL-all=1212-EX-31:2■35:30■36:1,2■37:1■38:22-1CH-2:20-2CH-1:5-EZR-10:30
BEZEK-all=966-J'G-1:4,5-1SA-11:8
BEZER-all=1221-DE-4:43-JOS-20:8■21:36-1CH-6:78■7:37
BICHRI-all=1075-2SA-20:1,2,6,7,10,13,21,22
BIDKAR-2KI-9:25(920)
BIGTHA-ES-1:10(903)
BIGTHAN-ES-2:21(904)
BIGTHANA-ES-6:2(904)
BIGVAI-all=902-EZR-2:2,14■8:14-NE-7:7,19■10:16
BILDAD-all=1085-JOB-2:11■8:1■18:1■25:1■42:9
BILEAM-1CH-6:70(1109)
BILGAH-all=1083-1CH-24:14-NE-12:5,18
BILGAI-NE-10:8(1084)
BILHAH-all=1090-GE-29:29■30:3,4,5,7■35:22,25■37:2■46:25-1CH-4:29■7:13
BILHAN-all=1092-GE-36:27-1CH-1:42■7:10^2
BILSHAN-EZR-2:2(1114)-NE-7:7(1114)
BIMHAL-1CH-7:33(1118)
BINEA-1CH-8:37(1150)■9:43(1150)
BINNUI-all=1131-EZR-8:33■10:30,38-NE-3:24■7:15■10:9■12:8
BIRSHA-GE-14:2(1306)
BIRZAVITH-1CH-7:31(1269)
BISHLAM-EZR-4:7(1312)
BITHIAH-1CH-4:18(1332)
BITHRON-2SA-2:29(1338)
BITHYNIA-AC-16:7(978)-1PE-1:1(978)
BIZJOTHJAH-JOS-15:28(964)
BIZTHA-ES-1:10(968)
BLASTUS-AC-12:20(986)
BOANERGES-M'R-3:17(993)
BOAZ-all=1162-RU-2:1,3,4,5,8,11,14,15,19,23■3:2,7■4:1^2,5,8,9,13,21-1KI-7:21-1CH-2:11,12-2CH-3:17
BOCHERU-all=1074-1CH-8:33■9:44
BOCHIM-J'G-2:1(1066),5(1066)
BOHAN-JOS-15:6(932)■18:17(932)
BOOZ-M'T-1:5^2(1003)-LU-3:32(1003)
BOSCATH-2KI-22:1(1218)
BOSOR-2PE-2:15(1007)
BOZEZ-1SA-14:4(949)
BOZKATH-JOS-15:39(1218)
BOZRAH-all=1224-GE-36:33-1CH-1:44-IS-34:6■63:1-JER-48:24■49:13,22-AM-1:12- MIC-2:12
BUKKI-all=1231-NU-34:22-1CH-6:5,51-EZR-7:4
BUKKIAH-1CH-25:4(1232),13(1232)
BUL-1KI-6:38(945)
BUNAH-1CH-2:25(946)
BUNNI-all=1137-NE-9:4■10:15■11:15
BUT-O.T.supplied■N.T.-all=235
BUZ-all=938-GE-22:21-1CH-5:14-JER-25:23
BUZI-EZE-1:3(941)
BUZITE-JOB-32:2(940),6(940)
BY-all supplied

C

CABBON-JOS-15:40(3522)
CABUL-JOS-19:27(3521)-1KI-9:13(3521)
CAESAR-all=2541-M'T-22:17,21-M'R-12:14,17-LU-2:1■3:1■20:22,25■23:2-JOH-19:12,15-AC-11:28■17:7■25:8,11,12^2,21■26:32■27:24■28:19
CAESAREA-all=2542-M'T-16:13-M'R-8:27-AC-8:40■9:30■10:1,24■11:11■12:19■18:22■21:8,16■23:23,33■25:1,4,6,13
CAESAR'S-all=2541-M'T-22:21^2-M'R-12:16,17-LU-20:24,25-JOH-19:12-AC-25:10-PH'P-4:22
CAIAPHAS-all=2503-M'T-26:3,57-LU-3:2-JOH-11:49■18:13,14,24,28-AC-4:6
CAIN-all=7014-GE-4:1,2,3,5^2,6,8^2,9,13,15^2,16,17,24,25-JOS-15:57■N.T.-all=2503-HEB-11:4-1JO-3:12-JUDE-11
CAINAN-all=7018-GE-5:9,10,12,13,14■N.T.-LU-3:36(2536),37(2536)
CALAH-GE-10:11(3625),12(3625)
CALCOL-1CH-2:6(3633)
CALEB-all=3612-NU-13:6,30■14:6,24,30,38■26:65■32:12■34:19-DE-1:36-JOS-14:6,13,14■15:13,14,16,17,18■21:12-J'G-1:12,14,15,20-1SA-25:3■30:14-1CH-2:18,19,42,49,50■4:15■6:56
CALEB-EPHRATAH-1CH-2:24(3613)
CALEB'S-all=3612-J'G-1:13■3:9-1CH-2:46,48
CALNEH-GE-10:10(3641)-AM-6:2(3641)
CALNO-IS-10:9(3641)
CALVARY-LU-23:33(2898)
CAMON-J'G-10:5(7056)
CANA-all=2580-JOH-2:1,11■4:46■21:2■16:1■subscr
CANAAN-all=3667-GE-9:18,22,25,26,27■10:6,15■11:31■12:5^2■13:12■16:3■17:8■23:2,19■28:1,6,8■31:18■33:18■35:6■36:2,5,6■37:1■42:5,7,13,29,32■44:8■45:17,25■46:6,12,31■47:1,4,13,14,15■48:3,7■49:30■50:5,13-EX-6:4■15:15■16:35-LE-14:34■18:3■25:38-NU-13:2,17■26:19■32:30,32■33:40,51■34:2^2,29■35:10,14-DE-32:49-JOS-5:12■14:1■21:2■22:9,10,11,32■24:3-J'G-3:1■4:2,23,24^2■5:19■21:12-1CH-1:8,13■16:18-PS-105:11■106:38■135:11-IS-19:18-EZE-16:3,29-ZEP-2:5■N.T.-M'T-15:22(5478)
CANAANITE-all=3669-GE-12:6■13:7■38:2-EX-23:28■33:2■34:11-NU-21:1■33:40-JOS-9:1■11:3■13:3-ZEC-14:21■N.T.-M'T-10:4(2581)-M'R-3:18(2581)
CANAANITES-all=3669-GE-10:18,19■15:21■24:3,37■34:30■50:11-EX-3:8,17■13:5,11■23:23-NU-13:29■14:25,43,45■21:3-DE-1:7■7:1■11:30■20:17-JOS-3:10■5:1■7:9■12:8■13:4■16:10^2■17:12,13,16,18■24:11-J'G-1:1,3,4,5,9,10,17,27,28,29^2,30,32,33■3:3,5-2SA-24:7-1KI-9:16-EZR-9:1-NE-9:8,24-OB-20
CANAANITESS-1CH-2:3(3669)
CANAANITISH-GE-46:10(3669)-EX-6:15(3669)
CANDACE-AC-8:27(2582)
CANNEH-EZE-27:23(3656)
CAPERNAUM-all=2584-M'T-4:13■8:5■11:23■17:24-M'R-1:21■2:1■9:33-LU-4:23,31■7:1■10:15-JOH-2:12■4:46■6:17,24,59
CAPHTHORIM-1CH-1:12(3732)
CAPHTOR-all=3731-DE-2:23-JER-47:4-AM-9:7
CAPHTORIM-GE-10:14(3732)
CAPHTORIMS-DE-2:23(3732)
CAPPADOCIA-AC-2:9(2587)-1PE-1:1(2587)
CARCAS-ES-1:10(3752)
CARCHEMISH-IS-10:9(3751)--JER-46:2(3751)
CAREAH-2KI-25:23(7143)
CARMEL-all=3760-JOS-12:22■15:55■19:26-1SA-15:12■25:2^2,5,7,40-1KI-18:19,20,42-2KI-2:25■4:25■19:23-2CH-26:10-SONG-7:5-IS-33:9■35:2■37:24-JER-46:18■50:19-AM-1:2■9:3-MIC-7:14-NA-1:4
CARMELITE-all=3761-1SA-30:5-2SA-2:2■3:3■23:35-1CH-11:37
CARMELITESS-1SA-27:3(3762)-1CH-3:1(3762)
CARMI-all=3756-GE-46:9-EX-6:14-NU-26:6-JOS-7:1,18-1CH-2:7■4:1■5:3
CARMITES-NU-26:6(3757)
CARPUS-2TI-4:13(2591)
CARSHENA-ES-1:14(3771)
CASIPHIA-EZR-8:17^2(3703)
CASLUHIM-GE-10:14(3695)-1CH-1:12(3695)
CASSIA-EX-30:24(6916)-PS-45:8(7102)-EZE-27:19(6916)
CASTOR-AC-28:11(1359)
CEDRON-JOH-18:1(2748)
CENCHREA-all=2747-AC-18:18-RO-16:1■subscr
CEPHAS-all=2786-JOH-1:42-1CO-1:12■3:22■9:5■15:5-GA-2:9
CHALCOL-1KI-4:31(3633)
CHALDAEANS-AC-7:4(5466)
CHALDEA-all=3778-JER-50:10■51:24,35-EZE-11:24■16:29■23:15,16
CHALDEANS-all=3778,a=3779-JOB-1:17-IS-23:13■43:14■47:1,5■48:14,20-JER-21:4,9■22:25■24:5■25:12■32:4,5,24,25,28,29,43■33:5■35:11■37:5,8,9,10,11,13,14■38:2,18,19,23■39:8■40:9,10■41:3,18■43:3■50:1,8,25,35,45■51:4,54■52:7,8a,14a,17a-EZE-1:3a■12:13a■23:14a,23a-DA-1:4a■2:2a,4a,5a,10a■3:8a■4:7a■5:7a,11a,30a■9:1-HAB-1:6
CHALDEANS'-JER-39:5(3778)
CHALDEES-all=3778-GE-11:28,31■15:7-2KI-24:2■25:4,5,10,13,24,25,26-2CH-36:17-NE-9:7
CHALDEES'-IS-13:19(3778)
CHANAAN-AC-7:11(5477)■13:19(5477)
CHARASHIM-1CH-4:14(2798)
CHARCHEMISH-2CH-35:20(3751)
CHARRAN-AC-7:2(5488),4(5488)
CHEBAR-all=3529-EZE-1:1,3■3:15,23■10:15,20,22■43:3
CHEDORLAOMER-all=3540-GE-14:1,4,5,9,17
CHELAL-EZR-10:30(3636)
CHELLUH-EZR-10:35(3622)
CHELUB-1CH-4:11(3620)■27:26(3620)
CHELUBAI-1CH-2:9(3621)
CHEMARIMS-ZEP-1:4(3649)
CHEMOSH-all=3645-NU-21:29-J'G-11:24-1KI-11:7,33-2KI-23:13-JER-48:7,13,46
CHENAANAH-all=3668-1KI-22:11,24-1CH-7:10-2CH-18:10,23
CHENANI-NE-9:4(3662)
CHENANIAH-all=3663-1CH-15:22,27■26:29
CHEPHAR-HAAMMONAI-JOS-18:24(3726)
CHEPHIRAH-all=3716-JOS-9:17■18:26-EZR-2:25-NE-7:29
CHERAN-GE-36:26(3763)-1CH-1:41(3763)
CHERETHIMS-EZE-25:16(3774)
CHERETHITES-all=3774-1SA-30:14-2SA-8:18■15:18■20:7,23-1KI-1:38(3746),44-1CH-18:17-ZEP-2:5
CHERITH-1KI-17:3(3747),5(3747)
CHERUB-EZR-2:59(3743)-NE-7:61(3743)
CHESALON-JOS-15:10(3693)
CHESED-GE-22:22(3777)
CHESIL-JOS-15:30(3686)
CHESULLOTH-JOS-19:18(3694)
CHEZIB-GE-38:5(3580)
CHIDON-1CH-13:9(3592)
CHILEAB-2SA-3:3(3609)
CHILION-RU-1:2(3630),5(3630)
CHILION'S-RU-4:9(3630)
CHILMAD-EZE-27:23(3638)
CHIMHAM-all=3643-2SA-19:37,38,40-JER-41:17
CHINNERETH-all=3672-NU-

34:11-DE-3:17-JOS-13:27■19:35

CHINNEROTH-JOS-11:2(3672)■12:3(3672)

CHIOS-AC-20:15(5508)

CHISLEU-NE-1:1(3691)-ZEC-7:1(3691)

CHISLON-NU-34:21(3692)

CHISLOTH-TABOR-JOS-19:12(3696)

CHITTIM-all=3794-NU-24:24-1SA-23:1,12-JER-2:10-EZE-27:6-DA-11:30

CHIUN-AM-5:26(5394)

CHLOE-1CO-1:11(5514)

CHORASHAN-1SA-30:30(3565)

CHORAZIN-M'T-11:21(5523)-LU-10:13(5523)

CHOZEBA-1CH-4:22(3758)

CHRIST-all=5547&marked-M'T-1:1,16,17,18■2:4■11:2■16:16,20■22:42■23:8,10■24:5,23■26:63,68■27:17,22-M'R-1:1■8:29■9:41■12:35■13:6,21■14:61■15:32-LU-2:11,26■3:15■4:41^{2}■9:20■20:41■22:67■23:2,35,39■24:26-JOH-1:17,20,25,41■3:28■4:25,29,42■6:69■7:26,27,31,41^{2},42■9:22■10:24■11:27■12:34■17:3■20:31-AC-2:30,31,36,38■3:6,18,20■4:10,26■5:42■8:5,12,37■9:20,22,34■10:36■11:17■15:11,26■16:18,31■17:3^{2}■18:5,28■19:4■20:21■24:24■26:23■28:31-RO-1:1,3,6,7,8,16■2:16■3:22,24■5:1,6,8,11,15,17,21■6:3,4,8,9,11,23■7:4,25■8:1,2,9,10,11,17,34,35,39■9:1,3,5■10:4,6,7■12:5■13:14■14:9,10,15,18■15:3,5,6,7,8,16,17,18,19,20,29■16:3,5,7,9,10,16,18,20,24,25,27-1CO-1:1,2^{2},3,4,6,7,8,9,10,12,13,17^{2},23,24,30■2:2,16■3:1,11,23■4:1,10,15^{2},17■5:4^{2},7■6:15^{2}■8:6,11,12■9:1,12,18,21■10:4,9,16^{2}■11:1,3^{2}■12:12,27■15:3,12,13,14,15,16,17,18,19,20,22,23,31,57■16:22,23,24-2CO-1:1,2,3,5^{2},19,21■2:10,14,15,17■3:3,4,14■4:4,5,6■5:10,14,16,17,18,19,20■6:15■8:9,23■9:13■10:1,5,14■11:2,3,10,13,23,31■12:2,9,19■13:3,5,14-GA-1:1,3,6,7,10,12,22■2:4,16^{3},17^{2},20^{2},21■3:1,13,14,16,17,22,24,26,27,28■4:7,14,19■5:1,2,4,6■6:2,12,14,15,18-EPH-1:1^{2},2,3^{2},5,10,12,17,20■2:5,6,7,10,12,13^{2},20■3:1,4,6,8,9,11,14,17,19,21■4:7,12,13,15,20■5:2,5,14,20,23,24,25,32■6:5,6,23,24-PH'P-1:1^{2},2,6,8,10,11,13,15,16,18,19,20,21,23,26,27,29■2:1,5,11,16,30■3:3,7,8^{2},9,12,14,18,20■4:7,13,19,21,23-COL-1:1,2^{2},3,4,7,24,27,28■2:2,5,6,8,11,17,20■3:1^{2},3,4,11,13,16,24■4:3,12-1TH-1:1^{2},3■2:6,14,19■3:2,11,13■4:16■5:9,18,23,28-2TH-1:1,2,8,12^{2}■2:1,2,14,16■3:5,6,12,18-1TI-1:1^{2},2,12,14,15,16■2:5,7■3:13■4:6■5:11,21■6:3,13,14-2TI-1:1^{2},2,9,10,13■2:1,3,8,10,19■3:12,15■4:1,22-TIT-1:1,4■2:13■3:6-PH'M-1,3,6,8,9,23,25-HEB-3:1,6,14■5:5■6:1■9:11,14,24,28■10:10■11:26■13:8,21-JAS-1:1■2:1-1PE-1:1,2,3^{2},7,11^{2},13,19■2:5,21■3:16,18,21■4:1,11,14■5:1,10,14-2PE-1:1^{2},8,11,14,16■2:20■3:18-1JO-1:3,7■2:1,22■3:23■4:2,3■5:1,6,20-2JO-3,7,9^{2}-JUDE-1^{2},4,17,21-RE-1:1,2,5,9^{2}■11:15■12:10,17■20:4,6■22:21

CHRIST'S-all=5547-RO-15:30-1CO-3:23■4:10■7:22■15:23-2CO-2:12■5:20■10:7^{3}■12:10-GA-3:29■5:24-EPH-4:32-PH'P-2:21-1PE-4:13

CHRISTS-M'T-24:24(5880)-M'R-13:22(5880)

CHRISTIAN-AC-26:28(5546)-1PE-4:16(5546)

CHRISTIANS-AC-11:26(5546)

CHRONICLES-1CH-1:t(1697,3117)-2CH-1:t(1697,3117)

CHUB-EZR-30:5(3552)

CHUN-1CH-18:8(3560)

CHUSHAN-RISHATHAIM-J'G-3:8^{2}(3573),10^{2}(3573)

CHUZA-LU-8:3(5529)

CILCICIA-all=2791-AC-6:9■15:23,41■21:39■22:3■23:34■27:5-GA-1:21

CINNEROTH-1KI-15:20(3672)

CIS-AC-13:21(2797)

CLAUDA-AC-27:16(2802)

CLAUDIA-2TI-4:21(2803)

CLAUDIUS-all=2804-AC-11:28■18:2■23:26

CLEMENT-PH'P-4:3(2815)

CLEOPAS-LU-24:18(2810)

CLEOPHAS-JOH-19:25(2832)

CNIDUS-AC-27:7(2834)

COLHOZEH-NE-3:15(3626)■11:5(3636)

COLOSSE-COL-1:2(2857)

COLOSSIANS-COL-1:t(2858), subscr.(2858)

CONANIAH-2CH-35:9(3562)

CONIAH-all=3659-JER-22:24,28■37:1

CONONIAH-2CH-1:12(3562),13(3562)

COOS-AC-21:1(2972)

CORE-JUDE-11(2879)

CORINTH-all=2882-AC-18:1■19:1-1CO-1:2-2CO-1:1,23-2TI-4:20

CORINTHIANS-all=2881-AC-18:8-1CO-1:t,subscr-2CO-1:t,6:11,subscr.

CORINTHUS-RO-subscr.(2882)

CORNELIUS-all=2883-AC-10:1,3,7,17,21,22,24,25,30,31

COSAM-LU-3:28(2973)

COZ-1CH-4:8(6976)

COZBI-NU-25:15(3579),18(3579)

CRESCENS-2TI-4:10(2913)

CRETE-all=2914-AC-27:7,12,13,21-TIT-1:5

CRETES-AC-2:11(2912)

CRETIANS-TIT-1:12(2912),subscr.(2912)

CRISPUS-AC-18:8(2921)-1CO-1:14(2921)

CUSH-all=3568-GE-10:6,7,8-1CH-1:8,9,10-PS-7:t-IS-11:11

CUSHAN-HAB-3:7(3572)

CUSHI-all=3569-2SA-18:21^{2},22,23,31,32^{2}-JER-36:14-ZEP-1:1

CUTH-2KI-17:30(3575)

CUTHAH-2KI-17:24(3575)

CYPRUS-all=2954-AC-4:36■11:19,20■13:4■ 15:39■ 21:3,16■ 27:4

CYRENE-all=2957-M'T-27:32-AC-2:10■11:20■13:1

CYRENIAN-M'R-15:21(2956)-LU-23:26(2956)

CYRENIANS-AC-6:9(2956)

CYRENIUS-LU-2:2(2958)

CYRUS-all=3566&marked-2CH-36:22^{2},23-EZR-1:1^{2},2,7,8■3:7■4:3,5■5:13^{2}(3567),14(3567),17(3567)■6:3(3567),14(3567)-IS-44:28■45:1-DA-1:21■6:28(3567)■10:1

D

DABAREH-JOS-21:28(1705)

DABBASHETH-JOS-19:11(1708)

DABERATH-JOS-19:12(1705)-1CH-6:72(1705)

DAGON-all=1712-J'G-16:23-1SA-5:2^{2},3^{2},4^{3},5^{2},7-1CH-10:10

DAGON'S-1SA-5:5(1712)

DALAIAH-1CH-3:24(1806)

DALMANUTHA-M'R-8:10(1148)

DALMATIA-2TIM-4:10(1149)

DALPHON-ES-9:7(1813)

DAMARIS-AC-17:34(1152)

DAMASCENE-2CO-11:32(1153)

DAMASCUS-all=1834&marked-GE-14:15■15:2-2SA-8:5,6-1KI-11:24^{2}■15:18■19:15■20:34-2KI-5:12■8:7,9■14:28■16:9,10^{2},11^{2},12-1CH-18:5-2CH-16:2■24:23■28:5,23-SONG-7:4-IS-7:8^{2}■8:4■10:9■17:1^{2},3-JER-49:23,24,27-EZE-27:18■47:16,17,18■48:1-AM-1:3,5■3:12(1833)■5:27-ZEC-9:1■**N.T.**-all=1154-AC-9:2,3,8,10,19,22,27■22:5,6,10,11■26:12,20-2CO-11:32-GA-1:17

DAN-all=1835-GE-14:14■30:6■35:25■46:23■49:16,17-EX-1:4■31:6■35:34■38:23-LE-24:11-NU-1:12,38,39■2:25^{2},31■7:66■10:25■13:12■26:42^{2}■34:22-DE-27:13■33:22■34:1-JOS-19:40,47^{4},48■21:5,23-J'G-1:34■5:17■13:25■18:2,16,22,23,25,26,29^{2},30^{2}■20:1-1SA-3:20-2SA-3:10■17:11■24:2,15-1KI-4:25■12:29,30■15:20-2KI-10:29-1CH-2:2■21:2■27:22-2CH-2:14■16:4■30:5-JER-4:15■8:16-EZE-27:19■48:1,2,32-AM-8:14

DANIEL-all=1841,a=1840-1CH-3:1a-EZR-8:2a-NE-10:6a-EZE-14:14a,20a■28:3a-DA-1:ta,6a,7a,8a,9a,10a,11^{2}a,17a,19a,21a■2:13,14,15,16,17,18,19^{2},20,24,25,26,27,46,47,48,49^{2}■4:8,19■5:12^{2},13^{3},17,29■6:2,3,4,5,10,11,13,14,16^{2},17,20^{3},21,23^{2},24,26,27,28■7:1,2,15,28■8:1a,15a,27a■9:2a,22a■10:1a,2a,7a,11a,12a■12:4a,5a,9a■**N.T.**-M'T-24:15(1158)-M'R-13:14(1158)

DANITES-all=1839-J'G-13:2■18:1,11-1CH-12:35

DANJAAN-2SA-24:6(1842)

DANNAH-JOS-15:49(1837)

DARA-1CH-2:6(1873)

DARDA-1KI-4:31(1862)

DARIUS-all=1867,a=1868-EZR-4:5,24a■5:5a,6a,7a■6:1a,12a,13a,14a,15a-NE-12:22-DA-5:31a■6:1a,6a,9a,25a,28a■9:1■11:1-HAG-1:1,15■2:10-ZEC-1:1,7■7:1

DARKON-EZR-2:56(1874)-NE-7:58(1874)

DATHAN-all=1885-NU-16:1,12,24,25,27^{2}■26:9^{2}-DE-11:6-PS-106:17

DAVID-all=1732-RU-4:17,22-1SA-16:13,19,20,21,22,23■17:12,14,15,17,20,22,23,26,28,29,31,32,33,34,37^{2},38,39^{3},41,42,43^{2},44,45,48^{2},49,50^{2},51,54,55,57,58■18:1,3,4,5,6,7,8,9,10,11^{2},12,14,16,17,18,19,20,21,22,23^{2},24,25^{2},26^{2},27^{2},28,29,30■19:1,2^{2},4^{2},5,7^{2},8,9,10^{2},12,14,15,18,19,20,22■20:1,3,4,5,6,10,11,12^{2},15,16,17,18,24,28,33,34,35,39,41^{2},42■21:1^{2},2,4,5,8,9,11,12■22:1,3,4,5^{2},6,14,17,20,21,22■23:1,2^{2},4,5^{2},6,7,8,9,10,12,13^{2},14,15^{2},16,18,19,24,25^{2},26^{3},28,29■24:1,2,3,4^{2},7,8^{2},9^{2},16^{2},17,22^{2}■25:1,4,5^{2},8,9,10,13^{3},14,20,21,22,23^{2},32,35,39^{2},40^{2},42,43■26:1,2,3,4,5^{2},6,7,8,9,10,12,13,14,15,17^{2},21,22,25^{3}■27:1,2,3^{2},4,5,7,8,9,10,11^{2},12■28:1,2^{2},17■29:2,3,5^{2},6,8,9,11■30:1,3,4,6^{2},7^{2},8,9,10,11,13,15,17,18^{2},19,20,21^{4},22,23,26,31-2SA-1:1^{2},2,3,4,5,11,13,14,15,16,17■2:1^{2},2,3,4^{2},5,10,11,13,15,17,31■3:1^{2},2,5,6,8,9,10,12,14,17,18^{2},19,20^{2},21^{2},22^{2},26^{2},28,31^{2},35^{2}■4:8,9,12■5:1,3^{2},4,6^{2},7^{2},8,9^{3},10,11^{2},12,13^{2},17^{3},19^{2},20^{2},21,23,25■6:1,2,5,8,9,10^{3},12^{3},14^{2},15,16^{2},17^{2},18,20^{2},21■7:5,8,17,18,20,26■8:1^{2},3,4^{2},5,6^{3},7,8,9,10,11,13,14,15^{2}■9:1,2,5,6^{2},7■10:2^{2},3^{2},5,6,7,17^{2},18■11:1^{2},2,3,4,5,6^{2},7,8,10^{2},11,12,13,14,17,18,22,23,25,27^{2}■12:1,7,13^{2},15,16^{2},17,18,19^{3},20,24,27,29,31■13:1^{2},7,21,30,37,39■15:13,14,22,30,31^{2},32,33■16:1,5,6^{2},10,11,13,23■17:1,16,17,21^{2},22,24,27,29■18:1,2,7,9,24■19:11,16,22,43■20:1,2,3,6,11,21,26■21:1^{2},3,7,11,12,15^{2},16,17,21,22■22:1,51■23:1^{2},8,9,13,14,15,16,23■24:1,10,11,12,13,14,17,18,19,21,22,24,25-1KI-1:1,8,11,13,28,31,32,37,43,47■2:1,10^{2},11,12,24,26,32,33,44,45■3:1,3,6,7,14■5:1,3,5,7■6:12■7:51■8:1,15,16,17,18,20,24,25,26,66■9:4,5,24■11:4,6,12,13,15,21,24,27,33,36,38^{2},39,43■12:16^{2},19,20,26■13:2■14:8^{2},31■15:3,5,8,11,24■22:50-2KI-8:19,24■9:28■12:21■14:3,20■15:7,38■16:2,20■17:21■18:3■20:5■21:7■22:2-1CH-2:15■3:1,9■4:31■6:31■7:2■9:22■10:14■11:1,3^{2},4,5^{3},6,7^{2},9,10,13,15,16,17,18^{2},25■12:1,8,16,17,18^{2},19,21,22,23,31,38^{2},39■13:1,2,5,6,8,11,12,13^{2}■14:1,2,3^{2},8^{3},10,11^{2},12,14,16,17■15:1,2,3,4,11,16,25,27^{2},29^{2}■16:1,2,7,43■17:1^{2},2,4,7,15,16,18,24■18:1,3,4^{2},5,6^{2},7,8,9,10,11,13,14,17■19:2^{3},3,5,6,8,17^{2},18,19■20:1,2,3^{2},8■21:1,2,5,8,10,11,13,16^{2},17,18^{2},19,21^{3},22,23,24,25,26,28,30■22:1,2,3,4,5^{2},7,17■23:1,6,25,27■24:3,31■25:1■26:26,31,32■27:18,23,24■28:1,2,11,19,20■29:1,9,10^{2},20,22,23,24,26,29-2CH-1:1,4^{2},8,9■2:3,7,12,14,17■3:1^{2}■5:1,2■6:4,6,7,8,10,15,16,17,42■7:6^{2},10,17,18■8:11^{2},14^{2}■9:31■10:16^{2},19■11:17,18■12:16■13:5,6,8■14:1■16:14■17:3■21:1,7^{2},12,20■23:3,18^{2}■24:16,25■27:9■28:1■29:2,25,26,27,30■30:26■32:5,30,33■33:7,14■34:2,3■35:3,4,15-EZR-3:10■8:2,20-NE-3:15,16■12:24,36,37^{2},45,46-PS-3:t■4:t■6:t■7:t■8:t■9:t■11:t■12:t■13:t■14:t■15:t■16:t■17:t■18:t,50■19:t■

20:t■21:t■22:t■23:t■24:t■25:t■26:t■27:t■28:t■29:t■30:t■31:t■32:t■34:t■35:t■36:t■37:t■38:t■39:t■40:t■41:t■51:t■52:t^2■53:t■54:t^2■55:t■56:t■57:t■58:t■59:t■60:t■61:t■62:t■63:t■64:t■65:t■68:t■69:t■70:t■72:20■78:70■86:t■89:3,20,35,49■101:t■103:t■108:t■109:t■110:t■122:t,5■124:t■131:t■132:1,11,17■133:t■138:t■139:t■140:t■141:t■142:t■143:t■144:t,10-PR-1:1-EC-1:1-SONG-4:4-IS-7:2,13■9:7■16:5■22:9,22■29:1■38:5■55:3-JER-17:25■21:12■22:2,4,30■23:5■29:16■30:9■33:15,17,21,22,26■36:30-EZE-34:23,24■37:24,25-HO-3:5-AM-6:5■9:11-ZEC-12:7,8^2,10,12■13:1■N.T.-all=1138-M'T-1:1,6,17^2,20■9:27■12:3,23■15:22■20:30,31■21:9,15■22:42,43,45-M'R-2:25■10:47,48■11:10■12:35,36,37-LU-1:27,32,69■2:4^2,11■3:31■6:3■18:38.39■20:42,44-JOH-7:42^2-AC-1:16■2:25,29,34■4:25■7:45■13:22^2,34,36■15:16-RO-1:3■4:6■11:9-2TI-2:8-HEB-4:7■11:32-RE-3:7■5:5■22:16

DAVID'S-all=1732-1SA-18:29■19:11^2■20:16,25,27■23:3■24:5■25:9,12,44■26:17■30:5,20-2SA-2:30■3:5■5:8■8:2,14,18■10:2,4■12:5,30■13:3,32■15:12,37■16:16■19:41■24:10,11-1KI-1:38■11:32■15:4-2KI-11:10■19:34■20:6-1CH-18:2,6,13■19:4■20:2,7■21:9■27:31,32-2CH-23:9-PS-132:10■145:t-IS-37:35-JER-13:13■N.T.-LU-20:41(1138)

DEBIR-all=1688-JOS-10:3,38,39■11:21■12:13■13:26■15:7,15^2,49■21:15-J'G-1:11^2-1CH-6:58

DEBORAH-all=1683-GE-35:8-J'G-4:4,5,9,10,14■5:1,7,12,15

DECAPOLIS-all=1179-M'T-4:25-M'R-5:20■7:31

DEDAN-all=1719-GE-10:7■25:3^2-1CH-1:9,32-JER-25:23■49:8-EZE-25:13■27:15,20■38:13

DEDANIM-IS-21:13(1720)

DEHAVITES-EZR-4:9(1723)

DEKAR-1KI-4:9(1857)

DELAIAH-all=1806-1CH-24:18-EZR-2:60-NE-6:10■7:62-JER-36:12,25

DELILAH-all=1807-J'G-16:4,6,10,12,13,18

DEMAS-all=1214-COL-4:14-2TI-4:10-PH'M-24

DEMETRIUS-all=1216-AC-19:24,38-3JO-12

DERBE-all=1191-AC-14:6,20■16:1■20:4

DEUEL-all=1845-NU-1:14■7:42,47■10:20

DEUTERONOMY-1:t(428,1697)

DIANA-all=735-AC-19:24,27,28,34,35

DIBLAIM-HO-1:3(1691)

DIBLATH-EZE-6:14(1689)

DIBON-all=1769-NU-21:30■32:3,34-JOS-13:9,17-NE-11:25-IS-15:2-JER-48:18,22

DIBON-GAD-NU-33:45(1769),46(1769)

DIBRI-LE-24:11(1704)

DIDYMUS-all=1324-JOH-11:16■20:24■21:2

DIKLAH-GE-10:27(1853)-1CH-1:21(1853)

DILEAN-JOS-15:38(1810)

DIMNAH-JOS-21:35(1829)

DIMON-IS-15:9^2(1775)

DIMONAH-JOS-15:22(1776)

DINAH-all=1783-GE-30:21■34:1,3,5,13,26■46:15

DINAH'S-GE-34:25(1783)

DINAITES-EZR-4:9(1784)

DINHABAH-GE-36:35(1838)-1CH-1:43(1838)

DIONYSIUS-AC-17:34(1354)

DIOTREPHES-3JO-9(1361)

DISHAN-all=1789-GE-36:21,28,30-1CH-1:38,42

DISHON-all=1788-GE-36:21,25,26,30-1CH-1:38,41^2

DIZAHAB-DE-1:1(1774)

DODAI-1CH-27:4(1739)

DODANIM-GE-10:4(1721)-1CH-1:7(1721)

DODAVAH-2CH-20:37(1735)

DODO-all=1734-J'G-10:1-2SA-23:9,24-1CH-11:12,26

DOEG-all=1673-1SA-21:7■22:9,18^2,22-PS-52:t

DOPHKAH-NU-33:12(1850),13(1850)

DOR-all=1756-JOS-11:2■12:23■17:11-J'G-1:27-1KI-4:11-1CH-7:29

DORCAS-AC-9:36(1393),39(1393)

DOTHAN-all=1886-GE-37:17^2-1KI-6:13

DRUSILLA-AC-24:24(1409)

DUMAH-all=1746-GE-25:14-JOS-15:25-1CH-1:30-IS-21:11

DURA-DA-3:1(1757)

E

EBAL-all=5858-GE-36:23-DE-11:29■27:4,13-JOS-8:30,33-1CH-1:22,40

EBED-all=5651-J'G-9:26,28,30,31,35-EZR-8:6

EBED-MELECH-all=5663-JER-38:7,8,10,11,12■39:16

EBENEZER-all=72-1SA-4:1■5:1■7:12

EBER-all=5677-GE-10:21,24,25■11:14,15,16,17-NU-24:24-1CH-1:18,19,25■8:12-NE-12:20

EBIASAPH-all=43-1CH-6:23,37■9:19

EBRONAH-NU-33:34(5684),35(5684)

ECCLESIASTES-EC-1:t^2(6953)

ED-supplied

EDAR-GE-35:21(5740)

EDEN-all=5731-GE-2:8,10,15■3:23,24■4:16-2KI-19:12-2CH-29:12■31:15-IS-37:12■51:3-EZE-27:23■28:13■31:9,16,18^2■36:35-JOE-2:3-AM-1:5

EDER-all=5740-JOS-15:21-1CH-23:23■24:30

EDOM-all=123-GE-25:30■32:3■36:1,8,16,17,19,21,31,32,43-EX-15:15-NU-20:14,18,20,21,23■21:4■24:18■33:37■34:3-JOS-15:1,21-J'G-5:4■11:17^2,18-1SA-14:47-2SA-8:14^3-1KI-9:26■11:14,15^2,16■22:47-2KI-3:8,9,12,20,26■8:20,22■14:7,10-1CH-1:43,51,54■18:11,13-2CH-8:17■25:20-PS-60:t■60:8,9■83:6■108:9,10■137:7-IS-11:14■63:1-JER-9:26■25:21■27:3■40:11■49:7,17,20,22-LA-4:21,22-EZE-25:12,13,14^2■32:29-DA-11:41-JOE-3:19-AM-1:6,9,11■2:1■9:12-OB-1,8-MAL-1:4

EDOMITE-all=130-DE-23:7-1SA-21:7■22:9,18-1KI-11:14-PS-52:t

EDOMITES-all=130-GE-36:9,43-1KI-11:1-2KI-8:21-1CH-18:12,13-2CH-21:8,9,10■25:14,19■28:17

EDREI-all=154-NU-21:33-DE-1:4■3:1,10-JOS-12:4■13:12,31■19:37

EGLAH-2SA-3:5(5698)-1CH-3:3(5698)

EGLAIM-IS-15:8(97)

EGLON-all=5700-JOS-10:3,5,23,34,36,37■12:12■15:39-J'G-3:12,14,15,17^2

EGYPT-all=4714&marked-GE-12:10,11,14■13:1,10■15:18■21:21■25:18■26:2■37:25,28,36■39:1■40:1^2,5■41:8^2,19,29,30,33,34,36,41,43,44,45,46^2,48,53,54,55,56,57■42:1,2,3■43:2,15■45:4,8,9,13,18,19,20,23,25,26■46:3,4,6,7,8,20,26,27^2■47:6,11,13,14,15,20,21,26,27,28,29,30■48:5^2■50:7,14,22,26-EX-1:1,5,8,15,17,18■2:23■3:7,10,11,12,16,17,18,19,20■4:18,19,20,21■5:4,12■6:11,13^2,26,27^2,28,29■7:3,4^2,5,11,19^2,21,22■8:5,6^2,7,16,17,24■9:4,6,9^2,18,22^2,23,24,25■10:2,7,12^2,13,14^2,15,19,21,22■11:1,3,4,5,6,9■12:1,12^3,13,17,27,29,30,39^2,40,41,42,51■13:3,8,9,14,15,16,17,18■14:5,7,8,11^2,12■16:1,3,6,32■17:3■18:1■19:1■20:2■22:21■23:9,15■29:46■32:1,4,7,8,11,23■33:1■34:18-LE-11:45■18:3■19:34,36■22:33■23:43■25:38,42,55■26:13,45-NU-1:1■3:13■8.17■9.1■11:5,18,20■13:22■14:3,4,19,22■15:41■20:5,15,16■21:5■22:5,11■23:22■24:8■26:4,59■32:11■33:1,38■34:5-DE-1:27,30■4:20,34,37,45,46■5:6,15■6:12,21^2,22■7:8,15,18■8:14■9:7,12,26■10:19,22■11:3^2,4,10■13:5,10■15:15■16:1,3^2,6,12■17:16■20:1■23:4■24:9,18,22■25:17■26:5,8■28:27,60,68■29:2,16,25■34:11-JOS-2:10■5:4^2,5,6,9■9:9■13:3■15:4,47■24:4,5,6,7,14,17,32-J'G-2:1,12■6:8,13■11:13,16■19:30-1SA-2:27■8:8■10:18■12:6,8^2■15:2,6,7■27:8■30:13(4713)-2SA-7:6,23-1KI-3:1■4:21,30■6:1■8:9,16,21,51,53,65■9:9,16■10:28,29■11:17,18,21,40^2■12:2^2,28■14:25-2KI-17:4,7^2,36■18:21^2,24■21:15■23:29,34■24:7^3■25:26-1CH-13:5■17:21-2CH-1:16,17■5:10■6:5■7:8,22■9:26,28■10:2^2■12:2,3,9■20:10■26:8■35:20■36:3,4^2-NE-9:9,18-PS-68:31■78:12,43,51■80:8■81:5,10■105:23,38■106:7,21■114:1■135:8,9■136:10-PR-7:16-IS-7:18■10:24,26■11:11,16■19:1^4,3,12,13,14,15,16,17,18,19,20,21,22,23^2,24,25■20:3,4,5■23:5■27:12,13■30:2^2,3■31:1■36:6^2,9■43:3■45:14■52:4-JER-2:6,18,36■7:22,25■9:26■11:4,7■16:14■23:7■24:8■25:19■26:21,22^2,23■31:32■32:20,21■34:13■37:5,7■41:17■42:14,15,16^2,17,18,19■43:2,7,11,12^2,13■44:1,8,12^2,13,14,15,24,26^2,27,28^2,30■46:2^2,8,11,13,14,17,19,20,24,25-EZE-17:15■19:4■20:5,6,7,8^2,9,10,36■23:3,8,19,27^2■27:7■29:2^2,3,6,9,10,12,19,20■30:4^2,6,8,9,10,11,13^2,15,16,18,19,21,22,25■31:2■32:2,12,15,16,18-DA-9:15■11:8,42,43-HO-2:15■7:11,16■8:13■9:3,6■11:1,5,11■12:1,9,13■13:4-JOE-3:19-AM-2:10■3:1,9■4:10■8:8■9:5,7-MIC-6:4■7:15-NA-3:9-HAG-2:5-ZEC-10:10,11■14:18,19■N.T.-all=125-M'T-2:13,14,15,19-AC-2:10■7:9,10^2,11,12,15,17,34^2,36,39,40■13:17-HEB-3:16■8:9■11:26,27-JUDE-5-RE-11:8

EGYPTIAN-all=4713&marked-GE-16:1,3■21:9■25:12■39:1,2-EX-1:19■2:11,12,14,19-LE-24:10-DE-23:7-1SA-30:11-2SA-23:21^2-1CH-2:34■11:23-IS-11:15(4714)■19:23(4714)■N.T.-all=124-AC-7:24,28■21:38

EGYPTIAN'S-all=4713-GE-39:5-2SA-23:21-1CH-11:23^2

EGYPTIANS-all=4714&marked-GE-12:12(4713),14(4713)■41:55,56■43:32^2(4713),32■45:2■46:34■47:15,20■50:3,11-EX-1:13■3:8,9,21,22■6:5,6,7■7:5,18,21,24■8:21,26^2■9:11■10:6■11:3,7■12:23,27,30,33,35,36■14:4,9,10,12^2,13,17,18,20,23,24^2,25^2,26,27^2,30^2,31■15:26■18:8,9,10^2■19:4■32:12-NU-14:13■20:15■33:3,4-DE-26:6(4713)-JOS-24:6,7(4713)-J'G-6:9■10:11-1SA-4:8■6:6■10:18-2KI-7:6-EZR-9:1(4713)-IS-19:2,4,21,24■20:4■30:7■31:3-JER-43:13-LA-5:6-EZE-16:26■23:21■29:12,13■30:23,26■N.T.-AC-7:22(124)-HEB-11:29(124)

EHI-GE-46:21(278)

EHUD-all=261-J'G-3:15,16,20^2,21,23,26■4:1 1CH-7:10■8:6

EKER-1CH-2:27(6134)

EKRON-all=6138-JOS-13:3■15:11,45,46■19:43-J'G-1:18-1SA-5:10^2■6:16,17■7:14■17:52^2-2KI-1:2,3,6,16-JER-25:20-AM-1:8-ZEP-2:4-ZEC-9:5,7

EKRONITES-JOS-13:3(6139)-1SA-5:10(6139)

ELADAH-1CH-7:20(497)

ELAH-all=425-GE-36:41-1SA-17:2,19■21:9-1KI-4:18■16:6,8,13,14-2KI-15:30■17:1■18:1,9-1CH-1:52■4:15^2■9:8

ELAM-all=5867-GE-10:22■14:1,9-1CH-1:17■8:24■26:3-EZR-2:7,31■8:7■10:2,26-NE-7:12,34■10:14■12:42-IS-11:11■21:2■22:6-JER-25:25■49:34,35,36^2,37,38,39-EZE-32:24-DA-8:2

ELAMITES-EZR-4:9(5962)■N.T-AC-2:9(1639)

ELASAH-EZR-10:22(501)-JER-29:3(501)

ELATH-all=359-DE-2:8-2KI-14:22■16:6^3

EL-BETHEL-GE-35:7(416)

ELDAAH-GE-25:4(420)-1CH-1:33(420)

ELDAD-NU-11:26(419),27(419)

ELEAD-1CH-7:21(496)

ELEALEH-all=501-NU-32:3,37-IS-15:4■16:9-JER-48:34

ELEASAH-all=501-1CH-2:39,40■8:37■9:43

ELEAZAR-all=499-EX-6:23,25■28:1-LE-10:6,12,16-NU-3:2,4,32■4:16■16:37,39■19:3,4■20:25,26,28^2■25:7,11■26:1,3,60,63■27:2,19,21,22■31:6,12,13,21,26,29,31,41,51,54■32:2,28■34:17-DE-10:6-JOS-14:1■17:4■19:51■21:1■22:13,31,32■24:33-J'G-20:28-1SA-7:1-2SA-23:9-1CH-6:3,4,50■9:20■11:12■23:21,22■24:1,2,3,4^2,5,6,28-EZR-7:5■8:33-NE-12:42■N.T-M'T-1:15(1648)
EL-ELOHE-ISRAEL-GE-33:20(415)
ELEPH-JOS-18:28(507)
ELHANAN-all=445-2SA-21:19■23:24-1CH-11:26■20:5
ELI-all=5941-1SA-1:3,9,12,13,14,17,25■2:11,12,20,22,27■3:1,2,5,6,8^2,9,12,14,15,16■4:4,11,13,14^2,15,16■14:3-1KI-2:27■N.T-M'T-27:46(2241)
ELIAB-all=446-NU-1:9■2:7■7:24,29■10:16■16:1,12■26:8,9-DE-11:6-1SA-16:6■17:13,28-1CH-2:13■6:27■12:9■15:18,20■16:5-2CH-11:18
ELIAB'S-1SA-17:28(446)
ELIADA-all=450-2SA-5:16-1CH-3:8-2CH-17:17
ELIADAH-1KI-11:23(450)
ELIAH-1CH-8:27(452)-EZR-10:26(452)
ELIAHBA-2SA-23:32(455)-1CH-11:33(455)
ELIAKIM-all=471-2KI-18:18,26,37■19:2■23:34-2CH-36:4-NE-12:41-IS-22:20■36:3,11,22■37:2■N.T-M'T-1:13(1662)-LU-3:30(1662)
ELIAM-2SA-11:3(463)■23:34(463)
ELIAS-all=2243-M'T-11:14■16:14■17:3,4,10,11,12■27:47,49-M'R-6:15■8:28■9:4,5,11,12,13■15:35,36-LU-1:17■4:25,26■9:8,19,30,33,54-JOH-1:21,25-RO-11:2-JAS-5:17
ELIASAPH-all=460-NU-1:14■2:14■3:24■7:42,47■10:20
ELIASHIB-all=475-1CH-3:24■24:12-EZR-10:6,24,27,36-NE-3:1,20,21^2■12:10^2,22,23■13:4,7,28
ELIATHAH-1CH-25:4(448),27(448)
ELIDAD-NU-34:21(449)
ELIEL-all=447-1CH-5:24■6:34■8:20,22■11:46,47■12:11■15:9,11-2CH-31:13
ELIENAI-1CH-8:20(462)
ELIEZER-all=461-GE-15:2-EX-18:4-1CH-7:8■15:24■23:15,17^2■26:25■27:16-2CH-20:37-EZR-8:16■10:18,23,31■N.T-LU-3:29(1663)
ELIHOENAI-EZR-8:4(454)
ELIHOREPH-1KI-4:3(456)
ELIHU-all=453-1SA-1:1-1CH-12:20■26:7■27:18-JOB-32:2,4,5,6■34:1■35:1■36:1
ELIJAH-all=452-1KI-17:1,13,15,16,18,22,23^2,24■18:1,2,7^2,8,11,14,15,16,17,21,22,25,27,30,31,36,40^2,41,42,46■19:1,2,9,13^2,19,20,21■21:17,20,28-2KI-1:3,4,8,10,12,13,15,17■2:1^2,2,4,6,8,9,11,13,14^2,15■3:11■9:36■10:10,17-2CH-21:12-EZR-10:21-MAL-4:5
ELIKA-2SA-23:25(470)
ELIM-all=362-EX-15:27■16:1^2-NU-33:9^2,10
ELIMELECH-all=458-RU-1:2,3■2:1,3
ELIMELECH'S-RU-4:3(458),9(458)
ELIOENAI-all=454-1CH-3:23,24■4:36■7:8■26:3-EZR-10:22,27-NE-12:41
ELIPHAL-1CH-11:35(465)
ELIPHALET-2SA-5:16(467)-1CH-14:7(467)
ELIPHAZ-all=464-GE-36:4,10,11,12^2,15,16-1CH-1:35,36-JOB-2:11■4:1■15:1■22:1■42:7,9
ELIPHELEH-1CH-15:18(465),21(465)
ELIPHELET-all=467-2SA-23:34-1CH-3:6,8■8:39-EZR-8:13■10:33
ELI'S-1SA-3:14(5941)
ELISABETH-all=1665-LU-1:5,7,13,24,36,40,41^2
ELISABETH'S-LU-1:57(1665)
ELISEUS-LU-4:27(1666)
ELISHA-all=477-1KI-19:16,17,19-2KI-2:1,2^2,3,4,5,9^2,12,14,15,19,22■3:11,13,14■4:1,2,8,17,32,38■5:8,9,10,20,25■6:1,12,17^2,18^2,19,20,21,31,32■7:1■8:1,4,5,7,10,13,14^2■9:1■13:14,15,16,17,20,21^2
ELISHAH-all=473-GE-10:4-1CH-1:7-EZE-27:7
ELISHAMA-all=476-NU-1:10■2:18■7:48,53■10:22-2SA-5:16-2KI-25:25-1CH-2:41■3:6,8■7:26■14:7-2CH-17:8-JER-36:12,20,21■41:1
ELISHAPHAT-2CH-23:1(478)
ELISHEBA-EX-6:23(472)
ELISHUA-2SA-5:15(474)-1CH-14:5(474)
ELIUD-M'T-1:14(1664),15(1664)
ELIZAPHAN-all=469-NU-3:30■34:25-1CH-15:8-2CH-29:13
ELIZUR-all=468-NU-1:5■2:10■7:30,35■10:18
ELKANAH-all=511-EX-6:24-1SA-1:1,4,8,19,21,23■2:11,20-1CH-6:23,25,26,27,34,35,36■9:16■12:6■15:23-2CH-28:7
ELKOHSHITE-NA-1:1(512)
ELLASAR-GE-14:1(495),9(495)
ELMODAM-LU-3:28(1678)
ELNAAM-1CH-11:46(493)
ELNATHAN-all=494-2KI-24:8-EZR-8:16^2-JER-26:22■36:12,25
ELOI-M'R-15:34(1682)
ELON-all=356-GE-26:34■36:2■46:14-NU-26:26-JOS-19:43-J'G-12:11,12
ELON-BETH-HANAN-1KI-4:9(358)
ELONITES-NU-26:26(440)
ELOTH-all=359-1KI-9:26-2CH-8:17■26:2
ELPAAL-all=508-1CH-8:11,12,18
ELPALET-1CH-1:15(467)■14:5(467)
EL-PARAN-GE-14:6(364)
ELTEKEH-JOS-19:44(514)■21:23(514)
ELTEKON-JOS-15:59(515)
ELTOLAD-JOS-15:30(513)■19:4(513)
ELUL-NE-6:15(435)
ELUZAI-1CH-12:5(498)
ELYMAS-AC-13:8(1681)
ELZABAD-1CH-12:12(443)■26:7(443)
ELZAPHAN-EX-6:22(469)-LE-10:4(469)
EMIMS-all=368-GE-14:5-DE-2:10,11
EMMANUEL-M'T-1:23(1684)
EMMAUS-LU-24:13(1695)
EMMOR-AC-7:16(1697)
ENAM-JOS-15:34(5879)
ENAN-all=5881-NU-1:15■2:29■7:78,83■10:27
ENDOR-all=5874-JOS-17:11-1SA-28:7-PS-83:10
EN-EGLAIM-EZE-47:10(5882)
EN-GANNIM-all=5873-JOS-15:34■19:21■21:29
ENGEDI-all=5872-JOS-15:62-1SA-23:29■24:1-2CH-20:2-SONG-1:14-EZE-47:10
EN-HADDAH-JOS-19:21(5876)
EN-HAKKORE-J'G-15:19(5875)
EN-HAZOR-JOS-19:37(5877)
EN-MISHPAT-GE-14:7(5880)
ENOCH-all=2585-GE-4:17^2,18■5:18,19,21,22,23,24■N.T.-all=1802-LU-3:37-HEB-11:5-JUDE-14
ENOS-all=583-GE-4:26■5:6,7,9,10,11■N.T-LU-3:38(1800)
ENOSH-1CH-1:1(583)
EN-RIMMON-NE-11:29(5884)
EN-ROGEL-all=5883-JOS-15:7■18:16-2SA-17:17-1KI-1:9
EN-SHEMESH-JOS-15:7(5885)■18:17(5885)
EN-TAPPUAH-JOS-17:7(5887)
EPAENETUS-RO-16:5(1866)
EPAPHRAS-all=1889-COL-1:7■4:12-PH'M-23
EPAPHRODITUS-all=1891-PH'M-2:25■4:18,subscr.
EPHAH-all=5891-GE-25:4-1CH-1:33■2:46,47-IS-60:6
EPHAI-JER-40:8(5778)
EPHER-all=6081-GE-25:4-1CH-1:33■4:17■5:24
EPHESDAMMIN-1SA-17:1(658)
EPHESIAN-AC-21:29(2180)
EPHESIANS-all=2180-AC-19:28,34,35-EPH-1:t^2,subs.-2TI-subs.
EPHESUS-all=2181-AC-18:19,21,24■19:1,17,26,35■20:16,17-1CO-15:32■16:8-EPH-1:1-1TI-1:3-2TI-1:18■4:12-RE-1:11■2:1
EPHLAL-1CH-2:37(654)
EPHOD-NU-34:23(641)
EPHRAIM-all=669-GE-41:52■46:20■48:1,5,13,17,20^2-NU-1:10,32,33■2:18^2,24■7:48■10:22■13:8■26:28,35,37■34:24-DE-33:17■34:2-JOS-14:4■16:4,5,8,9■17:8,9,15,17■19:50■20:7■21:5,20,21■24:30,33-J'G-1:29■2:9■3:27■4:5■5:14■7:24^2■8:1,2■10:1,9■12:1,4^3,15■17:1,8■18:2,13■19:1,16,18-2SA-1:1■9:4■14:22-2SA-2:9■13:23■18:6■20:21-1KI-4:8■12:25-2KI-5:22■14:13-1CH-6:66,67■7:20,22■9:3■12:30■27:10,14,20-2CH-13:4■15:8,9■17:2■19:4■25:7,10,23■28:7,12■30:1,10,18■31:1■34:6,9-NE-8:16■12:39-PS-60:7■78:9,67■80:2■108:8-IS-7:2,5,8,9,17■9:9,21■11:13^3■17:3■28:1,3-JER-4:15■7:15■31:6,9,18,20■50:19-EZE-37:16,19■48:5,6-HO-4:17■5:3^2,5,9,11,12,13,13^2,14■6:4,10■7:1,8^2,11■8:9,11■9:3,8,11,13^2,16■10:6,11^2■11:3,8,9,12■12:1,8,14■13:1,12■14:8-OB-1:19-ZEC-9:10,13■10:7■N.T-JOH-11:54(2187)
EPHRAIMITE-J'G-12:5(673)
EPHRAIMITES-all=669-JOS-16:10-J'G-12:4,5^2,6
EPHRAIM'S-all=669-GE-48:14,17■50:23-JOS-17:10
EPHRAIN-2CH-13:19(6085)
EPHRATAH-all=672-RU-4:11-1CH-2:50■4:4-PS-132:6-MIC-5:2
EPHRATH-all=672-GE-35:16,19■48:7^2-1CH-2:19
EPHRATHITE-all=673-1SA-1:1■17:12-1KI-11:26
EPHRATHITES-RU-1:2(673)
EPHRON-all=6085-GE-23:8,10^2,13,14,16^2,17■25:9■49:29,30■50:13-JOS-15:9
EPICUREANS-AC-17:18(1946)
ER-all=6147-GE-38:3,6,7■46:12^2-NU-26:19^2-1CH-2:3^2■4:21■N.T-LU-3:28(2262)
ERAN-NU-26:36(6197)
ERANITES-NU-26:36(6198)
ERASTUS-all=2037-AC-19:22-RO-16:23-2TI-4:20
ERECH-GE-10:10(751)
ERI-GE-46:16(6179)-NU-26:16(6179)
ERITES-NU-26:16(6180)
ESAIAS-all=2268-M'T-3:3■4:14■8:17■12:17■13:14■15:7-M'R-7:6-LU-3:4■4:17-JOH-1:23■12:38,39,41-AC-8:28,30■28:25-RO-9:27,29■10:16,20■15:12
ESAR-HADDON-all=634-2KI-19:37-EZR-4:2-IS-37:38
ESAU-all=6215-GE-25:25,27,28,29,30,32,34^2■26:34■27:1,5^2,6,11,15,19,21,22,24,30,32,34,37,38^2,41^2,42^2■28:6,8,9■32:3,4,6,8,11,13,17,18,19■33:1,4,9,15,16■35:1,29■36:1,2,4,5,6,8,9,10^2,14,15^2,19,40,43-DE-2:4,5,8,12,22,29-JOS-24:4^2-1CH-1:34,35-JER-49:8,10-OB-6,8,9,18^2,19,21-MAL-1:2,3■N.T.-all=2269-RO-9:13-HEB-11:20■12:26
ESAU'S-all=6215-GE-25:26■27:23■28:5■36:10,12,13,14,17^2,18^2
ESEK-GE-26:20(6320)
ESH-BAAL-1CH-8:33(792)■9:39(792)
ESH-BAN-GE-36:26(790)-1CH-1:41(790)
ESHCOL-all=812-GE-14:13,24-NU-13:23,24■32:9-DE-1:24
ESHEAN-JOS-15:52(824)
ESHEK-1CH-8:39(6232)
ESHKALONITES-JOS-13:3(832)
ESHTAOL-all=847-JOS-15:33■19:41-J'G-13:25■16:31■18:2,8,11
ESHTAULITES-1CH-2:53(848)
ESHTEMOA-all=851-JOS-21:14-1SA-30:28-1CH-4:17,19■6:57
ESHTEMOH-JOS-15:50(851)
ESHTON-1CH-4:11(850),12(850)
ESLI-LU-3:25(2069)
ESROM-M'T-1:3(2074)-LU-3:33(2074)
ESTHER-all=635-ES-1:t■2:7,8,10,11,15^2,16,17,20^2,22^2■4:5,8,9,10,13,15,17■5:1,2^3,3,4,5^2,6,7,12■6:14■7:1,2^2,3,5,6,7,8■8:1^2,2,3,4^2,7^2■9:12,13,25,29,31,32
ESTHER'S-all=635-ES-2:18■4:4,12
ETAM-all=5862-J'G-15:8,11-1CH-4:3,

32-**2CH**-11:6

ETHAM-all=864-**EX**-13:20-**NU**-33:6,7,8

ETHAN-all=387-**1KI**-4:31-**1CH**-2:6, 8■6:42,44■15:17,19-**PS**-89:t

ETHANIM-**1KI**-8:2(388)

ETHBAAL-**1KI**-16:31(856)

ETHER-**JOS**-15:42(6281)■19:7(6281)

ETHIOPIA-all=3568-**GE**-2:13 -**2KI**-19:9-**ES**-1:1■8:9-**JOB**-28:19 -**PS**-68:31■87:4-**IS**-18:1■20:3,5■37:9■ 43:3■45:14-**EZE**-29:10■30:4,5■38:5 -**NA**-3:9-**ZEP**-3:10■**N.T.**-**AC**-8:27(128)

ETHIOPIAN-all=3569-**NU**-12:1^{2} -**2CH**-14:9-**JER**-13:23■38:7,10,12■39:16

ETHIOPIANS-all=3569-**2CH**-12:3■ 14:12^{2},13■16:8■21:16-**1SA**-20:4-**JER**-46:9-**EZE**-30:9-**DA**-11:43-**AM**-9:7-**ZEP**-2:12■**N.T**-**AC**-8:27(128)

ETHNAN-**1CH**-4:7(869)

ETHNI-**1CH**-6:41(867)

EUBULUS-**2TI**-4:21(2103)

EUNICE-**2TI**-1:5(2131)

EUODIAS-**PH'P**-4:2(2136)

EUPHRATES-all=6578-**GE**-2:14■ 15:18-**DE**-1:7■11:24-**JOS**-1:4-**2SA**-8:3 -**2KI**-23:29■24:7-**1CH**-5:9■18:3-**2CH**-35:20-**JER**-13:4,5,6,7■46:2,6,10■51:63■ **N.T**-**RE**-9:14(2166)■16:12(2166)

EUROCLYDON-**AC**-27:14(2148)

EUTYCHUS-**AC**-20:9(2161)

EVE-**GE**-3:20(2332)■4:1(2332)■ **N.T**-**2CO**-11:3(2096)-**1TI**-2:13(2096)

EVI-**NU**-31:8(189)-**JOS**-13:21(189)

EVIL-MERODACH-**2KI**-25:27 (192)-**JER**-52:31(192)

EXODUS-**EX**-1:t(428,8031)

EZAR-**1CH**-1:38(687)

EZBAI-**1CH**-11:37(229)

EZBON-**GE**-46:16(675)-**1CH**-7:7(675)

EZEKIAS-**M'T**-1:9(1478),10(1478)

EZEKIEL-**EZE**-1:t,3(3168)■24:24(3168)

EZEL-**1SA**-20:19(237)

EZEM-**1CH**-4:29(6107)

EZER-all=687&marked-**GE**-36:21, 27,30-**1CH**-1:42■4:4(5829)■7:21(5827)■ 12:9(5829)-**NE**-3:19(5829)■12:42(5829)

EZION-GABER-all=6100-**NU**-33:35,36-**DE**-2:8-**2CH**-20:36

EZIONGEBER-all=6100-**1KI**-9:26■22:48-**2CH**-8:17

EZNITE-**2SA**-23:8(6112)

EZRA-all=5830-**1CH**-4:17-**EZR**-1:t■ 7:1,6,10,11,12,21,25■10:1,2,5,6,10,16 -**NE**-8:1,2,4,5,6,9,13■12:1,13,26,33,36

EZRAHITE-all=250-**1KI**-4:31-**PS**-88:t■89:t

EZRI-**1CH**-27:26(5836)

F

FELIX-all=5344-**AC**-23:24,26■24:3, 22,24,25,27■25:14

FELIX'-**AC**-24:27(5344)

FESTUS-all=5347-**AC**-24:27■25:1, 4,9,12,13,14,22,24■26:24,25,32

FESTUS'-**AC**-25:23(5347)

FOR-all=3588■**N.T.**-all=2135

FORTUNATUS-**1CO**-16:17(5414), subscr.(5414)

FROM-**O.T.**supplied■**N.T.**-all=1722

G

GAAL-all=1603-**J'G**-9:26,28,30,31,35, 36,37,39,41

GAASH-all=1608-**JOS**-24:30-**J'G**-2:9 -**2SA**-23:30-**1CH**-11:32

GABA-all=1387-**JOS**-18:24-**EZR**-2:26 -**NE**-7:30

GABBAI-**NE**-11:8(1373)

GABBATHA-**JOH**-19:13(1042)

GABRIEL-**DA**-8:16(1403)■9:21(1403)■ **N.T.**-**LU**-1:19(1043),26(1043)

GAD-all=1408-**GE**-30:11■35:26■46:16■ 49:19-**EX**-1:4-**NU**-1:14,24,25■2:14^{2}■7:42■ 10:20■13:15■26:15,18■32:1,2,6,25,29, 31,33,34■34:14-**DE**-27:13■33:20^{2}-**JOS**-4:12■13:24,28■18:7■20:8■21:7,38■22:9, 10,11,13,15,21,25,30,31,32,33,34-**1SA**-13:7■22:5-**2SA**-24:5,11,13,14,18,19-**1CH**-2:2■5:11■6:63,80■12:14■21:9,11,13,18, 19■29:29-**2CH**-29:25-**JER**-49:1-**EZE**-48:27,28,34-**RE**-7:5(1045)

GADARENES-all=1046-**M'R**-5:1 -**LU**-8:26,37

GADDI-**NU**-13:11(1426)

GADDIEL-**NU**-13:10(1427)

GADI-**2KI**-15:14(1424),17(1424)

GADITE-**2SA**-23:36(1425)

GADITES-all=1425-**DE**-3:12,16■ 4:43■29:8-**JOS**-1:12■12:6■13:8■22:1 -**2KI**-10:33-**1CH**-5:18,26■12:8,37■26:32

GAHAM-**GE**-22:24(1514)

GAHAR-**EZR**-2:47(1515)-**NE**-7:49(1515)

GAIUS-all=1050-**AC**-19:29■20:4-**RO**-16:23-**1CO**-1:14-**3JO**-1

GALAL-all=1559-**1CH**-9:15,16-**NE**-11:17

GALATIA-all=1053&marked-**AC**-16:6(1054)■18:23(1054)-**1CO**-16:1-**GA**-1:2-**2TI**-4:10-**1PE**-1:1

GALATIANS-all=1052-**GA**-1:t■3:1,subscr.

GALEED-**GE**-31:47(1567),48(1567)

GALILAEAN-all=1057-**M'R**-14:70 -**LU**-22:59■23:6

GALILAEANS-all=1057-**LU**-13:1, 2^{2}-**JOH**-4:45-**AC**-2:7

GALILEE-all=1551-**JOS**-20:7■ 21:32-**1KI**-9:11-**2KI**-15:29-**1CH**-6:76 -**IS**-9:1■**N.T.**all=1056-**M'T**-2:22■ 3:13■4:12,15,18,23,25■15:29■17:22■ 19:1■21:11■26:32,69■27:55■28:7,10,16 -**M'R**-1:9,14,16,28,39■3:7■6:21■7:31■ 9:30■14:28■15:41■16:7-**LU**-1:26■2:4, 39■3:1■4:14,31,44■5:17■8:26■17:11■ 23:5,6,49,55■24:6-**JOH**-1:43■2:1,11■ 4:3,43,45,46,47,54■6:1■7:1,9,41,52^{2}■12:21■ 21:2-**AC**-1:11■5:37■9:31■10:37■13:31

GALLIM-**1SA**-25:44(1554)-**IS**-10:30(1554)

GALLIO-all=1058-**AC**-18:12,14,17

GAMALIEL-all=1583-**NU**-1:10■ 2:20■7:54,59■10:23■**N.T.**-**AC**-5:34 (1059)■22:3(1059)

GAMMADIMS-**EZE**-27:11(1575)

GAMUL-**1CH**-24:17(1577)

GAREB-all=1619-**2SA**-23:38-**1CH**-11:40-**JER**-31:39

GARMITE-**1CH**-4:19(1636)

GASHMU-**NE**-6:6(1654)

GATAM-all=1609-**GE**-36:11,16 -**1CH**-1:36

GATH-all=1661-**JOS**-11:22-**1SA**-5:8■ 6:17■7:14■17:4,23,52■21:10,12■27:2, 3,4,11-**2SA**-1:20■15:18■21:20,22-**1KI**-2:39^{2},40^{2},41-**2KI**-12:17-**1CH**-7:21■ 8:13■18:1■20:6,8-**2CH**-11:8■26:6-**PS**-56:t-**AM**-6:2-**MIC**-1:10

GATHHEPHER-**2KI**-14:25(1662)

GATHRIMMON-all=1667-**JOS**-19:45■21:24,25-**1CH**-6:69

GAZA-all=5804-**GE**-10:19-**JOS**-10:41■ 11:22■15:47-**J'G**-1:18■6:4■16:1,21-**1SA**-6:17-**2KI**-18:8-**1CH**-7:28-**JER**-47:1,5 -**AM**-1:6,7-**ZEP**-2:4-**ZEC**-9:5^{2}■**N.T.** -**AC**-8:26(1048)

GAZATHITES-**JOS**-13:3(5841)

GAZER-all=1507-**2SA**-5:25-**1CH**-4:16

GAZEZ-**1CH**-2:46(1495)

GAZITES-**J'G**-16:2(5841)

GAZZAM-**EZR**-2:48(1502)-**NE**-7:51(1502)

GEBA-all=1387-**JOS**-21:17-**1SA**-13:3 -**2SA**-5:25-**1KI**-15:22-**2KI**-23:8-**1CH**-6:60■8:6-**2CH**-16:6-**NE**-11:31■12:29 -**IS**-10:29-**ZEC**-14:10

GEBAL-**PS**-83:7(1381)-**EZE**-27:9(1381)

GEBER-**1KI**-4:13(1398),19(1398)

GEBIM-**IS**-10:31(1374)

GEDALIAH-all=1436-**2KI**-25:22, 23,24,25-**1CH**-25:3,9-**EZR**-10:18-**JER**-38:1■39:14■40:5,6,7,8,9,11,12,13,14,15, 16■41:1,2,3,4,6,9,10,16,18■43:6-**ZEP**-1:1

GEDEON-**HEB**-11:32(1066)

GEDER-**JOS**-12:13(1445)

GEDERAH-**JOS**-15:36(1449)

GEDERATHITE-**1CH**-12:4(1452)

GEDERITE-**1CH**-27:28(1451)

GEDEROTH **JOS** 15:41(1450) -**2CH**-28:18(1450)

GEDEROTHAIM-**JOS**-5:36(1453)

GEDOR-all=1441-**JOS**-15:58-**1CH**-4:4,18,39■8:31■9:37■12:7

GEHAZI-all=1522-**2KI**-4:12,14,25, 27,29,31,36■5:20,21,25■8:4,5

GELILOTH-**JOS**-18:17(1553)

GEMALLI-**NU**-13:12(1582)

GEMARIAH-all=1587-**JER**-29:3■ 36:10,11,12,25

GENESIS-**GE**-1:t(7225)

GENNESARET-all=1082-**M'T**-14:34-**M'R**-6:53-**LU**-5:1

GENTILE-**RO**-2:9(1672),10(1672)

GENTILES-all=1471-**GE**-10:5 -**J'G**-4:2,13,16-**IS**-11:10■42:1,6■49:6, 22■54:3■60:3,5,11,16■61:6,9■62:2■ 66:12,19-**JER**-4:7■14:22■16:19■46:1 -**LA**-2:9-**EZE**-4:13-**HO**-8:8-**JOE**-3:9-**MIC**-5:8-**ZEC**-1:21-**MAL**-1:11■**N.T.**-all= 1484&marked-**M'T**-4:15■6:32■10:5,18■ 12:18,21■20:19,25-**M'R**-10:33,42-**LU**-2:32■18:32■21:24^{2}■22:25-**JOH**-7:35^{2} (1672)-**AC**-4:27■7:45■9:15■10:45■11:1, 18■13:42,46,47,48■14:2,5,27■15:3,7,12, 14,17,19,23■18:6■21:11,19,21,25■22:21■ 26:17,20,23■28:28-**RO**-1:13■2:14,24■ 3:9(1672),29■9:24,30■11:11,12,13^{2},25■ 15:9^{2},10,11,12^{2},16^{2},18,27■16:4-**1CO**-5:1■10:20,32(1672)■12:2,13(1672)-**GA**-2:2,8,12,14(1483),14,15■3:14-**EPH**-2:11■3:1,6,8■4:17-**COL**-1:27-**1TH**-2:16■4:5-**1TI**-2:7■3:16-**2TI**-1:11■4:17 -**1PE**-2:12■4:3-**3JO**-7-**RE**-11:2

GENUBATH-**1KI**-11:20^{2}(1592)

GERA-all=1617-**GE**-46:21-**J'G**-3:15 -**2SA**-16:5■19:16,18-**1KI**-2:8-**1CH**-8:3,5,7

GERAR-all=1642-**GE**-10:19■20:1, 2■26:1,6,17,20,26-**2CH**-14:13,14

GERGESENES-**M'T**-8:28(1086)

GERIZIM-all=1630-**DE**-11:29■ 27:12-**JOS**-8:33-**J'G**-9:7

GERSHOM-all=1648-**EX**-2:22■18:3 -**J'G**-18:30-**1CH**-6:16,17,20,43,62,71■ 15:7■23:15,16■26:24-**EZR**-8:2

GERSHON-all=1647-**GE**-46:11 -**EX**-6:16,17-**NU**-3:17,18,21,25■4:22, 28,38,41■7:7■10:17■26:57-**JOS**-21:6,27 -**1CH**-6:1■23:6

GERSHONITE-all=1649-**1CH**-26:21^{2}■29:8

GERSHONITES-all=1649-**NU**-3:21,23■3:24■4:24,27■26:57-**JOS**-21:33 -**1CH**-23:7-**2CH**-29:12

GESHAM-**1CH**-2:47(1529)

GESHEM-all=1654-**NE**-2:19■6:1,2

GESHUR-all=1650-**2SA**-3:3■13:37, 38■14:23,32■15:8-**1CH**-2:23■3:2

GESHURI-**DE**-3:14(1651)-**JOS**-13:2 (1651)

GESHURITES-all=1651-**JOS**-12:5■ 13:11,13^{2}-**1SA**-27:8

GETHER-**GE**-10:23(1666)-**1CH**-1:17(1666)

GETHSEMANE-**M'T**-26:36 (1068)-**M'R**-14:32(1068)

GEUEL-**NU**-13:15(1345)

GEZER-all=1507-**JOS**-10:33■12:12■ 16:3,10■21:21-**J'G**-1:29-**1KI**-9:15,16, 17-**1CH**-6:67■7:28■20:4

GEZRITES-**1SA**-27:8(1511)

GIAH-**1CH**-2:24(1520)

GIBBAR-**EZR**-2:20(5303)

GIBBETHON-all=1405-**JOS**-19:44■21:23-**1KI**-15:27^{2}■16:15,17

GIBEA-**1CH**-2:49(1388)

GIBEAH-all=1390-**JOS**-15:27-**J'G**-19:12,13,14,15,16■20:4,5,9,10,13,14,15, 19,20,21,25,29,30,31,33,34,36,37,43-**1SA**-10:26■11:4■13:2,15,16■14:2,5,1■15:34■ 22:6■23:19■26:1-**2SA**-6:3,4■21:6■23:29 -**1CH**-11:31-**2CH**-13:2-**IS**-10:29-**HO**-5:8■9:9■10:9^{2}

GIBEATH-**JOS**-18:28(1394)

GIBEATHITE-**1CH**-12:3(1395)

GIBEON-all=1391&marked-**JOS**-9:3, 17■10:1,2,4,5,6,10,12,41■11:19■18:25■ 21:17-**2SA**-2:12,13,16,24■3:30■20:8-**1KI**-3:4,5■9:2-**1CH**-8:29,29(25)■9:35,35(25)■ 14:16■16:39■21:29-**2CH**-1:3,13-**NE**-3:7■7:25-**IS**-28:21-**JER**-28:1■41:12,16

GIBEONITE-**1CH**-12:4(1393)-**NE**-3:7(1393)

GIBEONITES-all=1393-**2SA**-21:1, 2,3,4,9

GIBLITES-**JOS**-13:5(1382)

GIDDALTI-**1CH**-25:4(1437),29(1437)

GIDDEL-all=1435-**EZR**-2:47,56 -**NE**-7:49,58

GIDEON-all=1439-**J'G**-6:11,13,19,22^2,24,27,29,34,36,39■7:1,2,4,5,7,13,14,15,18,19,20,24,25■8:4,7,11,13,21,22,23,24,27^2,28,30,32,33,35

GIDEONI-all=1441-**NU**-1:11■2:22■7:60,65■10:24

GIDOM-**J'G**-20:45(1440)

GIHON-all=1521-**GE**-2:13-**1KI**-1:33,38,45-**2CH**-32:30■33:14

GILALAI-**NE**-12:36(1562)

GILBOA-all=1533-**1SA**-28:4■31:1,8-**2SA**-1:6,21■21:12-**1CH**-10:1,8

GILEAD-all=1568-**GE**-31:21,23,25■37:25■26:29,30■27:1■32:1,26,29,39,40■36:1-**DE**-2:36■3:10,12,13,15,16■4:43■34:1-**JOS**-12:2,5■13:11,25,31■17:1^2,3,5,6■20:8■21:38■22:9,13,15,32-**J'G**-5:17■7:3■10:4,8,17,18^2■11:1,5,7,8^2,9,10,11,29^3■12:4^2,5,7■20:1-**1SA**-13:7-**2SA**-2:9■17:26■24:6-**1KI**-4:13,19■17:1■22:3-**2KI**-10:33^2■15:29-**1CH**-2:21,22,23■5:9,10,14,16■6:80■7:14,17■26:31■27:21-**PS**-60:7■108:8-**SONG**-4:1■6:5-**JER**-8:22■22:6■46:11■50:19-**EZE**-47:18-**HO**-6:8■12:11-**AM**-1:3,13-**OB**-1:19-**MIC**-7:14-**ZEC**-10:10

GILEADITE-all=1569-**J'G**-10:3■11:1,40■12:7-**2SA**-17:27■19:31-**1KI**-2:7-**EZR**-2:61-**NE**-7:63

GILEADITES-all=1569-**NU**-26:29-**J'G**-12:4,5-**2KI**-15:25

GILEAD'S-**J'G**-11:2(1568)

GILGAL-all=1537-**DE**-11:30-**JOS**-4:19,20■5:9,10■9:6■10:6,7,9,15,43■12:23■14:6■15:7-**J'G**-2:1■3:19-**1SA**-7:16■10:8■11:14,15^2■13:4,7,8,12,15■15:12,21,33-**2SA**-19:15,40-**2KI**-2:1■4:38-**NE**-12:29-**HO**-4:15■9:15■12:11-**AM**-4:4■5:5^2-**MIC**-6:5

GILOH-**JOS**-15:51(1542)-**2SA**-15:12(1542)

GILONITE-**2SA**-15:12(1526)■23:34(1526)

GIMZO-**2CH**-28:18(1579)

GINATH-**1KI**-16:21(1527),22(1527)

GINNETHO-**NE**-12:4(1599)

GINNETHON-**NE**-10:6(1599)■12:16(1599)

GIRGASHITE-**1CH**-1:14(1622)

GIRGASHITES-all=1622-**GE**-15:21-**DE**-7:1-**JOS**-3:10■24:11-**NE**-9:8

GIRGASITE-**GE**-10:16

GISPA-**NE**-11:21(1658)

GITTAHHEPHER-**JOS**-19:13(1662)

GITTAIM-**2SA**-4:3(1664)-**NE**-11:33(1664)

GITTITE-all=1663-**2SA**-6:10,11■15:19,22■18:2■21:19-**1CH**-13:13■20:5

GITTITES-**JOS**-13:3(1663)-**2SA**-15:18(1663)

GITTITH-all=1665-**PS**-8:t■81:t■84:t

GIZONITE-**1CH**-11:34(1493)

GOATH-**JER**-31:39(1601)

GOB-**2SA**-21:18(1359),19(1359)

GOD-all=430,a=410,b=3069,c=426,d=433&marked-**GE**-1:1,2,3,4^2,5,6,7,8,9,10^2,11,12,14,16,17,18,20,21^2,22,24,25^2,26,27^2,28,29,31■2:2,3^2,4,5,7,8,9,15,16,18,19,21,22■3:1^2,3,5,8^2,9,13,14,21,22,23■4:25■5:1^2,22,24^2■6:2,4,5(3068),9,11,12,13,22■7:9,16■8:1^2,15■9:1,6,8,12,16,17,26,27■14:18a,19a,20a,22a■15:2b,8b■16:13a■17:1a,3,7,8,9,15,18,19,22,23■19:29^2■20:3,6,11,13,17■21:2,4,6,12,17^3,19,20,22,23,33a■22:1,3,8,9,12■24:3,7,12,27,42,48■25:11■26:24■27:20,28■28:3a,4,12,13^2,17,20,21■30:6,17,18,20,22,23■31:5,7,9,11,13a,16^2,24,29,42^2,50,53^2■32:1,9^2,28,30■33:5,10,11■35:1,1a,3a,5,7,9,10,11,11a,13,15■39:9■40:8■41:16,25,28,32^2,38,39,51,52■42:18,28■43:14a,23,29■44:16■45:5,7,8,9■46:1,2,3a,3■48:3a■9,11,15^2,20,21■49:25a■50:17,19,20,24,25-**EX**-1:17,20,21■2:23,24^2,25^2■3:1,4,6^4,11,12,13^2,14,15^3,16^2,18^2■4:5^3,16,20,27■5:1,3^2,8■6:2,3a,7^2■7:1,16■8:10,19,25,26,27,28■9:1,13,30■10:3,7,8,16,17,25,26■13:17^2,18,19■14:19■15:2a,2,26■16:12■17:9■18:1,4,5,12^2,15,16,19^2,21,23■19:3,17,19■20:1,2,5,5a,7,10,12,19,20,21■21:13■22:20■23:17(3068),19,25■24:10,11,13■29:45,46^2■31:3,18■32:11,16^2,27■34:6a,14^{2}a,23(3068),23,24,26■35:31-**LE**-2:13■4:22■11:44,45■18:2,4,21,30■19:2,3,4,10,12,14,25,31,32,34,36■20:7,24■21:6^3,7,8,12^2,17,21,22■22:25,33■23:14,22,28,40,43■24:15,22■25:17^2,36,38^2,43,55■26:1,12,13,44,45-**NU**-6:7■10:9,10^2■12:13a■15:40,41^3■16:9,22a,22■21:5■22:9,10,12,18,20,38■23:4,8a,19a,21,22a,23a,27■24:2,4a,8a,16a,23a■25:13■27:16-**DE**-1:6,10,11,19,20,21^2,25,26,30,31,32,41■2:7^2,29,30,33,36,37■3:3,18,20,21,22,24b,24a■4:1,2,3,4,5,7^2,10,19,21,23^2,24,24a,25,29,30,31,31a,32,33,34^2,35,39,40■5:2,6,9,9a,11,12,14,15^2,16^2,24^2,25,26,27^2,32,33■6:1,2,3,4,5,10,13,15,15a,15,16,17,20,24,25■7:1,2,6^2,9,9a,12,16,18,19^2,20,21,21a,22,23,25■8:2,5,6,7,10,11,14,18,19,20■9:3,4,5,6,7,16,21,23,26b■10:9,12^3,14,17,17a,20,21,22■11:1,2,12^2,13,22,25,27,28,29,31■12:1,4,5,7^2,9,10,11,12,15,18^3,20,21,27^2,28,29,31■13:3^2,4,5^2,10,12,16,18^2■14:1,2,21,23^2,24^2,25,26,29■15:4,5,6,7,10,14,15,18,19,20,21■16:1^2,2,5,6,7,8,10,10sup,10,11^2,15^2,16,17,18,20,21,22■17:1^2,2^2,8,12,14,15,19■18:5,7,9,12,13,14,15,16^2■19:1^2,2,3,8,9,10,14■20:1,4,13,14,16,17,18■21:1,5,10,23^2■22:5■23:5^3,14,18^2,20,21^2,23■24:4,9,13,18,19■25:15,16,18,19^2■26:1,2^2,3,4,5,7,10^2,11,13,14,16,17,19■27:2,3^2,5,6^2,7,9,10■28:1^2,2,8,9,13,15,45,47,52,53,58,62■29:6,10,12^2,13,15,18,25,29■30:1,2,3^2,4,5,6^2,7,9,10^2,16^2,20■31:3,6,11,12,13,17,26■32:3,4a,12a,15d,17d,18a,21a,39■33:1,26a,27-**JOS**-1:9,11,13,15,17■2:11■3:3,9,10a■4:5,23^2,24■7:7b,7sup,13,19,20■8:7,30■9:9,18,19,23,24■10:19,40,42■13:14,33■14:6,8,9,14■18:3,6■22:3,4,5,16,19,22a,24,29sup,29,33,34■23:3^2,5^2,8,10,11,13^2,14,15^2,16■24:1,2,17,18,19,19a,23,24,26,27-**J'G**-1:7■2:12■3:7,20■4:6,23■5:3,5■6:8,10,20,22b,26,31,36,39,40■7:14■8:3,33,34■9:7,9,13,23,27,46a,56,57■10:10■11:21,23,24^2■13:5,6^2,7,8,9^2,22■15:19■16:17,23^2,24,28b,28■18:5,10,31■20:2,18(1008),18,26(1008),27,31(1008)■21:2(1008),2,3-**RU**-1:16■2:12-**1SA**-1:17■2:2,3a,27,30■3:3^2,17■4:4,7,11,13,17,18,19,21,22■5:1,2,7^2,8^3,10^3,11^2■6:3,5,20■7:8■9:6,7,8,9,10,27■10:3,5,7,9,10,18,19,26■11:6■12:9,12,14,19■13:13■14:18^2,36,37,41,44,45sup,45■15:15,21,30■16:15,16,23■17:26,36,45,46■18:10■19:20,23■20:12■22:3,13,15■23:7,10,11,14,16■25:22,29,32,34■26:8■28:15■29:9■30:6,15-**2SA**-2:27■3:9,35■5:10■6:2,3,4,6,7^2,12^2■7:2,18b,19^{2}b,20b,22^2,23,24,25,26,27,28b,28,29b■9:3■10:12■12:7,16,22(3068)■14:11,13,14,16,17^2,20■15:24^2,25,29,32■16:23■18:28■19:13,27■21:14■22:3,7,22,30,31a,32a,32,33a,47,48a■23:1,3^2,5a■24:3,23,24-**1KI**-1:17,30,36,47,48■2:3,23,26b■3:5,7,11,28■4:29■5:3,4,5■8:15,17,23^2,25,26,27,28,53b,57,59,60,61,65■9:9■10:9,24■11:4,9,23,31,33^2■12:22^2■13:1,4,5,6^3,7,8,11,12,14^2,21^2,26,29,31■14:7,13■15:3,4,30■16:13,26,33■17:1,12,14,18,20,21,24■18:10,21,24^2,27,36^2,37,39^2■19:8,10,14■20:28^3■21:10,13■22:53-**2KI**-1:2,3^2,6^2,9,10,11,12^2,13,16^2■2:14■4:7,9,16,21,22,25^2,27^2,40,42■5:7,8,11,14,15^2,20■6:6,9,10,15,31■7:2,17,18,19■8:2,4,7,8,11■9:6■10:31■13:19■14:25■16:2■17:7,9,14,16,19,26^2,27,39■18:5,12,22■19:4^3,10,15^2,16,19^2,20,37■20:5■21:12,22■22:15,18■23:16,17,21-**1CH**-4:10^2■5:20,22,25^2,26■6:48,49■9:11,13,26,27■11:2,19■12:17,18,22■13:2,3,5,6,7,8,10,12^2,14■14:10,11,14,15,16■15:1,2^2,12,13,14,15,24,26■16:1^2,4,6,14,35,36,42■17:2,3,16,17^2,20,21,22,24^2,25,26■19:13■21:7,8,15,17^2,30■22:1,2,6,7,11,12,18,19^3■23:14,25,28■24:5,19■25:5^2,6■26:5,20,32■28:2,3,4,8^2,9,12,20^2,21■29:1^2,2,3^2,7,10,13,16,17,18,20^2-**2CH**-1:1,3,4,7,8,9,11■2:4^2,5,12■3:3■4:11,19■5:1,14■6:4,7,10,14,16,17,18,19,40,41^2,42■7:5,22■8:14■9:8^2,23■10:15■11:2,16^2■13:5,10,11,12^2,15,16,18■14:2,4,7,11^3■15:1,3,4,6,9,12,13,18■16:7■17:4■18:5,13,31■19:3,4,7■20:6^2,7,12,19,20,29,30,33■21:10,12■22:7,12■23:3,9■24:5,7,9,13,16,18,20^2,24,27■25:7,8^2,9^2,16,20,24■26:5^3,7,16,18■27:6■28:5,6,9,10,24^2,25■29:5,6,7,10,36■30:1,5,6,7,8,9,12,16,19^2,22■31:6,13,14,20,21^2■32:8,11,14,15d,15,16,17^2,19,21,29,31,■33:7,12^2,13,16,17,18^2■34:3,8,9,23,26,27,32^2,33^2■35:3,8,21^2,22■36:5,12,13^2,15,16,18,19,23^2-**EZR**-1:2,3^3,4,5■2:68■3:2^2,8,9■4:1,2,3^2,24c■5:1c,2^{2}c,5c,8c,11c,12c,13c,14c,15c,16c,17c■6:3c,5^{2}c,7^{2}c,8c,9c,10c,12^{2}c,14c,16c,17c,18c,21,22■7:6^2,9,12c,14c,15c,16c,18c,19^{2}c,20c,21c,23^{2}c,24c,25^{2}c,26c,27,28■8:17,18,21,22,23,25,28,30,31,33,35,36■9:4,5,6^2,8^2,9^2,10,13,15■10:1,2,3^2,6,9,11,14-**NE**-1:4,5,5a■2:4,8,12,18,20■4:4,9,15,20■5:9,13,15,19■6:10,12,14,16■7:2,5■8:6,8,9,16,18■9:3^2,4,5,7,17d,18,31a,32,32a■10:28,29,32■33,34^2,36^2,37,38,39■11:11,16,22■12:24,36,40,43,45,46■13:1,2,4,7,9,11,14^2,18,22,25,26^2,27,29,31-**JOB**-1:1,5,6,8,9,16,22■2:1,3,9,10■3:4d,23d■4:9d,17d■5:8a,8,17d■6:4d,8d,9d■8:3a,5a,13a,20a■9:2a,13d■10:2d■11:5d,6d,7d■12:4d,6a,6d■13:3a,7a,8a■15:4a,8d,11a,13a,25a■16:11a,20d,21d■18:21a■19:6d,21d,22a,26d■20:15a,29,29a■21:9d,14a,19d,22a■22:2a,12d,13a,17a,26d■23:16a■24:12d■25:4a■27:2a,3d,8d,9a,10d,11a,13a■28:23■29:2d,4d■31:2d,6d,14a,23a,28a■32:2,13a■33:4a,12d,14a,26d,29a■34:5a,9,10a,12a,23a,31a,37a■35:10d,13a■36:5a,22a,26a■37:5a,10a,14a,15d,22d■38:7,41a■39:17d■40:2d,9a,19a-**PS**-3:2,7■4:1■5:2,4a,10■7:1,3,9,10,11,11a■9:17■10:4sup,4,11a,12a,13■13:3■14:1,2,5■16:1a■17:6a■18:2a,6,21,28,29,30a,31d,31,32a,46,47a■19:1a■20:1,5,7■22:1a,2,10a■24:5■25:2,5,22■27:9■29:3a■30:2,12■31:5a,14■33:12■35:23,24■36:1,7■37:31■38:15,21■40:3,5,8,17■41:13■42:1,2,2a,2,3,4,5,6,8a,9a,10,11^2■43:1,2,4,4a,4,5^2■44:1,4,8,20,20a,21■45:2,6,7■46:1,4,5^2,7,10,11■47:1,5,6,7,8^2,9^2■48:1,3,8^2,9,10,14■49:7,15■50:1,2,3,6,7,14,16,22d,23■51:1,10,14^2,17^2■52:1a,5a,7,8^2■53:1,2^2,4,5^2,6■54:1,2,3,4■55:1,14,16,19a,19,23■56:1,4^2,7,9,10,11,12,13■57:1,2,2a,3,5,7,11■58:6,11■59:1,5^2,9,10^2,13,17^2■60:1,6,10^2,12■61:1,5,7■62:1,5,7^2,8,11^2■63:1,1a,11■64:1,7,9■65:1,5,9■66:1,3,5,8,10,16,19,20■67:1,3,5,6,7■68:1,2,3,4,5,6,7,8^2,9,10,15,16,17,18,19a,20a,20b,21,24,24a,26,28^2,31,32,34,35,35a,35■69:1,3,5,6b,6,13,29,30,32,35■70:1,4,5■71:4,5b,11,12,16b,17,18,19^2,22■72:1,18■73:1,11a,17a,26,28,28b■74:1,8a,10,12,22■75:1,7,9■76:1,6,9,11■77:1,3,9a,13,13a,13,14a,16■78:7,7a,8a,10,18a,19,19a,22,31,34a,35,35a,41a,56,59■79:1,9,10■80:3,4,7,14,19■81:1^2,4,9^{2}a,10■82:1,8■83:1,1a,12,13■84:2a,3,7,8^2,9,10,11■85:4,8a■86:2,10,12,14,15a■87:3■88:1■89:7a,8,26a■90:t,2a,17■91:2■92:13■94:1^{2}a,7,22,23■95:3a,7■98:3■99:5,8,8a,9^2■100:3■102:24a■104:1,21a,33■105:7■106:14a,21a,47,48■107:11a■108:1,5,7,11^2,13■109:1,21b,26■113:5■114:7d■115:2,3■116:5■118:27a,28a,28■119:115■122:9■123:2■135:2■136:2,26a■139:17a,19d,23a■140:6a,7b■141:8b■143:10■144:9,15■145:1■146:2,5a,5,10■147:1,7,12■149:6a■150:1a-**PR**-2:5,17■3:4■25:2■30:5d,9-**EC**-1:13■2:24,26sup,26■3:10,11,13,14^2,15,17,18■5:1,2,4,6,7,18,19^2,20■6:2^2■7:13,14,18,26,29■8:2,12,13,15,17■9:1,7■11:5,9■12:7,13,14-**IS**-1:10■2:3■3:15b■5:16a■7:7b,11,13■8:10a■8:19,21■9:6a■10:21a,23b,24b■12:2a■13:19■14:13a■17:6,10■21:10,17■22:5b,12b,14b,15b■24:15■25:1,8b,9■26:13■28:16b,22b,26■29:23■30:15b,18■31:3a■35:2,4^2■36:7■37:4^3,10,16^2,17,20,21,38■38:5■40:1,3,8,9,10b,18a,27,28■41:10,13,17■42:5a■43:3,10a,12sup,12a,■44:6,8d,8(6697),10a,15a,17^{2}a■45:3,5,14a,14,15a,15,18,20a,21,21a,22a■46:6a,9a,9■48:1,2,16b,17■49:4,5,22b■50:4b,5b,7b,9b,10■51:15,20,22■52:4b,7,

10,12■53:4■54:5,6■55:5,7■56:8b■57:21■58:2^{2}■59:2,13■60:9,19■61:1b,2,6,10,11b■62:3,5■64:4■65:13b,15b,16^{2}■66:9-JER-1:6b■2:17,19,19b,22b■3:13,21,22,23,25^{2}■4:10b■5:4,5,14,19,24■7:3,20b,21,23,28■8:14■9:15■10:10^{2}■11:3,4■13:12,16■14:13b,22■15:16■16:9,10■19:3,15■21:4■22:9■23:2,23^{2},36^{2}■24:5,7■25:15,27■26:13,16■27:4,21■28:2,14■29:4,8,21,25■30:2,9,22■31:1,6,18,23,33■32:14,15,17b,18a,25b,27,36,38■33:4■34:2,13■35:4,13,17^{2},18,19■37:3,7■38:17^{2}■39:16■40:2■42:2,3,4,5,6^{2},9,13,15,18,20^{3},21■43:1^{2},2,10■44:2,7^{2},11,25,26b■45:2■46:10^{2}b,25■48:1■49:5b■50:4,18,25b,28,31b,40■51:5,10,33,56a-LA-3:41a-EZE-1:1■2:4b■3:11b,27b■4:14b■5:5b,7b,8b,11b■6:3^{2}b,11b■7:2b,5b■8:1b,3,4■9:3,8b■10:5a■19,20■11:7b,8b,13b,16b,17b,20,21b,22,24■12:10b,19b,23b,25b,28^{2}b■13:3b,8^{2}b,9b,13b,16b,18b,20b■14:4b,6b,11,11b,14b,16b,18b,20b,21b,23b■15:6b,8b■16:3b,8b,14b,19b,23b,30b,36b,43b,48b,59b,63b■17:3b,9b,16b,19b,22b■18:3b,9b,23b,30b,32b■20:3^{2}b,5b,5,7,19,20,27b,30b,31b,33b,36b,39b,40b,44b,47b,49b■21:7b,13b,24b,26b,28b■22:3b,12b,19b,28b,31b■23:22b,28b,32b,34b,35b,46b,49b■24:3b,6b,9b,14b,21b,24b■25:3^{2}b,6b,8b,12b,13b,14b,15b,16b■26:3b,5b,7b,14b,15b,19b,21b■27:3b■28:2b,2a,2,2a,2,6b,6,9,9a,10b,12b,13,14,16,22b,24b,25b,26■29:3b,8b,13b,16b,19b,20b■30:2b,6b,10b,13b,22b■31:8^{2},9,10b,15b,18b■32:3b,8b,11b,14b,16b,31b,32b■33:11b,25b,27b■34:2b,8b,10b,11b,15b,17b,20b,24,30,30b,31,31b■35:3b,6b,11b,14b■36:2b,3b,4^{2}b,5b,6b,7b,13b,14b,15b,22b,23b,28,32b,33b,37b■37:3b,5b,9b,12b,19b,21b,23,27■38:3b,10b,14b,17b,18b,21b■39:1b,5b,8b,10b,13b,17b,20b,22,25b,28,29b■40:2■43:2,18b,19b,27b■44:2,6b,9b,12b,15b,27b■45:9^{2}b,15b,18b■46:1b,16b■47:13b,23b■48:29b-DA-1:2^{3},9,17■2:18c,19c,20c,23c,28c,37c,44c,45c,47c■3:15c,17c,25c,26c,28^{2}c,29^{2}c■4:2c,8c■5:3c,18c,21c,23c,26c■6:5c,7c,10c,11c,12c,16c,20c,22c,23c,26^{2}c■9:3,4,4a,9,10,11,13,14,15,17,18,19,20^{2}■10:12■11:32,36^{2}a,37,37d,38d,39d-HO-1:7,10a■2:23■3:5■4:1,6,12■5:4■6:6■7:10■8:2,6■9:1,8^{2},17■11:9a,12■12:3,5,6^{2},9■13:4^{2},16■14:1-JOE-1:13^{2},14,16■2:13,14,17,23,26,27■3:17-AM-1:8b■2:8■3:7b,8b,11b,13b,13■4:2b,5b,11,12,13■5:3b,14,15,16,26,27■6:8b,8,14■7:1b,2b,4^{2}b,5b,6b■8:1b,3b,9b,11b,14■9:5b,8b,15-OB-1b-JON-1:5,6,9■2:1,6■3:5,8,9,10^{2}■4:2a,6,7,8,9-MIC-1:2b■3:7■4:2,5^{2}■5:4■6:6,8■7:7^{2},10,17,18a-NA-1:2a-HAB-1:11,12,12(6697)■3:3d,18,19(136)-ZEP-1:7b■2:7,9■3:2,17-HAG-1:12^{2},14-ZEC-6:15■7:2(1008)■8:8,23■9:7,14b,16■10:6■11:4■12:5,8■13:9■14:5-MAL-1:9a■2:10a,11a,16,17■3:8,14,15,18■N.T.-all=2316,a=3361,1096&marked-M'T-1:23■3:9,16■4:3,4,6,7,10■5:8,9■6:24,30,33■8:29■9:8■12:4,28^{2}■14:33■15:3,4,6,31■16:16,23■19:6,17,24,26■21:12,31,43■22:16,21,29,30,31,32^{3},37■23:22■26:61,63^{2}■27:40,43^{2},46,54-M'R-1:1,14,15,24■2:7,12,26■3:11,35■4:11,26,30■5:7^{2}■7:8,9,13■8:33■9:1,47■10:6,9,14,15,18,23,24,25,27^{2}■11:22■12:14,17,24,26^{3},27^{2},29,30,32,34■13:19■14:25■15:34,39,43■16:19-LU-1:6,8,16,19,26,30,32,35,37,47,64,68,78■2:13,14,20,28,40,52■3:2,6,8,38■4:3,4,8,9,12,34,41,43■5:1,21,25,26■6:4,12,20■7:16^{2},28,29,30■8:1,10,11,21,28,39■9:2,11,20,27,43,60,62■10:9,11,27■11:20^{2},28,42,49■12:6,8,9,20,21,24,28,31■13:13,18,20,28,29■14:15■15:10■16:13,15^{2},16■17:15,18,20^{2},21■18:2,4,7,11,13,16,17,19,24,25,27,43^{2}■19:11,37■20:16a,21,25,36,37^{2},38■21:4,31■22:16,18,69,70■23:35,40,47,51■24:19,53-JOH-1:1,2,6,12,13,18,29,34,36,49,51■3:2^{2},3,5,16,17,18,21,33,34^{2},36■4:10,24■5:18^{2},25,42,44■6:27,28,29,33,45,46,69■7:17■8:40,41,42^{2},47^{2},54■9:3,16,24,29,31,31(2318),33,35■10:33,35,36■11:4^{2},22^{2},27,40,52■12:43■13:3,31,32^{2}■14:1■16:2,27,30■17:3■19:7■20:17,28,31■21:19-AC-1:3■2:11,17,22^{2},23,24,30,32,33,36,39,47■3:8,9,13^{2},15,18,21,22,25,26■4:10,19^{2},21,24^{2},31■5:4,29,30,31,32,39,39(2314)■6:2,7,11■7:2,6,7,9,17,25,32^{3},35,37,42,43,45,46^{2},55^{2},56■8:10,12,14,20,21,22,37■9:20■10:2^{2},3,4,15,22,22sup,28,31,33^{2},34,38^{2},40,41,42,46■11:1,9,17^{2},18^{2},23■12:5,22,23,24■13:5,7,16,17,21,23,26,30,33,36,37,43,44,46■14:15,22,26,27■15:4,7,8,10,12,14,18,19,40■16:14,17,25,34■17:13,23,24,29,30■18:7,11,13,21,26■19:8,11,20(2962)■20:21,24,25,27,28,32■21:19■22:3,14■23:1,3,9(2313)■24:14,15,16■26:6,8,18,20,22,29■27:23,24,25,35■28:6,15,23,28,31-RO-1:1,4,7^{2},8,9,10,16,17,18,19^{2},21^{2},23,24,25,26,28^{2},30(2319),32■2:2,3,4,5,11,13,16,17,23,24,29■3:2,3,4a,4,5^{2},6a,6,7,11,18,19,21,22,23,25^{2},29,30,31(3336,1096)■4:2,3,6,17,20^{2}■5:1,2,5,8,10,11,15■6:2a,10,11,13^{2},15a,17,22,23■7:4,7a,13a,22,25^{2}■8:3,7^{2},8,9,14^{2},16,17,19,21,27,28,31,33,34,39■9:5,6,8,11,14,14a,16,20,22,26■10:1,2,3,9,17■11:1,1a,2^{2},8,11a,21,22,23,29,30,32,33■12:1^{2},2,3■13:1^{2},2,4^{2}■14:3,4,6^{2},11,12,17,18,20,22■15:5,6,7,8,9,13,15,16,17,19,30,32,33■16:20,26,27-1CO-1:1,2,3,4^{2},9,14,18,20,21^{3},24,25^{2},27^{2},28,30■2:1,5,7^{2},9,10^{2},11^{2},12^{2},14■3:6,7,9,10,16^{2},17^{3},19■4:1,5,9,20■5:13■6:9,10,11,13,14,15a,19,20■7:7,15,17,19,24,40■8:3,4,6,8■9:9,21■10:5,13,20,31,32■11:3,7,12,13,16,22■12:3,6,18,24,28■14:2,18,25^{2},28,33,36■15:9,10^{2},15^{2},24,28,34,38,50,57-2CO-1:1^{2},2,3^{2},4,9,12,18,19,20^{2},21,23■2:14,15,17^{2}■3:3,5■4:2^{2},4^{2},6^{2},7,15■5:1,5,11,13,18,19,20^{2},21■6:1,4,7,16^{3}■7:1,6,12■8:1,5,16■9:7,8,11,12,13,14,15■10:4,5,13■11:7,11,31■12:2,3,19,21■13:4^{2},7,11,14-GA-1:1,3,4,10,13,15,20,24■2:6,17a,19,20,21■3:6,8,11,17,18,20,21,21a,26■4:4,6,7,8,9^{2},14■5:21■6:7,14a,16-EPH-1:1,2,3,17■2:4,8,10,12(112),16,19,22■3:2,7,9,10,19■4:6,13,18,24,30,32■5:1,2,5,6,20,21■6:6,11,13,17,23-PH'P-1:2,3,8,11,28■2:6^{2},9,11,13,15,27■3:3,9,14,15,19■4:6,7,9,18,19,20-COL-1:1,2,3,6,10,15,25^{2},27■2:2,12,19■3:1,3,6,12,15,17,22■4:3,11,12-1TH-1:1^{2},2,3,4,9^{2}■2:2^{2},4^{2},5,8,9,10,12,13^{3},14,15■3:2,9^{2},11,13■4:1,3,5,7,8,9(2312),14,16■5:9,18,23,23sup-2TH-1:1,2,3,4,5^{2},6,8,11,12■2:4^{3},11,13^{2},16■3:5-1TI-1:1,2,11,17■2:3,5^{2}■3:5,15^{2},16■4:3,4,5,10■5:4,5,21■6:1,11,13,17-2TI-1:1,2,3,6,7,8■2:9,15,19,25■3:4(5377),16(2315),17■4:1-TIT-1:1,2,3,4,7,16■2:5,10,11,13■3:4,8-PH'M-3,4-HEB-1:1,6,8,9■2:4,9,13,17■3:4,12■4:4,9,10,12,14■5:1,4,10,12,■6:1,3,5,6,7,10,13,17,18■7:1,3,19,25■8:5(5537),10■9:14^{2},20,24■10:7,9,12,21,29,31,36■11:3,4^{2},5^{2},6,10,16^{2},19,25,40■12:2,7,15,22,23,28,29■13:4,7,15,16,20-JAS-1:1,5,13^{2},20,27■2:5,19,23^{2}■3:9^{2}■4:4^{2},6,7,8-1PE-1:2,3,5,21^{2},23■2:4,5,10,12,15,16,17,19,20■3:4,5,15,17,18,20,21,22■4:2,6,10,11^{3},14,16,17^{2},19■5:2,5,6,10,12-2PE-1:1,2,17,21■2:4■3:5,12-1JO-1:5■2:5,14,17■3:1,2,8,9^{2},10^{2},17,20,21■4:1,2^{2},3,4,6^{2},7^{2},8,9^{2},10,11,12^{2},15^{2},16^{2},20^{2},21■5:1,2,3,4,5,9^{2},10^{3},11,12,13^{2},18^{2},19,20^{2}-2JO-3,9-3JO-11^{2}-JUDE-1,4^{2},21,25-RE-1:1,2,6,9■2:7,18■3:1,2,12^{4},14■4:5,8■5:6,9,10■6:9■7:2,3,10,11,12,15,17■8:2,4■9:4,13■10:7■11:1,4,11,13,16^{2},17,19■12:5,6,10^{2},17■13:6■14:4,5,7,10,12,19■15:1,2,3^{2},7,8■16:1,7,9,11,14,19,21■17:17^{2}■18:5,8,20■19:1,4,5,6,9,10,13,15,17■20:4,6,9,12■21:2,3^{3},4,7,10,11,22,23■22:1,3,5,6,9,18,19

GOD'S-all=430&marked-GE-28:22■30:2■32:2-NU-22:22-DE-1:17-2CH-20:15-NE-10:29-JOB-33:6(410)■35:2(410)■36:2(433)■N.T.-all=2316-M'T-5:34■22:21-M'R-12:17-LU-18:29■20:25-JOH-8:47-AC-23:4-RO-8:33■10:3■13:6-1CO-3:9^{2},23■6:20-TIT-1:1-1PE-5:3

GODS-all=430,a=426&marked-GE-3:5■31:30,32■35:2,4-EX-12:12■15:11(410)■18:11■20:3,23^{2}■22:28■23:13,24,32,33■32:1,4,8,23,31■34:15,15,16^{2},17-LE-19:4-NU-25:2^{2}■33:4-DE-4:28■5:7■6:14^{2}■7:4,16,25■8:19■10:17■11:16,28■12:2,3,30^{2},31^{2}■13:2,6,7,13■17:3■18:20■20:18■28:14,36,64■29:18,26^{2}■30:17■31:16,18,20■32:17,17sup,37-JOS-2:22■23:7,16■24:2,14,15^{2},16,20,23-J'G-2:3,12,17,19■3:6■5:8■6:10■10:6^{3},13,14,16■17:5■18:24-RU-1:15-1SA-4:8^{2}■6:5■7:3■8:8■17:43■26:19■28:13-2SA-7:23-1KI-9:6,9■11:2,4,8,10■12:28■14:9■18:24,25■19:2■20:10,23-2KI-5:17■17:7,29,31,33,35,37,38■18:33,34^{2},35■19:12,18^{2}■22:17-1CH-5:25■10:10■14:12■16:25,26-2CH-2:5■7:19,22■13:8,9■25:14^{2},15,20■28:23^{2},25■32:13,14,17,19■33:15■34:25-EZR-1:7-PS-82:1,6■86:8■95:3■96:4,5■97:7,9■135:5■136:2■138:1-IS-21:9■36:18,19^{2},20■37:12,19^{2}■41:23■42:17-JER-1:16■2:11,28^{2}■5:7,19■7:6,9,18■10:11(426)■11:10,12,13■13:10■16:11,13,20^{2}■19:4,13■22:9■25:6■32:29■35:15■43:12,13■44:3,5,8,15■46:25■48:35-DA-2:11a,47a■3:12a,14a,18a■4:8a,9a,18■5:4a,11^{2}a,14a,23a■11:8,36(410)-HO-3:1■14:3-NA-1:14-ZEP-2:11■N.T.-all=2316&marked-JOH-10:34,35-AC-7:40■14:11■17:18(1140)■19:26-1CO-8:5^{2}-GA-4:8

GOG-all=1463&marked-1CH-5:4-EZE-38:2,3,14,16,18■39:1^{2},11^{2}■N.T.-RE-20:8(1136)

GOLAN-all=1474-DE-4:43-JOS-20:8■21:27-1CH-6:71

GOLGOTHA-all=1115-M'T-27:33-M'R-15:22-JOH-19:17

GOLIATH-all=1555-1SA-17:4,23■21:9■22:10-2SA-21:19-1CH-20:5

GOMER-all=1586-GE-10:2,3-1CH-1:5,6-EZE-38:6-HO-1:3

GOMORRAH-all=6017-GE-10:19■13:10■14:2,8,10,11■18:20■19:24,28-DE-29:23■32:32-IS-1:9,10■13:19-JER-23:14■49:18■50:40-AM-4:11-ZEP-2:9

GOMORRHA-all=6017-M'T-10:15-M'R-6:11-RO-9:29-2PE-2:6-JUDE-7

GOSHEN-all=1657-GE-45:10■46:28^{2},29,34■47:1,4,6,27■50:8-EX-8:22■9:26-JOS-10:41■11:16■15:51

GOZAN-all=1470-2KI-17:6■18:11■19:12-1CH-5:26-IS-37:12

GRECIA-all=3120-DA-8:21■10:20■11:2

GRECIANS-JOE-3:6(3125)■N.T.-all=1675-AC-6:1■9:29■11:20

GREECE-ZEC-9:13(3120)-AC-20:2(1671)

GREEK-all=1672&marked-M'R-7:26(1674)-LU-23:38(1673)-JOH-19:20(1676)-AC-16:1,3■21:37(1676)-RO-1:16■10:12-GA-2:3■3:28-COL-3:11-RE-9:11(1673)

GREEKS-all=1672&marked-JOH-12:20-AC-14:1■17:4,12(1674)■18:4,17■19:10,17■20:21■21:28-RO-1:14-1CO-1:22,23,24

GUDGODAH-DE-10:7(1418)

GUNI-all=1476-GE-46:24-NU-26:48-1CH-5:15■7:13

GUNITES-NU-26:48(1477)

GUR-2KI-9:27(1483)

GURBAAL-2CH-26:7(1485)

H

HAAHASHTARI-1CH-4:6(326)

HABAIAH-EZR-2:61(2252)-NE-7:63(2252)

HABAKKUK-all=2265-HAB-1:t,1■3:1

HABAZINIAH-JER-35:3(2262)

HABOR-all=2249-2KI-17:6■18:11-1CH-5:26

HACHALIAH-NE-1:1(2446)■10:1(2446)

HACHILAH-all=2444-IS-23:19■26:1,3

HACHMONI-1CH-27:32(2453)

HACHMONITE-1CH-11:11(2453)

HADAD-all=1908-GE-36:35,36-1KI-11:14,17^{2},19,21^{2},25-1CH-1:30,46,47,50,51

HADADEZER-all=1909-2SA-8:3,

5,7,8,9,10^2,12-1KI-11;23

HADADRIMMON-ZEC-12:11(1910)

HADAR-GE-25:15(1924)■36:39(1924)

HADAREZER-all=1928-2SA-10:16^2, 19-1CH-18:3,5,7,8,9,10^2■19:16,19

HADASHAH-JOS-15:37(2322)

HADASSAH-ES-2:7(1919)

HADATTAH-JOS-15:25(2675)

HADID-all=2307-EZR-2:33-NE-7:37■11:34

HADLAI-2CH-28:12(2311)

HADORAM-all=1913-GE-10:27-1CH-1:21■18:10-2CH-10:18

HADRACH-ZEC-9:1(2317)

HAGAB-EZR-2:46(2285)

HAGABA-NE-7:48(2286)

HAGABAH-EZR-2:45(2286)

HAGAR-all=1904-GE-16:1,3,4,8,15^2,16■21:9,14,17^2■25:12

HAGARENES-PS-83:6(1905)

HAGARITES-all=1905-1CH-5:10,19,20

HAGERITE-1CH-27:31(1905)

HAGGAI-all=2292-EZR-5:1■6:14 **HAG**-1:t,1,3,12,13■2:1,10,13,14,20

HAGGERI-1CH-11—:38(1905)

HAGGI-GE-46:16(2291)-NU-26:15(2291) **HAGGIAH**-1CH-6:30(2293)

HAGGITES-NU-26:15(2291)

HAGGITH-all=2294-2SA-3:4-1KI-1:5,11■2:13-1CH-3:2

HAI-GE-12:8(5857)■13:3(5857)

HAKKATAN-EZR-8:12(6997)

HAKKOZ-1CH-24:10(6976)

HAKUPHA-EZR-2:51(2709)-NE-7:53(2709)

HALAH-all=2477-2KI-17:6■18:11-1CH-5:26

HALAK-JOS-11:17(2510)■12:7(2510)

HALHUL-JOS-15:58(2478)

HALI-JOS-19:25(2482)

HALLOHESH-NE-10:24(3873)

HALOHESH-NE-3:12(3873)

HAM-all=2526&marked-GE-5:32■6:10■7:13■9:18^2,22■10:1,6,20■14:5(1990)-1CH-1:4,8■4:40-PS-78:51■105:23,27■106:22

HAMAN-all=2001-ES-3:1,2,4,5^2,6,7,8,10,11,12,15■4:7■5:4,5^2,8,9^2,10,11,12,14■6:4,5,6^2,7,10,11,12,13,14■7:1,6^2,7,8,9^2,10■8:1,2^2,3,5,7■9:10,12,24

HAMAN'S-all=2001-ES-7:8■9:13,14

HAMATH-all=2574&marked-NU-13:21■34:8-JOS-13:5-J'G-3:3-2SA-8:9-1KI-8:65-2KI-14:25,28■17:24,30■18:34■19:13■23:33■25:21-1CH-18:3,9-2CH-7:8■8:4-IS-10:9■11:11■36:19■37:13-JER-39:5■49:23■52:9,27-EZE-47:16^2,17,20■48:1^2-AM-6:2(2579)-ZEC-9:2

HAMATHITE-GE-10:18(2577)-1CH-1:16(2577)

HAMATHZOBAH-2CH-8:3(2578)

HAMMATH-JOS-19:35(2575)

HAMMEDATHA-all=4099-ES-3:1,10■8:5■9:10,24

HAMMELECH-JER-36:26(4429)■38:6(4429)

HAMMOLEKETH-1CH-7:18(4447)

HAMMON-JOS-19:28(2540)-1CH-6:76(2540)

HAMMOTHDOR-JOS-21:32(2576)

HAMONAH-EZE-39:16(1997)

HAMONGOG-EZE-39:11(1996),15(1996)

HAMOR-all=2544-GE-33:19■34:2,4,6,8,13,18,20,24,26-JOS-24:32-J'G-9:28

HAMOR'S-GE-34:18(2544)

HAMUEL-1CH-4:26(2536)

HAMUL-all=2538-GE-46:12-NU-26:21-1CH-2:5

HAMULITES-NU-26:21(2539)

HAMUTAL-all=2537-2KI-23:31■24:18-JER-52:1

HANAMEEL-all=2601-JER-32:7,8,9,12

HANAN-all=2605-1CH-8:23,38■9:44■11:43-EZR-2:46-NE-7:49■8:7■10:10,22,26■13:13-JER-35:4

HANANEEL-all=2606-NE-3:1■12:39-JER-31:38-ZEC-14:10

HANANI-all=2607-1KI-16:1,7-1CH-25:4,25-2CH-16:7■19:2■20:34-EZR-10:20-NE-1:2■7:2■12:36

HANANIAH-all=2608-2CH-3:19,21■8:24■25:4,23-2CH-26:11-EZR-10:28-NE-3:8,30■7:2■10:23■12:12,41-JER-28:1,5,10,11,12,13,15^2,17■36:12■37:13-DA-1:6,7,11,19■2:17

HANES-IS-30:4(2609)

HANIEL-1CH-7:39(2592)

HANNAH-all=2584-1SA-1:2^2,5^2,8,9,13,15,19,20,22■2:1,21

HANNATHON-JOS-19:14(2615)

HANNIEL-NU-34:23(2592)

HANOCH-all=2585-GE-25:4■46:9-EX-6:14-NU-26:5-1CH-5:3

HANOCHITES-NU-26:5(2599)

HANUN-all=2586-2SA-10:1,2,3,4-1CH-19:2^2,3,4,6-NE-3:13,30

HAPHRAIM-JOS-19:19(2663)

HARA-1CH-5:26(2024)

HARADAH-NU-33:24(2732),25(2732)

HARAN-all=2771,a=2039-GE-11:26a,27a,28a,29a,31a,31,32■12:4,5■27:43■28:10■29:4-2KI-19:12-1CH-2:46^2■23:9a-IS-37:12-EZE-27:23

HARARITE-all=2043-2SA-23:11,33^2-1CH-11:34,35

HARBONA-ES-1:10(2726)

HARBONAH-ES-7:9(2726)

HAREPH-1CH-2:51(2780)

HARETH-1SA-22:5(2802)

HARHAIAH-NE-3:8(2736)

HARHAS-2KI-22:14(2745)

HARHUR-EZR-2:51(2144)-NE-7:53(2744)

HARIM-all=2766-1CH-24:8-EZR-2:32,39■10:21,31-NE-3:11■7:35,42■10:5,27■12:15

HARIPH-NE-7:24(2756)■10:19(2756)

HARNEPHER-1CH-7:36(2774)

HAROD-J'G-7:1(5878)

HARODITE-2SA-23:25(2733)

HAROEH-1CH-2:52(7204)

HARORITE-1CH-11:27(2033)

HAROSHETH-all=2800-J'G-4:2,13,16

HARSHA-EZR-2:52(2797)-NE-7:54(2797)

HARUM-1CH-4:8(2037)

HARUMAPH-NE-3:10(2739)

HARUPHITE-1CH-12:5(2741)

HARUZ-2KI-21:19(2743)

HASADIAH-1CH-3:20(2619)

HASENUAH-1CH-9:7(5574)

HASHABIAH-all=2811-1CH-6:45■9:14■25:3,19■26:30■27:17-2CH-35:9-EZR-8:19,24-NE-3:17■10:11■11:15,22■12:21,24

HASHABNAH-NE-10:25(2812)

HASHBANIAH-NE-3:10(2813)■9:5(2813)

HASHBADANA-NE-8:4(2806)

HASHEM-1CH-11:34(2044)

HASHMONAH-NU-33:29(2832),30(2832)

HASHUB-all=2815-NE-3:11,23■10:23■11:15

HASHUBAH-1CH-3:20(2807)

HASHUM-all=2828-EZR-2:19■10:33-NE-7:22■8:4■10:18

HASHUPHA-NE-7:46(2817)

HASRAH-2CH-34:22(2641)

HASSENAAH-NE-3:3(5574)

HASSHUB-1CH-9:14(2815)

HASUPHA-EZR-2:43(2817)

HATACH-all=2047-ES-4:5,6,9,10

HATHATH-1CH-14:13(2867)

HATIPHA-EZR-2:54(2412)-EZR-7:56(2412)

HATITA-EZR-2:42(2410)-NE-7:45(2410)

HATTIL-EZR-2:57(2411)-EZR-7:59(2411)

HATTUSH-all=2407-1CH-3:22-EZR-8:2-NE-3:10■10:4■12:2

HAURAN-EZR-47:16(2362),18(2362)

HAVILAH-all=2341-GE-2:11■10:7,29■25:18-1SA-15:7-1CH-1:9,23

HAVOTH-JAIR-NUM-22:41(2334)-J'G-10:4(2334)

HAZAEL-all=2371-1KI-19:15,17-2KI-8:8,9,12,13,15,28,29■9:14,15■10:32■12:17^2,18■13:3^2,22,24,25-2CH-22:5,6-AM-1:4

HAZAIAH-NE-11:5(2382)

HAZAR-ADDAR-NU-34:4(2692)

HAZAR-ENAN-all=2704&marked-NU-34:9,10-EZE-47:17(2703)■48:1

HAZAR-GADDAH-JOS-5:27(2693)

HAZAR-HATTICON-EZE-47:16(2694)

HAZAR-MAVETH-GE-10:26(2700)-1CH-1:20(2700)

HAZAR-SHUAL-all=2705-JOS-15:28■19:3-1CH-4:28-NE-11:27

HAZAR-SUSAH-JOS-19:5(2701)

HAZAR-SUSIM-1CH-4:31(2702)

HAZAZON-TAMAR-2CH-20:2(2688)

HAZELEL-PONI-1CH-4:3(6753)

HAZERIM-DE-2:23(2699)

HAZEROTH-all=2698-NU-11:35^2■12:16■33:17,18-DE-1:1

HAZEZON-TAMAR-GE-14:7(2688)

HAZIEL-1CH-23:9(2381)

HAZO-GE-22:22(2375)

HAZOR-all=2674-JOS-11:1,10^2,11,13■12:19■15:23,25(2675),25■19:36-J'G-4:2,17-1SA-12:9-1KI-9:15-2KI-15:29-NE-11:33-JER-49:28,30,33

HE-all=1931■N.T.-all=846

HEBER-all=2268&marked-GE-46:17-NU-26:45-J'G-4:11,17^2■5:24-1CH-4:18■5:13(5677)■7:31,32■8:17,22(5677)■N.T.-LU-8:35(1443)

HEBERITES-NU-26:45(2277)

HEBER'S-J'G-4:21(2268)

HEBREW-all=5680-GE-14:13■39:14,17■41:12-EX-1:15,16,19■2:7,11■21:2-DE-15:12-JER-34:9,14-JON-1:9■N.T.-all=1447&marked-LU-23:38(1444)-JOH-5:2■19:13,17,20-AC-21:40(1446)■22:2(1446)■26:14(1446)-PH'P-3:5(1446)-RE-9:11■16:16

HEBREWESS-JER-34:9(5680)

HEBREWS-all=5680-GE-40:15■43:32-EX-2:13■3:18■5:3■7:16■9:1,13■10:3-1SA-4:6,9■13:3,7,19■14:11,21■29:3■N.T.-all=1445-AC-6:1-2CO-11:22-PH'P-3:5

HEBREWS'-EX-2:6(5680)

HEBRON-all=2275-GE-13:18■23:2,19■35:27■37:14-EX-6:18-NU-3:19■13:22^2-JOS-10:3,5,23,36,39■11:21■12:10■14:13,14,15■15:13,54■19:28■20:7■21:11,13-J'G-1:10^2,20■16:3-1SA-30:31-2SA-2:1,3,11,32■3:2,5,19,20,22,27,32■4:1,8,12^2■5:1,3^2,5,13■15:7,9,10-1KI-2:11-1CH-2:42,43■3:1,4■6:2,18,55,57■11:1,3^2■12:23,38■15:9■23:12^2,19■29:27-2CH-11:10

HEBRONITES-all=2276-NU-3:27■26:58-1CH-26:23,30,31^2

HEGAI-ES-2:8^2(1896),15(1896)

HEGE-ES-2:3(1896)

HELAH-1CH-4:5(2458),7(2458)

HELAM-2SA-10:16(2431),17(2431)

HELBAH-J'G-1:31(2462)

HELBON-EZE-27:18(2463)

HELDAI-1CH-27:15(2469)-ZEC-6:10(2469)

HELEB-2SA-23:29(2460)

HELED-1CH-11:30(2466)

HELEK-NU-26:30(2507)-JOS-17:2(2507)

HELEKITES-NU-26:30(2516)

HELEM-1CH-7:35(2494)-ZEC-6:14(2494)

HELEPH-JOS-19:33(2501)

HELEZ-all=2503-2SA-23:26-1CH-2:39■11:27■27:10

HELI-LU-3:23(2242)

HELKAI-NE-12:15(2517)

HELKATH-JOS-19:25(2520)■21:31(2520)

HELKATH-HAZZURIM-2SA-2:16(2521)

HELON-all=2497-NU-1:9■2:7■7:24,29■10:16

HEMAM-GE-36:22(1967)

HEMAN-all=1968-1KI-4:31-1CH-2:6■6:33■15:17,19■16:41,42■25:1,4,5^2,6-2CH-5:12■29:14■35:15-PS-88:t

HEMATH-all=2574-1CH-2:55■13:5-AM-6:14

HEMDAN-GE-36:26(2533)

HEN-ZEC-6:14(2581)

HENA-all=2012-2KI-18:34■19:13-IS-37:13

HENADAD-all=2582-EZR-3:9-NE-3:18,24■10:9
HENOCH-1CH-1:3(2585),33(2585)
HEPHER-all=2660-NU-26:32,33■27:1-JOS-12:17■17:2,3-1KI-4:10-1CH-4:6■11:36
HEPERITES-NU-26:32(2662)
HEPHZIBAH-2KI-21:1(2657)-IS-62:4(2657)
HER-O.T.supplied■N.T.-all=1722
HERES-J'G-1:35(2776)
HERESH-1CH-9:15(2792)
HERMAS-RO-16:14(2057)
HERMES-RO-16:14(2060)
HERMOGENES-2TI-1:15(2061)
HERMON-all=2768-DE-3:8,9■4:48-JOS-11:3,17■12:1,5■13:5,11-1CH-5:23-PS-89:12■133:3-SONG-4:8
HERMONITES-PS-42:6(2769)
HEROD-all=2264-M'T-2:1,3,7,12,13,15,16,19,22■14:1,3,6-M'R-6:14,16,17,18,20,21,22■8:15-LU-1:5■3:1,19^2■9:7,9■13:31■23:7,8,11,12,15-AC-4:27■12:1,6,11,19,20,21■13:1
HERODIANS-all=2265-M'T-22:16-M'R-3:6■12:13
HERODIAS-all=2266-M'T-14:6-M'R-6:19,22-LU-3:19
HERODIAS'-M'T-14:3(2266)-M'R-6:17(2266)
HERODION-RO-16:11(2267)
HEROD'S-all=2264-M'T-14:6-LU-8:3■23:7-AC-23:35
HESED-1KI-4:10(2618)
HESHBON-all=2809-NU-1:25,26,27,28,30,34■32:3,37-DE-1:4■2:24,26,30■3:2,6■4:46■29:7-JOS-9:10■12:2,5■13:10,17,21,26,27■21:39-J'G-11:19,26-1CH-6:81-NE-9:22-SONG-7:4-IS-15:4■16:8,9-JER-48:2,34,45^2■49:3
HESHMON-JOS-15:27(2829)
HETH-all=2845-GE-10:15■23:3,5,7,10^2,16,18,20■25:10■27:46^2■49:32-1CH-1:13
HETHLON-EZE-47:15(2855)■48:1(2855)
HEZEKI-1CH-8:17(2395)
HEZEKIAH-all=2396-2KI-16:20■18:1,9,10,13,14^2,15,16^2,17,19,22,29,30,31,32,37■19:1,3,5,9,10,14^2,15,20■20:1,3,5,8,10,12^2,13^2,14^2,15,16,19,20,21■21:3-1CH-3:13,23■4:41-2CH-28:27■29:1,18,20,27,30,31,36■30:1,18,20,22,24■31:2,8,9,11,13,20■32:2,8,9,11,12,15,16,17,20,22,23,24,25,26^2,27,30^2,32,33■33:3-EZR-2:16-NE-7:21-PR-25:1-IS-1:1■36:1,2,4,7,14,15,16,18,22■37:1,3,5,9,10,14^2,15,21■38:1,2,3,5,9,22■39:1,2^2,3^2,4,5,8-JER-15:4■26:18,19-HO-1:1-MIC-1:1
HEZION-1KI-15:18(2383)
HEZIR-1CH-24:15(2387)-NE-10:20(2387)
HEZRAI-2SA-23:35(2695)
HEZRO-1CH-11:37(2695)
HEZRON-all=2696-GE-46:9,12-EX-6:14-NU-26:6,21-JOS-15:3,25-RU-4:18,19-1CH-2:5,9,18,21,24,25■4:1■5:3
HEZRONITES-NU-26:6(2697),21(2697)
HEZRON'S-1CH-2:24(2696)
HIDDAI-2SA-23:30(1914)
HIDDEKEL-all=2313-GE-2:14(2313)-DA-10:4(2313)
HIEL-1KI-16:34(2419)
HIERAPOLIS-COL-4:13(2404)
HILEN-1CH-6:58(2432)
HILKIAH-all=2518-2KI-18:18,26,37■22:4,8^2,10,12,14■23:4,24-1CH-6:13,45■9:11■26:11-2CH-34:9,14,15^2,18,20,22■35:8-EZR-7:1-NE-8:4■11:11■12:7,21-IS-22:20,22-JER-1:1■29:3
HILKIAH'S-IS-36:3(2518)
HILLEL-J'G-12:13(1985),15(1985)
HIM-O.T.supplied■N.T.-all=1722
HINNOM-all=2011-JOS-15:8^2■18:16^2-2KI-23:10-2CH-28:3■33:6-NE-11:30-JER-7:31,32■19:2,6■32:35
HIRAH-GE-38:1(2437),12(2437)
HIRAM-all=2438-2SA-5:11-1KI-5:1^2,2,7,8,10,11^2,12■7:13,40^2,45■9:11^2,12,14,27■10:11,22-1CH-14:1
HIRAM'S-1KI-5:18(2438)
HIS-O.T.supplied■N.T.-all=1722
HITTITE-all=2850-GE-23:10■25:9■26:34^2■36:2■49:29,30■50:13-EX-23:28■33:2■34:11-JOS-9:1■11:3-1SA-26:6-2SA-11:3,6,17,21,24■12:9,10■23:39-1KI-15:5-1CH-11:41-EZE-16:3,45
HITTITES-all=2850-GE-15:20-EX-3:8,17■13:5■23:23-NU-13:29-DE-7:1■20:17-JOS-1:4■3:10■12:8■24:11-J'G-1:26■3:5-1KI-9:20■10:29■11:1-2KI-7:6-2CH-1:17■8:7-EZR-9:1-NE-9:8
HIVITE-all=2340-GE-10:17■34:2■36:2-EX-23:28■33:2■34:11-JOS-9:1■11:3-1CH-1:15
HIVITES-all=2430-EX-3:8,17■13:5■23:23-DE-7:1■20:17-JOS-3:10■9:7■11:19■12:8■24:11-J'G-3:3,5-2SA-24:7-1KI-9:20-2CH-8:7
HIZKIAH-ZEP-1:1(2396)
HIZKIJAH-NE-10:17(2396)
HOBAB-NU-10:29(2246)-J'G-4:11(2246)
HOBAH-GE-14:15(2327)
HOD-1CH-7:37(1963)
HODAIAH-1CH-3:24(1939)
HODAVIAH-all=1938-1CH-5:24■9:7-EZR-2:40
HODESH-1CH-8:9(2321)
HODEVAH-NE-7:43(1937)
HODIAH-1CH-4:19(1940)
HODIJAH-all=1940-NE-8:7■9:5■10:10,13,18
HOGLAH-all=2295-NU-26:33■27:1■36:11-JOS-17:3
HOHAM-JOS-10:3(1944)
HOLON-all=2473-JOS-15:51■21:15-JER-48:21
HOMAM-1CH-1:39(1950)
HOPHNI-all=2652-1SA-1:3■2:34■4:4,11,17
HOR-all=2023-NU-20:22,23,25,27■21:4■33:37,38,39,41■34:7,8-DE-32:50
HORAM-JOS-10:33(2036)
HOREB-all=2722-EX-3:1■17:6■33:6-DE-1:2,6,19■4:10,15■5:2■9:8■18:16■29:1-1KI-8:9■19:8-2CH-5:10-PS-106:19-MAL-4:4
HOREM-JOS-19:38(2765)
HORHAGIDGAD-NU-33:32(2735),33(2735)
HORI-all=2753-GE-36:22,30-NU-13:5-1CH-1:39
HORIMS-DE-2:12(2752),22(2752)
HORITE-GE-36:20(2752)
HORITES-all=2752-GE-14:6■36:21,29
HORMAH-all=2767-NU-14:45■21:3-DE-1:44-JOS-12:14■15:30■19:14-J'G-1:17-1SA-30:30-1CH-4:30
HORONAIM-all=2773-IS-15:5-JER-48:3,5,34
HORONITE-all=2772-NE-2:10,19■13:28
HOSAH-all=2621-JOS-19:29-1CH-16:38■26:10,11,16
HOSEA-all=1954-HO-1:t,1,2^2
HOSHAIAH-all=1955-NE-12:32-JER-42:1■43:2
HOSHAMA-1CH-3:18(1953)
HOSHEA-all=1954-DE-32:44-2KI-15:30■17:1,3,4,6■18:1,9,10-1CH-27:20-NE-10:23
HOTHAM-1CH-7:32(2369)
HOTHAN-1CH-11:44(2369)
HOTHIR-1CH-25:4(1956),28(1956)
HUKKOK-JOS-19:34(2712)
HUKOK-1CH-6:75(2712)
HUL-GE-10:23(2343)-1CH-1:17(2343)
HULDAH-2KI-22:14(2468)-2CH-34:22(2468)
HUMTAH-JOS-15:54(2547)
HUPHAM-NU-26:39(2349)
HUPHAMITES-NU-26:39(2350)
HUPPAH-1CH-24:13(2647)
HUPPIM-all=2650-GE-46:21-1CH-7:12,15
HUR-all=2354-EX-17:10,12■24:14■31:2■35:30■38:32-NU-31:8-JOS-13:21-1KI-4:8-1CH-2:19,20,50■4:1,4-2CH-1:5-NE-3:9
HURAI-1CH-11:32(2360)
HURAM-all=2438&marked-1CH-8:5(2361)-2CH-2:3(2361),11,12(2361),13■4:11^2(2361),16(2361)■8:2,18■9:10,21
HURI-1CH-5:14(2359)
HUSHAH-1CH-4:4(2364)
HUSHAI-all=2365-2SA-15:32,37■16:16^2,17,18■17:5,6,7,8,14,15-1KI-4:16-1CH-27:33
HUSHAM-all=2367-GE-36:34,35-1CH-1:45,46
HUSHATHITE-all=2843-2SA-21:18■23:27-1CH-11:29■20:4■27:11
HUSHIM-all=2366-GE-46:23-1CH-7:12■8:8,11
HUZ-GE-22:21(5780)
HUZZAB-NA-2:7(5324)
HYMENAEUS-1TI-1:20(5211)-2TI-2:17(5211)

I

I-all=589■N.T.-all=1473
IBHAR-all=2984-2SA-5:15-1CH-3:6■14:5
IBLEAM-all=2991-JOS-17:11-J'G-1:27-2KI-9:27
IBNEIAH-1CH-9:8(2997)
IBNIJAH-1CH-9:8(2998)
IBRI-1CH-24:27(5681)
IBZAN-J'G-12:8(78),10(78)
ICHABOD-1SA-4:21(350)
ICABOD'S-1SA-14:3(350)
ICONIUM-all=2430-AC-13:51■14:1,19,21■16:2-2TI-3:11
IDALAH-JOS-19:15(3030)
IDBASH-1CH-4:3(3031)
IDDO-all=5714&marked-1KI-4:14-1CH-6:21■27:21(3035)-2CH-9:29(3260)■12:15■13:22-EZR-5:1■6:14■8:17^2(112)-NE-12:4,16-ZEC-1:1,7
IDUMAEA-M'R-3:8(2401)
IDUMEA-all=123-IS-34:5,6-EZE-35:15■36:5
IGAL-NU-13:7(3008)-2SA-23:36(3008)
IGDALIAH-JER-35:4(3012)
IGEAL-1CH-3:22(3008)
IIM-NU-33:45(5864)-JOS-15:29(5864)
IJEABARIM-NU-21:11(5863)■33:44(5863)
IJON-all=5859-1KI-15:20-2KI-15:29-2CH-16:4
IKKESH-all=6142-2SA-23:26-1CH-11:28■27:9
ILAI-1CH-11:29(5866)
ILLYRICUM-RO-15:19(2437)
IMLA-2CH-18:7(3229),8(3229)
IMLAH-1KI-22:8(3229),9(3229)
IMMANUEL-IS-7:14(6005)■8:8(6005)
IMMER-all=564-1CH-9:12■24:14-EZR-2:37,59■10:20-NE-3:29■7:40,61■11:13-JER-20:1
IMNA-1CH-7:35(3234)
IMNAH-1CH-7:30(3232)-2CH-31:14(3232)
IMRAH-1CH-7:36(3236)
IMRI-1CH-9:4(556)-NE-3:2(556)
IN-O.T.supplied■N.T.-all=1722
INDIA-ES-1:1(1912)■8:9(1912)
IPHEDEIAH-1CH-8:25(3301)
IR-1CH-7:12(5893)
IRA-all=5896-2SA-20:26■23:26,38-1CH-11:28,40■27:9
IRAD-GE-4:18^2(5897)
IRAM-GE-36:43(5902)-1CH-1:54(5902)
IRI-1CH-7:7(5901)
IRIJAH-JER-37:13(3376),14(3376)
IRNAHASH-1CH-4:12(5904)
IRON-JOS-19:38(3375)
IRPEEL-JOS-18:27(3416)
IRSHEMESH-JOS-19:41(5905)
IRU-1CH-4:15(5902)
IS-all=1961■N.T.-all=2076
ISAAC-all=3327&marked-GE-17:19,21■21:3,4,5,8,10,12■22:2,3,6,7,9■24:4,14,62,63,64,66,67^2■25:5,6,9,11^2,19^2,20,21,26,28■26:1,6,8,9^2,12,16,17,18,27,31,35■27:1,5,20,21,22,26,30^2,32,33,37,39,46■28:1,5,6,8,13■31:18,42,53■32:9■35:12,27^2,28,29■46:1■48:15,16■49:31■50:24-EX-2:24■3:6,15,16■4:5■6:3,8■32:13■33:1-LE-26:42-NU-32:11-DE-1:8■6:10■9:5,27■29:13■30:20■34:4-JOS-24:3,4-1KI-18:36-2KI-13:23-1CH-1:28,34^2■

16:16■29:18-**2CH**-30:6-**PS**-105:9(3446)-**JER**-33:26(3446)-**AM**-7:9(3446),16(3446)■**N.T.**-all=2664-**M'T**-1:2■8:11■22:32-**M'R**-12:26-**LU**-3:34■13:28■20:37-**AC**-3:13■7:8^2,32-**RO**-9:7,10-**GA**-4:28-**HEB**-11:9,17,18,20-**JAS**-2:21

ISAAC'S-all=3327-**GE**-26:19,20,25,32

ISAIAH-all=3740-**2KI**-19:2,5,6,20■20:1,4,7,8,9,11,14,16,19-**2CH**-26:22■32:20,32-**IS**-1:1■2:1■7:3■13:1■20:2,3■37:2,5,6,21■38:1,4,21■39:3,5,8

ISCAH-**GE**-11:29(3252)

ISCARIOT-all=2469-**M'T**-10:4■26:14-**M'R**-3:19■14:10-**LU**-6:16■22:3-**JOH**-6:71■12:4■13:3,26■14:22

ISHBAH-**1CH**-4:17(3431)

ISHBAK-**GE**-25:2(3435)-**1CH**-1:32(3435)

ISHBIBENOB-**2SA**-21:16(3432)

ISHBOSHETH-all=378-**2SA**-2:8,10,12,15■3:7,8,14,15■4:5,8^2,12

ISHI-all=3469&marked-**1CH**-2:31■4:20,42■5:24-**HO**-2:16(376)

ISHIAH-**1CH**-7:3(3449)

ISHIJAH-**EZR**-10:31(3449)

ISHMA-**1CH**-4:3(3457)

ISHMAEL-all=3458-**GE**-16:11,15,16■17:18,20,23,25,26■25:9,12,13^2,16,17■28:9^2-**2KI**-25:23,25-**1CH**-1:28,29,31■8:38■9:44-**2CH**-19:11■23:1-**EZR**-10:22-**JER**-40:8,14,15,16■41:1,2,3,6,7,8,9^2,10^2,11,12,13,14,15,16,18

ISHMAELITE-**1CH**-27:30(3459)

ISHMAELITES-**J'G**-8:24(3459)-**PS**-83:6(3459)

ISHMAEL'S-**GE**-36:3(3458)

ISHMAIAH-**1CH**-27:19(3460)

ISHMEELITE-**1CH**-2:17(3459)

ISHMEELITES-all=3459-**GE**-37:25,27,28■39:1

ISHMERAI-**1CH**-8:18(3461)

ISHOD-**1CH**-7:18(379)

ISHPAN-**1CH**-8:22(3473)

ISHTOB-**2SA**-10:6(382),8(382)

ISHUAH-**GE**-46:17(3438)

ISHUAI-**1CH**-7:30(3440)

ISHUI-**1SA**-14:49(3440)

ISMACHIAH-**2CH**-31:13(3253)

ISMAIAH-**1CH**-12:4(3460)

ISPAH-**1CH**-8:16(3472)

ISRAEL-all=3478&marked-**GE**-32:28,32■34:7■35:10^2,21,22^2■36:31■37:3,13■42:5■43:6,8,11■45:21,28■46:1,2,5,8,29,30■47:27,29,31■48:2,8,10,11,14,20,21■49:2,7,16,24,28■50:2,25-**EX**-1:1,7,9,12,13■2:23,25■3:9,10,11,13,14,15,16,18■4:22,29,31■5:1,2^2,14,15,19■6:5,6,9,11,12,13^2,14,26,27■7:2,4,5■9:4^2,6,26,35■10:20,23■11:7^2,10■12:3,6,15,19,21,27,28,31,35,37,40,42,47,50,51■13:2,18,19■14:2,3,5,8^2,10^2,15,16,19,20,22,25,29,30^2,31■15:1,19,22■16:1,2,3,6,9,10,12,15,17,31,35■17:1,5,6,7,8,11■18:1^2,9,12,25■19:1,2,3,6■20:22■24:1,4,5,9,10,11,17■25:2,22■27:20,21■28:1,9,11,12,21,29,30,38■29:28^2,43,45■30:12,16^2,31■31:13,16,17■32:4,8,13,20,27■33:5,6■34:23,27,30,32,34,35■35:1,4,20,29,30■36:3■39:6,7,14,32,42■40:36,38-**LE**-1:2■4:2,13■7:23,29,34^2,36,38■9:1,3■10:6,11,14■11:2■12:2■15:2,31■16:5,16,17,19,21,34■17:2,3,5,8,10,12,13,14■18:2■19:2■20:2^3■21:24■22:2,3,15,18^3,32■23:2,10,24,34,43,44■24:2,8,10,10(3481)(3481),15,23^2■25:2,33,46,55■26:46■27:2,34-**NU**-1:2,3,16,44,45^2,49,52,53,54■2:2,32,33,34■3:8,9,12^2,13,38,40,41^2,42,45,46,50■4:46■5:2,4^2,6,9,12■6:2,23,27■7:2,84■8:6,9,10,11,14,16^2,17,18,19^5,20^2■9:2,4,5,7,10,17^2,18,19,22■10:4,12,28,29,36■11:4,16,30■13:2,3,24,26,32■14:2,5,7,10,27,39■15:2,18,25,26,29,32,38■16:2,9^2,25,34,38,40,41■17:2,5,6,9,12■18:5,6,8,11,14,19,20,21,22,23,24^2,26,28,32■19:2,9,10,13■20:1,12,13,14,19,21^2,22,24,29■21:1^2,2,3,6,10,17,21,23^3,24,25^2,31■22:1,2,3■23:7,10,21,23^2■24:1,2,5,17,18■25:1,3^2,4,5,6^2,8^3,11^2,13■26:2^2,4,51,62^2,63,64■27:8,11,12,20,21■28:2■29:40■30:1■31:2,4,5,9,12,16,54■32:4,7,9,13,14,17,18,22,28■33:1,3,5,38,40,51■34:2,13,29■35:2,8,10,15,34■36:1,2,3,4,5,7^2,8^2,9,13-**DE**-1:1,3,38■2:12■3:18■4:1,44,45,46■5:1^2■6:3,4■9:1■10:6,12■11:6■13:11■17:4,12,20■18:1,6■19:13■20:3■21:8,21■22:19,21,22■23:17^2■24:7■25:6,7,10■26:15■27:1,9^2,14■29:1,2,10,21■31:1,7,9,11^2,19^2,22,23,30■32:8,45,49,51^2,52■33:1,5,10,21,28,29■34:8,9,10,12-**JOS**-1:2■2:2■3:1,7,9,12■4:4,5,7,8^2,12,14,21,22■5:1^2,2,3,6,10,12■6:1,18,23,25■7:1^2,6,8,11,12,13^2,15,16,19,20,23,24,25■8:10,14,15,17^2,21,22,24,27,30,31,32,33^2,35■9:2,6,7,17,18^2,19,26■10:1,4,10,11^2,12^2,14,15,20,21,24,29,30,31,32,34,36,38,40,42,43■11:5,6,8,13,14,16,19,20,21,22,23■12:1,6,7^2■13:6,13,14,22,33■14:1^2,5,10,14■17:13■18:1,2,3,10■19:49,51■20:2,9■21:1,3,8,41,43,45■22:9,11^2,12^2,13,14^2,16,18,20,21,22,24,30,31,32,33^2■23:1,2■24:1^2,2,9,23,31^2,32-**J'G**-1:1,28■2:4,6,7,10,11,14,20,22■3:1^2,2,4,5,7,8^2,9^2,10,12^2,13,14,15^2,27,30,31■4:1,3^2,4,5,6,23,24■5:2,3,5,7^2,8,9,11■6:1,2^2,3,4,6^2,7,8^2,14,15,36,37■7:2,8,14,15,23■8:22,27,28,33,34,35■9:22,55■10:1,2,3,6,7,8^2,9,10,11,15,16,17■11:4,5,13,15,16,17^2,19^2,20^2,21^3,23^2,25,26,27,33,39,40■12:7,8,9,11^2,13,14■13:1,5■14:4■15:20■16:31■17:6■18:1^2,19,29■19:1,12,29,30■20:1,2,3^2,6^2,7,10^2,11,12,13^2,14,17,18,19,20^2,22,23,24,25,26,27,29,30,31,32,33^2,34,35^2,36,38,39^2,41,42,48■21:1,3^3,5^2,6^2,8,15,17,18,24,25-**RU**-2:12■4:7^2,11,14-**1SA**-1:17■2:22,28^2,29,30,32■3:11,20■4:1^2,2^2,3,5,10^2,17,18,21,22■5:7,8^3,10,11■6:3,5■7:2,3,4,5,6,7^3,8,9,10^2,11,13,14^3,15,16,17■8:1,4,22■9:2,9,16,20,21■10:18^3,20■11:2,3,7,8,13,15■12:1■13:1,2,4^2,5,6,13,19■14:12,18,22,23,24,37,39,40,41,45,47,48■15:1,2,6,17^2,26,28,29,30,35■16:1■17:2,3,8,10,11,19,21,24,25^3,26,45,46,52,53■18:6,16,18■19:5■20:12■23:10,11,17■24:2,14,20■25:30,32,34■26:2,15,20■27:1,12■28:1,3,4,19^2■29:3■30:25■31:1^2,7^2-**2SA**-1:3,12,19,24■2:9,10,17,28■3:10,12,17,18,19,21,37,38■5:1,2^3,3^2,5,12,17■6:1,5,15,19,20,21■7:6,7^3,8,10,11,23,24,26,27■8:15■10:9,15,17,18,19^2■11:1,11■12:7^2,8,12■13:12,13■14:25■15:2,6^2,10,13■16:3,15,18,21,22■17:4,10,11,13,14,15,24,26■18:6,7,16,17■19:8,9,11,22^2,40,41,42,43^2■20:1,2,14,19^2,23■21:2^3,4,5,15,17,21■23:1,3,9■24:1^2,2,4,9,15,25-**1KI**-1:3,20,30,34,35,48■2:4,5,11,15,32■3:28■4:1,7,20,25■5:13■6:1^2,13^2■8:1^2,2,3,5,9,14^2,15,16^3,17,20^2,22,23,25^2,26,30,33,34,36,38,41,43,52,55,56,59,62,63,65,66■9:5^2,7^2,20,21,22■10:9^2■11:2,9,16,25^2,31,32,37,38,42■12:1,3,16^3,17,18,19,20^2,21,24,28,33■14:7^2,10,13^2,14,15^2,16^2,18,19,21,24■15:9,16,17,19,20,25^2,26,27,30^2,31,32,33,34■16:2^2,5,8,13^2,14,16^2,17,19,20,21,23,26^2,27,29^2,33^2■17:1,14■18:17,18,19,20,31,36^2■19:10,14,16,18■20:2,4,7,11,13,15,20,21,22,26,27^2,28,29,31^2,32,40,41,43■21:7,18,21,22,26■22:1,2,3,4,5,6,8,9,10,17,18,26,29,30^2,31,32,33,34,39,41,44,51^2,52,53-**2KI**-1:1,3,6,16,18■2:12■3:1,3,4,5,6,9,10,12,13^2,24,27■5:2,4,5,6,7,8^2,12,15■6:8,9,10,11,12^2,21,23,26■7:6,13■8:12,16,18,25,26■9:3,6^2,8,12,14,21■10:21,28,29,30,31^2,32^2,34,36■13:1,2,3,4,5^2,6,8,10,11,12,13,14^2,16,18,22,25■14:1,8,9,11,12,13,15,16,17,23,24,25^2,26^2,27,28^2,29■15:1,8,9,11,12,15,17,18,20,21,23,24,26,27,28,29,31,32■16:3^2,5,7■17:1,2,6,7,8^2,9,13,18,19,20,21^2,22,23^2,24,34■18:1,4,5,9,10,11■19:15,20,22■21:2,3,7,8,9,12■22:15,18■23:13,15,19,22^2,27■24:13-**1CH**-1:34,43■2:1,7■4:10■5:1^2,3,17,26■6:38,49,64■7:29■9:1^2■10:1^2,7■11:1,2^3,3^2,4,10^2■12:32,38^2,40■13:2^2,5,6,8■14:2^2,8■15:3,12,14,25,28■16:3,4,13,17,36,40■17:5,6^2,7,9,10,21,22,24■18:14■19:10,16,17,18,19■20:7■21:1^2,2,3,4,5,7,12,14^2■22:1,2,6,9,10,12,13,17■23:1,2,25■24:19■26:29,30■27:1,16,22,23,24■28:1,4^3,5,8■29:6,10,18,21,23,25^2,26,27,30-**2CH**-1:2^2,13■2:4,12,17■5:2^2,3,4,6,10■6:3^2,4,5^2,6,7,10^2,11,12,13,14,16^2,17,21,24,25,27,29,32,33■7:3,6,8,10,18■8:2,7,8,9,11■9:8,30■10:1,3,16^3,17,18,19■11:1,3,13,16^2■12:1,6,13■13:4,5^2,12,15,16,17,18■15:3,4,9,13,17■16:1,3,4,11■17:1,4■18:3,4,5,7,8,9,16,17,19,25,28,29^2,30,31,32,33,34■19:8■20:7,10,19,29,34,35■21:2,4,6,13■22:5■23:2■24:5,6,9,16■25:6,7^2,9,17,18,21,22,23,25,26■27:7■28:2,3,5,8,13,19,23,26,27■29:7,10,24^2,27■30:1^2,5^2,6^3,21,25^2,26■31:1^2,5,6,8■32:17,32■33:2,7,8,9,16,18^2■34:7,9,21,23,26,33^2■35:3^3,4,17,18^3,25,27■36:8,13-**EZR**-1:3■2:2,59,70■3:1,2,10,11■4:1,3^2■5:1(3479),11(3479)■6:14(3479),16(3479),17^2(3479),21^2,22■7:6,7,10,11,13(3479),15(3479),28■8:18,25,29,35^2■9:1,4,15■10:1,2,5,10,25-**NE**-1:6^2■2:10■7:7,61,73^2■8:1,14,17■9:1,2■10:33,39■11:3,20■12:47■13:2,3,18,26^2-**PS**-14:7^2■22:3,23■25:22■41:13■50:7■53:6^2■59:5■68:8,26,34,35■69:6■71:22■72:18■73:1■76:1■78:5,21,31,41,55,59,71■80:1■81:4,8,11,13■83:4■89:18■98:3■103:7■105:10,23■106:48■114:1,2■115:9,12■118:2■121:4■122:4■124:1■125:5■128:6■129:1■130:7,8■131:3■135:4,12,19■136:11,14,22■147:2,19■148:14■149:2-**PR**-1:1-**EC**-1:12-**SONG**-3:7-**IS**-1:3,4,24■4:2■5:7,19,24■7:1■8:14,18■9:8,12,14■10:17,20^2,22■11:12,16■12:6■14:1,2■17:3,6,7,9■19:24,25■21:10,17■24:15■27:6,12■29:19,23■30:11,12,15,29■31:1,6■37:16,21,23■40:27■41:8,14^2,16,17,20■42:24■43:1,3,14,15,22,28■44:1,5,6,21^2,23■45:3,4,11,15,17,25■46:3,13■47:4■48:1^2,2,12,17■49:3,5,6,7^2■52:12■54:5■55:5■56:8■60:9,14■63:7,16■66:20-**JER**-2:3,4,14,26,31■3:6,8,11,12,18,20,21,23■4:1■5:11,15■6:9■7:3,12,21■9:15,26■10:1,16■11:3,10,17■12:14■13:11,12■14:8■16:9,14,15■17:13■18:6^2,13■19:3,15■21:4■23:2,6,7,8,13■24:5■25:15,27■27:4,21■28:2,14■29:4,8,21,23,25■30:2,3,4,10■31:1,2,4,7,9,10,21,23,27,31,33,36,37■32:14,15,20,21,30^2,32,36■33:4,7,14,17■34:2,13■35:13,17,18,19■36:2■37:7■38:17■39:16■41:9■42:9,15,18■43:10■44:2,7,11,25■45:2■46:25,27■48:1,13,27■49:1,2■50:4,17,18,19,20,29,33■51:5^2,33,49-**LA**-2:1,3,5-**EZE**-2:3■3:1,4,5,7^2,17■4:3,4,5,13■5:4■6:2,3,5,11■7:2■8:4,6,10,11,12■9:3,8,9■10:19,20■11:5,10,11,13,15,17,22■12:6,9,10,19,22,23,24,27■13:2,4,5,9^2,16■14:1,4,5,6,7^2,9,11■17:2,23■18:2,3,6,15,25,29^2,30,31■19:1,9■20:1,3,5,13,27,30,31,38,39,40^2,42,44■21:2,3,12,25■22:6,18■24:21■25:3,6,14■27:17■28:24,25■29:6,16,21■33:7,10,11,20,24,28■34:2^2,13,14^2,30■35:5,12,15■36:1^2,4,6,8^2,10,12,17,21,22^2,32,37■37:11,12,16^2,19,21,22,28■38:8,14,16,17,18,19■39:2,4,7^2,9,11,12,17,22,23,25,29■40:2,4■43:2,7^2,10■44:2,6^2,9,10,12,15,22,28,29■45:6,8^2,9,15,16,17^2■47:13,18,21,22^2■48:11,19,29,31-**DA**-1:3■9:7,11,20-**HO**-1:1,4,5,6,10,11■3:1,4,5■4:1,15,16■5:1,3^2,5^2,9■6:10^2■7:1,10■8:2,3,6,8,14■9:1,7,10■10:1,6,8,9,15■11:1,8,12■12:12,13■13:1,9■14:1,5-**JOE**-2:27■3:2,16-**AM**-1:1^2■2:6,11■3:1,12,14■4:5,12^2■5:1,2,3,4,25■6:1,14■7:8,9,10^2,11,15,16,17■8:2■9:7^2,9,14-**OB**-20-**MIC**-1:5,13,14,15■2:12■3:1,8,9■5:1,2,3■6:2-**NA**-2:2-**ZEP**-2:9■3:13,14,15-**ZEC**-1:19■8:13■9:1■11:14■12:1-**MAL**-1:1,5■2:11,16■4:4■**N.T.**-all=2474&marked-**M'T**-2:6,20,21■8:10■9:33■10:6,23■15:24,31■19:28■27:9,42-**M'R**-12:29■15:32-**LU**-1:16,54,68,80■2:25,32,34■4:25,27■7:9■22:30■24:21-**JOH**-1:31,49■3:10■12:13-**AC**-1:6■2:22(2475),36■3:12(2475)■4:8,10,27■5:21,31,35(2475)■7:23,37,42■9:15■10:36■13:16(2475),17,23,24■21:28(2475)■28:20-**RO**-9:6,27^2,31■10:1,19,21■11:2,7,25,26-**1CO**-10:18-**2CO**-3:7,13-**GA**-6:16-**EPH**-2:12-**PH'P**-3:5-**HEB**-8:8,10■11:22-**RE**-2:14■7:4■21:12

ISRAELITE-**NU**-5:14(1121,3478)-**2SA**-17:25(3481)■**N.T.**-**JOH**-1:47(2475)-**RO**-11:1(2475)

ISRAELITES-all=3478&marked-**EX**-9:7-**LE**-23:42-**JOS**-3:17■8:24■13:6,13-**J'G**-20:21-**1SA**-2:14■13:20■14:21■25:1■

29:1-**2SA**-4:1-**2KI**-3:24■7:13-**1CH**-9:2■**N.T.**-**RO**-9:4(2475)-**2CO**-11:22(2475)

ISRAELITISH-all=3482-**LE**-24:10^2,11

ISRAEL'S-all=3478&marked-**GE**-48:13^2-**EX**-18:8-**NU**-1:20■31:30,42,47-**DE**-21:8-**2SA**-5:12-**2KI**-3:11

ISSACHAR-all=3485-**GE**-30:18■35:23■46:13■49:14-**EX**-1:3-**NU**-1:8,28,29■2:5^2■7:18■10:15■13:7■26:23,25■34:26-**DE**-27:12■33:18-**JOS**-17:10,11■19:17,23■21:6,28-**J'G**-5:15■10:1-**1KI**-4:17■15:27-**1CH**-2:1■6:62,72■7:1,5■12:32,40■26:5■27:18-**2CH**-30:18-**EZE**-48:25,26,33■**N.T.**-**RE**-7:7(2466)

ISSHIAH-**1CH**-4:21(3449),25(3449)

ISUAH-**1CH**-7:30(3440)

ISUI-**GE**-46:17(3440)

IT-**O.T.**supplied■**N.T.**-all=846

ITALIAN-**AC**-10:1(2483)

ITALY-all=2482-**AC**-18:2■27:1,6-**HEB**-13:24

ITHAI-**1CH**-11:31(2833)

ITHAMAR-all=385-**EX**-6:23■28:1■38:21-**LE**-10:6,12,16-**NU**-3:2,4■4:28,33■7:8■26:60-**1CH**-6:3■24:1,2,3,4^2,5,6-**EZR**-8:2

ITHIEL-**NE**-11:7(384)-**PR**-30:1(384)

ITHMAH-**1CH**-11:46(3495)

ITHNAN-**JOS**-15:23(3497)

ITHRA-**2SA**-17:25(3501)

ITHRAN-all=3506-**GE**-36:26-**1CH**-1:41■7:37

ITHREAM-**2SA**-3:5(3507)-**1CH**-3:3(3507)

ITHRITE-**2SA**-23:38(3505)-**1CH**-11:40(3505)

ITHRITES-**1CH**-2:53(3505)

ITTAHKAZIN-**JOS**-19:13(6278)

ITTAI-all=863-**2SA**-15:19,21,22^2■18:2,5,12■23:29

ITURAEA-**LU**-3:1(2484)

IVAH-all=5755-**2KI**-18:34■19:13-**IS**-37:13

IZEHAR-**NU**-3:19(3324)

IZEHARITES-**NU**-3:27(3325)

IZHAR-all=3324-**EX**-6:18,21-**NU**-16:1-**1CH**-6:2,18,38■23:12,18

IZHARITES-all=3325-**1CH**-24:22■26:23,29

IZRAHIAH-**1CH**-7:3^2(3156)

IZRAHITE-**1CH**-27:8(3155)

IZRI-**1CH**-25:11(3340)

J

JAAKAN-**DE**-10:6(3292)

JAAKOBAH-**1CH**-4:36(3291)

JAALA-**NE**-7:58(3279)

JAALAH-**EZR**-2:56(3279)

JAALAM-all=3281-**GE**-36:5,14,18-**1CH**-1:35

JAANAI-**1CH**-5:12(3285)

JAAREOREGIM-**2SA**-21:19(3296)

JAASAU-**EZR**-10:37(3299)

JAASIEL-**1CH**-27:21(3300)

JAAZANIAH-all=2970-**2KI**-25:23-**JER**-35:3-**EZE**-8:11■11:1

JAAZER-**NU**-21:32(3270)■32:35(3270)

JAAZIAH-**1CH**-24:26(3269),27(3269)

JAAZIEL-**1CH**-15:18(3268)

JABAL-**GE**-4:20(2989)

JABBOK-all=2999-**GE**-32:22-**NU**-21:24-**DE**-2:37■3:16-**JOS**-12:2-**J'G**-11:13,21

JABESH-all=3003-**1SA**-11:1,3,5,9,10■31:12,13-**2KI**-15:10,13,14-**1CH**-10:12^2

JABESHGILEAD-all=3003,1568-**J'G**-21:8,9,10,12,14-**1SA**-11:1,9■31:11-**2SA**-2:4,5■21:12-**1CH**-10:11

JABEZ-all=3258-**1CH**-2:55■4:9^2,10

JABIN-all=2985-**JOS**-11:1-**J'G**-4:2,17,23,24^2-**PS**-83:9

JABIN'S-**J'G**-4:7(2985)

JABNEEL-**JOS**-15:11(2995)■19:33(2995)

JABNEH-**2CH**-26:6(2996)

JACHAN-**1CH**-5:13(3275)

JACHIN-all=3199-**GE**-46:10-**EX**-6:15-**NU**-26:12-**1KI**-7:21-**1CH**-9:10■24:17-**2CH**-3:17-**NE**-11:10

JACHINITES-**NU**-26:12(3200)

JACOB-all=3290-**GE**-25:26,27,28,29,30,31,33^2,34■27:6,11,15,17,19,21,22,30^2,36,41^2,42,46■28:1,5,6,7,10,16,18,20■29:1,4,10^2,11,12,13,15,18,20,21,28■30:1^2,4,5,7,9,10,12,16,17,19,25,31,36^2,37,40,41■31:1,2,3,4,11,17,20,22,24,25^2,26,29,31,32,36^2,43,45,46,47,51,53,54■32:1,2,3,4,6,7,9,20,24,27,28,29,30■33:1,10,17,18■34:1,3,5^2,6,7,13,25,27,30■35:1,2,4^2,5,6,9,10^2,14,15,20,22,26,27^2■36:6■37:1,2,34■42:1^2,4,29,36■45:25,27■46:2,5^2,6,8,15,18,22,25,26,27■47:7^2,8,9,10,28^2■48:2,3■49:1,2,7,24,33■50:24-**EX**-1:1,5■2:24■3:6,15,16■4:5■6:3,8■19:3■33:1-**LE**-26:42-**NU**-23:7,10,21,23^2■24:5,17,19■32:11-**DE**-1:8■6:10■9:5,27■29:13■30:20■32:9■33:4,10,28■34:4-**JOS**-24:4^2,32-**1SA**-12:8-**2SA**-23:1-**1KI**-18:31-**2KI**-13:23■17:34-**1CH**-16:13,17-**PS**-14:7■20:1■22:23■24:6■44:4■46:7,11■47:4■53:6■59:13■75:9■76:6■77:15■78:5,21,71■79:7■81:1,4■84:8■85:1■87:2■94:7■99:4■105:6,10,23■114:1,7■132:2,5■135:4■146:5■147:19-**IS**-2:3,5,6■8:17■9:8■10:20,21■14:1^2■17:4■27:6,9■29:22^2,23■40:27■41:8,14,21■42:24■43:1,22,28■44:1,2,5,21,23■45:4,19■46:3■48:1,12,20■49:5,6,26■58:1,14■59:20■60:16■65:9-**JER**-2:4■5:20■10:16,25■30:10^2■31:7,11■33:26^2■46:27^2,28■51:9-**LA**-1:17■2:2,3-**EZE**-20:5■28:25■37:25■39:25-**HO**-10:11■12:2,12-**AM**-3:13■6:8■7:2,5■8:7■9:8-**OB**-10,17,18-**MIC**-1:5^2■2:7,12■3:1,8,9■4:2■5:7,8■7:20-**NA**-2:2-**MAL**-1:2■2:12■3:6■**N.T.**-all=2384-**M'T**-1:2,15,16■8:11■22:32-**M'R**-12:26-**LU**-1:33■3:34■13:28■20:37-**JOH**-4:5,12-**AC**-3:13■7:8,12,14,15,32,46-**RO**-9:13■11:26-**HEB**-11:9,20,21

JACOB'S-all=3290-**GE**-27:22■28:5■30:2,42■31:33■32:18,25,32■34:7,19■35:23■46:8,19,26-**JER**-30:7,18-**MAL**-1:2■**N.T.**-**JOH**-4:6(2384)

JADA-**1CH**-2:28(3047),32(3047)

JADAU-**EZR**-10:43(3035)

JADDUA-all=3037-**NE**-10:21■12:11,22

JADON-**NE**-3:7(3036)

JAEL-all=3278-**J'G**-4:17,18,21,22■5:6,24

JAGUR-**JOS**-15:21(3017)

JAH-**PS**-68:4(3050)

JAHATH-all=3189-**1CH**-4:2^2■6:20,43■23:10,11■24:22-**2CH**-34:12

JAHAZ-all=3096-**NU**-21:23-**DE**-2:32-**J'G**-11:20-**IS**-15:4-**JER**-48:34

JAHAZA-**JOS**-13:18(3096)

JAHAZAH-**JOS**-21:36(3096)-**JER**-48:21(3096)

JAHAZIAH-**EZR**-10:15(3167)

JAHAZIEL-all=3166-**1CH**-12:4■16:6■23:19■24:23-**2CH**-20:14-**EZR**-8:5

JAHDAI-**1CH**-2:47(3056)

JAHDIEL-**1CH**-5:24(3164)

JAHDO-**1CH**-5:14(3163)

JAHLEEL-**GE**-46:14(3177)-**NU**-26:26(3177)

JAHLEELITES-**NU**-26:26(3178)

JAHMAI-**1CH**-7:2(3181)

JAHZAH-**1CH**-6:78(3096)

JAHZEEL-**GE**-46:24(3183)-**NU**-26:48(3183)

JAHZEELITES-**NU**-26:48(3184)

JAHZERAH-**1CH**-9:12(3170)

JAHZIEL-**1CH**-7:13(3185)

JAIR-all=2971&marked-**NU**-32:41-**DE**-3:14-**JOS**-13:30-**J'G**-10:3,5-**1KI**-4:13-**1CH**-2:22,23■20:5(3265)-**ES**-2:5

JAIRITE-**2SA**-20:26(2972)

JAIRUS-**M'R**-5:22(2383)-**LU**-8:41(2383)

JAKAN-**1CH**-1:42(3292)

JAKEH-**PR**-30:1(3348)

JAKIM-**1CH**-8:19(3356)■24:12(3356)

JALON-**1CH**-4:17(3210)

JAMBRES-**2TI**-3:8(2387)

JAMES-all=2385-**M'T**-4:21■10:2,3■13:55■17:1■27:56-**M'R**-1:19,29■3:17,18■5:37■6:3■9:2■10:35,41■13:3■14:33■15:40■16:1-**LU**-5:10■6:14,15,16■8:51■9:28,54■24:10-**AC**-1:13^3■12:2,17■15:13■21:18-**1CO**-15:7-**GA**-1:19■2:9,12-**JAS**-1:t,1-**JUDE**-1

JAMIN-all=3226-**GE**-46:10-**EX**-6:15-**NU**-26:12-**1CH**-2:27■4:24-**NE**-8:7

JAMINITES-**NU**-26:12(3228)

JAMLECH-**1CH**-4:34(3230)

JANNA-**LU**-3:24(2388)

JANNES-**2TI**-3:8(2389)

JANOAH-**2KI**-15:29(3239)

JANOHAH-**JOS**-16:6(3239),7(3239)

JANUM-**JOS**-15:53(3241)

JAPHETH-all=3315-**GE**-5:32■6:10■7:13■9:18,23,27■10:1,2,21-**1CH**-1:4,5

JAPHIA-all=3309-**JOS**-10:3■19:12-**2SA**-5:15-**1CH**-3:7■14:6

JAPHLET-**1CH**-7:32(3310),33^2(3310)

JAPHLETI-**JOS**-16:3(3311)

JAPHO-**JOS**-19:46(3305)

JARAH-**1CH**-9:42(3294)

JAREB-**HO**-5:13(3377)■10:6(3377)

JARED-all=3382-**GE**-5:15,16,18,19,20■**N.T.**-**LU**-3:37(2391)

JARESIAH-**1CH**-8:27(3298)

JARHA-**1CH**-2:34(3398),35(3398)

JARIB-all=3402-**1CH**-4:24-**EZR**-8:16■10:18

JARMUTH-all=3412-**JOS**-10:3^2,5■12:11■15:35■21:29-**NE**-11:29

JAROAH-**1CH**-5:14(3386)

JASHEN-**2SA**-23:32(3464)

JASHER-**JOS**-10:13(3477)-**2SA**-1:18(3477)

JASHOBEAM-all=3434-**1CH**-11:11■12:6■27:2

JASHUB-all=3437-**NU**-26:24-**1CH**-7:1-**EZR**-10:29

JASHUBILEHEM-**1CH**-4:22(3433)

JASHUBITES-**NU**-26:24(3432)

JASIEL-all=supplied

JASON-all=2394-**AC**-17:5,6,7,9-**RO**-16:21

JATHNIEL-**1CH**-26:2(3496)

JATTIR-all=3492-**JOS**-15:48■21:14-**1SA**-30:27-**1CH**-6:57

JAVAN-all=3120-**GE**-10:2,4-**1CH**-1:5,7-**IS**-66:19-**EZE**-27:13,19

JAZER-all=3270-**NU**-32:1,3-**JOS**-13:25■21:39-**2SA**-24:5-**1CH**-6:81■26:31-**IS**-16:8,9-**JER**-48:32^2

JAZIZ-**1CH**-27:31(3151)

JEARIM-supplied

JEATERAI-**1CH**-6:21(2979)

JEBERECHIAH-**IS**-8:2(3000)

JEBUS-all=2982-**J'G**-19:10,11-**1CH**-11:4,5

JEBUSI-**JOS**-18:16(2983),28(2983)

JEBUSITE-all=2983-**GE**-10:16-**EX**-33:2■34:11-**JOS**-9:1■11:3■15:8-**2SA**-24:16,18-**1CH**-1:14■21:15,18,28-**2CH**-3:1-**ZEC**-9:7

JEBUSITES-all=2983-**GE**-15:21-**EX**-3:8,17■13:5■23:23-**NU**-13:29-**DE**-7:1■20:17-**JOS**-3:10■12:8■15:63^2■24:11-**J'G**-1:21^2■3:5■19:11-**2SA**-5:6,8-**1KI**-9:20-**1CH**-11:4,6-**2CH**-8:7-**EZR**-9:1-**NE**-9:8

JECAMIAH-**1CH**-3:18(3359)

JECHOLIAH-**2KI**-15:2(3203)

JECHONIAS-**M'T**-1:11(2423),12(2423)

JECOLIAH-**2CH**-26:3(3203)

JECONIAH-all=3204-**1CH**-3:16,17-**ES**-2:6-**JER**-24:1■27:20■28:4■29:2

JEDAIAH-all=3048-**1CH**-4:37(3042)■9:10■24:7-**EZR**-2:36-**NE**-3:10(3042)■7:39■11:10■12:6,7,19,21-**ZEC**-6:10,14

JEDIAEL-all=3043-**1CH**-7:6,10,11■11:45■12:20■26:2

JEDIDAH-**2KI**-22:1(3040)

JEDIDIAH-**2SA**-12:25(3041)

JEDUTHUN-all=3038-**1CH**-9:16■16:38,41,42^2■25:1,3^2,6-**2CH**-5:12■29:14■35:15-**NE**-11:17-**PS**-39:t■62:t■77:t

JEEZER-**NU**-26:30(372)

JEEZERITES-**NU**-26:30(373)

JEGARSAHADUTHA-**GE**-31:47(3026)

JEHALELEEL-**1CH**-4:16(3094)

JEHALELEL-**2CH**-29:12(3094)

JEHDEIAH-**1CH**-24:20(3165)■27:30(3165)

JEHEZEKEL-**1CH**-24:16(3168)

JEHIAH-**1CH**-15:24(3174)

JEHIEL-all=3171-**1CH**-9:35(3273)■11:44(3273)■15:18,20■16:5■23:8■27:32■29:8-**2CH**-21:2■29:14■31:13■35:8-**EZR**-8:9■10:2,21,26

JEHIELI-**1CH**-28:21(3172),22(3172)

JEHIZKIAH-**2CH**-28:12(3169)

JEHOADAH-**1CH**-8:36(3085)

JEHOADDAN-**2KI**-14:2(3086)-**2CH**-25:1(3086)

JEHOAHAZ-all=3059&marked-**2KI**-10:35■13:1,4,7,8,9,10,22,25^2■14:1(3099),8,17■23:30,31,34-**2CH**-21:17■25:17,23,25■36:1,2,4

JEHOASH-all=3060-**2KI**-11:21■12:1,2,4,6,7,18■13:10,25■14:8,9,11,13^2,15,16,17

JEHOHANAN-all=3076-**1CH**-26:3-**2CH**-17:15■23:1-**EZR**-10:28-**NE**-12:13,42

JEHOIACHIN-all=3078-**2KI**-24:6,8,12,15■25:27^2-**2CH**-36:8,9-**JER**-52:31^2

JEHOIACHIN'S-**EZE**-1:2(3112)

JEHOIADA-all=3111-**2SA**-8:18■20:23■23:20,22-**1KI**-1:8,26,32,36,38,44■2:25,29,34,35,46■4:4-**2KI**-11:4,9^2,15,17■12:2,7,9-**1CH**-11:22,24■12:27■18:17■27:5,34-**1CH**-22:11■23:1,8^2,9,11,14,16,18■24:2,3,6,12,14^2,15,17,20,22,25-**NE**-3:6-**JER**-29:26

JEHOIAKIM-all=3079-**2KI**-23:34,35,36■24:1,5,6,19-**1CH**-3:15,16-**2CH**-36:4,5,8-**JER**-1:3■22:18,24■24:1■25:1■26:1,21,22,23■27:1,20■28:4■35:1■36:1,9,28,29,30,32■37:1■45:1■46:2■52:2-**DA**-1:1,2

JEHOIARIB-**1CH**-9:10(3080)■24:7(3080)

JEHONADAB-**2KI**-10:15^2(3082),23(3082)

JEHONATHAN-all=3083-**1CH**-27:25-**2CH**-17:8-**NE**-12:18

JEHORAM-all=3088-**1KI**-22:50-**2KI**-1:17^2■3:1,6■8:16,25,29■9:24■12:18-**2CH**-17:8■21:1,3,4,5,9,16■22:1,5,6^2,7,11

JEHOSHABEATH-**2CH**-22:11^2(3090)

JEHOSHAPHAT-all=3092&marked-**2SA**-8:16■20:24-**1KI**-4:3,17■15:24■22:2,4^2,5,7,8^2,10,18,29,30,32^2,41,42,44,45,48,49^2,50,51-**2KI**-1:17■3:1,7,11,12^2,14■8:16^2■9:2,14■12:18-**1CH**-3:10■15:24(3046)■18:15-**2CH**-17:1,3,5,10,11,12■18:1,3,4,6,7^2,9,17,28,29,31^2■19:1,2,4,8■20:1,2,3,5,15,18,20,25,27,30,31,34,35,37■21:1,2^2,12■22:9-**JOE**-3:2,12

JEHOSHEBA-**2KI**-11:2(3089)

JEHOSHUA-**NU**-13:16(3091)

JEHOSHUAH-**1CH**-7:27(3091)

JEHOVAH-all=3068-**EX**-6:3-**PS**-83:18-**IS**-12:2■26:4

JEHOVAH-JIREH-**GE**-22:14(3070)

JEHOVAH-NISSI-**EX**-17:15(3071)

JEHOVAH-SHALOM-**J'G**-6:24(3073)

JEHOZABAD-all=3075-**2KI**-12:21-**1CH**-26:4-**2CH**-17:18■24:26

JEHOZADAK-**1CH**-6:14(3087),15(3087)

JEHU-all=3058-**1KI**-16:1,7,12■19:16,17^2-**2KI**-9:2,5,11,13,14,15,16,17,18,19,20,21,22^2,24,25,27,30,31■10:1,5,11,13,18^2,19,20,21,23,24,25,28,29,30,31,34,35,36■12:1■13:1■14:8■15:12-**1CH**-2:38■4:35■12:3-**2CH**-19:2■20:34■22:7,8,9■25:17-**HO**-1:4

JEHUBBAH-**1CH**-7:34(3160)

JEHUCAL-**JER**-37:3(3081)

JEHUD-**JOS**-19:45(3055)

JEHUDI-all=3605-**JER**-36:14,21^2,23

JEHUDIJAH-**1CH**-4:18(3057)

JEHUSH-**1CH**-8:39(3266)

JEIEL-all=3273-**1CH**-5:7■15:18,21■16:5^2-**2CH**-20:14■26:11■29:13■35:9-**EZR**-8:13■10:43

JEKABZEEL-**NE**-11:25(3343)

JEKAMEAM-**1CH**-23:19(3360)■24:23(3360)

JEKAMIAH-**1CH**-2:41(3359)

JEKUTHIEL-**1CH**-4:18(3354)

JEMIMA-**JOB**-42:14(3224)

JEMUEL-**GE**-46:10(3223)-**EX**-6:15(3223)

JEPHTHAE-**HEB**-11:32(2422)

JEPHTHAH-all=3316-**J'G**-11:1^2,2,3^2,5,6,7,8,9,10,11^2,12,13,14,15,28,29,30,32,34,40■12:1,2,4,7^2-**1SA**-12:11

JEPHUNNEH-all=3312-**NU**-13:6■14:6,30,38■26:65■32:12■34:19-**DE**-1:36-**JOS**-14:6,13,14■15:13■21:12-**1CH**-4:15■6:56■7:38

JERAH-**GE**-10:26(3392)-**1CH**-1:20(3392)

JERAHMEEL-all=3396-**1CH**-2:9,25,26,27,33,42■24:29-**JER**-36:26

JERAHMEELITES-**1SA**-27:10(3397)■30:29(3397)

JERED-**1CH**-1:2(3382)■4:18(3382)

JEREMAI-**EZR**-10:33(3413)

JEREMIAH-all=3414-**2KI**-23:31■24:18-**1CH**-5:24■12:4,10,13-**2CH**-35:25■36:12,21,22-**EZR**-1:1-**NE**-10:2■12:1,12,34-**JER**-1:t,1,11■7:1■11:1■14:1■18:1,18■19:14■20:1,2,3^2■21:1,3■24:3■25:1,2,13■26:7,8,9,12,20,24■27:1■28:5,6,11,12^2,15■29:1,27,29,30■30:1■32:1,2,6,26■33:1,19,23■34:1,6,8,12■35:1,3,12,18■36:1,4^2,5,8,10,19,26,27^2,32^2■37:2,3,4,6,12,13,14^2,15,16^2,17,18,21^2■38:1,6^3,7,9,10,11,12^2,13^2,14^2,15,16,17,19,20,24,27,28■39:11,14,15■40:1,2,6■42:2,4,5,7■43:1,2,6,8■44:1,15,20,24■45:1^2■46:1,13■47:1■49:34■50:1■51:59,60,61,64■52:1-**DA**-9:2

JEREMIAH'S-**JER**-28:10(3414)

JEREMIAS-**M'T**-16:14(2408)

JEREMOTH-all=3406-**1CH**-8:14■23:23■25:22-**EZR**-10:26,27

JEREMY-**M'T**-2:17(2408)■27:9(2408)

JERIAH-**1CH**-23:19(3404)■24:23(3404)

JERIBAI-**1CH**-11:46(3403)

JERICHO-all=3405-**NU**-22:1■26:3,63■31:12■33:48,50■34:15■35:1■36:13-**DE**-32:49■34:1,3-**JOS**-2:1,2,3■3:16■4:13,19■5:10,13■6:1,2,25,26■7:2■8:2■9:3■10:1,28,30■12:9■13:32■16:1^3,7■18:12,21■20:8■24:11^2-**2SA**-10:5-**1KI**-16:34-**2KI**-2:4^2,5,15,18■25:5-**1CH**-6:78■19:5-**2CH**-28:15-**EZR**-2:34-**NE**-3:2■7:36-**JER**-39:5■52:8■**N.T.**-all=2410-**M'T**-20:29-**M'R**-10:46-**LU**-10:30■18:35■19:1-**HEB**-11:30

JERIEL-**1CH**-7:2(3400)

JERIJAH-**1CH**-26:31(3404)

JERIMOTH-all=3406-**1CH**-7:7,8■12:5■24:30■25:4■27:19-**2CH**-11:18■31:13

JERIOTH-**1CH**-2:18(3408)

JEROBOAM-all=3379-**1KI**-11:26,28,29,31,40^2■12:2^2,3,12,15,20,25,26,32■13:1,4,33,34■14:1,2^2,5,6,7,10^3,11,13^2,14,16,19,20,30■15:1,6,7,9,25,29^2,30,34■16:2,3,7,19,26,31■21:22■22:52-**2KI**-3:3■9:9■10:29,31■13:2,6,11,13■14:16,23,24,27,28,29■15:1,8,9,18,24,28■17:21^2,22■23:15-**1CH**-5:17-**2CH**-9:29■10:2^2,3,12,15■11:4,14■12:15■13:1,2,3,4,6,8,13,15,19,20-**HO**-1:1-**AM**-1:1■7:9,10,11

JEROBOAM'S-**1KI**-14:4(3379),17(3379)

JEROHAM-all=3395-**1SA**-1:1-**1CH**-6:27,34■8:27■9:8,12■12:7■27:22-**2CH**-23:1-**NE**-11:12

JERUBBAAL-all=3378-**J'G**-6:32■7:1■8:29,35■9:1,2,5^2,16,19,24,28,57-**1SA**-12:11

JERUBBESHETH-**2SA**-11:21(3380)

JERUEL-**2CH**-20:16(3385)

JERUSALEM-all=3389a=3390-**JOS**-10:1,3,5,23■12:10■15:8,63^2■18:28-**J'G**-1:7,8,21^2■19:10-**1SA**-17:54-**2SA**-5:5,6,13,14■8:7■9:13■10:14■11:1,12■12:31■14:23,28■15:8,11,14,29,37■16:3,15■17:20■19:19,25,33,34■20:2,3,7,22■24:8,16-**1KI**-2:11,36,38,41■3:1,15■8:1■9:15,19■10:2,26,27■11:7,29,36,42■12:18,21,27,28■14:21,25■15:2,4^2,10■22:42-**2KI**-8:17,26■9:28■12:1,17,18■14:2^2,13^2,19,20■15:2^2,33■16:2,5■18:2,17^2,22^2,35■19:10,21,31■21:1,4,7,12,13^2,16,19■22:1,14■23:1,2,4,5,6,9,13,20,23,24,27,30,31,33,36■24:4,8^2,10,14,15,18,20■25:1,8,9,10-**1CH**-3:4,5■6:10,15,32■8:28,32■9:3,34,38■11:4■14:3,4■15:3■18:7■19:15■20:1,3■21:4,15,16■23:25■28:1■29:27-**2CH**-1:4,13,14,15■2:7,16■3:1■5:2■6:6■8:6■9:1,25,27,30■10:18■11:1,5,14,16■12:2,4,5,7,9,13^2■13:2■14:15■15:10■17:13■19:1,4,8^2■20:5,15,17,18,20,27^2,28,31■21:5,11,13,20■22:1,2■23:2■24:1,6,9,18,23■25:1^2,23^2,27■26:3^2,9,15■27:1,8■28:1,10,24,27■29:1,8■30:1,2,3,5,11,13,14,21,26^2■31:4■32:2,9^2,10,12,18,19,22,23,25,26,33■33:1,4,7,9,13,15,21■34:1,3,5,7,9,22,29,30,32^2■35:1,18,24^2■36:1,2,3,4,5,9,10,11,14,19,23-**EZR**-1:2,3^2,4,5,7,11■2:1,68■3:1,8^2■4:6,8a,12a,20a,23a,24a■5:1a,2a,14a,15a,16a,17a■6:3a,5^{2}a,9a,12a,18a■7:7,8,9,13a,14a,15a,16a,17a,19a,27■8:29,30,31,32■9:9■10:7^2,9-**NE**-1:2,3■2:11,12,13,17^2,20■3:8,9,12■4:7,8,22■6:7■7:2,3^2,6■8:15■11:1^2,2,3,4,6,22■12:27^2,28,29,43■13:6,7,15,16,19,20-**ES**-2:6-**PS**-51:18■68:29■79:1,3■102:21■116:19■122:2,3,6■125:2■128:5■135:21■137:5,6,7■147:2,12-**EC**-1:1,12,16■2:7,9-**SONG**-1:5■2:7■3:5,10■5:8,16■6:4■8:4-**IS**-1:1■2:1,3■3:1,8■4:3^2,4■5:3■7:1■8:14■10:10,11,12,32■22:10,21■24:23■27:13■28:14■30:19■31:5,9■33:20■36:2,7,20■37:10,22,32■40:2,9■41:27■44:26,28■51:17■52:1,2,9^2■62:6,7■64:10■65:18,19■66:10,13,20-**JER**-1:3,15■2:2■3:17^2■4:3,4,5,10,11,14,16■5:1■6:1,6,8■7:17,34■8:1,5■9:11■11:2,6,9,12,13■13:9,13,27■14:2,16■15:4,5■17:19,20,21,25,26,27^2■18:11■19:3,7,13■22:19■23:14,15■24:1,8■25:2,18■26:18■27:3,18,20^2,21■29:1^2,2^2,4,20,25■32:2,32,44■33:10,13,16■34:1,6,7,8,19■35:11^2,13,17■36:9^2,31■37:5^2,11,12■38:28^2■39:1,8■40:1■42:18■44:2,6,9,13,17,21■51:35,50■52:1,3,4,12,13,14,29-**LA**-1:7,8,17■2:10,13,15■4:12-**EZE**-4:1,7,16■5:5■8:3■9:4,8■11:15■12:10,19■13:16■14:21,22■15:6■16:2,3■17:12■21:2,20,22■22:19■23:4■24:2■26:2■33:21■36:38-**DA**-1:1■5:2a,3a■6:10a■9:2,7,12,16^2,25-**JOE**-2:32■3:1,6,16,17,20-**AM**-1:2■2:5-**OB**-11,20-**MIC**-1:1,5,9,12■3:10,12■4:2,8-**ZEP**-1:4,12■3:14,16-**ZEC**-1:12,14,16^2,17,19■2:2,4,12■3:2■7:7■8:3^2,4,8,15,22■9:9,10■12:2^2,3,5,6^2,7,8,9,10,11■13:1■14:2,4,8,10,11,12,14,16,17,21-**MAL**-2:11■3:4■**N.T.**-all=2419,a=2414-**M'T**-2:1a,3a■3:5a■4:25a■5:35a■15:1a■16:21a■20:17a,18a■21:1a,10a■23:37-**M'R**-1:5a■3:8a,22a■7:1a■10:32a,33a■11:1,11a,15a,27a■15:41a-**LU**-2:22a,25,38,41,42a,43,45■4:9■5:17■6:17■9:31,51,53■10:30■13:4,22,33,34■17:11■18:31a■19:11,28a■21:20,24■23:7a,28■24:13,18,33,47,49,52-**JOH**-1:19a■2:13a,23a■4:20a,21a,45a■5:1a,2a■7:25a■10:22a■11:18a,55a■12:12a-**AC**-1:4a,8,12^2,19■2:5,14■4:6,16■5:16,28■6:7■8:1a,14a,25,26,27■9:2,13,21,26,28■10:39■11:2a,22a,27a■12:25■13:13a,27,31■15:2,4■16:4■18:21a■19:21■20:16a,22■21:4,11,12,13,15,17a,31■22:5,17,18■23:11■24:11■25:1a,3,7a,9a,15a,20,24a■26:4a,10a,20a■28:17a-**RO**-15:19,25,26,31-**1CO**-16:3-**GA**-1:17a,18a■2:1a■4:25,26-**HEB**-12:22-**RE**-3:12■21:2,10

JERUSALEM'S-all=3389&-**1KI**-11:13,32-**1SA**-62:1

JERUSHA-**2KI**-15:33(3388)

JERUSHAH-**2CH**-27:1(3388)

JESAIAH-**1CH**-3:21(3470)-**NE**-11:7(3470)

JESHAIAH-all=3470-**1CH**-25:3,15■26:25-**EZR**-8:7,19

JESHANAH-**2CH**-13:19(3466)

JESHARELAH-**1CH**-25:14(3480)

JESHEBEAB-**1CH**-24:13(3434)

JESHER-**1CH**-2:18(3475)

JESHIMON-all=3452-**NU**-21:20■23:28-**1SA**-23:19,24■26:1,3

JESHISHAI-**1CH**-5:14(3454)

JESHOHAIAH-**1CH**-4:36(3439)

JESHUA-all=3442&marked-**2CH**-31:15-**EZR**-2:2,6,36,40■3:2,8,9■4:3■5:2(3443)■8:33(3443)■10:18-**NE**-3:19■7:7,11,39,43■8:7,17■9:4,5■10:9■11:26■12:1,7,8,10,24,26

JESHUAH-**1CH**-24:11(3442)

JESHURUN-all=3484-**DE**-32:15■33:5,26

JESIAH-**1CH**-12:6(3449)■23:20(3449)

JESIMIEL-**1CH**-4:36(3450)

JESSE-all=3448-RU-4:17,22-1SA-16:1,3,5,8,9,10^{2},11^{2},18,19,20,22■17:12,13,17,20,58■20:27,30,31■22:7,8,9,13■25:10-2SA-20:1■23:1-1KI-12:16-1CH-2:12,13■10:14■12:18■29:26-2CH-10:16■11:18-PS-72:20-IS-11:1,10■N.T.-all=2421-M'T-1:5,6-LU-3:32-AC-13:22-RO-15:12

JESUI-NU-26:44(3440)

JESUITES-NU-26:44(3441)

JESURUN-IS-44:2(3484)

JESUS-all=2424&marked-M'T-1:1,16,18,21,25■2:1■3:13,15,16■4:1,7,10,12,17,18,23■7:28■8:3,4,5,7,10,13,14,18,20,22,29,34■9:2,4,9,10,12,15,19,22,23,27,28,30,35■10:5■11:1,4,7,25■12:1,15,25■13:1,34,36,51,53,57■14:1,12,13,14,16,22,25,27,29,31■15:1,16,21,28,29,32,34■16:6,8,13,17,20,21,24■17:1,4,7,8,9,11,17,18,19,20,22,25,26■18:1,2,22■19:1,14,18,21,23,26,28■20:17,22,25,30,32,34■21:1,6,11,12,16,21,24,27,31,42■22:1,18,29,37,41■23:1■24:1,2,4■26:1,4,6,10,17,19,26,31,34,36,49,50^{2},51,52,55,57,59,63,64,69,71,75■27:1,11^{2},17,20,22,26,27,37,46,50,54,55,58■28:5,9,10,16,18-M'R-1:1,9,14,17,24,25,41,45■2:5,8,15^{2},17,19■3:7■5:6,7,13,15,19,20,21,27,30,36■6:4,30,34■7:27■8:1,17,27■9:2,4,5,8,23,25,27,39■10:5,14,18,21,23,24,27,29,32,38,39,42,47^{2},49,50,51,52^{2}■11:6,7,11,14,15,22,29,33^{2}■12:17,24,29,34,35,41■13:2,5■14:6,18,22,27,30,48,53,55,60,62,67,72■15:1,5,15,34,37,43■16:6-LU-1:31■2:21,27,43,52■3:21,23■4:1,4,8,12,14,34,35■5:10,12,19,22,31■6:3,9,11■7:3,4,6,9,19,22,40■8:28^{2},30,35^{2},38,39,40,45,46,50■9:33,36,41,42,43,47,50,58,60,62■10:21,29,30,37,41■13:2,12,14■14:3■17:13,17■18:16,19,22,24,37,38,40,42■19:3,5,9,35^{2}■20:8,34■22:47,48,51,52,63■23:8,20,25,26,28,34,42,43,46,52■24:3,15,19,36-JOH-1:17,29,36,37,38,42^{2},43,45,47,48,50■2:1,2,3,4,7,11,13,19,22,24■3:2,3,5,10,22■4:1,2,6,7,10,13,16,17,21,26,34,44,46,47,48,50^{2},53,54■5:1,6,8,13,14,15,16,17,19■6:1,3,5,10,11,14,15,17,19,22,24^{2},26,29,32,35,42,43,53,61,64,67,70■7:1,6,14,16,21,28,33,37,39,50(846)■8:1,6,9,10,11,12,14,19,20,21,25,28,31,34,39,42,49,54,58,59■9:3,11,14,35,37,39,41■10:6,7,23,25,32,34■11:4,5,9,13,14,17,20,21,23,25,30,32,33,35,38,39,40,41,44,45,46,51,54,56■12:1,3,7,11,12,14,16,21,22,23,30,35,36,44■13:1,3,7,8,10,21,23,26,27,29,31,36,38■14:6,9,23■16:19,31■17:1,3■18:1,2,4,5^{2},7,8,11,12,15^{2},19,20,22,23,28,32,33,34,36,37■19:1,5,9^{2},11,13,16,18,19,20,23,25,26,28,30,33,38^{3},39,40,42■20:2,12,14^{2},15,16,17,19,21,24,26,29,30,31■21:1,4^{2},5,7,10,12,13,14,15,17,20,21,22,23,25-AC-1:1,11,14,16,21■2:22,32,36,38■3:6,13,20,26■4:2,10,13,18,27,30,33■5:30,40,42■6:14■7:45,55,59■8:12,16,35,37■9:5,17,27,29,34■10:36,38■11:17,20■13:23,33■15:11,26■16:18,31■17:3,7,18■18:5,28■19:4,5,10,13^{2},15,17■20:21,24,35■21:13■22:8■25:19■26:9,15■28:23,31-RO-1:1,3,6,7,8■2:16■3:22,24,26■4:24■5:1,11,15,17,21■6:3,11,23■7:25■8:1,2,11,39■10:9■13:14■14:14■15:5,6,8,16,17,30■16:3,18,20,24,25,27-1CO-1:1,2^{2},3,4,7,8,9,10,30■2:2■3:11■4:15■5:4^{2},5■6:11■8:6■9:1■11:23■12:3^{2}■15:31,57■16:22,23,24-2CO-1:1,2,3,14,19■4:5,6,10^{2},11,14^{2}■5:18■8:9■11:4,31■13:5,14-GA-1:1,3,12■2:4,16^{2}■3:1,14,22,26,28■4:14■5:6■6:14,15,17,18-EPH-1:1^{2},2,3,5,15,17■2:6,7,10,13,20■3:1,9,11,14,21■4:21■5:20■6:23,24-PH'P-1:1^{2},2,6,8,11,19,26■2:5,10,11,19,21■3:3,8,12,14,20■4:7,19,21,23-COL-1:1,2,3,4,28■2:6■3:17■4:11-1TH-1:1^{2},3,10■2:14,15,19■3:11,13■4:1,2,14^{2}■5:9,18,23,28-2TH-1:1,2,7,8,12^{2}■2:1,14,16■3:6,12,18-1TI-1:1^{2},2,12,14,15,16■2:5■3:13■4:6■5:21■6:3,13,14-2TI-1:1^{2},2,9,10,13■2:1,3,8,10■3:12,15■4:1,22-TIT-1:1,4■2:13■3:6-PH'M-1,3,5,6,9,23,25-HEB-2:9■3:1■4:8,14■6:20■7:22■10:10,19■12:2,24■13:8,12,20,21-JAS-1:1■2:1-1PE-1:1,2,3^{2},7,13■2:5■3:21■4:11■5:10,14-2PE-1:1^{2},2,8,11,14,16■2:20■3:18-1JO-1:3,7■2:1,22■3:23■4:2,3,15■5:1,5,6,20-2JO-3,7-JUDE-1^{2},4,17,21-RE-1:1,2,5,9^{2}■12:17■14:12■17:6■19:10^{2}■20:4■22:16,20,21

JESUS'-all=2424-M'T-15:30■27:57-LU-5:8■8:41■10:39-JOH-12:9■13:23,25-2CO-4:5,11

JETHER-all=3500-J'G-8:20-1KI-2:5,32-1CH-2:17,32^{2}■4:17■7:38

JETHETH-GE-36:40(3509)-1CH-1:51(3509)

JETHLAH-JOS-19:42(3494)

JETHRO-all=3503-EX-3:1■4:18^{2}■18:1,2,5,6,9,10,12

JETUR-all=3195-GE-25:15-1CH-1:31■5:19

JEUEL-1CH-9:6(3262)

JEUSH-all=3266-GE-36:5,14,18-1CH-1:35■7:10■23:10,11-2CH-11:19

JEUZ-1CH-8:10(3263)

JEW-all=3064&marked-ES-2:5■3:4■5:13■6:10■8:7■9:29,31■10:3-JER-34:9-ZEC-8:23■N.T.-all=2453-JOH-4:9■18:35-AC-10:28■13:6■18:2,24■19:14,34■21:39■22:3-RO-1:16■2:9,10,17,28,29■3:1■10:12-1CO-9:20-GA-2:14■3:28-COL-3:11

JEWESS-AC-6:1(2453)■24:24(2453)

JEWISH-TIT-1:14(2451)

JEWRY-DA-5:13(3061)■N.T.-LU-23:5(2449)-JOH-7:1(2449)

JEWS-all=3064&marked-2KI-16:6■25:25-EZR-4:12(3062),23(3062)■5:1(3062),5(3062)■6:7^{2}(3062),8(3062),14(3062)-NE-1:2■2:16■4:1,2,12■5:1,8,17■6:6■13:23-ES-3:6,13■4:3,7,13,14,16■6:13■8:3,5,7,8,9^{2},11,13,16,17^{2},17(3054)■9:1^{2},2,3,5,6,10,12,13,15,16,18,19,20,22,23,24^{2},25,27,28,30■10:3-JER-32:12■38:19■40:11,12,15■41:3■44:1■52:28,30-DA-3:8,12■N.T.-all=2453&marked-M'T-2:2■27:11,29,37■28:15-M'R-7:3■15:2,9,12,18,26-LU-7:3■23:3,37,38,51-JOH-1:19■2:6,18,20■3:1,25■4:9,22■5:1,10,15,16,18■6:4,41,52■7:1,11,13,15,35■8:22,31,48,52,57■9:18,22^{2}■10:19,24,31,33■11:8,19,31,33,36,45,54■12:9,11■13:33■18:12,14,20,31,33,36,38,39■19:3,7,12,14,19,20,21^{3},31,38,40■20:19-AC-2:5,10■9:22,23■10:22,39■11:19■12:3,11■13:5,42,43,45,50■14:1^{2},2,4,5,13■16:3,20■17:1,5,10,13,17■18:2,4,5,12,14^{2},19,28■19:10,13,17,33■20:3,19,21■21:11,20,21,27■22:12,30■23:12,20,27,30■24:5,9,18,27■25:2,7,8,9,10,15,24■26:2,3,4,7,21■28:17,19,29-RO-3:9,29■9:24-1CO-1:22,23,24■9:20^{2}■10:32■12:13-2CO-11:24-GA-2:13,14(2452),14(2450),15-1TH-2:14-RE-2:9■3:9

JEWS'-all=3066&marked-2KI-18:26,28-2CH-32:18-NE-13:24-ES-3:10(3064)■8:1(3064)-ISA-36:11(3064),13(3064)■N.T.-all=2453&marked-JOH-2:13■7:2■11:55■19:42-GA-1:13(2454),14(2454)

JEZANIAH-JER-40:8(3153)■42:1(3153)

JEZEBEL-all=348-1KI-16:31■18:4,13■19:1,2■21:5,7,11,14,15^{2},23^{2},25-2KI-9:7,10,22,30,36,37^{2}■N.T.-RE-2:20(2403)

JEZEBEL'S-1KI-18:19(348)

JEZER-all=3337-GE-46:24-NU-26:49-1CH-7:13

JEZERITES-NU-26:49(3339)

JEZIAH-EZR-10:25(3150)

JEZIEL-1CH-12:3(3149)

JEZLIAH-1CH-8:18(3152)

JEZOAR-1CH-4:7(3328)

JEZRAHIAH-NE-12:42(3156)

JEZREEL-all=3157-JOS-15:56■17:16■19:18-J'G-6:33-1SA-25:43■29:1,11-2SA-2:9■4:4-1KI-4:12■18:45,46■21:1,23-2KI-8:29^{2}■9:10,15^{2},16,17,30,36,37■10:1,6,7,11-1CH-4:3-2CH-22:6^{2}-HO-1:4^{2},5,11■2:22

JEZREELITE-all=3158-1KI-21:1,4,6,7,15,16-2KI-9:21,25

JEZREELITESS-all=3159-1SA-27:3■30:5-2SA-2:2■3:2-1CH-3:1

JIBSAM-1CH-7:2(3005)

JIDLAPH-GE-22:22(3044)

JIMNA-NU-26:44(3232)

JIMNAH-GE-46:17(3232)

JIMNITES-NU-26:44(3232)

JIPHTAH-JOS-15:43(3316)

JIPHTHAH-EL-JOS-19:14(3317),27(3317)

JOAB-all=3097&marked-1SA-26:6-2SA-2:13,14^{2},18,22,24,26,27,28,30,32■3:22,23^{2},24,26,27,29^{2},30,31■8:16■10:7,9,13,14■11:1,6^{2},7,11,14,16,17,18,22,25■12:26,27■14:1,2,3,19^{2},20,21,22^{2},23,29,31,32,33■17:25■18:2,5,10,11,12,14,16^{2},20,21^{2},22^{2},29■19:1,5,13■20:9^{2},10,11^{2},13,15,16,17,20,21,22^{2},23■23:18,24,37■24:2,3,4^{2},9-1KI-1:7,19,41■2:5,22,28^{3},29,30,31,33■11:15,16,21-1CH-2:16,54(5854)■4:14■11:6,8,20,26,39■18:15■19:8,10,14,15■20:1^{2}■21:2,3,4^{2},5,6■26:28■27:7,24,34-EZR-2:6■8:9-NE-7:11-PS-60:t

JOAB'S-all=3097-2SA-14:30■17:25■18:2,15■20:7,8,10,11

JOAH-all=3098-2KI-18:18,26,37-1CH-6:21■26:4-2CH-29:12^{2}■34:8-IS-36:3,11,22

JOAHAZ-2CH-34:8(3098)

JOANNA-all=2489-LU-3:27■8:3■24:10

JOASH-all=3101&marked-J'G-6:11,29,30,31■7:14■8:13,29,32^{2}-1KI-22:26-2KI-11:2■12:19,20■13:1,9,10,12,13^{2},14,25■14:1^{2},3,17,23^{2},27-1H-3:11■4:22■7:8(3135)■12:3■27:28(3135)-2CH-18:25■22:11■24:1,4,22,24■25:17,18,21,23^{2},25^{2}-HO-1:1-AM-1:1

JOATHAM-M'T-1:9(2488)

JOB-all=347&marked-GE-46:13(3102)-JOB-1:t,1,5^{3},8,9,14,20,22■2:3,7,10■3:1,2■6:1■9:1■12:1■12:1■16:1■19:1■21:1■23:1■26:1■27:1■29:1■31:40■32:1,2,3,12■33:1,31■34:5,7,35,36■35:16■37:14■38:1■40:1,3,6■42:1,7^{2},8^{3},9,10^{2},12,15,16,17-EZE-14:14,20■N.T.-JAS-5:11(2492)

JOBAB-all=3103-GE-10:29■36:33,34-JOS-11:1-1CH-1:23,44,45■8:9,18

JOB'S-JOB-2:11(347)

JOCHEBED-EX-6:20(3115)-NU-26:59(3115)

JOED-NE-11:7(3133)

JOEL-all=3100-1SA-8:2-1CH-4:35■5:4,8,12■6:33,36■7:3■11:38■15:7,11,17■23:8■26:22■27:20-2CH-29:12-EZR-10:43-NE-11:9-JOE-1:t,1■N.T.-AC-2:16(2493)

JOELAH-1CH-12:7(3132)

JOEZER-1CH-12:6(3134)

JOGBEHAH-NU-32:35(3011)-J'G-8:11(3011)

JOGLI-NU-34:22(3020)

JOHA-1CH-8:16(3109)■11:45(3109)

JOHANAN-all=3110&marked-2KI-25:23-1CH-3:15,24■6:9,10■12:4,12-2CH-28:12(3076)-EZR-8:12■10:6(3076)-NE-6:18■12:22,23-JER-40:8,13,15,16■41:11,13,14,15,16■42:1,8■43:2,4,5

JOHN-all=2491-M'T-3:1,4,13,14■4:12,21■9:14■10:2■11:2,4,7,11,12,13,18■14:2,3,4,8,10■16:14■17:1,13■21:25,26,32-M'R-1:4,6,9,14,19,29■2:18^{2}■3:17■5:37■6:14,16,17,18,20,24,25■8:28■9:2,38■10:35,41■11:30,32■13:3■14:33-LU-1:13,60,63■3:2,15,16,20■5:10,33■6:14■7:18,19,20,22,24^{2},28,29,33■8:51■9:7,9,19,28,49,54■11:1■16:16■20:4,6■22:8-JOH-1:t,6,15,19,26,28,29,32,35,40■3:23,24,26,27■4:1■5:33,36■10:40,41^{2}-AC-1:5,13,22■3:1,3,4,11■4:6,13,19■8:14■10:37■11:16■12:2,12,25■13:5,13,24,25■15:37■18:25■19:4-GA-2:9-1JO-1:t-2JO-1:t-3JO-1:t-RE-1:t,1,4,9■21:2■22:8

JOHN'S-JOH-3:25(2491)-AC-19:3(2491)

JOIADA-all=3111-NE-12:10,10,11,22■13:28

JOIAKIM-all=3113-NE-12:10,12,26

JOIARIB-all=3114-EZR-8:16-NE-11:5,10■12:6,19

JOKDEAM-JOS-15:56(3347)

JOKIM-1CH-4:22(3137)

JOKMEAM-1CH-6:68(3361)

JOKNEAM-all=3362-JOS-12:22■19:11■21:34-1KI-4:12

JOKSHAN-all=3370-GE-25:2,3-1CH-1:32^{2}

JOKTAN-all=3355-GE-10:25,26,29-1CH-1:19,20,23

JOKTHEEL-JOS-15:38(3371) -2KI-14:7(3371)

JONA-JOH-1:42(2495)

JONADAB-all=3122&marked -2SA-13:3^2,5,32,35-JER-35:6,8(3082), 10,14(3082),16(3082),18(3082),19

JONAH-all=3124-2KI-14:25-JON-1:1, 3,5,7,15,17^2■2:1,10■3:1,3,4■4:1,5,6^2,8,9

JONAN-LU-3:30(2494)

JONAS-all=2495-M'T-12:39,40,41^2■ 16:4-LU-11:29,30,32^2-JOH-21:15,16,17

JONATHAN-all=3083,a=3129&marked-J'G-18:30a-1SA-13:2a,3a,16a, 22^{2}a■14:1a,3a,4a,6,8,12^{2}a,13^{2}a,14a,17a,21a, 27a,29a,39a,40a,41a,42^{2}a,43^{2}a,44a,45^{2}a, 49a■18:1^2,3,4■19:1a,2^2,4,6,7^2■20:1,3,4, 5,9,10,11,12,13,16,17,18,25,27,28,30,32, 33,34,35,37^2,38,39,40,42^2■23:16,18■31:2 -2SA-1:4,5,12,17,22,23,25,26■4:4^2■9:3, 6,7■15:27,36■17:17,20■21:7^2,12,13,14, 21■23:32-1KI-1:42a,43a-1CH-2:32a,33a■ 8:33,34■9:39,40■10:2a■11:34a■20:7■ 27:32-EZR-8:6■10:15-NE-12:11,14,35 -JER-37:15,20■40:8a

JONATHAN'S-all=3129-1SA-20:38 -2SA-9:1-JER-38:26

JONATH-ELEM-RECHOKIM -PS-56:t(3128)

JOPPA-all=3305-2CH-2:16-EZR-3:7-JON-1:3■N.T.-all=2445-AC-9:36, 38,42,23■10:5,8,23,32■11:5,13

JORAH-EZR-2:18(3139)

JORAI-1CH-5:13(3140)

JORAM-all=3141&marked-2SA-8:10-2KI-8:16,21,23,24,25,28^2,29^2■9:14^2, 15(3188),16^2,17(3188),21^2(3188),22 (3188),23(3188),29(3188)■11:2-1CH-3:11■26:25-2CH-22:5,7■N.T.-M'T-1:8(2496)

JORDAN-all=3383-GE-13:10,11■ 32:10■50:10,11-NU-13:29■22:1■26:3, 63■31:12■32:5,19^2,21,29,32■33:48,49,50, 51■34:12,15■35:1,10,14■36:13-DE-1:1,5■2:29■3:8,17,20,25,27■4:21,22,26, 41,46,47,49■9:1■11:30,31■12:10■27:2, 4,12■30:18■31:2,13■32:47-JOS-1:2,11, 14,15■2:7,10■3:1,8^2,11,13^2,14,15^2,17^2■ 4:1,3,5,7^3,8,9,10,16,17,18^2,19,20,22,23■ 5:1^2■7:7^2■9:1,10■12:1,7■13:8,23,27^2,32■ 14:3■15:5^2■16:1,7■17:5■18:7,12,19,20■ 19:22,33,34■20:8■22:4,7,10^2,11,25■ 23:4■24:8,11-J'G-3:28■5:17■7:24^2,25■ 8:4■10:8,9■11:13,22■12:5,6-1SA-13:7■ 31:7-2SA-2:29■10:17■17:22^2,24■19:15^2, 17,18,31^2,36,39,41■20:2■24:5-1KI-2:8■ 7:46■17:3,5-2KI-2:6,7,13■5:10,14■6:2, 4■7:15■10:33-1CH-6:78^2■12:15,37■ 19:17■26:30-2CH-4:17-JOB-40:23 -PS-42:6■114:3,5-IS-9:1-JER-12:5■ 49:19■50:44-EZE-47:18-ZEC-11:3■ N.T.-all=2446-M'T-3:5,6,13■4:15,25■ 19:1-M'R-1:5,9■3:8■10:1-LU-3:3■ 4:1-JOH-1:28■3:26■10:40

JORIM-LU-3:29(2497)

JORKOAM-1CH-2:44(3421)

JOSABAD-1CH-12:4(3107)

JOSAPHAT-M'T-1:8(2498)

JOSE-LU-3:29(2499)

JOSEDECH-all=3087-HAG-1:1, 12,14■2:2,4-ZEC-6:11

JOSEPH-all=3130&marked-GE-30:24,25■33:2,7■35:24■37:2^2,3,5,13,17, 23^2,28^3,29,33■39:1,2,4,6,7,10,21■40:3,4, 6,8,9,12,16,18,22,23■41:14,15,16,17,25, 39,41,44,45,46^2,49,50,51,54,55,56,57■ 42:6,7,8,9,14,18,23,25,36■43:15,16,17, 25,26,30■44:2,4,15■45:1^2,3,4^2,9,17,21, 26,27^2,28■46:4,19,20,27,28,29,30,31■ 47:1,5,7,11,12,14^2,15,16,17^2,20,23,26, 29■48:1,2,3,9,11,12,13,15,17,18,21■ 49:22,26■50:1,2,4,7,8,14,15,16,17^2,19, 22^2,23,24,25,26-EX-1:5,6,8■13:19-NU-1:10,32■13:7,11■26:28,37■27:1■32:33■ 34:23■36:1,5,12-DE-27:12■33:13,16 -JOS-14:4■16:1,4■17:1,2,14,16,17■18:5, 11■24:32^2-J'G-1:22,23,35-2SA-19:20 -1KI-11:28-1CH-2:2■5:1■7:29■25:2,9 -EZR-10:42-NE-12:14-PS-77:15■ 78:67■80:1■81:5(3084)■105:17-EZE-37:16,19■47:13■48:32-AM-5:6,15■6:6 -OB-18-ZEC-10:6■N.T.-all=2501 -M'T-1:16,18,19,20,24■2:13,19■27:57, 59-M'R-15:43,45-LU-1:27■2:4,16,33, 43■3:23,24,26,30■23:50-JOH-1:45■ 4:5■6:42■19:38-AC-1:23■7:9,13,14,18 -HEB-11:21,22-RE-7:8

JOSEPH'S-all=3130-GE-37:31■ 39:5,6,20,22■41:42,45■42:3,4,6■43:17, 18,19,24■44:14■45:16■48:8■50:15,23 -1CH-5:2■N.T.-LU-4:22(2501)-AC-7:13(2501)

JOSES-all=2500-M'T-13:55■27:56 -M'R-6:3■15:40,47-AC-4:36

JOSHAH-1CH-4:34(3144)

JOSAPHAT-1CH-11:43(3146)

JOSHAVIAH-1CH-11:46(3145)

JOSHBEKASHAH-1CH-25:4 (3436),24(3436)

JOSHUA-all=3091-EX-17:9,10,13, 14■24:13■32:17■33:11-NU-11:28■14:6, 30,38■26:65■27:18,22■32:12,28■34:17 -DE-1:38■3:21,28■31:3,7,14^2,23■34:9 -JOS-1:t,1,10,12,16■2:1,23,24■3:1,5,6,7, 9,10■4:1,4,5,8^2,9,10^2,14,15,17,20■5:2,3, 4,7,9,13^2,14,15^2■6:2,6,8,10,12,16,22,25^2, 26,27■7:2,3,6,7,10,16,19,20,22,23,24,25■ 8:1,3^2,9^2,10,13,15,16,18^2,21,23,26,27,28, 29,30,35■9:2,3,6,8^2,15,22,24,27■10:1,4,6, 7,8,9,12,15,17,18,20,21,22,24^2,25,26,27, 28,29,31,33,34,36,38,40,41,42,43■11:6, 7,9,10,12,13,15,16,18,21^2,23^2■12:7^2■13:1■ 14:1,6,13■15:13■17:4,14,15,17■18:3,8, 9,10^2■19:49,51■20:1■21:1■22:1,6,7^2■ 23:1,2■24:1,2,19,21,22,24,25,26,27,28, 29,31^2-J'G-1:1■2:6,7^2,8,21,23-1SA-6:14, 18-1KI-16:34-2KI-23:8-HAG-1:1,12, 14■2:2,4-ZEC-3:1,3,6,8,9■6:11

JOSIAH-all=2977-1KI-13:2-2KI-21:24,26■22:1,3■23:16,19,23,24,28,29, 30,34-1CH-3:14,15-2CH-33:25■34:1, 33■35:1,7,16,18,19,20^2,22,23,24,25^2,26■ 36:1-JER-1:2,3^2■3:6■22:11^2,18■25:1,3■ 26:1■27:1■35:1■36:1,2,9■37:1■45:1■ 46:2-ZEP-1:1-ZEC-6:10

JOSIAS-M'T-1:10(2502),11(2502)

JOSIBIAH-1CH-4:35(3143)

JOSIPHIAH-EZR-8:10(3131)

JOTBAH-2KI-21:19(3192)

JOTBATH-DE-10:7(3193)

JOTBATHAH-NU-33:33(3193), 34(3193)

JOTHAM-all=3147-J'G-9:5,7,21,57 -2KI-15:5,7,30,32,36,38■16:1-1CH-2:47■3:12■5:17-2CH-26:21,23■27:1,6,7,9 -IS-1:1■7:1-HO-1:1-MIC-1:1

JOZABAD-all=3107-1CH-12:20^2 -2CH-31:13■35:9-EZR-8:33■10:22,23 -NE-8:7■11:16

JOZACHAR-2KI-12:21(3108)

JOZADAK-all=3136-EZR-3:2,8■ 5:2■10:18-NE-12:26

JUBAL-GE-4:21(3106)

JUCAL-JER-38:1(3116)

JUDA-all=2455&marked-M'T-2:6^2 -M'R-6:3-LU-1:39(2448)■3:26,30,33 -HEB-7:14-RE-5:5■7:5

JUDAEA-all=2449&marked-M'T-2:1,5,22■3:1,5■4:25■19:1■24:16-M'R-1:5■3:7■10:1■13:14-LU-1:5,65■2:4■ 3:1■5:17■6:17■7:17■21:21-JOH-3:22■ 4:3,47,54■7:3■11:7-AC-1:8■2:9,14(2453)■ 8:1■9:31■10:37■11:1,29■12:19■15:1■ 21:10■26:20■28:21-RO-15:31-2CO-1:16-GA-1:22-1TH-2:14

JUDAH-all=3063&marked-GE-29:35■ 35:23■37:26■38:1,2,6,8,11,12,15,20,22, 23,24^2,26■43:3,8■44:14,16,18■46:12,28■ 49:8,9,10-EX-1:2■31:2■35:30■38:22 -NU-1:7,26,27■2:3^2,9■7:12■10:14■13:6■ 26:19,20,22■34:19-DE-27:12■33:7^2■ 34:2-JOS-7:1,16,17,18■11:21■14:6■ 15:1,12,13,20,21,63^2■18:5,11,14■19:1,9^2, 34■20:7■21:4,9,11-J'G-1:2,3,4,8,9,10,16, 17,18,19■10:9■15:9,10,11■17:7■18:12■ 20:18-RU-1:7■4:12-1SA-11:8■15:4■ 17:1,52■18:16■22:5■23:3,23■27:6,10■ 30:14,16,26-2SA-1:18■2:1,4^2,7,10,11■ 3:8,10■5:5^2■6:2■11:11■12:8■19:11,14, 15,16,40,41,42,43^2■20:2,4,5■21:2■24:1, 7,9-1KI-1:9,35■2:32■4:20,25■12:17,20, 21,23^2,27^2,32■13:1,12,14,21■14:21,22,29■ 15:1,7,9,17^2,22,23,25,28,33■16:8,10,15, 23,29■19:3■22:2,10,29,41,45,51-2KI-1:17■3:1,7,9,14■8:16^2,19,20,22,23,25, 29■9:16,21,27,29■10:13■12:18^2,19■13:1, 10,12■14:1,9,10,11^2,12,13,15,17,18,21, 22,23,28■15:1,6,8,13,17,23,27,32,36,37■ 16:1,19■17:1,13,18,19■18:1,5,13,14^2,16, 22■19:10,30■20:20■21:11^2,12,16,17,25■ 22:13,16,18■23:1,2,5^2,8,11,12,17,22,24, 26,27,28■24:2,3,5,12,20■25:21,22,27^2 -1CH-2:1,3^2,4,10■4:1,21,27,41■5:2,17■ 6:15,55,57,65■9:1,3,4■12:16,24■13:6■ 21:5■27:18■28:4^2-2CH-2:7■9:11■10:17■ 11:1,3^2,5,10,12,14,17,23■12:4,5,12■13:1, 13,14,15^3,16,18■14:4,5,6,7,8,12■15:2,8,9, 15■16:1^2,6,7,11■17:2^2,5,6,7,9^2,10,12,13, 14,19■18:3,9,28■19:1,5,11■20:3,4^2,5,13, 15,17,18,20,22,24,27,31,35■21:3,8,10,11^2, 12,13,17■22:1,6,8,10■23:2^2,8■24:5,6,9, 17,18,23■25:5^2,10,12,13,17,18,19,21^2,22, 23,25,26,28■26:1,2■27:4,7■28:6,9,10,17, 18,19^2,25,26■29:8,21■30:1,6,12,24,25^2■ 31:1^2,6^2,20■32:1,8,9^2,12,23,25,32,33■ 33:9,14,16■34:3,5,9,11,21,24,26,29,30■ 35:18,21,24,27■36:4,8,10,23-EZR-1:2, 3,5,8■2:1■3:9■4:1,4,6■5:1(3061)■7:14 (3061)■9:9■10:7,9,23-NE-1:2■2:5,7■ 4:10,16■5:14■6:7,17,18■7:6■11:3,4^2,9, 20,24,25,36■12:8,31,32,34,36,44■13:12, 15,16,17-ES-2:6-PS-48:11■60:7■63:t■ 68:27■69:35■76:1■78:68■97:8■108:8■ 114:2-PR-25:1-IS-1:1^2■2:1■3:1,8■5:3, 7■7:1,6,17■8:8■9:21■11:12,13^3■19:17■ 22:8,21■26:1■36:1,7■37:10,31■38:9■ 40:9■44:26■48:1■65:9-JER-1:1,3^2,15, 18■2:28■3:7,8,10,11,18■4:3,4,5,16■5:11, 20■7:2,17,30,34■8:1■9:11,26■10:22■ 11:2,6,9,10,12,13,17■15:14■13:9,11,19■ 14:2,19■15:4■17:1,19,20,25,26■18:11■ 19:3,4,7,13■20:4,5■21:7,11■22:1,2,6,11, 18,24,30■23:6■24:1^2,5,8■25:1^2,2,3,18■ 26:1,2,10,18^2,19^2■27:1,3,12,18,20^2,21■ 28:1,4^2■29:2,3,22■30:3,4■31:23,24,27,31■ 32:1,3,4,30,32^2,35,44■33:4,7,10,13,14,16■ 34:2,4,6,7^2,19,21,22■35:1,13,17■36:1,2, 3,6,9^2,28,29,30,31,32■37:1,7■39:1,4,6, 10■40:1,5,11,12,15■42:15,19■43:4,5^2,9 (3064)■44:2,6,7,9^2,11,12,14^2,17,21,24,26^2, 27,28^2,30■45:1■46:2■49:34■50:4,20,33■ 51:5,59■52:3,10,27,31^2-LA-1:3,15■2:2, 5■5:11-EZE-4:6■8:1,17■9:9■21:20■ 25:3,8,12■27:17■37:16,19■48:7,8,22,31 -DA-1:1,2,6■2:25(3061)■5:13(3061)■6:13 (3061)■9:7-HO-1:1,7,11■4:15■5:5,10, 12,13,14■6:4,11■8:14■10:11■11:12■12:2 -JOE-3:1,6,8,18,19,20-AM-1:1■2:4, 5■7:12^2-OB-12-MIC-1:1,5,9■5:2-NA-1:15-ZEP-1:1,4■2:7-HAG-1:1,14■ 2:2,21-ZEC-1:12,19,21^2■2:12■8:13, 15,19■9:7,13■10:3,6■11:14■12:2,4, 5,6,7^2■14:5,14,21-MAL-2:11^2■3:4■ N.T.-HEB-8:8(2455)

JUDAH'S-all=3063-GE-38:7,12 -JER-32:2■38:22

JUDAS-all=2455-M'T-1:2,3■10:4■ 13:55■26:14,25,47■27:3-M'R-3:19■ 14:10,43-LU-6:16^2■22:3,47,48-JOH-6:71■12:4■13:2,26,29■14:22■18:2,3,5 -AC-1:13,16,25■5:37■9:11■15:22,27,32

JUDE-JUDE-1:t(2455),1(2455)

JUDEA-EZR-5:8(3061)

JUDITH-GE-26:34(3067)

JULIA-RO-16:15(2456)

JULIUS-AC-27:1(2457),3(2457)

JUNIA-RO-16:7(2458)

JUPITER-AC-14:12(2203),13 (2203)■19:35(1356)

JUSHABHESED-1CH-3:20(3142)

JUSTUS-all=2459-AC-1:23■18:7 -COL-4:11

JUTTAH-JOS-15:55(3194)■ 21:16(3194)

K

KABZEEL-all=6909-JOS-15:21 -2SA-23:20-1CH-11:22

KADESH-all=6946-GE-14:7■16:14■ 20:1-NU-13:26■20:1,14,16,22■27:14■ 33:36,37-DE-1:46-J'G-11:16,17-PS-29:8-EZE-47:19■48:28

KADESH-BARNEA-all=6947

L

LOIS-**2TI**-1:5(3090)

LORD-all=3068,a=113,b=136,c=3050&marked-**GE**-2:4,5,7,8,9,15,16,18,19,21,22■3:1,8^2,9,13,14,21,22,23■4:1,3,4,6,9,13,15^2,16,26■5:29■6:3,6,7,8■7:1,5,16■8:20,21^2■9:26■10:9^2■11:5,6,8,9^2■12:1,4,7^2,8^2,17■13:4,10^2,13,14,18■14:22■15:1,2b,4,6,7,8b,18■16:2,5,7,9,10,11^2,13■17:1■18:1,3b,12a,13,14,17,19^2,20,22,26,27b,30b,31b,32b,33■19:13^2,14,16,18a,24^2,27■20:4b,18■21:1^2,33■22:11,14,15,16■23:6a,11a,15a■24:1,3,7,12,18a,21,26,27^2,31,35,40,42,44,48^2,50,51,52,56■25:21^2,22,23■26:2,12,22,24,25,28,29■27:7,20,27,29(1376),37(1376)■28:13^2,16,21■29:31,32,33,35■30:24,27,30■31:3,35a,49■32:4a,5a,9,18a■33:8a,13a,14^{2}a,15a■38:7^2,10■39:2,3^2,5^2,16a,21,23^2■40:1a■42:10a,30a,33a■44:5a,7a,16a,18a,19a,20a,22a,24a,33a■45:8a,9a■47:18^{3}a,25a■49:18-**EX**-3:2,4,7,15,16,18^2■4:1,2,4,5,6,10,10b,11^2,13b,14,19,21,22,24,27,28,30,31■5:1,2^2,3,17,21,22,22b■6:1,2,6,7,8,10,12,13,26,28,29^2,30■7:1,5,6,8,10,13,14,16,17^2,19,20,22,25■8:1^2,5,8^2,10,12,13,15,16,19,20^2,22,24,26,27,28,29^2,30,31■9:1^2,3,4,5^2,6,8,12^2,13^2,20,21,22,23^2,27,28,29,30,33,35■10:1,2,3,7,8,9,10,11,12,13,16,17,18,19,20,21,24,25,26^2,27■11:1,3,4,7,9,10■12:1,12,14,23^2,25,28,29,31,36,41,42^2,43,48,50,51■13:1,3,5,6,8,9,11,12,14,15^2,16,21■14:1,4,8,10,13,14,15,18,21,24,25,26,27,30,31^2■15:1^2,2,3,6^2,11,16,17,17b,18,19,21,25^2,26^2■16:3,4,6,7^2,8^3,9,10,11,12,15,16,23^2,25,28,29,32,33,34■17:1,2,4,5,7^2,14,16^2■18:1,8^2,9,10,11■19:3,7,8^2,9^2,10,11,18,20^2,21^2,22^2,23,24^2■20:2,5,7^2,10,11^2,12,22■22:11,20■23:17b,19,25■24:1,2,3^2,4,5,7,8,12,16,17■25:1■27:21■28:12,29,30^2,35,36,38■29:11,18^2,23,24,25^2,26,28,41,42,46^2■30:8,10,11,12,13,14,15,16,17,20,22,34,37■31:1,12,13,15,17■32:5,7,9,11^2,14,22a,27,29,30,31,33,35■33:1,5,7,11,12,17,19,21■34:1,4,5^2,6^2,9b,10,14,23b,24,26,27,28,32,34■35:1,2,4,5^2,10,22,29^2,30■36:1^2,2,5■38:22■39:1,5,7,21,26,29,30,31,32,42,43■40:1,16,19,21,23^2,25^2,27,29,32,34,35,38-**LE**-1:1,2,3,5,9,11,13,14,17■2:1,2,3,8,9,10,11^2,12,14,16■3:1,3,5,6,7,9,11,12,14■4:1,2,3,4^2,6,7,13,15^2,17,18,22,24,27,31,35■5:6,7,12,14,15^2,17,19■6:1,2,6,7,8,14,15,18,19,20,21,22,24,25■7:5,11,14,20,21,22,25,28,29^2,30^2,35^2,36,38^2■8:1,4,5,9,13,17,21^2,26,27,28,29^2,34,35,36■9:2,4^2,5,6^2,7,10,21,23,24■10:1,2^2,3,6,7,8,11,12,13,15^2,17,19^2■11:1,44,45■12:1,7■13:1■14:1,11,12,16,18,23,24,27,29,31,33■15:1,14,15,30■16:1^2,2,7,8,10,12,13,18,30,34■17:1,2,4^2,5^2,6^2,9■18:1,2,4,5,6,21,30■19:1,2,3,4,5,8,10,12,14,16,18,21,22,24,25,28,30,31,32,34,36,37■20:1,7,8,24,26■21:1,6,8,12,15,16,21,23■22:1,2,3^2,8,9,15,16,17,18,21,22^2,24,26,27,29,30,31,32,33■23:1,2,3,4,6,8,9,11,12,13,16,17,18^2,20^2,22,23,25,26,27,28,33,34,36^2,37^2,38^2,39,40,41,43,44■24:1,3,4,6,7,8,9,12,13,16,22,23■25:1,2,4,17,38,55■26:1,2,13,44,45,46■27:1,2,9^2,11,14,16,21,22,23,28^2,30,32,34-**NU**-1:1,19,48,54■2:1,33,34■3:1,4^2,5,11,13,14,16,39,40,41,42,44,45,51^2■4:1,17,21,37,41,45,49^2■5:1,4,5,6,8,11,16,18,21^2,25,30■6:1,2,5,6,8,12,14,16,17,20,21,22,24,25,26■7:3,4,11■8:1,3,4,5,10,11^2,12,13,20,21,22,23■9:1,5,7,8,9,10,13,14,18^2,19,20^2,23^4■10:1,9,10,13,29^2,32,33^2,34,35,36■11:1^3,2,3,10,11,16,18^2,20,23,24,25,28a,29,31,33^2■12:2^2,4,5,6,8,9,11a,13,14■13:1,3■14:3,8,9^2,10,11,13,14^2,16,17b,18,20,21,26,28,35,37,40,41,42,43^2,44■15:1,3^2,4,7,8,10,13,14,15,17,19,21,22,23^2,24,25^2,28,30,31,35,36,37,39,41^2■16:3^2,5,7^2,9,11,15,16,17,19,20,23,28,29,30^2,35,36,38,40^2,41,42,44,46■17:1,7,9,10,11,13■18:1,6,8,12,13,15,17,19^2,20,24,25,26,28,29■19:1,2,13,20■20:3,4,6,7,9,12,13,16,23,27■21:2,3,6,7^2,8,14,16,34■22:8,13,18,19,22,23,24,25,26,27,28,31^2,32,34,35■23:3,5,8,12,16,17,21,26■24:1,6,11,13^2■25:3,4^3,10,16■26:1,4,9,52,61,65■27:3,5,6,11,12,15,16,17,18,21,22,23■28:1,3,6,7,8,11,13,15,16,19,24,26,27■29:2,6,8,12,13,36,39,40■30:1,2,3,5,8,12,16■31:1,3,7,16^2,21,25,28,29,30,31,41,47^2,50^2,52,54■32:4,7,9,12,13,14,20,21,22^3,23,25a,27,27a,29,31,32■33:2,4^2,38,50■34:1,13,16,29■35:1,9,34■36:2,2^{2}a,2,5,6,10,13-**DE**-1:3,6,8,10,11,19,20,21^2,25,26,27,30,31,32,34,36,37,41^2,42,43,45^2■2:1,2,7^2,9,12,14,15,17,21,29,30,31,33,36,37■3:2,3,18,20^2,21^2,22,23,24b,26^2■4:1,2,3^2,4,5,7,10^2,12,14,15,19,20,21^2,23^2,24,25,27^2,29,30,31,34,35,39,40■5:2,3,4,5^2,6,9,11^2,12,14,15^2,16^2,22,24,25,27^2,28^2,32,33■6:1,2,3,4,5,10,12,13,15^2,16,17,18^2,19,20,21,22,24^2,25■7:1,2,4,6^2,7,8^2,9,12,15,16,18,19^2,20,21,22,23,25■8:1,2,3,5,6,7,10,11,14,18,19,20^2■9:3^2,4^3,5^2,6,7^2,8^2,9,10^2,11,12,13,16^2,18^2,19^2,20,22,23^2,24,25^2,26,26b,28■10:1,4^2,5,8^3,9^2,10^2,11,12^3,13,15,17,17,20,22■11:1,2,4,7,9,12^2,13,17,21,22,23,25,27,28,29,31■12:1,4,5,7^2,9,10,11^2,12,14,15,18^3,20,21^2,25,26,27^2,28,29,31^2■13:3^2,4,5^2,10,12,16,17,18^2■14:1,2^2,21,23^2,24^2,25,26,29■15:4^2,5,6,7,9,10,14,15,18,19,20^2,21■16:1^2,2^2,5,6,7,8,10,10sup,10,11^2,15^3,16^2,17,18,20,21,22■17:1^2,2^2,8,10,12,14,15,16,19■18:1,2,5^2,6,7^2,9,12^2,13,14,15,16^2,17,21,22^2■19:1^2,2,3,8,9,10,14,17■20:1,4,13,14,16,17,18■21:1,5^2,8,9,10,23■22:5■23:1,2^2,3^2,5^3,8,14,18^2,20,21^2,23■24:4^2,9,13,15,18,19■25:15,16,19^2■26:1,2^2,3^2,4,5,7^2,8,10^3,11,13,14,16,17,18,19■27:2,3^2,5,6^2,7,9,10,15■28:1^2,2,7,8^2,9^2,10,11^2,12,13^2,15,20,21,22,24,25,27,28,35,36,37,45,47,48,49,52,53,58,59,61,62,63^2,64,65,68■29:1,2,4,6,10,12^2,15,18,20^3,21,22,23,24,25,27,28,29■30:1,2,3^2,4,5,6^2,7,8,9^2,10^2,16^2,20^2■31:2,3^2,4,5,6,7,8,9,11,12,13,14,15,16,25,26,27,29■32:3,6,12,19,27,30,36,48■33:2,7,11,12,12sup,13,21,23,29■34:1,4,5^2,9,10,11-**JOS**-1:1^2,9,11,13^2,15^2,17■2:9,10,11,12,14,24■3:3,5,7,9,11a,13a,17■4:1,5,7,8,10,11,13,14,15,18,23^2,24^2■5:1,2,6^3,9,14,14a■6:2,6,7,8^2,11,12,13^2,16,17,19^2,24,26,27■7:1,6,7b,8b,10,13,14^3,15,19,20,23,25,26■8:1,7,8,18,27,30,31^2,33^2■9:9,14,18,19,24,27■10:8,10,11,12^2,14^2,19,25,30,32,40,42■11:6,8,9,12,15^2,20^2,23■12:6^2■13:1,8,14,33■14:2,5,6,7,8,9,10^2,12^3,14■15:13■17:4^2,14■18:3,6,7^2,8,10■19:50,51■20:1■21:2,3,8,43,44^2,45■22:2,3,4^2,5^2,9,16^3,17,18^2,19^3,22^2,23^2,24,25^3,27^2,28,29^3,31^3,34■23:1,3^2,5^2,8,9,10,11,13^2,14,15^3,16^2■24:2,7,14^2,15^2,16,17,18^2,19,20,21,22,23,24,26,27,29,31^2-**J'G**-1:1,2,4,19,22■2:1,4,5,7^2,8,10,11,12^2,13,14,15^2,16,17,18^3,20,22,23■3:1,4,7^2,8,9^2,10^2,12^3,15^2,25a■28■4:1,2,3,6,9,14^2,15,18a■5:2,3^2,4,5^2,9,11^2,13,23^3,31■6:1^2,6,7,8^2,10,11,12^2,13a,13^3,14,15b,16,21^2,22,22b,22,23,24,25,26,27,34■7:2,4,5,7,9,15,18,20,22■8:7,19,23,34■10:6^2,7,10,11,15,16■11:9,10,11,21,23,24,27,29,30,32,35,36^2■12:3■13:1^2,3,8^2,13,15,16^3,17,18,19,20,21^2,23,24,25■14:4,6,19■15:14,18■16:20,28,28b■17:2,3,13■18:6■19:18,26a,27a■20:1,18,23^3,26^2,27,28,35■21:3,5^2,7,8,15,19-**RU**-1:6,8,9,13,17,21^2■2:4^2,12^2,13a,20■3:10,13■4:11,12,13,14-**1SA**-1:3^2,5,6,7,9,10,11^2,12,15a,15,19^2,20,21,22,23,24,26^{2}a,26,27,28^3■2:1^2,2,3,6,7,10^2,11,12,17^2,18,20^2,21^2,25^2,26,27,30^2■3:1^2,3,4,6,7^2,8^2,9,10,11,15,18,19,20,21^3■4:3^2,4,5,6■5:3,4,6,9■6:1,2,8,11,14,15^2,17,18,19^2,20,21■7:1^2,2,3^2,4,5,6^2,8,9^3,10,12,13,17■8:6,7,10,18,21,22■9:15,17■10:1,6,17,18,19,22^2,24,25■11:7,13,15^2■12:3,5,6,7^2,8^2,9,10^2,11,12,13,14^3,15^3,16,17^2,18^3,19,20^2,22^2,23,24■13:12,13^2,14^3■14:6^2,10,12,23,33,34,35^2,39,41,45■15:1^2,2,10,11,13^2,15,16,17,18,19^2,20^2,21,22^2,23,24,25,26^2,28,30,31,33,35■16:1,2^2,4,5,7^3,8,9,10,12,13,14^2,16a,18■17:37^2,45,46,47■18:12,14,28■19:5,6,9■20:3,8,12,13^2,14,15,16,21,22,23,42^2■21:6,7■22:10,12a,17^2■23:2^2,4^2,10,11^2,12,18,21■24:4,6^2,8a,10,10a,12^2,15,18,19,21■25:24a,25^{2}a,26a,26^2,26a,27^{2}a,28,28^{2}a,28,29a,29,30,30a,31^{2}b,31,31a,32,34,38,39^2,41a,■26:10^2,11,12,15^{2}a,16,17a,18a,19a,19^3,20,23^2,24■28:6^2,10^2,16,17^2,18^2,19^2■29:6,8a■30:6,8,23,26-**2SA**-1:10a,12■2:1^2,5,5a,6■3:9,18,21a,28,39■4:8,8a,9■5:2,3,10,12,19^2,20,23,24,25■6:2,5,7,8,9^2,10,11^2,12,13,14,15,16^2,17^2,18,21^3■7:1,3,4,5,8,11,18,18b,19^{2}b,20b,22,24,25,26,27,28b,29b■8:6,11,14■9:11a■10:3a,12■11:9a,11^{2}a,13a,27■12:1,5,7,9,11,13^2,14,15,20,24,25■13:32a,33a■14:9a,11^2,12a,15a,17^{2}a,17,18a,19^{2}a,20a,22a■15:7,8^2,15a,21,21^{2}a,25,31■16:4a,8^2,9a,10,11,12^2,18■17:14^2■18:19,28,28a,31a,31,32a■19:7,19^{2}a,20a,26a,27^{2}a,28a,30a,35a,37a■20:19■21:1^2,3,6^2,9■22:1^2,2,4,7,14,16,19,21,22,25,29^2,31,32,42,47,50■23:2,10,12,16,17■24:1,3,3^{2}a,10^2,11,12,14,15,16^2,17,18,19,21a,21,22a,23,24,25^2-**1KI**-1:2^{2}a,11a,13a,17a,17,18a,20^{2}a,21a,24a,27^{2}a,29,30,31a,33a,36,36a,37,37^{2}a,43a,47a,48■2:3,4,8,15,23,24,26b,27^2,28,29,30,32,33,38a,42,43^2,44,45■3:1,2,3,5,7,10b,15,17a,26a■5:3^2,3,4,5^2,7,12■6:1,2,11,19,37■7:12,40,45,48,51^2■8:1,4,6,9,10,11^2,12,15,17,18,20^3,21,22,23,25,28,44,53b,54^2,56,57,59^2,60,61,62,63^2,64^2,65,66■9:1,2,3,8,9^2,10,15,25^2■10:1,5,9^2,12■11:2,4,6^2,9^2,10,11,14,23a,31■12:15^2,24^3,27,27a■13:1,2^2,3,5,6^2,9,17,18,20,21^3,26^3,32■14:5,7,11,13,14,15^2,18,21,22,24,26,28■15:3,4,5,11,14,15,18,26,29,30,34■16:1,7^2,12,13,19,25,26,30,33,34■17:1,2,5,8,12,14^2,16,20^2,21^2,22,24■18:1,3,4,7a,8a,10,10a,11a,12^2,13a,13,14a,15,18,21,22,24,30,31,32,36,37^2,38,39,46■19:4,7,9,10,11^5,12,14,15■20:4a,9a,13^2,14,28^3,35,36,42■21:3,17,19^2,20,23,25,26,28■22:5,6b,7,8,11,12,14^2,15,16,17,19^2,20,21,22,23^2,24,28,38,43,52,53-**2KI**-1:3,4,6,15,16,17■2:1,2^2,3,4^2,5,6^2,14,16,19a,21,24■3:2,10,11^2,12,13,14,15,16,17,18■4:1,16a,27,28a,30,33,43,44■5:1,3a,4a,11,16,17,18^2,20■6:12a,17^2,18,20^2,26a,27,33^2■7:1^2,2(7991),2,6b,16,17(7991),19(7991)19,■8:1,5a,8,10,12a,13,18,19,27■9:3,6^2,7,11a,12,25,26^3,36■10:10^3,16,17,23,30,31,32■11:3,4^2,7,10,13,15,17,18,19■12:2,4^2,9^2,10,11^2,12,13^2,14,16,18■13:2,3,4^2,5,11,23■14:3,6,14,24,25,26,27■15:3,5,9,12,18,24,28,34,35,37■16:2,3,8,14^2,18■17:2,7,8,9,11^2,12,13,14,15,16,17,18,19,20,21,23,25^2,28,32,33,34^2,35,36,39,41■18:3,5,6^2,7,12^2,15,16,22,23a,25^2,30^2,32,35■19:1,4^2,6,14^2,15^2,16^2,17,19^2,20,21,23a,31,32,33,35■20:1,2,3,4,5^2,8^2,9^2,11,16,17,19■21:2^2,4,5,6,7,9,10,12,16,20,22^2■22:2,3,4,5^2,8,9,13^2,15,16,18^2,19^2■23:2^2,3^2,4,6,7,9,11,12,16,21,23,24,25,26,27,32,37■24:2^2,3,4,9,13^3,19,20■25:13^2,16-**1CH**-2:3■6:15,31,32■9:19,20,23■10:13^2,14■11:2,3^2,9,10,14,18■12:23■13:2,6,10,11,14■14:2,10,17■15:2,3,12,13,14,15,25,26,28,29■16:2,4^2,7,8,10,11,14,23,25,26,28^2,29^2,31,33,34,36^2,37,39,40^2,41■17:1,4,7,10,16^2,17,19,20,22,23,24,26,27■18:6,11,13■19:13■21:3,3^{2}a,9,10,11,12^2,13,14,15^2,16,17,18^2,19,22,23a,24,26^2,27,28,29,30■22:1,5,6,7,8,11^2,12^2,13,14,16,18^2,19^4■23:4,5,13,24,25,28,30,31^2,32■24:19^2■25:3,6,7■26:12,22,27,30■27:23■28:2,4,5^2,8^2,9,10,12,13^2,18,19,20^2■29:1,5,8,9,10^2,11^2,16,18,20^3,21^2,22^2,23,25-**2CH**-1:1,3,5,6,9■2:1,4^2,11,12^2,14a,15a■3:1,1sup■4:16■5:1,2,7,10,13^3,14■6:1,4,7,8,10^3,11,12,14,16,17,19,41^2,42■7:1,2^2,3^2,4,6^2,7,10,11^2,12,21,22■8:1,11,12,16^2■9:4,8^2,11■10:15■11:2,4^2,14,16^2■12:1,2,5,6,7^2,9,11,12,13,14■13:5,6a,8,9,10^2,11^2,12,14,18,20■14:2,4,6,7,11^4,12,13,14■15:2,4,8^2,9,11,12,13,14,15■16:2,7,8,9,12■17:3,5,6,9,10,16■18:4,6,7,10,11,13,15,16,18^2,19,20^2,22^2,23,27,31■19:2^2,4,6,7^2,8,9,10,11^2■20:3,4^2,5,6,13,14,15,17^2,18,19,20,21^2,22,26,27,28,29,32,37■21:6,7,10,12,14,16,18■22:4,7,9■23:3,5,6^2,12,14,18^3,19,20■24:2,4,6,7,8,9,12^3,14^2,18,19,20^2,21,22,24^2■25:2,4,7,9,15,27■26:4,5,16^2,17,18^2,19,20,21■27:2^2,3,6■28:1,3,5,6,9^2,10,11,13,19^2,21,22,24,25■29:2,3,5,6^2,8,10,11,15^2,16^3,17^2,18,19,20,21,25^2,27,30,31^2,32,35■30:1^2,5,6,7,8^2,9^2,12,15,17,18,19,20,21^2,22^2■31:2,3,4,6,8,10^2,11,14,16,20■32:8,11,16,17,21,22,23,24,26■33:2^2,4^2,5,6,9,10,11,12,13,15^2,16^2,17,18,22,23■34:2,8,10^2,14^2,15,17,21^3,23,24,26^2,27,30^2,31^2,33^2■35:1,

2,3^{2},6,12,16^{2},26■36:5,7,9,10,12^{2},13,14,
15,16,18,21,22^{2},23^{2}-**EZR**-1:1^{2},2,3,5,7■
2:68■3:3,5^{2},6^{2},8,10^{2},11^{3}■4:1,3■6:21,22■
7:6^{2},10,11,27^{2},28■8:28^{2},29,35■9:5
,8,15■10:3b,11-**NE**-1:5,11b■3:5a■4:14b,
5:13■8:1,6^{2},9,10a,10,14■9:3^{2},4,5,6,7■
10:29,29a,34,35-**JOB**-1:6,7^{2},8,9,12^{2},
21^{2}■2:1^{2},2^{2},3,4,6,7■12:9■28:28b■
38:1■40:1,3,6■42:1,7^{2},9^{2},10^{2},11,12
-**PS**-1:2,6■2:2,4b,7,11■3:1,3,4,5,7,
8■4:3^{2},5,6,8■5:1,3,6,8,12■6:1,2^{2},3,4,
8,9^{2}■7:t,1,3,6,8^{2},17^{2}■8:1,1a,9,9a■9:1,7,9,
10,11,13,16,19,20■10:1,3,12,16,17■11:1,
4,5,7■12:1,3,4a,5,6,7■13:1,3,6■14:2,4,6,
7■15:1,4■16:2,2b,5,7,8■17:1,13,14■
18:t^{3},1,2,3,6,13,15,18,20,21,24,28,30,
31,41,46,49■19:7^{2},8^{2},9^{2},14■20:1,5,6,7,9■
21:1,7,9,13■22:8,19,23,26,27,30b■23:1,6■
24:3,5,8^{2},10■25:1,4,6,7,8,10,11,12,14,
15■26:1^{2},2,6,8,12■27:1^{2},4^{3},6,7,8,10,11,13,
14^{2}■28:1,5,6,7,8■29:1^{2},2^{2},3^{2},4^{2},5^{2},7,8^{2},9,
10^{2},11^{2}■30:1,2,3,4,7,8,8b,10^{2},12■31:1,5,6,9,
14,17,21,23^{2},24■32:2,5,10,11■33:1,2,4,
5,6,8,10,11,12,13,18,20,22■34:1,2,3,4,6,
7,8,9,10,11,15,16,17,18,19,22■35:1,5,6,
9,10,17b,22^{2},23b,24,27■36:t,5,6■37:3,4,
5,7,9,13b,17,18,20,23,24,28,33,34,39,40■
38:1,9b,15,15b,21,22b■39:4,7b,12■
40:1,3,4,5,9,11,13^{2},16,17b■41:1,2,3,4,
10,13■42:8■44:23b■45:11a■46:7,8,11■
47:2,5■48:1,8■50:1■51:15b■54:4b,6■
55:9b,16,22■56:10■57:9b■58:6■59:3,5,8,
11b■62:12b■64:10■66:18b■68:11b,16,
17b,18c,19b,20b,22b,26b,32b■69:6b,13,16,
31,33■70:1,5■71:1,5b,16b■72:18,73:20b,
28b■74:18■75:8■76:11■77:2b,7b,11c■
78:4,21,65b■79:5,12b■80:4,19■
81:10,15■83:16■84:1,2,3,8,11^{2},12■
85:1,7,8,12■86:1,3b,4b,5b,6,8b,9b,11,
12b,15b,17■87:2,6■88:1,9,13,14■
89:1,5,6^{2},8,8c,15,18,46,49b,50b,51,
52■90:1b,13,17■91:2,9■92:1,4,5,8,9,
13,15■93:1^{2},3,4,5■94:1,3,5,7c,11,12c,
14,17,18,22,23■95:1,3,6■96:1^{2},2,4,5,7^{2},8,
9,10,13■97:1,5,5a,8,9,10,12■98:1,2,4,5,6,
9■99:1,2,5,6,8,9^{2}■100:1,2,3,5■101:1,8■
102:t,1,12,15,16,18c,19,21,22■103:1,2,
6,8,13,17,19,20,21,22^{2}■104:1^{2},16,24,
31^{2},33,34,35,35c■105:1c,3c,4c,7c,19c,21a,
45c■106:1c,1,2,4,16,25,34,40,47,48,48c■
107:1,2,6,8,13,15,19,21,24,28,31,43■
108:3■109:14,15,20,21b,26,27,30■110:1,
1a,2,4,5b■111:1c,1,2,4,10■112:1c,1,7■
113:1c,1^{2},2,4,5,9c■114:7a■115:1,9,10,11,
12,13,14,15,17c,18^{2}c■116:1,4^{2},5,6,7,9,12,
13,14,15,16,17,18,19c■117:1,2,2c■118:1,
4,5^{2}c,6,7,8,9,10,11,12,13,14c,15,16^{2},17c,
18c,19c,20,24,25^{2},26^{2},27,29■119:1,12,
31,33,41,52,55,57,64,65,75,89,107,108,
126,137,145,149,151,156,159,166,169,
174■120:1,2■121:2,5^{2},7,8■122:1,4c,4,
9■123:2,3■124:1,2,6,8■125:1,2,4,5■
126:1,2,3,4■127:1^{2},3■128:1,4,5■129:4,8^{2}■
130:1,2b,3c,3b,5,6b,7^{2}■131:1,3■132:1,2,5,
8,11,13■133:3■134:1^{3},2,3■135:1c,1^{2},2,3c,
3,4c,5,5a,6,13^{2},14,19^{2},20^{2},21,21c■136:1,
3a■137:7■138:4,5^{2},6,8^{2}■139:1,4,21■140:1,
4,6^{2},7b,8,12■141:1,3,8b■142:1^{2},5■143:1,7,9,
11■144:1,3,5,15■145:3,8,9,10,14,17,18,20,
21■146:1c,1,2,5,7,8^{3},9,10,10c■147:1c,2,
5a,6,7,11,12,20c■148:1c,1,5,7,13,14c■
149:1c,1,4,9c■150:1c,6^{2}c-**PR**-1:7,29■2:5,
6■3:5,7,9,11,12,19,26,32,33■5:21■6:16■
8:13,22,35■9:10■10:3,22,27,29■11:1,20■
12:2,22■14:2,26,27■15:3,8,9,11,16,25,26,
29,33■16:1,2,3,4,5,6,7,9,20,33■17:3,15■
18:10,22■19:3,14,17,21,23■20:10,12,22,
23,24,27■21:1,2,3,30,31■22:2,4,12,14,
19,23■23:17■24:18,21■25:22■28:5,25■
29:13,25,26■30:9■31:30-**IS**-1:2,4,9,10,
11,18,20,24a,24,28■2:3^{2},5,10,11,12,17,
19,21■3:1a,1,8,13,14,15b,16,17b,17,18b■
4:2,4b,5■5:7,9,12,16,24,25■6:1b,3,5,8b,
11b,12■7:3,7b,10,11,12,14b,17,18,20b■
8:1,3,5,7b,11,13,17,18^{2}■9:7,8,11,13,14,
17b,19■10:12b,16a,16b,20,23b,24b,26,33a,
33■11:2^{2},3,9,11b,15■12:1,2c,4,5■13:4,5,
6,9,13■14:1,2,3,5,22^{2},23,24,27,32■16:13,
14■17:3,6■18:4,7^{2}■19:1,4^{2}a,4,12,14,16,
17,18,19^{2},20^{2},21^{3},22^{2},25■20:2,3■21:6b,8b,
10,16b,17■22:5b,12b,14,14b,15b,17,25^{2}■
23:9,11,17,18^{2}■24:1,3,14,15^{2},21,23■25:1,
6,8b,8,9,10■26:4,4c,8,10,11,12,13,15,16,
17,21■27:1,3,12,13■28:2b,5,13,14,16b,
21,22b,29■29:6,10,13b,15,19,22■30:1,9,
15b,18^{2},20b,26,27,29,30,31,32,33■31:1,
3,4^{2},5,9■32:6■33:2,5,6,10,21,22^{3}■34:2,6^{2},
16■35:2,10■36:7,10^{2},15^{2},18,20■37:1,4^{2},
6,14^{2},15,16,17^{2},18,20^{2},21,22,24b,32,33,
34,36■38:1,2,3,4,5,7^{2},11c,14,16b,20^{2},22■
39:5,6,8■40:3,5^{2},7,10b,13,27,28,31■41:4,
13,14,16,17,20,21■42:5,6,8,10,12,13,21,
24■43:1,3,10,11,12,14,15,16■44:2,5,6^{2},
23^{2},24^{2}■45:1,3,5,6,7,8,11,13,14,17,18^{2},
19,21,24,25■47:4■48:1,2,14,16b,17^{2},20,
22■49:1,4,5^{2},7^{2},8,13,14,14b,18,22b,23,25,
26■50:1,4b,5b,7b,9b,10^{2}■51:1,3^{2},9,11,13,
15^{2},17,20,22a,22■52:3,4b,5^{2},8,9,10,11,
12■53:1,6,10^{2}■54:1,5,6,8,10,13,17^{2}■55:5,6,
7,8,13■56:1,3^{2},4,6^{2},8b■57:19■58:5,8,9,
11,13,14^{2}■59:13,15,19^{2},20,21^{2}■60:1,2,6,
9,14,16,19,20,22■61:1b,1,2,3,6,8,9,10,
11b■62:2,3,4,6,8,9,11,12■63:7^{3},14,16,17■
64:8,9,12■65:7,8,11,13b,15b,23,25■66:1,
2,5^{2},6,9,12,14,15,16^{2},17,20^{3},21,22,23
-**JER**-1:2,4,6b,7,8,9^{2},11,12,13,14,15,19■
2:1,2,3^{2},4,5,6,8,9,12,17,19,19b,22b,29,
31,37■3:1,6,10,11,12^{2},13^{2},14,16^{2},17^{2},20,
21,22,23,25^{2}■4:1,2,3,4,8,9,10b,17,26,27■
5:2,3,4,5,9,11,12,14,15,18,19,22,24,29■
6:6,9,10,11,12,15,16,21,22,30■7:1,2^{2},3,4^{2},
11,13,19,20b,21,28,29,30,32■8:1,3,4,7,
8,9,12,13,14^{2},17,19■9:3,6,7,9,12,13,15,
17,20,22,23,24^{2},25■10:1,2,6,10,16,18,21,
23,24■11:1,3,5,6,9,11,16,17,18,20,21^{2},22■
12:1,3,12,13,14,16,17■13:1,2,3,5,6,8,9,
11,12,13,14,15,16,25■14:1,7,9,10^{2},11,
13b,14,15,20,22■15:1,2,3,6,9,11,15,16,
19,20■16:1,3,5^{2},9,10^{2},11,14^{2},15,16,19,21■
17:5^{2},7^{2},10,13^{2},14,15,19,20,21,24,26■
18:1,5,6,11,13,19,23■19:1,3^{2},6,11,12,14,
15■20:1,2,3,4,7,8,11,12,13,16■21:1,2^{2},4,
7,8,10,11,12,13,14■22:1,2,3,5,6,8,9,11,
16,18,18a,24,29,30■23:1,2^{2},4,5,6,7^{2},8,9,
11,12,15,16^{2},17,18,19,20,23,24^{2},28,29,30,
31,32^{2},33^{2},34,35^{2},36^{2},37^{2},38^{4}■24:1^{2},3,4,5,
7,8■25:3,4,5,7,8,9,12,15,17,27,28,29,30,
31^{2},32,33,36,37■26:1,2,4,7,8,9^{2},10,12,13^{2},
15,16,18,19^{2},20■27:1,2,4,8,11,13,15,16,
18^{3},19,21^{2},22■28:1,2,4,5,6,9,11,12,13,14,
15,16^{2}■29:4,7,8,9,10,11,14^{2},15,16,17,19^{2},
20,21,22,23,25,26^{2},30,31,32^{3}■30:1,2,3^{2},
4,5,8,9,10,11,12,17,18,21,23,24■31:1,2,
3,6,7^{2},10,11,12,14,15,16^{2},17,18,20,22,23^{2},
27,28,31,32,33,34^{2},35^{2},36,37^{2},38^{2},40■
32:1,3,5,6,8^{2},14,15,16,17b,18,25b,26,27,
28,30,36,42,44■33:1,2^{3},4,10,11^{4},12,13,
14,16,17,19,20,23,24,25■34:1,2^{2},4^{2},5a,5,8,
12^{2},13,17^{2},22■35:1,2,4,12,13^{2},17,18,19■
36:1,4,5,6,7^{2},8,9,10,11,26,27,29,30■37:2,
3,6,7,9,17,20a■38:2,3,9a,14,16,17,20,21■
39:15,16,17,18■40:1,2,3^{2}■41:5■42:2,3,4^{2},
5^{2},6^{2},7,9,11,13,15^{2},18,19,20^{3},21■43:1^{2},2,
4,7,8,10■44:2,7,11,16,21,22,23^{2},24,25,26^{2},
26b,29,30■45:2,3,4,5■46:1,5,10^{2}b,13,15,
18,23,25,26,28■47:1,2,4,6,7■48:1,8,10,
12,15,25,26,30,35,38,40,42,43,44,47■
49:1,2^{2},5b,6,7,12,13,14,16,18,20,26,28,
30,31,32,34,35,37,38,39■50:1,4^{2},5,7^{2},
10,13,14,15,18,20,21,24,25,25b,28,29,
30,31b,33,34,35,40,45■51:1,5,10^{2},
11^{2},12,14,19,24,25,26,29,33,36,39,45,
48,50,52,53,55,56,57,58,62■52:2,3,13,
17^{2},20-**LA**-1:5,9,11,12,14b,15^{2}b,17,18,
20■2:1b,2b,5b,6,7b,7,8,9,17,18b,
19b,20,20b■3:18,24,25,26,31b,36b,
37b,40,50,55,58b,59,61,64,66■4:11,
16,20■5:1,19,21-**EZE**-1:3^{2},28■2:4b■
3:11b,12,14,16,22,23,27b■4:13,
14b■5:5b,7b,8b,11b,13,15,17■6:1,3^{2}b,7,
10,11b,13,14■7:1,2b,4,5b,9,19,27■8:1b,
12^{2},16^{2}■9:4,8b,9^{2}■10:4,18■11:5^{2},7b,8b,
10,12,13b,14,15,16b,17b,21b,23,25■12:1,
8,10b,15,16,17,19b,20,21,23b,25,25b,26,
28^{2}b■13:1,2,3b,5,6,7,8^{2}b,9b,13b,14,16b,
18b,20b,21,23■14:2,4b,4,6b,7,8,9,11b,12,
14b,16b,18b,20b,21b,23b■15:1,6b,7,8b■
16:1,3b,8b,14b,19b,23b,30b,35,36b,43b,
48b,58,59b,62,63b■17:1,3b,9b,11,16b,19b,
21,22b,24^{2}■18:1,3b,9b,23b,25b,29b,30b,
32b■20:1,2,3^{2}b,5b,5,7,12,19,20,26,27b,
30b,31b,33b,36b,38,39b,40b,42,44,44b,
45,47,47b,48,49b■21:1,3,5,7b,8,9,13b,
17,18,24b,26b,28b,32■22:1,3b,12b,14,16,
17,19b,22,23,28b,28,31b■23:1,22b,28b,
32b,34b,35b,36,46b,49b■24:1,3b,6b,9b,
14,14b,15,20,21b,24b,27■25:1,3^{2}b,5,6b,
7,8b,11,12b,13b,14b,15b,16b,17■26:1,3b,
5b,6,7b,14,14b,15b,19b,21b■27:1,3b■
28:1,2b,6b,10b,11,12b,20,22b,22,23,24b,
25b,26■29:1,3b,6,8b,9,13b,16b,17,19b,20b,
21■30:1,2b,3,6,6b,8,10b,12,13b,19,20,22b,
25,26■31:1,10b,15b,18b■32:1,3b,8b,11b,
14b,15,16b,17,31b,32b■33:1,11b,17b,
20b,22,23,25b,27b,29,30■34:1,2b,7,8b,9,
10b,11b,15b,17b,20b,24^{2},27,30,30b,31b■
35:1,3b,4,6b,9,10,11b,12,14b,15■36:1,2b,
3b,4^{2}b,5b,6b,7b,11,13b,14b,15b,16,20,
22b,23,23b,32b,33b,36^{2},37b,38■37:1^{2},3b,
4,5b,6,9b,12b,13,14,14b,15,19b,21b,28■
38:1,3b,10b,14b,17b,18b,21b,23■39:1b,
5b,6,7,8b,10b,13b,17b,20b,22,25b,28,
29b■40:1,46■41:22■42:13■43:4,5,18b,
19b,24^{2},27b■44:2^{2},3,4,5^{2},6b,9b,12b,15b,
27b■45:1,4,9^{2}b,15b,18b,23■46:1b,3,4,9,
12,13,14,16b■47:13b,23b■48:9,10,14,
29b,35-**DA**-1:2b,10a■2:10(7229),47
(4756)■4:19(4756),24(4756)■5:23
(4756)■9:2,3b,4,4b,7b,8b,9b,10,13,14^{2},
15b,16b,19^{2}b,20■10:16a,17a,19a■12:8a
-**HO**-1:1,2^{3},4,7■2:13,16,20,21■3:1^{2},5^{2}■
4:1^{2},10,15,16■5:4,6,7■6:1,3■7:10■8:1,
13■9:4^{2},5,14■10:3,12■11:10,11■12:2,5^{2},
9,13,14a■13:4,15■14:1,2,9-**JOE**-1:1,9,
14^{2},15,19■2:1,11^{2},12,13,14,17^{2},18,19,21,
23,26,27,31,32^{3}■3:8,11,14,16^{2},17,18,21
-**AM**-1:2,3,5,6,8b,9,11,13,15■2:1,3,4^{2},6,
11,16■3:1,6,7b,8b,10,11b,12,13b,15■
4:2b,3,5b,6,8,9,10,11,13■5:3b,4,6,8,14,
15,16,16b,17,18^{2},20,27■6:8b,8,10,11,14■
7:1b,2b,3^{2},4^{2}b,5b,6,6b,7b,8,8b,15^{2},16,17■
8:1b,2,3b,7,9b,11b,11,12■9:1b,5b,6,7,8b,
8,12,13,15-**OB**-1b,1,4,8,15,18-**JON**-1:1,
3^{2},4,9,10,14^{3},16^{2},17■2:1,2,6,7,9,10■3:1,
3■4:2^{2},3,4,6,10-**MIC**-1:1,2^{2}b,3,12■2:3,5,
7,13■3:4,5,8,11^{2}■4:1,2^{2},4,5,6,7,10,12,13,
13a■5:4^{2},7,10■6:1,2,5,6,7,8■7:7,8,9,10,
17-**NA**-1:2^{3},3^{2},7,9,11,12,14■2:2,13■3:5
-**HAB**-1:2,12^{2}■2:2,13,14,20■3:2^{2},8,18,19
-**ZEP**-1:1,2,3,5,6^{2},7b,7^{2},10,12,14^{2},17■
2:2,3,5,7,9,10,11■3:2,5,8,9,12,15^{2},17,20
-**HAG**-1:1,2,3,5,7,8,9,12^{3},13,14^{2}■2:1,4^{3},
6,7,8,9^{2},10,11,14,15,17,20,23^{3}-**ZEC**-1:1,
2,3^{3},4^{2},6,7,9a,10,11,12^{2},13,14,16^{2},17^{2},20■
2:5,6^{2},8,9,10,11^{2},12,13■3:1,2^{3},5,6,7,9,10■
4:4a,5a,6^{2},8,9,10,13a,14a■5:4■6:4a,5a,9,
12^{2},13,14,15^{3}■7:1,2,3,4,7,8,9,12^{2},13■8:1,
2,3^{2},4,6^{2},7,9^{2},11,14^{2},17,18,19,20,21^{2},22^{2},
23■9:1^{2},4b,14,14b,15,16■10:1^{2},3,5,6,7,
12^{2}■11:4,5,6,11,13^{2},15■12:1^{2},4,5,7,8^{2}■
13:2,3,7,8,9■14:1,3,5,7,9^{2},12,13,16,17,
18,20,21^{2}-**MAL**-1:1,2^{2},4^{2},5,6,7,8,9,10,
11,12b,13^{2},14b,14■2:2,4,7,8,11,12^{2},13,14,
16^{2},17^{2}■3:1a,1,3,4,5,6,7,10,11,12,13,14,16^{3},
17■4:1,3,5■**N.T.**-all=2962&marked
-**M'T**-1:20,22,24■2:13,15,19■3:3■4:7,
10■5:33■7:21,22■8:2,6,8,21,25■9:28,38■
10:24,25■11:25■12:8■13:51■14:28,30■
15:22,25,27■16:22■17:4,15■18:21,25,26,
27,31,32,34■20:8,30,31,33■21:3,9,40■
22:37,43,44^{2},45■23:39■24:42,45,46,48,50■
25:11,19,20,21^{2},22,23^{2},24,26,37,44■26:22■
27:10■28:2,6-**M'R**-1:3■2:28■5:19■7:28■
9:24■10:51(4462)■11:3,9,10■12:9,
29,30,36^{2},37■13:20■16:19,20
-**LU**-1:6,9,11,15,16,17,25,28,
32,38,43,45,46,58,66,68,76■2:9^{2},
11,15,22,23^{2},24,29(1203),38,39■3:4■4
:8,12,18,19■5:8,12,17■6:5,46■7:6,13,
31■9:54,57,59,61■10:1,2,17,21,27,40■
11:1,39■12:36,37,41,42^{2},43,45,46■13:8,
15,23,25^{2},35■14:21,22,23■16:3,5,8■17:5,
6,37■18:6,41■19:8^{2},16,18,20,25,31,34,38■
20:13,15,37,42^{2},44■22:31,33,38,49,61^{2}■
23:42■24:3,34-**JOH**-1:23■4:1■6:23,34,
68■8:11■9:36,38■11:2,3,12,21,27,32,34
,39■12:13,38^{2}■13:6,9,13,14,16,25,36,37
■14:5,8,22■15:15,20■20:2,13,18,20,25,
28■21:7^{2},12,15,16,17,20,21-**AC**-1:6,21,
24■2:20,21,25,34^{2},36,39,47■3:19,22■4:24
(1203),26,29,33■5:9,14,19■7:30,31,33,37,
49,59,60■8:16,24,25,26,39■9:1,5^{2},6^{2},10^{2},

11,13,15,17,27,29,31,35,42■10:4,14,36, 48■11:8,16,17,20,21^{2},23,24■12:7,11,17, 23■13:2,10,11,12,47,48,49■14:3,23■15:11, 17^{2},26,35,36■16:10,14,15,31,32■17:24,27■ 18:8,9,25^{2}■19:5,10,13,17■20:19,21,24,35■ 21:13,14,20■22:8,10^{2},16,19■23:11■25:26■ 26:15■28:31-RO-1:3,7■4:8,24■5:1,11, 21■6:11,23■7:25■8:39■9:28,29■10:9,12, 13,16■11:3,34■12:11,19■13:14■14:6^{4},8^{2}, 9(2961),11,14■15:6,11,30■16:2,8,11,12^{2}, 13,18,20,22,24-1CO-1:2,3,7,8,9,10,31■ 2:8,16■3:5,20■4:4,5,17,19■5:4^{2},5■6:11, 13^{2},14,17■7:10,12,17,22,25^{2},32^{2},34,35,39■ 8:6■9:1^{2},2,5,14■10:21,22■11:11,23^{2},27^{2}, 32■12:3,5■14:21,37■15:31,47,57,58^{2}■ 16:7,10,19,22,23-2CO-1:2,3,14■2:12■ 3:16,17^{2},18^{2}■4:5,10,14■5:6,8,11■6:17, 18■8:5,9,19,21■10:8,17,18■11:17,31■ 12:1,8■13:10,14-GA-1:3■4:1■5:10■6:14, 17,18-EPH-1:2,3,15,17■2:21■3:11,14■ 4:1,5,17■5:8,10,17,19,20,22,29■6:1,4,7,8, 10,21,23,24-PH'P-1:2,14■2:11,19,24, 29■3:1,8,20■4:1,2,4,5,10,23-COL-1:2,3, 10■2:6■3:16,17,18,20,23,24^{2}■4:7, 17-1TH-1:1^{2},3,6,8■2:15,19■3:8,11, 12,13■4:1,2,6,15^{2},16,17^{2}■5:2,9,12,23,27, 28-2TH-1:1,2,7,8,9,12^{2}■2:1,8,13, 14,16■3:1,3,4,5,6,12,16^{2},18-1TI-1:1, 2,12,14■5:21■6:3,14,15-2TI-1:2,8,16, 18^{2}■2:7,14,19,22,24■3:11■4:1,8,14, 17,18,22-TIT-1:4-PH'M-3,5,16,20^{2}, 25-HEB-1:10■2:3■7:14,21■8:2,8,9,10, 11■10:16,30^{2}■12:5,6,14■13:6, 20-JAS-1:1,7,12■2:1,1sup■4:10,15■ 5:4,7,8,10,11^{2},14,15-1PE-1:3,25■2:3■ 3:6,12^{2},15-2PE-1:2,8,11,14,16■2:1 (1203),9,11,20■3:2,8,9,10,15,18-2JO- 3-JUDE-4^{2},5,9,14,17,21-RE-1:8■4:8, 11■6:10(1203)■11:8,15,17■14:13■15:3, 4■16:5,7■17:14■18:8■19:1,6,16■21:22■22:5,6,20,21

LORD'S-all=3068&marked-GE-40:7 (113)■44:8(113),9(113),16(113),18(113) -EX-9:29■12:11,27■13:9,12■32:26■35:21, 24-LE-3:16■16:9■23:5■27:26^{2},30-NU-11:23,29■18:28■31:37,38,39,40,41■ 32:10,13-DE-10:14■11:17■15:2■32:9 -JOS-1:15■5:15■22:19-J'G-11:31-1SA -2:8,24■14:3■16:6■17:47■18:17■22:21■ 24:6,10■26:9,11,16,23-2SA-1:14,16■ 19:21■20:6(113)■21:7-1KI-18:13-2KI-11:17■13:17-1CH-21:3(113)-2CH-7:2■ 23:16-PS-11:4■22:28■24:1■113:3■115:16■ 116:19■118:23■137:4-PR-16:11-IS-2:2■ 22:18(113)■34:8■40:2■42:19■44:5■59:1-JER-5:10■7:2■13:17■19:14■25:17■ 26:2^{2},10■27:16■28:3,6■36:6,8,10■51:6,7, 51-LA-2:22■3:22-EZE-8:14,16■10:4, 19■11:1-DA-9:17(136)-HO-9:3-JOE-1:9-OB-21-MIC-6:2,9-HAB-2:16 -ZEP-1:8,18■2:2,3-HAG-1:2,13^{2}■2:18 -ZEC-14:20■N.T.-all=2962&marked -M'T-21:42■25:18-M'R-12:11-LU-2:26■ 12:47■16:5-RO-14:8-1CO-7:22■10:21, 26,28■11:20(2960),26,29-GA-1:19 -1PE-2:13-RE-1:10(2960)

LO-RUHAMAH-HO-1:6(3819),8 (3819)

LOT-all=3876-GE-11:27,31■12:4,5■ 13:1,5,8,10,11^{2},12,14■14:12,16■19:1^{2},5, 6,9,10,12,14,15,18,23,29^{2},30,36-DE-2:9, 19-PS-83:8■N.T.-all=3091-LU-17:28, 29-2PE-2:7

LOTAN-all=3877-GE-36:20,22,29 -1CH-1:38,39

LOTAN'S-GE-36:22(3877)-1CH-1:39(3877)

LOT'S-GE-13:7(3876)

LUBIM-NA-3:9(3864)

LUBIMS-2CH-12:3(3864)■16:8(3864)

LUCAS-2CO-subscr.(3065)-PH'M-24(3065)

LUCIFER-IS-14:12(1966)

LUCIUS-AC-13:1(3066)-RO-16:21(3066)

LUD-all=3865-GE-10:22-1CH-1:17 -IS-66:19-EZE-27:10

LUDIM-GE-10:13(3866)-1CH-1:11(3866)

LUHITH-IS-15:5(3872)-JER-48:5(3872)

LUKE-all=3065-LU-1:t-COL-4:14 -2TI-4:11

LUZ-all=3870-GE-28:19■35:6■48:3 -JOS-16:2■18:13-J'G-1:23,26

LYCAONIA-AC-14:6(3071),11(3071)

LYCIA-AC-27:5(3073)

LYDDA-all=3069-AC-9:32,35,38

LYDIA-EZE-30:5(3865)■N.T.-AC-16:14(3070),40(3070)

LYDIANS-JER-46:9(3866)

LYSANIAS-LU-3:1(3078)

LYSIAS-all=3079-AC-23:26■24:7,22

LYSTRA-all=3082-AC-14:6,8,21■ 16:1,2-2TI-3:11

M

MAACAH-all=4601-2SA-3:3■10:6,8

MAACHAH-all=4601-GE-22:24 -1KI-2:39■15:2,10,13-1CH-2:48■3:2■ 7:15,16■8:29■9:35■11:43■19:7■27:16 -2CH-11:20,21,22■15:16

MAACHATHI-DE-3:14(4602)

MAACHATHITE-all=4602-2SA-23:34-2KI-25:23-1CH-4:19-JER-40:8

MAACHATHITES-all=4602 -JOS-12:5■13:11,13^{2}

MAADAI-EZR-10:34(4572)

MAADIAH-NE-12:5(4573)

MAAI-NE-12:36(4597)

MAALEH-ACRABBIM-JOS-15:3(4610)

MAARATH-JOS-15:59(4638)

MAASEIAH-all=4641&marked-1CH-15:18,20-2CH-23:1■26:11■28:7■34:8 -EZR-10:18,21,22,30-NE-3:23■8:4, 7■10:25■11:5,7■12:41,42-JER-21:1■29:21, 25■32:12(4271)■35:4■37:3■51:59(4271)

MAASIAI-1CH-9:12(4640)

MAATH-LU-3:26(3092)

MAAZ-1CH-2:27(4619)

MAAZIAH-1CH-24:18(4590)-NE-10:8(4590)

MACEDONIA-all=3109,a=3110 -AC-16:9a,9,10,12■18:5■19:21,22,29a■ 20:1,3-RO-15:26-1CO-16:5^{2},-2CO-1:16^{2}■ 2:13■7:5■8:1■9:2a,4a■11:9,subscr.-PH'P-4:15-1TH-1:7,8■4:10-1TI-1:3-TIT-subscr.

MACEDONIAN-AC-27:2(3110)

MACHBANAI-1CH-12:13(4344)

MACHBENAH-1CH-2:49(4343)

MACHI-NU-13:15(4352)

MACHIR-all=4353-GE-50:23-NU-26:29^{2}■27:1■32:39,40■36:1-DE-3:15 -JOS-13:31^{2}■17:1,3-J'G-5:14-2SA-9:4, 5■17:27-1CH-2:21,23■7:14,15,16,17

MACHIRITES-NU-26:29(4354)

MACHNADEBAI-EZR-10:40(4367)

MACHPELAH-all=4375-GE-23:9, 17,19■25:9■49:30■50:13

MADAI-GE-10:2(4074)-1CH-1:5(4074)

MADIAN-AC-7:29(3099)

MADMANNAH-JOS-15:31(4089) -1CH-2:49(4089)

MADMEN-JER-48:2(4886)

MADMENAH-IS-10:31(4088)

MADON-JOS-11:1(4068)■12:19(4068)

MAGBISH-EZR-2:30(4019)

MAGDALA-M'T-15:39(3093)

MAGDALENE-all=3094-M'T-27:56, 61■28:1-M'R-15:40,47■16:1,9-LU-8:2■ 24:10-JOH-19:25■20:1,18

MAGDIEL-GE-36:43(4025)-1CH-1:54(4025)

MAGOG-all=4031-GE-10:2-1CH-1:5-EZE-38:2■39:6-RE-20:8

MAGORMISSABIB-JER-20:3(4036)

MAGPIASH-NE-10:20(4047)

MAHALAH-1CH-7:18(4244)

MAHALALEEL-all=4111-GE-5:12, 13,15,16,17-1CH-1:2-NE-11:4

MAHALATH-GE-28:9(4258)-2CH-11:18(4258)-PS-53:t(4257)■88:t(4257)

MAHALI-EX-6:19(4249)

MAHANAIM-all=4266-GE-32:2 -JOS-13:26,30■21:38-2SA-2:8,12,29■ 17:24,27■19:32-1KI-2:8■4:14-1CH-6:80

MAHANEH-DAN-J'G-18:12(4265)

MAHARAI-all=4121-2SA-23:28 -1CH-11:30■27:13

MAHATH-all=4287-1CH-6:35 -2CH-29:12■31:13

MAHAVITE-1CH-11:46(4233)

MAHAZIOTH-1CH-25:4(4238), 30(4238)

MAHER-SHALAL-HASH-BAZ -IS-8:1(4122),3(4122)

MAHLAH-all=4244-NU-26:33■27:1■ 36:11-JOS-17:3

MAHLI-all=4249-NU-3:20-1CH-6:19, 29,47■23:21^{2},23■24:26,28,30-EZR-8:18

MAHLITES-NU-3:33(4250)■26:58(4250)

MAHLON-all=4248-RU-1:2,5■4:10

MAHLON'S-RU-4:9(4248)

MAHOL-1KI-4:31(4235)

MAKAZ-1KI-4:9(4739)

MAKHELOTH-NU-33:25(4721), 26(4721)

MAKKEDAH-all=4719-JOS-10:10, 16,17,21,28^{2},29■12:16■15:41

MAKTESH-ZEP-1:11(4389)

MALACHI-MAL-1:1(4401)

MALCHAM-1CH-8:9(4445)-ZEP-1:5(4445)

MALCHIAH-all=4441-1CH-6:40 -EZR-10:25,31-NE-3:14,31■8:4■11:12 -JER-38:1,6

MALCHIEL-all=4439-GE-46:17 -NU-26:45-1CH-7:31

MALCHIELITES-NU-26:45(4440)

MALCHIJAH-all=4441-1CH-9:12■ 24:9-EZR-10:25-NE-3:11■10:3■12:42

MALCHIRAM-1CH-3:18(4443)

MALCHI-SHUA-all=4444-1CH-8:33■ 9:39■10:2

MALCHUS-JOH-18:10(3124)

MALELEEL-LU-3:37(3121)

MALLOTHI-1CH-25:4(4413),26(4413)

MALLUCH-all=4409-1CH-6:44-EZR-10:29,32-NE-10:4,27■12:2

MAMRE-all=4471-GE-13:18■14:13, 24■18:1■23:17,19■25:9■35:27■49:30■50:13

MANAEN-AC-13:1(3127)

MANAHATH-all=4506-GE-36:23 -1CH-1:40■8:6

MANAHETHITES-1CH-2:52 (2679),54(2680)

MANASSEH-all=4519&marked -GE-41:51■46:20■48:1,5,13,14,20^{2}■50:23 -NU-1:10,34,35■2:20^{2}■7:54■10:23■13:11■ 26:28,29,34■27:1■32:33,39,40,41■34:14, 23■36:1,12-DE-3:13,14■29:8(4520)■ 33:17■34:2-JOS-1:12■4:12■12:6■13:7, 29^{2},31■14:4■16:4,9■17:1^{2},2^{2},3,5,6,7,8^{2},9^{2}, 11,12,17■18:7■20:8■21:5,6,25,27■22:1, 7,9,10,11,13,15,21,30,31-J'G-1:27■6:15, 35■7:23■11:29■18:30-1KI-4:13-2KI-20:21■21:1,9,11,16,17,18,20■23:12,26■ 24:3-1CH-3:13■5:18,23,26■6:61,62,70, 71■7:14,17,29■9:3■12:19,20^{2},31,37■26:32 (4520)■27:20,21-2CH-15:9■30:1,10, 11,18■31:1■32:33■33:1,9,10,11,13,18, 20,22^{2},23■34:6,9-EZR-10:30,33-PS-60:7■80:2■108:8-IS-9:21-JER-15:4 -EZE-48:4,5

MANASSEH'S-all=4519&marked -GE-48:14,17-JOS-17:6,10

MANASSES-all=3128-M'T-1:10^{2} -RE-7:6

MANASSITES-DE-4:43(4520) -J'G-12:4(4519)-2KI-10:33(4520)

MANOAH-all=4495-J'G-13:2,8,9^{2}, 11,12,13,15,16^{2},17,19^{2},20,21^{2},22■16:31

MAOCH-1SA-27:2(4582)

MAON-all=4584-JOS-15:55-1SA-23:24,25^{2}■25:2-1CH-2:45^{2}

MAONITES-J'G-10:12(4584)

MARA-RU-1:20(4755)

MARAH-all=4785-EX-15:23^{3}-NU-33:8,9

MARALAH-JOS-19:11(4831)

MARCUS-all=3138-COL-4:10 -PH'M-24-1PE-5:13

MARESHAH-all=4762-JOS-15:44 -1CH-2:42■4:21-2CH-11:8■14:9,10■ 20:37-MIC-1:15

MARK-all=3138-M'R-1:t-AC-12:12, 25■15:37,39-2TI-4:11

MAROTH-MIC-1:12(4796)

MARS'-AC-17:22(697)

MARSENA-ES-1:14(4826)

MARTHA-all=3136-LU-10:38,40, 41-JOH-11:1,5,19,20,21,24,30,39■12:2

MARY-all=3137-M'T-1:16,18,20■ 2:11■13:55■27:56^{2},61^{2}■28:1^{2}-M'R-6:3■ 15:40^{2},47^{2}■16:1,^{2},9-LU-1:27,30,34,38,

39,41,46,56■2:5,16,19,34■8:2■10:39,42■24:10^{2}-JOH-11:1,2,19,20,28,31,32,45■12:3■19:25^{2}■20:1,11,16,18-AC-1:14■12:12-RO-16:6

MASCHIL-all=7919-PS-32:t■42:t■44:t■45:t■52:t■53:t■54:t■55:t■74:t■78:t■88:t■89:t■142:t

MASH-GE-10:23(4851)

MASHAL-1CH-6:74(4913)

MASREKAH-GE-36:36(4957)-1CH-1:47(4957)

MASSA-all=4854-GE-25:14(4854)-1CH-1:30(4854)

MASSAH-all=4532-EX-17:7-DE-6:16■9:22■33:8

MATHUSALA-LU-3:37(3103)

MATRED-GE-36:36(4308)-1CH-1:50(4308)

MATRI-1SA-10:21(4309)

MATTAN-all=4977-2KI-11:18-2CH-23:17-JER-38:1

MATTANAH-NU-21:18(4980),19(4980)

MATTANIAH-all=4983-2KI-24:17-1CH-9:15■25:4,16-2CH-20:14■29:13-EZR-10:26,27,30,37-NE-11:17,22■12:8,25,35■13:13

MATTATHA-LU-3:31(3160)

MATTATHAH-EZR-10:33(4992)

MATTATHIAS-LU-3:25(3161),26(3161)

MATTENAI-all=4982-EZR-10:33,37-NE-12:19

MATTHAN-M'T-1:15(3157)

MATTHAT-LU-3:24(3158),29(3158)

MATTHEW-all=3156-M'T-1t■9:9■10:3-M'R-3:18-LU-6:15-AC-1:13

MATTHIAS-AC-1:23(3159),26(3159)

MATTITHIAH-all=4993-1CH-9:31■15:18,21■16:5■25:3,21-EZR-10:43-NE-8:4

MAZZAROTH-JOB-38:32(4216)

ME-O.T.supplied■N.T.-all=1691 or 3165

MEAH-NE-3:1(3968)■12:39(3968)

MEARAH-JOS-13:4(4632)

MEBUNNAI-2SA-23:27(4012)

MECHERATHITE-1CH-11:36(4382)

MEDAD-NU-11:26(4312),27(4312)

MEDAN-GE-25:2(4091)-1CH-1:32(4091)

MEDE-DA-11:1(4075)

MEDEBA-all=4311-NU-21:30-JOS-13:9,16-1CH-19:7-IS-15:2

MEDES-all=4074&marked-2KI-17:6■18:11-EZR-6:2-ES-1:19-IS-13:17-JER-25:25■51:11,28-DA-5:28(4076)■6:8(4076),12(4076),15(4076)■9:1■N.T.-AC-2:9(3370)

MEDIA-all=4074-ES-1:3,14,18■10:2-IS-21:2-DA-8:20

MEDIAN-DA-5:31(4077)

MEGIDDO-all=4023-JOS-12:21■17:11-J'G-1:27■5:19-1KI-4:12■9:15-2KI-9:27■23:29,30-1CH-7:29-2CH-35:22

MEGIDDON-ZEC-12:11(4023)

MEHETABEEL-NE-6:10(4105)

MEHETABEL-GE-36:39(4105)-1CH-1:50(4105)

MEHIDA-EZR-2:52(4240)-NE-7:54(4240)

MEHIR-1CH-4:11(4243)

MEHOLATHITE-1SA-18:19(4259)-2SA-21:8(4259)

MEHUJAEL-GE-4:18(4232)

MEHUMAN-ES-1:10(4104)

MEHUNIM-EZR-2:50(4586)

MEHUNIMS-2CH-26:7(4586)

ME-JARKON-JOS-19:46(4313)

MEKONAH-NE-11:28(4368)

MELATIAH-NE-3:7(4424)

MELCHI-LU-3:24(3197),28(3197)

MELCHIAH-JER-21:1(4441)

MELCHISEDEC-all=3198-HEB-5:6,10■6:20■7:1,10,11,15,17,21

MELCHI-SHUA-all=4444-1SA-14:49■31:2

MELCHIZEDEK-GE-14:18(4442)-PS-110:4(4442)

MELEA-LU-3:31(3190)

MELECH-1CH-8:35(4429)■9:41(4429)

MELICU-NE-12:14(4409)

MELITA-AC-28:1(3194)

MELZAR-DA-1:11(4453),16(4453)

MEMPHIS-HO-9:6(4644)

MEMUCAN-all=4462-ES-1:14,16,21

MENAHEM-all=4505-2KI-15:14,16,17,19,20,21,22,23

MENAN-LU-3:31(3104)

MEONENIM-J'G-9:37(6049)

MEONOTHAI-1CH-4:14(4587)

MEPHAATH-all=4158-JOS-13:18■21:37-1CH-6:79-JER-48:21

MEPHIBOSHETH-all=4648-2SA-4:4■9:6^{2},10,11,12^{2},13■16:1,4■19:24,25,30■21:7,8

MERAB-all=4764-1SA-14:49■18:17,19

MERAIAH-NE-12:12(4811)

MERAIOTH-all=4812-1CH-6:6,7,52■9:11-EZR-7:3-NE-11:11■12:15

MERARI-all=4847-GE-46:11-EX-6:16,19-NU-3:17,20,33^{2},35,36■4:29,33,42,45■7:8■10:17■26:57-JOS-21:7,34,40-1CH-6:1,16,19,29,44,47,63,77■9:14■15:6,17■23:6,21■24:26,27■26:10,19-2CH-29:12■34:12-EZR-8:19

MERARITES-NU-26:57(4848)

MERATHAIM-JER-50:21(4850)

MERCURIUS-AC-14:12(2060)

MERED-1CH-4:17(4778),18(4778)

MEREMOTH-all=4822-EZR-8:33■10:36-NE-3:4,21■10:5■12:3

MERES-ES-1:14(4825)

MERIBAH-all=4809-EX-17:7-NU-20:13,24■27:14-DE-33:8-PS-81:7

MERIBAH-KADESH-DE-32:51(4809,6946)

MERIB-BAAL-all=4807&marked-1CH-8:34^{2}■9:40,40(4810)

MERODACH-JER-50:2(4781)

MERODACH-BALADAN-IS-39:1(4757)

MEROM-JOS-11:5(4792),7(4792)

MERONOTHITE-1CH-27:30(4824)-NE-3:7(4824)

MEROZ-J'G-5:23(4789)

MESECH-PS-120:5(4902)

MESHA-GE-10:30(4331)-2KI-3:4(4337)-1CH-2:42(4338)■8:9(4331)

MESHACH-all=4336&marked-DA-1:7(4335)■2:49■3:12,13,14,16,19,20,22,23,26^{2},28,29,30

MESHECH-all=4902-GE-10:2-1CH-1:5,17-EZE-27:13■32:26■38:2,3■39:1

MESHELEMIAH-all=4920-1CH-9:21■26:1,2,9

MESHEZABEEL-all=4898-NE-3:4■10:21■11:24

MESHILLEMITH-1CH-9:12(4921)

MESHILLEMOTH-2CH-28:12(4919)-NE-11:13(4919)

MESHOBAD-1CH-4:34(4877)

MESHULLAM-all=4918-2KI-22:3-1CH-3:19■5:13■8:17■9:7,8,11,12-2CH-34:12-EZR-8:16■10:15,29-NE-3:4,6,30■6:18■8:4■10:7,20■11:7,11■12:13,16,25,33

MESHULLEMETH-2KI-21:19(4922)

MESOBAITE-1CH-11:47(4677)

MESOPOTAMIA-all=763-GE-24:10-DE-23:4-J'G-3:8,10-1CH-19:6■N.T.-AC-2:9(3318)■7:2(3318)

MESSIAH-DA-9:25(4899),26(4899)

MESSIAS-JOH-1:41(3323)■4:25(3323)

METHEGAMMAH-2SA-8:1(4965)

METHUSAEL-GE-4:18(4967)

METHUSELAH-all=4968-GE-5:21,22,25,26,27-1CH-1:3

MEUNIM-NE-7:52(4586)

MEZAHAB-GE-36:39(4314)-1CH-1:50(4314)

MIAMIN-EZR-10:25(4326)-NE-12:5(4326)

MIBHAR-1CH-11:38(4006)

MIBSAM-all=4017-GE-25:13-1CH-1:29■4:25

MIBZAR-GE-36:42(4014)-1CH-1:53(4014)

MICAH-all=4318&marked-J'G-17:1(4319),4(4319),5,8,9(4319),10(4319),12^{2},13■18:2,3,4,13,15,22,23,26,27-1CH-5:5■8:34,35■9:15(4316),40,41■23:20-2CH-34:20-JER-26:18(4320)-MIC-1:t■1:1

MICAH'S-all=4318-J'G-18:18,22,31

MICAIAH-all=4321&marked-1KI-22:8,9,13,14,15,24,25,26,28-2CH-18:7,8(4319),12,13,14(4318),23,24,25,27

MICHA-all=4316-2SA-9:12-NE-10:11■11:17,22

MICHAEL-all=4317-NU-13:13-1CH-5:13,14■6:40■7:3■8:16■12:20■27:18-2CH-21:2-EZR-8:8-DA-10:13,21■12:1■N.T.-JUDE-9(3413)-RE-12:7(3413)

MICHAH-all=4318-1CH-24:24^{2},25

MICHAIAH-2KI-22:12(4320)-2CH-13:2(4322)■17:7(4322)-NE-12:35(4320),41(4320)-JER-36:11(4321),13(4321)

MICHAL-all=4324-1SA-14:49■18:20,27,28■19:11,12,13,17^{2}■25:44-2SA-3:13,14■6:16,20,21,23■21:8-1CH-15:29

MICHMAS-EZR-2:27(4363)-NE-7:31(4363)

MICHMASH-all=4363-1SA-13:2,5,11,16,23■14:5,31-NE-11:31-IS-10:28

MICHMETHAH-JOS-16:6(4366)■17:7(4366)

MICHRI-1CH-9:8(4381)

MICHTAM-all=4387-PS-16:t■56:t■57:t■58:t■59:t■60:t

MIDDIN-JOS-15:61(4081)

MIDIAN-all=4080-GE-25:2,4■36:35-EX-2:15,16■3:1■4:19■18:1-NU-22:4,7■25:15,18■31:3,8^{2},9-JOS-13:21-J'G-6:1,2■7:8,13,14,15,25■8:3,5,12,22,26,28■9:17-1KI-11:18-1CH-1:32,33,46-IS-9:4■10:26■60:6-HAB-3:7

MIDIANITE-NU-10:29(4084)

MIDIANITES-all=4080&marked-GE-37:28(4084),36(4092)-NU-25:17(4084)■31:2(4084),3,7-J'G-6:2,3,6,7,11,13,14,16,33■7:1,2,7,12,23,24,25■8:1-PS-83:9

MIDIANITISH-all=4084-NU-25:6,14,15

MIGDAL-EL-JOS-19:38(4027)

MIGDAL-GAD-JOS-15:37(4028)

MIGDOL-all=4024-EX-14:2-NU-33:7-JER-44:1■46:14

MIGRON-1SA-14:2(4051)-IS-10:28(4051)

MIJAMIN-1CH-24:9(4326)-NE-10:7(4326)

MIKLOTH-all=4732-1CH-8:32■9:37,38■27:4

MIKNEIAH-1CH-15:18(4737),21(4737)

MILALAI-NE-12:36(4450)

MILCAH-all=4435-GE-11:29^{2}■22:20,23■24:15,24,47-NU-26:33■27:1■36:11-JOS-17:3

MILCOM-all=4445-1KI-11:5,33-2KI-23:13

MILETUM-2TI-4:20(3399)

MILETUS-AC-20:15(3399),17(3399)

MILLO-all=4407-J'G-9:6,20^{2}-2SA-5:9-1KI-9:15,24■11:27-2KI-12:20-1CH-11:8-2CH-32:5

MINIAMIN-all=4509-2CH-31:15-NE-12:17,41

MINNI-JER-51:27(4508)

MINNITH-J'G-11:33(4511)-EZE-27:17(4511)

MIPHKAD-NE-3:31(4663)

MIRIAM-all=4813-EX-15:20,21-NU-12:1,4,5,10^{2},15^{2}■20:1■26:59-DE-24:9-1CH-4:17■6:3-MIC-6:4

MIRMA-1CH-8:10(4821)

MISGAB-JER-48:1(4870)

MISHAEL-all=4332-EX-6:2-LE-10:4-NE-8:4-DA-1:6,7,11,19■2:17

MISHAL-JOS-21:30(4861)

MISHAM-1CH-8:12(4936)

MISHEAL-JOS-19:26(4861)

MISHMA-all=4927-GE-25:14-1CH-1:30■4:25,26

MISHMANNAH-1CH-12:10(4925)

MISHRAITES-1CH-2:53(4954)

MISPERETH-NE-7:7(4559)

MISREPHOTH-MAIM-JOS-11:8(4956)■13:6(4956)

MITHCAH-NU-33:28(4989),29(4989)

MITHNITE-1CH-11:43(4981)
MITHREDATH-EZR-1:8(4990)■4:7(4990)
MITYLENE-AC-20:14(3412)
MIZAR-PS-42:6(4706)
MIZPAH-all=4709&marked-GE-31:49-1KI-15:22-2KI-25:23,25-2CH-16:6-NE-3:7,15,19-JER-40:6(4708),8(4708),10(4708),12(4708),13(4708),15■41:1^2,3,6,10^2,14,16-HO-5:1
MIZPAR-EZR-2:2(4558)
MIZPEH-all=4709&marked-JOS-11:3,8(4708)■15:38(4708)■18:26(4708)-J'G-10:17■11:11,29^2(4708),34■20:1,3■21:1,5,8-1SA-7:5(4708),6,6(4708),7(4708),11,12,16■10:17■22:3(4708)
MIZRAIM-all=4714-GE-10:6,13-1CH-1:8,11
MIZZAH-all=4199-GE-36:13,17-1CH-1:37
MNASON-AC-21:16(3416)
MOAB-all=4124&marked-GE-19:37■36:35-EX-15:15-NU-21:11,13^2,15,20,26,28,29■22:1,3^2,4,7,8,10,14,21,36■23:6,7,17■24:17■25:1■26:3,63■31:12■33:44,48,49,50■35:1■36:13-DE-1:5■2:8,18■29:1■32:49■34:1,5,6,8-JOS-13:32■24:9-J'G-3:12,14,15,17,28,29,30■10:6■11:15,17,18^4,25-RU-1:1,2,4(4125),6^2,22■2:6■4:3-1SA-12:9■14:47■22:3^2,4-2SA-8:2,12■23:20-1KI-11:7-2KI-1:1■3:4,5,7^2,10,13,23,26-1CH-1:46■4:22■8:8■11:22■18:2,11-2CH-20:1,10,22,23-NE-13:23(4125)-PS-60:8■83:6■108:9-IS-11:14■15:1^3,2,4,5,8,9■16:2,4,6,7,11,12,13,14■25:10-JER-9:26■25:21■27:3■40:11■48:1,2,4,9,11,13,15,16,18,20^2,24,25,26,28,29,31^2,33,35,36,38^2,39^2,40,41,42,43,44,45,46,47^2-EZE-25:8,9,11-DA-11:41-AM-2:1,2^2-MIC-6:5-ZEP-2:8,9
MOABITE-all=4125-DE-23:3-1CH-11:46-NE-13:1
MOABITES-all=4124&marked-GE-19:37-NU-22:4-DE-2:9,11(4125),29(4125)-J'G-3:28-2SA-8:2-1KI-11:1,33-2KI-3:18,21,22,24^2■13:20■23:13■24:2-1CH-18:2-EZR-9:1
MOABITESS-all=4125-RU-1:22■2:2,21■4:5,10-2CH-24:26
MOABITISH-RU-2:6(4125)
MOADIAH-NE-12:17(4153)
MOLADAH-all=4137-JOS-15:26■19:2-1CH-4:28-NE-11:26
MOLECH-all=4432-LE-18:21■20:2,3,4,5-1KI-11:7-2KI-23:10-JER-32:35
MOLID-1CH-2:29(4140)
MOLOCH-AM-5:26(4432)■N.T.-AC-7:43(3434)
MORASTHITE-JER-26:18(4183)-MIC-1:1(4183)
MORDECAI-all=4782-EZR-2:2-NE-7:7-ES-2:5,7,10,11,15,19,20^2,21,22■3:2,3,5,6^3■4:1^2,4,5,6,7,9,10,12,13,15,17■5:9^2,13,14■6:2,3,4,10,11,12,13■7:9,10■8:1,2^2,7,9,15■9:3,4^2,20,23,29,31■10:2,3
MORDECAI'S-ES-2:22(4782)■3:4(4782)
MOREH-all=4176-GE-12:6-DE-11:30-J'G-7:1
MORESHETH-GATH-MIC-1:14(4182)
MORIAH-GE-22:2(4179)-2CH-3:1(4179)
MOSERA-DE-10:6(4149)
MOSEROTH-NU-33:30(4149),31(4149)
MOSES-all=4872-EX-2:10,11,14,15^2,17,21^2■3:1,3,4,6,11,13,14,15■4:1,3,4,10,14,18^2,19,20^2,21,27,28,29,30■5:1,4,20,22■6:1,2,9^2,10,12,13,20,26,27,28,29,30■7:1,6,7,8,10,14,19,20■8:1,5,8,9,12^2,13,16,20,25,26,29,30,31■9:1,8^2,10,11,12,13,22,23,27,29,33,35■10:1,3,8,9,12,13,16,21,22,24,25,29■11:1,3,4,9,10■12:1,21,28,31,35,43,50■13:1,3,19■14:1,11,13,15,21,26,27,31■15:1,22,24■16:2,4,6,8,9,11,15,19,20^2,22,24,25,28,32,33,34■17:2^2,3,4,5,6,9,10^2,11,14,15■18:1,5,6,7,8,13^2,15,24,25,26,27■19:3,7,8,9^2,10,14,17,19,20^2,21,23,25■20:19,20,21,22■24:1,2,3,4,6,8,9,12,13^2,15,16,18^2■25:1■30:11,17,22,34■31:1,12,18■32:1:1^2,7,9,11,17,21,23,25,26,28,29,30,31,33■33:1,5,7,8^2,9^2,11,12,17■34:1,4,8,27,29^2,30,31^2,33,34,35^2■35:1,4,20,29,30■36:2,3,5,6■38:21,22■39:1,5,7,21,26,29,31,32,33,42,43^2■40:1,16,18,19,21,23,25,27,29,31,32,33,35-LE-1:1■4:1■5:14■6:1,8,19,24■7:22,28,38■8:1,4,5,6,9,10,13^2,15,16,17,19,20,21^2,23,24^2,28,29^2,30,31,36■9:1,5,6,7,10,21,23■10:3,4,5,6,7,11,12,16,19,20■11:1■12:1■13:1■14:1,33■15:1■16:1,2,34■17:1■18:1■19:1■20:1■21:1,16,24■22:1,17,26■23:1,9,23,26,33,44■24:1,11,13,23^2■25:1■26:46■27:1,34-NU-1:1,17,19,44,48,54■2:1,33,34■3:1,5,11,14,16,38,39,40,42,44,49,51^2■4:1,17,21,34,37^2,41,45^2,46,49^2■5:1,4,11■6:1,22■7:1,4,6,11,89■8:1,3,4,5,20^2,22,23■9:1,4,5,6,8,9,23■10:1,13,29,35■11:2^2,10^2,11,16,21,23,24,27,28^2,29,30■12:1,2,3,4,7,8,11,13,14■13:1,3,16^2,17,26,30■14:2,5,11,13,26,36,39,41,44■15:1,17,22,23,33,35,36,37■16:2,3,4,8,12,15,16,18,20,23,25,28,36,40,41,42,43,44,46,47,50■17:1,6,7,8,9,10,11,12■18:25■19:1■20:2,3,6,7,9,10,11,12,14,23,27,28^2■21:5,7^2,8,9,16,32,34■25:4,5,6,10,16■26:1,3,4,9,52,59,63,64■27:2,5,6,11,12,15,18,22,23■28:1■29:40^2■30:1,16■31:1,3,6,7,12,13,14,15,21,25,31^2,41^2,42,47^2,48,49,51,54■32:2,6,20,25,28,29,33,40■33:1,2,50■34:1,13,16■35:1,9■36:1,5,10,13-DE-1:1,3,5■4:41,44,45,46■5:1■27:1,9,11■29:1,2■31:1,7,9,10,14^2,16,22,24,25,30■32:44,45,48■33:1,4■34:1,5,7,8^2,9^2,10,12-JOS-1:1,2,3,5,7,13,14,15,17^2■3:7■4:10,12,14■8:31^2,32,33,35■9:24■11:12,15^3,20,23■12:6^2■13:8^2,12,15,21,24,29,32,33■14:2,3,5,6,7,9,10,11■17:4■18:7■20:2■21:2,8■22:2,4,5,7,9■23:6■24:5-J'G-1:20■3:4■4:11-1SA-12:6,8-1KI-2:3■8:9,53,56-2KI-14:6■18:4,6,12■21:8■23:25-1CH-6:3,49■15:15■21:29■22:13■23:13,14,15■26:24-2CH-1:3■5:10■8:13■23:18■24:6,9■25:4■30:16■33:8■34:14■35:6,12-EZR-3:2■6:18(4873)■7:6-NE-1:7,8■8:1,14■9:14■10:29■13:1-PS-77:20■90:t■99:6■103:7■105:26■106:16,23,32-IS-63:11,12-JER-15:1-DA-9:11,13-MIC-6:4-MAL-4:4■N.T.-all=3475-M'T-8:4■17:3,4■19:7,8■22:24-M'R-1:44■7:10■9:4,5■10:3,4■12:19,26-LU-2:22■5:14■9:30,33■16:29,31■20:28,37■24:27,44-JOH-1:17,45■3:14■5:45,46■6:32■7:19,22^2,23■8:5■9:29-AC-3:22■6:11,14■7:20,22,29,31,32,35,37,40,44■13:39■15:1,5,21■21:21■26:22■28:23-RO-5:14■9:15■10:5,19-1CO-9:9■10:2-2CO-3:7,13,15-2TI-3:8-HEB-3:2,3,5,16■7:14■8:5■9:19■11:23,24■12:21-JUDE-9-RE-15:3
MOSES'-all=4872-EX-17:12■18:1,2^2,5,12^2,14,17■32:19■34:29,35-LE-8:29-NU-10:29-JOS-1:1-J'G-1:16■N.T.-all=3475-M'T-23:2-JOH-9:28-HEB-10:28
MOZA-all=4162-1CH-2:46■8:36,37■9:42,43
MOZAH-JOS-18:26(4681)
MUPPIM-GE-46:21(4649)
MUSHI-all=4187-EX-6:19-NU-3:20-1CH-6:19,47■23:21,23■24:26,30
MUSHITES-NU-3:33(4188)■26:58(4188)
MUTH-LABBEN-PS-9:t(4192)
MY-O.T.supplied■N.T.-all=1700 or 3450
MYRA-AC-27:5(3460)
MYSIA-AC-16:7(3463),8(3463)

N

NAAM-1CH-4:15(5277)
NAAMAH-all=5279-GE-4:22-JOS-15:41-1KI-14:21,31-2CH-12:13
NAAMAN-all=5283-GE-46:21-NU-26:40^2-2KI-5:1,6,9,11,17,20,21^2,23,27-1CH-8:4,7■N.T.-LU-4:27(3497)
NAAMAN'S-2KI-5:2(5283)
NAAMATHITE-all=5284-JOB-2:11■11:1■20:1■42:9
NAAMITES-NU-26:40(5280)
NAAMITES-NU-26:40(5280)
NAARAH-all=5292 1CH4:5,6^2
NAARAI-1CH-11:37(5293)
NAARAN-1CH-7:28(5295)
NAARATH-JOS-16:7(5292)
NAASHON-EX-6:23(5177)
NAASSON-M'T-1:4(3476)-LU-3:32(3476)
NABAL-all=5037-1SA-25:3,4,5,9,10,19,25^2,26,34,36,37,38,39^3■30:5-2SA-3:3
NABAL'S-all=5037-1SA-25:14,36■27:3-2SA-2:2
NABOTH-all=5022-1KI-21:1,2,3,4,6,7,8,9,12,13^2,14,15^3,16^2,18,19-2KI-9:21,25,26
NACHON'S-2SA-6:6(5225)
NACHOR-JOS-24:2(5152)■N.T.-LU-3:34(3493)
NADAB-all=5070-EX-6:23■24:1,9■28:1-LE-10:1-NU-3:2,4■26:60,61-1KI-14:20■15:25,27,31-1CH-2:28,30■6:3■8:30■9:36■24:1,2
NAGGE-LU-3:25(3471)
NAHALAL-JOS-21:35(5096)
NAHALIEL-NU-21:19^2(5160)
NAHALLAL-JOS-19:15(5096)
NAHALOL-J'G-1:30(5096)
NAHAM-1CH-4:19(5163)
NAHAMANI-NE-7:7(5167)
NAHARAI-1CH-11:39(5171)
NAHARI-2SA-23:37(5171)
NAHASH-all=5176-1SA-11:1^2,2■12:12-2SA-10:2■17:25,27-1CH-19:1,2
NAHATH-all=5184-GE-36:13,17-1CH-1:37■6:26-2CH-31:13
NAHBI-NU-13:14(5147)
NAHOR-all=5152-GE-11:22,23,24,25,26,27,29■22:20,23■24:10,15,24■29:5■31:53-1CH-1:26
NAHOR'S-GE-11:29(5152)■24:47(5152)
NAHSHON-all=5177-NU-1:7■2:3■7:12,17■10:14-RU-4:20-1CH-2:10,11
NAHUM-1:t(5151)■1:1(5151)
NAIN-LU-7:11(3484)
NAIOTH-all=5121-1SA-19:18,19,22,23^2■20:1
NAOMI-all=5281-RU-1:2,8,11,19,20,21,22■2:1,2,6,20^2,22■3:1■4:3,5,9,14,16,17
NAOMI'S-RU-1:3(5281)
NAPHISH-all=5305-GE-25:15-1CH-1:31
NAPHTALI-all=5321-GE-30:8■35:25■46:24■49:21-EX-1:4-NU-1:15,42,43■2:29^2■7:78■10:27■13:14■26:48,50■34:28-DE-27:13■33:23■34:2-JOS-19:32^2,39■20:7■21:6,32-J'G-1:33■4:6,10■5:18■6:35■7:23-1KI-4:15■7:14■15:20-2KI-15:29-1CH-2:2■6:62,76■7:13■12:34,40■27:19-2CH-16:4■34:6-PS-68:27-IS-9:1-EZE-48:3,4,34
NAPHTUHIM-all=5320-GE-10:13-1CH-1:11
NARCUSSIS-RO-16:11(3488)
NATHAN-all=5416-2SA-5:14■7:2,3■7:4,17■12:1,5,7,13^2,15,25■23:36-1KI-1:8,10,11,22,23,24,32,34,38,44,45■4:5^2-1CH-2:36■3:5■11:38■14:4■17:1,2,3,15■29:29-2CH-9:29■29:25-EZR-8:16■10:39-PS-51:t-ZEC-12:12■N.T.-LU-3:31(3481)
NATHANAEL-all=3482-JOH-1:45,46,47,48,49■21:2
NATHANMELECH-2KI-23:11(5419)
NAUM-LU-3:25(3486)
NAZARENE-M'T-2:23(3480)
NAZARENES-AC-24:5(3480)
NAZARETH-all=3478-M'T-2:23■4:13■21:11■26:71-M'R-1:9,24■10:47■14:67■16:6-LU-1:26■2:4,39,51■4:16,34■18:37■24:19-JOH-1:45,46■18:5,7■19:19-AC-2:22■3:6■4:10■6:14■10:38■22:8■26:9
NAZARITE-all=5139-NU-6:2,13,18,19,20,21-J'G-13:5,7■16:17
NAZARITES-all=5139-LA-4:7-AM-2:11,12
NEAH-JOS-19:13(5269)
NEAPOLIS-AC-16:11(3496)
NEARIAH-all=5294-1CH-3:22,23■4:42
NEBAI-NE-10:19(5109)
NEBAIOTH-1CH-1:29(5032)-

IS-60:7(5032)

NEBAJOTH-all=5032-GE-25:13■28:9■36:3

NEBALLAT-NE-11:34(5041)

NEBAT-all=5028-1KI-11:26■12:2,15■15:1■16:3,26,31■21:22■22:52-2KI-3:3■9:9■10:29■13:2,11■14:24■15:9,18,24,28■17:21■23:15-2CH-9:29■10:2,15■13:6

NEBO-all=5015-NU-32:3,38■33:47-DE-32:49■34:1-1CH-5:8-EZR-2:29■10:43-NE-7:33-IS-15:2■46:1-JER-48:1,22

NEBUCHADNEZZAR-all=5020,a=5019&marked-2KI-24:1a,10a,11a■25:1a,8a,22a-1CH-6:15a-2CH-36:6a,7a,10a,13a-EZR-1:7a■2:1a■5:12,14■6:5-NE-7:6a-ES-2:6a-JER-27:6a,8a,20a■28:3a,11a,14a■29:1a,3a■34:1■39:5-DA-1:1a,18a■2:1^{2}a,28,46■3:1,2^2,3^2,5,7,9,13,14,16,19,24,26,28■4:1,4,18,28■31,33,34,37■5:2,11,18

NEBUCHADREZZAR-all=5019-JER-21:2,7■22:25■24:1■25:1,9■29:21■32:1,28■35:11■37:1■39:1,11■43:10■44:30■46:2,13,26■49:28,30■50:17■51:34■52:4,12,28,29,30-EZE-26:7■29:18,19■30:10

NEBUSHASBAN-JER-39:13(5021)

NEBUZAR-ADAN-all=5018-2KI-25:8,11,20-JER-39:9,10,11,13■40:1■41:10■43:6■52:12,15,16,26,30

NECHO-all=5224-2CH-35:20,22■36:4

NEDABIAH-1CH-3:18(5072)

NEGINAH-PS-61:t(5058)

NEGINOTH-all=5058-PS-4:t■6:t■54:t■55:t■67:t■76:t

NEHELAMITE-all=5161-JER-29:24,31,32

NEHEMIAH-all=5166-EZR-2:2-NE-1:t,1:1■3:16■7:7■8:9■10:1■12:26,47

NEHILOTH-PS-5:t(5155)

NEHUM-NE-7:7(5149)

NEHUSHTA-2KI-24:8(5179)

NEHUSHTAN-2KI-18:4(5180)

NEIEL-JOS-19:27(5272)

NEKEB-JOS-19:33(5346)

NEKODA-all=5353-EZR-2:48,60-NE-7:50,62

NEMUEL-all=5241-NU-26:9,12-1CH-4:24

NEMUELITES-NU-26:12(5242)

NEPHEG-all=5298-EX-6:21-2SA-5:15-1CH-3:7■14:6

NEPHISH-1CH-5:19(5305)

NEPHISHESIM-NE-7:52(5300)

NEPHTHALIM-all=3508-M'T-4:13,15-RE-7:6

NEPHTOAH-all=5318-JOS-15:9■18:15

NEPHUSIM-EZR-2:50(5304)

NER-all=5369-1SA-14:50,51■26:5,14-2SA-2:8,12■3:23,25,28,37-1KI-2:5,32-1CH-8:33■9:36,39■26:28

NEREUS-RO-16:15(3517)

NERGAL-2KI-17:30(5370)

NERGAL-SHAREZER-all=5371-JER-39:3^2,13

NERI-LU-3:27(3518)

NERIAH-all=5374-JER-32:12,16■36:4,8,14,32■43:3,6■45:1■51:59

NERO-2TI-subscr.(3505)

NETHANEEL-all=5417-NU-1:8■2:5■7:18,23■10:15-1CH-2:14■15:24■24:6-2CH-17:7■35:9-EZR-10:22-NE-12:21,36

NETHANIAH-all=5418-2KI-25:23,25-1CH-25:2,12-2CH-17:8-JER-36:14■40:8,14,15■41:1,2,6,7,9,10,11,12,15,16,18

NETHINIMS-all=5411&marked-1CH-9:2-EZR-2:43,58,70■7:7,24(5412)■8:17,20^2-NE-3:26,31■7:46,60,73■10:28■11:3,21^2

NETOPHAH-EZR-2:22(5199)-NE-7:26(5199)

NETOPHATHI-NE-12:28(5200)

NETOPHATHITE-all=5200-2SA-23:28,29-2KI-25:23-1CH-11:30^2■27:13,15-JER-40:8

NETOPHATHITES-1CH-2:54(5200)■9:16(5200)

NEZIAH-EZR-2:54(5335)-NE-7:56(5335)

NEZIB-JOS-15:43(5334)

NIBHAZ-2KI-17:31(5026)

NIBSHAN-JOS-15:62(5044)

NICANOR-AC-6:5(3527)

NICODEMUS-all=3530-JOH-3:1,4,9■7:50■19:39

NICOLAITANS-RE-2:6(3531),15(3531)

NICOLAS-AC-6:5(3532)

NICOPOLIS-TIT-3:12(3533),subscr(3533)

NIGER-AC-13:1(3526)

NIMRAH-NU-32:3(5247)

NIMRIM-IS-15:6(5249)-JER-48:34(5249)

NIMROD-all=5248-GE-10:8,9-1CH-1:10-MIC-5:6

NIMSHI-all=5250-1KI-19:16-2KI-9:2,14,20-2CH-22:7

NINEVE-LU-11:32(3535)

NINEVEH-all=5210-GE-10:11,12-2KI-19:36-IS-37:37-JON-1:2■3:2,3^2,4,5,6,7■4:11-NA-1:1■2:8■3:7-ZEP-2:13■N.T.-M'T-12:41(3536)

NINEVITES-LU-11:30(3536)

NISAN-NE-2:1(5212)-ES-3:7(5212)

NISROCH-2CH-19:37(5268)-IS-37:38(5268)

NO-all=4996-JER-46:25-EZE-30:14,15,16-NA-3:8

NOADIAH-EZR-8:33(5129)-NE-6:14(5129)

NOAH-all=5146&marked-GE-5:29,30,32^2■6:8,9^3,10,13,22■7:1,5,6,7,9^2,13^2,15,23■8:1,6,11,13,15,18,20■9:1,8,17,18,19,20,24,28,29■10:1,32-NU-26:33(5270)■27:1(5270)■36:11(5270)-JOS-17:3(5270)-1CH-1:4-IS-54:9^2-EZE-14:14,20■N.T.-all=3575-HEB-11:7-1PE-3:202PE-2:5

NOAH'S-GE-7:11(5146),13(5146)

NOB-all=5011-1SA-21:1■22:9,11,19-NE-11:32-IS-10:32

NOBAH-all=5025-NU-32:42^2-J'G-8:11

NOD-GE-4:16(5113)

NODAB-1CH-5:19(5114)

NOE-all=3575-M'T-24:37,38-LU-3:36■17:26,27

NOGAH-1CH-3:7(5052)■14:6(5052)

NOHAH-1CH-8:2(5119)

NON-1CH-7:27(5126)

NOPH-all=5297-IS-19:13-JER-2:16■44:1■46:14,19-EZE-30:13,16

NOPHAH-NU-21:30(5302)

NOT-all=1722■N.T.-all=3756

NUMBERS-1:t(4057)

NUN-all=5126-EX-33:11-NU-11:28■13:8,16■14:6,30,38■26:65■27:18■32:12,28■34:17-DE-1:38■31:23■32:44■34:9-JOS-1:1■2:1,23■6:6■14:1■17:4■19:49,51■21:1■24:29-J'G-2:8-1KI-16:34-NE-8:17

NYMPHAS-COL-4:15(3564)

O

O-O.T.supplied■N.T.-all=5599

OBADIAH-all=5662-1KI-18:3^2,4,5,6,7,16-1CH-3:21■7:3■8:38■9:16,44■12:9■27:19-2CH-17:7■34:12-EZR-8:9-NE-10:5■12:25-OB-1:t,1

OBAL-GE-10:28(5745)

OBED-all=5744-RU-4:17,21,22-1CH-2:12,37,38■11:47■26:7-2CH-23:1■N.T.-M'T-1:5(5601)-LU-3:32(5601)

OBED-EDOM-all=5654-2SA-6:10,11^2,12^2-1CH-13:13,14^2■15:18,21,24,25■16:5:38^2■26:4,8^2,15-2CH-25:24

OBIL-1CH-27:30(179)

OBOTH-all=88-NU-21:10,11■33:43,44

OCRAN-all=5918-NU-1:13■2:27■7:72,77■10:26

ODED-all=5752-2CH-15:1,8■28:9

OF-all supplied

OG-all=5747-NU-21:33■32:33-DE-1:4■3:1,3,4,10,11,13■4:47■29:7■31:4-JOS-2:10■9:10■12:4■13:12,30,31-1KI-4:19-NE-9:22-PS-135:11■136:20

OHAD-GE-46:10(161)-EX-6:15(161)

OHEL-1CH-3:20(169)

OLIVET-2SA-15:30(2132)■N.T.-AC-1:12(1638)

OLYMPAS-RO-16:15(3632)

OMAR-all=201-GE-36:11,15-1CH-1:36

OMEGA-all=5598-RE-1:8,11■21:6■22:13

OMRI-all=6018-1KI-16:16,17,21,22^2,23,25,27,28,29^2,30-2KI-8:26-1CH-7:8■9:4■27:18-2CH-22:2-MIC-6:16

ON-all=204&marked-GE-41:45,50■46:20-NU-16:1(203)

ONAM-all=208-GE-36:23-1CH-1:40■2:26,28

ONAN-all=209-GE-38:4,8,9■46:12^2-NU-26:19^2-1CH-2:3

ONESIMUS-all=3682-COL-4:9 subscr.-PH'M-10,subscr.

ONESIPHORUS-2TI-1:16(3683)■4:19(3683)

ONO-all=207-1CH-8:12-EZR-2:33-NE-6:2■7:37■11:35

OPHEL-all=6077-2CH-27:3■33:14-NE-3:26,27■11:21

OPHIR-all=211-GE-10:29-1KI-9:28■10:11^2■22:48-1CH-1:23■29:4-2CH-8:18■9:10-JOB-22:24■28:16-PS-45:9-IS-13:12

OPHNI-JOS-18:24(6078)

OPHRAH-all=6084-JOS-18:23-J'G-6:11,24■8:27,32■9:5-1SA-13:17-1CH-4:14

OREB-all=6157-J'G-7:25^3■8:3-PS-83:11-IS-10:26

OREN-1CH-2:25(767)

ORION-all=3685-JOB-9:9■38:31-AM-5:8

ORNAN-all=771-1CH-21:15,18,20^2,21,22,23,24,25,28-2CH-3:1

ORPAH-RU-1:4(6204),14(6204)

OSEE-RO-9:25(5617)

OSHEA-NU-13:8(1954),16(1954)

OTHNI-1CH-26:7(6273)

OTHNIEL-all=6274-JOS-15:17-J'G-1:13■3:9,11-1CH-4:13^2■27:15

OUR-O.T.supplied■N.T.-all=2257

OUT-O.T.supplied■N.T.-all=3756

OZEM-1CH-2:15(684),25(684)

OZIAS-M'T-1:8(3604),9(3604)

OZNI-NU-26:16(244)

OZNITES-NU-26:16(244)

P

PAARAI-2SA-23:35(6474)

PACATIANA-1TI-subscr.(3818)

PADAN-GE-48:7(6307)

PADAN-ARAM-all=6307-GE-25:20■28:2,5,6,7■31:18■33:18■35:9,26■46:15

PADON-EZR-2:44(6303)-NE-7:47(6303)

PAGIEL-all=6295-NU-1:13■2:27■7:72,77■10:26

PAHATH-MOAB-all=6355-EZR-2:6■8:4■10:30-NE-3:11■7:11■10:14

PAI-1CH-1:50(6464)

PALAL-NE-3:25(6420)

PALESTINA-all=6429-EX-15:14-IS-14:29,31

PALESTINE-JOE-3:4(6429)

PALLU-all=6396-EX-6:14-NU-26:5,8-1CH-5:3

PALLUITES-NU-26:5(6384)

PALTI-NU-13:9(6406)

PALTIEL-NU-34:26(6409)

PALTITE-2SA-23:26(6407)

PAMPHYLIA-all=3828-AC-2:10■13:13■14:24■15:38■27:5

PANNAG-EZE-27:17(6438)

PAPHOS-AC-13:6(3974),13(3974)

PARAH-JOS-18:23(6511)

PARAN-all=6290-GE-21:21-NU-10:12■12:16■13:3,26-DE-1:1■33:2-1SA-25:1-1KI-11:18^2-HAB-3:3

PARBAR-1CH-26:18^2(6503)

PARMASHTA-ES-9:9(6534)

PARMENAS-AC-6:5(3937)

PARNACH-NU-34:25(6535)

PAROSH-all=6551-EZR-2:3■10:25-NE-3:25■7:8■10:14

PARSHANDATHA-ES-9:7(6577)

PARTHIANS-AC-2:9(3934)

PARUAH-1KI-4:17(6515)

PARVAIM-2CH-3:6(6516)

PASACH-1CH-7:33(6457)

PASDAMMIM-1CH-11:13(6450)

PASEAH-all=6454-**1CH**-4:12-**EZR**-2:49-**NE**-3:6

PASHUR-all=6583-**1CH**-9:12-**EZR**-2:38■10:22-**NE**-7:41■10:3■11:12-**JER**-20:1,2,3^{2},6■21:1■38:1^{2}

PATARA-**AC**-21:1(3959)

PATHROS-all=6624-**IS**-11:11-**JER**-44:1,15-**EZE**-29:14■30:14

PATHRUSIM-**GE**-10:14(6625)-**1CH**-1:12(6625)

PATMOS-**RE**-1:9(3963)

PATROBAS-**RO**-16:14(3969)

PAU-**GE**-36:39(6464)

PAUL-all=3972-**AC**-13:9,13,16,43,45,46,50■14:9,11,12,14,19■15:2^{2},12,22,25,35,36,38,40■16:3,9,14,17,18,19,25,28,29,36,37■17:2,4,10,13,14,15,16,22,33■18:1,5,9,12,14,18■19:1,4,6,11,13,15,21,26,30■20:1,7,9,10,13,16■21:4,13,18,26,29,30,32,37,39,40■22:25,28,30■23:1,3,5,6,10,11,12,14,16,17,18,20,24,31,33■24:1,10,23,24,26,27■25:2,4,6,7,9,10,19,21,23■26:1^{2},24,28,29■27:1,3,9,11,21,24,31,33,43■28:3,8,15,16,17,25,30-**RO**-1:t,1-**1CO**-1:t,1,12,13^{2}■3:4,5,22■16:21-**2CO**-1:t,1■10:1-**GA**-1:t,1■5:2-**EPH**-1:t,1■3:1-**PH'P**-1:t,1-**COL**-1:t,1,23■4:18-**1TH**-1:t,1■2:18-**2TH**-1:t,1■3:17-**1TI**-1:t,1-**2TI**-1:t,1,subscr.,**TIT**-1:t,1-**PH'M**-1:t,1,9,19-**HEB**-1:t-**2PE**-3:15

PAUL'S-all=3972-**AC**-19:29■20:37■21:8,11■23:16■25:14

PAULUS-**AC**-13:7(3972)

PEDAHEL-**NU**-34:28(6300)

PEDAHZUR-all=6301-**NU**-1:10■2:20■7:54,59■10:23

PEDAIAH-all=6305-**2KI**-23:36-**1CH**-3:18,19■27:20-**NE**-3:25■8:4■11:7■13:13

PEKAH-all=6492-**2KI**-15:25,27,29,30,31,32,37■16:1,5-**2CH**-28:6-**IS**-7:1

PEKAHIAH-all=6494-**2KI**-15:22,23,26

PEKOD-**JER**-50:21(6489)-**EZE**-23:23(6489)

PELAIAH-all=6411-**1CH**-3:24-**NE**-8:7■10:10

PELALIAH-**NE**-11:12(6421)

PELATIAH-all=6410-**1CH**-3:21■4:42-**NE**-10:22-**EZE**-11:1,13

PELEG-all=6389-**GE**-10:25■11:16,17,18,19-**1CH**-1:19,25

PELET-all=6404-**1CH**-2:47■12:3

PELETH-all=6431-**NU**-16:1-**1CH**-2:33

PELETHITES-all=6432-**2SA**-8:18■15:18■20:7,23-**1KI**-1:38,44-**1CH**-18:17

PELONITE-all=6397-**1CH**-11:27,36■27:10

PENIEL-**GE**-32:30(6439)

PENINNAH-all=6444-**1SA**-1:2^{2},4

PENUEL-all=6439-**GE**-32:31-**J'G**-8:8^{2},9,17-**1KI**-12:25-**1CH**-4:4■8:25

PEOR-all=6465-**NU**-23:28■25:18■31:16-**JOS**-22:17

PEOR'S-**NU**-25:18(6465)

PERAZIM-supplied

PERESH-**1CH**-7:16(6570)

PEREZ-all=6557-**1CH**-27:3-**NE**-11:4,6

PEREZUZZA-**1CH**-13:11(6560)

PEREZUZZAH-**2SA**-6:8(6560)

PERGA-all=4011-**AC**-13:13,14■14:25

PERGAMOS-**RE**-1:11(4010)■2:12(4010)

PERIDA-**NE**-7:57(6514)

PERIZZITE-all=6522-**GE**-13:7-**EX**-33:2■34:11-**JOS**-9:1■11:3

PERIZZITES-all=6522-**GE**-15:20■34:30-**EX**-3:8,17■23:23-**DE**-7:1■20:17-**JOS**-3:10■12:8■17:15■24:11-**J'G**-1:4,5■3:5-**1KI**-9:20-**2CH**-8:7-**EZR**-9:1-**NE**-9:8

PERSIA-all=6539&marked-**2CH**-36:20,22^{2},23-**EZR**-1:1^{2},2,8■3:7■4:3,5^{2},7,24(6540)■6:14(6540)■7:1■9:9-**ES**-1:3,14,18■10:2-**EZE**-27:10■38:5-**DA**-8:20■10:1,13^{2},20■11:2

PERSIAN-**NE**-12:22(6542)-**DA**-6:28(6523)

PERSIANS-all=6540&marked-**ES**-1:19(6539)-**DA**-5:28■6:8,12,15

PERSIS-**RO**-16:12(4069)

PERUDA-**EZR**-2:55(6514)

PETER-all=4074-**M'T**-4:18■10:2■14:28,29■15:15■16:16,18,22,23■17:1,4,24,26■18:21■19:27■26:33,35,37,40,58,69,73,75-**M'R**-3:16■5:37■8:29,32,33■9:2,5■10:28■11:21■13:3■14:29,33,37,54,66,67,70,72■16:7-**LU**-5:8■6:14■8:45,51■9:20,28,32,33■12:41■18:28■22:8,34,54,55,58,60,61^{2},62■24:12-**JOH**-1:44■6:68■13:6,8,9,24,36,37■18:10,11,15,16^{2},17,18,25,26,27■20:2,3,4,6■21:2,3,7^{2},11,15,17,20,21-**AC**-1:13,15■2:14,37,38■3:1,3,4,6,11,12■4:8,13,19■5:3,8,9,15,29■8:14,20■9:32,34,38,39,40^{2}■10:5,9,13,14,17,18,19,21,23,25,26,32,34,44,45,46■11:2,4,7,13■12:3,5,6,7,11,13,14,16,18■15:7-**GA**-1:8■2:7,8,11,14-**1PE**-1:t,1-**2PE**-1:t,1

PETER'S-all=4074-**M'T**-8:14-**JOH**-1:40■6:8-**AC**-12:14

PETHAHIAH-all=6611-**1CH**-24:16-**EZR**-10:23-**NE**-9:5■11:24

PETHOR-**NU**-22:5(6604)-**DE**-23:4(6604)

PETHUEL-**JOE**-1:1(6602)

PEULTHAI-**1CH**-26:5(6469)

PHALEC-**LU**-3:35(5317)

PHALLU-**GE**-46:9(6396)

PHALTI-**1SA**-25:44(6406)

PHALTIEL-**2SA**-3:15(6409)

PHANUEL-**LU**-2:36(5328)

PHARAOH-all=6547-**GE**-12:15^{2},17,18,20■39:1■40:2,13,14,17,19■41:1,4,7,8^{2},9,10,14^{2},15,16^{2},17,25^{3},28^{2},32,33,34,35,37,38,39,41,42,44,45,46^{2},55^{2}■42:15,16■44:18■45:2,8,16,17,21■46:5,31,33■47:1,2,3^{2},4,5,7,8,9,10^{2},11,19,20,22^{2},23,24,26■50:4^{2},6,7-**EX**-1:11,19,22■2:5,15^{2}■3:10,11■4:21,22■5:1,2,5,6,10,15,20,21,23■6:1,11,12,13,27,29,30■7:1,2,4,7,9^{2},10^{2},11,15,20,23■8:1,8,9,12^{2},15,19,20,24,25,28,29^{2},30,31,32■9:1,7^{2},8,10,12,13,20,27,33,34,35■10:1,3,6,8,16,18,24,28■11:1,5,8,9,10■12:29,30■13:15,17■14:3,4,5,8,9,10,17,18,28■15:19■18:4,8,10-**DE**-6:22■7:8,18■11:3■29:2■34:11-**1SA**-6:6-**1KI**-3:1■9:16■11:1,18,19,20,21,22-**1KI**-17:17■18:21■23:35^{2}-**1CH**-4:18-**2CH**-8:11-**NE**-9:10-**PS**-135:9■136:15-**IS**-19:11^{2}■30:2,3■36:6-**JER**-25:19■46:17,25^{2}■47:1-**EZE**-17:17■29:2,3■30:21,22,25■31:2,18■32:2,31^{2},32■**N.T.**-**AC**-7:10,13-**RO**-9:17

PHARAOHHOPHRA-**JER**-44:30(6548)

PHARAOHNECHO-**JER**-46:2(6549)

PHARAOHNECHOH-all=6549-**2KI**-23:29,33,34,35

PHARAOH'S-all=6547-**GE**-12:15■37:36■40:7,11^{3},13,20,21■45:16■47:14,20,25,26-**EX**-2:7,8,9,10■5:14■7:3,13,14,22■8:19■10:7,11,20,27■11:3,10■14:4,23■15:4-**DE**-6:21-**1SA**-2:27-**1KI**-3:1■7:8■9:24■11:20^{2}-**SONG**-1:9-**JER**-37:5,7,11■43:9-**EZE**-30:24■**N.T.**-**AC**-7:21(5328)-**HEB**-11:24(5328)

PHARES-**M'T**-1:3^{2}(5329)-**LU**-3:33(5329)

PHAREZ-all=6557-**GE**-38:29■46:12^{2}-**NU**-26:20,21-**RU**-4:12,18-**1CH**-2:4,5■4:1■9:4

PHAROSH-**EZR**-8:3(6551)

PHARPAR-**2KI**-5:12(6554)

PHARZITES-**NU**-26:20(6558)

PHASEAH-**NE**-7:51(6454)

PHEBE-**RO**-16:1,subscr.(5402)

PHENICE-**AC**-11:19(5402)■15:3(5402)■27:12(5405)

PHENICIA-**AC**-21:2(5402)

PHICHOL-all=6369-**GE**-21:22,23■26:26

PHILADELPHIA-**RE**-1:11(5359)■3:7(5359)

PHILEMON-all=5371-**PH'M**-1:t,1■subscr.

PHILETUS-**2TI**-2:17(5372)

PHILIP-all=5376-**M'T**-10:3-**M'R**-3:18-**LU**-3:1■6:14-**JOH**-1:43,44,45,46,48■6:5,7■12:21,22^{2}■14:8,9-**AC**-1:13■6:5■8:5,6,12,13,26,29,30,31,34,35,37,38,39,40■21:8

PHILIPPI-all=5375&marked-**M'T**-16:13(2542)-**M'R**-8:27(2542)-**AC**-16:12■20:6-**1CO**-subscr.-**2CO**-subscr.-**PH'P**-1:1-**1TH**-2:2

PHILIPPIANS-all=5374-**PH'P**-1:t■4:15,subscr.

PHILIP'S-all=5376-**M'T**-14:3-**M'R**-6:17-**LU**-3:19

PHILISTIA-all=6429-**PS**-60:8■87:4■108:9

PHILISTIM-**GE**-10:14(6430)

PHILISTINE-all=6430-**1SA**-17:8,10,11,16,23,26^{2},32,33,36,37,40,41,42,43^{2},44,45,48^{2},49,50^{2},51,54,55,57^{2}■18:6■19:5■21:9■22:10-**2SA**-21:17

PHILISTINES-all=6430-**GE**-21:32■26:1,8,14,15,18-**EX**-13:17■23:31-**JOS**-13:2,3-**J'G**-3:3,31■10:6,7,11■13:1,5■14:1,2,3,4^{2}■15:3,5,6^{2},9,11,12,14,20■16:5,8,9,12,14,18^{2},20,21,23,27,28,30-**1SA**-4:1^{2},2^{2},3,6,7,9,10,17■5:1,2,8,11■6:1,2,4,12,16,17,18,21■7:3,7^{3},8,10^{2},11,13^{2},14^{2}■9:16■10:5■12:9■13:3^{2},4^{2},5,11,12,16,17,19,20,23■14:11^{2},19,21,22,30,31,36,37,46^{2},47,52■17:1,2,3,4,19,21,23,46,51,52^{2},53■18:17,21,25^{2},27,30■19:8■23:1,2^{2},3,4,5,27,28■24:1■27:1,7,11■28:1,4,5,15,19^{2}■29:1,2,3^{2},4^{2},7,9,11^{2}■30:16■31:1^{2},2^{2},7,8,9,11-**2SA**-1:20■3:14,18■5:17^{2},18,19^{2},22,24,25■8:1^{2},12■19:9■21:12^{2},15^{2},18,19■23:9,10,11^{2},12,13,14,16-**1KI**-4:21■15:27■16:15-**2KI**-8:2,3■18:8-**1CH**-1:12■10:1^{2},2^{2},7,8,9,11■11:13^{2},14,15,18■12:19^{2}■14:8^{2},9,10,13,15,16■18:1^{2},11■20:4,5-**2CH**-9:26■17:11■21:16■26:6^{2},7■28:18-**PS**-56:t■83:7-**IS**-2:6■9:12■11:14-**JER**-25:20■47:1,4^{2}-**EZE**-16:27,57■25:15,16-**AM**-1:8■6:2■9:7-**OB**-19-**ZEP**-2:5-**ZEC**-9:6

PHILISTINES'-all=6430-**GE**-21:34-**1SA**-14:1,4-**1CH**-11:16

PHILOLOGUS-**RO**-16:15(5378)

PHINEHAS-all=6372-**EX**-6:25-**NU**-25:7,11■31:6-**JOS**-22:13,30,31,32■24:33-**J'G**-20:28-**1SA**-1:3■2:34■4:4,11,17■14:3-**1CH**-6:4,50■9:20-**EZR**-7:5■8:2,33-**PS**-106:30

PHINEHAS'-**1SA**-4:19(6372)

PHLEGON-**RO**-16:14(5393)

PHRYGIA-all=5435-**AC**-2:10■16:6■18:23-**1TI**-subscr.

PHURAH-**J'G**-7:10(6513),11(6513)

PHUT-**GE**-10:6(6316)-**EZE**-27:10(6316)

PHUVAH-**GE**-46:13(6312)

PHYGELLUS-**2TI**-1:15(5436)

PI-BESETH-**EZE**-30:17(6364)

PI-HAHIROTH-all=6367-**EX**-14:2,9-**NU**-33:7,8

PILATE-all=4091-**M'T**-27:2,13,17,22,24,58^{2},62,65-**M'R**-15:1,2,4,5,9,12,14,15,43,44-**LU**-3:1■13:1■23:1,3,4,6,11,12,13,20,24,52-**JOH**-18:29,31,33,35,37,38■19:1,4,5,6,8,10,12,13,15,19,21,22,31,38^{2}-**AC**-3:13■4:27■13:28-**1TI**-6:13

PILDASH-**GE**-22:22(6394)

PILEHA-**NE**-10:24(6401)

PILTAI-**NE**-12:17(6408)

PINON-**GE**-36:41(6373)-**1CH**-1:52(6373)

PIRAM-**JOS**-10:3(6502)

PIRATHON-**J'G**-12:15(6552)

PIRATHONITE-all=6553-**J'G**-12:13,15-**2SA**-23:30-**1CH**-11:31■27:14

PISGAH-all=6449-**NU**-21:20■23:14-**DE**-3:27■4:49■34:1

PISIDIA-**AC**-13:14(4099)■14:24(4099)

PISON-**GE**-2:11(6376)

PISPAH-**1CH**-7:38(6462)

PITHOM-**EX**-1:11(6619)

PITHON-**1CH**-8:35(6377)■9:41(6377)

PLEIADES-**JOB**-9:9(3598)■38:31(3598)

POCHERETH-**EZR**-2:57(6380)-**NE**-7:59(6380)

POLLUX-**AC**-28:11(1359)

PONTIUS-all=4194-**M'T**-27:2-**LU**-3:1-**AC**-4:27-**1TI**-6:13

PONTUS-all=4195-**AC**-2:9■18:2-**1PE**-1:1

PORATHA-**ES**-9:8(6334)

PORCIUS-**AC**-24:27(4201)

POTIPHAR-**GE**-37:36(6318)■39:1(6318)

POTIPHERAH-all=6319-GE-41:45,50■46:20
PRAETORIUM-M'R-15:16(4232)
PRISCA-2TI-4:19(4251)
PRISCILLA-all=4252-AC-18:2,18,26-RO-16:3-1CO-16:19
PROCHORUS-AC-6:5(4402)
PTOLEMAIS-AC-21:7(4424)
PUA-NU-26:23(6312)
PUAH-EX-1:15(6326)-J'G-10:1(6312)-1CH-7:1(6312)
PUBLIUS-AC-28:7(4196),8(4196)
PUDENS-2TI-4:21(4227)
PUHITES-1CH-2:53(6336)
PUL-all=6322-2KI-15:19^2-1CH-5:26-IS-66:19
PUNITES-NU-26:23(6324)
PUNON-NU-33:42(6325),43(6325)
PUT-1CH-1:8(3166)-NA-3:9(3166)
PUTEOLI-AC-28:13(4223)
PUTIEL-EX-6:25(6317)
PYGARG-DE-14:5(1787)

Q

QUARTUS-RO-16:23(2890)

R

RAAMAH-all=7484-GE-10:7^2-1CH-1:9^2-EZE-27:22
RAAMIAH-NE-7:7(7485)
RAAMSES-EX-1:11(7486)
RABBAH-all=7237-JOS-13:25■15:60-2SA-11:1■12:26,27,29■17:27-1CH-20:1^2-JER-49:2,3-EZE-25:5-AM-1:14
RABBATH-DE-3:11(7237)-EZE-21:20(7237)
RABBITH-JOS-19:20(7245)
RABBONI-JOH-20:16(4462)
RAB-MAG-JER-39:3(7248),13(7248)
RAB-SARIS-all=7249-2KI-18:17-JER-39:3,13
RAB-SHAKEH-all=7262-2KI-18:17,19,26,27,28,37■19:4,8
RABSHAKEH-all=7262-IS-36:2,4,11,12,13,22■37:4,8
RACHAB-M'T-1:5(4477)
RACHAL-1SA-30:29(7403)
RACHEL-all=7354-GE-29:6,9,10,11,12,16,17,18^2,20,25,28,29,30^2,31■30:1^2,2,6,8,14,15,22,25■31:4,14,19,32,34■33:1,2,7■35:16,19,24■46:19,22,25■48:7-RU-4:11■**N.T**-M'T-2:18(4478)
RACHEL'S-all=7354-GE-30:7■31:33■35:20,25-1SA-10:2
RADDAI-1CH-2:14(7288)
RAGAU-LU-3:35(4466)
RAGUEL-NU-10:29(7467)
RAHAB-all=7343=&marked-JOS-2:1,3■6:17,23,25-PS-87:4(7294)■89:10(7294)-IS-51:9(7294)■**N.T.**-HEB-11:31(4460)-JAS-2:25(4460)
RAHAM-1CH-2:44(7357)
RAHEL-JER-31:15(7354)
RAKEM-1CH-7:16(7552)
RAKKATH-JOS-19:35(7557)
RAKKON-JOS-19:46(7542)
RAM-all=7410-RU-4:19-1CH-2:9,10,25,27-JOB-32:2
RAMA-M'T-2:18(4471)
RAMAH-all=7414-JOS-18:25■19:29,36-J'G-4:5■19:13-1SA-1:19■2:11■7:17■8:4■15:34■16:13■19:18,19,22^2,23^2■20:1■22:6■25:1■28:3-1KI-15:17,21,22-2KI-8:29-2CH-16:1,5,6■22:6-EZR-2:26-NE-7:30■11:33-IS-10:29-JER-31:15■40:1-HO-5:8
RAMATH-JOS-19:8(7418)
RAMATHAIM-ZOPHIM-1SA-1:1(7436)
RAMATHITE-1CH-27:27(7435)
RAMATHLEHI-J'G-15:17(7437)
RAMATH-MIZEPH-JOS-13:26(7434)
RAMESES-all=7486-GE-47:11-EX-12:37-NU-33:3,5
RAMIAH-EZR-10:25(7422)
RAMOTH-all=7216&marked-DE-4:43-JOS-20:8■21:38-1SA-30:27(7418)-1KI-22:3-1CH-6:73,80-EZR-10:29(3406)
RAMOTH-GILEAD-all=7433-1KI-4:13■22:4,6,12,15,20,29-2KI-8:28■9:1,4,14-2CH-18:2,3,5,11,14,19,28■22:5
RAPHA-1CH-8:2(7498),37(7498)
RAPHU-NU-13:9(7505)
REAIA-1CH-5:5(7211)
REAIAH-all=7211-1CH-4:2-EZR-2:47-NE-7:50
REBA-NU-31:8(7254)-JOS-13:21(7254)
REBECCA-RO-9:10(4479)
REBEKAH-all=7259-GE-22:23■24:15,29,30,45,51,53,58,59,60,61^2,64,67■25:20,21,28■26:7,8,35■27:5,6,11,15,42,46■28:5■49:31
REBEKAH'S-GE-29:12(7259)■35:8(7259)
RECAH-1CH-4:12(7397)
RECHAB-all=7394-2SA-4:2,5,6,9-2KI-10:15,23-1CH-2:55-NE-3:14-JER-35:6,8,14,16,19
RECHABITES-all=7397-JER-35:2,3,5,18
RED-all=5488&marked-EX-10:19■13:18■15:4,22■23:31-NU-14:25■21:4,14(5492)■33:10,11-DE-1:1(5489),40■2:1■11:4-JOS-2:10■4:23■24:6-J'G-11:16-1KI-9:26-NE-9:9-PS-106:7,9,22■136:13,15-JER-49:21■**N.T.**-AC-7:36(2281)-HEB-11:29(2281)
REELAIAH-EZR-2:2(7480)
REGEM-1CH-2:47(7276)
REGEM-MELECH-ZEC-7:2(7278)
REHABIAH-all=7345-1CH-23:17^2■24:21■26:25
REHOB-all=7340-NU-13:21-JOS-19:28,30■21:31-J'G-1:31-2SA-8:3,12■10:8-1CH-6:75-NE-10:11
REHOBOAM-all=7346-1KI-11:43■12:1,3,6,12,17,18^2,21^2,23,27^2■14:21^2,25,27,29,30,31■15:6-1CH-3:10-2CH-9:31■10:1,3,6,12,13,17,18^2■11:1^2,3,5,17,18,21,22■12:1,2,5,10,13^2,15^2,16■13:7^2
REHOBOTH-all=7344-GE-10:11■26:22■36:37-1CH-1:48
REHUM-all=7348-EZR-2:2■4:8,9,17,23-NE-3:17■10:25■12:3
REI-1KI-1:8(7472)
REKEM-all=7552-NU-31:8-JOS-13:21■18:27-1CH-2:43,44
REMALIAH-all=7425-2KI-15:25,27,30,32,37■16:1,5-2CH-28:6-IS-7:1,4,5
REMALIAH'S-IS-7:9(7425)■8:6(7425)
REMETH-JOS-19:21(7432)
REMMON-JOS-19:7(7417)
REMMON-METHOAR-JOS-19:13(7417)
REMPHAN-AC-7:43(4481)
REPHAEL-1CH-26:7(7501)
REPHAH-1CH-7:25(7506)
REPHAIAH-all=7509-1CH-3:21■4:42■7:2■9:43-NE-3:9
REPHAIM-all=7497-2SA-5:18,22■23:13-1CH-11:15■14:19-IS-17:5
REPHAIMS-GE-14:5(7497)■15:20(7497)
REPHIDIM-all=7508-EX-17:1,8■19:2-NU-33:14,15
RESEN-GE-10:12(7449)
RESHEPH-1CH-7:25(7566)
REU-all=7466-GE-11:18,19,20,21-1CH-1:25
REUBEN-all=7205&marked-GE-29:32■30:14■35:22,23■37:21,22,29■42:22,37■46:8,9■48:5■49:3-EX-1:2■6:14^2-NU-1:5,20,21■2:10^2,16■7:30■10:18■13:4■16:1■26:5^2■32:1,2,6,25,29,31,33,37■34:14(7206)-DE-11:6■27:13■33:6-JOS-4:12■13:15,23^2■15:6■18:7,17■20:8■21:7,36■22:9,10,11,13,15,21,25,30,31,32,33,34-J'G-5:15,16-1CH-2:1■5:1,3,18■6:63,78-EZE-48:6,7,31■**N.T.**RE-7:5(4502)
REUBENITE-1CH-11:42(7206)
REUBENITES-all=7206-NU-26:7-DE-3:12,16■4:43■29:8-JOS-1:12■12:6■13:8■22:1-2KI-10:33-1CH-5:6,26■11:42■12:37■26:32■27:16
REUEL-all=7467-GE-36:4,10,13,17^2-EX-2:18■NU-2:14-1CH-1:35,37■9:8
REUMAH-GE-22:24(7208)
REZEPH-2KI-19:12(7530)-IS-37:12(7530)
REZIA-1CH-7:39(7525)
REZIN-all=7526-2KI-15:37■16:5,6,9-EZR-2:48-NE-7:50-IS-7:1,4,8■8:6■9:11
REZON-1KI-11:23(7331)
RHEGIUM-AC-28:13(4484)
RHESA-LU-3:27(4488)
RHODA-AC-12:13(4498)
RHODES-AC-21:1(4499)
RIBAI-2SA-23:29(7380)-1CH-11:31(7380)
RIBLAH-all=7247-NU-34:11-2KI-23:33■25:6,20,21-JER-39:5,6■52:9,10,26,27
RIMMON-all=7417-JOS-15:32-J'G-20:45,47^2■21:13-2SA-4:2,5,9-2KI-5:18^3-1CH-4:32■6:77-EC-14:10
RIMMON-PAREZ-NU-33:19(7428),20(7428)
RINNAH-1CH-4:20(7441)
RIPHATH-GE-10:3(7384)-1CH-1:6(7384)
RISSAH-NU-33:21(7446),22(7446)
RITHMAH-NU-33:18(7575),19(7575)
RIZPAH-all=7532-2SA-3:7■21:8,10,11
ROBOAM-M'T-1:7(4497)
ROGELIM-2SA-17:27(7274)■19:31(7274)
ROHGAH-1CH-7:34(7303)
ROMAMTI-EZER-1CH-25:4(7320),31(7320)
ROMAN-all=4514-AC-22:25,26,27,29■23:27
ROMANS-all=4514-JOH-11:48-AC-16:21,37,38■25:16■28:17-RO-1:t,subscr.
ROME-all=4516-AC-2:10■18:2■19:21■23:11■28:14,16-RO-1:7,15-GA-subscr.-EPH-subscr.-PH'P-subscr.-COL-subscr.-2TI-1:17,subscr.-PH'M-subscr.
ROSH-GE-46:21(7220)
RUFUS-M'R-15:21(4504)-RO-16:13(4504)
RUHAMAH-HO-2:1(7355)
RUMAH-2KI-23:36(7316)
RUTH-all=7327-RU-1:4,14,16,22■2:2,8,21,22■3:9■4:5,10,13■**N.T**-M'T-1:5(4503)

S

SABAOTH-RO-9:29(4519)-JAS-5:4(4519)
SABEANS-JOB-1:15(7614)-IS-45:14(5436)-EZE-23:42(5433)-JOE-3:8(7615)
SABTA-1CH-1:9(5454)
SABTAH-GE-10:7(5454)
SABTECHA-1CH-1:9(5455)
SABTECHAH-GE-10:7(5455)
SACAR-1CH-11:35(7940)■26:4(7940)
SADDUCEES-all=4523-M'T-3:7■16:1,6,11,12■22:23,34-M'R-12:18-LU-20:27-AC-4:1■5:17■23:6,7,8
SADOC-M'T-1:14(4524)
SALA-LU-3:35(4527)
SALAH-all=7974-GE-10:24■11:12,13,14,15
SALAMIS-AC-13:5(4529)
SALATHIEL-1CH-3:17(7597)■**N.T.**-all=4528-M'T-1:12^2-LU-3:27
SALCAH-all=5548-JOS-12:5■13:11-1CH-5:11
SALCHAH-DE-3:10(5548)
SALEM-GE-14:18(8004)-PS-76:2(8004)■**N.T.**-HEB-7:1(4532),2(4532)
SALIM-JOH-3:23(4530)
SALLAI-NE-11:8(5543)■12:20(5543)
SALLU-all=5543-1CH-9:7-NE-11:7■12:7
SALMA-all=8007-1CH-2:11,51,54
SALMON-RU-4:20(8009),21(8012)-PS-68:14(6726)■**N.T.**-all=4533-M'T-1:4,5-LU-3:32
SALMONE-AC-27:7(4534)
SALOME-M'R-15:40(4539)■16:1(4539)
SALU-NU-25:14(5543)
SAMARIA-all=8111&marked-1KI-13:32■16:24^2,28,29,32■18:2■20:1,10,17,34,43■21:1,18■22:10,37^2,38,51-2KI-1:2,3■2:25■3:1,6■5:3■6:19,20^2,24,25■7:1,18■10:1^2,12,17^2,35,36■13:1,6,9,10,13■14:14,16,23■15:8,13,14^2,17,23,25,27■17:1,5,6,24^2,26,28■18:9,10,34■21:13■23:18,19-2CH-18:2,9■22:9■25:13,24■28:8,9,15-EZR-4:10(8115),17(8115)-NE-4:2-IS-7:9^2■8:4■9:9■10:9,10,11■36:19-JER-23:13■31:5■41:5-EZE-16:46,51,53,55■23:4,33-HO-7:1■8:5,6■

10:5,7■13:16-AM-3:9,12■4:1■6:1■8:14-OB-19-MIC-1:1,5,6■N.T.-all=4540-LU-17:11-JOH-4:4,5,7,9^2-AC-1:8■8:1,5,9,14■9:31■15:3

SAMARITAN-all=4541-LU-10:33■17:16-JOH-8:48

SAMARITANS-2KI-17:29(8118)■N.T.-all=4541-M'T-10:5-LU-9:52-JOH-4:9,39,40-AC-8:25

SAMGAR-NEBO-JER-39:3(5562)

SAMLAH-all=8072-GE-36:36,37-1CH-1:47,48

SAMOS-AC-20:15(4544)

SAMOTHRACIA-AC-16:11(4543)

SAMSON-all=8123-J'G-13:24■14:1,3,5,7,10,12■15:1,3,4,6,7,10,11,12,16■16:1,2,3,6,7,9,10,12,13,14,20,23,25^2,26,27,28,29,30■N.T.-HEB-11:32(4546)

SAMSON'S-all=8123-J'G-14:15,16,20

SAMUEL-all=8050-1SA-1:t■1:20■2:18,21,26■3:1,3,4,6^2,7,8,9^2,10^2,11,15^2,16,18,19,20,21■4:1■7:3,5,6,8,9^2,10,12,13,15■8:1,4,6^2,7,10,19,21,22^2■9:14,15,17,18,19,22,23,24sup,24,26^2,27■10:1,9,14,15,16,17,20,24,25^2■11:7,12,14■12:1,6,11,18^2,19,20■13:8^2,10,11,13,15■15:1,10,11,12^2,13,14,16,17,20,22,24,26,27,28,31,32,33^2,34,35^2■16:1,2,4,7,8,10^2,11^2,13^2■19:18^2,20,22,24■25:1■28:3,11,12,14,15,16,20-2SA-1:t-1CH-6:28■9:22■11:3■26:28■29:29-2CH-35:18-PS-99:6-JER-15:1■N.T.-all=4545-AC-3:24■13:20-HEB-11:32

SANBALLAT-all=5571-NE-2:10,19■4:1,7■6:1,2,5,12,14■13:28

SANSANNAH-JOS-15:31(5578)

SAPH-2SA-21:18(5593)

SAPHIR-MIC-1:11(8208)

SAPPHIRA-AC-5:1(4551)

SARA-HEB-11:11(4564)-1PE-3:6(4564)

SARAH-all=8283-GE-17:15,17,19,21■18:6,9,10^2,11^2,12,13,14,15■20:2^2,14,16,18■21:1^2,2,3,6,7,9,12■23:1^2,2^2,19■24:36■25:10■49:31-NU-26:46(8294)-IS-51:2■N.T.-RO-9:9(4564)

SARAH'S-GE-24:67(8283)■25:12(8283)■N.T.-RO-4:19(4564)

SARAI-all=8297-GE-11:29,30,31■12:5,11,17■16:1,2^2,3,5,6^2,8■17:15^2

SARAI'S-GE-16:8(8297)

SARAPH-1CH-4:22(8315)

SARDIS-all=4554-RE-1:11■3:1,4

SARDITES-NU-26:26(5625)

SAREPTA-LU-4:26(4558)

SARGON-IS-20:1(5623)

SARID-JOS-19:10(8301),12(8301)

SARON-AC-9:35(4565)

SARSECHIM-JER-39:3(8310)

SARUCH-LU-3:35(4562)

SAUL-all=7586-GE-36:37,38-1SA-9:2,3,5,7,8,10,15,17,18,19,21,22,24^2,25,26^2,27■10:11,12,16,21,26■11:4,5^2,6,7,11,12,13,15^2■13:1,2^2,3,4^2,7,9,10,11,13,15,16,22^2■14:1,2,16,17,18,19^2,20,21,24,33,34,35,36,37,38,40,41^2,42,43,44,45,46,47,49,51,52^2■15:1,4,5,6,7,9,11,12^2,13,15,16,20,24,26,31^2,34^2,35^3■16:1,2,14,17,19,20,21,22,23^2■17:2,8,11,12,13,14,15,19,31,32,33,34,37,38,39,55,57,58■18:1,2,5^2,6,7,8,9,10,11,12^2,13,15,17^2,18,20,21^2,22,24,25^2,27,28,29^2,30■19:1,2,4,6^2,7,9,10,11,14,15,17^2,18,19,20^2,21^2,24■20:26,27,28,32,33■21:7^2,10,11■22:6^2,7,9,12,13,21,22■23:7^2,8,9,10,11,12,13,14,15,17^2,19,21,24,25^2,26^3,27,28■24:1,2,3,7^2,8^2,9,16^3,22■25:44■26:1,2,3^2,4,5^3,6,7,17,21,25^2■27:1^2,4■28:3,4,5,6,7,8,9,10,12^2,13,14,15^2,20,21,25■29:3,5■31:2,3,4^2,5,6,7,8,11,12-2SA-1:1,2,4,5,6,12,17,21,22,23,24■2:4,5,7,8,12,15■3:1^2,6^2,7,8,10■4:4,8^2,10■5:2■6:20,23■7:15■9:1,2,3,6,7,9■12:7■16:5,8■19:17,24■21:1,2,4,6,7^2,8^2,11,12^2,13,14■22:1-1CH-5:10■8:33^2■9:39^2■10:2^2,3,4^2,5,6,7,8,11,12,13■11:2■12:1,19^2,23,29^2■13:3■15:29■26:28-PS-18:t■52:t■54:t■57:t■59:t-IS-10:29■N.T.-all=4569-AC-7:58■8:1,3■9:1,4,8,11,17,19,22,24,26■11:25,30■12:25■13:1,2,7,9,21■22:7,13■26:14

SAUL'S-all=7586-1SA-9:3■10:14,15■14:50^2■16:15■18:5,10,19,20,23,28■19:2,10■20:25,30■23:16■24:4,5■26:12■31:2-2SA-2:8,10■3:13,14■4:1,2,4■6:16■9:9-1CH-12:2

SCEVA-AC-19:14(4630)

SCYTHIAN-COL-3:11(4658)

SEBA-all=5434-GE-10:7-1CH-1:9-PS-72:10-IS-43:3

SEBAT-ZEC-1:7(7627)

SECACAH-JOS-15:61(5527)

SECHU-1SA-19:22(7906)

SECUNDUS-AC-20:4(4580)

SEGUB-all=7687-1KI-16:34-1CH-2:21,22

SEIR-all=8165-GE-14:6■32:3■33:14,16■36:8,9,20,21,30-NU-24:18-DE-1:2,44■2:1,4,5,8,12,22,29■33:2-JOS-11:17■12:7■15:10■24:4-J'G-5:4-1CH-1:38■4:42-2CH-20:10,22,23^2■25:11,14-IS-21:11-EZE-25:8■35:2,3,7,15

SEIRATH-J'G-3:26(8167)

SELA-IS-16:1(5554)

SELAH-2KI-14:7(5554)

SELA-HAMMAHLEKOTH-1SA-23:28(5555)

SELED-1CH-2:30^2(5540)

SELEUCIA-AC-13:4(4581)

SEM-LU-3:36(4590)

SEMACHIAH-1CH-26:7(5565)

SEMEI-LU-3:26(4584)

SENAAH-EZR-2:35(5570)-NE-7:38(5570)

SENEH-1SA-14:4(5573)

SENIR-1CH-5:23(8149)-EZE-27:5(8149)

SENNACHERIB-all=5576-2KI-18:13■19:16,20,36-2CH-32:1,2,9,10,22-IS-36:1■37:17,21,37

SENUAH-NE-11:9(5574)

SEORIM-1CH-24:8(8188)

SEPHAR-GE-10:30(5611)

SEPHARAD-OB-20(5614)

SEPHARVAIM-all=5617-2KI-17:24,31■18:34■19:13-IS-36:19■37:13

SEPHARVITES-2KI-17:31(5616)

SERAH-GE-46:17(8294)-1CH-7:30(8294)

SERAIAH-all=8303-2SA-8:17-2KI-25:18,23-1CH-4:13,14,35■6:14-EZR-2:2■7:1-NE-10:2■11:11■12:1,12-JER-36:26■40:8■51:59^2,61■52:24

SERED-GE-46:14(5624)-NU-26:26(5624)

SERGIUS-AC-13:7(4588)

SERUG-all=8286-GE-11:20,21,22,23-1CH-1:26

SETH-all=8352-GE-4:25,26■5:3,4,6,7,8■N.T.-LU-3:38(4589)

SETHUR-NU-13:13(5639)

SHAALABBIN-JOS-19:42(8169)

SHAALBIM-J'G-1:35(8169)-1KI-4:9(8169)

SHAALBONITE-all=8170-2SA-23:32(8170)-1CH-11:33(8170)

SHAAPH-1CH-2:47(8174),49(8174)

SHAARAIM-1SA-17:52(8189)-1CH-4:31(8189)

SHAASHGAZ-ES-2:14(8190)

SHABBETHAI-all=7678-EZR-10:15-NE-8:7■11:16

SHACHIA-1CH-8:10(7634)

SHADRACH-all=7715&marked-DA-1:7(7714)■2:49■3:12,13,14,16,19,20,22,23,26^2,28,29,30

SHAGE-1CH-11:34(7681)

SHAHAR-PS-22:t(7837)

SHAHARAIM-1CH-8:8(7842)

SHAHAZIMAH-JOS-19:22(7831)

SHALEM-GE-33:18(8003)

SHALIM-1SA-9:4(8171)

SHALISHA-1SA-9:4(8031)

SHALL-all supplied

SHALLECHETH-1CH-26:16(7996)

SHALLUM-all=7967-2KI-15:10,13,14,15■22:14-1CH-2:40,41■3:15■4:25■6:12,13■7:13■9:17^2,19,31-2CH-28:12■34:22-EZR-2:42■7:2■10:24,42-NE-3:12■7:45-JER-22:11■32:7■35:4

SHALLUN-NE-3:15(7968)

SHALMAI-EZR-2:46(8073)-NE-7:48(8014)

SHALMAN-HO-10:14(8020)

SHALMANESER-2KI-17:3(8022)■18:9(8022)

SHALT-all supplied

SHAMA-1CH-11:44(8091)

SHAMED-1CH-8:12(8106)

SHAMER-1CH-6:46(8106)■7:34(8106)

SHAMGAR-J'G-3:31(8044)■5:6(8044)

SHAMHUTH-1CH-27:8(8049)

SHAMIR-all=8069&marked-JOS-15:48-J'G-10:1,2-1CH-24:24(8053)

SHAMMA-1CH-7:37(8037)

SHAMMAH-all=8048-GE-36:13,17-1SA-16:9■17:13-2SA-23:11,25,33-1CH-1:37

SHAMMAI-all=8060-1CH-2:28^2,32,44,45■4:17

SHAMMOTH-1CH-11:27(8054)

SHAMMUA-all=8051-NU-13:4-1CH-14:4-NE-11:17■12:18

SHAMMUAH-2SA-5:14(8051)

SHAMSHERAI-1CH-8:26(8125)

SHAPHAM-1CH-5:12(8223)

SHAPHAN-all=8227-2KI-22:3,8^2,9,10^2,12^2,14■25:22-2CH-34:8,15^2,16,18^2,20^2-JER-26:24■29:3■36:10,11,12■39:14■40:5,9,11■41:2■43:6-EZE-8:11

SHAPHAT-all=8202-NU-13:5-1KI-19:16,19-2KI-3:11■6:31-1CH-3:22■5:12■27:29

SHAPHER-NU-33:23(8234),24(8234)

SHARAI-EZR-10:40(8298)

SHARAIM-JOS-15:36(8189)

SHARAR-2SA-23:33(8325)

SHAREZER-2KI-19:37(8272)-IS-37:38(8272)

SHARON-all=8289-1CH-5:16■27:29-SONG-2:1-IS-33:9■35:2■65:10

SHARONITE-1CH-27:29(8290)

SHARUHEN-JOS-19:6(8287)

SHASHAI-EZR-10:40(8343)

SHASHAK-1CH-8:14(8349),25(8349)

SHAUL-all=7586-GE-46:10-EX-6:15-NU-26:13-1CH-1:48,49■4:24■6:24

SHAULITES-NU-26:13(7587)

SHAVEH-GE-14:5(7741),17(7740)

SHAVSHA-1CH-18:16(7798)

SHE-O.T.supplied■N.T.-all=3756

SHEAL-EZR-10:29(7594)

SHEALTIEL-all=7597-EZR-3:2,8■5:2-NE-12:1-HAG-1:1,12,14■2:2,23

SHEARIAH-1CH-8:38(8187)■9:44(8187)

SHEAR-JASHUB-IS-7:3(7610)

SHEBA-all=7614&marked-GE-10:7,28■25:3-JOS-19:2(7652)-2SA-20:1(7652),2(7652),6(7652),7(7652),10(7652),13(7652),21(7652),22(7652)-1KI-10:1,4,10,13-1CH-1:9,22,32■5:13(7652)-2CH-9:1,3,9,12-JOB-6:19-PS-72:10,15-IS-60:6-JER-6:20-EZE-27:22,23■38:13

SHEBAH-GE-26:33(7656)

SHEBAM-NU-32:3(7643)

SHEBANIAH-all=7645-1CH-15:24-NE-9:4,5■10:4,10,12■12:14

SHEBARIM-JOS-7:5(7671)

SHEBER-1CH-2:48(7669)

SHEBNA-all=7644-2KI-18:18,26,37■19:2-IS-22:15■36:3,11,22■37:2

SHEBUEL-all=7619-1CH-23:16■25:4■26:24

SECANIAH-1CH-24:11(7935)-2CH-31:15(7935)

SHECHANIAH-all=7935-1CH-3:21,22-EZR-8:3,5■10:2-NE-3:29■6:18■12:3

SHECHEM-all=7927&marked-GE-33:18■34:2,4,6,8,11,13,18,20,24,26■35:4■37:12,13,14-NU-26:31(7928)-JOS-17:2(7928),7■20:7■21:21■24:1,25,32^2-J'G-8:31■9:1,2,3,6^2,7,18,20^2,23^2,24,25,26^2,28^2,31,34,39,41,46,47,49,57■21:19-1KI-12:1^2,25-1CH-6:67■7:19(7928),28-2CH-10:1^2-PS-60:6■108:7-JER-41:5

SHECHEMITES-NU-26:31(7930)

SHECHEM'S-GE-33:19(7927)■34:26(7927)

SHEDEUR-all=7707-NU-1:5■2:10■7:30,35■10:18

SHEHARIAH-1CH-8:26(7841)

SHELAH-all=7956&marked-GE-38:5,11,14,26■46:12-NU-26:20-1CH-1:18(7974),24■2:3■4:21

SHELANITES-NU-26:20(8024)

SHELEMIAH-all=8018-1CH-26:14-EZR-10:39,41-NE-3:30■13:13-JER-36:14,26■37:3,13■38:1

SHELEPH-GE-10:26(8026)-1CH-1:20(8026)

SHELESH-1CH-7:35(8028)

SHELOMI-NU-34:27(8015)

SHELOMITH-all=8019&marked-LE-24:11-1CH-3:19■23:9(8013),18(9019)■26:25(8013),26(8013),28-2CH-11:20-EZR-8:10

SHELOMOTH-1CH-24:22(8013)

SHELUMIEL-all=8017-NU-1:6■2:12■7:36,41■10:19

SHEM-all=8035-GE-5:32■6:10■7:13■9:18,23,26,27■10:1,21,22,31■11:10^{2},11-1CH-1:4,17,24

SHEMA-all=8087-JOS-15:26-1CH-2:43,44■5:8■8:13-NE-8:4

SHEMAAH-1CH-12:3(8093)

SHEMAIAH-all=8098-1KI-12:22-1CH-3:22^{2}■4:37■5:4■9:14,16■15:8,11■24:6■26:4,6,7-2CH-11:2■12:5,7,15■17:8■29:14■31:15■35:9-EZR-8:13,16■10:21,31-NE-3:29■6:10■10:8■11:15■12:6,18,34,35,36,42-JER-26:20■29:24,31^{2},32■36:12

SHEMARIAH-all=8114-1CH-12:5-2CH-11:19-EZR-10:32,41

SHEMEBER-GE-14:2(8038)

SHEMER-1KI-16:24^{2}(8016)

SHEMIDA-all=8061-NU-26:32(8061)-JOS-17:2(8061)

SHEMIDAH-1CH-7:19(8061)

SHEMIDAITES-NU-26:32(8062)

SHEMINITH-all=8067-1CH-15:21-PS-6:t■12:t

SHEMIRAMOTH-all=8070-1CH-15:18,20■16:5-2CH-17:8

SHEMUEL-all=8050-NU-34:20-1CH-6:33■7:2

SHEN-1SA-7:12(8129)

SHENAZAR-1CH-3:18(8137)

SHENIR-DE-3:9(8149)-SONG-4:8(8149)

SHEPHAM-NU-34:10(8221),11(8221)

SHEPHATIAH-all=8203-2SA-3:4-1CH-3:3■9:8■12:5■27:16-2CH-21:2-EZR-2:4,57■8:8-NE-7:9,59■11:4-JER-38:1

SHEPHI-1CH-1:40(8195)

SHEPHO-GE-36:23(8195)

SHEPHUPHAN-1CH-8:5(8197)

SHERAH-1CH-7:24(7609)

SHEREBIAH-all=8274-EZR-8:18,24-NE-8:7■9:4,5■10:12■12:8,24

SHERESH-1CH-7:16(8329)

SHEREZER-ZEC-7:2(8272)

SHESHACH-JER-25:26(8347)■51:41(8347)

SHESHAI-all=8344-NU-13:22-JOS-15:14-J'G-1:10

SHESHAN-all=8348-1CH-2:31^{2},34^{2},35

SHESHBAZZAR-all=8339-EZR-1:8,11■5:14,16

SHETH-NU-24:17(8352)-1CH-1:1(8352)

SHETHAR-ES-1:14(8369)

SHETHAR-BOZNAI-all=8370-EZR-5:3,6■6:6,13

SHEVA-2SA-20:25(7724)-1CH-2:49(7724)

SHIBMAH-NU-32:38(7643)

SHICRON-JOS-15:11(7942)

SHIGGAION-PS-7:t(7692)

SHIGIONOTH-HAB-3:1(7692)

SHIHON-JOS-19:19(7866)

SHIHOR-1CH-13:5(7883)

SHIHOR-LIBNATH-JOS-19:26(7884)

SHILHI-1KI-22:42(7977)-2CH-20:31(7977)

SHILHIM-JOS-15:32(7978)

SHILLEM-GE-46:24(8006)-NU-26:49(8006)

SHILLEMITES-NU-26:49(8016)

SHILOAH-IS-8:6(7975)

SHILOH-all=7887&marked-GE-49:10(7886)-JOS-18:1,8,9,10■19:51■21:2■22:9,12-J'G-18:31■21:12,19,21^{2}-1SA-1:3,9,24■2:14■3:21^{2}■4:3,4,12■14:3-1KI-2:27■14:2,4-PS-78:60-JER-7:12,14■26:6,9■41:5

SHILONI-NE-11:5(8023)

SHILONITE-all=7888-1KI-11:29■12:15■15:29-2CH-9:29■10:15

SHILONITES-1CH-9:5(7888)

SHILSHAH-1CH-7:37(8030)

SHIMEA-all=8092-1CH-3:5■6:30,39■20:7

SHIMEAH-all=8093&marked-2SA-13:3,32■21:21(8096)-1CH-8:32

SHIMEAM-1CH-9:38(8043)

SHIMEATH-2KI-12:21(8100)-2CH-24:26(8100)

SHIMEATHITES-1CH-2:55(8101)

SHIMEI-all=8096&marked-NU-3:18-2SA-16:5,7,13■19:16,18,21,23-1KI-1:8■2:8,36,38^{2},39^{2},40^{2},41,42,44■4:18-1CH-3:19■4:26,27■5:4■6:17,29,42■23:7,9,10^{2}■25:17■27:27-2CH-29:14■31:12,13-EZR-10:23,33,38-ES-2:5-ZEC-12:13(8097)

SHIMEON-EZR-10:31(8095)

SHIMHI-1CH-8:21(8096)

SHIMI-EX-6:17(8096)

SHIMITES-NU-3:21(8097)

SHIMMA-1CH-2:13(8092)

SHIMON-1CH-4:20(7889)

SHIMRATH-1CH-8:21(8119)

SHIMRI-all=8113-1CH-4:37■11:45-2CH-29:13

SHIMRITH-2CH-24:26(8116)

SHIMROM-1CH-7:1(8110)

SHIMRON-all=8110-GE-46:13-NU-26:24-JOS-11:1■19:15

SHIMRONITES-NU-26:24(8117)

SHIMRON-MERON-JOS-12:20(8112)

SHIMSHAI-all=8124-EZR-4:8,9,17,23

SHINAB-GE-14:2(8134)

SHINAR-all=8152-GE-10:10■11:2■14:1,9-IS-11:11-DA-1:2-ZEC-5:11

SHIPHI-1CH-4:37(8230)

SHIPHMITE-1CH-27:27(8225)

SHIPHRAH-EX-1:15(8237)

SHIPHTAN-NU-34:24(8204)

SHISHA-1KI-4:3(7894)

SHISHAK-all=7895-1KI-11:40■14:25-2CH-12:2,5^{2},7,9

SHITRAI-1CH-27:29(7861)

SHITTAH-IS-41:19(7848)

SHITTIM-all=7851-NU-25:1-JOS-2:1■3:1-JOE-3:18-MIC-6:5

SHIZA-1CH-11:42(7877)

SHOA-EZE-23:23(7772)

SHOBAB-all=7727-2SA-5:14-1CH-2:18■3:5■14:4

SHOBACH-2SA-10:16(7731),18(7731)

SHOBAI-EZR-2:42(7630)-NE-7:45(7630)

SHOBAL-all=7732-GE-36:20,23,29-1CH-1:38,40■2:50,52■4:1,2

SHOBEK-NE-10:24(7733)

SHOBI-2SA-17:27(7629)

SHOCHO-2CH-28:18(7755)

SHOCHOH-1SA-17:1^{2},(7755)

SHOCO-2CH-11:7(7755)

SHOHAM-1CH-24:27(7719)

SHOMER-all=7763-2KI-12:21(7763)-1CH-7:32(7763)

SHOPHACH-1CH-19:16(7780),18(7780)

SHOPHAN-NU-32:35(5855)

SHOSHANNIM-PS-45:t(7799)■69:t(7799)

SHOSHANNIM-EDUTH-PS-80:t(7802)

SHUA-1CH-2:3(7770)■7:32(7774)

SHUAH-GE-25:2(7744)■38:2(7770),12(7770)-1CH-1:32(7744)■4:11(7746)

SHUAL-1SA-13:17(7777)-1CH-7:36(7777)

SHUBAEL-1CH-24:20(2619)■25:20(2619)

SHUHAM-NU-26:42(7748)

SHUHAMITES-NU-26:42(7749),43(7749)

SHUHITE-all=7747-JOB-2:11■8:1■18:1■25:1■42:9

SHULAMITE-SONG-6:13^{2}(7759)

SHUMATHITES-1CH-2:53(8126)

SHUNAMMITE-all=7767-1KI-1:3,15■2:17,21,22-2KI-4:12,25,36

SHUNEM-all=7766-JOS-19:18-1SA-28:4-2KI-4:8

SHUNI-GE-46:16(7764)-NU-26:15(7764)

SHUNITES-NU-26:15(7765)

SHUPHAM-NU-26:39(8197)

SHUPHAMITES-NU-26:39(7781)

SHUPPIM-all=8206-1CH-7:12,15■26:16

SHUR-all=7793-GE-16:7■20:1■25:18-EX-15:22-1SA-15:7■27:8

SHUSHAN-all=7800-NE-1:1-ES-1:2,5■2:3,5,8■3:15^{2}■4:8,16■8:14,15■9:6,11,12,13,14,15^{2},18-DA-8:2

SHUSHAN-EDUTH-PS-60:t(7802)

SHUTHALHITES-NU-26:35(8364)

SHUTHELAH-all=7803-NU-26:35,36-1CH-7:20,21

SIA-NE-7:47(5517)

SIAHA-EZR-2:44(5517)

SIBBECAI-1CH-11:29(5444)■27:11(5444)

SIBBECHAI-2SA-21:18(5444)-1CH-20:4(5444)

SIBBOLETH-J'G-12:6(5451)

SIBMAH-all=7643-JOS-13:19-IS-16:8,9-JER-48:32

SIBRAIM-EZE-47:16(5453)

SICHEM-GE-12:6(7927)

SIDDIM-all=7708-GE-14:3,8,10

SIDON-GE-10:15(6721),19(6721)■N.T.-all=4605-M'T-11:21,22■15:21-M'R-3:8■7:24,31-LU-4:26■6:17■10:13,14-AC-12:20■27:3

SIDONIANS-all=6722-DE-3:9-JOS-13:4,6-J'G-3:3-1KI-5:6

SIHON-all=5511-NU-21:21,23^{2},26,27,28,29,34■32:33-DE-1:4■2:24,26,30,31,32■3:2,6■4:46■29:7■31:4-JOS-2:10■9:10■12:2,5■13:10,21^{2},27-J'G-11:19,20^{2},21-1KI-4:19-NE-9:22-PS-135:11■136:19-JER-48:45

SIHOR-all=7883-JOS-13:3-IS-23:3-JER-2:18

SILAS-all=4609-AC-15:22,27,32,34,40■16:19,25,29■17:4,10,14,15■18:5

SILLA-2KI-12:20(5538)

SILOAH-NE-3:15(7975)

SILOAM-all=4611-LU-13:4-JOH-9:7,11

SILVANUS-all=4610-2CO-1:19-1TH-1:1-2TH-1:1-2PE-5:12

SIMEON-all=8095&marked-GE-29:33■34:25,30■35:23■42:24,36■43:23■46:10■48:5■49:5-EX-1:2■6:15^{2}-NU-1:6,22,23■2:12^{2}■7:36■10:19■13:5■26:12■34:20-DE-27:12-JOS-19:1^{2},8,9^{2}■21:4(8099),9-J'G-1:3^{2},17-1CH-2:1■4:24,42■6:65■12:25-2CH-15:9■34:6-EZE-48:24,25,33■N.T.-all=4826-LU-2:25,34■3:30-AC-13:1■15:14-RE-7:7

SIMEONITES-all=8099-NU-25:14■26:14-1CH-27:16

SIMON-all-4613-M'T-4:18■10:2,4■13:55■16:16,17■17:25■26:6■27:32-M'R-1:16,29,36■3:16,18■6:3■14:3,37■15:21-LU-5:4,5,8,10^{2}■6:14,15■7:40,43,44■22:31■23:26■24:34-JOH-1:40,41,42■6:8,68,71■13:6,9,24,26,36■18:10,15,25■20:2,6■21:2,3,7,11,15,16,17-AC-1:13■8:9,13,18,24■9:43■10:5,6,18,32^{2}■11:13-2PE-1:1

SIMON'S-all=4613-M'R-1:30-LU-4:38^{2}■5:3-JOH-12:4■13:2-AC-10:17

SIMRI-1CH-26:10(8113)

SIN-all=5512-EX-16:1■17:1-NU-33:11,12-EZE-30:15,16

SINA-all=4614-AC-7:30(4614),38(4614)

SINAI-all=5514-EX-16:1■19:1,2,11,18,20,23■24:16■31:18■34:2,4,29,32-LE-7:38^{2}■25:1■26:46■27:34-NU-1:1,19■3:1,4,14■9:1,5■10:12■26:64■28:6■33:15,16-DE-33:2-J'G-5:5-NE-9:13-PS-68:8,17■N.T.-GA-4:24(4614),25(4614)

SINIM-IS-49:12(5515)

SINITE-GE-10:17(5513)-1CH-1:15(5513)

SION-DE-4:48(7865)-PS-65:1(6726)■N.T.-all=4622-M'T-21:5-JOH-12:15-RO-9:33■11:26-HEB-12:22-1PE-2:6-RE-14:1

SIPHMOTH-1SA-30:28(8224)

SIPPAI-1CH-20:4(5598)

SIRAH-2SA-3:26(5626)

SIRION-DE-3:9(8304)-PS-29:6(8304)

SISAMAI-1CH-2:40(5581)

SISERA-all=5516-J'G-4:2,7,9,12,13,14,

15^{2},16,17,18,22^{2}■5:20,26,28,30-1SA-12:9-EZR-2:53-NE-7:55-PS-83:9

SITNAH-GE-26:21(7856)

SIVAN-ES-8:9(5510)

SMYRNA-RE-1:11(4667)■2:8(4668)

SO-2KI-17:4(5471)

SOCHO-1CH-4:18(7755)

SOCHOH-1KI-4:10(7755)

SOCOH-all=7755-JOS-15:35(7755),48(7755)

SODI-NU-13:10(5476)

SODOM-all=5467-GE-10:19■13:10,12,13■14:2,8,10,11,12,17,21,22■18:16,20,22,26■19:1^{2},4,24,28-DE-29:23■32:32-IS-1:9,10■3:9■13:19-JER-23:14■49:18■50:40-LA-4:6-EZE-16:46,48,49,53,55,56-AM-4:11-ZEP-2:9■N.T.-all=4670-M'T-10:15■11:23,24-M'R-6:11-LU-10:12■17:29-2PE-2:6-JUDE-7-RE-11:8

SODOMA-RO-9:29(4670)

SODOMITE-DE-23:17(6945)

SODOMITES-all=6945-1KI-14:24■15:12■22:46-2KI-23:7

SOLOMON-all=8010-2SA-5:14■12:24-1KI-1:10,11,12,13,17,19,21,26,30,33,34,37,38,39^{2},43,46,47,50,51^{3},52,53^{3}■2:1,12,13,17,19,22,23,25,27,29^{2},41,45,46■3:1,3,4,5,6,10,15■4:1,7,11,15,21^{2},25,26,27,29,34■5:1,2,7,8,10,11^{2},12^{2},13,15■6:2,11,14,21■7:1,8,13,14,40,45,47,48,51^{2}■8:1^{2},2,5,12,22,54,63,65■9:1,2,10,11^{2},12,15,17,19^{2},21,22,25,26,27,28■10:1,2,3,10,13^{2},14,16,21,23,24,26,28■11:1,2,4,5,6,7,9,11,14,25,27,28,31,40^{2},41^{2},42,43■12:2,6,21,23■14:21,26-2KI-21:7■23:13■24:13■25:16-1CH-3:5■6:10,32■14:4■18:8■22:5,6,7,9,17■23:1■28:5,6,9,11,20■29:1,19,22,23,24,25,28-2CH-1:1,2,3,5,6,7,8,11,13,14,16■2:1,2,3,11,17■3:1,3■4:11,16,18,19■5:1^{2},2,6■6:1,13■7:1,5,7^{2},8,10,11,12■8:1,2^{2},3,6^{2},8,9,11,12,16,17,18^{2}■9:1^{3},2^{2},3,9,10,12,13,14,15,20^{2},22,23,25,28,29,30,31■10:2,6■11:3,17^{2}■12:9■13:6,7■30:26■33:7■35:3,4-NE-12:45■13:26-PS-72:t■127:t-PR-1:1■10:1■25:1-SONG-1:5■3:9,11■8:11,12-JER-52:20■N.T.-all=4672-M'T-1:6,7■6:29■12:42^{2}-LU-1:31^{2}■12:27-AC-7:47

SOLOMON'S-all=8010-1KI-4:22,27,30■5:16,18■6:1■9:1,16,23■10:4,21■11:26-1CH-3:10-2CH-7:11■8:10-EZR-2:55,58-NE-7:57,60■11:3-SONG-1:1■3:7■N.T.-all=4672-JOH-10:23-AC-3:11■5:12

SOPATER-AC-20:4(4986)

SOPHERETH-EZR-2:55(5618)-NE-7:57(5618)

SOREK-J'G-16:4(7796)

SOSIPATER-RO-16:21(4989)

SOSTHENES-AC18:17(4988)-1CO-1:1(4988)

SOTAI-EZR-2:55(5479)-NE-7:57(5479)

SPAIN-RO-15:24(4681),28(4681)

STACHYS-RO-16:9(4720)

STEPHANAS-all=4734-1CO-1:16■16:15,17,subscr.

STEPHEN-all=4736-AC-6:5,8,9■7:59■8:2■11:19■22:20

STOICKS-AC-17:18(4770)

SUAH-1CH-7:36(5477)

SUCCOTH-all=5523-GE-33:17^{2}-EX-12:37■13:20-NU-33:5,6-JOS-13:27-J'G-8:5,6,8,14^{2},15,16-1KI-7:46-2CH-4:17-PS-60:6■108:7

SUCCOTH-BENOTH-2KI-17:30(5524)

SUCHATHITES-1CH-2:55(7756)

SUKKIIMS-2CH-12:3(5525)

SUR-2KI-11:6(5495)

SUSANCHITES-EZR-4:9(7801)

SUSANNA-LU-8:3(4677)

SUSI-NU-13:11(5485)

SYCHAR-JOH-4:5(4965)

SYCHEM-AC-7:16^{2}(4966)

SYENE-EZE-29:10(5482)■30:6(5482)

SYNTYCHE-PH'P-4:2(4941)

SYRACUSE-AC-28:12(4946)

SYRIA-all=758-J'G-10:6-2SA-8:6,12■15:8-1KI-10:29■11:25■15:18■19:15■20:1,20,22,23■22:1,3,31-2KI-5:1^{2},5■6:8,11,23,24■7:5■8:7,9,13,28,29■9:14,15■12:17,18■13:3,4,7,17,19^{2},22,24■15:37■16:5,6^{2},7-2CH-1:17■16:2,7^{2}■18:10,30■20:2■22:5,6■24:23■28:5,23-IS-7:1,2,4,5,8■17:3-EZE-16:57■27:16-HO-12:12-AM-1:5■N.T.-all=4947-M'T-4:24-LU-2:2-AC-15:23,41■18:18■20:3■21:3-GA-1:21

SYRIACK-DA-2:4(762)

SYRIA-DAMASCUS-1CH-18:6(758,1834)

SYRIA-MAACHAH-1CH-19:6(758)

SYRIAN-all=761&marked-GE-25:20^{2}■28:5■31:20,24-DE-26:5-2KI-5:20■18:26(762)-EZR-4:7^{2}(762)-IS-36:11(762)■N.T.-LU-4:27(4948)

SYRIANS-all=758&marked-2SA-8:5^{2},6,13■10:6^{2},8,9,11,13,14,15,16,17,18^{2},19-1KI-20:20,21,26,27,28,29■22:11,35-2KI-5:2■6:9■7:4,5,6,10,12,14,15,16■8:28(761),29(761)■9:15(761)■13:5,17■16:6■24:2-1CH-18:5^{2},6■19:10,12,14,15,16^{2},17,18^{2},19-2CH-18:34■22:5(761)■24:24-IS-9:12-JER-35:11-AM-9:7

SYROPHENICIAN-M'R-7:26(4949)

T

TAANACH-all=8590-JOS-12:21■17:11-J'G-1:27■5:19-1KI-4:12-1CH-7:29

TAANATHSHILOH-JOS-16:6(8387)

TABBAOTH-EZR-2:43(2884)-NE-7:46(2884)

TABBATH-J'G-7:22(2888)

TABEAL-IS-7:6(2870)

TABEEL-EZR-4:7(2870)

TABERAH-NU-11:3(8404)-DE-9:22(8404)

TABITHA-AC-9:36(5000),40(5000)

TABOR-all=8396-JOS-19:22-J'G-4:6,12,14■8:18-1SA-10:13-1CH-6:77-PS-89:12-JER-46:18-HO-5:1

TABRIMON-IKI-15:18(2886)

TACHMONITE-2SA-23:8(8461)

TADMOR-1KI-9:18(8412)-2CH-8:4(8412)

TAHAN-NU-26:35(8465)-1CH-7:25(8465)

TAHANITES-JER-2:16(8471)

TAHAPANES-JER-2:16(8471)

TAHATH-all=8480-NU-33:26,27-1CH-6:24,37■7:20^{2}

TAHPANHES-all=8471-JER-43:7,8,9■44:1■46:14

TAHPENES-1KI-11:19(4872),20^{2}(4872)

TAHREA-1CH-9:41(8475)

TAHTIM-HODSHI-2SA-24:6(8483)

TALITHA-M'R-5:41(5008)

TALMAI-all=8526-NU-13:22-JOS-15:14-J'G-1:10-2SA-3:3■13:37-1CH-3:2

TALMON-all=2929-1CH-9:17-EZR-2:42-NE-7:45■11:19■12:25

TAMAH-NE-7:55(8547)

TAMAR-all=8559-GE-38:6,11^{2},13,24-RU-4:12-2SA-13:1,2,4,5,6,7,8,10^{2},19,20,22,32■14:27-1CH-2:4■3:9-EZE-47:19■48:28

TAMMUZ-EZE-8:14(8542)

TANACH-JOS-21:25(8590)

TANHUMETH-2KI-25:23(8576)-JER-40:8(8576)

TAPHATH-1KI-4:11(2955)

TAPPUAH-all=8599-JOS-12:17■15:34■16:8■17:8^{2}-1CH-2:43

TARAH-NU-33:27(8646),28(8646)

TARALAH-JOS-18:27(8634)

TAREA-1CH-8:35(8390)

TARPELITES-EZR-4:9(2967)

TARSHISH-all=8656-GE-10:4-1CH-1:7-2CH-9:21^{2}■20:36,37-ES-1:14-PS-48:7■72:10-IS-2:16■23:1,6,10,14■60:9■66:19-JER-10:9-EZE-27:12,25■38:13-JON-1:3^{3}■4:2■

TARSUS-all=5109&marked-AC-9:11(5018),30■11:25■21:39(5108)■22:3

TARTAK-2KI-17:31(8662)

TARTAN-2KI-18:17(8661)-IS-20:1(8661)

TATNAI-all=8674-EZR-5:3,6■6:6,13

TEBAH-GE-22:24(2875)

TEBALIAH-1CH-26:11(2882)

TEBETH-ES-2:16(2887)

TEHAPHNEHES-EZE-30:18(8471)

TEHINNAH-1CH-4:12(8468)

TEKEL-all=8625-DA-5:25(8625),27(8625)

TEKOA-all=8620-1CH-2:24■4:5-2CH-11:6■20:20-JER-6:1-AM-1:1

TEKOAH-2SA-14:2(8620),4(8621),9(8621)

TEKOITE-all=8621-2SA-23:26-1CH-11:28■27:9

TEKOITES-NE-3:5(8621),27(8621)

TELABIB-EZE-3:15(8512)

TELAH-1CH-7:25(8520)

TELAIM-1SA-15:4(2923)

TELASSAR-IS-37:12(8515)

TELEM-JOS-15:24(2928)-EZR-10:24(2928)

TEL-HARESHA-NE-7:61(8521)

TEL-HARSA-EZR-2:59(8521)

TEL-MELAH-EZR-2:59(8528)-NE-7:61(8528)

TEMA-all=8485-GE-25:15-1CH-1:30-JOB-6:19-IS-21:14-JER-25:23

TEMAN-all=8487-GE-36:11,15,42-1CH-1:36,53-JER-49:7,20-EZE-25:13-AM-1:12-OB-9-HAB-3:3

TEMANI-GE-36:34(8489)

TEMANITE-all=8489-JOB-2:11■4:1■15:1■22:1■42:7,9

TEMANITES-1CH-1:45(8489)

TEMENI-1CH-4:6(8488)

TERAH-all=8646-GE-11:24,25,26,27^{2},28,31,32^{2}-JOS-24:2-1CH-1:26

TERESH-ES-2:21(8657)■6:2(8657)

TERTIUS-RO-16:22(5060)

TERTULLUS-AC-24:1(5061),2(5061)

THADDAEUS-M'T-10:3(2280)-M'R-3:18(2280)

THAHASH-GE-22:24(8477)

THAMAH-EZR-2:53(8547)

THAMAR- M'T-1:3(2283)

THARA-LU-3:34(2291)

THARSHISH-all=8659-1KI-10:22^{2},48-1CH-7:10

THAT-all=834or2088or3588■N.T.-all=1565or3754

THE-O.T.supplied■N.T.-all=3588

THEBEZ-all=8405-J'G-9:50^{2}-2SA-11:21

THEE-O.T.supplied■N.T.-all=4571

THEIR-O.T.supplied■N.T.-all=846

THELASAR-2KI-19:12(8515)

THEM-O.T.supplied■N.T.-all=846

THEOPHILUS-LU-1:3(2321)-AC-1:1(2321)

THESSALONIANS-all=2331-AC-20:4-1TH-1:t,1,subscr.-2TH-1:t,1,subscr.

THESSALONICA-all=2332&marked-AC-17:1,11,13■27:2(2331)-PH'P-4:16-2TI-4:10

THEUDAS-AC-5:36(2333)

THEY-all=4571■N.T.-all=846

THIMNATHAH-JOS-19:43(8553)

THOMAS-all=2381-M'T-10:3-M'R-3:18-LU-6:15-JOH-11:16■14:5■20:24,26,27,28,29■21:2-AC-1:13

THOU-all=859■N.T.-all=4771

THUMMIM-all=8550-EX-28:30-LE-8:8-DE-33:8-EZR-2:63-NE-7:65

THY-O.T.supplied■N.T.-all=4674 or 4675

THYATIRA-all=2363-AC-16:14-RE-1:11■2:18,24

TIBERIAS-all=5085-JOH-6:1,23■21:1

TIBERIUS-LU-3:1(5086)

TIBHATH-1CH-18:8(2880)

TIBNI-all=8402-1KI-16:21,22^{2}

TIDAL-GE-14:1(8413),9(8413)

TIGLATH-PILESER-all=8407-2KI-15:29■16:7,10

TIKVAH-2KI-22:14(8616)-EZR-10:15(8616)

TIKVATH-2CH-34:22(8616)

TILGATH-PILNESER-all=8407-1CH-5:6,26-2CH-28:20

TILON-1CH-4:20(8436)

TIMAEUS-M'R-10:46(5090)

TIMNA-all=8555-GE-36:12,22-1CH-1:36,39

TIMNAH-all=8553&marked-GE-36:40(8555)-JOS-15:10,57-1CH-1:51(8555)-2CH-28:18

TIMNATH-all=8553-GE-38:12,13,

14-**J'G**-14:1^2,2,5^2

TIMNATH-HERES-**J'G**-2:9(8556)

TIMNATH-SERAH-**JOS**-19:50(8556)■24:30(8556)

TIMNITE-**J'G**-15:6(8554)

TIMON-**AC**-6:5(5096)

TIMOTHEUS-all=5095-**AC**-16:1■17:14,15■18:5■19:22■20:4-**RO**-16:21-**1CO**-4:17■16:10,subscr.-**2CO**-1:19-**PH'P**-1:1■2:19-**COL**-1:1-**1TH**-1:1■3:2,6-**2TH**-1:1-**2TI**-subscr.

TIMOTHY-all=5095-**2CO**-1:1-**1TI**-1:t,2,18■6:20,subscr.-**2TI**-1:t,2-**PH'M**-1-**HEB**-13:23,subscr.

TIPHSAH-**1KI**-4:24(8607)-**2KI**-15:16(8607)

TIRAS-**GE**-10:2(8493)-**1CH**-1:5(8493)

TIRATHITES-**1CH**-2:55(8654)

TIRHAKAH-**2KI**-19:9(8640)-**IS**-37:9(8640)

TIRHANAH-**1CH**-2:48(8647)

TIRIA-**1CH**-4:16(8493)

TIRSHATHA-all=8660-**EZR**-2:63-**NE**-7:65,70■8:9■10:1

TIRZAH-all=8656-**NU**-26:33■27:1■36:11-**JOS**-12:24■17:3-**1KI**-14:17■15:21,33■16:6,8,9^2,15,17,23-**2KI**-16:14,16-**SONG**-6:4

TISHBITE-all=8664-**1KI**-17:1■21:17,28-**2KI**-1:3,8■9:36

TITUS-all=5103-**2CO**-2:13■7:6,13,14■8:6,16,23■12:18^2,subscr.-**GA**-2:1,3-**2TI**-4:10-**TIT**-1:t,4,subscr.

TIZITE-**1CH**-11:45(8491)

TO-**O.T.**supplied■**N.T.**-all=1519

TOAH-**1CH**-6:34(8430)

TOB-**J'G**-11:3(2897),5(2897)

TOB-ADONIJAH-**2CH**-17:8(2899)

TOBIAH-all=2900-**EZR**-2:60-**NE**-2:10,19■4:3,7■6:1,12,14,17^2,19■7:62■13:4,7,8

TOBIJAH-all=2900-**2CH**-17:8-**ZEC**-6:10,14

TOCHEN-**1CH**-4:32(8507)

TOGARMAH-all=8425-**GE**-10:3-**1CH**-1:6-**EZE**-27:14■38:16

TOHU-**1SA**-1:1(8459)

TOI-all=8583-**2SA**-8:9,10^2

TOLA-all=8439-**GE**-46:13-**NU**-6:23-**J'G**-10:1-**1CH**-7:1,2^2

TOLAD-**1CH**-4:29(8434)

TOLAITES-**NU**-26:23(8440)

TOPHEL-**DE**-1:1(8603)

TOPHET-all=8612&marked-**IS**-30:33(8613)-**JER**-7:31,32^2■19:6,11,12,13,14

TOPHETH-**2KI**-23:10(8612)

TOU-**1CH**-18:9(8583),10(8583)

TRACHONITIS-**LU**-3:1(5139)

TROAS-all=5174-**AC**-16:8,11■20:5,6-**2CO**-2:12-**2TI**-4:13

TROGYLLIUM-**AC**-20:15(5175)

TROPHIMUS-all=5161-**AC**-20:4■21:29-**2TI**-4:20

TRYPHENA-**RO**-16:12(5170)

TRYPHOSA-**RO**-16:12(5173)

TUBAL-all=8422-**GE**-10:2-**1CH**-1:5-**IS**-66:19-**EZE**-27:13■32:26■38:2,3■39:1

TUBAL-CAIN-**GE**-4:22^2(8423)

TYCHICUS-all=5190-**AC**-20:4-**EPH**-6:21,subscr.-**CO**-4:7■subscr.-**2TI**-4:12-**TIT**-3:12

TYRANNUS-**AC**-19:9(5181)

TYRE-all=6685&marked-**JOS**-19:29-**2SA**-5:11■24:7-**1KI**-5:1■7:13,14(6876)■9:11,12-**1CH**-14:1■22:4(6876)-**2CH**-2:3,11,14(6876)-**EZR**-3:7(6876)-**NE**-13:16(6876)-**PS**-45:12■83:7■87:4-**IS**-23:1,5,8,15^2,17-**JOE**-3:4■**N.T.**-all=5184&marked-**M'T**-11:21,22■15:21-**M'R**-3:8■7:24,31-**LU**-6:17■10:13,14-**AC**-12:20■21:3,7

TYRUS-all=6685-**JER**-25:22■27:3■47:4-**EZE**-26:2,3,4,7,15■27:2,3^2,8,32■28:2,12■29:18^2-**HO**-9:13-**AM**-1:9,10-**ZEC**-9:2,3

U

UCAL-**PR**-30:1(401)

UEL-**EZR**-10:34(177)

ULAI-**DA**-8:2(195),16(195)

ULAM-all=198-**1CH**-7:16,17■8:39,40

ULLA-**1CH**-7:39(5925)

UMMAH-**JOS**-19:30(5981)

UNNI-all=6042-**1CH**-15:18,20-**NE**-12:9

UNTO-**O.T.**supplied■**N.T.**-all=1519

UP-all=4605-**O.T.**supplied■**N.T.**-all=507

UPHAZ-**JER**-10:9(210)-**DA**-10:5(210)

UPON-all=5921-**O.T.**supplied■**N.T.**-all=1906

UR-all=218-**GE**-11:28,31■15:7-**1CH**-11:35-**NE**-9:7

URBANE-**RO**-16:9(3773)

URI-all=221-**EX**-31:2■35:30■38:22-**1KI**-4:19-**1CH**-2:20-**2CH**-1:5-**EZR**-10:24

URIAH-all=223-**2SA**-11:3,6^2,7,8^2,9,10^2,11,12^2,14,15,16,17,21,24,26■12:9,10■23:39-**1KI**-15:5-**1CH**-11:41-**EZR**-8:33-**IS**-8:2

URIAH'S-**2SA**-12:15(223)

URIAS-**M'T**-1:6(3744)

URIEL-all=222-**1CH**-6:24■15:5,11-**2CH**-13:2

URIJAH-all=223-**2KI**-16:10,11^2,15,16-**NE**-3:4,21■8:4-**JER**-26:20,21,23

US-**O.T.**supplied■**N.T.**-all=2248

UTHAI-**1CH**-9:4(5793)-**EZR**-8:14(5793)

UZ-all=5780-**GE**-10:23■36:28-**1CH**-1:17,42-**JOB**-1:1-**JER**-25:20-**LA**-4:21

UZAI-**NE**-3:25(186)

UZAL-**GE**-10:27(187)-**1CH**-1:21(187)

UZZA-all=5798-**2KI**-21:18,26-**1CH**-6:29■8:7■13:7,9,10,11-**EZR**-2:49-**NE**-7:51

UZZAH-all=5798-**2SA**-6:3,6,7,8

UZZENSHERAH-**1CH**-7:24(242)

UZZI-all=5813-**1CH**-6:5,6,51■7:2,3,7■9:8-**EZR**-7:4-**NE**-11:22■12:19,42

UZZIA-**1CH**-11:44(5814)

UZZIAH-all=5818-**2KI**-15:13,30,32,34-**1CH**-6:24■27:25-**2CH**-26:1,3,8,9,11,14,18^2,19,21,22,23■27:2-**EZR**-10:21-**NE**-11:4-**IS**-1:1■6:1■7:1-**HO**-1:1-**AM**-1:1-**ZEC**-14:5

UZZIEL-all=5816-**EX**-6:18,22-**LE**-10:4-**NU**-3:19,30-**1CH**-4:42■6:2,18■7:7■15:10■23:12,20■24:24■25:4-**2CH**-29:14-**NE**-3:8

UZZIELITES-**NU**-3:27(5817)-**1CH**-26:23(5817)

V

VAJEZATHA-**ES**-9:9(2055)

VANIAH-**EZR**-10:36(2057)

VASHNI-**1CH**-6:28(2059)

VASHTI-all=2060-**ES**-1:9,11,12,15,16,17,19■2:1,4,17

VOPHSI-**NU**-13:14(2058)

W

WAS-all=1961-■**N.T.**-all=2258

WE-all=587■**N.T.**-all=2249

WERE-all=1961■**N.T.**-all=2258

WITH-all=5973■**N.T.**-all=4862

Y

YE-all=859■**N.T.**-all=5210

YOU-all =supplied

Z

ZAANAIM-**J'G**-4:11(6815)

ZAANAN-**MIC**-1:11(6630)

ZAANANNIM-**JOS**-19:33(6815)

ZAAVAN-**GE**-36:27(2190)

ZABAD-all=2066-**1CH**-2:36,37■7:21■11:41-**2CH**-24:26-**EZR**-10:27,33,43

ZABBAI-all=2079-**EZR**-10:28-**NE**-3:20

ZABBUD-**EZR**-8:14(2072)

ZABDI-all=2067-**JOS**-1:1,17■7:18-**1CH**-8:19■27:27-**NE**-11:17

ZABDIEL-all=2068-**1CH**-27:2-**NE**-11:14

ZABUD-**1KI**-4:5(2071)

ZABULON-all=2194-**M'T**-4:13,15-**RE**-7:8

ZACCAI-all=2140-**EZR**-2:9-**NE**-7:14

ZACCHAEUS-all=2195-**LU**-19:2,5,8

ZACCHUR-**1CH**-4:26(2139)

ZACCUR-all=2139-**NU**-13:4-**1CH**-24:27■25:2,10-**NE**-3:2■10:12■12:35■13:13

ZACHARIAH-all=2148-**2KI**-14:29■15:8,11■18:2

ZACHARIAS-all=2197-**M'T**-23:35-**LU**-1:5,12,13,18,21,40,59,67■3:2■11:51

ZACHER-**1CH**-8:31(2144)

ZADOK-all=6659-**2SA**-8:17■15:24,25,27,29,35^2■17:15■18:19,22,27■19:11■20:25-**1KI**-1:8,26,32,34,38,39,44,45■2:35■4:2,4-**2KI**-15:33-**1CH**-6:8,12,53■9:11■12:28■15:11■16:39■18:16■24:3,6,31■27:17■29:22-**2CH**-27:1■31:10-**EZR**-7:2-**NE**-3:4,29■10:21■11:11■13:13-**EZE**-40:46■43:19■44:15■48:11

ZADOK'S-**2SA**-15:36(6659)

ZAHAM-**2CH**-11:19(2093)

ZAIR-**2KI**-8:21(6811)

ZALAPH-**NE**-3:30(6764)

ZALMON-all=6756-**J'G**-9:48-**2SA**-23:28

ZALMONAH-all=6758-**NU**-33:41,42

ZALMUNNA-all=6759-**J'G**-8:5,6,7,10,12^2,15^2,18,21^2-**PS**-83:11

ZAMZUMMIMS-**DE**-2:20(2157)

ZANOAH-all=2182-**JOS**-15:34,56-**1CH**-4:18-**NE**-3:13■11:30

ZAPHNATH-PAANEAH-**GE**-41:45(6847)

ZAPHON-**JOS**-13:27(6829)

ZARA-**M'T**-1:3(2196)

ZARAH-**GE**-38:30(2226)■46:12(2226)

ZAREAH-**NE**-11:29(6881)

ZAREATHITES-**1CH**-2:53(6882)

ZARED-**NU**-21:12(2218)

ZAREPHATH-all=6886-**1KI**-17:9,10-**OB**-20

ZARETAN-**JOS**-3:16(6891)

ZARETH-SHAHAR-**JOS**-13:19(6890)

ZARHITES-all=2227-**NU**-26:13,20-**JOS**-7:17^2-**1CH**-27:11,13

ZARTANAH-**1KI**-4:12(6891)

ZARTHAN-**1KI**-7:46(6891)

ZATTHU-**NE**-10:14(2240)

ZATTU-all=2240-**EZR**-2:8■10:27-**NE**-7:13

ZAVAN-**1CH**-1:42(2190)

ZAZA-**1CH**-2:33(2117)

ZEBADIAH-all=2069-**1CH**-8:15,17■12:7■26:2■27:7-**2CH**-17:8■19:11-**EZR**-8:8■10:20

ZEBAH-all=2078-**J'G**-8:5,6,7,10,12^2,15^2,18,21^2-**PS**-83:11

ZEBAIM-**EZR**-2:57(6380)-**NE**-7:59(6380)

ZEBEDEE-all=2199-**M'T**-4:21^2■10:2■26:37-**M'R**-1:19,20■3:17■10:35-**LU**-5:10-**JOH**-21:2

ZEBEDEE'S-**M'T**-20:20(2199)■27:56(2199)

ZEBINA-**EZR**-10:43(2081)

ZEBOIIM-**GE**-14:2(6636),8(6636)

ZEBOIM-all=6636&marked-**GE**-10:19-**DE**-29:23-**1SA**-13:18(6650)-**NE**-11:34(6650)-**HO**-11:8

ZEBUDAH-**2KI**-23:36(2081)

ZEBUL-all=2083-**J'G**-9:28,30,36^2,38,41

ZEBULONITE-**J'G**-12:11(2075),12(2075)

ZEBULUN-all=2074-**GE**-30:20■35:23■46:14■49:13-**EX**-1:3-**NU**-1:9,30,31■2:7^2■7:24■10:16■13:10■26:26■34:25-**DE**-27:13■33:18-**JOS**-19:10,16,27,34■21:7,34-**J'G**-1:30■4:6,10■5:14,18■6:35■12:12-**1CH**-2:1■6:63,77■12:33,40■27:19-**2CH**-30:10,11,18-**PS**-68:27-**IS**-9:1-**EZR**-48:26,27,33

ZEBULUNITES-**NU**-26:27(2075)

ZECHARIAH-all=2148-**1CH**-5:7■9:21,37■15:18,20,24■16:5■24:25■26:2,11,14■27:21-**2CH**-17:7■20:14■21:2■24:20■26:5■29:1,13■34:12■35:8-**EZR**-5:1■6:14■8:3,11,16■10:26-**NE**-8:4■11:4,5,12■12:16,35,41-**IS**-8:2-**ZEC**-1:t,1,7■7:1,8

ZEDAD-**NU**-34:8(6657)-**EZE**-47:15(6657)

ZEDEKIAH-all=6667-**1KI**-22:11,24-**2KI**-24:17,18,20■25:2,7^2-**1CH**-3:15,16-**2CH**-18:10,23■36:10,11-**JER**-1:3■21:1,3,7■24:8■27:3,12■28:1■29:3,21,22■32:1,3,4,5■34:2,4,6,8,21■36:12■37:1,3,17,18,

21■38:5,14,15,16,17,19,24■39:1,2,4,5,6■44:30■49:34■51:59■52:1,3,5,8,10,11

ZEDEKIAH'S-**JER**-39:7(6667)

ZEEB-all=2062-**J'G**-7:25^{3}■8:3-**PS**-83:11

ZELAH-**JOS**-18:28(6762)-**2SA**-21:14(6762)

ZELEK-**2SA**-23:37(6768)-**1CH**-11:39(6768)

ZELOPHEHAD-all=6765-**NU**-26:33^{2}■27:1,7■36:2,6,10,11-**JOS**-17:3-**1CH**-7:15

ZELOTES-**LU**-6:15(2208)-**AC**-1:13(2208)

ZELZAH-**1SA**-10:2(6766)

ZEMARAIM-**JOS**-18:22(6787)-**2CH**-13:4(6787)

ZEMARITE-**GE**-10:18(6786)-**1CH**-1:16(6786)

ZEMIRA-**1CH**-7:8(2160)

ZENAN-**JOS**-15:37(6799)

ZENAS-**TIT**-3:13(2211)

ZEPHANIAH-all=6846-**2KI**-25:18-**1CH**-6:36-**JER**-21:1■29:25,29■37:3■52:24-**ZEP**-1:t,1-**ZEC**-6:10,14

ZEPHATH-**J'G**-1:17(6857)

ZEPHATHAH-**2CH**-14:10(6859)

ZEPHI-**1CH**-1:36(6825)

ZEPHO-**GE**-36:11(6825),15(6825)

ZEPHON-**NU**-26:15(6827)

ZEPHONITES-**NU**-26:15(6831)

ZER-**JOS**-19:35(6863)

ZERAH-all=2226-**GE**-36:13,17,33-**NU**-26:13,20-**JOS**-7:1,18,24■22:20-**1CH**-1:37,44■2:4,6■4:24■6:21,41-**2CH**-14:9-**NE**-11:24

ZERAHIAH-all=2228-**1CH**-6:6,51-**EZR**-7:4■8:4

ZERED-all=2218-**DE**-2:13^{2},14

ZEREDA-**1KI**-11:26(6868)

ZEREDATHAH-**2CH**-4:17(6868)

ZERERATH-**J'G**-7:22(6888)

ZERESH-all=2238-**ES**-5:10,14■6:13^{2}

ZERETH-**1CH**-4:7(6889)

ZERI-**1CH**-25:3(6874)

ZEROR-**1SA**-9:1(6872)

ZERUAH-**1KI**-11:26(6871)

ZERUBBABEL-all=2216&marked-**1CH**-3:19^{2}-**EZR**-2:2■3:2,8■4:2,3■5:2(2217)-**NE**-7:7■12:1,47-**HAG**-1:1,12,14■2:2,4,21,23-**ZEC**-4:6,7,9,10

ZERUIAH-all=6870-**1SA**-26:6-**2SA**-2:13,18■3:39■8:16■14:1■16:9,10■17:25■18:2■19:21,22■21:17■23:18,37-**1KI**-1:7■2:5,22-**1CH**-2:16^{2}■11:6,39■18:12,15■26:28■27:24

ZETHAM-**1CH**-23:8(2241)■26:22(2241)

ZETHAN-**1CH**-7:10(2133)

ZETHAR-**ES**-1:10(2242)

ZIA-**1CH**-5:13(2127)

ZIBA-all=6717-**2SA**-9:2^{2},3,4,9,10,11,12■16:1,2^{2},3,4^{2}■19:17,29

ZIBEON-all=6649-**GE**-36:2,14,20,24^{2},29-**1CH**-1:38,40

ZIBIA-**1CH**-8:9(6644)

ZIBIAH-**2KI**-12:1(6645)-**2CH**-24:1(6645)

ZICHRI-all=2147-**EX**-6:21-**1CH**-8:19,23,27■9:15■26:25■27:16-**2CH**-17:16■23:1■28:7-**NE**-11:9■12:17

ZIDDIM-**JOS**-19:35(6661)

ZIDKIJAH-**NE**-10:1(6667)

ZIDON-all=6721&marked-**GE**-49:13-**JOS**-11:8■19:28-**J'G**-1:31■10:6■18:28-**2SA**-24:6-**1KI**-17:9-**1CH**-1:13-**EZR**-3:7(6722)-**IS**-23:2,4,12-**JER**-25:22■27:3■47:4-**EZE**-27:8■28:21,22-**JOE**-3:4-**ZEC**-9:2

ZIDONIANS-all=6722-**J'G**-10:12■18:7^{2}-**1KI**-11:1,5,33■16:31-**2KI**-23:13-**1CH**-22:4-**EZE**-32:30

ZIF-**1KI**-6:1(2099),37(2099)

ZIHA-all=6727-**EZR**-2:43-**NE**-7:46■11:21

ZIKLAG-all=6860-**JOS**-15:31■19:5-**1SA**-27:6^{2}■30:1^{3},14,26-**2SA**-1:1■4:10-**1CH**-4:30■12:1,20-**NE**-11:28

ZILLAH-all=6741-**GE**-4:19,22,23

ZILPAH-all=2153-**GE**-29:24■30:9,10,12■35:26■37:2■46:18

ZILTHAI-**1CH**-8:20(6769)■12:20(6769)

ZIMMAH-all=2155-**1CH**-6:20,42-**2CH**-29:12

ZIMRAN-**GE**-25:2(2175)-**1CH**-1:32(2175)

ZIMRI-all=2174-**NU**-25:14-**1KI**-16:9,10,12,15,16,18,20-**2KI**-9:31-**1CH**-2:6■8:36■9:42-**JER**-25:25

ZIN-all=6790-**NU**-13:21■20:1■27:14^{2}■33:36■34:3,4-**DE**-32:51-**JOS**-15:1,3

ZINA-**1CH**-23:10(2126)

ZION-all=6726-**2SA**-5:7-**1KI**-8:1-**2KI**-19:21,31-**1CH**-11:5-**2CH**-5:2-**PS**-2:6■9:11,14■14:7■20:2■48:2,11,12■50:2■51:18■53:6■69:35■74:2■76:2■78:68■84:7■87:2,5■97:8■99:2■102:13,16,21■110:2■125:1■126:1■128:5■129:5■132:13■133:3■134:3■135:21■137:1,3■146:10■147:12■149:2-**SONG**-3:11-**IS**-1:8,27■2:3■3:16,17■4:3,4,5■8:18■10:12,24,32■12:6■14:32■16:1■18:7■24:23■28:16■29:8■30:19■31:4,9■33:5,14,20■34:8■35:10■37:22,32■40:9■41:27■46:13■49:14■51:3,11,16■52:1,2,7,8■59:20■60:14■61:3■62:11■64:10■66:8-**JER**-3:14■4:6,31■6:2,23■8:19■9:19■14:19■26:18■30:17■31:6,12■50:5,28■51:10,24,35-**LA**-1:4,6,17■2:1,4,6,8,10,13,18■4:2,11,22■5:11,18-**JOE**-2:1,15,23,32■3:16,17,21-**AM**-1:2■6:1-**OB**-17,21-**MIC**-1:13■3:10,12■4:2,7,8,10,11,13-**ZEP**-3:14,16-**ZEC**-1:14,17■2:7,10■8:2,3■9:9,13

ZION'S-**IS**-62:1(2726)

ZIOR-**JOS**-15:54(6730)

ZIPH-all=2128-**JOS**-15:24,55-**1SA**-23:14,15,24■26:2^{2}-**1CH**-2:42■4:16-**2CH**-11:8

ZIPHAH-**1CH**-4:16(2129)

ZIPHIMS-**PS**-54:t(2130)

ZIPHION-**GE**-46:16(6837)

ZIPHITES-**1SA**-23:19(2130)■26:1(2130)

ZIPHRON-**NU**-34:9(2202)

ZIPPOR-all=6834-**NU**-22:2,4,10,16■23:18-**JOS**-24:9-**J'G**-11:25

ZIPPORAH-all=6855-**EX**-2:21■4:25■18:2

ZITHRI-**EX**-6:22(5644)

ZIZ-**2CH**-20:16(6732)

ZIZA-**1CH**-4:37(2124)-**2CH**-11:20(2124)

ZIZAH-**1CH**-23:11(2125)

ZOAN-all=6814-**NU**-13:22-**PS**-78:12,43-**IS**-19:11,13■30:4-**EZE**-30:14

ZOAR-all=6820-**GE**-13:10■14:2,8■19:22,23,30^{2}-**DE**-34:3-**IS**-15:5-**JER**-48:34

ZOBA-**2SA**-10:6(6678),8(6678)

ZOBAH-all=6678-**1SA**-14:47-**2SA**-8:3,5,12■23:36-**1KI**-11:23,24-**1CH**-18:3,5,9■19:6

ZOBEBAH-**1CH**-4:8(6637)

ZOHAR-all=6714-**GE**-23:8■25:9■46:10-**EX**-6:15

ZOHELETH-**1KI**-1:9(2120)

ZOHETH-**1CH**-4:20(2105)

ZOPHAH-**1CH**-7:35(6690),36(6690)

ZOPHAI-**1CH**-6:26(6689)

ZOPHAR-all=6691-**JOB**-2:11■11:1■20:1■42:9

ZOPHIM-**NU**-23:14(6839)

ZORAH-all=6881-**JOS**-19:41-**J'G**-13:2,25■16:31■18:2,8,11-**2CH**-11:10

ZORATHITES-**1CH**-4:2(6882)

ZOREAH-**JOS**-15:33(6881)

ZORITES-**1CH**-2:54(6882)

ZOROBABEL-all=2216-**M'T**-1:12,13-**LU**-3:27

ZUAR-all=6686-**NU**-1:8■2:5■7:18,23■10:15

ZUPH-all=6689-**1SA**-1:1■9:5-**1CH**-6:35

ZUR-all=6698-**NU**-25:15■31:8-**JOS**-13:21-**1CH**-8:30■9:36

ZURIEL-**NU**-3:35(6700)

ZURISHADDAI-all=6701-**NU**-1:6■2:12■7:36,41■10:19

ZUZIMS-**GE**-14:5(2104)

NOTES

STRONG'S DICTIONARY

OF THE WORDS IN THE HEBREW BIBLE

1. All the original words are treated in their alphabetical Hebrew order, and are numbered regularly from the first to the last, each being known throughout by its appropriate number. This renders reference easy without recourse to the Hebrew characters.
2. Next follows the precise pronunciation, according to the usual English mode of sounding syllables.
3. Then ensues a tracing of the etymology, radical meaning, and applied signification of the word, justly but tersely analyzed and expressed, with any other important peculiarities in this regard.
4. Finally (after the punctuation mark:–) are given all the different renderings of the word in the Authorized English Version (KJV), arranged in alphabetical order.

HEBREW

WRITING AND PRONOUNCING HEBREW:

The following explanations are sufficient to show the method of transliterating Hebrew words into English adopted in this *Dictionary*

1. The Hebrew is read *from right to left*. The Alphabet consists of 22 letters (and their variations), which are all regarded as *consonants*, being enunciated by the aid of certain "points" or marks, mostly beneath the letters, and which serve as *vowels*. There is no distinction of *capitals, italics*, etc.

2. The letters are as follows:

No.	Form.	Name.		transliteration and power.
1.	א	'Aleph	(*aw'-lef*)	', unappreciable
2.	ב	Bêyth	(*bayth*)	**b**
3.	ג	Gîymel	(*ghee'-mel*)	**g** hard = γ
4.	ד	Dâleth	(*daw'-leth*)	**d**
5.	ה	Hê'	(*hay*)	**h**, often quiescent
6.	ו	Vâv	(*vawv*)	**v**, or **w**, quiescent
7.	ז	Zayin	(*zah'-yin*)	**z**, as in *zeal*
8.	ח	Chêyth	(*khayth*)	German **ch** = χ (nearly *kh*)
9.	ט	Têyth	(*tayth*)	**t** = תּ
10.	י	Yôwd	(*yode*)	**y**, often quiescent
11.	כ final ך	Kaph	(*caf*)	**k** = ק
12.	ל	Lâmed	(*law'-med*)	**l**
13.	מ final ם	Mêm	(*mame*)	**m**
14.	נ final ן	Nûwn	(*noon*)	**n**
15.	ס	Çâmek	(*saw'-mek*)	ç = *s* sharp = שׂ
16.	ע	'Ayin	(*ah'-yin*)	ʽpeculiar*
17.	פ final ף	Phê'	(*fay*)	**ph** = *f* = φ
	פּ	Pê'	(*pay*)	**P**
18.	צ final ץ	Tsâdêy	(*tsaw-day'*)	**ts**
19.	ק	Qôwph	(*cofe*)	**q** = *k* = כ
20.	ר	Rêysh	(*raysh*)	**r**
21.	שׂ	Sîyn	(seen)	**s** sharp = ס = σ
	שׁ	Shîyn	(sheen)	**sh**
22.	ת	Thâv	(*thawv*)	**th**, as in *THin*=θ
	תּ	Tâv	(*tawv*)	**t** = ט = τ

* The letter *'Ayin*, owing to the difficulty experienced by Occidentals in pronouncing it accurately (it is a deep guttural sound, like that made in *gargling*), it is generally neglected (i.e. passed over silently) in reading. We have represented it to the eye (but not exactly to the ear) by the Greek *rough breathing* (for distinctness and typographical convenience, a reversed *apostrophe*) in order to distinguish it from *'Âleph*, which is likewise treated as silent, being similarly represented by the Greek *smooth breathing* (the *apostrophe*).

3. The *vowel-points* are the following:

(ָ) Qâmêts (*caw-mates'*) â, as in *All*

(ַ) Pattach (*pat'-takh*) a, as in *mAn*, (*fār*)

(ֲ) Sh

(ֲ) Sheᵉvâ'-Pattach (*she-vaw' pat'-takh*) ă, as in *hAt*

(ֵ) Tsêrêy (*tsay-ray'*) **ê**, as in *thEy* = η

(ֶ) Çegôwl (*seg-ole'*) { **e**, as in *thEir* / **e**, as in *mEn* = ϵ }

(ֱ) Shᵉvâ'-Çegôwl (*she-vaw' seg-ole'*) **ĕ**, as in *mEt*

(ְ) Shᵉvâ'† (*she-vaw'*) ᵉobscure, as in *avErage*; silent, as *e* in *madE*

(ִ) Chîyriq (*khee'-rik*) { **î**, as in *machIne*‡ / **i**, as in *supplIant*, (*mīsery, hĭt*) }

(ֹ) Chôwlem § (*kho'-lem*) { **ô**, as in *no*= ω

(ָ) Short Qâmêts ± **o**, as in *nor* = o }

(ֳ) Shᵉvà'-Qâmêts (*she-vaw' caw-mates'*) **ŏ**, as in *not*

(ּ) Shûwrêq * (*shoo-rake'*) **û**, as in *crUel*

(ֻ) Qĭbbūts * (*kib'-boots*) **u**, as in *fUll, rūde*

*The parenthesis-marks ( ) are given here in order to show the place of the vowel-points, whether below, above, or in the middle of the letter.

† *Silent* Shᵉvâ is not represented by any mark in our method of transliteration, as it is understood whenever there is no other vowel-point.

‡ *Chîyriq* is thus long only when it is followed by a quiescent *yôwd* (either expressed or implied).

§ *Chôwlem* is written *fully* only over *Vâv*, which is then quiescent (*ω*); but when used "defectively" (without the *Vâv*) it may be written either over the the left-hand corner of the letter to which it belongs, or over the right-hand corner of the following one.

± Short *Qâmêts* is found only in *unaccented syllables. ending with a consonant sound.*

4. A point in the bosom of a letter is called *Dâgêsh'*, and is of two kinds, which must be carefully distinguished.

a. Dâgêsh *lenè* occurs only in the letters, ב,ג,ד,כ,פ,ת, (technically vocalized *Bᵉgad'-Kᵉphath',*) when they *begin* a clause or sentence, or are preceded by a consonant *sound;* and simply has the affect of removing their aspiration. †

b. Dâgêsh *fortè* may occur in any letter except ח,א,ע ה, or ר; it is equivalent to *doubling* the letter, and at the same time it removes the aspiration of a Bᵉgad-Kᵉphath letter.‡

5. The *Maqqêph'* (־), like a *hyphen*, unites words only for the purpose of pronunciation (by removing the primary accent from all except the last of them), but does not affect their meaning or their grammatical construction.

* *shûwrêq* is written only in the bosom of *Vâv*. Sometimes it is said to be "defectively" written (without the *Vâv*), and then takes the form of *Qibbūts*, which in such cases is called *vicarious*.

† In our system of transliteration Dâgêsh *lenè* is represented only in the letters פ and ת, because elsewhere it does not affect the pronunciation (with most Hebraists).

‡ A point in the bosom of ה is called *Mappîyq* (*map-peek'*). It occurs only in the final vowelless letter of a few words, and we have represented it by *hh*. A Dâgêsh *fortè* in the bosom of ו may easily be distinguished from the vowel *Shûwrêq* by noticing that in the former case the letter has a proper vowel-point accompanying it.

It should be noted that both kinds of Dâgêsh are often omitted in writing (being then said to be *implied*), but (in the case at least of Dâgêsh *fortè*) the word is (by most Hebraists) pronounced the same as if it were present.

ABBREVIATIONS USED IN THE HEBREW AND GREEK DICTIONARIES

abb. = abbreviated
abbreviation
absol. = absolute(ly)
abstr. = abstract(ly)
acc. = accusative (case)
act. = active(ly)
adj. = adjective(ly)
adv. = adverb
adverbial(ly)
aff. = affix(ed)
alt. = alternate
anal. = analogy
app. = apparent(ly)
appl. = application(s)
arch. = architecture
architectural(ly)
art. = article
artif. = artificial(ly)
Ass. = Assyrian
Bab. = Babylon
Babylonia(n)
caus. = causative(ly)
cerem. = ceremonial(ly)
Chald. = Chaldaism
Chaldee
Chr. = Christian
coll. = collective(ly)
collat. = collateral(ly)
com. = compound
comp. = compare
comparative(ly)
comparison
compo. = composition
concr. = concrete(ly)
conj. = conjunction(al)(ly)
constr. = construct(ion)
constructive(ly)
contr. = contracted
contraction
cor. = corresponding(ly)
correl. = correlated
correlation
correlative(ly)
dat. = dative (case)
def. = definite(ly)
demonstr. = demonstrative
denom. = denominative(ly)
der. = derived
derivative(ly)
derivation
desc. = descendant(s)
dimin. = diminutive
E. = East
Eastern
eccl. = ecclesiastical
e.g = for example
Eg. = Egypt, Egyptians
ellip. = ellipsis
elliptical(ly)
emphat. = emphatic(ally)
equiv. = equivalent(ly)
err. = erroneous(ly)
error
euph. = euphemism
euphemistic(ally)
ext. = extension
exter. = external(ly)
esp. = especially
fem. = feminine
fig. = figurative(ly)
for. = foreign(er)
Gr. = Græcism
Greek
gen. = general(ly)
generic(al)(ly)
genitive
Heb. = Hebrew
i.e. = *id est*
that is
ident. = identical(ly)
immed. = immediate(ly)
imper. = imperative
imperf. = imperfect
impers. = impersonal(ly)
impl. = implication
incl. = including
inclusive(ly)
indef. = indefinite(ly)
(ness)
indiv. = individual(izing)
inf. = infinitive
inh. = inhabitant(s)
ins. = inserted
insep. = inseparable
intens. = intensive(ly)
interch. = interchange
interj. = interjection(al)(ly)
interp. = interposed
interrog. =
interrogative(ly)
intr. = intransitive(ly)
invol. = involuntarily
irreg. = irregular
Isr. = Israel(ite)(s)(ish)
Isr.s = Israelitess(es)
Jerus. = Jerusalem
Lat. = Latin
lit. = literal(ly)
masc. = masculine
marg. = margin
marginal reading
mean. = meaning
ment. = mental(ly)
mid. = middle
modif. = modified
modification
mor. = moral(ly)
mult. = multiplicative
mus. = musical
nat. = native, nature
natural(ly)
neg. = negative(ly)
obj. = object(ive)(ively)
obs. = obsolete
or. = origin(al)(ly)
ord. = ordinal
orth. = orthographical
Pal. = Palestine
par. = particle
part. = participle
pass. = passive(ly)
patron. = patronymic(al)(ly)
perh. = perhaps
perm. = permutation
Pers. = Persia(n)(s)
pers. = person(al)(ly)
pl. = plural
phys. = physical(ly)
pos. = positive(ly)
pref. = prefix(ed)
prep. = preposition(al)
pres. = present
prim. = primary
prob. = probable(ly)
prol. = prolonged
prolongation
pron. = pronominal(ly)
pronoun
prop. = properly
redupl. = reduplicated
reduplication
refl. = reflexive(ly)
rel. = relative(ly)
relig. = religion
religious(ly)
sec. = second(ary)(ily)
short. = shortened
shorter
signif. = signification
sing. = singular
spec. = specific(ally)
specially
spir. = spiritual(ly}
streng. = strengthen(ed)
(ing)
subj. = subject(ive)(ly)
sup. = superlative(ly)
symb. = symbolical(ly)
te. = technically
trans. = transitive(ly
transc. = transcription
transf. = transfer(ral)
(ing)
transp. = transposed
transposition
unc. = uncertain(ly)
un. = unused
var. = variation
voc. = vocative (case)
vol. = voluntarily

SIGNS EMPLOYED

+ (*addition*) denotes a rendering in the A.V. of one or more Heb. words in connection wiith the one under consideration.

X (*multiplication*) denotes a rendering in the A.V. that results from an idiom peculiar to the Heb.

( ) (parenthesis), in the renderings from the A.V., denotes a word or syllable sometimes given in connection with the principal word to which it is annexed.

[ ] (bracket), in the rendering from the A.V., denotes the inclusion of an additional word in the Heb.

Italics, at the end of a rendering from the A.V., denote an explanation of the variations from the usual form.

HEBREW DICTIONARY OF THE OLD TESTAMENT

HEBREW

א

1. אָב *awb*; a prim. word; *father*, in a lit and immed., or fig. and remote appl.):–chief, (fore-)father[-less], X patrimony, principal. Comp. names in "Abi-".

2. אַב *ab* (chald); cor. to 1:–father.

3. אֵב *abe;* from the same as 24; a *green* plant:–greenness, fruit.

4. אֵב *abe* (Chald); cor. to 3:–fruit.

5. אֲבַגְתָא *ab-ag-thaw';* of for. or.; *Abagtha*, a eunuch of Xerxes: –Abagtha.

6. אָבַד *aw-bad';* a prim. root; prop. to *wander* away, i.e. *lose* oneself; by impl. to *perish* (caus., *destroy*): –break, destroy(-uction), + not escape, fail, lose, (cause to, make) perish, spend, X and surely, take, be undone, X utterly, be void of, have no way to flee.

7. אֲבַד *ab-ad'* (chald); cor. to 6:–destroy, perish.

8. אֹבֵד *o-bade';* act.part. of 6; (concr.) *wretched* or (abstr.) *destruction*:–perish.

9. אֲבֵדָה *ab-ay-daw';* from 6; concr., something *lost;* abstr., *destruction*, i.e. Hades:–lost. Comp. 10.

10. אֲבַדֹּה *ab-ad-do';* the same as 9, miswritten for 11; a *perishing*:– destruction.

11. אֲבַדּוֹן *ab-ad-done';* intens. from 6; abstr., a *perishing;* concr., Hades:–destruction.

12. אַבְדָן *ab-dawn';* from 6; a *perishing*: – destruction.

13. אׇבְדַן *ob-dawn';* from 6; a *perishing*: – destruction.

14. אָבָה *aw-baw';* a prim. root; to *breathe* after, i.e. (fig.) to *be acquiescent*:–con-sent, rest content will, be willing.

15. אָבֶה *aw-beh';* from 14; *longing*:–desire

16. אֵבֶה *ay-beh';* from 14 (in the sense of *bending* towards); the *papyrus*:–swift.

17. אֲבוֹי *ab-o'ee;* from 14 (in the sense of *desiring*); *want:*–sorrow.

18. אֵבוּס *ay-booce';* from 75; a *manger* or *stall*:–crib.

19. אִבְחָה *ib-khaw';* from an un. root (app. mean. to *turn*); *brandishing* of a sword:–point.

20. אֲבַטִּחַ *ab-at-tee'-akh;* of unc. der.; a *melon* (only pl.):–melon.

21. אֲבִי *ab-ee';* from 1; *fatherly*; *Abi*, Hezekiah's mother:–Abi.

22. אֲבִיאֵל *ab-ee-ale';* from 1 and 410; *father* (i.e. *possessor*) *of God; Abiel,* the name of two Isr.:–*Abiel.*

23. אֲבִיאָסָף *ab-ee-aw-sawf';* from 1 and 622; *father of gathering* (i.e. *gatherer*); *Abiasaph*, an Isr.:–Abiasaph.

24. אָבִיב *aw-beeb';* from an un. root (mean. to *be tender*); *green*, i.e. a young ear of grain; hence, the name of the month *Abib* or Nisan:–Abib, ear, green ears of corn (not maize).

25. אֲבִי גִבְעוֹן *ab-ee' ghib-one';* from 1 and 1391; *father* (i.e. *founder*) *of Gibon*; *Abi-Gibon,* perh. an Isr.:–father of Gibeon.

26 אֲבִיגַיִל *ab-ee-gah'-yil;* אֲבִיגַל or short. *ab-ee-gal';* from 1 and 1524; *father* (i.e. *source*) *of joy*; *Abigail* or *Abigal*, the name of two Isr.s:–Abigal. **27**. אֲבִידָן *ab-ee-dawn';* from 1 and 1777; *father of judgment* (i.e. *judge*); *Abidan*, an Isr.:– Abidan.

28. אֲבִידָע *ab-ee-daw';* from 1 and 3045; *father of knowledge* (i.e. *knowing*); *Abida*, a son of Abraham by Keturah:–Abida, Abidah.

29. אֲבִיָּה *ab-ee-yaw';* אֲבִיָּהוּ or prol. *ab-ee-yaw'-hoo;* from 1 and 3050; *father* (i.e. *worshipper*) of *Jah; Abijah*, the name of several Isr. men and two Isr.s:–Abiah, Abijah.

30. אֲבִיהוּא *ab-ee-hoo';* from 1 and 1931; *father* (i.e. *worshipper) of Him* (i.e. *God*); *Abihu*, a son of Aaron:–Abihu.

31. אֲבִיהוּד *ab-ee-hood';* from 1 and 1935; *father* (i.e. *possessor*) *of renown; Abihud*, the name of two Isr.:–Abihud.

32. אֲבִיהַיִל *ab-ee-hah'-yil;* or (more correctly) אֲבִיחַיִל *ab-ee-khah'-yil;* from 1 and 2428; *father* (i.e. *possessor*) of *might*; *Abihail* or *Abichail*, the name of three Isr. and two Isr.s:–Abihail.

33. אֲבִי הָעֶזְרִי *ab-ee'-haw-ez-ree';* from 44 with the art. ins.; *father of the Ezrite*; an *Abiezrite* or desc. of Abiezer; –Abiezrite.

34. אֶבְיוֹן *eb-yone';* from 14, in the sense of *want* (esp. in feeling); *destitute*:–beggar, needy, poor (man).

35. אֲבִיּוֹנָה *ab-ee-yo-naw';* from 14; pro-vocative of *desire*; the *caper* berry (from its *stimulative* taste):–desire.

36. אֲבִיטוּב *ab-ee-toob';* from 1 and 2898; *father of goodness* (i.e. *good*); *Abitub*, an Isr.:–Abitub.

37. אֲבִיטַל *ab-ee-tal'* from 1 and 2919; *father of dew* (i.e. *fresh*); *Abital*, a wife of King David:–Abital.

38. אֲבִיָּם *ab-ee-yawm';* from 1 and 3220; *father of* (the) *sea* (i.e. *seaman*); *Abijam* (or Abijah), a king of Judah:–Abijam.

39. אֲבִימָאֵל *ab-ee-maw-ale';* from 1 and an elsewhere un. (prob. for.) word; *father of Mael* (app. some Arab tribe); *Abimael*, a son of Joktan:–Abimael.

40. אֲבִימֶלֶךְ *ab-ee-mel'-ek;* from 1 and 4428; *father of* (the) *king; Abimelek,* the name of two Philistine kings and of two Isr.:–Abimelech.

41. אֲבִינָדָב *ab-ee-naw-dawb'* from 1 and 5068; *father of generosity* (i.e. *liberal*); *Abinadab*, the name of four Isr.:–Abinadab.

42. אֲבִינֹעַם *ab-ee-no'-am;* from 1 and 5278; *father of pleasantness* (i.e. *gracious*); *Abinoam*, an Isr.:–Abinoam.

43. אֶבְיָסָף *eb-yaw-sawf';* contr. from 23; *Ebjasaph*, an Isr.:–Ebiasaph.

44. אֲבִיעֶזֶר *ab-ee-ay'-zer;* from 1 and 5829; *father of help* (i.e. *helpful*); *Abiezer,* the name of two Isr.:–Abiezer.

45. אֲבִי־עַלְבוֹן *ab-ee-al-bone';* from 1 and and an un. root of unc.. der.; prob., *father of strength* (i.e. *valiant*); *Abialbon,* an Isr.:–Abialbon.

46. אֲבִיר *aw-beer';* from 82; *mighty* (spoken of God):–mighty (one).

47. אַבִּיר *ab-beer';* for 46;–angel, bull, chiefest, mighty (one), stout[-hearted], strong (one), valiant.

48. אֲבִירָם *ab-ee-rawm';* from 1 and 7311; *father of height* (i.e. *lofty*);*Abiram*, the name of two Isr.:–Abiram.

49. אֲבִישַׁג *ab-ee-shag'* from 1 and 7686; *father of err.* (i.e. *blundering*); *Abishag*, a concubine of David:–Abishag.

50. אֲבִישׁוּעַ *ab-ee-shoo'-ah;* from 1 and 7771; *father of plenty* (i.e. *prosperous*); *Abishua*, the name of two Isr.:–Abishua.

51. אֲבִישׁוּר *ab-ee-shoor';* from 1 and 7791; *father of* (the) *wall* (i.e. perh. *mason*); *Abishur*, an Isr.:–Abishur.

52. אֲבִישַׁי *ab-ee-shah'ee;* or (short.) אַבְשַׁי *ab-shah'ee;* from 1 and 7862; *father of a gift* (i.e. prob. *generous*); *Abishai,* an Isr.:–Abishai.

53. אֲבִישָׁלוֹם *ab-ee-shaw-lome';* or (short.) אַבְשָׁלוֹם *ab-shaw- lome';* from 1 and 7965; *father of peace* (i.e. *friendly*); *Abshalom*, a son of David; also (the fuller form) a later Isr.:–Abishalom, Absalom.

54. אֶבְיָתָר *ab-yaw-thawr';* contr. from 1 and 3498; *father of abundance* (i.e. *liberal*); *Ebjathar*, an Isr.:–Abiathar.

55. אָבַךְ *aw-bak';* a prim. root; prob. to *coil* upward:–mount up.

56. אָבַל *aw-bal';* a prim. root; to *bewail*: – lament, mourn.

57. אָבֵל *aw-bale';* from 56; *lamenting*:–mourn(-er,-ing).

58. אָבֵל *aw-bale';* from an un. root(mean. to *be grassy*); a *meadow:*–plain. Comp. also the proper names beginning with Abel-.

59. אָבֵל *aw-bale';* from 58; a *meadow*; *Abel*,the name of two places in Pal..:–Abel.

60. אֵבֶל *ay'-bel;* from 56; *lamentation*:–mourning.

61. אֲבָל *ab-awl';* app. from 56 through the idea of *negation; nay,* i.e. *truly* or *yet*:–but, indeed, nevertheless, verily.

62. אָבֵל בֵּית־מַעֲכָה *aw-bale' bayth ma-a-kaw';* from 58 and 1004 and 4601; *meadow of Beth-Maakah*; *Abel of Beth-maakah*, a place in Pal.: –Abel-beth-maachah, Abel of Beth-maachah.

63. אָבֵל הַשִּׁטִּים *aw-bale' hash-shit-teem';* from 58 and the pl. of 7848, with the art. ins.; *meadow of the acacias; Abel hash-Shittim*, a place in Pal.:–Abel-shittim.

64. אָבֵל כְּרָמִים *aw-bale' ker-aw-meem';* from 58 and the pl. of 3754; *meadow of vineyards*; *Abel-Keramim*, a place in Pal.:–plain of the vineyards.

65. אָבֵל מְחוֹלָה *aw-bale' mekh-o-law';* from 58 and 4246; *meadow of dancing; Abel-Mecholah*, a place in Pal.:–Abel-meholah.

66. אָבֵל מַיִם *aw-bale' mah'-yim;* from 58 and 4325; *meadow of water; Abel-Majim,* a place in Pal.:–Abel-maim.

67. אָבֵל מִצְרַיִם *aw-bale' mits-rah'-yim;* from 58 and 4714; *meadow of Eg.*; *Abel-Mitsrajim*, a place in Pal.:–Abel-mizraim.

68. אֶבֶן *eh'-ben* from the root of 1129 through the mean. to *build*; *a stone*:–+ carbuncle, + mason, + plummet, [chalk-, hail-, head-, sling-]stone(-ny),(divers) weight(-s).

69. אֶבֶן *eh'-ben;* (Chald) cor. to 68:–stone.

70. אֹבֶן *o'ben;* from the same as 68; *a pair of stones* (only dual); a potter's *wheel* or a midwife's *stool* (consisting alike of two horizontal disks with a support between):–wheel, stool.

71. אֲבָנָה *ab-aw-naw';* perh. fem. of 68; *stony; Abanah*, a river near Damascus:–Abana. Comp. 549.

72. אֶבֶן הָעֵזֶר *eh'-ben haw-e'-zer;* from 68 and 5828 with the art. ins.; *stone of the help*; *Eben-ha-Ezer*, a place in Pal.:–Ebenezer.
73. אַבְנֵט *ab-nate';* of unc. der.; a *belt*: girdle.
74. אַבְנֵר *ab-nare';* or (fully) אֲבִינֵר 'Abiyner *ab-ee-nare';* from 1 and 5216; *father of light* (i.e. *enlightening*); *Abner*, an Isr.:–Abner.
75. אָבַס *aw-bas';* a prim. root; to *fodder*:–fatted, stalled.
76. אֲבַעְבֻּעָה *ab-ah-boo-aw';* (by redupl.) from an un. root (mean. to *belch* forth); an inflammatory *pustule* (as *eruption*):–blains.
77. אֶבֶץ *eh'-bets;* from an un. root prob. mean. to *gleam; conspicuous*; *Ebets,* a place in Pal.:–Abez.
78. אִבְצָן *ib-tsawn';* from the same as 76; *splendid; Ibtsan*, an Isr.:–Ibzan.
79. אָבַק *aw-bak';* a prim. root, prob. to *float* away (as vapor), but used only as denom. from 80; to *bedust*, i.e. *grapple*:– wrestle.
80. אָבָק *aw-bawk';* from root of 79; light particles (as *volatile*):–(small) dust, powder.
81. אֲבָקָה *ab-aw-kaw';* fem. of 80:–powder.
82. אָבַר *aw-bar';* a prim. root; to *soar*:–fly.
83. אֵבֶר *ay-ber';* from 82; a *pinion*:– [long-] wing(-ed).
84. אֶבְרָה *eb-raw';* fem. of 83:–feather, wing.
85. אַבְרָהָם *ab-raw-hawm';* contr. from 1 and an un. root (prob. mean. to *be populous*); *father of a multitude*; *Abraham*, the later name of Abram:–Abraham.
86. אַבְרֵךְ *ab-rake';* prob. an Eg. word mean. *kneel*:–bow the knee.
87. אַבְרָם *ab-rawm';* contr. from 48; *high father*; *Abram*, the or. name of Abraham:–Abram.
88. אֹבֹת *o-both';* pl. of 178; water-*skins*; *Oboth*, a place in the Desert:–Oboth.
89. אָגֵא *aw-gay';* of unc. der. [comp. 90]; *Agë*, an Isr.:–Agee.
90. אֲגַג *ag-ag';* or אֲגָג *ag-awg';* of unc. der. [comp. 89]; *flame*; *Agag*, a title of Amalekitish kings:–Agag.
91. אֲגָגִי *ag-aw-ghee';* patrial or patron. from 90; an *Agagite* or descendent (subj.) of Agag:–Agagite
92. אֲגֻדָּה *ag-ood-daw'* fem. pass.part. of an un. root (mean. to *bind*); a *band, bundle, knot*, or *arch*:–bunch, burden, troop.
93. אֱגוֹז *eg-oze';* prob of Pers. or.; a *nut*:–nut.
94. אָגוּר *aw-goor';* pass.part. of 103; *gathered* (i.e. *received* among the sages); *Agur*, a fanciful name for Solomon:–Agur.
95. אֲגוֹרָה *ag-o-raw'*; from the same as 94; prop. something *gathered*, i.e. perh. a *grain* or *berry*; used only of a small (silver) *coin*:–piece (of) silver.
96. אֵגֶל *eh'-ghel;* from an un. root (mean. to *flow* down or together as drops); a *reservoir*:–drop.
97. אֶגְלַיִם *eg-lah'-yim;* dual of 96; a *double pond*; *Eglajim*, a place in Moab:–Eglaim.
98. אֲגַם *ag-am'* from an un. root (mean. to *coll.* as water); a *marsh*; hence a *rush* (as growing in swamps); hence a *stockade* of reeds:–pond, pool, standing [water].
99. אָגֵם *aw-game'* prob. from the same as 98 (in the sense of *stagnant* water); fig., *sad*:–pond.
100. אַגְמוֹן *ag-mone'* from the same as 98; a marshy *pool* [others from a different root, a *kettle*]; by impl. a *rush* (as growing there); coll. a *rope* of rushes:–bulrush, caldron, hook, rush.
101. אַגָּן *ag-gawn';* prob. from 5059; a *bowl* (as *pounded* out hollow): basin, cup, goblet.
102. אֲגַף *ag-gawf;'* prob. from 5062 (through the idea of *impending*); a *cover* or *heap*; i.e. (only pl.) *wings* of an army, or *crowds* of troops:–bands.
103. אָגַר *aw-gar';* a prim. root; to *harvest*:–gather.
104. אִגְּרָה *ig-er-aw'* (Chald); of Pers. or.; an *epistle* (as carried by a state courier or postman):–letter.
105. אֲגַרְטָל *ag-ar-tawl';* of unc. der.; a *basin*:–charger.
106. אֶגְרֹף *eg-rofe';* from 1640 (in the sense of *grasping*); the *clenched* hand:–fist.
107. אִגֶּרֶת *ig-eh'-reth;* fem. of 104; an *epistle*:–letter.
108. אֵד ade from the same as 181 (in the sense of *enveloping*); a *fog*:– mist, vapor.
109. אָדַב *aw-dab';* a prim. root; to *languish*:–grieve.
110. אַדְבְּאֵל *ad-beh-ale';* prob. from 109 (in the sense of *chastisement*) and 410; *disciplined of God*; *Adbeël*, a son of Ishmael:–Adbeel.
111. אֲדַד *ad-ad';* prob. an orth. var. for 2301; *Adad* (or Hadad), an Edomite:–Hadad.
112. אִדּוֹ *id-do;* of unc. der.; *Iddo*, an Isr.:–Iddo.
113. אָדוֹן *aw-done';* or (short.) אָדֹן *aw-done';* from an un. root (mean. to *rule*); *sovereign,* i.e. *controller* (human or divine):– lord, master, owner. Comp. also names beginning with"Adoni-"
114. אַדּוֹן *ad-done';* prob. intens. for 113; *powerful*; *Addon*, app. an Isr.:–Addon.
115. אֲדוֹרַיִם *ad-o-rah'-yim;* dual from 142 (in the sense of *eminence*); *double mound; Adorajim*, a place in Pal.:–Adoraim.
116. אֱדַיִן *ed-ah'-yin* (Chald); of uncert der; *then* (of time):–now, that time, then.
117. אַדִּיר *ad-deer';* from 142; *wide* or (gen.) *large*; fig., *powerful*:–excellent, famous, gallant, glorious, goodly, lordly, mighty(-ier one), noble, principal, worthy.
118. אֲדַלְיָא *ad-al-yaw';* of Pers. der.; *Adalja*, a son of Haman:–Adalia.
119. אָדַם *aw-dam';* to *show blood* (in the face), i.e. *flush* or turn rosy:–be (dyed, made) red (ruddy).
120. אָדָם *aw-dawm';* from 119; *ruddy* i.e. a *human being* (an indiv. or the species, *mankind,* etc.):–X another, + hypocrite, + common sort, X low, man (mean, of low degree), person.
121. אָדָם *aw-dawm';* the same as 120; *Adam* the name of the first man, also of a place in Pal.:–Adam.
122. אָדֹם *aw-dome';* from 119; *rosy*:–red, ruddy.
123. אֱדֹם *ed-ome';* or (fully) אֱדוֹם *ed-ome';* from 122; *red* (see Ge. 25:25); *Edom*, the elder twin-brother of Jacob; hence the region (Idumaea) occupied by him:–Edom, Edomites, Idumea.
124. אֹדֶם *o'-dem;* from 119; *redness*, i.e. the *ruby, garnet*, or some other red gem:–sardius.
125. אֲדַמְדָּם *ad-am-dawm';* redupl. from 119; *reddish*:–(somewhat) reddish.
126. אַדְמָה *ad-maw';* contr. for 127; *earthy; Admah*, a place near the Dead Sea:–Admah.
127. אֲדָמָה *ad-aw-maw';* from 119; *soil* (from its gen. *redness*):–country, earth, ground, husband [-man] (-ry), land.
128. אֲדָמָה *ad-aw-maw';* the same as 127; *Adamah*, a place in Pal.:–Adamah.
129. אֲדָמִי *ad-aw-mee';* from 127; *earthy; Adami*, a place in Pal.:–Adami.
130. אֱדֹמִי *ed-o-mee';* or (fully) אֱדוֹמִי *ed-o-mee';* patron. from 123; an *Edomite*, or desc. from (or inh. of) Edom:–Edomite. See 726.
131. אֲדֻמִּים *ad-oom-meem';* pl. of 121; *red* spots; *Adummim*, a pass in Pal.:–Adummim.
132. אַדְמֹנִי *ad-mo-nee';* or (fully) אַדְמוֹנִי *ad-mo-nee';* from 119; *reddish* (of the hair or the complexion):–red, ruddy.
133. אַדְמָתָא *ad-maw-thaw';* prob. of Pers. der.: *Admatha*, a Pers. nobleman:–Admatha.
134. אֶדֶן *eh'-den;* from the same as 113 (in the sense of *strength*); a *basis* (of a building, a column, etc.):–foundation, socket.
135. אַדָּן *ad-dawn';* intens. from the same as 134; *firm*; *Addan*, an Isr.:–Addan.
136. אֲדֹנָי *ad-o-noy';* an emphat. form of 113; the *Lord* (used as a proper name of God only):–(my) Lord.
137. אֲדֹנִי־בֶזֶק *ad-o"-nee-beh'-zek;* from 113 and 966; *lord of Bezek*; *Adoni-Bezek*; a Canaanitish king:–Adoni-bezek.
138. אֲדֹנִיָּה *ad-o-nee-yaw';* or. (prol) אֲדֹנִיָּהוּ *ad-o-nee- yaw'-hoo;* from 113 and 3050; *lord* (i.e. worshipper) of Jah; *Adonijah,* the name of three Isr.:–Adonijah.
139. אֲדֹנִי־צֶדֶק *ad-o"-nee-tseh'-dek;* from 113 and 6664; *lord of justice*; *Adoni-Tsedek*, a Canaanitish king:–Adonizedec.
140. אֲדֹנִיקָם *ad-o-nee-kawm';* from 113 and 6965; *lord of rising* (i.e. *high*); *Adonikam*, the name of one or two Isr.:–Adonikam.
141. אֲדֹנִירָם *ad-o-nee-rawm';* from 113 and 7311; *lord of height*; *Adoniram*, an Isr.:–Adoniram.
142. אָדַר *aw-dar';* a prim. root; to *expand,* i.e. *be great* or (fig.) *magnificent*:–(become) glorious, honourable.
143. אֲדָר *ad-awr';* prob. of for. derivation; perh. mean. *fire*; *Adar*, the 12th Heb. month:–Adar.
144. אֲדָר *ad-awr'* (Chald); cor. to 143:–Adar.
145. אֶדֶר *eh'-der;* from 142; *amplitude,* i.e. (concr.) a *mantle*; also (fig.) *splendor*:–goodly, robe.
146. אַדָּר *ad-dawr';* intens. from 142; *ample*; *Addar*, a place in Pal.; also an Isr.:–Addar.
147. אִדַּר *id-dar'* (Chald.); intens., from a root cor. to 142; *ample*, i.e. a threshing-*floor*:–threshingfloor.
148. אֲדַרְגָּזֵר *ad-ar"-gaw-zare'* (Chald.); from the same as 147, and 1505; a *chief diviner*, or *astrologer*:–judge.
149. אַדְרַזְדָּא *ad-raz-daw'* (Chald.); prob. of Pers. or.; *quickly* or *carefully*:–diligently.
150. אֲדַרְכֹּן *ad-ar-kone';* of Pers. or.; a *daric* or Pers. coin:–dram.
151. אֲדֹרָם *ad-o-rawm';* contr. for 141; *Adoram* (or Adoniram), an Isr.:–Adoram.
152. אַדְרַמֶּלֶךְ *ad-ram-meh'-lek;* from 142 and 4428; *splendor of* (the) *king; Adrammelek*, the name of an Ass. idol, also of a son of Sennacherib:–Adrammelech.
153. אֶדְרָע *ed-raw'* (Chald.); an orth. var. for 1872; an *arm*, i.e. (fig.) *power*:–force.
154. אֶדְרֶעִי *ed-reh'-ee;* from the equiv. of 153; *mighty*; *Edrei*, the name of two places in Pal.:–Edrei.
155. אַדֶּרֶת *ad-deh'-reth;* fem. of 117; some-

thing *ample* (as a *large* vine, a *wide* dress); also the same as 145:–garment, glory, goodly, mantle, robe.
156. אָדַשׁ *aw-dash';* a prim. root; to *tread* out (grain):–thresh.
157. אָהַב *aw-hab';* or אָהֵב *aw-habe';* a prim. root; to *have affection* for (sexually or otherwise):–(be-)love(-d, -ly, -r), like, friend.
158. אַהַב *ah'-hab;* from 157; *affection* (in a good or a bad sense):–love(-r).
159. אֹהַב *o'-hab;* from 156; mean. the same as 158:–love.
160. אַהֲבָה *a-hab-aw;* fem. of 158 and mean. the same:–love.
161. אֹהַד *o'-had;* from an un. root mean. to be *united*; *unity*; Ohad, an Isr.:–Ohad.
162. אֲהָהּ *a-haw';* app. a prim. word ex-pressing *pain* exclamatorily; *Oh*!:–ah, alas.
163. אַהֲוָא *a-hav-aw';* prob. of for. or.; *Ahava*, a river of Babylonia:–Ahava.
164. אֵהוּד *ay-hood';* from the same as 161; *united; Ehud*, the name of two or three Isr.:–Ehud.
165. אֱהִי *e-hee';* app. an orth. var. for 346; *where:*–I will be (Ho. 13:10, 14) [*which is often the rendering of the same Heb. form from* 1961].
166. אָהַל *aw-hal';* a prim. root; to be *clear*:–shine.
167. אָהַל *aw-hal';* a denom. from 168; to *tent*:–pitch (remove) a tent.
168. אֹהֶל *o'-hel;* from 166; a *tent* (as *clearly* conspicuous from a distance):–covering, (dwelling)(place), home, tabernacle, tent.
169. אֹהֶל *o'-hel;* the same as 168; *Ohel*, an Isr.:–Ohel.
170. אָהֳלָה *o-hol-aw';* in form a fem. of 168, but in fact for אָהֳלָהּ *o-hol-aw';* from 168; *her tent* (i.e. idolatrous *sanctuary*); *Oholah*, a symbol. name for Samaria:–Aholah.
171. אָהֳלִיאָב *o"-hol-e-awb';* from 168 and 1; *tent of* (his) *father; Oholiab*, an Isr.:–Aholiab.
172. אָהֳלִיבָה *o"-hol-ee-baw';* (similarly with 170) for אָהֳלִיבָהּ *o"-hol-e-baw';* from 168; *my tent* (is) *in her; Oholibah*, a symbolic name for Judah:–Aholibah.
173. אָהֳלִיבָמָה *o"-hol-ee-baw-maw';* from 168 and 1116; *tent of* (the) *height; Oholibamah*, a wife of Esau:–Aholibamah.
174. אֲהָלִים *a-haw-leem';* or (fem.) אֲהָלוֹת *a-haw-loth';* (only used thus in the pl.); of for. or.; *aloe* wood (i.e. sticks):–(tree of lign-) aloes.
175. אַהֲרוֹן *a-har-one';* of unc. der.; *Aharon*, the brother of Moses:–Aaron.
176. אוֹ *o;* presumed to be the "constr." or genitival form of אַו *av*; short. for 185; *desire* (and so prob. in Pr. 31:4); hence (by way of alternative) *or*, also *if*:–also, and, either, if, at the least, X nor, or, otherwise, then, whether.
177. אוּאֵל *oo- ale';* from 176 and 410; *wish of God; Uel*, and Isr.:–Uel.
178. אוֹב *obe;* from the same as 1 (app. through the idea of *prattling* a father's name); prop. a *mumble*, i.e. a water *skin* (from its hollow sound); hence a *necromancer* (ventriloquist, as from a jar):–bottle, familiar spirit.
179. אוֹבִיל *o-beel';* prob. from 56; *mournful; Obil*, an Ishmaelite:–Obil.
180. אוּבָל *oo-bawl';* or (short.) אֻבָל *oo-bawl';* from 2986 (in the sense of 2988); a *stream*:–river.
181. אוּד *ood;* from an un. root mean. to *rake* together; a *poker* (for *turning* or *gathering* embers):–(fire-)brand.
182. אוֹדוֹת *o-doth';* or (short.) אֹדוֹת *o-doth'* (only thus in the pl.); from the same as 181; *turnings* (i.e. *occasions*); (adv.) on *account* of:–(be-)cause, concerning, sake.
183. אָוָה *aw-vaw';* a prim. root; to *wish* for:–covet, (greatly) desire, be desirous, long, lust (after).
184. אָוָה *aw-vaw';* a prim. root; to *extend* or *mark* out:–point out.
185. אַוָּה *av-vaw';* from 183; *longing*:–desire, lust after, pleasure.
186. אוּזַי *oo-zah'-ee;* perh. by perm. for 5813, *strong; Uzai*, an Isr.:–Uzai.
187. אוּזָל *oo-zawl';* of unc. der.; *Uzal*, a son of Joktan:–Uzal.
188. אוֹי *o'-ee;* prob. from 183 (in the sense of *crying* out after); *lamentation*; also interj. *Oh*!:–alas, woe.
189. אֱוִי *ev-ee';* prob. from 183; *desirous*; *Evi*, a Midianitish chief:–Evi.
190. אוֹיָה *o-yaw';* fem. of 188:–woe.
191. אֱוִיל *ev-eel';* from an un. root (mean. to be *perverse*); (fig.) *silly*:–fool(-ish) (man).
192. אֱוִיל מְרֹדַךְ *ev-eel' mer-o-dak'* of Chald. der. and prob. mean. *soldier of Merodak*; *Evil-Merodak*, a Babylonian king:–Evil-merodach.
193. אוּל *ool;* from an un. root mean. to *twist*, i.e. (by impl.) *be strong*; the *body* (as being *rolled* together); also *powerful*:–mighty, strength.
194. אוּלַי *oo-lah'ee;* or (short.) אֻלַי *oo-lah'ee;* from 176; *if not*; hence *perh.*:–if so be, may be, peradventure, unless.
195. אוּלַי *oo-lah'ee;* of Pers. der.; the *Ulai* (or Eulaeus), a river of Pers.:–Ulai.
196. אֱוִלִי *ev-ee-lee';* from 191; *silly, foolish*; hence (mor.) *impious*:–foolish.
197. אוּלָם *oo-lawm';* or (short.) אֻלָם *oo-lawm';* from 481 (in the sense of *tying*); a *vestibule* (as *bound* to the building):–porch.
198. אוּלָם *oo-lawm';* app., from 481 (in the sense of *dumbness*); *solitary*; *Ulam*, the name of two Isr.:–Ulam.
199. אוּלָם *oo-lawm';* app. a var. of 194; *however* or *on the contrary*:–as for, but, howbeit, in very deed, surely, truly, wherefore.
200. אִוֶּלֶת *iv-veh'-leth;* from the same as 191; *silliness*:–folly, foolishly(-ness).
201. אוֹמָר *o-mawr'* from 559; *talkative*; *Omar*, a grandson of Esau:–Omar.
202. אוֹן *ōne;* prob. from the same as 205 (in the sense of *effort*, but successful); *ability, power*, (fig.) *wealth*:–force, goods, might, strength, substance.
203. אוֹן *ōne;* the same as 202; *On*, an Isr.:–On.
204. אוֹן *ōne;* or (short.); אֹן *ōne*; of Eg. der.; *On*, a city of Eg.:–On.
205. אָוֶן *aw-ven';* from an un. root perh. mean. prop. to *pant* (hence, to *exert* oneself, usually in vain; to *come to naught*); strictly *nothingness*; also *trouble. vanity, wickedness*; spec. an *idol*:–affliction, evil, false, idol, iniquity, mischief, mourners(-ing), naught, sorrow, unjust, unrighteous, vain, vanity, wicked(-ness). Comp. 369.
206. אָוֶן *aw'-ven;* the same as 205; *idolatry*; *Aven*, the contemptuous synonym of three places, one in Coele-Syria, one in Eg. (On), and one in Pal. (Bethel):–Aven. See also 204, 1007.
207. אוֹנוֹ *o-no';* or (short.) אֹנוֹ *o-no';* prol. from 202; *strong; Ono*, a place in Pal.:–Ono.
208. אוֹנָם *o-nawm';* a var. of 209; *strong; Onam*, the name of an Edomite and of an Isr.:–Onam.
209. אוֹנָן *o-nawn';* a var. of 207; *strong; Onan*, a son of Judah:–Onan.
210. אוּפָז *oo-fawz';* perh. a corruption of 211; *Uphaz*, a famous gold region:–Uphaz.
211. אוֹפִיר *o-feer';* or (short) אֹפִיר *o-feer';* and אוֹפִר *o- feer';* of unc. der.; *Ophir*, the name of a son of Joktan, and of a gold region in the E.:–Ophir.
212. אוֹפָן *o-fawn';* or (short) אֹפָן *o-fawn';* from an un. root mean. to *revolve*; a *wheel*:–wheel.
213. אוּץ *oots;* a prim. root; to *press*; (by impl.) to *be close, hurry, withdraw*:–(make) haste(-n, -y), labor, be narrow.
214. אוֹצָר *o-tsaw';* from 686; a *depository*:–armory, cellar, garner, store(-house), treasure(-house) (-y).
215. אוֹר *ore;* a prim. root; *to be* (caus., *make*) *luminous* (lit. and metaphorically):–X break of day, glorious, kindle, (be, en-, give, show) light (-en, -ened), set on fire, shine.
216. אוֹר *ore;* from 215; *illumination* or (concr.) *luminary* (in every sense, incl. *lightning, happiness*, etc.):–bright, clear, + day, light (-ning), morning, sun.
217. אוּר *oor* from 215; *flame*; hence (in the pl.) the *E.* (as being the region of light):–fire, light. See also 224.
218. אוּר *oor;* the same as 217; *Ur,* a place in Chaldaea; also an Isr.:–Ur.
219. אוֹרָה *o-raw';* fem. of 216; *luminousness*, i.e. (fig.) *prosperity*; also a plant (as being *bright*):–herb, light.
220. אֲוֵרָה *av-ay-raw';* by transp. for 723; a *stall*:–cote.
221. אוּרִי *oo-ree';* from 217; *fiery; Uri*, the name of three Isr.:–Uri.
222. אוּרִיאֵל *oo-ree-ale';* from 217 and 410; *flame of God*; *Uriel*, the name of two Isr.:–Uriel.
223. אוּרִיָּה *oo-ree-yaw';* or (prol.) אוּרִיָּהוּ *oo-ree-yaw'-hoo;* from 217 and 3050; *flame* of *Jah*; *Urijah*, the name of one Hittite and five Isr.:–Uriah, Urijah.
224. אוּרִים *oo-reem';* pl of 217; *lights; Urim*, the oracular brilliancy of the figures in the high-priest's breastplate:–Urim.
225. אוּת *ooth;* a prim. root; prop. to *come*, i.e. (implied) to *assent*:–consent.
226. אוֹת *ōth;* prob. from 225 (in the sense of *appearing*); a *signal* (lit. or fig.), as a *flag, beacon, monument, omen, prodigy, evidence*, etc.:–mark, miracle, (en-)sign, token.
227. אָז *awz;* a demonstr. adv.; *at that time* or *place*; also as a conj., *therefore*:–beginning, for, from, hitherto, now, of old, once, since, then, at which time, yet.
228. אֲזָא *az-zaw'* (Chald.); or אֲזָה *az-aw'* (Chald.); to *kindle*; (by impl.) to *heat*:–heat, hot.
229. אֶזְבַּי *ez-bah'ee;* prob. from 231; *hyssop-like; Ezbai*, an Isr.:–Ezbai.
230. אֲזַד *az-zawd'* (Chald.); of unc. der.; firm:–be gone.
231. אֵזוֹב *ay-zobe';* prob. of for. der.; *hyssop*:–hyssop.
232. אֵזוֹר *ay-zore';* from 246; something *girt;* a *belt,* also a *band*:–girdle.
233. אֲזַי *az-ah'ee;* prob. from 227; *at that time*:–then.
234. אַזְכָּרָה *az-kaw-raw';* from 2142; a *reminder*;

HEBREW

spec. *remembrance-offering*:–memorial.
235. אָזַל *aw-zal'*; a prim. root; to *go away*, hence, to *disappear*:–fail, gad about, go to and fro.
236. אֲזַל *az-al'* (Chald.); the same as 235; to *depart*:–go (up).
237. אֶזֶל *eh'-zel*; from 235; *departure; Ezel*, a memorial stone in Pal.:–Ezel.
238. אָזַן *aw-zan'*; a prim. root; prob. to *expand*; but used only as a denom. from 241; to *broaden out the ear* (with the hand), i.e. (by impl.) to *listen*:–give (perceive by the) ear, hear(-ken). See 239.
239. אָזַן *aw-zan'*; a prim. root [rather ident. with 238 through the idea of *scales* as if two ears]; to *weigh*, i.e. (fig.) *ponder*:–give good heed.
240. אָזֵן *aw-zane'*; from 238; a *spade* or *paddle* (as having a *broad* end):–weapon.
241. אֹזֶן *o'-zen*; from 238; *broadness*. i.e. (concr.) the *ear* (from its form in man):–+ advertise, audience, + displease, ear, hearing, + show.
242. אֻזֵּן שֶׁאֱרָה *ooz-zane' sheh-er-aw'*; from 238 and 7609; *plat of Sheerah* (i.e. settled by him); *Uzzen-Sheërah*, a place in Pal.:–Uzzen-sherah.
243. אַזְנוֹת תָּבוֹר *az-noth' taw-bore'*; from 238 and 8396; *flats* (i.e. *tops*) of *Tabor* (i.e. situated on it); *Aznoth-Tabor*, a place in Pal.:–Aznoth-tabor.
244. אָזְנִי *oz-nee'*; from 241; *having* (quick) *ears; Ozni*, an Isr.; also an Oznite (coll.), his desc.:–Ozni, Oznites.
245. אֲזַנְיָה *az-an-yaw'*; from 238 and 3050; *heard* by *Jah*; *Azanjah*, an Isr.:–Azaniah.
246. אֲזִקִּים *az-ik-keem'*; a var. for 2131; *manacles*:–chains.
247. אָזַר *aw-zar'*; a prim. root; to *belt*:–bind (compass) about, gird (up, with).
248. אֶזְרוֹעַ *ez-ro'-a*; var. for 2220; the *arm*:–arm.
249. אֶזְרָח *ez-rawkh'*; from 2224 (in the sense of *springing up*); a spontaneous *growth*, i.e. *nat.* (tree or persons):–bay tree, (home-) born (in the land), of the (one's own) country (nation).
250. אֶזְרָחִי *ez-raw-khee'*; patron. from 2246; an *Ezrachite* or desc. of Zerach:–Ezrahite.
251. אָח *awkh*; a prim. word; a *brother* (used in the widest sense of lit. relationship and metaphorical affinity or resemblance [like1]):–another, brother(-ly); kindred, like, other. Comp. also the proper names beginning with "Ah-" or "Ahi-".
252. אַח *akh* (Chald.); cor. to 251:–brother.
253. אָח *awkh*; a var. for 162; *Oh*! (expressive of grief or surprise):–ah, alas.
254. אָח *awkh*; of unc. der.; a fire-*pot* or chafing dish:– hearth.
255. אֹחַ *o'-akh*; prob. from 253; a *howler* or lonesome wild animal:–doleful creature.
256. אַחְאָב *akh-awb'*; once (by contr.) אֶחָב *'Echab*; (Jer. 29:22) from 251 and 1; *brother* (i.e. *friend*) of (his) *father; Achab*, the name of a king of Isr. and of a prophet at Babylon:–Ahab.
257. אַחְבָּן *akh-bawn'*; from 251 and 995; *brother* (i.e. *possessor*) *of understanding*; *Achban*, an Isr.:–Ahban.
258. אָחַד *aw-khad'*; perh. a prim. root; to *unify*, i.e. (fig.) *coll.* (one's thoughts):–go one way or other.
259. אֶחָד *ekh-awd'*; a numeral from 258; prop. *united*, i.e. *one*; or (as an ord.) *first*:–a, alike, alone, altogether, and, any(-thing), apiece, a certain, [dai-]ly, each (one), + eleven, every, few, first, + highway, a man, once, one, only, other, some, together,
260. אָחוּ *aw'-khoo*; of unc. (perh. Eg.) der.; a *bulrush* or any marshy grass (particularly that along the Nile):–flag, meadow.
261. אֵחוּד *ay-khood'*; from 258; *united; Echud*, the name of three Isr.:–Ehud.
262. אַחְוָה *akh-vaw'*; from 2331 (in the sense of 2324); an *utterance*:– declaration.
263. אַחֲוָה *akh-av-aw'* (Chald.); cor. to 262; *solution* (of riddles):–showing.
264. אַחֲוָה *akh-av-aw'*; from 251; *fraternity*:–brotherhood.
265. אֲחוֹחַ *akh-o'-akh*; by redupl. from 251; *brotherly; Achoach*, an Isr.:–Ahoah.
266. אֲחוֹחִי *akh-o-khee'*; patron. from 264; an *Achochite* or desc. of Achoach:–Ahohite.
267. אֲחוּמַי *akh-oo-mah'-ee*; perh. from 251 and 4325; *brother* (i.e. *neighbour*) *of water*; *Achumai*, an Isr.:–Ahumai.
268. אָחוֹר *aw-khore'*; or (short) אָחֹר *aw-khore'*; from 299; the *hinder* part; hence (adv.) *behind, backward*; also (as facing north) the *West*:–after(-ward), back (part, -side,-ward), hereafter, (be-)hind(-er part), time to come, without.
269. אָחוֹת *aw-khoth'*; irreg. fem. of 251; a *sister* (used very widely [like 250], lit. and fig.):–(an-)other, sister, together.
270. אָחַז *aw-khaz'*; a prim. root; to *seize* (often with the accessory idea of holding in possession):–+ be affrighted, bar, (catch, lay, take) hold (back), come upon, fasten, handle, portion, (get, have or take) possess(-ion).
271. אָחָז *aw-khawz'*; from 270; *possessor; Achaz*, the name of a Jewish king and of an Isr.:–Ahaz.
272. אֲחֻזָּה *akh-ooz-zaw'*; fem. pass.part. from 270; something *seized*, i.e. a *possession* (esp. of land):–possession.
273. אַחְזַי *akh-zah'ee* from 270; *seizer*; *Achzai*, an Isr.:–Ahasai.
274. אֲחַזְיָה *akh-az-yaw'*; or (prol.) אֲחַזְיָהוּ *'Achazyahuw*; from 270 and 3050; *Jah has seized*; *Achazjah*, the name of a Jewish and an Isr. king:–Ahaziah.
275. אֲחֻזָּם *akh-ooz-zawm'*; from 270; *seizure; Achuzzam*, an Isr.:–Ahuzam.
276. אֲחֻזַּת *akh-ooz-zath'*; a var. of 272; *possession; Achuzzath*, a Philistine:–Ahuzzath.
277. אֲחִי *akh-ee'*; from 251; *brotherly; Achi*, the name of two Isr.:–Ahi.
278. אֵחִי *ay-khee'*; prob. the same as 277; *Echi*, an Isr.:–Ehi.
279. אֲחִיאָם *akh-ee-awm'*; from 251 and 517; *brother of* the *mother* (i.e. *uncle*); *Achiam*, an Isr.:–Ahiam.
280. אֲחִידָה *akh-ee-daw'* (Chald.); cor. to 2420, an *enigma*:–hard sentence.
281. אֲחִיָּה *akh-ee-yaw*; or (prol.) אֲחִיָּהוּ *akh-ee-yaw'-hoo*; from 251 and 3050; *brother* (i.e. *worshipper*) *of Jah; Achijah*, the name of nine Isr.:–Ahiah, Ahijah.
282. אֲחִיהוּד *akh-ee-hood'*; from 251 and 1935; *brother* (i.e. *possessor*) *of renown*; *Achihud*, an Isr.:–Ahihud.
283. אַחְיוֹ *akh-yo'*; prol. from 251; *brotherly; Achio*, the name of three Isr.:–Ahio.
284. אֲחִיחֻד *akh-ee-khood'*; from 251 and 2330; *brother of a riddle* (i.e. *mysterious*); *Achichud*, an Isr.:–Ahihud.
285. אֲחִיטוּב *akh-ee-toob'*; from 251 and 2898; *brother of goodness*; *Achitub*, the name of several priests:–Ahitub.
286. אֲחִילוּד *akh-ee-lood'*; from 251 and 3205; *brother of* one *born*; *Achilud*, an Isr.:–Ahilud.
287. אֲחִימוֹת *akh-ee-mōth'*; from 251 and 4191; *brother of death; Achimoth*, an Isr.:–Ahimoth.
288. אֲחִימֶלֶךְ *akh-ee-meh'-lek*; from 251 and 4428; *brother of* (the) *king; Achimelek*, the name of an Isr. and of a Hittite:–Ahimelech.
289. אֲחִימַן *akh-ee-man'*; or אֲחִימָן *akh-ee-mawn'*; from 251 and 4480; *brother of a portion* (i.e. *gift*); *Achiman*, the name of an Anakite and of an Isr.:–Ahiman.
290. אֲחִימַעַץ *akh-ee-mah'-ats*; from 251 and the equiv. of 4619; *brother of anger; Achimaats*, the name of three Isr.:–Ahimaaz.
291. אַחְיָן *akh-yawn'*; from 251; *brotherly; Achjan*, an Isr.:–Ahian.
292. אֲחִינָדָב *akh-ee-naw-dawb'*; from 251 and 5068; *brother of liberality; Achinadab*, an Isr.:–Ahinadab.
293. אֲחִינֹעַם *akh-ee-no'-am*; from 251 and 5278; *brother of pleasantness; Achinoam*, the name of two Isr.s:–Ahinoam.
294. אֲחִיסָמָךְ *akh-ee-saw-mawk"*; from 251 and 5564; *brother of support; Achisamak*, an Isr.:–Ahisamach.
295. אֲחִיעֶזֶר *akh-ee-eh'-zer*; from 251 and 5828; *brother of help; Achiezer*, the name of two Isr.:–Ahiezer.
296. אֲחִיקָם *akh-ee-kawm'*; from 251 and 6965; *brother of rising* (i.e. *high*); *Achikam*, an Isr.:–Ahikam.
297. אֲחִירָם *akh-ee-rawm'*; from 251 and 7311; *brother of height* (i.e. *high*); *Achiram*, an Isr.:–Ahiram.
298. אֲחִירָמִי *akh-ee-raw-mee'*; patron. from 297; an *Achiramite* or desc. (coll.) of *Achiram*:–Ahiramites.
299. אֲחִירַע *akh-ee-rah*; from 251 and 7451; *brother of wrong; Achira*, an Isr.:–Ahira.
300. אֲחִישַׁחַר *akh-ee-shakh'-ar*; from 251 and 7837; *brother of* (the) *dawn; Achishachar*, an Isr.:–Ahishar.
301. אֲחִישָׁר *akh-ee-shawr'*; from 251 and 7891; *brother of* (the) *singer; Achishar*, an Isr.:–Ahishar.
302. אֲחִיתֹפֶל *akh-ee-tho'-fel*; from 251 and 8602; *brother of folly; Achithophel*, an Isr.:–Ahithophel.
303. אַחְלָב *akh-lawb'*; from the same root as 2459; *fatness* (i.e. *fertile*); *Achlab*, a place in Pal.:–Ahlab.
304. אַחְלַי *akh-lah'ee*; the same as 305; *wishful; Achlai*, the name of an Isr.s and of an Isr.:–Ahlai.
305. אַחֲלַי *akh-al-ah'ee*; or אַחֲלֵי *akh-al-ay'*; prob from 253 and a var. of 3863; *would that!*:–O that, would God.
306. אַחְלָמָה *akh-law'-maw*; perh. from 2492 (and thus *dream-stone*); a gem, prob. the *amethyst*:–amethyst.
307. אַחְמְתָא *akh-me-thaw'*; of Pers. der.; *Achmetha* (i.e. *Ecbatana*), the summer capital of Pers.:–Achmetha.
308. אֲחַסְבַּי *akh-as-bah'ee*; of unc. der.; *Achasbai*, an Isr.:–Ahasbai.
309. אָחַר *aw-khar'*; a prim. root; to *loiter* (i.e. *be behind*); by impl. to *procrastinate*:–continue, defer, delay, hinder, be late (slack), stay (there), tarry (longer).

310. אַחַר *akh-ar';* from 309; prop. the *hind* part; gen. used as an adv. or conj., *after* (in various senses):–after (that,-ward), again, at, away from, back (from, -side), behind, beside, by, follow (after, -ing), forasmuch, from, hereafter, hinder end, + out (over) live, + persecute, posterity, pursuing, remnant, seeing, since, thence[-forth], when, with.

311. אַחַר *akh-ar'* (Chald.); cor. to 310; *after:*–[here-]after.

312. אַחֵר *akh-air'* from 309; prop. *hinder;* gen., *next, other,* etc.:–(an-)other man, following, next, strange.

313. אַחֵר *akh-air';* the same as 312; *Acher,* an Isr.:–Aher.

314. אַחֲרוֹן *akh-ar-one';* or (short); אַחֲרֹן *akh-ar-one';* from 309; *hinder;* gen., *late* or *last;* spec. (as facing the east) *western:*–after (-ward), to come, following, hind(-er, -ermost, -most), last, latter, rereward, ut(ter)most.

315. אַחְרַח *akh-rakh';* from 310 and 251; *after* (his) *brother: Achrach,* an Isr.:–Aharah.

316. אֲחַרְחֵל *akh-ar-kale';* from 310 and 2426; *behind* (the) *intrenchment* (i.e. *safe*); *Acharchel,* an Isr.:–Aharhel,

317. אָחֳרִי *okh-or-ee'* (Chald.); from 311; *other:*–(an-)other.

318. אָחֳרֵין *okh-or-ane'* (Chald.); or (short) אָחֳרֵן *okh-or-ane';* from 317; *last:*–at last.

319. אַחֲרִית *akh-ar-eeth';* from 310; the *last* or *end,* hence, the *future;* also *posterity:*–(last, latter) end (time), hinder (utter) -most, length, posterity, remnant, residue, reward.

320. אַחֲרִית *akh-ar-eeth'* (Chald.); from 311; the same as 319; *later:*–latter.

321. אָחֳרָן *okh-or-awn'* (Chald.); from 311; the same as 317; *other:*–(an-)other.

322. אֲחֹרַנִּית *akh-o-ran-neeth';* prol. from 268; *backwards:*–back (-ward, again).

323. אֲחַשְׁדַּרְפַּן *akh-ash-dar-pan';* of Pers. der.; a *satrap* or governor of a main province (of Pers.):–lieutenant.

324. אֲחַשְׁדַּרְפַּן *akh-ash-dar-pan'* (Chald.); cor. to 323:–prince.

325. אֲחַשְׁוֵרוֹשׁ *akh-ash-vay-rosh';* or (short) *akh-ash-rosh';* (Es. 10:1); of Pers. or.; *Achashverosh* (i.e. Ahasuerus or Artaxerxes, but in this case Xerxes), the title (rather than name) of a Pers. king:–Ahasuerus.

326. אֲחַשְׁתָּרִי *akh-ash-taw-ree';* prob. of Pers. der.; an *achastarite* (i.e. courier); the designation (rather than name) of an Isr.:–Haakashtari [*includ. the art.*].

327. אֲחַשְׁתְּרָן *akh-ash-taw-rawn';* of Pers. or.; a *mule:*–camel.

328. אַט *at;* from an un. root perh. mean. to *move softly;* (as a noun) a *necromancer* (from their soft incantations), (as an adv.) *gently:*–charmer, gently, secret, softly.

329. אָטָד *aw-tawd';* from an un. root prob. mean. to *pierce* or *make fast;* a *thorn*-tree (esp. the *buckthorn*):–Atad, bramble, thorn.

330. אֵטוּן *ay-toon';* from an un. root (prob. mean. to *bind*); prop. *twisted* (yarn), i.e. *tapestry:*–fine linen.

331. אָטַם *aw-tam';* a prim. root; to *close* (the lips or ears); by analogy to *contract* (a window by bevelled jambs):–narrow, shut, stop.

332. אָטַר *aw-tar;* a prim. root; to *close* up:–shut.

333. אָטֵר *aw-tare';* from 332; *maimed; Ater,* the name of three Isr.:–Ater.

334. אִטֵּר *it-tare';* from 332; *shut* up, i.e. *impeded* (as to the use of the right hand):–+ left-handed.

335. אַי *ah'ee;* perh. from 370; *where?* hence *how?:*–how, what, whence, where, whether, which (way).

336. אִי *ee;* prob. ident. with 335 (through the idea of a *query*); *not:*–island (Job 22:30).

337. אִי *ee;* short from 188; *alas!:*–woe.

338. אִי *ee;* prob. ident. with 337 (through the idea of a *doleful* sound); a *howler* (used only in the pl.), i.e. any solitary wild creature; –wild beast of the islands.

339. אִי *ee;* from 183; prop. a *habitable* spot (as *desirable*); dry *land,* a *coast,* an *island:*–country, isle, island.

340. אָיַב *aw-yab;* a prim. root; to *hate* (as one of an opposite tribe or party); hence to *be hostile:*–be an enemy.

341. אֹיֵב or (fully) אוֹיֵב *o-yabe';* act.part. of 340; *hating;* an *adversary:*–enemy, foe.

342. אֵיבָה *ay-baw';* from 340; *hostility:*–emnity, hatred.

343. אֵיד *ade;* from the same as 181 (in the sense of *bending* down); *oppression;* by impl. *misfortune, ruin:*–calamity, destruction.

344. אַיָּה *ah-yaw';* perh. from 337; the *screamer,* i.e. a *hawk:*–kite, vulture.

345. אַיָּה *ah-yaw';* the same as 344; *Ajah,* the name of two Isr.:–Aiah, Ajah.

346. אַיֵּה *ah-yay;* prol. from 335; *where?:*–where.

347. אִיּוֹב *ee-yobe';* from 340; *hated* (i.e. *persecuted*); *Ijob,* the patriarch famous for his patience:–Job.

348. אִיזֶבֶל *ee-zeh'-bel;* from 336 and 2083; *chaste; Izebel,* the wife of king Ahab:–Jezebel.

349. אֵיךְ *ake;* also אֵיכָה *ay-kaw';* and אֵיכָכָה *ay-kaw'-kah;* prol. from 335; *how?* or *how!;* also *where:*–how, what.

350. אִי־כָבוֹד *ee-kaw-bode';* from 336 and 3519; (there is) *no glory,* i.e. *inglorious; Ikabod,* a son of Phineas:–I-chabod.

351. אֵיכֹה *ay-ko;* prob. a var. for 349, but not as an interogative; *where:*–where.

352. אַיִל *ah'-yil;* from the same as 193; prop. *strength;* hence, anything *strong;* spec. a *chief* (politically); also a *ram* (from his strength); a *pilaster* (as a strong support); an *oak* or other strong tree:–mighty (man), lintel, oak, post, ram, tree.

353. אֱיָל *eh-yawl';* a var. of *352; strength:*–strength.

354. אַיָּל *ah-yawl';* an intens. form of 352 (in the sense of *ram*); a *stag* or male deer:–hart.

355. אַיָּלָה *ah-yaw-law';* fem. of 354; *a doe* or female deer:–hind.

356. אֵילוֹן *ay-lone';* or (short) ; אֵלוֹן *ay-lone';* or אֵילֹן *ay- lone';* from 352; *oak-grove; Elon,* the name of a place in Pal., and also of one Hittite, two Isr.:–Elon.

357. אַיָּלוֹן *ah-yaw-lone';* from 354; *deer-field; Ajalon,* the name of five places in Pal.:–Aijalon, Ajalon.

358. אֵילוֹן בֵּית חָנָן *ay-lone' bayth-chaw-nawn';* from 356, 1004, and 2603; *oak-grove of* (the) *house of favor; Elon of Beth-chanan,* a place in Pal.:–Elon-beth-hanan.

359. אֵילוֹת *ay-loth';* or אֵילַת *ay-lath';* from 352; *trees* or a *grove* (i.e. palms); *Eloth or Elath,* a place on the Red Sea:–Elath, Eloth.

360. אֱיָלוּת *eh-yaw-looth'* fem. of 353; *power;* by impl., *protection:*–strength.

361. אֵילָם *ay-lawm';* or (short) אֵלָם *ay-lawm';* or (fem.) אֵלַמָּה *ay-lam-maw';* prob. from 352; a *pillar-space* (or colonnade), i.e. a *pale* (or portico):–arch.

362. אֵילִם *ay-leem';* pl. of 352; palm-*trees; Elim,* a place in the Desert:–Elim.

363. אִילָן *ee-lawn'* (Chald.); cor. to 356; a *tree:*–tree.

364. אֵיל פָּארָן, *ale paw-rawn';* from 352 and 6290; *oak of Paran; El-Paran,* a portion of the district of Paran:–El-paran.

365. אַיֶּלֶת *ah-yeh'-leth;* the same as 355; a *doe:*–hind, Aijeleth.

366. אָיֹם *aw-yome';* from an un. root (mean. to *frighten*); *frightful:*–terrible.

367. אֵימָה ay-maw' or (short) אֵמָה *ay-maw';* from the same as 366; *fright;* concr., an *idol* (as a bugbear):–dread, fear, horror, idol, terrible, terror.

368. אֵימִים *ay-meem';* pl. of 367; *terrors; Emim,* an early Canaanitish (or Maobitish) tribe:–Emims.

369. אַיִן *ah'-yin;* as if from a prim. root mean. to *be nothing* or *not exist;* a *non-entity;* gen. used as a neg. particle:–else, except, fail, [father-]less, be gone, in[-curable], neither, never, no (where), none, nor, (any, thing), not, nothing, to nought, past, un[-searchable], well-nigh, without. Comp. 370.

370. אַיִן *ah-yin';* prob. ident. with 369 in the sense of *query* (comp. 336); *–where?* (only in connection with prep. pref., *whence*):–whence, where.

371. אִין *een;* app. a short. form of 369; but (like 370) an interrog.: is it *not?:*–not.

372. אִיעֶזֶר *ee-eh'-zer;* from 336 and 5828; *helpless; Iezer,* an Isr.:–Jeezer.

373. אִיעֶזְרִי *ee-ez-ree';* patron. from 372; an *Iezrite* or desc. of Iezer:–Jezerite.

374. אֵיפָה *ay-faw';* or (short) אֵפָה *ay-faw';* of Eg. der.; an *ephah* or measure for grain; hence, a *measure* in gen.:– ephah, (divers) measure(-s).

375. אֵיפֹה *ay-fo';* from 335 and 6311; *what place?;* also (of time) *when?;* or (of means) *how?;* –what manner, where.

376. אִישׁ *eesh;* contr. for 582 [or perh. rather from an un. root mean. to *be extant*]; a *man* as an indiv. or a male person; often used as an adjunct to a more def. term (and in such cases frequently not expressed in translation):–also, another, any (man), a certain, + champion, consent, each, every (one), fellow, (foot-, husband-)man, (good-, great, mighty) man, he, high (degree), him (that is), husband, man(-kind), + none, one, people, person, + steward, what (man) soever, whoso(-ever), worthy. Comp. 802.

377. אִישׁ *eesh;* denom. from 376; to *be a man,* i.e. act in a manly way:–show (one) self a man.

378. אִישׁ־בֹּשֶׁת *eesh-bo'-sheth;* from 376 and 1322; *man of shame*; *Ish-Bosheth,* a son of King Saul:–Ish-bosheth.

379. אִישְׁהוֹד *eesh-hode';* from 376 and 1935; *man of renown; Ishod,* an Isr.:–Ishod.

380. אִישׁוֹן *ee-shone';* dimin. from 376; the *little man* of the eye; the *pupil* or *ball;* hence, the *middle* (of night):–apple [of the eye], black, obscure.

381. אִישׁ־חַיִל *eesh-khah'-yil;* from 376 and 2428; *man of might;* by defect. transc. (2 Sa. 23:20) אִישׁ־חַי *eesh-khah'ee;* as if from 376 and 2416; *living man; Ish-chail* (or *Ish-chai*), an Isr.:–a valiant man.

382. אִישׁ־טוֹב *eesh-tobe';* from 376 and 2897;

HEBREW

man of Tob; Ish-Tob, a place in Pal.:–Ish-tob.
383. אִיתַי *ee-thah'ee* (Chald.); cor. to 3426; prop. *entity;* used only as a particle of affirmation, there *is:*–art thou, can, do ye, have, it be, there is (are), X we will not.
384. אִיתִיאֵל *eeth-ee-ale';* perh. from 837 and 410; *God has arrived; Ithiel,* the name of an Isr., also of a symb. person:–Ithiel.
385. אִיתָמָר *eeth-aw-mawr';* from 339 and 8558; *coast of* the *palm*-tree; *Ithamar,* a son of Aaron:–Ithamar.
386. אֵיתָן *ay-thawn';* or (short) אֵתָן *ay-thawn';* from an un. root (mean. to *continue*); *permanence;* hence (concr.) *permanent;* spec. a *chieftain:*–hard, mighty, rough, strength, strong.
387. אֵיתָן *ay-thawn';* the same as 386; *permanent; Ethan,* the name of four Isr.:–Ethan.
388. אֵיתָנִים *ay-thaw-neem';* pl. of 386; always with the art.; the *permanent* brooks; *Ethanim,* the name of a month:–Ethanim.
389. אַךְ *ak;* akin to 403; a particle of affirmation, *surely;* hence (by limitation) *only:*–also, in any wise, at least, but, certainly, even, howbeit, nevertheless, notwithstanding, only, save, surely, of a surety, truly, verily, + wherefore, yet (but).
390. אַכַּד *ak-kad';* from an un. root prob. mean. to *strengthen;* a *fortress; Accad,* a place in Babylon:–Accad.
391. אַכְזָב *ak-zawb'* from 3576; *falsehood*; by impl. *treachery:*–liar, lie.
392. אַכְזִיב *ak-zeeb';* from 391; *deceitful* (in the sense of a winter- torrent which *fails* in summer), *Akzib,* the name of two places in Pal.:–Achzib.
393. אַכְזָר *ak-zawr';* from an un. root (app. mean. to *act harshly*); *violent;* by impl. *deadly;* also (in a good sense) *brave:*–cruel, fierce.
394. אַכְזָרִי *ak-zawr-ree';* from 393; *terrible:*–cruel (one).
395. אַכְזְרִיּוּת *ak-ze-ree-ooth';* from 394; *fierceness:*–cruel.
396. אֲכִילָה *ak-ee-law';* fem. from 398; something *eatable,* i.e. *food:*–meat.
397. אָכִישׁ *aw-keesh';* of unc. der.; *Akish,* a Philistine king:–Achish.
398. אָכַל *aw-kal';* a prim. root; to *eat* (lit. or fig.):–X at all, burn up, consume, devour(-er, up), dine, eat(-er, up), feed (with), food, X freely, X in...wise(-deed, plenty), (lay) meat, X quite.
399. אֲכַל *ak-al'* (Chald.); cor. to 398:–+ accuse, devour, eat.
400. אֹכֶל *o'-kel;* from 398; *food:*–eating, food, meal[-time], meat, prey, victuals.
401. אֻכָל *oo-kawl;'* or אֻכָּל *ook-kawl';* app. from 398; *devoured; Ucal,* a fancy name:–Ucal.
402. אָכְלָה *ok-law';* fem. of 401; *food:*–consume, devour, eat, food, meat.
403. אָכֵן *aw-kane';* from 3559 [comp. 3651]; *firmly;* fig., *surely;* also (advers.) but:–but, certainly, nevertheless, surely, truly, verily.
404. אָכַף *aw-kaf';* a prim. root; app. mean. to *curve* (as with a burden); to *urge:*–crave.
405. אֶכֶף *eh'-kef;* from 404; a *load;* by impl., a *stroke* (others *dignity*):–hand.
406. אִכָּר *ik-kawr';* from an un. root mean. to *dig;* a *farmer:*–husbandman, ploughman.
407. אַכְשָׁף *ak-shawf';* from 3784; *fascination; Acshaph,* a place in Pal.:–Achshaph.
408. אַל *al;* neg. particle [akin to 3808]; *not* (the qualified negation, used as a deprecative); once (Job 24:25) as a noun, *nothing:*–nay, neither, + never, no ,nor, not, nothing [worth], rather than.
409. אַל *al* (Chald.); cor. to 408:–not.
410. אֵל *ale;* short. from 352; *strength;* as adj., *mighty;* esp. the *Almighty* (but used also of any *deity*):–God (god), X goodly, X great, idol, might(-y one), power, strong. Comp. names in "-el."
411. אֵל *ale;* demonstr. particle (but only in a pl. sense) *these* or *those:*–these, those. Comp. 428.
412. אֵל *ale* (Chald.); cor. to 411:–these.
413. אֵל ale; (but only used in the short. constr. form אֶל *el*); a prim. particle; prop. denoting motion *towards,* but occasionally used of a quiescent position, i.e. *near, with* or *among;* often in gen., to:–about, according to ,after, against, among, as for, at, because(-fore, -side), both...and, by, concerning, for, from, X hath, in(- to), near, (out) of, over, through, to (-ward), under, unto, upon, whether, with(-in).
414. אֵלָא *ay-law'* a var. of 424; *oak; Ela,* an Isr.:–Elah.
415. אֵל אֱלֹהֵי יִשְׂרָאֵל *ale el-o-hay' yis-raw-ale;* from 410 and 430 and 3478; the *mighty God of Jisrael; El-Elohi-Jisrael,* the title given to a consecrated spot by Jacob:–El-elohe-israel.
416. אֵל בֵּית-אֵל *ale bayth-ale';* from 410 and 1008; the *God of Bethel; El-Bethel,* the title given to a consecrated spot by Jacob:–El-beth-el.
417. אֶלְגָּבִישׁ *el-gaw-beesh';* from 410 and 1378; *hail* (as if a *great pearl*):–great hail[-stones].
418. אַלְגּוּמִּים *al-goom-meem';* by transposition for 484; sticks of *algum* wood:–algum[trees].
419. אֶלְדָּד *el-dad';* from 410 and 1730; *God has loved; Eldad,* an Isr.:–Eldad.
420. אֶלְדָּעָה *el-daw-aw';* from 410 and 3045; *God of knowledge; Eldaah,* a son of Midian:–Eldaah.
421. אָלָה *aw-law';* a prim. root [(rather ident. with 422 through the idea of *invocation*]; to *bewail:*–lament.
422. אָלָה *aw-law';* prim. root; prop. to *adjure*, i.e. (usually in a bad sense) *imprecate:*–adjure, curse, swear.
423. אָלָה *aw-law';* from 422; an *imprecation:*–curse, cursing, execration, oath, swearing.
424. אֵלָה *ay-law';* fem. of 352; an *oak* or other strong tree:–elm, oak, teil-tree.
425. אֵלָה *ay-law';* same as 424; *Elah,* the name of an Edomite, of four Isr., and also of a place in Pal.:–Elah.
426. אֱלָהּ *el-aw'* (Chald.); cor. to 433; *God:*–God, god.
427. אַלָּה *al-law';* a var. of 424:–oak.
428. אֵלֶּה *ale'-leh;* prol. from 411; *these* or *those:*–an- (the) other; one sort, so, some, such, them, these (same), they, this, those, thus, which, who(-m).
429. אֵלֶּה *ale'-leh* (Chald.); cor. to 428:–these.
430. אֱלֹהִים *el-o-heem';* pl. of 433; *gods* in the ordinary sense; but spec. used (in the pl. thus, esp. with the art.) of the supreme *God;* occasionally applied by way of deference to *magistrates;* and sometimes as a sup.:–angels, X exceeding, God (gods)(-dess, -ly), X (very) great, judges, X mighty.
431. אֲלוּ *al-oo'* (Chald.); prob. prol. from 412; *lo!:*–behold.
432. אִלּוּ *il-loo';* prob. from 408; *nay,* i.e. (softened) *if:*–but if, yea though.
433. אֱלוֹהַּ *el-o'-ah;* rarely (short.) אֱלֹהַּ *el-o'-ah;* prob. prol. (emphat.) from 410; a *deity* or the *Deity:*–God, god. See 430.
434. אֱלוּל *el-ool';* for 457; good for *nothing:*–thing of nought.
435. אֱלוּל *el-ool';* prob. of for. der.; *Elul,* the sixth Jewish month:–Elul.
436. אֵלוֹן *ay-lone';* prol. from 352; an *oak* or other strong tree:–plain. See also 356.
437. אַלּוֹן *al-lone';* a var. of 436:–oak.
438. אַלּוֹן *al-lone';* the same as 437; *Allon,* an Isr., also a place in Pal.:–Allon.
439. אַלּוֹן בָּכוּת *al-lone' baw-kooth';* from **437** and a var. of 1068; *oak of weeping; Allon-Bakuth,* a monument. tree:–Allon-bachuth.
440. אֵלוֹנִי *ay-lo-nee';* or rather (short) אֵלֹנִי *ay-lo-nee';* patron from 438; an *Elonite* or desc. (coll.) of Elon:–Elonites.
441. אַלּוּף *al-loof';* or (short) אַלֻּף *al-loof';* from 502; *familiar;* a *friend,* also *gentle;* hence, a *bullock* (as being tame; applied, although masc., to a *cow*); and so, a *chieftain* (as notable, like neat cattle):–captain, duke, (chief) friend, governor, guide, ox.
442. אָלוּשׁ *aw-loosh';* of unc. der.; *Alush,* a place in the Desert:–Alush.
443. אֶלְזָבָד *el-zaw-bawd';* from 410 and 2064; *God has bestowed; Elzabad,* the name of two Isr.:–Elzabad.
444. אָלַח *aw-lakh';* a prim. root; to *muddle,* i.e. (fig. and intr.) to *turn* (mor.) *corrupt:*–become filthy.
445. אֶלְחָנָן *el-khaw-nawn';* from 410 and 2603; *God* (is) *gracious; Elchanan,* an Isr.:–Elkanan.
446. אֱלִיאָב *el-ee-awb';* 410 and 1; *God of* (his) *father; Eliab,* the name of six Isr.:–Eliab.
447. אֱלִיאֵל *el-ee-ale';* from 410 repeated; *God of* (his) *God; Eliel,* the name of nine Isr.:–Eliel.
448. אֱלִיאָתָה *el-ee-aw-thaw';* or (contr.) אֱלִיָּתָה; *el-ee-yaw- thaw';* from 410 and 225; *God of* (his) *consent; Eliathah,* an Isr.:– Eliathah.
449. אֱלִידָד *el-ee-dawd';* from the same as 419; *God of* (his) *love; Elidad,* an Isr.:–Elidad.
450. אֶלְיָדָע *el-yaw-daw';* from 410 and 3045; *God* (is) *knowing; Eljada,* the name of two Isr. and of an Aramaean leader:–Eliada.
451. אַלְיָה *al-yaw';* from 422 (in the or. sense of *strength*); the *stout* part, i.e. the fat *tail* of the Oriental sheep:–rump.
452. אֵלִיָּה *ay-lee-yaw';* or prol. אֵלִיָּהוּ *ay-lee-yaw'-hoo;* from 410 and 3050; *God of Jehovah; Elijah,* the name of the famous prophet and of two other Isr.:–Elijah, Eliah.
453. אֱלִיהוּ *el-ee-hoo';* or (fully) אֱלִיהוּא *el-ee-hoo';* from 410 and 1931; *God of him; Elihu,* the name of one of Job's friends, and of three Isr.:–Elihu.
454. אֶלְיְהוֹעֵינַי *el-ye-ho-ay-nah'ee;* or (short) אֶלְיוֹעֵינַי *el-yo-ay-nah'ee;* from 413 and 3068 and 5869; *towards Jehovah* (are) *my eyes; Eljehoenai* or *Eljoenai,* the name of seven Isr.:–Elihoenai, Elionai.
455. אֶלְיַחְבָּא *el-yakh-baw';* from 410 and 2244; *God will hide; Eljachba,* an Isr.:–Eliahbah.
456. אֱלִיחֹרֶף *el-ee-kho'-ref;* from 410 and 2779; *God of autumn; Elichoreph,* an Isr.:–Elihoreph.

457. אֱלִיל *el-eel';* app. from 408; good for *nothing,* by anal. *vain* or *vanity;* spec. an *idol:*–idol, no value, thing of nought.
458. אֱלִימֶלֶךְ *el-ee-meh'-lek;* from 410 and 4428; *God of* (the) *king; Elimelek,* an Isr.:–Elimelech.
459. אִלֵּין *il-lane'* (Chald.); or short. אִלֵּן *il-lane';* prol. from 412; *these:*–the, these.
460. אֶלְיָסָף *el-yaw-sawf';* from 410 and 3254; *God* (is) *gatherer; Eljasaph,* the name of two Isr.:–Eliasaph.
461. אֱלִיעֶזֶר *el-ee-eh'-zer;* from 410 and 5828; *God of help; Eliezer,* the name of a Damascene and of ten Isr.:–Eliezer.
462. אֱלִיעֵינַי *el-ee-ay-nah'ee;* prob. contr. for 454; *Elienai,* an Isr.:–Elienai.
463. אֱלִיעָם *el-ee-awm';* from 410 and 5971; *God of* (the) *people; Eliam,* an Isr.:–Eliam.
464. אֱלִיפַז *el-ee-faz';* from 410 and 6337; *God of gold; Eliphaz,* the name of one of Job's friends, and of a son of Esau:–Eliphaz.
465. אֱלִיפָל *el-ee-fawl';* from 410 and 6419; *God of judgment; Eliphal,* an Isr.:–Eliphal.
466. אֱלִיפְלֵהוּ *el-ee-fe-lay'-hoo;* from 410 and 6395; *God of his distinction; Eliphelehu,* an Isr.:–Elipheleh.
467. אֱלִיפֶלֶט *el-ee-feh'-let;* or (short) אֶלְפֶּלֶט *el-peh'-let;* from 410 and 6405; *God of deliverance; Eliphelet* or *Elpelet,* the name of six Isr.:–Eliphalet, Eliphelet, Elpalet.
468. אֱלִיצוּר *el-ee-tsoor';* from 410 and 6697; *God of* (the) *rock; Elitsur,* an Isr.:–Elizur.
469. אֱלִיצָפָן *el-ee-tsaw-fawn';* or (short) אֶלְצָפָן *el-tsaw-fawn';* from 410 and 6845; *God of treasure; Elitsaphan* or *Eltsaphan,* an Isr.:–Elizaphan, Elzaphan.
470. אֱלִיקָא *el-ee-kaw';* from 410 and 6958; *God of rejection; Elika,* an Isr.:–Elika.
471. אֶלְיָקִים *el-yaw-keem';* from 410 and 6965; *God of raising; Eljakim,* the name of four Isr.:–Eliakim.
472. אֱלִישֶׁבַע *el-ee-sheh'-bah;* from 410 and 7651 (in the sense of 7650); *God of* (the) *oath; Elisheba,* the wife of Aaron:–Elisheba.
473. אֱלִישָׁה *el-ee-shaw';* prob. of for. der.; *Elishah,* a son of Javan:–Elishah
474. אֱלִישׁוּעַ *el-ee-shoo'-ah;* from 410 and 7769; *God of supplication* (or *of riches*); *Elishua,* the son of King David:–Elishua.
475. אֶלְיָשִׁיב *el-yaw-sheeb';* from 410 and 7725; *God will restore; Eljashib,* the name of six Isr.:–Eliashib.
476. אֱלִישָׁמָע *el-ee-shaw-maw';* from 410 and 8085; *God of hearing; Elishama,* the name of seven Isr.:–Elishama.
477. אֱלִישָׁע *el-ee-shaw';* contr. for 474; *Elisha,* the famous prophet:–Elisha.
478. אֱלִישָׁפָט *el-ee-shaw-fawt';* from 410 and 8199; *God of judgment; Elishaphat,* an Isr.:–Elishaphat.
479. אִלֵּךְ *il-lake'* (Chald.); prol. from 412; *these:*–these, those.
480. אַלְלַי *al-le-lah'ee;* by redupl. from 421; *alas!:*–woe.
481. אָלַם *aw-lam';* a prim. root; to *tie* fast; hence (of the mouth) to be *tongue-tied:*–bind, be dumb, put to silence.
482. אֵלֶם *ay'-lem;* from 481; *silence* (i.e. mute justice):–congregation. Comp. 3128.
483. אִלֵּם *il-lame';* from 481; *speechless:*–dumb (man).
484. אַלְמֻגִּים *al-moog-gheem';* prob. of for. der. (used thus only in the pl.); *almug* (i.e. prob. sandle-wood) sticks:–almug trees. Comp. 418.
485. אֲלֻמָּה *al-oom-maw';* or (masc.) אָלֻם *aw-loom';* pass.part. of 481; something *bound;* a *sheaf:*–sheaf.
486. אַלְמוֹדָד *al-mo-dawd';* prob. of for. der.:–*Almodad,* a son of Joktan:–Almodad.
487. אַלַּמֶּלֶךְ *al-lam-meh'-lek;* from 427 and 4428; *oak of* (the) *king; Allammelek,* a place in Pal.:–Alammelech.
488. אַלְמָן *al-mawn';* prol. from 481 in the sense of *bereavement; discarded* (as a divorced person):–forsaken.
489. אַלְמֹן *al-mone';* from 481 as in 488; *bereavement:*–widowhood.
490. אַלְמָנָה *al-maw-naw';* fem of 488; a *widow;* also a *desolate* place:–desolate house (palace), widow.
491. אַלְמָנוּת *al-maw-nooth';* fem. of 488; concr., a *widow;* abstr., *widowhood:*–widow, widowhood.
492. אַלְמֹנִי *al-mo-nee';* from 489 in the sense of *concealment; some* one (i.e. *so and so,* without giving the name of the pers. or place):–one, and such.
493. אֶלְנַעַם *el-nah'-am;* from 410 and 5276; *God* (is his) *delight; Elnaam,* an Isr.:–Elnaam.
494. אֶלְנָתָן *el-naw-thawn';* from 410 and 5414; *God* (is the) *giver; Elnathan,* the name of four Isr.:–Elnathan.
495.אֶלָּסָר *el-law-sawr';* prob. of for. der.; *Ellasar,* an early country of Asia:–Ellasar.
496. אֶלְעָד *el-awd';* from 410 and 5749; *God has testified; Elad,* an Isr.:–Elead.
497. אֶלְעָדָה *el-aw-daw';* from 410 and 5710; *God has decked; Eladah,* an Isr.:–Eladah.
498. אֶלְעוּזַי *el-oo-zah'ee;* from 410 and 5756 (in the sense of 5797); *God* (is) *defensive; Eluzai,* an Isr.:–Eluzai.
499. אֶלְעָזָר *el-aw-zawr;* from 410 and 5826; *God* (is) *helper; Elazar,* the name of seven Isr.:–Eleazar.
500. אֶלְעָלֵא *el-aw-lay';* or (more prop.) אֶלְעָלֵה *el-aw-lay';* from 410 and 5927; *God* (is) *going up; Elale* or *Elaleh,* a place east of the Jordan:–Elealeh.
501. אֶלְעָשָׂה *el-aw-saw';* from 410 and 6213; *God has made; Elasah,* the name of four Isr.:–Elasah, Eleasah.
502. אָלַף *aw-lof';* a prim. root, to *associate* with; hence, to *learn* (and caus. to *teach*):–learn, teach, utter.
503. אָלַף aw-laf'; denom. from 505; causative, to *make a thousandfold:*–bring forth thousands.
504. אֶלֶף *eh'-lef;* from 502; a *family;* also (from the sense of *yoking* or *taming*) an *ox* or *cow:*–family, kine, oxen.
505. אֶלֶף *eh'-lef;* the same as 504; a *thousand:*–thousand.
506. אֲלַף *al-af'* (Chald.); or אֶלֶף *eleph* (Chald.); cor. to 505:–thousand.
507. אֶלֶף *eh'-lef;* the same as 505; *Eleph,* a place in Pal.:–Eleph.
508. אֶלְפַּעַל *el-pah'-al;* from 410 and 6466; *God* (is) *act; Elpaal,* an Isr.:–Elpaal.
509. אָלַץ *aw-lats';* prim. root; to *press:*–urge.
510. אַלְקוּם *al-koom';* prob. from 408 and 6965; a *non-rising* (i.e. *resistlessness*):–no rising up.
511. אֶלְקָנָה *el-kaw-naw';* from 410 and 7069; *God has obtained; Elkanah,* the name of seven Isr.:–Elkanah.
512. אֶלְקֹשִׁי *el-ko-shee';* patrial from a name of unc. der.; an *Elkoshite* or nat. of Elkosh:–Elkoshite.
513. אֶלְתּוֹלַד *el-to-lad';* prob. from 410 and a masc. form of 8435 (comp. 8434); *God* (is) *generator; Eltolad,* a place in Pal.:– Eltolad.
514. אֶלְתְּקֵא *el-te-kay';* or (more prop.) אֶלְתְּקֵה *el-te-kay';* of unc. der.; *Eltekeh* or *Elteke,* a place in Pal.:– Eltekeh.
515. אֶלְתְּקֹן *el-te-kone';* from 410 and 8626; *God* (is) *straight; Eltekon,* a place in Pal.:–Eltekon.
516. אַל תַּשְׁחֵת *al tash-kayth';* from 408 and 7843; *Thou must not destroy;* prob. the opening words to a popular song:–Al-taschith.
517. אֵם *ame;* prim. word; a *mother* (as the *bond* of the family); in a wide sense (both lit. and fig. [like 1]:–dam, mother, X parting.
518. אִם *eem;* a prim. particle; used very widely as demonstr., *lo!;* interrog., *whether?;* or conditional, *if, although;* also *Oh that!, when;* hence, as a neg., *not:*–(and, can-, doubtless, if, that) (not), + but, either, + except, + more(-over if, than), neither, nevertheless, nor, oh that, or, + save (only, -ing), seeing, since, sith, + surely (no more, none, not), though, + of a truth, + unless, + verily, when, whereas, whether, while, + yet.
519. אָמָה *aw-maw';* app. a prim. word; a *maid-servant* or female slave:–(hand-) bondmaid(-woman), maid(-servant).
520. אַמָּה *am-maw';* prol. from 517; properly, a *mother* (i.e. *unit* of measure, or the *fore-arm* (below the elbow), i.e. a *cubit;* also a door-*base* (as a *bond* of the entrance):–cubit, + hundred [*by exchange for* 3967], measure, post.
521. אַמָּה *am-maw'* (Chald.); cor. to 520:–cubit.
522. אַמָּה *am-maw';* the same as 520; *Ammah,* a hill in Pal.:–Ammah.
523. אֻמָּה *oom-maw';* from the same as 517; a *collection,* i.e. community of persons:–nation, people.
524. אֻמָּה *oom-maw'* (Chald.); cor. to 523:–nation.
525. אָמוֹן *aw-mone';* from 539, prob. in the sense of *training; skilled,* i.e. an architect [like 542]–one brought up.
526. אָמוֹן *aw-mone';* the same as 525; *Amon,* the name of three Isr.:–Amon.
527. אָמוֹן *aw-mone';* a var. for 1995; a *throng* of people:–multitude.
528. אָמוֹן *aw-mone';* Eg. der.; *Amon* (i.e. Ammon or Amn), a deity of Eg. (used only as an adjunct of 4996):–multitude, populous.
529. אֵמוּן *ay-moon';* from 539; *established,* i.e. (fig.) *trusty;* also (abstr.) *trustworthiness:*–faith(-ful), truth.
530. אֱמוּנָה *em-oo-naw';* or (short) אֱמֻנָה *em-oo-naw';* fem. of 529; lit. *firmness;* fig. *security;* mor. *fidelity:*–faith(-ful, -ly, -ness, [man]), set office, stability, steady, truly, truth, verily.
531. אָמוֹץ *aw-mohts';* from 553; *strong; Amots,* an Isr.:–Amoz.
532. אָמִי *aw-mee';* an abbrev. for 526; *Ami,* an Isr.:–Ami.
533. אַמִּיץ *am-meets';* or (short) אַמִּץ *am-meets';* from 553; *strong* or (abstr.) *strength:*–courageous, mighty, strong (one).
534. אָמִיר *aw-meer';* app. from 559 (in the sense of *self- exaltation*); a *summit* (of a tree

HEBREW

or mountain:–bough, branch.
535. אָמַל *aw-mal';* a prim. root; to *droop;* by impl. to *be sick,* to *mourn:*–languish, be weak, wax feeble.
536. אֻמְלַל *oom-lal';* from 535; *sick:*–weak.
537. אֲמֵלָל *am-ay-lawl';* from 535; *languid:*–feeble.
538. אֲמָם *am-awm';* from 517; *gathering-spot; Amam,* a place in Pal.:–Amam.
539. אָמַן *aw-man';* a prim. root; prop. to *build up* or *support;* to *foster* as a parent or nurse; fig. to *render* (or *be*) *firm* or faithful, to *trust* or believe, to be *permanent* or quiet; mor. to *be true* or certain; to *go to the right hand:*–hence, assurance, believe, bring up, establish, + fail, be faithful (of long continuance, stedfast, sure, surely, trusty, verified), nurse, (-ing father), (put), trust, turn to the right.
540. אֲמַן *am-an'* (Chald.); cor. to 539:–believe, faithful, sure.
541. אָמַן *aw-man';* denom. from 3225; to take the *right hand* road:–turn to the right. See 539.
542. אָמָן *aw-mawn';* from 539 (in the sense of *training*); an *expert:*–cunning workman.
543. אָמֵן *aw-mane';* from 539; *sure;* abstr., *faithfulness;* adv., *truly:*–Amen, so be it, truth.
544. אֹמֶן *oh-men';* from 539; *verity:*–truth.
545. אָמְנָה *om-naw';* fem. of 544 (in the spec. sense of *training*); *tutelage:*–brought up.
546. אָמְנָה *om-naw';* form of 544 (in its usual sense); adv., *surely:*–indeed.
547. אֹמְנָה *om-me-naw';* fem. act.part. of 544 (in the or. sense of *supporting); a column:*–pillar.
548. אֲמָנָה *am-aw-naw'* of 543; something *fixed,* i.e. a *covenant.* an *allowance:*–certain portion, sure.
549. אֲמָנָה *am-aw-naw'* the same as 548; *Amanah,* a mountain near Damascus:–Amana.
550. אַמְנוֹן *am-nohn'* or אֲמִינוֹן *am-ee-nohn';* from 539; *faithful; Amnon* (or Aminon), a son of David:–Amnon.
551. אָמְנָם *om-nawm'* adv. from 544; *verily:*–indeed, no doubt, surely, (it is, of a) true(-ly, -th).
552. אֻמְנָם *oom-nawm';* an orth. var. of 551:–in (very) deed; of a surety.
553. אָמֵץ *aw-mats'* a prim. root; to *be alert,* phys. (on foot) or ment. (in courage):–confirm, be courageous (of good courage, stedfastly minded, strong, stronger), establish, fortify, harden, increase, prevail, strengthen (self), make strong (obstinate, speed).
554. אָמֹץ *aw-mohts'* prob. from 553; of a *strong* color, i.e. *red* (others fleet):–bay.
555. אֹמֶץ *o'-mets* from 553; *strength:*–stronger.
556. אַמְצָה *am-tsaw'* from 553; *force:*–strength.
557. אַמְצִי *am-tsee';* from 553; *strong; Amtsi, an Isr.:*–Amzi.
558. אֲמַצְיָה *am-ats-yaw';* or אֲמַצְיָהוּ *am-ats-yaw'-hoo;* from 553 and 3050; *strength of Jah; Amatsjah,* the name of four Isr.:–Amaziah.
559. אָמַר aw-*mar';* a prim. root; to *say* (used with great latitude):–answer, appoint, avouch, bid, boast self, call, certify, challenge, charge, + (at the, give) command(-ment), commune, consider, declare, demand, X desire, determine, X expressly, X indeed, X intend, name, X plainly, promise, publish, report, require, say, speak (against, of), X still, X suppose, talk, tell, term, X that is, X think, use (speech), utter, X verily, X yet.
560. אֲמַר *am-ar'* (Chald.); cor. to 559:–command, declare, say, speak, tell.
561. אֵמֶר *ay'-mer;* from 559; something *said:*–answer, X appointed unto him, saying, speech, word.
562. אֹמֶר *o'-mer;* the same as 561:–promise, speech, thing, word.
563. אִמַּר *im-mar'* (Chald.); perh. from 560 (in the sense of *bringing forth*); a *lamb:*–lamb.
564. אִמֵּר *im-mare';* from 559; *talkative; Immer,* the name of five Isr.:–Immer.
565. אִמְרָה *im-raw';* or אֶמְרָה *em-raw';* fem. of 561, and mean. the same:–commandment, speech, word.
566. אִמְרִי *im-ree'* from 564; *wordy; Imri,* the name of two Isr.:–Imri.
567. אֱמֹרִי *em-o-ree';* prob. a patron. from an un. name der. from 559 in the sense of *publicity,* i.e. prominence; thus, a *mountaineer;* an *Emorite,* one of the Canaanitish tribes:–Amorite.
568. אֲמַרְיָה *am-ar-yaw';* or prol. אֲמַרְיָהוּ *am-ar-yaw'-hoo;* from 559 and 3050; *Jah has said* (i.e. promised); *Amarjah,* the name of nine Isr.:–Amariah.
569. אַמְרָפֶל *am-raw-fel';* of unc. (perh. for.) der.; *Amraphel,* a king of Shinar:–Amraphel.
570. אֶמֶשׁ *eh'-mesh;* time *past,* i.e. *yesterday* or *last night:*–former time, yesterday(-night)
571. אֱמֶת *eh'-meth* contr. from 539; *stability;* (fig.) *certainty, truth, trustworthiness:*–assured(-ly), establishment, faithful, right, sure, true (-ly, -th), verity.
572. אַמְתַּחַת *am-takh'-ath;* from 4969; prop. something *expansive,* i.e. a *bag:*–sack.
573. אֲמִתַּי *am-it-tah'ee;* from 571; *veracious; Amittai,* an Isr.:–Amittai.
574. אֵמְתָּנִי *em-taw-nee'* Chald.); from a root cor. to that of 4975; *well-loined* (i.e. burly) or *mighty:*–terrible.
575. אָן *awn;* or אָנָה *aw-naw';* contr. from 370; *where*?; hence, *whither*?, *when*?; also *hither* and *thither:*–+ any (no) whither, now, here, whither(-soever).
576. אֲנָא *an-aw'* (Chald.); or אֲנָה *an-aw'* (Chald.); cor. to 589; I:–I, as for me.
577. אָנָּא *awn-naw;* or אָנָּה *awn-naw';* app. contr. from 160 and 4994; *oh now!:*–I (me) beseech (pray) thee, O.
578. אָנָה *aw-naw';* a prim. root; to *groan:*–lament, mourn.
579. אָנָה *aw-naw;* prim. root (perh. rather ident. with 578 through the idea of *contr.* in anguish); to *approach;* hence, to *meet* in various senses:–befall, deliver, happen, seek a quarrel.
580. אֲנוּ *an-oo';* contr. for 587; *we:*–we.
581. אִנּוּן *in-noon'* (Chald.); or (fem.) אִנִּין *in-neen'* (Chald.); cor. to 1992; *they:*–X are, them, these.
582. אֱנוֹשׁ *en-oshe';* from 605; prop. a *mortal* (and thus differing from the more dignified 120); hence, a *man* in gen. (singly or coll.):–another, X [blood-]thirsty, certain, chap[-man]; divers, fellow, X in the flower of their age, husband, (certain, mortal) man, people, person, servant, some (X of them), + stranger, those, + their trade. It is often unexpressed in the English versions, esp. when used in apposition with another word. Comp. 376.
583. אֱנוֹשׁ *en-ohsh';* the same as 582; *Enosh,* a son of Seth; –Enos.
584. אָנַח *aw-nakh';* a prim. root; to *sigh:*–groan, mourn, sigh.
585. אֲנָחָה *an-aw-khaw';* from 585; *sighing:*–groaning, mourn, sigh.
586. אֲנַחְנָא *an-akh'-naw;* Chald.) or אֲנַחְנָה *an-akh- naw';* cor. to 587; *we:*–we.
587. אֲנַחְנוּ *an-akh'-noo;* app. from 595; *we:*–ourselves, us, we.
588. אֲנָחֲרָת *an-aw-kha-rawth';* prob. from the same root as 5170; a *gorge* or narrow pass; *Anacharath,* a place in Pal.:–Anaharath.
589. אֲנִי *an-ee';* contr. from 595; *I:*–I, (as for) me, mine, myself, we, X which, X who.
590. אֳנִי *on-ee';* prob. from 579 (in the sense of *conveyance*); a *ship* or (coll.)a *fleet:*–galley, navy (of ships).
591. אֳנִיָּה *on-ee-yaw';* fem. of 590; a *ship:*–ship([-men]).
592. אֲנִיָּה *an-ee-yaw';* from 578; *groaning:*–lamentation, sorrow.
593. אֲנִיעָם *an-ee-awm';* from 578 and 5971; *groaning* of (the) *people; Aniam,* an Isr.:–Aniam.
594. אֲנָךְ *an-awk';* prob. from an un. root mean. to *be narrow;*a plumb-*line,* (a *hook*):–plumb-line.
595. אָנֹכִי *aw-no-kee';* sometimes aw-no'-kee; a prim. pro.; *I:*–I, me, X which.
596. אָנַן *aw-nan';* prim. root; to *mourn,* i.e. *complain:*–complain.
597. אָנַס *aw-nas';* to *insist:*–compel.
598. אֲנַס *an-as'* (Chald.); cor. to 597; fig., to *distress:*–trouble.
599. אָנַף *aw-naf';* prim. root; to *breathe* hard, i.e. *be enraged:*–be angry (displeased).
600. אֲנַף *an-af'* (Chald.); cor. to 639 (only in the pl. as a sing.); the *face:*–face, visage.
601. אֲנָפָה *an-aw-faw';* from 599; an unclean bird, perh. the *parrot* (from its *irascibility*):–heron.
602. אָנַק *aw-nak';* prim. root; to *shriek:*–cry, groan.
603. אֲנָקָה *an-aw-kaw';* from 602; *shrieking:*–crying out, groaning, sighing.
604. אֲנָקָה *an-aw-kaw';* the same as 603; some kind of lizard, prob. the *gecko* (from its *wail*):–ferret.
605. אָנַשׁ *aw-nash';* a prim. root; to *be frail, feeble,* or (fig.) *melancholy:*–desperate(-ly wicked), incurable, sick, woeful.
606. אֱנָשׁ *en-awsh'* (Chald.); or אֱנַשׁ *en-ash';* cor. to 582; a *man:*–man, + whosoever.
607. אַנְתָּה *an-taw'* (Chald.); cor. to 859; *thou:*–as for thee, thou.
608. אַנְתּוּן *an-toon'* (Chald.); pl. of 607; *ye:*–ye.
609. אָסָא *aw-saw';* of unc. der.; *Asa,* the name of a king and of a Levite:–Asa.
610. אָסוּךְ *aw-sook';* from 5480; *anointed,* i.e. an oil-*flask:*–pot.
611. אָסוֹן *aws-sone';* of unc. der.; *hurt:*–mischief.
612. אֵסוּר *ay-soor';* from 631; a *bond* (esp. *manacles* of a prisoner):–band, + prison.
613. אֱסוּר *es-oor'* (Chald.); cor. to 612:–band, imprisonment.
614. אָסִיף *aw-seef';* or אָסִף *aw-seef';* from 622; *gathered,* i.e. (abstr.) a *gathering* in of crops:–ingathering.
615. אָסִיר *aw-sere';* from 631; *bound,* i.e. a *captive:*–(those which are) bound, prisoner.
616. אַסִּיר *as-sere';* for 615: prisoner.
617. אַסִּיר *as-sere';* the same as 616; *prisoner; Assir,* the name of two Isr.:–Assir.
618. אָסָם *aw-sawm';* from an un. root mean. to *heap* together; a *storehouse* (only

in the pl.):–barn, storehouse.
619. אָסְנָה *as-naw';* of unc. der.; *Asnah,* one of the Nethinim:–Asnah.
620. אָסְנַפַּר *os-nap-par';* for. der.; *Osnappar,* an Ass. king:–Asnapper.
621. אָסְנַת *aw-se-nath';* of Eg. der.; *Asenath,* the wife of Joseph:–Asenath.
622. אָסַף *aw-saf';* a prim. root; to *gather* for any purpose; hence, to *receive, take away,* i.e. remove (destroy, leave behind, put up, restore, etc.):–assemble, bring, consume, destroy, felch, gather (in, together, up again), X gen., get (him), lose, put all together, receive, recover [another from leprosy], (be) rereward, X surely, take (away, into, up), X utterly, withdraw.
623. אָסָף *aw-sawf';* from 622; *collector; Asaph,* the name of three Isr., and of the family of the first:–Asaph.
624. אָסֻף *aw-soof';* pass.part. of 622; *collected* (only in the pl.), i.e. a *collection* of offerings):–threshold, Asuppim.
625. אֹסֶף *o'-sef;* from 622; a *collection* (of fruits):–gathering.
626. אֲסֵפָה *as-ay-faw';* from 622; a *collection* of people (only adv.):–X together.
627. אֲסֻפָּה *as-up-paw';* fem of 624.; a *collection* of (learned) men (only in the pl.):–assembly.
628. אֲסַפְסֻף *as-pes-oof';* by redupl. from 624; *gathered up together,* i.e. a promiscuous *assemblage* (of people):–mixt multitude.
629. אָסְפַּרְנָא *os-par-naw'* (Chald.); of Pers. der.; *diligently:*–fast, forthwith, speed(-ily).
630. אַסְפָּתָא *as-paw-thaw';* of Pers. der.; *Aspatha,* a son of Haman:–Aspatha.
631. אָסַר *aw-sar';* a prim. root; to *yoke* or *hitch;* by anal., to *fasten* in any sense, to *join* battle:–bind, fast, gird, harness, hold, keep, make ready, order, prepare, prison(-er), put in bonds, set in array, tie.
632. אֱסָר *es-sawr';* or אִסָּר *is-sawr';* from 631; an *obligation* or *vow* (of abstinence):–binding, bond.
633. אֱסָר *es-sawr'* (Chald.); cor. to 632 in a legal sense; an *interdict:*–decree.
634. אֵסַר־חַדּוֹן *ay-sar' chad-dohn';* of for. der.; *Esar-chaddon,* an Ass. king:–Esar-haddon.
635. אֶסְתֵּר *es-tare';* of Pers. der.; *Ester,* the Jewish heroine:–Esther.
636. אָע *aw* (Chald.); cor. to 6086; a *tree* or wood:–timber, wood.
637. אַף *af;* prim. particle; mean. *accession* (used as an adv. or conj.); *also* or *yea;* adversatively *though:*–also, + although, and (furthermore, yet), but, even, + how much less (more, rather than), moreover, with, yea.
638. אַף *af* (Chald.); cor. to 637:–also.
639. אַף *af;* from 599; prop. the *nose* or *nostril;* hence, the *face,* and occasionally a *person;* also (from the rapid breathing in passion) *ire:*–anger(-gry), + before, coun-tenance, face, + forebearing, forehead, + [long-] suffering, nose, nostril, snout, X worthy, wrath.
640. אָפַד *aw-fad';* a prim. root [rather a denom. from 646]; to *gird* on (the ephod):–bind, gird.
641. אֵפֹד *ay-fode';* the same as 646 short; *Ephod,* an Isr.:–Ephod.
642. אֲפֻדָּה *ay-food-daw';* fem. of 646; a *girding* on (of the ephod); hence, gen., a *plating* (of metal):–ephod, ornament.
643. אַפֶּדֶן *ap-peh'-den;* app. of for. der.; a *pavilion* or palace-tent:–palace.
644. אָפָה *aw-faw';* a prim. root; to *cook,* esp. to *bake:*–bake(-r, [-meats]).
645. אֵפוֹ *ay-fo';* or אֵפוֹא *ay-fo';* from 6311; strictly a demonstr. particle, *here;* but used of time, *now* or *then:*–here, now, where?
646. אֵפוֹד *ay-fode';* rarely אֵפֹד *ay-fode';* prob. of for. der.; a *girdle;* spec. the *ephod* or high-priest's shoulder- piece; also gen., an *image:*–ephod.
647. אֲפִיחַ *af-ee'-akh;* perh. from 6315; *breeze; Aphiach,* an Isr.:–Aphiah.
648. אָפִיל *aw-feel';* from the same as 651 (in the sense of *weakness*); *unripe:*–not grown up.
649. אַפַּיִם *ap-pah'-yim;* dual of 639; *two nostrils; Appajim,* an Isr.:–Appaim.
650. אָפִיק *aw-feek';* from 622; prop. *containing,* i.e. a *tube;* also a *bed* or *valley* of a stream; also a *strong* thing or a *hero:*–brook, channel, mighty, river, + scale, stream, strong piece.
651. אָפֵל *aw-fale';* from an un. root mean. to *set* as the sun; *dusky:*–very dark.
652. אֹפֶל *o'fel;* from the same as 651; *dusk:*–darkness, obscurity, privily.
653. אֲפֵלָה *af-ay-law';* fem. of 651; *duskiness,* fig., *misfortune;* concr., *concealment:*–dark, darkness, gloominess, X thick.
654. אֶפְלָל *ef-lawl';* from 6419; *judge; Ephlal,* an Isr.:–Ephlal.
655. אֹפֶן *o'-fen;* from an un. root mean. to *revolve;* a *turn,* i.e. a *season:*–+ fitly.
656. אָפֵס *aw-face';* prim. root; to *disappear,* i.e. *cease:*–be clean gone (at an end, brought to nought), fail.
657. אֶפֶס *eh'-fes;* from 656; *cessation,* i.e. an *end* (esp. of the earth); often used adv., *no further;* also (like 6466) the *ankle* (in the dual), as being the extremity of the leg or foot:–ankle, but (only), end, howbeit, less than nothing, nevertheless (where), no, none (beside), not (any, -withstanding), thing of nought, save(-ing), there, uttermost part, want, without (cause).
658. אֶפֶס דַּמִּים *eh'-fes dam-meem';* from 657 and the pl. of 1818; *boundary of blood-*drops; *Ephes-Dammim,* a place in Pal.:–Ephes-dammim.
659. אֶפַע *eh'-fah;* from an un. root prob. mean. to *breathe;* prop. a *breath,* i.e. *nothing:*–of nought.
660. אֶפְעֶה *ef-eh';* from 659 (in the sense of *hissing*); an *asp* or other venomous serpent:–viper.
661. אָפַף *aw-faf';* prim. root; to *surround:*–compass.
662. אָפַק *aw-fak';* a prim. root; to *contain,* i.e. (reflex.) *abstain:*–force (oneself), restrain.
663. אֲפֵק *af-ake';* or אֲפִיק *af-eek';* from 662 (in the sense of *strength*); *fortress; Aphek* (or *Aphik*), the name of three places in Pal.:–Aphek, Aphik.
664. אֲפֵקָה *af-ay-kaw';* fem. of 663; *fortress; Aphekah,* a place in Pal.:–Aphekah.
665. אֵפֶר *ay'-fer;* from an un. root mean. to *bestrew; ashes:*–ashes.
666. אֲפֵר *af-ayr';* from the same as 665 (in the sense of *covering*); a *turban:*–ashes.
667. אֶפְרֹחַ *ef-ro'-akh;* 6524 (in the sense of *bursting* the shell); the *brood* of a bird:–young (one).
668. אַפִּרְיוֹן *ap-pir-yone;* prob. of Eg. der.; a *palanquin:*–chariot.
669. אֶפְרַיִם *ef-rah'-yim;* dual of masc. form of 672; *double fruit; Ephrajim,* a son of Joseph; also the tribe descended from him, and its territory:–Ephraim, Ephraimites.
670. אֲפָרְסַי *af-aw-re-sah'ee* (Chald.); of for. or. (only in the pl.); an *Apherasite* or inh. of an unknown region of Assyria:– Apharsite.
671. אֲפַרְסְכַי *af-ar-sek-ah'ee* (Chald.); or אֲפַרְסַתְכַי *af-ar-sath-kah'ee;* of for. or. (only in the pl.); an *Apharsekite* or *Apharsathkite,* an unknown Ass. tribe:–Apharsachites, Apharasthchites.
672. אֶפְרָת *ef-rawth';* or אֶפְרָתָה *ef-raw'-thaw;* from 6509; *fruitfulness; Ephrath,* another name for Bethlehem; once (Ps. 132:6) perh. for *Ephraim;* also of an Isr. woman:–Ephrath, Ephratah.
673. אֶפְרָתִי *ef-rawth-ee';* patrial from 672; an *Ephrathite* or an *Ephraimite:*–Ephraimite, Ephrathite.
674. אַפְּתֹם *ap-pe-thome'* (Chald.); of Pers. or.; *revenue;* others *at the last:*–revenue.
675. אֶצְבּוֹן *ets-bone';* or אֶצְבֹּן *ets-bone';* of unc. der.; *Etsbon,* the name of two Isr.:–Ezbon.
676. אֶצְבַּע *ets-bah';* from the same as 6648 (in the sense of *grasping*); something to *sieze* with, i.e. a *finger;* by anal., a toe:–finger, toe.
677. אֶצְבַּע *ets-bah'* (Chald.); cor. to 676:–finger, toe.
678. אָצִיל *aw-tseel';* from 680 (in its sec. sense of *separation*); an *extremity* (Is. 41:9), also a *noble:*–chief man, noble.
679. אַצִּיל *ats-tseel';* from 680 (in its prim. sense of *uniting*); a *joint* of the hand (i.e. *knuckle*); also (according to some) a *party-wall* (Eze. 41:8):–[arm] hole, great.
680. אָצַל *aw-tsal';* a prim. root; prop. to *join;* used only as a denom. from 681; to *separate;* hence, to *select, refuse, contr. act:*–keep, reserve, straiten, take.
681. אֵצֶל *ay'-tsel;* from 680 (in the sense of *joining*); a *side;* (as a prep.) *near:*–at, (hard) by, (from) (beside), near (unto), toward, with. See also 1018.
682. אָצֵל *aw-tsale';* from 680; *noble; Atsel,* the name of an Isr., and of a place in Pal.:–Azal, Azel.
683. אֲצַלְיָהוּ *ats-al-yaw'-hoo;* from 680 and 3050 prol.; *Jah has reserved; Atsaljah,* an Isr.:–Azaliah.
684. אֹצֶם *o'-tsem;* from an un. root prob. mean. to be *strong; strength* (i.e. *strong*); *Otsem,* the name of two Isr.:–Ozem.
685. אֶצְעָדָה *ets-aw-daw';* a var. from 6807; prop. a *step-chain;* by anal., a *bracelet:*–bracelet, chain.
686. אָצַר *aw-tsar';* a prim. root; to *store* up:–(lay up in) store, + (make) treasure(-r).
687. אֵצֶר *ay'-tser;* from 686; *treasure; Etser,* an Idumaean:–Ezer.
688. אֶקְדָּח *ek-dawkh';* from 6916; *burning,* i.e. a *carbuncle* or other fiery gem:–carbuncle.
689. אַקּוֹ *ak-ko';* prob. from 602; *slender,* i.e. the *ibex:*–wild goat.
690. אֲרָא *ar-aw';* prob. for 738; *lion; Ara,* an Isr.:–Ara.
691. אֶרְאֵל *er-ale';* prob. for 739; a *hero* (coll.):–valiant one.
692. אַרְאֵלִי *ar-ay-lee';* from 691; *heroic; Areli* (or an *Arelite,* coll.), an Isr. and his desc.:–Areli, Arelites.
693. אָרַב *aw-rab';* a prim. root; to *lurk:*–(lie

HEBREW

in) ambush(-ment), lay (lie in) wait.

694. אָרָב *ar-awb';* from 693; *ambush; Arab,* a place in Pal.:–Arab.

695. אֶרֶב *eh'-reb;* from 693; *ambuscade:*–den, lie in wait.

696. אֹרֶב *o'-reb;* the same as 695:–wait.

697. אַרְבֶּה *ar-beh';* from 7235; a *locust* (from its rapid *increase*):– grasshopper, locust.

698. אׇרֳבָה *or-ob-aw';* fem. of 696 (only in the pl.); *ambuscades:*–spoils.

699. אֲרֻבָּה *ar-oob-baw';* fem. part. pass. of 693 (as if for *lurking*); a *lattice;* (by impl.) a *window, dove-cot* (because of the *pigeon-holes*), *chimney* (with its apertures for smoke), *sluice* (with openings for water):–chimney, window.

700. אֲרֻבּוֹת *ar-oob-both;* pl. of 699; *Arubboth,* a place in Pal.:–Aruboth.

701. אַרְבִּי *ar-bee';* patrial from 694; an *Arbite* or nat. of Arab:–Arbite.

702. אַרְבַּע *ar-bah';* masc. אַרְבָּעָה *ar-baw-aw';* from 7251; *four:*–four.

703. אַרְבַּע *ar-bah'* (Chald.); cor. to 702 *four:*–four.

704. אַרְבַּע *ar-bah';* the same as 702; *Arba,* one of the Anakim:–Arba.

705. אַרְבָּעִים *ar-baw-eem';* multiple of 702; *forty:*—forty.

706. אַרְבַּעְתַּיִם *ar-bah-tah'-yim;* dual of 702; *fourfold:*–fourfold.

707. אָרַג *aw-rag';* a prim. root; to *plait* or *weave:*–weaver(-r).

708. אֶרֶג *eh'-reg;* from 707; a *weaving;* a *braid;* also a *shuttle:*–beam, weaver's shuttle.

709. אַרְגֹּב *ar-gobe';* from the same as 7263; *stony; Argob,* a district of Pal.:–Argob.

710. אַרְגְּוָן *arg-ev-awn';* a var. for 713; *purple:*–purple.

711. אַרְגְּוָן *arg-ev-awn'* (Chald.); cor. to 710 –scarlet

712. אַרְגַּז *ar-gawz';* perh. from 7264 (in the sense of being *suspended*), a *box* (as a pannier):–coffer.

713. אַרְגָּמָן *ar-gaw-mawn';* of for. or.; *purple* (the color or the dyed stuff):–purple.

714. אַרְדְּ *ard;* from an un. root prob. mean. to *wander; fugitive; Ard;* the name of two Isr.:–Ard.

715. אַרְדּוֹן *ar-dohn';* from the same as 714; *roaming; Ardon,* an Isr.:–Ardon.

716. אַרְדִּי *ar-dee;* patron. from 714; an *Ardite* (coll.) or desc. of Ard:–Ardites.

717. אָרָה *aw-raw';* a prim. root; to *pluck:*–gather, pluck.

718. אֲרוּ *ar-oo'* (Chald.); prob. akin to 431; *lo!:*–behold,lo.

719. אַרְוַד *ar-vad';* prob. from 7300; a refuge for the *roving; Arvad,* an island-city of Pal.:–Arvad.

720. אֲרוֹד *ar-ode;* an orth. var. of 719; *fugitive; Arod,* an Isr.:–Arod.

721. אַרְוָדִי *ar-vaw-dee';* patrial from 719; an *Arvadite* or citizen of Arvad:–Arvadite.

722. אֲרוֹדִי *ar-o-dee';* patron. from 721; an *Arodite* or desc. of Arod:–Arodi, Arodites.

723. אֻרְוָה *oor-vaw';* or אֲרָיָה *ar-aw'-yah';* from 717 (in the sense of *feeding*); a *herding-place* for an animal:–stall.

724. אֲרוּכָה *ar-oo-kaw';* or אֲרֻכָה *ar-oo-kaw';* fem. pass.part. of 748 (in the sense of *restoring* to soundness); *wholeness* (lit. or fig.):–health, made up, perfected.

725. אֲרוּמָה *ar-oo-maw';* a var. of 7316; *height; Arumah,* a place in Pal.:–Arumah.

726. אֲרוֹמִי *ar-o-mee':*–Syrian.

727. אָרוֹן *aw-rone';* or אָרֹן *aw-rone';* from 717 (in the sense of *gathering*); a *box:*–ark, chest, coffin.

728. אֲרַוְנָה *ar-av-naw';* or (by transp.) אוֹרְנָה *ore-naw';* or אֲרַנְיָה *ar-nee-yaw';* all by orth. var. for 771; *Aravnah* (or *Arnijah* or *Ornah*), a Jebusite:–Araunah.

729. אָרַז *aw-raz';* a prim. root; to be *firm;* used only in the pass.part. as a denom. from 730; of *cedar:*–made of cedar.

730. אֶרֶז *eh-rez';* from 729; a *cedar* tree (from the tenacity of its roots):–cedar (tree).

731. אַרְזָה *ar-zaw';* fem of 730; *cedar* wainscoating:–cedar work.

732. אָרַח *aw-rakh';* a prim. root; to *travel:*–go, wayfaring (man).

733. אָרַח *aw-rakh';* from 732; *way faring; Arach,* the name of three Isr.: Arah.

734. אֹרַח *o'-rakh;* from 732; a well-trodden *road* (lit. or fig.); also a *caravan:*–manner, path, race, rank, traveller, troop, [by-, high-] way.

735. אֹרַח *o'-rakh* (Chald.); cor. to 734; a *road:*–way.

736. אֹרְחָה *o-rekh-aw';* fem. act.part. of 732; a *caravan:*–(travelling) company.

737. אֲרֻחָה *ar-oo-khaw';* fem. pass.part. of 732 (in the sense of *appointing*); a *ration* of food:–allowance, diet, dinner, victuals.

738. אֲרִי *ar-ee';* or (prol.) אַרְיֵה *ar-yay';* from 717 (in the sense of *violence*); a *lion:*–(young) lion, + pierce (from the marg.).

739. אֲרִיאֵל *ar-ee-ale';* or אֲרִאֵל *ar-ee-ale';* from 738 and 410*; lion of God;* i.e. *heroic:*–lionlike men.

740. אֲרִיאֵל *ar-ee-ale';* the same as 739; *Ariel,* a symb. name for Jerus., also the name of an Isr.:–Ariel.

741. אֲרִאֵיל *ar-ee-ale';* either by transp. for 739 or, more prob., an orth. var. for 2025; the *altar* of the temple:– altar.

742. אֲרִידַי *ar-ee-dah'-ee;* of Pers. or.; *Aridai,* a son of Haman:–Aridai.

743. אֲרִידָתָא *ar-ee-daw-thaw';* of Pers. or.; *Aridatha,* a son of Haman:–Aridatha.

744. אַרְיֵה *ar-yay';* (Chald.) cor. to 738:–lion.

745. אַרְיֵה *ar-yay'* the same as 738; *lion; Arjeh,* an Isr.:–Arieh.

746. אֲרִיוֹךְ *ar-yoke';* of for. or.; *Arjok,* the name of two Babylonians:–Arioch.

747. אֲרִיסַי *ar-ee-sah'-ee;* of Pers. or.; *Arisai,* a son of Haman:–Arisai.

748. אָרַךְ *aw-rak';* a prim. root; to *be* (caus., *make*) *long* (lit. or fig.):–defer, draw out, lengthen, (be, become, make, pro-)long, + (out-, over-) live, tarry (long).

749. אֲרַךְ *ar-ak'* (Chald.); prop. cor. to 748, but used only in the sense of *reaching* to a given point; to *suit:*–be meet.

750. אָרֵךְ *aw-rake';* from 748; *long:*–long[-suffering, -winged], patient, slow [to anger].

751. אֶרֶךְ *eh'-rek;* from 748; *length; Erek,* a place in Babylon:–Erech.

752. אָרֹךְ *aw-roke'* from 748; *long:*–long.

753. אֹרֶךְ *o'rek';* from 748; *length:*–+ forever, length, long.

754. אַרְכָּא *ar-kaw'* (Chald.); or אַרְכָה *ar-kaw';* from 749; *length:*–lengthening, prol..

755. אַרְכֻבָה *ar-koo-baw'* (Chald.); from an un. root cor. to 7392 (in the sense of *bending* the knee); the *knee:*–knee.

756. אַרְכְּוַי *ar-kev-ah'ee* (Chald.); patrial from 751; an *Arkevite* (coll.) or nat. of Erek:–Archevite.

757. אַרְכִּי *ar-kee';* patrial from another place (in Pal.) of similar name with 751; an *Arkite* or nat. of Erek:–Archi, Archite.

758. אֲרָם *arawm';* from the same as 759; the *highland; Aram* or Syria, and its inh.; also the name of the son of Shem, a grandson of Nahor, and of an Isr.:–Aram, Mesopotamia, Syria, Syrians.

759. אַרְמוֹן *ar-mone';* from an un. root (mean. to *be elevated*); a *citadel* (from its *height*):–castle, palace. Comp. 2038.

760. אֲרַם צוֹבָה *ar-am' tso-baw';* from 758 and 6678; *Aram of Tsoba* (or Coele-Syria):–Aram-zobah.

761. אֲרַמִּי *ar-am-mee';* patrial from 758; an *Aramite* or Aramaean:–Syrian, Aramitess.

762. אֲרָמִית *ar-aw-meeth';* fem. of 761; (only adv.)*in Aramean:*–in the Syrian language (tongue), in Syriac.

763. אֲרַם נַהֲרַיִם *ar-am' nah-har-ah'-yim;* from 758 and the dual of 5104; *Aram of* (the) *two rivers* (Euphrates and Tigris) or Mesopotamia:–Aham-naharaim, Mesopotamia.

764. אַרְמֹנִי *ar-mo-nee';* from 759; *palatial; Armoni,* an Isr.:–Armoni.

765. אֲרָן *ar-awn';* from 7442; *stridulous; Aran,* an Edomite:–Aran

766. אֹרֶן *o'-ren;* from the same as 765 (in the sense of *strength*); the *ash* tree (from its toughness):–ash.

767. אֹרֶן *o'-ren;* the same as 766; *Oren,* an Isr.:–Oren.

768. אַרְנֶבֶת *ar-neh'-beth;* of unc. der.; the *hare:*–hare.

769. אַרְנוֹן *ar-nohn';* or אַרְנֹן *ar-nohn';* from 7442; a *brawling* stream; the *Arnon,* a river east of the Jordan; also its territory:– Arnon.

770. אַרְנָן *ar-nawn';* prob. from the same as 769; *noisy; Arnan,* an Isr.:–Arnan.

771. אׇרְנָן *or-nawn';* prob. from 766; *strong; Ornan,* a Jebusite:–Ornan. See 728.

772. אֲרַע *ar-ah'* (Chald.); cor. to 776; the *earth;* by impl. (fig.) *low:*–earth, interior.

773. אַרְעִית *arh-eeth'* (Chald.);, fem. of 772; the *bottom:*–bottom.

774. אַרְפָּד *ar-pawd';* from 7502; *spread* out; *Arpad,* a place in Syria:–Arpad, Arphad.

775. אַרְפַּכְשַׁד *ar-pak-shad';* prob. of for. or.; *Arpakshad,* a son of Noah; also the region settled by him:–Arphaxad.

776. אֶרֶץ *eh'-rets;* from an un. root prob. mean. to be *firm;* the *earth* (at large, or partitively a *land*):–X common, country, earth, field, ground, land, X nations, way, + wilderness, world.

777. אַרְצָא *ar-tsaw';* from 776; *earthiness; Artsa,* an Isr.:–Arza.

778. אֲרַק *ar-ak'* (Chald.); by transmutation for 772; the *earth:*–earth.

779. אָרַר *awrar';* a prim. root; to *execrate:*–X bitterly curse.

780. אֲרָרַט *ar-aw-rat';* of for. or.; *Ararat* (or rather Armenia):–Ararat, Armenia.

781. אָרַשׂ *aw-ras';* a prim. root; to *engage* for matrimony:–betroth, espouse.

782. אֲרֶשֶׁת *ar-eh'-sheth;* from 781 (in the sense of *desiring* to possess); a *longing* for:–request.

783. אַרְתַּחְשַׁשְׁתָּא *ar-takh-shash-taw';* or אַרְתַּחְשַׁשְׁתְּ *ar-takh-shasht';* or by perm. אַרְתַּחְשַׁשְׂתְּא *ar-takh-shast';* of for. or.; *Artachshasta* (or Artaxerxes), a title (rather than name) of several Pers. kings:–Artaxerxes.
784. אֵשׁ *aysh;* a prim. word; *fire* (lit. or fig.):– burning, fiery, fire, flaming, hot.
785. אֶשָּׁא *aysh* (Chald.); cor. to 784:–flame.
786. אִשׁ eesh; ident. (in or. and formation) with 784; *entity,* used only adv., there *is* or *are:*–are there, none can. Comp. 3426.
787. אשׁ *ohsh* (Chald.); cor. (by transp. and abb) to 803; a *foundation:*–foundation.
788. אַשְׁבֵּל *ash-bale';* prob. from the same as 7640; *flowing*; *Ashbel,* an Isr.:–Ashbel.
789. אַשְׁבֵּלִי *ash-bay-lee';* patron. from 788; an *Ashbelite* (coll.) or desc. of Ashbel:–Ashbelites.
790. אֶשְׁבָּן *esh-bawn';* prob. from the same as 7644; *vigorous; Eshban,* an Idumaean:–Eshban.
791. אַשְׁבֵּעַ *ash-bay'-ah;* from 7650; *adjurer; Asbeä,* an Isr.:–Ashbea.
792. אֶשְׁבַּעַל *esh-bah'-al;* from 376 and 1168; *man of Baal; Eshbaal* (or Ishbosheth), a son of King Saul:–Eshbaal.
793. אֶשֶׁד *eh'-shed;* from an un. root mean. to *pour;* an *outpouring:*–stream.
794. אֲשֵׁדָה *ash-ay-daw';* fem. of 793; a *ravine:*–springs.
795. אַשְׁדּוֹד *ash-dode';* from 7703; *ravager; Ashdod,* a place in Pal.:–Ashdod
796. אַשְׁדּוֹדִי *ash-do-dee';* patrial from 795; an *Ashdodite* (often coll.) or inh. of Ashdod:–Ashdodites, of Ashdod.
797. אַשְׁדּוֹדִית *ash-do-deeth';* fem. of 796; (only adv.) *in the language of Ashdod:*–in the speech of Ashdod.
798. אַשְׁדּוֹת הַפִּסְגָּה *ash-doth' hap-pis-gaw'* from the pl. of 794 and 6449 with the art. interp.; *ravines of the Pisgah; Ashdoth-Pisgah,* a place east of the Jordan:–Ashdoth-pisgah.
799. אֶשְׁדָּת *esh-dawth';* from 784 and 1881; a *fire-law:*–fiery law.
800. אֶשָּׁה *esh-shaw'* fem. of 784; *fire:*–fire.
801. אִשָּׁה *ish-shaw';* the same as 800, but used in a liturgical sense; prop. a *burnt-offering;* but occasionally of any *sacrifice:*–(offering, sacrifice), (made) by fire.
802. אִשָּׁה *ish-shaw';* fem. of 376 or 582; irreg. pl., נָשִׁים *naw-sheem';* a *woman* (used in the same wide sense as 582):–[adulter]ess, each, every, female, X many, + none, one, + together, wife, woman. Often unexpressed in English.
803. אֲשׁוּיָה *ash-oo-yah';* fem. pass.part. from an un. root mean. to *found; foundation:*–foundation.
804. אַשּׁוּר *ash-shoor';* or אַשֻּׁר *ash-shoor';* app. from 833 (in the sense of *successful*); *Ashshur,* the second son of Shem; also his desc. and the country occupied by them (i.e. Assyria), its region and its empire:–Asshur, Assur, Assyria, Assyrians. See 838.
805. אֲשׁוּרִי *ash-oo-ree';* or אַשּׁוּרִי *ash-shoo-ree';* from a patrial word of the same form as 804; an *Ashurite* (coll.) or inh. of Ashur, a district in Pal.:–Asshurim, Ashurites.
806. אַשְׁחוּר *ash-khoor';* prob. from 7835; *black; Ashchur,* an Isr.:–Ashur.
807. אֲשִׁימָא *ash-ee-maw';* of for. or.; *Ashima,* a deity of Hamath:–Ashima.
808. אָשִׁישׁ *aw-sheesh';* from the same as 784 (in the sense of *pressing* down firmly; comp. 803); a (ruined) *foundation:*–foundation.
809. אֲשִׁישָׁה *ash-ee-shaw';* fem. of 808; something closely *pressed* together, i.e. a *cake* of raisins or other comfits:–flagon.
810. אֶשֶׁךְ *eh'-shek;* from an un. root (prob. mean. to *bunch* together); a *testicle* (as a *lump*):–stone.
811. אֶשְׁכּוֹל *esh-kole';* or אֶשְׁכֹּל *esh-kole';* prob. prol. from 810; a *bunch of grapes* or other fruit:–cluster (of grapes).
812. אֶשְׁכֹּל *esh-kole';* the same as 811; *Eshcol,* the name of an Amorite, also of a valley in Pal.:–Eshcol.
813. אַשְׁכְּנַז *ash-ken-az';* of for. or.; *Ashkenaz,* a Japhethite, also his desc.:–Ashkenaz.
814. אֶשְׁכָּר *esh-cawr';* for 7939; a *gratuity:*–gift, present.
815. אֵשֶׁל *ay'-shel;* from a root of unc. signif.; a *tamarisk* tree; by ext., a *grove* of any kind:–grove, tree.
816. אָשַׁם *aw-sham';* or אָשֵׁם *aw-shame';* a prim. root; to *be guilty;* by impl. to *be punished* or *perish:*–X certainly, be (-come, made) desolate, destroy, X greatly, be(-come, found, hold) guilty, offend (acknowledge offence), trespass.
817. אָשָׁם *aw-shawm';* from 816; *guilt;* by impl., a *fault;* also a *sin-offering:*–guiltiness, (offering for) sin, trespass (offering).
818. אָשֵׁם *aw-shame';* from 816; *guilty;* hence, *presenting* a *sin-offering:*–one which is faulty, guilty.
819. אַשְׁמָה *ash-maw';* fem. of 817; *guiltiness,* a *fault,* the *presentation* of a *sin-offering:*–offend, sin, (cause of) trespass (-ing, offering).
820. אַשְׁמָן *ash-mawn';* prob. from 8081; a *fat*-field:–desolate place.
821. אַשְׁמֻרָה *ash-moo-raw';* or אַשְׁמוּרָה *ash-moo-raw';* or אַשְׁמֹרֶת *ash-mo'-reth;* (fem.) from 8104; a night *watch:*–watch.
822. אֶשְׁנָב *esh-nawb';* app. from an un. root (prob. mean. to *leave interstices*); a latticed *window:*–casement, lattice.
823. אַשְׁנָה *ash-naw';* prob. a var. for 3466; *Ashnah,* the name of two places in Pal.:–Ashnah.
824. אֶשְׁעָן *esh-awn';* from 8172; *support; Eshan,* a place in Pal.:–Eshean.
825. אַשָּׁף *ash-shawf';* from an un. root (prob. mean. to *lisp,* i.e. *practice enchantment*); a *conjurer:*–astrologer.
826. אָשַׁף *ash-shawf'* (Chald.); cor. to 825:–astrologer.
827. אַשְׁפָּה *ash-paw';* perh. (fem.) from the same as 825 (in the sense of *covering*); a *quiver* or arrow-case:–quiver.
828. אַשְׁפְּנַז *ash-pen-az';* of for. or.; *Ashpenaz,* a Babylonian eunuch:–Ashpenaz.
829. אֶשְׁפָּר *esh-pawr';* of unc. der.; a measured *portion:*–good piece (of flesh).
830. אַשְׁפֹּת *ash-pohth';* or אַשְׁפּוֹת *ash-pohth';* or (contr.) שְׁפֹת *shef-ohth';* pl. of a noun of the same form as 827, from 8192 (in the sense of *scraping*); a heap of *rubbish* or *filth:*–dung (hill).
831. אַשְׁקְלוֹן *ash-kel-one';* prob. from 8254 in the sense of *weighing*-place (i.e. *mart*); *Ashkelon,* a place in Pal.:–Ashkelon, Askalon.
832. אֶשְׁקְלוֹנִי *esh-kel-o-nee';* patrial from 831; *Ashkelonite* (coll.) or inh. of Ashkelon:–Eshkalonites.
833. אָשַׁר *aw-shar';* or אָשֵׁר *aw-share';* a prim. root; to *be straight* (used in the widest sense, esp. to *be level, right, happy*); fig., to *go forward, be honest, prosper:*–(call, be) bless(-ed, happy), go, guide, lead, relieve.
834. אֲשֶׁר *ash-er';* a prim. rel. pron. (of every gender and number); *who, which, what, that;* also (as an adv. and a conj.) *when, where, how, because, in order that,* etc.:–X after, X alike, as (soon as), because, X every, for, + forasmuch, + from whence, + how(-soever), X if, (so) that ([thing]which, wherein), X though, + until, + whatsoever, when, where (+ -as, -in, -of, -on, -soever, -with), which, whilst, + whither(- soever), who(-m,-soever, -se). As it is indeclinable, it is often accompanied by the pers. pron. expletively, used to show the connection.
835. אֶשֶׁר *eh'-sher;* from 833; *happiness;* only in masc. pl. constr. as interj., how *happy!:*–blessed, happy.
836. אָשֵׁר *aw-share';* from 833, *happy; Asher,* a son of Jacob, and the tribe descended from him, with its territory; also a place in Pal.:–Asher
837. אֹשֶׁר *o'-sher;* from 833; *happiness:*– happy.
838. אָשֻׁר *aw-shoor';* or אַשֻּׁר *ash-shoor';* from 833 in the sense of *going;* a *step:*–going, step.
839. אֲשֻׁר *ash-oor';* contr. for 8391; the *cedar* tree or some other light elastic wood:–Ashurite.
840. אֲשַׂרְאֵל *as-ar-ale';* by orth. var. from 833 and 410; *right of God; Asarel,* an Isr.:–Asareel.
841. אֲשַׂרְאֵלָה *as-ar-ale'-aw;* from the same as 840; *right towards God; Asarelah,* an Isr.:–Asarelah. Comp. 3480.
842. אֲשֵׁרָה *ash-ay-raw';* or אֲשֵׁירָה *ash-ay-raw';* from 833; *happy; Asherah* (or Astarte) a Phoenician goddess; also an *image* of the same:– grove. Comp. 6253.
843. אָשֵׁרִי *aw-shay-ree';* patron. from 836; an *Asherite* (coll.) or desc. of Asher:–Asherites.
844. אַשְׂרִיאֵל *as-ree-ale';* an orth. var. for 840; *Asriel,* the name of two Isr.:–Ashriel, Asriel.
845. אַשְׂרְאֵלִי *as-ree-ale-ee';* patron. from 844; an *Asrielite* (coll.) or desc. of Asriel:–Asrielites.
846. אֻשַּׁרְנָא *oosh-ar-naw'* (Chald.); from a root cor. to 833; a *wall* (from its uprightness):–wall.
847. אֶשְׁתָּאֹל *esh-taw-ole';* or אֶשְׁתָּאוֹל *esh-taw-ole';* prob. from 7592; *intreaty; Eshtaol,* a place in Pal.:–Eshtaol.
848. אֶשְׁתָּאֻלִי *esh-taw-oo-lee';* patrial from 847; an *Eshtaolite* (coll.) or inh. of Eshtaol:–Eshtaulites.
849. אֶשְׁתַּדּוּר *esh-tad-dure'* (Chald.); from 7712 (in a bad sense); *rebellion:*–sedition.
850. אֶשְׁתּוֹן *esh-tone';* prob. from the same as 7764; *restful; Eshton,* an Isr.:–Eshton.
851. אֶשְׁתְּמֹעַ *esh-tem-o'-ah;* or אֶשְׁתְּמוֹעַ *esh-tem-o'-ah;* or אֶשְׁתְּמֹה *esh-tem-o';* from 8085 (in the sense of *obedience*); *Eshtemoa* or *Eshtemoh,* a place in Pal.:–Eshtemoa, Eshtemoh.
852. אָת *awth* (Chald.); cor. to 226; a *portent:*–sign.
853. אֵת *ayth;* app. contr. from 226 in the demonstr. sense of *entity;* prop. *self* (but gen. used to point out more def. the obj. of a verb or prep., *even* or *namely*):–[*as such unrepresented in English*].
854. אֵת *ayth;* prob. from 579; prop. *nearness*

HEBREW

(used only as a prep. or an adv.), *near;* hence, gen., *with, by, at, among,* etc.:–against, among, before, by, for, from, in(-to), (out) of, with. Often with another prep. pref.

855. אֵת *ayth;* of unc. der.; a *hoe* or other digging implement:–coulter, plowshare.

856. אֶתְבַּעַל *eth-bah'-al;* from 854 and 1168; *with Baal; Ethbaal,* a Phoenician king:–Ethbaal.

857. אָתָה *aw-thaw';* or אָתָא *aw-thaw';* a prim. root [collat. to 225 contr.]; to *arrive:*–(be-, things to) come (upon), bring.

858. אָתָה *aw-thaw'* (Chald.); or אָתָא *aw-thaw';* cor. to 857:–(be-)come, bring.

859. אַתָּה *at-taw';* or (short); אַתָּ *at-taw';* or אַת *ath;* fem. (irreg.) sometimes אַתִּי *at-tee';* pl. masc. אַתֶּם *at- tem';* fem. אַתֶּן *at-ten';* or אַתֵּנָה *at-tay'naw;* or אַתֵּנָּה *at-tane'-naw;* a prim. pron. of the sec. pers.; *thou* and *thee,* or (pl.) *ye* and *you:*–thee, thou, ye, you.

860. אָתוֹן *aw-thone';* prob. from the same as 386 (in the sense of *patience*); a female *ass* (from its docility):–(she) ass.

861. אַתּוּן *at-toon'* (Chald.); prob. from the cor. to 784; prob. a *fire-place,* i.e. *furnace:*–furnace.

862. אַתּוּק *at-tooke';* or אַתִּיק *at-teek';* from 5423 in the sense of *decreasing;* a *ledge* or offset in a building:–gallery.

863. אִתַּי *it-tah'ee;* or אִיתַי *ee-thah'ee;* from 854; near; *Ittai* or *Ithai,* the name of a Gittite and of an Isr.:–Ithai, Ittai.

864. אֵתָם *ay-thawm';* of Eg. der.; *Etham,* a place in the Desert:–Etham.

865. אֶתְמוֹל *eth -mole';* or אִתְמוֹל *ith-mole';* or אֶתְמוּל *eth- mool';* prob. from 853 or 854 and 4136; *heretofore;* def. *yesterday:*–+ before (that) time, + heretofore, of late (old), + times past, yester[day].

866. אֶתְנָה *eth-naw';* from 8566; a *present* (as the price of harlotry):–reward.

867. אֶתְנִי *eth-nee';* perh. from 866; *munificence; Ethni,* an Isr.:–Ethni.

868. אֶתְנַן *eth-nan';* the same as 866; a *gift* (as the price of harlotry or idolatry):–hire, reward.

869. אֶתְנַן *eth-nan';* the same as 868 in the sense of 867; *Ethnan,* an Isr.:–Ethnan.

870. אֲתַר *ath-ar';* (Chald.) from a root cor. to that of 871; a *place;* (adv.) *after:*–after, place.

871. אֲתָרִים *ath-aw-reem';* pl. from an un. root (prob. mean. to *step*); places; *Atharim,* a place near Pal.:–spies.

ב

872. בְּאָה *bĕ-aw';* from 935; an *entrance* to a building:–entry.

873. בְּאוּשׁ *be-oosh'* (Chald.); from 888; *wicked:*–bad.

874. בָּאַר *baw-ar';* a prim. root; to *dig;* by anal., to *engrave;* fig., to *explain:*–declare, (make) plain(-ly).

875. בְּאֵר *bĕ-ayr';* from 874; a *pit;* esp. a *well:*–pit, well.

876. בְּאֵר *bĕ-ayr';* the same as 875; Beër, a place in the Desert, also one in Pal.:–Beer.

877. בֹּאר *bore;* from 874; a *cistern:*–cistern.

878. בְּאֵרָא *bĕ-ay-raw';* from 875; a *well; Beëra,* an Isr.:–Beera.

879. בְּאֵר אֵלִים *be-ayr' ay-leem;* from 875 and the pl. of 410; *well of heroes; Beër-Elim,* a place in the Desert:–Beer-elim.

880. בְּאֵרָה *bĕ-ay-raw';* the same as 878; *Beërah,* an Isr.:–Beerah.

881. בְּאֵרוֹת *be-ay-rohth';* fem. pl. of 875; *wells; Beëroth,* a place in Pal.:–Beeroth.

882. בְּאֵרִי *bĕ-ay-ree';* from 875; *fountained; Beëri,* the name of a Hittite and of an Isr.:–Beeri.

883. בְּאֵר לַחַי רֹאִי *be-ayr' lakh-ah'ee ro-ee'* from 875 and 2416 (with pref.) and 7203; *well of a living* (One) *my Seer; Beër-Lachai-Roï,* a place in the Desert:–Beer-lahai-roi.

884. בְּאֵר שֶׁבַע *be-ayr' sheh'-bah;* from 875 and 7651 (in the sense of 7650); *well of an oath; Beër-Sheba,* a place in Pal.:–Beer-shebah.

885. בְּאֵרֹת בְּנֵי־יַעֲקַן *be-ay-roth' be-nay' yah-a-can';* from the fem. pl. of 875, and the pl. contr. of 1121, and 3292; *wells of* (the) *sons of Jaakan; Beeroth-Bene-Jaakan,* a place in the Desert:–Beeroth of the children of Jaakan.

886. בְּאֵרֹתִי *be-ay-ro-thee';* patrial from 881; a *Beërothite* or inh. of *Beëroth:*–Beerothite.

887. בָּאַשׁ *baw-ash';* a prim. root; to *smell* bad; fig., to *be offensive* mor.:–(make to) be abhorred (had in abomination, loathsome, odious), (cause a, make to) stink(-ing savour), X utterly.

888. בְּאֵשׁ *bĕ-aysh'* (Chald.); cor. to 887:–displease.

889. בְּאשׁ *be-oshe';* from 877; a *stench:*–stink.

890. בָּאְשָׁה *bosh-aw';* fem. of 889; *stink-weed* or any other noxious or useless plant:–cockle.

891. בְּאֻשִׁים *bĕ-oo-sheem';* pl. of 889; *poison-berries:*–wild grapes.

892. בָּבָה *baw-baw';* fem. act.part. of an un. root mean. to *hollow* out; something *hollowed* (as a *gate*), i.e. *pupil* of the eye:–apple [of the eye].

893. בֵּבַי *bay-bah'ee;* prob. of for. or.; *Bebai,* an Isr.:–Bebai.

894. בָּבֶל *baw-bel';* from 1101; *confusion; Babel* (i.e. Babylon), incl. Babylonia and the Babylonian empire:–Babel, Babylon.

895. בָּבֶל *baw-bel'* (Chald.); cor. to 894:–Babylon.

896. בַּבְלִי *bab-lee'* (Chald.); patrial from 895; a *Babylonian:*–Babylonia.

897. בַּג *bag;* a Pers. word; *food:*–spoil

898. בָּגַד *baw-gad';* a prim. root; to *cover* (with a garment); fig., to *act covertly;* by impl., to *pillage:*–deal deceitfully (treacherously, unfaith-fully), offend, transgress(-or), (depart), treacherous (dealer, -ly, man), unfaithful(-ly, man), X very.

899. בֶּגֶד *behg'-ed;* from 898; a *covering,* i.e. clothing; also *treachery* or *pillage:*–apparel, cloth(-es, -ing), garment, lap, rag, raiment, robe, X very [treacherously], vesture, wardrobe.

900. בֹּגְדוֹת *bohg-ed-ohth;* fem. pl. act.part. of 898; *treacheries:*– treacherous.

901. בָּגוֹד *baw-gode';* from 898; *treacherous:*–treacherous.

902. בִּגְוַי *big-vah'ee;* prob. of for. or.; *Bigvai,* an Isr.:–Bigvai.

903. בִּגְתָא *big-thaw';* of Pers. der.; *Bigtha,* a eunuch of Xerxes:–Bigtha.

904. בִּגְתָן *big-thawn';* or בִּגְתָנָא *big-thaw'naw;* of similar der. to 903; *Bigthan* or *Bigthana,* a eunuch of Xerxes:–Bigthan, Bigthana.

905. בַּד *bad;* from 909; prop. *separation;* by impl., a *part* of the body, *branch* of a tree, bar for carrying; fig., *chief* of a city; esp. (with prep. pref.) as an adv., *apart, only, besides:*–alone, apart, bar, besides, branch, by self, of each alike, except, only, part, staff, strength.

906. בַּד *bad;* perh. from 909 (in the sense of *divided* fibres); flaxen *thread* or yarn; hence, a *linen* garment:–linen.

907. בַּד *bad;* from 908; a *brag* or *lie;* also a *liar:*–liar, lie.

908. בָּדָא *baw-daw';* a prim. root; (fig.) to *invent:*–devise, feign.

909. בָּדַד *baw-dad';* a prim. root; to *divide,* i.e. (reflex.) *be solitary:*–alone.

910. בָּדָד *baw-dawd';* from 909; *separate;* adv., *separately:*–alone, desolate, only, solitary.

911. בְּדַד *bed-ad';* from 909; *separation; Bedad,* an Edomite:–Bedad

912. בֵּדְיָה *bay-de-yaw';* prob. short. for 5662; *servant of Jehovah; Bedejah,* an Isr.:–Bedeiah.

913. בְּדִיל *bed-eel';* from 914; *alloy* (because removed by smelting); by anal., *tin:*–+ plummet, tin.

914. בָּדַל *baw-dal';* a prim. root; to *divide* (in var. senses lit. or fig., *separate, distinguish, differ, select,* etc.):– (make, put) difference, divide (asunder), (make) separate (self, -ation), sever (out), X utterly.

915. בָּדָל *baw-dawl';* from 914; a *part:*–piece.

916. בְּדֹלַח *bed-o'-lakh;* prob. from 914; something in *pieces,* i.e. *bdellium,* a (fragrant) gum (perh. *amber*); others a pearl:–bdellium.

917. בְּדָן *bed-awn';* prob. short. for 5658; *servile; Bedan,* the name of two Isr.:–Bedan.

918. בָּדַק *baw-dak'* a prim. root; to *gap* open; used only as a denom. from 919; to *mend* a breach:–repair.

919. בֶּדֶק *beh'-dek;* from 918; a *gap* or *leak* (in a building or a ship):–breach, + calker.

920. בִּדְקַר *bid-car';* prob. from 1856 with a prep. pref.; *by stabbing,* i.e. *assassin; Bidkar,* an Isr.:–Bidkar.

921. בְּדַר *bed-ar'* (Chald.); cor. (by transp. to 6504); to *scatter:*–scatter.

922. בֹּהוּ *bo'-hoo;* from an un. root (mean. to *be empty*); a *vacuity,* i.e. (superficially) an undistinguishable *ruin:*–emptiness, void.

923. בַּהַט *bah'-hat;* from an un. root (prob. mean. to *glisten*); white *marble* or perh. *alabaster:*–red [marble].

924. בְּהִילוּ *bĕ-hee-loo'* (Chald.); from 927; a *hurry;* only adv., *hastily:*–in haste.

925. בָּהִיר *baw-here';* from an un. root (mean. to *be bright*); *shining:*–bright.

926. בָּהַל *baw-hal';* a prim. root; to *tremble* inwardly (or *palpitate*), i.e. (fig.) *be* (caus., *make*) (suddenly) *alarmed* or *agitated;* by impl. to *hasten* anxiously:–be (make) affrighted (afraid, amazed, dismayed, rash), (be, get, make) haste(-n, -y, -ily), (give) speedy(-ily), thrust out, trouble, vex.

927. בְּהַל *bĕ-hal'* (Chald.); cor. to 926; to *terrify, hasten:*–in haste, trouble.

928. בֶּהָלָה *beh-haw-law';* from 926; *panic, destruction:*–terror, trouble.

929. בְּהֵמָה *bĕ-hay-maw';* from an un. root (prob. mean. to be *mute*); prop. a *dumb* beast; esp. any large quadruped or *animal* (often coll.):–beast, cattle.

930. בְּהֵמוֹת *bĕ-hay-mōhth'* in form a pl. of 929, but really a sing. of Eg. der.; a *water-ox,* i.e. the *hippopotamus* or Nile-horse:–Behemoth.

931. בֹּהֶן *bo'-hen;* from an un. root app. mean. to *be thick;* the *thumb* of the hand or

great toe of the foot:–thumb, great toe.
932. בֹּהַן *bo'han;* an orth. var. of 931; *thumb; Bohan,* an Isr.:–Bohan.
933. בֹּהַק *bo'-hak;* from an un. root mean. to *be pale;* white *scurf:*–freckled spot.
934. בֹּהֶרֶת *bo-heh'-reth;* fem. act.part. of the same as 925; a *whitish* spot on the skin:–bright spot.
935. בּוֹא *bo;* a prim. root; to *go* or *come* (in a wide variety of appl.):–abide, apply, attain, X be, befall, + besiege, bring (forth, in, into, to pass), call, carry, X certainly, (cause, let, thing for) to come (against, in, out, upon, to pass), depart, X doubtless again, + eat, + employ, (cause to) enter (in, into, -tering, -trance, -try), be fallen, fetch, + follow, get, give, go (down, in, to war), grant, + have, X indeed, [in-] vade, lead, lift [up], mention, pull in, put, resort, run (down), send, set, X (well) stricken [in age], X surely, take (in), way.
936. בּוּז *booz;* a prim. root; to *disrespect:*–contemn, despise, X utterly.
937. בּוּז *booz;* from 936; *disrespect:*–contempt(-uously), despised, shamed.
938. בּוּז *booz;* the same as 937; *Buz,* the name of a son of Nahor, and of an Isr.:–Buz.
939. בּוּזָה *boo-zaw';* fem. pass.part. of 936; something *scorned;* an obj. of *contempt:*–despised.
940. בּוּזִי *boo-zee';* patron. from 938; a *Buzite* or desc. of Buz:–Buzite.
941. בּוּזִי *boo-zee';* the same as 940; *Buzi,* an Isr.:–Buzi.
942. בַּוַּי *bav-vah'ee;* prob. of Pers. or.; *Bavvai,* an Isr.:–Bavai.
943. בּוּךְ *book;* a prim. root; to *involve* (lit. or fig.):–be entangled, (perplexed).
944. בּוּל *bool;* for 2981; *produce* (of the earth, etc.):–food, stock.
945. בּוּל *bool;* the same as 944 (in the sense of *rain*); *Bul,* the eighth Heb. month:–Bul.
946. בּוּנָה *boo-naw';* from 995; *discretion; Bunah,* an Isr.:–Bunah.
947. בּוּס *boos;* a prim. root; to *trample* (lit. or fig.):–loath, tread (down, under [foot]), be polluted.
948. בּוּץ *boots;* from an un. root (of the same form) mean. to *bleach,* i.e. (intr.) *be white;* prob. *cotton* (of some sort):–fine (white) linen.
949. בּוֹצֵץ *bo-tsates';* from the same as 948; *shining; Botsets,* a rock near Michmash:–Bozez.
950. בּוּקָה *boo-kaw';* fem. pass.part. of an un. root (mean. to *be hollow*); *emptiness* (as adj.):–empty.
951. בּוֹקֵר *bo-kare';* prop. act.part. from 1239 as denom. from 1241; a *cattle-tender:*–herdman.
952. בּוּר *boor;* a prim. root; to *bore,* i.e. (fig.) *examine:*–declare.
953. בּוֹר *bore;* from 952 (in the sense of 877); a pit *hole* (esp. one used as a *cistern* or a *prison*):–cistern, dungeon, fountain, pit, well.
954. בּוֹשׁ *boosh;* a prim. root; prop. to *pale,* i.e. by impl. to *be ashamed;* also (by impl.) to *be disappointed* or *delayed:*–(be, make, bring to, cause, put to, with, a-)shamed(-d), be (put to) confounded(-fusion), become dry, delay, be long.
955. בּוּשָׁה *boo-shaw';* fem. part. pass. of 954; *shame:*–shame.
956. בּוּת *booth* (Chald.); app. denom. from 1005; to *lodge* over night:–pass the night.
957. בַּז *baz;* from 962; *plunder:*–booty, prey, spoil(-ed).
958. בָּזָא *baw-zaw';* a prim. root; prob. to *cleave:*–spoil
959. בָּזָה *baw-zaw';* a prim. root; to *disesteem:*–despise, disdain, contemn(-ptible), + think to scorn, vile person.
960. בָּזֹה *baw-zo';* from 959; *scorned:*–despise.
961. בִּזָּה *biz-zaw';* fem. of 957; booty:–prey, spoil.
962. בָּזַז *baw-zaz';* a prim. root; to *plunder:*–catch, gather, (take) for a prey, rob(-ber), spoil, take (away, spoil), X utterly.
963. בִּזָּיוֹן *biz-zaw-yone';* from 959:–*disesteem:*–contempt.
964. בִּזְיוֹתְיָה *biz-yo-thĕ-yaw';* from 959 and 3050; *contempts of Jah; Bizjothjah,* a place in Pal.:–Bizjothjah.
965. בָּזָק *baw-zawk';* from an un. root mean. to *lighten;* a *flash* of lightning:–flash of lightning.
966. בֶּזֶק *beh'-zek;* from 965; *lightning; Bezek,* a place in Pal.:–Bezek.
967. בָּזַר *baw-zar';* a prim. root; to *disperse:*–scatter
968. בִּזְּתָא *biz-thaw';* of Pers. or.; *Biztha,* a eunuch of Xerxes:–Biztha.
969. בָּחוֹן *baw-khone';* from 974; an *assayer* of metals:–tower.
970. בָּחוּר *baw-khoor';* or בָּחֻר *baw-khoor';* part. pass. of 977; prop. *selected,* i.e. a *youth* (often coll.):–(choice) young (man), chosen, X hole.
971. בַּחִין *bakh-een';* another form of 975; a watch-*tower* of besiegers:–tower.
972. בָּחִיר *baw-kheer';* from 977; *select:*–choose, chosen one, elect.
973. בָּחַל *baw-khal';* a prim. root; to *loathe:*–abhor, get hastily.
974. בָּחַן *baw-khan';* a prim. root; to *test* (esp. metals); gen. and fig., to *investigate:*–examine, prove, tempt, try (trial).
975. בַּחַן *bakh'-an;* from 974 (in the sense of keeping a *look-out*); a watch*tower:*–tower.
976. בֹּחַן *bo'-khan;* from 974; *trial:*–tried.
977. בָּחַר *baw-khar';* a prim. root; prop. to *try,* i.e. (by impl.) *select:*–acceptable, appoint, choose (choice), excellent, join, be rather, require.
978. בַּחֲרוּמִי *bakh-ar-oo-mee';* patrial from 980 (by transp.); a *Bacharumite* or inh. of Bachurim:–Baharumite.
979. בְּחֻרוֹת *bekh-oo-rothe';* or בְּחוּרוֹת *bekh-oo-roth';* fem. pl. of 970; also (masc. pl.) בְּחֻרִים *bekh-oo-reem'; youth* (coll. and abstr.):–young men, youth.
980. בַּחֻרִים *bakh-oo-reem';* or בַּחוּרִים *bakh-oo-reem';* masc. pl. of 970; *young men; Bachurim,* a place in Pal.:–Bahurim.
981. בָּטָא *baw-taw';* or בָּטָה *baw-taw';* a prim. root; to *babble;* hence, to *vociferate* angrily:–pronounce, speak (unadvisedly).
982. בָּטַח *baw-takh';* a prim. root; prop. to *hie* for refuge [but not so *precipitately* as 2620]; fig., to *trust,* be *confident* or *sure:*–be bold (confident, secure, sure), careless (one, woman), put confidence, (make to) hope, (put, make to) trust.
983. בֶּטַח *beh'takh;* from 982; prop. a place of *refuge;* abstr., *safety,* both the fact (*security*) and the feeling (*trust*); often (adv. with or without prep.) *safely:*–assurance, boldly, (without) care(-less), confidence, hope, safe (-ly, -ty), secure, surely.
984. בֶּטַח *beh'takh;* the same as 983; *Betach,* a place in Syria:–Betah.
985. בִּטְחָה *bit-khaw';* fem. of 984; *trust:*–confidence.
986. בִּטָּחוֹן *bit-taw-khone';* from 982; *trust:*–confidence, hope.
987. בַּטֻּחוֹת *bat-too-khōth';* fem. pl. from 982; *security:*–secure.
988. בָּטֵל *baw-tale';* a prim. root; to *desist* from labor:–cease.
989. בְּטֵל *bet-ale'* (Chald.); cor. to 988; to *stop:*–(cause, make to), cease, hinder.
990. בֶּטֶן *beh'-ten;* from an un. root prob. mean. to *be hollow;* the *belly,* esp. the *womb;* also the *bosom* or *body* of anything:–belly, body, + as they be born, + within, womb.
991. בֶּטֶן *beh'-ten;* the same as 990; *Beten.* a place in Pal.:–Beten.
992. בֹּטֶן *bo'-ten;* from 990; (only in pl.) a *pistachio*-nut (from its form):–nut.
993. בְּטֹנִים *bet-o-neem';* prob. pl. from 992; *hollows; Betonim,* a place in Pal.:–Betonim.
994. בִּי *bee;* perh. from 1158 (in the sense of *asking*); prop. a *request;* used only adv. (always with "my Lord"); *Oh that!; with leave,* or *if it please:*–alas, O, oh.
995. בִּין *bene;* a prim. root; to *separate* ment. (or *distinguish*), i.e. (gen.) *understand:*–attend, consider, be cunning, diligently, direct, discern, eloquent, feel, inform, instruct, have intelligence, know, look well to, mark, perceive, be prudent, regard, (can) skill(-ful), teach, think, (cause, make to, get, give, have) understand (-ing), view, (deal) wise(-ly, man).
996. בֵּין *bane;* (sometimes in the pl. masc. or fem.); prop. the constr. contr. form of an otherwise un. noun from 995; a *distinction;* but used only as a prep, *between* (repeated before each noun, often with other particles); also as a conj., *either...or:*–among, asunder, at, between (-twixt...and), + from (the widest), X in, out of, whether (it be...or), within.
997. בֵּין *bane* (Chald.); cor. to 996:–among, between.
998. בִּינָה *bee-naw';* from 995; *understanding:*–knowledge, mean., X perfectly, understanding, wisdom.
999. בִּינָה *bee-naw'* (Chald.); cor. to 998:–knowledge.
1000. בֵּיצָה *bay-tsaw';* from the same as 948; an *egg* (from its whiteness):–egg.
1001. בִּירָא *bee-raw'* (Chald.); cor. to 1002; a *palace:*–palace.
1002. בִּירָה *bee-raw';* of for. or.; a *castle* or *palace:*–palace.
1003 בִּירָנִית *bee-raw-neeth';* from 1002; a *fortress:*–castle.
1004. בַּיִת *bah'-yith;* prob. from 1129 abb; a *house* (in the greatest var. of appl., esp. *family,* etc.):–court, daughter, door, + dungeon, family, + forth of, X great as would contain, hangings, home[born], [winter] house(-hold), inside(-ward), palace, place, + prison, + steward, + tablet, temple, web, + within(-out).
1005. בַּיִת *bah-yith* (Chald.); cor. to 1004:–house.
1006. בַּיִת *bah'-yith;* the same as 1004; *Bajith,* a place in Pal.:–Bajith.
1007. בֵּית אָוֶן *bayth aw'-ven;* from 1004 and 205; *house of vanity; Beth-Aven,* a place in Pal.:–Beth-aven.
1008. בֵּית־אֵל *bayth-ale';* from 1004 and 410; *house of God; Beth-El,* a place in Pal.:–Beth-el.
1009. בֵּית אַרְבֵּאל *bayth ar-bale';* from 1004 and 695 and 410; *house of God's ambush;*

Beth-Arbel, a place in Pal.:–Beth-Arbel.
1010. בֵּית בַּעַל מְעוֹן *bayth bah'-al mĕ-own';* from 1004 and 1168 and 4583; *house of Baal* of (the) *habitation* of (app. by transp.); or (short.) בֵּית מְעוֹן *bayth mĕ-own'; house of habitation of* (Baal); *Beth-Baal-Meön,* a place in Pal.:–Beth-baal-meon. Comp. 1186 and 1194.
1011. בֵּית בִּרְאִי *bayth bir-ee';* from 1004 and 1254; *house of a creative* one; *Beth-Biri,* a place in Pal.:–Beth-birei.
1012. בֵּית בָּרָה *bayth baw-raw';* prob. from 1004 and 5679; *house of* (the) *ford; Beth-Barah,* a place in Pal.:–Beth-barah.
1013. בֵּית־גָּדֵר *bayth-gaw-dare';* from 1004 and 1447; *house of* (the) *wall; Beth-Gader,* a place in Pal.:–Beth-gader.
1014. בֵּית גָּמוּל *bayth gaw-mool';* from 1004 and the pass.part. of 1576; *house of* (the) *weaned; Beth-Gamul,* a place E. of the Jordan:–Beth-gamul.
1015. בֵּית דִּבְלָתַיִם *bayth dib-law-thah'-yim;* from 1004 and the dual of 1690; *house of* (the) *two figcakes; Beth-Diblathajim,* a place E. of the Jordan:–Beth-diblathaim.
1016. בֵּית־דָּגוֹן *bayth-daw-gohn';* from 1004 and 1712; *house of Dagon; Beth-Dagon,* the name of two places in Pal.:–Beth-dagon.
1017. בֵּית הָאֱלִי *bayth haw-el-ee';* patrial from 1008 with the art. interp.; a *Beth-elite,* or inh. of Bethel:–Bethelite.
1018. בֵּית הָאֵצֶל *bayth haw-ay'-tsel;* from 1004 and 681 with the art. interp.; *house of the side; Beth-ha-Etsel,* a place in Pal.:–Beth-ezel.
1019. בֵּית הַגִּלְגָּל *bayth hag-gil gawl';* from 1004 and 1537 with the art. interp.; *house of Gilgal* (or *rolling*); *Beth-hag-Gilgal,* a place in Pal.:–Beth-gilgal.
1020. בֵּית הַיְשִׁמוֹת *bayth hah-yesh-ee-mōth';* from 1004 and the pl. of 3451 with the art. interp.; *house of the deserts; Beth-ha-Jeshimoth,* a town E. of the Jordan:–Beth-jeshimoth.
1021. בֵּית הַכֶּרֶם *bayth hak-keh'-rem;* from 1004 and 3754 with the art. interp.; *house of the vineyard; Beth-hak-Kerem,* a place in Pal.:–Beth-haccerem.
1022. בֵּית הַלַּחְמִי *bayth hal-lakh-mee'* patrial from 1035 with the art. ins.; a *Beth-lechemite,* or nat. of Bethlechem:–Bethlehemite.
1023. בֵּית הַמֶּרְחָק *bayth ham-mer-khawk';* from 1004 and 4801 with the art. interp.; *house of the breadth; Beth-ham-Merchak,* a place in Pal.:–place that was far off.
1024. בֵּית הַמַּרְכָּבוֹת *bayth ham-mar-kaw-both;'* or (short.) בֵּית מַרְכָּבוֹת *bayth mar-kaw-both';* from 1004 and the pl. of 4818 (with or without the art. interp.); *place of* (the) *chariots; Beth-ham-Markaboth* or *Beth-Markaboth,* a place in Pal.:–Beth-marcaboth.
1025. בֵּית הָעֵמֶק *bayth haw-Ay'-mek;* from 1004 and 6010 with the art. interp.; *house of the valley; Beth-ha-Emek,* a place in Pal.:–Beth-emek.
1026. בֵּית הָעֲרָבָה *bayth haw-ar-aw-baw;* from 1004 and 6160 with the art. interp.; *house of the Desert; Beth-ha-Arabah,* a place in Pal.:–Beth-arabah.
1027. בֵּית הָרָם *bayth haw-rawm';* from 1004 and 7311 with the art. interp.; *house of the height; Beth-ha-Ram,* a place E. of the Jordan:–Beth-aram.
1028. בֵּית הָרָן *bayth haw-rawn';* prob. for 1027; *Beth-ha-Ran,* a place E. of the Jordan:–Beth-haran.
1029. בֵּית הַשִּׁטָּה *bayth hash-shit-taw';* from 1004 and 7848 with the art. interp.; *house of the acacia; Beth-hash-Shittah,* a place in Pal.:–Beth-shittah.
1030. בֵּית הַשִּׁמְשִׁי *bayth hash-shim-shee';* patrial from 1053 with the art. ins.; a *Beth-shimshite,* or inh. of Bethshemesh:–Bethshemite.
1031. בֵּית חָגְלָה *bayth chog-law';* from 1004 and the same as 2295; *house of a partridge; Beth-Choglah,* a place in Pal.:–Beth-hoglah.
1032. בֵּית חוֹרוֹן *bayth kho-rone';* from 1004 and 2356; *house of hollowness; Beth-Choron,* the name of two adjoining places in Pal.:–Beth-horon.
1033. בֵּית כַּר *bayth kar;* from 1004 and 3733; *house of pasture; Beth-Car,* a place in Pal.:–Beth-car.
1034. בֵּית לְבָאוֹת *bayth leb-aw-oth,'* from 1004 and the pl. of 3833; *house of lionesses; Beth-Lebaoth,* a place in Pal.:–Beth-lebaoth.
1035. בֵּית לֶחֶם *bayth leh'-khem,* from 1004 and 3899; *house of bread; Beth-Lechem,* a place in Pal.:–Beth-lehem.
1036. בֵּית לְעַפְרָה *bayth le-af-raw',* from 1004 and the fem. of 6083 (with prep. interp.); *house to* (i.e. *of*) *dust; Beth-le-Aphrah,* a place in Pal.:–house of Aphrah.
1037. בֵּית מִלּוֹא *bayth mil-lo',* or בֵּית מִלֹּא *bayth mil-lo';* from 1004 and 4407; *house of* (the) *rampart; Beth-Mill,* the name of two citadels:– house of Millo.
1038. בֵּית מַעֲכָה *bayth mah-ak-aw',* from 1004 and 4601; *house of Maakah; Beth-Maakah,* a place in Pal.:–Beth-maachah.
1039. בֵּית נִמְרָה *bayth nim-raw',* from 1004 and the fem. of 5246; *house of* (the) *leopard; Beth-Nimrah,* a place east of the Jordan:–Beth-Nimrah. Comp. 5247.
1040. בֵּית עֵדֶן *bayth ay'-den,* from 1004 and 5730; *house of pleasure; Beth-Eden,* a place in Syria:–Beth-eden.
1041. בֵּית עַזְמָוֶת *bayth az-maw'-veth,* from 1004 and 5820; *house of Azmaveth,* a place in Pal.:–Beth-az-maveth. Comp. 5820.
1042. בֵּית עֲנוֹת *bayth an-oth',* from 1004 and a pl. from 6030; *house of replies; Beth-Anoth,* a place in Pal.:–Beth-anoth.
1043. בֵּית עֲנָת *bayth an-awth,'* an orth. var. for 1042; *Beth-Anath,* a place in Pal.:–Beth-anath.
1044. בֵּית עֵקֶד *bayth ay'-ked,* from 1004 and a der. of 6123; *house of* (the) *binding* (for sheep-shearing); *Beth-Eked,* a place in Pal.:–shearing house.
1045. בֵּית עַשְׁתָּרוֹת *bayth ash-taw-roth';* from 1004 and 6252; *house of Ashtoreths;* Beth-Ashtaroth, a place in Pal.:–house of Ashtaroth. Comp. 1203, 6252.
1046. בֵּית פֶּלֶט *bayth peh'-let,* from 1004 and 6412; *house of escape; Beth-Palet,* a place in Pal.:–Beth-palet.
1047. בֵּית פְּעוֹר *bayth pĕ-ore',* from 1004 and 6465; *house of Peor; Beth-Peor,* a place E. of the Jordan:–Beth-peor.
1048. בֵּית פַּצֵּץ *bayth pats-tsates',* from 1004 and a der. from 6327; *house of dispersion; Beth-Patstsets,* a place in Pal.:–Beth-pazzez.
1049. בֵּית צוּר *bayth tsoor',* from 1004 and 6697; *house of* (the) *rock; Beth-Tsur,* a place in Pal.:–Beth-zur.
1050. בֵּית רְחוֹב *bayth rĕ-khobe',* from 1004 and 7339; *house of* (the) *street; Beth-Rechob,* a place in Pal.:–Beth-rehob.
1051. בֵּית רָפָא *bayth raw-faw',* from 1004 and 7497; *house of* (the) *giant; Beth-Rapha,* an Isr.:–Beth-rapha.
1052. בֵּית שְׁאָן *bayth shĕ-awn',* or בֵּית שָׁן *bayth shawn';* from 1004 and 7599; *house of ease; Beth-Shean* or *Beth-Shan,* a place in Pal.:–Beth-shean, Beth-Shan.
1053. בֵּית שֶׁמֶשׁ *bayth sheh'-mesh,* from 1004 and 8121; *house of* (the) *sun; Beth-Shemesh,* a place in Pal.:–Beth-shemesh.
1054. בֵּית תַּפּוּחַ *bayth tap-poo'-akh,* from 1004 and 8598; *house of* (the) *apple; Beth-Tappuach,* a place in Pal.:–Beth-tappuah.
1055. בִּיתָן *bee-thawn',* prob. from 1004; *a palace* (i.e. *large house*):–palace.
1056. בָּכָא *baw-kaw',* from 1058, *weeping; Baca,* a valley in Pal.:–Baca.
1057. בָּכָא *baw-kaw',* the same as 1056; the *weeping* tree (some gum-distilling tree, perh. the *balsam*):–mulberry tree.
1058. בָּכָה *baw-kaw',* a prim. root; to *weep;* gen. to *bemoan:*–X at all, bewail, complain, make lamentation, X more, mourn, X sore, X with tears, weep.
1059. בֶּכֶה *beh'-keh,* from 1058; a *weeping:*–X sore.
1060. בְּכוֹר *bek-ore',* from 1069; *firstborn;* hence, *chief:*–eldest (son), firstborn(-ling).
1061. בִּכּוּר *bik-koor',* from 1069; the *first-fruits* of the crop:–first fruit (-ripe [fig.]), hasty fruit.
1062. בְּכוֹרָה *bek-o-raw',* or (short) בְּכֹרָה *bek-o-raw';* fem. of 1060; the *firstling* of man or beast; abstr. *primogeniture:*–birthright, firstborn(-ling).
1063. בִּכּוּרָה *bik-koo-raw',* fem. of 1061; the *early* fig:–firstripe (fruit).
1064. בְּכוֹרַת *bek-o-rath',* fem. of 1062; *primogeniture; Bekorath,* an Isr.:–Bechorath.
1065. בְּכִי *bek-ee',* from 1058; a weeping; by anal., a *dripping:*–overflowing, X sore, (continual) weeping, wept.
1066. בֹּכִים *bo-keem',* pl. act.part. of 1058; (with the art.) the *weepers; Bo-kim,* a place in Pal.:–Bochim.
1067. בְּכִירָה *bek-ee-raw',* fem. from 1069; the *eldest* daughter:–firstborn.
1068. בְּכִית *bek-eeth',* from 1058; a weeping:–mourning.
1069. בָּכַר *baw-kar',* a prim. root; prop. to *burst* the womb, i.e. (caus.) *bear* or *make early fruit* (of woman or tree); also (as denom. from 1061) to *give the birthright:*–make firstborn, be firstling, bring forth first child (new fruit).
1070. בֶּכֶר *beh'-ker,* from 1069 (in the sense of *youth*); a young *camel:*– dromedary.
1071. בֶּכֶר *beh'-ker,* the same as 1070; *Beker,* the name of two Isr.:– Becher.
1072. בִּכְרָה *bik-raw',* fem. of 1070; a young *she-camel:*–dromedary.
1073. בַּכֻּרָה *bak-koo-raw',* by orth. var. for 1063; a *first-ripe fig:*–firstripe.
1074. בֹּכְרוּ *bo-ker-oo',* from 1069; *first-born; Bokeru,* an Isr.:–Bocheru.
1075. בִּכְרִי *bik-ree',* from 1069; *youth-ful; Bikri,* an Isr.:–Bichri.
1076. בַּכְרִי *bak-ree',* patron. from 1071; a *Bakrite* (coll.) or desc. of Beker:–Bachrites.
1077. בַּל *bal,* from 1086; prop. a *failure;* by impl. *nothing;* usually (adv.) *not* at all; also *lest:*–

lest, neither, no, none (that...), not (any), nothing.

1078. בֵּל *bale,* by contr. for 1168; *Bel,* the Baal of the Babylonians:–Bel.

1079. בָּל *bawl* (Chald.); from 1080; prop. *anxiety,* i.e. (by impl.) the *heart* (as its seat):–heart.

1080. בְּלָא *bel-aw'* (Chald.); cor. to 1086 (but used only in a ment. sense); to *afflict:*–wear out.

1081. בַּלְאֲדָן *bal-ad-awn',* from 1078 and 113 (contr.); *Bel* (is his) *lord; Baladan,* the name of a Babylonian prince:–Baladan.

1082. בָּלַג *baw-lag',* a prim. root; to *break off* or *loose* (in a favorable or unfavorable sense), i.e. *desist* (from grief) or *invade* (with destruction):–comfort, (recover) strength(-en).

1083. בִּלְגָּה *bil-gaw',* from 1082; *desistance; Bilgah,* the name of two Isr.:–Bilgah.

1084. בִּלְגַּי *bil-gah'ee,* from 1082; *desistant; Bilgai,* an Isr.:–Bilgai

1085. בִּלְדַּד *bil-dad',* of unc. der.; *Bildad,* one of Job's friends:–Bildad.

1086. בָּלָה *baw-law',* a prim. root; to *fail;* by impl. to *wear out, decay* (caus., consume, *spend*):–consume, enjoy long, become (make, wax) old, spend, waste.

1087. בָּלֶה *baw-leh',* from 1086; *worn out:*–old.

1088. בָּלָה *baw-law',* fem. of 1087; *failure; Balah,* a place in Pal.:–Balah.

1089. בָּלַהּ *baw-lah',* a prim. root [rather by transp. for 926]; to *palpitate;* hence, (caus.) to *terrify:*–trouble.

1090. בִּלְהָה *bil-haw',* from 1089; *timid; Bilhah,* the name of one of Jacob's concubines; also of a place in Pal.:–Bilhah.

1091. בַּלָּהָה *bal-law-haw',* from 1089; *alarm;* hence, *destruction:*–terror, trouble.

1092. בִּלְהָן *bil-hawn',* from 1089; *timid; Bilhan,* the name of an Edomite and of an Isr.:–Bilhan.

1093. בְּלוֹ *bel-o'* (Chald.); from a root cor. to 1086; *excise* (on articles consumed):–tribute.

1094. בְּלוֹא *bel-o',* or (fully) בְּלוֹי *bel-o'ee;* from 1086; (only in pl. constr.) *rags:*–old.

1095. בֵּלְטְשַׁאצַּר *bale-tesh-ats-tsar',* of for. der.; *Belteshatstsar,* the Babylonian name of Daniel:–Belteshazzar.

1096. בֵּלְטְשַׁאצַּר *bale-tesh-ats-tsar'* (Chald.); cor. to 1095:–Belteshazzar.

1097. בְּלִי *bel-ee',* from 1086; prop. *failure,* i.e. *nothing* or *destruction;* usually (with prep.) *without, not yet, because not, as long as,* etc.:–corruption, ig[norantly], for lack of, where no... is, so that no, none, not, un[awares], without.

1098. בְּלִיל *bel-eel',* from 1101; *mixed,* i.e. (spec.) *feed* (for cattle):–corn, fodder, provender.

1099. בְּלִימָה *bel-ee-mah';* from 1097 and 4100; (as indef.) *nothing whatever:*–nothing.

1100. בְּלִיַּעַל *bel-e-yah'-al,* from 1097 and 3276; *without profit, worthlessness;* by extension, *destruction, wickedness* (often in connection with 376, 802, 1121, etc.):–Belial, evil, naughty, ungodly (men), wicked.

1101. בָּלַל *baw-lal',* a prim. root; to *overflow* (spec. with oil.); by impl., to *mix;* also (denom. from 1098) to *fodder:*–anoint, confound, X fade, mingle, mix (self), give provender, temper.

1102. בָּלַם *baw-lam',* a prim. root; to *muzzle:*–be held in.

1103. בָּלַס *baw-las',* a prim. root; to *pinch* sycamore figs (a process necessary to ripen them):–gatherer.

1104. בָּלַע *baw'-lah,* a prim. root; to *make away with* (spec. by *swallowing*); gen., to *destroy:*–cover, destroy, devour, eat up, be at end, spend up, swallow down (up).

1105. בֶּלַע *beh-lah,* from 1104; a *gulp;* fig., *destruction:*–devouring, that which he hath swallowed up.

1106. בֶּלַע *beh'-lah,* the same as 1105; Bela, the name of a place, also of an Edomite and of two Isr.:–Bela.

1107. בִּלְעֲדֵי *bil-ad-ay',* or בַּלְעֲדֵי *bal-ad-ay';* constr. pl. from 1077 and 5703, *not till,* i.e. (as prep. or adv.) *except, without, besides:*–beside, not (in), save, without.

1108. בַּלְעִי *bel-ee',* patron. from 1106: a *Belaite* (coll.) or desc. of Bela:–Belaites.

1109. בִּלְעָם *bil-awm',* prob. from 1077 and 5971; *not* (of the) *people,* i.e. *foreigner; Bilam,* a Mesopotamian prophet; also a place in Pal.:–Balaam, Bileam.

1110. בָּלַק *baw-lak',* a prim. root; to *annihilate:*–(make) waste.

1111. בָּלָק *baw-lawk',* from 1110; *waster; Balak,* a Moabitish king:–Balak.

1112. בֵּלְשַׁאצַּר *bale-shats-tsar',* or בֵּלְאשַׁצַּר *bale-shats-tsar';* of for. or. (comp. 1095); *Belshatstsar,* a Babylonian king:–Belshazzar.

1113. בֵּלְשַׁאצַּר *bale-shats-tsar'* (Chald.); cor. to 1112:–Belshazzar.

1114. בִּלְשָׁן *bil-shawn',* of unc. der.; *Bilshan,* an Isr.:–Bilshan.

1115. בִּלְתִּי *bil-tee',* constr. fem. of 1086 (equiv. to 1097); prop. a *failure* of, i.e. (used only as a neg. particle, usually with a prep. pref.) *not, except, without, unless, besides, because not, until,* etc.:–because un[satiable], beside, but, + continual, except, from, lest, neither, no more, none, not, nothing, save, that no, without.

1116. בָּמָה *bam-maw',* from an un. root (mean. to *be high*); an *elevation:*–height, high place, wave.

1117. בָּמָה *baw-maw';* the same as 1116; *Bamah,* a place in Pal.:–Bamah. See also 1120.

1118. בִּמְהָל *bim-hawl',* prob. from 4107 with prep. pref.; *with pruning; Bimhal,* an Isr.:–Bimhal.

1119. בְּמוֹ *bem-o',* prol. for prep. pref.; *in, with, by,* etc.:–for, in into, through.

1120. בָּמוֹת *baw-moth',* pl. of 1116; *heights;* or (fully) בָּמוֹת בַּעַל *baw-moth' bah'-al;* from the same and 1168; *heights of Baal; Bamoth* or *Bamoth-Baal,* a place E. of the Jordan:–Bamoth, Bamoth-baal.

1121. בֵּן *bane,* from 1129; a *son* (as a *builder* of the family name), in the widest sense (of lit.and fig. relationship, incl. *grandson, subject, nation, quality* or *condition,* etc., [like 1, 251, etc.]):–+ afflicted, age, [Ahoh-] [Ammon-] [Hachmon-] [Lev-]ite, [anoint-]ed one, appointed to, (+) arrow, [Assyr-] [Babylon-] [Eg.-] [Grec-]ian, one born, bough, branch, breed, + (young) bullock, + (young) calf, X came up in, child, colt, X common, X corn, daughter, X of first, + firstborn, foal, + very fruitful, + postage, X in, + kid, + lamb, (+) man, meet, + mighty, + nephew, old, (+) people, + rebel, + robber, X servant born, X soldier, son, + spark, + steward, + stranger, X surely, them of, + tumultuous one, + valiant(-est), whelp, worthy, young (one), youth.

1122. בֵּן *bane;* the same as 1121; *Ben,* an Isr.:–Ben.

1123. בֵּן *bane* (Chald.); cor. to 1121:–child, son, young.

1124. בְּנָא *ben-aw'* (Chald.); or בְּנָה *ben-aw';* cor. to 1129; to *build:*–build, make.

1125. בֶּן־אֲבִינָדָב *ben-ab-ee"- naw-dawb,'* from 1121 and 40; (the) *son of Abinadab;* Ben-*Abinadab,* an Isr.:–the son of Abinadab.

1126. בֶּן־אוֹנִי *ben-o-nee';* from 1121 and 205; *son of my sorrow; Ben-Oni,* the or. name of Benjamin:–Ben-oni.

1127. בֶּן־גֶּבֶר *ben-gheh'-ber,* from 1121 and 1397; *son of* (the) *hero; Ben-Geber,* an Isr.:–the son of Geber.

1128. בֶּן־דֶּקֶר *ben-deh'-ker;* from 1121 and a der. of 1856; *son of piercing* (or *of a lance*); *Ben-Deker,* an Isr.:–the son of Dekar.

1129. בָּנָה *baw-naw';* a prim. root; to *build* (lit. and fig.):–(begin to) build(-er), obtain children, make, repair, set (up), X surely.

1130. בֶּן־הֲדַד *ben-had-ad',* from 1121 and 1908; *son of Hadad; Ben-Hadad,* the name of several Syrian kings:–Ben-hadad.

1131. בִּנּוּי *bin-noo'-ee;* from 1129; *built* up; *Binnui,* an Isr.:–Binnui.

1132. בֶּן־זוֹחֵת *ben-zo-khayth';* from 1121 and 2105; *son of Zocheth; Ben- Zocheth,* an Isr.:–Ben-zoketh.

1133. בֶּן־חוּר *ben-khoor';* from 1121 and 2354; *son of Chur; Ben-Chur,* an Isr.:–the son of Hur.

1134. בֶּן־חַיִל *ben-khah'-yil;* from 1121 and 2428; *son of might; Ben-Chail,* an Isr.:–Ben-hail.

1135. בֶּן־חָנָן *ben-khaw-nawn';* from 1121 and 2605; *son of Chanan; Ben-Chanan,* an Isr.:–Ben-hanan.

1136. בֶּן־חֶסֶד *ben-kheh'-sed;* from 1121 and 2617; *son of kindness; Ben-Chesed,* an Isr.:–the son of Hesed.

1137. בָּנִי *baw-nee;* from 1129; *built; Bani,* the name of five Isr.:–Bani.

1138. בֻּנִּי *boon-nee';* or (fuller) בּוּנִּי *boo-nee';* from 1129; *built; Bunni* or *Buni,* an Isr.:–Bunni.

1139. בְּנֵי־בְרַק *ben-ay'-ber-ak';* from the pl. constr. of 1121 and 1300*; sons of lightning, Bene-berak,* a place in Pal.:–Bene-barak.

1140. בִּנְיָה *bin-yaw';* fem. from 1129; a *structure:*–building.

1141. בְּנָיָה *ben-aw-yaw';* or (prol.) בְּנָיָהוּ *ben-aw-yaw'-hoo;* from 1129 and 3050; *Jah has built; Benajah,* the name of twelve Isr.:– Benaiah.

1142. בְּנֵי יַעֲקָן *ben-ay' yah-ak-awn'* from the pl. of 1121 and 3292; sons of Yaakan; Bene-Jaakan, a place in the Desert:–Bene-jaakan.

1143. בֵּינַיִם *bay-nah'-yim;* dual of 996; a *double interval,* i.e. the space between two armies:–+ champion.

1144. בִּנְיָמִין *bin-yaw-mene';* from 1121 and 3225; son of (the) *right* hand; *Binjamin, youngest son of Jacob;* also the tribe descended from him, and its territory:–Benjamin.

1145. בֶּן־יְמִינִי *ben-yem-ee-nee';* sometimes (with the art. ins.) בֶּן־הַיְמִינִי *ben-hah-yem-ee-nee';* with 376 ins. (1 Sa. 9:1) בֶּן־ אִישׁ יְמִינִי *ben-eesh' yem-ee-nee';* son of a man of Jemini; or short. (1 Sa. 9:4; Es. 2:5) אִישׁ יְמִינִי *eesh yem-ee-nee';* a man of Jemini, or (1 Sam. 20:1) simply יְמִינִי *yem-ee-nee';* a Jeminite; (pl. בְּנֵי יְמִינִי *ben-ay'yem-ee-nee';* patron from 1144; a *Benjaminite,* or descendent of Benjamin:–Benjamite, of Benjamin.

1146. בִּנְיָן *bin-yawn';* from 1129; an *edifice:*–building.

1147. בִּנְיָן *bin-yawn'* (Chald.); cor. to 1146:–

HEBREW

building.
1148. בְּנִינוּ *ben-ee-noo';* prob. from 1121 with pron. suff.; *our son; Beninu,* an Isr.:–Beninu.
1149. בְּנַס *ben-as'* (Chald.); of unc. affinity; to *be enraged:*–be angry.
1150. בִּנְעָא *bin-aw';* or בִּנְעָה *bin-aw';* of unc. der.; *Bina* or *Binah,* an Isr.:–Binea, Bineah.
1151. בֶּן־עַמִּי *ben-am-mee';* from 1121 and 5971 with pron. suffix; *son of my people; Ben-Ammi,* a son of Lot:–Ben-ammi.
1152. בְּסוֹדְיָה *bes-o-deh-yaw';* from 5475 and 3050 with prep. pref.; *in* (the) *counsel of Jehovah; Besodejah,* an Isr.:–Besodeiah.
1153. בְּסַי *bes-ah'-ee;* from 947; *domineering; Besai,* one of the Nethinim:–Besai.
1154. בֶּסֶר *beh'-ser;* from an un. root mean. to be sour; an immature grape:–unripe grape.
1155. בֹּסֶר *bo'ser;* from the same as 1154:–sour grape.
1156. בְּעָא *beh-aw'* (Chald.); or בְּעָה *beh-aw'* (Chald.); cor. to 1158; to *seek* or *ask:*–ask, desire, make [petition], pray, request, seek.
1157. בְּעַד *beh-ad';* from 5704 with prep. pref.; *in up to* or *over against;* gen. *at, beside, among, behind, for,* etc.:–about, at by (means of), for, over, through, up (-on), within.
1158. בָּעָה *baw-aw';* a prim. root; to *gush* over, i.e. to *swell;* (fig.) to *desire* earnestly; by impl. to *ask:*–cause, inquire, seek up, swell out, boil.
1159. בָּעוּ *baw-oo'* (Chald.); from 1156; a *request:*–petition.
1160. בְּעוֹר *beh-ore';* from 1197 (in the sense of *burning*); a *lamp; Beör,* the name of the father of an Edomitish king; also of that of Balaam:–Beor.
1161. בִּעוּתִים *be-oo-theme';* masc. pl. from 1204; *alarms:*–terrors.
1162. בֹּעַז *bo'az;* from an un. root of unc. mean.; *Boaz,* the ancestor of David; also the name of a pillar in front of the temple:–Boaz.
1163. בָּעַט *baw-at';* a prim. root; to *trample* down, i.e. (fig.) *despise:*–kick.
1164. בְּעִי *beh-ee';* from 1158; a *prayer:*–grave.
1165. בְּעִיר *beh-ere';* from 1197 (in the sense of *eating*): cattle:–beast, cattle.
1166. בָּעַל *baw-al';* a prim. root; to *be master;* hence, (as denom. from 1167) to *marry:*–have dominion (over), be husband, marry(-ried, X wife).
1167. בַּעַל *bah'-al;* from 1166; a *master;* hence, a *husband,* or (fig.) *owner* (often used with another noun in modif. of this latter sense):–+ archer, + babbler, + bird, captain, chief man, + confederate, + have to do, + dreamer, those to whom it is due, + furious, those that are given to it, great, + hairy, he that hath it, have, + horseman, husband, lord, man, + married, master, person, + sworn, they of.
1168. בַּעַל *bah'-al;* the same as 1167; *Baal,* a Phoenician deity:–Baal, [pl.] Baalim.
1169. בְּעֵל *beh-ale'* (Chald.); cor. to 1167:–+ chancellor.
1170. בַּעַל בְּרִית *bah'-al ber-eeth;* from 1168 and 1285; *Baal of* (the) *covenant; Baal-Berith,* a special deity of the Shechemites:–Baal-berith.
1171. בַּעַל גָּד *bah'-al gawd;* from 1168 and 1409; *Baal of Fortune; Baal-Gad,* a place in Syria:–Baal-gad.
1172. בַּעֲלָה *bah-al-aw';* fem. of 1167; a *mistress:*–that hath, mistress.
1173. בַּעֲלָה *bah-al-aw';* the same as 1172; *Baalah,* the name of three places in Pal.:–Baalah.
1174. בַּעַל הָמוֹן *bah'-al; haw-mone';* from 1167 and 1995; *possessor of a multitude; Baal-Hamon,* a place in Pal.:–Baal-hamon.
1175. בְּעָלוֹת *beh-aw-lōth';* pl. of 1172; *mistresses*; *Beäloth,* a place in Pal.:–Bealoth, in Aloth
1176. בַּעַל זְבוּב *bah'-al zeb-oob';* from 1168 and 2070; *Baal of* (the) *Fly; Baal-Zebub,* a special deity of the Ekronites:–Baal-zebub.
1177. בַּעַל חָנָן *bah'-al khaw-nawn';* from 1167 and 2603; *possessor of grace; Baal-Chanan,* the name of an Edomite, also of an Isr.:–Baal-hanan.
1178. בַּעַל חָצוֹר *bah'-al khaw-tsore';* from 1167 and a modif. of 2691; *possessor of a village; Baal-Chatsor,* a place in Pal.:–Baal-hazor.
1179. בַּעַל חֶרְמוֹן *bah'-al kher-mone';* from 1167 and 2768; *possessor of Hermon; Baal-Chermon,* a place in Pal.:–Baal-hermon.
1180. בַּעֲלִי *bah-al-ee';* from 1167 with pron. suff.; my master; *Baali,*–Baali.
1181. בַּעֲלֵי בָמוֹת *bah-al-ay' baw-mōth';* from the pl. of 1168 and the pl. of 1116; Baals of (the) heights; Baale-Bamoth, a place E. of the Jordan:–lords of the high places.
1182. בְּעֶלְיָדָע *beh-el-yaw-daw';* from 1168 and 3045; *Baal has known; Beëljada,* an Isr.:–Beeliada.
1183. בְּעַלְיָה *beh-al-yaw';* from 1167 and 3050; *Jah* (is) *master; Bealjah,* an Isr.:–Bealiah.
1184. בַּעֲלֵי יְהוּדָה *bah-al-ay' yeh-hoo-daw'* from the pl. of 1167 and 3063; *masters of Judah; Baale-Jehudah,* a place in Pal.:–Baale of Judah.
1185. בַּעֲלִיס *bah-al-ece';* prob. from a der. of 5965 with prep. pref.; *in exultation; Baalis,* an Ammonitish king:–Baalis.
1186. בַּעַל מְעוֹן *bah-al meh-one';* from 1168 and 4583; *Baal of* (the) *habitation* (of) [comp. 1010]; *Baal-Meön,* a place E. of the Jordan:–Baal-meon.
1187. בַּעַל פְּעוֹר *bah'-al peh-ore';* from 1168 and 6465; *Baal of Peor; Baal-Peör,* a Moabitish deity:–Baal-peor.
1188. בַּעַל פְּרָצִים *bah'-al; per-aw-tseem';* from 1167 and the pl. of 6556; *possessor of breaches; Baal-Peratsim,* a place in Pal.:–Baal-perazim.
1189. בַּעַל צְפוֹן *bah'-al tsef-one';* from 1168 and 6828 (in the sense of *cold*) *Baal of winter; Baal-Tsephon,* a place in Eqypt:–Baal-zephon.
1190. בַּעַל שָׁלִשָׁה *bah'-al shaw-lee-shaw';* from 1168 and 8031; *Baal of Shalishah, Baal-Shalishah,* a place in Pal.:–Baal-shalisha.
1191. בַּעֲלָת *bah-al-awth';* a modif. of 1172; *mistressship; Baalath,* a place in Pal.:–Baalath.
1192. בַּעֲלַת בְּאֵר *bah-al-ath' beh-ayr';* from 1172 and 875; *mistress of a well; Baalath-Beer,* a place in Pal.:–Baalath-beer.
1193. בַּעַל תָּמָר *bah'-al taw-mawr';* from 1167 and 8558; *possessor of* (the) *palm-tree; Baal-Tamar,* a place in Pal.:–Baal-tamar.
1194. בְּעֹן *beh-ohn';* prob. a contr. of 1010; *Beön,* a place E. of the Jordan:–Beon.
1195. בַּעֲנָא *bah-an-aw';* the same as 1196; Baana, the name of four Isr.:–Baana, Baanah.
1196. בַּעֲנָה *bah-an-aw';* from a der. of 6031 with prep. pref.; *in affliction:–Baanah,* the name of four Isr.:–Baanah.
1197. בָּעַר *baw-ar';* a prim. root; to *kindle,* i.e. *consume* (by fire or by eating); also (as denom. from 1198) to *be*(*-come*) *brutish:*–be brutish, bring (put, take) away, burn, (cause to) eat (up), feed, heat, kindle, set ([on fire]), waste.
1198. בַּעַר *bah'-ar;* from 1197; prop. *food* (as *consumed*); i.e. (by ext..) of cattle *brutishness;* (concr.) *stupid:*–brutish (person), foolish.
1199. בַּעֲרָא *bah-ar-aw';* from 1198; *brutish: Baara,* an Israelitish woman:–Baara.
1200. בְּעֵרָה *bĕ-ay-raw';* from 1197; a *burning:*–fire.
1201. בַּעְשָׁא *bah-shaw';* from an un. root mean. to *stink; offensiveness; Basha,* a king of Isr.:–Baasha.
1202. בַּעֲשֵׂיָה *bah-as-ay-yaw';* from 6213 and 3050 with a prep. pref.; *in* (the) *work of Jah; Baasejah,* an Isr.:–Baaseiah.
1203. בְּעֶשְׁתְּרָה *beh-esh-ter-aw';* from 6251 (as sing. of 6252) with a prep. pref.; *with Ashtoreth; Beështerah,* a place E. of the Jordan:–Beeshterah.
1204. בָּעַת *baw-ath';* a prim. root; to *fear:*–affright, be (make) afraid, terrify, trouble.
1205. בְּעָתָה *beh-aw-thaw';* from 1204; *fear:*–trouble.
1206. בֹּץ *botse;* prob. the same as 948; *mud* (as *whitish* clay):–mire.
1207. בִּצָּה *bits-tsaw';* intens. from 1206; a *swamp:*–fen, mire(-ry place).
1208. בָּצוֹר *baw-tsore';* from 1219; *inaccessible,* i.e. lofty:–vintage
1209. בֵּצַי *bay-tsah'-ee;* perh. the same as 1153; *Betsai,* the name of two Isr.:–Bezai.
1210. בָּצִיר *baw-tseer';* from 1219; *clipped,* i.e. the *grape crop:*–vintage.
1211. בֶּצֶל *beh'-tsel* from an un. root app. mean. to *peel*; an *onion:*–onion.
1212. בְּצַלְאֵל *bets-al-ale';* prob. from 6738 and 410 with a prep. pref.; *in* (the) *shadow* (i.e. protection) *of God; Betsalel,* the name of two Isr.:–Bezaleel.
1213. בַּצְלוּת *bats-looth';* or בַּצְלִית *bats-leeth';* from the same as 1211; a *peeling; Batsluth* or *Batslith,* an Isr.:–Bazlith, Bazluth.
1214. בָּצַע *baw-tsah';* a prim. root to *break* off, i.e. (usually) *plunder;* fig., to *finish,* or (intr.) *stop:*–(be) covet(-ous), cut (off), finish, fulfill, gain (greedily), get, be given to [covetousness], greedy, perform, be wounded.
1215. בֶּצַע *beh'-tsah;* from 1214; *plunder;* by ext., *gain* (usually unjust):–covetousness, (dishonest) gain, lucre, profit.
1216. בָּצֵק *baw-tsake';* a prim. root; perh. to *swell* up, i.e. *blister:*–swell.
1217. בָּצֵק *baw-tsake';* from 1216; *dough* (*as swelling by* fermentation):–dough, flour.
1218. בָּצְקַת *bots-cath';* from 1216; a *swell* of ground; *Botscath,* a place in Pal.:–Bozcath, Boskath.
1219. בָּצַר *baw-tsar';* a prim. root; to *clip off;* spec. (as denom. from 1210) to *gather* grapes; also to *be isolated* (i.e. *inaccessible by* height or fortification):–cut off, (de-) fenced, fortify, (grape) gather(-er), mighty things, restrain, strong, wall (up), withhold.
1220. בֶּצֶר *beh'-tser;* from 1219; strictly a *clipping,* i.e. *gold* (as *dug* out):–gold defence.

1221. בֶּצֶר *beh'-tser;* the same as 1220, an *inaccessible* spot; *Betser,* a place in Pal.; also an Isr.:–Bezer.
1222. בְּצַר *bets-ar';* another form for 1220; *gold:*–gold.
1223. בָּצְרָה *bots-raw';* fem. from 1219; an *enclosure,* i.e. *sheep-fold:*–Bozrah.
1224. בָּצְרָה *bots-raw';* the same as 1223; *Botsrah,* a place in Edom:–Bozrah.
1225. בִּצָּרוֹן *bits-tsaw-rone';* masc. intens. from 1219; a *fortress:*–stronghold.
1226. בַּצֹּרֶת *bats-tso'-reth';* fem. intens. from 1219; *restraint* (of rain), i.e. *drought:*–dearth, drought.
1227. בַּקְבּוּק *bak-book';* the same as 1228; *Bakbuk,* one of the *Nethinim:*–Bakbuk.
1228. בַּקְבֻּק *bak-book';* from 1238; a *bottle* (from the gurgling in *emptying*):–bottle, cruse.
1229. בַּקְבֻּקְיָה *bak-book-yaw';* from 1228 and 3050; *emptying* (i.e. *wasting*) *of Jah; Bakbukjah,* an Isr.:–Bakbukiah.
1230. בַּקְבַּקַּר *bak-bak-kar';* redupl. from 1239; *searcher; Bakbakkar,* an Isr.:–Bakbakkar.
1231. בֻּקִּי *book-kee';* from 1238; *wasteful; Bukki,* the name of two Isr.:–Bukki.
1232. בֻּקִּיָּה *book-kee-yaw';* from 1238 and 3050; *wasting of Jah; Bukkijah,* an Isr.:–Bukkiah.
1233. בְּקִיעַ *bek-ee'-ah;* from 1234; a *fissure:*–breach, cleft.
1234. בָּקַע *baw-kah';* a prim. root; to *cleave;* gen., to *rend, break, rip or open:*–make a breach, break forth (into, out, in pieces, through, up), be ready to burst, cleave (asunder), cut out, divide, hatch, rend (asunder), rip up, tear, win.
1235. בֶּקַע *beh'-kah;* from 1234; a *section* (half) of a shekel, i.e. a *beka* (a weight and a coin):–bekah, half a shekel.
1236. בִּקְעָא *bik-aw'* (Chald.); cor. to 1237:–plain.
1237. בִּקְעָה *bik-aw';* from 1234; prop. a *split,* i.e. a wide level *valley* between mountains:–plain, valley.
1238. בָּקַק *baw-kak';* a prim. root; to *pour* out, i.e. to *empty,* fig., to *depopulate;* by anal., to *spread* out (as a fruitful vine):–(make) empty (out), fail, X utterly, make void.
1239. בָּקַר *baw-kar;* a prim. root; prop. to *plough,* or (gen.) *break* forth, i.e. (fig.) to *inspect, admire, care for, consider:*–(make) inquire (-ry), (make) search, seek out.
1240. בְּקַר *bek-ar'* (Chald.); cor. to 1239:–inquire, make search.
1241. בָּקָר *baw-kawr';* from 1239; a *beeve* or animal of the ox kind of either gender (as used for *plowing*); coll., a *herd:*– beeve, bull (+ -ock), + calf, + cow, great [cattle], + heifer, herd, kine, ox.
1242. בֹּקֶר *bo'-ker;* from 1239; prop. *dawn* (as the *break* of day); gen., *morning:*–(+) day, early, morning, morrow.
1243. בַּקָּרָה *bak-kaw-raw';* intens. from 1239; a *looking after:*–seek out.
1244. בִּקֹּרֶת *bik-ko-reth;* from 1239; prop. *examination,* i.e. (by impl.) *punishment:*–scourged.
1245. בָּקַשׁ *baw-kash';* a prim. root; to *search* out (by any method, spec. in worship or prayer); by impl., to *strive after:*–ask, beg, beseech, desire, enquire, get, make inquisition, procure, (make) request, require, seek (for).
1246. בַּקָּשָׁה *bak-kaw-shaw';* from 1245; a *petition:*–request.
1247. בַּר *bar* (Chald.); cor. to 1121; a *son, grandson,* etc.:–X old, son.
1248. בַּר *bar;* borrowed (as a title) from 1247; the *heir* (app. to the throne):–son.
1249. בַּר *bar;* from 1305 (in its various senses); *beloved;* also *pure, empty:*–choice, clean, clear, pure.
1250. בָּר *bawr;* or בַּר *bar;* from 1305 (in the sense of *winnowing*); *grain* of any kind (even while standing in the field); by ext.. the open *country:*–corn, wheat.
1251. בַּר *bar* (Chald.); cor. to 1250; a *field:*–field.
1252. בֹּר *bore;* from 1305; *purity:*–cleanness, pureness.
1253. בֹּר *bore;* same as 1252; vegetable *lye* (from its *cleansing*); used as a *soap* for washing, or a *flux* for metals:–X never so, purely.
1254. בָּרָא *baw-raw';* prim. root; (absol.) to *create;* (qualified) to *cut* down (a wood), *select, feed* (as formative processes):–choose, create (creator), cut down, dispatch, do, make (fat).
1255. בְּרֹאדַךְ בַּלְאֲדָן *ber-o-dak' bal-ad-awn';* a var. of 4757; *Berodak-Baladan,* a Babylonian king:–Berodach-baladan.
1256. בְּרָאיָה *ber-aw-yaw;* from 1254 and 8050; *Jah has created; Berajah,* an Isr.:–Beraiah.
1257. בַּרְבֻּר *bar-boor';* by redupl. from 1250; a *fowl* (as fattened on *grain*):–fowl.
1258. בָּרַד *baw-rad';* a prim. root, to *hail:*–hail.
1259. בָּרָד *baw-rawd';* from 1258; *hail:*–hail ([stones]).
1260. בֶּרֶד *beh'red;* from 1258; *hail; Bered,* the name of a place south of Pal., also of an Isr.:–Bered.
1261. בָּרֹד *baw-rode';* 1258; *spotted* (as if with *hail*):–grisled.
1262. בָּרָה *baw-raw';* a prim. root; to *select;* also (as denom. from 1250) *to feed;* also (as equiv. to 1305) to *render clear* (Ec. 3:18):–choose, (cause to) eat, manifest, (give) meat.
1263. בָּרוּךְ *baw-rook';* pass.part. from 1288; *blessed; Baruk,* the name of three Isr.:–Baruch.
1264. בְּרוֹם *ber-ome';* prob. of for. or.; *damask* (stuff of variegated thread):–rich apparel.
1265. בְּרוֹשׁ *ber-osh';* of unc. der.; a *cypress* (?) tree; hence, a *lance* or a *mus.* instrument (as made of that wood):–fir (tree)
1266. בְּרוֹת *ber-oth';* a var. of 1265; the cypress (or some elastic tree):–fir.
1267. בָּרוּת *baw-rooth;* from 1262; *food:*–meat.
1268. בֵּרוֹתָה *bay-ro-thaw';* or בֵּרֹתַי *bay-ro-thah'-ee;* prob. from 1266; *cypress* or *cypresslike; Berothah* or *Berothai,* a place north of Pal.:–Berothah, Berothai.
1269. בִּרְזוֹת *beer-zoth';* prob. fem. pl. from an un. root (app. mean to *pierce*); *holes; Birzoth,* an Isr.:–Birzavith
1270. בַּרְזֶל *bar-zel';* perh. from the root of 1269; *iron* (as *cutting*); by ext., an iron *implement:*–(ax) head, iron.
1271. בַּרְזִלַּי *bar-zil-lah'-ee;* from 1270; *iron*-hearted; *Barzillai,* the name of three Isr.:–Barzillai.
1272. בָּרַח *baw-rakh';* a prim. root; to *bolt,* i.e. fig., to *flee* suddenly:–chase (away); drive away, fain, flee (away), put to flight, make haste, reach, run away, shoot.
1273. בַּרְחֻמִי *bar-khoo-mee';* by transp. for 978; a *Barchumite,* or nat. of *Bachurim:*–Barhumite.
1274. בְּרִי *ber-ee';* from 1262; *fat:*–fat.
1275. בֵּרִי *bay-ree';* prob. by contr. from 882; *Beri,* an Isr.:–Beri.
1276. בֵּרִי *bay-ree';* of unc. der.; (only in the pl. and with the art.) the *Berites,* a place in Pal.:–Berites.
1277. בָּרִיא *baw-ree';* from 1254 (in the sense of 1262); *fatted* or *plump:*–fat ([(fleshed], -ter), fed, firm, plenteous, rank.
1278. בְּרִיאָה *ber-ee-aw';* fem. from 1254; a *creation,* i.e. a *novelty:*–new thing.
1279. בִּרְיָה *beer-yaw';* fem. from 1262; *food:*–meat.
1280. בְּרִיחַ *ber-ee'-akh;* from 1272; a *bolt:*–bar, fugitive.
1281. בָּרִיחַ *baw-ree'-akh;* or (short) בָּרִחַ *baw-ree'-akh;* from 1272; a *fugitive,* i.e. the *serpent* (as *fleeing*), and the constellation by that name:–crooked, piercing.
1282. בָּרִיחַ *baw-ree'-akh;* the same as 1281; *Bariach,* an Isr.:–Bariah.
1283. בְּרִיעָה *ber-ee'-aw;* app. from the fem. of 7451 with a prep. pref.; *in trouble; Beriah,* the name of four Isr.:–Beriah.
1284. בְּרִיעִי *ber-ee-ee';* patron. from 1283; a *Beriite* (coll.) or desc. of Beriah:–Beerites.
1285. בְּרִית *ber-eeth';* from 1262 (in the sense of *cutting* [like 1254]); a *compact* (because made by passing between *pieces* of flesh):–confederacy, [con-]feder[-ate], covenant, league.
1286. בְּרִית *ber-eeth';* the same as 1285; *Berith,* a Shechemitish deity:–Berith.
1287. בֹּרִית *bo-reeth';* fem. of 1253; vegetable *alkali:*–sope.
1288. בָּרַךְ *baw-rak';* a prim. root; to *kneel;* by impl. to *bless* God (as an act of adoration), and (vice-versa) man (as a benefit); also (by euphem.) to *curse* (God or the king, as treason):–X abundantly, X altogether, X at all, blaspheme, bless, congratulate, curse, X greatly, X indeed, kneel (down), praise, salute, X still, thank.
1289. בְּרַךְ *ber-ak'* (Chald.); cor. to 1288:–bless, kneel.
1290. בֶּרֶךְ *beh'-rek;* from 1288; a *knee:*–knee.
1291. בֶּרֶךְ *beh'-rek* (Chald.); cor. to 1290:–knee.
1292. בָּרַכְאֵל *baw-rak-ale';* from 1288 and 410, *God has blessed; Barakel,* the father of one of Job's friends:–Barachel.
1293. בְּרָכָה *ber-aw-kaw';* 1288; *benediction;* by impl. *prosperity:*–blessing, liberal, pool, present.
1294. בְּרָכָה *ber-aw-kaw';* the same as 1293; *Berakah,* the name of an Isr., and also of a valley in Pal.:–Berachah.
1295. בְּרֵכָה *ber-ay-kaw';* from 1288; a *reservoir* (at which camels *kneel* as a resting-place):–(fish-)pool.
1296. בֶּרֶכְיָה *beh-rek-yaw';* or בֶּרֶכְיָהוּ *beh-rek-yaw'-hoo;* from 1290 and 3050; *knee* (i.e. *blessing*) of *Jah; Berekjah,* the name of six Isr.:–Berachiah, Berechiah.
1297. בְּרַם *ber-am'* (Chald.); perh. from 7313 with a prep. pref.; prop. *highly,* i.e. *surely;* but used adversatively, *however:*–but, nevertheless, yet.
1298. בֶּרַע *beh'-rah;* of unc. der.; *Bera,* a Sodomitish king:–Bera.
1299. בָּרַק *baw-rak';* a prim. root; to *lighten* (lightning):–cast forth.
1300. בָּרָק *baw-rawk';* from 1299; *lightning;* by anal., a *gleam;* concr., a *flashing* sword:–bright, glitter(-ing sword), lightning.
1301. בָּרָק *baw-rawk';* the same as 1300;

Barak, an Isr.:–Barak.
1302. בַּרְקוֹס *bar-kose';* of unc. der.; *Barkos,* one of the Nethimim:–Barkos.
1303. בַּרְקָן *bar-kan';* 1300; a *thorn* (perh. as burning *brightly*):–brier.
1304. בָּרֶקֶת *baw-reh'-keth;* or בָּרְקַת *baw-rek-ath';* from 1300; a gem (as *flashing*), perh. the *emerald:*–carbuncle.
1305. בָּרַר *baw-rar';* prim. root; to *clarify* (i.e. *brighten*), *examine, select:*–make bright, choice, chosen, cleanse (be clean), clearly, polished, (shew self) pure(-ify), purge (out).
1306. בִּרְשַׁע *beer-shah';* prob. from 7562 with a prep. pref.; *with wickedness;* Birsha, a king of Gomorrah:–Birsha.
1307. בֵּרֹתִי *bay-ro-thee';* patrial from 1268; a *Berothite,* or inh. of Berothai:–Berothite.
1308. בְּשׂוֹר *bes-ore';* from 1319; *cheerful; Besor,* a stream of Pal.:–Besor.
1309. בְּשׂוֹרָה *bes-o-raw';* or (short.) בְּשֹׂרָה *bes-o-raw';* fem. from 1319; glad *tidings;* by impl., *reward for good news:*–reward for tidings.
1310. בָּשַׁל *baw-shal';* a prim. root; prop. to *boil* up; hence, to *be done* in cooking; fig. to *ripen:*–bake, boil, bring forth, roast, seethe, sod (be sodden).
1311. בָּשֵׁל *baw-shale';* from 1310; *boiled:*–X at all, sodden.
1312. בִּשְׁלָם *bish-lawm';* of for. der.; *Bishlam,* a Pers.:–Bishlam.
1313. בָּשָׂם *baw-sawm';* from an un. root mean. to *be fragrant;* [comp. 5561] the *balsam* plant:–spice.
1314. בֶּשֶׂם *beh'-sem;* or בֹּשֶׂם *bo'-sem;* from the same as 1313; *fragrance;* by impl., *spicery;* also the *balsam* plant:–smell, spice, sweet (odour).
1315. בָּשְׂמַת *bos-math';* fem. of 1314 (the sec. form); *fragrance; Bosmath,* the name of a wife of Esau, and of a daughter of Solomon:– Bashemath, Basmath.
1316. בָּשָׁן *baw-shawn';* of unc. der.; *Bashan* (often with the art.), a region E. of the Jordan:–Bashan.
1317. בָּשְׁנָה *bosh-naw';* fem. from 954; *shamefulness:*–shame.
1318. בָּשַׁס *baw-shas';* a prim. root; to *trample* down:–tread.
1319. בָּשַׂר *baw-sar';* a prim. root; prop. to *be fresh,* i.e. *full* (*rosy,* (fig.) *cheerful*); to *announce* (glad news):–messenger, preach, publish, shew forth, (bear, bring, carry, preach, good, tell good) tidings.
1320. בָּשָׂר *baw-sawr';* from 1319; *flesh* (from its *freshness*); by ext., *body, person;* also (by euphem.) the *pudenda* of a man:–body, [fat, lean] flesh[-ed], kin, [man-]kind, + nakedness, self, skin.
1321. בְּשַׂר *bes-ar'* (Chald.); cor. to 1320:–flesh.
1322. בֹּשֶׁת *bo'-sheth;* from 954; *shame* (the feeling and the condition, as well as its cause); by impl. (spec.) an *idol:*–ashamed, confusion, + greatly, (put to) shame(-ful thing).
1323. בַּת *bath;* from 1129 (as fem. of 1121); a *daughter* (used in the same wide sense as other terms of relationship, lit. and fig.):–apple [of the eye], branch, company, daughter, X first, X old, + owl, town, village.
1324. בַּת *bath;* prob. from the same as 1327; a *bath* or Heb. measure (as a means of *division*) of liquids:–bath.
1325. בַּת *bath* (Chald.); cor. to 1324:–bath.
1326. בָּתָה *baw-thaw';* prob. an orth. var. for 1327; *desolation:*–waste.
1327. בַּתָּה *bat-taw';* fem. from an un. root (mean. to *break* in pieces); *desolation:*–desolate.
1328. בְּתוּאֵל *beth-oo-ale';* app. from the same as 1326 and 410; *destroyed of God; Bethuel,* the name of a nephew of Abraham, and of a place in Pal.:–Bethuel. Comp. 1329.
1329. בְּתוּל *beth-ool';* for 1328; *Bethul* (i.e. *Bethuel*), a place in Pal.:–Bethuel.
1330. בְּתוּלָה *beth-oo-law';* fem. pass. part. of an un. root mean. to *separate;* a *virgin* (from her *privacy*); sometimes (by continuation) a *bride;* also (fig.) a *city* or *state:*–maid, virgin.
1331. בְּתוּלִים *beth-oo-leem';* pl. of the same as 1330; (coll. and abstr.) *virginity;* by impl. and concr., the *tokens* of it:–X maid, virginity.
1332. בִּתְיָה *bith-yaw';* from 1323 and 3050; *daughter* (i.e. worshipper) *of Jah; Bithjah,* an Eg. woman:–Bithiah.
1333. בָּתַק *baw-thak';* a prim. root; to *cut* in pieces:–thrust through.
1334. בָּתַר *baw-thar';* a prim. root, to *chop* up:–divide.
1335. בֶּתֶר *beh'-ther;* from 1334; a *section:*–part, piece.
1336. בֶּתֶר *beh'-ther;* the same as 1335; *Bether,* a (craggy) place in Pal.:–Bether.
1337. בַּת רַבִּים *bath rab-beem';* from 1323 and a masc. pl. from 7227; the *daughter* (i.e. *city*) of *Rabbah:*–Bath-rabbim.
1338. בִּתְרוֹן *bith-rone';* from 1334; (with the art.) the *craggy* spot; *Bithron,* a place E. of the Jordan:–Bithron.
1339. בַּת-שֶׁבַע *bath-sheh'-bah;* from 1323 and 7651 (in the sense of 7650); *daughter of an oath; Bath-Sheba,* the mother of Solomon:–Bath-sheba.
1340. בַּת-שׁוּעַ *bath-shoo'-ah;* from 1323 and 7771; *daughter of wealth; Bath-shuä,* the same as 1339:–Bath-shua.

ג

1341. גֵּא *gay';* for 1343; *haughty:*–proud.
1342. גָּאָה *gaw-aw';* a prim. root; to *mount up;* hence, in gen., to *rise,* (fig.) be *majestic:*–gloriously, grow up, increase, be risen, triumph.
1343. גֵּאֶה *gay-eh';* from 1342; *lofty;* fig., *arrogant:*–proud.
1344. גֵּאָה *gay-aw';* fem. from 1342; *arrogance:*–pride.
1345. גְּאוּאֵל *gheh-oo-ale';* from 1342 and 410; *majesty of God; Geüel,* an Isr.:–Geuel.
1346. גַּאֲוָה *gah-av-aw';* from 1342; *arrogance* or *majesty;* by impl., (concr.) *or-nament:*–excellency, haughtiness, highness, pride, proudly, swelling.
1347. גָּאוֹן *gaw-ohn';* from 1342; the same as 1346:–arrogancy, excellency(-lent), majesty, pomp, pride, proud, swelling.
1348. גֵּאוּת *gay-ooth';* from 1342; the same as 1346:–excellent things, lifting up, majesty, pride, proudly, raging.
1349. גַּאֲיוֹן *gah-ah-yone';* from 1342: *haughty:*–proud.
1350. גָּאַל *gaw-al';* a prim. root, to *redeem* (according to the Oriental law of kinship), i.e. to *be the next of kin* (and as such to *buy back* a relative's property, *marry* his widow, etc.):–X in any wise, X at all, avenger, deliver, (do, perform the part of near, next) kinsfolk(-man), purchase, ransom, redeem(-er), revenger.
1351. גָּאַל *gaw-al';* a prim. root, [rather identified with 1350, through the idea of *freeing,* i.e. *repudiating*]; to *soil* or (fig.) *desecrate:*–defile, pollute, stain.
1352. גֹּאֶל *go'-el;* from 1351; *profanation:*–defile.
1353. גְּאֻלָּה *gheh-ool-law';* fem. pass.part. of 1350; *redemption* (incl. the right and the obj.); by impl., *relationship:*–kindred, redeem, redemption, right.
1354. גַּב *gab;* from an un. root mean. to *hollow* or *curve;* the *back* (as *rounded* [comp. 1460 and 1479]; by anal., the *top* or *rim,* a *boss,* a *vault, arch* of eye, *bulwarks,* etc.:–back, body, boss, eminent (higher) place, [eye]brows, nave, ring.
1355. גַּב *gab* (Chald.); cor. to 1354:–back.
1356. גֵּב *gabe;* from 1461; a *log* (as *cut* out); also *well* or *cistern* (as *dug*):–beam, ditch, pit.
1357. גֵּב *gabe;* prob. from 1461 [comp. 1462]; a *locust* (from its *cutting*):–locust.
1358. גֹּב *gobe* (Chald.); from a root cor. to 1461; a *pit* (for wild animals) (as *cut* out):–den.
1359. גֹּב *gobe;* or (fully) גּוֹב *gobe';* from 1461; *pit; Gob,* a place in Pal.:–Gob.
1360. גֶּבֶא *geh'-beh;* from an un. root mean. prob. to *coll.;* a *reservoir;* by anal., a *marsh:*–marish, pit.
1361. גָּבַהּ *gaw-bah';* a prim. root; to *soar,* i.e. *be lofty;* fig., to be *haughty:*–exalt, *be* haughty, be (make) high(-er), lift up, mount up, be proud, raise up great height, upward.
1362. גָּבָהּ *gaw-bawh';* from 1361; *lofty* (lit. or fig.):–high, proud.
1363. גֹּבַהּ *go'-bah;* from 1361; *elation, grandeur, arrogance:*–excellency,
1364. גָּבֹהַּ *gaw-bo'-ah;* or (fully) גָּבוֹהַּ *gaw-bo'-ah;* from 1361; *elevated* (or *elated*), *powerful, arrogant:*–haughty, height, high (-er), lofty, proud, X exceeding proudly.
1365. גַּבְהוּת *gab-hooth';* from 1361; *pride:*–loftiness, lofty.
1366. גְּבוּל *gheb-ool';* or (short) גְּבֻל *gheb-ool';* from 1379; prop. a cord (as *twisted*), i.e. (by impl.) a *boundary;* by ext. the *territory* inclosed:–border, bound, coast, X great, landmark, limit, quarter, space.
1367. גְּבוּלָה *gheb-oo-law';* (short) גְּבֻלָה *gheb-oo-law';* fem. of 1366; a *boundary, region:*–border, bound, coast, landmark. place.
1368. גִּבּוֹר *ghib-bore';* or (short) גִּבֹּר *ghib-bore';* intens. from the same as 1397; *powerful;* by impl., *warrior, tyrant:*–champion, chief, X excel, giant, man, mighty (man, one), strong (man), valiant man.
1369. גְּבוּרָה *gheb-oo-raw';* fem. pass.part. from the same as 1368; *force* (lit. or fig.); by impl., *valor, victory:*– force, mastery, might, mighty (act, power), power, strength.
1370. גְּבוּרָה *gheb-oo-raw'* (Chald.); cor. to 1369; *power:*–might.
1371. גִּבֵּחַ *ghib-bay'-akh;* from an un. root mean. to *be high* (in the forehead); *bald* in the forehead:–forehead bald.
1372. גַּבַּחַת *gab-bakh'-ath;* from the same as 1371; *baldness* in the forehead; by anal.,

a *bare spot* on the right side of cloth:–bald forehead, X without.
1373. גַּבַּי *gab-bah'ee;* from the same as 1354; *coll.:–Gabbai,* an Isr.:–Gabbai.
1374. גֵּבִים *gay-beem';* pl. of 1356; *cisterns; Gebim,* a place in Pal.:–Gebim.
1375. גְּבִיעַ *gheb-ee'-ah;* from an un. root (mean. to be *convex*); a *goblet*; by anal., the *calyx* of a flower:–house, cup, pot.
1376. גְּבִיר *gheb-eer';* from 1396; a *master:*–lord.
1377. גְּבִירָה *gheb-ee-raw';* fem. of 1376; a *mistress:*–queen
1378. גָּבִישׁ *gaw-beesh';* from an un. root (prob. mean. to *freeze*); *crystal* (from its resemblance to *ice*):–pearl.
1379. גָּבַל *gaw-bal';* a prim. root; prop. to *twist* as a rope; only (as a denom. from 1366) to *bound* (as by a line):–be border, set (bounds about).
1380. גְּבַל *gheb-al';* from 1379 (in the sense of a *chain* of hills); a *mountain; Gebal,* a place in Phoenicia:–Gebal.
1381. גְּבָל *gheb-awl';* the same as 1380; *Gebal,* a region in Idumaea:–Gebal.
1382. גִּבְלִי *ghib-lee';* patrial from 1380; a *Gebalite,* or inh. of Gebal:–Giblites, stone-squarer.
1383. גַּבְלֻת *gab-looth';* from 1379; a twisted *chain* or *lace:*–end.
1384. גִּבֵּן *gib-bane';* from an un. root mean. to be *arched* or *contr.; hunch-backed:*–crookbackt.
1385. גְּבִינָה *gheb-ee-naw';* fem. from the same as 1384; *curdled* milk:–cheese.
1386. גַּבְנֹן *gab-nohn';* from the same as 1384; a *hump* or *peak* of hills:–high.
1387. גֶּבַע *gheh'-bah;* from the same as 1375, a *hillock; Geba,* a place in Pal.:–Gaba, Geba, Gibeah.
1388. גִּבְעָא *ghib-aw';* by perm. for 1389; a *hill; Giba,* a place in Pal.:–Gibeah.
1389. גִּבְעָה *ghib-aw';* fem. from the same as 1387; a *hillock:*–hill, little hill.
1390. גִּבְעָה *ghib-aw';* the same as 1389; *Gibah;* the name of three places in Pal.:–Gibeah, the hill.
1391. גִּבְעוֹן *ghib-ohn';* from the same as 1387; *hilly; Gibon,* a place in Pal.:–Gibeon.
1392. גִּבְעֹל *ghib-ole';* prol. from 1375; the *calyx* of a flower:–bolled.
1393. גִּבְעֹנִי *ghib-o-nee'* patrial from 1391; a Gibonite, or inh. of Gibon:–Gibeonite.
1394. גִּבְעַת *ghib-ath';* from the same as 1375; *hilliness; Gibath:*–Gibeath.
1395. גִּבְעָתִי *ghib-aw-thee';* patrial from 1390; a *Gibathite,* or inh. of Gibath:–Gibeathite.
1396. גָּבַר *gaw-bar';* a prim. root; to *be strong;* by impl., to *prevail, act insolently:*–exceed, confirm, be great, be mighty, prevail, put to more [strength], strengthen, be stronger, be valiant.
1397. גֶּבֶר *gheh'-ber;* from 1396; prop. a *valiant* man or *warrior;* gen., a *person* simply:–every one, man, X mighty.
1398. גֶּבֶר *gheh'-ber;* the same as 1397; *Geber,* the name of two Isr.:–Geber.
1399. גְּבַר *gheb-ar';* from 1396; the same as 1397; a person:–man.
1400. גְּבַר *gheb-ar'* (Chald.); cor. to 1399:–certain, man.
1401. גִּבָּר *ghib-bawr'* (Chald.); intens. of 1400; *valiant,* or *warrior:*–mighty.
1402. גִּבָּר *ghib-bawr';* intens. of 1399; *Gibbar,* an Isr.:–Gibbar.
1403. גַּבְרִיאֵל *gab-ree-ale';* from 1397 and 410; *man of God; Gabriel,* an archangel:–Gabriel.
1404. גְּבֶרֶת *gheb-eh'-reth;* fem. of 1376; *mistress:*–lady, mistress.
1405. גִּבְּתוֹן *ghib-beth-one';* intens. from 1389; a *hilly* spot; *Gibbethon;* a place in Pal.:–Gibbethon.
1406. גָּג *gawg;* prob. by redupl. from 1342; a roof; by anal., the *top* of an altar:–roof (of the house), (house) top (of the house).
1407. גַּד *gad;* from 1413 (in the sense of cutting); coriander seed (from its furrows):–coriander.
1408. גַּד *gad;* a var. of 1409; *Fortune,* a Babylonian deity:–that troop.
1409. גָּד *gawd;* from 1464 (in the sense of *distributing*); *fortune:*–troop.
1410. גָּד *gawd;* from 1464; *Gad,* a son of Jacob, incl. his tribe and its territory; also a prophet:–Gad.
1411. גְּדָבָר *ghed-aw-bawr'* (Chald.); cor. to 1489; a *treasurer:*–treasurer.
1412. גֻּדְגֹּדָה *gud-go'-daw;* by redupl. from 1413 (in the sense of *cutting*) *cleft; Gudgodah,* a place in the Desert:–Gudgodah.
1413. גָּדַד *gaw-dad';* a prim. root (comp. 1464); to *crowd;* also to *gash* (as if by *pressing* into):–assemble (selves by troops), gather (selves together, self in troops), cut selves.
1414. גְּדַד *ghed-ad'* (Chald.); cor. to 1413; to *cut* down:–hew down.
1415. גָּדָה *gaw-daw';* from an un. root (mean. to *cut* off); a *border* of a river (as *cut* into by the stream):–bank.
1416. גְּדוּד *ghed-ood';* from 1413; a *crowd* (esp. of soldiers):–army, band (of men), company, troop (of robbers).
1417. גְּדוּד *ghed-ood';* or (fem.) גְּדֻדָה *ghed-oo-daw';* from 1413; a *furrow* (as *cut*):–furrow.
1418. גְּדוּדָה *ghed-oo-daw';* fem. part. pass. of 1413; an *incision:*–cutting.
1419. גָּדוֹל *gaw-dole';* or (short) גָּדֹל *gaw-dole';* from 1431; *great* (in any sense); hence, *older;* also *insolent:*–+ aloud, elder (-est), + exceeding(-ly), + far, (man of) great (man, matter, thing,-er,-ness), high, long, loud, mighty, more, much, noble, proud thing, X sore, (X) very.
1420. גְּדוּלָה *ghed-oo-law';* or (short) גְּדֻלָּה *ghed-ool-law';* or (less accurately) גְּדוּלָּה *ghed-ool-law';* fem. of 1419; *greatness;* (concr.) *mighty acts:*–dignity, great things(-ness), majesty.
1421. גִּדּוּף *ghid-doof';* or (short) גִּדֻּף *ghid-doof';* and (fem.) גִּדּוּפָה *ghid-doo-faw';* or גִּדֻּפָה *ghid-doo-faw';* from 1422; *vilification:*–reproach, reviling.
1422. גְּדוּפָה *ghed-oo-faw';* fem. pass.part. of 1442; a *revilement:*–taunt.
1423. גְּדִי *ghed-ee';* from the same as 1415; a young *goat* (from *browsing*):–kid.
1424. גָּדִי *gaw-dee';* from 1409; *fortunate; Gadi,* an Isr.:–Gadi.
1425. גָּדִי *gaw-dee';* patron. from 1410; a *Gadite* (coll.) or desc. of Gad:–Gadites, children of Gad.
1426. גַּדִּי *gad-dee';* intens. for 1424; *Gaddi,* an Isr.:–Gaddi.
1427. גַּדִּיאֵל *gad-dee-ale';* from 1409 and 410; *fortune of God; Gaddiel,* an Isr.:–Gaddiel.
1428. גִּדְיָה *ghid-yaw';* or גַּדְיָה *gad-yaw';* the same as 1415; a river *brink:*–bank.
1429. גְּדִיָּה *ghed-ee-yaw';* fem. of 1423; a young female *goat:*–kid.
1430. גָּדִישׁ *gaw-deesh';* from an un. root (mean. to *heap* up); a *stack* of sheaves; by anal., a *tomb:*–shock (stack) (of corn), tomb.
1431. גָּדַל *gaw-dal';* a prim. root; prop. to *twist* [comp. 1434], i.e. to *be* (caus. *make*) *large* (in various senses, as in body, mind, estate or honor, also in pride):–advance, boast, bring up, exceed, excellent, be(-come, do, give, make, wax), great(-er, come to... estate, + things), grow(up),increase, lift up, magnify(-ifical), be much set by, nourish (up), pass, promote, proudly [spoken], tower.
1432. גָּדֵל *gaw-dale';* from 1431; *large* (lit. or fig.):–great, grew.
1433. גֹּדֶל *go'-del;* from 1431; *magnitude* (lit. or fig.):– greatness, stout(-ness).
1434. גְּדִל *ghed-eel';* from 1431 (in the sense of *twisting*); *thread,* i.e. a *tassel* or *festoon:*–fringe, wreath.
1435. גִּדֵּל *ghid-dale';* from 1431; *stout; Giddel,* the name of one of the Nethinim, also of one of "Solomon's servants":–Giddel.
1436. גְּדַלְיָה *ghed-al-yaw';* or (prol.) גְּדַלְיָהוּ *ghed-al-yaw'-hoo;* from 1431 and 3050; *Jah has become great; Gedaljah,* the name of five Isr.:–Gedaliah.
1437. גִּדַּלְתִּי *ghid-dal'-tee;* from 1431; *I have made great; Giddalti,* an Isr.:–Giddalti.
1438. גָּדַע *gaw-dah';* a prim. root; to *fell* a tree; gen., to *destroy* anything:–cut (asunder, in sunder, down, off), hew down.
1439. גִּדְעוֹן *ghid-ohn';* from 1438; *feller* (i.e. *warrior*); *Gidon,* an Isr.:–Gideon.
1440. גִּדְעֹם *ghid-ohm';* from 1438; a *cutting* (i.e. *desolation*); *Gidom,* a place in Pal.:–Gidom.
1441. גִּדְעֹנִי *ghid-o-nee';* from 1438; warlike [comp. 1439]; *Gidoni,* an Isr.:–Gideoni.
1442. גָּדַף *gaw-daf';* a prim. root; to *hack* (with words), i.e. *revile:*–blaspheme, reproach.
1443. גָּדַר *gaw-dar';* a prim. root; to *wall* in or around:–close up, fence up, hedge, inclose, make up [a wall], mason, repairer.
1444. גֶּדֶר *gheh'-der;* from 1443; a *circumvallation:*–wall.
1445. גֶּדֶר *gheh'-der;* the same as 1444; *Geder,* a place in Pal.:–Geder.
1446. גְּדֹר *ghed-ore';* or (fully) גְּדוֹר *ghed-ore';* from 1443; *inclosure; Gedor,* a place in Pal.; also the name of three Isr.:–Gedor.
1447. גָּדֵר *gaw-dare';* from 1443; a *circumvallation;* by *impl.,* an *inclosure:*–fence, hedge, wall.
1448. גְּדֵרָה *ghed-ay-raw';* fem. of 1447; *enclosure* (esp. for flocks):–[sheep-] cote (fold) hedge, wall.
1449. גְּדֵרָה *ghed-ay-raw';* the same as 1448; (with the art.) *Gederah,* a place in Pal.:–Gederah, hedges.
1450. גְּדֵרוֹת *ghed-ay-rohth';* pl. of 1448; *walls; Gederoth,* a place in Pal.:–Gederoth.
1451. גְּדֵרִי *ghed-ay-ree';* patrial from 1445; a *Gederite,* or inh. of Geder:–Gederite.
1452. גְּדֵרָתִי *ghed-ay-raw-thee';* patrial from 1449; a *Gederathite,* or inh. of Gederah:–Gederathite.
1453. גְּדֵרֹתַיִם *ghed-ay-ro-thah'-yim;* dual of 1448; *double wall; Gederothajim,* a place in Pal.:–Gederothaim.
1454. גֵּה *gay;* prob. a clerical err. for 2088; *this:*–this.
1455. גָּהָה *gaw-haw';* a prim. root; to *remove*

(a bandage from a wound, i.e. *heal* it):–cure.
1456. גֵּהָה *gay-haw';* from 1455; a *cure:*–medicine.
1457. גָּהַר *gaw-har';* a prim. root; to *prostrate* oneself:–cast self down, stretch self.
1458. גַּו *gav;* another form for 1460; the *back:*–back.
1459. גַּו gav (Chald.); cor. to 1460; the middle:–midst, same, there- (where-) in.
1460. גֵּו *gave;* from 1342 [cor. to 1354]; the *back;* by anal., the *mid:*–+ among, back, body.
1461. גּוּב *goob;* a prim. root; to *dig:*–husbandman.
1462. גּוֹב *gobe;* from 1461; the *locust* (from its *grubbing* as a larvae):– grasshopper, X great.
1463. גּוֹג *gohg;* of unc. der.; *Gog,* the name of an Isr., also of some nothern nation:–Gog.
1464. גּוּד *goode;* a prim. root [akin to 1413]; to *crowd* upon, i.e. *attack:*–invade, overcome.
1465. גֵּוָה *gay-vaw';* fem. of 1460; the *back,* i.e. (by ext.) the *person:*–body.
1466. גֵּוָה *gay-vaw';* the same as 1465; *exaltation;* (fig.) *arrogance:*–lifting up, pride.
1467. גֵּוָה *gay-vaw'* (Chald.); cor. to 1466:–pride.
1468. גּוּז *gooz;* a prim. root [comp. 1494]; prop. to *shear* off; but used only in the (fig.) sense of *passing* rapidly:–bring, cut off.
1469. גּוֹזָל *go-zawl';* or (short) גֹּזָל *go-zawl';* from 1497; a *nestling* (as being comp. *nude* of feathers):–young (pigeon).
1470. גּוֹזָן go-zawn' prob. from 1468; a *quarry* (as a place of *cutting* stones); *Gozan,* a province of Assyria:–Gozan.
1471. גּוֹי *go'-ee;* rarely (short.) גֹּי *go'-ee;* app. from the same root as 1465 (in the sense of *massing*); a for. *nation;* hence, a *Gentile;* also (fig.) a *troop* of animals, or a *flight* of locusts:–Gentile, heathen, nation, people.
1472. גְּוִיָּה *ghev-ee-yaw';* prol. for 1465; a *body,* whether alive or dead:–(dead) body, carcase, corpse.
1473. גּוֹלָה *go-law';* or (short.) גֹּלָה *go-law';* act. part. fem. of 1540; *exile;* concr. and coll. *Exiles:*–(carried away), captive(-ity), removing.
1474. גּוֹלָן *go-lawn';* from 1473; *captive; Golan,* a place east of the Jordan:–Golan.
1475. גּוּמָּץ *goom-mawts';* of unc. der.; a *pit:*–pit.
1476. גּוּנִי *goo-nee';* prob. from 1598; *protected; Guni,* the name of two Isr.:–Guni.
1477. גּוּנִי *goo-nee';* patron. from 1476; a *Gunite* (coll. with art. pref.) or desc. of Guni:–Gunites.
1478. גָּוַע *gaw-vah';* a prim. root; to *breathe* out, i.e. (by impl.) *expire:*–die, be dead, give up the ghost, perish.
1479. גּוּף *goof;* a prim. root; prop. to *hollow* or *arch,* i.e. (fig.) *close;* to *shut:*–shut.
1480. גּוּפָה *goo-faw';* from 1479; a *corpse* (as *closed* to sense):–body.
1481. גּוּר *goor;* a prim. root; prop. to *turn* aside from the road (for a lodging or any other purpose), i.e. *sojourn* (as a guest); also to *shrink, fear* (as in a *strange* place); also to *gather* for hostility (as *afraid*):–abide, assemble, be afraid, dwell, fear, gather (together), inh., remain, sojourn, stand in awe, (be) stranger, X surely.
1482. גּוּר *goor;* or (short.) גֻּר *goor;* perh. from 1481; a *cub* (as still *abiding* in the lair), esp. of the lion:–whelp, young one.
1483. גּוּר *goor;* the same as 1482; *Gur,* a place in Pal.:–Gur.
1484. גּוֹר *gore;* or (fem.) גֹּרָה *go-raw';* a var. of 1482:–whelp.
1485. גּוּר־בַּעַל *goor-bah'-al;* from 1481 and 1168; *dwelling of Baal; Gur- Baal,* a place in Arabia:–Gur-baal.
1486. גּוֹרָל *go-rawl';* or (short.) גֹּרָל *go-ral';* from an un. root mean. to *be rough* (as stone); prop. a *pebble,* i.e. a *lot* (small stones being used for that purpose); fig., a *portion* or *destiny* (as if determined by lot):–lot.
1487. גּוּשׁ *goosh;* or rather (by perm.) גִּישׁ *gheesh;* of unc. der.; a *mass* of earth:–clod.
1488 גֵּז *gaze;* from 1494; a *fleece* (as *shorn*); also mown *grass:*–fleece, mowing, mown grass.
1489. גִּזְבָּר *ghiz-bawr';* of for. derivation; *treasurer:*–treasurer.
1490. גִּזְבָּר *ghiz-bawr'* (Chald.); cor. to 1489:–treasurer.
1491. גָּזָה *gaw-zaw';* a prim. root (akin to 1468); to *cut* off, i.e. *portion* out:–take.
1492. גַּזָּה *gaz-zaw';* fem. from 1494; a *fleece:*–fleece.
1493. גִּזוֹנִי *ghee-zo-nee';* patrial from the un. name of a place app. in Pal.; a *Gizonite* or inh. of Gizoh:–Gizonite.
1494. גָּזַז *gaw-zaz';* a prim. root (akin to 1468); to *cut* off; spec. to *shear* a flock or *shave* the hair; fig. to *destroy* an enemy:–cut off (down), poll, shave, ([sheep-]) shear(-er).
1495. גָּזֵז *gaw-zaze';* from 1494; *shearer; Gazez,* the name of two Isr.:–Gazez.
1496. גָּזִית *gaw-zeeth';* from 1491; something *cut,* i.e. *dressed* stone:–hewed, hewn stone, wrought.
1497. גָּזַל *gaw-zal';* a prim. root; to *pluck* off; spec. to *flay, strip* or *rob:*–catch, consume, exercise [robbery], pluck (off), rob, spoil, take away (by force, violence), tear.
1498. גָּזֵל *gaw-zale';* from 1497; *robbery,* or (concr.) *plunder:*–robbery, thing taken away by violence.
1499. גֵּזֶל ghe'-zel from 1497; *plunder,* i.e. *violence:*–violence, violent perverting. גֹּזָל gozal. See 1469.
1500. גְּזֵלָה *ghez-ay-law';* fem. of 1498 and mean the same:–that (he had robbed) [which he took violently away], spoil, violence.
1501. גָּזָם *gaw-zawm;* from an un. root mean. to *devour;* a kind of *locust:*–palmer-worm.
1502. גַּזָּם *gaz-zawm';* from the same as 1501; *devourer:–Gazzam,* one of the Nethinim:–Gazzam.
1503. גֶּזַע *geh'-zah;* from an un. root mean. to *cut* down (trees); the *trunk* or *stump* of a tree (as felled or as planted):–stem, stock.
1504. גָּזַר *gaw-zar';* a prim. root; to *cut* down or off; (fig.) to *destroy, divide, exclude,* or *decide:*–cut down (off), decree, divide, snatch.
1505. גְּזַר *ghez-ar'* (Chald.); cor. to 1504; to *quarry; determine:*–cut out, soothsayer.
1506. גֶּזֶר *gheh'-zer;* from 1504; something *cut* off; a *portion:*–part, piece.
1507. גֶּזֶר *gheh'-zer;* the same as 1506; *Gezer,* a place in Pal.:–Gazer, Gezer.
1508. גִּזְרָה *ghiz-raw';* fem. of 1506; the *figure* or person (as if *cut* out); also an *inclosure* (as *separated*):–polishing, separate place.
1509. גְּזֵרָה *ghez-ay-raw';* from 1504; a *desert* (as *separated*):–not inhabited.
1510. גְּזֵרָה *ghez-ay-raw'* (Chald.); from 1505 (as 1504); a *decree:*–decree.
1511. גִּזְרִי *ghiz-ree';* (in the marg.), patrial from 1507; a *Gezerite* (coll.) or inh. of Gezer; but better (as in the text) by transp. גִּרְזִי *gherzee';* patrial of 1630; a *Grizite* (coll.) or member of a nat. tribe in Pal.:–Gezrites.
1512. גָּחוֹן *gaw-khone';* prob. from 1518; the ext. *abdomen, belly* (as the *source* of the foetus [comp. 1521]):–belly.
1513. גֶּחֶל *geh'-khel;* or (fem.) גַּחֶלֶת *gahkheh'-leth;* from an un. root mean. to *glow* or *kindle;* an *ember:*–(burning) coal.
1514. גַּחַם *gah'-kham;* from an un. root mean. to *burn; flame; Gacham,* a son of Nahor:–Gaham.
1515. גַּחַר *gah'-khar;* from an un. root mean. to *hide; lurker; Gachar,* one of the Nethinim:–Gahar.
1516. גַּיְא *gah'-ee;* or (short.) גַּי *gah'-ee;* prob. (by transmutation) from the same root as 1466 (abb); a *gorge* (from its *lofty* sides; hence, narrow, but not a gully or winter-torrent):–valley.
1517. גִּיד *gheed;* prob. from 1464; a *thong* (as *compressing*); by anal., a *tendon:*–sinew.
1518. גִּיחַ *ghee'-akh;* or (short.) גֹּחַ *go'-akh;* a prim. root; to *gush* forth (as water), gen. to *issue:*–break forth, labor to bring forth, come forth, draw up, take out.
1519. גִּיחַ *ghee'-akh* (Chald.); or (short.) גּוּחַ *goo'- akh;* cor. to 1518; to *rush* forth:–strive.
1520. גִּיחַ *ghee'-akh;* from 1518; a *fountain; Giach,* a place in Pal.:–Giah.
1521. גִּיחוֹן *ghee-khone';* or (short.) גִּחוֹן *ghee-khone';* from 1518; *stream; Gichon,* a river of Paradise; also a valley (or pool) near Jerus.:–Gihon.
1522. גֵּיחֲזִי *gay-khah-zee';* or גֵּחֲזִי *gay-khahzee';* app. from 1516 and 2372; *valley of a visionary; Gechazi,* the servant of Elisha:–Gehazi.
1523. גִּיל *gheel;* or (by perm.) גּוּל *gool;* a prim. root; prop. to *spin* round (under the influence of any violent emotion), i.e. usually *rejoice,* or (as *cringing*) *fear:*–be glad, joy, be joyful, rejoice.
1524. גִּיל *gheel;* from 1523; a *revolution* (of time, i.e. an *age*); also *joy:*–X exceedingly, gladness, X greatly, joy, rejoice(-ing), sort.
1525. גִּילָה *ghee-law';* or גִּילַת *ghee-lath';* fem. of 1524; *joy:*–joy, rejoicing.
1526. גִּילֹנִי *ghee-lo-nee';* patrial from 1542; a *Gilonite* or inh. of Giloh:–Gilonite.
1527. גִּינַת *ghee-nath';* of unc. der.; *Ginath,* an Isr.:–Ginath.
1528. גִּיר *gheer* (Chald.); cor. to 1615; *lime:*–plaster.
1529. גֵּישָׁן *gay-shawn';* from the same as 1487; *lumpish; Geshan,* an Isr.:–Geshan.
1530. גַּל *gal;* from 1556; something *rolled,* i.e. a *heap* of stone or dung (pl. *ruins*), by anal., a *spring* of water (pl. *waves*):–billow, heap, spring, wave.
1531. גֹּל *gole;* from 1556; a *cup* for oil (as *round*):–bowl.
1532. גַּלָּב *gal-lawb';* from an un. root mean. to *shave;* a *barber:*–barber.
1533. גִּלְבֹּעַ *ghil-bo'-ah;* from 1530 and 1158; *fountain of ebullition; Gilboa,* a mountain of Pal.:–Gilboa.
1534. גַּלְגַּל *gal-gal';* by redupl. from 1556; a *wheel;* by anal., a *whirlwind;* also *dust* (as *whirled*):–heaven, rolling thing, wheel.
1535. גַּלְגַּל *gal-gal'* (Chald.); cor. to 1534; a

wheel:–wheel.
1536. גִּלְגָּל *ghil-gawl';* a var. of 1534:–wheel.
1537. גִּלְגָּל *ghil-gawl';* the same as 1536 (with the art. as a prop. noun); *Gilgal,* the name of three places in Pal.:–Gilgal. See also 1019.
1538. גֻּלְגֹּלֶת *gul-go'-leth;* by redupl. from 1556; a *skull* (as *round*); by impl., a *head* (in enumeration of persons):–head, every man, poll, skull.
1539. גֶּלֶד *ghe'-led;* from an un. root prob. mean. to *polish;* the (human) *skin* (as *smooth*):–*skin.*
1540. גָּלָה *gaw-law';* a prim. root; to *denude* (esp. in a disgraceful sense); by impl., to *exile* (captives being usually *stripped*); fig., to *reveal:*–+ advertise, appear, bewray, bring, (carry, lead, go) captive (into captivity), depart, disclose, discover, exile, be gone, open, X plainly, publish, remove, reveal, X shamelessly, shew, X surely, tell, uncover.
1541. גְּלָה *ghel-aw'* (Chald.); or גְּלָא *ghel-aw';* cor. to 1540:–bring over, carry away, reveal.
1542. גִּלֹה *ghee-lo';* or (fully) גִּילֹה *ghee-lo';* from 1540; *open; Giloh,* a place in Pal.:–Giloh.
1543. גֻּלָּה *gool-law';* fem. from 1556; a *fountain, bowl* or *globe* (all as *round*):–bowl, pommel, spring.
1544. גִּלּוּל *ghil-lool';* or (short.) גִּלֻּל *ghil-lool';* from 1556; prop. a *log* (as *round*); by impl., an *idol:*–idol.
1545. גְּלוֹם *ghel-ome';* from 1563; *clothing* (as *wrapped*):–clothes.
1546. גָּלוּת *gaw-looth';* fem. from 1540; captivity; concr., *exiles* (coll.):–(they that are carried away) captives(-ity).
1547. גָּלוּת *gaw-looth';* (Chald.); cor. to 1546:–captivity.
1548. גָּלַח *gaw-lakh';* a prim. root; prop. to *be bald,* i.e. (caus.) to *shave;* fig. to *lay waste:*–poll, shave (off).
1549. גִּלָּיוֹן *ghil-law-yone';* or גִּלְיוֹן *ghil-yone';* from 1540; a *tablet* for writing (as *bare*); by anal., a *mirror* (as a *plate*):–glass, roll.
1550. גָּלִיל *gaw-leel';* from 1556; a *valve* of a folding door (as *turning*); also a *ring* (as *round*):–folding, ring.
1551. גָּלִיל *gaw-leel';* or (prol.) גָּלִילָה *gaw-lee-law';* the same as 1550; a *circle* (with the art.); *Galil* (as a special *circuit*) in the North of Pal.:–Galilee.
1552. גְּלִילָה *ghel-ee-law';* fem. of 1550; a *circuit* or *region:*–border, coast, country.
1553. גְּלִילוֹת *ghel-ee-lowth';* pl. of 1552; *circles; Geliloth,* a place in Pal.:–Geliloth.
1554. גַּלִּים *gal-leem';* pl. of 1530; *springs; Gallim,* a place in Pal.:–Gallim.
1555. גָּלְיַת *gol-yath'* perh. from 1540; *exile; Goljath,* a Philistine:–Goliath.
1556. גָּלַל *gaw-lal'* a prim. root; to *roll* (lit. or fig.):–commit, remove, roll (away, down, together), run down, seek occasion, trust, wallow.
1557. גָּלָל *gaw-lawl';* from 1556; *dung* (as in *balls*):–dung.
1558. גָּלָל *gaw-lawl';* from 1556; a *circumstance* (as *rolled* around); only used adv., on *account* of:–because of, for (sake).
1559. גָּלָל *gaw-lawl';* from 1556, in the sense of 1560; *great; Galal,* the name of two Isr.:–Galal.
1560. גְּלָל *ghel-awl'* (Chald.); from a root cor. to 1556; *weight* or *size* (as if *rolled*):–great.
1561. גֵּלֶל *gay'-lel;* var. of 1557; *dung* (pl. *balls* of dung):–dung.
1562. גִּלֲלַי *ghe-lal-ah'-ee;* from 1561; *dungy; Gilalai,* an Isr.:–Gilalai.
1563. גָּלַם *gaw-lam';* a prim. root; to *fold:*–wrap together.
1564. גֹּלֶם *go'-lem;* from 1563; a *wrapped* (and unformed *mass,* i.e. as the *embryo*):–substance yet being unperfect.
1565. גַּלְמוּד *gal-mood';* prob. by prol. from 1563; *sterile* (as *wrapped* up too hard); fig., *desolate:*–desolate, solitary.
1566. גָּלַע *gaw-lah';* a prim. root; to be *obstinate:*–(inter-)meddle (with).
1567. גַּלְעֵד *gal-ade';* from 1530 and 5707; *heap of testimony; Galed,* a memorial cairn E. of the Jordan:–Galeed.
1568. גִּלְעָד *ghil-awd';* prob. from 1567; *Gilad,* a region E. of the Jordan; also the name of three Isr.:–Gilead, Gileadite.
1569. גִּלְעָדִי *ghil-aw-dee';* patron. from 1568; a *Giladite* or desc. of Gilad:–Gileadite.
1570. גָּלַשׁ *gaw-lash';* a prim. root; prob. to *caper* (as a goat):–appear.
1571. גַּם *gam;* by contr. from an un. root mean. to *gather;* prop. *assemblage;* used only adv. *also, even, yea, though;* often repeated as correl. *both...and:*–again, alike, also, (so much) as (soon), both (so)...and , but, either...or, even, for all, (in) likewise (manner), moreover, nay...neither, one, then(-refore), though, what, with, yea.
1572. גָּמָא *gaw-maw';* a prim. root (lit. or fig.) to *absorb:*–swallow, drink.
1573. גֹּמֶא *go'-meh;* fom 1572; prop. an *absorbent,* i.e. the *bulrush* (from its *porosity*); spec. the *papyrus:*–(bul-)rush.
1574. גֹּמֶד *go'-med;* from an un. root app. mean. to *grasp;* prop. a *span:*–cubit.
1575. גַּמָּד *gam-mawd';* from the same as 1574; a *warrior* (as *grasping* weapons):–Gammadims.
1576. גְּמוּל *ghem-ool';* from 1580; *treatment,* i.e. an *act* (of good or ill); by impl., *service* or *requital:*– +as hast served, benefit, desert, deserving, that which he hath given, recompense, reward.
1577. גָּמוּל *gaw-mool';* pass.part. of 1580; *rewarded; Gamul,* an Isr.:–Gamul. See also 1014.
1578. גְּמוּלָה *ghem-oo-law';* fem. of 1576; mean. the same:–deed, recompense, such a reward.
1579. גִּמְזוֹ *ghim-zo';* of unc. der.; Gimzo, a place in Pal.:–Gimzo.
1580. גָּמַל *gaw-mal';* a prim. root; to *treat* a person (well or ill), i.e. *benefit* or *requite;* by impl. (of *toil*), to *ripen,* i.e. (spec.) to *wean:*–bestow on, deal bountifully, do (good), recompense, requite, reward, ripen, + serve, mean, yield.
1581. גָּמָל *gaw-mawl';* app. from 1580 (in the sense of *labor* or *burden-bearing*); a *camel:*–camel.
1582. גְּמַלִּי *ghem-al-lee';* prob. from 1581; *camel-driver; Gemalli,* an Isr.:–Gemalli.
1583. גַּמְלִיאֵל *gam-lee-ale';* from 1580 and 410; *reward of God; Gamliel,* an Isr.:–Gamaliel.
1584. גָּמַר *gaw-mar';* a prim. root; to *end* (in the sense of *completion* or *failure*):–cease, come to an end, fail, perfect, perform.
1585. גְּמַר *ghem-ar';* (Chald.); cor. to 1584:–perfect.
1586. גֹּמֶר *go'-mer;* from 1584; *completion; Gomer,* the name of a son of Japheth and of his desc.; also of a Hebrewess:–Gomer.
1587. גְּמַרְיָה *ghem-ar-yaw';* or גְּמַרְיָהוּ *ghem-ar-yaw'-hoo;* from 1584 and 3050; *Jah has perfected; Gemarjah,* the name of two Isr.:–Gemariah.
1588. גַּן *gan;* from 1598; a *garden* (as *fenced*):–garden.
1589. גָּנַב *gaw-nab';* a prim. root; to *thieve* (lit. or fig.); by impl., to *deceive:*–carry away, X indeed, secretly bring, steal (away), get by stealth.
1590. גַּנָּב *gaw-nab';* from 1589; a *stealer:*–thief.
1591. גְּנֵבָה *ghen-ay-baw';* from 1589; *stealing,* i.e. (concr.) something *stolen:*–theft.
1592. גְּנֻבַת *ghen-oo-bath';* from 1589; *theft; Genubath,* an Edomitish prince:–Genubath.
1593. גַּנָּה *gan-naw';* fem. of 1588; a *garden:*–garden.
1594. גִּנָּה *ghin-naw';* another form for 1593:–garden.
1595. גֶּנֶז *gheh'-nez;* from an un. root mean. to *store; treasure;* by impl., a *coffer:*–chest, treasury.
1596. גְּנַז *ghen-az'* (Chald.); cor. to 1595; treasure:–treasure.
1597. גִּנְזַךְ *ghin-zak';* prol. from 1595; a *treasury:*–treasury.
1598. גָּנַן *gaw-nan';* prim. root; to *hedge* about, i.e. (gen.) *protect:*–defend.
1599. גִּנְּתוֹן *ghin-neth-one;* or גִּנְּתוֹ *ghin-neth-o';* from 1598; *gardener; Ginnethon* or *Ginnetho,* an Isr.:–Ginnetho, Ginnethon.
1600. גָּעָה *gaw-aw';* a prim. root; to *bellow* (as cattle):–low.
1601. גֹּעָה *go-aw';* fem. act.part. of 1600; *lowing; Goah,* a place near Jerus.:–Goath.
1602. גָּעַל *gaw-al';* a prim. root; to *detest;* by impl., to *reject:*–abhor, fail, lothe, vilely cast away.
1603. גַּעַל *gah'-al;* from 1602; *loathing;* Gaal, an Isr.:–Gaal.
1604. גֹּעַל *go'-al;* from 1602; *abhorrence:*–loathing.
1605. גָּעַר *gaw-ar';* a prim. root; to *chide:*–corrupt, rebuke, reprove.
1606. גְּעָרָה *gheh-aw-raw';* from 1605; a *chiding:*–rebuke(-ing), reproof.
1607. גָּעַשׁ *gaw-ash';* a prim. root to *agitate* violently:–move, shake, toss, trouble.
1608. גַּעַשׁ *ga'-ash;* from 1607; a *quaking; Gaash,* a hill in Pal.:–Gaash.
1609. גַּעְתָּם *gah-tawm';* of unc. der.; *Gatam,* an Edomite:–Gatam.
1610. גַּף *gaf;* from an un. root mean. to *arch;* the *back;* by ext. the *body* or self:–+ highest places, himself.
1611. גַּף *gaf* (Chald.); cor. to 1610; a *wing:*–wing.
1612. גֶּפֶן *gheh'-fen;* from an un. root mean. to *bend;* a *vine* (as *twining*), esp. the grape:–vine, tree.
1613. גֹּפֶר *go'-fer;* from an un. root, prob. mean. to *house in;* a kind of tree or wood (as used for *building*), app. the *cypress:*– gopher.
1614. גָּפְרִית *gof-reeth';* prob. fem. of 1613; prop. *cypress-resin;* by anal., *sulphur* (as equally inflammable):–brimstone.
1615. גִּר *gheer;* perh. from 3564; *lime* (from being *burned* in a kiln):–chalk-[stone].
1616. גֵּר *gare;* or (fully) גֵּיר *gare;* from 1481; prop. a *guest;* by impl., a *foreigner:*–alien, sojourner, stranger.
1617. גֵּרָא *gay-raw';* perh. from 1626; a

grain; Gera, the name of six Isr.:–Gera.
1618. גָּרָב *gaw-rawb';* from an un. root mean. to *scratch; scurf* (from *itching*):–scab, scurvy.
1619. גָּרֵב *gaw-rabe';* from the same as 1618; *scabby; Gareb,* the name of an Isr., also of a hill near Jerus.:–Gareb.
1620. גַּרְגַּר *gar-gar';* by redupl. from 1641; a *berry* (as if a pellet of *rumination*):–berry.
1621. גַּרְגְּרוֹת *gar-gher-owth';* fem. pl. from 1641; the *throat* (as used in *rumination*):–neck.
1622. גִּרְגָּשִׁי *ghir-gaw-shee';* patrial from an un. name [of unc. der.]; a *Girgashite,* one of the nat. tribes of Canaan:–Girgashite, Girgasite.
1623. גָּרַד *gaw-rad';* a prim. root; to *abrade:*–scrape.
1624. גָּרָה *gaw-raw';* a prim. root; prop. *to grate,* i.e. (fig.) to *anger:*–contend, meddle, stir up, strive.
1625. גֵּרָה *gay-raw';* from 1641; the *cud* (as *scraping* the throat):–cud.
1626. גֵּרָה *gay-raw';* from 1641 (as in 1625); prop. (like 1620) a *kernel* (round as if *scraped*), i.e. a *gerah* or small weight (and coin):– gerah.
1627. גָּרוֹן *gaw-rone';* or (short.) גָּרֹן *gaw-rone';* from 1641; the *throat* [comp. 1621] (as *roughened* by swallowing):–X aloud, mouth, neck, throat.
1628. גֵּרוּת *gay-rooth';* from 1481; a (temporary) *residence:*–habitation.
1629. גָּרַז *gaw-raz';* a prim. root; to *cut* off:–cut off.
1630. גְּרִזִים *gher-ee-zeem';* pl. of an un. noun from 1629 [comp. 1511], *cut* up (i.e. *rocky*); *Gerizim,* a mountain of Pal.:–Gerizim.
1631. גַּרְזֶן *gar-zen';* from 1629; an *axe:*–ax.
1632. גָּרֹל *gaw-role';* from the same as 1486; *harsh:*–man of great.
1633. גָּרַם *gaw-ram';* a prim. root; to be *spare* or *skeleton-like;* used only as a denom. from 1634; (caus.) to *bone,* i.e. *denude* (by ext., *craunch*) the bones:–gnaw the bones, break.
1634. גֶּרֶם *gheh'-rem;* from 1633; a *bone* (as the *skeleton* of the body); hence, *self,* i.e. (fig.) *very:*–bone, strong, top.
1635. גְּרַם *gheh'-rem* (Chald.); cor. to 1634; a *bone:*–bone.
1636. גַּרְמִי *gar-mee';* from 1634; *bony,* i.e. *strong:*–Garmite.
1637. גֹּרֶן *go'-ren;* from an un. root mean. to *smooth;* a threshing-*floor* (as made *even*); by anal., any open *area:*–(barn, corn, threshing-) floor, (threshing-, void) place.
1638. גָּרַס *gaw-ras';* a prim. root; to *crush;* also (intr. and fig.) to *dissolve:*–break.
1639. גָּרַע *gaw-rah';* a prim. root; to *scrape* off; by impl., to *shave, remove, lessen, withhold:*–abate, clip, (di-) minish, do (take) away, keep back, restrain, make small, withdraw.
1640. גָּרַף *gaw-raf';* a prim. root; to *bear* off violently:–sweep away.
1641. גָּרַר *gaw-rar';* a prim. root; to *drag* off roughly; by impl., to *bring up* the cud (i.e. *ruminate*); by anal., to *saw:*–catch, chew, X continuing, destroy, saw.
1642. גְּרָר *gher-awr';* prob. from 1641; a *rolling* country; *Gerar,* a Philistine city:–Gerar.
1643. גֶּרֶשׂ *gheh'-res;* from an un. root mean. to *husk;* a *kernel* (coll.), i.e. *grain:*–beaten corn.
1644. גָּרַשׁ *gaw-rash';* a prim. root; to drive out from a possession; esp. to *expatriate* or *divorce:*–cast up (out), divorced (woman), drive away (forth, out), expel, X surely put away, trouble, thrust out.
1645. גֶּרֶשׁ *gheh'-resh;* from 1644; *produce* (as if *expelled*):–put forth.
1646. גְּרֻשָׁה *gher-oo-shaw';* fem. pass.part. of 1644; (abstr.) *dispossession:*–exaction.
1647. גֵּרְשֹׁם *gay-resh-ome';* for 1648; *Gereshom,* the name of four Isr.:–Gershom.
1648. גֵּרְשׁוֹן *gay-resh-one';* or גֵּרְשׁוֹם *gay-resh-ome';* from 1644; a *refugee; Gereshon* or *Gereshom,* an Isr.:–Gershon, Gershom.
1649. גֵּרְשֻׁנִּי *gay-resh-oon-nee';* patron. from 1648; a *Gereshonite* or desc. of Gereshon:–Gershonite, sons of Gershon.
1650. גְּשׁוּר *ghesh-oor';* from an un. root (mean. to *join*); *bridge; Geshur,* a district of Syria:–Geshur, Geshurite.
1651. גְּשׁוּרִי *ghe-shoo-ree';* patrial from 1650; a *Geshurite* (also coll.) or inh. of Geshur:–Geshuri, Geshurites.
1652. גָּשַׁם *gaw-sham';* a prim. root; to *shower* violently:–(cause to) rain.
1653. גֶּשֶׁם *gheh'-shem;* from 1652; a *shower:*–rain, shower.
1654. גֶּשֶׁם *gheh'-shem* or (prol.) גַּשְׁמוּ *gash-moo';* the same as 1653; *Geshem* or *Gashmu,* an Arabian:–Geshem, Gashmu.
1655. גֶּשֶׁם *gheh'-shem* (Chald.); app. the same as 1653; used in a peculiar sense, the *body* (prob. for the [fig.] idea of a *hard* rain):–body.
1656. גֹּשֶׁם *go'-shem;* from 1652; equiv. to 1653:–rained upon.
1657. גֹּשֶׁן *go'-shen;* prob. of Eg. or.; *Goshen,* the residence of the Isr. in Eg.; also a place in Pal.:–Goshen.
1658. גִּשְׁפָּא *ghish-paw';* of unc. der.; *Gishpa,* an Isr.:–Gispa.
1659. גָּשַׁשׁ *gaw-shash';* a prim. root; app. to *feel* about:–grope.
1660. גַּת *gath;* prob. from 5059 (in the sense of *treading* out grapes); a wine-*press* (or vat for holding the grapes in pressing them):–(wine-)press (fat).
1661. גַּת *gath;* the same as 1660; *Gath,* a Philistine city:–Gath.
1662. גַּת־הַחֵפֶר *gath-hah-khay'-fer;* or (abridged) גִּתָּה־חֵפֶר *ghit-taw-khay'-fer;* from 1660 and 2658 with the art. ins.; *wine-press* of *(the) well; Gath-Chepher,* a place in Pal.:–Gath-kephr, Gittah-kephr.
1663. גִּתִּי *ghit-tee';* patrial from 1661; a *Gittite* or inh. of Gath:–Gittite.
1664. גִּתַּיִם *ghit-tah'-yim* dual of 1660; *double wine-press; Gittajim,* a place in Pal.:–Gittaim.
1665. גִּתִּית *ghit-teeth';* fem. of 1663; a *Gittite* harp:–Gittith.
1666. גֶּתֶר *gheh'-ther;* of unc. der.; *Gether,* a son of Aram, and the region settled by him:–Gether.
1667. גַּת־רִמּוֹן *gath-rim-mone';* from 1660 and 7416; *wine-press* of (the) *pomegranate; Gath-Rimmon,* a place in Pal.:–Gath-rimmon.

ד

1668. דָּא *daw* (Chald.); cor. to 2088; *this:*–one..another, this.
1669. דָּאַב *daw-ab';* a prim. root; to *pine:*–mourn, sorrow(-ful).
1670. דְּאָבָה *dĕh-aw-baw';* from 1669; prop. *pining;* by anal., *fear:*–sorrow.
1671. דְּאָבוֹן *dĕh-aw-bone';* from 1669; *pining:*–sorrow.
1672. דָּאַג *daw-ag';* a prim. root; be *anxious:*–be afraid (careful, sorry), sorrow, take thought.
1673. דֹּאֵג *do-ayg';* or (fully) דּוֹאֵג *do-ayg';* act. part. of 1672; *anxious; Doëg,* an Edomite:–Doeg.
1674. דְּאָגָה *dĕh-aw-gaw';* from 1672; *anxiety:*–care(-fulness), fear, heaviness, sorrow.
1675. דָּאָה *daw-aw';* a prim. root; to *dart,* i.e. *fly* rapidly:–fly.
1676. דָּאָה *daw-aw';* from 1675; the *kite* (from its rapid *flight*):–vulture. See 7201.
1677. דֹּב *dobe;* or (fully) דּוֹב *dobe;* from 1680; the *bear* (as slow):–bear.
1678. דֹּב *dobe* (Chald.); cor. to 1677:–bear.
1679. דֹּבֶא *do'-beh;* from an un. root (comp. 1680) (prob. mean. to *be sluggish,* i.e. *restful*); *quiet:*–strength.
1680. דָּבַב *daw-bab'* a prim. root (comp. 1679); to *move* slowly, i.e. *glide:*–cause to speak.
1681. דִּבָּה *dib-baw';* from 1680 (in the sense of *furtive* motion); *slander:*–defaming, evil report, infamy, slander.
1682. דְּבוֹרָה *deb-o-raw';* or (short.) דְּבֹרָה *deb-o-raw';* from 1696 (in the sense of *orderly* motion); the *bee* (from its *systematic* instincts):–bee.
1683. דְּבוֹרָה *deb-o-raw';* or (short.) דְּבֹרָה *deb-o-raw';* the same as 1682; *Deborah,* the name of two Hebrewesses:–Deborah.
1684. דְּבַח *deb-akh'* (Chald.); cor. to 2076; to *sacrifice* (an animal):–offer [sacrifice].
1685. דְּבַח *deb-akh'* (Chald.); from 1684; a *sacrifice:*–sacrifice.
1686. דִּבְיוֹן *dib-yone';* in the marg. for the textual reading, חֶרְיוֹן *kher-yone;* both (in the pl. only and) of unc. der.; prob. some cheap vegetable, perh. a bulbous root:–dove's dung.
1687. דְּבִיר *deb-eer'* or (short.) דְּבִר *deb-eer';* from 1696 (app. in the sense of *oracle*); the *shrine* or innermost part of the sanctuary:–oracle.
1688. דְּבִיר *deb-eer';* or (short.) דְּבִר (Jos. 13:26 [but see 3810]) *deb-eer';* the same as 1687; *Debir,* the name of an Amoritish king and of two places in Pal.:–Debir.
1689. דִּבְלָה *dib-law';* prob. an orth. err. for 7247; *Diblah,* a place in Syria:–Diblath.
1690. דְּבֵלָה *deb-ay-law';* from an un. root (akin to 2082) prob. mean. to *press* together; a *cake* of pressed figs:–cake (lump) of figs.
1691. דִּבְלַיִם *dib-lah'-yim;* dual from the masc. of 1690; *two cakes; Diblajim,* a symbolic name:–Diblaim.
1692. דָּבַק *daw-bak';* a prim. root; prop. to *impinge,* i.e. *cling* or *adhere;* fig., to *catch* by pursuit:–abide fast, cleave (fast together), follow close (hard after), be joined (together), keep (fast), overtake, pursue hard, stick, take.
1693. דְּבַק *deb-ak'* (Chald.); cor. to 1692; to *stick* to:–cleave.
1694. דֶּבֶק *deh'-bek;* from 1692; a *joint;* by impl., *solder:*–joint, solder.
1695. דָּבֵק *daw-bake';* from 1692; *adhering:*–cleave, joining, stick closer.
1696. דָּבַר *daw-bar';* a prim. root; perh. prop. to *arrange;* but used fig. (of words), to *speak;* rarely (in a destructive sense) to *subdue:*–answer, appoint, bid, command,

commune, declare, destroy, give, name, promise, pronounce, rehearse, say, speak, be spokesman, subdue, talk, teach, tell, think, use [entreaties], utter, X well, X work.

1697. דָּבָר *daw-bawr';* from 1696; a *word;* by impl., a *matter* (as *spoken* of) or *thing;* adv., a *cause:*–act, advice, affair, answer, X any such (thing), because of, book, business, care, case, cause, certain rate, + chronicles, commandment, X commune(-ication), + concern[-ing], + confer, counsel, + dearth, decree, deed, X disease, due, duty, effect, + eloquent, errand, [evil favoured-] ness, + glory, + harm, hurt, + iniquity, + judgment, language, + lying, manner, matter, message, [no] thing, oracle, X ought, X parts, + pertaining, + please, portion, + power, promise, provision, purpose, question, rate, reason, report, request, X (as hast) said, sake, saying, sentence, + sign, + so, some [uncleanness], somewhat to say, + song, speech, X spoken, talk, task, + that, X there done, thing (concerning), thought, + thus, tidings, what[-soever], + wherewith, which, word, work.

1698. דֶּבֶר *deh'-ber;* from 1696 (in the sense of *destroying*); a *pestilence:*–murrain, pestilence, plague.

1699. דֹּבֶר *do'-ber;* from 1696 (in its or. sense); a *pasture* (from its *arrangement* of the flock):–fold, manner.

1699'. דִּבֵּר *dib-bare;* for 1697:–word

1700. דִּבְרָה *dib-raw'* fem. of 1697; a *reason, suit or style:*–cause, end, estate, order, regard.

1701. דִּבְרָה *dib-raw';* (Chald.); cor. to 1700:–intent, sake.

1702. דֹּבְרָה *do-ber-aw';* fem. act.part. of 1696 in the sense of *driving* [comp. 1699]; a *raft:*–float.

1703. דַּבָּרָה *dab-baw-raw';* intens. from 1696; a *word:*–word.

1704. דִּבְרִי *dib-ree';* from 1697; *wordy; Dibri,* an Isr.:–Dibri.

1705. דָּבְרַת *daw-ber-ath';* from 1697 (perh. in the sense of 1699); *Daberath,* a place in Pal.:–Dabareh, Daberath.

1706. דְּבַשׁ *deb-ash';* from an un. root mean. to *be gummy; honey* (from its *stickiness*); by anal., *syrup:*–honey([-comb]).

1707. דַּבֶּשֶׁת *dab-beh'-sheth;* intens. from the same as 1706; a sticky *mass,* i.e. the *hump* of a camel:–hunch [of a camel].

1708. דַּבֶּשֶׁת *dab-beh'-sheth;* the same as 1707; *Dabbesheth,* a place in Pal.:–Dabbesheth.

1709. דָּג *dawg;* or (fully) דָּאג (Nehemiah 13:16) *dawg;* from 1711; a *fish* (as *prolific*); or perh. rather from 1672 (as *timid*); but still better from 1672 (in the sense of *squirming,* i.e. moving by the vibratory action of the tail); a *fish* (often used coll.):–fish.

1710. דָּגָה *daw-gaw';* fem. of 1709, and mean. the same:–fish.

1711. דָּגָה *daw-gaw';* a prim. root; to *move rapidly;* used only as a denom. from 1709; to *spawn,* i.e. *become numerous:*–grow.

1712. דָּגוֹן *daw-gohn';* from 1709; the *fish-god; Dagon,* a Philistine deity:–Dagon.

1713. דָּגַל *daw-gal';* a prim. root; to *flaunt,* i.e. *raise a flag;* fig., to *be conspicuous:*–(set up, with) banners, chiefest.

1714. דֶּגֶל *deh'-gel;* from 1713; a *flag:*–banner, standard.

1715. דָּגָן *daw-gawn';* from 1711; prop. *increase,* i.e. *grain:*–corn ([floor]), wheat.

1716. דָּגַר *daw-gar';* a prim. root, to *brood* over eggs or young:–gather, sit.

1717. דַּד *dad;* app. from the same as 1730; the *breast* (as the seat of *love,* or from its shape):–breast, teat.

1718. דָּדָה *daw-daw';* a doubtful root; to *walk gently:*–go (softly, with).

1719. דְּדָן *ded-awn';* or (prol.) דְּדָנֶה (Eze. 25:13) *deh-daw'-neh;* of unc. der.; *Dedan,* the name of two Cushites and of their territory:–Dedan.

1720. דְּדָנִים *ded-aw-neem';* pl. of 1719 (as patrial); *Dedanites,* the desc. or inh. of Dedan:–Dedanim.

1721. דֹּדָנִים *do-daw-neem';* or (by orth. err.) רֹדָנִים 1 Ch.. 1:7) *ro-daw-neem;* a pl. of unc. der.; *Dodanites,* or desc. of a son of Javan:–Dodanim.

1722. דְּהַב *deh-hab'* (Chald.); cor. to 2091; *gold:*–gold(-en).

1723. דַּהֲוָא *dah-hav-aw'* (Chald.); of unc. der.; *Dahava,* a people colonized in Samaria:–Dehavites.

1724. דָּהַם *daw-ham';* a prim. root (comp. 1740); to *be dumb,* i.e. (fig.) *dumbfounded:*–astonished.

1725. דָּהַר *daw-har';* a prim. root; to *curvet* or move irregularly:–panse.

1726. דַּהֲהַר *dah-hah-har';* by redupl. from 1725; a *gallop:*–pransing.

1727. דּוּב *doob;* a prim. root; to *mope,* i.e. (fig.) *pine:*– sorrow.

1728. דַּוָּג *dav-vawg';* an orth. var. of 1709 as a denom. [1771]; a *fisherman:*–fisher.

1729. דּוּגָה *doo-gaw';* fem. from the same as 1728; prop. *fishery,* i.e. a *hook* for fishing:–fish [hook].

1730. דּוֹד *dode;* or (short.) דֹּד *dode;* from an un. root mean. prop. to *boil,* i.e. (fig.) to *love;* by impl., a *love-token, lover, friend;* spec. an *uncle:*–(well-)beloved, father's brother, love, uncle.

1731. דּוּד *dood;* from the same as 1730; a *pot* (for *boiling*); also (by resemblance of shape) a *basket:*–basket, caldron, kettle, (seething) pot.

1732. דָּוִד *daw-veed';* rarely (fully); דָּוִיד *daw-veed';* from the same as 1730; *loving; David,* the youngest son of Jesse:–David.

1733. דּוֹדָה *do-daw';* fem. of 1730; an *aunt:*–aunt, father's sister, uncle's wife.

1734. דּוֹדוֹ *do-do';* from 1730; *loving; Dodo,* the name of three Isr.:–Dodo.

1735. דּוֹדָוָהוּ *do-daw-vaw'-hoo;* from 1730 and 3050; *love of Jah; Dodavah,* an Isr.:–Dodavah.

1736. דּוּדַי *doo-dah'-ee;* from 1731; a *boiler* or *basket;* also the *mandrake* (as an *aphrodisiac*):–basket, mandrake.

1737. דּוֹדַי *do-dah'ee;* formed like 1736; *amatory; Dodai,* an Isr.:–Dodai.

1738. דָּוָה *daw-vaw';* a prim. root; to *be sick* (as if in menstruation):–infirmity.

1739. דָּוֶה *daw-veh';* from 1738; *sick* (esp. in menstruation):–faint, menstruous cloth, she that is sick, having sickness.

1740. דּוּחַ *doo'-akh;* a prim. root; to *thrust* away; fig., to *cleanse:*–cast out, purge, wash.

1741. דְּוַי *dev-ah'ee;* from 1739; *sickness;* fig., *loathing:*–languishing, sorrowful.

1742. דַּוָּי *dav-voy';* from 1739; *sick;* fig., *troubled:*–faint.

1743. דּוּךְ *dook;* a prim. root; to *bruise* in a mortar:–beat.

1744. דּוּכִיפַת *doo-kee-fath';* of unc. der.; the *hoopoe* or else the *grouse:*–lapwing.

1745. דּוּמָה *doo-maw';* from an un. root mean. to *be dumb* (comp. 1820); *silence;* fig., *death:*–silence.

1746. דּוּמָה *doo-maw';* the same as 1745; *Dumah,* a tribe and region of Arabia:–Dumah.

1747. דּוּמִיָּה *doo-me-yaw';* rom 1820; *stillness;* adv., *silently;* abstr. *quiet, trust:*–silence, silent, waiteth.

1748. דּוּמָם *doo-mawm';* from 1826; *still;* adv., *silently:*–dumb, silent, quietly wait.

1749. דּוֹנַג *do-nag';* of unc. der.; *wax :*–wax.

1750. דּוּץ *doots;* a prim. root; to *leap:*–be turned.

1751. דּוּק *dook* (Chald.); cor. to 1854; to *crumble:*–be broken to pieces.

1752. דּוּר *dure;* a prim. root; prop. to *gyrate* (or move in a circle), i.e. to *remain:*–dwell.

1753. דּוּר *dure* (Chald.); cor. to 1752; to *reside:*–dwell.

1754. דּוּר *dure;* from 1752; a *circle, ball* or *pile:*–ball, turn, round about.

1755. דּוֹר *dore;* or (short.) דֹּר *dore;* from 1752; prop. a *revolution* of time, i.e. an *age* or generation; also a *dwelling:*–age, X evermore, generation, [n-]ever, posterity.

1756. דּוֹר *dore;* or (by perm.) דֹּאר (Jos. 17:11; 1 Kings 4:11) *dore;* from 1755; *dwelling; Dor,* a place in Pal.:–Dor.

1757. דּוּרָא *doo-raw'* (Chald.); prob. from 1753; *circle* or *dwelling; Dura,* a place in Babylonia:–Dura.

1758. דּוּשׁ *doosh;* or דּוֹשׁ *dosh;* or דִּישׁ *deesh;* a prim. root; to *trample* or *thresh:*–break, tear, thresh, tread out (down), at grass .

1759. דּוּשׁ *doosh* (Chald.); cor. to 1758; to *trample:*–tread down.

1760. דָּחָה *daw-khaw';* or (Jer. 23:12) דָּחַח *daw-khakh';* a prim. root; to *push* down:–chase, drive away (on), overthrow, outcast, X sore, thrust, totter.

1761. דַּחֲוָה *dakh-av-aw'* (Chald.); from the equiv. of 1760; prob. a mus. *instrument* (as being *struck*):–instrument of music.

1762. דְּחִי *deh-khee';* from 1760; a *push,* i.e. (by impl.) a *fall:*–falling.

1763. דְּחַל *deh-khal'* (Chald.); cor. to 2119; to *slink,* i.e. (by impl.) to *fear,* or (caus.) be *formidable:*–make afraid, dreadful, fear, terrible.

1764. דֹּחַן *do'-khan;* of unc. der.; *millet:*–millet.

1765. דָּחַף *daw-khaf';* a prim. root; to *urge,* i.e. *hasten:*–(be) haste(-ned), pressed on.

1766. דָּחַק *daw-khak';* a prim. root; to *press,* i.e. *oppress:*–thrust, vex.

1767. דַּי *dahee;* of unc. der.; *enough* (as noun or adv.), used chiefly with prep. in phrases:–able, according to, after (ability), among, as (oft as), (more than) enough, from, in, since, (much as is) sufficient(-ly), too much, very, when.

1768. דִּי *dee* (Chald.); app. for 1668; *that,* used as rel. conj., and esp. (with a prep.) in adv. phrases; also as prep. *of:*–X as, but, for (-asmuch +), + now, of, seeing, than, that, therefore, until, + what (-soever), when, which, whom, whose.

1769. דִּיבוֹן *dee-bone';* or (short.) דִּיבֹן *dee-bone';* from 1727; *pining:*–*Dibon,* the name of three places in Pal.:–Dibon. [*Also, with* 1410 *added,* Dibon-gad.]

1770. דִּיג *deeg;* denom. from 1709; to *fish:*–fish.
1771. דַּיָּג *dah-yawg';* from 1770; a *fisherman:*–fisher.
1772. דַּיָּה *dah-yaw';* intens. from 1675; a *falcon* (from its *rapid* flight):–vulture.
1773. דְּיוֹ *deh-yo';* of unc. der.; *ink:*–ink.
1774. דִּי זָהָב *dee zaw-hawb';* as if from 1768 and 2091; *of gold*; *Dizahab,* a place in the Desert:–Dizahab.
1775. דִּימוֹן *dee-mone';* perh. for 1769; *Dimon,* a place in Pal.:–Dimon.
1776. דִּימוֹנָה *dee-mo-naw';* fem. of 1775; *Dimonah,* a place in Pal.:–Dimonah.
1777. דִּין *deen;* or (Ge. 6:3) דּוּן *doon;* a prim. root [comp. 113]; *to rule;* by impl. to *judge* (as umpire); also to *strive* (as at law):–contend, execute (judgment), judge, minister judgment, plead (the cause), at strife, strive.
1778. דִּין *deen* (Chald.); cor. to 1777; *judge:*–judge.
1779. דִּין *deen;* or (Job 19:29) דּוּן *doon;* from 1777; *judgment* (the suit, justice, sentence or tribunal); by impl. also *strife:*–cause, judgment, plea, strife.
1780. דִּין *deen* (Chald.); cor. to 1779:–judgment.
1781. דַּיָּן *dah-yawn';* from 1777; a *judge* or *advocate:*–judge.
1782. דַּיָּן *dah-yawn'* (Chald.); cor. to 1781:–judge.
1783. דִּינָה *dee-naw';* fem. of 1779; *justice; Dinah,* the daughter of Jacob:–Dinah.
1784. דִּינַי *dee-nah'ee* (Chald.); patrial from unc. prim.; a *Dinaite* or inh. of some unknown Assyria province:–Dinaite.
1785. דָּיֵק *daw-yake';* from a root cor. to 1751; a *battering*-tower:–fort.
1786. דַּיִשׁ *day'-yish;* from 1758*; threshing*-time:–threshing.
1787. דִּישׁוֹן, דִּשׁוֹן, דִּשֹׁן or דִּשֹׁן *dee-shone';* the same as 1788; *Dishon,* the name of two Edomites:–Dishon.
1788. דִּישֹׁן *dee-shone';* from 1758; the *leaper,* i.e. an *antelope:*–pygarg.
1789. דִּישָׁן *dee-shawn';* another form of 1787 *Dishan,* an Edomite:–Dishan, Dishon.
1790. דַּךְ *dak;* from an un. root (comp. 1794); *crushed,* i.e. (fig.) *injured:*–afflicted, oppressed.
1791. דֵּךְ *dake* (Chald.); or דָּךְ *dawk;* prol. from 1668; *this:*–the same, this.
1792. דָּכָא *daw-kaw';* a prim. root (comp. 1794); to *crumble;* trans., to *bruise* (lit. or fig.):–beat to pieces, break (in pieces), bruise, contrite, crush, destroy, humble, oppress, smite.
1793. דַּכָּא *dak-kaw';* from 1792; *crushed* (lit. *powder,* or fig., *contrite*):–contrite, destruction.
1794. דָּכָה *daw-kaw';* a prim. root (comp. 1790, 1792); to *collapse* (phys. or ment.):–break (sore), contrite, crouch.
1795. דַּכָּה *dak-kaw';* from 1794 like 1793; *mutilated:*–+ wounded.
1796. דֳּכִי *dok-ee';* from 1794; a *dashing* of surf:–wave.
1797. דִּכֵּן *dik-kane'* (Chald.); prol. from 1791; *this:*–same, that, this.
1798. דְּכַר *dek-ar'* (Chald.); cor. to 2145; prop. a *male,* i.e. of sheep:–ram.
1799. דִּכְרוֹן *dik-rone'* (Chald.); or דָּכְרָן *dok-rawn'* (Chald.); cor. to 2146; a *register:*–record.
1800. דַּל *dal;* from 1809; prop. *dangling,* i.e. (by impl.) *weak* or *thin:*–lean, needy, poor (man), weaker.
1801. דָּלַג *daw-lag';* a prim. root; to *spring:*–leap.
1802. דָּלָה *daw-law';* a prim. root (comp. 1809); prop. to *dangle,* i.e. to *let down* a bucket (for *drawing* out water); fig., to *deliver:*–draw (out), X enough, lift up.
1803. דַּלָּה *dal-law';* from 1802; prop. something *dangling,* i.e. a loose *thread* or *hair;* fig., *indigent:*–hair, pining sickness, poor(-est sort).
1804. דָּלַח *daw-lakh';* a prim. root; to *roil* water:–trouble.
1805. דְּלִי *del-ee';* or דֳּלִי *dol-ee';* from 1802; a *pail* or *jar* (for *drawing* water):–bucket.
1806. דְּלָיָה *del-aw-yaw';* or (prol.) דְּלָיָהוּ *del-aw-yaw'-hoo;* from 1802 and 3050; *Jah has delivered; Delajah,* the name of five Isr.:–Dalaiah, Delaiah.
1807. דְּלִילָה *del-ee-law';* from 1809; *languishing:–Delilah,* a Philistine woman:–Delilah.
1808. דָּלִית *daw-lee-yaw';* from 1802; something *dangling,* i.e. a *bough:*–branch.
1809. דָּלַל *daw-lal';* a prim. root (comp. 1802); to *slacken* or *be feeble;* fig., to *be oppressed:*–bring low, dry up, be emptied, be not equal, fail, be impoverished, be made thin.
1810. דִּלְעָן *dil-awn';* of unc. der.; *Dilan,* a place in Pal.:–Dilean.
1811. דָּלַף *daw-laf';* a prim. root; to *drip*; by impl., to *weep:*–drop through, melt, pour out.
1812. דֶּלֶף *deh'-lef;* from 1811; a *dripping:*–dropping.
1813. דַּלְפוֹן *dal-fone';* from 1811; *dripping; Dalphon,* a son of Haman:–Dalphon.
1814. דָּלַק *daw-lak';* a prim. root; to *flame* (lit. or fig.):–burning, chase, inflame, kindle, persecute(-or), pursue hotly.
1815. דְּלַק *del-ak'* (Chald.); cor. to 1814:–burn.
1816. דַּלֶּקֶת *dal-lek'-keth;* from 1814; a *burning* fever:–inflammation.
1817. דֶּלֶת *deh'-leth;* from 1802; something *swinging,* i.e. the *valve* of a door:–door (two-leaved), gate, leaf, lid. [In Ps. 141:3, *dâl,* irreg.].
1818. דָּם *dawm;* from 1826 (comp. 119); *blood* (as that which when shed causes *death*) of man or an animal; by anal., the *juice* of the grape; fig. (esp. in the pl.) *bloodshed* (i.e. *drops* of blood):–blood(-y, -guiltiness, [-thirsty], + innocent.
1819. דָּמָה *daw-maw';* a prim. root; to comp.; by impl., to *resemble, liken, consider:*–comp., devise, (be) like(-n), mean, think, use similitudes.
1820 דָּמָה *daw-maw';* a prim. root; to be *dumb* or *silent;* hence, to *fail* or *perish;* trans. to *destroy:*–cease, be cut down (off), destroy, be brought to silence, be undone, X utterly.
1821. דְּמָה *dem-aw'* (Chald.); cor. to 1819; to *resemble:*–be like.
1822. דֻּמָּה *doom-maw';* from 1820; *desolation;* concr., *desolate:*–destroy.
1823. דְּמוּת *dem-ooth';* from 1819; *resemblance;* concr., *model, shape;* adv., *like:*–fashion, like (-ness, as), manner, similitude.
1824. דְּמִי *dem-ee';* or דֳּמִי *dom-ee';* from 1820; *quiet:*–cutting off, rest, silence.
1825. דִּמְיוֹן *dim-yone';* from 1819; *resemblance:*–X like.
1826. דָּמַם *daw-man';* a prim root [comp. 1724, 1820]; to *be dumb;* by impl., to *be astonished,* to *stop;* also to *perish:*–cease, be cut down (off), forbear, hold peace, quiet self, rest, be silent, keep (put to) silence, be (stand) still, tarry, wait.
1827. דְּמָמָה *dem-aw-maw';* fem. from 1826; *quiet:*–calm, silence, still.
1828. דֹּמֶן *do'-men;* of unc. der.; *manure:*–dung.
1829. דִּמְנָה *dim-naw';* fem. from the same as 1828; a *dung-heap; Dimnah,* a place in Pal.:–Dimnah.
1830. דָּמַע *daw-mah';* a prim. root; to *weep:*–X sore, weep.
1831. דֶּמַע *deh'-mah;* from 1830; a *tear;* fig., *juice:*–liquor.
1832. דִּמְעָה *dim-aw';* fem. of 1831; *weeping:*–tears.
1833. דְּמֶשֶׁק *dem-eh'-shek;* by orth. var. from 1834*; damask* (as a fabric of Damascus):–in Damascus.
1834. דַּמֶּשֶׂק *dam-meh'-sek;* or דּוּמֶשֶׂק *doo-meh'-sek;* or דַּרְמֶשֶׂק *dar-meh'-sek;* of for. or.; *Damascus,* a city of Syria:–Damascus.
1835. דָּן *dawn;* from 1777; *judge; Dan,* one of the sons of Jacob; also the tribe descended from him, and its territory; likewise a place in Pal. colonized by them:–Dan.
1836. דֵּן *dane* (Chald.); an orth. var. of 1791; *this:*–[afore-]time, + after this manner, here [-after], one...another, such, there[-fore], these, this (matter), + thus, where[-fore], which.
1837. דַּנָּה *dan-naw';* of unc. der.; *Dannah,* a place in Pal.:–Dannah.
1838. דִּנְהָבָה *din-haw-baw';* of unc. der.; *Dinhabah,* an Edomitish town:–Dinhaban.
1839. דָּנִי *daw-nee';* patron. from 1835; a *Danite* (often coll.) or desc. (or inh.) of Dan:–Danites, of Dan.
1840. דָּנִיֵּאל *daw-nee-yale';* in Eze. דָּנִאֵל *daw-nee-ale';* from 1835 and 410; *judge of God; Daniel* or *Danijel,* the name of two Isr.:–Daniel.
1841. דָּנִיֵּאל *daw-nee-yale'* (Chald.); cor. to 1840; *Danijel,* the Heb. prophet:–Daniel.
1842. דָּן יַעַן *dawn yah'-an;* from 1835 and (app.) 3282; *judge of purpose; Dan-Jaan,* a place in Pal.:–Dan-jaan.
1843. דֵּעַ *day'-ah;* from 3045; *knowledge:*–knowledge, opinion.
1844. דֵּעָה *day-aw';* fem. of 1843; *knowledge:*–knowledge.
1845. דְּעוּאֵל *deh-oo-ale';* from 3045 and 410; *known of God; Deüel,* an Isr.:–Deuel.
1846. דָּעַךְ *daw-ak';* a prim. root; to *be extinguished;* fig., to *expire* or *be dried up:*–be extinct, consumed, put out, quenched.
1847. דַּעַת *dah'-ath;* from 3045; *knowledge:*–cunning, [ig-]norantly, know(-ledge),[un-] awares (wittingly).
1848. דֳּפִי *dof'-ee* from an un. root (mean. to *push* over); a *stumbling*-block: –slanderest.
1849. דָּפַק *daw-fak';* a prim. root; to *knock;* by anal., to *press* severely:–beat, knock, overdrive.
1850. דָּפְקָה *dof-kaw';* from 1849; a *knock; Dophkah,* a place in the Desert:–Dophkah.
1851. דַּק *dak;* from 1854; *crushed,* i.e. (by impl.) *small* or *thin:*–dwarf, lean[-fleshed], very little thing, small, thin.
1852. דֹּק *doke;* from 1854; something *crumbling,* i.e. *fine* (as a *thin* cloth):–curtain.
1853. דִּקְלָה *dik-law';* of for. or.; *Diklah,* a region of Arabia:–Diklah.
1854. דָּקַק *daw-kak';* a prim. root [comp. 1915]; to *crush* (or intr.) *crumble:*–beat in pieces (small), bruise, make dust, (into) X powder, (be, very) small, stamp (small).
1855. דְּקַק *dek-ak'* (Chald.); cor. to 1854; to *crumble* or (trans.) *crush:*–break to pieces.

1856. דָּקַר *daw-kar';* a prim. root; to *stab;* by anal., to *starve;* fig., to *revile:*–pierce, strike (thrust) through, wound.
1857. דֶּקֶר *deh'-ker;* from 1856; a *stab; Deker,* an Isr.:–Dekar.
1858. דַּר *dar;* app. from the same as 1865; prop. a *pearl* (from its sheen as rapidly *turned*); by anal., *pearl-stone,* i.e. mother-of-pearl or alabaster:–X white.
1859. דָּר *dawr* (Chald.); cor. to 1755; an *age:*–generation.
1860. דְּרָאוֹן *der-aw-one';* or דֵּרָאוֹן *day-raw-one;* from an un. root (mean. to *repulse*); an obj. of *aversion:*–abhorring, contempt.
1861. דָּרְבוֹן *dor-bone';* [also *dor-bawn'*]; of unc. der.; a *goad:*–goad.
1862. דַּרְדַּע *dar-dah';* app. from 1858 and 1843; *pearl of knowledge; Darda,* an Isr.:–Darda.
1863. דַּרְדַּר *dar-dar';* of unc. der.; a *thorn:*–thistle.
1864. דָּרוֹם *daw-rome';* of unc. der.; the *south;* poet. the *south wind:*–south.
1865. דְּרוֹר *der-ore';* from an un. root (mean. to *move rapidly*); *freedom;* hence, *spontaneity* of outflow, and so *clear:*–liberty, pure.
1866. דְּרוֹר *der-ore';* the same as 1865, applied to a bird; the *swift,* a kind of swallow:–swallow.
1867. דָּרְיָוֶשׁ *daw-reh-yaw-vaysh';* of Pers. or.; *Darejavesh,* a title (rather than name) of several Pers. kings:–Darius.
1868. דָּרְיָוֶשׁ *daw-reh-yaw-vaysh'* (Chald.); cor. to 1867:–Darius.
1869. דָּרַךְ *daw-rak';* a prim. root; to *tread;* by impl., to *walk;* also to *string* a bow (by treading on it in bending):–archer, bend, come, draw, go (over), guide, lead (forth), thresh, tread (down), walk.
1870. דֶּרֶךְ *deh'-rek;* from 1869; a *road* (as *trodden*); fig., a *course* of life or *mode* of action, often adv.:–along, away, because of, + by, conversation, custom, [east-]ward, journey, manner, passenger, through, toward, [high-] [path-]way [-side], whither [-soever].
1871. דַּרְכְּמוֹן *dar-kem-one';* of Pers. or.; a "*drachma,*" or coin:–dram.
1872. דְּרָע *der-aw'* (Chald.); cor. to 2220; an *arm:*–arm.
1873. דָּרַע *daw-rah';* prob. a contr.from 1862; *Dara,* an Isr.:–Dara.
1874. דַּרְקוֹן *dar-kone';* of unc. der.; *Darkon,* one of "Solomon's servants":–Darkon.
1875. דָּרַשׁ *daw-rash';* a prim. root; prop. to *tread* or *frequent;* usually to *follow* (for pursuit or search); by impl., to *seek* or *ask;* spec. to *worship:*–ask, X at all, care for, X diligently, inquire, make inquisition, [necro-]mancer, question, require, search, seek [for, out], X surely.
1876. דָּשָׁא *daw-shaw';* a prim. root; to *sprout:*–bring forth, spring.
1877. דֶּשֶׁא *deh'-sheh;* from 1876; a *sprout;* by anal., *grass:*–(tender) grass, green, (tender)herb.
1878. דָּשֵׁן *daw-shane';* a prim. root; to *be fat;* trans., to *fatten* (or regard as fat); spec. to *anoint;* fig., to *satisfy;* denom. (from 1880) to *remove* (fat) *ashes* (of sacrifices):–accept, anoint, take away the (receive) ashes (from), make (wax) fat.
1879. דָּשֵׁן *daw-shane';* from 1878; *fat;* fig., *rich, fertile:*–fat.
1880. דֶּשֶׁן *deh'-shen;* from 1878; the *fat;* abstr. *fatness,* i.e. (fig.) *abundance;* spec. the (fatty) *ashes* of sacrifices:– ashes, fatness.
1881. דָּת *dawth;* of unc. (perh. for.) der.: a royal *edict* or statute:–commandment, commission, decree, law, manner.
1882. דָּת *dawth;* (Chald.); cor. to 1881; decree, law.
1883. דֶּתֶא *deh'-thay* (Chald.); cor. to 1877:–tender grass.
1884. דְּתָבָר *deth-aw-bawr'* (Chald.); of Pers. or.; mean. one *skilled in law;* a *judge:*–counsellor.
1885. דָּתָן *daw-thawn';* of unc. der.; *Dathan,* an Isr.:–Dathan.
1886. דֹּתָן *do'-thawn;* or (Chald. dual) דֹּתַיִן (Ge. 37:17) *do-thah'-yin;* of unc. der.; *Dothan,* a place in Pal.:–Dothan.

ה

1887. הֵא *hay;* a prim. particle; *lo!:*–behold, lo.
1888. הֵא *hay* (Chald.); or הָא *haw* (Chald.); cor. to 1887:–even, lo.
1889. הֶאָח *heh-awkh';* from 1887 and 253; *aha!:*–ah, aha, ha.
1890. הַבְהָב *hab-hawb';* by redupl. from 3051; *gift* (in sacrifice), i.e. *holocaust:*–offering.
1891. הָבַל *haw-bal';* a prim. root; to *be vain* in act, word, or expectation; spec. to *lead astray:*–be (become, make) vain.
1892. הֶבֶל *heh'bel;* or (rarely in the abs.) הֲבֵל *hab-ale';* from 1891; *emptiness* or *vanity;* fig., something *transitory* and *unsatisfactory;* often used as an adv.:–X altogether, vain, vanity.
1893. הֶבֶל *heh'-bel;* the same as 1892; *Hebel,* the son of Adam:–Abel.
1894. הֹבֶן *ho'-ben;* only in pl., from an un. root mean. to *be hard; ebony:*–ebony.
1895. הָבַר *haw-bar';* a prim. root of unc. (perh. for.) der.; to *be a horoscopist:*–+ (astro-)loger.
1896. הֵגֵא *hay-gay';* or (by perm.) הֵגַי *hay-gah'-ee;* prob. of Pers. or.; *Hege* or *Hegai,* a eunuch of Xerxes:–Hegai, Hege.
1897. הָגָה *haw-gaw';* a prim. root [comp. 1901]; to *murmur* (in pleasure or anger); by impl., to *ponder:*–imagine, meditate, mourn, mutter, roar, X sore, speak, study, talk, utter.
1898. הָגָה *haw-gaw';* a prim. root; to *remove:*–stay, stay away.
1899. הֶגֶה *heh'-geh;* from 1897; a *muttering* (in sighing, thought, or as thunder):–mourning, sound, tale.
1900. הָגוּת *haw-gooth';* from 1897; *musing:*–meditation.
1901. הָגִיג *haw-gheeg';* from an un. root akin to 1897; prop. a *murmur,* i.e. *complaint:*–meditation, musing.
1902. הִגָּיוֹן *hig-gaw-yone';* intens. from 1897; a *murmuring* sound, i.e. a mus. notation (prob. similar to the modern *affettuoso* to indicate solemnity of movement); by impl., a *machination:*–device, Higgaion, meditation, solemn sound.
1903. הָגִין *haw-gheen';* of unc. der.; perh. *suitable* or *turning:*–directly.
1904. הָגָר *haw-gawr';* of unc. (perh. for.) der.; *Hagar,* the mother of Ishmael:–Hagar.
1905. הַגְרִי *hag-ree';* or (prol.) הַגְרִיא *hag-ree';* perh. patron. from 1904; a *Hagrite* or member of a certain Arabian clan:–Hagarene, Hagarite, Haggeri.
1906. הֵד *hade;* for 1959; a *shout:*–sounding again.
1907. הַדָּבָר *had-daw-bawr'* (Chald.); prob. of for. or.; a *vizier:*–counsellor.
1908. הֲדַד *had-ad';* prob. of for. or. [comp. 111]; *Hadad,* the name of an idol, and of several kings of Edom:–Hadad.
1909. הֲדַדְעֶזֶר *had-ad-eh'-zer;* from 1908 and 5828; *Hadad* (is his) *help; Hadadezer,* a Syrian king:–Hadadezer. Comp. 1928.
1910. הֲדַדְרִמּוֹן *had-ad-rim-mone';* from 1908 and 7417; *Hadad-Rimmon,* a place in Pal.:–Hadad-rimmon.
1911. הָדָה *haw-daw';* a prim. root [comp. 3034]; to *stretch forth* the hand:–put.
1912. הֹדּוּ *ho'-doo;* of for. or.; *Hodu* (i.e. Hindû-stan):–India.
1913. הֲדוֹרָם *had-o-rawm'* or הֲדֹרָם *had-o-rawm';* prob. of for. der.; *Hadoram,* a son of Joktan, and the tribe descended from him:– Hadoram.
1914. הִדַּי *hid-dah'ee;* of unc. der.; *Hiddai,* an Isr.:–Hiddai.
1915. הָדַךְ *haw-dak';* a prim. root [comp. 1854]; to *crush* with the foot:–tread down.
1916. הֲדֹם *had-ome';* from an un. root mean. to *stamp* upon; a foot-stool:–[foot-] stool.
1917. הַדָּם *had-dawm'* (Chald.); from a root cor. to that of 1916; something *stamped* to pieces, i.e. a *bit:*–piece.
1918. הֲדַס *had-as';* of unc. der.; the *myrtle:*–myrtle (tree).
1919. הֲדַסָּה *had-as-saw'* fem. of 1918; *Hadassah* (or Esther):–Hadassah.
1920. הָדַף *haw-daf';* a prim root; to *push* away or down:–cast away (out), drive, expel, thrust (away).
1921. הָדַר *haw-dar'* a prim. root; to *swell* up (lit. or fig., act.or pass.); by impl., to *favor* or *honour, be high* or *proud:*–countenance, crooked place, glorious, honour, put forth.
1922. הֲדַר *had-ar'* (Chald.); cor. to 1921; to *magnify* (fig.):–glorify, honour.
1923. הֲדַר *had-ar'* (Chald.); from 1922; *magnificence:*–honour, majesty.
1924. הֲדַר *had-ar';* the same as 1926; *Hadar,* an Edomite:–Hadar.
1925. הֶדֶר *heh'-der;* from 1921; *honour;* used (fig.) for the *capital* city (Jerus.):–glory.
1926. הָדָר *haw-dawr';* from 1921; *magnificence,* i.e. ornament or splendor:–beauty, comeliness, excellency, glorious, glory, goodly, honour, majesty.
1927. הֲדָרָה *had-aw-raw';* fem. of 1926; *decoration:*–beauty, honour.
1928. הֲדַרְעֶזֶר *had-ar-eh'-zer;* from 1924 and 5828; *Hadar* (i.e. *Hadad,* 1908) is his *help; Hadarezer* (i.e. Hadadezer, 1909), a Syrian king:–Hadarezer.
1929. הָהּ *haw;* a short. form of 162; ah! expressing grief:–woe worth.
1930. הוֹ *ho;* by perm. from 1929; *oh!:*–alas.
1931. הוּא *hoo;* of which the fem. (beyond the Pentateuch) is הִיא *he;* a prim. word, the third pers. pron. sing., he (*she* or *it*); only expressed when emphat. or without a verb; also (intens.) *self,* or (esp. with the art.) the same; sometimes (as demonstr.) *this* or *that;* occasionally (instead of copula) *as* or *are:*–he, as for her, him(-self), it, the same, she (herself), such, that (...it), these, they, this, those, which (is), who.
1932. הוּא *hoo* (Chald.); or (fem.) הִיא *he;* cor. to 1931:–X are, it, this.
1933. הָוָא *haw-vaw';* or הָוָה *haw-vaw';* a prim. root [comp. 183, 1961] supposed to mean prop. to *breathe;* to *be* (in the sense of

existence):–be, X have.
1934. הֲוָא *hav-aw'* (Chald.); or הֲוָה *hav-aw'* (Chald.); cor. to 1933; to *exist;* used in a great variety of appl. (esp. in connection with other words):–be, become, + behold, + came (to pass), + cease, + cleave, + consider, + do, + give, + have, + judge, + keep, + labour, + mingle (self), + put, + see, + seek, + set, + slay, + take heed, tremble, + walk, + would.
1935. הוֹד *hode;* from an un. root; *grandeur* (i.e. an imposing form and appearance):–beauty,comeliness,excellency, glorious, glory, goodly, honour, majesty.
1936. הוֹד *hode;* the same as 1935*; Hod,* an Isr.:–Hod.
1937. הוֹדְוָה *ho-dev-aw';* a form of 1938; *Hodevah* (or Hodevjah), an Isr.:–Hodevah.
1938. הוֹדַוְיָה *ho-dav-yaw';* from 1935 and 3050; *majesty of Jah; Hodavjah,* the name of three Isr.:–Hodaviah.
1939. הוֹדַיְוָהוּ *ho-dah-yeh-vaw'-hoo;* a form of 1938; *Hodajvah,* an Isr.:–Hodaiah.
1940. הוֹדִיָּה *ho-dee-yaw';* a form for the fem. of 3064; a *Jewess:*–Hodiah.
1941. הוֹדִיָּה *ho-dee-yaw';* a form of 1938; *Hodijah,* the name of three Isr.:–Hodijah.
1942. הַוָּה *hav-vaw';* from 1933 (in the sense of eagerly *coveting* and *rushing* upon; by impl., of *falling*); *desire;* also *ruin:*–calamity, iniquity, mischief, mischievous (thing), naughtiness, naughty, noisome, perverse thing, substance, very wickedness.
1943. הֹוָה *ho-vaw'*; another form for 1942; *ruin*:–mischief.
1944. הוֹהָם *ho-hawm';* of unc. der.; *Hoham,* a Canaanitish king:–Hoham.
1945. הוֹי *hoh'ee;* a prol. form of 1930 [akin to 188]; *oh!:*–ah, alas, ho, O, woe.
1946. הוּךְ *hook* (Chald.); cor. to 1981; to *go;* caus., to *bring:*–bring again, come, go (up).
1947. הוֹלֵלָה *ho-lay-law';* fem. act.part.of 1984; *folly:*–madness.
1948. הוֹלֵלוּת *ho-lay-looth';* from act.part.of 1984; *folly:*–madness.
1949. הוּם *hoom;* a prim. root [comp. 2000]; to *make an uproar,* or *agitate* greatly:–destroy, move, make a noise, put, ring again.
1950. הוֹמָם *ho-mawm';* from 2000; *raging; Homam,* an Edomitish chieftain:–Homam. Comp. 1967.
1951. הוּן *hoon;* a prim. root; prop. to be *naught,* i.e. (fig.) to *be* (caus., act) *light:*–be ready.
1952. הוֹן *hone;* from the same as 1951 in the sense of 202; *wealth;* by impl., *enough:*–enough, + for nought, riches, substance, wealth.
1953. הוֹשָׁמָע *ho-shaw-maw';* from 3068 and 8085; *Jehovah has heard; Hoshama,* an Isr.:–Hoshama.
1954. הוֹשֵׁעַ *ho-shay'-ah; from 3467; deliverer*; *Hosheä,* the name of five Isr.:–Hosea, Hoshea, Oshea.
1955. הוֹשַׁעְיָה *ho-shah-yaw';* from 3467 and 3050; *Jah has saved; Hoshajah,* the name of two Isr.:–Hoshaiah.
1956. הוֹתִיר *ho-theer';* from 3498; *he has caused to remain; Hothir,* an Isr.:–Hothir.
1957. הָזָה *haw-zaw';* a prim. root (comp. 2372); to *dream:*–sleep.
1958. הִי *he;* for 5092; *lamentation:*–woe. (For הִיא *hee,* see 1931, 1932.)
1959. הֵידָד *hay-dawd';* from an un. root (mean. to *shout*); *acclamation:*–shout(-ing).
1960. הֻיְּדָה *hoo-yed-aw';* from the same as 1959; prop. an *acclaim,* i.e. a *choir* of singers:–thanksgiving.
1961. הָיָה *haw-yaw;* a prim. root [comp. 1933]; to *exist,* i.e. *be* or *become, come to pass* (always emphat., and not a mere copula or auxiliary):–beacon, X altogether, be(-come), accomplished, committed, like), break, cause, come (to pass), do, faint, fall, + follow, happen, X have, last, pertain, quit (one-)self, require, X use.
1962. הַיָּה *hah-yaw';* another form for 1943; *ruin:*–calamity.
1963. הֵיךְ *hake;* another form for 349; *how?:*–how.
1964. הֵיכָל *hay-kawl';* prob. from 3201 (in the sense of *capacity*); a large public building, such as a *palace* or *temple:*–palace, temple.
1965. הֵיכַל *hay-kal'* (Chald.); cor. to 1964:–palace, temple.
1966. הֵילֵל *hay-lale';* from 1984 (in the sense of *brightness*):–lucifer.
1967. הֵימָם *hay-mawm';* another form for 1950; *Hemam,* an Idumaean:–Hemam.
1968. הֵימָן *hay-mawn';* prob. from 539; *faithful; Heman,* the name of at least two Isr.:–Heman.
1969. הִין *heen;* prob. of Eg. or.; a *hin* or liquid measure:–hin.
1970. הָכַר *haw-kar';* a prim. root; app. to *injure:*–make self strange.
1971. הַכָּרָה *hak-kaw-raw';* from 5234; *respect,* i.e. partiality:–shew.
1972. הָלָא *haw-law';* prob. denom. from 1973; to *remove* or be *remote:*–cast far off.
1973. הָלְאָה *haw-leh-aw';* from the prim. form of the art. [הַל hal]; *to the distance,* i.e. *far away;* also (of time) *thus far:*–back, beyond, (hence,-) forward, hitherto, thenceforth, yonder.
1974. הִלּוּל *hil-lool';* from 1984 (in the sense of *rejoicing*); a *celebration* of thanksgiving for harvest:–merry, praise.
1975. הַלָּז *hal-lawz';* from 1976; *this* or *that:*–side, that, this.
1976. הַלָּזֶה *hal-law-zeh';* from the art. [see 1973] and 2088; *this very:*–this.
1977. הַלֵּזוּ *hal-lay-zoo';* another form of 1976; *that:*–this.
1978. הָלִיךְ *haw-leek';* from 1980; a *walk,* i.e. (by impl.) a *step:*–step.
1979. הֲלִיכָה *hal-ee-kaw';* fem. of 1978; a *walking;* by impl., a *procession* or *march,* a *caravan:*–company, going, walk, way.
1980. הָלַךְ *haw-lak';* akin to 3212; a prim. root; to *walk* (in a great variety of appl., lit. and fig.):–(all) along, apace, behave (self), come, (on) continually, be conversant, depart, + be eased, enter, exercise (self), + follow, forth, forward, get, go (about, abroad, along, away, forward, on, out, up and down), + greater, grow, be wont to haunt, lead, march, X more and more, move (self), needs, on, pass (away), be at the point, quite, run (along), + send, speedily, spread, still, surely, + tale-bearer, + travel(-ler), walk (abroad, on, to and fro, up and down, to places), wander, wax, way-] faring man, X be weak, whirl.
1981. הֲלַךְ *hal-ak'* (Chald.); cor. to 1980 [comp. 1946]; to *walk:*–walk.
1982. הֵלֶךְ *hay'-lek;* from 1980; prop. a *journey,* i.e. (by impl.) a *wayfarer;* also a *flowing:*–X dropped, traveller.
1983. הֲלָךְ *hal-awk'* (Chald.); from 1981; prop. a *journey,* i.e. (by impl.) *toll* on goods at a road:–custom.
1984. הָלַל *haw-lal';* a prim. root; to *be clear* (or. of sound, but usually of color); to *shine;* hence, to *make a show,* to *boast;* and thus to *be* (clamorously) *foolish;* to *rave;* caus., to *celebrate;* also to *stultify:*–(make) boast (self), celebrate, commend, (deal, make), fool(- ish, -ly), glory, give [light], be (make, feign self) mad (against), give in marriage, [sing, be worthy of] praise, rage, renowned, shine.
1985. הִלֵּל *hil-layl';* from 1984; *praising* (namely God); *Hillel,* an Isr.:–Hillel.
1986. הָלַם *haw-lam';* a prim. root; to *strike* down; by impl., to *hammer, stamp, conquer, disband:*–beat (down), break (down), overcome, smite (with the hammer).
1987. הֶלֶם *hay'-lem;* from 1986; *smiter; Helem,* the name of two Isr.:–Helem.
1988. הֲלֹם *hal-ome';* from the art. [see 1973]; *hither:*–here, hither(-[to]), thither.
1989. הַלְמוּת *hal-mooth'* from 1986; a *hammer* (or *mallet*):–hammer.
1990. הָם *hawm;* of unc. der.; *Ham,* a region of Pal.:–Ham.
1991. הֵם *haym;* from 1993; *abundance,* i.e. *wealth:*–any of theirs.
1992. הֵם *haym;* or (prol.) הֵמָּה *haym'-maw;* masc. pl. from 1981; *they* (only used when emphat.):–it, like, X (how, so) many (soever, more as) they (be), (the) same, X so, X such, their, them, these, they, those, which, who, whom, withal, ye.
1993. הָמָה *haw-maw';* a prim. root [comp. 1949]; to *make a loud sound* like Engl. "hum"); by impl., to *be in great commotion* or *tumult,* to *rage, war, moan, clamor:*–clamorous, concourse, cry aloud, be disquieted, loud, mourn, be moved, make a noise, rage, roar, sound, be troubled, make in tumult, tumultuous, be in an uproar.
1994. הִמּוֹ *him-mo'* (Chald.); or (prol.) הִמּוֹן *him-mone';* cor. to 1992; *they:*–X are, them, those.
1995. הָמוֹן *haw-mone';* or הָמֹן (Eze. 5:7) *haw-mone';* from 1993; a *noise, tumult, crowd;* also *disquietude, wealth:*–abundance, company, many, multitude, multiply, noise, riches, rumbling, sounding, store, tumult.
1996. הֲמוֹן גּוֹג *ham-one' gohg;* from 1995 and 1463; the *multitude of Gog;* the fanciful name of an emblematic place in Pal.:–Hamogog.
1997. הֲמוֹנָה *ham-o-naw';* fem. of 1995; *multitude; hamonah,* the same as 1996:–Hamonah.
1998. הֶמְיָה *hem-yaw';* from 1993; *sound:*–noise.
1999. הֲמֻלָּה *ham-ool-law';* or (too fully) הֲמוּלָּה (Jer. ll:l6) *ham-ool-law';* fem. pass. part. of an un. root mean. to *rush* (as rain with a windy roar); a *sound:*–speech, tumult.
2000. הָמַם *haw-mam';* a prim. root [comp. 1949, 1993]; prop. to *put in commotion;* by impl., to *disturb, drive, destroy:*–break, consume, crush, destroy, discomfit, trouble, vex.
2001. הָמָן *haw-mawn';* of for. derivation; *Haman,* a Pers. vizier:–Haman.
2002. הַמְנִיךְ *ham-neek'* (Chald.); but the text is הֲמוּנֵךְ *ham-oo-nayk';* of for. or.; a *necklace:*–chain.
2003. הָמָס *haw-mawce';* from an un. root app. mean. to *crackle;* a dry *twig* or *brushwood:*–melting.
2004. הֵן *hane;* fem. pl. from 1931; *they* (only used when emphat.):– X in, such like, (with) them, thereby, therein, (more than)

they, wherein, in which, whom, withal.
2005. הֵן *hane;* a prim. particle; *lo!*; also (as expressing surprise) *if:*–behold, if, lo, though.
2006. הֵן *hane* (Chald.); cor. to 2005: *lo!* also *there*[-fore], [un-]*less, whether, but, if:*–(that) if, or, whether.
2007. הֵנָּה *hane'-naw;* prol. for 2004; *themselves* (often used emphat. for the copula, also in indirect relation):–X in, X such (and such things), their, (into) them, thence, therein, these, they (had), on this side, whose, wherein.
2008. הֵנָּה *hane'-naw;* from 2004; *hither* or *thither* (but used both of place and time):–here, hither[-to], now, on this (that) side, + since, this (that) way, thitherward, + thus far, to...fro, + yet.
2009. הִנֵּה *hin-nay';* prol. for 2005; *lo!:*–behold, lo, see.
2010. הֲנָחָה *han-aw-khaw';* from 5117; *permission* of rest, i.e. *quiet:*–release.
2011. הִנֹּם *hin-nome';* prob. of for. or.; *Hinnom,* app. a Jebusite:–Hinnom.
2012. הֵנַע *hay-nah';* prob. of for. derivation; *Hena,* a place app. in Mesopotamia:–Hena.
2013. הָסָה *haw-saw';* a prim. root; to *hush:*–hold peace (tongue), (keep) silence, be silent, still.
2014. הֲפֻגָה *haf-oo-gaw';* from 6313; *relaxation:*–intermission.
2015. הָפַךְ *haw-fak';* a prim. root; to *turn* about or over; by impl., to *change, overturn, return, pervert:*–X become, change, come, be converted, give, make (a bed), overthrow (-turn), perverse, retire, tumble, turn (again, aside, back, to the contrary, every way).
2016. הֶפֶךְ *heh'-fek;* or הֵפֶךְ *hay'-fek;* from 2015; a *turn,* i.e. the *reverse:*–contrary.
2017. הֹפֶךְ *ho'-fek;* from 2015; an *upset,* i.e. (abstr.) *perversity:*–turning of things upside down.
2018. הֲפֵכָה *haf-ay-kaw';* fem. of 2016; *destruction:*–overthrow.
2019. הֲפַכְפַּךְ *haf-ak-pak';* by redupl. from 2015; *very perverse:*–froward.
2020. הַצָּלָה *hats-tsaw-law';* from 5337; *rescue:*–deliverance.
2021. הֹצֶן *ho'-tsen;* from an un. root mean. app. to *be sharp* or *strong;* a *weapon* of war:–chariot.
2022. הַר *har;* a short. form of 2042; a *mountain* or *range* of hills (sometimes used fig.):–hill (country), mount(-ain), X promotion.
2023. הֹר *hore;* another form of 2022; *mountain; Hor,* the name of a peak in Idumaea and of one in Syria:–Hor.
2024. הָרָא *haw-raw';* perh. from 2022; *mountainousness; Hara,* a region of Media:–Hara.
2025. הַרְאֵל *har-ale';* from 2022 and 410; *mount of God;* fig., the *altar* of burnt-offering:–altar. Comp. 739.
2026. הָרַג *haw-rag';* a prim. root; to *smite* with deadly intent:–destroy, out of hand, kill, murder(-er), put to [death], make [slaughter], slay(-er), X surely.
2027. הֶרֶג *heh'-reg;* from 2026; *slaughter:*–be slain, slaughter.
2028. הֲרֵגָה *har-ay-gaw';* fem. of 2027; *slaughter:*–slaughter.
2029. הָרָה *haw-raw';* a prim. root; to *be* (or *become*) *pregnant, conceive* (lit. or fig.):–been, be with child, conceive, progenitor.
2030. הָרֶה *haw-reh';* or הָרִי (Ho. 14:1) *haw-ree';* from 2029; *pregnant:*–(be, woman) with child, conceive, X great.
2031. הַרְהֹר *har-hor';* (Chald.); from a root cor. to 2029; a ment. *conception:*–thought.
2032. הֵרוֹן *hay-rone';* or הֵרָיוֹן *hay-raw-yone';* from 2029; *pregnancy:*–conception.
2033. הֲרוֹרִי *har-o-ree';* another form for 2043; a *Harorite* or mountaineer:–Harorite.
2034. הֲרִיסָה *har-ee-saw';* from 2040; something *demolished:*–ruin.
2035. הֲרִיסוּת *har-ee-sooth';* from 2040; *demolition:*–destruction.
2036. הֹרָם *ho-rawm';* from an un. root (mean. to *tower* up); *high; Horam,* a Canaanitish king:–Horam.
2037. הָרֻם *haw-room';* pass.part. of the same as 2036; *high; Harum,* an Isr.:–Harum.
2038. הַרְמוֹן *har-mone';* from the same as 2036; a *castle* (from its height):–palace.
2039. הָרָן *haw-rawn';* perh. from 2022; *mountaineer; Haran,* the name of two men:–Haran.
2040. הָרַס *haw-ras';* a prim. root; to *pull* down or in pieces, *break, destroy:*–beat down, break (down, through), destroy, overthrow, pluck down, pull down, ruin, throw down, X utterly.
2041. הֶרֶס *heh'-res;* from 2040; *demolition:*–destruction.
2042. הָרָר *haw-rawr';* from an un. root mean. to *loom* up; a *mountain:*–hill, mount(-ain).
2043. הֲרָרִי *hah-raw-ree';* or הָרָרִי or (2 Sa. 23:11) *haw-raw-ree';* or הָאֲרָרִי (2 Sa. 23:34, (last clause), *haw-raw-ree';* app. from 2042; a *mountaineer:*–Hararite.
2044. הָשֵׁם *haw-shame';* perh. from the same as 2828; *wealthy; Hashem,* an Isr.:–Hashem.
2045. הַשְׁמָעוּת *hashmaw-ooth';* from 8085; *announcement:*–to cause to hear.
2046. הִתּוּךְ *hit-took';* from 5413; a *melting:*–is melted.
2047. הֲתָךְ *hath-awk';* prob. of for. or.; *Hathak,* a Pers. eunuch:–Hatach.
2048. הָתַל *haw-thal';* a prim. root; to *deride;* by impl., to *cheat:*–deal deceitfully, deceive, mock.
2049. הָתֹל *haw-thole';* from 2048 (only in pl. coll.); a *derision:*–mocker.
2050. הָתַת *haw-thath';* a prim. root; prop. to *break* in upon, i.e. to *assail:*–imagine mischief.

ו

2051. וְדָן *ved-awn';* perh. for 5730; Vedan (or Aden), a place in Arabia:–Dan also.
2052. וָהֵב *vaw-habe';* of unc. der.; *Vaheb,* a place in Moab:–what he did.
2053. וָו *vaw';* prob. a *hook* (the name of the sixth Heb. letter):–hook.
2054. וָזָר *vaw-zawr';* presumed to be from an un. root mean. to *bear* guilt; *crime:*–X strange.
2055. וַיְזָתָא *vah-yez-aw'-thaw;* of for. or.; *Vajezatha,* a son of Haman:–Vajezatha.
2056. וָלָד *vaw-lawd';* for 3206; a *boy:*–child.
2057. וַנְיָה *van-yaw';* perh. for 6043; *Vanjah,* an Isr.:–Vaniah.
2058. וָפְסִי *vof-see';* prob. from 3254; *additional; Vophsi,* an Isr.:–Vophsi.
2059. וַשְׁנִי *vash-nee';* prob. from 3461; *weak; Vashni,* an Isr.:–Vashni.
2060. וַשְׁתִּי *vash-tee';* of Pers. or.; *Vashti,* the queen of Xerxes:–Vashti.

ז

2061. זְאֵב *zeh-abe';* from an un. root mean. to *be yellow;* a *wolf:*–wolf.
2062. זְאֵב *zeh-abe';* the same as 2061; *Zeëb,* a Midianitish prince:–Zeeb.
2063. זֹאת *zothe';* irreg. fem. of 2089; *this* (often used adv.):– hereby (-in, -with), it, likewise, the one (other, same), she, so (much), such (deed), that, therefore, these, this (thing), thus.
2064. זָבַד *zaw-bad';* a prim. root; to *confer:*–endure.
2065. זֶבֶד *zeh'-bed;* from 2064; a *gift:*–dowry.
2066. זָבָד *zaw-bawd';* from 2064; *giver; Zabad,* the name of seven Isr.:–Zabad.
2067. זַבְדִּי *zab-dee';* from 2065; *giving; Zabdi,* the name of four Isr.:–Zabdi.
2068. זַבְדִּיאֵל *zab-dee-ale';* from 2065 and 410; *gift of God: Zabdiel,* the name of two Isr.:–Zabdiel.
2069. זְבַדְיָה *zeb-ad-yaw';* or זְבַדְיָהוּ *zeb-ad-yaw'-hoo;* from 2064 and 3050; *Jah has given; Zebadjah,* the name of nine Isr.:–Zebadiah.
2070. זְבוּב *zeb-oob';* from an un. root (mean. to *flit*); a *fly* (esp. one of a stinging nat.):–fly.
2071. זָבוּד *zaw-bood';* from 2064; *given, Zabud,* an Isr.:–Zabud.
2072. זַבּוּד *zab-bood';* a form of 2071; *given; Zabbud,* an Isr.:–Zabbud.
2073. זְבוּל *ze-bool';* or זְבֻל *zeb-ool';* from 2082; a *residence:*–dwell in, dwelling, habitation.
2074. זְבוּלוּן *zeb-oo-loon';* or זְבֻלוּן *zeb-oo-loon';* or זְבוּלֻן *zeb-oo-loon';* from 2082; *habitation; Zebulon,* a son of Jacob; also his territory and tribe:–Zebulun.
2075. זְבוּלֹנִי *zeb-oo-lo-nee';* patron. from 2074; a *Zebulonite* or desc. of Zebulun:–Zebulonite.
2076. זָבַח *zaw-bakh';* a prim. root; to *slaughter* an animal (usually in sacrifice):–kill, offer, (do) sacrifice, slay.
2077. זֶבַח *zeh'-bakh;* from 2076; prop. a *slaughter,* i.e. the *flesh* of an animal; by impl., a *sacrifice* (the victim or the act):–offer(- ing), sacrifice.
2078. זֶבַח *zeh'-bakh;* the same as 2077; *sacrifice; Zebach,* a Midianitish prince:–Zebah.
2079. זַבַּי *zab-bah'-ee;* prob. by orth. err. for 2140; *Zabbai* (or Zaccai), an Isr.:–Zabbai.
2080. זְבִידָה *zeb-ee-daw';* fem. from 2064; *giving; Zebidah,* an Isr.s:–Zebudah.
2081. זְבִינָא *zeb-ee-naw';* from an un. root (mean. to *purchase*); *gainfulness; Zebina,* an Isr.:–Zebina.
2082. זָבַל *zaw-bal';* a prim. root; app. prop. to *inclose,* i.e. to *reside:*–dwell with.
2083. זְבֻל *zeb-ool'* the same as 2073; *dwelling; Zebul,* an Isr.:–Zebul. Comp. 2073.
2084. זְבַן *zeb-an'* (Chald.); cor. to the root of 2081; to *acquire* by purchase:–gain.
2085. זָג *zawg;* from an un. root prob. mean. to *inclose;* the *skin* of a grape:–husk.
2086. זֵד *zade';* from 2102; *arrogant:*–presumptuous, proud.
2087. זָדוֹן *zaw-done';* from 2102; *arrogance:*–presumptuously, pride, proud (man).
2088. זֶה *zeh;* a prim. word; the masc. demonstr. pron., *this* or *that:*–he, X hence, X here, it(-self), X now, X of him, the one...the other, X than the other, (X out of) the (self) same, such (a one) that, these, this (hath, man), on this side...on that side, X thus, very,

which. Comp. 2063, 2090, 2097, 2098.
2089. זֶה *zeh;* (1 Sa. by perm.for 7716; a *sheep:*–lamb.
2090. זֹה *zo;* for 2088; *this* or *that:*–as well as another, it, this, that, thus and thus.
2091. זָהָב *zaw-hawb';* from an un. root mean. to *shimmer; gold,* fig., something *gold-colored* (i.e. yellow), as *oil,* a *clear sky:*– gold(-en), fair weather.
2092. זָהַם *zaw-ham';* a prim. root; to be *rancid,* i.e. (trans.) to *loathe:*–abhor.
2093. זַהַם *zah'-ham;* from 2092; *loathing; Zaham,* an Isr.:–Zaham.
2094. זָהַר *zaw-har';* a prim. root; to *gleam;* fig., to *enlighten* (by caution):–admonish, shine, teach, (give) warn(-ing).
2095. זְהַר *zeh-har'* (Chald.); cor. to 2094; (pass.) *be admonished:*–take heed.
2096. זֹהַר *zo'-har;* from 2094; *brilliancy:*–brightness.
2097. זוֹ *zo;* for 2088; *this* or *that:*–that, this.
2098. זוּ *zoo;* for 2088; *this* or *that:*–that, this, X wherein, which, whom.
2099. זִו *zeev';* prob. from an un. root mean. to *be prominent;* prop. *brightness* [comp. 2122], i.e. (fig.) the month of *flowers; Ziv* (cor. to Ijar or May):–Zif.
2100. זוּב *zoob;* a prim. root; to *flow* freely (as water), i.e. (spec.) to *have a* (sexual) *flux;* fig., to *waste* away; also to *overflow:*–flow, gush out, have a (running) issue, pine away, run.
2101. זוֹב *zobe;* from 2100; a seminal or menstrual *flux:*–issue.
2102. זוּד *zood;* or (by perm.) זִיד *zeed;* a prim. root; to *seethe;* fig., to *be insolent:*–be proud, deal proudly, presume, (come) presumptuously, sod.
2103. זוּד *zood* (Chald.); cor. to 2102; to *be proud:*–in pride.
2104. זוּזִים *zoo-zeem';* pl. prob. from the same as 2123; *prominent; Zuzites,* an aboriginal tribe of Pal.:–Zuzims.
2105. זוֹחֵת *zo-khayth';* of unc. or.; *Zocheth,* an Isr.:–Zoheth.
2106. זָוִית *zaw-veeth';* app. from the same root as 2099 (in the sense of *prominence*); an *angle* (as *projecting*), i.e. (by impl.) a *corner-column* (or *anta*):–corner(stone).
2107. זוּל *zool;* a prim. root [comp. 2151]; prob. to *shake* out, i.e. (by impl.) to *scatter* profusely; fig., to *treat lightly:*–lavish, despise.
2108. זוּלָה *zoo-law';* from 2107; prob. *scattering,* i.e. *removal;* used adv., *except:*–beside, but, only, save.
2109 זוּן *zoon;* a prim. root; perh. prop. to *be plump,* i.e. (trans.) to *nourish:*–feed.
2110. זוּן *zoon* (Chald.); cor. to 2109:–feed.
2111. זוּעַ *zoo'-ah* a prim. root; prop. to *shake* off, i.e. (fig.) to *agitate* (as with fear):–move, tremble, vex.
2112. זוּעַ *zoo'-ah* (Chald.); cor. to 2111; to *shake* (with fear):–tremble.
2113. זְוָעָה *zev-aw-aw';* from 2111; *agitation, fear:*–be removed, trouble, vexation. Comp. 2189.
2114. זוּר *zoor;* a prim. root; to *turn* aside (esp. for lodging); hence to *be a foreigner, strange, profane;* spec. (act.part.) to *commit adultery:*–(come from) another (man, place), fanner, go away, (e-)strange(-r, thing, woman).
2115. זוּר *zoor;* a prim. root [comp. 6695]; to *press* together, *tighten:*–close, rush, thrust together.
2116. זוּרֶה *zoo-reh';* from 2115; *trodden* on:–that which is crushed.
2117. זָזָא *zaw-zaw';* prob. from the root of 2123; *prominent; Zaza,* an Isr.:–Zaza.
2118. זָחַח *zaw-khakh';* a prim. root; to *shove* or *displace:*–loose.
2119. זָחַל *zaw-khal';* a prim. root; to *crawl;* by impl., to *fear:*–be afraid, serpent, worm.
2120. זֹחֶלֶת *zo-kheh'-leth;* fem. act.part. of 2119; *crawling* (i.e. *serpent*); *Zocheleth,* a boundary stone in. Pal.:–Zoheleth.
2121. זֵידוֹן *zay-dohn';* from 2102; *boiling* of water, i.e. *wave:*–proud.
2122. זִיו *zeev* (Chald.); cor. to 2099; (fig.) *cheerfulness:*–brightness, countenance.
2123. זִיז *zeez;* from an un. root app. mean. to *be conspicuous; fulness* of the breast; also a moving *creature:*–abundance, wild beast.
2124. זִיזָא *zee-zaw';* app. from the same as 2123; *prominence; Ziza,* the name of two Isr.:–Ziza.
2125. זִיזָה *zee-zaw';* another form for 2124; *Zizah,* an Isr.:–Zizah.
2126. זִינָא *zee-naw';* from 2109; well-*fed;* or perh. an orth. err. for 2124; *Zina,* an Isr.:–Zina.
2127. זִיעַ *zee'-ah;* from 2111; *agitation; Zia,* an Isr.:–Zia.
2128. זִיף *zeef;* from the same as 2203; *flowing; Ziph,* the name of a place in Pal.; also of an Isr.:–Ziph.
2129. זִיפָה *zee-faw';* fem. of 2128; a *flowing; Ziphah,* an Isr.:–Ziphah.
2130. זִיפִי *zee-fee';* patrial from 2128; a *Ziphite* or inh. of Ziph:–Ziphim, Ziphite.
2131. זִיקָה (Is. 50:11) *zee-kaw';* (fem.); and זִק *zeek;* or זֵק *zake;* from 2187; prop. what *leaps* forth, i.e. *flash* of fire, or a burning *arrow;* also (from the or. sense of the root) a *bond:*–chain, fetter, firebrand, spark.
2132. זַיִת *zay'-yith;* prob. from an un. root [akin to 2099]; an *olive* (as yielding *illuminating* oil), the tree, the branch or the berry:–olive (tree, -yard), Olivet.
2133. זֵיתָן *zay-thawn';* from 2132; *olive* grove; *Zethan,* an Isr.:–Zethan.
2134. זַךְ *zak;* from 2141; *clear:*–clean, pure.
2135. זָכָה *zaw-kaw';* a prim. root [comp. 2141]; to *be translucent;* fig., to *be innocent:*–be (make) clean, cleanse, be clear, count pure.
2136. זָכוּ *zaw-koo'* (Chald.); from a root cor. to 2135; *purity:*–innocency.
2137. זְכוּכִית *zek-oo-keeth;* from 2135; prop. *transparency,* i.e. *glass:*–crystal.
2138. זָכוּר *zaw-koor';* prop. pass.part. of 2142, but used for 2145; a *male* (of man or animals):–males, men-children.
2139. זַכּוּר *zaw-koor';* from 2142; *mindful; Zakkur,* the name of seven Isr.:–Zaccur, Zacchur.
2140. זַכַּי *zak-kah'-ee;* from 2141; *pure; Zakkai,* an Isr.:–Zaccai.
2141. זָכַךְ *zaw-kak';* a prim. root [comp. 2135]; to *be transparent* or *clean* (phys. or mor.):–be (make) clean, be pure(-r).
2142. זָכַר *zaw-kar';* a prim. root; prop. to *mark* (so as to be recognized), i.e. to *remember;* by impl., to *mention;* also (as denom. from 2145) to *be male:*–X burn [incense], X earnestly, *be male,* (make) mention (of), be mindful, recount, record(-er), remember, make to be remembered, bring (call, come, keep, put) to (in) remembrance, X still, think on, X well.
2143. זֵכֶר *zay'-ker;* or זֶכֶר *zeh'-ker;* from 2142; a *memento,* abstr. *recollection* (rarely if ever); by impl., *commemoration:*–memorial, memory, remembrance, scent.
2144. זֶכֶר *zeh'-ker;* the same as 2143; *Zeker,* an Isr.:–Zeker.
2145. זָכָר *zaw-kawr';* from 2142; prop. *remembered,* i.e. a *male* (of man or animals, as being the most noteworthy sex):–X him, male, man(child, -kind).
2146. זִכְרוֹן *zik-rone';* from 2142; a *memento* (or memorable thing, day or writing):–memorial, record.
2147. זִכְרִי *zik-ree';* from 2142; *memorable; Zicri,* the name of twelve Isr.:–Zichri.
2148. זְכַרְיָה *zek-ar-yaw';* or זְכַרְיָהוּ *zek-ar-yaw'-hoo;* from 2142 and 3050; *Jah has remembered; Zecarjah,* the name of twenty-nine Isr.:–Zachariah, Zechariah.
2149. זֻלּוּת *zool-looth';* from 2151; prop. a *shaking,* i.e. perh. a *tempest:*–vilest.
2150. זַלְזַל *zal-zal';* by redupl. from 2151*; tremulous,* i.e. a *twig:*–sprig.
2151. זָלַל *zaw-lal';* a prim. root (comp. 2107); to *shake* (as in the wind), i.e. to *quake;* fig., to *be loose* mor., *worthless* or *prodigal:*–blow down, glutton, riotous (eater), vile.
2152. זַלְעָפָה *zal-aw-faw';* or זִלְעָפָה *zil-aw-faw';* from 2196; a *glow* (of wind or anger); also a *famine* (as *consuming*):–horrible, horror, terrible.
2153. זִלְפָּה *zil-paw;* from an un. root app. mean. to *trickle,* as myrrh; fragrant *dropping; Zilpah,* Leah's maid:–Zilpah.
2154. זִמָּה *zim-maw';* or זַמָּה *zam-maw';* from 2161; a *plan,* esp. a bad one:–heinous crime, lewd(-ly, -ness), mischief, purpose, thought, wicked (device, mind, -ness).
2155. זִמָּה *zim-maw';* the same as 2154; *Zimmah,* the name of two Isr.:–Zimmah.
2156. זְמוֹרָה *zem-o-raw';* or זְמֹרָה *zem-o-raw'* (fem.); and זְמֹר *zem-ore'* (masc.); from 2168; a *twig* (as *pruned*):–vine, branch, slip.
2157. זַמְזֹם *zam-zome';* from 2161; *intriguing;* a *Zamzumite,* or nat. tribe of Pal.:–Zamzummim.
2158. זָמִיר *zaw-meer';* or זָמִר *zaw-meer';* and (fem.) זְמִרָה *zem-ee-raw';* from 2167; a *song* to be accompanied with instrumental music:–psalm(-ist), singing, song.
2159. זָמִיר *zaw-meer';* from 2168; a *twig* (as *pruned*):–branch.
2160. זְמִירָה *zem-ee-raw';* fem. of 2158; *song; Zemirah,* an Isr.:–Zemira.
2161. זָמַם *zaw-mam';* a prim. root; to *plan,* usually in a bad sense:–consider, devise, imagine, plot, purpose, think (evil).
2162. זָמָם *zaw-mawm';* from 2161; a *plot:*–wicked device.
2163. זָמַן *zaw-man';* a prim. root; to *fix* (a time):–appoint.
2164. זְמַן *zem-an'* (Chald.); cor. to 2163; to *agree* (on a time and place):–prepare.
2165. זְמָן *zem-awn';* from 2163; an *appointed* occasion:–season, time.
2166. זְמָן *zem-awn'* (Chald.); from 2165; the same as 2165:–season, time.
2167. זָמַר *zaw-mar';* a prim. root [perh. ident. with 2168 through the idea of *striking* with the fingers]; prop. to *touch* the strings or parts of a mus. instrument, i.e. *play* upon it; to make *music,* accompanied by the voice; hence to *celebrate* in song and music:–give praise, sing forth praises, psalms.

2168. זָמַר *zaw-mar';* a prim. root [comp. 2167, 5568, 6785]; to *trim* (a vine):–prune.
2169. זֶמֶר *zeh'-mer;* app. from 2167 or 2168; a *gazelle* (from its lightly *touching* the ground):–chamois.
2170. זְמָר *zem-awr'* (Chald.); from a root cor. to 2167; instrumental *music*:–musick.
2171. זַמָּר *zam-mawr'* (Chald.); from the same as 2170; an instrumental *musician*:–singer.
2172. זִמְרָה *zim-raw';* from 2167; a *mus.* piece or *song* to be accompanied by an instrument:–melody, psalm.
2173. זִמְרָה *zim-raw';* from 2168; pruned (i.e. *choice*) fruit:–best fruit.
2174. זִמְרִי *zim-ree';* from 2167; *mus.; Zimri,* the name of five Isr., and of an Arabian tribe:–Zimri.
2175. זִמְרָן *zim-rawn';* from 2167; *musical; Zimran,* a son of Abraham by Keturah:–Zimran.
2176. זִמְרָת *zim-rawth'* from 2167; instrument. *music*; by impl., *praise*:–song.
2177. זַן *zan;* from 2109; prop. *nourished* (or fully *developed*), i.e. a *form* or *sort:*–divers kinds, X all manner of store.
2178. זַן *zan* (Chald.); cor. to 2177; *sort:*–kind.
2179. זָנַב *zaw-nab';* a prim. root mean. to *wag;* used only as a denom. from 2180; to *curtail,* i.e. *cut* off the rear:–smite the hindmost.
2180. זָנָב *zaw-nawb';* from 2179 (in the or. sense of *flapping*); the *tail* (lit. or fig.):–tail.
2181. זָנָה *zaw-naw';* a prim. root [highly-fed and therefore *wanton*]; to *commit adultery* (usually of the female, and less often of simple fornication, rarely of involuntary ravishment); fig., to *commit idolatry* (the Jewish people being regarded as the spouse of Jehovah):–(cause to) commit fornication, X continually, X great, (be an, play the) harlot, (cause to be, play the) whore, (commit, fall to) whoredom, (cause to) go a-whoring, whorish.
2182. זָנוֹחַ *zaw-no'-akh;* from 2186; *rejected; Zanoach,* the name of two places in Pal.:–Zanoah.
2183. זְנוּן *zaw-noon';* from 2181; *adultery;* fig., *idolatry:*–whoredom.
2184. זְנוּת *zen-ooth';* from 2181; adultery, i.e. (fig.) *infidelity, idolatry:*–whoredom.
2185. זֹנוֹת *zo-noth';* regarded by some as if from 2109 or an un. root, and applied to military *equipments;* –armour.
2186. זָנַח *zaw-nakh';* a prim. root mean. to *push* aside, i.e. *reject, forsake, fail:*–cast away (off), remove far away (off).
2187. זָנַק *zaw-nak';* a prim. root; prop. to *draw together* the feet (as an animal about to dart upon its prey), i.e. to *spring* forward:– leap.
2188. זֵעָה *zay-aw';* from 2111 (in the sense of 3154); *perspiration:*–sweat.
2189. זַעֲוָה *zah-av-aw';* by transp. for 2113; *agitation, maltreatment:*–X removed, trouble.
2190. זַעֲוָן *zah-av-awn';* from 2111; *disquiet; Zaavan,* an *Idumaean:*–Zaavan.
2191. זְעֵיר *zeh-ayr';* from an un. root [akin (by perm.] to 6819), mean. to *dwindle; small:*–little.
2192. זְעֵיר *zeh-ayr'* (Chald.); cor. to 2191:–*little.*
2193. זָעַךְ *zaw-ak';* a prim. root; to *extinguish:*–be extinct.
2194. זָעַם *zaw-am';* a prim. root; prop. to *foam* at the mouth, i.e. to *be enraged:*–abhor, abominable, (be) angry, defy, (have) indignation.
2195. זַעַם *zah'-am;* from 2194; strictly *froth* at the mouth, i.e. (fig.) *fury* (esp. of God's displeasure with sin):–angry, indignation, rage.
2196. זָעַף *zaw-af';* a prim. root; prop. to *boil* up, i.e. (fig.) to *be peevish* or *angry:*–fret, sad, worse liking, be wroth.
2197. זַעַף *zah'-af;* from 2196; *anger:*–indignation, rage(-ing), wrath.
2198. זָעֵף *zaw-afe';* from 2196; *angry:*–displeased.
2199. זָעַק *zaw-ak';* a prim. root; to *shriek* (from anguish or danger); by anal., (as a herald) to *announce* or *convene* publicly:–assemble, call (together), (make a) cry (out), come with such a company, gather (together), cause to be proclaimed.
2200. זְעִק *zek'-eek* (Chald.); cor. to 2199; to *make an outcry:*–cry.
2201. זַעַק *zah'-ak;* and (fem.) זְעָקָה *zeh-aw-kaw';* from 2199; a *shriek* or *outcry:*–cry(-ing).
2202. זִפְרֹן *zi-frone';* from an un. root (mean. to *be fragrant*); *Ziphron,* a place in Pal.:–Ziphron.
2203. זֶפֶת *zeh'-feth;* from an un. root (mean. to *liquify*); *asphalt* (from its tendency to *soften* in the sun):–pitch.
2204. זָקֵן *zaw-kane';* a prim. root; to *be old:*–aged man, be (wax) old (man).
2205. זָקֵן *zaw-kane';* from 2204; *old:*–aged, ancient (man), elder(-est), old (man, men and...women), senator.
2206. זָקָן *zaw-kawn';* from 2204; the *beard* (as indicating *age*):–beard.
2207. זֹקֶן *zo'-ken;* from 2204; old *age:*–age.
2208. זָקֻן *zaw-koon';* prop. pass.part. of 2204 (used only in the pl. as a noun); *old* age:–old age.
2209. זִקְנָה *zik-naw';* fem. of 2205; old *age:*–old (age).
2210 זָקַף *zaw-kaf';* a prim. root; to *lift,* i.e. (fig.) *comfort:*–raise (up).
2211. זְקַף *zek-af'* (Chald.); cor. to 2210; to *hang,* i.e. *impale:*–set up.
2212. זָקַק *zaw-kak';* a prim. root; to *strain,* (fig.) *extract, clarify:*–fine, pour down, purge, purify, refine.
2213. זֵר *zare;* from 2237 (in the sense of *scattering*); a *chaplet* (as *spread* around the top), i.e. (spec.) a border *moulding:*–crown.
2214. זָרָא *zaw-raw';* from 2114 (in the sense of *estrangement*) [comp. 2219]; *disgust:*–loathsome.
2215. זָרַב *zaw-rab';* a prim. root; to *flow* away:–wax warm.
2216. זְרֻבָּבֶל *zer-oob-baw-bel';* from 2215 and 894; *descended of* (i.e. from) *Babylon,* i.e. born there; *Zerubbabel,* an Isr.:–Zerubbabel.
2217. זְרֻבָּבֶל *zer-oob-baw-bel'* (Chald.); cor. to 2216:–Zerubbabel.
2218. זֶרֶד *zeh'-red;* from an un. root mean. to be *exuberant* in growth; lined with *shrubbery; Zered,* a brook E. of the Dead Sea:–Zared, Zered.
2219. זָרָה *zaw-raw';* a prim. root (comp. 2114); to *toss* about; by impl., to *diffuse, winnow:*–cast away, compass, disperse, fan, scatter (away), spread, strew, winnow.
2220. זְרוֹעַ *zer-o'-ah;* or (short.) זְרֹעַ *zer-o'-ah;* and (fem.) זְרוֹעָה *zer-o-aw';* or זְרֹעָה *zer-o-aw';* from 2232; the *arm* (as *stretched* out), or (of animals) the *foreleg;* fig., *force:*–arm, + help, mighty, power, shoulder, strength.
2221. זֵרוּעַ *zay-roo'-ah;* from 2232; something *sown,* i.e. a *plant:*–sowing, thing that is sown.
2222. זַרְזִיף *zar-zeef';* by redupl. from an unused root mean. to *flow*; a *pouring rain:*–water.
2223. זַרְזִיר *zar-zeer'* by redupl. from 2115; prop. tightly *girt*, i.e. prob. a *racer*, or some fleet animal (as being *slender* in the waist):–+ greyhound.
2224. זָרַח *zaw-rakh'* a prim. root; prop. to *irradiate* (or shoot forth beams), i.e. to *rise* (as the sun); spec., to *appear* (as a symptom of leprosy):–arise, rise (up), as soon as it is up.
2225. זֶרַח *zeh'-rakh* from 2224; a *rising* of light:–rising.
2226. זֶרַח *zeh'-rakh* the same as 2225; *Zerach,* the name of three Isr., also of an Idumaean and an Ethiopian prince:–Zarah, Zerah.
2227. זַרְחִי *zar-khee'* patron. from 2226; a *Zarchite* or desc. of Zerach:–Zarchite.
2228. זְרַחְיָה *zer-akh-yaw'* from 2225 and 3050; Jah has risen: Zerachjah, the name of two Isr.:–Zerahiah.
2229. זָרַם *zaw-ram';*a prim. root; to *gush* (as water):–carry away as with a flood, pour out.
2230. זֶרֶם *zeh'-rem* from 2229; a *gush* of water:–flood, overflowing, shower, storm, tempest.
2231. זִרְמָה *zir-maw'* fem. of 2230; a *gushing* of fluid (semen):–issue.
2232. זָרַע *zaw-rah'* a prim. root; to *sow*; fig., to *disseminate, plant, fructify:*–bear, conceive seed, set with sow(-er), yield.
2233. זֶרַע *zeh'-rah* from 2232; seed; fig., *fruit, plant, sowing-time, posterity:*–X carnally, child, fruitful, seed(-time), sowing- time.
2234. זְרַע *zer-ah'* (Chald.); cor. to 2233; *posterity:*–seed.
2235. זֵרֹעַ *zay-ro'-ah* or זֵרְעֹן *zay-raw-ohn';* from 2232; something *sown* (only in the pl.), i.e. a *vegetable* (as food):–pulse.
2236. זָרַק *zaw-rak'* a prim. root; to *sprinkle* (fluid or solid particles):–be here and there, scatter, sprinkle, strew.
2237. זָרַר *zaw-rar'* a prim. root (comp. 2114); perh. to *diffuse,* i.e. (spec.) to *sneeze:*–sneeze.
2238. זֶרֶשׁ *zeh'-resh* of Pers. or.; *Zeresh,* Haman's wife:–Zeresh.
2239. זֶרֶת *zeh'-reth* from 2219; the *spread* of the fingers, i.e. a *span:*–span.
2240. זַתּוּא *zat-too'* of unc. der.; *Zattu,* an Isr.:–Zattu.
2241. זֵתָם *zay-thawm'* app. a var. for 2133; *Zetham,* an Isr.:–Zetham.
2242. זֵתַר *zay-thar'* of Pers. or.; *Zethar,* a eunuch of Xerxes:–Zethar.

ח

2243. חֹב *khobe* by contr. from 2245; prop. a *cherisher*, i.e. the *bosom:*–bosom.
2244. חָבָא *khaw-baw'* a prim. root [comp. 2245]; to *secrete:*–X held, hide (self), do secretly.
2245. חָבַב *khaw-bab';*a prim. root [comp. 2244, 2247]; prop. to *hide* (as in the bosom), i.e. to *cherish* (with affection):–love.
2246. חֹבָב *kho-bawb';* from 2245; *cherished*; *Chobab*, father-in-law of Moses:–Hobab.
2247. חָבָה *khaw-bah';* a prim. root (comp. 2245); to *secrete:*–hide (self).
2248. חֲבוּלָה *khab-oo-law'* (Chald.); from 2255; prop. *overthrown,* i.e. (mor.) *crime:*–hurt.
2249. חָבוֹר *khaw-bore';* from 2266; *united*; *Chabor*, a river of Assyria:–Habor.
2250. חַבּוּרָה *khab-boo-raw';* or חַבֻּרָה *khab-boo-raw';* or חֲבֻרָה *khab-oo-raw';* from 2266; prop. *bound* (with stripes), i.e. a *weal*

HEBREW

(or black-and-blue mark itself):–blueness, bruise, hurt, stripe, wound.
2251. חָבַט *khaw-bat';* a prim. root; to *knock* out or off:–beat (off, out), thresh.
2252. חֲבַיָה *khab-ah-yaw';* or חֲבָיָה *khab-aw-yaw';* from 2247 and 3050; *Jah has hidden; Chabajah,* an Isr.:–Habaiah.
2253. חֶבְיוֹן *kheb-yone';* from 2247; a *concealment*:–hiding.
2254. חָבַל *khaw-bal';* a prim. root; to *wind* tightly (as a rope), i.e. to *bind*; spec., by a *pledge;* fig., to *pervert, destroy*; also to *writhe* in pain (esp. of parturition):–X at all, band, bring forth, (deal) corrupt(-ly), destroy, offend, lay to (take a) pledge, spoil, travail, X very, withhold.
2255. חֲבַל *khab-al'* (Chald.); cor. to 2254; to *ruin*:–destroy, hurt.
2256. חֶבֶל *kheh'-bel;* or חֵבֶל *khay'-bel*; from 2254; a *rope* (as *twisted*), esp. a measuring *line;* by impl., a *district* or *inheritance* (as *measured*); or a *noose* (as of *cords*); fig., a *company* (as if *tied* together); also a *throe* (esp. of parturition); also *ruin*:–band, coast, company, cord, country, destruction, line, lot, pain, pang, portion, region, rope, snare, sorrow, tackling.
2257. חֲבַל *khab-al'* (Chald.); from 2255; *harm* (pers. or pecuniary):–damage, hurt.
2258. חֲבֹל *khab-ole';* or (fem.) חֲבֹלָה *khab-o-law';* from 2254; a *pawn* (as security for debt):–pledge.
2259. חֹבֵל *kho-bale';* act.part. from 2254 (in the sense of handling *ropes*); a *sailor*:–pilot, shipmaster.
2260. חִבֵּל *khib-bale';* from 2254 (in the sense of furnished with *ropes*); a *mast*:–mast.
2261. חֲבַצֶּלֶת *khab-ats-tseh'-leth;* of unc. derivation; prob. *meadow-saffron*:–rose.
2262. חֲבַצִּנְיָה *khab-ats-tsan-yaw';* of unc. der.; *Chabatstsanjah*, a Rechabite:–Habazaniah.
2263. חָבַק *khaw-bak';* a prim. root; to *clasp* (the hands or in embrace):–embrace, fold.
2264. חִבֻּק *khib-book';* from 2263; a *clasping* of the hands (in idleness):–fold.
2265. חֲבַקּוּק *khab-ak-kook';* by redupl. from 2263; *embrace; Chabakkuk*, the prophet:–Habakkuk.
2266. חָבַר *khaw-bar';* a prim. root; to *join* (lit. or fig.); spec. (by means of spells) to *fascinate*:–charm(-er), be compact, couple (together), have fellowship with, heap up, join (self, together), league.
2267. חֶבֶר *kheh'-ber;* from 2266; a *society*; also a spell:–+ charmer (-ing), company, enchantment, X wide.
2268. חֶבֶר *kheh'-ber;* the same as 2267; *community; Cheber*, the name of a Kenite and of three Isr.:–Heber.
2269. חֲבַר *khab-ar'* (Chald.); from a root cor. to 2266; an *associate*:–companion, fellow.
2270. חָבֵר *khaw-bare';* from 2266; an *associate*:–companion, fellow, knit together.
2271. חַבָּר *khab-bawr';* from 2266; a *partner*:–companion.
2272. חֲבַרְבֻּרָה *khab-ar-boo-raw';* by reduplication from 2266; a *streak* (like a *line*), as on the tiger:–spot.
2273. חַבְרָה *khab-raw'* (Chald.); fem. of 2269; an *associate*:–other.
2274. חֶבְרָה *kheb-raw';* fem. of 2267; *association*:–company.
2275. חֶבְרוֹן *kheb-rone';* from 2267; seat of *association; Chebron*, a place in Pal., also the name of two Isr.:–Hebron.
2276. חֶבְרוֹנִי *kheb-ro-nee';* or חֶבְרֹנִי *kheb-ro-nee';* patron. from 2275; *Chebronite* (coll.), an inh. of Chebron:–Hebronites.
2277. חֶבְרִי *kheb-ree';* patron. from 2268; a *Chebrite* (coll.) or desc. of Cheber:–Heberites.
2278. חֲבֶרֶת *khab-eh'-reth;* fem. of 2270; a *consort*:–companion.
2279. חֹבֶרֶת *kho-beh'-reth;* fem. act.part. of 2266; a *joint*:–which coupleth, coupling.
2280. חָבַשׁ *khaw-bash';* a prim. root; to *wrap* firmly (esp. a turban, compress, or *saddle*); fig., to *stop*, to *rule*:–bind (up), gird about, govern, healer, put, saddle, wrap about.
2281. חֲבִת *khaw-bayth';* from an un. root prob. mean. to *cook* [comp. 4227]; something *fried,* prob. a griddle-*cake*:–pan.
2282. חַג *khag;* or חָג *khawg*; from 2287; a *festival,* or a *victim* therefor:–(solemn) feast (day), sacrifice, solemnity.
2283. חָגָא *khaw-gaw';* from an un. root mean. to *revolve* [comp. 2287]; prop. *vertigo,* i.e. (fig.) *fear:*–terror.
2284. חָגָב *khaw-gawb';* of unc. der.; a *locust:*–locust.
2285. חָגָב *khaw-gawb';* the same as 2284; *locust; Chagab,* one of the Nethinim:–Hagab.
2286. חֲגָבָא *khag-aw-baw';* or חֲגָבָה *khag-aw-baw';* fem. of 2285; locust; *Chagaba* or *Chagabah,* one of the Nethinim:–Hagaba, Hagabah.
2287. חָגַג *khaw-gag';* a prim. root [comp. 2283, 2328]; prop. to move in a *circle,* i.e. (spec.) to *march* in a sacred procession, to *observe* a festival; by impl., to *be giddy:*–celebrate, dance, (keep, hold) a (solemn) feast (holiday), reel to and fro.
2288. חֲגָו *khag-awv'* from an un. root mean. to take *refuge;* a *rift* in rocks:–cleft.
2289. חָגוֹר *khaw-gore';* from 2296; *belted:*–girded with.
2290. חֲגוֹר *khag-ore';* or חֲגֹר *khag-ore';* and (fem.) חֲגוֹרָה *khag-o-raw';* or חֲגֹרָה *khag-o-raw';* from 2296; a *belt* (for the waist):–apron, armour, gird(-le).
2291. חַגִּי *khag-ghee';* from 2287; *festive, Chaggi,* an Isr.; also (patron.) a *Chaggite,* or desc. of the same:–Haggi, Haggites.
2292. חַגַּי *khag-gah'-ee;* from 2282; *festive; Chaggai,* a Heb. prophet:–Haggai.
2293. חַגִּיָּה *khag-ghee-yaw';* from 2282 and 3050; *festival of Jah; Chaggijah,* an Isr.:–Haggiah.
2294. חַגִּית *khag-gheeth';* fem. of 2291; *festive; Chaggith,* a wife of David:–Haggith.
2295. חָגְלָה *khog-law';* of unc. der.; prob. a *partridge; Choglah,* an Isr.s:–Hoglah. See also 1031.
2296. חָגַר *khaw-gar';* a prim. root; to *gird* on (as a belt, armor, etc.):–be able to put on, be afraid, appointed, gird, restrain, X on every side.
2297. חַד *khad;* abridged from 259; *one:*–one.
2298. חַד *khad* (Chald.); cor. to 2297; as cardinal *one;* as art. *single;* as an ord., *first;* adv., at *once:*–a, first, one, together.
2299. חַד *khad;* from 2300; *sharp:*–sharp.
2300. חָדַד *khaw-dad'* a prim. root; to be (caus., *make) sharp* or (fig.) *severe:*–be fierce, sharpen.
2301. חֲדַד *khad-ad';* from 2300; *fierce; Chadad,* an Ishmaelite:–Hadad.
2302. חָדָה *khaw-daw';* a prim. root; to *rejoice:*–make glad, be joined, rejoice.
2303. חַדּוּד *khad-dood';* from 2300; a *point:*–sharp.
2304. חֶדְוָה *khed-vaw';* from 2302; *rejoicing:*–gladness, joy.
2305. חֶדְוָה *khed-vaw'* (Chald.); cor. to 2304:–joy.
2306. חֲדִי *khad-ee'* (Chald.); cor. to 2373; a *breast:*–breast.
2307. חָדִיד khaw-deed' from 2300; a *peak; Chadid,* a place in Pal.:–Hadid.
2308. חָדַל *khaw-dal';* a prim. root; prop. to be *flabby,* i.e. (by impl.) *desist;* (fig.) *be lacking or idle:*–cease, end, fall, forbear, forsake, leave (off), let alone, rest, be unoccupied, want.
2309. חֶדֶל *kheh'-del;* from 2308; *rest,* i.e. the state of the *dead:*–world.
2310. חָדֵל *khaw-dale';* from 2308; *vacant,* i.e. *ceasing* or *destitute:*–he that forbeareth, frail, rejected.
2311. חַדְלַי *khad-lah'-ee;* from 2309*; idle; Chadlai,* an Isr.:–Hadlai.
2312. חֵדֶק *khay'-dek;* from an un. root mean. to *sting;* a *prickly* plant:–brier, thorn.
2313. חִדֶּקֶל *khid-deh'-kel;* prob. of for. or.; the *Chiddekel* (or Tigris) river:–Hiddekel.
2314. חָדַר *khaw-dar';* a prim. root; prop. to *inclose* (as a room), i.e. (by anal.,) to *beset* (as in a siege):–enter a privy chamber.
2315. חֶדֶר *kheh'-der;* from 2314; an *apartment* (usually lit.):–([be] inner) chamber, innermost(-ward) part, parlour, + south, X within
2316. חֲדַר *khad-ar';* another form for 2315; *chamber; Chadar,* an Ishmaelite:–Hadar.
2317. חַדְרָךְ *khad-rawk';* of unc. der.; *Chadrak,* a Syrian deity:–Hadrach.
2318. חָדַשׁ *khaw-dash';'* a prim. root; to *be new;* caus., to *rebuild:*–renew, repair.
2319. חָדָשׁ *khaw-dawsh';* from 2318; *new:*–fresh, new thing.
2320. חֹדֶשׁ *kho'-desh;* from 2318; the *new* moon; by impl., a *month:*–month(-ly), new moon.
2321. חֹדֶשׁ *kho'-desh;* the same as 2320; *Chodesh,* an Isr.s:–Hodesh.
2322. חֲדָשָׁה *khad-aw-shaw';* fem. of 2319; *new; Chadashah,* a place in Pal.:–Hadashah.
2323. חֲדַת *khad-ath'* (Chald.); cor. to 2319; *new:*–new.
2324. חֲוָא *khav-aw'* (Chald.); cor. to 2331; to *show:*–shew.
2325. חוּב *khoob;* also חָיַב *khaw-yab';* a prim. root; prop. perh. to *tie,* i.e. (fig. and refl.) to *owe,* or (by impl.) to *forfeit:*–make endanger.
2326. חוֹב *khobe;* from 2325; *debt:*–debtor.
2327. חוֹבָה *kho-baw';* fem. act.part. of 2247; *hiding place; Chobah,* a place in Syria:–Hobah.
2328. חוּג *khoog;* a prim. root [comp. 2287]; to describe a *circle:*–compass.
2329. חוּג *khoog;* from 2328; a *circle:*–circle, circuit, compass.
2330. חוּד *khood;* a prim. root; prop. to *tie* a knot, i.e. (fig.) to *propound* a riddle:–put forth.
2331. חָוָה *khaw-vah';* a prim. root; [comp. 2324, 2421]; prop. to *live*; by impl. (intens.) to *declare* or *show:*–show.
2332. חַוָּה *khav-vaw';* caus. from 2331; *life-giver; Chavvah* (or Eve), the first woman:–Eve.
2333. חַוָּה *khav-vaw';* prop. the same as 2332 (*life-giving,* i.e. *living-place*); by impl., an encampment or *village:*–(small) town.

2334. חַוּוֹת יָעִיר *khav-vothe' yaw-eer';* from the pl. of 2333 and a modif. of 3265; *hamlets of Jair,* a region of Pal.:–[Bashan-] Havoth-jair.
2335. חוֹזַי *kho-zah'-ee;* from 2374; *visionary; Chozai,* an Isr.:–the seers.
2336. חוֹחַ *kho'-akh;* from an un. root app. mean. to *pierce; a thorn;* by anal., a *ring* for the nose:–bramble, thistle, thorn.
2337. חָוָח *khaw-vawkh';* perh. the same as 2336; a *dell or crevice* (as if *pierced* in the earth):–thicket.
2338. חוּט *khoot* (Chald.); cor. to the root of 2339, perh. as a denom.; to *string* together, i.e. (fig.) to *repair:*–join.
2339. חוּט *khoot;* from an un. root prob. mean. to *sew;* a *string;* by impl., a measuring *tape:*–cord, fillet, line, thread.
2340. חִוִּי *khiv-vee';* perh. from 2333; a *villager*; a *Chivvite,* one of the aboriginal tribes of Pal.:–Hivite.
2341. חֲוִילָה *khav-ee-law';* prob. from 2342; *circular; Chavilah,* the name of two or three eastern regions; also perh. of two men:–Havilah.
2342. חוּל *khool;* or חִיל *kheel;* a prim. root; prop. to *twist* or *whirl* (in a circular or spiral manner), i.e. (spec.) to *dance,* to *writhe* in pain (esp. of parturition) or fear; fig., to *wait,* to *pervert:*–bear, (make to) bring forth, (make to) calve, dance, drive away, fall grievously (with pain), fear, form, great, grieve, (be) grievous, hope, look, make, be in pain, be much (sore) pained, rest, shake, shapen, (be) sorrow(-ful), stay, tarry, travail (with pain), tremble, trust, wait carefully (patiently), be wounded.
2343. חוּל *khool;* from 2342; a *circle; Chul,* a son of Aram; also the region settled by him:–Hul.
2344. חוֹל *khole;* from 2342; *sand* (*as round* or whirling particles):–sand.
2345. חוּם *khoom;* from an un. root mean. to *be warm,* i.e. (by impl.) *sunburnt* or *swarthy* (blackish):–brown.
2346. חוֹמָה *kho-maw';* fem. act.part. of an un. root app. mean. to *join;* a *wall* of protection:–wall, walled.
2347. חוּס *khoos;* a prim. root; prop. to *cover,* i.e. (fig.) to *compassionate:*–pity, regard, spare.
2348. חוֹף *khofe;* from an un. root mean. to *cover;* a *cove* (as a *sheltered* bay):–coast [of the sea], haven, shore, sea-]side.
2349. חוּפָּם *khoo-fawm';* from the same as 2348; *protection: Chupham,* an Isr.:–Hupham.
2350. חוּפָמִי *khoo-faw-mee';* patron. from 2349; a *Chuphamite* or desc. of Chupham:–Huphamites.
2351. חוּץ *khoots;* or (short.) חֻץ *khoots;* (both forms fem. in the pl.) from an un. root mean. to *sever;* prop. *separate* by a wall, i.e. *outside, outdoors:*–abroad, field, forth, highway, more, out(-side, -ward), street, without.
2352. חוּר *khoor;* or (short.) חֻר *khoor;* from an un. root prob. mean. to *bore;* the *crevice* of a serpent; the *cell* of a prison:–hole.
2353. חוּר *khoor;* from 2357; *white* linen:–white.
2354. חוּר *khoor;* the same as 2353 or 2352; *Chur,* the name of four Isr. and one Midianite:–Hur.
2355. חוֹר *khore;* the same as 2353; *white* linen:–network. Comp. 2715.
2356. חוֹר *khore;* or (short.) חֹר *khore;* the same as 2352; a *cavity, socket, den:*–cave, hole.
2357. חָוַר *khaw-var';* a prim. root; to *blanch* (as with shame):–wax pale.
2358. חִוָּר *khiv-vawr'* (Chald.);; from a root cor. to 2357; *white:*–white.
2359. חוּרִי *khoo-ree';* prob. from 2353; *linen*-worker; *Churi,* an Isr.:–Huri.
2360. חוּרַי *khoo-rah'ee;* prob. an orth. var. for 2359; *Churai,* an Isr.:–Hurai.
2361. חוּרָם *khoo-rawm';* prob. from 2353; *whiteness,* i.e. noble; *Churam,* the name of an Isr. and two Syrians:–Huram. Comp. 2438.
2362. חַוְרָן *khav-rawn';* app. from 2357 (in the sense of 2352); *cavernous; Chavran,* a region E. of the Jordan:–Hauran.
2363. חוּשׁ *koosh;* a prim. root; to *hurry;* fig., to *be eager* with excitement or enjoyment:–(make) haste(-n), ready.
2364. חוּשָׁה *khoo-shaw';* from 2363; *haste; Chushah,* an Isr.:–Hushah.
2365. חוּשַׁי *khoo-shah'-ee;* from 2363; *hasty; Chushai,* an Isr.:–Hushai.
2366. חוּשִׁים *khoo-sheem';* or חֻשִׁים *khoo-shem';* or חֻשִׁם *khoo- sheem';* pl. from 2363; *hasters; Chushim,* the name of three Isr.:–Hushim.
2367. חוּשָׁם *khoo-shawm';* or חֻשָׁם *khoo-shawm';* from 2363; *hastily; Chusham,* an Idumaean:–Husham.
2368. חוֹתָם *kho-thawm'* or חֹתָם *kho-thawm';* from 2856; a *signature*-ring:–seal, signet.
2369. חוֹתָם *kho-thawm';* the same as 2368; *seal; Chotham,* the name of two Isr.:–Hotham, Hothan.
2370. חֲזָא *khaz-aw'* (Chald.); or חֲזָה *khaz-aw';* cor. to 2372; to *gaze* upon; ment. to *dream, be usual* (i.e. *seem*):–behold, have [a dream], see, be wont.
2371. חֲזָאֵל *khaz-aw-ale';* or חֲזָהאֵל *khaz-aw-ale';* from 2372 and 410; *God has seen; Chazael,* a king of Syria:–Hazael.
2372. חָזָה *khaw-zaw';* a prim. root; to *gaze* at; ment., to *perceive, contemplate* (with pleasure); spec., to *have a vision of:*–behold, look, prophesy, provide, see.
2373. חָזֶה *khaw-zeh';* from 2372; the *breast* (as most *seen* in front):–breast.
2374. חֹזֶה *kho-zeh';* act.part. of 2372; a *beholder* in vision; also a *compact* (as *looked upon* with approval):–agreement, prophet, see that, seer, [star-]gazer.
2375. חֲזוֹ *khaz-o';* from 2372; *seer; Chazo,* a nephew of Abraham:–Hazo.
2376. חֵזוּ *khay'-zev* (Chald.); from 2370; a *sight:*–look, vision.
2377. חָזוֹן *khaw-zone';* from 2372; a *sight* (ment.), i.e. a *dream, revelation,* or *oracle:*–vision.
2378. חָזוֹת *khaw-zoth';* from 2372; a *revelation:*–vision.
2379. חֲזוֹת *khaz-oth'* (Chald.); from 2370; a *view:*–sight.
2380. חָזוּת *khaw-zooth';* from 2372; a *look;* hence (fig.) striking *appearance, revelation,* or (by impl.) *compact:*–agreement, notable (one), vision.
2381. חֲזִיאֵל *khaz-ee-ale';* from 2372 and 410; *seen of God; Chaziel,* a Levite:–Haziel.
2382. חֲזָיָה *khaz-aw-yaw';* from 2372 and 3050; *Jah has seen; Chazajah,* an Isr.:–Hazaiah.
2383. חֶזְיוֹן *khez-yone';* from 2372; *vision; Chezjon,* a Syrian:–Hezion.
2384. חִזָּיוֹן *khiz-zaw-yone';* from 2372; a *revelation,* expectation by *dream:*–vision.
2385. חֲזִיז *khaw-zeez';* from an un. root mean. to *glare;* a *flash* of lightning:–bright cloud, lightning.
2386. חֲזִיר *khaz-eer';* from an un. root prob. mean. to *enclose;* a *hog* (perh. as *penned*):–boar, swine.
2387. חֵזִיר *khay-zeer';* from the same as 2386; perh. *protected; Chezir,* the name of two Isr.:–Hezir.
2388. חָזַק *khaw-zak';* a prim. root; to *fasten* upon; hence, to *seize, be strong* (fig., *courageous,* caus. *strengthen, cure, help, repair, fortify*), *obstinate;* to *bind, restrain, conquer:*–aid, amend, X calker, catch, cleave, confirm, be constant, constrain, continue, be of good (take) courage(-ous, -ly), encourage (self), be established, fasten, force, fortify, make hard, harden, help, (lay) hold (fast), lean, maintain, play the man, mend, become (wax) mighty, prevail, be recovered, repair, retain, seize, be (wax) sore, strengthen (self), be stout, be (make, shew, wax) strong(-er), be sure, take (hold), be urgent, behave self valiantly, withstand.
2389. חָזָק *khaw-zawk';* from 2388; *strong* (usu. in a bad sense, *hard, bold, violent*):–harder, hottest, + impudent, loud, mighty, sore, stiff [-hearted], strong(-er).
2390. חָזֵק *khaw-zake';* from 2388; *powerful:*–X wax louder, stronger.
2391. חֵזֶק *khay'-zek;* from 2388; *help:*–strength.
2392. חֹזֶק *kho'-zek;* from 2388; *power:*–strength.
2393. חֶזְקָה *khez-kaw';* fem. of 2391; prevailing *power:*–strength(- en self), (was) strong.
2394. חָזְקָה *khoz-kaw';* fem. of 2392; *vehemence* (usually in a bad sense):–force, mightily, repair, sharply.
2395. חִזְקִי *khiz-kee';* from 2388; *strong; Chizki,* an Isr.:–Hezeki.
2396. חִזְקִיָּה *khiz-kee-yaw';* or חִזְקִיָּהוּ *khiz-kee-yaw'-hoo;* also יְחִזְקִיָּה *yekh-iz-kee-yaw'* or יְחִזְקִיָּהוּ *yekh-iz-kee-yaw'-hoo; from* 2388 and 3050; *strengthened of Jah; Chizkijah,* a king of Judah, also the name of two other Isr.:–Hezekiah, Hizkiah, Hizkijah. Comp. 3169.
2397. חָח *khawkh;* once (Eze. 29:4) חָחִי *khakh-ee';* from the same as 2336; a *ring* for the nose (or lips):–bracelet, chain, hook.
2398. חָטָא *khaw-taw';* a prim. root; prop. to *miss;* hence (fig. and gen.) to *sin;* by inference, to *forfeit, lack, expiate, repent,* (caus.) *lead astray, condemn:*–bear the blame, cleanse, commit [sin], by fault, harm he hath done, loss, miss, (make) offend(-er), offer for sin, purge, purify (self), make reconciliation, (cause, make) sin(-ful, -ness), trespass.
2399. חֵטְא *khate;* from 2398; a crime or its *penalty:*–fault, X grievously, offence, (punishment of) sin.
2400. חַטָּא *khat-taw';* intens. from 2398; a *criminal,* or one accounted *guilty:*–offender, sinful, sinner.
2401. חֲטָאָה *khat-aw-aw';* fem. of 2399; an *offence,* or a *sacrifice* for it:–sin (offering).
2402. חַטָּאָה *khat-taw-aw'* (Chald.); cor. to 2401; an *offence,* and the *penalty* or *sacrifice* for it:–sin (offering).
2403. חַטָּאָה *khat-taw-aw'* or חַטָּאת *khat-tawth';* from 2398; an *offence* (sometimes habitual *sinfulness*), and its penalty, occasion, sacrifice, or expiation; also (concr.) an *offender:*–punishment (of sin), purifying(-fication for sin), sin(-ner, offering).
2404. חָטַב *khaw-tab'* a prim. root; to *chop* or *carve* wood:–cut down, hew(-er), polish.

2405. חֲטֻבָה *khat-oo-baw'* fem. pass.part. of 2404; prop. a *carving*; hence, a *tapestry* (as figured):–carved.
2406. חִטָּה *khit-taw';* of unc. der.; *wheat,* whether the grain or the plant:–wheat(-en).
2407. חַטּוּשׁ *khat-toosh'* from an un. root of unc. signif.; *Chattush*, the name of four or five Isr.:–Hattush.
2408. חֲטִי *khat-ee'* (Chald.); from a root cor. to 2398; an *offence:*–sin.
2409. חַטָּיָא *khat-taw-yaw'* (Chald.);; from the same as 2408; an *expiation:*–sin offering.
2410. חֲטִיטָא *khat-ee-taw';* from an un. root app. mean. to *dig* out; *explorer*; Chatita, a temple porter:–Hatita.
2411. חַטִּיל *khat-teel';* from an un. root app. mean. to *wave; fluctuating; Chattil,* one of "Solomon's servants":–Hattil.
2412. חֲטִיפָא *khat-ee-faw';* from 2414; *robber; Chatipha*, one of the Nethinim:–Hatipha.
2413. חָטַם *khaw-tam';* a prim. root; to *stop:*–refrain.
2414. חָטַף *khaw-taf';* a prim. root; to *clutch;* hence, to *seize* as a prisoner:–catch.
2415. חֹטֶר *kho'-ter;* from an un. root of unc. signif.; a *twig:*–rod.
2416. חַי *khah'-ee;* from 2421; *alive;* hence, *raw* (flesh); *fresh* (plant, water, year), *strong;* also (as noun, esp. in the fem. sing. and masc. pl.) *life* (or living thing), whether lit. or fig.:–+ age, alive, appetite, (wild) beast, company, congregation, life(-time), live(-ly), living (creature, thing), maintenance, + merry, multitude, + (be) old, quick, raw, running, springing, troop.
2417. חַי *khah'-ee* (Chald.); from 2418; *alive;* also (as noun in pl.) *life:*–life, that liveth, living.
2418. חֲיָא *hah-yaw'* (Chald.); or חֲיָה *khah-yaw';* cor. to 2421; to *live:*–live, keep alive.
2419. חִיאֵל *khee-ale';* from 2416 and 410; *living of God; Chiel,* an Isr.:–Hiel.
2420. חִידָה *khee-daw';* from 2330; a *puzzle,* hence, a *trick, conundrum,* sententious *maxim:*–dark saying (sentence, speech), hard question, proverb, riddle.
2421. חָיָה *khaw-yaw';* a prim. root[comp. 2331, 2421]; to *live,* whether lit. or fig.; caus., to *revive:*–keep (leave, make) alive, X certainly, give (promise) life, (let, suffer to) live, nourish up, preserve (alive), quicken, recover, repair, restore (to life), revive, (X God) save (alive, life, lives), X surely, be whole.
2422. חָיֶה *khaw-yeh;* from 2421; *vigorous:*–lively.
2423. חֵיוָא *khay-vaw'* (Chald.); from 2418; an *animal:*–beast.
2424. חַיּוּת *khah-yooth';* from 2421; *life:*–X living.
2425. חָיַי *khaw-yah'-ee;* a prim. root [comp. 2421]; to *live;* caus. to *revive:*–live, save life.
2426. חֵיל *khale;* or (short.) חֵל *khale;* a collat. form of 2428; an *army;* also (by anal.,) an *intrenchment:*–army, bulwark, host, + poor, rampart, trench, wall.
2427. חִיל *kheel;* and; (fem.) חִילָה *khee-law';* from 2342; a *throe* (expectant of childbirth):–pain, pang, sorrow.
2428. חַיִל *khah'-yil;* from 2342; prob. a *force,* whether of men, means or other resources; an *army, wealth, virtue, valor, strength:*–able, activity, (+) army, band of men (soldiers), company, (great) forces, goods, host, might, power, riches, strength, strong, substance, train, (+)valiant(-ly), valour, virtuous(-ly), war, worthy(-ily).
2429. חַיִל *khah'-yil* (Chald.); cor. to 2428; an *army,* or *strength:*–aloud, army, X most [mighty], power.
2430. חֵילָה *khay-law';* fem. of 2428; an *intrenchment:*–bulwark.
2431. חֵילָם *khay-lawm';* or חֵלָאם *khay-lawm';* from 2428; *fortress; Chelam,* a place E. of Pal.:–Helam.
2432. חִילֵז *khee-lane';* from 2428; *fortress; Chilen,* a place in Pal.:–Hilen.
2433. חִין *kheen;* another form for 2580; *beauty:*–comely.
2434. חַיִץ *khah'-yits;* another form for 2351; a *wall:*–wall.
2435. חִיצוֹן *khee-tsone';* from 2434; prop. the (outer) *wall side;* hence, *exterior;* fig., *secular* (as opposed to sacred):–outer, outward, utter, without.
2436. חֵיק *khake;* or חֵק *khake;* and חוֹק *khoke;* from an un. root, app. mean. to *inclose;* the *bosom* (lit. or fig.):–bosom, bottom, lap, midst, within.
2437. חִירָה *khee-raw';* from 2357 in the sense of *splendor; Chirah,* an Adullamite:–Hirah.
2438. חִירָם *khee-rawm';* or חִירוֹם *khee-rome';* another form of 2361; *Chiram* or *Chirom,* the name of two Tyrians:–Hiram, Huram.
2439. חִישׁ *kheesh*; another form of 2363; to *hurry:*–make haste.
2440. חִישׁ *kheesh*; from 2439; prop. a *hurry;* hence (adv.) *quickly:*–soon.
2441. חֵךְ *khake;* prob. from 2596 in the sense of *tasting;* prop. the *palate* or inside of the mouth; hence, the *mouth* itself (as the organ of speech, taste and kissing):–(roof of the) mouth, taste.
2442. חָכָה *khaw-kaw';* a prim. root [app. akin to 2707 through the idea of *piercing*]; prop. to *adhere* to; hence, to await:–long, tarry, wait.
2443. חַכָּה *khak-kaw';* prob. from 2442; a *hook* (as *adhering*):–angle, hook.
2444. חֲכִילָה *khak-ee-law';* from the same as 2447; *dark; Chakilah,* a hill in Pal.:–Hachilah.
2445. חַכִּים *khak-keem'* (Chald.); from a root cor. to 2449; *wise,* i.e. a *Magian:*–wise.
2446. חֲכַלְיָה *khak-al-yaw';* from the base of 2447 and 3050; *darkness of Jah; Chakaljah,* an Isr.:–Hachaliah.
2447. חַכְלִיל *khak-leel';* by redupl. from an un. root app. mean. to *be dark;* darkly *flashing* (only of the eyes); in a good sense, *brilliant* (as stimulated by wine):–red.
2448. חַכְלִלוּת *khak-lee-looth';* from 2447; *flash* (of the eyes); in a bad sense, *blearedness:*–redness.
2449. חָכַם *khaw-kam';* a prim. root, to *be wise* (in mind, word or act):–X exceeding, teach wisdom, be (make self, shew self) wise, deal (never so) wisely, make wiser.
2450. חָכָם *khaw-kawm';* from 2449; *wise,* (i.e. intelligent, skilful or artful):–cunning (man), subtil, ([un-]), wise([hearted], man).
2451. חָכְמָה *khok-maw';* from 2449; *wisdom* (in a good sense):–skilful, wisdom, wisely, wit.
2452. חָכְמָה *khok-maw'* (Chald.); cor. to 2451; *wisdom:*–wisdom.
2453. חַכְמוֹנִי *khak-mo-nee';* from 2449; *skilful*; *Chakmoni*, an Isr.:–Hachmoni, Hachmonite.
2454. חָכְמוֹת *khok-moth';* or חַכְמוֹת *khak-moth';* collat. forms of 2451; *wisdom:*–wisdom, every wise [woman].
2455. חֹל *khole;* from 2490; prop. *exposed;* hence, *profane:*–common, profane (place), unholy.
2456. חָלָא *khaw-law'* a prim. root [comp. 2470]; to *be sick:*–be diseased.
2457. חֶלְאָה *khel-aw';* from 2456; prop. *disease;* hence, *rust:*–scum.
2458. חֶלְאָה *khel-aw';* the same as 2457; *Chelah,* an Isr.s:–Helah.
2459. חֶלֶב *kheh'-leb;* or חֵלֶב *khay'-leb;* from an un. root mean. to *be fat; fat,* whether lit. or fig.; hence, the *richest* or *choice* part:–X best, fat(-ness), X finest, grease, marrow.
2460. חֵלֶב *khay'-leb;* the same as 2459; *fatness; Cheleb,* an Isr.:–Heleb.
2461. חָלָב *khaw-lawb';* from the same as 2459; *milk* (as the *richness* of kine):–+ cheese, milk, sucking.
2462. חֶלְבָּה *khel-baw';* fem. of 2459; *fertility: Chelbah,* a place in Pal.:–Helbah.
2463. חֶלְבּוֹן *khel-bone';* from 2459; *fruitful; Chelbon,* a place in Syria:–Helbon.
2464. חֶלְבְּנָה *khel-ben-aw';* from 2459; *galbanam,* an odorous gum (as if *fatty*):–galbanum.
2465. חֶלֶד *kheh'-led;* from an un. root app. mean. to *glide* swiftly; *life* (as a *fleeting* portion of time); hence, the *world* (as *transient*):–age, short time, world.
2466. חֵלֶד *khay'-led;* the same as 2465; *Cheled,* an Isr.:–Heled.
2467. חֹלֶד *kho'-led;* from the same as 2465; a *weasel* (from its *gliding* motion):–weasel.
2468. חֻלְדָּה *khool-daw';* fem. of 2467; *Chuldah,* an Isr.s:–Huldah.
2469. חֶלְדַּי *khel-dah'-ee;* from 2466; *worldliness; Cheldai,* the name of two Isr.:–Heldai.
2470. חָלָה *khaw-law';* a prim. root [comp. 2342, 2470, 2490]; prop. to *be rubbed* or *worn;* hence (fig.) to *be weak, sick, afflicted;* or (caus.) to *grieve, make sick;* also to *stroke* (in flattering), *entreat:*–beseech, (be) diseased, (put to) grief, be grieved, (be) grievous, infirmity, intreat, lay to, put to pain, X pray, make prayer, be (fall, make) sick, sore, be sorry, make suit (X supplication), woman in travail, be (become) weak, be wounded.
2471. חַלָּה *khal-law';* from 2490; a *cake* (as usually *punctured*):–cake.
2472. חֲלוֹם *khal-ome';* or (short.) חֲלֹם *khal-ome';* from 2492; a *dream:*–dream(-er).
2473. חֹלוֹן *kho-lone';* or (short.) חֹלֹן *kho-lone';* prob. from 2344; *sandy; Cholon,* the name of two places in Pal.:–Holon.
2474. חַלּוֹן, *khal-lone';* a *window* (as *perforated*):–window.
2475. חֲלוֹף *khal-ofe';* from 2498; prop. *surviving;* by impl. (coll.) *orphans:*–X destruction.
2476. חֲלוּשָׁה *khal-oo-shaw';* fem. pass.part. of 2522; *defeat:*–being overcome.
2477. חֲלַח *khal-akh';* prob. of for. or.; *Chalach,* a region of Assyria:–Halah.
2478. חַלְחוּל *khal-khool';* by redupl. from 2342; *contorted; Chalchul,* a place in Pal.:–Halhul.
2479. חַלְחָלָה *khal-khaw-law';* fem. from the same as 2478; *writhing* (in childbirth); by impl., *terror:*–(great, much) pain.
2480. חָלַט *khaw-lat';* a prim. root; to *snatch* at:–catch.
2481. חֲלִי *khal-ee';* from 2470; a *trinket* (as *polished*):–jewel, ornament.
2482. חֲלִי *khal-ee';* the same as 2481; *Chali,*

a place in Pal.:–Hali.
2483. חֳלִי *khol-ee'*; from 2470; *malady, anxiety, calamity*:–disease, grief, (is) sick(-ness).
2484. חֶלְיָה *khel-yaw'*; fem. of 2481; a *trinket*:–jewel.
2485. חָלִיל *khaw-leel'*; from 2490; a *flute* (as *perforated*):–pipe.
2486. חָלִילָה *khaw-lee'-law*; or חָלִלָה *khaw-lee'-law*; a directive from 2490; lit. *for a profaned* thing; used (interj.) *far be it!*:–be far, (X God) forbid.
2487. חֲלִיפָה *khal-ee-faw'*; from 2498; *alternation*:–change, course.
2488. חֲלִיצָה *khal-ee-tsaw'*; from 2503; *spoil*:–armour.
2489. חֵלְכָא *hay-lek-aw'*; or חֵלְכָה *khay-lek-aw'*; app. from an un. root prob. mean. to *be dark* or (fig.) *unhappy*; a *wretch*, i.e. unfortunate:–poor.
2490. חָלַל *khaw-lal'*; a prim. root [comp. 2470]; prop. to *bore*, i.e. (by impl.) to *wound*, to *dissolve*; fig., to *profane* (a pers., place or thing), to *break* (one's word), to *begin* (as if by an "opening wedge"); denom. (from 2485) to *play* (the flute):–begin (X men began), defile, X break, defile, X eat (as common things), X first, X gather the grape thereof, X take inheritance, pipe, player on instruments, pollute, (cast as) profane (self), prostitute, slay (slain), sorrow, stain, wound.
2491. חָלָל *khaw-lawl'*; from 2490; *pierced* (esp. to death); fig., *polluted*:–kill, profane, slain (man), X slew, (deadly) wounded.
2492. חָלַם *khaw-lam'*; a prim. root; prop. to *bind* firmly, i.e. (by impl.) to *be* (caus. to *make*) *plump*; also (through the fig. sense of *dumbness*) to *dream*:–(cause to) dream(-er), be in good liking, recover.
2493. חֵלֶם *khay'-lem* (Chald.); from a root cor. to 2492; a *dream*:–dream.
2494. חֵלֶם *khay'lem*; from 2492; a *dream*; *Chelem*, an Isr.:–Helem. Comp. 2469.
2495. חַלָּמוּת *khal-law-mooth'*; from 2492 (in the sense of *insipidity*); prob. *purslain*:–egg.
2496. חַלָּמִישׁ *klal-law-meesh'*; prob. from 2492 (in the sense of *hardness*); *flint*:–flint(-y), rock.
2497. חֵלֹן *khay-lone'*; from 2428; *strong*; *Chelon*, an Isr.:–Helon.
2498. חָלַף *khaw-laf'*; a prim. root; prop. to *slide* by, i.e. (by impl.) to *hasten away, pass on, spring* up, *pierce* or *change*:–abolish, alter, change, cut off, go on forward, grow up, be over, pass (away, on, through), renew, sprout, strike through.
2499. חֲלַף *khal-af'* (Chald.); cor. to 2498; to *pass* on (of time):–pass.
2500. חֵלֶף *klay'-lef*; from 2498; prop. *exchange*; hence (as prep.) *instead* of:–X for.
2501. חֶלֶף *kheh'lef* the same as 2500; *change*; *Cheleph*, a place in Pal.:–Heleph.
2502. חָלַץ *khaw-lats'* a prim. root; to *pull* off; hence (intens.) to *strip*, (reflex.) to *depart*; by impl., to *deliver, equip* (for fight); *present, strengthen*:–arm (self), (go, ready) armed (X man, soldier), deliver, draw out, make fat, loose, (ready) prepared, put off, take away, withdraw self.
2503. חֶלֶץ *kheh'-lets* or חֵלֶץ *khay'-lets*; from 2502; perh., *strength*; *Chelets*, the name of two Isr.:–Helez.
2504. חָלָץ *khaw-lawts'* from 2502 (in the sense of *strength*); only in the dual; the *loins* (as the seat of vigor):–loins, reins.
2505. חָלַק *khaw-lak'* a prim. root; to be smooth (fig.); by impl. (as smooth stones were used for *lots*) to *apportion* or *separate*:–deal, distribute, divide, flatter, give, (have, im-)part(-ner), take away a portion, receive, separate self, (be) smooth(-er).
2506. חֵלֶק *khay'lek*; from 2505; prop. *smoothness* (of the tongue); also an *allotment*:–flattery, inheritance, part, X partake, portion.
2507. חֵלֶק *khay'-lek*; the same as 2506; *portion*; *Chelek*, an Isr.:–Helek.
2508. חֲלָק *khal-awk'* (Chald.); from a root cor. to 2505; a *part*:–portion.
2509. חָלָק *khaw-lawk'*; from 2505; *smooth* (esp. of tongue):–flattering, smooth.
2510. חָלָק *khaw-lawk'*; the same as 2509; *bare*; *Chalak*, a mountain of Idumaea:–Halak.
2511. חַלָּק *khal-lawk'*; from 2505; *smooth*:–smooth.
2512. חַלֻּק *khal-look'*; from 2505; *smooth*:–smooth.
2513. חֶלְקָה *khel-kaw'*; fem. of 2506; prop. *smoothness*; fig., *flattery*; also an *allotment*:–field, flattering(-ry), ground, parcel, part, piece of land ([ground]), plat, portion, slippery place, smooth (thing).
2514. חֲלַקָּה *khal-ak-kaw'*; fem. from 2505; flattery:–flattery.
2515. חֲלֻקָּה *khal-ook-kaw'*; fem. of 2512; a *distribution*:–division.
2516. חֶלְקִי *khel-kee'*; patron. from 2507; a *Chelkite* or desc. of Chelek:–Helkites.
2517. חֶלְקַי *khel-kah'ee*; from 2505; *apportioned*; *Chelkai*, an Isr.:–Helkai.
2518. חִלְקִיָּה *khil-kee-yaw'*; or חִלְקִיָּהוּ *khil-kee-yaw'-hoo'*; from 2506 and 3050; *portion of Jah*; *Chilhijah*, the name of eight Isr.:– Hillkiah.
2519. חֲלַקְלַקָּה *khal-ak-lak-kaw'*; by reduplication from 2505; prop. something *very smooth*; i.e. a *treacherous* spot; fig., *blandishment*:–flattery, slippery.
2520. חֶלְקַת *khel-kath'*; a form of 2513; *smoothness*; *Chelkath*, a place in Pal.:–Helkath.
2521. חֶלְקַת הַצֻּרִים *khel-kath' hats-tsoo-reem'*; from 2520 and the pl. of 6697, with the art. ins.; *smoothness of the rocks*; *Chelkath Hats-tsurim*, a place in Pal.:–Helkath-hazzurim.
2522. חָלַשׁ *khaw-lash'*; a prim. root; to *prostrate*; by impl., to *overthrow, decay*:–discomfit, waste away, weaken.
2523. חַלָּשׁ *khal-lawsh'*; from 2522; *frail*:–weak.
2524. חָם *khawm*; from the same as 2346; a *father-in-law* (as in *affinity*):–father in law.
2525. חָם *khawm*; from 2552; *hot*:–hot, warm.
2526. חָם *khawm*; the same as 2525; *hot* (from the tropical habitat); *Cham*, a son of Noah; also (as a patron.) his desc. or their country:–Ham.
2527. חֹם *khome*; from 2552; *heat*:–heat, to be hot (warm).
2528. חֱמָא *khem-aw'* (Chald.); or חֱמָה *khem-aw'*; cor. to 2534; *anger*:–fury.
2529. חֶמְאָה *khem-aw'*; or (short.) חֵמָה *khay-maw'*; from the same root as 2346; curdled *milk* or *cheese*:–butter.
2530. חָמַד *khaw-mad'*; a prim. root; to *delight* in:–beauty, greatly beloved, covet, delectable thing, (X great) delight, desire, goodly, lust, (be) pleasant (thing), precious (thing).
2531. חֶמֶד *kheh'-med*; from 2530; *delight*:–desirable, pleasant.
2532. חֶמְדָּה *khem-daw'*; fem. of 2531; *delight*:–desire, goodly, pleasant, precious.
2533. חֶמְדָּן *khem-dawn'*; from 2531; *pleasant*; *Chemdan*, an Idumaean:–Hemdan.
2534. חֵמָה *khay-maw'*; or (Da. 11:44) חֵמָא *khay-maw'*; from 3179; *heat*; fig., *anger, poison* (from its *fever*):–anger, bottles, hot displeasure, furious(-ly, -ry), heat, indignation, poison, rage, wrath(-ful). See 2529.
2535. חַמָּה *kham-maw'*; from 2525; *heat*; by impl., the *sun*:–heat, sun.
2536. חַמּוּאֵל *kham-moo-ale'*; from 2535 and 410; *anger of God*; *Chammuel*, an Isr.:–Hamuel.
2537. חֲמוּטַל *kham-oo-tal'*; or חֲמִיטַל *kham-ee-tal'*; from 2524 and 2919; *father-in-law of dew*; *Chamutal* or *Chamital*, an Isr.s:– Hamutal.
2538. חָמוּל, *khaw-mool'*; from 2550; *pitied*; *Chamul*, an Isr.:–Hamul.
2539. חָמוּלִי *khaw-moo-lee'*; patron. from 2538: a *Chamulite* (coll.) or desc. of Chamul:–Hamulites.
2540. חַמּוֹן *kham-mone'*; from 2552; *warm* spring; *Chammon*, the name of two places in Pal.:–Hammon.
2541. חָמוֹץ *khaw-motse'*; from 2556; prop. *violent*; by impl., a *robber*:–oppressed.
2542. חַמּוּק *kham-mook'*; from 2559; a *wrapping*, i.e. *drawers*:–joints.
2543. חֲמוֹר *kham-ore'*; or (short.) חֲמֹר *kham-ore*; from 2560; a male *ass* (from its dun *red*):–(he)ass.
2544. חֲמוֹר *kham-ore'*; the same as 2543; *ass*; *Chamor*, a Canaanite:–Hamor.
2545. חֲמוֹת *kham-oth'*; or (short.) חֲמֹת *kham-oth'*; fem. of 2524; a *mother-in-law*:–mother in law.
2546. חֹמֶט *kho'met*; from an un. root prob. mean., to *lie low*; a *lizard* (as *creeping*):–snail.
2547. חֻמְטָה *khoom-taw'*; fem. of 2546; *low*; *Chumtah*, a place in Pal.:–Humtah.
2548. חָמִיץ *khaw-meets'*; from 2556; *seasoned*, i.e. *salt* provender:–clean.
2549. חֲמִישִׁי *kham-ee-shee'*; or חֲמִשִּׁי *kham-ish-shee'*; ord. from 2568; *fifth*; also a *fifth*:–fifth (part).
2550. חָמַל *khaw-mal'*; a prim. root; to *commiserate*; by impl., to *spare*:–have compassion, (have) pity, spare.
2551. חֶמְלָה *khem-law'*; from 2550; *commiseration*:–merciful, pity.
2552. חָמַם *khaw-mam'*; a prim. root; to *be hot* (lit. or fig.):–enflame self, get (have) heat, be (wax) hot, (be, wax) warm (self, at).
2553. חַמָּן *kham-mawn'*; from 2535; a *sun-pillar*:–idol, image.
2554. חָמַס *khaw-mas'*; a prim. root; to be *violent*; by impl., to *maltreat*:–make bare, shake off, violate, do violence, take away violently, wrong, imagine wrongfully.
2555. חָמָס *khaw-mawce'*; from 2554; *violence*; by impl., *wrong*; by meton. unjust *gain*:–cruel(-ty), damage, false, injustice, X oppressor, unrighteous, violence (against, done), violent (dealing), wrong.
2556. חָמֵץ *khaw-mates'*; a prim. root; to *be pungent*; i.e. in taste (*sour*, i.e. lit. *fermented*, or fig., *harsh*), in color (*dazzling*):–cruel (man), dyed, be grieved, leavened.
2557. חָמֵץ *khaw-mates'*; from 2556; *ferment*,

HEBREW

(fig.) *extortion:*–leaven, leavened (bread).
2558. חֹמֶץ *kho'-mets;* from 2556; *vinegar:*–vinegar.
2559. חָמַק *khaw-mak';* a prim. root; prop. to *enwrap;* hence, to *depart* (i.e. turn about):–go about, withdraw self.
2560. חָמַר *khaw-mar';* a prim. root; prop. to *boil* up; hence, to *ferment* (with scum); to *glow* (with redness); as denom. (from 2564) to *smear* with pitch:–daub, befoul, be red, trouble.
2561. חֶמֶר *kheh'-mer;* from 2560; *wine* (as *fermenting*):–X pure, red wine.
2562. חֲמַר *kham-ar'* (Chald.); cor. to 2561; *wine:*–wine.
2563. חֹמֶר *kho'mer;* from 2560; prop. a *bubbling* up, i.e. of water, a *wave;* of earth, *mire* or *clay* (cement); also a *heap;* hence, a *chomer* or dry measure:–clay, heap, homer, mire, mortar.
2564. חֵמָר *khay-mawr';* from 2560; *bitumen* (as *rising* to the surface):–slime(-pit).
2565. חֲמֹרָה *kham-o-raw';* from 2560 (comp. 2563); a *heap:*–heap.
2566. חַמְרָן *kham-rawn';* from 2560; *red; Chamran,* an Idumaean:–Amran.
2567. חָמַשׁ *khaw-mash';* a denom. from 2568; to *tax a fifth:*–take up the fifth part.
2568. חָמֵשׁ *khaw-maysh';* masc. חֲמִשָּׁה *kham-ish-shaw;* a prim. numeral; *five:*–fif[-teen], fifth, five (X apiece).
2569. חֹמֶשׁ *kho'-mesh;* from 2567; a *fifth* tax:–fifth part.
2570. חֹמֶשׁ *kho'-mesh;* from an un. root prob. mean., to *be stout;* the *abdomen* (as *obese*):–fifth[rib].
2571. חָמֻשׁ *khaw-moosh';* pass.part. of the same as 2570; *staunch,* i.e. able-bodied *soldiers:*–armed (men), harnessed.
2572. חֲמִשִּׁים *kham-ish-sheem';* multiple of 2568; *fifty:*–fifty.
2573. חֵמֶת *klay'-meth;* from the same as 2346; a skin *bottle* (as *tied* up):–bottle.
2574. חֲמָת *kham-awth';* from the same as 2346; *walled; Chamath,* a place in Syria:–Hamath, Hemath.
2575. חַמַּת *klam-math';* a var. for the first part of 2576; *hot* springs; *Chammath,* a place in Pal.:–Hammath.
2576. חַמֹּת דֹּאר *kham-moth' dore;* from the pl. of 2535 and 1756; *hot* springs of *Dor; Chammath-Dor,* a place in Pal.:–Hamath-Dor.
2577. חֲמָתִי *kham-aw-thee';* patrial from 2574; a *Chamathite* or nat. of *Chamath:*–Hamathite.
2578. חֲמַת צוֹבָה *kham-ath' tso-baw';* from 2574 and 6678; *Chamath of Tsobah; Chamath-Tsobah;* prob. the same as 2574:–Hamath-Zobah.
2579. חֲמַת רַבָּה *kham-ath' rab-baw';* from 2574 and 7237; *Chamath of Rabbah; Chamath-Rabbah,* prob. the same as 2574.
2580. חֵן *khane;* from 2603; *graciousness,* i.e. subj. (*kindness, favor*) or obj. (*beauty*):–favour, grace(-ious), pleasant, precious, [well-]favoured.
2581. חֵן *khane;* the same as 2580; *grace; Chen,* a fig. name for an Isr.:–Hen.
2582. חֵנָדָד *khay-naw-dawd';* prob. from 2580 and 1908; *favor of Hadad; Chenadad,* an Isr.:–Henadad.
2583. חָנָה *khaw-naw';* a prim. root [comp. 2603]; prop. to *incline;* by impl., to *decline* (of the slanting rays of evening); spec., to *pitch* a tent; gen. to *encamp* (for abode or siege):–abide (in tents), camp, dwell, encamp, grow to an end, lie, pitch (tent), rest in tent.
2584. חַנָּה *khan-naw'* from 2603; *favored; Channah,* an Isr.s:–Hannah.
2585. חֲנוֹךְ *khan-oke';* from 2596; *initiated; Chanok,* an antediluvian patriach:–Enoch.
2586. חָנוּן *khaw-noon';* from 2603; *favored; Chanun,* the name of an Ammonite and of two Isr.:–Hanun.
2587. חַנּוּן *khan-noon';* from 2603; *gracious:*–gracious.
2588. חָנוּת *khaw-nooth';* from 2583; prop. a *vault* or *cell* (with an arch); by impl., a *prison:*–cabin.
2589. חַנּוֹת *klan-noth';* from 2603 (in the sense of *prayer*); *supplication:*–be gracious, intreated.
2590. חָנַט *khaw-nat';* a prim. root; to *spice;* by impl., to *embalm;* also to *ripen:*–embalm, put forth.
2591. חִנְטָא *khint-taw'* (Chald.); cor. to 2406; *wheat:*–wheat.
2592. חַנִּיאֵל *khan-nee-ale';* from 2603 and 410; *favor of* God; *Channiel,* the name of two Isr.:–Hanniel.
2593. חָנִיךְ *kaw-neek';* from 2596; *initiated;* i.e. *practiced:*–trained.
2594. חֲנִינָה *khan-ee-naw';* from 2603; *graciousness:*–favour.
2595. חֲנִית *khan-eeth';* from 2583; a lance (for *thrusting,* like *pitching* a tent):–javelin, spear.
2596. חָנַךְ *khaw-nak';* a prim. root; prop. to *narrow* [comp. 2614]; fig., to *initiate* or *discipline:*–dedicate, train up.
2597. חֲנֻכָּא *chan-ook-kaw'* (Chald.); cor. to 2598; *consecration:*–dedication.
2598. חֲנֻכָּה *khan-ook-kaw';* from 2596; *initiation,* i.e. *consecration:*–dedicating(-tion).
2599. חֲנֹכִי *khan-o-kee';* patron. from 2585; a *Chanokite* (coll.) or desc. of Chanok:–Hanochites.
2600. חִנָּם *khin-nawm';* from 2580; *gratis,* i.e. devoid of cost, reason or advantage:–without a cause (cost, wages), causeless, to cost nothing, free(-ly), innocent, for nothing (nought, in vain.
2601. חֲנַמְאֵל *khan-am-ale';* prob. by orth. var. for 2606; *Chanamel,* an Isr.
2602. חֲנָמָל *khan-aw-mawl';* of unc. derivation; perh. the aphis or plantlouse:–frost.
2603. חָנַן *khaw-nan';* a prim. root [comp. 2583]; prop. to *bend* or stoop in kindness to an inferior; to *favor, bestow;* caus. to *implore* (i.e. move to favor by petition):–beseech, X fair, (be, find, shew) favour(-able), be (deal, give, grant (gracious(-ly), intreat, (be) merciful, have (shew) mercy (on, upon), have pity upon, pray, make supplication, X very.
2604. חֲנַן *khan-an'* (Chald.); cor. to 2603; to *favor* or (caus.) to *entreat:*–shew mercy, make supplication.
2605. חָנָן *khaw-nawn';* from 2603; *favor; Chanan,* the name of seven Isr.:–Canan.
2606. חֲנַנְאֵל *khan-an-ale';* from 2603 and 410; *God has favored; Chananel,* prob. an Isr., from whom a tower of Jerus. was named:–Hananeel.
2607. חֲנָנִי *khan-aw-nee';* from 2603; *gracious; Chanani,* the name of six Isr.:–Hanani.
2608. חֲנַנְיָה *khan-an-yaw';* or חֲנַנְיָהוּ *khan-an-yaw'-hoo;* from 2603 and 3050; *Jah has favored; Chananjah,* the name of thirteen Isr.:–Hananiah.
2609. חָנֵס *khaw-nace';* of Eg. der.; *Chanes,* a place in Eg.:–Hanes.
2610. חָנֵף *khaw-nafe';* a prim. root; to *soil,* esp. in a mor. sense:–corrupt, defile, X greatly, pollute, profane.
2611. חָנֵף *khaw-nafe';* from 2610; *soiled* (i.e. with sin), *impious:*– hypocrite(-ical).
2612. חֹנֶף *kho'-nef;* from 2610; mor. *filth,* i.e. *wickedness:*–hypocrisy.
2613. חֲנֻפָּה *khan-oo-faw';* fem. from 2610; *impiety:*–profaneness.
2614. חָנַק *khaw-nak';* a prim. root [comp. 2596]; to *be narrow;* by impl., to *throttle,* or (reflex.) to *choke* oneself to death (by a rope):–hang self, strangle.
2615. חַנָּתֹן *khan-naw-thone';* prob.from 2603; *favored; Channathon,* a place in Pal.:–Hannathon.
2616. חָסַד *khaw-sad';* a prim. root; prop. perh. to *bow* (the neck only [comp. 2603] in courtesy to an equal), i.e. to *be kind;* also (by euphem. [comp. 1288], but rarely) to *reprove:*–shew self merciful, put to shame.
2617. חֶסֶד *kheh'-sed;* from 2616; *kindness;* by impl. (towards God) *piety:* rarely (by opposition) *reproof,* or (subj..) *beauty:*–favour, good deed(-liness, -ness), kindly, (loving-)kindness, merciful (kindness), mercy, pity, reproach, wicked thing.
2618. חֶסֶד *kheh'-sed;* the same as 2617: *favor; Chesed,* an Isr.:–Hesed.
2619. חֲסַדְיָה *khas-ad-yaw';* from 2617 and 3050; *Jah has favored: Chasadjah,* an Isr.:–Hasadiah.
2620. חָסָה *khaw-saw';* a prim. root; to *flee* for protection [comp. 982]; fig., to *confide* in:–have hope, make refuge, (put) trust.
2621. חֹסָה *kho-saw';* from 2620. *hopeful; Chosah,* an Isr.; also a place in Pal.:–Hosah.
2622 חָסוּת *khaw-sooth';* from 2620; *confidence:*–trust.
2623. חָסִיד *khaw-seed';* from 2616; prop. *kind,* i.e. (relig.) *pious* (a saint):–godly (man), good, holy (one), merciful, saint, [un-]godly.
2624. חֲסִידָה *khas-ee-daw';* fem. of 2623; the *kind* (maternal) bird, i.e. a *stork:*–X feather, stork.
2625. חָסִיל *khaw-seel';* from 2628; the *ravager,* i.e. a *locust:*–caterpillar.
2626. חֲסִין *khas-een';* from 2630; prop. *firm,* i.e. (by impl.) *mighty:*–strong.
2627. חַסִּיר *khas-seer'* (Chald.); from a root cor. to 2637; *deficient:*–wanting.
2628. חָסַל *khaw-sal';* a prim. root; to *eat* off:–consume.
2629. חָסַם *khaw-sam';* a prim. root; to *muzzle;* by anal., to *stop* the nose:–muzzle, stop.
2630. חָסַן *khaw-san';* a prim. root; prop. to (*be*) *compact;* by impl., to *hoard:*–lay up.
2631. חֲסַן *khas-an'* (Chald.); cor. to 2630; to *hold* in occupancy:–possess.
2632. חֵסֶן *hay'-sen* (Chald.); from 2631; *strength:*–power.
2633. חֹסֶן *kho'-sen;* from 2630; *wealth:*–riches, strength, treasure.
2634. חָסֹן *khaw-sone';* from 2630; *powerful:*–strong.
2635. חֲסַף *khas-af'* (Chald.); from a root cor. to that of 2636; a *clod:*–clay.
2636. חַסְפַּס *khas-pas';* redupl. from an un. root mean. app. to *peel;* a *shred* or *scale:*–

round thing.
2637. חָסֵר *khaw-sare';* a prim. root; to *lack;* by impl., to *fail, want, lessen:*–be abated, bereave, decrease, (cause to) fail, (have) lack, make lower, want.
2638. חָסֵר *khaw-sare';* from 2637; lacking; hence, *without:*–destitute, fail, lack, have need, void, want.
2639. חֶסֶר *kheh'-ser;* from 2637; *lack;* hence, *destitution:*–poverty, want.
2640. חֹסֶר *kho'-ser* from 2637; *poverty:*–in want of.
2641. חַסְרָה *khas-raw';* from 2637; *want:*–*Chasrah,* an Isr.:–Hasrah.
2642. חֶסְרוֹן *khes-rone';* from 2637; *deficiency:*–wanting.
2643. חַף *khaf;* from 2653 (in the mor. sense of *covered* from soil); *pure:*–innocent.
2644. חָפָא *khaw-faw';* an orth. var. of 2645; prop. to *cover,* i.e. (in a sinister sense) to *act covertly:*–do secretly.
2645. חָפָה *khaw-faw';* a prim. root [comp. 2644, 2653]; to *cover;* by impl., to *veil,* to *encase, protect:*–ceil, cover, overlay.
2646. חֻפָּה *khoop-paw';* from 2645; a *canopy:*–chamber, closet, defence.
2647. חֻפָּה *khoop-paw';* the same as 2646; *Chuppah,* an Isr.:–Huppah.
2648. חָפַז *khaw-faz';* a prim. root; prop. to *start* up suddenly, i.e. (by impl.) to *hasten* away, to *fear:*–(make) haste (away), tremble.
2649. חִפָּזוֹן *khip-paw-zone';* from 2468; *hasty flight:*–haste.
2650. חֻפִּים *khoop-peem';* pl. of 2646 [comp. 2349]; *Chuppim,* an Isr.:–Huppim.
2651. חֹפֶן *kho'-fen;* from an un. root of unc. signif.; a *fist* (only in the dual):–fists, (both) hands, hand[-ful].
2652. חָפְנִי *khof-nee';* from 2651; perh. *pugilist; Chophni,* an Isr.:–Hophni.
2653. חָפַף *khaw-faf';* a prim. root [comp. 2645, 3182]; to *cover* (in protection):–cover.
2654. חָפֵץ *khaw-fates';* a prim. root; properly, to *incline* to; by impl. (lit. but rarely) to *bend;* fig., to *be pleased* with, *desire:*–X any at all, (have, take) delight, desire, favour, like, move, be (well) pleased, have pleasure, will, would.
2655. חָפֵץ *khaw-fates';* from 2654; *pleased* with:–delight in, desire, favour, please, have pleasure, whosoever would, willing, wish.
2656. חֵפֶץ *khay'-fets;* from 2654; *pleasure;* hence (abstr.) *desire;* concr., a *valuable* thing; hence (by ext.) a *matter* (as something in mind):–acceptable, delight(-some), desire, things desired, matter, pleasant(-ure), purpose, willingly.
2657. חֶפְצִי בָהּ *khef-tsee' baw;* from 2656 with suffixes; *my delight* (is) *in her; Cheptsi-bah,* a fanciful name for Pal.:–Hephzi-bah.
2658. חָפַר *khaw-far';* a prim. root; prop. to *pry* into; by impl., to *delve,* to *explore:*–dig, paw, search out, seek.
2659. חָפֵר *khaw-fare';* a prim. root [perh. rath. the same as 2658 through the idea of *detection*]: to *blush;* fig., to *be ashamed, disappointed;* caus., to *shame, reproach:*–be *ashamed,* be confounded, be brought to confusion (unto shame), come (be put to) shame, bring reproach.
2660. חֵפֶר *khay'-fer;* from 2658 or 2659; a *pit* or *shame*; *Chepher,* a place in Pal.; also the name of three Isr.:–Hepher.
2661. חֲפֹר *khaf-ore';* from 2658; a *hole;* only in connection with 6512, which ought rather to be joined as one word, thus חֲפַרְפֵּרָה *khaf-ar-pay-raw';* by redupl. from 2658; a *burrower,* i.e. prob. a *rat:*–+ mole.
2662. חֶפְרִי *khef-ree';* patron. from 2660; a *Chephrite* (coll.) or desc. of *Chepher:*–Hepherites.
2663. חֲפָרַיִם *khaf-aw-rah'-yim;* dual of 2660; *double pit; Chapharajim,* a place in Pal.:–Haphraim.
2664. חָפַשׂ *khaw-fas';* a prim. root; to *seek;* caus., to *conceal* oneself (i.e. let be sought), or *mask:*–change, (make) diligent (search), disguise self, hide, search (for, out).
2665. חֵפֶשׂ *khay'-fes;* from 2664; something *covert,* i.e. a *trick:*–search.
2666. חָפַשׁ *khaw-fash';* a prim. root; to *spread* loose; fig., to *manumit:*–be free.
2667. חֹפֶשׁ *kho'-fesh;* from 2666; something *spread* loosely, i.e. a *carpet:*–precious.
2668. חֻפְשָׁה *khoof-shaw';* from 2666; *liberty* (from slavery):–freedom.
2669. חָפְשׁוּת *khof-shooth';* and חָפְשִׁית *khof-sheeth';* from 2666; *prostration* by sickness (with 1004, a *hospital*):–several.
2670. חָפְשִׁי *khof-shee';* from 2666; *exempt* (from bondage, tax or care):–free, liberty.
2671. חֵץ *khayts;* from 2686; prop. a *piercer,* i.e. an *arrow;* by impl., a *wound;* fig., (of God) thunder-bolt; (by interch. for 6086) the *shaft* of a spear:–+ archer, arrow, dart, shaft, staff, wound.
2672. חָצַב *khaw-tsab';* or חָצֵב *khaw-tsabe';* a primitive root ; to *cut* or carve (wood), stone or other material); by impl., to *hew, split, square, quarry, engrave:*–cut, dig, divide, grave, hew (out, -er), made, mason.
2673. חָצָה *khaw-tsaw'* a prim. root [comp. 2086]; to *cut* or *split* in two; to *halve:*–divide, X live out half, reach to the midst, part.
2674. חָצוֹר *khaw-tsore';* a coll. Form of 2691; *village; Chatsor,* the name (thus simply) of two places in Pal. and of one in Arabia:– Hazor.
2675. חָצוֹר חֲדַתָּה *khaw-tsore' khad-at-taw';* from 2674 and a Chaldaizing form of the fem. of 2319 [comp. 2323]; *new Chatsor,* a place in Pal.:–Hazor, Hadattah [*as if two places*].
2676. חֲצוֹת *khaw-tsoth';* from 2673; the *middle* (of the night):–mid[-night].
2677. חֵצִי *khay-tsee';* from 2673; the half or *middle:*–*half, middle,* mid[-night], midst, part, two parts.
2678. חִצִּי *khits-tsee';* or חֵצִי *chay-tsee;* prol. from 2671; an *arrow:*–arrow.
2679. חֲצִי הַמְּנֻחוֹת *chat-tsee' men-oo-khoth'* from 2677 and the pl. of 4496, with the art. interp.; *midst of the resting-places; Chatsi-ham-Menuchoth,* an Isr.:–half of the Manahethites.
2680. חֲצִי הַמְּנַחְתִּי *khat-see' ham-men-akh-tee';* patron. from 2679; a *Chatsi-ham-Menachtite* or desc. of Chatsi-ham-Menuchoth:–half of the Manahethites.
2681. חָצִיר *khaw-tseer';* a collat. form of 2691; a *court* or *abode:*–court.
2682. חָצִיר *khaw-tseer';* perh. or. the same as 2681, from the *greenness* of a courtyard; *grass;* also a *leek* (coll.):–grass, hay, herb, leek.
2683. חֵצֶן *khay'-tsen;* from an un. root mean. to hold *firmly;* the *bosom* (as *comprised* between the arms):–bosom.
2684. חֹצֶן *kho'tsen;* a collat. form of 2683, and mean. the same:–arm, lap.
2685. חֲצַף *khats-af'* (Chald.); a prim. root; prop. to *shear* or cut close; fig., to *be severe:*–hasty, be urgent.
2686. חָצַץ *khaw-tsats';* a prim. root [comp. 2673]; prop. to *chop* into, pierce or sever; hence, to *curtail,* to *distribute* (into ranks); as denom. from 2671, to *shoot* an arrow:–archer, X bands, cut off in the midst.
2687. חָצָץ *khaw-tsawts'* from 2687; prop. something *cutting;* hence, *gravel* (as *grit*); also (like 2671) an *arrow:*–arrow, gravel (stone).
2688. חַצְצוֹן תָּמָר *khats-ets-one' taw-mawr';* or חַצֲצֹן תָּמָר *khats-ats-one' taw-mawr';* from 2686 and 8558; *division* [i.e. perh. *row*] of (the) *palm-tree; Chatsetson-tamar,* a place in Pal.:–Hazezon- tamar.
2689. חֲצֹצְרָה *khats-o-tser-aw';* by reduplication from 2690; a *trumpet* (from its *sundered* or quavering note):–trumpet(-er).
2690. חָצַר *khaw-tsar';* a prim. root; prop. to *surround* with a stockade, and thus *separate* from the open country; but used only in the redupl. form חֲצֹצֵר *khast-o-tsare';* or (2 Chronicles 5:12) חֲצֹרֵר *khats-o-rare';* as dem. from 2689; to *trumpet,* i.e. blow on that instrument:–blow, sound, trumpeter.
2691. חָצֵר *khaw-tsare';* (masc. and fem.); from 2690 in its or. sense; a *yard* (as *inclosed* by a fence); also a *hamlet* (as similarly *surrounded* with walls):–court, tower, village.
2692. חֲצַר אַדָּר *khats-ar' addawr';* from 2691 and 146; (the) *village of Addar; Chatsar-Addar,* a place in Pal.:–Hazar-addar.
2693. חֲצַר גַּדָּה *khats-ar'gad-daw';* from 2691 and a fem. of 1408; (the) *village of* (female) *Fortune; Chatsar-Gaddah,* a place in Pal.:–Hazar-gaddah.
2694. חֲצַר הַתִּיכוֹן *khats-ar' hat-tee-kone';* from 2691 and 8484 with the art. interp.; *village of the middle; Chatsar-hat-Tikon,* a place in Pal.:–Hazar-hatticon.
2695. חֶצְרוֹ *khets-ro';* by an orth. var. for 2696; *inclosure; Chetsro,* an Isr.:–Hezro, Hezrai.
2696. חֶצְרוֹן *khets-rone';* from 2691; *court-yard; Chetsron,* the name of a place in Pal.; also of two Isr.:–Hezron.
2697. חֶצְרוֹנִי *khets-ro-nee';* patron. from 2696; a *Chetsronite* or (coll.) desc. of Chetsron:–Hezronites.
2698. חֲצֵרוֹת *khats-ay-roth';* fem. pl. of 2691; *yards; Chatseroth,* a place in Pal.:–Hazeroth.
2699. חֲצֵרִים *khats-ay-reem';* pl. masc. of 2691; *yards; Chatserim,* a place in Pal.:–Hazerim.
2700. חֲצַרְמָוֶת *khats-ar-maw'-veth;* from 2691 and 4194; *village of death; Chatsarmaveth,* a place in Arabia:–Hazarmaveth.
2701. חֲצַר סוּסָה *khats-ar'soo-saw';* from 2691 and 5484; *village of cavalry; Chatsar-Susah,* a place in Pal.:–Hazar-susah.
2702. חֲצַר סוּסִים *khats-ar' soo-seem';* from 2691 and the pl. of 5483; *village of horses; Chatsar-Susim,* a place in Pal.:–Hazar-susim.
2703. חֲצַר עֵינוֹן *khats-ar' ay-nōne';* from 2691 and a der. of 5869; *village of springs; Chatsar-Enon,* a place in Pal.:–Hazar-enon.
2704. חֲצַר עֵינָן *khats-ar' ay-nawn';* from 2691 and the same as 5881; *village of springs; Chatsar-Enan,* a place in Pal.:–Hazar-enan.
2705. חֲצַר שׁוּעָל *khats-ar' shoo-awl';* from 2691 and 7776; *village of* (the) *fox; Chatsar-Shual,* a place in Pal.:–Hazar-shual.
2706. חֹק *khoke;* from 2710; an *enactment;*

hence, an *appointment* (of time, space, quantity, labor or usage):–appointed, bound, commandment, convenient, custom, decree(-d), due, law, measure, X necessary, ordinance (-nary), portion, set time, statute, task.

2707. חָקָה *khaw-kaw';* a prim. root; to *carve;* by impl., to *delineate;* also to *entrench:*–carved work, portrayed, set a print.

2708. חֻקָּה *khook-kaw';* fem. of 2706, and mean. substantially the same:–appointed, custom, manner, ordinance, site, statute.

2709. חֲקוּפָא *khah-oo-faw';* from an un. root prob. mean. to *bend; crooked; Chakupha,* one of the Nethinim:–Hakupha.

2710. חָקַק *khaw-kak';* a prim. root; prop. to *hack,* i.e. *engrave* (Judges 5:14, to *be a scribe* simply); by impl., to *enact* (laws being *cut* in stone or metal tablets) or (gen.) *prescribe:*–appoint, decree, governor, grave, lawgiver, note, pourtray, print, set.

2711. חֵקֶק *khay'-kek;* from 2710; an *enactment,* a *resolution:*–decree, thought.

2712. חֻקֹּק *khook-koke';* or (fully) חוּקֹק *khoo-koke';* from 2710; *appointed; Chukkok* or *Chukok,* a place in Pal.:–Hukkok, Hukok.

2713. חָקַר *khaw-kar';* a prim. root; prop. to *penetrate;* hence, to *examine* intimately:–find out, (make) search (out), seek (out), sound, try.

2714. חֵקֶר *khay'-ker;* from 2713; *examination, enumeration, deliberation:*–finding out, number, [un-]search(-able, -ed, out, -ing).

2715. חֹר *khore;* or חוֹר (fully) *khore;* from 2787; prop. *white* or *pure* (from the *cleansing* or *shining* power of fire [comp. 2751]; hence (fig.) *noble* (in rank):–noble.

2716. חֶרֶא *kheh'-reh;* from an un. (and vulgar) root prob. mean. to *evacuate* the bowels: *excrement:*–dung. Also חֲרִי *khar-ee'.*

2717. חָרַב *khaw-rab'* or חָרֵב *khaw-rabe';* a prim. root; to *parch* (through drought) i.e. (by anal.,) to *desolate, destroy, kill:*– decay, (be) desolate, destroy(-er), (be) dry (up), slay, X surely, (lay, lie, make) waste.

2718. חֲרַב *khar-ab'* (Chald.); a root cor. to 2717; to *demolish:*–destroy.

2719. חֶרֶב *kheh'-reb;* from 2717; *drought;* also a *cutting* instrument (from its *destructive* effect), as a *knife, sword,* or other sharp implement:–axe, dagger, knife, mattock, sword, tool.

2720. חָרֵב *khaw-rabe';* from 2717; *parched* or *ruined:*–desolate, dry, waste.

2721. חֹרֶב *kho'-reb;* a collat. form of 2719; *drought* or *desolation:*–desolation, drought, dry, heat, X utterly, waste.

2722. חֹרֵב *kho-rabe';* from 2717; *desolate; Choreb,* a (generic) name for the Sinaitic mountains:–Horeb.

2723. חָרְבָּה *khor-baw';* fem. of 2721; prop. *drought,* i.e. (by impl.) a *desolation:*–decayed place, desolate (place, -tion), destruction, (laid) waste (place).

2724. חָרָבָה *khaw-raw-baw';* fem. of 2720; a *desert:*–dry (ground, land).

2725. חֲרָבוֹן *khar-aw-bone';* from 2717; parching *heat:*–drought.

2726. חַרְבוֹנָא *khar-bo-naw';* or חַרְבוֹנָה *khar-bo-naw';* of Pers. or.; *Charbona* or *Charbonah,* a eunuch of Xerxes:–Harbona, Harbonah.

2727. חָרַג *khaw-rag';* a prim. root; prop. to *leap* suddenly, i.e. (by impl.) to *be dismayed:*–be afraid.

2728. חַרְגֹּל *khar-gole';* from 2727; the *leaping* insect, i.e. a *locust:*–beetle.

2729. חָרַד *khaw-rad';* a prim. root; to *shudder* with terror; hence, to *fear;* also to *hasten* (with anxiety):–be (make) afraid, be careful, discomfit, fray (away), quake, tremble.

2730. חָרֵד *khaw-rade';* from 2729; *fearful;* also *reverential:*–afraid, trembling.

2731. חֲרָדָה *khar-aw-daw';* fem. of 2730; *fear, anxiety:*–care, X exceedingly, fear, quaking, trembling.

2732. חֲרָדָה *khar-aw-daw';* the same as 2731; *Charadah,* a place in the Desert:–Haradah.

2733. חֲרֹדִי *khar-o-dee';* patrial from a der. of 2729 [comp. 5878]; a *Charodite,* or inh. of *Charod:*–Harodite.

2734. חָרָה *khaw-raw';* a prim. root [comp. 2787]; to *glow* or grow warm; fig. (usually) to *blaze* up, of anger, zeal, jealousy:–be angry, burn, be displeased, X earnestly, fret self, grieve, be (wax) hot, be incensed, kindle, X very, be wroth. See 8474.

2735. חֹר הַגִּדְגָּד *khore hag-ghid-gawd';* from 2356 and a collat. (masc.) form of 1412, with the art. interp.; *hole of the cleft: Chor-hag-Gidgad,* a place in the Desert:–Hor-hagidgad.

2736. חַרְהֲיָה *khar-hah-yaw';* from 2734 and 3050; *fearing Jah; Charhajah,* an Isr.:–Harhaiah.

2737. חָרוּז *khaw-rooz';* from an un. root mean. to *perforate;* prop. *pierced,* i.e. *a bead* of pearl, gems or jewels (as strung):–chain.

2738. חָרוּל *khaw-rool';* or (short.) חָרֻל *khaw-rool';* app., a pass.part. of an un. root prob. mean. to *be prickly;* prop. *pointed,* i.e. a *bramble* or other thorny weed: nettle.

2739. חֲרוּמַף *khar-oo-maf';* from pass.part. of 2763 and 639; *snub-nosed; Charumaph,* an Isr.:–Harumaph.

2740. חָרוֹן *khaw-rone';* or (short.) חָרֹן *khaw-rone';* from 2734; a *burning* of anger:–sore displeasure, fierce(-ness), fury, (fierce) wrath(-ful).

2741. חֲרוּפִי *khar-oo-fee';* a patrial from (prob.) a collat. form of 2756; a *Charuphite* or inh. of Charuph (or Chariph):–Haruphite.

2742. חָרוּץ *khaw-roots';* or חָרֻץ *khaw-roots';* pass.part. of 2782; prop. *incised* or (act.) *incisive;* hence (as noun masc. or fem.) a *trench* (as dug), *gold* (as mined), a *threshing-sledge* (having sharp teeth); (fig.) *determination;* also *eager:*–decision, diligent, (fine) gold, pointed things, sharp, threshing instrument, wall.

2743. חָרוּץ *khaw-roots';* he same as 2742; *earnest; Charuts,* an Isr.:–Haruz.

2744. חַרְחוּר *khar-khoor';* a fuller form of 2746; *inflammation; Charchur,* one of the Nethinim:–Harhur.

2745. חַרְחַס *khar-khas';* from the same as 2775; perh. *shining; Charchas,* an Isr.:–Harhas.

2746. חַרְחֻר *khar-khoor';* from 2787; *fever* (as *hot*):–extreme burning.

2747. חֶרֶט *kheh'-ret;* from a prim. root mean. to *engrave;* a *chisel* or *graver;* also a *style* for writing:–graving tool, pen.

2748. חַרְטֹם *khar-tome';* from the same as 2747; a *horoscopist* (as *drawing* magical lines or circles):–magician.

2749. חַרְטֹם *khar-tome'* (Chald.); the same as 2748:–magician.

2750. חֳרִי *khor-ee';* from 2734; a *burning* (i.e. intense) anger:–fierce, X great, heat.

2751. חֹרִי *kho-ree';* from the same as 2353; *white* bread:–white.

2752. חֹרִי *kho-ree';* from 2356; *cave-dweller* or troglodyte; a *Chorite* or aboriginal Idumaean:–Horims, Horites.

2753. חֹרִי *kho-ree';* or חוֹרִי *kho-ree';* the same as 2752; *Chori,* the name of two men:–Hori.

2754. חָרִיט *khaw-reet';* or חָרִט *khaw-reet';* from the same as 2747; prop. *cut* out (or *hollow*), i.e. (by impl.) a *pocket:*–bag, crisping pin.

2755. חֲרֵי־יוֹנִים *khar-ay'-yo-neem';* from the pl. of 2716 and the pl. of 3123; *excrements of doves* [or perh. rather the pl. of a single word *khar-aw-yone';* of similar or unc. der.,] prob. a kind of vegetable:–doves' dung.

2756. חָרִיף *khaw-reef';* from 2778; *autumnal; Chariph,* the name of two Isr.:–Hariph.

2757. חָרִיץ *khaw-reets';* or חָרִץ *khaw-reets';* from 2782; prop. *incisure* or (pass.) *incised* [comp. 2742]; hence, a *threshing-sledge* (with *sharp* teeth): also a *slice* (as cut):–+ cheese, harrow.

2758. חָרִישׁ *khaw-reesh';* from 2790; *ploughing* or its season:–earing (time), ground.

2759. חֲרִישִׁי *khar-ee-shee';* from 2790 in the sense of *silence; quiet,* i.e. *sultry* (as fem. noun, the *sirocco* or hot east wind):–vehement.

2760. חָרַךְ *khaw-rak';* a prim. root; to *braid* (i.e. to *entangle* or snare) or *catch* (game) in a net:–roast.

2761. חֲרַךְ *khar-ak'* (Chald.); a root prob. allied to the equiv. of 2787; to *scorch:*–singe.

2762. חֶרֶךְ *kheh'-rek;* from 2760; prop. a *net,* i.e. (by anal.) *lattice:*–lattice.

2763. חָרַם *khaw-ram';* a prim. root; to *seclude;* spec. (by a ban) to *devote* to relig. uses (esp. destruction); phys. and refl., to be *blunt* as to the nose:–make accursed, consecrate, (utterly) destroy, devote, forfeit, have a flat nose, utterly (slay, make away).

2764. חֵרֶם *khay'-rem;* or (Zecheriah 14:11) חֶרֶם *kheh'-rem;* from 2763; phys. (as *shutting in*) a *net* (either lit. or fig.); usually a *doomed* obj.; abstr. *extermination:*–(ac-)curse(-d, -d thing), dedicated thing, things which should have been utterly destroyed, (appointed to) utter destruction, devoted (thing), net.

2765. חֳרֵם *khor-ame';* from 2763; *devoted; Chorem,* a place in Pal.:–Horem.

2766. חָרִם *khaw-reem';* from 2763; *snub-nosed; Charim,* an Isr.:–Harim.

2767. חָרְמָה *khor-maw';* from 2763; *devoted; Chormah,* a place in Pal.:–Hormah.

2768. חֶרְמוֹן *kher-mone';* from 2763; *abrupt; Chermon,* a mount of Pal.:–Hermon.

2769. חֶרְמוֹנִים *kher-mo-neem';* pl. of 2768; *Hermons,* i.e. its peaks:–the Hermonites.

2770. חֶרְמֵשׁ *kher-mashe';* from 2763; a *sickle* (as *cutting*):–sickle.

2771. חָרָן *kaw-rawn';* from 2787; *parched; Charan,* the name of a man and also of a place:–Haran.

2772. חֹרֹנִי *kho-ro-nee';* patrial from 2773; a *Choronite* or inh. of Choronaim:–Horonite.

2773. חֹרֹנַיִם *kho-ro-nah'-yim;* dual of a der. from 2356; *double cave-town; Choronajim,* a place in Moab:–Horonaim.

2774. חַרְנֶפֶר *khar-neh'fer;* of unc. der.; *Charnepher,* an Isr.:–Harnepher.

2775. חֶרֶס *kheh'-res;* or (with a directive enclitic) חַרְסָה *khar'- saw;* from an un. root mean. to *scrape;* the *itch;* also [perh. from the mediating idea of 2777] the *sun:*–itch, sun.

2776. חֶרֶס *kheh'-res;* the same as 2775; *shining; Cheres,* a mountain in Pal.:–Heres.

2777. חַרְסוּת *khar-sooth';* from 2775 (app. in the sense of a red *tile* used for scraping); a *potsherd,* i.e. (by impl.) a *pottery;* the name of a gate at Jerus.:–east.

2778. חָרַף *khaw-raf';* a prim. root; to *pull* off, i.e. (by impl.) to *expose* (as by *stripping*); spec., to *betroth* (as if a surrender); fig., to carp at, i.e. *defame;* denom. (from 2779) to spend the *winter:*–betroth, blaspheme, defy, jeopard, rail, reproach, upbraid.

2779. חֹרֶף *kho'-ref;* from 2778; prop. the *crop* gathered, i.e. (by impl.) the *autumn* (and winter) season; fig., *ripeness* of age:–cold, winter ([-house]), youth.

2780. חָרֵף *khaw-rafe';* from 2778; *reproachful; Chareph,* an Isr.:–Hareph.

2781. חֶרְפָּה *kher-paw';* from 2778; *contumely, disgrace,* the *pudenda:*–rebuke, reproach(-fully), shame.

2782. חָרַץ *khaw-rats';* a prim. root; prop. to *point* sharply, i.e. (lit.) to *wound;* fig., to *be alert,* to *decide:*–bestir self, decide, decree, determine, maim, move.

2783. חֲרַץ *khar-ats'* (Chald.); from a root cor. to 2782 in the sense of *vigor;* the *loin* (as the seat of strength):–loin.

2784. חַרְצֻבָּה *khar-tsoob-baw';* of unc. der.; a *fetter;* fig., a *pain:*–band.

2785. חַרְצַן *kchar-tsan';* from 2782; a *sour* grape (as *sharp* in taste):–kernel.

2786. חָרַק *khaw-rak';* a prim. root; to *grate* the teeth:–gnash.

2787. חָרַר *khaw-rar';* a prim. root; to *glow,* i.e. lit. (to *melt, burn, dry* up) or fig. (to *show* or *incite passion:*–be angry, burn, dry, kindle.

2788. חָרֵר *khaw-rare';* from 2787; *arid:*–parched place.

2789. חֶרֶשׂ *kheh'-res;* a collat. form mediating between 2775 and 2791; a piece of *pottery:*–earth(-en), (pot-)sherd, + stone.

2790. חָרַשׁ *khaw-rash';* a prim. root; to *scratch,* i.e. (by impl.) to *engrave, plough;* hence (from the use of tools) to *fabricate* (of any material); fig., to *devise* (in a bad sense); hence (from the idea of secrecy) to be *silent,* to *let alone;* hence (by impl.) to *be deaf* (as an accompaniment of dumbness):–X altogether, cease, conceal, be deaf, devise, ear, graven, imagine, leave off speaking, hold peace, plow(-er, man), be quiet, rest, practise secretly, keep silence, be silent, speak not a word, be still, hold tongue, worker.

2791. חֶרֶשׁ *kheh'-resh;* from 2790; magical *craft;* also *silence:*–cunning, secretly.

2792. חֶרֶשׁ *kheh'-resh;* the same as 2791:–*Cheresh,* a Levite:–Heresh.

2793. חֹרֶשׁ *kho'-resh;* from 2790; a *forest* (perh. as furnishing the material for fabric):–bough, forest, shroud, wood.

2794. חֹרֵשׁ *kho-rashe';* act.part. of 2790; a *fabricator* or mechanic:–artificer.

2795. חֵרֵשׁ *khay-rashe';* from 2790; *deaf* (whether lit. or spir.):–deaf.

2796. חָרָשׁ *khaw-rawsh'* from 2790; a *fabricator* or any material:–artificer, (+) carpenter, craftsman, engraver, maker, + mason, skilful, (+) smith, worker, workman, such as wrought.

2797. חַרְשָׁא *khar-shaw';* from 2792; *magician; Charsha,* one of the Nethinim:–Harsha.

2798. חֲרָשִׁים *khar-aw-sheem';* pl. of 2796; *mechanics,* the name of a valley in Jerus.:–Charashim, craftsmen.

2799. חֲרֹשֶׁת *khar-o'-sheth;* from 2790; mechanical *work:*–carving, cutting.

2800. חֲרֹשֶׁת *khar-o'-sheth;* the same as 2799; *Charosheth,* a place in Pal.:–Harosheth.

2801. חָרַת *khaw-rath';* a prim. root; to *engrave:*–graven.

2802. חֶרֶת *kheh'-reth;* from 2801 [but equiv. to 2793]; *forest; Chereth,* a thicket in Pal.:–Hereth.

2803. חָשַׁב *khaw-shab';* a prim. root; prop. to *plait* or interpenetrate, i.e. (lit.) to *weave* or (gen.) to *fabricate;* fig., to *plot* or contrive (usually in a malicious sense); hence (from the ment. effort) to *think, regard, value, compute:*–(make) account (of), conceive, consider, count, cunning (man, work, workman), devise, esteem, find out, forecast, hold, imagine, impute, invent, be like, mean, purpose, reckon(-ing be made), regard, think.

2804. חֲשַׁב *khash-ab'* (Chald.); cor. to **2803**; to *regard:*–repute.

2805. חֵשֶׁב *khay'-sheb;* from 2803; a *belt* or strap (as being interlaced):–curious girdle.

2806. חַשְׁבַּדָּנָה *khash-bad-daw'-naw;* from 2803 and 1777; *considerate judge; Chasbaddanah,* an Isr.:–Hasbadana.

2807. חֲשֻׁבָה *khash-oo-baw';* from 2803; *estimation; Cashubah,* an Isr.:–Hashubah.

2808. חֶשְׁבּוֹן *khesh-bone';* from 2803; prop. *contrivance;* by impl., *intelligence:*–account, device, reason.

2809. חֶשְׁבּוֹן *khesh-bone';* the same as 2808; *Cheshbon,* a place E. of the Jordan:–Heshbon.

2810. חִשָּׁבוֹן *khish-shaw-bone';* from 2803; a *contrivance,* i.e. actual (a warlike *machine*) or ment. (a *machination*):–engine, invention.

2811. חֲשַׁבְיָה *khash-ab-yaw';* or חֲשַׁבְיָהוּ *khash-ab-yaw'-hoo;* from 2803 and 3050; *Jah has regarded; Chashabjah,* the name of nine Isr.:–Hashabiah.

2812. חֲשַׁבְנָה *khash-ab-naw';* fem. of 2808; *inventiveness; Chashnah,* an Isr.:–Hashabnah.

2813. חֲשַׁבְנְיָה *khash-ab-neh-yaw';* from 2808 and 3050; *thought of Jah; Chashabnejah,* the name of two Isr.:–Hashabniah.

2814. חָשָׁה *khaw-shaw';* a prim. root; to *hush* or keep quiet:–hold peace, keep silence, be silent, (be) still.

2815. חַשּׁוּב *khash-shoob';* from 2803; *intelligent; Chashshub,* the name of two or three Isr.:–Hashub, Hasshub.

2816. חֲשׁוֹךְ *khash-oke'* (Chald.); from a root cor. to 2821; the *dark:*–darkness.

2817. חֲשׂוּפָא *khas-oo-faw';* or חֲשֻׂפָא *khas-oo-faw';* from 2834; *nakedness; Chasupha,* one of the Nethinim:–Hashupha, Hasupha.

2818. חֲשַׁח *khash-akh'* (Chald.); a collat. root to one cor. to 2363 in the sense of *readiness;* to *be necessary* (from the idea of *convenience*) or (trans.) to *need:*–careful, have need of.

2819. חַשְׁחוּת *khash-khooth';* from a root cor. to 2818; *necessity:*–be needful.

2820. חָשַׂךְ *khaw-sak';* a prim. root; to *restrain* or (reflex.) *refrain;* by impl., to *refuse, spare, preserve;* also (by interch. with 2821) to *observe:*–assuage, X darken, forbear, hinder, hold back, keep (back), punish, refrain, reserve, spare, withhold.

2821. חָשַׁךְ *khaw-shak';* a prim. root; to *be dark* (as withholding light); trans., to *darken:*–be black, be (make) dark, darken, cause darkness, be dim, hide.

2822. חֹשֶׁךְ *kho-shek';* from 2821; the *dark;* hence (lit.) *darkness;* fig., *misery, destruction, death, ignorance, sorrow, wickedness:*–dark (-ness), night, obscurity.

2823. חָשֹׁךְ *khaw-shoke';* from 2821; *dark* (fig., i.e. *obscure*):–mean.

2824. חֶשְׁכָה *khesh-kaw';* from 2821; *darkness:*–dark.

2825. חֲשֵׁכָה *khash-ay-kaw';* or חֲשֵׁיכָה *khash-ay-kaw';* from 2821; *darkness;* fig., *misery:*–darkness.

2826. חָשַׁל *khaw-shal';* a prim. root; to *make* (intr. be) *unsteady,* i.e. *weak:*–feeble.

2827. חֲשַׁל *khash-al'* (Chald.); a root cor. to 2826; to *weaken,* i.e. *crush:*–subdue.

2828. חָשֻׁם *khaw-shoom';* from the same as 2831; *enriched; Chashum,* the name of two or three Isr.:–Hashum.

2829 חֶשְׁמוֹן *khesh-mone';* the same as 2831; *opulent; Cheshmon,* a place in Pal.:–Heshmon.

2830. חַשְׁמַל *khash-mal';* of unc. der. prob. *bronze* or polished spectrum metal:–amber.

2831. חַשְׁמַן *khash-man';* from an un. root (prob. mean. *firm* or *capacious* in resources); app. *wealthy:*–princes.

2832. חַשְׁמֹנָה *khash-mo-naw';* fem. of 2831; *fertile; Chasmonah,* a place in the Desert:–Hashmonah.

2833. חֹשֶׁן *kho'-shen;* from an un. root prob. mean. to *contain* or *sparkle;* perh. a *pocket* (as holding the Urim and Thummim), or *rich* (as containing gems), used only of the *gorget* of the highpriest:–breastplate.

2834. חָשַׂף *khaw-saf';* a prim. root; to *strip* off, i.e. gen. to *make naked* (for exertion or in disgrace), to *drain* away or *bail* up (a liquid):–make bare, clean, discover, draw out, take, uncover.

2835. חָשִׂף *khaw-seef';* from 2834; prop. *drawn off,* i.e. separated; hence, a small *company* (as divided from the rest):–little flock.

2836. חָשַׁק *khaw-shak';* a prim. root; to *cling,* i.e. *join,* (fig.) to *love, delight* in; ellip. (or by interch. for 2820) to *deliver:*–have a delight, (have a) desire, fillet, long, set (in) love.

2837. חֵשֶׁק *khay'-shek;* from 2836; *delight:*–desire, pleasure.

2838. חָשֻׁק *khaw-shook';* or חָשׁוּק *khaw-shook';* past part. of 2836; *attached,* i.e. a fence-*rail* or rod connecting the posts or pillars:–fillet.

2839. חִשֻּׁק *khish-shook';* from 2836; *conjoined,* i.e. a wheel-*spoke* or rod connecting the hub with the rim:–felloe.

2840. חִשֻּׁר *khish-shoor';* from an un. root mean. to *bind* together; *combined,* i.e. the *nave* or hub of a wheel (as holding the spokes together):–spoke.

2841. חַשְׁרָה *khash-raw';* from the same as 2840; prop. a *combination* or gathering, i.e. of watery *clouds:*–dark.

2842. חָשַׁשׁ *khaw-shash';* by var. for 7179; dry *grass:*–chaff.

2843. חֻשָׁתִי *khoo-shaw-thee';* patron. from 2364; a *Chushathite* or desc. of Chushah:–Hushathite.

2844. חַת *khath;* from 2865; concr., *crushed;* also *afraid;* abstr., *terror:*–broken, dismayed, dread, fear.

2845. חֵת *khayth;* from 2865; *terror; Cheth,* an aboriginal Canaanite:–Heth.

2846. חָתָה *khaw-thaw';* a prim. root; to lay *hold* of; esp. to *pick* up fire:–heap, take (away).

2847. חִתָּה *khit-taw';* from 2865; *fear:*–terror.
2848. חִתּוּל *khit-tool';* from 2853; *swathed,* i.e. a *bandage:*–roller.
2849. חַתְחַת *khath-khath';* from 2844; *terror:*–fear.
2850. חִתִּי *khit-tee';* patron. from 2845; a *Chittite,* or desc. of Cheth:–Hittite, Hittities.
2851. חִתִּית *khit-teeth';* from 2865; *fear:*–terror.
2852. חָתַךְ *khaw-thak';* a prim. root; prop. to *cut* off, i.e. (fig.) to *decree:*–determine.
2853. חָתַל *khaw-thal';* a prim. root; to *swathe:*–X at all, swaddle.
2854. חֲתֻלָּה *khath-ool-law';* from 2853; a *swathing* cloth (fig.):–swaddling band.
2855. חֶתְלֹן *kheth-lone';* from 2853; *enswathed; Chethlon,* a place in Pal.:–Hethlon.
2856. חָתַם *khaw-tham';* a prim. root; to *close* up; esp. to *seal:*–make an end, mark, seal (up), stop.
2857. חֲתַם *khath-am'* (Chald.); a root cor. to 2856; to *seal:*–seal.
2858. חֹתֶמֶת *kho-the-meth;* fem. act.part. of 2856; a *seal:*–signet.
2859. חָתַן *khaw-than';* a prim. root; to *give* (a daughter) *away* in marriage; hence (gen.) to *contract affinity* by marriage:–join in affinity, father in law, make marriages, mother in law, son in law.
2860. חָתָן *khaw-thawn';* from 2859; a *relative* by marriage (esp. through the bride); fig., a *circumcised* child (as a species of relig. espousal):–bridegroom, husband, son in law.
2861. חֲתֻנָּה *khath-oon-naw';* from 2859; a *wedding:*–espousal.
2862. חָתַף *khaw-thaf';* a prim. root; to *clutch:*–take away.
2863. חֶתֶף *kheh'-thef;* from 2862; prop. *rapine;* fig., *robbery:*–prey.
2864. חָתַר *khaw-thar';* a prim. root; to *force* a passage, as by burglary; fig., with oars:–dig (through), row.
2865. חָתַת *khaw-thath';* a prim. root; prop. to *prostrate*; hence, to *break* down, either (lit.) by violence, or (fig.) by confusion and fear:–abolish, affright, be (make) afraid, amaze, beat down, discourage, (cause to) dismay, go down, scare, terrify.
2866. חֲתַת *khath-ath';* from 2865; *dismay:*–casting down.
2867. חֲתַת *khath-ath';* the same as 2866; *Chathath,* an Isr.:–Hathath.

ט

2868. טְאֵב *teh-abe'* (Chald.); a prim. root; to *rejoice:*–be glad.
2869. טָב *tawb* (Chald.); from 2868; the same as 2896; *good:*–fine, good.
2870. טָבְאֵל *taw-beh-ale';* from 2895 and 410; *pleasing* (to) *God*; *Tabeël,* the name of a Syrian and of a Pers.:–Tabeal, Tabeel.
2871. טָבוּל *taw-bool';* pass.part. of 2881; prop. *dyed,* i.e. a *turban* (prob. as of *colored* stuff):–dyed attire.
2872. טַבּוּר *tab-boor';* from an un. root mean. to *pile* up; prop. *accumulated*; i.e. (by impl.) a *summit:*–middle, midst.
2873. טָבַח *taw-bakh';* a prim. root; to *slaughter* (animals or men):–kill, (make) slaughter, slay.
2874. טֶבַח *teh'-bakh;* from 2873; prop. something *slaughtered;* hence, a *beast* (or *meat,* as butchered); abstr. *butchery* (or concr., a place of slaughter):–X beast, slaughter, X slay, X sore.
2875. טֶבַח *teh'-bakh;* the same as 2874; *massacre; Tebach,* the name of a Mesopotamian and of an Isr.:–Tebah.
2876. טַבָּח *tab-bawkh';* from 2873; prop. a *butcher;* hence, a *lifeguardsman* (because he was acting as an executioner); also a *cook* (usually slaughtering the animal for food):–cook, guard.
2877. טַבָּח *tab-bawkh'* (Chald.); the same as 2876; a *lifeguardsman:*–guard.
2878. טִבְחָה *tib-khaw';* fem. of 2874 and mean. the same:–flesh, slaughter.
2879. טַבָּחָה *tab-baw-khaw';* fem. of 2876; a female *cook:*–cook.
2880. טִבְחַת *tib-khath';* from 2878; *slaughter; Tibchath,* a place in Syria:–Tibhath.
2881. טָבַל *taw-bal';* a prim. root; to *dip,* to immerse:–dip, plunge.
2882. טְבַלְיָהוּ *teb-al-yaw'-hoo;* from 2881 and 3050; *Jah has dipped; Tebaljah,* an Isr.:–Tebaliah.
2883. טָבַע *taw-bah';* a prim. root; to *sink:*–drown, fasten, settle, sink.
2884. טַבָּעוֹת *tab-baw-othe';* pl. of 2885; *rings; Tabbaoth,* one of the Nethinim:–Tabaoth.
2885. טַבַּעַת *tab-bah'-ath;* from 2883; prop. a *seal* (as *sunk* into the wax), i.e. *signet* (for sealing); hence (gen.) a *ring* of any kind:–ring.
2886. טַבְרִמּוֹן *tab-rim-mone';* from 2895 and 7417; *pleasing* (to) *Rimmon; Tabrimmon,* a Syrian:–Tabrimmon.
2887. טֵבֵת *tay'-beth;* prob. of for. der.; *Tebeth,* the tenth Heb. month:–Tebeth.
2888. טַבַּת *tab-bath';* of unc. der.; *Tabbath,* a place E. of the Jordan:–Tabbath.
2889. טָהוֹר *taw-hore';* or טָהֹר *taw-hore';* from 2891; *pure* (in a phys., chemical, cerem. or mor. sense):–clean, fair, pure(-ness).
2890. טְהוֹר *teh-hore';* from 2891; *purity:*–pureness.
2891. טָהֵר *taw-hare';* a prim. root; prop. to *be bright;* i.e. (by impl.) to *be pure* (phys. *sound, clear, unadulterated;* Levitically *uncontaminated;* mor., *innocent* or *holy*):–be (make, make self, pronounce) clean, cleanse (self), purge, purify(-ier, self).
2892. טֹהַר *to'-har;* from 2891; lit. *brightness;* cerem. *purification:*–clearness, glory, purifying.
2893. טָהֳרָה *toh-or-aw'* fem. of 2892; cerem. *purification;* mor. *purity:*– X is cleansed, cleansing, purification(-fying).
2894. טוּא *too;* a prim. root; to *sweep away:*–sweep.
2895. טוֹב *tobe;* a prim. root, to *be* (trans., *do* or *make*) *good* (or *well*) in the widest sense:–be (do) better, cheer, be (do, seem) good, (make) goodly, X please, (be, do, go, play) well.
2896. טוֹב *tobe;* from 2895; *good* (as an adj.) in the widest sense; used likewise as a noun, both in the masc. and the fem., the sing. and the pl. (*good,* a *good* or *good* thing, a *good* man or woman; the *good, goods* or *good* things, *good* men or women), also as an adv. (*well*):–beautiful, best, better, bountiful, cheerful, at ease, X fair (word), (be in) favour, fine, glad, good (deed, -lier, -liest, -ly, -ness, -s), graciously, joyful, kindly, kindness, liketh (best), loving, merry, X most, pleasant, + pleaseth, pleasure, precious, prosperity, ready, sweet, wealth, welfare, (be) well ([-favoured]).
2897. טוֹב *tobe;* the same as 2896; *good; Tob,* a region app. E. of the Jordan:–Tob.
2898. טוּב *toob;* from 2895; *good* (as a noun), in the widest sense, esp. *goodness* (sup. concr., the *best*), *beauty, gladness, welfare:*–fair, gladness, good(-ness, thing, -s), joy, go well with.
2899. טוֹב אֲדֹנִיָּהוּ *tobe ado-nee-yah'-hoo;* from 2896 and 138; *pleasing* (to) *Adonijah; Tob-Adonijah,* an Isr.:–Tob-adonijah.
2900. טוֹבִיָּה *to-bee-yaw';* or טוֹבִיָּהוּ *to-bee-yaw'-hoo;* from 2896 and 3050; *goodness of Jehovah; Tobijah,* the name of three Isr. and of one Samaritan:–Tobiah, Tobijah.
2901. טָוָה *taw-vaw';* a prim. root; to *spin:*–spin.
2902. טוּחַ *too'-akh;* a prim. root; to *smear,* esp. with lime:–daub, overlay, plaister, smut.
2903. טוֹטָפָה *to-faw-faw';* from an un. root mean. to *go around* or *bind;* a *fillet* for the forehead:–frontlet.
2904. טוּל *tool;* a prim. root; to *pitch* over or *reel;* hence (trans.) to *cast* down or out:–carry away, (utterly) cast (down, forth, out), send out.
2905. טוּר *toor;* from an un. root mean. to *range* in a regular manner; a *row;* hence, a *wall:*–row.
2906. טוּר *toor* (Chald.); cor. to 6697; a *rock* or hill:–mountain.
2907. טוּשׂ *toos;* a prim. root; to *pounce* as a bird of prey:–haste.
2908. טְוָת *tev-awth'* (Chald.); from a root cor. to 2901; *hunger* (as *twisting*):–fasting.
2909. טָחָה *taw-khaw';* a prim. root; to *stretch* a bow, as an *archer:*–[bow-]shot.
2910. טֻחָה *too-khaw';* from 2909 (or 2902) in the sense of *overlaying;* (in the pl. only) the *kidneys* (as being *covered*); hence (fig.) the inmost *thought:*–inward parts.
2911. טְחוֹן *tekh-one';* from 2912; a hand *mill;* hence, a *millstone:*–to grind.
2912. טָחַן *taw-khan';* a prim. root; to *grind* meal; hence, to be a *concubine* (that being their employment):–grind(-er).
2913. טַחֲנָה *takh-an-aw';* from 2912; a hand *mill;* hence (fig.) *chewing:*–grinding.
2914. טְחֹר *tekh-ore';* from an un. root mean. to *burn;* a *boil* or ulcer (from the inflammation), esp. a tumor in the anus or pudenda (the piles):–emerod.
2915. טִיחַ *tee'akh;* from (the equiv. of) 2902; mortar or *plaster:*–daubing.
2916. טִיט *teet;* from an un. root mean. app. to *be sticky* [rath. perh. a denom. from 2894, through the idea of dirt to be *swept* away]; *mud* or *clay;* fig., *calamity:*–clay, dirt, mire.
2917. טִין *teen* (Chald.); perh., by interch., for a word cor. to 2916; *clay:*–miry.
2918. טִירָה *tee-raw';* fem. of (an equiv. to) 2905; a *wall;* hence, a *fortress* or a *hamlet:*–(goodly) castle, habitation, palace, row.
2919. טַל *tal;* from 2926; *dew* (as *covering* vegetation):–dew.
2920. טַל *tal* (Chald.); the same as 2919:–dew.
2921. טָלָא *taw-law';* a prim. root; prop. to *cover* with pieces; i.e. (by impl.) to *spot* or *variegate* (as tapestry):–clouted, with divers colours, spotted.
2922. טְלָא *tel-aw';* app. from 2921 in the (or.) sense of *covering* (for protection); a lamb [comp. 2924]:–lamb.
2923. טְלָאִים *tel-aw-eem';* from the pl. of 2922; *lambs; Telaim,* a place in Pal.:–Telaim.
2924. טָלֶה *taw-leh';* by var. for 2922; a *lamb:*–lamb.
2925. טַלְטֵלָה *tal-tay-law';* from 2904; *overthrow* or *rejection:*–captivity.
2926. טָלַל *taw-lal';* a prim. root; prop. to *strew* over, i.e. (by impl.) to *cover* in or

plate (with beams):–cover.
2927. טְלַל *tel-al'* (Chald.); cor. to 2926; to *cover* with shade:–have a shadow.
2928. טֶלֶם *teh'-lem;* from an un. root mean. to *break* up or treat violently; *oppression; Telem,* the name of a place in Idumaea, also of a temple doorkeeper:–Telem.
2929. טַלְמוֹן *tal-mone';* from the same as 2728; *oppressive; Talmon,* a temple doorkeeper:–Talmon.
2930. טָמֵא *taw-may';* a prim. root; to *be foul,* esp. in a cerem. or mor. sense (*contaminated*):–defile (self), pollute (self), be (make, make self, pronounce) unclean, X utterly.
2931. טָמֵא *taw-may';* from 2930; *foul* in a relig. sense:–defiled, + infamous, polluted (-tion), unclean.
2932. טֻמְאָה *toom-aw';* from 2930; relig. *impurity:*–filthiness, unclean(-ness).
2933. טָמָה *taw-maw';* a collat. form of 2930; to *be impure* in a relig. sense:–be defiled, be reputed vile.
2934. טָמַן *taw-man';* a prim. root; to *hide* (by *covering* over):–hide, lay privily, in secret.
2935. טֶנֶא *teh'-neh;* from an un. root prob. mean. to *weave;* a *basket* (of interlaced osiers):–basket.
2936. טָנַף *taw-naf';* a prim. root; to *soil:*–defile.
2937. טָעָה *taw-aw';* a prim. root; to *wander;* caus. to *lead astray:*–seduce.
2938. טָעַם *taw-am';* a prim. root; to *taste;* fig., to *perceive:*–X but, perceive, taste.
2939. טְעֵם *teh-am'* (Chald.); cor. to 2938; to *taste;* caus. to *feed:*–make to eat, feed.
2940. טַעַם *tah'-am;* from 2938; prop. a *taste,* i.e. (fig.) *perception;* by impl., *intelligence;* trans., a *mandate:*– advice, behaviour, decree, discretion, judgment, reason, taste, understanding.
2941. טַעַם *tah'-am* (Chald.); from 2939; prop. a *taste,* i.e. (as in 2940) a judicial *sentence:*–account, X to be commanded, commandment, matter.
2942. טְעֵם *teh-ame'* (Chald.); from 2939, and equiv. to 2941; prop. *flavor;* fig., *judgment* (both subj. and obj.); hence, *account* (both subj. and obj.):–+ chancellor, + command, commandment, decree, + regard, taste, wisdom.
2943. טָעַן *taw-an';* a prim. root; to *load* a beast:–lade.
2944. טָעַן *taw-an';* a prim. root; to *stab:*–thrust through.
2945. טַף *taf;* from 2952 (perh. referring to the *tripping* gait of children); a *family* (mostly used coll. in the sing.):–(little) children (ones), families.
2946. טָפַח *taw-fakh';* a prim. root; to *flatten* out or *extend* (as a tent); fig., to *nurse* a child (as *promotive* of growth); or perh. a denom. from 2947, from *dandling* on the palms:–span, swaddle.
2947. טֶפַח *tay'-fakh;* from 2946; a *spread* of the hand, i.e. a *palm-breadth* (not "span" of the fingers); arch., a *corbel* (as a supporting palm):–coping, hand-breadth.
2948. טֹפַח *to'-fakh;* from 2946 (the same as 2947):–hand-breadth (broad).
2949. טִפֻּחַ *tip-pookh';* from 2946; *nursing:*–span long.
2950. טָפַל *taw-fal';* a prim. root; prop. to *stick* on as a patch; fig., to *impute* falsely:–forge(-r), sew up.
2951. טִפְסַר *tif-sar';* of for. der.; a military *governor:*–captain.
2952. טָפַף *taw-faf';* a prim. root; app. to *trip* (with short steps) coquettishly:–mince.
2953. טְפַר *tef-ar'* (Chald.); from a root cor. to 6852, and mean. the same as 6856; a finger-*nail;* also a *hoof* or *claw:*–nail.
2954. טָפַשׁ *taw-fash';* a prim. root; prop. app. to *be thick;* fig., to *be stupid:*–be fat.
2955. טָפַת *taw-fath';* prob. from 5197; a *dropping* (of ointment); *Taphath,* an Isr.s:–Taphath.
2956. טָרַד *taw-rad';* a prim. root; to *drive* on; fig., to *follow* close:–continual.
2957. טְרַד *ter-ad'* (Chald.); cor. to 2956; to *expel:*–drive.
2958. טְרוֹם *ter-ome';* a var. of 2962; *not yet:*–before.
2959. טָרַח *taw-rakh';* a prim. root; to *overburden:*–weary.
2960. טֹרַח *to'-rakh;* from 2959; a *burden:*–cumbrance, trouble.
2961. טָרִי *taw-ree';* from an un. root app. mean. to *be moist;* prop. *dripping;* hence, *fresh* (i.e. recently made such):–new, putrefying.
2962. טֶרֶם *teh'-rem;* from an un. root app. mean. to *interrupt* or *suspend;* prop. *non-occurrence;* used adv., *not yet* or *before:*–before, ere, not yet.
2963. טָרַף *taw-raf';* a prim. root; to *pluck* off or *pull* to pieces; caus. to *supply* with food (as in morsels):–catch, X without doubt, feed, ravin, rend in pieces, X surely, tear (in pieces).
2964. טֶרֶף *teh'-ref;* from 2963; something *torn,* i.e. a fragment, e.g. a *fresh* leaf, *prey, food:*–leaf, meat, prey, spoil.
2965. טָרָף *taw-rawf';* from 2963; recently *torn* off, i.e. *fresh:*–pluckt off.
2966. טְרֵפָה *ter-ay-faw';* fem. (coll.) of 2964; *prey,* i.e. flocks devoured by animals:–ravin, (that which was) torn (of beasts, in pieces).
2967. טַרְפְּלַי *tar-pel-ah'-ee* (Chald.); from a name of for. der.; a *Tarpelite* (coll.) or inh. of Tarpel, a place in Assyria:–Tarpelites.

י

2968. יָאַב *yaw-ab';* a prim. root; to *desire:*–long.
2969. יָאָה *yaw-aw';* a prim. root; to *be suitable:*–appertain.
2970. יַאֲזַנְיָה *yah-az-an-yaw';* or יַאֲזַנְיָהוּ *yah-az-an-yaw'-hoo;* from 238 and 3050; *heard of Jah; Jaazanjah,* the name of four Isr.:–Jaazaniah. Comp. 3153.
2971. יָאִיר *yaw-ere';* from 215; *enlightener; Jaïr,* the name of four Isr.:–Jair.
2972. יָאִרִי *yaw-ee-ree';* patron. from 2971; a *Jaïrite* or desc. of Jair:–Jairite.
2973. יָאַל *yaw-al';* a prim. root; prop. to *be slack,* i.e. (fig.) to *be foolish:*–dote, be (become, do) foolish(-ly).
2974. יָאַל *yaw-al';* a prim. root [prob. rather the same as 2973 through the idea of ment. *weakness*]; prop. to *yield,* esp. *assent;* hence (pos.) to *undertake* as an act of volition:–assay, begin, be content, please, take upon, X willingly, would.
2975. יְאֹר *yeh-ore';* of Eg. or.; a *channel,* e.g. a fosse, canal, shaft; spec. the *Nile,* as the one river of Eg., incl. its collat. trenches; also the *Tigris,* as the main river of Assyria:–brook, flood, river, stream.
2976. יָאַשׁ *yaw-ash';* a prim. root; to *desist,* i.e. (fig.) to *despond:*–(cause to) despair, one that is desperate, be no hope.
2977. יֹאשִׁיָּה *yo-shee-yaw';* or יֹאשִׁיָּהוּ *yo-she-yaw'-hoo;* from the same root as 803 and 3050; *founded of Jah; Joshijah,* the name of two Isr.:– Josiah.
2978. יְאִתוֹן *yeh-ee-thone';* from 857; an *entry:*–entrance.
2979. יְאָתְרַי *yeh-aw-ther-ah'ee;* from the same as 871; *stepping;* Jeätherai, an Isr.:–Jeaterai.
2980. יָבַב *yaw-bab;* a prim. root; to *bawl:*–cry out.
2981. יְבוּל *yeb-ool';* from 2986; *produce,* i.e. a *crop* or (fig.) *wealth:*–fruit, increase.
2982. יְבוּס *yeb-oos';* from 947; *trodden,* i.e. threshing-place; *Jebus,* the aboriginal name of Jerus.:–Jebus.
2983. יְבוּסִי *yeb-oo-see';* patrial from 2982; a *Jebusite* or inh. of Jebus:–Jebusite(-s).
2984. יִבְחַר *yib-khar';* from 977; *choice; Jibchar,* an Isr.:–Ibhar.
2985. יָבִין *yaw-bene';* from 995; *intelligent; Jabin,* the name of two Canaanitish kings:–Jabin.
2986. יָבַל *yaw-bal';* a prim. root; prop. to *flow;* caus., to *bring* (esp. with pomp):–bring (forth), carry, lead (forth).
2987. יְבַל *yeb-al'* (Chald.); cor. to 2986; to *bring:*–bring, carry.
2988. יָבָל *yaw-bawl';* from 2986; a *stream:*–[water-]course, stream.
2989. יָבָל *yaw-bawl';* the same as 2988; *Jabal,* an antediluvian:–Jabal.
2990. יַבֵּל *yab-bale';* from 2986; having *running* sores:–wen.
2991. יִבְלְעָם *yib-leh-awm'* from 1104 and 5971; *devouring* people; Jibleäm, a place in Pal.:–Ibleam.
2992. יָבַם *yaw-bam';* a prim. root of doubtful mean.; used only as a denom. from 2993; to *marry* a (deceased) brother's widow:–perform the duty of a husband's brother, marry.
2993. יָבָם *yaw-bawm';* from (the or. of) 2992; a *brother-in-law:*–husband's brother.
2994. יְבֵמֶת *yeb-ay'-meth;* fem. part. of 2992; a *sister-in-law:*–brother's wife, sister in law.
2995. יַבְנְאֵל *yab-neh-ale';* from 1129 and 410:*built of God; Jabneël,* the name of two places in Pal.:–Jabneel.
2996. יַבְנֶה *yab-neh';* from 1129; a *building; Jabneh,* a place in Pal.:–Jabneh.
2997. יִבְנְיָה *yib-neh-yaw';* from 1129 and 3050; *built of Jah; Jibnejah,* an Isr.:–Ibneiah.
2998. יִבְנִיָּה *yib-nee-yaw';* from 1129 and 3050; *building of Jah; Jibnijah,* an Isr.:–Ibnijah.
2999. יַבֹּק *yab-boke';* prob. from 1238; *pouring* forth; *Jabbok,* a river east of the Jordan:–Jabbok.
3000. יְבֶרֶכְיָהוּ *yeb-eh-rek-yaw'-hoo;* from 1288 and 3050: *blessed of Jah; Jeberekjah,* an Isr.:–Jeberechiah.
3001. יָבֵשׁ *yaw-bashe';* a prim. root; to *be ashamed, confused* or *disappointed;* also (as failing) to *dry* up (as water) or *wither* (as herbage):–be ashamed, clean, be confounded, (make) dry (up), (do) shame (-fully), X utterly, wither (away).
3002. יָבֵשׁ *yaw-bashe';* from 3001; *dry:*–dried (away), dry.
3003. יָבֵשׁ *yaw-bashe';* the same as 3002 (also יָבֵישׁ *yaw-bashe';* often with the addition of 1568, i.e. *Jabesh of Gilad*); *Jabesh,* the name of an Isr. and of a place in Pal.:–Jabesh (-[Gilead]).
3004. יַבָּשָׁה *yab-baw-shaw';* from 3001; dry

ground:–*dry* (ground, land).

3005. יִבְשָׂם *yib-sawm'*; from the same as 1314; *fragrant; Jibsam*, an Isr.:–Jibsam.

3006. יַבָּשָׁה *yab-beh'-sheth;* a var. of 3004; *dry* ground:–dry land.

3007. יַבֶּשֶׁת *yab-beh'-sheth* (Chald.); cor. to 3006; *dry* land:–earth.

3008. יִגְאָל *yig-awl'*; from 1350; *avenger; Jigal,* the name of three Isr.:–Igal, Igeal.

3009. יָגַב *yaw-gab'*; a prim. root; to *dig* or plow:–husbandman.

3010. יָגֵב *yaw-gabe'*; from 3009; a plowed *field:*–field.

3011. יָגְבְּהָה *yog-beh-haw'*; fem. from 1361; *hillock; Jogbehah,* a place E. of the Jordan:–Jogbehah.

3012. יִגְדַּלְיָהוּ *yig-dal-yaw'-hoo;* from 1431 and 3050; *magnified of Jah; Jigdaljah,* an Isr.:–Igdaliah.

3013. יָגָה *yaw-gaw';* a prim. root; to *grieve:*–afflict, cause grief, grieve, sorrowful, vex.

3014. יָגָה *yaw-gaw';* a prim. root [prob. rather the same as 3013 through the common idea of *dissatisfaction*]; to *push* away:–be removed.

3015. יָגוֹן *yaw-gohn';* from 3013; *affliction:*–grief, sorrow.

3016. יָגוֹר *yaw-gore';* from 3025; *fearful:*–afraid, fearest.

3017. יָגוּר *yaw-goor';* prob. from 1481; a *lodging; Jagur,* a place in Pal.:–Jagur.

3018. יְגִיעַ *yeg-ee'-ah;* from 3021; *toil;* hence, a *work, produce, property* (as the result of labor):–labour, work.

3019. יָגִיעַ *yaw-ghee'-ah;* from 3021; *tired:*–weary.

3020. יָגְלִי *yog-lee';* from 1540; *exiled; Jogli,* an Isr.:–Jogli.

3021. יָגַע *yaw-gah';* a prim. root; prop. to *gasp;* hence, to *be exhausted,* to *tire,* to *toil:*–faint, (make to) labour, (be) weary.

3022. יָגָע *yaw-gaw';* from 3021; *earnings* (as the product of toil):–that which he laboured for.

3023. יָגֵעַ *yaw-gay'-ah;* from 3021; *tired;* hence (trans.) *tiresome:*–full of labour, weary.

3024. יְגִעָה *yeg-ee-aw';* fem. of 3019; *fatigue:*–weariness.

3025. יָגֹר *yaw-gore';* a prim. root; to *fear:*–be afraid, fear.

3026. יְגַר שָׂהֲדוּתָא *yegar' sah-had-oo-thaw'* (Chald.); from a word der. from an un. root (mean. to *gather*) and a der. of a root cor. to 7717; *heap of the testimony; Jegar-Sahadutha,* a cairn E. of the Jordan:–Jegar-Sahadutha.

3027. יָד *yawd;* a prim. word; a *hand* (the *open* one [indicating *power, means, direction,* etc.], in distinction from 3709, the *closed* one); used (as noun, adv., etc.) in a great variety of appl., both lit. and fig., both proximate and remote [as follows]:–(+ be) able, X about, + armholes, at, axletree, because of, beside, border, X bounty, + broad, [broken-] handed, X by, charge, coast, + consecrate, + creditor, custody, debt, dominion, X enough, + fellowship, force, X from, hand [-staves, -y work], X he, himself, X in, labour, + large, ledge, [left-]handed, means, X mine, ministry, near, X of, X order, ordinance, X our, parts, pain, power, X presumptuously, service, side, sore, state, stay, draw with strength, stroke, + swear, terror, X thee, X by them, X themselves, X thine own, X thou, through, X throwing, + thumb, times, X to, X under, X us, X wait on, [way-]side, where, + wide, X with (him, me, you), work, + yield, X yourselves.

3028. יַד *yad* (Chald.); cor. to 3027:–hand, power.

3029. יְדָא *yed-aw'* (Chald.); cor. to 3034; to *praise:*–(give) thank(-s).

3030. יִדְאֲלָה *yid-al-aw';* of unc. der.; *Jidalah,* a place in Pal.:–Idalah.

3031. יִדְבָּשׁ *yid-bawsh';* from the same as 1706; perh. *honeyed; Jidbash,* an Isr.:–Idbash.

3032. יָדַד *yaw-dad';* a prim. root; prop. to *handle* [comp. 3034], i.e. to *throw,* e.g. lots:–cast.

3033. יְדִדוּת *yed-ee-dooth';* from 3039; prop. *affection;* concr., a *darling* obj.:–dearly beloved.

3034. יָדָה *yaw-daw';* a prim. root; used only as denom. from 3027; lit., to *use* (i.e. hold out) *the hand;* phys., to *throw* (a stone, an arrow) at or away; esp. to *revere* or *worship* (with extended hands); intens., to *bemoan* (by wringing the hands):–cast (out), (make) confess(-ion), praise, shoot, (give) thank(-ful, -s, -sgiving).

3035. יִדּוֹ *yid-do';* from 3034; *praised; Jiddo,* an Isr.:–Iddo.

3036. יָדוֹן *yaw-done';* from 3034; *thankful; Jadon,* an Isr.:–Jadon.

3037. יַדּוּעַ *yad-doo'-ah;* from 3045; *knowing; Jaddüä,* the name of two Isr.:–Jaddua.

3038. יְדוּתוּן *yed-oo-thoon';* or יְדֻתוּן *yed-oo-thoon';* or יְדִיתוּן *yed-ee-thoon';* prob. from 3034; *laudatory; Jeduthun,* an Isr.:–Jeduthun.

3039. יְדִיד *yed-eed';* from the same as 1730; *loved:*–amiable, (well-)beloved, loves.

3040. יְדִידָה *yed-ee-daw';* fem. of 3039; *beloved; Jedidah,* an Isr.s:–Jedidah.

3041. יְדִידְיָה *yed-ee-deh-yaw';* from 3039 and 3050; *beloved of Jah; Jedidejah,* a name of Solomon:–Jedidiah.

3042. יְדָיָה *yed-aw-yaw';* from 3034 and 3050; *praised of Jah; Jedajah,* the name of two Isr.:–Jedaiah.

3043. יְדִיעֲאֵל *yed-ee-ah-ale';* from 3045 and 410; *knowing God; Jediaël,* the name of three Isr.:–Jediael.

3044. יִדְלָף *yid-lawf';* from 1811; *tearful; Jidlaph,* a Mesopotamian:–Jidlaph.

3045. יָדַע *yaw-dah';* a prim. root; to *know* (prop. to ascertain by *seeing*); used in a great variety of senses, fig., lit., euphem. and inferentially (incl. *observation, care, recognition;* and caus., *instruction, designation, punishment,* etc.) [as follow]:–acknowledge, acquaintance(-ted with), advise, answer, appoint, assuredly, be aware, [un-]awares, can[-not], certainly, comprehend, consider, X could they, cunning, declare, be diligent, (can, cause to) discern, discover, endued with, familiar friend, famous, feel, can have, be [ig-]norant, instruct, kinsfolk, kinsman, (cause to let, make) know, (come to give, have, take) knowledge, have [knowledge], (be, make, make to be, make self) known, + be learned, + lie by man, mark, perceive, privy to, X prognosticator, regard, have respect, skilful, shew, can (man of) skill, be sure, of a surety, teach, (can) tell, understand, have [understanding], X will be, wist, wit, wot.

3046. יְדַע *yed-ah'* (Chald.); cor. to 3045:–certify, know, make known, teach.

3047. יָדָע *yaw-daw';* from 3045; *knowing; Jada,* an Isr.:–Jada.

3048. יְדַעְיָה *yed-ah-yaw';* from 3045 and 3050; *Jah has known; Jedajah,* the name of two Isr.:–Jedaiah.

3049. יִדְּעֹנִי *yid-deh-o-nee';* from 3045; prop. a *knowing* one; spec., a *conjurer;* (by impl) a *ghost:*–wizard.

3050. יָהּ *yaw*; contr. for 3068, and mean. the same; *Jah,* the sacred name:–Jah, the Lord, most vehement. Comp. names in "-iah," "- jah".

3051. יָהַב *yaw-hab';* a prim. root; to *give* (whether lit. or fig.); gen., to *put;* imper. (refl.) *come:*–ascribe, bring, come on, give, go, set, take.

3052. יְהַב *yeh-hab'* (Chald.); cor. to 3051:–deliver, give, lay, + prolong, pay, yield.

3053. יְהָב *ye-hawb';* from 3051; prop. what is *given* (by Providence), i.e. a *lot:*–burden.

3054. יָהַד *yaw-had';* denom. from a form cor. to 3061; to *Judaize,* i.e. become Jewish:–become Jews.

3055. יְהֻד *yeh-hood';* a briefer form of one cor. to 3061; *Jehud,* a place in Pal.:–Jehud.

3056. יֶהְדַּי *yeh-dah'-ee;* perh. from a form cor. to 3061; *Judaistic; Jehdai,* an Isr.:–Jehdai.

3057. יְהֻדִיָּה *yeh-hoo-dee-yaw';* fem. of 3064; *Jehudijah,* a *Jewess:*–Jehudijah.

3058. יֵהוּא *yay-hoo';* from 3068 and 1931; *Jehovah* (is) *He; Jehu,* the name of five Isr.:–Jehu.

3059. יְהוֹאָחָז *yeh-ho-aw-khawz';* from 3068 and 270; *Jehovah-seized; Jehoächaz,* the name of three Isr.:–Jehoahaz. Comp. 3099.

3060. יְהוֹאָשׁ *yeh-ho-awsh';* from 3068 and (perh.) 784; *Jehovah-fired; Jehoäsh,* the name of two Isr. kings:–Jehoash. Comp. 3101.

3061. יְהוּד *yeh-hood'* (Chald.); contr. from a form cor. to 3063; prop. *Judah,* hence, *Judæa:*–Jewry, Judah, Judea.

3062. יְהוּדָאִי *yeh-hoo-daw-ee'* (Chald.); patrial from 3061; a *Jehudaïte* (or Judaite), i.e. Jew:–Jew.

3063. יְהוּדָה *yeh-hoo-daw';* from 3034; *celebrated; Jehudah* (or Judah), the name of five Isr.; also of the tribe descended from the first, and of its territory:–Judah.

3064. יְהוּדִי *yeh-hoo-dee'* patron. from 3063; a *Jehudite* (i.e. Judaite or Jew), or desc. of Jehudah (i.e. Judah):–Jew.

3065. יְהוּדִי *yeh-hoo-dee';* the same as 3064; *Jehudi,* an Isr.:–Jehudi.

3066. יְהוּדִית *yeh-hoo-deeth';* fem. of 3064; the *Jewish* (used adv.) language:–in the Jews' language.

3067. יְהוּדִית *yeh-hoo-deeth';* the same as 3066; *Jewess; Jehudith,* a Canaanitess:–Judith.

3068. יְהֹוָה *yeh-ho-vaw';* from 1961; (the) self-*Existent* or Eternal; *Jehovah,* Jewish national name of God:–Jehovah, the Lord. Comp. 3050, 3069.

3069. יְהֹוִה *yeh-ho-vee';* a var. of 3068 [used after 136, and pronounced by Jews as 430, in order to prevent the repetition of the same sound, since they elsewhere pronounce 3068 as 136]:–God.

3070. יְהֹוָה יִרְאֶה *yeh-ho-vaw' yir-eh';* from 3068 and 7200; *Jehovah will see* (to it); *Jehovah-Jireh,* a symb. name for Mount Moriah:–Jehovah-jireh.

3071. יְהֹוָה נִסִּי *yeh-ho-vaw' nis-see';* from 3068 and 5251 with the pron.suffix; *Jehovah* (is) *my banner; Jehovah-Nissi,* a symb. name of an altar in the Desert:–Jehovah-nissi.

3072. יְהֹוָה צִדְקֵנוּ *ye-ho-vaw' tsid-kay'-noo;*

from 3068 and 6664 with pron. suffix; *Jehovah* (is) *our right; Jehovah-Tsidkenu,* a symb. epithet of the Messiah and of Jerus.:–the Lord our righteousness.

3073. יְהֹוָה שָׁלוֹם *yeh-ho-vaw' shaw-lome';* from 3068 and 7965; *Jehovah* (is) *peace; Jehovah-Shalom,* a symb. name of an altar in Pal.:–Jehovah-shalom.

3074. יְהֹוָה שָׁמָּה *yeh-ho-vaw' shawm'-maw;* from 3068 and 8033 with directive enclitic; *Jehovah* (is) *thither; Jehovah-Shammah,* a symbolic title of Jerus.:–Jehovah-shammah.

3075. יְהוֹזָבָד *yeh-ho-zaw-bawd';* from 3068 and 2064; *Jehovah-endowed; Jehozabad,* the name of three Isr.:–Jehozabad. Comp. 3107.

3076. יְהוֹחָנָן *yeh-ho-khaw-nawn';* from 3068 and 2603; *Jehovah-favored; Jehochanan,* the name of eight Isr.:–Jehohanan, Johanan. Comp. 3110.

3077. יְהוֹיָדָע *yeh-ho-yaw-daw';* from 3068 and 3045; *Jehovah-known; Jehojada,* the name of three Isr.:–Jehoiada. Comp. 3111.

3078. יְהוֹיָכִין *yeh-ho-yaw-keen';* from 3068 and 3559; *Jehovah will establish; Jehojakin,* a Jewish king:–Jehoiachin. Comp. 3112.

3079. יְהוֹיָקִים *yeh-ho-yaw-keem';* from 3068 abb. and 6965; *Jehovah will raise; Jehojakim,* a Jewish king:–Jehoiakim. Comp. 3113.

3080. יְהוֹיָרִיב *yeh-ho-yaw-reeb';* from 3068 and 7378; *Jehovah will contend; Jehojarib,* the name of two Isr.:–Jehoiarib. Comp. 3114.

3081. יְהוּכַל *yeh-hoo-kal';* from 3201; *potent; Jehukal,* an Isr.:–Jehucal. Comp. 3116.

3082. יְהוֹנָדָב *yeh-ho-naw-dawb';* from 3068 and 5068; *Jehovah-largessed; Jehonadab,* the name of an Isr. and of an Arab:–Jehonadab, Jonadab. Comp. 3122.

3083. יְהוֹנָתָן *yeh-ho-naw-thawn';* from 3068 and 5414; *Jehovah-given; Jehonathan,* the name of four Isr.:–Jonathan. Comp. 3129.

3084. יְהוֹסֵף *yeh-ho-safe';* a fuller form of 3130; *Jehoseph* (i.e. Joseph), a son of Jacob:–Joseph.

3085. יְהוֹעַדָּה *yeh-ho-ad-daw';* from 3068 and 5710; *Jehovah-adorned; Jehoäddah,* an Isr.:–Jehoada.

3086. יְהוֹעַדִּין *yeh-ho-ad-deen';* or יְהוֹעַדָּן *yeh-ho-ad-dawn';* from 3068 and 5727; *Jehovah-pleased; Jehoäddin* or *Jehoäddan,* an Isr.s:–Jehoaddan.

3087. יְהוֹצָדָק *yeh-ho-tsaw-dawk';* from 3068 and 6663; *Jehovah-righted; Jehotsadak,* an Isr.:–Jehozadek, Josedech. Comp. 3136.

3088. יְהוֹרָם *yeh-ho-rawm';* from 3068 and 7311; *Jehovah-raised; Jehoram,* the name of a Syrian and of three Isr.:–Jehoram, Joram. Comp. 3141.

3089. יְהוֹשֶׁבַע *yeh-ho-sheh'-bah;* from 3068 and 7650; *Jehovah-sworn; Jehosheba,* an Isr.s:–Jehosheba. Comp. 3090.

3090. יְהוֹשַׁבְעַת *yeh-ho-shab-ath';* a form of 3089; *Jehoshabath,* an Isr.s:–Jehoshabeath.

3091. יְהוֹשׁוּעַ *yeh-ho-shoo'-ah;* or יְהוֹשֻׁעַ *yeh-ho-shoo'-ah;* from 3068 and 3467; *Jehovah-saved; Jehoshuä* (i.e. Joshua), the Jewish leader:–Jehoshua, Jehoshuah, Joshua. Comp. 1954, 3442.

3092. יְהוֹשָׁפָט *yeh-ho-shaw-fawt';* from 3068 and 8199; *Jehovah-judged; Jehoshaphat,* the name of six Isr.; also of a valley near Jerus.:–Jehoshaphat. Comp. 3146.

3093. יָהִיר *yaw-here';* prob. from the same as 2022; *elated;* hence, *arrogant:*–haughty, proud.

3094. יְהַלֶּלְאֵל *yeh-hal-lel-ale';* from 1984 and 410; *praising God; Jehallelel,* the name of two Isr.:–Jehaleleel, Jehalelel.

3095. יַהֲלֹם *yah-hal-ome';* from 1986 (in the sense of *hardness*); a precious stone, prob. *onyx:*–diamond.

3096. יַהַץ *yah'-hats;* or יַהְצָה *yah'-tsaw;* or (fem.) יַהְצָה *yah-tsaw';* from an un. root mean. to *stamp;* perh. *threshing*-floor; *Jahats* or *Jahtsah,* a place E. of the Jordan:–Jahaz, Jahazah, Jahzah.

3097. יוֹאָב *yo-awb';* from 3068 and 1; *Jehovah-fathered; Joäb,* the name of three Isr.:–Joab.

3098. יוֹאָח *yo-awkh';* from 3068 and 251; *Jehovah-brothered; Joach,* the name of four Isr.:–Joah.

3099. יוֹאָחָז *yo-aw-khawz';* a form of 3059; Joächaz, the name of two Isr.:–Jehoahaz, Joahaz.

3100. יוֹאֵל *yo-ale';* from 3068 and 410; *Jehovah* (is his) *God; Joël,* the name of twelve Isr.:–Joel.

3101. יוֹאָשׁ *yo-awsh';* or יֹאָשׁ *yo-awsh'* (2 Ch..24:1); a form of 3060; *Joäsh,* the name of six Isr.:–Joash.

3102. יוֹב *yobe;* perh. a form of 3103, but more prob. by err. transc. for 3437; *Job,* an Isr.:–Job.

3103. יוֹבָב *yo-bawb';* from 2980; *howler; Jobab,* the name of two Isr. and of three foreigners:–Jobab.

3104. יוֹבֵל *yo-bale';* or יֹבֵל *yob-ale';* app. from 2986; the *blast* of a horn (from its *continuous* sound); spec., the *signal* of the silver trumpets; hence, the instrument itself and the festival thus introduced:–jubile, ram's horn, trumpet.

3105. יוּבַל *yoo-bal';* from 2986; a *stream:*–river.

3106. יוּבָל *yoo-bawl';* from 2986; *stream; Jubal,* an antediluvian:–Jubal.

3107. יוֹזָבָד *yo-zaw-bawd';* a form of 3075; *Jozabad,* the name of ten Isr.:–Josabad, Jozabad.

3108. יוֹזָכָר *yo-zaw-kawr';* from 3068 and 2142; *Jehovah-remembered; Jozacar,* an Isr.:–Jozachar.

3109. יוֹחָא *yo-khaw';* prob. from 3068 and a var. of 2421; *Jehovah-revived; Jocha,* the name of two Isr.:–Joha.

3110. יוֹחָנָן *yo-khaw-nawn';* a form of 3076; *Jochanan,* the name of nine Isr.:–Johanan.

3111. יוֹיָדָע *yo-yaw-daw';* a form of 3077; *Jojada,* the name of two Isr.:–Jehoiada, Joiada.

3112. יוֹיָכִין *yo-yaw-keen';* a form of 3078; *Jojakin,* an Isr. king:–Jehoiachin.

3113. יוֹיָקִים *yo-yaw-keem';* a form of 3079; *Jojakim,* an Isr.:–Joiakim. Comp. 3137.

3114. יוֹיָרִיב *yo-yaw-reeb';* a form of 3080; *Jojarib,* the name of four Isr.:–Joiarib.

3115. יוֹכֶבֶד *yo-keh'-bed;* from 3068 contr. and 3513; *Jehovah-gloried; Jokebed,* the mother of Moses:–Jochebed.

3116. יוּכַל *yoo-kal';* a form of 3081; *Jukal,* an Isr.:–Jucal.

3117. יוֹם *yome;* from an un. root mean. to *be hot;* a *day* (as the *warm* hours), whether lit. (from sunrise to sunset, or from one sunset to the next), or fig. (a space of time defined by an associated term), [often used adv.]:–age, + always, + chronicles, continually (-ance), daily, ([birth-], each, to) day, (now a, two) days (agone), + elder, X end, + evening, + (for) ever(-lasting, -more), X full, life, as (so) long as (... live), (even) now, + old, + outlived, + perpetually, presently, + remaineth, X required, season, X since, space, then, (process of) time, + as at other times, + in trouble, weather, (as) when, (a, the, within a) while (that), X whole (+ age), (full) year(-ly), + younger.

3118. יוֹם *yome* (Chald.); cor. to 3117; a *day:*–day (by day), time.

3119. יוֹמָם *yo-mawm';* from 3117; daily:–*daily,* (by, in the) day(-time).

3120. יָוָן *yaw-vawn';* prob. from the same as 3196; *effervescing* (i.e. hot and active); *Javan,* the name of a son of Joktan, and of the race (*Ionians,* i.e. Gr.) descended from him, with their territory; also of a place in Arabia:–Javan.

3121. יָוֵן *yaw-ven';* from the same as 3196; prop. *dregs* (as *effervescing*); hence, *mud:*–mire, miry.

3122. יוֹנָדָב *yo-naw-dawb';* a form of 3082; *Jonadab,* the name of an Isr. and of a Rechabite:–Jonadab.

3123. יוֹנָה *yo-naw';* prob. from the same as 3196; a *dove* (app. from the *warmth* of their mating):–dove, pigeon.

3124. יוֹנָה *yo-naw';* the same as 3123; *Jonah,* an Isr.:–Jonah.

3125. יְוָנִי *yev-aw-nee';* patron. from 3121; a *Jevanite,* or desc. of Javan:–Grecian.

3126. יוֹנֵק *yo-nake';* act.part. of 3243; a *sucker;* hence, a *twig* (of a tree felled and sprouting):–tender plant.

3127. יוֹנֶקֶת *yo-neh'-keth;* fem. of 3126; a *sprout:*–(tender) branch, young twig.

3128. יוֹנַת אֵלֶם רְחֹקִים *yo-nath' ay'-lem rekh-o-keem';* from 3123 and 482 and the pl. of 7350; *dove of* (the) *silence* (i.e. *dumb* Isr.) of (i.e. among) *distances* (i.e. strangers); the title of a Psalm (used for a name of its melody):–Jonath-elem-rechokim.

3129. יוֹנָתָן *yo-naw-thawn';* a form of 3083; *Jonathan,* the name of ten Isr.:–Jonathan.

3130. יוֹסֵף *yo-safe';* future of 3254; *let him add* (or perh. simply act.part. *adding*); *Joseph,* the name of seven Isr.:–Joseph. Comp. 3084.

3131. יוֹסִפְיָה *yo-sif-yaw';* from act.part. of 3254 and 3050; *Jah* (is) *adding; Josiphjah,* an Isr.:–Josiphiah.

3132. יוֹעֵאלָה *yo-ay-law';* perh. fem. act.part. of 3276; *furthermore; Joelah,* an Isr.:–Joelah.

3133. יוֹעֵד *yo-ade';* app. the act.part. of 3259; *appointer; Joed,* an Isr.:–Joed.

3134. יוֹעֶזֶר *yo-eh'-zer;* from 3068 and 5828; *Jehovah* (is his) *help; Joezer,* an Isr.:–Joezer.

3135. יוֹעָשׁ *yo-awsh';* from 3068 and 5789; *Jehovah-hastened; Joash,* the name of two Isr.:–Joash.

3136. יוֹצָדָק *yo-tsaw-dawk';* a form of 3087; *Jotsadak,* an Isr.:–Jozadak.

3137. יוֹקִים *yo-keem';* a form of 3113; *Jokim,* an Isr.:–Jokim.

3138. יוֹרֶה *yo-reh';* act.part. of 3384; *sprinkling;* hence, a *sprinkling* (or autumnal showers):–first rain, former [rain].

3139. יוֹרָה *yo-raw';* from 3384; *rainy; Jorah,* an Isr.:–Jorah.

3140. יוֹרַי *yo-rah'-ee;* from 3384; *rainy; Jorai,* an Isr.:–Jorai.

3141. יוֹרָם *yo-rawm';* a form of 3088; *Joram,* the name of three Isr. and one Syrian:–Joram.

3142. יוּשַׁב חֶסֶד *yoo-shab' kheh'-sed;* from 7725 and 2617; *kindness will be returned; Jushab-Chesed,* an Isr.:–Jushab-hesed.

3143. יוֹשִׁבְיָה *yo-shib-yaw';* from 3427 and 3050; *Jehovah will cause to dwell;*

Josibjah, an Isr.:–Josibiah.
3144. יוֹשָׁה *yo-shaw';* prob. a form of 3145; *Joshah,* an Isr.:–Joshah.
3145. יוֹשַׁוְיָה *yo-shav-yaw';* from 3068 and 7737; *Jehovah-set; Joshavjah,* an Isr.:–Joshaviah. Comp. 3144.
3146. יוֹשָׁפָט *yo-shaw-fawt';* a form of 3092; *Joshaphat,* an Isr.:–Joshaphat.
3147. יוֹתָם *yo-thawm';* from 3068 and 8535; *Jehovah* (is) *perfect; Jotham,* the name of three Isr.:–Jotham.
3148. יוֹתֵר *yo-thare';* act.part. of 3498; prop. *redundant;* hence, *over and above,* as adj., noun, adv. or conj. [as follows]:–better, more (-over), over, profit.
3149. יְזַוְאֵל *yez-av-ale';* from an un. root (mean. to *sprinkle*) and 410; *sprinkled of God; Jezavel,* an Isr.:–Jeziel .
3150. יִזִּיָּה *yiz-zee-yaw';* from the same as the first part of 3149 and 3050; *sprinkled of Jah; Jizzijah,* an Isr.:–Jeziah.
3151. יָזִיז *yaw-zeez';* from the same as 2123; *he will make prominent; Jaziz,* an Isr.:–Jaziz.
3152. יִזְלִיאָה *yiz-lee-aw';* perh. from an un. root (mean. to *draw up*); *he will draw out; Jizliah,* an Isr.:–Jezliah.
3153. יְזַנְיָה *yez-an-yaw';* or יְזַנְיָהוּ *yez-an-yaw'-hoo;* prob. for 2970; *Jezanjah,* an Isr.:–Jezaniah.
3154. יֶזַע *yeh'-zah;* from an un. root mean to *ooze; sweat,* i.e. (by impl.) a *sweating* dress:–any thing that causeth sweat.
3155. יִזְרָח *yiz-rawkh';* a var. for 250; a *Jizrach* (i.e. Ezrachite or Zarchite) or desc. of Zerach:–Izrahite.
3156. יִזְרַחְיָה *yiz-rakh-yaw';* from 2224 and 3050; *Jah will shine; Jizrachjah,* the name of two Isr.:–Izrahiah, Jezrahiah.
3157. יִזְרְעֶאל *yiz-reh-ale';* from 2232 and 410; *God will sow; Jizreël,* the name of two places in Pal. and of two Isr.:–Jezreel.
3158. יִזְרְעֵאלִי *yiz-reh-ay-lee';* patron. from 3157; a *Jizreëlite* or nat. of Jizreel:–Jezreelite.
3159. יִזְרְעֵאלִית *yiz-reh-ay-leeth';* fem. of 3158; a *Jezreëlitess:*–Jezreelitess.
3160. יְחֻבָּה *yekh-oob-baw';* from 2247; *hidden; Jechubbah,* an Isr.:–Jehubbah.
3161. יָחַד *yaw-khad';* a prim. root; to *be* (or become) *one:*–join, unite.
3162. יַחַד *yakh'-ad* from 3161; prop. a *unit,* i.e. (adv.) *unitedly:*–alike, at all (once), both, likewise, only, (al-) together, withal.
3163. יַחְדּוֹ *yakh-doe';* from 3162 with pron. suffix; *his unity,* i.e. (adv.) *together; Jachdo,* an Isr.:–Jabdo.
3164. יַחְדִּיאֵל *yakh-dee-ale';* from 3162 and 410; *unity of God; Jachdiel,* an Isr.:–Jahdiel.
3165. יֶחְדִּיָּהוּ *yekh-dee-yaw'-hoo;* from 3162 and 3050; *unity of Jah; Jechdijah,* the name of two Isr.:–Jehdeiah.
3166. יַחֲזִיאֵל *yakh-az-ee-ale';* from 2372 and 410; *beheld of God; Jachaziël,* the name of five Isr.:–Jahaziel, Jahziel.
3167. יַחְזְיָה *yakh-zeh-yaw';* from 2372 and 3050; *Jah will behold; Jachzejah,* an Isr.:–Jahaziah.
3168. יְחֶזְקֵאל *yekh-ez-kale';* from 2388 and 410; *God will strengthen; Jechezkel,* the name of two Isr.:–Ezekiel, Jehezekel.
3169. יְחִזְקִיָּה *yekh-iz-kee-yaw';* or יְחִזְקִיָּהוּ *yekh-iz-kee-yaw'- hoo;* from 3388 and 3050; *strengthened of Jah; Jechizkijah,* the name of five Isr.:–Hezekiah, Jehizkiah. Comp. 2396.
3170. יַחְזֵרָה *yakh-zay-raw';* from the same as 2386; perh. *protection; Jachzerah,* an Isr.:–Jahzerah.
3171. יְחִיאֵל *yekh-ee-ale';* or (2 Ch.. 29:14) יְחַוְאֵל *yekh-av-ale';* from 2421 and 410; *God will live; Jechiël* (or *Jechavel*), the name of eight Isr.:–Jehiel.
3172. יְחִיאֵלִי *yekh-ee-ay-lee';* patron. from 3171; a *Jechiëlite* or desc. of Jechiel:–Jehieli.
3173. יָחִיד *yaw-kheed';* from 3161; prop. *united,* i.e. *sole;* by impl., *beloved;* also *lonely;* (fem.) the *life* (as not to be replaced):–darling, desolate, only (child, son), solitary.
3174. יְחִיָּה *yekh-ee-yaw';* from 2421 and 3050; *Jah will live; Jechijah,* an Isr.:–Jehiah.
3175. יָחִיל *yaw-kheel';* from 3176; *expectant:*–should hope.
3176. יָחַל *yaw-chal';* a prim. root; to *wait;* by impl., to *be patient, hope:*–(cause to, have, make to) hope, be pained, stay, tarry, trust, wait.
3177. יַחְלְאֵל *yakh-leh-ale';* from 3176 and 410; *expectant of God; Jachleël,* an Isr.:–Jahleel.
3178. יַחְלְאֵלִי *yakh-leh-ay-lee';* patron. from 3177; a *Jachleëlite* or desc. of Jachleel:–Jahleelites.
3179. יָחַם *yaw-kham';* a prim. root; prob. to *be hot;* fig., to *conceive:*–get heat, be hot, conceive, be warm.
3180. יַחְמוּר *yakh-moor';* from 2560; a kind of *deer* (from the color; comp. 2543):–fallow deer.
3181. יַחְמַי *yakh-mah'-ee;* prob. from 3179; *hot; Jachmai,* an Isr.:–Jahmai.
3182. יָחֵף *yaw-khafe';* from an un. root mean. to *take off the shoes; unsandalled:*–barefoot, being unshod.
3183. יַחְצְאֵל *yakh-tseh-ale';* from 2673 and 410; *God will allot; Jachtseël,* an Isr.:–Jahzeel. Comp. 3185.
3184. יַחְצְאֵלִי *yakh-tseh-ay-lee';* patron. from 3183; a *Jachtseëlite* (coll.) or desc. of Jachtseel:–Jahzeelites.
3185. יַחְצִיאֵל *yakh-tsee-ale';* from 2673 and 410; *allotted of God; Jachtsiël,* an Isr.:–Jahziel. Comp. 3183.
3186. יָחַר *yaw-khar';* a prim. root; to *delay:*–tarry longer.
3187. יָחַשׂ *yaw-khas';* a prim. root; to *sprout;* used only as denom. from 3188; to *enroll* by pedigree:–(number after, number throughout the) genealogy (to be reckoned), be reckoned by genealogies.
3188. יַחַשׂ *yakh'-as;* from 3187; a *pedigree* or family list (as *growing* spontaneously):–genealogy.
3189. יַחַת *yakh'-ath;* from 3161; *unity; Jachath,* the name of four Isr.:–Jahath.
3190. יָטַב *yaw-tab';* a prim. root; to be (caus.) *make well,* lit. (*sound, beautiful*) or fig. (*happy, successful, right*):–be accepted, amend, use aright, benefit, be (make) better, seem best, make cheerful, be comely, + be content, diligent(-ly), dress, earnestly, find favour, give, be glad, do (be, make) good([-ness]), be (make) merry, please (+ well), shew more [kindness], skilfully, X very small, surely, make sweet, thoroughly, tire, trim, very, be (can, deal, entreat, go, have) well [said, seen].
3191. יְטַב *yet-ab'* (Chald.); cor. to 3190:–seem good.
3192. יָטְבָה *yot-baw';* from 3190; *pleasantness; Jotbah,* a place in Pal.:–Jotbah.
3193. יָטְבָתָה *yot-baw'-thaw;* from 3192; *Jotbathah,* a place in the Desert:–Jotbath, Jotbathah.
3194. יֻטָּה *yoo-taw';* or יוּטָה *yoo-taw';* from 5186; *extended; Juttah* (or *Jutah*), a place in Pal.:–Juttah.
3195. יְטוּר *yet-oor'* prob. from the same as 2905; *encircled;* (i.e. inclosed); *Jetur,* a son of Ishmael:–Jetur.
3196. יַיִן *yah'-yin;* from an un. root mean. to *effervesce; wine* (as fermented); by impl., *intoxication:*–banqueting, wine, wine[-bibber].
3197. יַךְ *yak;* by err. transc. for 3027; a *hand* or *side:*–[way-]side.
3198. יָכַח *yaw-kahh';* a prim. root; to *be right* (i.e. correct); reciprocally, to *argue;* caus., to *decide, justify* or *convict:*–appoint, argue, chasten, convince, correct(-ion), daysman, dispute, judge, maintain, plead, reason (together), rebuke, reprove(-r), surely, in any wise.
3199. יָכִין *yaw-keen';* from 3559; *he* (or *it*) *will establish; Jakin,* the name of three Isr. and of a temple pillar:–Jachin.
3200. יָכִינִי *yaw-kee-nee';* patron. from 3199; a *Jakinite* (coll.) or desc. of Jakin:–Jachinites.
3201. יָכֹל *yaw-kole';* or (fuller) יָכוֹל *yaw-kole';* a prim. root; to *be able,* lit. (*can, could*) or mor. (*may, might*):–be able, any at all (ways), attain, can (away with, [-not]), could, endure, might, overcome, have power, prevail, still, suffer.
3202. יְכֵל *yek-ale'* (Chald.); or יְכִיל *yek-eel';* to 3201:–be able, can, couldest, prevail.
3203. יְכָלְיָה *yek-ol-yaw';* and יְכָלְיָהוּ *yek-ol-yaw'-hoo;* or (2 Chronicles 26:3) *yek-ee-leh-yaw';* from 3201 and 3050; *Jah will enable; Jekoljah* or *Jekiljah,* an Isr.s:–Jecholiah, Jecoliah.
3204. יְכָנְיָה *yek-on-yaw';* and יְכָנְיָהוּ *yek-on-yaw'-hoo;* or (Jeremiah 27:20) יְכוֹנְיָה *yek-o-neh-yaw';* from 3559 and 3050; *Jah will establish; Jekonjah,* a Jewish king:–Jeconiah. Comp. 3659.
3205. יָלַד *yaw-lad';* a prim. root; to *bear* young; caus., to *beget;* medically, to *act as midwife;* spec., to *show lineage:*–bear, beget, birth ([-day]), born, (make to) bring forth (children, young), bring up, calve, child, come, be delivered (of a child), time of delivery, gender, hatch, labour, (do the office of a) midwife, declare pedigrees, be the son of, (woman in, woman that) travail(-eth, -ing woman).
3206. יֶלֶד *yeh'-led;* from 3205; something *born,* i.e. a *lad* or *offspring:*–boy, child, fruit, son, young man (one).
3207. יַלְדָּה *yal-daw';* fem. of 3206; a *lass:*–damsel, girl.
3208. יַלְדוּת *yal-dooth';* abstr. from 3206; *boyhood* (or *girlhood*):–childhood, youth.
3209. יִלּוֹד *yil-lode';* pass. from 3205; *born:*–born.
3210. יָלוֹן *yaw-lone';* from 3885; *lodging; Jalon,* an Isr.:–Jalon.
3211. יָלִיד *yaw-leed';* from 3205; *born:*–([home-])born, child, son.
3212. יָלַךְ *yaw-lak';* a prim. root [comp. 1980]; to *walk* (lit. or fig.); caus., to *carry* (in various senses):–X again, away, bear, bring, carry (away), come (away), depart, flow, + follow (-ing), get (away, hence, him), (cause to, made) go (away, -ing, -ne, one's way, out), grow, lead (forth), let down, march, prosper, + pursue, cause to run, spread, take away ([-journey]), vanish, (cause to) walk(-ing), wax, X be weak.
3213. יָלַל *yaw-lal';* a prim. root; to *howl* (with a wailing tone) or *yell* (with a boisterous one):–(make to) howl, be howling.

3214. יְלֵל *yel-ale'*; from 3213; a *howl;*-howling.

3215. יְלָלָה *yel-aw-law'*; fem. of 3214; a *howling.*

3216. . יָלַע *yaw-lah'*; a prim. root; to *blurt* or utter inconsiderately:–devour.

3217. יַלֶּפֶת *yal-leh'-feth;* from an un. root app. mean. to *stick* or *scrape; scurf* or *tetter:*–scabbed.

3218. יֶלֶק *yeh'-lek;* from an un. root mean. to *lick* up; a *devourer;* spec., the young *locust:*–cankerworm, caterpillar.

3219. יַלְקוּט *yal-koot';* from 3950; a travel-ling *pouch* (as if for gleanings):–scrip.

3220. יָם *yawm;* from an un. root mean. to *roar;* a *sea* (as breaking in *noisy* surf) or large body of water; spec. (with the art.), the *Mediterranean Sea;* sometimes a large *river,* or an artifical *basin;* locally, the *west,* or (rarely) the *south:*–sea (X -faring man, [-shore]), south, west (-ern, side, -ward).

3221. יָם *yawm* (Chald.); cor. to 3220:–sea.

3222. יֵם *yame;* from the same as 3117; a *warm* spring:–mule.

3223. יְמוּאֵל *yem-oo-ale';* from 3117 and 410; *day of God; Jemuel,* an Isr.:–Jemuel.

3224. יְמִימָה *yem-ee-maw';* perh. from the same as 3117; prop. *warm,* i.e. *affectionate;* hence, *dove* [comp. 3123]; *Jemimah,* one of Job's daughters:–Jemimah.

3225. יָמִין *yaw-meen';* from 3231; the *right* hand or side (leg, eye) of a person or other obj. (as the *stronger* and more dexterous); locally, the *south:*–+ left-handed, right (hand, side), south.

3226. יָמִין *yaw-meen';* the same as 3225; *Jamin,* the name of three Isr.:–Jamin. See also 1144.

3227. יְמִינִי *yem-ee-nee';* for 3225; *right:*–(on the) right (hand).

3228. יְמִינִי *yem-ee-nee';* patron. from 3226; a *Jeminite* (coll.) or desc. of Jamin:–Jaminites. See also 1145.

3229. יִמְלָא *yeem-law';* or יִמְלָה *yim-law';* from 4390; *full; Jimla* or *Jimlah,* an Isr.:–Imla, Imlah.

3230. יַמְלֵךְ *yam-lake';* from 4427; *he will make king; Jamlek,* an Isr.:–Jamlech.

3231. יָמַן *yaw-man';* a prim. root; to be (phys.) *right* (i.e. firm); but used only as denom. from 3225 and trans., to *be right-handed* or *take the right-hand side:*–go (turn) to (on, use) the right hand.

3232. יִמְנָה *yim-naw';* from 3231; *prosperity* (as betokened by the *right* hand); *Jimnah,* the name of two Isr.; also (with the art.) of the posterity of one of them:–Imna, Imnah, Jimnah, Jimnites.

3233. יְמָנִי *yem-aw-nee';* from 3231; *right* (i.e. at the right hand):–(on the) right (hand).

3234. יִמְנָע *yim-naw';* from 4513; *he will restrain; Jimna,* an Isr.:–Imna.

3235. יָמַר *yaw-mar';* a prim. root; to *exchange;* by impl., to *change places:*–boast selves, change.

3236. יִמְרָה *yim-raw'* prob. from 3235; *interchange; Jimrah,* an Isr.:– Imrah.

3237. יָמַשׁ *yaw-mash';* a prim. root; to *touch:*–feel.

3238. יָנָה *yaw-naw';* a prim. root; to *rage* or *be violent:* by impl., to *suppress,* to *maltreat:*–destroy, (thrust out by) oppress(-ing, -ion, -or), proud, vex, do violence.

3239. יָנוֹחַ *yaw-no'-akh;* or (with enclitic) יָנוֹחָה *yaw-no'-khaw;* from 3240; *quiet; Janoäch* or *Janochah,* or a place in Pal.:–Janoah, Janohah.

3240. יָנַח *yaw-nakh';* a prim. root; to *deposit;* by impl., to *allow to stay:*–bestow, cast down, lay (down, up), leave (off), let alone (remain), pacify, place, put, set (down), suffer, withdraw, withhold.

3241. יָנִים *yaw-neem';* from 5123; *asleep; Janim,* a place in Pal.:–Janum .

3242. יְנִיקָה *yen-ee-kaw';* from 3243; a *sucker* or sapling:–young twig.

3243. יָנַק *yaw-nak';* a prim. root; to *suck;* caus., to *give milk:*–milch, nurse(-ing mother), (give, make to) suck(-ing child, -ling).

3244. יַנְשׁוּף *yan-shoof';* or יַנְשׁוֹף *yan-shofe';* app. from 5398; an unclean (acquatic) bird; prob. the *heron* (perh. from its *blowing* cry, or because the *night*-heron is meant [comp. 5399]):–(great) owl.

3245. יָסַד *yaw-sad';* a prim. root; to set (lit. or fig.); intens., to *found;* refl., to *sit* down together, i.e. *settle, consult:*–appoint, take counsel, establish, (lay the, lay for a) found (-ation), instruct, lay, ordain, set, X sure.

3246. יְסֻד *yes-ood';* from 3245; a *foundation* (fig., i.e. *beginning*):–X began.

3247. יְסוֹד *yes-ode';* from 3245; a *foundation* (lit. or fig.):–bottom, foundation, repairing.

3248. יְסוּדָה *yes-oo-daw';* fem. of 3246; a *foundation:*–foundation.

3249. יָסוּר *yaw-soor'* from 5493; *departing:*–they that depart

3250. יִסּוֹר *yis-sore';* from 3256; a *reprover:*–instruct.

3251. יָסַךְ *yaw-sak';* a prim. root; to *pour* (intr.):–be poured.

3252. יִסְכָּה *yis-kaw';* from an un. root mean. to *watch; observant; Jiskah,* sister of Lot:–Iscah.

3253. יִסְמַכְיָהוּ *yis-mak-yaw-hoo';* from 5564 and 3050; *Jah will sustain; Jismakjah,* an Isr.:–Ismachiah.

3254. יָסַף *yaw-saf';* a prim. root; to *add or augment* (often adv., to *continue* to do a thing):–add, X again, X any more, X cease, X come more, + conceive again, continue, exceed, X further, X gather together, get more, give moreover, X henceforth, increase (more and more), join, X longer (bring, do, make, much, put), X (the, much, yet) more (and more), proceed (further), prolong, put, be [strong-] er, X yet, yield.

3255. יְסַף *yes-af'* (Chald.); cor. to 3254:–add.

3256. יָסַר *yaw-sar';* a prim. root; to *chastise,* lit. (with blows) or fig. (with words); hence, to *instruct:*–bind, chasten, chastise, correct, instruct, punish, reform, reprove, sore, teach.

3257. יָע *yaw;* from 3261; a *shovel:*–shovel.

3258. יַעְבֵּץ *yah-bates';* from an un. root prob. mean. to *grieve; sorrowful; Jabets,* the name of an Isr., and also of a place in Pal.:–Jabez.

3259. יָעַד *yaw-ad';* a prim. root; to *fix* upon (by agreement or appointment); by impl., to *meet* (at a stated time), to *summon* (to trial), to *direct* (in a certain quarter or position), to *engage* (for marriage):–agree,(make an) appoint(-ment, a time), assemble (selves), betroth, gather (selves, together), meet (together), set (a time).

3260. יֶעְדִּי *yed-ee';* from 3259; *appointed; Jedi,* an Isr.:–Iddo See 3035.

3261. יָעָה *yaw-aw';* a prim. root; app. to *brush* aside:–sweep away.

3262. יְעוּאֵל *yeh-oo-ale';* from 3261 and 410; *carried away of God; Jeüel,* the name of four Isr.:–Jehiel, Jeiel, Jeuel. Comp. 3273.

3263. יְעוּץ *yeh-oots';* from 5779; *counsellor; Jeüts,* an Isr.:–Jeuz.

3264. יָעוֹר *yaw-ore';* a var. of 3298; a *forest:*–wood.

3265. יָעוּר *yaw-oor';* app. the pass.part. of the same as 3293; *wooded; Jaür,* an Isr.:–Jair.

3266. יְעוּשׁ *yeh-oosh';* from 5789; *hasty; Jeüsh,* the name of an Edomite and of four Isr.:–Jehush, Jeush. Comp. 3274.

3267. יָעַז *yaw-az';* a prim. root; to be *bold* or *obstinate:* fierce.

3268. יַעֲזִיאֵל *yah-az-ee-ale';* from 3267 and 410; *emboldened of God; Jaaziël,* an Isr.:–Jaaziel.

3269. יַעֲזִיָּהוּ *yah-az-ee-yaw'-hoo;* from 3267 and 3050; *emboldened of Jah; Jaazijah,* an Isr.:–Jaaziah.

3270. יַעְזֵיר *yah-az-ayr';* or יַעְזֵר *yah-zare';* from 5826; *helpful; Jaazer* or *Jazer,* a place E. of the Jordan:–Jaazer, Jazer.

3271. יָעַט *yaw-at';* a prim. root; to *clothe:*–cover.

3272. יְעַט *yeh-at'* (Chald.); cor. to 3289; to *counsel;* refl., to *consult:*–counsellor, consult together.

3273. יְעִיאֵל *yeh-ee-ale';* from 3261 and 410; *carried away of God; Jeïel,* the name of six Isr.:–Jeiel, Jehiel. Comp. 3262.

3274. יְעִישׁ *yeh-eesh';* from 5789; *hasty; Jeïsh,* the name of an Edomite and of an Isr.:–Jeush . Comp. 3266.

3275. יַעְכָּן *yah-kawn';* from the same as 5912; *troublesome; Jakan,* an Isr.:–Jachan.

3276. יָעַל *yaw-al';* a prim. root; prop. to *ascend;* fig., to *be valuable* (obj.: *useful,* subj.: *benefited*):–X at all, set forward, can do good, (be, have) profit, (able).

3277. יָעֵל *yaw-ale';* from 3276; an *ibex* (as *climbing*):–wild goat.

3278. יָעֵל *yaw-ale';* the same as 3277; *Jaël,* a Canaanite:–Jael.

3279. יַעֲלָא *yah-al-aw';* or יַעֲלָה *yah-al-aw';* the same as 3280 or direct from 3276; *Jaala* or *Jaalah,* one of the Nethinim:–Jaala, Jaalah.

3280. יַעֲלָה *yah-al-aw';* fem. of 3277:–roe.

3281. יַעְלָם *yah-lawm';* from 5956; *occult; Jalam,* an Edomite:–Jalam.

3282. יַעַן *yah'-an;* from an un. root mean. to *pay attention;* prop. *heed;* by impl., *purpose* (sake or account); used adv. to indicate the *reason* or cause:–because (that), forasmuch (+ as), seeing then, + that, + wheras, + why.

3283. יָעֵן *yaw-ane';* from the same as 3282; the *ostrich* (prob. from its *answering* cry:–ostrich.

3284. יַעֲנָה *yah-an-aw';* fem. of 3283, and mean. the same:–+ owl.

3285. יַעֲנַי *yah-an-ah'ee;* from the same as 3283; *responsive; Jaanai,* an Isr.:–Jaanai.

3286. יָעַף *yaw-af';* a prim. root; to *tire* (as if from wearisome *flight*):–faint, cause to fly, (be) weary (self).

3287. יָעֵף *yaw-afe';* from 3286; *fatigued;* fig., *exhausted:*–faint, weary.

3288. יְעָף *yeh-awf';* from 3286; *fatigue* (adv., utterly *exhausted*):–swiftly.

3289. יָעַץ *yaw-ats';* a prim. root; to *advise;* refl., to *deliberate* or *resolve:*–advertise, take advise, advise (well), consult, (give, take) counsel (-lor), determine, devise, guide, purpose.

3290. יַעֲקֹב *yah-ak-obe';* from 6117; *heel-catcher* (i.e. supplanter); *Jaakob,* the Isr. patriarch:–Jacob.

3291. יַעֲקֹבָה *yah-ak-o'-baw;* from 3290; *Jaakobah,* an Isr.:–Jaakobah.

3292. יַעֲקָן *yah-ak-awn';* from the same as 6130; *Jaakan,* an Idumaean:–Jaakan. Comp. 1142.

3293. יַעַר *yah'-ar;* from an un. root prob. mean. to *thicken* with verdure; a *copse* of bushes; hence, a *forest;* hence, *honey* in the *comb* (as hived in trees):–[honey-]comb, forest, wood.
3294. יַעְרָה *yah-raw';* a form of 3295; *Jarah,* an Isr.:–Jarah.
3295. יַעֲרָה *yah-ar-aw';* fem. of 3293, and mean. the same:–[honey-] comb, forest.
3296. יַעֲרֵי אֹרְגִים *yah-ar-ay' o-reg-eem';* from the pl. of 3293and the masc. pl. act. part. of 707; *woods* of *weavers; Jaare-Oregim,* an Isr.:–Jaare-oregim.
3297. יְעָרִים *yeh-aw-reem';* pl. of 3293; *forests; Jeärim,* a place in Pal.:–Jearim. Comp. 7157.
3298. יַעֲרֶשְׁיָה *yah-ar-esh-yaw';* from an un. root of unc. signif. and 3050; *Jaareshjah,* an Isr.:–Jaresiah.
3299. יַעֲשׂוֹ *yah-as-oo';* from 6213; *they will do; Jaasu,* an Isr.:–Jaasau.
3300. יַעֲשִׂיאֵל *yah-as-ee-ale';* from 6213 and 410; *made of God; Jaasiel,* an Isr.:–Jaasiel, Jasiel.
3301. יִפְדְיָה *yif-deh-yaw';* from 6299 and 3050; *Jah will liberate; Jiphdejah,* an Isr.:–Iphedeiah.
3302. יָפָה *yaw-faw';* a prim. root; prop. to *be bright,* i.e. (by impl.) *beautiful:*–be beautiful, be (make self) fair(-r), deck.
3303. יָפֶה *yaw-feh';* from 3302; *beautiful* (lit. or fig.):–+ beautiful, beauty, comely, fair(-est, one), + goodly, pleasant, well.
3304. יְפֵה־פִיָּה *yef-eh' fee-yaw';* from 3302 by redupl.; *very beautiful:*–very fair.
3305. יָפוֹ *yaw-fo';* or יָפוֹא (Ezra 3:7) *yaw-fo';* from 3302; *beautiful; Japho,* a place in Pal.:–Japha, Joppa.
3306. יָפַח *yaw-fakh';* a prim. root; prop. to *breathe* hard, i.e. (by impl.) to *sigh:*–bewail self.
3307. יָפֵחַ *yaw-fay'-akh;* from 3306; prop. *puffing,* i.e. (fig.) *meditating:*–such as breathe out.
3308. יֳפִי *yof-ee';* from 3302; *beauty:*–beauty.
3309. יָפִיעַ *yaw-fee'-ah;* from 3313; *bright; Japhia,* the name of a Canaanite, an Isr., and a place in Pal.:–Japhia.
3310. יַפְלֵט *yaf-late';* from 6403; *he will deliver; Japhlet,* an Isr.:–Japhlet.
3311. יַפְלֵטִי *yaf-lay-tee';* patron. from 3310; a *Japhletite* or desc. of Japhlet:–Japhleti.
3312. יְפֻנֶּה *yef-oon-neh';* from 6437; *he will be prepared; Jephunneh,* the name of two Isr.:–Jephunneh.
3313. יָפַע *yaw-fah';* a prim. root; to *shine:*–be light, shew self, (cause to) shine (forth).
3314. יִפְעָה *yif-aw';* from 3313; *splendor* or (fig.) *beauty:*–brightness.
3315. יֶפֶת *yeh'-feth;* from 6601; *expansion;* Jepheth, a son of Noah; also his posterity:–Japheth.
3316. יִפְתָּח *yif-tawkh';* from 6605; *he will open; Jiphtach,* an Isr.; also a place in Pal.:–Jephthah, Jiphtah.
3317. יִפְתַּח־אֵל *yif-tach-ale';* from 6605 and 410; *God will open; Jiphtach-el,* a place in Pal.:–Jiphthah-el.
3318. יָצָא *yaw-tsaw';* a prim. root; to *go* (caus., *bring*) *out,* in a great variety of appl., lit. and fig., direct and proximate:–X after, appear, X assuredly, bear out, X begotten, break out, bring forth (out, up), carry out, come (abroad, out, thereat, without), + be condemned, depart(-ing, -ure), draw forth, in the end, escape, exact, fail, fall (out), fetch forth (out), get away (forth, hence, out), (able to, cause to, let) go abroad (forth, on, out), going out, grow, have forth (out), issue out, lay (lie) out, lead out, pluck out, proceed, pull out, put away, be risen, X scarce, send with commandment, shoot forth, spread, spring out, stand out, X still, X surely, take forth (out), at any time, X to [and fro], utter.
3319. יְצָא *yets-aw'* (Chald.); cor. to 3318:–finish.
3320. יָצַב *yaw-tsab';* a prim. root; to *place* (any thing so as to stay); refl., to *station, offer, continue:*–present selves, remaining, resort, set (selves), (be able to, can, with-) stand (fast, forth, -ing, still, up).
3321. יְצַב *yets-abe'* (Chald.); cor. to 3320; to *be firm;* hence, to *speak surely:*–truth.
3322. יָצַג *yaw-tsag';* a prim. root; to *place* permanently:–establish, leave, make, present, put, set, stay.
3323. יִצְהָר *yits-hawr';* from 6671; *oil* (as producing *light*); fig., *anointing:*–+ anointed oil.
3324. יִצְהָר *yits-hawr';* the same as 3323; *Jitshar,* an Isr.:–Izhar.
3325. יִצְהָרִי *yits-haw-ree';* patron. from 3324; a *Jitsharite* or desc. of *Jitshar:*–Izeharites, Izharites.
3326. יָצוּעַ *yaw-tsoo'-ah;* pass.part. of 3331; *spread,* i.e. a *bed;* (arch.) an *extension,* i.e. *wing* or *lean-to* (a single story or coll.):–bed, chamber, couch.
3327. יִצְחָק *yits-khawk';* from 6711; *laughter* (i.e. *mockery*); *Jitschak* (or Isaac), son of Abraham:–Isaac. Comp. 3446.
3328. יִצְחַר *yits-khar';* from the same as 6713; *he will shine; Jitschar,* an Isr.:–and Zehoar.
3329. יָצִיא *yaw-tsee';* from 3318; *issue,* i.e. offspring:–those that came forth.
3330. יַצִּיב *yats-tseeb'* (Chald.); from 3321; *fixed, sure;* concr., *certainty:*–certain(-ty), true, truth.
3331. יָצַע *yaw-tsah';* a prim. root; to *strew* as a surface:–make [one's] bed, X lie, spread.
3332. יָצַק *yaw-tsak';* a prim. root; prop. to *pour* out (trans. or intr.); by impl., to *melt* or *cast* as metal; by ext., to *place* firmly, to *stiffen* or grow hard:–cast, cleave fast, be (as) firm, grow, be hard, lay out, molten, overflow, pour (out), run out, set down, stedfast.
3333. יְצֻקָה *yets-oo-kaw';* pass.part. fem. of 3332; *poured* out, i.e. *run* into a mould:–when it was cast.
3334. יָצַר *yaw-tsar';* a prim. root; to *press* (intr.), i.e. *be narrow;* fig., be *in distress:*–be distressed, be narrow, be straitened (in straits), be vexed.
3335. יָצַר *yaw-tsar';* prob. ident. with 3334 (through the *squeezing* into shape); ([comp. 3331]); to *mould* into a form; esp. as a *potter;* fig., to *determine* (i.e. form a resolution):–X earthen, fashion, form, frame, make(-r), potter, purpose.
3336. יֵצֶר *yay'-tser;* from 3335; a *form;* fig., *conception* (i.e. purpose):–frame, thing framed, imagination, mind, work.
3337. יֵצֶר *yay-tser;* the same as 3336; *Jetser,* an Isr.:–Jezer.
3338. יָצֻר *yaw-tsoor';* pass.part. of 3335; *structure,* i.e. limb or part:–member.
3339. יִצְרִי *yits-ree';* from 3335; *formative; Jitsri,* an Isr.:–Isri.
3340. יִצְרִי *yits-ree';* patron. from 3337; a *Jitsrite* (coll.) or desc. of Jetser:–Jezerites.
3341. יָצַת *yaw-tsath';* a prim. root; to *burn* or *set on fire;* fig., to *desolate:*–burn (up), be desolate, set (on) fire ([fire]), kindle.
3342. יֶקֶב *yeh'-keb;* from an un. root mean. to *excavate;* a *trough* (as dug out); spec., a wine-*vat* (whether the lower one, into which the juice drains; or the upper, in which the grapes are crushed):–fats, presses, press-fat, wine(-press).
3343. יְקַבְצְאֵל *yek-ab-tseh-ale';* from 6908 and 410; *God will gather; Jekabtseël,* a place in Pal.:–Jekabzeel. Comp. 6909.
3344. יָקַד *yaw-kad';* a prim. root; to *burn:*–(be) burn(-ing), X from the hearth, kindle.
3345. יְקַד *yek-ad'* (Chald.); cor. to 3344:–burning.
3346. יְקֵדָא *yek-ay-daw'* (Chald.); from 3345; a *conflagration:*–burning.
3347. יָקְדְעָם *yok-deh-awm';* from 3344 and 5971; *burning of* (the) *people; Jokdeäm,* a place in Pal.:–Jokdeam.
3348. יָקֶה *yaw-keh';* from an un. root prob. mean. to *obey; obedient; Jakeh,:*–Jakeh.
3349. יִקָּהָה *yik-kaw-haw';* from the same as 3348; *obedience:*–gathering, to obey.
3350. יְקוֹד *yek-ode';* from 3344; a *burning:*–burning.
3351. יְקוּם *yek-oom';* from 6965; prop. *standing* (extant), i.e. by impl., a *living thing:*–(living) substance.
3352. יָקוֹשׁ *yaw-koshe';* from 3369; prop. *entangling;* hence, a *snarer:*–fowler.
3353. יָקוּשׁ *yaw-koosh';* pass.part. of 3369; prop. *entangled,* i.e. by impl. (intr.) a *snare,* or (trans.) a *snarer:*–fowler, snare.
3354. יְקוּתִיאֵל *yek-ooth-ee'-ale;* from the same as 3348 and 410; *obedience of God; Jekuthiël,* an Isr.:–Jekuthiel.
3355. יָקְטָן *yok-tawn';* from 6994; *he will be made little; Joktan,* an Arabian patriarch:–Joktan.
3356. יָקִים *yaw-keem';* from 6965; *he will raise; Jakim,* the name of two Isr.:–Jakim. Comp. 3079.
3357. יַקִּיר *yak-keer';* from 3365; *precious:*–dear.
3358. יַקִּיר *yak-keer';* (Chald.) cor. to 3357:–noble, rare.
3359. יְקַמְיָה *yek-am-yaw';* from 6965 and 3050; *Jah will rise; Jekamjah,* the name of two Isr.:–Jekamiah. Comp. 3079.
3360. יְקַמְעָם *yek-am'-awm;* from 6965 and 5971; (the) *people will rise; Jekamam,* an Isr.:–Jekameam. Comp. 3079, 3361.
3361. יָקְמְעָם *yok-meh-awm';* from 6965 and 5971; (the) *people will be raised; Jokmeäm,* a place in Pal.:–Jokmeam. Comp. 3360, 3362.
3362. יָקְנְעָם *yok-neh-awm';* from 6969 and 5971; (the) *people will be lamented; Jokneäm,* a place in Pal.:–Jokneam.
3363. יָקַע *yaw-kah';* a prim. root; prop. to *sever* oneself, i.e. (by impl.) to *be dislocated;* fig., to *abandon;* caus., to *impale* (and thus allow to drop to pieces by *rotting*):–be alienated, depart, hang (up), be out of joint.
3364. יָקַץ *yaw-kats';* a prim. root; to *awake* (intr.):–(be) awake(-d).
3365. יָקַר *yaw-kar';* a prim. root; prop. app., to *be heavy,* i.e. (fig.) *valuable;* caus., to *make rare* (fig., to *inhibit*):–be (make) precious, be prized, be set by, withdraw.
3366. יְקָר *yek-awr';* from 3365; *value,* i.e. (concr.) *wealth;* abstr., *costliness, dignity:*–honour, precious (things), price.
3367. יְקָר *yek-awr'* (Chald.); cor. to 3366:–glory, honour.
3368. יָקָר *yaw-kawr';* from 3365; *valuable* (obj. or subj.):–brightness, clear, costly, excellent, fat,

honourable women, precious, reputation.
3369. יָקֹשׁ *yaw-koshe';* a prim. root; to *ensnare* (lit. or fig.):–fowler (lay a) snare.
3370. יָקְשָׁן *yok-shawn';* from 3369; *insidious; Jokshan,* an Arabian patriarch:–Jokshan.
3371. יָקְתְאֵל *yok-theh-ale';* prob. from the same as 3348 and 410; *veneration of God* [comp. 3354]; Joktheël, the name of a place in Pal., and of one in Idumaea:–Joktheel.
3372. יָרֵא *yaw-ray';* a prim. root; to *fear;* mor., to *revere;* caus. to *frighten:*–affright, be (make) afraid, dread(-ful), (put in) fear (-ful, -fully, -ing), (be had in) reverence (-end), X see, terrible (act, -ness, thing).
3373. יָרֵא *yaw-ray';* from 3372; *fearing;* mor., *reverent:*–afraid, fear (-ful).
3374. יִרְאָה *yir-aw';* fem. of 3373; *fear* (also used as inf.); mor., *reverence:*–X dreadful, X exceedingly, fear(-fulness).
3375. יִרְאוֹן *yir-ohn';* from 3372; *fearfulness; Jiron,* a place in Pal:–Iron.
3376. יִרְאִיָּיה *yir-ee-yaw';* from 3373 and 3050; *fearful of Jah; Jirijah,* an Isr.:–Irijah.
3377. יָרֵב *yaw-rabe';* from 7378; *he will contend; Jareb,* –Jareb. Comp. 3402.
3378. יְרֻבַּעַל *yer-oob-bah'-al;* from 7378 and 1168; *Baal will contend; Jerubbaal,* a symbol. name of Gideon:–Jerubbaal.
3379. יָרָבְעָם *yaw-rob-awm';* from 7378 and 5971; (the) *people will contend; Jarobam,* the name of two Isr. kings:–Jeroboam.
3380. יְרֻבֶּשֶׁת *yer-oob-beh'-sheth;* from 7378 and 1322; *shame* (i.e. the idol) *will contend; Jerubbesheth,* a symbol. name for Gideon:–Jerubbesheth.
3381. יָרַד *yaw-rad';* a prim. root; to descend (lit., to go *downwards;* or conventionally to a lower region, as the shore, a boundary, the enemy, etc.; or fig., to *fall*); caus., to *bring down* (in all the above appl.):–X abundantly, bring down, carry down, cast down, (cause to) come (-ing) down, fall (down), get down, go(-ing) down(-ward), hang down, X indeed, let down, light (down), put down (off), (cause to, let) run down, sink, subdue, take down.
3382. יֶרֶד *yeh'-red;* from 3381; a *descent; Jered,* the name of an antediluvian, and of an Isr.:–Jared.
3383. יַרְדֵּן *yar-dane';* from 3381; a *descender; Jarden,* the principal river of Pal.:–Jordan.
3384. יָרָה *yaw-raw';* or (2 Chr. 26:15) יָרָא *yaw-raw';* a prim. root; prop. to *flow* as water (i.e. to *rain*); trans., to *lay* or *throw* (esp. an arrow, i.e. to *shoot*); fig., to *point* out (as if by *aiming* the finger), to *teach:*–(+) archer, cast, direct, inform, instruct, lay, shew, shoot, teach(-er,-ing), through.
3385. יְרוּאֵל *yer-oo-ale';* from 3384 and 410; *founded of God; Jeruel,* a place in Pal.:–Jeruel.
3386. יָרוֹחַ *yaw-ro'-akh;* perh. denom. from 3394; (born at the) new *moon; Jaroäch,* an Isr.:–Jaroah.
3387. יָרוֹק *yaw-roke';* from 3417; *green,* i.e. an herb:–green thing.
3388. יְרוּשָׁא *yer-oo-shaw';* or יְרוּשָׁה *yer-oo-shaw';* fem. pass.part. of 3423; *possessed;Jerusha* or *Jerushah,* an Isr.s:–Jerusha, Jerushah.
3389. יְרוּשָׁלַםִ *yer-oo-shaw-lah'-im;* rarely יְרוּשָׁלַיִם *shaw-lah'-yim;* a dual (in allusion to its two main hills; prob. from (the pass. part. of) 3384 and 7999; *founded peaceful; Jerushalaïm* or *Jerushalem,* the capital city of Pal.:–Jerusalem
3390. יְרוּשְׁלֵם *yer-oo-shaw-lame';* cor. to 3389:–Jerusalem
3391. יֶרַח *yeh'-rakh;* from a un. root of unc. signif.; a *lunation,* i.e. *month:*–month, moon.
3392. יֶרַח *yeh'-rakh;* the same as 3391; *Jerach,* an Arabian patriarch:–Jerah.
3393. יְרַח *yeh-rakh'* (Chald.); cor. to 3391; a *month:*–month.
3394. יָרֵחַ *yaw-ray'-akh;* from the same as 3391; the *moon:*–moon. יָרֵחַ. See 3405.
3395. יְרֹחָם *yer-o-khawm';* from 7355; *compassionate; Jerocham,* the name of seven or eight Isr.:–Jeroham.
3396. יְרַחְמְאֵל *yer-akh-meh-ale';* from 7355 and 410; *God will compassionate; Jerachmeël,* the name of three Isr.:–Jerahmeel.
3397. יְרַחְמְאֵלִי *yer-akh-meh-ay-lee';* patron. from 3396; a *Jerachmeëlite* or desc. of Jerachmeel:–Jerahmeelites.
3398. יַרְחָע *yar-khaw';* prob. of Eg. or.; *Jarcha,* an Eg.:–Jarha.
3399. יָרַט *yaw-rat';* a prim. root; to *precipitate or hurl (rush)* headlong; (intr.) to *be rash:*–be perverse, turn over.
3400. יְרִיאֵל *yer-ee-ale';* from 3384 and 410; *thrown of God; Jeriël,* an Isr.:–Jeriel. Comp. 3385.
3401. יָרִיב *yaw-rebe';* from 7378; lit., *he will contend;* prop. adj., *contentious;* used as noun, an *adversary:*–that content(-eth), that strive.
3402. יָרִיב *yaw-rebe';* the same as 3401; *Jarib,* the name of three Isr.:–Jarib.
3403. יְרִיבַי *yer-eeb-ah'ee;* from 3401; *contentious; Jeribai,* an Isr.:–Jeribai.
3404. יְרִיָּה *yer-ee-yaw';* or יְרִיָּהוּ *yer-ee-yaw'-hoo;* from 3384 and 3050; *Jah will throw; Jerijah,* an Isr.:–Jeriah, Jerijah.
3405. יְרִיחוֹ *yer-ee-kho';* or יְרֵחוֹ *yer-ay-kho';* or var. (1 Kings 16:34) יְרִיחֹה *yer-ee-kho';* perh. from 3394; *its month;* or else from 7306; *fragrant; Jericho* or *Jerecho,* a place in Pal.:–Jericho.
3406. יְרִימוֹת *yer-ee-mohth';* or יְרֵימוֹת *yer-ay-mohth';* or יְרֵמוֹת *yer-ay-mohth';* fem. pl. from 7311; *elevations; Jerimoth* or *Jeremoth,* the name of twelve Isr.:–Jermoth, Jerimoth, and Ramoth.
3407. יְרִיעָה *yer-ee-aw';* from 3415; a *hanging* (as *tremulous*):–curtain.
3408. יְרִיעוֹת *yer-ee-ohth';* pl. of 3407; *curtains; Jerioth,* an Isr.s:–Jerioth.
3409. יָרֵךְ *yaw-rake';* from an un. root mean. to *be soft;* the *thigh* (from its fleshy *softness*); by euphem. the *generative parts;* fig., a *shank, flank, side:*–X body, loins, shaft, side, thigh.
3410. יַרְכָא *yar-kaw'* (Chald.); cor. to 3411; a *thigh:*–thigh.
3411. יְרֵכָה *yer-ay-kaw';* fem. of 3409; prop. the flank; but used only fig., the rear or recess:–border, coast, part, quarter, side.
3412 יַרְמוּת *yar-mooth';* from 7311; *elevation; Jarmuth,* the name of two places in Pal.:–Jarmuth.
3413. יְרֵמַי *yer-ay-mah'-ee;* from 7311; *elevated; Jeremai,* an Isr.:–Jeremai.
3414. יִרְמְיָה *yir-meh-yaw';* or יִרְמְיָהוּ *yir-meh-yaw'-hoo;* from 7311 and 3050; *Jah will rise; Jirmejah,* the name of eight or nine Isr.:–Jeremiah.
3415. יָרַע *yaw-rah';* a prim. root; prop. to *be broken* up (with any violent action) i.e. (fig.) to *fear:*–be grievous [*only* Is. 15:4; *the rest belong* to 7489].
3416. יִרְפְּאֵל *yir-peh-ale';* from 7495 and 410; *God will heal; Jirpeël,* a place in Pal.:–Irpeel.
3417. יָרַק *yaw-rak';* a prim. root; to *spit:*–X but, spit.
3418. יֶרֶק *yeh'-rek;* from 3417 (in the sense of *vacuity* of color); prop. *pallor,* i.e. hence, the yellowish *green* of young and sickly vegetation; concr., *verdure,* i.e. grass or vegetation:–grass, green (thing).
3419. יָרָק *yaw-rawk';* from the same as 3418; prop. *green;* concr., a *vegetable:*–green, herbs.
3420. יֵרָקוֹן *yay-raw-kone';* from 3418; *paleness,* whether of persons (from fright), or of plants (from drought):–greenish, yellow.
3421. יָרְקְעָם *yor-keh-awm';* from 7324 and 5971; *people will be poured forth; Jorkeäm,* a place in Pal.:–Jorkeam.
3422. יְרַקְרַק *yer-ak-rak';* from the same as 3418; *yellowishness:*–greenish, yellow.
3423. יָרַשׁ *yaw-rash';* or יָרֵשׁ *yaw-raysh';* a prim. root; to *occupy* (by *driving* out previous tenants, and *possessing* in their place); by impl., to *seize,* to *rob,* to *inherit;* also to *expel,* to *impoverish,* to *ruin:*–cast out, consume, destroy, disinherit, dispossess, drive(-ing) out, enjoy, expel, X without fail, (give to, leave for) inherit(-ance, -or) + magistrate, be (make) poor, come to poverty, (give to, make to) possess, get (have) in (take) possession, seize upon, succeed, X utterly.
3424. יְרֵשָׁה *yer-ay-shaw';* from 3423; *occupancy:*–possession.
3425. יְרֻשָּׁה *yer-oosh-shaw';* from 3423; something *occupied;* a *conquest;* also a *patrimony:*–heritage, inheritance, possession.
3426. יֵשׁ *yaysh;* perh. from an un. root mean. to *stand* out, or *exist; entity;* used adv. or as a copula for the substantive verb (1961); there *is* or *are* (or any other form of the verb to be, as may suit the connection):–(there) are, (he, it, shall, there, there may, there shall, there should) be, thou do, had, hast, (which) hath, (I, shalt, that) have, (he, it, there) is, substance, it (there) was, (there) were, ye will, thou wilt, wouldest.
3427. יָשַׁב *yaw-shab';* a prim. root; prop. to *sit* down (spec. as judge. in ambush, in quiet); by impl., to *dwell,* to *remain;* caus., to *settle,* to *marry:*–(make to) abide(-ing), continue, (cause to, make to) dwell(-ing), ease self, endure, establish, X fail, habitation, haunt, (make to) inhabit(-ant), make to keep [house], lurking, X marry(-ing), (bring again to) place, remain, return, seat, set(- tle), (down-) sit(-down, still, -ting down, -ting [place] -uate), take, tarry.
3428. יֶשֶׁבְאָב *yeh-sheb-awb';* from 3427 and 1; *seat of* (his) *father; Jeshebab,* an Isr.:–Jeshebeab.
3429. ישֵׁב בַּשֶּׁבֶת *yo-shabe' bash-sheh'-beth;* from the act.part. of 3427 and 7674, with a prep. and the art. interp.; *sitting in the seat; Josheb-bash-Shebeth,* an Isr.:–that sat in the seat.
3430. יִשְׁבּוֹ בְּנֹב *yish-bo'beh-nobe;* from 3427 and 5011, with a pron. suffix and a prep. interp.; *his dwelling* (is) *in Nob; Jishbo-be-Nob,* a Philistine:–Ishbi-benob .
3431. יִשְׁבַּח *yish-bakh';* from 7623; *he will praise; Jishbach,* an Isr.:–Ishbah.
3432. יָשֻׁבִי *yaw-shoo-bee';* patron. from 3437; a *Jashubite,* or desc. of Jashub:–Jashubites.
3433. יָשֻׁבִי לֶחֶם *yaw-shoo-bee' leh'-khem;* from 7725 and 3899; *returner of bread;*

HEBREW

Jashubi-Lechem, an Isr.:–Jashubi-lehem. [Prob. the text should be pointed יֹשְׁבֵי לֶחֶם yo-*sheh-bay' leh'-khem,* and rendered "(they were) inh. of Lechem," i.e. of Bethlehem (by contr.). Comp. 3902].

3434. יָשָׁבְעָם *yaw-shob-awm';* from 7725 and 5971; *people will return; Jashobam,* the name of two or three Isr.:–Jashobeam.

3435. יִשְׁבָּק *yish-bawk';* from an un. root cor. to 7662; *he will leave; Jishbak,* a son of Abraham:–Ishbak.

3436. יָשְׁבְּקָשָׁה *yosh-bek-aw-shaw;* from 3427 and 7186; *a hard seat; Joshbekashah,* an Isr.:–Joshbekashah.

3437. יָשׁוּב *yaw-shoob';* or יָשִׁיב *yaw-sheeb';* from 7725; *he will return; Jashub,* the name of two Isr.:–Jashub.

3438. יִשְׁוָה *yish-vaw';* from 7737; *he will level; Jishvah,* an Isr.:–Ishvah, Isvah.

3439. יְשׁוֹחָיָה *yesh-o-khaw-yaw';* from the same as 3445 and 3050; *Jah will empty; Jeshochajah,* an Isr.:–Jeshoaiah.

3440. יִשְׁוִי *yish-vee';* from 7737; *level; Jishvi,* the name of two Isr.:–Ishuai, Ishvi, Isui, Jesui.

3441. יִשְׁוִי *yish-vee';* patron. from 3440; a *Jishvite* (coll.) or desc. of Jishvi:–Jesuites.

3442. יֵשׁוּעַ *yay-shoo'-ah;* for 3091; *he will save; Jeshua,* the name of ten Isr., also of a place in Pal.:–Jeshua.

3443. יֵשׁוּעַ *yay-shoo'-ah* (Chald.); cor. to 3442:–Jeshua.

3444. יְשׁוּעָה *yesh-oo'-aw;* fem. pass.part. of 3467; something *saved,* i.e. (abstr.) *deliverance;* hence, *aid, victory, prosperity:*–deliverance, health, help(-ing), salvation, save, saving (health), welfare.

3445. יֶשַׁח *yeh'-shakh;* from an un. root mean. to *gape* (as the empty stomach); *hunger:*–casting down.

3446. יִשְׂחָק *yis-khawk';* from 7831; *he will laugh; Jischak,* the heir of Abraham:–Isaac. Comp. 3327.

3447. יָשַׁט *yaw-shat';* a prim. root; to *extend:*–hold out.

3448. יִשַׁי *yee-shah'-ee;* by Chald. אִישַׁי *ee-shah'-ee;* from the same as 3426; *extant; Jishai,* David's father:–Jesse.

3449. יִשִּׁיָּה *yish-shee-yaw';* or יִשִּׁיָּהוּ *yish-shee-yaw'-hoo;* from 5383 and 3050; *Jah will lend; Jishshijah,* the name of five Isr.:–Ishiah, Isshiah, Ishijah, Jesiah.

3450. יְשִׂימָאֵל *yes-eem-aw-ale';* from 7760 and 410; *God will place; Jesimaël,* an Isr.:–Jesimael.

3451. יְשִׁימָה *yesh-ee-maw';* from 3456; *desolation:*–let death seize .

3452. יְשִׁימוֹן *yesh-ee-mone';* from 3456; a *desolation:*–desert, Jeshimon, solitary, wilderness.

3453. יָשִׁישׁ *yaw-sheesh';* from 3486; an *old* man:–(very) aged (man), ancient, very old.

3454 יְשִׁישַׁי *yesh-ee-shah'-ee;* from 3453; *aged; Jeshishai,* an Isr.:–Jeshishai.

3455. יָשַׂם *yaw-sam';* a prim root; to *place;* intr., to *be placed:*–be put (set).

3456. יָשַׁם *yaw-sham';* a prim. root; to *lie waste:*–be desolate.

3457. יִשְׁמָא *yish-maw';* from 3456; *desolate; Jishma,* an Isr.:–Ishma.

3458. יִשְׁמָעֵאל *yish-maw-ale';* from 8085 and 410; *God will hear; Jishmael,* the name of Abraham's oldest son, and of five Isr.:–Ishmael.

3459. יִשְׁמְעֵאלִי *yish-maw-ay-lee';* patron. from 3458; a *Jishmaëlite* or desc. of Jishmael:–Ishmaelite.

3460. יִשְׁמַעְיָה *yish-mah-yaw';* or יִשְׁמַעְיָהוּ *yish-mah-yaw'-hoo;* from 8085 and 3050; *Jah will hear; Jishmajah,* the name of two Isr.:–Ishmaiah.

3461. יִשְׁמְרַי *yish-mer-ah'-ee;* from 8104; *preservative; Jishmerai,* an Isr.:–Ishmerai.

3462. יָשֵׁן *yaw-shane';* a prim. root; prop. to *be slack* or *languid,* i.e. (by impl.) *sleep* (fig., to *die*); also to *grow old, stale* or *inveterate:*–old (store), remain long, (make to) sleep.

3463. יָשֵׁן *yaw-shane';* from 3462; *sleepy:*–asleep, (one out of) sleep(-eth, -ing), slept.

3464. יָשֵׁן *yaw-shane';* the same as 3463; *Jashen,* an Isr.:–Jashen.

3465. יָשָׁן *yaw-shawn';* from 3462; *old:*–old.

3466. יְשָׁנָה *yesh-aw-naw';* fem. of 3465; *Jeshanah,* a place in Pal.:–Jeshanah.

3467. יָשַׁע *yaw-shah';* a prim. root; prop. to *be open, wide* or *free,* i.e. (by impl.) to *be safe;* caus., to *free* or *succor:*–X at all, avenging, defend, deliver(-er), help, preserve, rescue, be safe, bring (having) salvation, save(-iour), get victory.

3468. יֶשַׁע *yeh'-shah;* or יֵשַׁע *yay'-shah;* from 3467; *liberty, deliverance, prosperity:*–safety, salvation, saving.

3469. יִשְׁעִי *yish-ee';* from 3467; *saving; Jishi,* the name of four Isr.:–Ishi.

3470. יְשַׁעְיָה *yesh-ah-yaw';* or יְשַׁעְיָהוּ *yesh-ah-yaw'-hoo*; from 3467 and 3050; *Jah has saved; Jeshajah,* the name of seven Isr.:–Isaiah, Jesaiah, Jeshaiah.

3471. יָשְׁפֵה *yaw-shef-ay';* from an un. root mean. to *polish;* a gem supposed to be *jasper* (from the resemblance in name):–jasper.

3472. יִשְׁפָּה *yish-paw';* perh. from 8192; *he will scratch; Jishpah,* an Isr.:–Ispah.

3473. יִשְׁפָּן *yish-pawn';* prob. from the same as 8227; *he will hide; Jishpan,* an Isr.:–Ishpan.

3474. יָשַׁר *yaw-shar';* a prim. root; to *be straight* or *even;* fig., to *be* (caus., to *make*) *right, pleasant, prosperous:*–direct, fit, seem good (meet), + please (will), be (esteem, go) right (on), bring (look, make, take the) straight (way), be upright(-ly).

3475. יֵשֶׁר *yay'-sher;* from 3474; the *right; Jesher,* an Isr.:–Jesher.

3476. יֹשֶׁר *yo'-sher;* from 3474; the *right:*–equity, meet, right, upright(-ness).

3477. יָשָׁר *yaw-shawr';* from 3474; *straight* (lit. or fig.):–convenient, equity, Jasher, just, meet (-est), + pleased well right(-eous), straight, (most) upright(-ly, -ness).

3478. יִשְׂרָאֵל *yis-raw-ale';* from 8280 and 410; *he will rule as God; Jisraël,* Jacob; also (typically) of his posterity: –Israel.

3479. יִשְׂרָאֵל *yis-raw-ale'* (Chald.); cor. to 3478:–Israel

3480. יְשַׂרְאֵלָה *yes-ar-ale'-aw;* by var. from 3477 and 410 with directive enclitic; *right towards God; Jesarelah,* an Isr.:–Jesharelah.

3481. יִשְׂרְאֵלִי *yis-reh-ay-lee';* patron. from 3478; a *Jiseëlite* or desc. of Jisael:–of Israel, Israelite.

3482 יִשְׂרְאֵלִית *yis-reh-ay-leeth';* fem. of 3481; a *Jisreëlitess* or female desc. of Jisrael:–Israelitish.

3483. יִשְׁרָה *yish-raw';* fem. or 3477; *rectitude:*–uprightness.

3484. יְשֻׁרוּן *yesh-oo-roon';* from 3474; *upright; Jeshurun:*–Jeshurun.

3485. יִשָּׂשכָר *yis-saw-kawr';* (strictly *yis-saws-kawr'*); from 5375 and 7939; *he will bring a reward; Jissaskar,* a son of Jacob:–Issachar.

3486 יָשֵׁשׁ *yaw-shaysh';* from an un. root mean. to *blanch; gray*-haired, i.e. an *aged* man:–stoop for age.

3487. יַת *yath* (Chald.); cor. to 853; a sign of the obj. of a verb: + whom.

3488. יְתִב *yeth-eeb'* (Chald.); cor. to 3427; to *sit* or *dwell:*–dwell, (be) set, sit.

3489. יָתֵד *yaw-thade';* from an un. root mean. to *pin* through or fast; a *peg:*–nail, paddle, pin, stake.

3490. יָתוֹם *yaw-thome';* from an un. root mean. to *be lonely;* a *bereaved* person:–fatherless (child), orphan.

3491. יָתוּר *yaw-thoor';* pass.part. of 3498; prop. what is *left,* i.e. (by impl.) a *gleaning:*–range.

3492. יַתִּיר *yat-teer';* from 3498; *redundant; Jattir,* a place in Pal.:–Jattir.

3493. יַתִּיר *yat-teer'* (Chald.); cor. to 3492; *pre-eminent;* as an adv., *very:*–exceeding (-ly), excellent.

3494. יִתְלָה *yith-law';* prob. from 8518; *it will hang,* i.e. be high; *Jithlah,* a place in Pal.:–Jethlah.

3495. יִתְמָה *yith-maw';* from the same as 3490; *orphanage; Jithmah,* an Isr.:–Ithmah.

3496. יַתְנִיאֵל *yath-nee-ale';* from an un. root mean. to *endure,* and 410; *continued of God; Jathniël,* an Isr.:–Jathniel.

3497. יִתְנָן *yith-nawn';* from the same as 8577; *extensive; Jithnan,* a place in Pal.:–Ithnan.

3498. יָתַר *yaw-thar';* a prim. root; to *jut* over or *exceed;* by impl., to *excel;* (intr.) to *remain* or be *left;* caus., to *leave, cause to abound, preserve:*–excel, leave (a remnant), left behind, too much, make plenteous, preserve, (be, let) remain(-der, -ing, - nant), reserve, residue, rest.

3499. יֶתֶר *yeh'-ther;* from 3498; prop. an *overhanging,* i.e. (by impl.) an *excess, superiority, remainder;* also a small *rope* (as hanging free):–+ abundant, cord, exceeding, excellency(-ent), what they leave, that hath left, plentifully, remnant, residue, rest, string, with.

3500. יֶתֶר *yeh'-ther;* the same as 3499; *Jether,* the name of five or six Isr. and of one Midianite:–Jether, Jethro. Comp. 3503.

3501. יִתְרָא *yith-raw';* by var. for 3502; *Jithra,* an Isr. (or Ishmaelite):–Ithra.

3502. יִתְרָה *yith-raw';* fem. of 3499; prop. *excellence,* i.e. (by impl.) *wealth:*–abundance, riches.

3503. יִתְרוֹ *yith-ro';* from 3499 with pron. suffix; *his excellence; Jethro,* Moses' father-in-law:–Jethro. Comp. 3500.

3504. יִתְרוֹן *yith-rone'* from 3498; *preeminence, gain:*–better, excellency(-leth), profit(-able).

3505. יִתְרִי *yith-ree';* patron. from 3500; a *Jithrite* or desc. of Jether:–Ithrite.

3506. יִתְרָן *yith-rawn';* from 3498; *excellent; Jithran,* the name of an Edomite and of an Isr.:–Ithran.

3507. יִתְרְעָם *yith-reh-awm';* from 3499 and 5971; *excellence of people; Jithreäm,* a son of David:–Ithream.

3508. יֹתֶרֶת *yo-theh'-reth;* fem. act.part. of 3498; the *lobe* or *flap* of the liver (as if redundant or outhanging):–caul.

3509. יְתֵת *yeh-thayth';* of unc. der.; *Jetheth,* an Edomite:–Jetheth.

כ

3510. כָּאַב *kaw-ab';* a prim. root; prop. to feel

pain; by impl., to *grieve;* fig., to *spoil:*–grieving, mar, have pain, make sad (sore), (be) sorrowful.
3511. כְּאֵב *keh-abe';* from 3510; *suffering* (phys. or ment.), *adversity:*–grief, pain, sorrow.
3512. כָּאָה *kaw-aw';* a prim. root; to *despond:* caus., to *deject:*–broken, be grieved, make sad.
3513. כָּבַד *kaw-bad';* or כָּבֵד *kaw-bade';* a prim. root; to *be heavy,* i.e. in a bad sense (*burdensome, severe, dull*) or in a good sense (*numerous, rich, honorable*; caus., to *make weighty* (in the same two senses):–abounding with, more grievously afflict, boast, be chargeable, X be dim, glorify, be (make) glorious (things), glory, (very) great, be grievous, harden, be (make) heavy, be heavier, lay heavily, (bring to, come to, do, get, be had in) honour (self), (be) honourable (man), lade, X more be laid, make self many, nobles, prevail, promote (to honour), be rich, be (go) sore, stop.
3514. כֹּבֶד *ko'-bed;* from 3513; *weight, multitude, vehemence:*–grievousness, heavy, great number.
3515. כָּבֵד *kaw-bade';* from 3513; *heavy;* fig. in a good sense (*numerous*) or in a bad sense (*severe, difficult, stupid*):–(so) great, grievous, hard(-ened), (too) heavy(-ier), laden, much, slow, sore, thick.
3516. כָּבֵד *kaw-bade';* the same as 3515; the *liver* (as the *heaviest* of the viscera):–liver.
3517. כְּבֵדֻת *keb-ay-dooth';* fem. of 3515; *difficulty:*–X heavily.
3518. כָּבָה *kaw-baw;* a prim. root; to *expire* or (caus.) to *extinguish* (fire, light, anger):–go (put) out, quench.
3519. כָּבוֹד *kaw-bode';* כָּבֹד rarely *kaw-bode';* from 3513; prop. *weight,* but only fig. in a good sense, *splendor* or *copiousness:*–glorious(-ly), glory, honour(-able).
3520. כְּבוּדָּה *keb-ood-daw';* irreg. fem. pass. part. of 3513; *weightiness,* i.e. *magnificence, wealth:*–carriage, all glorious, stately.
3521. כָּבוּל *kaw-bool';* from the same as 3525 in the sense of *limitation; sterile; Cabul,* the name of two places in Pal.:–Cabul.
3522. כַּבּוֹן *kab-bone';* from an un. root mean. to *heap* up; *hilly; Cabon,* a place in Pal.:–Cabbon.
3523. כְּבִיר *keb-eer;* from 3527 in the or. sense of *plaiting;* a *matrass* (of intertwined materials):–pillow.
3524. כַּבִּיר *kab-beer';* from 3527; *vast,* whether in extent (fig., of power, *mighty;* of time, *aged*), or in number, *many:*–+ feeble, mighty, most, much, strong, valiant.
3525. כֶּבֶל *keh'-bel;* from an un. root mean. to *twine* or braid together; a *fetter:*–fetter.
3526. כָּבַס *kaw-bas';* a prim. root; to *trample;* hence, to *wash* (prop. by stamping with the feet), whether lit. (incl. the *fulling* process) or fig.:–fuller, wash(-ing).
3527. כָּבַר *kaw-bar';* prim. root; prop. to *plait* together, i.e. (fig.) to *augment* (esp. in number or quantity, to *accumulate*):–in abundance, multiply.
3528. כְּבָר *keb-awr';* from 3527; prop. *extent* of time, i.e. a *great while;* hence, *long ago, formerly, hitherto:*–already, (seeing that which), now.
3529. כְּבָר *keb-awr';* the same as 3528; *length; Kebar,* a river of Mesopotamia:–Chebar. Comp. 2249.
3530. כִּבְרָה *kib-raw';* fem. of 3528; prop. *length,* i.e. a *measure* (of unc. dimension):–X little.
3531. כְּבָרָה *keb-aw-raw';* from 3527 in its or. sense; a *sieve* (as netted):–sieve.
3532. כֶּבֶשׂ *keh-bes';* from an un. root mean. to *dominate;* a *ram* (just old enough to *butt*):–lamb, sheep.
3533. כָּבַשׁ *kaw-bash';* a prim. root; to *tread* down; hence, neg., to *disregard;* pos., to *conquer, subjugate, violate:*–bring into bondage, force, keep under, subdue, bring into subjection.
3534. כֶּבֶשׁ *keh'-besh;* from 3533; a *footstool* (as trodden upon):–footstool.
3535. כִּבְשָׂה *kib-saw';* or כַּבְשָׂה *kab-saw';* fem. of 3532; a *ewe:*–(ewe) lamb.
3536. כִּבְשָׁן *kib-shawn';* from 3533; a smelting *furnace* (as reducing metals):–furnace.
3537. כַּד *kad;* from an un. root mean. to *deepen;* prop. a *pail;* but gen. of earthenware; a *jar* for domestic purposes:–barrel, pitcher.
3538. כְּדַב *ked-ab'* (Chald.); from a root cor. to 3576; *false:*–lying.
3539. כַּדְכֹּד *kad-kobe';* from the same as 3537 in the sense of *striking fire* from a metal forged; a *sparkling* gem, prob. the ruby:–agate.
3540. כְּדָרְלָעֹמֶר *ked-or-law-o'-mer;* of for. or.; *Kedorlaomer,* an early Pers. king:–Chedorlaomer.
3541. כֹּה *ko;* from the pref. k and 1931; prop. *like this,* i.e. by impl., (of manner) *thus* (or *so*); also (of place) *here* (or *hither*); or (of time) *now:*–also, here, + hitherto, like, on the other side, so (and much), such, on that manner, (on) this (manner, side, way, way and that way), + mean while, yonder.
3542. כָּה *kaw* (Chald.); cor. to 3541:–hitherto.
3543. כָּהָה *kaw-haw';* a prim. root; to *be weak,* i.e. (fig.) to *despond* (caus., *rebuke*), or (of light, the eye) to *grow dull:*– darken, be dim, fail, faint, restrain, X utterly.
3544. כֵּהֶה *kay-heh';* from 3543; *feeble, obscure:*–somewhat dark, darkish, wax dim, heaviness, smoking.
3545. כֵּהָה *kay-haw';* fem. of 3544; prop. a *weakening;* fig., *alleviation,* i.e. cure:–healing.
3546. כְּהַל *keh-hal'* (Chald.); a root cor. to 3201 and 3557; to *be able:*–be able, could.
3547. כָּהַן *kaw-han';* a prim. root, app. mean. to *mediate* in relig. services; but used only as denom. from 3548; to *officiate* as a priest; fig., to *put on regalia:*–deck, be (do the office of a, execute the, minister in the) priest('s office).
3548. כֹּהֵן *ko-hane';* act.part. of 3547; lit., one *officiating,* a *priest;* also (by courtesy) an *acting priest* (although a layman):–chief ruler, X own, priest, prince, principal officer.
3549. כָּהֵן *kaw-hane'* (Chald.); cor. to 3548:–priest.
3550. כְּהֻנָּה *keh-hoon-naw';* from 3547; *priesthood:*–priesthood, priest's office.
3551. כַּו *kav* (Chald.); from a root cor. to 3854 in the sense of *piercing;* a *window* (as a perforation):–window.
3552. כּוּב *koob;* of for. der.; *Kub,* a country near Eg.:–Chub.
3553. כּוֹבַע *ko'-bah;* from an un. root mean. to be *high* or *rounded;* a *helmet* (as *arched*):–helmet. Comp. 6959.
3554. כָּוָה *kaw-vaw';* a prim. root; prop. to *prick* or *penetrate;* hence, to *blister* (as smarting or eating into):–burn.
3555. כְּוִיָּה *kev-ee-yaw';* from 3554; a *branding:*–burning.
3556. כּוֹכָב *ko-kawb';* prob. from the same as 3522 (in the sense of *rolling*) or 3554 (in the sense of *blazing*); a *star* (as *round* or as *shining*); fig., a *prince:*–star([-gazer]).
3557. כּוּל *kool;* a prim. root; prop. to *keep in;* hence, to *measure;* fig., to *maintain* (in various senses):–(be able to, can) abide, bear, comprehend, contain, feed, forbearing, guide, hold(-ing in), nourish (-er), be present, make provision, receive, sustain, provide sustenance (victuals).
3558. כּוּמָז *koo-mawz';* from an un. root mean. to *store* away; a *jewel* (prob. gold beads):–tablet.
3559. כּוּן *koon;* a prim. root; prop. to *be erect* (i.e. stand perpendicular); hence (caus.) to *set up,* in a great variety of appl., whether lit. (*establish, fix, prepare, apply*), or fig. (*appoint, render sure, proper* or *prosperous*):–certain(-ty), confirm, direct, faithfulness, fashion, fasten, firm, be fitted, be fixed, frame, be meet, ordain, order, perfect, (make) preparation, prepare (self), provide, make provision, (be, make) ready, right, set (aright, fast, forth), be stable, (e-)stablish, stand, tarry, X very deed.
3560. כּוּן *koon;* prob. from 3559; *established; Kun,* a place in Syria:–Chun.
3561. כַּוָּן *kav-vawn';* from 3559; something *prepared,* i.e. a sacrificial *wafer:*–cake.
3562. כּוֹנַנְיָהוּ *ko-nan-yaw'-hoo;* from 3559 and 3050; *Jah has sustained; Conanjah,* the name of two Isr.:–Conaniah, Cononiah. Comp. 3663.
3563. כּוֹס *koce;* from an un. root mean. to *hold* together; a *cup* (as a container), often fig., a *lot* (as if a potion); also some unclean bird, prob. an *owl* (perh. from the cup-like cavity of its eye):–cup, (small) owl. Comp. 3599.
3564. כּוּר *koor;* from an un. root mean. prop. to *dig* through; a *pot* or *furnace* (as if excavated):–furnace. Comp. 3600.
3565. כּוֹר עָשָׁן *kore aw-shawn';* from 3564 and 6227; *furnace of smoke; Cor-Ashan,* a place in Pal.:–Chor-ashan.
3566. כּוֹרֶשׁ *ko'-resh;* or (Ezra 1:1[last time],2) כֹּרֶשׁ *ko'-resh;* from the Pers.; Koresh (or Cyrus), the Pers. king:–Cyrus.
3567. כּוֹרֶשׁ *ko'-resh*(Chald.); cor. to 3566:–Cyrus.
3568. כּוּשׁ *koosh;* prob. of for. or.; *Cush* (or Ethiopia), the name of a son of Ham, and of his territory; also of an Isr.:–Chush, Cush, Ethiopia.
3569. כּוּשִׁי *koo-shee';* patron. from 3568; a *Cushite,* or desc. of Cush:–Cushi, Cushite, Ethiopian(-s).
3570. כּוּשִׁי *koo-shee';* the same as 3569; *Cushi,* the name of two Isr.:–Cushi.
3571. כּוּשִׁית *koo-sheeth';* fem. of 3569; a *Cushite* woman:–Ethiopian.
3572. כּוּשָׁן *koo-shawn';* perh. from 3568; *Cushan,* a region of Arabia:–Cushan.
3573. כּוּשַׁן רִשְׁעָתַיִם *koo-shan' rish-aw-thah'-yim;* app. from 3572 and the dual of 7564; *Cushan of double wickedness; Cushan-Rishathajim,* a Mesopotamian king:–Chushan-rishathayim.
3574. כּוֹשָׁרָה *ko-shaw-raw';* from 3787; *prosperity;* in pl. *freedom:*–X chain.
3575. כּוּת *kooth;* or (fem.) כּוּתָה *koo-thaw';* of for. or.; *Cuth* or *Cuthah,* a province of Assyria:–Cuth.
3576. כָּזַב *kaw-zab';* a prim. root; to *lie* (i.e. *deceive*), lit. or fig.:–fail, (be found a, make a) liar, lie, lying, be in vain.
3577. כָּזָב *kaw-zawb';* from 3576; *falsehood;* lit. (*untruth*) or fig. (*idol*):–deceitful, false, leasing, + liar, lie, lying.
3578. כֹּזְבָא *ko-zeb-aw';* from 3576; *falla-*

HEBREW

cious; Cozeba, a place in Pal.:–Choseba.

3579. כָּזְבִּי *koz-bee';* from 3576; *false; Cozbi,* a Midianitess:–Cozbi.

3580. כְּזִיב *kez-eeb';* from 3576; *falsified; Kezib,* a place in Pal.:–Chezib.

3581. כֹּחַ *ko'-akh;* or (Da. 11:6) כּוֹחַ *ko'-akh;* from an un. root mean. to *be firm; vigor,* lit. (*force,* in a good or a bad sense) or fig. (*capacity, means, produce*); also (from its hardiness) a large *lizard:*–ability, able, chameleon, force, fruits, might, power(-ful), strength, substance, wealth.

3582. כָּחַד *kaw-khad';* a prim. root; to *secrete,* by act or word; hence (intens.) to *destroy:*–conceal, cut down (off), desolate, hide.

3583. כָּחַל *kaw-khal';* a prim. root; to *paint* (with stibium):–paint.

3584. כָּחַשׁ *kaw-khash';* a prim. root; to *be untrue,* in word (to *lie, feign, disown*) or deed (to *disappoint, fail, cringe*):–deceive, deny, dissemble, fail, deal falsely, be found liars, (be-)lie, lying, submit selves.

3585. כַּחַשׁ *kakh'-ash;* from 3584; lit., a *failure* of flesh, i.e. *emaciation*; fig., *hypocrisy:*–leanness, lies, lying.

3586. כֶּחָשׁ *kekh-awsh';* from 3584; *faithless:*–lying.

3587. כִּי *kee;* from 3554; a *brand* or *scar:*–burning.

3588. כִּי *kee;* a prim. particle [the full form of the prep. pref.] indicating *causal* relations of all kinds, antecedent or consequent; (by impl.) very widely used as a rel. conj. or adv. [as below;] often largely modif. by other particles annexed:–and, + (forasmuch, inasmuch, where-)as, assured [-ly], + but, certainly, doubtless, + else, even, + except, for, how, (because, in, so, than) that, + nevertheless, now, rightly, seeing, since, surely, then, therefore, + (al-)though, + till, truly, + until, when, whether, while, whom, yea, yet.

3589. כִּיד *keed;* from a prim. root mean. to *strike:* a *crushing;* fig., *calamity:*–destruction.

3590. כִּידוֹד *kee-dode';* from the same as 3589 [comp. 3539]; prop. something *struck* off, i.e. a *spark* (as struck):–spark.

3591. כִּידוֹן *kee-dohn';* from the same as 3589; prop. something to *strike* with, i.e. a *dart* (perh. smaller that 2595):–lance, shield, spear, target.

3592. כִּידוֹן *kee-dohn';* the same as 3591; *Kidon,* a place in Pal.:–Chidon.

3593. כִּידוֹר *kee-dore';* of unc. der.; perh. *tumult:*–battle.

3594. כִּיּוּן *kee-yoon';* from 3559; prop. a *statue,* i.e. idol; but used (by euphem.) for some heathen deity (perh. cor. to Priapus or Baal-peor):–Chiun.

3595. כִּיּוֹר *kee-yore';* or כִּיֹּר *kee-yore';* from the same as 3564; prop. something *round* (as *excavated* or *bored*), i.e. a chafing-*dish* for coals or a *caldron* for cooking; hence (from similarity of form) a *washbowl;* also (for the same reason) a *pulpit* or platform:–hearth, laver, pan, scaffold.

3596. כִּילַי *kee-lah'-ee;* or כֵּלַי *kay-lah'-ee;* from 3557 in the sense of *withholding; niggardly:*–churl.

3597. כֵּילַף *kay-laf';* from an un. root mean. to *clap* or strike with noise; a *club* or sledge-hammer:–hammer.

3598. כִּימָה *kee-maw';* from the same as 3558; a *cluster* of stars, i.e. the *Pleiades:*–Pleiades, seven stars.

3599. כִּיס *keece;* a form for 3563; a *cup;* also a *bag* for money or weights:–bag, cup, purse.

3600. כִּיר *keer;* a form for 3564 (only in the dual); a cooking *range* (consisting of two parallel stones, across which the boiler is set):–ranges for pots.

3601. כִּישׁוֹר *kee-shore';* from 3787; lit., a *director,* i.e. the *spindle* or shank of a distaff (6418), by which it is twirled:–spindle.

3602. כָּכָה *kaw'-kaw;* from 3541; *just so,* referring to the previous or following context:–after that (this) manner, this matter, (even) so, in such a case, thus.

3603. כִּכָּר *kik-kawr';* from 3769; a *circle,* i.e. (by impl.) a circumjacent *tract* or region, esp. the *Ghôr* or valley of the Jordan; also a (round) *loaf;* also a *talent* (or large [round] coin):–loaf, morsel, piece, plain, talent.

3604. כִּכַּר *kik-kare'* (Chald.); cor. to 3603; a *talent:*–talent.

3605 כֹּל *kole;* or (Jer. 33:8) כּוֹל *kole;* from 3634; prop. the *whole;* hence, *all, any* or *every* (in the sing. only, but often in a pl. sense):–(in) all (manner, [ye]), altogether, any (manner), enough, every (one, place, thing), howsoever, as many as, [no-]thing, ought, whatsoever, (the) whole, whoso(-ever).

3606. כֹּל *kole* (Chald.); cor. to 3605:–all, any, + (forasmuch) as, + be-(for this) cause, every, + no (manner, -ne), + there (where)-fore, + though, what (where, who)-soever, (the) whole.

3607. כָּלָא *kaw-law';* a prim. root; to *restrict,* by act (*hold* back or in) or word (*prohibit*):–finish, forbid, keep (back), refrain, restrain, retain, shut up, be stayed, withhold.

3608. כֶּלֶא *keh'-leh;* from 3607; a *prison:*–prison. Comp. 3610, 3628.

3609. כִּלְאָב *kil-awb';* app. from 3607 and 1; *restraint of* (his) *father; Kilab,* an Isr.:–Chileab.

3610. כִּלְאַיִם *kil-ah'-yim;* dual of 3608 in the or. sense of *separation; two heterogeneities:*–divers seeds (-e kinds), mingled (seed).

3611. כֶּלֶב *keh'-leb;* from an un. root means. to *yelp,* or else to *attack;* a *dog;* hence (by euphem.) a male *prostitute:*–dog.

3612. כָּלֵב *kaw-labe';* perh. a form of 3611, or else from the same root in the sense of *forcible; Caleb,* the name of three Isr.:–Caleb.

3613. כָּלֵב אֶפְרָתָה *kaw-labe' ef-raw'-thaw;* from 3612 and 672; *Caleb- Ephrathah,* a place in Eg. (if the text is correct):–Caleb-ephrathah.

3614. כָּלִבּוֹ *kaw-lib-bo';* prob. by err. transc. for כָּלֵבִּי *kaw-lay-bee';* patron. from 3612; a *Calebite* or desc. of Caleb:–of the house of Caleb.

3615. כָּלָה *kaw-law';* a prim. root; to *end,* whether intr. (to *cease, be finished, perish*) or trans. (to *complete, prepare, consume*):–accomplish, cease, consume (away), determine, destroy (utterly), be (when ... were) done, (be an) end (of), expire, (cause to) fail, faint, finish, fulfil, X fully, X have, leave (off), long, bring to pass, wholly reap, make clean riddance, spend, quite take away, waste.

3616. כָּלֶה kaw-leh'; from 3615; *pining:*–fail.

3617. כָּלָה *kaw-law';* from 3615; a *completion;* adv., *completely;* also *destruction:*–altogether, (be, utterly) consume(-d), consummation(-ption), was determined, (full, utter) end, riddance.

3618. כַּלָּה *kal-law';* from 3634; a *bride* (as if *perfect*); hence, a *son's wife:*–bride, daughter-in-law, spouse.

3619. כְּלוּב *kel-oob';* from the same as 3611; a bird-*trap* (as furnished with a *clap*-stick or treadle to spring it); hence, a *basket* (as resembling a wicker cage):–basket, cage.

3620. כְּלוּב *kel-oob';* the same as 3619; *Kelub,* the name of two Isr.:–Chelub.

3621. כְּלוּבַי *kel-oo-bay'-ee;* a form of 3612; *Kelubai,* an Isr.:–Chelubai.

3622. כְּלוּהַי *kel-oo-hah'-ee;* from 3615; *completed; Keluhai,* an Isr.:–Chelluh.

3623. כְּלוּלָה *kel-oo-law';* denom. pass.part. from 3618; *bridehood* (only in the pl.):–espousal.

3624. כֶּלַח *keh'-lakh;* from an un. root mean. to *be complete; maturity:*–full (old) age.

3625. כֶּלַח *keh'-lakh;* the same as 3624; *Kelach,* a place in Assyria:–Calah.

3626. כָּל־חֹזֶה *kol-kho-zeh';* from 3605 and 2374; *every seer; Col- Chozeh,* an Isr.:–Col-hozeh.

3627. כְּלִי *kel-ee';* from 3615; something *prepared,* i.e. any *apparatus* (as an implement, utensil, dress, vessel or weapon):–armour ([-bearer]), artillery, bag, carriage, + furnish, furniture, instrument, jewel, that is made of, X one from another, that which pertaineth, pot, + psaltery, sack, stuff, thing, tool, vessel, ware, weapon, + whatsoever.

3628. כְּלִיא *kel-ee';* or כְּלוּא *kel-oo';* from 3607 [comp. 3608]; a *prison:*–prison.

3629. כִּלְיָה *kil-yaw';* fem. of 3627 (only in the pl.); a *kidney* (as an essential *organ*); fig., the *mind* (as the interior self):–kidneys, reins.

3630. כִּלְיוֹן *kil-yone';* a form of 3631; *Kiljon,* an Isr.:–Chilion.

3631. כִּלָּיוֹן *kil-law-yone';* from 3615; *pining, destruction:*–consumption, failing.

3632. כָּלִיל *kaw-leel';* from 3634; complete; as noun, the *whole* (spec., a sacrifice *entirely consumed*); as adv., *fully:*–all, every whit, flame, perfect(-ion), utterly, whole burnt offering (sacrifice), wholly.

3633. כַּלְכֹּל *kal-kole';* from 3557; *sustenance; Calcol,* an Isr.:–Calcol, Chalcol.

3634. כָּלַל *kaw-lal';* a prim. root; to *complete:*–(make) perfect.

3635. כְּלַל *kel-al';* (Chald.) cor. to 3634; to *complete:*–finish, make (set) up

3636. כְּלָל *kel-awl';* from 3634; *complete; Kelal,* an Isr.:–Chelal.

3637. כָּלַם *kaw-lawm';* a prim. root; prop. to *wound;* but only fig., to *taunt* or *insult:*–be (make) ashamed, blush, be confounded, be put to confusion, hurt, reproach, (do, put to) shame.

3638. כִּלְמַד *kil-mawd';* of for. der.; *Kilmad,* a place app. in the Assyrian empire:–Chilmad.

3639. כְּלִמָּה *kel-im-maw';* from 3637; *disgrace:*–confusion, dishonour, reproach, shame.

3640. כְּלִמּוּת *kel-im-mooth';* from 3639; *disgrace:*–shame.

3641. כַּלְנֶה *kal-neh';* or כַּלְנֵה *kal-nay';* also כַּלְנוֹ *kal-no';* of for. der.; *Calneh* or *Calno,* a place in the Assyrian empire:–Calneh, Calno. Comp. 3656.

3642. כָּמַהּ *kaw-mah;* a prim. root; to *pine* after:–long.

3643. כִּמְהָם *kim-hawm';* from 3642; *pining; Kimham,* an Isr.:–Chimham.

3644. כְּמוֹ *kem-o';* or כָּמוֹ *kaw-mo';* a form of the pref. "*k*-", but used separately [comp. 3651]; *as, thus, so:*–according to, (such) as (it were, well as), in comp. of, like (as, to, unto), thus, when, worth.

3645. כְּמוֹשׁ *kem-oshe';* or (Jer. 48:7) כְּמִישׁ *kem-eesh';* from an un. root mean. to

subdue; the *powerful; Kemosh,* the god of the Moabites:–Chemosh.
3646. כַּמֹּן *kam-mone';* from an un. root mean. to *store* up or *preserve;* "*cummin*" (from its use as a *condiment*):–cummin.
3647. כָּמַס *kaw-mas';* a prim. root; to *store* away, i.e. (fig.) in the memory:–lay up in store.
3648 כָּמַר *kaw-mar';* a prim. root; prop. to *intertwine* or *contract,* i.e. (by impl.) to *shrivel* (as with heat); fig., to *be* deeply *affected* with passion (love or pity):–be black, be kindled, yearn.
3649. כָּמָר *kaw-mawr';* from 3648; prop., an *ascetic* (as if *shrunk* with self-maceration), i.e. an idolatrous *priest* (only in pl.):–Chemarims (idolatrous) priests.
3650. כִּמְרִיר *kim-reer';* redupl. from 3648; *obscuration* (as if from *shrinkage* of light, i.e. an *eclipse* (only in pl.):–blackness.
3651. כֵּן *kane;* from 3559; prop. *set* upright; hence (fig. as adj.) *just;* but usually (as adv. or conj.) *rightly* or *so* (in various appl. to manner, time and relation; often with other particles):–+ after that (this, -ward, -wards), as ... as, + [for-] asmuch as yet, + be (for which) cause, + following, howbeit, in (the) like (manner, -wise), X the more, right, (even) so, state, straightway, such (thing), surely, + there (where)-fore, this, thus, true, well, X you.
3652. כֵּן *kane* (Chald.); cor. to 3651; *so:*–thus.
3653. כֵּן *kane;* the same as 3651, used as a noun; a *stand,* i.e. pedestal or station:–base, estate, foot, office, place, well.
3654. כֵּן *kane;* from 3661 in the sense of *fastening;* a *gnat* (from infixing its sting; used only in pl. [and irreg. in Ex. 8:17,18; Heb. 13:14]):–lice, X manner.
3655. כָּנָה *kaw-naw';* a prim. root; to *address* by an additional name; hence, to *eulogize:*–give flattering titles, surname (himself).
3656. כַּנֵּה *kan-neh';* for 3641; *Canneh,* a place in Assyria:–Canneh.
3657. כַּנָּה *kaw-naw';* from 3661; a *plant* (as *set*):–X vineyard.
3658. כִּנּוֹר *kin-nore';* from a un. root mean. to *twang;* a *harp:*–harp.
3659. כָּנְיָהוּ *kon-yaw'-hoo;* for 3204; *Conjah,* an Isr. king:–Coniah.
3660. כְּנֵמָא *ken-ay-maw'* (Chald.); cor. to 3644; *so* or *thus:*–so, (in) this manner (sort), thus.
3661. כָּנַן *kaw-nan';* a prim. root; to *set* out, i.e. *plant:*–X vineyard.
3662. כְּנָנִי *ken-aw-nee';* from 3661; *planted; Kenani,* an Isr.:–Chenani.
3663. כְּנַנְיָה *ken-an-yaw';* or כְּנַנְיָהוּ *ken-an-yaw'-hoo};* from 3661 and 3050; *Jah has planted; Kenanjah,* an Isr.:–Chenaniah.
3664. כָּנַס *kaw-nas';* a prim. root; to *collect;* hence, to *enfold:*–gather (together), heap up, wrap self.
3665. כָּנַע *kaw-nah';* a prim. root; prop. to *bend* the knee; hence, to *humiliate, vanquish:*–bring down (low), into subjection, under, humble (self), subdue.
3666. כִּנְעָה *kin-aw';* from 3665 in the sense of *folding* [comp. 3664]; a *package:*–wares.
3667. כְּנַעַן *ken-ah'-an;* from 3665; *humiliated; Kenaan,* a son a Ham; also the country inhabited by him:–Canaan, merchant, traffick.
3668. כְּנַעֲנָה *ken-ah-an-aw';* fem. of 3667; *Kenaanah,* the name of two Isr.:–Chenaanah.
3669. כְּנַעֲנִי *ken-ah-an-ee';* patrial from 3667; a *Kenaanite* or inh. of Kenaan; by impl., a *pedlar* (the Canaanites standing for their neighbors the Ishmaelites, who conducted mercantile caravans):–Canaanite, merchant, trafficker.
3670. כָּנַף *kaw-naf';* a prim. root; prop. to *project* laterally, i.e. prob. (refl.) to *withdraw:*–be removed.
3671. כָּנָף *kaw-nawf';* from 3670; an *edge* or *extremity;* spec. (of a bird or army) a *wing,* (of a garment or bed-clothing) a *flap,* (of the earth) a *quarter,* (of a building) a *pinnacle:*–+ bird, border, corner, end, feather[-ed], X flying, + (one an-)other, overspreading, X quarters, skirt, X sort, uttermost part, wing([-ed]).
3672. כִּנְּרוֹת *kin-ner-oth';* or כִּנֶּרֶת *kin-neh'-reth;* respectively pl. and sing. fem. from the same as 3658; perh. *harp*-shaped; *Kinneroth* or *Kinnereth,* a place in Pal.:–Chinnereth, Chinneroth, Cinneroth.
3673. כָּנַשׁ *kaw-nash'* (Chald.); cor. to 3664; to *assemble:*–gather together.
3674. כְּנָת *ken-awth';* from 3655; a *colleague* (as having the same title):–companion.
3675. כְּנָת *ken-awth'* (Chald.); cor. to 3674:–companion.
3676. כֵּס *kace;* app. a contr. for 3678, for 5251:–sworn.
3677. כֶּסֶא *keh'-seh;* or כֶּסֶה *keh'-seh;* app. from 3680; prop. *fulness* or the *full moon,* i.e. its festival:–(time) appointed.
3678. כִּסֵּא *kis-say';* or כִּסֵּה *kis-say';* from 3680; prop. *covered,* i.e. a *throne* (as *canopied*):–seat, stool, throne.
3679. כַּסְדַּי *kas-dah'-ee;* for 3778:–Chaldean.
3680. כָּסָה *kaw-saw';* a prim. root; prop. to *plump,* i.e. *fill up* hollows; by impl., to *cover* (for clothing or secrecy):–clad self, close, clothe, conceal, cover (self), (flee to) hide, overwhelm. Comp. 3780.
3681. כָּסוּי *kaw-soo'-ee;* pass.part. of 3680; prop. *covered,* i.e. (as noun) a *covering:*–covering.
3682. כְּסוּת *kes-ooth';* from 3680; a *cover* (garment); fig., a *veiling:*–covering, raiment, vesture.
3683. כָּסַח *kaw-sakh';* a prim. root; to *cut off:*–cut down (up).
3684. כְּסִיל *kes-eel';* from 3688; prop. *fat,* i.e. (fig.) stupid or *silly:*–fool(-ish).
3685. כְּסִיל *kes-eel';* the same as 3684; any notable *constellation;* spec. *Orion* (as if a *burly* one):–constellation, Orion.
3686. כְּסִיל *kes-eel';* the same as 3684; *Kesil,* a place in Pal.:–Chesil.
3687. כְּסִילוּת *kes-eel-ooth';* from 3684; *silliness* –foolish.
3688. כָּסַל *kaw-sal';* a prim. root; prop. to *be fat,* i.e. (fig.) *silly:*–be foolish.
3689. כֶּסֶל *keh'-sel;* from 3688; prop. *fatness,* i.e. by impl. (lit.) the *loin* (as the seat of the leaf *fat*) or (gen.) the *viscera;* also (fig.) *silliness* or (in a good sense) *trust:*–confidence, flank, folly, hope, loin.
3690. כִּסְלָה *kis-law';* fem. of 3689; in a good sense, *trust;* in a bad one, *silliness:*–confidence, folly.
3691. כִּסְלֵו *kis-lave';* prob. of for. or.; *Kisleu,* the 9th Heb. Month:–Chisleu.
3692. כִּסְלוֹן *kis-lone';* from 3688; *hopeful; Kislon,* an Isr.:–Chislon.
3693. כְּסָלוֹן *kes-aw-lone';* from 3688; *fertile; Kesalon,* a place in Pal.:–Chesalon.
3694. כְּסֻלּוֹת *kes-ool-loth';* fem. pl. of pass. part. of 3688; *fattened; Kesulloth,* a place in Pal.:–Chesulloth.
3695. כַּסְלֻחִים *kas-loo'-kheem;* a pl. prob. of for. der.; *Casluchim,* a people cognate to the Eg.:–Casluhim.
3696. כִּסְלֹת תָּבֹר *kis-loth' taw-bore';* from the fem. pl. of 3689 and 8396; *flanks of Tabor; Kisloth-Tabor,* a place in Pal.:–Chisloth- tabor.
3697. כָּסַם *kaw-sam';* a prim. root; to *shear:*–X only, poll. Comp. 3765.
3698. כֻּסֶּמֶת *koos-seh'-meth;* from 3697; *spelt* (from its bristliness as if just *shorn*):–fitches, rie.
3699. כָּסַס *kaw-sas';* a prim. root; to *estimate:*–make count.
3700. כָּסַף *kaw-saf';* a prim. root; prop. to become *pale,* i.e. (by impl.) to *pine* after; also to *fear:*–[have] desire, be greedy, long, sore.
3701. כֶּסֶף *keh'-sef;* from 3700; *silver* (from its *pale* color); by impl., *money:*–money, price, silver(-ling).
3702. כְּסַף *kes-af'* (Chald.); cor. to 3701:–money, silver.
3703. כָּסִפְיָא *kaw-sif-yaw';* perh. from 3701; *silvery; Casiphja,* a place in Bab.:–Casiphia.
3704. כֶּסֶת *keh'-seth;* from 3680; a *cushion* or pillow (as *covering* a seat or bed):–pillow.
3705. כְּעַן *keh-an'* (Chald.); prob. from 3652; *now:*–now.
3706. כְּעֶנֶת *keh-eh'-neth* (Chald.); or כְּעֶת *keh-eth';* fem. of 3705; *thus* (only in the formula "and *so forth*"):–at such a time.
3707. כָּעַס *kaw-as';* a prim. root; to *trouble;* by impl., to *grieve, rage, be indignant:*–be angry, be grieved, take indignation, provoke (to anger, unto wrath), have sorrow, vex, be wroth.
3708 כַּעַס *kah'-as;* or (in Job). כַּעַשׂ *kah'-as;* from 3707; *vexation:*–anger, angry, grief, indignation, provocation, provoking, X sore, sorrow, spite, wrath.
3709. כַּף *kaf;* from 3721; the hollow *hand* or palm (so of the *paw* of an animal, of the *sole,* and even of the *bowl* of a dish or sling, the *handle* of a bolt, the *leaves* of a palm-tree); fig., *power:*–branch, + foot, hand ([-ful], -dle, [-led]), hollow, middle, palm, paw, power, sole, spoon.
3710. כֵּף *kafe;* from 3721; a hollow *rock:*–rock.
3711. כָּפָה *kaw-faw';* a prim. root; prop. to *bend,* i.e. (fig.) to *tame* or subdue:–pacify.
3712. כִּפָּה *kip-paw';* fem. of 3709; a *leaf* of a palm-tree:–branch.
3713. כְּפוֹר *kef-ore';* from 3722; prop. a *cover,* i.e. (by impl.) a *tankard* (or *covered* goblet); also white *frost* (as *covering* the ground):–bason, hoar(-y) frost.
3714. כָּפִיס *kaw-fece';* from an un. root mean. to *connect;* a *girder:*–beam.
3715. כְּפִיר *kef-eer';* from 3722; *a village* (as *covered* in by walls); also a young *lion* (perh. as *covered* with a mane):–(young) lion, village. Comp. 3723.
3716. כְּפִירָה *kef-ee-raw';* fem. of 3715; the *village* (always with the art.); *Kephirah,* a place in Pal.:–Chephirah.
3717. כָּפַל *kaw-fal';* a prim. root; to *fold* together; fig., to *repeat:*–double.
3718. כֶּפֶל *keh'-fel;* from 3717; a *duplicate:*–double.
3719. כָּפַן *kaw-fan';* a prim. root; to *bend:*–bend.
3720. כָּפָן *kaw-fawn';* from 3719; *hunger* (as

making to *stoop* with emptiness and pain):–famine.

3721. כָּפַף *kaw-faf'*; a prim. root; to *curve:* –bow down (self).

3722. כָּפַר *kaw-far'*; a prim. root; to *cover* (spec. with bitumen); fig., to *expiate* or *condone,* to *placate* or *cancel:*–appease, make (an atonement, cleanse, disannul, forgive, be merciful, pacify, pardon, purge (away), put off, (make) reconcile(-liation).

3723. כָּפָר *kaw-fawr'*; from 3722; a *village* (as *protected* by walls):–village. Comp. 3715.

3724. כֹּפֶר *ko'-fer;* from 3722; prop. a *cover,* i.e. (lit.) a *village* (as *covered* in); (spec.) *bitumen* (as used for *coating*), and the *henna* plant (as used for *dyeing*); fig., a *redemption-price:*–bribe, camphire, pitch, ransom, satisfaction, sum of money, village.

3725. כִּפֻּר *kip-poor';* from 3722; *expiation* (only in pl.):–atonement.

3726. כְּפַר הָעַמּוֹנִי *kef-ar'; haw-am-mo-nee';* from 3723 and 5984, with the art. interp.; *village of the Ammonite; Kefar-ha-Ammoni,* a place in Pal.:–Chefar-haamonai.

3727. כַּפֹּרֶת *kap-po'-reth;* from 3722; a *lid* (used only of the *cover* of the sacred Ark):–mercy seat.

3728. כָּפַשׁ *kaw-fash';* a prim. root; to *tread* down; fig., to *humiliate:*–cover.

3729. כְּפַת *kef-ath'* (Chald.); a root of unc. correspondence; to *fetter:*–bind.

3730. כַּפְתֹּר *kaf-tore';* or (Am. 9:1) כַּפְתּוֹר *kaf-tore';* prob. from an un. root mean. to *encircle;* a *chaplet;* but used only in an architectonic sense, i.e. the *capital* of a column, or a wreath-like *button* or *disk* on the candelabrum:–knop, (upper) lintel.

3731. כַּפְתֹּר *kaf-tore';* or (Am. 9:7) כַּפְתּוֹר *kaf-tore';* app. the same as 3730; *Caphtor* (i.e. a *wreath*-shaped island), the or. seat of the Philistines:–Caphtor.

3732. כַּפְתֹּרִי *kaf-to-ree';* patrial from 3731; a *Caphtorite* (coll.) or nat. of Caphtor:–Caphthorim, Caphtorim(-s).

3733. כַּר *kar;* from 3769 in the sense of *plumpness;* a *ram* (as *full-grown* and *fat*), incl. a *battering-ram* (as *butting*); hence, a *meadow* (as *for sheep*); also a *pad* or camel's saddle (as *puffed out*):–captain, furniture, lamb, (large) pasture, ram. See also 1033, 3746.

3734. כֹּר *kore;* from the same as 3564; prop. a deep round *vessel,* i.e. (spec.) a *cor* or measure for things dry:–cor, measure. Chald. the same.

3735. כָּרָא *kaw-raw'* (Chald.); prob. cor. to 3738 in the sense of *piercing* (fig.); to *grieve:*–be grieved.

3736. כַּרְבֵּל *kar-bale';* from the same as 3525; to *gird* or *clothe:*–clothed.

3737. כַּרְבְּלָא *kar-bel-aw'* (Chald.); from a verb cor. to that of 3736; a *mantle:*–hat.

3738. כָּרָה *kaw-raw';* a prim. root; prop. to *dig;* fig., to *plot;* gen., to *bore* or open:–dig, X make (a banquet), open.

3739. כָּרָה *kaw-raw';* usually assigned as a prim. root, but prob. only a special appl. of 3738 (through the common idea of *planning* implied in a bargain); to *purchase:*–buy, prepare.

3740. כֵּרָה *kay-raw';* from 3739; a *purchase:*–provision.

3741. כָּרָה *kaw-raw';* fem. of 3733; a *meadow:*–cottage.

3742. כְּרוּב *ker-oob';* of unc. der.; a *cherub* or imaginary figure:–cherub, [*pl.*] cherubims.

3743. כְּרוּב *ker-oob';* the same as 3742; *Kerub,* a place in Bab.:–Cherub.

3744. כָּרוֹז *kaw-roze'* (Chald.); from 3745; a *herald:*–herald.

3745. כְּרַז *ker-az'* (Chald.); prob. of Gr. or. (κηρύσσω) to *proclaim:*–make a proclamation.

3746. כָּרִי *kaw-ree';* perh. an abridged pl. of 3733 in the sense of *leader* (of the flock); a *life-guardsman:*–captains, Cherethites.

3747. כְּרִית *ker-eeth';* from 3772; a *cut; Kerith,* a brook of Pal.:–Cherith.

3748. כְּרִיתוּת *ker-ee-thooth';* from 3772; a *cutting* (of the matrimonial bond), i.e. *divorce:*–divorce(-ment).

3749. כַּרְכֹּב *kar-kobe';* expanded from the same as 3522; a *rim* or top :–compass.

3750. כַּרְכֹּם *kar-kome';* prob. of for. or.; the *crocus:*–saffron.

3751. כַּרְכְּמִישׁ *kar-kem-eesh';* of for. der.; *Karkemish,* a place in Syria:–Carchemish.

3752. כַּרְכַּס *kar-kas';* of Pers. or.; *Karkas,* a eunuch of Xerxes:–Carcas.

3753. כַּרְכָּרָה *kar-kaw-raw';* from 3769; a *dromedary* (from its *rapid* motion as if dancing):–swift beast.

3754. כֶּרֶם *keh'-rem;* from an un. root of unc. mean.; a *garden* or *vineyard:*–vines, (increase of the) vineyard(-s), vintage. See also 1021.

3755. כֹּרֵם *ko-rame';* act.part. of an imaginary denom. from 3754; a *vinedresser:*–vine dresser [*as one or two words*].

3756. כַּרְמִי *kar-mee';* from 3754; *gardener; Karmi,* the name of three Isr.:–Carmi.

3757. כַּרְמִי *kar-mee';* patron. from 3756; a *Karmite* or desc. of *Karmi:*–Carmites.

3758. כַּרְמִיל *kar-meele';* prob. of for. or.; *carmine,* a deep red:–crimson.

3759. כַּרְמֶל *kar-mel';* from 3754; a planted *field* (garden, orchard, vineyard or park); by impl., garden *produce:*–full (green) ears (of corn), fruitful field (place), plentiful (field).

3760. כַּרְמֶל *kar-mel';* the same as 3759; *Karmel,* the name of a hill and of a town in Pal.:–Carmel, fruitful (plentiful) field, (place).

3761. כַּרְמְלִי *kar-mel-ee';* patron from 3760; a *Karmelite* or inh. of Karmel (the town):–Carmelite.

3762. כַּרְמְלִית *kar-mel-eeth';* fem. of 3761; a *Karmelitess* or female inh. of Karmel:–Carmelitess.

3763. כְּרָן *ker-awn';* of unc. der.; *Keran,* an aboriginal Idumaean:–Cheran.

3764. כָּרְסֵא *kor-say'* (Chald.); cor. to 3678; a *throne:*–throne.

3765. כִּרְסֵם *kir-same';* from 3697; to *lay waste:*–waste.

3766. כָּרַע *kaw-rah';* a prim. root; to *bend* the knee; by impl., to *sink,* to *prostrate:*–bow (down, self), bring down (low), cast down, couch, fall, feeble, kneeling, sink, smite (stoop) down, subdue, X very.

3767 כָּרָע *kaw-raw';* from 3766; the *leg* (from the knee to the ankle) of men or locusts (only in the dual):–leg.

3768. כַּרְפַּס *kar-pas';* of for. or.; *byssus* or fine vegetable wool:–green.

3769. כָּרַר *kaw-rar';* a prim. root; to *dance* (i.e. *whirl*):–dance(-ing).

3770. כְּרֵשׂ *ker-ace';* by var. from 7164; the *paunch* or belly (as *swelling* out):–belly.

3771. כַּרְשְׁנָא *kar-shen-aw';* of for. or.; *Karshena,* a courtier of Xerxes:–Carshena.

3772. כָּרַת *kaw-rath';* a prim. root; to *cut* (off, down or asunder); by impl., to *destroy* or *consume;* spec., to *covenant* (i.e. make an alliance or bargain, or. by *cutting* flesh and passing between the pieces):–be chewed, be con-[feder]-ate, covenant, cut (down, off), destroy, fail, feller, be freed, hew (down), make a league ([covenant]), X lose, perish, X utterly, X want.

3773. כָּרֻתָה *kaw-rooth-aw';* pass.part. fem. of 3772; something *cut,* i.e. a hewn *timber:*–beam.

3774. כְּרֵתִי *ker-ay-thee';* prob. from 3772 in the sense of *executioner;* a *Kerethite* or *life-guardsman* [comp. 2876] (only coll. in the sing. as pl.):–Cherethims, Cherethites.

3775. כֶּשֶׂב *keh'-seb;* app. by transp. for 3532; a young *sheep:*–lamb.

3776. כִּשְׂבָּה *kis-baw';* fem. of 3775; a young *ewe:*–lamb.

3777. כֶּשֶׂד *keh'-sed;* from an un. root of unc. mean.; *Kesed,* a relative of Abraham:–Chesed.

3778. כַּשְׂדִּי *kas-dee';* (occasionally with enclitic) כַּשְׂדִּימָה *kas-dee'-maw;* towards the *Kasdites:*–into Chaldea), patron. from 3777 (only in the pl.); a *Kasdite,* or desc. of Kesed; by impl., a *Chaldæan* (as if so descended); also an *astrologer* (as if proverbial of that people:–Chaldeans, Chaldees, inh. of Chaldea.

3779. כַּשְׂדַּי *kas-dah'-ee* (Chald.); cor. to 3778; a *Chaldaean* or inh. of Chaldaea; by impl., a *Magian* or professional astrologer:–Chaldean.

3780. כָּשָׂה *kaw-saw';* a prim. root; to *grow fat* (i.e. be *covered* with flesh):–be covered. Comp. 3680.

3781. כַּשִּׁיל *kash-sheel';* from 3782; prop. a *feller,* i.e. an *axe:*–ax.

3782. כָּשַׁל *kaw-shal';* a prim. root; to *totter* or *waver* (through weakness of the legs, esp. the ankle); by impl., to *falter, stumble,* faint or fall:–bereave, cast down, be decayed, (cause to) fail, (cause, make to) fall (down, -ing), feeble, be (the) ruin(-ed, of), (be) overthrown, (cause to) stumble, X utterly, be weak.

3783. כִּשָּׁלוֹן *kish-shaw-lone';* from 3782; prop. a *tottering,* i.e. *ruin:*–fall.

3784. כָּשַׁף *kaw-shaf';* a prim. root; prop. to *whisper* a spell, i.e. to *inchant* or practise magic:–sorcerer, (use) witch(-craft).

3785. כֶּשֶׁף *keh'-shef;* from 3784; *magic:*–sorcery, witchcraft.

3786. כַּשָּׁף *kash-shawf';* from 3784; a *magician:*–sorcerer.

3787. כָּשֵׁר *kaw-share';* a prim. root prop. to be *straight* or *right;* by impl., to *be acceptable;* also to *succeed* or prosper:–direct, be right, prosper.

3788. כִּשְׁרוֹן *kish-rone';* from 3787; *success, advantage:*–equity, good, right.

3789. כָּתַב *kaw-thab';* a prim. root; to *grave,* by impl., to *write* (describe, inscribe, prescribe, subscribe):–describe, record, prescribe, subscribe, write(-ing, -ten).

3790. כְּתַב *keth-ab'* (Chald.); cor. to 3789:–write(-ten).

3791. כָּתָב *kaw-thawb';* from 3789; something *written,* i.e. a *writing, record* or *book:*–register, scripture, writing.

3792. כְּתָב *keth-awb'* (Chald.); cor. to 3791:–prescribing, writing(-ten).

3793. כְּתֹבֶת *keth-o'-beth;* from 3789; a *letter* or other *mark* branded on the skin:–X any [mark].

3794. כִּתִּי *kit-tee';* or כִּתִּיִּי *kit-tee-ee';* patrial from an un. name denoting Cyprus (only in the pl.); a *Kittite* or Cypriote; hence, an *islander* in gen., i.e. the Gr. or Romans on the shores opposite Pal.:–Chittim, Kittim.

3795. כָּתִית *kaw-theeth';* from 3807; *beaten,* i.e. pure (oil):–beaten.

3796. כֹּתֶל *ko'-thel;* from an un. root mean. to *compact;* a wall (as *gathering* inmates):–wall.

3797. כְּתַל *keth-al'* (Chald.); cor. to 3796:–wall.

3798. כִּתְלִישׁ *kith-leesh';* from 3796 and 376; *wall of a man; Kithlish,* a place in Pal.:–Kithlish.

3799. כָּתַם *kaw-tham';* a prim. root; prop. to *carve* or *engrave,* i.e. (by impl.) to *inscribe* indclibly:–mark.

3800. כֶּתֶם *keh'-them;* from 3799; prop. something *carved* out, i.e. *ore;* hence, *gold* (pure as or. mined):–([most] fine, pure) gold(-en wedge).

3801. כְּתֹנֶת *keth-o'-neth;* or כֻּתֹּנֶת *koot-to'-neth;* from an un. root mean. to *cover* [comp. 3802]; a *shirt:*–coat, garment, robe.

3802. כָּתֵף *kaw-thafe';* from an un. root mean. to *clothe;* the *shoulder* (proper, i.e. upper end of the arm; as being the spot where the garments hang); fig., *side-piece* or lateral projection of anything:–arm, corner, shoulder(-piece), side, undersetter.

3803. כָּתַר *kaw-thar';* a prim. root; to *enclose;* hence (in a friendly sense) to *crown,* (in a hostile one) to *besiege;* also to *wait* (as restraining oneself):–beset round, compass about, be crowned inclose round, suffer.

3804. כֶּתֶר *keh'-ther;* from 3803; prop. a *circlet,* i.e. a *diadem:*–crown.

3805. כֹּתֶרֶת *ko-theh'-reth;* fem. act.part. of 3803; the *capital* of a column:–chapiter.

3806. כָּתַשׁ *kaw-thash';* a prim. root; to *butt* or *pound:*–bray.

3807. כָּתַת *kaw-thath';* a prim. root; to *bruise* or violently *strike:*–beat (down, to pieces), break in pieces, crushed, destroy, discomfit, smite, stamp.

ל

3808. לֹא *lo;* or לוֹא *lo;* or לֹה (De. 3:11) *lo;* a prim. particle; *not* (the simple or abs. negation); by impl., *no;* often used with other particles (as follows):–X before, + or else, ere, + except, ig-[norant], much, less, nay, neither, never, no([-ne], -r, [-thing]), (X as though...,[can-], for) not (out of), of nought, otherwise, out of, + surely, + as truly as, + of a truth, + verily, for want, + whether, without.

3809. לָא *law* (Chald.); or לָה (Chald.) (Da. 4:32), *law;* cor. to 3808:–or even, neither, no (-ne, -r), ([can-])not, as nothing, without.

3810. לֹא דְבַר *lo deb-ar';* or לוֹ דְבַר (2 Sa. 9:4,5), *lo deb-ar';* or (Jos. 13:26), לִדְבִר *lid-beer';* [prob. rather לֹדְבַר *lo-deb-ar'*]; from 3808 and 1699; *pastureless; Lo-Debar,* a place in Pal.:–Debir, Lo-debar.

3811. לָאָה *law-aw';* a prim. root; to *tire;* (fig.) to *be* (or *make*) *disgusted:*–faint, grieve, lothe, (be, make) weary (selves).

3812. לֵאָה *lay-aw';* from 3811; *weary; Leah,* a wife of Jacob:–Leah.

3813. לָאַט *law-at';* a prim. root; to *muffle:*–cover.

3814. לָאט *lawt;* from 3813 (or perh. for act.part. of 3874); prop. *muffled,* i.e. *silently:*–softly.

3815. לָאֵל *law-ale';* from the prep. pref. and 410; (belonging*) to God; Laël* an Isr.:–Lael.

3816. לְאֹם *leh-ome';* or לְאוֹם *leh-ome';* from an un. root mean. to *gather;* a *community:*–nation, people.

3817. לְאֻמִּים *leh-oom-meem';* pl. of 3816; *communities; Leüm mim,* an Arabian:–Leummim.

3818. לֹא עַמִּי *lo am-mee';* from 3808 and 5971 with pron. suffix; *not my people; Lo-Ammi,* the a son of Hosea:–Lo-ammi.

3819. לֹא רֻחָמָה *lo roo-khaw-maw';* from 3808 and 7355; *not pitied; Lo- Ruchamah,* a daughter of Hosea:–Lo-ruhamah.

3820. לֵב *labe;* a form of 3824; the *heart;* also used (fig.) very widely for the feelings, the will and even the intellect; likewise for the *centre* of anything:–+ care for, comfortably, consent, X considered, courag[-eous], friend [-ly], ([broken-], [hard-], [merry-], [stiff-], [stout-], double) heart([-ed]), X heed, X I, kindly, midst, mind(-ed), X regard([-ed]), X themselves, X unawares, understanding, X well, willingly, wisdom.

3821. לֵב *labe* (Chald.); cor. to 3820:–heart.

3822. לְבָאוֹת *leb-aw-oth';* pl. of 3833; *lionesses; Lebaoth,* a place in Pal.:–Lebaoth. See also 1034.

3823. לָבַב *law-bab';* a prim. root; prop. to *be enclosed* (as if with *fat*); by impl. (as denom. from 3824) to *unheart,* i.e. (in a good sense) *transport* (with love), or (in a bad sense) *stultify;* also (as denom. from 3834) to *make cakes:*–make cakes, ravish, be wise.

3824. לֵבָב *lay-bawb';* from 3823; the *heart* (as the most interior organ); used also like 3820:– + bethink themselves, breast, comfortably, courage, ([faint], [tender-] heart([-ed]), midst, mind, X unawares, understanding.

3825. לְבַב *leb-ab'* (Chald.); cor. to 3824:–heart.

3826. לִבָּה *lib-baw';* fem. of 3820; the *heart:*–heart.

3827. לַבָּה *lab-baw';* for 3852; *flame:*–flame.

3828. לְבוֹנָה *leb-o-naw';* or לְבֹנָה *leb-o-naw';* from 3836; *frankincense* (from its *whiteness* or perh. that of its smoke):–(frank-) incense.

3829. לְבוֹנָה *leb-o-naw';* the same as 3828; *Lebonah,* a place in Pal.:–Lebonah.

3830. לְבוּשׁ *leb-oosh';* or לְבֻשׁ *leb-oosh';* from 3847; a *garment* (lit. or fig.); by impl. (euphem.) a *wife:*–apparel, clothed with, clothing, garment, raiment, vestment, vesture.

3831. לְבוּשׁ *leb-oosh'* (Chald.); cor. to 3830 :–garment.

3832. לָבַט *law-bat';* a prim. root; to *overthrow;* intr., to *fall:*–fall.

3833. לָבִיא *law-bee';* or (Eze. 19:2) לְבִיָּא *leb-ee-yaw';* irreg. masc. pl. לְבָאִים *leb-aw-eem';* irreg. fem. pl. לְבָאוֹת *leb-aw-oth';* from an un. root men. to *roar;* a *lion* (prop. a *lioness* as the fiercer [although not a *roarer;* comp. 738]):–(great, old, stout) lion, lioness, young [lion].

3834. לָבִיבָה *law-bee-baw';* or rather לְבִבָה *leb-ee-baw';* from 3823 in its or. sense of *fatness* (or perh. of *folding*); a *cake* (either as *fried* or *turned*):–cake.

3835. לָבַן *law-ban';* a prim. root; to *be* (or *become*) *white;* also (as denom. from 3843) to *make bricks:*–make brick, be (made, make) white(-r).

3836. לָבָן *law-bawn';* or (Ge. 49:12) לָבֵן *law-bane';* from 3835; *white:*–white.

3837. לָבָן *law-bawn';* the same as 3836; *Laban,* a Mesopotamian; also a place in the Desert:–Laban.

3838. לְבָנָא *leb-aw-naw';* or לְבָנָה *leb-aw-naw';* the same as 3842; *Lebana* or *Lebanah,* one of the Nethinim:–Lebana, Lebanah.

3839. לִבְנֶה *lib-neh';* from 3835; some sort of *whitish* tree, perh. the *storax:*–poplar.

3840. לִבְנָה *lib-naw';* from 3835; properly, *whiteness,* i.e. (by impl.) *transparency:*–paved.

3841. לִבְנָה *lib-naw';* the same as 3839; *Libnah,* a place in the Desert and one in Pal.:–Libnah.

3842. לְבָנָה *leb-aw-naw';* from 3835; prop. (the) *white,* i.e. the *moon:*–moon. See also 3838.

3843. לְבֵנָה *leb-ay-naw';* from 3835; a *brick* (from the *whiteness* of the clay):–(altar of) brick, tile.

3844. לְבָנוֹן *leb-aw-nohn';* from 3825; (the) *white* mountain (from its snow); *Lebanon,* a mountain range in Pal.:–Lebanon.

3845. לִבְנִי *lib-nee';* from 3835; *white; Libni,* an Isr.:–Libni.

3846. לִבְנִי *lib-nee';* patron. from 3845; a *Libnite* or desc. of Libni (coll.):–Libnites.

3847. לָבַשׁ *law-bash';* or לָבֵשׁ *law-bashe';* a prim. root; prop. *wrap* around, i.e. (by impl.) to *put on* a garment or *clothe* (oneself, or another), lit. or fig.:–(in) apparel, arm, array (self), clothe (self), come upon, put (on, upon), wear.

3848. לְבַשׁ *leb-ash'* (Chald.); cor. to 3847:–clothe.

3849. לֹג *lohg;* from an un. root app. mean. to *deepen* or *hollow* [like 3537]; a log or measure for liquids:–log [of oil].

3850. לֹד *lode;* from an un. root of unc. signif.; *Lod,* a place in Pal.:–Lod.

3851. לַהַב *lah'-hab;* from an usused root mean. to *gleam;* a *flash;* fig., a sharply polished *blade* or *point* of a weapon:–blade, bright, flame, glittering.

3852. לֶהָבָה *leh-aw-baw';* or לַהֶבֶת *lah-eh'-beth;* fem. of 3851, and mean. the same:–flame(-ming), head [of a spear].

3853. לְהָבִים *leh-haw-beem';* pl. of 3851; *flames; Lehabim,* a son of Mizrain, and his desc.:–Lehabim.

3854. לַהַג *lah'-hag;* from an un. root mean. to *be eager;* intense ment. *application:*–study.

3855. לַהַד *lah'-had;* from an un. root mean. to *glow* [comp. 3851] or else to *be earnest* [comp. 3854]; *Lahad,* an Isr.:–Lahad.

3856. לָהַהּ *law-hah';* a prim. root mean. prop. to *burn,* i.e. (by impl.) to *be rabid* (fig., *insane*); also (from the *exhaustion* of frenzy) to *languish:*–faint, mad.

3857. לָהַט *law-hat';* a prim. root; prop. to *lick,* i.e. (by impl.) to *blaze:*–burn (up), set on fire, flaming, kindle.

3858. לַהַט *lah'-hat;* from 3857; a *blaze;* also (from the idea of *enwrapping*) *magic* (as *covert*):–flaming, enchantment.

3859. לָהַם *law-ham';* a prim. root; prop. to *burn* in, i.e. (fig.) to *rankle:*–wound.

3860. לָהֵן *law-hane';* from the prep. pref. mean. *to* or *for* and 2005; popularly *for if;* hence, *therefore:*–for them

3861. לָהֵן *law-hane';* (Chald.) cor. to 3860; *therefore;* also *except:*–but, except, save, therefore, wherefore.

3862. לַהֲקָה *lah-hak-aw';* prob. from an un. root mean. to *gather;* an *assembly:*–company.

3863. לוּא *loo;* or לֻא *loo;* or לוּ *loo;* a

HEBREW

conditional particle; *if;* by impl. (interj. as a wish) *would that!:*–if (haply), peradventure, I pray thee, though, I would, would God (that).
3864. לוּבִי *loo-bee';* or לֻבִּי *loob-bee';* patrial from a name prob. der. from an un. root mean. to *thirst,* i.e. a *dry* region; app. a *Libyan* or inh. of interior Africa (only in pl.):–Lubim(-s), Libyans.
3865. לוּד *lood;* prob. of for. der.; *Lud,* the name of two nations:–Lud, Lydia.
3866. לוּדִי *loo-dee';* or לוּדִיִּי *loo-dee-ee';* patrial from 3865; a *Ludite* or inh. of Lud (only in pl.):–Ludim. Lydians.
3867. לָוָה *law-vaw';* a prim. root; prop. to *twine,* i.e. (by impl.) to *unite,* to *remain;* also to *borrow* (as a form of *obligation*) or (caus.) to *lend:*–abide with, borrow(-er), cleave, join (self), lend(-er).
3868. לוּז *looz;* a prim. root; to *turn* aside [comp. 3867, 3874 and 3885], i.e. (lit.) to *depart,* (fig.) *be perverse:*–depart, orward, perverse(-ness).
3869. לוּז *looz;* prob. of for. or.; some kind of *nut*-tree, perh. the *almond:*–hazel.
3870. לוּז *looz;* prob. from 3869 (as growing there); *Luz,* the name of two places in Pal.:–Luz.
3871. לוּחַ *loo'-akh;* or לֻחַ *loo'-akh;* from a prim. root; prob. mean. to *glisten;* a *tablet* (as *polished*), of stone, wood or metal:–board, plate, table.
3872. לוּחִית *loo-kheeth';* or לֻחוֹת (Jer. 48:5) *loo-khoth';* from the same as 3871; *floored; Luchith,* a place E. of the Jordan:–Luhith.
3873. לוֹחֵשׁ *lo-khashe';* act.part. of 3907; (the) *enchanter; Lochesh,* an Isr.:–Hallohesh, Haloshesh [*incl. the art.*].
3874. לוּט *loot;* a prim. root; to *wrap* up:–cast, wrap.
3875. לוֹט *lote;* from 3874; a *veil:*–covering.
3876. לוֹט *lote;* the same as 3875; *Lot,* Abraham's nephew:–Lot.
3877. לוֹטָן *lo-tawn';* from 3875; *covering; Lotan,* an Idumaean:–Lotan.
3878. לֵוִי *lay-vee';* from 3867; *attached; Levi,* a son of Jacob:–Levi. See also 3879, 3881.
3879. לֵוִי *lay-vee'* (Chald.); cor. to 3880:–Levite.
3880. לִוְיָה *liv-yaw';* from 3867; something *attached,* i.e. a *wreath:*–ornament.
3881. לֵוִיִּי *lay-vee-ee';* or לֵוִי *lay-vee';* patron. from 3878; a *Levite* or desc. of Levi:–Levite.
3882. לִוְיָתָן *liv-yaw-thawn';* from 3867; a *wreathed* animal, i.e. a *serpent* (esp. the *crocodile* or some other large sea-monster); fig., the constellation of the *dragon;* also as a symbol of *Bab.:*–leviathan, mourning.
3883. לוּל *lool;* from an un. root mean. to *fold* back; a *spiral* step:–winding stair. Comp. 3924.
3884. לוּלֵא *loo-lay';* or לוּלֵי *loo lay';* from 3863 and 3808; *if not:*–except, had not, if (...not), unless, were it not that.
3885. לוּן *loon;* or לִין *leen;* a prim. root; to *stop* (usually over night); by impl., to *stay* permanently; hence (in a bad sense) to be *obstinate* (esp. in words, to *complain*):–abide (all night), continue, dwell, endure, grudge, be left, lie all night, (cause to) lodge (all night, in, -ing, this night), (make to) murmur, remain, tarry (all night, that night).
3886. לוּעַ *loo'-ah;* a prim. root; to *gulp;* fig., to *be rash:*–swallow down (up).
3887. לוּץ *loots;* a prim. root; prop. to *make mouths* at, i.e. to *scoff;* hence (from the effort to pronounce a for. language) to *interpret,* or (gen.) *intercede:*–ambassador, have in derision, interpreter, make a mock, mocker, scorn(-er,-ful), teacher.
3888. לוּשׁ *loosh;* a prim. root; to *knead:*–knead.
3889. לוּשׁ *loosh;* from 3888; *kneading; Lush,* a place in Pal.:–Laish Comp. 3919.
3890. לְוָת *lev-awth'* (Chald.); from a root cor. to 3867; prop. *adhesion,* i.e. (as prep.) *with:*–X thee.
3891. לְזוּת *lez-ooth';* from 3868; *perverseness:*–perverse.
3892. לַח *lakh;* from an un. root mean. to *be new; fresh,* i.e. un. or undried:–green, moist.
3893. לֵחַ *lay'-akh;* from the same as 3892; *freshness,* i.e. vigor:–nat. force.
3894. לָחוּם *law-khoom';* or לָחֻם *law-khoom';* pass.part. of 3898; prop. *eaten,* i.e. *food;* also *flesh,* i.e. *body:*–while...is eating, flesh.
3895. לְחִי *lekh-ee';* from an un. root mean. to *be soft;* the *cheek* (from its *fleshiness*); hence, the *jaw*-bone:–cheek (bone), jaw (bone).
3896. לֶחִי *lekh'-ee;* a form of 3895; *Lechi,* a place in Pal.:–Lehi. Comp. also 7437.
3897. לָחַךְ *law-khak';* a prim. root; to *lick:*–lick (up).
3898. לָחַם *law-kham';* a prim. root; to *feed* on; fig., to *consume;* by impl., to *battle* (as *destruction*):–devour, eat, X ever, fight (-ing), overcome, prevail, (make) war(-ring).
3899. לֶחֶם *lekh'-em;* from 3898; *food* (for man or beast), esp. *bread,* or *grain* (for making it):–([shew-])bread, X eat, food, fruit, loaf, meat, victuals. See also 1036.
3900. לְחֶם *lekh-em'* (Chald.); cor. to 3899:–feast.
3901. לָחֶם *law-khem';* from 3898, *battle:*–war.
3902. לַחְמִי *lakh-mee';* from 3899; *foodful; Lachmi,* an Isr.; or rather prob. a brief form for 1022:– Lahmi. See also 3433.
3903. לַחְמָס *lakh-maws';* prob. by err. transc.. for לַחְמָם *lakh-mawm';* from 3899; *food-like; Lachmam* or *Lachmas,* a place in Pal.:–Lahmam.
3904. לְחֵנָה *lekh-ay-naw'* (Chald.); from an un. root of unc. mean.; a *concubine:*–concubine.
3905. לָחַץ *law-khats';* a prim. root; prop. to *press,* i.e. (fig.) to *distress:*–afflict, crush, force, hold fast, oppress(-or), thrust self.
3906. לַחַץ *lakh'-ats;* from 3905; *distress:*–affliction, oppression.
3907. לָחַשׁ *law-khash';* a prim. root; to *whisper;* by impl., to *mumble* a spell (as a magician):–charmer, whisper (together).
3908. לַחַשׁ *lakh'-ash;* from 3907; prop. a *whisper,* i.e. by impl., (in a good sense) a private *prayer,* (in a bad one) an *incantation;* concr., an *amulet:*–charmed, earring, enchantment, orator, prayer.
3909. לָט *lawt;* a form of 3814 or else part. from 3874; prop. *covered,* i.e. *secret;* by impl., *incantation;* also *secrecy* or (adv.) *covertly:*–enchantment, privily, secretly, softly.
3910. לֹט *lote;* prob. from 3874; a *gum* (from its sticky nat.), prob. *ladanum:*–myrrh.
3911. לְטָאָה *let-aw-aw';* from an un. root mean. to *hide;* a kind of *lizard* (from its *covert* habits):–lizard.
3912. לְטוּשִׁם *let-oo-sheem;* masc. pl. of pass. part. of 3913; *hammered* (i.e. *oppressed*) ones; *Letushim,* an Arabian tribe:–Letushim.
3913. לָטַשׁ *law-tash';* a prim. root; prop. to *hammer* out (an edge), i.e. to *sharpen:*–instructer, sharp(-en), whet.
3914. לֹיָה *lo-yaw';* a form of 3880; a *wreath:*–addition.
3915. לַיִל *lah'-yil;* or (Is. 21:11) לֵיל *lale;* also לַיְלָה *lah'- yel-aw;* from the same as 3883; prop. a *twist* (away of the light), i.e. *night;* fig., *adversity:*–([mid-]) night (season).
3916. לֵילְיָא *lay-leh-yaw'* (Chald.); cor. to 3815:–night.
3917. לִילִית *lee-leeth';* from 3915; a *night* spectre:–screech owl.
3918. לַיִשׁ *lah'-yish;* from 3888 in the sense of *crushing;* a lion (from his destructive *blows*):–(old)lion.
3919. לַיִשׁ *lah'-yish;* the same as 3918; *Laïsh,* the name of two places in Pal.:–Laish. Comp. 3889.
3920. לָכַד *law-kad';* a prim. root; to *catch* (in a net, trap or pit); gen., to *capture* or occupy; also to *choose* (by lot); fig., to *cohere:*–X at all, catch (self), be frozen, be holden, stick together, take.
3921. לֶכֶד *leh'ked;* from 3920; something to *capture* with, i.e. a *noose:*–being taken.
3922. לֵכָה *lay-kaw';* from 3212; a *journey; Lekah,* a place in Pal.:–Lecah.
3923. לָכִישׁ *law-keesh';* from an un. root of unc. mean.; *Lakish,* a place in Pal.:–Lachish.
3924. לֻלָאָה *loo-law-aw';* from the same as 3883; *a loop:*–loop.
3925. לָמַד *law-mad';* a prim. root; prop. to *goad,* i.e. (by impl.) to *teach* (the rod being an Oriental *incentive*):[un-] accustomed, X diligently, expert, instruct, learn, skilful, teach(-er, -ing).
3926. לְמוֹ *lem-o';* a prol. and separable form of the prep. pref.; *to* or *for:*–at, for, to, upon.
3927. לְמוּאֵל *lem-oo-ale';* or לְמוֹאֵל *lem-o-ale';* from 3926 and 410; (belonging) *to God; Lemuël* or *Lemoël:*–Lemuel.
3928. לִמּוּד *lim-mood';* or לִמֻּד *lim-mood';* from 3925; *instructed:*–accustomed, disciple, learned, taught, used.
3929. לֶמֶךְ *leh'-mek;* from an un. root of unc. mean.; *Lemek,* the name of two antediluvian patriarchs:–Lamech.
3930. לֹעַ *lo'ah;* from 3886; the *gullet:*–throat.
3931. לָעַב *law-ab';* a prim. root; to *deride:*–mock.
3932. לָעַג *law-ag';* a prim. root; to *deride;* by impl. (as if imitating a foreigner) to *speak unintelligibly:*–have in derision, laugh (to scorn), mock (on), stammering.
3933. לַעַג *lah'-ag;* from 3932; *derision, scoffing:*–derision, scorn (-ing).
3934. לָעֵג *law-ayg';* from 3932; a *buffoon;* also a *foreigner:*–mocker, stammering.
3935. לַעְדָּה *lah-daw';* from an un. root of unc. mean.; *Ladah,* an Isr.:–Laadah.
3936. לַעְדָּן *lah-dawn';* from the same as 3935; *Ladan,* the name of two Isr.:–Laadan.
3937. לָעַז *law-az';* a prim. root; to *speak in a for. tongue:*–strange language.
3938. לָעַט *law-at';* a prim. root; to *swallow* greedily; caus., to *feed:*–feed.
3939. לַעֲנָה *lah-an-aw';* from an un. root supposed to mean to *curse; wormwood* (regarded as *poisonous,* and therefore *accursed*):–hemlock, wormwood.
3940. לַפִּיד *lap-peed';* or לַפִּד *lap-peed';* from an un. root prob. mean. to *shine;* a *flambeau, lamp* or *flame:*–(fire-) brand,

(burning) lamp, lightning, torch.
3941. לַפִּידוֹת *lap-pee-doth';* fem. pl. of 3940; *Lappidoth,* the husband of Deborah:–Lappidoth.
3942. לִפְנַי *lif-nah'ee;* from the prep. pref. (*to* or *for*) and 6440; *anterior:*–before.
3943. לָפַת *law-fath';* a prim. root; prop. to *bend,* i.e. (by impl.) to *clasp;* also (refl.) to *turn* around or aside:–take hold, turn aside (self).
3944. לָצוֹן *law-tsone';* from 3887; *derision:*–scornful(-ning).
3945. לָצַץ *law-tsats';* a prim. root; to *deride:*–scorn.
3946. לַקּוּם *lak-koom';* from an un. root thought to mean to *stop* up by a barricade; perh. *fortification; Lakkum,* a place in Pal.:–Lakum.
3947. לָקַח *law-kakh';* a prim. root; to *take* (in the widest variety of appl.):–accept, bring, buy, carry away, drawn, fetch, get, infold, X many, mingle, place, receive (-ing), reserve, seize, send for, take (away, -ing, up), use, win.
3948. לֶקַח *leh'-kakh;* from 3947; prop. something *received,* i.e. (ment.) *instruction* (whether on the part of the teacher or hearer); also (in an act. and sinister sense) *inveiglement:*–doctrine, learning, fair speech.
3949. לִקְחִי *lik-khee';* from 3947; *learned; Likchi,* an Isr.:–Likhi.
3950. לָקַט *law-kat';* a prim. root; prop. to *pick* up, i.e. (gen.) to *gather;* spec., to *glean:*–gather (up), glean.
3951. לֶקֶט *leh'-ket;* from 3950; the *gleaning:*–gleaning.
3952. לָקַק *law-kak';* a prim. root; to *lick* or *lap:*–lap, lick.
3953. לָקַשׁ *law-kash';* a prim. root; to *gather* the *after* crop:–gather.
3954. לֶקֶשׁ *leh'-kesh;* from 3953; the *after crop:*–latter growth.
3955. לְשַׁד *lesh-ad';* from an un. root of unc. mean.; app. *juice,* i.e. (fig.) *vigor;* also a sweet or fat *cake:*–fresh, moisture.
3956. לָשׁוֹן *law-shone';* or לָשֹׁן *law-shone';* also (in pl.) fem. לְשֹׁנָה *lesh-o-naw';* from 3960; the *tongue* (of man or animals), used lit. (as the instrument of licking, eating, or speech), and fig. (speech, an ingot, a fork of flame, a cove of water):–+ babbler, bay, + evil speaker, language, talker, tongue, wedge.
3957. לִשְׁכָּה *lish-kaw';* from an un. root of unc. mean.; a *room* in a building (whether for storage, eating, or lodging):–chamber, parlour. Comp. 5393.
3958. לֶשֶׁם *leh'-shem;* from an un. root of unc. mean.; a *gem,* perh. the *jacinth:*–ligure.
3959. לֶשֶׁם *leh'-shem;* the same as 3958; *Leshem,* a place in Pal.:–Leshem.
3960. לָשַׁן *law-shan';* a prim. root; prop. to *lick;* but used only as a denom. from 3956; to *wag the tongue,* i.e. to *calumniate:*–accuse, slander.
3961. לִשָּׁן *lish-shawn'* (Chald.); cor. to 3956; *speech,* i.e. a *nation:*–language.
3962. לֶשַׁע *leh'-shah;* from an un. root thought to mean to *break* through; a boiling *spring; Lesha,* a place prob. E. of the Jordan:–Lasha.
3963. לֶתֶךְ *leh'-thek;* from an un. root; a *measure* for things dry:–half homer.

מ

3964. מָא maw (Chald.); cor. to 4100; (as indef.) that:–+ what.
3965. מַאֲבוּס *mah-ab-ooce';* from 75; a *granary:*–storehouse.
3966. מְאֹד *meh-ode';* from the same as 181; prop. *vehemence,* i.e. (with or without prep.) *vehemently;* by impl., *wholly, speedily,* etc. (often with other words as an intens. or sup.; esp. when repeated):–diligently, esp., exceeding(-ly), far, fast, good, great(-ly), X louder and louder, might(-ily, -y), (so) much, quickly, (so) sore, utterly, very (+ much, sore), well.
3967. מֵאָה *may-aw';* or מֵאיָה *may-yaw';* prob. a prim. numeral; a *hundred;* also as a mult. and a fraction:–hundred ([-fold], -th), + sixscore.
3968. מֵאָה *may-aw';* the same as 3967; *Meäh,* a tower in Jerus.:–Meah.
3969. מְאָה *meh-aw'* (Chald.); cor. to 3967:–hundred.
3970. מַאֲוַי *mah-av-ah'ee;* from 183; a *desire:*–desire.
3971. מאוּם *moom;* usually מוּם *moom;* as if pass.part. from an un. root prob. mean. to *stain;* a *blemish* (phys.or mor.):–blemish, blot, spot.
3972. מְאוּמָה *meh-oo'-maw;* app. a form of 3971; prop. a *speck* or *point,* i.e. (by impl.) *something;* with neg., *nothing:*–fault, + no (-ught), ought, somewhat, any ([no-])thing.
3973. מָאוֹס *maw-oce';* from 3988; *refuse:*–refuse.
3974. מָאוֹר *maw-ore';* or מָאֹר *aw-ore';* also (in pl.) fem. מְאוֹרָה *meh-o-raw';* or מְאֹרָה *meh-o-raw';* from 215; prop. a *luminous* body or *luminary* i.e. (abstr.) *light* (as an element): fig., *brightness,* i.e. *cheerfulness;* spec., a *chandelier:*–bright, light.
3975. מְאוּרָה *meh-oo-raw';* fem. pass.part. of 215; something *lighted,* i.e. an *aperture;* by impl., a *crevice* or *hole* (of a serpent):–den.
3976. מֹאזֵן *mo-zane';* from 239; (only in the dual) a pair of *scales:*–balances.
3977. מֹאזֵן *mo-zane'* (Chald.); cor. to 3976:–balances.
3978. מַאֲכָל *mah-ak-awl';* from 398; an *eatable* (incl. provender, flesh and fruit):–food, fruit, ([bake-]) meat(-s), victual.
3979. מַאֲכֶלֶת *mah-ak-eh'-leth;* from 398; something to *eat* with, i.e. a *knife:*–knife.
3980. מַאֲכֹלֶת *mah-ak-o'-leth;* from 398; something *eaten* (by fire), i.e. *fuel:*–fuel.
3981. מַאֲמָץ *mah-am-awts';* from 553; *strength,* i.e. (pl.) *resources:*–force.
3982. מַאֲמַר *mah-am-ar';* from 559; something (authoritatively) *said,* i.e. an *edict:*–commandment, decree.
3983. מֵאמַר *may-mar'* (Chald.); cor. to 3982:–appointment, word.
3984. מָאן *mawn* (Chald.); prob. from a root cor. to 579 in the sense of an *inclosure* by sides; a *utensil:*–vessel.
3985. מָאֵן *maw-ane';* a prim. root; to *refuse:*–refuse, X utterly.
3986. מָאֵן *maw-ane';* from 3985; *unwilling:*–refuse.
3987. מֵאֵן *may-ane';* from 3985; refractory:–refuse.
3988. מָאַס *maw-as';* a prim. root; to *spurn;* also (intr.) to *disappear:*–abhor, cast away (off), contemn, despise, disdain, (become) loathe(some), melt away, refuse, reject, reprobate, X utterly, vile person.
3989. מַאֲפֶה *mah-af-eh';* from 644; something *baked,* i.e. a *batch:*–baken.
3990. מַאֲפֵל *mah-af-ale';* from the same as 651; something *opaque:*–darkness.
3991. מַאְפֵּלְיָה *mah-af-ay-leh-yaw';* prol. fem. of 3990; *opaqueness:*–darkness.
3992. מָאַר *maw-ar';* a prim. root; to *be bitter* or (caus.) to *embitter,* i.e. *be painful:*–fretting, picking.
3993. מַאֲרָב *mah-ar-awb';* from 693; an *ambuscade:*–lie in ambush, ambushment, lurking place, lying in wait.
3994. מְאֵרָה *meh-ay-raw';* from 779; an *execration:*–curse.
3995. מִבְדָּלָה *mib-daw-law';* from 914; a *separation,* i.e. (concr.) a *separate place:*–separate.
3996. מָבוֹא *maw-bo';* from 935; an *entrance* (the place or the act); spec. (with or without 8121) *sunset* or the *west;* also (adv. with prep.) *towards:*–by which came, as cometh, in coming, as men enter into, entering, entrance into, entry, where goeth, going down, + westward. Comp. 4126.
3997. מְבוֹאָה *meb-o-aw';* fem. of 3996; a *haven:*–entry.
3998. מְבוּכָה *meb-oo-kaw';* from 943; *perplexity:*–perplexity.
3999. מַבּוּל *mab-bool';* from 2986 in the sense of *flowing;* a *deluge:*–flood.
4000. מָבוֹן *maw-bone';* from 995; *instructing:*–taught.
4001. מְבוּסָה *meb-oo-saw';* from 947; a *trampling:*–treading (trodden) down (under foot).
4002. מַבּוּעַ *mab-boo'-ah;* from 5042; a *fountain:*–fountain, spring.
4003. מְבוּקָה *meb-oo-kah';* from the same as 950; *emptiness:*–void.
4004. מִבְחוֹר *mib-khore';* from 977; *select,* i.e. well fortified:–choice.
4005. מִבְחָר *mib-khawr';* from 977; *select,* i.e. best:–choice(-st), chosen.
4006. מִבְחָר *mib-khawr';* the same as 4005; *Mibchar,* an Isr.:–Mibhar.
4007. מַבָּט *mab-bawt';* or מֶבָּט *meb-bawt';* from 5027; something *expected,* i.e. (abstr.) *expectation:*–expectation.
4008. מִבְטָא *mib-taw';* from 981; a rash *utterance* (hasty vow):–(that which ...) uttered (out of).
4009. מִבְטָח *mib-tawkh';* from 982; prop. a *refuge,* i.e. (obj.) *security,* or (subj.) *assurance:*–confidence, hope, sure, trust.
4010. מַבְלִיגִית *mab-leeg-eeth';* from 1082; *desistance* (or rather *desolation*):–comfort self.
4011. מִבְנֶה *mib-neh';* from 1129; a *building:*–frame.
4012. מְבֻנַּי *meb-oon-nah'-ee;* from 1129; *built* up; *Mebunnai* an Isr.:–Mebunnai.
4013. מִבְצָר *mib-tsawr';* also (in pl.) fem. (Da. 11:15) מִבְצָרָה *mib-tsaw-raw';* from 1219; a *fortification, castle,* or *fortified* city; fig., a *defender:*–(de-, most) fenced, fortress, (most) strong (hold).
4014. מִבְצָר *mib-tsawr';* the same as 4013; *Mibtsar,* an Idumaean:–Mibzar.
4015. מִבְרָח *mib-rawkh';* from 1272; a *refugee:*–fugitive.
4016. מָבוּשׁ *maw-boosh';* from 954; (pl.) the (male) *pudenda:*–secrets.
4017. מִבְשָׂם *mib-sawm';* from the same as 1314; *fragrant; Mibsam,* the name of an Ishmaelite and of an Isr.:–Mibsam.
4018. מְבַשְּׁלָה *meb-ash-shel-aw';* from 1310;

a cooking *hearth:*–boiling-place.
4019. מַגְבִּישׁ *mag-beesh';* from the same as 1378; *stiffening; Magbish,* an Isr., or a place in Pal.:–Magbish.
4020. מִגְבָּלָה *mig-baw-law';* from 1379; a *border:*–end.
4021. מִגְבָּעָה *mig-baw-aw';* from the same as 1389; a *cap* (as *hemispherical*):–bonnet.
4022. מֶגֶד *meh'-ghed;* from an un. root prob. mean. to be *eminent;* prop. a *distinguished* thing; hence something *valuable,* as a product or fruit:–pleasant, precious fruit (thing).
4023. מְגִדּוֹן *meg-id-done';* (Zec. 12:11) or מְגִדּוֹ *meg-id-do';* from 1413; *rendezvous; Megiddon* or *Megiddo,* a place in Pal.:–Megiddo, Megiddon.
4024. מִגְדּוֹל *mig-dole';* or מִגְדֹּל *mig-dole';* prob. of Eg. or.; *Migdol,* a place in Eg.:–Migdol, tower.
4025. מַגְדִּיאֵל *mag-dee-ale';* from 4022 and 410; *preciousness of God; Magdiël,* an Idumaean:–Magdiel.
4026. מִגְדָּל *mig-dawl';* also (in pl.) fem. מִגְדָּלָה *mig-daw-law';* from 1431; a *tower* (from its size or height); by anal., a *rostrum;* fig., a (pyramidal) *bed* of flowers:–castle, flower, tower.
4027. מִגְדַּל־אֵל *mig-dal-ale';* from 4026 and 410; *tower of God; Migdal-El,* a place in Pal.:–Migdal-el.
4028. מִגְדַּל־גָּד *migdal-gawd';* from 4026 and 1408; *tower of Fortune; Migdal-Gad,* a place in Pal.:–Migdal-gad.
4029. מִגְדַּל־עֵדֶר *mig-dal'-ay'-der;* from 4026 and 5739; *tower of a flock; Migdal-Eder,* a place in Pal.:–Migdal-eder, tower of the flock.
4030. מִגְדָּנָה *mig-daw-naw';* from the same as 4022; *preciousness,* i.e. a *gem:*–precious thing, present.
4031. מָגוֹג *maw-gogue'* from 1463; *Magog,* a son of Japheth; also a barbarous northern region:–Magog.
4032. מָגוֹר *maw-gore';* or (La. 2:22) מָגוּר *maw-goor';* from 1481 in the sense of *fearing;* a *fright* (obj. or subj.):–fear, terror. Comp. 4036.
4033. מָגוּר *maw-goor';* or מָגֻר *maw-goor';* from 1481 in the sense of *lodging;* a temporary *abode;* by ext., a permanent *residence:*–dwelling, pilgrimage, where sojourn, be a stranger. Comp. 4032.
4034. מְגוֹרָה *meg-o-raw';* fem. of 4032; *affright:* –fear.
4035. מְגוּרָה *meg-oo-raw';* fem. of 4032 or of 4033; a *fright;* also a *granary:*–barn, fear.
4036. מָגוֹר מִסָּבִיב *maw-gore' mis-saw-beeb';* from 4032 and 5439 with the prep. ins.; *affright from around; Magor-mis-Sabib,* a symbolic name of Pashur:–Magor-missabib.
4037. מַגְזֵרָה *mag-zay-raw';* from 1504; a *cutting* implement, i.e. a *blade:*–axe.
4038. מַגָּל *mag-gawl';* from an un. root mean. to *reap;* a *sickle:*–sickle.
4039. מְגִלָּה *meg-il-law';* from 1556; a *roll:*–roll, volume.
4040. מְגִלָּה *meg-il-law'* (Chald.); cor. to 4039:–roll.
4041. מְגַמָּה *meg-am-maw';* from the same as 1571; prop. *accumulation,* i.e. *impulse* or *direction:*–sup up.
4042. מָגַן *maw-gan';* a denom. from 4043; prop. to *shield; encompass* with; fig., to *rescue,* to hand safely *over* (i.e. *surrender*):–deliver.
4043. מָגֵן *maw-gane';* also (in pl.) fem. מְגִנָּה *meg-in-naw';* from 1598; a *shield* (i.e. the small one or *buckler*); fig., a *protector;* also the scaly *hide* of the crocodile:–X armed, buckler, defence, ruler, + scale, shield.
4044. מְגִנָּה *meg-in-naw';* from 4042; a *covering* (in a bad sense), i.e. *blindness* or obduracy:–sorrow. See also 4043.
4045. מִגְעֶרֶת *mig-eh'-reth;* from 1605; *reproof* (i.e. curse):–rebuke.
4046. מַגֵּפָה *mag-gay-faw';* from 5062; a *pestilence;* by anal., *defeat:*–(X be) plague(-d), slaughter, stroke.
4047. מַגְפִּיעָשׁ *mag-pee-awsh';* app. from 1479 or 5062 and 6211; *exterminator of* (the) *moth; Magpiash,* an Isr.:–Magpiash.
4048. מָגַר *maw-gar';* a prim. root; to *yield up;* intens., to *precipitate:*–cast down, terror.
4049. מְגַר *meg-ar'* (Chald.); cor. to 4048; to *overthrow:*–destroy.
4050. מְגֵרָה *meg-ay-raw';* from 1641; a *saw:*–axe, saw.
4051. מִגְרוֹן *mig-rone';* from 4048; *precipice; Migron,* a place in Pal.:–Migron.
4052. מִגְרָעָה *mig-raw-aw';* from 1639; a *ledge* or offset:–narrowed rest.
4053. מִגְרָפָה *mig-raw-faw';* from 1640; something *thrown off* (by the spade), i.e. a *clod:*–clod.
4054. מִגְרָשׁ *mig-rawsh';* also (in pl.) fem. (Eze. 27:28) מִגְרָשָׁה *mig-raw-shaw';* from 1644; a *suburb* (i.e. open country whither flocks are *driven* from pasture); hence, the *area* around a building, or the *margin* of the sea:–cast out, suburb.
4055. מַד *mad;* or מֵד *made;* from 4058; prop. *extent,* i.e. *height;* also a measure; by impl., a *vesture* (as measured); also a *carpet:*–armour, clothes, garment, judgment, measure, raiment, stature.
4056. מַדְבַּח *mad-bakh'* (Chald.); from 1684; a sacrificial *altar:*–altar.
4057. מִדְבָּר *mid-bawr';* from 1696 in the sense of *driving;* a *pasture* (i.e. open field, whither cattle are driven); by impl., a *desert;* also *speech* (incl. its organs):–desert, south, speech, wilderness.
4058. מָדַד *maw-dad';* a prim. root: prop. to *stretch;* by impl., to *measure* (as if by *stretching* a line); fig., to *be extended:*–measure, mete, stretch self.
4059. מִדַּד *mid-dad';* from 5074; *flight:*–be gone.
4060. מִדָּה *mid-daw';* fem. of 4055; prop. *extension,* i.e. height or breadth; also a *measure* (incl. its standard); hence a *portion* (as measured) or a *vestment;* spec., *tribute* (as measured):–garment, measure(-ing, meteyard, piece, size, (great) stature, tribute, wide.
4061. מִדָּה *mid-daw'* (Chald.); or מִנְדָּה *min-daw';* cor. to 4060; *tribute* in money:–toll, tribute.
4062. מַדְהֵבָה *mad-hay-baw';* perh. from the equiv. of 1722; *goldmaking,* i.e. *exactness:*–golden city.
4063. מֶדֶו *meh'-dev';* from an un. root mean. to *stretch;* prop. *extent,* i.e. *measure;* by impl., a *dress* (as measured):–garment.
4064. מַדְוֶה *mad-veh';* from 1738; *sickness:*–disease.
4065. מַדּוּחַ *mad-doo'akh;* from 5080; *seduction:*–cause of banishment.
4066. מָדוֹן *maw-dohn';* from 1777; a *contest* or quarrel:–brawling, contention(-ous), discord, strife. Comp. 4079, 4090.
4067. מָדוֹן *maw-dohn';* from the same as 4063; *extensiveness,* i.e. height:–stature.
4068. מָדוֹן *maw-dohn';* the same as 4067; *Madon,* a place in Pal.:–Madon.
4069. מַדּוּעַ *mad-doo'-ah;* or מַדֻּעַ *mad-doo'-ah;* from 4100 and the pass.part. of 3045; *what* (is) *known?;* i.e. (by impl.) (adv.) *why?:*–how, wherefore, why.
4070. מְדוֹר *med-ore'* (Chald.); or מְדֹר *med-ore';* or מְדָר *med-awr';* from 1753; a *dwelling:*–dwelling.
4071. מְדוּרָה *med-oo-raw';* or מְדֻרָה *med-oo-raw';* from 1752 in the sense of *accumulation;* a *pile* of fuel:–pile (for fire).
4072. מִדְחֶה *mid-kheh';* from 1760; *overthrow:*–ruin.
4073. מְדַחְפָה *med-akh-faw';* from 1765; a *push,* i.e. ruin:–overthrow.
4074. מָדַי *maw-dah'-ee;* of for. *derivation; Madai,* a country of central Asia:–Madai, Medes, Media.
4075. מָדַי *maw-dah'-ee;* patrial from 4074; a *Madian* or nat. of Madai:–Mede.
4076. מָדַי *maw-dah'-ee* (Chald.); cor. to 4074:–Mede(-s).
4077. מָדַי *maw-dah'-ee* (Chald.); cor. to 4075:–Median.
4078. מַדַּי *mad-dah'-ee;* from 4100 and 1767; what (is) *enough,* i.e. *sufficiently:*–sufficiently.
4079. מִדְיָן *mid-yawn';* a var. for 4066:–brawling, contention(-ous).
4080. מִדְיָן *mid-yawn';* the same as 4079; *Midjan,* a son of Abraham; also his country and (coll.) his desc.:–Midian, Midianite.
4081. מִדִּין *mid-deen';* a var. for 4080:–Middin.
4082. מְדִינָה *med-ee-naw';* from 1777; prop. a *judgeship,* i.e. *jurisdiction;* by impl., a *district* (as ruled by a judge); gen., a *region:*–(X every) province.
4083. מְדִינָה *med-ee-naw'* (Chald.); cor. to 4082:–province.
4084. מִדְיָנִי *mid-yaw-nee';* patron. or patrial from 4080; a *Midjanite* or descend. (nat.) of Midjan:–Midianite. Comp. 4092.
4085. מְדֹכָה *med-o-kaw';* from 1743; a *mortar:*–mortar.
4086. מַדְמֵן *mad-mane';* from the same as 1828; *dunghill; Madmen,* a place in Pal.:–Madmen.
4087. מַדְמֵנָה *mad-may-naw';* fem. from the same as 1828; a *dunghill:*–dunghill.
4088. מַדְמֵנָה *mad-may-naw';* the same as 4087; *Madmenah,* a place in Pal.:–Madmenah.
4089. מַדְמַנָּה *mad-man-naw';* a var. for 4087; *Madmannah,* a place in Pal.:–Madmannah.
4090. מְדָן *med-awn';* a form of 4066:–discord, strife.
4091. מְדָן *med-awn';* the same as 4090; *Medan,* a son of Abraham:–Medan.
4092. מְדָנִי *med-aw-nee';* a var. of 4084:–Midianite.
4093. מַדָּע *mad-daw';* or מַדַּע *mad-dah';* from 3045; *intelligence* or *consciousness:*–knowledge, science, thought.
4094. מַדְקָרָה *mad-kaw-raw';* from 1856; a *wound:*–piercing.
4095. מַדְרֵגָה *mad-ray-gaw';* from an un. root mean. to *step;* prop. a *step;* by impl., a *steep* or inaccessible place:–stair, steep place.
4096. מִדְרָךְ *mid-rawk';* from 1869; a *treading,* i.e. a place for stepping on:–[foot-] breadth.
4097. מִדְרָשׁ *mid-rawsh';* from 1875; prop. an *investigation,* i.e. (by impl.) a *treatise* or elaborate compilation:–story.

4098. מְדֻשָׁה *med-oosh-shaw';* from 1758; a *threshing,* i.e. (concr. and fig.) *down-trodden* people:–threshing.
4099. מְדָתָא *med-aw-thaw';* of Pers. or.; *Medatha,* the father of Haman:–Hammedatha [*incl. the art.*].
4100. מָה *maw;* or מַה *mah;* or מָ *maw;* or מַ *mah;* also מֶה *meh;* a prim. particle; prop. interrog. *what?* (incl. *how? why? when?*); but also exclamation, *what!* (incl. *how!*), or indef. *what* (incl. *whatever,* and even rel., *that which*); often used with prefixes in various adv. or conjunctive senses:–how (long, oft, [-soever]), [no-]thing, what (end, good, purpose, thing), whereby(-fore, -in, -to, -with), (for) why.
4101. מָה *maw* (Chald.); cor. to 4100:–how great (mighty), that which, what (-soever), why.
4102. מָהַהּ *maw-hah';* app. a denom. from 4100; prop. to *question* or hesitate, i.e. (by impl.) to *be reluctant:*–delay, linger, stay selves, tarry.
4103. מְהוּמָה *meh-hoo-maw';* from 1949; *confusion* or uproar:–destruction, discomfiture, trouble, tumult, vexation, vexed.
4104. מְהוּמָן *Meh-hoo-mawn';* of Pers. or.; *Mehuman,* a eunuch of Xerxes:–Mehuman.
4105. מְהֵיטַבְאֵל *meh-hay-tab-ale';* from 3190 (augmented) and 410; *bettered of God; Mehetabel,* the name of an Edomitish man and woman:–Mehetabeel, Mehetabel.
4106. מָהִיר *maw-here';* or מָהִר *maw-here';* from 4116; *quick;* hence, *skilful:*–diligent, hasty, ready.
4107. מָהַל *maw-hal';* a prim. root; prop. to *cut down* or *reduce,* i.e. by impl., to *adulterate:*–mixed.
4108. מַהְלֵךְ *mah-lake';* from 1980; a *walking* (pl. coll.), i.e. *access:*–place to walk.
4109. מַהֲלָךְ *mah-hal-awk';* from 1980; a *walk,* i.e. a *passage* or a *distance:*–journey, walk.
4110. מַהֲלָל *mah-hal-awl';* from 1984; *fame:*–praise.
4111. מַהֲלַלְאֵל *mah-hal-al-ale';* from 4110 and 410; *praise of God; Mahalalel,* the name of an antediluvian patriarch and of an Isr.:–Mahalaleel.
4112. מַהֲלֻמָּה *mah-hal-oom-maw';* from 1986; a *blow:*–stripe, stroke.
4113. מַהֲמֹרָה *mah-ham-o-raw';* from an un. root; perh. an *abyss:*–deep pit.
4114. מַהְפֵּכָה *mah-pay-kaw';* from 2015; a *destruction:*–when...overthrew, overthrow(-n).
4115. מַהְפֶּכֶת *mah-peh'-keth;* from 2015; a *wrench,* i.e. the *stocks:*–prison, stocks.
4116. מָהַר *maw-har';* a prim. root; prop. to be *liquid* or *flow* easily, i.e. (by impl.); to *hurry* (in a good or a bad sense); often used (with another verb) adv., *promptly:*–be carried headlong, fearful, (cause to make, in, make) haste(-n, -ily), (be) hasty, (fetch, make ready) X quickly, rash, X shortly, (be so) X soon, make speed, X speedily, X straight-way, X suddenly, swift.
4117. מָהַר *maw-har';* a prim. root (perh. rather the same as 4116 through the idea of *readiness* in assent); to *bargain* (for a wife), i.e. to *wed:*–endow, X surely.
4118. מַהֵר *mah-hare';* from 4116; prop. *hurrying;* hence (adv.) *in a hurry:*–hasteth, hastily, at once, quickly, soon, speedily, suddenly.
4119. מֹהַר *mo'-har;* from 4117; a *price* (for a wife):–dowry.
4120. מְהֵרָה *meh-hay-raw';* fem. of 4118; prop. a *hurry;* hence (adv.) *promptly:*–hastily, quickly, shortly, soon, make (with) speed(-ily), swiftly.
4121. מַהֲרַי *mah-har-ah'-ee;* from 4116; *hasty; Maharai,* an Isr.:–Maharai.
4122. מַהֵר שָׁלָל חָשׁ בַּז *mah-hare' shaw-lawl' khawsh baz;* from 4118 and 7998 and 2363 and 957; *hasting* (is he [the enemy] to the) *booty, swift* (to the) *prey; Maher-Shalal-Chash-Baz;* the symb. name of the son of Isaiah:–Maher-sha-lal-bash-baz.
4123. מַהֲתַלָּה *mah-hath-al-law';* from 2048; a *delusion:*–deceit.
4124. מוֹאָב *mo-awb;* from a prol. form of the prep. pref. m- and 1; *from* (her [the mother's]) *father;* Moäb, an incestuous son of Lot; also his territory and desc.:–Moab.
4125. מוֹאָבִי *mo-aw-bee';* מוֹאָבִיָּה fem. *mo-aw-bee-yaw';* or מוֹאָבִית *mo-aw-beeth';* patron. from 4124; *Moäbite* or *Moäbitess,* i.e. a desc. from Moab:–(woman) of Moab, Moabite(-ish, -ss).
4126. מוֹבָא *mo-baw';* by transp. for 3996; an *entrance:*–coming.
4127. מוּג *moog;* a prim. root; to *melt,* i.e. lit. (to *soften,* flow down, *disappear*), or fig. (to *fear, faint*):–consume, dissolve, (be) faint.
4128. מוּד *mood;* a prim. root; to *shake:*–measure.
4129. מוֹדַע *mo-dah';* or rather מֹדָע *mo-daw';* from 3045; an *acquaintance:*–kinswoman.
4130. מוֹדַעַת *mo-dah'-ath;* from 3045; *acquaintance:*–kindred.
4131. מוֹט *mote;* a prim. root; to *waver;* by impl., to *slip, shake, fall:*–be carried, cast, be out of course, be fallen in decay, X exceedingly, fall(-ing down), be (re-)moved, be ready, shake, slide, slip.
4132. מוֹט *mote;* from 4131; a *wavering,* i.e. *fall;* by impl., a *pole* (as shaking); hence, a *yoke* (as essentially a bent pole):–bar, be moved, staff, yoke.
4133. מוֹטָה *mo-taw';* fem. of 4132; a *pole;* by impl., an *ox-bow;* hence, a *yoke* (either lit. or fig.):–bands, heavy, staves, yoke.
4134. מוּךְ *mook;* a prim. root; to *become thin,* i.e. (fig.) *be impoverished:*–be (waxen) poor(-er).
4135. מוּל *mool;* a prim. root; to *cut* short, i.e. *curtail* (spec. the prepuce, i.e. to *circumcise*); by impl., to *blunt;* fig., to *destroy:*–circumcise(-ing), selves), cut down (in pieces), destroy, X must needs.
4136. מוּל *mool;* or מוֹל (Deuteronomy 1:1) מוֹאל *mole;* or (Nehemiah 12:38) מֻל *mole;* or (Numbers 22:5) *mool;* from 4135; prop. *abrupt,* i.e. a *precipice;* by impl., the *front;* used only adv. (with prep. pref.) *opposite:*–(over) against, before, [fore-]front, from, [God-] ward, toward, with.
4137. מוֹלָדָה *mo-law-daw';* from 3205; *birth; Moladah,* a place in Pal.:–Moladah.
4138. מוֹלֶדֶת *mo-leh'-deth;* from 3205; *nativity* (pl. *birth-place*); by impl., *lineage, native country;* also *offspring, family:*–begotten, born, issue, kindred, nat.(-ity).
4139. מוּלָה *moo-law';* from 4135; *circumcision:*–circumcision.
4140. מוֹלִיד *mo-leed';* from 3205; *genitor; Molid,* an Isr.:–Molid.
4141. מוּסָב *moo-sawb';* from 5437; a *turn,* i.e. *circuit* (of a building):–winding about.
4142. מוּסַבָּה *moo-sab-baw';* or מֻסַבָּה *moo-sab-baw';* fem. of 4141; a *reversal,* i.e. the *backside* (of a gem), *fold* (of a double-leaved door), *transmutation* (of a name):–being changed, inclosed, be set, turning.
4143. מוּסָד *moo-sawd';* from 3245; a *foundation:*–foundation.
4144. מוֹסָד *mo-sawd';* from 3245; a *foundation:*–foundation.
4145. מוּסָדָה *moo-saw-daw';* fem. of 4143; a *foundation;* fig., an *appointment:*–foundation, grounded. Comp. 4328.
4146. מוֹסָדָה *mo-saw-daw';* מֹסָדָה *mo-saw-daw';* fem. of 4144; a *foundation:*–foundation.
4147. מוֹסֵר *mo-sare';* also (in pl.) fem. מוֹסֵרָה *mo-say-raw';* or מֹסְרָה *mo-ser-aw';* from 3256; prop. *chastisement,* i.e. (by impl.) a *halter;* fig., *restraint:*–band, bond.
4148. מוּסָר *moo-sawr';* from 3256; prop. *chastisement;* fig., *reproof, warning* or *instruction;* also *restraint:*–bond, chastening ([-eth]), chastisement, check, correction, discipline, doctrine, instruction, rebuke.
4149. מוֹסֵרָה *mo-say-raw';* or (pl.) מֹסְרוֹת *mo-ser-othe'* fem. of 4147; *correction* or *corrections; Moserah* or *Moseroth,* a place in the Desert:–Mosera, Moseroth.
4150. מוֹעֵד *mo-ade';* or מֹעֵד *mo-ade';* or (fem.) (2 Chronicles 8:13) מוֹעָדָה *mo-aw-daw';* from 3259; prop. an *appointment,* i.e. a fixed *time* or season; spec., a *festival;* conventionally a *year;* by impl., an *assembly* (as convened for a def. purpose); te. the *congregation;* by ext., the *place of meeting;* also a *signal* (as appointed beforehand):–appointed (sign, time), (place of, solemn) assembly, congregation, (set, solemn) feast, (appointed, due) season, solemn (-ity), synogogue, (set) time (appointed).
4151. מוֹעָד *mo-awd';* from 3259; prop. an *assembly* [as in 4150]; fig., a *troop:*–appointed time.
4152. מוּעָדָה *moo-aw-daw';* from 3259; an *appointed* place, i.e. *asylum:*–appointed.
4153. מוֹעַדְיָה *mo-ad-yaw';* from 4151 and 3050; *assembly of Jah; Moädjah,* an Isr.:–Moadiah. Comp. 4573.
4154. מוּעֶדֶת *moo-ay'-deth;* fem. pass.part. of 4571; prop. *made to slip,* i.e. *dislocated:*–out of joint.
4155. מוּעָף *moo-awf';* from 5774; prop. *covered,* i.e. *dark;* abstr., *obscurity,* i.e. *distress:*–dimness.
4156. מוֹעֵצָה *mo-ay-tsaw';* from 3289; a *purpose:*–counsel, device.
4157. מוּעָקָה *moo-aw-kaw';* from 5781; *pressure,* i.e. (fig.) *distress:*–affliction.
4158. מוֹפַעַת *mo-fah'-ath;* (Jer. 48:21 or מֵיפַעַת *may-fah'-ath;* or מֵפַעַת *may-fah'-ath;* from 3313; *illuminative; Mophaath* or *Mephaath,* a place in Pal.:–Mephaath.
4159. מוֹפֵת *mo-faith';* or מֹפֵת *mo-faith';* from 3302 in the sense of *conspicuousness;* a *miracle;* by impl., a *token* or *omen:*–miracle, sign, wonder(-ed at).
4160. מוּץ *moots;* a prim. root; to *press,* i.e. (fig.) to *oppress:*–extortioner.
4161. מוֹצָא *mo-tsaw';* or מֹצָא *mo-tsaw';* from 3318; a *going forth,* i.e. (the act) an *egress,* or (the place) an *exit;* hence, a *source* or *product;* spec., *dawn,* the *rising* of the sun (the *E.*), *exportation, utterance,* a *gate,* a *fountain,* a *mine,* a *meadow* (as producing grass):–brought out, bud, that which came

HEBREW

out, east, going forth, goings out, that which (thing that) is gone out, outgoing, proceeded out, spring, vein, [water-]course [springs].
4162. מוֹצָא *mo-tsaw';* the same as 4161; *Motsa,* the name of two Isr.:–Moza.
4163. מוֹצָאָה *mo-tsaw-aw';* fem. of 4161; a family *descent;* also a *sewer* (marg.; comp. 6675):–draught house; going forth.
4164. מוּצַק *moo-tsak';* or מוּצָק *moo-tsawk';* from 3332; *narrowness;* fig., *distress:*–anguish, is straitened, straitness.
4165. מוּצָק *moo-tsawk';* from 5694; prop. *fusion,* i.e. lit., a *casting* (of metal); fig., a *mass* (of clay):–casting, hardness.
4166. מוּצָקָה *moo-tsaw-kaw';* or מֻצָּקָה *moo-tsaw-kaw';* from 3332; prop. something *poured* out, i.e. a *casting* (of metal); by impl., a *tube* (as cast):–when it was cast, pipe.
4167. מוּק *mook;* a prim. root; to *jeer,* i.e. (intens.) *blaspheme:*–be corrupt.
4168. מוֹקֵד *mo-kade';* from 3344; a *fire* or *fuel;* abstr., a *conflagration:*–burning, hearth.
4169. מוֹקְדָה *mo-ked-aw';* fem. of 4168; *fuel:*–burning.
4170. מוֹקֵשׁ *mo-kashe';* or מֹקֵשׁ *mo-kashe';* from 3369; a *noose* (for catching animals) (lit. or fig.): by impl., a *hook* (for the nose):–be ensnared, gin, (is) snare(-d), trap.
4171. מוּר *moor;* a prim. root; to *alter;* by impl., to *barter,* to *dispose of:*–X at all, (ex-) change, remove.
4172. מוֹרָא *mo-raw';* or מֹרָא *mo-raw';* or (Ps. 9:20) מוֹרָה *mo-raw';* from 3372; *fear;* by impl., a *fearful* thing or deed:–dread, (that ought to be) fear(-ed), terribleness, terror.
4173. מוֹרַג *mo-rag';* or מֹרַג *mo-rag';* from an un. root mean. to *triturate;* a threshing *sledge:*–threshing instrument.
4174. מוֹרָד *mo-rawd';* from 3381; a *descent;* as arch., an ornament. *appendage,* perh. a *festoon:*–going down, steep place, thin work.
4175. מוֹרֶה *mo-reh';* from 3384; an *archer;* also *teacher* or *teaching;* also the *early rain* [see 3138]:–(early) rain.
4176. מוֹרֶה *mo-reh';* or מֹרֶה *mo-reh';* the same as 4175; *Moreh,* a Canaanite; also a hill (perh. named from him):–Moreh.
4177. מוֹרָה *mo-raw';* from 4171 in the sense of *shearing;* a *razor:*–razor.
4178. מוֹרָט *mo-rawt';* from 3399; *obstinate,* i.e. independent:–peeled.
4179. מוֹרִיָּה *mo-ree-yaw';* or מֹרִיָּה *mo-ree-yaw';* from 7200 and 3050; *seen of Jah; Morijah,* a hill in Pal.:–Moriah.
4180. מוֹרָשׁ *mo-rawsh';* from 3423; a *possession;* fig., *delight:*– possession, thought.
4181. מוֹרָשָׁה *mo-raw-shaw';* fem. of 4180; a *possession:*–heritage, inheritance, possession.
4182. מוֹרֶשֶׁת גַּת *mo-reh'-sheth gath;* from 3423 and 1661; *possession of Gath; Moresheth-Gath,* a place in Pal.:–Moresheth-gath.
4183. מוֹרַשְׁתִּי *mo-rash-tee';* patrial from 4182; a *Morashtite* or inh. of Moresheth-Gath:–Morashthite.
4184. מוּשׁ *moosh;* a prim. root; to *touch:*–feel, handle.
4185 מוּשׁ *moosh;* a prim. root (perh. rather the same as 4184 through the idea of receding by *contact*); to *withdraw* (both lit. and fig., whether intr. or trans.):–cease, depart, go back, remove, take away.
4186. מוֹשָׁב *mo-shawb';* or מֹשָׁב *mo-shawb';* from 3427; a *seat;* fig., a *site;* abstr., a *session;* by ext. an *abode* (the place or the time); by impl., *population:*–assembly, dwell in, dwelling(-place), wherein (that) dwelt (in), inhabited place, seat, sitting, situation, sojourning.
4187. מוּשִׁי *moo-shee';* or מֻשִּׁי *mush-shee';* from 4184; *sensitive; Mushi,* a Levite:–Mushi.
4188. מוּשִׁי *moo-shee';* patron. from 4187; a *Mushite* (coll.) or desc. of Mushi:–Mushites.
4189. מוֹשְׁכָה *mo-shek-aw';* act part. fem. of 4900; something *drawing,* i.e. (fig.) a *cord:*–band.
4190. מוֹשָׁעָה *mo-shaw-aw';* from 3467; *deliverance:*–salvation.
4191. מוּת *mooth;* a prim. root: to *die* (lit. or fig.); caus., to *kill:*–X at all, X crying, (be) dead (body, man, one), (put to, worthy of) death, destroy(-er), (cause to, be like to, must) die, kill, necro[-mancer], X must needs, slay, X surely, X very suddenly, X in [no] wise.
4192. מוּת *mooth;* (Psalm 48:14) or מוּת לַבֵּן *mooth lab-bane';* from 4191 and 1121 with the prep. and art. interp.; "*To die for the son*", prob. the title of a popular song:–death, Muthlabben.
4193. מוֹת *mohth* (Chald.); cor. to 4194; *death:*–death.
4194. מָוֶת *maw'-veth;* from 4191; *death* (nat. or violent); concr., the *dead,* their place or state (*hades*); fig., *pestilence, ruin:*–(be) dead([-ly]), death, die(-d).
4195. מוֹתָר *mo-thar';* from 3498; lit., *gain;* fig., *superiority:*–plenteousness, preeminence, profit.
4196. מִזְבֵּחַ *miz-bay'-akh;* from 2076; an *altar:*–altar.
4197. מֶזֶג *meh'-zeg;* from an un. root mean. to *mingle* (water with wine); *tempered* wine:–liquor.
4198. מָזֶה *maw-zeh';* from an un. root mean. to *suck* out; *exhausted:*–burnt.
4199. מִזָּה *miz-zaw';* prob. from an un. root mean. to *faint* with fear; *terror; Mizzah,* an Edomite:–Mizzah.
4200. מֶזֶו *meh'-zev;* prob. from an un. root mean. to *gather* in; a *granary:*–garner.
4201. מְזוּזָה *mez-oo-zaw';* or מְזֻזָה *mez-oo-zaw';* from the same as 2123; a *door-post* (as *prominent*):–(door, side) post.
4202. מָזוֹן *maw-zone';* from 2109; *food:*–meat, victual.
4203. מָזוֹן *maw-zone'* (Chald.); cor. to 4202:–meat
4204. מָזוֹר *maw-zore';* from 2114 in the sense of *turning aside* from truth; *treachery,* i.e. a *plot:*–wound.
4205. מָזוֹר *maw-zore';* or מָזֹר *maw-zore';* from 2115 in the sense of *binding* up; a *bandage,* i.e. remedy; hence, a *sore* (as needing a compress):–bound up, wound.
4206. מָזִיחַ *maw-zee'-akh;* or מֵזַח *may-zakh';* from 2118; a *belt* (as movable):–girdle, strength.
4207. מַזְלֵג *maz-layg';* or (fem.) מִזְלָגָה *miz-law-gaw';* from an un. root mean. to *draw* up; a *fork:*–fleshhook.
4208. מַזָּלָה *maz-zaw-law';* app. from 5140 in the sense of *raining;* a *constellation,* i.e. Zodiacal sign (perh. as affecting the weather):–planet. Comp. 4216.
4209. מְזִמָּה *mez-im-maw';* from 2161; a *plan,* usually evil (*machination*), sometimes good (*sagacity*):–(wicked) device, discretion, intent, witty invention, lewdness, mischievous (device), thought, wickedly.
4210. מִזְמוֹר *miz-more';* from 2167; prop. instrumental *music;* by impl., a *poem* set to notes:–psalm.
4211. מַזְמֵרָה *maz-may-raw';* from 2168; a *pruning-knife:*–pruning-hook.
4212. מְזַמְּרָה *mez-am-mer-aw';* from 2168; a *tweezer* (only in the pl.):–snuffers.
4213. מִזְעָר *miz-awr';* from the same as 2191; *fewness;* by impl., as sup. *diminutiveness:*–few, X very.
4214. מִזְרֶה *miz-reh';* from 2219; a winnowing *shovel* (as scattering the chaff):–fan.
4215. מְזָרֶה *mez-aw-reh';* app. from 2219; prop. a *scatterer,* i.e. the north *wind* (as dispersing clouds; only in pl.):–north.
4216. מַזָּרָה *maz-zaw-raw';* app. from 5144 in the sense of *distinction;* some noted *constellation* (only in the pl.), perh. coll., the *zodiac:*–Mazzoroth. Comp. 4208.
4217. מִזְרָח *miz-rawkh';* from 2224; *sunrise,* i.e. the east:–*east* (side, -ward), (sun-)rising (of the sun).
4218. מִזְרָע *miz-raw';* from 2232; a planted *field:*–thing sown.
4219 מִזְרָק *miz-rawk';* from 2236; a *bowl* (as if for sprinkling):–bason, bowl.
4220. מֵחַ *may'-akh;* from 4229 in the sense of *greasing; fat;* fig., *rich:*–fatling (one).
4221. מֹחַ *mo'-akh;* from the same as 4220; *fat,* i.e. marrow:–marrow.
4222. מָחָא *maw-khaw';* a prim. root; to *rub* or *strike* the hands together (in exultation):–clap.
4223. מְחָא *mekh-aw'* (Chald.); cor. to 4222; to *strike* in pieces; also to *arrest;* spec. to *impale:*–hang, smite, stay.
4224. מַחֲבֵא *makh-ab-ay';* or מַחֲבֹא *makh-ab-o';* from 2244; a *refuge:*–hiding (lurking) place.
4225. מַחְבֶּרֶת *makh-beh'-reth;* from 2266; a *junction,* i.e. seam or sewed piece:–coupling.
4226. מְחַבְּרָה *mekh-ab-ber-aw';* from 2266; a *joiner,* i.e. brace or cramp:–coupling, joining.
4227. מַחֲבַת *makh-ab-ath';* from the same as 2281; a *pan* for baking in:–pan.
4228. מַחֲגֹרֶת *makh-ag-o'-reth';* from 2296 a *girdle:*–girding.
4229. מָחָה *maw-khaw';* a prim. root; prop. to *stroke* or *rub;* by impl., to *erase;* also to *smooth* (as if with oil), i.e. *grease* or make fat; also to *touch,* i.e. reach to:–abolish, blot out, destroy, full of marrow, put out, reach unto, X utterly, wipe (away, out).
4230. מְחוּגָה *mekh-oo-gaw';* from 2328; an instrument for marking a circle, i.e. *compasses:*–compass.
4231. מָחוֹז *maw-khoze';* from an un. root mean. to *enclose;* a *harbor* (as *shut* in by the shore):–haven.
4232. מְחוּיָאֵל *mekh-oo-yaw-ale';* or מְחִיָּיאֵל *mekh-ee-yaw-ale';* from 4229 and 410; *smitten of God; Mechujael* or *Mechijael,* an antediluvian patriarch:–Mehujael.
4233. מַחֲוִים *makh-av-eem';* app. a patrial, but from an unknown place (in the pl. only for a sing.); a *Machavite* or inh. of some place named Machaveh:–Mahavite.
4234. מָחוֹל *maw-khole';* from 2342; a (round) *dance:*–dance(-cing).
4235. מָחוֹל *maw-khole';* the same as 4234; *dancing; Machol,* an Isr.:–Mahol.
4236. מַחֲזֶה *makh-az-eh'* from 2372; a *vision:*–vision.

4237. מֶחֱזָה *mekh-ez-aw';* from 2372; a *window:*–light.
4238. מַחֲזִיאוֹת *makh-az-ee-oth';* fem. pl. from 2372; *visions; Machazioth,* an Isr.:–Mahazioth.
4239. מְחִי *mekh-ee';* from 4229; a *stroke,* i.e. battering-*ram:*–engines.
4240. מְחִידָא *mek-ee-daw';* from 2330; *junction; Mechida,* one of the Nethinim:–Mehida.
4241. מִחְיָה *mikh-yaw';* from 2421; *preservation of life;* hence, *sustenance;* also the live flesh, i.e. the *quick:*–preserve life, quick, recover selves, reviving, sustenance, victuals.
4242. מְחִיר *mekk-eer';* from an un. root mean. to *buy; price, payment, wages:*–gain, hire, price, sold, worth.
4243. מְחִיר *mekh-eer';* the same as 4242; *price; Mechir,* an Isr.:–Mehir.
4244. מַחְלָה *makh-law';* from 2470; *sick-ness; Machlah,* the name app. of two Isr.s:–Mahlah.
4245. מַחֲלֶה *makh-al-eh';* or (fem.) מַחֲלָה *makk-al-aw';* from 2470; *sickness:*–disease, infirmity, sickness.
4246. מְחֹלָה *mek-o-law';* fem. of 4284; a *dance:*–company, dances(-cing).
4247. מְחִלָּה *mekh-il-law';* from 2490; a *cavern* (as if excavated):–cave.
4248. מַחְלוֹן *makh-lone';* from 2470; *sick; Machlon,* an Isr.:–Mahlon.
4249. מַחְלִי makh-lee'; from 2470; sick; *Machli,* the name of two Isr.:–Mahli.
4250. מַחְלִי *makh-lee';* patron. from 4249; a *Machlite* or (coll.) desc. of Machli:–Mahlites.
4251. מַחֲלֻי *makh-loo'-ee;* from 2470; a *disease:*–disease.
4252. מַחֲלָף *makh-al-awf';* from 2498; a (sacrificial) *knife* (as *gliding* through the flesh):–knife.
4253. מַחְלָפָה *makh-law-faw';* from 2498; a *ringlet* of hair (as *gliding* over each other):–lock.
4254. מַחֲלָצָה *makh-al-aw-tsaw';* from 2502; a *mantle* (as easily *drawn off*):–changeable suit of apparel, change of raiment.
4255. מַחְלְקָה *makh-lek-aw'* (Chald.); cor. to 4256; a *section* (of the Levites):–course.
4256. מַחֲלֹקֶת *makh-al-o'-keth;* from 2505; a *section* (of Levites, people or soldiers):–company, course, division, portion. See also 5555.
4257. מַחֲלַת *makh-al-ath';* from 2470; *sickness; Machalath,* prob. the title (initial word) of a popular song:–Mahalath.
4258. מָחֲלַת *makh-al-ath';* the same as 4257; *sickness; Machalath,* the name of an Ishmaelitess and of an Isr.s:–Mahalath.
4259. מְחֹלָתִי *mekh-o-law-thee';* patrial from 65; a *Mecholathite* or inh. of Abel-Mecholah:–Mecholathite.
4260. מַחֲמָאָה *makh-am-aw-aw';* a denom. from 2529; something *buttery* (i.e. unctuous and pleasant), as (fig.) *flattery:*–X than butter.
4261. מַחְמָד *makh-mawd';* from 2530; *delightful;* hence, a *delight,* i.e. obj. of affection or desire:–beloved, desire, goodly, lovely, pleasant (thing).
4262. מַחְמֻד *makh-mood';* or מַחְמוּד *makh-mood';* from 2530; *desired;* hence, a *valuable:*–pleasant thing.
4263. מַחְמָל *makh-mawl';* from 2550; prop. *sympathy;* (by paronomasia with 4261) *delight:*–pitieth.
4264. מַחֲנֶה *makh-an-eh';* from 2583; an *encampment* (of travellers or troops); hence, an *army,* whether lit. (of soldiers) or fig. (of dancers, angels, cattle, locusts, stars; or even the sacred courts):– army, band, battle, camp, company, drove, host, tents.
4265. מַחֲנֵה־דָן *makh-an-ay'-dawn;* from 4264 and 1835; *camp of Dan; Machaneh-Dan,* a place in Pal.:–Mahaneh-dan.
4266. מַחֲנַיִם *makh-an-ah'-yim;* dual of 4264; *double camp; Machanajim,* a place in Pal.:–Mahanaim.
4267. מַחֲנָק *makh-an-ak';* from 2614: *choking:*–strangling.
4268. מַחֲסֶה *makh-as-eh';* or מַחְסֶה *makh-seh';* from 2620; a *shelter* (lit. or fig.):–hope, (place of) refuge, shelter, trust.
4269. מַחְסוֹם *makh-sohm';* from 2629; a *muzzle:*–bridle.
4270. מַחְסוֹר *makh-sore';* or מַחְסֹר makh-sore'; from 2637; *deficiency;* hence, *impoverishment:*–lack, need, penury, poor, poverty, want.
4271. מַחְסֵיָה *makh-say-yaw';* from 4268 and 3050; *refuge of* (i.e. *in) Jah; Machsejah,* an Isr.:–Maaseiah.
4272. מָחַץ *maw-khats';* a prim. root; to *dash* asunder; by impl., to *crush, smash* or violently *plunge;* fig., to *subdue* or *destroy:*–dip, pierce (through), smite (through), strike through, wound.
4273. מַחַץ *makh'-ats;* from 4272; a *contusion:*–stroke.
4274. מַחְצֵב *makh-tsabe';* from 2672; prop. a *hewing;* concr., a *quarry:*–hewed(-n).
4275. מֶחֱצָה *mekh-ets-aw';* from 2673; a *halving:*–half.
4276. מַחֲצִית *makh-ats-eeth';* from 2673; a *halving* or the *middle:*–half (so much), mid[-day].
4277. מָחַק *maw-khak';* a prim. root; to *crush:*–smite off.
4278. מֶחְקָר *mekh-kawr';* from 2713; prop. *scrutinized,* i.e. (by impl.) a *recess:*–deep place.
4279. מָחָר *maw-khar';* prob. from 309; prop. *deferred,* i.e. the *morrow;* usually (adv.) *tomorrow;* indef., *hereafter:*–time to come, tomorrow.
4280. מַחֲרָאָה *makh-ar-aw-aw';* from the same as 2716; a *sink:*–draught house.
4281. מַחֲרֵשָׁה *makh-ar-ay-shaw';* from 2790; prob. a *pick*-axe:–mattock.
4282. מַחֲרֶשֶׁת *makh-ar-eh'-sheth;* from 2790; prob. a *hoe:*–share.
4283. מָחֳרָת *mokh-or-awth';* or מָחֳרָתָם (1 Sa. 30:17) *mokh-or-aw-thawm';* fem. from the same as 4279; the *morrow* or (adv.) *tomorrow:*–morrow, next day.
4284. מַחֲשָׁבָה *makh-ash-aw-baw';* or מַחֲשֶׁבֶת *makh-ash-eh'-beth;* from 2803; a *contrivance,* i.e. (concr.) a *texture, machine,* or (abstr.) *intention, plan* (whether bad, a *plot;* or good, *advice*):–cunning (work), curious work, device(-sed), imagination, invented, means, purpose, thought.
4285. מַחְשָׁךְ *makh-shawk';* from 2821; *darkness;* concr., a *dark place:*–dark(-ess, place).
4286. מַחְשֹׂף *makh-sofe';* from 2834; a *peeling:*–made appear.
4287. מַחַת *makh'-ath;* prob. from 4229; *erasure; Machath,* the name of two Isr.:–Mahath.
4288. מְחִתָּה *mekh-it-taw';* from 2846; prop. a *dissolution;* concr., a *ruin,* or (abstr.) *consternation:*–destruction, dismaying, ruin, terror.
4289. מַחְתָּה *makh-taw';* the same as 4288 in the sense of *removal;* a *pan* for live coals:–censer, firepan, snuffdish.
4290. מַחְתֶּרֶת *makh-teh'-reth;* from 2864; a *burglary;* fig., *unexpected examination:*–breaking up, secret search.
4291. מְטָא *met-aw'* (Chald.); or מְטָה *met-aw';* app. cor. to 4672 in the intr. sense of being found *present;* to *arrive, extend* or *happen:*–come, reach.
4292. מַטְאֲטֵא *mat-at-ay';* app. a denom. from 2916; a *broom* (as removing *dirt* [(comp. Engl. "to dust", i.e. remove dust]):–besom.
4293. מַטְבֵּחַ *mat-bay'-akh;* from 2873; *slaughter:*–slaughter.
4294. מַטֶּה *mat-teh';* or (fem.) מַטָּה *mat-taw';* from 5186; a *branch* (as *extending*); fig., a *tribe;* also a *rod,* whether for chastising (fig., *correction*), ruling (a *sceptre*), throwing (a *lance*), or walking (a *staff;* fig., a *support* of life, e.g. bread):–rod, staff, tribe.
4295. מַטָּה *mat'-taw;* from 5786 with directive enclitic appended; *downward, below* or *beneath;* often adv. with or without prefixes:–beneath, down(-ward), less, very low, under(-neath).
4296. מִטָּה *mit-taw';* from 5186; a *bed* (as *extended*) for sleeping or eating; by anal., a *sofa, litter* or *bier:*–bed(-[chamber]), bier.
4297. מֻטֶּה *moot-teh';* from 5186; a *stretching,* i.e. *distortion* (fig., *iniquity*):–perverseness.
4298. מֻטָּה *moot-taw';* from 5186; *expansion:*–stretching out.
4299. מַטְוֶה *mat-veh';* from 2901; something *spun:*–spun.
4300. מְטִיל *met-eel';* from 2904 in the sense of *hammering* out; an iron *bar* (as *forged*):–bar.
4301. מַטְמוֹן *mat-mone';* or מַטְמֹן *mat-mone';* or מַטְמֻן *mat-moon';* from 2934; a *secret* storehouse; hence, a *secreted* valuable (buried); gen. *money:*–hidden riches, (hid) treasure(-s).
4302. מַטָּע *mat-taw'* from 5193; something *planted,* i.e. the place (a *garden* or vineyard), or the thing (a *plant,* fig. or men); by impl., the act, *planting:*–plant(-ation, -ing).
4303. מַטְעָם *mat-am';* or (fem.) מַטְעַמָּה *mat-am-maw';* from 2938; a *delicacy:*–dainty (meat), savoury meat.
4304. מִטְפַּחַת *mit-pakh'-ath;* from 2946; a wide *cloak* (for a woman):–vail, wimple.
4305. מָטַר *maw-tar';* a prim. root; to *rain:*–(cause to) rain (upon).
4306. מָטָר *maw-tawr';* from 4305; *rain:*–rain.
4307. מַטָּרָא *mat-taw-raw';* or מַטָּרָה *mat-taw-raw';* from 5201; a *jail* (as a *guard*-house); also an *aim* (as being closely *watched*):–mark, prison.
4308. מַטְרֵד *mat-rade';* from 2956; *propulsive; Matred,* an Edomitess:–Matred.
4309. מַטְרִי *mat-ree';* from 4305; *rainy; Matri,* an Isr.:–Matri.
4310. מִי *me;* an interrog. pron. of persons, as 4100 is of things, *who?* (occasionally, by a peculiar idiom, of things); also (indef.) *whoever;* often used in oblique const. with pref. or suffix:–any (man), X he, X him, + O that! what, which, who(-m, -se, -soever), + would to God.
4311. מֵידְבָא *may-deb-aw';* from 4325 and 1679; *water of quiet; Medeba,* a place in Pal.:–Medeba.
4312. מֵידָד *may-dawd';* from 3032 in the sense of *loving; affectionate; Medad,* an Isr.:–Medad.
4313. מֵי הַיַּרְקוֹן *may hah"-ee-yar-kone';* from 4325 and 3420 with the art. interp.; *water of the yellowness; Me-haj-Jarkon,* a place in Pal.:–Me-jarkon.
4314. מֵי זָהָב *may zaw-hawb';* from 4325

and 2091, *water of gold; Me-Zahab,* an Edomite:–Mezahab.
4315. מֵיטָב *may-tawb';* from 3190; the *best part:*–best.
4316. מִיכָא *mee-kaw';* a var. for 4318; *Mica,* the name of two Isr.:–Micha.
4317. מִיכָאֵל *me-kaw-ale';* from 4310 and (the pref. der. from) 3588 and 410; *who* (is) *like God?; Mikael,* the name of an archangel and of nine Isr.:–Michael.
4318. מִיכָה *mee-kaw';* an abbrev. of 4320; *Micah,* the name of seven Isr.:–Micah, Micaiah, Michah.
4319. מִיכָהוּ *me-kaw'-hoo;* a contr.. for 4321; *Mikehu,* an Isr. prophet:–Micaiah (2 Chronicles 18:8).
4320. מִיכָיָה *me-kaw-yaw';* from 4310 and (the pref. der. from) 3588 and 3050; *who (is) like Jah?; Micajah,* the name of two Isr.:–Micah, Michaiah. Comp. 4318.
4321. מִיכָיְהוּ *me-kaw-yeh-hoo';* or (Jeremiah 36:11) מִכָיְהוּ *me-kaw-yeh-hoo';* abb. for 4322; *Mikajah,* the name of three Isr.:–Micah, Micaiah, Michaiah.
4322. מִיכָיָהוּ *me-kaw-yaw'-hoo;* for 4320; *Mikajah,* the name of an Isr. and an Isr.s:–Michaiah.
4323. מִיכָל *me-kawl';* from 3201; prop. a *container,* i.e. a *streamlet:*–brook.
4324. מִיכָל *me-kawl';* app. the same as 4323; *rivulet; Mikal,* Saul's daughter:–Michal.
4325. מַיִם *mah'-yim;* dual of a prim. noun (but used in a sing. sense); *water;* fig., *juice;* by euphem., *urine, semen:*–+ piss, wasting, water(-ing, [-course, -flood, -spring]).
4326. מִיָּמִן *me-yaw-meem';* a form for 4509; *Mijamin,* the name of three Isr.:–Miamin, Mijamin.
4327. מִין *meen;* from an un. root mean. to *portion* out; a *sort,* i.e. *species:*–kind. Comp. 4480.
4328. מְיֻסָּדָה *meh-yoos-saw-daw';* prop. fem. pass.part. of 3245; something *founded,* i.e. a *foundation:*–foundation.
4329. מֵיסָךְ *may-sawk';* from 5526; a *portico* (as *covered*):–covert.
4330. מִיץ *meets;* from 4160; *pressure:*–churning, forcing, wringing.
4331. מֵישָׁא *may-shaw';* from 4185; *departure; Mesha,* a place in Arabia; also an Isr.:–Mesha.
4332. מִישָׁאֵל *mee-shaw-ale';* from 4310 and 410 with the abb. insep. rel. [see 834] interp.; *who* (is) *what God* (is)?; *Mishaël,* the name of three Isr.:–Mishael.
4333. מִישָׁאֵל *mee-shaw-ale'* (Chald.); cor. to 4332; *Mishaël,* an Isr.:–Mishael.
4334. מִישׁוֹר *mee-shore';* or מִישֹׁר *mee-shore';* from 3474; a *level,* i.e. a *plain* (often used [with the art. pref.] as a prop. name of certain districts); fig., *concord;* also *straightness,* i.e. (fig.) *justice* (sometimes adv., *justly*):–equity, even place, plain, right(-eously), (made) straight, uprightness.
4335. מֵישַׁךְ *may-shak';* borrowed from 4336; *Meshak,* an Isr.:–Meshak.
4336. מֵישַׁךְ *may-shak'* (Chald.); of for. or. and doubtful significance; *Meshak,* the Babylonian name of 4333:–Meshak.
4337. מֵישָׁע *may-shah';* from 3467; *safety; Mesha,* an Isr.:–Mesha.
4338. מֵישַׁע *may-shaw';* a var. for 4337; *safety; Mesha,* a Moabite:–Mesha.
4339. מֵישָׁר *may-shawr';* from 3474; *evenness,* i.e. (fig.) *prosperity* or *concord;* also *straightness,* i.e. (fig.) *rectitude* (only in pl. with sing. sense; often adv.):–agreement, aright, that are equal, equity, (things that are) right(-eously, things), sweetly, upright(-ly, -ness).
4340. מֵיתָר *may-thar';* from 3498; a *cord* (of a tent) [comp. 3499] or *string* (of a bow):–cord, string.
4341. מַכְאֹב *mak-obe';* sometimes מַכְאוֹב *mak-obe';* also (fem. Isaiah 53:3*)* מַכְאֹבָה *mak-o-baw';* from 3510; *anguish* or (fig.) *affliction:*–grief, pain, sorrow.
4342. מַכְבִּיר *mak-beer';* trans. part. of 3527; *plenty:*–abundance.
4343. מַכְבֵּנָא *mak-bay-naw';* from the same as 3522; *knoll; Macbena,* a place in Pal. settled by him:–Machbenah.
4344. מַכְבַּנַּי *mak-ban-nah'-ee;* patrial from 4343; a *Macbannite* or nat. of Macbena:–Machbanai.
4345. מִכְבָּר *mak-bare';* from 3527 in the sense of *covering* [comp. 3531]; a *grate:*–grate.
4346. מַכְבָּר *mak-bawr';* from 3527 in the sense of *covering;* a cloth (as *netted* [comp. 4345]):–thick cloth.
4347. מַכָּה *mak-kaw';* or (masc.) מַכֶּה *makkeh';* (pl. only) from 5221; a *blow* (in 2 Chronicles 2:10, of the flail); by impl., a *wound;* fig., *carnage,* also *pestilence:*–beaten, blow, plague, slaughter, smote, X sore, stripe, stroke, wound([-ed]).
4348. מִכְוָה *mik-vaw';* from 3554; a *burn:*–that burneth, burning.
4349. מָכוֹן *maw-kone';* from 3559; prop. a *fixture,* i.e. a *basis;* gen. a *place,* esp. as an *abode:*–foundation, habitation, (dwelling-, settled) place.
4350. מְכוֹנָה *mek-o-naw';* or מְכֹנָה *mek-o-naw';* fem. of 4349; a *pedestal,* also a *spot:*–base.
4351. מְכוּרָה *mek-oo-raw';* or מְכֹרָה *mek-o-raw';* from the same as 3564 in the sense of *digging; origin* (as if a mine):–birth, habitation, nativity.
4352. מָכִי *maw-kee';* prob. from 4134; *pining; Maki,* an Isr.:–Machi.
4353. מָכִיר *maw-keer';* from 4376; *salesman; Makir,* an Isr.:–Machir.
4354. מָכִירִי *maw-kee-ree';* patron. from 4353; a *Makirite* or descend. of Makir:–of Machir.
4355. מָכַךְ *maw-kak';* a prim. root; to *tumble* (in ruins); fig., to *perish:*–be brought low, decay.
4356. מִכְלָאָה *mik-law-aw';* or מִכְלָה *mik-law';* from 3607; a *pen* (for flocks):–([sheep-]) fold. Comp. 4357.
4357. מִכְלָה *mik-law';* from 3615; *completion* (in pl. concr. adv., *wholly*):–perfect. Comp. 4356.
4358. מִכְלוֹל *mik-lole';* from 3634; *perfection* (i.e. concr. adv., *splendidly*):–most gorgeously, all sorts.
4359. מִכְלָל *mik-lawl';* from 3634; *perfection* (of beauty):–perfection.
4360. מִכְלֻל *mik-lool';* from 3634; something *perfect,* i.e. a splendid *garment:*–all sorts.
4361. מַכֹּלֶת *mak-ko'-leth;* from 398; *nourishment:*–food.
4362. מִכְמָן *mik-man';* from the same as 3646 in the sense of *hiding; treasure* (as *hidden*):–treasure.
4363 מִכְמָס *mik-maws';* (Ezra 2:27; Ne. 7:31) or מִכְמָשׁ *mik-mawsh';* or (Ne. 11:31), מִכְמַשׁ *mik-mash';* from 3647; *hidden; Mikmas* or *Mikmash,* a place in Pal.:–Mikmas, Mikmash.
4364. מַכְמָר *mak-mawr';* or מִכְמֹר *mik-more';* from 3648 in the sense of *blackening* by heat; a (hunter's) *net* (as *dark* from concealment):–net.
4365. מִכְמֶרֶת *mik-meh'-reth;* or מִכְמֹרֶת *mik-mo'-reth;* fem. of 4364; a (fisher's) *net:*–drag, net.
4366. מִכְמְתָת *mik-meth-awth';* app. from an un. root mean. to *hide; concealment; Mikmethath,* a place in Pal.:–Michmethath.
4367. מַכְנַדְבַי *mak-nad-bah'-ee;* from 4100 and 5068 with a particle interp.; *what* (is) *like* (a) *liberal* (man)?; *Maknadbai,* an Isr.:–Machnadebai.
4368. מְכֹנָה *mek-o-naw';* the same as 4350; a *base; Mekonah,* a place in Pal.:–Mekonah.
4369. מְכֻנָה *mek-oo-naw';* the same as 4350; a *spot:*–base.
4370. מִכְנָס *mik-nawce';* from 3647 in the sense of *hiding;* (only in dual) *drawers* (from *concealing* the private parts):–breeches.
4371. מֶכֶס *meh'-kes;* prob. from an un. root mean. to *enumerate;* an *assessment* (as based upon a *census*):–tribute.
4372. מִכְסֶה *mik-seh';* from 3680; a *covering,* i.e. weather-*boarding:*–covering.
4373. מִכְסָה *mik-saw';* fem. of 4371; an *enumeration;* by impl., a *valuation:*–number, worth.
4374. מְכַסֶּה *mek-as-seh';* from 3680; a *covering,* i.e. *garment;* spec., a *coverlet* (for a bed), an *awning* (from the sun); also the *omentum* (as covering the intestines):–clothing, to cover, that which covereth.
4375. מַכְפֵּלָה *mak-pay-law';* from 3717; a *fold; Makpelah,* a place in Pal.:–Machpelah.
4376. מָכַר *maw-kar';* a prim. root; to *sell,* lit. (as merchandise, a daughter in marriage, into slavery), or fig. (to *surrender*):–X at all, sell (away, -er, self).
4377. מֶכֶר *meh'-ker;* from 4376; *merchandise;* also *value:*–pay, price, ware.
4378. מַכָּר *mak-kawr';* from 5234; an *acquaintance:*–acquaintance.
4379. מִכְרֶה *mik-reh';* from 3738; a *pit* (for salt):–[salt-]pit.
4380. מְכֵרָה *mek-ay-raw';* prob. from the same as 3564 in the sense of *stabbing;* a *sword:*–habitation.
4381. מִכְרִי *mik-ree';* from 4376; *salesman; Mikri,* an Isr.:–Michri.
4382. מְכֵרָתִי *mek-ay-raw-thee';* patrial from an un. name (the same as 4380) of a place in Pal.: a *Mekerathite,* or inh. of Mekerah:–Mecherathite.
4383. מִכְשׁוֹל *mik-shole';* or מִכְשֹׁל *mik-shole';* masc. from 3782; a *stumbling-block,* lit. or fig. (*obstacle, enticement* [spec. an idol], *scruple*):–caused to fall, offence, X [no-]thing offered, ruin, stumbling-block.
4384. מַכְשֵׁלָה *mak-shay-law';* fem. from 3782; a *stumbling-block,* but only fig. (*fall, enticement* [idol]):–ruin, stumbling-block.
4385. מִכְתָּב *mik-tawb';* from 3789; a thing *written,* the *characters,* or a *document* (letter, copy, edict, poem):–writing.
4386. מְכִתָּה *mek-it-taw';* from 3807; a *fracture:*–bursting.
4387. מִכְתָּם *mik-tawm';* from 3799; an *engraving,* i.e. (te.) a *poem:*–Michtam.
4388. מַכְתֵּשׁ *mak-taysh';* from 3806; a *mortar;* by anal., a *socket* (of a tooth):–hollow place, mortar.
4389. מַכְתֵּשׁ *mak-taysh';* the same as 4388;

dell; the *Maktesh,* a place in Jerus.:–Maktesh.

4390. מָלֵא *maw-lay';* or (Es. 7:5) מָלָא *maw-law';* a prim. root, to *fill* or (intr.) *be full* of, in a wide appl. (lit. and fig.):–accomplish, confirm, + consecrate, be at an end, be expired, be fenced, fill, fulfil, (be, become, X draw, give in, go) full(-ly, -ly set, tale), [over-] flow, ullness, furnish, gather (selves, together), presume, replenish, satisfy, set, space, take a [hand-] full, + have wholly.

4391. מְלָא *mel-aw'* (Chald.); cor. to 4390; to *fill:*–fill, be full.

4392. מָלֵא *maw-lay';* from 4390; *full* (lit. or fig.) or *filling* (lit.); also (concr.) *fulness;* adv., *fully:*–X she that was with child, fill(-ed, -ed with), full(-ly), multitude, as is worth.

4393. מְלֹא *mel-o';* rarely מְלוֹא *mel-o';* or (Ezekiel 41:8), מְלוֹ *mel-o';* from 4390; *fullness* (lit. or fig.):–X all along, X all that is (there-)in, fill, (X that whereof...was) full, fullness, [hand-] full, multitude.

4394. מִלֻּא *mil-loo';* from 4390; a *fulfilling* (only in pl.), i.e. (lit.) a *setting* (of gems), or (te.) *consecration* (also concr., a dedicatory *sacrifice*):–consecration, be set.

4395. מְלֵאָה *mel-ay-aw';* fem. of 4392; something *fulfilled,* i.e. *abundance* (of produce):–(first of ripe) fruit, fullness.

4396. מִלֻּאָה *mil-loo-aw';* fem. of 4394; a *filling,* i.e. *setting* (of gems):–inclosing, setting.

4397. מַלְאָךְ *mal-awk';* from an un. root mean. to *despatch* as a deputy; a *messenger;* spec., of God, i.e. an *angel* (also a prophet, priest or teacher):–ambassador, angel, king, messenger.

4398. מַלְאַךְ *mal-ak'* (Chald.); cor. to 4397; an *angel:*–angel.

4399. מְלָאכָה *mel-aw-kaw';* from the same as 4397; prop. *deputyship,* i.e. ministry; gen., *employment* (never servile) or work (abstr. or concr.); also *property* (as the result of *labor*):–business, + cattle, + industrious, occupation, (+ -pied), + officer, thing (made), use, (manner of) work([-man], -manship).

4400. מַלְאֲכוּת *mal-ak-ooth';* from the same as 4397; a *message:*–message.

4401. מַלְאָכִי *mal-aw-kee';* from the same as 4397; *ministrative; Malaki,* a prophet:–Malachi.

4402. מִלֵּאת *mil-layth';* from 4390; *fulness,* i.e. (concr.) a *plump* socket (of the eye):–X fitly.

4403. מַלְבּוּשׁ *mal-boosh';* or מַלְבֻּשׁ *mal-boosh';* from 3847; a *garment,* or (coll.) *clothing:*–apparel, raiment, vestment.

4404. מַלְבֵּן *mal-bane';* from 3835 (denom.); a *brick-kiln:*–brickkiln.

4405. מִלָּה *mil-law';* from 4448 (pl. masc. as if from מִלֶּה *mil-leh';* a word; coll., a *discourse;* fig., a *topic:*–+ answer, by-word, matter, any thing (what) to say, to speak(-ing), speak, talking, word.

4406. מִלָּה *mil-law'* (Chald.); cor. to 4405; a *word, command, discourse,* or *subject:*–commandment, matter, thing word.

4407. מִלּוֹא *mil-lo';* or (2 Kings 12:20) מִלֹּא *mil-lo';* from 4390; a *rampart* (as *filled* in), i.e. the *citadel:*–Millo. See also 1037.

4408. מַלּוּחַ *mal-loo'-akh;* from 4414; *sea-purslain* (from its *saltness*):–mallows.

4409. מַלּוּךְ *mal-luke';* or (Ne. 12:14) מְלוּכִי *mal-loo-kee';* from 4427; *remnant; Malluk,* the name of five Isr.:–Malluch, Melichu .

4410. מְלוּכָה *mel-oo-kaw';* fem. Pass.part. of 4427; something *ruled,* i.e. a *realm:*–kingdom, king's, X royal.

4411. מָלוֹן *maw-lone';* from 3885; a *lodgment,* i.e. *caravanserai* or *encampment:*–inn, place where...lodge, lodging (place).

4412. מְלוּנָה *mel-oo-naw';* fem. from 3885; a *hut,* a *hammock:*–cottage, lodge.

4413. מַלּוֹתִי *mal-lo'-thee;* app. from 4448; *I have talked* (i.e. *loquacious*):–*Mallothi,* an Isr.:–Mallothi.

4414. מָלַח *maw-lakh';* a prim. root; prop. to *rub* to pieces or pulverize; intr., to *disappear* as dust; also (as denom. from 4417) to *salt* whether internally (to *season* with salt) or ext. (to *rub* with salt):–X at all, salt, season, temper together, vanish away.

4415. מְלַח *mel-akh'* (Chald.); cor. to 4414; to *eat* salt, i.e. (gen.) *subsist:*–+ have maintenance.

4416. מְלַח *mel-akh'* (Chald.); from 4415; *salt:*–+ maintenance, salt.

4417. מֶלַח *meh'-lakh;* from 4414; prop. *powder,* i.e. (spec.) *salt* (as easily pulverized and dissolved:–salt([-pit]).

4418. מָלָח *maw-lawkh';* from 4414 in its or. sense; a *rag* or old garment:–rotten rag.

4419. מַלָּח *mal-lawkh';* from 4414 in its second. sense; a *sailor* (as following "the salt"):–mariner.

4420. מְלֵחָה *mel-ay-khaw';* from 4414 (in its denom. sense); prop. *salted* (i.e. land [776 being understood]), i.e. a *desert:*–barren land(-ness), salt [land].

4421. מִלְחָמָה *mil-khaw-maw';* from 3898 (in the sense of *fighting*); a *battle* (i.e. the *engagement*); gen., *war* (i.e. *warfare*):–battle, fight(-ing), war([-rior]).

4422. מָלַט *maw-lat';* a prim. root; prop. to *be smooth,* i.e. (by impl.) to *escape* (as if by *slipperiness*); caus., to *release* or *rescue;* spec., to *bring forth* young, *emit* sparks:–deliver (self), escape, lay, leap out, let alone, let go, preserve, save, X speedily, X surely.

4423. מֶלֶט *meh'-let;* from 4422, *cement* (from its plastic *smoothness*):–clay.

4424. מְלַטְיָה *mel-at-yaw';* from 4423 and 3050; (whom) *Jah has delivered; Melatjah,* a Gibeonite:–Melatiah.

4425. מְלִילָה *mel-ee-law';* from 4449 (in the sense of *cropping* [comp. 4135]); a *head* of grain (as *cut* off):–ear.

4426. מְלִיצָה *mel-ee-tsaw';* from 3887; an *aphorism;* also a *satire:*–interpretation, taunting.

4427. מָלַךְ *maw-lak';* a prim. root; to *reign;* inceptively, to *ascend* the *throne;* caus., to *induct* into royalty; hence (by impl.) to *take counsel:*–consult, X indeed, be (make, set a, set up) king, be (make) queen, (begin to, make to) reign(-ing), rule, X surely.

4428. מֶלֶךְ *meh'-lek;* from 4427; a *king:*–king, royal.

4429. מֶלֶךְ *meh'-lek;* the same as 4428; *king; Melek,* the name of two Isr.:–Melech, Hammelech [*by incl. the art.*].

4430. מֶלֶךְ *meh'-lek* (Chald.); cor. to 4428; a *king:*–king, royal.

4431. מְלַךְ *mel-ak'* (Chald.); from a root cor. to 4427 in the sense of *consultation: advice:*–counsel.

4432. מֹלֶךְ *mo'-lek;* from 4427; *Molek* (i.e. king), the chief deity of the Ammonites:–Molech. Comp. 4445.

4433. מַלְכָּא *mal-kaw'* (Chald.); cor. to 4436; a *queen:*–queen.

4434. מַלְכֹּדֶת *mal-ko'-deth;* from 3920; a *snare:*–trap.

4435. מִלְכָּה *mil-kaw';* a form of 4436; *queen; Milcah,* the name of a Hebrewess and of an Isr.:–Milcah.

4436. מַלְכָּה *mal-kaw';* fem. of 4428; a *queen:*–queen.

4437. מַלְכוּ *mal-koo'* (Chald.); cor. to 4438; *dominion* (abstr. or concr.):–kingdom, kingly, realm, reign.

4438. מַלְכוּת *mal-kooth';* or מַלְכֻת *mal-kooth';* or (in pl.) מַלְכֻיָּה *mal-koo-yah';* from 4427; a *rule;* concr., a *dominion:*–empire, kingdom, realm, reign, royal.

4439. מַלְכִּיאֵל *mal-kee-ale';* from 4428 and 410; *king of* (i.e. appointed by) *God; Malkiël,* an Isr.:–Malchiel.

4440. מַלְכִּיאֵלִי *mal-kee-ay-lee';* patron. from 4439; a *Malkiëlite* or desc. of Malkiel:–Malchielite.

4441. מַלְכִּיָּה *mal-kee-yaw';* or (Jer. 38:6), מַלְכִּיָּהוּ *mal-kee-yaw'-hoo;* from 4428 and 3050; *king of* (i.e. appointed by) *Jah; Malkijah,* the name of ten Isr.:–Malchiah, Malchijah.

4442. מַלְכִּי־צֶדֶק *mal-kee-tseh'-dek;* from 4428 and 6664; *king of right; Malki-Tsedek,* an early king in Pal.:–Melchizedek.

4443. מַלְכִּירָם *mal-kee-rawm';* from 4428 and 7311; *king of* a *high one* (i.e. of exaltation); *Malkiram,* an Isr.:–Malchiram.

4444. מַלְכִּישׁוּעַ *mal-kee-shoo'-ah;* from 4428 and 7769; *king of wealth; Malkishua,* an Isr.:–Malchishua.

4445. מַלְכָּם *mal-kawm';* or מִלְכּוֹם *mil-kome';* from 4428 for 4432; *Malcam* or *Milcom,* the national idol of the Ammonites:–Malcham, Milcom.

4446. מְלֶכֶת *mel-eh'-keth;* from 4427; a *queen:*–queen.

4447. מֹלֶכֶת *mo-leh'-keth;* fem. act.part. of 4427; *queen; Moleketh,* an Isr.s:–Hammoleketh [*incl. the art.*].

4448. מָלַל *maw-lal';* a prim. root; to *speak* (mostly poetical) or *say:*–say, speak, utter.

4449. מְלַל *mel-al'* (Chald.); cor. to 4448; to *speak:*–say, speak(-ing).

4450. מִלֲלַי *mee-lal-ah'-ee;* from 4448; *talkative; Milalai,* an Isr.:–Milalai.

4451. מַלְמָד *mal-mawd';* from 3925; a *goad* for oxen:–goad.

4452. מָלַץ *maw-lats';* a prim. root; to *be smooth,* i.e. (fig.) *pleasant:*–be sweet.

4453. מֶלְצַר *mel-tsawr';* of Pers. der.; the *butler* or other officer in the Babylonian court:–Melzar.

4454. מָלַק *maw-lak';* a prim. root; to *crack* a joint; by impl., to *wring* –wring off.

4455. מַלְקוֹחַ *mal-ko'-akh;* from 3947; trans. (in dual) the *jaws* (as taking food); intr., *spoil* [and captives] (as taken):–booty, jaws, prey.

4456. מַלְקוֹשׁ *mal-koshe';* from 3953; the spring *rain* (comp. 3954); fig., *eloquence:*–latter rain.

4457. מֶלְקָח *mel-kawkh';* or מַלְקָח *mal-kawkh';* from 3947; (only in dual) *tweezers:*–snuffers, tongs.

4458. מֶלְתָּחָה *mel-taw-khaw';* from an un. root mean. to *spread* out; a *wardrobe* (i.e. room where clothing is *spread*):–vestry.

4459. מַלְתָּעָה *mal-taw-aw';* transp. for 4973; a *grinder,* i.e. back *tooth:*–great tooth.

4460. מַמְּגֻרָה *mam-meg-oo-raw';* from 4048 (in the sense of *depositing*); a *granary:*–barn.

4461. מֵמַד *may-mad';* from 4058; a *measure:*–

HEBREW

measure.
4462. מְמוּכָן *mem-oo-kawn';* or (transp.) (Es. 1:16) מוֹמְכָן *mo-moo-kawn';* of Pers. der.; *Memucan* or *Momucan,* a Pers. satrap:–Memucan.
4463. מָמוֹת *maw-mothe';* from 4191; a mortal *disease;* concr., a *corpse:*–death.
4464. מַמְזֵר *mam-zare';* from an un. root mean. to *alienate;* a *mongrel,* i.e. born of a Jewish father and a heathen mother:–bastard.
4465. מִמְכָּר *mim-kawr';* from 4376; *merchandise;* abstr., a *selling:*–X ought, (that which cometh of) sale, that which...sold, ware.
4466. מִמְכֶּרֶת *mim-keh'-reth;* fem. of 4465; a *sale:*–+ sold as.
4467. מַמְלָכָה *mam-law-kaw';* from 4427; *dominion,* i.e. (abstr.) the estate (*rule*) or (concr.) the country (*realm*):–kingdom, king's, reign, royal.
4468. מַמְלָכוּת *mam-law-kooth';* a form of 4467 and equiv. to it:–kingdom, reign.
4469. מַמְסָךְ *mam-sawk';* from 4537; *mixture,* i.e. (spec.) wine *mixed* (with water or spices):–drink-offering, mixed wine.
4470. מֶמֶר *meh'-mer;* from an un. root mean. to *grieve; sorrow:*–bitterness.
4471. מַמְרֵא *mam-ray';* from 4754 (in the sense of *vigor*); *lusty; Mamre,* an Amorite:–Mamre.
4472. מַמְרֹר *mam-rore';* from 4843; a *bitterness,* i.e. (fig.) calamity:–bitterness.
4473. מִמְשַׁח *mim-shakh';* from 4886, in the sense of *expansion; outspread* (i.e. with outstretched wings):–anointed.
4474. מִמְשָׁל *mim-shawl';* from 4910; a *ruler* or (abstr.) *rule:*–dominion, that ruled.
4475. מֶמְשָׁלָה *mem-shaw-law';* fem. of 4474; *rule;* also (concr. in pl.) a *realm* or a *ruler:*–dominion, government, power, to rule.
4476. מִמְשָׁק *mim-shawk';* from the same as 4943; a *possession:*–breeding.
4477. מַמְתַּק *mam-tak';* from 4985; something *sweet* (lit. or fig.):–(most) sweet.
4478. מָן *mawn;* from 4100; lit., a *whatness* (so to speak), i.e. *manna* (so called from the question about it):–manna.
4479. מָן *mawn* (Chald.); from 4101; *who* or *what* (prop. interrog., hence, also indef. and rel.):–what, who(-msoever, + -so).
4480. מִן *min;* or מִנִּי *min-nee';* or (constr. pl.) מִנֵּי *min-nay';* (Isaiah 30:11); for 4482; prop. a *part* of; hence (prep.), *from* or *out of* in many senses (as follows):–above, after, among, at, because of, by (reason of), from (among), in, X neither, X nor, (out) of, over, since, X then, through, X whether, with.
4481. מִן *min* (Chald.); cor. to 4480:–according, after, + because, + before, by, for, from, X him, X more than, (out) of, part, since, X these, to, upon, + when.
4482. מֵן *mane;* from an un. root mean. to *apportion;* a *part;* hence, a mus. *chord* (as parted into strings):–in [the same] (Psalm 68:23), stringed instrument (Psalm 150:4), whereby (Psalm 45:8).
4483. מְנָא *men-aw'* (Chald.); or מְנָה *men-aw'* (Chald.); cor. to 4487; to *count, appoint:*–number, ordain, set.
4484. מְנֵא *men-ay'* (Chald.); pass.part. of 4483; *numbered:*–Mene.
4485. מַנְגִּינָה *man-ghee-naw';* from 5059; a *satire:*–music.
4486. מַנְדַּע *man-dah'* (Chald.); cor. to 4093; *wisdom* or *intelligence:*–knowledge, reason, understanding.
4487. מָנָה *maw-naw';* a prim. root; prop. to *weigh* out; by impl., to *allot* or constitute officially; also to *enumerate* or enroll:–appoint, count, number, prepare, set, tell.
4488. מָנֶה *maw-neh';* from 4487; prop. a fixed *weight* or measured amount, i.e. (te.) a *maneh* or mina:–maneh, pound.
4489. מֹנֶה *mo-neh';* from 4487; prop. something *weighed* out, i.e. (fig.) a *portion* of time, i.e. an *instance:*–time.
4490. מָנָה *maw-naw';* from 4487; prop. something *weighed* out, i.e. (gen.) a *division;* spec. (of food) a *ration;* also a *lot:*–such things as belonged, part, portion.
4491. מִנְהָג *min-hawg';* from 5090; the *driving* (of a chariot):–driving.
4492. מִנְהָרָה *min-haw-raw';* from 5102; prop. a *channel* or fissure, i.e. (by impl.) a *cavern:*–den.
4493. מָנוֹד *maw-node';* from 5110 a *nodding* or *toss* (of the head in derision):–shaking.
4494. מָנוֹחַ *maw-no'-akh;* from 5117; *quiet,* i.e. (concr.) a *settled spot*, or (fig.) a *home:*–(place of) rest.
4495. מָנוֹחַ *maw-no'-akh;* the same as 4494; *rest; Manoäch,* an Isr.:–Manoah.
4496. מְנוּחָה *men-oo-khaw';* or מְנֻחָה *men-oo-khaw';* fem. of 4495; *repose* or (adv.) *peacefully;* fig., *consolation* (spec., *matrimony*); hence (concr.) an *abode:*–comfortable, ease, quiet, rest(-ing place), still.
4497. מָנוֹן *maw-nohn';* from 5125; a *continuator,* i.e. *heir:*–son.
4498. מָנוֹס *maw-noce';* from 5127; a *retreat* (lit. or fig.); abstr., a *fleeing:*–X apace, escape, way to flee, flight, refuge.
4499. מְנוּסָה *men-oo-saw';* or מְנֻסָה *men-oo-saw';* fem. of 4498; *retreat:*–fleeing, flight.
4500. מָנוֹר *maw-nore';* from 5214; a *yoke* (prop. for *ploughing*), i.e. the *frame* of a loom:–beam.
4501. מְנוֹרָה *men-o-raw';* or מְנֹרָה *men-o-raw';* fem. of 4500 (in the or. sense of 5216); a *chandelier:*–candlestick.
4502. מִנְּזָר *min-ez-awr';* from 5144; a *prince:*–crowned.
4503. מִנְחָה *min-khaw';* from an un. root mean. to *apportion,* i.e. *bestow;* a *donation;* euphem., *tribute;* spec. a sacrificial *offering* (usually bloodless and voluntary):–gift, oblation, (meat) offering, present, sacrifice.
4504. מִנְחָה *min-khaw'* (Chald.); cor. to 4503; a sacrificial *offering:*–oblation, meat offering.
4505. מְנַחֵם *men-akh-ame';* from 5162; *comforter; Menachem,* an Isr.:–Menahem.
4506. מָנַחַת *maw-nakh'-ath;* from 5117; *rest; Manachath,* the name of an Edomite and of a place in Moab:–Manahath.
4507. מְנִי *men-ee';* from 4487; the *Apportioner,* i.e. Fate (as an idol):–number.
4508. מִנִּי *min-nee';* of for. der.; *Minni,* an Armenian province:–Minni.
4509. מִנְיָמִין *min-yaw-meen';* from 4480 and 3225; *from* (the) *right hand; Minjamin,* the name of two Isr.:–Miniamin. Comp. 4326.
4510. מִנְיָן *min-yawn'* (Chald.); from 4483; *enumeration:*–number.
4511. מִנִּית *min-neeth';* from the same as 4482; *enumeration; Minnith,* a place E. of the Jordan:–Minnith.
4512. מִנְלֶה *min-leh';* from 5239; *completion,* i.e. (in produce) *wealth:*–perfection.
4513. מָנַע *maw-nah';* a prim. root; to *debar* (neg. or pos.) from benefit or injury:–deny, keep (back), refrain, restrain, withhold.
4514. מַנְעוּל *man-ool';* or מַנְעֻל *man-ool';* from 5274; a *bolt:*–lock.
4515. מִנְעָל *man-awl';* from 5274; a *bolt:*–shoe.
4516. מַנְעַם *man-am';* from 5276; a *delicacy:*–dainty.
4517. מְנַעַנְעַ *men-ah-nah';* from 5128; a *sistrum* (so called from its *rattling* sound):–cornet.
4518. מְנַקִּית *men-ak-keeth';* from 5352; a *sacrificial basin* (for holding blood):–bowl.
4519. מְנַשֶּׁה *men-ash-sheh';* from 5382; *causing to forget; Menashsheh,* a grandson of Jacob, also the tribe descended from him, and its territory:–Manasseh.
4520. מְנַשִּׁי *men-ash-shee';* from 4519; a *Menashshite* or desc. of Menashsheh:–of Manasseh, Manassites.
4521. מְנָת *men-awth';* from 4487; an *allotment* (by courtesy, law or providence):–portion.
4522. מַס *mas;* or מִס *mees;* from 4549; prop. a burden (as causing to *faint*), i.e. a *tax* in the form of forced *labor:*–discomfited, levy, task [-master], tribute(-tary).
4523. מָס *mawce;* from 4549; *fainting,* i.e. (fig.) *disconsolate:*–is afflicted.
4524. מֵסַב *may-sab';* pl. masc. מְסִבִּים *mes-ib-beem';* or fem. מְסִבּוֹת *mes-ib-bohth';* from 5437; a *divan* (as enclosing the room); abstr. (adv.) *around:*–that compass about, (place) round about, at table.
4525. מַסְגֵּר *mas-gare';* from 5462; a *fastener,* i.e. (of a person) a *smith,* (of a thing) a *prison:*–prison, smith.
4526. מִסְגֶּרֶת *mis-gheh'-reth;* from 5462; something *enclosing,* i.e. a *margin* (of a region, of a panel); concr., a *stronghold:*–border, close place, hole.
4527. מַסַּד *mas-sad';* from 3245; a *foundation:*–foundation.
4528. מִסְדְּרוֹן *mis-der-ohn';* from the same as 5468; a *colonnade* or internal portico (from its *rows* of pillars):–porch.
4529. מָסָה *maw-saw';* a prim. root; to *dissolve:*–make to consume away, (make to) melt, water.
4530. מִסָּה *mis-saw';* from 4549 (in the sense of *flowing*); *abundance,* i.e. (adv.) *liberally:* tribute.
4531. מַסָּה *mas-saw';* from 5254; a *testing,* of men (judicial) or of God (querulous):–temptation, trial.
4532. מַסָּה *mas-saw';* the same as 4531; *Massah,* a place in the Desert:–Massah.
4533. מַסְוֶה *mas-veh';* app. from an un. root mean. to *cover;* a *veil:*–vail.
4534. מְסוּכָה *mes-oo-kaw';* for 4881; a *hedge:*–thorn hedge.
4535. מַסָּח *mas-sawkh';* from 5255 in the sense of *staving* off; a *cordon,* (adv.) or (as a) military *barrier:*–broken down.
4536. מִסְחָר *mis-khawr';* from 5503; *trade:*–traffic.
4537. מָסַךְ *maw-sak';* a prim. root; to *mix,* esp. wine (with spices):–mingle.
4538. מֶסֶךְ *meh'-sek;* from 4537; a *mixture,* i.e. of wine with spices:–mixture.
4539. מָסָךְ *maw-sawk';* from 5526; a *cover,* i.e. *veil:*–covering, curtain, hanging.
4540. מְסֻכָּה *mes-ook-kaw';* from 5526; a *covering,* i.e. garniture:–covering.
4541. מַסֵּכָה *mas-say-kaw';* from 5258; prop.

a *pouring* over, i.e. *fusion* of metal (esp. a *cast* image); by impl., a *libation,* i.e. league; concr. a *coverlet* (as if *poured* out):–covering, molten (image), vail.

4542. מִסְכֵּן *mis-kane';* from 5531; *indigent:*–poor (man).

4543. מִסְכְּנָה *mis-ken-aw';* by transp. from 3664; a *magazine:*–store (-house), treasure.

4544. מִסְכֵּנֻת *mis-kay-nooth';* from 4542; *indigence:*–scarceness.

4545. מַסֶּכֶת *mas-seh'-keth;* from 5259 in the sense of *spreading* out; something *expanded,* i.e. the *warp* in a loom (as *stretched* out to receive the woof):–web.

4546. מְסִלָּה *mes-il-law';* from 5549; a *thoroughfare* (as *turnpiked*), lit. or fig.; spec. a *viaduct,* a *staircase:*–causeway, course, highway, path, terrace.

4547. מַסְלוּל *mas-lool';* from 5549; a *thoroughfare* (as turnpiked):–highway.

4548. מַסְמֵר *mas-mare';* or מִסְמֵר *mis-mare';* also (fem.) מַסְמְרָה *mas-mer-aw';* or מִסְמְרָה *mis-mer-aw';* or even (Ec. 12:11) מַשְׂמְרָה *mas-mer-aw';* from 5568; a *peg* (as *bristling* from the surface):–nail.

4549. מָסַס *maw-sas';* a prim. root; to *liquefy;* fig., to *waste* (with disease), to *faint* (with fatigue, fear or grief):–discourage, faint, be loosed, melt (away), refuse, X utterly.

4550. מַסַּע *mas-sah';* from 5265; a *departure* (from *striking* the tents), i.e. march (not necessarily a single day's travel); by impl., a *station* (or point of *departure*):–journey(-ing).

4551. מַסָּע *mas-saw';* from 5265 in the sense of *projecting;* a *missile* (spear or arrow); also a *quarry* (whence stones are, as it were, *ejected*):–before it was brought, dart.

4552. מִסְעָד *mis-awd';* from 5582; a *balustrade* (for stairs):–pillar.

4553. מִסְפֵּד *mis-pade';* from 5594; a *lamentation:*–lamentation, one mourneth, mourning, wailing.

4554. מִסְפּוֹא *mis-po';* from an un. root mean. to *collect; fodder:*–provender.

4555. מִסְפָּחָה *mis-paw-khaw';* from 5596; a *veil* (as *spread* out):–kerchief.

4556. מִסְפַּחַת *mis-pakh'-ath;* from 5596; *scruf* (as *spreading* over the surface):–scab.

4557. מִסְפָּר *mis-pawr';* from 5608; a *number,* def. (arithmetical) or indef. (large, *innumerable;* small, a *few*); also (abstr.) *narration:*–+ abundance, account, X all, X few, [in-]finite, (certain) number(-ed), tale, telling, + time.

4558. מִסְפָּר *mis-pawr';* the same as 4457; *number; Mispar,* an Isr.:–Mizpar. Comp. 4559.

4559. מִסְפֶּרֶת *mis-peh'-reth;* fem. of 4437; *enumeration; Mispereth,* an Isr.:–Mispereth. Comp. 4458.

4560. מָסַר *maw-sar';* a prim. root; to *sunder,* i.e. (trans.) *set apart,* or (reflex.) *apostatize:*–commit, deliver.

4561. מֹסָר *mo-sawr';* from 3256; *admonition:*–instruction.

4562. מָסֹרֶת *maw-so'-reth;* from 631; a *band:*–bond.

4563. מִסְתּוֹר *mis-tore';* from 5641; a *refuge:*–covert.

4564. מַסְתֵּר *mas-tare';* from 5641; prop. a *hider,* i.e. (abstr.) a hiding, i.e. *aversion:*–hid.

4565. מִסְתָּר *mis-tawr';* from 5641; prop. a *concealer,* i.e. a *covert:*–secret(-ly, place).

4566. מַעְבָּד *mah-bawd';* from 5647; an *act:*–work.

4567. מַעְבָד *mah-bawd'* (Chald.); cor. to 4566; an *act:*–work.

4568. מַעֲבֶה *mah-ab-eh';* from 5666; prop. *compact* (part of soil), i.e. *loam:*–clay.

4569. מַעֲבָר *mah-ab-awr';* or fem. מַעֲבָרָה *mah-ab-aw-raw';* from 5674; a *crossing*-place (of a river, a *ford;* of a mountain, a *pass*); abstr., a *transit,* i.e. (fig.) *overwhelming:*–ford, place where...pass, passage.

4570. מַעְגָּל *mah-gawl';* or fem. מַעְגָּלָה *mah-gaw-law';* from the same as 5696; a *track* (lit. or fig.); also a *rampart* (as *circular*):–going, path, trench, way([-side]).

4571. מָעַד *maw-ad';* a prim. root; to *waver:*–make to shake, slide, slip.

4572. מַעֲדַי *mah-ad-ah'-ee;* from 5710; *ornament.; Maadai,* an Isr.:–Maadai.

4573. מַעַדְיָה *mah-ad-yaw';* from 5710 and 3050; *ornament of Jah; Maadjah,* an Isr.:–Maadiah. Comp. 4153.

4574. מַעֲדָן *mah-ad-awn';* or (fem.) מַעֲדַנָּה *mah-ad-an-naw';* from 5727; a *delicacy* or (abstr.) *pleasure* (adv., *cheerfully*):–dainty, delicately, delight.

4575. מַעֲדַנָּה *mah-ad-an-naw';* by trans. from 6029; a *bond,* i.e. *group:*–influence.

4576. מַעְדֵּר *mah-dare';* from 5737; a (weeding) *hoe:*–mattock.

4577. מְעָה *meh-aw'* (Chald.); or מְעָא *meh-aw'* (Chald.); cor. to 4578; only in pl. the *bowels:*–belly.

4578. מֵעֶה *may-aw';* from an un. root prob. mean. to *be soft;* used only in pl. the *intestines,* or (coll.) the *abdomen,* fig., *sympathy;* by impl., a *vest;* by ext. the *stomach,* the *uterus* (or of men, the seat of generation), the *heart* (fig.):–belly, bowels, X heart, womb.

4579. מֵעָה *may-aw';* fem. of 4578; the *belly,* i.e. (fig.) interior:–gravel.

4580. מָעוֹג *maw-ogue';* from 5746; a *cake* of bread (with 3934 a *table-buffoon,* i.e. *parasite*):–cake, feast.

4581. מָעוֹז *maw-oze';* (also מָעוּז *maw-ooz'*); or מָעֹז *maw-oze'* (also מָעֻז *maw-ooz';* from 5810; a *fortified* place; fig., a *defence:*–force, fort(-ress), rock, strength(-en), (X most) strong (hold).

4582. מָעוֹךְ *maw-oke';* from 4600; *oppressed; Maok,* a Philistine:–Maoch.

4583. מָעוֹן *maw-ohn';* or (1 Chronicles 4:41) מָעִין *maw-een';* from the same as 5772; an *abode,* of God (the Tabernacle or the Temple), men (their home) or animals (their lair); hence, a *retreat* (asylum):–den, dwelling([-]place), habitation.

4584. מָעוֹן *maw-ohn';* the same as 4583; a *residence; Maon,* the name of an Isr. and of a place in Pal.:–Maon, Maonites. Comp. 1010, 4586.

4585. מְעוֹנָה *meh-o-naw';* or מְעֹנָה *meh-o-naw';* fem. of 4583, and mean. the same:–den, habitation, (dwelling) place, refuge.

4586. מְעוּנִי *meh-oo-nee';* or מְעִינִי *meh-ee-nee';* prob. patrial from 4584; a *Meünite,* or inh. of Maon (only in pl.):–Mehunim(-s), Meunim.

4587. מְעוֹנֹתַי *meh-o-no-thah'-ee;* pl. of 4585; *habitative; Meonothai,* an Isr.:–Meonothai.

4588. מָעוּף *maw-off';* from 5774 in the sense of *covering* with shade [comp. 4155]; *darkness:*–dimness.

4589. מָעוֹר *maw-ore';* from 5783; *nakedness,* i.e. (in pl.) the *pudenda:*–nakedness.

4590. מַעַזְיָה *mah-az-yaw';* or מַעַזְיָהוּ *mah-az-yaw'-hoo;* prob. from 5756 (in the sense of *protection*) and 3050; *rescue of Jah; Maazjah,* the name of two Isr.:–Maaziah.

4591. מָעַט *maw-at';* a prim. root; prop. to *pare* off, i.e. *lessen;* intr., to *be* (or caus., to *make*) *small* or *few* (or fig., *ineffective*):–suffer to decrease, diminish, (be, X borrow a, give, make) few (in number, -ness), gather least (little), be (seem) little, (X give the) less, be minished, bring to nothing.

4592. מְעַט *meh-at';* or מְעָט *meh-awt';* from 4591; a *little* or *few* (often adv. or comp.):–almost (some, very) few(-er, -est), lightly, little (while), (very) small (matter, thing), some, soon, X very.

4593. מֹעָט *maw-ote';* pass. adj. of 4591; *thinned* (as to the edge), i.e. *sharp:*–wrapped up.

4594. מַעֲטֶה *mah-at-eh';* from 5844; a *vestment:*–garment.

4595. מַעֲטָפָה *mah-at-aw-faw';* from 5848; a *cloak:*–mantle.

4596. מְעִי *meh-ee';* from 5753; a *pile* of rubbish (as *contorted*), i.e. a *ruin* (comp. 5856):–heap.

4597. מָעַי *maw-ah'-ee;* prob. from 4578; *sympathetic; Maai,* an Isr.:–Maai.

4598. מְעִיל *meh-eel';* from 4603 in the sense of *covering;* a *robe* (i.e. upper and outer *garment*):–cloke, coat, mantle, robe.

4599. מַעְיָן *mah-yawn';* or מַעְיְנוֹ (Ps. 114:8) *mah-yen-o';* or (fem.) מַעְיָנָה *mah-yaw-naw';* from 5869 (as a denom. in the sense of a *spring*); a *fountain* (also coll.), fig., a *source* (of satisfaction):–fountain, spring, well.

4600. מָעַךְ *maw-ak';* a prim. root; to *press,* i.e. to *pierce, emasculate, handle:*–bruised, stuck, be pressed.

4601. מַעֲכָה *mah-ak-aw';* or מַעֲכָת (Jos. 13:13) *mah-ak-awth';* from 4600; *depression; Maakah* (or *Maakath*), the name of a place in Syria, also of a Mesopotamian, of three Isr., and of four Isr.s and one Syrian woman:–Maachah, Maachathites. See also 1038.

4602. מַעֲכָתִי *mah-ak-aw-thee';* patrial from 4601; a *Maakathite,* or inh. of Maakah:–Maachathite.

4603. מָעַל *maw-al';* a prim. root; prop. to *cover* up; used only fig., to *act covertly,* i.e. *treacherously:*–transgress, (commit, do a) trespass(-ing).

4604. מַעַל *mah'-al;* from 4603; *treachery,* i.e. sin:–falsehood, grievously, sore, transgression, trespass, X very.

4605. מַעַל *mah'al;* from 5927; prop. the *upper* part, used only adv. with pref. *upward, above, overhead, from the top,* etc.:– above, exceeding(-ly), forward, on (X very) high, over, up(-on, -ward), very.

4606. מֵעָל *may-awl'* (Chald.); from 5954; (only in pl. as sing.) the *setting* (of the sun):–going down.

4607. מֹעַל *mo'-al;* from 5927; a *raising* (of the hands):–lifting up.

4608. מַעֲלֶה *mah-al-eh';* from 5927; an *elevation,* i.e. (concr.) *acclivity* or *platform;* abstr. (the relation or state) a *rise* or (fig.) *priority:*–ascent, before, chiefest, cliff, that goeth up, going up, hill, mounting up, stairs.

4609. מַעֲלָה *mah-al-aw';* fem. of 4608; *elevation,* i.e. the act (lit., a *journey* to a higher place, fig., a *thought* arising), or (concr.) the condition (lit., a *step* or *grade*-mark, fig., a *superiority* of station); spec. a climactic *progression* (in certain Psalms):–things that come up, (high) degree, deal, go up, stair, step, story.

4610. מַעֲלֵה עַקְרַבִּים *mah-al-ay'; ak-rab-beem'* from 4608 and (the pl. of) 6137; *Steep of Scorpions,* a place in the Desert:–Maaleh-accrabim, the ascent (going up) of Akrabbim.
4611. מַעֲלָל *mah-al-awl';* from 5953; an *act* (good or bad):–doing, endeavour, invention, work.
4612. מַעֲמָד *mah-am-awd';* from 5975; (fig.) a *position:*–attendance, office, place, state.
4613. מָעֳמָד *moh-om-awd';* from 5975; lit., a *foothold:*–standing.
4614. מַעֲמָסָה *mah-am-aw-saw';* from 6006; *burdensomeness:*–burdensome.
4615. מַעֲמָק *mah-am-awk';* from 6009; a *deep:*–deep, depth.
4616. מַעַן *mah'-an;* from 6030; prop. *heed,* i.e. *purpose;* used only adv., *on account of* (as a motive or an aim), teleologically, *in order that:*–because of, to the end (intent) that, for (to,... 's sake), + lest, that, to.
4617. מַעֲנֶה *mah-an-eh';* from 6030; a *reply* (favorable or contradictory):–answer, X himself.
4618. מַעֲנָה *mah-an-aw';* from 6031, in the sense of *depression* or *tilling;* a *furrow:*–+ acre, furrow.
4619. מַעַץ *mah'-ats;* from 6095; *closure;* Maats, an Isr.:–Maaz.
4620. מַעֲצֵבָה *mah-ats-ay-baw'* from 6087; *anguish:*–sorrow.
4621. מַעֲצָד *mah-ats-awd';* from an usused root mean. to *hew;* an *axe:*–ax, tongs.
4622. מַעְצוֹר *mah-tsore';* from 6113; obj., a *hindrance:*–restraint.
4623. מַעְצָר *mah-tsawr'* from 6113; subj., *control:*–rule.
4624. מַעֲקֶה *mah-ak-eh';* from an un. root mean. to *repress;* a *parapet:*–battlement.
4625. מַעֲקָשׁ *mah-ak-awsh';* from 6140; a *crook* (in a road):–crooked thing.
4626. מַעַר *mah'-ar;* from 6168; a *nude* place, i.e. (lit.) the *pudenda,* or (fig.) a vacant *space:*–nakedness, proportion.
4627. מַעֲרָב *mah-ar-awb';* from 6148, in the sense of *trading; traffic;* by impl., mercantile *goods:*–market, merchandise.
4628. מַעֲרָב *mah-ar-awb';* or (fem.) מַעֲרָבָה *mah-ar-aw-baw';* from 6150, in the sense of *shading;* the *west* (as a region of the *evening* sun):–west.
4629. מַעֲרֶה *mah-ar-eh';* from 6168; a *nude* place, i.e. a *common:*–meadows.
4630. מַעֲרָה *mah-ar-aw';* fem. of 4629; an *open* spot:–army .
4631. מְעָרָה *meh-aw-raw';* from 5783; a *cavern* (as dark):–cave, den, hole.
4632. מְעָרָה *meh-aw-raw'* the same as 4631; *cave; Meärah,* a place in Pal.:– Mearah.
4633. מַעֲרָךְ *mah-ar-awk';* from 6186; an *arrangement,* i.e. (fig.) ment. *disposition:*–preparation.
4634. מַעֲרָכָה *mah-ar-aw-kaw';* fem. of 4633; an *arrangement;* concr., a *pile;* spec. a military *array:*–army, fight, be set in order, ordered place, rank, row.
4635. מַעֲרֶכֶת *mah-ar-eh'-keth;* from 6186; an *arrangement,* i.e. (concr.) a *pile* (of loaves):–row, shewbread.
4636. מַעֲרֹם *mah-ar-ome';* from 6191, in the sense of *stripping; bare:*–naked.
4637. מַעֲרָצָה *mah-ar-aw-tsaw';* from 6206; *violence:*–terror.
4638. מַעֲרָת *mah-ar-awth';* a form of 4630; *waste; Maarath,* a place in Pal.:–Maarath.
4639. מַעֲשֶׂה *mah-as-eh'* from 6213; an *action* (good or bad); gen., a *transaction;* abstr., *activity;* by impl., a *product* (spec., a *poem*) or (gen.) *property:*–act, art, + bakemeat, business, deed, do(-ing), labor, thing made, ware of making, occupation, thing offered, operation, possession, X well, ([handy-, needle-, net-]) work(ing, -manship), wrought.
4640. מַעֲשַׂי *mah-as-ah'ee;* from 6213; *operative; Maasai,* an Isr.:–Maasiai.
4641. מַעֲשֵׂיָה *mah-as-ay-yaw';* or מַעֲשֵׂיָהוּ *mah-as-ay-yaw'-hoo;* from 4639 and 3050; *work of Jah; Maasejah,* the name of sixteen Isr.:–Maaseiah.
4642. מַעֲשַׁקָּה *mah-ash-ak-kaw';* from 6231; *oppression:*–oppression, X oppressor.
4643. מַעֲשֵׂר *mah-as-ayr';* or מַעֲשַׂר *mah-as-ar';* and (in pl.) fem. מַעַשְׂרָה *mah-as-raw';* from 6240; a *tenth;* esp. a *tithe:*– tenth (part), tithe(-ing).
4644. מֹף *mofe;* of Eg. or.: Moph, the capital of Lower Eg.:– Memphis. Comp. 5297.
4645. מִפְגָּע *mif-gaw';* from 6293; an *object of attack:*–mark.
4646. מַפָּח *map-pawkh';* from 5301; a *breathing out* (of life), i.e. expiring:–giving up.
4647. מַפֻּחַ *map-poo'-akh;* from 5301; the *bellows* (i.e. *blower*) of a forge:–bellows.
4648. מְפִיבֹשֶׁת מְפִבֹשֶׁת *mef-ee-bo'-sheth;* or *mef-ee-bo'-sheth;* prob. from 6284 and 1322; *dispeller of shame*; *Mephibosheth,* the name of two Isr.:–Mephibosheth.
4649. מֻפִּים *moop-peem';* a pl. app. from 5130; *wavings; Muppim,* an Isr.:–Muppim. Comp. 8206.
4650. מֵפִיץ *may-feets';* from 6327; a *breaker,* i.e. mallet:–maul.
4651. מַפָּל *map-pawl';* from 5307; a *falling* off, i.e. chaff; also something *pendulous,* i.e. a flap:–flake, refuse.
4652. מִפְלָאָה *mif-law-aw';* from 6381; a *miracle:*–wondrous work.
4653. מִפְלַגָּה *mif-lag-gaw';* from 6385; a *classification:*–division.
4654. מַפָּלָה *map-paw-law';* or מַפֵּלָה *map-pay-law';* from 5307; something *fallen,* i.e. a *ruin:*–ruin(-ous).
4655. מִפְלָט *mif-lawt';* from 6403; an *escape:*–escape.
4656. מִפְלֶצֶת *mif-leh'-tseth;* from 6426; a *terror,* i.e. an idol:–idol.
4657. מִפְלָשׂ *mif-lawce';* from an un. root mean. to *balance;* a *poising:*–balancing.
4658. מַפֶּלֶת *map-peh'-leth;* from 5307; *fall,* i.e. *decadence;* concr., a *ruin;* spec. a *carcase:*–carcase, fall, ruin.
4659 מִפְעָל *mif-awl';* or (fem.) מִפְעָלָה *mif-aw-law';* from 6466; a *performance:*–work.
4660. מַפָּץ *map-pawts';* from 5310; a *smiting* to pieces:–slaughter.
4661. מַפֵּץ *map-pates';* from 5310; a *smiter,* i.e. a war *club:*–battle ax.
4662. מִפְקָד *mif-kawd';* from 6485; an *appointment,* i.e. *mandate;* concr., a designated *spot;* spec., a *census:*–appointed place, commandment, number.
4663. מִפְקָד *mif-kawd';* the same as 4662; *assignment; Miphkad,* the name of a gate in Jerus.:–Miphkad.
4664. מִפְרָץ *mif-rawts';* from 6555; a *break* (in the shore), i.e. a *haven:*–breach.
4665. מַפְרֶקֶת *mif-reh'-keth;* from 6561; prop. a *fracture,* i.e. *joint* (*vertebrae*) of the neck:–neck.
4666. מִפְרָשׂ *mif-rawce';* from 6566; an *expansion:*–that which...spreadest forth, spreading.
4667. מִפְשָׂעָה *mif-saw-aw';* from 6585; a *stride,* i.e. (by euphem.) the *crotch:*–buttocks.
4668. מַפְתֵּחַ *maf-tay'-akh;* from 6605; an *opener,* i.e. a *key:*–key.
4669. מִפְתָּח *mif-tawkh';* from 6605; an *aperture,* i.e. (fig.) *utterance:*–opening.
4670. מִפְתָּן *mif-tawn';* from the same as 6620; a *stretcher,* i.e. a *sill:*–threshold.
4671. מֹץ *motes;* or (Zep. 2:2) מוֹץ *motes;* from 4160; *chaff* (as *pressed* out, i.e. *winnowed* or [rather] threshed loose):–chaff.
4672. מָצָא *maw-tsaw';* a prim. root; prop. to *come* forth to, i.e. *appear* or *exist;* trans., to *attain,* i.e. *find* or *acquire;* fig., to *occur, meet* or *be present:*–+ be able, befall, being, catch, X certainly, (cause to) come (on, to, to hand), deliver, be enough (cause to) find(-ing, occasion, out), get (hold upon), X have (here), be here, hit, be left, light (up-)on, meet (with), X occasion serve, (be) present, ready, speed, suffice, take hold on.
4673. מַצָּב *mats-tsawb';* from 5324; a fixed *spot;* fig., an *office,* a military *post:*–garrison, station, place where...stood.
4674. מֻצָּב *moots-tsawb';* from 5324; a *station,* i.e. military *post:*–mount.
4675. מַצָּבָה *mats-tsaw-baw';* or מִצָּבָה *mits-tsaw-baw';* fem. of 4673; a military *guard:*–army, garrison.
4676. מַצֵּבָה *mats-tsay-baw';* fem. (caus.) part. of 5324; something *stationed,* i.e. a *column* or (memorial *stone*); by anal., an *idol:*–garrison, (standing) image, pillar.
4677. מְצֹבָיָה *mets-o-baw-yaw';* app. from 4672 and 3050; *found of Jah; Metsobajah,* a place in Pal.:–Mesobaite.
4678. מַצֶּבֶת *mats-tseh'-beth;* from 5324; something *stationary,* i.e. a monumental *stone;* also the *stock* of a tree:–pillar, substance.
4679. מְצַד *mets-ad';* or מְצָד *mets-awd';* or (fem.) מְצָדָה *mets-aw-daw';* from 6679; a *fastness* (as a *covert* of ambush):–castle, fort, (strong) hold, munition.
4680. מָצָה *maw-tsaw';* a prim. root; to *suck* out; by impl., to *drain,* to *squeeze* out:–suck, wring (out).
4681. מֹצָה *mo-tsaw';* act.part. fem. of 4680; *drained; Motsah,* a place in Pal.:–Mozah.
4682. מַצָּה *mats-tsaw';* from 4711 in the sense of *greedily* devouring for sweetness; prop. *sweetness;* concr., *sweet* (i.e. not soured or bittered with yeast); spec., an *unfermented cake* or loaf, or (ellip.) the festival of *Passover* (because no leaven was then used):–unleaved (bread, cake), without leaven.
4683. מַצָּה *mats-tsaw';* from 5327; a *quarrel:*–contention, debate, strife.
4684. מַצְהָלָה *mats-haw-law';* from 6670; a *whinnying* (through impatience for battle or lust):–neighing.
4685. מָצוֹד *maw-tsode';* or (fem.) מְצוֹדָה *mets-o-daw';* or מְצֹדָה *mets-o-daw';* from 6679; a *net* (for *capturing* animals or fishes):–also a *fastness* or (besieging) *tower:*–bulwark, hold, munition, net, snare.
4686. מָצוּד *maw-tsood';* or (fem.) מְצוּדָה *mets-oo-daw';* or מְצֻדָה *mets-oo-daw';* for 4685; a *net,* or (abstr.) *capture;* also a *fastness;* –castle, defense, fort(-ress), (strong) hold, be

hunted, net, snare, strong place.

4687. מִצְוָה *mits-vaw';* from 6680; a *command,* whether human or divine (coll., the *Law*):–(which was) commanded(-ment), law, ordinance, precept.

4688. מְצוֹלָה *mets-o-law';* or מְצֹלָה *mets-o-law';* also מְצוּלָה *mets-oo-law';* or מְצֻלָה *mets-oo-law';* from the same as 6683; a *deep* place (of water or mud):–bottom, deep, depth.

4689. מָצוֹק *maw-tsoke';* from 6693; a *narrow* place, i.e. (abstr. and fig.) *confinement* or *disability:*–anguish, distress, straitness.

4690. מָצוּק *maw-tsook';* or מָצֻק *maw-tsook';* from 6693; something *narrow,* i.e. a *column* or *hill*top:–pillar, situate.

4691. מְצוּקָה *mets-oo-kaw';* or מְצֻקָה *mets-oo-kaw';* fem. of 4690; *narrowness,* i.e. (fig.) *trouble:*–anguish, distress.

4692. מָצוֹר *maw-tsore';* or מָצוּר maw-tsoor'; from 6696; something *hemming* in, i.e. (obj.) a *mound* (of besiegers), (abstr.) a *siege,* (fig.) *distress;* or (subj.) a *fastness:*–besieged, bulwark, defence, fenced, fortress, siege, strong (hold), tower.

4693. מָצוֹר *maw-tsore';* the same as 4692 in the sense of a *limit; Eg.* (as the *border* of Pal.):–besieged places, defense, fortified.

4694. מְצוּרָה *mets-oo-raw';* or מְצֻרָה *mets-oo-raw';* fem. of 4692; a *hemming* in, i.e. (obj.) a *mound* (of siege), or (subj.) a *rampart* (of protection), (abstr.) *fortification:*–fenced (city, fort, munition, strong hold.

4695. מַצּוּת *mats-tsooth';* from 5327; a *quarrel:*–that contended.

4696. מֵצַח *may'-tsakh;* from an un. root mean. to be *clear,* i.e. *conspicuous;* the *forehead* (as *open* and *prominent*):–brow, forehead, + impudent.

4697. מִצְחָה *mits-khaw';* from the same as 4696; a *shin-piece* of armor (as *prominent*), only pl.:–greaves.

4698. מְצִלָּה *mets-il-law';* from 6750; a *tinkler,* i.e. a *bell:*–bell.

4699. מְצֻלָּה *mets-ool-law';* from 6751; *shade:*–bottom.

4700. מְצֵלֶת *mets-ay'-leth;* from 6750; (only dual) double *tinklers,* i.e. cymbals:–cymbals.

4701. מִצְנֶפֶת *mits-neh'-feth;* from 6801; a *tiara,* i.e. official *turban* (of a king or high priest):–diadem, mitre.

4702. מַצָּע *mats-tsaw';* from 3331; a *couch:*–bed.

4703. מִצְעָד *mits-awd';* from 6805; a *step;* fig., *companionship:*–going, step.

4704. מִצְּעִירָה *mits-tseh-ee-raw';* fem. of 4705; prop. *littleness;* concr., *diminuative:*–little.

4705. מִצְעָר *mits-awr';* from 6819; *petty* (in size or number); adv., a *short* (time):–little one (while), small.

4706. מִצְעָר *mits-awr';* the same as 4705; *Mitsar,* a peak of Lebanon:–Mizar.

4707. מִצְפֶּה *mits-peh';* from 6822; an *observatory,* esp. for military purposes:–watch tower.

4708. מִצְפֶּה *mits-peh'* the same as 4707; *Mitspeh,* the name of five places in Pal.:–Mizpeh, watch tower. Comp. 4709.

4709. מִצְפָּה *mits-paw';* fem. of 4708; *Mitspah,* the name of two places in Pal.:–Mitspah. [This seems rather to be only an orthographic var. of 4708 when "in pause".]

4710. מִצְפֻּן *mits-poon';* from 6845; a *secret* (place or thing, perh., *treasure*):–hidden thing.

4711. מָצַץ *maw-tsats';* a prim. root; to *suck:*–milk.

4712. מֵצַר *may-tsar';* from 6896; something *tight,* i.e. (fig.) *trouble:*–distress, pain, strait.

4713. מִצְרִי *mits-ree';* from 4714; a *Mitsrite,* or inh. of Mitsrajim:–Eg., of Egypt

4714. מִצְרַיִם *mits-rah'-yim;* dual of 4693; *Mitsrajim,* i.e. Upper and Lower Eg.:–Egypt, Egyptians, Mizraim.

4715. מִצְרֵף *mits-rafe';* from 6884; a *crucible:* –fining pot.

4716. מַק *mak;* from 4743; prop. a *melting,* i.e. *putridity:*– rottenness, stink.

4717. מַקָּבָה *mak-kaw-baw';* from 5344; prop. a *perforatrix,* i.e. a *hammer* (as *piercing*):–hammer.

4718. מַקֶּבֶת *mak-keh'-beth;* from 5344; prop. a *perforator,* i.e. a *hammer* (as *piercing*); also (intr.) a *perforation,* i.e. a *quarry:*–hammer, hole.

4719. מַקֵּדָה *mak-kay-daw';* from the same as 5348 in the denom. sense of *herding* (comp. 5349); *fold; Makkedah,* a place in Pal.:–Makkedah.

4720. מִקְדָּשׁ *mik-dawsh';* or (Ex. 15:17) מִקְּדָּשׁ *mik-ked-awsh';* from 6942; a *consecrated* thing or place, esp., a *palace, sanctuary* (whether of Jehovah or of idols) or *asylum:*–chapel, hallowed part, holy place, sanctuary.

4721. מַקְהֵל *mak-hale';* or (fem.) מַקְהֵלָה *mak-hay-law';* from 6950; an *assembly:*–congregation.

4722. מַקְהֵלֹת *mak-hay-loth';* pl. of 4721 (fem.); *assemblies; Makheloth,* a place in the Desert:–Makheloth.

4723. מִקְוֶה *mik-veh';* or מִקְוֵה (1 Kings 10:28) *mik-vay';* or מִקְוֵא (2 Ch.. 1:16) *mik-vay';* from 6960; something *waited* for, i.e. *confidence* (obj. or subj.); also a *collection,* i.e. (of water) a *pond,* or (of men and horses) a *caravan* or *drove:*–abiding, gathering together, hope, linen yarn, plenty [of water], pool.

4724. מִקְוָה *mik-vaw';* fem. of 4723; a *collection,* i.e. (of water) a *reservoir:*–ditch.

4725. מָקוֹם *maw-kome';* or מָקֹם *maw-kome';* also (fem.) מְקוֹמָה *mek-o-mah';* or מְקֹמָה *mek-o-mah';* from 6965; prop. a *standing,* i.e. a *spot;* but used widely of a *locality* (gen. or spec.); also (fig.) of a *condition* (of body or mind):–country, X home, X open, place, room, space, X whither[-soever].

4726. מָקוֹר *maw-kore';* or מָקֹר *maw-kore';* from 6979; prop. something *dug,* i.e. a (gen.) *source* (of water, even when nat. flowing; also of tears, blood [by euphem., of the female *pudenda*]; fig., of happiness, wisdom, progeny):–fountain, issue, spring, well(-spring).

4727. מִקָּח *mik-kawkh';* from 3947; *reception:*–taking.

4728. מַקָּחָה *mak-kaw-khaw';* from 3947; something *received,* i.e. *merchandise* (purchased):–ware.

4729. מִקְטָר *mik-tawr';* from 6999; something to *fume* (incense) on i.e. a *hearth* place:–to burn...upon.

4730. מִקְטֶרֶת *mik-teh'-reth;* fem. of 4729; something to *fume* (incense) in, i.e. a *coal-pan:*–censer.

4731. מַקֵּל *mak-kale;* or (fem.) מַקְּלָה *mak-kel-aw';* from an un. root mean. app. to *germinate;* a *shoot,* i.e. *stick* (with leaves on, or for walking, striking, guiding, divining):–rod, ([hand-])staff.

4732; מִקְלוֹת *mik-lohth';* (or perh. *mik-kel-ohth'*) pl. of (fem.) 4731; *rods; Mikloth,* a place in the Desert:–Mikloth.

4733. מִקְלָט *mik-lawt';* from 7038 in the sense of *taking* in; an *asylum* (as a *receptacle*):–refuge.

4734. מִקְלַעַת *mik-lah'-ath;* from 7049; a *sculpture* (prob. in bas-relief):–carved (figure), carving, graving.

4735. מִקְנֶה *mik-neh';* from 7069; something *bought,* i.e. *property,* but only live *stock;* abstr., *acquisition:*–cattle, flock, herd, possession, purchase, substance.

4736. מִקְנָה *mik-naw';* fem. of 4735; prop. a *buying,* i.e. *acquisition;* concr., a piece of *property* (land or living); also the *sum* paid:–(he that is) bought, possession, piece, purchase.

4737. מִקְנֵיָהוּ *mik-nay-yaw'-hoo;* from 4735 and 3050; *possession of Jah; Miknejah,* an Isr.:–Mikneiah.

4738. מִקְסָם *mik-sawn';* from 7080; an *augury:*–divination.

4739. מָקַץ *maw-kats';* from 7112; *end; Makats,* a place in Pal.:–Makaz.

4740. מַקְצוֹעַ *mak-tso'-ah;* or מַקְצֹעַ *mak-tso-ah;* or (fem.) מַקְצֹעָה *mak-tso-aw';* from 7106 in the denom. sense of *bending;* an *angle* or recess:–corner, turning.

4741. מַקְצֻעָה *mak-tsoo-aw';* from 7106; a *scraper,* i.e. a carving *chisel:*–plane.

4742. מְקֻצְעָה *mek-oots-aw';* from 7106 in the denom. sense of *bending;* an *angle:*–corner.

4743. מָקַק *maw-kak';* a prim. root; to *melt;* fig., to *flow, dwindle, vanish:*–consume away, be corrupt, dissolve, pine away.

4744. מִקְרָא *mik-raw';* from 7121; something *called* out, i.e. a public *meeting* (the act, the persons, or the place); also a *rehearsal:*–assembly, calling, convocation, reading.

4745. מִקְרֶה *mik-reh';* from 7136; something with, i.e. an *accident* or *fortune:*–something befallen, befalleth, chance, event, hap(-peneth).

4746. מְקָרֶה *mek-aw-reh';* from 7136; prop. something *meeting,* i.e. a *frame* (of timbers):–building.

4747. מְקֵרָה *mek-ay-raw';* from the same as 7119; a *cooling* off:–X summer.

4748. מִקְשֶׁה *mik-sheh';* from 7185 in the sense of *knotting* up round and hard; something *turned* (rounded), i.e. a *curl* (of tresses):–X well [set] hair.

4749. מִקְשָׁה *mik-shaw';* fem. of 4748; *rounded* work, i.e. moulded by *hammering* (*repousse*):–beaten (out of one piece, work), upright, whole piece.

4750. מִקְשָׁה *mik-shaw';* denom. from 7180; lit., a *cucumbered* field, i.e. a *cucumber* patch:–garden of cucumbers.

4751. מַר *mar;* or (fem.) מָרָה *maw-raw';* from 4843; *bitter* (lit. or fig.); also (as noun) *bitterness,* or (adv.) *bitterly:*–+ angry, bitter (-ly, -ness), chafed, discontented, X great, heavy.

4752. מַר *mar;* from 4843 in its or. sense of *distillation;* a *drop:*–drop.

4753. מֹר *mor;* or מוֹר *more;* from 4843; *myrrh* (as *distilling* in drops, and also as *bitter*):–myrrh

4754. מָרָא *maw-raw';* a prim. root; to *rebel;* hence (through the idea of *maltreating*) to *whip,* i.e. *lash* (self with wings, as the ostrich in running):–be filthy, lift up self.

4755. מָרָא *maw-raw';* for 4751 fem.; *bitter; Mara,* a symbolic name of Naomi:–Mara.

4756. מָרֵא *maw-ray'* (Chald.); from a root cor. to 4754 in the sense of *domineering;* a *master:*–lord, Lord.

4757. מְרֹאדַךְ בַּלְאֲדָן *mer-o-dak' bal-aw-dawn';* of for. der.; *Merodak-Baladan,* a Babylonian king:–Merodach-baladan. Comp. 4781.

4758. מַרְאֶה *mar-eh';* from 7200; a *view* (the act of seeing); also an *appearance* (the thing seen), whether (real) a *shape* (esp. if handsome, *comeliness;* often pl. the *looks*), or (ment.) a *vision:*–X app., appearance(-reth), X as soon as beautiful(-ly), countenance, fair, favoured, form, goodly, to look (up) on (to), look[-eth], pattern, to see, seem, sight, visage, vision.

4759. מַרְאָה *mar-aw';* fem. of 4758; a *vision;* also (caus.) a *mirror:*–looking glass, vision.

4760. מֻרְאָה *moor-aw';* app. fem. pass. caus. part. of 7200; something *conspicuous,* i.e. the *craw* of a bird (from its *prominence*):–crop.

4761. מַרְאָשָׁה *mar-aw-shaw';* denom. from 7218; prop. *headship,* i.e. (pl. for coll.) *dominion:*–principality.

4762. מַרְאֵשָׁה *mar-ay-shaw';* or מָרֵשָׁה *mar-ay-shaw';* formed like 4761; *summit; Mareshah,* the name of two Isr. and of a place in Pal.:–Mareshah.

4763. מְרַאֲשָׁה *mer-ah-ash-aw';* formed like 4761; prop. a *headpiece,* i.e. (pl. for adv.) *at* (or *as*) the *head-rest* (or pillow):–bolster, head, pillow. Comp. 4772.

4764. מֵרָב *may-rawb';* from 7231; *increase; Merab,* a daughter of Saul:–Merab.

4765. מַרְבַד *mar-bad';* from 7234; a *coverlet:*–covering of tapestry.

4766. מַרְבֶּה *mar-beh';* from 7235; prop. *increasing;* as noun, *greatness,* or (adv.) *greatly:*–great, increase.

4767. מִרְבָּה *meer-baw';* from 7235; *abundance,* i.e. a great quantity:–much.

4768. מַרְבִּית *mar-beeth';* from 7235; a *multitude;* also *offspring;* spec. *interest* (on capital):–greatest part, greatness, increase, multitude.

4769. מַרְבֵּץ *mar-bates';* from 7257; a *reclining* place, i.e. *fold* (for flocks):–couching place, place to lie down.

4770. מַרְבֵּק *mar-bake';* from an un. root mean. to *tie* up; a *stall* (for cattle):–X fat (-ted), stall.

4771. מַרְגּוֹעַ *mar-go'-ah;* from 7280; a *resting* place:–rest.

4772. מַרְגְּלָה *mar-ghel-aw';* denom. from 7272; (pl. for coll.) a *footpiece,* i.e. (adv.) *at the foot,* or (direct.) the *foot* itself:–feet. Comp. 4763.

4773. מַרְגֵּמָה *mar-gay-maw';* from 7275; a *stone*-heap:–sling.

4774. מַרְגֵּעָה *mar-gay-aw';* from 7280; *rest:*–refreshing.

4775. מָרַד *maw-rad';* a prim. root; to rebel:–*rebel*(-lious).

4776. מְרַד *mer-ad'* (Chald.); from a root cor. to 4775; *rebellion:*–rebellion.

4777. מֶרֶד *meh'-red;* from 4775; *rebellion:*–rebellion.

4778. מֶרֶד *meh'-red;* the same as 4777; *Mered,* an Isr.:–Mered.

4779. מָרָד *maw-rawd'* (Chald.); from the same as 4776; *rebellious:*–rebellious.

4780. מַרְדּוּת *mar-dooth';* from 4775; *rebelliousness:*–X rebellious.

4781. מְרֹדָךְ *mer-o-dawk';* of for. der.; *Merodak,* a Babylonian idol:–Merodach. Comp. 4757.

4782. מָרְדְּכַי *mor-dek-ah'-ee;* of for. der.; *Mordecai,* an Isr.:–Mordecai.

4783. מֻרְדָּף *moor-dawf';* from 7291; *persecuted:*–persecuted.

4784. מָרָה *maw-raw';* a prim. root; to *be* (caus., *make*) *bitter* (or unpleasant); (fig.) to *rebel* (or resist; caus., to *provoke*):–bitter, change, be disobedient, disobey, grievously, provocation, provoke(-ing), (be) rebel (against, -lious).

4785. מָרָה *maw-raw';* the same as 4751 fem.; *bitter; Marah,* a place in the Desert:–Marah.

4786. מֹרָה *mo-raw';* from 4843; *bitterness,* i.e. (fig.) *trouble:*–grief.

4787. מָרָּה *mor-raw';* a form of 4786; *trouble:*–bitterness.

4788. מָרוּד *maw-rood';* from 7300 in the sense of *maltreatment;* an *outcast;* (abstr.) *destitution:*–cast out, misery.

4789. מֵרוֹז *may-roze';* of unc. der.; *Meroz,* a place in Pal.:–Meroz.

4790 מְרוֹחַ *mer-o-akh';* from 4799; *bruised,* i.e. *emasculated:*–broken.

4791. מָרוֹם *maw-rome';* from 7311; *altitude,* i.e. concr. (an *elevated place*), abstr. (*elevation,*) fig. (*elation*), or adv. (*aloft*):–(far) above, dignity, haughty, height, (most, on) high (one, place), loftily, upward.

4792. מֵרוֹם *may-rome';* formed like 4791; *height; Merom,* a lake in Pal.:–Merom.

4793. מֵרוֹץ *may-rotes';* from 7323; a *run* (the trial of speed):–race.

4794. מְרוּצָה *mer-oo-tsaw';* or מְרֻצָה *mer-oo-tsaw';* fem. of 4793; a *race* (the act), whether the manner or the progress:–course, running. Comp. 4835.

4795. מָרוּק *maw-rook';* from 4838; prop. *rubbed;* but used abstr., a *rubbing* (with perfumery):–purification.

4796. מָרוֹת *maw-rohth';* pl. of 4751 fem.; *bitter* springs; *Maroth,* a place in Pal.:–Maroth.

4797. מִרְזַח *meer-zakh';* from an un. root mean. to *scream;* a *cry,* i.e. (of joy), a *revel:*–banquet.

4798. מַרְזֵחַ *mar-zay'-akh;* formed like 4797; a *cry,* i.e. (of grief) a *lamentation:*–mourning.

4799. מָרַח *maw-rakh';* a prim. root; prop. to *soften* by rubbing or pressure; hence (medicinally) to *apply* as an emollient:–lay for a plaister.

4800. מֶרְחָב *mer-khawb';* from 7337; *enlargement,* either lit. (an *open space,* usually in a good sense), or fig. (*liberty*):–breadth, large place (room).

4801. מֶרְחָק *mer-khawk';* from 7368; *remoteness,* i.e. (concr.) a *distant* place; often (adv.) *from afar:*–(a-, dwell in, very) far (country, off). See also 1023.

4802. מַרְחֶשֶׁת *mar-kheh'-sheth;* from 7370; a *stew*-pan:–fryingpan.

4803. מָרַט *maw-rat';* a prim. root; to *polish;* by impl., to *make bald* (the head), to *gall* (the shoulder); also, to *sharpen:*–bright, furbish, (have his) hair (be) fallen off, peeled, pluck off (hair).

4804. מְרַט *mer-at'* (Chald.); cor. to 4803; to *pull* off:–be plucked.

4805. מְרִי *mer-ee';* from 4784; *bitterness,* i.e. (fig.) *rebellion;* concr., *bitter,* or *rebellious:*–bitter, (most) rebel(-lion, -lious).

4806. מְרִיא *mer-ee';* from 4754 in the sense of *grossness,* through the idea of *domineering* (comp. 4756); *stall-fed;* often (as noun) a *beeve:*–fat (fed) beast (cattle, -ling).

4807. מְרִיב בַּעַל *mer-eeb' bah'-al;* from 7378 and 1168; *quarreller of Baal, Merib-Baal,* an epithet of Gideon:–Merib-baal. Comp. 4810.

4808. מְרִיבָה *mer-ee-baw';* from 7378; *quarrel:*–provocation, strife.

4809. מְרִיבָה *mer-ee-baw';* the same as 4808; *Meribah,* the name of two places in the Desert:–Meribah.

4810. מְרִי בַעַל *mer-ee' bah'-al;* from 4805 and 1168; *rebellion of* (i.e. *against*) *Baal; Meri-Baal,* an epithet of Gideon:–Meri-baal. Comp. 4807.

4811. מְרָיָה *mer-aw-yaw';* from 4784; *rebellion; Merajah,* an Isr.:–Meraiah. Comp. 3236.

4812. מְרָיוֹת *mer-aw-yohth';* pl. of 4811; *rebellious; Merajoth,* the name of two Isr.:–Meraioth.

4813. מִרְיָם *meer-yawm';* from 4805; *rebelliously; Mirjam,* the name of two Isr.s:–Miriam.

4814. מְרִירוּת *mer-ee-rooth';* from 4843; *bitterness,* i.e. (fig.) *grief:*–bitterness.

4815. מְרִירִי *mer-ee-ree';* from 4843; *bitter,* i.e. *poisonous:*–bitter.

4816. מֹרֶךְ *mo'-rek;* perh. from 7401; *softness,* i.e. (fig.) *fear:*–faintness.

4817. מֶרְכָּב *mer-kawb';* from 7392; a *chariot;* also a *seat* (in a vehicle):–chariot, covering, saddle.

4818. מֶרְכָּבָה *mer-kaw-baw';* fem. of 4817; a *chariot:*–chariot. See also 1024.

4819. מַרְכֹּלֶת *mar-ko'-leth;* from 7402; a *mart:*–merchandise.

4820. מִרְמָה *meer-maw';* from 7411 in the sense of *deceiving; fraud:*–craft, deceit (-ful, -fully), false, feigned, guile, subtilly, treachery.

4821. מִרְמָה *meer-maw';* the same as 4820; *Mirmah,* an Isr.:–Mirma.

4822. מְרֵמוֹת *mer-ay-mohth';* pl. from 7311; *heights; Meremoth,* the name of two Isr.:–Meremoth.

4823. מִרְמָס *meer-mawce';* from 7429; *abasement* (the act or the thing):–tread (down) -ing, (to be) trodden (down) under foot.

4824. מֵרֹנֹתִי *may-ro-no-thee';* patrial from an un. noun; a *Meronothite,* or inh. of some (otherwise unknown) Meronoth.:–Meronothite.

4825. מֶרֶס *meh'-res;* of for. der.; *Meres,* a Pers.:–Meres.

4826. מַרְסְנָא *mar-sen-aw';* of for. der.; *Marsena,* a Pers.:–Marsena.

4827. מֵרַע *may-rah';* from 7489; used as (abstr.) noun, *wickedness:*–do mischief.

4828. מֵרֵעַ *may-ray'-ah;* from 7462 in the sense of *companionship;* a *friend:*–companion, friend.

4829. מִרְעֶה *meer-eh';* from 7462 in the sense of *feeding; pasture* (the place or the act); also the *haunt* of wild animals:–feeding place, pasture.

4830. מִרְעִית *meer-eeth';* from 7462 in the sense of *feeding; pasturage;* concr., a *flock:*–flock, pasture.

4831. מַרְעֲלָה *mar-al-aw';* from 7477; perh., *earthquake; Maralah,* a place in Pal.:–Maralah.

4832. מַרְפֵּא *mar-pay';* from 7495; prop. *curative,* i.e. lit. (concr.) a *medicine,* or (abstr.) a *cure;* fig. (concr.) *deliverance,* or (abstr.) *placidity:*–([in-])cure(-able), healing(-lth), remedy, sound, wholesome, yielding.

4833. מִרְפָּשׂ *meer-paws';* from 7515; *muddled* water:–that which...have fouled.

4834. מָרַץ *maw-rats';* a prim. root; prop. to *press,* i.e. (fig.) to be *pungent* or vehement; to *irritate:*–embolden, be forcible, grievous, sore.

4835. מְרֻצָה *mer-oo-tsaw';* from 7533; *oppression:*–violence. See also 4794.
4836. מַרְצֵעַ *mar-tsay'-ah;* from 7527; an *awl:*–aul.
4837. מַרְצֶפֶת *mar-tseh'-feth;* from 7528; a *pavement:*–pavement.
4838. מָרַק *maw-rak';* a prim. root; to *polish;* by impl., to *sharpen;* also to *rinse:*–bright, furbish, scour.
4839. מָרָק *maw-rawk';* from 4838; *soup* (as if a *rinsing*):–broth. See also 6564.
4840. מֶרְקָח *mer-kawkh';* from 7543; a *spicy* herb:–X sweet.
4841. מֶרְקָחָה *mer-kaw-khaw';* fem. of 4840; abstr., a *seasoning* (with spicery); concr., *unguent-kettle* (for preparing spiced oil):–pot of ointment, X well.
4842. מִרְקַחַת *meer-kakh'-ath;* from 7543; an aromatic *unguent;* also an *unguent-pot:*–prepared by the apothecaries' art, compound, ointment.
4843. מָרַר *maw-rar';* a prim. root; prop. to *trickle* [see 4752]; but used only as a denom. from 4751; to *be* (caus., *make*) *bitter* (lit. or fig.):–(be, be in, deal, have, make) bitter (-ly, -ness), be moved with choler, (be, have sorely, it) grieved(-eth), provoke, vex.
4844. מְרֹר *mer-ore';* מְרוֹר or *mer-ore';* from 4843; a *bitter* herb:– bitter(-ness).
4845. מְרֵרָה *mer-ay-raw';* from 4843; *bile* (from its bitterness):–gall.
4846. מְרֹרָה *mer-o-raw';* or מְרוֹרָה *mer-o-raw';* from 4843; prop. *bitterness;* concr., a *bitter thing;* spec. *bile;* also *venom* (of a serpent):–bitter (thing), gall.
4847. מְרָרִי *mer-aw-ree';* from 4843; *bitter; Merari,* an Isr.:–Merari. See also 4848.
4848. מְרָרִי *mer-aw-ree';* from 4847; a *Merarite* (coll.), or decendants of Merari:–Merarites.
4849. מִרְשַׁעַת *meer-shah'-ath;* from 7561; a female *wicked doer:*–wicked woman.
4850. מְרָתַיִם *mer-aw-thah'-yim;* dual of 4751 fem.; *double bitterness; Merathajim,* an epithet of Babylon:–Merathaim.
4851. מַשׁ *mash;* of for. der.; *Mash,* a son of Aram, and the people descended from him:–Mash.
4852. מֵשָׁא *may-shaw';* of for. der.; *Mesha,* a place in Arabia:–Mesha.
4853. מַשָּׂא *mas-saw';* from 5375; a *burden;* spec., *tribute,* or (abstr.) *porterage;* fig., an *utterance,* chiefly a *doom,* esp. *singing;* ment., *desire:*–burden, carry away, prophecy, X they set, song, tribute.
4854. מַשָּׂא *mas-saw';* the same as 4853; *burden*; *Massa,* a son of Ishmael:–Massa.
4855. מַשָּׁא *mash-shaw';* from 5383; a *loan;* by impl., *interest* on a debt:–exaction, usury.
4856. מַשֹּׂא *mas-so';* from 5375; *partiality* (as a *lifting* up):–respect.
4857. מַשְׁאָב *mash-awb';* from 7579; a *trough* for cattle to drink from:–place of drawing water.
4858. מַשָּׂאָה *mas-saw-aw';* from 5375; a *conflagration* (from the *rising* of smoke):–burden.
4859. מַשָּׁאָה *mash-shaw-aw';* fem. of 4855; a *loan:*–X any[- thing], debt.
4860. מַשָּׁאוֹן *mash-shaw-ohn';* from 5377; *dissimulation:*–deceit.
4861. מִשְׁאָל *mish-awl';* from 7592; *request; Mishal,* a place in Pal.:–Mishal, Misheal. Comp. 4913.
4862. מִשְׁאָלָה *mish-aw-law';* from 7592; a *request:*–desire, petition
4863. מִשְׁאֶרֶת *mish-eh'-reth;* from 7604 in the or. sense of *swelling;* a *kneading-trough* (in which the dough *rises*):–kneading trough, store.
4864. מַשְׂאֵת *mas-ayth';* from 5375; prop. (abstr.) a *raising* (as of the hands in prayer), or *rising* (of flame); fig. an *utterance;* concr., a *beacon* (as *raised*); a *present* (as taken), *mess,* or *tribute;* fig. a *reproach* (as a burden):–burden, collection, sign of fire, (great) flame, gift, lifting up, mess, oblation, reward.
4865. מִשְׁבְּצָה *mish-bets-aw';* from 7660; a *brocade;* by anal., a (reticulated) *setting* of a gem:–ouch, wrought.
4866. מִשְׁבֵּר *mish-bare';* from 7665; the *orifice* of the womb (from which the fetus *breaks* forth):–birth, breaking forth.
4867. מִשְׁבָּר *mish-bawr';* from 7665; a *breaker* (of the sea):–billow, wave.
4868. מִשְׁבָּת *mish-bawth';* from 7673; *cessation,* i.e. destruction:–sabbath.
4869. מִשְׂגָּב *mis-gawb';* from 7682; prop. a *cliff* (or other *lofty* or *inaccessible* place); abstr., *altitude;* fig., a *refuge:*– defence, high fort (tower), refuge, Misgab, a place in Moab:–Misgab.
4870. מִשְׁגֶּה *mish-geh';* from 7686; an *err.:*–oversight.
4871. מָשָׁה *maw-shaw';* a prim. root; to *pull* out (lit. or fig.):–draw(out).
4872. מֹשֶׁה *mo-sheh';* from 4871; *drawing* out (of the water), i.e. *rescued; Mosheh,* the Isr. lawgiver:–Moses.
4873. מֹשֶׁה *mo-sheh'* (Chald.); cor. to 4872:–Moses.
4874. מַשֶּׁה *mash-sheh';* from 5383; a *debt:*– + creditor.
4875. מְשׁוֹאָה *mesh-o-aw';* or מְשֹׁאָה *mesh-o-aw';* from the same as 7722; (a) *ruin*, abstr. (the act) or concr. (the wreck):–desolation, waste.
4876. מַשּׁוּאָה *mash-shoo-aw';* or מַשֻּׁאָה *mash-shoo-aw';* for 4875; *ruin:*–desolation, destruction.
4877. מְשׁוֹבָב *mesh-o-bawb';* from 7725; *returned; Meshobab,* an Isr.:–Meshobab.
4878. מְשׁוּבָה *mesh-oo-baw';* or מְשֻׁבָה *mesh-oo-baw';* from 7725; *apostasy:*–backsliding, turning away.
4879. מְשׁוּגָה *mesh-oo-gaw';* from an un. root mean. to *stray; mistake:*–err.
4880. מָשׁוֹט *maw-shote';* or מִשּׁוֹט *mish-shote';* from 7751; an *oar:*–oar.
4881. מְשׂוּכָה *mes-oo-kaw';* or מְשֻׂכָה *mes-oo-kaw'; from* 7753; *a hedge:*–hedge.
4882. מְשׁוּסָה *mesh-oo-saw';* from an un. root mean. to *plunder; spoilation:*–spoil.
4883. מַשּׂוֹר *mas-sore';* from an un. root mean. to *rasp;* a *saw:*–saw.
4884. מְשׂוּרָה *mes-oo-raw';* from an un. root mean. app. to *divide;* a *measure* (for liquids):–measure.
4885. מָשׂוֹשׂ *maw-soce';* from 7797; *delight,* concr. (the cause or obj.) or abstr. (the feeling):–joy, mirth, rejoice.
4886. מָשַׁח *maw-shakh';* a prim. root; to *rub* with oil, i.e. to *anoint;* by impl., to *consecrate;* also to *paint:*–anoint, paint.
4887. מְשַׁח *mesh-akh'* (Chald.); from a root cor. to 4886; *oil:*–oil.
4888. מִשְׁחָה *meesh-khaw';* or מָשְׁחָה *mosh-khaw';* from 4886; *unction* (the act); by impl., a consecratory *gift:*–(to be) anointed(-ing), ointment.
4889. מַשְׁחִית *mash-kheeth';* from 7843; *destructive,* i.e. (as noun) *destruction*, lit. (spec. a *snare*) or fig. (*corruption*):–corruption, (to) destroy(-ing), destruction, trap, X utterly.
4890. מִשְׂחָק *mis-khawk';* from 7831; a *laughing*-stock:–scorn.
4891. מִשְׁחָר *mish-khawr';* from 7836 in the sense of day *breaking; dawn:*–morning.
4892. מַשְׁחֵת *mash-khayth';* for 4889; *destruction:*–destroying.
4893. מִשְׁחָת *mish-khawth';* or מָשְׁחָת *mosh-khawth';* from 7843; *disfigurement:*–corruption, marred.
4894. מִשְׁטוֹחַ *mish-to'-akh;* or מִשְׁטַח *mish-takh';* from 7849; a *spreading*-place:–(to) spread (forth, -ing, upon).
4895. מַשְׂטֵמָה *mas-tay-maw';* from the same as 7850; *enmity:*–hatred.
4896. מִשְׁטָר *mish-tawr';* from 7860; *jurisdiction:*–dominion.
4897. מֶשִׁי *meh'-shee;* from 4871; *silk* (as *drawn* from the cocoon):–silk.
4898. מְשֵׁיזַבְאֵל *mesh-ay-zab-ale';* from an equiv. to 7804 and 410; *delivered of God; Meshezabel,* an Isr.:–Meshezabeel.
4899. מָשִׁיחַ *maw-shee'-akh;* from 4886; *anointed;* usually a *consecrated* person (as a king, priest, or saint); spec., the *Messiah:*–anointed, Messiah.
4900. מָשַׁךְ *maw-shak';* a prim. root; to *draw,* used in a great variety of appl. (incl. to *sow,* to *sound,* to *prolong,* to *develop,* to *march,* to *remove,* to *delay,* to *be tall,* etc.):–draw (along, out), continue, defer, extend, forbear, X give, handle, make (pro-, sound) long, X sow, scatter, stretch out.
4901. מֶשֶׁךְ *meh'shek;* from 4900; a *sowing;* also a *possession:*–precious, price.
4902. מֶשֶׁךְ *meh'-shek;* the same in form as 4901, but prob. of for. der.; *Meshek,* a son of Japheth, and the people descended from him:–Mesech, Meshech.
4903. מִשְׁכַּב *mish-kab'* (Chald.); cor. to 4904; a *bed:*–bed.
4904. מִשְׁכָּב *mish-kawb';* from 7901; a *bed* (fig., a *bier*); abstr., *sleep*; by euphem., carnal *intercourse:*–bed([-chamber]), couch, lieth (lying) with.
4905. מַשְׂכִּיל *mas-keel';* from 7919; *instructive,* i.e. a *didactic* poem:–Maschil.
4906. מַשְׂכִּית *mas-keeth';* from the same as 7906; a *figure* (carved on stone, the wall, or any obj.); fig., *imagination:*–conceit, image(-ry), picture, X wish.
4907. מִשְׁכַּן *mish-kan';* (Chald.) cor. to 4908; *residence:*–habitation.
4908. מִשְׁכָּן *mish-kawn';* from 7931; a *residence* (incl. a shepherd's *hut,* the *lair* of animals, fig., the *grave;* also the *Temple*); spec., the *Tabernacle* (prop. its wooden walls):–dwelleth, dwelling (place), habitation, tabernacle, tent.
4909. מַשְׂכֹּרֶת *mas-koh'-reth;* from 7936; *wages* or a *reward:*–reward, wages.
4910. מָשַׁל *maw-shal';* a prim. root; to *rule:*–(have, make to have) dominion, governor, X indeed, reign, (bear, cause to, have) rule (-ing, -r), have power.
4911. מָשַׁל *maw-shal';* denom. from 4912; to *liken,* i.e. (trans.) to use fig. language (an allegory, adage, song or the like); intr., to

resemble:–be(-come) like, comp., use (as a) proverb, speak (in proverbs), utter.

4912. מָשָׁל *maw-shawl';* app. from 4910 in some or. sense of *superiority* in ment. action; prop. a pithy *maxim,* usually of metaphorical nat.; hence, a *simile* (as an adage, poem, discourse):–byword, like, parable, proverb.

4913. מָשָׁל *maw-shawl';* for 4861; *Mashal,* a place in Pal.:–Mashal.

4914. מְשֹׁל *mesh-ol';* from 4911; a *satire:*–byword.

4915. מֹשֶׁל *mo'-shel;* (1) from 4910; *empire;* (2) from 4911; a *parallel:*–dominion, like.

4916. מִשְׁלוֹחַ *mish-lo'-akh;* or מִשְׁלֹחַ *mish-lo'-akh;* also מִשְׁלָח *mish-lawkh';* from 7971; a *sending* out, i.e. (abstr.) *presentation* (favorable), or *seizure* (unfavorable); also (concr.) a place of *dismissal,* or a *business* to be discharged:–to lay, to put, sending (forth), to set.

4917. מִשְׁלַחַת *mish-lakh'-ath;* fem. of 4916; a *mission,* i.e. (abstr.) and favorable) *release,* or (concr. and unfavorable) an *army:*–discharge, sending.

4918. מְשֻׁלָּם *mesh-ool-lawm';* from 7999; *allied; Meshullam,* the name of seventeen Isr.:–Meshullam.

4919. מְשִׁלֵּמוֹת *mesh-il-lay-mohth';* pl. from 7999; *reconciliations:–Meshillemoth,* an Isr.:–Meshillemoth. Comp. 4921.

4920. מְשֶׁלֶמְיָה *mesh-eh-lem-yaw';* or מְשֶׁלֶמְיָהוּ *mesh-eh-lem-yaw'-hoo;* from 7999 and 3050; *ally of Jah; Meshelemjah,* an Isr.:–Meshelemiah.

4921. מְשִׁלֵּמִית *mesh-il-lay-meeth';* from 7999; *reconciliation; Meshillemith,* an Isr.:–Meshillemith. Comp. 4919.

4922. מְשֻׁלֶּמֶת *mesh-ool-leh'-meth';* fem. of 4918; *Meshullemeth,* an Isr.s:–Meshullemeth.

4923. מְשַׁמָּה *mesh-am-maw';* from 8074; a *waste* or *amazement:*–astonishment, desolate.

4924. מַשְׁמָן *mash-mawn';* from 8080; *fat,* i.e. (lit. and abstr.) *fatness;* but usually (fig. and concr.) a *rich* dish, a *fertile* field, a *robust* man:–fat (one, -ness, -test, -test place).

4925. מִשְׁמַנָּה *mish-man-naw';* from 8080; *fatness; Mashmannah,* an Isr.:–Mishmannah.

4926. מִשְׁמָע *mish-maw';* from 8085; a *report:*–hearing.

4927. מִשְׁמָע *mish-maw';* the same as 4926; *Mishma,* the name of a son of Ishmael, and of an Isr.:–Mishma.

4928 מִשְׁמַעַת *mish-mah'-ath;* fem. of 4926 *audience,* i.e. the royal *court;* also *obedience,* i.e. (concr.) *subject:* bidding, guard, obey.

4929. מִשְׁמָר *mish-mawr';* from 8104; a *guard* (the man, the post or the *prison*); a *deposit* (fig.); also (as observed) a *usage* (abstr.), or an *example* (concr.):–diligence, guard, office, prison, ward, watch.

4930. מַשְׂמְרָה *mas-mer-aw';* for 4548 fem.; a *peg:*–nail.

4931. מִשְׁמֶרֶת *mish-meh'-reth;* fem. of 4929; *watch,* i.e. the act (*custody*), or (concr.) the *sentry,* the *post;* obj. *preservation,* or (concr.) *safe;* fig. *observance,* i.e. (abstr.) *duty* or (obj.) a *usage* or *party:*–charge, keep, or to be kept, office, ordinace, safeguard, ward, watch.

4932. מִשְׁנֶה *mish-neh';* from 8138; prop. a *repetition,* i.e. a *duplicate* (*copy* of a document), or a *double* (in amount); by impl., a *second* (in order, rank, age, quality or location):–college, copy, double, fatlings, next, second (order), twice as much.

4933. מְשִׁסָּה *mesh-is-saw';* from 8155; *plunder:*–booty, spoil.

4934. מִשְׁעוֹל *mish-ole';* from the same as 8168; a *hollow,* i.e. a narrow passage:–path.

4935. מִשְׁעִי *mish-ee';* prob. from 8159; *inspection:*–to supple.

4936. מִשְׁעָם *mish-awm';* app. from 8159; *inspection; Misham,* an Isr.:–Misham.

4937. מִשְׁעֵן *mish-ane';* or מִשְׁעָן *mish-awn';* from 8172; a *support* (concr.), i.e. (fig.) a *protector* or *sustenance:*–stay.

4938. מִשְׁעֵנָה *mish-ay-naw';* or מִשְׁעֶנֶת *mish-eh'-neth;* fem. of 4937; *support* (abstr.), i.e. (fig.) *sustenance* or (concr.) a *walking-stick:*–staff.

4939. מִשְׂפָּח *mis-pawkh';* from 5596; *slaughter:*–oppression.

4940. מִשְׁפָּחָה *mish-paw-khaw';* from 8192 [comp. 8198]; a *family,* i.e. circle of relatives; fig., a *class* (of persons), a *species* (of animals) or *sort* (of things); by ext. a *tribe* or *people:*–family, kind(-red).

4941. מִשְׁפָּט *mish-pawt';* from 8199; prop. a *verdict* (favorable or unfavorable) pronounced judicially, esp. a *sentence* or formal decree (human or [participant's] divine *law,* indiv. or coll.), incl. the act, the place, the suit, the crime, and the penalty; abstr., *justice,* incl. a participant's *right* or *privilege* (statutory or customary), or even a *style:*–+ adversary, ceremony, charge, X crime, custom, desert, determination, discretion, disposing, due, fashion, form, to be judged, judgment, just (-ice, -ly), (manner of) law(-ful), manner, measure, (due) order, ordinance, right, sentence, usest, X worthy, + wrong.

4942. מִשְׁפָּת *mish-pawth';* from 8192; a *stall* for cattle (only dual):–burden, sheepfold.

4943. מֶשֶׁק *meh'-shek;* from an un. root mean. to *hold; possession:*–+ steward.

4944. מַשָּׁק *mash-shawk';* from 8264; a *traversing,* i.e. rapid *motion:*–running to and fro.

4945. מַשְׁקֶה *mash-keh';* from 8248; prop. causing to *drink,* i.e. a *butler;* by impl. (intr.), *drink* (itself); fig., a *well-watered* region:–butler(-ship), cupbearer, drink(-ing), fat pasture, watered.

4946. מִשְׁקוֹל *mish-kole';* from 8254; *weight:*–weight.

4947. מַשְׁקוֹף *mash-kofe';* from 8259 in its or. sense of *overhanging;* a *lintel:*–lintel.

4948. מִשְׁקָל *mish-kawl';* from 8254; *weight* (numerically estimated); hence, *weighing* (the act):–(full) weight.

4949. מִשְׁקֶלֶת *mish-keh'-leth;* or מִשְׁקֹלֶת *mish-ko'-leth;* fem. of 4948 or 4947; a *weight,* i.e. a *plummet* (with line attached):–plummet.

4950. מִשְׁקָע *mish-kaw';* from 8257; a *settling* place (of water), i.e. a pond:–deep.

4951. מִשְׂרָה *mis-raw';* from 8280; *empire:*–government.

4952. מִשְׁרָה *mish-raw';* from 8281 in the sense of *loosening; maceration,* i.e. steeped *juice:*–liquor.

4953. מַשְׁרוֹקִי *mash-ro-kee'* (Chald.); from a root cor. to 8319; a (mus.) *pipe* (from its *whistling* sound):–flute.

4954. מִשְׁרָעִי *mish-raw-ee';* patrial from an un. noun from an un. root; prob. mean. to *stretch* out; ext.; a *Mishraite,* or inh. (coll.) of Mishra:–Mishraites.

4955. מִשְׂרָפָה *mis-raw-faw';* from 8313; *combustion,* i.e. *cremation* (of a corpse), or *calcination* (of lime):–burning.

4956. מִשְׂרְפוֹת מַיִם *mis-ref-ohth' mah'-yim;* from the pl. of 4955 and 4325; *burnings of water; Misrephoth-Majim,* a place in Pal.:–Misrephoth-mayim.

4957. מַשְׂרֵקָה *mas-ray-kaw';* a form for 7796 used denom.; *vineyard; Masrekah,* a place in Idumaea:–Masrekah.

4958. מַשְׂרֵת *mas-rayth';* app. from an un. root mean. to *perforate,* i.e. hollow out; a *pan:*–pan.

4959. מָשַׁשׁ *maw-shash';* a prim. root; to *feel* of; by impl., to *grope:*–feel, grope, search.

4960. מִשְׁתֶּה *mish-teh';* from 8354; *drink,* by impl., *drinking* (the act); also (by impl.) a *banquet* or (gen.) feast:–banquet, drank, drink, feast([-ed], -ing).

4961. מִשְׁתֵּה *mish-teh'* (Chald.); cor. to 4960; a *banquet:*–banquet.

4962. מַת *math;* from the same as 4970; prop. an *adult* (as of full length); by impl., a *man* (only in the pl.):–+ few, X friends, men, persons, X small.

4963. מַתְבֵּן *math-bane';* denom. from 8401; *straw* in the heap:–straw.

4964. מֶתֶג *meh-theg;* from an un. root mean. to *curb;* a *bit:*–bit, bridle.

4965. מֶתֶג הָאַמָּה *meh'-theg haw-am-maw';* from 4964 and 520 with the art. interp.; *bit of the metropolis; Metheg-ha-Ammah,* an epithet of Gath:–Metheg-ammah.

4966. מָתוֹק *maw-thoke';* or מָתוּק *maw-thook';* from 4985; *sweet:*–sweet(-er, -ness).

4967. מְתוּשָׁאֵל *meth-oo-shaw-ale';* from 4962 and 410, with the rel. interp.; *man who* (is) *of God; Methusaël,* an antediluvian patriarch:–Methusael.

4968. מְתוּשֶׁלַח *meth-oo-sheh'-lakh;* from 4962 and 7973; *man of a dart; Methushelach,* an antediluvian patriarch:–Methuselah.

4969. מָתַח *maw-thakh';* a prim. root; to *stretch* out:–spread out.

4970. מָתַי *maw-thah'ee;* from an un. root mean. to *extend;* prop. *extent* (of time); but used only adv. (esp. with other particle prefixes), *when* (either rel. or interrog.):–long, when.

4971. מַתְכֹּנֶת *math-ko'-neth;* or מַתְכֻּנֶת *math-koo'-neth;* from 8505 in the transferred sense of *measuring; proportion* (in size, number or ingredients):–composition, mea-sure, state, tale.

4972. מַתְּלָאָה *mat-tel-aw-aw';* from 4100 and 8513; *what a trouble!:*–what a weariness.

4973. מְתַלְּעָה *meth-al-leh-aw';* contr. from 3216; prop. a *biter,* i.e. a tooth:–cheek (jaw) tooth, jaw.

4974. מְתֹם *meth-ohm';* from 8552; *wholesomeness;* also (adv.) *completely:*–men [*by reading* 4962], soundness.

4975. מֹתֶן *mo'-then;* from an un. root mean. to *be slender;* prop. the *waist* or small of the back; only in pl. the *loins:*–+ greyhound, loins, side.

4976. מַתָּן *mat-tawn';* from 5414; a *present:*–gift, to give, reward.

4977. מַתָּן *mat-tawn';* the same as 4976; *Mattan,* the name of a priest of Baal, and of an Isr.:–Mattan.

4978. מַתְּנָא *mat-ten-aw'* (Chald.); cor. to 4979:–gift.

4979. מַתָּנָה *mat-taw-naw';* fem. of 4976; a

present; spec. (in a good sense), a sacrificial *offering,* (in a bad sense) a *bribe:*–gift.

4980. מַתָּנָה *mat-taw-naw';* the same as 4979; *Mattanah,* a place in the Desert:–Mattanah.

4981. מִתְנִי *mith-nee';* prob. patrial from an un. noun mean. *slenderness;* a mithnite, or inh. of Methen:–Mithnite.

4982. מַתְּנַי *mat-ten-ah'ee;* from 4976; *liberal; Mattenai,;* the name of three Isr.:–Mattenai.

4983. מַתַּנְיָה *mat-tan-yaw';* or מַתַּנְיָהוּ *mat-tan-yaw'-hoo;* from 4976 and 3050; *gift of Jah; Mattanjah,* the name of ten Isr.:–Mattaniah.

4984. מִתְנַשֵּׂא *mith-nas-say';* from 5375; (used as abstr.) supreme *exaltation:*–exalted.

4985. מָתַק *maw-thak';* a prim. root; to *suck,* by impl., to *relish,* or (intr.) *be sweet:*–be (made, X take) sweet.

4986. מֶתֶק *meh'-thek;* from 4985; fig., *pleasantness* (of discourse):–sweetness.

4987. מֹתֶק *mo'-thek;* from 4985; *sweetness:*–sweetness.

4988. מָתָק *maw-thawk';* from 4985; a *dainty,* i.e. (gen.) *food:*–feed sweetly

4989. מִתְקָה *mith-kaw';* fem. of 4987; *sweetness; Mithkah,* a place in the Desert:–Mithcah.

4990. מִתְרְדָת *mith-red-awth';* of Pers. or.; *Mithredath,* the name of two Pers.:–Mithredath.

4991. מַתָּת *mat-tawth';* fem. of 4976 abb. form; a *present:*–gift.

4992. מַתַּתָּה *mat-tat-taw';* for 4993; *gift of Jah; Mattattah,* an Isr.:–Mattathah.

4993. מַתִּתְיָה *mat-tith-yaw';* or מַתִּתְיָהוּ *mat-tith-yaw'-hoo;* from 4991 and 3050; *gift of Jah; Mattithjah,* the name of four Isr.:–Mattithiah.

נ

4994. נָא *naw;* a prim. particle of incitement and entreaty, which may usually be rendered: *I pray,now,* or *then;* added mostly to verbs (in the imper. or future), or to interj., occasionally to an adv. or conj.:–I beseech (pray) thee (you), go to, now, oh.

4995. נָא *naw;* app. from 5106 in the sense of *harshness* from refusal; prop. *tough,* i.e. *uncooked* (flesh):–raw.

4996. נֹא *no;* of Eg. or.; *No* (i.e. *Thebes*), the capital of Upper Eg.:–No. Comp. 528.

4997. נֹאד *node;* or נאוֹד *node;* also (fem.) נֹאדָה *no-daw';* from an un. root a (skin or leather) *bag* (for fluids):–bottle.

4998. נָאָה *naw-aw';* a prim. root; prop. to *be at home,* i.e. (by impl.) to be *pleasant* (or *suitable*), i.e. *beautiful:*–be beautiful, become, be comely.

4999. נָאָה *naw-aw';* from 4998; a *home;* fig., a *pasture:*–habitation, house, pasture, pleasant place.

5000. נָאוֶה *naw-veh';* from 4998 or 5116; *suitable,* or *beautiful:*–becometh, comely, seemly.

5001. נָאַם *naw-am;* a prim. root; prop. to *whisper,* i.e. (by impl.) to *utter* as a oracle:–say.

5002. נְאֻם *neh-oom';* from 5001; an *oracle:*–(hath) said, saith.

5003. נָאַף *naw-af';* a prim. root; to *commit adultery;* fig., to *apostatize:*–adulterer (-ess), commit(-ing) adultery, woman that breaketh wedlock.

5004. נִאֻף *nee-oof';* from 5003; *adultery:*–adultery.

5005. נַאֲפוּף *nah-af-oof';* from 5003; *adultery:*–adultery.

5006. נָאַץ *naw-ats';* a prim. root; to *scorn;* –abhor, (give occasion to) blaspheme, contemn, despise, X great, provoke.

5007. נְאָצָה *neh-aw-tsaw';* or נֶאָצָה *neh-aw-tsaw';* from 5006; *scorn:*–blasphemy.

5008. נָאַק *naw-ak';* a prim. root; to *groan:*–groan.

5009. נְאָקָה *neh-aw-kaw';* from 5008; a *groan:*–groaning.

5010. נָאַר *naw-ar';* a prim. root; to *reject:*–abhor, make void.

5011. נֹב *nobe;* the same as 5108; *fruit; Nob,* a place in Pal.:–Nob.

5012. נָבָא *naw-baw';* a prim. root; to *prophesy,* i.e. speak (or sing) by inspiration (in prediction or simple discourse):–prophesy (-ing), make self a prophet.

5013. נְבָא *neb-aw'* (Chald.); cor. to 5012:–prophesy.

5014. נָבַב *naw-bab';* a prim. root; to *pierce;* to *be hollow,* or (fig.) *foolish:*–hollow, vain.

5015. נְבוֹ *neb-o';* prob. of for. der.; *Nebo,* the name of a Bab. deity, also of a mountain in Moab, and of a place in Pal.:–Nebo.

5016. נְבוּאָה *neb-oo-aw';* from 5012; a *prediction* (spoken or written):–prophecy.

5017. נְבוּאָה *neb-oo-aw* (Chald.); cor. to 5016; inspired *teaching:*–prophesying.

5018. נְבוּזַרְאֲדָן *neb-oo-zar-ad-awn';* of for. or.; *Nebuzaradan,* a Babylonian gen.:–Nebuzaradan.

5019. נְבוּכַדְנֶאצַּר *neb-oo-kad-nets-tsar';* or (2 Kings 24:1, 10) נְבֻכַדְנֶאצַּר *neb-oo-kad-nets-tsar';* or (Es. 2:6; Daniel 1:18) נְבוּכַדְנֶצַּר *neb-oo-kad-nets-tsar';* or נְבוּכַדְרֶאצַּר *neb-oo-kad-rets-tsar';* or נְבוּכַדְרֶאצּוֹר (Ezra 2:1; Jeremiah 49:28) *neb-oo-kad-rets-tsore';* or for. der.; *Nebukadnetstsar* (or *-retstsar,* or *-retstsor*), king of Babylon:–Nebuchadnezzar, Nebuchadrezzar.

5020. נְבוּכַדְנֶצַּר *neb-oo-kad-nets-tsar'* (Chald.); cor. to 5019:–Nebuchadnezzar.

5021. נְבוּשַׁזְבָּן *neb-oo-shaz-bawn';* of for. der.; *Nebushazban,* Nebuchadnezzar's chief eunuch:–Nebushazban.

5022. נָבוֹת *naw-both';* fem. pl. from the same as 5011; *fruits; Naboth,* an Isr.:–Naboth.

5023. נְבִזְבָּה *neb-iz-baw'* (Chald.); of unc. der.; a *largess:*–reward.

5024. נָבַח *naw-bakh';* a prim. root; to *bark* (as a dog):–bark.

5025. נֹבַח *no'-bach;* from 5024; a *bark; Nobach,* the name of an Isr., and of a place E. of the Jordan:–Nobah.

5026. נִבְחַז *nib-khaz';* of for. or.; *Nibchaz,* a deity of the Avites:–Nibhaz.

5027. נָבַט *naw-bat';* a prim. root; to *scan,* i.e. look intently at; by impl., to *regard* with pleasure, favor or care:–(cause to) behold, consider, look (down), regard, have respect, see.

5028. נְבָט *neb-awt';* from 5027; *regard; Nebat,* the father of Jeroboam I:–Nebat.

5029. נְבִיא *neb-ee'* (Chald.); cor. to 5030; a *prophet:*–prophet.

5030. נָבִיא *naw-bee';* from 5012; a *prophet* or (gen.) *inspired* man:–prophecy, that prophesy, prophet.

5031. נְבִיאָה *neb-ee-yaw';* fem. of 5030; a *prophetess* or (gen.) *inspired* woman; by impl., a *poetess;* by association a *prophet's wife:*–prophetess.

5032. נְבָיוֹת *neb-aw-yoth';* or נְבָיֹת *neb-aw-yoth';* fem. pl. from 5107; *fruitfulnesses; Nebajoth,* a son of Ismael, and the country settled by him:–Nebaioth, Nebajoth.

5033. נֵבֶךְ *nay'-bek;* from an un. root mean. to *burst* forth; a *fountain:*–spring.

5034. נָבֵל *naw-bale';* a prim. root; to *wilt;* gen., to *fall* away, *fail, faint;* fig., to *be foolish* or (mor.) *wicked;* caus., to *despise, disgrace:*–disgrace, dishounour, lightly esteem, fade (away, -ing), fall (down, -ling, off), do foolishly, come to nought, X surely, make vile, wither.

5035. נֶבֶל *neh'-bel;* or נֵבֶל *nay'-bel;* from 5034; a skin-*bag* for liquids (from *collapsing* when empty); hence, a *vase* (as similar in shape when full); also a *lyre* (as having a body of like form):–bottle, pitcher, psaltery, vessel, viol.

5036. נָבָל *naw-bawl';* from 5034; *stupid; wicked* (esp. *impious*):– fool(-ish, -ish man, -ish woman), vile person.

5037. נָבָל *naw-bawl';* the same as 5036; *dolt; Nabal,* an Isr.:–Nabal.

5038. נְבֵלָה *neb-ay-law';* from 5034; a *flabby* thing, i.e. a *carcase* or *carrion* (human or bestial, often coll.); fig., an *idol:*–(dead) body, (dead) carcase, dead of itself, which died, (beast) that (which) dieth of itself.

5039. נְבָלָה *neb-aw-law';* fem. of 5036; *foolishness,* i.e. (mor.) *wickedness;* concr., a *crime;* by ext., *punishment:*–folly, vile, villany.

5040. נַבְלוּת *nab-looth';* from 5036; prop. *disgrace,* i.e. the (female) *pudenda:*–lewdness.

5041. נְבַלָּט *neb-al-lawt';* app. from 5036 and 3909; *foolish secrecy; Neballat,* a place in Pal.:–Neballat.

5042. נָבַע *naw-bah';* a prim. root; to *gush* forth; fig., to *utter* (good or bad words); spec., to *emit* (a foul odor):–belch out, flowing, pour out, send forth, utter (abundantly).

5043. נֶבְרְשָׁא *neb-reh-shaw'* (Chald.); from an un. root mean. to *shine;* a *light;* pl. (coll.) a *chandelier:*–candlestick.

5044. נִבְשָׁן *nib-shawn';* of unc. der.; *Nibshan,* a place in Pal.:–Nibshan.

5045. נֶגֶב *neh'-gheb;* from an un. root mean. to *be parched;* the *south* (from its drought); spec., the *Negeb* or southern district of Judah, occasionally, *Eg.* (as south to Pal.):–south (country, side, -ward).

5046. נָגַד *naw-gad';* a prim. root; prop. to *front,* i.e. stand boldly out opposite; by impl. (caus.), to *manifest;* fig., to *announce* (always by word of mouth to one present); spec., to *expose, predict, explain, praise:*–bewray, X certainly, certify, declare(-ing), denounce, expound, X fully, messenger, plainly, profess, rehearse, report, shew (forth), speak, X surely, tell, utter.

5047. נְגַד *neg-ad';* (Chald.) cor. to 5046; to *flow* (through the idea of *clearing* the way):–issue.

5048. נֶגֶד *neh'-ghed;* from 5046; a *front,* i.e. part opposite; spec. a *counterpart,* or mate; usually (adv., esp. with prep.) *over against* or *before:*–about, (over) against, X aloof, X far (off), X from, over, presence, X other side, sight, X to view.

5049. נֶגֶד *neh'-ghed* (Chald.); cor. to 5048; *opposite:*–toward.

5050. נָגַהּ *naw-gah';* a prim. root; to *glitter;* caus., to *illuminate:*–(en-)lighten, (cause to) shine.

5051. נֹגַהּ *no'-gah;* from 5050; *brilliancy* (lit. or fig.):–bright(-ness), light, (clear) shining.

5052. נֹגַהּ *no'-gah;* the same as 5051; *Nogah,* a son of David:–Nogah.

5053. נֹגַהּ *no'-gah* (Chald.); cor. to 5051; *dawn:*–morning.

5054. נְגֹהָה *neg-o-haw';* fem. of 5051; *splendor*:–brightness.

5055. נָגַח *naw-gakh';* a prim. root; to *but* with the horns; fig., to *war* against:–gore, push (down, -ing).

5056. נַגָּח *nag-gawkh';* from 5055; *butting*, i.e. *vicious*:–used (wont) to push.

5057. נָגִיד *naw-gheed';* or נָגִד *naw-gheed';* from 5046; a *commander* (as occupying the *front*), civil, military or relig.; gen. (abstr., pl.), *honorable* themes:–captain, chief, excellent thing, (chief) governor, leader, noble, prince, (chief) ruler.

5058. נְגִינָה *neg-ee-naw';* or נְגִינַת (Ps. 61 : title) *neg-ee-nath';* from 5059; prop. instrumental *music*; by impl. a stringed *instrument*; by ext., a *poem* set to music; spec., an *epigram*:–stringed instrument, musick, Neginoth [*pl.*], song.

5059. נָגַן *naw-gan';* a prim. root; prop. to *thrum*, i.e. *beat* a tune with the fingers; exp. to *play* on a stringed instrument; hence (gen.), to *make music*:–player on instruments, sing to the stringed instruments, melody, ministrel, play(-er, -ing).

5060. נָגַע *naw-gah';* a prim. root; prop. to *touch*, i.e. *lay the hand upon* (for any purpose; euphem., to *lie with* a woman); by impl., to *reach* (fig., to *arrive, acquire*); violently, to *strike* (punish, defeat, destroy, etc.):–beat, (X be able to) bring (down), cast, come (nigh), draw near (nigh), get up, happen, join, near, plague, reach (up), smite, strike, touch.

5061. נֶגַע *neh'-gah;* from 5060; a *blow* (fig., *infliction*); also (by impl.) a *spot* (concr., a *leprous* person or dress):–plague, sore, stricken, stripe, stroke, wound.

5062. נָגַף *naw-gaf';* a prim. root; to *push, gore, defeat, stub* (the toe), *inflict* (a disease):–beat, dash, hurt, plague, slay, smite (down), strike, stumble, X surely, put to the worse.

5063. נֶגֶף *neh'-ghef;* from 5062; a *trip* (of the foot); fig., an *infliction* (of disease):–plague, stumbling.

5064. נָגַר *naw-gar';* a prim. root; to *flow;* fig., to *stretch* out; caus., to *pour* out or down; fig., to *deliver* over:–fall, flow away, pour down (out), run, shed, spilt, trickle down.

5065. נָגַשׂ *naw-gas';* a prim. root; to *drive* (an animal, a workman, a debtor, an army); by impl., to *tax, harass, tyrannize*:–distress, driver, exact(-or), oppress(-or), X raiser of taxes, taskmaster.

5066. נָגַשׁ *naw-gash';* a prim. root; to *be* or *come* (caus., *bring*) *near* (for any purpose); euphem., to *lie with* a woman; as an enemy, to *attack*; relig. to *worship*; caus., to *present*; fig., to *adduce* an argument; by reversal, to *stand back*:–(make to) approach (nigh), bring (forth, hither, near), (cause to) come (hither, near, nigh), give place, go hard (up), (be, draw, go) near (nigh), offer, overtake, present, put, stand.

5067. נֵד *nade*; from 5110 in the sense of *piling* up; a *mound*, i.e. *wave*:–heap.

5068. נָדַב *naw-dab';* a prim. root; to *impel*; hence, to *volunteer* (as a soldier), to *present* spontaneously:–offer freely, be (give, make, offer self) willing(-ly).

5069. נְדַב *ned-ab'* (Chald.); cor. to 5068; *be* (or *give*) *liberal*(*-ly*):–(be minded of...own) freewill (offering), offer freely (willingly).

5070. נָדָב *naw-dawb';* from 5068; *liberal; Nadab*, the name of four Isr.:–Nadab.

5071. נְדָבָה *ned-aw-baw';* from 5068; prop. (abstr.) *spontaneity*, or (act.) *spontaneous*; also (concr.) a *spontaneous* or (by inference, in pl.) *abundant* gift:–free (-will) offering, freely, plentiful, voluntary (-ily, offering), willing(-ly), offering).

5072. נְדַבְיָה *ned-ab-yaw';* from 5068 and 3050; *largess of Jah; Nedabjah*, an Isr.:–Nedabiah.

5073. נִדְבָּךְ *nid-bawk'* (Chald.); from a root mean. to *stick*; a *layer* (of building materials):–row.

5074. נָדַד *naw-dad';* a prim. root; prop. to *wave* to and fro (rarely to *flap* up and down); fig., to *rove, flee*, or (caus.) to *drive* away:–chase (away), X could not, depart, flee (X apace, away), (re-)move, thrust away, wander (abroad, -er, -ing).

5075. נְדַד *ned-ad'* (Chald.); cor. to 5074; to *depart*:–go from.

5076. נָדֻד *naw-dood'* pass.part. of 5074; prop. *tossed*; abstr., a *rolling* (on the bed):–tossing to and fro.

5077. נָדָה *naw-daw';* or נָדָא (2 Kings 17:21) *naw-daw';* a prim. root; prop. to *toss*; fig., to *exclude*, i.e. banish, postpone, prohibit:–cast out, drive, put far away.

5078. נֵדֶה *nay'-deh* from 5077 in the sense of freely *flinging* money; a *bounty* (for prostitution):–gifts.

5079. נִדָּה *nid-daw';* from 5074; prop. *rejection*; by impl., *impurity*, esp. pers. (menstruation) or mor. (idolatry, incest):–X far, filthiness, X flowers, menstruous (woman), put apart, X removed (woman), separation, set apart, unclean(-ness, thing, with filthiness).

5080. נָדַח *naw-dakh';* a prim. root; to *push* off; used in a great variety of appl., lit. and fig. (to expel, mislead, strike, inflict, etc.):–banish, bring, cast down (out), chase, compel, draw away, drive (away, out, quite), fetch a stroke, force, go away, outcast, thrust away (out), withdraw.

5081. נָדִיב *naw-deeb';* from 5068; prop. *voluntary*, i.e. generous; hence, *magnanimous*; as noun, a *grandee* (sometimes a *tyrant*):–free, liberal (things), noble, prince, willing ([hearted]).

5082. נְדִיבָה *ned-ee-baw';* fem. of 5081; prop. *nobility*, i.e. reputation:–soul.

5083. נָדָן *naw-dawn';* prob. from an un. root mean. to *give*; a *present* (for prostitution):–gift.

5084. נָדָן *naw-dawn';* of unc. der.; a *sheath* (of a sword):–sheath.

5085. נִדְנֶה *nid-neh'* (Chald.); from the same as 5084; a *sheath*; fig., the *body* (as the receptacle of the soul):–body.

5086. נָדַף *naw-daf';* a prim. root; to *shove* asunder, i.e. *disperse*:–drive (away, to and fro), thrust down, shaken, tossed to and fro.

5087. נָדַר *naw-dar';* a prim. root; to *promise* (pos., to do or give something to God):–(make a) vow.

5088. נֶדֶר *neh'-der*; or נֵדֶר *nay'-der*; from 5087; a *promise* (to God); also (concr.) a thing *promised*:–vow([-ed]).

5089. נֹהַּ *no'-ah;* from an un. root mean. to *lament; lamentation*:–wailing.

5090. נָהַג *naw-hag';* a prim. root; to *drive* forth (a person, an animal or chariot), i.e. *lead, carry away*; refl., to *proceed* (i.e. impel or guide oneself); also (from the *panting* induced by effort), to *sigh*:–acquaint, bring (away), carry away, drive (away), lead (away, forth), (be) guide, lead (away, forth).

5091. נָהָה *naw-haw';* a prim. root; to *groan*, i.e. *bewail*; hence (through the idea of *crying* aloud), to *assemble* (as if on proclamation):–lament, wail.

5092. נְהִי *neh-hee';* from 5091; an *elegy*:–lamentation, wailing.

5093. נִהְיָה *nih-yaw';* fem. of 5092; *lamentation*:–doleful.

5094. נְהִיר *neh-heere'* (Chald.); or נַהִירוּ *neh-hee-roo'* (Chald.); from the same as 5105; *illumination*, i.e. (fig.) wisdom:–light.

5095. נָהַל *naw-hal';* a prim. root; prop. to run with a *sparkle*, i.e. *flow*; hence (trans.), to *conduct*, and (by inference) to *protect, sustain*:–carry, feed, guide, lead (gently, on).

5096. נַהֲלָל *nah-hal-awl';* or נַהֲלֹל *nah-hal-ole';* the same as 5097; *Nahalal* or *Nahalol*, a place in Pal.:–Nahalal, Nahallal, Nahalol.

5097. נַהֲלֹל *nah-hal-ole';* from 5095; *pasture*:–bush.

5098. נָהַם *naw-ham';* a prim. root; to *growl*:–mourn, roar(-ing).

5099. נַהַם *nah'-ham;* from 5098; a *snarl*:–roaring.

5100. נְהָמָה *neh-haw-maw';* fem. of 5099; *snarling*:–disquietness, roaring.

5101. נָהַק *naw-hak*; a prim. root; to *bray* (as an ass), *scream* (from hunger):–bray.

5102. נָהַר *naw-har';* a prim. root; to *sparkle*, i.e. (fig.) be *cheerful*; hence (from the *sheen* of a running stream) to *flow*, i.e. (fig.) assemble:–flow (together), be lightened.

5103. נְהַר *neh-har'* (Chald.); from a root cor. to 5102; a *river*, esp. the Euphrates:–river, stream.

5104. נָהָר *naw-hawr';* from 5102; a *stream* (incl. the *sea*; exp. the Nile, Euphrates, etc.); fig., *prosperity*:–flood, river.

5105. נְהָרָה *neh-haw-raw';* from 5102 in its or. sense; *daylight*:–light.

5106. נוּא *noo*; a prim. root; to *refuse, forbid, dissuade*, or *neutralize*:–break, disallow, discourage, make of none effect.

5107. נוּב *noob*; a prim. root; to *germinate*, i.e. (fig.) to (caus., *make*) *flourish*; also (of words), to *utter*:–bring forth (fruit), make cheerful, increase.

5108. נוֹב *nobe*; or נֵיב *nabe*; from 5107; *produce*, lit. or fig.:–fruit.

5109. נוֹבַי *no-bah'ee;* from 5108; *fruitful; Nobai*, an Isr.:–Nebai .

5110. נוּד *nood;* a prim. root; to *nod*, i.e. waver; fig., to *wander, flee, disappear*; also (from shaking the head in sympathy), to *console, deplore*, or (from *tossing* the head in scorn) *taunt*:–bemoan, flee, get, mourn, make to move, take pity, remove, shake, skip for joy, be sorry, vagabond, way, wandering.

5111. נוּד *nood* (Chald.); cor. to 5116; to *flee*:–get away.

5112. נוֹד *node*; [only defect. נֹד *node*]; from 5110; *exile*:–wandering.

5113. נוֹד *node*; the same as 5112; *vagrancy*; *Nod*, the land of Cain:–Nod.

5114. נוֹדָב *no-dawb';* from 5068; *noble; Nodab*, an Arab tribe:–Nodab.

5115. נָוָה *naw-vaw';* a prim. root; to *rest* (as at home); caus. (through the implied idea of *beauty* [comp. 5116]), to *celebrate* (with praises):–keep at home, prepare an habitation.

5116. נָוֶה *naw-veh';* or נָוָה (fem.) *naw-vaw';* from 5115; (adj.) at *home*; hence (by impl.

of satisfaction) *lovely*; also (noun) a *home*, of God (temple), men (residence), flocks (pasture), or wild animals (*den*):–comely, dwelling (place), fold, habitation, pleasant place, sheepcote, stable, tarried.

5117. נוּחַ *noo'-akh*; a prim. root; to *rest*, i.e. *settle* down; used in a great variety of appl., lit. and fig., intr., trans. and caus. (to *dwell, stay, let fall, place, let alone, withdraw, give comfort*, etc.):–cease, be confederate, lay, let down, (be) quiet, remain, (cause to, be at, give, have, make to) rest, set down. Comp. 3241.

5118. נוּחַ *noo'-akh*; or נוֹחַ *no'-akh*; from 5117; *quiet*:–rest(-ed, -ing place).

5119. נוֹחָה *no-chaw'*; fem. of 5118; *quietude; Nochah*, an Isr.:–Nohah.

5120. נוּט *noot*; to *quake*:–be moved.

5121. נָוִית *naw-veeth'*; from 5115; *residence*; *Navith*, a place in Pal.:–Naioth .

5122. נְוָלוּ *nev-aw-loo'* (Chald.); נְוָלִי *nev-aw-lee'* (Chald.); from an un. root prob. mean. to be *foul*; a *sink*:–dunghill.

5123. נוּם *noom*; a prim. root; to slumber (from drowsiness):–sleep, *slumber*.

5124. נוּמָה *noo-maw'* from 5123; *sleepiness*:–drowsiness.

5125. נוּן *noon*; a prim. root; to *resprout*, i.e. propagate by shoots; fig., to *be perpetual*:–be continued.

5126. נוּן *noon*; or נוֹן (1 Ch.. 7:27) *nohn*; from 5125; *perpetuity*, *Nun* or *Non*, the father of Joshua:–Non, Nun.

5127. נוּס *noos*; a prim root; to *flit*, i.e. *vanish* away (subside, escape; caus., chase, impel, deliver):–X abate, away, be displayed, (make to) flee (away, -ing), put to flight, X hide, lift up a standard.

5128. נוּעַ *noo'-ah*; a prim. root; to *waver*, in a great variety of appl., lit. and fig. (as subjoined):–continually, fugitive, X make, to [go] up and down, be gone away, (be) move (-able, -d), be promoted, reel, remove, scatter, set, shake, sift, stagger, to and fro, be vagabond, wag, (make) wander (up and down).

5129. נוֹעַדְיָה *no-ad-yaw'*; from 3259 and 3050; *convened of Jah*; *Noadjah*, the name of an Isr., and a false prophetess:–Noadiah.

5130. נוּף *noof*; a prim. root; to *quiver* (i.e. *vibrate* up and down, or *rock* to and fro); used in a great variety of appl. (incl. sprinkling, beckoning, rubbing, bastinadoing, sawing, waving, etc.):–lift up, move, offer, perfume, send, shake, sift, strike, wave.

5131. נוֹף *nofe*; from 5130; *elevation*:–situation. Comp. 5297.

5132. נוּץ *noots*; a prim. root; prop. to *flash*; hence, to *blossom* (from the brilliancy of color); also, to *fly* away (from the quickness of motion):–flee away, bud (forth).

5133. נוֹצָה *no-tsaw'*; or נֹצָה *no-tsaw'*; fem. act.part. of 5327 in the sense of *flying*; a *pinion* (or wing feather); often (coll.) *plumage*:–feather(-s), ostrich.

5134. נוּק *nook*; a prim. root; to *suckle*:–nurse.

5135. נוּר *noor* (Chald.); from an un. root (cor. to that of 5216) mean. to *shine; fire*:–fiery, fire.

5136. נוּשׁ *noosh;* a prim. root; to be *sick*, i.e. (fig.) *distressed*:–be full of heaviness.

5137. נָזָה *naw-zaw'*; a prim. root; to *spirt*, i.e. *besprinkle* (esp. in expiation):–sprinkle.

5138. נָזִיד *naw-zeed'*; from 2102; something *boiled*, i.e. *soup*:–pottage.

5139. נָזִיר *naw-zeer'*; or נָזִר *naw-zeer'*; from 5144; *separate*, i.e. consecrated (as *prince*, a *Nazirite*); hence (fig. from the latter) an *unpruned* vine (like an unshorn Nazirite):–Nazarite, separate(-d), vine undressed.

5140. נָזַל *naw-zal'*; a prim. root; to *drip*, or *shed* by trickling:–distil, drop, flood, (cause to) flow(-ing), gush out, melt, pour (down), running water, stream.

5141. נֶזֶם *neh'-zem*; from an un. root of unc. mean.; a nose-*ring*:–earring, jewel.

5142. נְזַק *nez-ak'* (Chald.); cor. to the root of 5143; to *suffer* (caus., *inflict*) *loss*:–have (en-)damage, hurt(-ful).

5143. נֵזֶק *nay'zek*; from an un. root mean. to *injure; loss*:–damage.

5144. נָזַר *naw-zar'*; a prim. root; to *hold aloof*, i.e. (intr.) *abstain* (from food and drink, from impurity, and even from divine worship [i.e. *apostatize*]); spec., to *set apart* (to sacred purposes), i.e. *devote*:–consecrate, separate(-ing, self).

5145. נֶזֶר *neh'-zer*; or נֵזֶר *nay'-zer;* from 5144; prop. something *set apart*, i.e. (abstr.) *dedication* (of a priet or Nazirite); hence (concr.) unshorn *locks*; also (by impl.) a *chaplet* (esp. of royalty):–consecration, crown, hair, separation.

5146. נֹחַ *no'-akh;* the same as 5118; *rest*; *Noäch*, the patriarch of the flood:–Noah.

5147. נַחְבִּי *nakh-bee'*; from 2247; *occult; Nachbi*, an Isr.:–Nakbi.

5148. נָחָה *naw-khaw'*; a prim. root; to *guide;* by impl., to *transport* (into exile, or as colonists):–bestow, bring, govern, guide, lead (forth), put, straiten.

5149. נְחוּם *neh-khoom'*; from 5162; *comforted; Nechum*, an Isr.:–Nehum.

5150. נִחוּם *nee-khoom'*; or נִחֻם *nee-khoom'*; from 5162; prop. *consoled*; abstr., *solace*:–comfort(-able), repenting.

5151. נַחוּם *nakh-oom'*; from 5162; *comfortable; Nachum*, an Isr. prophet:–Nahum.

5152. נָחוֹר *naw-khore'*; from the same as 5170; *snorer; Nachor*, the name of the grandfather and a brother of Abraham:–Nahor.

5153. נָחוּשׁ *naw-khoosh'*; app. pass.part. of 5172 (perh. in the sense of *ringing*, i.e. bell-metal; or from the *red* color of the throat of a serpent [5175, as denom.] when hissing); *coppery*, i.e. (fig.) hard:–of brass.

5154. נְחוּשָׁה *nekh-oo-shaw'*; or נְחֻשָׁה *nekh-oo-shaw'*; fem. of 5153; *copper*:–brass, steel. Comp. 5176.

5155. נְחִילָה *nekh-ee-law'*; prob. denom. from 2485; a *flute*:–[*pl.*] Nehiloth.

5156. נְחִיר *nekh-eer'*; from the same as 5170; a *nostril*:–[*dual*] nostrils.

5157. נָחַל *naw-khal'*; a prim. root; to *inherit* (as a [fig.] mode of descent), or (gen.) to *occupy*; caus., to *bequeath*, or (gen.) *distribute, instate*:–divide, have ([inheritance]), take as a heritage, (cause to, give to, make to) inherit, (distribute for, divide [for, for an, by], give for, have, leave for, take [for]) inheritance, (have in, cause to, be made to) possess(-ion).

5158. נַחַל *nakh'-al*; or נַחְלָה (fem.) (Psalm 124:4) *nakh'-law*; or נַחֲלָה (Ezekiel 47:19; 48:28) *nakh-al-aw'*; from 5157 in its or. sense; a *stream*, esp. a winter *torrent*; (by impl.) a (narrow) *valley* (in which a brook runs); also a *shaft* (of a mine):–brook, flood, river, stream, valley.

5159. נַחֲלָה *nakh-al-aw'*; from 5157 (in its usual sense); prop. something *inherited*, i.e. (abstr.) *occupancy*, or (concr.) an *heirloom*; gen. an *estate, patrimony* or *portion*:–heritage, to inherit, inheritance, possession. Comp. 5158.

5160. נַחֲלִיאֵל *nakh-al-ee-ale'*; from 5158 and 410; *valley of God*; *Nachaliël*, a place in the Desert:–Nahaliel.

5161. נֶחֱלָמִי *nekh-el-aw-mee'*; app. a patron. from an un. name (app. pass.part. of 2492); *dreamed*; a *Nechelamite*, or desc. of Nechlam:–Nehelamite.

5162. נָחַם *naw-kham'*; a prim. root; prop. to *sigh*, i.e. *breathe* strongly; by impl., to *be sorry*, i.e. (in a favorable sense) to *pity, console* or (refl.) *rue*; or (unfavorably) to *avenge* (oneself):–comfort (self), ease [one's self], repent(-er,-ing, self).

5163. נַחַם *nakh'-am*; from 5162; *consolation; Nacham*, an Isr.:–Naham.

5164. נֹחַם *no'-kham*; from 5162; *ruefulness*, i.e. desistance:–repentance.

5165. נֶחָמָה *nekh-aw-maw'* from 5162; *consolation*:–comfort.

5166. נְחֶמְיָה *nekh-em-yaw'*; from 5162 and 3050; *consolation of Jah*; *Nechemjah*, the name of three Isr.:–Nehemiah.

5167. נַחֲמָנִי *nakh-am-aw-nee'*; from 5162; *consolatory; Nachamani*, an Isr.:–Nahamani.

5168. נַחְנוּ *nakh-noo'*; for 587; *we*:–we.

5169. נָחַץ *naw-khats'*; a prim. root; to be *urgent*:–require haste.

5170. נַחַר *nakh'-ar*; and (fem.) נַחֲרָה *nakh-ar-aw'*; from an un. root mean. to *snort* or *snore*; a snorting:–nostrils, snorting.

5171. נַחֲרַי *nakh-ar-ah'-ee*; or נַחְרַי *nakh-rah'-ee*; from the same as 5170; *snorer; Nacharai* or *Nachrai*, an Isr.:–Naharai, Nahari.

5172. נָחַשׁ *naw-khash'*; a prim. root; prop. to *hiss*, i.e. *whisper* a (magic) spell; gen., to *prognosticate*:–X certainly, divine, enchanter, (use) X enchantment, learn by experience, X indeed, diligently observe.

5173. נַחַשׁ *nakh'-ash*; from 5172; an *incantation* or *augury*:–enchantment.

5174. נְחָשׁ *nekh-awsh'* (Chald.); cor. to 5154; *copper*:–brass.

5175. נָחָשׁ *naw-khawsh'*; from 5172; a *snake* (from its *hiss*):–serpent.

5176. נָחָשׁ *naw-khawsh'*; the same as 5175; *Nachash*, the name of two persons app. non-Isr.:–Nahash.

5177. נַחְשׁוֹן *nakh-shone'*; from 5172; *enchanter; Nachshon*, an Isr.:–Naashon, Nahshon.

5178. נְחֹשֶׁת *nekh-o'-sheth*; for 5154; *copper*, hence, something made of that metal, i.e. *coin*, a *fetter*; fig., *base* (as compared with gold or silver):–brasen, brass, chain, copper, fetter (of brass), filthiness, steel.

5179. נְחֻשְׁתָּא *nekh-oosh-taw'*; from 5178; *copper; Nechushta*, an Isr.s:–Nehushta.

5180. נְחֻשְׁתָּן *nekh-oosh-tawn'*; from 5178; something made of *copper*, i.e. the copper *serpent* of the Desert:–Nehushtan.

5181. נָחַת *naw-khath'*; a prim. root; to *sink*, i.e. *descend*; caus., to *press* or *lead* down:–be broken, (cause to) come down, enter, go down, press sore, settle, stick fast.

5182. נְחַת *nekh-ath'* (Chald.); cor. to 5181; to *descend*; caus., to *bring away, deposit, depose*:–

carry, come down, depose, lay up, place.
5183. נַחַת *nakh'-ath*; from 5182; a *descent*, i.e. imposition, unfavorable (*punishment*) or favorable (*food*); also (intr.; perh. from 5117), *restfulness*:–lighting down, quiet (-ness), to rest, be set on.
5184. נַחַת *nakh'-ath*; the same as 5183; *quiet*; *Nachath*, the name of an Edomite and of two Isr.:–Nahath.
5185. נָחֵת *naw-khayth'*; from 5181; *descending*:–come down.
5186. נָטָה *naw-taw'*; a prim. root; to *stretch* or spread out; by impl., to *bend* away (incl. mor. deflection); used in a great variety of appl. (as follows):–+ afternoon, apply, bow (down, -ing), carry aside, decline, deliver, extend, go down, be gone, incline, intend, lay, let down, offer, outstretched, overthrown, pervert, pitch, prolong, put away, shew, spread (out), stretch (forth, out), take (aside), turn (aside, away), wrest, cause to yield.
5187. נְטִיל *net-eel'*; from 5190; *laden*:–that bear.
5188. נְטִיפָה *net-ee-faw'*; from 5197; a *pendant* for the ears (esp. of pearls):–chain, collar.
5189. נְטִישָׁה *net-ee-shaw'*; from 5203; a *tendril* (as an offshoot):–battlement, branch, plant.
5190. נָטַל *naw-tal'*; a prim root; to *lift*; by impl., to *impose*:–bear, offer, take up.
5191. נְטַל *net-al'* (Chald.); cor. to 5190; to *raise*:–take up.
5192. נֵטֶל *nay'-tel*; from 5190; a *burden*:–weighty.
5193. נָטַע *naw-tah'*; a prim. root; prop. to *strike* in, i.e. *fix*; spec., to *plant* (lit. or fig.):–fastened, plant(- er).
5194. נֶטַע *neh'-tah*; from 5193; a *plant*; coll., a *plantation*; abstr., a *planting*:–plant.
5195. נָטִיעַ *naw-tee'-ah*; from 5193; a *plant*:–plant.
5196. נְטָעִים *net-aw-eem'*; pl. of 5194; *Netaïm*, a place in Pal.:–plants.
5197. נָטַף *naw-taf'*; a prim. root; to *ooze*, i.e. *distil* gradually; by impl., to *fall in drops*; fig., to *speak* by inspiration:–drop(-ping), prophesy(-et).
5198. נָטָף *naw-tawf'*; from 5197; a *drop*; spec., an aromatic *gum* (prob. *stacte*):–drop, stacte.
5199. נְטֹפָה *net-o-faw'*; from 5197; *distillation; Netophah*, a place in Pal.:–Netophah.
5200. נְטֹפָתִי *net-o-faw-thee'*; patron. from 5199; a *Netophathite*, or inh. of Netophah:–Netophathite.
5201. נָטַר *naw-tar'*; a prim. root; to *guard*; fig., to *cherish* (anger):–bear grudge, keep(-er), reserve.
5202. נְטַר *net-ar'* (Chald.); cor. to 5201; to *retain*:–keep.
5203. נָטַשׁ *naw-tash'*; a prim. root; prop. to *pound*, i.e. *smite*; by impl. (as if beating out, and thus expanding) to *disperse*; also, to *thrust* off, down, out or upon (incl., *reject, let alone, permit, remit*, etc.):–cast off, drawn, let fall, forsake, join [battle], leave (off), lie still, loose, spread (self) abroad, stretch out, suffer.
5204. נִי *nee*; a doubtful word; app. from 5091; *lamentation*:– wailing.
5205. נִיד *need*; from 5110; *motion* (of the lips in speech):–moving.
5206. נִידָה *nee-daw'*; fem. of 5205; *removal*, i.e. exile:–removed.
5207. נִיחוֹחַ *nee-kho'-akh;* or נִיחֹחַ *nee-kho'-akh*; from 5117; prop. *restful*, i.e. *pleasant*; abstr., *delight*:–sweet (odour).
5208. נִיחוֹחַ *nee-kho'-akh* (Chald.); or נִיחֹחַ (short.) *nee-kho'-akh* (Chald.); cor. to 5207; *pleasure*:–sweet odour (savour).
5209. נִין *neen*; from 5125; *progeny*:–son.
5210. נִינְוֵה *nee-nev-ay'*; of for. or.; *Nineveh*, the capital of Assyria:–Nineveh.
5211. נִיס *neece*; from 5127; *fugitive*:–that fleeth.
5212. נִיסָן *nee-sawn';* prob. of for. or.; *Nisan*, the first month of the Jewish sacred year:–Nisan.
5213. נִיצוֹץ *nee-tsotes';* from 5340; a *spark*:–spark.
5214. נִיר *neer;* a root prob. ident. with that of 5216, through the idea of the *gleam* of a fresh furrow; to *till* the soil:–break up.
5215. נִיר *neer*; or נִר *neer;* from 5214; prop. *ploughing,* i.e. (concr.) freshly *plowed* land:–fallow ground, plowing, tillage.
5216. נִיר *neer*; or נִר *neer*; also נֵיר *nare*; or נֵר *nare*; or (fem.) נֵרָה *nay-raw'*; from a prim. root [see 5214; 5135] prop. mean. to *glisten*; a *lamp* (i.e. the burner) or *light* (lit. or fig.):–candle, lamp, light.
5217. נָכָא *naw-kaw'*; a prim. root; to *smite*, i.e. *drive* away:–be viler.
5218. נָכֵא *naw-kay';* or נָכָא *naw-kaw*; from 5217; *smitten*, i.e. (fig.) *afflicted*:–broken, stricken, wounded.
5219. נְכֹאת *nek-ohth';* from 5218; prop. a *smiting*, i.e. (concr.) an aromatic *gum* [perh. *styrax*] (as *powdered*):–spicery(-ces).
5220. נֶכֶד *neh'-ked*; from an un. root mean. to *propagate*; *offspring*:–nephew, son's son.
5221. נָכָה *naw-kaw'*; a prim. root; to *strike* (lightly or severely, lit. or fig.):–beat, cast forth, clap, give [wounds], X go forward, X indeed, kill, make [slaughter], murderer, punish, slaughter, slay(-er, -ing), smite(-r, -ing), strike, be stricken, (give) stripes, X surely, wound.
5222. נֵכֶה *nay-keh'*; from 5221; a *smiter*, i.e. (fig.) *traducer*:–abject.
5223. נָכֶה *naw-keh'*; *smitten*, i.e. (lit.) maimed, or (fig.) dejected:–contrite, lame.
5224. נְכוֹ *nek-o'*; prob. of Eg. or.; *Neko*, an Eg. King:–Necho. Comp. 6549.
5225. נָכוֹן *naw-kone';* from 3559; *prepared; Nakon*, prob. an Isr.:–Nachon.
5226. נֵכַח *nay'-kakh*; from an un. root mean. to *be straightforward*; prop. the *fore* part; used adv., *opposite*:–before, over against.
5227. נֹכַח *no'-kakh*; from the same as 5226; prop. the *front* part; used adv. (esp. with prep.), *opposite, in front of, forward, in behalf of*:–(over) against, before, direct[-ly], for, right (on).
5228. נָכֹחַ *naw-ko'-akh*; from the same as 5226; *straightforward*, i.e. (fig.), *equitable, correct*, or (abstr.), *integrity*:–plain, right, uprightness.
5229. נְכֹחָה *nek-o-khaw';* fem. of 5228; prop. *straightforwardness*, i.e. (fig.) *integrity*, or (concr.) a *truth*:–equity, right (thing), uprightness.
5230. נָכַל *naw-kal';* a prim root; to *defraud*, i.e. *act treacherously*:–beguile, conspire, deceiver, deal subtilly.
5231. נֵכֶל *nay'-kel*; from 5230; *deceit*:–wile.
5232. נְכַס *nek-as'* (Chald.); cor. to 5233:–goods.
5233. נֶכֶס *neh'-kes*; from an un. root mean. to *accumulate; treasure*:–riches, wealth.
5234. נָכַר *naw-kar';* a prim. root; prop. to *scrutinize*, i.e. look intently at; hence (with *recognition* implied), to *acknowledge, be acquainted with, care for, respect, revere*, or (with *suspicion* implied), to *disregard, ignore*, be *strange* toward, *reject, resign, dissimulate* (as if ignorant or disowning):–acknowledge, X could, deliver, discern, dissemble, estrange, feign self to be another, know, take knowledge (notice), perceive, regard, (have) respect, behave (make) self strange(-ly).
5235. נֶכֶר *neh'-ker*; or נֹכֶר *no'-ker*; from 5234; something *strange*, i.e. unexpected *calamity*:–strange.
5236. נֵכָר *nay-kawr';* from 5234; for., or (concr.) a *foreigner*, or (abstr.) *heathendom*:–alien, strange (+ -er).
5237. נָכְרִי *nok-ree';* from 5235 (sec. form); *strange*, in a variety of degrees and appl. (*for., non-relative, adulterous, different, wonderful*):–alien, foreigner, out-landish, strange(-r, woman).
5238. נְכֹת *nek-oth';* prob. for 5219; *spicery*, i.e. (gen.) *valuables*:–precious things.
5239. נָלָה *naw-law'*; app. a prim. root; to *complete*:–make an end.
5240. נְמִבְזֶה *nem-ib-zeh';* from 959, *despised*:–vile.
5241. נְמוּאֵל *nem-oo-ale';* app. for 3223; *Nemuel*, the name of two Isr.:–Nemuel.
5242. נְמוּאֵלִי *nem-oo-ay-lee'*; from 5241; a *Nemuelite*, or desc. of Nemuel:–Nemuelite.
5243. נָמַל *naw-mal'*; a prim. root; to *become clipped* or (spec.) *circumcised*:–(branch to) be cut down (off), circumcise.
5244. נְמָלָה *nem-aw-law';* fem. from 5243; an *ant* (prob. from its almost *bisected* form):–ant.
5245. נְמַר *nem-ar'* (Chald.); cor. to 5246:–leopard.
5246. נָמֵר *naw-mare'*; from an un. root mean. prop. to *filtrate*, i.e. *be limpid* [comp 5247 and 5249]; and thus to *spot* or *stain* as if by dripping; a *leopard* (from its stripes):–leopard.
5247. נִמְרָה *nim-raw';* from the same as 5246; *clear* water; *Nimrah*, a place E. of the Jordan:–Nimrah. See also 1039, 5249.
5248. נִמְרוֹד *nim-rode'*; or נִמְרֹד *nim-rode'*; prob. of for. or.; *Nimrod*, a son of Cush:–Nimrod.
5249. נִמְרִים *nim-reem'*; pl. of a masc. cor. to 5247; *clear* waters; *Nimrim*, a place E. of the Jordan:–Nimrim. Comp. 1039.
5250. נִמְשִׁי *nim-shee'*; prob. from 4871; *extricated; Nimshi*, the (grand-)father of Jehu:–Nimshi.
5251. נֵס *nace;* from 5264; a *flag;* also a *sail;* by impl., a *flagstaff;* gen. a *signal;* fig., a *token*:–banner, pole, sail, (en-)sign, standard.
5252. נְסִבָּה *nes-ib-baw';* fem. part.pass. of 5437; prop. an *environment,* i.e. *circumstance* or *turn* of affairs:–cause.
5253. נָסַג *naw-sag'*; a prim. root; to *retreat*:–departing away, remove, take (hold), turn away.
5254. נָסָה *naw-saw'*; a prim. root; to *test;* by impl., to *attempt*:–adventure, assay, prove, tempt, try.
5255. נָסַח *naw-sakh';* a prim. root; to *tear* away:–destroy,pluck,root.
5256. נְסַח *nes-akh'* (Chald.); cor. to 5255:–pull down.
5257. נְסִיךְ *nes-eek'*; from 5258; prop. something *poured* out, i.e. a *libation;* also a molten *image;* by impl., a *prince* (as *anointed*):–drink offering, duke, prince(ipal).
5258. נָסַךְ *naw-sak'* ;a prim. root; to *pour* out, esp. a libation, or to *cast* (metal); by anal., to *anoint* a king:–cover, melt, offer,

(cause to) pour (out), set (up).

5259. נָסַךְ *naw-sak'*; a prim. root [prob. ident. with 5258 through the idea of fusion]; to *interweave,* i.e. (fig.) to *overspread:*–that is spread.

5260. נְסַךְ *nes-ak'* (Chald.); cor. to 5258; to *pour* out a libation:–offer.

5261. נְסַךְ *nes-ak'* (Chald.); cor. to 5262; a *libation:*–drink offering.

5262. נֶסֶךְ *neh'-sek*; or נֵסֶךְ *nay'-sek;* from 5258; a *libation;* also a *cast idol:*–cover, drink offering, molten image.

5263. נָסַס *naw-sas';* a prim. root; to *wane,* i.e. *be sick.*

5264. נָסַס *naw-sas'*; a prim. root; to *gleam* from afar, i.e. to *be conspicuous* as a signal; or rather perh. a denom. from 5251 [and ident. with 5263, through the idea of a flag as *fluttering* in the wind]; to *raise a beacon:*–lift up as an ensign, standard bearer.

5265. נָסַע *naw-sah'*; a primitive root; prop. to *pull* up, esp. the tent-pins, i.e. *start* on a journey:–cause to blow, bring, get, (make to) go (away, forth, forward, onward, out), (take) journey, march, remove, set aside (forward), X still, be on his (go their) way.

5266. נָסַק *naw-sak';* a prim. root; to *go* up:–ascend.

5267. נְסַק *nes-ak'* (Chald.); cor. to 5266:–take up.

5268. נִסְרֹךְ *nis-roke'*; of for. or.; *Nisrok,* a Babylonian idol:–Nisroch.

5269. נֵעָה *nay-aw';* from 5128; *motion; Neäh,* a place in Pal.:–Neah.

5270. נֹעָה *no-aw'*; from 5218; *movement; Noäh,* an Isr.s:–Noah.

5271. נָעוּר *naw-oor';* or נָעֻר *naw-oor';* and (fem.) נְעֻרָה *neh- oo-raw';* prop. pass.part. from 5288 as denom.; (only in pl. coll. or emphat. form) *youth,* the state (*juvenility*) or the persons (*young* people):–childhood, youth.

5272. נְעִיאֵל *neh-ee-ale'*; from 5128 and 410; *moved of God; Neïel,* a place in Pal.:–Neiel.

5273. נָעִים *naw-eem';* from 5276; *delightful* (obj. or subj., lit. or fig.):–pleasant(-ure), sweet.

5274. נָעַל *naw-al';* a prim. root; prop. to *fasten* up, i.e. with a bar or cord; hence (denom. from 5275), to *sandal,* i.e. furnish with slippers:–bolt, inclose, lock, shoe, shut up.

5275. נַעַל *nah'-al*; or (fem.) נַעֲלָה *nah-al-aw';* from 5274; prop. a sandal *tongue;* by ext. a *sandal* or slipper (sometimes as a symbol of occupancy, a refusal to marry, or of something valueless):–dryshod, (pair of) shoe([-latchet], -s).

5276. נָעֵם *naw-ame';* a prim. root; to *be agreeable* (lit. or fig.):–pass in beauty, be delight, be pleasant, be sweet.

5277. נַעַם *nah'-am*; from 5276; *pleasure; Naam,* an Isr.:–Naam.

5278. נֹעַם *no'-am*; from 5276; *agreeableness,* i.e. *delight, suitableness, splendor* or *grace:*–beauty, pleasant(-ness).

5279. נַעֲמָה *nah-am-aw';* fem. of 5277; *pleasantness; Naamah,* the name of an antediluvian woman, of an Ammonitess, and of a place in Pal.:–Naamah.

5280. נַעֲמִי *nah-am-ee';* patron. from 5283; a *Naamanite,* or desc. of Naaman (coll.):–Naamites.

5281. נָעֳמִי *no-om-ee';* from 5278; *pleasant; Noömi,* an Isr.s:–Naomi.

5282. נַעֲמָן *nah-am-awn'*; from 5276; *pleasantness* (pl. as concr.):–pleasant.

5283. נַעֲמָן *nah-am-awn'*; the same as 5282; *Naaman,* the name of an Isr. and of a Damascene:–Naaman.

5284. נַעֲמָתִי *nah-am-aw-thee'*; patrial from a place cor. in name (but not ident.) with 5279; a *Naamathite,* or inh. of Naamah:–Naamathite.

5285. נַעֲצוּץ *nah-ats-oots';* from an un. root mean. to *prick;* prob. a *brier;* by impl., a *thicket* of thorny bushes:–thorn.

5286. נָעַר *naw-ar';* a prim. root; to *growl:*–yell.

5287. נָעַר *naw-ar'*; a prim. root [prob. ident. with 5286, through the idea of the *rustling* of mane, which usually accompanies the lion's roar]; to *tumble* about:–shake (off, out, self), overthrow, toss up and down.

5288. נַעַר *nah'-ar*; from 5287; (concr.) a *boy* (as active), from the age of infancy to adolescence; by impl., a *servant;* also (by interch. of sex), a *girl* (of similar latitude in age):–babe, boy, child, damsel, lad, servant, young (man).

5289. נַעַר *nah'-ar*; from 5287 in its der. sense of *tossing* about; a *wanderer:*–young one.

5290. נֹעַר *no'-ar*; from 5287; (abstr.) *boyhood* [comp. 5288]:–child, youth.

5291. נַעֲרָה *nah-ar-aw'*; fem. of 5288; a *girl* (from infancy to adolescence):–damsel, maid(-en), young (woman).

5292. נַעֲרָה *nah-ar-aw'*; the same as 5291; *Naarah,* the name of an Isr.s, and of a place in Pal.:–Naarah, Naarath.

5293. נַעֲרַי *nah-ar-ah'-ee* from 5288; *youthful; Naarai,* an Isr.:–Naarai.

5294. נְעַרְיָה *neh-ar-yaw'*; from 5288 and 3050; *servant of Jah; Neärjah,* the name of two Isr.:–Neariah.

5295. נַעֲרָן *nah-ar-awn'*; from 5288; *juvenile; Naaran,* a place in Pal.:–Naaran.

5296. נְעֹרֶת *neh-o'-reth*; from 5287; something *shaken* out, i.e. *tow* (as the refuse of flax):–tow.

5297. נֹף *nofe*; a var. of 4644; *Noph,* the capital of Upper Eg.:–Noph.

5298. נֶפֶג *neh'-feg*; from an un. root prob. mean. to *spring* forth; a *sprout; Nepheg,* the name of two Isr.:–Nepheg.

5299. נָפָה *naw-faw';* from 5130 in the sense of *lifting;* a *height;* also a *sieve:*–border, coast, region, sieve.

5300. נְפוּשְׁסִים *nef-oo-shes-eem'*; for 5304; *Nephushesim,* a Temple- servant:–Nephisesim .

5301. נָפַח *naw-fakh';* a prim. root; to *puff,* in various appl. (lit., to *inflate, blow* hard, *scatter, kindle, expire;* fig., to *disesteem*):–blow, breath, give up, cause to lose [life], seething, snuff.

5302. נֹפַח *no'-fakh*; from 5301; a *gust; Nophach,* a place in Moab:–Nophah.

5303. נְפִיל *nef-eel'*; or נְפִל *nef-eel';* from 5307; prop. a *feller,* i.e. a *bully* or *tyrant:*–giant.

5304. נְפִיסִים *nef-ee-seem'*; pl. from an un. root mean. to *scatter; expansions; Nephisim,* a Temple-servant:–Nephusim .

5305. נָפִישׁ *naw-feesh';* from 5314; *refreshed; Naphish,* a son of Ishmael, and his posterity:–Naphish.

5306. נֹפֶךְ *no'-fek*; from an un. root mean. to *glisten; shining;* a gem, prob. the *garnet:*–emerald.

5307. נָפַל *naw-fal'*; a prim. root; to *fall,* in a great variety of appl. (intr. or caus., lit. or fig.):–be accepted, cast (down, self, [lots], out), cease, die, divide (by lot), (let) fail, (cause to, let, make, ready to) fall (away, down, -en, -ing), fell(-ing), fugitive, have [inheritance], inferior, be judged, lay (along), (cause to) lie down, light (down), be (X hast) lost, lying, overthrow, overwhelm, perish, present(-ed, -ing), (make to) rot, slay, smite out, X surely, throw down.

5308. נְפַל *nef-al'* (Chald.); cor. to 5307:–fall (down), have occasion.

5309. נֶפֶל *neh'-fel;* or נֵפֶל *nay'-fel;* from 5307; something *fallen,* i.e. an *abortion:*–untimely birth.

5310. נָפַץ *naw-fats';* a prim. root; to *dash* to pieces, or *scatter:*–be beaten in sunder, break (in pieces), broken, dash (in pieces), cause to be discharged, dispersed, be overspread, scatter.

5311. נֶפֶץ *neh'-fets*; from 5310; a *storm* (as dispersing):–scattering.

5312. נְפַק *nef-ak'* (Chald.); a prim. root; to *issue;* caus., to *bring out:*–come (go, take) forth (out).

5313. נִפְקָה *nif-kaw'* (Chald.); from 5312; an *outgo,* i.e. expense:–expense.

5314. נָפַשׁ *naw-fash';* a prim. root; to *breathe;* pass., to *be breathed* upon, i.e. (fig.) *refreshed* (as if by a current of air):–(be) refresh selves(-ed).

5315. נֶפֶשׁ *neh'-fesh*; from 5314; prop. a *breathing* creature, i.e. *animal* of (abstr.) *vitality;* used very widely in a lit., accommodated or fig. sense (bodily or ment.):–any, appetite, beast, body, breath, creature, X dead(-ly), desire, X [dis-] contented, X fish, ghost, + greedy, he, heart(-y), (hath, X jeopardy of) life (X in jeopardy), lust, man, me, mind, mortally, one, own, person, pleasure, (her-, him-, my-, thy-) self, them (your)-selves, + slay, soul, + tablet, they, thing, (X she) will, X would have it.

5316. נֶפֶת *neh'-feth*; for 5299; a *height:*–country.

5317. נֹפֶת *no'-feth*; from 5130 in the sense of *shaking* to pieces; a *dripping* i.e. of *honey* (from the comb):–honeycomb.

5318. נֶפְתּוֹחַ *nef-to'-akh;* from 6605; *opened,* i.e. a *spring; Nephtoäch,* a place in Pal.:–Neptoah.

5319. נַפְתּוּל *naf-tool';* from 6617; prop. *wrestled*; but used (in the pl.) trans., a *struggle*:–wrestling.

5320. נַפְתֻּחִים *naf-too-kheem*; pl. of for. or., *Naphtuchim,* an Eg. tribe:–Naptuhim.

5321. נַפְתָּלִי *naf-taw-lee';* from 6617; *my wrestling; Naphtali,* a son of Jacob, with the tribe descended from him, and its territory:–Naphtali.

5322. נֵץ *nayts*; from 5340; a *flower* (from its *brilliancy*); also a hawk (from it *flashing* speed); –blossom, hawk.

5323. נָצָא *naw-tsaw';* a prim. root; to *go away*; –flee.

5324. נָצַב *naw-tsab';* a prim root; to *station,* in various appl. (lit. or fig.):–appointed, deputy, erect, establish, X Huzzah, lay, officer, pillar, present, rear up, set (over, up), settle, sharpen, establish, (make to) stand (-ing, still, up, upright), best state.

5325. נִצָּב *nits-tsawb';* pass.part. of 5324; *fixed,* i.e. a *handle:*–haft.

5326. נִצְבָּה *nits-baw'* (Chald.); from a root cor. to 5324; *fixedness,* i.e. *firmness:*–strength.

5327. נָצָה *naw-tsaw';* a prim. root; prop. to *go forth,* i.e. (by impl.) to *be expelled,* and (consequently) *desolate*; caus., to lay *waste;* also (spec.), to *quarrel*:–be laid waste,

runinous, strive (together).
5328. נִצָּה *nits-tsaw';* fem. of 5322; a *blossom*; –flower.
5329. נָצַח *naw-tsakh';* a prim. root; prop. to *glitter* from afar, i.e. to be *eminent* (as a superintendent, esp. of the Temple services and its music); also (as denom. from 5331), to *be permanent*:–excel, chief musician (singer), oversee(-r), set forward.
5330. נְצַח *nets-akh'* (Chald.); cor. to 5329; to *become chief*:–be preferred.
5331. נֶצַח *neh'-tsakh;* or נֵצַח *nay'-tsakh;* from 5329; prop. a *goal,* i.e. the bright obj. at a distance travelled towards; hence (fig.), *splendor,* or (subj.) *truthfulness,* or (obj.) *confidence;* but usually (adv.), *continually* (i.e. to the most distant point of view):–alway(-s), constantly, end, (+n-) ever(more), perpetual, strength, victory.
5332. נֵצַח *nay'-tsakh*; prob. ident. with 5331, through the idea of *brilliancy* of color; *juice* of the grape (as blood red):–blood, strength.
5333. נְצִיב *nets-eeb';* or נְצִב *nets-eeb';* from 5324; something *stationary,* i.e. a *prefect,* a military *post,* a *statue*:–garrison, officer, pillar.
5334. נְצִיב *nets-eeb';* the same as 5333; *station; Netsib,* a place in Pal.:–Nezib.
5335. נְצִיחַ *nets-ee'-akh;* from 5329; *conspicuous; Netsiach,* a Temple- servant:–Neziah.
5336. נָצִיר *naw-tsere';* from 5341; prop. *conservative;* but used pass., *delivered*:–preserved.
5337. נָצַל *naw-tsal';* a prim. root; to *snatch* away, whether in a good or a bad sense:–X at all, defend, deliver (self), escape, X without fail, part, pluck, preserve, recover, rescue, rid, save, spoil, strip, X surely, take (out).
5338. נְצַל *nets-al'* (Chald.); cor. to 5337; to *extricate*:–deliver, rescue.
5339. נִצָּן *nits-tsawn';* from 5322; a *blossom*:–flower.
5340. נָצַץ *naw-tsats';* a prim. root; to *glare,* i.e. *be bright*- colored:–sparkle.
5341. נָצַר *naw-tsar';* a prim. root; to *guard,* in a good sense (to *protect, maintain, obey,* etc.) or a bad one (to *conceal,* etc.):– besieged, hidden thing, keep(-er, -ing), monument, observe, preserve(-r), subtil, watcher(-man).
5342. נֵצֶר *nay'-tser;* from 5341 in the sense of *greenness* as a striking color; a *shoot;* fig., a *desc.*:–branch.
5343. נְקֵא *nek-ay'* (Chald.); from a root cor. to 5352; *clean*:–pure.
5344. נָקַב *naw-kab';* a prim. root; to *puncture,* lit. (to *perforate,* with more or less violence) or fig. (to *specify, designate, libel*):–appoint, blaspheme, bore, curse, express, with holes, name, pierce, strike through.
5345. נֶקֶב *neh'keb;* a *bezel* (for a gem):–pipe.
5346. נֶקֶב *neh'-keb;* the same as 5345; *dell; Nekeb,* a place in Pal.:–Nekeb.
5347. נְקֵבָה *nek-ay-baw';* from 5344; *female* (from the sexual form):–female woman.
5348.נָקֹד *naw-kode';* from an un. root mean. to *mark* (by *puncturing* or *branding*); *spotted*:–speckled.
5349. נֹקֵד *no-kade';* act.part. from the same as 5348; a *spotter* (of sheep or cattle), i.e. the owner or tender (who thus marks them):–herdman, sheepmaster.
5350. נִקֻּד *nik-kood';* from the same as 5348; a *crumb* (as *broken* to spots); also a *biscuit* (as *pricked*):–cracknel, mouldy.
5351. נְקֻדָּה *ned-ood-daw';* fem. of 5348; a *boss*:–stud.
5352. נָקָה *naw-kaw';* a prim. root; to *be* (or *make*) *clean* (lit. or fig.); by impl. (in an adverse sense) to *be bare,* i.e. *extirpated*:–acquit X at all, X altogether, be blameless, cleanse, (be) clear(-ing), cut off, be desolate, be free, be (hold) guiltless, be (X utterly, X wholly.
5353. נְקוֹדָא *nek-o-daw';* fem. of 5348 (in the fig. sense of *marked*); *distinction; Nekoda,* a Temple-servant:–Nekoda.
5354. נָקַט *naw-kat';* a prim. root; to *loathe*:–weary.
5355. נָקִי *naw-kee';* or (Joel 4:19; Jonah 1 :14), נָקִיא *naw-kee';* from 5352; *innocent*:–blameless, clean, clear, exempted, free, guiltless, innocent, quit.
5356. נִקָּיוֹן *nik-kaw-yone';* or נִקָּיֹן *nik-kaw-yone';* from 5352; *clearness* (lit. or fig.):–cleanness, innocency.
5357. נָקִיק *naw-keek';* from an un. root mean. to *bore;* a *cleft*:–hole.
5358. נָקַם *naw-kam';* a prim. root; to *grudge,* i.e. *avenge* or *punish*:–avenge(-r, self), punish, revenge (self), X surely, take vengeance.
5359. נָקָם *naw-kawm';* from 5358; *revenge*:–+ avenged, quarrel, vengeance.
5360. נְקָמָה *nek-aw-maw';* fem. of 5359; *avengement,* whether the act of the passion:–+ avenge, revenge(-ing), vengeance.
5361. נָקַע *naw-kah';* a prim. root; to *feel aversion*:–be alienated.
5362. נָקַף *naw-kaf';* a prim. root; to *strike* with more or less violence (*beat, fell, corrode*); by impl. (of attack) to *knock together,* i.e. *surround* or *circulate*:–compass (about, -ing), cut down, destroy, go round (about), inclose, round.
5363. נֹקֶף *no'-kef;* from 5362; a *threshing* (of olives):–shaking.
5364. נִקְפָּה *nik-paw';* from 5362; prob. a *rope* (as *encircling*):–rent.
5365. נָקַר *naw-kar';* a prim. root; to *bore* (*penetrate, quarry*):–dig, pick out, pierce, put (thrust) out.
5366. נְקָרָה *nek-aw-raw';* from 5365, a *fissure*:–cleft, clift.
5367. נָקַשׁ *naw-kash';* a prim. root; to *entrap* (with a noose), lit. or fig.:–catch (lay a) snare.
5368. נְקַשׁ *nek-ash'* (Chald.); cor. to 5367; but used in the sense of 5362; to *knock*:–smote.
5369. נֵר *nare;* the same as 5216; *lamp; Ner,* an Isr.:–Ner.
5370. נֵרְגַל *nare-gal';* of for. or.; *Nergal,* a Cuthite deity:–Nergal.
5371. נֵרְגַל שַׁרְאֶצֶר *nare-gal' shar-eh'-tser;* from 5370 and 8272; *Nergal-Sharetser,* the name of two Babylonians:–Nergal-sharezer.
5372. נִרְגָּן *neer-gawn';* from an un. root mean. to *roll* to pieces; a *slanderer*:–talebearer, whisperer.
5373. נֵרְדְּ *nayrd;* of for. or.; *nard,* an aromatic:–spikenard.
5374. נֵרִיָּה *nay-ree-yaw';* or נֵרִיָּהוּ *nay-ree-yaw'-hoo;* from 5216 and 3050; *light of Jah; Nerijah,* an Isr.:–Neriah.
5375. נָשָׂא *naw-saw';* or נָסָה (Psalm 4:6 [7]) *naw-saw';* a prim. root; to *lift,* in a great variety of appl., lit. and fig., absol. and rel. (as follows):–accept, advance, arise, (able to, [armor], suffer to) bear(-er, up), bring (forth), burn, carry (away), cast, contain, desire, ease, exact, exalt (self), extol, fetch, forgive, furnish, further, give, go on, help, high, hold up, honorable (+ man), lade, lay, lift (self) up, lofty, marry, magnify, X needs, obtain, pardon, raise (up), receive, regard, respect, set (up), spare, stir up, + swear, take (away, up), X utterly, wear, yield.
5376. נְשָׂא *nes-aw'* (Chald.); cor. to 5375:–carry away, make insurrection, take.
5377. נָשָׁא *naw-shaw';* a prim. root; to *lead astray,* i.e. (ment.) to *delude,* or (mor.) to *seduce*:–beguile, deceive, X greatly, X utterly.
5378. נָשָׁא *naw-shaw';* a prim. root [perh. ident. with 5377, through the idea of *imposition*]; to *lend* on interest; by impl., to *dun* for debt:–X debt, exact, giver of usury.
5379. נִשֵּׂאת *nis-sayth';* pass.part. fem. of 5375; something *taken,* i.e. a *present*:–gift.
5380. נָשַׁב *naw-shab';* a prim. root; to *blow;* by impl., to *disperse*:–(cause to) blow, drive away.
5381. נָשַׂג *naw-sag';* a prim. root; to *reach* (lit. or fig.):–ability, be able, attain (unto), (be able to, can) get, lay at, put, reach, remove, wax rich, X surely, (over-)take (hold of, on, upon).
5382. נָשָׁה *naw-shaw';* a prim. root; to *forget;* fig., to *neglect;* caus., to *remit, remove*:–forget, deprive, exact.
5383. נָשָׁה *naw-shaw';* a prim. root [rather ident. with 5382, in the sense of 5378]; to *lend* or (by reciprocity) *borrow* on security or interest:–creditor, exact, extortioner, lend, usurer, lend on (taker on) usury.
5384. נָשֶׁה *naw-sheh';* from 5382, in the sense of *failure; rheumatic* or *crippled* (from the incident to Jacob):–which shrank.
5385. נְשׂוּאָה *nes-oo-aw';* or נְשֻׂאָה rather, *nes-oo-aw';* fem.. pass.part. of 5375; something *borne,* i.e. a *load*:–carriage.
5386. נְשִׁי *nesh-ee';* from 5383; a *debt*:–debt.
5387. נָשִׂיא *naw-see';* or נָשִׂא *naw-see';* from 5375; prop. an *exalted* one, i.e. a *king* or *sheik;* also a rising *mist*:–captain, chief, cloud, governor, prince, ruler, vapour.
5388. נְשִׁיָּה *nesh-ee-yaw';* from 5382; *oblivion*:–forgetfulness.
5389. נָשִׁין *naw-sheen'* (Chald.); irreg. pl. fem. of 606:–women.
5390. נְשִׁיקָה *nesh-ee-kaw';* from 5401; a *kiss*:–kiss.
5391. נָשַׁךְ *naw-shak';* a prim. root; to *strike* with a sting (as a serpent); fig., to *oppress* with interest on a loan:–bite, lend upon usury.
5392. נֶשֶׁךְ *neh'-shek;* from 5391; *interest* on a debt:–usury.
5393. נִשְׁכָּה *nish-kaw';* for 3957; a *cell*:–chamber.
5394. נָשַׁל *naw-shal';* a prim. root; to *pluck* off, i.e. *divest, eject* or *drop*:–cast (out), drive, loose, put off (out), slip.
5395. נָשַׁם *naw-sham';* a prim. root; prop. to *blow* away, i.e. *destroy*:–destroy.
5396. נִשְׁמָא *nish-maw'* (Chald.); cor. to 5397; vital *breath*:–breath.
5397. נְשָׁמָה *nesh-aw-maw';* from 5395; a *puff,* i.e. *wind,* angry or vital *breath,* divine *inspiration, intellect.* or (concr.) an *animal*:–blast, (that) breath(-eth), inspiration, soul, spirit.
5398. נָשַׁף *naw-shaf';* a prim. root; to *breeze,* i.e. *blow* up fresh (as the wind):–blow.
5399. נֶשֶׁף *neh'-shef;* from 5398; prop. a *breeze,* i.e. (by impl.) *dusk* (when the evening breeze prevails):–dark, dawning of the day (morning), night, twilight.
5400. נָשַׂק *naw-sak';* a prim. root; to *catch* fire:–burn, kindle.

5401. נָשַׁק *naw-shak'*; a prim. root [ident. with 5400, through the idea of *fastening* up; comp. 2388, 2836]; to *kiss*, lit. or fig. (*touch*); also (as a mode of *attachment*), to *equip* with weapons:–armed (men), rule, kiss, that touched.

5402. נֶשֶׁק *neh'-shek;* or נֵשֶׁק *nay'-shek*; from 5401; military *equipment*, i.e. (coll.) *arms* (offensive or defensive), or (concr.) an *arsenal*:–armed men, armour(-y), battle, harness, weapon.

5403. נְשַׁר *nesh-ar'* (Chald.); cor. to 5404; an *eagle*:–eagle.

5404. נֶשֶׁר *neh'-sher*; from an un. root mean. to *lacerate*; the *eagle* (or other large bird of prey):–eagle.

5405. נָשַׁת *naw-shath'*; a prim. root; prop. to *eliminate*, i.e. (intr.) to *dry* up:–fail.

5406. נִשְׁתְּוָן *nish-tev-awn'*; prob. of Pers. or.; an *epistle*:–letter.

5407. נִשְׁתְּוָן *nish-tev-awn'* (Chald.); cor. to 5406:–letter.

5408. נָתַח *naw-thakh'*; a prim. root; to *dismember*:–cut (in pieces), divide, hew in pieces.

5409. נֵתַח *nay'-thakh*; from 5408; a *fragment*:–part, piece.

5410. נָתִיב *naw-theeb'*; or (fem.) נְתִיבָה *neth-ee-baw'*; or נְתִבָה (Jeremiah 6:16) *neth-ee-baw'*; from an un. root mean. to *tramp*; a (beaten) *track*:–path([-way]), X travel[-ler], way.

5411. נָתִין *naw-theen'*; or נָתוּן (Ezra 8:17) *naw-thoon'*; (the proper form as pass.part.), from 5414; one *given*, i.e. (in the pl. only) the *Nethinim*, or Temple-servants (as *given* to that duty):–Nethinims.

5412. נְתִין *netheen'* (Chald.); cor. to 5411:–Nethinims.

5413. נָתַךְ *naw-thak'*; a prim. root; to *flow* forth (lit. or fig.); by impl., to *liquify*:–drop, gather (together), melt, pour (forth, out).

5414. נָתַן *naw-than'*; a prim. root; to *give*, used with greatest latitude of appl. (*put, make*, etc.):–add, apply, appoint, ascribe, assign, X avenge, X be ([healed]), bestow, bring (forth, hither), cast, cause, charge, come, commit, consider, count, + cry, deliver (up), direct, distribute, do, X doubtless, X without fail, fasten, frame, X get, give (forth, over, up), grant, hang (up), X have, X indeed, lay (unto charge, up), (give) leave, lend, let (out), + lie, lift up, make, + O that, occupy, offer, ordain, pay, perform, place, pour, print, X pull , put (forth), recompense, render, requite, restore, send (out), set (forth), shew, shoot forth (up), + sing, + slander, strike, [sub-]mit, suffer, X surely, X take, thrust, trade, turn, utter, + weep, + willingly, + withdraw, + would (to) God, yield.

5415. נְתַן *neth-an'* (Chald.); cor. to 5414; *give*:–bestow, give pay.

5416. נָתָן *naw-thawn';* from 5414; *given; Nathan*, the name of five Isr.:–Nathan.

5417. נְתַנְאֵל *neth-an-ale'*; from 5414 and 410; *given of God; Nethanel*, the name of ten Isr.:–Nethaneel.

5418. נְתַנְיָה *neth-an-yaw';* or נְתַנְיָהוּ *neth-an-yaw'-hoo*; from 5414 and 3050; *given of Jah; Nethanjah*, the name of four Isr.:–Nethaniah.

5419. נְתַן־מֶלֶךְ *neth-an' meh'-lek*; from 5414 and 4428; *given of* (the) *king; Nethan-Melek*, an Isr.:–Nathan-melech.

5420. נָתַס *naw-thas'*; a prim. root; to *tear* up:–mar.

5421. נָתַע *naw-thah';* for 5422; to *tear* out:–break.

5422. נָתַץ *naw-thats'*; a prim. root; to *tear* down:–beat down, break down (out), cast down, destroy, overthrow, pull down, throw down.

5423. נָתַק *naw-thak'*; a prim. root; to *tear* off:–break (off), burst, draw (away), lift up, pluck (away, off), pull (out), root out.

5424. נֶתֶק *neh'-thek;* from 5423; *scurf*:–(dry) scall.

5425. נָתַר *naw-thar'*; a prim. root; to *jump*, i.e. *be* violently *agitated*; caus., to *terrify, shake* off, *untie*:–drive asunder, leap, (let) loose, X make, move, undo.

5426. נְתַר *neth-ar'* (Chald.); cor. to 5425:–shake off.

5427. נֶתֶר *neh'-ther*; from 5425; mineral *potash* (so called from *effervescing* with acid):–nitre.

5428. נָתַשׁ *naw-thash'*; a prim. root; to *tear* away:–destroy, forsake, pluck (out, up, by the roots), pull up, root out (up), X utterly.

ס

5429. סְאָה *seh-aw;'* from an un. root mean. to *define*; a *seäh*, or certain measure (as *determinative*) for grain:–measure.

5430. סְאוֹן *seh-own'*; from 5431; perh. a military *boot* (as a protection from *mud*:–battle.

5431. סָאַן *saw-an';* a prim. root; to *be miry*; used only as denom. from 5430; to *shoe*, i.e. (act.part.) a *soldier* shod:–warrior.

5432. סַאסְאָה *sah-seh-aw';* for 5429; *measurement*, i.e. *moderation*:–measure.

5433. סָבָא *saw-baw';* a prim. root; to *quaff* to satiety, i.e. *become tipsy*:–drunkard, fill self, Sabean, [wine-]bibber.

5434. סְבָא *seb-aw'*; of for. or.; *Seba*, a son of Cush, and the country settled by him:–Seba.

5435. סֹבֶא *so'-beh;* from 5433; *potation*, concr. (*wine*), or abstr. (*carousal*):–drink, drunken, wine.

5436. סְבָאִי *seb-aw-ee'*; patrial from 5434; a *Sebaite*, or inh. of Seba:–Sabean.

5437. סָבַב *saw-bab';* a prim. root; to *revolve, surround*, or *border*; used in various appl., lit. and fig. (as follows):–bring, cast, fetch, lead, make, walk, X whirl, X round about, be about on every side, apply, avoid, beset (about), besiege, bring again, carry (about), change, cause to come about, X circuit, (fetch a) compass (about, round), drive, environ, X on every side, beset (close, come, compass, go, stand) round about, inclose, remove, return, set, sit down, turn (self) (about, aside, away, back).

5438. סִבָּה *sib-baw'*; from 5437; a (providential) *turn* (of affairs):–cause.

5439. סָבִיב *saw-beeb'*; or (fem.) סְבִיבָה *seb-ee-baw'*; from 5437; (as noun) *a circle, neighbour*, or *environs*; but chiefly (as adv., with or without prep.) *around*:–(place, round) about, circuit, compass, on every side.

5440. סָבַךְ *saw-bak'*; a prim. root; to *entwine*:–fold together, wrap.

5441. סֹבֶךְ *so'-bek;* from 5440; a *copse*:–thicket.

5442. סְבָךְ *seb-awk';* from 5440, a *copse*:–thick(-et).

5443. סַבְּכָא *sab-bek-aw'* (Chald.); or שַׂבְּכָא *sab-bek-aw'* (Chald.); from a root cor. to 5440; a *lyre*:–sackbut.

5444. סִבְּכַי *sib-bek-ah'-ee*; from 5440; *copse-like; Sibbecai*, an Isr.:–Sibbecai, Sibbechai.

5445. סָבַל *saw-bal'*; a prim. root; to *carry* (lit. or fig.), or (refl.) *be burdensome*; spec., to *be gravid*:–bear, be a burden, carry, strong to labour.

5446. סְבַל *seb-al'* (Chald.); cor. to 5445; to *erect*:–strongly laid.

5447. סֵבֶל *say'-bel*; from 5445; a *load* (lit. or fig.):–burden, charge.

5448. סֹבֶל *so'-bel*; [only in the form סֻבָּל *soob-bawl'*;] from 5445; a *load* (fig.):–burden.

5449. סַבָּל *sab-bawl';* from 5445; a *porter*:–(to bear, bearer of) burden(-s).

5450. סְבָלָה *seb-aw-law';* from 5447; *porterage*:–burden.

5451. סִבֹּלֶת *sib-bo'-leth*; for 7641; an *ear* of grain:–Sibboleth.

5452. סְבַר *seb-ar'* (Chald.); a prim. root; to *bear in mind*, i.e. *hope*:–think.

5453. סִבְרַיִם *sib-rah'-yim*; dual from a root cor. to 5452; *double hope; Sibrajim*, a place in Syria:–Sibraim.

5454. סַבְתָּא *sab-taw';* or סַבְתָּה *sab-taw'*; prob. of for. der.; *Sabta* or *Sabtah*, the name of a son of Cush, and the country occupied by his posterity:–Sabta, Sabtah.

5455. סַבְתְּכָא *sab-tek-aw'*; prob. of for. der.; *Sabteca*, the name of a son of Cush, and the region settled by him:–Sabtecha, Sabtechah.

5456. סָגַד *saw-gad';* a prim. root; to *prostrate* oneself (in homage):–fall down.

5457. סְגִד *seg-eed'* (Chald.); cor. to 5456:–worship.

5458. סְגוֹר from 5462; prop. *shut* up, i.e. the *breast* (as inclosing the heart); also *gold* (as gen. *shut* up safely):–caul, gold.

5459. סְגֻלָּה *seg-ool-law'*; fem. pass.part. of an un. root mean. to *shut* up; *wealth* (as closely *shut* up):–jewel, peculiar (treasure), proper good, special.

5460. סְגַן *seg-an'* (Chald.); cor. to 5461:–governor.

5461. סָגָן *saw-gawn';* from an un. root mean. to *superintend*; a *prefect* of a province:–prince, ruler.

5462. סָגַר *saw-gar';* a prim. root; to *shut* up; fig., to *surrender*:–close up, deliver (up), give over (up), inclose, X pure, repair, shut (in, self, out, up, up together), stop, X straitly.

5463. סְגַר *seg-ar'* (Chald.); cor. to 5462:–shut up.

5464. סַגְרִיר *sag-reed'*; prob. from 5462 in the sense of *sweeping* away; a pouring rain:–very rainy.

5465. סַד *sad*; from an un. root mean. to *estop*; the *stocks*:–stocks.

5466. סָדִין *saw-deen';* from an un. root mean. to *envelop*; a *wrapper*, i.e. *shirt*:–fine linen, sheet.

5467. סְדֹם *sed-ome'*; from an un. root mean. to *scorch*; *burnt* (i.e. *volcanic* or *bituminous*) district; Sedom, a place near the Dead Sea:– Sodom.

5468. סֶדֶר *seh'-der*; from an un. root mean. to *arrange; order*:–order.

5469. סַהַר *cah'-har*; from an un. root mean. to *be round; roundness*:–round.

5470. סֹהַר *so'-har;* from the same as 5469; a *dungeon* (as *surrounded* by walls):–prison.

5471. סוֹא *so*; of for. der.; *So*, an Eg. king:–So.

5472. סוּג *soog*; a prim. root; prop. to *flinch*, i.e. (by impl.) to *go back*, lit. (to *retreat*) or fig. (to *apostatize*):–backslider, drive, go back, turn (away, back).

5473. סוּג *soog*; a prim. root [prob. rather ident. with 5472 through the idea of *shrinking* from a hedge; comp. 7735]; to *hem* in,

i.e. *bind*:–set about.
5474. סוּגַר *soo-gar'*; from 5462; an *inclosure*, i.e. *cage* (for an animal):–ward.
5475. סוֹד *sode*; from 3245; a *session,* i.e. *company* of persons (in close deliberation); by impl., *intimacy, consultation*, a *secret*:–assembly, counsel, inward, secret (counsel).
5476. סוֹדִי *so-dee'*; from 5475; a *confidant; Sodi*, an Isr.:–Sodi.
5477. סוּחַ *soo'-akh*; from an un. root mean. to *wipe* away; *sweeping*; *Suäch*, an Isr.:–Suah.
5478. סוּחָה *soo-khaw'*; from the same as 5477; something *swept* away, i.e. *filth*:–torn.
5479. סוֹטַי *so-tah'-ee*; from 7750; *roving*; *Sotai*, one of the Nethinim:–Sotai.
5480. סוּךְ *sook*; a prim. root; prop. to *smear* over (with oil), i.e. *anoint*:–anoint (self), X at all.
5481. סוּמְפּוֹנְיָה *soom-po-neh-yaw'* (Chald.); or סוּמְפֹּנְיָה *soom-po-neh-yaw'* (Chald.); or (Da. 3:10) סִיפֹּנְיָא *see-fo-neh-yaw'* (Chald.); of Gr. or.; (συμφωνία) a *bagpipe* (with a double pipe):–dulcimer.
5482. סְוֵנֵה *sev-ay-nay'*; [rather to be written סְוֵנָה *sev-ay'-naw*; for סְוֵן *sev-ane'*; i.e *to Seven*]; of Eg. der.; *Seven*, a place in Upper Eg.:–Syene.
5483. סוּס *soos;* or סֻס *soos*; from an un. root mean. to *skip* (prop. for joy); a *horse* (as leaping); also a *swallow* (from its rapid *flight*):–crane, horse([-back, -hoof]). Comp. 6571.
5484. סוּסָה *soo-saw';* fem. of 5483; a *mare*:–company of horses.
5485. סוּסִי *soo-see';* from 5483; *horse-like; Susi*, an Isr.:–Susi.
5486. סוּף *soof*; a prim. root; to *snatch* away, i.e. *terminate*:–consume, have an end, perish, X be utterly.
5487. סוּף *soof* (Chald.); cor. to 5486; to *come to an end*:– consume, fulfill.
5488. סוּף *soof;* prob. of Eg. or.; a reed, esp. the *papyrus*:–flag, Red [sea], weed. Comp. 5489.
5489. סוּף *soof;* for 5488 (by ellip. of 3220); the *Reed* (*Sea*):–Red Sea.
5490. סוֹף *sofe;* from 5486; a *termination*:–conclusion, end, hinder part.
5491. סוֹף *sofe* (Chald.); cor. to 5490:–end.
5492. סוּפָה *soo-faw';* from 5486; a *hurricane*:–Red Sea, storm, tempest, whirlwind, Red sea.
5493. סוּר *soor;* or שׂוּר (Ho. 9:12) *soor*; a prim. root; to *turn* off (lit. or fig.):–be[-head], bring, call back, decline, depart, eschew, get [you], go (aside), X grievous, lay away (by), leave undone, be past, pluck away, put (away, down), rebel, remove (to and fro), revolt, X be sour, take (away, off), turn (aside, away, in), withdraw, be without.
5494. סוּר *soor*; prob. pass.part. of 5493; *turned* off, i.e. *deteriorated*:–degenerate.
5495. סוּר *soor*; the same as 5494; *Sur*, a gate of the temple:–Sur.
5496. סוּת *sooth*; perh. denom. from 7898; prop. to *prick*, i.e. (fig.) stimulate; by impl., to *seduce*:–entice, move, persuade, provoke, remove, set on, stir up, take away.
5497. סוּת *sooth*; prob. from the same root as 4533; *covering*, i.e. *clothing*:–clothes.
5498. סָחַב *saw-khab'*; a prim. root; to *trail* along:–draw (out), tear.
5499. סְחָבָה *seh-khaw-baw'*; from 5498; a *rag*:–cast clout.
5500. סָחָה *saw-khaw'*; a prim. root; to *sweep* away:–scrape.
5501. סְחִי *seh-khee'*; from 5500; *refuse* (as *swept* off):–offscouring.
5502. סָחַף *saw-khaf'*; a prim. root; to *scrape* off:–sweep (away).
5503. סָחַר *saw-khar'*; a prim. root; to *travel* round (spec. as a *pedlar*); intens., to *palpitate*:–go about, merchant(-man), occupy with, pant, trade, traffick.
5504. סַחַר *sakh'-ar*; from 5503; *profit* (from trade):–merchandise.
5505. סָחַר *saw-khar'*; from 5503; an *emporium*; abstr., *profit* (from trade):–mart, merchandise.
5506. סְחֹרָה *sekh-o-raw';* from 5503: *traffic*:–merchandise.
5507. סֹחֵרָה *so-khay-raw'*; prop. act.part. fem. of 5503; something *surrounding* the person, i.e. a *shield*:–buckler.
5508. סֹחֶרֶת *so-kheh'-reth*; similar to 5507; prob. a (black) *tile* (or *tessara*) for laying borders with:–black marble.
5509. סִיג *seeg*; or סוּג (Eze. 22:18) *soog*; from 5472 in the sense of *refuse*; *scoria*:–dross.
5510. סִיוָן *see-vawn'*; prob. of Pers. or.; *Sivan*, the third Heb. month:–Sivan.
5511. סִיחוֹן *see-khone';* or סִיחֹן *see-khone'*; from the same as 5477; *tempestuous; Sichon*, an Amoritish king:–Sihon.
5512. סִין *seen*; of unc. der.; *Sin* the name of an Eg. town and (prob.) desert adjoining:–Sin.
5513. סִינִי *see-nee';* from an otherwise unknown name of a man; a *Sinite*, or desc. of one of the sons of Canaan:–Sinite.
5514. סִינַי *see-nah'-ee*; of unc. der.; *Sinai*, mountain of Arabia:–Sinai.
5515. סִינִים *see-neem';* pl. of an otherwise unknown name; *Sinim*, a distant Oriental region:–Sinim.
5516. סִיסְרָא *see-ser-aw'*; of unc. der.; *Sisera*, the name of a Canaanitish king and of one of the Nethinim:–Sisera.
5517. סִיעָא *see-ah'*; or סִיעֲהָא *see-ah-haw'*; from an un. root mean. to *converse*; *congregation*; *Sia* or *Siaha*, one of the Nethinim:– Sia, Siaha.
5518. סִיר *seer*; or (fem.) סִירָה *see-raw'*; or סִרָה (Jeremiah 52:18) *see-raw'*; from a prim. root mean. to *boil* up; a *pot*; also a *thorn* (as springing up rapidly); by impl., a *hook*:–caldron, fishhook, pan, ([wash-])pot, thorn.
5519. סָךְ *sawk*; from 5526; prop. a *thicket* of men, i.e. a *crowd*:– multitude.
5520. סֹךְ *soke*; from 5526; a *hut* (as of *entwined* boughs); also a *lair*:– covert, den, pavilion, tabernacle.
5521. סֻכָּה *sook-kaw';* fem of 5520; a *hut* or *lair*:–booth, cottage, covert, pavilion, tabernacle, tent.
5522. סִכּוּת *sik-kooth'*; fem. of 5519; an (idolatrous) *booth*:–tabernacle.
5523. סֻכּוֹת *sook-kohth'*; or סֻכֹּת *sook-kohth'*; pl. of 5521; *booths*; *Succoth,* the name of a place in Eg. and of three in Pal.:– Succoth.
5524. סֻכּוֹת בְּנוֹת *sook-kohth' ben-ohth'*; from 5523 and the (irreg.) pl. of 1323; *booths of (the) daughters; brothels*, i.e. idolatrous *tents* for impure purpose:–Succoth-benoth.
5525. סֻכִּי *sook-kee';* patrial; from an unknown name (perh. 5520); a *Sukkite*, or inh. of some place near Eg. (i.e. *hut-dwellers*):–Sukkiims.
5526. סָכַךְ *saw-kak';* or שָׂכַךְ (Ex. 33:22) *saw-kak'*; a prim. root; prop. to *entwine* as a screen; by impl., to *fence* in, *cover* over, (fig.) *protect*:–cover, defence, defend, hedge in, join together, set, shut up.
5527. סְכָכָה *sek-aw-kaw';* from 5526; *inclosure*; *Secacah*, a place in Pal.:–Secacah.
5528. סָכַל *saw-kal';* for 3688; to be *silly*:–do (make, play the, turn into) fool(-ish, -ishly, -ishness).
5529. סֶכֶל *seh'-kel*; from 5528; *silliness*; concr. and coll., *dolts*:–folly.
5530. סָכָל *saw-kawl'*; from 5528; *silly*:–fool(-ish), sottish.
5531. סִכְלוּת *sik-looth'*; or שִׂכְלוּת (Ec. 1:17) *sik-looth'*; from 5528; *silliness*:–folly, foolishness.
5532. סָכַן *saw-kan';* a prim. root; to *be familiar* with; by impl., to *minister* to, *be serviceable* to, to *cherish be customary*:–acquaint (self), be advantage, X ever, (be, [un-])profit(-able), treasurer, be wont.
5533. סָכַן *saw-kan';* prob. a denom. from 7915; prop. *to cut*, i.e. *damage*; also to *grow* (caus., *make*) *poor*:–endanger, impoverish.
5534. סָכַר *saw-kar';* a prim. root; to *shut* up; by impl., to *surrender*:–stop, give over. See also 5462, 7936.
5535. סָכַת *saw-kath';* a prim. root to *be silent*; by impl., to *observe* quietly:–take heed.
5536. סַל *sal;* from 5549; prop. a willow *twig* (as *pendulous*), i.e. an *osier*; but only as woven into a *basket*:–basket.
5537. סָלָא *saw-law';* a prim. root; to *suspend* in a balance, i.e. *weigh*:–comp..
5538. סִלָּא *sil-law'*; from 5549; *an embankment; Silla*, a place in Jerus.:–Silla.
5539. סָלַד *saw-lad'*; a prim. root; prob. to *leap* (with joy), i.e. *exult*:–harden self.
5540. סֶלֶד *seh'-led*; from 5539; *exultation*; *Seled*, an Isr.:–Seled.
5541. סָלָה *saw-law'*; a prim. root; to *hang up*, i.e. *weigh*, or (fig.) *contemn*:–tread down (under foot), value.
5542. סֶלָה *seh'-law*; from 5541; *suspension* (of music), i.e. *pause*:–Selah.
5543. סַלּוּ *sal-loo'*; or סַלּוּא *sal-loo'*; or סָלוּא *sal-loo'*; or סַלַּי *sal-lah'-ee*; from 5541; *weighed*; *Sallu* or *Sallai*, the name of two Isr.:–Sallai, Sallu, Salu.
5544. סִלּוֹן *sil-lone'*; or סַלּוֹן *sal-one';* from 5541; a *prickle* (as if *pendulous*); brier, thorn.
5545. סָלַח *saw-lakh';* a prim. root; to *forgive*:–forgive, pardon, spare.
5546. סַלָּח *saw-lawkh'*; from 5545; *placable*: ready to forgive.
5547. סְלִיחָה *sel-ee-khaw'*; from 5545; *pardon*:–forgiveness, pardon.
5548. סַלְכָה *sal-kaw';* from an un. root. mean. to *walk; walking; Salcah*, a place E. of the Jordan:–Salcah, Salchah.
5549. סָלַל *saw-lal';* a prim. root; to *mound* up (esp. a turnpike); fig., to *exalt*; refl., to *oppose* (as by a dam):–cast up, exalt (self), extol, make plain, raise up.
5550. סֹלְלָה *so-lel-aw'*; or סוֹלְלָה *so-lel-aw';* act.part. fem. of 5549, but used pass.; a military *mound*, i.e. *rampart* of besiegers:–bank, mount.
5551. סֻלָּם *sool-lawm'*; from 5549; a *staircase*:–ladder.
5552. סַלְסִלָּה *sal-sil-law'*; from 5541; a *twig* (as *pendulous*):–basket.
5553. סֶלַע *seh'-lah*; from an un. root mean. to be *lofty*; a craggy *rock*, lit. or fig. (a *fortress*):–(ragged) rock, stone(-ny), strong hold.
5554. סֶלַע *seh'-lah*; the same as 5553; *Sela*,

the rock-city of Idumaea:–rock, Sela(-h).
5555. סֶלַע הַמַּחְלְקוֹת *seh'-lah ham-makh-lek-oth'*; from 5553 and the pl. of 4256 with the art. interp.; *rock of the divisions; Sela-ham-Machlekoth*, a place in Pal.:–Sela-hammalekoth.
5556. סָלְעָם *sol-awm'*; app. from the same as 5553 in the sense of *crushing* as with a rock, i.e. consuming; a kind of *locust* (from its *destructiveness*):–bald locust.
5557. סָלַף *saw-laf'*; a prim. root; prop. to *wrench*, i.e. (fig.) to *subvert*:–overthrow, pervert.
5558. סֶלֶף *seh'-lef*; from 5557; *distortion*, i.e. (fig.) *viciousness*:–perverseness.
5559. סְלִק *sel-eek'* (Chald.); a prim. root; to *ascend*:–come (up).
5560. סֹלֶת *so'-leth*; from an un. root mean. to *strip*; *flour* (as *chipped* off):–(fine) flour, meal.
5561. סַם *sam'*; from an un. root mean. to *smell* sweet; an *aroma*:– sweet (spice).
5562. סַמְגַּר נְבוֹ *sam-gar' neb-o'*; of for. or.; *Samgar-Nebo*, a Babylonian gen.:–Samgar-nebo.
5563. סְמָדַר *sem-aw-dar'*; of unc. der.; a vine *blossom*; used also adv., *abloom*:–tender grape.
5564. סָמַךְ *saw-mak'*; a prim. root; to *prop* (lit. or fig.); refl., to *lean* upon or *take hold* of (in a favorable or unfavorable sense):–bear up, establish, (up-)hold, lay, lean, lie hard, put, rest self, set self, stand fast, stay (self), sustain.
5565. סְמַכְיָהוּ *sem-ak-yaw'-hoo*; from 5564 and 3050; *supported* of *Jah; Semakjah*, an Isr.:–Semachiah.
5566. סֶמֶל *seh'-mel*; or סֵמֶל *say'-mel*; from an un. root mean. to *resemble*; a *likeness*:–figure, idol, image.
5567. סָמַן *saw-man'*; a prim. root; to *designate*:–appointed.
5568. סָמַר *saw-mar'*; a prim. root; to *be erect*, i.e. *bristle* as hair:–stand up, tremble.
5569. סָמָר *saw-mawr'*; from 5568; *bristling*, i.e. *shaggy*:–rough.
5570. סְנָאָה *sen-aw-aw'*; from an un. root mean. to *prick*; *thorny*; *Senaah*, a place in Pal.:–Senaah, Hassenaah [*with the art.*].
5571. סַנְבַלַּט *san-bal-lat'*; of for. or.; *Sanballat*, a Pers. satrap of Samaria:–Sanballat.
5572. סְנֶה *sen-eh'*; from an un. root mean. to *prick*; a *bramble*:–bush.
5573. סֶנֶה *seh-neh'*; the same s 5572; *thorn*; *Seneh*, a crag in Pal.:–Seneh.
5574. סְנוּאָה *sen-oo-aw'*; or סְנֻאָה *sen-oo-aw'*; from the same as 5570; *pointed*; (used with the art. as a proper name) *Senuah*, the name of two Isr.:–Hasenuah [*incl. the art*], Senuah.
5575. סַנְוֵר *san-vare'*; of unc. der.; (in pl.) *blindness*:–blindness.
5576. סַנְחֵרִיב *san-khay-reeb'*; of for. or.; *Sancherib*, an Assyrian king:–Sennacherib.
5577. סַנְסִן *san-seen'*; from an un. root mean. to be *pointed*; a *twig* (as *tapering*):–bough.
5578. סַנְסַנָּה *san-san-naw'*; fem. of a form of 5577; a *bough; Sansannah*, a place in Pal.:–Sansannah.
5579. סְנַפִּיר *sen-ap-peer'*; of unc. der.; a *fin* (coll.):–fins.
5580. סָס *sawce*; from the same as 5483; a *moth* (from the *agility* of the fly):–moth.
5581. סִסְמָי *sis-mah'-ee*; of unc. der.; *Sismai*, an Isr.:–Sisamai.
5582. סָעַד *saw-ad'*; a prim. root; to *support* (mostly fig.):–comfort, establish, hold up, refresh self, strengthen, be upholden.
5583. סְעַד *seh-ad'* (Chald.); cor. to 5582; to *aid*:–helping.
5584. סָעָה *saw-aw'*; a prim. root; to *rush*:–storm.
5585. סָעִיף *saw-eef'*; from 5586; a *fissure* (of rocks); also a *bough* (as *subdivided*):–(outmost) branch, clift, top.
5586. סָעַף *saw-af'*; a prim. root; prop. to *divide* up; but used only as denom. from 5585, to *disbranch* (a tree):–top.
5587. סָעִף *saw-eef'*; or שָׂעִף *saw-eef'*; from 5586; *divided* (in mind), i.e. (abstr.) a *sentiment*:–opinion.
5588. סֵעֵף *say-afe'*; from 5586 *divided* (in mind), i.e. (concr.) a *skeptic*:–thought.
5589. סְעַפָּה *seh-ap-paw'*; fem. of 5585; a *twig or branch*:–bough. Comp. 5634.
5590. סָעַר *saw-ar'*; a prim. root; to *rush* upon; by impl., to *toss* (trans. or intr., lit. or fig.):–be (toss with) tempest(-uous), be sore, troubled, come out as a (drive with the, scatter with a) whirlwind.
5591. סַעַר *sah'-ar*; or (fem.) סְעָרָה *seh-aw-raw'*; from 5590; a *hurricane*:–storm(-y), tempest, whirlwind.
5592. סַף *saf*; from 5605, in its or. sense of *containing*; a *vestibule* (as a *limit*); also a *dish* (for holding blood or wine):–bason, bowl, cup, door (post), gate, post, threshold.
5593. סַף *saf*; the same as 5592; *Saph*, a Philistine:–Saph. Comp. 5598.
5594. סָפַד *saw-fad'*; a prim. root; prop. to *tear* the hair and *beat* the breasts (as Orientals do in grief); gen. to *lament*; by impl., to *wail*:–lament, mourn(-er), wail.
5595. סָפָה *saw-faw'*; a prim. root; prop. to *scrape* (lit., to *shave*; but usually fig.) together (i.e. to *accumulate* or *increase*) or away (i.e. to *scatter, remove*, or *ruin*; intr., to *perish*):–add, augment, consume, destroy, heap, join, perish, put.
5596. סָפַח *saw-fakh'* or שָׂפַח (Isaiah 3:17) *saw-fakh'*; a prim. root; prop. to *scrape* out, but in certain peculiar senses (of *removal* or *association*):–abiding, gather together, cleave, smite with the scab.
5597. סַפַּחַת *sap-pakh'-ath*; from 5596; the *mange* (as making the hair fall off):–scab.
5598. סִפַּי *sip-pah'-ee*; from 5592; *bason-like*; *Sippai*, a Philistine:–Sippai. Comp. 5593.
5599. סָפִיחַ *saw-fee'-akh*; from 5596; something (spontaneously) *falling* off, i.e. a *self-sown* crop; fig., a *freshet*:–(such) things as (which) grow (of themselves), which groweth of its own accord (itself).
5600. סְפִינָה *sef-ee-naw'*; from 5603; a (sea-going) *vessel* (as *ceiled* with a deck):–ship.
5601. סַפִּיר *sap-peer'*; from 5608; a *gem* (perh. used for *scratching* other substances), prob. the *sapphire*:–sapphire.
5602. סֵפֶל *say'-fel*; from an un. root mean. to *depress*; a *basin* (as *deepened* out):–bowl, dish.
5603. סָפַן *saw-fan'*; a prim. root; to *hide* by covering; spec., to *roof* (pass.part. as noun, a *roof*) or *wainscot*; fig., to *reserve*:–cieled, cover, seated.
5604. סִפֻּן *sip-poon'*; from 5603; a *wainscot*:–cieling.
5605. סָפַף *saw-faf'*; a prim. root; prop. to *snatch* away, i.e. *terminate*; but used only as denom. from 5592 (in the sense of a *vestibule*), to *wait* at the *threshold*:–be a doorkeeper.
5606. סָפַק *saw-fak'*; or שָׂפַק (1 Kings 20:10; Job 27:23; Isaiah 2:6) *saw-fak'*; a prim. root; to *clap* the hands (in token of compact, derision, grief, indignation, or punishment); by impl. of satisfaction, to *be enough*; by impl. of excess, to *vomit*:–clap, smite, strike, suffice, wallow.
5607. סֵפֶק *say'-fek*; or שֶׂפֶק (Job 20:22; 36:18) *seh'-fek*; from 5606; *chastisement*; also *satiety*:–stroke, sufficiency.
5608. סָפַר *saw-far'*; a prim. root; prop. to *score* with a mark as a tally or record, i.e. (by impl.) to *inscribe*, and also to *enumerate*; intens., to *recount*, i.e. *celebrate*:–commune, (ac-)count; declare, number, + penknife, reckon, scribe, shew forth, speak, talk, tell (out), writer.
5609. סְפַר *sef-ar'* (Chald.); from a root cor. to 5608; a *book*:–book, roll.
5610. סְפָר *sef-awr'*; from 5608; a *census*:–numbering.
5611. סְפָר *sef-awr'*; the same as 5610; *Sephar*, a place in Arabia:–Sephar.
5612. סֵפֶר *say'-fer*; or (fem.) סִפְרָה (Ps. 56:8 [9]) *sif-raw'*; from 5608; prop. *writing* (the art or a document); by impl., a *book*:–bill, book, evidence, X learn[-ed] (-ing), letter, register, scroll.
5613. סָפֵר *saw-fare'* (Chald.); from the same as 5609; a *scribe* (secular or sacred):–scribe.
5614. סְפָרָד *sef-aw-rawd'*; of for. der.; *Sepharad*, a region of Assyria:–Sepharad.
5615. סְפֹרָה *sef-o-raw'*; from 5608; a *numeration*:–number.
5616. סְפַרְוִי *sef-ar-vee'*; patrial from 5617; a *Sepharvite* or inh. of Sepharvain:–Sepharvite.
5617. סְפַרְוַיִם (dual), *sef-ar-vah'-yim*; or (pl.) סְפָרִים *sef-aw-reem'*; of for. der.; *Sepharvajim* or *Sepharim*, a place in Assyria:– Sepharvaim.
5618. סֹפֶרֶת *so-feh'-reth*; fem. act.part. of 5608; a *scribe* (prop. female); *Sophereth*, a temple servant:–Sophereth.
5619. סָקַל *saw-kal'*; a prim. root; prop. to *be weighty*; but used only in the sense of *lapidation* or its contrary (as if a *de*lapidation):–(cast, gather out, throw) stone(-s), X surely.
5620. סַר *sar*; contr. from 5637; *peevish*:–heavy, sad.
5621. סָרָב *saw-rawb'*; from an un. root mean. to *sting*; a thistle:–brier.
5622. סַרְבַּל *sar-bal'* (Chald.); of unc. der.; a *cloak*:–coat.
5623. סַרְגּוֹן *sar-gone'*; of for. der.; *Sargon*, an Assyrian king:–Sargon.
5624. סֶרֶד *seh'-red*; from a prim. root mean. to *tremble*; *trembling*; *Sered*, an Isr.:–Sered.
5625. סַרְדִּי *sar-dee'*; patron from 5624; a *Seredite* (coll.) or desc. of Sered:–Sardites.
5626. סִרָה *see-raw'*; from 5493; *departure*; *Sirah*, a cistern so-called:–Sirah. See also 5518.
5627. סָרָה *saw-raw'*; from 5493; *apostasy*, *crime*; fig., *remission*:–X continual, rebellion, revolt([-ed]), turn away, wrong.
5628. סָרַח *saw-rakh'*; a prim. root; to *extend* (even to *excess*):–exceeding, hand, spread, stretch self, banish.
5629. סֶרַח *seh'-rakh*; from 5628; a *redundancy*:–remnant.
5630. סִרְיוֹן *sir-yone'*; for 8302; a coat of *mail*:–brigandine.
5631. סָרִיס *saw-reece'*; or סָרִס *saw-reece'*; from an un. root mean. to *castrate*; a *eunuch*; by impl., *valet* (esp. of the female

apartments), and thus, a *minister* of state:–chamberlain, eunuch, officer. Comp. 7249.
5632. סָרֵךְ *saw-rake'* (Chald.); of for. or.; an *emir:*–president.
5633. סֶרֶן *seh'-ren*; from an un. root of unc. mean.; an *axle;* fig., a *peer:*–lord, plate.
5634. סַרְעַפָּה *sar-ap-paw'*; for 5589; a *twig:*–bough.
5635. סָרַף *saw-raf'*; a prim. root; to *cremate,* i.e. to *be* (near) *of kin* (such being privileged to kindle the pyre):–burn.
5636. סַרְפָּד *sar-pawd';* from 5635; a *nettle* (as stinging like a *burn*):–brier.
5637. סָרַר *saw-rar';* a prim. root; to *turn* away, i.e. (mor.) *be refractory:*–X away, backsliding, rebellious, revolter(-ing), slide back, stubborn, withdrew.
5638. סְתָו *seth-awv'*; from an un. root mean. to *hide; winter* (as the dark season):–winter.
5639. סְתוּר *seth-oor'*; from 5641; *hidden; Sethur,* an Isr.:–Sethur.
5640. סָתַם *saw-tham'*; or שָׂתַם (Numbers 24:15) *saw-tham';* a prim. root; to *stop* up; by impl., to *repair;* fig., to *keep secret:*–closed up, hidden, secret, shut out (up), stop.
5641. סָתַר *saw-thar'*; a prim. root; to *hide* (by covering), lit. or fig.:–be absent, keep close, conceal, hide (self), (keep) secret, X surely.
5642. סְתַר *seth-ar'* (Chald.); cor. to 5641; to *conceal;* fig., to *demolish:*–destroy, secret thing.
5643. סֵתֶר *say'-ther*; or (fem.) סִתְרָה (De. 32:38), *sith-raw';* from 5641; a *cover* (in a good or a bad, a lit. or a fig. sense):–backbiting, covering, covert, X disguise[-th], hiding place, privily, protection, secret(-ly, place).
5644. סִתְרִי *sith-ree'*; from 5643; *protective; Sithri,* an Isr.,:–Zithri.

ע

5645. עָב *awb*; (masc. and fem.); from 5743; prop. an *envelope,* i.e. *darkness* (or *density,* 2 Ch.. 4:17); spec., a (scud) *cloud;* also a *copse:*–clay, (thick) cloud, X thick, thicket. Comp. 5672.
5646. עָב *awb*; or עֹב *obe;* from an un. root mean. to *cover;* prop. equiv. to 5645; but used only as an arch. term, an *architrave* (as *shading* the pillars):–thick (beam, plant).
5647. עָבַד *aw-bad';* a prim. root; to *work* (in any sense); by impl., to *serve, till,* (caus.) *enslave,* etc.:–X be, keep in bondage, be bondmen, bond-service, compel, do, dress, ear, execute, + husbandman, keep, labour(-ing man, bring to pass, (cause to, make to) serve(-ing, self), (be, become) servant(-s), do (use) service, till(-er), transgress (set a) work, be wrought, worshipper.
5648. עֲבַד *ab-bad'* (Chald.); cor. to 5647; to *do, make, prepare, keep,* etc.:–X cut, do, execute, go on, make, move, work.
5649. עֲבַד *ab-bad'* (Chald.); from 5648; a *servant:*–servant.
5650. עֶבֶד *eh'-bed*; from 5647; a *servant:*–X bondage, bondman, [bond-] servant, (man-) servant.
5651. עֶבֶד *eh'-bed*; the same as 5650; *Ebed,* the name of two Isr.:–Ebed.
5652. עֲבָד *ab-awd'*; from 5647; a *deed:*–work.
5653. עַבְדָּא *ab-daw'*; from 5647; *work; Abda,* the name of two Isr.:–Abda.
5654. עֹבֵד אֱדוֹם *o-bade' ed-ome';* from the act. part. of 5647 and 123; *worker of Edom; Obed-Edom,* the name of five Isr.:–Obed-edom.
5655. עַבְדְּאֵל *ab-deh-ale'*; from 5647 and 410; *serving God; Abdeël,* an Isr.: Abdeel. Comp. 5661.
5656. עֲבֹדָה *ab-o-daw';* or עֲבוֹדָה *ab-o-daw';* from 5647; *work* of any kind:–act, bondage, + bondservant, effect, labour, ministering (-try), office, service(-ile, -itude), tillage, use, work, X wrought.
5657. עֲבֻדָּה *ab-ood-daw';* pass.part. of 5647; something *wrought,* i.e. (concr.) *service:*–household, store of servants.
5658. עַבְדוֹן *ab-dohn'*; from 5647; *servitude; Abdon,* the name of a place in Pal. and of four Isr.:–Abdon. Comp. 5683.
5659. עַבְדוּת *ab-dooth'*; from 5647; *servitude:*–bondage
5660. עַבְדִּי *ab-dee'*; from 5647; *serviceable; Abdi,* the name of two Isr.:–Abdi.
5661. עַבְדִיאֵל *ab-dee-ale'*; from 5650 and 410; *servant of God; Abdiël,* an Isr.:–Abdiel. Comp. 5655.
5662. עֹבַדְיָה *o-bad-yaw'*; or עֹבַדְיָהוּ *o-bad-yaw'-hoo;* act.part. of 5647 and 3050; *serving Jah; Obadjah,* the name of thirteen Isr.:–Obadiah.
5663. עֶבֶד־מֶלֶךְ *eh'-bed meh'-lek*; from 5650 and 4428; *servant of a king; Ebed-Melek,* a eunuch of Zedekeah:–Ebed-melech.
5664. עֲבֵד נְגוֹ *ab-ade' neg-o';* the same as 5665; *Abed-Nego,* the Babylonian name of one of Daniel's companions:–Abed-nego.
5665. עֲבֵד נְגוֹא *ab-ade' neg-o'* (Chald.); of for. or.; *Abed-Nego,* the name of Azariah:–Abed-nego.
5666. עָבָה *aw-baw';* a prim. root; to *be dense:*–be (grow) thick(-er).
5667. עֲבוֹט *ab-ote';* or עֲבֹט *ab-ote';* from 5670; a *pawn:*–pledge.
5668. עָבוּר *aw-boor'*; or עָבֻר *aw-boor';* pass. part. of 5674; prop. *crossed,* i.e. (abstr.) *transit;* used only adv., on *account* of, in *order* that:–because of, for (...'s sake), (intent) that, to.
5669. עָבוּר *aw-boor'*; the same as 5668; *passed,* i.e. *kept* over; used only of *stored* grain:–old corn.
5670. עָבַט *aw-bat'*; a prim. root; to *pawn*; caus., to *lend* (on security); fig., to *entangle:*–borrow, break [*ranks*], fetch [a *pledge*], lend, X surely.
5671. עַבְטִיט *ab-teet';* from 5670; something *pledged,* i.e. (coll.) *pawned* goods:–thick clay.
5672. עֲבִי *ab-ee';* or עֳבִי *ob-ee';* from 5666; *density,* i.e. *depth* or *width:*–thick(-ness). Comp. 5645.
5673. עֲבִידָה *ab-ee-daw'* (Chald.); from 5648; *labor* or *business:*–affairs, service, work.
5674. עָבַר *aw-bar';* a prim. root; to *cross* over; used very widely of any *transition* (lit. or fig.; trans., intr., intens., caus.); spec., to *cover* (in copulation):–alienate, alter, X at all, beyond, bring (over, through), carry over, (over-)come (on, over), conduct (over), convey over, current, deliver, do away, enter, escape, fail, gender, get over, (make) go (away, beyond, by, forth, his way, in, on, over, through), have away (more), lay, meddle, overrun, make partition, (cause to, give, make to, over) pass(-age, along, away, beyond, by, -enger, on, out, over, through), (cause to, make) + proclaim(-amation), perish, provoke to anger, put away, rage, + raiser of taxes, remove, send over, set apart, + shave, cause to (make) sound, X speedily, X sweet smelling, take (away), (make to) transgress(-or), translate, turn away, [way-] faring man, be wrath.
5675. עֲבַר *ab-ar'* (Chald.); cor. to 5676:–beyond, this side.
5676. עֵבֶר *ay'-ber*; from 5674; prop. a region *across;* but used only adv. (with or without a prep.) on the *opposite* side (esp. of the Jordan; ususally mean. the *east*):–X against, beyond, by, X from, over, passage, quarter, (other, this) side, straight.
5677. עֵבֶר *ay'-ber;* the same as 5676; *Eber,* the name of two patriarchs and four Isr.:–Eber, Heber.
5678. עֶבְרָה *eb-raw'*; fem. of 5676; an *outburst* of passion:–anger, rage, wrath.
5679. עֲבָרָה *ab-aw-raw'*; from 5674; a *crossing*-place:–ferry, plain .
5680. עִבְרִי *ib-ree'*; patron. from 5677; an *Eberite* (i.e. Hebrew) or desc. of Eber:–Hebrew(-ess, woman).
5681. עִבְרִי *ib-ree';* the same as 5680; *Ibri,* an Isr.:–Ibri.
5682. עֲבָרִים *ab-aw-reem'*; pl. of 5676; regions *beyond; Abarim,* a place in Pal.:–Abarim, passages.
5683. עֶבְרֹן *eb-rone'*; from 5676; *transitional; Ebron,* a place in Pal.:–Hebron.
5684. עֶבְרֹנָה *eb-raw;* fem. of 5683; *Ebronah,* place in the Desert:–Ebronah.
5685. עָבַשׁ *aw-bash';* a prim. root; to *dry* up:–be rotten.
5686. עָבַת *aw-bath';* a prim. root; to *interlace,* i.e. (fig.) to *pervert:*–wrap up.
5687. עָבֹת *aw-both'* or עָבוֹת *aw-both'*; from 5686; *intwined,* i.e. *dense:*–thick.
5688. עֲבֹת *ab-oth';* or עֲבוֹת *ab-oth'*; or עֲבֹתָה (fem.) *ab-oth-aw'*; the same as 5687; something *intwined,* i.e. a *string, wreath* or *foliage:*–band, cord, rope, thick bough (branch), wreathen (chain).
5689. עָגַב *aw-gab';* a prim. root; to *breathe* after, i.e. to *love* (sensually):–dote, lover.
5690. עֶגֶב *eh'-gheb;* from 5689; *love* (concr.), i.e. *amative* words:–much love, very lovely.
5691. עֲגָבָה *ag-aw-baw';* from 5689; *love* (abstr.), i.e. *amorousness:*–inordinate love.
5692. עֻגָּה *oog-gaw';* from 5746; an *ash-cake* (as *round*):–cake (upon the hearth).
5693. עָגוּר *aw-goor';* pass. part [but with act. sense] of an un. root mean. to *twitter:* prob. the *swallow:*–swallow.
5694. עָגִיל *aw-gheel';* from the same as 5696; something *round,* i.e. a *ring* (for the ears):–earring.
5695. עֵגֶל *ay-ghel*; from the same as 5696; a (male) *calf* (as *frisking* round), esp. one nearly grown (i.e. a *steer*):–bullock, calf.
5696. עָגֹל *aw-gole';* or עָגוֹל *aw-gole'*; from an un. root mean. to *revolve, circular:*–round.
5697. עֶגְלָה *eg-law'*; fem. of 5695; a (female) *calf,* esp. one nearly grown (i.e. a *heifer*):–calf, cow, heifer.
5698. עֶגְלָה *eg-law'*; the same as 5697; *Eglah,* a wife of David:–Eglah.
5699. עֲגָלָה *ag-aw-law'*; from the same as 5696; something *revolving,* i.e. a wheeled *vehicle:*–cart, chariot, wagon
5700. עֶגְלוֹן *eg-lawn'*; from 5695; *vituline*; *Eglon,* the name of a place in Pal. and of a Moabitish king:–Eglon.
5701. עָגַם *aw-gam'*; a prim. root; to *be sad:*–grieve.
5702. עָגַן *aw-gan';* a prim. root; to *debar,* i.e. from marriage:–stay.
5703. עַד *ad*; from 5710; prop. a (peremptory) *terminus,* i.e. (by impl.) *duration,* in the sense of *advance* or *perpetuity* (substantially

as a noun, either with or without a prep.):–eternity, ever(-lasting, -more), old, perpetually, + world without end.

5704. עַד *ad*; prop. the same as 5703 (used as a prep., adv. or conj.; esp. with a prep.); *as far* (or *long*, or *much*) *as*, whether of space (*even unto*) or time (*during, while, until*) or degree (*equally with*):–against, and, as, at, before, by (that), even (to), for(-asmuch as), [hither-]to, + how long, into, as long (much) as, (so) that, till, toward, until, when, while, (+ as) yet.

5705. עַד *ad* (Chald.); cor. to 5704:–X and, at, for, [hither-]to, on till, (un-) to, until, within.

5706. עַד *ad;* the same as 5703 in the sense of the *aim* of an attack; *booty:*–prey.

5707. עֵד *ayd*; contr. from 5749 ; concr., a *witness*; abstr., *testimony*; spec., a *recorder*, i.e. *prince:*–witness.

5708. עֵד *ayd*; from an un. root mean. to *set* a period [comp. 5710, 5749]; the *menstrual* flux (as periodical); by impl. (in pl.) *soiling:*–filthy.

5709. עֲדָא *ad-aw'* (Chald.) or עֲדָה *ad-aw'* (Chald.); cor. to 5710:–alter, depart, pass (away), remove, take (away).

5710. עָדָה *aw-daw'*; a prim. root; to *advance*, i.e. *pass* on or *continue*; caus., to *remove*; spec., to *bedeck* (i.e. bring an ornament upon):–adorn, deck (self), pass by, take away.

5711. עָדָה *aw-daw'*; from 5710; *ornament; Adah*, the name of two women:–Adah.

5712. עֵדָה *ay-daw'*; fem. of 5707 in the or. sense of *fixture*; a stated *assemblage* (spec., a *concourse*, or gen., a *family* or *crowd*):–assembly, company, congregation, multitude, people, swarm. Comp. 5713.

5713. עֵדָה *ay-daw'*; fem. of 5707 in its te. sense; *testimony:*– testimony, witness. Comp. 5712.

5714. עִדּוֹ *id-do'*; or עִדּוֹא *id-do'*; or עִדִּיא *id-dee'*; from 5710; *timely; Iddo* (or *Iddi*), the name of five Isr.:–Iddo. Comp. 3035, 3260.

5715. עֵדוּת *ay-dooth'*; fem. of 5707; *testimony:*–testimony, witness.

5716. עֲדִי *ad-ee'*; from 5710 in the sense of *trappings*; *finery*; gen. an *outfit*; spec., a *headstall:*–X excellent, mouth, ornament.

5717. עֲדִיאֵל *ad-ee-ale'*; from 5716 and 410; *ornament of God*; *Adiël*, the name of three Isr.:–Adiel.

5718. עֲדָיָה *ad-aw-yaw'*; or עֲדָיָהוּ *ad-aw-yaw'-hoo*; from 5710 and 3050; *Jah has adorned; Adajah*, the name of eight Isr.:–Adaiah.

5719. עָדִין *aw-deen'*; from 5727; *voluptuous:*–given to pleasures.

5720. עָדִין *aw-deen'*; the same as 5719; *Adin*, the name of two Isr.:–Adin.

5721. עֲדִינָא *ad-ee-naw';* from 5719; *effeminacy; Adina*, an Isr.:–Adina.

5722. עֲדִינוֹ *ad-ee-no';* prob. from 5719 in the or. sense of *slender* (i.e. a *spear*); his *spear:*–Adino.

5723. עֲדִיתַיִם *ad-ee-thah'-yim;* dual of a fem. of 5706; *double prey; Adithajim*, a place in Pal.:–Adithaim.

5724. עַדְלַי *ad-lah'-ee;* prob. from an un. root of unc. mean.; *Adlai*, an Isr.:–Adlai.

5725. עֲדֻלָּם *ad-ool-lawm';* prob. from the pass.part. of the same as 5724; *Adullam*, a place in Pal.:–Adullam.

5726. עֲדֻלָּמִי *ad-ool-law-mee';* patrial from 5725; an *Adullamite* or nat. of Adullam:–Adullamite.

5727. עָדַן *aw-dan';* a prim. root; to be *soft* or *pleasant*; fig. and refl., to *live voluptuously:*–delight self.

5728. עֲדֶן *ad-en';* or עֲדֶנָה *ad-en'-naw*; from 5704 and 2004; *till now:*–yet.

5729. עֶדֶן *eh'-den;* from 5727; *pleasure; Eden*, a place in Mesopotamia:–Eden.

5730. עֵדֶן *ay'-den;* or (fem.) עֶדְנָה *ed-naw'*; from 5727; *pleasure:*–delicate, delight, *pleasure*. See also 1040.

5731. עֵדֶן *ay'-den;* the same as 5730 (masc.); *Eden*, the region of Adam's home:–Eden.

5732. עִדָּן *id-dawn'* (Chald.); from a root cor. to that of 5708; a set *time*; te., a *year:*–time.

5733. עַדְנָא *ad-naw';* from 5727; *pleasure; Adna*, the name of two Isr.:–Adna.

5734. עַדְנָה *ad-naw';* from 5727; *pleasure; Adnah*, the name of two Isr.:–Adnah.

5735. עֲדְעָדָה *ad-aw-daw';* from 5712; *festival; Adadah*, a place in Pal.:–Adadah.

5736. עָדַף *aw-daf';* a prim. root; to *be* (caus., *have*) *redundant:*–be more, odd number, be (have) over (and above), overplus, remain.

5737. עָדַר *aw-dar';* a prim. root; to *arrange*, as a battle, a vineyard (to *hoe*); hence, to *muster* and so to *miss* (or find *wanting*):–dig, fail, keep (rank), lack.

5738. עֶדֶר *eh'-der;* from 5737; an *arrangement* (i.e. drove); *Eder*, an Isr.:–Ader.

5739. עֵדֶר *ay'-der;* from 5737; an *arrangement*, i.e. *muster* (of animals):–drove, flock, herd.

5740. עֵדֶר *ay'-der;* the same as 5739 *Eder*, the name of an Isr. and of two places in Pal.:–Edar, Eder.

5741. עַדְרִיאֵל *ad-ree-ale';* from 5739 and 410; *flock of God; Adriel*, an Isr.:–Adriel.

5742. עָדָשׁ *aw-dawsh';* from an un. root of unc. mean.; a *lentil:*–lentile.

5743. עוּב *oob* a prim. root; to be *dense* or *dark*, i.e. to *becloud:*–cover with a cloud.

5744. עוֹבֵד *o-bade';* act.part. of 5647; *serving; Obed*, the name of five Isr.:–Obed.

5745. עוֹבָל *o-bawl';* of for. der.; *Obal*, a son of Joktan:–Obal.

5746. עוּג *oog;* a prim. root; prop. to *gyrate;* but used only as a denom. from 5692, to *bake* (round cakes on the hearth):–bake.

5747. עוֹג *ogue* prob. from 5746; *round; Og*, a king of Bashan:–Og.

5748. עוּגָב *oo-gawb';* or עֻגָּב *oog-gawb';* from 5689 in the or. sense of *breathing;* a *reed*-instrument of music:–organ.

5749. עוּד *ood;* a prim. root; to *duplicate* or *repeat;* by impl., to *protest, testify* (as by reiteration); intens., to *encompass, restore* (as a sort of redupl.):–admonish,charge, earnestly, lift up, protest, call (take) to record, relieve, rob, solemnly, stand upright, testify, give warning, (bear, call to, give, take to) witness.

5750. עוֹד *ode;* or עֹד *ode;* from 5749; prop. *iteration* or *continuance;* used only adv. (with or without prep.), *again, repeatedly, still, more:*– again, X all life long, at all, besides, but, else, further(-more), henceforth, (any) longer, (any) more(-over), X once, since, (be) still, when, (good, the) while (having being), (as, because, whether, while) yet (within).

5751. עוֹד *ode* (Chald.); cor. to 5750:–while.

5752. עוֹדֵד *o-dade';* or עֹדֵד *o-dade';* from 5749; *reiteration; Oded,* the name of two Isr.:–Oded.

5753. עָוָה *aw-vaw';* a prim. root; to *crook*, lit. or fig. (as follows):–do amiss, bow down, make crooked, commit iniquity, pervert, (do) perverse(-ly), trouble, X turn, do wickedly, do wrong.

5754. עַוָּה *av-vaw';* intens. from 5753 abb; *overthrow:*–X overturn.

5755. עִוָּה *iv-vaw';* or עַוָּא (2 Kings 17:24) *av-vaw';* for 5754; *Ivvah* or *Avva,* a region of Assyria:–Ava, Ivah.

5756. עוּז *ooz;* a prim. root; to *be strong;* caus., to *strengthen,* i.e. (fig.) to *save* (by flight):–gather (self, self to flee), retire.

5757. עַוִּי *av-vee';* patrial from 5755; an *Avvite* or nat. of Avvah (only pl.):–Avims, Avites.

5758. עִוְיָא *iv-yaw'* (Chald.); from a root cor. to 5753; *perverseness:*–iniquity.

5759. עֲוִיל *av-eel';* from 5764; a *babe:*–young child, little one.

5760. עֲוִיל *av-eel';* from 5765; *perverse* (mor.):–ungodly.

5761. עַוִּים *av-veem';* pl. of 5757; *Avvim* (as inhabited by Avvites), a place in Pal. (with the art. pref.):–Avim.

5762. עֲוִית *av-veeth';* or [perh. עַיּוֹת *ah-yoth',* as if pl. of 5857] עַיּוּת *ah-yooth';* from 5753; *ruin*; *Avvith* (or *Avvoth*), a place in Pal.:–Avith.

5763. עוּל *ool;* a prim. root; to *suckle,* i.e. *give milk:*–milch, (ewe great) with young.

5764. עוּל *ool*; from 5763; a *babe:*–sucking child, infant.

5765. עָוַל *aw-val';* a prim. root; to *distort* (mor.):–deal unjustly, unrighteous.

5766. עֶוֶל *eh'-vel;* or עָוֶל *aw'-vel;* and (fem.) עַוְלָה *av-law';* or עוֹלָה *o-law';* or עֹלָה *o-law';* from 5765; (mor.) *evil:*–iniquity, perverseness, unjust(-ly), unrighteousness(-ly); wicked(-ness).

5767. עַוָּל *av-vawl';* intens. from 5765; *evil* (mor.):–unjust, unrighteous, wicked.

5768. עוֹלֵל *o-lale'* or עֹלָל *o-lawl';* from 5763; a *suckling:*–babe, (young) child, infant, little one.

5769. עוֹלָם *o-lawm';* or עֹלָם *o-lawm';* from 5956; prop. *concealed,* i.e. the *vanishing* point; gen., time *out of mind* (past or future), i.e. (practically) *eternity;* freq., adv. (esp. with prep. pref.) *always:*–alway(-s), ancient (time), any more, continuance, eternal, (for, [n-]) ever(-lasting, -more, of old), lasting, long (time), (of) old (time), perpetual, at any time, (beginning of the) world (+ without end). Comp. 5331, 5703.

5770. עָוַן *aw-van';* denom. from 5869; to *watch* (with jealosy):–eye.+

5771. עָוֹן *aw-vone';* or עָווֹן (2 Kings 7:9; Psalm 51:5 [7]) *aw-vone';* from 5753; *perversity,* i.e. (mor.) *evil:*–fault, iniquity, mischief, punishment (of iniquity), sin.

5772. עוֹנָה *o-naw';* from an un. root app. mean. to *dwell* together; sexual (*cohabitation*):–duty of marriage.

5773. עַוְעֶה *av-eh';* from 5753; *perversity:*–X perverse.

5774. עוּף *oof;* a prim. root; to *cover* (with wings or obscurity); hence (as denom. from 5775) to *fly;* also (by impl. of dimness) to *faint* (from the darkness of swooning):–brandish, be (wax) faint, flee away, fly (away), X set, shine forth, weary.

5775. עוֹף *ofe;* from 5774; a *bird* (as *covered* with feathers, or rather as *covering* with wings), often coll.:–bird, that flieth, flying, fowl.

5776. עוֹף *ofe* (Chald.); cor. to 5775:–fowl.

5777. עוֹפֶרֶת *o-feh'-reth;* or עֹפֶרֶת *o-feh'-reth;* fem. part. act. of 6080; *lead* (from its *dusty* color):–lead.

5778. עוֹפַי *o-fah'-ee;* from 5775; *birdlike; Ephai,* an Isr.:–Ephai [*from marg.*].

5779. עוּץ *oots* a prim. root; to *consult:*–take

advice ([counsel] together).
5780. עוּץ *oots;* app. from 5779; *consultation; Uts,* a son of Aram, also a Seirite, and the regions settled by them.:–Uz.
5781. עוּק *ook;* a prim. root; to *pack:*–be pressed.
5782. עוּר *oor;* a prim. root [rather ident. with 5783 through the idea of *opening* the eyes]; to *wake* (lit. or fig.):–(a-)wake(-n, up), lift up (self), X master, raise (up), stir up (self).
5783. עוּר *oor;* a prim. root; to (*be*) *bare:*–be made naked.
5784. עוּר *oor* (Chald.); *chaff* (as the *naked* husk):–chaff.
5785. עוֹר *ore;* from 5783; *skin* (as *naked*); by impl., *hide, leather:*–hide, leather, skin.
5786. עָוַר *aw-var';* a prim. root (rather denom. from 5785 through the idea of a *film* over the eyes); to *blind:*–blind, put out. See also 5895.
5787. עִוֵּר *iv-vare';* intens. from 5786; *blind* (lit. or fig.):–blind (men, people).
5788. עִוָּרוֹן *iv-vaw-rone';* and (fem.) עַוֶּרֶת *av-veh'-reth;* from 5787; *blindness:*–blind(-ness).
5789. עוּשׁ *oosh;* a prim. root; to *hasten:*–assemble self.
5790. עוּת *ooth;* for 5789; to *hasten,* i.e. *succor:*–speak in season.
5791. עָוַת *aw-vath';* a prim. root; to *wrest:*–bow self, (make) crooked., falsifying, over-throw, deal perversely, pervert, subvert, turn upside down.
5792. עַוָּתָה *av-vaw-thaw';* from 5791; *oppression:*–wrong.
5793. עוּתַי *oo-thah'-ee;* from 5790; *succoring; Uthai,* the name of two Isr.:–Uthai.
5794. עַז *az;* from 5810; *strong, vehement, harsh:*–fierce, + greedy, mighty, power, roughly, strong.
5795. עֵז *aze;* from 5810; a she-*goat* (as *strong*), but masc. in pl. (which also is used ellipt. for *goat's hair*):–(she) goat, kid.
5796. עֵז *aze* (Chald.); cor. to 5795:–goat.
5797. עֹז *oze;* or (fully) עוֹז *oze;* from 5810; *strength* in various appl. (*force, security, majesty, praise*):–boldness, loud, might, power, strength, strong.
5798. עֻזָּא *ooz-zaw';* or עֻזָּה *ooz-zaw';* fem. of 5797; *strength; Uzza* or *Uzzah,* the name of five Isr.:–Uzza, Uzzah.
5799. עֲזָאזֵל *az-aw-zale';* from 5795 and 235; *goat of departure;* the *scapegoat:*–scapegoat.
5800. עָזַב *aw-zab';* a prim. root; to *loosen,* i.e. *relinquish, permit,* etc.:–commit self, fail, forsake, fortify, help, leave (destitute, off), refuse, X surely.
5801. עִזָּבוֹן *iz-zaw-bone';* from 5800 in the sense of *letting go* (for a price, i.e. *selling*); *trade,* i.e. the place (*mart*) or the payment (*revenue*):–fair, ware.
5802. עַזְבּוּק *az-book';* from 5794 and the root of 950; *stern depopulator; Azbuk,* an Isr.:–Azbuk.
5803. עַזְגָּד *az-gawd';* from 5794 and 1409; *stern troop; Azgad,* an Isr.:–Azgad.
5804. עַזָּה *az-zaw';* fem. of 5794; *strong; Azzah,* a place in Pal.:–Azzah, Gaza.
5805. עֲזוּבָה *az-oo-baw';* fem. pass.part. of 5800; *desertion* (of inh.):–forsaking.
5806. עֲזוּבָה *az-oo-baw';* the same as 5805; *Azubah,* the name of two Isr.s:–Azubah.
5807. עֱזוּז *ez-ooz';* from 5810; *forcibleness:*–might, strength.
5808. עִזּוּז *iz-zooz';* from 5810; *forcible;* coll. and concr., an *army:*–power, strong.
5809. עַזּוּר *az-zoor';* or עַזֻּר *az-zoor';* from 5826; *helpful; Azzur,* the name of three Isr.:–Azur, Azzur.
5810. עָזַז *aw-zaz';* a prim. root; to *be stout* (lit. or fig.):–harden, impudent, prevail, strengthen (self), be strong.
5811. עָזָז *aw-zawz';* from 5810; *strong; Azaz,* an Isr.:–Azaz.
5812. עֲזַזְיָהוּ *az-az-yaw'-hoo;* from 5810 and 3050; *Jah has strengthened; Azazjah,* the name of three Isr.:–Azaziah.
5813. עֻזִּי *ooz-zee'* from 5810; *forceful; Uzzi,* the name of six Isr.:–Uzzi.
5814. עֻזִּיָּא *ooz-zee-yaw';* perh. for 5818; *Uzzija,* an Isr.:–Uzzia.
5815. עֲזִיאֵל *az-ee-ale' from 5756 and 410; strengthened of God; Aziël,* an Isr.:–Aziel. Comp. 3268.
5816. עֻזִּיאֵל *ooz-zee-ale';* from 5797 and 410; *strength of God; Uzziël,* the name of six Isr.:–Uzziel.
5817. עָזִּיאֵלִי *oz-zee-ay-lee';* patron. from 5816; an *Uzziëlite* (coll.) or desc. of Uzziel:–Uzzielites.
5818. עֻזִּיָּה *ooz-zee-yaw';* or עֻזִּיָּהוּ *ooz-zee-yaw'-hoo;* from 5797 and 3050; *strength of Jah; Uzzijah,* the name of five Isr.:–Uzziah.
5819. עֲזִיזָא *az-ee-zaw';* from 5756; *strengthfulness; Aziza,* an Isr.:–Aziza.
5820. עַזְמָוֶת *az-maw'-veth;* from 5794 and 4194; *strong one of death; Azmaveth,* the name of three Isr. and of a place in Pal.:–Azmaveth. See also 1041.
5821. עַזָּן *az-zawn';* from 5794; *strong* one; *Azzan,* an Isr.:–Azzan.
5822. עָזְנִיָּה *oz-nee-yaw';* prob. fem. of 5797; prob. the *sea-eagle* (from its *strength*):–ospray.
5823. עָזַק *aw-zak';* a prim. root; to *grub* over:–fence about.
5824. עִזְקָא *iz-kaw'* (Chald.); from a root cor. to 5823; a *signet*-ring (as engraved):–signet.
5825. עֲזֵקָה *az-ay-kaw';* from 5823; *tilled; Azekah,* a place in Pal.:–Azekah.
5826. עָזַר *aw-zar';* a prim. root; to *surround,* i.e. *protect* or *aid:*–help, succour.
5827. עֶזֶר *eh'-zer;* from 5826; *help; Ezer,* the name of two Isr.:–Ezer. Comp. 5829.
5828. עֵזֶר *ay'-zer;* from 5826; *aid:*–help.
5829. עֵזֶר *ay'-zer;* the same as 5828; *Ezer,* the name of four Isr.:–Ezer. Comp. 5827.
5830. עֶזְרָא *ez-raw';* a var. of 5833; *Ezra,* an Isr.:–Ezra.
5831. עֶזְרָא *ez-raw'* (Chald.); cor. to 5830; *Ezra,* an Isr. –Ezra.
5832. עֲזַרְאֵל *az-ar-ale';* from 5826 and 410; *God has helped; Azarel,* the name of five Isr.:–Azarael, Azareel.
5833. עֶזְרָה *ez-raw';* or (Ps. 60:11 [13]; 108:12 [13]) עֶזְרָת *ez-rawth';* fem. of 5828; *aid:*–help(-ed, -er).
5834. עֶזְרָה *ez-raw';* the same as 5833; *Ezrah,* an Isr.:–Ezrah.
5835. עֲזָרָה *az-aw-raw';* from 5826 in its or. mean. of *surrounding;* an *inclosure;* also a *border:*–court, settle.
5836. עֶזְרִי *ez-ree';* from 5828; *helpful; Ezri,* an Isr.:–Ezri.
5837. עַזְרִיאֵל *az-ree-ale';* from 5828 and 410; *help of God; Azriël,* the name of three Isr.:–Azriel.
5838. עֲזַרְיָה *az-ar-yaw';* or עֲזַרְיָהוּ *az-ar-yaw'-hoo;* from 5826 and 3050; *Jah has helped; Azarjah,* the name of nineteen Isr.:–Azariah.
5839. עֲזַרְיָה *az-ar-yaw'* (Chald.); cor. to 5838; *Azarjah,* one of Daniel's companions:–Azariah.
5840. עַזְרִיקָם *az-ree-kawm';* from 5828 and act.part. of 6965; *help of an enemy; Azrikam,* the name of four Isr.:–Azrikam.
5841. עַזָּתִי *az-zaw-thee';* patrial from 5804; an *Azzathite* or inh. of Azzah:–Gazathite, Gazite.
5842. עֵט *ate* from 5860 (contr.) in the sense of *swooping,* i.e. *side-long stroke;* a *stylus* or marking stick:–pen.
5843. עֵטָא *ay-taw'* (Chald.); from 3272; *prudence:*–counsel.
5844. עָטָה *aw-taw';* a prim. root; to *wrap,* i.e. *cover, veil, cloth,* or *roll:*–array self, be clad, (put a) cover (-ing, self), fill, put on, X surely, turn aside.
5845. עֲטִין *at-een';* from an un. root mean. app. to *contain;* a *receptacle* (for milk, i.e. *pail;* fig., *breast*):–breast.
5846. עֲטִישָׁה *at-ee-shaw';* from an un. root mean. to *sneeze; sneezing:*–sneezing.
5847. עֲטַלֵּף *at-al-lafe';* of unc. der.; a *bat:*–bat.
5848. עָטַף *aw-taf';* a prim. root; to *shroud,* i.e. *clothe* (whether trans. or reflex.); hence (from the idea of *darkness*) to *languish:*– cover (over), fail, faint, feebler, hide self, be overwhelmed, swoon.
5849. עָטַר *aw-tar';* a prim. root; to *encircle* (for attack or protection); esp. to *crown* (lit. or fig.):–compass, crown.
5850. עֲטָרָה *at-aw-raw';* from 5849; a *crown:*–crown.
5851. עֲטָרָה *at-aw-raw';* the same as 5850; *Atarah,* an Isr.s:–Atarah.
5852. עֲטָרוֹת *at-aw-roth';* or עֲטָרֹת *at-aw-roth';* pl. of 5850; *Ataroth,* the name (thus simply) of two places in Pal.:–Ataroth.
5853. עַטְרוֹת אַדָּר *at-roth' ad-dawr';* from the same as 5852 and 146; *crowns of Addar; Atroth-Addar,* a place in Pal.: –Ataroth-adar(-addar).
5854. עַטְרוֹת בֵּית יוֹאָב *at-roth' bayth yo-awb';* from the same as 5852 and 1004 and 3097; *crowns of the house of Joäb; Atroth-beth-Joäb,* a place in Pal.:–Ataroth the house of Joab.
5855. עַטְרוֹת שׁוֹפָן *at-roth' sho-fawn';* from the same as 5852 and a name otherwise un. [being from the same as 8226] mean. *hidden; crowns of Shophan; Atroth-Shophan,* a place in Pal.:–Atroth, Shophan [*as if two places*].
5856. עִי *ee;* from 5753; a *ruin* (as if overturned):–heap.
5857. עַי *ah'ee;* or עַיָּא (fem.) (Ne. 11:31) *ah-yaw';* or (Isaiah 10:28) עַיָּת *ah-yawth';* for 5856; *Ai, Aja* or *Ajath,* a place in Pal.:–Ai, Aija, Aijath, Hai.
5858. עֵיבָל *ay-bawl';* perh. from an un. root prob. mean. to be *bald; bare; Ebal,* a mountain of Pal.:–Ebal.
5859. עִיּוֹן *ee-yone';* from 5856; *ruin; Ijon,* a place in Pal.:–Ijon.
5860. עִיט *eet;* a prim. root; to *swoop* down upon (lit. or fig.):–fly, rail.
5861. עַיִט *ah'-yit;* from 5860; a *hawk* or other bird of prey:–bird, fowl, ravenous (bird).
5862. עֵיטָם *ay-tawm';* from 5861; *hawk-ground; Etam,* a place in Pal.:–Etam.
5863. עִיֵּי הָעֲבָרִים *ee-yay'; haw-ab-aw-reem'* from the pl. of 5856 and the pl. of the act. part. of 5674 with the art. interp.; *ruins of the passers; Ije-ha-Abarim,* a place near Pal.:–Ije-abarim.
5864. עִיִּים *ee-yeem';* pl. of 5856; *ruins; Ijim,* a place in the Desert.:–Iim.

5865. עִילוֹם *ay-lome';* for 5769:–ever.
5866. עִילַי *ee-lah'-ee;* from 5927; *elevated; Ilai,* an Isr.:–Ilai.
5867. עֵילָם *ay-lawm';* or (Ezra 10:2; Jeremiah 49:36) עוֹלָם *o-lawm';* prob. from 5956; *hidden,* i.e. *distant; Elam,* a son of Shem and his descendants, with their country; also of six Isr.:–Elam.
5868. עֲיָם *ah-yawm';* of doubtful or. and authenticity; prob. mean. *strength:*–mighty.
5869. עַיִן *ah'-yin;* prob. a prim. word; an *eye* (lit. or fig.); by anal., a *fountain* (as the *eye* of the landscape):–affliction, outward appearance, + before, + think best, colour, conceit, + be content, countenance, + displease, eye([-brow], [-d], -sight), face, + favour, fountain, furrow X him, + humble, knowledge, look, (+ well), X me, open(-ly), + (not) please, presence, + regard, resemblance, sight, X thee, X them, + think, X us, well, X you(-rselves).
5870. עַיִן *ah'-yin* (Chald.); cor. to 5869; an *eye:*–eye.
5871. עַיִן *ah'-yin;* the same as 5869; *fountain; Ajin,* the name (thus simply) of two places in Pal.:–Ain.
5872. עֵין גֶּדִי *ane geh'-dee;* from 5869 and 1423; *fountain of a kid; En-Gedi,* a place in Pal.:–En-gedi.
5873. עֵין גַּנִּים *ane gan-neem';* from 5869 and the pl. of 1588; *fountain of gardens; En-Gannim,* a place in Pal.:–En-gannim.
5874. עֵין־דּאר *ane-dore';* or עֵין דּוֹר *ane dore;* or עֵין־דֹּר *ane-dore';* from 5869 and 1755; *fountain of dwelling; En-Dor,* a place in Pal.:–En-dor.
5875. עֵין הַקּוֹרֵא *ane-hak-ko-ray';* from 5869 and the act.part. of 7121; *fountain of* One *calling; En-hak-Kore,* a place near Pal.:–En-hakhore.
5876. עֵין חַדָּה *ane khad-daw';* from 5869 and the fem. of a der. from 2300; *fountain of sharpness; En-Chaddah,* a place in Pal.:–En-haddah.
5877.עֵין חָצוֹר *ane khaw-tsore';* from 5869 and the same as 2674; *fountain of a village; En-Chatsor,* a place in Pal.:–En-hazor.
5878. עֵין חֲרֹד *ane khar-ode';* from 5869 and a der. of 2729; *fountain of trembling; En-Charod,* a place in Pal.:–well of Harod.
5879. עֵינַיִם *ay-nah'-yim;* or עֵינָם *ay-nawm';* dual of 5869; *double fountain; Enajim* or *Enam,* a place in Pal.:–Enaim, openly (Genesis 38:21).
5880. עֵין מִשְׁפָּט *ane mish-pawt';* from 5869 and 4941; *fountain of judgment; En-Mishpat,* a place near Pal.:–En-mishpat.
5881. עֵינָן *ay-nawn';* from 5869; *having eyes; Enan,* an Isr.:–Enan. Comp. 2704.
5882. עֵין עֶגְלַיִם *ane eg-lah'-yim;* 5869 and the dual of 5695; *fountain of two calves; En-Eglajim,* a place in Pal.:–En-eglaim.
5883. עֵין רֹגֵל *ane ro-gale';* from 5869 and the act.part. of 7270; *fountain of a traveller; En-Rogel,* a place near Jerus.:–En-rogel.
5884. עֵין רִמּוֹן *ane rim-mone';* from 5869 and 7416; *fountain of a pomegranate; En-Rimmon,* a place in Pal.:–En-rimmon.
5885. עֵין שֶׁמֶשׁ *ane sheh'-mesh;* from 5869 and 8121; *fountain of* the *sun; En-Shemesh,* a place in Pal.:–En-shemesh.
5886. עֵין תַּנִּים *ane tan-neem';* from 5869 and the pl. of 8565; *fountain of jackals; En-Tannim,* a pool near Jerus.: –dragon well.
5887. עֵין תַּפּוּחַ *ane tap-poo'-akh;* from 5869 and 8598; *fountain of an apple-tree; En-Tappuäch,* a place in Pal.:–En-tappuah.
5888. עָיֵף *aw-yafe';* a prim. root; to *languish:*–be wearied.
5889. עָיֵף *aw-yafe';* from 5888; *languid:*–faint, thirsty, weary.
5890. עֵיפָה *ay-faw';* fem. from 5774; *obscurity* (as if from *covering*):–darkness.
5891. עֵיפָה *ay-faw';* the same as 5890; *Ephah,* the name of a son of Midian, and of the region settled by him; also of an Isr. and of an Isr.:–Ephah.
5892. עִיר *eer;* or (in the pl.) עָר *awr;* or (Judges 10:4) עָיַר *aw-yar';* from 5782 a *city* (a place guarded by *waking* or a watch) in the widest sense (even of a mere *encampment* or *post*):–Ai, city, court, town.
5893. עִיר *eer;* the same as 5892; *Ir,* an Isr.:–Ir.
5894. עִיר *eer* (Chald.); from a root cor. to 5782; a *watcher,* i.e. an *angel* (as guardian):–watcher.
5895. עַיִר *ah'-yeer;* from 5782 in the sense of *raising* (i.e. *bearing* a burden); prop. a young *ass* (as just broken to a load); hence an ass-*colt:*–(ass) colt, foal, young ass.
5896. עִירָא *ee-raw';* from 5782; *wakefulness; Ira,* the name of three Isr.:–Ira.
5897. עִירָד *ee-rawd';* from the same as 6166; *fugitive; Irad,* an antediluvian:–Irad.
5898. עִיר הַמֶּלַח *eer; ham-meh'-lakh* from 5892 and 4417 with the art. of substance interp.; *city of* (*the*) *salt; Ir-ham-Melach,* a place near Pal.:–the city of salt.
5899. עִיר הַתְּמָרִים *eer hat-tem-aw-reem';* from 5892 and the pl. of 8558 with the art. interpolated; *city of the palmtrees; Ir-hat-Temarim,* a place in Pal.:–the city of palmtrees.
5900. עִירוּ *ee-roo';* from 5892; a *citizen; Iru,* an Isr.:–Iru.
5901. עִירִי *ee-ree';* from 5892; *urbane; Iri,* an Isr.:–Iri.
5902. עִירָם *ee-rawm';* from 5892; *city-wise; Iram,* an Idumaean:–Iram.
5903. עֵירֹם *ay-rome';* or עֵרֹם *ay-rome';* from 6191; *nudity:*–naked(-ness).
5904. עִיר נָחָשׁ *eer naw-khawsh';* from 5892 and 5175; *city of a serpent; Ir-Nachash,* a place in Pal.:–Ir-nahash.
5905. עִיר שֶׁמֶשׁ *eer sheh'-mesh;* from 5892 and 8121; *city of* the *sun; Ir-Shemesh,* a place in Pal.:–Ir-shemesh.
5906 עַיִשׁ *ah'-yish;* or . עָשׁ *awsh;* from 5789; the constellation of the Great *Bear* (perh. from its *migration* through the heavens):– Arcturus.
5907. עַכְבּוֹר *ak-bore';* prob. for 5909; *Akbor,* the name of an Idumaean and of two Isr.:–Achbor.
5908. עַכָּבִישׁ *ak-kaw-beesh';* prob. from an un. root in the lit. sense of *entangling;* a *spider* (as *weaving* a network):–spider.
5909. עַכְבָּר *ak-bawr';* prob. from the same as 5908 in the sec. sense of *attacking;* a *mouse* (as *nibbling*):–mouse.
5910. עַכּוֹ *ak-ko'* app. from an un. root mean. to *hem* in; *Akko* (from its situation on a *bay*):–Accho.
5911. עָכוֹר *aw-kore';* from 5916; *troubled; Akor,* the name of a place in Pal.:–Achor.
5912. עָכָן *aw-kawn';* from an un. root mean. to *trouble; troublesome; Akan,* an Isr.:–Achan. Comp. 5917.
5913. עָכַס *aw-kas';* a prim. root; prop. to *tie,* spec., with fetters; but used only as denom. from 5914; to put *on anklets:*–make a tinkling ornament.
5914. עֶכֶס *eh'-kes;* from 5913; a *fetter;* hence, an *anklet:*–stocks, tinkling ornament.
5915. עַכְסָה *ak-saw';* fem. of 5914; *anklet; Aksah,* an Isr.s:–Achsah.
5916. עָכַר *aw-kar';* a prim. root; prop. to *roil* water; fig., to *disturb* or *afflict:*–trouble, stir.
5917. עָכָר *aw-kawr';* from 5916; *troublesome; Akar,* an Isr.:–Achar. Comp. 5912.
5918. עָכְרָן *ok-rawn';* from 5916; *muddler; Okran,* an Isr.:–Ocran.
5919. עַכְשׁוּב *ak-shoob';* prob. from an un. root mean. to *coil;* an *asp* (from lurking *coiled* up):–adder.
5920. עַל *al;* from 5927; prop. the *top;* spec., the *Highest* (i.e. *God*); also (adv.) *aloft,* to *Jehovah:*–above, high, most High.
5921. עַל *al;* prop. the same as 5920 used as a prep. (in the sing. or pl. often with pref., or as conj. with a particle following); *above, over, upon,* or *against* (yet always in this last relation with a downward aspect) in a great variety of appl. (as follow):–above, according to(-ly), after, (as) against, among, and, X as, at, because of, beside (the rest of), between, beyond the time, X both and, by (reason of), X had the charge of, concerning for, in (that), (forth, out) of, (from) (off), (up-)on, over, than, through (-out), to, touching, X with.
5922. עַל *al* (Chald.); cor. to 5921:–about, against, concerning, for, [there-] fore, from, in, X more, of, (there-, up-) on, (in-)to, + why with.
5923. עֹל *ole;* or עוֹל *ole;* from 5953; a *yoke* (as *imposed* on the neck), lit. or fig.:–yoke.
5924. עֵלָּא *ale-law'* (Chald.); from 5922; *above:*–over.
5925. עֻלָּא *ool-law';* fem. of 5923; *burden; Ulla,* an Isr.:–Ulla.
5926. עִלֵּג *il-layg';* from an un. root mean. to *stutter; stuttering:*–stammerer.
5927. עָלָה *aw-law';* a prim. root; to *ascend,* intr. (*be high*) or act. (*mount*); used in a great variety of senses, prim. and sec., lit. and fig. (as follows):–arise (up), (cause to) ascend up, at once, break [*the day*] (up), bring (up), (cause to) burn, carry up, cast up, + shew, climb (up), (cause to, make to) come (up), cut off, dawn, depart, exalt, excel, fall, fetch up, get up, (make to) go (away, up); grow (over) increase, lay, leap, levy, lift (self) up, light, [make] up, X mention, mount up, offer, make to pay, + perfect, prefer, put (on), raise, recover, restore, (make to) rise (up), scale, set (up), shoot forth (up), (begin to) spring (up), stir up, take away (up), work.
5928. עֲלָה *al-law'* (Chald.); cor. to 5930; a *holocaust:*–burnt offering.
5929. עָלֶה *aw-leh';* from 5927; a *leaf* (*as coming up* on a tree); coll., *foliage:*–branch, leaf.
5930. עֹלָה *o-law';* or עוֹלָה *o-law';* fem. act. part. of 5927; a *step* or (coll., *stairs,* as *ascending*); usually a *holocaust* (as *going up* in smoke):–ascent, burnt offering (sacrifice), go up to. See also 5766.
5931. עִלָּה *il-law'* (Chald.); fem. from a root cor. to 5927; a *pretext* (as *arising* artif.):–occasion.
5932. עַלְוָה *al-vaw';* for 5766; mor. *perverseness:*–iniquity.
5933. עַלְוָה *al-vaw';* or עַלְיָה *al-yaw';* the same as 5932; *Alvah* or *Aljah,* an Idumaean:–Aliah, Alvah.
5934. עָלוּם *aw-loom';* pass.part. of 5956 in the denom. sense of 5958; (only in pl. as abstr.) *adolescence;* fig., *vigor:*–youth.

HEBREW

5935. עַלְוָן *al-vawn';* or עַלְיָן *al-yawn';* from 5927; *lofty; Alvan* or *Aljan,* an Idumaean:–Alian, Alvan.
5936. *2* עֲלוּקָה
5937. עָלַז *aw-laz';* a prim. root; to *jump* for joy, i.e. *exult:*–be joyful, rejoice, triumph.
5938. עָלֵז *aw-laze';* from 5937; *exultant:*–that rejoiceth.
5939. עֲלָטָה *al-aw-taw';* fem. from an un. root mean. to *cover; dusk:*–dark, twilight.
5940. עֱלִי *el-ee';* from 5927; a *pestle* (as *lifted*):–pestle.
5941. עֵלִי *ay-lee';* from 5927; *lofty; Eli,* an Isr. high-priest:–Eli.
5942. עִלִּי *il-lee';* from 5927; *high*; i.e. comp.:–upper.
5943. עִלַּי *il-lah'-ee* (Chald.); cor. to 5942; *supreme* (i.e. *God*):–(most) high.
5944. עֲלִיָּה *al-ee-yaw';* fem. from 5927; something *lofty,* i.e. a *stair-way;* also a *second-story* room (or even one on the roof); fig., the *sky:*–ascent, (upper) chamber, going up, loft, parlour.
5945. עֶלְיוֹן *el-yone';* from 5927; an *elevation,* i.e. (adj.) *lofty* (comp.); as title, the *Supreme:*–(Most, on) high(-er, -est), upper(-most).
5946. עֶלְיוֹן *el-yone'* (Chald.); cor. to 5945; the *Supreme:*–Most high.
5947. עַלִּיז *al-leez';* from 5937; *exultant:*–joyous, (that) rejoice(-ing)
5948. עֲלִיל *al-eel';* from 5953 in the sense of *completing;* prob. a *crucible* (as *working* over the metal):–furnace.
5949. עֲלִילָה *al-ee-law';* or עֲלִלָה *al-ee-law';* from 5953 in the sense of *effecting;* an *exploit* (of God), or a *performance* (of man, often in a bad sense); by impl., an *opportunity:*–act(-ion), deed, doing, invention, occasion, work.
5950. עֲלִילִיָּה *al-ee-lee-yaw';* for 5949; (miraculous) *execution:*–work.
5951. עֲלִיצוּת *al-ee-tsooth';* from 5970; *exultation:*–rejoicing.
5952. עַלִּית *al-leeth';* from 5927; a *second-story* room:–chamber. Comp. 5944.
5953. עָלַל *aw-lal';* a prim. root; to *effect* thoroughly; spec., to *glean* (also fig.); by impl. (in a bad sense) to *overdo,* i.e. maltreat, be saucy to, pain, impose (also lit.):–abuse, affect, X child, defile, do, glean, mock, practise, thoroughly, work (wonderfully).
5954. עֲלַל *al-al'* (Chald.); cor. to 5953 (in the sense of *thrusting* oneself in), to *enter;* caus., to *introduce:*–bring in, come in, go in.
5955. עֹלֵלָה *o-lay-law';* fem. act.part. of 5953; only in pl. *gleanings*; by ext. *gleaning-time:*–(gleaning) (of the) grapes, grapegleanings.
5956. עָלַם *aw-lam;'* a prim. root; to *veil* from sight, i.e. *conceal* (lit. or fig.):–X any ways, blind, dissembler, hide (self), secret (thing).
5957. עָלַם *aw-lam'* (Chald.); cor. to 5769; *remote* time, i.e. the *future* or *past* indef.; often adv., *forever:*–for ([n-])ever(lasting), old.
5958. עֶלֶם *eh'-lem;* from 5956; prop. something *kept out of sight* [comp. 5959], i.e. a *lad:*–young man, stripling.
5959. עַלְמָה *al-maw';* fem. of 5958; a *lass* (as *veiled* or private):–damsel, maid, virgin.
5960. עַלְמוֹן *al-mone';* from 5956; *hidden; Almon,* a place in Pal. See also 5963.
5961. עֲלָמוֹת *al-aw-moth';* pl. of 5959; prop. *girls,* i.e. the *soprano* or female voice, perh. *falsetto:*–Alamoth.
5962. עַלְמִי *al-mee'* (Chald.); patrial from a name cor. to 5867 contr.; an *Elamite* or inh. of Elam:–Elamite.
5963. עַלְמֹן דִּבְלָתָיְמָה *al-mone'; dib-law-thaw'-yem-aw* from the same as 5960 and the dual of 1690 [comp. 1015] with enclitic of direction; *Almon towards Diblathajim; Almon-Diblathajemah,* a place in Moab:–Almon-dilathaim.
5964. עָלֶמֶת *aw-leh'-meth;* from 5956; a *covering; Alemeth,* the name of a place in Pal. and of two Isr.:–Alameth, Alemeth.
5965. עָלַס *aw-las';* a prim. root; to *leap* for joy, i.e. *exult, wave* joyously:–X peacock, rejoice, solace self.
5966. עָלַע *aw-lah'* a prim root; to *sip* up:–suck up.
5967. עֲלַע *al-ah'* (Chald.); cor. to 6763; a *rib:*–rib.
5968. עָלַף *aw-laf';* a prim. root; to *veil* or *cover;* fig., to *be languid:*–faint, overlaid, wrap self.
5969. עֻלְפֶּה *ool-peh';* from 5968; an *envelope,* i.e. (fig.) *mourning:*–fainted.
5970. עָלַץ *aw-lats';* a prim. root; to *jump* for joy, i.e. *exult:*–be joyful, rejoice, triumph.
5971. עַם *am*; from 6004; a *people* (as a congregated *unit*); spec., a *tribe* (as those of Isr.); hence (coll.) *troops* or *attendants;* fig., a *flock:*–folk, men, nation, people.
5972. עַם *am* (Chald.); cor. to 5971:–people.
5973. עִם *eem*; from 6004; adv. or prep., *with* (i.e. in *conjunction* with), in varied appl.; spec., *equally with;* often with prep. pref. (and then usually unrepresented in English):–accompanying, against, and, as (X long as), before, beside, by (reason of), for all, from (among, between), in, like, more than, of, (un-)to, with(-al).
5974. עִם *eem* (Chald.); cor. to 5973:–by, from, like, to(-ward), with.
5975. עָמַד *aw-mad';* a prim. root; to *stand,* in various relations (lit. and fig., intr. and trans.) :–abide (behind), appoint, arise, cease, confirm, continue, dwell, be employed, endure, establish, leave, make, ordain, be [over], place, (be) present (self), raise up, remain, repair, + serve, set (forth, over, -tle, up), (make to, make to be at a, with-)stand (by, fast, firm, still, up), (be at a) stay (up), tarry.
5976. עָמַד *aw-mad';* for 4571; to *shake:*–be at a stand.
5977. עֹמֶד *o'-med*; from 5975; a *spot* (as being *fixed*):–place, (+ where) stood, upright.
5978. עִמָּד *im-mawd'*; prol. for 5973; along *with:*–against, by, from, + me, + mine, of, + that I take, unto, upon, with(-in.)
5979. עֶמְדָּה *em-daw'*; from 5975; a *station,* i.e. domicile:–standing.
5980. עֻמָּה *oom-maw';* from 6004; *conjunction,* i.e. *society;* mostly adv. or prep. (with prep. pref.), *near, beside, along with:*–(over) against, at, beside, hard by, in points.
5981. עֻמָּה *oom-maw';* the same as 5980; *association; Ummah,* a place in Pal.:–Ummah.
5982. עַמּוּד *am-mood';* or עַמֻּד *am-mood';* from 5975; a *column* (*as standing*); also a *stand,* i.e. platform:–X apiece, pillar.
5983. עַמּוֹן *am-mone';* from 5971; *tribal,* i.e. *inbred; Ammon,* a son of Lot; also his posterity and their country:–Ammon, Ammonites.
5984. עַמּוֹנִי *am-mo-nee';* patron. from 5983; an *Ammonite* or (the adj.) *Ammonitish:*–Ammonite(-s).
5985. עַמּוֹנִית *am-mo-neeth';* fem. of 5984; an *Ammonitess:*–Ammonite(-ss).
5986. עָמוֹס *aw-moce';* from 6006; *burdensome; Amos,* an Isr. prophet:–Amos.
5987. עָמוֹק *aw-moke';* from 6009; *deep; Amok,* an Isr.:–Amok.
5988. עַמִּיאֵל *am-mee-ale';* from 5971 and 410; *people of God; Ammiël,* the name of three or four Isr.:–Ammiel.
5989. עַמִּיהוּד *am-mee-hood'*; from 5971 and 1935; *people of splendor; Ammihud,* the name of three Isr.:–Ammihud.
5990. עַמִּיזָבָד *am-mee-zaw-bawd';* from 5971 and 2064; *people of endowment; Ammizabad,* an Isr.:–Ammizabad.
5991. עַמִּיחוּר *am-mee-khoor'* from 5971 and 2353; *people of nobility; Ammichur,* a Syrian prince:–Ammihud
5992. עַמִּינָדָב *am-mee-naw-dawb';* from 5971 and 5068; *people of liberality; Amminadab,* the name of four Isr.:–Amminadab.
5993. עַמִּי נָדִיב *am-mee'; naw-deeb';* from 5971 and 5081; *my people* (is) *liberal; Ammi-Nadib,* prob. an Isr.:–Amminadib.
5994. עֲמִיק *am-eek'* (Chald.); cor. to 6012; *profound,* i.e. unsearchable, deep.
5995. עָמִיר *aw-meer';* from 6014; a *bunch* of grain:–handful, sheaf.
5996. עַמִּישַׁדַּי *am-mee-shad-dah'ee;* from 5971 and 7706; *people of* (the) *Almighty; Ammishaddai,* an Isr.:–Ammishaddai.
5997. עָמִית *aw-meeth';* from a prim. root mean. to *associate; companionship;* hence (concr.) a *comrade* or kindred
5998. עָמַל *aw-mal';* a prim. root; to *toil,* i.e. *work severely* and with irksomeness:–[take] labour (in).
5999. עָמָל *aw-mawl';* from 5998; *toil,* i.e. *wearing effort;* hence, *worry,* whether of body or mind:–grievance(-vousness), iniquity, labour, mischief, miserable (-sery), pain(-ful), perverseness, sorrow, toil, travail, trouble, wearisome, wickedness.
6000. עָמָל *aw-mawl';* the same as 5999; *Amal,* an Isr.:–Amal.
6001. עָמֵל *aw-male';* from 5998; *toiling;* concr., a *laborer;* fig., *sorrowful:*–that laboureth, that is a misery, had taken [labour], wicked, workman.
6002. עֲמָלֵק *am-aw-lake';* prob. of for. or.; *Amalek,* a desc. of Esau; also his posterity and their country:–Amalek.
6003. עֲמָלֵקִי *am-aw-lay-kee';* patron. from 6002; an *Amalekite* (or coll. the *Amalekites*) or desc. of Amalek:–Amalekite(-s).
6004. עָמַם *aw-mam';* a prim. root; to *associate;* by impl., to *overshadow* (by *huddling* together):–become dim, hide.
6005. עִמָּנוּאֵל *im-maw-noo-ale';* from 5973 and 410 with a pron. suffix ins.; *with us* (is) *God; Immanuel,* a type name of Isaiah's son:–Immanuel.
6006. עָמַס *aw-mas';* or עָמַשׂ *aw-mas';* a prim. root; to *load,* i.e. *impose* a burden (or fig., infliction):–be borne, (heavy) burden (self), lade, load, put.
6007. עֲמַסְיָה *am-as-yaw';* from 6006 and 3050; *Jah has loaded; Amasjah,* an Isr.:–Amasiah.
6008. עַמְעָד *am-awd';* from 5971 and 5703; *people of time; Amad,* a place in Pal.:–Amad.
6009. עָמַק *aw-mak';* a prim. root; to *be* (caus., *make*) *deep* (lit. or fig.):–(be, have, make, seek) deep(-ly), depth, be profound.

6010. עֵמֶק *ay'-mek;* from 6009; a *vale* (i.e. broad *depression*):–dale, vale, valley [*often used as a part of proper names*]. See also 1025.
6011. עֹמֶק *o'-mek;* from 6009; *depth:*–depth.
6012. עָמֵק *aw-make';* from 6009; *deep* (lit. or fig.):–deeper, depth, strange.
6013. עָמֹק *aw-moke';* from 6009; *deep* (lit. or fig.):–(X exceeding) deep (thing).
6014. עָמַר *aw-mar';* a prim. root; prop. app. to *heap;* fig., to *chastise* (as if *piling* blows); spec. (as denom. from 6016) to *gather* grain:–bind sheaves, make merchandise of.
6015. עֲמַר *am-ar'* (Chald.); cor. to 6785; *wool:*–wool.
6016. עֹמֶר *o'-mer;* from 6014; prop. a *heap,* i.e. a *sheaf;* also an *omer,* as a dry measure:–omer, sheaf.
6017. עֲמֹרָה *am-o-raw';* from 6014; a (ruined) *heap; Amorah,* a place in Pal.:–Gomorrah.
6018. עָמְרִי *om-ree';* from 6014; *heaping; Omri,* an Isr.:–Omri.
6019. עַמְרָם *am-rawm';* prob. from 5971 and 7311; *high people; Amram,* the name of two Isr.:–Amram.
6020. עַמְרָמִי *am-raw-mee';* from 6019; an *Amramite* or desc. of Amram:–Amramite.
6021. עֲמָשָׂא *am-aw-saw';* from 6006; *burden; Amasa,* the name of two Isr.:–Amasa.
6022. עֲמָשַׂי *am-aw-sah'-ee;* from 6006; *burdensome; Amasai,* the name of three Isr.:–Amasai.
6023. עֲמַשְׁסַי *am-ash-sah'-ee;* prob. from 6006; *burdensome; Amashsay,* an Isr.:–Amashai.
6024. עֲנָב *an-awb';* from the same as 6025; *fruit; Anab,* a place in Pal.:–Anab.
6025. עֵנָב *ay-nawb';* from an un. root prob. mean. to *bear* fruit; a *grape:*–(ripe) grape, wine.
6026. עָנַג *aw-nag';* a prim. root; to be *soft* or pliable, i.e. (fig.) *effeminate* or luxurious:–delicate(-ness), (have) delight (self), sport self.
6027. עֹנֶג *o'-neg;* from 6026; *luxury:*–delight, pleasant.
6028. עָנֹג *aw-nogue';* from 6026; *luxurious:*–delicate.
6029. עָנַד *aw-nad'* a prim. root; to *lace* fast:–bind, tie.
6030. עָנָה *aw-naw';* a prim. root; prop. to *eye* or (gen.) to *heed,* i.e. *pay attention;* by impl., to *respond;* by ext. to *begin* to speak; spec. to *sing, shout, testify, announce:*–give account, afflict (cause to, give) answer, bring low cry, hear, Leannoth, lift up, say, X scholar, (give a) shout, sing (together by course), speak, testify, utter, (bear) witness. See also 1042, 1043.
6031. עָנָה *aw-naw';* a prim. root [possibly rather ident. with 6030 through the idea of *looking* down or *browbeating*]; to *depress* lit. or fig., trans. or intr. (in various appl., as follows):–abase self, afflict(-ion, self), answer chasten self, deal hardly with, defile, exercise, force, gentleness, humble (self), hurt, ravish, sing speak, submit self, weaken, X in any wise.
6032. עֲנָה *an-aw'* (Chald.); cor. to 6030:–answer,
6033. עֲנָה *an-aw'* (Chald.); cor. to 6031:–poor.
6034. עֲנָה *an-aw';* prob. from 6030; an *answer; Anah,* the name of two Edomites and one Edomitess:–Anah.
6035. עָנָו *aw-nawv'* or [by intermixture with 6041] עָנָיו *aw-nawv';* from 6031; *depressed* (fig.), in mind (*gentle*) or circumstances (*needy,* esp. *saintly*):–humble, lowly, meek, poor. Comp. 6041.
6036. עָנוּב *aw-noob';* pass.part. from the same as 6025; *borne* (as fruit); *Anub,* an Isr.:–Anub.
6037. עַנְוָה *an-vaw';* fem. of 6035; *mildness* (royal); also (concr.) *oppressed:*–gentleness, meekness.
6038. עֲנָוָה *an-aw-vaw';* from 6035; *condescension,* human and subj. (*modesty*), or divine and obj. (*clemency*):–gentleness, humility, meekness.
6039. עֱנוּת *en-ooth';* from 6031; *affliction:*–affliction.
6040. עֳנִי *on-ee';* from 6031; *depression,* i.e. misery:–afflicted(-ion), trouble.
6041. עָנִי *aw-nee';* from 6031; *depressed,* in mind or circumstances [practically the same as 6035, 6035 subj. and 6041 obj.]:–afflicted, humble, lowly, needy, poor.
6042. עֻנִּי *oon-nee';* from 6031; *afflicted; Unni,* the name of two Isr.:–Unni.
6043. עֲנָיָה *an-aw-yaw';* from 6030; *Jah has answered; Anajah,* the name of two Isr.:–Anaiah.
6044. עָנִים *aw-neem';* for pl. of 5869; *fountains; Anim,* a place in Pal.:–Anim.
6045. עִנְיָן *in-yawn';* from 6031; *ado,* i.e. (gen.) *employment* or (spec.) an *affair:*–business, travail.
6046. עָנֵם *aw-name';* from the dual of 5869; *two fountains; Anem,* a place in Pal.:– Anem.
6047. עֲנָמִים *an-aw-meem';* as if pl. of some Eg. word; *Anamim,* a son of Mizraim and his desc., with their country:–Anamim.
6048. עֲנַמֶּלֶךְ *an-am-meh'-lek;* of for. or.; *Anammelek,* an Assyrian deity:–Anammelech.
6049. עָנַן *aw-nan';* a prim. root; to *cover;* used only as a denom. from 6051, to *cloud* over; fig., to *act covertly,* i.e. practise magic:–X bring, enchanter, Meonemin, observe(-r of) times, soothsayer, sorcerer.
6050. עֲנַן *an-an'* (Chald.); cor. to 6051:–cloud.
6051. עָנָן *aw-nawn';* from 6049; a *cloud* (as *covering* the sky), i.e. the *nimbus* or thunder-cloud:–cloud(-y).
6052. עָנָן *aw-nawn';* the same as 6051; *cloud; Anan,* an Isr.:–Anan.
6053. עֲנָנָה *an-aw-naw';* fem. of 6051; *cloudiness:*–cloud.
6054. עֲנָנִי *an-aw-nee';* from 6051; *cloudy; Anani,* an Isr.:–Anani.
6055. עֲנַנְיָה *an-an-yaw';* from 6049 and 3050; *Jah has covered; Ananjah,* the name of an Isr. and of a place in Pal.:–Ananiah.
6056. עֲנַף *an-af'* (Chald.); or עֶנֶף *eh'-nef;* cor. to 6057:–bough, branch.
6057. עָנָף *aw-nawf';* from an un. root mean. to *cover;* a *twig* (as *covering* the limbs):–bough, branch.
6058. עָנֵף *aw-nafe';* from the same as 6057; *branching:*–full of branches.
6059. עָנַק *aw-nak';* a prim. root; prop. to *choke;* used only as denom. from 6060, to *collar,* i.e. adorn with a necklace; fig., to *fit out* with supplies:–compass about as a chain, furnish, liberally.
6060. עָנָק *aw-nawk';* from 6059; a *necklace* (as if *strangling*):–chain.
6061. עָנָק *aw-nawk';* the same as 6060; *Anak,* a Canaanite:–Anak.
6062. עֲנָקִי *an-aw-kee';* patron. from 6061; an *Anakite* or desc. of Anak:–Anakim.
6063. עָנֵר *aw-nare';* prob. for 5288; *Aner,* a Amorite, also a place in Pal.:–Aner.
6064. עָנַשׁ *aw-nash';* a prim. root; prop. to *urge;* by impl., to *inflict* a penalty, spec., to *fine:*–amerce, condemn, punish, X surely.
6065. עֲנַשׁ *an-ash'* (Chald.); cor. to 6066; a *mulct:*–confiscation.
6066. עֹנֶשׁ *o'-nesh;* from 6064; a *fine:*–punishment, tribute
6067. עֲנָת *an-awth';* from 6030; *answer; Anath,* an Isr.:–Anath.
6068. עֲנָתוֹת, *an-aw-thoth';* pl. of 6067; *Anathoth,* the name of two Isr., also of a place in Pal:–Anathoth.
6069. עַנְתֹתִי *an-tho-thee';* or עַנְּתוֹתִי *an-ne-tho-thee';* patrial from 6068; a *Antothite* or inh. of Anathoth:–of Anathoth, Anethothite, Anetothite, Antothite.
6070. עַנְתֹתִיָּה *an-tho-thee-yaw';* from the same as 6068 and 3050; *answers of Jah; Anthothijah,* an Isr.:–Antothijah.
6071. עָסִיס *aw-sees';* from 6072; *must* or fresh grape-juice (as just *trodden* out):–juice, new (sweet) wine.
6072. עָסַס *aw-sas';* a prim. root; to *squeeze* out juice; fig., to *trample:*–tread down.
6073. עֳפֶא *of-eh';* from an un. root mean. to *cover;* a *bough* (as covering the tree):–branch.
6074. עֳפִי *of-ee'* (Chald.); cor. to 6073; a *twig;* bough, i.e. (coll.) *foliage:*–leaves.
6075. עָפַל *aw-fal';* a prim. root; to *swell;* fig., *be elated:*–be lifted up, presume.
6076. עֹפֶל *o'-fel;* from 6075; a *tower;* also a *mound,* i.e. fortress:–emerod, fort, strong hold, tower.
6077. עֹפֶל *o'-fel;* the same as 6076; *Ophel,* a ridge in Jerus.:–Ophel.
6078. עָפְנִי *of-nee';* from an un. noun [denoting a place in Pal.; from an un. root of unc. mean.]; an *Ophnite* (coll.) or inh. of Ophen:–Ophni.
6079. עַפְעַף *af-af';* from 5774; an *eyelash* (as *fluttering*); fig., morning *ray:*–dawning, eye-lid.
6080. עָפַר *aw-far';* a prim. root; mean. either to *be gray* or perh. rather to *pulverize;* used only as denom. from 6083, to *be dust:*–cast [dust].
6081. עֵפֶר *ay'-fer;* prob. a var. of 6082; *gazelle; Epher,* the name of an Arabian and of two Isr.:–Epher.
6082. עֹפֶר *o'-fer;* from 6080; a *fawn* (from the *dusty* color):–young roe [hart].
6083. עָפָר *aw-fawr';* from 6080; *dust* (as *powdered* or *gray*); hence, *clay, earth, mud:*–ashes, dust, earth, ground, morter, powder, rubbish.
6084. עָפְרָה *of-raw';* fem. of 6082; *female fawn; Ophrah,* the name of an Isr. and of two places in Pal.:–Ophrah.
6085. עֶפְרוֹן *ef-rone';* from the same as 6081; *fawn-like; Ephron,* the name of a Canaanite and of two places in Pal.:–Ephron, Ephrain
6086. עֵץ *ates;* from 6095; a *tree* (from its *firmness*); hence, *wood* (pl. *sticks*):–+ carpenter, gallows, helve, + pine, plank, staff, stalk, stick, stock, timber, tree, wood.
6087. עָצַב *aw-tsab';* a prim. root; prop. to *carve,* i.e. *fabricate* or *fashion;* hence (in a bad sense) to *worry, pain* or *anger:*– displease, grieve, hurt, make, be sorry, vex, worship, wrest.
6088. עֲצַב *ats-ab'* (Chald.); cor. to 6087; to *afflict:*–lamentable.

6089. עֶצֶב *eh'-tseb;* from 6087; an earthen *vessel;* usually (painful) *toil;* also a *pang* (whether of body or mind): grievous, idol, labor, sorrow.
6090. עֹצֶב *o'-tseb;* a var. of 6089; an *idol* (as fashioned); also *pain* (bodily or ment.):–idol, sorrow, X wicked.
6091. עָצָב *aw-tsawb';* from 6087; an (idolatrous) *image:*–idol, image.
6092. עָצֵב *aw-tsabe';* from 6087; a (hired) *workman:*–labour.
6093. עִצָּבוֹן *its-tsaw-bone';* from 6087; *worrisomeness,* i.e. *labor* or *pain:*–sorrow, toil.
6094. עַצֶּבֶת *ats-tseh'-beth* from 6087; an *idol;* also, *a pain* or *wound:*–sorrow, wound.
6095. עָצָה *aw-tsaw';* a prim. root; prop. to *fasten* (or *make firm*), i.e. to *close* (the eyes):–shut.
6096. עָצֶה *aw-tseh';* from 6095; the *spine* (as giving *firmness* to the body):–backbone.
6097. עֵצָה *ay-tsaw';* fem. of 6086; *timber:*–trees.
6098. עֵצָה *ay-tsaw';* from 3289; *advice;* by impl., *plan;* also *prudence:*–advice, advisement, counsel(-[l or]), purpose.
6099. עָצוּם *aw-tsoom';* or עָצֻם *aw-tsoom';* pass. part. of 6105; *powerful* (spec., a *paw*); by impl., *numerous:*–+ feeble, great, mighty, must, strong.
6100. עֶצְיוֹן גֶּבֶר *ets-yone' gheh'ber;* (short.) עֶצְיֹן *Etsyon Geber;* from 6096 and 1397; *backbone-like of a man; Etsjon-Geber,* a place on the Red Sea:–Ezion-geber.
6101. עָצַל *aw-tsal';* a prim. root; to *lean* idly, i.e. to be *indolent* or *slack:*–be slothful.
6102. עָצֵל *aw-tsale';* from 6101; *indolent:*–slothful, sluggard.
6103. עַצְלָה *ats-law';* fem. of 6102; (as abstr.) *indolence:*–slothfulness.
6104. עַצְלוּת *ats-looth';* from 6101; *indolence:*–idleness.
6105. עָצַם *aw-tsam';* a prim. root; to *bind* fast, i.e. *close* (the eyes); intr., to *be* (caus., *make*) *powerful* or *numerous*; denom. (from 6106) to *crunch* the bones:–break the bones, close, be great, be increased, be (wax) mighty(-ier), be more, shut, be (-come, make) strong(-er).
6106. עֶצֶם *eh'tsem;* from 6105; a *bone* (as *strong*); by ext., the *body;* fig., the *substance,* i.e. (as pron.) *selfsame:*–body, bone, X life, (self-)same, strength, X very.
6107. עֶצֶם *eh'-tsem;* the same as 6106; *bone; Etsem,* a place in Pal.:–Azem, Ezem.
6108. עֹצֶם *o'-tsem;* from 6105; *power;* hence, *body:*–might, strong, substance.
6109. עָצְמָה *ots-maw';* fem. of 6108; *powerfulness;* by ext., *numerousness:*–abundance, strength.
6110. עַצֻּמָה *ats-tsoo-maw'* fem. of 6099; a *bulwark,* i.e. (fig.) argument:–strong.
6111. עַצְמוֹן *ats-mone'* or עַצְמֹן *ats-mone';* from 6107; *bone-like*; *Atsmon*, a place near Pal.:–Azmon.
6112. עֵצֶן *ay'-tsen*; from an un. root mean. to *be sharp* or *strong*; a *spear:*–Eznite.
6113. עָצַר *aw-tsar';* a prim. root; to *inclose*; by anal., to *hold back*; also to *maintain, rule, assemble:*–X be able, close up, detain, fast, keep (self close, still), prevail, recover, refrain, X reign, restrain, retain, shut (up), slack, stay, stop, withhold (self).
6114. עֶצֶר *eh'-tser*; from 6113; *restraint:*–+ magistrate.
6115. עֹצֶר *o'-tser;* from 6113; *closure*; also *constraint:*–X barren, oppression, X prison.
6116. עֲצָרָה *ats-aw-raw';* or עֲצֶרֶת *ats-eh'-reth;* from 6113; an *assembly,* esp. on a *festival* or *holiday:*–(solemn) assembly (meeting).
6117. עָקַב *aw-kab';* a prim. root; prop. to *swell* out or up; used only as denom. from 6119, to *seize by the heel*; fig., to *circumvent* (as if *tripping* up the heels); also to *restrain* (as if holding by the heel):–take by the heel, stay, supplant, X utterly.
6118. עֵקֶב *ay'-keb;* from 6117 in the sense of 6119; a *heel,* i.e. (fig.) the *last* of anything (used adv., *for ever*); also *result,* i.e. *compensation*; and so (adv. with prep. or rel.) on *account* of:–X because, by, end, for, if, reward.
6119. עָקֵב *aw-kabe';* or (fem.) עִקְּבָה *ik-keb-aw';* from 6117; a heel (as *protuberant*); hence, a *track*; fig., the *rear* (of an army):–heel, [horse-] hoof, last, lier in wait, (foot-) step.
6120. עָקֵב *aw-kabe';* from 6117 in its denom. sense; a *lier in wait:*–heel.
6121. עָקֹב *aw-kobe';* from 6117; in the or. sense, a *knoll* (as *swelling* up); in the denom. sense (trans.) *fraudulent* or (intr.) *tricked:*–crooked, deceitful, polluted.
6122. עָקְבָה *ok-baw';* fem. of an un. form from 6117 mean. a *trick; trickery:*–subtilty.
6123. עָקַד *aw-kad';* a prim. root; to *tie* with thongs:–bind.
6124. עָקֹד *aw-kode';* from 6123; *striped* (with *bands*):–ring straked.
6125. עָקָה *aw-kaw';* from 5781; *constraint:*–oppression.
6126. עַקּוּב *ak-koob';* from 6117; *insidious; Akkub,* the name of five Isr.:–Akkub.
6127. עָקַל *aw-kal'* a prim. root; to *wrest:*–wrong.
6128. עֲקַלְקַל *ak-al-kal'* from 6127; *winding:*–by [-way], crooked way.
6129. עֲקַלָּתוֹן *ak-al-law-thone';* from 6127; *tortuous:*–crooked.
6130. עָקָן *aw-kawn';* from an un. root mean. to *twist; tortuous; Akan,* an Idummaean:–Akan. Comp. 3292.
6131. עֲקַר *aw-ar'* (Chald.); a prim. root; to *pluck* up (esp. by the roots); spec., to *hamstring*; fig., to *exterminate:*–dig down, hough, pluck up, root up.
6132. עֲקַר *ay'-kar* (Chald.); cor. to 6131:–pluck up by the roots.
6133. עֵקֶר *ay'-ker;* from 6131. fig., a *transplanted* person, i.e. naturalized citizen:–stock.
6134. עֵקֶר *ay'-ker;* the same as 6133; *Eker,* an Isr.:–Eker.
6135. עָקָר *aw-kawr';* from 6131; *sterile* (as if *extirpated* in the generative organs):–(X male or female) barren (woman).
6136. עִקַּר *ik-kar'* (Chald.); from 6132; a *stock:*–stump.
6137. עַקְרָב *ak-rawb';* of unc. der.; a *scorpion*; fig., a *scourge* or knotted whip:–scorpion.
6138. עֶקְרוֹן *ek-rone';* from 6131; *eradication; Ekron,* a place in Pal.:–Ekron.
6139. עֶקְרוֹנִי *ek-ro-nee';* or עֶקְרֹנִי *ek-ro-nee';* patrial from 6138; an *Ekronite* or inh. of Ekron:–Ekronite.
6140. עָקַשׁ *aw-kash';* a prim. root; to *knot* or *distort*; fig., to *pervert* (act or declare perverse):–make crooked, (prove, that is) perverse(-rt).
6141. עִקֵּשׁ *ik-kashe';* from 6140; *distorted*; hence, *false:*–crooked, froward, perverse.
6142. עִקֵּשׁ *ik-kashe';* the same as 6141; perverse; *Ikkesh*, an Isr.:–Ikkesh.
6143. עִקְּשׁוּת *ik-kesh-ooth';* from 6141; *perversity:* –X froward.
6144. עָר *awr;* the same as 5892; a *city*; Ar, a place in Moab:–Ar.
6145. עָר *awr*; from 5782; a *foe* (as *watchful* for mischief):–enemy.
6146. עָר *awr* (Chald.); cor. to 6145:–enemy.
6147. עֵר *ayr;* from 5782; *watchful*; Er, the name of two Isr.:–Er.
6148. עָרַב *aw-rab';* a prim. root; to *braid,* i.e. *intermix*; te., to *traffic* (as if by barter); also or *give* to *be security* (as a kind of exchange):–engage, (inter-)meddle (with), mingle (self), mortgage, occupy, give pledges, be(-come, put in) surety, undertake.
6149. עָרֵב *aw-rabe';* a prim. root [ident. with 6148 through the idea of close *association*]; to be *agreeable:*–be pleasant (-ing), take pleasure in, be sweet.
6150. עָרַב *aw-rab';* a prim. root [ident. with 6148 through the idea of *covering* with a texture]; to grow *dusky* at sundown:–be darkened, (toward) evening.
6151. עֲרַב *ar-ab'* (Chald.); cor. to 6148; to *commingle:*–mingle (self), mix.
6152. עֲרָב *ar-awb';* or עֲרַב *ar-ab';* from 6150 in the fig. sense of *sterility; Arab* (i.e. *Arabia*), a country E. of Pal.:–Arabia.
6153. עֶרֶב *eh'-reb;* from 6150; *dusk:*–+ day, even(-ing, tide), night.
6154. עֵרֶב *ay'-reb;* or (1 Kings 10:15), (with the art. pref.) עֶרֶב *eh'-reb;* from 6148; the *web* (or transverse threads of cloth); also a *mixture,* (or *mongrel* race):–Arabia, mingled people, mixed (multitude), woof.
6155. עָרָב *aw-rawb';* from 6148; a *willow* (from the use of osiers as wattles):–willow.
6156. עָרֵב *aw-rabe';* from 6149; *pleasant:*–sweet.
6157. עָרֹב *aw-robe';* from 6148; a *mosquito* (from its *swarming*):–divers sorts of flies, swarm.
6158. עֹרֵב *o-rabe';* or עוֹרֵב *o-rabe';* from 6150; a *raven* (from its *dusky* hue):–raven.
6159. עֹרֵב *o-rabe';* or עוֹרֵב *o-rabe';* the same as 6158; *Oreb,* the name of a Midianite and of the cliff near the Jordan:–Oreb.
6160. עֲרָבָה *ar-aw-baw';* from 6150 (in the sense of *sterility*); a *desert;* esp. (with the art. pref.) the (gen.) sterile valley of the Jordan and its continuation to the Red Sea:–Arabah, champaign, desert, evening, heaven, plain, wilderness. See also 1026.
6161. עֲרֻבָּה *ar-oob-baw';* fem. pass.part. of 6048 in the sense of a *bargain* or *exchange;* something given as *security,* i.e. (lit.) a *token* (of safety) or (metaphorically) a *bondsman:*–pledge, surety.
6162. עֲרָבוֹן *ar-aw-bone';* from 6148 (in the sense of *exchange*); a *pawn* (given as security):–pledge.
6163. עֲרָבִי *ar-aw-bee';* or עַרְבִי *ar-bee';* patrial from 6152; an *Arabian* or inh. of Arab (i.e. Arabia):–Arabian.
6164. עַרְבָתִי *ar-baw-thee';* patrial from 1026; an *Arbathite* or inh. of (Beth-) Arabah:–Arbahite.
6165. עָרַג *aw-rag';* a prim. root; to *long* for:–cry, pant.
6166. עֲרָד *ar-awd';* from an un. root mean. to *sequester* itself; *fugitive; Arad,* the name of a place near Pal., also of a Canaanite and an Isr.:–Arad.

6167. עֲרָד, *ar-awd'* (Chald.); cor. to 6171; an *onager:*–wild ass.

6168. עָרָה *aw-raw';* a prim. root; to *be* (caus., *make*) *bare;* hence, to *empty, pour* out, *demolish:*–leave destitute, discover, empty, make naked, pour (out), rase, spread self, uncover.

6169. עָרָה *aw-raw';* fem. from 6168; a *naked* (i.e. level) plot:–paper reed.

6170. עֲרוּגָה *ar-oo-gaw';* or עֲרֻגָה *ar-oo-gaw';* fem. pass.part. of 6165; something *piled* up (as if [fig.] *raised* by ment. aspiration), i.e. a *parterre:*–bed, furrow.

6171. עָרוֹד *aw-rode';* from the same as 6166; an *onager* (from his *lonesome* habits):–wild ass.

6172. עֶרְוָה *er-vaw';* from 6168; *nudity,* lit. (esp. the *pudenda*) or fig. (*disgrace, blemish*):–nakedness, shame, unclean(-ness).

6173. עַרְוָה *ar-vaw'* (Chald.); cor. to 6172; *nakedness,* i.e. (fig.) *impoverishment:*–dishonor.

6174. עָרוֹם *aw-rome';* or עָרֹם *aw-rome';* from 6191 (in its or. sense); *nude,* either partially or totally:–naked.

6175. עָרוּם *aw-room';* pass.part. of 6191; *cunning* (usually in a bad sense):–crafty, prudent, subtil.

6176. עֲרוֹעֵר *ar-o-ayr';* or עַרְעָר *ar-awr';* from 6209 redupl.; a *juniper* (from its *nudity* of situation):–health.

6177. עֲרוֹעֵר *ar-o-ayr';* or עֲרֹעֵר *ar-o-ayr';* or עַרְעוֹר *ar-ore';* the same as 6176; *nudity* of situation; *Aroër,* the name of three places in or near Pal.:–Aroer.

6178. עָרוּץ *aw-roots';* pass.part. of 6206; *feared,* i.e. (concr.) a *horrible* place or *chasm:*–cliffs.

6179. עֵרִי *ay-ree';* from 5782; *watchful; Eri,* an Isr.:–Eri.

6180. עֵרִי *ay-ree';* patron. of 6179; a *Erite* (coll.) or desc. of Eri:–Erites.

6181. עֶרְיָה *er-yaw';* for 6172; *nudity:*–bare, naked, X quite.

6182. עֲרִיסָה *ar-ee-saw';* from an un. root mean. to *comminute; meal:*–dough.

6183. עָרִיף *aw-reef';* from 6201; the *sky* (as *dropping* at the horizon):–heaven.

6184. עָרִיץ *aw-reets';* from 6206; *fearful,* i.e. *powerful* or *tyrannical:*–mighty, oppressor, in great power, strong, terrible, violent.

6185. עֲרִירִי *ar-e-ree';* from 6209; *bare,* i.e. destitute (of children):–childless.

6186. עָרַךְ *aw-rak';* a prim. root; to set in a *row,* i.e. *arrange,* put in *order* (in a very wide variety of appl.):–put (set) (the battle, self) in array, comp., direct, equal, esteem, estimate, expert [in war], furnish, handle, join [battle], ordain, (lay, put, reckon up, set) (in) order, prepare, tax, value.

6187. עֵרֶךְ *eh'rek;* from 6186; a *pile, equipment, estimate:*–equal, estimation, (things that are set in) order, price, proportion, X set at, suit, taxation, X valuest.

6188. עָרֵל *aw-rale';* a prim. root; prop. to *strip;* but used as denom. from 6189; to *expose* or *remove* the *prepuce,* whether lit. (to *go naked*) or fig. (to *refrain* from using):–count uncircumcised, foreskin to be uncovered.

6189. עָרֵל *aw-rale';* from 6188; prop. *exposed,* i.e. projecting loose (as to the prepuce); used only te., *uncircumcised* (i.e. still having the prepuce uncurtailed):–uncircumcised (person).

6190. עָרְלָה *or-law';* fem. of 6189; the *prepuce:*–foreskin, + uncircumcised.

6191. עָרַם *aw-ram';* a prim. root; prop. to *be* (or *make*) *bare;* but used only in the der. sense (through the idea perh. of *smoothness*) to *be cunning* (usually in a bad sense):–X very, beware, take crafty [counsel], be prudent, deal subtilly.

6192. עָרַם *aw-ram';* a prim. root; to *pile* up:–gather together.

6193. עֹרֶם *o'-rem;* from 6191; a *stratagem:*–craftiness.

6194. עָרֵם *aw-rame';* (Jer. 50:26 or (fem.) עֲרֵמָה *ar-ay-maw';* from 6192; a *heap;* spec., a *sheaf:*–heap (of corn), sheaf.

6195. עָרְמָה *or-maw';* fem. of 6193; *trickery;* or (in a good sense) *discretion:*–guile, prudence, subtilty, wilily, wisdom.

6196. עַרְמוֹן *ar-mone';* prob. from 6191; the *plane* tree (from its *smooth* and shed bark):–chestnut tree.

6197. עֵרָן *ay-rawn';* prob. from 5782; *watchful; Eran,* an Isr.:–Eran.

6198. עֵרָנִי *ay-raw-nee';* patron. from 6197; an *Eranite* or desc. (coll.) of Eran:–Eranites.

6199. עַרְעָר *ar-awr';* from 6209; *naked,* i.e. (fig.) *poor:*–destitute. See also 6176.

6200. עֲרֹעֵרִי *ar-o-ay-ree';* patron. from 6177; an *Aroërite* or inh. of Aroër:–Aroerite.

6201. עָרַף *aw-raf';* a prim. root; to *droop;* hence, to *drip:*–drop (down).

6202. עָרַף *aw-raf';* a prim. root [ident. with 6201 through the idea of *sloping*]; prop. to *bend* downward; but used only as a denom. from 6203, to *break the neck;* hence (fig.) to *destroy:*–that is beheaded, break down, break (cut off, strike off) neck.

6203. עֹרֶף *o-ref';* from 6202; the *nape* or *back* of the neck (as *declining*); hence, the *back* gen. (whether lit. or fig.):– back ([stiff-])neck([-ed]).

6204. עָרְפָּה *or-paw';* fem. of 6203; *mane; Orpah,* a Moabites:–Orpah.

6205. עֲרָפֶל *ar-aw-fel';* prob. from 6201; *gloom* (as of a *lowering* sky):–(gross, thick) dark (cloud, -ness).

6206. עָרַץ *aw-rats';* a prim. root; to *awe* or (intr.) to *dread;* hence, to *harass:*–be affrighted (afraid, dread, feared, terrified), break, dread, fear, oppress, prevail, shake terribly.

6207. עָרַק *aw-rak';* a prim. root; to *gnaw,* i.e. (fig.) *eat* (by hyberbole); also (part.) a *pain:*–fleeing, sinew.

6208. עַרְקִי *ar-kee';* patrial from an un. name mean. a *tush;* an *Arkite* or inh. of Erek:–Arkite.

6209. עָרַר *aw-rar';* a prim. root; to *bare;* fig., to *demolish:*–make bare, break, raise up, X utterly.

6210. עֶרֶשׂ *eh'res;* from an un. root mean. perh. to *arch;* a *couch* (prop. with a *canopy*):–bed (-stead), couch.

6211. עָשׁ *awsh;* from 6244; a *moth:*–moth. See also 5906.

6211'. עֲשַׂב *as-ab'* (Chald.); 6212:–grass.

6212. עֶשֶׂב *eh'seb;* from an un. root mean. to *glisten* (or *be green*); *grass* (or any tender shoot):–grass, herb.

6213. עָשָׂה *aw-saw';* a prim. root; to *do* or *make,* in the broadest sense and widest appl. (as follows):–accomplish, advance, appoint, apt, be at, become, bear, bestow, bring forth, bruise, be busy, X certainly, have the charge of, commit, deal (with), deck, + displease, do, (ready) dress (-ed), (put in) execute(-ion), exercise, fashion, + feast, [fight-]ing man, + finish, fit, fly, follow, fulfill, furnish, gather, get, go about, govern, grant, great, + hinder, hold ([a feast]), X indeed, + be industrious, + journey, keep, labour, maintain, make, be meet, observe, be occupied, offer, + officer, pare, bring (come) to pass, perform, pracise, prepare, procure, provide, put, requite, X sacrifice, serve, set, shew, X sin, spend, X surely, take, X thoroughly, trim, X very, + vex, be [warr-]ior, work(-man), yield, use.

6214. עֲשָׂהאֵל *as-aw-ale';* from 6213 and 410; *God has made; Asahel,* the name of four Isr.:–Asahel.

6215. עֵשָׂו *ay-sawv';* app. a form of the pass. part. of 6213 in the or. sense of *handling; rough* (i.e. sensibly *felt*); *Esav,* a son of Isaac, including his posterity:–Esau.

6216. עָשׁוֹק *aw-shoke';* from 6231; *oppressive* (as noun, a *tyrant*):–oppressor.

6217. עָשׁוּק *aw-shook';* or עָשֻׁק *aw-shook';* pass.part. of 6231; used in pl. masc. as abstr., *tyranny:*–oppressed(-ion).

6218. עָשׂוֹר *aw-sore';* or עָשֹׂר *aw-sore';* from 6235; *ten;* by abbrev. ten *strings,* and so a *decachord:*–(instrument of) ten (strings, -th).

6219. עָשׁוֹת *aw-shoth';* from 6245; *shining,* i.e. polished:–bright.

6220. עַשְׁוָת *ash-vawth';* for 6219; *bright; Ashvath,* an Isr.:–Ashvath.

6221. עֲשִׂיאֵל *as-ee-ale';* from 6213 and 410; *made of God; Asiël,* an Isr.:–Asiel.

6222. עֲשָׂיָה *aw-saw-yaw';* from 6213 and 3050; *Jah has made; Asajah,* the name of three or four Isr.:–Asaiah.

6223 עָשִׁיר *aw-sheer';* from 6238; *rich,* whether lit. or fig. (*noble*):–rich (man).

6224. עֲשִׂירִי *as-ee-ree';* from 6235; *tenth;* by abb, *tenth month* or (fem.) *part:*–tenth (part).

6225. עָשַׁן *aw-shan';* a prim. root; to *smoke,* whether lit. or fig.:–be angry (be on a) smoke.

6226. עָשֵׁן *aw-shane';* from 6225; *smoky:*–smoking.

6227. עָשָׁן *aw-shawn';* from 6225; *smoke,* lit. or fig. (*vapor, dust, anger*):–smoke(-ing).

6228. עָשָׁן *aw-shawn';* the same as 6227; *Ashan,* a place in Pal.:–Ashan.

6229. עָשַׂק *aw-sak;* a prim. root (ident. with 6231); to *press upon,* i.e. *quarrel;* –strive with.

6230. עֵשֶׂק *ay'sek;* from 6229; *strife:*–Esek.

6231. עָשַׁק *aw-shak';* a prim. root (comp. 6229); to *press* upon, i.e. *oppress, defraud, violate, overflow:*–get deceitfully, deceive, defraud, drink up, (use) oppress([-ion]), -or), do violence (wrong).

6232. עֵשֶׁק *ay-shek';* from 6231; *oppression; Eshek,* an Isr.:–Eshek.

6233. עֹשֶׁק *o'-shek;* from 6231; *injury, fraud,* (subj.) *distress,* (concr.) *unjust gain:*–cruelly, extortion, oppression, thing [deceitfully gotten].

6234. עָשְׁקָה *osh-kaw';* fem. of 6233; *anguish:*–oppressed.

6235. עֶשֶׂר *eh'ser;* masc. of term עֲשָׂרָה *as-aw-raw';* from 6237; *ten* (as an *accumulation* to the extent of the digits):–ten, [fif-, seven-]teen.

6236. עֲשַׂר *as-ar'* (Chald.); masc. עַשְׂרָה *as-raw'* (Chald.); cor. to 6235; ten:–ten, + twelve.

6237. עָשַׂר *aw-sar';* a prim. root (ident. with 6238); to *accumulate;* but used only as denom. from 6235; to *tithe,* i.e. to take or give a tenth:–X surely, give (take) the tenth, (have, take) tithe(-ing, -s), X truly.

6238. עָשַׁר *aw-shar';* a prim. root; prop. to *accumulate;* chiefly (spec.) to *grow* (caus., *make*) *rich:*–be(-come, en-, make, make self, wax) rich, make (1 Kings 22:48). See 6240.

6239. עֹשֶׁר *o'-sher;* from 6238; *wealth:*–X far [richer], riches.
6240. עָשָׂר *aw-sawr';* for 6235; *ten* (only in combination),i.e.*-teen;*also(ord.)*-teenth:*–[eigh-, fif-, four-, nine-, seven-, six-, thir-]teen(-th), + eleven(-th), + sixscore thousand, + twelve(-th).
6241. עִשָּׂרוֹן *is-saw-rone';* or עִשָּׂרֹן *is-saw-rone';* from 6235; (fractional) a *tenth* part:–tenth deal.
6242. עֶשְׂרִים *es-reem';* from 6235; *twenty;* also (ord.) *twentieth:*–[six-]score, twenty(-ieth).
6243. עֶשְׂרִין *es-reen'* (Chald.); cor. to 6242:–twenty.
6244. עָשֵׁשׁ *aw-shaysh';* a prim. root; prob. to *shrink,* i.e. *fail:*–be consumed.
6245. עָשַׁת *aw-shath';* a prim. root; prob. to be *sleek,* i.e. *glossy;* hence (through the idea of *polishing*) to *excogitate* (as if *forming* in the mind):–shine, think.
6246. עֲשִׁת *ash-eeth'* (Chald.); cor. to 6245; to *purpose:*–think.
6247. עֶשֶׁת *eh'-sheth;* from 6245; a *fabric:*–bright.
6248. עַשְׁתּוּת *ash-tooth';* from 6245; *cogitation:*–thought.
6249. עַשְׁתֵּי *ash-tay';* app. masc. pl. const. of 6247 in the sense of an *afterthought* (used only in connection with 6240 in lieu of 259) *eleven* or (ord.) *eleventh:*–+ eleven(-th).
6250. עֶשְׁתֹּנָה *esh-to-naw';* from 6245; *thinking:*–thought.
6251. עַשְׁתְּרָה *ash-ter-aw';* prob. from 6238; *increase:*–flock.
6252. עַשְׁתָּרוֹת *ash-taw-roth';* or עַשְׁתָּרֹת *ash-taw-roth';* pl. of 6251; *Ashtaroth,* the name of a Sidonian deity, and of a place E. of the Jordan:–Ashtaroth, Astaroth. See also 1045, 6253, 6255.
6253. עַשְׁתֹּרֶת *ash-to'reth;* prob. for 6251; *Ashtoreth,* the Phoenician goddess of love (and *increase*):–Ashtoreth.
6254. עַשְׁתְּרָתִי *ash-ter-aw-thee';* patrial from 6252; an *Ashterathite;* or inh. of Ashtaroth:–Ashterathite.
6255. עַשְׁתְּרֹת קַרְנַיִם *ash-ter-oth' kar-nah'-yim;* from 6252 and the dual of 7161; *Ashtaroth of* (the) *double horns* (a symbol of the deity); *Ashteroth-Karnaïm,* a place E. of the Jordan:–Ashtoreth Karnaim.
6256. עֵת *ayth;* from 5703; *time,* esp. (adv. with prep.) *now, when,* etc.:–+ after, [al-]ways, X certain, + continually, + evening, long, (due) season, so [long] as, [even-, evening-, noon-] tide, ([meal-]), what) time, when.
6257. עָתַד *aw-thad';* a prim. root; to *prepare:*–make fit, be ready to become.
6258. עַתָּה *at-taw';* from 6256; at *this time,* whether adv., conj. or expletive:–henceforth, now, straightway, this time, whereas.
6259. עָתוּד *aw-thood';* pass.part. of 6257; *prepared:*–ready.
6260. עַתּוּד *at-tood';* or עַתֻּד *at-tood';* from 6257; *prepared,* i.e. *full grown;* spoken only (in pl.) of *he-goats,* or (fig.) *leaders* of the people:–chief one, (he) goat, ram.
6261. עִתִּי *it-tee';* from 6256; *timely:*–fit.
6262. עַתַּי *at-tah'ee;* for 6261; *Attai,* the name of three Isr.:–Attai.
6263. עֲתִיד *ath-eed'* (Chald.); cor. to 6264; *prepared:*–ready.
6264. עָתִיד *aw-theed';* from 6257; *prepared;* by impl., *skilful;* fem. pl. the *future;* also *treasure:*–things that shall come, ready, treasures.
6265. עֲתָיָה *ath-aw-yaw';* from 5790 and 3050; *Jah has helped; Athajah,* an Isr.:–Athaiah.
6266. עָתִיק *aw-theek';* from 6275; prop. *antique,* i.e. *venerable* or *splendid:*–durable.
6267. עַתִּיק *at-teek';* from 6275; *removed,* i.e. *weaned;* also *antique:*–ancient, drawn.
6268. עַתִּיק *at-teek'* (Chald.); cor. to 6267; *venerable:*–ancient.
6269. עֲתָךְ *ath-awk';* from an un. root mean. to *sojourn; lodging; Athak,* a place in Pal.:–Athach.
6270. עַתְלַי *ath-lah'ee;* from an un. root mean. to *compress; constringent; Athlai,* an Isr.:–Athlai.
6271. עֲתַלְיָה *ath-al-yaw';* or עֲתַלְיָהוּ *ath-al-yaw'-hoo;* from the same as 6270 and 3050; *Jah has constrained; Athaljah,* the name of an Isr.s and two Isr.:–Athaliah.
6272. עָתַם *aw-tham;* a prim. root; prob. to *glow,* i.e. (fig.) *be desolated:*–be darkened.
6273. עָתְנִי *oth-nee';* from an un. root mean. to *force; forcible; Othni,* an Isr.:–Othni.
6274. עָתְנִיאֵל *oth-nee-ale';* from the same as 6273 and 410; *force of God; Othniël,* an Isr.:–Othniel.
6275. עָתַק *aw-thak';* a prim. root; to *remove* (intr. or trans.) fig., to *grow old;* spec., to *transcribe:*–copy out, leave off, become (wax) old, remove.
6276. עָתֵק *aw-thake';* from 6275; *antique,* i.e. *valued:*–durable.
6277. עָתָק *aw-thawk';* from 6275 in the sense of *license; impudent:*–arrogancy, grievous (hard) things, stiff.
6278. עֵת קָצִין *ayth kaw-tseen';* from 6256 and 7011; *time of a judge; Eth-Katsin,* a place in Pal.:–Ittah-kazin
6279. עָתַר *aw-thar'* a prim. root [rather denom. from 6281]; to burn *incense* in worship, i.e. *intercede* (reciprocally, *listen* to prayer):–intreat, (make) pray(-er).
6280. עָתַר *aw-thar';* a prim. root; to be (caus., *make*) *abundant:*–deceitful, multiply.
6281. עֶתֶר *eh'ther;* from 6280; *abundance; Ether,* a place in Pal.:–Ether.
6282. עָתָר *aw-thawr';* from 6280; *incense* (as increasing to a *volume* of smoke); hence (from 6279) a *worshipper:*–suppliant, thick.
6283. עֲתֶרֶת *ath-eh'-reth;* from 6280; *copiousness:*–abundance.

פ

6284. פָּאָה *paw-aw';* a prim. root; to *puff,* i.e. *blow* away:–scatter into corners.
6285. פֵּאָה *pay-aw';* fem. of 6311; prop. *mouth* in a fig. sense, i.e. *direction, region, extremity:*–corner, end, quarter, side.
6286. פָּאַר *paw-ar';* a prim. root; to *gleam,* i.e. (caus.) *embellish;* fig., to *boast;* also to *explain* (i.e. make clear) oneself; denom. from 6288, to *shake* a tree:–beautify, boast self, go over the boughs, glorify (self), glory, vaunt self.
6287. פְּאֵר *peh-ayr';* from 6286; an *embellishment,* i.e. fancy *head-dress:*–beauty, bonnet, goodly, ornament, tire.
6288. פְּאֹרָה *peh-o-raw';* or פֹּרָאה *po-raw';* פֻּארָה *poo-raw';* from 6286; prop. *ornamentation,* i.e. (pl.) *foliage* (incl. the limbs) as *bright* green:–bough, branch, sprig.
6289. פָּארוּר *paw-roor';* from 6286; prop. *illuminated,* i.e. a *glow;* as noun, a *flush* (of anxiety):–blackness.
6290. פָּארָן *paw-rawn';* from 6286; *ornament.; Paran,* a desert of Arabia:–Paran.
6291. פַּג *pag;* from an un. root mean. to *be torpid,* i.e. *crude;* an *unripe* fig:–green fig.
6292. פִּגּוּל *pig-gool';* or פִּגֻּל *pig-gool';* from an un. root mean. to *stink;* prop. *fetid,* i.e. (fig.) *unclean* (cerem.):–abominable(-tion, thing).
6293. פָּגַע *paw-gah';* a prim. root; to *impinge,* by accident or violence, or (fig.) by importunity:–come (betwixt), cause to entreat, fall (upon), make intercession, intercessor, intreat, lay, light [upon], meet (together), pray, reach, run.
6294. פֶּגַע *peh'-gah;* from 6293; *impact* (casual):–chance, occurent.
6295. פַּגְעִיאֵל *pag-ee-ale';* from 6294 and 410; *accident of God; Pagiël,* an Isr.:–Pagiel.
6296. פָּגַר *paw-gar';* a prim. root; to *relax,* i.e. become *exhausted:*–be faint.
6297. פֶּגֶר *peh'gher;* from 6296; a *carcase* (as *limp*), whether of man or beast; fig., an idolatrous *image:*–carcase, corpse, dead body.
6298. פָּגַשׁ *paw-gash';* a prim. root; to *come in contact with,* whether by accident or violence; fig., to *concur:*–meet (with, together).
6299. פָּדָה *paw-daw';* a prim. root; to *sever,* i.e. *ransom;* gen. to *release, preserve:*–X at all, deliver, X by any means, ransom, (that are to be, let be) redeem(-ed), rescue, X surely.
6300. פְּדַהְאֵל *ped-ah-ale';* from 6299 and 410; *God has ransomed; Pedahel,* an Isr.:–Pedahel.
6301. פְּדָהצוּר *ped-aw-tsoor';* from 6299 and 6697; a *rock* (i.e. God) *has ransomed; Pedahtsur,* an Isr.:–Pedahzur.
6302. פָּדוּי *paw-doo'ee;* pass.part. of 6299. *ransomed* (and so occurring under 6299); as abstr. (in pl. masc.) a *ransom:*–(that are) to be (that were) redeemed.
6303. פָּדוֹן *paw-done';* from 6299; *ransom; Padon,* one of the Nethinim:– Padon.
6304. פְּדוּת *ped-ooth';* or פְּדֻת *ped-ooth';* from 6929; *distinction;* also *deliverance:*–division, redeem, redemption.
6305. פְּדָיָה *ped-aw-yaw';* or פְּדָיָהוּ *ped-aw-yaw'-hoo;* from 6299 and 3050; *Jah has ransomed; Pedajah,* the name of six Isr.:–Pedaiah.
6306. פִּדְיוֹם *pid-yome';* or פִּדְיֹם *pid-yome';* also פִּדְיוֹן *pid-yone';* or פִּדְיֹן *pid-yone';* from 6299; a *ransom:*–ransom, that were redeemed, redemption.
6307. פַּדָּן *pad-dawn';* from an un. root mean. to *extend;* a *plateau;* or פַּדַּן אֲרָם *pad-dan' ar-awm';* from the same and 758; the *table-land of Aram; Paddan* or *Paddan-Aram,* a region of Syria:–Padan, Padan-aram.
6308. פָּדַע *paw-dah';* a prim. root; to *retrieve:*–deliver.
6309. פֶּדֶר *peh'der;* from an un. root mean. to *be greasy; suet:*–fat.
6310. פֶּה *peh;* from 6284; the *mouth* (as the means of *blowing*), whether lit. or fig. (particularly *speech*); spec. *edge, portion or side;* adv. (with prep.) *according to:*–accord (-ing as, -ing to), after, appointment, assent, collar, command(-ment), X eat, edge, end, entry, + file, hole, X in, mind, mouth, part, portion, X (should) say(-ing), sentence, skirt, sound, speech, X spoken, talk, tenor, X to, + two-edged, wish, word.
6311. פֹּה *po;* or פֹּא (Job 38:11) *po;* or פּוֹ *po;* prob. from a prim. insep. particle פּ p (of demonstr. force) and 1931; *this place* (French içi), i.e. *here* or *hence:*–here, hither,

the one (other, this, that) side.
6312. פּוּאָה *poo-aw';* or פֻּוָּה *poov-vaw';* from 6284; a *blast; Puäh* or *Puvvah,* the name of two Isr.:–Phuvah, Pua, Puah.
6313. פּוּג *poog;* a prim. root; to *be sluggish:*–cease, be feeble, faint, be slacked.
6314. פּוּגָה *poo-gaw';* from 6313; *intermission:*–rest.
6315. פּוּחַ *poo'akh;* a prim. root; to *puff,* i.e. blow with the breath or air; hence, to *fan* (as a breeze), to *utter,* to *kindle* (a fire), to *scoff:*–blow (upon), break, puff, bring into a snare, speak, utter.
6316. פּוּט *poot;* of for. or.; *Put,* a son of Ham, also the name of his desc. or their region, and of a Pers. tribe:–Phut, Put.
6317. פּוּטִיאֵל *poo-tee-ale';* from an un. root (prob. mean. to *disparage*) and 410; *contempt of God; Putiël,* an Isr.:–Putiel.
6318. פּוֹטִיפַר *po-tee-far';* of Eg. der.; *Potiphar,* an Eg.:–Potiphar.
6319. פּוֹטִי פֶרַע *po-tee feh'-rah;* of Eg. der.; *Poti-Phera,* an Eg.:–Poti-pherah.
6320. פּוּךְ *pook;* from an un. root mean. to *paint; dye* (spec., *stibium* for the eyes):–fair colours, glistering, paint[-ed] (-ing).
6321. פּוֹל *pole;* from an un. root mean. to *be thick;* a *bean* (as *plump*):–beans.
6322. פּוּל *pool;* of for. or.; *Pul,* the name of an Ass. king and of an Ethiopian tribe:–Pul.
6323. פּוּן *poon;* a prim. root mean. to *turn,* i.e. *be perplexed:*–be distracted.
6324. פּוּנִי *poo-nee';* patron. from an un. name mean. a *turn;* a *Punite* (coll.) or de-scendants of an unknown Pun:–Punites.
6325. פּוּנֹן *poo-none';* from 6323; *perplexity; Punon,* a place in the Desert:–Punon.
6326. פּוּעָה *poo-aw';* from an un. root mean. to *glitter; brilliancy;* Puäh, an Isr.s:–Puah.
6327. פּוּץ *poots;* a prim. root; to *dash* in pieces, lit. or fig. (esp. to *disperse*):–break (dash, shake) in (to) pieces, cast (abroad), disperse (selves), drive, retire, scatter (abroad), spread abroad.
6328. פּוּק *pook;* a prim. root; to *waver:*–stumble, move.
6329. פּוּק *pook;* a prim. root (ident. with 6328 through the idea of *dropping* out; comp. 5312); to *issue,* i.e. *furnish;* caus., to *secure;* fig., to *succeed:*–afford, draw out, further, get, obtain.
6330. פּוּקָה *poo-kaw';* from 6328; a *stumbling-block:*–grief.
6331. פּוּר *poor;* a prim. root; to *crush:*–break, bring to nought, X utterly take.
6332. פּוּר *poor;* also (pl.) פּוּרִים *poo-reem';* or פֻּרִים *poo-reem';* from 6331; a lot (as by means of a *broken* piece):–Pur, Purim.
6333. פּוּרָה *poo-raw';* from 6331; a *wine*-press (as *crushing* the grapes):–winepress.
6334. פּוֹרָתָא *po-raw-thaw';* of Pers. or.; *Poratha,* a son of Haman:–Poratha.
6335. פּוּשׁ *poosh;* a prim. root; to *spread;* fig., *act proudly:*–grow up, be grown fat, spread selves, be scattered.
6336. פּוּתִי *poo-thee';* patron. from an un. name mean. a *hinge;* a *Puthite* (coll.) or desc. of an unknown Puth:–Puhites (*as if from* 6312).
6337. פָּז *pawz;* from 6338; *pure* (gold); hence, *gold* itself (as refined):–fine (pure) gold.
6338. פָּזַז *paw-zaz';* a prim. root; to *refine* (gold):–best [gold].
6339. פָּזַז *paw-zaz';* a prim. root (rather ident. with 6338); to *solidify* (as if by *refining*); also to *spring* (as if *separating* the limbs):–leap, be made strong.
6340. פָּזַר *paw-zar';* a prim. root; to *scatter,* whether in enmity or bounty:–disperse, scatter (abroad).
6341. פַּח *pakh;* from 6351; a (metallic) *sheet* (as *pounded* thin); also a spring *net* (as spread out like a *lamina*):–gin, (thin) plate, snare.
6342. פָּחַד *paw-kkad';* a prim. root; to *be startled* (by a sudden alarm); hence, to *fear* in gen.:–be afraid, stand in awe, (be in) fear, make to shake.
6343. פַּחַד *pakh'-ad;* from 6342; a (sudden) *alarm;* (prop. the obj. feared, by impl., the feeling):–dread(-ful), fear, (thing) great [fear, -ly feared], terror.
6344. פַּחַד *pakh'-ad;* the same as 6343; a *testicle* (as a cause of *shame* akin to fear):–stone.
6345. פַּחְדָּה *pakh-daw';* fem. of 6343; *alarm* (i.e. *awe*):–fear.
6346. פֶּחָה *peh-khaw';* of for. or.; a *prefect* (of a city or small district):–captain, deputy, governor
6347. פֶּחָה *peh-khaw'* (Chald.); cor. to 6346:–captain, governor.
6348. פָּחַז *paw-khaz';* a prim. root; to *bubble* up or *froth* (as boiling water), i.e. (fig.) to *be unimportant:*–light.
6349. פַּחַז *pakh'-az;* from 6348; *ebullition,* i.e. froth (fig., lust):–unstable.
6350. פַּחֲזוּת *pakh-az-ooth';* from 6348; *frivolity:*–lightness.
6351. פָּחַח *paw-khakh';* a prim. root; to *batter* out; but used only as denom. from 6341, to *spread a net:*–be snared.
6352. פֶּחָם *peh-khawm';* perh. from an un. root prob. mean. to *be black;* a *coal,* whether charred or live:–coals.
6353. פֶּחָר *peh-khawr'* (Chald.); from an un. root prob. mean. to *fashion;* a *potter:*–potter.
6354. פַּחַת *pakh'-ath;* prob. from an un. root app. mean. to *dig;* a *pit,* esp. for catching animals:–hole, pit, snare.
6355. פַּחַת מוֹאָב *pakh'-ath mo-awb';* from 6354 and 4124; *pit of Moäb; Pachath-Moäb,* an Isr.:–Pahath-moab.
6356. פְּחֶתֶת *pekh-eh'-theth;* from the same as 6354; a *hole* (by mildew in a garment):–fret inward.
6357. פִּטְדָה *pit-daw';* of for. der.; a *gem,* prob. the *topaz:*–topaz.
6358 פָּטוּר *paw-toor';* pass.part. of 6362; *opened,* i.e. (as noun) a *bud:*–open.
6359. פָּטִיר *paw-teer';* from 6362; *open,* i.e. *unoccupied:*–free.
6360. פַּטִּישׁ *pat-teesh';* intens. from an un. root mean. to *pound;* a *hammer:*–hammer.
6361. פַּטִּישׁ *pat-teesh'* (Chald.); from a root cor. to that of 6360; a *gown* (as if *hammered* out wide):–hose.
6362. פָּטַר *paw-tar';* a prim. root; to *cleave* or burst through, i.e. (caus.) to *emit,* whether lit. or fig. (*gape*):–dismiss, free, let (shoot) out, slip away.
6363. פֶּטֶר *peh'-ter;* or פִּטְרָה *pit-raw';* from 6362; a *fissure,* i.e. (concr.) *firstling* (as *opening* the matrix):–firstling, openeth, such as open.
6364. פִּי־בֶסֶת *pee beh'-seth;* of Eg. or.; *Pi-Beseth,* a place in Eg.:–Pi-beseth.
6365. פִּיד *peed;* from an un. root prob. mean. to *pierce;* (fig.) *misfortune:*–destruction, ruin.
6366. פֵּיָה *pay-aw';* or פִּיָה *pee-yaw';* fem. of 6310; an *edge:*– (two-)edge(-d).
6367. פִּי הַחִירֹת *pee hah-khee-roth';* from 6310 and the fem. pl. of a noun (from the same root as 2356), with the art. interpolated; *mouth of the gorges; Pi-ha-Chiroth,* a place in Eg.:–Pi-hahiroth. [In Numbers 14:19 without Pi-.]
6368. פִּיחַ pee'-akh from 6315; a *powder* (as easily *puffed* away), i.e. *ashes* or *dust:*–ashes.
6369. פִּיכֹל *pee-kole';* app. from 6310 and 3605; *mouth of all; Picol,* a Philistine:–Phichol.
6370. פִּילֶגֶשׁ *pee-leh'-ghesh;* or פִּלֶגֶשׁ *pee-leh'-ghesh;* of unc. der.; a *concubine;* also (masc.) a *paramour:*–concubine, paramour.
6371. פִּימָה *pee-maw';* prob. from an un. root mean. to *be plump; obesity:*–collops.
6372. פִּינְחָס *pee-nekh-aws';* app. from 6310 and a var. of 5175; *mouth of a serpent; Pinechas,* the name of three Isr.:–Phinehas
6373. פִּינֹן *pee-none';* prob. the same as 6325; *Pinon,* an Idumaean:–Pinon.
6374. פִּיפִיָּה *pee-fee-yaw';* for 6366; an *edge* or *tooth:*–tooth, X two-edged.
6375. פִּיק *peek;* from 6329; a *tottering:*–smite together.
6376. פִּישׁוֹן *pee-shone';* from 6335; *dispersive; Pishon,* a river of Eden:–Pison.
6377. פִּיתוֹן *pee-thone';* prob. from the same as 6596; *expansive; Pithon,* an Isr.:–Pithon.
6378. פַּךְ *pak;* from 6379; a *flask* (from which a liquid may *flow*):–box, vial.
6379. פָּכָה *paw-kaw'* a prim. root; to *pour:*–run out.
6380. פֹּכֶרֶת צְבָיִים *po-keh'-reth; tseb-aw-yeem';* from the act.part. (of the same form as the first word) fem. of an un. root (mean. to *entrap*) and pl. of 6643; *trap of gazelles; Pokereth-Tsebajim,* one of the "servants of Solomon":–Pochereth of Zebaim.
6381. פָּלָא *paw-law';* a prim. root; prop. perh. to *separate,* i.e. *distinguish* (lit. or fig.); by impl., to *be* (caus., *make*) *great, difficult, wonderful:*–accomplish, (arise...too, be too) hard, hidden, things too high, (be, do, do a, shew) marvelous (-ly, -els, things, work), miracles, perform, separate, make sing., (be, great, make) wonderful(-ers, -ly, things, works), wondrous (things, works, -ly).
6382. פֶּלֶא *peh'-leh;* from 6381; a *miracle:*–marvellous thing, wonder(-ful, -fully).
6383. פִּלְאִי *pil-ee';* or פָּלִיא *paw-lee';* from 6381; *remarkable:*–secret, wonderful.
6384. פַּלֻּאִי *pal-loo-ee';* patron. from 6396; a *Palluïte* (coll.) or desc. of Pallu:–Palluites.
6385. פָּלַג *paw-lag';* a prim. root; to *split* (lit. or fig.):–divide.
6386. פְּלַג *pel-ag'* (Chald.); cor. to 6385:–divided.
6387. פְּלַג *pel-ag'* (Chald.); from 6386; a *half:*–dividing.
6388. פֶּלֶג *peh'-leg;* from 6385; a *rill* (i.e. small *channel* of water, as in irrigation):–river, stream.
6389. פֶּלֶג *peh'-leg;* the same as 6388; *earthquake; Peleg,* a son of Shem:–Peleg.
6390. פְּלַגָּה *pel-ag-gaw';* from 6385; a *runlet,* i.e. *gully:*–division, river.
6391. פְּלֻגָּה *pel-oog-gaw';* from 6385; a *section:*–division.
6392. פְּלֻגָּה *pel-oog-gaw'* (Chald.); cor. to 6391:–division.
6393. פְּלָדָה *pel-aw-daw';* from an un-

HEBREW

used root mean. to *divide;* a *cleaver,* i.e. iron *armature* (of a chariot):–torch.
6394. פִּלְדָּשׁ *pil-dawsh';* of unc. der.; *Pildash,* a relative of Abraham:–Pildash.
6395. פָּלָה *paw-law';* a prim. root; to *distinguish* (lit. or fig.):–put a difference, show marvellous, separate, set apart, sever, make wonderfully.
6396. פַּלּוּא *pal-loo';* from 6395; *distinguished; Pallu,* an Isr.:–Pallu, Phallu.
6397. פְּלוֹנִי *pel-o-nee';* patron. from an un. name (from 6395) mean. *separate;* a *Pelonite* or inh. of an unknown Palon:– Pelonite.
6398. פָּלַח *paw-lakh';* a prim. root; to *slice,* i.e. *break* open or *pierce:*–bring forth, cleave, cut, shred, strike through.
6399. פְּלַח *pel-akh'* (Chald.); cor. to 6398; to *serve* or worship:–minister, serve.
6400. פֶּלַח *peh'-lakh;* from 6398; a *slice:*–piece.
6401. פִּלְחָא *pil-khaw';* from 6400; *slicing; Pilcha,* an Isr.:–Pilcha.
6402. פָּלְחָן *pol-khawn'* (Chald.); from 6399; *worship:*–service.
6403. פָּלַט *paw-lat';* a prim. root; to *slip* out, i.e. *escape;* caus., to *deliver:*–calve, carry away safe, deliver, (cause to) escape.
6404. פֶּלֶט *peh'-let;* from 6403; *escape; Pelet,* the name of two Isr.:–Pelet. See also 1046.
6405. פַּלֵּט *pal-late';* from 6403; *escape:*–deliverance, escape.
6406. פַּלְטִי *pal-tee';* from 6403; *delivered; Palti,* the name of two Isr.:–Palti, Phalti
6407. פַּלְטִי *pal-tee';* patron. from 6406; a Paltite or desc. of Palti:–Paltite.
6408. פִּלְטַי *pil-tah'-ee;* for 6407; *Piltai,* an Isr.:–Piltai.
6409. פַּלְטִיאֵל *pal-tee-ale';* from the same as 6404 and 410; *deliverance of God; Paltiël,* the name of two Isr.:–Paltiel, Phaltiel
6410. פְּלַטְיָה *pel-at-yaw';* or פְּלַטְיָהוּ *pel-at-yaw'-hoo;* from 6403 and 3050; *Jah has delivered; Pelatjah,* the name of four Isr.:–Pelatiah.
6411. פְּלָיָה *pel-aw-yaw';* or פְּלָאיָה *pel-aw-yaw';* from 6381 and 3050; *Jah has distinguished; Pelajah,* the name of three Isr.:–Pelaiah.
6412. פָּלִיט *paw-leet';* or פָּלֵיט *paw-late';* or פָּלֵט *paw-late';* from 6403; a *refugee:*–(that have) escape(-d, -th), fugitive.
6413. פְּלֵיטָה *pel-ay-taw';* or פְּלֵטָה *pel-ay-taw';* fem. of 6412; *deliverance;* concr., an *escaped* portion:–deliverance, (that is) escape(-d), remnant.
6414. פָּלִיל *paw-leel';* from 6419; a *magistrate:*–judge.
6415. פְּלִילָה *pel-ee-law';* fem. of 6414; *justice:*–judgment.
6416. פְּלִילִי *pel-ee-lee';* from 6414; *judicial:*–judge.
6417. פְּלִילִיָּה *pel-ee-lee-yaw';* fem. of 6416; *judicature:*–judgment.
6418. פֶּלֶךְ *peh'-lek;* from an un. root mean. to *be round;* a *circuit* (i.e. *district*); also a *spindle* (as *whirled*); hence, a *crutch:*–(di-) staff, part.
6419. פָּלַל *paw-lal';* a prim. root; to *judge* (officially or ment.); by ext., to *intercede, pray:*–intreat, judge(-ment), (make) pray(-er, -ing), make supplication.
6420. פָּלָל *paw-lawl';* from 6419; *judge; Palal,* an Isr.:–Palal.
6421. פְּלַלְיָה *pel-al-yaw';* from 6419 and 3050; *Jah has judged; Pelaljah,* an Isr.:–Pelaliah.
6422. פַּלְמוֹנִי *pal-mo-nee';* prob. for 6423; a *certain* one, i.e. so-and-so:–certain.
6423. פְּלֹנִי *pel-o-nee';* from 6395; *such* a *one,* i.e. a specified *person:*–such.
6424. פָּלַס *paw-las';* a prim. root; prop. to *roll* flat, i.e. *prepare* (a road); also to *revolve,* i.e. *weigh* (ment.):–make, ponder, weigh.
6425. פֶּלֶס *peh'-les;* from 6424; a *balance:*–scales, weight.
6426. פָּלַץ *paw-lats';* a prim. root; prop. perh. to *rend,* i.e. (by impl.) to *quiver:*–tremble.
6427. פַּלָּצוּת *pal-law-tsooth';* from 6426; *affright:*–fearfulness, horror, trembling.
6428. פָּלַשׁ *paw-lash';* a prim. root; to *roll* (in dust):–roll (wallow) self.
6429. פְּלֶשֶׁת *pel-eh'-sheth;* from 6428; *rolling,* i.e. *migratory; Pelesheth,* a region of Syria:–Palestina, Pal., Philistia, Philistines.
6430. פְּלִשְׁתִּי *pel-ish-tee';* patrial from 6429; a *Pelishtite* or inh. of Pelesheth:–Philistine.
6431. פֶּלֶת *peh'-leth;* from an un. root mean. to *flee; swiftness; Peleth,* the name of two Isr.:–Peleth.
6432. פְּלֵתִי, *pel-ay-thee';* from the same form as 6431; a *courier* (coll.) or official *messenger:*–Pelethites.
6433. פֻּם *poom* (Chald.); prob. for 6310; the *mouth* (lit. or fig.):–mouth.
6434. פֵּן *pane;* from an un. root mean. to *turn;* an *angle* (of a street or wall):–corner.
6435. פֵּן *pane;* from 6437; prop. *removal;* used only (in the const.) adv. as conj., *lest:*–(lest) (peradventure), that...not.
6436. פַּנַּג *pan-nag';* of unc. der.; prob. *pastry:*–Pannag.
6437. פָּנָה *paw-naw';* a prim. root; to *turn;* by impl., to *face,* i.e. *appear, look,* etc.:–appear, at [even-]tide, behold, cast out, come on, X corner, dawning, empty, go away, lie, look, mark, pass away, prepare, regard, (have) respect (to), (re-)turn (aside, away, back, face, self), X right [early].
6438. פִּנָּה *pin-naw';* fem. of 6434; an *angle;* by impl., a *pinnacle;* fig., a *chieftain:*–bulwark, chief, corner, stay, tower.
6439. פְּנוּאֵל *pen-oo-ale';* or (more prop.) פְּנִיאֵל *pen-ee-ale';* from 6437 and 410; *face of God; Penuël* or *Peniël,* a place E. of Jordan; also (as Penuel) the name of two Isr.:–Peniel, Penuel.
6440. פָּנִים *paw-neem';* pl. (but always as sing.) of an un. noun [פָּנֶה *paw-neh';* from 6437]; the *face* (as the part that *turns*); used in a great variety of appl. (lit. and fig.); also (with prep. pref.) as a prep. (*before,* etc.):–+ accept, a-(be-)fore(-time), against, anger, X as (long as), at, + battle, + because (of), + beseech, countenance, edge, + employ, endure, + enquire, face, favour, fear of, for, forefront(-part), form(-er time, -ward), from, front, heaviness, X him(-self), + honourable, + impudent, + in, it, look[-eth] (-s), X me, + meet, X more than, mouth, of, off, (of) old (time), X on, open, + out of, over against, the partial, person, + please, presence, propect, was purposed, by reason of, + regard, right forth, + serve, X shewbread, sight, state, straight, + street, X thee, X them(-selves), through (+ -out), till, time(-s) past, (un-)to(-ward), + upon, upside (+ down), with(- in, + -stand), X ye, X you.
6441. פְּנִימָה *pen-ee'-maw;* from 6440 with directive enclitic; *faceward,* i.e. *indoors:*–(with-)in(-ner part, -ward).
6442. פְּנִימִי *pen-ee-mee';* from 6440; *interior:*–(with-)in(-ner, -ward).
6443. פָּנִין *paw-neen';* or פָּנִי *paw-nee';* from the same as 6434; prob. a *pearl* (as *round*):–ruby.
6444. פְּנִנָּה *pen-in-naw';* prob. fem. from 6443 contr.; *Peninnah,* an Isr.s:–Peninnah.
6445. פָּנַק *paw-nak';* a prim. root; to *enervate:*–bring up.
6446. פַּס *pas;* from 6461; prop. the *palm* (of the hand) or *sole* (of the foot) [comp. 6447]; by impl. (pl.) a *long and sleeved* tunic (perh. simply a *wide* one; from the or. sense of the root, i.e. of *many breadths*):–(divers) colours.
6447. פַּס *pas* (Chald.); from a root cor. to 6461; the *palm* (of the hand, as being *spread* out):–part.
6448. פָּסַג *paw-sag';* a prim. root; to *cut up,* i.e. (fig.) *contemplate:*–consider.
6449. פִּסְגָּה *pis-gaw';* from 6448; a *cleft; Pisgah,* a mt. E. of Jordan:–Pisgah.
6450. פַּס דַּמִּים *pas dam-meem';* from 6446 and the pl. of 1818; *palm* (i.e. *dell*) *of bloodshed; Pas-Dammim,* a place in Pal.:–Pas-dammim. Comp. 658.
6451. פִּסָּה *pis-saw';* from 6461; *expansion,* i.e. *abundance:*–handful.
6452. פָּסַח *paw-sakh';* a prim. root; to *hop,* i.e. (fig.) *skip* over (or *spare*); by impl., to *hesitate;* also (lit.) to *limp,* to *dance:*–halt, become lame, leap, pass over.
6453. פֶּסַח *peh'-sakh;* from 6452; a *pretermission,* i.e. *exemption;* used only techically of the Jewish *Passover* (the festival or the victim):–passover (offering).
6454. פָּסֵחַ *paw-say'-akh;* from 6452; *limping; Paseäch,* the name of two Isr.:–Paseah, Phaseah.
6455. פִּסֵּחַ *pis-say'-akh;* from 6452; *lame:*–lame.
6456. פְּסִיל *pes-eel';* from 6458; an *idol:*–carved (graven) image, quarry.
6457. פָּסַךְ *paw-sak';* from an un. root mean. to *divide; divider; Pasak,* an Isr.:–Pasach.
6458. פָּסַל *paw-sal';* a prim. root; to *carve,* whether wood or stone:–grave, hew.
6459. פֶּסֶל *peh'-sel;* from 6458; an *idol:*–carved (graven) image.
6460. פְּסַנְטֵרִין *pes-an-tay-reen'* (Chald.); or פְּסַנְתֵּרִין *pes-an-tay-reen';* a transliteration of the Gr. *ψαλτήριον psaltēriŏn;* a *lyre:*–psaltery.
6461. פָּסַס *paw-sas';* a prim. root; prob. to *disperse,* i.e. (intr.) *disappear:*–cease.
6462. פִּסְפָּה *pis-paw';* perh. from 6461; *dispersion; Pispah,* an Isr.:–Pispah.
6463. פָּעָה *paw-aw';* a prim. root; to *scream:*–cry.
6464. פָּעוּ *paw-oo';* or פָּעִי *paw-ee';* from 6463; *screaming; Paü* or *Paï,* a place in Edom:–Pai, Pau.
6465. פְּעוֹר *peh-ore';* from 6473; a *gap;* Peör, a mountain E. of Jordan; also (for 1187) a deity worshipped there:–Peor. See also 1047.
6466. פָּעַל *paw-al';* a prim. root; to *do* or *make* (systematically and habitually), esp. to *practise:*–commit, [evil-] do(-er), make(-r), ordain, work(-er).
6467. פֹּעַל *po'-al;* from 6466; an *act* or *work* (concr.):–act, deed, do, getting, maker, work.
6468. פְּעֻלָּה *peh-ool-law';* fem. pass.part. of 6466; (abstr.) *work:*–labour, reward, wages, work.
6469. פְּעֻלְּתַי *peh-ool-leh-thah'-ee;* from 6468; *laborious; Peüllethai,* an Isr.:–Peulthai.
6470. פָּעַם *paw-am';* a prim. root; to *tap,* i.e. beat regularly; hence (gen.) to *impel* or *agitate:*–move, trouble.

6471. פַּעַם *pah'-am;* or (fem.) פַּעֲמָה *pah-am-aw';* from 6470; a *stroke,* lit. or fig. (in various appl., as follows):–anvil, corner, foot(-step), going, [hundred-]fold, X now, (this) + once, order, rank, step, + thrice, ([often-]), second, this, two) time(-s), twice, wheel.
6472. פַּעֲמֹן *pah-am-one';* from 6471; a *bell* (as *struck*):–bell.
6473. פָּעַר *paw-ar';* a prim. root; to *yawn,* i.e. *open* wide (lit. or fig.):–gape, open (wide).
6474. פַּעֲרַי *pah-ar-ah'-ee;* from 6473; *yawning; Paarai,* an Isr.:–Paarai.
6475. פָּצָה *paw-tsaw';* a prim. root; to *rend,* i.e. *open* (esp. the mouth):–deliver, gape, open, rid, utter.
6476. פָּצַח *paw-tsakh';* a prim. root; to *break* out (in joyful sound):–break (forth, forth into joy), make a loud noise.
6477. פְּצִירָה *pets-ee-raw';* from 6484; *bluntness:*–+ file.
6478. פָּצַל *paw-tsal';* a prim. root; to *peel:*–pill.
6479. פְּצָלָה *pets-aw-law';* from 6478; a *peeling:*–strake.
6480. פָּצַם *paw-tsam';* a prim. root; to *rend* (by earthquake):–break.
6481. פָּצַע *paw-tsah';* a prim. root; to *split,* i.e. *wound:*–wound.
6482. פֶּצַע *peh'-tsah;* from 6481; a *wound:*– wound(-ing).
6483. פִּצֵּץ *pits-tsates';* from an un. root mean. to *dissever; dispersive; Pitstsets,* a priest:–Apses (*incl. the art.*).
6484. פָּצַר *paw-tsar';* prim. root; to *peck* at, i.e.(fig.) *stun* or *dull:*–press, urge, stubbornness.
6485. פָּקַד *paw-kad';* a prim. root; to visit (with friendly or hostile intent); by anal., to *oversee, muster, charge, care for, miss, deposit,* etc.:– appoint, X at all, avenge, bestow, (appoint to have the, give a) charge, commit, count, deliver to keep, be empty, enjoin, go see, hurt, do judgment, lack, lay up, look, make, X by any means, miss, number, officer, (make) overseer, have (the) oversight, punish, reckon, (call to) remember (-brance), set (over), sum, X surely, visit, want.
6486. פְּקֻדָּה *pek-ood-daw';* fem. pass.part. of 6485; *visitation* (in many senses, chiefly official):–account, (that have the) charge, custody, that which... laid up, numbers, office(-r), ordering, oversight, + prison, reckoning, visitation.
6487. פִּקָּדוֹן *pik-kaw-done';* from 6485; a *deposit:*–that which was delivered (to keep), store.
6488. פְּקִדֻת *pek-ee-dooth';* from 6496; *supervision:*–ward.
6489. פְּקוֹד *pek-ode';* from 6485; *punishment; Pekod,* a symb. name for Bab.:–Pekod.
6490. פִּקּוּד *pik-kood';* or פִּקֻּד *pik-kood';* from 6485; prop. *appointed,* i.e. a *mandate* (of God; pl. only, coll., for the *Law*):– commandment, precept, statute.
6491. פָּקַח *paw-kakh';* a prim. root; to *open* (the senses, esp. the eyes); fig., to *be observant:*–open.
6492. פֶּקַח *peh'-kakh;* from 6491; *watch; Pekach,* an Isr. king:–Pekah.
6493. פִּקֵּחַ *peh'-kakh;* from 6491; *watch; Pekach,* an Isr. king:–Pekah.
6494. פְּקַחְיָה *pek-akh-yaw';* from 6491 and 3050; *Jah has observed; Pekachjah,* an Isr. king:–Pekahiah.
6495. פְּקַח־קוֹחַ *pek-akh-ko'-akh;* from 6491 redoubled; *opening* (of a dungeon), i.e. *jail-delivery* (fig., *salvation* for sin):–opening of the prison.
6496. פָּקִיד *paw-keed';* from 6485; a *superintendent* (civil, military or relig.):–which had the charge, governor, office, overseer, [that] was set.
6497. פֶּקַע *peh'-kah;* from an un. root mean. to *burst;* only used as an arch. term of an ornament similar to 6498, a *semi-globe:*–knop.
6498. פַּקֻּעָה *pak-koo-aw';* from the same as 6497; the *wild cucumber* (from *splitting* open to shed its seeds):–gourd.
6499. פַּר *par;* or פָּר *pawr;* from 6565; a *bullock* (app. as *breaking* forth in wild strength, or perh. as *dividing* the hoof):–(+ young) bull(-ock), calf, ox.
6500. פָּרָא *paw-raw';* a prim. root; to *bear fruit:*–be fruitful.
6501. פֶּרֶא *peh'-reh;* or (Jeremiah 2:24) פֶּרֶה *peh'-reh;* from 6500 in the sec. sense of *running* wild; the *onager:*–wild (ass).
6502. פִּרְאָם *pir-awm';* from 6501; *wildly; Piram,* a Canaanite:–Piram.
6503. פַּרְבָּר *par-bawr';* or פַּרְוָר *par-vawr';* of for. or.; *Parbar* or *Parvar,* a quarter of Jerus.:–Parbar, suburb.
6504. פָּרַד *paw-rad';* a prim. root; to *break* through, i.e. *spread* or *separate* (oneself):– disperse, divide, be out of joint, part, scatter (abroad), separate (self), sever self, stretch, sunder.
6505. פֶּרֶד *peh'-red;* from 6504; a *mule* (perh. from his *lonely* habits):–mule.
6506. פִּרְדָּה *pir-daw';* fem. of 6505; a *she-mule:*–mule.
6507. פְּרֻדָה *per-oo-daw';* fem. pass.part. of 6504; something *separated,* i.e. a *kernel:*–seed.
6508. פַּרְדֵּס *par-dace';* of for. or.; a *park:*– forest, orchard.
6509. פָּרָה *paw-raw';* a prim. root; to *bear fruit* (lit. or fig.):–bear, bring forth (fruit), (be, cause to be, make) fruitful, grow, increase.
6510. פָּרָה *paw-raw';* fem. of 6499; a *heifer:*–cow, heifer, kine.
6511. פָּרָה *paw-raw';* the same as 6510; *Parah,* a place in Pal.:–Parah.
6512. פֵּרָה *pay-raw';* from 6331; a *hole* (as *broken,* i.e. dug):–+ mole. Comp. 2661.
6513. פֻּרָה *poo-raw';* for 6288; *foliage; Purah,* an Isr.:–Phurah.
6514. פְּרוּדָא *per-oo-daw';* or פְּרִידָא *per-ee-daw';* from 6504; *dispersion; Peruda* or *Perida,* one of "Solomon's servants":–Perida, Peruda.
6515. פָּרוּחַ *paw-roo'-akh;* pass.part. of 6524; *blossomed; Paruäch,* an Isr.:–Paruah.
6516. פַּרְוַיִם *par-vah'-yim;* of for. or.; *Parvajim,* an Oriental region:–Parvaim.
6517. פָּרוּר *paw-roor';* pass.part. of 6565 in the sense of *spreading* out [comp. 6524]; a *skillet* (as *flat* or *deep*):–pan, pot.
6518. פָּרָז *paw-rawz';* from an un. root mean. to *separate,* i.e. *decide;* a *chieftain:*–village.
6519. פְּרָזָה *per-aw-zaw';* from the same as 6518; an *open* country:–(unwalled) town (without walls), unwalled village.
6520. פְּרָזוֹן *per-aw-zone';* from the same as 6518; *magistracy,* i.e. *leadership* (also concr., *chieftains*):–village.
6521. פְּרָזִי *per-aw-zee';* or פְּרוֹזִי *per-o-zee';* from 6519; a *rustic:*–village.
6522. פְּרִזִּי *per-iz-zee';* for 6521; inh. *of the open country;* a *Perizzite,* one of the Canaanitish tribes:–Perizzite.
6523. פַּרְזֶל *par-zel'* (Chald.); cor. to 1270; *iron:*–iron.
6524. פָּרַח *paw-rakh';* a prim. root; to *break* forth as a bud, i.e. *bloom;* gen., to *spread;* spec., to *fly* (as extending the wings); fig., to *flourish:*–X abroad, X abundantly, blossom, break f\orth (out), bud, flourish, make fly, grow, spread, spring (up).
6525. פֶּרַח *peh'-rakh;* from 6524; a *calyx* (nat. or artif.); gen., *bloom:*–blossom, bud, flower.
6526. פִּרְחַח *pir-khakh';* from 6524; *progeny,* i.e. a *brood:*–youth.
6527. פָּרַט *paw-rat';* a prim. root; to *scatter* words, i.e. *prate* (or *hum*):–chant.
6528. פֶּרֶט *peh'-ret;* from 6527; a *stray* or *single* berry:–grape.
6529. פְּרִי *per-ee';* from 6509; *fruit* (lit. or fig.):–bough, ([first-]) fruit([-ful), reward.
6530. פְּרִיץ *per-eets';* from 6555; *violent,* i.e. a *tyrant:*–destroyer, ravenous, robber.
6531. פֶּרֶךְ *peh'-rek;* from an un. root mean. to *break* apart; *fracture,* i.e. *severity:*–cruelty, rigour.
6532. פֹּרֶכֶת *po-reh'-keth;* fem. act.part. of the same as 6531; a *separatrix,* i.e. (the sacred) *screen:*–vail.
6533. פָּרַם *paw-ram';* a prim. root; to *tear:*–rend.
6534. פַּרְמַשְׁתָּא *par-mash-taw';* of Pers. or.; *Parmashta,* a son of Haman:–Parmasta.
6535. פַּרְנַךְ *par-nak';* of unc. der.; *Parnak,* an Isr.:–Parnach.
6536. פָּרַס *paw-ras';* a prim. root; to *break* in pieces, i.e. (usually without violence) to *split, distribute:*–deal, divide, have hoofs, part, tear.
6537. פְּרַס *per-as'* (Chald.); cor. to 6536; to *split* up:–divide, [U-] pharsin.
6538. פֶּרֶס *peh'-res;* from 6536; a *claw;* also a kind of *eagle:*–claw, ossifrage.
6539. פָּרַס *paw-ras';* of for. or.; *Paras* (i.e. *Pers.*), an E. country, incl. its inh.:–Pers., Persians.
6540. פָּרַס *paw-ras'* (Chald.); cor. to 6539:– Pers., Persians.
6541. פַּרְסָה *par-saw';* fem. of 6538; a *claw* or split *hoof:*–claw, [cloven-]footed, hoof.
6542. פַּרְסִי *par-see';* patrial from 6539; a *Parsite* (i.e. *Pers.*), or inh. of Peres:–Pers..
6543. פַּרְסִי *par-see'* (Chald.); cor. to 6542:– Persian
6544. פָּרַע *paw-rah';* a prim. root; to *loosen;* by impl., to *expose, dismiss;* fig., *absolve, begin:*–avenge, avoid, bare, go back, let, (make) naked, set at nought, perish, refuse, uncover.
6545. פֶּרַע *peh'-rah;* from 6544; the *hair* (as *dishevelled*):–locks.
6546. פַּרְעָה *par-aw';* fem. of 6545 (in the sense of *beginning*); *leadership* (pl. concr., *leaders*):–+ avenging, revenge.
6547. פַּרְעֹה *par-o';* of Eg. der.; *Paroh,* a gen. title of Eg. kings:–Pharaoh.
6548. פַּרְעֹה חָפְרַע *par-o' khof-rah';* of Eg. der.; *Paroh-Chophra,* an Eg. king:–Pharaoh-hophra.
6549. פַּרְעֹה נְכֹה *par-o' nek-o';* or פַּרְעֹה נְכוֹ *par-o'nek-o';* of Eg. der.; Paroh-Nekoh (or -Neko), an Eg. king:–Pharaoh-necho, Pharaoh-nechoh.
6550. פַּרְעֹשׁ *par-oshe';* prob. from 6544 and 6211; a *flea* (as the *isolated insect*):–flea.
6551. פַּרְעֹשׁ *par-oshe';* the same as 6550; *Parosh,* the name of our Isr.:–Parosh, Pharosh.
6552. פִּרְעָתוֹן *pir-aw-thone';* from 6546; *chieftaincy; Pirathon,* a place in Pal.:–Pirathon.
6553. פִּרְעָתוֹנִי *pir-aw-tho-nee';* or פִּרְעָתֹנִי *pir-aw-tho-nee';* patrial from 6552; a *Pirathonite* or inh. of Pirathon:–Pirathonite.
6554. פַּרְפַּר *par-par';* prob. from 6565 in the

HEBREW

sense of *rushing; rapid; Parpar,* a river of Syria:–Pharpar.

6555. פָּרַץ *paw-rats';* a prim. root; to *break* out (in many appl., direct and indirect, lit. and fig.):–X abroad, (make a) breach, break (away, down, -er, forth, in, up), burst out, come (spread) abroad, compel, disperse, grow, increase, open, press, scatter, urge.

6556. פֶּרֶץ *peh'-rets;* from 6555; a *break* (lit. or fig.):–breach, breaking forth (in), X forth, gap.

6557. פֶּרֶץ *peh'-rets;* the same as 6556; Perets, the name of two Isr.:–Perez, Pharez.

6558. פַּרְצִי *par-tsee';* patron. from 6557; a *Partsite* (coll.) or desc. of Perets:–Pharzites.

6559. פְּרָצִים *per-aw-tseem';* pl. of 6556; *breaks;* Peratsim, a mountain in Pal.:–Perazim.

6560. פֶּרֶץ עֻזָּא *peh'-rets ooz-zaw';* from 6556 and 5798; *break of Uzza; Perets-Uzza,* a place in Pal.:–Perez-uzza.

6561. פָּרַק *paw-rak';* a prim. root; to *break* off or *crunch;* fig., to *deliver:*–break (off), deliver, redeem, rend (in pieces), tear in pieces.

6562. פְּרַק *per-ak'* (Chald.); cor. to 6561; to *discontinue:*–break off.

6563. פֶּרֶק *peh'-rek;* from 6561; *rapine;* also a *fork* (in roads):–crossway, robbery.

6564. פָּרָק *paw-rawk';* from 6561; *soup* (as full of *crumbed* meat):–broth. See also 4832.

6565. פָּרַר *paw-rar';* a prim. root; to *break* up (usually fig., i.e. to *violate, frustrate:*–X any ways, break (asunder), cast off, cause to cease, X clean, defeat, disannul, disappoint, dissolve, divide, make of none effect, fail, frustrate, bring (come) to nought, X utterly, make void.

6566. פָּרַשׂ *paw-ras';* a prim. root; to *break* apart, *disperse,* etc.:–break, chop in pieces, lay open, scatter, spread (abroad, forth, selves, out), stretch (forth, out).

6567. פָּרַשׁ *paw-rash';* a prim. root; to *separate,* lit. (to *disperse*) or fig. (to *specify*); also (by impl.) to *wound:*–scatter, declare, distinctly, shew, sting.

6568. פְּרַשׁ *per-ash'* (Chald.); cor. to 6567; to *specify:*–distinctly.

6569. פֶּרֶשׁ *peh'-resh;* from 6567; *excrement* (as *eliminated*):–dung.

6570. פֶּרֶשׁ *peh'-resh;* the same as 6569; *Peresh,* an Isr.:–Peresh.

6571. פָּרָשׁ *paw-rawsh';* from 6567; a *steed* (as *stretched* out to a vehicle, not single nor for mounting [comp. 5483]); also (by impl.) a *driver* (in a chariot), i.e. (coll.) cavalry:–horseman.

6572. פַּרְשֶׁגֶן *par-sheh'-ghen; or* פַּתְשֶׁגֶן *path-sheh'-gen;* of for. or.; a *transcript:*–copy.

6573. פַּרְשֶׁגֶן *par-sheh'-ghen* (Chald.); cor. to 6572:–copy.

6574. פַּרְשְׁדֹן *par-shed-one';* perh. by compounding 6567 and 6504 (in the sense of *straddling*) [comp. 6576]; the *crotch* (or *anus*):–dirt.

6575. פָּרָשָׁה *paw-raw-shaw';* from 6567; *exposition* :–declaration, sum.

6576. פַּרְשֵׁז *par-shaze';* a root app. formed by compounding 6567 and that of 6518 [comp. 6574]; to *expand:*–spread.

6577. פַּרְשַׁנְדָּתָא *par-shan-daw-thaw';* of Pers. or.; *Parshandatha,* a son of Haman:–Parshandatha.

6578. פְּרָת *per-awth';* from an un. root mean. to *break* forth; *rushing; Perath* (i.e. *Euphrates*), a river of the E.:–Euphrates.

6579. פַּרְתַּם *par-tam';* of Pers. or.; a *grandee:*–(most) noble, prince.

6580. פַּשׁ *pash;* prob. from an un. root mean. to *disintegrate; stupidity* (as a result of *grossness* or of *degeneracy*):–extremity.

6581. פָּשָׂה *paw-saw';* a prim. root; to *spread:*–spread.

6582. פָּשַׁח *paw-shakh';* a prim. root; to *tear* in pieces:–pull in pieces.

6583. פַּשְׁחוּר *pash-khoor';* prob. from 6582; *liberation; Pashchur,* the name of four Isr.:–Pashur.

6584. פָּשַׁט *paw-shat';* a prim. root; to *spread* out (i.e. *deploy* in hostile array); by anal., to *strip* (i.e. *unclothe, plunder, flay,* etc.):–fall upon, flay, invade, make an invasion, pull off, put off, make a road, run upon, rush, set, spoil, spread selves (abroad), strip (off, self).

6585. פָּשַׂע *paw-sah';* a prim. root; to *stride* (from *spreading* the legs), i.e. *rush* upon:–go.

6586. פָּשַׁע *paw-shah';* a prim. root [rather ident. with 6585 through the idea of *expansion*]; to *break* away (from just authority), i.e. *trespass, apostatize, quarrel:*–offend, rebel, revolt, transgress(-ion, -or).

6587. פֶּשַׂע *peh'-sah;* from 6585; a *stride:*–step.

6588. פֶּשַׁע *peh'-shah;* from 6586; a *revolt* (national, mor. or relig.):–rebellion, sin, transgression, trespass.

6589. פָּשַׂק *paw-sak;* a prim. root; to *dispart* (the feet or lips), i.e. *become licentious:*–open (wide).

6590. פְּשַׁר pesh-ar' (Chald.); cor. to 6622; to *interpret:*–make [interpretations], interpreting.

6591. פְּשַׁר *pesh-ar'* (Chald.); from 6590; an *interpretation:*–interpretation.

6592. פֵּשֶׁר *pay'-sher;* cor. to 6591:–interpretation.

6593. פִּשְׁתֶּה *pish-teh';* from the same as 6580 as in the sense of *comminuting; linen* (i.e. the thread, as *carded*):–flax, linen.

6594. פִּשְׁתָּה *pish-taw';* fem. of 6593; *flax;* by impl., a *wick:*–flax, tow.

6595. פַּת *path;* from 6626; a *bit:*–meat, morsel, piece.

6596. פֹּת *pohth;* or (Eze. 13:19) פֹּתָה *po-thaw';* from an un. root mean. to *open;* a *hole,* i.e. *hinge* or the female *pudenda:*–hinge, secret part.

6597. פִּתְאוֹם *pith-ome';* or פִּתְאֹם *pith-ome';* from 6621; *instantly:*–straightway, sudden(-ly).

6598. פַּתְבַּג *pathbag';* of Pers. or.; a *dainty:*–portion (provision) of meat.

6599. פִּתְגָּם *pith-gawm';* of Pers. or.; a (judicial) *sentence:*–decree, sentence.

6600. פִּתְגָּם *pith-gawm';* (Chald.) cor. to 6599; a *word, answer, letter* or *decree:*–answer, letter, matter, word.

6601. פָּתָה *paw-thaw';* a prim. root; to *open,* i.e. *be* (caus., *make*) *roomy;* usually fig. (in a ment. or mor. sense) to *be* (caus., *make*) *simple* or (in a sinister way) *delude:*–allure, deceive, enlarge, entice, flatter, persuade, silly (one).

6602. פְּתוּאֵל *peth-oo-ale';* from 6601 and 410; *enlarged of God; Pethuël,* an Isr.:–Pethuel.

6603. פִּתּוּחַ *pit-too'-akh;* or פִּתֻּחַ *pit-too'-akh;* pass.part. of 6605; *sculpture* (in low or high relief or even intaglio):–carved (work) (are, en-)grave(-ing, -n).

6604. פְּתוֹר *peth-ore';* of for. or.; *Pethor,* a place in Mesopotamia:–Pethor.

6605. פָּתַח *paw-thakh';* a prim. root; to *open* wide (lit. or fig.); spec., to *loosen, begin, plough, carve:*–appear, break forth, draw (out), let go free, (en-)grave(-n), loose (self), (be, be set) open(-ing), put off, ungird, unstop, have vent.

6606. פְּתַח *peth-akh'* (Chald.); cor. to 6605; to *open:*–open.

6607. פֶּתַח *peh'-thakh;* from 6605; an *opening* (lit.), i.e. *door* (*gate*) or *entrance* way:–door, entering (in), entrance (-ry), gate, opening, place.

6608. פֵּתַח *pay'-thakh;* from 6605; *opening* (fig.) i.e. *disclosure:*–entrance.

6609. פְּתִחָה *peth-ee-khaw';* from 6605; something *opened,* i.e. a *drawn* sword:–drawn sword.

6610. פִּתְחוֹן *pith-khone';* from 6605; *opening* (the act):–open(-ing).

6611. פְּתַחְיָה *peth-akh-yaw';* from 6605 and 3050; *Jah has opened; Pethachjah,* the name of four Isr.:–Pethakiah.

6612. פְּתִי *peth-ee';* or פֶּתִי *peh'-thee;* or פְּתָאִי *peth-aw-ee';* from 6601; *silly* (i.e. *seducible*):–foolish, simple(-icity, one).

6613. פְּתַי *peth-ah'-ee* (Chald.); from a root cor. to 6601; *open,* i.e. (as noun) *width:*–breadth.

6614. פְּתִיגִיל *peth-eeg-eel';* of unc. der.; prob. a figured *mantle* for holidays:–stomacher.

6615. פְּתַיּוּת *peth-ah-yooth';* from 6612; *silliness* (i.e. *seducibility*):–simple.

6616. פָּתִיל *paw-theel';* from 6617; *twine:*–bound, bracelet, lace, line, ribband, thread, wire.

6617. פָּתַל *paw-thal';* a prim. root; to *twine,* i.e. (lit.) to *struggle* or (fig.) *be* (mor.) *tortuous:*–(shew self) froward, shew self unsavoury, wrestle.

6618. פְּתַלְתֹּל *peth-al-tole';* from 6617; *tortuous* (i.e. crafty):–crooked.

6619. פִּתֹם *pee-thome';* of Eg. der.; *Pithom,* a place in Eg.:–Pithom.

6620. פֶּתֶן *peh'-then;* from an un. root mean. to *twist;* an *asp* (from its *contortions*):–adder.

6621. פֶּתַע *peh'-thah;* from an un. root mean. to *open* (the eyes); a *wink,* i.e. *moment* [comp. 6597] (used only [with or without prep.] adv., *quickly* or *unexpectedly*):–at an instant, suddenly, X very.

6622. פָּתַר *paw-thar';* a prim. root; to *open* up, i.e. (fig.) *interpret* (a dream):–interpret(-ation, -er).

6623. פִּתְרוֹן *pith-rone';* or פִּתְרֹן *pith-rone';* from 6622; *interpretation* (of a dream):–interpretation.

6624. פַּתְרוֹס *path-roce';* of Eg. der.; *Pathros,* a part of Eg.:–Pathros.

6625. פַּתְרֻסִי *path-roo-see';* patrial from 6624; a *Pathrusite,* or inh. of Pathros:–Pathrusim.

6626. פָּתַת *paw-thath';* a prim. root; to *open,* i.e. *break:*–part.

צ

6627. צָאָה *tsaw-aw';* from 3318; *issue,* i.e. (human) *excrement:*–that (which) cometh from (out).

6628. צֶאֱל *tseh'-el;* from an un. root mean. to be *slender;* the *lotus* tree:–shady tree.

6629. צֹאן *tsone* or (Psalm 144:13) *tseh-one';* from an un. root mean. to *migrate;* a coll. name for a *flock* (of sheep or goats); also fig. (of men):–(small) cattle, flock (+ -s), lamb (+ -s), sheep([-cote, -fold, -shearer, -herds]).

6630. צַאֲנָן *tsah-an-awn';* from the same as 6629 used denom.; *sheep* pasture; *Zaanan,* a place in Pal.:–Zaanan.

6631. צֶאֱצָא *tseh-ets-aw';* from 3318; *issue,* i.e. *produce, children:*–that which cometh forth (out), offspring.

6632. צָב *tsawb;* from an un. root mean. to *establish;* a *palanquin* or *canopy* (as a *fixture*); also a species of *lizard* (prob. as clinging *fast*):–covered, litter, tortoise.

6633. צָבָא *tsaw-baw';* a prim. root; to *mass* (an army or servants):–assemble, fight,

perform, muster, wait upon, war.
6634. צְבָא *tseb-aw'* (Chald.); cor. to 6623 in the fig. sense of *summoning* one's wishes; to *please:*–will, would.
6635. צָבָא *tsaw-baw';* or (fem.) צְבָאָה *tseb-aw-aw';* from 6633; a *mass* of persons (or fig., things), esp. reg. organized for war (an *army*); by impl., a *campaign,* lit. or fig. (spec., *hardship, worship*):–appointed time, (+) army, (+) battle, company, host, service, soldiers, waiting upon, war(-fare).
6636. צְבֹאִים *tseb-o-eem';* or (more correctly) צְבִיִּים *tseb-ee-yeem';* or צְבִיִם *tseb-ee-yeem';* pl. of 6643; *gazelles; Tseboïm* or *Tsebijim,* a place in Pal.:–Zeboiim, Zeboim.
6637. צֹבֵבָה *tso-bay-baw';* fem. act.part. of the same as 6632; the *canopier* (with the art.); *Tsobebah,* an Isr.s:–Zobebah.
6638. צָבָה *tsaw-baw';* a prim. root; to *amass,* i.e. *grow turgid;* spec., to *array* an army against:–fight swell.
6639. צָבֶה *tsaw-beh';* from 6638; *turgid:*–swell.
6640. צְבוּ *tseb-oo'* (Chald.); from 6634; prop. *will;* concr., an *affair* (as a matter of *determination*):–purpose.
6641. צָבוּעַ *tsaw-boo'-ah;* pass.part. of the same as 6648; *dyed* (in stripes), i.e. the *hyena:*–speckled.
6642. צָבַט *tsaw-bat';* a prim. root; to *grasp,* i.e. *hand* out:–reach.
6643. צְבִי *tseb-ee';* from 6638 in the sense of *prominence; splendor* (as *conspicuous*); also a *gazelle* (as *beautiful*):–beautiful(-ty), glorious (-ry), goodly, pleasant, roe(-buck).
6644. צִבְיָא *tsib-yaw';* for 6645; *Tsibja,* an Isr.:–Zibia.
6645 צִבְיָה *tsib-yaw'* for 6646; *Tsibjah,* an Isr.s:–Zibiah.
6646. צְבִיָּה *tseb-ee-yaw';* fem. of 6643; a *female* gazelle:–roe.
6647. צְבַע *tseb-ah'* (Chald.); a root cor. to that of 6648; to *dip:*–wet.
6648. צֶבַע *tseh'-bah;* from an un. root mean. to *dip* (into coloring fluid); a *dye:*–divers, colours.
6649. צִבְעוֹן *tsib-one';* from the same as 6648; *variegated; Tsibon,* an Idumaean:–Zibeon.
6650. צְבֹעִים *tseb-o-eem';* pl. of 6641; *hyenas; Tseboïm,* a place in Pal.:–Zeboim.
6651. צָבַר *tsaw-bar';* a prim. root; to *aggregate:*–gather (together), heap (up), lay up.
6652. צִבֻּר *tsib-boor';* from 6551; a *pile:*–heap.
6653. צֶבֶת *tseh'-beth;* from an un. root app. mean. to *grip;* a *lock* of stalks:–handful.
6654. צַד *tsad;* contr.. from an un. root mean. to *sidle* off; a *side;* fig., an *adversary:*–(be-)side.
6655. צַד *tsad* (Chald.); cor. to 6654; used adv. (with prep.) at or upon the *side* of:–against, concerning.
6656 צְדָא *tsed-aw'* (Chald.); from an un. root cor. to 6658 in the sense of *intentness;* a (sinister) design:–true.
6657. צְדָד *tsed-awd';* from the same as 6654; a *siding; Tsedad,* a place near Pal.:–Zedad.
6658. צָדָה *tsaw-daw';* a prim. root; to *chase;* by impl., to *desolate:*–destroy, hunt, lie in wait.
6659. צָדוֹק *tsaw-doke';* from 6663; *just; Tsadok,* the name of eight or nine Isr.:–Zadok.
6660. צְדִיָּה *tsed-ee-yaw';* from 6658; *design* [comp. 6656]:–lying in wait.
6661. צִדִּים *tsid-deem';* pl. of 6654; *sides; Tsiddim* (with the art.), a place in Pal.:–Ziddim.
6662. צַדִּיק *tsad-deek';* from 6663; *just:*–just, lawful, righteous (man).
6663. צָדַק *tsaw-dak';* a prim. root; to *be* (caus., *make*) *right* (in a mor. or forensic sense):–cleanse, clear self, (be, do) just(-ice, -ify, -ify self), (be turn to) righteous(-ness).
6664. צֶדֶק *tseh'-dek;* from 6663; the *right* (nat., mor. or legal); also (abstr.) *equity* or (fig.) *prosperity:*–X even, (X that which is altogether) just(-ice), ([un-])right(-eous) (cause, -ly, - ness).
6665. צִדְקָה *tsid-kaw'* (Chald.); cor. to 6666; *beneficence:*– righteousness.
6666. צְדָקָה *tsed-aw-kaw';* from 6663; *rightness* (abstr.), subj. (*rectitude*), obj. (*justice*), mor. (*virtue*) or fig. (*prosperity*):–justice, moderately, right(-eous) (act, -ly, -ness).
6667. צִדְקִיָּה *tsid-kee-yaw';* or צִדְקִיָּהוּ *tsid-kee-yaw'-hoo;* from 6664 and 3050; *right of Jah; Tsidkijah,* the name of six Isr.:–Zedekiah, Zidkijah.
6668. צָהַב *tsaw-hab';* a prim. root; to *glitter,* i.e. *be golden* in color:–X fine.
6669. צָהֹב *tsaw-obe';* from 6668; *golden* in color:–yellow.
6670. צָהַל *tsaw-hal';* a prim root; to *gleam,* i.e. (fig.) *be cheerful;* by transf. to *sound* clear (of various animal or human expressions):–bellow, cry aloud (out), lift up, neigh, rejoice, make to shine, shout.
6671. צָהַר *tsaw-har';* a prim. root; to *glisten;* used only as denom. from 3323, to *press* out *oil:*–make oil.
6672. צֹהַר *tso'-har;* from 6671; a *light* (i.e. *window*): dual *double light,* i.e. *noon:*–midday, noon(-day, -tide), window.
6673. צַו *tsav;* or צָו *tsawv;* from 6680; an *injunction:*–commandment, precept.
6674. צוֹא *tso;* or צֹא *tso;* from an un. root mean. to *issue; soiled* (as if *excrementitious*):–filthy.
6675. צוֹאָה *tso-aw';* or צֹאָה *tso-aw':* fem. of 6674; *excrement;* gen., *dirt;* fig., *pollution:*–dung, filth(-iness).
6676. צַוַּאר *tsav-var'* (Chald.); cor. to 6677:–neck.
6677. צַוָּאר *tsav-vawr';* or (Nehemiah 3:5) צַוָּר *tsav-vawr';* or (Song. 4:9) צַוְּרֹן *tsav-vaw-rone';* צַוָּארָה or (fem.) (Micah 2:3) *tsav-vaw-raw';* intens. from 6696 in the sense of *binding;* the back of the *neck* (as that on which burdens are *bound*):–neck.
6678. צוֹבָא *tso-baw';* or צוֹבָה *tso-baw';* or צֹבָה *tso-baw';* from an un. root mean. to *station;* a *station; Zoba* or *Zobah,* a region of Syria:–Zoba, Zobah.
6679. צוּד *tsood;* a prim. root; to *lie* alongside (i.e. in wait); by impl., to *catch* an animal (fig., men); (denom. from 6718) to *victual* (for a journey):–chase, hunt, sore, take (provision).
6680. צָוָה *tsaw-vaw';* a prim. root; (intens.) to *constitute, enjoin:*–appoint, (for-)bid, (give a) charge, (give a, give in, send with) command (-er, -ment), send a messenger, put, (set) in order.
6681. צָוַח *tsaw-vakh';* a prim. root; to *screech* (exultingly):–shout.
6682. צְוָחָה *tsev-aw-khaw';* from 6681; a *screech* (of anguish):–cry(-ing).
6683. צוּלָה *tsoo-law';* from an un. root mean. to *sink:* an *abyss* (of the sea):–deep.
6684. צוּם *tsoom;* a prim. root; to *cover* over (the mouth), i.e. to *fast:*–X at all, fast.
6685. צוֹם *tsome;* or צֹם *tsome;* from from 6684; a *fast:*–fast(-ing).
6686. צוּעָר *tsoo-awr';* from 6819; *small; Tsuär,* an Isr.:–Zuar.
6687. צוּף *tsoof;* a prim. root; to *overflow:*–(make to over-) flow, swim.
6688. צוּף *tsoof;* from 6687; *comb* of honey (from *dripping*):–honeycomb.
6689. צוּף *tsoof;* or צוֹפַי *tso-fah'-ee;* or צִיף *tseef;* from 6688; *honey-comb; Tsuph* or *Tsophai* or *Tsiph,* the name of an Isr. and of a place in Pal.:–Zophai, Zuph.
6690. צוֹפַח *tso-fakh';* from an un. root mean. to *expand, breadth; Tsophach,* an Isr.:–Zophah.
6691. צוֹפַר *tso-far';* from 6852; *departing; Tsophar,* a friend of Job:–Zophar.
6692. צוּץ *tsoots* a prim. root; to *twinkle,* i.e. *glance;* by anal., to *blossom* (fig., *flourish*):–bloom, blossom, flourish, shew self.
6693. צוּק *tsook;* a prim. root; to *compress,* i.e. (fig.) *oppress, distress:*–constrain, distress, lie sore, (op-)press(-or), straiten.
6694. צוּק *tsook;* a prim. root [rather ident. with 6693 through the idea of *narrowness* (of orifice)]; to *pour* out, i.e. (fig.) *smelt, utter:*–be molten, pour
6695. צוֹק *tsoke;* or (fem.) צוּקָה *tsoo-kaw';* from 6693; a *strait,* i.e. (fig.) *distress:*–anguish, X troublous.
6696. צוּר *tsoor;* a prim. root; to *cramp,* i.e. *confine* (in many appl., lit. and fig., formative or hostile):–adversary, assault, beset, besiege, bind (up), cast, distress, fashion, fortify, inclose, lay siege, put up in bags.
6697. צוּר *tsoor;* or צֻר *tsoor;* from 6696; prop. a *cliff* (or sharp rock, as *compressed*); gen., a *rock* or *boulder;* fig., a *refuge;* also an *edge* (as *precipitous*):–edge, X (mighty) God (one), rock, X sharp, stone, X strength, X strong. See also 1049.
6698. צוּר *tsoor;* the same as 6697; *rock; Tsur,* the name of a Midianite and of an Isr.:–Zur.
6699. צוּרָה *tsoo-raw';* fem. of 6697; a *rock* (Job 28:10); also a *form* (as if *pressed* out):–form, rock.
6700. צוּרִיאֵל *tsoo-ree-ale';* from 6697 and 410; *rock of God; Tsuriël,* an Isr.:–Zuriel.
6701. צוּרִישַׁדַּי *tsoo-ree-shad-dah'-ee;* from 6697 and 7706; *rock of* (the) *Almighty; Tsurishaddai,* an Isr.:–Zurishaddai.
6702. צוּת *tsooth;* a prim. root; to *blaze:*–burn.
6703. צַח *tsakh;* from 6705; *dazzling,* i.e. *sunny, bright,* (fig.) *evident:*–clear, dry, plainly, white.
6704. צִחֶה *tsee-kheh';* from an un. root mean. to *glow; parched:*–dried up.
6705. צָחַח *tsaw-khakh';* a prim. root; to *glare,* i.e. be *dazzling* white:–be whiter.
6706. צְחִיחַ *tsekh-ee'-akh;* from 6705; *glaring,* i.e. *exposed* to the bright sun:–higher place, top.
6707. צְחִיחָה *tsekh-ee-khaw';* fem. of 6706; a *parched* region, i.e. the *desert:*–dry land.
6708. צְחִיחִי *tsekh-ee-khee';* from 6706; *bare* spot, i.e. in the *glaring* sun:–higher place.
6709. צַחֲנָה *tsakh-an-aw';* from an un. root mean. to *putrefy; stench:*–ill savour.
6710. צַחְצָחָה *tsakh-tsaw-khaw';* from 6705; a *dry* place, i.e. *desert:*–drought.
6711. צָחַק *tsaw-khak';* a prim. root; to *laugh* outright (in merriment or scorn); by impl., to *sport:*–laugh, mock, play, make sport.
6712. צְחֹק *tsekh-oke';* from 6711; *laughter* (in pleasure or derision):–laugh(-ed to scorn).
6713. צַחַר *tsakh'-ar;* from an un. root mean. to *dazzle; sheen,* i.e. *whiteness:*–white.

HEBREW

6714. צֹחַר *tso'-khar;* from the same as 6713; *whiteness; Tsochar,* the name of a Hittite and of an Isr.:–Zohar. Comp. 3328.
6715. צָחֹר *tsaw-khore';* from the same as 6713; *white:*–white.
6716. צִי *tsee;* from 6680; a *ship* (as a *fixture*):–ship.
6717. צִיבָא *tsee-baw';* from the same as 6678; *station; Tsiba,* an Isr.:–Ziba.
6718. צַיִד *tsah'-yid;* from a form of 6679 and mean. the same; the *chase;* also *game* (thus taken); (gen.) *lunch* (esp. for a journey):–X catcheth, food, X hunter, (that which he took in) hunting, venison, victuals.
6719. צַיָּד *tsah'-yawd;* from the same as 6718; a *huntsman:*–hunter.
6720. צֵידָה *tsay-daw';* or צֵדָה *tsay-daw';* fem. of 6718; *food:*–meat, provision, venison, victuals.
6721. צִידוֹן *tsee-done';* or צִידֹן *tsee-done';* from 6679 in the sense of *catching* fish; *fishery; Tsidon,* the name of a son of Canaan, and of a place in Pal.:–Sidon, Zidon.
6722. צִידֹנִי (or צִדֹנִי) *tsee-do-nee';* patrial from 6721; a *Tsidonian* or inh. of Tsidon:–Sidonian, of Sidon, Zidonian.
6723. צִיָּה *tsee-yaw';* from an un. root mean. to *parch; aridity;* concr., a *desert:*–barren, drought, dry (land, place), solitary place, wilderness.
6724. צִיוֹן *tsee-yone';* from the same as 6723; a *desert:*–dry place.
6725. צִיּוּן *tsee-yoon';* from the same as 6723 in the sense of *conspicuousness* [comp. 5329]; a monument. or guiding *pillar:*–sign, title, waymark.
6726. צִיּוֹן *tsee-yone';* the same (regularly) as 6725; *Tsijon* (as a permanent *capital*), a mountain of Jerus.:–Zion.
6727. צִיחָא *tsee-khaw';* or צִחָא *tsee-khaw';* as if fem. of 6704; *drought; Tsicha,* the name of two Nethinim:–Ziha.
6728. צִיִּי *tsee-ee';* from the same as 6723; a *desert-dweller,* i.e. *nomad* or wild *beast:*–wild beast of the desert, that dwell in (inhabiting) the wilderness.
6729. צִינֹק *tsee-noke';* from an un. root mean. to *confine;* the *pillory:*–stocks.
6730. צִיעֹר *tsee-ore';* from 6819; *small; Tsior,* a place in Pal.:–Zior.
6731. צִיץ *tseets;* or צִץ *tseets;* from 6692; prop. *glistening,* i.e. a burnished *plate;* also a *flower* (as *bright*-colored); a *wing* (as *gleaming* in the air):–blossom, flower, plate, wing.
6732. צִיץ *tseets;* the same as 6731; *bloom; Tsits,* a place in Pal.:–Ziz.
6733. צִיצָה *tsee-tsaw';* fem. of 6731; a *flower:*–flower.
6734. צִיצִת *tsee-tseeth';* fem. of 6731; a *floral* or *wing*-like projection, i.e. a *forelock* of hair, a *tassel:*–fringe, lock.
6735. צִיר *tseer;* from 6696; a *hinge* (as *pressed* in turning); also a *throe* (as a phys. or ment. *pressure*); also a *herald* or errand-doer (as *constrained* by the principal):–ambassador, hinge, messenger, pain, pang, sorrow. Comp. 6736.
6736. צִיר *tseer;* the same as 6735; a *form* (of beauty; as if *pressed* out, i.e. carved); hence, an (idolatrous) *image:*–beauty, idol.
6737. צִיַּר *tsaw-yar';* a denom. from 6735 in the sense of *ambassador;* to *make an errand,* i.e. *betake* oneself:–make as if...had been ambassador.
6738. צֵל *tsale;* from 6751; *shade,* whether lit. or fig.:–defence, shade(-ow).
6739. צְלָא *tsel-aw'* (Chald.); prob. cor. to 6760 in the sense of *bowing; pray:*–pray.
6740. צָלָה *tsaw-law';* a prim. root; to *roast:*–roast.
6741. צִלָּה *tsil-law';* fem. of 6738; *Tsillah,* an antediluvian woman:–Zillah.
6742. צְלוּל *tsel-ool';* from 6749 in the sense of *rolling;* a (round or flattened) *cake:*–cake.
6743. צָלַח *tsaw-lakh';* or צָלֵחַ *tsaw-lay'-akh;* a prim. root; to *push* forward, in various senses (lit. or fig., trans. or intr.):–break out, come (mightily), go over, be good, be meet, be profitable, (cause to, effect, make to, send) prosper(-ity, -ous, - ously).
6744. צְלַח *tsel-akh'* (Chald.); cor. to 6743; to *advance* (trans. or intr.):–promote, prosper.
6745. צֵלָחָה *tsay-law-khaw';* from 6743; something *protracted* or flattened out, i.e. a *platter:*–pan.
6746. צְלֹחִית *tsel-o-kheeth';* from 6743; some-thing *prolonged* or tall, i.e. a *vial* or salt-*cellar:*–cruse.
6747. צַלַּחַת *tsal-lakh'-ath;* from 6743; something *advanced* or deep, i.e. a *bowl;* fig., the *bosom:*–bosom, dish.
6748. צָלִי *tsaw-lee';* pass.part. of 6740; *roasted:*–roast.
6749. צָלַל *tsaw-lal';* a prim. root; prop. to *tumble* down, i.e. *settle* by a waving motion:–sink. Comp. 6750, 6751.
6750. צָלַל *tsaw-lal';* a prim. root [rather ident. with 6749 through the idea of *vibration*]; to *tinkle,* i.e. *rattle* together (as the ears in *reddening* with shame, or the teeth in *chattering* with fear):–quiver, tingle.
6751. צָלַל *tsaw-lal';* a prim. root [rather ident. with 6749 through the idea of *hovering* over (comp. 6754)]; to *shade,* as twilight or an opaque obj.:–begin to be dark, shadowing.
6752. צֵלֶל *tsay'-lel;* from 6751; *shade:*–shadow.
6753. צְלֶלְפּוֹנִי *tsel-el-po-nee';* from 6752 and the act.part. of 6437; *shade-facing; Tselelponi,* an Isr.s:–Hazelelponi [incl. the art.].
6754. צֶלֶם *tseh'-lem;* from an un. root mean. to *shade;* a *phantom,* i.e. (fig.) *illusion, resemblance;* hence, a representative *figure,* esp. an *idol:*–image, vain shew.
6755. צֶלֶם *tseh'-lem* (Chald.); or צְלֵם *tsel-em'* (Chald.); cor. to 6754; an idolatrous *figure:*–form, image.
6756. צַלְמוֹן *tsal-mone';* from 6754; *shady; Tsalmon,* the name of a place in Pal. and of an Isr.:–Zalmon.
6757. צַלְמָוֶת *tsal-maw'-veth;* from 6738 and 4194; *shade of death,* i.e. the *grave* (fig., *calamity*):–shadow of death.
6758. צַלְמֹנָה *tsal-mo-naw';* fem. of 6757; *shadiness; Tsalmonah,* a place in the Desert:–Zalmonah.
6759. צַלְמֻנָּע *tsal-moon-naw';* from 6738 and 4513; *shade has been denied; Tsalmunna,* a Midianite:–Zalmunna.
6760. צָלַע *tsaw-lah';* a prim. root: prob. to *curve;* used only as denom. from 6763, to *limp* (as if *one-sided*):–halt.
6761. צֶלַע *tseh'-lah;* from 6760; a limping or *fall* (fig.):–adversity, halt(-ing).
6762. צֶלַע *tseh'-lah;* the same as 6761; *Tsela,* a place in Pal.:–Zelah.
6763. צֵלָע *tsay-law';* or (fem.) צַלְעָה *tsal-aw';* from 6760; a *rib* (as *curved*), lit. (of the body) or fig. (of a door, i.e. *leaf*); hence, a *side,* lit. (of a person) or fig. (of an obj. or the sky, i.e. *quarter*); arch., a (esp. floor or ceiling) *timber* or *plank* (single or coll., i.e. a *flooring*):–beam, board, chamber, corner, leaf, plank, rib, side (chamber).
6764. צָלָף *tsaw-lawf';* from an un. root of unknown mean.; *Tsalaph,* an Isr.:–Zalaph.
6765. צְלָפְחָד *tsel-of-chawd';* from the same as 6764 and 259; *Tselophchad,* an Isr.:–Zelophehad.
6766. צֶלְצַח *tsel-tsakh';* from 6738 and 6703; *clear shade; Tseltsach,* a place in Pal.:–Zelzah.
6767. צְלָצַל *tsel-aw-tsal';* from 6750 redupl.; a *clatter,* i.e. (abstr.) *whirring* (of wings); (concr.) a *cricket;* also a *harpoon* (as *rattling*), a *cymbal* (as *clanging*):–cymbal, locust, shadowing, spear.
6768. צֶלֶק *tseh'-lek;* from an un. root mean. to *split; fissure; Tselek,* an Isr.:–Zelek.
6769. צִלְּתַי *tsil-leth-ah'-ee;* from the fem. of 6738; *shady; Tsillethai,* the name of two Isr.:–Zilthai.
6770. צָמֵא *tsaw-may';* a prim. root; to *thirst* (lit. or fig.):–(be a-, suffer) thirst(-y).
6771. צָמֵא *tsaw-may';* from 6770; *thirsty* (lit. or fig.):–(that) thirst(-eth, -y).
6772. צָמָא *tsaw-maw';* from 6770; *thirst* (lit. or fig.):–thirst(-y).
6773. צִמְאָה *tsim-aw';* fem. of 6772; *thirst* (fig., of *libidinousnes*):–thirst.
6774. צִמָּאוֹן *tsim-maw-one';* from 6771; a *thirsty* place, i.e. *desert:*–drought, dry ground, thirsty land.
6775. צָמַד *tsaw-mad';* a prim. root; to *link,* i.e. *gird;* fig., to *serve,* (ment.) *contrive:*–fasten, frame, join (self).
6776. צֶמֶד *tseh'-med;* a *yoke* or *team* (i.e. pair); hence, an *acre* (i.e. day's task for a yoke of cattle to plough):–acre, couple, X together, two [asses], yoke (of oxen).
6777. צַמָּה *tsam-maw';* from an un. root mean. to *fasten* on; a *veil:*–locks.
6778. צַמּוּק *tsam-mook;* 'from 6784; a cake of *dried* grapes:–bunch (cluster) of raisins.
6779. צָמַח *tsaw-makh';* a prim. root; to *sprout* (trans. or intr., lit. or fig.):–bear, bring forth, (cause to, make to) bud (forth), (cause to, make to) grow (again, up), (cause to) spring (forth, up).
6780. צֶמַח *tseh'-makh;* from 6779; a *sprout* (usually concr.), lit. or fig.:–branch, bud, that which (where) grew (upon), spring(-ing).
6781. צָמִיד *tsaw-meed'* or צָמִד *tsaw-meed';* from 6775; a *bracelet* or *arm-clasp;* gen., a *lid:*–bracelet, covering.
6782. צַמִּים *tsam-meem';* from the same as 6777; a *noose* (as *fastening*); fig., *destruction:*–robber.
6783. צְמִיתֻת *tsem-ee-thooth'; or* צְמִתֻת *tsem-ee-thooth';* from 6789; *excision,* i.e. *destruction;* used only (adv.) with prep. pref. to *extinction,* i.e. *perpetually:*–ever.
6784. צָמַק *tsaw-mak';* a prim. root; to *dry* up:–dry.
6785. צֶמֶר *tseh'-mer;* from an un. root prob. mean. to be *shaggy; wool:*–wool(-len).
6786. צְמָרִי *tsem-aw-ree';* patrial from an unused name of a place in Pal.; a *Tsemarite* or branch of the Canaanites:–Zemarite.
6787. צְמָרַיִם *tsem-aw-rah'-yim;* dual of 6785; *double fleece; Tsemarajim,* a place in Pal.:–Zemaraim.
6788. צַמֶּרֶת *tsam-meh'-reth;* from the same as 6785; *fleeciness,* i.e. *foliage:*–highest branch, top.
6789. צָמַת *tsaw-math';* a prim. root; to *extirpate*

(lit. or fig.):–consume, cut off, destroy, vanish.

6790. צִן *tseen;* from an un. root mean. to *prick;* a *crag; Tsin,* a part of the Desert:–Zin.

6791. צֵן *tsane;* from an un. root mean. to be *prickly;* a *thorn; hence,* a cactus-*hedge:*–thorn.

6792. צֹנֵא *tso-nay';* or צֹנֶה *tso-neh';* for 6629; a *flock:*–sheep.

6793. צִנָּה *tsin-naw';* fem. of 6791; a hook (as *pointed*); also a (large) *shield* (as if guarding by *prickliness*); also *cold* (as *piercing*):– buckler, cold, hook, shield, target.

6794. צִנּוּר *tsin-noor';* from an un. root perh. mean. to *be hollow;* a *culvert:*–gutter, water-spout.

6795. צָנַח *tsaw-nakh';* a prim. root; to *alight;* (trans.) to *cause* to *descend,* i.e. *drive* down:–fasten, light [from off].

6796. צָנִין *tsaw-neen';* or צָנִן *tsaw-neen';* from the same as 6791; a *thorn:*–thorn.

6797. צָנִיף *tsaw-neef';* or צָנוֹף *tsaw-nofe';* or (fem.) צָנִיפָה *tsaw-nee-faw';* from 6801; a *head-dress* (i.e. piece of cloth *wrapped* around):–diadem, hood, mitre.

6798. צָנַם *tsaw-nam';* a prim. root; to *blast* or *shrink:*–withered.

6799. צְנָן *tsen-awn';* prob. for 6630; *Tsenan,* a place near Pal.:–Zenan.

6800. צָנַע *tsaw-nah';* a prim. root; to *humiliate:*–humbly, lowly.

6801. צָנַף *tsaw-naf';* a prim. root; to *wrap,* i.e. *roll* or *dress:*–be attired, X surely, violently turn.

6802. צְנֵפָה *tsen-ay-faw';* from 6801; a *ball:*–X toss.

6803. צִנְצֶנֶת *tsin-tseh'-neth;* from the same as 6791; a *vase* (prob. a vial *tapering* at the top):–pot.

6804. צַנְתָּרָה *tsan-taw-raw';* prob. from the same as 6794; a *tube:*–pipe.

6805. צָעַד *tsaw-ad';* a prim. root; to *pace,* i.e. *step* regularly; (upward) to *mount;* (along) to *march;* (down and caus.) to *hurl:*– bring, go, march (through), run over.

6806. צַעַד *tsah'-ad;* from 6804; a *pace* or regular *step:*–pace, step.

6807. צְעָדָה *tseh-aw-daw';* fem. of 6806; a *march;* (concr.) an (ornament.) *ankle-chain:*–going, ornament of the legs.

6808. צָעָה *tsaw-aw';* a prim. root; to *tip* over (for the purpose of *spilling* or *pouring* out), i.e. (fig.) *depopulate;* by impl., to *imprison* or *conquer;* (refl.) to *lie down* (for coitus):–captive exile, travelling, (cause to) wander(-er).

6809. צָעִיף *tsaw-eef';* from an un. root mean. to *wrap* over; a *veil:*–vail.

6810. צָעִיר *tsaw-eer';* or צָעוֹר *tsaw-ore';* from 6819; *little;* (in number) *few;* (in age) *young,* (in value) *ignoble:*–least, little (one), small (one), + young(-er, -est).

6811. צָעִיר *tsaw-eer';* the same as 6810; *Tsaïr,* a place in Idumaea:–Zair.

6812. צְעִירָה *tseh-ee-raw';* fem. of 6810; *smallness* (of age), i.e. *juvenility:*–youth.

6813. צָעַן *tsaw-an';* a prim. root; to *load* up (beasts), i.e. to *migrate:*–be taken down.

6814. צֹעַן *tso'-an;* of Eg. der.; *Tsoän,* a place in Eg.:–Zoan.

6815. צַעֲנַנִּים *tsah-an-an-neem';* or (dual) צַעֲנַיִם *tsah-an-ah'-yim;* pl. from 6813; *removals; Tsaanannim* or *Tsaanajim,* a place in Pal.:–Zaannannim, Zaanaim.

6816. צַעֲצֻעַ *tsah-tsoo'-ah;* from an un. root mean. to *bestrew* with carvings; *sculpture:*–image [work].

6817. צָעַק *tsaw-ak';* a prim. root; to *shriek;* (by impl.) to *proclaim* (an assembly):–X at all, call together, cry (out), gather (selves) (together).

6818. צַעֲקָה *tsah-ak-aw';* from 6817; a *shriek:*–cry(-ing).

6819. צָעַר *tsaw-ar';* a prim. root; to be *small,* i.e. (fig.) *ignoble:*–be brought low, little one, be small.

6820. צֹעַר *tso'ar;* from 6819; *little; Tsoär,* a place E. of the Jordan:–Zoar.

6821. צָפַד *tsaw-fad';* a prim. root; to *adhere:*–cleave.

6822. צָפָה *tsaw-faw';* a prim. root; prop. to *lean* forward, i.e. to *peer* into the distance; by impl., to *observe, await:*–behold, espy, look up (well), wait for, (keep the) watch(-man).

6823. צָפָה *tsaw-faw';* a prim. root [prob. rather ident. with 6822 through the idea of *expansion* in outlook, transferring to action]; to *sheet* over (esp. with metal):–cover, overlay.

6824. צָפָה *tsaw-faw';* from 6823; an *inundation* (as *covering*):–X swimmest.

6825. צְפוֹ *tsef-o';* or צְפִי *tsef-ee';* from 6822; *observant; Tsepho* or *Tsephi,* an Idumaean:–Zephi, Zepho.

6826. צִפּוּי *tsip-poo'-ee;* from 6823; *encasement* (with metal):–covering, overlaying.

6827. צְפוֹן *tsef-one';* prob. for 6837; *Tsephon,* an Isr.:–Zephon.

6828. צָפוֹן *tsaw-fone';* or צָפֹן *tsaw-fone';* from 6845; prop. *hidden,* i.e. *dark;* used only of the *north* as a quarter (*gloomy* and *unknown*):–north(-ern, side, -ward, wind).

6829. צָפוֹן *tsaw-fone';* the same as 6828; *boreal; Tsaphon,* a place in Pal.:–Zaphon.

6830. צְפוֹנִי *tsef-o-nee';* from 6828; *northern:*–northern.

6831. צְפוֹנִי *tsef-o-nee';* patron. from 6827; a *Tsephonite,* or (coll.) desc. of Tsephon:–Zephonites.

6832. צְפוּעַ *tsef-oo'-ah;* from the same as 6848; *excrement* (as *protruded*):–dung.

6833. צִפּוֹר *tsip-pore';* or צִפֹּר *tsip-pore';* from 6852; a little *bird* (as *hopping*):–bird, fowl, sparrow.

6834. צִפּוֹר *tsip-pore';* the same as 6833; *Tsippor,* a Moabite:–Zippor.

6835. צַפַּחַת *tsap-pakh'-ath;* from an un. root mean. to *expand;* a *saucer* (as *flat*):–cruse.

6836. צְפִיָּה *tsef-ee-yaw';* from 6822; *watchfulness:*–watching.

6837. צִפְיוֹן *tsif-yone';* from 6822; *watch*-tower; *Tsiphjon,* an Isr.:–Ziphion. Comp. 6827.

6838. צַפִּיחִת *tsap-pee-kheeth';* from the same as 6835; a flat thin *cake:*–wafer.

6839. צֹפִים *tso-feem';* pl. of act.part. of 6822; *watchers; Tsophim,* a place E. of the Jordan:–Zophim.

6840. צָפִין *tsaw-feen';* from 6845; a *treasure* (as *hidden*):–hid.

6841. צְפִיר *tsef-eer'* (Chald.); cor. to 6842; a he-*goat:*–he [goat].

6842. צָפִיר *tsaw-feer';* from 6852; a male *goat* (as *prancing*):–(he) goat.

6843. צְפִירָה *tsef-ee-raw';* fem. formed like 6842; a *crown* (as *encircling* the head); also a *turn* of affairs (i.e. *mishap*):–diadem, morning.

6844. צָפִית *tsaw-feeth';* from 6822; a *sentry:*–watchtower.

6845. צָפַן *tsaw-fan';* a prim. root; to *hide* (by *covering* over); by impl., to *hoard* or *reserve;* fig. to *deny;* spec. (favorably) to *protect,* (unfavorably) to *lurk:*–esteem, hide(-den one, self), lay up, lurk (be set) privily, (keep) secret(-ly, place).

6846. צְפַנְיָה *tsef-an-yaw';* or צְפַנְיָהוּ *tsef-an-yaw'-hoo;* from 6845 and 3050; *Jah has secreted; Tsephanjah,* the name of four Isr.:–Zephaniah.

6847. צָפְנַת פַּעְנֵחַ *tsof-nath' pah-nay'-akh;* of Eg. der.; *Tsophnath-Paneäch,* Joseph's Eg. name:–Zaphnath-paaneah.

6848. צֶפַע *tseh'-fah* or צִפְעֹנִי *tsif-o-nee';* from an un. root mean. to *extrude;* a *viper* (as *thrusting* out the tongue, i.e. *hissing*):–adder, cockatrice.

6849. צְפִעָה *tsef-ee-aw';* fem. from the same as 6848; an *outcast* thing:–issue.

6850. צָפַף *tsaw-faf';* a prim. root; to *coo* or *chirp* (as a bird):–chatter, peep, whisper.

6851. צַפְצָפָה *tsaf-tsaw-faw';* from 6687; a *willow* (as growing in *overflowed* places):–willow tree.

6852. צָפַר *tsaw-far';* a prim. root; to *skip* about, i.e. *return:*–depart early.

6853. צְפַר *tsef-ar'* (Chald.); cor. to 6833; a *bird:*–bird.

6854. צְפַרְדֵּעַ *tsef-ar-day'-ah;* from 6852 and a word elsewhere un. mean. a *swamp;* a *marsh-leaper,* i.e. *frog:*–frog.

6855. צִפֹּרָה *tsip-po-raw';* fem. of 6833; *bird; Tsipporah,* Moses' wife:–Zipporah.

6856. צִפֹּרֶן *tsip-po'-ren;* from 6852 (in the denom. sense [from 6833] of *scratching*); prop. a *claw,* i.e. (human) *nail;* also the *point* of a style (or pen, tipped with adamant):–nail, point.

6857. צְפַת *tsef-ath';* from 6822; *watch*-tower; *Tsephath,* a place in Pal.:–Zephath.

6858. צֶפֶת *tseh'-feth;* from an un. root mean. to *encircle;* a *capital* of a column:–chapiter.

6859. צְפָתָה *tsef-aw'-thaw;* the same as 6857; *Tsephathah,* a place in Pal.:–Zephathah.

6860. צִקְלַג *tsik-lag';* or צִיקְלַג (1 Chronicles 12:1,20) *tsee-kel-ag';* of unc. der.: *Tsiklag* or *Tsikelag,* a place in Pal.:–Ziklag.

6861. צִקְלֹן *tsik-lone';* from an un. root mean. to *wind;* a *sack* (as *tied* at the mouth):–husk.

6862. צַר *tsar;* or צָר *tsawr;* from 6887; *narrow;* (as a noun) a *tight* place (usually fig., i.e. *trouble*); also a *pebble* (as in 6864); (trans.) an *opponent* (as *crowding*):–adversary, afflicted (-tion), anguish, close, distress, enemy, flint, foe, narrow, small, sorrow, strait, tribulation, trouble.

6863. צֵר *tsare;* from 6887; *rock; Tser,* a place in Pal.:–Zer.

6864. צֹר *tsore;* from 6696; a *stone* (as if *pressed* hard or to a point); (by impl., of use) a *knife:*–flint, sharp stone.

6865. צֹר *tsore;* or צוֹר *tsore;* the same as 6864; a *rock; Tsor,* a place in Pal.:–Tyre, Tyrus.

6866. צָרַב *tsaw-rab';* a prim. root; to *burn:*–burn.

6867. צָרֶבֶת *saw-reh'-beth;* from 6686; *conflagration* (of fire or disease):–burning, inflammation.

6868. צְרֵדָה *tser-ay-daw';* or צְרֵדָתָה *tser-ay-daw'-thaw;* app. from an un. root mean. to *pierce; puncture; Tseredah,* a place in Pal.:–Zereda, Zeredathah.

6869. צָרָה *tsaw-raw';* fem. of 6862; *tightness* (i.e. fig., *trouble*); trans., a female *rival:*–adversary, adversity, affliction, anguish, distress, tribulation, trouble.

6870. צְרוּיָה *tser-oo-yaw';* fem. pass.part. from the same as 6875; *wounded; Tserujah,* an Isr.s:–Zeruiah.

6871. צְרוּעָה *tser-oo-aw';* fem. pass.part. of 6879; *leprous; Tseruäh,* an Isr.s:–Zeruah.

6872. צְרוֹר *tser-ore';* or (short.) צְרֹר *tser-ore';* from 6887; a *parcel* (as *packed* up); also a

kernel or *particle* (as if a *package*):–bag, X bendeth, bundle, least grain, small stone.
6873. צָרַח *tsaw-rakh'*; a prim. root; to *be clear* (in tone, i.e. *shrill*), i.e. to *whoop*:–cry, roar.
6874. צְרִי *tser-ee'*; the same as 6875; *Tseri*, an Isr.:–Zeri. Comp. 3340.
6875. צְרִי *tser-ee'*; or צֳרִי *tsor-ee'*; from an un. root mean. to *crack* [as by *pressure*], hence, to *leak*; *distillation*, i.e. *balsam*:–balm.
6876. צֹרִי *tso-ree'*; patrial from 6865; a *Tsorite* or inh. of Tsor (i.e. *Syrian*):–(man) of Tyre.
6877. צְרִיחַ *tser-ee'-akh*; from 6873 in the sense of *clearness* of vision; a *citadel*:–high place, hold.
6878. צֹרֶךְ *tso'-rek*; from an un. root mean. to *need*; *need*:–need.
6879. צָרַע *tsaw-rah'* a prim. root; to *scourge*, i.e. (intr. and fig.) to *be stricken with leprosy*:–leper, leprous.
6880. צִרְעָה *tsir-aw'*; from 6879; a *wasp* (as *stinging*):–hornet.
6881. צָרְעָה *tsor-aw'*; app. another form for 6880; *Tsorah*, a place in Pal.:–Zareah, Zorah, Zoreah.
6882 צָרְעִי *tsor-ee'*; or צָרְעָתִי *tsor-aw-thee'*; patrial from 6881; a *Tsorite* or *Tsorathite*, i.e. inh. of Tsorah:–Zorites, Zareathites, Zorathites.
6883. צָרַעַת *tsaw-rah'-ath*; from 6879; *leprosy*:–leprosy.
6884. צָרַף *tsaw-raf'* a prim. root; to *fuse* (metal), i.e. *refine* (lit. or fig.):–cast, (re-)fine(-er), founder, goldsmith, melt, pure, purge away, try.
6885. צֹרְפִי *tso-ref-ee'*; from 6884; *refiner*; *Tsorephi* (with the art.), an Isr.:–goldsmith's.
6886. צָרְפַת *tsaq-ref-ath'*; from 6884; *refinement*; *Tsarephath*, a place in Pal.:–Zarephath.
6887. צָרַר *tsaw-rar'*; a prim. root; to *cramp*, lit. or fig., trans. or intr. (as follows):–adversary, (be in) afflict(-ion), beseige, bind (up), (be in, bring) distress, enemy, narrower, oppress, pangs, shut up, be in a strait (trouble), vex.
6888. צְרֵרָה *tser-ay-raw'*; app. by err. transc. for 6868; *Tsererah* for *Tseredah*:–Zererath.
6889. צֶרֶת *tseh'-reth*; perh. from 6671; *splendor*; *Tsereth*, an Isr.:–Zereth.
6890. צֶרֶת הַשַּׁחַר *tseh'-reth hash-shakh'-ar*; from the same as 6889 and 7837 with the art. interp.; *splendor of the dawn*; *Tsereth-hash-Shachar*, a place in Pal.:–Zareth-shahar.
6891. צָרְתָן tsaw-reth-awn'; perh. for 6868; *Tsarethan*, a place in Pal.:–Zarthan.

ק

6892. קֵא *kay*; or קִיא *kee*; from 6958; *vomit*:–vomit.
6893. קָאַת *kaw-ath'*; from 6958; prob. the *pelican* (from *vomiting*):–cormorant.
6894. קַב *kab*; from 6895; a *hollow*, i.e. vessel used as a (dry) *measure*:–cab.
6895. קָבַב *kaw-bab'*; a prim. root; to *scoop* out, i.e. (fig.) to *malign* or *execrate* (i.e. *stab* with words):–X at all, curse.
6896. קֵבָה *kay-baw'* from 6895; the *paunch* (as a *cavity*) or first stomach of ruminants:–maw.
6897. קֹבָה *ko'-baw*; from 6895; the *abdomen* (as a cavity):–belly.
6898. קֻבָּה *koob-baw'*; from 6895; a *pavilion* (as a domed *cavity*):–tent.
6899. קִבּוּץ *kib-boots'*; from 6908; a *throng*:–company.
6900. קְבוּרָה *keb-oo-raw'*; or קְבֻרָה *keb-oo-raw'*; fem. pass.part. of 6912; *sepulture*; (concr.) a *sepulchre*:–burial, burying place, grave, sepulchre.
6901. קָבַל *kaw-bal'*; a prim. root; to *admit*, i.e. *take* (lit. or fig.):–choose, (take) hold, receive, (under-)take.
6902. קְבַל *keb-al'* (Chald.); cor. to 6901; to *acquire*:–receive, take.
6903. קְבֵל *keb-ale'* (Chald.); or קֳבֵל *kob-ale'* (Chald.); (cor. to 6905; (adv.) *in front of*; usually (with other particles) *on account of*, *so* as, *since*, *hence*:–+ according to, + as, + because, before, + for this cause, + forasmuch as, + by this means, over against, by reason of, + that, + therefore, + though, + wherefore.
6904. קֹבֶל *ko'-bel*; from 6901 in the sense of *confronting* (as standing *opposite* in order to receive); a *battering*-ram:–war.
6905. קָבָל *kaw-bawl'*; from 6901 in the sense of *opposite* [see 6904]; the *presence*, i.e. (adv.) *in front of*:–before.
6906. קָבַע *kaw-bah'*; a prim. root; to *cover*, i.e. (fig.) *defraud*:–rob, spoil.
6907. קֻבַּעַת *koob-bah'-ath*; from 6906; a *goblet* (as deep like a *cover*):–dregs.
6908. קָבַץ *kaw-bats'*; a prim. root; to *grasp*, i.e. *collect*:–assemble (selves), gather (bring) (together, selves together, up), heap, resort, X surely, take up.
6909. קַבְצְאֵל *kab-tseh-ale'*; from 6908 and 410; *God has gathered*; *Kabtseël*, a place in Pal.:–Kabzeel. Comp. 3343.
6910. קְבֻצָה *keb-oo-tsaw'*; fem. pass.part. of 6908; a *hoard*:–X gather.
6911. קִבְצַיִם *kib-tsah'-yim*; dual from 6908; a *double heap*; *Kibtsajim*, a place in Pal.:–Kibzaim.
6912. קָבַר *kaw-bar'*; a prim. root; to *inter*:–X in any wise, bury(-ier).
6913. קֶבֶר *keh'-ber*; or (fem.) קִבְרָה *kib-raw'*; from 6912; a *sepulchre*:–burying place, grave, sepulchre.
6914. קִבְרוֹת הַתַּאֲוָה *kib-roth' hat-tah-av-aw'*; from the fem. pl. of 6913 and 8378 with the art. interp.; *graves of the longing*; *Kibroth-hat-Taavh*, a place in the Desert:–Kibroth-hattaavah.
6915. קָדַד *kaw-dad'*; a prim. root; to *shrivel* up, i.e. *contract* or *bend* the body (or neck) in deference:–bow (down) (the) head, stoop.
6916. קִדָּה *kid-daw'*; from 6915; *cassia* bark (as in *shrivelled* rolls):–cassia.
6917. קָדוּם *kaw-doom'*; pass.part. of 6923; a *pristine* hero:–ancient.
6918. קָדוֹשׁ *kaw-doshe'*; or קָדֹשׁ *kaw-doshe'*; from 6942; *sacred* (cerem. or mor.); (as noun) *God* (by eminence), an *angel*, a *saint*, a *sanctuary*:–holy (One), saint.
6919. קָדַח *kaw-dakh'*; a prim. root to *inflame*:–burn, kindle.
6920. קַדַּחַת *kad-dakh'-ath*; from 6919; *inflammation*, i.e. febrile disease:–burning ague, fever.
6921. קָדִים *kaw-deem'*; or קָדִם kaw-deem'; from 6923; the *fore* or front part; hence (by orientation) the *E.* (often adv., *eastward*, for brevity the east *wind*):–east(-ward, wind).
6922. קַדִּישׁ *kad-deesh'* (Chald.); cor. to 6918. –holy (One), saint.
6923. קָדַם *kaw-dam'*; a prim. root; to *project* (one self), i.e. *precede*; hence, to *anticipate*, *hasten*, *meet* (usually for help):–come (go, [flee]) before, + disappoint, meet, prevent.
6924. קֶדֶם *keh'-dem*; or קֵדְמָה *kayd'-maw*; from 6923; the *front*, of place (absol., the *fore part*, rel. the *E.*) or time (*antiquity*); often used adv. (*before*, *anciently*, *eastward*):–aforetime, ancient (time), before, east (end, part, side, -ward), eternal, X ever (-lasting), forward, old, past. Comp. 6926.
6925. קֳדָם *kod-awm'* (Chald.); or (Daniel 7:13) קֱדָם *ked-awm'*; cor. to 6924; *before*:–before, X from, X I (thought), X me, + of, X it pleased, presence.
6926. קִדְמָה *kid-maw'*; fem. of 6924; the *forward* part (or rel.) *E.* (often adv., on the *east* or *in front*):–east(-ward).
6927. קַדְמָה *kad-maw'*; from 6923; *priority* (in time); also used adv. (*before*):–afore, antiquity, former (old) estate.
6928. קַדְמָה *kad-maw'* (Chald.); cor. to 6927; *former* time:– afore[-time], ago.
6929. קֵדְמָה *kayd'-maw*; from 6923; *precedence*; *Kedemah*, a son of Ishmael:–Kedemah.
6930. קַדְמוֹן *kad-mone'*; from 6923; *eastern*:–east.
6931. קַדְמוֹנִי *kad-mo-nee'*; or קַדְמֹנִי *kad-mo-nee'*; from 6930; (of time) *anterior* or (of place) *oriental*:–former, ancient, they that went before, east, (thing of) old.
6932. קְדֵמוֹת *ked-ay-mothe'*; from 6923; *beginnings*; *Kedemoth*, a place in eastern Pal.:–Kedemoth.
6933. קַדְמַי *kad-mah'-ee* (Chald.); from a root cor. to 6923; *first*:–first.
6934. קַדְמִיאֵל *kad-mee-ale'*; from 6924 and 410; *presence of God*; *Kadmiël*, the name of three Isr.:–Kadmiel.
6935. קַדְמֹנִי *kad-mo-nee'*; the same as 6931; *ancient*, i.e. aboriginal; *Kadmonite* (coll.), the name of a tribe in Pal.:– Kadmonites.
6936. קָדְקֹד *kod-kode'*; from 6915; the *crown* of the head (as the part most *bowed*):–crown (of the head), pate, scalp, top of the head.
6937. קָדַר *kaw-dar'*; a prim. root; to *be ashy*, i.e. *dark*-colored; by impl., to *mourn* (in sackcloth or sordid garments):–be black (-ish), be (make) dark(-en), X heavily, (cause to) mourn.
6938. קֵדָר *kay-dawr'*; from 6937; *dusky* (of the skin or the tent); *Kedar*, a son of Ishmael; also (coll.) *Bedouin* (as his desc. or representatives):–Kedar.
6939. קִדְרוֹן *kid-rone'*; from 6937; *dusky* place; *Kidron*, a brook near Jerus.:–Kidron.
6940. קַדְרוּת *kad-rooth'* from 6937; *duskiness*:–blackness.
6941. קְדֹרַנִּית *ked-o-ran-neeth'*; adv. from 6937; *blackish ones* (i.e. *in sackcloth*); used adv., in *mourning* weeds:–mournfully.
6942. קָדַשׁ *kaw-dash'*; a prim. root; to *be* (caus., *make*, *pronounce* or *observe* as) *clean* (cerem. or mor.):–appoint, bid, consecrate, dedicate, defile, hallow, (be, keep) holy(-er, place), keep, prepare, proclaim, purify, sanctify(-ied one, self), X wholly.
6943. קֶדֶשׁ *keh'-desh*; from 6942; a *sanctum*; *Kedesh*, the name of four places in Pal.:–Kedesh.
6944. קֹדֶשׁ *ko'-desh*; from 6942; a *sacred* place or thing; rarely abstr., *sanctity*:–consecrated (thing), dedicated (thing), hallowed (thing), holiness, (X most) holy (X day, portion, thing), saint, sanctuary.
6945. קָדֵשׁ *kaw-dashe'*; from 6942; a (quasi) *sacred* person, i.e. (te.) a (male) *devotee* (by prostitution) to licentious idolatry:–sodomite, unclean.

6946. קָדֵשׁ *kaw-dashe'*; the same as 6945; *sanctuary; Kadesh,* a place in the Desert:–Kadesh. Comp. 6947.

6947. קָדֵשׁ בַּרְנֵעַ *kaw-dashe' bar-nay'-ah;* from the same as 6946 and an otherwise un. word (app. compounded of a correspondent to 1251 and a der. of 5128) mean. *desert of a fugitive; Kadesh* of (the) *Wilderness of Wandering; Kadesh-Barneä,* a place in the Desert:–Kadesh-barnea.

6948. קְדֵשָׁה *ked-ay-shaw';* fem. of 6945; a female *devotee* (i.e. *prostitute*):–harlot, whore.

6949. קָהָה *kaw-haw';* a prim. root; to be *dull*:–be set on edge, be blunt.

6950. קָהַל *kaw-hal';* a prim. root; to *convoke*:–assemble (selves) (together), gather (selves) (together).

6951. קָהָל *kaw-hawl'; from* 6950; *assemblage* (usually concr.):–assembly, company, congregation, multitude.

6952. קְהִלָּה *keh-hil-law';* from 6950; an *assemblage*:–assembly, congregation.

6953. קֹהֶלֶת *ko-heh'-leth;* fem. of act.part. from 6950; a (female) *assembler* (i.e. lecturer): abstr., *preaching* (used as a "nom de plume", *Koheleth*):–preacher.

6954. קְהֵלָתָה *keh-hay-law'-thaw;* from 6950; *convocation; Kehelathah,* a place in the Desert:–Kehelathah.

6955. קְהָת *keh-hawth';* from an un. root mean. to *ally* oneself; *allied*; *Kehath*, an Isr.:–Kohath.

6956. קֳהָתִי *ko-haw-thee';* patron. from 6955; a *Kohathite* (coll.) or desc. of Kehath:–Kohathites.

6957. קַו *kav;* or קָו *kawv;* from 6960 [comp. 6961]; a *cord* (as *connecting*), esp. for measuring; fig., a *rule*; also a *rim*, a mus. *string* or *accord*:–line. Comp. 6978.

6958. קוֹא *ko;* or קָיָה *kawah;* (Jer. 25:27) *kaw-yaw';* a prim. root; to *vomit*:–spue (out), vomit (out, up, up again).

6959. קוֹבַע *ko'-bah;* or *ko-bah';* a form collat. to 3553; a *helmet*:–helmet.

6960. קָוָה *kaw-vaw';* a prim. root; to *bind* together (perh. by *twisting*), i.e. *coll.*; (fig.) to *expect*:–gather (together), look, patiently, tarry, wait (for, on, upon).

6961. קָוֶה *kaw-veh';* from 6960; a (measuring) *cord* (as if for *binding*):–line.

6962. קוּט *koot;* a prim. root; prop. to *cut off*, i.e. (fig.) *detest*:–be grieved, loathe self.

6963. קוֹל *kole;* or קֹל *kole;* from an un. root mean. to *call* aloud; a *voice* or *sound*:–+ aloud, bleating, crackling, cry (+ out), fame, lightness, lowing, noise, + hold peace, [pro-]claim, proclamation, + sing, sound, + spark, thunder(-ing), voice, + yell.

6964. קוֹלָיָה *ko-law-yaw';* from 6963 and 3050; *voice of Jah; Kolajah,* the name of two Isr.:–Kolaiah.

6965. קוּם *koom;* a prim. root; to *rise* (in various appl., lit., fig., intens. and caus.):–abide, accomplish, X be clearer, confirm, continue, decree, X be dim, endure, X enemy, enjoin, get up, make good, help, hold, (help to) lift up (again), make, X but newly, ordain, perform, pitch, raise (up), rear (up), remain, (a-)rise (up) (again, against), rouse up, set (up), (e-)stablish, (make to) stand (up), stir up, strengthen, succeed, (as-, make) sure(-ly), (be) up(-hold, - rising).

6966. קוּם *koom* (Chald.); cor. to 6965:–appoint, establish, make, raise up self, (a-) rise (up), (make to) stand, set (up).

6967. קוֹמָה *ko-maw';* from 6965; *height*:–X along, height, high, stature, tall.

6968. קוֹמְמִיּוּת *ko-mem-ee-yooth';* from 6965; *elevation*, i.e. (adv.) *erectly* (fig.):–upright.

6969. קוּן *koon;* a prim. root; to *strike;* a mus. note, i.e. *chant* or *wail* (at a funeral):–lament, mourning woman.

6970. קוֹעַ *ko'-ah;* prob. from 6972 in the or. sense of *cutting* off; *curtailment*; *Koä*, a region of Bab.:–Koa.

6971. קוֹף *kofe;* or קֹף *kofe;* prob. of for. or.; a *monkey*:–ape.

6972. קוּץ *koots;* a prim. root; to *clip* off; used only as denom. from 7019; to *spend the harvest* season:–summer.

6973. קוּץ *koots;* a prim. root [rather ident. with 6972 through the idea of *severing* oneself from (comp. 6962]); to be (caus., *make*) *disgusted* or *anxious*:–abhor, be distressed, be grieved, loathe, vex, be weary.

6974. קוּץ *koots;* a prim. root [rather ident. with 6972 through the idea of *abruptness* in starting up from sleep (comp. 3364)]; to *awake* (lit. or fig.):–arise, (be) (a-)wake, watch.

6975. קוֹץ *kotse;* or קֹץ *kotse;* from 6972 (in the sense of *pricking*); a *thorn*:–thorn.

6976. קוֹץ *kotse;* the same as 6975; *Kots,* the name of two Isr.:–Koz, Hakkoz [*incl. the art.*].

6977. קְוֻצָּה *kev-oots-tsaw';* fem. pass.part. of 6972 in its or. sense; a *forelock* (as *shorn*):–lock.

6978. קַו־קַו *kav-kav';* from 6957 (in the sense of a *fastening*); *stalwart*:–X meted out.

6979. קוּר *koor;* a prim. root; to *trench;* by impl., to *throw forth;* also (denom. from 7023) to *wall up,* whether lit. (to *build* a wall) or fig. (to *estop*):–break down, cast out, destroy, dig.

6980. קוּר *koor;* from 6979; (only pl.) *trenches,* i.e. a *web* (as if so formed):–web.

6981. קוֹרֵא *ko-ray';* or (1 Chronicles 26:1) קֹרֵא *ko-ray';* act.part. of 7121; crier; *Kore,* the name of two Isr.:–Kore.

6982. קוֹרָה *ko-raw'* or קֹרָה *ko-raw';* from 6979; a *rafter* (forming *trenches* as it were); by impl., a *roof*:–beam, roof.

6983. קוֹשׁ *koshe;* a prim. root; to *bend;* used only as denom. for 3369, to *set a trap*:–lay a snare.

6984. קוּשָׁיָהוּ *koo-shaw-yaw'-hoo;* from the pass.part. of 6983 and 3050; *entrapped of Jah; Kushajah,* an Isr.:–Kushaiah.

6985. קַט *kat;* from 6990 in the sense of *abbreviation;* a *little*, i.e. (adv.) *merely*:–very.

6986. קֶטֶב *keh'-teb* from an un. root mean. to *cut* off; *ruin*:–destroying, destruction.

6987. קֹטֶב *ko'-teb* from the same as 6986; *extermination*:–destruction.

6988. קְטוֹרָה *ket-o-raw'* from 6999; *perfume*:–incense.

6989. קְטוּרָה *ket-oo-raw'* fem. pass.part. of 6999; *perfumed; Keturah,* a wife of Abraham:–Keturah.

6990. קָטַט *kaw-tat';* a prim. root; to *clip* off, i.e. (fig.) *destroy*:–be cut off.

6991. קָטַל *kaw-tal';* a prim. root; prop. to *cut* off, i.e. (fig.) *put to death*:–kill, slay.

6992. קְטַל *ket-al'* (Chald.); cor. to 6991; to *kill*:–slay.

6993. קֶטֶל *keh'-tel;* from 6991; a violent *death*:–slaughter.

6994. קָטֹן *kaw-tone';* a prim. root [rather denom. from 6996]; to *diminish,* i.e. *be* (caus., *make*) *diminutive* or (fig.) *of no account*:–be a (make) small (thing), be not worthy.

6995. קֹטֶן *ko'-ten;* from 6994; a *pettiness,* i.e. the *little finger*:–little finger.

6996. קָטָן *kaw-tawn';* or קָטֹן *kaw-tone';* from 6962; *abbreviated,* i.e. *diminutive,* lit. (in quantity, size or number) or fig. (in age or importance):–least, less(-er), little (one), small(-est, one, quantity, thing), young(-er, -est).

6997. קָטָן *kaw-tawn';* the same as 6996; *small; Katan,* an Isr.:–Hakkatan (incl. the art.).

6998. קָטַף *kaw-taf';* a prim. root; to *strip* off:–crop off, cut down (up), pluck.

6999. קָטַר *kaw-tar';* a prim. root [rather ident. with 7000 through the idea of fumigation in a *close* place and perh. thus *driving* out the occupants]; to *smoke*, i.e. turn into fragrance by fire (esp. as an act of worship):–burn (incense, sacrifice) (upon), (altar for) incense, kindle, offer (incense, a sacrifice).

7000. קָטַר *kaw-tar';* a prim. root; to *inclose*:–join.

7001. קְטַר *ket-ar'* (Chald.); from a root cor. to 7000; a *knot* (as *tied* up), i.e. (fig.) a *riddle*; also a *vertebra* (as if a knot):–doubt, joint.

7002. קִטֵּר *kit-tare';* from 6999; *perfume*:–incense.

7003. קִטְרוֹן *kit-rone';* from 6999; *fumigative*; *Kitron,* a place in Pal.:–Kitron.

7004. קְטֹרֶת *ket-o'-reth;* from 6999; a *fumigation*:–(sweet) incense, perfume.

7005. קַטָּת *kat-tawth';* from 6996; *littleness*; *Kattath,* a place in Pal.:–Kattath.

7006. קָיָא *kaw-yaw';* a prim. root; to *vomit*:–spue.

7007. קַיִט *kah'-yit* (Chald.); cor. to 7019; *harvest*:–summer.

7008. קִיטוֹר *kee-tore';* or קִיטֹר *kee-tore';* from 6999; a *fume*, i.e. *cloud*:–smoke, vapour.

7009. קִים *keem;* from 6965; an *opponent* (as *rising* against one), i.e. (coll.) enemies:–substance.

7010. קְיָם *keh-yawm'* (Chald.); from 6966; an *edict* (as *arising* in law):–decree, statute.

7011. קַיָּם *kah-yawm'* (Chald.); from 6966; *permanent* (as *rising* firmly):–stedfast, sure.

7012. קִימָה *kee-maw';* from 6965; an *arising*:–rising up.

7013. קַיִן *kah'-yin;* from 6969 in the or. sense of *fixity*; a *lance* (as *striking fast*):–spear.

7014. קַיִן *kah'-yin;* the same as 7013 (with a play upon the affinity to 7069); *Kajin,* the name of the first child, also of a place in Pal., and of an Oriental tribe:–Cain, Kenite(-s).

7015. קִינָה *kee-naw';* from 6969; a *dirge* (as accompanied by *beating* the breasts or on instruments):–lamentation.

7016. קִינָה *kee-naw';* the same as 7015; *Kinah,* a place in Pal.:–Kinah.

7017. קֵינִי *kay-nee';* or (1 Ch.. 2:55) קִינִי *kee-nee';* patron. from 7014; a *Kenite* or member of the tribe of Kajin:–Kenite.

7018. קֵינָן *kay-nawn';* from the same as 7064; *fixed*; *Kenan,* an antediluvian:–Cainan, Kenan.

7019. קַיִץ *kah'-yits;* from 6972; harvest (as the *crop*), whether the product (grain or fruit) or the (dry) season:–summer (fruit, house).

7020. קִיצוֹן *kee-tsone';* from 6972; *terminal*:–out- (utter-)most.

7021. קִיקָיוֹן *kee-kaw-yone';* perh. from 7006; the *gourd* (as *nauseous*):–gourd.

7022. קִיקָלוֹן *kee-kaw-lone';* from 7036; intense *disgrace*:–shameful spewing.

7023. קִיר keer; or קִר (Is. 22:5) keer; or (fem.) קִירָה *kee-raw'*; from 6979; a *wall* (as built in a *trench*):–+ mason, side, town, X very, wall.
7024. קִיר *keer* the same as 7023; *fortress*; *Kir*, a place in Ass.; also one in Moab:–Kir. Comp. 7025.
7025. קִיר חֶרֶשׂ *keer kheh'-res*; or (fem. of the latter word) קִיר חֲרֶשֶׂת *keer khar-eh'-seth;* from 7023 and 2789; *fortress of earthenware; Kir-Cheres* or *Kir-Chareseth*, a place in Moab:–Kir-haraseth, Kir-hareseth, Kir-haresh, Kir-heres.
7026. קֵירֹס *kay-roce'*; or קֵרֹס *kay-roce'*; from the same as 7166; *ankled*; *Keros*, one of the Nethinim:–Keros.
7027. קִישׁ *keesh;* from 6983; a *bow*; *Kish*, the name of five Isr.:–Kish.
7028. קִישׁוֹן *kee-shone'*; from 6983; *winding*; *Kishon*, a river of Pal.:–Kishon, Kison.
7029. קִישִׁי *kee-shee'*; from 6983; *bowed*; *Kishi*, an Isr.:–Kishi.
7030. קִיתָרֹס *kee-thaw-roce'* (Chald.); of Gr. or.;(ςιραθίκ) a *lyre*:–harp.
7031. קַל *kal*; contr. from 7043; *light*; (by impl.) *rapid* (also adv.):–light, swift(-ly).
7032. קָל *kawl* (Chald.); cor. to 6963:–sound, voice.
7033. קָלָה *kaw-law'* a prim. root [rather ident. with 7034 through the idea of *shrinkage* by heat]; to *toast*, i.e. *scorch* partially or slowly:–dried, loathsome, parch, roast.
7034. קָלָה *kaw-law';* a prim. root; to be *light* (as implied in *rapid* motion), but fig., only (*be* [caus., *hold*] in *contempt*):–base, contemn, despise, lightly esteem, set light, seem vile.
7035. קָלַהּ *kaw-lah';* for 6950; to *assemble*:–gather together.
7036. קָלוֹן *kaw-lone';* from 7034; *disgrace*; (by impl.) the *pudenda*:– confusion, dishonour, ignominy, reproach, shame.
7037. קַלַּחַת *kal-lakh'-ath*; app. but a form for 6747; a *kettle*:–caldron.
7038. קָלַט *kaw-lat'*; a prim. root; to *maim*:–lacking in his parts.
7039. קָלִי *kaw-lee'* or קָלִיא *kaw-lee'*; from 7033; *roasted* ears of grain:–parched corn.
7040. קַלַּי *kal-lah'-ee*; from 7043; *frivolous*; *Kallai*, an Isr.:–Kallai..
7041. קֵלָיָה *kay-law-yaw'*; from 7034; *insignificance*; *Kelajah*, an Isr.:–Kelaiah.
7042. קְלִיטָא *kel-ee-taw';* rom 7038; *maiming; Kelita,* the name of three Israelites:–Kelita.
7043. קָלַל *kaw-lal'*; a prim. root; to be (caus., *make*) *light*, lit. (*swift, small, sharp*, etc.) or fig. (*easy, trifling, vile*, etc.):–abate, make bright, bring into contempt, (ac-)curse, despise, (be) ease(-y, -ier), (be a, make, make somewhat, move, seem a, set) light(-en, -er, -ly, -ly afflict, -ly esteem, thing), X slight[-ly], be swift(-er), (be, be more, make, re-) vile, whet.
7044. קָלָל *kaw-lawl';* from 7043; *brightened* (as if *sharpened*):–burnished, polished.
7045. קְלָלָה *kel-aw-law'*; from 7043; *vilification*:–(ac-)curse(-d, -ing).
7046. קָלַס *kaw-las';* a prim. root; to *disparage*, i.e. ridicule:–mock, scoff, scorn.
7047. קֶלֶס *keh'-les*; from 7046; a *laughing-stock*:–derision.
7048. קַלָּסָה *kal-law-saw'*; intens. from 7046; *ridicule*:–mocking.
7049. קָלַע *kaw-lah';* a prim. root: to sling: also to *carve* (as if a *circular* motion, or into *light* forms):–carve, sling (out).
7050. קֶלַע *keh'-lah*; from 7049; a *sling*; also a (door) *screen* (as if *slung* across), or the *valve* (of the door) itself:–hanging, leaf, sling.
7051. קַלָּע *kal-law';* intens. from 7049; a *slinger*:–slinger.
7052. קְלֹקֵל *kel-o-kale'*; from 7043; *insubstantial*:–light.
7053. קִלְּשׁוֹן *kil-lesh-one';* from an un. root mean. to *prick*; a *prong*, i.e. hay-fork:–fork.
7054. קָמָה *kaw-maw'*; fem. of act.part. of 6965; something that *rises*, i.e. a *stalk* of grain:–(standing) corn, grown up, stalk.
7055. קְמוּאֵל *kem-oo-ale'* from 6965 and 410; *raised of God*; *Kemuël*, the name of a relative of Abraham, and of two Isr.:–Kemuel.
7056. קָמוֹן *kaw-mone';* from 6965; an *elevation*; *Kamon*, a place E. of the Jordan:–Camon.
7057. קִמּוֹשׁ *kim-moshe';* or קִימוֹשׁ *kee-moshe'*; from an un. root mean. to *sting*; a *prickly* plant:–nettle. Comp. 7063.
7058. קֶמַח *keh'-makh*; from an un. root prob. mean. to *grind*; *flour*:–flour, meal.
7059. קָמַט *kaw-mat';* a prim. root; to *pluck*, i.e. destroy:–cut down, fill with wrinkles.
7060. קָמַל *kaw-mal'*; a prim. root; to *wither*: –hew down, wither.
7061. קָמַץ *kaw-mats';* a prim. root; to *grasp* with the hand:–take an handful.
7062. קֹמֶץ *ko'mets;* from 7061; a *grasp*, i.e. *handful*:–handful.
7063. קִמָּשׁוֹן *kim-maw-shone'*; from the same as 7057; a *prickly* plant:–thorn.
7064. קֵן *kane*; contr. from 7077; a *nest* (as *fixed*), sometimes incl. the *nestlings*; fig., a *chamber* or *dwelling*:–nest, room.
7065. קָנָא *kaw-naw';* a prim. root; to *be* (caus., *make*) *zealous*, i.e. (in a bad sense) *jealous* or *envious*:–(be) envy(-ious), be (move to, provoke to) jealous(-y), X very, (be) zeal(-ous).
7066. קְנָה *ken-aw'* (Chald.); cor. to 7069; to *purchase*:–buy.
7067. קַנָּא *kan-naw';* from 7065; *jealous*:–jealous. Comp. 7072.
7068. קִנְאָה *kin-aw'* from 7065; *jealousy* or *envy*:–envy(-ied), jealousy, X sake, zeal.
7069. קָנָה *kaw-naw';* a prim. root; to *erect,* i.e. *create;* by ext. to *procure,* esp. by purchase (caus. *sell;* by impl. to *own*:–attain, buy (-er), teach to keep cattle, get, provoke to jealousy, possess (-or), purchase, recover, redeem, X surely, X verily.
7070. קָנֶה *kaw-neh'* from 7069; a *reed* (as *erect*); by resemblance a *rod* (esp. for measuring), *shaft, tube*, stem, the *radius* (of the arm), *beam* (of a steelyard):–balance, bone, branch, calamus, cane, reed, X spearman, stalk.
7071. קָנָה *kaw-naw';* feminine of 7070; *reediness; Kanah*, the name of a stream and of a place in Pal.:–Kanah.
7072. קַנּוֹא *kan-no';* for 7067; *jealous* or *angry*:–jealous.
7073. קְנַז *ken-az'* prob. from an un. root mean. to *hunt; hunter; Kenaz*, the name of an Edomite and of two Isr.:–Kenaz.
7074. קְנִזִּי *ken-iz-zee'* patron. from 7073, a *Kenizzite* or desc. of Kenaz:–Kenezite, Kenizzites.
7075. קִנְיָן *kin-yawn'*; from 7069; *creation*, i.e. (concr.) *creatures*; also *acquisition, purchase, wealth*:–getting, goods, X with money, riches, substance.
7076. קִנָּמוֹן *kin-naw-mone';* from an un. root (mean. to *erect*); *cinnamon* bark (as in *upright* rolls):–cinnamon.
7077. קָנַן *kaw-nan';* a prim. root; to *erect*; but used only as denom. from 7064; to *nestle*, i.e. *build* or *occupy* as a nest:– make...nest.
7078. קֶנֶץ *keh'-nets*; from an un. root prob. mean. to *wrench; perversion*:–end.
7079. קְנָת *ken-awth'* from 7069; *possession*; *Kenath*, a place E. of the Jordan:–Kenath.
7080. קָסַם *kaw-sam';* a prim. root; prop. to *distribute*, i.e. *determine* by lot or magical scroll; by impl., to *divine*:–divine(-r, -ation), prudent, soothsayer, use [divination].
7081. קֶסֶם *keh'-sem*; from 7080; a *lot:* also *divination* (incl. its *fee*), *oracle*:–(reward of) divination, divine sentence, witchcraft.
7082. קָסַס *kaw-sas'*; a prim. root; to *lop* off:–cut off.
7083. קֶסֶת *keh'-seth*; from the same as 3563 (or as 7185); prop. a *cup*, i.e. an *ink-stand*:–inkhorn.
7084. קְעִילָה *keh-ee-law'*; perh. from 7049 in the sense of *inclosing*; *citadel*; *Keïlah*, a place in Pal.:–Keilah.
7085. קַעֲקַע *kah-ak-ah'*; from the same as 6970; an *incision* or gash:–+ mark.
7086. קְעָרָה *keh-aw-raw'*; prob. from 7167; a *bowl* (as *cut* out hollow):–charger, dish.
7087. קָפָא *kaw-faw'*; a prim. root; to *shrink*, i.e. *thicken* (as unracked wine, curdled milk, clouded sky, frozen water):–congeal, curdle, dark, settle.
7088. קָפַד *kaw-fad'*; a prim. root; to *contract*, i.e. roll together:–cut off.
7089. קְפָדָה *kef-aw-daw'*; from 7088; *shrinking*, i.e., terror:–destruction.
7090. קִפּוֹד *kip-pode'*; or קִפֹּד *kip-pode'*; from 7088; a species of bird, perh. the *bittern* (from its *contracted* form):–bittern.
7091. קִפּוֹז *kip-poze'*; from an un. root mean. to *contract*, i.e. *spring* forward; an *arrow-snake* (as *darting* on its prey):–great owl.
7092. קָפַץ *kaw-fats'*; a prim. root; to *draw together*, i.e. close; by impl., to *leap* (by *contracting* the limbs); spec., to *die* (from *gathering* up the feet):–shut (up), skip, stop, take out of the way.
7093. קֵץ *kates*; contr. from 7112; an *extremity*; adv. (with prep. pref.) *after*:–+ after, (utmost) border, end, [in-]finite, X process.
7094. קָצַב *kaw-tsab';* a prim. root; to *clip*, or (gen.) *chop*:–cut down, shorn.
7095. קֶצֶב *keh'-tseb* from 7094; *shape* (as if *cut out*); *base* (as if there *cut* off):–bottom, size.
7096. קָצָה *kaw-tsaw'* a prim. root; to *cut* off; (fig.) to *destroy*; (partially) to *scrape* off:–cut off, cut short, scrape (off).
7097. קָצֶה *kaw-tseh';* or (neg. only) קֵצֶה *kay'-tseh*; from 7096; an *extremity* (used in a great variety of appl. and idioms; comp. 7093):–X after, border, brim, brink, edge, end, [in-]finite, frontier, outmost coast, quarter, shore, (out-)side, X some, ut(-ter-)most (part).
7098. קָצָה *kaw-tsaw'* fem. of 7097; a *termination* (used like 7097):–coast, corner, (selv-)edge, lowest, (uttermost) part.
7099. קֶצֶו *keh'-tsev*; and (fem.) קִצְוָה *kits-vaw'*; from 7096; a *limit* (used like 7097, but with less variety):–end, edge, uttermost part.
7100. קֶצַח *keh'-tsakh*; from an un. root app. mean. to *incise*; *fennelflower* (from its

pungency):–fitches.

7101. קָצִין *kaw-tseen';* from 7096 in the sense of *determining*; a *magistrate* (as *deciding*) or other *leader*:–captain, guide, prince, ruler. Comp. 6278.

7102. קְצִיעָה *kets-ee-aw'*; from 7106; *cassia* (as *peeled*; pl. the bark):–cassia.

7103. קְצִיעָה *kets-ee-aw'*; the same as 7102; *Ketsiah*, a daughter of Job:–Kezia.

7104. קְצִיץ *kets-eets'* from 7112; *abrupt*; Keziz, a valley in Pal.:–Keziz.

7105. קָצִיר *kaw-tseer'*; from 7114; *severed*, i.e. *harvest* (as *reaped*), the crop, the time, the reaper, or fig.; also a *limb* (of a tree, or simply *foliage*):–bough, branch, harvest (man).

7106. קָצַע *kaw-tsah'*; a prim. root; to *strip* off, i.e. (partially) *scrape;* by impl., to *segregate* (as an angle):–cause to scrape, corner.

7107. קָצַף *kaw-tsaf';* a prim. root; to *crack* off, i.e. (fig.) *burst* out in rage:–(be) anger (-ry), displease, fret self, (provoke to) wrath (come), be wroth.

7108. קְצַף *kets-af'* (Chald.); cor. to 7107; to *become enraged*:–be furious.

7109. קְצַף *kets-af'* (Chald.); from 7108; *rage*:–wrath.

7110. קֶצֶף *keh'-tsef*; from 7107; a *splinter* (as *chipped* off); fig., *rage* or *strife*:–foam, indignation, X sore, wrath.

7111. קְצָפָה *kets-aw-faw'*; from 7107; a *fragment*:–bark[-ed].

7112. קָצַץ *kaw-tsats'*; a prim. root; to *chop* off (lit. or fig.):–cut (asunder, in pieces, in sunder, off), X utmost.

7113. קְצַץ *kets-ats'* (Chald.); cor. to 7112:–cut off.

7114. קָצַר *kaw-tsar'*; a prim. root; to *dock* off, i.e. *curtail* (trans. or intr., lit. or fig.); esp. to *harvest* (grass or grain):–X at all, cut down, much discouraged, grieve, harvestman, lothe, mourn, reap(-er), (be, wax) short(-en, -er), straiten, trouble, vex.

7115. קֹצֶר *ko'-tser*; from 7114; *shortness* (of spirit), i.e. impatience:–anguish.

7116. קָצֵר *kaw-tsare'*; from 7114; *short* (whether in size, number, life, strength or temper):–few, hasty, small, soon.

7117. קְצָת *kets-awth'*; from 7096; a *termination* (lit. or fig.); also (by impl.) a *portion*; adv. (with prep. pref.) *after*:–end, part, X some.

7118. קְצָת *kets-awth'* (Chald.); cor. to 7117:–end, partly.

7119. קַר *kar;* contr. from an un. root mean. to *chill*; *cool*; fig., *quiet*:–cold, excellent.

7120. קֹר *kore*; from the same as 7119; *cold*:–cold.

7121. קָרָא *kaw-raw';* a prim. root [rather ident. with 7122 through the idea of *accosting* a person met]; to *call* out to (i.e. prop. *address* by name, but used in a wide variety of appl.):–bewray [self], that are bidden, call (for, forth, self, upon), cry (unto), (be) famous, guest, invite, mention, (give) name, preach, (make) proclaim(-ation), pronounce, publish, read, renowned, say.

7122. קָרָא *kaw-raw'*; a prim. root: to *encounter*, whether accidentally or in a hostile manner:–befall, (by) chance, (cause to) come (upon), fall out, happen, meet.

7123. קְרָא *ker-aw'* (Chald.); cor. to 7121:–call, cry, read.

7124. קֹרֵא *ko-ray'*; prop. act.part. of 7121; a *caller*, i.e. *partridge* (from its *cry*):–partridge. See also 6981.

7125. קִרְאָה *keer-aw';* from 7122; an *encountering*, accidental, friendly or hostile (also adv., *opposite*):–X against (he come), help, meet, seek, X to, X in the way.

7126. קָרַב *kaw-rab'*; a prim. root; to *approach* (caus., *bring near*) for whatever purpose:–(cause to) approach, (cause to) bring (forth, near), (cause to) come (near, nigh), (cause to) draw near (nigh), go (near), be at hand, join, be near, offer, present, produce, make ready, stand, take.

7127. קְרֵב *ker-abe'* (Chald.); cor. to 7126:–approach, come (near, nigh), draw near.

7128. קְרָב *ker-awb';* from 7126; hostile *encounter*:–battle, war.

7129. קְרָב *ker-awb'* (Chald.); cor. to 7128:–war.

7130. קֶרֶב *keh'-reb*; from 7126; prop. the *nearest* part, i.e. the *center*, whether lit., fig. or adv. (esp. with prep.):–X among, X before, bowels, X unto charge, + eat (up), X heart, X him, X in, inward (X -ly, part, -s, thought), midst, + out of, purtenance, X therein, X through, X within self.

7131. קָרֵב *kaw-rabe'* from 7126; *near*:–approach, come (near, nigh), draw near.

7132. קְרָבָה *ker-aw-baw'* from 7126; *approach*:–approaching, draw near.

7133. קָרְבָּן *kor-bawn'*; or קֻרְבָּן *koor-bawn'*; from 7126; something *brought near* the altar, i.e. a sacrificial *present*:–oblation, that is offered, offering.

7134. קַרְדֹּם *kar-dome'* perh. from 6923 in the sense of *striking* upon; an *axe*:–ax.

7135. קָרָה *kaw-raw'* fem. of 7119; *coolness*:–cold.

7136. קָרָה *kaw-raw'*; a prim. root; to *light upon* (chiefly by accident); caus., to *bring about*; spec., to *impose* timbers (for roof or floor):–appoint, lay (make) beams, befall, bring, come (to pass unto), floor, [hap] was, happen (unto), meet, send good speed.

7137. קָרֶה *kaw-reh'*; from 7136; an (unfortunate) *occurrence*, i.e. some accidental (cerem.) *disqualification*:–uncleanness that chanceth.

7138. קָרוֹב *kaw-robe'*; or קָרֹב *kaw-robe'*; from 7126; *near* (in place, kindred or time):–allied, approach, at hand, + any of kin, kinsfold(-sman), (that is) near (of kin), neighbour, (that is) next, (them that come) nigh (at hand), more ready, short(-ly).

7139. קָרַח *kaw-rakh';* a prim. root; to *depilate*:–make (self) bald.

7140. קֶרַח *keh'-rakh*; or קֹרַח *ko'-rakh*; from 7139; *ice* (as if bald, i.e. *smooth*); hence, *hail*; by resemblance, rock *crystal*:–crystal, frost, ice.

7141. קֹרַח *ko'rakh*; from 7139; *ice; Korach*, the name of two Edomites and three Isr.:–Korah.

7142. קֵרֵחַ *kay-ray'-akh*; from 7139; *bald* (on the back of the head):–bald (head).

7143. קָרֵחַ *kaw-ray'-akh*; from 7139; *bald; Kareäch*, an Isr.:–Careah, Kareah.

7144. קָרְחָה *kor-khaw'*; or (Eze. 27:31) קָרְחָא *kor-khaw'*; from 7139; *baldness*:–bald(-ness), X utterly.

7145. קָרְחִי *kor-khee'*; patron. from 7141; a *Korchite* (coll.) or desc. of Korach:–Korahite, Korathite, sons of Kore, Korhite.

7146. קָרַחַת *kaw-rakh'-ath*; from 7139; a *bald* spot (on the back of the head); fig., a *threadbare* spot (on the back side of the cloth):–bald head, bare within.

7147. קְרִי *ker-ee'*; from 7136; hostile *encounter*:–contrary.

7148. קָרִיא *kaw-ree'*; from 7121; *called*, i.e. *select*:–famous, renowned.

7149. קִרְיָא *keer-yaw'* (Chald.); קִרְיָה or *keer-yaw'* (Chald.); cor. to 7151:–city.

7150. קְרִיאָה *ker-ee-aw'*; from 7121; a *proclamation*:–preaching.

7151. קִרְיָה *kir-yaw'*; from 7136 in the sense of *flooring*, i.e. building; a *city*:–city.

7152. קְרִיּוֹת *ker-ee-yoth';* pl. of 7151; *buildings; Kerioth*, the name of two places in Pal.:–Kerioth, Kirioth.

7153. קִרְיַת אַרְבַּע *keer-yath' ar-bah';* or (with the art. interp.) קִרְיַת הָאַרְבַּע (Ne. 11:25) *keer-yath' haw-ar-bah'*; from 7151 and 704 or 702; *city of Arba*, or *city of the four* (giants); *Kirjath-Arba* or *Kirjath-ha-Arba*, a place in Pal.:–Kirjath-arba.

7154. קִרְיַת בַּעַל *keer-yath' bah'-al;* from 7151 and 1168; *city of Baal; Kirjath-Baal*, a place in Pal.:–Kirjath-baal.

7155. קִרְיַת חֻצוֹת *keer-yath' khoo-tsoth';* from 7151 and the fem. pl. of 2351; *city of streets; Kirjath-Chutsoth*, a place in Moab:–Kirjath-huzoth.

7156. קִרְיָתַיִם *keer-yaw-thah'-yim*; dual of 7151; *double city; Kirjathaïm*, the name of two placed in Pal.:–Kiriathaim, Kirjathaim.

7157. קִרְיַת יְעָרִים *keer-yath' yeh-aw-reem';* or (Jer. 26:20) with the art. interp.; or (Jos. 18:28) simply the former part of the word; or קִרְיַת עָרִים *keer-yath' aw-reem'*; from 7151 and the pl. of 3293 or 5892; *city of forests*, or *city of towns; Kirjath-Jeärim* or *Kirjath-Arim*, a place in Pal.:–Kirjath, Kirjath-jearim, Kirjath-arim.

7158. קִרְיַת סַנָּה *keer-yath' san-naw';* or קִרְיַת סֵפֶר *keer-yath' say-fer*; from 7151 and a simpler fem. from the same as 5577, or (for the latter name) 5612; *city of branches*, or *of a book*; *Kirjath-Sannah* or *Kirjath-Sepher*, a place in Pal.:–Kirjath-sannah, Kirjath-sepher.

7159. קָרַם *kaw-ram'*; a prim. root; to *cover*:–cover.

7160. קָרַן *kaw-ran';* a prim. root; to *push* or gore; used only as denom. from 7161, to *shoot out horns*; fig., *rays*:–have horns, shine.

7161. קֶרֶן *keh'-ren*; from 7160; a *horn* (as *projecting*); by impl., a *flask, cornet*; by resembl. an elephant's *tooth* (i.e. *ivory*), a *corner* (of the altar), a *peak* (of a mountain), a *ray* (of light); fig., *power*:–X hill, horn.

7162. קֶרֶן, *keh'-ren* (Chald.); cor. to 7161; a *horn* (lit. or for sound):–horn, cornet.

7163. קֶרֶן הַפּוּךְ *keh'-ren hap-pook'*; from 7161 and 6320; *horn of cosmetic*; *Keren-hap-Puk*, one of Job's daughters:–Keren-happuch.

7164. קָרַס *kaw-ras'*; a prim. root; prop. to *protrude*; used only as denom. from 7165 (for alliteration with 7167), to *hunch*, i.e. be hump-backed:–stoop.

7165. קֶרֶס *keh'-res*; from 7164; a *knob* or belaying-pin (from its swelling form):–tache.

7166. קַרְסֹל *kar-sole'*; from 7164; an *ankle* (as a *protuberance* or joint):–foot.

7167. קָרַע *kaw-rah'*; a prim. root; to *rend*, lit. or fig. (*revile*, *paint* the eyes, as if enlarging them):–cut out, rend, X surely, tear.

7168. קֶרַע *keh'-rah*; from 7167; a *rag*:–piece, rag.

7169. קָרַץ *kaw-rats'*; a prim. root; to *pinch*, i.e. (partially) to *bite* the lips, *blink* the

eyes (as a gesture of malice), or (fully) to *squeeze* off (a piece of clay in order to mould a vessel from it):–form, move, wink.
7170. קְרַץ *ker-ats'* (Chald.); cor. to 7171 in the sense of a *bit* (to "eat the *morsels* of" any one, i.e. *chew* him up [fig.] by *slander*):–+ accuse.
7171. קֶרֶץ *keh'-rets*; from 7169; *extirpation* (as if by *constriction*):–destruction.
7172. קַרְקַע *kar-kah'*;from 7167; *floor* (as if a pavement of pieces or *tesseræ*), of a building or the sea:–bottom, (X one side of the) floor.
7173. קַרְקַע *kar-kah'*; the same as 7172; *ground-floor*; *Karka* (with the art. pref.), a place in Pal.:–Karkaa.
7174. קַרְקֹר *kar-kore'*; from 6979; *foundation*; *Karkor*, a place E. of the Jordan:–Karkor.
7175. קֶרֶשׁ *keh'-resh*; from an un. root mean. to *split* off; a *slab* or plank; by impl., a *deck* of a ship:–bench, board.
7176. קֶרֶת *keh'-reth*; from 7136 in the sense of building; a *city*:–city.
7177. קַרְתָּה *kar-taw'*; from 7176; city; *Kartah*, a place in Pal.:–Kartah.
7178. קַרְתָּן *kar-tawn'*; from 7176; *city-plot*; *Kartan*, a place in Pal.:–Kartan.
7179. קַשׁ *kash;* from 7197; *straw* (as dry):–stubble.
7180. קִשֻּׁא *kish-shoo';* from an un. root (mean. to be *hard*); a *cucumber* (from the difficulty of *digestion*):–cucumber.
7181. קָשַׁב *kaw-shab';* a prim. root; to *prick up* the ears, i.e. *hearken*:–attend, (cause to) hear (-ken), give heed, incline, mark (well), regard.
7182. קֶשֶׁב *keh'-sheb*; from 7181; a *hearkening*:–X diligently, hearing, much heed, that regarded.
7183. קַשָּׁב *kash-shawb'*; or קַשֻּׁב *kash-shoob'*; from 7181; *hearkening*:–attent(-ive).
7184. קָשָׂה *kaw-saw'*; or קַשְׂוָה *kas-vaw'*; from an un. root mean. to be *round*; a *jug* (from its shape):–cover, cup.
7185. קָשָׁה *kaw-shaw'*; a prim. root; prop. to be *dense*, i.e. tough or *severe* (in various appl.):–be cruel, be fiercer, make grievous, be ([ask a], be in, have, seem, would) hard (-en, [labour], -ly, thing), be sore, (be, make) stiff(-en, [-necked]).
7186. קָשֶׁה *kaw-sheh'* from 7185; *severe* (in various appl.):–churlish, cruel, grievous, hard([-hearted], thing), heavy, + impudent, obstinate, prevailed, rough(-ly), sore, sorrowful, stiff([necked]), stubborn, + in trouble.
7187. קְשׁוֹט *kesh-ote'* (Chald.); or קְשֹׁט *kesh-ote'* (Chald.); cor. to 7189; *fidelity*:–truth.
7188. קָשַׁח *kaw-shakh'*; a prim. root; to *be* (caus., *make*) *unfeeling*:–harden.
7189. קֹשֶׁט *ko'-shet;* or קֹשְׁט *kosht;* from an un. root mean. to *balance*; *equity* (as evenly *weighed*), i.e. *reality*:–truth.
7190. קְשִׁי *kesh-ee';* from 7185; *obstinacy*:–stubbornness.
7191. קִשְׁיוֹן *kish-yone'*; from 7190; *hard ground*; *Kishjon*, a place in Pal.:–Kishion, Keshon.
7192. קְשִׂיטָה *kes-ee-taw';* from an un. root (prob. mean. to *weigh* out); an *ingot* (as def. *estimated* and stamped for a coin):–piece of money (silver).
7193. קַשְׂקֶשֶׂת *kas-keh'-seth;* by redupl. from an un. root mean. to *shale* off as bark; a *scale* (of a fish); hence a coat of *mail* (as composed of or covered with jointed *plates* of metal):–mail, scale.
7194. קָשַׁר *kaw-shar'*; a prim. root: to *tie*, phys. (*gird, confine, compact*) or ment. (in *love, league*):–bind (up), (make a) conspire (-acy, -ator), join together, knit, stronger, work [(treason)].
7195. קֶשֶׁר *keh'-sher*; from 7194; an (unlawful) *alliance*:–confederacy, conspiracy, treason.
7196. קִשֻּׁר *kish-shoor'*; from 7194; an (ornament.) *girdle* (for women):–attire, headband.
7197. קָשַׁשׁ *kaw-shash';* a prim. root; to *become sapless* through drought; used only as denom. from 7179; to *forage* for straw, stubble or wood; fig., to *assemble*:–gather (selves) (together).
7198. קֶשֶׁת *keh'-sheth*; from 7185 in the or. sense (of 6983) of *bending*: a *bow*, for *shooting* (hence, fig., *strength*) or the *iris*:–X arch(-er), + arrow, bow([-man, -shot]).
7199. קַשָּׁת *kash-shawth'*; intens. (as denom.) from 7198; a *bowman*:–X archer.

ר

7200. רָאָה *raw-aw';* a prim. root; to *see*, lit. or fig. (in numerous appl., direct and implied, trans., intr. and caus.):–advise self, appear, approve, behold, X certainly, consider, discern, (make to) enjoy, have experience, gaze, take heed, X indeed, X joyfully, lo, look (on, one another, one on another, one upon another, out, up, upon), mark, meet, X be near, perceive, present, provide, regard, (have) respect, (fore-, cause to, let) see(-r,-m, one another), shew (self), X sight of others, (e-)spy, stare, X surely, X think, view, visions.
7201. רָאָה *raw-aw';* from 7200; a *bird* of prey (prob. the *vulture*, from its sharp *sight*):–glede. Comp. 1676.
7202. רָאֶה *raw-eh';* from 7200; *seeing*, i.e. experiencing:–see.
7203. רֹאֶה *ro-eh'*; act.part. of 7200; a *seer* (as often rendered); but also (abstr.) a *vision*:–vision.
7204. רֹאֶה *ro-ay'*; for 7203; *prophet*; *Roëh*, an Isr.:–Haroeh (*incl. the art.*).
7205. רְאוּבֵן *reh-oo-bane'*; from the imper. of 7200 and 1121; *see* ye a *son*; *Reüben*, a son of Jacob:–Reuben.
7206. רְאוּבֵנִי *reh-oob-ay-nee'*; patron. from 7205; a *Reübenite* or desc. of Reuben:–children of Reubën, Reubenites.
7207. רַאֲוָה *rah-av-aw'* from 7200; *sight*, i.e. satisfaction:–behold.
7208. רְאוּמָה *reh-oo-maw'*; fem. past.part. of 7213; *raised*; *Reümah*, a Syrian woman:–Reumah.
7209. רְאִי *reh-ee';* from 7200; a *mirror* (as *seen*):–looking glass.
7210. רֳאִי *ro-ee';*from 7200; sight, whether abstr. (*vision*) or concr. (a *spectacle*):–gazingstock, look to, (that) see(-th).
7211. רְאָיָה *reh-aw-yaw';* from 7200 and 3050; *Jah has seen; Reäjah*, the name of three Isr.:–Reaia, Reaiah.
7212. רְאִית *reh-eeth'* from 7200; *sight*:–beholding.
7213. רָאַם *raw-am';* a prim. root; to *rise*:–be lifted up.
7214. רְאֵם *reh-ame'* or רְאֵים *reh-ame'*; or רֵים *rame*; or רֵם *rame*; from 7213; a wild *bull* (from its *conspicuousness*):–unicorn.
7215. רָאמָה *raw-maw';* from 7213; something *high* in value, i.e. perh. *coral*:–coral.
7216. רָאמוֹת *raw-moth'* or רָאמֹת *raw-moth'*; pl. of 7215; *heights; Ramoth*, the name of two places in Pal.:–Ramoth.
7217. רֵאשׁ *raysh* (Chald.); cor. to 7218; the *head;* fig., the *sum*:–chief, head, sum.
7218. רֹאשׁ *roshe;* from an un. root app. mean. to *shake;* the *head* (as most easily *shaken*), whether lit. or fig. (in many appl., of place, time, rank, itc.):–band, beginning, captain, chapiter, chief(-est place, man, things), company, end, X every [man], excellent, first, forefront, ([be-])head, height, (on) high(-est part, [priest]), X lead, X poor, principal, ruler, sum, top.
7219. רֹאשׁ *roshe*; or (De. 32:32) רוֹשׁ *roshe;* app. the same as 7218; a poisonous *plant*, prob. the *poppy* (from its conspicuous *head*); gen. *poison* (even of serpents):–gall, hemlock, poison, venom.
7220. רֹאשׁ *roshe;* robably the same as 7218; *Rosh*, the name of an Isr. and of a for. nation:–Rosh.
7221. רִאשָׁה *ree-shaw'* from the same as 7218; a *beginning*:–beginning.
7222. רֹאשָׁה *ro-shaw'* fem. of 7218; the *head*:–head[-stone].
7223. רִאשׁוֹן *ree-shone';* or רִאשֹׁן *ree-shone'*; from 7221; *first*, in place, time or rank (as adj. or noun):–ancestor, (that were) before (-time), beginning, eldest, first, fore[-father] (-most), former (thing), of old time, past.
7224. רִאשֹׁנִי *ree-sho-nee'*; from 7223; *first*:–first.
7225. רֵאשִׁית *ray-sheeth'*; from the same as 7218; the *first*, in place, time, order or rank (spec., a *firstfruit*):–beginning, chief(-est), first(-fruits, part, time), principal thing.
7226. רַאֲשֹׁת *rah-ash-oth'*; from 7218; a *pillow* (being for the *head*):–bolster.
7227. רַב *rab* by contr. from 7231; *abundant* (in quantity, size, age, number, rank, quality):–(in) abound(-undance, -ant, -antly), captain, elder, enough, exceedingly, full, great(-ly, man, one), increase, long (enough, [time]), (do, have) many(-ifold, things, a time), ([ship-]) master, mighty, more, (too, very) much, multiply(-tude), officer, often [-times], plenteous, populous, prince, process [of time], suffice(-lent).
7228. רַב *rab*; by contr. from 7232; an *archer* [or perh. the same as 7227]:–archer.
7229. רַב *rab* (Chald.); cor. to 7227:–captain, chief, great, lord, master, stout.
7230. רֹב *robe*; from 7231; *abundance* (in any respect):–abundance(-antly), all, X common [sort], excellent, great(-ly,-ness, number), huge, be increased, long, many, more in number, most, much, multitude, plenty(-ifully), X very [age].
7231. רָבַב *raw-bab'*; a prim. root; prop. to *cast* together [comp. 7241], i.e. *increase*, esp. in number; also (as denom. from 7233) to *multiply by the myriad*:–increase, be many (-ifold), be more, multiply, ten thousands.
7232. רָבַב *raw-bab';* a prim. root [rather ident. with 7231 through the idea of *projection*]; to *shoot* an arrow:–shoot.
7233. רְבָבָה *reb-aw-baw'*; from 7231; *abundance* (in number), i.e. (spec.) a *myriad* (whether def. or indef.):–many, million, X multiply, ten thousand.
7234. רָבַד *raw-bad'* a prim. root; to *spread*:–deck.
7235. רָבָה *raw-baw'*; a prim. root; to *increase* (in whatever respect):–[bring in] abundance (X -antly), + archer, be in authority, bring up, X continue, enlarge, excel, exceeding(-ly), be full of, (be, make) great(-er, -ly, X -ness), grow up,

heap, increase, be long, (be, give, have, make, use) many (a time), (any, be, give, give the, have) more (in number), (ask, be, be so, gather, over, take, yield) much (greater, more), (make to) multiply, nourish, plenty(-eous), X process [of time], sore, store, thoroughly, very.

7236. רְבָה *reb-aw'* (Chald.); cor. to 7235:–make a great man, grow.

7237. רַבָּה *rab-baw'*; fem. of 7227; *great; Rabbah,* the name of two places in Pal., E. and West:–Rabbah, Rabbath.

7238. רְבוּ *reb-oo'* (Chald.); from a root cor. to 7235; *increase* (of dignity):–greatness, majesty.

7239. רִבּוֹא *rib-bo'*; from 7231; or רִבּוֹא *rib-bo'* from 7231; a *myriad,* i.e. indef., *large number*:–great things, ten ([eight]-een, [for]-ty, + sixscore, + threescore, X twenty, (twen)-ty) thousand.

7240. רִבּוֹ *rib-bo'* (Chald.); cor. to 7239:–X ten thousand times ten thousand.

7241. רָבִיב *raw-beeb'*; from 7231; a *rain* (as an *accumulation* of drops):–shower.

7242. רָבִיד *raw-beed'*; from 7234; a *collar* (as *spread* around the neck):–chain.

7243. רְבִיעִי *reb-ee-ee'*; or רְבִעִי *reb-ee-ee'*; from 7251; *fourth*; also (fractionally) a *fourth*:–foursquare, fourth (part).

7244. רְבִיעַי *reb-ee-ah'-ee* (Chald.); cor. to 7243 – fourth.

7245. רַבִּית *rab-beeth'*; from 7231; *multitude; Rabbith,* a place in Pal.:–Rabbith.

7246. רָבַךְ *raw-bak'*; a prim. root; to *soak* (bread in oil):–baken, (that which is) fried.

7247. רִבְלָה *rib-law'*; from an un. root mean. to be *fruitful; fertile; Riblah,* a place in Syria:–Riblah.

7248. רַב־מָג *rab-mawg'*; from 7227 and a for. word for a Magian; *chief Magian; Rab-Mag,* a Bab. official:–Rab-mag.

7249. רַב־סָרִיס *rab-saw-reece'*; from 7227 and a for. word for a eunuch; *chief chamberlain*; *Rab-Saris,* a Babylonian official:–Rab-saris.

7250. רָבַע *raw-bah'*; a prim. root; to *squat* or *lie* out flat, i.e. (spec.) in copulation:–let gender, lie down.

7251. רָבַע *raw-bah'*; a prim. root [rather ident. with 7250 through the idea of *sprawling* "at all fours" (or possibly the reverse is the order of deriv.); comp. 702]; prop. to *be four* (sided); used only as denom. of 7253; to be *quadrate*:–(four-)square(-d).

7252. רֶבַע *reh'-bah*; from 7250; *prostration* (for sleep):–lying down.

7253. רֶבַע *reh'-bah*; from 7251; a *fourth* (part or side):–fourth part, side, square.

7254. רֶבַע *reh'-bah*; the same as 7253; *Reba,* a Midianite:–Reba.

7255. רֹבַע *ro'-bah*; from 7251; a *quarter*:–fourth part.

7256. רִבֵּעַ *rib-bay'-ah*; from 7251; a desc. of the *fourth* generation, i.e. *great great grandchild*:–fourth.

7257. רָבַץ *raw-bats'*; a prim. root; to *crouch* (on all four legs folded, like a recumbent animal); be impl., to recline, repose, *brood, lurk, imbed*:–crouch (down), fall down, make a fold, lay, (cause to, make to) lie (down), make to rest, sit.

7258. רֶבֶץ *reh'-bets*; from 7257; a *couch* or place of repose:–where each lay, lie down in, resting place.

7259. רִבְקָה *rib-kaw'*; from an un. root prob. mean. to *clog* by tying up the fetlock; *fettering* (by beauty); *Ribkah,* the wife of Isaac:– Rebekah.

7260. רַבְרַב *rab-rab'* (Chald.); from 7229; *huge* (in size); *domineering* (in character):–(very) great (things).

7261. רַבְרְבָן *rab-reb-awn'* (Chald.); from 7260; a *magnate*:–lord, prince.

7262. רַבְשָׁקֵה *rab-shaw-kay'* from 7227 and 8248; *chief butler; Rabshakeh,* a Bab. official:–Rabshakeh.

7263. רֶגֶב *reh'-gheb*; from an un. root mean. to *pile* together; a *lump* of clay:–clod.

7264. רָגַז *raw-gaz'*; a prim. root; to *quiver* (with any violent emotion, esp. anger or fear):–be afraid, stand in awe, disquiet, fall out, fret, move, provoke, quake, rage, shake, tremble, trouble, be wroth.

7265. רְגַז *reg-az'* (Chald.); cor. to 7264:–provoke unto wrath.

7266. רְגַז *reg-az'* (Chald.); from 7265; violent *anger*:–rage.

7267. רֹגֶז *ro'-ghez*; from 7264; *commotion, restlessness* (of a horse), *crash* (of thunder), *disquiet, anger*:–fear, noise, rage, trouble (-ing), wrath.

7268. רַגָּז *rag-gawz'*; intens. from 7264; *timid*:–trembling.

7269. רָגְזָה *rog-zaw'*; fem. of 7267; *trepidation*:–trembling.

7270. רָגַל *raw-gal'*; a prim. root; to *walk* along; but only in spec., appl., to *reconnoiter,* to *be a tale-bearer* (i.e. slander); also (as denom. from 7272) to *lead about*:–backbite, search, slander, (e-) spy (out), teach to go, view.

7271. רְגַל *reg-al'* (Chald.); cor. to 7272:–foot.

7272. רֶגֶל *reh'-gel*; from 7270; a *foot* (as used in *walking*); by impl., a *step*; by euphem. the *pudenda*:–X be able to endure, X according as, X after, X coming, X follow, ([broken-]) foot([-ed, -stool]), X great toe, X haunt, X journey, leg, + piss, + possession, time.

7273. רַגְלִי *rag-lee'*; from 7272; a *footman* (soldier):–(on) foot(- man).

7274. רֹגְלִים *ro-gel-eem'*; pl. of act.part. of 7270; *fullers* (as *tramping* the cloth in washing); *Rogelim,* a place E. of the Jordan:– Rogelim.

7275. רָגַם *raw-gam'*; a prim. root [comp. 7263, 7321, 7551]; to *cast* together (stones), i.e. to *lapidate*:–X certainly, stone.

7276. רֶגֶם *reh'-gem*; from 7275; stone*heap*; *Regem,* an Isr.:–Regem.

7277. רִגְמָה *rig-maw'*; fem. of the same as 7276; a *pile* (of stones), i.e. (fig.) a *throng*:–council.

7278. רֶגֶם מֶלֶךְ *reh'-gem meh'-lek*; from 7276 and 4428; *king's heap; Regem-Melek,* an Isr.:–Regem-melech.

7279. רָגַן *raw-gan'*; a prim. root; to *grumble,* i.e. *rebel*:–murmur.

7280. רָגַע *raw-gah'*; a prim. root; prop. to *toss* violently and suddenly (the sea with waves, the skin with boils); fig. (in a favorable manner) to *settle,* i.e. quiet; spec., to *wink* (from the motion of the eye-lids):–break, divide, find ease, be a moment, (cause, give, make to) rest, make suddenly.

7281. רֶגַע *reh'-gah*; from 7280. a *wink* (of the eyes), i.e. a very *short space* of time:–instant, moment, space, suddenly.

7282. רָגֵעַ *raw-gay'-ah*; from 7280; *restful,* i.e. peaceable:–that are quiet.

7283. רָגַשׁ *raw-gash'*; a prim. root; to be *tumultuous*:–rage.

7284. רְגַשׁ *reg-ash'* (Chald.); cor. to 7283; to *gather* tumultuously:–assemble (together).

7285. רֶגֶשׁ *reh'-ghesh*; or (fem.) רִגְשָׁה *rig-shaw'*; from 7283; a tumultuous *crowd*:–company, insurrection.

7286. רָדַד *raw-dad'*; prim. root; to *tread* in pieces, i.e. (fig.) to *conquer*, or (spec.) to *overlay*:–spend, spread, subdue.

7287. רָדָה *raw-daw'*; a prim. root; to *tread* down, i.e. *subjugate*; spec., to *crumble* off:–(come to, make to) have dominion, prevail against, reign, (bear, make to) rule,(-r, over), take.

7288. רַדַּי *rad-dah'-ee*; intens. from 7287; *domineering; Raddai,* an Isr.:–Raddai.

7289. רָדִיד *raw-deed'*; from 7286 in the sense of *spreading*; a *veil* (as expanded):–vail, veil.

7290. רָדַם *raw-dam'*; a prim. root; to *stun,* i.e. *stupefy* (with sleep or death):–(be fast a-, be in a deep, cast into a dead, that) sleep(-er, -eth).

7291. רָדַף *raw-daf'*; a prim. root; to *run after* (usually with hostile intent; fig. [of time] *gone by*):–chase, put to flight, follow (after, on), hunt, (be under) persecute(-ion, -or), pursue(-r).

7292. רָהַב *raw-hab'*; a prim. root; to *urge* severely, i.e. (fig.) *importune, embolden, capture, act insolently*:–overcome, behave self proudly, make sure, strengthen.

7293. רַהַב *rah'-hab*; from 7292, *bluster* (*-er*):–proud, strength.

7294. רַהַב *rah'-hab*; the same as 7293; *Rahab* (i.e. *boaster*), an epithet of Eg.:–Rahab.

7295. רָהָב *raw-hawb'*; from 7292; *insolent*:–proud.

7296. רֹהַב *ro'-hab*; from 7292; *pride*:–strength.

7297. רָהָה *raw-haw'*; a prim. root; to *fear*:–be afraid.

7298. רַהַט *rah'-hat*; from an un. root app. mean. to *hollow out*; a *channel* or watering-box; by resemblance a *ringlet* of hair (as forming parallel lines):–gallery, gutter, trough.

7299. רֵו *rave* (Chald.); from a root cor. to 7200; *aspect*:–form.

7300. רוּד *rood*; a prim. root; to *tramp* about, i.e. *ramble* (free or disconsolate):–have the dominion, be lord, mourn, rule.

7301. רָוָה *raw-vaw'*; a prim. root; to *slake* the thirst (occasionally of other appetites):–bathe, make drunk, (take the) fill, satiate, (abundantly) satisfy, soak, water (abundantly).

7302. רָוֶה *raw-veh'*; from 7301; *sated* (with drink):–drunkenness, watered.

7303. רוֹהֲגָה *ro-hag-aw'*; from an un. root prob. mean. to *cry* out; *outcry;* Rohagah, an Isr.:–Rohgah.

7304. רָוַח *raw-vakh'*; a prim. root [rather ident. with 7306]; prop. to *breathe* freely, i.e. *revive*; by impl., to *have ample room*:–be refreshed, large.

7305. רֶוַח *reh'-vakh* from 7304; *room,* lit. (an *interval*) or fig. (*deliverance*):–enlargement, space.

7306. רוּחַ *roo'-akh*; a prim. root; prop. to *blow,* i.e. *breathe;* only (lit.) to *smell* or (by impl., *perceive* (fig., to *anticipate, enjoy*):–accept, smell, X touch, make of quick understanding.

7307. רוּחַ *roo'-akh*; from 7306; *wind;* by resemblance *breath,* i.e. a sensible (or even violent) exhalation; fig., *life, anger, unsubstantiality;* by ext., a *region* of the sky*;* by resemblance *spirit,* but only of

HEBREW

a rational being (incl. its expression and functions):–air, anger, blast, breath, X cool, courage, mind, X quarter, X side, spirit ([-ual]), tempest, X vain, ([whirl-]) wind(-y).
7308. רוּחַ *roo'-akh* (Chald.); cor. to 7307:–mind, spirit, wind.
7309. רְוָחָה *rev-aw-khaw';* fem. of 7305; *relief:*–breathing, respite.
7310. רְוָיָה *rev-aw-yaw';* from 7301; *satisfaction:*–runneth over, wealthy.
7311. רוּם *room;* a prim. root; to *be high* actively, to *rise* or *raise* (in various appl., lit. or fig.):–bring up, exalt (self), extol, give, go up, haughty, heave (up), (be, lift up on, make on, set up on, too) high(-er, one), hold up, levy, lift(-er) up, (be) lofty, (X a-)loud, mount up, offer (up), + presumptuously, (be) promote(-ion), proud, set up, tall(-er), take (away, off, up), breed worms.
7312. רוּם *room*; or רֻם *room;* from 7311; (lit.) *elevation* or (fig.) *elation:*–haughtiness, height, X high.
7313. רוּם *room* (Chald.); cor. to 7311; (fig. only):– extol, lift up (self), set up.
7314. רוּם *room* (Chald.); from 7313; (lit.) *altitude:*–height.
7315. רוֹם *rome;* from 7311; *elevation,* i.e. (adv.) *aloft:*–on high.
7316. רוּמָה *roo-maw';* from 7311; *height; Rumah,* a place in Pal.:–Rumah.
7317. רוֹמָה *ro-maw';* fem. of 7315; *elation,* i.e. (adv.) *proudly:*–haughtily.
7318. רוֹמָם *ro-mawm';* from 7426; *exaltation,* i.e. (fig. and spec.) *praise:*–be extolled.
7319. רוֹמְמָה *ro-mem-aw';* fem. act.part. of 7426; *exaltation,* i.e. *praise:*–high.
7320. רוֹמַמְתִּי עֶזֶר *ro-mam'-tee eh'-zer;* (or רֹמַמְתִּי *Ro-mam'-tee* from 7311 and 5828; *I have raised* up a *help; Romamti-Ezer,* an Isr.:–Romamti- ezer.
7321. רוּעַ *roo-ah';* a prim. root; to *mar* (esp. by breaking); fig., to *split* the ears (with sound), i.e. *shout* (for alarm or joy):–blow an alarm, cry (alarm, aloud, out), destroy, make a joyful noise, smart, shout (for joy), sound an alarm, triumph.
7322. רוּף *roof;* a prim. root; prop. to *triturate* (in a mortar), i.e. (fig.) to *agitate* (by concussion):–tremble.
7323. רוּץ *roots;* a prim. root; to *run* (for whatever reason, esp. to *rush*):–break down, divide speedily, footman, guard, bring hastily, (make) run (away, through), post stretch out.
7324. רוּק *rook*; a prim. root; to *pour* out (lit. or fig.), i.e. *empty:*–X arm, cast out, draw (out), (make) empty, pour forth (out).
7325. רוּר *roor*; a prim. root; to *slaver* (with spittle), i.e. (by anal.) to *emit* a fluid (ulcerous or nat.):–run.
7326. רוּשׁ *roosh*; a prim. root; to be *destitute:*–lack, needy, (make self) poor (man).
7327. רוּת *rooth*; prob. for 7468; *friend; Ruth,* a Moabitess:–Ruth.
7328. רָז *rawz* (Chald.); from an un. root prob. mean. to *attenuate*, i.e. (fig.) *hide*; a *mystery:*–secret.
7329. רָזָה *raw-zaw';* a prim. root; to *emaciate*, i.e. *make* (become) *thin* (lit. or fig.):–famish, wax lean.
7330. רָזֶה *raw-zeh';* from 7329; *thin:*–lean.
7331. רְזוֹן *rez-one'* from 7336; *prince; Rezon,* a Syrian:–Rezon.
7332. רָזוֹן *raw-zone';* from 7329; *thinness:*–leanness, X scant.
7333. רָזוֹן *raw-zone';* from 7336; a *dignitary:*–prince.
7334. רָזִי *raw-zee';* from 7329; *thinness:*–leanness.
7335. רָזַם *raw-zam';* a prim. root; to *twinkle* the eye (in mockery): wink.
7336. רָזַן *raw-zan';* a prim. root; prob. to be *heavy,* i.e. (fig.) *honorable:*–prince, ruler.
7337. רָחַב *raw-khab';* a prim. root; to *broaden* (intr. or trans., lit. or fig.):–be an en-(make) large(-ing), make room, make (open) wide.
7338. רַחַב *rakh'-ab;* from 7337; a *width:*–breadth, broad place.
7339. רְחֹב *rekh-obe';* or רְחוֹב *rekh-obe';* from 7337; a *width,* i.e. (concr.) *avenue* or *area:*–broad place (way), street. See also 1050.
7340. רְחֹב *rekh-obe';* or רְחוֹב *rekh-obe';* the same as 7339; *Rechob,* the name of a place in Syria, also of a Syrian and an Isr.:–Rehob.
7341. רֹחַב *ro'-khab;* from 7337; *width* (lit. or fig.):–breadth, broad, largeness, thickness, wideness.
7342. רָחָב *raw-khawb';* from 7337; *roomy,* in any (or every) direction, lit. or fig.:–broad, large, at liberty, proud, wide.
7343. רָחָב *raw-khawb';* the same as 7342; *proud; Rachab,* a Canaanitess:–Rahab.
7344. רְחֹבוֹת *rekh-o-both';* or רְחֹבֹת *rekh-o-both';* pl. of 7339; *streets; Rechoboth,* a place in Assyria and one in Pal.:– Rehoboth.
7345. רְחַבְיָה *rekh-ab-yaw';* or רְחַבְיָהוּ *rek-ab-yaw'-hoo;* from 7337 and 3050; *Jah has enlarged; Rechabjah,* an Isr.:–Rehabiah.
7346. רְחַבְעָם *rekh-ab-awm';* from 7337 and 5971; a *people has enlarged; Rechabam,* an Isr. king:–Rehoboam.
7347. רֵחֶה *ray-kheh';* from an un. root mean. to *pulverize*; a *mill*-stone:–mill (stone).
7348. רְחוּם *rekh-oom';* a form of 7349; *Rechum,* the name of a Pers. and of three Isr.:–Rehum.
7350. רָחוֹק *raw-khoke';* or רָחֹק *raw-khoke';* from 7368; *remote,* lit. or fig., of place or time; spec., *precious*; often used adv. (with prep.):–(a-)far (abroad, off), long ago, of old, space, great while to come.
7351. רְחִיט *rekh-eet';* from the same as 7298; a *panel* (as resembling a *trough*):–rafter.
7352. רַחִיק *rakh-eek'* (Chald.); cor. to 7350:–far.
7353. רָחֵל *raw-kale';* from an un. root mean. to *journey*; a *ewe* [the *females* being the predominant element of a flock] (as a good *traveller*):–ewe, sheep.
7354. רָחֵל *raw-khale';* the same as 7353; *Rachel,* a wife of Jacob:–Rachel.
7355. רָחַם *raw-kham';* a prim. root; to *fondle*; by impl., to *love*, esp. to *compassionate:*–have compassion (on, upon), love, (find, have, obtain, shew) mercy(-iful, on, upon), (have) pity, Ruhamah, X surely.
7356. רַחַם *rakh'-am;* from 7355; *compassion* (in the pl.); by ext., the *womb* (as *cherishing* the fetus); by impl., a *maiden:*– bowels, compassion, damsel, tender love, (great, tender) mercy, pity, womb.
7357. רַחַם *rakh'-am;* the same as 7356; *pity; Racham,* an Isr.:–Raham.
7358. רֶחֶם *rekh'-em;* from 7355; the *womb* [comp. 7356]:–matrix, womb.
7359. רְחֵם *rekh-ame'* (Chald.); cor. to 7356; (pl.) *pity:*–mercy.
7360. רָחָם *raw-khawm';* or רָחָמָה (fem.) *raw-khaw-maw';* from 7355; a kind of *vulture* (supposed to be *tender* towards its young):–gier- eagle.
7361. רַחֲמָה *rakh-am-aw';* fem. of 7356; a *maiden:*–damsel.
7362. רַחְמָנִי *rakh-maw-nee';* from 7355; *compassionate:*–pitiful.
7363. רָחַף *raw-khaf';* a prim. root; to *brood*; by impl., to be *relaxed:*–flutter, move, shake.
7364. רָחַץ *raw-khats';* a prim. root; to *lave* (the whole or a part of a thing):–bathe (self), wash (self).
7365. רְחַץ *rekh-ats'* (Chald.); cor. to 7364 [prob. through the accessory idea of *ministering* as a servant at the bath]; to *attend* upon:–trust.
7366. רַחַץ *rakh'-ats;* from 7364; a *bath:*–wash[-pot].
7367. רַחְצָה *rakh-tsaw';* fem. of 7366; a *bathing* place:–washing.
7368. רָחַק *raw-khak';* a prim. root; to *widen* (in any direction), i.e. (intr.) *recede* or (trans.) *remove* (lit. or fig., of place or relation):–(a-, be, cast, drive, get, go, keep [self], put, remove, be too, [wander], withdraw) far (away, off), loose, X refrain, very, (be) a good way (off).
7369. רָחֵק *raw-khake';* from 7368; *remote:*–that are far.
7370. רָחַשׁ *raw-khash';* a prim. root; to *gush:*–indite.
7371. רַחַת *rakh'-ath;* from 7306; a *winnowing*-fork (as *blowing* the chaff away):–shovel.
7372. רָטַב *raw-tab';* a prim. root; to *be moist:*–be wet.
7373. רָטֹב *raw-tobe';* from 7372; *moist* (with sap):–green.
7374. רֶטֶט *reh'-tet;* from an un. root mean. to *tremble; terror:*–fear.
7375. רֻטֲפַשׁ *roo-taf-ash';* a root compounded from 7373 and 2954; to be *rejuvenated:*–be fresh.
7376. רָטַשׁ *raw-tash';* a prim. root; to *dash* down:–dash (in pieces).
7377. רִי *ree;* from 7301; *irrigation,* i.e. a shower:–watering.
7378. רִיב *reeb;* or רוּב *roob;* a prim. root; prop. to *toss,* i.e. *grapple*; mostly fig., to *wrangle,* i.e. *hold* a *controversy*; (by impl.) to *defend:*–adversary, chide, complain, contend, debate, X ever, X lay wait, plead, rebuke, strive, X thoroughly.
7379. רִיב *reeb; or* רִב *reeb;* from 7378; a *contest* (personal or legal):–+ adversary, cause, chiding, contend(-tion), controversy, multitude, pleading, strife, strive(-ing), suit.
7380. רִיבַי *ree-bah'-ee;* from 7378; *contentious*; *Ribai,* an Isr.:–Ribai.
7381. רֵיחַ *ray'-akh;* from 7306; *odor* (as if *blown*):–savour, scent, smell.
7382. רֵיחַ *ray'-akh* (Chald.); cor. to 7381:–smell.
7383. רִיפָה *ree-faw'* or רִפָה *ree-faw';* from 7322; (only pl.), *grits* (as *pounded*):–ground corn, wheat.
7384. רִיפַת *ree-fath'* or (prob. by orth. err.) דִּיפַת *dee-fath';* of for. or.; *Riphath,* a grandson of Japheth and his desc.:–Riphath.
7385. רִיק *reek* from 7324; *emptiness*; fig., a *worthless* thing; adv., *in vain:*–empty, to no purpose, (in) vain (thing), vanity.
7386. רֵיק *rake* or רֵק (short.) *rake*; from 7324; *empty*; fig., *worthless:*–*emptied*(-ty), vain (fellow, man).

7387. רֵיקָם *ray-kawm'* from 7386; *emptily*; fig. (obj.) *ineffectually*, (subj.) *undeservedly*:–without cause, empty, in vain, void.
7388. רִיר *reer* from 7325; *saliva*; by resemblance, *broth*:–spittle, white [of an egg].
7389. רֵישׁ *raysh* or רֵאשׁ *raysh*; or רִישׁ *reesh*; from 7326; *poverty*:–poverty.
7390. רַךְ *rak* from 7401; *tender* (lit. or fig.); by impl., *weak*:–faint([-hearted], soft, tender ([-hearted], one), weak.
7391. רֹךְ *roke*; from 7401; *softness* (fig.):–tenderness.
7392. רָכַב *raw-kab'*; a prim. root; to *ride* (on an animal or in a vehicle); caus., to *place upon* (for riding or gen.), to *despatch*:–bring (on [horse-] back), carry, get [oneself] up, on [horse-] back, put, (cause to, make to) ride (in a chariot, on,-r), set.
7393. רֶכֶב *reh'-keb*; from 7392; a *vehicle*; by impl., a *team*; by ext., *cavalry*; by anal. a *rider*, i.e. the upper millstone:–chariot, (upper) millstone, multitude wagon.
7394. רֵכָב *ray-kawb'*; from 7392; *rider*; *Rekab*, the name of two Arabs and of two Isr.:–Rechab.
7395. רַכָּב *rak-kawb'*; from 7392; a *charioteer*:–chariot man, driver of a chariot, horseman.
7396. רִכְבָּה *rik-baw'*; fem. of 7393; a *chariot* (coll.):–chariots.
7397. רֵכָה *ray-kaw'*; prob. fem. from 7401; *softness; Rekah*, a place in Pal.:–Rechah.
7398. רְכוּב *rek-oob'*; from pass.part. of 7392; a *vehicle* (as *ridden* on):–chariot.
7399. רְכוּשׁ *rek-oosh'*; or רְכֻשׁ *rek-oosh'*; from pass.part. of 7408; *property* (as *gathered*):–good, riches, substance.
7400. רָכִיל *raw-keel'*; from 7402 a *scandal-monger* (as *travelling* about):–slander, carry tales, talebearer.
7401. רָכַךְ *raw-kak'*; a prim. root; to *soften* (intr. or trans.), used fig.:–(be) faint ([-hearted]), mollify, (be, make) soft(-er), be tender.
7402. רָכַל *raw-kal'*; a prim. root; to *travel* for trading:–(spice) merchant.
7403. רָכָל *raw-kawl'*; from 7402; *merchant; Rakal*, a place in Pal.:–Rachal.
7404. רְכֻלָּה *rek-ool-law'*; fem. pass.part. of 7402; *trade* (as *peddled*):–merchandise, traffic.
7405. רָכַס *raw-kas'*; a prim. root; to *tie*:–bind.
7406. רֶכֶס *reh'-kes* from 7405; a mountain *ridge* (as of *tied* summits):–rough place.
7407. רֹכֶס *ro'-kes*; from 7405; a *snare* (as of *tied* meshes):–pride.
7408. רָכַשׁ *raw-kash'*; a prim. root; to *lay up*, i.e. coll.:–gather, get.
7409. רֶכֶשׁ *reh'-kesh*; from 7408; a *relay* of animals on a post-route (as *stored* up for that purpose); by impl., a *courser*:–dromedary, mule, swift beast.
7410. רָם *rawm*; act.part. of 7311; *high; Ram*, the name of an Arabian and of an Isr.:–Ram. See also 1027.
7411. רָמָה *raw-maw'*; a prim. root; to *hurl;* spec., to *shoot;* fig., to *delude* or *betray* (as if causing to fall):–beguile, betray, [bow-] man, carry, deceive, throw.
7412. רְמָה *rem-aw'* (Chald.); cor. to 7411; to *throw, set,* (fig.) *assess*:–cast (down), impose.
7413. רָמָה *raw-maw'*; fem. act.part. of 7311; a *height* (as a seat of idolatry):–high place.
7414. רָמָה *raw-maw'*; the same as 7413; *Ramah*, the name of four places in Pal.:–Ramah.
7415. רִמָּה *rim-maw'* from 7426 in the sense of *breading* [comp. 7311]; a *maggot* (as rapidly *bred*), lit. or fig.:–worm.
7416. רִמּוֹן *rim-mone'*; or רִמֹּן *rim-mone'*; from 7426; a *pomegranate,* the tree (from its *upright* growth) or the fruit (also an artif. ornament):–pomegranate.
7417. רִמּוֹן *rim-mone'*; or (short.) רִמֹּן *rim-mone'*; or (1 Chronicles 6:62 [77]) רִמּוֹנוֹ *rim-mo-no'*; the same as 7416; *Rimmon,* the name of a Syrian deity, also of five places in Pal.:–Remmon, Rimmon. The addition "-methoar" (Jos. 19:13) is הַמְּתֹאָר *ham-meth-o-awr';* pass.part. of 8388 with the art.; *the* (one) *marked off,* i.e. *which pertains.*
7418. רָמוֹת־נֶגֶב *raw-moth-neh'-gheb;* or רָמַת נֶגֶב *raw'-math neh'-gheb;* from the pl. or const. form of 7413 and 5045; *heights* (or *height*) *of* the *South; Ramoth-Negeb* or *Ramath-Negeb,* a place in Pal.:–south Ramoth, Ramath of the south.
7419. רָמוּת *raw-mooth'* from 7311; a *heap* (of carcases):–height.
7420. רֹמַח *ro'-makh;* from an un. root mean. to *hurl;* a *lance* (as *thrown*); esp. the iron *point:*–buckler, javelin, lancet, spear.
7421. רַמִּי *ram-mee;* for 761; a *Ramite,* i.e. Aramaean:–Syrian.
7422. רַמְיָה *ram-yaw';* from 7311 and 3050; *Jah has raised; Ramjah,* an Isr.:–Ramiah.
7423. רְמִיָּה *rem-ee-yaw';* from 7411; *remissness, treachery:*–deceit(-ful, -fully), false, guile, idle, slack, slothful.
7424. רַמָּךְ *ram-mawk';* of for. or.; a brood *mare:*–dromedary.
7425. רְמַלְיָהוּ *rem-al-yaw'-hoo;* from an un. root and 3050 (perh. mean. to *deck*); *Jah has bedecked; Remaljah,* an Isr.:–Remaliah.
7426. רָמַם *raw-mam';* a prim. root; to *rise* (lit. or fig.):–exalt, get [oneself] up, lift up (self), mount up.
7427. רֹמֵמֻת *ro-may-mooth';* from the act. part. of 7426; *exaltation:*–lifting up of self.
7428. רִמֹּן פֶּרֶץ *rim-mone' peh'-rets;* from 7416 and 6556; *pomegranate of the breach; Rimmon-Perets,* a place in the Desert:–Rimmon-parez.
7429. רָמַס *raw-mas'* a prim. root; to *tread* upon (as a potter, in walking or abusively):–oppressor, stamp upon, trample (under feet), tread (down, upon).
7430. רָמַשׂ *raw-mas';* a prim. root; prop. to *glide* swiftly, i.e. to *crawl* or *move* with short steps; by anal. to *swarm:*–creep, move.
7431. רֶמֶשׂ *reh'-mes;* from 7430; a *reptile* or any other rapidly moving animal:–that creepeth, creeping (moving) thing.
7432. רֶמֶת *reh'-meth;* from 7411; *height; Remeth,* a place in Pal.:–Remeth.
7433. רָמֹת (or רָמוֹת) גִּלְעָד *raw-moth';* (2 Chronicles 22:5) *raw-moth' gil-awd';* from the pl. of 7413 and 1568*; heights of Gilad; Ramoth-Gilad,* a place E. of the Jordan:–Ramoth-gilead, Ramoth in Gilead. See also 7216.
7434. רָמַת הַמִּצְפֶּה *raw-math' ham-mits-peh';* from 7413 and 4707 with the art. interpolated; *height of the watch-tower; Ramath-ham-Mitspeh,* a place in Pal.:–Ramath-mizpeh.
7435. רָמָתִי *raw-maw-thee';* patron. of 7414; a Ramathite or inh. of Ramah:–Ramathite.
7436. רָמָתַיִם צוֹפִים *raw-maw-thah'-yim tso-feem';* from the dual of 7413 and the pl. of the act.part. of 6822; *double height of watchers; Ramathajim-Tsophim,* a place in Pal.:–Ramathaimzophim.
7437. רָמַת לֶחִי *raw'-math lekh'-ee;* from 7413 and 3895; *height of* a *jaw-bone; Ramath-Lechi,* a place in Pal.:–Ramath-lehi.
7438. רֹן *rone;* from 7442; a *shout* (of deliverance):–song.
7439. רָנָה *raw-naw';* a prim. root; to *whiz:*–rattle.
7440. רִנָּה *rin-naw';* from 7442; prop. a *creaking* (or shrill sound), i.e. *shout* (of joy or grief):–cry, gladness, joy, proclamation, rejoicing, shouting, sing(-ing), triumph.
7441. רִנָּה *rin-naw';* the same as 7440; *Rinnah,* an Isr.:–Rinnah.
7442. רָנַן *raw-nan';* a prim. root; prop. to *creak* (or emit a stridulous sound), i.e. to *shout* (usually for joy):–aloud for joy, cry out, be joyful (greatly, make to) rejoice, (cause to) shout (for joy), (cause to) sing (aloud, for joy, out), triumph..
7443. רֶנֶן *reh'-nen;* from 7442; an *ostrich* (from its *wail*):–X goodly.
7444. רַנֵּן *ran-nane';* intens. from 7442; *shouting* (for joy):–singing.
7445. רְנָנָה *ren-aw-naw';* from 7442; a *shout* (for joy):–joyful (voice), singing, triumphing.
7446. רִסָּה *ris-saw';* from 7450; a *ruin* (as *dripping* to pieces); *Rissah,* a place in the Desert:–Rissah.
7447. רָסִיס *raw-sees';* from 7450; prop. *dripping* to pieces, i.e. a *ruin;* also a dew-*drop:*–breach, drop.
7448. רֶסֶן *reh'-sen;* from an un. root mean. to *curb;* a *halter* (as *restraining*); by impl., the *jaw:*–bridle.
7449. רֶסֶן reh'-sen the same as 7448; *Resen,* a place in Ass.:–Resen.
7450. רָסַס *raw-sas';* a prim. root; to *comminute;* used only as denom. from 7447, to *moisten* (with drops):–temper.
7451. רַע *rah;* from 7489; *bad* or (as noun) evil (nat. or mor.):– adversity, affliction, bad, calamity, + displease (-ure), distress, evil([-favouredness], man, thing), + exceedingly, X great, grief(-vous), harm, heavy, hurt(-ful), ill (favoured), + mark, mischief(-vous), misery, naught(-ty), noisome, + not please, sad(-ly), sore, sorrow, trouble, vex, wicked(-ly, -ness, one), worse(-st), wretchedness, wrong. [incl. fem. רָעָה *raw-awh*; as adj. or noun.].
7452. רֵעַ *ray'-ah;* from 7321; a *crash* (of thunder), *noise* (of war), *shout* (of joy):–X aloud, noise, shouted.
7453. רֵעַ *ray'-ah;* or רֵיעַ *ray'-ah;* from 7462; an *associate* (more or less close):–brother, companion, fellow, friend, husband, lover, neighbour, X (an-)other.
7454. רֵעַ *ray'-ah;* from 7462; a *thought* (as *association* of ideas):–thought.
7455. רֹעַ *ro'-ah;* from 7489; *badness* (as *marring*), phys. or mor.:–X be so bad, badness, (X be so) evil, naughtiness, sadness, sorrow, wickedness.
7456. רָעֵב *raw-abe';* a prim. root; to *hunger:*–(suffer to) famish, (be, have, suffer, suffer to) hunger(-ry).
7457. רָעֵב *raw-abe';* from 7456; *hungry*

(more or less intensely):–hunger bitten, hungry.
7458. רָעָב *raw-awb'*; from 7456; *hunger* (more or less extensive):–dearth, famine, + famished, hunger.
7459. רְעָבוֹן *reh-aw-bone'* from 7456; *famine:*–famine.
7460. רָעַד *raw-ad';* a prim. root: to *shudder* (more or less violently):–tremble.
7461. רַעַד *rah'-ad;* or (fem.) רְעָדָה *reh-aw-daw';* from 7460; a *shudder:*–trembling.
7462. רָעָה *raw-aw';* a prim. root; to *tend* a flock; i.e. *pasture* it; intr., to *graze* (lit. or fig.); gen. to *rule;* by ext., to *associate* with (as a friend):–X break, companion, keep company with, devour, eat up, evil entreat, feed, use as a friend, make friendship with, herdman, keep [sheep](-er), pastor, + shearing house, shepherd, wander, waste.
7463. רֵעֶה *ray-eh';* from 7462; a (male) *companion:*–friend.
7464. רֵעָה *ray'-aw;* fem. of 7453; a female *associate:*–companion, fellow.
7465. רֹעָה *ro-aw';* for 7455; *breakage:*–broken, utterly.
7466. רְעוּ *reh-oo';* for 7471 in the sense of 7453; *friend; Reü,* a postdiluvian patriarch:–Reu.
7467. רְעוּאֵל *reh-oo-ale';* from the same as 7466 and 410; *friend of God; Reüel,* the name of Moses' father-in-law, also of an Edomite and an Isr.:–Raguel, Reuel.
7468. רְעוּת *reh-ooth';* from 7462 in the sense of 7453; a female *associate;* gen. an *additional* one:–+ another, mate, neighbour.
7469. רְעוּת *reh-ooth';* prob. from 7462; a *feeding* upon, i.e. grasping after:–vexation.
7470. רְעוּת *reh-ooth'* (Chald.); cor. to 7469; *desire:*–pleasure, will.
7471. רְעִי *reh-ee';* from 7462; *pasture:*–pasture.
7472. רֵעִי *ray-ee';* from 7453; *social; Reï,* an Isr.:–Rei.
7473. רֹעִי *ro-ee';* from act.part. of 7462; *pastoral;* as noun, a *shepherd:*–shepherd.
7474. רַעְיָה *rah-yaw'; fem.* of 7453; a female *associate:*–fellow, love.
7475. רַעְיוֹן *rah-yone';* from 7462 in the sense of 7469; *desire:*–vexation.
7476. רַעְיוֹן *rah-yone'* (Chald.); cor. to 7475; a *grasp.* i.e. (fig.) ment. *conception:*–cogitation, thought.
7477. רָעַל *raw-al';* a prim. root; to *reel,* i.e. (fig.) to *brandish:*–terribly shake.
7478. רַעַל *rah'-al;* from 7477; a *reeling* (from intoxication):–trembling.
7479. רַעֲלָה *rah-al-aw';* fem. of 7478; a long *veil* (as *fluttering*):–muffler.
7480. רְעֵלָיָה *reh-ay-law-yaw';* from 7477 and 3050; *made to tremble* (i.e. *fearful*) *of Jah; Reëlajah,* an Isr.:–Reeliah.
7481. רָעַם *raw-am';* a prim. root; to *tumble,* i.e. be violently *agitated;* spec., to *crash* (of thunder); fig., to *irritate* (with anger):–make to fret, roar, thunder, trouble.
7482. רַעַם *rah'am*; from 7481; a *peal* of thunder:–thunder.
7483. רַעְמָה *rah-maw';* fem. of 7482; the *mane* of a horse (as *quivering* in the wind):–thunder.
7484. רַעְמָה *rah-maw';* the same as 7483; *Ramah,* the name of a grandson of Ham, and of a place (perh. Founded by him):–Raamah.
7485. רַעַמְיָה *rah-am-yaw';* from 7481 and 3050; *Jah has shaken; Raamjah,* an Isr.:–Raamiah.
7486. רַעְמְסֵס *rah-mes-ace';* or רַעַמְסֵס *rah-am-sace';* of Eg. or.; *Rameses* or *Raamses,* a place in Eg.:–Raamses, Rameses.
7487. רַעֲנָן *rah-an-nan'* (Chald.); cor. to 7488; *green,* i.e. (fig.) *prosperous;* –flourishing.
7488. רַעֲנָן *rah-an-awn';* from an un. root mean. to *be green; verdant;* by anal., *new;* fig., *prosperous:*–green, flourishing.
7489. רָעַע *raw-ah';* a prim. root; prop. to *spoil* (lit., by *breaking* to pieces); fig., to *make* (or *be*) *good for nothing,* i.e. *bad* (phys., socially or mor.):–afflict, associate selves, break (down, in pieces), + displease, (be, bring, do) evil (doer, entreat, man), show self friendly, do harm, (do) hurt, (behave self, deal) ill, X indeed, do mischief, punish, still, vex, (do) wicked (doer, -ly), be (deal, do) worse.
7490. רְעַע *reh-ah'* (Chald.); cor. to 7489:–break, bruise.
7491. רָעַף *raw-af'* a prim. root; to *drip:*–distil, drop (down).
7492. רָעַץ *raw-ats'* a prim. root; to *break* in pieces; fig., *harass:*–dash in pieces, vex.
7493. רָעַשׁ *raw-ash;* a prim. root; to *undulate* (as the earth, the sky, etc.; also a field of grain), partic. through fear; spec., to *spring* (as a locust):–make afraid, (re-)move, quake, (make to) shake, (make to) tremble.
7494. רַעַשׁ *rah'-ash;* from 7493; *vibration, bounding, uproar:*–commotion, confused noise, earthquake, fierceness, quaking, rattling, rushing, shaking.
7495. רָפָא *raw-faw';* or רָפָה *raw-faw';* a prim. root; prop. to *mend* (by stitching), i.e. (fig.) to *cure:*–cure, (cause to) heal, physician, repair, X thoroughly, make whole. See 7503.
7496. רָפָא *raw-faw';* from 7495 in the sense of 7503; prop. *lax,* i.e. (fig.) a *ghost* (as *dead;* in pl. only):–dead, deceased.
7497. רָפָא *raw-faw'* or רָפָה *raw-faw';* from 7495 in the sense of *invigorating;* a *giant:*–giant, Rapha, Rephaim(-s). See also 1051.
7498. רָפָא *raw-faw';* or רָפָה *raw-faw';* prob. the same as 7497; *giant; Rapha* or *Raphah,* the name of two Isr.:–Rapha.
7499. רְפֻאָה *ref-oo-aw';* fem. pass.part. of 7495; a *medicament:*–heal[-ed], medicine..
7500. רִפְאוּת *rif-ooth';* from 7495; a *cure:*–health.
7501. רְפָאֵל *ref-aw-ale';* from 7495 and 410; *God has cured*; *Rephaël*, an Isr.:–Rephael.
7502. רָפַד *raw-fad';* a prim. root; to *spread* (a bed); by impl., to *refresh:*–comfort, make [a bed], spread.
7503. רָפָה *raw-faw';* a prim. root; to *slacken* (in many appl., lit. or fig.):–abate, cease, consume, draw [toward evening], fail, (be) faint, be (wax) feeble, forsake, idle, leave, let alone (go, down), (be) slack, stay, be still, be slothful, (be) weak(-en). See 7495.
7504. רָפֶה *raw-feh';* from 7503; *slack* (in body or mind):–weak
7505. רָפוּא *raw-foo';* pass.part. of 7495; *cured; Raphu,* an Isr.:–Raphu.
7506. רֶפַח *reh'-fakh* from an un. root app. mean. to *sustain; support; Rephach,* an Isr.:–Rephah.
7507. רְפִידָה *ref-ee-daw';* from 7502; a *railing* (as *spread* along):–bottom.
7508. רְפִידִים *ref-ee-deem';* pl. of the masc. of the same as 7507; *ballusters; Rephidim,* a place in the Desert:–Rephidim.
7509. רְפָיָה *ref-aw-yaw';* from 7495 and 3050; *Jah has cured; Rephajah,* the name of five Isr.:–Rephaiah.
7510. רִפְיוֹן *rif-yone';* from 7503; *slackness:*–feebleness.
7511. רָפַס *raw-fas';* a prim. root; to *trample,* i.e. *prostrate:*–humble self, submit self.
7512. רְפַס *ref-as'* (Chald.); cor. to 7511:–stamp.
7513. רַפְסֹדָה *raf-so-daw';* from 7511; a *raft* (as *flat* on the water):–flote.
7514. רָפַק *raw-fak';* a prim. root; to *recline:*–lean.
7515. רָפַשׂ *raw-fas';* a prim. root; to *trample,* i.e. *roil* water:–foul, trouble.
7516. רֶפֶשׁ *reh'-fesh;* from 7515; *mud* (as *roiled*):–mire.
7517. רֶפֶת *reh'-feth;* prob. from 7503; a *stall* for cattle (from their *resting* there):–stall.
7518. רַץ *rats;* contr. from 7533; a *fragment:*–piece.
7519. רָצָא *raw-tsaw';* a prim. root; to *run;* also to *delight* in:–accept, run.
7520. רָצַד *raw-tsad';* a prim. root; prob. to *look askant,* i.e. (fig.) *be jealous:*–leap.
7521. רָצָה *raw-tsaw';* a prim. root; to *be pleased with*; spec., to *satisfy* a debt:–(be) accept(-able), accomplish, set affection, approve, consent with, delight (self), enjoy, (be, have a) favour (-able), like, observe, pardon, (be, have, take) please(-ure), reconcile self.
7522. רָצוֹן *raw-tsone';* or רָצֹן *raw-tsone';* from 7521; *delight* (esp. as shown):–(be) acceptable(-ance, -ed), delight, desire, favour, (good) pleasure, (own, self, voluntary) will, as...(what) would.
7523. רָצַח *raw-tsakh';* a prim. root; prop. to *dash* in pieces, i.e. *kill* (a human being), esp. to *murder:*–put to death, kill, (man-) slay(-er), murder(-er).
7524. רֶצַח *reh-tsakh;* from 7523; a *crushing;* spec., a *murder*-cry:–slaughter, sword.
7525. רִצְיָא *rits-yaw';* from 7521; *delight; Ritsjah,* an Isr.:–Rezia.
7526. רְצִין *rets-een';* prob. for 7522; *Retsin,* the name of a Syrian and of an Isr.:–Rezin.
7527. רָצַע *raw-tsah';* a prim. root; to *pierce:*–bore.
7528. רָצַף *raw-tsaf';* a denom. from 7529; to *tessellate,* i.e. embroider (as if with bright stones):–pave.
7529. רֶצֶף *reh'-tsef;* for 7565; a red-hot *stone* (for baking):–coal.
7530. רֶצֶף *reh'-tsef;* the same as 7529; *Retseph,* a place in Assyrian:–Rezeph.
7531. רִצְפָּה *rits-paw';* fem. of 7529; a hot *stone;* also a tessellated *pavement:*–live coal, pavement.
7532. רִצְפָּה *rits-paw';* the same as 7531; *Ritspah,* an Isr.s:–Rizpah.
7533. רָצַץ *raw-tsats';* a prim. root; to *crack* in pieces, lit. or fig.:–break, bruise, crush, discourage, oppress, struggle together.
7534. רַק *rak;* from 7556 in its or. sense; *emaciated* (as if *flattened* out):–lean([-fleshed]), thin.
7535. רַק *rak;* the same as 7534 as a noun; prop. *leanness,* i.e. (fig.) limitation; only adv., *merely,* or conj., *although:*–but, even, except, howbeit howsoever, at the least, nevertheless, nothing but, notwithstanding, only, save, so [that], surely, yet (so), in any wise.
7536. רֹק *roke;* from 7556; *spittle:*–spit (-ting, -tle).
7537. רָקַב *raw-kab';* a prim. root; to *decay* (as by worm-eating):–rot.

7538. רָקָב *raw-kawb';* from 7537; *decay* (by *caries*):–rottenness (thing).
7539. רִקָּבוֹן *rik-kaw-bone';* from 7538; *decay* (by caries):–rotten.
7540. רָקַד *raw-kad';* a prim. root; prop. to *stamp,* i.e. to *spring* about (wildly or for joy):–dance, jump, leap, skip.
7541. רַקָּה *rak-kaw';* fem. of 7534; prop. *thinness,* i.e. the *side* of the head:–temple.
7542. רַקּוֹן *rak-kone';* from 7534; *thinness; Rakkon,* a place in Pal.:–Rakkon.
7543. רָקַח *raw-kakh';* a prim. root; to *perfume:*–apothecary, compound, make [ointment], prepare, spice.
7544. רֶקַח *reh'-kakh;* from 7543; prop. *perfumery,* i.e. (by impl.) *spicery* (for flavor):–spiced.
7545. רֹקַח *ro'-kakh;* from 7542; an *aromatic:*–confection, ointment.
7546. רַקָּח *rak-kawkh';* from 7543; a male *perfumer:*–apothecary.
7547. רַקֻּחַ *rak-koo'-akh;* from 7543; a *scented* substance:–perfume.
7548. רַקָּחָה *rak-kaw-khaw';* fem. of 7547; a female *perfumer:*–confectioner.
7549. רָקִיעַ *raw-kee'-ah;* from 7554; prop. an *expanse,* i.e. the *firmament* or (app.) visible arch of the sky:–firmament.
7550. רָקִיק *raw-keek';* from, 7556 in its or. sense; a thin *cake:* –cake, wafer.
7551. רָקַם *raw-kam';* a prim. root; to *variegate* color, i.e. *embroider;* by impl., to *fabricate:*–embroiderer, needlework, curiously work.
7552. רֶקֶם *reh'-kem* from 7551; *versi-color; Rekem,* the name of a place in Pal., also of a Midianite and an Isr.:–Rekem.
7553. רִקְמָה *rik-maw';* from 7551; *variegation* of color; spec., *embroidery:*–broidered (work), divers colours, (raiment of) needlework (on both sides).
7554. רָקַע *raw-kah'* a prim. root; to *pound* the earth (as a sign of passion); by anal. to *expand* (by hammering); by impl., to *overlay* (with thin sheets of metal):–beat, make broad, spread abroad (forth, over, out, into plates), stamp, stretch.
7555. רִקֻּעַ *rik-koo'-ah;* from 7554; *beaten* out, i.e. a (metallic) *plate:*–broad.
7556. רָקַק *raw-kak';* a prim. root; to *spit:*–spit.
7557. רַקַּת *rak-kath';* from 7556 in its or. sense of *diffusing;* a *beach* (as *expanded* shingle); *Rakkath,* a place in Pal.:–Rakkath.
7558. רִשְׁיוֹן *rish-yone';* from an un. root mean. to *have leave;* a *permit:*–grant.
7559. רָשַׁם *raw-sham'* a prim. root; to *record:*–note.
7560. רְשַׁם *resh-am'* (Chald.); cor. to 7559:–sign, write.
7561. רָשַׁע *raw-shah'* a prim. root; to *be* (caus., *do* or *declare*) *wrong;* by impl., to *disturb, violate:*–condemn, make trouble, vex, be (commit, deal, depart, do) wicked(-ly, -ness).
7562. רֶשַׁע *reh'-shah;* from 7561; a *wrong* (esp. mor.):–iniquity, wicked(-ness).
7563. רָשָׁע *raw-shaw'* from 7561; mor. *wrong;* concr., an (act.) *bad* person:–+ condemned, guilty, ungodly, wicked (man), that did wrong.
7564. רִשְׁעָה *rish-aw'* fem. of 7562; *wrong* (esp. mor.):–fault, wickedly(-ness).
7565. רֶשֶׁף *reh'-shef* from 8313; a live *coal;* by anal. *lightning;* fig., an *arrow,* (as *flashing* through the air); spec., *fever:*–arrow, (burning) coal, burning heat, + spark, hot thunderbolt.
7566. רֶשֶׁף *reh'-shef;* the same as 7565; *Resheph,* an Isr.:–Resheph.
7567. רָשַׁשׁ *raw-shash'* a prim. root; to *demolish:*–impoverish.
7568. רֶשֶׁת *reh'-sheth;* from 3423; a *net* (as *catching* animals):–net(-work).
7569. רַתּוֹק *rat-toke';* from 7576; a *chain:*–chain.
7570. רָתַח *raw-thakh';* a prim. root; to *boil:*–boil.
7571. רֶתַח *reh'-thakh;* from 7570; a *boiling:*–X [boil] well.
7572. רַתִּיקָה *rat-tee-kaw';* from 7576; a *chain:*–chain.
7573. רָתַם *raw-tham';* a prim. root; to *yoke* up (to the pole of a vehicle):–bind.
7574. רֶתֶם *reh'-them;* or רֹתֶם *ro'-them;* from 7573; the Spanish *broom* (from its pole-like stems):–juniper (tree).
7575. רִתְמָה *rith-maw';* fem. of 7574; *Rithmah,* a place in the Desert:–Rithmah.
7576. רָתַק *raw-thak'* a prim. root; to *fasten:*–bind.
7577. רְתֻקָה *reth-oo-kaw';* fem. pass.part. of 7576; something *fastened,* i.e. a *chain:*–chain.
7578. רְתֵת *reth-ayth';* for 7374; *terror:*–trembling.

ש

7579. שָׁאַב *shaw-ab';* a prim. root; to *bale* up water:–(woman to) draw(-er, water).
7580. שָׁאַג *shaw-ag';* a prim. root; to *rumble* or *moan:*–X mightily, roar.
7581. שְׁאָגָה *sheh-aw-gaw'* from 7580; a *rumbling* or *moan:*–roaring..
7582. שָׁאָה *shaw-aw';* a prim. root; to *rush;* by impl., to *desolate:*–be desolate, (make a) rush(-ing), (lay) waste.
7583. שָׁאָה *shaw-aw';* a prim. root [ident. with 7582 through the idea of *whirling* to giddiness]; to *stun,* i.e. (intr.) be *astonished:*–wonder.
7584. שַׁאֲוָה *shah-av-aw'* from 7582; a *tempest* (as *rushing*):–desolation.
7585. שְׁאוֹל *sheh-ole';* or שְׁאֹל *sheh-ole';* from 7592; *Hades;* or the world of the dead (as if a subterranean *retreat*), incl. its accessories and inmates:–grave, hell, pit.
7586. שָׁאוּל *shaw-ool';* pass.part. of 7592; *asked; Shaül,* the name of an Edomite and two Isr.:–Saul, Shaul.
7587. שָׁאוּלִי *shaw-oo-lee';* patron. from 7856; a *Shaülite* or desc. of Shaul:–Shaulites.
7588. שָׁאוֹן *shaw-one';* from 7582; *uproar* (as of *rushing*); by impl., *destruction:*–X horrible, noise, pomp, rushing, tumult (X -uous).
7589. שְׁאָט *sheh-awt';* from an un. root mean. to *push* aside; *contempt:*–despite(-ful).
7590. שָׁאט *shawt;* for act.part of 7750 [comp. 7589]; one *contemning:*–that (which) despise(-d).
7591. שְׁאִיָּה *sheh-ee-yaw';* from 7582; *desolation:*–destruction.
7592. שָׁאַל *shaw-al';* or שָׁאֵל *shaw-ale';* a prim. root; to *inquire;* by impl., to *request;* by ext., to *demand:*–ask (counsel, on), beg, borrow, lay to charge, consult, demand, desire, X earnestly, enquire, + greet, obtain leave, lend, pray, request, require, + salute, X straitly, X surely, wish.
7593. שְׁאֵל *sheh-ale'* (Chald.); cor. to 7592:–ask, demand, require.
7594. שְׁאָל *sheh-awl';* from 7592; *request; Sheäl,* an Isr.:–Sheal.
7595. שְׁאֵלָא *sheh-ay-law'* (Chald.); from 7593; prop. a *question* (at law), i.e. judicial *decision* or mandate:–demand.
7596. שְׁאֵלָה *sheh-ay-law';* or שֵׁלָה (1 Sa. 1:17) *shay-law';* from 7592; a *petition;* by impl., a *loan:*–loan, petition, request.
7597. שְׁאַלְתִּיאֵל *sheh-al-tee-ale';* or שַׁלְתִּיאֵל *shal-tee-ale';* from 7592 and 410; *I have asked God; Sheältiël,* an Isr.:–Shalthiel, Shealtiel.
7598. שְׁאַלְתִּיאֵל *sheh-al-tee-ale'* (Chald.); cor. to 7597:–Shealtiel.
7599. שָׁאַן *shaw-an'* a prim. root; to *loll,* i.e. *be peaceful:*–be at ease, be quiet, rest. See also 1052.
7600. שַׁאֲנָן *shah-an-awn';* from 7599; *secure;* in a bad sense, *haughty:*–that is at ease, quiet, tumult. Comp. 7946.
7601. שָׁאַס *shaw-as';* a prim. root; to *plunder:*–spoil.
7602. שָׁאַף *shaw-af';* a prim. root; to *inhale* eagerly; fig., to *covet;* by impl., to *be angry;* also to *hasten:*–desire (earnestly), devour, haste, pant, snuff up, swallow up.
7603. שְׂאֹר *seh-ore';* from 7604; *barm* or yeast-cake (as *swelling* by fermentation):–leaven.
7604. שָׁאַר *shaw-ar';* a prim. root; prop. to *swell* up, i.e. *be* (caus., *make*) *redundant:*–leave, (be) left, let, remain, remnant, reserve, the rest.
7605. שְׁאָר *sheh-awr';* from 7604; a *remainder:*–X other, remnant, residue, rest.
7606. שְׁאָר *sheh-awr'* (Chald.); cor. to 7605:–X whatsoever more, residue, rest.
7607. שְׁאֵר *sheh-ayr';* from 7604; *flesh* (as *swelling out*), as living or for food; gen. *food* of any kind; fig., *kindred* by blood:–body, flesh, food, (near) kin(-sman, -swoman), near (nigh) [of kin].
7608. שַׁאֲרָה *shah-ar-aw';* fem. of 7607; female *kindred* by blood:–near kinswomen.
7609. שֶׁאֱרָה *sheh-er-aw';* the same as 7608; *Sheërah,* an Isr.s:–Sherah.
7610. שְׁאָר יָשׁוּב *sheh-awr' yaw-shoob';* from 7605 and 7725; a *remnant will return; Sheär-Jashub,* the symbolic name of one of Isaiah's sons:–Shear-jashub.
7611. שְׁאֵרִית *sheh-ay-reeth';* from 7604; a *remainder* or residual (surviving, final) portion:–that had escaped, be left, posterity, remain(-der), remnant, residue, rest.
7612. שֵׁאת *shayth;* from 7582; *devastation:*–desolation.
7613. שְׂאֵת *seh-ayth';* from 5375; an *elevation* or leprous scab; fig., *elation* or cheerfulness; *exaltation* in rank or character:–be accepted, dignity, excellency, highness, raise up self, rising.
7614. שְׁבָא *sheb-aw';* of for. or.; *Sheba,* the name of three early progenitors of tribes and of an Ethiopian district:–Sheba, Sabeans.
7615. שְׁבָאִי *sheb-aw-ee';* patron. from 7614; a *Shebaïte* or desc. of Sheba:–Sabean.
7616. שָׁבָב *shaw-bawb';* from an un. root mean. to *break* up; a *fragment,* i.e. *ruin:*–broken in pieces.
7617. שָׁבָה *shaw-baw';* a prim. root; to *transport* into captivity:–(bring away, carry, carry away, lead, lead away, take) captive (-s), drive (take) away.
7618. שְׁבוֹ *sheb-oo';* from an un. root (prob. ident. with that of 7617 through the idea of *subdivision* into flashes or streamers [comp. 7632] mean. to *flame;* a *gem* (from its sparkle), prob. the *agate:*–agate.
7619. שְׁבוּאֵל *sheb-oo-ale';* or שׁוּבָאֵל *shoo-baw-ale';* from 7617 (abb.) or 7725 and 410; *captive* (or *returned*) *of God; Shebuël* or *Shubaël,* the name of two Isr.:–Shebuel, Shubael.

7620. שָׁבוּעַ *shaw-boo'-ah;* or שָׁבֻעַ *shaw-boo'-ah;* also (fem.) שְׁבֻעָה *sheb-oo-aw';* prop. pass.part. of 7650 as a denom. of 7651; lit., *sevened,* i.e. a *week* (spec., of years):–seven, week.
7621. שְׁבוּעָה *sheb-oo-aw';* fem. pass.part. of 7650; prop. something *sworn,* i.e. an *oath:*–curse, oath, X sworn.
7622. שְׁבוּת *sheb-ooth';* or שְׁבִית *sheb-eeth';* from 7617; *exile,* concr., *prisoners;* fig., a *former state* of prosperity:– captive(-ity).
7623. שָׁבַח *shaw-bakh';* a prim. root; prop. to *address* in a loud tone, i.e. (spec.) *loud;* fig., to *pacify* (as if by words):–commend, glory, keep in, praise, still, triumph.
7624. שְׁבַח *sheb-akh'* (Chald.); cor. to 7623; to *adulate,* i.e. *adore:*–praise.
7625. שְׁבַט *sheb-at'* (Chald.); cor. to 7626; a *clan:*–tribe.
7626. שֵׁבֶט *shay'-bet;* from an un. root prob. mean. to *branch* off; a *scion,* i.e. (lit.) a *stick* (for punishing, writing, fighting, ruling, walking, etc.) or (fig.) a *clan:*–X correction, dart, rod, sceptre, staff, tribe.
7627. שְׁבָט *sheb-awt';* of for. or.; *Shebat,* a Jewish month:–Sebat.
7628. שְׁבִי *sheb-ee';* from 7618; *exiled; captured;* as noun, *exile* (abstr. or concr. and coll.); by ext., *booty:*–captive(-ity), prisoners, X take away, that was taken.
7629. שֹׁבִי *sho-bee';* from 7617; *captor; Shobi,* an Ammonite:–Shobi.
7630. שֹׁבַי *sho-bah'-ee;* for 7629; *Shobai,* an Isr.:–Shobai.
7631. שְׁבִיב *seb-eeb'* (Chald.); cor. to 7632:–flame.
7632. שָׁבִיב *shaw-beeb';* from the same as 7616; *flame* (as *split* into tongues):–spark.
7633. שִׁבְיָה *shib-yaw';* fem. of 7628; *exile* (abstr. or concr. and coll.):–captives(-ity).
7634. שָׁבְיָה *shob-yaw';* fem. of the same as 7629; *captivation; Shobjah,* an Isr.:–Shachia.
7635. שָׁבִיל *shaw-beel';* from the same as 7640; a *track* or passage-way (as if *flowing* along):–path.
7636. שָׁבִיס *shaw-beece';* from an un. root mean. to *interweave;* a *netting* for the hair:–caul.
7637. שְׁבִיעִי *sheb-ee-ee';* or שְׁבִעִי *sheb-ee-ee';* ord. from 7657; *seventh:*–seventh (time).
7638. שָׂבָךְ *saw-bawk';* from an un. root mean. to *intwine;* a *netting* (ornament to the capital of a column):–net.
7639. שְׂבָכָה *seb-aw-kaw';* fem. of 7638; a *net-work,* i.e (in hunting) a *snare,* (in arch.) a *ballustrade;* also a *reticulated* ornament to a pillar:–checker, lattice, network, snare, wreath(-enwork).
7640. שֹׁבֶל *show'-bel;* from an un. root mean. to *flow;* a lady's *train* (as *trailing* after her):–leg.
7641. שִׁבֹּל *shib-bole;* or (fem.) שִׁבֹּלֶת *shib-bo'-leth;* from the same as 7640; a *stream* (as *flowing*); also an *ear* of grain (as *growing* out); by anal., a *branch:*–branch, channel, ear (of corn), ([water-])flood, Shibboleth. Comp. 5451.
7642. שַׁבְלוּל *shab-lool';* from the same as 7640; a *snail* (as if *floating* in its own slime):–snail.
7643. שְׂבָם *seb-awm';* or (fem.) שִׂבְמָה *sib-maw';* prob. from 1313; *spice; Sebam* or *Sibmah,* a place in Moab:–Shebam, Shibmah, Sibmah.
7644. שֶׁבְנָא *sheb-naw';* or שֶׁבְנָה *sheb-naw';* from an un. root mean. to *grow; growth; Shebna* or *Shebnah,* an Isr.:–Shebna, Shebnah.
7645. שְׁבַנְיָה *sheb-an-yaw';* or שְׁבַנְיָהוּ *sheb-an-yaw'-hoo;* from the same as 7644 and 3050; *Jah has grown* (i.e. *prospered*); *Shebanjah,* the name of three or four Isr.:–Shebaniah.
7646. שָׂבַע *saw-bah';* or שָׂבֵעַ *saw-bay'-ah;* a prim. root; to *sate,* i.e. *fill* to satisfaction (lit. or fig.):–have enough, fill (full, self, with), be (to the) full (of), have plenty of, be satiate, satisfy (with), suffice, be weary of.
7647. שָׂבָע *saw-baw';* from 7646; *copiousness:*–abundance, plenteous(-ness,-ly).
7648. שֹׂבַע *so'-bah;* from 7646; *satisfaction* (of food or [fig.] joy):–fill, full(-ness), satisfying, be satisfied.
7649. שָׂבֵעַ *saw-bay'-ah;* from 7646; *satiated* (in a pleasant or disagreeable sense):–full (of), satisfied (with).
7650. שָׁבַע *shaw-bah';* a prim. root; propr. to be *complete,* but used only as a denom. from 7651; to *seven* oneself, i.e. *swear* (as if by repeating a declaration seven times):–adjure, charge (by an oath, with an oath), take an oath, X straitly, (cause to, make to) swear.
7651. שֶׁבַע *sheh'-bah;* or (masc.) שִׁבְעָה *shib-aw';* from 7650; a prim. cardinal number; *seven* (as the sacred *full* one); also (adv.) *seven times;* by impl., a *week;* by ext., an *indef.* number:–by) seven[-fold],-s, [-teen, -teenth, [-th, times). Comp. 7658.
7652. שֶׁבַע *sheh'-bah;* the same as 7651; *seven; Sheba,* the name of a place in Pal., and of two Isr.:–Sheba.
7653. שִׂבְעָה *sib-aw'* fem. of 7647; *satiety:*–fulness.
7654. שָׂבְעָה *sob-aw';* fem. of 7648; *satiety:*–(to have) enough, X till...be full, [un-] satiable, satisfy, X sufficiently.
7655. שִׁבְעָה *shib-aw'* (Chald.); cor. to 7651:–seven (times).
7656. שִׁבְעָה *shib-aw'* masc. of 7651; *seven (-th); Shebah,* a well in Pal.:–Shebah.
7657. שִׁבְעִים *shib-eem';* multiple of 7651; seventy:–*seventy,* threescore and ten (+ -teen).
7658. שִׁבְעָנָה *shib-aw-naw';* prol. for the masc. of 7651; *seven:*–seven.
7659. שִׁבְעָתַיִם *shib-aw-thah'-yim* dual (adv.) of 7651; *seven-times:*–seven(-fold, times).
7660. שָׁבַץ *shaw-bats';* a prim. root; to *interweave* (colored) threads in squares; by impl. (of *reticulation*) to *inchase* gems in gold:–embroider, set.
7661. שָׁבָץ *shaw-bawts';* from 7660; *entanglement,* i.e. (fig.) *perplexity:*–anguish.
7662. שְׁבַק *sheb-ak'* (Chald.); cor. to the root of 7733; to *quit,* i.e. allow to remain:–leave, let alone.
7663. שָׂבַר *saw-bar';* שָׁבַר (Nehemiah 2:13, 15) *shaw-bar';* a prim. root; to *scrutinize;* by impl. (of *watching*) to *expect* (with hope and patience):–hope, tarry, view, wait.
7664 שֵׂבֶר *say'-ber* from 7663; *expectation:*–hope.
7665. שָׁבַר *shaw-bar';* a prim. root; to *burst* (lit. or fig.):–break (down, off, in pieces, up), broken([-hearted]), bring to the birth, crush, destroy, hurt, quench, X quite, tear, view.
7666. שָׁבַר *shaw-bar';* denom. from 7668; to *deal* in grain:–buy, sell.
7667. שֶׁבֶר *sheh'-ber;* or שֵׁבֶר *shay'-ber;* from 7665; a *fracture,* fig., *ruin;* spec., a *solution* (of a dream):–affliction, breach, breaking, broken [-footed, -handed], bruise, crashing, destruction, hurt, interpretation, vexation.
7668. שֶׁבֶר *sheh'-ber;* the same as 7667; *grain* (as if *broken* into kernels):–corn, victuals.
7669. שֶׁבֶר *sheh'-ber* the same as 7667; *Sheber,* an Isr.:–Sheber.
7670. שִׁבְרוֹן *shib-rone';* from 7665; *rupture,* i.e. a *pang;* fig., ruin:–breaking, destruction.
7671. שְׁבָרִים *sheb-aw-reem';* pl. of 7667; *ruins; Shebarim,* a place in Pal.:–Shebarim.
7672. שְׁבַשׁ *sheb-ash'* (Chald.); cor. to 7660; to *entangle,* i.e. *perplex:*–be astonished.
7673. שָׁבַת *shaw-bath';* a prim. root; to *repose,* i.e. *desist* from exertion; used in many implied relations (caus., fig. or spec.):–(cause to, let, make to) cease, celebrate, cause (make) to fail, keep (sabbath), suffer to be lacking, leave, put away (down), (make to) rest, rid, still, take away.
7674. שֶׁבֶת *sheh'-beth;* from 7673; *rest, interruption, cessation:*–cease, sit still, loss of time.
7675. שֶׁבֶת *sheh'-beth;* inf. of 3427; prop. *session;* but used also concr., an *abode* or *locality:*–place, seat. Comp. 3429.
7676. שַׁבָּת *shab-bawth';* intens. from 7673; *intermission,* i.e (spec.) the *Sabbath:*–(+ every) sabbath.
7677. שַׁבָּתוֹן *shab-baw-thone';* from 7676; a *sabbatism* or special holiday:–rest, sabbath.
7678. שַׁבְּתַי *shab-beth-ah'-ee;* from 7676; *restful; Shabbethai,* the name of three Isr.:–Shabbethai.
7679. שָׂגָא *saw-gaw';* a prim. root; to *grow,* i.e. (caus.) to *enlarge,* (fig.) *laud:*–increase, magnify.
7680. שְׂגָא *seg-aw'* (Chald.); cor. to 7679; to *increase:*–grow, be multiplied.
7681. שָׁגֶה *shaw-gay'* prob. from 7686; *erring; Shage,* an Isr.:–Shage.
7682. שָׂגַב *saw-gab';* a primitive root; to *be* (caus., *make*) *lofty,* esp. *inaccessible;* by impl., *safe, strong;* used lit. and fig.:–defend, exalt, be excellent, (be, set on) high, lofty, be safe, set up (on high), be too strong.
7683. שָׁגַג *shaw-gag';* a prim. root; to *stray,* i.e. (fig.) *sin* (with more or less apology):–X also for that, deceived, err, go astray, sin ignorantly.
7684. שְׁגָגָה *sheg-aw-gaw';* from 7683; a *mistake* or inadvertent *transgression:*–error, ignorance, at unawares; unwittingly.
7685. שָׂגָה *saw-gaw'* a prim. root; to *enlarge* (esp. upward, also fig.):–grow (up), increase.
7686. שָׁגָה *shaw-gaw';* a prim. root; to *stray* (caus., *mislead*), usually (fig.) to *mistake,* esp. (mor.) to *transgress;* by ext. (through the idea of intoxication) to *reel,* (fig.) be *enraptured:*–(cause to) go astray, deceive, err, be ravished, sin through ignorance, (let, make to) wander.
7687. שְׂגוּב *seg-oob';* from 7682; *aloft; Segub,* the name of two Isr.:–Segub.
7688. שָׁגַח *shaw-gakh'* a prim. root; to *peep,* i.e. *glance* sharply at:–look (narrowly).
7689. שַׂגִּיא *sag-ghee';* from 7679; (sup.) *mighty:*–excellent, great.
7690. שַׂגִּיא *sag-ghee'* (Chald.); cor. to 7689; *large* (in size, quantity or number, also adv.):–exceeding, great(-ly); many, much, sore, very.
7691. שְׁגִיאָה *sheg-ee-aw';* from 7686; a mor. *mistake:*–err..
7692. שִׁגָּיוֹן *shig-gaw-yone'* or שִׁגָּיֹנָה *shig-gaw-yo-naw';* from 7686; prop. *aberration,* i.e. (te.) a *dithyramb* or rambling poem:–Shiggaion, Shigionoth.
7693. שָׁגַל *shaw-gal';* a prim. root; to *copulate* with:–lie with, ravish.

7694. שֵׁגָל *shay-gawl'* from 7693; a *queen* (from cohabitation):–queen.
7695. שֵׁגָל *shay-gawl'* (Chald.); cor. to 7694; a (legitimate) *queen*:–wife.
7696. שָׁגַע *shaw-gah'*; a prim. root; to *rave* through insanity:–(be, play the) mad (man).
7697. שִׁגָּעוֹן *shig-gaw-yone'*; from 7696; *craziness*:–furiously, madness.
7698. שֶׁגֶר *sheh'-ger*; from an un. root prob. mean. to *eject*; the *fetus* (as finally *expelled*):–that cometh of, increase.
7699. שַׁד *shad*; or שֹׁד *shode*; prob. from 7736 (in its or. sense) contr.; the *breast* of a woman or animal (as *bulging*):–breast, pap, teat.
7700. שֵׁד *shade;* from 7736; a *dæmon* (as *malignant*):–devil.
7701. שֹׁד *shode;* or (Job 5:21) שׁוֹד *shode;* from 7736; *violence, ravage:*–desolation, destruction, oppression, robbery, spoil(-ed, -er, - ing), wasting.
7702. שָׂדַד *saw-dad';* a prim. root; to *abrade*, i.e. *harrow* a field:–break clods, harrow.
7703. שָׁדַד *shaw-dad';* a prim. root; prop. to *be burly,* i.e. (fig.) *powerful* (pass., *impregnable*); by impl., to *ravage:*–dead, destroy(-er), oppress, robber, spoil(-er), X utterly, (lay) waste.
7704. שָׂדֶה *saw-deh';* or שָׂדַי *saw-dah'-ee;* from an un. root mean. to *spread* out; a *field* (as *flat*):–country, field, ground, land, soil, X wild.
7705. שִׁדָּה *shid-dah';* from 7703; a *wife* (as *mistress* of the house):–X all sorts, mus. instrument.
7706. שַׁדַּי *shad-dah'-ee* from 7703; the *Almighty:*–Almighty.
7707. שְׁדֵיאוּר *shed-ay-oor';* from the same as 7704 and 217; *spreader of light; Shedejur,* an Israelite:–Shedeur.
7708. שִׂדִּים *sid-deem';* pl. from the same as 7704; *flats; Siddim,* a valley in Pal.:–Siddim.
7709 שְׁדֵמָה *shed-ay-maw';* app. from 7704; a cultivated *field;* – blasted, field.
7710. שָׁדַף *shaw-daf';* a prim. root; to *scorch*:–blast.
7711. שְׁדֵפָה *shed-ay-faw'; or* שִׁדָּפוֹן *shid-daw-fone';* from 7710; *blight:*–blasted(-ing).
7712. שְׁדַר *shed-ar'* (Chald.); a prim. root; to *endeavor:*–labour.
7713. שְׂדֵרָה *sed-ay-raw';* from an un. root mean. to *regulate;* a *row,* i.e. *rank* (of soldiers), *story* (of rooms):–board, range.
7714. שַׁדְרַךְ *shad-rak';* prob. of for. or.; *Shadrak,* the Bab. name of one of Daniel's companions:–Shadrach.
7715. שַׁדְרַךְ *shad-rak'* (Chald.); the same as 7714:–Shadrach.
7716. שֶׂה *seh;* or שֵׂי *say;* prob. from 7582 through the idea of *pushing* out to graze; a member of a flock, i.e. a *sheep* or *goat:*–(lesser, small) cattle, ewe, goat, lamb, sheep. Comp. 2089.
7717. שָׂהֵד *saw-hade';* from an un. root mean. to *testify;* a *witness:*–record.
7718. שֹׁהַם *sho'-ham;* from an un. root prob. mean to *blanch;* a gem, prob. the *beryl* (from its *pale* green color):–onyx.
7719. שֹׁהַם *sho'-ham;* the same as 7718; *Shoham,* an Isr.:–Shoham.
7720. שַׂהֲרֹן *sah-har-one';* from the same as 5469; a round *pendant* for the neck:–ornament, round tire like the moon.
7721. שׂוֹא *so;* from an un. root (akin to 5375 and 7722) mean. to *rise*; a *rising*:–arise.
7722. שׁוֹא *sho*; or (fem.) שׁוֹאָה *sho-aw'*; or שֹׁאָה *sho-aw'*; from an un. root mean. to *rush* over; a *tempest*; by implication, *devastation*:–desolate(-ion), destroy, destruction, storm, wasteness.
7723. שָׁוְא *shawv;* or *shav;* from the same as 7722 in the sense of *desolating; evil* (as *destructive*), lit. (*ruin*) or mor. (esp. *guile*); fig. *idolatry* (as false, subj.), *uselessness* (as deceptive, obj.; also adv., in *vain*):–false (-ly), lie, lying, vain, vanity.
7724. שְׁוָא *shev-aw';* from the same as 7723; *false; Sheva,* an Isr.:–Sheva.
7725. שׁוּב *shoob;* a prim. root; to *turn* back (hence, away) trans. or intr., lit. or fig. (not necessarily with the idea of *return* to the starting point); gen. to *retreat;* often adv., *again:*–([break, build, circumcise, dig, do anything, do evil, feed, lay down, lie down, lodge, make, rejoice, send, take, weep]) X again, (cause to) answer (+ again), X in any case (wise), X at all, averse, bring (again, back, home again), call [to mind], carry again (back), cease, X certainly, come again (back), X consider, + continually, convert, deliver (again), + deny, draw back, fetch home again, X fro, get [oneself] (back) again, X give (again), go again (back, home), [go] out, hinder, let, [see] more, X needs, be past, X pay, pervert, pull in again, put (again, up again), recall, recompense, recover, refresh, relieve, render (again), requite, rescue, restore, retrieve, (cause to, make to) return, reverse, reward, + say nay, send back, set again, slide back, still, X surely, take back (off), (cause to, make to) turn (again, self again, away, back, back again, backward, from, off), withdraw.
7726. שׁוֹבָב *sho-bawb';* from 7725; *apostate,* i.e. idolatrous:–backsliding, frowardly, turn away.
7727. שׁוֹבָב *sho-bawb';* the same as 7726; *rebellious; Shobab,* the name of two Isr.:–Shobab.
7728. שׁוֹבֵב *sho-babe';* from 7725; *apostate,* i.e. heathenish or (actually) heathen:–backsliding.
7729. שׁוּבָה *shoo-baw';* from 7725; a *return:*–returning.
7730. שׂוֹבֶךְ *so'-bek;* for 5441; a *thicket,* i.e. interlaced branches:–thick boughs.
7731. שׁוֹבָךְ *sho-bawk'* perh. for 7730; *Shobak,* a Syrian:–Shobach.
7732. שׁוֹבָל *sho-bawl';* from the same as 7640; *overflowing; Shobal,* the name of an Edomite and two Isr.:–Shobal.
7733. שׁוֹבֵק *sho-bake';* act.part. from a prim. root mean. to *leave* (comp. 7662); *forsaking; Shobek,* an Isr.:–Shobek.
7734. שׂוּג *soog;* a prim. root; to *retreat:*–turn back.
7735. שׂוּג *soog;* a prim. root; to *hedge* in:–make to grow.
7736. שׁוּד *shood;* a prim. root; prop. to *swell* up, i.e. fig. (by impl. of *insolence*) to *devastate:*–waste.
7737. שָׁוָה *shaw-vaw';* a prim. root; prop. to *level,* i.e. *equalize;* fig., to *resemble;* by impl., to *adjust* (i.e. counterbalance, be suitable, compose, place, yield, etc.):–avail, behave, bring forth, comp., countervail, (be, make) equal, lay, be (make, a-)like, make plain, profit, reckon.
7738. שָׁוָה *shaw-vaw';* a prim. root; to *destroy:*–X substance
7739. שְׁוָה *shev-aw'* (Chald.); cor. to 7737; to *resemble:*–make like.
7740. שָׁוֵה *shaw-vay';* from 7737; *plain; Shaveh,* a place in Pal.:–Shaveh.
7741. שָׁוֵה קִרְיָתַיִם *shaw-vay' kir-yaw-thah'-yim;* from the same as 7740 and the dual of 7151; *plain of a double city; Shaveh-Kirjathajim,* a place E. of the Jordan:–Shaveh Kiriathaim.
7742. שׂוּחַ *soo'-akh;* a prim. root; to *muse* pensively:–meditate.
7743. שׁוּחַ *shoo'-akh;* a prim. root; to *sink,* lit. or fig.:–bow down, incline, humble.
7744. שׁוּחַ *shoo'-akh;* from 7743; *dell; Shuäch,* a son of Abraham:–Shuah.
7745. שׁוּחָה *shoo-khaw';* from 7743; a *chasm:*–ditch, pit.
7746. שׁוּחָה *shoo-khaw';* the same as 7745; *Shuchah,* an Isr.:–Shuah.
7747. שׁוּחִי *shoo-khee';* patron. from 7744; a *Shuchite* or desc. of Shuach:–Shuhite.
7748. שׁוּחָם *shoo-khawm';* from 7743; *humbly; Shucham,* an Isr.:–Shuham.
7749. שׁוּחָמִי *shoo-khaw-mee';* patron. from 7748; a *Shuchamite* (coll.):–Shuhamites.
7750. שׂוּט *soot;* or (by perm.) סוּט *soot;* a prim. root; to *detrude,* i.e. (intr. and fig.) *become derelict* (wrongly practise; namely, idolatry):–turn aside to.
7751. שׁוּט *shoot;* a prim. root; prop. to *push* forth; (but used only fig.) to *lash,* i.e. (the sea with oars) to *row;* by impl., to *travel:*–go (about, through, to and fro), mariner, rower, run to and fro.
7752. שׁוֹט *shote;* from 7751; a *lash* (lit. or fig.):–scourge, whip.
7753. שׂוּךְ *sook;* a prim. root; to *entwine,* i.e. *shut* in (for formation, protection or restraint):–fence, (make an) hedge (up).
7754. שׂוֹךְ *soke;* or (fem.) שׂוֹכָה *so-kaw';* from 7753; a *branch* (as *interleaved*):–bough.
7755. שׂוֹכֹה *so-ko';* or שֹׂכֹה *so-ko';* or שׂוֹכוֹ *so-ko';* from 7753; *Sokoh* or *Soko,* the name of two places in Pal.:–Shocho, Shochoh, Sochoh, Soco, Socoh.
7756. שׂוּכָתִי *soo-kaw-thee';* prob. patron. from a name cor. to 7754 (fem.); a *Sukathite* or desc. of an unknown Isr. named Sukah:–Suchathite.
7757. שׁוּל *shool;* from an un. root mean. to *hang* down; a *skirt;* by impl., a bottom *edge:*–hem, skirt, train.
7758. שׁוֹלָל *sho-lawl';* or (Micah 1:8) שֵׁילָל *shay-lawl';* from 7997; *nude* (esp. bare-foot); by impl., *captive:*–spoiled, stripped.
7759. שׁוּלַמִּית *shoo-lam-meeth';* from 7999; *peaceful* (with the art. always pref., making it a pet name); the *Shulammith,* an epithet of Solomon's queen:–Shulamite.
7760. שׂוּם *soom;* or שִׂים *seem;* a prim. root; to *put* (used in a great variety of appl., lit., fig., inferentially, and ellip.):–X any wise, appoint, bring, call [a name], care, cast in, change, charge, commit, consider, convey, determine, + disguise, dispose, do, get, give, heap up, hold, impute, lay (down, up), leave, look, make (out), mark, + name, X on, ordain, order, + paint, place, preserve, purpose, put (on), + regard, rehearse, reward, (cause to) set (on, up), shew, + stedfastly, take, X tell, + tread down, ([over-]turn, X wholly, work.
7761. שׂוּם *soom* (Chald.); cor. to 7760:–+ command, give, lay, make, + name, + regard, set.
7762. שׁוּם *shoom;* from an un. root mean. to *exhale; garlic* (from its rank *odor*):–garlic.
7763. שׁוֹמֵר *sho-mare';* or שֹׁמֵר *sho-mare';* act.part. of 8104; *keeper; Shomer,* the name

of two Isr.:–Shomer.
7764. שׁוּנִי *shoo-nee'* from an un. root mean. to rest; quiet; Shuni, an Isr.:–Shuni.
7765. שׁוּנִי *shoo-nee'* patron. from 7764; a *Shunite* (coll.) or desc. of Shuni:–Shunites.
7766. שׁוּנֵם *shoo-name';* prob. from the same as 7764; *quietly; Shunem,* a place in Pal:–Shunem.
7767. שׁוּנַמִּית *shoo-nam-meeth';* patrial from 7766; a *Shunammitess,* or female inh. of Shunem:–Shunamite.
7768. שָׁוַע *shaw-vah';* a prim. root; prop. to *be free;* but used only caus. and refl., to *halloo* (for help, i.e. *freedom* from some trouble):–cry (aloud, out), shout.
7769. שׁוּעַ *shoo'-ah;* from 7768; a *halloo:*–cry, riches.
7770. שׁוּעַ *shoo'-ah;* the same as 7769; *Shuä,* a Canaanite:–Shua, Shuah.
7771. שׁוֹעַ *sho'-ah;* from 7768 in the or. sense of *freedom;* a *noble,* i.e. *liberal, opulent;* also (as noun in the der. sense) a *halloo:*–bountiful, crying, rich.
7772. שׁוֹעַ *sho'-ah;* the same as 7771; *rich; Shoä,* an Oriental people:–Shoa.
7773. שֶׁוַע *sheh'-vah*; from 7768; a *halloo:*–cry.
7774. שׁוּעָא *shoo-aw';* from 7768; *wealth; Shuä,* an Isr.s:–Shua.
7775. שַׁוְעָה *shav-aw';* fem. of 7773; a *hallooing:*–crying.
7776. שׁוּעָל *shoo-awl';* or שֻׁעָל *shoo-awl';* from the same as 8168; a *jackal* (as a *burrower*):–fox.
7777. שׁוּעָל *shoo-awl';* the same as 7776; *Shuäl,* the name of an Isr. and of a place in Pal.:–Shual.
7778. שׁוֹעֵר *sho-are';* or שֹׁעֵר *sho-are':* act.part. of 8176 (as denom. from 8179); a *janitor:*–doorkeeper, porter.
7779. שׁוּף *shoof;* a prim. root; prop. to *gape,* i.e. *snap* at; fig., to *overwhelm:*–break, bruise, cover.
7780. שׁוֹפָךְ *sho-fawk';* from 8210; *poured; Shophak,* a Syrian:–Shophach.
7781. שׁוּפָמִי *shoo-faw-mee';* patron. from 8197; a *Shuphamite* (coll.) or desc. of Shephupham:–Shuphamite.
7782. שׁוֹפָר *sho-far';* or שֹׁפָר *sho-far';* from 8231 in the or. sense of *incising;* a *cornet* (as giving a *clear* sound) or curved horn:–cornet, trumpet.
7783. שׁוּק *shook;* a prim. root; to *run* after or over, i.e. *overflow:*–overflow, water.
7784. שׁוּק *shook;* from 7783; a *street* (as *run* over):–street.
7785. שׁוֹק *shoke;* from 7783; the (lower) *leg* (as a *runner*):–hip, leg, shoulder, thigh.
7786. שׂוּר *soor;* a prim. root; prop. to *vanquish;* by impl., to *rule* (caus., *crown*):–make princes, have power, reign. See 5493.
7787. שׂוּר soor; a prim. root [rather ident. with 7786 through the idea of *reducing* to pieces; comp. 4883]; to *saw:*–cut.
7788. שׁוּר *shoor;* a prim. root; prop. to *turn,* i.e. *travel* about (as a harlot or a merchant):–go, sing. See also 7891.
7789. שׁוּר *shoor;* a prim. root [rather ident. with 7788 through the idea of *going round* for inspection]; to *spy* out, i.e. (gen.) *survey,* (for evil) *lurk for,* (for good) *care for:*–behold, lay wait, look, observe, perceive, regard, see.
7790. שׁוּר *shoor;* from 7889; a *foe* (as *lying in wait*):–enemy.
7791. שׁוּר *shoor;* from 7788; a *wall* (as *going about*):–wall.
7792. שׁוּר *shoor* (Chald.); cor. to 7791:–wall.
7793. שׁוּר *shoor;* the same as 7791; *Shur,* a region of the Desert:–Shur.
7794. שׁוֹר *shore;* from 7788; a *bullock* (as a *traveller*):–bull(-ock), cow, ox, wall.
7795. שׂוֹרָה *so-raw';* from 7786 in the prim. sense of 5493; prop. a *ring,* i.e. (by anal.) a *row* (adv.):–principal.
7796. שׂוֹרֵק *so-rake';* the same as 8321; a *vine; Sorek,* a valley in Pal.:–Sorek.
7797. שׂוּשׂ *soos;* or שִׂישׂ *sece*; a prim. root; to *be bright,* i.e. *cheerful:*–be glad, X greatly, joy, make mirth, rejoice.
7798. שַׁוְשָׁא *shav-shaw'*; from 7797; *joyful; Shavsha,* an Isr.:–Shavsha.
7799. שׁוּשַׁן *shoo-shan';* or שׁוֹשַׁן *sho-shawn';* or שֹׁשַׁן *sho-shawn';* and (fem.) שׁוֹשַׁנָּה *sho-shan-naw';* from 7797; a *lily* (from its *whiteness*), as a flower of arch. ornament; also a (straight) *trumpet* (from the *tubular* shape): lily, Shoshannim.
7800. שׁוּשַׁן *shoo-shan';* the same as 7799; *Shushan,* a place in Pers.:–Shushan.
7801. שׁוּשַׁנְכִי *shoo-shan-kee'* (Chald.); of for. or.; a *Shushankite* (coll.) or inh. of some unknown place in Ass.:–Susanchites.
7802. שׁוּשַׁן עֵדוּת *shoo-shan' ay-dooth';* or (pl. of former) שׁוֹשַׁנִּים עֵדוּת *sho-shan-neem' ay-dooth';* from 7799 and 5715; *lily* (or *trumpet*) of *assemblage*; *Shushan-Eduth* or *Shoshannim-Eduth,* the title of a popular song:–Shoshannim-Eduth, Shushan-eduth.
7803. שׁוּתֶלַח *shoo-theh'-lakh*; prob. from 7582 and the same as 8520; *crash of breakage; Shuthelach,* the name of two Isr.:–Shuthelah.
7804. שְׁזַב *shez-ab'* (Chald.); cor. to 5800; to *leave,* i.e. (caus.) *free*:–deliver.
7805. שָׁזַף *shaw-zaf'* a prim. root; to *tan* (by sun-burning); fig. (as if by a piercing ray) to *scan*:–look up, see.
7806. שָׁזַר *shaw-zar';* a prim. root; to *twist* (a thread of straw):–twine.
7807. שַׁח *shakh*; from 7817; *sunk,* i.e. *downcast*:–+ humble.
7808. שֵׂחַ *say'-akh;* for 7879; *communion,* i.e. (refl.) *meditation*:–thought.
7809. שָׁחַד *shaw-khad'*; a prim. root; to *donate*, i.e. *bribe*:–hire, give a reward.
7810. שַׁחַד *shakh'-ad;* from 7809; a *donation* (venal or redemptive):–bribe(-ry), gift, present, reward.
7811. שָׂחָה *saw-khaw'*; a prim. root; to *swim*; caus., to *inundate*:–(make to) swim.
7812. שָׁחָה *shaw-khaw';* a prim. root; to *depress,* i.e. *prostrate* (esp. refl., in homage to royalty or God):–bow (self) down, crouch, fall down (flat), humbly beseech, do (make) obeisance, do reverence, make to stoop, worship.
7813. שָׂחוּ *saw'-khoo*; from 7811; a *pond* (for *swimming*):–to swim in.
7814. שְׂחוֹק *sekh-oke';* or שְׂחֹק *sekh-oke';* from 7832; *laughter* (in merriment or defiance):–derision, laughter(-ed to scorn, -ing), mocked, sport.
7815. שְׁחוֹר *shekh-ore'*; from 7835; *dinginess,* i.e. perh. *soot*:–coal.
7816. שְׁחוּת *shekh-ooth'*; from 7812; *pit*:–pit.
7817. שָׁחַח *shaw-khakh'*; a prim. root; to *sink* or *depress* (refl. or caus.):–bend, bow (down), bring (cast) down, couch, humble self, be (bring) low, stoop.
7818. שָׂחַט *saw-khat'*; a prim. root; to *tread* out, i.e. *squeeze* (grapes):–press.
7819. שָׁחַט *shaw-khat';* a prim. root; to *slaughter* (in sacrifice or massacre):–kill, offer, shoot out, slay, slaughter.
7820. שָׁחַט *shaw-khat'*; a prim. root [ident. with 7819 through the idea of *striking*]; to *hammer* out:–beat.
7821. שְׁחִיטָה *shekh-ee-taw';* from 7819; *slaughter*:–killing.
7822. שְׁחִין *shekh-een'*; from an un. root prob. mean. to *burn*; *inflammation*, i.e. an *ulcer*;–boil, botch.
7823. שָׁחִיס *shaw-khece';* or סָחִישׁ *saw-kheesh'*; from an un. root app. mean. to *sprout*; *after-growth*:–(that) which springeth of the same.
7824. שָׁחִיף *shaw-kheef;'* from the same as 7828; a *board* (as *chipped* thin):–cieled with.
7825. שְׁחִית *shekh-eeth'* from 7812; a *pit*-fall (lit. or fig.):–destruction, pit.
7826. שַׁחַל *shakh'-al;* from an un. root prob. mean. to *roar*; a *lion* (from his characteristic *roar*):–(fierce) lion.
7827. שְׁחֵלֶת *shekh-ay'-leth*; app. from the same as 7826 through some obscure idea, perh. that of *peeling* off by concussion of sound; a *scale* or shell, i.e. the aromatic *mussel*.:–onycha.
7828. שַׁחַף *shakh'-af*; from an un. root mean. to *peel*, i.e. *emaciate*; the *gull* (as *thin*):–cuckoo.
7829. שַׁחֶפֶת *shakh-eh'-feth;* from the same as 7828; *emaciation*:–consumption.
7830. שַׁחַץ *shakh'-ats*; from an un. root app. mean. to *strut*; *haughtiness* (as evinced by the attitude):–X lion, pride.
7831. שַׁחֲצוֹם *shakh-ats-ome';* from the same as 7830; *proudly; Shachatsom,* a place in Pal.:–Shahazimah.
7832. שָׂחַק *saw-khak';* a prim. root; to *laugh* (in pleasure or detraction); by impl., to *play*:–deride, have in derision, laugh, make merry, mock(-er), play, rejoice, (laugh to) scorn, be in (make) sport.
7833. שָׁחַק *shaw-khak';* a prim. root; to *comminute* (by trituration or attrition):–beat, wear.
7834. שַׁחַק *shakh'-ak* from 7833; a *powder* (as *beaten* small): by anal., a thin *vapor*; by ext., the *firmament*:–cloud, small dust, heaven, sky.
7835. שָׁחַר *shaw-khar';* a prim. root [ident. with 7836 through the idea of the *duskiness* of early dawn]; to be *dim* or dark (in color):–be black.
7836. שָׁחַר *shaw-khar'*; a prim. root; prop. to *dawn*, i.e. (fig.) be (up) *early* at any task (with the impl. of earnestness); by ext., to *search* for (with painstaking):–[do something] betimes, enquire early, rise (seek) betimes, seek diligently) early, in the morning).
7837. שַׁחַר *shakh'-ar*; from 7836; *dawn* (lit., fig. or adv.):–day(-spring), early, light, morning, whence riseth.
7838. שָׁחֹר *shaw-khore'*; or שָׁחוֹר *shaw-khore'*; from 7835; prop. *dusky*, but also (absol.) *jetty*:–black.
7839. שַׁחֲרוּת *shakh-ar-ooth'*; from 7836; a *dawning*, i.e. (fig.) *juvenescence*:–youth.
7840. שְׁחַרְחֹרֶת *shekh-ar-kho'-reth*; from 7835; *swarthy*:–black.

7841. שְׁחַרְיָה *shekh-ar-yaw'*; from 7836 and 3050; Jah *has sought; Shecharjah*, an Isr.:–Shehariah.
7842. שַׁחֲרַיִם *shakh-ar-ah'-yim*; dual of 7837; *double dawn; Shacharajim*, an Isr.:–Shaharaim.
7843. שָׁחַת *shaw-khath'*; a prim. root; to *decay*, i.e. (caus.) *ruin* (lit. or fig.):–batter, cast off, corrupt(-er, thing), destroy(-er, -uction), lose, mar, perish, spill, spoiler, X utterly, waste(-r).
7844. שְׁחַת *shekh-ath'* (Chald.); cor. to 7843:–corrupt, fault.
7845. שַׁחַת *shakh'-ath*; from 7743; a *pit* (esp. as a trap); fig., *destruction*:–corruption, destruction, ditch, grave, pit.
7846. שֵׂט *sayte;* or סֵט *sayt*; from 7750; a *departure* from right, i.e. *sin*:–revolter, that turn aside.
7847. שָׂטָה *saw-taw';* a prim. root; to *deviate* from duty:–decline, go aside, turn.
7848. שִׁטָּה *shit-taw'*; fem. of a der. [only in the pl. שִׁטִּים *shit-teem'*; mean. the *sticks* of wood] from the same as 7850; the *acacia* (from its *scourging* thorns):–shittah, shittim. See also 1029.
7849. שָׁטַח *shaw-takh'*; a prim. root; to *expand*:–all abroad, enlarge, spread, stretch out.
7850. שֹׁטֵט *sho-tate'* act.part. of an otherwise un. root mean. (prop. to *pierce*; but only as a denom. from 7752) to *flog*; a *goad*:–scourge.
7851. שִׁטִּים *shit-teem'*; the same as the pl. of 7848; *acacia* trees; *Shittim*, a place E. of the Jordan:–Shittim.
7852. שָׂטַם *saw-tam'*; a prim. root; prop. to *lurk* for, i.e. *persecute*:–hate, oppose self against.
7853. שָׂטַן *saw-tan'*; a prim. root; to *attack*, (fig.) *accuse*:–(be an) adversary, resist.
7854. שָׂטָן *saw-tawn'*; from 7853; an *opponent*; esp. (with the art. pref.) *Satan*, the arch-enemy of good:–adversary, Satan, withstand.
7855. שִׂטְנָה *sit-naw';* from 7853; *opposition* (by letter):–accusation.
7856. שִׂטְנָה *sit-naw'*; the same as 7855; *Sitnah*, the name of a well in Pal:–Sitnah.
7857. שָׁטַף *shaw-taf'*; a prim. root; to *gush*; by impl., to *inundate, cleanse*; by anal., to *gallop, conquer*:–drown, (over-)flow(-whelm, rinse, run, rush, (throughly) wash (away).
7858. שֶׁטֶף *sheh'-tef;* or שֵׁטֶף *shay'-tef*; from 7857; a *deluge* (lit. or fig.):–flood, outrageous, overflowing.
7859. שְׁטַר *shet-ar'* (Chald.); of unc. der.; a *side*:–side.
7860. שֹׁטֵר *sho-tare'*; act.part. of an other-wise un. root prob. mean. to *write*; prop. a *scribe*, i.e. (by anal. or impl.) an official *superintendent* or *magistrate*:–officer, overseer, ruler.
7861. שִׁטְרַי *shit-rah'-ee*; from the same as 7860; *magisterial; Shitrai*, an Isr.:–Shitrai.
7862. שַׁי *shah'-ee*; prob. from 7737; a *gift* (as *available*):–present.
7863. שִׂיא *see;* from the same as 7721 by perm.; *elevation*:– excellency.
7864. שְׁיָא *sheh-yaw'*; for 7724; *Sheja*, an Isr.:–Sheva.
7865. שִׂיאֹן *see-ohn';* from 7863; *peak; Sion*, the summit of Mt. Hermon:–Sion.
7866. שִׁיאוֹן *shee-ohn'*; from the same as 7722; *ruin; Shijon*, a place in Pal. –Shihon.
7867. שִׂיב *seeb*; a prim. root; prop. to *become aged*, i.e. (by impl.) to *grow gray*:–(be) grayheaded.
7868. שִׂיב *seeb* (Chald.); cor. to 7867:–elder.
7869. שֵׂיב *sabe;* from 7867; old *age*:–age.
7870. שִׁיבָה *shee-baw'* by perm. from 7725; a *return* (of property):–captivity.
7871. שִׁיבָה *shee-baw'*; from 3427; *residence*:–while...lay.
7872. שֵׂיבָה *say-baw'*; fem. of 7869; old *age*:–(be) gray (grey hoar,-y) hairs (head, -ed), old age.
7873. שִׂיג *seeg*; from 7734; a *withdrawal* (into a private place):–pursuing.
7874. שִׂיד *seed*; a prim. root prob. mean. to *boil* up (comp. 7736); used only as denom. from 7875; to *plaster*:–plaister.
7875. שִׂיד *seed;* from 7874; lime (as *boiling* when slacked):–lime, plaister.
7876. שָׁיָה *shaw-yaw'*; a prim. root; to *keep* in memory:–be unmindful. [Render Deuteronomy 32:18, "A Rock bore thee, *thou must recollect*; and (yet) thou hast forgotten," etc.]
7877. שִׁיזָא *shee-zaw'*; of unknown der.; *Shiza*, an Is.:–Shiza.
7878. שִׂיחַ *see'-akh;* a prim. root; to *ponder*, i.e. (by impl.) *converse* (with oneself, and hence, aloud) or (trans.) *utter*:–commune, complain, declare, meditate, muse, pray, speak, talk (with).
7879. שִׂיחַ *see'-akh*; from 7878; a *contemplation*; by impl., an *utterance*:–babbling, communication, complaint, meditation, prayer, talk.
7880. שִׂיחַ *see'-akh* from 7878; a *shoot* (as if *uttered* or put forth), i.e. (gen.) *shrubbery*:–bush, plant, shrub.
7881. שִׂיחָה *see-khaw'* fem. of 7879; *reflection*; be ext., *devotion*:–meditation, prayer.
7882. שִׁיחָה *shee-khaw'*; for 7745; a *pit*-fall:–pit.
7883. שִׁיחוֹר *shee-khore';* or שִׁחוֹר *shee-khore'*; or שִׁחֹר *shee-khore'*; prob. from 7835; *dark*, i.e. *turbid*; *Shichor*, a stream of Eg.:–Shihor, Sihor.
7884. שִׁיחוֹר לִבְנָת *shee-khore'; lib-nawth;'* from the same as 7883 and 3835; *darkish whiteness*; *Shichor-Libnath*, a stream of Pal.:–Shihor-libnath.
7885. שַׁיִט *shay'-yit*; from 7751; an *oar*; also (comp. 7752) a *scourge* (fig.):–oar, scourge.
7886. שִׁילֹה *shee-lo'*; from 7951; *tranquil; Shiloh*, an epithet of the Messiah:–Shiloh.
7887. שִׁילֹה *shee-lo'*; or שִׁלֹה *shee-lo'*; or שִׁילוֹ *shee-lo'*; or שִׁלוֹ *shee-lo'*; from the same as 7886; *Shiloh*, a place in Pal.:–Shiloh.
7888. שִׁילוֹנִי *shee-lo-nee'*; or שִׁילֹנִי *shee-lo-nee'*; or שִׁלֹנִי *shee-lo-nee'*; from 7887; a *Shilonite* or inh. of Shiloh:–Shilonite.
7889. שִׁימוֹן *shee-mone'*; app. for 3452; *desert; Shimon*, an Isr.:–Shimon.
7890. שַׁיִן *shah'-yin*; from an un. root mean. to *urinate; urine*:–piss.
7891. שִׁיר *sheer*; or (the or. form) שׁוּר (1 Sa. 18:6) *shoor*; a prim. root [ident. with 7788 through the idea of strolling minstrelsy]; to *sing*:–sing(-er, -ing man, -ing woman).
7892. שִׁיר *sheer*; or fem. שִׁירָה *shee-raw'*; from 7891; a *song*; abstr., *singing*:–mus.(-ick), X sing(-er, -ing), song.
7893. שַׁיִשׁ *shah'-yish*; from an un. root mean. to *bleach*, i.e. *whiten*; *white*, i.e. *marble*. See 8336.
7894. שִׁישָׁא *shee-shaw'*; from the same as 7893; *whiteness; Shisha*, an Isr.:–Shisha.
7895. שִׁישַׁק *shee-shak';* or שׁוּשַׁק *shoo-shak'*; of Eg. der.; *Shishak*, an Eg. king:–Shishak.
7896. שִׁית *sheeth*; a prim. root; to *place* (in a very wide appl.):–apply, appoint, array, bring, consider, lay (up), let alone, X look, make, mark, put (on), + regard, set, shew, be stayed, X take.
7897. שִׁית *sheeth*; from 7896; a *dress* (as *put* on):–attire.
7898. שַׁיִת *shah'-yith*; from 7896; *scrub* or *trash*, i.e. wild *growth* of weeds or briers (as if *put* on the field):–thorns.
7899. שֵׂךְ *sake*; from 5526 in the sense of 7753; a *brier* (as of a hedge):–prick.
7900. שֹׂךְ *soke*; from 5526 in the sense of 7753; a *booth* (as *interlaced*):–tabernacle.
7901. שָׁכַב *shaw-kab'*; a prim. root; to *lie* down (for rest, sexual connection, decease or any other purpose):–X at all, cast down, ([over-])lay (self) (down), (make to) lie (down, down to sleep, still with), lodge, ravish, take rest, sleep, stay.
7902. שְׁכָבָה *shek-aw-baw'*; from 7901; a *lying* down (of dew, or for the sexual act):–X carnally, copulation, X lay, seed.
7903. שְׁכֹבֶת *shek-o'-beth*; from 7901; a (sexual) *lying* with:–X lie.
7904. שָׁכָה *shaw-kaw';* a prim. root; to *roam* (through lust):–in the morning.
7905. שֻׂכָּה *sook-kaw'*; fem. of 7900 in the sense of 7899; a *dart* (as pointed like a *thorn*):–barbed iron.
7906. שֵׂכוּ *say'-koo*; from an un. root app. mean. to *surmount*; an *observatory* (with the art.); *Seku*, a place in Pal.:–Sechu.
7907. שֶׂכְוִי *sek-vee'*; from the same as 7906; *observant*, i.e. (concr.) the *mind*:–heart.
7908. שְׁכוֹל *shek-ole'*; inf. of 7921; *bereavement*:–loss of children, spoiling.
7909. שַׁכּוּל *shak-kool';* or שַׁכֻּל *shak-kool'*; from 7921; *bereaved*:–barren, bereaved (robbed) of children (whelps).
7910. שִׁכּוֹר *shik-kore';* or שִׁכֹּר *shik-kore'*; from 7937; *intoxicated*, as a state or a habit:–drunk(-ard, -en, -en man).
7911. שָׁכַח *shaw-kakh'*; or שָׁכֵחַ *shaw-kay'-akh*; a prim. root; to *mislay*, i.e. to *be oblivious* of, from want of memory or attention:–X at all, (cause to) forget.
7912. שְׁכַח *shek-akh'* (Chald.); cor. to 7911 through the idea of disclosure of a *covered* or *forgotten* thing; to *discover* (lit. or fig.):–find.
7913. שָׁכֵחַ *shaw-kay'-akh;* from 7911; *oblivious*:–forget.
7914. שְׂכִיָּה *sek-ee-yaw';* fem. from the same as 7906; a *conspicuous* obj.:–picture.
7915. שַׂכִּין *sak-keen';* intens. perh. from the same as 7906 in the sense of 7753; a *knife* (as *pointed* or edged):–knife.
7916. שָׂכִיר *saw-keer';* from 7936; a man at *wages* by the day or year:–hired (man, servant), hireling.
7917. שְׂכִירָה *sek-ee-raw'* fem. of 7916; a *hiring*:–that is hired.
7918. שָׁכַךְ *shaw-kak'*; a prim. root; to *weave* (i.e. *lay*) a trap; fig., (through the idea of *secreting*) to *allay* (passions; phys., *abate* a flood):–appease, assuage, make to cease, pacify, set.
7919. שָׂכַל *saw-kal'*; a prim. root; to *be* (caus., *make* or *act*) *circumspect* and hence, *intelligent*:–consider, expert, instruct, prosper, (deal) prudent(-ly), (give) skill(-ful), have good success, teach, (have, make to) understand(-ing), wisdom, (be, behave self, consider, make) wise(- ly), guide wittingly.
7920. שְׂכַל *sek-al'* (Chald.); cor. to 7919:–consider.
7921. שָׁכֹל *shaw-kole'* a prim. root; prop. to

miscarry, i.e. *suffer abortion*; by anal., to *bereave* (lit. or fig.):–bereave (of children), barren, cast calf (fruit, young), be (make) childless, deprive, destroy, X expect, lose children, miscarry, rob of children, spoil.
7922. שֶׂכֶל *seh'-kel;* or שֵׂכֶל *say'-kel*; from 7919; *intelligence*; by impl., *success*:–discretion, knowledge, policy, prudence, sense, understanding, wisdom, wise.
7923. שִׁכֻּלִים *shik-koo-leem'*; pl. from 7921; *childlessness* (by continued bereavements):–to have after loss of others.
7924. שׇׂכְלְתָנוּ *sok-leth-aw-noo'* (Chald.); from 7920; *intelligence*:–understanding.
7925. שָׁכַם *shaw-kam*'; a prim. root; prop. to *incline* (the shoulder to a burden); but used only as denom. from 7926; lit., to *load up* (on the back of man or beast), i.e. to *start early* in the morning:–(arise, be up, get [oneself] up, rise up) early (betimes), morning.
7926. שְׁכֶם *shek-em';* from 7925; the *neck* (between the shoulders) as the place of burdens; fig., the *spur* of a hill:–back, X consent, portion, shoulder.
7927. שְׁכֶם *shek-em*'; the same as 7926; *ridge*; *Shekem*, a place in Pal.:–Shechem.
7928. שֶׁכֶם *sheh'-kem*. for 7926; *Shekem*, the name of a Hivite and two Isr.:–Shechem.
7929. שִׁכְמָה *shik-maw'*. fem. of 7926; the *shoulder*-bone:–shoulder blade.
7930. שִׁכְמִי *shik-mee'*; patron. from 7928; a *Shikmite* (coll.), or desc. of Shekem:–Shichemites.
7931. שָׁכַן *shaw-kan'* a prim. root [app. akin (by transmission) to 7901 through the idea of *lodging*; comp. 5531, 7925]; to *reside* or permanently stay (lit. or fig.):–abide, continue, (cause to, make to) dwell(-er), have habitation, inhabit, lay, place, (cause to) remain, rest, set (up).
7932. שְׁכַן *shek-an'* (Chald.); cor. to 7931:–cause to dwell, have habitation.
7933. שֶׁכֶן *sheh'-ken*; from 7931; a *residence*:–habitation.
7934. שָׁכֵן *shaw-kane'*; from 7931; a *resident*; by ext., a fellow-*citizen*:–inhabitant, neighbour, nigh.
7935. שְׁכַנְיָה *shek-an-yaw'* or (prol.) שְׁכַנְיָהוּ *shek-an-yaw'-hoo*; from 7931 and 3050; *Jah has dwelt; Shekanjah*, the name of nine Isr.:–Shecaniah, Shechaniah.
7936. שָׂכַר *saw-kar';* or (by perm.) (Ezra 4:5) סָכַר *saw-kar';* a prim. root [app. akin (by prosthesis) to 3739 through the idea of temporary *purchase;* comp. 7937]; to hire:–earn wages, hire (out self), reward, X surely.
7937. שָׁכַר *shaw-kar';* a prim. root; to *become tipsy;* in a qualified sense, to *satiate* with a stimulating drink or (fig.) influence:–(be filled with) drink (abundantly), (be, make) drunk(-en), be merry. [Sup. of 8248.]
7938. שֶׂכֶר *seh'-ker;* from 7936; *wages:*–reward, sluices.
7939. שָׂכָר *saw-kawr';* from 7936; *payment* of contract; concr., *salary, fare, maintenance;* by impl., *compensation, benefit:*–hire, price, reward[-ed], wages, worth.
7940. שָׂכָר *saw-kar';* the same as 7939; *recompense; Sakar*, the name of two Isr.:–Sacar.
7941. שֵׁכָר *shay-kawr';* from 7937; an *intoxicant,* i.e. intensely alcoholic *liquor:*–strong drink, + drunkard, strong wine.
7942. שִׁכְּרוֹן *shik-ker-one';* for 7943; *drunkenness, Shikkeron,* a place in Pal.:–Shicron.
7943. שִׁכָּרוֹן *shik-kaw-rone';* from 7937; *intoxication:*–(be) drunken(-ness).
7944. שַׁל *shal;* from 7952 abbrev.; a *fault:*–err..
7945. שֶׁל *shel;* for the rel. 834; used with prep. pref., and often followed by some pron. affix; on *account* of, *whatsoever, whichsoever:*–cause, sake.
7946. שַׁלְאֲנָן *shal-an-awn';* for 7600; *tranquil:*–being at ease.
7947. שָׁלַב *shaw-lab'* a prim. root; to *space* off; intens. (*evenly*) to make *equidistant:*–equally distant, set in order.
7948. שָׁלָב *shaw-lawb';* from 7947; a *spacer* or raised *interval,* i.e. the *stile* in a frame or panel:–ledge.
7949. שָׁלַג *shaw-lag';* a prim. root; prop. mean. to be *white;* used only as denom. from 7950; to be *snow-white* (with the linen clothing of the slain):–be as snow.
7950. שֶׁלֶג *sheh'-leg;* from 7949; *snow* (prob. from its *whiteness*):–snow(-y).
7951. שָׁלָה *shaw-law';* or (Job 3:26) שָׁלַו *shaw-lav';* a prim. root; to be *tranquil,* i.e. *secure* or *successful:*–be happy, prosper, be in safety.
7952. שָׁלָה *shaw-law';* a prim. root [prob. ident. with 7953 through the idea of *educing*); to *mislead:*–deceive, be negligent.
7953. שָׁלָה *shaw-law';* a prim. root [rather cognate (by contr.) to the base of 5394, 7997 and their congeners through the idea of *extracting*]; to *draw* out or off, i.e. *remove* (the soul by death):–take away.
7954. שְׁלָה *shel-aw'* (Chald.); cor. to 7951; to *be secure:*–at rest.
7955. שָׁלָה *shaw-law'* (Chald.); from a root cor. to 7952; a *wrong:*–thing amiss.
7956. שֵׁלָה *shay-law';* the same as 7596 (short.); *request; Shelah,* the name of a postdiluvian patriarch and of an Isr.:–Shelah.
7957. שַׁלְהֶבֶת *shal-heh'-beth;* from the same as 3851 with sibilant pref.; a *flare* of fire:–(flaming) flame.
7958. שְׂלָו *sel-awv';* or שְׂלָיו *sel-awv';* by orth. var. from 7951 through the idea of *sluggishness;* the *quail* coll. (as *slow* in flight from its weight):–quails.
7959. שֶׁלֶו *sheh'-lev;* from 7951; *security:*–prosperity.
7960. שָׁלוּ *shaw-loo'* (Chald.); or שָׁלוּת *shaw-looth'* (Chald.); from the same as 7955; a *fault:*–err., X fail, thing amiss.
7961. שָׁלֵו *shaw-lave';* or שָׁלֵיו *shaw-lave';* fem. שְׁלֵוָה *shel-ay-vaw';* from 7951; *tranquil;* (in a bad sense) *careless;* abstr., *security:*–(being) at ease, peaceable, (in) prosper(-ity), quiet(-ness), wealthy.
7962. שַׁלְוָה *shal-vaw';* from 7951; *security* (genuine or false):–abundance, peace(-ably), prosperity, quietness.
7963. שְׁלֵוָה *shel-ay-vaw'* (Chald.); cor. to 7962; *safety:*–tranquillity. See also 7961.
7964. שִׁלּוּחַ *shil-loo'-akh;* or שִׁלֻּחַ *shil-loo'-akh;* from 7971; (only in pl.) a *dismissal,* i.e. (of a wife) *divorce* (esp. the document); also (of a daughter) *dower:*–presents, have sent back.
7965. שָׁלוֹם *shaw-lome';* or שָׁלֹם *shaw-lome';* from 7999; *safe,* i.e. (fig.) *well, happy, friendly;* also (abstr.) *welfare,* i.e. health, prosperity, peace:–X do, familiar, X fare, favour, + friend, X great, (good) health, (X perfect, such as be at) peace(-able, -ably), prosper(-ity, -ous), rest, safe (-ty), salute, welfare, (X all is, be) well, X wholly.
7966. שִׁלּוּם *shil-loom';* or שִׁלֻּם *shil-loom';* from 7999; a *requital,* i.e. (secure) *retribution,* (venal) a *fee:*–recompense, reward.
7967. שַׁלּוּם *shal-loom';* or (short.) שַׁלֻּם *shal-loom';* the same as 7966; *Shallum,* the name of fourteen Isr.:–Shallum.
7968. שַׁלּוּן *shal-loon';* prob. for 7967; *Shallun,* an Isr.:–Shallum.
7969. שָׁלוֹשׁ *shaw-loshe';* or שָׁלֹשׁ *shaw-loshe';* masc. שְׁלוֹשָׁה *shel-o-shaw';* or שְׁלֹשָׁה *shel-o-shaw';* a prim. number; *three;* occasionally (ord.) *third,* or (multipl.) *thrice:*–+ fork, + often[-times], third, thir[-teen,-teenth], three, + thrice. Comp. 7991.
7970. שְׁלוֹשִׁים *shel-o-sheem';* or שְׁלֹשִׁים *shel-o-sheem';* multiple of 7969; *thirty;* or (ord.) *thirtieth:*–thirty, thirtieth. Comp. 7991.
7971. שָׁלַח *shaw-lakh';* a prim. root; to *send* away, for, or out (in a great variety of appl.):–X any wise, appoint, bring (on the way), cast (away, out), conduct, X earnestly, forsake, give (up), grow long, lay, leave, let depart (down, go, loose), push away, put (away, forth, in, out), reach forth, send (away, forth, out), set, shoot (forth, out), sow, spread, stretch forth (out).
7972. שְׁלַח *shel-akh'* (Chald.); cor. to 7971:–put, send.
7973. שֶׁלַח *sheh'-lakh;* from 7971; a *missile* of attack, i.e. *spear;* also (fig.) a *shoot* of growth; i.e. *branch:*–dart, plant, X put off, sword, weapon.
7974. שֶׁלַח *sheh'-lakh;* the same as 7973; *Shelach,* a postdiluvian patriarch:–Salah, Shelah. Comp. 7975.
7975. שִׁלֹּחַ *shee-lo'-akh;* or (in imitation of 7974) שֶׁלַח (Ne. 3:15) *sheh'-lakh;* from 7971; *rill*; *Shiloach,* a fountain of Jerus.:– Shiloah, Siloah.
7976. שִׁלֻּחָה *shil-loo-khaw';* fem. of 7964; a *shoot:*–branch.
7977. שִׁלְחִי *shil-khee';* from 7973; *missive,* i.e. *armed; Shilchi,* an Isr.:–Shilhi.
7978. שִׁלְחִים *shil-kheem';* pl. of 7973; *javelins* or *sprouts; Shilchim,* a place in Pal.:–Shilhim.
7979. שֻׁלְחָן *shool-khawn';* from 7971; a *table* (as *spread* out); by impl., a *meal:*–table.
7980. שָׁלַט *shaw-lat';* a prim. root; to *dominate,* i.e. *govern;* by impl., to *permit:*–(bear, have) rule, have dominion, give (have) power.
7981. שְׁלֵט *shel-ate'* (Chald.); cor. to 7980:–have the mastery, have power, bear rule, be (make) ruler.
7982. שֶׁלֶט *sheh'-let;* from 7980; prob. a *shield* (as *controlling,* i.e. protecting the person):–shield.
7983. שִׁלְטוֹן *shil-tone'* (Chald.); from 7980; a *potentate;* –power.
7984. שִׁלְטוֹן *shil-tone'* (Chald.); or שִׁלְטֹן *shil-tone';* cor. to 7983:–ruler.
7985. שׇׁלְטָן *shol-tawn'* (Chald.); from 7981; *empire* (abstr. or concr.):–dominion.
7986. שַׁלֶּטֶת *shal-leh'-teth;* fem. from 7980; a *vixen:*–imperious.
7987. שְׁלִי *shel-ee';* from 7951; *privacy:* –+ quietly.
7988. שִׁלְיָה *shil-yaw';* fem. from 7953; a *fetus* or *babe* (as *extruded* in birth):–young one.
7989. שַׁלִּיט *shal-leet';* from 7980; *potent;* concr., a *prince* or *warrior:*–governor, mighty, that hath power, ruler.
7990. שַׁלִּיט *shal-leet'* (Chald.); cor. to 7989; *mighty;* abstr., *permission;* concr., a

premier:–captain, be lawful, rule(- r).

7991. שָׁלִישׁ *shaw-leesh'*; or (1 Ch.. 11:11; 12:18) שָׁלוֹשׁ *shaw-loshe'*; or (2 Sa. 23:13) שָׁלִשׁ *shaw-loshe'*; from 7969; a *triple*, i.e. (as a mus. instrument) a *triangle* (or perh. rather *three*-stringed lute); also (as an indef., great quantity) a *three*-fold measure (perh. a *treble* ephah); also (as an officer) a gen. of the *third* rank (upward, i.e. the highest):–captain, instrument of musick, (great) lord, (great) measure, prince, three.

7992. שְׁלִישִׁי *shel-ee-shee'*; ord. from 7969; *third*; fem. a *third* (part); by ext., a *third* (day, year or time); spec., a *third*-story cell):–third (part, rank, time), three (years old).

7993. שָׁלַךְ *shaw-lak*; a prim. root; to *throw* out, down or away (lit. or fig.):–adventure, cast (away, down, forth, off, out), hurl, pluck, throw.

7994. שָׁלָךְ *shaw-lawk'*; from 7993; *bird of prey*, usually thought to be the *pelican* (from *casting* itself into the sea):–cormorant.

7995. שַׁלֶּכֶת *shal-leh'-keth*; from 7993; a *felling* (of trees):–when cast.

7996. שַׁלֶּכֶת *shal-leh'-keth*; the same as 7995; *Shalleketh*, a gate in Jerus.:–Shalleketh.

7997. שָׁלַל *shaw-lal'*; a prim. root; to *drop* or *strip*; by impl., to *plunder*:–let fall, make self a prey, X of purpose, (make a, [take]) spoil.

7998. שָׁלָל *shaw-lawl'*; from 7997; *booty*:–prey, spoil.

7999. שָׁלַם *shaw-lam'*; a prim. root; to *be safe* (in mind, body or estate); fig., to *be* (caus., *make*) *completed*; by impl., to *be friendly*; by ext., to *reciprocate*. (in various appl.):–make amends, (make an) end, finish, full, give again, make good, (re-)pay (again), (make) (to) (be at) peace (-able), that is perfect, perform, (make) prosper(-ous), recompense, render, requite, make restitution, restore, reward, X surely.

8000. שְׁלַם *shel-am'* (Chald.); cor. to 7999; to *complete*, to *restore*:–deliver, finish.

8001. שְׁלָם *shel-awm'* (Chald.); cor. to 7965; *prosperity*:–peace.

8002. שֶׁלֶם *sheh'-lem* from 7999; prop. *requital*, i.e. a (voluntary) sacrifice in *thanks*:–peace offering.

8003. שָׁלֵם *shaw-lame'*; from 7999; *complete* (lit. or fig.); esp. *friendly*:–full, just, made ready, peaceable, perfect(-ed), quiet, Shalem, whole.

8004. שָׁלֵם *shaw-lame'*; the same as 8003; *peaceful*; *Shalem*, an early name of Jerus.:–Salem.

8005. שִׁלֵּם *shil-lame'*; from 7999; *requital*:–recompense.

8006. שִׁלֵּם *shil-lame'*; the same as 8005; *Shillem*, an Isr.:–Shillem.

8007. שַׂלְמָא *sal-maw'*; prob. for 8008; *clothing*; *Salma*, the name of two Isr.:–Salma.

8008. שַׂלְמָה *sal-maw'*; transp. for 8071; a *dress*:–clothes, garment, raiment.

8009. שַׂלְמָה *sal-maw'* the same as 8008; *clothing*; *Salmah*, an Isr.:–Salmon. Comp. 8012.

8010. שְׁלֹמֹה *shel-o-mo'*; from 7965; *peaceful*; *Shelomah*, David's successor:–Solomon.

8011. שִׁלֻּמָה *shil-loo-maw'*; fem. of 7966; *retribution*:–recompense.

8012. שַׂלְמוֹן *sal-mone'*; from 8008; *investiture*; *Salmon*, an Isr.:–Salmon. Comp. 8009.

8013. שְׁלֹמוֹת *shel-o-moth'*; fem. pl. of 7965; *pacifications*; *Shelomoth*, the name of two Isr.:–Shelomith, Shelomoth. Comp. 8019.

8014. שַׂלְמַי *sal-mah'-ee*; from 8008; *clothed*; *Salmai*, an Isr.:–Shalmai.

8015. שְׁלֹמִי *shel-o-mee'*; from 7965; *peaceable*; *Shelomi*, an Isr.:–Shelomi.

8016. שִׁלֵּמִי *shil-lay-mee;'* patron. from 8006; a *Shilemite* (coll.) or desc. of Shillem:–Shillemites.

8017. שְׁלֻמִיאֵל *shel-oo-mee-ale'*; from 7965 and 410; *peace of God*; *Shelumiël*, an Isr.:–Shelumiel.

8018. שֶׁלֶמְיָה *shel-em-yaw'*; or שֶׁלֶמְיָהוּ *shel-em-yaw'-hoo*; from 8002 and 3050; *thank-offering of Jah*; *Shelemjah*, the name of nine Isr.:–Shelemiah.

8019. שְׁלֹמִית *shel-o-meeth'*; or שְׁלוֹמִית (Ezra 8:10) *shel-o-meeth'*; from 7965; *peaceableness*; *Shelomith*, the name of five Isr. and three Isr.s:–Shelomith.

8020. שַׁלְמַן *shal-man'* of for. der.; *Shalman*, a king app. of Assyria:–Shalman. Comp. 8022.

8021. שַׁלְמֹן *shal-mone'*; from 7999; a *bribe*:–reward.

8022. שַׁלְמַנְאֶסֶר *shal-man-eh'-ser*; of for. der.; *Shalmaneser*, an Ass. king:–Shalmaneser. Comp 8020.

8023. שִׁילֹנִי *shee-lo-nee'*; the same as 7888; *Shiloni*, an Isr.:–Shiloni.

8024. שֵׁלָנִי *shay-law-nee'*; from 7956; a *Shelanite* (coll.), or desc. of Shelah:–Shelanites.

8025. שָׁלַף *saw-laf'*; a prim. root; to *pull* out, up or off:–draw (off), grow up, pluck off.

8026. שֶׁלֶף *sheh'-lef*; from 8025; *extract*; *Sheleph*, a son of Jokthan:–Sheleph.

8027. שָׁלַשׁ *shaw-lash'*; a prim. root perh. or. to *intensify*, i.e. *treble*; but app. used only as denom. from 7969, to *be* (caus., *make*) *triplicate* (by restoration, in portions, strands, days or years):–do the third time, (divide into, stay) three (days, -fold, parts, years old).

8028. שֶׁלֶשׁ *sheh'-lesh*; from 8027; *triplet*; *Shelesh*, an Isr.:–Shelesh.

8029. שִׁלֵּשׁ *shil-laysh'*; from 8027; a desc. of the *third* degree, i.e. *great grandchild*:–third [generation].

8030. שִׁלְשָׁה *shil-shaw'*; fem. from the same as 8028; *triplication*; *Shilshah*, an Isr.:–Shilshah.

8031. שָׁלִשָׁה *shaw-lee-shaw'*; fem. from 8027; *trebled* land; *Shalishah*, a place in Pal.:–Shalisha.

8032. שִׁלְשׁוֹם *shil-shome'*; or שִׁלְשֹׁם *shil-shome'*; from the same as 8028; *trebly*, i.e. (in time) *day before yesterday*:–+ before (that time, -time), excellent things, + heretofore, three days, + time past.

8033. שָׁם *shawm*; a prim. particle [rather from the rel. pron., 834]; *there* (transferring to time) *then*; often *thither*, or *thence*:–in it, + thence, there (-in, + of, + out), + thither, + whither.

8034. שֵׁם *shame*; a prim. word [perh. rather from 7760 through the idea of def. and conspicuous *position*; comp. 8064]; an *appellation*, as a mark or memorial of individuality; by impl. *honor, authority, character*:–+ base, [in-]fame[-ous], named(-d), renown, report.

8035. שֵׁם *shame*; the same as 8034; *name*; *Shem*, a son of Noah (often includ. his posterity):–Sem, Shem.

8036. שֻׁם *shoom* (Chald.); cor. to 8034:–name.

8037. שַׁמָּא *sham-maw'*; from 8074; *desolation*; *Shamma*, an Isr.:–Shamma.

8038. שֶׁמְאֵבֶר *shem-ay'-ber*; app. from 8034 and 83; *name of pinion*, i.e. *illustrious*; *Shemeber*, a king of Zeboim:–Shemeber.

8039. שִׁמְאָה *shim-aw'*; perh. for 8093; *Shimah*, an Isr.:–Shimah. Comp. 8043.

8040. שְׂמֹאול *sem-ole'*; or שְׂמֹאל *sem-ole'*; a prim. word [rather perh. from the same as 8071 (by insertion of the א) through the idea of *wrapping* up]; prop. *dark* (as *enveloped*), i.e. the *north*; hence (by orientation), the *left* hand:–left (hand, side).

8041. שָׂמַאל *saw-mal'*; a primitive root [rather denom. from 8040]; to use the *left* hand or pass in that direction):–(go, turn) (on the, to the) left.

8042. שְׂמָאלִי *sem-aw-lee'*; from 8040; situated on the *left* side:–left.

8043. שִׁמְאָם *shim-awm'*; for 8039 [comp. 38]; *Shimam*, an Isr.:–Shimeam.

8044. שַׁמְגַּר *sham-gar'*; of unc. der.; *Shamgar*, an Isr. judge:–Shamgar.

8045. שָׁמַד *shaw-mad'*; a prim. root; to *desolate*:–destroy(-uction), bring to nought, overthrow, perish, pluck down, X utterly.

8046. שְׁמַד *shem-ad'* (Chald.); cor. to 8045:–consume.

8047. שַׁמָּה *sham-maw'*; from 8074; *ruin*; by impl., *consternation*:–astonishment, desolate(-ion), waste, wonderful thing.

8048. שַׁמָּה *sham-maw'*; the same as 8047; *Shammah*, the name of an Edomite and four Isr.:–Shammah.

8049. שַׁמְהוּת *sham-hooth'*; for 8048; *desolation*; *Shamhuth*, an Isr.:–Shamhuth.

8050. שְׁמוּאֵל *shem-oo-ale'*; from the pass. part. of 8085 and 410; *heard of God*; *Shemuël*, the name of three Isr.:–Samuel, Shemuel.

8051. שַׁמּוּעַ *sham-moo'-ah*; from 8074; *renowned*; *Shammua*, the name of four Isr.:–Shammua, Shammuah.

8052. שְׁמוּעָה *shem-oo-aw'*; fem. pass. part. of 8074; something *heard*, i.e. an *announcement*:–bruit, doctrine, fame, mentioned, news, report, rumor, tidings.

8053. שָׁמוּר *shaw-moor'*; pass.part. of 8103; *observed*; *Shamur*, an Isr.:–Shamir.

8054. שַׁמּוֹת *sham-moth'*; pl. of 8047; *ruins*; *Shammoth*, an Isr.:–Shamoth.

8055. שָׂמַח *saw-makh'*; a prim. root; prob. to *brighten* up, i.e. (fig.) *be* (caus., *make*) *blithe* or *gleesome*:–cheer up, be (make) glad, (have, make) joy(-ful), be (make) merry, (cause to, make to) rejoice, X very.

8056. שָׂמֵחַ *saw-may'-akh*; from 8055; *blithe* or *gleeful*:–(be) glad, joyful, (making) merry([-hearted], -ily), rejoice(-ing).

8057. שִׂמְחָה *sim-khaw'*; from 8056; *blithesomeness* or *glee*, (relig. or festival):–X exceeding(-ly), *gladness*, joy(-fulness), mirth, pleasure, rejoice(-ing).

8058. שָׁמַט *shaw-mat'*; a prim. root; to *fling* down; incipiently to *jostle*; fig., to *let alone, desist, remit*:–discontinue, overthrow, release, let rest, shake, stumble, throw down.

8059. שְׁמִטָּה *shem-it-taw'*; from 8058; *remission* (of debt) or *suspension* of labor):–release.

8060. שַׁמַּי *sham-mah'-ee*; from 8073; *destructive*; *Shammai*, the name of three Isr.:–Shammai.

8061. שְׁמִידָע *shem-ee-daw'*; app. from 8034 and 3045; *name of knowing*; *Shemida*, an Isr.:–Shemida, Shemidah.

8062. שְׁמִידָעִי *shem-ee-daw-ee'*; patron. from 8061; a *Shemidaïte* (coll.) or desc. of

Shemida:–Shemidaites.
8063. שְׂמִיכָה *sem-ee-kaw'*; from 5564; a *rug* (as *sustaining* the Oriental sitter):–mantle.
8064. שָׁמַיִם *shaw-mah'-yim*; dual of an un. sing. שָׁמֶה *shaw-meh'*; from an un. root mean. to be *lofty*; the *sky* (as *aloft*; the dual perh. alluding to the visible arch in which the clouds move, as well as to the higher ether where the celestial bodies revolve):–air, X astrologer, heaven(-s).
8065. שְׁמַיִן *shaw-mah'-yin* (Chald.); cor. to 8064:–heaven.
8066. שְׁמִינִי *shem-ee-nee';* from 8083; *eight*:–eight.
8067. שְׁמִינִית *shem-ee-neeth'*; fem. of 8066; prob. an *eight*-stringed lyre:–Sheminith.
8068. שָׁמִיר sh*aw-meer'*; from 8104 in the or. sense of *pricking*; a *thorn*; also (from its *keenness* for scratching) a gem, prob. the *diamond*:–adamant (stone), brier, diamond.
8069. שָׁמִיר *shaw-meer'*; the same as 8068; *Shamir*, the name of two places in Pal.:–Shamir. Comp. 8053.
8070. שְׁמִירָמוֹת *shem-ee-raw-moth'*; or שְׁמָרִימוֹת *shem-aw-ree-moth'*; prob. from 8034 and pl. of 7413; *name of heights; Shemiramoth*, the name of two Isr.:–Shemiramoth.
8071. שִׂמְלָה *sim-law'*; perh. by perm. for the fem. of 5566 (through the idea of a *cover* assuming the shape of the obj. beneath); a *dress*, esp. a *mantle*:–apparel, cloth(-es, -ing), garment, raiment. Comp. 8008.
8072. שַׂמְלָה *sam-law'*; prob. for the same as 8071; *Samlah*, an Edomite:–Samlah.
8073. שַׁמְלַי *sham-lah'-ee*; for 8014; *Shamlai*, one of the Nethinim:–Shalmai.
8074. שָׁמֵם *shaw-mame'*; a prim. root; to *stun* (or intr., *grow numb*), i.e. *devastate* or (fig.) *stupefy* (both usually in a pass. sense):–make amazed, be astonied, (be an) astonish (-ment), (be, bring into, unto, lay, lie, make) desolate(-ion, places), be destitute, destroy (self), (lay, lie, make) waste, wonder.
8075. שְׁמַם *shem-am'* (Chald.); cor. to 8074:–be astonied.
8076. שָׁמֵם *shaw-mame'*; from 8074; *ruined*:–desolate.
8077. שְׁמָמָה *shem-aw-maw'* or שִׁמֲמָה *shee-mam-aw'*; fem. of 8076; *devastation*; fig., *astonishment*:–(laid, X most) desolate (-ion), waste.
8078. שִׁמָּמוֹן *shim-maw-mone'*; from 8074; *stupefaction*:–astonishment.
8079. שְׂמָמִית *sem-aw-meeth';* prob. from 8074 (in the sense of *poisoning*); a *lizard* (from the superstition of its *noxiousness*):–spider.
8080. שָׁמַן *shaw-man';* a prim. root; to *shine*, i.e. (by anal.) *be* (caus., *make*) *oily* or *gross*:–become (make, wax) fat.
8081. שֶׁמֶן *sheh'-men*; from 8080; *grease*, esp. liquid (as from the olive, often perfumed); fig., *richness*:–anointing, X fat (things), X fruitful, oil([-ed]), ointment, olive, + pine.
8082. שָׁמֵן *shaw-mane'*; from 8080; *greasy*, i.e. *gross*; fig., *rich*:–fat, lusty, plenteous.
8083. שְׁמֹנֶה *shem-o-neh'*; or שְׁמוֹנֶה *shem-o-neh'*; fem. שְׁמֹנָה *shem-o-naw'*; or שְׁמוֹנָה *shem-o-naw'*; app. from 8082 through the idea of *plumpness*; a cardinal number, *eight* (as if a *surplus* above the "perfect" seven); also (as ord.) *eighth*:–eight([-een, -eenth]), eighth.
8084. שְׁמֹנִים *shem-o-neem'*; or שְׁמוֹנִים *shem-o-neem'*; mult. from 8083; *eighty*, also *eightieth*:–eighty(-ieth), fourscore.
8085. שָׁמַע *shaw-mah'*; a prim. root; to *hear* intelligently (often with impl. of attention, obedience, etc.; caus., to *tell*, etc.):–X attentively, call (gather) together, X carefully, X certainly, consent, consider, be content, declare, X diligently, discern, give ear, (cause to, let, make to) hear (-ken, tell), X indeed, listen, make (a) noise, (be) obedient, obey, perceive, (make a) proclaim(-ation), publish, regard, report, shew (forth), (make a) sound, X surely, tell, understand, whosoever [heareth], witness.
8086. שְׁמַע *shem-ah'* (Chald.); cor. to 8085:–hear, obey.
8087. שֶׁמַע *sheh'-mah*; for the same as 8088; *Shema*, the name of a place in Pal. and of four Isr.:–Shema.
8088. שֵׁמַע *shay'-mah*; from 8085; something *heard*, i.e. a *sound*, *rumor*, *announcement*; abstr., *audience*:–bruit, fame, hear(-ing), loud, report, speech, tidings.
8089. שֹׁמַע *sho'-mah*; from 8085; a *report*:–fame.
8090. שְׁמָע *shem-aw';* for 8087; *Shema*, a place in Pal.:–Shema.
8091. שָׁמָע *shaw-maw'*; from 8085; *obedient; Shama*, an Isr.:–Shama.
8092. שִׁמְעָא *shim-aw'*;for 8093; *Shima*, the name of four Isr.:–Shimea, Shimei, Shamma.
8093. שִׁמְעָה *shim-aw'*; fem. of 8088; *annunciation; Shimah*, an Isr.:–Shimeah.
8094. שְׁמָעָה *shem-aw-aw'*; for 8093; *Shemaah*, an Isr.:–Shemaah.
8095. שִׁמְעוֹן *shim-one'*; from 8085; *hearing; Shimon*, one of Jacob's sons, also the tribe descended from him:–Simeon.
8096. שִׁמְעִי *shim-ee'*; from 8088; *famous*; *Shimi*, the name of twenty Isr.:–Shimeah, Shimei, Shimhi, Shimi.
8097. שִׁמְעִי *shim-ee'*; patron. from 8096; a *Shimite* (coll.) or desc. of Shimi:–of Shimi, Shimites.
8098. שְׁמַעְיָה *shem-aw-yaw'*; or שְׁמַעְיָהוּ *shem-aw-yaw'-hoo*; from 8085 and 3050; *Jah has heard; Shemajah*, the name of twenty-five Isr.:–Shemaiah.
8099. שִׁמְעֹנִי *shim-o-nee';* patron. from 8095; a *Shimonite* (coll.) or desc. of Shimon:–tribe of Simeon, Simeonites.
8100. שִׁמְעָת *shim-awth'*; fem. of 8088; *annunciation; Shimath*, an Ammonitess:–Shimath.
8101. שִׁמְעָתִי *shim-aw-thee';* patron. from 8093; a *Shimathite* (coll.) or desc. of Shimah:–Shimeathites.
8102. שֶׁמֶץ *sheh'-mets;* from an un. root mean. to *emit* a sound; an *inkling*:–a little.
8103. שִׁמְצָה *shim-tsaw'*; fem. of 8102; scornful *whispering* (of hostile spectators):–shame.
8104. שָׁמַר *shaw-mar'*; a prim. root; prop. to *hedge* about (as with thorns), i.e. *guard*; gen., to *protect, attend* to, etc.:–beware, be circumspect, take heed (to self), keep(-er, self), mark, look narrowly, observe, preserve, regard, reserve, save (self), sure, (that lay) wait (for), watch(-man).
8105. שֶׁמֶר *sheh'-mer*; from 8104; something *preserved*, i.e. the *settlings* (pl. only) of wine:–dregs, (wines on the) lees.
8106. שֶׁמֶר *sheh'-mer;* the same as 8105; *Shemer*, the name of three Isr.:–Shamer, Shemer.
8107. שִׁמֻּר *shim-moor'*; from 8104; an *observance*:–X be (much) observed.
8108. שָׁמְרָה *shom-raw'*; fem. of an un. noun from 8104 mean. a *guard; watchfulness*:–watch.
8109. שְׁמֻרָה *shem-oo-raw'*; fem. of pass.part. of 8104; something *guarded*, i.e. an *eye-lid*:–waking.
8110. שִׁמְרוֹן *shim-rone'*; from 8105 in its or. sense; *guardianship; Shimron*, the name of an Isr. and of a place in Pal.:–Shimron.
8111. שֹׁמְרוֹן *sho-mer-one'*; from the act.part. of 8104; *watch-station; Shomeron*, a place in Pal.:–Samaria.
8112. שִׁמְרוֹן מְראוֹן *shim-rone' mer-one'* from 8110 and a der. of 4754; *guard of lashing;Shimron-Meron*, a place in Pal.:–Shimon-meron.
8113. שִׁמְרִי *shim-ree'*; from 8105 in its or. sense; *watchful; Shimri*, the name of four Isr.:–Shimri.
8114. שְׁמַרְיָה *shem-ar-yaw';* or שְׁמַרְיָהוּ *shem-ar-yaw'-hoo*; from 8104 and 3050; *Jah has guarded; Shemarjah*, the name of four Isr.:–Shamariah, Shemariah.
8115. שָׁמְרַיִן *shom-rah'-yin* (Chald.); cor. to 8111; *Shomraïn*, a place in Pal.:–Samaria.
8116. שִׁמְרִית *shim-reeth';* fem. of 8113; *female guard*; *Shimrith*, a Moabitess:–Shimrith.
8117. שִׁמְרֹנִי *shim-ro-nee'*; patron. from 8110; a *Shimronite* (coll.) or desc. of Shimron:–Shimronites.
8118. שֹׁמְרֹנִי *sho-mer-o-nee'*; patrial from 8111; a *Shomeronite* (coll.) or inh. of Shomeron:–Samaritans.
8119. שִׁמְרָת *shim-rawth'*; from 8104; *guardship; Shimrath*, an Isr.:–Shimrath.
8120. שְׁמַשׁ *shem-ash'* (Chald.); cor. to the root of 8121 through the idea of *activity* implied in day-light; to *serve*:–minister.
8121. שֶׁמֶשׁ *sheh'-mesh*; from an un. root mean. to be *brilliant*; the *sun*; by impl., the *east*; fig., a *ray*, i.e. (arch.) a notched *battlement*:–+ east side(-ward), sun ([rising]), + west(-ward), window. See also 1053.
8122. שֶׁמֶשׁ *sheh'-mesh* (Chald.); cor. to 8121; the *sun*:–sun.
8123. שִׁמְשׁוֹן *shim-shone'*; from 8121; *sunlight; Shimshon*, an Isr.:–Samson.
8124. שִׁמְשַׁי *shim-shah'-ee* (Chald.); from 8122; *sunny; Shimshai*, a Samaritan:–Shimshai.
8125. שַׁמְשְׁרַי *sham-sher-ah'-ee;* app. from 8121; *sunlike; Shamsherai*, an Isr.:–Shamsherai.
8126. שֻׁמָתִי *shoo-maw-thee';* patron. from an un. name from 7762 prob. mean. *garlic*-smell; a *Shumathite* (coll.) or desc. of Shumah:–Shumathites.
8127. שֵׁן *shane*; from 8150; a tooth (as *sharp*); spec. (for 8143) *ivory*; fig., a *cliff*:–crag, X forefront, ivory, X sharp, tooth.
8128. שֵׁן *shane* (Chald.); cor. to 8127; a *tooth*:–tooth.
8129. שֵׁן *shane;* the same as 8127; *crag; Shen*, a place in Pal.:–Shen.
8130. שָׂנֵא *saw-nay;'* a prim. root; to *hate* (pers.):–enemy, foe, (be) hate(-ful,-r), odious, X utterly.
8131. שְׂנֵא *sen-ay'* (Chald.); cor. to 8130:–hate.
8132. שָׁנָה *shaw-naw;'* a prim. root; to *alter*:–change.
8133. שְׁנָא *shen-aw'* (Chald.); cor. to 8132:–alter, change, (be) diverse.

8134. שִׁנְאָב *shin-awb'*; prob. from 8132 and 1; a *father has turned; Shinab*, a Canaanite:–Shinab.
8135. שִׂנְאָה *sin-aw'*; from 8130; *hate*:–+ exceedingly, hate(-ful, -red).
8136. שִׁנְאָן *shin-awn'*; from 8132; *change*, i.e. *repetition*:–X angels.
8137. שֶׁנְאַצַּר *shen-ats-tsar'*; app. of Bab. or.; *Shenatstsar*, an Isr.:–Senazar.
8138. שָׁנָה *shaw-naw'*; a prim. root; to *fold*, i.e. *duplicate* (lit. or fig.); by impl., to *transmute* (trans. or intr.):–do (speak, strike) again, alter, double, (be given to) change, disguise, (be) diverse, pervert, prefer, repeat, return, do the second time.
8139. שְׁנָה *shen-aw'* (Chald.); cor. to 8142:–sleep.
8140. שְׁנָה *shen-aw'* (Chald.); cor. to 8141:–year.
8141. שָׁנֶה *shaw-neh'*; (in pl. only) or (fem.) שָׁנָה *shaw-naw'*; from 8138; a *year* (as a *revolution* of time):–+ whole age, X long, + old, year(X -ly).
8142. שֵׁנָה *shay-naw'*; or שֵׁנָא *shay-naw'*; (Ps. 127:2)from 3462; *sleep*:–sleep.
8143. שֶׁנְהַבִּים *shen-hab-beem'*; from 8127 and the pl. app. of a for. word; prob., *tooth of elephants*, i.e. *ivory tusk*:–ivory.
8144. שָׁנִי *shaw-nee'*; of unc. der.; *crimson*, prop. the insect or its color, also stuff dyed with it:–crimson, scarlet (thread).
8145. שֵׁנִי *shay-nee'*; from 8138; prop. *double*, i.e. *second*; also adv., *again*:–again, either [of them], (an-)other, second (time).
8146. שָׂנִיא *saw-nee'*; from 8130; *hated*:–hated.
8147. שְׁנַיִם *shen-ah'-yim*; dual of 8145; fem. שְׁתַּיִם *shet-tah'-yim*; *two*; also (as ord.) *twofold*:–both, couple, double, second, twain, + twelfth, + twelve, + twenty (sixscore) thousand, twice, two.
8148. שְׁנִינָה *shen-ee-naw'*; from 8150; something *pointed*, i.e. a *gibe*:–byword, taunt.
8149. שְׁנִיר *shen-eer'*; or שְׂנִיר *sen-eer'*; from an un. root mean. to be *pointed; peak*; *Shenir* or *Senir*, a summit of Lebanon:–Senir, Shenir.
8150. שָׁנַן *shaw-nan'*; a prim. root; to *point* (trans. or intr.); intens., to *pierce*; fig., to *inculcate*:–prick, sharp(-en), teach diligently, whet.
8151. שָׁנַס *shaw-nas'*; a prim. root; to *compress* (with a belt):–gird up.
8152. שִׁנְעָר *shin-awr'*; prob. of for. der.; *Shinar*, a plain in Babylonia:–Shinar.
8153. שְׁנָת *shen-awth'*; from 3462; *sleep*:–sleep.
8154. שָׁסָה *shaw-saw'*; or שָׁשָׂה (Is. 10:13) *shaw-saw'*; a prim. root; to *plunder*:–destroyer, rob, spoil(-er).
8155. שָׁסַס *shaw-sas'*; a prim. root; to *plunder*:–rifle, spoil.
8156. שָׁסַע *shaw-sah'*; a prim. root; to *split* or *tear*; fig., to *upbraid*:–cleave, (be) cloven ([footed]), rend, stay.
8157. שֶׁסַע *sheh'-sah*; from 8156; a *fissure*:–cleft, clovenfooted.
8158. שָׁסַף *shaw-saf'*; a prim. root; to *cut* in pieces, i.e. slaughter:–hew in pieces.
8159. שָׁעָה *shaw-aw'*; a prim. root; to *gaze* at or about (prop. for help); by impl., to *inspect, consider, compassionate, be nonplussed* (as looking around in amazement) or *bewildered*:–depart, be dim, be dismayed, look (away), regard, have respect, spare, turn.
8160. שָׁעָה *shaw-aw'* (Chald.); from a root cor. to 8159; prop. a *look*, i.e. a *moment*:–hour.
8161. שַׁעֲטָה *shah'-at-aw*; fem. from an un. root mean. to *stamp*; a *clatter* (of hoofs):–stamping.
8162. שַׁעַטְנֵז *shah-at-naze'*; prob. of for. der.; *linsey-woolsey*, i.e. cloth of linen and wool carded and spun together:–garment of divers sorts, linen and wollen.
8163. שָׂעִיר *saw-eer'*; or שָׂעִר *saw-eer'*; from 8175; *shaggy*; as noun, a *he-goat*; by anal., a *faun*:–devil, goat, hairy, kid, rough, satyr.
8164. שָׂעִיר *saw-eer'*; formed the same as 8163; a *shower* (as *tempestuous*):–small rain.
8165. שֵׂעִיר *say-eer'*; formed like 8163; *rough*; *Seïr*, a mountain of Idumaea and its aboriginal occupants, also one in Pal.:–Seir.
8166. שְׂעִירָה *seh-ee-raw'*; fem. of 8163; a *she-goat*:–kid.
8167. שְׂעִירָה *seh-ee-raw'*; formed as 8166; *roughness; Seïrah*, a place in Pal.:–Seirath.
8168. שֹׁעַל *sho'-al*; from an un. root mean. to *hollow* out; the *palm*; by ext., a *handful*:–handful, hollow of the hand.
8169. שַׁעַלְבִים *shah-al-beem'*; or שַׁעֲלַבִּין *shah-al-ab-been'*; pl. from 7776; *fox-holes; Shaalbim* or *Shaalabbin*, a place in Pal.:–Shaalabbin, Shaalbim.
8170. שַׁעַלְבֹנִי *shah-al-bo-nee'*; patrial from 8169; a *Shaalbonite* or inh. of Shaalbin:–Shaalbonite.
8171. שַׁעֲלִים *shah-al-eem'*; pl. of 7776; *foxes; Shaalim*, a place in Pal.:–Shalim.
8172. שָׁעַן *shaw-an'*; a prim. root; to *support* one's self:–lean, lie, rely, rest (on, self), stay.
8173. שָׁעַע *shaw-ah'*; a prim. root; (in a good acceptation) to *look* upon (with complacency), i.e. *fondle, please* or *amuse* (self); (in a bad one) to *look* about (in dismay), i.e. *stare*:–cry (out) dandle, delight (self), play, shut.
8174. שַׁעַף *shah'-af*; from 5586; *fluctuation; Shaaph*, the name of two Isr.:–Shaaph.
8175. שָׂעַר *saw-ar'*; a prim. root; to *storm*; by impl., to *shiver*, i.e. *fear*:–be (horribly) afraid, fear, hurl as a storm, be tempestuous, come like (take away as with) a whirlwind.
8176. שָׁעַר *shaw-ar'*; a prim. root; to *split* or *open*, i.e. (lit., but only as denom. from 8179) to *act as gate-keeper* (see 7778): (fig.) to *estimate*:–think.
8177. שְׂעַר *seh-ar'* (Chald.); cor. to 8181; *hair*:–hair.
8178. שַׂעַר *sah'-ar* from 8175; a *tempest*; also a *terror*:–affrighted, X horribly, X sore, storm. See 8181.
8179. שַׁעַר *shah'-ar*; from 8176 in its or. sense; an *opening*, i.e. *door* or *gate*:–city, door, gate, port (X -er).
8180. שַׁעַר, *shah'-ar* from 8176; a *measure* (as a *section*):–[hundred-]fold.
8181. שֵׂעָר *say-awr'*; or שַׂעַר *sah'-ar*;(Isaiah 7:20) from 8175 in the sense of *dishevelling; hair* (as if *tossed* or *bristling*):–hair(-y), X rough.
8182. שֹׁעָר *sho-awr'*; from 8176; *harsh* or *horrid*, i.e. *offensive*:–vile.
8183. שְׂעָרָה *seh-aw-raw'* fem. of 8178; a *hurricane*:–storm, tempest.
8184. שְׂעֹרָה *seh-o-raw'*; or שְׂעוֹרָה *seh-o-raw'* (fem. mean. *the plant*); and (masc. mean. the *grain*); also שְׂעֹר *seh-ore'*; or שְׂעוֹר *seh-ore'*; from 8175 in the sense of *roughness; barley* (as *villose*):–barley.
8185. שַׂעֲרָה *sah-ar-aw'*; fem. of 8181; *hairiness*:–hair.
8186. שַׁעֲרוּרָה *shah-ar-oo-raw'*; or שַׁעֲרִירִיָּה *shah-ar-ee-ree-yaw'*; or שַׁעֲרֻרִת *shah-ar-oo-reeth'*; fem. from 8176 in the sense of 8175; something *fearful*:–horrible thing.
8187. שְׁעַרְיָה *sheh-ar-yaw'*; from 8176 and 3050; *Jah has stormed; Sheärjah*, an Isr.:–Sheariah.
8188. שְׂעֹרִים *seh-o-reem'*; masc. pl. of 8184; *barley* grains; *Seörim*, an Isr.:–Seorim.
8189. שַׁעֲרַיִם *shah-ar-ah'-yim*; dual of 8179; *double gates; Shaarajim*, a place in Pal.:–Shaaraim.
8190. שַׁעַשְׁגַז *shah-ash-gaz'*; of Pers. der.; *Shaashgaz*, a eunuch of Xerxes:–Shaashgaz.
8191. שַׁעְשֻׁעַ *shah-shoo'-ah*; from 8173; *enjoyment*:–delight, pleasure.
8192. שָׁפָה *shaw-faw'*; a prim. root; to *abrade*, i.e. *bare*:–high, stick out.
8193. שָׂפָה *saw-faw'*; or (in dual and pl.) שֶׂפֶת *sef-eth'*; prob. from 5595 or 8192 through the idea of *termination* (comp. 5490); the *lip* (as a nat. boundary); by impl., *language*; by anal., a *margin* (of a vessel, water, cloth, etc.):–band, bank, binding, border, brim, brink, edge, language, lip, prating, ([sea-])shore, side, speech, talk, [vain]words.
8194. שָׁפָה *shaw-faw'*; from 8192 in the sense of *clarifying*; a *cheese* (as *strained* from the whey):–cheese.
8195. שְׁפוֹ *shef-o'*; or שְׁפִי *shef-ee'*; from 8192; *baldness* [comp. 8205]; *Shepho* or *Shephi*, an Idumaean:–Shephi, Shepho.
8196. שְׁפוֹט *shef-ote'*; or שְׁפוּט *shef-oot'*; from 8199; a judicial *sentence*, i.e. *punishment*:–judgment.
8197. שְׁפוּפָם *shef-oo-fawm'*; or שְׁפוּפָן *shef-oo-fawn'*; from the same as 8207; *serpent-like; Shephupham* or *Shephuphan*, an Isr.:–Shephuphan, Shupham.
8198. שִׁפְחָה *shif-khaw'*; fem. from an un. root mean. to *spread* out (as a *family*; see 4940); a *female slave* (as a member of the *household*):–(bond-, hand-)maid(-en, -servant), wench, bondwoman, womanservant.
8199. שָׁפַט *shaw-fat'*; a prim. root; to *judge*, i.e. pronounce *sentence* (for or against); by impl., to *vindicate* or *punish*; by ext., to *govern*; pass., to *litigate* (lit. or fig.):–+ avenge, X that condemn, contend, defend, execute (judgment), (be a) judge(-ment), X needs, plead, reason, rule.
8200. שְׁפַט *shef-at'* (Chald.); cor. to 8199; to *judge*:–magistrate.
8201. שֶׁפֶט *sheh'-fet*; from 8199; a *sentence*, i.e. *infliction*:–judgment.
8202. שָׁפָט *shaw-fawt'*; from 8199; *judge; Shaphat*, the name of four Isr.:–Shaphat.
8203. שְׁפַטְיָה *shef-at-yaw'*; or שְׁפַטְיָהוּ *shef-at-yaw'-hoo*; from 8199 and 3050; *Jah has judged; Shephatjah*, the name of ten Isr.:–Shephatiah.
8204. שִׁפְטָן *shif-tawn'*; from 8199; *judge-like; Shiphtan*, an Isr.:–Shiphtan.
8205. שְׁפִי *shef-ee'*; from 8192; *bareness*; concr., a *bare* hill or plain:–high place, stick out.
8206. שֻׁפִּים *shoop-peem'*; pl. of an un. noun from the same as 8207 and mean. the same; *serpents; Shuppim*, an Isr.:–Shuppim.
8207. שְׁפִיפֹן *shef-ee-fone'*; from an un. root mean. the same as 7779; a kind of *serpent* (as *snapping*), prob. the *cerastes* or horned adder:–adder.
8208. שָׁפִיר *shaf-eer'*; from 8231; *beautiful; Shaphir*, a place in Pal.:–Saphir.
8209. שַׁפִּיר *shap-peer'* (Chald.); intens. of a form cor. to 8208; *beautiful*:–fair.
8210. שָׁפַךְ *shaw-fak'*; a prim. root; to *spill*

forth (blood, a libation, liquid metal; or even a solid, i.e. to *mound* up); also (fig.) to *expend* (life, soul, complaint, money, etc.); intens., to *sprawl* out:–cast (up), gush out, pour (out), shed(-der, out), slip.
8211. שֶׁפֶךְ *sheh'-fek*; from 8210; an *emptying* place, e.g. an ash-*heap*:–are poured out.
8212. שָׁפְכָה *shof-kaw'*; fem. of a der. from 8210; a *pipe* (for *pouring* forth, e.g. wine), i.e. the *penis*:–privy member.
8213. שָׁפֵל *shaw-fale'*; a prim. root; to *depress* or *sink* (esp. fig., to *humiliate*, intr. or trans.):–abase, bring (cast, put) down, debase, humble (self), be (bring, lay, make, put) low(-er).
8214. שְׁפַל *shef-al'* (Chald.); cor. to 8213:–abase, humble, put down, subdue.
8215. שְׁפַל *shef-al'* (Chald.); from 8214; *low*:–basest.
8216. שֵׁפֶל *shay'-fel*; from 8213; an *humble* rank:–low estate (place).
8217. שָׁפָל *shaw-fawl'*; from 8213; *depressed*, lit. or fig.:–base(-st), humble, low(-er, -ly).
8218. שִׁפְלָה *shif-law'*; fem. of 8216; *depression*:–low place.
8219. שְׁפֵלָה *shef-ay-law'*; from 8213; *Lowland*, i.e. (with the art.) the maritime slope of Pal.:–low country, (low) plain, vale(-ley).
8220. שִׁפְלוּת *shif-looth'*; from 8213; *remissness*:–idleness.
8221. שְׁפָם *shef-awm'*; prob. from 8192; *bare* spot; *Shepham*, a place in or near Pal.:–Shepham.
8222. שָׂפָם *saw-fawm'*; from 8193; the *beard* (as a *lip-piece*):–beard, (upper) lip.
8223. שָׁפָם *shaw-fawm'*; formed like 8221; *baldly*; *Shapham*, an Isr.:–Shapham.
8224. שִׂפְמוֹת *sif-moth'*; fem. pl. of 8221; *Siphmoth*, a place in Pal.:–Siphmoth.
8225. שִׁפְמִי *shif-mee'*; patrial from 8221; a *Shiphmite* or inh. of Shepham:–Shiphmite.
8226. סָפַן *saw-fan'*; a prim. root; to *conceal* (as a valuable):–treasure.
8227. שָׁפָן *shaw-fawn'*; from 8226; a species of *rock-rabbit* (from its *hiding*), i.e. prob. the *hyrax*:–coney.
8228. שֶׁפַע *sheh'-fah*; from an un. root mean. to *abound; resources*:–abundance.
8229. שִׁפְעָה *shif-aw'*; fem. of 8228; *copiousness*:–abundance, company, multitude.
8230. שִׁפְעִי *shif-ee'*; from 8228; *copious; Shiphi*, an Isr.:–Shiphi.
8231. שָׁפַר *shaw-far'*; a prim. root; to *glisten*, i.e. (fig.) *be* (caus., *make*) *fair*:–X goodly.
8232. שְׁפַר *shef-ar'* (Chald.); cor. to 8231; to *be beautiful*:–be acceptable, please, + think good.
8233. שֶׁפֶר *sheh'-fer* from 8231; *beauty*:–X goodly.
8234. שֶׁפֶר *sheh'-fer*; the same as 8233; *Shepher*, a place in the Desert:–Shapper.
8235. שִׁפְרָה *shif-raw'*; from 8231; *brightness*:–garnish.
8236. שִׁפְרָה *shif-raw'*; the same as 8235; *Shiphrah*, an Isr.s:–Shiphrah.
8237. שַׁפְרוּר *shaf-roor'* from 8231; *splendid*, i.e. a *tapestry* or canopy:–royal pavilion.
8238. שְׁפַרְפַר *shef-ar-far'* (Chald.); from 8231; the *dawn* (as *brilliant* with aurora):–X very early in the morning.
8239. שָׁפַת *shaw-fath'*; a prim. root; to locate, i.e. (gen.) *hang* on or (fig.) *establish, reduce*:–bring, ordain, set on.
8240. שָׁפָת *shaw-fawth'*; from 8239; a (double) *stall* (for cattle); also a (two-pronged) *hook* (for flaying animals on):–hook, pot.
8241. שֶׁצֶף *sheh'-tsef*; from 7857 (for alliteration with 7110); an *outburst* (of anger):–little.
8242. שַׂק *sak*; from 8264; prop. a *mesh* (as allowing a liquid to *run* through), i.e. coarse loose cloth or *sacking* (used in mourning and for bagging); hence, a *bag* (for grain, etc.):–sack(-cloth, -clothes).
8243. שָׁק *shawk* (Chald.); cor. to 7785; the *leg*:–leg.
8244. שָׂקַד *saw-kad'*; a prim. root; to *fasten*:–bind.
8245. שָׁקַד *shaw-kad'* a prim. root; to be *alert*, i.e. *sleepless*; hence to *be on the lookout* (whether for good or ill):–hasten, remain, wake, watch (for).
8246. שָׁקַד *shaw-kad'* a denom. from 8247; to be (intens., *make*) *almond-shaped*:–make like (unto, after the fashion of) almonds.
8247. שָׁקֵד *shaw-kade'*; from 8245; the *almond* (tree or nut; as being the *earliest* in bloom):–almond (tree).
8248. שָׁקָה *shaw-kaw'*; a prim. root; to *quaff*, i.e. (caus.) to *irrigate* or *furnish* a *potion* to:–cause to (give, give to, let, make to) drink, drown, moisten, water. See 7937, 8354.
8249. שִׁקֻּו *shif-koov'*; from 8248; (pl. coll.) a *draught*:–drink.
8250. שִׁקּוּי *shik-koo'-ee*; from 8248; a *beverage*; *moisture*, i.e. (fig.) *refreshment*:–drink, marrow.
8251. שִׁקּוּץ *shik-koots'*; or שִׁקֻּץ *shik-koots'*; from 8262; *disgusting*, i.e. *filthy*; esp. *idolatrous* or (concr.) an *idol*:– abominable filth (idol, -ation), detestable (thing).
8252. שָׁקַט *shaw-kat'*; a prim. root; to *repose* (usually fig.):–appease, idleness, (at, be at, be in, give) quiet(-ness), (be at, be in, give, have, take) rest, settle, be still.
8253. שֶׁקֶט *sheh'-ket* from 8252; *tranquillity*:–quietness.
8254. שָׁקַל *shaw-kal'*; a prim. root; to *suspend* or *poise* (esp. in trade):–pay, receive(-r), spend, X throughly, weigh.
8255. שֶׁקֶל *sheh'-kel* from 8254; prob. a *weight*; used as a commercial standard:–shekel.
8256. שָׁקָם *shaw-kawm'*; or שִׁקְמָה (fem.) *shik-maw'*; of unc. der.; a *sycamore* (usually the tree):–sycamore (fruit, tree).
8257. שָׁקַע *shaw-kah'*; (Am. 8:8); a prim. root; to *subside*; by impl., to *be overflowed, cease*; caus., to *abate, subdue*:–make deep, let down, drown, quench, sink.
8258. שְׁקַעֲרוּרָה *shek-ah-roo-raw'*; from 8257; a *depression*:–hollow strake.
8259. שָׁקַף *shaw-kaf'* a prim. root; prop. to *lean out* (of a window), i.e. (by impl.) *peep* or *gaze* (pass., *be a spectacle*):–appear, look (down, forth, out).
8260. שֶׁקֶף *sheh'-kef*; from 8259; a *loophole* (for *looking out*), to admit light and air:–window.
8261. שָׁקֻף *shaw-koof'*; pass.part. of 8259; an *embrasure* or opening (comp. 8260) with bevelled jam:–light, window.
8262. שָׁקַץ *shaw-kats'*; a prim. root; to be *filthy*, i.e. (intens.) to *loathe, pollute*:–abhor, make abominable, have in abomination, detest, X utterly.
8263. שֶׁקֶץ *sheh'-kets*; from 8262; *filth*, i.e. (fig. and spec.) an *idolatrous* obj.:–abominable(-tion).
8264. שָׁקַק *shaw-kak'*; a prim. root; to *course* (like a beast of prey); by impl., to *seek* greedily:–have appetite, justle one against another, long, range, run (to and fro).
8265. שָׂקַר *saw-kar'*; a prim. root; to *ogle*, i.e. *blink* coquettishly:–wanton.
8266. שָׁקַר *shaw-kar'*; a prim. root; to *cheat, i.e. be untrue* (usually in words):–fail, deal falsely, lie.
8267. שֶׁקֶר *sheh'-ker*; from 8266; an *untruth*; by impl., a *sham* (often adv.):–without a cause, deceit(-ful), false(-hood, -ly), feignedly, liar, + lie, lying, vain (thing), wrongfully.
8268. שֹׁקֶת *sho'-keth*; from 8248; a *trough* (for *watering*):–trough.
8269. שַׂר *sar*; from 8323; a *head* person (of any rank or class):–captain (that had rule), chief (captain), gen., governor, keeper, lord, ([-task-])master, prince(-ipal), ruler, steward.
8270. שֹׁר *shore*; from 8324; a *string* (as *twisted* [comp. 8306]), i.e. (spec.) the umbilical cord (also fig., as the centre of strength):–navel.
8271. שְׁרֵא *sher-ay'* (Chald.); a root cor. to that of 8293; to *free, separate*; fig., to *unravel, commence*; by impl. (of unloading beasts) to *reside*:–begin, dissolve, dwell, loose.
8272. שַׁרְאֶצֶר *shar-eh'-tser*; of for. der.; *Sharetser*, the name of an Ass. and an Isr.:–Sharezer.
8273. שָׁרָב *shaw-rawb'*; from an un. root mean. to *glare*; quivering *glow* (of the air), esp. the *mirage*:–heat, parched ground.
8274. שֵׁרֵבְיָה *shay-rayb-yaw'*; from 8273 and 3050; *Jah has brought heat; Sherebjah*, the name of two Isr.:–Sherebiah.
8275. שַׁרְבִיט *shar-beet'*; for 7626; a *rod* of empire:–sceptre.
8276. שָׂרַג *saw-rag'*; a prim. root; to *intwine*:–wrap together, wreath.
8277. שָׂרַד *saw-rad'*; a prim. root; prop. to *puncture* (comp. 8279), i.e. (fig. through the idea of *slipping* out) to *escape* or survive:–remain.
8278. שְׂרָד *ser-awd'*; from 8277; *stitching* (as *pierced* with a needle):–service.
8279. שֶׂרֶד *seh'-red*; from 8277; a (carpenter's) *scribing-awl* (for *pricking* or scratching measurements):–line.
8280. שָׂרָה *saw-raw'*; a prim. root; to *prevail*:–have power (as a prince).
8281. שָׁרָה *shaw-raw'*; a prim. root; to *free*:–direct.
8282. שָׂרָה, *saw-raw'*; fem. of 8269; a *mistress*, i.e. female noble:–lady, princess, queen.
8283. שָׂרָה *saw-raw'*; the same as 8282; *Sarah*, Abraham's wife:–Sarah.
8284. שָׁרָה *shaw-raw'*; prob. fem. of 7791; a *fortification* (lit. or fig.):–sing, wall.
8285. שֵׁרָה *shay-raw'*; from 8324 in its or. sense of *pressing*; a wrist-*band* (as *compact* or *clasping*):–bracelet.
8286. שְׂרוּג *ser-oog'*; from 8276; *tendril*; *Serug*, a postdiluvian patriarch:–Serug.
8287. שָׁרוּחֶן *shaw-roo-khen'*; prob. from 8281 (in the sense of *dwelling* (comp. 8271) and 2580; *abode of pleasure; Sharuchen*, a place in Pal.:–Sharuhen.
8288. שְׂרוֹךְ, *ser-oke'*; from 8308; a *thong* (as *laced* or *tied*):–([shoe-]) latchet.
8289. שָׁרוֹן *shaw-rone'*; prob. abridged from 3474; *plain, Sharon*, the name of a place in Pal.:–Lasharon, Sharon.
8290. שָׁרוֹנִי *shaw-ro-nee'* patrial from 8289; a *Sharonite* or inh. of Sharon:–Sharonite.
8291. שַׂרוּק *sar-ook'*; pass.part. from the same as 8321; a *grapevine*:–principal plant.

See 8320, 8321.
8292. שְׁרוּקָה, *sher-oo-kaw';* or (by perm.) שְׁרִיקָה *sher-ee- kaw'*; fem. pass.part. of 8319; a *whistling* (in scorn); by anal., a *piping*:–bleating, hissing.
8293. שֵׁרוּת *shay-rooth'*; from 8281 abb; *freedom*:–remnant.
8294. שֶׂרַח *seh'-rakh*; by perm. for 5629; *superfluity; Serach*, an Isr.s:–Sarah, Serah.
8295. שָׂרַט *saw-rat'*; a prim. root; to *gash*: –cut in pieces, make [(cuttings] pieces.
8296. שֶׂרֶט *seh'-ret* and שָׂרֶטֶת *saw-reh'-teth*; from 8295; an *incision*:–cutting.
8297. שָׂרַי *saw-rah'-ee;* from 8269; *dominative; Sarai*, the wife of Abraham:–Sarai.
8298. שָׁרַי *shaw-rah'-ee*; prob. from 8324; *hostile; Sharay*, an Isr.:–Sharai.
8299. שָׂרִיג *saw-reeg'*; from 8276; a *tendril* (as *entwining*):–branch.
8300. שָׂרִיד *saw-reed'*; from 8277; a *survivor*:–X alive, left, remain(-ing), remnant, rest.
8301. שָׂרִיד *saw-reed';* the same as 8300; *Sarid*, a place in Pal.:–Sarid.
8302. שִׁרְיוֹן *shir-yone';* or שִׁרְיֹן *shir-yone'*; and שִׁרְיָן *shir-yawn'*; also (fem.) שִׁרְיָה *shir-yaw'*; and שִׁרְיֹנָה *shir-yo-naw'*; from 8281 in the or. sense of *turning*; a *corslet* (as if *twisted*):–breastplate, coat of mail, habergeon, harness. See 5630.
8303. שִׁרְיוֹן *shir-yone'*; and שִׂרְיֹן *sir-yone'*; the same as 8304 (i.e. *sheeted* with snow); *Shirjon* or *Sirjon*, a peak of the Lebanon:–Sirion.
8304. שְׂרָיָה *ser-aw-yaw';* or שְׂרָיָהוּ *ser-aw-yaw'-hoo*; from 8280 and 3050; *Jah has prevailed; Serajah*, the name of nine Isr.:–Seraiah.
8305. שְׂרִיקָה *ser-ee-kaw'*; from the same as 8321 in the or. sense of *piercing; hetchelling* (or combing flax), i.e. (concr.) *tow* (by ext., *linen* cloth):–fine.
8306. שָׁרִיר *shaw-reer'*; from 8324 in the or. sense as in 8270 (comp. 8326); a *cord*, i.e. (by anal.) *sinew*:–navel.
8307. שְׁרִירוּת, *sher-ee-rooth';* from 8324 in the sense of *twisted*, i.e. *firm; obstinacy*:–imagination, lust.
8308. שָׂרַךְ *saw-rak'*; a prim. root; to *interlace*:–traverse.
8309. שְׁרֵמָה *sher-ay-maw'*; prob. by an orth. err. for 7709; a *common*:–field.
8310. שַׂרְסְכִים *sar-seh-keem'*; of for. der.; *Sarsekim*, a Babylonian gen.:–Sarsechim.
8311. שָׂרַע *saw-rah';* a prim. root; to *prolong*, i.e. (reflex) *be deformed* by excess of members:–stretch out self, (have any) superfluous thing.
8312. שַׂרְעַף *sar-af'*; for 5587; *cogitation*:–thought.
8313. שָׂרַף *saw-raf'*; a prim. root; to *be* (caus., *set*) *on fire*:–(cause to, make a) burn([-ing], up) kindle, X utterly.
8314. שָׂרָף *saw-rawf'*; from 8313; *burning*, i.e. (fig.) *poisonous* (serpent); spec., a *saraph* or symb. creature (from their copper color):–fiery (serpent), seraph.
8315. שָׂרָף *saw-raf'*; the same as 8314; *Saraph*, an Isr.:–Saraph.
8316. שְׂרֵפָה *ser-ay-faw'*; from 8313; *cremation*:–burning.
8317. שָׁרַץ *shaw-rats';* a prim. root; to *wriggle*, i.e. (by impl.) *swarm* or *abound*:–breed (bring forth, increase) abundantly (in abundance), creep, move.
8318. שֶׁרֶץ *sheh'-rets*; from 8317; a *swarm*, i.e. act.mass of minute animals:–creep(-ing thing), move(-ing creature).
8319. שָׁרַק *shaw-rak'*; a prim. root; prop. to *be shrill*, i.e. to whistle or *hiss* (as a call or in scorn):–hiss.
8320. שָׂרֻק *saw-rook'*; from 8319; *bright red* (as *piercing* to the sight), i.e. *bay*:–speckled. See 8291.
8321. שֹׂרֵק *so-rake'*; or שׂוֹרֵק *so-rake'*; and (fem.) שֹׂרֵקָה *so-ray-kaw'*; from 8319 in the sense of *redness* (comp. 8320); a *vine* stock (prop. one yielding *purple* grapes, the richest variety):–choice(-st, noble) wine. Comp. 8291.
8322. שְׁרֵקָה *sher-ay-kaw'*; from 8319; a *derision*:–hissing.
8323. שָׂרַר *saw-rar'*; a prim. root; to *have* (trans., *exercise*; refl., *get*) *dominion*:–X altogether, make self a prince, (bear) rule.
8324. שָׁרַר *shaw-rar'*; a prim. root; to *be hostile* (only act.part. an *opponent*):–enemy.
8325. שָׁרָר *shaw-rawr'*; from 8324; *hostile; Sharar*, an Isr.:–Sharar.
8326. שֹׁרֶר *sho'-rer;* from 8324 in the sense of *twisting* (comp. 8270); the umbilical *cord*, i.e. (by ext.) a *bodice*:–navel.
8327. שָׁרַשׁ *shaw-rash'*; a prim. root; to *root*, i.e. strike into the soil, or (by impl.) to pluck from it:–(take, cause to take) root (out).
8328. שֶׁרֶשׁ *sheh'-resh*; from 8327; a *root* (lit. or fig.):–bottom, deep, heel, root.
8329. שֶׁרֶשׁ *sheh'-resh*; the same as 8328; *Sheresh*, an Isr.:–Sharesh.
8330. שֹׁרֶשׁ *sho'-resh* (Chald; cor. to 8328:–root.
8331. שַׁרְשָׁה *shar-shaw'* from 8327; a *chain* (as *rooted*, i.e. *linked*):–chain. Comp. 8333.
8332. שְׁרֹשׁוּ *sher-o-shoo'* (Chald.); from a root cor. to 8327; *eradication*, i.e. (fig.) *exile*:–banishment.
8333. שַׁרְשְׁרָה *shar-sher-aw'*; from 8327 (comp. 8331); a *chain*; (arch.) prob. a *garland*:–chain.
8334. שָׁרַת *shaw-rath'*; a prim. root; to *attend* as a menial or worshipper; fig., to *contribute* to:–minister (unto), (do) serve (-ant, -ice, -itor), wait on.
8335. שָׁרֵת *shaw-rayth'*; inf. of 8334; *service* (in the Temple):–minister(-ry).
8336. שֵׁשׁ *shaysh*; or (for alliteration with 4897) שְׁשִׁי *shesh-ee'*; for 7893; *bleached* stuff, i.e. *white* linen or (by anal.) marble:–X blue, fine ([twined]) linen, marble, silk.
8337. שֵׁשׁ *shaysh*; masc. שִׁשָּׁה *shish-shaw'*; a prim. number; *six* (as an overplus [see 7797] beyond five or the fingers of the hand); as ord. *sixth*:–six([-teen, -teenth]), sixth.
8338. שָׁשָׁא *shaw-shaw'*; a prim. root; app., to *annihilate*:–leave by the sixth part
8339. שֵׁשְׁבַּצַּר *shaysh-bats-tsar'*; of for. der.; *Sheshbatstsar*, Zerubbabel's Pers. name:–Sheshbazzar.
8340. שֵׁשְׁבַּצַּר *shaysh-bats-tsar'* (Chald.); cor. to 8339:–Sheshbazzar.
8341. שָׁשָׁה *shaw-shaw'*; a denom. from 8337; to *sixth* or divide into sixths:–give the sixth part.
8342. שָׂשׂוֹן *saw-sone'*; or שָׂשֹׂן *saw-sone';* from 7797; *cheerfulness*; spec., *welcome*:–gladness, joy, mirth, rejoicing.
8343. שָׁשַׁי *shaw-shah'-ee;* perh. from 8336; *whitish; Shashai*, an Isr.:–Shashai.
8344. שֵׁשַׁי *shay-shah'-ee*; prob. for 8343; *Sheshai*, a Canaanite:–Sheshai.
8345. שִׁשִּׁי *shish-shee';* from 8337; *sixth*, ord. or (fem.) fractional:–sixth (part).
8346. שִׁשִּׁים *shish-sheem';* multiple of 8337; *sixty*:–sixty, three score.
8347. שֵׁשַׁךְ *shay-shak'*; of for. der.; *Sheshak*, a symbol. name of Babylon:–Sheshach.
8348. שֵׁשָׁן *shay-shawn'*; perh. for 7799; *lily; Sheshan*, an Isr.:–Sheshan.
8349. שָׁשַׁק *shaw-shak'*; prob. from the base of 7785; *pedestrian; Shashak*, an Isr.:–Shashak.
8350. שָׁשַׁר *shaw-shar'*; perh. from the base of 8324 in the sense of that of 8320; *red* ochre (from its *piercing* color):–vermillion.
8351. שֵׁת *shayth*; (Nu. 24:17) from 7582; *tumult*:–Sheth.
8352. שֵׁת *shayth;* from 7896; put, i.e. *substituted; Sheth*, third son of Adam:–Seth, Sheth.
8353. שֵׁת *shayth* (Chald.); or שִׁת *sheeth* (Chald.); cor. to 8337:–six(-th).
8354. שָׁתָה *shaw-thaw'*; a prim. root; to *imbibe* (lit. or fig.):–X assuredly, banquet, X certainly, drink(-er,-ing), drunk (X-ard), surely. [Prop. intens. of 8248.]
8355. שְׁתָה *sheth-aw'* (Chald.); cor. to 8354:–drink.
8356. שָׁתָה *shaw-thaw'*; from 7896; a *basis*, i.e. (fig.) political or mor. *support*:–foundation, purpose.
8357. שֵׁתָה *shay-thaw';* from 7896; the *seat* (of the person):–buttock.
8358. שְׁתִי *sheth-ee'*; from 8354; *intoxicaion*:–drunkenness.
8359. שְׁתִי *sheth-ee'*; from 7896; a *fixture*, i.e. the *warp* in weaving:–warp.
8360. שְׁתִיָּה *sheth-ee-yaw'*; fem. of 8358; *potation*:–drinking.
8361. שִׁתִּין *shit-teen'* (Chald.); cor. to 8346 [comp. 8353]; *sixty*:–threescore.
8362. שָׁתַל *shaw-thal';* a prim. root; to *transplant*:–plant.
8363. שְׁתִל *sheth-eel'*; from 8362; a *sprig* (as if *transplanted*), i.e. *sucker*:–plant.
8364. שֻׁתַלְחִי *shoo-thal-khee';* patron. from 7803; a *Shuthalchite* (coll.) or desc. of Shuthelach:–Shuthalhites.
8365. שָׁתַם *shaw-tham'*; a prim. root; to *unveil* (fig.):–be open.
8366 שָׁתַן *shaw-than'*; a prim. root; (caus.) to *make water*, i.e. *urinate*:–piss..
8367. שָׁתַק *shaw-thak'*; a prim. root; to *subside*:–be calm, cease, be quiet.
8368. שָׂתַר *saw-thar'*; a prim. root; to *break* out (as an eruption):–have in [one's]secret parts.
8369. שֵׁתָר *shay-thawr'*; of for. der.; *Shethar*, a Pers. satrap:–Shethar.
8370. שְׁתַר בּוֹזְנַי *sheth-ar' bo-zen-ah'-ee;* of for. der.; *Shethar-Bozenai*, a Pers. officer:–Shethar-boznai.
8371. שָׁתַת *shaw-thath'*; a prim. root; to *place*, i.e. *array*; reflex. to *lie*:–be laid, set.

ת

8372. תָּא *taw*; and (fem.) תָּאָה (Eze. 40:12) *taw-aw'*; from (the base of) 8376; a *room* (as *circumscribed*):–(little) chamber.
8373. תָּאַב *taw-ab'*; a prim. root; to *desire*:–long.
8374. תָּאַב *taw-ab'*; a prim. root [prob. ident. with 8373 through the idea of *puffing* disdainfully at; comp. 340]; to *loathe* (mor.):–abhor.
8375. תַּאֲבָה *tah-ab-aw'*; from 8374 [comp. 15]; *desire*:–longing
8376. תָּאָה *taw-aw'*; a prim. root; to *mark* off,

i.e. (intens.) *designate*:–point out.

8377. תְּאוֹ *teh-o'*;and תּוֹא (the or. form) *toh*; from 8376; a species of *antelope* (prob. from the white *stripe* on the cheek):–wild bull (ox).

8378. תַּאֲוָה *tah-av-aw'*; from 183 (abb); a *longing*; by impl., a *delight* (subj., *satisfaction*, obj., a *charm*):–dainty, desire, X exceedingly, X greedily, lust(ing), pleasant. See also 6914.

8379. תַּאֲוָה *tah-av-aw'*; from 8376; a *limit*, i.e. full extent:–utmost bound.

8380. תָּאוֹם *taw-ome'*; or תָּאֹם *taw-ome'*; from 8382; a *twin* (in pl. only), lit. or fig.:–twins.

8381. תַּאֲלָה *tah-al-aw'*; from 422; an *imprecation*:–curse.

8382. תָּאַם *taw-am'*; a prim. root; to *be complete*; but used only as denom. from 8380, to *be* (caus., *make*) *twinned*, i.e. (fig.) *duplicate* or (arch.) *jointed*:–coupled (together), bear twins.

8383. תְּאֻן *teh-oon'*; from 205; *naughtiness*, i.e. *toil*:–lie.

8384. תְּאֵן *teh-ane'*; or (in the sing., fem.) תְּאֵנָה *teh-ay-naw'*; perh. of for. der.; the *fig* (tree or fruit):–fig (tree).

8385. תַּאֲנָה *tah-an-aw'*; or תֹּאֲנָה *to-an-aw'*; from 579; an *opportunity* or (subj.) *purpose*:–occasion.

8386. תַּאֲנִיָּה *tah-an-ee-yaw'*; from 578; *lamentation*:–heaviness, mourning.

8387. תַּאֲנַת שִׁלֹה *tah-an-ath' shee-lo'*; from 8385 and 7887; *approach of Shiloh; Taanath-Shiloh*, a place in Pal.:–Taanath-shiloh.

8388. תָּאַר *taw-ar'*; a prim. root; to *delineate*; reflex. to *extend*:–be drawn, mark out, [Rimmon-]methoar [by *union with* 7417].

8389. תֹּאַר *to'-ar*; from 8388; *outline*, i.e. *figure* or *appearance*:–+ beautiful, X comely, countenance, + fair, X favoured, form, X goodly, X resemble, visage.

8390. תַּאֲרֵעַ *tah-ar-ay'-ah*; perh. from 772; *Taareä*, an Isr.:–Tarea. See 8475.

8391. תְּאַשּׁוּר *teh-ash-shoor'*; from 833; a species of *cedar* (from its *erectness*):–box (tree).

8392. תֵּבָה *tay-baw'*; perh. of for. der.; a *box*:–ark.

8393. תְּבוּאָה *teb-oo-aw'*; from 935; *income*, i.e. *produce* (lit. or fig.):–fruit, gain, increase, revenue.

8394. תָּבוּן *taw-boon'* and (fem.) תְּבוּנָה *teb-oo-naw'*; or תּוֹבֻנָה *to-boo-naw'*; from 995; *intelligence*; by impl., an *argument*; by ext., *caprice*:–discretion, reason, skilfulness, understanding, wisdom.

8395. תְּבוּסָה *teb-oo-saw'*; from 947; a *treading down*, i.e. *ruin*:–destruction.

8396. תָּבוֹר *taw-bore'*; from a root cor. to 8406; *broken* region; *Tabor*, a mountain in Pal., also a city adjacent:–Tabor.

8397. תֶּבֶל *teh'-bel* app. from 1101; *mixture*, i.e. *unnatural* bestiality:–confusion.

8398. תֵּבֵל *tay-bale'* from 2986; the *earth* (as *moist* and therefore inhabited); by ext., the *globe*; by impl., its *inh.*; spec., a partic. *land*, as Babylonia, Pal.:–habitable part, world.

8399. תַּבְלִית *tab-leeth'*; from 1086; *consumption*:–destruction.

8400. תְּבַלֻּל *teb-al-lool'*; from 1101 in the or. sense of *flowing*: a *cataract* (in the eye):–blemish.

8401. תֶּבֶן *teh'-ben* prob. from 1129; prop. *material*, i.e. (spec.) refuse *haum* or stalks of grain (as *chopped* in threshing and used for fodder):–chaff, straw, stubble.

8402. תִּבְנִי *tib-nee'*; from 8401; *strawy; Tibni*, an Isr.:–Tibni.

8403. תַּבְנִית *tab-neeth'*; from 1129; *structure*; by impl., a *model*, *resemblance*:–figure, form, likeness, pattern, similitude.

8404. תַּבְעֵרָה *tab-ay-raw'*; from 1197; *burning; Taberah*, a place in the Desert:–Taberah.

8405. תֵּבֵץ *tay-bates'*; from the same as 948; *whiteness*; *Tebets*, a place in Pal.:–Thebez.

8406. תְּבַר *teb-ar'* (Chald.); cor. to 7665; to be *fragile* (fig.):–broken.

8407. תִּגְלַת פִּלְאֶסֶר *tig-lath' pil-eh'-ser* or תִּגְלַת פְּלֶסֶר *tig-lath pel-eh-ser*; or תִּלְגַת פִּלְנְאֶסֶר *til-gath' pil-neh-eh'-ser* or תִּלְגַת פִּלְנֶסֶר *til-gath' pil-neh'-ser*; of for. der.; *Tiglath-Pileser* or *Tilgath-pilneser*, an Assyr. king:–Tiglath-pileser, Tilgath- pilneser.

8408. תַּגְמוּל *tag-mool'*; from 1580; a *bestowment*:–benefit.

8409. תִּגְרָה *tig-raw'*; from 1624; *strife*, i.e. *infliction*:–blow.

8410. תִּדְהָר *tid-hawr'*; app. from 1725; *enduring*; a species of hard-wood or *lasting* tree (perh. *oak*):–pine (tree).

8411. תְּדִירָא *ted-ee-raw'* (Chald.); from 1753 in the or. sense of *enduring; permanence*, i.e. (adv.) *constantly*:–continually.

8412. תַּדְמֹר *tad-more'*; or תַּמֹּר (1 Kings 9:18) *tam-more'*; app. from 8558; *palm-city*; *Tadmor*, a place near Pal.:–Tadmor.

8413. תִּדְעָל *tid-awl'*; perh. from 1763; *fearfulness; Tidal*, a Canaanite:–Tidal.

8414. תֹּהוּ *to'-hoo;* from an un. root mean. to lie *waste*; a *desolation* (of surface), i.e. *desert*; fig., a *worthless* thing; adv., in *vain*:–confusion, empty place, without form, nothing, (thing of) nought, vain, vanity, waste, wilderness.

8415. תְּהוֹם *teh-home'*; or תְּהֹם *teh-home';* (usually fem.) from 1949; an *abyss* (as a *surging* mass of water), esp. the *deep* (the *main* sea or the subterranean *water-supply*):–deep (place), depth.

8416. תְּהִלָּה *teh-hil-law'*; from 1984; *laudation*; spec. (concr.) a *hymn*:–praise.

8417. תָּהֳלָה *to-hol-aw';* fem. of an un. noun (app. from 1984) mean. *bluster; braggadocio*, i.e. (by impl.) *fatuity*:–folly.

8418. תַּהֲלֻכָה *tah-hal-oo-kaw';* from 1980; a *procession*:–X went.

8419. תַּהְפֻּכָה *tah-poo-kaw';* from 2015; a *perversity* or *fraud*:–(very) froward(-ness, thing), perverse thing.

8420. תָּו *tawv*; from 8427; a *mark*; by impl., a *signature*:–desire, mark.

8421. תּוּב *toob* (Chald.); cor. to 7725, to *come back*; spec. (trans. and ellip.) to *reply*:–answer, restore, return (an answer).

8422. תּוּבַל *too-bal'* or תֻּבַל *too-bal'*; prob. of for. der.; *Tubal*, a postdiluvian patriarch and his posterity:–Tubal.

8423. תּוּבַל קַיִן *too-bal' kah'-yin;* app. from 2986 (comp. 2981) and 7014; *offspring of Cain; Tubal-Kajin*, an antidiluvian patriarch:–Tubal-cain.

8424. תּוּגָה *too-gaw';* from 3013; *depression* (of spirits); concr. a *grief*:–heaviness, sorrow.

8425. תּוֹגַרְמָה *to-gar-maw';* or תֹּגַרְמָה *to-gar-maw'*; prob. of for. der.; *Togarmah*, a son of Gomer and his posterity:–Togarmah.

8426. תּוֹדָה *to-daw';* from 3034; prop. an *ext.* of the hand, i.e. (by impl.) *avowal*, or (usually) *adoration*; spec., a *choir* of worshippers:–confession, (sacrifice of) praise, thanks(-giving, offering).

8427. תָּוָה *taw-vaw';* a prim. root; to *mark* out, i.e. (prim.) *scratch* or (def.) *imprint*: –scrabble, set [a mark].

8428. תָּוָה *taw-vaw'*; a prim. root [or perh. ident. with 8427 through a similar idea from *scraping* to pieces]; to *grieve*:–limit.

8429. תְּוַהּ *tev-ah'* (Chald.); cor. to 8539 or perh. to 7582 through the idea of *sweeping* to ruin [comp. 8428]; to *amaze*, i.e. (reflex. by impl.) *take alarm*:–be astonied.

8430. תּוֹחַ *to'-akh*; from an un. root mean. to *depress; humble; Toäch*, an Isr.:–Toah.

8431. תּוֹחֶלֶת *to-kheh'-leth*; from 3176; *expectation*:–hope.

8432. תָּוֶךְ *taw'-vek*; from an un. root mean. to *sever*; a *bisection*, i.e. (by impl.) the *centre*:–among(-st), X between, half, X (there-, where-), in(-to), middle, mid(-night), midst (among), X out (of), X through, X with(-in).

8433. תּוֹכֵחָה *to-kay-khaw'*; and תּוֹכַחַת *to-kakh'-ath*; from 3198; *chastisement*; fig. (by words) *correction, refutation, proof* (even in defence):–argument, X chastened, correction, reasoning, rebuke, reproof, X be (often) reproved.

8434. תּוֹלָד *to-lawd'*; from 3205; *posterity; Tolad*, a place in *Pal.*:–*Tolad*. Comp. 513.

8435. תּוֹלְדָה *to-led-aw'*; or תֹּלְדָה *to-led-aw'*; from 3205; (pl. only) *descent*, i.e. *family*; (fig.) *history*:–birth, generations.

8436. תּוּלוֹן *too-lone'*; from 8524; *suspension; Tulon*, an Isr.:–Tilon.

8437. תּוֹלָל *to-lawl'*; from 3213; *causing* to *howl*, i.e. an *oppressor*:–that wasted.

8438. תּוֹלָע *to-law'*; and (fem.) תּוֹלֵעָה *to-lay-aw'*; or תּוֹלַעַת *to-lah'-ath*; or תֹּלַעַת *to-lah'-ath*; from 3216; a *maggot* (as *voracious*); spec. (often with ellip. of 8144) the crimson-*grub*, but used only (in this connection) of the color from it, and cloths dyed therewith:–crimson, scarlet, worm.

8439. תּוֹלָע *to-law'* the same as 8438; *worm; Tola*, the name of two Isr.:–Tola.

8440. תּוֹלָעִי *to-law-ee';* patron. from 8439; a *Tolaite* (coll.) or desc. of Tola:–Tolaïtes.

8441. תּוֹעֵבָה *to-ay-baw'*; or תֹּעֵבָה *to-ay-baw'*; fem. act.part. of 8581; prop. something *disgusting* (mor.), i.e. (as noun) an *abhorrence*; esp. *idolatry* or (concr.) an *idol*:–abominable (custom, thing), abomination.

8442. תּוֹעָה, *to-aw'*; fem. act.part. of 8582; *mistake*, i.e. (mor.) *impiety*, or (political) *injury*:–err., hinder.

8443. תּוֹעָפָה *to-aw-faw'*; from 3286; (only in pl. coll.) *weariness*, i.e. (by impl.) *toil* (*treasure* so obtained) or *speed*:–plenty, strength.

8444. תּוֹצָאָה *to-tsaw-aw'*; or תֹּצָאָה *to-tsaw-aw'*; from 3318; (only in pl. coll.) *exit*, i.e. (geographical) *boundary*, or (fig.) *deliverance*, (act.) *source*:–border(-s), going(-s) forth (out), issues, outgoings.

8445. תּוֹקַהַת *to-kah'-ath*; from the same as 3349; *obedience; Tokahath*, an Isr.:–Tikvath (by correction for 8616).

8446. תּוּר *toor*; a prim. root; to *meander* (caus., *guide*) about, esp. for trade or reconnoitring:–chap[-man], sent to descry, be excellent, merchant[-man], search (out), seek, (e-)spy (out).

8447. תּוֹר *tore*; or תֹּר *tore;* from 8446; a *succession*, i.e. a *string* or (abstr.) *order*:–border, row, turn.

8448. תּוֹר *tore*; prob. the same as 8447; a *manner* (as a sort of *turn*):–estate.

8449. תּוֹר *tore*; or תֹּר *tore*; prob. the same as

8447; a *ring*-dove, often (fig.) as a term of endearment:–(turtle) dove.

8450. תּוֹר *tore* (Chald.); cor. (by perm.) to 7794; a *bull*:–bullock, ox.

8451. תּוֹרָה *to-raw'*; or תֹּרָה *to-raw'*; from 3384; a *precept* or *statute*, esp. the *Decalogue* or *Pentateuch*:–law.

8452. תּוֹרָה *to-raw'*; prob. fem. of 8448; a *custom*:–manner.

8453. תּוֹשָׁב *to-shawb'*; or תֹּשָׁב (1 Kings 17:1) *to-shawb'*; from 3427; a *dweller* (but not outlandish [(5237)]); esp. (as distinguished from a nat. citizen [act.part. of 3427] and a temporary inmate [1616] or mere lodger [3885]) resident *alien*:–foreigner, inhabitant, sojourner, stranger.

8454. תּוּשִׁיָּה *too-shee-yaw'*; or תֻּשִׁיָּה *too-shee-yaw'*; from an un. root prob. mean. to *substantiate*; *support* or (by impl.) *ability*, i.e. (direct) *help*, (in purpose) an *undertaking*, (intellectual) *understanding*:–enterprise, that which (thing as it) is, substance, (sound) wisdom, working.

8455. תּוֹתָח *to-thawkh'*; from an un. root mean. to *smite*; a *club*:–darts.

8456. תָּזַז *taw-zaz'* a prim. root; to *lop* off:–cut down.

8457. תַּזְנוּת *taz-nooth'*; or תַּזְנֻת *taz-nooth'*; from 2181; *harlotry*, i.e. (fig.) *idolatry*:–fornication, whoredom.

8458. תַּחְבֻּלָה *takh-boo-law'*; or תַּחְבּוּלָה *takh-boo-law'*; from 2254 as denom. from 2256; (only in pl.) prop. *steerage* (as a management of *ropes*), i.e. (fig.) *guidance* or (by impl.) a *plan*:–good advice, (wise) counsels.

8459. תֹּחוּ *to'-khoo*; from an un. root mean. to *depress*; *abasement*; *Tochu*, an Isr.:–Tohu.

8460. תְּחוֹת *tekh-oth'* (Chald.); or תְּחֹת *tekh-oth'* (Chald.); cor. to 8478; *beneath*:–under.

8461. תַּחְכְּמֹנִי *takh-kem-o-nee'*; prob. for 2453; *sagacious*; *Tachkemoni*, an Isr.:–Tachmonite.

8462. תְּחִלָּה *tekh-il-law'*; from 2490 in the sense of *opening*; a *commencement*; rel. *or.* (adv., -ly):–begin(-ning), first (time).

8463. תַּחֲלוּא *takh-al-oo'*; or תַּחֲלֻא *takh-al-oo'*; from 2456; a *malady*:–disease, X grievous, (that are) sick(-ness).

8464. תַּחְמָס *takh-mawce'*; from 2554; a species of unclean bird (from its *violence*), perh. an *owl*:–night hawk.

8465. תַּחַן *takh'-an*; prob. from 2583; *station*; *Tachan*, the name of two Isr.:–Tahan.

8466. תַּחֲנָה *takh-an-aw'*; from 2583; (only pl. coll.) an *encampment*:–camp.

8467. תְּחִנָּה *tekh-in-naw'*; from 2603; *graciousness*; caus., *entreaty*:–favour, grace, supplication.

8468. תְּחִנָּה *tekh-in-naw'*; the same as 8467; *Techinnah*, an Isr.:–Tehinnah.

8469. תַּחֲנוּן *takh-an-oon'*; or (fem.) תַּחֲנוּנָה *takh-an-oo-naw'*; from 2603; earnest *prayer*:–intreaty, supplication.

8470. תַּחֲנִי *takh-an-ee'*; patron. from 8465; a *Tachanite* (coll.) or desc. of Tachan:–Tahanites.

8471. תַּחְפַּנְחֵס *takh-pan-khace'*; or תְּחַפְנְחֵס (Eze. 30:18) *tekh-af-nekh-ace'*; or תַּחְפְּנֵס (Jeremiah 2:16) *takh-pen-ace'*; of Eg. der.; *Tachpanches, Techaphneches* or *Tachpenes*, a place in Eg.:–Tahapanes, Tahpanhes, Tehaphnehes.

8472. תַּחְפְּנֵיס *takh-pen-ace'*; of Eg. der.; *Tachpenes*, an Eg. woman: –Tahpenes.

8473. תַּחֲרָא *takh-ar-aw'*; from 2734 in the or. sense of 2352 or 2353; a linen *corslet* (as *white* or *hollow*):–habergeon.

8474. תַּחָרָה *takh-aw-raw'*; a facitious root from 2734 through the idea of the *heat* of jealousy; to *vie* with a rival:–close, contend.

8475. תַּחְרֵעַ *takh-ray'-ah*; for 8390; *Tachreä*, an Isr.:–Tahrea.

8476. תַּחַשׁ *takh'-ash*; prob. of for. der.; a (clean) animal with fur, prob. a species of *antelope*:–badger.

8477. תַּחַשׁ *takh'-ash*; the same as 8476; *Tachash*, a relative of Abraham:–Thahash.

8478. תַּחַת *takh'-ath*; from the same as 8430; the *bottom* (as *depressed*); only adv., *below* (often with prep. pref. *underneath*), in *lieu of*, etc.:–as, beneath, X flat, in(-stead), (same) place (where... is), room, for...sake, stead of, under, X unto, X when...was mine, whereas, [where-]fore, with.

8479. תַּחַת *takh'-ath*; (Chald.); cor. to 8478:–under.

8480. תַּחַת *takh'-ath* the same as 8478; *Tachath*, the name of a place in the Desert, also of three Isr.:–Tahath.

8481. תַּחְתּוֹן *takh-tone'*; or תַּחְתֹּן *takh-tone'*; from 8478; *bottommost*:–lower(-est), nether(-most).

8482. תַּחְתִּי *takh-tee'*; from 8478; *lowermost*; as noun (fem. pl.) the *depths* (fig., a *pit*, the *womb*):–low (parts, -er, -er parts, -est), nether (part).

8483. תַּחְתִּים חָדְשִׁי *takh-teem' khod-shee'*; app. from the pl. masc. of 8482 or 8478 and 2320; *lower* (ones) *monthly*; *Tachtim-Chodshi*, a place in Pal.:–Tahtim-hodshi.

8484. תִּיכוֹן *tee-kone'*; or תִּיכֹן *tee-kone'*; from 8432; *central*:–middle(-most), midst.

8485. תֵּימָא *tay-maw'*; or תֵּמָא *tay-maw'*; prob. of for. der.; *Tema*, a son of Ishmael, and the region settled by him:–Tema.

8486. תֵּימָן *tay-mawn'*; or תֵּמָן *tay-mawn'*; denom. from 3225; the *south* (as being on the *right* hand of a person facing the east):–south (side, -ward, wind).

8487. תֵּימָן *tay-mawn'*; or תֵּמָן *tay-mawn'*; the same as 8486; *Teman*, the name of two Edomites, and of the region and desc. of one of them:–south, Teman.

8488. תֵּימְנִי *tay-men-ee'*; prob. for 8489; *Temeni*, an Isr.:–Temeni.

8489. תֵּימָנִי *tay-maw-nee'*; patron. from 8487; a *Temanite* or desc. of Teman:–Temani, Temanite.

8490. תִּימָרָה *tee-maw-raw'*; or תִּמָרָה *tee-maw-raw'*; from the same as 8558; a *column*, i.e. cloud:–pillar.

8491. תִּיצִי *tee-tsee'*; patrial or patron. from an un. noun of unc. mean.; a *Titsite* or desc. or inh. of an unknown Tits:–Tizite.

8492. תִּירוֹשׁ *tee-roshe'*; or תִּירֹשׁ *tee-roshe'*; from 3423 in the sense of *expulsion; must* or fresh grape-juice (as just *squeezed* out); by impl. (rarely) fermented *wine*:–(new, sweet) wine.

8493. תִּירְיָא *tee-reh-yaw'*; prob. from 3372; *fearful, Tirja*, an Isr.:–Tiria.

8494. תִּירָס *tee-rawce'*; prob. of for. der.; *Tiras*, a son of Japheth:–Tiras.

8495. תַּיִשׁ *tah'-yeesh* from an un. root mean. to *butt*; a *buck* or he-goat (as given to *butting*):–he goat.

8496 תֹּךְ *toke*; or תּוֹךְ (Ps. 72:14) *toke;* from the same base as 8432 (in the sense of *cutting* to pieces); *oppression*:–deceit, fraud.

8497. תָּכָה *taw-kaw';* a prim. root; to *strew*, i.e. *encamp*:–sit down.

8498. תְּכוּנָה *tek-oo-naw'*; fem. pass.part. of 8505; *adjustment*, i.e. *structure*; by impl., *equipage*:–fashion, store.

8499. תְּכוּנָה *tek-oo-naw'*; from 3559; or prob. ident. with 8498; something *arranged* or *fixed*, i.e. a *place*:–seat.

8500. תֻּכִּי *took-kee'*; or תּוּכִּי *took-kee'*; prob. of for. der.; some imported creature, prob. a *peacock*:–peacock.

8501. תָּכָךְ *taw-kawk';* from an un. root mean. to *dissever*, i.e. crush:–deceitful.

8502. תִּכְלָה *tik-law'*; from 3615; *completeness*:–perfection.

8503. תַּכְלִית *tak-leeth';* from 3615; *completion*; by impl., an *extremity*:–end, perfect(-ion).

8504. תְּכֵלֶת *tek-ay'-leth;* prob. for 7827; the cerulean *mussel*, i.e. the color (*violet*) obtained therefrom or stuff dyed therewith:–blue.

8505. תָּכַן *taw-kan';* a prim. root; to balance, i.e. *measure* out (by weight or dimension); fig., *arrange, equalize*, through the idea of *levelling* (ment. *estimate, test*):–bear up, direct, be ([un-]) equal, mete, ponder, tell, weigh.

8506. תֹּכֶן *to'-ken*; from 8505; a fixed *quantity*:–measure, tale.

8507. תֹּכֶן *to'-ken*; the same as 8506; *Token*, a place in Pal.:–Tochen.

8508. תָּכְנִית *tok-neeth'*; from 8506; *admeasurement*, i.e. *consummation*:–pattern, sum.

8509. תַּכְרִיךְ *tak-reek'*; app. from an un. root mean. to *encompass*; a *wrapper* or robe:–garment.

8510. תֵּל *tale*; by contr. from 8524; a *mound*:–heap, X strength.

8511. תָּלָא *taw-law'*; a prim. root; to *suspend*; fig. (through *hesitation*) to be *unc.*; by impl. (of ment. *dependence*) to *habituate*:–be bent, hang (in doubt).

8512. תֵּל אָבִיב *tale aw-beeb';* from 8510 and 24; *mound* of *green* growth; *Tel-Abib*, a place in Chaldaea:–Tel-abib.

8513. תְּלָאָה *tel-aw-aw'*; from 3811; *distress*:–travail, travel, trouble.

8514. תַּלְאוּבָה *tal-oo-baw'*; from 3851; *desiccation*: –great drought.

8515. תְּלַאשָּׂר *tel-as-sar'*; or תְּלַשָּׂר *tel-as-sar'*; of for. der.; *Telassar*, a region of Assyria:–Telassar.

8516. תַּלְבֹּשֶׁת *tal-bo'-sheth*; from 3847; a *garment*:–clothing.

8517. תְּלַג *tel-ag'* (Chald.); cor. to 7950; *snow*:–snow.

8518. תָּלָה *taw-law'*; a prim. root; to *suspend* (esp. to *gibbet*):–hang (up).

8519. תְּלוּנָּה *tel-oo-naw'* or תְּלֻנָּה *tel-oon-naw'*; from 3885 in the sense of *obstinacy*; a *grumbling*:–murmuring.

8520. תֶּלַח *teh'-lakh*; prob. from an un. root mean. to *dissever; breach; Telach*, an Isr.:–Telah.

8521. תֵּל חַרְשָׁא *tale khar-shaw';* from 8510 and the fem. of 2798; *mound of workmanship*; *Tel-Charsha*, a place in Babylonia:–Tel-haresha, Tel-harsa.

8522. תְּלִי *tel-ee';* prob. from 8518; a *quiver* (as *slung*):–quiver.

8523. תְּלִיתַי *tel-ee-thah'-ee* (Chald.); or תַּלְתִּי *tal-tee'* (Chald.); ord. from 8532; *third*:–third.

8524. תָּלַל *taw-lal'*; a prim. root; to *pile* up, i.e. *elevate*:–eminent. Comp. 2048.

8525. תֶּלֶם *teh'-lem*; from an un. root mean. to *accumulate*; a *bank* or *terrace*:–furrow, ridge.

8526. תַּלְמַי *tal-mah'-ee*; from 8525; *ridged; Talmai*, the name of a Canaanite and a

HEBREW

Syrian:–Talmai.
8527. תַּלְמִיד *tal-meed'*; from 3925; a *pupil*:–scholar.
8528. תֵּל מֶלַח *tale meh'-lakh*; from 8510 and 4417; *mound of salt*; *Tel-Melach*, a place in Babylonia:–Tel-melah.
8529. תָּלַע *taw-law'*; a denom. from 8438; to *crimson*, i.e. dye that color:–X scarlet.
8530. תַּלְפִּיָּה *tal-pee-yaw'*; fem. from an un. root mean. to *tower*; something *tall*, i.e. (pl. coll.) *slenderness*:–armoury.
8531. תְּלַת *tel-ath'* (Chald.); from 8532; a *tertiary* rank:–third.
8532. תְּלָת *tel-awth'* (Chald.); masc. תְּלָתָה *tel-aw-thaw'* (Chald.); or תְּלָתָא *tel-aw-thaw'* (Chald.); cor. to 7969; *three* or *third*:–third, three.
8533. תְּלָתִין *tel-aw-theen'* (Chald.); mult. of 8532; *ten times three*:–thirty.
8534. תַּלְתַּל *tal-tal'*; by redupl., from 8524 through the idea of *vibration*; a trailing *bough* (as *pendulous*):–bushy.
8535. תָּם *tawm*; from 8552; *complete*; usually (mor.) *pious*; spec., *gentle*, *dear*:–coupled together, perfect, plain, undefiled, upright.
8536. תָּם *tawm* (Chald.); cor. to 8033; *there*:–X thence, there, X where.
8537. תֹּם *tome;* from 8552; *completeness*; fig., *prosperity*; usually (mor.) *innocence*:–full, integrity, perfect(-ion), simplicity, upright(-ly, -ness), at a venture. See 8550.
8538. תֻּמָּה *toom-maw'*; fem. of 8537; *innocence*:–integrity.
8539. תָּמַהּ *taw-mah'*; a prim. root; to be in *consternation*:–be amazed, be astonished, marvel(-lously), wonder.
8540. תְּמַהּ *tem-ah'* (Chald.); from a root cor. to 8539; a *miracle*:–wonder.
8541. תִּמָּהוֹן *tim-maw-hone';* from 8539; *consternation*:–astonishment.
8542. תַּמּוּז *tam-mooz'*; of unc. der.; *Tammuz*, a Phoenician deity:–Tammuz.
8543. תְּמוֹל *tem-ole'*; or תְּמֹל *tem-ole'*; prob. for 865; prop. *ago*, i.e. a (short or long) *time since*; esp. *yesterday*, or (with 8032) *day before* yesterday:–+before (-time), + these [three] days, + heretofore, + time past, yesterday.
8544. תְּמוּנָה *tem-oo-naw'*; or תְּמֻנָה *tem-oo-naw'*; from 4327; *something portioned* (i.e. *fashioned*) out, as a *shape*, i.e. (indef.) *phantom*, or (spec.) *embodiment*, or (fig.) *manifestation* (of favor):–image, likeness, similitude.
8545. תְּמוּרָה *tem-oo-raw'*; from 4171; *barter, compensation*:–(ex-)change(-ing), recompense, restitution.
8546. תְּמוּתָה *tem-oo-thaw'*; from 4191; *execution* (as a doom):–death, die.
8547. תֶּמַח *teh'-makh*; of unc. der.; *Temach*, one of the Nethinim:–Tamah, Thamah.
8548. תָּמִיד *taw-meed'*; from an un. root mean. to *stretch*; prop. *continuance* (as indef. *ext.*); but used only (attributively as adjective) *constant* (or adv., *constantly*); ellipt. the *regular* (daily) sacrifice:–alway(-s), continual (employment, -ly), daily, ([n-])ever(-more), perpetual.
8549. תָּמִים *taw-meem';* from 8552; *entire* (lit., fig. or mor.); also (as noun) *integrity, truth*:–without blemish, complete, full, perfect, sincerely (-ity), sound, without spot, undefiled, upright(-ly), whole.
8550. תֻּמִּים *toom-meem'*; pl. of 8537; *perfections*, i.e. (te.) one of the epithets of the obj. in the high-priest's breastplate as an emblem of *complete* Truth:–Thummim.
8551. תָּמַךְ *taw-mak'*; a prim. root; to *sustain*; by impl., to *obtain, keep fast*; fig., to *help, follow close*:–(take, up-)hold (up), maintain, retain, stay (up).
8552. תָּמַם *taw-mam';* a prim. root; to *complete*, in a good or a bad sense, lit., or fig., trans. or intr. (as follows):–accomplish, cease, be clean [pass-] ed, consume, have done, (come to an, have an, make an) end, fail, come to the full, be all gone, X be all here, be (make) perfect, be spent, sum, be (shew self) upright, be wasted, whole.
8553. תִּמְנָה *tim-naw'*; from 4487; a *portion* assigned; *Timnah*, the name of two places in Pal.:–Timnah, Timnath, Thimnathah.
8554. תִּמְנִי *tim-nee'*; patrial from 8553; a *Timnite* or inh. of Timnah:–Timnite.
8555. תִּמְנָע *tim-naw'*; from 4513*; restraint; Timna*, the name of two Edomites:–Timna, Timnah.
8556. תִּמְנַת חֶרֶס *tim-nath kheh'-res*; or תִּמְנַת סֶרַח *tim-nath seh'-rakh*; from 8553 and 2775; portion *of* (the) *sun; Timnath-Cheres*, a place in Pal.:–Timnath-heres, Timnath-serah.
8557. תֶּמֶס *teh'-mes*; from 4529; *liquefaction, i.e. disappearance*:–melt.
8558. תָּמָר *taw-mawr'* from an un. root mean. to be *erect*; a *palm* tree:–palm (tree).
8559. תָּמָר *taw-mawr'*; the same as 8558; *Tamar*, the name of three women and a place:–Tamar.
8560. תֹּמֶר *to'-mer;* from the same root as 8558; a *palm* trunk:–palm tree.
8561. תִּמֹּר *tim-more'*; (pl. only or תִּמֹּרָה (fem.) *tim-mo-raw'*; (sing. and pl.) from the same root as 8558; (arch.) a *palm*-like pilaster (i.e. umbellate):–palm tree.
8562. תַּמְרוּק *tam-rook'*; or תַּמְרֻק *tam-rook'*; or תַּמְרִיק *tam-reek'*; from 4838; prop. a *scouring*, i.e. *soap* or *perfumery* for the bath; fig., a *detergent*:–X cleanse, (thing for) purification(-fying).
8563. תַּמְרוּר *tam-roor'*; from 4843; *bitterness* (pl. as coll.):–X most bitter(-ly).
8564. תַּמְרוּר *tam-roor'*; from the same root as 8558; an *erection*, i.e. *pillar* (prob. for a guide-board):–high heap.
8565. תַּן *tan*; from an un. root prob. mean. to *elongate*; a *monster*, i.e. a *sea-serpent* (or other huge marine animal); also a *jackal* (or other hideous land animal):–dragon, whale. Comp. 8577.
8566. תָּנָה *taw-naw'*; a prim. root; to *present* (a mercenary inducement), i.e. *bargain* with (a harlot):–hire.
8567. תָּנָה *taw-naw'*; a prim. root [ident. with 8566 through the idea of *attributing* honor]; to *ascribe* (praise), i.e. *celebrate, commemorate*:–lament, rehearse.
8568. תַּנָּה *tan-naw'*; prob. fem. of 8565; a female *jackal*:–dragon.
8569. תְּנוּאָה *ten-oo-aw'*; from 5106; *alienation*; by impl., *enmity*:–breach of promise, occasion.
8570. תְּנוּבָה *ten-oo-baw'*; from 5107; *produce*:–fruit, increase.
8571. תְּנוּךְ *ten-ook';* perh. from the same as 594 through the idea of *protraction*; a *pinnacle*, i.e. *extremity*:–tip.
8572. תְּנוּמָה *ten-oo-maw'*; from 5123; *drowsiness*, i.e. *sleep*:–slumber(-ing).
8573. תְּנוּפָה *ten-oo-faw'*; from 5130; a *brandishing* (in threat); by impl., *tumult*; spec., the official *undulation* of sacrificial offerings:–offering, shaking, wave (offering).
8574. תַּנּוּר *tan-noor;'* from 5216; a *fire-pot*:–furnace, oven.
8575. תַּנְחוּם *tan-khoom';* or תַּנְחֻם *tan-khoom'*; and תַּנְחוּמָה (fem.) *tan-khoo-maw'*; from 5162; *compassion, solace*:–comfort, consolation.
8576. תַּנְחֻמֶת *tan-khoo'-meth*; for 8575 (fem.); *Tanchumeth*, an Isr.:–Tanhumeth.
8577. תַּנִּין *tan-neen';* or תַּנִּים (Eze. 29:3) *tan-neem'*; intens. from the same as 8565; a marine or land *monster*, i.e. *sea-serpent* or *jackal*:–dragon, sea-monster, serpent, whale.
8578. תִּנְיָן *tin-yawn'* (Chald.); cor. to 8147; *second*:–second.
8579. תִּנְיָנוּת *tin-yaw-nooth'* (Chald.); from 8578; a *second time*:–again.
8580. תַּנְשֶׁמֶת *tan-sheh'-meth;* from 5395; prop. a hard *breather*, i.e. the name of two unclean creatures, a lizard and a bird (both perh. from changing color through their *irascibility*), prob. the *tree-toad* and the *water-hen*:–mole, swan.
8581. תָּעַב *taw-ab'*; a prim. root; to *loathe*, i.e. (mor.) *detest*:–(make to be) abhor(-red),(be, commit more, do) abominable(-y), X utterly.
8582. תָּעָה *taw-aw'*; a prim. root; to *vacillate*, i.e. *reel* or *stray* (lit. or fig.); also caus. of both:–(cause to) go astray, deceive, dissemble, (cause to, make to) err, pant, seduce, (make to) stagger, (cause to) wander, be out of the way.
8583. תֹּעוּ *to'-oo*; or תֹּעִי *to'-ee*; from 8582; *err., Toü* or *Toï*, a Syrian king:–Toi, Tou.
8584. תְּעוּדָה *teh-oo-daw'*; from 5749; *attestation*, i.e. a *precept, usage*:–testimony.
8585. תְּעָלָה *teh-aw-law';* from 5927; a *channel* (into which water is *raised* for irrigation); also a *bandage* or *plaster* (as placed *upon* a wound):–conduit, cured, healing, little river, trench, watercourse.
8586. תַּעֲלוּל *tah-al-ool'*; from 5953; *caprice* (as a fit *coming on*), i.e. *vexation*; concr. a *tyrant*:–babe, delusion.
8587. תַּעֲלֻמָּה *tah-al-oom-maw';* from 5956; a *secret*:–thing that is hid, secret.
8588. תַּעֲנוּג *tah-an-oog'*; or תַּעֲנֻג *tah-an-oog'*; and תַּעֲנֻגָה (fem.) *tah-ah-oog-aw'*; from 6026; *luxury*:–delicate, delight, pleasant.
8589. תַּעֲנִית *tah-an-eeth';* from 6031; *affliction* (of self), i.e. *fasting*:–heaviness.
8590. תַּעֲנָךְ *tah-an-awk';* or תַּעְנָךְ *tah-nawk'*; of unc. der.; *Taanak* or *Tanak*, a place in Pal.:–Taanach, Tanach.
8591. תָּעַע *taw-ah'*; a prim. root; to *cheat*; by anal., to *maltreat*:–deceive, misuse.
8592. תַּעֲצֻמָה *tah-ats-oo-maw';* from 6105; *might* (pl. coll.):–power.
8593. תַּעַר *tah'-ar;* from 6168; a *knife* or *razor* (as *making* bare): also a *scabbard* (as *being bare*, i.e. empty):–[pen-] knife, razor, scabbard, shave, sheath.
8594. תַּעֲרֻבָה *tah-ar-oo-baw';* from 6148; *suretyship*, i.e. (concr.) a *pledge*:–+ hostage.
8595. תַּעְתֻּעַ *tah-too'-ah*; from 8591; a *fraud*:–err..
8596. תֹּף *tofe*; from 8608 contr.; a *tambourine*:–tabret, timbrel.
8597. תִּפְאָרָה *tif-aw-raw'*; or תִּפְאֶרֶת *tif-eh'-reth*; from 6286; *ornament* (abstr. or concr., lit. or fig.):–beauty(-iful), bravery, comely, fair,

glory(-ious), honour, majesty.

8598. תַּפּוּחַ *tap-poo'-akh*; from 5301; an *apple* (from its *fragrance*), i.e. the fruit or the tree (prob. includ. others of the *pome* order, as the quince, the orange, etc.):–apple (tree). See also 1054.

8599. תַּפּוּחַ *tap-poo'-akh*; the same as 8598; *Tappuäch*, the name of two places in Pal., also of an Isr.:–Tappuah.

8600. תְּפוֹצָה *tef-o-tsaw'*; from 6327; a *dispersal*:–dispersion.

8601. תֻּפִין *too-feen'*; from 644; *cookery*, i.e. (concr.) a *cake*:–baked piece.

8602. תָּפֵל *taw-fale'*; from an un. root mean. to *smear*, *plaster* (as *gummy*) or *slime*; (fig.) *frivolity*:–foolish things, unsavoury, untempered.

8603. תֹּפֶל *to'-fel*; from the same as 8602; *quagmire*; *Tophel*, a place near the Desert:–Tophel.

8604. תִּפְלָה *tif-law'*; from the same as 8602; *frivolity*:–folly, foolishly.

8605. תְּפִלָּה *tef-il-law'*; from 6419; *intercession*, *supplication*; by impl., a *hymn*:–prayer.

8606. תִּפְלֶצֶת *tif-leh'-tseth*; from 6426; *fearfulness*:–terrible.

8607. תִּפְסַח *tif-sakh'*; from 6452; *ford*; *Tiphsach*, a place in Mesopotamia:–Tipsah.

8608. תָּפַף *taw-faf'*; a prim. root; to *drum*, i.e. play (as) on the tambourine:–taber, play with timbrels.

8609. תָּפַר *taw-far'*; a prim. root; to *sew*:–(women that) sew (together).

8610. תָּפַשׂ *taw-fas'*; a prim. root; to *manipulate*, i.e. *seize*; chiefly to *capture*, *wield*, spec., to *overlay*; fig., to *use* unwarrantably:–catch, handle, (lay, take) hold (on, over), stop, X surely, surprise, take.

8611. תֹּפֶת *to'-feth*; from the base of 8608; a *smiting*, i.e. (fig.) *contempt*:–tabret.

8612. תֹּפֶת *to'-feth*; the same as 8611; *Topheth*, a place near Jerus.:–Tophet, Topheth.

8613. תָּפְתֶּה *tof-teh'*; prob. a form of 8612; *Tophteh*, a place of cremation:–Tophet.

8614. תִּפְתַּי *tif-tah'-ee* (Chald.); perh. from 8199; *judicial*, i.e. a *lawyer*:–sheriff.

8615. תִּקְוָה *tik-vaw'*; from 6960; lit., a *cord* (as an *attachment* [comp. 6961]); fig., *expectancy*:–expectation([-ted]), hope, live, thing that I long for.

8616. תִּקְוָה *tik-vaw'*; the same as 8615; *Tikvah*, the name of two Isr.:–Tikvah.

8617. תְּקוּמָה *tek-oo-maw'*; from 6965; *resistfulness*:–power to stand.

8618. תְּקוֹמֵם *tek-o-mame'*; from 6965; an *opponent*:–rise up against.

8619. תָּקוֹעַ *taw-ko'-ah*; from 8628 (in the mus. sense); a *trumpet*:–trumpet.

8620. תְּקוֹעַ *tek-o'-ah*; a form of 8619; *Tekoä*, a place in Pal.:–Tekoa, Tekoah.

8621. תְּקוֹעִי *tek-o-ee'*; or תְּקֹעִי *tek-o-ee'*; patron. from 8620; a *Tekoïte* or inh. of Tekoah:–Tekoite.

8622. תְּקוּפָה *tek-oo-faw'*; or תְּקֻפָה *tek-oo-faw'*; from 5362; a *revolution*, i.e. (of the sun) *course*, (of time) *lapse*:–circuit, come about, end.

8623. תַּקִּיף *tak-keef'*; from 8630; *powerful*:–mightier.

8624. תַּקִּיף *tak-keef'* (Chald.); cor. to 8623:–mighty, strong.

8625. תְּקַל *tek-al'* (Chald.); cor. to 8254; to *balance*:–Tekel, be weighed.

8626. תָּקַן *taw-kan'*; a prim. root; to *equalize*, i.e. *straighten* (intr. or trans.); fig., to *compose*:–set in order, make straight.

8627. תְּקַן *tek-an'* (Chald.); cor. to 8626; to *straighten* up, i.e. *confirm*:–establish.

8628. תָּקַע *taw-kah'*; a prim. root; to *clatter*, i.e. *slap* (the hands together), *clang* (an instrument); by anal., to *drive* (a nail or tent-pin, a dart, etc.); by impl., to *become bondsman* by handclasping):–blow ([a trumpet]), cast, clap, fasten, pitch [tent], smite, sound, strike, X suretiship, thrust.

8629. תֵּקַע, *tay-kah'*; from 8628; a *blast* of a trumpet:–sound.

8630. תָּקַף *taw-kaf'*; a prim. root; to *overpower*:–prevail (against).

8631. תְּקֵף *tek-afe'* (Chald.); cor. to 8630; to *become* (caus., *make*) *mighty* or (fig.) *obstinate*:–make firm, harden, be(-come) strong.

8632. תְּקֹף *tek-ofe'* (Chald.); cor. to 8633; *power*:–might, strength.

8633. תֹּקֶף *to'-kef*; from 8630; *might* or (fig.) *positiveness*:–authority, power, strength.

8634. תַּרְאֲלָה *tar-al-aw'*; prob. for 8653; a *reeling*; *Taralah*, a place in Pal.:–Taralah.

8635. תַּרְבּוּת *tar-booth'*; from 7235; *multiplication*, i.e. *progeny*:–increase.

8636. תַּרְבִּית *tar-beeth'*; from 7235; *multiplication*, i.e. *percentage* or *bonus* in addition to principal:–increase, unjust gain.

8637. תִּרְגַּל *teer-gal'*; a denom. from 7270; to *cause to walk*:–teach to go.

8638. תִּרְגֵּם *teer-gam'*; a denom. from 7275 in the sense of *throwing* over; to *transfer*, i.e. *translate*:–interpret.

8639. תַּרְדֵּמָה *tar-day-maw'*; from 7290; a *lethargy* or (by impl.) *trance*:–deep sleep.

8640. תִּרְהָקָה *teer-haw'-kaw*; of for. der.; *Tirhakah*, a king of Kush:–Tirhakah.

8641. תְּרוּמָה *ter-oo-maw'*; or תְּרֻמָה (De. 12:11) *ter-oo-maw'*; from 7311; a *present* (as offered *up*), esp. in *sacrifice* or as *tribute*:–gift, heave offering ([shoulder]), oblation, offered(-ing).

8642. תְּרוּמִיָּה, *ter-oo-mee-yaw'*; formed as 8641; a sacrificial *offering*:–oblation.

8643. תְּרוּעָה *ter-oo-aw'*; from 7321; *clamor*, i.e. *acclamation* of joy or a *battle-cry*; esp. *clangor* of trumpets, as an *alarum*:–alarm, blow(-ing) (of, the) (trumpets), joy, jubile, loudnoise, rejoicing, shout(-ing), (high, joyful) sound(-ing).

8644. תְּרוּפָה *ter-oo-faw'*; from 7322 in the sense of its congener 7495; a *remedy*:–medicine.

8645. תִּרְזָה *teer-zaw'*; prob. from 7329; a species of tree (app. from its *slenderness*), perh. the *cypress*:–cypress.

8646. תֶּרַח *teh'-rakh*; of unc. der.; *Terach*, the father of Abraham; also a place in the Desert:–Tarah, Terah.

8647. תִּרְחֲנָה *teer-khan-aw'*; of unc. der.; *Tirchanah*, an Isr.:–Tirhanah.

8648. תְּרֵין *ter-ane'* (Chald.); fem. תַּרְתֵּין *tar-tane'*; cor. to 8147; *two*:–second, + twelve, two.

8649. תָּרְמָה *tor-maw'*; and תַּרְמוּת *tar-mooth'*; or תַּרְמִית *tar-meeth'*; from 7411; *fraud*:–deceit(-ful), privily.

8650. תֹּרֶן *to'-ren*; prob. for 766; a *pole* (as a mast or flag-staff):–beacon, mast.

8651. תְּרַע *ter-ah'* (Chald.); cor. to 8179; a *door*; by impl., a *palace*:–gate mouth.

8652. תָּרָע *taw-raw'* (Chald.); from 8651; a *doorkeeper*:–porter.

8653. תַּרְעֵלָה *tar-ay-law'* from 7477; *reeling*:–astonishment, trembling.

8654. תִּרְעָתִי *teer-aw-thee'*; patrial from an un. name mean. *gate*; a *Tirathite* or inh. of an unknown Tirah:–Tirathite.

8655. תְּרָפִים *ter-aw-feme'*; pl. from 7495; a *healer*; *Teraphim* (sing. or pl.) a family idol:–idols(-atry), images, teraphim.

8656. תִּרְצָה *teer-tsaw'*; from 7521; *delightsomeness*; *Tirtsah*, a place in Pal.; also an Isr.s:–Tirzah.

8657. תֶּרֶשׁ *teh'-resh*; of for. der.; *Teresh*, a eunuch of Xerxes:–Teresh.

8658. תַּרְשִׁישׁ *tar-sheesh'*; prob. of for. der. [comp. 8659]; a gem, perh. the *topaz*:–beryl.

8659. תַּרְשִׁישׁ *tar-sheesh'*; prob. the same as 8658 (as the region of the stone, or the reverse); *Tarshish*, a place on the Mediterranean, hence, the ephithet of a *merchant* vessel (as if for or from that port); also the name of a Pers. and of an Isr.:–Tarshish, Tharshish.

8660. תִּרְשָׁתָא *teer-shaw-thaw'*; of for. der.; the title of a Pers. deputy or *governor*:–Tirshatha.

8661. תַּרְתָּן *tar-tawn'*; of for. der.; *Tartan*, an Ass.:–Tartan.

8662. תַּרְתָּק, *tar-tawk'*; of for. der.; *Tartak*, a deity of the Avvites:–Tartak.

8663. תְּשֻׁאָה *tesh-oo-aw'*; from 7722; a *crashing* or loud *clamor*:–crying, noise, shouting, stir.

8664. תִּשְׁבִּי *tish-bee'*; patrial from an unused name mean. *recourse*; a *Tishbite* or inh. of Tishbeh (in Gilead):–Tishbite.

8665. תַּשְׁבֵּץ *tash-bates'*; from 7660; *checkered* stuff (as *reticulated*):–broidered.

8666. תְּשׁוּבָה *tesh-oo-baw'*; or תְּשֻׁבָה *tesh-oo-baw'*; from 7725; a *recurrence* (of time or place); a *reply* (as *returned*):–answer, be expired, return.

8667. תְּשׂוּמֶת *tes-oo-meth'*; from 7760; a *deposit*, i.e. *pledging*:–+ fellowship.

8668. תְּשׁוּעָה *tesh-oo-aw'*; or תְּשֻׁעָה *tesh-oo-aw'*; from 7768 in the sense of 3467; *rescue* (lit. or fig., pers., national or spir.):–deliverance, help, safety, salvation, victory.

8669. תְּשׁוּקָה *tesh-oo-kaw'*; from 7783 in the or. sense of *stretching* out after; a *longing*:–desire.

8670. תְּשׁוּרָה *tesh-oo-raw'*; from 7788 in the sense of *arrival*; a *gift*:–present.

8671. תְּשִׁיעִי *tesh-ee-ee'*; ord. from 8672; *ninth*:–ninth.

8672. תֵּשַׁע *tay'-shah*; or (masc.) תִּשְׁעָה *tish-aw'*; perh. from 8159 through the idea of a *turn* to the next or full number ten; *nine* or (ord.) *ninth*:–nine (+ -teen, + -teenth, -th).

8673. תִּשְׁעִים *tish-eem'*; multiple from 8672; *ninety*:–ninety.

8674. תַּתְּנַי *tat-ten-ah'-ee*; of for. der.; *Tattenai*, a Pers.:–Tatnai.

HEBREW

PLACES WHERE THE HEBREW AND THE ENGLISH BIBLES DIFFER IN THE DIVISION OF CHAPTERS AND VERSES

	English	*Hebrew*
Genesis	31:55 32: 1–32	32:1 2–33
Exodus	8: 1–4 5–32 22: 1 2–31	7:26–29 8: 1–28 21:37 22: 1–30
Leviticus	6: 1–7 8–30	5:20–26 6: 1–23
Numbers	16:36–50 17: 1–13 26: 1(first clause) 29:40 30: 1–16	17: 1–15 16–28 25:19 30: 1 2–17
Deuteronomy	5:18–33 12:32 13: 1–18 22:30 23: 1–25 29: 1 2–29	5:17–30 13: 1 2–19 23: 1 2–26 28:69 29: 1–28
Joshua	21: 36, 37 38–45	(not in most copies) 21:36–43
1 Samuel	19: 2 (first clause) 20:42 21: 1–15 23:29 24: 1–22	19: 1 21: 1 2–16 24: 1 2–23
2 Samuel	17:28(first word) 18:33 19: 1–43	29 (middle) 19: 1 2–44
1 Kings	4:21–34 5: 1–18 18:33 (1. half) 20: 2 (1. half) 22:22 (f, clause) 43 (last half) 44–53	5: 1–14 15–32 18:34 (first half) 20: 3 (first half) 22:21 (1. cl) 44 45–54
2 Kings	11:21 12: 1–21	12: 1 2–22
1 Chronicles	6: 1–15 16–81	5:27–41 6: 1–66
2 Chronicles	2: 1 2–18 14: 1 2–15	1:18 2: 1–17 13:23 14: 1–14
Nehemiah	4: 1–6 7–23 9:38 10: 1–39	3:33–38 4: 1–17 10: 1 2–40

	English	*Hebrew*
Job	41:1–8 9–34	40:25–32 41: 1–26
Psalms For Psalms with Titles, the Title in the English is considered v.1 in the Hebrew Bible.		
Ecclesiastes	5: 1 2–20	4:17 5: 1–19
Canticles (Song of S)	6:13 7: 1–13	7: 1 2–14
Isaiah	9: 1 2–21 64: 1 2:21	8:23 9: 1–20 63:19 64: 1–11
Jeremiah	9: 1 2–26	8:23 9: 1–25
Ezekiel	20:45–49 21: 1–32	21: 1–5 6–37
Daniel	4: 1–3 4–37 5:31 6: 1–28	3:31–33 4: 1–34 6: 1 2–29
Hosea	1:10, 11 2: 1–23 11:12 12: 1–14 13:16 14: 1–9	2: 1, 2 3–25 12: 1 2–15 14: 1 2–10
Joel	2:28–32 3: 1–21	3: 1–5 4: 1–21
Jonah	1:17 2: 1–10	2: 1 2–11
Micah	5: 1 2–15	4:14 5: 1–14
Nahum	1:15 2: 1–13	2: 1 2–14
Zechariah	1: 18 2: 1–13	2: 1–4 2–17
Malachi	4: 1–6	3:19–24

STRONG'S DICTIONARY

OF THE WORDS IN THE GREEK NEW TESTAMENT

1. All the original words are treated in their alphabetical Greek order, and are numbered regularly from the first to the last, each being known throughout by its appropriate number. This renders reference easy without recourse to the Greek characters.
2. Next follows the precise pronunciation, according to the usual English mode of sounding syllables.
3. Then ensues a tracing of the etymology, radical meaning, and applied significations of the word, justly but tersely analyzed and expressed, with any other important peculiarities in this regard.
4. Finally (after the punctuation mark:–) are given all the different renderings of the word in the Authorized English Version, arranged in alphabetical order.

WRITING AND PRONOUNCING GREEK:

The *Alphabe*t is as follows:

No.	Form.	Name.	Transliteration and power.
1.	Α α	Alpha (*al'-fah*)	a, as in *Arm* or [*mAn**
2.	Β β	Bēta (*bay'-tah*)	b
3.	Γ γ	Gamma (*gam'-mah*)	g hard †
4.	Δ δ	Dĕlta (*del'-tah*)	d
5.	Ε ε	Ĕpsilŏn (*ep'-see-lon*)	ĕ, as in *mEt*
6.	Ζ ζ	Zēta (*dzay'-tah*)	z, as in *aDZe*‡
7.	Η η	Ēta (*ay'-tah*)	ē, as in *thEy*
8.	Θ θ or ϑ	Thēta (*thay'-tah*)	th,as in *THin*§
9.	Ι ι	Iōta (*ee-o'-tah*)	i, as in *machIne*±
10.	Κ κ or ϰ	Kappa (*cap'-pah*)	k
11.	Λ λ	Lambda (*lamb'-dah*)	l
12.	Μ μ	Mu (*moo*)	m
13.	Ν ν	Nu (*noo*)	n
14.	Ξ ξ	Xi (*ksee*)	x = *ks*
15.	Ο ο	Omikrŏn (*om'-e-cron*)	ŏ, as in *not*
16.	Π π	Pi (*pee*)	P
17.	Ρ ρ	Rhō (*hro*)	r
18.	Σ σ, final ς	Sigma (*sig'-mah*)	s sharp
19.	Τ τ	Tau (*tŏw*)	t ¶
20.	Υ υ	Upsilŏn (*u'-pse-lon*)	u, as in *full*
21.	Φ ϕ	Phi (*fee*)	ph=*f*
22.	Χ χ	Chi (*khee*)	German ch*
23.	Ψ ψ	Psi (*psee*)	ps
24.	Ω ω	Omĕga (*o'-meg-ah*)	ō, as in *no*.

* a, when *final*, or before ρ final or followed by any *other* consonant, is sounded like a in *Arm*; elsewhere like a in *mAn*.

† γ, when followed by γ, κ, χ, or ξ, is sounded like *ng* in *kiNG*.

‡ ζ is always sounded like *dz*.

§ θ never has the guttural sound, like th in *THis*.

± ι has the sound of *ee* when it *ends* an *accented* syllable; in other situations a more obscure sound, like i in *amIable* or *Imbecile*.

¶ τ never has a sibilant sound, like *t* in *naTion, naTure*.

2. the mark ‘, placed over the *initial* vowel of a word, is called the *Rough Breathing*, and is equivalent to the English *h*, by which we have accordingly represented it. Its *absence* over an initial vowl is indicated by the mark’, called the *Smooth Breathing*, which is unappreciable or silent, and is therefore not represented in out method of transliteration. †

3. The following are the Greek *diphthongs*, properly so called: ‡

Form.	Transliteration and power.	Form.	Transliteration and power.
αι	ai, (*ah'ee*) [ă + ē]	αυ	ow, as in *nOW*
ει	ei, as in *hEIght*	ευ	eu, as in *fEUd*
οι	oi, as in *oIl*	ου	ou, as in *through*
υι	we, as in *sWEet*		

*From the difficulty of producing the true sound of χ, it is generally sounded like *k*.

† These signs are placed over the *second* vowel of a *diphthong*. The same is true of the accents. The *Rough* Breathing always belongs to υ initial.

The Rough Breathing is always used with *ρ*, when it begins a word. If this letter be doubled in middle of a word, the first takes the Smooth, and the second the Rough, Breathing.

As these signs cannot conveniently be written over the first letter of a word, when a *capital*, they are in such cases placed *before* it. This observation applies also to the *accents*. The aspiration *always* begins the syllable.

Occasionally, in consequence of a contraction (*crasis*), the Smooth Breathing is made to stand in the middle of a word, and is then called *coro'nis*.

‡ The above are combinations of two *short* vowels, and are pronounced like their respective elements, but in more rapid succession than otherwise. Thus αι is midway between *i* in *hIgh* and ay in *sAY*.

Beside these, there are what are called *improper* diphthongs, in which the former is a *long* vowel. In these,

ᾳ sounds like a	ηυ sounds like η + υ
ῃ " " η	ωυ " " ω + υ
ῳ " " ω	

the second vowel, when ι, is written *under* the first (unless that be a capital), and is *silent;* when υ, it is sounded separately. When the initial is a capital, the ι is placed after it, but does not take the breathing nor accent.

The sign ¨, called *diaer'esis*, placed over the *latter* of two vowels, indicates that they do *not* form a diphthong.

4. The *accent* (stress of voice) falls on the syllable where it is written.* It is of three forms: the *acute* (ʹ), which is the only true accent; the *grave* (ˋ) which is substitute; and the *circumflex* (ˆor˜), which is the union of the two. The acute may stand on any one of the last *three* syllables, and in case it occurs on the final syllable before another word in the same sentence, it is written as a grave. The grave is understood (but never written as such) on every other syllable. The circumflex is written on every syllable (necessarily the last or next to the last one of a word), formed by the contradiction of the two syllables, of which the *first* would properly have the acute.

5. The following *punctuation*-marks are used: the coma (,), the semicolon (·), the colon or period (.), the interrogation-point(;), and by some editors, also the exclamation-point, parentheses and quotation-marks.

*Every word (except a few monosyllables, called *Aton'ics*) must have one accent; several small words (called *Enclit'ics*) throw their accent (always as an acute) on the last syllable of the preceding word (in addition to its own accent, which still has the principal stress), where this is possible.

SIGNS EMPLOYED

+ (*addition*) denotes a rendering in the A.V. of one or more Gr. words in connection wiith the one under consideration.

X (*multiplication*) denotes a rendering in the A.V. that results from an idiom peculiar to the Gr.

( ) (*parenthesis*), in the renderings from the A.V., denotes a word or syllable sometimes given in connection with the principal word to which it is annexed.

[ ] (*bracket*), in the rendering from the A.V., denotes the inclusion of an additional word in the Gr.

Italics, at the end of a rendering from the A.V., denote an explanation of the variations from the usual form.

FOR ABBREVIATIONS USED, SEE 1ST PAGE OF HEBREW

GREEK DICTIONARY OF THE NEW TESTAMENT

A.

1. Α α *al'-fah;* of Heb. or.; the first letter of the alphabet; fig. only (from its use as a numeral) the *first:*–Alpha. Often used (usually άν an, before a vowel) also in compo. (as a contr. from *427*) in the sense of *privation;* so, in many words, beginning with this letter; occasionally in the sense of *union* (as a contr. of *260*).
2. ʼΑρών *ah-ar-ōhn';* of Heb. or. [175]; *Aaron,* the brother of Moses:–Aaron.
3. ʼΑβαδδών *ab-ad-dōhn';* of Heb. or. [11]; a destroying *angel:*–Abaddon.
4. ἀβαρής *ab-ar-ace;'* from *1* (as a neg. par.) and *922*; *weightless*, i.e. (fig.) *not burdensome:*–from being burdensome.
5. ʼΑββᾶ *ab-bah';* of Chald. or. [2]; *father* (as a voc.):–Abba.
6. ʼΆβελ *ab'-el;* of Heb. or. [1893]; *Abel*, the son of Adam:–Abel.
7. ʼΑβια *ab-ee-ah';* of Heb. or. [29]; *Abijah*, the name of two Isr.:–Abia.
8. ʼΑβιάθαρ *ab-ee-ath'-ar;* of Heb. or. [54]; *Abiathar,* an Isr.:–Abiathar.
9. ʼΑβιληνή *ab-ee-lay-nay';* of for. or. [comp. 58]; *Abilene*, a region of Syria:–Abilene.
10. ʼΑβιούδ *ab-ee-ood';* of Heb. or. [31]; *Abihud*, an Isr.:–Abiud.
11. ʼΑβραάμ *ab-rah-am';* of Heb. or. [85]; Abraham, the Heb. patriarch:–Abraham. [In Acts 7:16 the text should prob. read *Jacob*.]
12. ἄβυσσος *ab'-us-sos;* from *1* (as a neg. par.) and a var. of *1037; depthless*, i.e. (spec.) (infernal) "*abyss*":–deep, (bottomless) pit.
13. ʼΆγαβος *ag'-ab-os;* of Heb. or. [comp. 2285]; *Agabus* an Isr.:–Agabus.
14. ἀγαθοεργέω *ag-ath-er-gheh'-o;* from *18* and *2041*; to *work* good:–do good.
15. ἀγαθοποιέω *ag-ath-op-oy-eh'-o;* from *17;* to *be a well-doer* (as a favor or a duty):–(when) do good (well).
16. ἀγαθοποιΐα *ag-ath-op-oy-ee'-ah;* from *17; well-doing*, i.e. *virtue:*–well-doing.
17. ἀγαθοποιός *ag-ath-op-oy-os';* from *18* and *4160;* a *well-doer*, i.e. *virtuous:*–them that do well.
18. ἀγαθός, *ag ag-ath-os';* a prim. word; "*good* " (in any sense, often as noun):–benefit, good(-s, things), well. Comp. *2570*.
19. ἀγαθωσύνη *ag-ath-o-soo'-nay;* from *18*; *goodness*, i.e. *virtue* or *beneficence:*–goodness.
20. ἀγαλλιασις *ag-al-lee'-as-is;* from *21*; *exultation*; spec. *welcome:*–gladness, exceeding) joy.
21.ἀγαλλιάω *ag-al-lee-ah'-o;* from ἄγαν (*much*) and *242*; prop. to *jump for joy*, i.e. *exult:*–be (exceeding) glad, with exceeding joy, rejoice (greatly).
22. ἄγαμος *ag'-am-os;* from *1* (as a neg. par.) and *1062*; *unmarried:*–unmarried.
23. ἀγανακτέω *ag-an-ak-teh'-o;* from ἄγαν (*much*) and ἄχθος, (*grief;* akin to the base of *43*);to *be greatly afflicted*, i.e. (fig.) *indignant:*–be much (sore) displeased, have (be moved with, with) indignation.
24. ἀγανάκτησις *ag-an-ak'-tay-sis;* from *23*; *indignation:*–indignation.
25. ἀγαπάω *ag-ap-ah'-o;* perh. from ἄγαν, agan (*much*) [or comp. 5689]; to *love* (in a social or mor. sense):–(be-)love(-ed). Comp. *5368*.
26. ἀγάπη *ag-ah'-pay;* from *25*; *love*, i.e. *affection* or *benevolence;* spec. (pl.) a *love-feast:*–(feast of) charity([-ably]), dear, love.
27. ἀγαπητός *ag-ap-ay-tos;'* from *25; beloved:*–dearly, well) beloved, dear.
28. ʼΆγαρ *ag'-ar;* of Heb. or. [1904]; *Hagar*, the concubine of Abraham:–Hagar.
29. ἀγγαρεύω *ang-ar-yew'-o;* of for. or. [comp. 104]; prop. to *be a courier,* i.e. (by impl.) to *press* into public service:–compel (to go).
30. ἀγγεῖον *ang-eye'-on;* from ἄγγος (a *pail*, perh. as *bent;* comp. the base of *43*); a *receptacle:*–vessel.
31. ἀγγελία *ang-el-ee'-ah; from 32*; an *announcement*, i.e. (by impl.) *precept:*–message.
32. ἄγγελος *ang'-el-os;* from ἀγγέλλω [prob. der. from *71;* comp. *34*] (to *bring tidings*); a *messenger;* esp. an "*angel* "; by impl. a *pastor:*–angel, messenger.
33. ἄγε *ag'-eh;* imper. of *71*; prop. *lead*, i.e. *come* on:–go to.
34. ἀγέλη *ag-el'-ay;* from *71* [comp. *32*]; a *drove:*–herd.
35. ἀγενεαλόγητος *ag-en-eh-al-og'-ay-tos;* from *1* (as neg. par.) and *1075*; *unregistered* as to birth:–without descent.
36. ἀγενής *ag-en-ace';* from *1* (as neg. par.) and *1085*; prop. *without kin*, i.e. (of unknown descent, and by impl.) *ignoble:*–base things.
37. ἁγιάζω *hag-ee-ad'-zo;* from *40;* to *make holy,* i.e. (cer.) *purify* or *consecrate;* (ment.) to *venerate:*–hallow, be holy, sanctify.
38. ἁγιασμός *hag-ee-as-mos';* from *37;* prop. *purification*, i.e. (the state) *purity;* concr. (by Heb.) a *purifier:*–holiness, sanctification.
39. ἅγιον *hag'-ee-on;* neut. of *40;* a *sacred* thing (i.e. spot):–holiest (of all), holy place, sanctuary.
40. ἅγιος *hag'-ee-os;* from ἅγος (an *awful* thing) (comp. *53*, 2282); *sacred* (phys. *pure*, mor. *blameless* or *relig*., cer., *consecrated*):–(most) holy (one, thing), saint.
41. ἁγιότης *hag-ee-ot'-ace;* from *40*; *sanctity* (i.e. prop. the state):–holiness.
42. ἁγιωσύνη *hag-ee-o-soo'-nay;* from *40*; *sacredness* (i.e. prop. the quality):–holiness.
43. ἀγκάλη *ang-kal'-ay;* from ἄγκος (a *bend*, "ache"); an *arm* (as *curved*):–arm.
44. ἄγκιστρον *ang'-kis-tron* from the same as *43;* a *hook* (as *bent*):–hook.
45. ἄγκυρα *ang'-koo-rah;* from the same as *43;* an "*anchor*" (as *crooked*):–anchor.
46. ἄγναφος *ag'-naf-os;* from *1* (as a neg. par.) and the same as *1102;* prop. *unfulled*, i.e. (by impl.) *new* (cloth):–new.
47. ἁγνεία *hag-ni'-ah;* from *53*; *cleanliness* (the quality), i.e. (spec.) *chastity:*–purity.
48. ἁγνίζω *hag-nid'-zo;* from *53*; to *make clean,* i.e. (fig.) *sanctify* (cer. or mor.):–purify (self).
49. ἁγνισμός *hag-nis-mos';* from *48*; a *cleansing* (the act), i.e. (cer.) *lustration:*–purification.
50. ἀγνοέω *ag-no-eh'-o;* from *1* (as a neg. par.) and *3539; =not to know* (through lack of information or intelligence); by impl. to *ignore* (through disinclination):–(be) ignorant(-ly), not know, not understand, unknown.
51. ἀγνόημα *ag-no'–ay-mah;* from *50;* a thing *ignored*, i.e. *shortcoming:*–error.
52. ἄγνοια *ag'-noy-ah;* from *50*; *ignorance* (prop. the quality):–ignorance.
53. ἁγνός *hag-nos;'* from the same as *40*; prop. *clean*, i.e. (fig.) *innocent, modest*, *perfect*:–chaste, clean, pure.
54. ἁγνότης *hag-not'-ace;* from *53; cleanness* (the state), i.e. (fig *blamelessness:*–pureness.
55. ἁγνῶς *hag-noce';* adv. from *53; purely*, i.e. *honestly:*–sincerely.
56. ἀγνωσία *ag-no-see'-ah;* from *1* (as neg. par.) and *1108; ignorance* (prop. the state):–ignorance, not the knowledge.
57. ἄγνωστος *ag'-noce-tos';* from *1* (as neg. par.) and *1110; unknown:*–unknown.
58. ἀγορά *ag-or-ah';* from ἀγείρω (to *gather;* prob. akin to *1453*); prop. the *town-square* (as a place of public resort); by impl. a *market* or *thoroughfare:*–market(-place), street.
59. ἀγοράζω *ag-or-ad'-zo;* from *58;* prop. to *go to market,* i.e. (by impl.) to *purchase;* spec. to *redeem*:–buy, redeem.
60. ἀγοραῖος *ag-or-ah'-yos;* from *58; relating to the market-place,* i.e. *forensic* (times); by impl. *vulgar:*–baser sort, low.
61. ἄγρα *ag'-rah;* from *71;* (abstr.) a *catching* (of fish); also (concr.) a *haul* (of fish):–draught.
62. ἀγράμματος *ag-ram-mat-os;* from *1* (as neg. par.) and *1121; unlettered,* i.e. *illiterate:*–unlearned.
63. ἀγραυλέω *ag-row-leh'-o;* from *68* and *832* (in the sense of *833*); to *camp out:*–abide in the field.
64. ἀγρεύω *ag-rew'-o;* from *61;* to *hunt,* i.e. (fig.) to *entrap:*–catch.
65. ἀγριέλαιος *ag-ree-el'-ah-yos;* from *66* and *1636*; an *oleaster:*–olive tree (which is) wild. ἄγριος *ag'-ree-os;* from *68; wild* (as pertaining to the *country*), lit. (*nat.*) or fig. (*fierce*):–wild, raging.
67. Ἀγρίππας *ag-rip'-pas;* app. from *66* and *2462; wild-horse* tamer; *Agrippas*, one of the Herods:–Agrippa.
68. ἀγρός *ag-ros';* from *71;* a *field* (as a *drive* for cattle); gen. case, the *country;* spec. a *farm*, i.e. *hamlet:*–country, farm, piece of ground, land.
69. ἀγρυπνέω *ag-roop-neh'-o;* ultimately

from *1* (as neg. par.) and *5258;* to *be sleepless,* i.e. *keep awake:*–watch.

70. ἀγρυπνία *ag-roop-nee'-ah;* from *69;* *sleeplessness,* i.e. a *keeping awake:*–watch.

71. ἄγω *ag'-o;* a prim. verb; prop. to *lead;* by impl. to *bring, drive,* (refl.) *go,* (spec.) *pass* (time), or (fig.) *induce:*–be, bring (forth), carry, (let) go, keep, lead away, be open.

72. ἀγωγή *ag-o-gay';* redupl. from *71;* a *bringing* up, i.e. *mode of living:*–manner of life.

73. ἀγών *ag-one';* from *71;* prop. a place of *assembly* (as if *led*), i.e. (by impl.) a *contest* (held there); fig. an *effort* or *anxiety:*–conflict, contention, fight, race.

74. ἀγωνία *ag-o-nee'-ah;* from *73;* a *struggle* (prop. the state), i.e. (fig.) *anguish:*–agony.

75. ἀγωνίζομαι *ag-o-nid'-zom-ahee;* from *73;* to *struggle,* lit. (to *compete* for a prize), fig. (to *contend* with an adversary), or gen. case (to *endeavor* to accomplish something):–fight, labor fervently, strive.

76. 'Αδάμ *ad-am';* of Heb. or. [121]; *Adam,* the first man; typically (of Jesus) *man* (as his representative):–Adam.

77. ἀδάπανος *ad-ap'-an-os;* from *1* (as neg. par.); and *1160;* *costless,* i.e. *gratuitous:*–without expense.

78. 'Αδδί *ad-dee';* prob. of Heb. or. [comp. 5716]; *Addi,* an Isr.:–Addi.

79. ἀδελφή *ad-el-fay';* fem of *80;* a *sister* (nat. or eccl.):–sister.

80. ἀδελφός *ad-el-fos';* from *1* (as a connective par.) and δελφύς (the *womb*); a *brother* (lit. or fig.) near or remote [much like 1]:–brother.

81. ἀδελφότης *ad-el-fot'-ace;* from *80*; *brotherhood* prop. the feeling of *brother-liness*), i.e. the (Chr.) *fraternity:*–brethren, brotherhood.

82. ἄδηλος *ad'-ay-los;* from *1* (as a neg. par.) and 1212; *hidden,* fig. *indistinct:*–appear not, uncertain.

83. ἀδηλότης *ad-ay-lot'-ace;* from *82;* *uncertainty:*–X uncertain.

84. ἀδήλως *ad-ay'-loc;* adv. from 82; *uncert.:*–uncertainly.

85. ἀδημονέω *ad-ay-mon-eh'-o;* from a der. of ἁδέω (to be *sated* to loathing); to *be in distress* (of mind):–be full of heaviness, be very heavy.

86. ᾅδης *hah'-dace;* from *1* (as neg. par.) and 1492; prop. *unseen,* i.e. "*Hades*" or the place (state) of departed souls:–grave, hell.

87. ἀδιάκριτος *ad-ee-ak-'ree-tos;* from *1* (as a neg. par.) and a der. of *1252;* prop. *undistinguished,* i.e. (act.) *impartial:*–without partiality.

88. ἀδιάλειπτος *ad-ee-al'-ipe-tos;* from *1* (as a neg. par.) and a der. of a com. of *1223* and *3007;* *unintermitted,* i.e. *permanent:*–without ceasing, continual.

89. ἀδιαλείπτως *ad-ee-al-ipe'-toce;* adv. from *88;* *uninterruptedly,* i.e. *without omission* (on an appropriate occasion):–without ceasing.

90. ἀδιαφθορία *ad-ee-af-thor-ee'-ah;* from a der. of a com. of *1* (as a neg. par.) and a der. of *1311;* *incorruptibleness,* i.e. (fig.) *purity* (of doctrine):–uncorruptness.

91. ἀδικέω *ad-ee-keh'-o;* from 94; to *be unjust,* i.e. (act.) *do wrong* (mor. socially or phys.):–hurt, injure, be an offender, be unjust, (do, suffer, take) wrong.

92. ἀδίκημα *ad-eek'-ay-mah;* from *91;* a *wrong* done:–evil doing, iniquity, matter of wrong.

93. ἀδικία *ad-ee-kee'-ah;* from *94;* (legal) *injustice* (prop. the quality, by impl. the act); mor. *wrongfulness* (of character, life or act):–iniquity, unjust, unrighteousness, wrong.

94. ἄδικο *ad'-ee-kos;* from *1* (as a neg. par.) and *1349;* *unjust*; by ext. *wicked*; by impl. *treacherous;* spec. *heathen:*–unjust, unrighteous.

95. ἀδίκως *ad-ee'-koc;* adv. from *94;* *unjustly:*–wrongfully.

96. ἀδόκιμος *ad-ok'-ee-mos;* from *1* (as a neg. par.) and *1384;* *unapproved,* i.e. *rejected;* by impl. *worthless* (lit. or mor.):–castaway, rejected, reprobate.

97. ἄδολος *ad'-ol-os;* from *1* (as a neg. par.) and *1388;* *undeceitful,* i.e. (fig.) *unadulterated:*–sincere.

98. 'Αδραμυττηνός *ad-ram-oot-tay-nos';* from 'Αδραμύττειον (a place in Asia Minor); *Adramyttene* or belonging to Adramyttium:–of Adramyttium.

99. 'Αδρίας *ad ad-ree'-as;* from 'Αδρία (a place near its shore); the *Adriatic* sea (incl. the Ionian):–Adria.

100. ἁδρότης *had-rot'-ace;* from ἁδρός (stout); *plumpness,* i.e. (fig.) *liberality:*–abundance.

101. ἀδυνατέω *ad-oo-nat-eh'-o;* from *102;* to *be unable,* i.e. (pass.) *impossible:*–be impossible.

102. ἀδύνατος *ad-oo'-nat-os;* from *1* (as a neg. par.) and *1415;* unable, i.e. *weak* (lit. or fig.); pass. *impossible:*–could not do, impossible, impotent, not possible, weak.

103. ᾄδω *ad'-o;* a prim. Verb; to *sing:*–sing.

104. ἀεί, *ah-eye';* from an obs. prim. noun (app. mean. continued *duration*); "*ever*;" by qualification *regularly;* by impl. *earnestly;* --always, ever.

105. ἀετός *ah-et-os';* from the same as *109;* an *eagle* (from its *wind*-like flight):–eagle.

106. ἄζυμος *ad'-zoo-mos;* from *1* (as a neg. par.) and *2219;* *unleavened,* i.e. (fig.) *uncorrupted*; (in the neutral pl.) spec.. (by impl.) the *Passover* week:–unleavened (bread).

107. 'Αζώρ *ad-zore';* of Heb. or. [comp. 5809]; *Azor,* an Isr.:–Azor.

108. Ἄζωτος *ad'-zo-tos;* of Heb. or. [795]; *Azotus* (i.e. Ashdod), a place in Pal.:–Azotus.

109. ἀήρ *ah-ayr';* from ἄημι aemi (to *breathe* unconsciously, i.e. *respire;* by anal. to *blow*); "air" (as nat. *circumambient*):–air. Comp. *5594.*

110. ἀθανασία *ath-an-as-ee'-ah;* from a com. of *1* (as a neg. par.) and *2288;* *deathlessness:*–immortality.

111. ἀθέμιτος *ath-em'-ee-tos;* from *1* (as a neg. par.) and a der. of θέμις (*statute;* from the base of *5087*); *illegal;* by impl. *flagitious:*–abominable, unlawful thing.

112. ἄθεος *ath'-eh-os;* from *1* (as a neg. par.) and *2316;* *godless:*–without God.

113. ἄθεσμος *ath'-es-mos;* from *1* (as a neg. par.) and a der. of *5087* (in the sense of *enacting*); *lawless*, i.e. (by impl.) *criminal:*–wicked.

114. ἀθετέω *ath-et-eh'-o;* from a com. of *1* (as a neg. par.) and a der. of *5087;* to *set aside,* i.e. (by impl.) to *disesteem, neutralize* or *violate:*–cast off, despise, disannul, frustrate, bring to nought, reject.

115. ἀθέτησις *ath-et'-ay-sis;* from *114;* *cancel-lation* (lit. or fig.):–disannulling, put away.

116. 'Αθῆναι *ath-ay-nahee;* pl. of 'Αθήνη (the goddess of wisdom, who was reputed to have founded the city); *Athenae*, the capitol of Greece:– Athens.

117. 'Αθηναῖος *ath-ay-nah'-yos;* from *116;* an *Athenaean* or inh. of Athenae:–Athenian.

118. ἀθλέω *ath-leh'-o;* from ἄθλος (a *contest* in the public lists); to *contend* in the competitive games:–strive.

119. ἄθλησις *ath'-lay-sis;* from *118;* a *struggle* (fig.):–fight.

120. ἀθυμέω *ath-oo-meh'-o;* from a com. of *1* (as a neg. par.) and *2372;* to *be spiritless*, i.e. *disheartened:*–be dismayed.

121. ἄθωος *ath'-o-os;* from *1* (as a neg. par.) and prob. a der. of *5087* (mean. a *penalty*); *not guilty:*–innocent.

122. αἴγειος *ah'-ee-ghi-os;* from αἴξ (a *goat*); belonging to a *goat:*–goat.

123. αἰγιαλός *ahee-ghee-al-os';* from ἀΐσσω; (to rush) and *251* (in the sense of the *sea*); a *beach* (on which the *waves dash*):–shore.

124. Αἰγύπτιος *ahee-goop'-tee-os;* from *125;* an *Ægyptian* or inh. of Ægyptus:–Egyptian.

125. Αἴγυπτος *ah'-ee-goop-tos;* of unc. der.; *Ægyptus*, the land of the Nile:–Egypt.

126. ἀΐδιος *ah-id'-ee-os;* from *104;* *everduring* (forward and backward, or forward only):–eternal, everlasting.

127. αἰδώς *ahee-doce';* perh. from *1* (as a neg. par.) and *1492* (through the idea of *downcast* eyes); *bashfulness*, i.e. (towards men), *modesty* or (towards God) *awe:*–reverence, shamefacedness.

128. Αἰθίοψ *ahee-thee'-ops;* from Αἴθω aitho (to *scorch*) and ὤψ (the *face*, from *3700*); an *Æthiopian* (as a *blackamoor*):–Ethiopian.

129. αἷμα *hah'-ee-mah;* of unc. der.; *blood,* lit. (of men or animals), fig. (the *juice* of grapes) or spec. (the atoning *blood* of Christ); by impl. *bloodshed,* also *kindred:*–blood.

130. αἱματεκχυσία *hahee-mat-ek-khoo-see'-ah;* from *129* and a der. of *1632;* an *effusion* of *blood:*–shedding of blood.

131. αἱμοῤῥέω *hahee-mor-hreh'-o;* from *129* and *4482*; to *flow blood,* i.e. *have a hemorrhage:*–diseased with an issue of blood.

132. Αἰνέας *ahee-neh'-as;* of unc. der.; Aeneas, an Isr.:–Aeneas.

133. αἴνεσις *ah'-ee-nes-is;* from *134;* a

GREEK

praising (the act), i.e. (spec.) a *thank* (-offering): –praise.

134. αἰνέω *ahee-neh'-o;* from *136;* to *praise* (God):–praise.

135. αἴνιγμα *ah'-ee-nig-ma;* from a der. of *136* (in its prim. sense); an *obscure* saying ("enigma"), i.e. (abstr.) *obscureness:*–X darkly.

136. αἶνος *ah'-ee-nos;* app. a prime word; prop. a *story,* but used in the sense of *1868; praise* (of God):–praise.

137. Αἰνών *ahee-nohn';* of Heb. or. [a der. of 5869, *place of springs*]; *Ænon,* a place in Pal.:–Ænon.

138. αἱρέομαι *hahee-reh'-om-ahee;* prob. akin to *142;* to *take for oneself,* i.e. to *prefer:*–choose. Some of the forms are borrowed from a cognate ἕλλομαι *hel'-lom-ahee;* which is otherwise obs.

139. αἵρεσις *hah'-ee-res-is;* from *138;* prop. a *choice,* i.e. (spec.) a *party* or (abstr.) *disunion:*–heresy [*which is the Gr. word itself*], sect.

140. αἱρετίζω *hahee-ret-id'-zo;* from a der. of *138;* to *make a choice:*–choose.

141. αἱρετικός *hahee-ret-ee-kos';* from the same as *140;* a *schismatic:*–heretic [*the Gr. word itself*].

142. αἴρω *ah'-ee-ro;* a prim. verb; to *lift;* by impl. to *take up* or *away;* fig. to *raise* (the voice), *keep in suspense* (the mind), spec. to *sail* away (i.e. *weigh anchor*); by Heb. [comp. 5375] to *expiate* sin:–away with, bear (up), carry, lift up, loose, make to doubt, put away, remove, take (away, up).

143. αἰσθάνομαι *ahee-sthan'-om-ahee;* of unc. der.; to *apprehend* (prop. by the senses):–perceive.

144. αἴσθησις *ah'-ee-sthay-sis;* from *143; perception,* i.e. (fig.) *discernment:*–judgment.

145. αἰσθητήριον *ahee-sthay-tay'-ree-on;* from a der. of *143;* prop. an *organ of perception,* i.e. (fig.) *judgment:*–senses.

146. αἰσχροκερδής *ahee-skhrok-er-dace';* from *150* and κέρδος (*gain*); *sordid:*–given to (greedy of) filthy lucre.

147. αἰσχροκερδῶς *ahee-skhrok-er-doce';* adv. from *146; sordidly:*–for filthy lucre's sake.

148. αἰσχρολογία *ahee-skhrol-og-ee'-ah;* from *150* and *3056; vile conversation:*–filthy communication.

149. αἰσχρόν *ahee-skhron';* neut. of *150;* a *shameful* thing, i.e. *indecorum:*–shame.

150. αἰσχρός *ahee-skhros';* from the same as *153; shameful,* i.e. *base* (spec. *venal*):–filthy.

151. αἰσχρότης *ahee-skhrot'-ace;* from *150; shamefulness,* i.e. *obscenity:*–filthiness.

152. αἰσχύνη *ahee-skhoo'-nay;* from *153; shame* or *disgrace* (abstr. or concr.):–dishonesty, shame.

153. αἰσχύνομαι *ahee-skhoo'-no;* from αἶσχος (*disfigurement,* i.e. *disgrace*); to *feel shame* (for oneself):–be ashamed.

154. αἰτέω *ahee-teh'-o;* of unc. der.; to *ask* (in gen. case):–ask, beg, call for, crave, desire, require. Comp. *4441.*

155. αἴτημα *ah'-ee-tay-mah;* from *154;* a *thing asked* or (abstr.) an *asking:*–petition, request, required.

156. αἰτία *ahee-tee'-a;* from the same as *154;* a *cause* (as if *asked* for), i.e. (logical) *reason* (motive, matter), (legal) *crime* (alleged or proved):–accusation, case, cause, crime, fault, [wh-]ere[-fore].

157. αἰτίαμα *ahee-tee'-am-ah;* from a der. of *156;* a *thing charged:*–complaint.

158. αἴτιον *ah'-ee-tee-on;* neut. of *159;* a *reason* or *crime* [like 156]:–cause, fault.

159. αἴτιος *ah'-ee-tee-os;* from the same as *154; caus.* i.e. (concr.) a *causer:*–author.

160. αἰφνίδιος *aheef-nid'-ee-os;* from a com. of *1* (as a neg. par.) and *5316* comp. *1810*] (mean. *non-app.*); *unexpected,* i.e. (adv.) *suddenly:*–sudden, unawares.

161. αἰχμαλωσία *aheekh-mal-o-see'-ah;* from *164; captivity:*–captivity.

162. αἰχμαλωτεύω *aheekh-mal-o-tew'-o;* from *164;* to *capture* like *163*]:–lead captive.

163. αἰχμαλωτίζω *aheekh-mal-o-tid'-zo;* from *164;* to *make captive:*–lead away captive, bring into captivity.

164. αἰχμαλωτός *aheekh-mal-o-tos';* from αἰχμή (a *spear*) and a der. of the same as *259;* prop. a *prisoner of war,* i.e. (gen. case) a *captive:*–captive.

165. αἰών *ahee-ohn';* from the same as *104;* prop. an *age;* by ext., *perpetuity* (also past); by impl. the *world;* spec. (Jewish) a Messianic period (pres. or fut.):–age, course, eternal, (for) ever(-more), [n-]ever, (beginning of the, while the) world (began, without end). Comp. 5550.

166. αἰώνιος *ahee-o'-nee-os;* from *165; perpetual* (also used of past time, or past and fut. as well):–eternal, for ever, everlasting, world (began).

167. ἀκαθαρσία *ak-ath-ar-see'-ah;* from *169; impurity* (the quality), phys. or mor.:–uncleanness.

168. ἀκαθάρτης *ak-ath-ar'-tace;* from *169; impurity* (the state), mor.:–filthiness.

169. ἀκάθαρτος *ak-ath'-ar-tos;* from *1* (as a neg. par.) and a presumed der. of *2508* (mean. *cleansed*); *impure* (cer., mor. [*lewd*] or spec. [*demonic*]):–foul, unclean.

170. ἀκαιρέομαι *ak-ahee-reh'-om-ahee;* from a com. of *1* (as a neg. par.) and *2540* (mean. *unseasonable*); to *be inopportune* (for oneself), i.e. to *fail of a proper occasion:*–lack opportunity.

171. ἀκαίρως *ak-ah'-ee-roce;* adv. from the same as *170; inopportunely:*–out of season.

172. ἄκακος *ak'-ak-os;* from *1* (as a neg. par.) and *2556; not bad,* i.e. (obj.) *innocent* or (subj.) *unsuspecting:*–harmless, simple.

173. ἄκακος *ak'-an-thah;* prob. from the same as *188;* a *thorn:*–thorn.

174. ἀκάνθινος *ak-an'-thee-nos;* from *173; thorny:*–of thorns.

175. ἄκαρπος *ak'-ar-pos;* from *1* (as a neg. par.) and *2590; barren* (lit. or fig.):–without fruit, unfruitful.

176. ἀκατάγνωστος *ak-at-ag'-noce-tos;* from *1* (as a neg. par.) and a der. of *2607; unblamable:*–that cannot be condemned.

177. ἀκατακάλυπτος *ak-at-ak-al'-oop-tos;* from *1* (as a neg. par.) and a der. of a com. of *2596* and *2572; unveiled:*–uncovered.

178. ἀκατάκριτος *ak-at-ak'-ree-tos;* from *1* (as a neg. par.) and a der. of *2632; without* (legal) *trial:*–uncondemned.

179. ἀκατάλυτος *ak-at-al'-oo-tos;* from *1* (as a neg. par.) and a der. of *2647; indissoluble,* i.e. (fig.) *permanent:*–endless.

180. ἀκατάπαυστος *ak-at-ap'-ow-stos;* from *1* (as a neg. par.) and a der. of *2664; unrefraining:*–that cannot cease.

181. ἀκαταστασία *ak-at-as-tah-see'-ah;* from *182; instability,* i.e. *disorder:*–commotion, confusion, tumult.

182. ἀκατάστατος *ak-at-as'-tat-os;* from *1* (as a neg. par.) and a der. of *2525; inconstant:*–unstable.

183. ἀκατάσχετος *ak-at-as'-khet-os;* from *1* (as a neg. par.) and a der. of *2722; unrestrainable:*–unruly.

184. Ἀκελδαμά *ak-el-dam-ah';* of Chald. or. [mean. *field of blood*; cor. to 2506 and 1818]; *Akeldama,* a place near Jerus.:–Aceldama.

185. ἀκέραιος *ak-er'-ah-yos;* from *1* (as a neg. par.) and a presumed der. of *2767; unmixed,* i.e. (fig.) *innocent:*–harmless, simple.

186. ἀκλινής *ak-lee-nace';* from *1* (as a neg. par.) and *2827; not leaning,* i.e. (fig.) *firm:*–without wavering.

187. ἀκμάζω *ak-mad'-zo;* from the same as *188;* to *make a point,* i.e. (fig.) *mature:*–be fully ripe.

188. ἀκμήν *ak-mane';* acc. of a noun ("*acme*") akin to ἀκή (a *point*) and mean. the same; adv. *just* now, i.e. *still:*–yet.

189. ἀκοή *ak-o-ay';* from *191*; *hearing* (the act, the sense or the thing heard):–audience, ear, fame, which ye heard, hearing, preached, report, rumor.

190. ἀκολουθέω *ak-ol-oo-theh'-o;* from *1* (as a par. of union) and κέλευθος (a *road*); prop. to be *in the same way with,* i.e. to *accompany* (spec. as a disciple):–follow, reach.

191. ἀκούω *ak-oo'-o;* a prim. verb; to *hear* (in various senses):–give (in the) audience (of), come (to the ears), ([shall]) hear(-er, -ken), be noised, be reported, understand.

192. ἀκρασία *ak-ras-ee'-a;* from *193*; *want of self-restraint:*–excess, incontinency.

193. ἀκράτης *ak-rat'-ace;* from *1* (as a neg. par.) and *2904; powerless,* i.e. *without self-control:*–incontinent.

194. ἄκρατος *ak'-rat-os;* from *1* (as a neg. par.) and a presumed der. of *2767; undiluted:*–without mixture.

195. ἀκρίβεια *ak-ree'-bi-ah;* from the same as *196; exactness:*–perfect manner.

196. ἀκρίβέστατος *ak-ree-bes'-ta-tos;* sup. of ἀκρίβης (a der. of the same as *206); most exact:*–most straitest.

197. ἀκριβέστερον *ak-ree-bes'-ter-on;* neut.

of the comp. of the same as *196;* (adv.) *more exactly:*–more perfect(-ly).

198. ἀκριβόω *ak-ree-bo'-o;* from the same as *196;* to *be exact,* i.e. *ascertain:*–enquire diligently.

199. ἀκριβῶς *ak-ree-boce';* adv. from the same as *196; exactly:*–circumspectly, diligently, perfect(-ly).

200. ἀκρίς *ak-rece';* app. from the same as *206;* a *locust* (as *pointed,* or as *lighting* on the *top* of vegetation):–locust.

201. ἀκροατήριον *ak-ro-at-ay'-ree-on;* from *202;* an *audience-room:*–place of hearing.

202. ἀκροατής *ak-ro-at-ace';* from ἀκροάομαι (to *listen;* app. an intens. of *191*); a *hearer* (merely):–hearer.

203. ἀκροβυστία *ak-rob-oos-tee'-ah;* from *206* and prob. a modif. form of πόσθη (the *penis* or male sexual organ); the *prepuce;* by aplication, an *uncircumcised* (i.e. *gentile,* fig. *unregenerate*) state or pers.:–not circumcised, uncircumcised [with *2192*], uncircumcision.

204. ἀκρογωνιαῖος *ak-rog-o-nee-ah'-yos;* from *206* and *1137;* belonging to the extreme *corner:*–chief corner.

205. ἀκροθίνιον *ak-roth-in'-ee-on;* from *206* and θίς this (a *heap*); prop. (in the pl.) the *top of the heap,* i.e. (by impl.) *best of the booty:*–spoils.

206. ἄκρον *ak'-ron;* neut. of an adj. prob. akin to the base of *188;* the *extremity:*–one end... other, tip, top, uttermost part.

207. Ἀκύλας *ak-oo'-las;* prob. for Lat. *aquila* (an *eagle*); *Akulas,* an Isr.:–Aquila.

208. ἀκυρόω *ak-oo-ro'-o;* from *1* (as a neg. par.) and *2964;* to *invalidate:*–disannul, make of none effect.

209. ἀκωλύτως *ak-o-loo'-toce;* adv. from a com. of *1* (as a neg. par.) and a der. of *2967;* in *an unhindered manner,* i.e. *freely:*–no man forbidding him.

210. ἄκων *ak'-ohn;* from *1* (as a neg. par.) and *1635; unwilling:*–against the will.

211. ἀλάβαστρον *al-ab'-as-tron;* neut. of ἀλάβαστρος (of unc. der.), the name of a stone; prop. an "*alabaster*" box, i.e. (by ext.) a perfume *vase* (of any material):–(alabaster) box.

212. ἀλαζονεία *al-ad-zon-i'-a;* from *213; braggadocio,* i.e. (by impl.) *self-confidence:*–boasting, pride.

213. ἀλαζών *al-ad-zone';* from ἄλη (*vagrancy*); *braggart:*–boaster.

214. ἀλαλάζω *al-al-ad'-zo;* from ἀλαλή (a *shout,* "*halloo*"); to *vociferate,* i.e. (by impl.) to *wail;* fig. to *clang:*–tinkle, wail.

215. ἀλάλητος *al-al'-ay-tos;* from *1* (as a neg. par.) and a der. of *2980; unspeakable:*–unutterable, which cannot be uttered.

216. ἄλαλος *al'-al-os;* from *1* (as a neg. par.) and *2980; mute:*–dumb.

217. ἅλας *hal'-as;* from *251; salt;* fig. *prudence:*–salt.

218. ἀλείφω *al-i'-fo;* from *1* (as par. of union) and the base of *3045;* to *oil* (with perfume):–anoint.

219. ἀλεκτοροφωνία *al-ek-tor-of-o-nee'-ah;* from *220* and *5456; cock-crow,* i.e. the third night-watch:–cockcrowing.

220. ἀλέκτωρ *al-ek'-tore;* from ἀλέκω (to *ward* off); a *cock* or male fowl:–cock.

221. Ἀλεξανδρεύς *al-ex-and-reuce';* from Ἀλεξάνδρεια (the city so called); an *Alexandreian* or inh. of Alexandria:–of Alexandria, Alexandrian.

222. Ἀλεξανδρίνος *al-ex-an-dree'-nos;* from the same as 221; *Alexandrine,* or belonging to Alexandria:–of Alexandria.

223. Ἀλέξανδρος *al-ex'-an-dros;* from the same as (the first part of) *220* and *435; man-defender; Alexander,* the name of three Isr. and one other man:–Alexander.

224. ἄλευρον *al'-yoo-ron;* from ἀλέω (to *grind*); *flour:*–meal.

225. ἀλήθεια *al-ay'-thi-a;* from *227; truth:*–true, X truly, truth, verity.

226. ἀληθεύω *al-ayth-yoo'-o;* from *227;* to *be true* (in doctrine and profession):–speak (tell) the truth.

227. ἀληθής *al-ay-thace';* from *1* (as a neg. par.) and *2990; true* (as *not concealing*):–true, truly, truth.

228. ἀληθινός *al-ay-thee-nos';* from *227; truthful:*–true.

229. ἀλήθω *al-ay'-tho;* the same as *224;* to *grind:*–grind.

230. ἀληθῶς *al-ay-thoce';* adv. from *227; truly:*–indeed, surely, of a surety, truly, of a (in) truth, verily, very.

231. ἁλιεύς *hal-ee-yoos';* from *251;* a *sailor* (as engaged on the *salt* water), i.e. (by impl.) a *fisher:*–fisher(-man).

232. ἁλιεύω *hal-ee-yoo'-o;* from *231;* to *be a fisher,* i.e. (by impl.) to *fish:*–go a-fishing.

233. ἁλίζω *hal-id'-zo;* from *251;* to *salt:*–salt.

234. ἀλίσγεμα *al-is'-ghem-ah;* from ἀλισγέω (to *soil*); (cer.) *defilement:*–pollution.

235. ἀλλά *al-lah';* neut. pl. of *243;* prop. *other* things, i.e. (adv.) *contrariwise* (in many relations):–and, but (even), howbeit, indeed, nay, nevertheless, no, notwithstanding, save, therefore, yea, yet.

236. ἀλλάσσω *al-las'-so;* from *243;* to *make different:*–change.

237. ἀλλαχόθεν *al-lakh-oth'-en;* from *243; from elsewhere:*–some other way.

238. ἀλληγορέω *al-lay-gor-eh'-o;* from *243* and ἀγορέω (to *harangue* [comp. *58*]); to *allegorize:*–be an allegory [*the Gr. word itself*].

239 ἀλληλουΐα *al-lay-loo'-ee-ah;* of Heb. or. [imper. of 1984 and 3050]; *praise ye Jah!,* an adoring exclamation:–alleluiah.

240. ἀλλήλων *al-lay'-lone;* gen. pl. from *243* redupl.; *one another:*–each other, mutual, one another, (the other), (them-, your-)selves, (selves) together [*sometimes with 3326 or 4314*].

241. ἀλλογενής *al-log-en-ace';* from *243* and *1085; for.* i.e. not a Jew:–stranger.

242. ἅλλομαι *hal'-lom-ahee;* mid. of app. a prim. verb; to *jump;* fig. to *gush:*–leap, spring up.

243. ἄλλος *al'-los* prim. word; "*else,*" i.e. *different* (in many appl.):–more, one (another), (an-, some an-)other(-s, -wise).

244. ἀλλοτριεπίσκοπο *al-lot-ree-ep-is'-kop-os;* from *245* and *1985*; *overseeing others' affairs,* i.e. a *meddler* (spec. in Gentile customs):–busybody in other men's matters.

245. ἀλλότριος *al-lot'-ree-os;* from *243; another's,* i.e. not one's own; by ext. *for. not akin, hostile:*–alien, (an-)other (man's, men's), strange(-r).

246. ἀλλόφυλος *al-lof'-oo-los;* from *243* and *5443; for.* i.e. (spec.) *Gentile:*–one of another nation.

247. ἄλλως *al'-loce;* adv. from *243; differently:*–otherwise.

248. ἀλοάω *al-o-ah'-o;* from the same as *257;* to *tread* out grain:–thresh, tread out the corn.

249. ἄλογος *al'-og-os;* from *1* (as a neg. par.) and *3056; irrational:*–brute, unreasonable.

250. ἀλοή *al-o-ay';* of for. or. (comp. 174); *aloes* (the gum):–aloes.

251. ἅλς *halce;* a prim. word; "*salt*":–salt.

252. ἁλυκός *hal-oo-kos';* from *251; briny:*–salt.

253. ἀλυπότερος *al-oo-pot'-er-os;* comparison of a com. of *1* (as a neg. par.) and *3077; more without grief:*–less sorrowful.

254. ἅλυσις *hal'-oo-sis;* of unc. der.; a *fetter* or *manacle:*–bonds, chain.

255. ἀλυσιτελής *al-oo-sit-el-ace';* from *1* (as a neg. par.) and the base of *3081; gainless,* i.e. (by impl.) *pernicious:*–unprofitable.

256. Ἀλφαῖος *al-fah'-yos;* of Heb. or. (comp. 2501); *Alphoeus,* an Isr.:–Alpheus.

257. ἅλων *hal'-ohn;* prob. from the base of *1507;* a threshing-*floor* (as *rolled* hard), i.e. (fig.) the *grain* (and chaff, as just threshed):–floor.

258. ἀλώπηξ *al-o'-pakes;* of unc. der.; a *fox,* i.e. (fig.) a *cunning* pers.:–fox.

259. ἅλωσις *hal'-o-sis;* from a coll. form of *138; capture,* be taken.

260. ἅμα *ham'-ah;* a prim. par.; prop. *at the "same" time,* but freely used as a prep. or adv. denoting close association:–also, and, together, with(-al).

261. ἀμαθής *am-ath-ace';* from *1* (as a neg. par.) and *3129; ignorant:*–unlearned.

262. ἀμαράντινος *am-ar-an'-tee-nos;* from *263; "amaranthine",* i.e. (by impl.) *fadeless:*–that fadeth not away.

263. ἀμάραντος *am-ar'-an-tos;* from *1* (as a neg. par.) and a presumed der. of *3133; unfading,* i.e. (by impl.) *perpetual:*–that fadeth not away.

264. ἁμαρτάνω *ham-ar-tan'-o;* perh. from *1* (as a neg. par.) and the base of *3313;* prop. to *miss* the mark (and so *not share* in the prize), i.e. (fig.) to *err,* esp. (mor.) to *sin.*–for your faults, offend, sin, trespass.

265. ἁμάρτημα *ham-ar'-tay-mah;* from *264;* a *sin* (prop. concr.):–sin.

266. ἁμαρτία *ham-ar-tee'-ah;* from *264;* a *sin* (prop. abstr.):–offence, sin(-ful).

267. ἀμάρτυρος *am-ar'-too-ros;* from *1* (as

GREEK

a neg. par.) and a form of *3144; unattested:*–without witness.

268. ἁμαρτωλός *ham-ar-to-los'*; from *264; sinful*, i.e. a *sinner:*–sinful, sinner.

269. ἄμαχος *am'-akh-os;* from *1* (as a neg. par.) and *3163; peaceable:*–not a brawler.

270. ἀμάω *am-ah'-o;* from *260;* prop. to *collect,* i.e. (by impl.) *reap:*–reap down.

271. ἀμέθυστος *am-eth'-oos-tos;* from *1* (as a neg. par.) and a der. of *3184;* the "*amethyst*" (supposed to *prevent intoxication*):–amethyst.

272. ἀμελέω *am-el-eh'-o;* from *1* (as a neg. par.) and *3199;* to *be careless* of:–make light of, neglect, be negligent, not regard.

273. ἄμεμπτος *am'-emp-tos;* from *1* (as a neg. par.) and a der. of *3201; irreproachable:*–blameless,faultless, unblamable.

274. ἀμέμπτως *am-emp'-toce;* adv. from *273; faultlessly:*–blameless, unblamably.

275. ἀμέριμνος *am-er'-im-nos;* from *1* (as a neg. par.) and *3308; not anxious:*–without care(-fulness), secure.

276. ἀμετάθετος *am-et-ath'-et-os;* from *1* (as a neg. par.) and a der. of *3346; unchangeable,* or (neut. as abstr.) *unchangeability:*–immutable(-ility).

277. ἀμετακίνητος *am-et-ak-in'-ay-tos;* from *1* (as a neg. par.) and a der. of *3334; immovable:*–unmovable.

278. ἀμεταμέλητος *am-et-am-el'-ay-tos;* from *1* (as a neg. par.) and a presumed der. of *3338; irrevocable:*–without repentance, not to be repented of.

279. ἀμετανόητος *am-et-an-o'-ay-tos;* from *1* (as a neg. par.) and a presumed der. of *3340; unrepentant:*–impenitent.

280. ἄμετρος *am'-et-ros;* from *1* (as a neg. par.) and *3358; immoderate:*–(thing) without measure.

281. ἀμήν *am-ane';* of Heb. or. [543]; prop. *firm,* i.e. (fig.) *trustworthy;* adv. *surely* (often as interj. *so be it*):–amen, verily.

282. ἀμήτωρ *am-ay'-tore;* from *1* (as a neg. par.) and *3384; motherless,* i.e. of *unknown maternity:*–without mother.

283. ἀμίαντος *am-ee'-an-tos;* from *1* (as a neg. par.) and a der. of *3392; unsoiled,* i.e. (fig.) *pure:*–undefiled.

284. Ἀμιναδάβ *am-ee-nad-ab';* of Heb. or. [5992]; *Aminadab,* an Isr.:–Aminadab.

285. ἄμμος *am'-mos;* perh. from *260; sand* (as *heaped* on the beach):–sand.

286. ἀμνός *am-nos';* app. a prim. word; a *lamb:*–lamb.

287. ἀμοιβή *am-oy-bay';* from ἀμείβω (to *exchange*); *requital:*–requite.

288. ἄμπελος *am'-pel-os;* prob. from the base of *297* and that of *257;* a *vine* (as *coiling about* a support):–vine.

289. ἀμπελουργός *am-pel-oor-gos';* from *288* and *2041;* a *vine-worker,* i.e. *pruner:*–vine-dresser.

290. ἀμπελών *am-pel-ohn';* from *288;* a *vineyard:*–vineyard.

291. Ἀμπλίας *am-plee'-as;* contr. for Lat. *ampliatus* [*enlarged*]; *Amplias*, a Rom. Chr.:–Amplias.

292. ἀμύνομαι *am-oo'-nom-ahee;* mid. of a prim. verb; to *ward off* (for oneself), i.e. *protect:*–defend.

293. ἀμφίβληστρον *am-fib'-lace-tron;* from a com. of the base of *297* and *906;* a (fishing) *net* (as *thrown about* the fish):–net.

294. ἀμφιέννυμι *am-fee-en'-noo-mee;* from the base of *297* and ἕννυμι (to *invest*); to *enrobe:*–clothe.

295. Ἀμφίπολις *am-fip'-ol-is;* from the base of *297* and *4172;* a *city surrounded* by a river; *Amphipolis,* a place in Macedonia:–Amphipolis

296. ἄμφοδον *am'-fod-on;* from the base of *297* and *3598;* a *fork* in the road:–where two ways meet.

297. ἀμφότερος *am-fot'-er-os;* comp. of ἀμφί amphi (*around*); (in pl.) *both:*–both.

298. ἀμώμητος, *am-o'-may-tos;* from 1 (as a neg. par.) and a der. of *3469; unblamable:*–blameless.

299. ἄμωμος *am'-o-mos;* from *1* (as a neg. par.) and *3470; unblemished* (lit. or fig.):–without blame (blemish, fault, spot), faultless, unblamable.

300. Ἀμών *am-one';* of Heb. or. [526]; *Amon,* an Isr.:–Amon.

301. Ἀμώς, *am-oce'* of Heb. or. [531]; *Amos,* an Isr.:–Amos.

302. ἄν*an;* a prim. par., denoting a supposition, wish, possibility or uncertainty:–[what-, where-, wither-, who]-soever]. Usually unexpressed except by the subjunctive or potential mood. Also contr. for 1437.

303. ἀνά *an-ah';* a prim. prep. and adv.; prop. *up;* but (by ext.) used (distributively) *severally,* or (locally) *at* (etc.):–and, apiece, by, each, every (man), in, through. In com. (as a pref.) it often means (by impl.) *repetition, intensity, reversal,* etc.

304. ἀναβαθμός *an-ab-ath-mos';* from *305* [comp. *898*]; a *stairway:*–stairs.

305. ἀναβαίνω *an-ab-ah'-ee-no;* from *303* and the base of *939;* to *go up* (lit. or fig.):–arise, ascend (up), climb (go, grow, rise, spring) up, come (up).

306. ἀναβάλλομαι *an-ab-al'-lom-ahee;* mid. from *303* and *906;* to *put off* (for oneself):–defer.

307. ἀναβιβάζω *an-ab-ee-bad'-zo;* from *303* and a der. of the base of *939;* to *cause to go up,* i.e. *haul* (a net):–draw.

308. ἀναβλέπω *an-ab-lep'-o;* from *303* and *991;* to *look up;* by impl. to *recover sight:*–look (up), see, receive sight.

309. ἀνάβλεψις *an-ab'-lep-sis;* from *308; restoration of sight:*–recovery of sight.

310. ἀναβοάω *an-ab-o-ah'-o;* from *303* and *994;* to *halloo:*–cry (aloud, out).

311. ἀναβολή *an-ab-ol-ay';* from *306;* a *putting off:*–delay.

312. ἀναγγέλλω *an-ang-el'-lo;* from *303* and the base of *32;* to *announce* (in detail):–declare, rehearse, report, show, speak, tell.

313. ἀναγεννάω *an-ag-en-nah'-o;* from *303* and *1080;* to *beget* or (by ext.) *bear* (again):–beget, (bear) X (again).

314. ἀναγινώσκω *an-ag-in-oce'-ko;* from *303* and *1097;* to *know again*, i.e. (by ext.) to *read:*–read.

315. ἀναγκάζω *an-ang-kad'-zo;* from *318;* to *necessitate:*–compel, constrain.

316. ἀναγκαῖος *an-ang-kah'-yos* from *318; necessary;* by impl. *close* (of kin):–near, necessary, necessity, needful.

317. ἀναγκαστῶς *an-ang-kas-toce';* adv. from a der. of *315; compulsorily:*–by constraint.

318. ἀναγκή *an-ang-kay';* from *303* and the base of *43; constraint* (lit. or fig.); by impl. *distress:*–distress, must needs, (of) necessity(-sary), needeth, needful.

319. ἀναγνωρίζομαι *an-ag-no-rid'-zom-ahee;* mid. from *303* and *1107;* to *make* (oneself) *known:*–be made known.

320. ἀνάγνωσις *an-ag'-no-sis;* from *314;* (the act of) *reading:*–reading

321. ἀνάγω *an-ag'-o;* from *303* and *71;* to *lead up;* by ext. to *bring out;* spec. to *sail* away:–bring (again, forth, up again), depart, launch (forth), lead (up), loose, offer, sail, set forth, take up.

322. ἀναδείκνυμι *an-ad-ike'-noo-mee;* from *303* and *1166;* to *exhibit,* i.e. (by impl.) to *indicate, appoint:*–appoint, shew.

323. ἀνάδειξις *an-ad'-ike-sis;* from *322;* (the act of) *exhibition:*–shewing.

324. ἀναδέχομαι *an-ad-ekh'-om-ahee;* from *303* and *1209;* to *entertain* (as a guest):–receive.

325. ἀναδίδωμι *an-ad-eed'-om-ee;* from *303* and *1325;* to *hand over:*–deliver.

326. ἀναζάω *an-ad-zah'-o;* to *recover life* (lit. or fig.):–(be a-)live again, revive.

327. ἀναζητέω *an-ad-zay-teh'-o;* from *303* and *2212;* to *search* out:–seek.

328. ἀναζώννυμι *an-ad-zone'-noo-mee;* from *303* and *2224;* to *gird afresh:*–gird up.

329. ἀναζωπυρέω *an-ad-zo-poor-eh'-o;* from *303* and a com. of the base of *2226* and *4442;* to *re-enkindle:*–stir up.

330. ἀναθάλλω *an-ath-al'-lo;* from *303* and θάλλω (to *flourish*); to *revive:*–flourish again.

331. ἀνάθεμα *an-ath'-em-ah;* from *394;* a (relig.) *ban* or (concr.) *excommunicated* (thing or pers.):–accused, anathema, curse, X great.

332. ἀναθεματίζω *an-ath-em-at-id'-zo;* from *331;* to *declare* or *vow* under penalty of execration:–(bind under a) curse, bind with an oath.

333. ἀναθεωρέω *an-ath-eh-o-reh'-o;* from *303* and *2334;* to *look again* (i.e. *attentively*) at (lit. or fig.):–behold, consider.

334. ἀνάθημα *an-ath'-ay-mah;* from *394* [like *331*, but in a good sense]; a *votive* offering:–gift.

335. ἀναίδεια *an-ah'-ee-die-ah';* from a com. of *1* (as a neg. par. [comp. 427]) and *127; impudence,* i.e. (by impl.) *importunity:*–importunity.

336. ἀναίρεσις *an-ah'-ee-res-is;* from *337;* (the act of) *killing:*–death.

337. ἀναιρέω *an-ahee-reh'-o*; from *303* and (the act. of) *138;* to *take up,* i.e. *adopt;* by impl. to *take away* (violently), i.e. *abolish, murder:*–put to death, kill, slay, take away, take up.

338. ἀναίτιος *an-ah'-ee-tee-os;* from *1* (as a neg. par.) and *159* (in the sense of *156*); *innocent:*–blameless, guiltless.

339. ἀνακαθίζω *an-ak-ath-id'-zo;* from *303* and *2523;* prop. to *set up,* i.e. (refl.) to *sit up:*–sit up.

340. ἀνακαινίζω *an-ak-ahee-nid'-zo;* from *303* and a der. of *2537;* to *restore:*–renew.

341. ἀνακαινόω *an-ak-ahee-no'-o;* from *303* and a der. of *2537;* to *renovate:*–renew.

342. ἀνακαίνωσις *an-ak-ah'-ee-no-sis;* from *341; renovation:*–renewing.

343. ἀνακαλύπτω *an-ak-al-oop'-to;* from *303* (in the sense of *reversal*) and *2572;* to *unveil:*–open, ([un-]) taken away.

344. ἀνακάμπτω *an-ak-amp'-to;* from *303* and *2578;* to *turn back:*–(re-)turn.

345. ἀνακεῖμαι *an-ak-i'-mahee;* from *303* and *2749;* to *recline* (as a corpse or at a meal):–guest, lean, lie, sit (down, at meat), at the table.

346. ἀνακεφαλαίομαι *an-ak-ef-al-ah'-ee-om-ahee;* from *303* and *2775* (in its or. sense); to *sum up:*–briefly comprehend, gather together in one.

347. ἀνακλίνω *an-ak-lee'-no;* from *303* and *2827;* to *lean back:*–lay, (make) sit down.

348. ἀνακόπτω *an-ak-op'-to;* from *303* and *2875;* to *beat back,* i.e. *check:*–hinder.

349. ἀνακράζω *an-ak-rad'-zo;* from *303* and *2896;* to *scream up* (aloud):–cry out.

350. ἀνακρίνω *an-ak-ree'-no;* from *303* and *2919;* prop. to *scrutinize*, i.e. (by impl.) *investigate, interrogate, determine:*–ask, question, discern, examine, judge, search.

351. ἀνάκρισις, *an-ak'-ree-sis;* from *350;* a (judicial) *investigation:*–examination.

352. ἀνακύπτω *an-ak-oop'-to;* from *303* (in the sense of *reversal*) and *2955;* to *unbend,* i.e. *rise;* fig. *be elated:*–lift up, look up.

353. ἀναλαμβάνω *an-al-am-ban'-o;* from *303* and *2983;* to *take up:*–receive up, take (in, unto, up).

354. ἀνάληψις *an-al'-ape-sis;* from *353; ascension:*–taking up.

355. ἀναλίσκω *an-al-is'-ko; from 303 and a form of the alt. of 138*; prop. to *use up,* i.e. *destroy:*–consume.

356. ἀναλογία *an-al-og-ee'-ah;* from a com. of *303* and *3056; proportion:*–proportion.

357. ἀναλογίζομαι *an-al-og-id'-zom-ahee;* mid. from *356;* to *estimate,* i.e. (fig.) *contemplate:*–consider.

358. ἄναλος *an'-al-os;* from *1* (as a neg. par.) and *251; saltless,* i.e. *insipid:*–X lose saltness.

359. ἀνάλυσις *an-al'-oo-sis;* from *360; departure:*–departure.

360. ἀναλύω *an-al-oo'-o;* from *303* and *3089;* to *break up,* i.e. *depart* (lit. or fig.):–depart, return.

361. ἀναμάρτητος *an-am-ar'-tay-tos;* from *1* (as a neg. par.) and a presumed der. of *264; sinless:*–i.e. that is without sin.

362. ἀναμένω *an-am-en'-o;* from *303* and *3306;* to *await:*–wait for.

363. ἀναμιμνήσκω *an-am-im-nace'-ko;* from *303* and *3403;* to *remind;* (refl.) to *recollect:*–call to mind, (bring to, call to, put in), remember(-brance).

364. ἀνάμνησις *an-am'-nay-sis;* from *363; recollection:*–*remembrance* (again).

365. ἀνανεόω *an-an-neh-o'-o;* from *303* and a der. of *3501;* to *renovate,* i.e. *reform:*–renew.

366. ἀνανήφω *an-an-ay'-fo;* from *303* and *3525;* to become *sober again,* i.e. (fig.) *regain* (one's) *senses:*–recover self.

367. Ἀνανίας *an-an-ee'-as;* of Heb. or. [2608]; *Ananias,* the name of three Isr.:–Ananias.

368. ἀναντίῤῥητος *an-an-tir'-hray-tos* from *1* (as a neg. par.) and a presumed der. of a com. of *473* and *4483; indisputable:*–cannot be spoken against.

369. ἀναντιῤῥήτως *an-an-tir-hray'-toce;* adv. from *368; promptly:*–without gainsaying.

370. ἀνάξιος *an-ax'-ee-os;* from *1* (as a neg. par.) and *514; unfit:*–unworthy.

371. ἀναξίως, *an-ax-ee'-oce;* adv. from *370; irreverently:*–unworthily.

372. ἀνάπαυσις *an-ap'-ow-sis;* from *373; intermission;* by impl. *recreation:*–rest.

373. ἀναπαύω *an-ap-ow'-o;* from *303* and *3973;* (refl.) to *repose* (lit. or fig. [*be exempt*], *remain*); by impl. to *refresh:*–take ease, refresh, (give, take) rest.

374. ἀναπείθω *an-ap-i'-tho;* from *303* and *3982;* to *incite:*–persuade.

375. ἀναπέμπω *an-ap-em'-po;* from *303* and *3992;* to *send up* or *back:*–send (again).

376. ἀνάπηρος *an-ap'-ay-ros;* from *303* (in the sense of *intensity*) and πῆρος (*maimed*); *crippled:*–maimed.

377. ἀναπίπτω *an-ap-ip'-to;* from *303* and *4098;* to *fall back,* i.e. *lie down, lean back:*–lean, sit down (to meat).

378. ἀναπληρόω *an-ap-lay-ro'-o;* from *303* and *4137;* to *complete;* by impl. to *occupy, supply;* fig. to *accomplish* (by coincidence or obedience):–fill up, fulfill, occupy, supply.

379. ἀναπολόγητος *an-ap-ol-og'-ay-tos;* from *1* (as a neg. par.) and a presumed der. of *626; indefensible:*–without an excuse, inexcusable.

380. ἀναπτύσσω *an-ap-toos'-o;* from *303* (in the sense of *reversal*) and *4428;* to *unroll* (a scroll or volume):–open.

381. ἀνάπτω *an-ap'-to;* from *303* and *681;* to *enkindle:*–kindle, light.

382. ἀναρίθμητος *an-ar-ith'-may-tos;* from *1* (as a neg. par.) and a der. of *705; unnumbered,* i.e. *without number:*–innumerable.

383. ἀνασείω *an-as-i'-o;* from *303* and *4579;* fig. to *excite:*–move, stir up.

384. ἀνασκευάζω *an-ask-yoo-ad'-zo;* from *303* (in the sense of *reversal*) and a der. of *4632;* prop. to *pack up* (baggage), i.e. (by impl. and fig.) to *upset:*–subvert.

385. ἀνασπάω *an-as-pah'-o;* from *303* and *4685;* to *take up* or *extricate:*–draw up, pull out.

386. ἀνάστασις *an-as'-tas-is;* from *450*; a *standing up* again, i.e. (lit.) a *resurrection* from death (indiv., gen. case or by impl. [its author]), or (fig.) a (mor.) *recovery* (of spir. truth):–raised to life again, resurrection, rise from the dead, that should rise, rising again.

387. ἀναστατόω *an-as-tat-o'-o;* from a der. of 450 (in the sense of *removal*); prop. to *drive out* of home, i.e. (by impl.) to *disturb* (lit. or fig.):–trouble, turn upside down, make an uproar.

388. ἀνασταυρόω *an-as-tow-ro'-o;* from *303* and *4717;* to *recrucify* (fig.):–crucify afresh.

389. ἀναστενάζω *an-as-ten-ad'-zo;* from *303* and *4727;* to *sigh deeply:*–sigh deeply.

390. ἀναστρέφω *an-as-tref'-o;* from *303* and *4762;* to *overturn*; also to *return;* by impl. to *busy* oneself, i.e. *remain, live:*–abide, behave self, have conversation, live, overthrow, pass, return, be used.

391. ἀναστροφή *an-as-trof-ay';* from *390; behavior:*–conversation.

392. ἀνατάσσομαι *an-at-as'-som-ahee;* from *303* and the mid. of *5021;* to *arrange:*–set in order.

393. ἀνατέλλω *an-at-el'-lo;* from *303* and the base of *5056;* to (*cause* to) *arise:*–(a-, make to) rise, at the rising of, spring (up), be up.

394. ἀνατίθεμαι *an-at-ith'-em-ahee;* from *303* and the mid. of *5087;* to *set forth* (for oneself), i.e *propound:*–communicate, declare.

395. ἀνατολή *an-at-ol-ay';* from *393;* a *rising* of light, i.e. *dawn* (fig.); by impl. the *E.* (also in pl.):–dayspring, east, rising.

396. ἀνατρέπω *an-at-rep'-o;* from *303* and the base of *5157;* to *overturn* (fig.):–overthrow, subvert.

397. ἀνατρέφω *an-at-ref'-o;* from *303* and *5142;* to *rear* (phys. or ment.):–bring up, nourish (up).

398. ἀναφαίνω *an-af-ah'-ee-no;* from *303* and *5316;* to *show*, i.e. (*refl.*) *appear,* or pass. to *have pointed* out:–(should) appear, discover.

399. ἀναφέρω *an-af-er'-o;* from *303* and *5342;* to *take up* (lit. or fig.):–bear, bring (carry, lead) up, offer (up).

400. ἀναφωνέω *an-af-o-neh'-o;* from *303* and *5455;* to *exclaim:*–speak out.

401. ἀνάχυσις *an-akh'-oo-sis;* from a com. of *303* and χέω (to *pour*); prop. *effusion,* i.e. (fig.) *license:*–excess.

402. ἀναχωρέω *an-akh-o-reh'-o;* from *303* and *5562;* to *retire:*–depart, give place, go (turn) aside, withdraw self.

403. ἀνάψυξις *an-aps'-ook-sis;* from *404;* prop. a *recovery of breath,* i.e. (fig.) *revival:*–*revival*.

404. ἀναψύχω *an-aps-oo'-kho;* from *303* and *5594;* prop. to *cool off,* i.e. (fig.) *relieve:*–refresh.

405. ἀνδραποδιστής *an-drap-od-is-tace';* from a der. of a com. of *435* and *4228;* an *enslaver* (as bringing *men* to his *feet*):–menstealer.

406. Ἀνδρέας *an-dreh'-as;* from *435; manly;*

GREEK

Andreas, an Isr.:–Andrew.

407. ἀνδρίζομαι *an-drid'-zom-ahee;* mid. from *435;* to *act manly:*–quit like men.

408. Ἀνδρόνικος *an-dron'-ee-kos;* from *435* and *3534; man of victory; Andronicos,* an Isr.:–Adronicus.

409. ἀνδροφόνος *an-drof-on'-os;* from *435* and *5408;* a *murderer:*–manslayer.

410. ανέγκλητος *an-eng'-klay-tos;* from *1* (as a neg. par.) and a der. of *1458; unaccused,* i.e. (by impl.) *irreproachable:*–blameless.

411. ἀνεκδιήγητος *an-ek-dee-ay'-gay-tos;* from *1* (as a neg. par.) and a presumed der. of *1555; not expounded* in full, i.e. *indescribable:*–unspeakable.

412. ἀνεκλάλητος *an-ek-lal'-ay-tos;* from *1* (as a neg. par.) and a presumed der. of *1583; not spoken out,* i.e. (by impl.) *unutterable:*–unspeakable.

413. ἀνέκλειπτος *an-ek'-lipe-tos;* from *1* (as a neg. par.) and a presumed der. of *1587; not left out,* i.e. (by impl.) *inexhaustible:*–that faileth not.

414. ἀνεκτότερος *an-ek-tot'-er-os;* comp. of a der. of *430; more endurable:*–more tolerable.

415. ἀνελεήμων *an-eleh-ay'-mone;* from *1* (as a neg. par.) and *1655; merciless:*–unmerciful.

416. ἀνεμίζω *an-em-id'-zo; from 417;* to *toss with the wind:*–drive with the wind.

417. ἄνεμος, *an'-em-os;* from the base of *109; wind;* (pl.) by impl. (the four) *quarters* (of the earth):–wind.

418. ἀνένδεκτος *an-en'-dek-tos;* from *1* (as a neg. par.) and a der. of the same as 1735; *unadmitted,* i.e. (by impl.) *not supposable:*–impossible.

419. ἀνεξερεύνητος *an-ex-er-yoo'-nay-tos;* from *1* (as a neg. par.) and a presumed der. of *1830; not searched out,* i.e. (by impl.) *inscrutable:*–unsearchable.

420. ἀνεξίκακος *an-ex-ik'-ak-os;* from *430* and *2556; enduring of ill,* i.e. *forbearing:*–patient.

421. ἀνεξιχνίαστος *an-ex-ikh-nee'-as-tos;* from *1* (as a neg. par.) and a presumed der. of a com. of *1537* and a der. of *2487; not tracked out,* i.e. (by impl.) *untraceable:*–past finding out; unsearchable.

422. ἀνεπαίσχυντος *an-ep-ah'-ee-skhoon-tos;* from *1* (as a neg. par.) and a presumed der. of a com. of *1909* and *153; not ashamed,* i.e. (by impl.) *irreprehensible:*–that needeth not to be ashamed.

423. ἀνεπίληπτος *an-ep-eel'-ape-tos;* from *1* (as a neg. par.) and a der. of *1949; not arrested,* i.e. (by impl.)*inculpable:*–blameless, unrebukeable.

424. ἀνέρχομαι *an-erkh'-om-ahee;* from *303* and *2064;* to *ascend:*–go up.

425. ἄνεσις *an'-es-is;* from *447; relaxation* or (fig.) *relief:*–eased, liberty, rest.

426. ἀνετάζω *an-et-ad'-zo;* from *303* and ἐτάζω (to *test*); to *investigate* (judicially):–(should have) examine(-d).

427. ἄνευ *an'-yoo;* a prim. par.; *without:*–without. Comp. *1*.

428. ἀνεύθετος *an-yoo'-the-tos;* from *1* (as a neg. par.) and *2111; not well set,* i.e. *inconvenient:*–not commodious.

429. ἀνευρίσκω *an-yoo-ris'-ko;* from *303* and *2147;* to *find out:*–find.

430. ἀνέχομαι *an-ekh'-om-ahe;* mid. from *303* and *2192;* to *hold oneself up* against, i.e. (fig.) *put up* with:–bear with, endure, forbear, suffer.

431. ἀνέψιος *an-eps'-ee-os;* from *1* (as a par. of union) and an obs. νέπος (a *brood*); prop. *akin,* i.e. (spec.) a *cousin:*–sister's son.

432. ἄνηθον *an'-ay-thon;* prob. of for. or.; *dill:*–anise.

433. ἀνήκω *an-ay'-ko;* from *303* and *2240;* to *attain* to, i.e. (fig.) *be proper:*–convenient, be fit.

434. ἀνήμερος *an-ay'-mer-os;* from *1* (as a neg. par.) and ἥμερος (*lame*); *savage:*–fierce.

435. ἀνήρ *an'-ayr;* a prim. word [comp. *444*]; a *man* (prop. as an indiv. male):–fellow, husband, man, sir.

436. ἀνθίστημι *anth-is'-tay-mee;* from *473* and *2476;* to *stand against*, i.e. *oppose:*–resist, withstand.

437. ἀνθομολογέομαι *anth-om-ol-og-eh'-om-ahee;* from *473* and the mid. of *3670;* to *confess in turn,* i.e. *respond* in praise:–give thanks.

438. ἄνθος *anth'-os;* a prim. word; a *blossom:*–flower.

439. ἀνθρακιά *anth-rak-ee-ah';* from *440;* a bed of burning *coals:*–fire of coals.

440. ἄνθραξ *anth'-rax;* of unc. der.; a live *coal:*–coal of fire.

441. ἀνθρωπάρεσκος *anth-ro-par'-es-ko;* from *444* and *700; man-courting,* i.e. *fawning:*–men-pleaser.

442. ἀνθρώπινος *anth-ro'-pee-nos;* from *444; human:*–human, common to man, man[-kind], [man-]kind, men's, after the manner of men.

443. ἀνθρωποκτόνος *anth-ro-pok-ton'-os;* from *444* and κτείνω (to *kill*); a *manslayer:*–murderer. Comp. *5406*.

444. ἄνθρωπος *anth'-ro-pos;* from *435* and ὤψ (the *countenance;* from *3700*); *man-faced,* i.e. a *human* being:–cert., man.

445. ἀνθυπατεύω *anth-oo-pat-yoo'-o;* from *446;* to *act as proconsul:*–be the deputy.

446. ἀνθύπατος *anth-oo'-pat-os;* from *473* and a sup. of *5228; instead* of the *highest* officer, i.e. (spec.) a Rom. *proconsul:*–deputy.

447. ἀνίημι *an-ee'-ay-mee;* from *303* and ἵημι (to *send*); to *let up,* i.e. (lit.) *slacken* or (fig.) *desert, desist* from:–forbear, leave, loose.

448. ἀνίλεως *an-ee'-leh-oce;* from *1* (as a neg. par.) and *2436; inexorable:*–without mercy.

449. ἄνιπτος *an'-ip-tos;* from *1* (as a neg. par.) and a presumed der. of *3538; without ablution:–unwashen.*

450. ἀνίστημι *an-is'-tay-mee;* from *303* and *2476;* to *stand up* (lit. or fig. trans. or intr.):–arise, lift up, raise up (again), rise (again), stand up(-right).

451. Ἄννα *an'-nah;* of Heb. or. [2584]; *Anna,* an Isr.s:–Anna.

452. Ἄννας *an'-nas;* of Heb. or. [2608]; *Annas* (i.e. *367*), an Isr.:–Annas.

453. ἀνόητος *an-o'-ay-tos;* from *1* (as a neg. par.) and a der. of *3539; unintelligent;* by impl. *sensual:*–fool(-ish), unwise.

454. ανοια *an'-oy-ah;* from a com. of *1* (as a neg. par.) and *3563; stupidity;* by impl. *rage:*–folly, madness.

455. ἀνοίγω *an-oy'-go;* from *303* and οἴγω (to *open*); to *open up* (lit. or fig. in various appl.):–open.

456. ἀνοικοδομέω *an-oy-kod-om-eh'-o;* from *303* and *3618;* to *rebuild:*–build again.

457. ἄνοιξις *an'-oix-is;* from *455; opening* (throat):–X open.

458. ἀνομία *an-om-ee'-ah;* from *459; illegality,* i.e. *violation of law* or (gen. case) *wickedness:*–iniquity, X transgress(-ion of) the law, unrighteousness.

459. ἄνομος *an'-om-os;* from *1* (as a neg. par.) and *3551; lawless,* i.e. (neg.) *not subject to* (the Jewish) *law;* (by impl. a *Gentile*), or (pos.) *wicked:*–without law, lawless, transgressor, unlawful, wicked.

460. ἀνόμως *an-om'-oce;* adv. from *459; lawlessly,* i.e. (spec.) *not amenable* to (the Jewish) *law:*–without law.

461. ἀνορθόω *an-orth-o'-o;* from *303* and a der. of the base of *3717;* to *straighten up:*–lift (set) up, make straight.

462. ἀνόσιος *an-os'-ee-os;* from *1* (as a neg. par.) and *3741; wicked:*–unholy.

463. ἀνοχή *an-okh-ay';* from *430; self-restraint,* i.e. *tolerance:*–forbearance.

464. ἀνταγωνίζομαι *an-tag-o-nid'-zom-ahee;* from *473* and *75;* to *struggle against* (fig.) ["antagonize"]:–strive against.

465. ἀντάλλαγμα *an-tal'-ag-mah;* from a com. of *473* and *236;* an *equivalent* or *ransom:*–in exchange.

466. ἀνταναπληρόω *an-tan-ap-lay-ro'-o;* from 473 and *378;* to *supplement:*–fill up.

467. ἀνταποδίδωμι *an-tap-od-ee'-do-mee;* from *473* and *591;* to *requite* (good or evil):–recompense, render, repay.

468. ἀνταπόδομα *an-tap-od'-om-ah;* from *467;* a *requital* (prop. the thing):–recompense.

469. ἀνταπόδοσις *an-tap-od'-os-is* from *467; requital* (prop. the act):–reward.

470. ἀνταποκρίνομαι *an-tap-ok-ree'-nom-ahee;* from *473* and *611;* to *contradict* or *dispute:*–answer again, reply against.

471. ἀντέπω *an-tep'-o;* from *473* and *2036;* to *refute* or *deny:*–gainsay, say against.

472. ἀντέχομαι *an-tekh'-om-ahee;* from *473* and the mid. of *2192;* to *hold* oneself *opposite* to, i.e. (by impl.) *adhere to;* by ext. to *care for:*–hold fast, hold to, support.

473. ἀντί *an-tee';* a prim. par.; *opposite,* i.e. *instead* or *because* of (rarely *in addition* to):–for, in the room of. Often used in compo. to denote *contrast, requital, substitution, correspondence,* etc.

474. ἀντιβάλλω *an-tee-bal'-lo; from 473 and 906;* to *bandy:*–have.

475. ἀντιδιατίθεμαι *an-tee-dee-at-eeth'-em-ahee;* from *473* and *1303;* to *set oneself opposite,* i.e. *be disputatious:*–that oppose themselves.
476. ἀντίδικος *an-tid'-ee-kos;* from *473* and *1349;* an *opponent* (in a lawsuit); spec. *Satan* (as the arch-enemy):–adversary.
477. ἀντίθεσις *an-tith'-es-is;* from a com. of *473* and *5087; opposition,* i.e. a *conflict* (of theories):–opposition.
478. ἀντικαθίστημι *an-tee-kath-is'-tay-mee;* from *473* and *2525;* to *set down* (troops) *against,* i.e. *withstand:*–resist.
479. ἀντικαλέω *an-tee-kal-eh'-o;* from *473* and *2564;* to *invite in return:*–bid again.
480. ἀντίκειμαι *an-tik'-i-mahee;* from *473* and *2749;* to *lie opposite,* i.e. *be adverse* (fig. *repugnant*) to:–adversary, be contrary, oppose.
481. ἀντικρύ *an-tee-kroo';* prol. from *473; opposite:*–over against.
482. ἀντιλαμβάνομαι *an-tee-lam-ban'-om-ahee;* from *473* and the mid. of *2983;* to *take* hold of *in turn,* i.e. *succor;* also to *participate:*–help, partaker, support.
483. ἀντίλεγω *an-til'-eg-o;* from *473* and *3004;* to *dispute, refuse:*–answer again, contradict, deny, gainsay(-er), speak against.
484. ἀντίληψις *an-til'-ape-sis;* from *482; relief:*–help.
485. ἀντιλογία *an-tee-log-ee'-ah;* from a der. of *483; dispute, disobedience:*–contradiction, gainsaying, strife.
486. ἀντιλοιδορέω *an-tee-loy-dor-eh'-o;* from *473* and *3058;* to *rail in reply:*–revile again.
487. ἀντίλυτρον *an-til'-oo-tron;* from *473* and *3083;* a *redemption-price:*–ransom.
488. ἀντιμετρέω *an-tee-met-reh'-o;* from *473* and *3354;* to *mete in return:*–measure again.
489. ἀντιμισθία *an-tee-mis-thee'-ah;* from a com. of *473* and *3408; requital, correspondence:*–recompense.
490. Ἀντιόχεια *an-tee-okh'-i-ah;* from Ἀντίοχος (a Syrian king); *Antiochīa,* a place in Syria:–Antioch.
491. Ἀντιοχεύς *an-tee-okh-yoos';* from *490; an Antiochian* or inh. of Antiochia:–of Antioch.
492. ἀντιπαρέρχομαι *an-tee-par-er'-khom-ahee;* from *473* and *3928;* to *go along opposite:*–pass by on the other side.
493. Ἀντίπας *an-tee'-pas;* contr. for a com. of *473* and a der. of *3962; Antipas,* a Chr.:–Antipas.
494. Ἀντιπατρίς *an-tip-at-rece';* from the same as *493; Antipatris,* a place in Pal.:–Antipatris.
495. ἀντιπέραν *an-tee-per'-an;* from *473* and *4008; on the opposite side:*–over against.
496. ἀντιπίπτω *an-tee-pip'-to;* from *473* and *4098* (incl. its alt.); to *oppose:*–resist.
497. ἀντιστρατεύομαι *an-tee-strat-yoo'-om-ahee;* from *473* and *4754;* (fig.) to *attack,* i.e. (by impl.) *destroy:*–war against.
498. ἀντιτάσσομαι *an-tee-tas'-som-ahee;* from *473* and the mid. of *5021;* to *range oneself against,* i.e. *oppose:*–oppose themselves, resist
499. ἀντίτυπον *an-teet'-oo-pon;* neut. of a com. of *473* and *5179; cor.* ("antitype"), i.e. a *representative, counterpart:*–(like) figure (whereunto).
500. ἀντίχριστος *an-tee'-khris-tos;* from *473* and *5547;* an *opponent of the Messiah:*–antichrist.
501. ἀντλέω *ant-leh-o;* from ἄντλος (the *hold* of a ship); to *bale* up (prop. bilge water), i.e. *dip* water (with a bucket, pitcher, etc.):–draw (out).
502. ἄντλημα *ant'-lay-mah;* from *501;* a *baling-vessel:*–thing to draw with.
503. ἀντοφθαλμέω *ant-of-thal-meh'-o;* from a com. of *473* and *3788;* to *face:*–bear up into.
504. ἄνυδρος *an'-oo-dros;* from *1* (as a neg. par.) and *5204; waterless,* i.e. *dry:*–dry, without water.
505. ἀνυπόκριτος *an-oo-pok'-ree-tos;* from *1* (as a neg. par.) and a presumed der. of *5271; undissembled,* i.e. *sincere:*–without dissimulation (hypocrisy), unfeigned.
506. ἀνυπότακτος *an-oo-pot'-ak-tos;* from *1* (as a neg. par.) and a presumed der. of *5293; unsubdued,* i.e. *insubordinate* (in fact or temper):–disobedient, i.e. not put under, unruly.
507. ἄνω *an'-o;* adv. from *473; upward* or *on the top:*–above, brim, high, up.
508. ἀνώγεον *an-ogue'-eh-on;* from *507* and *1093; above* the *ground,* i.e. (prop.) the *second floor* of a building; used for a *dome* or a *balcony* on the upper story:–upper room.
509. ἄνωθεν *an'-o-then;* from *507; from above;* by anal. *from the first;* by impl. *anew:*–from above, again, from the beginning (very first), the top.
510. ἀνωτερικός *an-o-ter-ee-kos';* from *511; superior,* i.e. (locally) *more remote:*–upper.
511. ἀνώτερος *an-o'-ter-os;* comp. degree of *507; upper,* i.e. (neut. as adv.) to a *more conspicuous* place, in a *former* part of the book:–above, higher.
512. ἀνωφέλες *an-o-fel'-ace* from *1* (as a neg. par.) and the base of *5624; useless* or (neut.) *inutility:*–unprofitable(-ness).
513. ἀξίνη *ax-ee'-nay;* prob. from ἄγνυμι (to *break;* comp. *4486*); an *axe:*–axe.
514. ἄξιος *ax'-ee-os;* prob. from *71; deserving, comparable* or *suitable* (as if *drawing* praise):–due reward, meet, [un-]worthy.
515. ἀξιόω *ax-ee-o'-o;* from *514;* to *deem entitled* or *fit:*–desire, think good, count (think) worthy.
516. ἀξίως *ax-ee'-oce;* adv. from *514; appropriately:*–as becometh, after a godly sort, worthily(-thy).
517. ἀόρατος *ah-or'-at-os;* from *1* (as a neg. par.) and *3707; invisible:*–invisible (thing).
518. ἀπαγγέλλω *ap-ang-el'-lo;* from *575* and the base of *32;* to *announce:*–bring word (again), declare, report, shew (again), tell.
519. ἀπάγχομαι *ap-ang'-khom-ahee;* from *575* and ἄγχω (to *choke;* akin to the base of *43*); to *strangle oneself off* (i.e. to death):–hang himself.
520. ἀπάγω *ap-ag'-o;* from *575* and *71;* to *take off* (in various senses):–bring, carry away, lead (away), put to death, take away.
521. ἀπαίδευτος *ap-ah'-ee-dyoo-tos;* from *1* (as a neg. par.) and a der. of *3811; uninstructed,* i.e. (fig.) *stupid:*–unlearned.
522. ἀπαίρω *ap-ah'-ee-ro;* from *575* and *142;* to *lift off,* i.e. *remove:*–take (away).
523. ἀπαιτέω *ap-ah'-ee-teh-o;* from *575* and *154;* to *demand back:*–ask again, require.
524. ἀπα λγέω, *ap-alg-eh'-o;* from *575* and ἀλγέω (to *smart*); to *grieve out,* i.e. *become apathetic:*–be past feeling.
525. ἀπαλλάσσω *ap-al-las'-so;* from *575* and *236;* to *change away,* i.e. *release,* (refl.) *remove:*–deliver, depart.
526. ἀπαλλοτριόω *ap-al-lot-ree-o'-o;* from *575* and a der. of *245;* to *estrange away,* i.e. (pass. and fig.) to *be non-participant:*–alienate, be alien.
527. ἀπαλός *ap-al-os';* of unc. der.; *soft:*–tender.
528. ἀπαντάω *ap-an-tah'-o;* from *575* and a der. of *473;* to *meet away,* i.e. *encounter:*–meet.
529. ἀπάντησις *ap-an'-tay-sis;* from *528*; a (friendly) *encounter:*–meet.
530. ἅπαξ *hap'-ax;* from *537; one* (or a *single*) *time* (numerically or conclusively):–once.
531. ἀπαράβατος *ap-ar-ab'-at-os;* from *1* (as a neg. par.) and a der. of *3845; not passing away,* i.e. *untransferable* (perpetual):– unchangeable.
532. ἀπαρασκεύαστος *ap-ar-ask-yoo'-as-tos;* from *1* (as a neg. par.) and a der. of *3903; unready:*–unprepared.
533. ἀπαρνέομαι *ap-ar-neh'-om-ahee;* from *575* and *720;* to *deny utterly,* i.e. *disown, abstain:*–deny.
534. ἀπάρτι *ap-ar'-tee;* from *575* and *737; from now,* i.e. *henceforth* (*already*):–from henceforth.
535. ἀπαρτισμός *ap-ar-tis-mos';* from a der. of *534; completion:*–finishing.
536. ἀπαρχή *ap-ar-khay';* from a com. of *575* and *756;* a *beginning* of *sacrifice,* i.e. the (Jewish) *first-fruit* (fig.):–first-fruits.
537. ἅπας *hap'-as;* from *1* (as a par. of union) and *3956;* absol. *all* or (sing.) *every* one:–all (things), every (one), whole.
538. ἀπατάω *ap-at-ah'-o;* of unc. der.; to *cheat,* i.e. *delude:*–deceive.
539. ἀπάτη *ap-at'-ay;* from *538; delusion:*–deceit(-ful, -fulness), deceivableness(-ving).
540. ἀπάτωρ *ap-at'-ore;* from *1* (as a neg. par.) and *3962; fatherless,* i.e. *of unrecorded paternity:*–without father.
541. ἀπαύγασμα *ap-ow'-gas-mah;* from a com. of *575* and *826;* an *off-flash,* i.e. *effulgence:*–brightness.
542. ἀπείδω *ap-i'-do;* from *575* and the same as *1492;* to *see* fully:–see.
543. ἀπείθεια *ap-i'-thi-ah;* from *545; disbelief* (obstinate and rebellious):–disobedience, unbelief.
544. ἀπειθέω *ap-i-theh'-o;* from *545;* to *disbelieve* (wilfully and perversely):–not believe, disobedient, obey not, unbelieving.
545. ἀπειθής *ap-i-thace';* from *1* (as a neg. par.) and *3982; unpersuadable,* i.e.

GREEK

contumacious:–disobedient.

546. ἀπειλέω *ap-i-leh'-o;* of unc. der.; to *menace;* by impl. to *forbid:*–threaten.

547. ἀπειλή *ap-i-lay';* from *546;* a *menace:*–X straitly, threatening. .

548. ἄπειμι *ap'-i-mee;* from *575* and *1510;* to *be away:*–be absent. Comp. 549.

549. ἄπειμι *ap'-i-mee;* from *575* and εἶμι (to *go*); to *go away:*–go. Comp. *548*.

550. ἀπειπόμην *ap-i-pom'-ane;* refl. past of a com. of *575* and *2036;* to *say off* for oneself, i.e. *disown:*–renounce.

551. ἀπείραστος *ap-i'-ras-tos;* from *1* (as a neg. par.) and a presumed der. of *3987; untried,* i.e. *not temptable:*–not to be tempted.

552. ἄπειρος *ap'-i-ros;* from *1* (as a neg. par.) and *3984; inexperienced,* i.e. *ignorant:*–unskilful.

553. ἀπεκδέχομαι, *ap-ek-dekh'-om-ahee;* from *575* and *1551;* to *expect fully:*–look (wait) for.

554. ἀπεκδύομαι *ap-ek-doo'-om-ahee;* mid. from *575* and *1562;* to *divest wholly* oneself, or (for oneself) *despoil:*–put off, spoil.

555. ἀπέκδυσις *ap-ek'-doo-sis;* from *554; divestment:*–putting off.

556. ἀπελαύνω *ap-el-ow'-no;* from *575* and *1643;* to *dismiss:*–drive.

557. ἀπελεγμός *ap-el-eg-mos';* from a com. of *575* and *1651; refutation,* i.e. (by impl.) *contempt:*–nought.

558. ἀπελεύθερος *ap-el-yoo'-ther-os;* from *575* and *1658;* one *freed away,* i.e. a *freedman:*–freeman.

559. Ἀπελλῆς *ap-el-lace';* of Lat. or.; *Apelles,* a Chr.:–Apelles.

560. ἀπελπίζω *ap-el-pid'-zo;* from *575* and *1679;* to *hope out,* i.e. *fully expect:*–hope for again.

561. ἀπέναντι *ap-en'-an-tee;* from *575* and *1725; from in front,* i.e. *opposite, before* or *against:*–before, contrary, over against, in the presence of.

562. ἀπέραντος *ap-er'-an-tos;* from *1* (as a neg. par.) and a sec. der. of *4008; unfinished,* i.e. (by impl.) *interminable:*–endless.

563. ἀπερισπάστως *ap-er-is-pas-toce';* adv. from a com. of *1* (as a neg. part.) and a presumed der. of *4049; undistractedly,* i.e. *free from* (domestic) *solicitude:*–without distraction.

564. ἀπερίτμητος *ap-er-eet'-may-tos;* from *1* (as a neg. par.) and a presumed der. of *4059; uncircumcised* (fig.):–uncircumcised.

565. ἀπέρχομαι *ap-erkh'-om-ahee;* from *575* and *2064;* to *go off* (i.e. *depart*), *aside* (i.e. *apart*) or *behind* (i.e. *follow*), lit. or fig.:–come, depart, go (aside, away, back, out, ... ways), pass away, be past.

566. ἀπέχει *ap-ekh'-i;* third pers. sing. pres. ind. act. of *568* used impers.; *it is sufficient:*–it is enough.

567. ἀπέχομαι *ap-ekh'-om-ahee;* mid. (refl.) of *568;* to *hold oneself off,* i.e. *refrain:*–abstain.

568. ἀπέχω *ap-ekh'-o;* from *575* and *2192;* (act.) to *have out,* i.e. *receive in full;* (intr.) to *keep* (oneself) *away,* i.e. *be distant* (lit. or fig.):–be, have, receive.

569. ἀπιστέω *ap-is-teh'-o;* from *571;* to *be unbelieving,* i.e. (trans.) *disbelieve,* or (by impl.) *disobey:*–believe not.

570. ἀπιστία *ap-is-tee'-ah;* from *571; faithlessness,* i.e. (neg.) *disbelief* (*want of* Chr. *faith*), or (pos.) *unfaithfulness* (*disobedience*):–unbelief.

571. ἄπιστος *ap'-is-tos;* from *1* (as a neg. par.) and *4103;* (act.) *disbelieving,* i.e. *without* Chr. *faith* (spec. a *heathen*); (pass.) *untrustworthy* (pers.), or *incredible* (thing):–that believeth not, faithless, incredible thing, infidel, unbeliever(-ing).

572. ἁπλότης *hap-lot'-ace;* from *573; singleness,* i.e. (subj.) *sincerity* (*without dissimulation* or *self-seeking*), or (obj.) *generosity* (*copious bestowal*):–bountifulness, liberal(-ity), simplicity, singleness.

573. ἁπλοῦς *hap-looce*'; prob. from *1* (as a par. of union) and the base of *4120;* prop. *folded together,* i.e. *single* (fig. *clear*):–single.

574. ἁπλῶς *hap-loce';* adv. from *573* (in the obj. sense of *572*); *bountifully;* --liberally.

575. ἀπό *apo;* a prim. par.; *"off,"* i.e. *away* (from something near), in various senses (of place, time, or relation; lit. or fig.):–(X here-) after, ago, at, because of, before, by (the space of), for(-th), from, in, (out) of, off, (up-) on(-ce), since, with. In compo. (as a pref.) it usually denotes *separation, departure, cessation, completion, reversal,* etc.

576. ἀποβαίνω *ap-ob-ah'-ee-no;* from *575* and the base of *939;* lit. to *disembark;* fig. to *eventuate:*–become, go out, turn.

577. ἀποβάλλω *ap-ob-al'-lo;* from *575* and *906;* to *throw off;* fig. to *lose:*–cast away.

578. ἀποβλέπω *ap-ob-lep'-o;* from *575* and *991;* to *look away* from everything else, i.e. (fig.) intently *regard:*–have respect.

579. ἀπόβλητος *ap-ob'-lay-tos;* from *577; cast off,* i.e. (fig.) such as to *be rejected:*–be refused.

580. ἀποβολή *ap-ob-ol-ay*'; from *577; rejection;* fig. *loss:*–casting away, loss.

581. ἀπογενόμενος *ap-og-en-om'-en-os;* past part. of a com. of *575* and *1096; absent,* i.e. *deceased* (fig. *renounced*):–being dead.

582. ἀπογραφή *ap-og-raf-ay';* from *583;* an *enrollment;* by impl. an *assessment:*–taxing.

583. ἀπογράφω *ap-og-raf'-o;* from *575* and *1125;* to *write off* (a copy or list), i.e. *enrol:*–tax, write.

584. ἀποδείκνυμι *ap-od-ike'-noo-mee;* from *575* and *1166;* to *show off,* i.e. *exhibit;* fig. to *demonstrate,* i.e. *accredit:*–(ap-) prove, set forth, shew.

585. ἀπόδειξις *ap-od'-ike-sis;* from *584; manifestation:*–demonstration.

586. ἀποδεκατόω *ap-od-ek-at-o'-o;* from *575* and *1183;* to *tithe* (as debtor or creditor):–(give, pay, take) tithe.

587. ἀπόδεκτος *ap-od'-ek-tos;* from *588; accepted*, i.e. *agreeable:*–acceptable.

588. ἀποδέχομαι *ap-od-ekh'-om-ahee;* from *575* and *1209;* to *take fully,* i.e. *welcome* (persons), *approve* (things):–accept, receive (gladly).

589. ἀποδημέω *ap-od-ay-meh'-o;* from *590;* to *go abroad,* i.e. *visit* a *for. land:*–go (travel) into a far country, journey.

590. ἀπόδημος *ap-od'-ay-mos;* from *575* and *1218; absent from* one's own *people,* i.e. a *for. traveller:*–taking a far journey.

591. ἀποδίδωμι *ap-od-eed'-o-mee;* from *575* and *1325;* to *give away,* i.e. *up, over, back,* etc. (in various appl.):–deliver (again), give (again), (re-)pay(-ment be made), perform, recompense, render, requite, restore, reward, sell, yield.

592. ἀποδιορίζω *ap-od-ee-or-id'-zo;* from *575* and a com. of *223* and *3724;* to *disjoin* (by a boundary, fig. a party):–separate.

593. ἀποδοκιμάζω *ap-od-ok-ee-mad'-zo;* from *575* and *1381;* to *disapprove,* i.e. (by impl.) to *repudiate:*–disallow, reject.

594. ἀποδοχή *ap-od-okh-ay';* from *588; acceptance:*–acceptation.

595. ἀπόθεσις *ap-oth'-es-is;* from *659;* a *laying aside* (lit. or fig.):–putting away (off).

596. ἀποθήκη *ap-oth-ay'-kay;* from *659;* a *repository,* i.e. *granary:*–barn, garner.

597. ἀποθησαυρίζω *ap-oth-ay-sow-rid'-zo;* from *575* and *2343;* to *treasure away:*–lay up in store.

598. ἀποθλίβω *ap-oth-lee'-bo;* from *575* and *2346;* to *crowd* (from every side):–press.

599. ἀποθνήσκω *ap-oth-nace'-ko;* from *575* and *2348;* to *die* off (lit. or fig.):–be dead, death, die, lie a-dying, be slain (X with).

600. ἀποκαθίστημι *ap-ok-ath-is'-tay-mee;* from *575* and *2525;* to *reconstitute* (in health, home or organization):–restore (again).

601. ἀποκαλύπτω *ap-ok-al-oop'-to;* from *575* and *2572;* to *take off the cover,* i.e. *disclose:*–reveal.

602. ἀποκάλυψις *ap-ok-al'-oop-sis;* from *601; disclosure:*–appearing, coming, lighten, manifestation, be revealed, revelation.

603. ἀποκαραδοκία *ap-ok-ar-ad-ok-ee'-ah;* from a comp. of *575* and a comp. of κάρα (the *head*) and *1380* (in the sense of *watching*); *intense anticipation:*–earnest expectation.

604. ἀποκαταλλάσσω *ap-ok-at-al-las'-so;* from *575* and *2644;* to *reconcile fully:*–reconcile.

605. ἀποκατάστασις *ap-ok-at-as'-tas-is;* from *600; reconstitution:*–restitution.

606. ἀπόκειμαι *ap-ok'-i-mahee;* from *575* and *2749;* to *be reserved;* fig. to *await:*–be appointed, (be) laid up.

607. ἀποκεφαλίζω *ap-ok-ef-al-id'-zo* from *575* and *2776;* to *decapitate:*–behead.

608. ἀποκλείω *ap-ok-li'-o;* from *575* and *2808;* to *close fully:*–shut up.

609. ἀποκόπτω *ap-ok-op'-to;* from *575* and *2875;* to *amputate;* refl. (by irony) to *mutilate* (the privy parts):–cut off. Comp. 2699.

610. ἀπόκριμα *ap-ok'-ree-mah;* from *611* (in its orig. sense of *judging*); a judicial *decision:*–sentence.

611. ἀποκρίνομαι *ap-ok-ree'-nom-ahee;* from *575* and κρινω; to *conclude for oneself,* i.e. (by

impl.) to *respond;* by Heb. [comp. 6030] to *begin to speak* (where an address is expected):–answer.
612. ἀπόκρισις *ap-ok'-ree-sis;* from *611; a response:*–answer.
613. ἀποκρύπτω *ap-ok-roop'-to;* from *575* and *2928;* to *conceal away* (i.e. *fully*); fig. to *keep secret:*–hide.
614. ἀπόκρυφος *ap-ok'-roo-fos;* from *613; secret;* by impl. *treasured:*–hid, kept secret.
615. ἀποκτείνω *ap-ok-ti'-no;* from *575* and κτείνω (to *slay*); to *kill* outright; fig. to *destroy:*–put to death, kill, slay.
616. ἀποκυέω *ap-ok-oo-eh'-o;* from *575* and the base of *2949;* to *breed forth,* i.e. (by transf.) to *generate* (fig.):–beget, bring forth.
617. ἀποκυλίω *ap-ok-oo-lee'-o;* from *575* and *2947;* to *roll away:*–roll away (back).
618. ἀπολαμβάνω *ap-ol-am-ban'-o;* from *575* and *2983;* to *receive* (*spec.* in *full*, or as a host); also to *take aside:*–receive, take.
619. ἀπόλαυσις *ap-ol'-ow-sis;* from a com. of *575* and λαύω *123* (to *enjoy*); full *enjoyment:*–enjoy(-ment).
620. ἀπολείπω *ap-ol-ipe'-o;* from *575* and *3007;* to *leave* behind (pass. *remain*); by impl. to *forsake:*–leave, remain.
621. ἀπολείχω *ap-ol-i'-kho;* from *575* and λείχω (to "*lick*"); to *lick* clean:–lick.
622. ἀπόλλυμι *ap-ol'-loo-mee;* from *575* and the base of *3639;* to *destroy fully* (refl. to *perish,* or *lose*), lit. or fig.:–destroy, die, lose, mar, perish.
623. Ἀπολλύων *ap-ol-loo'-ohn;* act. part. of *622;* a *destroyer* (i.e. *Satan*):–Apollyon.
624. Ἀπολλωνία *ap-ol-lo-nee'-ah;* from the pagan deity Ἀπόλλων (i.e. the *sun;* from *622*); *Apollonia,* a place in Macedonia:–Apollonia.
625. Ἀπολλώς *ap-ol-loce;'* prob. from the same as *624; Apollos,* an Isr.:–Apollos.
626. ἀπολογέομαι *ap-ol-og-eh'-om-ahee;* mid. from a com. of *575* and *3056;* to give an *account* (legal *plea*) of oneself, i.e. *exculpate* (self):–answer (for self), make defence, excuse (self), speak for self.
627. ἀπολογία *ap-ol-og-ee'-ah;* as *626;* a *plea* ("apology"):–answer (for self), clearing of self, defence.
628. ἀπολούω *ap-ol-oo'-o;* from *575* and *3068;* to *wash* fully, i.e. (fig.) *have remitted* (refl.):–wash (away).
629. ἀπολύτρωσις *ap-ol-oo'-tro-sis;* from a com. of *575* and *3083;* (the act) *ransom* in full, i.e. (fig.) *riddance,* or (spec.) Chr. *salvation:*–deliverance, redemption.
630. ἀπολύω *ap-ol-oo'-o;* from *575* and *3089; to free* fully, i.e. (lit.) *relieve, release, dismiss* (refl. *depart*), or (fig.) *let die, pardon* or (spec.) *divorce:*–(let) depart, dismiss, divorce, forgive, let go, loose, put (send) away, release, set at liberty.
631. ἀπομάσσομαι *ap-om-as'-som-ahee;* mid. from *575* and μάσσω masso (to *squeeze, knead, smear*); to *scrape away:*–wipe off.
632. ἀπονέμω *ap-on-em'-o;* from *575* and the base of *3551;* to *apportion,* i.e. *bestow:*–give.
633. ἀπονίπτω *ap-on-ip'-to;* from *575* and *3538;* to *wash off* (refl. one's own hands symb.):–wash.
634. ἀποπίπτω *ap-op-ip'-to;* from *575* and *4098;* to *fall off:*–fall.
635. ἀποπλανάω *ap-op-lan-ah'-o;* from *575* and *4105;* to *lead astray* (fig.); pass. to *stray* (from truth):–err, seduce.
636. ἀποπλέω *ap-op-leh'-o;* from *575* and *4126;* to *set sail:*–sail away.
637. ἀποπλύνω *ap-op-loo'-no;* from *575* and *4150;* to *rinse off:*–wash.
638. ἀποπνίγω *ap-op-nee'-go;* from *575* and *4155;* to *stifle* (by drowning or overgrowth):–choke.
639. ἀπορέω *ap-or-eh'-o;* from a comp. of *1* (as a neg. par.) and the base of *4198;* to *have no way* out, i.e. *be at a loss* (ment.):– (stand in) doubt, be perplexed.
640. ἀπορία *ap-or-ee'-a;* from the same as *639;* a (state of) *quandary:*–perplexity.
641. ἀποῤῥίπτω *ap-or-hrip'-to;* from *575* and *4496;* to *hurl off,* i.e. *precipitate* (oneself):–cast.
642. ἀπορφανίζω *ap-or-fan-id'-zo;* from *575* and a der. of *3737;* to *bereave wholly,* i.e. (fig.) *separate* (from intercourse):–take.
643. ἀποσκευάζω *ap-osk-yoo-ad'-zo;* from *575* and a der. of *4632;* to *pack up* (one's) *baggage:*–take up... carriages.
644. ἀποσκίασμα *ap-os-kee'-as-mah;* from a comp. of *575* and a der. of *4639;* a *shading off,* i.e. *obscuration:*–shadow.
645. ἀποσπάω *ap-os-pah'-o;* from *575* and *4685;* to *drag forth,* i.e. (lit.) *unsheathe* (a sword), or rel. (with a degree of force implied) *retire* (pers. or factiously):–(with-) draw (away), after we were gotten from.
646. ἀποστασία *ap-os-tas-ee'-ah;* fem. of the same as *647; defection* from truth (prop. the state) ["apostasy"]:–falling away, forsake.
647. ἀποστάσιον *ap-os-tas'-ee-on;* neut. of a (presumed) adj. from a der. of *868;* prop. something *separative,* i.e. (spec.) *divorce:*–(writing of) divorcement.
648. ἀποστεγάζω *ap-os-teg-ad'-zo;* from *575* and a der. of *4721;* to *unroof:*–uncover.
649. ἀποστέλλω *ap-os-tel'-lo;* from *575* and *4724; set apart,* i.e. (by impl.) to *send out* (prop. on a mission) lit. or fig.:–put in, send (away, forth, out), set [at liberty].
650. ἀποστερέω *ap-os-ter-eh'-o;* from *575* and στερέω (to *deprive*); to *despoil:*–defraud, destitute, kept back by fraud.
651. ἀποστολή *ap-os-tol-ay';* from *649; commission,* i.e. (spec.) *apostolate:*–apostleship.
652. ἀπόστολος *ap-os'-tol-os;* from *649;* a *delegate;* spec. an *ambassador* of the Gospel; officially a *commissioner* of Christ ("*apostle*") (with miraculous powers):–apostle, messenger, he that is sent.
653. ἀποστοματίζω *ap-os-tom-at-id'-zo;* from *575* and a (presumed) der. of *4750;* to *speak off-hand* (prop. *dictate*), i.e. to *catechize* (in an invidious manner):–provoke to speak.
654. ἀποστρέφω *ap-os-tref'-o;* from *575* and *4762;* to *turn away* or *back* (lit. or fig.):–bring again, pervert, turn away (from).
655. ἀποστυγέω *ap-os-toog-eh'-o;* from *575* and the base of *4767;* to *detest* utterly:–abhor.
656. ἀποσυνάγωγος *ap-os-oon-ag'-o-gos;* from *575* and *4864; excommunicated:*–(put) out of the synagogue(-s).
657. ἀποτάσσομαι *ap-ot-as'-som-ahee;* mid. from *575* and *5021;* lit. to *say adieu* (by departing or dismissing); fig. to *renounce:*–bid farewell, forsake, take leave, send away.
658. ἀποτελέω *ap-ot-el-eh'-o;* from *575* and *5055;* to *complete entirely,* i.e. *consummate:*–finish.
659. ἀποτίθημι *ap-ot-eeth'-ay-mee;* from *575* and *5087;* to *put away* (lit. or fig.):–cast off, lay apart (aside, down), put away (off).
660. ἀποτινάσσω *ap-ot-in-as'-so;* from *575* and τινάσσω (to *jostle*); to *brush off:*–shake off.
661. ἀποτίνω *ap-ot-ee'-no;* from *575* and *5099;* to *pay* in full:–repay.
662. ἀποτολμάω *ap-ot-ol-mah'-o;* from *575* and *5111;* to *venture* plainly:–be very bold.
663. ἀποτομία *ap-ot-om-ee'-ah;* from the base of *664;* (fig.) *decisiveness,* i.e. *rigor:*–severity.
664. ἀποτόμως *ap-ot-om'-oce;* adv. from a der. of a comp. of *575* and τέμνω (to *cut*); *abruptly,* i.e. *peremptorily:*–sharply(-ness).
665. ἀποτρέπω *ap-ot-rep'-o;* from *575* and the base of *5157;* to *deflect,* i.e. (refl.) *avoid:*–turn away.
666. ἀπουσία *ap-oo-see'-ah;* from the part. of *548;* a *being away:*–absence.
667. ἀποφέρω *ap-of-er'-o;* from *575* and *5342;* to *bear off* (lit. or rel.):–bring, carry (away).
668. ἀποφεύγω *ap-of-yoo'-go;* from *575* and *5343;* (fig.) to *escape:*–escape.
669. ἀποφθέγγομαι *ap-of-theng'-om-ahee;* from *575* and *5350;* to *enunciate* plainly, i.e. *declare:*–say, speak forth, utterance.
670. ἀποφορτίζομαι *ap-of-or-tid'-zom-ahee;* from *575* and the mid. of *5412;* to *unload:*–unlade.
671. ἀπόχρησις *ap-okh'-ray-sis;* from a comp. of *575* and *5530;* the act of *using up,* i.e. *consumption:*–using.
672. ἀποχωρέω *ap-okh-o-reh'-o;* from *575* and *5562;* to *go away:*–depart.
673. ἀποχωρίζω *ap-okh-o-rid'-zo;* from *575* and *5563;* to *rend apart;* refl. to *separate:*–depart (asunder).
674. ἀποψύχω *ap-ops-oo'-kho;* from *575* and *5594;* to *breathe out,* i.e. *faint:*–hearts failing.
675. Ἄππιος *ap'-pee-os;* of Lat. or.; (in the gen. i.e. possessive case) of *Appius,* the name of a Rom.:–Appii.
676. ἀπρόσιτος *ap-ros'-ee-tos;* from *1* (as a neg. par.) and a der. of a comp. of *4314* and εἶμι (to *go*); *inaccessible:*–which no man can approach.
677. ἀπρόσκοπος *ap-ros'-kop-os;* from *1* (as a neg. par.) and a presumed der. of *4350;* act. *inoffensive,* i.e. *not leading into sin;* pass. *faultless,* i.e. *not led into sin:*–none

GREEK

(void of, without) offence.

678. ἀπροσωπολήπτως *ap-ros-o-pol-ape'-tos;* adv. from a com. of *1* (as a neg. par.) and a presumed der. of a presumed com. of *4383* and *2983* [comp. *4381*]; in a way *not accepting* the *pers.*, i.e. *impartially:*–without respect of persons.

679. ἄπταιστος *ap-tah'-ee-stos;* from *1* (as a neg. par.) and a der. of *4417; not stumbling,* i.e. (fig.) *without sin:*–from falling.

680. ἅπτομαι *hap'-tom-ahee;* refl. of *681;* prop. to *attach* oneself to, i.e. to *touch* (in many implied relations):–touch.

681. ἅπτω *hap'-to;* a prim. verb; prop. to *fasten* to, i.e. (spec.) to *set* on fire:–kindle, light.

682. 'Απφία *ap-fee'-a;* prob. of for. or.; *Apphia,* a woman of Collosae:–Apphia.

683. ἀπωθέομαι *ap-o-theh'-om-ahee;* from *575* and the mid. of ὠθέω or ὤθω (to *shove*); to *push off,* fig. to *reject:*–cast away, put away (from), thrust away (from).

684. ἀπώλεια *ap-o'-li-a;* from a presumed der. of *622; ruin* or *loss* (phys. spir. or eternal):–damnable(-nation), destruction, die, perdition, X perish, pernicious ways, waste.

685. ἀρά *ar-ah';* prob. from *142;* prop. *prayer* (as *lifted* to Heaven), i.e. (by impl.) *imprecation:*–curse.'

686. ἄρα *ar'-ah;* prob. from *142* (through the idea of *drawing* a conclusion); a par. denoting an *inference* more or less decisive (as follows):–haply, (what) manner (of man), no doubt, perh. so be, then, therefore, truly, wherefore. Often used in connection with other par., *esp. 1065* or *3767* (after) or *1487* (before). Comp. also *687*.

687. ἆρα *ar'-ah;* a form of *686,* denoting an *interrogation* to which a neg. answer is presumed:–therefore.

688. 'Αραβία *ar-ab-ee'-ah;* of Heb. or. [6152]; *Arabia,* a region of Asia:–Arabia.

689. 'Αράμ *ar-am';* of Heb. or. [7410]; *Aram* (i.e. *Ram*), an Isr.:–Aram.

690. Ἄραψ *ar'-aps;* from *688;* an *Arab* or native of Arabia:–Arabian.

691. ἀργέω *arg-eh'-o;* from *692;* to *be idle,* i.e. (fig.) to *delay:*–linger.

692. ἀργός *ar-gos';* from *1* (as a neg. par.) and *2041; inact.,* i.e. *unemployed;* (by impl.) *lazy, useless:*–barren, idle, slow.

693. ἀργύρεος *ar-goo'-reh-os;* from *696;* made *of silver:*–(of) silver.

694. ἀργύριον *ar-goo'-ree-on;* neut. of a presumed der. of *696; silvery,* i.e. (by impl.) *cash;* spec. a *silverling* (i.e. *drachma* or *shekel*):–money, (piece of) silver (piece).

695. ἀργυροκόπος *ar-goo-rok-op'-os;* from *696* and *2875;* a *beater* (i.e. *worker*) *of silver:*–silversmith.

696. ἄργυρος *ar'-goo-ros;* from ἀργός (*shining*); *silver* (the metal, in the articles or coin):–silver.

697. Ἄρειος Παγος *ar'-i-os pag'-os;* from Ἄρης (the name of the Gr. deity of war) and a der. of *4078; rock of Ares,* a place in Athens:–Areopagus, Mars' Hill.

698. 'Αρεοπαγίτης *ar-eh-op-ag-ee'-tace;* from *697;* an *Areopagite* or member of the court held on Mars' Hill:–Areopagite.

699. ἀρέσκεια *ar-es'-ki-ah;* from a der. of *700; complaisance:*–pleasing.

700. ἀρέσκω *ar-es'-ko;* prob. from *142* (through the idea of *exciting* emotion); to *be agreeable* (or by impl. to seek to be so):–please.

701. ἀρεστός *ar-es-tos';* from *700; agreeable;* by impl. *fit:*–(things that) please(-ing), reason.

702. 'Αρέτας *ar-et'-as;* of for. or.; *Aretas,* an Arabian:–Aretas.

703. ἀρέτη *ar-et'-ay;* from the same as *730;* prop. *manliness* (*valor*), i.e. *excellence* (intrinsic or attributed):–praise, virtue.

704. ἀρήν *ar-ane';* perh. the same as *730;* a *lamb* (as a *male*):–lamb.

705. ἀριθμέω *ar-ith-meh'-o;* from *706;* to *enumerate* or *count:*–number.

706. ἀριθμός *ar-ith-mos';* from *142;* a *number* (as reckoned *up*):–number.

707. 'Αριμαθαία *ar-ee-math-ah'-ee-ah;* of Heb. or. [7414]; *Arimathaea* (or *Ramah*), a place in Pal.:–Arimathaea.

708. 'Αρισταρχος *ar-is'-tar-khos;* from the same as *712* and *757; best ruling; Aristarchus,* a Macedonian:–Aristarchus.

709. ἀριστάω *ar-is-tah'-o;* from *712;* to *take the principle meal:*–dine.

710. ἀριστερός *ar-is-ter-os';* app. a comp. of the same as *712;* the *left* hand (as *second-best*):–left [hand].

711. 'Αριστόβουλος *ar-is-tob'-oo-los;* from the same as *712* and *1012; best counselling; Aristoboulus,* a Chr.:–Aristobulus.

712. ἄριστον *ar'-is-ton;* app. neut. of a sup. from the same as *730;* the *best* meal [or *breakfast;* perh. from ἦρι ("*early*")], i.e. *luncheon:*–dinner.

713. ἀρκετός *ar-ket-os';* from *714; satisfactory:*–enough, suffice (-ient).

714. ἀρκέω *ar-keh'-o;* app. a prim. verb [but prob. akin to *142* through the idea of *raising* a barrier]; prop. to *ward off,* i.e. (by impl.) to *avail* (fig. *be satisfactory*]:–be content, be enough, suffice, be sufficient.

715. ἄρκτος *ark'-tos;* prob. from *714;* a bear (as *obstructing* by ferocity):–bear.

716. ἅρμα *har'-mah;* prob. from *142* [perh. with *1* (as a par. of union) pref.]; a *chariot* (as *raised* or fitted *together* [comp. *719*]):-chariot.

717. 'Αρμαγεδδών *ar-mag-ed-dohn';* of Heb. or. [2022 and 4023]; *Armageddon* (or *Har-Meggiddon*),a symbol name:–Armageddon.

718. ἁρμόζω *har-mod'-zo;* from *719;* to *joint,* i.e. (fig.) to *woo* (refl. to *betroth*):–espouse.

719. ἁρμός *har-mos';* from the same as *716;* an *articulation* (of the body):–joint.

720. ἀρνέομαι *ar-neh'-om-ahee;* perh. from *1* (as a neg. par.) and the mid. of *4483;* to *contradict,* i.e. *disavow, reject, abnegate:*–deny, refuse.

721. ἀρνίον *ar-nee'-on;* dim. from *704;* a *lambkin:*–lamb.

722. ἀροτριόω *ar-ot-ree-o'-o;* from *723;* to *plough:*– plow.

723. ἄροτρον *ar'-ot-ron;* from ἀρόω (to *till*); a *plough:*– plow..

724. ἁρπαγή *har-pag-ay';* from *726; pillage* (prop. abstr.):–extortion, ravening, spoiling.

725. ἁρπαγμός *har-pag-mos';* from *726; plunder* (prop. concr.):–robbery.

726. ἁρπάζω *har-pad'-zo;* from a der. of *138;* to *seize* (in various appl.):–catch (away, up), pluck, pull, take (by force).

727. ἅρπαξ *har'-pax;* from *726; rapacious:*–extortion, ravening.

728. ἀῤῥαβών *ar-hrab-ohn';* of Heb. or. [6162]; a *pledge,* i.e. part of the purchase-money or property given in advance as *security* for the rest:–earnest.

729. ἄῤῥαφος *ar'-hhraf-os;* from *1* (as a neg. par.) and a presumed der. of the same as *4476; unsewed,* i.e. of a single piece:–without seam.

730. ἄῤῥην *ar'-hrane;* or αρσην *ar-sane;* prob. from *142; male* (as stronger for *lifting*):–male, man.

731. ἄῤῥητος *ar'-hray-tos;* from *1* (as a neg. par.) and the same as *4490; unsaid,* i.e. (by impl.) *inexpressible:*–unspeakable.

732. ἄῤῥωστος *ar'-hroce-tos;* from *1* (as a neg. par.) and a presumed der. of *4517; infirm:*–sick (folk, -ly).

733. ἀρσενοκοίτης *ar-sen-ok-oy'-tace;* from *730* and *2845;* a *sodomite:*–abuser of (that defile) self with mankind.

734. 'Αρτεμάς *ar-tem-as';* contr. from a comp. of *735* and *1435; gift of Artemis; Artemas* (or *Artemidorus*), a Chr.:–Artemas.

735. Ἄρτεμις *ar'-tem-is;* prob. from the same as *736; prompt; Artemis,* the name of a Grecian goddess borrowed by the Asiatics for one of their deities:–Diana.

736. ἀρτέμων *ar-tem'-ohn;* from a der. of *737;* prop. something *ready* [or else more remotely from *142* (comp. *740*); something *hung* up], i.e. (spec.) the *topsail* (rather *foresail* or *jib*) of a vessel:–mainsail.

737. ἄρτι *ar'-tee;* adv. from a der. of *142* (comp. *740*) through the idea of *suspension;* just *now:*–this day (hour), hence[-forth], here [-after], hither[-to], (even) now, (this) present.

738. ἀρτιγέννητος *ar-teeg-en'-nay-tos;* from *737* and *1084; just born,* i.e. (fig.) a *young convert:*–new born.

739. ἄρτιος *ar'-tee-os;* from *737; fresh,* i.e. (by impl.) *complete:*–perfect.

740. ἄρτος *ar'-tos;* from *142; bread* (as *raised*) or a *loaf:*–(shew-)bread, loaf.

741. ἀρτύω *ar-too'-o;* from a presumed der. of *142;* to *prepare,* i.e. *spice* (with *stimulating* condiments):–season.

742. 'Αρφαξάδ *ar-fax-ad';* of Heb. or. [775]; Arphaxad, a post-diluvian patriarch:–Arphaxad.

743. ἀρχάγγελος *ar-khang'-el-os;* from *757* and *32;* a *chief angel:*–archangel.

744. ἀρχαῖος *ar-khah'-yos;* from *746; origional* or *primeval:*–(them of) old (time).

745. 'Αρχέλαος *ar-khel'-ah-os;* from *757* and *2994; people-ruling; Archelaus,* a

Jewish king:–Archelaus.

746. ἀρχή *ar-khay';* from *756;* (prop. abstr.) a *commencement,* or (concr.) *chief* (in various appl. of order, time, place, or rank):–beginning, corner, (at the, the) first (estate), magistrate, power, principality, principle, rule.

747. ἀρχηγός *ar-khay-gos';* from *746* and *71;* a *chief leader:*–author, captain, prince.

748. ἀρχιερατικός *ar-khee-er-at-ee-kos';* from *746* and a der. of *2413; high-priestly:*–of the high-priest.

749. ἀρχιερεύς *ar-khee-er-yuce';* from *746* and *2409;* the *high-priest* (lit. of the Jews, typ. Christ); by ext. a *chief priest:*–chief (high) priest, chief of the priests.

750. ἀρχιποίμην *ar-khee-poy'-mane;* from *746* and *4166;* a *head shepherd:*–chief shepherd.

751. Ἄρχιππος *ar'-khip-pos;* from *746* and *2462; horse-ruler; Archippus,* a Chr.:–Archippus.

752. ἀρχισυνάγωγος *ar-khee-soon-ag'-o-gos;* from *746* and *4864; director* of the *synagogue* services:–(chief) ruler of the synagogue.

753. ἀρχιτέκτων *ar-khee-tek'-tone; 5045;* a *chief constructor,* i.e. "*architect*":–masterbuilder.

754. ἀρχιτελώνης *ar-khee-tel-o'-nace;* from *746* and *5057;* a *principle tax-gatherer:*–chief among the publicans.

755. ἀρχιτρίκλινος *ar-khee-tree'-klee-nos;* from *746* and a com. of *5140* and *2827* (a *dinner-bed,* because composed of three couches); *director of* the *entertainment:*–governor (ruler) of the feast.

756. ἄρχομαι *ar'-khom-ahee;* mid. of *757* (through the impl. of *precedence*); to *commence* (in order of time):–(rehearse from the) begin(-ning).

757. ἄρχω *ar'-kho;* a prim. verb; to be *first* (in political rank or power):–reign (rule) over.

758. ἄρχων *ar'-khone;* pres. part. of *757;* a *first* (in rank or power):–chief (ruler), magistrate, prince, ruler.

759. ἄρωμα *ar'-o-mah;* from *142* (in the sense of *sending* off scent); an *aromatic:*–(sweet) spice.

760. Ἀσά *as-ah';* of Heb. or. [609]; *Asa,* an Isr.:–Asa.

761. ἀσάλευτος *as-al'-yoo-tos;* from *1* (as a neg. par.) and a der. of *4531; unshaken,* i.e. (by impl.) *immovable* (fig.):–which cannot be moved, unmovable.

762. ἄσβεστος *as'-bes-tos;* from *1* (as a neg. par.) and a der. of *4570; not extinguished,* i.e. (by impl.) *perpetual:*–not to be quenched, unquenchable.

763. ἀσέβεια *as-eb'-i-ah;* from *765; impiety,* i.e. (by impl.) *wickedness:*–ungodly(-liness).

764. ἀσεβέω *as-eb-eh'-o* from *765;* to be (by impl. act) *impious* or *wicked:*–commit (live, that after should live) ungodly.

765. ἀσεβής *as-eb-ace';* from *1* (as a neg. par.) and a presumed der. of *4576; irreverent,* i.e. (by ext.) *impious* or *wicked:*– ungodly (man).

766. ἀσέλγεια *as-elg'-i-a;* from a comp. of *1* (as a neg. par.) and a presumed σελγής (of unc. der. but app. mean. *continent*); *licentiousness* (sometimes incl. other vices):–filthy, lasciviousness, wantonness.

767. ἄσημος *as'-ay-mos;* from *1* (as a neg. par.) and the base of *4591; unmarked,* i.e. (fig.) *ignoble:*–mean.

768. Ἀσήρ *as-ayr';* of Heb. or. [836]; *Aser* (i.e. *Asher*), an Isr. tribe:–Aser.

769. ἀσθένεια *as-then'-i-ah;* from *772; feebleness* (of mind or body); by impl. *malady;* mor. *frailty:*–disease, infirmity, sickness, weakness.

770. ἀσθενέω *as-then-eh'-o;* from *772;* to *be feeble* (in any sense):–be diseased, impotent folk (man), (be) sick, (be, be made) weak.

771. ἀσθένημα *as-then'-ay-mah;* from *770;* a *scruple* of conscience:–infirmity.

772. ἀσθενής *as-then-ace';* from *1* (as a neg. par.) and the base of *4599; strengthless* (in various appl., lit. fig. and mor.):–more feeble, impotent, sick, without streng., weak(-er, -ness, thing).

773. Ἀσία *as-ee'-ah;* of unc. der.; *Asia,* i.e. *Asia Minor,* or (usually) only its western shore:–Asia.

774. Ἀσιανός, *as-ee-an-os';* from *773;* an *Asian* (i.e. *Asiatic*) or an inh. of Asia:–of Asia.

775. Ἀσιάρχης *as-ee-ar'-khace;* from *773* and *746;* an *Asiarch* or president of the public festivities in a city of Asia Minor:–chief of Asia.

776. ἀσιτία *as-ee-tee'-ah;* from *777; fasting* (the state):–abstinence.

777. ἄσιτος *as'-ee-tos;* from *1* (as a neg. par.) and *4621; without* (taking) *food:*–fasting.

778. ἀσκέω *as-keh'-o;* prob. from the same as *4632;* to *elaborate,* i.e. (fig.) *train* (by impl. *strive*):–exercise.

779. ἀσκός *as-kos';* from the same as *778;* a leathern (or skin) *bag* used as a bottle:–bottle.

780. ἀσμένως *as-men'-oce;* adv. from a der. of the base of *2237; with pleasure:*–gladly.

781. ἄσοφος *as'-of-os;* from *1* (as a neg. par.) and *4680; unwise:*–fool.

782. ἀσπάζομαι *as-pad'-zom-ahee;* from *1* (as a par. of union) and a presumed form of *4685;* to *enfold* in the arms, i.e. (by impl.) to *salute,* (fig.) to *welcome:*–embrace, greet, salute, take leave.

783. ἀσπασμός *as-pas-mos';* from *782;* a *greeting* (in pers. or by letter):–greeting, salutation.

784. ἄσπιλος *as'-pee-los;* from *1* (as a neg. par.) and *4695; unblemished* (phys. or mor.):–without spot, unspotted.

785. ἀσπίς *as-pece';* of unc. der.; a *buckler* (or *round* shield); used of a serpent (as *coiling* itself), prob. the "*asp*":–asp.

786. ἄσπονδος *as'-pon-dos;* from *1* (as a neg. par.) and a der. of *4689;* lit. *without libation* (which usually accompanied a treaty), i.e. (by impl.) *truceless:*–implacable, truce-breaker.

787. ἀσσάριον *as-sar'-ee-on;* of Lat. or.; an *assarius* or *as,* a Rom. coin:–farthing.

788. ἆσσον *as'-son;* neut. comp. of the base of *1451; more nearly,* i.e. *very near:*–close.

789. Ἄσσος *as'-sos* prob. of for. or.; *Assus,* a city of Asia Minor:–Assos.

790. ἀστατέω *as-tat-eh'-o;* from *1* (as a neg. par.) and a der. of *2476;* to *be non-stationary,* i.e. (fig.) *homeless:*–have no cert. dwelling-place.

791. ἀστεῖος *as-ti'-os;* from ἄστυ (a *city*); *urbane,* i.e. (by impl.) *handsome:*–proper, fair.

792. ἀστήρ *as-tare';* prob. from the base of *4766;* a *star* (as *strown* over the sky), lit. or fig.:–star.

793. ἀστήρικτος *as-tay'-rik-tos;* from *1* (as a neg. par.) and a presumed der. of *4741; unfixed,* i.e. (fig.) *vacillating:*–unstable.

794. ἄστοργος *as'-tor-gos;* from *1* (as a neg. par.) and a presumed der. of στέργω (to *cherish* affectionately); *hard-hearted* towards kindred:–without nat. affection.

795. ἀστοχέω *as-tokh-eh'-o;* from a comp. of *1* (as a neg. par.) and στοιχος (an *aim*); to *miss* the mark, i.e. (fig.) *deviate* from truth:–err, swerve.

796. ἀστραπή *as-trap-ay';* from *797; lightning;* by anal. *glare:*–lightning, bright shining.

797. ἀστράπτω *as-trap'-to;* prob. from *792;* to *flash* as lightning:–lighten, shine.

798. ἄστρον *as'-tron;* neut. from *792;* prop. a *constellation;* put for a single *star* (nat. or artif.):–star.

799. Ἀσύγκριτος *as-oong'-kree-tos;* from *1* (as a neg. par.) and a der. of *4793; incomparable; Asyncritus,* a Chr.:–Asyncritos.

800. ἀσύμφωνος *as-oom'-fo-nos;* from *1* (as a neg. par.) and *4859; inharmonious* (fig.):–agree not.

801. ἀσύνετος *as-oon'-ay-tos;* from *1* (as a neg. par.) and *4908; unintelligent;* by impl. *wicked:*–foolish, without understanding.

802. ἀσύνθετος *as-oon'-thet-os;* from *1* (as a neg. par.) and a der. of *4934;* prop. *not agreed,* i.e. *treacherous* to compacts:– covenant-breaker.

803. ἀσφάλεια *as-fal'-i-ah;* from *804; security* (lit. or fig.):–certainty, safety.

804. ἀσφαλής *as-fal-ace';* from *1* (as a neg. par.) and σφφαλλω (to "*fail*"); *secure* (lit. or fig.):–cert.(-ty), safe, sure.

805. ἀσφαλίζω *as-fal-id'-zo;* from *804;* to *render secure:*–make fast (sure).

806. ἀσφαλῶς *as-fal-oce';* adv. from *804; securely* (lit. or fig.):–assuredly, safely.

807. ἀσχημονέω *as-kay-mon-eh'-o;* from *809;* to *be* (i.e. *act*) *unbecoming:*–behave self uncomely (unseemly).

808. ἀσχημοσύνη *as-kay-mos-oo'-nay;* from *809;* an *indecency;* by impl. the *pudenda:*–shame, that which is unseemly.

809. ἀσχήμων *as-kay'-mone;* from *1* (as a neg. par.) and a presumed der. of *2192* (in the sense of its congener *4976*); prop. *shapeless,* i.e. (fig.) *inelegant:*–uncomely.

810. ἀσωτία *as-o-tee'-ah;* from a com. of *1* (as a neg. par.) and a presumed der. of *4982;* prop. *unsavedness,* i.e. (by impl.) *profligacy:*–excess, riot.

811. ἀσώτως *as-o'-toce;* adv. from the same as *810; dissolutely:*–riotous.

812. ἀτακτέω *at-ak-teh'-o;* from *813;* to be (i.e. *act*) *irreg.:*–behave self disorderly.

813. ἄτακτος *at'-ak-tos;* from *1* (as a neg. par.) and a der. of *5021; unarranged,* i.e. (by impl.)

insubordinate (relig.):–unruly.

814. ἀτάκτως *at-ak'-toce;* adv. from *813, irreg.* (mor.):–disorderly.

815. ατεκνος *at'-ek-no;* from *1* (as a neg. par.) and *5043; childless:*–childless, without children.

816. ἀτενίζω *at-en-id'-zo;* from a com. of *1* (as a par. of union) and τείνω (to *stretch*); to *gaze* intently:–behold earnestly (stedfastly), fasten (eyes), look (earnestly, stedfastly, up stedfastly), set eyes.

817. ἄτερ *at'-er* a par. prob. akin to *427; aloof,* i.e. *apart* from (lit. or fig.):–in the absence of, without.

818. ἀτιμάζω *at-im-ad'-zo;* from *820;* to *render infamous,* i.e. (by impl.) *contemn* or *maltreat:*–despise, dishonour, suffer shame, entreat shamefully.

819. ἀτιμία *at-ee-mee'-ah;* from *820; infamy,* i.e. (subj.) comp. *indignity,* (obj.) *disgrace:*–dishonour, reproach, shame, vile.

820. ἄτιμος *at'-ee-mos;* from *1* (as a neg. par.) and *5092;* (neg.) *unhonoured* or (pos.) *dishonoured:*–despised, without honour, less honourable [*comp. degree*].

821. ἀτιμόω *at-ee-mo'-o;* from *820;* used like *818,* to *maltreat:*–handle shamefully.

822. ἀτμίς *at-mece';* from the same as *109; mist:*–vapour.

823. ἄτομος *at'-om-os;* from *1* (as a neg. par.) and the base of *5114; uncut,* i.e. (by impl.) *indivisible* [an "*atom*" of time]:– moment.

824. ἄτοπος *at'-op-os;* from *1* (as a neg. par.) and *5117; out of place,* i.e. (fig.) *improper, injurious, wicked:*–amiss, harm, unreasonable.

825. ᾿Αττάλεια *at-tal'-i-ah;* from Ἄτταλος (a king of Pergamus); *Attaleia,* a place in Pamphylia:–Attalia.

826. αὐγάζω *ow-gad'-zo;* from *827;* to *beam* forth (fig.):–shine.

827. αὐγή *owg'-ay;* of unc. der.; a *ray* of light, i.e. (by impl.) *radiance, dawn:*–break of day.

828. Αὔγουστος *ow'-goos-tos;* from Lat. ["august"]; *Augustus,* a title of the Rom. emperor:–Augustus.

829. αὐθάδης *ow-thad'-ace;* from *846* and the base of *2237; self-pleasing,* i.e. *arrogant:*–self-willed.

830. αὐθαίρετος *ow-thah'-ee-ret-os;* from *846* and the same as *140; self-chosen,* i.e. (by impl.) *voluntarily:*–of own accord, willing of self.

831. αὐθεντέω *ow-then-teh'-o;* from a com. of *846* and an obs. ἕντης (a *worker*); to *act of oneself,* i.e. (fig.) *dominate:*–usurp authority over.

832. αὐλέω *ow-leh'-o;* from *836;* to play the *flute:*–pipe.

833. αὐλή *ow-lay';* from the same as *109;* a *yard* (as open to the *wind*); by impl. a *mansion:*–court, ([sheep-]) fold, hall, palace.

834. αὐλητής *ow-lay-tace';* from *832;* a *flute-player:*–minstrel, piper.

835. αὐλίζομαι τηὶς, *ow-lid'-zom-ahee;* mid. from *833;* to *pass the night* (prop. in the open air):–abide, lodge.

836. αὐλός *ow-los';* from the same as *109;* a *flute* (as *blown*):–pipe.

837. αὐξάνω *owx-an'-o;* a prol. form of a prim. verb; to *grow* ("*wax*"), i.e. *enlarge* (lit. or fig. act. or pass.):–grow (up), (give the) increase.

838. αὔξησις *owx'-ay-sis;* from *837; growth:*–increase.

839. αὔριον *ow'-ree-on;* from a der. of the same as *109* (mean. a *breeze,* i.e. the morning *air*); prop. *fresh,* i.e. (adv. with ell. of *2250*) *to-morrow:*–(to-)morrow, next day.

840. αὐστηρός *ow-stay-ros';* from a (presumed) der. of the same as *109* (mean. *blown*); *rough* (prop. as a *gale*), i.e. (fig.) *severe:*–austere.

841. αὐτάρκεια *ow-tar'-ki-ah;* from *842; self-satisfaction,* i.e. (abstr.) *contentedness,* or (concr.) a *competence:*–contentment, sufficiency.

842. αὐτάρκης *ow-tar'-kace;* from *846* and *714; self-complacent,* i.e. *contented:*–content.

843. αὐτοκατάκριτος *ow-tok-at-ak'-ree-tos;* from *846* and a der. or *2632; self-condemned:*–condemned of self.

844. αὐτόματος *ow-tom'-at-os;* from *846* and the same as *3155; self-moved* ["automatic"], i.e. *spontaneous:*–of own accord, of self.

845. αὐτόπτης *ow-top'-tace;* from *846* and *3700; self-seeing,* i.e. an *eye-witness:*–eye-witness.

846. αὐτός *ow-tos';* from the par. αὖ, [perh. akin to the base of *109* through the idea of a *baffling* wind] (*backward*);

the refl. pron. *self,* used (alone or in the comp. *1438*) of the third pers., and (with the proper pers. pron.) of the other persons:–her, it(-self), one, the other, (mine) own, said, ([self-], the) same, ([him-, my-, thy-]) self, [your-]selves, she, that, their(-s), them(-selves), there[-at, - by, -in, -into, -of, -on, -with], they, (these) things, this (man), those, together, very, which. Comp. *848*.

847. αὐτοῦ *ow-too';* gen. (i.e. possessive) of *846,* used as an adv. of location; prop. belonging to the *same* spot, i.e. *in this* (or *that*) *place:*–(t-)here.

848. αὑτοῦ *how-too';* contr. for *1438; self* (in some oblique case or refl. relation):–her (own), (of) him(-self), his (own), of it, thee, their (own), them(-selves), they.

849. αὐτόχειρ *ow-tokh'-ire;* from *846* and *5495; self-handed,* i.e. doing *pers.:*–with ... own hands.

850. αὐχμηρός *owkh-may-ros';* from αὐχμός [prob. from a base akin to that of *109*] (*dust,* as *dried* by wind); prop. *dirty,* i.e. (by impl.) *obscure:*–dark .

851. ἀφαιρέω *af-ahee-reh'-o;* from *575* and *138;* to *remove* (lit. or fig.):–cut (smite) off, take away.

852. ἀφανής *af-an-ace';* from *1* (as a neg. par.) and *5316; non-app.*):–i.e. not manifest.

853. ἀφανίζω *af-an-id'-zo;* from *852; to render unapparent,* i.e. (act.) *consume* (*becloud*), or pass. *disappear* (*be destroyed*):–corrupt, disfigure, perish, vanish away.

854. ἀφανισμός *af-an-is-mos';* from *853; disappearance,* i.e. (fig.) *abrogation:*–vanish away.

855. ἄφαντος *af'-an-tos;* from *1* (as a neg. par.) and a der. of *5316; non-manifested,* i.e. *invisible:*–vanished out of sight.

856. ἀφεδρών *af-ed-rone';* from a com. of *575* and the base of *1476;* a place of *sitting apart,* i.e. a *privy:*–draught.

857. ἀφειδία *af-i-dee'-ah;* from a com. of *1* (as a neg. par.) and *5339; unsparingness,* i.e. *austerity* (*asceticism*):–neglecting.

858. ἀφελότης *af-el-ot'-ace;* from a com. of *1* (as a neg. par.) and φέλλος (in the sense of a *stone* as *stubbing* the foot); *smoothness,* i.e. (fig.) *simplicity:*–singleness.

859. ἄφεσις *af'-es-is;* from *863; freedom;* (fig.) *pardon:*–deliverance, forgiveness, liberty, remission.

860. ἁφή *haf-ay';* from *680;* prob. a *ligament* (as *fastening*):–joint.

861. ἀφθαρσία *af-thar-see'-ah;* from *862; incorruptibility;* gen. *unending existence;* (fig.) *genuineness:*–immortality, incorruption, sincerity.

862. ἄφθαρτος *af'-thar-tos;* from *1* (as a neg. par.) and a der. of *5351; undecaying* (in essence or continuance):–not (in-, un-) corruptible, immortal.

863. ἀφίημι *af-ee'-ay-mee;* from *575* and ἵημι (to *send;* an intens. form of εἶμι, to go); to *send forth,* in various appl. (as follow):–cry, forgive, forsake, lay aside, leave, let (alone, be, go, have), omit, put (send) away, remit, suffer, yield up.

864. ἀφικνέομαι *af-ik-neh'-om-ahee;* from *575* and the base of *2425;* to *go* (i.e. *spread*) *forth* (by rumor):–come abroad.

865. ἀφιλάγαθος *af-il-ag'-ath-os* from *1* (as a neg. par.) and *5358; hostile to virtue:*–despiser of those that are good.

866. ἀφιλάργυρος *af-il-ar'-goo-ros;* from *1* (as a neg. par.) and *5366; unavaricious:*–without covetousness, not greedy of filthy lucre.

867. ἄφιξις *af'-ix-is;* from *864;* prop. *arrival,* i.e. (by impl.) *departure:*–departing.

868. ἀφίστημι *af-is'-tay-mee* from *575* and *2476;* to *remove,* i.e. (act.) *instigate* to revolt; usually (refl.) to *desist, desert,* etc.:–depart, draw (fall) away, refrain, withdraw self.

869. ἄφνω *af'-no;* adv. from *852* (contr.); *unawares,* i.e. *unexpectedly:*–suddenly.

870. ἀφόβως *af-ob'-oce;* adv. from a com. of *1* (as a neg. par.) and *5401; fearlessly:*–without fear.

871. ἀφομοιόω *af-om-oy-o'-o;* from *575* and *3666;* to *assimilate* closely:–make like.

872. ἀφοράω *af-or-ah'-o* from *575* and *3708;* to *consider* attentively:–look.

873. ἀφορίζω *af-or-id'-zo;* from 575 and 3724; to *set off* by boundary, i.e. (fig.) *limit, exclude, appoint,* etc.:–divide, separate, sever.

874. ἀφορμή *af-or-may';* from a comp. of *575* and *3729;* a *starting*-point, i.e. (fig.) an *opportunity:*–occasion.

875. ἀφρίζω *af-rid'-zo;* from *876;* to *froth* at the mouth (in epilepsy):–foam.

876. ἀφρός *af-ros';* app. a prim. word;

froth, i.e. *slaver:*–foaming.

877. ἀφροσύνη *af-ros-oo'-nay;* from *878; senselessness,* i.e. (euph.) *egotism;* (mor.) *recklessness:*–folly, foolishly(-ness).

878. ἄφρων *af'-rone;* from *1* (as a neg. par.) and *5424;* prop. *mindless,* i.e. *stupid,* (by impl.) *ignorant,* (spec.) *egotistic,* (practically) *rash,* or (mor.) *unbelieving:*–fool(-ish), unwise.

879. ἀφυπνόω *af-oop-no'-o;* from a com. of *575* and *5258;* prop. to *become awake,* i.e. (by impl.) to *drop* (off) in slumber:–fall asleep.

880. ἄφωνος *af'-o-nos;* from *1* (as a neg. par.) and *5456; voiceless,* i.e. *mute* (by nature or choice); fig. *unmeaning:*–dumb, without signification.

881. 'Αχάζ *akh-adz';* of Heb. or. [271]; *Achaz,* an Isr.:–Achaz.

882. 'Αχαΐα *ach-ah-ee'-ah;* of unc. der.; *Achaïa* (i.e. *Greece*), a country of Europe:–Achaia.

883. 'Αχαϊκός *ach-ah-ee-kos';* from *882;* an *Achaïan; Achaïcus,* a Chr.:–Achaicus.

884. ἀχάριστος *ach-ar'-is-tos;* from *1* (as a neg. par.) and a presumed der. of *5483; thankless,* i.e. *ungrateful:*–unthankful.

885. 'Αχείμ *akh-ime';* prob. of Heb. or. [comp. 3137]; *Achim,* an Isr.:–Achim.

886. ἀχειροποίητος, *akh-i-rop-oy'-ay-tos;* from *1* (as a neg. par.) and *5499; unmanufactured,* i.e. *inartificial:*–made without (not made with) hands.

887. ἀχλύς *akh-looce';* of unc. der.; *dimness* of sight, i.e. (prob.) a *cataract:*–mist.

888. ἀχρεῖος *akh-ri'-osv* from *1* (as a neg. par.) and a der. of *5534* [comp. *5532*]; *useless,* i.e. (euph.) *unmeritorious:*–unprofitable.

889. ἀχρειόω *akh-ri-o'-o;* from 888; to *render useless,* i.e. *spoil:*–become unprofitable.

890. ἄχρηστος *akh'-race-tos;* from *1* (as a neg. par.) and *5543; inefficient,* i.e. (by impl.) *detrimental:*–unprofitable.

891. ἄχρι *akh'-ree;*or ἄχρις, *akh'-rece;* akin to *206* (through the idea of a *terminus*); (of time) *until* or (of place) *up to:*–as far as, for, in(-to), till, (even, un-)to, until, while. Comp. *3360.*

892. ἄχυρον *akh'-oo-ron;* perh. remotely from χέω (to *shed* forth); *chaff* (as *diffusive*):–chaffin.

893. ἀψευδής *aps-yoo-dace';* from *1* (as a neg. par.) and *5579; veracious:*–that cannot lie.

894. ἄψινθος *ap'-sin-thos;* of unc. der.; *wormwood* (as a type of *bitterness,* i.e. [fig.] *calamity*):–wormwood.

895. ἄψυχος *ap'-soo-khos;* from *1* (as a neg. par.) and *5590; lifeless,* i.e. *inanimate* (mechanical):–without life.

B

896. Βάαλ *bah'-al;* of Heb. or. [1168]; *Baal,* a Phoenician deity (used as a symbol of idolatry):–Baal.

897. Βαβυλών *bab-oo-lone';* of Heb. or. [894]; *Bab.,* the capitol of Chaldaea (lit. or fig. [as a type of tyranny]):– Babylon

898. βαθμός *bath-mos';* from the same as *899;* a *step,* i.e. (fig.) *grade* (of dignity):–degree.

899. βάθος *bath'-os;* from the same as *901; profundity,* i.e. (by impl.) *extent;* (fig.) *mystery:*–deep(-ness, things), depth.

900. βαθύνω *bath-oo'-no;* from *901;* to *deepen:*–deep.

901. βαθύς *bath-oos';* from the base of *939; profound* (as *going* down), lit. or fig.:–deep, very early.

902. βαΐον *bah-ee'-on;* a dim. of a der. prob. of the base of *939;* a palm *twig* (as *going* out far):–branch.

903. Βαλαάμ *bal-ah-am';* of Heb. or. [1109]; *Balaam,* a Mesopotamian (symbolic of a false teacher):–Balaam.

904. Βαλάκ *bal-ak';* of Heb. or. [1111]; *Balak,* a Moabite:–Balac.

905. βαλάντιον *bal-an'-tee-on;* prob. remotely from *906* (as a *depository*); a *pouch* (for money):–bag, purse.

906. βάλλω *bal'-lo;* a prim. verb; to *throw* (in various appl., more or less violent or intense):–arise, cast (out), X dung, lay, lie, pour, put (up), send, strike, throw (down), thrust. Comp. *4496.*

907. βαπτίζω *bap-tid'-zo;* from a der. of *911;* to *make whelmed* (i.e. *fully wet*); used only (in the N.T.) of cer. *ablution,* esp. (tech.) of the ordinance of Chr. *baptism:*–Baptist, baptize, wash.

908. βάπτισμα *bap'-tis-mah;* from *907; baptism* (tech. or fig.):–baptism.

909. βαπτισμός *bap-tis-mos';* from *907; ablution* (cer. or Chr.):–baptism, washing.

910. Βαπτιστής *bap-tis-tace';* from *907;* a *baptizer,* as an epithet of Christ's forerunner:–Baptist.

911. βάπτω *bap'-to;* a prim. verb; to *whelm,* i.e. cover wholly with a fluid; in the N.T. only in a qualified or spec. sense, i.e. (lit.) to *moisten* (a part of one's pers.), or (by impl.) to *stain* (as with dye):–dip.

912. Βαραββᾶς *bar-ab-bas';* of Chald. or. [1347 and 5]; *son of Abba; Bar-abbas,* an Isr.:–Barabbas.

913. Βαράκ *bar-ak';* of Heb. or. [1301]; *Barak,* an Isr.:–Barak.

914. Βαραχίας *bar-akh-ee'-as;* of Heb. or. [1296]; *Barachias* (i.e. *Berechijah*), an Isr.:–Barachias.

915. βάρβαρος *bar'-bar-os;* of unc. der.; a *foreigner* (i.e. *non-Gr.*):–barbarian(-rous).

916. βαρέω *bar-eh'-o;* from *926;* to *weigh* down (fig.):–burden, charge, heavy, press.

917. βαρέως *bar-eh'-oce* adv. from *926; heavily* (fig.):–dull.

918. Βαρθολομαῖος *bar-thol-om-ah'-yos;* of Chald. or. [1247 and 8526]; *son of Tolmai; Bar-tholomoeus,* a Chr. apostle:–Bartholomeus.

919. βαριησοῦς *bar-ee-ay-sooce';* of Chald. or. [1247 and 3091]; *son of Jesus* (or *Joshua*); *Bar-jesus,* an Isr.:–Barjesus.

920. ΒαριΓωνᾶς *bar-ee-oo-nas'* of Chald. or. [1247 and 3124]; *son of Jonas* (or *Jonah*); *Bar-jonas,* an Isr.:–Bar-jona.

921. Βαρνάβας *bar-nab'-as;* of Chald. or. [1247 and 5029]; *son of Nabas* (i.e. *prophecy*); *Barnabas,* an Isr.:–Barnabas.

922. βάρος *bar'-os;* prob. from the same as *939* (through the notion of *going* down; comp. *899*); *weight;* in the N.T. only, fig. a *load, abundance, authority:*–burden(-some), weight.

923. Βαρσαβᾶς *bar-sab-as';* of Chald. or. [1247 and prob. 6634]; *son of Sabas* (or *Tsaba*); *Bar-sabas,* the name of two Isr.:–Barsabas.

924. Βαρτιμαῖος *bar-tim-ah'-yos;* of Chald. or. [1247 and 2931]; *son of Timoeus* (or the *unclean*); *Bar-timoeus,* an Isr.:–Bartimaeus.

925. βαρύνω *bar-oo'-no;* from *926;* to *burden* (fig.):–overcharge.

926. βαρυς *bar-ooce';* from the same as *922; weighty,* i.e. (fig) *burdensome, grave:*–grievous, heavy, weightier.

927. βαρύτιμος *bar-oo'-tim-os;* from *926* and *5092;* highly *valuable:*–very precious.

928. βασανίζω *bas-an-id'-zo* from *931;* to *torture:*–pain, toil, torment, toss, vex.

929. βασανισμός *bas-an-is-mos';* from *928; torture:*–torment.

930. βασανιστής *bas-an-is-tace';* from *928;* a *torturer:*–tormentor.

931. βάσανος *bas'-an-os;* perh. remotely from the same as *939* (through the notion of *going* to the bottom); a *touch-stone,* i.e. (by anal.) *torture:*–torment.

932. βασιλεία *bas-il-i'-ah;* from *935;* prop. *royalty,* i.e. (abstr.) *rule,* or (concr.) a *realm* (lit. or fig.):–kingdom, + reign.

933. βασίλειον *bas-il'-i-on;* neut. of *934;* a *palace:*–king's court.

934. βασίλειος *bas-il'-i-os;* from *935; kingly* (in nature):–royal.

935. βασιλεύς *bas-il-yooce';* prob. from *939* (through the notion of a *foundation* of power); a *sovereign* (abstr., rel. or fig.):–king.

936. βασιλεύω *bas-il-yoo'-o;* from *935;* to *rule* (lit. or fig.):–king, reign.

937. βασιλικός *bas-il-ee-kos';* from *935; regal* (in relation), i.e. (lit.) belonging to (or befitting) the sovereign (as land, dress, or a *courtier*), or (fig.) *preeminent:*–king's, nobleman, royal.

938. βασίλισσα *bas-il'-is-sah;* or. from *936;* a *queen:*–queen.

939. βάσις *bas'-ece;* from βαίνω (to *walk*); a *pace* ("base"), i.e. (by impl.) the *foot:*–foot.

940. βασκαίνω *bas-kah'-ee-no;* akin to *5335;* to *malign,* i.e. (by ext.) to *fascinate* (by false representations):–bewitch.

941. βαστάζω *bas-tad'-zo;* perh. remotely der. from the base of *939* (through the idea of *removal*); to *lift,* lit. or fig. (*endure, declare, sustain, receive,* etc.):–bear, carry, take up.

942. βάτος *bat'-os;* of unc. der.; a *brier* shrub:–bramble, bush.

943. βάτος *bat'-os;* of Heb. or. (1324); a *bath,* or measure for liquids:–measure

944. βάτραχος *bat'-rakh-os;* of unc. der.; a *frog:*–frog.

945. βαττολογέω *bat-tol-og-eh'-o;* from

Βαττος (a proverbial stammerer) and *3056;* to *stutter,* i.e. (by impl.) to *prate* tediously:–use vain repetitions.
946. βδέλυγμα *bdel'-oog-mah;* from *948;* a *detestation,* i.e. (spec.) *idolatry:*–abomination.
947. βδελυκτός *bdel-ook-tos';* from *948; detestable,* i.e. (spec.) *idolatrous:*–abominable.
948. βδελύσσω *bdel-oos'-so;* from a (presumed) der. of βδέω (to *stink*); to *be disgusted,* i.e. (by impl.) *detest* (esp. of idolatry):–abhor, abominable.
949. βέβαιος *beb'-ah-yos;* from the base of *939* (through the idea of *basality*); *stable* (lit. or fig.):–firm, of force, stedfast, sure.
950. βεβαιόω *beb-ah-yo'-o;* from *949;* to *stabilitate* (fig.):–confirm, (e-)stablish.
951. βεβαίωσις *beb-ah'-yo-sis;* from *950; stabiliment:*–confirmation.
952. βέβηλος *beb'-ay-los;* from the base of 939 and βηλός (a *threshold*); *accessible* (as by *crossing* the *door-way*), i.e. (by impl. of Jewish notions) *heathenish, wicked:*–profane (pers.).
953. βεβηλόω *beb-ay-lo'-o;* from *952;* to *desecrate:*–profane.
954. Βεελζεβούλ *beh-el-zeb-ool';* of Chald. or. [by parody on 1176]; *dung-god; Beelzebul,* a name of Satan:–Beelzebub.
955. Βελίαλ *bel-ee'-al;* of Heb. or. [1100]; *worthlessness; Belial,* as an epithet of Satan:–Belial.
956. βέλος *bel'-os;* from *906;* a *missile,* i.e. *spear* or *arrow:*–dart
957. βελτίον *bel-tee'-on;* neut. of a com. of a der. of *906* (used for the comp. of *18*); *better:*–very well.
958. Βενιαμίν *ben-ee-am-een';* of Heb. or. [1144]; *Benjamin,* an Isr.:–Benjamin.
959. Βερνίκη *ber-nee'-kay;* from a provincial form of *5342* and *3529; victorious; Bernicè,* a member of the Herodian family:–Bernice.
960. Βέροια *ber'-oy-ah;* perh. a provincial from a der. of *4008* [*Peroea,* i.e. the region *beyond* the coast-line]; *Beroea,* a place in Macedonia:–Berea.
961. Βεροιαῖος *ber-oy-ah'-yos;* from *960;* a *Beroeoean* or native of Beroea:–of Berea.
962. Βηθαβαρά *bay-thab-ar-ah';* of Heb. or. [1004 and 5679]; *ferry-house; Bethabara* (i.e. *Bethabarah*), a place on the Jordan:–Bethabara.
963. Βηθανία *bay-than-ee'-ah;* of Chald. or.; *date-house; Beth-any,* a place in Pal.:–Bethany.
964. Βηθεσδά *bay-thes-dah';* of Chald. or. [comp. 1004 and 2617]; *house of kindness; Beth-esda,* a pool in Jerus.:–Bethesda.
965. Βηθλεέμ *bayth-leh-em';* of Heb. or. [1036]; *Bethleem* (i.e. *Beth-lechem*), a place in Pal.:–Bethlehem.
966. Βηθσαϊδά *bayth-sahee-dah';* of Chald. or. [comp. 1004 and 6719]; *fishing-house; Bethsaïda,* a place in Pal.:–Bethsaida.
967. Βηθφαγή *bayth-fag-ay';* of Chald. or. [comp. 1004 and 6291]; *fig-house; Beth-phagè,* a place in Pal.:–Bethphage.
968. βῆμα *bay'-ma;* from the base of *939;* a *step,* i.e. *foot-breath;* by impl. a *rostrum,* i.e. a *tribunal:*–judgment-seat, set [foot] on, throne.
969. βήρυλλος *bay'-rool-los;* of unc. der.; a "*beryl*":–beryl.
970. βία *bee'-ah;* prob. akin to *979* (through the idea of *vital* activity); *force:*–violence.
971. βιάζω *bee-ad'-zo;* from *970;* to *force,* i.e. (refl.) to *crowd oneself* (into), or (pass.) to *be seized:*–press, suffer violence.
972. βίαιος *bee'-ah-yos;* from *970; violent:*–mighty.
973. βιαστής *bee-as-tace';* from *971;* a *forcer,* i.e. (fig.) *energetic:*–violent.
974. βιβλιαρίδιον *bib-lee-ar-id'-ee-on;* a dim. of *975;* a *booklet:*–little book.
975. βιβλίον *bib-lee'-on;* a dim. of *976;* a *roll:*–bill, book, scroll, writing.
976. βίβλος *bib'-los;* prop. the inner *bark* of the papyrus plant, i.e. (by impl.) a *sheet* or *scroll* of writing:–book.
977. βιβρώσκω *bib-ro'-sko;* a redupl. and prol. form of an obs. prim. verb [perh. caus. of *1006*]; to *eat:*–eat.
978. Βιθυνία *bee-thoo-nee'-ah;* of unc. der.; *Bithynia,* a region of Asia:–Bithynia.
979. βίος *bee'-os;* a prim. word; *life,* i.e. (lit.) the present state of existence; by impl. the means of *livelihood:*–good, life, living.
980. βιόω *bee-o'-o;* from 979; to *spend* existence:–live.
981. Βίωσις *bee'-o-sis;* from *980; living* (prop. the act, by impl. the mode):–manner of life.
982. βιωτικός *bee-o-tee-kos';* from a der. of *980; relating* to the present *existence:*–of (pertaining to, things that pertain to) this life.
983. βλαβερός *blab-er-os';* from *984; injurious:*–hurtful.
984. βλάπτω *blap'-to;* a prim. verb; prop. to *hinder,* i.e. (by impl.) to *injure:*–hurt.
985. βλαστάνω *blas-tan'-o;* from βλαστός (a *sprout*); to *germinate;* by impl. to *yield* fruit:–bring forth, bud, spring (up).
986. Βλάστος *blas'-tos;* perh. the same as the base of *985; Blastus,* an officer of Herod Agrippa:–Blastus.
987. βλασφημέω *blas-fay-meh'-o;* from 989; to *vilify;* spec. to *speak impiously:*–(speak) blaspheme(-er, -mously, -my), defame, rail on, revile, speak evil.
988. βλασφημία *blas-fay-me'-ah;* from *989;* vilification (esp. against God):–blasphemy, evil speaking, railing.
989. βλάσφημος *blas'-fay-mos;* from a der. of *984* and *5345; scurrilious,* i.e. *calumnious* (against man), or (spec.) *impious* (against God):–blasphemer(-mous), railing.
990. βλέμμα *blem'-mah;* from *991; vision* (prop. concr.; by impl. abstr.):–seeing.
991. βλέπω *blep'-o;* a prim. verb; to *look* at (lit. or fig.):–behold, beware, lie, look (on, to), perceive, regard, see, sight, take heed. Comp. *3700.*
992. βλητέος *blay-teh'-os;* from *906;* fit *to be cast* (i.e. *applied*):–must be put.
993. Βοανεργές *bo-an-erg-es';* of Chald. or. [1123 and 7266]; *sons of commotion; Boänerges,* an epithet of two of the apostles:–Boanerges.'
994. βοάω *bo-ah'-o;* app. a prol. form of a prim. verb; to *halloo,* i.e. *shout* (for help or in a tumultuous way):–cry.
995. βοή *bo-ay';* from *994;* a *halloo,* i.e. *call* (for aid, etc.):–cry.
996. βοήθεια *bo-ay'-thi-ah;* from *998; aid;* spec. a rope or chain for frapping a vessel:–help.
997. βοηθέω *bo-ay-theh'-o;* from 998; to *aid* or *relieve:*–help, succor.
998. βοηθός *bo-ay-thos';* from *995* and θέω (to *run*); a *succorer:*–helper.
999. βόθυνος *both'-oo-nos;* akin to *900;* a *hole* (in the ground); spec. a *cistern:*–ditch, pit.
1000. βολή *bol-ay';* from *906;* a *throw* (as a measure of distance):–cast.
1001. βολίζω *bol-id'-zo;* from *1002;* to heave the lead:–sound.
1002. βολίς *bol-ece';* from *906;* a *missile,* i.e. *javelin:*–dart.
1003. Βοόζ *bo-oz';* of Heb. or. [1162]; *Boöz* (i.e. Boäz), an Isr.:–Booz.
1004. βόρβορος *bor'-bor-os;* of unc. der.; *mud:*–mire.
1005. βορῥᾶς *bor-hras';* of unc. der.; the *north* (prop. wind):–north.
1006. Βόσκω *bos'-ko;* a prol. form of a prim. verb [comp. *977, 1016*]; to *pasture;* by ext. to, *fodder;* refl. to *graze:*–feed, keep.
1007. Βοσόρ *bos-or';* of Heb. or. [1160]; Bosor [i.e. *Beör*], a Moabite:–Bosor
1008. βοτάνη *bot-an'-ay;* from *1006; herbage* (as if for *grazing*):–herb.
1009. βότρυς *bot'-rooce;* of unc. der.; a *bunch* (of grapes):–(vine) cluster (of the vine).
1010. βουλευτής *bool-yoo-tace';* from *1011;* an *adviser,* i.e. (spec.) a *councillor* or member of the Jewish Sanhedrin:–counsellor.
1011. βουλεύω *bool-yoo'-o;* from *1012;* to *advise,* i.e. (refl.) *deliberate,* or (by impl.) *resolve:*–consult, take counsel, determine, be minded, purpose.
1012. βουλή *boo-lay';* from *1014; volition,* i.e. (obj.) *advice,* or (by impl.) *purpose:*–+ advise, counsel, will.
1013. βούλημα *boo'-lay-mah;* from *1014;* a *resolve:*–purpose, will.
1014. βούλομαι *boo'-lom-ahee;* mid. of a prim. verb; to "*will,*" i.e. (refl.) *be willing:*–be disposed, minded, intend, list, (be, of own) will (-ing). Comp. *2309.*
1015. βουνός *boo-nos';* prob. of for. or.; a *hillock:*–hill.
1016. βοῦς *booce;* prob. from the base of *1006;* an *ox* (as *grazing*), i.e. an animal of that species ("beef"):–ox.
1017. βραβεῖον *brab-i'-on;* from βραβεύς (an *umpire;* of unc. der.); an *award* (of arbitration), i.e. (spec.) a *prize* in the public games:–prize.
1018. βραβεύω *brab-yoo'-o;* from the same as *1017;* to *arbitrate,* i.e. (gen. case) to *govern* (fig. *prevail*):–rule.
1019. βραδύνω *brad-oo'-no;* from *1021;* to

delay:–be slack, tarry.
1020. βραδυπλοέω *brad-oo-plo-eh'-o;* from *1021* and a prol. form of *4126;* to *sail slowly:*–sail slowly.
1021. βραδύς *brad-ooce';* of unc. affin.; *slow;* fig. *dull:*–slow.
1022. βραδύτης *brad-oo'-tace;* from *1021; tardiness:*–slackness.
1023. βραχίων *brakh-ee'-own;* prop. comp. of *1024,* but app. in the sense of βράσσω (to *wield*); the *arm,* i.e. (fig.) *streng.:*–arm.
1024. βραχύς *brakh-ooce';* of unc. affin.; *short* (of time, place, quantity, or number):–few words, little (space, while).
1025. βρέφος *bref'-os;* of unc. affin.; an *infant* (prop. unborn) lit. or fig.:–babe, (young) child, infant.
1026. βρέχω *brekh'-o;* a prim. verb; to *moisten* (esp. by a shower):–(send) rain, wash.
1027. βροντή *bron-tay;* akin to βρέμω (to *roar*); *thunder:*–thunder(-ing).
1028. βροχή *brokh-ay';* from *1026; rain:*–rain.
1029. βρόχος *brokh'-os;* of unc. der.; a *noose:*–snare.
1030. βρυγμός *broog-mos';* from *1031;* a *grating* (of the teeth):–gnashing.
1031. βρύχω *broo'-kho;* a prim. verb; to *grate* the teeth (in pain or rage):–gnash.
1032. βρύω *broo'-o;* a prim. verb; to *swell* out, i.e. (by impl.) to *gush:*–send forth.
1033. βρῶμα *bro'-mah;* from the base of *977; food* (lit. or fig.), esp. (cer.) articles allowed or forbidden by the Jewish law:–meat, victuals.
1034. βρώσιμος *bro'-sim-os;* from *1035; eatable:*–meat.
1035. βρῶσις *bro'-sis;* from the base of *977;* (abstr.) *eating* (lit. or fig.); by ext. (concr.) *food* (lit. or fig.):–eating, food, meat.
1036. βυθίζω *boo-thid'-zo;* from *1037;* to *sink;* by impl. to *drown:*–begin to sink, drown.
1037. βυθός *boo-thos';* a var. of *899; depth,* i.e. (by impl.) the *sea:*–deep.
1038. βυρσεύς *boorce-yooce';* from βυρσα (a *hide*); a *tanner:*–tanner.
1039. βυσσινος *boos'-see-nos;* from *1040;* made of *linen* (neut. a linen *cloth*):–fine linen.
1040. βύσσος *boos'-sos;* of Heb. or. [948]; white *linen:*–fine linen.
1041. βῶμος *bo'-mos;* from the base of *939;* prop. a *stand,* i.e. (spec.) an *altar:*–altar.

Γ

1042. γαββαθά *gab-bath-ah';* of Heb. or. [comp. 1355]; *the knoll; gabbatha,* a vernacular term for the Rom. tribunal in Jerus.:– Gabbatha.
1043. Γαβριήλ *gab-ree-ale';* of Heb. or. [1403]; *Gabriel,* an archangel:–Gabriel.
1044. γάγγραινα *gang'-grahee-nah;* from γραίνω (to *gnaw*); an *ulcer* ("gangrene"):–canker.
1045. Γάδ *gad;* of Heb. or. [1410]; *Gad,* a tribe of Isr.:–Gad.
1046. Γαδαρηνός *gad-ar-ay-nos';* from Γαδαρά (a town E. of the Jordan); a *Gadarene* or inh. of Gadara:–Gadarene.
1047. γάζα *gad'-zah;* of for. or.; a *treasure:*–treasure.
1048. Γάζα *gad'-zah;* of Heb. or. [5804]; *Gazah* (i.e. 'Azzah), a place in Pal.:–Gaza.
1049. γαζοφυλάκιον *gad-zof-oo-lak'-ee-on;* from *1047* and *5438;* a *treasure-house,* i.e. a court in the temple for the collection-boxes:–treasury.
1050. Γάϊος *gah'-ee-os;* of Lat. or.; Gaïus (i.e. *Caius*), a Chr.:–Gaius.
1051. γάλα *gal'-ah;* of unc. affin.; *milk* (fig.):–milk.
1052. Γαλάτης *gal-at'-ace;* from *1053;* a *Galatian* or inh. of Galatia:–Galatian.
1053. Γαλατία *gal-at-ee'-ah;* of for. or.; *Galatia,* a region of Asia:–Galatia.
1054. Γαλατικός *gal-at-ee-kos';* from *1053; Galatic* or relating to Galatia:–of Galatia.
1055. γαλήνη *gal-ay'-nay;* of unc. der.; *tranquillity:*–calm.
1056. Γαλιλαία *gal-il-ah'-yah;* of Heb. or. [1551]; *Galiloea* (i.e. the heathen *circle*), a region of Pal.:–Galilee.
1057. Γαλιλαῖος *gal-ee-lah'-yos;* from *1056; Galilean* or belonging to Galilea:–Galilean, of Galilee.
1058. Γαλλίων *gal-lee'-own;* of Lat. or.; *Gallion* (i.e. *Gallio*), a Rom. officer:–Gallio.
1059. Γαμαλιήλ *gam-al-ee-ale';* of Heb. or. [1583]; *Gamaliel* (i.e. *Gamliel*), an Isr.:–Gamaliel.
1060. γαμέω *gam-eh'-o;* from *1062;* to *wed* (of either sex):–marry (a wife).
1061. γαμίσκω *gam-is'-ko;* from *1062;* to *espouse* (a daughter to a husband):–give in marriage.
1062. γάμος *gam'-os;* of unc. affin.; *nuptials:*–marriage, wedding.
1063. γάρ *gar;* a prim. par.; prop. assigning a *reason* (used in argument, explanation or intensification; often with other par.):–and, as, because (that), but, even, for, indeed, no doubt, seeing, then, therefore, verily, what, why, yet.
1064. γαστήρ *gas-tare';* of unc. der.; the *stomach;* by anal. the *matrix;* fig. a *gourmand:*–belly, + with child, womb.
1065. γέ *gheh;* a prim. par. of *emphasis* or *qualification* (often used with other par. pref.):–and besides, doubtless, at least, yet.
1066. Γεδεών *ghed-eh-own';* of Heb. or. [1439]; *Gedeon* (i.e. *Gid[e]on*), an Isr.:–Gedeon.
1067. γέεννα *gheh'-en-nah;* of Heb. or. [1516 and 2011]; *valley of* (the son of) *Hinnom; ge-henna* (or *Ge-Hinnom*), a valley of Jerus. used (fig.) as a name for the place (or state) of everlasting punishment:–hell.
1068. Γεθσημανή *gheth-say-man-ay';* of Heb. or. [comp. 1660 and 8081]; *oil-press; Gethsemane,* a garden near Jerus.:–Gethsemane.
1069. γείτων *ghi'-tone;* from *1093;* a *neighbour* (as adjoining one's *ground*); by impl. a *friend:*–neighbour.
1070. γελάω *ghel-ah'-o;* of unc. affin.; to *laugh* (as a sign of joy or satisfaction):–laugh.
1071. γέλως *ghel'-os;* from *1070; laughter* (as a mark of gratification):–laughter.
1072. γεμίζω, *ghem-id'-zo;* trans. from *1073;* to *fill* entirely:–fill (be) full.
1073. γέμω, *ghem'-o;* a prim. verb; to *swell* out, i.e. *be full:*–be full.
1074. γενεά, *ghen-eh-ah';* from (a presumed der. of) *1085;* a *generation;* by impl. an *age* (the period or the persons):–age, generation, nation, time.
1075. γενεαλογέω *ghen-eh-al-og-eh'-o;* from *1074* and *3056;* to *reckon by generations,* i.e. *trace in genealogy:*–count by descent.
1076. γενεαλογία *ghen-eh-al-og-ee'-ah;* from the same as *1075; tracing by generations,* i.e. "*genealogy*":–genealogy.
1077. γενέσια *ghen-es'-ee-a;* neut. pl. of a der. of *1078; birthday* ceremonies:–birthday.
1078. γένεσις *ghen'-es-is;* from the same as *1074; nativity;* fig. *nature:*–generation, nature(-ral).
1079. γενετή *ghen-et-ay;* fem. of a presumed der. of the base of *1074; birth:*–birth.
1080. γεννάω *ghen-nah'-o;* from a var. of *1085;* to *procreate* (prop. of the father, but by ext. of the mother); fig. to *regenerate:*–bear, beget, be born, bring forth, conceive, be delivered of, gender, make, spring.
1081. γέννημα *ghen'-nay-mah;* from *1080; offspring;* by anal. *produce* (lit. or fig.):–fruit, generation.
1082. Γεννησαρέτ *ghen-nay-sar-et';* of Heb. or. [comp. 3672]; *Gennesaret* (i.e. *Kinnereth*), a lake and plain in Pal.:–Gennesaret.
1083. γέννησις *ghen'-nay-sis;* from *1080; nativity:*–birth
1084. γεννητός *ghen-nay-tos';* from *1080; born:*–they that are born.
1085. γένος *ghen'-os;* from *1096;* "*kin*" (abstr. or concr. lit. or fig. indiv. or coll.):–born, country(-man), diversity, generation, kind(-red), nation, offspring, stock.
1086. Γεργεσηνός *gher-ghes-ay-nos';* of Heb. or. [1622]; a *Gergesene* (i.e. *Girgashite*) or one of the aborigines of Pal.:–Gergesene.
1087. γερουσία *gher-oo-see'-ah;* from *1088;* the *eldership,* i.e. (coll.) the Jewish *Sanhedrin:*–senate.
1088. γέρων *gher'-own;* of unc. affin. [comp. *1094*]; *aged:*–old.
1089. γεύομαι *ghyoo'-om-ahee;* a prim. verb; to *taste;* by impl. to *eat;* fig. to *experience* (good or ill):–eat, taste.
1090. γεωργέω *gheh-or-gheh'-o;* from *1092;* to *till* (the soil):–dress.
1091. γεώργιον *gheh-ore'-ghee-on;* neut. of a (presumed) der. of *1092; cultivable,* i.e. a *farm:*–husbandry.
1092. γεωργός *gheh-ore-gos';* from *1093* and the base of *2041;* a *land-worker,* i.e. *farmer:*–husbandman.
1093. γῆ *ghay;* contr. from a prim. word; *soil;* by ext. a *region,* or the solid part or the whole of the *terrene* globe (incl. the occupants in each appl.):–country, earth

GREEK

(-ly), ground, land, world.
1094. γῆρας *ghay'-ras;* akin to *1088; senility:*–old age.
1095. γηράσκω *ghay-ras'-ko;* from *1094;* to *be senescent:*–be (wax) old.
1096. γίνομαι *ghin'-om-aheea;* prol. and mid. form of a prim. verb; to *cause to be* ("*gen*"*erate*), i.e. (refl.) to *become* (*come into being*), used with great latitude (lit. fig. intens. etc.):–arise, be assembled, be (-come, -fall, -have self), be brought (to pass), (be) come (to pass), continue, be divided, draw, be ended, fall, be finished, follow, be found, be fulfilled, + God forbid, grow, happen, have, be kept, be made, be married, be ordained to be, partake, pass, be performed, be published, require, seem, be showed, X soon as it was, sound, be taken, be turned, use, wax, will, would, be wrought.
1097. γινώσκω *ghin-oce'-koa;* a prol. form of a prim. verb; to "*know*" (absol.) in a great variety of appl. and with many implications (as follow, with others not thus clearly expressed):–allow, be aware (of), feel, (have) know(-ledge), perceive, be resolved, can speak, be sure, understand.
1098 γλεῦκος *glyoo'-kos;* akin to *1099; sweet* wine, i.e. (prop.) *must* (fresh juice), but used of the more saccharine (and therefore highly inebriating) fermented *wine:*–new wine.
1099. γλυκύς *gloo-koos';* of unc. affin.; *sweet* (i.e. not bitter nor salt):–sweet, fresh.
1100. γλῶσσα *gloce-sah';* of unc. affin.; the *tongue;* by impl. a *language* (spec. one nat. unacquired):–tongue.
1101. γλωσσόκομον *gloce-sok'-om-on;* from *1100* and the base of *2889;* prop. a *case* (to keep mouthpieces of wind-instruments in) i.e. (by ext.) a *casket* or (spec.) *purse:*–bag.
1102. γναφεύς *gnaf-yuce';* by var. for a der. from κναπτω (to *tease* cloth); a cloth-*dresser:*–fuller.
1103. γνήσιος *gnay'-see-os;* from the same as *1077; legitimate* (of birth), i.e. *genuine:*–own, sincerity, true.
1104. γνησίως *gnay-see'-ose;* adv. from *1103 genuinely,* i.e. *really:*–naturally
1105. γνόφος *gnof'-os;* akin to *3509; gloom* (as of a storm):–blackness.
1106. γνώμη *gno'-may;* from *1097; cognition,* i.e. (subj.) *opinion,* or (obj.) *resolve* (*counsel, consent,* etc.):–advice, + agree, judgment, mind, purpose, will.
1107. γνωρίζω *gno-rid'-zo;* from a der. of *1097;* to *make known;* subj. to *know;*–certify, declare, make known, give to understand, do to wit, wot.
1108. γνῶσις *gno'-sis;* from *1097; knowing* (the act), i.e. (by impl.) *knowledge:*–knowledge, science.
1109. γνώστης *gnoce'-tace;* from *1097;* a *knower:*–expert.
1110. γνωστός *gnoce-tos';* from *1097;* well-*known:*–acquaintance, (which may be) known, notable.
1111. γογγύζω *gong-good'-zo;* of unc. der.; to *grumble:*–murmur.
1112. γογγυσμός *gong-goos-mos';* from *1111;* a *grumbling:*–grudging, murmuring.
1113. γογγυστής *gong-goos-tace';* from *1111;* a *grumbler:*–murmurer.
1114. γόης *go'-ace;* from γοάω (to *wail*); prop. a *wizard* (as *muttering* spells), i.e. (by impl.) an *imposter:*–seducer.
1115. Γολγοθᾶ *gol-goth-ah';* of Chald. or. [comp. 1538]; *the skull; Golgotha,* a knoll near Jerus.:–Golgotha.
1116. Γόμορρα *gom'-or-hrhah;* of Heb. or. [6017] *Gomorrha* (i.e. *'Amorah*), a place near the Dead Sea:–Gomorrha.
1117. γόμος *gom'-os;* from *1073;* a *load* (as *filling*), i.e. (spec.) a *cargo,* or (by ext.) *wares:*–burden, merchandise.
1118. γονεύς *gon-yooce';* from the base of *1096;* a *parent:*–parent.
1119. γονύ *gon-oo';* of unc. affin.; the "*knee*":–knee(X -l).
1120. γονυπετέω *gon-oo-pet-eh'-o;* from a com. of *1119* and the alt. of *4098;* to *fall* on the *knee:*–bow the knee, kneel down.
1121. γράμμα *gram'-mah;* from *1125;* a *writing,* i.e. a *letter, note, epistle, book,* etc.; pl. *learning:*–bill, learning, letter, scripture, writing, written.
1122. γραμματεύς *gram-mat-yooce';* from 1121; a *writer,* i.e. (professionally) *scribe* or *secretary:*–scribe, town-clerk.
1123. γραπτός *grap-tos';* from *1125;in-scribed* (fig.):–written.
1124. γραφή *graf-ay';* from *1125;* a *document,* i.e. holy *Writ* (or its contents or a statement in it):–scripture.
1125. γράφω *graf'-o;* a prim. verb; to "*grave*", esp. to *write;* fig. to *describe:*–describe, write (-ing, -ten).
1126. γραώδης *grah-o'-dace;* from γραῦς (an *old woman*) and *1491; crone-like,* i.e. *silly:*–old wives'.
1127. γρηγορεύω *gray-gor-yoo'-o;* from *1453;* to *keep awake,* i.e. *watch* (lit. or fig.):–be vigilant, wake, (be) watch(-ful).
1128. γυμνάζω *goom-nad'-zo;* from *1131;* to *practise naked* (in the games), i.e. *train* (fig.):–exercise.
1129. γυμνασία *goom-nas-ee'-ah;* from *1128; training,* i.e. (fig.) *asceticism:*–exercise.
1130. γυμνητεύω *goom-nayt-yoo'-o;* from a der. of *1131;* to *strip,* i.e. (refl.) *go poorly clad:*–be naked.
1131. γυμνός *goom-nos';* of unc. affin.; *nude* (absol. or rel. lit. or fig.):–naked.
1132. γυμνότης *goom-not'-ace;* from *1131; nudity* (absol. or comp.):–nakedness.
1133. γυναικάριον *goo-nahee-kar'-ee-on;* a dimin. from *1135;* a *little* (i.e. *foolish*) *woman:*–silly woman.
1134. γυναικεῖος *goo-nahee-ki'-os;* from *1135; fem.:*–wife.
1135. γυνή *goo-nay';* prob. from the base of *1096;* a *woman;* spec. a *wife:*–wife, woman.
1136. Γώγ *gogue;* of Heb. or. [1463]; *Gog,* a symbolic name for some fut. Antichrist:–Gog.
1137. γωνία *go-nee'-ah;* prob. akin to *1119;* an *angle:*–corner, quarter.

Δ

1138. Δαβίδ *dab-eed';* of Heb. or. [1732]; *Dabid* (i.e. *David*), the Isr. king:–David.
1139. δαιμονίζομαι *dahee-mon-id'-zom-ahee;* mid. from *1142;* to *be exercised by a demon:*–have a (be vexed with, be possessed with) devil(-s).
1140. δαιμόνιον *dahee-mon'-ee-on;* neut. of a der. of *1142;* a *demonic being;* --devil, god.
1141. δαιμονιώδης *dahee-mon-ee-o'-dace;* from *1140* and *1142; demon-like:*–devilish.
1142. δαίμων *dah'-ee-mown;* from δαίω (to *distribute* fortunes); a *demon* or supernatural spirit (of a bad nature):–devil.
1143. δάκνω *dak'-no;* a prol. form of a prim. root: to *bite,* i.e. (fig.) *thwart:*–bite.
1144. δάκρυ *dak'-roo; or* δάκρυον *dak'-roo-on;* of unc. affin.; a *tear:*–tear.
1145. δακρύω *dak-roo'-o;* from *1144;* to *shed tears:*–weep. Comp. *2799.*
1146. δακτύλιος *dak-too'-lee-os;* from *1147;* a *finger*-ring:–ring.
1147. δάκτυλος *dak'-too-los;* prob. from *1176;* a *finger:*–finger.
1148. Δαλμανουθά *dal-man-oo-thah';* prob. of chald. or.; *Dalmanūtha,* a place in Pal.:–Dalmanutha.
1149. Δαλματία *dal-mat-ee'-ah;* prob. of for. der.; *Dalmatia,* a region of Europe:–Dalmatia.
1150. δαμάζω *dam-ad'-zo;* a var. of an obs. prim. of the same mean.; to *tame:*–tame
1151. δάμαλις *dam'-al-is;* prob. from the base of *1150;* a *heifer* (as *tame*):–heifer.
1152. Δάμαρις *dam'-ar-is;* prob. from the base of *1150;* perh. *gentle; Damaris,* an Athenian woman:–Damaris.
1153. Δαμασκηνός *dam-as-kay-nos';* from *1154;* a *Damascene* or inh. of Damascus:–Damascene.
1154. Δαμασκός *dam-as-kos';* of Heb. or. [1834] *Damascus,* a city of Syria:–Damascus.
1155. δανείζω *dan-ide'-zo;* from *1156;* to *loan* on interest; refl. to *borrow:*–borrow, lend.
1156. δάνειον *dan'-i-on;* from δάνος (a *gift*); prob. akin to the base of *1325;* a *loan:*–debt.
1157. δανειστής *dan-ice-tace';* from *1155;* a *lender:*–creditor.
1158. Δανιήλ *dan-ee-ale';* of Heb. or. [1840] *Daniel,* an Isr.:–Daniel.
1159. δαπανάω, *dap-an-ah'-o;* from *1160;* to *expend,* i.e. (in a good sense) to *incur cost,* or (in a bad one) to *waste:*–be at charges, consume, spend.
1160. δαπάνη *dap-an'-ay;* from δαπτω (to *devour*); *expense* (as *consuming*):–cost.
1161. δέ *deh;* a prim. par. (adversative or continuative); *but, and,* etc.:–also, and, but, moreover, now [*often unexpressed in English*].
1162. δέησις *deh'-ay-sis;* from *1189;* a *petition:*–prayer, request, supplication.

1163. δεῖ *die;* 3d pers. sing. act. pres. of *1210;* also δεόν *deh-on';* neut. act. part. of the same; both used impers.; *it is* (*was,* etc.) *necessary* (as *binding*):–behoved, be meet, must (needs), (be) need(-ful), ought, should.
1164. δεῖγμα *digh'-mah;* from the base of *1166;* a *specimen* (as *shown*):–example
1165. δειγματίζω *digh-mat-id'-zo;* from *1164;* to *exhibit:*–make a shew.
1166. δεικνύω *dike-noo'-o;* a prol. form of an obs. prim. of the same mean.; to *show* (lit. or fig.):–shew.
1167. δειλία *di-lee'-ah;* from *1169; timidity:*–fear.
1168. δειλιάω *di-lee-ah'-o;* from *1167;* to *be timid:*–be afraid.
1169. δειλός *di-los';* from δέος (*dread*); *timid,* i.e. (by impl.) *faithless:*–fearful.
1170. δεῖνα *di'-nah;* prob. from the same as *1171* (through the idea of forgetting the name as *fearful,* i.e. *strange*); *so and so* (when the pers. is not specified):–such a man.
1171. δεινῶς *di-noce';* adv. from a der. of the same as *1169; terribly,* i.e. *excessively:*–grievously, vehemently.
1172. δειπνέω *dipe-neh'-o;* from *1173;* to *dine,* i.e. take the principle (or evening) meal:–sup (X -er).
1173. δεῖπνον *dipe'-non;* from the same as *1160; dinner,* i.e. the chief meal (usually in the evening):–feast, supper.
1174. δεισιδαιμονέστερος *dice-ee-dahee-mon-es'-ter-os;* the com. of a der. of the base of *1169* and *1142; more relig.* than others:–too superstitious.
1175. δεισιδαιμονία *dice-ee-dahee-mon-ee'-ah;* from the same as *1174; religion:*–superstition.
1176. δέκα *dek'-ah;* a prim. number; *ten:*–[eight-]een, ten.
1177. δεκαδύο *dek-ad-oo'-o;* from *1176* and *1417; two* and *ten,* i.e. *twelve:*–twelve.
1178. δεκαπέντε *dek-ap-en'-teh;* from *1176* and *4002; ten* and *five,* i.e. *fifteen:*–fifteen.
1179. Δεκάπολις *dek-ap'-ol-is;* from *1176* and *4172;* the *ten-city* region; the *Decapolis,* a district in Syria:–Decapolis.
1180. δεκατέσσαρες *dek-at-es'-sar-es;* from *1176* and *5064; ten* and *four,* i.e. *fourteen:*–fourteen.
1181. δεκάτη *dek-at'-ay;* fem. of *1182;* a *tenth,* i.e. as a percentage or (tech.) *tithe:*–tenth (part), tithe.
1182. δέκατος *dek'-at-os;* ord. from *1176; tenth:*–tenth.
1183. δεκατόω *dek-at-o'-o;* from *1181;* to *tithe,* i.e. to *give* or *take* a *tenth:*–pay (receive) tithes.
1184. δεκτός *dek-tos';* from *1209; approved;* (fig.) *propitious:*– accepted(-table).
1185. δελεάζω *del-eh-ad'-zo;* from the base of *1388;* to *entrap,* i.e. (fig.) *delude:*–allure, beguile, entice.
1186. δένδρον *den'-dron;* prob. from δρύς (an *oak*); a *tree:*–tree.
1187. δεξιολάβος *dex-ee-ol-ab'-os;* from *1188* and *2983;* a *guardsman* (as if *taking the right*) or light-armed soldier:–spearman
1188. δεξιός *dex-ee-os';* from *1209;* the *right* side or (fem.) hand (as that which usually *takes*):–right (hand, side).
1189. δέομαι *deh'-om-ahee;* mid. of *1210;* to *beg* (as *binding oneself*), i.e. *petition:*–beseech, pray (to), make request. Comp. 4441.
1190. Δερβαῖος *der-bah'-ee-os;* from *1191;* a *Derbæan* or inh. of Derbe:–of Derbe.
1191. Δέρβη *der-bay';* of for. or.; Derbè, a place in Asia Minor:–Derbe.
1192. δέρμα *der'-mah;* from 1194; a hide:–skin.
1193. δερμάτινος *der-mat'-ee-nos;* from *1192;* made of *hide:*–leathern, of a skin.
1194. δέρω *der'-o;* a prim. verb; prop. to *flay,* i.e. (by impl.) to *scourge,* or (by anal.) to *thrash:*–beat, smite.
1195. δεσμεύω *des-myoo'-o;* from a (presumed) der. of *1196;* to *be a binder* (*captor*), i.e. to *enchain* (a prisoner), to *tie on* (a load):– bind.
1196. δεσμέω *des-meh'-o;* from *1199;* to *tie,* i.e. *shackle:*–bind.
1197. δεσμή *des-may';* from *1196;* a *bundle:*–bundle.
1198. δέσμιος *des'-mee-os;* from *1199;* a *captive* (as *bound*):–in bonds, prisoner.
1199. δεσμόν *des-mon';* δεσμός *des-mos';* neut. and masc. respectively from *1210;* a *band* i.e. *ligament* (of the body) or *shackle* (of a prisoner); fig. an *impediment* or *disability:*–band, bond, chain, string.
1200. δεσμοφύλαξ *des-mof-oo'-lax;* from *1199* and *5441;* a *jailer* (as *guarding the prisoners*):–*jailer,* keeper of the prison.
1201. δεσμωτήριον *des-mo-tay'-ree-on;* from a der. of *1199* (equiv. to *1196*); a *place of bondage,* i.e. a *dungeon:*–prison.
1202. δεσμώτης *des-mo'-tace;* from the same as *1201;* pass. a *captive:*–prisoner.
1203. δεσπότης *des-pot'-ace;* perh. from *1210* and πόσις (a *husband*); an absol. *ruler* ("despot"):–Lord, master.
1204. δεῦρο *dyoo'-ro;* of unc. affin.; *here;* used also imper. *hither!;* and of time, *hitherto:*–come (hither), hither[-to].
1205 δεῦτε *dyoo'-teh;* from *1204* and an imper. form of εἶμι (*to go*); *come hither!:*–come, X follow.
1206. δευτεραῖος *dyoo-ter-ah'-yos;* from *1208; sec.,* i.e. (spec.) on the *sec.* day:–next day.
1207. δευτερόπρωτος *dyoo-ter-op'-ro-tos;* from *1208* and *4413; second-first,* i.e. (spec.) a designation of the Sabbath immed. after the Paschal week (being the *second* after Passover day, and the *first* of the seven Sabbaths intervening before Pentecost):–second ... after the first.
1208. δεύτερος *dyoo'-ter-os;* as the comp. of *1417;* (ord.) *second* (in time, place, or rank; also adv.):–afterward, again, second(-arily, time)
1209. δέχομαι *dekh'-om-ahee;* mid. of a prim. verb; to *receive* (in various appl., lit. or fig.):–accept, receive, take. Comp. *2983.*
1210. δέω *deh'-o;* a prim. verb; to *bind* (in various appl., lit. or fig.):–bind, be in bonds, knit, tie, wind. See also *1163, 1189.*
1211. δή *day;* prob. akin to *1161;* a par. of emphasis or explicitness; *now, then,* etc.:–also, and, doubtless, now, therefore.
1212. δῆλος *day'-los;* of unc. der.; *clear:*–+ bewray, cert., evident, manifest.
1213. δηλόω *day-lo'-o;* from *1212;* to *make plain* (by words):–declare, shew, signify.
1214. Δημᾶς *day-mas';* prob. for *1216; Demas,* a Chr.:–Demas.
1215. δημηγορέω *day-may-gor-eh'-o;* from a com. of *1218* and *58;* to *be a people-gatherer,* i.e. to *address* a public assembly:–make an oration.
1216. Δημήτριος *day-may'-tree-os;* from Δημήτηρ (*Ceres*); *Demetrius,* the name of an Ephesian and of a Chr.:–Demetrius.
1217. δημιουργός *day-me-oor-gos';* from *1218* and *2041;* a *worker* for the *people,* i.e. *mechanic* (*spoken* of the *Creator*):–maker.
1218. δῆμος *day'-mos;* from *1210;* the *public* (as *bound* together socially):–people.
1219. δημόσιος *day-mos'ee-os;* from *1218; public;* (fem.sing. dat. as adv.) *in public:*–common, openly, publickly.
1220. δηνάριον *day-nar'-ee-on;* of Lat. or.; a *denarius* (or *ten asses*):–pence, penny[-worth].
1221. δήποτε *day'-pot-eh;* from *1211* and *4218;* a par. of generalization; *indeed, at any time:*–(what-)soever.
1222. δήπου *day'-poo;* from *1211* and *4225;* a par. of asseveration; *indeed doubtless:*–verily.
1223. διά *dee-ah';* a prim. prep. denoting the *channel* of an act; *through* (in very wide appl., local, causal, or occasional):–after, always, among, at, to avoid, because of (that), briefly, by, for (cause) ... fore, from, in, by occasion of, of, by reason of, for sake, that, thereby, therefore, X though, through(-out), to, wherefore, with (-in). In compo. it retains the same general import.
1224. διαβαίνω *dee-ab-ah'-ee-no;* from 1223 and the base of *939;* to *cross:*–come over, pass (through).
1225. διαβάλλω *dee-ab-al'-lo;* from *1223* and *906;* (fig.) to *traduce:*–accuse.
1226. διαβεβαιόομαι *dee-ab-eb-ahee-o'-om-ahee* mid. of a com. of *1223* and *950;* to *confirm thoroughly* (by words), i.e. *asseverate:*–affirm constantly.
1227. διαβλέπω *dee-ab-lep'-o;* from *1223* and *991;* to *look through,* i.e. *recover* full *vision:*–see clearly.
1228. διάβολος *dee-ab'-ol-os;* from *1225;* a *traducer;* spec. *Satan* [comp. 7854]:–false accuser, devil, slanderer.
1229. διαγγέλλω *de-ang-gel'-lo;* from *1223* and the base of *32;* to *herald thoroughly:*–declare, preach, signify.
1230. διαγίνομαι *dee-ag-in'-om-ahee;* from *1223* and *1096;* to *elapse meanwhile:*–X after, be past, be spent.
1231. διαγινώσκω *dee-ag-in-o'-sko;* from *1223* and *1097;* to *know thoroughly,* i.e. *ascertain exactly:*–(would) enquire, know the uttermost.

GREEK

1232. διαγνωρίζω *dee-ag-no-rid'-zo;* from *1123* and *1107;* to *tell abroad:*–make known.
1233. διάγνωσις *dee-ag'-no-sis;* from *1231;* (magisterial) *examination* ("diagnosis"):–hearing.
1234. διαγογγύζω *dee-ag-ong-good'-zo;* from *1223* and *1111;* to *complain throughout* a crowd:–murmur.
1235. διαγρηγορέω *dee-ag-ray-gor-eh'-o;* from *1223* and *1127;* to *waken thoroughly:*–be awake.
1236. διάγω *dee-ag'-o;* from *1223* and *71;* to *pass* time or life:–lead life, living.
1237. διαδέχομαι *dee-ad-ekh'-om-ahee;* from *1223* and *1209;* to *receive in turn,* i.e. (fig.) *succeed to:*–come after.
1238. διάδημα *dee-ad'-ay-mah;* from a com. of *1223* and *1210;* a "*diadem*" (as *bound about* the head):–crown. Comp. *4735.*
1239. διαδίδωμι *dee-ad-id'-o-mee;* from *1223* and *1325;* to *give throughout* a crowd, i.e. *deal out;* also to *deliver* over (as to a successor):–(make) distribute(-ion), divide, give.
1240. διάδοχος *dee-ad'-okh-os;* from *1237;* a *successor* in office:–room.
1241. διαζώννυμι *dee-az-own'-noo-mee;* from *1223* and *2224;* to *gird tightly:*–gird.
1242. διαθήκη *dee-ath-ay'-kay;* from *1303;* prop. a *disposition,* i.e. (spec.) a *contract* (esp. a devisory *will*):–covenant, testament.
1243. διαίρεσις *dee-ah'-ee-res-is;* from *1244;* a *distinction* or (concr.) *variety:*–difference, diversity.
1244. διαιρέω *dee-ahee-reh'-o;* from *1223* and *138;* to *separate,* i.e. *distribute:*–divide.
1245. διακαθαρίζω *dee-ak-ath-ar-id'-zo;* from *1223* and *2511;* to *cleanse perfectly,* i.e. (spec.) *winnow:*–thoroughly purge.
1246. διακατελέγχομαι *dee-ak-at-el-eng'-khom-ahee;* mid. from *1223* and a com. of *2596* and *1651;* to *prove downright,* i.e. *confute:*–convince.
1247. διακονέω *dee-ak-on-eh'-o;* from *1249;* to *be an attendant,* i.e. *wait upon* (menially or as a host, friend, or [fig.] teacher); tech., to *act as a* Chr. *deacon:*–(ad-)minister (unto), serve, use the office of a deacon.
1248. διακονία *dee-ak-on-ee'-ah;* from *1249;* *attendance* (as a servant, etc.); fig. (eleemosynary) *aid,* (official) *service* (esp. of the Chr. teacher, or tech. of the *diaconate*):–(ad-)minister(-ing, -tration, -try), office, relief, service(-ing).
1249. διάκονος *dee-ak'-on-os;* prob. from an obs. διάκω(to *run* on errands; comp. *1377*); an *attendant,* i.e. (gen. case) a *waiter* (at table or in other menial duties); spec. a Chr. *teacher* and *pastor* (tech., a *deacon* or *deaconess*):–deacon, minister, servant.
1250. διακόσιοι *dee-ak-os'-ee-oy;* from *1364* and *1540;* *two hundred:*–two hundred.
1251. διακούομαι *dee-ak-oo'-om-ahee;* mid. from *1223* and *191;* to *hear throughout,* i.e. *patiently listen* (to a prisoner's plea):–hear.
1252. διακρίνω *dee-ak-ree'-no;* from *1223* and *2919;* to *separate thoroughly,* i.e. (lit. and refl.) to *withdraw* from, or (by impl.) *oppose;* fig. to *discriminate* (by impl. *decide*), or (refl.) *hesitate:*–contend, make (to) differ (-ence), discern, doubt, judge, be partial, stagger, waver.
1253. διάκρισις *dee-ak'-ree-sis;* from *1252;* judicial *estimation:*–discern(-ing), disputation.
1254. διακωλύω *dee-ak-o-loo'-o;* from *1223* and *2967;* to *hinder altogether,* i.e. *utterly prohibit:*–forbid.
1255. διαλαλέω *dee-al-al-eh'-o;* from *1223* and *2980;* to *talk throughout* a company, i.e. *converse* or (gen. case) *publish:*–commune, noise abroad.
1256. διαλέγομαι *dee-al-eg'-om-ahee;* mid. from *1223* and *3004;* to *say thoroughly,* i.e. *discuss* (in argument or exhortation):–dispute, preach (unto), reason (with), speak.
1257. διαλείπω *dee-al-i'-po;* from *1223* and *3007;* to *leave off in the mid.* i.e. *intermit:*–cease.
1258. διάλεκτος *dee-al'-ek-tos;* from *1256;* a (mode of) *discourse,* i.e. "*dialect*":–language, tongue.
1259. διαλλάσσω *dee-al-las'-so;* from *1223* and *236;* to *change thoroughly,* i.e. (ment.) to *conciliate:*–reconcile.
1260. διαλογίζομαι *dee-al-og-id'-zom-ahee;* from *1223* and *3049;* to *reckon thoroughly,* i.e. (gen. case) to *deliberate* (by reflection or discussion):–cast in mind, consider, dispute, muse, reason, think.
1261. διαλογισμός *dee-al-og-is-mos';* from *1260;* *discussion,* i.e. (internal) *consideration* (by impl. *purpose*), or (exter.) *debate:*–dispute, doubtful(-ing), imagination, reasoning, thought.
1262. διαλύω *dee-al-oo'-o;* from *1223* and *3089;* to *dissolve utterly:*–scatter.
1263. διαμαρτύρομαι *dee-am-ar-too'-rom-ahee;* from *1223* and *3140;* to *attest* or *protest earnestly,* or (by impl.) *hortatively:*–charge, testify (unto), witness.
1264. διαμάχομαι *dee-am-akh'-om-ahee;* from *1223* and *3164;* to *fight fiercely* (in altercation):–strive.
1265. διαμένω *dee-am-en'-o;* from *1223* and *3306;* to *stay constantly* (in being or relation):–continue, remain.
1266. διαμερίζω *dee-am-er-id'-zo;* from *1223* and *3307;* to *partition thoroughly* (lit. in distribution, fig. in dissension):–cloven, divide, part.
1267. διαμερισμός *dee-am-er-is-mos';* from *1266;* *disunion* (of opinion and conduct):–division.
1268. διανέμω *dee-an-em'-o;* from *1223* and the base of *3551;* to *distribute,* i.e. (of information) to *disseminate:*–spread.
1269. διανεύω *dee-an-yoo'-o;* from *1223* and *3506;* to *nod* (or *express* by signs) *across* an intervening space:–beckon.
1270. διανόημα *dee-an-o'-ay-mah;* from a com. of *1223* and *3539;* something *thought through,* i.e. a *sentimenwt:*–thought.
1271. διάνοια *dee-an'-oy-ah;* from *1223* and *3563;* *deep thought,* prop. the faculty (*mind* or its *disposition*), by impl. its exercise:–imagination, mind, understanding.
1272. διανοίγω *dee-an-oy'-go;* from *1223* and *455;* to *open thoroughly,* lit. (as a first-born) or fig. (to *expound*):–open.
1273. διανυκτερεύω *dee-an-ook-ter-yoo'-o;* from *1223* and a der. of *3571;* to *sit up the whole night:*–continue all night.
1274. διανύω *dee-an-oo'-o;* from *1223* and ἀνύω (to *effect*); to *accomplish thoroughly:*–finish.
1275. διαπαντός *dee-ap-an-tos';* from *1223* and the gen. case of *3956;* *through all* time, i.e. (adv.) *constantly:*–alway(-s), continually.
1276. διαπεράω *dee-ap-er-ah'-o;* from *1223* and a der. of the base of *4008;* to *cross entirely:*–go over, pass (over), sail over.
1277. διαπλέω *dee-ap-leh'-o;* from *1223* and *4126;* to *sail through:*–sail over.
1278. διαπονέω *dee-ap-on-eh'-o;* from *1223* and a der. of *4192;* to *toil through,* i.e. (pass.) *be worried:*–be grieved.
1279. διαπορεύομαι *dee-ap-or-yoo'-om-ahee;* from *1223* and *4198;* to *travel through:*–go through, journey in, pass by.
1280. διαπορέω *dee-ap-or-eh'-o;* from *1223* and *639;* to *be thoroughly nonplussed:*–(be in) doubt, be (much) perplexed.
1281. διαπραγματεύομαι *dee-ap-rag-mat-yoo'-om-ahee;* from *1223* and *4231;* to *thoroughly occupy oneself,* i.e. (trans. and by impl.) to *earn* in business:–gain by trading.
1282. διαπρίω *dee-ap-ree'-o;* from *1223* and the base of *4249;* to *saw asunder,* i.e. (fig.) to *exasperate:*–cut (to the heart)
1283. διαρπάζω *dee-ar-pad'-zo;* from *1223* and *726;* to *seize asunder,* i.e. *plunder:*–spoil.
1284. διαῤῥήσσω *dee-ar-hrayce'-so;* from *1223* and *4486;* to *tear asunder:*–break, rend.
1285. διάσαφέω *dee-as-af-eh'-o;* from *1223* and σαφής (*clear*); to *clear thoroughly,* i.e. (fig.) *declare:*–tell unto.
1286. διασείω *dee-as-i'-o;* from *1223* and *4579;* to *shake thoroughly,* i.e. (fig.) to *intimidate:*–do violence to.
1287. διασκορπίζω *dee-as-kor-pid'-zo;* from *1223* and *4650;* to *dissipate,* i.e. (gen. case) to *rout* or *separate;* spec. to *winnow;* fig. to *squander:*–disperse, scatter (abroad), strew, waste.
1288. διασπάω *dee-as-pah'-o;* from *1223* and *4685;* to *draw apart,* i.e. *sever* or *dismember:*–pluck asunder, pull in pieces.
1289. διασπείρω *dee-as-pi'-ro;* from *1223* and *4687;* to *sow throughout,* i.e. (fig.) *distribute* in for. lands:–scatter abroad.
1290. διασπορά *dee-as-por-ah';* from *1289;* *dispersion,* i.e. (spec. and concr.) the (converted) Isr. *resident* in Gentile countries:–(which are) scattered (abroad).
1291. διαστέλλομαι *dee-as-tel'-lom-ahee;* mid. from *1223* and *4724;* to *set* (oneself) *apart* (fig. *distinguish*), i.e. (by impl.) to *enjoin:*–charge, that which was (give) commanded(-ment).
1292. διάστημα *dee-as'-tay-mah;* from *1339;* an *interval:*–space.

1293. διαστολή *dee-as-tol-ay'*; from *1291*; a *var.*:–difference, distinction.

1294. διαστρέφω *dee-as-tref'-o*; from *1223* and *4762*; to *distort*, i.e. (fig.) *misinterpret*, or (mor.) *corrupt*:–perverse(-rt), turn away.

1295. διασώζω *dee-as-odze'-o*, from *1223* and *4982*; to *save thoroughly*, i.e. (by impl. or anal.) to *cure*, *preserve*, *rescue*, etc.:–bring safe, escape (safe), heal, make perfectly whole, save.

1296. διαταγή *dee-at-ag-ay'*; from *1299*; *arrangement*, i.e. *institution*:–instrumentality.

1297. διάταγμα *dee-at'-ag-mah*; from *1299*; an *arrangement*, i.e. (authoritative) *edict*:–commandment.

1298. διαταράσσω *dee-at-ar-as'-so*; from *1223* and *5015*; to *disturb wholly*, i.e. *agitate* (with alarm):–trouble.

1299. διατάσσω *dee-at-as'-so*; from *1223* and *5021*; to *arrange thoroughly*, i.e. (spec.) *institute*, *prescribe*, etc.:–appoint, command, give, (set in) order, ordain.

1300. διατελέω *dee-at-el-eh'-o*; from *1223* and *5055*; to *accomplish thoroughly*, i.e. (subj.) to *persist*:–continue.

1301. διατηρέω *dee-at-ay-reh'-o*; from *1223* and *5083*; to *watch thoroughly*, i.e. (pos. and trans.) to *observe* strictly, or (neg. and refl.) to *avoid* wholly:–keep.

1302. διατί *dee-at-ee'*; from *1223* and *5101*; *through what cause?*, i.e. *why?*:–wherefore, why.

1303. διατίθεμαι *dee-at-ith'-em-ahee*; mid. from *1223* and *5087*; to *put apart*, i.e. (fig.) *dispose* (by assignment, compact, or bequest):–appoint, make, testator.

1304. διατρίβω *dee-at-ree'-bo*; from *1223* and the base of *5147*; to *wear through* (time), i.e. *remain*:–abide, be, continue, tarry.

1305. διατροφή *dee-at-rof-ay'*; from a comp. of *1223* and *5142*; *nourishment*:–food.

1306. διαυγάζω *dee-ow-gad'-zo*; from *1223* and *826*; to *glimmer through*, i.e. *break* (as day):–dawn.

1307. διαφανής *dee-af-an-ace'*; from *1223* and *5316*; *appearing through*, i.e. "*diaphanous*":–transparent.

1308. διαφέρω *dee-af-er'-o*; from *1223* and *5342*; to *bear through*, i.e. (lit.) *transport*; usually to *bear apart*, i.e. (obj.) to *toss about* (fig. *report*); subj. to "*differ*," or (by impl.) *surpass*:–be better, carry, differ from, drive up and down, be (more) excellent, make matter, publish, be of more value.

1309. διαφεύγω *dee-af-yoo'-go*; from *1223* and *5343*; to *flee through*, i.e. *escape*:–escape.

1310. διαφημίζω *dee-af-ay-mid'-zo*; from *1223* and a der. of *5345*; to *report thoroughly*, i.e. *divulgate*:–blaze abroad, commonly report, spread abroad, fame.

1311. διαφθείρω *dee-af-thi'-ro*; from *1225* and *5351*; to *rot thoroughly*, i.e. (by impl.) to *ruin* (pass. *decay* utterly, fig. *pervert*):–corrupt, destroy, perish.

1312. διαφθορά *dee-af-thor-ah'*; from *1311*; *decay*:–corruption.

1313. διάφορος *dee-af'-or-os*; from *1308*; *varying*; also *surpassing*:–differing, divers, more excellent.

1314. διαφυλάσσω *dee-af-oo-las'-so*; from *1223* and *5442*; to *guard thoroughly*, i.e. *protect*:–keep.

1315. διαχειρίζομαι *dee-akh-i-rid'-zom-ahee*; from *1223* and a der. of *5495*; to *handle thoroughly*, i.e. *lay* violent *hands* upon:–kill, slay.

1316. διαχωρίζομαι *dee-akh-o-rid'-zom-ahee*; from *1223* and the mid. of *5563*; to *remove* (oneself) *wholly*, i.e. *retire*:–depart.

1317. διδακτικός *did-ak-tik-os'*; from *1318*; *instructive* ("didactic"):–apt to teach.

1318. διδακτός *did-ak-tos'*; from *1321*; (subj.) *instructed*, or (obj.) *communicated* by teaching:–taught, which ... teacheth.

1319. διδασκαλία *did-as-kal-ee'-ah*; from *1320*; *instruction* (the function or the information):–doctrine, learning, teaching.

1320. διδάσκαλος *did-as'-kal-os*; from *1321*; an *instructor* (gen. case or spec.):–doctor, master, teacher.

1321. διδάσκω *did-as'-ko*; a prol. (caus.) form of a prim. verb δάω (to *learn*); to *teach* (in the same broad appl.):–teach.

1322. διδαχή *did-akh-ay'*; from *1321*; *instruction* (the act or the matter):–doctrine, hath been taught.

1323. δίδραχμον *did'-rakh-mon*; from *1364* and *1406*; a *double drachma* (*didrachm*):–tribute

1324. Δίδυμος *did'-oo-mos*; prol. from *1364*; *double*, i.e. *twin*; *Didymus*, a Chr.:–Didymus.

1325. δίδωμι *did'-o-mee*; a prol. form of a prim. verb (which is used as an alternative in most of the tenses); to *give* (used in a very wide appl., prop. or by impl. lit. or fig.; greatly modif. by the connection):–adventure, bestow, bring forth, commit, deliver (up), give, grant, hinder, make, minister, number, offer, have power, put, receive, set, shew, smite (+ with the hand), strike (+ with the palm of the hand), suffer, take, utter, yield.

1326. διεγείρω *dee-eg-i'-ro*; from *1223* and *1453*; to *wake fully*; i.e. *arouse* (lit. or fig.):–arise, awake, raise, stir up.

1327. διέξοδος *dee-ex'-od-os*; from *1223* and *1841*; an *outlet through*, i.e. prob. an open *square* (from which roads diverge):–highway.

1328. διερμηνευτής *dee-er-main-yoo-tace'*; from *1329*; an *explainer*:–interpreter.

1329. διερμηνεύω *dee-er-main-yoo'-o*; from *1223* and *2059*; to *explain thoroughly*, by impl. to *translate*:–expound, interpret(-ation).

1330. διέρχομαι *dee-er'-khom-ahee*; from *1223* and *2064*; to *traverse* (lit.):–come, depart, go (about, abroad, everywhere, over, through, throughout), pass (by, over, through, throughout), pierce through, travel, walk through.

1331. διερωτάω *dee-er-o-tah'-o*; from *1223* and *2065*; to *question throughout*, i.e. *ascertain* by interrogation:–make enquiry for.

1332. διετής *dee-et-ace'*; from *1364* and *2094*; *of two years* (in age):–two years old.

1333. διετία *dee-et-ee'-a*; from *1332*; a space of *two years* (*biennium*):–two years.

1334. διηγέομαι *dee-ayg-eh'-om-ahee*; from *1223* and *2233*; to *relate fully*:–declare, shew, tell.

1335. διήγεσις *dee-ayg'-es-is*; from *1334*; a *recital*:–declaration.

1336. διηνεκές *dee-ay-nek-es'*; neut. of a com. of *1223* and a der. of an alt. of *5342*; *carried through*, i.e. (adv. with *1519* and *3588* pref.) *perpetually*:–+ continually, for ever.

1337. διθάλασσος *dee-thal'-as-sos*; from *1364* and *2281*; *having two seas*, i.e. a *sound* with a double outlet:–where two seas meet.

1338. διϊκνέομαι *dee-ik-neh'-om-ahee*; from *1223* and the base of *2425*; to *reach through*, i.e. *penetrate*:–pierce.

1339. διΐστημι *dee-is'-tay-mee*; from *1223* and *2476*; to *stand apart*, i.e. (refl.) to *remove*, *intervene*:–go further, be parted, after the space of.

1340. διϊσχυρίζομαι *dee-is-khoo-rid'-zom-ahee*; from *1223* and a der. of *2478*; to *stout* it *through*, i.e. *asservate*:–confidently (constantly) affirm.

1341. δικαιοκρισία *dik-ah-yok-ris-ee'-ah*; from *1342* and *2920*; a *just sentence*:–righteous judgment.

1342. δίκαιος *dik'-ah-yos*; from *1349*; *equitable* (in character or act); by impl. *innocent*, *holy* (absol. or rel.):–just, meet, right(-eous).

1343. δικαιοσύνη *dik-ah-yos-oo'-nay*; from *1342*; *equity* (of character or act); spec. (Chr.) *justification*:–righteousness.

1344. δικαιόω *dik-ah-yo'-o*; from *1342*; to *render* (i.e. *show* or *regard* as) *just* or *innocent*:–free, justify(-ier), be righteous.

1345. δικαίωμα *dik-ah'-yo-mah*; from *1344*; an *equitable deed*; by impl. a *statute* or *decision*:–judgment, justification, ordinance, righteousness.

1346. δικαίως *dik-ah'-yoce*; adv. from *1342*; *equitably*:–justly, (to) righteously(-ness).

1347. δικαίωσις *dik-ah'-yo-sis*; from *1344*; *aquittal* (for Christ's sake):–justification.

1348. δικαστής *dik-as-tace'*; from a der. of *1349*; a *judger*:–judge.

1349. δίκη *dee'-kay*; prob. from *1166*; *right* (as self-*evident*), i.e. *justice* (the principle, a decision, or its execution):–judgment, punish, vengeance.

1350. δίκτυον *dik'-too-on*; prob. from a prim. verb δίκω (to *cast*); a *seine* (for fishing):–net.

1351. δίλογος *dil'-og-os*; from *1364* and *3056*; *equivocal*, i.e. telling a different story:–double-tongued.

1352. διό *dee-o'*; from *1223* and *3739*; *through which* thing, i.e. *consequently*:–for which cause, therefore, wherefore.

1353. διοδεύω *dee-od-yoo'-o*; from *1223* and *3593*; to *travel through*:–go throughout, pass through.

1354. Διονύσιος *dee-on-oo'-see-os*; from Διόνυσος (*Bacchus*); *reveller*; *Dionysius*, an Athenian:–Dionysius.

1355. διόπερ *dee-op'-er*; from *1352* and *4007*; *on which very account*:–wherefore.

1356. διοπετής *dee-op-et'-ace*; from the alt. of *2203* and the alt. of *4098*; *sky-fallen* (i.e. an *aerolite*):–which fell down from Jupiter.

GREEK

1357. διόρθωσις *dee-or'-tho-sis;* from a com. of *1223* and a der. of *3717,* mean. to *straighten thoroughly; rectification,* i.e. (spec.) the Messianic *restauration:*–reformation.
1358. διορύσσω *dee-or-oos'-so;* from *1223* and *3736;* to *penetrate* burglariously:–break through (up).
1359. Διόσκουροι *dee-os'-koo-roy;* from the alt. of *2203* and a form of the base of *2877; sons of Jupiter,* i.e. the twins *Dioscuri:*–Castor and Pollux.
1360. διότι *dee-ot'-ee;* from *1223* and *3754; on the very account that,* or *inasmuch as*:–because (that), for, therefore.
1361. Διοτρεφής *dee-ot-ref-ace';* from the alt. of *2203* and *5142; Jove-nourished; Diotrephes,* an opponent of Christianity:–Diotrephes.
1362. διπλοῦς *dip-looce';* from *1364* and (prob.) the base of *4119; two-fold*:–double, two-fold more.
1363. διπλόω *dip-lo'-o;* from *1362;* to *render two-fold:*–double.
1364. δίς *dece* adv. from *1417; twice:*–again, twice.
1365. διστάζω *dis-tad'-zo;* from *1364;* prop. to *duplicate,* i.e. (ment.) to *waver* (in opinion):–doubt
1366. δίστομος *dis'-tom-os;* from *1364* and *4750; double-edged:*–with two edges, two-edged.
1367. δισχίλιοι *dis-khil'-ee-oy;* from *1364* and *5507; two thousand:*–two thousand.
1368. διϋλίζω *dee-oo-lid'-zo;* from *1223* and ὑλίζω *hoo-lid'-zo* (to *filter*); to *strain out:*–strain at [*prob. by misprint*].
1369. διχάζω *dee-khad'-zo;* from a der. of *1364;* to *make apart,* i.e. *sunder* (fig. *alienate*):–set at variance.
1370. διχοστασία *dee-khos-tas-ee'-ah;* from a der. of *1364* and *4714; disunion,* i.e. (fig.) *dissension:*–division, sedition.
1371. διχοτομέω *dee-khot-om-eh'-o;* from a com. of a der. of *1364* and a der. of τέμνω (to *cut*); to *bisect,* i.e. (by ext.) to *flog* severely:–cut asunder (in sunder).
1372. διψάω *dip-sah'-o;* from a var. of *1373;* to *thirst* for (lit. or fig.):–(be, be a-)thirst(-y).
1373. δίψος *dip'-sos;* of unc. affin.; *thirst:*–thirst.
1374. δίψυχος *dip'-soo-khos;* from *1364* and *5590; two-spirited,* i.e. *vacillating* (in opinion or purpose):–double minded.
1375. διωγμός *dee-ogue-mos';* from *1377; persecution:*–persecution.
1376. διώκτης *dee-oke'-tace;* from *1377;* a *persecutor:*–persecutor.
1377. διώκω *dee-o'-ko;* a prol. (and caus.) form of a prim. verb δίω (to *flee;* comp. the base of *1169* and *1249*); to *pursue* (lit. or fig.); by impl. to *persecute:*–ensue, follow (after), given to, (suffer) persecute(-ion), press forward.
1378. δόγμα *dog'-mah;* from the base of *1380;* a *law* (civil, cer. or eccl.):–decree, ordinance.
1379. δογματίζω *dog-mat-id'-zo;* from *1378;* to *prescribe* by statute, i.e. (refl.) to *submit* to, cer. *rule:*–be subject to ordinances.
1380. δοκέω *dok-eh'-o;* prol. form of a prim. verb, δόκω dok'-o (used only as an alt. in cert. tenses; comp. the base of *1166*) of the same mean.; to *think;* by impl. to *seem* (truthfully or uncert.):–be accounted, (of own) please(-ure), be of reputation, seem (good), suppose, think, trow.
1381. δοκιμάζω *dok-im-ad'-zo;* from *1384;* to *test* (lit. or fig.); by impl. to *approve:*–allow, discern, examine, X like, (ap-)prove, try.
1382. δοκιμή *dok-ee-may';* from the same as *1384; test* (abstr. or concr.); by impl. *trustiness:*–experience(-riment), proof, trial.
1383. δοκίμιον *dok-im'-ee-on;* neut. of a presumed der. of *1382;* a *testing;* by impl. *trustworthiness:*–trial, trying.
1384. δόκιμος *dok'-ee-mos;* from *1380;* prop. *acceptable* (*current* after assayal), i.e. *approved:*–approved, tried.
1385. δοκός *dok-os';* from *1209* (through the idea of *holding* up); a *stick* of timber:–beam.
1386. δόλιος *dol'-ee-os;* from *1388; guileful:*–deceitful.
1387. δολιόω *dol-ee-o'-o;* from *1386;* to *be guileful*:–use deceit.
1388. δόλος *dol'-os;* from an obs. prim. verb, δέλλω (prob. mean. to *decoy;* comp. *1185*); a *trick* (*bait*), i.e. (fig.) *wile:*–craft, deceit, guile, subtilty.
1389. δολόω *dol-o'-o;* from *1388;* to *ensnare,* i.e. (fig.) *adulterate:*–handle deceitfully.
1390. δόμα *dom'-ah;* from the base of *1325;* a *present:*–gift.
1391. δόξα *dox'-ah;* from the base of *1380; glory* (as very *app.*), in a wide appl. (lit. or fig. obj. or subj.):–dignity, glory(-ious), honour, praise, worship.
1392. δοξάζω *dox-ad'-zo;* from *1391;* to *render* (or *esteem*) *glorious* (in a wide appl.):–(make) glorify(-ious), full of (have) glory, honour, magnify.
1393. Δορκάς *dor-kas'; gazelle; Dorcas,* a Chr. woman:–Dorcas.
1394. δόσις *dos'-is;* from the base of *1325;* a *giving;* by impl. (concr.) a *gift:*–gift, giving.
1395. δότης *dot'-ace;* from the base of *1325;* a *giver:*–giver.
1396. δουλαγωγέω *doo-lag-ogue-eh'-o;* from a presumed com. of *1401* and *71;* to *be a slave-driver,* i.e. to *enslave* (fig. subdue):–bring into subjection.
1397. δουλεία *doo-li'-ah;* from *1398; slavery* (cer. or fig.):–bondage.
1398. δουλεύω *dool-yoo'-o;* from *1401;* to *be a slave* to (lit. or fig. invol. or vol.):–be in bondage, (do) serve(-ice).
1399. δούλη *doo'-lay;* fem. of *1401;* a *female slave* (invol. or vol.):–handmaid(-en).
1400. δοῦλον *doo'-lon;* neut. of *1401; subservient:*–servant.
1401. δοῦλος *doo'-los;* from *1210;* a *slave* (lit. or fig. invol. or vol.; frequently, therefore in a qualified sense of *subjection* or *subserviency*):–bond(-man), servant.
1402. δουλόω *doo-lo'-o;* from *1401;* to *enslave* (lit. or fig.):–bring into (be under) bondage, X given, become (make) servant.
1403. δοχή *dokh-ay';* from *1209;* a *reception,* i.e. convivial *entertainment:*–feast.
1404. δράκων *drak'-own;* prob. from an alt. form of δέρκομαι (to *look*); a fabulous kind of *serpent* (perh. as supposed to *fascinate*):–dragon.
1405. δράσσομαι *dras'-som-ahee;* perh. akin to the base of *1404* (through the idea of *capturing*); to *grasp,* i.e. (fig.) *entrap:*–take.
1406. δραχμή *drakh-may';* from *1405;* a *drachma* or (silver) coin (as handled):–piece (of silver).
1407. δρέπανον *drep'-an-on;* from δρέπω (to *pluck*); a gathering *hook* (esp. for harvesting):–sickle.
1408. δρόμος *drom'-os;* from the alt. of *5143;* a *race,* i.e. (fig.) *career:*–course.
1409. Δρούσιλλα *droo'-sil-lah;* a fem. dim. of *Drusus* (a Rom. name); *Drusilla,* a member of the Herodian family:–Drusilla.
1410. δύναμαι *doo'-nam-ahee;* of unc. affin.; to *be able* or *possible:*–be able, can (do, + -not), could, may, might, be possible, be of power.
1411. δύναμις *doo'-nam-is;* from *1410; force* (lit. or fig.); *spec.* miraculous *power* (usually by impl. a *miracle* itself):–ability, abundance, mean. might(-ily, -y, -y deed), (worker of) miracle(-s), power, streng., violence, mighty (wonderful) work.
1412. δυναμόω *doo-nam-o'-o;* from *1411;* to *enable:*–strengthen.
1413. δυνάστης *doo-nas'-tace;* from *1410;* a *ruler* or *officer:*–of great authority, mighty, potentate.
1414. δυνατέω *doo-nat-eh'-o;* from *1415;* to *be efficient* (fig.):–be mighty.
1415. δυνατός *doo-nat-os';* from *1410; powerful* or *capable* (lit. or fig.); neut. *possible:*–able, could, (i.e.) mighty (man), possible, power, strong.
1416. δύνω *doo'-no;* or δῦμι *doo'-mee;* prol. forms of an obs. prim. δύω *doo'-o* (to *sink*) to *go "down":*–set.
1417. δύο *doo'-o;* a prim. numeral; "*two*":–both, twain, two.
1418. δυσ- *doos-;* a prim. insep. par. of unc. der.; used only in compo. as a pref.; *hard,* i.e. *with difficulty:*–+ hard, + grievous, etc.
1419. δυσβάστακτος *doos-bas'-tak-tos;* from *1418* and a der. of *941; oppressive:*–grievous to be borne.
1420. δυσεντερία *doos-en-ter-ee'-ah;* from *1418* and a comp. of *1787* (mean. a *bowel*); a "*dysentery*":–bloody flux.
1421. δυσερμήνευτος *doos-er-mane'-yoo-tos;* from *1418* and a presumed der. of *2059; difficult of explanation:*–hard to be uttered.
1422. δύσκολος *doos'-kol-os;* from *1418* and κόλον (*food*); prop. *fastidious about eating* (*peevish*), i.e. (gen. case) *impracticable:*–hard.
1423. δυσκόλως *doos-kol'-oce;* adv. from *1422; impracticably:*–hardly.

1424. δυσμή *doos-may';* from *1416;* the sun-*set,* i.e. (by impl.) the *western* region:–west.
1425. δυσνόητος *doos-no'-ay-tos;* from *1418* and a der. of *3539; difficult of perception:*–hard to be understood.
1426. δυσφημία *doos-fay-mee'-ah;* from a com. of *1418* and *5345; defamation:*–evil report.
1427. δώδεκα *do'-dek-ah;* from *1417* and *1176; two* and *ten,* i.e. a *dozen:*–twelve.
1428. δωδέκατος *do-dek'-at-os;* from *1427; twelfth:*–twelfth.
1429. δωδεκάφυλον *do-dek-af'-oo-lon;* from *1427* and *5443;* the *commonwealth* of Israel:–twelve tribes.
1430. δῶμα *do'-mah;* from δέμο (to *build*); prop. an *edifice,* i.e. (spec.) a *roof:*–housetop.
1431. δωρεά *do-reh-ah';* from *1435;* a *gratuity:*–gift.
1432. δωρεάν *do-reh-an';* acc. of *1431* as adv.; *gratuitously* (lit. or fig.):–without a cause, freely, for naught, in vain.
1433. δωρέομαι *do-reh'-om-ahee;* mid. from *1435;* to *bestow* gratuitously:–give.
1434. δωρημα *do'-ray-mah;* from *1433;* a *bestowment:*–gift.
1435. δῶρον *do'-ron;* a *present;* spec. a *sacrifice:*–gift, offering.

E

1436. ἔα *eh'-ah;* app. imper. of *1439;* prop. *let it be,* i.e. (as interj.) *aha!:*–let alone.
1437. ἐάν *eh-an';* from *1487* and *302;* a *conditional* par.; *in case* that, *provided,* etc.; often used in connection with other par. to denote *indef.* or *uncertainty:*–before, but, except, (and) if, (if) so, (what-, whither-) soever, though, when (-soever), whether (or), to whom, [who-]so(-ever). See *3361.*
1438. ἑαυτοῦ *heh-ow-too';* (incl. all the other cases); from a refl. pron. otherwise obs. and the gen. (dat. or acc.) of *846; him- (her-, it-, them-,* also [in conj. with the pers. pron. of the other persons] *my-, thy-, our-, your-) self (selves),* etc.:–alone, her (own, -self), (he) himself, his (own), itself, one (to) another, our (thine) own (-selves), + that she had, their (own, own selves), (of) them(-selves), they, thyself, you, your (own, own conceits, own selves, -selves).
1439. ἐάω *eh-ah'-o;* of unc. affin.; to *let be,* i.e. *permit* or *leave* alone:–commit, leave, let (alone), suffer. See also *1436.*
1440. ἑβδομήκοντα *heb-dom-ay'-kon-tah;* from *1442* and a modif. form of *1176; seventy:*–seventy, three score and ten.
1441. ἑβδομηκοντακίς *heb-dom-ay-kon-tak-is;* multiple adv. from *1440; seventy times:*–seventy times.
1442. ἕβδομος *heb'-dom-os;* ord. from *2033; seventh:*–seventh.
1443. Ἐβέρ *eb-er';* of Heb. or. [5677]; *Eber,* a patriarch:–Eber.
1444. Ἑβραϊκός *heb-rah-ee-kos';* from *1443;Hebraïc* or the *Jewish* language:–Heb.
1445. Ἑβραῖος *heb-rah'-yos;* from *1443;* a *Hebræan* (i.e. Heb.) or *Jew:*–Heb..
1446. Ἑβραΐς *heb-rah-is';* from *1443;* the *Hebraistic* (i.e. *Heb.*) or *Jewish* (*Chald.*) *language:*–Heb..
1447. Ἑβραϊστί *heb-rah-is-tee';* adv. from *1446; Hebraistically* or in the Jewish (Chald.) language:–in (the) Heb. (tongue).
1448. ἐγγίζω *eng-id'-zo;* from *1451;* to make *near,* i.e. (refl.) *approach:*–approach, be at hand, come (draw) near, be (come, draw) nigh.
1449. ἐγγράφω *eng-graf'-o;* from *1722* and *1125;* to "*engrave*", i.e. *inscribe:*–write (in).
1450. ἔγγυος *eng'-goo-os;* from *1722* and γυῖον (a *limb*); *pledged* (as if *articulated* by a member), i.e. a *bondsman:*–surety.
1451. ἐγγύς *eng-goos';* from a prim. verb ἄγχω (to *squeeze* or *throttle;* akin to the base of *43*); *near* (lit. or fig. of place or time):–from , at hand, near, nigh (at hand, unto), ready.
1452. ἐγγύτερον *eng-goo'-ter-on;* neut. of the comp. of *1451; nearer:*–nearer.
1453. ἐγείρω *eg-i'-ro;* prob. akin to the base of *58* (through the idea of *collecting* one's faculties); to *waken* (trans. or intr.), i.e. *rouse* (lit. from sleep, from sitting or lying, from disease, from death; or fig. from obscurity, inactivity, ruins, n, up), rear up, (a-)rise (again, up), stand, take up.
1454. ἔγερσις *eg'-er-sis;* from 1453; a *resurgence* (from death):–resurrection.
1455. ἐγκάθετος *eng-kath'-et-os;* from *1722* and a der. of *2524; subinduced,* i.e.onexistence):–awake, lift (up), raise (again surreptitiously *suborned* as a lier-in-wait:–spy.
1456. ἐγκαίνια *eng-kah'-ee-nee-ah;* neut. pl. of a presumed com. from *1722* and *2537; innovatives,* i.e. (spec.) *renewal* (of religeous services after the Antiochian interruption):–dedication.
1457. ἐγκαινίζω *eng-kahee-nid'-zo;* from *1456;* to *renew,* i.e. *inaugurate:*–consecrate, dedicate.
1458. ἐγκαλέω *eng-kal-eh'-o;* from *1722* and *2564;* to *call in* (as a debt or demand), i.e. *bring to account* (*charge, criminate,* etc.):–accuse, call in question, implead, lay to the charge.
1459. ἐγκαταλείπω *eng-kat-al-i'-po;* from *1722* and *2641;* to *leave behind in* some place, i.e. (in a good sense) *let remain over,* or (in a bad sense) to *desert:*–forsake, leave.
1460. ἐγκατοικέω *eng-kat-oy-keh'-o;* from *1722* and *2730;* to *settle down in* a place, i.e. *reside:*–dwell among.
1461. ἐγκεντρίζω *eng-ken-trid'-zo;* from *1722* and a der. of *2759;* to *prick in,* i.e. *ingraft:*–graff in(-to).
1462. ἔγκλημα *eng'-klay-mah;* from *1458;* an *accusation,* i.e. *offence* alleged:–crime laid against, laid to charge.
1463. ἐγκομβόομαι *eng-kom-bo'-om-ahee;* mid. from *1722* and κομβόω (to *gird*); to *engirdle* oneself (for labor), i.e. fig. (the apron as being a badge of servitude) to *wear* (in token of mutual deference):–be clothed with.
1464. ἐγκοπή *eng-kop-ay';* from *1465;* a *hindrance:*–X hinder.
1465. ἐγκόπτω *eng-kop'-to;* from *1722* and *2875;* to *cut into,* i.e. (fig.) *impede, detain:*–hinder, be tedious unto.
1466. ἐγκράτεια *eng-krat'-i-ah;* from *1468; self-control* (esp. *continence*):–temperance.
1467. ἐγκρατεύομαι *eng-krat-yoo'-om-ahee;* mid. from *1468;* to *exercise self-restraint* (in diet and chastity):–can([-not]) contain, be temperate.
1468. ἐγκρατής *eng-krat-ace';* from *1722* and *2904; strong in* a thing (*masterful*), i.e. (fig. and refl.) *self-controlled* (in appetite, etc.):–temperate.
1469. ἐγκρίνω *eng-kree'-no;* from *1722* and *2919;* to *judge in,* i.e. *count* among:–make of the number.
1470. ἐγκρύπτω *eng-kroop'-to;* from *1722* and *2928;* to *conceal in,* i.e. *incorporate with:*–hid in.
1471. ἔγκυος *eng'-koo-os;* from *1722* and the base of *2949; swelling in*side, i.e. *pregnant:*–great with child.
1472. ἐγκρίω *eng-khree'-o;* from *1722* and *5548;* to *rub in* (oil), i.e. *besmear:*–anoint.
1473. ἐγώ *eg-o';* a prim. pron. of the first pers. *I* (only expressed when emphat.):–I, me. For the other cases and the pl. see *1691, 1698, 1700, 2248, 2249, 2254, 2257,* etc.
1474. ἐδαφίζω *ed-af-id'-zo;* from *1475;* to *raze:*–lay even with the ground.
1475. ἔδαφος *ed'-af-os;* from the base of *1476;* a *basis* (*bottom*), i.e. the *soil:*–ground.
1476. ἑδαῖος *hed-rah'-yos;* from a der. of ἕζομαι (to *sit*); *sedentary,* i.e. (by impl.) *immovable:*–settled, stedfast.
1477. ἑδραίωμα *hed-rah'-yo-mah;* from a der. of *1476;* a *support,* i.e. (fig.) *basis:*–ground.
1478. Ἐζεκίας *ed-zek-ee'-as;* of Heb. or. [2396]; *Ezekias* (i.e. *Hezekeiah*), an Isr.:–Ezekias.
1479. ἐθελοθρησκεία *eth-el-oth-race-ki'-ah;* from *2309* and *2356; vol.* (*arbitrary* and *unwarranted*) *piety,* i.e. *sanctimony:*–will worship.
1480. ἐθίζω *eth-id'-zo;* from *1485;* to *accustom,* i.e. (neut. pass. part.) *customary:*–custom.
1481. ἐθνάρχης *eth-nar'-khace;* from *1484* and *746;* the *governor* [not king] of *a district:*–ethnarch.
1482. ἐθνικός *eth-nee-kos';* from *1484; national* ("*ethnic*"), i.e. (spec.) a *Gentile:*–heathen (man).
1483. ἐθνικῶς *eth-nee-koce';* adv. from *1482; as a Gentile:*–after the manner of Gentiles.
1484. ἔθνος *eth'-nos;* prob. from *1486;* a *race* (as of the same *habit*), i.e. a *tribe;* spec. a *for.* (*non-Jewish*) one (usually, by impl. *pagan*):–Gentile, heathen, nation, people.
1485. ἔθος *eth'-os;* from *1486;* a *usage* (prescribed by habit or law):–custom, manner, be wont.
1486. ἔθω *eth'-o;* a prim. verb; to *be used* (by

GREEK

habit or conventionality); neut. perfect part. *usage:*–be custom (manner, wont).
1487. εἰ *i;* a prim. par. of conditionality; *if, whether, that,* etc.:–forasmuchas, if, that, ([al]-) though, whether. Often used in connection or compo. with other par., esp. as in *1489, 1490, 1499, 1508, 1509, 1512, 1513, 1536, 1537.* See also *1437.*
1488. εἶ *i;* sec. pers. sing. pres. of *1510;* thou *art:*–art, be.
1489. εἴγε *i'-gheh;* from *1487* and *1065; if indeed, seeing that, unless,* (with neg.) *otherwise:*–if (so be that, yet).
1490. εἰ δὲ μή(γε), *i deh may'-(gheh)* from *1487, 1161,* and *3361* (sometimes with *1065* added); *but if not:*–(or) else, if (not, otherwise), otherwise.
1491. εἶδος *i'-dos;* from *1492;* a *view,* i.e. *form* (lit. or fig.):– appearance, fashion, shape, sight.
1492. εἴδω *i'-do;* a prim. verb; used only in cert. past tenses, the others being borrowed from the equiv. *3700* and *3708;* prop. to *see* (lit. or fig.); by impl. (in the perfect tense only) to *know:*–be aware, behold, X can (+ not tell), consider, (have) know(-ledge), look (on), perceive, see, be sure, tell, understand, wish, wot. Comp. *3700.*
1493. εἰδωλεῖον *i-do-li'-on;* neut. of a presumed der. of *1497;* an *image-fane:*– idol's temple.
1494. εἰδωλόθυτον *i-do-loth'-oo-ton;* neut. of a com. of *1497* and a presumed der. of *2380;* an *image-sacrifice,* i.e. part of an *idolatrous offering:*–(meat, thing i.e.) offered (in sacrifice, sacrificed) to (unto) idols.
1495. εἰδωλολατρεία *i-do-lol-at-ri'-ah;* from *1497* and *2999; image-worship* (lit. or fig.):–idolatry.
1496. εἰδωλολάτρης *i-do-lol-at'-race;* from *1497* and the base of *3000;* an *image-(servant* or) *worshipper* (lit. or fig.):–idolater.
1497. εἴδωλον *i'-do-lon;* from *1491;* an *image* (i.e. for worship); by impl. a heathen *god,* or (pl.) the *worship* of such:–idol.
1498. εἴην *i'-ane;* optative (i.e. English subjunctive) pres. of *1510* (incl. the other pers.); *might* (*could, would,* or *should) be:*– mean, + perish, should be, was, were.
1499. εἰ καί *i kahee;* from *1487* and *2532; if also* (or *even*):–if (that), though.
1500. εἰκῆ *i-kay';* prob. from *1502* (through the idea of *failure*); *idly,* i.e. *without reason* (or *effect*):–without a cause, (in) vain(-ly).
1501. εἴκοσι *i'-kos-ee;* of unc. affin.; a *score:*– twenty.
1502. εἴκω *i'-ko;* app. a prim. verb; prop. to *be weak,* i.e. *yield:*–give place.
1503. εἴκω *i'-ko;* app. a prim. verb [perh. akin to *1502* through the idea of *faintness* as a copy]; to *resemble:*–be like.
1504. εἰκών *i-kone';* from *1503;* a *likeness,* i.e. (lit.) *statue, profile,* or (fig.) *representation, resemblance:*–image.
1505. εἰλικρίνεια *i-lik-ree'-ni-ah;* from *1506;* *clearness,* i.e. (by impl.) *purity* (fig.):–sincerity.
1506. εἰλικρινής *i-lik-ree-nace';* from εἵλη (the sun's *ray*) and *2919; judged* by *sunlight,* i.e. tested as *genuine* (fig.):–pure, sincere.
1507. εἱλίσσω *hi-lis'-so;* a prol. form of a prim. but defective verb εἴλω (of the same mean.); to *coil* or *wrap:*–roll together. See also *1667.*
1508. ἐὶ μή *i may;* from *1487* and *3361; if not:*–but, except (that), if not, more than, save (only) that, saving, till.
1509. εἰ μή τι *i may tee;* from *1508* and the neut. of *5100; if not somewhat:*–except.
1510. εἰμί *i-mee';* the first pers. sing. pres. ind.; a prol. form of a prim. and defective verb; I *exist* (used only when emphat.):–am, have been, X it is I, was. See also *1488, 1498, 1511, 1527, 2258, 2071, 2070, 2075, 2076, 2771, 2468, 5600.*
1511. εἶναι *i'-nahee;* pres. infin. from *1510; to exist:*–am, are. come, is, X lust after, X please well, there is, to be, was.
1512. εἴ περ *iper;* from *1487* and *4007; if perh.:*–if so be (that), seeing, though.
1513. εἴ πως *ipoce;* from *1487* and *4458; if somehow:*–if by any means.
1514. εἰρηνεύω *i-rane-yoo'-o;* from *1515;* to *be* (*act*) *peaceful:*–be at (have, live in) peace, live peaceably.
1515. εἰρήνη *i-ray'-nay;* prob. from a prim. verb εἴρω (to *join*); *peace* (lit. or fig.); by impl. *prosperity:*–one, peace, quietness, rest, + set at one again.
1516. εἰρηνικός *i-ray-nee-kos';* from *1515; pacific;* by impl. *salutary:*–peaceable.
1517. εἰρηνοποιέω *i-ray-nop-oy-eh'-o;* from *1518;* to *be a peace-maker,* i.e. (fig.) to *harmonize:*–make peace.
1518. εἰρηνοποιός *i-ray-nop-oy-os';* from *1515* and *4160; pacificatory,* i.e. (subj.) *peaceable:*–peacemaker
1519. εἰς *ice;* a prim. prep.; *to* or *into* (indicating the point reached or entered), of place, time, or (fig.) purpose (result, etc.); also in adv. phrases:–(abundant-)ly, against, among, as, at, [back-]ward, before, by, concerning, + continual, + far more exceeding, for [intent, purpose], fore, + forth, in (among, at, unto, -so much that, -to), to the intent that, + of one mind, + never, of, (up-)on, + perish, + set at one again, (so) that, therefore(-unto), throughout, til, to (be, the end, -ward), (here-) until(-to), ...ward, [where-] fore, with. Often used in compo. with the same general import, but only with verbs (etc.) expressing motion (lit. or fig.).
1520. εἷς *hice;* (incl. the neut. [etc.] ἕν hen); a prim. numeral; *one:*–a(-n, -ny, cert.), + abundantly, man, one (another), only, other, some. See also *1527, 3367, 3391, 3762.*
1521. εἰσάγω *ice-ag'-o;* from *1519* and *71;* to *introduce* (lit. or fig.):–bring in(-to), (+ was to) lead into.
1522. εἰσακούω *ice-ak-oo'-o;* from *1519* and *191;* to *listen* to:–hear.
1523. εἰσδέχομαι *ice-dekh'-om-ahee;* from *1519* and *1209;* to *take into* one's favor:–receive.
1524. εἴσειμι *ice'-i-mee;* from *1519* and εἶμι (to *go*); to *enter:*–enter (go) into.
1525. εἰσέρχομαι *ice-er'-khom-ahee;* from *1519* and *2064;* to *enter* (lit. or fig.):–X arise, come (in, into), enter in(-to), go in (through).
1526. εἰσί *i-see';* 3d pers. pl. pres. ind. of 1510; they *are:*–agree, are, be, dure, X is, were.
1527. εἷς καθ εἷς *hice kath hice;* from *1520* repeated with *2596* ins.; *severally:*–one by one.
1528. εἰσκαλέω *ice-kal-eh'-o;* from *1519* and *2564;* to *invite* in:–call in.
1529. εἴσοδος *ice'-od-os;* from *1519* and *3598;* an *entrance* (lit. or fig.):–coming, enter(-ing) in (to).
1530. εἰσπηδάω *ice-pay-dah'-o;* from *1519* and πηδάω (to *leap*); to *rush in:*–run (spring) in.
1531. εἰσπορεύομαι *ice-por-yoo'-om-ahee;* from *1519* and *4198;* to *enter* (lit. or fig.):–come (enter) in, go into.
1532. εἰστρέχω *ice-trekh'-o;* from *1519* and *5143;* to *hasten inward:*–run in.
1533. εἰσφέρω *ice-fer'-o;* from *1519* and *5342;* to *carry inward* (lit. or fig.):–bring (in), lead into.
1534. εἶτα *i'-tah;* of unc. affin.; a par. of *succession* (in time or logical enumeration), *then, moreover:*–after that(-ward), further-more, then. See also *1899.*
1535. εἴτε *i'-teh;* from *1487* and *5037; if too:*–if, or, whether.
1536. εἴ τις *i tis;* from *1487* and *5100; if any:*–he that, if a(-ny) man('s thing, from any, ought), whether any, whosoever.
1537. ἐκ *ek;* or ἐξ *ex;* prim. prep. denoting *or.* (the point *whence* action or motion proceeds), *from, out* (of place, time, or cause; lit. or fig.; dir. or remote):–after, among, x are, at, betwixt (-yond), by (the means of), exceedingly, (+ abundantly above), for(- th), from (among, forth, up), + grudgingly, + heartily, x heavenly, x hereby, + very highly, in, ...ly, (because, by reason) of, off (from), on, out among (from, of), over, since, X thenceforth, through, X unto, X vehemently, with (-out). Often used in compo., with the same general import; often of *completion.*
1538. ἕκαστος *hek'-as-tos;* as if a sup. of ἕκας (*afar*); *each* or *every:*–any, both, each (one), every (man, one, woman), particularly.
1539. ἑκάστοτε *hek-as'-tot-eh;* as if from *1538* and *5119;* at *every time:*–always.
1540. ἑκατόν *hek-at-on';* of unc. affin.; a *hundred:*–hundred.
1541. ἑκατονταέτης *hek-at-on-tah-et'-ace;* from *1540* and *2094; centenarian:*–hundred years old.
1542. ἑκατονταπλασίων *hek-at-on-ta-plah-see'-own;* from *1540* and a presumed der. of *4111;* a *hundred times:*–hundredfold.
1543. ἑκατοντάρχης *hek-at-on-tar'-khace; or* ἑκατόνταρχος *hek-at-on-tar' hos* from *1540* and *757;* the *captain of one hundred men:*–centurion.
1544. ἐκβάλλω *ek-bal'-lo;* from *1537* and

906; to *eject* (lit. or fig.):–bring forth, cast (forth, out), drive (out), expel, leave, pluck (pull, take, thrust) out, put forth (out), send away (forth, out).

1545. ἔκβασις *ek'-bas-is;* from a com. of *1537* and the base of *939* (mean. to *go out*); an *exit* (lit. or fig.):–end, way to escape.

1546. ἐκβολή *ek-bol-ay';* from *1544; ejection,* i.e. (spec.) a *throwing overboard* of the cargo:–+ lighten the ship.

1547. ἐκγαμίζω *ek-gam-id'-zo;* from *1537* and a form of *1061* [comp. *1548*]; to *marry off* a daughter:–give in marriage.

1548. ἐκγαμίσκω *ek-gam-is'-ko;* from *1537* and *1061;* the same as *1547:*–give in marriage.

1549. ἔκγονον *ek'-gon-on;* neut. of a der. of a com. of *1537* and *1096;* a *desc.,* i.e. (spec.) *grandchild:*–nephew.

1550. ἐκδαπανάω *ek-dap-an-ah'-o;* from *1537* and *1159;* to *expend* (wholly), i.e. (fig.) *exhaust:*–spend.

1551. ἐκδέχομαι *ek-dekh'-om-ahee;* from *1537* and *1209;* to *accept from* some source, i.e. (by impl.) to *await:*–expect, look (tarry) for, wait (for).

1552. ἔκδηλος *ek'-day-los;* from *1537* and *1212; wholly evident:*–manifest.

1553. ἐκδημέω *ek-day-meh'-o;* from a com. of *1537* and *1218;* to *emigrate,* i.e. (fig.) *vacate* or *quit:*–be absent.

1554. ἐκδίδωμὶ *ek-did-o'-mee;* from *1537* and *1325;* to *give forth,* i.e. (spec.) to *lease:*–let forth (out).

1555. ἐκδιηγέομαι *ek-dee-ayg-eh'-om-ahee;* from *1537* and a com. of *1223* and *2233;* to *narrate* through wholly:–declare

1556. ἐκδικέω *ek-dik-eh'-o;* from *1558;* to *vindicate, retaliate, punish:*–a (re-)venge.

1557. ἐκδίκησις *ek-dik'-ay-sis;* from *1556; vindication, retribution:*–(a-, re-)venge(-ance), punishment.

1558. ἔκδικος *ek'-dik-os;* from *1537* and *1349;* carrying *justice out,* i.e. a *punisher:*–a (re-)venger.

1559. ἐκδιώκω *ek-dee-o'-ko;* from *1537* and *1377;* to *pursue out,* i.e. *expel* or *persecute* implacably:–persecute.

1560. ἔκδοτος *ek'-dot-os;* from *1537* and a der. of *1325; given out* or *over,* i.e. *surrendered:*–delivered.

1561. ἐκδοχή *ek-dokh-ay';* from *1551; expectation:*–looking for

1562. ἐκδύω *ek-doo'-o;* from *1537* and the base of *1416;* to cause to *sink out* of, i.e. (spec. as of clothing) to *divest:*–strip, take off from, unclothe.

1563. ἐκεῖ *ek-i';* of unc. affin.; *there;* by ext., *thither:*–there, thither(-ward), (to) yonder (place).

1564. ἐκεῖθεν *ek-i'-then;* from *1563; thence:*–from that place, (from) thence, there.

1565. ἐκεῖνος *ek-i'-nos;* from *1563; that* one (or [neut.] thing); often intensified by the art. pref.:–he, it, the other (same), selfsame, that (same, very), X their, X them, they, this, those. See also *3778.*

1566. ἐκεῖσε *ek-i'-seh;* from *1563; thither:*–there.

1567 ἐκζητέω *ek-zayteh'-o;* from *1537* and *2212;* to *search out,* i.e. (fig.) *investigate, crave, demand,* (by Heb.) *worship:*–en- (re-) quire, seek after (carefully, diligently).

1568. ἐκθαμβέω *ek-tham-beh'-o;* from *1569;* to *astonish* utterly:–affright, greatly (sore) amaze.

1569. ἔκθαμβος *ek'-tham-bos;* from *1537* and *2285; utterly astounded:*–greatly wondering.

1570. ἔκθαμβος *ek'-thet-os;* from *1537* and a der. of *5087; put out,* i.e. *exposed* to perish:–cast out.

1571. ἐκκαθαίρω *ek-kath-ah'-ee-ro;* from *1537* and *2508;* to *cleanse thoroughly:*–purge (out).

1572. ἐκκαίω *ek-kah'-yo;* from *1537* and *2545;* to *inflame* deeply:–burn.

1573. ἐκκακέω *ek-kak-eh'-o;* from *1537* and *2556;* to *be* (*bad* or) *weak,* i.e. (by impl.) to *fail* (in heart):–faint, be weary.

1574. ἐκκεντέω *ek-ken-teh'-o;* from *1537* and the base of *2759;* to *transfix:*–pierce.

1575. ἐκκλάὼ *ek-klah'-o;* from *1537* and *2806;* to *exscind:*–break off.

1576. ἐκκλείω *ek-kli'-o;* from *1537* and *2808;* to *shut out* (lit. or fig.):–exclude.

1577. ἐκκλησία *ek-klay-see'-ah;* from a com. of *1537* and a der. of 2564; a *calling out,* i.e. (concr.) a popular *meeting,* esp. a relig. *congregation* (Jewish *synagogue,* or Chr. community of members on earth or saints in heaven or both):–assembly, church.

1578. ἐκκλίνω *ek-klee'-no;* from *1537* and *2827;* to *deviate,* i.e. (absol.) to *shun* (lit. or fig.), or (rel.) to *decline* (from piety):–avoid, eschew, go out of the way.

1579. ἐκκολυμβάω *ek-kol-oom-bah'-o;* from *1537* and *2860;* to *escape* by *swimming:*–swim out.

1580. ἐκκομίζω *ek-kom-id'-zo;* from *1537* and *2865;* to *bear forth* (to burial):–carry out.

1581. ἐκκόπτω *ek-kop'-to;* from *1537* and *2875;* to *exscind;* fig. to *frustrate:*–cut down (off, out), hew down, hinder.

1582. ἐκκρέμαμαι *ek-krem'-am-ahee;* mid. from *1537* and *2910;* to *hang upon* the lips of a speaker, i.e. *listen closely:*–be very attentive.

1583. ἐκλαλέω *ek-lal-eh'-o;* from 1537 and *2980;* to *divulge:*–tell.

1584. ἐκλάμπω *ek-lam'-po;* from *1537* and *2989;* to *be resplendent:*–shine forth.

1585. ἐκλανθάνομαι *ek-lan-than'-om-ahee;* mid. from *1537* and *2990;* to *be* utterly *oblivious* of:–forget.

1586. ἐκλέγομαι *ek-leg'-om-ahee;* mid. from *1537* and *3004* (in its prim. sense); to *select:*–make choice, choose (out), chosen.

1587. ἐκλείπω *ek-li'-po;* from *1537* and *3007;* to *omit,* i.e. (by impl.) *cease* (*die*):–fail.

1588. ἐκλεκτός *ek-lek-tos';* from *1586; select;* by impl. *favorite:*–chosen, elect.

1589. ἐκλογή *ek-log-ay';* from *1586;* (divine) *selection* (abstr. or concr.):–chosen, election.

1590. ἐκλύω *ek-loo'-o;* from *1537* and *3089;* to *relax* (lit. or fig.):–faint.

1591. ἐκμάσσω *ek-mas'-so;* from *1537* and the base of *3145;* to *knead out,* i.e. (by anal.) to *wipe dry:*–wipe.

1592. ἐκμυκτερίζω *ek-mook-ter-id'-zo;* from *1537* and *3456;* to *sneer* outright at:–deride.

1593. ἐκνεύω *ek-nyoo'-o;* from *1537* and *3506;* (by anal.) to *slip off,* i.e. quietly *withdraw:*–convey self away.

1594. ἐκνήφω *ek-nay'-fo;* from *1537* and *3525;* (fig.) to *rouse* (oneself) *out* of stupor:–awake.

1595. ἑκούσιον *hek-oo'-see-on;* neut. of a der. from *1635; voluntariness:*–willingly.

1596. ἑκουσίως *hek-oo-see'-oce;* adv. from the same as *1595; vol.:*–wilfully, willingly.

1597. ἔκπαλαι *ek'-pal-ahee;* from *1537* and *3819; long ago, for a long while:*–of a long time, of old.

1598. ἐκπειράζω *ek-pi-rad'-zo;* from *1537* and *3985;* to *test thoroughly:*–tempt.

1599. ἐκπέμπω *ek-pem'-po;* from *1537* and *3992;* to *despatch:*–send away (forth).

1600. ἐκπετάννυμι *ek-pet-an'-noo-mee;* from *1537* and a form of *4072;* to *fly out,* i.e. (by anal.) to *extend:*–stretch forth.

1601. ἐκπίπτω *ek-pip'-to;* from *1537* and *4098;* to *drop away;* spec. *be driven out* of one's course; fig. to *lose, become inefficient:*–be cast, fail, fall (away, off), take none effect.

1602. ἐκπλέω *ek-pleh'-o;* from *1537* and *4126;* to *depart* by ship:–sail (away, thence).

1603. ἐκπληρόω *ek-play-ro'-o;* from *1537* and *4137;* to *accomplish* entirely:–fulfill.

1604. ἐκπλήρωσις *ek-play'-ro-sis;* from *1603; completion:*–accomplishment.

1605. ἐκπλήσσω *ek-place'-so;* from *1537* and *4141;* to *strike* with astonishment:–amaze, astonish.

1606. ἐκπνέω *ek-pneh'-o;* from *1537* and *4154;* to *expire:*–give up the ghost.

1607. ἐκπορεύομαι *ek-por-yoo'-om-ahee;* from *1537* and *4198;* to *depart, be discharged, proceed, project:*–come (forth, out of), depart, go (forth, out), issue, proceed (out of).

1608. ἐκπορνεύὼ *ek-porn-yoo'-o;* from *1537* and *4203;* to *be utterly unchaste:*–give self over to fornication.

1609. ἐκπτύω *ek-ptoo'-o;* from *1537* and *4429;* to *spit out,* i.e. (fig.) *spurn:*–reject.

1610. ἐκριζόω *ek-rid-zo'-o;* from *1537* and *4492;* to *uproot:*–pluck up by the root, root up.

1611. ἔκστασις *ek'-stas-is;* from *1839;* a *displacement* of the mind, i.e. *bewilderment,* "*ecstasy*":–+ be amazed, amazement, astonishment, trance.

1612. ἐκστρέφω *ek-stref'-o;* from *1537* and *4762;* to *pervert* (fig.):–subvert.

1613. ἐκταράσσω *ek-tar-as'-so;* from *1537* and *5015;* to *disturb wholly:*–exceedingly trouble.

1614. ἐκτείνω *ek-ti'-no;* from *1537* and τείνω (to *stretch*); to *extend:*–cast, put forth, stretch forth (out).

1615. ἐκτελέω *ek-tel-eh'-o;* from *1537* and *5055;* to *complete* fully:–finish.

1616. ἐκτένεια *ek-ten'-i-ah;* from *1618; intentness:*–X instantly.

GREEK

1617. ἐκτενέστερον *ek-ten-es'-ter-on;* neut. of the comp. of *1618; more intently:*–more earnestly.

1618. ἐκτενής *ek-ten-ace';* from *1614; intent:*–without ceasing, fervent.

1619. ἐκτενῶς *ek-ten-oce';* adv. from *1618; intently:*–fervently.

1620. ἐκτίθημι *ek-tith'-ay-mee;* from *1537* and *5087;* to *expose;* fig. to *declare:*–cast out, expound.

1621. ἐκτινάσσω *ek-tin-as'-so;* from *1537* and τιναὶσσω (to swing); to *shake* violently:–shake (off).

1622. ἐκτός *ek-tos';* from *1537;* the *exterior;* fig. (as a prep.) *aside from, besides:*–but, except(-ed), other than, out of, outside, unless, without.

1623. ἕκτος *hek'-tos;* ord. from *1803; sixth:*–sixth.

1624. ἐκτρέπω *ek-trep'-o;* from *1537* and the base of 5157; to *deflect,* i.e. *turn away* (lit. or fig.):–avoid, turn (aside, out of the way).

1625. ἐκτρέφω *ek-tref'-o;* from *1537* and *5142;* to *rear up* to maturity, i.e. (gen. case) to *cherish* or *train:*–bring up, nourish.

1626. ἔκτρωμα *ek'-tro-mah;* from a comp. of *1537* and τιτρώσκω (to *wound*); a *miscarriage* (*abortion*), i.e. (by anal.) *untimely birth*:–born out of due time.

1627. ἐκφέρω *ek-fer'-o;* from *1537* and *5342;* to *bear out* (lit. or fig.):–bear, bring forth, carry forth (out).

1628. ἐκφεύγω *ek-fyoo'-go;* from *1537* and *5343;* to *flee out:*–escape, flee.

1629. ἐκφοβέω *ek-fob-eh'-o;* from *1537* and *5399;* to *frighten utterly:*–terrify.

1630. ἔκφοβος *ek'-fob-os;* from *1537* and *5401; frightened out* of one's wits: sore afraid, exceedingly fear.

1631. ἐκφύω *ek-foo'-o;* from *1537* and *5453;* to *sprout up:*–put forth.

1632. ἐκχέω *ek-kheh'-o;* or (by var.) ἐκχύνω *ek-khoo'-no;* from *1537* and χέω (to *pour*); to *pour forth;* fig. to *bestow:*–gush (pour) out, run greedily (out), shed (abroad, forth), spill.

1633. ἐκχωρέω from *1537* and *5562;* to *depart:*–depart out.

1634. ἐκψύχω *ek-psoo'-kho;* from *1537* and *5594;* to *expire:*–give (yield) up the ghost.

1635. ἑκών *hek-own';* of unc. affin.; *voluntarily:*–willingly.

1636. ἐλαία *el-ah'-yah;* fem. of a presumed der. from an obs. prim.; an *olive* (the tree or the fruit):–olive (berry, tree).

1637. ἔλαιον *el'-ah-yon;* neut. of the same as *1636;* olive *oil:*–oil.

1638. ἐλαιών *el-ah-yone';* from *1636;* an *olive-orchard,* i.e. (spec.) the *Mount of Olives:*–Olivet.

1639. Ἐλαμίτης *el-am-ee'-tace;* of Heb. or. [5867]; an *Elamite* or Pers.:–Elamite.

1640. ἐλάσσων *el-as'-sone* or ἐλάττων comp. of the same as *1646; smaller* (in size, quantity, age or quality):–less, under, worse, younger.

1641. ἐλαττονέω *el-at-ton-eh-o;* from *1640;* to *diminish,* i.e. *fall short:*–have lack.

1642. ἐλαττόω *el-at-to'-o;* from *1640;* to *lessen* (in rank or influence):–decrease, make lower.

1643. ἐλαύνω *el-ow'-no;* a prol. form of a prim. verb (obs. except in cert. tenses as an alternative of this) of unc. affin.; to *push* (as wind, oars or demonical power):–carry, drive, row.

1644. ἐλαφρία *el-af-ree'-ah; from 1645; levity* (fig.), i.e. *fickleness:*–lightness.

1645. ἐλαφρός *el-af-ros';* prob. akin to *1643* and the base of *1640; light,* i.e. *easy:*–light.

1646. ἐλάχιστος *el-akh'-is-tos;* sup. of ἔλαχυς (*short*); used as equiv. to *3398; least* (in size, amount, dignity, etc.):–least, very little (small), smallest.

1647. ἐλαχιστότερος *el-akh-is-tot'-er-os;* comp. of *1646; far less:*–less than the least.

1648. Ἐλεάζαρ *el-eh-ad'-zar;* of Heb. or. [499]; *Eleazar,* an Isr.:–Eleazar.

1649. ἔλεγξις *el'-eng-xis;* from *1651; refutation,* i.e. *reproof:*–rebuke.

1650. ἔλεγχος *el'-eng-khos;* from *1651; proof, conviction:*–evidence, reproof.

1651. ἐλέγχω *el-eng'-kho;* of unc. affin.; to *confute, admonish:*–convict, convince, tell a fault, rebuke, reprove.

1652. ἐλεεινός *el-eh-i-nos';* from *1656; pitiable:*–miserable.

1653. ἐλεέω *el-eh-eh'-o;* from *1656;* to *compassionate* (by word or deed, spec. by divine grace):–have compassion (pity on), have (obtain, receive, shew) mercy (on).

1654. ἐλεημοσύνη *el-eh-ay-mos-oo'-nay;* from *1656; compassionateness,* i.e. (as exercised towards the poor) *beneficence,* or (concr.) a *benefaction:*–alms(-deeds).

1655. ἐλεήμων *el-eh-ay'-mone;* from 1653; *compassionate* (act.):–merciful.

1656. ἔλεος *el'-eh-os;* of unc. affin.; *compassion* (human or divine, esp. act.):–(+ tender) mercy.

1657. ἐλευθερία *el-yoo-ther-ee'-ah;* from *1658; freedom* (legitimate or licentious, chiefly mor. or cer.):–liberty.

1658. ἐλεύθερος *el-yoo'-ther-os;* prob. from the alt. of *2064; unrestrained* (to *go* at pleasure), i.e. (as a citizen) *not a slave* (whether *freeborn* or *manumitted*), or (gen. case) *exempt* (from obligation or liability):–free (man, woman), at liberty.

1659. ἐλευθερόω *el-yoo-ther-o'-o;* from *1658;* to *liberate,* i.e. (fig.) to *exempt* (from mor. cer. or mortal liability):–deliver, make free.

1660. ἔλευσις *el'-yoo-sis;* from the alt. of *2064;* an *advent:*–coming.

1661. ἐλεφάντινος *el-ef-an'-tee-nos;* from ἔλεφας (an "*elephant*"); *elephantine,* i.e. (by impl.) composed of *ivory:*–of ivory.

1662. Ἐλιακείμ *el-ee-ahm'* or Ἐλιακίμ *el-ee-ak-ime';* of Heb. or. [471]; *Eliakim,* an Isr.:–Eliakim.

1663. Ἐλιέζερ *el-ee-ed'-zer;* of Heb. or. [461]; *Eliezer,* an Isr.:–Eliezer.

1664. Ἐλιούδ *el-ee-ood';* of Heb. or. [410 and 1935]; *God of majesty; Eliud,* an Isr.:–Eliud.

1665. Ἐλισάβετ *el-ee-sab'-et;* of Heb. or. [472]; *Elisabet,* an Isr.s:–Elisabeth.

1666. Ἐλισσαῖος *el-is-sah'-yos;* of Heb. or. [477]; *Elissaeus,* an Isr.:–Elissaeus.

1667. ἑλίσσω *hel-is'-so* a form of *1507;* to *coil* or *wrap:*–fold up.

1668. ἕλκος *hel'-kos;* prob. from *1670;* an *ulcer* (as if drawn together):–sore.

1669. ἑλκόω *hel-ko'-o;* from 1668; to *cause to ulcerate,* i.e. (pass.) *be ulcerous:*–full of sores.

1670. ἑλκύω *hel-koo'-o;* or ἕλκω *hel'-ko;* prob. akin to *138;* to *drag* (lit. or fig.):–draw. Comp. *1667.*

1671. Ἑλλάς *hel-las'* of unc. affin.; *Hellas* (or *Greece*), a country of Europe:–Greece.

1672. Ἕλλην *hel'-lane;* from *1671;* a *Hellen* (*Grecian*) or inh. of Hellas; by ext. a *Gr.-speaking* pers., esp. a *non-Jew:*– Gentile, Greek.

1673. Ἑλληνικός *hel-lay-nee-kos';* from *1672; Hellenic,* i.e. *Grecian* (in language):–Greek.

1674. Ἑλληνίς *hel-lay-nis';* fem. or. of *1672;* a *Grecian* (i.e. *non-Jewish*) woman:–Greek.

1675. Ἑλληνιστής *hel-lay-nis-tace';* from a der. of *1672;* a *Hellenist* or Gr.-speaking Jew:–Grecian.

1676. Ἑλληνιστί *hel-lay-nis-tee';* adv. from the same as *1675*; *Hellenistically,* i.e. in the Grecian language:–Gr..

1677. ἐλλογέω *el-log-eh'-o;* from *1722* and *3056* (in the sense of *account*); to *reckon in,* i.e. *attribute:*–impute, put on account.

1678. Ἐλμωδάμ *el-mo-dam';* of Heb. or. [perh. for 486]; *Elmodam,* an Isr.:–Elmodam.

1679. ἐλπίζω *el-pid'-zo;* from *1680;* to *expect* or *confide:*–(have, thing) hope(-d) (for), trust.

1680. ἐλπίς *'el-pece';* from a prim. ἔλπω (to *anticipate,* usually with pleasure); *expectation* (abstr. or concr.) or *confidence:*–faith, hope.

1681. Ἐλύμας *el-oo'-mas;* of for. or.; *Elymas,* a wizard:–Elymas.

1682. ἐλοΐ *el-o-ee';* of Chald. or. [426 with pron. suffix] *my* God:–Eloi.

1683. ἐμαυτοῦ *em-ow-too';* gen. com. of *1700* and *846; of myself* so likewise the dat. ἐμαυτῷ *em-ow-to',* and acc. ἐμαυτόν *em-ow-ton:*–me, mine own (self), myself.

1684. ἐμβαίνω *em-ba'-hee-no;* from *1722* and the base of *939;* to *walk* on, i.e. *embark* (aboard a vessel), *reach* (a pool):–come (get) into, enter (into), go (up) into, step in, take ship.

1685. ἐμβάλλω *em-bal'-lo;* from *1722* and *906;* to *throw on,* i.e. (fig.) *subject* to (eternal punishment):–cast into.

1686. ἐμβάπτω *em-bap'-to;* from *1722* and *911;* to *whelm on,* i.e. *wet* (a part of the pers., etc.) by contact with a fluid:–dip.

1687. ἐμβατεύω *em-bat-yoo'-o;* from *1722* and a presumed der. of the base of *939;* equiv. to *1684;* to *intrude on* (fig.):–intrude into.

1688. ἐμβιβάζω *em-bib-ad'-zo;* from *1722* and βιβάζω (to *mount;* caus. of *1684*); to *place on,* i.e. *transfer* (aboard a vessel):–put in.

1689. ἐμβλέπω *em-blep'-o;* from *1722* and *991;* to *look on,* i.e. (rel.) to *observe* fixedly, or (absol.) to *discern* clearly:–behold, gaze up, look upon, (could) see.
1690. ἐμβριμάομαι *em-brim-ah'-om-ahee;* from *1722* and βριμάομαι (to *snort* with anger); to have *indignation on,* i.e. (trans.) to *blame,* (intr.) to *sigh* with chagrin, (spec.) to sternly *enjoin:*–straitly charge, groan, murmur against.
1691. ἐμέ *em-eh';* a prol. form of *3165; me:*–I, me, my (-self).
1692. ἐμέω *em-eh'-o;* of unc. affin.; to *vomit:*–(will) spue.
1693. ἐμμαίνομαι *em-mah'-ee-nom-ahee;* from *1722* and *3105;* to *rave on,* i.e. *rage at:*–be mad against.
1694. Ἐμμανουήλ *em-man-oo-ale';* of Heb. or. [6005]; *God with us; Emmanuel,* a name of Christ:–Emmanuel.
1695. Ἐμμαούς *em-mah-ooce';* prob. of Heb. or. [comp. 3222]; *Emmaüs,* a place in Pal.:–Emmaus.
1696. ἐμμένω *em-men'-o;* from *1722* and *3306;* to *stay* in the same place, i.e. (fig.) *persevere:*–continue.
1697. Ἐμμόρ *em-mor';* of Heb. or. [2544]; *Emmor* (i.e. *Chamor*), a Canaanite:–Emmor.
1698. ἐμοί *em-oy';* a prol. form of *3427*; to *me:*–I, me, mine, my.
1699. ἐμός *em-os';* from the oblique cases of *1473* (*1698, 1700, 1691*); *my:*–of me, mine (own), my.
1700. ἐμοῦ *em-oo';* a prol. form *of* 3450; of *me:*–me, mine, my.
1701. ἐμπαιγμός *emp-aheeg-mos';* from *1702*; *derision:*–mocking.
1702. ἐμπαίζω *emp-aheed'-zo;* from *1722* and *3815;* to *jeer at,* i.e. *deride:*–mock.
1703. ἐμπαίκτης *emp-aheek-tace';* from *1702;* a *derider,* i.e. (by impl.) a *false teacher:*–mocker, scoffer.
1704. ἐμπεριπατέω *em-per-ee-pat-eh'-o;* from *1722* and *4043;* to *perambulate on* a place, i.e. (fig.) to *be occupied among* persons:–walk in.
1705. ἐμπίπλημι *em-pip'-lay-mee;* or ἐμπλήθω *em-play'-tho;* from *1722* and the base of *4118;* to *fill in* (*up*), i.e. (by impl.) to *satisfy* (lit. or fig.):–fill.
1706. ἐμπίπτω *em-pip'-to;* from *1722* and *4098;* to *fall on,* i.e. (lit.) to *be entrapped by,* or (fig.) *be overwhelmed with:*–fall among (into).
1707. ἐμπλέκω *em-plek'-o;* from *1722* and *4120;* to *entwine,* i.e. (fig.) *involve* with:–entangle (in, self with).
1708. ἐμπλοκή *em-plok-ay';* from *1707;* elaborate *braiding* of the hair:–plaiting.
1709. ἐμπνέω *emp-neh'-o;* from *1722* and *4154;* to *inhale,* i.e. (fig.) to *be animated by* (*bent upon*):–breathe.
1710. ἐμπορεύομαι *em-por-yoo'-om-ahee;* from *1722* and *4198;* to *travel in* (a country as a pedlar), i.e. (by impl.) to *trade:*–buy and sell, make merchandise.
1711. ἐμπορία *em-por-ee'-ah;* or. from *1713; traffic:*–merchandise.
1712. ἐμπόριον *em-por'-ee-on;* neut. from *1713;* a *mart* ("*emporium*"):–merchandise.
1713. ἔμπορος *em'-por-os;* from *1722* and the base of *4198;* a (wholesale) *tradesman:*–merchant.
1714. ἐμπρήθω *em-pray'-tho;* from *1722* and πρήθω (to *blow* a flame); to *enkindle,* i.e. *set on fire:*–burn up.
1715. ἔμπροσθεν *em'-pros-then;* from *1722* and *4314; in front of* (in place [lit. or fig.] or time):–against, at, before, (in presence, sight) of.
1716. ἐμπτύω *emp-too'-o;* from *1722* and *4429;* to *spit at* or *on:*–spit (upon).
1717. ἐμφανής *em-fan-ace';* from a com. of *1722* and *5316; app. in* self:–manifest, openly.
1718. ἐμφανίζω *em-fan-id'-zo;* from *1717;* to *exhibit* (in pers.) or *disclose* (by words):–appear, declare (plainly), inform, (will) manifest, shew, signify.
1719. ἔμφοβος *em'-fob-os;* from *1722* and *5401; in fear,* i.e. *alarmed:*–affrighted, afraid, tremble.
1720. ἐμφυσάω *em-foo-sah'-o;* from *1722* and φυσάω (to *puff*) [comp. *5453*]; to *blow* at or *on:*–breathe on.
1721. ἔμφυτος *em'-foo-tos;* from *1722* and a der. of *5453; implanted* (fig.):–engrafted.
1722. ἐν *en;* a prim. prep. denoting (fixed) *position* (in place, time or state), and (by impl.) *instrumentality* (medially or constr.), i.e. a relation of *rest* (intermediate between *1519* and *1537*); "*in,*" *at,* (up-)*on, by,* etc.:–about, after, against, + almost, X altogether, among, X as, at, before, between, (here-)by (+ all means), for (... sake of), + give self wholly to, (here-)in(-to, -wardly), X mightily, (because) of, (up-)on, [open-]ly, X outwardly, one, X quickly, X shortly, [speedi-]ly, X that,X there (-in, -on), through(-out), (un-)to(-ward), under, when, where(-with), while, with(-in). Often used in com., with substantially the same import; rarely with verbs of motion, and then not to indicate direction, except (ell.) by a separate (and different) prep.
1723. ἐναγκαλίζομαι *en-ang-kal-id'-zom-ahee;* from *1722* and a der. of *43;* to *take in* one's *arms,* i.e. *embrace:*–take up in arms.
1724. ἐνάλιος *en-al'-ee-os;* from *1722* and *251; in* the *sea,* i.e. *marine:*–thing in the sea.
1725. ἔναντι *en'-an-tee;* from *1722* and *473; in front* (i.e. fig. *presence*) *of:*–before.
1726. ἐναντίον *en-an-tee'-on;* neut. of *1727;* (adv.) *in* the *presence* (*view*) *of:*–before, in the presence of.
1727. ἐναντίος *en-an-tee'-os;* from *1725; opposite;* fig. *antagonistic:*–(over) against, contrary.
1728. ἐνάρχομαι *en-ar'-khom-ahee;* from *1722* and *756;* to *commence on:*–rule.
1729. ἐνδεής *en-deh-ace';* from a com. of *1722* and *1210* (in the sense of *lacking*); *deficient in:*–lacking.
1730. ἔνδειγμα *en'-dighe-mah;* from *1731;* an *indication* (concr.):–manifest token.
1731. ἐνδείκνυμι *en-dike'-noo-mee;* from *1722* and *1166;* to *indicate* (by word or act):–do, show (forth).
1732. ἔνδειξις *en'-dike-sis;* from *1731; indication* (abstr.):–declare, evident token, proof.
1733. ἕνδεκα *hen'-dek-ah;* from (the neut. of) *1520* and *1176; one* and *ten,* i.e. *eleven:*–eleven.
1734. ἑνδέκατος *hen-dek'-at-os;* ord. from *1733; eleventh:*–eleventh.
1735. ἐνδέχεται *en-dekh'-et-ahee;* third pers. sing. pres. of a com. of *1722* and *1209;* (impers.) *it is accepted in,* i.e. *admitted* (*possible*):–can (+ not) be.
1736. ἐνδημέω *en-day-meh'-o;* from a com. of *1722* and *1218;* to *be in* one's own *country,* i.e. *home* (fig.):–be at home (present).
1737. ἐνδιδύσκω *en-did-oos'-ko;* a prol. form of *1746;* to *invest* (with a garment):–clothe in, wear.
1738. ἔνδικος *en'-dee-kos;* from *1722* and *1349; in* the *right,* i.e. *equitable:*–just.
1739. ἐνδόμησις *en-dom'-ay-sis;* from a com. of *1722* and a der. of the base of *1218;* a *housing in* (*residence*), i.e. *structure:*–building.
1740. ἐνδοξάζω *en-dox-ad'-zo;* from *1741;* to *glorify:*–glorify.
1741. ἔνδοξος *en'-dox-os;* from *1722* and *1391; in glory,* i.e. *splendid,* (fig.) *noble:*–glorious, gorgeous[-ly], honourable.
1742. ἔνδυμα *en'-doo-mah;* from *1746; apparel* (esp. the outer *robe*):–clothing, garment, raiment.
1743. ἐνδυναμόω *en-doo-nam-o'-o;* from *1722* and *1412;* to *empower:*–enable, (increase in) streng.(-en), be (make) strong.
1744. ἐνδύνω *en-doo'-no;* from *1772* and *1416;* to *sink* (by impl. *wrap* [comp. *1746*]) *on,* i.e. (fig.) *sneak:*–creep.
1745. ἔνδυσις *en'-doo-sis;* from *1746; investment* with clothing:–putting on.
1746. ἐνδύω *en-doo'-o;* from *1722* and *1416* (in the sense of *sinking* into a garment); to *invest* with clothing (lit. or fig.):–array, clothe (with), endue, have (put) on.
1747. ἐνέδρα *en-ed'-rah;* fem. from *1722* and the base of *1476;* an *ambuscade,* i.e. (fig.) murderous *purpose:*–lay wait. See also 1749.
1748. ἐνεδρεύω *en-ed-ryoo'-o;* from *1747;* to *lurk,* i.e. (fig.) *plot* assassination:–lay wait for.
1749. ἔνεδρον *en'-ed-ron;* neut. of the same as *1747;* an *ambush,* i.e. (fig.) murderous *design:*–lying in wait.
1750. ἐνειλέω *en-i-leh'-o;* from *1772* and the base of *1507;* to *enwrap:*–wrap in.
1751. ἔνειμι *en'-i-mee;* from *1772* and *1510;* to *be within* (neut. part. pl.):–such things as ... have. See also*1762.*
1752. ἕνεκα *hen'-ek-ah;* or ἕνεκεν *hen'-ek-en;* or εἵνεκεν *hi'-nek-en;* of unc. affin.; *on account of:*–because, for (cause, sake), (where-) fore, by reason of, that.
1753. ἐνέργεια *en-erg'-i-ah;* from *1756; efficiency* ("energy"):–operation, strong,

(effectual) working.

1754. ἐνεργέω *en-erg-eh'-o;* from *1756;* to be *act., efficient:*–do, (be) effectual (fervent), be mighty in, shew forth self, work (effectually in).

1755. ἐνέργημα *en-erg'-ay-mah;* from *1754;* an *effect:*–operation, working.

1756. ἐνεργής *en-er-gace';* from *1722* and *2041; act., operative:*–effectual, powerful.

1757. ἐνευλογέω *en-yoo-log-eh'-o;* from *1722* and *2127;* to *confer a benefit on:*–bless.

1758. ἐνέχω *en-ekh'-o;* from *1722* and *2192;* to *hold in* or *upon,* i.e. *ensnare;* by impl. to *keep a grudge:*–entangle with, have a quarrel against, urge.

1759. ἐνθάδε *en-thad'-eh;* from a prol. form of *1722;* prop. *within,* i.e. (of place) *here, hither:*–(t-)here, hither.

1760. ἐνθυμέομαι *en-thoo-meh'-om-ahee;* from a com. of *1722* and *2372;* to *be inspirited,* i.e. *ponder:*–think.

1761. ἐνθύμησις *en-thoo'-may-sis;* from *1760; deliberation:*–device, thought.

1762. ἔνι *en'-ee* contr. for the third pers. sing. pres. ind. of *1751;* impers., *there is* in or among:–be, (there) is.

1763. ἐνιαυτός *en-ee-ow-tos';* prol. from a prim. ἔνος (a *year*); a *year:*–year.

1764. ἐνίστημι *en-is'-tay-mee;* from *1722* and *2476;* to *place on* hand, i.e. (refl.) *impend,* (part.) be *instant:*–come, be at hand, present

1765. ἐνισχύω *en-is-khoo'-o;* from *1722* and *2480;* to *invigorate* (trans. or refl.):–strengthen.

1766. ἔνατος *en'-nat-os;* ord. from *1767; ninth:*–ninth.

1767. ἐννέα *en-neh'-ah;* a prim. number; *nine:*–nine.

1768. ἐννενηκονταεννέα *en-nen-ay-kon-tah-en-neh'-ah;* from a (tenth) multiple of *1767* and *1767* itself; *ninety-nine:*–ninety and nine.

1769. ἐννεός *en-neh-os';* from *1770; dumb* (as *making signs*), i.e. *silent* from astonishment:–speechless.

1770. ἐννεύω *en-nyoo'-o;* from *1722* and *3506;* to *nod at,* i.e. *beckon* or *communicate by gesture:*–make signs.

1771. ἔννοια *en'-noy-ah;* from a com. of *1722* and *3563; thoughtfulness,* i.e. mor. *understanding:*–intent, mind.

1772. ἔννομος *en'-nom-os;* from *1722* and *3551;* (subj.) *legal,* or (obj.) *subject* to:–lawful, under law.

1773. ἔννυχον *en'-noo-khon;* neut. of a com. of *1722* and *3571;* (adv.) *by night:*–before day.

1774. ἐνοικέω *en-oy-keh'-o;* from *1722* and *3611;* to *inhabit* (fig.):–dwell in.

1775. ἑνότης *hen-ot-ace';* from *1520; oneness,* i.e. (fig.) *unanimity:*–unity.

1776. ἐνοχλέω *en-okh-leh'-o;* from *1722* and *3791;* to *crowd in,* i.e. (fig.) to *annoy:*–trouble.

1777. ἔνοχος *en'-okh-os;* from *1758; liable* to (a condition, penalty or imputation):–in danger of, guilty of, subject to.

1778. ἔνταλμα *en'-tal-mah;* from *1781;* an *injunction,* i.e. relig. *precept:*–commandment.

1779. ἐνταφιάζῳ *en-taf-ee-ad'-zo;* from a com. of *1722* and *5028;* to *inswathe* with cerements for interment:–bury.

1780. ἐνταφιασμός *en-taf-ee-as-mos';* from *1779; preparation* for interment:–burying.

1781. ἐντέλλομαι *en-tel'-lom-ahee;* from *1722* and the base of *5056;* to *enjoin:*–(give) charge, (give) command(-ments), injoin.

1782. ἐντεῦθεν *ent-yoo'-then;* from the same as *1759; hence* (lit. or fig.); (repeated) *on both sides:*–(from) hence, on either side.

1783. ἔντευξις *ent'-yook-sis;* from *1793;* an *interview,* i.e. (spec.) *supplication:*–intercession, prayer.

1784. ἔντιμος *en'-tee-mos;* from *1722* and *5092; valued* (fig.):–dear, more honourable, precious, in reputation.

1785. ἐντολή *en-tol-ay';* from *1781*; *injunction,* i.e. an authoritative *prescription:*–commandment, precept.

1786. ἐντόπιος *en-top'-ee-os;* from *1722* and *5117;* a *resident:*–of that place.

1787. ἐντός *en-tos';* from *1722; inside* (adv. or noun):–within.

1788. ἐντρέπω *en-trep'-o;* from *1722* and the base of *5157;* to *invert,* i.e. (fig. and refl.) in a good sense, to *respect;* or in a bad one, to *confound:*–regard, (give) reference, shame.

1789. ἐντρέφω *en-tref'-o;* from *1722* and *5142;* (fig.) to *educate:*–nourish up in.

1790. ἔντρομος *en'-trom-os;* from *1722* and *5156; terrified:*–X quake, X trembled.

1791. ἐντροπή *en-trop-ay';* from *1788; confusion:*–shame.

1792. ἐντρυφάω *en-troo-fah'-o;* from *1722* and *5171;* to *revel in:*–sporting selves.

1793. ἐντυγχάνω *en-toong-khan'-o;* from *1722* and *5177;* to *chance upon,* i.e. (by impl.) *confer with;* by ext. to *entreat* (in favor or against):–deal with, make intercession.

1794. ἐντυλίσσω *en-too-lis'-so;* from *1722* and τυλίσσω (to *twist;* prob. akin to 1507); to *entwine,* i.e. *wind* up in:–wrap in (together).

1795. ἐντυπόω *en-too-po'-o;* from *1722* and a der. of *5179;* to *enstamp,* i.e. *engrave:*–engrave.

1796. ἐνυβρίζω *en-oo-brid'-zo;* from *1722* and *5195;* to *insult:*–do despite unto.

1797. ἐνυπνιάζομαι *en-oop-nee-ad'-zom-ahee;* mid. from *1798;* to *dream:*–dream(-er).

1798. ἐνύπνιον *en-oop'-nee-on;* from *1722* and *5258;* something seen *in sleep,* i.e. a *dream* (*vision* in a dream):–dream.

1799. ἐνώπιον *en-o'-pee-on;* neut. of a com. of *1722* and a der. of *3700; in* the *face* of (lit. or fig.):–before, in the presence (sight) of, to.

1800. 'Ενώς *en-oce';* of Heb. or. [583]; *Enos* (i.e. *Enosh*), a patriarch:–Enos.

1801. ἐνωτίζομαι *en-o-tid'-zom-ahee;* mid. from a com. of *1722* and *3775;* to take *in one's ear,* i.e. to *listen:*–hearken.

1802. 'Ενώχ *en-oke';* of Heb. or. [2585]; *Enoch* (i.e. *Chanok*), an antediluvian:–Enoch.

1803. ἕξ *hex* a prim. numeral; *six:*–six.

1804. ἐξαγγέλλω *ex-ang-el'-lo;* from *1537* and the base of *32;* to *publish,* i.e. *celebrate:*–shew forth.

1805. ἐξαγοράζω *ex-ag-or-ad'-zo;* from *1537* and *59;* to *buy up,* i.e. *ransom;* fig. to *rescue* from loss (*improve* opportunity):–redeem.

1806. ἐξάγω *ex-ag'-o;* from *1537* and *71;* to *lead forth:*–bring forth (out), fetch (lead) out.

1807. ἐξαιρέω *ex-ahee-reh'-o;* from *1537* and *138;* act., to *tear out;* mid., to *select;* fig. to *release:*–deliver, pluck out, rescue.

1808. ἐξαίρω *ex-ah'-ee-ro;* from *1537* and *142;* to *remove:*–put (take) away.

1809. ἐξαιτέομαι *ex-ahee-teh'-om-ahee;* mid. from *1537* and *154;* to *demand* (for trial):–desire.

1810. ἐξαίφνης *ex-ah'-eef-nace;* from *1537* and the base of *160;* of a *sudden* (*unexpectedly*):–suddenly. Comp. *1819.*

1811. ἐξακολουθέω *ex-ak-ol-oo-theh'-o;* from *1537* and *190;* to *follow out,* i.e. (fig.) to *imitate, obey,* yield to:–follow.

1812. ἑξακόσιοι *hex-ak-os'-ee-oy;* pl. ord. from *1803* and *1540; six hundred:*–six hundred.

1813. ἐξαλείφω *ex-al-i'-fo;* from *1537* and *218;* to *smear out,* i.e. *obliterate* (*erase* tears, fig. *pardon* sin):–blot out, wipe away.

1814. ἐξάλλομαι *ex-al'-lom-ahee;* from *1537* and *242;* to *spring forth:*–leap up.

1815. ἐξανάστασις *ex-an-as'-tas-is;* from *1817;* a *rising from* death:–resurrection.

1816. ἐξανατέλλω *ex-an-at-el'-lo;* from *1537* and *393;* to *start up out* of the ground, i.e. *germinate:*–spring up.

1817. ἐξανίστημι *ex-an-is'-tay-mee;* from *1537* and *450;* obj., to *produce,* i.e. (fig.) *beget;* subj. to *arise,* i.e. (fig.) *object:*–raise (rise) up.

1818. ἐξαπατάω *ex-ap-at-ah'-o;* from *1537* and *538;* to *seduce wholly:*–beguile, deceive.

1819. ἐξάπινα *ex-ap'-ee-nah;* from *1537* and a der. of the same as *160; of* a *sudden,* i.e. *unexpectedly:*–suddenly. Comp. *1810.*

1820. ἐξαπορέομαι *ex-ap-or-eh'-om-ahee;* mid. from *1537* and *639;* to *be utterly at a loss,* i.e. *despond:*–(in) despair.

1821. ἐξαποστέλλω *ex-ap-os-tel'-lo;* from *1537* and *649;* to *send away forth,* i.e. (on a mission) to *despatch,* or (peremptorily) to *dismiss:*–send (away, forth, out).

1822. ἐξαρτίζω *ex-ar-tid'-zo;* from *1537* and a der. of *739;* to *finish out* (time); fig. to *equip fully* (a teacher):–accomplish, thoroughly furnish.

1823. ἐξαστράπτῳ *ex-as-trap'-to;* from *1537* and *797;* to *lighten forth,* i.e. (fig.) to *be radiant* (of very white garments):–glistening.

1824. ἐξαύτης *ex-ow'-tace;* from *1537* and the gen. sing. fem. of *846* (*5610* being understood); *from that* hour, i.e. *instantly:*–by and by, immed., presently, straightway.

1825. ἐξεγείρω *ex-eg-i'-ro;* from *1537* and *1453;* to *rouse fully,* i.e. (fig.) to *resuscitate* (from death), *release* (from infliction):–raise up.

1826. ἔξειμι *ex'-i-mee;* from *1537* and εἶμι (to *go*); to *issue,* i.e. *leave* (a place), *escape* (to the shore):–depart, get [*to land*], go out.
1827. ἐξελέγχω *ex-el-eng'-kho;* from *1537* and *1651;* to *convict fully,* i.e. (by impl.) to *punish:*–convince.
1828. ἐξέλκω *ex-el'-ko;* from *1537* and *1670;* to *drag forth,* i.e. (fig.) to *entice* (to sin):–draw away.
1829. ἐξέραμα *ex-er'-am-ah;* from a comp. of *1537* and a presumed ἐραω (to *spue*); *vomit,* i.e. *food disgorged:*–vomit.
1830. ἐξερευνάω *ex-er-yoo-nah'-o;* from *1537* and *2045;* to *explore* (fig.):–search diligently.
1831. ἐξέρχομαι *ex-er'-khom-ahee;* from *1537* and *2064;* to *issue* (lit. or fig.):–come (forth, out), depart (out of), escape, get out, go (abroad, away, forth, out, thence), proceed (forth), spread abroad.
1832. ἔξεστι *ex'-es-tee;* third pers. sing. pres. ind. of a com. of *1537* and *1510;* so also ἐξόν *ex-on';* neut. pres. part. of the same (with or without some form of 1510 expressed); impers., *it is right* (through the fig. idea of *being out* in public):–be lawful, let, X may(-est).
1833. ἐξετάζω *ex-et-ad'-zo;* from *1537* and ἐτάζω (to *examine*); to *test thoroughly* (by questions), i.e. *ascertain* or *interrogate:*–ask, enquire, search.
1834. ἐξηγέομαί *ex-ayg-eh'-om-ahee;* from *1537* and *2233;* to *consider out* (aloud), i.e. *rehearse, unfold:*–declare, tell.
1835. ἑξήκοντα *hex-ay'-kon-tah;* the tenth multiple of *1803; sixty:*–sixty[-fold], threescore.
from 1537 and 2233; to consider out (aloud), i.e. rehearse, unfold:–declare, tell.
1836. ἑξῆς *hex-ace';* from *2192* (in the sense of *taking hold* of, i.e. *adjoining*); *successive:*–after, following, X morrow, next.
1837. ἐξηχέομαι *ex-ay-kheh'-om-ahee;* mid. from *1537* and *2278;* to "*echo*" *forth,* i.e. *resound* (be generally *reported*):–sound forth.
1838. ἕξις *hex'-is;* from *2192; habit,* i.e. (by impl.) *practice:*–use.
1839. ἐξίστημι *ex-is'-tay-mee;* from *1537* and *2476;* to *put* (*stand*) *out* of wits, i.e. *astound,* or (refl.) *become astounded, insane:*–amaze, be (make) astonished, be beside self (selves), bewitch, wonder.
1840. ἐξισχύω *ex-is-khoo'-o;* from *1537* and *2480;* to *have full streng.,* i.e. *be entirely competent:*–be able.
1841. ἔξοδος *ex'-od-os;* from *1537* and *3598;* an *exit,* i.e. (fig.) *death:*–decease, departing.
1842. ἐξολοθρεύω *ex-ol-oth-ryoo'-o;* from *1537* and *3645;* to *extirpate:*–destroy.
1843. ἐξομολογέω *ex-om-ol-og-eh'-o;* from *1537* and *3670;* to *acknowledge* or (by impl. of *assent*) *agree fully:*–confess, profess, promise.
1844. ἐξορκίζω *ex-or-kid'-zo;* from *1537* and *3726;* to *exact an oath,* i.e. *conjure:*–adjure.
1845. ἐξορκιστής *ex-or-kis-tace';* from *1844; one that binds by an oath* (or *spell*), i.e. (by impl.) an "*exorcist*" (*conjurer*):–exorcist.
1846. ἐξορύσσω *ex-or-oos'-so;* from *1537* and *3736;* to *dig out,* i.e. (by ext.) to *extract* (an eye), *remove* (roofing):–break up, pluck out.
1847. ἐξουδενόω *ex-oo-den-o'-o;* from *1537* and a der. of the neut. of *3762;* to *make utterly nothing of,* i.e. *despise:*–set at nought. See also *1848.*
1848. ἐξουθενέω *ex-oo-then-eh'-o;* a var. of *1847* and mean. the same:–contemptible, despise, least esteemed, set at nought.
1849. ἐξουσία *ex-oo-see'-ah;* from *1832* (in the sense of *ability*); *privilege,* i.e. (subj.) *force, capacity, competency, freedom,* or (obj.) *mastery* (concr. *magistrate, superhuman, potentate, token of control*), delegated *influence:*–authority, jurisdiction, liberty, power, right, strength.
1850. ἐξουσιάζω *ex-oo-see-ad'-zo;* from *1849;* to *control:*–exercise authority upon, bring under the (have) power of.
1851. ἐξοχή *ex-okh-ay';* from a com. of *1537* and *2192* (mean. to *stand out*); *prominence* (fig.):–principal.
1852. ἐξυπνίζω *ex-oop-nid'-zo;* from *1853;* to *waken:*–awake out of sleep.
1853. ἔξυπνος *ex'-oop-nos;* from *1537* and *5258; awake:*–X out of sleep.
1854. ἔξω *ex'-o;* adv. from *1537; out(-side, of doors),* lit. or fig.:–away, forth, (with-)out (of, -ward), strange.
1855. ἔξωθεν *ex'-o-then;* from *1854; external* (*-ly*):–out(-side, -ward, - wardly), (from) without.
1856. ἐξωθέω *ex-o-theh'-o;* or ἐξώθω *ex-o'-tho;* from *1537* and ὠθέω (to *push*); to *expel;* by impl. to *propel:*–drive out, thrust in.
1857. ἐξώτερος *ex-o'-ter-os;* comp. of *1854; exterior:*–outer.
1858. ἑορτάζω *heh-or-tad'-zo;* from *1859;* to *observe a festival:*–keep the feast.
1859. ἑορτή *heh-or-tay';* of unc. affin.; *a festival:*–feast, holyday.
1860. ἐπαγγελία *ep-ang-el-ee'-ah;* from 1861; an *announcement* (for information, assent or pledge; esp. a divine *assurance* of good):–message, promise.
1861. ἐπαγγέλλω *ep-ang-el'-lo;* from *1909* and the base of *32;* to *announce upon* (refl.), i.e. (by impl.) to *engage* to do something, to *assert* something respecting oneself:–profess, (make) promise.
1862. ἐπάγγελμα *ep-ang'-el-mah;* from *1861;* a *self-committal* (by *assurance* of conferring some good):–promise.
1863. ἐπάγω *ep-ag'-o;* from *1909* and *71;* to *superinduce,* i.e. *inflict* (an evil), *charge* (a crime):–bring upon.
1864. ἐπαγωνίζομαι *ep-ag-o-nid'-zom-ahee;* from *1909* and *75;* to *struggle for:*–earnestly contend for.
1865. ἐπαθροίζω *ep-ath-roid'-zo;* from *1909* and ἀθροίζω (to *assemble*); to *accumulate:*–gather thick together.
1866. Ἐπαίνετος *ep-a'-hee-net-os;* from *1867; praised; Epaenetus,* a Chr.:–Epenetus.
1867. ἐπαινέω *ep-ahee-neh'-o;* from *1909* and *134;* to *applaud:*–commend, laud, praise.
1868. ἔπαινος *ep'-ahee-nos;* from *1909* and the base of *134; laudation;* concr. a *commendable thing:*–praise.
1869. ἐπαίρω *ep-ahee'-ro;* from *1909* and *142;* to *raise up* (lit. or fig.):–exalt self, poise (lift, take) up.
1870. ἐπαισχύνομαι *ep-ahee-skhoo'-nom-ahee;* from *1909* and *153;* to *feel shame for* something:–be ashamed.
1871. ἐπαιτέω *ep-ahee-teh'-o;* from *1909* and *154;* to *ask for:*–beg.
1872. ἐπακολουθέω *ep-ak-ol-oo-theh'-o;* from *1909* and *190;* to *accompany:*–follow (after).
1873. ἐπακούω *ep-ak-oo'-o;* from *1909* and *191;* to *hearken* (favorably) *to:*–hear.
1874. ἐπακροάομαι *ep-ak-ro-ah'-om-ahee;* from *1909* and the base of *202;* to *listen* (intently) *to:*–hear.
1875. ἐπάν *ep-an';* from *1909* and *302;* a par. of indef. contemporaneousness; *whenever, as soon as:*–when.
1876. ἐπάναγκες *ep-an'-ang-kes;* neut. of a presumed com. of *1909* and *318;* (adv.) *on necessity,* i.e. *necessarily:*–necessary.
1877. επανάγω *ep-an-ag'-o;* from *1909* and *321;* to *lead up on,* i.e. (technical) to *put out* (to sea); (intrans.) to *return:*–launch (thrust) out, return.
1878. ἐπαναμιμνήσκω *ep-an-ah-mim-nace'-ko;* from *1909* and *363;* to *remind of:*–put in mind.
1879. ἐπαναπαύομαι *ep-an-ah-pow'-om-ahee;* mid. from *1909* and *373;* to *settle on;* lit. (*remain*) or fig. (*rely*):–rest in (upon).
1880. ἐπανέρχομαι *ep-an-er'-khom-ahee; from 1909* and *424;* to *come up on,* i.e. *return:*–come again, return.
1881. ἐπανίσταμαι *ep-an-is'-tam-ahee;* mid. from *1909* and *450*; *to stand up on,* i.e. (fig.) to *attack:*–rise up against.
1882. ἐπανόρθωσις *ep-an-or'-tho-sis;* from a com. of *1909* and *461;* a *straightening up again,* i.e. (fig.) *rectification* (*reformation*):– correction.
1883. ἐπάνω *ep-an'-o;* from *1909* and *507; up above,* i.e. *over* or *on* (of place, amount, rank, etc.):–above, more than, (up-)on, over.
1884. ἐπαρκέω *ep-ar-keh'-o;* from *1909* and *714;* to *avail for,* i.e. *help:*–relieve.
1885. ἐπαρχία *ep-ar-khee'-ah;* from a com. of *1909* and *757* (mean. a *governor* of a district, "eparch"); a spec. *region* of government, i.e. a Rom. *præfecture:*–province.
1886. ἔπαυλις *ep'-ow-lis;* from *1909* and an equiv. of *833;* a *hut over* the head, i.e. a *dwelling:*–habitation
1887. ἐπαύριον *ep-ow'-ree-on;* from *1909* and *839;* occurring *on* the *succeeding* day, i.e. (*2250* being implied) *to-morrow:*–day following, morrow, next day (after).
1888. ἐπαυτοφώρῳ *ep-ow-tof-o'-ro;* from *1909* and *846* and (the dat. sing. of) a der. of φώρ (a *thief*); *in theft itself,* i.e. (by anal.) *in actual crime:*–in the very act.
1889. Ἐπαφρᾶς *ep-af-ras';* contr. from *1891; Epaphras,* a Chr.:–Epaphras.
1890. ἐπαφρίζω *ep-af-rid'-zo;* from *1909*

GREEK

and *875;* to *foam upon,* i.e. (fig.) to *exhibit* (a vile passion):–foam out.

1891. Ἐπαφρόδιτος *ep-af-rod'-ee-tos;* from *1909* (in the sense of *devoted* to) and Ἀφροδίτη (*Venus*); *Epaphroditus,* a Chr.:–Epaphroditus. Comp. *1889.*

1892. ἐπεγείρω *ep-eg-i'-ro;* from *1909* and *1453;* to *rouse upon,* i.e. (fig.) to *excite* against:–raise, stir up.

1893. ἐπεί *ep-i';* from *1909* and *1487; thereupon,* i.e. *since* (of time or cause):–because, else, for that (then, -asmuch as), otherwise, seeing that, since, when.

1894. ἐπειδή *ep-i-day';* from *1893* and *1211; since now,* i.e. (of time) *when,* or (of cause) *whereas:*–after that, because, for (that, -asmuch as), seeing, since.

1895. ἐπειδήπερ *ep-i-day'-per;* from *1894* and *4007; since indeed* (of cause):–forasmuch.

1896. ἐπεῖδον *ep-i'-don;* and other moods and persons of the same tense; from *1909* and *1492;* to *regard* (favorably or otherwise):–behold, look upon.

1897. ἐπείπερ *ep-i'-per;* from *1893* and *4007; since* indeed (of cause):–seeing.

1898. ἐπεισαγωγή *ep-ice-ag-o-gay';* from a com. of *1909* and *1521;* a *super-introduction:*–bringing in.

1899. ἔπειτα *ep'-i-tah;* from *1909* and *1534; thereafter:*–after that(-ward), then.

1900. ἐπέκεινα *ep-ek'-i-nah;* from *1909* and (the acc. pl. neut. of) *1565; upon those* parts of, i.e. *on the further side of:*–beyond.

1901. ἐπεκτείνομαι *ep-ek-ti'-nom-ahee;* mid. from *1909* and *1614;* to *stretch* (oneself) forward *upon:*–reach forth.

1902. ἐπενδύομαι *ep-en-doo'-om-ahee;* mid. from *1909* and *1746;* to *invest upon* oneself:–be clothed upon.

1903. ἐπενδύτης *ep-en-doo'-tace;* from *1902;* a *wrapper,* i.e. outer garment:–fisher's coat.

1904. ἐπέρχομαι *ep-er'-khom-ahee;* from *1909* and *2064;* to *supervene,* i.e. *arrive, occur, impend, attack,* (fig.) *influence:*–come (in, upon).

1905. ἐπερωτάω *ep-er-o-tah'-o;* from *1909* and *2065;* to *ask for,* i.e. *inquire, seek:*–ask (after, questions), demand, desire, question.

1906. ἐπερώτημα *ep-er-o'-tay-mah;* from *1905;* an *inquiry:*–answer.

1907. ἐπέχω *ep-ekh'-o;* from *1909* and *2192;* to *hold upon,* i.e. (by impl.) to *retain;* (by ext.) to *detain;* (with impl. of 3563) to *pay attention to:*–give (take) heed unto, hold forth, mark, stay.

1908. ἐπηρεάζω *ep-ay-reh-ad'-zo;* from a comp. of *1909* and (prob.) ἀρειά (*threats*); to *insult, slander:*–use despitefully, falsely accuse.

1909. ἐπί *ep-ee';* a prim. prep. prop. mean. *superimposition* (of time, place, order, etc.), as a relation of *distribution* [with the gen.], i.e. *over, upon,* etc.; of *rest* (with the dat.) *at, on,* etc.; of *direction* (with the acc.) *towards, upon,* etc.:–about (the times), above, after, against, among, as long as (touching), at, beside, X have charge of, (be-, [where-])fore, in (a place, as much as, the time of, -to), (because) of, (up-)on (behalf of), over, (by, for) the space of, through(-out), (un-) to(-ward), with. In com. it retains essentially the same import, *at, upon,* etc. (lit. or fig.).

1910. ἐπιβαίνω *ep-ee-bah'-ee-no;* from *1909* and the base of *939;* to *walk upon,* i.e. *mount, ascend, embark, arrive:*–come (into), enter into, go abroad, sit upon, take ship.

1911. ἐπιβάλλω *ep-ee-bal'-lo;* from *1909* and *906;* to *throw upon* (lit. or fig. trans. or refl.; usually with more or less force); spec. (with *1438* implied) to *reflect;* impers., to *belong to:*–beat into, cast (up-)on, fall, lay (on), put (unto), stretch forth, think on.

1912. ἐπιβαρέω *ep-ee-bar-eh'-o;* from *1909* and *916;* to *be heavy upon,* i.e. (pecuniarily) to *be expensive to;* fig. to *be severe towards:*–be chargeable to, overcharge.

1913. ἐπιβιβάζω *ep-ee-bee-bad'-zo;* from *1909* and a redupl. der. of the base of *939* [comp. *307*] to *cause to mount* (an animal):–set on.

1914. ἐπιβλέπω *ep-ee-blep'-o;* from *1909* and *991;* to *gaze at* (with favor, pity or partiality):–look upon, regard, have respect to.

1915. ἐπίβλημα *ep-ib'-lay-mah;* from *1911;* a *patch:*–piece.

1916. ἐπιβοάω *ep-ee-bo-ah'-o;* from *1909* and *994;* to *exclaim against:*–cry.

1917. ἐπιβουλή *ep-ee-boo-lay';* from a presumed com. of *1909* and *1014;* a *plan against* someone, i.e. a *plot:*–laying (lying) in wait.

1918. ἐπιγαμβρεύω *ep-ee-gam-bryoo'-o;* from *1909* and a der. of *1062;* to *form affin. with,* i.e. (spec.) in a levirate way:–marry.

1919. ἐπίγειος *ep-ig'-i-os;* from *1909* and *1093; worldly* (phys. or mor.):–earthly, in earth, terrestrial.

1920. ἐπιγίνομαι *ep-ig-in'-om-ahee;* from *1909* and *1096;* to *arrive upon,* i.e. *spring up* (as a wind):–blow

1921. ἐπιγινώσκω *ep-ig-in-oce'-ko;* from *1909* and *1097;* to *know upon* some mark, i.e. *recognize;* by impl. to *become fully acquainted with,* to *acknowledge:*–(ac-,have, take)know(-ledge, well), perceive.

1922. ἐπίγνωσις *ep-ig'-no-sis;* from *1921; recognition,* i.e. (by impl.) full *discernment, acknowledgement:*–(ac-) knowledge (-ing, - ment).

1923. ἐπιγραφή *ep-ig-raf-ay';* from *1924;* an *inscription:*–superscription.

1924. ἐπιγράφω *ep-ee-graf'-o;* from *1909* and *1125;* to *inscribe* (phys. or ment.):–*inscription,* write in (over, thereon).

1925. ἐπιδείκνυμι *ep-ee-dike'-noo-mee;* from *1909* and *1166;* to *exhibit* (phys. or ment.):–shew

1926. ἐπιδέχομαι *ep-ee-dekh'-om-ahee;* from *1909* and *1209;* to *admit* (as a guest or [fig.] teacher):–receive.

1927. ἐπιδημέω *ep-ee-day-meh'-o;* from a com. of *1909* and *1218;* to *make oneself at home,* i.e. (by ext.) to *reside* (in a for. country):–[be] dwelling (which were) there, stranger.

1928. ἐπιδιατάσσομαι *ep-ee-dee-ah-tas'-som-ahee;* mid. from *1909* and *1299;* to *appoint besides,* i.e. *supplement* (as a codicil):–add to.

1929. ἐπιδίδωμι *ep-ee-did'-o-mee;* from *1909* and *1325;* to *give over* (by hand or surrender):–deliver unto, give, let (+ [her drive]), offer.

1930. ἐπιδιορθόω *ep-ee-dee-or-tho'-o;* from *1909* and a der. of *3717;* to *straighten further,* i.e. (fig.) *arrange additionally:*–set in order.

1931. ἐπιδύω *ep-ee-doo'-o;* from *1909* and *1416;* to *set* fully (as the sun):–go down.

1932. ἐπιείκεια *ep-ee-i'-ki-ah;* from *1933; suitableness,* i.e. (by impl.) *equity, mildness:*–clemency, gentleness.

1933. ἐπιεικής *ep-ee-i-kace';* from *1909* and *1503; appropriate,* i.e. (by impl.) *mild:*–gentle, moderation, patient.

1934. ἐπιζητέω *ep-eed-zay-teh'-o;* from *1909* and *2212;* to *search* (*inquire*) *for;* intens., to *demand,* to *crave:*–desire, enquire, seek (after, for).

1935. ἐπιθανάτιος *ep-ee-than-at'-ee-os;* from *1909* and *2288;* doomed *to death:*–appointed to death.

1936. ἐπίθεσις *ep-ith'-es-is;* from *2007;* an *imposition* (of hands officially):–laying (putting) on.

1937. ἐπιθυμέω *ep-ee-thoo-meh'-o;* from *1909* and *2372;* to set the *heart upon,* i.e. *long* for (rightfully or otherwise):–covet, desire, would fain, lust (after).

1938. ἐπιθυμητής *ep-ee-thoo-may-tace';* from *1937;* a *craver:*–+ lust after.

1939. ἐπιθυμία *ep-ee-thoo-mee'-ah;* from *1937;* a *longing* (esp. for what is forbidden):–concupiscence, desire, lust (after).

1940. ἐπικαθίζω *ep-ee-kath-id'-zo;* from *1909* and *2523;* to *seat upon:*–set on.

1941. ἐπικαλέομαι *ep-ee-kal-eh'-om-ahee;* mid. from *1909* and *2564;* to *entitle;* by impl. to *invoke* (for aid, worship, testimony, decision, etc.):–appeal (unto), call (on, upon), surname.

1942. ἐπικάλυμα *ep-ee-kal'-oo-mah;* from *1943;* a *covering,* i.e. (fig.) *pretext:*–cloke.

1943. ἐπικαλύπτω *ep-ee-kal-oop'-to;* from *1909* and *2572;* to *conceal,* i.e. (fig.) *forgive:*–cover.

1944. ἐπικατάρατος *ep-ee-kat-ar'-at-os;* from 1909 and a der. of 2672; *imprecated,* i.e. *execrable:*–accursed.

1945. ἐπίκιμαι *ep-ik'-i-mahee;* from *1909* and *2749;* to *rest upon* (lit. or fig.):–impose, be instant, (be) laid (there-, up-) on, (when) lay (on), lie (on), press upon

1946. Ἐπικούρειος *ep-ee-koo'-ri-os;* from Ἐπίκουρος [comp. 1947] (a noted philosopher); an *Epicurean* or follower of Epicurus:–Epicurean

1947. ἐπικουρία *ep-ee-koo-ree'-ah;* from a com. of *1909* and a (prol.) form of the base of *2877* (in the sense of *servant*); *assistance:*–help.

1948. ἐπικρίνω *ep-ee-kree'-no;* from *1909* and *2919;* to *adjudge:*–give sentence.

1949. ἐπιλαμβάνομαι *ep-ee-lam-ban'-om-ahee;* mid. from *1909* and *2983;* to *seize* (for help, injury, attainment, or any other purpose; lit. or fig.):–catch, lay hold (up-) on, take (by, hold of, on).

1950. ἐπιλανθάνομαι *ep-ee-lan-than'-om-ahee;* mid. from *1909* and *2990;* to *lose out* of mind; by impl. to *neglect:*–(be) forget(-ful of).

1951. ἐπιλέγομαι *ep-ee-leg'-om-ahee;* mid. from *1909* and *3004;* to *surname, select:*–call, choose.

1952. ἐπιλείπω *ep-ee-li'-po;* from *1909* and *3007;* to *leave upon,* i.e. (fig.) to *be insufficient for:*–fail.

1953. ἐπιλησμονή *ep-ee-lace-mon-ay';* from a der. of *1950; negligence:*–X forgetful.

1954. ἐπίλοιπος *ep-il'-oy-pos;* from *1909* and *3062; left over,* i.e. *remaining:*–rest.

1955. ἐπίλυσις *ep-il'-oo-sis;* from *1956; explanation,* i.e. *appl.:*–interpretation.

1956. ἐπιλύω *ep-ee-loo'-o;* from *1909* and *3089;* to *solve further,* i.e. (fig.) to *explain, decide:*–determine, expound.

1957. ἐπιμαρτυρέω *ep-ee-mar-too-reh'-o;* from *1909* and *3140;* to *attest further,* i.e. *corroborate:*–testify.

1958. ἐπιμέλεια *ep-ee-mel'-i-ah;* from *1959; carefulness,* i.e. kind *attention* (*hospitality*):–+ refresh self.

1959. ἐπιμελέομαι *ep-ee-mel-eh'-om-ahee;* mid. from *1909* and the same as *3199;* to *care for* (phys. or otherwise):–take care of.

1960. ἐπιμελῶς *ep-ee-mel-oce';* adv. from a der. of *1959; carefully:*–diligently.

1961. ἐπιμένω *ep-ee-men'-o;* from *1909* and *3306;* to *stay over,* i.e. *remain* (fig. *persevere*):–abide (in), continue (in), tarry.

1962. ἐπινεύω *ep-een-yoo'-o;* from *1909* and *3506;* to *nod at,* i.e. (by impl.) to *assent:*–consent.

1963. ἐπίνοια *ep-in'-oy-ah;* from *1909* and *3563; attention* of the mind, i.e. (by impl.) *purpose:*–thought.

1964. ἐπιορκέω *ep-ee-or-keh'-o;* from *1965;* to *commit perjury:*–forswear self.

1965. ἐπίορκος *ep-ee'-or-kos;* from *1909* and *3727; on oath,* i.e. (falsely) a *forswearer:*–perjured pers..

1966. ἐπιοῦσα *ep-ee-oo'-sah;* or. sing. part. of a comp. of *1909* and εἶμι (to *go*); *supervening,* i.e. (*2250* or *3571* being expressed or implied) the *ensuing* day or night:–following, next.

1967. ἐπιούσιος *ep-ee-oo'-see-os;* perh. from the same as *1966; tomorrow's;* but more prob. from *1909* and a der. of the pres. part. or. of *1510;* for *subsistence,* i.e. *needful:*–daily.

1968. ἐπιπίπτω *ep-ee-pip'-to;* from *1909* and *4098*; to *embrace* (with affection) or *seize* (with more or less violence; lit. or fig.):–fall into (on, upon) lie on, press upon.

1969. ἐπιπλήσσω *ep-ee-place'-so;* from *1909* and *4141;* to *chastise,* i.e. (with words) to *upbraid:*–rebuke.

1970. ἐπιπνίγω *ep-ee-pnee'-go;* from *1909* and *4155;* to *throttle upon,* i.e. (fig.) *overgrow:*–choke.

1971. ἐπιποθέω *ep-ee-poth-eh'-o;* from *1909* and ποθέω (to *yearn*); to *dote upon,* i.e. *intensely crave* possession (lawfully or wrongfully):–(earnestly) desire (greatly), (greatly) long (after), lust.

1972. ἐπιπόθησις *ep-ee-poth'-ay-sis;* from *1971;* a *longing for:*–earnest (vehement) desire.

1973. ἐπιπόθητος *ep-ee-poth'-ay-tos;* from *1909* and a der. of the latter part of *1971; yearned upon,* i.e. *greatly loved:*–longed for.

1974. ἐπιποθία *ep-ee-poth-ee'-ah;* from *1971; intense longing:*–great desire.

1975. ἐπιπορεύομαι *ep-ee-por-yoo'-om-ahee;* from *1909* and *4198;* to *journey further,* i.e. *travel on* (*reach*):–come.

1976. ἐπιῤῥάπτω *ep-ir-hrap'-to';* from *1909* and the base of *4476;* to *stitch upon,* i.e. *fasten* with the needle:–sew on.

1977. ἐπιῤῥίπτω *ep-ir-hrip'-to;* from *1909* and *4496;* to *throw upon* (lit. or fig.):–cast upon. **1978**. ἐπίσημος *ep-is'-ay-mos;* from *1909* and some form of the base of *4591; remarkable,* i.e. (fig.) *eminent:*–notable, of note.

1979. ἐπισιτισμός *ep-ee-sit-is-mos';* from a com. of *1909* and a der. of *4621;* a *provisioning,* i.e. (concr.) *food:*–victuals.

1980. ἐπισκέπτομαι *ep-ee-skep'-tom-ahee;* mid. from *1909* and the base of *4649;* to *inspect,* i.e. (by impl.) to *select;* by ext., to *go to see, relieve:*–look out, visit.

1981. ἐπισκηνόω *ep-ee-skay-no'-o;* from *1909* and *4637;* to *tent upon,* i.e. (fig.) *abide with :*–rest upon.

1982. ἐπισκιάζω *ep-ee-skee-ad'-zo;* from *1909* and a der. of *4639;* to *cast a shade upon,* i.e. (by anal.) to *envelop* in a haze of brilliancy; fig. to *invest* with preternatural influence:–overshadow.

1983. ἐπισκοπέω *ep-ee-skop-eh'-o;* from *1909* and *4648;* to *oversee;* by impl. to *beware:*–look diligently, take the oversight.

1984. ἐπισκοπή *ep-is-kop-ay';* from *1980; inspection* (for relief); by impl. *superintendence;* spec. the Chr. "*episcopate*":–the office of a "bishop", bishoprick, visitation.

1985. ἐπίσκοπος *ep-is'-kop-os;* from *1909* and *4649* (in the sense of *1983*); a *superintendent,* i.e. Chr. officer in gen. case charge of a (or the) church (lit. or fig.):–bishop, overseer.

1986. ἐπισπάομαι *ep-ee-spah'-om-ahee;* from *1909* and *4685;* to *draw over,* i.e. (with *203* implied) *efface* the mark of *circumcision* (by recovering with the foreskin):–become uncircumcised.

1987. ἐπίσταμαι *ep-is'-tam-ahee;* app. a mid. of *2186* (with *3563* implied); to *put* the mind *upon,* i.e. *comprehend,* or *be acquainted with:*–know, understand.

1988. ἐπιστάτης *ep-is-tat'-ace;* from *1909* and a presumed der. of *2476;* an *appointee over,* i.e. *commander* (*teacher*):–master.

1989. ἐπιστέλλω *ep-ee-stel'-lo;* from *1909* and *4724;* to *enjoin* (by writing), i.e. (gen. case) to *communicate by letter* (for any purpose):–write (a letter, unto).

1990. ἐπιστήμων a *ep-ee-stay'-mone;* from *1987; intelligent:*–endued with knowledge.

1991. ἐπιστηρίζω *ep-ee-stay-rid'-zo;* from *1909* and *4741;* to *support further,* i.e. *reëstablish:*–confirm, strengthen.

1992. ἐπιστολή *ep-is-tol-ay';* from *1989;* a *written message:*–"epistle," letter.

1993. ἐπιστομίζω *ep-ee-stom-id'-zo;* from *1909* and *4750;* to put something *over* the *mouth,* i.e. (fig.) to *silence:*–stop mouths.

1994. ἐπιστρέφω *ep-ee-stref'-o;* from *1909* and *4762;* to *revert* (lit. fig. or mor.):–come (go) again, convert, (re-)turn (about, again).

1995. ἐπιστροφή *ep-is-trof-ay';* from *1994; reversion,* i.e. mor. *revolution:*–conversion.

1996. ἐπισυνάγω *ep-ee-soon-ag'-o;* from *1909* and *4863;* to *collect upon* the same place:–gather (together).

1997. ἐπισυναγωγή *ep-ee-soon-ag-o-gay';* from *1996;* a complete *collection;* esp. a Chr. *meeting* (for worship):–assembling (gathering) together.

1998. ἐπισυντρέχω *ep-ee-soon-trekh'-o;* from *1909* and *4936;* to *hasten together upon* one place (or a particular occasion):–come running together.

1999. ἐπισύστασις *ep-ee-soo'-stas-is;* from the mid. of a com. of *1909* and *4921;* a *conspiracy,* i.e. *concourse* (riotous or friendly):–that which cometh upon, + raising up.

2000. ἐπισφαλής *ep-ee-sfal-ace';* from a com. of *1909* and σφάλλω (to *trip*); fig. *insecure:*–dangerous.

2001. ἐπισχύω *ep-is-khoo'-o;* from *1909* and *2480;* to *avail further,* i.e. (fig.) *insist stoutly:*–be the more fierce.

2002. ἐπισωρεύω *ep-ee-so-ryoo'-o;* from *1909* and *4987;* to *accumulate further,* i.e. (fig.) *seek* additionally:–heap.

2003. ἐπιταγή *ep-ee-tag-ay';* from *2004;* an *injunction* or *decree;* by impl. *authoritativeness:*–authority, commandment.

2004. ἐπιτάσσω *ep-ee-tas'-so;* from *1909* and *5021;* to *arrange upon,* i.e. *order:*–charge, command, injoin.

2005. ἐπιτελέω *ep-ee-tel-eh'-o;* from *1909* and *5055;* to *fulfill further* (or *completely*), i.e. *execute;* by impl. to *terminate, undergo:*–accomplish, do, finish, (make) (perfect), perform(X -ance).

2006. ἐπιτήδειος *ep-ee-tay'-di-os;* from ἐπιτηδεὶς (*enough*); *serviceable,* i.e. (by impl.) *requisite:*–things which are needful.

2007. ἐπιτίθημι *ep-ee-tith'-ay-mee;* from *1909* and *5087;* to *impose* (in a friendly or hostile sense):–add unto, lade, lay upon, put (up) on, set on (up), + surname, X wound.

2008. ἐπιτιμάω *ep-ee-tee-mah'-o;* from *1909* and *5091;* to *tax upon,* i.e. *censure* or *admonish;* by impl. *forbid:*–(straitly) charge, rebuke.

2009. ἐπιτιμία *ep-ee-tee-mee'-ah;* from a com. of *1909* and *5092;* prop. *esteem,* i.e. *citizenship;* used (in the sense of *2008*) of a *penalty:*–punishment.

2010. ἐπιτρέπω *ep-ee-trep'-o;* from *1909*

GREEK

and the base of *5157;* to *turn over* (*transfer*), i.e. *allow:*–give leave (liberty, license), let, permit, suffer.

2011. ἐπιτροπή *ep-ee-trop-ay';* from *2010; permission,* i.e. (by impl.) full *power:*–commission.

2012. ἐπίτροπος *ep-it'-rop-os;* from *1909* and *5158* (in the sense of *2011*); a *commissioner,* i.e. domestic *manager, guardian:*–steward, tutor.

2013. ἐπιτυγχάνω *ep-ee-toong-khan'-o;* from *1909* and *5177;* to *chance upon,* i.e. (by impl.) to *attain:*–obtain.

2014. ἐπιφαίνω *ep-ee-fah'-ee-no;* from *1909* and *5316;* to *shine upon,* i.e. *become* (lit.) *visible* or (fig.) *known:*–appear, give light.

2015. ἐπιφάνεια *ep-if-an'-i-ah;* from *2016;* a *manifestation,* i.e. (spec.) the *advent* of Christ (past or fut.):–appearing, brightness.

2016. ἐπιφανής *ep-if-an-ace';* from *2014; conspicuous,* i.e. (fig.) *memorable:*–notable.

2017. ἐπιφαύω *ep-ee-fow'-o;* a form of 2014; to *illuminate* (fig.):–give light.

2018. ἐπιφέρω *ep-ee-fer'-o;* from *1909* and *5342;* to *bear upon* (or *further*), i.e. *adduce* (pers. or judicially [*accuse, inflict*]), *superinduce:*–add, bring (against), take.

2019. ἐπιφωνέω *ep-ee-fo-neh'-o;* from *1909* and *5455;* to *call at* something, i.e. *exclaim:*–cry (against), give a shout.

2020. ἐπιφώσκω *ep-ee-foce'-ko;* a form of *2017;* to begin to *grow light:*–begin to dawn, X draw on.

2021. ἐπιχειρέω *ep-ee-khi-reh'-o;* from *1909* and *5495;* to put the *hand upon,* i.e. *undertake:*–go about, take in hand (upon).

2022. ἐπιχέω *ep-ee-kheh'-o;* from *1909* and χέω (to *pour*); –to *pour upon:*–pour in.

2023. ἐπιχορηγέω *ep-ee-khor-ayg-eh'-o;* from *1909* and *5524;* to *furnish besides,* i.e. fully *supply,* (fig.) *aid* or *contribute:*–add, minister (nourishment, unto).

2024. ἐπιχορηγία *ep-ee-khor-ayg-ee'-ah;* from *2023; contribution:*–supply.

2025. ἐπιχρίω *ep-ee-khree'-o;* from *1909* and *5548;* to *smear over:*–anoint.

2026. ἐποικοδομέω *ep-oy-kod-om-eh'-o;* from *1909* and *3618;* to *build upon,* i.e. (fig.) to *rear up:*–build thereon (thereupon, on, upon).

2027. ἐποκέλλω *ep-ok-el'-lo;* from *1909* and ὀκέλλω (to *urge*); to *drive upon* the shore, i.e. to *beach* a vessel:–run aground.

2028. ἐπονομάζω *ep-on-om-ad'-zo;* from *1909* and *3687;* to *name further,* i.e. *denominate:*–call.

2029. ἐποπτεύω *ep-opt-yoo'-o;* from *1909* and a der. of *3700;* to *inspect,* i.e. *watch:*–behold.

2030. ἐποπτης *ep-op'-tace;* from *1909* and a presumed der. of *3700;* a *looker-on:*–eye-witness. from 2036; a word:–X say.

2031. ἔπος *ep'-os;* from *2036;* a *word:*–X say.

2032. ἐπουράνιος *ep-oo-ran'-ee-os;* from *1909* and *3772; above* the *sky:*–celestial, (in) heaven(-ly), high.

2033. ἑπτά *hep-tah';* a prim. number; *seven:*–seven.

2034. ἑπτακίς *hep-tak-is';* adv. from *2033; seven times:*–seven times.

2035. ἑπτακισχίλιοι *hep-tak-is-khil'-ee-y;* from *2034* and *5507; seven times* a *thousand:*–seven thousand.

2036. ἔπω *ep'-o;* a prim. verb (used only in the def. past tense, the others being borrowed from *2046, 4483,* and *5346*); to *speak* or *say* (by word or writing):–answer, bid, bring word, call, command, grant, say (on), speak, tell. Comp. *3004.*

2037. Ἔραστος *er'-as-tos;* from ἐράω (to *love*); *beloved; Erastus,* a Chr.:–Erastus

2038. ἐργάζομαι *er-gad'-zom-ahee;* mid. from *2041;* to *toil* (as a task, occupation, etc.), (by impl.) *effect, be engaged in* or *with,* etc.:–commit, do, labor for, minister about, trade (by), work.

2039. ἐργασία *er-gas-ee'-ah;* from *2040; occupation;* by impl. *profit, pains:*–craft, diligence, gain, work.

2040. ἐργάτης *er-gat'-ace;* from *2041;* a *toiler;* fig. a *teacher:*–labourer, worker(-men).

2041. ἔργον *er'-gon;* from a prim. (but obs.) ἔργω (to *work*); *toil* (as an effort or occupation); by impl. an *act:*–deed, doing, labour, work.

2042. ἐρεθίζω *er-eth-id'-zo;* from a presumed prol. form of *2054;* to *stimulate* (esp. to anger):–provoke.

2043. ἐρείδω *er-i'-do;* of obscure affin.; to prop, i.e. (refl.) *get fast:*–stick fast.

2044. ἐρεύγομαι *er-yoog'-om-ahee;* of unc. affin.; to *belch,* i.e. (fig.) to *speak out:*–utter.

2045. ἐρευνάω *er-yoo-nah'-o;* app. from *2046* (through the idea of *inquiry*); to *seek,* i.e. (fig.) to *investigate:*–search

2046. ἐρέω *er-eh'-o;* prob. a fuller form of *4483;* an alt. for *2036* in cert. tenses; to *utter,* i.e. *speak* or *say:*–call, say, speak (of), tell.

2047. ἐρημία *er-ay-mee'-ah;* from *2048; solitude* (concr.):–desert, wilderness.

2048. ἔρημος *er'-ay-mos;* of unc. affin.; *lonesome,* i.e. (by impl.) *waste* (usually as a noun, *5561* being implied):–desert, desolate, solitary, wilderness.

2049. ἐρημόω *er-ay-mo'-o;* from *2048;* to *lay waste* (lit. or fig.):–(bring to, make) desolate(-ion), come to nought.

2050. ἐρήμωσις *er-ay'-mo-sis;* from *2049; despoliation:*–desolation.

2051. ἐρίζω *er-id'-zo;* from *2054;* to *wrangle:*–strive.

2052. ἐριθεία *er-ith-i'-ah;* perh. as the same as *2042;* prop. *intrigue,* i.e. (by impl.) *faction:*–contention(-ious), strife.

2053. ἔριον *er'-ee-on;* of obscure affin.; *wool:*–wool.

2054. ἔρις *er'-is;* of unc. affin.; a *quarrel,* i.e. (by impl.) *wrangling:*–contention, debate, strife, variance.

2055. ἐρίφιον *er-if'-ee-on;* from *2056;* a *kidling,* i.e. (gen. case) *goat* (symb., *wicked* pers.):–goat.

2056. ἔριφος *er'-if-os;* perh. from the same as *2053* (through the idea of *hairiness*); a *kid* or (gen. case) *goat:*–goat, kid.

2057. Ἑρμᾶς *her-mas';* prob. from *2060; Hermas,* a Chr.:–Hermas.

2058. ἑρμηνεία *her-may-ni'-ah;* from the same as *2059; translation:*–interpretation.

2059. ἑρμηνεύω *her-mayn-yoo'-o;* from a presumed der. of *2060* (as the god of language); to *translate:*–interpret.

2060. Ἑρμῆς *her-mace';* perh. from *2046; Hermes,* the name of the messenger of the Gr. deities; also of a Chr.:–Hermes, Mercury.

2061. Ἑρμογένης *her-mog-en'-ace;* from *2060* and *1096; born of Hermes; Hermogenes,* an apostate Chr.:–Hermogenes.

2062. ἑρπετόν *her-pet-on';* neut. of a der. of ἕρπω (to *creep*); a *reptile,* i.e. (by Heb. [comp. 7431]) a small *animal:*–creeping thing, serpent.

2063. ἐρυθρός *er-oo-thros';* of unc. affin.; *red,* i.e. (with *2281*) the *Red* Sea:–red.

2064. ἔρχομαι *er'-khom-ahee;* mid. of a prim. verb (used only in the pres. and imperf. tenses, the others being supplied by a kindred [mid.] ἐλεύθομαι *el-yoo'-thom-ahee;* or [act.] ἔλθω *el'-tho,* which do not otherwise occur) to *come* or *go* (in a great variety of appl., lit. and fig.):–accompany, appear, bring, come, enter, fall out, go, grow, X light, X next, pass, resort, be set.

2065. ἐρωτάω *er-o-tah'-o;* app. from *2046* [comp. *2045*]; to *interrogate;* by impl. to *request:*–ask, beseech, desire, intreat, pray. Comp. *4441*

2066. ἐσθής *es-thace' ;* from ἕννυμι (to *clothe*); *dress:*–apparel, clothing, raiment, robe.

2067. ἔσθησις *es'-thay-sis;* from a der. of *2066; clothing* (concr.):–government.

2068. ἐσθίω *es-thee'-o;* streng. for a prim. ἔδω (to *eat*); used only in cert. tenses, the rest being supplied by *5315;* to *eat* (usually lit.):–devour, eat, live.

2069. Ἐσλί *es-lee';* of Heb. or. [prob. for 454]; *Esli,* an Isr.:–Esli.

2070. ἐσμέν *es-men';* first pers. pl. ind. of *1510;* we *are:*–are, be, have our being, X have hope, + [the gospel] was [preached unto] us.

2071. ἔσομαι *es'-om-ahee;* fut. of *1510; will be:*–shall (should) be (have), (shall) come (to pass), X may have, X fall, what would follow, X live long, X sojourn.

2072. ἔσοπτρον *es'-op-tron;* from *1519* and a presumed der. of *3700;* a *mirror* (for *looking into*):–glass. Comp. *2734.*

2073. ἑσπέρα *hes-per'-ah;* or. of an adj. ἑσπερός (*evening*); the *eve* (*5610* being implied):–evening(-tide).

2074. Ἐσρώμ *es-rome;* of Heb. or. [2696]; *Esrom* (i.e. *Chetsron*), an Isr.:–Esrom.

2075. ἐστέ *es-teh';* sec. pers. pl. pres. ind. of *1510;* ye *are:*–be, have been, belong.

2076. ἐστί *es-tee';* third pers. sing. pres. ind. of *1510;* he (she or it) *is;* also (with neut. pl.) they *are:*–are, be(-long), call, X can[-not], come, consisteth, X dure for a while, + follow, X have, (that) is (to say), make, meaneth, X must needs, + profit, + remaineth, + wrestle.

2077. ἔστω *es'-to;* sec. pers. sing. pres. imper. of *1510; be* thou; also ἔστωσαν *es'-to-san;* third pers. of the same let them *be:*–be.

2078. ἔσχατος *es'-khat-os;* a sup. prob. from *2192* (in the sense of *contiguity*); *farthest, final* (of place or time):–ends of, last, latter end, lowest, uttermost.

2079. ἐσχάτως *es-khat'-oce;* adv. from *2078; finally,* i.e. (with *2192*) *at the extremity* of life:–point of death.

2080. ἔσω *es'-o;* from *1519; inside* (as prep. or adj.):–(with-)in(-ner, -to, -ward).

2081. ἔσωθεν *es'-o-then;* from *2080; from inside;* also used as equiv. to *2080* (*inside*):–inward(-ly), (from) within, without.

2082. ἐσώτερος *es-o'-ter-os;* comp. of *2080; interior:*–inner, within.

2083. ἑταῖρος *het-ah'-ee-ros;* from ἔτης (a *clansman*); a *comrade:*–fellow, friend.

2084. ἑτερόγλωσσος *het-er-og'-loce-sos;* from *2087* and *1100; other-tongued,* i.e. a *foreigner:*–man of other tongue.

2085. ἑτεροδιδασκαλέω *het-er-od-id-as-kal-eh'-o;* from *2087* and *1320;* to *instruct differently:*–teach other doctrine(-wise).

2086. ἑτεροζυγέω *het-er-od-zoog-eh'-o;* from a com. of *2087* and *2218;* to *yoke* up *differently,* i.e. (fig.) to *associate discordantly:*–unequally yoke together with.

2087. ἕτερος *het'-er-os;* of unc. affin.; (an-, the) *other* or *different:*–altered, else, next (day), one, (an-) other, some, strange.

2088. ἑτέρως *het-er'-oce;* adv. from *2087; differently:*–otherwise.

2089. ἔτι *et'-ee;* perh. akin to *2094;* "*yet,*" *still* (of time or degree):–after that, also, ever, (any) further, (t-)henceforth (more), hereafter, (any) longer, (any) more(-one), now, still, yet.

2090. ἑτοιμάζω *het-oy-mad'-zo;* from *2092;* to *prepare:*–prepare, provide, make ready. Comp. *2680.*

2091. ἑτοιμασία *het-oy-mas-ee'-ah;* from *2090; preparation:*–preparation.

2092. ἕτοιμος *het-oy'-mos;* from an old noun ἕτεος (*fitness*); *adjusted,* i.e. *ready:*–prepared, (made) ready(-iness, to our hand).

2093. ἑτοίμως *het'-oy-moce;* adv. from *2092;* in *readiness:*–ready.

2094. ἔτος *et'-os;* app. a prim. word; a *year:*–year.

2095. εὖ *yoo;* neut. of a prim. εὖς (*good*); (adv.) *well:*–good, well (done).

2096. Εὔα *yoo'-ah;* of Heb. or. [2332]; *Eua* (or *Eva,* i.e. *Chavvah*), the first woman:–Eve.

2097. εὐαγγελίζω *yoo-ang-ghel-id'-zo;* from *2095* and *32;* to *announce good* news ("evangelize") esp. The gospel:–declare, bring (declare, show) glad (good) tidings, preach (the gospel).

2098. εὐαγγέλιον *yoo-ang-ghel'-ee-on;* from the same as *2097;* a *good message,* i.e. the *gospel:*–gospel.

2099. εὐαγγελιστής *yoo-ang-ghel-is-tace';* from *2097;* a *preacher* of the gospel:–evangelist.

2100. εὐαρεστέω *yoo-ar-es-teh'-o;* from *2101;* to *gratify entirely:*–please (well).

2101. εὐάρεστος *yoo-ar'-es-tos;* from *2095* and *701; fully agreeable:*–acceptable(-ted), well pleasing.

2102. εὐαρέστως *yoo-ar-es'-toce;* adv. from *2101; quite agreeably:*–acceptably, + please well.

2103. Εὔβουλος *yoo'-boo-los;* from *2095* and *1014; good-willer; Eubulus,* a Chr.:–Eubulus.

2104. εὐγένης *yoog-en'-ace;* from *2095* and *1096; well born,* i.e. (lit.) *high* in rank, or (fig.) *generous:*–more noble, nobleman.

2105. εὐδία *yoo-dee'-ah;* fem. from *2095* and the alt. of *2203* (as the god of the weather); a *clear sky,* i.e. *fine weather:*–fair weather.

2106. εὐδοκέω *yoo-dok-eh'-o;* from *2095* and *1380;* to *think well* of, i.e. *approve* (an act); spec. to *approbate* (a pers. or thing):–think good, (be well) please(-d), be the good (have, take) pleasure, be willing.

2107. εὐδοκία *yoo-dok-ee'-ah;* from a presumed com. of *2095* and the base of *1380; satisfaction,* i.e. (subj.) *delight,* or (obj.) *kindness, wish, purpose:*–desire, good pleasure (will), X seem good.

2108. εὐεργεσία *yoo-erg-es-ee'-ah;* from *2110; beneficence* (gen. case or spec.):–benefit, good deed done.

2109. εὐεργετέω *yoo-erg-et-eh'-o;* from *2110;* to *be philanthropic:*–do good.

2110. εὐεργέτης *yoo-erg-et'-ace;* from *2095* and the base of *2041;* a *worker of good,* i.e. (spec.) a *philanthropist:*–benefactor.

2111. εὔθετος *yoo'-thet-os;* from *2095* and a der. of *5087; well placed,* i.e. (fig.) *appropriate:*–fit, meet.

2112. εὐθέως *yoo-theh'-oce;* adv. from *2117; dir.,* i.e. *at once* or *soon:*–anon, as soon as, forthwith, immed., shortly, straightway.

2113. εὐθυδρομέω *yoo-thoo-drom-eh'-o;* from *2117* and *1408;* to *lay a straight course,* i.e. *sail dir.:*–(come) with a straight course.

2114. εὐθυμέω *yoo-thoo-meh'-o;* from *2115;* to *cheer up,* i.e. (intr.) *be cheerful;* neut. comp. (adv.) *more cheerfully:*–be of good cheer (merry).

2115. εὔθυμος *yoo'-thoo-mos;* from *2095* and *2372;* in *fine spirits,* i.e. *cheerful:*–of good cheer, the more cheerfully.

2116. εὐθύνω *yoo-thoo'-no;* from *2117;* to *straighten* (*level*); tech., to *steer:*–governor, make straight.

2117. εὐθύς *yoo-thoos';* perh. from *2095* and *5087; straight,* i.e. (lit.) *level,* or (fig.) *true;* adv. (of time) *at once:*–anon, by and by, forthwith, immed., straightway.

2118. εὐθύτης *yoo-thoo'-tace;* from *2117; rectitude:*–righteousness.

2119. εὐκαιρέω *yoo-kahee-reh'-o;* from *2121;* to *have good time,* i.e. *opportunity* or *leisure:*–have leisure (convenient time), spend time.

2120. εὐκαιρία *yoo-kahee-ree'-ah;* from *2121;* a *favorable occasion:*–opportunity.

2121. εὔκαιρος *yoo'-kahee-ros;* from *2095* and *2540; well-timed,* i.e. *opportune:*–convenient, in time of need.

2122. εὐκαίρως *yoo-kah'-ee-roce;* adv. from *2121; opportunely:*–conveniently, in season.

2123 εὐκοπώτερος *yoo-kop-o'-ter-os;* comp. of a com. of *2095* and *2873; better for toil,* i.e. *more facile:*–easier.

2124. εὐλάβεια *yoo-lab'-i-ah;* from *2126;* prop. *caution,* i.e. (relig.) *reverence* (*piety*); by impl. *dread* (concr.):–fear(-ed).

2125. εὐλαβέομαι *yoo-lab-eh'-om-ahee;* mid. from *2126;* to *be circumspect,* i.e. (by impl.) to *be apprehensive;* relig., to *reverence:*–(moved with) fear.

2126. εὐλαβής *yoo-lab-ace'; from 2095* and *2983; taking well* (*carefully*), i.e. *circumspect* (relig., *pious*):–devout.

2127. εὐλογέω *yoo-log-eh'-o;* from a com. of *2095* and *3056;* to *speak well of,* i.e. (relig.) to *bless* (*thank* or *invoke a benediction upon, prosper*):–bless, praise.

2128. εὐλογητός *yoo-log-ay-tos';* from *2127; adorable:*–blessed.

2129. εὐλογία *yoo-log-ee'-ah;* from the same as *2127; fine speaking,* i.e. *elegance of language; commendation* ("*eulogy*"), i.e. (reverentially) *adoration;* relig., *benediction;* by impl. *consecration;* by ext., *benefit* or *largess:*–blessing (a matter of) bounty (X-tifully), fair speech.

2130. εὐμετάδοτος *yoo-met-ad'-ot-os;* from *2095* and a presumed der. of *3330; good at imparting,* i.e. *liberal:*–ready to distribute.

2131. Εὐνίκη *yoo-nee'-kay;* from *2095* and *3529; victorious; Eunice,* a Jewess:–Eunice.

2132. εὐνόεω *yoo-no-eh'-o;* from a com. of *2095* and *3563;* to *be well-minded,* i.e. *reconcile:*–agree.

2133. εὔνοια *yoo'-noy-ah;* from the same as *2132; kindness;* euph., *conjugal duty:*–benevolence, good will.

2134. εὐνουχίζω *yoo-noo-khid'-zo;* from *2135;* to *castrate* (fig. *live unmarried*):–make...eunuch.

2135. εὐνοῦχος *yoo-noo'-khos;* from εὐνή (a *bed*) and *2192*; a *castrated* pers. (such being employed in Oriental bed-chambers); by ext. an *impotent* or *unmarried* man; by impl. a *chamberlain* (*state-officer*):–eunuch.

2136. Εὐοδία *yoo-od-ee'-ah;* from the same as *2137; fine traveling*; *Euodia,* a Chr. Woman:–Euodias.

2137. εὐοδόω *yoo-od-o'-o;* from a com. of *2095* and *3598;* to *help* on the *road,* i.e. (pass.) *Succeed in reaching;* fig. to *succeed* in business affairs:–(have a) prosper(-ous journey).

2138. εὐπειθής *yoo-pi-thace*'; from *2095* and *3982; good* for *persuasion,* i.e. (intr.) *complaint:*–easy to be intreated.

2139. εὐπερίστατος *yoo-per-is'-tat-os;* from *2095* and a der. of a presumed com. of *4012* and *2476; well standing around,* i.e. (a *competitor*) *thwarting* (a racer) in every direction (fig. of sin in gen. case):–which doth so easily beset.

GREEK

2140. εὐποιΐα *yoo-poy-ee'-ah;* from a com. of *2095* and *4160; well-doing,* i.e. *beneficence:*–to do good.

2141. εὐπορέω *yoo-por-eh'-o;* from a com. of *2090* and the base of *4197;* (intr.) to *be good* for *passing* through, i.e. (fig.) *have* pecuniary *means:*–ability.

2142. εὐπορία *yoo-por-ee'-ah;* from the same as *2141;* pecuniary *resources:*–wealth.

2143. εὐπρέπεια *yoo-prep'-i-ah;* from a com. of *2095* and *4241; good suitableness,* i.e. *gracefulness:*–grace.

2144. εὐπρόσδεκτος *yoo-pros'-dek-tos;* from *2095* and a der. of *4327; well-received,* i.e. *approved, favorable:*–acceptable(-ted).

2145. εὐπρόσεδρος *yoo-pros'-ed-ros;* from *2095* and the same as *4332; sitting well towards,* i.e. (fig.) *assiduous* (neut., *diligent service*):–X attend upon.

2146. εὐπροσωπέω *yoo-pros-o-peh'-o;* from a com. of *2095* and *4383;* to *be of good countenance,* i.e. (fig.) to *make a display:*–make a fair show.

2147. εὑρίσκω *hyoo-ris'-ko;* a prol. form of a prim εὕρω *hyoo'-ro* which (together with another cognate form) εὑ ρέω *hyoo-reh'-o;* is used for it in all the tenses except the pres. and imperf. ; to *find* (lit. or fig.):–find, get, obtain, perceive, see.

2148. Εὐροκλύδων *yoo-rok-loo'-dohn;* from Εὖρος (the *E.* wind) and *2830;* a *storm from the E.* (or southeast), i.e. (in modern phrase) a *Levanter:*–Euroklydon.

2149. εὐρύχωρος *yoo-roo'-kho-ros;* from εὐρύς (*wide*) and *5561; spacious:*–broad.

2150. εὐσέβεια *yoo-seb'-i-ah;* from *2152; piety;* spec. the *gospel* scheme:–godliness, holiness.

2151. εὐσεβέω *yoo-seb-eh'-o;* from *2152;* to *be pious,* i.e. (towards God) to *worship,* or (towards parents) to *respect* (*support*):–show piety, worship.

2152. εὐσεβής *yoo-seb-ace';* from *2095* and *4576; well-reverent,* i.e. *pious:*–devout, godly.

2153. εὐσεβῶς *yoo-seb-oce';* adv. from *2152; piously:*–godly.

2154. εὔσημος *yoo'-say-mos;* from *2095* and the base of *4591; well indicated,* i.e. (fig.) *significant:*–easy to be understood.

2155. εὔσπλαγχνος *yoo'-splangkh-nos;* from *2095* and *4698; well compassioned,* i.e. *sympathetic:*–pitiful, tender-hearted.

2156. εὐσχημόνως *yoo-skhay-mon'-oce;* adv. from *2158; decorously:*–decently, honestly.

2157. εὐσχημοσύνη *yoo-skhay-mos-oo'-nay;* from *2158; decorousness:*–comeliness.

2158. εὐσχήμων *yoo-skhay'-mone;* from *2095* and *4976; well-formed,* i.e. (fig.) *decorous, noble* (in rank):–comely, honourable.

2159. εὐτόνως *yoo-ton'-oce;* adv. from a com. of *2095* and a der. of τείνω (to *stretch*); *in a well-strung manner,* i.e. (fig.) *intensely* (in a good sense, *cogently;* in a bad one, *fiercely*):–mightily, vehemently.

2160. εὐτραπελία *yoo-trap-el-ee'-ah;* from a com. of *2095* and a der. of the base of *5157* (mean. *well-turned,* i.e. *ready at repartee, jocose*); *witticism,* i.e. (in a vulgar sense) *ribaldry:*–jesting.

2161. Εὔτυχος *yoo'-too-khos;* from *2095* and a der. of *5177; well- fated,* i.e. *fortunate; Eutychus,* a young man:–Eutychus.

2162. εὐφημία *yoo-fay-mee'-ah;* from *2163; good language* ("*euphemy*"), i.e. *praise* (*repute*):–good report.

2163. εὔφημος *yoo'-fay-mos;* from *2095* and *5345; well spoken of,* i.e. *reputable:*–of good report

2164. εὐφορέω *yoo-for-eh'-o;* from *2095* and *5409;* to *bear well,* i.e. *be fertile:*–bring forth abundantly.

2165. εὐφραίνω *yoo-frah'-ee-no;* from *2095* and *5424;* to *put* (mid. or pass. *be*) *in a good* frame of *mind,* i.e. *rejoice:*–fare, make glad, be (make) merry, rejoice.

2166. Εὐφράτης *yoo-frat'-ace;* of for. or. [comp. 6578]; *Euphrates,* a river of Asia:–Euphrates.

2167. εὐφροσύνη *yoo-fros-oo'-nay;* from the same as *2165; joyfulness:*–gladness, joy.

2168. εὐχαριστέω *yoo-khar-is-teh'-o;* from *2170;* to *be grateful,* i.e. (act.) to *express gratitude* (towards); spec. to *say grace* at a meal:–(give) thank(-ful, -s).

2169. εὐχαριστία *yoo-khar-is-tee'-ah;* from *2170; gratitude;* act., *grateful language* (to God, as an act of worship):–thankfulness, (giving of) thanks(-giving).

2170. εὐχάριστος *yoo-khar'-is-tos;* from *2095* and a der. of *5483; well favored,* i.e. (by impl.) *grateful:*–thankful.

2171. εὐχή *yoo-khay';* from *2172;* prop. a *wish,* expressed as a *petition* to God, or in *votive* obligation:–prayer, vow.

2172. εὔχομαι *yoo'-khom-ahee;* mid. of a prim. verb; to *wish;* by impl. to *pray* to God:–pray, will, wish.

2173. εὔχρηστος *yoo'-khrays-tos;* from *2095* and *5543; easily used,* i.e. *useful:*–profitable, meet for use.

2174. εὐψυχέω *yoo-psoo-kheh'-o;* from a com. of *2095* and *5590;* to *be in good spirits,* i.e. *feel encouraged:*–be of good comfort.

2175. εὐωδία *yoo-o-dee'-ah;* from a com. of *2095* and a der. of *3605; good-scentedness,* i.e. *fragrance:*–sweet savour (smell, -smelling).

2176. εὐώνυμος *yoo-o'-noo-mos;* from *2095* and *3686;* prop. *well-named* (*good-omened*), i.e. the *left* (which was the *lucky* side among the pagan Greeks); neut. as adv. *at the left* hand:–(on the) left.

2177. ἐφάλλομαι *ef-al'-lom-ahee;* from *1909* and *242;* to *spring upon:*–leap on.

2178. ἐφάπαξ *ef-ap'-ax;* from *1909* and *530; upon one occasion* (only):–(at) once (for all).

2179. Ἐφεσῖνος *ef-es-ee'-nos;* from *2181; Ephesine,* or situated at Ephesus:–of Ephesus.

2180. Ἐφέσιος *ef-es'-ee-os;* from *2181;* an *Ephesian* or inh. of Ephesus:–Ephesian, of Ephesus.

2181. Ἔφεσος *ef'-es-os;* prob. of for. or.; *Ephesus,* a city of Asia Minor:–Ephesus.

2182. ἐφευρέτης *ef-yoo-ret'-ace;* from a com. of *1909* and *2147;* a *discoverer,* i.e. *contriver:*–inventor.

2183. ἐφημερία *ef-ay-mer-ee'-ah;* from *2184; diurnality,* i.e. (spec.) the quotidian *rotation* or *class* of the Jewish priests' service at the Temple, as distributed by families:–course.

2184. ἐφήμερος *ef-ay'-mer-os;* from *1909* and *2250; for a day* ("ephemeral"), i.e. *diurnal:*–daily.

2185. ἐφικνέομαι *ef-ik-neh'-om-ahee;* from *1909* and a cognate of *2240;* to *arrive upon,* i.e. *extend to:*–reach.

2186. ἐφίστημι *ef-is'-tay-mee;* from *1909* and *2476;* to *stand upon,* i.e. *be present* (in various appl., friendly or otherwise, usually lit.):–assault, come (in, to, unto, upon), be at hand (instant), present, stand (before, by, over).

2187. Ἐφραΐμ *ef-rah-im';* of Heb. or. [669 or better 6085]; *Ephraïm,* a place in Pal.:–Ephraim.

2188. ἐφφαθά *ef-fath-ah';* of Chald. or. [6606]; *be opened!:*–Ephphatha.

2189. ἔχθρα *ekh'-thrah;* fem. of *2190; hostility;* by impl. a reason for *opposition:*–enmity, hatred.

2190. ἐχθρός *ekh-thros';* from a prim. ἔχθω (to *hate*); *hateful* (pass. *odious,* or act., *hostile*); usually as a noun, an *adversary* (esp. *Satan*):–enemy, foe.

2191. ἔχιδνα *ekh'-id-nah;* of unc. or.; an *adder* or other poisonous snake (lit. or fig.):–viper.

2192. ἔχω *ekh'-o;* (includ. an alt. form σχέω *skheh'-o;* used in cert. tenses only); a prim. verb; to *hold* (used in very various appl., lit. or fig., dir. or remote; such as *possession; ability, contiuity, relation, or condition*):–be (able, X hold, possessed with), accompany, + begin to amend, can(+ -not), X conceive, count, diseased, do + eat, + enjoy, + fear, following, have, hold, keep, + lack, + go to law, lie, + must needs, + of necessity, + need, next, + recover, + reign, + rest, + return, X sick, take for, + tremble, + uncircumcised, use.

2193. ἕως *heh'-oce;* of unc. affin.; a conj., prep. and adv. of continuance, *until* (of time and place):–even (until, unto), (as) far (as), how long, (un-)til(-l), (hither-, un-, up) to, while(-s).

Z

2194. Ζαβουλών *dzab-oo-lone';* of Heb. or. [2074]; *Zabulon* (i.e. *Zebulon*), a region of Pal.:–Zabulon.

2195. Ζακχαῖος *dzak-chah'-ee-yos;* of Heb. or. [comp. 2140]; *Zacchaeus,* an Isr.:–Zacchaeus.

2196. Ζαρά *dzar-ah';* of Heb. or. [2226]; *Zara,* (i.e. *Zerach*), an Isr.:–Zara.

2197. Ζαχαρίας *dzakh-ar-ee'-as;* of Heb. or. [2148]; *Zacharias* (i.e. *Zechariah*), the name of two Isr.:–Zacharias.

2198. ζάω *dzah'-o;* a prim. verb; to *live* (lit. or fig.):–life(-time), (a-)live(-ly), quick.

2199. Ζεβεδαῖος *dzeb-ed-ah'-yos;* of Heb. or. [comp. 2067] *Zebedaeus,* an Isr.:–Zebedee.

2200. ζεστός *dzes-tos';* from *2204; boiled,* i.e.

(by impl.) *calid* (fig. *fervent*):–hot.

2201. ζεῦγος *dzyoo'-gos;* from the same as *2218;* a *couple,* i.e. a *team* (of oxen yoked together) or *brace* (of birds tied together):–yoke, pair.

2202. ζευκτηρία *dzook-tay-ree'-ah;* fem. of a der. (at the sec. stage) from the same as *2218;* a *fastening* (*tiller-rope*):–band.

2203. Ζεύς *dzyooce;* of unc. affin.; in the oblique cases there is used instead of it a (prob. cognate) name Δίς *deece,* which is otherwise obs. *Zeus* or *Dis* (among the Latins, *Jupiter* or *Jove*), the supreme deity of the Greeks:–Jupiter.

2204. ζέω *dzeh'-o;* a prim. verb; to *be hot* (*boil,* of liquids; or *glow,* of solids), i.e. (fig.) *be fervid* (*earnest*):–be fervent.

2205. ζῆος *dzay'-los;* from *2204;* prop. *heat,* i.e. (fig.) "*zeal*" (in a favorable sense, *ardor;* in an unfavorable one, *jealousy,* as of a husband [fig. of God], or an enemy, *malice*):–emulation, envy (-ing), fervent mind, indignation, jealousy, zeal.

2206. ζηλόω *dzay-lo'-o;* from *2205;* to *have warmth* of feeling for or against:–affect, covet (earnestly), (have) desire, (move with) envy, be jealous over, (be) zealous(-ly affect).

2207. ζηλωτής *dzay-lo-tace';* from *2206;* a "*zealot*":–zealous.

2208. Ζηλωτής *dzay-lo-tace';* the same as *2208;* a *Zealot,* i.e. (spec.) *partisan* for Jewish political independence:–Zelotes.

2209. ζημία *dzay-mee'-ah;* prob. akin to the base of *1150* (through the idea of *violence*); *detriment:*–damage, loss.

2210. ζημιόω *dzay-mee-o'-o;* from *2209;* to *injure,* i.e. (refl. or pass.) to *experience detriment:*–be cast away, receive damage, lose, suffer loss.

2211. Ζηνᾶς *dzay-nas';* prob. contr. from a poetic form of *2203* and *1435; Jove-given; Zenas,* a Chr.:–Zenas.

2212. ζητέω *dzay-teh'-o;* of unc. affin.; to *seek* (lit. or fig.); spec. (by Heb.) to *worship* (God), or (in a bad sense) to *plot* (against life):–be (go) about, desire, endeavour, enquire (for), require, (X will) seek (after, for, means). Comp. *4441.*

2213. ζήτημα *dzay'-tay-mah;* from *2212;* a *search* (prop. concr.), i.e. (in words) a *debate:*–question.

2214. ζήτησις *dzay'-tay-sis;* from *2212;* a *searching* (prop. the act), i.e. a *dispute* or its *theme:*–question.

2215. ζιζάνιον *dziz-an'-ee-on;* of unc. or.; *darnel* or false grain:–tares.

2216. Ζοροβάβελ *dzor-ob-ab'-el;* of Heb. or. [2216]; *Zorobabel* (i.e. *Zerubbabel*), an Isr.:–Zorobabel.

2217. ζόφος *dzof'-os;* akin to the base of *3509; gloom* (as shrouding like a *cloud*):–blackness, darkness, mist.

2218. ζυγός *dzoo-gos';* from the root of ζεύγνυμι (to *join,* esp. by a "yoke"); a *coupling,* i.e. (fig.) *servitude* (a *law* or *obligation*); also (lit.) the *beam* of the balance (as *connecting* the scales):–pair of balances, yoke.

2219. ζύμη *dzoo'-may;* prob. from *2204; ferment* (as if *boiling* up):–leaven.

2220. ζυμόω *dzoo-mo'-o;* from *2219;* to *cause to ferment:*–leaven.

2221. ζωγρέω *dzogue-reh'-o;* from the same as *2226* and *64;* to *take alive* (*make a prisoner of war*), i.e. (fig.) to *capture or ensnare:*–take captive, catch.

2222. ζωή *dzo-ay';* from *2198; life* (lit. or fig.):–life(-time). Comp. *5590.*

2223. ζώνη *dzo'-nay;* prob. akin to the base of *2218;* a *belt;* by impl. a *pocket:*–girdle, purse.

2224. ζώννυμι *dzone'-noo-mi;* from *2223;* to *bind about* (esp. with a belt):–gird.

2225. ζωογονέω *dzo-og-on-eh'-o;* from the same as *2226* and a der. of *1096;* to *engender alive,* i.e. (by anal.) to *rescue* (pass. *be saved*) from death:–live, preserve.

2226. ζῶον *dzo'-on;* neut. of a der. of *2198;* a *live* thing, i.e. an *animal:*–beast.

2227. ζωοποιέω *dzo-op-oy-eh'-o;* from the same as *2226* and *4160;* to (*re-*)*vitalize* (lit. or fig.):–make alive, give life, quicken.

H

2228. ἤ *ay;* a prim. par. of distinction between two connected terms; disjunctive, *or;* comp., *than:*–and, but (either), (n-) either, except it be, (n-)or (else), rather, save, than, that, what, yea. Often used in connection with other par.. Comp. esp. *2235, 2260, 2273.*

2229. ἦ *ay;* an adv. of *confirmation;* perh. intens. of *2228;* used only (in the N.T.) before *3303; assuredly:*–surely.

2230. ἡγεμονεύω *hayg-em-on-yoo'-o;* from *2232;* to *act as ruler:*–be governor.

2231. ἡγεμονία *hayg-em-on-ee'-ah;* from *2232; government,* i.e. (in time) official *term:*–reign.

2232. ἡγεμών *hayg-em-ohn';* from *2233;* a *leader,* i.e. *chief* pers. (or fig. place) of a province:–governor, prince, ruler.

2233. ἡγέομα *hayg-eh'-om-ahee;* mid. of a (presumed) streng. form of *71;* to *lead,* i.e. *command* (with official authority); fig. to *deem,* i.e. *consider:*–account, (be) chief, count, esteem, governor, judge, have the rule over, suppose, think.

2234. ἡδέως *hay-deh'-oce;* adv. from a der. of the base of *2237; sweetly,* i.e. (fig.) *with pleasure:*–gladly.

2235. ἤδη *ay'-day;* app. from *2228* (or possibly *2229*) and *1211; even now:*–already, (even) now (already), by this time.

2236. ἥδιστα *hay'-dis-tah;* neut. pl. of the sup. of the same as *2234; with great pleasure:*–most (very) gladly.

2237. ἡδονή *hay-don-ay';* from ἁνδάνω (to *please*); sensual *delight;* by impl. *desire:*–lust, pleasure.

2238. ἡδύοσμον *hay-doo'-os-mon;* neut. of the com. of the same as *2234* and *3744;* a *sweet-scented* plant, i.e. *mint:*–mint.

2239. ἦθος *ay'-thos;* a streng. form of *1485; usage,* i.e. (pl.) mor. *habits:*–manners.

2240. ἥκω *hay'-ko;* a prim. verb; to *arrive,* i.e. *be present* (lit. or fig.):–come.

2241. ἠλί *ay-lee';* of Heb. or. [410 with pron. suffix]; *my God:*–Eli.

2242. Ἡλί *hay-lee';* of Heb. or. [5941]; *Heli* (i.e. *Eli*), an Isr.:–Heli.

2243. Ἡλίας *hay-lee'-as;* of Heb. or. [452]; *Helias* (i.e. *Elijah*), an Isr.:–Elias.

2244. ἡλικία *hay-lik-ee'-ah;* from the same as *2245; maturity* (in years or size):–age, stature.

2245. ἡλίκος *hay-lee'-kos;* from ἧλιξ (a *comrade,* i.e. one of the same age); *as big as,* i.e. (interjectively) *how much:*–how (what) great.

2246. ἥλιος *hay'-lee-os;* from ἕλη(a *ray;* perh. akin to the alt. of *138*); the *sun;* by impl. *light:*–+ east, sun.

2247. ἧλος *hay'-los;* of unc. affin.; a *stud,* i.e. *spike:*–nail.

2248. ἡμ ᾶς *hay-mas';* acc. pl. of *1473; us:*–our, us, we.

2249. ἡμεῖς *hay-mice';* nom. pl. of *1473; we* (only used when emphat.):–us, we (ourselves).

2250. ἡμέρα *hay-mer'-ah;* fem. (with *5610* implied) of a der. of ἧμαι (to *sit;* akin to the base of *1476*) mean. *tame,* i.e. *gentle; day,* i.e. (lit.) the time space between dawn and dark, or the whole 24 hours (but several days were usually reckoned by the Jews as inclusive of the parts of both extremes); fig. a *period* (always defined more or less clearly by the context):–age, + alway, (mid-) day (by day, [-ly]), + for ever, judgment, (day) time, while, years.

2251. ἡμέτερος *hay-met'-er-os;* from *2349; our:*–our, your.

2252. ἤμην *ay'-mane;* a prol. form of *2358;* I *was:*–be, was.

2253. ἡμιθανής *hay-mee-than-ace';* from a presumed com. of the base of *2255* and *2348; half dead,* i.e. *entirely exhausted:*–half dead.

2254. ἡμῖν *hay-meen';* dat. pl. of *1473; to* (or *for, with, by*) *us:*–our, (for) us, we.

2255. ἥμισυ *hay'-mee-soo;* neut. of a der. from an insep. pref. akin to *260* (through the idea of *partition* involved in *connection*) and mean. *semi-;* (as noun) *half:*–half.

2256. ἡμιώριον *hay-mee-o'-ree-on;* from the base of *2255* and *5610;* a *half-hour:*–half an hour.

2257. ἡμῶν *hay-mone';* gen. case pl. of *1473; of* (or *from*) *us:*–our (company), us, we.

2258. ἦν *ane;* imperf. of *1510; I* (*thou,* etc.) *was* (*wast* or *were*):–+ agree, be, X have (+ charge of), hold, use, was(-t), were.

2259. ἡνίκα *hay-nee'-kah;* of unc. affin.; *at which time:*–when.

2260. ἤπερ *ay'-per;* from *2228* and *4007; than at all* (or *than perh. than indeed*):–than.

2261. ἤπιος *ay'-pee-os;* prob. from *2031;* prop. *affable,* i.e. *mild* or *kind:*–gentle.

2262. Ἤρ *ayr;* of Heb. or. [6147]; *Er,* an

GREEK

Isr.:–Er.

2263. ἤρεμος *ay'-rem-os;* perh. by transp. from *2048* (through the idea of *stillness*); *tranquil:*–quiet.

2264. Ἡρώδης *hay-ro'-dace;* com. of ἥρως (a "*hero*") and *1491; heroic; Herodes,* the name of four Jewish kings:–Herod.

2265. Ἡρωδιανοί *hay-ro-dee-an-oy;* pl. of a der. of *2264; Herodians,* i.e. partisans of Herod:–Herodians.

2266. Ἡρωδιάς *hay-ro-dee-as';* from *2264; Herodias,* a woman of the Heodian family:–Herodias.

2267. Ἡρωδίων *hay-ro-dee'-ohn;* from *2264; Herodion,* a Chr.:–Herodion.

2268. Ἡσαΐας *hay-sah-ee'-as;* of Heb. or. [3470]; *Hesaias* (i.e. *Jeshajah*), an Isr.:–Esaias.

2269. Ἡσαῦ *ay-sow';* of Heb. or. [6215]; *Esau,* an Edomite:–Esau.

2270. ἡσυχάζω *hay-soo-khad'-zo;* from the same as *2272;* to *keep still* (intr.), i.e. *refrain* from labor, meddlesomeness or speech:–cease, hold peace, be quiet, rest.

2271. ἡσυχία *hay-soo-khee'-ah;* fem. of *2272;* (as noun) *stillness,* i.e. desistance from bustle or language:–quietness, silence.

2272. ἡσύχιος *hay-soo'-khee-os;* a prol. form of a com. prob. of a der. of the base of *1476* and perh. *2192;* prop. *keeping* one's *seat* (*sedentary*), i.e. (by impl.) *still* (*undisturbed,undisturbing*):–peaceable, quiet.

2273. ἤτοι *ay'-toy;* from *2228* and *5104; either indeed:*–whether.

2274. ἡττάω *hayt-tah'-o;* from the same as *2276;* to *make worse,* i.e. *vanquish* (lit. or fig.); by impl. to *rate lower:*–be inferior, overcome.

2275. ἥττημα *hayt'-tay-mah;* from *2274;* a *deterioration,* i.e. (obj.) *failure* or (subj.) *loss:*–diminishing, fault.

2276. ἧττον *hate'-ton;* neut. of comp. of ἧκα (*slightly*) used for that of *2556; worse* (as noun); by impl. *less* (as adv.):–less, worse.

2277. ἤτω *ay'-to;* third pers. sing. imper. of *1510; let him* (or *it*) *be:*–let ... be.

2278. ἠχέω *ay-kheh'-o;* from *2279;* to *make a* loud *noise,* i.e. *reverberate:*–roar, sound.

2279. ἦχος *ay'-khos;* of unc. affin.; a loud or confused *noise* ("*echo*"), i.e. *roar;* fig. a *rumor:*–fame, sound.

Θ

2280. Θαδδαῖος *thad-dah'-yos;* of unc. or.; *Thaddaeus,* one of the Apostles:–Thaddaeus.

2281. θάλασσα *thal'-as-sah;* prob. prol. from *251;* the *sea* (gen. case or spec.):–sea.

2282. θάλπω *thal'-po;* prob. akin to θαλλω (to *warm*); to *brood,* i.e. (fig.) to *foster:*–cherish.

2283. Θάμαρ *tham'-ar;* of Heb. or. [8559]; *Thamar* (i.e. *Tamar*), an Isr.s:–Thamar.

2284. θαμβέω *tham-beh'-o;* from *2285;* to *stupefy* (with surprise), i.e. *astound:*–amaze, astonish.

2285. θάμβος *tham'-bos;* akin to an obs. ταφω (to *dumbfound*); *stupefaction* (by surprise), i.e. *astonishment:*–X amazed, + astonished, wonder.

2286. θανάσιμος *than-as'-ee-mos;* from *2288; fatal,* i.e. *poisonous:*–deadly.

2287. θανατήφορος *than-at-ay'-for-os;* from (the fem. form of) *2288* and *5342; death-bearing,* i.e. *fatal:*–deadly.

2288. θάνατος *than'-at-os;* from *2348;* (prop. an adj. used as a noun) *death* (lit. or fig.):–X deadly, (be...) death.

2289. θανατόω *than-at-o'-o;* from *2288* to *kill* (lit. or fig.):–become dead, (cause to be) put to death, kill, mortify.

2290. θάπτω *thap'-to;* a prim. verb; to *celebrate funeral rites,* i.e. *inter:*–bury.

2291. Θάρα *thar'-ah;* of Heb. or. [8646]; *Thara* (i.e. *Terach*), the father of Abraham:–Thara.

2292. θαρρέω *thar-hreh'-o;* another form for *2293;* to *exercise courage:*–be bold, X boldly, have confidence, be confident. Comp. *5111.*

2293. θαρσέω *thar-seh'-o;* from *2294;* to *have courage:*–be of good cheer (comfort). Comp. *2292.*

2294. θάρσος *thar'-sos;* akin (by transp.) to θράσος (*daring*); *boldness* (subj.):–courage.

2295. θαῦμα *thou'-mah;* app. from a form of *2300; wonder* (prop. concr.; but by impl. abstr.):–admiration.

2296. θαυμάζω *thou-mad'-zo;* from *2295;* to *wonder;* by impl. to *admire:*–admire, have in admiration, marvel, wonder.

2297. θαυμάσιος *thow-mas'-ee-os;* from *2295; wondrous,* i.e. (neut. as noun) a *miracle:*–wonderful thing.

2298. θαυμαστός *thow-mas-tos';* from *2296; wondered* at, i.e. (by impl.) *wonderful:*–marvel(-lous).

2299. θεά *theh-ah';* fem. of *2316;* a female *deity:*–goddess.

2300. θεάομαι *theh-ah'-om-ahee;* a prol. form of a prim. verb; to *look* closely at, i.e. (by impl.) *perceive* (lit. or fig.); by ext. to *visit:*–behold, look (upon), see. Comp. *3700.*

2301. θεατρίζω *theh-at-rid'-zo;* from *2302;* to *expose as a spectacle:*–make a gazing stock.

2302. θέατρον *theh'-at-ron;* from *2300; a place for public show* ("*theatre*"), i.e. general *audience-room;* by impl. a *show* itself (fig.):–spectacle, theatre.

2303. θεῖον *thi'-on;* prob. neut. of *2304* (in its or. sense of *flashing*); *sulphur:*–brimstone.

2304. θεῖος *thi'-os;* from *2316; godlike* (neut. as noun, *divinity*): - divine, godhead.

2305. θειότης *thi-ot'-ace;* from *2304; divinity* (abstr.):–godhead.

2306. θειώδης *thi-o'-dace;* from *2303* and *1491; sulphur-like,* i.e. *sulphurous:*–brimstone.

2307. θέλημα *thel'-ay-mah;* from the prol. form of *2309;* a *determination* (prop. the thing), i.e. (act.) *choice* (spec. *purpose, decree;* abstr., *volition*) or pass. *inclination:*– desire, pleasure, will.

2308. θέλησις *thel'-ay-sis;* from *2309; determination* (prop. the act), i.e. *option:*–will.

2309. θέλω *thel'-o;* or ἐθέλω *eth-el'-o;* in cert. tenses θελέω *thel-eh'-o; and* ἐθελέω *eth-el-eh'-o,* which are otherwise obs.; app. streng. from the alt. form of *138;* to *determine* (as an act. *option* from subj. impulse; whereas *1014* prop. denotes rather a pass. *acquiescence* in obj. considerations), i.e. *choose* or *prefer* (lit. or fig.); by impl. to *wish,* i.e. *be inclined* to (sometimes adv. *gladly*); impers. for the fut. tense, to *be about to;* by Heb. to *delight in:*–desire, be disposed (forward), intend, list, love, mean, please, have rather, (be) will (have, -ling, - ling[-ly]).

2310. θεμέλιος *them-el'-ee-os;* from a der. of *5087;* something *put* down, i.e. a *substruction* (of a building, etc.), (lit. or fig.):–foundation.

2311. θεμελιόω *them-el-ee-o'-o;* from *2310;* to *lay a basis* for, i.e. (lit.) *erect,* or (fig.) *consolidate:*–(lay the) found(- ation), ground, settle.

2312. θεοδίδακτος *theh-od-id'-ak-tos;* from *2316* and *1321; divinely instructed:*–taught of God.

2312' θεολόγος *theh-ol-og'-os;* from *2316* and *3004;* a "*theologian*":–divine.

2313. θεομαχέω *theh-o-makh-eh'-o;* from *2314;* to *resist deity:*–fight against God.

2314. θεόμαχος *theh-om'-akh-os;* from *2316* and *3164;* an *opponent of deity:*–to fight against God.

2315. θεόπνευστος *theh-op'-nyoo-stos;* from *2316* and a presumed der. of *4154; divinely breathed* in:–given by inspiration of God.

2316. θεός *theh'-os;* of unc. affin.; a *deity,* esp. (with *3588*) the supreme *Divinity;* fig. a *magistrate;* by Heb. *very:*–X exceeding, God, god[-ly, -ward].

2317. θεοσέβεια *theh-os-eb'-i-ah;* from *2318; devoutness,* i.e. *piety:*–godliness.

2318. θεοσεβής *theh-os-eb-ace';* from *2316* and *4576; reverent of God,* i.e. *pious:*–worshipper of God.

2319. θεοστυγής *theh-os-too-gace';* from *2316* and the base of *4767; hateful to God,* i.e. *impious:*–hater of God.

2320. θεότης *theh-ot'-ace;* from *2316; divinity* (abstr.):–godhead.

2321. Θεόφιλος *theh-of'-il-os;* from *2316* and *5384; friend of God; Theophilus,* a Chr.:–Theophilus.

2322. θεραπεία *ther-ap-i'-ah;* from *2323; attendance* (spec. medical, i.e. *cure*); fig. and coll. *domestics:*–healing, household.

2323. θεραπεύω *ther-ap-yoo'-o;* from the same as *2324;* to *wait upon* menially, i.e. (fig.) to *adore* (God), or (spec.) to *relieve* (of disease):–cure, heal, worship.

2324. θεράπων *ther-ap'-ohn;* app. a part. from an otherwise obs. der. of the base of *2330;* a menial *attendant* (as if *cherishing*):–servant.

2325. θερίζω *ther-id'-zo;* from *2330* (in the sense of the *crop*); to *harvest:*–reap.

2326. θερισμός *ther-is-mos';* from *2325; reaping,* i.e. the *crop:*–harvest.

2327. θεριστής *ther-is-tace';* from *2325;* a *harvester:*–reaper.

2328. θερμαίνω *ther-mah'-ee-no;* from

2329; to *heat* (oneself):–(be) warm(-ed, self).
2329. θέρμη *ther'-may;* from the base of *2330; warmth:*–heat.
2330. θέρος *ther'-os;* from a prim. θέρω (to *heat*); prop. *heat,* i.e. *summer:*–summer.
2331. Θεσσαλονικεύς *thes-sal-on-ik-yoos';* from *2332;* a *Thessalonican,* i.e. inh. of Thessalonice:–Thessalonian.
2332. Θεσσαλονίκη *thes-sal-on-ee'-kay;* from Θεσσαλός (a *Thessalian*) and *3529; Thessalonice,* a place in Asia Minor:–Thessalonica.
2333. Θευδᾶς *thyoo-das';* of unc. or.; *Theudas,* an Isr.:–Theudas.
2334. θεωρέω *theh-o-reh'-o;* from a der. of *2300* (perh. by addition of *3708*); to *be a spectator* of, i.e. *discern,* (lit. fig. [*experience*] or intens. [*acknowledge*]):–behold, consider, look on, perceive, see. Comp. *3700.*
2335. θεωρία *theh-o-ree'-ah;* from the same as *2334; spectatorship,* i.e. (concr.) a *spectacle:*–sight.
2336. θήκη *thay'-kay;* from *5087;* a *receptacle,* i.e. *scabbard:*–sheath.
2337. θηλάζω *thay-lad'-zo;* from θηλή (the *nipple*); to *suckle;* (by impl.) to *suck:*–(give) suck(-ling).
2338. θῆλυς *thay'-loos* from the same as *2337; female:*–female, woman.
2339. θήρα *thay'-rah;* from θήρ (a wild *animal,* as *game*); *hunting,* i.e. (fig.) *destruction:*–trap.
2340. θηρεύω *thay-ryoo'-o;* from *2339;* to *hunt* (an animal), i.e. (fig.) to *carp at:*–catch.
2341. θηριομαχέω *thay-ree-om-akh-eh'-o;* from a com. of *2342* and *3164;* to be a *beast-fighter* (in the gladiatorial show), i.e. (fig.) to *encounter* (furious men):–fight with wild beasts.
2342. θηρίον *thay-ree'-on;* dim. from the same as *2339;* a *dangerous animal:*–(venomous, wild) beast.
2343. θησαυρίζω *thay-sow-rid'-zo;* from *2344;* to *amass* or *reserve* (lit. or fig.):–lay up (treasure), (keep) in store, (heap) treasure (together, up).
2344. θησαυρός *thay-sow-ros';* from *5087;* a *deposit,* i.e. *wealth* (lit. or fig.):–treasure.
2345. θιγγάνω *thing-gan'-o;* a prol. form of an obs. prim. θίγω (to *finger*); to *manipulate,* i.e. *have to do with;* by impl. to *injure:*–handle, touch.
2346. θλίβω *thlee'-bo;* akin to the base of *5147;* to *crowd* (lit. or fig.):–afflict, narrow, throng, suffer tribulation, trouble.
2347. θλίψις *thlip'-sis;* from *2346; pressure* (lit. or fig.):–afflicted(-tion), anguish, burdened, persecution, tribulation, trouble.
2348. θνήσκω *thnay'-sko;* a streng. form of a simpler prim. θάνω *than'-o* (which is used for it only in cert. tenses); to *die* (lit. or fig.):–be dead, die.
2349. θνητός *thnay-tos';* from *2348; liable to die:*–mortal(-ity).
2350. θορυβέω *thor-oo-beh'-o;* from *2351;* to *be in tumult,* i.e. *disturb, clamor:*–make ado (a noise), trouble self, set on an uproar.
2351. θόρυβος *thor'-oo-bos;* from the base of *2360;* a *disturbance:*–tumult, uproar.
2352. θραύω *throw'-o;* a prim. verb; to *crush:*–bruise. Comp. *4486.*
2353. θρέμμα *threm'-mah;* from *5142; stock* (as *raised* on a farm):–cattle.
2354. θρηνέω *thray-neh'-o;* from *2355;* to *bewail:*–lament, mourn.
2355. θρῆνος *thray'-nos;* from the base of *2360; wailing:*–lamentation.
2356. θρησκεία *thrace-ki'-ah;* from a der. of *2357;* cer. *observance:*–religion, worshipping.
2357.θρῆσκος *thrace'-kos;* prob. from the base of *2360; ceremonious* in worship (as *demonstr.*), i.e. *pious:*–religious.
2358. θριαμβεύω *three-am-byoo'-o;* from a prol. com. of the base of *2360;* and a der. of *680;* to *make an acclamatory procession,* i.e. (fig.) to *conquer* or (by Heb.) to *give victory:*–(cause) to triumph (over).
2359. θρίξ *threeks;* gen. case τριχός etc.; of unc. der.; *hair:*–hair. Comp. *2864.*
2360. θροέω *thro-eh'-o;* from θρέομαι (to *wail;*) to *clamor,* i.e. (by impl.) to *frighten:*–trouble.
2361. θρόμβος *throm'-bos;* perh. from *5142* (in the sense of *thickening*); a *clot:*–great drop.
2362. θρόνος *thron'-os;* from θράω (to *sit*); a stately *seat* ("*throne*"); by impl. *power* or (concr.) a *potentate:*–seat, throne.
2363. Θυάτειρα *thoo-at'-i-rah;* of unc. der.; *Thyatira,* a place in Asia Minor:–Thyatira.
2364. θυγάτηρ *thoo-gat'-air;* app. a prim. word (comp. "daughter"); a *female child,* or (by Heb.) *desc.* (or *inh.*):–daughter.
2365. θυγάτριον *thoo-gat'-ree-on;* from *2364;* a *daughterling:*–little (young) daughter.
2366. θύελλα *thoo'-el-lah;* from *2380* (in the sense of *blowing*) a storm:–tempest.
2367. θύϊνος *thoo'-ee-nos;* from a der. of *2380* (in the sense of *blowing;* denoting a cert. *fragrant* tree); made of *citron*-wood:–thyine.
2368. θυμίαμα *thoo-mee'-am-ah;* from *2370;* an *aroma,* i.e. fragrant *powder* burnt in relig. service; by impl. the *burning* itself:–incense, odour.
2369. θυμιαστήριον *thoo-mee-as-tay'-ree-on;* from a der. of *2370;* a *place of fumigation,* i.e. the *alter* of *incense* (in the Temple):–censer.
2370. θυμιάω *thoo-mee-ah'-o;* from a der. of *2380* (in the sense of *smoking*); to *fumigate,* i.e. *offer* aromatic *fumes:*–burn incense.
2371. θυμομαχέω *thoo-mom-akh-eh'-o;* from a presumed com. of *2372* and *3164;* to *be in a furious fight,* i.e. (fig.) to *be exasperated:*–be highly displeased.
2372. θυμός *thoo-mos';* from *2380; passion* (as if *breathing* hard):–fierceness, indignation, wrath. Comp. *5590.*
2373. θυμόω *thoo-mo'-o;* from *2372;* to *put in a passion,* i.e. *enrage:*–be wroth.
2374. θύρα *thoo'-rah;* app. a prim. word [comp. "door"]; a *portal* or entrance (the opening or the closure, lit. or fig.):–door, gate.
2375. θυρεός *thoo-reh-os';* from *2374;* a large *shield* (as *door*-shaped):–shield.
2376. θυρίς *thoo-rece';* from *2374;* an *aperture,* i.e. *window:*–window.
2377. θυρωρός *thoo-ro-ros';* from *2374* and οὖρος (a *watcher*); a *gate-warden:*–that kept the door, porter.
2378. θυσία *thoo-see'-ah;* from *2380; sacrifice* (the act or the victim, lit. or fig.):–sacrifice.
2379. θυσιαστήριον *thoo-see-as-tay'-ree-on;* from a der. of *2378;* a *place of sacrifice,* i.e. an *altar* (spec. or gen. case, lit. or fig.):–altar.
2380. θύω *thoo'-o;* a prim. verb; prop. to *rush* (*breathe* hard, *blow, smoke*), i.e. (by impl.) to *sacrifice* (prop. by fire, but gen. case); by ext. to *immolate* (*slaughter* for any purpose):–kill, (do) sacrifice, slay.
2381. Θωμᾶς *tho-mas';* of Chald. or. [comp. 8380]; *the twin; Thomas,* a Chr.:–Thomas.
2382. θώραξ *tho'-rax;* of unc. affin.; the *chest* ("*thorax*"), i.e. (by impl.) a *corslet:*–breast-plate.

I

2383. Ἰάειρος *ee-ah'-i-ros;* of Heb. or. [2971]; *Jăīrus* (i.e. *Jair*), an Isr.:–Jairus.
2384. Ἰακώβ *ee-ak-obe';* of Heb. or. [3290]; *Jacob* (i.e. *Ja`akob*), the progenitor of the Isr.:–also an Isr.:–Jacob.
2385. Ἰάκωβος *ee-ak'-o-bos;* the same as *2384* Graecized; *Jacobus,* the name of three Isr.:–James.
2386. ἴαμα *ee'-am-ah;* from *2390;* a *cure* (the effect):–healing.
2387. Ἰαμβρῆς *ee-am-brace';* of Eg. or.; *Jambres,* an Eg.:–Jambres.
2388. Ἰαννά *ee-an-nah';* prob. of Heb. or. [comp. 3238]; *Janna,* an Isr.:–Janna.
2389. Ἰαννῆς *ee-an-nace'* of Eg. or.; *Jannes,* an Eg.:–Jannes.
2390. ἰάομαι *ee-ah'-om-ahee;* mid. of app. a prim. verb; to *cure* (lit. or fig.):–heal, make whole.
2391. Ἰάρεδ *ee-ar'-ed;* of Heb. or. [3382]; *Jared* (i.e. *Jered*), an antediluvian:–Jared.
2392. ἴασις *ee'-as-is;* from *2390; curing* (the act):–cure, heal (-ing).
2393. ἴασπις *ee'-as-pis;* prob. of for. or. [see 3471]; "*jasper*", a gem:–jasper.
2394. Ἰάσων *ee-as'-oan;* fut. act. part. masc. of *2390; about to cure; Jason,* a Chr.:–Jason.
2395. ἰατρός *ee-at-ros';* from 2390; a *physician:*–physician.
2396. ἴδε *id'-eh;* sec. pers. sing. imper. act. of *1492;* used as an interj. to denote *surprise; lo!:*–behold, lo, see.
2397. ἰδέα *id-eh'-ah;* from *1492;* a *sight* [comp. fig. "idea"], i.e. *aspect:*–countenance.
2398. ἴδιος *id'-ee-os;* of unc. affin.; *pertaining to self,* i.e. one's *own;* by impl. *private* or *separate:*–X his acquaintance, when they were alone, apart, aside, due, his (own, proper, several), home, (her, our, thine, your) own (business), private(-ly), proper, severally, their (own).
2399. ἰδιώτης *id-ee-o'-tace;* from *2398;* a

GREEK

private pers., i.e. (by impl.) an *ignoramus* (comp. "idiot"):–ignorant, rude, unlearned.

2400. ἰδού *id-oo';* sec. pers. sing. imper. mid. of *1492;* used as imper. *lo!:*–behold, lo, see.

2401. Ἰδουμαία *id-oo-mah'-yah;* of Heb. or. [123]; *Idumaea* (i.e. *Edom*), a region E. (and South) of Pal.:–Idumaea.

2402. ἱδρώς *hid-roce';* a streng. form of a prim. ἴδος (*sweat*): *perspiration:*–sweat.

2403. Ἰεζαβήλ *ee-ed-zab-ale';* of Heb. or. [348]; *Jezabel* (i.e. *Jezebel*), a Tyrian woman (used as a synonym of a termagant or false teacher):–Jezabel.

2404. Ἱεράπολις *hee-er-ap'-ol-is;* from *2413* and *4172*; *holy city; Hierapolis,* a place in Asia Minor:–Hierapolis.

2405. ἱερατεία *hee-er-at-i'-ah;* from *2407; priestliness,* i.e. the *sacerdotal function:*–office of the priesthood, priest's office.

2406. ἱεράτευμα *hee-er-at'-yoo-mah;* from *2407;* the *priestly fraternity,* i.e. *sacerdotal order* (fig.):–priesthood.

2407. ἱερατεύω *hee-er-at-yoo'-o;* prol. from *2409; to be a priest,* i.e. *perform his functions:*–execute the priest's office.

2408. Ἱερεμίας, *hee-er-em-ee'-as;* of Heb. or. [3414]; *Hieremias* (i.e. *Jermijah*), an Isr.:–Jeremiah.

2409. ἱερεύς *hee-er-yooce';* from *2413;* a *priest* (lit. or fig.):–(high) priest.

2410. Ἱεριχώ *hee-er-ee-kho';* of Heb. or. [3405]; *Jericho,* a place in Pal.:–Jericho.

2411. ἱερόν *hee-er-on';* neut. of *2413;* a *sacred* place, i.e. the entire precincts (whereas *3485* denotes the central *sanctuary* itself) of the *Temple* (at Jerus. or elsewhere):–temple.

2412. ἱεροπρεπής *hee-er-op-rep-ace'*; from *2413* and the same as *4241; reverent:*–as becometh holiness.

2413. ἱερός *hee-er-os';* of unc. affin.; *sacred:*–holy.

2414. Ἱεροσόλυμα *hee-er-os-ol'-oo-mah;* of Heb. or. [3389]; *Hierosolyma* (i.e. *Jerushalaïm*), the capitol of Pal.:–Jerusalem. Comp. *2419.*

2415. Ἱεροσολυμίτης *hee-er-os-ol-oo-mee'-tace;* from *2414*; a *Hierosolymite,* i.e. inh. of Hierosolyma:–of Jerusalem.

2416. ἱεροσυλέω *hee-er-os-ool-eh'-o;* from *2417;* to *be a temple-robber* (fig.):–commit sacrilege.

2417. ἱερόσυλος *hee-er-os'-oo-los;* from *2411* and *4813;* a *temple-despoiler:*–robber of churches.

2418. ἱερουργέω *hee-er-oorg-eh'-o;* from a com. of *2411* and the base of *2041;* to *be a temple-worker,* i.e. *officiate as a priest* (fig.):–minister.

2419. Ἱερουσαλήμ *hee-er-oo-sal-ame';* of Heb. or. [3389]; *Hierusalem* (i.e. *Jerushalem*), the capitol of Pal.:–Jerusalem. Comp. *2414.*

2420. ἱερωσύνη *hee-er-o-soo'-nay;* from *2413; sacredness,* i.e. (by impl.) the *priestly office:*–priesthood.

2421. Ἰεσσαί *es-es-sah'-ee;* of Heb. or. [3448]; *Jessae* (i.e. *Jishai*), an Isr.:–Jesse.

2422. Ἰεφθάε *ee-ef-thah'-eh;* of Heb. or. [3316]; *Jephthaë* (i.e. *Jiphtach),* an Isr.:–Jephthah.

2423. Ἰεχονίας *ee-ekh-on-ee'-as;* of Heb. or. [3204]; *Jechonias* (i.e. *Jekonjah*), an Isr.:–Jechonias.

2424. Ἰησοῦς *ee-ay-sooce';* of Heb. or. [3091]; *Jesus* (i.e. *Jehoshua*), the name of our Lord and two (three) other Isr.:–Jesus.

2425. ἱκανός *hik-an-os';* from ἵκω [ἱκάνω or ἱκνέομαι akin to *2240*] (to *arrive*); *competent* (as if *coming* in season), i.e. *ample* (in amount) or *fit* (in character):–able, + content, enough, good, great, large, long (while), many, meet, much, security, sore, sufficient, worthy.

2426. ἱκανότης *hik-an-ot'-ace;* from *2425; ability:*–sufficiency.

2427. ἱκανόω *hik-an-o'-o;* from *2425;* to *enable,* i.e. *qualify:*–make able (meet).

2428. ἱκετηρία *hik-et-ay-ree'-ah;* from a der. of the base of *2425* (through the idea of *approaching* for a favor); *intreaty:*–supplication.

2429. ἰκμάς *hik-mas';* of unc. affin.; *dampness:*–moisture.

2430. Ἰκόνιον *ee-kon'-ee-on;* perh. from *1504; image-like; Iconium,* a place in Asia Minor:–Iconium.

2431. ἱλαρός *hil-ar-os';* from the same as *2436; propitious* or *merry* ("*hilarious*"), i.e. *prompt* or *willing*:–cheerful.

2432. ἱλαρότης *hil-ar-ot'-ace;* from *2431; alacrity:*–cheerfulness.

2433. ἱλάσκομαι *hil-as'-kom-ahee;* mid. from the same as *2436;* to *conciliate,* i.e. (trans.) to *atone* for (sin), or (intr.) *be propitious:*–be merciful, make reconciliation for.

2434. ἱλασμός *hil-as-mos'; atonement,* i.e. (concr.) an *expiator:*–propitiation.

2435. ἱλαστήριον *hil-as-tay'-ree-on;* neut. of a der. of *2433;* an *expiatory* (place or thing), i.e. (concr.) an atoning *victim,* or (spec.) the *lid* of the Ark (in the Temple):–mercyseat, propitiation.

2436. ἵλεως *hil'-eh-oce;* perh. from the alt. form of *138; cheerful* (as *attract.*), i.e. *propitious;* adv. (by Heb.) God be *gracious!,* i.e. (in averting some calamity) *far* be it:–be it far, merciful.

2437. Ἰλλυρικόν *il-loo-ree-kon';* neut. of an adj. from a name of unc. der.: (the) *Illyrican* (shore), i.e. (as a name itself) *Illyricum,* a region of Europe:–Illyricum.

2438. ἱμάς *hee-mas';* perh. from the same as *260;* a *strap,* i.e. (spec.) the *tie* (of a sandal) or the *lash* (of a scourge):–latchet, thong.

2439. ἱματίζω *him-at-id'-zo;* from *2440;* to *dress:*–clothe.

2440. ἱμάτιον *him-at'-ee-on;* neut. of a presumed der. of ἕννυμι (to *put on*); a *dress* (inner or outer):–apparel, cloke, clothes, garment, raiment, robe, vesture.

2441. ἱματισμός *him-at-is-mos';* from *2439*; *clothing:*–apparel (X –led), array, raiment, vesture.

2442. ἱμείρομαι *him-i'-rom-ahee;* mid. from ἵμερος (a *yearning;* of unc. affin.); to *long for:*–be affectionately desirous.

2443. ἵνα *hin'-ah;* prob. from the same as the former part of *1438* (through the *demonstr.* idea; comp. *3588*); in order *that* (denoting the *purpose* or the *result*):–albeit, because, to the intent (that), lest, so as, (so) that, (for) to. Comp. *3363.*

2444. ἱνατί *hin-at-ee';* from *2443* and *5101; for what* reason?, i.e. *why?:*–wherefore, why.

2445. Ἰόππη *ee-op'-pay;* of Heb. or. [3305]; *Joppe* (i.e. *Japho*), a place in Pal.:–Joppa.

2446. Ἰορδάνης *ee-or-dan'-ace;* of Heb. or. [3383]; the *Jordanes* (i.e. *Jarden*), a river of Pal.:–Jordan.

2447. ἰός *ee-os';* perh. from εἶμι (to *go*) or ἵημι (to *send*); *rust* (as if *emitted* by metals); also *venom* (as *emitted* by serpents):–poison, rust.

2448. Ἰουδά *ee-oo-dah';* of Heb. or. [3063 or perh. 3194]; *Judah* (i.e. *Jehudah* or *Juttah*), a part of (or place in) Pal.:–Judah.

2449. Ἰουδαία *ee-oo-dah'-yah;* fem. of *2453* (with *1093* implied); the *Judaean* land (i.e. *Judaea*), a region of Pal.:–Judaea.

2450. Ἰουδαΐζω *ee-oo-dah-id'-zo;* from *2453;* to *become a Judaean,* i.e. "*Judaize*":–live as the Jews.

2451. Ἰουδαϊκός *ee-oo-dah-ee-kos';* from *2453; Judaïc,* i.e. *resembling a Judaean:*–Jewish.

2452. Ἰουδαϊκῶς *ee-oo-dah-ee-koce';* adv. from *2451; Judaïcally* or *in a manner resembling a Judaean:*–as do the Jews.

2453. Ἰουδαῖος *ee-oo-dah'-yos;* from *2448* (in the sense of *2455* as a country); *Judaean,* i.e. belonging to *Jehudah:*–Jew(-ess), of Judaea.

2454. Ἰουδαϊσμός *ee-oo-dah-is-mos'*; from *2450; "Judaïsm"*, i.e. the *Jewish faith* and usages:–Jews' religion.

2455. Ἰουδάς *ee-oo-das';* of Heb. or. [3063]; *Judas* (i.e. *Jehudah*), the name of ten Isr.; also of the posterity of one of them and its region:–Juda(-h, -s); Jude.

2456. Ἰουλία *ee-oo-lee'-ah;* fem. of the same as *2457; Julia,* a Chr. Woman:–Julia.

2457. Ἰούλιος *ee-oo'-lee-os;* of Lat. or.; *Julius*, a centurion:–Julius.

2458. Ἰουνίας *ee-oo-nee'-as;* of Lat. or.; *Junias,* a Chr.:–Junias.

2459. Ἰοῦστος *ee-ooce'-tos* of Lat. or. ("*just*"); *Justus,* the name of three Chr.:–Justus.

2460. ἱππεύς *hip-yooce';* from *2462;* an *equestrian,* i.e. member of a *cavalry* corps:–horseman.

2461. ἱππικόν *hip-pee-kon';* neut. of a der. of *2462;* the *cavalry* force:–horse[-men].

2462. ἵππος *hip'-pos;* of unc. affin.; a *horse:*–horse.

2463. ἶρις *ee'-ris;* perh. from *2046* (as a symbol of the female *messenger* of the pagan deities); a *rainbow* ("*iris*"):–rainbow.

2464. Ισαάκ *ee-sah-ak';* of Heb. or. [3327]; *Isaac* (i.e. *Jitschak*), the son of Abraham:–Isaac.

2465. ἰσάγγελος *ee-sang'-el-los;* from

2470 and *32; like an angel,* i.e. *angelic:*–equal unto the angels.

2466. Ἰσαχάρ *ee-sakh-ar'*; of Heb. or. [3485]; *Isachar* (i.e. *Jissaskar*), a son of Jacob (fig. his desc.):–Issachar.

2467. ἴσημι *is'-ay-mee;* assumed by some as the base of cert. irreg. forms of *1492;* to *know:*–know.

2468. ἴσθι *is'-thee;* sec. pers. imper. pres. of *1510; be* thou:–+ agree, be, X give thyself wholly to.

2469. Ἰσκαριώτης *is-kar-ee-o'-tace;* of Heb. or. [prob. 377 and 7149]; *inh. of Kerioth; Iscariotes* (i.e. *Keriothite*), an epithet of Judas the traitor:–Iscariot.

2470. ἴσος *ee'-sos* prob. from *1492* (through the idea of *seeming*); *similar* (in amount and kind):–+ agree, as much, equal, like.

2471. ἰσότης *ee-sot'-ace; likeness* (in condition or proportion); by impl. *equity:*–equal(-ity).

2472. ἰσότιμος *ee-sot'-ee-mos;* from *2470* and *5092; of equal value* or *honor:*–like precious.

2473. ἰσόψυχος *ee-sop'-soo-khos;* from *2470* and *5590; of similar spirit:*–likeminded.

2474. Ἰσραήλ *is-rah-ale';* of Heb. or. [3478]; *Israel* (i.e. *Jisrael*), the adopted name of Jacob, incl. his desc. (lit. or fig.):–Israel.

2475. Ἰσραηλίτης *is-rah-ale-ee'-tace;* from *2474;* an "*Isr.*", i.e. desc. of Israel (lit. or fig.):–Isr.

2476. ἵστημι *his'-tay-mee;* a prol. form of a prim. στάω *stah'-o* (of the same mean. and used for it in cert. tenses); to *stand* (trans. or intr.), used in various appl. (lit. or fig.):–abide, appoint, bring, continue, covenant, establish, hold up, lay, present, set (up), stanch, stand (by, forth, still, up). Comp. *5087.*

2477. ἱστορέω *his-tor-eh'-o;* from a der. of *1492;* to *be knowing* (*learned*), i.e. (by impl.) to *visit* for information (*interview*):–see.

2478. ἰσχυρός *is-khoo-ros';* from *2479; forcible* (lit. or fig.):–boisterous, mighty(-ier), powerful, strong(-er, man), valiant.

2479. ἰσχύς *is-khoos';* from a der. of ἰς his (*force;* comp. ἔσχον, a form of *2192*); *forcefulness* (lit. or fig.):–ability, might[-ily], power, strength.

2480. ἰσχύω *is-khoo'-o;* from *2479;* to *have* (or *exercise*) *force* (lit. or fig.):–be able, avail, can do([-not]), could, be good, might, prevail, be of strength, be whole, + much work.

2481. ἴσως *ee'-soce;* adv. from *2470; likely,* i.e. *perh.:*–it may be.

2482. Ἰταλία *ee-tal-ee'-ah;* prob. of for. or.; *Italia,* a region of Europe:–Italy.

2483. Ἰταλικός *ee-tal-ee-kos';* from *2482; Italic,* i.e. belonging to Italia:–Italian.

2484. Ἰτουραία *ee-too-rah'-yah;* of Heb. or. [3195]; *Ituraea* (i.e. *Jetur*), a region of Pal.:–Ituraea.

2485. ἰχθύδιον *ikh-thoo'-dee-on;* dim. from *2486;* a *petty fish:*–little (small) fish.

2486. ἰχθύς *ikh-thoos'* of unc. affin.; a *fish:*–fish.

2487. ἴχνος *ikh'-nos;* from ἰκνέομαι (to *arrive;* comp. *2240*); a *track* (fig.):–step.

2488. Ἰωάθαμ *ee-o-ath'-am;* of Heb. or. [3147]; *Joatham* (i.e. *Jotham*), an Isr.:–Joatham.

2489. Ἰωάννα *ee-o-an'-nah;* fem. of the same as *2491; Joanna,* a Chr.:–Joanna.

2490. Ἰωαννᾶς *ee-o-an-nas';* a form of *2491; Joannas,* an Isr.:–Joannas.

2491. Ἰωάννης *ee-o-an'-nace;* of Heb. or. [3110]; *Joannes* (i.e. *Jochanan*), the name of four Isr.:–John.

2492. Ἰώβ *ee-obe';* of Heb. or. [347]; *Job* (i.e. *Ijob*), a patriarch:–Job.

2493. Ἰωήλ *ee-o-ale';* of Heb. or. [3100]; *Joel,* an Isr.:–Joel.

2494. Ἰωνάν, *ee-o-nan';* prob. for *2491* or *2495; Jonan,* an Isr.:–Jonan.

2495. Ἰωνᾶν *ee-o-nas';* of Heb. or. [3124]; *Jonas* (i.e. *Jonah*), the name of two Isr.:–Jonas.

2496. Ἰωράμ *ee-o-ram';* of Heb. or. [3141]; *Joram,* an Isr.:–Joram.

2497. Ἰωρείμ *ee-o-rime';* perh. for *2496; Jorim,* an Isr.:–Jorim.

2498. Ἰωσαφάτ *ee-o-saf-at';* of Heb. or. [3092]; *Josaphat* (i.e. *Jehoshaphat*), an Isr.:–Josaphat.

2499. Ἰωσή *ee-o-say';* gen. case of *2500; Jose,* an Isr.:–Jose.

2500. Ἰωσῆς *ee-o-sace';* perh. for *2501; Joses,* the name of two Isr.:–Joses. Comp. *2499.*

2501. Ἰωσήφ *ee-o-safe';* of Heb. or. [3130]; *Joseph,* the name of seven Isr.:–Joseph.

2502. Ἰωσίας *ee-o-see'-as;* of Heb. or. [2977]; *Josias* (i.e. *Joshiah*), an Isr.:–Josias.

2503. ἰῶτα *ee-o'-tah;* of Heb. or. [the tenth letter of the Heb. alphabet]; "*iota*", the name of the ninth letter of the Gr. alphabet, put (fig.) for a very small part of anything:–jot.

K

2504. κἀγώ *kag-o';* from *2532* and *1473;* (so also the dat. κἀμοί *kam-oy',* and acc. κἀμέ *kam-eh'*)*and* (or *also, even,* etc.) I, (*to*) *me:*–(and, even, even so, so) I (also, in like wise), both me, me also.

2505. καθά *kath-ah';* from *2596* and the neut. pl. of *3739; according to which* things, i.e. *just as:*–as.

2506. καθαίρεσις *kath-ah'-ee-res-is;* from *2507; demolition;* fig. *extinction:*–destruction, pulling down.

2507. καθαιρέω *kath-ahee-reh'-o;* from *2596* and *138* (incl. its alt.); to *lower* (or with violence) *demolish* (lit. or fig.):–cast (pull, put, take) down, destroy.

2508. καθαίρω *kath-ah'-ee-ro;* from *2513;* to *cleanse,* i.e. (spec.) to *prune;* fig. to *expiate:*–purge.

2509. καθάπερ *kath-ap'-er;* from *2505* and *4007; exactly as:*–(even, as well) as.

2510. καθάπτω *kath-ap'-to* from *2596* and *680;* to *seize upon:*–fasten on.

2511. καθαρίζω *kath-ar-id'-zo;* from *2513;* to *cleanse* (lit. or fig.):–(make) clean(-se), purge, purify.

2512. καθαρισμός *kath-ar-is-mos';* from *2511;* a *washing* off, i.e. (cer.) *ablution,* (mor.) *expiation:*–cleansing, + purge, purification(-fying).

2513. καθαρός *kath-ar-os';* of unc. affin.; *clean* (lit. or fig.):–clean, clear, pure.

2514. καθαρότης *kath-ar-ot'-ace;* from *2513; cleanness* (cer.):–purification.

2515. καθέδρα *kath-ed'-rah;* from *2596* and the same as *1476;* a *bench* (lit. or fig.):–seat.

2516. καθέζομαι *kath-ed'-zom-ahee;* from *2596* and the base of *1476;* to *sit down:*–sit.

2517. καθεξῆς *kath-ex-ace';* from *2596* and *1836; thereafter,* i.e. *consecutively;* as a noun (by ell. of noun) a *subsequent* pers. or time:–after(-ward), by (in) order.

2518. καθεύδω *kath-yoo'-do;* from *2596* and εὕδω (to *sleep*); to lie *down* to *rest,* i.e. (by impl.) to *fall asleep* (lit. or fig.):–(be a-)sleep.

2519. καθηγητής *kath-ayg-ay-tace';* from a com. of *2596* and *2233;* a *guide,* i.e. (fig.) a *teacher:*–master.

2520. καθήκω *kath-ay'-ko;* from *2596* and *2240;* to *reach to,* i.e. (neut. of pres. act. part., fig. as adj.) *becoming:*– convenient, fit.

2521. κάθημαι *kath'-ay-mahee;* from *2596;* and ἧμαι (to *sit;* akin to the base of *1476*); to *sit down;* fig. to *remain, reside:*–dwell, sit (by, down).

2522. καθημερινός *kath-ay-mer-ee-nos';* from *2596* and *2250; quotidian:*–daily.

2523. καθίζω *kath-id'-zo;* another (act.) form for *2516;* to *seat down,* i.e. *set* (fig. *appoint*); intr., to *sit* (down); fig. to *settle* (*hover, dwell*):–continue, set, sit (down), tarry.

2524. καθίημι *kath-ee'-ay-mee;* from *2596;* and ἵημι (to *send*); to *lower:*–let down.

2525. καθίστημι *kath-is'-tay-mee;* from *2596* and *2476;* to *place down* (permanently), i.e. (fig.) to *designate, constitute, convoy:*–appoint, be, conduct, make, ordain, set.

2526. καθό *kath-o';* from *2596* and *3739; according to which* thing, i.e. *precisely as, in proportion as:*–according to that, (inasmuch) as.

2526'. καθολικός *kath-ol-ee-kos';* from *2527; universal:*– general.

2527. καθόλου *kath-ol'-oo;* from *2596* and *3650; on* the *whole,* i.e. *entirely:*–at all.

2528. καθοπλίζω *kath-op-lid'-zo;* from *2596;* and *3695;* to *equip fully* with armor:–arm.

2529. καθοράω *kath-or-ah'-o;* from *2596* and *3708;* to *behold fully,* i.e. (fig.) *distinctly apprehend:*–clearly see.

2530. καθότι *kath-ot'-ee;* from *2596;* and *3739* and *5100; according to which cert.* thing, i.e. as *far* (or *inasmuch*) *as:*–(according, forasmuch) as, because (that).

2531. καθώς *kath-oce';* from *2596* and *5613; just* (or *inasmuch*) *as, that:*–according to, (according, even) as, how, when.

2532. καί *kahee;* app., a prim. par., having a *copulative* and sometimes also a *cumulative* force; *and, also, even, so then, too,* etc.; often used in connection (or compo.) with other par. or small words:–and, also, both, but, even, for, if, indeed, likewise. moreover, or, so, that, then, therefore, when, yea, yet.

GREEK

2533. Καϊάφας *kah-ee-af'-as;* of Chald. or.; *the dell; Caïaphas* (i.e. *Cajepha*), an Isr.:–Caiaphas.
2534. καίγε *kah'-ee-gheh;* from *2532* and *1065; and at least* (or *even, indeed*):–and, at least.
2535. Κάϊν *kah'-in;* of Heb. or. [7014]; *Caïn,* (i.e. *Cajin*), the son of Adam:–Cain.
2536. Καϊνάν *kah-ee-nan';* of Heb. or. [7018]; *Caïnan* (i.e. *Kenan*), the name of two patriarchs:–Cainan.
2537. καινός *kahee-nos';* of unc. affin.; *new* (esp. in *freshness;* while *3501* is prop. so with respect to *age:*–new.
2538. καινότης *kahee-not'-ace* from *2537; renewal* (fig.):–newness.
2539. καίπερ *kah'-ee-per;* from *2532* and *4007; and indeed,* i.e. *nevertheless* or *notwithstanding:*–and yet, although.
2540. καιρός *kahee-ros';* of unc. affin.; an *occasion,* i.e. *set* or *proper* time:–X always, opportunity, (convenient, due) season, (due, short, while) time, a while. Comp. *5550.*
2541. Καῖσαρ *kah'-ee-sar;* of Lat. or.; *Caesar,* a title of the Rom. emperor:–Caesar.
2542. Καισάρεια *kahee-sar'-i-a;* from *2541*; *Caesaria,* the name of two places in Pal.:–Caesarea.
2543. καίτοι *kah'-ee-toy;* from *2532* and *5104; and yet,* i.e. *nevertheless:*–although.
2544. καίτοιγε *kah'-ee-toyg-eh* from *2543* and *1065; and yet indeed,* i.e. *although really:*–nevertheless, though.
2545. καίω *kah'-yo;* app. a prim. verb; to *set on fire,* i.e. *kindle* or (by impl.) *consume:*–burn, light.
2546. κἀκεῖ *kak-i';* from *2532* and *1563; likewise in that place:*–and there, there (thither) also.
2547. κἀκεῖθεν *kak-i'-then;* from *2532* and *1564; likewise from that place* (or *time*):–and afterward (from) (thence), thence also.
2548. κἀκεῖνος *kak-i'-nos;* from *2532* and *1565; likewise that* (or *those*):–and him (other, them), even he, him also, them (also), (and) they.
2549. κακία *kak-ee'-ah;* from *2556; badness,* i.e. (subj.) *depravity,* or (act.) *malignity,* or pass. *trouble:*–evil, malice (-iousness), naughtiness, wickedness.
2550. κακοήθεια *kak-o-ay'-thi-ah;* from a com. of *2556* and *2239; bad character,* i.e. (spec.) *mischievousness:*–malignity.
2551. κακολογέω, *kak-ol-og-eh'-o;* from a com. of *2556* and *3056;* to *revile:*–curse, speak evil of.
2552. κακοπάθεια *kak-op-ath'-i-ah;* from a com. of *2256* and *3806; hardship:*–suffering affliction.
2553. κακοπαθέω *kak-op-ath-eh'-o;* from the same as *2552;* to *undergo hardship:*–be afflicted, endure afflictions (hardness), suffer trouble.
2554. κακοποιέω *kak-op-oy-eh'-o;* from *2555;* to *be a bad-doer,* i.e. (obj.) to *injure,* or (gen.) to *sin:*–do(ing) evil.
2555. κακοποιός *kak-op-oy-os';* from *2556* and *4160;* a *bad-doer;* (spec.), a *criminal:*–evil-doer, malefactor.
2556. κακός *kak-os';* app. a prim. word; *worthless* (*intrinsically,* such; whereas *4190* prop. refers to *effects*), i.e. (subj.) *depraved,* or (obj.) *injurious:*–bad, evil, harm, ill, noisome, wicked.
2557. κακοῦργος *kak-oor'-gos;* from *2556* and the base of *2041;* a *wrong-doer,* i.e. *criminal:*–evil-doer, malefactor.
2558. κακουχέω *kak-oo-kheh'-o;* from a presumed com. of *2556* and *2192;* to *maltreat:*–which suffer adversity, torment.
2559. κακόω *kak-o'-o;* from *2556;* to *injure;* fig. to *exasperate:*–make evil affected, entreat evil, harm, hurt, vex.
2560. κακῶς *kak-oce';* from *2556; badly* (phys. or mor.):–amiss, diseased, evil, grievously, miserably, sick, sore.
2561. κάκωσις *kak'-o-sis;* from *2559; maltreatment:*–affliction.
2562. καλάμη *kal-am'-ay;* fem. of *2563;* a *stalk* of grain, i.e. (coll.) *stubble:*–stubble.
2563. κάλαμος *kal'-am-os;* of unc. affin.; a *reed* (the plant or its stem, or that of a similar plant); by impl. a *pen:*–pen, reed.
2564. καλέω *kal-eh'-o;* akin to the base of *2753;* to "*call*" (prop. aloud, but used in a variety of appl., dir. or otherwise):–bid, call (forth), (whose, whose sur-)name (was [called]).
2565. καλλιέλαιος *kal-le-el'-ah-yos;* from the base of *2566* and *1636;* a *cultivated olive* tree, i.e. a *domesticated* or *improved* one:–good olive tree.
2566. καλλίον *kal-lee'-on;* neut. of the (irreg.) comp. of *2570;* (adv.) *better* than many:–very well.
2567. καλοδιδάσκαλος *kal-od-id-as'-kal-os;* from *2570* and *1320;* a *teacher* of the *right:*–teacher of good things.
2568. Καλοί Λιμένες *kal-oy' lee-men'-es;* pl. of *2570* and *3040; Good Harbors,* i.e. *Fairhaven,* a bay of Crete:–fair havens.
2569. καλοποιέω *kal-op-oy-eh'-o;* from *2570* and *4160;* to *do well,* i.e. live virtuously:–well doing.
2570. καλός *kal-os';* of unc. affin.; prop. *beautiful,* but chiefly (fig.) *good* (lit. or mor.), i.e. *valuable* or *virtuous* (for *appearance* or *use,* and thus distinguished from *18,* which is prop. *intrinsic*):–X better, fair, good(-ly), honest, meet, well, worthy.
2571. κάλυμα *kal'-oo-mah;* from *2572;* a *cover,* i.e. *veil:*–vail.
2572. καλύπτω *kal-oop'-to;* akin to *2813* and *2928;* to *cover* up (lit. or fig.):–cover, hide.
2573. καλῶς *kal-oce';* adv. from *2570; well* (usually mor.):–(in a) good (place), honestly, + recover, (full) well.
2574. κάμηλος *kam'-ay-los;* of Heb. or. [1581]); a "*camel*":–camel.
2575. κάμινος *kam'-ee-nos;* prob. from *2545;* a *furnace:*–furnace.
2576. καμμύω *kam-moo'-o;* from a com. of *2596* and the base of *3466;* to *shut down,* i.e. *close* the eyes:–close.
2577. κάμνω *kam'-no;* app. a prim. verb; prop. to *toil,* i.e. (by impl.) to *tire* (fig. *faint, sicken*):–faint, sick, be wearied.
2578. κάμπτω *kamp'-to;* app. a prim. verb; to *bend:*–bow.
2579. κἄν *kan;* from *2532* and *1437; and* (or *even*) *if:*–and (also) if (so much as), if but, at the least, though, yet.
2580. Κανᾶ *kan-ah';* of Heb. or. [comp. 7071]; *Cana,* a place in Pal.:–Cana.
2581. Κανανίτης *kan-an-ee'-tace;* of Chald. or. [comp. 7067]; *zealous; Cananitès,* an epithet:–Canaanite [*by mistake for a der. from 5477*].
2582. Κανδάκη *kan-dak'-ay;* of for. or.:–*Candacë,* an Eg. queen:–Candace.
2583. κανών *kan-ohn';* from κάνη *kane* (a straight *reed,* i.e. *rod*); a *rule* ("*canon*"), i.e. (fig.) a *standard* (of faith and practice); by impl. a *boundary,* i.e. (fig.) a *sphere* (of activity):–line, rule.
2584. Καπερναούμ *cap-er-nah-oom';* of Heb. or. [prob. 3723 and 5151]; *Capernaüm* (i.e. *Caphanachum*), a place in Pal.:–Capernaum.
2585. καπηλεύω *kap-ale-yoo'*-o; from κάπηλος kapelos (a *huckster*); to *retail,* i.e. (by impl.) to *adulterate* (fig.):–corrupt.
2586. καπνός *kap-nos';* of unc. affin.; *smoke:*–smoke.
2587. Καππαδοκία *kap-pad-ok-ee'-ah;* of for. or.; *Cappadocia,* a region of Asia Minor: –Cappadocia.
2588. καρδία *kar-dee'-ah;* prol. from a prim. κάρ (Lat. cor, "*heart*"); the *heart,* i.e. (fig.) the *thoughts* or *feelings* (*mind*); also (by anal.) the *mid.:*–(+ broken-)heart(-ed).
2589. καρδιογνώστης *kar-dee-og-noce'-tace;* from *2588* and *1097;* a *heart-knower:*–which knowest the hearts.
2590. καρπός *kar-pos';* prob. from the base of *726; fruit* (as *plucked*), lit. or fig.:–fruit.
2591. Κάρπος *kar'-pos;* perh. for *2590; Carpus,* prob. a Chr.:–Carpus.
2592. καρποφορέω *kar-pof-or-eh'-o;* from 2593*;* to *be fertile* (lit. or fig.):–be (bear, bring forth) fruit(-ful).
2593. καρποφόρος *kar-pof-or'-os;* from *2590* and *5342; fruitbearing* (fig.):–fruitful.
2594. καρτερέω *kar-ter-eh'-o;* from a der. of *2904* (transp.); to *be strong,* i.e. (fig.) *steadfast* (*patient*):–endure.
2595. κάρφος *kar'-fos;* from κάρφω (to *wither*); a dry *twig* or *straw:*–mote.
2596. κατά *kat-ah';* a prim. par.; (prep.ally) *down* (in place or time), in varied relations (according to the case [gen., dat. or acc.] with which it is joined):–about, according as (to), after, against, (when they were) X alone, among, and, X apart, (even, like) as (concerning, pertaining to touching), X aside, at, before, beyond, by, to the charge of, [charita-]bly, concerning, + covered, [dai-]ly,

down, every, (+ far more) exceeding, X more excellent, for, from ... to, godly, in(-asmuch, divers, every, -to, respect of), ... by, after the manner of, + by any means, beyond (out of) measure, X mightily, more, X nat., of (up-)on (X part), out (of every), over against, (+ your) X own, + particularly, so, through(-oughout, -oughout every), thus, (un-)to(-gether, -ward), X uttermost, where(-by), with. In compo. it retains many of these appl., and frequently denotes *opposition, distribution,* or *intensity.*

2597. καταβαίνω *kat-ab-ah'-ee-no;* from *2596* and the base of *939;* to *descend* (lit. or fig.):–come (get, go, step) down, fall (down).

2598. καταβάλλω *kat-ab-al'-lo;* from *2596* and *906;* to *throw down:*–cast down,descend, fall (down), lay.

2599. καταβαρέω *kat-ab-ar-eh'-o;* from *2596* and *916*; to *impose upon*:–burden.

2600. κατάβασις *kat-ab'-as-is;* from *2597;* a *declivity:*–descent.

2601. καταβιβάζω *kat-ab-ib-ad'-zo;* from *2596* and a der. of the base of *939*; to *cause to go down,* i.e. *precipitate*:–bring (thrust) down.

2602. καταβολή *kat-ab-ol-ay*'; from *2598*; a *deposition,* i.e. *founding;* fig. *conception:*–conceive, foundation.

2603. καταβραβεύω *kat-ab-rab-yoo'-o;* from *2596* and *1018* (in its or. sense); to *award* the price *against,* i.e. (fig.) to *defraud* (of salvation):–beguile of reward.

2604. καταγγελεύς *kat-ang-gel-yooce*'; from *2605*; a *proclaimer*:–setter forth.

2605. καταγγέλλω *kat-ang-gel'-lo;* from *2596* and the base of *32*; to *proclaim, promulgate:*–declare, preach, shew, speak of, teach.

2606. καταγελάω *kat-ag-el-ah'-o;* to *laugh down,* i.e. *deride*:–laugh to scorn.

2607. καταγινώσκω *kat-ag-in-o'-sko;* from *2596* and *1097;* to *note against,* i.e. *find fault with:*–blame, condemn.

2608. κατάγνυμι *kat-ag'-noo-mee;* from *2596* and the base of *4486*; to *rend in pieces*, i.e. *crack apart:*–break.

2609. κατάγω *kat-ag'-o;* from *2596* and *71;* to *lead down;* spec. to *moor* a vessel:–bring (down, forth), (bring to) land, touch.

2610. καταγωνίζομαι *kat-ag-o-nid'-zom-ahee;* from *2596* and *75;* to *struggle against,* i.e. (by impl.) to *overcome:*–subdue.

2611. καταδέω *kat-ad-eh'-o;* from *2596* and *1210;* to *tie down,* i.e. *bandage* (a wound):–bind up.

2612. κατάδηλος *kat-ad'-ay-los;* from *2596* intens. and *1212; manifest:*–far more evident.

2613. καταδικάζω *kat-ad-ik-ad'-zo;* from *2596* and a der. of *1349;* to *adjudge against,* i.e. *pronounce guilty:*–condemn.

2614. καταδιώκω *kat-ad-ee-o'-ko;* from *2596* and *1377;* to *hunt down,* i.e. *search for:*–follow after.

2615. καταδουλόω *kat-ad-oo-lo'-o;* from *2596* and *1402;* to *enslave utterly:*–bring into bondage.

2616. καταδυναστεύω *kat-ad-oo-nas-tyoo'-o;* from *2596* and a der. of *1413;* to *exercise dominion against,* i.e. *oppress:*–oppress.

2617. καταισχύνω *kat-ahee-skhoo'-no;* from *2596* and *153;* to *shame down,* i.e. *disgrace* or (by impl.) *put to the blush:*–confound, dishonour, (be a-, make a-) shame(-d).

2618. κατακαίω *kat-ak-ah'-ee-o;* from *2596* and *2545;* to *burn down* (to the ground), i.e. *consume wholly:*–burn (up,utterly).

2619. κατακαλύπτω *kat-ak-al-oop'-to;* from *2596* and *2572;* to *cover wholly,* i.e. *veil:*–cover, hide.

2620. κατακαυχάομαι *kat-ak-ow-khah'-om-ahee;* from *2596* and *2744;* to *exult against* (i.e. *over*):–boast (against), glory, rejoice against.

2621. κατάκειμαι *kat-ak'-i-mahee;* from *2596* and *2749;* to *lie down,* i.e. (by impl.) *be sick;* spec. to *recline* at a meal:–keep, lie, sit at meat (down).

2622. κατακλάω *kat-ak-lah'-o;* from *2596* and *2806;* to *break down,* i.e. *divide:*–break.

2623. κατακλείω *kat-ak-li'-o;* from *2596* and *2808;* to *shut down* (in a dungeon), i.e. *incarcerate:*–shut up.

2624. κατακληροδοτέω *kat-ak-lay-rod-ot-eh'-o;* from *2596* and a der. of a com. of *2819* and *1325;* to *be a giver of lots to each,* i.e. (by impl.) to *apportion an estate:*–divide by lot.

2625. κατακλίνω *kat-ak-lee'-no;* from *2596* and *2827; to recline down*, i.e. (spec.) to *take a place* at table:–(make) sit down (at meat).

2626. κατακλύζω *kat-ak-lood'-zo;* from *2596* and the base of *2830;* to *dash* (*wash*) *down,* i.e. (by impl.) to *deluge:*–overflow.

2627. κατακλυσμός *kat-ak-looce-mos'*; from *2626;* an *inundation:*–flood.

2628. κατακολουθέω *kat-ak-ol-oo-theh'-o;* from *2596* and *190;* to *accompany closely:*–follow (after).

2629. κατακόπτω *kat-ak-op'-to;* from *2596* and *2875;* to *chop down,* i.e. *mangle:*–cut.

2630. κατακρημνίζω *kat-ak-rame-nid'-zo;* from *2596* and a der. of *2911;* to *precipitate down:*–cast down headlong.

2631. κατάκριμα *kat-ak'-ree-mah;* from *2632;* an *adverse sentence* (the verdict):–condemnation.

2632. κατακρίνω *kat-ak-ree'-no;* from *2596* and *2919;* to *judge against,* i.e. *sentence:*–condemn, damn.

2633. κατάκρισις *kat-ak'-ree-sis;* from *2632; sentencing adversely* (the act):–condemn(-ation).

2634. κατακυριεύω *kat-ak-oo-ree-yoo'-o*; from *2596* and *2961;* to *lord against,* i.e. *control, subjugate:*–exercise dominion over (lordship), be lord over, overcome.

2635. καταλαλέω *kat-al-al-eh'-o;* from *2637;* to *be a traducer,* i.e. to *slander:*–speak against (evil of).

2636. καταλαλία *kat-al-al-ee'-ah;* from *2637; defamation:*–backbiting, evil speaking.

2637. κατάλαλος *kat-al'-al-os;* from *2596* and the base of *2980; talkative against,* i.e. a *slanderer:*–backbiter.

2638. καταλαμβάνω *kat-al-am-ban'-o;* from *2596* and *2983;* to *take eagerly,* i.e. *seize, possess,* etc. (lit. or fig.):–apprehend, attain, come upon, comprehend, find, obtain, perceive, (over-)take.

2639. καταλέγω *kat-al-eg'-o;* from *2596* and *3004* (in its or. mean.); to *lay down,* i.e. (fig.) to *enrol:*–take into the number.

2640. κατάλειμμα *kat-al'-ime-mah;* from *2641;* a *remainder,* i.e. (by impl.) a *few:*–remnant.

2641. καταλείπω *kat-al-i'-po;* from *2596* and *3007;* to *leave down,* i.e. *behind;* by impl. to *abandon, have remaining:*–forsake, leave, reserve.

2642. καταλιθάζω *kat-al-ith-ad'-zo;* from *2596* and *3034;* to *stone down,* i.e. to *death:*–stone.

2643. καταλλαγή *kat-al-lag-ay';* from *2644; exchange* (fig. *adjustment*), i.e. *restoration* to (the divine) favor:–atonement, reconciliation(-ing).

2644. καταλλάσσω *kat-al-las'-so;* from *2596* and *236;* to *change mutually,* i.e. (fig.) to *com.* a difference:–reconcile.

2645. κατάλοιπος *kat-al'-oy-pos;* from *2596* and *3062; left down* (*behind*), i.e *remaining* (pl. the *rest*):–residue.

2646. κατάλυμα *kat-al'-oo-mah;* from *2647;* prop. a *dissolution* (breaking up of a journey), i.e. (by impl.) a *lodging-place:*–guestchamber, inn.

2647. καταλύω *kat-al-oo'-o;* from *2596* and *3089;* to *loosen down* (*disintegrate*), i.e. (by impl.) to *demolish* (lit. or fig.); spec. [comp. *2646*] to *halt* for the night:–destroy, dissolve, be guest, lodge, come to nought, overthrow, throw down.

2648. καταμανθάνω *kat-am-an-than'-o;* from *2596* and *3129;* to *learn thoroughly,* i.e. (by impl.) to *note carefully:*–consider.

2649. καταμαρτυρέω *kat-am-ar-too-reh'-o;* from *2596* and *3140;* to *testify against:*–witness against.

2650. καταμένω *kat-am-en'-o;* from *2596* and *3306;* to *stay fully,* i.e. *reside:*–abide.

2651. καταμόνας *kat-am-on'-as;* from *2596* and acc. pl. fem. of *3441* (with *5561* implied); *according to sole* places, i.e. (adv.) *separately:*–alone.

2652. κατανάθεμα *kat-an-ath'-em-ah;* from *2596* (intens.) and *331;* an *imprecation:*–curse.

2653. καταναθεματίζω *kat-an-ath-em-at-id'-zo;* from *2596* (intens.) and *332;* to *imprecate:*–curse.

2654. καταναλίσκω *kat-an-al-is'-ko;* from *2596* and *355;* to *consume utterly:*–consume.

2655. καταναρκάω *kat-an-ar-kah'-o;* from *2596* and ναρκάω (to *be numb*); to *grow utterly torpid,* i.e. (by impl.) *slothful* (fig. *expensive*):–be burdensome (chargeable).

2656. κατανεύω *kat-an-yoo'-o;* from *2596* and *3506;* to *nod down* (*towards*), i.e. (by anal.) to *make signs* to:–beckon.

2657. κατανοέω *kat-an-o-eh'-o;* from *2596* and *3539;* to *observe fully:*–behold, consider, discover, perceive.

2658. καταντάω *kat-an-tah'-o;* from *2596* and a der. of *473;* to *meet against,* i.e. *arrive* at (lit. or fig.):–attain, come.

2659. κατάνυξις *kat-an'-oox-is;* from *2660;* a *prickling* (sensation, as of the limbs *asleep*), i.e. (by impl. [perh. by some confusion with *3506* or even with *3571*]) *stupor* (*lethargy*):–slumber.

2660. κατανύσσω *kat-an-oos'-so;* from *2596* and *3572;* to *pierce thoroughly,* i.e. (fig.) to *agitate* violently ("sting to the quick"):–prick.

2661. καταξιόω *kat-ax-ee-o'-o;* from *2596* and *515;* to *deem entirely deserving:*–(ac-) count worthy.

2662. καταπατέω *kat-ap-at-eh'-o;* from *2596* and *3961;* to *trample down;* fig. to *reject* with disdain:–trample, tread (down, underfoot).

2663. κατάπαυσις *kat-ap'-ow-sis;* from *2664;* *reposing down,* i.e. (by Heb.) *abode:*–rest.

2664. καταπαύω *kat-ap-ow'-o;* from *2596* and *3973;* to *settle down,* i.e. (lit.) to *colonize,* or (fig.) to (*cause to*) *desist:*–cease, (give) rest(-rain).

2665. καταπέτασμα *kat-ap-et'-as-mah;* from a comp. of *2596* and a congener of *4072;* something *spread thoroughly,* i.e. (spec.) the door *screen* (to the Most Holy Place) in the Jewish Temple:–vail.

2666. καταπίνω *kat-ap-ee'-no;* from *2596* and *4095;* to *drink down,* i.e. *gulp entire* (lit. or fig.):–devour, drown, swallow (up).

2667. καταπίπτω *kat-ap-ip'-to;* from *2596* and *4098;* to *fall down:*–fall (down).

2668. καταπλέω *kat-ap-leh'-o;* from *2596* and *4126;* to *sail down* upon a place, i.e. to *land* at:–arrive.

2669. καταπονέω *kat-ap-on-eh'-o;* from *2596* and a der. of *4192;* to *labor down,* i.e. *wear with toil* (fig. *harass*):–oppress, vex.

2670. καταποντίζω *kat-ap-on-tid'-zo;* from *2596* and a der. of the same as *4195;* to *plunge down,* i.e. *submerge:*–drown, sink.

2671. κατάρα *kat-ar'-ah;* from *2596* (intens.) and *685; imprecation, execration:*–curse(-d, ing).

2672. καταράομαι *kat-ar-ah'-om-ahee;* mid. from *2671;* to *execrate;* by anal. to *doom:*–curse.

2673. καταργέω *kat-arg-eh'-o;* from *2596* and *691;* to *be* (*render*) *entirely idle* (*useless*), lit. or fig.:–abolish, cease, cumber, deliver, destroy, do away, become (make) of no (none, without) effect, fail, loose, bring (come) to nought, put away (down), vanish away, make void.

2674. καταριθμέω *kat-ar-ith-meh'-o;* from *2596* and *705;* to *reckon among:*–number with.

2675. καταρτίζω *kat-ar-tid'-zo;* from *2596* and a der. of *739;* to *complete thoroughly,* i.e. *repair* (lit. or fig.) or *adjust:*–fit, frame, mend, (make) perfect(-ly join together), prepare, restore.

2676. κατάρτισις *kat-ar'-tis-is;* from *2675;* *thorough equipment* (subj.):–perfection.

2677. καταρτισμός, *kat-ar-tis-mos';* from *2675; complete furnishing* (obj.):–perfecting.

2678. κατασείω *kat-as-i'-o;* from *2596* and *4579;* to *sway downward,* i.e. *make a signal:*–beckon.

2679. κατασκάπτω *kat-as-kap'-to;* from *2596* and *4626;* to *undermine,* i.e. (by impl.) *destroy:*–dig down, ruin.

2680 κατασκευάζω *kat-ask-yoo-ad'-zo;* from *2596* and a der. of *4632;* to *prepare thoroughly* (prop. by exter. *equipment;* whereas *2090* refers rather to internal *fitness*); by impl. to *construct, create:*–build, make, ordain, prepare.

2681. κατασκηνόω *kat-as-kay-no'-o;* from *2596* and *4637;* to *camp down,* i.e. *haunt;* fig. to *remain:*–lodge, rest.

2682. κατασκήνωσις *kat-as-kay'-no-sis;* from *2681;* an *encamping,* i.e. (fig.) a *perch:*–nest.

2683. κατασκιάζω *kat-as-kee-ad'-zo;* from *2596* and a der. of *4639;* to *overshade,* i.e. *cover:*–shadow.

2684. κατασκοπέω *kat-as-kop-eh'-o;* from *2685;* to *be a sentinel,* i.e. to *inspect* insidiously:–spy out.

2685. κατάσκοπος *kat-as'-kop-os;* from *2596* (intens.) and *4649* (in the sense of a *watcher*); a *reconnoiterer:*–spy.

2686. κατασοφίζομαι *kat-as-of-id'-zom-ahee;* mid. from *2596* and *4679;* to *be crafty against,* i.e. *circumvent:*–deal subtilly with.

2687. καταστέλλω *kat-as-tel'-lo;* from *2596* and *4724;* to *put down,* i.e. *quell:*–appease, quiet.

2688. κατάστημα *kat-as'-tay-mah;* from *2525;* prop. a *position* or *condition,* i.e. (subj.) *demeanor:*–behaviour.

2689. καταστολή *kat-as-tol-ay';* from *2687;* a *deposit,* i.e. (spec.) *costume:*–apparel.

2690. καταστρέφω *kat-as-tref'-o;* from *2596* and *4762;* to *turn upside down*, i.e. *upset:*–overthrow.

2691. καταστρηνιάω *kat-as-tray-nee-ah'-o;* from *2596* and *4763;* to *become voluptuous against:*–begin to wax wanton against.

2692. καταστροφή *kat-as-trof-ay';* from *2690;* an *overturn* ("*catastrophe*"), i.e. *demolition;* fig. *apostasy:*–overthrow, subverting.

2693. καταστρώννυμι *kat-as-trone'-noo-mee;* from *2596* and *4766;* to *strew down,* i.e. (by impl.) to *prostrate* (*slay*):–overthrow.

2694. κατασύρω *kat-as-oo'-ro;* from *2596* and *4951;* to *drag down,* i.e. *arrest* judicially:–hale.

2695. κατασφάττω *kat-as-fat'-to;* from *2596* and *4969;* to *kill down,* i.e. *slaughter:*–slay.

2696. κατασφραγίζω *kat-as-frag-id'-zo;* from *2596* and *4972;* to *seal closely:*–seal.

2697. κατάσχεσις *kat-as'-khes-is;* from *2722;* a *holding down,* i.e. *occupancy:*–possession.

2698. κατατίθημι *kat-at-ith'-ay-mee;* from *2596* and *5087;* to *place down*, i.e. *deposit* (lit. or fig.):–do, lay, shew.

2699. κατατομή *kat-at-om-ay';* from a com. of *2596* and τέμνω (to *cut*); a *cutting down* (*off*), i.e. *mutilation* (ironically):–concision. Comp. *609*.

2700. κατατοξεύω *kat-at-ox-yoo'-o;* from *2596* and a der. of *5115;* to *shoot down* with an arrow or other missile:–thrust through.

2701. κατατρέχω *kat-at-rekh'-o;* from *2596* and *5143;* to *run down,* i.e. *hasten* from a tower:–run down.

2702. καταφέρω *kat-af-er'-o;* from *2596* and *5342* (incl. its alt.); to *bear down,* i.e. (fig.) *overcome* (with drowsiness); spec. to *cast* a vote:–fall, give, sink down.

2703. καταφεύγω *kat-af-yoo'-go;* from *2596* and *5343;* to *flee down* (*away*):–flee.

2704. καταφθείρω *kat-af-thi'-ro;* from *2596* and *5351;* to *spoil entirely,* i.e. (lit.) to *destroy;* or (fig.) to *deprave:*–corrupt, utterly perish.

2705. καταφιλέω *kat-af-ee-leh'-o;* from *2596* and *5368;* to *kiss earnestly:*–kiss.

2706. καταφρονέω *kat-af-ron-eh'-o;* from *2596* and *5426;* to *think against,* i.e. *disesteem:*–despise.

2707. καταφροντής *kat-af-ron-tace';* from *2706;* a *contemner:*–despiser.

2708. καταχέω *kat-akh-eh'-o;* from *2596* and χέω (to *pour*); to *pour down* (*out*):–pour.

2709. καταχθόνιος *kat-akh-thon'-ee-os;* from *2596* and χθών (the *ground*); *subterranean,* i.e. *infernal* (belonging to the world of departed spirits):–under the earth.

2710. καταχράομαι *kat-akh-rah'-om-ahee;* from *2596* and *5530;* to *overuse,* i.e. *misuse:*–abuse.

2711. καταψύχω *kat-ap-soo'-kho;* from *2596* and *5594;* to *cool down* (*off*), i.e. *refresh:*–cool.

2712. κατείδωλος *kat-i'-do-los;* from *2596* (intens.) and *1497; utterly idolatrous:*–wholly given to idolatry.

2713. κατέναντι *kat-en'-an-tee;* from *2596* and *1725; dir. opposite:*–before, over against.

2714. κατενώπιον *kat-en-o'-pee-on;* from *2596* and *1799; dir. in front of:*–before (the presence of), in the sight of.

2715. κατεξουσιάζω *kat-ex-oo-see-ad'-zo;* from *2596* and *1850;* to *have* (*wield*) *full privilege over:*–exercise authority.

2716. κατεργάζομαι *kat-er-gad'-zom-ahee;* from *2596* and *2038;* to *work fully*, i.e. *accomplish;* by impl. to *finish, fashion:*–cause, to (deed), perform, work (out).

2718. κατέρχομαι *kat-er'-khom-ahee;* from *2596* and *2064* (incl. its alt.); to *come* (or *go*) *down* (lit. or fig.):–come (down), depart, descend, go down, land.

2719. κατεσθίω *kat-es-thee'-o;* from *2596* and *2068* (incl. its alt.); to *eat down,* i.e. *devour* (lit. or fig.):–devour.

2720. κατευθύνω *kat-yoo-thoo'-no;* from *2596* and *2116;* to *straighten fully,* i.e. (fig.) *dir.:*–guide, dir.

2721. κατεφίστημι *kat-ef-is'-tay-mee;* from *2596* and *2186;* to *stand over against,* i.e. *rush upon* (*assault*):–make insurrection against.

2722. κατέχω *kat-ekh'-o;* from *2596* and *2192;* to *hold down* (*fast*), in various appl. (lit. or fig.):–have, hold (fast), keep (in memory), let, X make toward, possess, retain, seize on, stay, take, withhold.

2723. κατηγορέω *kat-ay-gor-eh'-o;* from *2725;* to *be a plaintiff,* i.e. to *charge* with some offence:–accuse, object.

2724. κατηγορία *kat-ay-gor-ee'-ah;* from *2725;* a *complaint* ("category"), i.e. criminal *charge:*–accusation (X -ed).

2725. κατήγορος *kat-ay'-gor-os;* from *2596* and *58;* *against* one in the *assembly,* i.e. a *complainant* at law; spec. *Satan:*–accuser.

2726. κατήφεια *kat-ay'-fi-ah;* from a comp. of *2596* and perh. a der. of the base of *5316* (mean. *downcast* in look); *demureness,* i.e. (by impl.) *sadness:*–heaviness.

2727. κατηχέω *kat-ay-kheh'-o;* from *2596* and *2279;* to *sound down* into the ears, i.e. (by impl.) to *indoctrinate* ("catechize") or (gen. case) to *apprise* of:–inform, instruct, teach.

2728. κατιόω *kat-ee-o'-o;* from *2596* and a der. of *2447;* to *rust down,* i.e. *corrode:*–canker.

2729. κατισχύω *kat-is-khoo'-o;* from *2596* and *2480;* to *overpower:*–prevail (against).

2730. κατοικέω, *kat-oy-keh'-o;* from *2596* and *3611;* to *house permanently,* i.e. *reside* (lit. or fig.):–dwell(-er), inh.(-ter).

2731. κατοίκησις *kat-oy'-kay-sis;* from *2730;* *residence* (prop. the act; but by impl. concr. the mansion):–dwelling.

2732. κατοικητήριον *kat-oy-kay-tay'-ree-on;* from a der. of *2730;* a *dwelling-place:*–habitation

2733. κατοικία *kat-oy-kee'-ah; residence* (prop. the condition; but by impl. the abode itself):–habitation.

2734. κατοπτρίζομαι *kat-op-trid'-zom-ahee;* mid. from a comp. of *2596* and a der. of *3700* [comp. *2072*]; *to mirror oneself,* i.e. to *see reflected* (fig.):–behold as in a glass.

2735. κατόρθωμα *kat-or'-tho-mah;* from a com. of *2596* and a der. of *3717* [comp. *1357*]; something *made fully upright,* i.e. (fig.) *rectification* (spec. *good* public *administration*):–very worthy deed.

2736. κάτω *kat'-o;* also (comp.) *kat-o-ter'-o* [comp. 2737]; adv. from *2596;* *downwards:*–beneath, bottom, down, under.

2737. κατώτερος *kat-o'-ter-os;* comp. from *2736;* *inferior* (locally, of Hades):–lower.

2738. καῦμα *kow'-mah;* from *2545;* prop. a *burn* (concr.), but used (abstr.) of a *glow:*–heat.

2739. καυματίζω *kow-mat-id'-zo;* from *2738;* to *burn:*–scorch.

2740. καῦσις *kow'-sis;* from *2545;* *burning* (the act):–be burned.

2741. καυσόω *kow-so'-o;* from *2740;* to *set on fire:*–with fervent heat.

2742. καύσων *kow'-sone;* from *2741;* a *glare:*–(burning) heat.

2743. καυτηριάζω *kow-tay-ree-ad'-zo;* from a der. of *2545;* to *brand* ("*cauterize*"), i.e. (by impl.) to *render unsensitive* (fig.):–sear with a hot iron.

2744. καυχάομαι *kow-khah'-om-ahee;* from some (obs.) base akin to that of αὐχέω (to *boast*) and *2172;* to *vaunt* (in a good or a bad sense):–(make) boast, glory, joy, rejoice.

2745. καύχημα *kow'-khay-mah;* from *2744;* a *boast* (prop. the object; by impl. the act) in a good or a bad sense:–boasting, (whereof) to glory (of), glorying, rejoice(-ing).

2746. καύχησις *kow'-khay-sis;* from *2744;* *boasting* (prop. the act; by impl. the object), in a good or a bad sense:–boasting, whereof I may glory, glorying, rejoicing.

2747. Κεγχρεαί *keng-khreh-a'-hee;* prob. from κέγχρος (*millet*); *Cenchreae,* a port of Corinth:–Cencrea.

2748. Κεδρών *ked-rone';* of Heb. or. [6939]; *Cedron* (i.e. *Kidron*), a brook near Jerus.:–Cedron.

2749. κεῖμαι *ki'-mahee;* mid. of a prim. verb; to *lie* outstretched (lit. or fig.):–be (appointed, laid up, made, set), lay, lie. Comp. *5087.*

2750. κειρία *ki-ree'-ah;* of unc. affin.; a *swathe,* i.e. *winding-sheet:*–graveclothes.

2751. κείρω *ki'-ro;* a prim. verb; to *shear:*–shear(-er).

2752. κέλευμα *kel'-yoo-mah;* from *2753;* a *cry* of incitement:–shout.

2753. κελεύω *kel-yoo'-o;* from a prim. κέλλω (to *urge* on); "hail"; to *incite* by word, i.e. *order:*–bid, (at, give) command(-ment).

2754. κενοδοξία *ken-od-ox-ee'-ah;* from *2755;* *empty glorying,* i.e. *self-conceit:*–vain-glory.

2755. κενόδοξος *ken-od'-ox-os;* from *2756* and *1391;* *vainly glorifying,* i.e. *self-conceited:*–desirous of vain-glory.

2756. κενός *ken-os';* app. a prim.word; *empty* (lit. or fig.):–empty, (in) vain.

2757. κενοφωνία, *ken-of-o-nee'-ah;* from a presumed com. of *2756* and *5456;* *empty sounding,* i.e. *fruitless discussion:*–vain.

2758. κενόω *ken-o'-o;* from *2756*; to *make empty,* i.e. (fig.) to *abase, neutralize, falsify:*–make (of none effect, of no reputation, void), be in vain.

2759. κέντρον *ken'-tron;'* from κεντέω (to *prick*); a *point* ("centre"), i.e. a *sting* (fig. *poison*) or *goad* (fig. divine *impulse*):–prick, sting.

2760. κεντυρίων *ken-too-ree'-ohn;* of Lat. or.; a *centurion,* i.e. *captain* of one hundred soldiers:–centurion.

2761. κενῶς *ken-oce';* adv. from *2756;* *vainly,* i.e. *to no purpose:*–in vain.

2762. κεραία *ker-ah'-yah;* fem. of a presumed der. of the base of *2768;* something *horn-like,* i.e. (spec.) the *apex* of a Heb. letter (fig. the least *par.*):–tittle.

2763. κεραμεύς *ker-am-yooce';* from *2766;* a *potter:*–potter.

2764. κεραμικός *ker-am-ik-os';* from *2766;* *made of clay,* i.e. *earthen:*–of a potter.

2765. κεράμιον *ker-am'-ee-on;* neut. of a presumed der. of *2766;* an *earthenware* vessel, i.e. *jar:*–pitcher.

2766. κέραμος *ker'-am-os;* prob. from the base of *2767* (through the idea of *mixing* clay and water); *earthenware,* i.e. a *tile* (by anal. a *thin* roof or *awning*):–tiling.

2767. κεράννυμι *ker-an'-noo-mee;* prol. form of a more prim. κεράω *ker-ah'-o* (which is used in cert. tenses); to *mingle,* i.e. (by impl.) to *pour* out (for drinking):–fill, pour out. Comp. *3396.*

2768. κέρας *ker'-as;* from a prim. κάρ (the *hair* of the head); a *horn* (lit. or fig.):–horn.

2769. κεράτιον *ker-at'-ee-on;* neut. of a presumed der. of *2768;* something *horned,* i.e. (spec.) the *pod* of the carob-tree:–husk.

2770. κερδαίνω *ker-dah'-ee-no;* from *2771;* to *gain* (lit. or fig.):–(get) gain, win.

2771. κέρδος *ker'-dos;* of unc. affin.; *gain* (pecuniary or gen. case):–gain, lucre.

2772. κέρμα, *ker'-mah;* from *2751;* a *clipping* (*bit*), i.e. (spec.) a *coin:*–money.

2773. κερματιστής *ker-mat-is-tace';* from a der. of *2772;* a *handler of coins,* i.e. *money-broker:*–changer of money.

2774. κεφάλαιον *kef-al'-ah-yon;* neut. of a der. of *2776;* a *principal* thing, i.e. *main point;* spec. an *amount* (of money):–sum.

2775. κεφαλαιόω *kef-al-ahee-o'-o;* from the same as *2774;* (spec.) to *strike on the head:*–wound in the head.

2776. κεφαλή *kef-al-ay';* from the prim. κάπτω (in the sense of *seizing*); the *head* (as the part most readily *taken* hold of), lit. or fig.:–head.

2777. κεφαλίς *kef-al-is';* from *2776;* prop. a *knob,* i.e. (by impl.) a *roll* (by ext. from the *end* of a stick on which the manuscript was rolled):–volume.

2778. κῆσος *kane'-sos;* of Lat. or.; prop. an *enrollment* ("*census*"), i.e. (by impl.) a *tax:*–tribute.

2779. κῆπος *kay'-pos;* of unc. affin.; a *garden:*–garden.

2780. κηπουρός *kay-poo-ros;* from *2779* and οὖρος (a *warden*); a *garden-keeper,* i.e. *gardener:*–gardener.

2781. κηρίον *kay-ree'-on;* dim. from κηός (*wax*); a *cell* for honey, i.e. (coll.) the *comb:*–[honey-]comb.

2782. κήρυγμα *kay'-roog-mah;* from *2784;* a *proclamation* (esp. of the gospel; by impl. the *gospel* itself):–preaching.

2783. κήρυξ *kay'-roox;* from *2784;* a *herald,* i.e. of divine truth (esp. of the gospel):–preacher.

2784. κηρύσσω *kay-roos'-so;* of unc. affin.; to *herald* (as a public *crier*), esp. divine truth (the gospel):–preacher(-er), proclaim, publish.

2785. κῆτος *kay'-tos;* prob. from the base of *5490;* a huge *fish* (as *gaping* for prey):–whale.

2786. Κηφᾶς, *kay-fas';* of Chald. or. [comp. 3710]; *the Rock; Cephas* (i.e. *Kepha*), a surname of Peter:–Cephas.

2787. κιβωτός *kib-o-tos';* of unc. der.; a *box,* i.e. the sacred *ark* and that of Noah:–ark.

2788. κιθάρα *kith-ar'-ah;* of unc. affin.; a *lyre:*–harp.

2789. κιθαρίζω *kith-ar-id'-zo;* from *2788;* to *play on a lyre:*–harp.

2790. κιθαρῳδός *kith-ar-o'-dos;* from *2788* and a der. of the same as *5603;* a *lyre-singer(-player)*, i.e. *harpist:*–harper.
2791. Κιλικία *kil-ik-ee'-ah;* prob. of for. or.; *Cilicia,* a region of Asia Minor:–Cilicia.
2792. κινάμωμον *kin-am'-o-mon;* of for. or. [comp. 7076;] *cinnamon:*–cinnamon.
2793. κινδυνέυω *kin-doon-yoo'-o;* from *2794*; to *undergo peril:*–be in danger, be (stand) in jeopardy.
2794. κίνδυνος *kin'-doo-nos;* of unc. der.; *danger:*–peril.
2795. κινέω *kin-eh'-o;* from κίω (poetic for εἶμι to *go*); to *stir* (trans.), lit. or fig.:–(re-) move(-r), way.
2796. κίνησις *kin'-ay-sis;* from *2795;* a *stirring:*–moving.
2797. Κίς, *kis;* of Heb. or. [7027]; *Cis* (i.e. *Kish*), an Isr.:–Cis.
2798. κλάδος *klad'-os;* from *2806;* a *twig* or *bough* (as if broken off):– branch.
2799. κλαίω *klah'-yo;* of unc. affin.; to *sob,* i.e. *wail* aloud (whereas *1145* is rather to *cry* silently):–bewail, weep.
2800. κλάσις *klas'-is;* from *2806; fracture* (the act):–breaking.
2801. κλάσμα *klas'-mah;* from *2806;* a *piece* (*bit*):–broken, fragment.
2802. Κλαύδη *klow'-day;* of unc. der.; *Claude,* an island near Crete:–Clauda.
2803. Κλαυδία *klow-dee'-ah;* fem. of *2804; Claudia,* a Chr. woman:–Claudia.
2804. Κλαύδιος *klow'-dee-os;* of Lat. or.; *Claudius,* the name of two Romans:–Claudius.
2805. κλαυθμός *klowth-mos';* from *2799; lamentation:*–wailing, weeping, X wept.
2806. κλάω *klah'-o;* a prim. verb; to *break* (spec. of bread):–break.
2807. κλείς *klice;* from *2808;* a *key* (as *shutting* a lock), lit. or fig.:–key.
2808. κλείω *kli'-o;* a prim. verb; to *close* (lit. or fig.):–shut (up).
2809. κλέμμα *klem'-mah;* from *2813; stealing* (prop. the thing stolen, but used of the act):–theft.
2810. Κλεόπας *kleh-op'-as;* prob. contr. from Κλεόπατρος (com. of *2811* and *3962*); *Cleopas,* a Chr.:–Cleopas.
2811. κλέος *kleh'-os;* from a short. form of *2564; renown* (as if *being called*):–glory.
2812. κλέπτης *klep'-tace;* from *2813;* a *stealer* (lit. or fig.):–thief. Comp. *3027.*
2813. κλέπτω *klep'-to;* a prim. verb; to *filch:*–steal.
2814. κλῆμα *kaly'-mah;* from *2806;* a *limb* or *shoot* (as if *broken* off):–branch.
2815. Κλήμης *klay'-mace* of Lat. or.; *merciful; Clemes* (i.e. *Clemens*), a Chr.:–Clement.
2816. κληρονομέω *klay-ron-om-eh'-o;* from *2818;* to *be* an *heir* to (lit. or fig.):–be heir, (obtain by) inherit(-ance).
2817. κληρονομία *klay-ron-om-ee'-ah;* from *2818; heirship,* i.e. (concr.) a *patrimony* or (gen. case) a *possession:*–inheritance.
2818. κληρονόμος *klay-ron-om'-os;* from *2819* and the base of *3551* (in its or. sense of *partitioning,* i.e. (refl.) *getting* by apportionment); a *sharer by lot,* i.e. *inheritor* (lit. or fig.); by impl. a *possessor:*–heir.
2819. κλῆρος *klay'-ros;* prob. from *2806* (through the idea of using *bits* of wood, etc., for the purpose; a *die* (for drawing chances); by impl. a *portion* (as if so secured); by ext., an *acquisition* (esp. a *patrimony,* fig.):–heritage, inheritance, lot, part.
2820. κληρόω *klay-ro-o;* from *2819;* to *allot,* i.e. (fig.) to *assign* (a privilege):–obtain an inheritance.
2821. κλσις *klay'-sis;* from a short. form of *2564;* an *invitation* (fig.):–calling.
2822. κλητός *klay-tos'* from the same as *2821; invited,* i.e. *appointed,* or (spec.), a *saint:*–called.
2823. κλίβανος *klib'-an-os;* of unc. der.; an earthen *pot* used for baking in:–oven.
2824. κλίμα *klee'-mah;* from *2827;* a *slope,* i.e. (spec.) a "*clime*" or *tract* of country:–part, region.
2825. κλίνη *klee'-nay;* from *2827;* a *couch* (for sleep, sickness, sitting or eating):–bed, table.
2826. κλινίδιον *klin-id'-ee-on;* neut. of a presumed der. of *2825;* a *pallet* or *little couch:*–bed.
2827. κλίνω *klee'-no;* a prim. verb; to *slant* or *slope,* i.e. *incline* or *recline* (lit. or fig.):–bow (down), be far spent, lay, turn to flight, wear away.
2828. κλισία *klee-see'-ah;* from a der. of *2827;* prop. *reclination,* i.e. (concr. and spec.), a *party* at a meal:–company.
2829. κλοπή *klop-ay';* from *2813; stealing:*–theft.
2830. κλύδων *kloo'-dohn;* from κλύζω (to *billow* or *dash* over); a *surge* of the sea (lit. or fig.):–raging, wave.
2831. κλυδωνίζομαι *kloo-do-nid'-zom-ahee;* mid. from *2830;* to *surge,* i.e. (fig.) to *fluctuate:*–toss to and fro.
2832. Κλωπᾶς *klo-pas';* of Chald. or. (cor. to *256*); *Clopas,* an Isr.:–Cleophas.
2833. κνήθω *knay'-tho;* from a prim. κνᾶω (to *scrape*); to *scratch,* i.e. (by impl.) to *tickle:*–X itching.
2834. Κνίδος *knee'-dos;* prob. of for. or.; *Cnidus,* a place in Asia Minor:–Cnidus.
2835. κοδράντης *kod-ran'-tace;* of Lat. or.; a *quadrans,* i.e. the fourth part of an as:–farthing.
2836. κοιλία *koy-lee'-ah;* from κοῖλο ("*hollow*"); a *cavity,* i.e. (esp.) the *abdomen;* by impl. the *matrix;* fig. the *heart:*–belly, womb.
2837. κοιμάω *koy-mah'-o;* from *2749;* to *put to sleep,* i.e. (pass. or refl.) to *slumber;* fig. to *decease:*–(be a-, fall a-, fall on) sleep, be dead.
2838. κοίμησις *koy'-may-sis;* from *2837; sleeping,* i.e. (by impl.) *repose:*–taking of rest.
2839. κοινός *koy-nos';* prob. from *4862; common,* i.e. (lit.) shared by all or several, or (cer.) *profane:*–common, defiled, un-clean, unholy.
2840. κοινόω *koy-no'-o;* from *2839;* to *make* (or *consider*) *profane* (cer.):–call common, defile, pollute, unclean.
2841. κοινωνέω *koy-no-neh'-o;* from *2844;* to *share* with others (obj. or subj.):–communicate, distribute, be partaker.
2842. κοινωνία *koy-nohn-ee'-ah;* from *2844; partnership,* i.e. (lit.) *participation,* or (social) *intercourse,* or (pecuniary) *benefaction:*–(to) communicate(-ation), communion, (contri-) distribution, fellowship.
2843. κοινωνικός *koy-no-nee-kos';* from *2844; communicative,* i.e. (pecuniarily) *liberal:*–willing to communicate.
2844. κοινωνός *koy-no-nos';* from *2839;* a *sharer,* i.e. *associate:*–companion, X fellowship, partaker, partner.
2845. κοίτη *koy'-tay;* from *2749;* a *couch;* by ext., *cohabitation;* by impl. the male *sperm:*–bed, chambering, X conceive.
2846. κοιτών *koy-tone';* from *2845;* a *bedroom:*–+ chamberlain.
2847. κόκκινος *kok'-kee-nos;* from *2848* (from the *kernel*-shape of the insect); *crimson*-colored:–scarlet (colour, coloured).
2848. κόκκος, *kok'-kos;* app. a prim. word; a *kernel* of seed:–corn, grain.
2849. κολάζω *kol-ad'-zo;* from κόλος (*dwarf*); prop. to *curtail,* i.e. (fig.) to *chastise* (or *reserve* for infliction):–punish.
2850. κολακεία *kol-ak-i'-ah;* from a der. of κόλαξ (a *fawner*); *flattery:*–X flattering.
2851. κόλασις *kol'-as-is;* from 2849; penal *infliction:*–punishment, torment.
2852. κολαφίζω *kol-af-id'-zo;* from a der. of the base of *2849;* to *rap* with the fist:–buffet.
2853. κολλάω *kol-lah'-o;* from κόλλα ("*glue*"); to *glue,* i.e. (pass. or refl.) to *stick* (fig.):–cleave, join (self), keep company.
2854. κολλούριον *kol-loo'-ree-on;* neut. of a presumed der. of κολλύρα (a *cake;* prob akin to the base of *2853*); prop. a *poultice* (as made of or in the form of *crackers*), i.e. (by anal.) a *plaster:*– eyesalve.
2855. κολλυβιστής *kol-loo-bis-tace';* from a presumed der. of κόλλυβος (a small *coin;* prob. akin to *2854*); a *coin-dealer:*–(money-) changer.
2856. κολοβόω *kol-ob-o'-o;* from a der. of the base of *2849;* to *dock,* i.e. (fig.) *abridge:*–shorten.
2857. Κολοσσαί *kol-os-sah'-ee;* app. or. pl. of κολοσσοός ("*colossal*"); *Colossae,* a place in Asia Minor:–Colosse.
2858. Κολοσσαεύς *kol-os-sayoos';* from *2857;* a *Colossaean,* i.e. inh. of Colossae:–Colossian.
2859. κόλπος *kol'-pos;* app. a prim. word; the *bosom;* by anal. a *bay:*–bosom, creek.
2860. κολυμβάω *kol-oom-bah'-o;* from κόλυμβος (a *diver*); to *plunge* into water:–swim.
2861. κολυμβήθρα *kol-oom-bay'-thrah;*

from *2860* a *diving-place,* i.e. *pond* for bathing (or swimming):–pool.

2862. κολωνία *kol-o-nee'-ah;* of Lat. or.; a Rom. "*colony*" for veterans:–colony.

2863. κομάω *kom-ah'-o;* from 2864; to wear *tresses* of hair:–have long hair.

2864. κόμη *kom'-ay;* app. from the same as *2865;* the *hair* of the head (*locks,* as *ornamental,* and thus differing from *2359;* which prop. denotes merely the *scalp*):–hair.

2865. κομίζω *kom-id'-zo;* from a prim. κομέω (to *tend,* i.e. take care of); prop. to *provide* for, i.e. (by impl.) to *carry* off (as if from harm; gen. case *obtain*):–bring, receive.

2866. κομψότερον *komp-sot'-er-on;* neut. comp. of a der. of the base of *2865* (mean. prop. *well dressed,* i.e. *nice*); fig. *convalescent:*–+ began to amend.

2867. κονιάω *kon-ee-ah'-o;* from κονία (*dust;* by anal. *lime*); to *whitewash:*–whiten.

2868. κονιορτός *kon-ee-or-tos';* from the base of *2867* and ὄρνμι (to "*rouse*"); *pulverulence* (as *blown* about):–dust.

2869. κοπάζω *kop-ad'-zo;* from *2873;* to *tire,* i.e. (fig.) to *relax:*–cease.

2870. κοπετός *kop-et-os';* from 2875; *mourning* (prop. by *beating* the breast):–lamentation.

2871. κοπή *kop-ay';* from *2875; cutting,* i.e. *carnage:*–slaughter.

2872. κοπιάω *kop-ee-ah'-o* from a der. of *2873;* to *feel fatigue;* by impl. to *work hard:*–(bestow) labour, toil, be wearied.

2873. κόπος *kop'-os;* from *2875;* a *cut,* i.e. (by anal.) *toil* (as *reducing* the strength), lit. or fig.; by impl. *pains:*–labour, + trouble, weariness.

2874. κοπρία *kop-ree'-ah;* from κόπρος (*ordure;* perh. akin to *2875*); *manure:*–dung(-hill).

2875. κόπτω *kop'-to;* a prim. verb; to "*chop*"; spec. to *beat* the breast in grief:–cut down, lament, mourn, (be-)wail. Comp. the base of *5114*.

2876. κόραξ *kor'-ax;* perh. from *2880;* a *crow* (from its *voracity*):–raven.

2877. κοράσιον *kor-as'-ee-on;* neut. of a presumed der. of κόρη (a *maiden*); a (little) *girl:*–damsel, maid.

2878. κορβᾶν *kor-ban';* and κορβανᾶς *kor-ban-as';* of Heb. and Chald. or. respectively [7133]; a votive *offering* and the *offering;* a *consecrated present* (to the Temple fund); by ext. (the latter term) the *Treasury* itself, i.e. the room where the contribution boxes stood:–Corban, treasury.

2879. Κορέ *kor-eh';* of Heb. or. [7141]; *Corè* (i.e. *Korach*), an Isr.:–Core.

2880. κορέννυμι *kor-en'-noo-mee;* a prim. verb; to *cram,* i.e. *glut* or *sate:*–eat enough, full.

2881. Κορίνθιος *kor-in'-thee-os;* from *2882;* a *Corinthian,* i.e. inh. of Corinth:–Corinthian.

2882. Κόρινθος *kor'-in-thos;* of unc. der.; *Corinthus,* a city of Greece:–Corinth.

2883. Κορνήλιος *kor-nay'-lee-os* of Lat. or.; *Cornelius,* a Rom.:–Cornelius.

2884. κόρος *kor'-os;* of Heb. or. [3734]; a *cor,*i.e. a specific measure:–measure.

2885. κοσμέω *kos-meh'-o;* from *2889;* to *put in* proper *order,* i.e. *decorate* (lit. or fig.); spec. to *snuff* (a wick):–adorn, garnish, trim.

2886. κοσμικός *kos-mee-kos';* from *2889* (in its sec. sense); *terrene* ("*cosmic*"), lit. (*mundane*) or fig. (*corrupt*):–worldly.

2887. κόσμιος *kos'-mee-os;* from *2889* (in its prim. sense); *orderly,* i.e. *decorous:*–of good behaviour, modest.

2888. κοσμοκράτωρ *kos-mok-rat'-ore;* from *2889* and *2902;* a *world-ruler,* an epithet of Satan:–ruler.

2889. κόσμος *kos'-mos;* prob. from the base of *2865; orderly arrangement,* i.e. *decoration;* by impl. the *world* (in a wide or narrow sense, incl. its inh., lit. or fig. [mor.]):–adorning, world.

2890. Κούαρτος *koo'-ar-tos;* of Lat. or. (*fourth*); *Quartus,* a Chr.:–Quartus.

2891. κοῦμι *koo'-mee;* of Chald. or. [6966]; *cumi* (i.e. *rise!*):–cumi.

2892. κουστωδία *koos-to-dee'-ah;* of Lat. or.; "*custody*", i.e. a Rom. *sentry:*–watch.

2893. κουφίζω *koo-fid'-zo;* from κοῦφος (*light* in weight); to *unload:*–lighten.

2894. κόφινος *kof'-ee-nos;* of unc. der.; a (small) *basket:*–basket.

2895. κράββατος *krab'-bat-os;* prob. of for. or.; a *mattress:*–bed.

2896. κράζω *krad'-zo;* a prim. verb; prop. to "*croak*" (as a raven) or *scream,* i.e. (gen. case) to *call* aloud (*shriek, exclaim, intreat*):–cry (out).

2897. κραιπάλη *krahee-pal'-ay;* prob. from the same as *726;* prop. a *headache* (as a *seizure* of pain) from drunkenness, i.e. (by impl.) a *debauch* (by anal. a *glut*):–surfeiting.

2898. κρανίον *kran-ee'-on;* dim. of a der. of the base of *2768;* a *skull* ("*cranium*"):–Calvary, skull.

2899. κράσπεδον *kras'-ped-on;* of unc. der.; a *margin,* i.e. (spec.), a *fringe* or *tassel:*–border, hem.

2900. κραταιός *krat-ah-yos';* from *2904; powerful:*–mighty.

2901. κραταιόω *krat-ah-yo'-o;* from *2900;* to *empower,* i.e. pass. *Increase in vigor:*–be strengthened, be (wax) strong.

2902. κρατέω *krat-eh'-o ;* from *2904;* to *use strength,* i.e. *seize* or *retain* (lit. or fig.):–hold (by, fast), keep, lay hand (hold) on, obtain, retain, take (by).

2903. κράτιστος *krat'-is-tos;* sup. of a der. of *2904; strongest,* i.e. (in dignity) *very honorable:*–most excellent (noble).

2904. κράτος *krat'-os;* perh. a prim. word; *vigor* ["great"] (lit. or fig.):–dominion, might[-ily], power, strength

2905. κραυγάζω *krow-gad'-zo;* from *2906;* to *clamor:*–cry out.

2906. κραυγή *krow-gay';* from 2896; an *outcry* (in notification, tumult or grief):–clamour, cry(-ing).

2907. κρέας *kreh'-as;* perh. a prim. word; (butcher's) *meat:*–flesh.

2908. κρεῖσσον *krice'-son;* neut. of an alt. form of *2909;* (as noun) *better,* i.e. *greater advantage:*–better.

2909. κρειττων *krite'-tohn;* comp. of a der. of *2904; stronger,* i.e. (fig.) *better,* i.e. *nobler:*–best, better.

2910. κρεμάννυμι *krem-an'-noo-mee;* a prol. form of a prim. verb; to *hang:*–hang.

2911. κρημνός *krame-nos';* from *2910; overhanging,* i.e. a *precipice:*–steep place.

2912. Κρής *krace;* from *2914;* a *Cretan,* i.e. inh. of Crete:–Crete, Cretian.

2913. Κρήσκης *krace'-kace;* of Lat. or.; *growing; Cresces* (i.e. *Crescens*), a Chr.:–Crescens.

2914. Κρήτη *kray'-tay;* of unc. der.; *Cretè,* an island in the Mediterranean:–Crete.

2915. κριθή *kree-thay';* of unc. der.; *barley:*–barley.

2916. κρίθινος *kree'-thee-nos;* from *2915;* consisting of *barley:*–barley.

2917. κρίμα *kree'-mah;* from *2919;* a *decision* (the function or the effect, for or against ["crime"]):–avenge, condemned, condemnation, damnation, + go to law, judgment.

2918. κρίνον *kree'-non;* perh. a prim word; *a lily:*–lily.

2919. κρίνω *kree'-no;* prop. to *distinguish,* i.e. *decide* (ment. or judicially); by impl. to *try, condemn, punish:*–avenge, conclude, condemn, damn, decree, determine, esteem, judge, go to (sue at the) law, ordain, call in question, sentence to, think.

2920. κρίσις *kree'-sis;* decision (subj. or obj., for or against); by ext., a *tribunal;* by impl. *justice* (esp. divine *law*):–accusation, condemnation, damnation, judgment.

2921. Κρίσπος *kris'-pos;* of Lat. or.; "*crisp*"; *Crispus,* a Corinthian:–Crispus.

2922. κριτήριον *kree-tay'-ree-on;* neut. of a presumed der. of *2923;* a rule of judging ("*criterion*"), i.e. (by impl.) a *tribunal:*–to judge, judgment (seat).

2923. κριτής *kree-tace;* from *2919;* a *judge* (gen. case or spec.):–judge.

2924. κριτικός *krit-ee-kos';* from *2923; decisive* ("*critical*"), i.e. *discriminative:*–discerner.

2925. κρούω *kroo'-o;* app. a prim. verb; to *rap:*–knock.

2926. κρυπτή *kroop-tay';* fem. of *2927;* a *hidden* place, i.e. *cellar* ("*crypt*"):–secret.

2927. κρυπτός *kroop-tos';* from *2928; concealed,* i.e. *private:*–hid(-den), inward [-ly], secret.

2928. κρύπτω *kroop'-to;* a prim. verb;to *conceal* (prop. by *covering*):–hide (self), keep secret, secret[-ly].

2929. κρυσταλλίζω *kroos-tal-lid'-z;* from *2930;* to *make* (i.e. intr., *resemble*) *ice* ("crystallize"):–be clear as crystal.

2930. κρύσταλλος *kroos'-tal-los;* from a der. of κρύος (*frost*); *ice,* i.e. (by anal.) rock "*crystal*":–crystal.

2931. κρυφῆ *kroo-fay';* adv. from *2928; privately:*–in secret.

2932. κτάομαι *ktah'-om-ahee;* a prim. verb; to *get,* i.e. *acquire* (by any means; *own*):–obtain, possess, provide, purchase.

2933. κτῆμα *ktay'-mah;* from *2932;* an *acquirement,* i.e. *estate:*–possession.

2934. κτῆνος *ktay'-nos;* from *2932; property,* i.e. (spec.) a domestic *animal:*–beast.

2935. κτήτωρ *ktay'-tore;* from *2932;* an *owner:*–possessor.

2936. κτίζω *ktid'-zo;* prob. Akin to *2932* (through the idea of *proprietorship* of the *manufacturer*); to *fabricate,* i.e. *found* (*form* or.):–create, Creator, make.

2937. κτίσις *ktis'-is;* from *2936;* or. *formation* (prop. the act; by impl. the thing, lit. or fig.):–building, creation, creature, ordinance.

2938. κτίσμα *ktis'-mah;* from *2936;* an or. *formation* (concr.), i.e. *product* (created thing):–creature.

2939. κτιστής *ktis-tace';* from *2936;* a *founder,* i.e. *God* (as author of all things):–Creator.

2940. κυβεία *koo-bi'-ah;* from κύβος (a "*cube*", i.e. *die* for playing); *gambling,* i.e. (fig.) *artifice* or *fraud:*–sleight.

2941. κυβέρνησις *koo-ber'-nay-sis;* from κυβερνάω (of Lat. or., to *steer*); *pilotage,* i.e. (fig.) *directorship* (in the church):–government.

2942. κυβερνήτης *koo-ber-nay'-tace;* from the same as *2941; helmsman,* i.e. (by impl.) *captain:*–(ship) master.

2943. κυκλόθεν *koo-kloth'-en;* adv. from the same as *2945; from* the *circle,* i.e. *all around:*–(round) about.

2944. κυκλόω *koo-klo'-o;* from the same as 2945; to *encircle,* i.e. *surround:*–compass (about), come (stand) round about.

2945. κύκλῳ *koo'-klo;* as if dat. of κύκλος (*a ring,* "*cycle*"; akin to *2947*); i.e. *in a circle* (by impl. of *1722*), i.e. (adv.) *all around:*–round about.

2946. κύλισμα *koo'-lis-mah;* from *2947;* a *wallow* (the effect of *rolling*), i.e. *filth:*–wallowing.

2947. κυλιόω *koo-lee-o'-o;* from the base of *2949* (through the idea of *circularity;* comp. *2945, 1507*); to *roll* about:–wallow.

2948. κυλλός *kool-los';* from the same as *2947; rocking* about, i.e. *crippled* (*maimed,* in feet or hands):–maimed.

2949. κῦμα, *koo'-mah;* from κύω (to *swell* [with young], i.e. *bend, curve*); a *billow* (as *bursting* or *toppling*):–wave.

2950. κύμβαλον *koom'-bal-on;* from a der. of the base of *2949;* a "*cymbal*" (as *hollow*):–cymbal.

2951. κύμινον *koo'-min-on;* of for. or. [comp. *3646*]; *dill* or *fennel* ("umin"):–cummin.

2952. κυνάριον *koo-nar'-ee-on;* neut. of a presumed der. of *2965;* a *puppy:*–dog.

2953. Κύπριος *koo'-pree-os;* from *2954;* a *Cyprian* (*Cypriot*), i.e. inh. of Cyprus:–of Cyprus.

2954. Κύπρος *koo'-pros;* of unc. or.; *Cyprus,* an island in the Mediterranean:–Cyprus.

2955. κύπτω *koop'-to;* prob. from the base of *2949;* to *bend* forward:–stoop (down).

2956. Κυρηναῖος *koo-ray-nah'-yos;* from *2957;* i.e. *Cyrenaean,* i.e. inh. of Cyrene:–of Cyrene, Cyrenian.

2957. Κυρήνη *koo-ray'-nay;* of unc. der.; *Cyrenë,* a region of Africa:–Cyrene.

2958. Κυρήνιος *koo-ray'-nee-os;* of Lat. or.; *Cyrenius* (i.e. *Quirinus*), a Rom.:–Cyrenius.

2959. Κυρία *koo-ree'-ah;* fem. Of *2962; Cyria,* a Chr. Woman:–lady.

2960. κυριακός *koo-ree-ak-os';* from *2962; belonging to* the *Lord* (Jehovah or Jesus):–Lord's.

2961. κυριεύω *ko-ree-yoo'-o;* from *2962;* to *rule:*–have dominion over, lord, be lord of, exercise lordship over.

2962. κύριος *koo'-ree-os;* from κῦρος (*supremacy*); *supreme* in authority, i.e. (as noun) *controller;* by impl. *Master* (as a respectful title):– God, Lord, master, Sir.

2963. κυριότης *koo-ree-ot'-ace;* from *2962; mastery,* i.e. (concr. and coll.) *rulers:*–dominion, government.

2964. κυρόω *koo-ro'-o;* from the same as *2962;* to *make authoritative,* i.e. *ratify:*–confirm.

2965. κύων *koo'-ohn;* a prim. word; a *dog* ["*hound*"] (lit. or fig.):–dog.

2966. κῶλον *ko'-lon;* from the base of *2849;* a *limb* of the body (as if *lopped*):–carcase.

2967. κωλύω *ko-loo'-o;* from the base of *2849;* to *estop,* i.e. *prevent* (by word or act):–forbid, hinder, keep from, let, not suffer, withstand.

2968. κώμη *ko'-may;* from *2749;* a *hamlet* (as if *laid* down):–town, village.

2969. κωμόπολις, *ko-mop'-ol-is;* from *2968* and *4172;* an unwalled *city:*–town.

2970. κῶμος *ko'-mos;* from 2749; a *carousal* (as if *letting* loose):–revelling, rioting.

2971. κώνωψ, *ko'-nopes;* app. a der. of the base of *2759* and a der. of *3700;* a *mosquito* (from its *stinging proboscis*):–gnat.

2972. Κῶς *koce;* of unc. or.; *Cos,* an island in the Mediterranean:–Cos.

2973. Κωσάμ *ko-sam';* of Heb. or. [comp. 7081]; *Cosam* (i.e. *Kosam*) an Isr.:–Cosam.

2974. κωφός *ko-fos';* from *2875; blunted,* i.e. (fig.) of hearing (*deaf*) or speech (*dumb*):–deaf, dumb, speechless.

Λ

2975. λαγχάνω *lang-khan'-o;* a prol. form of a prim. verb, which is only used as an alt. in cert. tenses; to *lot,* i.e. *determine* (by impl. *receive*) esp. by lot:–his lot be, cast lots, obtain.

2976. Λάζαρος *lad'-zar-os;* prob. of Heb. or. [499]; *Lazarus* (i.e. *Elazar*), the name of two Isr. (one imaginary):–Lazarus.

2977. λάθρα *lath'-rah;* adv. from *2990; privately:*–privily, secretly.

2978. λαῖλαψ *lah'-ee-laps;* of unc. der.; a *whirlwind* (*squall*):–storm, tempest.

2979. λακτίζω *lak-tid'-zo;* from adv. λάξ (*heelwise*); to *recalcitrate:*–kick.

2980. λαλέω *lal-eh'-o;* a prol. form of an otherwise obs. verb; to *talk,* i.e. *utter* words:–preach, say, speak (after), talk, tell, utter. Comp. *3004.*

2981. λαλιά *lal-ee-ah';* from *2980; talk:*–saying, speech.

2982. λαμά *lam-ah';* or λαμμᾶ *lam-mah';* of Heb. or. [*4100* with prep.al pref.]; *lama* (i.e. *why*):–lama.

2983. λαμβάνω *lam-ban'-o;* a prol. form of a prim. verb, which is use only as an alt. in cert. tenses; to *take* (in very many appl., lit. and fig. [prop. obj. or act., to *get hold* of; whereas *1209* is rather subj. or pass. to *have offered* to one; while *138* is more violent, to *seize* or *remove*]):–accept, + be amazed, assay, attain, bring, X when I call, catch, come on (X unto), + forget, have, hold, obtain, receive (X after), take (away, up).

2984. Λάμεχ, *lam'-ekh;* of Heb. or. [3929]; *Lamech* (i.e. *Lemek*), a patriarch:–Lamech.

2985. λαμπάς *lam-pas';* from *2989;* a "*lamp*" or *flambeau:*–lamp, light, torch.

2986. λαμπρός *lam-pros';* from the same as *2985; radiant;* by anal. *limpid; fig. magnificent* or *sumptuous* (in appearance):–bright, clear, gay, goodly, gorgeous, white.

2987. λαμπρότης *lam-prot'-ace;* from *2896; brilliancy:*–brightness.

2988. λαμπρῶς *lam-proce';* adv. from *2986; brilliantly,* i.e. fig. *luxuriously:*–sumptuously.

2989. λάμπω *lam'-po;* a prim. verb; to *beam,* i.e. *radiate* brilliancy (lit. or fig.):–give light, shine.

2990. λανθάνω *lan-than'-o;* a prol. form of a prim. verb, which is used only as an alt. in cert. tenses; to *lie hid* (lit. or fig.); often used adv. *unwittingly:*–be hid, be ignorant of, unawares.

2991. λαξευτός *lax-yoo-tos';* from a com. of λᾶς (a *stone*) and the base of *3584* (in its or. sense of *scraping*); *rock-quarried:*–hewn in stone.

2992. λαός *lah-os';* app. a prim. word; a *people* (in general; thus differing from *1218,* which denotes one's *own* populace):–people.

2993. Λαοδίκεια *lah-od-ik'-i-ah;* from a com. of *2992* and *1349; Laodicia,* a place in Asia Minor:–Laodicea.

2994. Λαοδικεύς *lah-od-ik-yooce;* from *2993;* a *Laodicean,* i.e. inh. of Laodicia:–Laodicean.

2995. λάρυγξ, *lar'-oongks;* of unc. der.; the *throat* ("*larynx*"):–throat.

2996. Λασαία *las-ah'-yah;* of unc. or.; *Lasaea,* a place in Crete:–Lasea.

2997. λάσχω *las'-kho;* a streng. form of a prim. verb, which only occurs in this and another prol. form as alt. in cert. tenses; to *crack* open (from a fall):–burst asunder.

2998. λατομέω *lat-om-eh'-o;* from the same as the first part of *2991* and the base of *5114;* to *quarry:*–hew.

2999. λατρεία *lat-ri'-ah;* from *3000; ministration* of God, i.e. *worship:*–(divine) service.

3000. λατρεύω *lat-ryoo'-o;* from λάτρις (a hired *menial*); to *minister* (to God), i.e.

render relig. *homage:*–serve, do the service, worship(-per).

3001. λάχανον *lakh'-an-on;* from λαχαίνω (to *dig*); a *vegetable:*–herb.

3002. Λεββαῖος *leb-bah'-yos;* of unc. or.; *Lebbaeus,* a Chr.:–Lebbaeus.

3003. λεγεών *leg-eh-ohn';* of Lat. or.; a "*legion*", i.e. Rom. *regiment* (fig.):–legion.

3004. λέγω *leg'-o* a prim. verb; prop. to "*lay*" forth, i.e. (fig.) *relate* (in words [usually of systematic or set *discourse;* whereas *2036* and *5346* generally refer to an *indiv.* expression or speech respectively; while *4483* is prop. to *break silence* merely, and *2980* means an *extended* or random harangue]); by impl. to *mean:*–ask, bid, boast, call, describe, give out, name, put forth, say(-ing, on), shew, speak, tell, utter.

3005. λεῖμμα *lime'-mah;* from *3007;* a *remainder:*–remnant.

3006. λεῖος *li'-os;* app. a prim. word; *smooth,* i.e. "*level*":–smooth.

3007. λείπω *li'-po;* a prim. verb; to *leave,* i.e. (intr. or pass.) to *fail* or *be absent:*–be destitute (wanting), lack.

3008. λειτουργέω *li-toorg-eh'-o;* from *3011;* to be a *public servant,* i.e. (by anal.) to *perform* relig. or charitable *functions* (*worship, obey, relieve*):–minister.

3009. λειτουργία *li-toorg-ee'-ah;* from *3008; public function* (as priest ["liturgy"] or almsgiver):–ministration(-try), service.

3010. λειτουργικός *li-toorg-ik-os';* from the same as *3008; functional publicly* ("liturgic"); i.e. *beneficient:*–ministering

3011. λειτουργός *li-toorg-os';* from a der. of *2992* and *2041;* a *public servant,* i.e. a *functionary* in the Temple or Gospel, or (gen. case) a *worshipper* (of God) or *benefactor* (of man):–minister(-ed).

3012. λέντιον *len'-tee-on;* of Lat. or.; a "*linen*" cloth, i.e. *apron:*–towel.

3013. λεπίς *lep-is';* from λέπω (to *peel*); a *flake:*–scale.

3014. λέπρα, *lep'-rah;* from the same as *3013; scaliness,* i.e. "*leprosy*":–leprosy.

3015. λεπρός, *lep-ros';* from the same as *3014; scaly,* i.e. *leprous* (a *leper*):–leper.

3016. λεπτόν, *lep-ton';* neut. of a der. of the same as *3013;* something *scaled* (*light*), i.e. a small *coin:*–mite.

3017.Λευΐ *lyoo'-ee;* of Heb. or. [(3878]; *Levi,* the name of three Isr.:–Levi. Comp. *3018.*

3018. Λευΐς *lyoo-is';* a form of *3017; Lewis* (i.e. *Levi*), a Chr.:–Levi.

3019. Λευΐτης *lyoo-ee'-tace;* from *3017*; a *Levite,* i.e. desc. of Levi:–Levite.

3020. Λευϊτικός *lyoo-it'-ee-kos;* from *3019; Levitic,* i.e. relating to the Levites:–Levitical.

3021. λευκαίνω *lyoo-kah'-ee-no;* from *3022;* to *whiten:*–make white, whiten.

3022. λευκός *lyoo-kos;'* from λύκη *luke* ("*light*"); *white:*–white.

3023. λεών *leh-ohn';* a prim. word; a "*lion*":–lion.

3024. λήθη *lay'-thay* from *2990; forgetfulness:*–+ forget.

3025. ληνός *lay-nos';* app. a prim. word; a *trough,* i.e. *wine-vat:*–winepress.

3026. λῆρος *lay'-ros;* app. a prim. word; *twaddle,* i.e. an *incredible* story:–idle tale.

3027. λῃστής *lace-tace';* from ληΐζομαι (to *plunder*); a *brigand:*–robber, thief.

3028. λῆψις *lape'-sis;* from *2983; receipt* (the act):–receiving.

3029. λίαν *lee'-an;* of unc. affin.; *much* (adv.):–exceeding, great(-ly), sore, very (+ chiefest).

3030. λίβανος *lib'-an-os* of for. or. [*3828*]; the incense-tree, i.e. (by impl.) *incense* itself:–frankincense.

3031. λιβανωτός *lib-an-o-tos';* from *3030; frankincense,* i.e. (by ext.) a *censer* for burning it:–censer.

3032. Λιβερτῖνος *lib-er-tee'-nos;* of Lat. or.; a Rom. *freedman:*–Libertine.

3033. Λιβύη *lib-oo'-ay;* prob. from *3047; Libye,* a region of Africa:–Libya.

3034. λιθάζω *lith-ad'-zo;* from *3037;* to *lapidate:*–stone.

3035. λίθινος *lith-ee'-nos;* from *3037; stony,* i.e. made of *stone:*–of stone.

3036. λιθοβολέω *lith-ob-ol-eh'-o;* from a com. of *3037* and *906;* to *throw stones,* i.e. *lapidate:*–stone, cast stones.

3037. λίθος *lee'-thos;* app. a prim. word; a *stone* (lit. or fig.):–(mill-, stumbling-)stone.

3038. λιθόστρωτος *lith-os'-tro-tos;* from *3037* and a der. of *4766; stone-strewed,* i.e. a tessellated *mosaic* on which the Rom. tribunal was placed:–Pavement.

3039. λικμάω *lik-mah'-o;* from λικμός, the equiv. of λίκνον (a winnowing *fan* or basket); to *winnow,* i.e. (by anal.), to *triturate:*–grind to powder.

3040. λιμήν *lee-mane';* app. a prim. word; a *harbor:*–haven. Comp. *2568.*

3041. λίμνη *lim'-nay* prob. from *3040* (through the idea of nearness of shore); a *pond* (large or small):–lake.

3042. λιμός *lee-mos';* prob. from *3007* (through the idea of *destitution*); a *scarcity* of food:–dearth, famine, hunger.

3043. λίνον *lee'-non;* prob. a prim. word; *flax,* i.e. (by impl.) "*linen*":–linen.

3044. Λῖνος, *lee'-nos;* perh. from *3043; Linus,* a Chr.:–Linus.

3045. λιπαρός *lip-ar-os';* from λίπος (*grease*); *fat,* i.e. (fig.) *sumptuous:*–dainty.

3046. λίτρα *lee'-trah;* of Lat. or. (*libra*); a *pound* in weight:–pound.

3047. λίψ *leeps;* prob. from λείβω (to *pour* a "libation"); the *south*(- west) wind (as bringing rain, i.e. (by ext.) the *south* quarter):–southwest.

3048. λογία *log-ee'-ah;* from *3056* (in the commercial sense); a *contribution:*–collection, gathering.

3049. λογίζομαι *log-id'-zom-ahee;* mid. from *3056;* to *take an inventory,* i.e. *estimate* (lit. or fig.):–conclude, (ac-)count (of), + despise, esteem, impute, lay, number, reason, reckon, suppose, think (on).

3050. λογικός *log-ik-os';* from *3056; rational* ("*logical*"):–reasonable, of the word.

3051. λόγιον *log'-ee-on;* neut. of *3052;* an *utterance* (of God):–oracle.

3052. λόγιος *log'-ee-os;* from *3056; fluent,* i.e. an *orator:*–eloquent.

3053. λογισμός *log-is-mos'* from *3049; computation,* i.e. (fig.) *reasoning* (*conscience, conceit*):–imagination, thought.

3054. λογομαχέω *log-om-akh-eh'-o;* from a com. of *3056* and *3164;* to *be disputatious* (on trifles):–strive about words.

3055. λογομαχία *log-om-akh-ee'-ah;* from the same as *3054; disputation* about trifles ("*logomachy*"):–strife of words.

3056. λόγος *log'-os;* from *3004;* something *said* (incl. the *thought*); by impl. a *topic* (subject of discourse), also *reasoning* (the ment. faculty) or *motive;* by ext., a *computation;* spec. (with the art. in John) the Divine *Expression* (i.e. *Christ*):–account, cause, communication, X concerning, doctrine, fame, X have to do, intent, matter, mouth, preaching, question, reason, + reckon, remove, say(-ing), shew, X speaker, speech, talk, thing, + none of these things move me, tidings, treatise, utterance, word, work.

3057. λόγχη *long'-khay;* perh. a prim. word; a "*lance*":–spear.

3058. λοιδορέω *loy-dor-eh'-o;* from *3060;* to *reproach,* i.e. *vilify:*–revile.

3059. λοιδορία *loy-dor-ee'-ah;* from *3060;* slander or *vituperation:*–railing, reproach[-fully].

3060. λοίδορος *loy'-dor-os;* from λοιδός (*mischief*); *abusive,* i.e. a *blackguard:*–railer, reviler.

3061. λοιμός *loy'-mos;* of unc. affin.; a *plague* (lit. the *disease,* or fig. a *pest*):–pestilence(-t).

3062. λοιποί *loy-poy';* masc. pl. of a der. of *3007; remaining* ones:–other, which remain, remnant, residue, rest.

3063. λοιπόν *loy-pon';* neut. sing. of the same as *3062;* something *remaining* (adv.):–besides, finally, furthermore, (from) henceforth, moreover, now, + it remaineth, then.

3064. λοιποῦ *loy-poo';* gen. case sing. of the same as *3062; remaining* time:–from henceforth.

3065. Λουκᾶς *loo-kas';* contr. from Lat. *Lucanus; Lucas,* a Chr.:–Lucas, Luke.

3066. Λούκιος *loo'-kee-os;* of Lat. or.; *illuminative; Lucius,* a Chr.:–Lucius.

3067. λουτρόν *loo-tron';* from *3068;* a *bath,* i.e. (fig.), *baptism:*–washing.

3068. λούω *loo'-o;* a prim. verb; to *bathe* (the *whole* pers.; whereas *3538* means to wet a *part* only, and *4150* to wash, cleanse *garments* exclusively):–wash.

3069. Λύδδα *lud'-dah;* of Heb. or. [3850]; *Lydda* (i.e. *Lod*), a place in Pal.:–Lydda.

3070. Λυδία *loo-dee'-ah;* prop. or. of Λυδιος [of for. or.] (a *Lydian,* in Asia Minor); *Lydia,* a Chr. woman: -Lydia.

3071. Λυκαονία *loo-kah-on-ee'-ah;* perh. remotely from *3074; Lycaonia,* a region of Asia Minor:–Lycaonia.
3072. Λυκαονιστί *loo-kah-on-is-tee';* adv. from a der. of *3071; Lycaonistically,* i.e. in the language of the Lycaonians:–in the speech of Lycaonia.
3073. Λυκία *loo-kee'-ah;* prob. remotely from *3074; Lycia,* a province of Asia Minor:–Lycia.
3074. λύκος *loo'-kos;* perh. akin to the base of *3022* (from the *whitish* hair); a *wolf:*–wolf.
3075. λυμαίνομαι *loo-mah'-ee-nom-ahee;* mid. from a prob. der. of *3089* (mean. *filth*); prop. to *soil,* i.e. (fig.) *insult* (*maltreat*):–make havock of.
3076. λυπέω *loo-peh'-o;* from *3077;* to *distress;* refl. or pass. to *be sad:*–cause grief, grieve, be in heaviness, (be) sorrow (-ful), be (make) sorry.
3077. λύπη *loo'-pay;* app. a prim. word; *sadness:*–grief, grievous, + grudgingly, heaviness, sorrow.
3078. Λυσανίας *loo-san-ee'-as;* from *3080* and ἀνία (*trouble*); *grief-dispelling; Lysanias,* a governor of Abilene:–Lysanias.
3079. Λυσίας *loo-see'-as;* of unc. affin.; *Lysias,* a Rom.:–Lysias.
3080. λύσις *loo'-sis;* from *3089;* a *loosening,* i.e. (spec.), *divorce:*–to be loosed.
3081. λυσιτελεῖ *loo-sit-el-i';* third pers. sing. pres. ind. act. of a der. of a com. of *3080* and *5056;* impers., it *answers* the *purpose*, i.e. is *advantageous:*–it is better.
3082. Λύστρα *loos'-trah;* of unc. or.; *Lystra,* a place in Asia Minor:–Lystra.
3083. λύτρον *loo'-tron;* from *3089;* something to *loosen* with, i.e. a redemption *price* (fig. *atonement*):–ransom.
3084. λυτρόω *loo-tro'-o;* from *3083;* to *ransom* (lit. or fig.):–redeem.
3085. λύτρωσις *loo'-tro-sis*; from *3084;* a *ransoming* (fig.):–+ redeemed, redemption.
3086. λυτρωτής *loo-tro-tace';* from *3084;* a *redeemer* (fig.):–deliverer.
3087. λυχνία *lookh-nee'-ah;* from *3088;* a *lamp-stand*
3088. λύχνος *lookh'-nos;* from the base of *3022;* a portable *lamp* or other *illuminator* (lit. or fig.):–candle, light.
3089. λύω *loo'-o;* a prim. verb; to "*loosen*" (lit. or fig.):–break (up), destroy, dissolve, (un-) loose, melt, put off. Comp. 4486.
3090. Λωΐς *lo-ece';* of unc. or.; *Loïs,* a Chr. woman:–Lois.
3091. Λώτ *lote;* of Heb. or.[3876]; *Lot,* a patriarch:–Lot.

M

3092. Μαάθ *mah-ath*'; prob. of Heb. or.; *Maath,* an Isr.:–Maath.
3093. Μαγδαλά *mag-dal-ah';* of Chald. or. [comp. 4026]; *the tower; Magdala* (i.e. *Migdala*), a place in Pal.:–Magdala.
3094. Μαγδαληνή *mag-dal-ay-nay';* or. of a der. of *3093;* a female *Magdalene,* i.e. inh. of Magdala:–Magdalene.
3095. μαγεία *mag-i'-ah;* from *3096;* "*magic*":–sorcery.
3096. μαγεύω *mag-yoo'-o;* from *3097;* to *practice magic:*–use sorcery.
3097. μάγος mag'-os of for. or. [7248]; a *Magian,* i.e. Oriental *scientist;* by impl. a *magician:*–sorcerer, wise man.
3098. Μαγώγ *mag-ogue';* of Heb. or. [4031]; *Magog,* a for. nation, i.e. (fig.) an Antichristian party:–Magog.
3099. Μαδιάν mad-ee-on' of Heb. or. [4080]; *Madian* (i.e. *Midian*), a region of Arabia:–Madian.
3100. Μαδιάν *math-ayt-yoo'-o;* from *3101;* intr., to *become a pupil;* trans., to *disciple,* i.e. enrol as scholar:–be disciple, instruct, teach.
3101. μαθητής *math-ay-tes'* from *3129;* a *learner,* i.e. *pupil:*–disciple.
3102. μαθήτρια *math-ay'-tree-ah* or. from *3101;* a female *pupil:*–disciple.
3103. Μαθουσάλα *math-oo-sal'-ah;* of Heb. or. [4968]; *Mathusala* (i.e. *Methushelach*), an antediluvian:–Mathusala.
3104. Μαϊνάν *mahee-nan';* prob. of Heb. or.; *Maïnan,* an Isr.:–Mainan.
3105. μαίνομαι *mah'-ee-nom-ahee;* mid. from a prim. μάω (to *long* for; through the idea of insensate *craving*); to *rave* as a "maniac":–be beside self (mad).
3106. μακαρίζω *mak-ar-id'-zo;* from *3107;* to *beatify,* i.e. *pronounce* (or *esteem*) *fortunate:*–call blessed, count happy.
3107. μακάριος *mak-ar'-ee-os;* a prol. form of the poetical μάκαρ (mean. the same); supremely *blest;* by ext., *fortunate, well off:*–blessed, happy(X -ier).
3108. μακαρισμός *mak-ar-is-mos';* from *3106; beatification,* i.e. *attribution of good fortune:*–blessedness.
3109. Μακεδονία *mak-ed-on-ee'-ah;* from *3110; Macedonia,* a region of Greece:–Macedonia.
3110. Μακεδών *mak-ed'-ohn;* of unc. der.; a *Macedon* (*Macedonian*), i.e. inh. of Macedonia:–of Macedonia, Macedonian.
3111. μάκελλον *mak'-el-lon;* of Lat. or. (*macellum);* a *butcher's stall, meat market* or *provision-shop:*–shambles.
3112. μακράν *mak-ran';* or. acc. sing. of *3117* (*3598* being implied); *at a distance* (lit. or fig.):–(a-)far (off), good (great) way off.
3113. μακρόθεν *mak-roth'-en;* adv. from *3117; from a distance* or *afar:*–afar off, from far.
3114. μακροθυμέω *mak-roth-oo-meh'-o;* from the same as *3116;* to *be long-spirited,* i.e.(obj.) *forbearing* or (subj.) *patient:*–bear (suffer) long, be longsuffering, have (long) patience, be patient, patiently endure.
3115. μακροθυμία *mak-roth-oo-mee'-ah;* from the same as *3116; longanimity,* i.e. (obj.) *forbearance* or (subj.) *fortitude:*–longsuffering, patience.
3116. μακροθυμώς *mak-roth-oo-moce';* adv. of a com. of *3117* and *2372;* with *long* (*enduring*) *temper,* i.e. *leniently:*–patiently.
3117. μακρός *mak-ros';* from *3372; long* (in place [*distant*] or time [neut. pl.]):–far, long.
3118. μακροχρόνιος *mak-rokh-ron'-ee-os;* from *3117* and *5550; long-timed,* i.e. *long-lived:*–live long.
3119. μαλακία *mal-ak-ee'-ah;* from *3120; softness,* i.e. *enervation* (*debility*):–disease.
3120. μαλακός *mal-ak-os';* of unc. affin.; *soft,* i.e. *fine* (clothing); fig. a *catamite:*–effeminate, soft.
3121. Μαλελεήλ *mal-el-eh-ale';* of Heb. or. [4111]; *Maleleël* (i.e. *Mahalalel*), an antediluvian:–Maleleel.
3122. μάλιστα *mal'-is-tah;* neut. pl. of the sup. of an app. prim. adv. μάλα (*very*); (adv.) *most* (*in the greatest degree*) or *particularly:*–chiefly, most of all, (e-) spec..
3123. μᾶλλον *mal'-lon;* neut. of the comp. of the same as *3122;* (adv.) *more* (*in a greater degree*) or *rather:*–+ better, X far, (the) more (and more), (so) much (the more), rather.
3124. Μάλχος *mal'-khos;* of Heb. or. [4429]; *Malchus,* an Isr.:–Malchus.
3125. μάμμη *mam'-may;* of nat. or. ["mammy"]; a *grandmother:*–grandmother.
3126. μαμμωνᾶς *mam-mo-nas'* of Chald. or. (*confidence,* i.e. *wealth,* personified); *mammonas,* i.e. *avarice* (deified):–mammon.
3127. Μαναήν *man-ah-ane;'* of unc. or.; *Manaën,* a Chr.:–Manaen.
3128. Μανασσῆς *man-as-sace';* of Heb. or. [4519]; *Mannasses* (i.e. *Menashsheh*), an Isr.:–Manasses.
3129. μανθάνω *man-than'-o;* prol. from a prim. verb, another form of which, μαθέω, is used as an alt. in cert. tenses; to *learn* (in any way):–learn, understand.
3130. μανία *man-ee'-ah;* from *3105; craziness*:–[+ make] X mad.
3131. μάννα man'-nah; of Heb. or. [4478]; *manna* (i.e. *man*), an edible gum:–manna.
3132. μαντεύομαι *mant-yoo'-om-ahee;* from a der. of *3105* (mean. a *prophet,* as supposed to *rave* through *inspiration*); to *divine,* i.e. *utter spells* (under pretense of foretelling:–by soothsaying.
3133. μαραίνω *mar-ah'-ee-no;* of unc. affin.; to *extinguish* (as fire), i.e. (fig. and pass.) to *pass away:*–fade away.
3134. μαράν ἀθά, *mar'-an ath'-ah;* of Chald. or. (mean. *our Lord has come*); *maranatha,* i.e. an exclamation of the approaching *divine judgment:*–Maran-atha.
3135. μαργαρίτης *mar-gar-ee'-tace;* from μάργαρος (a pearl-*oyster*); a *pearl:*–pearl.
3136. Μάρθα *mar'-thah;* prob. of Chald. or. (mean. *mistress*); *Martha,* a Chr. woman:–Martha.
3137. Μαρία *mar-ee'-ah;* or Μαριάμ *mar-ee-am';* of Heb. or. [4813]; *Maria* or *Mariam* (i.e. *Mirjam*), the name of six Chr. females:– Mary.
3138. Μάρκος *mar'-kos* of Lat. or.; *Marcus,* a Chr.:–Marcus, Mark.

3139. μάρμαρος *mar'-mar-os;* from μαρμαίρω (to *glisten*); *marble* (as sparkling *white*):–marble.
3140. μαρτυρέω *mar-too-reh'-o;* from *3144;* to *be a witness,* i.e. *testify* (lit. or fig.):–charge, give [evidence], bear record, have (obtain, of) good (honest) report, be well reported of, testify, give (have) testimony, (be, bear, give, obtain) witness.
3141. μαρτυρία *mar-too-ree'-ah;* from *3144; evidence* given (judicially or gen. case):–record, report, testimony, witness.
3142. μαρτύριον *mar-too'-ree-on;* neut. of a presumed der. of *3144;* something *evidential,* i.e. (gen. case) *evidence* given or (spec.), the *Decalogue* (in the sacred Tabernacle):–to be testified, testimony, witness.
3143. μαρτύρομαι *mar-too'-rom-ahee;* mid. from *3144;* to be *adduced* as *a witness,* i.e. (fig.) to *obtest* (in affirmation or exhortation):–take to record, testify.
3144. μάρτυς *mar'-toos;* of unc. affin.; a *witness* (lit. [judicially] or fig. [gen. case]); by anal. a "*martyr*":– martyr, record, witness.
3145. μασσάομαι *mas-sah'-om-ahee;* from a prim. μάσσω (to *handle* or *squeeze*); to *chew:*–gnaw.
3146. μαστιγόω *mas-tig-o'-o;* from *3148;* to *flog* (lit. or fig.):–scourge.
3147. μαστίζω *mas-tid'-zo;* from *3149;* to *whip* (lit.):–scourge.
3148. μάστιξ *mas'-tix;* prob. from the base of *3145* (through the idea of *contact*); a *whip* (lit. the Rom. *flagellum* for criminals; fig. a *disease*):–plague, scourging.
3149. μαστός *mas-tos';* from the base of *3145;* a (prop. female) *breast* (as if *kneaded* up):–pap.
3150. ματαιολογία *mat-ah-yol-og-ee'-ah;* from *3151; random talk,* i.e. *babble:*–vain jangling.
3151. ματαιολόγος *mat-ah-yol-og'-os;* from *3152* and *3004;* an *idle* (i.e. *senseless* or *mischievous*) *talker,* i.e. a *wrangler:*–vain talker.
3152. μάταιος *mat'-ah-yos;* from the base of *3155; empty,* i.e. (lit.) *profitless,* or (spec.), an *idol:*–vain, vanity.
3153. ματαιότης *mat-ah-yot'-ace;* from *3152; inutility;* fig. *transientness;* mor. *depravity:*–vanity.
3154. ματαιόω *mat-ah-yo'-o;* from *3152;* to *render* (pass. *become*) *foolish,* i.e. (mor.) *wicked* or (spec.), *idolatrous:*–become vain.
3155. μάτην *mat'-ane;* acc. of a der. of the base of *3145* (through the idea of tentative *manipulation,* i.e. unsuccessful *search,* or else of *punishment*); *folly,* i.e. (adv.) *to no purpose:*–in vain.
3156. Ματθαῖος *mat-thah'-yos;* a short. form of *3161; Matthaeus* (i.e. *Matthitjah*), an Isr. and a Chr.:–Matthew.
3157. Ματθάν *mat-than';* of Heb. or. [4977]; *Mathan* (i.e. *Mattan*), an Isr.:–Matthan.
3158. Ματθάτ *mat-that';* prob. a short. form of *3161; Matthat* (i.e. *Mattithjah*), the name of two Isr.:–Mathat.
3159. Ματθίας *mat-thee'-as;* app. a short. form of *3161; Matthias* (i.e. *Mattithjah*), an Isr.:–Matthias.
3160. Ματταθά *mat-tath-ah';* prob. a short. form of *3161* [comp. 4992]; *Mattatha* (i.e. *Mattithjah*), an Isr.:–Mattatha.
3161. Ματταθίας *mat-tath-ee'-as;* of Heb. or. [4993]; *Mattathias* (i.e. *Mattithjah*), an Isr. and a Chr.:–Mattathias.
3162. μάχαιρα *makh'-ahee-rah;* prob. or. of a presumed der. of *3163;* a *knife,* i.e. *dirk;* fig. *war,* judicial *punishment:*–sword.
3163. μάχη *makh'-ay;* from *3164;* a *battle,* i.e. (fig.) *controversy:*–fighting, strive, striving.
3164. μάχομαι *makh'-om-ahee;* mid. of an app. prim. verb; to *war,* i.e. (fig.) to *quarrel, dispute:*–fight, strive.
3165. μέ *meh;* a short. (and prob. or.ally) from of *1691; me:*–I, me, my.
3166. μεγαλαυχέω *meg-al-ow-kheh'-o;* from a comp. of *3173* and αὐχέω (to *boast;* akin to *837* and *2744*); to *talk big,* i.e. *be grandiloquent* (*arrogant, egotistic*):–boast great things.
3167. μεγαλεῖος *meg-al-i'-os;* from *3173; magnificent,* i.e. (neut., pl. as noun) a conspicuous *favor,* or (subj.) *perfection:*–great things, wonderful works.
3168. μεγαλειότης *meg-al-i-ot'-ace;* from *3167; superbness,* i.e. *glory* or *splendor:*–magnificence, majesty, mighty power.
3169. μεγαλοπρεπής *meg-al-op-rep-ace';* from *3173* and *4241; befitting greatness* or *magnificence* (*majestic*):–excellent.
3170. μεγαλύνω *meg-al-oo'-no;* from *3173;* to *make* (or *declare*) *great,* i.e. *increase* or (fig.) *extol:*–enlarge, magnify, shew great.
3171. μεγάλως *meg-al'-oce;* adv. from *3173; much:*–greatly.
3172. μεγαλωσύνη *meg-al-o-soo'-nay;* from *3173; greatness,* i.e. (fig.) *divinity* (often *God* himself):–majesty.
3173. μέγας *meg'-as;* [incl. the prol. forms, or. μεγάλη pl. μεiγάλοι, etc.; comp. also *3176, 3187*]; *big* (lit. or fig. in a very wide appl.):–(+ fear) exceedingly, great(-est), high, large, loud, mighty, + (be) sore (afraid), strong, X to years.
3174. μέγεθος *meg'-eth-os;* from *3173; magnitude* (fig.):–greatness.
3175. μεγιστᾶνες *meg-is-tan'-es;* pl. from *3176; grandees:*–great men, lords.
3176. μέγιστος *meg'-is-tos;* sup. of *3173; greatest* or *very great:*–exceeding great.
3177. μεθερμηνεύω *meth-er-mane-yoo'-o;* from *3326* and *2059;* to *explain over,* i.e. *translate:*–(by) interpret(-ation).
3178. μέθη *meth'-ay;* app. a prim. word; an *intoxicant,* i.e. (by impl.) *intoxication:*–drunkenness.
3179. μεθίστημι *meth-is'-tay-mee;*or (1 Co. 13:2) μεθιστάνω *meth-is-tan'-o;* from *3326* and *2476;* to *transfer,* i.e. *carry away, depose* or (fig.) *exchange, seduce:*–put out, remove, translate, turn away.
3180. μεθοδεία *meth-od-i'-ah;* from a com. of *3326* and *3593* [comp. "method"]; *travelling over,* i.e. *travesty* (*trickery*):–wile, lie in wait.
3181. μεθόριος *meth-or'-ee-os;* from *3326* and *3725; bounded alongside,* i.e. *contiguous* (neut. pl. as noun, *frontier*):–border.
3182. μεθύσκω *meth-oos'-ko;* a prol. (trans.) form of *3184;* to *intoxicate:*–be drunk(-en).
3183. μέθυσος *meth'-oo-sos;* from *3184; tipsy,* i.e. (as noun) a *sot:*–drunkard.
3184. μεθύω *meth-oo'-o;* from another form of *3178;* to *drink* to *intoxication,* i.e. *get drunk:*–drink well, make (be) drunk(-en).
3185. μεῖζον *mide'-zon;* neut. of *3187;* (adv.) in *greater* degree:–the more.
3186. μειζότερος *mide-zot'-er-os;* continued comp. of *3187; still larger* (fig.):–greater.
3187. μείζων *mide'-zone;* irreg. comp. of *3173; larger* (lit. or fig. spec. in age):–elder, greater(-est), more.
3188. μέλαν *mel'-an;* neut. of *3189* as noun; *ink:*–ink.
3189. μέλας *mel'-as;* app. a prim. word; *black:*–black.
3190. Μελεᾶς *mel-eh-as';* of unc. or.; *Meleas,* an Isr.:–Meleas.
3191. μελετάω *mel-et-ah'-o;* from a presumed der. of *3199;* to *take care of,* i.e. (by impl.) *revolve* in the mind:–imagine, (pre-) meditate.
3192. μέλι *mel'-ee;* app. a prim. word; *honey:*–honey.
3193. μελίσσιος *mel-is'-see-os;* from *3192; relating to honey,* i.e. *bee* (comb):–honeycomb.
3194. Μελίτη *mel-ee'-tay;* of unc. or.; *Melita,* an island in the Mediterranean:–Melita.
3195. μέλλω *mel'-lo;* a streng. form of *3199* (through the idea of *expectation*); to *intend,* i.e. *be about* to be, do, or suffer something (of persons or things, esp. events; in the sense of *purpose, duty, necessity, probability, possibility,* or *hesitation*):–about, after that, be (almost), (that which is, things, + which was for) to come, intend, was to (be), mean, mind, be at the point, (be) ready, + return, shall (begin), (which, that) should (after, afterwards, hereafter) tarry, which was for, will, would, be yet.
3196. μέλος *mel'-os;* of unc. affin.; a *limb* or *part* of the body:–member.
3197. Μελχί, *mel-khee';* of Heb. or. [4428 with pron. suffix, *my king*]; *Melchi* (i.e. *Malki*), the name of two Isr.:–Melchi.
3198. Μελχισεδέκ, *mel-khis-ed-ek';* of Heb. or. [4442]; *Melchisedek* (i.e. *Malkitsedek*), a patriarch:–Melchisedec.
3199. μέλω *mel'-o;* a prim. verb; to *be of interest* to, i.e. to *concern* (only third pers. sing. pres. ind. used impers., *it matters*):–(take) care.
3200. μεμβράνα *mem-bran'-ah;* of Lat. or. ("*membrane*"); a (written) sheep-*skin:*–parchment.
3201. μέμφομαι *mem'-fom-ahee;* mid. of an app. prim. verb; to *blame:*–find fault.
3202. μεμψίμοιρος *mem-psim'-oy-ros;* from

GREEK

a presumed der. of *3201* and μοῖρα (*fate;* akin to the base of *3313*); *blaming fate,* i.e. *querulous* (*discontented*):–complainer.

3303. μέν *men;* a prim. par.; prop. ind. of *affirmation* or *concession* (*in fact*); usually followed by a *contrasted* clause with *1161* (*this* one, the *former,* etc.):–even, indeed, so, some, truly, verily. Often com. with other par. in an *intens.* or *asseverative* sense.

3304. μενοῦνγε *men-oon'-geh;* from *3203* and *3767* and *1065; so then at least:*–nay but, yea doubtless (rather, verily).

3305. μέντοι *men'-toy;* from *3303* and *5104; indeed though,* i.e. *however:*–also, but, howbeit, nevertheless, yet.

3306. μένω *men'-o;* a prim. verb; to *stay* (in a given place, state, relation or expectancy):–abide, continue, dwell, endure, be present, remain, stand, tarry (for), X thine own.

3307. μερίζω *mer-id'-zo;* from *3313;* to *part,* i.e. (lit.) to *apportion, bestow, share,* or (fig.) to *disunite, differ:*–deal, be difference between, distribute, divide, give part.

3308. μέριμνα *mer'-im-nah;* from *3307* (through the idea of *distraction*); *solicitude:*–care.

3309. μεριμνάω *mer-im-nah'-o;* from *3308;* to *be anxious* about:–(be, have) care(-ful), take thought.

3310. μερίς *mer-ece';* fem. of *3313;* a *portion,* i.e. *province, share* or (abstr.) *participation:*–part (X -akers).

3311. μερισμός *mer-is-mos';* from *3307;* a *separation* or *distribution:*–dividing asunder, gift.

3312. μεριστής *mer-is-tace';* from *3307;* an *apportioner* (*administrator*):–divider.

3313. μέρος *mer'-os;* from an obs. but more prim. form of μείρομαι (to *get* as a *section* or *allotment*); a *division* or *share* (lit. or fig. in a wide appl.):–behalf, course, coast, craft, particular (+ -ly), part (+ -ly), piece, portion, respect, side, some sort(-what).

3314. μεσημβρία *mes-ame-bree'-ah;* from *3319* and *2250; midday;* by impl. the *south:*–noon, south.

3315. μεσιτεύω *mes-it-yoo'-o;* from *3316;* to *interpose* (as arbiter), i.e (by impl.) to *ratify* (as surety):–confirm.

3316. μεσίτης *mes-ee'-tace;* from *3319;* a *go-between,* i.e. (simply) an *internunciator,* or (by impl.) a *reconciler* (*intercessor*):–mediator.

3317. μεσονύκτιον *mes-on-ook'-tee-on;* neut. of com. of *3319* and *3571; midnight* (esp. as a watch):–midnight.

3318. Μεσοποταμία *mes-op-ot-am-ee'-ah;* from *3319* and *4215; Mesopotamia* (as lying between the Euphrates and the Tigris; comp. 763), a region of Asia:–Mesopotamia.

3319. μέσος *mes'-os;* from *3326; mid.* (as an adj. or [neut.] noun):–among, X before them, between, + forth, mid [-day, -night], midst, way.

3320. μεσότοιχον *mes-ot'-oy-khon;* from *3319* and *5109;* a *partition* (fig.):–middle wall.

3321. μεσουράνημα, *mes-oo-ran'-ay-mah;* from a presumed com. of *3319* and *3772; mid-sky:*–midst of heaven.

3322. μεσόω *mes-o'-o;* from *3319;* to *form* the *mid.,* i.e. (in point of time), to *be half-way* over:–be about the midst.

3323. Μεσσίας *mes-see'-as;* of Heb. or. [4899]; the *Messias* (i.e. *Mashiach*), or Christ:–Messias.

3324. μεστός *mes-tos';* of unc. der.:–*replete* (lit. or fig.):–full.

3325. μεστόω *mes-to'-o;* from *3324;* to *replenish,* i.e. (by impl.) to *intoxicate:*–fill.

3326. μετά *met-ah';* a prim. prep. (often used adv.); prop. denoting *accompaniment;* "*amid*" (local or causal); modif. variously according to the case (gen. *association,* or acc. *succession*) with which it is joined; occupying an intermediate position between *575* or *1537* and *1519* or *4314;* less intimate than *1722* and less close than *4862*):–after(-ward), X that he again, against, among, X and, + follow, hence, hereafter, in, of, (up-)on, + our, X and setting, since, (un-)to, + together, when, with (+ -out). Often used in compo., in substantially the same relations of *participation* or *proximity,* and *transfer* or *sequence.*

3327. μεταβίνω *met-ab-ah'-ee-no;* from *3326* and the base of *939;* to *change place:*–depart, go, pass, remove.

3328. μεταβάλλω *met-ab-al'-lo;* from *3326* and *906;* to *throw over,* i.e. (mid. fig.) to *turn about* in opinion:–change mind.

3329. μετάγω *met-ag'-o;* from *3326* and *718;* to *lead over,* i.e. *transfer* (*dir.*):–turn about.

3330. μεταδίδωμι *met-ad-id'-o-mee;* from *3326* and *1325;* to *give over,* i.e. *share:*–give, impart.

3331. μετάθεσις *met-ath'-es-is;* from *3346; transp.,* i.e. *transferral* (to heaven), *disestablishment* (of a law):–change, removing, translation.

3332. μεταίρω *met-ah'-ee-ro;* from *3326* and *142;* to *betake* oneself, i.e. *remove* (locally):–depart.

3333. μετακαλέω *met-ak-al-eh'-o;* from *3326* and *2564;* to *call elsewhere,* i.e. *summon:*–call (for, hither).

3334. μετακινέω *met-ak-ee-neh'-o;* from *3326* and *2795;* to *stir* to a place *elsewhere,* i.e. *remove* (fig.):–move away.

3335. μεταλαμβάνω *met-al-am-ban'-o;* from *3326* and *2983;* to *participate;* gen. case, to *accept* (and use):–eat, have, be partaker, receive, take.

3336. μετάληψις *met-al'-ape-sis;* from *3335; participation:*–taking.

3337. μεταλλάσσω *met-al-las'-so;* from *3326* and *236;* to *exchange:*–change.

3338. μεταμέλλομαι *met-am-el'-lom-ahee;* from 3326 and the mid. of *3199;* to *care afterwards,* i.e. *regret:*–repent (self).

3339. μεταμορφόω *met-am-or-fo'-o;* from *3326* and *3445;* to *transform* (lit. or fig. "metamorphose"):–change, transfigure, transform.

3340. μετανοέω *met-an-o-eh'-o;* from *3326* and *3539;* to *think differently* or *afterwards,* i.e. *reconsider* (mor. *feel compunction*):–repent.

3341. μετάνοια *met-an'-oy-ah;* from *3340;* (subj.) *compunction* (for guilt, incl. *reformation*); by impl. *reversal* (of [another's] decision:–repentance.

3342. μεταξύ *met-ax-oo';* from *3326* and a form of *4862; betwixt* (of place or pers.); (of time) as adj., *intervening,* or (by impl.) *adjoining:*–between, mean while, next.

3343. μεταπέμπω *met-ap-emp'-o;* from *3326* and *3992;* to *send* from *elsewhere,* i.e. (mid.) to *summon* or *invite:*–call (send) for.

3344. μεταστρέφω, *met-as-tref'-o;* from *3326* and *4762;* to *turn across,* i.e. *transmute* or (fig.) *corrupt:*–pervert, turn.

3345. μετασχηματίζω *met-askh-ay-mat-id'-zo;* from *3326* and a der. of *4976;* to *transfigure* or *disguise;* fig. to *apply* (by accommodation):–transfer, transform (self); to *change*

3346. μετατίθημι *met-at-ith'-ay-mee;* from *3326* and *5087;* to *transfer,* i.e. (lit.) *transport,* (by impl.) *exchange,* (refl.) *change sides,* or (fig.) *pervert:*–carry over, change, remove, translate, turn.

3347. μετέπειτα *met-ep'-i-tah;* from *3326* and *1899; thereafter:*–afterward.

3348. μετέχω *met-ekh'-o;* from *3326* and *2192;* to *share* or *participate;* by impl. *belong* to, *eat* (or *drink*):–be partaker, pertain, take part, use.

3349. μετεωρίζω *met-eh-o-rid'-zo;* from a com. of *3326* and a coll. form of *142* or perh. rather *109* (comp. "meteor"); to *raise in mid-air,* i.e. (fig.) *suspend* (pass. *fluctuate* or *be anxious*):–be of doubtful mind.

3350. μετοικεσία *met-oy-kes-ee'-ah;* from a der. of a com. of *3326* and *3624;* a *change of abode,* i.e. (spec.), *expatriation:*–X brought, carried(-ying) away (in-)to.

3351. μετοικίζω *met-oy-kid'-zo;* from the same as *3350;* to *transfer* as a *settler* or *captive,* i.e *colonize* or *exile:*–carry away, remove into.

3352. μετοχή *met-okh-ay';* from *3348; participation,* i.e. *intercourse:*–fellowship.

3353. μέτοχος *met'-okh-os;* from *3348; participant,* i.e. (as noun) a *sharer;* by impl. an *associate:*–fellow, partaker, partner.

3354. μετρέω *met-reh'-o;* from *3358;* to *measure* (i.e. ascertain in size by a fixed standard); by impl. to *admeasure* (i.e. allot by rule):–fig. to *estimate:*–measure, mete.

3355. μετρητής *met-ray-tace';* from *3354;* a *measurer,* i.e. (spec.), a cert. standard *measure* of capacity for liquids:–firkin.

3356. μετριοπαθέω *met-ree-op-ath-eh'-o;* from a com. of the base of *3357* and *3806;* to *be moderate in passion,* i.e. *gentle* (to *treat indulgently*):–have compassion.

3357. μετρίως *met-ree'-oce;* adv. from a der. of *3358; moderately,* i.e. *slightly:*–a little.

3358. μέτρον *met'-ron;* an app. prim. word; a *measure* ("metre"), lit. or fig.; by impl. a limited *portion* (*degree*):– measure.

3359. μέτωπον *met'-o-pon;* from *3326* and ὤψ (the *face*); the *forehead* (as *opposite* the *countenance*):–forehead.

3360. μέχρι *mekh'-ree* or μεχρίς *mekh-ris'*; from *3372*; *as far as*, i.e. *up to* a cert. point (as a prep., of extent [denoting the *terminus*, whereas *891* refers esp. to the *space* of time or place intervening] or conj.):–till, (un-) to, until.

3361. μή *may*; a prim. par. of qualified *negation* (whereas *3756* expresses an absol. denial); (adv.) *not*, (conj.) *lest*; also (as an interrog. implying a *neg*. answer [whereas *3756* expects an *affirmative* one]) *whether*:–any but (that), X forbear, + God forbid, + lack, lest, neither, never, no (X wise in), none, nor, [can-]not, nothing, that not, un[-taken], without. Often used in com. in substantially the same relations. See also *3362, 3363, 3364, 3372, 3373, 3375, 3378*.

3362. ἐάν μή *eh-an' may* i.e. *1437* and *3361*; *if not*, i.e. *unless*:–X before, but, except, if, no, (if, + whosoever) not.

3363. ἵνα μή *hin'-ah may*; i.e. *2443* and *3361*; *in order* (or *so*) *that not*:–albeit not, lest, that, no(-t, [-thing]).

3364. οὐ μή *oo may*; i.e. *3756* and *3361*; a double neg. streng. the denial; *not at all*:–any more, at all, by any (no) means, neither, never, no (at all), in no case (wise), nor ever, not (at all, in any wise). Comp. *3378*.

3365. μηδαμῶς *may-dam-oce'* adv. from a com. of *3361* and ἀμός (*somebody*); by no means:–not so

3366. μηδέ *may-deh'*; from *3361* and *1161*; *but not, not even*; in a continued negation, *nor*:–neither, nor (yet), (no) not (once, so much as).

3367. μηδείς *may-dice'*; include. the irreg. fem. μηδεμία *may-dem-ee'-ah*, and the neut. μηδέν *may-den'*; from *3361* and *1520*; *not even one* (man, woman, thing):–any (man, thing), no (man), none, not (at all, any man, a whit), nothing, + without delay.

3368. μηδέποτε *may-dep'-ot-eh*; from *3366* and *4218*; *not even ever*:–never.

3369. μηδέπω *may-dep'-o*; from *3366* and *4452*; *not even yet*:–not yet.

3370. Μῆδος *may'-dos*; of for. or. [comp. *4074*]; a *Median*, or inh. of Media:–Mede.

3371. μηκέτι *may-ket'-ee*; from *3361* and *2089*; *no further*:–any longer, (not) henceforth, hereafter, no henceforward (longer, more, soon), not any more.

3372. μηκος *may'-kos*; prob. akin to *3173*; *length* (lit. or fig.) length.

3373. μηκύνω *may-koo'-no* from *3372*; to *lengthen*, i.e. (mid.) to *enlarge*:–grow up.

3374. μηλωτή *may-lo-tay'*; from μῆλον (a *sheep*); a *sheep-skin*:–sheepskin.

3375. μήν *mane*; a stronger form of *3303*; a par. of affirmation (only with *2229*); *assuredly*:–+ surely.

3376. μήν *mane*; a prim. word; a *month*:–month.

3377. μηνύω *may-noo'-o*; prob. from the same base as *3145* and *3415* (i.e. μάω to *strive*); to *disclose* (through the idea of ment. *effort* and thus calling to *mind*), i.e. *report, declare, intimate*:–shew, tell.

3378. μὴ οὐκ *may ook*; i.e. *3361* and *3756*; as interrog. and neg., *is it not that?*:–neither (followed by *no*), + never, not. Comp. *3364*.

3379. μήποτε *may'-pot-eh*; or μή ποτε, *may pot'-eh*; from *3361* and *4218*; *not ever*; also *if* (or *lest*) *ever* (or *perh*.):–if peradventure, lest (at any time, haply), not at all, whether or not.

3380. μήπω *may'-po*; from *3361* and *4452*; *not yet*:–not yet.

3381. μήπως *may'-poce*; or μή πως *may poce*; from *3361* and *4458*; *lest somehow*:–lest (by any means, by some means, haply, perh.).

3382. μηρός *may-ros'*; perh. a prim. word; a *thigh*:–thigh.

3383. μήτε *may'-teh*; from *3361* and *5037*; *not too*, i.e. (in continued negation) *neither* or *nor*; also, *not even*:–neither, (n-)or, so as much.

3384. μήτηρ *may'-tare*; app. a prim. word; a "*mother*" (lit. or fig. immed. or remote):–mother.

3385. μήτι *may'-tee*; from *3361* and the neut. of *5100*; *whether at all*:–not [*the par. usually not expressed, except by the form of the question*].

3386. μήτιγε *may'-tig-eh*; from *3385* and *1065*; *not at all then*, i.e. *not to say* (*the rather still*):–how much more.

3387. μήτις *may'-tis*; or μή τις *may tis*; from 3361 and 5100; *whether any*:–any [*sometimes unexpressed except by the simple interrog. form of the sentence*].

3388. μήτρα *may'-trah*; from *3384*; the *matrix*:–womb.

3389. μητραλῴας *may-tral-o'-as*; from *3384* and the base of *257*; a *mother-thresher*, i.e. *matricide*:–murderer of mothers.

3390. μητρόπολις *may-trop'-ol-is*; from *3384* and *4172*; a *mother city*, i.e. "*metropolis*":–chiefest city.

3391. μία *mee'-ah*; irreg. fem. of *1520*; *one* or *first*:–a (cert.), + agree, first, one, X other.

3392. μιαίνω *me-ah'-ee-no*; perh. a prim. verb; to *sully* or *taint*, i.e. *contaminate* (cer. or mor.):–defile.

3393. μίασμα *mee'-as-mah*; from *3392* ("*miasma*"); (mor.) *foulness* (prop. the effect):–pollution.

3394. μιασμός *mee-as-mos'*; from *3392*; (mor.) *contamination* (prop. the act):–uncleanness.

3395. μίγμα *mig'-mah*; from *3396*; a *com.*:–mixture.

3396. μίγνυμι *mig'-noo-mee*; a prim. verb; to *mix*:–mingle.

3397. μικρόν *mik-ron'*; masc. or neut. sing. of *3398* (as noun); a *small* space of *time* or *degree*:–a (little) (while).

3398. μικρός *mik-ros'*; incl. the comp. μικρότερος, *mik-rot'-er-os*; app. a prim. word; *small* (in size, quantity, number or (fig.) dignity):–least, less, little, small.

3399. Μίλητος *mil'-ay-tos*; of unc. or.; *Miletus*, a city of Asia Minor:–Miletus.

3400. μίλιον *mil'-ee-on*; of Lat. or.; a *thousand* paces, i.e. a "*mile*":–mile.

3401. μιμέομαι *mim-eh'-om-ahee*; mid. from μῖμος (a "*mimic*"); to *imitate*:–follow.

3402. μιμητής *mim-ay-tace'*; from *3401*; an *imitator*:–follower.

3403. μιμνήσκω *mim-nace'-ko*; a prol. form of *3415* (from which some of the tenses are borrowed); to *remind*, i.e. (mid.) to *recall* to *mind*:–be mindful, remember.

3404. μισέω *mis-eh'-o*; from a prim. μῖσος (*hatred*); to *detest* (esp. to *persecute*); by ext., to *love less*:–hate(-ful).

3405. μισθαποδοσία *mis-thap-od-os-ee'-ah*; from *3406*; *requital* (good or bad):–recompence of reward.

3406. μισθαποδότης *mis-thap-od-ot'-ace*; from *3409* and *591*; a *renumerator*:–rewarder.

3407. μίσθιος *mis'-thee-os*; from *3408*; a *wage-earner*:–hired servant.

3408. μισθός *mis-thos'*; app. a prim. word; *pay* for service (lit. or fig.), good or bad:–hire, reward, wages.

3409. μισθόω *mis-tho'-o*; from *3408*; to *let* out for *wages*, i.e. (mid.) to *hire*:–hire.

3410. μίσθωμα *mis'-tho-mah*; from *3409*; a *rented* building:–hired house.

3411. μισθωτός *mis-tho-tos'*; from *3409*; a *wage-worker* (good or bad):–hired servant, hireling.

3412. Μιτυλήνη *mit-oo-lay'-nay*; for μυτιλήνη (*abounding in shell-fish*); *Mitylene* (or *Mytilene*), a town on the island of Lesbos:–Mitylene.

3413. Μιχαήλ *mikh-ah-ale'*; of Heb. or. [4317]; *Michaël*, an archangel:–Michael.

3414. μνᾶ *mnah*; of Lat. or.; a *mna* (i.e. *mina*), a cert. *weight*:– pound.

3415. μνάομαι, *mnah'-om-ahee*; mid. of a der. of *3306* or perh. of the base of *3145* (through the idea of *fixture* in the mind or of ment. *grasp*); to *bear in mind*, i.e. *recollect*; by impl. to *reward* or *punish*:–be mindful, remember, come (have) in remembrance. Comp. *3403*.

3416. Μνάσων *mnah'-sohn*; of unc. or.; *Mnason*, a Chr.:–Mnason.

3417. μνεία *mni'-ah*; from *3415* or *3403*; *recollection*; by impl. *recital*:–mention, remembrance.

3418. μνῆμα *mnay'-mah*; from *3415*; a memorial, i.e. sepulchral *monument* (*burial-place*):–grave, sepulchre, tomb.

3419. μνημεῖον *mnay-mi'-on*; from *3420*; a *remembrance*, i.e. *cenotaph* (*place of interment*):–grave, sepulchre, tomb.

3420. μνήμη *mnay'-may*; from *3403*; *memory*:–remembrance.

3421. μνημονεύω *mnay-mon-yoo'-o*; from a der. of *3420*; to *exercise memory*, i.e. *recollect*; by impl. to *punish*; also to *rehearse*:–make mention; be mindful, remember.

3422. μνημόσυνον *mnay-mos'-oo-non*; from *3421*; a *reminder* (*memorandum*), i.e. *record*:–memorial.

3423. μνηστεύω *mnace-tyoo'-o*; from a der. of *3415*; to *give a souvenir* (engagement present),

i.e. *betroth:*–espouse.
3424. μογιλάλος *mog-il-al'-os;* from *3425* and *2980; hardly talking,* i.e. *dumb* (*tongue-tied*):–having an impediment in his speech.
3425. μόγις *mog'-is;* adv. from a prim. μόγος (*toil*); *with difficulty:*–hardly.
3426. μόδιος *mod'-ee-os;* of Lat. or.; a *modius,* i.e. cert. measure for things dry (the quantity or the utensil):–bushel.
3427. μοί *moy;* the simpler form of *1698; to me:*–I, me, mine, my.
3428. μοιχαλίς *moy-khal-is';* a prol. form of the fem. of *3432;* an *adulteress* (lit. or fig.):–adulteress(-ous, -y).
3429. μοιχάω *moy-khah'-o;* from *3432;* (mid.) to *commit adultery:*–commit adultery.
3430. μοιχεία *moy-khi'-ah;* from *3431; adultery:*–adultery.
3431. μοιχεύω *moy-khyoo'-o;* from *3432;* to *commit adultery:*–commit adultery.
3432. μοιχός *moy-khos';* perh. a prim. word; a (male) *paramour;* fig. *apostate:*–adulterer.
3433. μόλις *mol'-is;* prob. by var. for *3425; with difficulty:*–hardly, scarce(-ly), + with much work.
3434. Μολόχ *mol-okh';* of Heb. or. [4432]; *Moloch* (i.e. *Molek*), an idol:–Moloch.
3435. μολύνω *mol-oo'-no;* prob. from *3189;* to *soil* (fig.):–defile.
3436. μολυσμός *mol-oos-mos';* from *3435;* a *stain;* i.e. (fig.) *immorality:*–filthiness.
3437. μομφή *mom-fay';* from *3201; blame,* i.e. (by impl.), a *fault:*–quarrel.
3438. μονή *mon-ay';* from *3306;* a *staying,* i.e. *residence* (the act or the place):–abode, mansion.
3439. μονογενής *mon-og-en-ace';* from *3441* and *1096; only-born,* i.e. *sole:*–only (begotten, child).
3440. μόνον *mon'-on;* neut. of *3441* as adv.; *merely:*–alone, but, only.
3441. μόνος *mon'-os;* prob. from *3306; remaining,* i.e. *sole* or *single;* by impl. *mere:*–alone, only, by themselves.
3442. μονόφθαλμος *mon-of'-thal-mos;* from *3441* and *3788; one-eyed:*–with one eye.
3443. μονόω *mon-o'-o;* from *3441;* to *isolate,* i.e. *bereave:*–be desolate.
3444. μορφή *mor-fay';* perh. from the base of *3313* (through the idea of *adjustment* of parts); *shape;* fig. *nature:*–form.
3445. μορφόω *mor-fo'-o;* from the same as *3444;* to *fashion* (fig.):–form.
3446. μόρφωσις *mor'-fo-sis;* from *3445; formation,* i.e. (by impl.), *appearance* (*semblance* or [concr.] *formula*):–form.
3447. μοσχοποιέω *mos-khop-oy-eh'-o;* from *3448* and *4160;* to *fabricate* the image of a *bullock:*–make a calf.
3448. μόσχος *mos'-khos;* prob. streng. for ὄσχος (a *shoot*); a young *bullock:*–calf.
3449. μόχθος *mokh'-thos;* from the base of *3425; toil,* i.e. (by impl.) *sadness:*–painfulness, travail.
3450. μοῦ *moo;* the simpler form of *1700; of me:*–I, me, mine (own), my.
3451. μουσικός *moo-sik-os';* from Μοῦσα (a *Muse*); "*musical*", i.e. (as noun) a *minstrel:*–musician.
3452. μυελός *moo-el-os';* perh. a prim. word; the *marrow:*–marrow.
3453. μυέω *moo-eh'-o;* from the base of *3466;* to *initiate,* i.e. (by impl.) to *teach:*–instruct.
3454. μῦθος *moo'-thos;* perh. from the same as *3453* (through the idea of *tuition*); a *tale,* i.e. *fiction* ("*myth*"):–fable.
3455. μυκάομαι *moo-kah'-om-ahee;* from a presumed der. of μύζω (to "*moo*"); to *bellow* (*roar*):–roar.
3456. μυκτηρίζω *mook-tay-rid'-zo;* from a der. of the base of *3455* (mean. *snout,* as that whence *lowing* proceeds); to *make mouths* at, i.e. *ridicule:*–mock.
3457. μυλικός *moo-lee-kos';* from *3458; belonging to a mill:*–mill[-stone].
3458. μύλος *moo'-los;* prob. ultimately from the base of 3433 (through the idea of *hardship*); a "*mill*", i.e. (by impl.), a *grinder* (*millstone*):–millstone.
3459. μύλων *moo'-lone;* from *3458;* a *mill-house:*–mill.
3460. Μύρα *moo'-rah;* of unc. der.; *Myra,* a place in Asia Minor:–Myra.
3461. μυρίας *moo-ree'-as;* from *3463;* a *ten-thousand;* by ext., a "*myriad*" or indef. number:–ten thousand.
3462. μυρίζω *moo-rid'-zo;* from *3464;* to *apply* (perfumed) *unguent* to:–anoint.
3463. μύριοι *moo'-ree-oi;* pl. of an app. prim. word (prop. mean. *very many*); *ten thousand;* by ext., *innumerably* many:–ten thousand.
3464. μύρον *moo'-ron;* prob. of for. or. [comp. *4753, 4666*]; "*myrrh*", i.e. (by impl.) *perfumed oil:*–ointment.
3465. Μυσία *moo-see'-ah;* of unc. or.; *Mysia,* a region of Asia Minor:–Mysia.
3466. μυστήριον *moos-tay'-ree-on;* from a der. of μύω (to *shut* the mouth); a *secret* or "*mystery*" (through the idea of *silence* imposed by *initiation* into relig. rites):–mystery.
3467. μυωπάζω *moo-ope-ad'-zo;* from a com. of the base of *3466* and ωψ (the *face:* from *3700*); to *shut* the *eyes,* i.e. *blink* (*see indistinctly*):–cannot see far off.
3468. μώλωψ *mo'-lopes;* from μῶλος ("*moil*"; prob. akin to the base of *3433*) and prob. ὤψ (the *face;* from *3700*); a *mole* ("black eye") or *blow-mark*:–stripe.
3469. μωμάομαι *mo-mah'-om-ahee;* from *3470;* to *carp* at, i.e. *censure* (*discredit*):–blame.
3470. μῶμος *mo'-mos;* perh. from *3201;* a *flaw* or *blot,* i.e. (fig.) *disgraceful* pers.:–blemish.
3471. μωραίνω *mo-rah'-ee-no;* from *3474;* to *become insipid;* fig. to *make* (pass. *act*) as a *simpleton:*–become fool, make foolish, lose savour.
3472. μωρία *mo-ree'-ah;* from *3474; silliness,* i.e. *absurdity:*–foolishness.
3473. μωρολογία *mo-rol-og-ee'-ah;* from a comp. of *3474* and *3004; silly talk,* i.e. *buffoonery:*–foolish talking.
3474. μωρός *mo-ros';* prob. from the base of *3466; dull* or *stupid* (as if *shut* up), i.e. *heedless,* (mor.) *blockhead,* (app.) *absurd:*–fool(-ish, X -ishness).
3475. Μωσεύς *moce-yoos';* or Μωσῆς *mo-sace';* or Μωϋσῆς *mo-oo-sace';* of Heb. or.; [4872]; *Moseus, Moses,* or *Moüses* (i.e. *Mosheh*), the Heb. lawgiver:–Moses.

N

3476. Ναασσών *nah-as-sone';* of Heb. or. [5177]; *Naasson* (i.e. *Nachshon*), an Isr.:–Naasson.
3477. Ναγγαί *nang-gah'-ee;* prob. of Heb. or. [comp. 5052]; *Nangae* (i.e. perh. *Nogach*), an Isr.:–Nagge.
3478. Ναζαρέθ *nad-zar-eth';* or Ναζαρέτ *nad-zar-et';* of unc. der.; *Nazareth* or *Nazaret,* a place in Pal.:–Nazareth.
3479. Ναζαρηνός *nad-zar-ay-nos';* from *3478;* a *Nazarene,* i.e. inh. of Nazareth:–of Nazareth.
3480. Ναζωραῖος *nad-zo-rah'-yos* from *3478;* a *Nazoraean,* i.e. inh. of Nazareth:–Nazarene, of Nazareth.
3481. Ναθάν *nath-an';* of Heb. or. [5416]; *Nathan,* an Isr.:–Nathan.
3482. Ναθαναήλ *nath-an-ah-ale';* of Heb. or. [5417]; *Nathanaël* (i.e. *Nathanel*), an Isr. and Chr.:–Nathanael.
3483. ναί *nahee;* a prim. par. of strong affirmation; *yes:*–even so, surely, truth, verily, yea, yes.
3484. Ναΐν *nah-in';* prob. of Heb. or. [comp. 4999]; *Naïn,* a place in Pal.:–Nain.
3485. ναός *nah-os';* from a prim. ναίω (to *dwell*); a *fane, shrine, temple:*–shrine, temple. Comp. *2411.*
3486. Ναούμ *nah-oom';* of Heb. or. [5151]; *Naüm* (i.e. *Nachum*), an Isr.:–Naum.
3487. νάρδος *nar'dos;* of for. or. [comp. 5373]; "*nard*":–[spike-]nard.
3488. Νάρκισσος *nar'-kis-sos;* a flower of the same name, from ναρκη (*stupefaction,* as a "narcotic"); *Narcissus,* a Rom.:–Narcissus.
3489. ναυαγέω *now-ag-eh'-o;* from a com. of *3491* and *71;* to *be shipwrecked* (*stranded,* "navigate"), lit. or fig.:–make (suffer) shipwreck.
3490. ναύκληρος *now'-klay-ros;* from *3491* and *2819* ("clerk"); a *captain:*–owner of a ship.
3491. ναῦς *nowce;* from νάω or νέω (to *float*); a *boat* (of any size):–ship.
3492. ναύτης *now'-tace;* from *3491;* a *boatman,* i.e. *seaman:*–sailor, shipman.
3493. Ναχώρ *nakh-ore';* of Heb. or. [5152]; *Nachor,* the grandfather of Abraham:–Nachor.
3494. νεανίας *neh-an-ee'-as;* from a der. of *3501;* a *youth* (up to about forty years):–young man.
3495. νεανίσκος *neh-an-is'-kos;* from the same as *3494;* a *youth* (under forty):–young man.

3496. Νεάπολις *neh-ap'-ol-is;* from *3501* and *4172; new town; Neäpolis*, a place in Macedonia:–Neapolis.

3497. Νεεμάν *neh-eh-man';* of Heb. or. [5283]; *Neëman* (i.e. *Naaman*), a Syrian:–Naaman.

3498. νεκρός *nek-ros';* from an app. prim. νέκυς (a *corpse*); *dead* (lit. or fig.; also as noun):–dead.

3499. νεκρόω *nek-ro'-o;* from *3498;* to *deaden*, i.e. (fig.) to *subdue:*–be dead, mortify.

3500. νέκρωσις *nek'-ro-sis;* from *3499; decease;* fig. *impotency:*–deadness, dying.

3501. νέος neh'-os; incl. the comp. νεώτερος *neh-o'-ter-os;* a prim. word; "*new*", i.e. (of persons) *youthful*, or (of things) *fresh;* fig. *regenerate:*–new, young.

3502. νεοσσός *neh-os-sos';* from *3501;* a *youngling* (*nestling*):–young.

3503. νεότης *neh-ot'-ace;* from *3501; newness*, i.e. *youthfulness:*–youth.

3504. νεόφυτος *neh-of'-oo-tos;* from *3501* and a der. of *5453; newly planted*, i.e. (fig.) a *young convert* ("*neophyte*"):–novice.

3505. Νέρων *ner'-ohn;* of Lat. or.; *Neron* (i.e. *Nero*), a Rom. emperor:–Nero.

3506. νεύω *nyoo'-o* app. a prim. verb; to "*nod*", i.e. (by anal.) to *signal:*–beckon.

3507. νεφέλη *nef-el'-ay;* from *3509;* prop. *cloudiness*, i.e. (concr.) a *cloud:*–cloud.

3508. Νεφθαλείμ *nef-thal-ime';* of Heb. or. [5321]; *Nephthaleim* (i.e. *Naphthali*), a tribe in Pal.:–Nephthalim.

3509. νέφος *nef'-os* app. a prim. word; a *cloud:*–cloud.

3510. νεφρός *nef-ros';* of unc. affin.; a *kidney* (pl.), i.e. (fig.) the inmost *mind:*–reins.

3511. νεωκόρος *neh-o-kor'-os;* from a form of *3485* and κορέω (to *sweep*); a *temple-servant*, i.e. (by impl.) a *votary:*–worshipper.

3512. νεωτερικός *neh-o-ter'-ik-os;* from the comp. of *3501; appertaining to younger* persons, i.e. *juvenile:*–youthful.

3513. νή *nay;* prob. an intens. form of *3483;* a par. of attestation (accompanied by the object invoked or appealed to in confirmation); *as sure as:*–I protest by.

3514. νήθω *nay'-tho;* from νέω (of like mean.); to *spin:*–spin.

3515. νηπιάζω *nay-pee-ad'-zo;* from *3516;* to *act* as *a babe*, i.e. (fig.) *innocently:*–be a child.

3516. νήπιος *nay'-pee-os;* from an obs. par. νη- *ne-* (implying *negation*) and *2031; not speaking*, i.e. an *infant* (*minor*); fig. a *simple-minded* pers., an *immature* Chr.:–babe, child (+ -ish).

3517. Νηρεύς *nare-yoos'* app. from a der. of the base of *3491* (mean. *wet*); *Nereus*, a Chr.:–Nereus.

3518. Νηρί *nay-ree';* of Heb. or. [5374]; *Neri* (i.e. *Nerijah*), an Isr.:–Neri.

3519. νησίον *nay-see'-on;* dim. of *3520;* an *islet:*–island.

3520. νῆσος *nay'-sos;* prob. from the base of *3491;* an *island:*–island, isle.

3521. νηστεία *nace-ti'-ah;* from *3522; abstinence* (from lack of food, or vol. and relig.); spec. the *fast* of the Day of Atonement:– fast(-ing).

3522. νηστεύω *nace-tyoo'-o;* from *3523;* to *abstain* from food (relig.):–fast.

3523. νῆστις *nace'-tis;* from the inseparable neg. par. νη *ne-* (*not*) and *2068; not eating*, i.e. *abstinent* from food (relig.):–fasting.

3524. νηφάλεος *nay-fal'-eh-os* νηφάλιος *nay-fal'-ee-os;* from *3525; sober*, i.e. (fig.) *circumspect:*–sober, vigilant.

3525. νήφω *nay'-fo;* of unc. affin.: to *abstain* from wine (*keep sober*), i.e. (fig.) *be discreet:*–be sober, watch.

3526. Νίγερ *neeg'-er;* of Lat. or.; *black; Niger*, a Chr.:–Niger.

3527. Νικάνωρ *nik-an'-ore;* prob. from *3528; victorious; Nicanor*, a Chr.:–Nicanor.

3528. νικάω *nik-ah'-o;* from *3529;* to *subdue* (lit. or fig.):–conquer, overcome, prevail, get the victory.

3529. νίκη *nee'-kay;* app. a prim. word; *conquest* (abstr.), i.e. (fig.) the *means of success:*–victory.

3530. Νικόδημος *nik-od'-ay-mos;* from *3534* and *1218; victorious* among his *people; Nicodemus*, an Isr.:–Nicodemus.

3531. Νικολαΐτης *nik-ol-ah-ee'-tace;* from *3532;* a *Nicolaïte*, i.e. adherent of *Nicolaüs:–Nicolaitane.*

3532. Νικόλαος *nik-ol'-ah-os';* from *3534* and *2994; victorious* over the *people; Nicolaüs*: a heretic:–Nicolaus.

3533. Νικόπολις *nik-op'-ol-is;* from *3534* and *4172; victorious city; Nicopolis*, a place in Macedonia:–Nicopolis.

3534. νῖκος *nee'-kos;* from *3529;* a *conquest* (concr.), i.e. (by impl.) *triumph:*–victory.

3535. Νινευΐ *nin-yoo-ee';* of Heb. or. [5210]; *Ninevi* (i.e. *Nineveh*), the capital of Assyria:–Nineve.

3536. Νινευΐτης *nin-yoo-ee'-tace;* from *3535;* a *Ninevite*, i.e. inh. of Nineveh:–of Nineve, Ninevite.

3537. νιπτήρ *nip-tare';* from *3538;* a *ewer:*–bason.

3538. νίπτω *nip'-to;* to *cleanse* (esp. the hands or the feet or the face); cer., to *perform ablution:*–wash. Comp. *3068*.

3539. νοιέω *noy-eh'-o;* from *3563;* to *exercise* the *mind* (*observe*), i.e. (fig.) to *comprehend, heed:*–consider, perceive, think, understand.

3540. νόημα *no'-ay-mah;* from *3539;* a *perception*, i.e. *purpose*, or (by impl.) the *intellect, disposition*, itself:–device, mind, thought.

3541. νόθος *noth'-os;* of unc. affin.; a *spurious* or *illegitimate* son:–bastard.

3542. νομή *nom-ay';* fem. from the same as *3551; pasture*, i.e. (the act) *feeding* (fig. *spreading* of a gangrene), or (the food) *pasturage:*–X eat, pasture.

3543. νομίζω *nom-id'-zo;* from *3551;* prop. to *do* by *law* (*usage*), i.e. to *accustom* (pass. *be usual*); by ext., to *deem* or *regard:*–suppose, thing, be wont.

3544. νομικός *nom-ik-os';* from *3551; according* (or *pertaining*) *to law*, i.e. *legal* (cer.); as noun, an *expert in* the (Mosaic) *law:*–about the law, lawyer.

3545. νομίμως *nom-im'-oce;* adv. from a der. of *3551; legitimately* (spec. agreeably to the rules of the lists):–lawfully.

3546. νόμισμα *nom'-is-mah;* from *3543; what is reckoned* as of value (after the Lat. *numisma*), i.e. current *coin:*–money.

3547. νομοδιδάσκαλος *nom-od-id-as'-kal-os;* from *3551* and *1320;* an *expounder of* the (Jewish) *law*, i.e. a *Rabbi:*–doctor (teacher) of the law.

3548. νομοθεσία *nom-oth-es-ee'-ah;* from *3550; legislation* (spec. the *institution of* the Mosaic *code*):–giving of the law.

3549. νομοθετέω *nom-oth-et-eh'-o;* from *3550;* to *legislate*, i.e. pass. to *have* (the Mosaic) *enactments* injoined, *be sanctioned* (by them):–establish, receive the law.

3550. νομοθέτης *nom-oth-et'-ace;* from *3551* and a der. of *5087;* a *legislator:*–lawgiver.

3551. νόμος *nom'-os;* from a prim. νέμω (to *parcel* out, esp. *food* or *grazing* to animals); *law* (through the idea of prescriptive *usage*), gen. case (*regulation*), spec. (of Moses [incl. the volume] also of the Gospel), or fig. (a *principle*):–law.

3552. νοσέω *nos-eh'-o;* from *3554;* to *be sick*, i.e. (by impl. of a diseased appetite) to *hanker* after (fig. to *harp* upon):–dote.

3553. νόσημα *nos'-ay-ma;* from *3552;* an *ailment:*–disease.

3554. νόσος *nos'-os;* of unc. affin.; a *malady* (rarely fig. of mor. *disability*):–disease, infirmity, sickness.

3555. νοσσιά *nos-see-ah';* from *3502;* a *brood* (of chickens):–brood.

3556. νοσσίον *nos-see'-on;* dim. of 3502; a *birdling:*–chicken.

3557. νοσφίζομαι *nos-fid'-zom-ahee;* mid. from νοσφί (*apart* or *clandestinely*); to *sequestrate* for oneself, i.e. *embezzle:*–keep back, purloin.

3558. νότος *not'-os;* of unc. affin.; the *south*(*-west*) *wind;* by ext., the *southern quarter* itself:–south (wind).

3559. νουθεσία *noo-thes-ee'-ah;* from *3563* and a der. of *5087;* calling *attention* to, i.e. (by impl.) mild *rebuke* or *warning:*–admonition.

3560. νουθετέω *noo-thet-eh'-o;* from the same as *3559;* to *put in mind*, i.e. (by impl.) to *caution* or *reprove* gently:–admonish, warn.

3561. νουμηνία *noo-may-nee'-ah;* fem. of a com. of *3501* and *3376* (as noun by impl. of *2250*); the festival of *new moon:*–new moon.

3562. νουνεχῶς *noon-ekh-oce';* adv. from a comp. of the acc. of *3563* and *2192;* in a *mind-having* way, i.e. *prudently:*–discreetly.

3563. νοῦς *nooce;* prob. from the base of *1097;* the *intellect*, i.e. *mind* (divine or human; in thought, feeling, or will); by impl. *mean.:*–mind, understanding. Comp. *5590*.

GREEK

3564. Νυμφᾶς *noom-fas'*; prob. contr. for a com. of *3565* and *1435; nymph-given* (i.e. *-born*); *Nymphas*, a Chr.:–Nymphas.

3565. νύμφη *noom-fay'*; from a prim. but obs. verb νύπτω (to *veil* as a bride; comp. Lat. "*nupto,*" to *marry*); a young *married* woman (as *veiled*), incl. a *betrothed* girl; by impl. a *son's wife*:–bride, daughter in law.

3566. νυμφίος *noom-fee'-os; from 3565;* a *bride-groom* (lit. or fig.):–bridegroom.

3567. νυμφών *noom-fohn'; from 3565;* the *bridal* room:–bridechamber.

3568. νῦν *noon;* a prim. par. of pres. time; "*now*" (as adv. of date, a transition or emphasis); also as noun or adj. *pres.* or *immed.*:–henceforth, + hereafter, of late, soon, present, this (time). See also *3569, 3570*.

3569. τανῦν *tan-oon';* or τά νύν *tah-oon';* from neut. pl. of *3588* and *3568; the* things *now,* i.e. (adv.) *at present*:–(but) now.

3570. νυνί *noo-nee';* a prol. form of *3568* for emphasis; *just now*:–now.

3571. νύξ *noox;* a prim. word; "*night*" (lit. or fig.):– (mid-)night.

3572. νύσσω *noos'-so;* app. a prim. word; to *prick* ("nudge"):–pierce.

3573. νυστάζω *noos-tad'-zo;* from a presumed der. of *3506;* to *nod,* i.e.(by impl.) to *fall asleep;* fig. to *delay*:–slumber.

3574. νυχθήμερον *nookh-thay'-mer-on;* from *3571* and *2250;* a *day-and-night,* i.e. full *day* of twenty-four hours:–night and day.

3575. Νῶε *no'-eh;* of Heb. or. [5146]; *Noë,* (i.e. *Noäch),* a patriarch:–Noe.

3576. νωθρός *no-thros';* from a der. of *3541; sluggish,* i.e. (lit.) *lazy,* or (fig.) *stupid*:–dull, slothful.

3577. νῶτος *no'-tos;* of unc. affin.; the *back*:–back.

Ξ

3578. ξενία *xen-ee'-ah;* from *3581; hospitality,* i.e. (by impl.) a *place of entertainment*:–lodging.

3579. ξενίζω *xen-id'-zo;* from *3581;* to *be a host* (pass. a *guest*); by impl. *be* (*make, appear*) *strange*:–entertain, lodge, (think it) strange.

3580. ξενοδοχέω *xen-od-okh-eh'-o;* from a com. of *3581* and *1209;* to *be hospitable*:–lodge strangers.

3581. ξένος *xen'-os;* app. a prim. word; *for.* (lit. *alien,* or fig. *novel*); by impl. a *guest* or (vice-versa) *entertainer*:–host, strange(-r).

3582. ξέστης *xes'-tace;* as if from ξέω (prop. to *smooth;* by impl. [of *friction*] to *boil* or *heat*); a *vessel* (as *fashioned* or for *cooking*) [or perh. by corruption from the Lat. *sextarius,* the *sixth* of a modius, i.e. about a *pint*], i.e. (spec.), a *measure* for liquids or solids, (by anal. a *pitcher*):–pot.

3583. ξηραίνω *xay-rah'-ee-no;* from *3584;* to *desiccate;* by impl. to *shrivel,* to *mature*:–dry up, pine away, be ripe, wither (away).

3584. ξηρός *xay-ros';* from the base of *3582* (through the idea of *scorching*); *arid;* by impl. *shrunken, earth* (as opposed to water):–dry land, withered.

3585. ξύλινος *xoo'-lin-os;* from *3586; wooden*:–of wood.

3586. ξύλον *xoo'-lon;* from another form of the base of *3582; timber* (as fuel or material); by impl. a *stick, club* or *tree* or other wooden article or substance:–staff, stocks, tree, wood.

3587. ξυράω *xoo-rah'-o;* from a der. of the same as *3586* (mean. a *razor*); to *shave* or "*shear*" the hair:–shave.

O

3588. ὁ *hŏ;* includ.the fem. ἡ *Hay;* and the neut. τό *tŏ,* in all their inflections; the def. art.; *the* (sometimes to be supplied, at others omitted, in English idiom):–the, this, that, one, he, she, it, etc.

3589. ὀγδοήκοντα *og-do-ay'-kon-tah;* from 3590; *ten times eight*:–fourscore.

3590. ὄγδοος *og'-do-os;* from *3638;* the *eighth*:–eighth.

3591. ὄγκος *ong'-kos;* prob. from the same as *43;* a *mass* (as *bending* or *bulging* by its load), i.e. *burden* (*hindrance*):–weight.

3592. ὅδε *hod'-eh;* includ.the fem. ἥδε, *hay'-deh;* and the neut. τόδε *tod'-e;* from *3588* and *1161;* the *same,* i.e. *this* or *that* one (pl. *these* or *those*); often used as a pers. pron.:–he, she, such, these, thus.

3593. ὁδεύω *hod-yoo'-o;* from *3598;* to *travel*:–journey.

3594. ὁδηγέω *hod-ayg-eh'-o;* from *3595;* to *show* the *way* (lit. or fig. [teach]):–guide, lead.

3595. ὁδηγός *hod-ayg-os';* from *3598* and *2233;* a *conductor* (lit. or fig. [teacher]):–guide, leader.

3596. ὁδοιπορέω *hod-oy-por-eh'-o;* from a com. of *3598* and *4198;* to *be a wayfarer,* i.e. *travel*:–go on a journey.

3597. ὁδοιπορία *hod-oy-por-ee'-ah;* from the same as *3596; travel*:–journey(-ing).

3598. ὁδός *hod-os';* app. a prim. word; a *road;* by impl. a *progress* (the route, act or distance); fig. a *mode* or *means*:–journey, (high-)way.

3599. ὀδούς *od-ooce;* perh. from the base of *2068;* a "*tooth*":–tooth.

3600. ὀδυνάω *od-oo-nah'-o* from *3601;* to *grieve*:–sorrow, torment.

3601. ὀδύνη *od-oo'-nay;* from *1416; grief* (as *dejecting*):–sorrow.

3602. ὀδυρμός *od-oor-mos';* from a der. of the base of *1416; moaning,* i.e. *lamentation*:–mourning.

3603. ὅ εστι *ho es-tee';* from the neut. of *3739* and the third pers. sing. pres. ind. of *1510; which is*:–called, which is (make), i.e. (to say).

3604. 'Οζίας *od-zee'-as;* of Heb. or. [5818]; *Ozias* (i.e. *Uzzijah*), an Isr.:–Ozias.

3605. ὄζω *od'-zo;* a prim. verb (in a streng. form); to *scent* (usually an ill "odor"): stink.

3606. ὅθεν *hoth'-en;* from 3739 with the directive enclitic of source; *from which* place or source or cause (adv. or conj.):–from thence, (from) whence, where(-by, -fore, -upon).

3607. ὀθόνη *oth-on'-ay;* of unc. affin.; a *linen* cloth, i.e. (esp.) a *sail*:–sheet.

3608. ὀθόνιον *oth-on'-ee-on;* neut. of a presumed der. of *3607;* a linen *bandage*:–linen clothes.

3609. οἰκεῖος *oy-ki'-os;* from *3624; domestic,* i.e. (as noun), a *rel. adherent*:–(those) of the (his own) house(-hold).

3610. οἰκέτης *oy-ket'-ace;* from *3611;* a fellow *resident,* i.e. menial *domestic*:–(household) servant.

3611. οἰκέω *oy-keh'-o;* from *3624;* to *occupy a house*, i.e. *reside* (fig. *inhabit, remain, inhere*); by impl. to *cohabit*:–dwell. See also *3625*.

3612. οἴκημα *oy'-kay-mah;* from *3611;* a *tenement,* i.e. (spec.), a *jail*:–prison.

3613. οἰκητήριον *oy-kay-tay'-ree-on;* neut. of a presumed der. of *3611* (equiv. to *3612*); a *residence* (lit. or fig.):–habitation, house.

3614. οἰκία *oy-kee'-ah;* from *3624;* prop. *residence* (abstr.), but usually (concr.) an *abode* (lit. or fig.); by impl. a *family* (esp. *domestics*):–home, house(-hold).

3615. οἰκιακός *oy-kee-ak-os';* from *3614; familiar,* i.e. (as noun) *relatives*:–they (them) of (his own) household.

3616. οἰκοδεσποτέω *oy-kod-es-pot-eh'-o;* from *3617;* to *be* the *head* of (i.e. *rule*) a *family*:–guide the house.

3617. οἰκοδεσπότης *oy-kod-es-pot'-ace;* from *3624* and *1203; the head of a family*:–goodman (of the house), householder, master of the house.

3618. οἰκοδομέω *oy-kod-om-eh'-o;* from the same as *3619;* to *be* a *house-builder,* i.e. *construct* or (fig.) *confirm*:–(be in) build (-er, -ing, up), edify, embolden.

3619. οἰκοδομή *oy-kod-om-ay';* fem. (abstr.) of a com. of *3624* and the base of *1430; architecture,* i.e. (concr.) a *structure;* fig. *confirmation*:–building, edify(-ication, -ing).

3620. οἰκοδομία *oy-kod-om-ee'-ah;* from the same as *3619; confirmation*:–edifying.

3621. οἰκονομέω *oy-kon-om-eh'-o;* from *3623;* to *manage* (a house, i.e. an estate):–be steward.

3622. οἰκονομία *oy-kon-om-ee'-ah;* from *3623; administration* (of a household or estate); spec. a (relig.) "*economy*":–dispensation, stewardship.

3623. οἰκονόμος *oy-kon-om'-os;* from *3624* and the base of *3551;* a *house-distributor* (i.e. *manager*), or *overseer,* i.e. an employee in that capacity; by ext., a fiscal *agent* (*treasurer*); fig. a *preacher* (of the Gospel):–chamberlain, governor, steward.

3624. οἶκος *oy'-kos;* of unc. affin.; a *dwelling* (more or less extensive, lit. or fig.); by impl. a *family* (more or less related, lit. or fig.):–home, house(-hold), temple.

3625. οἰκουμένη *oy-kou-men'-ay;* fem. part. pres. pass. of *3611* (as noun, by impl.

of 1093); *land,* i.e. the (terrene part of the) *globe;* spec. the Rom. *empire:*–earth, world.

3626. οἰκουρός *oy-koo-ros';* from *3624* and οὖρος (a *guard;* be "ware"); a *stayer at home*, i.e. *domestically inclined* (a "good housekeeper"):–keeper at home.

3627. οἰκτείρω *oyk-ti'-ro;* (also incertain tenses) prol. οἰκτερέω *oyk-ter-eh'-o;* from οἶκτος (*pity*); to *exercise pity:*–have compassion on.

3628. οἰκτιρμός *oyk-tir-mos';* from *3627; pity:* mercy.

3629. οἰκτίρμων *oyk-tir'-mone;* from 3627; *compassionate:*–merciful, of tender mercy.

3630. οἰνοπότης *oy-nop-ot'-ac;* from *3631* and a der. of the alt. of *4095;* a *tippler:*–winebibber.

3631. οἶνος *oy'-nos* a prim. word (or perh. of Heb. or. [3196]); "*wine*" (lit. or fig.):–wine.

3632. οἰνοφλυγία *oy-nof-loog-ee'-ah;* from *3631* and a form of the base of *5397;* an *overflow* (or surplus) of *wine,* i.e. *vinolency* (*drunkenness*):–excess of wine.

3633. οἴομαι *oy'-om-ahee;* or (short.) οἶμαι *oy'-mahee;* app. from *3634;* to *make like* (oneself), i.e. *imagine* (*be of* the *opinion*):–suppose, think.

3634. οἷος *hoy'-os;* prob. akin to *3588, 3739,* and *3745; such* or *what sort* of (as a correl. or exclamation); esp. the neut. (adv.) with neg., not *so:*–so (as), such as, what (manner of), which.

3635. ὀκνέω *ok-neh'-o;* from ὄκνος (*hesitation*); to *be slow* (fig. *loath*):–delay.

3636. ὀκνηρός *ok-nay-ros';* from *3635; tardy,* i.e. *indolent;* (fig.) *irksome:*–grievous, slothful.

3637. ὀκταήμερος *ok-tah-ay'-mer-os;* from *3638* and *2250;* an *eight-day* old pers. or act:–the eighth day.

3638. ὀκτώ, *ok-to';* a prim. numeral; "*eight*":–eight.

3639. ὄλεθρος *ol'-eth-ros;* from a prim. ὄλλυμι ollumi (to *destroy;* a prol. form); *ruin,* i.e. *death, punishment:*–destruction.

3640. ὀλιγόπιστος *ol-ig-op'-is-tos;* from *3641* and 4102; *incredulous,* i.e. *lacking confidence* (in Christ):–of little faith.

3641. ὀλίγος *ol-ee'-gos;* of unc. affin.; *puny* (in extent, degree, number, duration or value); esp. neut. (adv.) *somewhat:*–+ almost, brief[-ly], few, (a) little, + long, a season, short, small, a while.

3642. ὀλιγόψυχος *ol-ig-op'-soo-khos;* from *3641* and *5590; little-spirited,* i.e. *faint-hearted:*–feebleminded.

3643. ὀλιγωρέω *ol-ig-o-reh'-o;* from a com. of *3641* and ὥρα ("*care*"); to *have little regard* for, i.e. to *disesteem:*–despise.

3644. ὀλοθρευτής *ol-oth-ryoo-tace';* from *3645;* a *ruiner,* i.e. (spec.), a venomous *serpent:*–destroyer.

3645 ὀλοθρεύω *ol-oth-ryoo'-o;* from *3639;* to *spoil,* i.e. *slay:*–destroy.

3646. ὁλοκαύτωμα *hol-ok-ow'-to-mah;* from a der. of a com. of *3650* and a der. of *2545;* a *wholly-consumed* sacrifice ("holocaust"):–(whole) burnt offering.

3647. ὁλοκληρία *hol-ok-lay-ree'-ah;* from *3648; integrity,* i.e. phys. *wholeness:*–perfect soundness.

3648. ὁλόκληρος *hol'-ok'-lay-ros;* from *3650* and *2819; complete* in every *part,* i.e. perfectly *sound* (in body):–entire, whole.

3649. ὀλολύζω *ol-ol-ood'-zo;* a redupl. prim. verb; to "*howl*" or "*halloo*", i.e. *shriek:*–howl.

3650. ὅλος *hol'-os;* a prim. word; "*whole*" or "*all*", i.e. *complete* (in extent, amount, time or degree), esp. (neut.) as noun or adv.:–all, altogether, every whit, + throughout, whole.

3651. ὁλοτελής *hol-ot-el-ace';* from *3650* and *5056; complete* to the *end,* i.e. *absol. perfect:*–wholly.

3652. 'Ολυμπᾶς *ol-oom-pas';* prob. a contr. from 'Ολυμπιόδωρος (*Olympian-bestowed,* i.e. *heaven-descended*); *Olympas,* a Chr.:–Olympas.

3653. ὄλυνθος *ol'-oon-thos;* of unc. der.; an *unripe* (because out of season) *fig:*–untimely fig.

3654. ὅλως *hol'-oce;* adv. from *3650; completely,* i.e. *altogether;* (by anal.), *everywhere;* (neg.) not *by any means:*–at all, commonly, utterly.

3655. ὄμβρος *om'-bros;* of unc. affin.; a thunder *storm:*–shower.

3656. ὁμιλέω *hom-il-eh'-o;* from *3658;* to *be in company* with, i.e. (by impl.) to *converse:*–commune, talk.

3657. ὁμιλία *hom-il-ee'-ah;* from *3658; companionship* ("homily"), i.e. (by impl.) *intercourse:*–communication.

3658. ὅμιλος *hom'-il-os* from the base of *3674* and a der. of the alt. of *138* (mean. a *crowd*); *association together,* i.e. a *multitude:*–company.

3659. ὄμμα *om'-mah;* from *3700;* a *sight,* i.e. (by impl.) the *eye:*–eye.

3660. ὀμνύω *om-noo'-o;* a prol. form of a prim. but obs. ὄμω for which another prol. form (ὀμόω *om-o'-o*) is used in cert. tenses. to *swear,* i.e. *take* (or *declare on*) *oath:* –swear.

3661. ὁμοθυμαδόν *hom-oth-oo-mad-on';* adv. from a com. of the base of *3674* and *2372; unanimously:*–with one accord (mind).

3662. ὁμοιάζω *hom-oy-ad'-zo;* from *3664;* to *resemble:*–agree.

3663. ὁμοιοπαθής *hom-oy-op-ath-ace';* from *3664* and the alt. of *3958; similarly affected:*–of (subject to) like passions.

3664. ὅμοιος *hom'-oy-os;* from the base of *3674; similar* (in appearance or character):–like, + manner.

3665. ὁμοιότης *hom-oy-ot'-ace;* from *3664; resemblance:*–like as, similitude.

3666. ὁμοιόω *hom-oy-o'-o;* from *3664;* to *assimilate,* i.e. *comp.;* pass. to *become similar:*–be (make) like, (in the) liken(-ess), resemble.

3667. ὁμοίωμα *hom-oy'-o-mah;* from *3666;* a *form;* abstr., *resemblance:*–made like to, likeness, shape, similitude.

3668. ὁμοίως *hom-oy'-oce;* adv. from *3664; similarly:*–likewise, so.

3669. ὁμοίωσις *hom-oy'-o-sis;* from *3666; assimilation,* i.e. *resemblance:*–similitude.

3670. ὁμολογέω *hom-ol-og-eh'-o;* from a com. of the base of *3674* and *3056;* to *assent,* i.e. *covenant, acknowledge:*–con- (pro-)fess, confession is made, give thanks, promise.

3671. ὁμολογία *hom-ol-og-ee'-ah;* from the same as *3670; acknowledgment:*–con- (pro-) fession, professed.

3672. ὁμολογουμένως *hom-ol-og-ow-men-oce;* adv. of pres. pass. part. of *3670; confessedly:*–without controversy.

3673. ὁμότεχνος *hom-ot'-ekh-nos;* from the base of *3674* and *5078;* a *fellow-artificer:*–of the same craft.

3674. ὁμοῦ *hom-oo';* gen. of ὁμός (the *same;* akin to *260*) as adv.; *at* the *same* place or time:–together.

3675. ὁμόφρων *hom-of'-rone;* from the base of *3674* and *5424; like-minded,* i.e. *harmonious:*–of one mind.

3676. ὅμως *hom'-oce;* adv. from the base of *3674; at* the *same* time, i.e. (conj.) *notwithstanding, yet still:*–and even, nevertheless, though but.

3677. ὄναρ *on'-ar;* of unc. der.; a *dream:*–dream.

3678. ὀνάριον *on-ar'-ee-on;* neut. of a presumed der. of *3688;* a *little ass:*–young ass.

3679. ὀνειδίζω *on-i-did'-zo;* from *3681;* to *defame,* i.e. *rail at, chide, taunt:*–cast in teeth, (suffer) reproach, revile, upbraid.

3680. ὀνειδισμός *on-i-dis-mos';* from *3679; contumely:*–reproach.

3681. ὄνειδος *on'-i-dos;* prob. akin to the base of *3686; notoriety,* i.e. a *taunt* (*disgrace*):–reproach.

3682. 'Ονήσιμος *on-ay'-sim-os;* from *3685; profitable; Onesimus,* a Chr.:–Onesimus.

3683. 'Ονησίφορος *on-ay-sif'-or-os;* from a der. of *3685* and *5411; profit-bearer; Onesiphorus,* a Chr.:–Onespiphorus.

3684. ὀνικός *on-ik-os';* from *3688; belonging* to an *ass,* i.e. *large* (so as to be turned by a ass):–millstone.

3685. ὀνίνημι *on-in'-ay-mee;* a prol. form of an app. prim. verb (ὄνομαι to *slur*); for which another prol. form (ὀνάω onao) is used as an alt. in some tenses [unless indeed it be ident. with the base of *3686* through the idea of *notoriety*]; to *gratify,* i.e. (mid.) to *derive pleasure* or *advantage* from:– have joy.

3686. ὄνομα *on'-om-ah;* from a presumed der. of the base of *1097* (comp. *3685*); a "*name*" (lit. or fig.) [*authority, character*]:–called, (+ sur-) name(-d).

3687. ὀνομάζω *on-om-ad'-zo;* from *3686;* to *name,* i.e. *assign an appellation;* by ext., to *utter, mention, profess:*–call, name.

3688. ὄνος *on'-os;* app. a prim. word; a *donkey:*–an ass.

3689. ὄντως *on'-toce;* adv. of the oblique cases of *5607; really:*–certainly, clean,

GREEK

indeed, of a truth, verily.

3690. ὄξος *oz-os;* from *3691; vinegar,* i.e. *sour* wine:–vinegar.

3691. ὀξύς *oz-oos';* prob. akin to the base of *188* ["*acid*"]; *keen;* by anal. *rapid:*–sharp, swift.

3692. ὀπή *op-ay';* prob. from *3700;* a *hole* (as if for light), i.e. *cavern;* by anal. a *spring* (of water):–cave, place.

3693. ὄπισθεν *op'-is-then;* from ὄπις (*regard;* from *3700*) with enclitic of source; *from the rear* (as a secure *aspect*), i.e. *at* the *back* (adv. and prep. of place or time):–after, backside, behind.

3694. ὀπίσω *op-is'-o;* from the same as *3693* with enclitic of direction; *to* the *back,* i.e. *aback* (as adv. or prep. of time or place; or as noun):–after, back(-ward), (+ get) behind, + follow.

3695. ὁπλίζω *hop-lid'-zo;* from *3696;* to *equip* (with weapons [mid. and fig.]):–arm self.

3696. ὅπλον *hop'-lon;* prob. from a prim. ἕπω (to be *busy* about); an *implement* or *utensil* or *tool* (lit. or fig. esp. offensive for war):–armour, instrument, weapon.

3697. ὁποῖος *hop-oy'-os;* from *3739* and *4169;* of *what* kind *that,* i.e. *how* (as) *great* (*excellent*) (spec. as an indef. correl. to the antecedent *5108* of quality):–what manner (sort) of, such as whatsoever.

3698. ὁπότε *hop-ot'-eh;* from *3739* and *4218; what*(-ever) *then,* i.e. (of time) *as soon as:*–when.

3699. ὅπου *hop'-oo;* from *3739* and 4225; *what*(-ever) where, i.e. *at whichever* spot:–in what place, where(-as, -soever), whither (+ soever).

3700. ὀπτάνομαι *op-tan'-om-ahee;* a (mid.) prol. form of the prim. (mid.) ὄπτομαι *op-tom-ahee* which is used for it in cert. tenses; and both as alt. of *3708;* to *gaze* (i.e. with wide-open eyes, as at something remarkable; and thus differing from *991,* which denotes simply *vol.* observation; and from *1492,* which expresses merely mechanical, pass. or casual vision; while *2300,* and still more emphat. its intens. *2334,* signifies an earnest but more continued *inspection;* and *4648* a watching *from a distance*):–appear, look, see, shew self.

3701. ὀπτασία *op-tas-ee'-ah;* from a presumed der. of *3700; visuality,* i.e. (concr.) an *apparition:*–vision.

3702. ὀπτός *op-tos';* from an obs. verb akin to ἕψω (to "*steep*"); *cooked,* i.e. *roasted:*–broiled.

3703. ὀπώρα *op-o'-rah;* app. from the base of *3796* and *5610;* prop. *even-tide* of the (summer) season (*dog-days*), i.e. (by impl.) *ripe* fruit:–fruit.

3704. ὅπως *hop'-oce;* from *3739* and *4459; what*(-ever) *how,* i.e. *in* the *manner that* (as adv. or conj. of coincidence, intentional or actual):–because, how, (so) that, to, when.

3705. ὅραμα *hor'-am-ah;* from *3708; something gazed at,* i.e. a *spectacle* (esp. supernatural):–sight, vision.

3706. ὅρασις *hor'-as-is;* from *3708;* the act of *gazing,* i.e. (exter.) an *aspect* or (internally) an inspired *appearance:*–sight, vision.

3707. ὁρατός *hor-at-os';* from *3708; gazed at,* i.e. (by impl.) *capable of being seen:*–visible.

3708. ὁράω *hor-ah'-o;* prop. to *stare* at [comp. *3700*], i.e. (by impl.) to *discern* clearly (phys. or ment.); by ext., to *attend* to; by Heb., to *experience;* pass. to *appear:*–behold, perceive, see, take heed.

3709. ὀργή *or-gay';* from *3713;* prop. *desire* (as a *reaching* forth or *excitement* of the mind), i.e. (by anal.), violent *passion* (*ire,* or [justifiable] *abhorrence*); by impl. *punishment:*–anger, indignation, vengeance, wrath.

3710. ὀργίζω *or-gid'-zo;* from *3709;* to *provoke* or *enrage,* i.e. (pass.) *become exasperated:*–be angry (wroth).

3711. ὀργίλος *org-ee'-los;* from *3709; irascible:*–soon angry.

3712. ὀργυιά *org-wee-ah';* from *3713;* a *stretch* of the arms, i.e. a *fathom:*–fathom.

3713. ὀρέγομαι *or-eg'-om-ahee;* mid. of app. a prol. form of an obs. prim. [comp. *3735*]; to *stretch* oneself, i.e. *reach* out after (*long* for):–covet after, desire.

3714. ὀρεινός *or-i-nos;* from *3735; mountainous,* i.e. (fem. by impl. of *5561*) the *Highlands* (of Judaea):–hill country.

3715. ὄρεξις *or'-ex-is;* from *3713; excitement* of the mind, i.e. *longing* after:–lust.

3716. ὀρθοποδέω *or-thop-od-eh'-o;* from a com. of *3717* and *4228;* to *be straight-footed,* i.e. (fig.) to *go dir.* forward:–walk uprightly.

3717. ὀρθός *or-thos';* prob. from the base of *3735; right* (as *rising*), i.e. (perpendicularly) *erect* (fig. *honest*), or (horizontally) *level* or *dir.:*–straight, upright.

3718. ὀρθοτομέω *or-thot-om-eh'-o;* from a com. of *3717* and the base of *5114,* to *make* a *straight cut,* i.e. (fig.) to *dissect* (*expound*) *correctly* (the divine message):–rightly divide.

3719. ὀρθρίζω *or-thrid'-zo;* from *3722;* to use the *dawn,* i.e. (by impl.) to *repair betimes:*–come early in the morning.

3720. ὀρθρινός *or-thrin-os';* from *3722; relating to* the *dawn,* i.e. *matutinal* :–morning.

3721. ὄρθριος *or'-three-os;* from *3722; in* the *dawn,* i.e. up *at day-break:*–early.

3722. ὄρθρος *or'-thros;* from the same as *3735; dawn* (as *sun-rise, rising* of light); by ext., *morn:*–early in the morning.

3723. ὀρθῶς *or-thoce';* adv. from *3717; in* a *straight* manner, i.e. (fig.) *correctly* (also mor.):–plain, right(-ly).

3724. ὁρίζω *hor-id'-zo;* from *3725;* to *mark* out or *bound* ("horizon"), i.e. (fig.) to *appoint, decree, specify:*–declare, determine, limit, ordain.

3725. ὅριον *hor'-ee-on;* neut. of a der. of an app. prim. ὅρος (a *bound* or *limit*); a *boundary*-line, i.e. (by impl.) a *frontier* (*region*):–border, coast.

3726. ὁρκίζω *hor-kid'-zo;* from *3727;* to *put on oath,* i.e. *make swear;* by anal. to solemnly *enjoin:*–adjure, charge.

3727. ὅρκος *hor'-kos;* from ἕρκος (a *fence;* perh. akin to *3725*); a *limit,* i.e. (sacred) *restraint* (spec. an *oath*):–oath.

3728. ὁρκωμοσία *hor-ko-mos-ee'ah;* from a comp. of *3727* and a der. of *3660; asseveration on oath:*–oath.

3729. ὁρμάω *hor-mah'-o;* from *3730;* to *start, spur* or *urge* on, i.e. (refl.) to *dash* or *plunge:*–run (violently), rush.

3730. ὁρμή *hor-may'* of unc. affin.; a violent *impulse,* i.e. *onset:*–assault.

3731. ὅρμημα *hor'-may-mah;* from *3730;* an *attack,* i.e. (abstr.) *precipitancy:*–violence.

3732. ὄρνεον *or'-neh-on;* neut. of a presumed der. of *3733;* a *birdling:*–bird, fowl.

3733. ὄρνις *or'-nis;* prob. from a prol. form of the base of *3735;* a *bird* (as *rising* in the air), i.e. (spec.), a *hen* (or female domestic fowl):–hen.

3734. ὁροθεσία *hor-oth-es-ee'-ah;* from a com. of the base of *3725* and a der. of *5087;* a *limit-placing,* i.e. (concr.) *boundary-line:*–bound.

3735. ὄρος *or'-os;* prob. from an obs. ὄρω (to *rise* or "*rear*"; perh. akin to *142;* comp. *3733*); a *mountain* (as *lifting* itself above the plain): -hill, mount(-ain).

3736. ὀρύσσω *or-oos'-so;* app. a prim. verb; to "*burrow*" in the ground, i.e. *dig:*–dig.

3737. ὀρφανός *or-fan-os;'* of unc. affin.; *bereaved* ("*orphan*"), i.e. *parentless:*–comfortless, fatherless.

3738. ὀρχέομαι *or-kheh'-om-ahee;* mid. from ὄρχος (a *row* or *ring*); to *dance* (from the *ranklike* or *regular* motion):–dance.

3739 ὅς *hos;* includ. fem. ἥ *hay* and neut. ὅ *ho* prob. a prim. word (or perh. a form of the art. *3588*); the rel. (sometimes demonstr.) pron., *who, which, what, that*: -one, (an-, the) other, some, that, what, which, who (-m, -se), etc. See also *3757*

3740. ὁσάκις *hos-ak'-is;* multiple adv. from *3739; how* (i.e. with *302, so*) *many times* as:–as oft(-en) as.

3741. ὅσιος *hos'-ee-os;* of unc. affin.; prop. *right* (by intrinsic or divine character; thus distinguished from *1342,* which refers rather to *human* statutes and relations; from *2413,* which denotes formal *consecration;* and from *40,* which relates to *purity* from defilement), i.e. *hallowed* (*pious, sacred, sure*):–holy, mercy, shalt be.

3742. ὁσιότης *hos-ee-ot'-ace;* from *3741; piety:*–holiness.

3743. ὁσίως *hos-ee-oce;'* adv. from *3741; piously:*–holily.

3744. ὀσμή *os-may';* from *3605; fragrance* (lit. or fig.):–odour, savour.

3745. ὅσος *hos'-os;* by redupl. from *3739; as* (*much, great, long,* etc.) *as:*–all (that), as (long, many, much) (as), how great (many, much), [in-] as much as, so many as, that (ever), the more, those things, what (great,-soever), wheresoever, where-withsoever, which, X while, who(-soever).

3746. ὅσπερ *hos'-per;* from *3739* and *4007; who esp.:*–whomsoever.
3747. ὀστέον *os-teh'-on;* or contr. ὀστοῦν of unc. affin.; a *bone:*–bone.
3748. ὅστις *hos'-tis;* incl. the fem. ἥτις *hay'-tis;* and the neut. ὅ,τι, *ho-tee* from *3739* and *5100; which some,* i.e. *any that;* also (def.) *which same:*–X and (they), (such) as, (they) that, in that they, what (-soever), whereas ye, (they) which, who(-soever). Comp. *3754.*
3749. ὀστράκινος *os-tra'-kin-os;* from ὄστρακον ("oyster") (a *tile,* i.e. *terra cotta*); *earthen*-ware, i.e. *clayey;* by impl. *frail:*–of earth, earthen.
3750. ὄσφρησις *os'-fray-sis;* from a der. of *3605; smell* (the sense):–smelling.
3751. ὀσφύς *os-foos';* of unc. affin.; the *loin* (exter.), i.e. the *hip;* internally (by ext.) *procreative power:*–loin.
3752. ὅταν *hot'-an;* from *3753* and *302; whenever* (implying *hypothesis* or more or less *unc.*); also caus. (conj.) *inasmuch as:*–as long (soon) as, that, + till, when(-soever), while.
3753. ὅτε *hot'-eh;* from *3739* and *5037;* at *which* (thing) *too,* i.e. *when:*–after (that), as soon as, that, when, while. ὅ, τε *ho,t'-eh,* also fem, ἥ τε *hay'-teh;* and neut. τό τε *tot'-eh;* simply the art. *3588* folowed by *5037;* so written (in some editions) to distinguish them from *3752* and *5119.*
3754. ὅτι *hot'-ee;* neut. of *3748* as conj.; demonstr., that (sometimes redundant); caus., *because:*–as concerning that, as though, because (that), for (that), how (that), (in) that, though, why.
3755. ὅτου *hot'-oo;* for the gen. of *3748* (as adv.); during *which same* time, i.e. *whilst:*–whiles.
3756. οὐ *oo;* also (before a vowel)and οὐκ *ook;* and (before a aspirate) οὐχ *ookh;* a prim. word; the absol. neg. [comp. 3361] adv.; *no* or *not:*–+ long, nay, neither, never, no (X man), none, [can-]not, + nothing, + spec. un([-worthy]), when, + without, + yet but. See also *3364, 3372.*
3757. οὗ *hoo;* gen. of *3739* as adv.; at *which* place, i.e. *where:*–where(-in), whither ([-soever]).
3758. οὐά *oo-ah';* a prim. exclamation of surprise; "*ah*":–ah.
3759. οὐαί *oo-ah'-ee;* a prim. exclamation of grief; "*woe*":–alas, woe.
3760. οὐδαμῶς *oo-dam-oce';* adv. from (the fem.) of *3762; by no means:*–not.
3761. οὐδέ *oo-deh';* from *3756* and *1161; not however,* i.e. *neither, nor, not even:*–neither (indeed), never, no (more, nor, not), nor (yet), (also, even, then) not (even, so much as), + nothing, so much as.
3762. οὐδείς *oo-dice';* incl. the fem. οὐδεμία *oo-dem-ee'-ah* and the neut. οὐδέν *oo-den';* from *3761* and *1520; not even one* (man, woman or thing), i.e. *none, nobody, nothing:*–any (man), aught, man, neither any (thing), never (man), no (man), none (+ of these things), not (any, at all, -thing), nought.
3763. οὐδέποτε *oo-dep'-ot-eh;* from *3761* and *4218; not even at any time,* i.e. *never at all:*–neither at any time, never, nothing at any time.
3764. οὐδέπω *oo-dep'-o;* from *3761* and 4452; *not even yet:*–as yet not, never before (yet), (not) yet.
3765. οὐκέτι *ook-et'-ee;* also (separately) οὐκ ἔτι *ook-et'-ee* from *3756* and *2089; not yet, no longer:*–after that (not), (not) any more, henceforth (hereafter) not, no longer (more), not as yet (now), now no more (not), yet (not).
3766. οὐκοῦν *ook-oon';* from *3756* and *3767;* is it *not therefore* that, i.e. (affirmatively) *hence* or *so:*–then.
3767. οὖν *oon* app. a prim. word; (adv.) *certainly,* or (conj.) *accordingly:*–and (so, truly), but, now (then), so (likewise then), then, therefore, verily, wherefore.
3768. οὔπω *oo'-po;* from *3756* and *4452; not yet:*–hitherto not, (no...) as yet, not yet.
3769. οὐρά *oo-rah'* app. a prim. word; a *tail:*–tail.
3770. οὐράνιος *oo-ran'-ee-os;* from *3772; celestial,* i.e. *belonging to* or *coming from* the *sky:*–heavenly.
3771. οὐρανόθεν *oo-ran-oth'-en;* from *3772* and the enclitic of source; *from* the *sky:*–from heaven.
3772. οὐρανός *oo-ran-os';* perh. from the same as 3735 (through the idea of *elevation*); the *sky;* by ext., *heaven* (as the abode of God); by impl. *happiness, power, eternity;* spec. the Gospel (*Christianity*):–air, heaven(-ly), sky.
3773. Οὐρβανός, *oor-ban-os';* of Lat. or.; *Urbanus* (*of* the *city,* "*urbane*"), a Chr.:–Urbanus.
3774. Οὐρίας *oo-ree'-as;* of Heb. or. [223]; *Urias* (i.e. *Urijah*), a Hittite:–Urias.
3775. οὖς *ooce* app. a prim. word; the *ear* (phys. or ment.):–ear.
3776. οὐσία *oo-see'-ah;* from the fem. of *5607; substance,* i.e. *property* (*possessions*):–goods, substance.
3777. οὔτε *oo'-teh;* from *3756* and *5037; not too,* i.e. *neither* or *nor;* by anal. *not even:*–neither, none, nor (yet), (no, yet) not, nothing.
3778. οὗτος *hoo'-tos;* include nom. masc. plur. οὗτοι *hoo'-toy;* nom fem. sing. αὕτη *how'-ta* and nom. fem plur. αὗται *how'-tahee;* from the art. *3588* and *846; the he* (*she* or it), i.e. *this* or *that* (often with art. repeated):–he (it was that), hereof, it, she, such as, the same, these, they, this (man, same, woman), which, who.
3779. οὕτω *hoo'-to;* or, before a vowel οὕτως *hoo'-toce;* adv. from *3778; in this way* (referring to what precedes or follows):–after that, after (in) this manner, as, even (so), for all that, like(-wise), no more, on this fashion(-wise), so (in like manner), thus, what.
3780. οὐχί *oo-khee';* intens. of *3756; not indeed:*–nay, not.
3781. ὀφειλέτης *of-i-let'-ace;* from *3784;* an *ower,* i.e. pers. *indebted;* fig. a *delinquent;* mor. a *transgressor* (against God):–debtor, which owed, sinner.
3782. ὀφειλή *of-i-lay';* from *3784; indebtedness,* i.e. (concr.) a *sum* owed; fig. *obligation,* i.e. (conjugal) *duty:*–debt, due.
3783. ὀφείλημα *of-i'-lay-mah;* from (the alt. of) *3784; something owed,* i.e. (fig.) a *due;* mor. a *fault:*–debt.
3784. ὀφείλω *of-i'-lo;* or (in cert. tenses) its prol. form ὀφειλέω *of-i-leh'-o;* prob. from the base of *3786* (through the idea of *accruing*); to *owe* (pecuniarily); fig. to *be under obligation* (*ought, must, should*); mor. to *fail* in duty:–behove, be bound, (be) debt(-or), (be) due(-ty), be guilty (indebted), (must) need(-s), ought, owe, should. See also *3785.*
3785. ὄφελον *of'-el-on;* first pers. sing. of a past tense of *3784;* I *ought* (*wish*), i.e. (interj.) *oh that!:*–would (to God).
3786. ὄφελος *of'-el-os;* from ὀφέλλω ophello (to *heap* up, i.e. *accumulate* or *benefit*); *gain:*–advantageth,profit.
3787. ὀφθαλμοδουλεία *of-thal-mod-oo-li'-ah;* from *3788* and *1397; sight-labor,* i.e. that needs watching (*remissness*):–eye-service.
3788. ὀφθαλμός *of-thal-mos';* from *3700;* the *eye* (lit. or fig.); by impl. *vision;* fig. *envy* (from the jealous side-glance):–eye, sight.
3789. ὄφις *of'-is;* prob. from *3700* (through the idea of *sharpness* of vision); a *snake,* fig. (as a type of sly cunning) an artful *malicious* pers., esp. *Satan:*–serpent.
3790. ὀφρύς *of-roos';* perh. from *3700* (through the idea of the shading or proximity to the organ of *vision*); the eye-"*brow*" or *forehead,* i.e. (fig.) the *brink* of a precipice:–brow.
3791. ὀχλέω *okh-leh'-o;* from *3793;* to *mob,* i.e. (by impl.) to *harass:*–vex.
3792. ὀχλοποιέω *okh-lop-oy-eh'-o;* from *3793* and *4160;* to *make a crowd,* i.e. *raise a* public *disturbance:*–gather a company.
3793. ὄχλος *okh'los;* from a der. of *2192* (mean. a *vehicle*); a *throng* (as *borne* along); by impl. the *rabble;* by ext., a *class* of people; fig. a *riot:*–company, multitude, number (of people), people, press.
3794. ὀχύρωμα *okh-oo'-ro-mah;* from a remote der. of *2192* (mean. to *fortify,* through the idea of *holding* safely); a *castle* (fig. *argument*):–stronghold.
3795. ὀψάριον *op-sar'-ee-on;* neut. of a presumed der. of the base of *3702;* a *relish* to other food (as if cooked *sauce*), i.e. (spec.), *fish* (presumably salted and dried as a condiment):–fish.
3796. ὀψέ *op-seh';* from the same as *3694* (through the idea of *backwardness*); (adv.) *late* in the day; by ext., *after the close* of the day:–(at) even, in the end.
3797. ὄψιμος *op'-sim-os;* from *3796; later,* i.e. *vernal* (showering):–latter.
3798. ὄψιος *op'-see-os;* from *3796; late;* fem. (as noun) *afternoon* (early eve) or *nightfall* (later eve):–even(-ing, [-tide]).

GREEK

3799. ὄψις *op'-sis;* from *3700;* prop. *sight* (the act), i.e. (by impl.) the *visage*, an exter. *show:*–appearance, countenance, face.

3800. ὀψώνιον *op-so'-nee-on;* neut. of a presumed der. of the same as *3795; rations* for a soldier, i.e. (by ext.) his *stipend* or *pay:*– wages.

3801. ὁ ὢν καί ὁ ἦν καί ὁ ἐρχ όμενος *ho own kahee ho ane ho kahee er-khom'-en-os;* a phrase combining *3588* with the pres. part. and imperf. of *1510* and the pres. part. of *2064* by means of *2532*; *the* one *being and the* one that *was and the* one *coming*, i.e. *the Eternal*, as a divine epithet of Christ. which art (is, was), and (which) wast (is, was), and art (is) to come (shalt be).

Π

3802. παγιδεύω *pag-id-yoo'-o;* from *3803;* to *ensnare* (fig.):–entangle.

3803. παγίς *pag-ece';* from *4078;* a *trap* (as *fastened* by a noose or notch); fig. a *trick* or *statagem* (*temptation*):–snare.

3804. πάθημα *path'-ay-mah;* from a presumed der. of *3806;* something *undergone,* i.e. *hardship* or *pain;* subj. an *emotion* or *influence:*– affection, affliction, motion, suffering.

3805. παθητός *path-ay-tos';* from the same as *3804; liable* (i.e. *doomed) to* experience *pain:*–suffer.

3806. πάθος *path'-os;* from the alt. of *3958;* prop. *suffering* ("*pathos*"), i.e. (subj.) a *passion* (esp. *concupiscence*):– (inordinate) affection, lust.

3807. παιδαγωγός *pahee-dag-o-gos';* from *3816* and a redupl. form of *71;* a *boy-leader,* i.e. a servant whose office it was to take the children to school; (by impl. [fig.] a *tutor* ["*paedagogue*"]):– instructor, schoolmaster.

3808. παιδάριον *pahee-dar'-ee-on;* neut. of a presumed der. of *3816; a little boy:*–child, lad.

3809. παιδεία *pahee-di'-ah;* from *3811; tutorage,* i.e. *education* or *training;* by impl. disciplinary *correction:*–chastening, chastisement, instruction, nurture.

3810. παιδευτής *pahee-dyoo-tace;'* from *3811;* a *trainer,* i.e. *teacher* or (by impl.) *discipliner:*–which corrected, instructor.

3811. παιδεύω *pahee-dyoo'-o;* from *3816;* to *train* up a child, i.e. *educate,* or (by impl.), *discipline* (by punishment):– chasten(-ise), instruct, learn, teach.

3812. παιδιόθεν *pahee-dee-oth'-en;* adv. (of *source*) from *3813; from infancy:*–of a child.

3813. παιδίον *pahee-dee'-o;* neut. dimin. of *3816;* a *childling* (of either sex), i.e. (prop.), an infant, or (by ext.) a half-grown *boy* or girl; fig. an *immature* Chr.:–(little, young) child, damsel.

3814. παιδίσκη *pahee-dis'-kay;* fem. dimin. of 3816; a *girl,* i.e. (spec.), a *female slave* or *servant:*–bondmaid(-woman), damsel, maid(-en).

3815. παίζω *paheed'-zo;* from *3816;* to *sport* (as a boy):–play.

3816. παῖς *paheece* perh. from *3817;* a *boy* (as often *beaten* with impunity), or (by anal.), a *girl,* and (gen.) a *child;* spec. a *slave* or *servant* (esp. a *minister* to a king; and by eminence to God):–child, maid(-en), (man) servant, son, young man.

3817. παίω *pah'-yo;* a prim. verb; to *hit* (as if by a single blow and less violently than *5180*); spec. to *sting* (as a scorpion):–smite, strike.

3818. Πακατιανή *pak-at-ee-an-ay';* fem. of an adj. of unc. der.; *Pacatianian,* a section of Phrygia:–Pacatiana.

3819. πάλαι *pal'-ahee;* prob. another form for *3825* (through the idea of *retrocession*); (adv.) *formerly,* or (by rel.) *sometime since;* (ell. as adj.) *ancient:*–any while, a great while ago, (of) old, in time past.

3820. παλαιός *pal-ah-yos';* from *3819;* antique, i.e. *not recent, worn out:*–old.

3821. παλαιότης *pal-ah-yot'-ace;* from *3820; antiquatedness:*–oldness.

3822. παλαιόω *pal-ah-yo'-o;* from *3820;* to *make* (pass. *become*) *worn out,* or *declare obs.:*–decay, make (wax) old.

3823. πάλη *pal'-ay;* from πάλλω (to *vibrate;* another form for *906*); *wrestling:*–+ wrestle.

3824. παλιγγενεσία *pal-ing-ghen-es-ee'-ah;* from *3825* and *1078;* (spir.) *rebirth* (the state or the act), i.e. (fig.) spir. *renovation;* spec. Messianic *restoration:*–regeneration.

3825. πάλιν *pal'-in;* prob. from the same as *3823* (through the idea of *oscillatory* repetition); (adv.) *anew,* i.e. (of place) *back,* (of time) *once more,* or (conj.) *furthermore* or *on the other hand:*–again.

3826. παμπληθεί *pam-play-thi';* dat. (adv.) of a com. of *3956* and *4128; in full multitude,* i.e. *concertedly* or *simultaneously:*–all at once.

3827. πάμπολυς *pam-pol-ooce;* from *3956* and *4183; full many,* i.e. *immense:*–very great.

3828. Παμφυλία *pam-fool-ee'-ah;* from a com. of *3956* and *5443; every-tribal,* i.e. *heterogeneous* (*5561* being implied); *Pamphylia,* a region of Asia Minor:–Pamphylia.

3829. πανδοχεῖον *pan-dokk-i'-on;* neut. of a presumed com. of *3956* and a der. of *1209; all-receptive,* i.e. a public *lodging*-place (*caravanserai* or *khan*):–inn.

3830. πανδοχεύς *pan-dokh-yoos';* from the same as *3829;* an *innkeeper* (*warden* of *a caravanserai*):–host.

3831. πανήγυρις *pan-ay'-goo-ris;* from *3956* and a der. of *58;* a *mass-meeting,* i.e. (fig.) *universal companionship:*–gen. assembly.

3832. πανοικί *pan-oy-kee';* adv. from *3956* and *3624; with* the *whole family:*–with all his house.

3833. πανοπλία *pan-op-lee'-ah;* from a com. of *3956* and *3696; full armor* ("*panoply*"):–all (whole) armour.

3834. πανουργία *pan-oorg-ee'-ah;* from *3835; adroitness,* i.e. (in a bad sense) *trickery* or *sophistry:*–(cunning) craftiness, subtilty.

3835. πανοῦργος *pan-oor'-gos;* from *3956* and *2041; all-working,* i.e. *adroit* (*shrewd*):–crafty.

3836. πανταχόθεν *pan-takh-oth'-en;* adv. (of *source*) from *3837; from all* directions:– from every quarter.

3837. πανταχοῦ *pan-takh-oo';* gen. (as adv. of *place*) of a presumed der. of *3956; universally:*–in all places, everywhere.

3838. παντελής *pan-tel-ace';* from *3956* and *5056; full-ended,* i.e. *entire* (neut. as noun, *completion*):–+ in [no] wise, uttermost.

3839. πάντη *pan'-tay;* adv. (of *manner*) from *3956; wholly:*–always.

3840. παντόθεν *pan-toth'-en;* adv. (of *source*)from *3956; from* (i.e. *on*) *all* sides:– on every side, round about.

3841. παντοκράτωρ *pan-tok-rat'-ore;* from *3956* and *2904;* the *all-ruling,* i.e. *God* (as absol. and universal *sovereign*):–Almighty, Omnipotent.

3842. πάντοτε *pan'-tot-eh;* from *3956* and *3753; every when,* i.e. *at all* times:–alway (-s), ever(-more).

3843. πάντως *pan'-toce;* adv. from *3956; entirely;* spec. *at all events,* (with neg. following) *in* no *event:*–by all means, altogether, at all, needs, no doubt, in [no] wise, surely.

3844. παρά *par-ah';* a prim. prep.; prop. *near;* i.e. (with gen.) *from beside* (lit. or fig.), (with dat.) *at* (or *in*) the *vicinity* of (obj. or subj.), (with acc.) to the *proximity* with (local [esp. *beyond* or *opposed* to] or causal [*on account* of]:–above, against, among, at, before, by, contrary to, X friend, from, + give [such things as they], + that [she] had, X his, in, more than, nigh unto, (out) of, past, save, side...by, in the sight of, than, [there-]fore, with. In com. it retains the same variety of appl.

3845. παραβαίνω *par-ab-ah'-ee-no;* from *3844* and the base of *939;* to *go contrary to,* i.e. *violate* a command:–(by) transgress(-ion).

3846. παραβάλλω *par-ab-al'-lo;* from *3844* and *906;* to *throw alongside,* i.e. (refl.) to *reach* a place, or (fig.) to *liken:*–arrive, compare.

3847. παράβασις *par-ab'-as-is;* from *3845; violation:*–breaking, transgression.

3848. παραβάτης *par-ab-at'-ace;* from *3845;* a *violator:*–breaker, transgress(-or).

3849. παραβιάζομαι *par-ab-ee-ad'-zom-ahee;* from *3844* and the mid. of *971;* to *force contrary* to (nature), i.e. *compel* (by entreaty):–constrain.

3850. παραβολή *par-ab-ol-ay';* from *3846;* a *similitude* ("*parable*"), i.e. (symb.) *fictitious narrative* (of common life conveying a mor.), *apothegm* or *adage:*– comparison, figure, parable, proverb.

3851. παραβουλεύομαι *par-ab-ool-yoo'-om-ahee;* from *3844* and the mid. of *1011;* to *misconsult,* i.e. *disregard:*–not (to) regard(-ing).

3852. παραγγελία *par-ang-gel-ee'-ah;* from *3853;* a *mandate:*–charge, command.

3853. παραγγέλλω *par-ang-gel'-lo;* from *3844* and the base of *32;* to *transmit a message,* i.e. (by impl.) to *enjoin:*–(give in) charge, (give) command(-ment), declare.

3854. παραγίνομαι *par-ag-in'-om-ahee;* from *3844* and *1096;* to *become near,* i.e. *approach* (*have arrived*); by impl. to *appear* publicly:–come, go, be present.

3855. παράγω *par-ag'-o;* from 3844 and 71; to lead near, i.e. (refl. or intrans.) to go along or away:–depart, pass (away, by, forth).
3856. παραδειγματίζω *par-ad-igue-mat-id'-zo;* from 3844 and 1165; to show alongside (the public), i.e. expose to infamy:–make a public example, put to an open shame.
3857. παράδεισος *par-ad'-i-sos;* of Oriental or. [comp. 6508]; a park, i.e. (spec.), an Eden (place of fut. happiness, "paradise"):–paradise.
3858. παραδέχομαι *par-ad-ekh'-om-ahee;* from 3844 and 1209; to accept near, i.e. admit or (by impl.) delight in:–receive.
3859. παραδιατριβή *par-ad-ee-at-ree-bay';* from a com. of 3844 and 1304; misemployment, i.e. meddlesomeness:–perverse disputing.
3860. παραδίδωμι *par-ad-id'-o-mee;* from 3844 and 1325; to surrender, i.e yield up, intrust, transmit:–betray, bring forth, cast, commit, deliver (up), give (over, up), hazard, put in prison, recommend.
3861. παράδοξος *par-ad'-ox-os;* from 3844 and 1391 (in the sense of seeming); contrary to expectation, i.e. extraordinary ("paradox"):–strange.
3862. παράδοσις *par-ad'-os-is;* from 3860; transmission, i.e. (concr.) a precept; spec. the Jewish traditionary law:–ordinance, tradition.
3863. παραζηλόω *par-ad-zay-lo'-o;* from 3844 and 2206; to stimulate alongside, i.e. excite to rivalry:–provoke to emulation (jealousy).
3864. παραθαλάσσιος *par-ath-al-as'-see-os;* from 3844 and 2281; along the sea, i.e. maritime (lacustrine):–upon the sea coast.
3865. παραθεωρέω *par-ath-eh-o-reh'-o;* from 3844 and 2334; to overlook or disregard:–neglect.
3866. παραθήκη *par-ath-ay'-kay;* from 3908; a deposit, i.e. (fig.) trust:–committed unto.
3867. παραινέω *par-ahee-neh'-o;* from 3844 and 134; to mispraise, i.e. recommend or advise (a different course):–admonish, exhort.
3868. παραιτέομαι *par-ahee-teh'-om-ahee;* from 3844 and the mid. of 154; to beg off, i.e. deprecate, decline, shun:–avoid, (make) excuse, intreat, refuse, reject.
3869. παρακαθίζω *par-ak-ath-id'-zo;* from 3844 and 2523; to sit down near:–sit.
3870. παρακαλέω *par-ak-al-eh'-o;* from 3844 and 2564; to call near, i.e. invite, invoke (by imploration, hortation or consolation):–beseech, call for, (be of good) comfort, desire, (give) exhort(-ation), intreat, pray.
3871. παρακαλύπτω *par-ak-al-oop'-to;* from 3844 and 2572; to cover alongside, i.e. veil (fig.):–hide.
3872. παρακαταθήκη *par-ak-at-ath-ay'-kay;* from a com. of 3844 and 2698; something put down alongside, i.e. a deposit (sacred trust):–that (thing) which is committed (un-)to (trust).
3873. παράκειμαι *par-ak'-i-mahee;* from 3844 and 2749; to lie near, i.e. be at hand (fig. be prompt or easy):–be present.
3874. παράκλησις *par-ak'-lay-sis;* from 3870; imploration, hortation, solace:–comfort, consolation, exhortation, intreaty.
3875. παράκλητος *par-ak'-lay-tos;* an intercessor, consoler:–advocate, comforter.
3876. παρακοή *par-ak-o-ay';* from 3878; inattention, i.e. (by impl.) disobedience:–disobedience.
3877. παρακολουθέω *par-ak-ol-oo-theh'-o;* from 3844 and 190; to follow near, i.e. (fig.) attend (as a result), trace out, conform to:–attain, follow, fully know, have understanding.
3878. παρακούω *par-ak-oo'-o;* from 3844 and 191; to mishear, i.e. (by impl.) to disobey:–neglect to hear.
3879. παρακύπτω *par-ak-oop'-to;* from 3844 and 2955; to bend beside, i.e. lean over (so as to peer within):–look (into), stoop down.
3880. παραλαμβάνω *par-al-am-ban'-o;* from 3844 and 2983; to receive near, i.e. associate with oneself (in any familiar or intimate act or relation); by anal. to assume an office; fig. to learn:–receive, take (unto, with).
3881. παραλέγομαι *par-al-eg'-om-ahee;* from 3844 and the mid. of 3004 (in its or. sense); (spec.), to lay one's course near, i.e. sail past:–pass, sail by.
3882. παράλιος *par-al'-ee-os;* from 3844 and 251; beside the salt (sea), i.e. maritime:–sea coast.
3883. παραλλαγή *par-al-lag-ay';* from a com. of 3844 and 236; transmutation (of phase or orbit), i.e. (fig.) fickleness: variableness.
3884. παραλογίζομαι *par-al-og-id'-zom-ahee;* from 3844 and 3049; to misreckon, i.e. delude :–beguile, deceive.
3885. παραλυτικός *par-al-oo-tee-kos';* from a der. of 3886; as if dissolved, i.e. "paralytic":–that had (sick of) the palsy.
3886. παραλύω *par-al-oo'-o;* from 3844 and 3089; to loosen beside, i.e. relax (perfect pass. part., paralyzed or enfeebled):–feeble, sick of the (taken with) palsy.
3887. παραμένω, *par-am-en'-o;* from 3844 and 3306; to stay near, i.e. remain (lit. tarry; or fig. be permanent, persevere):–abide, continue.
3888. παραμυθέομαι *par-am-oo-theh'-om-ahee;* from 3844 and the mid. of a der. of 3454; to relate near, i.e. (by impl.) encourage, console:–comfort.
3889. παραμυθία *par-am-oo-thee'-ah;* from 3888; consolation (prop. abstr.):–comfort.
3890. παραμύθιον *par-am-oo'-thee-on;* neut. of 3889; consolation (prop. concr.):–comfort.
3891. παρανομέω *par-an-om-eh'-o;* from a com. of 3844 and 3551; to be opposed to law, i.e. to transgress:–contrary to law.
3892. παρανομία *par-an-om-ee'-ah;* from the same as 3891; transgression: iniquity.
3893. παραπικραίνω *par-ap-ik-rah'-ee-no;* from 3844 and 4087; to embitter alongside, i.e. (fig.) to exasperate:–provoke.
3894. παραπικρασμός *par-ap-ik-ras-mos';* from 3893; irritation:–provocation.
3895. παραπιπτω *par-ap-ip'-to;* from 3844 and 4098; to fall aside, i.e. (fig.) to apostatize:–fall away.
3896. παραπλέω *par-ap-leh'-o;* from 3844 and 4126; to sail near:–sail by.
3897. παραπλήσιον *par-ap-lay'-see-on;* neut. of a com. of 3844 and the base of 4139 (as adv.); close by, i.e. (fig.) almost:–nigh unto.
3898. παραπλησίως *par-ap-lay-see'-oce;* adv. from the same as 3897; in a manner near by, i.e. (fig.) similarly:–likewise.
3899. παραπορεύομαι *par-ap-or-yoo'-om-ahee;* from 3844 and 4198; to travel near:–go, pass (by).
3900. παράπτωμα *par-ap'-to-mah;* from 3895; a side-slip (lapse or deviation), i.e. (unintentional) error or (wilful) transgression:–fall, fault, offence, sin, trespass.
3901. παραρρυέω *par-ar-hroo-eh'-o;* from 3844 and the alt. of 4482; to flow by, i.e. (fig.) carelessly pass (miss):–let slip.
3902. παράσημος *par-as'-ay-mos;* from 3844 and the base of 4591; side-marked, i.e. labelled (with a badge [figure-head] of a ship):–sign.
3903. παρασκευάζω *par-ask-yoo-ad'-zo;* from 3844 and a der. of 4632; to furnish aside, i.e. get ready:–prepare self, be (make) ready.
3904. παρασκευή *par-ask-yoo-ay';* as if from 3903; readiness:–preparation.
3905. παρατείνω *par-at-i'-no;* from 3844 and τείνω (to stretch); to extend along, i.e. prolong (in point of time):–continue.
3906. παρατηρέω *par-at-ay-reh'-o;* from 3844 and 5083; to inspect alongside, i.e. note insidiously or scrupulously:–observe, watch.
3907. παρατήρησις *par-at-ay'-ray-sis;* from 3906; inspection, i.e. ocular evidence:–obervation.
3908. παρατίθημι *par-at-ith'-ay-mee;* from 3844 and 5087; to place alongside, i.e. present (food, truth); by impl. to deposit (as a trust or for protection):–allege, commend, commit (the keeping of), put forth, set before.
3909. παρατυγχάνω *par-at-oong-khan'-o;* from 3844 and 5177; to chance near, i.e. fall in with:–meet with.
3910. παραυτίκα *par-ow-tee'-kah;* from 3844 and a der. of 846; at the very instant, i.e. momentary:–but for a moment.
3911. παραφέρω *par-af-er'-o;* from 3844 and 5342 (incl. its alt. forms); to bear along or aside, i.e. carry off (lit. or fig.); by impl. to avert:–remove, take away.
3912. παραφρονέω *par-af-ron-eh'-o;* from 3844 and 5426; to misthink, i.e. be insane (silly):–as a fool.
3913. παραφρονία *par-af-ron-ee'-ah;* from 3912; insanity, i.e. foolhardiness:–madness.
3914. παραχειμάζω *par-akh-i-mad'-zo;* from 3844 and 5492; to winter near, i.e. stay with over the rainy season:–winter.
3915. παραχειμασία *par-akh-i-mas-ee'-ah;* from 3914; a wintering over:–winter in.
3916. παραχρῆμα *par-akh-ray'-mah;* from 3844 and 5536 (in its or. sense); at the thing itself, i.e. instantly:–forthwith,

immediately, presently, straightway, soon.

3917. πάρδαλις *par'-dal-is;* fem. of πάρδος (a *panther*); a *leopard:*–leopard.

3918. πάρειμι *par'-i-mee;* from *3844* and *1510* (incl. its various forms); to *be near,* i.e. *at hand;* neut. pres. part. (sing.) *time being,* or (pl.) *property:*–come, X have, be here, + lack, (be here) present.

3919. παρεισάγω *par-ice-ag'-o;* from *3844* and *1521;* to *lead in aside,* i.e. *introduce surreptitiously:*–privily bring in.

3920. παρείσακτος *par-ice'-ak-tos;* from *3919; smuggled in:* unawares brought in.

3921. παρεισδύνω *par-ice-doo'-no;* from *3844* and a com. of *1519* and *1416;* to *settle in alongside,* i.e. *lodge stealthily:*–creep in unawares.

3922. παρεισέρχομαι *par-ice-er'-khom-ahee;* from *3844* and *1525;* to *come in alongside,* i.e. *supervene additionally* or *steathily:*–come in privily, enter.

3923. παρεισφέρω *par-ice-fer'-o;* from *3844* and *1533;* to *bear in alongside,* i.e. *introduce simultaneously:*–give.

3924. παρεκτός *par-ek-tos';* from *3844* and *1622; near outside,* i.e. *besides:*–except, saving, without.

3925. παρεμβολή *par-em-bol-ay';* from a com. of *3844* and *1685;* a *throwing in beside* (*juxtaposition*), i.e. (*spec.*), *battle-array, encampment* or *barracks* (tower Antonia):–army, camp, castle.

3926. παρενοχλέω *par-en-okh-leh'-o;* from *3844* and *1776;* to *harass further,* i.e. *annoy:*–trouble.

3927. παρεπίδημος *par-ep-id'-ay-mos;* from 3844 and the base of *1927;* an *alien alongside,* i.e. a *resident foreigner:*–pilgrim, stranger.

3928. παρέρχομαι *par-er'-khom-ahee;* from *3844* and *2064;* to *come near* or *aside,* i.e. to *approach* (*arrive*), *go by* (or *away*), (fig.) *perish* or *neglect,* (caus.) *avert:*–come (forth), go, pass (away, by, over), past, transgress.

3929. πάρεσις *par'-es-is;* from *2935; praetermission,* i.e. *toleration:*–remission.

3930. παρέχω *par-ekh'-o;* from *3844* and *2192;* to *hold near,* i.e. *present, afford, exhibit, furnish occasion:*–bring, do, give, keep, minister, offer, shew, + trouble.

3931. παρηγορία *par-ay-gor-ee'-ah;* from a com. of *3844* and a der. of *58* (mean. to *harangue* an assembly); an *address alongside,* i.e. (spec.), *consolation:*–comfort.

3932. παρθενία *par-then-ee'-ah;* from *3933; maidenhood:*–virginity

3933. παρθένος *par-then'-os;* of unknown or.; a *maiden;* by impl. an *unmarried daughter:*–virgin.

3934. Πάρθος *par'-thos;* prob. of for. or.; a *Parthian,* i.e. inh. of Parthia:–Parthian.

3935. παρίημι *par-ee'-ay-mi;* from *3844* and ἵημι (to *send*); to *let by,* i.e. *relax:*–hang down.

3936. παρίστημι *par-is'-tay-mee;* or prol. παριστάνω *par-is'-tan-o;* or prol. from *3844* and *2476;* to *stand beside,* i.e. (trans.) to *exhibit, proffer,* (spec.), *recommend,* (fig.) *substantiate;* or (intrans.) to *be at hand* (or *ready*), *aid:*–assist, bring before, command, commend, give presently, present, prove, provide, shew, stand (before, by, here, up, with), yield.

3937. Παρμενᾶς *par-men-as';* prob. by contr. for Παρμενίδης (a der. of a com. of *3844* and *3306*); *constant; Parmenas,* a Chr.:–Parmenas.

3938. πάροδος *par'-od-os;* from *3844* and *3598;* a *by-road,* i.e. (act.) a *route:*–way.

3939. παροικέω *par-oy-keh'-o;* from *3844* and *3611;* to *dwell near,* i.e. *reside* as a *foreigner:*–sojourn in, be a stranger.

3940. παροικία *par-oy-kee'-ah;* from *3941; for. residence:*–sojourning, X as strangers.

3941. πάροικος *par'-oy-kos;* from *3844* and *3624;* having a *home near,* i.e. (as noun) a *by-dweller* (*alien resident*):–foreigner, sojourn, stranger.

3942. παροιμία *par-oy-mee'-ah;* from a com. of *3844* and perh. a der. of *3633;* app. a state *alongside of supposition,* i.e. (concr.) an *adage;* spec. an enigmatical or fictitious *illustration:*–parable, proverb.

3943. πάροινος *par'-oy-nos;* from *3844* and *3631;* staying *near wine,* i.e. *tippling* (a *toper*):–given to wine.

3944. παροίχομαι *par-oy'-khom-ahee;* from *3844* and οἴχομαι (to *depart*); to *escape along,* i.e. *be gone:*–past.

3945. παρομοιάζω *par-om-oy-ad'-zo;* from *3946;* to *resemble:*–be like unto.

3946. παρόμοιος *par-om'-oy-os;* from *3844* and *3664; alike nearly,* i.e. *similar:*–like.

3947. παροξύνω *par-ox-oo'-no;* from *3844* and a der. of *3691;* to *sharpen alongside,* i.e. (fig.) to *exasperate:*–easily provoke, stir.

3948. παροξυσμός *par-ox-oos-mos';* from *3947* ("*paroxysm*"); *incitement* (to good), or *dispute* (in anger):–contention, provoke unto.

3949. παροργίζω *par-org-id'-zo;* from *3844* and *3710;* to *anger alongside,* i.e. *enrage:*–anger, provoke to wrath.

3950. παροργισμός *par-org-is-mos;* from *3949; rage:*–wrath.

3951. παροτρύνω *par-ot-roo'-no;* from *3844* and ὀτρύνω (to *spur*); to *urge along,* i.e. *stimulate* (to hostility):–stir up.

3952. παρουσία *par-oo-see'-ah;* from the pres. part. of *3918;* a *being near,* i.e. *advent* (often, *return;* spec. of Christ to punish Jerus. or finally the wicked); (by impl.) phys. *aspect:*–coming, presence.

3953. παροψίς *par-op-sis';* from *3844* and the base of *3795;* a *side-dish* (the receptacle):–platter.

3954. παῤῥησία *par-rhay-see'-ah;* from *3956* and a der. of *4483; all* out-*spokenness,* i.e. *frankness, bluntness, publicity;* by impl. *assurance:*–bold (X -ly, -ness, -ness of speech), confidence, X freely, X openly, X plainly(-ness).

3955. παῤῥησιάζομαι *par-hray-see-ad'-zom-ahee;* mid. from *3954;* to *be frank* in utterance, or *confident* in spirit and demeanor:–be (wax) bold, (preach, speak) boldly.

3956. πᾶς *pas;* incl. all the forms of declension; app. a prim. word; *all, any, every,* the *whole:*–all (manner of, means), alway(-s), any (one), X daily, + ever, every (one, way), as many as, + no(-thing), X thoroughly, whatsoever, whole, whosoever.

3957. πάσχα *pas'-khah;* of Chald. or. [comp. *6453*]; the *Passover* (the meal, the day, the festival or the spec. sacrifices connected with it):–Easter, Passover.

3958. πάσχω *pas'-kho;* include. the forms πάθω *path'-o* and πένθω, *penth'-o;* app. a prim. verb to *experience* a sensation or impression (usually painful):–feel, passion, suffer, vex.

3959. Πάταρα *pat'-ar-ah;* prob. of for. or.; *Patara,* a place in Asia Minor:–Patara.

3960. πατάσσω *pat-as'-so;* prob. prol. from *3817;* to *knock* (gently or with a weapon or fatally):–smite, strike. Comp. *5180.*

3961. πατέω *pat-eh'-o;* from a der. prob. of *3817* (mean. a "*path*"); to *trample* (lit. or fig.):–tread (down, under foot).

3962. πατήρ *pat-ayr';* app. a prim. word; a "*father*" (lit. or fig. near or more remote):–father, parent.

3963. Πάτμος *pat'-mos;* of unc. der.; *Patmus,* an islet in the Mediterranean:–Patmos.

3964. πατραλῴας *pat-ral-o'-as;* from *3962* and the same as the latter part of *3389;* a *parricide:*–murderer of fathers.

3965. πατριά *pat-ree-ah';* as if fem. of a der. of *3962*; paternal *descent,* i.e. (concr.) a *group* of families or a whole race (*nation*):–family, kindred, lineage.

3966. πατριάρχης *pat-ree-arkh'-ace;* from *3965* and *757;* a *progenitor* ("patriarch"):–patriarch.

3967. πατρικός *pat-ree-kos';* from *3962; paternal,* i.e. *ancestral:*–of fathers.

3968. πατρίς *pat-rece';* from *3962;* a *father-land,* i.e. *native town;* (fig.) heavenly *home:*–(own) country.

3969. Πατρόβας *pat-rob'-as;* perh. a contr. for Πατρόβιος (a com. of *3962* and *979*); *father's life; Patrobas,* a Chr.:–Patrobas.

3970. πατροπαράδοτος *pat-rop-ar-ad'-ot-os;* from *3962* and a der. of *3860* (in the sense of *handing over* or *down*); *traditionary:*–received by tradition from fathers.

3971. πατρῷος *pat-ro'-os;* from *3962; paternal,* i.e. *hereditary:*–of fathers.

3972. Παῦλος *pow'-los;* of Lat. or.; (*little;* but remotely from a der. of *3973,* mean. the same); *Paulus,* the name of a Rom. and of an apostle:–Paul, Paulus.

3973. παύω *pow'-o;* a prim. verb ("*pause*"); to *stop* (trans. or intrans.), i.e. *restrain, quit, desist, come to an end:*–cease, leave, refrain.

3974. Πάφος *paf'-os;* of unc. der.; *Paphus,* a place in Cyprus:–Paphos.

3975. παχύνω *pakh-oo'-no;* from a der. of *4078* (mean. *thick*); to *thicken,* i.e. (by impl.) to *fatten* (fig. *stupefy* or *render callous*):–wax gross.

3976. πέδη *ped'-ay;* ultimately from *4228;* a *shackle* for the feet:–fetter.

3977. πεδινός *ped-ee-nos';* from a der. of *4228* (mean. the *ground*); *level* (as easy for the *feet*):–plain.

3978. πεζεύω *ped-zyoo'-o;* from the same as *3979;* to *foot a* journey, i.e. *travel* by land:–go afoot.

3979.πεζῇ *ped-zay';* dat. fem. of a der. of *4228* (as adv.); *foot-wise,* i.e. by *walking:*–a-(on) foot.

3980. πειθαρχέω *pi-tharkh-eh'-o;* from a com. of *3982* and *757;* to *be persuaded* by a *ruler,* i.e. (gen.) to *submit* to authority; by anal. to *conform* to advice:–hearken, obey (magistrates).

3981. πειθός *pi-thos';* from *3982; persuasive:*–enticing.

3982. πείθω *pi'-tho;* a prim. verb; to *convince* (by argument, true or false); by anal. to *pacify* or *conciliate* (by other fair means); refl. or pass. to *assent* (to evidence or authority), to *rely* (by inward certainty):–agree, assure, believe, have confidence, be (wax) conflent, make friend, obey, persuade, trust, yield.

3983. πεινάω *pi-nah'-o;* from the same as *3993* (through the idea of pinching *toil;* "*pine*"); to *famish* (absol. or comp.); fig. to *crave:*–be an hungered, hungry.

3984. πεῖρα *pi'-rah;* from the base of *4008* (through the idea of *piercing*); a *test,* i.e. *attempt, experience:*–assaying, trial.

3985. πειράζω *pi-rad'-zo;* from *3984;* to *test* (obj.), i.e. *endeavor, scrutinize, entice, discipline:*–assay, examine, go about, prove, tempt(-er), try.

3986. πειρασμός *pi-ras-mos';* from *3985;* a putting to *proof* (by experiment [of good], *experience* [of evil], solicitation, discipline or provocation); by impl. *adversity:*–temptation, X try.

3987. πειράω *pi-rah'-o;* from *3984;* to *test* (subj.), i.e. (refl.) to *attempt:*–assay.

3988. πεισμονή *pice-mon-ay';* from a presumed der. of *3982; persuadableness,* i.e. *credulity:*–persuasion.

3989. πέλαγος *pel'-ag-os;* of unc. affin.; deep or open *sea,* i.e. the *main:*–depth, sea.

3990. πελεκίζω *pel-ek-id'-zo;* from a der. of *4141* (mean. an *axe*); to *chop* off (the head), i.e. *truncate:*–behead.

3991. πέμπτος *pemp'-tos* from *4002; fifth:*–fifth.

3992. πέμπω *pem'-po;* app. a prim. verb; to *dispatch* (from the subj. view or point of *departure,* whereas ἵημι [as a stronger form of εἶμι] refers rather to the obj. point or *terminus ad quem,* and *4724* denotes prop. the *orderly* motion involved), esp. on a temporary errand; also to *transmit, bestow,* or *wield:*–send, thrust in.

3993. πένης, *pen'-ace;* from a prim. πένω (to *toil* for daily subsistence); *starving,* i.e. *indigent:*–poor. Comp. *4434.*

3994. πενθερά *pen-ther-ah';* fem. of *3995;* a *wife's mother:*–mother in law, wife's mother.

3995. πενθερός *pen-ther-os';* of unc. affin.; a *wife's father:*–father in law.

3996. πενθέω *pen-theh'-o;* from *3997;* to *grieve* (the feeling or the act):–mourn, (be-)wail.

3997. πένθος *pen'-thos;* streng. from the alt. of *3958; grief:*–mourning, sorrow.

3998. πεντιχρός *pen-ikh-ros';* prol. from the base of *3993; necessitous:*–poor.

3999. πεντακίς *pen-tak-ece'* mult. adv. from *4002; five times:*–five times.

4000. πεντακισχίλιοι *pen-tak-is-khil'-ee-oy;* from *3999* and *5507; five times a thousand:*–five thousand.

4001. πεντακόσιοι *pen-tak-os'-ee-oy;* from *4002* and *1540; five hundred:*–five hundred.

4002. πέντε *pen'-the;* a prim. number; "*five*":–five.

4003. πεντεκαιδέκατος *pen-tek-ahee-ded'-at-os;* from *4002* and *2532* and *1182; five* and *tenth:*–fifteenth.

4004. πεντήκοντα *pen-tay'-kon-tah;* mult. of *4002; fifty:*–fifty.

4005. πεντηκοστή *pen-tay-kos-tay';* fem. of the ord. of *4004; fiftieth* (*2250* being implied) from Passover, i.e. the festival of "*Pentecost*":–Pentecost.

4006. πεποίθησις *pep-oy'-thay-sis;* from the perfect of the alt. of *3958; reliance:*–confidence, trust.

4007. περ *per;* from the base of *4008;* an enclitic par. significant of *abundance* (*thoroughness*), i.e. *emphasis; much, very* or *ever:*–[whom-]soever.

4008. πέραν *per'-an;* app. acc. of an obs. der. of πείρω (to "*pierce*"); *through* (as adv. or prep.), i.e. *across:*–beyond, farther (other) side, over.

4009. πέρας *per'-as;* from the same as *4008;* an *extremity:*–end, ut-(ter-)most part.

4010. Πέργαμος *per'-gam-os;* from *4444; fortified; Pergamus,* a place in Asia Minor:–Pergamos.

4011. Πέργη *perg'-ay;* prob. from the same as *4010;* a *tower; Perga,* a place in Asia Minor:–Perga.

4012. περί *per-ee';* from the base of *4008;* prop. *through* (all *over*), i.e. *around;* fig. *with respect* to; used in various appl., of place, cause or time (with the gen. denoting the *subject* or *occasion* or *superl.* point; with the acc. the *locality, circuit, matter, circumstance* or gen. *period*):–(there-) about, above, against, at, on behalf of, X and his company, which concern, (as) concerning, for, X how it will go with, ([there-,where-]) of, on, over, pertaining (to), for sake, X (e-)state, (as) touching, [where-]by (in), with. In comp., it retains substantially the same mean. of circuit (*around*), excess (*beyond*), or completeness (*through*).

4013. περιάγω *per-ee-ag'-o;* from *4012* and *71;* to *take around* (as a companion); refl. to *walk around:*–compass, go (round) about, lead about.

4014. περιαιρέω *per-ee-ahee-reh'-o;* from *4012* and *138* (incl. its alt.); to *remove* all *around,* i.e. *unveil, cast off* (anchor); fig. to *expiate:*–take away (up).

4015. περιαστράπτω *per-ee-as-trap'-to;* from *4012* and *797;* to *flash* all *around,* i.e. *envelop in light:*–shine round (about).

4016. περιβάλλω *per-ee-bal'-lo;* from *4012* and *906;* to *throw* all *around,* i.e. *invest* (with a palisade or with clothing):–array, cast about, clothe(-d me), put on.

4017. περιβλέπω *per-ee-blep'-o;* from *4012* and *991;* to *look* all *around:*–look (round) about (on).

4018. περιβόλαιον *per-ib-ol'-ah-yon;* neut. of a presumed der. of *4016;* something *thrown around* one, i.e. a *mantle, veil:*–covering, vesture.

4019. περιδέω *per-ee-deh'-o;* from *4012* and *1210;* to *bind around* one, i.e. *enwrap:*–bind about.

4020. περιεργάζομαι *per-ee-er-gad'-zom-ahee;* from *4012* and *2038;* to *work* all *around,* i.e. *bustle about* (*meddle*):–be a busybody.

4021. περίεργος *per-ee'-er-gos;* from *4012* and *2041; working all around,* i.e. *officious* (*meddlesome,* neut. pl. *magic*):–busybody, curious arts.

4022. περιέρχομαι *per-ee-er'-khom-ahee;* from *4012* and *2064* (incl. its alt.); to *come* all *around,* i.e. *stroll, vacillate, veer:*–fetch a compass, vagabond, wandering about.

4023. περιέχω *per-ee-ekh'-o;* from *4012* and *2192;* to *hold* all *around,* i.e. *include, clasp* (fig.):–+ astonished, contain, after [this manner].

4024. περιζώννυμι *per-id-zone'-noo-mee;* from *4012* and *2224;* to *gird* all *around,* i.e. (mid. or pass.) to *fasten on one's belt* (lit. or fig.):–gird (about, self).

4025. περίθεσις *per-ith'-es-is;* from *4060;* a *putting* all *around,* i.e. *decorating* oneself with:–wearing.

4026. περιΐστημι *per-ee-is'-tay-mee;* from *4012* and *2476;* to *stand* all *around,* i.e. (near) to *be a bystander,* or (aloof) to *keep away* from:–avoid, shun, stand by (round about).

4027. περικάθρμα *per-ee-kath'-ar-mah;* from a comp. of *4012* and *2508;* something *cleaned* off all *around,* i.e. *refuse* (fig.):–filth.

4028. περικαλύπτω *per-ee-kal-oop'-to;* from 4012 and 2572; to *cover* all *around,* i.e. *entirely* (the face, a surface):–blindfold, cover, overlay.

4029. περίκειμαι *per-ik'-i-mahee;* from *4012* and *2749;* to *lie* all *around,* i.e. *inclose, encircle, hamper* (lit. or fig.):–be bound (compassed) with, hang about.

4030. περικεφαλαία *per-ee-kef-al-ah'-yah;* fem. of a comp. of *4012* and *2776; encirclement of* the *head,* i.e. a *helmet:*–helmet.

4031. περικρατής *per-ee-krat-ace';* from *4012* and *2904; strong* all *around,* i.e. a *master* (*manager*):–+ come by.

4032. περικρύπτω *per-ee-kroop'-to;* from *4012* and *2928;* to *conceal* all *around,* i.e. *entirely:*–hide.

4033. περικυκλόω *per-ee-koo-klo'-o;* from

GREEK

4012 and *2944;* to *encircle* all *around,* i.e. *blockade completely:*–compass round.

4034. περιλάμπω *per-ee-lam'-po;* from *4012* and *2989;* to *illuminate* all *around,* i.e. *invest with a halo:*–shine round about.

4035. περιλείπω *per-ee-li'-po;* from *4012* and *3007;* to *leave* all *around,* i.e. pass. *survive:*–remain.

4036. περίλυπος *per-il'-oo-pos;* from *4012* and *3077; grieved* all *around,* i.e. *intensely sad:*–exceeding (very) sorry(-owful).

4037. περιμένω *per-ee-men'-o;* from *4012* and *3306;* to *stay around,* i.e. *await:*–wait for.

4038. πέριξ *per'-ix* adv. from *4012;* all *around,* i.e. (as an adj.) *circumjacent:*–round about.

4039. περιοικέω *per-ee-oy-keh'-o;* from *4012* and *3611;* to *reside around,* i.e. *be* a *neighbor:*–dwell round about.

4040. περίοικος *per-ee'-oy-kos;* from *4012* and *3624; housed around,* i.e. *neighboring* (used ell. as a noun):–neighbour.

4041. περιούσιος, *per-ee-oo'-see-os;* from the pres. part. fem. of a com. of *4012* and *1510; being beyond* usual, i.e. *spec.* (one's *own*):–peculiar.

4042. περιοχή *per-ee-okh-ay';* from *4023;* a *being held around,* i.e. (concr.) a *passage* (of Scripture, as *circumscribed*):–place.

4043. περιπατέω *per-ee-pat-eh'-o;* from *4012* and *3961;* to *tread* all *around,* i.e. *walk* at large (esp. as proof of ability); fig. to *live, deport oneself, follow* (as a companion or votary):–go, be occupied with, walk (about).

4044. περιπείρω *per-ee-pi'-ro;* from *4012* and the base of *4008;* to *penetrate entirely,* i.e. *transfix* (fig.):–pierce through.

4045. περιπίπτω *per-ee-pip'-to;* from *4012* and *4098;* to *fall* into something i.e. all *around,* i.e. *light among* or *upon, be surrounded with:*–fall among (into).

4046. περιποιέομαι *per-ee-poy-eh'-om-ahee;* mid. from *4012* and *4160;* to *make around oneself,* i.e. *acquire* (*buy*):–purchase.

4047. περιποίησις *per-ee-poy'-ay-sis;* from *4046; acquisition* (the act or the thing); by ext., *preservation:*–obtain(-ing), peculiar, purchased, possession, saving.

4048. περιῤῥήγνυμι *per-ir-hrayg'-noo-mee;* from *4012* and *4486;* to *tear* all *around,* i.e. *completely away:*–rend off.

4049. περισπάω *per-ee-spah'-o;* from *4012* and *4685;* to *drag* all *around,* i.e. (fig.) to *distract* (with care):–cumber.

4050. περισσεία *per-is-si'-ah;* from *4052; surplusage,* i.e. *superabundance:*–abundance (-ant, [-ly]), superfluity.

4051. περίσσευμα *per-is'-syoo-mah;* from *4052;* a *surplus,* or *superabundance:*–abundance, that was left, over and above.

4052. περισσεύω *per-is-syoo'-o;* from *4053;* to *superabound* (in quantity or quality), *be in excess, be superfluous;* also (trans.) to *cause to superabound* or *excel:*–(make, more) abound, (have, have more) abundance (be more) abundant, be the better, enough and to spare, exceed, excel, increase, be left, redound, remain (over and above).

4053. περισσός *per-is-sos';* from *4012* (in the sense of *beyond*); *superabundant* (in quantity) or *superior* (in quality); by impl. *excessive;* adv. (with *1537*) *violently;* neut. (as noun) *preeminence:*–exceeding abundantly above, more abundantly, advantage, exceedingly, very highly, beyond measure, more, superfluous, vehement[-ly].

4054. περισσότερον *per-is-sot'-er-on;* neut. of *4055* (as adv.); in a *more superabundant* way:–more abundantly, a great deal, far more.

4055. περισσότερος *per-is-sot'-er-os;* comp. of *4053; more superabundant* (in number, degree or character):–more abundant, greater (much) more, overmuch.

4056. περισσοτέρως *per-is-sot-er'-oce;* adv. from *4055; more superabundantly:*–more abundant(-ly), X the more earnest, (more) exceedingly, more frequent, much more, the rather.

4057. περισσῶς *per-is-soce';* adv. from *4053; superabundantly:*–exceedingly, out of measure, the more.

4058. περιστερά *per-is-ter-ah';* of unc. der.; a *pigeon:*–dove, pigeon.

4059. περιτέμνω *per-ee-tem'-no;* from *4012* and the base of *5114;* to *cut around,* i.e. (spec.) to *circumcise:*–circumcise.

4060. περιτίθημι *per-ee-tith'-ay-mee;* from *4012* and *5087;* to *place around;* by impl. to *present:*–bestow upon, hedge round about, put about (on, upon), set about.

4061. περιτομή *per-it-om-ay';* from *4059; circumcision* (the rite, the condition or the people, lit. or fig.):–X circumcised, circumcision.

4062. περιτρέπω *per-ee-trep'-o;* from *4012* and the base of *5157;* to *turn around,* i.e. (ment.) to *craze:*–+ make mad.

4063. περιτρέχω *per-ee-trekh'-o;* from *4012* and *5143* (incl. its alt.); to *run around,* i.e. *traverse:*–run through.

4064. περιφέρω *per-ee-fer'-o;* from *4012* and *5342;* to *convey around,* i.e. *transport hither and thither:*–bear (carry) about.

4065. περιφρονέω *per-ee-fron-eh'-o;* from *4012* and *5426;* to *think beyond,* i.e. *depreciate* (*contemn*):–despise.

4066. περίχωρος *per-ikh'-o-ros;* from *4012* and *5561; around* the *region,* i.e. *circumjacent* (as noun, with *1093* implied *vicinity*):–country (round) about, region (that lieth) round about.

4067. περίψωμα *per-ip'-so-mah;* from a comp. of *4012* and ψάω (to *rub*); something *brushed* all *around,* i.e. *off-scrapings* (fig. *scum*):–offscouring.

4068. περπερεύομαι *per-per-yoo'-om-ahee;* mid. from πέρπερος (*braggart;* perh. by redupl. of the base of *4008*); to *boast:*–vaunt itself.

4069. Περσίς *per-sece';* a *Pers.* woman; *Persis,* a Chr. female:–Persis.

4070. πέυσι *per'-oo-si;* adv. from *4009;* the *by-gone,* i.e. (as noun) *last year:*–+ a year ago.

4071. πετεινόν *pet-i-non';* neut. of a der. of *4072;* a *flying* animal, i.e. *bird:*–bird, fowl.

4072. πετομαι *pet'-om-ahee; or prol.* πετάομαι *pet-ah'-om-ahee;* or contr. πτάομαι *ptah'-om-ahee;* mid. of a prim. verb; to *fly:*–fly(-ing).

4073. πέτρα *pet'-ra;* fem. of the same as *4074;* a (mass of) *rock* (lit. or fig.):–rock.

4074. Πέτρος *pet'-ros;* app. a prim. word; a (piece of) *rock* (larger than *3037*); as a name, *Petrus,* an apostle:–Peter, rock. comp. *2786.*

4075. πετρώδης *pet-ro'-dace;* from *4073* and *1491; rock-like,* i.e. *rocky:*–stony.

4076. πήγανον *pay'-gan-on;* from *4078; rue* (from its *thick* or *fleshy* leaves):–rue.

4077. πηγή *pay-gay';* prob. from *4078* (through the idea of *gushing* plumply); a *fount* (lit. or fig.), i.e. *source* or *supply* (of water, blood, enjoyment) (not necessarily the original spring):–fountain, well.

4078. πήγνυμι *payg'-noo-mee;* a prol. form of a prim. verb (which in its simpler form occurs only as an alt. in cert. tenses); to *fix* ("*peg*"), i.e. (spec.) to *set up* (a tent):–pitch.

4079. πηδάλιον *pay-dal'-ee-on;* neut. of a (presumed) der. of πηδόν pedon (the *blade* of an oar; from the same as *3976*); a "*pedal*", i.e. *helm:*–rudder.

4080. πηλίκος *pay-lee'-kos;* a quantitative form (the fem.) of the base of *4225; how much* (as an indef.), i.e. in size or (fig.) dignity:–how great (large).

4081. πηλός *pay-los';* perh. a prim. word; *clay:*–clay.

4082. πήρα *pay'-rah;* of unc. affin.; a *wallet* or leather *pouch* for food:–scrip.

4083. πῆχυς *pay'-khoos;* of unc. affin.; the *fore-arm,* i.e. (as a measure) a *cubit:*–cubit.

4084. πιάζω *pee-ad'-zo;* prob. another form of *971;* to *squeeze,* i.e. *seize* (gently by the hand [*press*], or officially [*arrest*], or in hunting [*capture*]):–apprehend, catch, lay hand on, take. Comp. *4085.*

4085. πιέζω *pee-ed'-zo;* another form for *4084;* to *pack:*–press down.

4086. πιθανολογία *pith-an-ol-og-ee'-ah;* from a com. of a der. of *3982* and *3056; persuasive language:*–enticing words.

4087. πικραίνω *pik-rah'-ee-no;* from *4089;* to *embitter* (lit. or fig.):–be (make) bitter.

4088. πικρία *pik-ree'-ah;* from *4089; acridity* (esp. *poison*), lit. or fig.:–bitterness.

4089. πικρός *pik-ros';* perh. from *4078* (through the idea of *piercing*); *sharp* (*pungent*), i.e. *acrid* (lit. or fig.):–bitter.

4090. πικρῶς *pik-roce';* adv. from *4089; bitterly,* i.e. (fig.) *violently:*–bitterly.

4091. Πιλάτος *pil-at'-os;* of Lat. or.; *close-pressed,* i.e. *firm; Pilatus,* a Rom.:–Pilate.

4092. πίμπρημι *pim'-pray-mee;*a redupl. and prol. form of a prim. word, πρέω *preh'-o;*(which occurs only as an alt. in cert. tenses); to *fire,* i.e. *burn* (fig. and pass. *become inflamed* with fever):–be (X should have) swollen.

4093. πινακίδιον *pin-ak-id'-ee-on;* dimin. of *4094;* a *tablet* (for writing on):–writing table.

4094. πίναξ *pin'-ax* app. a form of *4109;* a *plate:*–charger, platter.

4095. πίνω *pee'-no;* a prol. form of πίω *pee'-o*; which (together with another form πόω *po'-o;*) occurs only as an alt. in cert. tenses; to *imbibe* (lit. or fig.):–drink.

4096. πιότης *pee-ot'-ace;* from πίων (*fat;* perh. akin to the alt. of *4095* through the idea of *repletion*); *plumpness,* i.e. (by impl.) *richness* (*oiliness*):–fatness.

4097. πιπράσκω *pip-ras'-ko;* a redupl.and prol. form of πράω (which occurs only as an alt. in cert. tenses); contr. from περάω *phah-o;* (to *traverse;* from the base of *4008*); to *traffic* (by *travelling*), i.e. *dispose* of as merchandise or into slavery (lit. or fig.):–sell.

4098. πίπτω *pip'-to;* a redupl. and contr. form of πέτω *pet'-o* (which occurs only as an alt. in cert. tenses); prob. akin to *4072* through the idea of *alighting;* to *fall* (lit. or fig.):–fail, fall (down), light on.

4099. Πισιδία *pis-id-ee'-ah;* prob. of for. or.; *Pisidia,* a region of Asia Minor:–Pisidia.

4100. πιστεύω *pist-yoo'-o;* from *4102;* to have *faith* (in, upon, or with respect to, a person or thing), i.e. *credit;* by impl. to *entrust* (esp. one's spir. well-being to Christ):–believe(-r), commit (to trust), put in trust with.

4101. πιστικός *pis-tik-os';* from *4102; trustworthy,* i.e. *genuine* (*unadulterated*):–spike-[nard].

4102. πίστις *pis'-tis;* from *3982; persuasion,* i.e. *credence;* mor. *conviction* (of *relig.* truth, or the truthfulness of God or a relig. teacher), esp. *reliance* upon Christ for salvation; abstr., *constancy* in such profession; by ext., the system of relig. (Gospel) *truth* itself:–assurance, belief, believe, faith, fidelity.

4103. πιστός *pis-tos';* from *3982;* obj., *trustworthy;* subj. *trustful:*–believe(-ing, -r), faithful(-ly), sure, true.

4104. πιστόω *pis-to'-o;* from *4103;* to *assure:*–assure of.

4105. πλανάω *plan-ah'-o;* from *4106;* to (prop. *cause* to) *roam* (from safety, truth, or virtue):–go astray, deceive, err, seduce, wander, be out of the way.

4106. πλάνη *plan'-ay;* fem. of *4108* (as abstr.); obj., *fraudulence;* subj. a *straying* from orthodoxy or piety:–deceit, to deceive, delusion, error.

4107. πλανήτης *plan-ay'-tace;* from *4108;* a *rover* ("planet"), i.e. (fig.) an *erratic* teacher:–wandering.

4108. πλάνος *plan'-os;* of unc. affin.; *roving* (as a *tramp*), i.e. (by impl.) an *impostor* or *misleader;* --deceiver, seducing.

4109. πλάξ *plax;* from *4111;* a *moulding-board,* i.e. *flat* surface ("*plate*", or *tablet,* lit. or fig.):–table.

4110. πλάσμα *plas'-mah;* from *4111;* something *moulded:*–thing formed.

4111. πλάσσω a prim. verb; to *mould,* i.e. *shape* or *fabricate:*–form.

4112. πλαστός *plas-tos';* from *4111; moulded,* i.e. (by impl.) *artif.* or (fig.) *fictitious* (*false*):–feigned.

4113. πλατεῖα *plat-i'-ah;* fem. of *4116;* a *wide* "*plat*" or "*place*", i.e. open *square:*–street.

4114. πλάτος *plat'-os;* from *4116; width:*–breadth.

4115. πλατύνω *plat-oo'-no;* from *4116*; to *widen* (lit. or fig.):–make broad, enlarge.

4116. πλατύς *plat-oos'* from *4111;* spread out "*flat*" ("plot"), i.e. *broad:*–wide.

4117. πλέγμα *pleg'-mah;* from *4120;* a *plait* (of hair):–broidered hair.

4118. πλεῖστος *plice'-tos;* irreg. superl. of *4183;* the *largest number* or *very large:*–very great, most.

4119. πλείων *pli-own;* neut. πλεῖον *pli-on;* or πλέον *pleh-on* comp. of *4183;* more in quantity, number, or quality; also (in pl.) the *major portion:*–X above, + exceed, more excellent, further, (very) great(-er), long(-er), (very) many, greater (more) part, + yet but.

4120. πλέκω *plek'-o;* a prim. word; to *twine* or *braid*:–plait.

4121. πλεονάζω *pleh-on-ad'-zo;* from *4119;* to *do, make* or *be more,* i.e. *increase* (trans. or intrans.); by ext., to *superabound:*–abound, abundant, make to increase, have over.

4122. πλεονεκτέω *pleh-on-ek-teh'-o;* from *4123;* to *be covetous,* i.e. (by impl.) to *over-reach:*–get an advantage, defraud, make a gain.

4123. πλεονέκτης *pleh-on-ek'-tace;* from *4119* and *2192; holding* (*desiring*) *more,* i.e. *eager for gain* (*avaricious,* hence a *defrauder*):–covetous.

4124. πλεονεξία *pleh-on-ex-ee'-ah;* from *4123; avarice,* i.e. (by impl.) *fraudulency, extortion:*–covetous(-ness) practices, greediness.

4125. πλευρά *plyoo-rah';* of unc. affin.; a *rib,* i.e. (by ext.) *side:*–side.

4126. πλέω *pleh'-o;* another form for πλεύω *plyoo'-o,* which is used as an alt.in cert. tenses; prob. a form of *4150* (through the idea of *plunging* through the water); to *pass* in a vessel:–sail. See also *4130.*

4127. πληγή *play-gay';* from *4141;* a *stroke;* by impl. a *wound;* fig. a *calamity:*–plague, stripe, wound(-ed).

4128. πλῆθος *play'-thos;* from *4130;* a *fulness,* i.e. a *large number, throng, populace:*–bundle, company, multitude.

4129. πληθύνω *play-thoo'-no;* from another form of *4128;* to *increase* (trans. or intrans.):–abound, multiply.

4130. πλήθω *play'-tho;* a prol. form of a prim. word πλέω *pleh'-o;* (which appears only as an alt. in cert. tenses and in the redupl. form of πίμπλημι) to "*fill*" (lit. or fig. [*imbue, influence*, supply]); spec. to *fulfil* (time):–accomplish, full (...come), furnish.

4131. πλήκτης *plake'-tace;* from 4141; a *smiter,* i.e. *pugnacious* (*quarrelsome*):–striker.

4132. πλημμύρα *plame-moo'-rah;* prol. from 4130; *flood-tide,* i.e. (by anal.) a *freshet:*–flood.

4133. πλήν *plane;* from *4119; moreover* (*besides*), i.e. *albeit, save that, rather, yet:*–but (rather), except, nevertheless, notwithstanding, save, than.

4134. πλήρης *play'-race;* from *4130; replete,* or *covered* over; by anal. *complete:*–full.

4135. πληροφορέω *play-rof-or-eh'-o;* from *4134* and *5409;* to *carry* out *fully* (in evidence), i.e. *completely assure* (or *convince*), *entirely accomplish:*–most surely believe, fully know (persuade), make full proof of.

4136. πληροφορία *play-rof-or-ee'-ah*; from *4135; entire confidence:*–(full) assurance.

4137. πληρόω *play-ro'-o;* from *4134;* to *make replete,* i.e. (lit.) to *cram* (a net), *level* up (a hollow), or (fig.) to *furnish* (or *imbue, diffuse, influence*), *satisfy, execute* (an office), *finish* (a period or task), *verify* (or *coincide* with a prediction), etc.:–accomplish, X after, (be) complete, end, expire, fill (up), fulfil, (be, make) full (come), fully preach, perfect, supply.

4138. πλήρωμα *play'-ro-mah;* from *4137; repletion* or *completion,* i.e. (subj.) what *fills* (as contents, supplement, copiousness, multitude), or (obj.) what is *filled* (as container, performance, period):–which is put in to fill up, piece that filled up, fulfilling, full, fulness.

4139. πλησίον *play-see'-on;* neut. of a der. of πέλας (*near*); (adv.) *close* by; as noun, a *neighbor,* i.e. *fellow* (as man, countryman, Chr. or friend):–near, neighbour.

4140. πλησμονή *place-mon-ay';* from a presumed der. of *4130;* a *filling* up, i.e. (fig.) *gratification:*–satisfying.

4141. πλήσσω *place'-so;* app. another form of *4111* (through the idea of *flattening* out); to *pound,* i.e. (fig.) to *inflict* with (calamity):–smite. Comp. *5180.*

4142. πλοιάριον *ploy-ar'-ee-on;* neut. of a presumed der. of *4143;* a *boat:*–boat, little (small) ship.

4143. πλοῖν *ploy'-on;* from *4126;* a *sailer,* i.e. *vessel:*–ship(-ing).

4144. πλόος *plo'-os;* from *4126;* a *sail,* i.e. *navigation:*–course, sailing, voyage.

4145. πλούσιος *ploo'-see-os;* from *4149; wealthy;* fig. *abounding* with:–rich.

4146. πλουσίως *ploo-see'-oce;* adv. from *4145; copiously:*–abundantly, richly.

4147. πλουτέω *ploo-teh'-o;* from *4148;* to *be* (or *become*) *wealthy* (lit. or fig.):–be increased with goods, (be made, wax) rich.

4148. πλουτίζω *ploo-tid'-zo;* from *4149;* to *make wealthy* (fig.):–en- (make) rich.

4149. πλοῦτος *ploo'-tos;* from the base of *4130; wealth* (as *fulness*), i.e. (lit.) *money, possessions,* or (fig.) *abundance, richness,* (spec.), valuable *bestowment:*–riches.

4150. πλύνω *ploo'-no;* a prol. form of an obs. πλύω (to "*flow*"); to "*plunge*", i.e. *launder* clothing:–wash. comp. *3068, 3538.*

4151. πνεῦμα *pnyoo'-mah;* from *4154;* a

GREEK

current of air, i.e. *breath* (*blast*) or a *breeze;* by anal. or fig. a *spirit,* i.e. (human) the rational *soul,* (by impl.) *vital principle,* ment. *disposition,* etc., or (superhuman) an *angel, demon,* or (divine) *God,* Christ's *spirit,* the Holy *Spirit:*–ghost, life, spirit(-ual, -ually), mind. Comp. *5590.*

4152. πνευματικός *pnyoo-mat-ik-os';* from *4151; non-carnal,* i.e. (humanly) *ethereal* (as opposed to gross), or (demoniacally) a *spirit* (concr.), or (divinely) *supernatural, regenerate, religious:*–spiritual. Comp. 5591.

4153. πνευματικῶς *pnyoo-mat-ik-oce';* adv. from *4152; non-phys.* i.e. *divinely, fig.:*–spiritually.

4154. πνέω *pneh'-o;* a prim. word; to *breathe* hard, i.e. *breeze:*–blow. Comp. *5594.*

4155. πνίγω *pnee'-go;* streng. from *4154;* to *wheeze,* i.e. (caus., by impl.) to *throttle* or *strangle* (*drown*):–choke, take by the throat.

4156. πνικτός *pnik-tos';* from *4155; throttled,* i.e. (neut. concr.) an animal *choked* to death (*not bled*):–strangled.

4157. πνοή *pno-ay';* from *4154; respiration,* a *breeze:*–breath, wind.

4158. ποδήρης *pod-ay'-race* from *4228* and another element of unc. affin.; a *dress* (*2066* implied) *reaching* the *ankles:*–garment down to the foot.

4159. πόθεν *poth'-en;* from the base of *4213* with enclitic adv. of or., *from which* (as interrog.) or *what* (as rel.) place, state, source or cause:–whence.

4160. ποιέω *poy-eh'-o;* app. a prol. form of an obs. prim.; to *make* or *do* (in a very wide appl., more or less dir.):–abide, + agree, appoint, X avenge, + band together, be, bear, + bewray, bring (forth), cast out, cause, commit, + content, continue, deal, + without any delay, (would) do (-ing), execute, exercise, fulfil, gain, give, have, hold, X journeying, keep, + lay wait, + lighten the ship, make, X mean, + none of these things move me, observe, ordain, perform, provide, + have purged, purpose, put, + raising up, X secure, shew, X shoot out, spend, take, tarry, + transgress the law, work, yield. Comp. *4238.*

4161. ποίημα *poy'-ay-mah;* from *4160;* a *product,* i.e. *fabric* (lit. or fig.):–thing i.e. made, workmanship.

4162. ποίησις *poy'-ay-sis;* from *4160; action,* i.e. *performance* (of the law):–deed.

4163. ποιητής *poy-ay-tace'* from *4160;* a *performer;* spec. a "*poet*":–doer, poet.

4164. ποικίλος *poy-kee'-los;* of unc. der.; *motley,* i.e. *various* in character:–divers, manifold.

4165. ποιμαίνω *poy-mah'-ee-no;* from *4166;* to *tend* as a shepherd of (fig. *superviser*):–feed (cattle), rule.

4166. ποιμήν *poy-mane';* of unc. affin.; a *shepherd* (lit. or fig.):–shepherd, pastor.

4167. ποίμνη *poym'-nay;* contr. from *4165;* a *flock* (lit. or fig.):–flock, fold.

4168. ποίμνιον *poym'-nee-on;* neut. of a presumed der. of *4167;* a *flock,* i.e. (fig.) *group* (of believers):–flock.

4169. ποῖος *poy'-os* from the base of *4226* and *3634;* indiv. interrog. (of character) *what* sort of, or (of number) *which* one:–what (manner of), which.

4170. πολεμέω *pol-em-eh'-o;* from *4171;* to *be* (engaged) in *warfare,* i.e. to *battle* (lit. or fig.): -fight, (make) war.

4171. πόλεμος *pol'-em-os;* from πέλομαι (to *bustle*); *warfare* (lit. or fig.; a single encounter or a series):–battle, fight, war.

4172. πόλις *pol'-is;* prob. from the same as *4171,* or perh. from *4183;* a *town* (prop. with walls, of greater or less size):–city.

4173. πολιτάρχης *pol-it-ar'-khace;* from *4172* and *757;* a *town-officer,* i.e. *magistrate:*–ruler of the city.

4174. πολιτεία *pol-ee-ti'-ah;* from *4177* ("*polity*"); *citizenship;* concr. a *community:*–commonwealth, freedom.

4175. πολίτευμα *pol-it'-yoo-mah;* from *4176;* a *community,* i.e. (abstr.) *citizenship* (fig.):–conversation.

4176. πολιτεύομαι *pol-it-yoo'-om-ahee;* mid. of a der. of *4177;* to *behave* as a citizen (fig.):–let conversation be, live.

4177. πολίτης *pol-ee'-tace;* from *4172;* a *townsman:*–citizen.

4178. πολλάκις *pol-lak'-is;* mult. adv. from *4183; many times,* i.e. *frequently:*–oft(-en, -entimes, -times).

4179. πολλαπλασίων *pol-lap-las-ee'-ohn;* from 4183 and prob. a der. of *4120; manifold,* i.e. (neut. as noun) *very much more:*–manifold more.

4180. πολυλογία *pol-oo-log-ee'-ah;* from a com. of *4183* and *3056; loquacity,* i.e. *prolixity:*–much speaking.

4181. πολυμέρως *pol-oo-mer'-oce;* adv. from a com. of *4183* and *3313; in many portions,* i.e. *variously* as to time and agency (*piecemeal*):–at sundry times.

4182. πολυποίκιλος *pol-oo-poy'-kil-os;* from *4183* and *4164; much variegated,* i.e. *multifarious:*–manifold.

4183. πολύς *pol-oos';* incl. the forms from the alt. πολλός pollos; (sing.) *much* (in any respect) or (pl.) *many;* neut. (sing.) as adv. *largely;* neut. (pl.) as adv. or noun *often, mostly, largely:*–abundant, + altogether, common, + far (passed, spent), (+ be of a) great (age, deal, -ly, while), long, many, much, oft(-en [-times]), plenteous, sore, straitly. Comp. *4118, 4119.*

4184. πολύσπλαγχνος *pol-oo'-splankh-nos;* from *4183* and *4698* (fig.); *extremely compassionate:*–very pitiful.

4185. πολυτελής *pol-oo-tel-ace';* from *4183* and *5056; extremely expensive:*–costly, very precious, of great price.

4186. πολύτιμος *pol-oot'-ee-mos;* from *4183* and *5092; extremely valuable:*–very costly, of great price.

4187. πολυτρόπως *pol-oot-rop'-oce;* adv. from a com. of *4183* and *5158; in many ways,* i.e. *variously* as to method or form:–in divers manners.

4188. πόμα *pom'-ah;* from the alt. of *4095;* a *beverage:*–drink.

4189. πονηρία *pon-ay-ree'-ah;* from *4190; depravity,* i.e. (spec.), *malice;* pl. (concr.) *plots, sins:*–iniquity, wickedness.

4190. πονηρός *pon-ay-ros';* from a der. of *4192; hurtful,* i.e. *evil* (prop. in effect or influence, and thus differing from 2556, which refers rather to *essential* character, as well as from *4550,* which indicates *degeneracy* from or. virtue); fig. *calamitous;* also pass. *ill,* i.e. *diseased;* but esp. (mor.) *culpable,* i.e. *derelict, vicious, facinorous;* neut. (sing.) *mischief, malice,* or (pl.) *guilt;* masc. (sing.) the *devil,* or (pl.) *sinners:*–bad, evil, grievous, harm, lewd, malicious, wicked(-ness). See also *4191.*

4191. πονηρότερος *pon-ay-rot'-er-os;* comp. of *4190; more evil:*–more wicked.

4192. πόνος *pon'-os;* from the base of *3993; toil,* i.e. (by impl.) *anguish:*–pain.

4193. Ποντικός *pon-tik-os';* from *4195;* a *Pontican,* i.e. native of Pontus:–born in Pontus.

4194. Πόντιος *pon'-tee-os* of Lat. or.; app. *bridged; Pontius,* a Rom.:–Pontius.

4195. Πόντος *pon'-tos;* a *sea; Pontus,* a region of Asia Minor:–Pontus.

4196. Πόπλιος *pop'-lee-os;* of Lat. or.; app. "*popular*"; *Poplius* (i.e. *Publius*), a Rom.:–Publius.

4197. πορεία *por-i'-ah;* from *4198; travel* (by land); fig. (pl.) *proceedings,* i.e. *career:*–journey[-ing], ways.

4198. πορεύομαι *por-yoo'-om-ahee;* mid. from a der. of the same as *3984;* to *traverse,* i.e. *travel* (lit. or fig.; esp. to *remove* [fig. *die*], *live,* etc.); --depart, go (away, forth, one's way, up), (make a, take a) journey, walk.

4199. πορθέω *por-theh'-o;* prol. from πέρθω (to *sack*); to *ravage* (fig.):–destroy, waste.

4200. πορισμός *por-is-mos';* from a der. of πόρος poros (a *way,* i.e. *means*); *furnishing* (*procuring*), i.e. (by impl.) *money-getting* (*acquisition*):–gain.

4201. Πόρκιος *por'-kee-os;* of Lat. or.; app. *swinish; Porcius,* a Rom.:–Porcius.

4202. πορνεία *por-ni'-ah* from *4203; harlotry* (incl. *adultery* and *incest*); fig. *idolatry:*–fornication.

4203. πορνεύω *porn-yoo'-o;* from *4204;* to *act* the *harlot,* i.e. (lit.) *indulge* unlawful *lust* (of either sex), or (fig.) *practise idolatry:*–commit (fornication).

4204. πόρνη *por'-nay* fem. of *4205;* a *strumpet;* fig. an *idolater:*–harlot, whore.

4205. πόρνος *por'-nos;* from πέρνημι (to *sell;* akin to the base of *4097*); a (male) *prostitute* (as *venal*), i.e. (by anal.) a *debauchee* (*libertine*):–fornicator, whoremonger.

4206. πόρρω *por'-rho;* adv. from *4253; forwards,* i.e. *at a distance:*–far, a great way off. See also *4207.*

4207. πόρρωθεν *por'-rho-then;* from *4206* with adv. enclitic of source; *from far,* or (by impl.) *at a distance,* i.e. *distantly:*–afar off.

4208. πορρωτέρω *por-rho-ter'-o;* adv. comp. of *4206; further,* i.e. *a greater distance:*–further.

4209. πορφύρα *por-foo'-rah;* of Lat. or.; the "*purple*" mussel, i.e. (by impl.) the *red-blue* color itself, and finally a garment dyed with it:–purple.
4210. πορφυροῦς *por-foo-rooce';* from *4209; purpureal,* i.e. *bluish red:*–purple.
4211. πορφυρόπωλις *por-foo-rop'-o-lis;* fem. of a com. of *4209* and *4453;* a *female trader in purple* cloth:–seller of purple.
4212. ποσάκις *pos-ak'-is;* mult. from *4214; how many times:*–how oft(-en).
4213. πόσις *pos'-is;* from the alt. of *4095;* a *drinking* (the act), i.e. (concr.) a *draught:*–drink.
4214. πόσος *pos'-os;* from an absol. πός (*who, what*) and *3739;* interrog. pron. (of amount) *how much* (*large, long* or [pl.] *many*):–how great (long, many), what.
4215. ποταμός *pot-am-os';* prob. from a der. of the alt. of *4095* (comp. *4224*); a *current, brook* or *freshet* (as *drinkable*), i.e. *running water:*–flood, river, stream, water.
4216. ποταμοφόρητος *pot-am-of-or'-ay-tos;* from *4215* and a der. of *5409; river-borne,* i.e. *overwhelmed by a stream:*–carried away of the flood.
4217. ποταπός *pot-ap-os';* app. from *4219* and the base of *4226;* interrog., *whatever,* i.e. of *what possible* sort:–what (manner of).
4218. ποτέ *pot-eh';* from the base of *4225* and *5037;* indef. adv. at *some time, ever:*–afore-(any, some-)time(-s), at length (the last), (+ n-)ever, in the old time, in time past, once, when.
4219. πότε *pot'-eh;* from the base of *4226* and *5037;* interrog. adv. at *what time:*–+ how long, when.
4220. πότερον *pot'-er-on;* neut. of a comp. of the base of *4226;* interrog. as adv. *which* (of two), i.e. *is it* this or that:–whether.
4221. ποτήριον *pot-ay'-ree-on;* neut. of a der. of the alt. of *4095;* a *drinking-vessel;* by ext., the contents thereof, i.e. a *cupful* (*draught*); fig. a *lot* or *fate:*–cup.
4222. ποτίζω *pot-id'-zo;* from a der. of the alt. of *4095;* to *furnish drink, irrigate:*–give (make) to drink, feed, water.
4223. Ποτίολοι *pot-ee'-ol-oy;* of Lat. or.; *little wells,* i.e. *mineral springs; Potioli* (i.e. *Puteoli*), a place in Italy:–Puteoli.
4224. πότος *pot'-os;* from the alt. of *4095;* a *drinking-bout* or *carousal:*–banqueting.
4225. πού *poo;* gen. case of an indef. pron. πός (*some*) otherwise obs. (comp. *4214*); as adv. of place, *somewhere,* i.e. *nearly:*–about, a cert. place.
4226. ποῦ *poo;* gen. of an interrog. pron. πός (*what*) otherwise obs. (perh. the same as *4225* used with the rising slide of inquiry); as adv. of place; *at* (by impl. *to*) *what* locality:–where, whither.
4227. Πούδης *poo'-dace;* of Lat. or.; *modest; Pudes* (i.e. *Pudens*), a Chr.:–Pudens.
4228. πούς *pooce;* a prim. word; a "*foot*" (fig. or lit.):–foot(-stool).
4229. πρᾶγμα *prag'-mah;* from *4238;* a *deed;* by impl. an *affair;* by ext., an *object* (material):–business, matter, thing, work.
4230. πραγματεία *prag-mat-i'-ah;* from *4231;* a *transaction,* i.e. *negotiation:*–affair.
4231. πραγματεύομαι *prag-mat-yoo'-om-ahee;* from *4229;* to *busy oneself* with, i.e. to *trade:*–occupy.
4232. πραιτώριον *prahee-to'-ree-on;* of Lat. or.; the *praetorium* or governor's *courtroom* (sometimes incl. the whole *edifice* and *camp*):–(common, judgment) hall (of judgment), palace, praetorium.
4233. πράκτωρ *prak'-tore;* from a der. of *4238;* a *practiser,* i.e. (spec.), an official *collector:*–officer.
4234. πρᾶξις *prax'-is;* from *4238; practice,* i.e. (concr.) an *act;* by ext., a *function:*–deed, office, work.
4235. πρᾷος *prah'-os;* a form of *4239,* used in cert. parts; *gentle,* i.e. *humble:*–meek.
4236. πρᾳότης *prah-ot'-ace;* from *4235; gentleness,* by impl. *humility:*–meekness.
4237. πρασιά *pras-ee-ah';* perh. from πράσον prason (a *leek,* and so an *onion-patch*); a garden *plot,* i.e. (by impl. of regular *beds*) a *row* (repeated in pl. by Heb., to indicate an arrangement):–in ranks.
4238. πράσσω *pras'-so;* a prim. verb; to "*practise*", i.e. *perform repeatedly* or *habitually* (thus differing from *4160*, which prop. refers to a *single* act); by impl. to *execute, accomplish,* etc.; spec. to *collect* (dues), *fare* (pers.):–commit, deeds, do, exact, keep, require, use arts.
4239. πραΰς *prah-ooce';* app. a prim. word; *mild,* i.e. (by impl.) *humble:*–meek. See also *4235*.
4240. πραΰτης *prah-oo'-tace;* from *4239; mildness,* i.e. (by impl.) *humility:*–meekness.
4241. πρέπω *prep'-o;* app. a prim. verb; to *tower* up (*be conspicuous*), i.e. (by impl.) to *be suitable* or *proper* (third pers. sing. pres. ind., often used impers., it is *fit* or *right*):–become, comely.
4242. πρεσβεία *pres-bi'-ah;* from *4243; seniority* (*eldership*), i.e. (by impl.) an *embassy* (concr. *ambassadors*):–ambassage, message.
4243. πρεσβεύω *pres-byoo'-o;* from the base of *4245;* to be a *senior,* i.e. (by impl.) *act as a representative* (fig. *preacher*):–be an ambassador.
4244. πρεσβυτέριον *pres-boo-ter'-ee-on;* neut. of a presumed der. of *4245;* the *order of elders,* i.e. (spec.), Isr. *Sanhedrin* or Chr. "*presbytery*":–(estate of) elder(-s), presbytery.
4245. πρεσβύτερος *pres-boo'-ter-os;* comp. of πρέσβυς (*elderly*); *older;* as noun, a *senior;* spec. an Isr. *Sanhedrist* (also fig. member of the celestial council) or Chr. "*presbyter*":– elder(-est), old.
4246. πρεσβύτης *pres-boo'-tace;* from the same as *4245;* an *old man:*–aged (man), old man.
4247. πρεσβῦτις *pres-boo'-tis;* fem. of *4246;* an *old woman:*–aged woman.
4248. πρηνής *pray-nace';* from *4253; leaning* (*falling*) *forward* ("*prone*"), i.e. *head foremost:*–headlong.
4249. πρίζω *prid'-zo;* a streng. form of a prim. πρίω (to *saw*); to *saw* in two:–saw asunder.
4250. πρίν *prin;* adv. from *4253; prior, sooner:*–before (that), ere.
4251. Πρίσκα *pris'-kah;* of Lat. or.; fem. of Priscus, *ancient; Priska,* a Chr. woman:–Prisca. See also *4252*.
4252. Πρίσκιλλα *pris'-cil-lah;* dimin. of *4251; Priscilla* (i.e. *little Prisca*), a Chr. woman:–Priscilla.
4253. πρό *pro;* a prim. prep.; "*fore*", i.e. *in front of, prior* (fig. *superior*) *to:*–above, ago, before, or ever. In the comp., it retains the same significations.
4254. προάγω *pro-ag'-o;* from *4253* and *71;* to *lead forward* (magisterially); intrans., to *precede* (in place or time [part., *previous*]):–bring (forth, out), go before.
4255. προαιρέομαι *pro-ahee-reh'-om-ahee;* from *4253* and *138* to *choose* for oneself *before* another thing (*prefer*), i.e. (by impl.) to *propose* (*intend*):–purpose.
4256. προαιτιάομαι *pro-ahee-tee-ah'-om-ahee;* from *4253* and a der. of *156;* to *accuse already,* i.e. *previously charge:*–prove before.
4257. προακούω *pro-ak-oo'-o;* from *4253* and *191;* to *hear already,* i.e. *anticipate:*–hear before.
4258. προαμαρτάνω *pro-am-ar-tan'-o;* from *4253* and *264;* to *sin previously* (to conversion):–sin already, heretofore sin.
4259. προαύλιον *pro-ow'-lee-on;* neut. of a presumed com. of *4253* and *833;* a *forecourt,* i.e. *vestibule* (*alley-way*):–porch.
4260. προβαίνω *prob-ah'-ee-no;* from *4253* and the base of *939;* to *walk forward,* i.e. *advance* (lit. or in years):–+ be of a great age, go farther (on), be well stricken.
4261. προβάλλω *prob-al'-lo;* from *4253* and *906;* to *throw forward,* i.e. *push to the front, germinate:*–put forward, shoot forth.
4262. προβατικός *prob-at-ik-os;'* from *4263; relating to sheep,* i.e. (a *gate*) through which they were led into Jerus.:–sheep (market).
4263. πρόβατον *prob'-at-on;* prop. neut. of a presumed der. of *4260; something that walks forward* (a *quadruped*), i.e. (spec.), a *sheep* (lit. or fig.):–sheep([-fold]).
4264. προβιβάζω *prob-ib-ad'-zo;* from *4253* and a redupl. form of *971;* to *force forward,* i.e. *bring to the front, instigate:*–draw, before instruct.
4265. προβλέπω *prob-lep'-o;* from *4253* and *991;* to *look* out *beforehand,* i.e. *furnish in advance:*–provide.
4266. προγίνομαι *prog-in'-om-ahee;* from *4253* and *1096;* to *be already,* i.e. *have previousy transpired:*–be past.
4267. προγινώσκω *prog-in-oce'-ko;* from *4253* and *1097;* to *know beforehand,* i.e. *foresee:*–foreknow (ordain), know (before).
4268. πρόγνωσις *prog'-no-sis;* from *4267;*

GREEK

forethought:–foreknowledge.

4269. πρόγονος *prog'-on-os;* from *4266;* an *ancestor,* (*grand-*)*parent:*–forefather, parent.

4270. προγράφω *prog-raf'-o;* from *4253* and *1125;* to *write previously;* fig. to *announce, prescribe:*–before ordain, evidently set forth, write (afore, aforetime).

4271. πρόδηλος *prod'-ay-los;* from *4253* and *1212; plain before* all men, i.e. *obvious:*–evident, manifest (open) beforehand.

4272. προδίδωμι *prod-id'-o-mee;* from *4253* and *1325;* to *give before* the other party has given:–first give.

4273. προδότης *prod-ot'-ace;* from *4272* (in the sense of *giving forward* into another's [the enemy's] hands); a *surrender:*–betrayer, traitor.

4274. πρόδρομος *prod'-rom-os;* from the alt. of *4390;* a *runner ahead,* i.e. *scout* (fig. *precursor*):–forerunner.

4275. προείδω *pro-i'-do;* from *4253* and *1492; foresee:*–foresee, saw before.

4276. προελπίζω *pro-el-pid'-zo;* from *4253* and *1679;* to *hope in advance* of other confirmation:–first trust.

4277. προέπω *pro-ep'-o;* from *4253* and *2036;* to *say already,* to *predict:*–forewarn, say (speak, tell) before. Comp. *4280.*

4278. προενάρχομαι *pro-en-ar'-khom-ahee;* from *4253* and *1728;* to *commence already:*–begin (before).

4279. προεπαγγέλλομαι *pro-ep-ang-ghel'-lom-ahee;* mid. from *4253* and *1861;* to *promise of old:*–promise before.

4280. προερέω *pro-er-eh'-o;* from *4253* and *2046;* used as alt. of *4277;* to *say already, predict:*–foretell, say (speak, tell) before.

4281. προέρχομαι *pro-er'-khom-ahee;* from *4253* and *2064* (incl. its alt.); to *go onward, precede* (in place or time):–go before (farther, forward), outgo, pass on.

4282. προετοιμάζω *pro-et-oy-mad'-zo;* from *4253* and *2090;* to *fit* up in *advance* (lit. or fig.):–ordain before, prepare afore.

4283. προευαγγελίζομαι *pro-yoo-ang-ghel-id'-zom-ahee;* mid. from *4253* and *2097;* to *announce* glad news in *advance:*–preach before the gospel.

4284. προέχομαι *pro-ekh-om-ahee;* mid. from *4253* and *2192;* to *hold* oneself *before* others, i.e. (fig.) to *excel:*–be better.

4285. προηγέομαι *pro-ay-geh'-om-ahee;* from *4253* and *2233;* to *lead the way* for others, i.e. *show deference:*–prefer.

4286. πρόθεσις *proth'-es-is;* from *4388;* a *setting forth,* i.e. (fig.) *proposal* (*intention*); spec. the *show*-bread (in the Temple) as *exposed* before God:–purpose, shew[-bread].

4287. προθέσμιος *proth-es'-mee-os;* from *4253* and a der. of *5087; fixed beforehand,* i.e. (fem. with *2250* implied) a *designated* day:–time appointed.

4288. προθυμία *proth-oo-mee'-ah;* from *4289; predisposition,* i.e. *alacrity:*–forwardness of mind, readiness (of mind), ready (willing) mind.

4289. πρόθυμος *proth'-oo-mos;* from *4253* and *2372; forward* in *spirit,* i.e. *predisposed;* neut. (as noun) *alacrity:*–ready, willing.

4290. προθύμως *proth-oo'-moce;* adv. from *4289; with alacrity:*–willingly.

4291. προΐστημι *pro-is'-tay-mee;* from *4253* and *2476;* to *stand before,* i.e. (in rank) to *preside,* or (by impl.) to *practise:*–maintain, be over, rule.

4292. προκαλέομαι *prok-al-eh'-om-ahee;* mid. from *4253* and *2564;* to *call forth to oneself* (*challenge*), i.e. (by impl.) to *irritate:*–provoke.

4293. προκαταγγέλλω *prok-at-ang-ghel'-lo;* from *4253* and *2605;* to *anounce beforehand,* i.e. *predict, promise:*–foretell, have notice, (shew) before.

4294. προκαταρτίζω *prok-at-ar-tid'-zo;* from *4253* and *2675;* to *prepare in advance:*–make up beforehand.

4295. πρόκειμαι *prok'-i-mahee;* from *4253* and *2749;* to *lie before* the view, i.e. (fig.) to *be present..* (to the mind), to *stand forth* (as an example or reward):–be first, set before (forth).

4296. προκηρύσσω *prok-ay-rooce'-so;* from *4253* and *2784;* to *herald* (i.e. *proclaim*) *in advance:*–before (first) preach.

4297. προκοπή *prok-op-ay';* from *4298; progress,* i.e. *advancement* (subj. or obj.):–furtherance, profit.

4298. προκόπτω *prok-op'-to;* from *4253* and *2875;* to *drive forward* (as if by beating), i.e. (fig. and intrans.) to *advance* (in amount, to *grow;* in time, to *be well along*):–increase, proceed, profit, be far spent, wax.

4299. πρόκριμα *prok'-ree-mah;* from a com. of *4253* and *2919;* a *prejudgment* (*prejudice*), i.e. *prepossession:*–prefer one before another.

4300. προκυρόω *prok-oo-ro'-o;* from *4253* and *2964;* to *ratify previously:*–confirm before.

4301. προλαμβάνω *prol-am-ban'-o;* from *4253* and *2983;* to *take in advance,* i.e. (lit.) *eat before* others have an opportunity; (fig.) to *anticipate, surprise:*–come aforehand, overtake, take before.

4302. προλέγω *prol-eg'-o;* from *4253* and *3004;* to say *beforehand,* i.e. *predict, forewarn:*–foretell, tell before.

4303. προμαρτύρομαι *prom-ar-too'-rom-ahee;* from *4253* and *3143;* to *be a witness in advance* i.e. *predict:*–testify beforehand.

4304. προμελετάω *prom-el-et-ah'-o;* from *4253* and *3191;* to *premeditate:*–meditate before.

4305. προμεριμνάω *prom-er-im-nah'-o* from *4253* and *3309;* to *care* (anxiously) *in advance:*–take thought beforehand.

4306. προνοέω *pron-o-eh'-o;* from *4253* and *3539;* to *consider in advance,* i.e. *look* out for *beforehand* (act., by way of *maintenance* for others; mid. by way of *circumspection* for oneself):–provide (for).

4307. πρόνοια *pron'-oy-ah;* from *4306; forethought,* i.e. provident *care* or *supply:*–providence, provision.

4308. προοράω *pro-or-ah'-o* from *4253* and *3708;* to *behold in advance,* i.e. (act.) to *notice* (another) *previously,* or (mid.) to *keep in* (one's own) *view:*–foresee, see before.

4309. προορίζω *pro-or-id'-zo;* from *4253* and *3724;* to *limit in advance,* i.e. (fig.) *predetermine:*–determine before, ordain, predestinate.

4310. προπάσχω *prop-as'-kho;* from *4253* and *3958;* to *undergo* hardship *previously:*–suffer before.

4311. προπέμπω *prop-em'-po;* from *4253* and *3992;* to *send forward,* i.e. *escort* or *aid* in travel:–accompany, bring (forward) on journey (way), conduct forth.

4312. προπετής *prop-et-ace';* from a com. of *4253* and *4098; falling forward,* i.e. *headlong* (fig. *precipitate*):–heady, rash[-ly].

4313. προπορεύομαι *prop-or-yoo'-om-ahee;* from *4253* and *4198;* to *precede* (as guide or herald):–go before.

4314. πρός *pros;* a streng. form of *4253;* a prep. of direction; *forward to,* i.e. *toward* (with the gen. *the side* of, i.e. *pertaining to;* with the dat., *by the side of,* i.e. *near to;* usually with the acc., the place, time, occasion, or respect, which is the *destination* of the relation, i.e. *whither* or *for* which it is predicated):–about, according to, against, among, at, because of, before, between, [where-]by, for, X at thy house, in, for intent, nigh unto, of, which pertain to, that, to (the end that), + together, to ([you]) -ward, unto, with(-in). In compo.. it denotes essentially the same appl., namely, motion *towards,* accession *to,* or nearness *at.*

4315. προσάββατον *pros-ab'-bat-on;* from *4253* and *4521;* a *fore-sabbath,* i.e. the *Sabbath-eve:*–day before the sabbath. Comp. *3904.*

4316. προσαγορεύω *pros-ag-or-yoo'-o;* from *4314* and a der. of *58* (mean to *harangue*); to *address,* i.e. salute by *name:*–call.

4317. προσάγω *pros-ag'-o;* from *4314* and *71;* to *lead towards,* i.e. (trans.) to *conduct near* (*summon, present*), or (intrans.) to *approach:*–bring, draw near.

4318. προσαγωγή *pros-ag-ogue-ay';* from *4317* (comp. *72*); *admission:*–access.

4319. προσαιτέω *pros-ahee-teh'-o;* from *4314* and *154;* to *ask repeatedly* (importune), i.e. *solicit:*–beg.

4320. προσαναβαίνω *pros-an-ab-ah'-ee-no;* from *4314* and *305;* to *ascend farther,* i.e. *be promoted* (*take an upper* [*more honorable*] *seat*):–go up.

4321. προσαναλίσκω *pros-an-al-is'-ko;* from *4314* and *355;* to *expend further:*–spend.

4322. προσαναπληρόω *pros-an-ap-lay-ro'-o;* from *4314* and *378;* to *fill up further,* i.e. *furnish fully:*–supply.

4323. προσανατίθημι *pros-an-at-ith'-ay-mee;* from *4314* and *394;* to *lay up in addition,* i.e. (mid. and fig.) to *impart* or (by impl.) to *consult:*–in conference add, confer.

4324. προσαπειλέω *pros-ap-i-leh'-o;* from *4314* and *546;* to *menace additionally:*–i.e.

threaten further.

4325. προσδαπανάω *pros-dap-an-ah'-o;* from *4314* and *1159;* to *expend additionally:*–spend more.

4326. προσδέομαι *pros-deh'-om-ahee;* from *4314* and *1189;* to *require additionally,* i.e. *want further:*–need.

4327. προσδέχομαι *pros-dekh'-om-ahee;* from *4314* and *1209;* to *admit* (to intercourse, hospitality, credence, or [fig.] endurance); by impl. to *await* (with confidence or patience):–accept, allow, look (wait) for, take.

4328. προσδοκάω *pros-dok-ah'-o;* from *4314* and δοκεύω (to *watch*); to *anticipate* (in thought, hope or fear); by impl. to *await:*–(be in) expect (-ation), look (for), when looked, tarry, wait for.

4329. προσδοκία *pros-dok-ee'-ah;* from *4328; apprehension* (of evil); by impl. *infliction* anticipated:–expectation, looking after.

4330. προσεάω *pros-eh-ah'-o;* from *4314* and *1439;* to *permit further* progress:–suffer.

4331. προσεγγίζω *pros-eng-ghid'-zo;* from *4314* and *1448;* to *approach near:*–come nigh.

4332. προσεδρεύω *pros-ed-ryoo'-o;* from a com. of *4314* and the base of *1476;* to *sit near,* i.e. *attend* as a servant:–wait at.

4333. προσεργάζομαι *pros-er-gad'-zom-ahee;* from *4314* and *2038;* to *work additionally,* i.e. (by impl.) *acquire besides:*–gain.

4334. προσέρχομαι *pros-er'-khom-ahee ;* from *4314* and *2064* (incl. its alt.); to *approach,* i.e. (lit.) *come near, visit,* or (fig.) *worship, assent to:*–(as soon as he) come (unto), come thereunto, consent, draw near, go (near, to, unto).

4335. προσευχή *pros-yoo-khay';* from *4336; prayer* (*worship*); by impl. an *oratory* (*chapel*):–X pray earnestly, prayer.

4336. προσεύχομαι *pros-yoo'-khom-ahee;* from *4314* and *2172;* to *pray to* God, i.e. *supplicate, worship:*–pray (X earnestly, for), make prayer.

4337. προσέχω *pros-ekh'-o;* from *4314* and *2192;* (fig.) to *hold* the mind (*3563* implied) *towards,* i.e. *pay attention to, be cautious about, apply oneself* to, *adhere to:*–(give) attend(-ance, -ance at, -ance to, unto), beware, be given to, give (take) heed (to unto); have regard.

4338. προσηλόω *pros-ay-lo'-o;* from *4314* and a der. of *2247; to peg to,* i.e. *spike* fast:–nail to.

4339. προσήλυτος *pros-ay'-loo-tos* ;from the alt. of *4334;* an *arriver* from a for. region, i.e. (spec.), an *acceder* (*convert*) to Judaism ("*proselyte*"):–proselyte.

4340. πρόσκαιρος *pros'-kahee-ros;* from *4314* and *2540; for* the *occasion* only, i.e. *temporary:*–dur-[eth] for awhile, endure for a time, for a season, temporal.

4341. προσκαλέομαι *pros-kal-eh'-om-ahee ;* mid. from *4314* and *2564;* to *call toward oneself,* i.e. *summon, invite:*–call (for, to, unto).

4342. προσκαρτερέω *pros-kar-ter-eh'-o;* from *4314* and *2594;* to *be earnest towards,* i.e. (to a thing) to *persevere, be constantly* diligent, or (in a place) to *attend* assiduously all the exercises, or (to a pers.) to *adhere* closely *to* (as a servitor):–attend (give self) continually (upon), continue (in, instant in, with), wait on (continually).

4343. προσκαρτέρησις *pros-kar-ter'-ay-sis;* from *4342; persistancy:*–perseverance.

4344. προσκεφάλαιον *pros-kef-al'-ahee-on;* neut. of a presumed comp. of *4314* and *2776*; something *for* the *head,* i.e. a *cushion:*–pillow.

4345. προσκληρόω *pros-klay-ro'-o;* from *4314* and *2820;* to *give* a common *lot to,* i.e. (fig.) to *associate with:*–consort with.

4346. πρόσκλισις *pros'-klis-is;* from a com. of *4314* and *2827;* a *leaning towards,* i.e. (fig.) *proclivity* (*favoritism*):–partiality.

4347. προσκολλάω *pros-kol-lah'-o;* from *4314* and *2853;* to *glue to,* i.e. (fig.) to *adhere:*–cleave, join (self).

4348. πρόσκομμα *pros'-kom-mah;* from *4350;* a *stub,* i.e. (fig.) *occasion of apostasy:*–offence, stumbling(-block, [-stone]).

4349. προσκοπή *pros-kop-ay';* from *4350;* a *stumbling,* i.e. (fig. and concr.) *occasion of sin:*–offence.

4350. προσκόπτω *pros-kop'-to;* from *4314* and *2875;* to *strike at,* i.e. *surge against* (as water); spec. to *stub on,* i.e. *trip up* (lit. or fig.):–beat upon, dash, stumble (at).

4351. προσκυλίω *pros-koo-lee'-o;* from *4314* and *2947;* to *roll towards,* i.e. *block against:*–roll (to).

4352. προσκυνέω *pros-koo-neh'-o;* from *4314* and a prob. der. of *2965* (mean. to *kiss,* like a dog *licking* his master's hand); to *fawn* or *crouch to,* i.e. (lit. or fig.) *prostrate* oneself in homage (*do reverence* to, *adore*):–worship.

4353. προσκυνητής *pros-koo-nay-tace';* from *4352;* an *adorer:*–worshipper.

4354. προσλαλέω *pros-lal-eh'-o;* from *4314* and 2980; to *talk to,* i.e. *converse with:*–speak to (with).

4355. προσλαμβάνω *pros-lam-ban'-o;* from *4314* and *2983;* to *take to* oneself, i.e. *use* (food), *lead* (aside), *admit* (to friendship or hospitality):–receive, take (unto).

4356. πρόσληψις *pros'-lape-sis;* from *4355; admission:*–receiving.

4357. προσμένω *pros-men'-o;* from *4314* and *3306;* to *stay further,* i.e. *remain* in a place, with a pers.; fig. to *adhere* to, *persevere* in:–abide still, be with, cleave unto, continue in (with).

4358. προσορμίζω *pros-or-mid'-zo;* from *4314* and a der. of the same as *3730* (mean. to *tie* [*anchor*] or *lull*); to *moor to,* i.e. (by impl.) *land at:*–draw to the shore.

4359. προσοφείλω *pros-of-i'-lo;* from *4314* and *3784;* to *be indebted additionally:*–over besides.

4360. προσοχθίζω *pros-okh-thid'-zo;* from *4314* and a form of όχθέω (to *be vexed* with something irksome); to *feel indignant at:*–be grieved with.

4361. πρόσπεινος *pros'-pi-nos;* from *4314* and the same as *3983; hungering further,* i.e. *intensely hungry:*–very hungry.

4362. προσπήγνυμι *pros-payg'-noo-mee;* from *4314* and *4078;* to *fasten to,* i.e. (spec.), to *impale* (on a cross):–crucify.

4363. προσπίπτω *pros-pip'-to;* from *4314* and *4098;* to *fall towards,* i.e. (gently) *prostrate* oneself (in supplication or homage), or (violently) to *rush* upon (in storm):–beat upon, fall (down) at (before).

4364. προσποιέομαι *pros-poy-eh'-om-ahee;* mid. from *4314* and *4160; to do forward for oneself,* i.e. *pretend* (as if about to do a thing):–make as though.

4365. προσπορεύομαι *pros-por-yoo'-om-ahee;* from *4314* and *4198;* to *journey towards,* i.e. *approach* [not the same as 4313]:–go before.

4366. προσρήγνυμι *pros-rayg'-noo-mee;* from *4314* and *4486;* to *tear towards,* i.e. *burst upon* (as a tempest or flood):–beat vehemently against (upon).

4367. προστάσσω *pros-tas'-so;* from *4314* and *5021;* to *arrange towards,* i.e. (fig.) *enjoin:*–bid, command.

4368. προστάτις, *pros-tat'-is;* fem. of a der. of *4291;* a *patroness,* i.e. *assistant:*–succourer.

4369. προστίθημι *pros-tith'-ay-mee;* from *4314* and *5087;* to *place additionally,* i.e. *lay beside, annex, repeat:*–add, again, give more, increase, lay unto, proceed further, speak to any more.

4370. προστρέχω *pros-trekh'-o;* from *4314* and *5143* (incl. its alt.); to *run towards,* i.e. *hasten* to meet or join:–run (thither to, to).

4371. προσφάγιον *pros-fag'-ee-on;* neut. of a presumed der. of a com. of *4314* and *5315;* something *eaten in addition* to bread, i.e. a *relish* (spec. fish; comp. *3795*):–meat.

4372. πρόσφατος *pros'-fat-os;* from *4253* and a der. of *4969*; *previously* (*recently*) *slain* (*fresh*), i.e. (fig.) *lately made:*–new.

4373. προσφάτως *pros-fat'-oce;* adv. from *4372; recently:*–lately.

4374. προσφέρω *pros-fer'-o;* from *4314* and *5342* (incl. its alt.); to *bear towards,* i.e. *lead to, tender* (esp. to God), *treat:*–bring (to, unto), deal with, do, offer (unto, up), present, unto, put to.

4375. προσφιλής *pros-fee-lace';* from a presumed com. of *4314* and *5368; friendly towards,* i.e. *acceptable:*–lovely.

4376. προσφορά *pros-for-ah';* from *4374; presentation;* concr. an *oblation* (bloodless) or *sacrifice:*–offering (up).

4377. προσφωνέω *pros-fo-neh'-o;* from *4314* and *5455;* to *sound towards,* i.e. *address, exclaim, summon:*–call unto, speak (un-)to.

4378. πρόσχυσις *pros'-khoo-sis;* from a comp. of *4314* and χέω cheo (to *pour*); a *shedding forth,* i.e. *affusion:*–sprinkling.

4379. προσψαύω *pros-psow'-o;* from *4314* and ψαύω (to *touch*); to *impinge,* i.e. *lay a finger on* (in order to relieve):–touch.

4380. προσωποληπτέω *pros-o-pol-ape-teh'-o;* from *4381;* to *favor an individual,* i.e. *show partiality:*–have respect to persons.

4381. προσωπολήπτης *pros-o-pol-ape'-*

GREEK

tace; from *4383* and *2983;* an *accepter of a face* (*indiv.*), i.e. (spec.), one *exhibiting partiality:*–respecter of persons.

4382. προσωποληψία *pros-o-pol-ape-see'-ah;* from *4381; partiality,* i.e. *favoritism:*–respect of persons.

4383. πρόσωπον *pros'-o-pon;* from *4314* and ὤψ (the *visage,* from *3700*); the *front* (as being *towards view*), i.e. the *countenance, aspect, appearance, surface;* by impl. *presence, person.:*–(outward) appearance, X before, countenance, face, fashion, (men's) pers., presence.

4384. προτάσσω *prot-as'-so;* from *4253* and *5021;* to *pre-arrange,* i.e. *prescribe:*–before appoint.

4385. προτείνω *prot-i'-no;* from *4253* and τείνω (to *stretch*); to *protend,* i.e. *tie prostrate* (for scourging):–bind.

4386. πρότερον *prot'-er-on;* neut. of *4387* as adv. (with or without the art.); *previously:*–before, (at the) first, former.

4387. πρότερος *prot'-er-os;* comp. of *4253; prior* or *previous:*–former.

4388. προτίθεμαι *prot-ith'-em-ahee;* mid. from *4253* and *5087;* to *place before,* i.e. (for oneself) to *exhibit;* (to oneself) to *propose* (*determine*):–purpose, set forth.

4389. προτρέπομαι *prot-rep'-om-ahee;* mid. from *4253* and the base of *5157;* to *turn forward* for oneself, i.e. *encourage:*–exhort.

4390. προτρέχω *prot-rekh'-o;* from *4253* and *5143* (incl. its alt.); to *run forward,* i.e. *outstrip, precede:*–outrun, run before.

4391. προϋπάρχω *pro-oop-ar'-kho;* from *4253* and *5225;* to *exist before,* i.e. (adv.) to *be* or *do* something *previously:*–+ be before(-time).

4392. πρόφασις *prof'-as-is;* from a com. of *4253* and *5316;* an *outward showing,* i.e. *pretext:*–cloke, colour, pretence, show.

4393. προφέρω *prof-er'-o;* from *4253* and *5342;* to *bear forward,* i.e. *produce:*–bring forth.

4394. προφητεία *prof-ay-ti'-ah;* from *4396* ("*prophecy*"); *prediction* (scriptural or other):–prophecy, prophesying.

4395. προφητεύω *prof-ate-yoo'-o;* from *4396;* to *foretell* events, *divine, speak* under *inspiration, exercise* the prophetic *office:*–prophesy.

4396. προφήτης *prof-ay'-tace;* from a com. of *4253* and *5346;* a *foreteller* ("*prophet*"); by anal. an *inspired speaker;* by ext., a *poet:*–prophet.

4397. προφητικός *prof-ay-tik-os';* from *4396; pertaining to a foreteller* ("*prophetic*"):–of prophecy, of the prophets.

4398. προφῆτις *prof-ay'-tis;* fem. of *4396;* a *female foreteller* or an *inspired woman:*–prophetess.

4399. προφθάνω *prof-than'-o;* from *4253* and *5348;* to *get* an *earlier start of,* i.e. *anticipate:*–prevent.

4400. προχειρίζομαι *prokh-i-rid'-zom-ahee;* mid. from *4253* and a der. of *5495;* to *handle* for oneself *in advance,* i.e. (fig.) to *purpose:*–choose, make.

4401. προχειροτονέω *prokh-i-rot-on-eh'-o;* from *4253* and *5500;* to *elect in advance:*–choose before.

4402. Πρόχορος *prokh'-or-os;* from *4253* and *5525;* *before* the *dance; Prochorus,* a Chr.:–Prochorus.

4403. πρύμνα *proom'-nah;* fem. of πρυμνύς prumnus (*hindmost*); the *stern* of a ship:–hinder part, stern.

4404. πρωΐ *pro-ee';* adv. from *4253;* at *dawn;* by impl. the *day-break* watch:–early (in the morning), (in the) morning.

4405. πρωΐα *pro-ee'-ah;* fem. of a der. of *4404* as noun; *day-dawn:*–early, morning.

4406. πρώϊμος *pro'-ee-mos;* from *4404; dawning,* i.e. (by anal.) *autumnal* (showering, the first of the rainy season):–early.

4407. πρωϊνός *pro-ee-nos';* from *4404;* pertaining to the *dawn,* i.e. *matutinal:*–morning.

4408. πρώρα *pro'-ra;* fem. of a presumed der. of *4253* as noun; the *prow,* i.e. forward part of a vessel:–forepart(-ship).

4409. πρωτεύω *prote-yoo'-o;* from *4413;* to *be first* (in rank or influence):–have the preeminence.

4410. πρωτοκαθεδρία *pro-tok-ath-ed-ree'-ah;* from *4413* and *2515;* a *sitting first* (in the front row), i.e. *preeminence* in council:–chief (highest, uppermost) seat.

4411. πρωτοκλισία *pro-tok-lis-ee'-ah;* from *4413* and *2828;* a *reclining first* (in the place of honor) at the dinner-bed, i.e. *preeminence* at meals:–chief (highest, uppermost) room.

4412. πρῶτον *pro'-ton;* neut. of *4413* as adv. (with or without *3588*); *firstly* (in time, place, order, or importance):–before, at the beginning, chiefly (at, at the) first (of all).

4413. πρῶτος *pro'-tos;* contr. superl. of *4253; foremost* (in time, place, order or importance):–before, beginning, best, chief(-est), first (of all), former.

4414. πρωτοστάτης *pro-tos-tat'-ace;* from *4413* and *2476;* one *standing first* in the ranks, i.e. a *captain* (*champion*):–ringleader.

4415. πρωτοτόκια *pro-tot-ok'-ee-ah;* from *4416; primogeniture* (as a privilege):–birthright.

4416. πρωτοτόκος *pro-tot-ok'-os;* from *4413* and the alt. of *5088; first-born* (usually as noun, lit. or fig.):–firstbegotten(-born).

4417. πταίω *ptah'-yo;* a form of *4098;* to *trip,* i.e. (fig.) to *err, sin, fail* (of salvation):–fall, offend, stumble.

4418. πτέρνα *pter'-nah;* of unc. der.; the *heel* (fig.):–heel.

4419. πτερύγιον *pter-oog'-ee-on;* neut. of a presumed der. of *4420;* a *winglet,* i.e. (fig.) *extremity* (top corner):–pinnacle.

4420. πτέρυξ *pter'-oox;* from a der. of *4072* (mean. a *feather*); a *wing:*–wing.

4421. πτηνόν *ptay-non';* contr. for *4071;* a *bird:*–bird.

4422. πτοέω *pto-eh'-o;* prob. akin to the alt. of *4098* (through the idea of causing to *fall*) or to *4072* (through that of causing to *fly* away); to *scare:*–frighten.

4423. πτόησις *pto'-ay-sis;* from *4422; alarm:*–amazement.

4424. Πτολεμαΐς *ptol-em-ah-is';* from Πτολεμαῖος (*Ptolemy,* after whom it was named); *Ptolemaïs,* a place in Pal.:–Ptolemais.

4425. πτύον *ptoo'-on;* from *4429;* a *winnowing-fork* (as *scattering* like spittle):–fan.

4426. πτύρω *ptoo'-ro;* from a presumed der. of *4429* (and thus akin to *4422*); to *frighten:*–terrify.

4427. πτύσμα, *ptoos'-mah;* from *4429; saliva:*–spittle.

4428. πτύσσω *ptoos'-so;* prob. akin to πετάννυμι (to *spread;* and thus app. allied to *4072* through the idea of *expansion,* and to *4429* through that of *flattening;* comp. *3961*); to *fold,* i.e. *furl* a scroll:–close.

4429. πτύω *ptoo'-o;* a prim. verb (comp. *4428*); to *spit:*–spit.

4430. πτῶμα *pto'-mah;* from the alt. of *4098;* a *ruin,* i.e. (spec.), lifeless *body* (*corpse, carrion*):–dead body, carcase, corpse.

4431. πτῶσις *pto'-sis;* from the alt. of *4098;* a *crash,* i.e. *downfall* (lit. or fig.):–fall.

4432. πτωχεία *pto-khi'-ah;* from *4433; beggary,* i.e. *indigence* (lit. or fig.):–poverty.

4433. πτωχεύω *pto-khyoo'-o;* from *4434;* to *be a beggar,* i.e. (by impl.) to *become indigent* (fig.):–become poor.

4434. πτωχός *pto-khos';* from πτώσσω *ptosso* (to *crouch*); akin to *4422* and the alt. of *4098*); a *beggar* (as cringing), i.e. *pauper* (strictly denoting absol. or public *mendicancy,* although also used in a qualified or rel. sense; whereas *3993* prop. means only *straitened* circumstances in private), lit. (often as noun) or fig. (*distressed*):–beggar(-ly), poor.

4435. πυγμή *poog-may';* from a prim. πύξ (the *fist* as a weapon); the clenched *hand,* i.e. (only in dat. as adv.) *with* the *fist* (hard *scrubbing*):–oft.

4436. Πύθων *poo'-thone;* from Πυθώ (the name of the region where Delphi, the seat of the famous *oracle,* was located); a *Python,* i.e. (by anal. with the supposed *diviner* there) *inspiration* (*soothsaying*):–divination.

4437. πυκνός *pook-nos';* from the same as *4635; clasped* (*thick*), i.e. (fig.) *frequent;* neut. pl. (as adv.) *frequently:*–often(-er).

4438. πυκτέω *pook-teh'-o;* from a der. of the same as *4435;* to *box* (with the fist), i.e. *contend* (as a boxer) at the games (fig.):–fight.

4439. πύλη *poo'-lay;* app. a prim. word; a *gate,* i.e. the leaf or wing of a folding *entrance* (lit. or fig.):–gate.

4440. πυλών *poo-lone';* from *4439;* a *gate-way, door-way* of a building or city; by impl. a *portal* or *vestibule:*–gate, porch.

4441. πυνθάνομαι *poon-than'-om-ahee;* mid. prol. from a prim. πύθω (which occurs only as an alt. in cert. tenses); to *question,* i.e. *ascertain* by inquiry (as a matter of *information* merely; and thus differing from *2065,* which prop. means a *request* as a favor; and from *154,* which is strictly a *demand* of something due;

as well as from *2212,* which implies a *search* for something hidden; and from *1189,* which involves the idea of urgent *need*); by impl. to *learn* (by casual intelligence):–ask, demand, enquire, understand.

4442. πῦρ *poor;* a prim. word; "*fire*" (lit. or fig. spec. *lightning*):–fiery, fire.

4443. πυρά *poo-rah';* from *4442;* a *fire* (concr.):–fire.

4444. πύργος *poor'-gos;* app. a prim. word ("*burgh*"); a *tower* or *castle:*–tower.

4445. πυρέσσω *poo-res'-so;* from *4443;* to *be on fire,* i.e. (spec.), to *have a fever:*–be sick of a fever.

4446. πυρετός *poo-ret-os';* from *4445; inflamed,* i.e. (by impl.) *feverish* (as noun, *fever*):–fever.

4447. πύρινος *poo'-ree-nos;* from *4443; fiery,* i.e. (by impl.) *flaming:*–of fire.

4448. πυρόω *poo-ro'-o;* from 4442; to *kindle,* i.e. pass. to *be ignited, glow* (lit.), *be refined* (by impl.), or (fig.) to *be inflamed* (with anger, grief, lust):–burn, fiery, be on fire, try.

4449. πυῤῥάζω *poor-hrad'-zo;* from *4450;* to *redden* (intrans.):–be red.

4450. πυῤῥός *poor-hros';* from *4442; fire-like,* i.e. (spec.), *flame-colored:*–red.

4451. πύρωσις *poo'-ro-sis;* from *4448; ignition,* i.e. (spec.), *smelting* (fig. *conflagration, calamity* as a *test*):–burning, trial.

4452. -πω *po;* another form of the base of *4458;* an enclitic par. of indef.; *yet, even;* used only in the com. See *3369, 3380, 3764, 3768, 4455.*

4453. πωλέω *po-leh'-o;* prob. ultimately from πέλομαι (to *be busy,* to *trade*); to *barter* (as a *pedlar*), i.e. to *sell:*–sell, whatever is sold.

4454. πῶλος *po'-los;* app. a prim. word; a "*foal*" or "*filly*", i.e. (spec.), a *young ass:*–colt.

4455. πώποτε *po'-pot-e;* from *4452* and *4218; at any time,* i.e. (with neg. par.) *at no time:*–at any time, + never (...to any man), + yet, never man.

4456. πωρόω *po-ro'-o;* app. from πῶρος (a kind of *stone*); to *petrify,* i.e. (fig.) to *indurate* (*render stupid* or *callous*):–blind, harden.

4457. πώρωσις *po'-ro-sis;* from *4456; stupidity* or *callousness:*–blindness, hardness.

4458. -πώς *poce;* adv. from the base of 4225; an enclitic par. of indef. of manner; *somehow* or any*how;* used only in compo.:–haply, by any (some) means, perhaps. See *1513, 3381.* Comp. *4459.*

4459. πῶς *poce;* adv. from the base of *4226;* an interrog. par. of manner; *in what way?* (sometimes the question is indirect, *how?*); also as exclamation, *how* much!:–how, after (by) what manner (means), that. [*Occasionally unexpressed in English*].

P

4460. 'Ραάβ *hrah-ab*'; of Heb. or. [7343]; *Raab* (i.e. *Rachab*), a Canaanitess:–Rahab. See also *4477.*

4461. ῥαββί *hrab-bee';* of Heb. or. [7227 with pron. suffix]; *my master,* i.e *Rabbi,* as an official title of honor:–Master, Rabbi.

4462. ῥαββονί *hrab-bon-ee';* or ῥαββουνί *hrab-boo-nee';* of Chald. or.; cor. to *4461:*–Lord, Rabboni.

4463. ῥαβδίζω *hrab-did'-zo;* from *4464;* to *strike with a stick,* i.e. *bastinado:*–beat (with rods).

4464. ῥάβδος *hrab'-dos;* from the base of *4474;* a *stick* or *wand* (as a *cudgel,* a *cane* or a *baton* of royalty):–rod, sceptre, staff.

4465. ῥαβδοῦχος *hrab-doo'-khos;* from *4464* and *2192;* a *rod-* (the Lat. *fasces*) *holder,* i.e. a Rom. *lictor* (*constable* or *executioner*):–serjeant.

4466. 'Ραγαῦ *hrag-ow';* of Heb. or. [7466]; *Ragau* (i.e. *Reü*), a patriarch:–Ragau.

4467. ῥᾳδιούργημα *hrad-ee-oorg'-ay-mah;* from a comp. of ῥᾴδιος (*easy,* i.e. *reckless*) and *2041; easy-going behavior,* i.e. (by ext.) a *crime:*–lewdness.

4468. ῥᾳδιουργία *hrad-ee-oorg-ee'-a;* from the same as *4467; recklessness,* i.e. (by ext.) *malignity:*–mischief.

4469. ῥακά *rhak-ah';* of Chald. or. [comp. 7386]; O *empty* one, i.e. thou *worthless* (as a term of utter vilification):–Raca.

4470. ῥάκος *hrak'-os;* from *4486;* a "*rag,*" i.e. *piece* of cloth:–cloth.

4471. 'Ραμᾶ *hram-ah';* of Heb. or. [7414]; *Rama* (i.e. *Ramah*), a place in Pal.:–Rama.

4472. ῥαντίζω *hran-tid'-zo;* from a der. of ῥαίνω (to *sprinkle*); to *render besprinkled,* i.e. *asperse* (cer. or fig.):– sprinkle.

4473. ῥαντισμός *hran-tis-mos'* from *4472; aspersion* (cer. or fig.):–sprinkling.

4474. ῥαπίζω *hrap-id'-zo;* from a der. of a prim. ῥέπω (to let *fall,* "*rap*"); to *slap:*–smite (with the palm of the hand). Comp. *5180.*

4475. ῥάπισμα *hrap'-is-mah;* from *4474;* a *slap:*–(+ strike with the) palm of the hand, smite with the hand.

4476. ῥαφίς *hraf-ece';* from a prim. ῥάπτω (to *sew;* perh. rather akin to the base of *4474* through the idea of *puncturing*); a *needle:*– needle.

4477. 'Ραχάβ *hrakh-ab';* from the same as *4460; Rachab,* a Canaanitess:–Rachab.

4478. 'Ραχήλ *hrakh-ale';* of Heb. or. [7354]; *Rachel,* the wife of Jacob:–Rachel.

4479. 'Ρεβέκκα *hreb-bek'-kah;* of Heb. or. ([259]; *Rebecca* (i.e. *Ribkah*), the wife of Isaac:–Rebecca.

4480. ῥέδα *hred'-ah;* of Lat. or.; a *rheda,* i.e. four-wheeled *carriage* (*wagon* for riding):–chariot.

4481. 'Ρεμφάν *hrem-fan';* by incorrect transliteration for a word of Heb. or. [3594]; *Remphan* (i.e. *Kijun*), an Eg. idol:–Remphan.

4482. ῥέω *hreh'-o;* a prim. verb; for some tenses of which a prol. form ῥεύω *hryoo'-o* is used to *flow* ("*run*"; as water):–flow.

4483. ῥέω *hreh'-o;* for cert. tenses of which a prol. form ἐρέω *er-eh'-o* is used; both as alt. for *2036* perh. akin (or ident.) with *4482* (through the idea of *pouring* forth); to *utter,* i.e. *speak* or *say:*–command, make, say, speak (of). Comp. *3004.*

4484. 'Ρήγιον *hrayg'-ee-on;* of Lat. or.; *Rhegium,* a place in Italy:–Rhegium.

4485. ῥῆγμα *hrayg'-mah;* from *4486;* something *torn,* i.e. a *fragment* (by impl. and abstr., a *fall*):–ruin.

4486. ῥήγνυμι *hrayg'-noo-mee;* or ῥήσσω *hrace'-so* both are prol. forms of ῥήκω (which appears only in cert. forms, and is itself prob. a streng. form of ἄγνυμι [see in *2608*]) to "*break,*" "*wreck*" or "*crack*", i.e. (esp.) to *sunder* (by *separation* of the parts; *2608* being its intens. [with the prep. in compo.], and *2352* a *shattering* to minute fragments; but not a *reduction* to the constituent par., like *3089*) or *disrupt, lacerate;* by impl. to *convulse* (with *spasms*); fig. to *give vent* to joyful emotions:–break (forth), burst, rend, tear.

4487. ῥῆμα *hray'-mah;* from *4483;* an *utterance* (indiv., coll. or spec.); by impl. a *matter* or *topic* (esp. of narration, command or dispute); with a neg. *naught* whatever:–+ evil, + nothing, saying, word.

4488. 'Ρησά *hray-sah';* prob. of Heb. or. [app. for 7509]; *Resa* (i.e. *Rephajah*), an Isr.:–Rhesa.

4489. ῥήτωρ *hray'-tore;* from *4483;* a *speaker,* i.e. (by impl.) a forensic *advocate:*–orator.

4490. ῥητῶς *hray-toce';* adv. from a der. of *4483;* out-*spokenly,* i.e. *distinctly:*–expressly.

4491. ῥίζα, *hrid'-zah;* app. a prim. word; a "*root*" (lit. or fig.):–root.

4492. ῥιζόω *hrid-zo'-o;* from *4491;* to *root* (fig. *become stable*):–root.

4493. ῥιπή *hree-pay';* from 4496; a *jerk* (of the eye, i.e. [by anal.] an *instant*):–twinkling.

4494. ῥιπίζω *hrip-id'-zo;* from a der. of *4496* (mean. a *fan* or *bellows*); to *breeze up,* i.e. (by anal.) to *agitate* (into waves):–toss.

4495. ῥιπτέω *hrip-teh'-o;* from a der. of *4496;* to *toss* up:–cast off.

4496. ῥίπτω *hrip'-to;* a prim. verb (perh. rather akin to the base of *4474,* through the idea of sudden *motion*); to *fling* (prop. with a quick *toss,* thus differing from *906,* which denotes a *deliberate* hurl; and from τείνω [see in *1614*], which indicates an *extended* projection); by qualification, to *deposit* (as if a load); by ext., to *disperse:*–cast (down, out), scatter abroad, throw.

4497. 'Ροβοάμ *hrob-o-am';* of Heb. or. [7346]; *Roboäm* (i.e. *Rechobam*), an Isr.:–Roboam.

4498. 'Ρόδη *hrod'-ay;* prob. for ῥοδή (a *rose*); *Rodè,* a servant girl:–Rhoda.

4499. 'Ρόδος *hrod'-os;* prob. from ῥόδον (a *rose*); *Rhodus,* an island of the Mediterranean:–Rhodes.

4500. ῥοιζηδόν *hroyd-zay-don';* adv. from a der. of ῥοῖζος (a *whir*); *whizzingly,* i.e. *with a crash:*–with a great noise.

4501. ῥομφαία *hrom-fah'-yah;* prob. of for. or.; a *sabre,* i.e. a long and broad *cutlass* (any *weapon* of the kind, lit. or fig.):–sword.

GREEK

4502. Ῥουβήν *hroo-bane';* of Heb. or. [7205]; *Ruben* (i.e. *Reuben*), an Isr.:–Reuben.
4503. Ῥούθ *hrooth;* of Heb. or. [7327]; *Ruth,* a Moabitess:–Ruth.
4504. Ροῦφος *hroo'-fos;* of Lat. or.; *red; Rufus,* a Chr.:–Rufus.
4505. ῥύμη *hroo'-may;* prol. from *4506* in its or. sense; an *alley* or *avenue* (as crowded):–lane, street.
4506. ῥύομαι *rhoo'-om-ahee;* mid. of an obs. verb, akin to *4482* (through the idea of a *current;* comp. *4511*); to *rush* or *draw* (for oneself), i.e. *rescue:*–deliver(-er).
4507. ῥυπαρία *hroo-par-ee'-ah;* from *4508; dirtiness* (mor.):–filthiness.
4508. ῥυπαρός *rhoo-par-os';* from *4509; dirty,* i.e. (rel.) *cheap* or *shabby;* mor. *wicked:*–vile.
4509. ῥύπος *hroo'-pos;* of unc. affin.; *dirt,* i.e. (mor.) *depravity:*–filth.
4510 ῥυπόω *rhoo-po'-o;* from *4509;* to *soil,* i.e. (intrans.) to *become dirty* (mor.):–be filthy.
4511. ῥύσις *hroo'-sis;* from *4506* in the sense of its congener *4482;* a *flux* (of blood):–issue.
4512. ῥυτίς *hroo-tece';* from *4506;* a *fold* (as *drawing* together), i.e. a *wrinkle* (esp. on the face):–wrinkle.
4513. Ῥωμαϊκός *rho-mah-ee-kos';* from *4514; Romaïc,* i.e. *Lat.:*–Latin.
4514. Ῥωμαῖος *hro-mah'-yos;* from *4516; Romaean,* i.e. *Rom.* (as noun):–Roman, of Rome.
4515. Ῥωμαϊστί *hro-mah-is-tee';* adv. from a presumed der. of *4516; Romaïstically,* i.e. in the *Latin.* language:–Latin.
4516. Ῥώμη *hro'-may;* from the base of *4517; strength; Roma,* the capital of Italy:–Rome.
4517. ῥώννυμι *hrone'-noo-mee;* prol. from ῥώομαι (to *dart;* prob. akin to *4506*); to *strengthen,* i.e. (impers. pass.) *have health* (as a parting exclamation, *good-bye*):–farewell.

Σ

4518. σαβαχθανί *sab-akh-than-ee';* of Chald. or [7662 with pron. suffix]; *thou hast left me; sabachthani* (i.e. *shebakthani*), a cry of distress:–sabachthani.
4519. σαβαώθ *sab-ah-owth';* of Heb. or. [6635 in fem. pl.]; *armies; sabaoth* (i.e. *tsebaoth*), a military epithet of God:–sabaoth.
4520. σαββατισμός *sab-bat-is-mos';* from a der. of *4521;* a "*sabbatism*", i.e. (fig.) the *repose* of Christianity (as a type of heaven):–rest.
4521. σάββατον *sab'-bat-on;* of Heb. or. [7676]; the *Sabbath* (i.e. *Shabbath*), or day of weekly *repose* from secular avocations (also the observance or institution itself); by ext., a *se'nnight,* i.e. the interval between two Sabbaths; likewise the pl. in all the above appl.:–sabbath (day), week.
4522. σαγήνη *sag-ay'-nay;* from a der. of σάττω (to *equip*) mean. *furniture,* esp. a *pack-saddle* (which in the E. is merely a bag of *netted* rope); a "*seine*" for fishing:–net.
4523. Σαδδουκαῖος *sad-doo-kah'-yos;* prob. from *4524;* a *Sadducaean* (i.e. *Tsadokian*), or follower of a cert. heretical Isr.:–Sadducee.
4524. Σαδώκ *sad-oke';* of Heb. or. [6659]; *Sadoc* (i.e. *Tsadok*), an Isr.:–Sadoc.
4525. σαίνω *sah'-ee-no;* akin to *4579;* to *wag* (as a dog its tail fawningly), i.e. (gen.) to *shake* (fig. *disturb*):–move.
4526. σάκκος *sak'-kos;* of Heb. or. [8242]; "*sack*"-*cloth,* i.e. *mohair* (the material or garments made of it, worn as a sign of grief):– sackcloth.
4527. Σαλά *sal-ah';* of Heb. or. [7974]; Sala (i.e. *Shelach*), a patriarch:–Sala.
4528. Σαλαθιήλ *sal-ath-ee-ale';* of Heb. or. [7597]; *Salathiël* (i.e. *Sheältiël*), an Isr.:–Salathiel.
4529. Σαλαμίς *sal-am-ece';* prob. from *4535* (from the *surge* on the shore); *Salamis,* a place in Cyprus:–Salamis.
4530. Σαλαίμ *sal-ime'* prob. from the same as *4531; Salim,* a place in Pal.:–Salim.
4531. σαλεύω *sal-yoo'-o;* from *4535;* to *waver,* i.e. *agitate, rock, topple* or (by impl.) *destroy;* fig. to *disturb, incite:*–move, shake (together), which can[-not] be shaken, stir up.
4532. Σαλήμ *sal-ame';* of Heb. or. [8004]; *Salem* (i.e. *Shalem*), a place in Pal.:–Salem.
4533. Σαλμών *sal-mone';* of Heb. or. [8012]; *Salmon,* an Isr.:–Salmon.
4534. Σαλμώνη *sal-mo'-nay;* perh. of similar or. to *4529; Salmone,* a place in Crete:–Salmone.
4535. σάλος *sal'-os;* prob. from the base of *4525;* a *vibration,* i.e. (spec.), *billow:*–wave.
4536. σάλπιγξ *sal'-pinx;* perh. from *4535* (through the idea of *quavering* or *reverberation*); a *trumpet:*–trump(-et).
4537. σαλπίζω *sal-pid'-zo;* from 4536; to *trumpet,* i.e. *sound a blast* (lit. or fig.):–(which are yet to) sound (a trumpet).
4538. σαλπιστή, *sal-pis-tace';* from *4537;* a *trumpeter:*–trumpeter.
4539. Σαλώμη *sal-o'-may;* prob. of Heb. or. [fem. from *7965*]; *Salomè* (i.e. *Shelomah*), an Isr.:–Salome.
4540. Σαμάρεια *sam-ar'-i-ah;* of Heb. or. [8111]; *Samaria* (i.e. *Shomeron*), a city and region of Pal.:–Samaria.
4541. Σαμαρείτης *sam-ar-i'-tace;* from *4540;* a *Samarite,* i.e. inh. of Samaria:–Samaritan.
4542. Σαμαρεῖτις *sam-ar-i'-tis;* fem. of *4541;* a *Samaritess,* i.e. woman of Samaria:–of Samaria.
4543. Σαμοθρᾴκη *sam-oth-rak'-ay;* from *4544* and Θρᾴκη (*Thrace*); *Samo-thrace* (*Samos of Thrace*), an island in the Mediterranean:–Samothracia.
4544. Σάμος *sam'-os;* of unc. affin.; *Samus,* an island of the Mediterranean:–Samos.
4545. Σαμουήλ *sam-oo-ale';* of Heb. or. [8050]; *Samuel* (i.e. *Shemuel*), an Isr.:–Samuel.
4546. Σαμψών *samp-sone'* of Heb. or. [8123]; *Sampson* (i.e. *Shimshon*), an Isr.:–Samson.
4547. σανδάλιον *san-dal'-ee-on;* neut. of a der. of σάνδαλον (a "*sandal*"; of unc. or.); a *slipper* or *sole-pad:*–sandal.
4548. σανίς *san-ece';* of unc. affin.; a *plank:*–board.
4549. Σαούλ *sah-ool';* of Heb. or. [7586]; *Saül* (i.e. *Shaül*), the Jewish name of Paul:–Saul. Comp. *4569.*
4550. σαπρός *sap-ros';* from *4595*; *rotten,* i.e. *worthless* (lit. or mor.):–bad, corrupt. Comp. *4190.*
4551. Σαπφείρη *sap-fi'-ray;* fem. of *4552; Sapphire,* an Isr.:–Sapphira.
4552. σάπφειρος *sap'-fi-ros;* of Heb. or. [5601]; a "*sapphire*" or *lapis-lazuli* gem:–sapphire.
4553. σαργάνη *sar-gan'-ay;* app. of Heb. or. [8276]; a *basket* (as *interwoven* or *wicker*-work:–basket.
4554. Σάρδεις *sar'-dice;* pl. of unc. der.; *Sardis,* a place in Asia Minor:–Sardis.
4555. σάρδινος *sar'-dee-nos;* from the same as *4556;* sardine [*3037* being implied], i.e. a gem, so called:–sardine.
4556. σάρδιος *sar'-dee-os;* prop. an adj. from an unc. base; *sardian* (*3037* being implied), i.e. (as noun) the gem so called:–sardius.
4557. σαρδόνυξ *sar-don'-oox;* from the base of *4556* and ὄνυξ (the *nail* of a finger; hence the "*onyx*" stone); a "*sardonyx*", i.e. the gem so called:– sardonyx.
4558. Σάρεπτα *sar'-ep-tah;* of Heb. or. [6886]; *Sarepta* (i.e. *Tsarephath*), a place in Pal.:–Sarepta.
4559. σαρκικός *sar-kee-kos';* from *4561; pertaining to flesh,* i.e. (by ext.) *bodily, temporal,* or (by impl.) *animal, unregenerate:*–carnal, fleshly.
4560. σάρκινος *sar'-kee-nos;* from *4561;* similar to *flesh,* i.e. (by anal.) *soft:*–fleshly.
4561. σάρξ *sarx;* prob. from the base of *4563; flesh* (as *stripped* of the skin), i.e. (strictly) the *meat* of an animal (as food), or (by ext.) the *body* (as opposed to the soul [or spirit], or as the symbol of what is exter., or as the means of kindred), or (by impl.) *human nature* (with its frailties [phys. or mor.] and passions), or (spec.), a *human being* (as such):–carnal(-ly, + -ly minded), flesh([-ly]).
4562. Σαρούχ *sa-rooch';* of Heb. or. [8286]; *Saruch* (i.e. *Serug*), a patriarch:–Saruch.
4563. σαρόω *sar-o'-o;* from a der. of σαίρω (to *brush* off; akin to *4951*); mean. a *broom;* to *sweep:*–sweep.
4564. Σάῤῥα *sar'-hrah;* of Heb. or. (8283); Sarra (i.e. *Sarah*), the wife of Abraham:–Sara, Sarah.
4565. Σάρων *sar'-one;* of Heb. or. [8289]; *Saron* (i.e. *Sharon*), a district of Pal.:–Saron.
4566. Σατᾶν *sat-an';* of Heb. or. [7854]; *Satan,* i.e. the *devil:*–Satan. Comp. *4567.*
4567. Σατανᾶς *sat-an-as';* of Chald. or. cor. to *4566* (with the def. aff.); *the accuser,* i.e. the *devil:*–Satan.
4568. σάτον *sat'-on;* of Heb. or. [5429]; a cert. *measure* for things dry:–measure.
4569. Σαῦλος *sow'-los;* of Heb. or., the same as *4549; Saulus* (i.e. *Shaül*), the

Jewish name of *Paul:*–Saul.

4570. σβέννυμι *sben'-noo-mee;* a prol. form of an app. prim. verb; to *extinguish* (lit. or fig.):–go out, quench.

4571. σέ *seh* acc. sing. of *4771; thee:*–thee, thou, X thy house.

4572. σεαυτοῦ *seh-ow-too';* the gen. *4571* and *846* dat. of the same, σεαυτῷ *seh-ow-to';* and acc. σεαυτόν *se-ow-ton';* likewise contr. σαυτοῦ *sow-too';* σαυτῷ, *sow-to';* and σαυτόν *sow-ton';* respectively, *of* (*with, to*) *thyself:*–thee, thine own self, (thou) thy (-self).

4573. σεβάζομαι *seb-ad'-zom-ahee;* mid. from a der. of *4576;* to *venerate,* i.e. *adore:*–worship.

4574. σέβασμα, *seb'-as-mah;* from *4573;* something *adored,* i.e. an *object of worship* (god, altar, etc):–devotion, i.e. worshipped.

4575. σεβαστός *seb-as-tos';* from *4573; venerable* (*august*), i.e. (as noun) a title of the Rom. *Emperor,* or (as adj.) *imperial:*–Augustus(-').

4576. σέβομαι *seb'-om-ahee;* mid. of an app. prim. verb; to *revere,* i.e. *adore:*–devout, religious, worship.

4577. σειρά *si-rah';* prob. from *4951* through its congener εἴρω (to *fasten;* akin to *138*); a *chain* (as *binding* or *drawing*):–chain.

4578. σεισμός *sice-mos';* from *4579;* a *commotion,* i.e. (of the air) a *gale,* (of the ground) an *earthquake:*–earthquake, tempest.

4579. σείω *si'-o;* app. a prim. verb; to *rock* (*vibrate,* prop. sideways or to and fro), i.e. (gen.) to *agitate* (in any direction; cause to *tremble*); fig. to throw into a *tremor* (of fear or concern):–move, quake, shake.

4580. Σεκοῦνδος *sek-oon'-dos;* of Lat. or.; "*second*"; *Secundus,* a Chr.:–Secundus.

4581. Σελεύκεια *sel-yook'-i-ah;* from Σέλευκος (*Seleucus,* a Syrian king); *Seleuceia,* a place in Syria:–Seleucia.

4582. σελήνη *sel-ay'-nay;* from σέλας (*brilliancy;* prob. akin to the alt. of *138,* through the idea of *attractiveness*); the *moon:*–moon.

4583. σεληνιάζομαι *sel-ay-nee-ad'-zom-ahee;* mid. or pass. from a presumed der. of *4582;* to *be moon-struck,* i.e. *crazy:*–be lunatic.

4584. Σεμεΐ *sem-eh-ee';* of Heb. or. [8096]; *Semeï* (i.e. *Shimi*), an Isr.:–Semei.

4585. σεμίδαλις *sem-id'-al-is;* prob. of for. or.; fine wheaten *flour:*–fine flour.

4586. σεμνός *sem-nos';* from *4576; venerable,* i.e. *honorable:*–grave, honest.

4587. σεμνότης *sem-not'-ace;* from *4586; venerableness,* i.e. *probity:*–gravity, honesty.

4588. Σέργιος *serg'-ee-os;* of Lat. or.; *Sergius,* a Rom.:–Sergius.

4589. Σήθ *sayth;* of Heb. or. [8352]; *Seth* (i.e. *Sheth*), a patriarch:–Seth.

4590. Σήμ *Sem; same;* of Heb. or. [8035]; *Sem* (i.e. *Shem*), a patriarch:– Sem.

4591. σημαίνω *say-mah'-ee-no;* from σῆμα sema (a *mark;* of unc. der.); to *indicate:*–signify.

4592. σημεῖον *say-mi'-on;* neut. of a presumed der. of the base of *4591;* an *indication,* esp. cer. or supernaturally:–miracle, sign, token, wonder.

4593. σημειόν *say-mi-o'-o;* from *4592;* to *distinguish,* i.e. *mark* (for avoidance):–note.

4594. σήμερον *say'-mer-on;* neut. (as adv.) of a presumed com. of the art. *3588* (τ changed to σ) and *2250;* on the (i.e. *this*) day (or *night* current or just passed); gen. *now* (i.e. at *present, hitherto*):–this (to-)day.

4595. σήπω *say'-po;* app. a prim. verb; to *putrefy,* i.e. (fig.) *perish:*–be corrupted.

4596. σηρικός *say-ree-kos';* from Σήρ (an Indian tribe from whom *silk* was procured; hence the name of the *silk-worm*); *Seric,* i.e. *silken* (neut. as noun, a *silky* fabric):–silk.

4597. σής *sace;* app. of Heb. or. [5580]; a *moth:*–moth.

4598. σητόβρωτος *say-tob'-ro-tos;* from *4597* and a der. of *977; moth-eaten:*–motheaten.

4599. σθενόω *sthen-o'-o;* from σθένος (bodily *vigor;* prob. akin to the base of *2476*); to *strengthen,* i.e. (fig.) *confirm* (in spir. knowledge and power):–strengthen.

4600. σιαγών *see-ag-one';* of unc. der.; the *jaw*-bone, i.e. (by impl.) the *cheek* or side of the face:–cheek.

4601. σιγάω *see-gah'-o;* from *4602;* to *keep silent* (trans. or intrans.):–keep close (secret, silence), hold peace.

4602. σιγή *see-gay';* app. from σίζω (to *hiss,* i.e. *hist* or *hush*); *silence:*–silence. Comp. *4623.*

4603. σιδήρεος, *sid-ay'-reh-os;* from *4604;* made of *iron:*–(of) iron.

4604. σίδηρος *sid'-ay-ros;* of unc. der.; *iron:*–iron.

4605. Σιδών *sid-one';* of Heb. or. [6721]; *Sidon* (i.e. *Tsidon*), a place in Pal.:–Sidon.

4606. Σιδώνιος *sid-o'-nee-os;* from *4605;* a *Sidonian,* i.e. inh. of Sidon:–of Sidon.

4607. σικάριος *sik-ar'-ee-os;* of Lat. or.; a *dagger-man* or *assassin;* a *freebooter* (Jewish *fanatic* outlawed by the Romans):–murderer. Comp. *5406.*

4608. σίκερα *sik'-er-ah;* of Heb. or. [7941]; an *intoxicant,* i.e. intensely fermented *liquor:*–strong drink.

4609. Σίλας *see'-las;* contr. for *4610; Silas,* a Chr.:–Silas.

4610. Σίλας *sil-oo-an-os';* of Lat. or.; "*silvan*"; *Silvanus,* a Chr.:–Silvanus. Comp. *4609.*

4611. Σιλωάμ *sil-o-am';* of Heb. or. [7975]; *Siloäm* (i.e. *Shiloäch*), a pool of Jerus.:–Siloam.

4612. σιμικίνθιον *sim-ee-kin'-thee-on;* of Lat. or.; a *semicinctium* or *half-girding,* i.e. narrow covering (*apron*):–apron.

4613. Σίμων *see'-mone;* of Heb. or. [8095]; *Simon* (i.e. *Shimon*), the name of nine Isr.:–Simon. Comp. *4826.*

4614. Σινᾶ *see-nah';* of Heb. or. [5514]; *Sina* (i.e. *Sinai*), a mountain in Arabia:–Sina.

4615. σίναπι *sin'-ap-ee;* perh. from σίνομαι (to *hurt,* i.e. *sting*); *mustard* (the plant):–mustard.

4616. σινδών *sin-done';* of unc. (perh. for.) or.; *byssos,* i.e. bleached *linen* (the cloth or a garment of it):–(fine) linen (cloth).

4617. σινιάζω *sin-ee-ad'-zo;* from σινιον (a *sieve*); to *riddle* (fig.):–sift.

4618. σιτευτός *sit-yoo-tos';* from a der. of *4621; grain-fed,* i.e. *fattened:*–fatted.

4619. σιτιστός *sit-is-tos';* from a der. of *4621; grained,* i.e. *fatted:*–fatling.

4620. σιτόμετρον *sit-om'-et-ron;* from *4621* and *3358;* a *grain-measure,* i.e. (by impl.) *ration* (*allowance* of food):–portion of meat.

4621. σῖτος *see'-tos;* plur. irreg. neut. σίτα *see'-tah;* of unc. der.; *grain,* esp. *wheat:*–corn, wheat.

4622. Σιών *see-own';* of Heb. or. [6726]; *Sion* (i.e. *Tsijon*), a hill of Jerus.; fig. the *Church* (militant or triumphant):–Sion.

4623. σιωπάω *see-o-pah'-o;* from σιωπή (*silence,* i.e. a *hush;* prop. *muteness,* i.e. *invol.* stillness, or *inability* to speak; and thus differing from *4602,* which is rather a vol. *refusal* or *indisposition* to speak, although the terms are often used synonymously); to *be dumb* (but not *deaf* also, like *2974* prop.); fig. to *be calm* (as *quiet* water):–dumb, (hold) peace.

4624. σκανδαλίζω *skan-dal-id'-zo* from *4625;* to *entrap,* i.e. *trip* up (fig. *stumble* (trans.) or *entice* to sin, apostasy or displeasure):–(make to) offend.

4625. σκάνδαλον *skan'-dal-on;* ("*scandal*"); prob. from a der. of *2578;* a *trap-stick* (*bent* sapling), i.e. *snare* (fig. *cause* of displeasure or sin):–occasion to fall (of stumbling), offence, thing that offends, stumblingblock.

4626. σκάπτω *skap'-to;* app. a prim. verb; to *dig:*–dig.

4627. σκάφη *skaf'-ay;* a "*skiff*" (as if *dug* out), or *yawl* (carried aboard a large vessel for landing):–boat.

4628. σκέλος *skel'-os;* app. from σκέλλω (to *parch;* through the idea of *leanness*); the *leg* (as *lank*):–leg.

4629. σκέπασμα *skep'-as-mah;* from a der. of σκέπας (a *covering;* perh. akin to the base of *4649* through the idea of *noticeableness*); *clothing:*–raiment.

4630. Σκευᾶς *skyoo-as';* app. of Lat. or.; *left-handed; Scevas* (i.e. *Scoevus*), an Isr.:–Sceva.

4631. σκευή *skyoo-ay';* from *4632; furniture,* i.e. spare *tackle:*–tackling.

4632. σκεῦος *skyoo'-os;* of unc. affin.; a *vessel, implement, equipment* or *apparatus* (lit. or fig. [spec. a *wife* as contributing to the usefulness of the husband]):–goods, sail, stuff, vessel.

4633. σκηνή *skay-nay';* app. akin to *4632* and *4639;* a *tent* or cloth hut (lit. or fig.):–habitation, tabernacle.

4634. σκηνοπηγία *skay-nop-ayg-ee'-ah;* from *4636* and *4078;* the *Festival of Tabernacles* (so called from the custom of erecting booths for temporary homes):–tabernacles.

4635. σκηνοποιός *skay-nop-oy-os';* from *4633* and *4160;* a *manufacturer of tents:*–tent-maker.

4636. σκῆνος *skay'-nos;* from *4633;* a *hut* or temporary residence, i.e. (fig.) the human *body* (as the abode of the spirit):–tabernacle.

GREEK

4637. σκηνόω *skay-no'-o;* from *4636;* to *tent* or *encamp,* i.e. (fig.) to *occupy* (as a mansion) or (spec.), to *reside* (as God did in the Tabernacle of old, a symbol of protection and communion):– dwell.

4638. σκήνωμα *skay'-no-mah;* from *4637;* an *encampment,* i.e. (fig.) the *Temple* (as God's residence), the *body* (as a tenement for the soul):– tabernacle.

4639. σκία *skee'-ah;* app. a prim. word; "*shade*" or a shadow (lit. or fig. [darkness of *error* or an *adumbration*]):– shadow.

4640. σκιρτάω *skeer-tah'-o;* akin to σκαίρω (to *skip*); to *jump,* i.e. sympathetically *move* (as the *quickening* of a fetus):–leap (for joy).

4641. σκληροκαρδία *sklay-rok-ar-dee'-ah;* fem. of a com. of *4642* and *2588; hard-heartedness,* i.e. (spec.), *destitution* of (spir.) *perception:*–hardness of heart.

4642. σκληρός *sklay-ros';* from the base of *4628; dry,* i.e. *hard* or *tough* (fig. *harsh, severe*):–fierce, hard.

4643. σκληρότης *sklay-rot'-ace;* from *4642; callousness,* i.e. (fig.) *stubbornness:*–hardness.

4644. σκληροτράχηλος *sklay-rot-rakh'-ay-los;* from *4642* and *5137; hardnaped,* i.e. (fig.) *obstinate:*–stiffnecked.

4645. σκληρύνω *sklay-roo'-no;* from *4642;* to *indurate,* i.e. (fig.) *render stubborn:*–harden.

4646. σκολιός *skol-ee-os';* from the base of *4628; warped,* i.e. *winding;* fig. *perverse:*–crooked, froward, untoward.

4647. σκόλοψ *skol'-ops;* perh. from the base of *4628* and *3700; withered* at the *front,* i.e. a *point* or *prickle* (fig. a bodily *annoyance* or *disability*):–thorn.

4648. σκοπέω *skop-eh'-o;* from *4649;* to take *aim* at (*spy*), i.e. (fig.) *regard:*–consider, take heed, look at (on), mark. Comp. *3700.*

4649. σκοπός *skop-os'* ("scope") from σκέπτομαι (to *peer* about ["skeptic"]; perh. akin to *4626* through the idea of *concealment;* comp. *4629*); a *watch* (*sentry* or *scout*), i.e. (by impl.) a *goal:*–mark.

4650. σκορπίζω *skor-pid'-zo;* app. from the same as *4651* (through the idea of *penetrating*); to *dissipate,* i.e. (fig.) *put to flight, waste, be liberal:*–disperse abroad, scatter (abroad).

4651. σκορπίος *skor-pee'-os;* prob. from an obs. σκέρπω (perh. streng. from the base of *4649* and mean. to *pierce*); a "*scorpion*" (from its *sting*):–scorpion.

4652. σκοτεινός *skot-i-nos';* from *4655; opaque,* i.e. (fig.) *benighted:*–dark, full of darkness.

4653. σκοτία *skot-ee'-ah;* from *4655; dimness, obscurity* (lit. or fig.):–dark(-ness).

4654. σκοτίζω *skot-id-zo;* from *4655;* to *obscure* (lit. or fig.):–darken.

4655. σκότος *skot'-os* from the base of *4639; shadiness,* i.e. *obscurity* (lit. or fig.):–darkness.

4656. σκοτόω *skot-o'-o;* from *4655;* to *obscure* or *blind* (lit. or fig.):–be full of darkness.

4657. σκύβαλον *skoo'-bal-on;* neut. of a presumed der. of *1519* and *2965* and *906;* what is *thrown to* the *dogs,* i.e. *refuse* (*ordure*):–dung.

4658. Σκύθης *skoo'-thace;* prob. of for. or.; a *Scythene* or *Scythian,* i.e. (by impl.) a *savage:*–Scythian.

4659. σκυθρωπός *skoo-thro-pos';* from σκυθρός (sullen) and a der. of *3700; angry-visaged,* i.e. *gloomy* or affecting a mournful appearance:–of a sad countenance.

4660. σκύλλω *skool'-lo* app. a prim. verb; to *flay,* i.e. (fig.) to *harass:*–trouble(self).

4661. σκῦλον *skoo'-lon;* neut. from *4660;* something *stripped* (as a *hide*), i.e. *booty:*–spoil.

4662. σκωληκόβρωτος *sko-lay-kob'-ro-tos;* from *4663* and a der. of *977; worm-eaten,* i.e. *diseased with maggots:*–eaten of worms.

4663. σκώληξ *sko'-lakes;* of unc. der.; a *grub, maggot* or *earth-worm:*–worm.

4664. σμαράγδινος *smar-ag'-dee-nos;* from *4665;* consisting *of emerald:*–emerald.

4665. σμάραγδος *smar'-ag-dos;* of unc. der.; the *emerald* or green gem so called:–emerald.

4666. σμύρνα *smoor'-nah;* app. streng. for *3464; myrrh:*–myrrh.

4667. Σμύρνα *smoor'-nah;* the same as *4666; Smyrna,* a place in Asia Minor:–Smyrna.

4668. Σμυρναῖος *smoor-nah'-yos;* from *4667;* a *Smyrnoean:*–in Smyrna.

4669. σμυρνίζω *smoor-nid'-zo;* from *4667;* to *tincture with myrrh,* i.e. *embitter* (as a narcotic):–mingle with myrrh.

4670. Σόδομα *sod'-om-ah;* pl. of Heb. or. [5467]; *Sodoma* (i.e. *Sedom*), a place in Pal.:–Sodom.

4671. σοί *soy;* dat. of *4771; to thee:*–thee, thine own, thou, thy.

4672. Σολομών or Σολομῶν*; sol-om-one';* of Heb. or. [8010]; *Solomon* (i.e. *Shelomoh*), the son of David:–Solomon.

4673. σορός *sor-os';* prob. akin to the base of *4987;* a funereal receptacle (*urn, coffin*), i.e. (by anal.) a *bier:*–bier.

4674. σός *sos;* from *4771; thine:*–thine (own), thy (friend).

4675. σοῦ *soo;* gen. of *4771; of thee,* thy:–X home, thee, thine (own), thou, thy.

4676. σουδάριον *soo-dar'-ee-on;* of Lat. or.; a *sudarium* (*sweat-cloth*), i.e. *towel* (for wiping the perspiration from the face, or binding the face of a corpse):–handkerchief, napkin.

4677. Σουσάννα *soo-san'-nah;* of Heb. or. [7799 fem.]; *lily; Susannah* (i.e. *Shoshannah*), an Isr.:–Susanna.

4678. σοφία *sof-ee'-ah;* from *4680; wisdom* (higher or lower, worldly or spir.):–wisdom.

4679.σοφίζω *sof-id'-zo;* from *4680;* to *render wise;* in a sinister acceptation, to *form "sophisms",* i.e. *continue plausible error:*–cunningly devised, make wise.

4680. σοφός *sof-os';* akin to σαφής saphēs (*clear*); wise (in a most gen. appl.):–wise. Comp. *5429.*

4681. Σπανία *span-ee'-ah;* prob. of for. or.; *Spania,* a region of Europe:–Spain.

4682. σπαράσσω *spar-as'-so;* prol. from σπαίρω spairo (to *grasp;* app. streng. from *4685* through the idea of *spasmodic* contr.); to *mangle,* i.e. *convluse* with epilepsy:–rend, tear.

4683. σπαργανόω *spar-gan-o'-o;* from σπάργανον sparganon (a *strip;* from a der. of the base of *4682* mean. to *strap* or *wrap* with strips); to *swathe* (an infant after the Oriental custom):–wrap in swaddling clothes.

4684. σπαταλάω *spat-al-ah'-o;* from σπατάλη spatale (*luxury*); to *be voluptuous:*–live in pleasure, be wanton.

4685. σπάω *spah'-o* a prim. verb; to *draw:*–draw (out).

4686. σπεῖρα *spi'-rah;* of immed. Lat. or., but ultimately a der. of *138* in the sense of its cognate *1507;* a *coil* (*spira,* "spire"), i.e. (fig.) a *mass* of men (a Rom. military *cohort;* also [by anal.] a *squad* of Levitical janitors):–band.

4687. σπείρω *spi'-ro;* prob. streng. from *4685* (through the idea of *extending*); to *scatter,* i.e. *sow* (lit. or fig.):–sow(- er), receive seed.

4688. σπεκουλάτωρ *spek-oo-lat'-ore;* of Lat. or.; a *speculator,* i.e. military *scout* (*spy* or [by ext.] *life-guardsman*):–executioner.

4689. σπένδω *spen'-do;* app. a prim. verb; to *pour* out as a libation, i.e. (fig.) to *devote* (one's life or blood, as a sacrifice) ("*spend*"):–(be ready to) be offered.

4690. σπέρμα *sper'-mah;* from *4687;* something *sown,* i.e. *seed* (incl. the male "*sperm*"); by impl. *offspring;* spec. a *remnant* (fig. as if kept over for planting):–issue, seed.

4691. σπερμολόγος *sper-mol-og'-os;* from *4690* and *3004; a seed-picker* (as the crow), i.e. (fig.) a *sponger, loafer* (spec. a *gossip* or *trifler* in talk):–babbler.

4692. σπεύδω *spyoo'-do;* prob. streng. from *4228;* to "*speed*" ("study"), i.e. *urge* on (diligently or earnestly); by impl. to *await* eagerly:–(make, with) haste unto.

4693. σπήλαιον *spay'-lah-yon;* neut. of a presumed der. of σπέος spĕŏs (a *grotto*); a *cavern;* by impl. a *hiding-place* or *resort:*–cave, den.

4694. σπιλάς *spee-las';* of unc. der.; a *ledge* or *reef* of rock in the sea:–spot [by confusion with *4696*].

4695. σπιλόω *spee-lo'-o;* from *4696;* to *stain* or *soil* (lit. or fig.):–defile, spot.

4696. σπίλος *spee'-los;* of unc. der.; a *stain* or *blemish,* i.e. (fig.) *defect, disgrace:*–spot.

4697. σπλαγχνίζομαι *splangkh-nid'-zom-ahee;* mid. from *4698;* to have the *bowels* yearn, i.e. (fig.) *feel sympathy,* to *pity:*–have (be moved with) compassion.

4698. σπλάγχνον *splangkh'-non;* prob. streng. from σπλήν splēn (the "*spleen*"); an *intestine* (pl.); fig. *pity* or *sympathy:*–bowels, inward affection, + tender mercy.

4699. σπόγγος *spong'-gos;* perh. of for. or.; a "*sponge*":–spunge.

4700. σποδός *spod-os';* of unc. der.; *ashes:*–ashes.

4701. σπορά *spor-ah';* from *4687;* a *sowing,* i.e. (by impl.) *parentage:*–seed.
4702. σπόριμος *spor'-ee-mos;* from *4703; sown,* i.e. (neut. pl.) a planted *field:*–corn(-field).
4703. σπόρος *spro'-os;* from *4687;* a *scattering* (of seed), i.e. (concr.) *seed* (as sown):–seed (X sown).
4704. σπουδάζω *spoo-dad'-zo;* from *4710;* to *use speed,* i.e. to *make effort, be prompt* or *earnest:*–do (give) diligence, be diligent (forward), endeavour, labour, study.
4705. σπουδαῖος *spoo-dah'-yos;* from *4710; prompt, energetic, earnest:*–diligent.
4706. σπουδαιότερον *spoo-dah-yot'-er-on;* neut. of *4707* as adv.; *more earnestly* than others), i.e. very *promptly:*–very diligently.
4707. σπουδαιότερος *spoo-dah-yot'-er-os;* comp. of *4705; more prompt, more earnest:*–more diligent (forward).
4708. σπουδαιοτέρως *spoo-dah-yot-er'-oce;* adv. from *4707; more speedily,* i.e. *sooner* than otherwise:–more carefully.
4709. σπουδαίως *spoo-dah'-yoce;* adv. from *4705; earnestly, promptly:–diligently, instantly.*
4710. σπουδή *spoo-day';* from *4692;* "*speed*", i.e. (by impl.) *despatch, eagerness, earnestness:*–business, (earnest) care(-fulness), diligence, forwardness, haste.
4711. σπυρίς *spoo-rece';* from *4687* (as woven); a *hamper* or *lunch-receptacle:*–basket.
4712. στάδιον *stad'-ee-on;* (or masc. plur.) στάδιος *stad'-ee-os* from the base of *2476* (as *fixed*); a *stade* or cert. measure of distance; by impl. a *stadium* or *race-course:*–furlong, race.
4713. στάμνος *stam'-nos;* from the base of *2476* (as *stationary*); a *jar* or earthen *tank:*–pot.
4714. στάσις *stas'-is* from the base of *2476;* a *standing* (prop. the act), i.e. (by anal.) *position* (*existence*); by impl. a popular *uprising;* fig. *controversy:*–dissension, insurrection, X standing, uproar.
4715. στατήρ *stat-air';* from the base of *2746;* a *stander* (*standard* of value), i.e. (spec.), a *stater* or cert. coin:–piece of money.
4716. σταυρός *stŏw-ros';* from the base of *2476;* a *stake* or *post* (as *set* upright), i.e. (spec.), a *pole* or *cross* (as an instrument of capital punishment); fig. *exposure to death,* i.e. *self-denial;* by impl. the *atonement* of Christ:–cross.
4717. σταυρόω *stŏw-rŏ'-o;* from *4716;* to *impale* on the cross; fig. to *extinguish* (*subdue*) passion or selfishness:–crucify.
4718. σταφυλή *staf-oo-lay';* prob. from the base of *4735;* a *cluster* of grapes (as if *intertwined*):–grapes.
4719. στάχυς *stakh'-oos;* from the base of *2476;* a *head* of grain (as *standing* out from the stalk):–ear (of corn).
4720. Στάχυς *stakh'-oos;* the same as *4719; Stachys,* a Chr.:–Stachys.
4721. στέγη *steg'-ay;* streng. from a prim. τέγος tĕgŏs (a "*thatch*" or "*deck*" of a building); a *roof:*–roof.
4722. στέγω *steg'-o;* from *4721;* to *roof* over, i.e. (fig.) to *cover* with silence (*endure* patiently):–(for-)bear, suffer.
4723. στεῖρος *sti'-ros;* a contr. from *4731* (as *stiff* and *unnatural*); "*sterile*":–barren.
4724. στέλλω *stel'-lo;* prob. streng. from the base of *2476;* prop. to *set* fast ("*stall*"), i.e. (fig.) to *repress* (refl. *abstain* from associating with):–avoid, withdraw self.
4725. στέμμα *stem'-mah;* from the base of *4735;* a *wreath* for show:–garland.
4726. στεναγμός *sten-ag-mos';* from *4727;* a *sigh:*–groaning.
4727. στενάζω *sten-ad'-zo;* from *4728;* to *make* (intrans., *be*) *in straits,* i.e. (by impl.) to *sigh, murmur, pray* inaudibly:–with grief, groan, grudge, sigh.
4728. στενός *sten-os';* prob. from the base of *2476; narrow* (from obstacles *standing* close about):–strait.
4729. στενοχωρέω *sten-okh-o-reh'-o;* from the same as *4730;* to *hem* in closely, i.e. (fig.) *cramp:*–distress, straiten.
4730. στενοχωρία *sten-okh-o-ree'-ah;* from a com. of *4728* and *5561; narrowness of room,* i.e. (fig.) *calamity:*–anguish, distress.
4731. στερεός *ster-eh-os';* from *2476; stiff,* i.e. *solid, stable* (lit. or fig.):–stedfast, strong, sure.
4732. στερεόω *ster-eh-ŏ'-o* from *4731;* to *solidify,* i.e. *confirm* (lit. or fig.):–establish, receive strength, make strong.
4733. στερέωμα *ster-eh'-o-mah;* from *4732;* something *established,* i.e. (abstr.) *confirmation* (*stability*):–stedfastness.
4734. Στεφανᾶς *stef-an-as';* prob. contr. for στεφανωτός stĕphanōtŏs (crowned; from *4737*); *Stephanas,* a Chr.:–Stephanas.
4735. στέφανος *stef'-an-os;* from an app. prim. στέφω stĕphō (to *twine* or *wreathe*); a *chaplet* (as a badge of royalty, a prize in the public games or a symbol of honor gen.; but more conspicuous and elaborate than the simple *fillet, 1238*), lit. or fig.:–crown.
4736. Στέφανος *stef'-an-os;* the same as *4735; Stephanus,* a Chr.:–Stephen.
4737. στεφανόω *stef-an-ŏ'-o;* from *4735;* to *adorn with* an honorary *wreath* (lit. or fig.):–crown.
4738. στῆθος *stay'-thos;* from *2476* (as *standing* prominently); the (entire exter.) *bosom,* i.e. *chest:*–breast.
4739. στήκω *stay'-ko;* from the perfect tense of *2476;* to *be stationary,* i.e. (fig.) to *persevere:*–stand (fast).
4740. στηριγμός *stay-rig-mos';* from *4741; stability* (fig.):–stedfastness.
4741. στηρίζω *stay-rid'-zo;* from a presumed der. of *2476* (like *4731*); to *set fast,* i.e. (lit.) to *turn resolutely* in a cert. direction, or (fig.) to *confirm:*–fix, (e-)stablish, stedfastly set, strengthen.
4742. στίγμα *stig'-mah;* from a prim. στίζω stizō (to "*stick*", i.e. *prick*); a *mark* incised or punched (for recognition of ownership), i.e. (fig.) *scar* of service:–mark.
4743. στιγμή *stig-may';* fem. of *4742;* a *point* of *time,* i.e. an *instant:*–moment.
4744. στίλβω *stil'-bo;* app. a prim. verb; to *gleam,* i.e. *flash* intensely:–shining.
4745. στοά *stŏ-ah';* prob. from *2476;* a *colonnade* or interior *piazza:*–porch.
4746. στοιβάς *stoy-bas';* from a prim. στείβω stĕibō (to "*step*" or "*stamp*"); a *spread* (as if *tramped* flat) of loose materials for a couch, i.e. (by impl.) a *bough* of a tree so employed:–branch.
4747. στοιχεῖον *stoy-khi'-on;* neut. of a presumed der. of the base of *4748;* something *orderly* in arrangement, i.e. (by impl.) a *serial* (*basal, fundamental, initial*) constituent (lit.), proposition (fig.):–element, principle, rudiment.
4748. στοιχέω *stoy-kheh'-o;* from a der. of στείχω stĕichō (to *range* in regular line); to *march* in (military) rank (*keep step*), i.e. (fig.) to *conform* to virtue and piety:–walk (orderly).
4749. στολή *stol-ay';* from *4724; equipment,* i.e. (spec.), a "*stole*" or long-fitting *gown* (as a mark of dignity):–long clothing (garment), (long) robe.
4750. στόμα *stom'-a* prob. streng. from a presumed der. of the base of *5114;* the *mouth* (as if a *gash* in the face); by impl. *language* (and its relations); fig. an *opening* (in the earth); spec. the *front* or *edge* (of a weapon):–edge, face, mouth.
4751. στόμαχος *stom'-akh-os;* from *4750;* an *orifice* (the *gullet*), i.e. (spec.), the "*stomach*":–stomach.
4752. στρατεία *strat-i'-ah;* from *4754;* military *service,* i.e. (fig.) the apostolic *career* (as one of hardship and danger):–warfare.
4753. στράτευμα *strat'-yoo-mah;* from *4754;* an *armament,* i.e. (by impl.) a body of *troops* (more or less extensive or systematic):–army, soldier, man of war.
4754. στρατεύομαι *strat-yoo'-om-ahee;* mid. from the base of *4756;* to serve in a military campaign; fig. to *execute* the *apostolate* (with its arduous duties and functions), to *contend* with carnal inclinations:–soldier, (go to) war(-fare).
4755. στρατηγός *strat-ay-gos';* from the base of *4756* and *71* or *2233;* a *general* i.e. (by impl. or anal.) a (military) *governor* (*praetor*), the *chief* (*praefect*) of the (Levitical) temple-wardens:–captain, magistrate.
4756. στρατία *strat-ee'-ah;* fem. of a der. of στρατός stratŏs (an *army;* from the base of *4766,* as *encamped*); *camp-likeness,* i.e. an *army,* i.e. (fig.) the *angels,* the celestial *luminaries:*–host.
4757. στρατιώτης *strat-ee-o'-tace;* from a presumed der. of the same as *4756;* a *camper-out,* i.e. a (common) *warrior* (lit. or fig.):–soldier.
4758. στρατολογέω *strat-ol-og-eh'-o;* from a com. of the base of *4756* and *3004* (in its or. sense); to *gather* (or *select*) as a *warrior,* i.e. *enlist* in the army:–choose to be a soldier.
4759. στρατοπεδάρχης *strat-op-ed-ar'-khace;* from *4760* and *757;* a *ruler of an army,* i.e. (spec.), a Praetorian *praefect:*–captain of the guard.
4760. στρατόπεδον *strat-op'-ed-on;* from the base of *4756* and the same as *3977;* a *camping-ground,* i.e. (by impl.) a body of

GREEK

troops:–army.

4761. στρεβλόω *streb-lŏ'-o;* from a der. of *4762;* to *wrench,* i.e. (spec.), to *torture* (by the rack), but only fig. to *pervert:*– wrest.

4762. στρέφω *stref'-o* streng. from the base of *5157;* to *twist,* i.e. *turn* quite around or *reverse* (lit. or fig.):–convert, turn (again, back again, self, self about).

4763. στρηνιάω *stray-nee-ah'-o;* from a presumed der. of *4764;* to *be luxurious:*– live deliciously.

4764. στρῆνος *stray'-nos;* akin to *4731;* a "*straining*", "*strenuousness*" or "strength", i.e. (fig.) *luxury* (*voluptuousness*):–delicacy.

4765. στρουθίον *stroo-thee'-on;* dimin. of στρουθός strŏuthŏs (a *sparrow*); a *little sparrow:*–sparrow.

4766. στρώννυμι *strone'-noo-mee;* or simpler στρωννύω *strone'-noo-o;* prol. from a still simpler form, στρόω *strŏ'-o* (used only as an alt. in cert. tenses; prob. akin to *4731* through the idea of *positing*); to "*strew,*" i.e. *spread* (as a carpet or couch):–make bed, furnish, spread, strew.

4767. στυγνητός *stoog-nay-tos';* from a der. of an obs. app. prim. στύγω stugō (to *hate*); *hated,* i.e. *odious:*–hateful.

4768. στυγνάζω *stoog-nad'-zo;* from the same as *4767;* to *render gloomy,* i.e. (by impl.) *glower (be overcast* with clouds, or *sombreness* of speech):–lower, be sad.

4769. στύλος *stoo'-los* from στύω stuō (to *stiffen;* prop. akin to the base of *2476*); a *post* ("*style*"), i.e. (fig.) *support:*–pillar.

4770. Στωϊκός *sto-ik-os'* from *4745;* a "*Stoic*" (as occupying a particular porch in Athens), i.e. adherent of a certain philosophy:–Stoick.

4771. σύ *soo* the pers. pron. of the sec. pers. sing.; *thou:*– thou. See also *4571, 4671, 4675;* and for the pl. *5209, 5210, 5213, 5216.*

4772. συγγένεια *soong-ghen'-i-ah;* from 4773; *relationship,* i.e. (concr.) *relatives:*–kindred.

4773. συγγενής *soong-ghen-ace';* from *4862* and *1085;* a *relative* (by blood); by ext., a fellow *countryman:*–cousin, kin (-sfolk, -sman).

4774. συγγνώμη *soong-gno'-may;* from a com. of *4862* and *1097; fellow knowledge,* i.e. *concession:*–permission.

4775. συγκάθημαι *soong-kath'-ay-mahee;* from *4862* and *2521;* to *seat oneself* in company *with:*–sit with.

4776. συγκαθίζω *soong-kath-id'-zo;* from *4862* and *2523;* to *give* (or *take*) a *seat* in company *with:*–(make) sit (down) together.

4777. συγκακοπαθέω *soong-kak-op-ath-eh'-o; from 4862* and *2553;* to *suffer hardship* in company *with:*–be partaker of afflictions.

4778. συγκακουχέω *soong-kak-oo-kheh'-o;* from *4862* and *2558;* to *maltreat* in company *with,* i.e. pass. *endure persecution together:*–suffer affliction with.

4779. συγκαλέω *soong-kal-eh'-o;* from *4862* and *2564;* to *convoke:*–call together.

4780. συγκαλύπτω *soong-kal-oop'-to;* from *4862* and *2572;* to *conceal altogether:*–cover.

4781. συγκάμπτω *soong-kamp'-to;* from *4862* and *2578;* to *bend together,* i.e. (fig.) to *afflict:*–bow down.

4782. συγκαταβαίνω *soong-kat-ab-ah'-ee-no;* from *4862* and *2597;* to *descend* in company *with:*–go down with.

4783. συγκατάθεσις *soong-kat-ath'-es-is;* from *4784;* a *deposition* (of sentiment) in company *with,* i.e. (fig.) *accord* with:–agreement.

4784. συγκατατίθεμαι *soong-kat-at-ith'-em-ahee;* mid from *4862* and *2698;* to *deposit* (one's vote or opinion) in company *with,* i.e. (fig.) to *accord* with:–consent.

4785. συγκαταψηφίζω *soong-kat-aps-ay-fid'-zo;* from *4862* and a com. of *2596* and *5585;* to *count down* in company *with,* i.e. *enroll among:*–number with.

4786. συγκερννυμι *soong-ker-an'-noo-mee;* from *4862* and *2767;* to *commingle,* i.e. (fig.) to *combine* or *assimilate:*–mix with, temper together.

4787. συγκινέω *soong-kin-eh'-o;* from *4682* and *2795;* to *move together,* i.e. (spec.), to *excite* as a mass (to sedition):–stir up.

4788. συγκλείω *soong-kli'-o;* from *4862* and *2808;* to *shut together,* i.e. *include* or (fig.) *embrace* in a common subjection to:– conclude, inclose, shut up.

4789. συγκληρονόμος *soong-klay-ron-om'-os;* from *4862* and *2818;* a *co-heir,* i.e. (by anal.) *participant in common:*–fellow (joint)-heir, heir together, heir with.

4790. συγκοινωνέω *soong-koy-no-neh'-o;* from *4862* and *2841;* to *share* in company *with,* i.e. *co-participate* in:–communicate (have fellowship) with, be partaker of.

4791. συγκοινωνός *soong-koy-no-nos';* from *4862* and *2844;* a *co-participant:*– companion, partake(-r, -r with).

4792. συγκομίζω *soong-kom-id'-zo;* from *4862* and *2865;* to *convey together,* i.e. *collect* or *bear* away in company *with* others:–carry.

4793. συγκρίνω *soong-kree'-no;* from *4862* and *2919;* to *judge* of one thing in connection *with* another, i.e. *combine* (spir. ideas with appropriate expressions) or *collate* (one person with another by way of contrast or resemblance):–compare. among (with).

4794. συγκύπτω *soong-koop'-to;* from *4862* and *2955;* to *stoop altogether,* i.e. be *completely overcome* by:–bow together.

4795. συγκυρία *soong-koo-ree'-ah;* from a com. of *4862* and κυρέω kurĕō (to *light* or *happen;* from the base of *2962*); *concurrence,* i.e. *accident:*–chance.

4796. συγχαίρω *soong-khah'-ee-ro;* from *4862* and *5463;* to *sympathize in gladness, congratulate:*–rejoice in (with).

4797. συγχέω *soong-kheh'-o;* or συγχύνω *soong-khoo'-no;* from *4862* and χέω chĕō (to *pour*) or its alt.; to *commingle* promiscuously, i.e. (fig.) to *throw* (an assembly) *into disorder,* to *perplex* (the mind):–confound, confuse, stir up, be in an uproar.

4798. συγχράομαι *soong-khrah'-om-ahee;* from *4862* and *5530;* to *use jointly,* i.e. (by impl.) to *hold intercourse in common:*–have dealings with.

4799. σύγχυσις *soong'-khoo-sis;* from *4797; commixture,* i.e. (fig.) riotous *disturbance:*–confusion.

4800. συζάω *sood-zah'-o;* from *4862* and *2198;* to continue to *live* in common *with,* i.e. *co-survive* (lit. or fig.):–live with.

4801. συζεύγνυμι *sood-zyoog'-noo-mee;* from *4862* and the base of *2201;* to *yoke together,* i.e. (fig.) *conjoin* (in marriage):–join together.

4802. συζητέω *sood-zay-teh'-o;* from *4862* and *2212;* to investigate *jointly,* i.e. *discuss, controvert, cavil:*–dispute (with), enquire, question (with), reason (together).

4803. συζήτησις *sood-zay'-tay-sis;* from *4802; mutual questioning,* i.e. *discussion:*– disputation(-ting), reasoning.

4804. συζητητής *sood-zay-tay-tace';* from *4802;* a *disputant,* i.e. *sophist:*–disputer.

4805. σύζυγος *sood'-zoo-gos;* from *4801; co-yoked,* i.e. (fig.) as noun, a *colleague;* prob. rather as a proper name; *Syzygus,* a Chr.:–yokefellow.

4806. σύζωοποιέω *sood-zo-op-oy-eh'-o;* from *4862* and *2227;* to *reanimate conjointly* with (fig.):–quicken together with.

4807. συκάμινος *soo-kam'-ee-nos;* of Heb. or. [8256] in imitation of *4809;* a *sycamore*-fig tree:–sycamine tree.

4808. συκῆ *soo-kay';* from *4810;* a *fig-tree:*–fig tree.

4809. συκομωραία *soo-kom-o-rah'-yah;* from *4810* and μόρον mŏrŏn (the *mulberry*); the "*sycamore*"-fig tree:–sycamore tree. Comp. *4807.*

4810. σῦκον *soo'-kon;* app. a prim. word; a *fig:*–fig.

4811. συκοφαντέω *soo-kof-an-teh'-o;* from a com. of *4810* and a der. of *5316;* to *be a fig-informer* (reporter of the law forbidding the exportation of figs from Greece), "*sycophant*", i.e. (gen. and by ext.) to *defraud* (*exact* unlawfully, *extort*):–accuse falsely, take by false accusation.

4812. συλαγωγέω *soo-lag-ogue-eh'-o;* from the base of *4813* and (the redupl. form of) *71;* to *lead* away as *booty,* i.e. (fig.) *seduce:*–spoil.

4813. συλάω *soo-lah'-o;* from a der. of σύλλω sullō (to *strip;* prob. akin to *138;* comp. *4661*); to *despoil:*–rob.

4814. συλλαλέω *sool-lal-eh'-o;* from *4862* and *2980;* to *talk together,* i.e. *converse:*– commune (confer, talk) with, speak among.

4815. συλλαμβάνω *sool-lam-ban'-o;* from *4862* and *2983;* to *clasp,* i.e. *seize* (*arrest, capture*); spec. to *conceive* (lit. or fig.); by impl. to *aid:*–catch, conceive, help, take.

4816. συλλέγω *sool-leg'-o;* from *4862* and *3004* in its or. sense; to *collect:*–gather (together, up).

4817. συλλογίζομαι *sool-log-id'-zom-ahee;*

from *4862* and *3049;* to *reckon together* (with oneself), i.e. *deliberate:*–reason with.
4818. συλλυπέω *sool-loop-eh'-o;* from *4862* and *3076;* to *afflict jointly,* i.e. (pass.) *sorrow at* (on account of) someone:–be grieved.
4819. συμβαίνω *soom-bah'-ee-no;* from *4862* and the base of *939;* to *walk* (fig. *transpire*) *together,* i.e. *concur* (*take place*):–be(-fall), happen (unto).
4820. συμβάλλω *soom-bal'-lo;* from *4862* and *906;* to *combine,* i.e. (in speaking) to *converse, consult, dispute,* (ment.) to *consider,* (by impl.) to *aid,* (pers.) to *join, attack:*–confer, encounter, help, make, meet with, ponder.
4821. συμβασιλεύω *soom-bas-il-yoo'-o;* from *4862* and *936;* to *be co-regent* (fig.):–reign with.
4822. συμβιβάζω *soom-bib-ad'-zo;* from *4862* and βιβάζω bibazō (to *force;* caus. [by redupl.] of the base of *939*); to *drive together,* i.e. *unite* (in association or affection), (ment.) to *infer, show, teach:*–compact, assuredly gather, intrust, knit together, prove.
4823. συμβουλεύω *soom-bool-yoo'-o;* from *4862* and *1011;* to *give* (or *take*) *advice jointly,* i.e. *recommend, deliberate* or *determine:*–consult.
4824. συμβούλιον *soom-boo'-lee-on;* neut. of a presumed der. of *4825; advisement;* spec. a *deliberative* body, i.e. the provincial *assessors* or lay-court:–consultation, counsel, council.
4825. σύμβουλος *soom'-boo-los;* from *4862* and *1012;* a *consultor,* i.e. *adviser:*–counsellor.
4826. Συμεών *soom-eh-one'* from the same as *4613; Symeon* (i.e. *Shimon*), the name of five Isr.:–Simeon, Simon.
4827. συμμαθητής *soom-math-ay-tace';* from a com. of *4862* and *3129;* a *co-learner* (of Christianity):–fellow disciple.
4828. συμμαρτυρέω *soom-mar-too-reh'-o;* from *4862* and *3140;* to *testify jointly,* i.e. *corroborate* by (concurrent) evidence:–testify unto, (also) bear witness (with).
4829. συμμερίζομαι *soom-mer-id'-zom-ahee;* mid. from *4862* and *3307;* to *share jointly,* i.e. *participate* in:–be partaker with.
4830. συμμέτοχος *soom-met'-okh-os;* from *4862* and *3353;* a *co-participant:*–partaker.
4831. συμμιμητής *soom-mim-ay-tace';* from a presumed com. of *4862* and *3401;* a *co-imitator,* i.e. *fellow votary:*–follower together.
4832. συμμορφός *soom-mor-fos';* from *4862* and *3444; jointly formed,* i.e. (fig.) *similar:*–conformed to, fashioned like unto.
4833. συμμορφόω, *soom-mor-fo'-o;* from *4832;* to *render like,* i.e. (fig.) to *assimilate:*–make conformable unto.
4834. συμπαθέω *soom-path-eh'-o;* from *4835;* to *feel* "*sympathy*" with, i.e. (by impl.) to *commiserate:*–have compassion, be touched with a feeling of.
4835. συμπαθής *soom-path-ace';* from *4841; having a fellow-feeling* ("*sympathetic*"), i.e. (by impl.) *mutually commiserative:*–having compassion one of another.
4836. συμπαραγίνομαι *soom-par-ag-in'-om-ahee;* from *4862* and *3854;* to *be present together,* i.e. to *convene;* by impl. to *appear in aid:*–come together, stand with.
4837. συμπαρακαλέω *soom-par-ak-al-eh'-o;* from *4862* and *3870;* to *console jointly:*–comfort together.
4838. συμπαραλαμβάνω *soom-par-al-am-ban'-o* from *4862* and *3880;* to *take along in company:*–take with.
4839. συμπαραμένω *soom-par-am-en'-o;* from *4862* and *3887;* to *remain in company,* i.e. *still live:*–continue with.
4840. συμπάρειμι *soom-par'-i-mee;* from *4862* and *3918;* to *be at hand together,* i.e. *now present:*–be here present with.
4841. συμπάάσχω *soom-pas'-kho;* from *4862* and *3958* (incl. its alt.); to *experience pain jointly* or of the *same kind* (spec. *persecution;* to "*sympathize*"):–suffer with.
4842. συμπέμπω *soom-pem'-po;* from *4862* and *3992;* to *despatch in company:*–send with.
4843. συμπεριλαμβάνω *soom-per-ee-lam-ban'-o;* from *4862* and a com. of *4012* and *2983;* to *take by enclosing altogether,* i.e. *earnestly throw the arms about one:*–embrace.
4844. συμπίνω *soom-pee'-no;* from *4862* and *4095;* to *partake a beverage in company:*–drink with.
4845. συμπληρόω *soom-play-rŏ'-o;* from *4862* and *4137;* to *implenish completely,* i.e. (of space) to *swamp* (a boat), or (of time) to *accomplish* (pass. be *complete*):–(fully) come, fill up.
4846. συμπίγω *soom-pnee'-go;* from *4862* and *4155;* to *strangle completely,* i.e. (lit.) to *drown,* or (fig.) to *crowd:*–choke, throng.
4847. συμπολίτης *soom-pol-ee'-tace;* from *4862* and *4177;* a *native of the same town,* i.e. (fig.) *co-religionist* (*fellow-Chr.*):–fellow-citizen.
4848. συμπορεύομαι *soom-por-yoo'-om-ahee;* from *4862* and *4198;* to *journey together;* by impl. to *assemble:*–go with, resort.
4849. συμπόσιον *soom-pos'-ee-on;* neut. of a der. of the alt. of *4844;* a *drinking*-party ("*symposium*"), i.e. (by ext.) a *room* of guests:–company.
4850. συμπρεσβύτερος *soom-pres-boo'-ter-os;* from *4862* and *4245;* a *co-presbyter:*–presbyter, also an elder.
4851. συμφέρω *soom-fer'-o;* from *4862* and *5342* (incl. its alt.); to *bear together* (*contribute*), i.e. (lit.) to *collect,* or (fig.) to *conduce;* esp. (neut. part. as a noun) *advantage:*–be better for, bring together, be expedient (for), be good, (be) profit(-able for).
4852. σύμφημι *soom'-fay-mee;* from *4862* and *5346;* to *say jointly,* i.e. *assent to:*–consent unto.
4853. συμφυλέτης *soom-foo-let'-ace;* from *4862* and a der. of *5443;* a *co-tribesman,* i.e. *native of the same country:*–countryman.
4854. σύμφυτος *soom'-foo-tos;* from *4862* and a der. of *5453; grown* along *with* (*connate*), i.e. (fig.) closely *united* to:–planted together.
4855. συμφύω *soom-foo'-o;* from *4862* and *5453;* pass. to *grow jointly:*–spring up with.
4856. συμφωνέω *soom-fo-neh'-o* from *4859;* to be *harmonious,* i.e. (fig.) to *accord* (*be suitable, concur*) or *stipulate* (by compact):–agree (together, with).
4857. συμφώνησις *soom-fo'-nay-sis;* from *4856; accordance:*–concord.
4858. συμφωνία *soom-fo-nee'-ah;* from *4859;* unison of sound ("*symphony*"), i.e. a *concert* of instruments (harmonious *note*):–music.
4859. σύμφωνος *soom'-fo-nos;* from *4862* and *5456; sounding together* (*alike*), i.e. (fig.) *accordant* (neut. as noun, *agreement*):– consent.
4860. συμψηφίζω *soom-psay-fid'-zo;* from *4862* and *5585;* to *compute jointly:*–reckon.
4861. συìμψυχος *soom'-psoo-khos;* from *4862* and *5590; co-spirited,* i.e. *similar in sentiment:*–like-minded.
4862. σύν *soon;* a prim. prep. denoting *union; with* or *together* (but much closer than *3326* or *3844*), i.e. by association, companionship, process, resemblance, possession, instrumentality, addition, etc.:–beside, with. In compo. it has similar appl., incl. *completeness.*
4863. συνάγω *soon-ag'-o;* from *4862* and *71;* to *lead together,* i.e. *collect* or *convene;* spec. to *entertain* (hospitably):–+ accompany, assemble (selves, together), bestow, come together, gather (selves together, up, together), lead into, resort, take in.
4864. συναγωγή *soon-ag-o-gay';* from (the redupl. form of) *4863;* an *assemblage* of persons; spec. a Jewish "*synagogue*" (the meeting or the place); by anal. a Chr. *church:*–assembly, congregation, synagogue.
4865. συναγωνίζομαι *soon-ag-o-nid'-zom-ahee;* from *4862* and *75;* to *struggle* in company *with,* i.e. (fig.) to *be a partner* (*assistant*):–strive together with.
4866. συναθλέω *soon-ath-leh'-o* from *4862* and *118;* to *wrestle* in company *with,* i.e. (fig.) to *seek jointly:*–labour with, strive together for.
4867. συναθροίζω *soon-ath-royd'-zo;* from *4862* and ἀθροίζω athrŏizō (to *hoard*); to *convene:*–call (gather) together.
4868. συναίρω *soon-ah'-ee-ro;* from *4862* and *142;* to *make up together,* i.e. (fig.) to *compute* (an account):–reckon, take.
4869. συναιχμάλωτος *soon-aheekh-mal'-o-tos;* from *4862* and *164;* a *co-captive:*–fellowprisoner
4870. συνακολουθέω *soon-ak-ol-oo-theh'-o;* from *4862* and *190;* to *accompany:*–follow.
4871. συναλίζω *soon-al-id'-zo* from *4862* and ἁλίζω halizō (to *throng*); to *accumulate,* i.e. *convene:*–assemble together.
4872. συναναβαίνω *soon-an-ab-ah'-ee-no;* from *4862* and *305;* to *ascend* in company *with:*–come up with.
4873. συνανάκειμαι *soon-an-ak'-i-mahee;* from *4862* and *345;* to *recline* in company *with* (at a meal):–sit (down, at the table, together) with (at meat).
4874. συναναμίγνυμι *soon-an-am-ig'-noo-mee;* from *4862* and a com. of *303* and *3396;* to

GREEK

mix up together, i.e. (fig.) *associate with:*–(have, keep) company (with).

4875. συναναπαύομαι *soon-an-ap-ŏw'-om-ahee;* mid. from *4862* and *373;* to *recruit oneself* in company *with:*–refresh with.

4876. συναντάω *soon-an-tah'-o;* from *4862* and a der. of *473;* to *meet with;* fig. to *occur:*–befall, meet.

4877. συνάντησις *soon-an'-tay-sis;* from *4876;* a *meeting with:*–meet.

4878. συναντιλαμβάνομαι *soon-an-tee-lam-ban'-om-ahee* from *4862* and *482;* to *take* hold of *opposite together,* i.e. *co-operate* (*assist*):–help.

4879. συναπάγω *soon-ap-ag'-o;* from *4862* and *520;* to *take off together,* i.e. *transport with* (*seduce,* pass. *yield*):–carry (lead) away with, condescend.

4880. συναποθνήσκω *soon-ap-oth-nace'-ko;* from *4862* and *599;* to *decease* (lit.) in company *with,* or (fig.), similarly *to:*–be dead (die) with.

4881. συναπόλλυμι *soon-ap-ol'-loo-mee;* from *4862* and *622;* to *destroy* (mid. or pass. be *slain*) in company *with:*–perish with.

4882. συναποστέλλω *soon-ap-os-tel'-lo;* from *4862* and *649;* to *despatch* (on an errand) in company *with:*–send with.

4883. συναρμολογέω *soon-ar-mol-og-eh'-o;* from *4862* and a der. of a com. of *719* and *3004* (in its or. sense of *laying*); to *render close-jointed together,* i.e. *organize compactly:*–be fitly framed (joined) together.

4884. συναρπάζω *soon-ar-pad'-zo* from *4862* and *726;* to *snatch together,* i.e. *seize:*–catch.

4885. συναυξάνω *soon-ŏwx-an'-o;* from *4862* and *837;* to *increase* (*grow up*) *together:*–grow together.

4886. σύνδεσμος *soon'-des-mos;* from *4862* and *1199;* a *joint tie,* i.e. *ligament,* (fig.) *uniting principle, control:*–band, bond.

4887. συνδέω *soon-deh'-o;* from *4862* and *1210;* to *bind with,* i.e. (pass.) *be a fellow-prisoner* (fig.):–be bound with.

4888. συνδοξάζω *soon-dox-ad'-zo;* from *4862* and *1392;* to *exalt* to dignity in company (i.e. *similarly*) *with:*–glorify together.

4889. σύνδουλος *soon'-doo-los;* from *4862* and *1401;* a *co-slave,* i.e. *servitor* or *ministrant of the same master* (human or divine):–*fellowservant.*

4890. συνδρομή *soon-drom-ay';* from (the alt. of) *4936;* a *running together,* i.e. (riotous) *concourse:*–run together.

4891. συνεγείρω *soon-eg-i'-ro;* from *4862* and *1453;* to *rouse* (from death) in company *with,* i.e. (fig.) to *revivify* (spirtually) in resemblance to:–raise up together, rise with.

4892. συνέδριον *soon-ed'-ree-on;* neut. of a presumed der. of a com. of *4862* and the base of *1476;* a *joint session,* i.e. (spec.), the Jewish *Sanhedrin;* by anal. a subordinate *tribunal:*–council.

4893. συνείδησις *soon-i'-day-sis;* from a prol. form of *4894; co-perception,* i.e. moral *consciousness:*–conscience.

4894. συνείδω *soon-i'-do;* from *4862* and *1492;* to *see completely;* used (like its prim.) only in two past tenses, respectively mean. *to understand* or *become aware,* and to *be conscious* or (clandestinely) *informed of:*–consider, know, be privy, be ware of.

4895. σύνειμι *soon'-i-mee;* from *4862* and *1510* (incl. its various inflections); to *be* in company *with,* i.e. *present* at the time:–be with.

4896. σύνειμι *soon'-i-mee;* from *4862* and εἶμι ĕimi (to *go*); to *assemble:*–gather together.

4897. συνεισέρχομαι *soon-ice-er'-khom-ahee;* from *4862* and *1525;* to *enter* in company *with:*–go in with, go with into.

4898. συνέκδημος *soon-ek'-day-mos;* from *4862* and the base of *1553;* a *co-absentee* from home, i.e. *fellow-traveller:*–companion in travel, travel with.

4899. συνεκλεκτός *soon-ek-lek-tos';* from a com. of *4862* and *1586; chosen* in company *with,* i.e. *co-elect* (*fellow Christian*):–elected together with.

4900. συνελαύνω *soon-el-ow'-no;* from *4862* and *1643;* to *drive together,* i.e. (fig.) *exhort* (to reconciliation):–+ set at one again.

4901. συνεπιμαρτυρέω *soon-ep-ee-mar-too-reh'-o;* from *4862* and *1957;* to *testify further jointly,* i.e. *unite in adding evidence:*–also bear witness.

4902. συνέπομαι *soon-ep'-om-ahee;* mid. from *4862* and a prim. ἕπω hĕpō (to *follow*); to *attend* (*travel*) in company *with:*–accompany.

4903. συνεργέω *soon-erg-eh'-o;* from *4904;* to be a *fellow-worker,* i.e. *co-operate:*–help (work) with, work(-er) together.

4904. συνεργός *soon-er-gos';* from a presumed com. of *4862* and the base of *2041;* a *co-laborer,* i.e. *coadjutor:*–companion in labour, (fellow-)helper(-labourer, -worker), labourer together with, workfellow.

4905. συνέρχομαι *soon-er'-khom-ahee;* from *4862* and *2064;* to *convene, depart* in company *with, associate* with, or (spec.), *cohabit* (conjugally):–accompany, assemble (with), come (together), come (company, go) with, resort.

4906. συνεσθίω *soon-es-thee'-o;* from *4862* and *2068* (incl. its alt.); to *take food* in company *with:*–eat with.

4907. σύνεσις *soon'-es-is;* from *4920;* a ment. *putting together,* i.e. *intelligence* or (concr.) the *intellect:*–knowledge, understanding.

4908. συνετός *soon-et'-os;* from *4920;* ment. *put* (or *putting*) *together,* i.e. *sagacious:*–prudent. Comp. *5429.*

4909. συνευδοκέω *soon-yoo-dok-eh'-o;* from *4862* and *2106;* to *think well of in common,* i.e. *assent* to, *feel gratified with:*–allow, assent, be pleased, have pleasure.

4910. συνευωχέω *soon-yoo-o-kheh'-o;* from *4862* and a der. of a presumed com. of *2095* and a der. of *2192* (mean. to *be in good condition,* i.e. [by impl.] to *fare well,* or *feast*); to *entertain* sumptuously in company *with,* i.e. (mid. or pass.) to *revel* together:–feast with.

4911. συνεφίστημι *soon-ef-is'-tay-mee;* from *4862* and *2186;* to *stand up together,* i.e. to *resist* (or *assault*) *jointly:*–rise up together.

4912. συνέχω *soon-ekh'-o;* from *4862* and *2192;* to *hold together,* i.e. to *compress* (the ears, with a crowd or siege) or *arrest* (a prisoner); fig. to *compel, perplex, afflict, preoccupy:*–constrain, hold, keep in, press, lie sick of, stop, be in a strait, straiten, be taken with, throng.

4913. συνήδομαι *soon-ay'-dom-ahee;* mid. from *4862* and the base of *2237;* to *rejoice* in *with* oneself, i.e. *feel satisfaction* concerning:–delight.

4914. συνήθεια *soon-ay'-thi-ah;* from a com. of *4862* and *2239; mutual habituation,* i.e. *usage:*–custom.

4915. συνηλικιώτης *soon-ay-lik-ee-o'-tace;* from *4862* and a der. of *2244;* a *co-aged* person, i.e. *alike* in years:–equal.

4916. συνθάπτω *soon-thap'-to;* from *4862* and *2290*; to *inter* in company *with,* i.e. (fig.) to *assimilate* spir. (to Christ by a sepulture as to sin):–bury with.

4917. συνθλάω *soon-thlah'-o;* from *4862* and θλάω thlaō (to *crush*); to *dash together,* i.e. *shatter:*–break.

4918. συνθλίβω *soon-thlee'-bo;* from *4862* and *2346;* to *compress,* i.e. *crowd* on all sides:–throng.

4919. συνθρύπτω *soon-throop'-to;* from *4862* and θρύπτω thruptō (to *crumble*); to *crush together,* i.e. (fig.) to *dispirit:*–break.

4920. συνίημι *soon-ee'-ay-mee;* from *4862* and ἵημι hiēmi (to *send*); to *put together,* i.e. (ment.) to *comprehend;* by impl. to *act piously:*–consider, understand, be wise.

4921. συνιστάω *soon-is-tah'-o;* or (streng.) συνιστάνω *soon-is-tan'-o;* or συνίστημι *soon-is-tay'-mee;* from *4862* and *2476* (incl. its coll. forms); to *set together,* i.e. (by impl.) to *introduce* (favorably), or (fig.) to *exhibit;* intrans., to *stand near,* or (fig.) to *constitute:*–approve, commend, consist, make, stand (with).

4922. συνοδεύω *soon-od-yoo'-o;* from *4862* and *3593;* to *travel* in company *with:*–journey with.

4923. συνοδία *soon-od-ee'-ah;* from a com. of *4862* and *3598* ("*synod*"); *companionship* on a journey, i.e. (by impl.), a *caravan:*–company.

4924. συνοικέω *soon-oy-keh'-o* from *4862* and *3611;* to *reside together* (as a family):–dwell together.

4925. συνοικοδομέω *soon-oy-kod-om-eh'-o;* from *4862* and *3618;* to *construct,* i.e. pass. to *compose* (in company with other Christians, fig.):–build together.

4926. συνομιλέω *soon-om-il-eh'-o;* from *4862* and *3656;* to *converse* mutually:–talk with.

4927. συνομορέω *soon-om-or-eh'-o;* from *4862* and a der. of a com. of the base of *3674* and the base of *3725;* to *border together,* i.e. *adjoin:*–join hard.

4928. συνόχη *soon-okh-ay';* from *4912;*

restraint, i.e. (fig.) *anxiety:*–anguish, distress.
4929. συντάσσω *soon-tas-so;* from *4862* and *5021;* to *arrange jointly,* i.e. (fig.) to *dir.:*–appoint.
4930. συντέλεια *soon-tel'-i-ah;* from *4931; entire completion,* i.e. *consummation* (of a dispensation):–end.
4931. συντελέω *soon-tel-eh'-o;* from 4862 and 5055; to *complete entirely;* gen. to *execute* (lit. or fig.):–end, finish, fulfil, make.
4932. συντέμνω *soon-tem'-no;* from *4862* and the base of *5114;* to *contract* by cutting, i.e. (fig.) *do concisely* (*speedily*):–(cut) short
4933. συντηρέω *soon-tay-reh'-o;* from *4862* and *5083;* to *keep* closely *together,* i.e. (by impl.) to *conserve* (from ruin); ment., to *remember* (and *obey*):–keep, observe, preserve.
4934. συντίθεμαι *soon-tith'-em-ahee;* mid. from *4862* and *5087;* to *place jointly,* i.e. (fig.) to *consent* (*bargain, stipulate*), *concur:*–agree, assent, covenant.
4935. συντόμως *soon-tom'-oce* adv. from a der. of *4932; concisely* (*briefly*):–a few words.
4936. συντρέχω *soon-trekh'-o;* from *4862* and *5143* (incl. its alt.); to *rush together* (hastily *assemble*) or *headlong* (fig.):–run (together, with).
4937. συντρίβω *soon-tree'-bo;* from *4862* and the base of *5147;* to *crush completely,* i.e. to *shatter* (lit. or fig.):–break (in pieces), broken to shivers (+ -hearted), bruise.
4938. σύντριμμα *soon-trim'-mah;* from *4937; concussion* or utter *fracture* (prop. concr.), i.e. complete *ruin:*–destruction.
4939. σύντροφος *soon'-trof-os;* from *4862* and *5162* (in a pass. sense); a *fellow-nursling,* i.e. *comrade:*–brought up with.
4940. συντυγχάνω *soon-toong-khan'-o;* from *4862* and *5177;* to *chance together,* i.e. *meet* with (*reach*):–come at.
4941. Συντύχη *soon-too'-khay;* from *4940;* an *accident; Syntyche,* a Chr. female:–Syntyche.
4942. συνυποκρίνομαι *soon-oo-pok-rin'-om-ahee;* from *4862* and *5271;* to *act hypocritically* in concert *with:*–dissemble with.
4943. συνυπουργέω *soon-oop-oorg-eh'-o;* from *4862* and a der. of a com. of *5259* and the base of *2041;* to *be a co-auxiliary,* i.e. *assist:*–help together.
4944. συνωδίνω *soon-o-dee'-no;* from *4862* and *5605;* to *have* (parturition) *pangs* in company (concert, simultaneously) *with,* i.e. (fig.) to *sympathize* (in expectation of relief from suffering):–travail in pain together.
4945. συνωμοσία *soon-o-mos-ee'-ah;* from a com. of *4862* and *3660;* a *swearing together,* i.e. (by impl.) a *plot:*–conspiracy.
4946. Συράκουσαι *soo-rak'-oo-sahee;* pl. of unc. der.; *Syracuse,* the capital of Sicily:–Syracuse.
4947. Συρία *soo-ree'-ah;* prob. of Heb. or. [6865]; *Syria* (i.e. *Tsyria* or *Tyre*), a region of Asia:–Syria.
4948. Σύρος *soo'-ros;* from the same as *4947;* a *Syran* (i.e. prob. *Tyrian*), a native of Syria:–Syrian.
4949. Συροφοίνισσα *soo-rof-oy'-nis-sah;* fem. of a com. of *4948* and the same as *5403;* a *Syro-phoenician* woman, i.e. a female native of Phoenicia in Syria:–Syrophenician.
4950. σύρτις *soor'-tis;* from *4951;* a *shoal* (from the sand *drawn* thither by the waves), i.e. the *Syrtis* Major or great bay on the north coast of Africa:–quicksands.
4951. σύρω *soo'-ro;* prob. akin to *138;* to *trail:*–drag, draw, hale.
4952. συσπαράσσω *soos-par-as'-so;* from *4862* and 4682; to *rend completely,* i.e. (by anal.) to *convulse* violently:–throw down.
4953. σύσσημον *soos'-say-mon;* neut. of a com. of *4862* and the base of *4591*; a *sign in common,* i.e. preconcerted *signal:*–token.
4954. σύσσωμος *soos'-so-mos;* from *4862* and *4983; of a joint body,* i.e. (fig.) a *fellow-member* of the Christian community:–of the same body.
4955. συστασιαστής *soos-tas-ee-as-tace';* from a com. of *4862* and a der. of *4714;* a *fellow-insurgent:*–make insurrection with.
4956. συστατικός *soos-tat-ee-kos';* from a der. of *4921; introductory,* i.e. *recommendatory:*–of commendation.
4957. συσταυρόω *soos-tow-rŏ'-o;* from *4862* and *4717;* to *impale* in company *with* (lit. or fig.):–crucify with.
4958. συστέλλω *soos-tel'-lo;* from *4862* and *4724;* to *send* (*draw*) *together,* i.e. *enwrap* (*enshroud* a corpse for burial), *contract* (an interval):– short, wind up.
4959. συστενάζω *soos-ten-ad'-zo;* from *4862* and *4727;* to *moan jointly,* i.e. (fig.) *experience a common calamity:*–groan together.
4960. συστοιχέω *soos-toy-kheh'-o;* from *4862* and *4748;* to *file together* (as soldiers in ranks), i.e. (fig.) to *correspond* to:–answer to.
4961. συστρατιώτης *soos-trat-ee-o'-tace;* from *4862* and *4757;* a *co-campaigner,* i.e. (fig.) an *associate* in Christian toil:–fellowsoldier.
4962. συστρέφω *soos-tref'-o;* from *4862* and *4762;* to *twist together,* i.e. *collect* (a bundle, a crowd):–gather.
4963. συστροφή *soos-trof-ay';* from *4962;* a *twisting together,* i.e. (fig.) a secret *coalition,* riotous *crowd:*–+ band together, concourse.
4964. συσχηματίζω *soos-khay-mat-id'-zo;* from *4862* and a der. of *4976;* to *fashion alike,* i.e. *conform* to the same pattern (fig.):–conform to, fashion self according to.
4965. Συχάρ *soo-khar';* of Heb. or. [7941]; *Sychar* (i.e. *Shekar*), a place in Pal.:–Sychar.
4966. Συχέμ *soo-khem';* of Heb. or. [7927]; *Sychem* (i.e. *Shekem*), the name of a Canaanite and of a place in Pal.:–Sychem.
4967. σφαγή *sfag-ay';* from *4969; butchery* (of animals for food or sacrifice, or [fig.] of men [*destruction*):–slaughter.
4968. σφάγιον *sfag'-ee-on;* neut. of a der. of *4967;* a *victim* (in sacrifice):–slain beast.
4969. σφάζω *sfad'-zo;* a prim. verb; to *butcher* (esp. an animal for food or in sacrifice) or (gen.) to *slaughter,* or (spec.), to *maim* (violently):–kill, slay, wound.
4970. σφόδρα *sfod'-rah;* neut. pl. of σφοδρός sphŏdrŏs (*violent;* of unc. der.) as adv.; *vehemently,* i.e. in a *high degree, much:*– exceeding(-ly), greatly, sore, very.
4971. σφοδρῶς *sfod-roce';* adv. from the same as *4970; very much:*–exceedingly.
4972. σφραγίζω *sfrag-id'-zo;* from *4973;* to *stamp* (with a signet or private mark) for security or preservation (lit. or fig.); by impl. to *keep secret,* to *attest:*–(set a, set to) seal up, stop.
4973. σφραγίς *sfrag-ece';* prob. streng. from 5420; a *signet* (as *fencing* in or protecting from misappropriation); by impl. the *stamp* impressed (as a mark of privacy, or genuineness), lit. or fig.:–seal.
4974. σφυρόν *sfoo-ron';* neut. of a presumed der. prob. of the same as σφαῖρα sphaira (a *ball,* "*sphere*"; comp. the fem. σφυρα sphura, a *hammer*); the *ankle* (as *globular*):–ancle bone.
4975. σχεδόν *skhed-on';* neut. of a presumed der. of the alt. of *2192* as adv.; *nigh,* i.e. *nearly:*–almost.
4976. σχῆμα *skhay'-mah;* from the alt. of *2192;* a *figure* (as a *mode* or *circumstance*), i.e. (by impl.) exter. *condition:*–fashion.
4977. σχίζω *skhid'-zo;* app. a prim. verb; to *split* or *sever* (lit. or fig.):–break, divide, open, rend, make a rent.
4978. σχίσμα *skhis'-mah;* from *4977;* a *split* or *gap* ("*schism*"), lit. or fig.:–division, rent, schism.
4979. σχοινίον *skhoy-nee'-on;* dimin. of σχοῖνος schŏinŏs (a *rush* or *flag*-plant; of unc. der.); a *rushlet,* i.e. *grass-withe* or *tie* (gen.):–small cord, rope.
4980. σχολάζω *skhol-ad'-zo;* from *4981;* to *take a holiday,* i.e. *be at leisure* for (by impl. *devote oneself* wholly to); fig. to *be vacant* (of a house):–empty, give self.
4981. σχολή *skhol-ay';* prob. fem. of a presumed der. of the alt. of *2192;* prop. *loitering* (as a *withholding* of oneself from work) or *leisure,* i.e. (by impl.) a "*school*" (as *vacation* from phys. employment):–school.
4982. σώζω *sode'-zo;* from a prim. word σῶς sōs (contr. for the obso. σάος saŏs, "*safe*"); *sode'-zo* to *save,* i.e. *deliver* or *protect* (lit. or fig.):–heal, preserve, save (self), do well, be (make) whole.
4983. σῶμα *so'-mah;* from *4982;* the *body* (as a *sound* whole), used in a very wide appl., lit. or fig.:–bodily, body, slave.
4984. σωματικός *so-mat-ee-kos';* from *4983; corporeal* or *physical:*–bodily.
4985. σωματικῶς *so-mat-ee-koce';* adv. from *4984; corporeally* or *physically:*–bodily.
4986. Σώπατρος *so'-pat-ros;* from the base of *4982* and *3962;* of a *safe father; Sopatrus,* a Christian:–Sopater. Comp. *4989*.
4987. σωρεύω *sore-yoo'-o;* from another form of *4673;* to *pile* up (lit. or fig.):–heap, load.
4988. Σωσθένης *soce-then'-ace;* from the base of *4982* and that of *4599; of safe strength;*

GREEK

Sosthenes, a Chr.:–Sosthenes.
4989. Σωσίπατρος *so-sip'-at-ros;* prol. for *4986; Sosipatrus,* a Chr.:–Sosipater.
4990. σωτήρ *so-tare';* from *4982;* a *deliverer,* i.e. God or Christ:–saviour.
4991. σωτηρία *so-tay-ree'-ah;* fem. of a der. of *4990* as (prop. abstr.) noun; *rescue* or *safety* (phys. or mor.):–deliver, health, salvation, save, saving.
4992. σωτήριον *so-tay'-ree-on;* neut. of the same as *4991* as (prop. concr.) noun; *defender* or (by impl.) *defence:*–salvation.
4993. σωφρονέω *so-fron-eh'-o;* from *4998;* to *be of sound mind,* i.e. *sane,* (fig.) *moderate:*–be in right mind, be sober (minded), soberly.
4994. σωφρονίζω *so-fron-id'-zo;* from *4998*; to *make of sound mind,* i.e. (fig.) to *discipline* or *correct:*–teach to be sober.
4995. σωφρονισμος *so-fron-is-mos';* from *4994; discipline,* i.e. *self-control:*–sound mind.
4996. σωφρόνως *so-fron'-oce;* adv. from *4998; with sound mind,* i.e. *moderately:*–soberly.
4997. σωφροσύνη *so-fros-oo'-nay;* from *4998; soundness of mind,* i.e. (lit.) *sanity* or (fig.) *self-control:*–soberness, sobriety.
4998. σώφρων *so'-frone;* from the base of *4982* and that of *5424; safe* (*sound*) in *mind,* i.e. *self-controlled* (*moderate* as to opinion or passion):–discreet, sober, temperate.

T

4999. Ταβέρναι *tab-er'-nahee;* pl. of Lat. or.; *huts* or *wooden-walled* buildings; *Tabernoe:*–taverns.
5000. Ταβιθά *tab-ee-thah';* of Chald. or. [comp. *6646*]; *the gazelle; Tabitha* (i.e. *Tabjetha*), a Chr. female:–Tabitha.
5001. τάγμα *tag'-mah;* from *5021;* something orderly in *arrangement* (a *troop*), i.e. (fig.) a *series* or *succession:*–order.
5002. τακτός *tak-tos';* from *5021; arranged,* i.e. *appointed* or *stated:*–set.
5003. ταλαιπωρέω *tal-ahee-po-reh'-o;* from *5005;* to *be wretched,* i.e. *realize* one's own *misery:*–be afflicted.
5004. ταλαιπωρία *tal-ahee-po-ree'-ah;* from *5005; wretchedness,* i.e. *calamity:*–misery.
5005. ταλαίπωρος *tal-ah'-ee-po-ros;* from the base of *5007* and a der. of the base of *3984; enduring trial,* i.e. *miserable:*–wretched.
5006. ταλαντιαῖος *tal-an-tee-ah'-yos;* from *5007; talent-like* in weight:–weight of a talent.
5007. τάλαντον *tal'-an-ton;* neut. of a presumed der. of the or. form of τλάω tlaō (to *bear;* equiv. to *5342*); a *balance* (as *supporting* weights), i.e. (by impl.) a cert. *weight* (and thence a *coin* or rather *sum* of money) or "*talent*":–talent.
5008. ταλιθά *tal-ee-thah';* of Chald. or. [comp. 2924]; the *fresh,* i.e. young *girl; talitha* (O *maiden*):–talitha.
5009. ταμεῖον *tam-i'-on;* neut. contr. of a presumed der. of ταμίας tamias (a *dispenser* or *distributor;* akin to τέμνω temnō, to *cut*); a *dispensary* or *magazine,* i.e. a chamber on the ground-floor or interior of an Oriental house (gen. used for *storage* or *privacy,* a spot for retirement):–secret chamber, closet, storehouse.
5010. τάξις *tax'-is;* from *5021;* regular arrangement, i.e. (in time) fixed *succession* (of rank or character), official *dignity:*–order.
5011. ταπεινός *tap-i-nos';* of unc. der.; *depressed,* i.e. (fig.) *humiliated* (in circumstances or disposition):–base, cast down, humble, of low degree (estate), lowly.
5012. ταπεινοφροσύνη *tap-i-nof-ros-oo'-nay;* from a com. of *5011* and the base of *5424; humiliation of mind,* i.e. *modesty:*–humbleness of mind, humility (of mind, loneliness (of mind).
5013. ταπεινόω *tap-i-no'-o;* from *5011;* to *depress;* fig. to *humiliate* (in condition or heart):–abase, bring low, humble (self).
5014. ταπείνωσις *tap-i'-no-sis;* from *5013; depression* (in rank or feeling):–humiliation, be made low, low estate, vile.
5015. ταράσσω *tar-as'-so;* of unc. affin.; to *stir* or *agitate* (*roil* water):–trouble.
5016. ταραχή *tar-akh-ay';* fem. from *5015; disturbance,* i.e. (of water) *roiling,* or (of a mob) *sedition:*–trouble(-ing).
5017. τάραχος *tar'-akh-os;* masc. from *5015;* a *disturbance,* i.e. (popular) *tumult:*–stir.
5018. Ταρσεύς *tar-syoos';* from *5019;* a *Tarsean,* i.e. native of Tarsus:–of Tarsus.
5019. Ταρσός, *tar-sos';* perh. the same as ταρσός tarsŏs (a *flat* basket); *Tarsus,* a place in Asia Minor:–Tarsus.
5020. ταρταρόω *tar-tar-ŏ'-o;* from Τάρταρος Tartarŏs (the deepest *abyss* of Hades); to *incarcerate* in eternal torment:–cast down to hell.
5021. τάσσω *tas'-so;* a prol. form of a prim. verb (which latter appears only in cert. tenses); to *arrange* in an orderly manner, i.e. *assign* or *dispose* (to a cert. position or lot):–addict, appoint, determine, ordain, set.
5022. ταῦρος *tŏw'-ros;* app. a prim. word [comp. 8450, "*steer*"]; a *bullock:*–bull, ox.
5023. ταῦτα *tŏw'-tah;* nom. or acc. neut. pl. of *3778; these* things:–+ afterward, follow, + hereafter, X him, the same, so, such, that, then, these, they, this, those, thus.
5024. ταὐτά *tow-tah';* neut. pl. of *3588* and *846* as adv.; in *the same* way:–even thus, (manner) like, so.
5025. ταύταις *tow'-taheece;* and ταύτας *tŏw'-tas;* dat. and acc. fem. pl. respectively of *3778;* (*to* or *with* or *by,* etc.) *these:*–hence, that, then, these, those.
5026. ταύτῃ *tŏw'-tay;* and ταύτην *tŏw'-tane;* ταύτης *tŏw'-tace;* dat. acc. and gen. respectively of the fem. sing. of *3778;* (*towards* or *of*) *this:*–her, + hereof, it, that, + thereby, the (same), this (same).
5027. ταφή *taf-ay';* fem. from *2290; burial* (the act):–X bury.
5028. τάφος *taf'-os;* masc. from *2290;* a *grave* (the place of interment):–sepulchre, tomb.
5029. τάχα *takh'-ah;* as if neut. pl. of *5036* (adv.); *shortly,* i.e. (fig.) *possibly:*–peradventure(-haps).
5030. ταχέως *takh-eh'-oce;* adv. from *5036; briefly,* i.e. (in time) *speedily,* or (in manner) *rapidly:*–hastily, quickly, shortly, soon, suddenly.
5031. ταχινός *takh-ee-nos';* from *5034; curt,* i.e. *impending:*–shortly, swift.
5032. τάχιον *takh'-ee-on;* neut. sing. of the comp. of *5036* (as adv.); *more swiftly,* i.e. (in manner) *more rapidly,* or (in time) *more speedily:*–out (run), quickly, shortly, sooner.
5033. τάχιστα *takh'-is-tah;* neut. pl. of the superl. of *5036* (as adv.); *most quickly,* i.e. (with *5613* pref.) *as soon* as possible:–+ with all speed.
5034. τάχος *takh'-os;* from the same as *5036;* a *brief* space (of time), i.e. (with *1722* pref.) in haste:–+ quickly, + shortly, + speedily.
5035. ταχύ *takh-oo';* neut. sing. of *5036* (as adv.); *shortly,* i.e. *without delay, soon,* or (by surprise) *suddenly,* or (by impl. of ease) *readily:*–lightly, quickly.
5036. ταχύς *takh-oos';* of unc. affin.; *fleet,* i.e. (fig.) *prompt* or *ready:*–swift.
5037. τε *teh;* a prim. par. (enclitic) of connection or addition; *both* or *also* (prop. as correl. of *2532*):–also, and, both, even, then, whether. Often used in compo., usually as the latter part.
5038. τεῖχος *ti'-khos;* akin to the base of *5088;* a *wall* (as *formative* of a house):–wall.
5039. τεκμήριον *tek-may'-ree-on;* neut. of a presumed der. of τεκμάρ tĕkmar (a *goal* or fixed *limit*); a *token* (as *defining* a fact), i.e. *criterion* of certainty:–infallible proof.
5040. τεκνίον *tek-nee'-on;* dimin. of *5043;* an *infant,* i.e. (pl. fig.) *darlings* (Christian *converts*):–little children.
5041. τεκογονέω *tek-nog-on-eh'-o;* from a com. of *5043* and the base of *1096;* to *be a child-bearer,* i.e. *parent* (*mother*):–bear children.
5042. τεκνογονία *tek-nog-on-ee'-ah;* from the same as *5041; childbirth* (*parentage*), i.e. (by impl.) *maternity* (the performance of *maternal duties*):–childbearing.
5043. τέκνον *tek'-non;* from the base of *5098*; a *child* (as *produced*):–child, daughter, son.
5044. τεκνοτροφέω *tek-not-rof-eh'-o;* from a com. of *5043* and *5142;* to *be a childrearer,* i.e. *fulfil* the duties of *a female parent:*–bring up children.
5045. τέκτων *tek'-tone;* from the base of *5098;* an *artificer* (as *producer* of fabrics), i.e. (spec.), a *craftsman* in wood:–carpenter.
5046. τέλειος *tel'-i-os;* from *5056; complete* (in various appl. of labor, growth, ment. and mor. character, etc.); neut. (as noun, with *3588*) *completeness:*–of full age, man, perfect.
5047. τελειότης *tel-i-ot'-ace;* from *5046;* (the state) *completeness* (ment. or mor.):–perfection(-ness).
5048. τελειόω *tel-i-ŏ'-o;* from *5046;* to *complete,* i.e. (lit.) *accomplish,* or (fig.) *consummate* (in character):–consecrate, finish, fulfil, make) perfect.
5049. τελείως *tel-i'-oce;* adv. from *5046; completely,* i.e. (of hope) *without wavering:*–to the end.

5050. τελείωσις *tel-i'-o-sis;* from *5448;* (the act) *completion,* i.e. (of prophecy) *verification,* or (of expiation) *absolution:*–perfection, performance.
5051. τελειωτής *tel-i-o-tace';* from *5048;* a *completer,* i.e. *consummater:*–finisher.
5052. τελεσφορέω *tel-es-for-eh'-o;* from a com. of *5056* and *5342;* to *be a bearer to completion* (maturity), i.e. to *ripen* fruit (fig.):–bring fruit to perfection.
5053. τελευτάω *tel-yoo-tah'-o;* from a presumed der. of *5055;* to *finish* life (by impl. of *979*), i.e. *expire* (*demise*):–be dead, decease, die.
5054. τελευτή *tel-yoo-tay';* from *5053;* *decease:*–death.
5055. τελέω *tel-eh'-o;* from *5056;* to *end,* i.e. *complete, execute, conclude, discharge* (a debt):–accomplish, make an end, expire, fill up, finish, go over, pay, perform.
5056. τέλος *tel'-os;* from a prim. τέλλω tĕllō (to *set out* for a def. point or *goal*); prop. the point aimed at as a *limit,* i.e. (by impl.) the *conclusion* of an act or state (*term.* [lit. fig. or indef.], *result* [immed., ultimate or prophetic], *purpose*); spec. an *impost* or *levy* (as *paid*):–+ continual, custom, end (-ing), finally, uttermost. Comp. *5411.*
5057. τελώνης *tel-o'-nace;* from *5056* and *5608;* a *tax-farmer,* i.e. *collector* of public *revenue:*–publican.
5058. τελώνιον *tel-o'-nee-on;* neut. of a presumed der. of *5057;* a *tax-gatherer's* place of business:–receipt of custom.
5059. τέρας *ter'-as;* of unc. affin.; a *prodigy* or *omen:*–wonder.
5060. Τέρτιος *ter'-tee-os;* of Lat. or.; *third; Tertius,* a Chr.:–Tertius.
5061. Τέρτυλλος *ter'-tool-los;* of unc. der.; *Tertullus,* a Rom.:–Tertullus.
5062. Τεσσαράκοντα *tes-sar-ak'-on-tah;* the decade of *5064; forty:*–forty.
5063. Τεσσαρακονταετής *tes-sar-ak-on-tah-et-ace';* from 5062 and 2094; *of forty years* of age:–(+ full, of) forty years (old).
5064. τέσσαρες *tes'-sar-es;* neut. τέσσαρα *tes'-sar-ah;* a pl. number; *four:*–four.
5065. τεσσαρεσκαιδέκατος *tes-sar-es-kahee-dek'-at-os;* from *5064* and *2532* and *1182; fourteenth:*–fourteenth.
5066. τεταρταῖος *tet-ar-tah'-yos;* from *5064;* pertaining to the *fourth* day:–four days.
5067. τέταρτος *tet'-ar-tos;* ord. from *5064; fourth:*–four(-th).
5068. τετράγωνος *tet-rag'-o-nos;* from *5064* and *1137; four-cornered,* i.e. *square:*–foursquare.
5069. τετράδιον *tet-rad'-ee-on;* neut. of a presumed der. of τέτρας tetras (a *tetrad;* from *5064*); a *quaternion* or squad (picket) of four Rom. soldiers:–quaternion.
5070.τετρακισχ *tet-rak-is-khil'-ee-oy;* from the mult. adv. of *5064* and *5507; four times a thousand:*–four thousand.
5071.τετρακόσιοι *tet-rak-os'-ee-oy;* neut. τετρακόσια *tet-rak-os'-ee-ah;* pl. from *5064* and *1540; four hundred:*–four hundred.
5072. τετράμηνον *tet-ram'-ay-non;* neut. of a com. of *5064* and *3376;* a *four months'* space:–four months.
5073. τετραπλόος *tet-rap-lŏ'-os;* from *5064* and a der. of the base of *4118; quadruple:*–fourfold.
5074. τετράπους *tet-rap'-ooce;* from *5064* and *4228;* a *quadruped:*–fourfooted beast.
5075. τετραρχέω *tet-rar-kheh'-o;* from *5076;* to *be a tetrarch:*–(be) tetrarch.
5076. τετράρχης *tet-rar'-khace;* from *5064* and *757;* the *ruler of a fourth* part of a country ("*tetrarch*"):–tetrarch.
5077. τεφρόω *tef-rŏ'-o;* from τέφρα tephra (*ashes*); to *incinerate,* i.e. *consume:*–turn to ashes.
5078. τέχνη *tekh'-nay;* from the base of *5088; art* (as *productive*), i.e. (spec.), a *trade,* or (gen.) *skill:*–art, craft, occupation.
5079. τεχνίτης *tekh-nee'-tace;* from *5078;* an *artisan;* fig. a *founder* (*Creator*):–builder, craftsman.
5080. τήκω *tay'-ko;* app. a prim. verb; to *liquefy:*–melt.
5081. τηλαυγῶς *tay-lŏw-goce';* adv. from a com. of a der. of *5056* and *827;* in a *far-shining* manner, i.e. *plainly:*–clearly.
5082. τηλικοῦτος *tay-lik-oo'-tos;* fem. τηλικαύτη *tay-lik-ŏw'-tay* from a com. of *3588* with *2245* and *3778; such as this,* i.e. (in [fig.] magnitude) *so vast:*–so great, so mighty.
5083. τηρέω *tay-reh'-o;* from τηρός tĕrŏs (a *watch;* perh. akin to *2334*); to *guard* (from *loss* or *injury,* prop. by keeping *the eye* upon; and thus differing from *5442,* which is prop. to *prevent* escaping; and from *2892,* which implies a *fortress* or full military lines of apparatus), i.e. to *note* (a prophecy; fig. to *fulfil* a command); by impl. to *detain* (in custody; fig. to *maintain*); by ext., to *withhold* (for pers. ends; fig. to *keep unmarried*):–hold fast, keep(- er), (pre-, re-)serve, watch.
5084. τήρησις *tay'-ray-sis;* from *5083;* a *watching,* i.e. (fig.) *observance,* or (concr.) a *prison:*–hold.
5085. Τιβεριάς *tib-er-ee-as';* from *5086; Tiberias,* the name of a town and a lake in Pal.:–Tiberias.
5086. Τιβέριος *tib-er'-ee-os;* of Lat. or.; prob. *pertaining to the* river *Tiberis* or *Tiber; Tiberius,* a Rom. emperor:–Tiberius.
5087. τίθημι *tith'-ay-mee;* a prol. form of a prim. θεω *theh'-o* (which is used only as an alt. in cert. tenses); *to place* (in the widest appl., lit. and fig.; prop. in a pass. or horizontal posture, and thus different from *2476,* which prop. denotes an upright and act. position, while *2749* is prop. refl. and utterly prostrate):–+ advise, appoint, bow, commit, conceive, give, X kneel down, lay (aside, down, up), make, ordain, purpose, put, set (forth), settle, sink down.
5088. τίκτω *tik'-to;* a streng. form of a prim. τέκω *tek'-o* (which is used only as alt. in cert. tenses); to *produce* (from seed, as a mother, a plant, the earth, etc.), lit. or fig.:–bear, be born, bring forth, be delivered, be in travail.
5089. τίλλω *til'-lo;* perh. akin to the alt. of *138,* and thus to *4951;* to *pull* off:–pluck.
5090. Τίμαιος *tim'-ah-yos;* prob. of Chald. or. [comp. *2931*]; *Timoeus* (i.e. *Timay*), an Isr.:–Timaeus.
5091. τιμάω *tim-ah'-o;* from *5093;* to *prize,* i.e. *fix* a *valuation* upon; by impl. to *revere:*–honour, value.
5092. τιμή *tee-may';* from *5099;* a *value,* i.e. *money* paid, or (concr. and coll.) *valuables;* by anal. *esteem* (esp. of the highest degree), or the *dignity* itself:–honour, precious, price, some.
5093. τίμιος *tim'-ee-os;* include. the comp. τιμιώτερος *tim-ee-o'-ter-os* and the superl. τίμιώτατος *tim-ee-o'-tat-os;* from *5092; valuable,* i.e. (obj.) *costly,* or (subj.) *honored, esteemed,* or (fig.) *beloved:*–dear, honourable, (more, most) precious, had in reputation.
5094. τιμιότης *tim-ee-ot'-ace;* from *5093; expensiveness,* i.e. (by impl.) *magnificence:*–costliness.
5095. Τιμόθεος *tee-moth'-eh-os;* from *5092* and *2316; dear to God; Timotheus,* a Chr.:–Timotheus, Timothy.
5096. Τίμων *tee'-mone;* from *5092; valuable; Timon,* a Chr.:–Timon.
5097. τιμωρέω *tim-o-reh'-o;* from a com. of 5092 and οὖρος ŏurŏs (a guard); prop. to *protect* one's *honor,* i.e. to *avenge* (*inflict* a *penalty*):–punish.
5098. τιμωρία *tee-mo-ree'-ah;* from *5097; vindication,* i.e. (by impl.) a *penalty:*–punishment.
5099. τίνω *tee'-no;* streng. for a prim. word τίω *tee'-o* (which is only used as an alt. in cert. tenses) to *pay* a price, i.e. as a *penalty:*–be punished with.
5100. τὶς *tis;* an enclitic indef. pron.; *some* or *any* pers. or object:–a (kind of), any (man, thing, thing at all), cert. (thing), divers, he (every) man, one (X thing), ought, + partly, some (man, -body, - thing, -what), (+ that no-)thing, what(-soever), X wherewith, whom[-soever], whose([-soever]).
5101. τίς *tis;* prob. emphat. of *5100;* an interrog. pron., *who, which* or *what* (in dir. or indirect questions):–every man, how (much), + no(-ne, thing), what (manner, thing), where ([-by, -fore, -of, -unto, - with, -withal]), whether, which, who(-m, -se), why.
5102. τίτλος *tit'-los;* of Lat. or.; a *titulus* or "*title*" (*placard*):–title.
5103. Τίτος *tee'-tos;* of Lat. or. but unc. significance; *Titus,* a Chr.:–Titus.
5104. τοί *toy;* prob. for the dat. of *3588;* an enclitic par. of *asseveration* by way of contrast; *in sooth:*–[*used only with other par. in the comp., as 2544, 3305, 5105, 5106,* etc.]
5105. τοιγαροῦν *toy-gar-oon';* from *5104* and *1063* and *3767; truly for then,* i.e. *consequently:*–there-(where-)fore.
5106. τοίνυν *toy'-noon;* from *5104* and *3568; truly now,* i.e. *accordingly:*–then, therefore.
5107. τοιόσδε *toy-os'-deh* (incl. the other

inflections); from a der. of *5104* and *1161; such-like then*, i.e. *so great:*–such.
5108. τοιοῦτος *toy-oo'-tos;* (incl. the other inflections); from *5104* and *3778; truly this,* i.e. *of this sort* (to denote character or individuality):–like, such (an one).
5109. τοῖχος *toy'-khos;* another form of *5038;* a *wall:*–wall.
5110. τόκος *tok'-os;* from the base of *5088; interest* on money loaned (as a *produce*):–usury.
5111. τολμάω *tol-mah'-o;* from τόλμα tŏlma (*boldness;* prob. itself from the base of *5056* through the idea of *extreme* conduct); to *venture* (obj. or in *act;* while *2292* is rather subj. or in *feeling*); by impl. to be *courageous:*–be bold, boldly, dare, durst.
5112. τολμηρότερον *tol-may-rot'-er-on;* neut. of the comp. of a der. of the base of *5111* (as adv.); *more daringly,* i.e. *with greater confidence* than otherwise:–the more boldly.
5113. τολμητής *tol-may-tace';* from *5111;* a *daring* (*audacious*) man:–presumptuous.
5114. τομώτερος *tom-o'-ter-os;* comp. of a der. of the prim. τέμνω tĕmnō (to *cut;* more comprehensive or decisive than 2875, as if by a *single* stroke; whereas that implies repeated blows, like *hacking*); *more keen:*–sharper.
5115. τόξον *tox'-on;* from the base of *5088;* a *bow* (app. as the simplest fabric):–bow.
5116. τοπάζιον *top-ad'-zee-on;* neut. of a presumed der. (alt.) of τόπαζος tŏpazŏs (a "*topaz*"; of unc. or.); a gem, prob. the *chrysolite:*–topaz.
5117. τόπος *top'-os;* app. a prim. word; a *spot* (gen. in *space,* but limited by occupancy; whereas 5561 is a large but part. *locality*), i.e. *location* (as a position, home, tract, etc.); fig. *condition, opportunity;* spec. a *scabbard:*–coast, licence, place, X plain, quarter, + rock, room, where.
5118. τοσοῦτος *tos-oo'-tos*; from τόσος tŏsŏs (*so much;* app. from *3588* and *3739*) and *3778* (incl. its var.); so *vast as this,* i.e. *such* (in quantity, amount, number of space):–as large, so great (long, many, much), these many.
5119. τότε *tot'-eh;* from (the neut. of) *3588* and *3753; the when,* i.e. *at the time* that (of the past or fut., also in consecution):–that time, then.
5120. τοῦ *too;* prop. the gen. of *3588;* sometimes used for *5127; of this person:*–his.
5121. τούναντίον *too-nan-tee'-on;* contr. for the neut. of *3588* and *1726; on the contrary:*–contrariwise.
5122. τοὔνομα *too'-no-mah;* contr. for the neut. of *3588* and *3686; the name* (is):–named.
5123. τουτέστι *toot-es'-tee;* contr. for *5124* and *2076; i.e.:*–i.e. (to say).
5124. τοῦτο *too'-tŏ;* neut. sing. nom. or acc. of *3778;* that thing:–here [-unto], it, partly, self[-same], so, that (intent), the same, there[-fore, -unto], this, thus, where[-fore].
5125. τούτοις *too'-toice;* dat. pl. masc. or neut. of *3778;* to (*for, in, with* or *by*) *these* (persons or things):–such, them, there[-in, -with], these, this, those.
5126. τοῦτον *too'-ton;* acc. sing. masc. of *3778; this* (pers., as obj. of verb or prep.):–him, the same, that, this.
5127. τούτου *too'-too;* gen. sing. masc. or neut. of *3778; of* (*from* or *concerning*) *this* (pers. or thing):–here[-by], him, it, + such manner of, that, thence[-forth], thereabout, this, thus.
5128. τούτους *too'-tooce;* acc. pl. masc. of *3778; these* (persons, as obj. of verb or prep.):–such, them, these, this.
5129. τούτῳ *too'-to;* dat. sing. masc. or neut. of 3778; to (*in, with* or *by*) *this* (pers. or thing):–here-[by, -in], him, one, the same, there[-in], this.
5130. τούτων *too'-tone;* gen. pl. masc. or neut. of 3778; *of* [*from* or *concerning*] *these* (persons or things):–such, their, these (things), they, this sort, those.
5131. τράγος *trag'-os;* from the base of *5176,* a *he-goat* (as a *gnawer*):–goat.
5132. τράπεζα *trap'-ed-zah;* prob. contr. from 5064 and 3979; a *table* or *stool* (as being *four-legged*), usually for food (fig. a *meal*); also a *counter* for money (fig. a broker's *office* for loans at interest):–bank, meat, table.
5133. τραπεζίτης *trap-ed-zee'-tace;* from *5132;* a money-*broker* or *banker:*–exchanger.
5134. τραῦμα *trŏw'-mah;* from the base of τιτρώσκω titrosko (to *wound;* akin to the base of *2352, 5147, 5149,* etc.); a *wound:*–wound.
5135. τραυματίζω *trŏw-mat-id'-zo;* from *5134;* to *inflict a wound:*–wound.
5136. τραχηλίζω *trakh-ay-lid'-zo;* from *5137;* to *seize* by *the throat* or *neck,* i.e. to *expose* the *gullet* of a victim for killing (gen. to *lay bare*):–opened.
5137. τράχηλος *trakh'-ay-los;* prob. from *5143* (through the idea of *mobility*); the *throat* (*neck*), i.e. (fig.) *life:*–neck.
5138. τραχύς *trakh-oos';* perh. streng. from the base of *4486* (as if *jagged* by rents); *uneven, rocky* (*reefy*):–rock, rough.
5139. Τραχωντις *trakh-o-nee'-tis;* from a der. of *5138; rough* district; *Trachonitis,* a region of Syria:–Trachonitis.
5140. τρεῖς *trice; neut.* τρία *tree'-ah;* a prim. (pl.) number; "*three*":–three.
5141. τρέμω *trem'-o;* streng. from a prim. τρέω trĕō (to "*dread*", "*terrify*"); to "*tremble*" or *fear:*–be afraid, trembling.
5142. τρέφω *tref'-o;* a prim. verb (prop. θρέφω thrĕphō; but perh. streng. from the base of *5157* through the idea of *convolution*); prop. to *stiffen,* i.e. *fatten* (by impl. to *cherish* [with food, etc.], *pamper, rear*):–bring up, feed, nourish.
5143. τρέχω *trekh'-o;* app. a prim. verb (prop. θρέχω thrĕchō comp. *2359*); which uses δρέμω *drem'-o* (the base of *1408*) as alt. in cert. tenses; to *run* or *walk hastily* (lit. or fig.):–have course, run.
5144. τριάκοντα *tree-ak'-on-tah;* the decade of *5140; thirty:*–thirty.
5145. τριακόσιοι *tree-ak-os'-ee-oy;* pl. from *5140* and *1540; three hundred:*–three hundred.
5146. τρίβολος *trib'-ol-os;* from *5140* and *956;* prop. a *crow-foot* (*three-pronged* obstruction in war), i.e. (by anal.) a *thorny* plant (*caltrop*):–brier, thistle.
5147. τρίβος *tree'-bos;* from τρίβω tribo (to "*rub*"; akin to τείρω tĕirō, τρύω truō and the base of *5131, 5134*); a *rut* or worn *track:*–path.
5148. τριετία *tree-et-ee'-ah;* from a com. of *5140* and *2094;* a *three years' period* (*triennium*):–space of three years.
5149. τρίζω *trid'-zo;* app. a prim. verb; to *creak* (*squeak*), i.e. (by anal.) to *grate* the teeth (in frenzy):–gnash.
5150. τρίμηνον *trim'-ay-non;* neut. of a com. of *5140* and *3376* as noun; a *three months'* space:–three months.
5151. τρίς *trece*; adv. from *5140; three times:*–three times, thrice.
5152.τρίστεγον *tris'-teg-on;* neut. of a com. of *5140* and *4721* as noun; a *third roof* (*story*):–third loft.
5153. τρισχίλιοι *tris-khil'-ee-oy;* from *5151* and *5507; three times a thousand:*–three thousand.
5154. τρίτος *tree'-tos;* ord. from *5140; third;* neut. (as noun) a *third part,* or (as adv.) a (or the) *third* time, *thirdly:*–third(-ly).
5155. τρίχινος *trikh'-ee-nos;* from *2359; hairy,* i.e. made *of hair* (*mohair*):–of hair.
5156. τρόμος *trom'-os;* from *5141;* a "*trembling*", i.e. quaking with *fear:*–+ tremble(-ing).
5157. τροπή *trop-ay';* from an app. prim. τρέπω trepo (to *turn*); a *turn* ("trope"), i.e. *revolution* (fig. *var.*):–turning.
5158. τρόπος *trop'-os;* from the same as *5157;* a *turn,* i.e. (by impl.) *mode* or *style* (esp. with prep. or rel. pref. as adv. *like*); fig. *deportment* or *character:*–(even) as, conversation, [+ like] manner, (+ by any) means, way.
5159. τροποφορέω *trop-of-or-eh'-o;* from *5158* and *5409;* to *endure* one's *habits:*–suffer the manners.
5160. τροφή *trof-ay';* from *5142; nourishment* (lit. or fig.); by impl. *rations* (*wages*):–food, meat.
5161. Τρόφιμος *trof'-ee-mos;* from *5160; nutritive; Trophimus,* a Chr.:–Trophimus.
5162. τροφός *trof-os';* from *5142;* a *nourisher,* i.e. *nurse:*–nurse.
5163. τροχιά *trokh-ee-ah';* from *5164;* a *track* (as a wheel-*rut*), i.e. (fig.) a *course* of conduct:–path.
5164.τροχός *trokh-os';* from *5143;* a *wheel* (as a *runner*), i.e. (fig.) a *circuit* of phys. effects:–course.
5165. τρύβλιον *troob'-lee-on;* neut. of a presumed der. of unc. affin.; a *bowl:*–dish.
5166. τρυγάω *troo-gah'-o;* from a der. of τρύγω trugo (to *dry*) mean. ripe *fruit* (as if *dry*); to *collect* the vintage:–gather.
5167.τρυγών *troo-gone';* from, *troo-gone'* from τρύζω truzo (to *murmur;* akin to *5149,*

but denoting a *duller* sound); a *turtle-dove* (as *cooing*):–turtle-dove.
5168. τρυμαλιά *troo-mal-ee-ah';* from a der. of τρύω truo (to *wear* away; akin to the base of *5134, 5147* and *5176*); an *orifice,* i.e. needle's *eye:*–eye. Comp. *5169.*
5169.τρύπημα *troo'-pay-mah;* from a der. of the base of *5168;* an *aperture,* i.e. a needle's *eye:*–eye.
5170. Τρύφαινα *troo'-fahee-nah;* from *5172; luxurious; Tryphoena,* a Chr. woman:–Tryphena.
5171. τρυφάω *troo-fah'-o;* from *5172;* to *indulge in luxury:*–live in pleasure.
5172. τρυφή *troo-fay';* from θρύπτω thrupto (to *break* up or [fig.] *enfeeble,* esp. the mind and body by indulgence); *effeminacy,* i.e. *luxury* or *debauchery:*–delicately, riot.
5173. Τρυφῶσα *troo-fo'-sah;* from *5172; luxuriating; Tryphosa,* a Chr. female:–Tryphosa.
5174.Τρωάς *tro-as';* from Τρος Tros (a *Trojan*); the *Troad* (or plain of Troy), i.e. *Troas*, a place in Asia Minor:–Troas.
5175. Τρωγύλλιον *tro-gool'-lee-on;* of unc. der.; *Trogyllium,* a place in Asia Minor:–Trogyllium.
5176. τρώγω *tro'-go;* prob. streng. from a coll. form of the base of *5134* and *5147* through the idea of *corrosion* or *wear;* or perh. rather of a base of *5167* and *5149* through the idea of a *craunching* sound; to *gnaw* or *chew,* i.e. (gen.) to *eat:*–eat.
5177.τυγχάνω *toong-khan'-o;* prob. for an obs. τύχω tucho (for which the mid. of another alt. τεύχω teucho (to *make ready* or *bring to pass*) is used in cert. tenses; akin to the base of *5088* through the idea of *effecting;* prop. to *affect;* or (spec.), to *hit* or *light upon* (as a mark to be reached), i.e. (trans.) to *attain* or *secure* an object or end, or (intrans.) to *happen* (as if *meeting* with); but in the latter appl. only impers. (with *1487*), i.e. *perchance;* or (pres. part.) as adj., *usual* (as if commonly *met with,* with *3756, extraordinary*), neut. (as adv.) *perh.;* or (with another verb) as adv. by *accident* (*as it were*):–be, chance, enjoy, little, obtain, X refresh...self, + spec. Comp. *5180.*
5178. τυμπανίζω *toom-pan-id'-zo;* from a der. of *5180* (mean. a *drum,* "*tympanum*"); to stretch on an instrument of *torture* resembling a drum, and thus *beat* to death:–torture.
5179. τύπος *too'-pos;* from *5180;* a *die* (as *struck*), i.e. (by impl.) a *stamp* or *scar;* by anal. a *shape,* i.e. a *statue,* (fig.) *style* or *resemblance;* spec. a *sampler* ("*type*"), i.e. a *model* (for imitation) or *instance* (for warning):–en-(ex-)ample, fashion, figure, form, manner, pattern, print.
5180. τύπτω *toop'-to;* a prim. verb (in a streng. form); to "*thump*", i.e. *cudgel* or *pummel* (prop. with a stick or *bastinado*), but in any case by *repeated* blows; thus differing from *3817* and *3960,* which denote a [usually single] blow with the hand or any instrument, or 4141 with the *fist* [or a *hammer*], or *4474* with the *palm;* as well as from *5177,* an *accidental* collision); by impl. to *punish;* fig. to *offend* (the conscience):–beat, smite, strike, wound.
5181. Τύραννος *too'-ran-nos;* a provincial form of the der. of the base of *2962;* a "*tyrant*"; *Tyrannus,* an Ephesian:–Tyrannus.
5182. τυρβάζω *toor-bad'-zo;* from τύρβη turbe (Lat. *turba,* a *crowd;* akin to *2351*); to *make* "*turbid*", i.e. *disturb:*–trouble.
5183. Τύριος *too'-ree-os;* from *5184;* a *Tyrian,* i.e. inh. of Tyrus:–of Tyre.
5184. Τύρος *too'-ros;* of Heb. or. [6865]: *Tyrus* (i.e. *Tsor*), a place in Pal.:–Tyre.
5185. τυφλός *toof-los';* from, *5187; opaque* (as if *smoky*), i.e. (by anal.) *blind* (phys. or ment.):–blind.
5186. τυφλόω *toof-lo'-o;* from *5185;* to *make blind,* i.e. (fig.) to *obscure:*–blind.
5187. τυφόω *toof-o'-o;* from a der. of *5188;* to envelop with *smoke,* i.e. (fig.) to *inflate* with self-conceit:–high-minded, be lifted up with pride, be proud.
5188. τυφώ *too'-fo;* app. a prim. verb; to make a *smoke,* i.e. slowly *consume* without flame:–smoke.
5189. τυφωνικός *too-fo-nee-kos*'; from a der. of *5188; stormy* (as if *smoky*):–tempestuous.
5190. Τυχικός *too-khee-kos';* from a der. of *5177; fortuitous,* i.e. *fortunate; Tychicus,* a Chr.:–Tychicus.

Y

5191. ὑακίνθινος *hoo-ak-in'-thee-nos;* from *5192;* "*hyacinthine*" or "*jacinthine*", i.e. deep *blue:*–jacinth.
5192. ὑάκινθος *hoo-ak'-in-thos;* of unc. der.; the "*hyacinth*" or "*jacinth*", i.e. some gem of a deep *blue* color, prob. the *zirkon:*– jacinth.
5193. ὑάλινος *hoo-al'-ee-nos;* from *5194; glassy,* i.e. *transparent:*–of glass.
5194. ὕαλος *hoo'-al-os;* perh. from the same as *5205* (as being transparent like *rain*); *glass:*–glass.
5195. ὑβρίζω *hoo-brid'-zo;* from *5196;* to *exercise violence,* i.e. *abuse:*–use despitefully, reproach, entreat shamefully (spitefully).
5196. ὕβρις *hoo'-bris;* from *5228; insolence* (as *over*-bearing), i.e. *insult, injury:*–harm, hurt, reproach.
5197. ὑβριστής *hoo-bris-tace'* from *5195;* an *insulter,* i.e. *maltreater:*–despiteful, injurious.
5198. ὑγιαίνω *hoog-ee-ah'-ee-no* from *5199;* to *have* sound *health,* i.e. *be well* (in body); fig. to be *uncorrupt* (*true* in doctrine):–be in health, (be safe and) sound, (be) whole(-some).
5199. ὑγιής *hoog-ee-ace';* from the base of *837; healthy,* i.e. *well* (in body); fig. *true* (in doctrine):–sound, whole.
5200. ὑγρός *hoo-gros';* from the base of *5205; wet* (as if with *rain*), i.e. (by impl.) *sappy* (*fresh*):–green.
5201. ὑδριά *hoo-dree-ah';* from *5204;* a *water-jar,* i.e. receptacle for family supply:–water-pot.
5202. ὑδροποτέω *hoo-drop-ot-eh'-o;* from a com. of 5204 and a der. of *4095;* to *be* a *water-drinker,* i.e. to *abstain from vinous beverages:*–drink water.
5203. ὑδρωπικός *hoo-dro-pik-os';* from a com. of 5204 and a der. of *3700* (as if *looking watery*); to *be* "*dropsical*":–have the dropsy.
5204. ὕδωρ *hoo'-dore; gen.* ὕδατος hudatos, from the base of *5205; water* (as if *rainy*) lit. or fig.:–water.
5205. ὑετός *hoo-et-os';* from a prim. ὕω huo (to *rain*); *rain,* esp. a *shower:*–rain.
5206. υἱοθεσία *hwee-oth-es-ee'-ah;* from a presumed com. of *5207* and a der. of *5087;* the *placing* as a *son,* i.e. *adoption* (fig. Chr. *sonship* in respect to God):–adoption (of children, of sons).
5207. υἱός *hwee-os';* app. a prim. word; a "*son*" (sometimes of animals), used very widely of immed., remote or fig. kinship:–child, foal, son.
5208. ὕλη *hoo-lay';* perh. akin to *3586;* a *forest,* i.e. (by impl.) *fuel:*–matter.
5209. ὑμᾶς *hoo-mas';* acc. of *5210; you* (as the obj. of a verb or prep.):–ye, you (+ -ward), your (+ own).
5210. ὑμεῖς *hoo-mice';* irreg. pl. of *4771; you* (as subj. of verb):–ye (yourselves), you.
5211. Ὑμεναῖος *hoo-men-ah'-yos;* from Ὑμήν Humen (the god of *weddings*); "*hymeneal*"; *Hymeneus,* an opponent of Christianity:–Hymenaeus.
5212. ὑμέτερος *hoo-met'-er-os;* from *5210; yours,* i.e. *pertaining to you:*–your (own).
5213. ὑμῖν *hoo-min';* irreg. dat. of *5210;* to (*with* or *by*) *you:*–ye, you, your(-selves).
5214. ὑμνέω *hoom-neh'-o;* from *5215;* to *hymn,* i.e. sing a relig. ode; by impl. to *celebrate* (God) in song:–sing a hymn (praise unto).
5215. ὕμνος *hoom'-nos;* app. from a simpler (obs.) form of ὕδέω hudeo (to *celebrate;* prob. akin to 103; comp. *5667*); a "*hymn*" or relig. ode (one of the Psalms):–hymn.
5216. ὑμῶν *hoo-mone';* gen. case of 5210; *of* (*from* or *concerning*) *you:*–ye, you, your (own, -selves).
5217. ὑπάγω *hoop-ag'-o;* from *5259* and *71;* to *lead* (oneself) *under,* i.e. *withdraw* or *retire* (as if *sinking* out of sight), lit. or fig.:–depart, get hence, go (a-)way.
5218. ὑπακοή *hoop-ak-o-ay';* from *5219; attentive hearkening,* i.e. (by impl.) *compliance* or *submission:*–obedience, (make) obedient, obey(-ing).
5219. ὑπακούω *hoop-ak-oo'-o;* from *5259* and *191;* to *hear under* (as a *subordinate*), i.e. to *listen attentively;* by impl. to *heed* or *conform* to a command or authority:–hearken, be obedient to, obey.
5220.ὕπανδρος *hoop'-an-dros;* from *5259* and *435;* in subjection *under* a *man,* i.e. a *married* woman:–which hath an husband.
5221. ὑπαντάω *hoop-an-tah'-o;* from *5259* and a der. of *473;* to *go opposite* (*meet*) *under* (*quietly*), i.e. to *encounter, fall in with:*–(go to) meet.
5222. ὑπάντησις *hoop-an'-tay-sis;* from *5221;* an *encounter* or *concurrence* (with *1519* for inf., in order to *fall in with*):–meeting.

GREEK

5223. ὕπαρξις *hoop'-arx-is;* from *5225; existency* or *proprietorship,* i.e. (concr.) *property, wealth:*–goods, substance.
5224. ὑπάρχοντα *hoop-ar'-khon-tah;* neut. pl. of pres. part. act. of *5225* as noun; things *extant* or *in hand,* i.e. *property* or *possessions:*–goods, that which one has, things which (one) possesseth, substance, that hast.
5225. ὑπάρχω *hoop-ar'-kho;* from *5259* and *756; to begin under* (*quietly*), i.e. *come into existence* (*be present* or *at hand*); expletively, to *exist* (as copula or subordinate to an adj., part., adv. or prep., or as an auxiliary to a principal (verb):–after, behave, live.
5226. ὑπείκω *hoop-i'-ko;* from *5259* and εἴκω eiko (to *yield,* be *"weak"*); to *surrender:*–submit self.
5227. ὑπεναντίος *hoop-en-an-tee'-os;* from *5259* and *1727; under* (*covertly*) *contrary* to, i.e. *opposed* or (as noun) an *opponent:*–adversary, against.
5228. ὑπέρ *hoop-er';* a prim. prep.; *"over"*, i.e. (with the gen. case) of place, *above, beyond, across,* or causal, *for* the sake of, *instead, regarding;* with the acc. *superior to,* more *than:*–(+ exceeding, abundantly) above, in (on) behalf of, beyond, by, + very chiefest, concerning, exceeding (above, -ly), for, + very highly, more (than), of, over, on the part of, for sake of, in stead, than, to(-ward), very. In compo., it retains many of the above appl.
5229. ὑπεραίρομαι *hoop-er-ah'-ee-rom-ahee;* mid. from *5228* and *142;* to *raise* oneself *over,* i.e. (fig.) to *become haughty:*–exalt self, be exalted above measure.
5230. ὑπέρακμος *hoop-er'-ak-mos;* from *5228* and the base of *188; beyond* the *"acme"*, i.e. fig. (of a daughter) *past* the *bloom* (*prime*) of youth:–+ pass the flower of (her) age.
5231. ὑπεράνω *hoop-er-an'-o;* from *5228* and *507; above upward,* i.e. *greatly higher* (in place or rank):–far above, over.
5232. ὑπεραυξάνω *hoop-er-owx-an'-o;* from *5228* and *837;* to *increase above* ordinary degree:–grow exceedingly.
5233. ὑπερβαίνω *hoop-er-bah'-ee-no;* from *5228* and the base of *939;* to *transcend,* i.e. (fig.) to *overreach:*–go beyond.
5234. ὑπερβαλλόντως *hoop-er-bal-lon'-toce;* adv. from pres. part. act. of *5235; excessively:*–beyond measure.
5235. ὑπερβάλλω *hoop-er-bal'-lo;* from *5228* and *906;* to *throw beyond* the usual mark, i.e. (fig.) to *surpass* (only act. part. *supereminent*):–exceeding, excel, pass.
5236. ὑπερβολή *hoop-er-bol-ay';* from *5235;* a *throwing beyond* others, i.e. (fig.) *supereminence;* adv. (with 1519 or 2596) *pre-eminently:*–abundance, (far more) exceeding, excellency, more excellent, beyond (out of) measure.
5237. υπερείδω *hoop-er-i'-do;* from *5228* and *1492;* to *overlook,* i.e. *not punish:*–wink at.
5238. ὑπερέκεινα *hoop-er-ek'-i-nah;* from *5228* and the neut. pl. of *1565; above those* parts, i.e. *still farther:*–beyond.
5239. ὑπερεκτείνω *hoop-er-ek-ti'-no;* from *5228* and *1614;* to *extend inordinately:*–stretch beyond.
5240. ὑπερεκχύνω *hoop-er-ek-khoo'-no;* from 5228 and the alt. form of 1632; to *pour out over,* i.e. pass. to *overflow:*–run over.
5241. ὑπερεντυγχάνω *hoop-er-en-toong-khan'-o;* from *5228* and *1793;* to intercede *in behalf of:*–make intercession for
5242. ὑπερέχω *hoop-er-ekh'-o;* from *5228* and *2192;* to *hold oneself above,* i.e. (fig.) to *excel*; part. (as adj., or neut. as noun) *superior, superiority:*–better, excellency, higher, pass, supreme.
5243. ὑπερηφανία *hoop-er-ay-fan-ee'-ah;* from *5244; haughtiness:*–pride.
5244. ὑπερήφανος *hoop-er-ay'-fan-os;* from *5228* and *5316; appearing above* others (*conspicuous*), i.e. (fig.) *haughty:*–proud.
5245. ὑπερνικάω *hoop-er-nik-ah'-o;* from 5228 and 3528; to *vanquish beyond,* i.e. *gain* a decisive *victory:*–more than conquer.
5246. ὑπέρογκος *hoop-er'-ong-kos;* from *5228* and *3591; bulging over,* i.e. (fig.) *insolent:*–great swelling.
5247. ὑπεροχή *hoop-er-okh-ay';* from *5242; prominence,* i.e. (fig.) *superiority* (in rank or character):–authority, excellency.
5248. ὑπερπερισσεύω *hoop-er-per-is-syoo'-o;* from *5228* and *4052;* to *superabound:*–abound much more, exceeding.
5249. ὑπερπερισσῶς *hoop-er-per-is-soce';* from *5228* and *4057; superabundantly,* i.e. *exceedingly:*–beyond measure.
5250. ὑπερπλεονάζω *hoop-er-pleh-on-ad'-zo;* from *5228* and *4121;* to *superabound:*–be exceeding abundant.
5251. ὑπερυψόω *hoop-er-oop-so'-o;* from *5228* and *5312;* to *elevate above* others, i.e. *raise* to the *highest* position:–highly exalt.
5252. ὑπερφρονέω *hoop-er-fron-eh'-o;* from *5228* and *5426;* to *esteem* oneself *overmuch,* i.e. *be vain* or *arrogant:*–think more highly.
5253. ὑπερῷον *hoop-er-o'-on;* neut. of a der. of *5228;* a *higher* part of the house, i.e. apartment in the *third story:*–upper chamber (room).
5254. ὑπέχω *hoop-ekh'-o;* from *5259* and *2192;* to *hold* oneself *under,* i.e. *endure* with patience:–suffer.
5255. ὑπήκοος *hoop-ay'-ko-os;* from *5219; attentively listening,* i.e. (by impl.) *submissive:*–obedient.
5256. ὑπηρετέω *hoop-ay-ret-eh'-o;* from *5257;* to *be a subordinate,* i.e. (by impl.) *subserve:*–minister (unto), serve.
5257. ὑπηρέτης *hoop-ay-ret'-ace;* from *5259* and a der. of ἐρέσσω eresso (to *row*); an *under-oarsman,* i.e. (gen.) *subordinate* (*assistant, sexton, constable*):–minister, officer, servant.
5258. ὕπνος *hoop'-nos;* from an obs. prim. (perh. akin to *5259* through the idea of *subsilience*); *sleep,* i.e. (fig.) spir. *torpor:*–sleep.
5259. ὑπό *hoop-o';* a prim. prep.; *under,* i.e. (with the gen. case) of place (*beneath*), or with verbs (the agency or means, *through*); (with the acc.) of place (whither [*underneath*] or where [below]) or time (when [*at*]):–among, by, from, in, of, under, with. In compo., it retains the same gen. appl., esp. of *inferior* position or condition, and spec. *covertly* or *moderately.*
5260. ὑποβάλλω *hoop-ob-al'-lo;* from *5259* and *906;* to *throw* in *stealthily,* i.e. *introduce* by collusion:–suborn.
5261. ὑπογραμμός *hoop-og-ram-mos';* from a com. of *5259* and *1125;* an *underwriting,* i.e. *copy* for imitation (fig.):–example.
5262. ὑπόδειγμα *hoop-od'-igue-mah;* from *5263;* an *exhibit* for imitation or warning (fig. *specimen, adumbration*):–en-(ex-)ample, pattern.
5263. ὑποδείκνυμι *hoop-od-ike'-noo-mee;* from *5259* and *1166;* to *exhibit under* the eyes, i.e. (fig.) to *exemplify* (*instruct, admonish*):–show, (fore-) warn.
5264. ὑποδέχομαι *hoop-od-ekh'-om-ahee;* from *5259* and *1209;* to *admit under* one's roof, i.e. *entertain* hospitably:–receive.
5265. ὑποδέω *hoop-od-eh'-o;* from *5259* and *1210;* to *bind under* one's feet, i.e. *put on* shoes or sandals:–bind on, (be) shod.
5266. ὑπόδημα *hoop-od'-ay-mah;* from *5265;* something *bound under* the feet, i.e. a *shoe* or *sandal:*–shoe.
5267. ὑπόδικος *hoop-od'-ee-kos;* from 5259 and *1349; under sentence,* i.e. (by impl.) *condemned:*–guilty.
5268. ὑποζύγιον *hoop-od-zoog'-ee-on;* neut. of a com. of *5259* and *2218;* an animal *under* the *yoke* (*draught-beast*), i.e. (spec.), a *donkey:*–ass.
5269. ὑποζώννυμι *hoop-od-zone'-noo-mee;* from *5259* and *2224;* to *gird under,* i.e. *frap* (a vessel with cables across the keel, sides and deck):–undergirt.
5270. ὑποκάτω *hoop-ok-at'-o;* from *5259* and *2736; down under,* i.e. *beneath:*–under.
5271. ὑποκρίνομαι *hoop-ok-rin'-om-ahee;* mid. from *5259* and *2919;* to *decide* (*speak* or *act*) *under* a false part, i.e. (fig.) *dissemble* (*pretend*):–feign.
5272. ὑπόκρισις *hoop-ok'-ree-sis;* from *5271; acting under* a feigned part, i.e. (fig.) *deceit* ("*hypocrisy*"):–condemnation, dissimulation, hypocrisy.
5273. ὑποκριτής *hoop-ok-ree-tace';* from *5271;* an *actor under* an assumed character (*stage-player*), i.e. (fig.) a *dissembler* ("*hypocrite*":–hypocrite.
5274. ὑπολαμβάνω *hoop-ol-am-ban'-o;* from *5259* and *2983;* to *take* from *below,* i.e. *carry upward;* fig. to *take up,* i.e. *continue* a discourse or topic; ment., to *assume* (*presume*):–answer, receive, suppose.
5275. ὑπολείπω *hoop-ol-i'-po;* from *5295* and *3007;* to *leave under* (*behind*), i.e. (pass.) to *remain* (*survive*):–be left.
5276. ὑπολήνιον *hoop-ol-ay'-nee-on;* neut. of a presumed com. of *5259* and *3025;* vessel or receptacle *under* the *press,* i.e. lower *wine-vat:*–winefat.
5277. ὑπολιμπάνω *hoop-ol-im-pan'-o;* a

prol. form for *5275;* to *leave behind,* i.e. *bequeath:*–leave.
5278. ὑπομένω *hoop-om-en'-o;* from *5259* and *3306;* to *stay under* (*behind*), i.e. *remain;* fig. to *undergo,* i.e. *bear* (trials), *have fortitude, persevere:*–abide, endure, (take) patient(-ly), suffer, tarry behind.
5279. ὑπομιμνήσκω *hoop-om-im-nace'-ko;* from *5259* and *3403;* to *remind quietly,* i.e. *suggest* to the (mid., one's own) memory:–put in mind, remember, bring to (put in) remembrance.
5280. ὑπόμνησις *hoop-om'-nay-sis;* from *5279;* a *reminding* or (refl.) *recollection:*–remembrance.
5281. ὑπομονή *hoop-om-on-ay';* from *5278;* cheerful (or hopeful) *endurance, constancy:*–enduring, patience, patient continuance (waiting).
5282. ὑπονοέω *hoop-on-o-eh'-o;* from *5259* and *3539;* to *think under* (*privately*), i.e. to *surmise* or *conjecture:*–think, suppose, deem.
5283. ὑπόνοια *hoop-on'-oy-ah;* from *5282; suspicion:*–surmising.
5284. ὑποπλέω *hoop-op-leh'-o;* from *5259* and *4126;* to *sail under* the lee of:–sail under.
5285. ὑποπλέω *hoop-op-neh'-o;* from *5259* and *4154;* to *breathe gently,* i.e. *breeze:*–blow softly.
5286. ὑποπόδιον *hoop-op-od'-ee-on;* neut. of a com. of *5259* and *4228;* something *under* the *feet,* i.e. a *foot-rest (fig.):*–footstool
5287. ὑπόστασις *hoop-os'-tas-is;* from a com. of *5259* and *2476;* a *setting under* (*support*), i.e. (fig.) concr. *essence,* or abstr., *assurance* (obj. or subj.):–confidence, confident, pers., substance.
5288. ὑποστέλλω *hoop-os-tel'-lo;* from *5259* and *4724;* to *withhold under* (*out of sight*), i.e. (refl.) to *cower* or *shrink,* (fig.) to *conceal* (*reserve*):–draw (keep) back, shun, withdraw.
5289. ὑποστολή *hoop-os-tol-ay';* from *5288; shrinkage* (*timidity*), i.e. (by impl.) *apostasy:*–draw back.
5290. ὑποστρέφω *hoop-os-tref'-o;* from *5259* and *4762;* to *turn under* (*behind*), i.e. to *return* (lit. or fig.):–come again, return (again, back again), turn back (again).
5291. ὑποστρώννυμι *hoop-os-trone'-noo-mee;* from *5259* and *4766;* to *strew underneath* (the feet as a carpet):–spread.
5292. ὑποταγή *hoop-ot-ag-ay';* from *5293; subordination:*–subjection.
5293. ὑποτάσσω *hoop-ot-as'-so;* from *5259* and *5021;* to *subordinate;* refl. to *obey:*–be under obedience (obedient), put under, subdue unto, (be, make) subject (to, unto), be (put) in subjection (to, under), submit self unto.
5294. ὑποτίθημι *hoop-ot-ith'-ay-mee;* from *5259* and *5087;* to *place underneath,* i.e. (fig.) to *hazard,* (refl.) to *suggest:*–lay down, put in remembrance.
5295. ὑποτρέχω *hoop-ot-rekh'-o;* from *5259* and *5143* (incl. its alt.); to *run under,* i.e. (spec.), to *sail past:*–run under.
5296. ὑποτύπωσις *hoop-ot-oop'-o-sis;* from a com. of *5259* and a der. of *5179; typification under* (*after*), i.e. (concr.) a *sketch* (fig.) for imitation:–form, pattern.
5297. ὑποφέρω *hoop-of-er'-o;* from *5259* and *5342;* to *bear* from *underneath,* i.e. (fig.) to *undergo* hardship:–bear, endure.
5298. ὑποχωρέω *hoop-okh-o-reh'-o;* from *5259* and *5562;* to *vacate down,* i.e. *retire* quietly:–go aside, withdraw self.
5299. ὑπωπιάζω *hoop-o-pee-ad'-zo;* from a com. of *5259* and a der. of *3700;* to hit *under* the *eye* (*buffet* or *disable* an antagonist as a pugilist), i.e. (fig.) to *tease* or *annoy* (into compliance), *subdue* (one's passions):–keep under, weary.
5300. ὗς *hoos;* app. a prim. word; a *hog* ("*swine*"):–sow.
5301. ὕσσωπος *hoos'-so-pos;* of for. or. [*231*]; "*hyssop*":–hyssop.
5302. ὑστερέω *hoos-ter-eh'-o;* from 5306; to *be later*, i.e. (by impl.) to be *inferior*; gen. to *fall short* (*be deficient*):–come behind (short), be destitute, fail, lack, suffer need, (be in) want, be the worse.
5303. ὑστέρημα *hoos-ter'-ay-mah;* from 5302; a *deficit*; spec. *poverty:*–that which is behind, (that which was) lack(-ing), penury, want.
5304. ὑστέρησις *hoos-ter'-ay-sis;* a *falling short,* i.e. (spec.), *penury:*–want.
5305. ὕστερον *hoos'-ter-on;* neut. of *5306* as adv.; *more lately*, i.e. *eventually:*–afterward, (at the) last (of all).
5306. ὕστερος *hoos'-ter-os;* comp. from 5259 (in the sense of *behind*); *later:*–latter.
5307. ὑφαντός *hoo-fan-tos';* from ὑφαίνω huphaino to *weave*; *woven*, i.e. (perh.) *knitted:*–woven.
5308. ὑψηλός *hoop-say-los';* from 5311; *lofty* (in place or character):–high(-er, -ly) (esteemed).
5309. ὑψηλοφρονέω *hoop-say-lo-fron-eh'-o;* from a com. of 5308 and 5424; to be *lofty* in mind, i.e. arrogant:–be highminded.
5310. ὕψιστος *hoop'-sis-tos;* superl. from the base of 5311; *highest*, i.e. (masc. sing.) the *Supreme* (God), or (neut. pl.) the *heavens:*–most high, highest.
5311. ὕψος *hoop'-sos;* from a der. of 5228; *elevation*, i.e. (abstr.) *altitude*, (spec.), the *sky*, or (fig.) *dignity:*–be exalted, height, (on) high.
5312. ὑψόω *hoop-so'-o;* from 5311; to *elevate* (lit. or fig.):–exalt, lift up.
5313. ὕψωμα *hoop'-so-mah;* from 5312; an *elevated* place or thing, i.e. (abstr.) *altitude*, or (by impl.) a *barrier* (fig.):– height, high thing.

Φ

5314. φάγος *fag'-os;* from 5315; a *glutton:*–gluttonous.
5315. φάγω *fag'-o;* a prim. verb (used as an alt. of *2068* in cert. tenses); to *eat* (lit. or fig.):–eat, meat.
5316. φαίνω *fah'-ee-no;* prol. for the base of *5457;* to *lighten* (*shine*), i.e. *show* (trans. or intr., lit. or fig.):– appear, seem, be seen, shine, X think.
5317. Φάλεκ *fal'-ek;* of Heb. or. [6389]; *Phalek* (i.e. *Peleg*), a patriarch:–Phalec.
5318. φανερός *fan-er-os';* from *5316; shining,* i.e. *apparent* (lit. or fig.); neut. (as adv.) *publicly, externally:*–abroad, + appear, known, manifest, open [+ -ly], outward [+ -ly].
5319. φανερόω *fan-er-o'-o;* from *5318;* to *render apparent* (lit. or fig.):–appear, manifestly declare, (make) manifest (forth), shew (self).
5320. φανερῶς *fan-er-oce';* adv. from *5318; plainly,* i.e. *clearly* or *publicly:*–evidently, openly.
5321. φανέρωσις *fan-er'-o-sis;* from *5319; exhibition,* i.e. (fig.) *expression,* (by ext.) a *bestowment:*–manifestation.
5322. φανός *fan-os';* from *5316;* a *lightener,* i.e. *light; lantern:*–lantern.
5323. Φανουήλ *fan-oo-ale';* of Heb. or. [6439]; *Phanuël* (i.e. *Penuël*), an Isr.:–Phanuel.
5324. φαντάζω *fan-tad'-zo;* from a der. of *5316;* to *make apparent,* i.e. pass. to *appear* (neut. part. as noun, a *spectacle*):–sight.
5325. φαντασία *fan-tas-ee'-ah;* from a der. of *5324;* (prop. abstr.) a (vain) *show* ("fantasy"):–pomp.
5326. φάντασμα *fan'-tas-mah;* from *5324;* (prop. concr.) a (mere) *show* ("phantasm"), i.e. *spectre:*–spirit.
5327. φάραγξ *far'-anx;* prop. streng. from the base of *4008* or rather of *4486;* a *gap* or *chasm,* i.e. *ravine* (*winter-torrent*):–valley.
5328. Φαραώ *far-ah-o';* of for. or. [6547]; *Pharaö* (i.e. *Pharoh*), an Eg. king:–Pharaoh.
5329. Φαρές *far-es';* of Heb. or. [6557]; *Phares* (i.e. *Perets*), an Isr.:–Phares.
5330. Φαρισαῖος *far-is-ah'-yos;* of Heb. or. [comp. 6567]; a *separatist,* i.e. exclusively *religious;* a *Pharisean,* i.e. Jewish sectary:–Pharisee.
5331. φαρμακεία *far-mak-i'-ah;* from *5332; medication* ("pharmacy"), i.e. (by ext.) *magic* (lit. or fig.):–sorcery, witchcraft.
5332. φαρμακεύς *far-mak-yoos';* from φάρμακον *pharmakon* (a *drug,* i.e. spell-giving *potion*); a *druggist* ("pharmacist") or *poisoner,* i.e. (by ext.) a *magician:*–sorcerer.
5333. φαρμακός *far-mak-os';* the same as *5332:*–sorcerer.
5334. φάσις *fas'-is;* from *5346* (not the same as "phase", which is from *5316*); a *saying,* i.e. *report:*–tidings.
5335. φάσκω *fas'-ko;* prol. from the same as *5346;* to *assert:*–affirm, profess, say.
5336. φάτνη *fat'-nay;* from πατέομαι pateomai (to *eat*); a *crib* (for fodder):–manager, stall.
5337. φαῦλος *fow'-los;* app. a prim. word; "*foul*" or "*flawy*", i.e. (fig.) *wicked:*–evil.
5338. φέγγος *feng'-gos;* prob. akin to the base of *5457* [comp. *5350*]; *brilliancy:*–light.
5339. φείδομαι *fi'-dom-ahee;* of unc. affin.; to *be chary* of, i.e. (subj.) to *abstain* or (obj.) to *treat leniently:*–forbear, spare.
5340. φειδομένως *fi-dom-en'-oce;* adv. from part. of *5339; abstemiously,* i.e.

GREEK

stingily:–sparingly.
5341. φελόνης *fel-on'-ace;* by transp. for a der. prob. of *5316* (as *showing* outside the other garments); a *mantle* (*surtout*):– cloke.
5342. φέρω *fer'-o;* a prim. verb (for which other and app. not cognate ones are used in cert. tenses only; namely οἴω *oy'-o* and ἐνέγκω *en-eng'-ko*) a prim. verb--for which other, and app. not cognate ones are used in cert. tenses only; namely, oio oy'-o; and enegko en-eng'-ko to "*bear*" or *carry* (in a very wide appl., lit. and fig. as follows):–be, bear, bring (forth), carry, come, + let her drive, be driven, endure, go on, lay, lead, move, reach, rushing, uphold.
5343. φεύγω *fyoo'-go;* app. a prim. verb; to *run away* (lit. or fig.); by impl. to *shun;* by anal. to *vanish:*–escape, flee (away).
5344. Φῆλιξ *fay'-lix;* of Lat. or.; *happy; Phelix* (i.e. *Felix*), a Rom.:–Felix.
5345. φήμη *fay'-may;* from *5346;* a *saying,* i.e. *rumor* ("fame"):–fame.
5346. φημί *fay-mee';* prop. the same as the base of 5457 and 5316; to *show* or *make known* one's thoughts, i.e. *speak* or *say:*– affirm, say. Comp. *3004*.
5347. Φῆστος *face'-tos;* of Lat. der.; *festal; Phestus* (i.e. *Festus*), a Rom.:–Festus.
5348. φθάνω *fthan'-o;* app. a prim. verb; to *be beforehand,* i.e. *anticipate* or *precede;* by ext., to *have arrived* at:–(already) attain, come, prevent.
5349. φθαρτός *fthar-tos';* from *5351; decayed,* i.e. (by impl.) *perishable:*–corruptible.
5350. φθέγγομαι *ftheng'-gom-ahee;* prob. akin to *5338* and thus to *5346;* to *utter* a clear sound, i.e. (gen.) to *proclaim:*–speak.
5351.φθείρω *fthi'-ro;* prob. streng. from φθίω phthio (to *pine* or *waste*); prop. to *shrivel* or *wither,* i.e. to *spoil* (by any process) or (gen.) to *ruin* (esp. fig. by mor. influences, to *deprave*):–corrupt (self), defile, destroy.
5352. φθινοπωριός *fthin-op-o-ree-nos';* from der. of φθίνω phthino (to *wane;* akin to the base of *5351*) and *3703* (mean. *late autumn*); *autumnal* (as *stripped* of leaves):– whose fruit withereth.
5353. φθόγγος *ftong'-gos;* from *5350; utterance,* i.e. a *mus.* note (vocal or instrumental):–sound.
5354. φθονέω *fthon-eh'-o;* from *5355;* to *be jealous* of:–envy.
5355. φθόνος *fthon'-os;* prob. akin to the base of *5351; ill-will* (as *detraction*), i.e. *jealousy* (*spite*):–envy.
5356. φθορά *fthor-ah';* from *5351; decay,* i.e. *ruin* (spontaneous or inflicted, lit. or fig.):–corruption, destroy, perish.
5357. φιάλη *fee-al'-ay;* of unc. affin.; a broad shallow *cup* ("phial"):–vial.
5358. φιλάγαθος *fil-ag'-ath-os;* from *5384* and *18; fond to good,* i.e. a *promoter of virtue:*–love of good men.
5359. Φιλαδέλφεια *fil-ad-el'-fee-ah;* from Φιλάδελφος Philadelphos (the same as *5361*), a king of Pergamos; *Philadelphia,* a place in Asia Minor:–Philadelphia.
5360.φιλαδελφία *fil-ad-el-fee'-ah;* from *5361; fraternal affection:*–brotherly love (kindness), love of the brethren.
5361. φιλάδελφος *fil-ad'-el-fos;* from *5384* and *80; fond of brethren,* i.e. *fraternal:*– love as brethren.
5362. φίλανδρος *fil'-an-dros;* from *5384* and *435; fond of man,* i.e. *affectionate* as a wife:–love their husbands.
5363. φιλανθρωπία *fil-an-thro-pee'-ah;* from the same as *5364; fondness of mankind,* i.e. *benevolence* ("*philanthropy*"):– kindness, love towards man.
5364. φιλανθρώπως *fil-an-thro'-poce;* adv. from a com. of *5384* and *444; fondly to man* ("philanthropically"), i.e. *humanely:*–courteously.
5365. φιλαργυρία *fil-ar-goo-ree'-ah;* from *5366; avarice:*–love of money.
5366. φιλάργυρος *fil-ar'-goo-ros;* from *5384* and *696; fond of silver* (*money*), i.e. *avaricious:*–covetous.
5367. φίλαυτος *fil'-ow-tos;* from *5384* and *846; fond of self,* i.e. *selfish:*–lover of own self.
5368. φιλέω *fil-eh'-o;* from 5384; to *be a friend to* (*fond* of [an indiv. or an object]), i.e. *have affection* for (denoting *personal* attachment, as a matter of sentiment or feeling; while *25* is wider, embracing esp. the judgment and the *deliberate* assent of the will as a matter of principle, duty and propriety: the two thus stand related very much as *2309* and *1014*, or as *2372* and *3563* respectively; the former being chiefly of the *heart* and the latter of the *head*); spec. to *kiss* (as a mark of tenderness):–kiss, love.
5369. φιλήδονος *fil-ay'-don-os;* from *5384* and *2237; fond of pleasure,* i.e. *voluptuous:*–lover of pleasure.
5370. φίλημα *fil'-ay-mah;* from 5368; a *kiss:*–kiss.
5371. Φιλήμων *fil-ay'-mone;* from *5368; friendly; Philemon,* a Chr.:–Philemon.
5372. Φιλητός *fil-ay-tos';* from *5368; amiable; Philetus,* an opposer of Christianity:–Philetus.
5373. φιλία *fil-ee'-ah;* from *5384; fondness:*–friendship.
5374. Φιλιππήσιος *fil-ip-pay'-see-os;* from *5375;* a *Philippesian* (*Philippian*), i.e. native of Philippi:–Philippian.
5375. Φίλιπποι *fil'-ip-poy;* pl. of *5376; Philippi,* a place in Macedonia:–Philippi.
5376. Φίλιππος *fil'-ip-pos;* from *5384* and *2462; fond of horses; Philippus,* the name of four Isr.:–Philip.
5377. φιλόθεος *fil-oth'-eh-os;* from *5384* and *2316; fond of God,* i.e. *pious:*–lover of God.
5378. Φιλόλογος *fil-ol'-og-os;* from *5384* and *3056; fond of words,* i.e. *talkative* (*argumentative, learned,* "*philological*"); *Philologus,* a Chr.:–Philologus.
5379. φιλονεικία *fil-on-i-kee'-ah;* from *5380; quarrelsomeness,* i.e. a *dispute:*–strife.
5380. φιλόνεικος *fil-on'-i-kos;* from *5384 and* νεῖκος, *neikos* (a *quarrel;* prob. akin to *3534*); *fond of strife,* i.e. *disputatious:*–contentious.
5381. φιλονεξία *fil-ox-en-ee'-ah;* from *5382; hospitableness:*–entertain strangers, hospitality.
5382. φιλόξενος *fil-ox'-en-os;* from *5384* and *3581; fond of guests,* i.e. *hospitable:*– given to (lover of, use) hospitality.
5383. φιλοπρωτεύω *fil-op-rote-yoo'-o;* from a com. of *5384* and *4413;* to *be fond of being first,* i.e. *ambitious* of distinction:–love to have the preeminence.
5384. φίλος *fee'-los;* prop. *dear,* i.e. a *friend;* act., *fond,* i.e. *friendly* (still as a noun, an *associate, neighbor,* etc.):–friend.
5385. φιλοσοφία *fil-os-of-ee'-ah;* from *5386;* "*philosophy*", i.e. (spec.), Jewish *sophistry:*–philosophy.
5386. φιλόσοφος *fil-os'-of-os;* from *5384* and *4680; fond of wise* things, i.e. a "*philosopher*":–philosopher.
5387. φιλόστοργος *fil-os'-tor-gos;* from *5384* and στοργή storge (*cherishing* one's kindred, esp. parents or children); *fond of* nat. *relatives,* i.e. *fraternal* towards fellow Chr.:–kindly affectioned.
5388. φιλότεκνος *fil-ot'-ek-nos;* from *5384* and *5043; fond of* one's *children,* i.e. *maternal:*–love their children.
5389. φιλοτιμέομαι *fil-ot-im-eh'-om-ahee;* mid. from a com. of *5384* and *5092;* to be *fond of honor,* i.e. *emulous* (*eager* or *earnest* to do something):–labour, strive, study.
5390. φιλοφρόνως *fil-of-ron'-oce;* adv. from *5391; with friendliness of mind,* i.e. *kindly:*–courteously.
5391.φιλόφρων *fil-of'-rone;* from *5384* and *5424; friendly of mind,* i.e. *kind:*–courteous.
5392. φιμόω *fee-mo'-o;* from φιμός phimos (a *muzzle*); to *muzzle:*–muzzle.
5393. Φλέγων *fleg'-one;* act. part. of the base of *5395; blazing; Phlegon,* a Chr.:–Phlegon.
5394. φλογίζω *flog-id'-zo;* from *5395;* to *cause a blaze,* i.e. *ignite* (fig. to *inflame* with passion):–set on fire.
5395. φλόξ *flox;* from a prim. φλέγω phlego (to "*flash*" or "*flame*"); a *blaze:*–flame(-ing).
5396. φλυαρέω *floo-ar-eh'-o;* from *5397;* to *be* a *babbler* or *trifler,* i.e. (by impl.) to *berate* idly or mischievously:–prate against.
5397. φλύαρος *floo'-ar-os;* from φλύω phluo (to *bubble*); a *garrulous* person, i.e. *prater:*–tattler.
5398. φοβερός *fob-er-os'* from *5401; frightful,* i.e. (obj.) *formidable:*–fearful, terrible.
5399. φοβέω *fob-eh'-o;* from *5401;* to *frighten,* i.e. pass. to *be alarmed;* by anal. to *be in awe* of, i.e. *revere:*–be (+ sore) afraid, fear (exceedingly), reverence.
5400. φόβητρον *fob'-ay-tron;* neut. of a der. of *5399;* a *frightening* thing, i.e. *terrific* portent:–fearful sight.
5401. φόβος *fob'-os;* from a prim. φέβομαι phebomai (to *be* put in *fear*); *alarm* or *fright:*– be afraid, + exceedingly, fear, terror.
5402. Φοίβη *foy'-bay;* fem. of Φοῖβος phoibos (*bright;* prob. akin to the base of

5457); *Phoebe,* a Chr. woman:–Phebe.

5403. Φοινίκη *foy-nee'-kay;* from *5404; palm*-country; *Phoenice* (or *Phoenicia*), a region of Pal.:–Phenice, Phenicia.

5404. φοῖνιξ *foy'-nix;* of unc. der.; a *palm*-tree:–palm (tree).

5405. Φοῖνιξ *foy'-nix;* prob. the same as *5404; Phoenix,* a place in Crete:–Phenice.

5406. φονεύς *fon-yooce';* from *5408;* a *murderer* (always of *criminal* [or at least *intentional*] homicide; which *443* does not necessarily imply; while *4607* is a spec. term for a *public* bandit):–murderer.

5407. φονεύω *fon-yoo'-o;* from *5406;* to *be a murderer* (of):–kill, do murder, slay.

5408. φόνος *fon'-os;* from an obs. prim. φένω pheno (to *slay*); *murder:*–murder, + be slain with, slaughter.

5409. φορέω *for-eh'-o;* from *5411;* to *have a burden,* i.e. (by anal.) to *wear* as clothing or a constant accompaniment:–bear, wear.

5410. Φόρον *for'-on;* of Lat. or.; a *forum* or market-place; only in comp. with *675;* a *station* on the Appian road:–forum.

5411. φόρος *for'-os;* from *5342;* a *load* (as *borne*), i.e. (fig.) a *tax* (prop. an indiv. *assessment* on persons or property; whereas *5056* is usually a gen. *toll* on goods or travel):–tribute.

5412. φορτίζω *for-tid'-zo;* from *5414;* to *load* up (prop. as a vessel or animal), i.e. (fig.) to *overburden* with cer. (or spir. anxiety):–lade, be heavy laden.

5413. φορτίον *for-tee'-on;* dimin. of *5414;* an *invoice* (as part of *freight*), i.e. (fig.) a *task* or *service:*–burden.

5414. φόρτος *for'-tos;* from *5342;* something *carried,* i.e. the *cargo* of a ship:–lading.

5415. Φορτουνάτος *for-too-nat'-os;* of Lat. or.; "*fortunate*"; *Fortunatus,* a Chr.:–Fortunatus.

5416. φραγέλλιον *frag-el'-le-on;* neut. of a der. from the base of *5417;* a *whip,* i.e. Rom. *lash* as a public punishment:–scourge.

5417. φραγελλόω *frag-el-lo'-o;* from a presumed equiv. of the Lat. *flagellum;* to *whip,* i.e. *lash* as a public punishment:–scourge.

5418. φραγμός *frag-mos';* from *5420;* a *fence,* or inclosing *barrier* (lit. or fig.):–hedge (+ round about), partition.

5419. φράζω *frad'-zo;* prob. akin to 5420 through the idea of *defining;* to *indicate* (by word or act), i.e. (spec.), to *expound:*– declare.

5420. φράσσω *fras'-so;* app. a streng. form of the base of *5424;* to *fence* or inclose, i.e. (spec.), to *block* up (fig. to *silence*):–stop.

5421. φρέαρ *freh'-ar;* of unc. der.; a *hole* in the ground (dug for obtaining or holding water or other purposes), i.e. a *cistern* or *well;* fig. an *abyss* (as a *prison*):–well, pit.

5422. φρεναπατάω *fren-ap-at-ah'-o;* from 5423; to *be a mind-misleader,* i.e. *delude:*–deceive.

5423. φρεναπάτης *fren-ap-at'-ace;* from *5424* and *539;* a *mind-misleader,* i.e. *seducer:*–deceiver.

5424. φρήν *frane;* prob. from an obs. φράω phrao (to *rein* in or *curb;* comp. *5420*); the *midrif* (as a *partition* of the body), i.e. (fig. and by impl. of sympathy) the *feelings* (or sensitive nature; by ext. [also in the pl.] the *mind* or cognitive faculties):–understanding.

5425. φρίσσω *fris'-so;* app. a prim. verb; to "*bristle*" or *chill,* i.e. *shudder* (*fear*):–tremble.

5426. φρονέω *fron-eh'-o;* from *5424;* to *exercise* the *mind,* i.e. *entertain* or have a *sentiment* or *opinion;* by impl. to *be* (ment.) *disposed* (more or less earnestly in a cert. direction); intens., to *interest oneself* in (with concern or obedience):–set the affection on, (be) care(-ful), (be like-, + be of one, + be of the same, + let this) mind(-ed), regard, savour, think.

5427. φρόνημα *fron'-ay-mah;* from *5426;* (ment.) *inclination* or *purpose:*–(be, + be carnally, + be spiritually) mind(-ed).

5428. φρόνησις *fron'-ay-sis;* from *5426;* ment. *action* or *activity,* i.e. intellectual or mor. *insight:*–prudence, wisdom.

5429. φρόνιμος *fron'-ee-mos;* from *5424; thoughtful,* i.e. *sagacious* or *discreet* (implying a *cautious* character; while *4680* denotes *practical* skill or acumen; and *4908* indicates rather *intelligence* or ment. acquirement); in a bad sense *conceited* (also in the comp.):–wise(-r).

5430. φρονίμως *fron-im'-oce;* adv. from *5429; prudently:*–wisely.

5431. φροντίζω *fron-tid'-zo;* from a der. of *5424;* to *exercise thought,* i.e. *be anxious:*–be careful.

5432. φρουρέω *froo-reh'-o;* from a com. of *4253* and *3708;* to *be a watcher in advance,* i.e. to *mount guard* as a sentinel (*post spies* at gates); fig. to *hem in, protect:*–keep (with a garrison). Comp. *5083.*

5433. φρυάσσω *froo-as'-so;* akin to *1032, 1031;* to *snort* (as a spirited horse), i.e. (fig.) to *make a tumult:*–rage.

5434. φρύγανον *froo'-gan-on;* neut. of a presumed der. of φρύγω, phrugo (to *roast* or *parch;* akin to the base of *5395*); something *desiccated,* i.e. a dry *twig:*–stick.

5435. Φρυγία *froog-ee'-ah;* prob. of for. or.; *Phrygia,* a region of Asia Minor:–Phrygia.

5436. Φύγελλος *foog'-el-los;* prob. from *5343; fugitive; Phygellus,* an apostate Chr.:–Phygellus.

5437. φυγή *foog-ay';* from *5343;* a *fleeing,* i.e. *escape:*–flight.

5438. φυλακή *foo-lak-ay';* from *5442;* a *guarding* or (concr. *guard*), the act, the pers.; fig. the place, the condition, or (spec.), the time (as a division of day or night), lit. or fig.:–cage, hold, (im-)prison(-ment), ward, watch.

5439 φυλακίζω *foo-lak-id'-zo;* from *5441;* to *incarcerate:*–imprison.

5440. φυλακτήριον *foo-lak-tay'-ree-on;* neut. of a der. of *5442;* a *guard-case,* i.e. "*phylactery*" for wearing slips of Scripture texts:– phylactery.

5441. φύλαξ *foo'-lax;* from *5442;* a *watcher* or *sentry:*–keeper.

5442. φυλάσσω *foo-las'-so* prob. from *5443* through the idea of *isolation;* to *watch,* i.e. *be on guard* (lit. of fig.); by impl. to *preserve, obey, avoid:*–beware, keep (self), observe, save. Comp. *5083.*

5443. φυλή *foo-lay';* from *5453* (comp. *5444*); an *offshoot,* i.e. *race* or *clan:*–kindred, tribe.

5444. φύλλον *fool'-lon;* from the same as *5443;* a *sprout,* i.e. *leaf:*–leaf.

5445. φύραμα *foo'-ram-ah;* from a prol. form of φύρω phuro (to *mix* a liquid with a solid; perh. akin to *5453* through the idea of *swelling* in bulk), mean to *knead;* a *mass* of dough:–lump.

5446. φυσικός *foo-see-kos';* from *5449;* "*physically*", i.e. (by impl.) *instinctive:*–natural Comp. *5591.*

5447. φυσικῶς *foo-see-koce';* adv. from *5446;* "*physically*", i.e. (by impl.) *instinctively:*–natural

5448. φυσιόω *foo-see-o'-o;* from *5449* in the prim. sense of *blowing;* to *inflate,* i.e. (fig.) *make proud* (*haughty*):–puff up.

5449. φύσις *foo'-sis;* from *5453;* growth (by *germination* or *expansion*), i.e. (by impl.) nat. *production* (lineal *descent*); by ext., a *genus* or *sort;* fig. native *disposition, constitution* or *usage:*–[man-] kind, nature[-al].

5450. φυσίωσις *foo-see'-o-sis;* from *5448; inflation,* i.e. (fig.) *haughtiness:*–swelling.

5451. φυτεία *foo-ti'-ah* from *5452;* trans-*planting,* i.e. (concr.) a *shrub* or *vegetable:*–plant.

5452. φυτεύω *foot-yoo'-o;* from a der. of *5453;* to *set out* in the earth, i.e. *implant;* fig. to *instil* doctrine:–plant.

5453. φύω *foo'-o;* a prim. verb; prob. or., to "*puff*" or *blow,* i.e. to *swell* up; but only used in the implied sense, to *germinate* or *grow* (*sprout, produce*), lit. or fig.:–spring (up).

5454. φωλεός *fo-leh-os';* of unc. der.; a *burrow* or *lurking-place:*–hole.

5455 φωνέω *fo-neh'-o;* from *5456;* to emit a *sound* (animal, human or instrumental); by impl. to *address* in words or by name, also in imitation:–call (for), crow, cry.

5456. φωνή *fo-nay';* prob. akin to *5316* through the idea of *disclosure;* a *tone* (articulate, bestial or artif.); by impl. an *address* (for any purpose), *saying* or *language:*–noise, sound, voice.

5457. φῶς *foce;* from an obs. φάω phao (to *shine* or make *manifest,* esp. by *rays;* comp. *5316, 5346*); *luminousness* (in the widest appl., nat. or artif., abstr. or concr. lit. or fig.):–fire, light.

5458. φωστήρ *foce-tare';* from *5457;* an *illuminator,* i.e. (concr.) a *luminary,* or (abstr.) *brilliancy:*–light.

5459.φωσφόρος *foce-for'-os;* from *5457* and *5342; light-bearing* ("phosphorus"), i.e. (spec.), the *morning-star* (fig.):–day star.

5460. φωτεινός *fo-ti-nos';* from *5457; lustrous,* i.e. *transparent* or *well-illuminated* (fig.):–bright, full of light.

5461. φωτίζω *fo-tid'-zo;* from *5457;* to *shed rays,* i.e. to *shine* or (trans.) to *brighten* up (lit. or fig.):–enlighten, illuminate, (bring to, give) light, make to see.

5462 φωτισμός *fo-tis-mos';* from *5461; illumination* (fig.):–light.

X

5463. χαίρω *khah'-ee-ro;* a prim. verb; to be "*cheer*"*ful,* i.e. calmly *happy* or well-off; impers., esp. as salutation (on meeting or parting), *be well:*–farewell, be glad, God speed, greeting, hall, joy(- fully), rejoice.
5464. χάλαζα *khal'-ad-zah;* prob. from *5465; hail:*–hail.
5465. χαλάω *khal-ah'-o;* from the base of *5490;* to *lower* (as into a *void*):–let down, strike.
5466. Χαλδαῖος *khal-dah'-yos;* prob. of Heb. or [3778]; a *Chaldoean* (i.e. *Kasdi*), or native or the region of the lower Euphrates:–Chaldaean.
5467. χαλεπός *khal-ep-os';* perh. from *5465* through the idea of *reducing* the streng.; *difficult,* i.e. *dangerous,* or (by impl.) *furious:*–fierce, perilous.
5468. χαλιναγωγέω *khal-in-ag-ogue-eh'-o;* from a comp. of *5469* and the redupl. form of *71;* to be a *bit-leader,* i.e. to *curb* (fig.):–bridle.
5469. χαλινός *khal-ee-nos'* from *5465;* a *curb* or *head-stall* (as *curbing* the spirit):–bit, bridle.
5470. χάλκεος *khal'-keh-os;* from *5475; coppery:*–brass.
5471. χαλκεύς *khalk-yooce';* from *5475;* a *copper-worker* or *brazier:*–coppersmith.
5472. χαλκηδών *khal-kay-dohn';* from *5475* and perh. *1491; copper-like,* i.e. "*chalcedony*":–chalcedony.
5473. χαλκίον *khal-kee'-on;* dimin. from 5475; a *copper dish:*–brazen vessel.
5474. χαλκολίβανον *khal-kol-ib'-an-on;* neut. of a com. of *5475* and *3030* (in the implied mean of *whiteness* or *brilliancy*); *burnished copper,* an alloy of copper (or gold) and silver having a brilliant lustre:–fine brass.
5475. χαλκός *khal-kos';* perh. from *5465* through the idea of *hollowing* out as a vessel (this metal being chiefly used for that purpose); *copper* (the substance, or some implement or coin made of it):–brass, money.
5476. χαμαί *kham-ah-ee;* adv. perh. from the base of *5490* through the idea of a *fissure* in the soil; *earthward,* i.e. *prostrate:*–on (to) the ground.
5477. Χαναάν *khan-ah-an';* of Heb. or. [3667]; *Chanaan* (i.e. *Kenaan*), the early name of Pal.:–Chanaan.
5478. Χαναναῖος *khan-ah-an-ah'-yos;* from *5477;* a *Chanaanoean* (i.e. *Kenaanite*), or native of gentile Pal.:–of Canaan.
5479. χαρά *khar-ah';* from *5463; cheerfulness,* i.e. calm *delight:*–gladness, X greatly, (X be exceeding) joy(-ful, -fully, -fulness, -ous).
5480. χάραγμα *khar'-ag-mah;* from the same as *5482*; a *scratch* or *etching*, i.e. *stamp* (as a *badge* of servitude), or *scupltured* figure (*statue*):–graven, mark.
5481. χαρακτήρ *khar-ak-tare';* from the same as *5482;* a *graver* (the tool or the pers.), i.e. (by impl.) *engraving* (["*character*"], the figure stamped, i.e. an exact *copy* or [fig.] *representation*):–express image.
5482. χάραξ *khar'-ax;* from charasso (to *sharpen* to a point; akin to *1125* through the idea of *scratching*); a *stake*, i.e. (by impl.) a *palisade* or *rampart* (military *mound* for circumvallation in a siege):–trench.
5483. χαρίζομαι *khar-id'-zom-ahee;* mid. from *5485*; to grant as a *favor,* i.e. gratuitously, in kindness, pardon or rescue:–deliver, (frankly) forgive, (freely) give, grant.
5484. χάριν *khar'-in;* acc. of *5485* as prep.; through *favor* of, i.e. *on account* of:–be-(for) cause of, for sake of, +...fore, X reproachfully.
5485. χάρις *khar'-ece;* from *5463*; *graciousness* (as *gratifying*), of manner or act (abstr. or concr.; lit. fig. or spir.; esp. the divine influence upon the heart, and its reflection in the life; incl. *gratitude*):–acceptable, benefit, favour, gift, grace(-ious), joy, liberality, pleasure, thank(-s, -worthy).
5486. χάρισμα *khar'-is-mah;* from *5483;* a (divine) *gratuity,* i.e. *deliverance* (from danger or passion); (spec.), a (spir.) endowment, i.e. (subj.) relig. *qualification,* or (obj.) miraculous *faculty:*–(free) gift.
5487. χαριτόω *khar-ee-to'-o;* from *5485;* to *grace,* i.e. indue with spec. *honor:*–make accepted, be highly favoured.
5488. Χαῤῥάν *khar-hran';* of Heb. or. [2771]; *Charrhan* (i.e. Charan), a place in Mesopotamia:–Charran.
5489. χάρτης *khar'-tace;* from the same as *5482;* a *sheet* ("chart") of writing-material (as to be *scribbled* over):–paper.
5490. χσμα *khas'-mah;* from a form of an obs. prim. χάω chao (to "*gape*" or "*yawn*"); a "*chasm*" or *vacancy* (impassable interval):–gulf.
5491. χεῖλος *khi'-los;* from a form of the same as *5490;* a *lip* (as a *pouring* place); fig. a *margin* (of water):–lip, shore.
5492.χειμάζω *khi-mad'-zo;* from the same as *5494;* to *storm*, i.e. pass. to *labor under* a *gale:*–be tossed with tempest.
5493. χείμαῤῥος *khi'-mar-hros;* from the base of 5494 and *4482;* a *storm-runlet*, i.e. *winter-torrent:*–brook.
5494. χειμών *khi-mone';* from a der. of χέω cheo (to *pour*; akin to the base of 5490 through the idea of a *channel*), mean. a *storm* (as *pouring* rain); by impl. the *rainy* season, i.e. *winter:*–tempest, foul weather, winter.
5495. χείρ *khire;* perh. from the base of *5494* in the sense of its congener the base of *5490* (through the idea of *hollowness* for grasping); the *hand* (lit. or fig. (*power*); esp. (by Heb.) a *means* or *instrument*):–hand.
5496. χειραγωγέω *khi-rag-ogue-eh'-o;* from *5497;* to be a *hand-leader*, i.e. to *guide* (a blind pers.):–lead by the hand.
5497. χειραγωγός *khi-rag-o-gos';* from *5495* and a redupl. form of *71;* a *hand-leader,* i.e. pers. *conductor* (of a blind pers.):–some to lead by the hand.
5498. χειρόγραφον *khi-rog'-raf-on;* neut. of a com. of *5495* and *1125;* something *hand-written* ("*chirograph*"), i.e. a *manuscript* (spec. a legal *document* or *bond* [fig.]):–handwriting.
5499. χειροποίητος *khi-rop-oy'-ay-tos;* from *5495* and a der. of *4160*; *manufactured,* i.e. of *human construction:*–made by (make with) hands.
5500. χειροτονέω *khi-rot-on-eh'*-o; from a comp. of *5495* and τείνω teino (to stretch); to be a *hand-reacher* or *voter* (by raising the hand), i.e. (gen.) to *select* or *appoint*:–choose, ordain.
5501. χείρων *khi'-rone;* irreg. comp. of *2556*; from an obs. equiv. χέρης cheres (of unc. der.); *more evil* or *aggravated* (phys. ment. or mor.):–sorer, worse.
5502. χερουβίμ *kher-oo-beem';* pl. of Heb. or. (*3742*); "*cherubim*" (i.e. *cherubs* or *kerubim*):–cherubims.
5503. χήρα *khay'-rah;* fem. of a presumed der. app. from the base of *5490* through the idea of *deficiency*; a widow (as *lacking* a husband), lit. or fig.:–widow.
5504. χθές *khthes;* of unc. der.; "*yesterday*"; by ext., *in time past* or *hitherto:*–yesterday.
5505. χιλιάς *khil-ee-as';* from *5507*; *one thousand* ("*chiliad*"):–thousand.
5506. χιλίαρχος *khil-ee'-ar-khos;* from *5507* and *757*; the *commander of* a *thousand* soldiers ("*chiliarch*"); i.e. *colonel*:–(chief, high) captain.
5507. χίλιοι *khil'-ee-oy;* pl. of unc. affin.; a *thousand*:–thousand.
5508. Χίος *khee'-os;* of unc. der.; *Chios*, an island in the Mediterranean:–Chios.
5509.χιτών *khee-tone';* of for. or. (3801); a *tunic* or *shirt:*–clothes, coat, garment.
5510. χιών *khee-one';* perh. akin to the base of *5490 (5465)* or *5494* (as *descending* or *empty*); *snow:*–snow.
5511. χλαμύς *khlam-ooce';* of unc. der.; a military *cloak*:–robe.
5512. χλευάζω *khlyoo-ad'-zo;* from a der. prob. of *5491*; to *throw out* the *lip*, i.e. *jeer* at:–mock.
5513. χλιαρός *khlee-ar-os';* from χλίω chlio (to *warm*); *tepid*:–lukewarm.
5514. Χλόη *khlo'-ay;* fem. of app. a prim. word; "*green*"; *Chloë*, a Chr. female:–Chloe.
5515. χλωρός *khlo-ros';* from the same as *5514*; *greenish*, i.e. *verdant*, *dun-colored*:–green, pale.
5516. χξς *khee xee stig'-ma;* the 22nd, 14th and an obs. letter (*4742* as a *cross*) of the Gr. alphabet (intermediate between the 5th and 6th), used as numbers; denoting respectively 600, 60 and 6; 666 as a numeral:–six hundred threescore and six.
5517. χοϊκός *kho-ik-os';* from *5522*; *dusty* or *dirty* (*soil*-like), i.e. (by impl.) *terrene:*–earthy.
5518. χοῖνιξ *khoy'-nix;* of unc. der.; a *choenix* or cert. dry measure:–measure.
5519. χοῖρος *khoy'-ros;* of unc. der.; a *hog:*–swine.
5520. χολάω *khol-ah'-o;* from *5521*; to

be *bilious*, i.e. (by impl.) *irritable* (*enraged*, "choleric"):–be angry.

5521. χολή *khol-ay';* fem. of an equiv. perh. akin to the same as *5514* (from the *greenish* hue); *"gall"* or *bile*, i.e. (by anal.) *poison* or an *anodyne* (wormwood, poppy, etc.):–gall.

5522. χόος *kho'-os;* from the base of *5494*; a *heap* (as *poured* out), i.e. *rubbish;* loose *dirt:*–dust.

5523. Χοραζίν *khor-ad-zin';* of unc. der.; *Chorazin*, a place in Pal.:–Chorazin.

5524. χορηγέω *khor-ayg-eh'-o;* from a com. of *5525* and *71*; to be a *dance-leader*, i.e. (gen.) to *furnish:*–give, minister.

5525. χορός *khor-os';* of unc. der.; a *ring*, i.e. round *dance* ("choir"):–dancing.

5526. χορτάζω *khor-tad'-zo;* from *5528*; to *fodder*, i.e. (gen.) to *gorge* (*supply food* in abundance):–feed, fill, satisfy.

5527. χόρτασμα *khor'-tas-mah;* from *5526*; *forage*, i.e. *food:*–sustenance.

5528. χόρτος *khor'-tos;* app. a prim. word; a "*court*" or "*garden*", i.e. (by impl. of *pasture*) *herbage* or *vegetation:*–blade, grass, hay.

5529. Χουζᾶς *khood-zas';* of unc. or.; *Chuzas*, an officer of Herod:–Chuza.

5530. χράομαι *khrah'-om-ahee;* mid. of a prim. verb (perh. rather from *5495*, to *handle*); to *furnish* what is needed; (give an *oracle*, "*graze*" [touch slightly], *light* upon, etc.), i.e. (by impl.) to *employ* or (by ext.) to *act towards* one in a given manner:–entreat, use. Comp. *5531*; *5534*.

5531. χράω *khrah'-o;* prob. the same as the base of 5530; to *loan:*–lend.

5532. χρεία *khri'-ah;* from the base of *5530* or *5534*; *employment*, i.e. an *affair;* also (by impl.) *occasion, demand, requirement* or *destitution:*–business, lack, necessary(-ity), need(-ful), use, want.

5533. χρεωφειλέτης *khreh-o-fi-let'-ace;* from a der. of *5531* and *3781*; a *loan-ower,* i.e. *indebted* pers.:–debtor.

5534. χρή *khray;* third pers. sing. of the same as 5530 or 5531 used impers.; it *needs* (*must* or *should*) be:–ought.

5535. χρῄζω *khrade'-zo;* from *5532*; to *make* (i.e. *have*) *necessity*, i.e. *be in want* of:–(have) need.

5536. χρῆμα *khray'-mah;* something *useful* or *needed,* i.e. *wealth, price:*–money, riches.

5537. χρηματίζω, *khray-mat-id'-zo;* from *5536*; to *utter an oracle* (comp. the or. sense of *5530*), i.e. divinely *intimate*; by impl. (comp. the secular sense of *5532*) to constitute a *firm* for business, i.e. (gen.) *bear* as a *title:*–be called, be admonished (warned) of God, reveal, speak.

5538. χρηματισμος *khray-mat-is-mos';* from *5537*; a divine *response* or *revelation:*–answer of God.

5539. χρήσιμος *khray'-see-mos;* from *5540; serviceable:*–profit.

5540. χρῆσις *khray'-sis;* from *5530*; *employment,* i.e. (spec.), sexual *intercourse* (as an *occupation* of the body):–use.

5541. χρηστεῦομαι *khraste-yoo'-om-ahee;* mid. from *5543*; to *show oneself useful*, i.e. *act benevolently:*–be kind.

5542. χρηστολογία *khrase-tol-og-ee'-ah;* from a com. of *5543* and *3004; fair speech,* i.e. *plausibility:*–good words.

5543. χρηστός *khrase-tos';* from *5530; employed,* i.e. (by impl.) *useful* (in manner or morals):–better, easy, good(-ness), gracious, kind.

5544. χρηστότης *khray-stot'-ace;* from *5543; usefulness,* i.e. mor. *excellence* (in character or demeanor):–gentleness, good(-ness), kindness.

5545. χρίσμα *khris'-mah;* from *5548*; an *unguent* or *smearing,* i.e. (fig.) the spec. *endowment* ("chrism") of the Holy Spirit:–anointing, unction.

5546. Χριστιανός *khris-tee-an-os';* from *5547*; a *Chr.*, i.e. follower of Christ:–Christian.

5547. Χριστός *khris-tos';* from *5548*; *anointed*, i.e. the *Messiah*, an epithet of Jesus:–Christ.

5548. χρίω *khree'-o;* prob. akin to *5530* through the idea of *contact;* to *smear* or *rub* with oil, i.e. (by impl.) to *consecrate* to an office or relig. service:–anoint.

5549. χρονίζω *khron-id'-zo;* from *5550;* to *take time,* i.e. *linger:*–delay, tarry.

5550. χρόνος *khron'-os;* of unc. der.; a space of *time* (in gen. and thus prop. distinguished from 2540, which designates a *fixed* or spec. occasion; and from *165*, which denotes a particular *period*) or *interval;* by ext., an indiv. *opportunity;* by impl. *delay:*–+ years old, season, space, (X often-)time(-s), (a) while.

5551. χρονοτριβέω *khron-ot-rib-eh'-o;* from a presumed com. of *5550* and the base of *5147*; to be a *time-wearer,* i.e. to *procrastinate* (*linger*):–spend time.

5552. χρύσεος *khroo'-seh-os;* from *5557*; made of *gold:*–of gold, golden.

5553. χρυσίον *khroo-see'-on;* dimin. of *5557*; a *golden* article, i.e. gold plating, ornament, or coin:–gold.

5554. χρυσοδακτύλιος *khroo-sod-ak-too'-lee-os;* from *5557* and *1146*; *gold-ringed,* i.e. *wearing* a golden finger-ring or similar *jewelry:*–with a gold ring.

5555. χρυσόλιθος *khroo-sol'-ee-thos;* from *5557* and *3037*; *gold-stone,* i.e. a *yellow gem* (*"chrysolite"*):–chrysolite.

5556. χρυσόπρασος *khroo-sop'-ras-os;* from *5557* and πράσον prason (a *leek*); a *greenish-yellow* gem (*"chrysoprase"*):–chrysoprase.

5557. χρυσός *khroo-sos';* perh. from the base of *5530* (through the idea of the *utility* of the metal); *gold;* by ext., a *golden* article, as an ornament or coin:–gold.

5558. χρυσόω *khroo-so'-o;* from *5557*; to *gild,* i.e. *bespangle* with golden ornaments:–deck.

5559. χρώς *khroce;* prob. akin to the base of *5530* through the idea of *handling;* the *body* (prop. its *surface* or *skin*):–body.

5560. χωλός *kho-los';* app. a prim. word; *"halt"*, i.e. *limping:*–cripple, halt, lame.

5561. χώρα *kho'-rah;* fem. of a der. of the base of *5490* through the idea of *empty* expanse; *room,* i.e. a space of *territory* (more or less extensive; often incl. its inh.):–coast, county, fields, ground, land, region. Comp. *5117*.

5562. χωρέω *kho-reh'-o;* from *5561*; to *be* in (*give*) *space*, i.e. (intrans.) to *pass, enter,* or (trans.) to *hold, admit* (lit. or fig.):–come, contain, go, have place, (can, be room to) receive.

5563. χωρίζω *kho-rid'-zo;* from *5561*; to *place room* between, i.e. *part*; refl. to *go away:*–depart, put asunder, separate.

5564. χωρίον *kho-ree'-on;* dimin. of *5561*; a *spot* or *plot* of ground:–field, land, parcel of ground, place, possession.

5565. χωρίς *kho-rece';* adv. from *5561*; at a *space,* i.e. *separately* or *apart* from (often as prep.):–beside, by itself, without.

5566. χῶρος *kho'-ros;* of Lat. or.; the *north-west* wind:–north west.

Ψ

5567. ψάλλω *psal'-lo;* prob. streng. from ψάωpsao (to *rub* or *touch* the surface; comp. *5597*); to *twitch* or *twang,* i.e. to *play* on a stringed instrument (*celebrate* the divine worship *with music* and accompanying odes):–make melody, sing (psalms).

5568. ψαλμός *psal-mos';* from *5567*; a set piece of *music,* i.e. a sacred *ode* (accompanied with the voice, harp or other instrument; a "*psalm*"); coll., the book of the Psalms:–psalm. Comp. *5603*.

5569. ψευδάδελφος *psyoo-dad'-el-fos;* from *5571* and *80*; a *spurious brother*, i.e. *pretended associate:*–false brethren.

5570. ψευδαπόστολος *psyoo-dap-os'-tol-os;* from *5571* and *652*; a *spurious apostle,* i.e. *pretended pracher:*–false teacher.

5571. ψευδής *psyoo-dace' ;* from *5574*; *untrue,* i.e. *err., deceitful, wicked:*–false, liar.

5572. ψευδοδιδάσκαλος *psyoo-dod-id-as'-kal-os;* from *5571* and *1320*; a *spurious teacher,* i.e. *propagator* of *err.* Chr. *doctrine:*–false teacher.

5573. ψευδολόγος *psyoo-dol-og'-os;* from *5571* and *3004*; *mendacious,* i.e. *promulgating err.* Chr. *doctrine:*–speaking lies.

5574. ψεύδομαι *psyoo'-dom-ahee;* mid. of an app. prim. verb; to *utter an untruth* or attempt to *deceive* by falsehood:–falsely, lie.

5575. ψευδομάρτυρ *psyoo-dom-ar'-toor;* from *5571* and a kindred form of *3144*; a *spurious witness,* i.e. *bearer of untrue testimony:*–false witness.

5576. ψευδομαρτυρέω *psyoo-dom-ar-too-reh'-o;* from 5575; to be an *untrue testifier,* i.e. offer *falsehood in evidence:*–be a false witness.

5577. ψευδομαρτυρία *psyoo-dom-ar-too-ree'-ah;* from 5575; *untrue testimony:*–false witness.

5578. ψευδοπροφήτης *psyoo-dop-rof-ay'-tace;* from 5571 and *4396;* a *spurious prophet,* i.e. *pretended foreteller* or relig. *impostor:*–false prophet.

GREEK

5579. ψεῦδος *psyoo'-dos;* from *5574*; a *falsehood:*–lie, lying.
5580. ψευδόχριστος *psyoo-dokh'-ris-tos;* from *5571* and 5547; a *spurious Messiah:*–false Christ.
5581. ψευδώνυμος *psyoo-do'-noo-mos;* from *5571* and 3686; *untruly named:*–falsely so called.
5582. ψεῦσμα *psyoos'-mah;* from *5574*; a *fabrication,* i.e. *falsehood:*–lie.
5583. ψεύστης *psyoos-tace';* from *5574;* a *falsifier:*–liar.
5584. ψηλαφάω *psay-laf-ah'-o;* from the base of *5567* (comp. *5586*); to *manipulate,* i.e. *verify* by contact; fig. to *search* for:–feel after, handle, touch.
5585.ψηφίζω *psay-fid'-zo;* from *5586*; to *use pebbles* in enumeration, i.e. (gen.) to *compute:*–count.
5586. ψῆφος *psay'-fos;* from the same as *5584*; a *pebble* (as worn smooth by *handling*), i.e. (by impl. of use as a *counter* or *ballot*) a *verdict* (of acquittal) or *ticket* (of admission); a *vote:*–stone, voice.
5587. ψιθυρισμός *psith-oo-ris-mos';* from a der. of ψίθος psithos (a *whisper*; by impl. a *slander*; prob. akin to *5574*); *whispering*, i.e. secret *detraction:*–whispering.
5588. ψιθυριστής *psith-oo-ris-tace';* from the same as 5587; a secret *calumniator:*–whisperer.
5589. ψιχίον *psikh-ee'-on;* dimin. from a der. of the base of *5567* (mean. a *crumb*); a *little bit* or *morsel:*–crumb.
5590. ψυχή *psoo-khay';* from *5594; breath*, i.e. (by impl.) *spirit,* abstr. or concr. (the *animal* sentient principle only; thus distinguished on the one hand from *4151*, which is the rational and immortal *soul*; and on the other from *2222,* which is mere *vitality*, even of plants: these terms thus exactly correspond respectively to the Heb. 5315, 7307 and 2416):–heart (+ -ily), life, mind, soul, + us, + you.
5591. ψυχικός *psoo-khee-kos';* from *5590*; *sensitive*, i.e. *animate* (in distinction on the one hand from *4152*, which is the higher or *renovated* nature; and on the other from *5446*, which is the lower or *bestial* nature):–nat., sensual.
5592. ψύχος *psoo'-khos;* from *5594; coolness:*–cold.
5593. ψυχρός *psoo-chros';* from *5592*; *chilly* (lit. or fig.):–cold.
5594. ψύχω *psoo'-kho;* a prim. verb; to *breathe* (*vol.* but *gently*, thus differing on the one hand from *4154*, which denotes prop. a *forcible* respiration; and on the other from the base of *109,* which refers prop. to an inanimate *breeze*), i.e. (by impl. of reduction of temperature by evaporation) to *chill* (fig.):–wax cold.
5595. ψωμίζω *pso-mid'-zo;* from the base of *5596*; to *supply* with *bits,* i.e. (gen.) to *nourish:*–(bestow to) feed.
5596. ψωμίον *pso-mee'-on;* dimin. from a der. of the base of 5597; a *crumb* or *morsel* (as if *rubbed* off), i.e. a *mouthful:*–sop.
5597. ψώχω *pso'-kho;* prol. from the same base as *5567*; to *triturate*, i.e. (by anal.) to *rub* out (kernels from husks with the fingers or hand):–rub.

Ω

5598. Ω *o'-meg-ah;* the last letter of the Gr. alphabet, i.e. (fig.) the *finality:*–Omega.
5599. ὦ *o;* a prim. interj.; as a sign of the voc. case, O; as a note of exclamation, *oh:*–O.
5600. ὦ *o;* incl. the oblique forms, as well as ᾖς *ace ace*; ᾖ *ay* etc.; the subjunctive of *1510*; (*may, might, can, could, would, should, must*, etc.; also with 1487 and its comp., as well as with other par.) be:–+ appear, are, (may, might, should) be, X have, is, + pass the flower of her age, should stand, were.
5601. 'Ωβήδ *o-bade';* of Heb. or. (5744); *Obed*, an Isr.:–Obed.
5602. ὧδε *ho'-deh;* from an adv. form of *3592; in this* same spot, i.e. *here* or *hither:*–here, hither, (in) this place, there.
5603. ᾠδή *o-day';* from *103*; a *chant* or "*ode*" (the gen. term for any words sung; while *5215* denotes esp. a *relig.* metrical compo., and *5568* still more spec. a Heb. cantillation):–song.
5604. ὠδίν *o-deen';* akin to *3601*; a *pang* or *throe*, esp. of childbirth:–pain, sorrow, travail.
5605. ὠδίνω *o-dee'-no;* from *5604*; to *experience* the *pains* of parturition (lit. or fig.):–travail in (birth).
5606. ὦμος *o'-mos;* perh.. from the alt. of *5342;* the *shoulder* (as that on which burdens are *borne*):–shoulder.
5607. ὤν *oan;* includ. the fem. οὖσα, *oo'-sah* and the neut. ὄν, *on;* pres. part. of *1510*; *being:*–be, come, have.
5608. ὠνέομαι *o-neh'-om-ahee;* mid. voice from an app. prim. ὦνος, onos (a *sum* or *price*); to *purchase* (synonymous with the earlier *4092*):– buy.
5609. ᾠόν *o-on';* app. a prim. word; an "*egg*":–egg.
5610. ὥρα *ho'-rah;* app. a prim. word; an "*hour*" (lit. or fig.):–day, hour, instant, season, X short, [even-]tide, (high) time.
5611. ὡραῖος *ho-rah'-yos;* from *5610*; *belonging* to the right *hour* or *season* (*timely*), i.e. (by impl.) *flourishing* (*beauteous* [fig.]):–beautiful.
5612. ὠρύομαι *o-roo'-om-ahee;* mid. of an app. prim. verb; to "*roar*":–roar.
5613. ὡς *hoce;* prob. adv. of comp. from *3739*; *which how*, i.e. *in that manner* (very variously used, as follows):–about, after (that), (according) as (it had been, it were), as soon (as), even as (like), for, how (greatly), like (as, unto), since, so (that), that, to wit, unto, when[-soever], while, X with all speed.
5614. ὡσαννά *ho-san-nah';* of Heb. or. [3467 and 4994]; *oh save!; hosanna* (i.e. *hoshia-na*), an exclamation of adoration:–hosanna.
5615. ὡσαύτως *ho-sow'-toce;* from *5613* and an adv. from *846*; *as thus*, i.e. *in the same way:*–even so, likewise, after the same (in like) manner.
5616. ὡσεί *ho-si';* from *5613* and *1487*; as *if:*–about, as (it had been, it were), like (as).
5617. 'Ωσηέ *ho-say-eh';* of Heb. or. [1954]; *Hoseë* (i.e. *Hosheä*), an Isr.:–Osee.
5618. ὥσπερ *hoce'-per;* from *5613* and *4007*; *just as*, i.e. *exactly like:*–(even, like) as.
5619. ὡσπερεί *hoce-per-i';* from *5618* and *1487; just as if*, i.e. as *it were:*–as.
5620. ὥστε *hoce'-teh;* from *5613* and *5037*; *so too*, i.e. *thus therefore* (in various relations of *consecution*, as follow):–(insomuch) as, so that (then), (insomuch) that, therefore, to, wherefore.
5621. ὠτίον *o-tee'-on;* dimin. of *3775*; an *earlet*, i.e. *one* of the ears, or perh. the *lobe* of the ear:–ear.
5622. ὠφέλεια *o-fel'-i-ah;* from a der. of the base of *5624*; *usefulness*, i.e. *benefit:*–advantage, profit.
5623. ὠφελέω *o-fel-eh'-o;* from the same as *5622*; to *be useful*, i.e. to *benefit:*–advantage, better, prevail, profit.
5624. ὠφέλιμος *o-fel'-ee-mos;* from a form of *3786*; *helpful* or *serviceable*, i.e. *advantageous:*–profit(-able).

VARIATIONS

IN THE NUMBERING OF VERSES IN THE GREEK AND ENGLISH NEW TESTAMENT

English	Greek
Mark 13:8 (last clause)	(first clauses) 9
Luke 22:66 (last word)	(first word) 67
John 1:38 (all after first clause)	39
John 1:39-51	40-52
Acts 4:6 (last clause)	(in) 5
Acts 13:33 (former half)	(latter half) 32
1 Peter 2:8 (first two clauses)	(last two clauses) 7